THE AUTHORITY SINCE 1868

THE WORLD ALMANAC®
AND BOOK OF FACTS
2008

WORLD ALMANAC BOOKS

THE WORLD ALMANAC®
AND BOOK OF FACTS
2008

Editorial Director: C. Alan Joyce
Managing Editor: Elizabeth J. Lazzara
Editor: Sarah Janssen
Associate Editors: M. L. Liu, Andrew Steinitz
Desktop Publishing Associate: Sean Westmoreland
Index Editor: Nan Badgett
Contributing Editors: G. A. Clark, Helen A. Gaudette, Geoffrey M. Horn, Michael J. Kaufman, Lisa Renaud, George W. Smith, Vincent G. Spadafora and Donald Young
Research: Maximillian Del Rey, Trevor S. Hagstrom, Anikka Sellz, Kelly A. Walker
Desktop Publishing Assistant: Lanya Fisher
Associate Publisher/Photo Research: Edward A. Thomas

READERS DIGEST TRADE PUBLISHING
President and Publisher: Harold Clarke
Vice President, Director of Sales & Marketing: Stacey Ashton

Cover: Bill SMITH STUDIO

We acknowledge with thanks the many helpful letters and e-mails from readers of THE WORLD ALMANAC. Because of the volume of mail, it is not possible to reply to each one. However, every communication is read by the editors, and all suggestions receive careful attention. THE WORLD ALMANAC's e-mail address is Walmanac@waegroup.com.

The first edition of THE WORLD ALMANAC, a 120-page volume with 12 pages of advertising, was published by the *New York World* in 1868. Annual publication was suspended in 1876. Joseph Pulitzer, publisher of the *New York World*, revived THE WORLD ALMANAC in 1886 with the goal of making it a "compendium of universal knowledge." It has been published annually since then. THE WORLD ALMANAC does not decide wagers.

PHOTOS: Front Cover: AP Images: Michael Phelps sets new men's 200m Individual Medley world record in Melbourne, Australia, Mar. 29, 2007; women and children in the Gouroukoum refugee camp in eastern Chad, Mar. 28, 2007; Penelope Cruz on the red carpet at the 79th Academy Awards, Los Angeles, Feb. 25, 2007. **Back cover:** AP Images: U.S. Capitol building; iStockPhoto: China. **Tabs:** AP Images: Debate; Photodisc/BSS image: gold bars, circuit board; ©2007 JupiterImages: vials, movie reels, flag, golf tee; Corel Stock Photo Library/BSS Image: crowd, UN flag. **Text Pages:** NOAA: pgs. 304, 489; ©2007 Jupiterimages Corporation: p. 473, Fulton p. 476, 660, 661, 664, 667-669; Library of Congress: p. 474, Willard, Lewis & Clark p. 476, 477-483, Parks p. 484, 485, O'Connor p. 487, pgs. 671-676, Yalta p. 677; NASA: Glenn p. 484, Challenger p. 488, Aldrin p. 679, Mir p. 684; Dept. of Energy: Three Mile Island p. 487; U.S. State Dept.: Albright p. 490, Rice p. 684; U.S. Navy: p. 491; U.S. Coast Guard: p 493; © Edward A. Thomas: Hieroglyphics p. 659; NARA: Pearl Harbor p. 677; Jimmy Carter Library & Museum: Carter portrait p. 525, 680; Ronald Reagan Presidential Library p. 681; George Bush Presidential Library: Thatcher p. 682; DoD: Zemin p. 682; European Parliament Photoservice: Merkel p. 685. U.S. Presidents pgs. 517-526 Library of Congress, unless otherwise indicated; ©1967 by Dover Publications: J. Adams, Jackson, Harrison, Arthur, Harrison, McKinley, Harding, Hoover, Eisenhower; Lyndon B. Johnson Library: L. Johnson, Gerald R. Ford Museum: Ford; Eric Draper-The White House: G. W. Bush.

Library of Congress Catalog Card Number 4-3781
International Standard Serial Number (ISSN) 0084-1382
Softcover ISBN-10: 1-60057-072-0; ISBN-13: 978-1-60057-072-8
Hardcover ISBN-10: 1-60057-073-9; ISBN-13: 978-1-60057-073-5
Otabind Library Edition ISBN-10: 1-60057-097-6; 978-1-60057-097-1

The softcover and hardcover editions are distributed to the book trade by Simon & Schuster.
The Otabind Special Edition is distributed by World Almanac Education, (800) 321-1147.
Printed in the United States of America

WORLD ALMANAC BOOKS
A Reader's Digest Company
512 Seventh Avenue
New York, NY 10018
www.WorldAlmanac.com

CONTENTS

THE TOP TEN NEWS TOPICS OF 2007

1. Iraq. Pres. George W. Bush Jan. 10 outlined a new war strategy, notable for a so-called "surge" of some 30,000 additional troops intended to contain ongoing insurgent violence in Iraq. The announcement came as counterinsurgency expert Gen. David Petraeus, Pres. Bush's nominee to command the multinational forces in Iraq, was preparing to take over the war's military leadership; he was confirmed by the Senate Jan. 26. Pres. Bush vetoed Congress's Iraq war funding bill, which contained a timetable for withdrawal, May 1, but approved a version of the bill with no withdrawal timetable May 25. Gen. Petraeus testified before Congress Sept. 10-11 that the troop surge had been effective.

The Iraqi interior ministry said it was expelling private security company Blackwater USA Sept. 17, following an allegedly unprovoked shooting incident that had killed 17 Iraqi civilians, sparking debate in the U.S. on the military's jurisdiction over private security contractors. As of Oct. 10, the Defense Dept. had confirmed 3,820 U.S. military deaths in Iraq since the 2003 invasion; the total number of coalition deaths was at 4,123. Iraq Body Count, a group monitoring international press reports, estimated the number of civilian deaths from violence at 74,982 as of Oct. 12.

2. Economy. The U.S. housing market started to crumble as foreclosure rates spiked in 2007. Many of the foreclosures came on adjustable-rate "subprime" mortgages, which often had low initial rates that escalated rapidly and were typically issued to borrowers with poor credit histories. Market turbulence spread internationally, as fears spread that banks that had invested in the U.S. housing market had been weakened by the turmoil in the mortgage industry. In response to the housing and credit crises and the concurrent volatile markets, which reflected fears of recession, the Federal Reserve Sept. 18 cut the federal-funds interest rate ½ percent, to 4.75%.

3. Domestic Politics. The 110th Congress convened with Democratic majorities in both chambers for the first time since 1994, with the House of Representatives led by Rep. Nancy Pelosi (D, CA), the first woman Speaker of the House. Some Democratic-sponsored measures passed handily, including an increase to the federal minimum wage and new ethics rules, but Bush exercised his veto on others, notably a stem cell research bill, a measure on Iraq, and a bill to expand health care coverage for children.

The Bush Administration faced several political crises, including the March 6 conviction of vice-presidential aide I. Lewis "Scooter" Libby and controversy over the firing of federal prosecutors in 2006. Several key members of the administration, including Attorney Gen. Alberto Gonzales and presidential advisor Karl Rove, resigned within weeks of each other in Aug. 2007. Candidates for the Democratic and Republican nominations for president in 2008 staked out positions on issues, especially the war in Iraq, that were unlikely to be resolved under the Bush administration.

4. Europe. France and Britain underwent leadership changes for the first time in more than 10 years. Nicolas Sarkozy, a member of France's conservative party, took office May 16, succeeding Pres. Jacques Chirac, who had served for 12 years. British Prime Min. Tony Blair resigned June 27 after more than a decade in office; Gordon Brown, who had won leadership of Blair's Labour party in May, succeeded him. Two days after Brown became prime minister, British police thwarted two terrorist car bombs set to go off in central London. Two men, believed to be associated with al-Qaeda, crashed an SUV into the main terminal at Scotland's Glasgow Airport June 30, and Britain raised its terrorism threat alert to its highest level for several days.

5. Product Recalls. Consumer confidence sank as multiple high-profile products were recalled in 2007. Thousands of pets were thought to have died after eating pet food that had been made with tainted Chinese wheat flour; 60 million cans and pouches of food were recalled. Mattel Inc. recalled 21 million Chinese-made toys in Aug. and Sept., but later took responsibility for design defects in a majority of the recalled toys. Other imported products manufactured or packaged in China, such as toothpaste and seafood, were also subject to multi-million dollar recalls.

6. Global Warming. The Intergovernmental Panel on Climate Change (IPCC) Feb. 2 released *Climate Change 2007*, its latest review of climate-related scientific research. The panel called evidence supporting global warming "unequivocal" and said that it was 90 percent likely that human activities, such as fossil fuel consumption, were largely responsible. Additional reports in Apr. and May projected the global impact that climate change could have over the course of the century, by creating water shortages, decreasing crop yields, and increasing the risk of extinction for many plant and animal species.

7. Nuclear Programs. North Korea agreed Feb. 13 to cease its nuclear programs in exchange for an international aid package. Under the deal—reached with the U.S., China, Japan, Russia, and South Korea—North Korea would shut down its main nuclear facility and readmit nuclear inspectors. A second part to the agreement, announced Oct. 3, set out a specific timetable for complete denuclearization.

In violation of United Nations resolutions, Iran continued to enrich uranium for its nuclear program, which many members of the international community believed was ultimately intended for use in weapons; the UN imposed additional sanctions March 24 in response. Iran announced Aug. 26 that it had developed a "smart bomb" that would be used "against our enemies when the time comes."

8. Virginia Tech Shooting. In the worst school shooting in U.S. history, 33 people, including the shooter, were killed Apr. 16 at Virginia Tech in Blacksburg, VA. Seung-Hui Cho, a student at the university, opened fire in a campus dormitory and in a classroom building before committing suicide. A state panel later criticized the university for not addressing Cho's mental health problems before the tragedy, and for not responding quickly enough to notify students and secure the school after the shooting began.

9. Myanmar. The Myanmar (Burma) military junta cracked down on a burgeoning antigovernment movement, violently breaking up demonstrations and killing at least 9 people (according to the state-run media) Sept. 27. Antigovernment protests had escalated throughout the month, sparked by an Aug. cut in gas subsidies that more than doubled prices in the impoverished nation. Demonstrations culminated Sept. 24 when an estimated 100,000 protesters, led by some 20,000 Buddhist monks and nuns, marched against the military junta in Yangon (Rangoon). Pres. George W. Bush announced stricter Treasury Dept. sanctions for Myanmar at the opening of the UN General Assembly Sept. 25.

10. Bridge Disaster. An arterial highway bridge over the Mississippi River in Minneapolis, MN, collapsed during evening rush hour Aug. 1, killing 13 people and dropping over 50 cars into the river. Part of Interstate 35W, the 8-lane bridge was being repaired at the time of its collapse. In 2005, the federal government had called the bridge "structurally deficient" and in possible need of replacement.

THE WORLD
AT A GLANCE

Number Ones

Nation most dependent on **nuclear energy** . . . . France, 78.1% of electricity is nuclear-generated *(p. 109)*

World's most popular **tourist destination** . . . . France, 79.1 million arrivals in 2006 *(p. 79)*

Top-selling **passenger car** in the U.S. . . . . Toyota Camry, 448,445 (5.8% of car sales in 2006) *(p. 75)*

Most popular **luxury car color** in the U.S. . . . . Black, 22% of 2006 model year cars *(p. 75)*

Top-selling **light truck** in the U.S. . . . . Ford F-Series, 744,996 (8.5% of truck sales in 2006) *(p. 75)*

Most popular **light truck color** in the U.S. . . . . White, 25% of 2006 model year trucks *(p. 75)*

Nations with the most legally-mandated **paid days off** per year. . . . . Austria and Portugal, 35 days *(p. 82)*

Nation hosting the most **refugees** . . . . Pakistan, 2.2 million, mostly from Afghanistan, in 2006 *(p. 850)*

Nation that produced the most **refugees** . . . . Afghanistan, 3.3 million in 2006 *(p. 850)*

Top country for U.S. **foreign adoptions** . . . . China, 6,520 in 2006 *(p. 159)*

Nation that gave the most **foreign development aid**,
    as a percentage of its gross national income . . . . Sweden, 1.03% in 2006 *(p. 850)*

Recipient of most U.S. **military financing** . . . . Israel, $2.3 billion in 2006 *(p. 125)*

World's largest **bank company** . . . . UBS AG Zurich, $1.96 trillion in assets, 2006 *(p. 57)*

Fastest **roller coaster** in the world . . . . Kingda Ka, 128 mph (Six Flags Great Adventure, Jackson, NJ) *(p. 83)*

Airline that carried the most passengers. . . . . American Airlines, 98.1 million in 2006 *(p. 81)*

Busiest **airport** outside of the U.S.,
    by passenger traffic . . . . Heathrow Airport (London, UK), 67.5 million passengers in 2006 *(p. 81)*

Busiest **U.S. airport** by passenger traffic . . . . Hartsfield-Jackson Airport (Atlanta, GA), 84.8 million passengers in 2006 *(p. 81)*

Busiest **U.S. port** . . . . Port of South Louisiana, 212.2 million tons handled in 2005 *(p. 70)*

Most-visited **shopping website** . . . . eBay, 79.8 million visitors in July 2007 alone *(p. 366)*

Most prescribed class of **drugs** in U.S. doctor's offices . . . . Antidepressants, 107 million prescriptions in 2005 *(p. 135)*

Surprising Facts

The Rolling Stones had four of the 10 **highest-grossing North American concert tours** since 1985. *(p. 239)*

Car companies spent more on advertising than any other industry in 2006: $19.8 billion. *(p. 245)*

Swimmer Michael Phelps set **five new world records** in 5 days in 2007. *(p. 966)*

U.S. farmers grew **726.7 million pounds of tobacco** in 2006—less than half the quantity of tobacco grown in 1990. *(p. 88)*

Of the estimated 24.5 million **internally displaced persons** (IDPs) worldwide in 2006, 70% to 80% were women and children. *(p. 850)*

The United Kingdom had $303.2 billion worth of **direct investments** in the U.S. in 2006, the highest of any country. *(p. 72)*

One of the **deadliest disasters in human history** was the 1918-19 flu pandemic, which killed 50 to 100 million people worldwide. *(p. 308)*

Two U.S. **governors accept no salary** for their office: California's Arnold Schwarzenegger and New Jersey's Jon Corzine *(p. 442)*

In 2007, scientists successfully resuscitated microbes that had been **frozen in ice for a million years**. *(p. 265)*

Former Negro League pitcher Silas Simmons, believed to have been the **longest-living professional baseball player** ever, died in 2007 at age 111. *(p. 31)*

California's gross domestic product in 2006 was $1.73 trillion. If it was its own country, it would have the **10th largest economy in the world**, smaller than Russia's but larger than Brazil's. *(p. 577)*

If all circulating U.S. dollars and coins were equally distributed among the nation's population, **everyone would receive $2,688.** *(p. 52)*

Harvard University Library holds 15.6 million volumes, second in the U.S. only to the Library of Congress in the size of its collection. *(p. 404)*

Changing Times

1910-2005: Total **fat consumption** per capita in the U.S. was 37.7 pounds in 1910. It climbed to a whopping 85.5 pounds by 2005. *(p. 87)*

1940-2005: The **average monthly Social Security** check in 1940 was for $18.29 ($255.19 in 2005 dollars); in 2005, the average monthly check was for $915.71. *(p. 378)*

1950-2006: The United States' share of **total world motor vehicle production** fell from 75.7% in 1950 to 16% in 2006—though it still ranked as the second leading motor vehicle producing nation in 2006 (behind Japan). *(p. 73)*

1955-2005: The number of **cars registered in the U.S.** rose from 52.1 million to 136.6 million, a 161.9% increase over 50 years. *(p. 76)*

1975-2006: The U.S. posted a **trade surplus of $9.1 billion** in 1975. By 2006, the U.S. trade balance had slipped to a deficit of $817.3 billion. *(p. 68)*

1990-2005: **China's annual energy consumption** grew 249% in the past 15 years, from 27 quadrillion Btu in 1990 to 67 quadrillion Btu in 2005. *(p. 105)*

1990-2006: The amount Americans spent annually on **casino gambling** ballooned 610%, from $11.5 billion in 1990 to $81.6 billion in 2006. *(p. 46)*

2002-2006: The number of **cross-utility vehicles** (lighter, smaller SUVs) sold in the U.S. rose from 1.2 million in 2002 to 2.4 million in 2006, an increase of 94.7%. *(p. 75)*

1997-2006: The number of **violent crimes** in the U.S. declined from 1.6 million in 1997 to 1.4 million in 2006, a drop of 13.3%. *(p. 111)*

2007 World Almanac News Quiz

1. What South American nation was struck Aug. 15 by an 8.0 magnitude earthquake that killed more than 500 people?

- a. Bolivia
- b. Peru
- c. Colombia
- d. Brazil

2. On July 4, which city won its bid to host the 2014 Winter Olympics?

- a. PyeongChang, S. Korea
- b. Munich, Germany
- c. London, UK
- d. Sochi, Russia

3. Which contender for the Republican presidential nomination paused while giving a speech to the National Rifle Association (NRA) to take a phone call from his wife?

- a. Rudy Giuliani
- b. Mitt Romney
- c. John McCain
- d. Barack Obama

4. The U.S. Women's soccer team had been undefeated in 51 games when it was shut out, 4-0, in the World Cup semi-finals Sept. 27. What team defeated them?

- a. North Korea
- b. Norway
- c. Brazil
- d. Mexico

5. What company sued Apple Jan. 10 over the use of its iPhone trademark?

- a. Microsoft
- b. Cisco
- c. Verizon
- d. Oracle

6. Which July debate did three of the four major Republican candidates decline to attend, citing "scheduling conflicts"?

- a. PBS All-American Forum
- b. CNN/YouTube debate
- c. Telemundo debate
- d. MSNBC debate

7. On July 15, what Major League Baseball team experienced its 10,000th franchise loss (the first time a professional U.S. sports team had reached that milestone)?

- a. St. Louis Cardinals
- b. Philadelphia Phillies
- c. Detroit Tigers
- d. New York Yankees

8. A record number of women held office in the U.S. government in 2007. When the 110th Congress convened in January, how many women were in the House and Senate?

- a. 75 in the House / 15 in the Senate.
- b. 50 in the House / 10 in the Senate.
- c. 102 in the House / 14 in the Senate.
- d. 74 in the House / 16 in the Senate.

9. What does the "I" in former White House aide I. Scooter Libby's name stand for?

- a. Irving
- b. Ishmael
- c. Isaac
- d. Ingmar

10. Gerald Ford was the fourth former U.S. president to reach 90 years of age. Which president was the first?

- a. Ronald Reagan
- b. Herbert Hoover
- c. John Adams
- d. Harry Truman

11. David Beckham accepted a $250 million contract and left which European team to play soccer for the Los Angeles Galaxy?

- a. Real Madrid
- b. Manchester United
- c. AC Milan
- d. Liverpool Football Club

12. Which nation became the first in Africa to legalize same-sex marriage?

- a. Egypt
- b. Zambia
- c. South Africa
- d. Algeria

13. With Tiger Woods's PGA Championship victory Aug. 12, how many major tournaments had he won in his career?

- a. 10
- b. 13
- c. 5
- d. 15

14. Which Japanese prime minister—the first born after World War II—announced his resignation Sept. 12, after less than a year in office?

- a. Yasuhiro Nakasone
- b. Yasuo Fukuda
- c. Ichiro Suzuki
- d. Shinzo Abe

15. Which U.S. big-city mayor announced in June that he was leaving the Republican Party to become an independent?

- a. Richard M. Daley (Chicago, IL)
- b. Michael Bloomberg (New York, NY)
- c. Antonio Villaraigosa (Los Angeles, CA)
- d. Tom Leppert (Dallas, TX)

16. British Prime Minister Tony Blair stepped down June 27 after how many years in office?

- a. 12
- b. 9
- c. 15
- d. 10

17. Who became the new secretary general of the United Nations, on Jan. 1?

- a. Ban Ki-moon
- b. U Thant
- c. Kofi Annan
- d. Kim Jong-il

18. Who did Columbia University president Lee Bollinger describe as a "petty and cruel dictator," before yielding the podium to him at a Sept. 24 public forum?

- a. Syrian president Bashar al-Assad
- b. Iranian president Mahmoud Ahmadinejad
- c. Zimbabwe president Robert Mugabe
- d. Russian president Vladimir Putin

19. What musical act won 5 Grammys Feb. 12, including record, song, and album of the year?

- a. Red Hot Chili Peppers
- b. The Black Eyed Peas
- c. U2
- d. Dixie Chicks

20. France and the UK gained, respectively, a new president and prime minister in mid-2007. Who were they?

- a. Ségolène Royal and Gordon Brown
- b. Jacques Chirac and John Major
- c. Nicolas Sarkozy and Gordon Brown
- d. Nicolas Sarkozy and Margaret Thatcher

Scoring Guide: You . . .	
0-5: snooze through news	**11-15:** are a news junkie
6-10: skim the headlines	**16+:** should send us your resume

Answers: 1 b, 2 d, 3 a, 4 c, 5 b, 6 a, 7 b, 8 d, 9 a, 10 c, 11 a, 12 c, 13 b, 14 d, 15 b, 16 d, 17 a, 18 b, 19 d, 20 c

The Almanac in the Internet Age

With respect to the long and distinguished history of the *Encyclopædia Britannica*, *Funk and Wagnalls New Encyclopedia*, and other great, traditional encyclopedia-makers, I have a confession to make:

I love Wikipedia.

Which is not to say that I think it is the ultimate reference tool; I wouldn't use it as my only source of facts, any more than I would get all my news from *The Daily Show*, or eat only at McDonald's. Wikipedia has many shortcomings: the article on Britney Spears is as long as the one on St. Augustine; articles on contentious subjects like the Israeli-Palestinian conflict may be edited thousands of times an hour, often by irrational and grammatically-challenged editors; and as Wikipedia's audience grows, so does the number of pranksters who intentionally add false information to its articles.

Still, the project is undeniably fascinating—perhaps less for its content than as a sign of a larger phenomenon: who knew there were so many frustrated, amateur reference book editors in the world? The editors of *The World Almanac* know all too well that making reference books is, as the old saying goes, like making sausage: you may appreciate the results, but you don't want to watch the process. So it has been a perpetual source of amazement to see so many people willing, for free, to make the sausage: to participate in the laborious work of producing an accurate encyclopedia article or statistical chart.

It's doubtful that the average Wikipedia contributor follows the same rigorous process of researching, reviewing, fact-checking, cross-referencing, and copy editing that goes into each edition of *The World Almanac* (or any other traditional reference book). But thanks to teams of editors who spotlight and clean-up articles, a great many Wikipedia articles are—if lacking in polish, balance, and style—surprisingly accurate, and often quite excellent sources of links to better-written and more authoritative original sources. In its role as a filter for the wide, wild Internet, it has few equals, especially when it comes to current or particularly obtuse topics.

So what place does a book like *The World Almanac* have in the Internet age, when you can type a celebrity's name into Google or Wikipedia and summon up not only his or her birthplace and date, but also a complete filmography and photos from that celebrity's most recent Caribbean vacation?

The Almanac in History

I'll admit, it's a challenge. Mention that you work for *The World Almanac* these days, and there's a fair chance that you'll get this response:

"Wow, so you write about, like, planting crops and weather predictions, right?"

We don't, of course, but the confusion with more traditional-style almanacs is understandable. *The World Almanac* has been published almost continuously for 140 years, and it is the descendant of almanacs many hundreds of years older than that. The first almanac published in America was *An Almanac for New England* for the year 1639, and from that time through the 18th century, almanacs sold more copies each year than any other type of book in the country.

Most almanacs of this era were collections of miscellaneous information, including weather predictions, proverbs, jokes, practical advice, and household tips. The best-known of them is, of course, Benjamin Franklin's *Poor Richard's Almanac*, published from 1733 to 1758. For its first 15 years, Franklin's almanac contained only 24 pages: six pages of introductory matter, a page for each month of the year, and another six pages of general information. In its last 10 years of publication, it expanded to a whopping 36 pages. But Franklin used those few pages to refine the traditional almanac into a new type of literature, a printed work that would serve as a practical, educational, and inspirational companion throughout the year.

Unfortunately, when people hear the world "almanac" today, this is still the type of book they think of. We are often confused with our venerable cousin, *The Old Farmer's Almanac*—probably the last of the great traditional almanacs still in print—but *The World Almanac* and others have evolved into something different.

The Almanac Under Fire

The almanac, as a literary form and a reference source, has faced challenges before. For example, Henry III of France decreed in 1579 that almanac makers could no longer include predictions of the future in their books, because those predictions had grown increasingly gruesome and frightening—especially in predicting the deaths of kings.

As recently as 2003, almanacs were singled out by the FBI as containing information that terrorists could use "to assist with target selection and pre-operational planning." Police were warned to watch for people carrying almanacs, especially if they were "annotated in suspicious ways." For anyone with a passing familiarity with *The World Almanac* and its ilk, the alert was laughable, and served mainly to show how little most people know about the contents of a modern almanac. Most of the information singled out as potentially dangerous—data about tall buildings, bridges, and other important structures—appears in *The World Almanac* as brief entries detailing locations, heights, and spans. All these facts are culled from public sources, and are almost certainly of more use to students, architecture buffs, and crossword puzzle fanatics than to terrorists.

Even more recently, we've suffered at the hands of Stephen Colbert, whose solo television debut in 2005 featured an extended rant against not only reference books—"All fact, no heart"—but against facts in general. Even though the assault comes from a character who is merely a parody of bellicose TV punditry, the accusation seems to mirror some real sentiments in society that favor "truthiness" over truth—or, to borrow a term from his second season, "factiness" over facts. As editors of "The Book of Facts," we obviously take this to heart.

So how does a book like *The World Almanac* survive, in a world where terabytes of information are a mouse-click away, where reference books can be tagged as suspicious and dangerous tools, and where people rely more on "gut feelings" than rational, informed discussion? By doing much the same thing it has done for the past 140 years: by filtering through massive quantities of data to bring its readers only the most essential statistics, in readable format; by delivering authoritative, reliable facts and practical information; and by avoiding, as much as is humanly possible, the modern urge to editorialize and manipulate data to support a particular point of view.

In compiling each new edition, we stumble across countless surprises and unexpected revelations about the world; a casual flip through the pages of this volume should let you follow that same journey of surprise and discovery. As we close this 140th anniversary edition (and turn immediately to begin work on the 141st), we offer our thanks for your support, and our sincere hope that you will continue to find *The World Almanac* to be a trusted, impartial, reliable, and entertaining resource for facts, whatever your interests may be.

– C. Alan Joyce
and the Editors of *The World Almanac 2008*

2008 ELECTION GUIDE

2008 Election Overview

As in 2000 and 2004, the 2008 election season is shaping up to be another closely-fought contest, with one major difference: for the first time since 1952, there will be no sitting or former president or vice president running on either party's ticket, leaving the field open for an incredibly diverse array of candidates. Although the Democratic party made significant gains in the last midterm election, House, Senate, and governor races are likely to be close and hotly contested.

Past pre-election editions of the *World Almanac* have contained profiles of major presidential candidates, but because this year's field is so volatile and likely to be narrowed down very early in 2008, this edition instead offers a more general overview of what is at stake in this election. It also provides a cross-referenced guide to using the World Almanac itself as a daily source for background, historical context, and up-to-date, unbiased facts about some of the most important issues in the 2007-08 campaigns.

Major Parties

Republican Party
(Rep. Nat'l Committee)
310 First Street, SE
Washington, DC 20003
202.863.8790
www.gop.com

Democratic Party
(Dem. Nat'l Committee)
430 S. Capitol St. SE
Washington, DC 20003
202-863-8000
www.democrats.org

Green Party (U.S.)
1711 18th Street NW
Washington, DC 20009
202-319-7191
www.gp.org

Libertarian Party
2600 Virginia Ave, NW
Suite 200
Washington, DC 20037
800-353-2887
www.lp.org

Caucuses and Primaries: New Rules Transform "Super Tuesday"

In the U.S., before a candidate can run for president as the official representative of a major political party, they must prove themselves in state caucuses, primary elections, and finally (if ceremonially) at their party's national convention.

For decades, mid-February polls in Iowa and New Hampshire provided an early reading on the viability of each candidate's campaign, and typically had a major influence on the rest of the campaign season. Candidates who performed well in those states' polls tended to receive more support and funding from other states; candidates who did poorly tended to withdraw from the race. In 1988, however, 16 states moved their primary election dates to a single day ("Super Tuesday") in March, diluting the influence of the early caucuses—and prompting Iowa and New

Hampshire to reschedule their votes even earlier in the year.

This one-upmanship continued through 2007, and by mid-year a majority of states had pushed their primary election date to February or earlier. In 2008, the Iowa caucus and New Hampshire primary are scheduled for Jan. 3 and 19, respectively. A handful of other states have scheduled their primaries for January, and at least 20 states have scheduled (or at press time, were in the process of scheduling) their primaries for Feb. 5 ("Super Duper Tuesday"). As a result, the 2008 primary season is likely to be one of the shortest in history. A convincing win on Feb. 5 could all but guarantee a single candidate's party nomination, since a majority of delegates to the national conventions are chosen in states that hold primaries.

Scheduled Primary Debates
(as of Oct. 15, 2007)

Republican
November 6, 2007: Ames, IA
November 28, 2007: St. Petersburg, FL
January 5, 2008: Johnston, IA
January 10, 2008: Myrtle Beach, SC
January 30, 2008: Los Angeles, CA

Democratic
November 15, 2007: Las Vegas, NV
December 10, 2007: Los Angeles, CA
January 6, 2008: Johnson County, IA
January 15, 2008: Las Vegas, NV
January 31, 2008: Los Angeles, CA

Caucus and Primary Dates, 2008

Republican

Jan. 5: WY[1]
Jan. 14: IA[1]
Jan. 15: MI
Jan. 19: NV[1], SC
Jan. 22: NH
Jan. 29: FL
Feb. 1: ME[1]
Feb. 5, "Super Duper Tuesday": AL, AK, AZ, AR, CA, CO, CT, DE, GA, IL, MN, MO, MT[3], NC[3], NJ, NY, ND, OK, PA[3], TN, UT, WV[2]
Feb. 9: KS[1], LA, WA[1]

Feb. 12: DC, MD, VA
Feb. 19: WA, WI
Feb. 24: PR
March 4: MA, OH, RI, TX, VT
March 11: MS
May 6: IN
May 13: NE, WV
May 17: HI[2]
May 20: KY, OR
May 27: ID
June 3: NM, SD
June 28: NE[2]

Democratic

Jan. 14: IA[1]
Jan. 15: MI
Jan. 19: NV[1]
Jan. 22: NH
Jan. 29: FL, SC
Feb. 5, "Super Duper Tuesday": AL, AK[1], AZ, AR, CA, CO[1], CT, DE, GA, ID[1], IL, KS[1], MN[1], MO, NC[3], NJ, NM, NY, ND[1], OK, PA[3], TN, UT
Feb. 9: LA, NE[1], VI[1], WA[1]

Feb. 10: ME[1]
Feb. 12: DC, MD, VA
Feb. 19: HI[1], WI
March 4: MA, OH, RI, TX, VT
March 8: WY[1]
March 10: AS[1]
March 11: MS
May 3: Guam[1]
May 6: IN
May 13: NE, WV
May 20: KY, OR
June 3: MT, SD

(1) Caucus. (2) Convention. (3) Considering change to Feb. 5, as of Oct. 15, 2007.

National Conventions, 2008

May 23-26, 2008: Libertarian, Denver, CO
July 10-13, 2008: Green, Chicago, IL

August 25-28, 2008: Democratic, Denver, CO
September 1-4, 2008: Republican, Saint Paul, MN.

Key Election Dates

(Note: Deadline to register to vote in most states is approximately 30 days before primary or general election dates)

November 4, 2008: Election Day, all 50 states and the District of Columbia.

December 15, 2008: Members of U.S. Electoral College meet in each state to cast votes for President and Vice President.

January 6, 2009: Electoral votes officially tallied before both Houses of Congress.

January 20, 2009: Inauguration Day.

The 2008 Elections at a Glance: State by State

This table provides a major-party breakdown of U.S. House seats, Senate seats, and governorships that will be up for re-election in 2008. It also offers a quick reference to likely "swing states" in the 2008 presidential election. *Margin of victory* columns show the number of popular votes that separated the winning party from the runner-up; that margin is also represented as a percentage of all popular votes cast in the state. Thus, in Alabama, the Republican ticket won by 482,461 votes, or 25.6% of all popular votes cast in the state, marking it as a fairly secure Republican stronghold.

States where the margin of victory was 5% or less are in **boldface**; a relatively small shift in candidate preference could have easily swung the state election—and in some cases, the national election—in the opposite direction (for example, the Republican ticket won Ohio by only 2.1% of votes cast in the state.) Many of these states, which could easily swing either way in the next election, were likely to be closely contested throughout the campaign.

| | Presidential Election, 2004 | | | | | Seats up for re-election in 2008 | | | | | | |
	Total popular votes cast	D Margin of victory Pop. votes (% of state total)	Electoral Votes D	Electoral Votes R	R Margin of Victory Pop. votes (% of state total)		House D	House R	Senate D	Senate R	Governor D	Governor R
AL	1,883,449			9	482,461 (25.6%)	AL	2	5		1		
AK	312,598			3	79,864 (25.5%)	AK		1		1		
AZ	2,012,585			10	210,770 (10.5%)	AZ	4	4				
AR	1,054,945			6	102,945 (9.8%)	AR	3	1	1			
CA	12,421,852	1,235,659 (9.9%)	55			CA	34	19				
CO	**2,130,330**			9	**99,523 (4.7%)**	CO	4	3		1[1]		
CT	1,578,769	163,662 (10.4%)	7			CT	4	1				
DE	375,190	28,492 (7.6%)	3			DE		1	1		1	
DC	227,586	181,714 (79.8%)	3			DC						
FL	**7,609,810**			27	**380,978 (5.0%)**	FL	9	16				
GA	3,301,875			15	548,105 (16.6%)	GA	6	7		1		
HI	429,013	37,517 (8.7%)	4			HI	2					
ID	598,447			4	228,137 (38.1%)	ID		2		1[1]		
IL	5,274,322	545,604 (10.3%)	21			IL	10	9	1			
IN	2,468,002			11	510,427 (20.7%)	IN	5	4				1
IA	1,506,908			7	10,059 (0.7%)	IA	3	2	1			
KS	1,187,756			6	301,463 (25.4%)	KS	2	2		1		
KY	1,795,882			8	356,706 (19.9%)	KY	2	4		1		
LA	1,943,106			9	281,870 (14.5%)	LA	2	5	1			
ME	740,752	66,641 (9.0%)	4			ME	2			1		
MD	2,386,678	309,790 (13.0%)	10			MD	6	2				
MA	2,912,388	732,691 (25.2%)	12			MA	10		1			
MI	**4,839,252**	**165,437 (3.4%)**	17			MI	6	9	1			
MN	**2,828,387**	**98,319 (3.5%)**	9[2]			MN	5	3		1		
MS	1,152,145			6	226,887 (19.7%)	MS	2	2		1		
MO	2,731,364			11	196,542 (7.2%)	MO	4	5				1
MT	450,445			3	92,353 (20.5%)	MT	1	1	1		1	
NE	778,186			5	258,486 (33.2%)	NE		3		1[1]		
NV	**829,587**			5	**21,500 (2.6%)**	NV	1	2				
NH	**677,738**	**9,274 (1.4%)**	4			NH	2			1	1	
NJ	3,611,691	241,427 (6.7%)	15			NJ	7	6	1			
NM	**756,304**			5	**5,988 (0.8%)**	NM	1	2		1[1]		
NY	7,391,036	1,351,713 (18.3%)	31			NY	23	6				
NC	3,501,007			15	435,317 (12.4%)	NC	7	6		1	1	
ND	312,833			3	85,599 (27.4%)	ND	1					1
OH	**5,627,908**			20	**118,601 (2.1%)**	OH	7	11				
OK	1,463,758			7	455,826 (31.1%)	OK	1	4		1		
OR	**1,836,782**	**76,332 (4.2%)**	7			OR	4	1		1		
PA	**5,769,590**	**144,248 (2.5%)**	21			PA	11	8				
RI	437,134	90,719 (20.8%)	4			RI	2		1			
SC	1,617,730			8	276,275 (17.1%)	SC	2	4		1		
SD	388,215			3	83,340 (21.5%)	SD	1		1			
TN	2,437,319			11	347,898 (14.3%)	TN	5	4		1		
TX	7,410,765			34	1,694,213 (22.9%)	TX	13	19		1		
UT	927,844			5	422,543 (45.5%)	UT	1	2				1
VT	312,309	62,887 (20.1%)	3			VT	1					1
VA	3,198,367			13	262,217 (8.2%)	VA	3	8		1[1]		
WA	2,859,084	205,307 (7.2%)	11			WA	6	3			1	
WV	755,887			5	97,237 (12.9%)	WV	2	1	1		1	
WI	**2,997,007**	**11,384 (0.4%)**	10			WI	5	3				
WY	243,428			3	96,853 (39.8%)	WY		1		2		
Total	**122,295,345**		**251**	**286**	**3,012,166 (4.9%)**	**Total**	**233**	**202**	**12**	**22**	**6**	**5**

(1) Sitting senator announced plans to retire at end of current term. (2) One Minnesota elector voted for Democratic vice-presidential candidate Sen. John Edwards (D, NC) for both president and vice president.

Election Issues

These page are a quick reference guide to facts about selected issues that are likely to figure prominently in the 2008 election, drawn from the pages of *The World Almanac 2008*. Page numbers in *italics* refer to pages that offer more in-depth statistical information and historical context for each topic.

Key Domestic Issues in 2008

Jobs and Poverty

The percent of Americans below the poverty level hit a record low in 2000, at 11.3%. It has hovered between 12% and 13% since then. In 2006, the average income for a family of four living in poverty was $20,614. It was $10,294 for an individual. *(pp. 44-45)*

- In June 2007, the unemployment rate for blacks in the U.S. was 9.0%—more than double the rate for whites, and nearly triple the rate for Asians. *(p. 97)*
- The percent of elderly workers in the U.S. labor force plummeted throughout the 20th century, but has been climbing since 1990—rising from 16.3% of men and 8.6% of women 65 and older in that year, to 19.8% of men and 11.5% of women in 2005. *(p. 102)*
- 42.1% of children in a family without a father were living in poverty in 2006, versus 16.9% with a father present. However, the percentage living in poverty is still lower than in years prior to 2000. *(p. 45)*
- In 2006, nearly 1 in 4 blacks in the U.S. were living in poverty. *(p. 44)*

Social Security and Welfare

Entitlement programs—including Social Security, Medicare, and other programs that guarantee benefits provided certain requirements are met—are one of the federal government's biggest expenses. The federal government spent more on Social Security in 2006 than on any other single government program ($548.5 bil). Since 1996 legislation overhauled the welfare system to create Temporary Assistance for Needy Families (TANF), a federal program offering block grant assistance to states, welfare is no longer an entitlement program. *(pp. 53, 490)*

- An estimated 46.6 million Americans received Social Security or Supplemental Security income in 2006. The trust funds that support Social Security may not be able to support the current monthly benefit levels as the population ages *(pp. 377-378)*.
- 37.2 million Americans, or 12.4% of the population, were age 65 and older in 2006. *(p. 598)*
- 71.5 million Americans, or 19.7% of the population, will be age 65 or older by 2030. *(p. 598)*
- For Americans born after 1960, the age at which full retirement benefits are available has been raised to 67. *(p. 374)*
- In 1997, the first year of the TANF program, there were 10.9 million recipients of TANF benefits; in 2005, there were only 4.5 mil recipients. But in 1997, the program spent only $19.0 bil; in 2005, the TANF program cost $25.6 bil, despite having less than half the number of recipients. *(p. 380)*
- In 1997, the average TANF monthly expenditure per family was $402. By 2005, the average was up to $1,110. *(p. 380)*

Crime

Though violent crimes in the U.S. increased in 2006 for the second year in a row, violent crime rates were still much lower than they were a decade earlier. Between 1997 and 2006, the number of violent crimes nationwide dropped 13.3%. The number of property crime (burglary, larceny-theft, and motor vehicle theft) decreased for the 4th consecutive year in 2006. *(p. 110-11)*

- The national violent crime rate in 2006 was 473.5 per 100,000 residents. The South had the highest rate of any region (547.5). The rate of violent crime was lowest in Maine—only 115.5 offenses per 100,000 state residents. *(p. 112)*
- Drug abuse violations accounted for more arrests (1.4 million, or 13.2% of all arrests) than any other category of crime in 2006. *(p. 114)*
- Alaska experienced the largest increase in its prison population, with a 9.4% increase between 2005 and 2006. Louisiana had the highest incarceration rate in mid-2006—835 prisoners for every 100,000 residents. *(p. 114)*
- Between 1977, when the death penalty was reinstated, through the end of 2006, 1,057 people were executed. Lethal injection was the most common method of execution. Only 12 states did not allow capital punishment. *(p. 113)*
- 8,380 hate crimes were reported in 2005. 38.2% of all reported hate crime offenses, and more than half of all offenses motivated by race, were anti-black. 68.5% of reported hate crime offenses motivated by religion were anti-Jewish. *(p. 115)*

Education

Fourth graders in the U.S. scored an average of 518 on an international math assessment test in 2003, below the level of fourth graders in many other industrialized countries. Eighth graders performed similarly on a math assessment test administered the same year. *(p. 397)*

- In the 2004-05 school year, about 92% of the country's 53.2 million kids ages 5-17 attended public elementary (pre-kindergarten through grade 8) or secondary (grades 9-12) schools in the U.S. *(p. 395)*
- As of fall 2005, Vermont had the lowest student-teacher ratio in the nation; the state's public school system had 10.5 students for every teacher, but also had one of the lowest public school populations (94,600). In contrast, Utah employed on average one teacher for every 23 public school students, the highest ratio of any state. *(p. 396)*
- In 2005-06, students attending private universities typically paid $18,862 in tuition and fees, for an increase of about 502.6% over the past 25 years. *(p. 400)*
- Of all bachelor's degrees conferred since 1990, more have gone to women than men. *(p. 401)*

Environment

The U.S. accounts for more carbon dioxide emissions from fossil fuel consumption than any other nation. Although the U.S. has maintained this number-one ranking since 1980, China's emissions have risen 224%. *(p. 281)*

- The total amount of U.S. greenhouse gas emissions from human activities—not including carbon dioxide absorbed by forests or other means—increased 16.3% between 1990 and 2005. Carbon dioxide accounted for 83.9% of these emissions. *(pp. 281, 283)*
- The warmest year on record (through 2006) was 2005, with an average global temperature of 58.1°F. *(p. 284)*
- As of Aug. 2007, there were 1,301 hazardous waste sites in the U.S. New Jersey had the most, with 117, 114 of which qualified for Superfund financing. *(p. 284)*
- As of Sept. 2007, 1,921 plant and animal species found in the U.S. had been designated as threatened and/or endangered by the Fish and Wildlife Service. *(p. 287)*
- The amount spent by the federal government on conservation and land management increased from $6.2 bil in 2005 to $7.8 bil in 2006—still lower than the $9.8 bil spent each year from 2002-04. *(p. 53)*

Key International Issues in 2008

Energy and Oil

The U.S. produced (71.03 quadrillion Btu) and consumed (99.87 quadrillion Btu) more energy than any other nation in 2006 *(p. 104)*.

- About 84.8% of the energy Americans consume comes from fossil fuels. 6.8% of the energy Americans consume is renewable. *(p. 104)*
- Crude oil accounted for 12.1% of all U.S. imports in 2006. The U.S.'s biggest suppliers of crude oil are Canada and Mexico, followed closely by Saudi Arabia, Venezuela, and Nigeria. *(pp. 68, 108)*

Immigration

There were an estimated 11.6 million illegal immigrants in the U.S. in 2006. Of that number, about 56.9% were born in Mexico. 1.3 million legal immigrants were admitted to the country in 2006. *(pp. 597, 601)*

- Almost a quarter (24.5%) of the illegal immigrant population resided in California. An estimated 14.2% lived in Texas and 8.5% were in Florida. *(p. 601)*
- In 2006, four states—Hawaii, California, Texas, and New Mexico—were "majority-minority," i.e., minorities made up more than 50% of the population. *(p. 588)*
- About 12.1% of the U.S. population in 2005 were foreign born; almost one-third of the foreign-born population claimed Mexico as their country of origin. People from China, the second most common country of origin, made up only 4.9% of the foreign-born population. *(p. 597)*

Trade

The U.S. trade surplus in 1975 was $9.1 billion; by 2006 the trade balance had fallen to –$817.3 billion, the largest deficit to date. While the U.S. made $1 trillion in exports, it spent $1.9 trillion on imports. *(p. 68)*

- In 2006, vehicles were one of the largest categories of U.S. exports, valued at $83.5 billion; yet the U.S. imported far more vehicles from other countries—valued at nearly $212 billion. General Motors and Ford posted net losses in 2006, the only companies among the 25 largest in the U.S. to do so. *(pp. 48, 68)*
- In 2006, the U.S. trade deficit with Canada was $71.8 billion, and with Mexico, it was $64.3 billion. *(p. 69)*
- Foreign direct investments in the U.S. totalled $1.8 trillion in 2006. The U.S. had $2.4 trillion worth of direct investments abroad. *(p. 72)*

Afghanistan

Located in southwestern Asia, mountainous Afghanistan has known war for more than three decades. *(pp. 468, 744-45)*

- Afghanistan is one of the world's poorest countries, with a yearly gross domestic product estimated at only $800 per person. The government of Pres. Hamid Karzai has been unable to stamp out the poppy crop, which provides about 93% of the world's illicit opium. *(pp. 745, 848)*
- Because of war, millions of people have fled Afghanistan to neighboring Pakistan. Many Afghan refugees now live in Pakistan, Iran, and Russia. *(p. 850)*
- The U.S. still has more than 24,800 troops in Afghanistan. But the Taliban may be making a comeback. *(pp. 24, 121)*

Iran

The Islamic Republic of Iran shares borders with Afghanistan, Pakistan, and Iraq. *(pp. 468, 783)*

- 89% of Iranians are Shiite Muslims, following the Shi'a branch of Islam. *(p. 719)*
- One of the world's leading petroleum producers, Iran has reserves of at least 132 bil barrels of oil and 965 tril cu ft of natural gas. Sanctions prevent the U.S. from importing oil from Iran. *(p. 107)*
- Tensions between Iran and the U.S. stem, in part, from the hostage crisis of 1979-81, when followers of the Ayatollah Khomeini held 52 Americans captive. *(p. 487)*
- The U.S. has accused Iran of aiding Shiite militias in Iraq *(pp. 16, 17)* and supporting Lebanese Hezbollah fighters against Israel *(p. 786)*. Pres. Mahmoud Ahmadinejad has defied UN sanctions against Iran's nuclear program. *(pp. 19, 20)*

Iraq

With reserves estimated at 115 bil barrels of crude oil, Iraq has long been one of the top petroleum producers in the Middle East. *(pp. 108, 468)*

- Since 1991 the U.S. has fought two wars in Iraq. The 1st war, led by Pres. George H.W. Bush, ousted Iraq from Kuwait. The 2nd war, launched by his son, Pres. George W. Bush, ousted the regime of Iraqi dictator Saddam Hussein. *(pp. 131, 682, 684)*
- Pres. Bush declared May 1, 2003, that major combat operations in Iraq were over. But a civil war between Shiites and Sunnis, fighting between Shiite factions, and attacks against coalition forces by Sunni insurgents have engulfed Iraq in a complex, bloody conflict. *(pp. 12-28, 492, 719)*
- Since 2003 the U.S. has spent at least $450 bil on the war in Iraq, and more than 3,700 U.S. service members have been killed there. *(pp. 128, 784)*
- Many war critics embraced the recommendations of the Iraq Study Group *(p. 14)* In Sept. 2007, Gen. David Petraeus reported positive military results from a U.S. troop "surge" in Iraq. *(pp. 26, 27)* But progress toward political reconciliation remains slow *(p. 26)*

North Korea

Since the late 1940s, North Korea and South Korea have divided Asia's Korean Peninsula. *(p. 469)*

- The U.S. has 27,114 troops stationed on the Korean Peninsula, although that number has been declining. *(p. 121)*
- Communist North Korea remains isolated and poor, with a yearly GDP of only $1,800 per person. But its military ranks among the world's largest, with 1.1 mil active-duty troops and 4.7 mil reserves. *(pp. 124, 790)*
- In 2002, Pres. Bush said North Korea was part of an "axis of evil." *(p. 491)* But recently, in 6-nation talks, the U.S. has been willing to negotiate with the North Koreans *(p. 17)*. UN sanctions *(p. 12)* helped pressure North Korea to begin shutting down its nuclear program. *(p. 24)*

China

China is an ancient country in Asia, with a history spanning thousands of years. Today, the People's Republic of China has a population of over 1.3 bil, or about 1 of every 5 people on earth. *(pp. 468-69, 760-61, 847)*

- China has recently come under fire for exporting dangerous or defective products. *(pp. 4, 25)*
- U.S. relations with China's Communist government improved dramatically under Pres. Nixon, who was the 1st U.S. president to visit China. *(pp. 486, 524)*
- With a gross domestic product of over $10.1 tril, China ranks 2nd only to the U.S. Its economy has been growing at a rate of 10.7% yearly, but GDP per capita is only $7,700, much lower than that of the U.S. *(pp. 760, 848)*
- China also ranks 2nd to the U.S. as both a producer and consumer of energy *(p. 105)*.

CHRONOLOGY OF EVENTS

Reported Month by Month, Oct. 14, 2006, to Oct. 12, 2007

October 14-31, 2006

National

U.S. Population Hits 300 Million—Based on calculations by the U.S. Census Bureau, the U.S. population reached a total of 300 mil on the morning of Oct. 17; only China (1.3 bil) and India (1.1 bil) had more people. The U.S. had attained a population of 100 mil in 1915 and 200 mil in 1967. An accelerated rate of immigration contributed to the more rapid climb in population in recent decades.

Dow Jones Average Tops 12,000—The Dow Jones Industrial Average, an index of 30 major stocks, closed at record-breaking levels throughout October. On Oct. 19 the Dow closed above 12,000 for the first time, at 12,011.73. The Dow set a new all-time high on Oct. 26 at 12,163.66.

Prior to October 2006, the Dow's record high was 11,722.98, on Jan. 14, 2000. The current leg of the stock rebound had begun in July 2006 when a decline in crude oil futures, resulting in lower gasoline prices, stimulated investing. Despite the Dow's new milestone, broader stock market indexes remained below their all-time highs.

Ex-Enron CEO Sentenced to 24 Years in Prison—Jeffrey Skilling, the former CEO of Enron Corp., was sentenced, Oct. 23, to 24 years and 4 months in prison following his May 2006 conviction for fraud, conspiracy, and insider trading. Judge Simeon Lake, in U.S. District Court in Houston, also ordered that Skilling's $60 mil in assets be liquidated, with $45 mil going into a restitution fund for victims of Enron's bankruptcy. Skilling was appealing the sentence.

Congressman's Messages to Boys Are Investigated—The U.S. House of Representatives and the FBI began investigations into electronic messages sent by Rep. Mark Foley (R, FL) to teenage boys who had served as pages on Capitol Hill. On Oct. 24 House Speaker J. Dennis Hastert (R, IL) and Rep. Thomas Reynolds (NY), chairman of the National Republican Congressional Committee, testified behind closed doors before the House Ethics Committee. The committee also heard from House staff members and others who had made conflicting public statements concerning what House leaders knew about Foley's activities and when they knew it. Foley had abruptly resigned his House seat after ABC News first revealed the sexually explicit content of some of the messages.

New Jersey Court Backs Equal Rights for Gay Couples—New Jersey's 7-member Supreme Court concluded unanimously in the case of *Lewis v. Harris* Oct. 25 that, under the state constitution, gay couples were entitled to all the rights and benefits accorded to opposite-sex married couples. Four of the judges held that the state legislature must decide whether gay unions would be designated as marriage or by some other term. Three dissenting judges argued that any legal status other than marriage for same-sex couples would be discriminatory.

International

UN Imposes Sanctions on North Korea—Following North Korea's announcement that it had conducted an underground test of an atomic weapon, the UN Security Council Oct. 14 approved unanimously a resolution imposing sanctions on that country. The Council demanded that North Korea abandon its nuclear weapons program and suspend ballistic missile development, and that it return to multilateral talks with its neighbors and the U.S. The resolution barred trade with North Korea in materials that could be used to make weapons of mass destruction or military equipment capable of delivering them. It also asked governments to inspect goods going in and out of North Korea. The U.S. Oct. 16 confirmed that North Korea had tested a nuclear weapon, based on radioactive air samples, but said that it had been unusually small, with a blast of less than one kiloton.

Situation in Iraq Brings Calls for New Strategy—As evidence mounted that the U.S.-led coalition's effort to control violence in Iraq was failing, demands grew in the U.S. for a new strategic approach. The U.S. military acknowledged Oct. 19 that a 12-week campaign in Baghdad against insurgents and sectarian militias had failed to reduce violence. The Mahdi Army, a militia led by radical Shiite cleric Moqtada al-Sadr, briefly seized the city of Amara on Oct. 20, and then yielded it to the Iraqi army.

Pres. George W. Bush, at a press conference Oct. 25, insisted the U.S. was still "winning" the war, but said he was "not satisfied" with the situation in Iraq and that he was willing to adjust tactics. U.S. military deaths in October 2006 totaled 105, the highest monthly figure since October 2005.

General

Frontier Nun Canonized by Pope—Mother Theodore Guerin (1798-1856), a French-born nun who established schools and orphanages on the American frontier, was canonized along with 3 others by Pope Benedict XVI Oct. 15. Guerin established Saint Mary-of-the-Woods College, a women's college in Indiana, in 1841; by the time of her death she had established many more schools and orphanages throughout the state. Others canonized included a priest and a nun from Italy and a bishop from Mexico.

St. Louis Cardinals Win First World Series in 24 Years—The St. Louis Cardinals won their 10th franchise World Series, 4 games to 1, defeating the Detroit Tigers 4-2 in Game 5 in St. Louis Oct. 27. It was the Cardinals' first World Series win since 1982. The Cardinals had an 83-78 regular-season record, the poorest of any team that had ever gone on to win the Series. Tony La Russa managed the Cards, and shortstop David Eckstein was named most valuable player.

Mission to Repair the Hubble Space Telescope—NASA announced Oct. 31 that it would send a space shuttle to repair the 16-year-old Hubble Telescope. Without repair, the Hubble was expected to function for no more than a few more years. After the 2003 *Columbia* disaster, when the shuttle burned up on re-entry, a mission to fix the orbiting observatory was deemed too risky. With new shuttle safety mechanisms in place, NASA changed course and ordered a *Discovery* mission to repair Hubble in 2008. The crew will add two new cameras, replace batteries, and upgrade sensors and stabilizing equipment, extending the life of the telescope through at least 2013.

November 2006

National

Democrats Win Control of Both Houses of Congress—Democrats made big gains in the Nov. 7 midterm elections, taking majority control of the U.S. Senate and House and picking up 6 state governorships. Public displeasure with the Iraq war appeared to be the single most important factor in the election, but other hotly debated issues included corruption, immigration, and the uneven economic recovery.

In Ohio, incumbent Republican Sen. Mike DeWine lost to Democrat Sherrod Brown. In Pennsylvania, Democrat Bob Casey Jr., son of a popular former governor, easily defeated 2-term Sen. Rick Santorum (R), a leading conservative voice in the Senate. In Rhode Island, Sheldon Whitehouse (D), a former state attorney general, defeated Sen. Lincoln Chafee, a Republican moderate.

In a narrow, 7,000-vote upset in Virginia, Democrat Jim Webb, former Navy secretary under Pres. Ronald Reagan, edged out Republican incumbent Sen. George Allen. Allen had been damaged by remarks, made on the campaign trail in August, that were widely perceived as racially insensitive. In Montana, Jon Tester (D), president of the state senate and a moderate on some social issues, thwarted a 4th-term bid by Sen. Conrad Burns (R), who was hurt by his ties to convicted lobbyist Jack Abramoff. In Missouri, Democratic state auditor Claire McCaskill (D) unseated Sen. Jim Talent (R) in another close race.

Running as an independent and as a supporter of the Iraq war, Sen. Joseph Lieberman was reelected in Connecticut, defeating Ned Lamont, an antiwar candidate who had won the Democratic primary. Lieberman said he would caucus with the Democrats. U.S. Rep. Bernie Sanders, a self-described "democratic socialist" elected to the Senate from Vermont as an independent, said he would also ally himself with the Democrats. The Republicans held the open Senate seat in Tennessee, where former Chattanooga Mayor Bob Corker Jr. defeated U.S. Rep. Harold Ford Jr. In all, the Democrats, along with Democrat-leaning independents, came away with a 51-49 majority in the Senate.

Without losing a single seat, the Democrats took about 30 House seats from the Republicans. Democratic gains were scattered across the country, led by 4 in Pennsylvania and 3 each in Indiana and upstate New York. In 3 districts where Republican House members—Tom DeLay (TX), Bob Ney (OH), and Mark Foley (FL)—had resigned because of scandals, Democratic candidates won. Other Republicans touched by scandal—Richard Pombo (CA), Don Sherwood (PA), and Curt Weldon (PA)—ran for re-election but were defeated. Jim Leach (IA), Charles Bass (NH), and Nancy Johnson (CT) were among long-time GOP stalwarts who lost. The Democrats ended up with 231 House seats to the Republicans' 202. Two seats were still undecided at month's end.

In gubernatorial races, there were sweeping victories for state Atty. Gen. Eliot Spitzer (D) in New York and U.S. Rep. Ted Strickland (D) in Ohio. Other Democratic wins came in Arkansas, Colorado, Maryland, and Massachusetts, where former U.S. assistant attorney general Deval Patrick became the nation's 2nd black governor since Reconstruction. As a result of the election, 28 governors were Democrats, and 22 were Republicans.

A wide range of ballot propositions were considered in 37 states. Voters in 7 states approved state constitutional amendments banning same-sex marriages. In Arizona, however, that prohibition failed narrowly, the first time any state referendum had rejected a gay marriage ban. South Dakota voters overturned a controversial new state law that forbade almost all abortions. In Missouri, a state constitutional amendment to protect stem-cell research was ratified narrowly. Michigan voters passed a measure restricting affirmative action. Six states approved minimum-wage increases, and 8 states enacted restrictions on state and local government powers of eminent domain.

Sec. of Defense Donald Rumsfeld Resigns—Sec. of Defense Donald Rumsfeld, whose handling of the Iraq war had been criticized by supporters as well as opponents of the war, resigned Nov. 8, the day after the midterm elections. In making the announcement, Pres. Bush said that both he and Rumsfeld agreed that it was time for "a fresh perspective" on Iraq. Bush introduced Robert Gates, a former Director of Central Intelligence, as his nominee to succeed Rumsfeld.

New Leaders for the New Congress—Washington, DC, was in a state of transition throughout November. The outgoing 109th Congress returned for a post-election "lame duck" session with the Republicans still in a majority. In bipartisan gestures, Pres. Bush met Nov. 9 with House Democratic leader Nancy Pelosi and Nov. 10 with Senate Democratic leader Harry Reid. On Nov. 14, the Democratic Senate caucus chose Reid to be Senate majority leader in the new Congress. Sen. Richard Durbin (IL) was named majority whip.

House Democrats made history Nov. 16 when, as expected, they elected Pelosi as their candidate for Speaker of the House in the 110th Congress, placing her in line to become the first female House Speaker in U.S. history. Pelosi backed John Murtha (PA), a longtime ally and an outspoken advocate of U.S. withdrawal from Iraq, for the position of majority leader, but the caucus, by 149-86, chose Steny Hoyer (MD). James Clyburn (SC), an African-American, was elected majority whip.

Republican senators Nov. 15 chose Mitch McConnell (KY) to be minority leader; Bill Frist (TN), the incumbent majority leader, had not sought re-election to his Senate seat. By a margin of one vote, the Republicans chose Trent Lott (MS) as minority whip; Lott previously served as majority leader from 1996 to 2001, and then as minority leader until 2002, when he resigned after making remarks that some viewed as sympathetic to the South's history of racial segregation.

House Republicans chose their leaders Nov. 17. Speaker J. Dennis Hastert (IL), criticized for his handling of the Mark Foley scandal, had announced that he would not seek a leadership position. Republicans elected John Boehner (OH) as minority leader and Roy Blunt (MO) as minority whip. Adam Putnam (FL), 32, was elected conference chairman.

International

Iraq's Ex-Pres. Saddam Hussein Sentenced to Death—Saddam Hussein, who had been ousted as president of Iraq during the U.S.-led invasion in 2003, was unanimously sentenced Nov. 5 to death by hanging. The 5-judge Iraqi High Tribunal found him guilty in connection with the 1982 execution of 148 men and boys in the Shiite town of Dujail. The brutal reprisal had come after a failed attempt on Hussein's life. Seven other men were on trial for the same crime. Three—including Hussein's half-brother, Barzan Ibrahim al-Hassan al-Tikriti—were also sentenced to death. One defendant was sentenced to life in prison, three others received 15-year terms, and one defendant was acquitted.

Pres. Bush Travels to Asia—Pres. George W. Bush focused heavily on North Korea in discussions with Asian leaders, during a trip that began in Singapore Nov. 16. Arriving in Vietnam Nov. 17, he toured Ho Chi Minh City and met with Vietnamese leaders. At the 21-nation Asia Pacific Economic Cooperation (APEC) forum in Hanoi, Nov. 18-19, Bush lobbied unsuccessfully for tougher action against North Korea. The APEC did, however, call on North Korea to end its nuclear weapons program. In Jakarta, the capital of Indonesia, Bush met Nov. 20 with Pres. Susilo Bambang Yudhoyono.

Ortega, Former Foe of U.S., Regains Power in Nicaragua—Daniel Ortega, the former president of Nicaragua, whom the U.S. sought to overthrow in the 1980s, was elected president Nov. 5 with only 38% of the total vote. He had been one of the leaders of the Sandinista movement that overthrew Nicaragua's government in 1979. The U.S. had provided financial backing to Contra rebels who sought to topple Ortega's Marxist junta. Elected president in 1984, Ortega was voted out in another election in 1990, and failed in 2 subsequent elections to reclaim the presidency.

Bomber Kills 42 Military Trainees in Pakistan—A suicide bomber Nov. 8 detonated explosives killing 42 Pakistani soldiers who were being trained at a base in Dargai, Pakistan; local Taliban insurgents claimed responsibility. The worst such attack in the country's history, it was believed to be a reprisal for an Oct. 30 missile attack by the Pakistani government on a suspected terrorist training facility, which resulted in at least 80 deaths.

Israeli Shelling Kills 19 in Gaza—Sporadic violence continued along the northern edge of the Gaza Strip. On Nov. 8, at least 11 Israeli artillery shells hit the town of Beit Hanoun, killing 19 Palestinians and wounding 50. On Nov. 11 the U.S. vetoed a UN Security Council resolution condemning the attack. The General Assembly, by a 156-7 vote Nov. 17, officially "deplored" Israel's military offensive in Gaza and called for an end to all violence between Israel and Palestine.

Civilian Death Toll Rises in Iraq; U.S. Continues to Reassess Strategy—The Iraq interior ministry said Nov. 2 that 1,289 Iraqi civilians had been killed in October. A UN report released Nov. 22 put the total number of Iraqis killed in October at 3,709, a monthly record. In the Shiite district of Sadr City, in Baghdad, Nov. 23, car bombs and an artillery shell killed more than 200 and wounded many more.

Gen. John Abizaid, head of the U.S. Central Command and leader of U.S. forces in the Middle East, told the Senate Armed Services Committee Nov. 15 that the Bush administration had not sent enough troops to Iraq after Pres. Saddam Hussein was ousted in 2003. He also said that more U.S. troops would be needed to train Iraqi troops. Abizaid opposed setting a timetable for U.S. withdrawal, saying it would limit the flexibility of U.S. commanders in Iraq.

Iraq and Syria re-established diplomatic relations, which were broken in 1982 when Syria backed Iran in its war with Iraq, Nov. 21 when Syria's foreign minister visited Baghdad.

A total of 70 U.S. troops were killed in Iraq throughout November. Six U.S. soldiers were killed in action in Afghanistan.

Former Russian Spy Dies from Poisoning in London—Former Russian KGB intelligence agent Aleksandr Litvinenko, who had sought asylum in Great Britain in 2000, died Nov. 23 of radiation poisoning. Doctors confirmed Nov. 24 that the substance used to poison Litvinenko was polonium-210, a radioactive substance that in tiny doses can be lethal. They stated that Litvinenko had probably been poisoned on Nov. 1. The former agent, a critic of the Russian government, had been looking into the murder in October of a Russian journalist. Relatives said that from his deathbed, Litvinenko had accused Pres. Vladimir Putin of Russia of being behind his poisoning. By Nov. 30, traces of radioactivity had been found at 12 sites around London.

Lebanese Cabinet Minister Assassinated—Gunmen killed Lebanese Minister of Industry Pierre Gemayel and one of his bodyguards in Beirut Nov. 21. Gemayel, whose father had been president, was the latest in a series of anti-Syrian leaders to be assassinated. Pres. Bush called for an international investigation of the murder and said Nov. 21 that the U.S. would support Lebanon's efforts to resist attempts by Syria, Iran, and others to destabilize the country.

General

Evangelical Leader Resigns, Admits "Immorality"— Pastor Ted Haggard, president of the National Association of Evangelicals, resigned Nov. 2 after a former male prostitute made public accusations against him. Haggard, who also resigned as pastor of the 14,000-member New Life Church in Colorado Springs, CO, had denied the claims made by Mike Jones, who said that Haggard had paid him for sex about once a month for 3 years, and that Haggard had also bought methamphetamines through him. Jones said that he revealed his relationship with Haggard because the pastor had publicly endorsed a Colorado ballot proposal to ban same-sex marriage in the state. In a letter to his congregation Nov. 5, Haggard, who is married and has 5 children, called himself "a deceiver and a liar." The gay-marriage ban passed Nov. 7 with a 55% majority.

December 2006
National

John Bolton Resigns as U.S. Envoy to UN—Pres. George W. Bush announced Dec. 4 that he had accepted John Bolton's resignation as U.S. ambassador to the UN. Bolton had taken the position as a recess appointment by Pres. Bush Aug. 1, 2005, and it was apparent that the new Democratic-controlled Senate would not make his appointment permanent. Known for his blunt approach, Bolton had been a resolute supporter of Bush administration policies and a harsh critic of the UN bureaucracy.

Gates Confirmed as Sec. of Defense—The U.S. Senate confirmed Robert Gates as Secretary of Defense Dec. 6, in a 95-2 vote. During confirmation hearings before the Senate Armed Services Committee a day earlier, Gates was asked if the U.S. was winning the war in Iraq, to which he responded "No, sir." He later added that the war was not yet being lost either. Sworn in on Dec. 18, he flew to Iraq Dec. 20 to assess the military situation there. He said that senior military commanders were concerned that sending more U.S. troops to Iraq would delay the day when the Iraqi government would assume responsibility for its security.

Last Voting in House Elections Gives Democrats a 31-Seat Gain—With the conclusion of several runoff elections, the Democrats emerged from the midterm elections with 233 U.S. House seats, with 202 going to Republicans. This was a net gain of 31 seats for the Democrats. Rep. William Jefferson (D, LA) won a runoff Dec. 9 to retain his seat. He had gained notoriety when the FBI, while investigating his financial dealings, found $90,000 in his refrigerator. In a runoff in Texas Dec. 12, Rep. Henry Bonilla (R) lost his seat to Ciro Rodriguez (D).

Edwards, Kucinich Enter Presidential Race—Rep. Dennis Kucinich (D, OH), who had sought the Democratic presidential nomination in 2004, said Dec. 12 that he would try again in 2008. A staunch liberal, he had opposed the invasion of Iraq from the beginning and had been a vocal opponent of U.S. conduct of the war. Former Sen. John Edwards (NC), the 2004 Democratic nominee for vice president, announced his 2008 candidacy on Dec. 28.

U.S. Agents Crack Down on Illegal Immigrants—On Dec. 12, more than 1,000 Immigration and Customs Enforcement (ICE) agents raided six Swift & Co. meatpacking plants in Greeley, CO; Grand Island, NE; Cactus, TX; Hyrum, UT; Marshalltown, IA; and Worthington, MN. They arrested 1,282 undocumented workers. The raid was part of a 10-month investigation into identity theft by illegal immigrants. No charges were filed against the company, but 65 immigrants were charged with criminal violations related to document fraud.

International

Chávez Reelected in Venezuela—Pres. Hugo Chávez of Venezuela was reelected on Dec. 3, winning 63% of the vote. Chávez had long criticized Pres. Bush and U.S. foreign policy. In power since early 1999, Chávez has sought to lead a coalition of left-wing governments in Latin America and to tighten ties with the government of Iran.

Commission Calls Situation in Iraq "Grave and Deteriorating"; Saddam Hussein Is Executed—A bipartisan commission, the Iraq Study Group, concluded Dec. 6 that the military and political situation in Iraq was "grave and deteriorating." In its long-awaited report, the commission noted the pervasive violence and corruption, the inadequacy of Iraqi security forces, and the "sectarian prism" through which Iraqi leaders saw the nation's problems. The bipartisan panel, established by Congress, was chaired by former Sec. of State James Baker III (R) and Former U.S. Rep. Lee Hamilton (D, IN).

The commission offered 79 recommendations for the U.S.-led coalition to create a stable and democratic Iraq, and recommended that the U.S. aim to withdraw all combat forces not necessary for force protection from Iraq by early 2008.

On Dec. 26, an Iraqi appeals court upheld a death sentence against Saddam Hussein for crimes against humanity. Iraqi officials moved quickly to carry out the sentence, and Hussein was hanged Dec. 30 in a Justice Ministry building in northern Baghdad. Shortly after the execution, in multiple attacks apparently carried out by Hussein loyalists, four car bombs in Shiite areas of Baghdad and a nearby town killed more than 70 people and wounded dozens more.

The U.S. military death toll in Iraq in December totaled 115, of whom more than 60% were killed by improvised explosive devices, or IEDs. The December figure brought the number of U.S. military deaths in Iraq to more than 3,000 since the war began.

Ex-Pres. Pinochet of Chile Dies—Gen. Augusto Pinochet, who had seized power in Chile in 1973 ruled the country for 17 years, died Dec. 10. During the bloody 1973 coup, the Pinochet junta had ousted a democratically elected left-wing regime; as many as 3,000 were killed, and many others disappeared. In recent years, authorities had charged Pinochet in connection with human rights abuses.

Iranian Moderates and Reformers Gain in Elections— Elections in Iran Dec. 15 strengthened the hand of reformers and moderates, at the expense of conservative clerics and Pres. Mahmoud Ahmadinejad. The voting was for local councils and the Assembly of Experts, which advises the country's supreme leader. At Amirkabir University in Tehran, Dec. 11, students had heckled Ahmadinejad, thrown firecrackers, and kicked his car in the first major open protest against the president.

On Dec. 23, the UN Security Council passed a resolution banning the import to or export from Iran of materials and technology needed for nuclear enriching or reprocessing activities or for the manufacture of atomic weapons and ballistic missiles. It also froze the financial assets of 12 Iranians and 10 institutions linked to the nuclear program.

Islamists Flee Somali Capital—The ongoing conflict in Somalia entered a new phase Dec. 27 when Islamists fled Mogadishu, the Somali capital, one day before troops from Somalia's transitional government and forces from neighboring Ethiopia took command of the city. The fall of Mogadishu capped a series of recent reverses for the Islamists, who had captured the capital in June 2006 and had governed there as the Supreme Islamic Courts Council.

4 Marines Charged With Murder of 24 Iraqi Civilians—Military prosecutors Dec. 21 charged 4 Marines with the murder of 24 Iraqi civilians in the village of Haditha in 2005. Four officers were charged with related dereliction of duty and failure to report accurate information about the deaths up the chain of command.

Gas Line Explosion Kills 260 in Nigeria—An explosion in a gasoline pipeline in Lagos, the capital of Nigeria, killed at least 260 people Dec. 26. Thieves had been tapping the pipeline, stealing gasoline to resell it.

General

Death of Princess Diana Found to Be an Accident—A British investigation, Operation Paget, concluded Dec. 14 that the death of Princess Diana in 1997 was an accident and that no conspiracy or foul play was involved. She and her boyfriend, Emad Mohamed (Dodi) al-Fayed and their driver, Henri Paul, were killed when their car crashed in a tunnel in Paris while they were being pursued by paparazzi. Former London Police Commissioner Lord Stevens headed the inquiry. The report said that the driver's blood alcohol level was 3 times the legal limit in France.

Episcopal Congregations Vote to Secede—A long dispute within the Episcopal Church over its attitude toward homosexuals led to a walkout of some congregations. The Episcopal Church is the U.S. branch of the 79-mil member worldwide Anglican Communion. Conservative Episcopalians had been displeased by the consecration in 2003 of an openly gay bishop in New Hampshire and by the celebration of same-sex weddings in some congregations. On Dec. 17, 2 large Virginia parishes and 7 smaller Virginia churches voted to pull out. In all, more than 40 congregations had seceded since 2003.

Former Pres. Gerald Ford Dies at 93—Gerald R. Ford, the 38th president of the United States, died on Dec. 26 at his home in Rancho Mirage, CA, at the age of 93. He had been hospitalized with pneumonia in January and had returned to the hospital in October. Pres. George W. Bush led the nation in tributes, praising Ford had for "his quiet integrity, common sense, and kind instincts." Ford lived longer than any other president, exceeding the lifespan of Ronald Reagan by 45 days.

Rape Charges Against Duke Athletes Are Dropped—Recently reelected Durham, NC, District Atty. Michael Nifong announced Dec. 22 that he was dropping rape charges against 3 former members of the Duke University lacrosse team. He said he would continue to press kidnapping and sexual offense charges against the 3. The accuser originally said she was attacked at a team party in March while performing as a stripper. On Dec. 21, the accuser said she could not testify with certainty that she was raped.

U.S. Economy at a Glance: Calendar Year 2006	
Unemployment rate	4.6%
Consumer prices (change over 2005)	+2.5%
Trade deficit	$763.6 bil
Dow Jones closing (year end)	12,463.15
Dow Jones highest close (Dec. 27)	12,510.57
Dow Jones lowest close (Jan. 20)	10,667.39
GDP (change over 2005)	+2.9%

January 2007

National

Former Pres. Gerald Ford Buried in Michigan—National and world dignitaries Jan. 2 attended a funeral ceremony in Washington's National Cathedral for former Pres. Gerald R. Ford. Pres. George W. Bush, former Pres. George H.W. Bush, former Sec. of State Henry Kissinger, and former NBC news anchor Tom Brokaw gave eulogies. Former presidents Jimmy Carter and Bill Clinton also attended. Ford was buried Jan. 3 at the Gerald R. Ford Presidential Museum in Grand Rapids, MI.

Congress Convenes With Democrats in Control—The 110th Congress met for the first time Jan. 4 with the Democrats holding majorities in both the Senate and House. The House elected Rep. Nancy Pelosi (D, CA) as Speaker. Pelosi is the first woman to hold the office. Sen. Harry Reid (D, NV) was elected majority leader of the Senate.

Absent from the Senate was Sen. Tim Johnson (D, SD), who had been hospitalized since Dec. 13, 2006, after suffering a life-threatening brain hemorrhage. His condition was upgraded from critical to fair on Jan. 9. Doctors reported Jan. 19 that Johnson, who retained his Senate seat, had begun receiving physical, occupational, and speech therapy.

Pelosi had pledged that the Democrats would take a number of actions within the first 100 working hours after assuming House control. The House approved Jan. 4, 430-1, new ethics rules forbidding its members from accepting gifts or paid travel from lobbyists. The new rules also required members to identify themselves when they modify legislation by inserting so-called earmarks, or spending for special pet projects for their districts. The Senate Jan. 18 adopted similar rules.

Bush Makes Changes in His Administration—With his popularity slipping to new lows, Pres. Bush made changes in his administration. He said Jan. 5 that Director of National Intelligence John Negroponte would become Deputy Secretary of State. Negroponte had held the intelligence post for just 19 months, from the time the position was created. Bush said he would nominate Adm. John McConnell (ret.), former head of the National Security Agency, to replace Negroponte.

Sec. of State Condoleezza Rice said that Zalmay Khalilzad, currently ambassador to Iraq, would replace John Bolton as ambassador to the UN. Ryan Crocker, ambassador to Pakistan, would replace Khalilzad.

On Jan. 9, Bush named Fred Fielding to succeed Harriet Miers as White House counsel. Fielding had previously served in the Nixon and Reagan administrations.

Early Candidates Declare for the 2008 Presidential Race—The 2008 presidential race nearly became a stampede as a number of aspirants, both front-runners and dark horses, made early overtures. On Jan. 3, outgoing Republican governor of Massachusetts Mitt Romney announced that he was filing papers to set up an exploratory committee to consider a run. Sen. Christopher Dodd (CT) said Jan. 11 that he would seek the Democratic nomination. Sen. Barack Obama (IL) announced Jan. 16 that he was forming an exploratory committee to consider a run for the Democratic nomination.

In an email to supporters Jan. 20, Sen. Hillary Rodham Clinton (D, NY) declared her intention to seek her party's nomination. Clinton, wife of former Pres. Bill Clinton, had just been reelected to the Senate. She was leading in national polls of Democrats for the nomination.

Sen. Sam Brownback (KS), a fiscal conservative, announced Jan. 20 that he would seek the Republican nomination. Gov. Bill Richardson (NM) joined the Democratic field on Jan. 21. On Jan. 28, former Gov. Mike Huckabee of Arkansas (R), a Baptist minister, announced that he was forming an exploratory committee. Rep. Duncan Hunter (CA), former chair of the House Armed Services Committee and a supporter of the war in Iraq, declared his candidacy Jan. 25 for the GOP nomination. Sen. Joe Biden (D, DE), chair of the Senate Foreign Relations Committee, announced Jan. 31 on NBC's *Meet the Press* that he would seek his party's nomination.

Bush Troop "Surge" Plan for Iraq Stirs Furor in Congress—Pres. Bush announced Jan. 10 that he was sending more than 20,000 additional troops to Iraq. Most would be deployed in Baghdad, the capital, in support of Iraqi security forces who were struggling to curtail sectarian violence there. Some 4,000 U.S. personnel would be sent to Anbar Province, where Sunni Muslim insurgents and terrorists affiliated with al-Qaeda had created chaos. Bush said he had told Pres. Nouri Kamel al-Maliki and other Iraqi leaders that they must meet certain benchmarks, including passing a new law on oil revenue sharing and providing more support for reconstruction projects, in order for U.S. aid to continue.

Pres. Bush's Iraq proposal, which was generally labeled a troop "surge," set off intense debate in Congress. Almost all Democrats opposed it, and Republicans were divided. Lt. Gen. David Petraeus, whom Pres. Bush had named to become the new top U.S. commander in Iraq, warned the Senate Armed Services Committee Jan. 23 that the situation in Iraq was "dire" but not hopeless. He strongly backed Bush's planned troop increase. The Senate on Jan. 26 unanimously confirmed the Petraeus appointment.

On Jan. 24 the Senate Foreign Relations Committee adopted, 12-9, a resolution opposing the troop surge. One Republican, Chuck Hagel (NE), joined the Democrats in favor of the resolution.

Court to Oversee Controversial Wiretapping—The Bush administration announced Jan. 17 that henceforth a court established under the 1978 Foreign Intelligence Surveillance Act (FISA) would have jurisdiction over the National Security Agency's wiretapping program. At issue was the monitoring of international communications between people in the U.S. and suspected terrorists. The Justice Dept. said that the FISA court could act with the necessary speed to approve wiretap warrants. The administration, which had previously rejected any such role for the FISA court, had come under heavy fire over the last year for its practice of warrantless wiretapping.

Ex-Congressman Sentenced to Prison—On Jan. 19, U.S. District Court Judge Ellen S. Huvelle in Washington sentenced former U.S. Rep. Bob Ney (R, OH) to 2.5 years in prison. He was the only member of Congress to plead guilty in connection with the Jack Abramoff lobbying scandal. Ney had admitted that he had taken bribes from Abramoff and others in exchange for official favors.

Trial of Ex-Aide to Vice President Begins—I. Lewis "Scooter" Libby, former chief of staff to Vice Pres. Dick Cheney, went on trial Jan. 23 in Washington, DC, on five counts of perjury and obstruction of justice. The investigation, by special prosecutor Patrick Fitzgerald, had been launched to determine who had revealed to the press that Valerie Plame Wilson was employed by the CIA as an undercover agent. Libby himself was not accused of leaking that information. His lawyer, Theodore Wells, asserted in his opening statement that Libby had been made a scapegoat by the White House to protect Karl Rove, Pres. Bush's top political adviser.

Former *New York Times* reporter Judith Miller testified Jan. 31 that Libby had spoken with her about Plame's CIA connections several weeks before Libby claimed to have heard Plame's name from another reporter.

Bush Gives Annual "State of the Union" Address—Pres. Bush delivered his State of the Union address to a joint session of Congress Jan. 23. It was the first time during his presidency that both houses were under Democratic control. Bush appealed to Congress to back his proposal to increase troop strength in Iraq, emphasizing that the U.S. could not afford to fail there. On the domestic front, Bush called for a 20% cut in gasoline consumption over the next 10 years. He also warned of "the serious challenge of global climate change," and appealed to Congress to reform immigration laws and work toward a balanced federal budget.

In the Democratic response to the address, Sen. Jim Webb (VA) criticized the president for "recklessly" waging war in Iraq, and urged that a formula be found "that will in short order allow our combat forces to leave Iraq."

International

U.S. Gunship Attacks Islamists in Somalia—On Jan. 1, forces of the Somali transitional government, joined by Ethiopian troops, captured Kismayo, an Indian Ocean port town and the last stronghold of Islamists who had ruled as the Supreme Islamic Courts Council. As the Islamists fled, U.S. Navy warships of the 5th Fleet, based in Bahrain, began patrolling the coast to prevent any from escaping by sea. After Kenya closed its northern border Jan. 3, the Islamists were trapped in the southern tip of Somalia.

In Mogadishu, the Ethiopians were met with violent demonstrations on Jan. 6. During the night of Jan. 7-8, a U.S. helicopter gunship attacked sites in southern Somalia. The U.S. Defense Dept. said Jan. 9 that al-Qaeda leaders were thought to be in the area, but a U.S. official said Jan. 11 that none of the main targets had been killed. Ethiopian troops began to withdraw from Somalia on Jan. 23.

Ban Ki-moon Becomes UN Secretary General—Ban Ki-moon of South Korea took office Jan. 1 as the UN's 8th secretary general. Ban succeeded Kofi Annan of Ghana, whose 2nd term expired the previous day. After receiving a master's degree in public administration from the Kennedy School of Government at Harvard Univ. in 1985, Ban went to work in the South Korean ministry of foreign affairs, and served as foreign minister from Jan. 2004 through Oct. 2006.

Bulgaria, Romania Join European Union—Membership in the European Union grew to 27 countries and 489 mil people Jan. 1 when Bulgaria and Romania joined. Also Jan. 1, Slovenia officially adopted the euro as its standard of currency, becoming the 13th EU country to do so.

Venezuelan President to Nationalize Major Companies—Pres. Hugo Chávez of Venezuela announced Jan. 8 that he would nationalize the country's telecommunications and electric power industries, which had been controlled by U.S. companies Verizon Communications Inc. and the AES Group, respectively. Chávez was sworn in for a 3rd presidential term Jan. 10. On Jan. 30, the Venezuelan congress voted to give Chávez the power to rule by decree over the next 18 months, allowing him to consolidate his control over the economy.

Fighting Continues in Iraq; 34,000 Iraqis Killed in 2006—The UN reported Jan. 16 that in 2006, about 34,000 Iraqis had met violent deaths as a result of fighting and terror attacks in Iraq. According to the U.S., another 2,800 civilians were killed in Jan.

U.S. Secretary of State Condoleezza Rice said Jan. 12 that Pres. Bush had authorized recent raids on Iranians in Iraq. The administration believed that Iran was providing weapons and training to Shiites in Iraq. At least 70 Iraqis were killed Jan. 16

when 2 car bombs and a suicide bomber struck at the main gate of Mustansiriya University as students were leaving classes. On Jan. 17, the Iraqi government announced that it had arrested several dozen leaders of a powerful Shiite militia, the Mahdi Army, led by anti-American cleric Moqtada al-Sadr. At least 88 Iraqis died Jan. 22 when 2 car bombs exploded in a Baghdad market. In a major battle near Najaf, in southern Iraq, Jan. 28, U.S. and Iraqi forces killed at least 250 enemy fighters. The U.S. military death toll for the month was 84.

General

Florida Upsets Ohio State for NCAA Football Title—After leading in the polls and computer ratings throughout the 2006 college football season, the Ohio State Buckeyes lost to the Florida Gators, 41-14, in the NCAA Division I-A title game in Glendale, AZ, Jan. 38. The Buckeyes' Ted Ginn returned the opening kickoff 93 yards for a touchdown, but Florida, led by quarterback Chris Leak, was ahead 34-14 at the half. Leak completed 25 of 36 passes for 212 yards and a touchdown. Florida, which finished 13-1, was coached by Urban Meyer.

Beckham to L.A. Galaxy—English soccer star David Beckham inked a five-year $250 mil deal with the L.A. Galaxy Jan. 11. The deal called for the 31-year-old Beckham, a midfielder with Real Madrid in Spain, to join the Galaxy in the summer after Madrid's season ended.

February 2007

National

Submitting Budget, Bush Sees an End to Deficits—Pres. Bush Feb. 5 presented a $2.9 tril federal budget to Congress for the 2008 fiscal year, which would begin Oct. 1, 2007. Based on his plan, he predicted an end to federal budget deficits by 2012, without any tax increases. In his budget, Bush proposed holding most domestic programs that were not related to security to an annual increase of 1%, below the rate of inflation. He proposed outright cuts in the budgets of 8 agencies, including the Dept. of Education. Other proposed cuts included reducing projected spending growth for so-called entitlement programs, namely Social Security, Medicare, and Medicaid.

Overall, the budget called for a 4.2% increase in total federal spending in fiscal year 2008. Proposed funding for the regular Department of Defense budget rose by 11% to $481.4 bil, and an additional $141.7 bil was proposed for the wars in Iraq and Afghanistan. Bush again urged that tax cuts adopted in 2001 and 2003, which were scheduled to expire in 2010, be made permanent.

Trial of Ex-Aide to Cheney Goes to Jury—Jurors in the trial of I. Lewis "Scooter" Libby began deliberations Feb. 21. Before that, they had heard testimony from several witnesses who contradicted what Libby had told federal investigators and a grand jury. NBC News *Meet the Press* anchor Tim Russert testified Feb. 7-8 that he did not speak with Libby about Valerie Plame, contradicting Libby's grand jury testimony that he had learned about her employment at the CIA from Russert. Libby's lawyers announced Feb. 13 that neither he nor Vice Pres. Dick Cheney would testify. U.S. District Judge Reggie Walton Feb. 26 dismissed a juror who had been exposed to outside information about the case.

International

Rival Palestinian Factions Form Unity Government—The ongoing, violent conflict between Palestinian political factions Fatah and Hamas gave way, at least temporarily, to a unity government Feb. 8. In Mecca, Saudi Arabia, an agreement was reached between Palestinian Authority Pres. Mahmoud Abbas, who was representing the Fatah political party, and Premier Ismail Haniya and Khaled Meshal, both leaders of Hamas. The Hamas-controlled Palestinian cabinet resigned Feb. 15 to make way for the unity government.

Fighting between the factions in the Gaza Strip Feb. 1-4 had left about 30 dead and 200 wounded. Representatives of the UN, the EU, the U.S., and Russia demanded Feb. 2 that Hamas recognize Israel's right to exist, adhere to previous agreements with Israel, and renounce violence.

UN Authorizes Peacekeeping Force in Somalia—The UN Security Council gave unanimous approval Feb. 20 to a resolution authorizing an 8,000-member African Union (AU) peacekeeping mission to ensure security and stability in Somalia. Uganda pledged to contribute about 1,500 peacekeepers, but commitments from other African countries lagged.

16 U.S. Intelligence Agencies Issue Iraq Intelligence Report—The U.S. Intelligence Community, comprising 16 U.S. intelligence agencies, issued a new National Intelligence Estimate (NIE) on Iraq Feb. 2. Four pages of the classified report were released to the public. The NIE noted that the complex conflict in Iraq involved a "civil war" between Shiites and Sunnis, fights between Shiite factions, attacks against coalition forces by the Sunni jihadist group al-Qaeda in Iraq and other insurgents, and violence perpetrated by criminal elements. The NIE doubted that the violence would be ended by the Iraqi government or military, or by U.S. troops, but warned that a quick U.S. departure would "almost certainly" bring more sectarian conflict.

Deadliest Insurgent Attack Since Invasion, Other Violence in Iraq—In one of the deadliest attacks since the U.S. invasion, a truck bomb exploded in a Baghdad market in a predominantly Shiite area Feb. 3, killing at least 135 and wounding more than 300. On Feb. 12, 4 car bombs at a market in a largely Shiite area of Baghdad killed 70 and wounded 120. Two similar bombs in a market Feb. 18 killed 60. In a brazen new tactic, insurgents Feb. 19 attacked an American combat outpost north of Baghdad, killing 2 soldiers and wounding 17. Insurgents also began using car and truck bombs to disperse chlorine gas, setting off two separate "dirty" bombs over two days, Feb. 21-22. A truck bomb exploded next to a Sunni mosque in Ramadi Feb. 24, killing at least 36. A bomber killed at least 50 near a Baghdad university Feb. 25.

On Feb. 21, British Prime Min. Tony Blair announced that up to 1,600 (of 7,100) British troops would be withdrawn from Iraq within a few months. Coalition forces in Iraq at the end of Feb. included 135,000 U.S. troops and 14,000 allied personnel; 79 U.S. troops were killed during the month.

Iran's Role in Iraq Conflict Scrutinized—U.S. officials in Baghdad Feb. 11 presented evidence suggesting that the Iranian government was supplying Iraqi Shiite militants with weapons. The officials displayed components of explosively formed penetrators, or EFPs, that could tear through armored vehicles and that had killed 170 Americans in Iraq. The officials noted that recent raids in Baghdad had netted 6 members, including a chief of operations, of the Quds Force, an elite unit of Iran's Revolutionary Guard. Gen. Peter Pace, chairman of the Joint Chiefs of Staff, said Feb. 13 that although some bomb components had been manufactured in Iran, no direct link could be made to the Iranian government.

Russian President Criticizes U.S. Foreign Policy—On Feb. 10 at the Munich Conference on Security Policy, Russian Pres. Vladimir Putin declared that the U.S. was destabilizing relations by "an almost uncontained hyper-use of military force." He warned that the U.S. was provoking a new nuclear arms race and, referring to NATO's continuing growth, asked "Against whom is this expansion directed?"

North Korea Agrees to Shut Down Nuclear Facility—North Korea, the U.S., China, Japan, Russia, and South Korea reached an agreement Feb. 13, in Beijing, China, whereby North Korea would "freeze" its main nuclear facility at Yongbyon and readmit inspectors from the International Atomic Energy Agency. These would be the first steps toward North Korea giving up its nuclear weapons program. In return, North Korea would get 50,000 tons of fuel oil as part of what would become a $400 mil package of energy and economic aid.

Vice President Targeted in Taliban Attack—On Feb. 27, a Taliban suicide bomber near the entrance to Bagram Air Base, the main U.S. military base in Afghanistan, killed at least 23 and wounded 24. The Taliban claimed that Vice Pres. Dick Cheney, who was a safe distance from the blast, was the target of the attack.

General

Scientists Blame Global Warming on Human Activity—Hundreds of scientists participating in a UN-sponsored study concluded—with more than a 90% certainty—in a Feb. 2 report that human activity was the main factor contributing to global warming. The Intergovernmental Panel on Climate Change said it was "very likely" that greenhouse gases, mostly created by the burning of fossil fuels, were the culprits. Their report projected that during the next century temperatures would rise by anywhere from 3.2-7.0°F (1.8-4.0°C)

and that sea levels would rise between 7 and 23 inches (18-59 cm). The scientists foresaw significant changes in agriculture, natural ecosystems, and precipitation patterns, as well as more intense natural disasters.

Indianapolis Colts Win Super Bowl XLI—The championship of the National Football League went to the Indianapolis Colts Feb. 4 when they defeated the Chicago Bears, 29-17, in a rainy Super Bowl XLI in Miami, FL. Colts quarterback Peyton Manning completed 25 of 38 passes for 247 yards and a touchdown, and Adam Vinatieri kicked 3 field goals. Colts coach Tony Dungy and Bears coach Lovie Smith were the first African American coaches to lead teams to the Super Bowl.

Astronaut Arrested—Navy Capt. Lisa Marie Nowak became the first active NASA astronaut to be charged with a felony, after a Feb. 5 incident in which Nowak reportedly drove from Houston, TX, to Orlando, FL, to confront Air Force Capt. Colleen Shipman, whom Nowak viewed as a rival for the affections of another astronaut, Navy Cmdr. William Oefelein. Nowak allegedly approached Shipman, who was in her car at Orlando International Airport, attacked her with pepper spray through a car window, and tried to pull her from the vehicle. Police said Nowak was carrying a mallet, knife, and BB gun. Nowak, 43 and the mother of three children, had made one trip into space, aboard the shuttle *Discovery* in 2006. She filed a written plea of not guilty in Orlando, FL, Feb. 13, to charges that included attempted kidnapping.

Anna Nicole Smith's Death Leads to Legal Tangle—Anna Nicole Smith, an actress, model, and tabloid figure, died at age 39 on Feb. 8. Her body was found in her room at the Seminole Hard Rock Café Hotel and Casino in Hollywood, FL. On Mar. 26, the Broward County (FL) medical examiner's office said that Smith had died from an accidental overdose of chloral hydrate and other sedatives.

Born Vickie Lynn Hogan in Houston, TX, Smith had married young and had a son, Daniel, before divorcing. She met and married the oil billionaire J. Howard Marshall II in 1994; she was 26 and he 89. After his death 14 months later, his son, E. Pierce Marshall, and Smith became locked in a legal battle over the estate that she won in the U.S. Supreme Court in May 2006.

Dixie Chicks Win 5 Grammy Awards—The Dixie Chicks, a country music trio, won 5 Grammys at the annual awards ceremony of the National Academy of Recording Arts and Sciences in Los Angeles, Feb. 11. They swept the top three awards, including record and song of the year (for "Not Ready to Make Nice") and album of the year (for *Taking the Long Way*). The song had been written in response to an incident in 2003 when lead singer Natalie Maines told a London audience that the band was "ashamed the president of the U.S. is from Texas." When the remark was publicized, group members received death threats and saw their airplay on radio plummet. The Red Hot Chili Peppers won 4 Grammys, including best rock album for *Stadium Arcadium*.

Director Martin Scorsese Finally Wins an Oscar—Film director Martin Scorsese, who had been nominated for a best director Academy Award 5 times, finally received the honor Feb. 25 for his film *The Departed*, which was also named the best picture of 2006 at the annual Academy Awards ceremony in Los Angeles, CA. Helen Mirren received the best actress award for her portrayal of Elizabeth II in *The Queen*. Forest Whitaker was named best actor for his role as the Ugandan dictator Idi Amin in *The Last King of Scotland. An Inconvenient Truth*, a documentary about global warming that spotlighted former Vice President Al Gore, won the Oscar for best documentary feature.

March 2007
National

Poor Care for Wounded Soldiers Results in Dismissals—Reports of dilapidated quarters and bureaucratic delays that affected hospital care at Walter Reed Army Medical Center in Washington, DC, resulted in the dismissal of leading military officials involved. The Walter Reed Center provides care for soldiers and veterans, many of whom are recovering from wounds sustained in combat.

Maj. Gen. George Weightman, the commander at Walter Reed, was removed from his post by the Army on Mar. 1. Lt. Gen. Kevin Kiley, the Army's surgeon general, was named temporary commander the same day. However, Defense Sec. Robert Gates Mar. 2 rejected the appointment of Kiley, because he had in the past ignored complaints about conditions at the hospital, which included problems with mold, mice, and roaches. Gates in turn appointed Maj. Gen. Eric Schoomaker as commander of the facility. In addition, Gates Mar. 2 removed Sec. of the Army Francis Harvey for mishandling reports concerning poor treatment of soldiers at Walter Reed.

On Mar. 6, Pres. George W. Bush announced that he had appointed former Sen. Bob Dole and former Sec. of Health and Human Services Donna Shalala to head a commission to review military health care. In a speech given at Walter Reed Mar. 30, Bush apologized for the shoddy conditions at the center and promised to "fix the problem."

Cheney's Former Chief of Staff Convicted of Perjury, Obstruction—A U.S. District Court jury in Washington, DC, found I. Lewis "Scooter" Libby, former chief of staff for Vice Pres. Dick Cheney, guilty Mar. 6 on 4 of 5 counts of perjury and obstructing justice. Though not charged with leaking the name of undercover CIA agent Valerie Plame Wilson, Libby was convicted of obstructing a federal investigation by making false statements about his conversations with reporters. Cheney, Mar. 6, and Bush, Mar. 7, said they were saddened by Libby's conviction.

Wilson testified Mar. 16 before a House committee, asserting that her name and identity were carelessly and recklessly abused by senior government officials in a way that "jeopardized and even destroyed entire networks of foreign agents, who in turn risk their own lives to provide the United States with needed intelligence."

U.S. Attorney General Snarled in Dispute Over Dismissals—U.S. Attorney Gen. Alberto Gonzales found himself drawn into a growing scandal over the firing of 8 U.S. attorneys in 2006. The Justice Dept. had claimed that the dismissals were generally based on performance issues and were not politically motivated.

Six of the dismissed attorneys—David Iglesias, John McKay, H. E. (Bud) Cummins, Carol Lam, Daniel Bogden, and Paul Charlton—appeared before House and Senate Judiciary committees Mar. 6. Iglesias testified that Sen. Pete Domenici and Rep. Heather Wilson, both New Mexico Republicans, had asked him about the status of an investigation targeting alleged corruption by New Mexico Democrats. According to Iglesias, both expressed dismay when told that the investigation would not be concluded before the Nov. 2006 elections. Congressional rules bar members from contacting prosecutors about investigations.

The Justice Dept. had previously acknowledged that Cummins, former U.S. attorney in Arkansas, had been removed to allow the appointment of Timothy Griffin, an assistant to Karl Rove. Griffin removed his name from consideration Feb. 15 because he felt that Democratic senators would block his confirmation.

Kyle Sampson, Gonzales' chief of staff, resigned Mar. 12. According to emails released by the Justice Dept., he had coordinated the dismissals with then White House counsel Harriet Miers. Another email revealed that Sampson had planned to install Griffin in Arkansas under a provision of the Patriot Act that would not require Senate confirmation.

Gonzales in a press conference Mar. 13 acknowledged that "mistakes were made" in the dismissal of the attorneys. He denied that he had been involved in any discussions about what was going on. Bush, Mar. 14, said that the removal of the attorneys had been appropriate but that the explanation of the dismissals before Congress had been mishandled.

Sampson, testifying before the Senate Judiciary Committee Mar. 29, said Gonzales had been briefed regularly for 2 years on the removal of federal prosecutors, and that Gonzales and Miers made the final decision on whether to dismiss the attorneys.

Justice Dept. Says FBI Abused Patriot Act—The inspector general of the Justice Dept. issued a report Mar. 9 asserting that the FBI had misused the Patriot Act while gathering information on thousands of U.S. citizens and foreign nationals. The internal audit found that the FBI had understated the use of national security letters, which were used to get phone records, email addresses, and other data without court approval, on people with suspected links to terrorism and espio-

nage. The audit also said that "exigent letters," used when the need for information was urgent, had often been used in nonemergency situations.

Edwards to Stay in Presidential Race Despite Wife's Cancer—Former Sen. John Edwards (D, NC) announced Mar. 22 that his wife, Elizabeth, had been diagnosed with a recurrence of breast cancer, which had first been discovered in 2004. He said he would continue to be a candidate for the 2008 Democratic presidential nomination.

Former Interior Dept. Official Pleads Guilty in Abramoff Scandal—On Mar. 23, Stephen Griles, deputy secretary of the Interior during Pres. Bush's first term, pleaded guilty to lying under oath to the Senate Interior Affairs Committee to cover up his ties with convicted lobbyist Jack Abramoff. Griles had told the committee in 2005 that he had "no special relationship" with Abramoff. However, since then an email from Abramoff surfaced, which referred to Griles as "our guy" at Interior. On June 26, Griles was sentenced to 10 months in prison.

Pentagon Rebukes 4 Generals in Pat Tillman Case—The Pentagon announced Mar. 26 the result of an internal investigation into the 2004 death in Afghanistan of U.S. soldier Pat Tillman, who had given up a pro football career to serve in the Army after the 2001 terror attacks. The report recommended that 9 officers be disciplined for not promptly disclosing that Tillman had been killed accidentally by other U.S. soldiers rather than by enemy fire.

International

Insurgents Target Pilgrims in Iraq—Sunni insurgents Mar. 4-7 killed and wounded hundreds of Shiite Muslim pilgrims traveling to the holy city of Karbala in Iraq. A bombing in Hilla Mar. 4 killed 4, while 8 more were found dead in the western half of Baghdad. Several attacks by gunmen Mar. 5 killed at least 7 pilgrims in Baghdad. Five more were killed in the Diyala province. The worst attack came Mar. 6, in Hilla, where 2 suicide bombers killed at least 77 pilgrims and wounded at least 125 more. Other attacks Mar. 7 resulted in the deaths of nearly 40 pilgrims.

U.S. and Iraqi Government Troops Sweep Sadr City; Other Iraq News—Some 1,100 U.S. and Iraqi soldiers began to conduct security sweeps in the Sadr City neighborhood of Baghdad, a stronghold of the anti-American Shiite cleric Moqtada al-Sadr, Mar. 4. The soldiers conducted door-to-door searches, and set up checkpoints along the way. There were no reports of significant clashes. The Iraqi military said Mar. 14 that since the new U.S. security effort had begun in Baghdad, the violence in the capital had declined sharply. The U.S. military death toll during the month was 82.

In other Iraq news, two bombings in a Shiite area of Tal Afar Mar. 27 killed 83; in retaliation, gunmen shot 70 Sunnis. On Mar. 29, 5 suicide bombers struck Shiite marketplaces in Baghdad and areas north of the capital, killing 125; the overall death toll in Iraq that day was 181.

In a short speech Mar. 19 marking the 4th anniversary of the beginning of the war, Pres. Bush said he saw some gains from the recent troop surge, but said it would take months for the operation to show real progress. On Mar. 20 in Baghdad, former Iraqi Vice Pres. Taha Yassin Ramadan was hanged for his part in the deaths of 148 Shiites in Dujail in 1982.

In a speech to members of the Arab League in Riyadh, Mar. 28, King Abdullah of Saudi Arabia said that the U.S. occupation of Iraq was illegal.

Bush Tours Latin America—On the eve of his 5-nation tour of Latin America, Pres. Bush Mar. 5 pledged hundreds of millions of dollars in financial aid to poor people in the region. Bush arrived in São Paulo, Brazil, Mar. 8, and on Mar. 9, after a meeting with Pres. Luiz Inacio Lula da Silva, the two leaders completed an agreement aimed at increasing their countries' development of ethanol as a fuel alternative to gas and oil. Bush continued his trip, Mar. 10-13, with a succession of summit meetings in Uruguay, Colombia, Guatemala, and Mexico.

Captured Terrorist Says He Planned 2001 Attacks on U.S.—Khalid Sheikh Mohammed, a prisoner long suspected by the U.S. of masterminding the attacks of Sept. 11, 2001, confessed Mar. 10 that he did in fact plan them. Mohammed, who had been captured in Pakistan in 2003 and then held incommunicado in secret CIA facilities, made his confession during a military hearing at the U.S. prison and naval base at

Guantánamo Bay, Cuba. Through a representative, Mohammed said, "I was responsible for the 9/11 operation, from A to Z." His confession was made public on Mar. 14.

Mohammed said he was also responsible, wholly or in part, for some 30 other attacks and plots, including the 1993 bombing of New York's World Trade Center, Richard Reid's attempt to bomb a transatlantic flight in 2001, the Indonesian nightclub bombing in 2002, and the Mombasa, Kenya, hotel bombing in 2002. Some of his schemes were not carried out, including alleged assassination attempts against former presidents Jimmy Carter and Bill Clinton and Pope John Paul II.

Mohammed declared that he and other detainees had been tortured while in CIA custody and had made false statements as a result. In response to questions at the hearing, however, he said his confession that day was not made in response to any threat or coercion.

U.S. and Iranian Diplomats Meet in Baghdad—Diplomatic delegations from the U.S. and Iran met in Baghdad Mar. 10 during a conference called by Iraqi leaders to seek help in ending the bloodshed there. All 6 of Iraq's neighbors, the 5 permanent members of the UN Security Council, and 3 international organizations participated. Although the Bush administration had vowed not to talk with the Iranian regime, representatives of the 2 countries did exchange concerns about Iran's nuclear program, alleged Iranian participation in the Iraqi conflict, and the recent U.S. seizure of Iranian diplomats. Iraq's neighbors agreed to work together to control the problems that were fueling sectarian and terrorist violence in Iraq.

Iran Seizes 15 British Troops at Sea—Eight British sailors and 7 marines were seized at gunpoint Mar. 23 by Iran's Revolutionary Guard, an elite corps affiliated with Iran's ruling clergy. The 14 men and one woman were part of a UN-mandated force patrolling the Persian Gulf. They had just searched a cargo ship in Shatt al-Arab, a disputed waterway between Iraq and Iran, before they were seized. Iran charged that the 15, who were in 2 inflatable boats, were in Iranian waters. The UK denied the accusation and insisted the troops were operating in Iraqi territorial waters.

On Mar. 24, the UN Security Council, 15-0, approved tougher sanctions aimed at persuading Iran to suspend uranium enrichment and resume negotiations on its nuclear program. The Council resolution strengthened financial sanctions approved in December 2006.

General

Prosecutors File Lesser Charge Against Astronaut—Prosecutors in Orlando, FL, Mar. 2, charged astronaut Lisa Marie Nowak with attempted kidnapping with intent to commit bodily harm toward Air Force Capt. Colleen Shipman. Nowak, who viewed Shipman as a rival for the affections of Navy Comdr. William Oefelein, had confronted Shipman Feb. 5 at Orlando International Airport. A charge of attempted murder, recommended by police, was not filed. On Mar. 7, NASA terminated Nowak's service as an astronaut. Nowak formally entered a plea of not guilty Mar. 22.

U.S. Economy at a Glance: March 2007	
Unemployment rate	4.4%
Consumer prices (change over 2006)	+2.8%
Trade deficit (12 months through Mar.)	$746.4 bil
Dow Jones closing, 1st quarter	12,354.35
Dow Jones highest close 1st quarter (Feb. 20)	12,786.64
Dow Jones lowest close 1st quarter (Mar. 5)	12,050.41
1st quarter GDP growth (annual rate)	+0.6%

April 2007
National

Presidential Campaign Funds Break First-Quarter Records—Campaign contributions reported by several presidential candidates in the first quarter of 2007 broke records for that period. Sen. Hillary Clinton (NY) led the Democrats with $26 mil as of Apr. 1, to which she added $10 mil from her U.S. Senate reelection campaign account. Sen. Barack Obama (D, IL) reported Apr. 4 that he had raised $25 mil, receiving money from about 100,000 donors, twice the number of those who gave to Clinton. Former Sen. John Edwards (D, NC) reported $14 mil in contributions as of Apr. 1.

Former Gov. Mitt Romney (R, MA) led the Republican slate with campaign funds of $20.6 mil as of Apr. 2. Former New York City Mayor Rudy Giuliani followed with $16 mil,

and Sen. John McCain (R, AZ) reported $13.7 mil. McCain, who had not yet formally joined the race, announced his candidacy Apr. 25.

Supreme Court Rules that EPA Can Regulate Greenhouse Gases—On Apr. 2, the Supreme Court held, 5-4, that under the Clean Air Act the U.S. Environmental Protection Agency had the power to regulate the emission of "greenhouse gases" by motor vehicles, and that the EPA would have to provide a science-based rationale if it chose not to do so. The Bush administration contended that the Clean Air Act did not allow the EPA to regulate greenhouse gases such as carbon dioxide, and that even if it did, any enforcement authority would be discretionary.

Talk Show Host Fired After He Insults Female Athletes—Don Imus, host of the radio talk show "Imus in the Morning," who had developed a wide following over 30 years, lost his job after making a sexually and racially offensive remark on the air Apr. 4 about the predominantly black Rutgers University women's basketball team. Rutgers had just lost the national championship game to Tennessee. Imus's morning talk show, whose guests included many political leaders and journalists, was simulcast on CBS Radio and cable channel MSNBC. NBC, Apr. 11, and then CBS, Apr. 12, announced that they were canceling the show. Imus had repeatedly apologized for his remark, and met directly Apr. 12 with the Rutgers team and coach C. Vivian Stringer at the governor's mansion in Princeton, NJ.

Pressure Grows on Attorney General to Resign—Congress in April pressed an investigation into the firing of 8 federal prosecutors in 2006, amid growing demands that U.S. Attorney Gen. Alberto Gonzales step down. On Apr. 6, Monica Goodling, counsel to the attorney general and White House liaison, became the 3rd official to resign as a result of the inquiry. She had said that if called to testify she would refuse. The House Judiciary Committee Apr. 10 subpoenaed all Justice Dept. records related to the dismissals.

On Apr. 19, Gonzales testified before the Senate Judiciary Committee. Committee members of both parties were openly skeptical as Gonzales repeatedly said he could not recall key details surrounding the firings.

Shooting Rampage at Virginia Tech Leaves 33 Dead—A senior at Virginia Tech shot 27 students and 5 faculty members to death on Apr. 16 before he shot himself fatally. All the deaths occurred on the university campus in Blacksburg, VA. 24 others were injured in what was thought to be the worst shooting rampage in U.S. history.

The killer was identified Apr. 17 as Seung-Hui Cho, 23, a permanent legal resident of the U.S. who was born in South Korea. Cho used 2 semiautomatic guns in his killing spree; he had passed required background checks.

The spree began at about 7:15 A.M. when Cho entered a dormitory and killed 2 students. Investigators on the scene believed that the shootings had involved a domestic dispute and that the perpetrator probably had fled the area. No classes were canceled on the 2,600-acre campus, although at 9:26 A.M. a campus-wide email sent by school administrators reported the shootings and warned students and faculty to be cautious. At about 9:45 A.M. Cho entered Norris Hall, a classroom building some distance from the first shootings, and went from classroom to classroom shooting victims at random. Liviu Librescu, 76, a professor of engineering and a Holocaust survivor, blocked his classroom door as some students jumped from windows, before he himself was killed.

On Apr. 18, NBC received at its New York City offices a package Cho had mailed from a Blacksburg post office at 9:01 a.m. on the day of the rampage. The contents included a long, rambling video statement in which Cho blamed others for his actions and described himself as a martyr. Classes at the university resumed Apr. 23, but Norris Hall remained closed for the rest of the semester.

Supreme Court Upholds Ban on "Partial-Birth" Abortion—On Apr. 18 the Supreme Court upheld, 5-4, a federal law enacted in 2003 that banned a procedure commonly called partial-birth abortion. The medical name for the rare procedure is intact dilation and extraction, and it is usually performed late in the pregnancy. This decision marked the first time the Court had supported a ban on a particular abortion technique; the Court also broke new ground in upholding an abortion restriction that made no exception for the mother's health. In his majority opinion, Justice Anthony Kennedy asserted that the government "has a legitimate and substantial interest in preserving and promoting fetal life."

Dow Industrials Close Above 13,000—On Apr. 25, the Dow Jones industrial average closed above 13,000 for the first time in its history. Investors were encouraged by strong company earnings reports. The Dow closed the day at 13,089.89.

International

House Speaker Pelosi Meets with Syrian President—U.S. House Speaker Nancy Pelosi led a delegation of House members that met with Syrian political leaders, including Pres. Bashar al-Assad, in Damascus, Syria, Apr. 3-4. The six other House members present included 5 Democrats and one Republican. After the Apr. 4 meeting, Pelosi told reporters that Assad had said he was ready to resume peace talks with Israel, and that she had relayed a message to Assad from Prime Min. Ehud Olmert of Israel that he too was ready to talk. Israeli officials said Apr. 4 that talks were possible only if Syria ended its support of the militant groups Hamas and Hezbollah. Both U.S. Pres. Bush and Vice Pres. Cheney criticized Pelosi's meeting with Assad, with whom the administration had no current direct diplomatic contacts. During their Mideast trip, the House members also visited Israel, Lebanon, and Saudi Arabia.

Iran Frees 15 British Crew Members After 13 Days—Iranian Pres. Mahmoud Ahmadinejad Apr. 5 freed all 15 members of a British Navy crew that Iranian units had seized in the Persian Gulf on Mar. 23. Through Apr. 3, Iran had broadcast statements by the sailors and marines in which they said that they had entered Iranian waters. After meeting with Ahmadinejad and then flying home to the UK, the crew members held a news conference Apr. 6 in which they said they had been outnumbered by their captors and that resistance would have been futile. The crew members also said that they were subjected to aggressive interrogations, and were coerced into making favorable statements to the media about their treatment and their alleged guilt.

Limited Progress Reported in Iraq—Reports from the U.S. military Apr. 4 claimed that sectarian violence in Iraq had declined in March over the previous month by 26%. Gen. David Petraeus, the top U.S. military commander, noted that while the stepped-up security effort was showing progress in Baghdad, the capital, attacks continued to occur elsewhere.

A suicide truck bomb rigged with chlorine gas exploded April 6 in Ramadi, killing 27, many of whom were children. In Baghdad, on Apr. 12, in a shocking breach of the heavily fortified Green Zone, a suicide bombing in a cafeteria adjacent to Iraq's parliament killed a member of the legislature and wounded 22. In one especially bloody attack, 127 were killed and 148 were wounded Apr. 18 in a suicide car bomb explosion near a Baghdad market; in all, at least 233 people were killed or found dead in Baghdad and elsewhere in Iraq that day. Nine U.S. soldiers in the 82nd Airborne Division were killed and 20 were wounded in a suicide car bombing in Diyala Province Apr. 23. A total of 104 U.S. troops died in Iraq during the month.

Longer Tours for U.S. Troops—Defense Secretary Robert Gates announced Apr. 11 that the standard tour of duty for Army soldiers in Iraq and Afghanistan would be increased from 12 to 15 months, in order to maintain the necessary force levels and sustain the troop "surge" in Iraq. Congressional democrats assailed the move, saying that it would hurt morale among the troops.

New UN Report Paints Grim Picture on Climate Change—A report from the UN-sponsored Intergovernmental Panel on Climate Change, issued Apr. 6, forecast the consequences of the worldwide buildup in greenhouse gases. The findings represented the consensus of hundreds of scientists and gained the endorsement of 120 countries. The report said that if greenhouse gas emissions continued at present levels, temperatures and sea levels would continue to rise, drowning islands and coastal areas. Other results would include severe droughts, more hunger and disease, and the potential extinction of up to 30% of the world's species. The panel recommended that governments begin preparing for the effects of climate change, and warned that as many as 50 mil environmental refugees could be created by 2010.

Iran Announces New Advances in Nuclear Program—Pres. Ahmadinejad announced Apr. 9 that Iran had the ability to produce uranium for use in nuclear power generation on an industrial scale. He said that opposition from the UN would not deter Iran from continuing its program.

Bombs Kill 33 in Algerian Capital—A group with known ties to al-Qaeda claimed responsibility for two Apr. 11 bombings that killed 33 and wounded 200 in Algiers, the capital of Algeria. One bomb exploded near the Government Palace office of Prime Min. Abdelaziz Belkhadem, who was not there. The other bombing occurred at a police station in an eastern suburb of Algiers.

Verdict Reached in British Terror Trial—A British judge in London Apr. 30 sentenced 5 men to life in prison after they were convicted of plotting bombing attacks across the United Kingdom. The men, who were officially charged with plotting to cause an explosion likely to endanger life, were arrested in 2004. During the trial, links were found between the accused and the Islamists responsible for the July 7, 2005, terrorist attacks in London that left 56 people dead, including 4 suicide bombers.

Report Criticizes Israeli Prime Minister—An official Israeli government commission Apr. 30 harshly criticized Prime Min. Ehud Olmert for "severe failures" of leadership during the 2006 conflict against Hezbollah in Lebanon, which ended in an apparent stalemate. The report did not call on Olmert to resign, however, but he refused to do so. The commission also rebuked Lt. Gen. Dan Halutz, who was chief of staff during the Lebanon war, and Defense Min. Amir Peretz. Halutz had resigned Jan. 16. Peretz lost his Labor Party leadership in a primary election May 28 and gave up the defense portfolio June 15.

General

Florida Repeats as NCAA Men's Basketball Champion; Lady Vols Take Home Women's Title—The Florida Gators, led by coach Billy Donovan, won the NCAA Division I men's basketball title Apr. 2 for the 2nd year in a row. With the same starting lineup as the previous season, they defeated Ohio State, 84-75, in the title game in Atlanta. Forward Corey Brewer, who scored 13 points, was named most outstanding player of the Final Four.

The Tennessee Lady Vols took the women's NCAA title Apr. 3, defeating Rutgers, 59-46, in the final in Cleveland. It was the 7th title for Tennessee coach Pat Summitt. Tennessee forward Candace Parker, who scored 17 points in the game, was named the most outstanding player in the Final Four.

Zach Johnson Wins Masters Title—Zach Johnson won the Masters golf tournament in Augusta, GA, Apr. 8, with a one-over-par total of 289. That equaled the highest number of strokes ever made by a Masters winner. Four-time Masters winner Tiger Woods was among 3 players who tied for 2nd place at 291.

Charges Against 3 Duke Lacrosse Players Dropped—North Carolina Attorney Gen. Roy Cooper announced Apr. 11 that all charges had been dropped in a sexual-assault case involving 3 members of the Duke Univ. men's lacrosse team. Cooper called Durham County District Atty. Michael Nifong, who had brought the case in 2006, a "rogue prosecutor." On June 16, an ethics panel of the state bar association disbarred Nifong.

May 2007

National

6 Accused of Planning to Kill Soldiers at Fort Dix—Six Muslim men who had been arrested by the FBI May 7 were charged in U.S. District Court in Camden, NJ, May 8—5 for conspiring to kill U.S. soldiers at Fort Dix in New Jersey, and the 6th on a related weapons charge. Officials said that the men had been arrested after they attempted to purchase automatic weapons from FBI informants. The accused were described as "Islamic militants" who had no formal link to al-Qaeda, but were inspired by the terrorist network's ideology.

Chrysler to Return to U.S. Ownership—The German company DaimlerChrysler AG announced May 14 that it would sell 80.1% of its Chrysler division to a private equity firm based in New York City. The company, Cerberus Capital Management L.P., would pay $7.4 bil for the stock. Daimler-Benz AG had bought Chrysler in 1998, but the merger was largely regarded as a failure.

Bush Names "War Czar" for Iraq, Afghanistan—Pres. Bush May 15 appointed Lt. Gen. Douglas Lute to coordinate operations in Iraq and Afghanistan. Lute, who had directed operations for the Joint Chiefs of Staff, was confirmed June 28 by the Senate, 94-4.

Senators Hear of Confrontation Over Surveillance Program—Members of the Senate Judiciary Committee were told May 15 of a confrontation in 2004 between White House aides and top Justice Dept officials. Former Deputy Atty. Gen. James Comey described a dispute within the Bush administration concerning an unnamed program that provided for secret surveillance of U.S. citizens by the National Security Agency without court warrants. Then-Atty. Gen. John Ashcroft, who at the time was ill in a hospital, thought the program was illegal, as did Comey.

Comey said that he, Ashcroft, and Mueller were ready to resign, but that Bush on Mar. 12 ordered changes in the program that the Justice Dept. had demanded. Gonzales had testified under oath in 2006 that there was no "serious disagreement" within the administration on the NSA program.

Monica Goodling, who had resigned as Justice Dept. liaison to the White House, testified before the House Judiciary Committee May 23 admitted that she had "crossed the line" when she had questioned job candidates about their partisan political backgrounds while interviewing them for positions at the Justice Dept. and as assistant U.S. attorneys.

Congress OKs Iraq War Funding, Minimum Wage Hike—The Senate and House May 24 approved a new, 4-month, Iraq and Afghanistan war-funding bill that did not include a timetable for the withdrawal of U.S. troops from Iraq. However, the bill did require that the Iraqi government meet a series of benchmarks as conditions for continued U.S. reconstruction aid. The vote in the Senate was 80-14 and in the House 280-142. Pres. Bush signed the measure May 25.

As part of the agreement on war funding, both houses also approved an increase in the national minimum wage. It would rise from the current $5.15 per hour to $7.25 in 3 stages over 2 years.

Pres. Bush May 1 had vetoed a funding bill that did include a timetable for withdrawal from Iraq. The House May 2 voted 222-203 to override the veto, a margin far short of the two-thirds majority required. The Senate May 16 rejected, 67-29, a bill to end funding for U.S. military efforts in Iraq by April 2008.

International

Killing of Afghan Civilians by U.S. Forces Reported—Afghan officials investigating a U.S. operation in Shindand reported May 2 that 42 Afghan civilians had been killed. Pres. Hamid Karzai rebuked U.S. and NATO forces for not making more of an effort to prevent civilian casualties. On May 8, U.S. Col. Jack Nicholson expressed remorse for the killings in March of Afghan civilians by U.S. Marines. He said 19 had died and that the U.S. had paid $2,000 each to the victims' families. Afghan officials said May 9 that U.S. air strikes had killed 21 more civilians in Sarwan Qala on May 8. Residents said May 10 that the death toll might have been 50 or more.

U.S. Steps Up Diplomatic Efforts on Iraq—Representatives of 60 nations met in Egypt May 3-4 to discuss the future of Iraq. Sec. of State Condoleezza Rice May 3 met with Foreign Min. Walid Mouallem of Syria—the first contact between the two countries at that diplomatic level in 2 years. UN Sec. Gen. Ban Ki-moon, who was also in Egypt, said May 3 that Iraq's creditors had agreed to cancel $30 bil in debt. The conference attendees agreed May 4 to work to stop the flow of fighters and weapons into Iraq.

Sarkozy Wins French Presidential Election—Nicolas Sarkozy, representing the center-right Union for a Popular Movement, was elected president of France in a runoff election May 6, succeeding outgoing Pres. Jacques Chirac, who had held the office for 12 years. Sarkozy defeated Socialist Party candidate Ségolène Royal by a margin of 53% to 47%.

After serving as mayor of Neuilly-sur-Seine, an affluent Paris suburb, Sarkozy had entered the National Assembly and cabinet, eventually serving as budget minister, interior minister, and finance minister. He was sworn in as president May 16. His choice for premier, François Fillon, took office May

17. After his victory, Sarkozy signaled that he would take a friendlier stance than Chirac toward the U.S.

Protestant and Catholic Adversaries Share Power in Northern Ireland—Northern Ireland, also known as Ulster, installed a new government May 8, implementing a landmark power-sharing agreement between Protestant and Catholic parties that had been announced Mar. 26. The Rev. Ian Paisley, the Protestant leader who supported continued union with Britain, was sworn in as first minister, and Martin McGuinness, deputy leader of Sinn Fein, took the oath as deputy first minister. On May 3 the Ulster Volunteer Force, the biggest unionist paramilitary organization, said it would abandon violence and put away its weapons.

Political and Military Developments in Iraq—Army Maj. Gen. Benjamin Mixon, commander of U.S. forces north of Baghdad, said May 11 that he needed more troops, and he called the Iraqi government corrupt and nonfunctional. A Defense Dept. report said May 15 that 100,000 to 300,000 barrels of Iraqi oil went unaccounted for each day, representing a daily loss of $5 mil to $15 mil. The report also said that attacks on troops and civilians were near an all-time high. After being out of the public eye for months, the radical Shiite cleric Moqtada al-Sadr spoke in a mosque in Kufa, south of Baghdad, May 25, renewing his denunciation of the U.S. military presence.

The total number of U.S. soldiers killed in Iraq in May was 127, with nearly 65% dying from improvised explosive devices, or IEDs. The monthly total was the highest in more than 2 years. The "surge" brought the total number of U.S. troops in Iraq to 149,700, while the number of allied forces declined to about 12,100.

Taliban Commander Killed in Afghanistan—U.S.-led forces May 12 killed Mullah Dadullah, the top Taliban commander in southern and southeastern Afghanistan. An ethnic Pashtun, Dadullah had helped oust the Soviet Union from Afghanistan.

Factional Conflict in Gaza Involves Israel—The strife between the Fatah and Hamas Palestinian factions in Gaza intensified May 13 when a Fatah security official and his bodyguard were killed. Within a few days 40 Palestinians were dead from violent exchanges. On May 15, Hamas militants fired rockets into southern Israel, prompting Israeli air strikes on Hamas targets that killed 8. Air attacks continued, killing 5 Palestinians on May 18. Another air attack May 20 killed 8 at the home of a Hamas member of Parliament, including 3 of his brothers. Israeli bombs killed 5 Palestinians May 26.

President of World Bank Forced to Resign—Paul Wolfowitz announced May 17 that he would step down as president of the World Bank effective June 30. For months, allegations had circulated that Wolfowitz had arranged a salary increase and promotion for his romantic partner, Shaha Ali Riza, which made her the highest paid employee in the U.S. State Dept. Although he insisted he had acted ethically and with the bank board's knowledge and approval, on May 14 a bank investigatory panel found that Wolfowitz had violated the bank's code of conduct.

On May 30, Bush announced that he had chosen Robert Zoellick, an executive with Goldman Sachs and a former U.S. trade representative, to succeed Wolfowitz.

Bush Toughens Economic Sanctions Against Sudan—Pres. Bush May 29 rebuked the government of Sudan for not cooperating with international efforts to end the humanitarian crisis in the country's Darfur region. He had warned that he would act if Pres. Omar Hassan Al-Bashir did not allow full deployment of UN peacekeepers, allow aid to reach Darfur, and stop supporting the murderous *janjaweed* militias. Bush said he would enforce economic sanctions against some 100 Sudanese companies, and push for a UN resolution to impose a broad arms embargo on Sudan.

New President Inaugurated in Nigeria—On May 29, for the first time ever in Nigeria's history, a civilian president was succeeded by another civilian. Umaru Musa Yar'Adua was inaugurated to succeed Olusegun Obasanjo, who was not eligible for another term. Yar'Adua had won the Apr. 21 presidential election with about 70% of the vote, but monitors from the European Union concluded that the vote fell "far short of basic international and regional standards for democratic elections."

General

Triple Crown Eludes Thoroughbred Horses Again—No thoroughbred horse claimed the Triple Crown of racing for 2007. Street Sense, the 9-2 favorite, ridden by Calvin Borel, won the Kentucky Derby, the first Triple Crown event, on May 5, finishing in 2 minutes, 2.17 seconds. On May 19, however, Street Sense lost in a photo finish to Curlin in the Preakness Stakes, at Pimlico Race Course, Baltimore. Curlin, ridden by Robby Albarado, stumbled at the gate but came on strong in the stretch, equaling the stakes record of 1 minute, 53.46 seconds.

Tornado Destroys Kansas Town, Kills 11—With winds as high as 205 mph, a tornado leveled almost all of the southwestern Kansas town of Greensburg May 4, killing 11. Gov. Kathleen Sebelius (D) said May 7 that the deployment of Kansas National Guard units to Iraq and Afghanistan, which stretched the Guard's resources, had slowed the relief effort. Pres. George W. Bush visited Greensburg May 9.

Franchitti Wins Indianapolis 500, Ended Early by Downpour—Dario Franchitti of Scotland won the 91st Indianapolis 500 May 27. The race was cut short when a downpour stopped the contest after 166 of the scheduled 200 laps. An earlier rainfall after 113 laps had delayed the race for 3 hours. The lead changed hands frequently, and a downpour a few minutes earlier would have brought a different result. This was Franchitti's 1st Indy 500 win in 5 starts.

June 2007

National

Four Charged in Alleged Plot to Bomb New York Airport—Authorities June 4 charged 4 men with plotting to blow up fuel tanks and pipelines at John F. Kennedy International Airport in New York City. Russell Defreitas, who was thought to be the ringleader of the group, had been arrested in Brooklyn, NY, June 1. The U.S. citizen and native of Guyana had been a cargo handler at the airport in the 1990s. In Trinidad and Tobago, 2 men (Kareem Ibrahim and Abdul Kadir) were arrested June 1, and another (Abdel Nur) turned himself in June 5. All four were indicted on June 29.

Ex-Aide to Cheney Sentenced to 30 Months in Prison—U.S. District Court Judge Reggie Walton June 5 sentenced I. Lewis "Scooter" Libby, a former vice-presidential aide, to 30 months in prison for lying to federal investigators and obstructing justice. Walton also fined Libby $250,000.

Immigration Reform Bill Fails in Senate—Voting on a comprehensive immigration reform bill was stalled June 7 when supporters were unable to move to a final vote. Supporters got only 45 of the 60 votes needed to end debate. Although Pres. Bush backed the bill, only 7 Republicans supported it. Sen. Harry Reid (D, NV), the majority leader, temporarily withdrew the bill from consideration. Bush met with GOP senators June 13 and sought to assure them that the bill would provide the enhanced border security that many of their constituents were demanding. He announced June 14 that he would spend an additional $4.4 bil to protect U.S. borders. The bill was revived June 26 by a 64-35 vote, with 24 Republicans in the majority, but failed to secure enough votes to end debate (46-53) on June 28. Reasons for the failure were split: some believed immigrants' rights weren't ensured, while others thought the bill would guarantee amnesty to illegal immigrants.

Chairman of Joint Chiefs to Be Replaced—Sec. of Defense Robert Gates announced June 8 that he would not renominate Marine Gen. Peter Pace, chairman of the Joint Chiefs of Staff, for a 2nd term. Pace was the first chairman in more than 40 years to serve only one 2-year term. Gates said that he had consulted senators from both parties and had concluded that renominating Pace would result in a divisive confirmation hearing related to the conduct of the Iraq war. Pres. Bush said he would accept Gates' recommendation that he nominate Adm. Michael Mullen, chief of naval operations, to succeed Pace. Mullen was confirmed by the Senate Aug. 3 and sworn in Oct. 1.

Supreme Court Rules on McCain-Feingold—The Supreme Court ruled June 25 in a 5-4 decision that a portion of the McCain-Feingold campaign finance law was unconstitutional. Under a provision of the law, corporations, interest groups (including activist organizations), and unions could not run any political advertising in the last 30 days before a primary election or the last 60 days before a general election. Chief Justice John Roberts, writing for the majority, held that the only ads that could be kept off the air during those periods were those that were "susceptible of no reasonable interpretation other than as an appeal to vote for or against a specific candidate."

International

Putin Warns U.S. on Missile Defense Bases—On June 1, Pres. Vladimir Putin warned the U.S. that if it went ahead with plans to place missile defense bases in Eastern Europe, Russia would target European sites with its own missiles. Pres. Bush said June 5 that the missile plans were a "purely defensive measure." At a private meeting during the Group of Eight (G-8) summit in Germany, Putin proposed to Bush that the U.S. use a Russian-managed radar base in Azerbaijan to guard against a missile attack from Iran.

U.S. Troop "Surge" in Iraq Assessed—A Defense Dept. quarterly report released June 13 said that a joint U.S.-Iraqi security drive had reduced violence in Baghdad and Anbar Province but that attacks were up elsewhere. Suicide attacks had more than doubled from January to March, and attacks utilizing explosively formed penetrators (EFPs) against U.S. forces were at a record high in April.

A military spokesman June 15 said that the U.S. "surge," which had begun in February, was complete. U.S. forces had been increased by 28,500 to an overall strength of about 160,000. Army Lt. Gen. Raymond Odierno, the No. 2 commander in Iraq, said June 17 that 40% of Baghdad was "really very safe on a routine basis." On June 19, 10,000 Americans and 3,000 Iraqis, supported by 2 Sunni units that had turned against the Sunni jihadist group known as al-Qaeda in Iraq, began an offensive against a jihadist stronghold in the Baquba area. U.S. troop deaths in June totaled 100.

Leaders of Industrial Nations Meet in Germany—Heads of government of the world's leading industrial nations, the Group of Eight (G-8), met in Heiligendamm, Germany. In a joint statement June 7, the leaders agreed to "seriously consider" a proposal from the European Union, Canada, and Japan that global greenhouse gas emissions be cut in half by 2050. German Chancellor Angela Merkel had wanted each nation to commit to cutting its own emissions by 50% by 2050. On June 8, the G-8 leaders agreed to commit $60 bil to fight AIDS, malaria, and tuberculosis in developing countries.

Hamas Wins Bloody Struggle to Control Gaza Strip—The Palestinian Authority violently split in June as Hamas, which opposes Israel's right to exist, seized control of the Gaza Strip on June 14 after fighting with Fatah left more than 100 dead. In Gaza City, Hamas captured the police station June 13 and the president's compound June 14. Some Fatah officials were reportedly executed.

On June 14, Pres. Mahmoud Abbas dissolved the Fatah-Hamas unity government; dismissed the Hamas prime minister, Ismail Haniya; and declared a state of emergency. On June 15 he named Salam Fayyad as prime minister. Hamas rejected the new government. U.S. Sec. of State Condoleezza Rice said June 18 that Bush fully supported Abbas and the U.S. would resume full assistance to his government. On June 30, Hamas rejected Fatah's call for an international force to be sent to Gaza to supervise early elections.

"Chemical Ali" Sentenced to Hang in Iraq—The Iraqi High Tribunal June 24 sentenced Ali Hassan al-Majid, known by the nickname "Chemical Ali," to be executed by hanging. Al-Majid, cousin of the late Pres. Saddam Hussein, was convicted of genocide, war crimes, and crimes against humanity. He had overseen the poison gas attacks that killed thousands of Kurds in 1987-88.

Tony Blair Steps Down as British Prime Minister—Prime Min. Tony Blair of Great Britain submitted his resignation to Queen Elizabeth II on June 27; he had announced his retirement May 10, after a decade in power. Blair was immediately called on to serve as envoy for the so-called quartet—the UN, European Union, Russia, and the U.S.—that has sought to mediate peace talks between Israel and the Palestinians. In the UK, Gordon Brown, a Labour stalwart who had been Blair's powerful chancellor of the exchequer, was invited to form a new government. Prime Min. Brown named his cabinet the following day.

Suspected Bomb Plot Pushes Britain to "Critical" Alert Level—British police defused two car bombs in London's theatre district June 29, the first of them just a few hours after new Prime Minister Gordon Brown named his cabinet. Police reported that the bombs were designed to be set off by remote control using cell phones, but that multiple calls to at least one of the cars had failed to trigger a detonation. The next day, June 30, a four-wheel-drive vehicle exploded at Glasgow airport after being driven into the main terminal. The passenger of the vehicle was arrested and charged with conspiring to cause explosions; the driver, an Indian engineer, was hospitalized for severe burns. Immediately following the explosion, Britain raised its national alert level to "critical," indicating that new attacks were expected imminently; the U.S. security level remained unchanged, but security was increased at many U.S. airports in advance of the busy July 4 holiday

General

Anaheim Wins National Hockey League Title—The Anaheim (CA) Ducks defeated the Ottawa Senators, 6-2, June 6 to win the Stanley Cup. The Ducks, coached by Randy Carlyle, beat out the Senators 4 games to 1 to win their first NHL title. Scott Niedermayer, an Anaheim defenseman, was named the most valuable player of the playoffs.

Filly Wins Belmont Stakes—On June 9, for the 1st time since 1905, a filly, Rags to Riches, won the Belmont Stakes. The winner, ridden by jockey John Velazquez, covered the 1.5-mile distance in 2 minutes and 28.74 seconds.

San Antonio Wins NBA Title in a 4-Game Sweep—The San Antonio Spurs June 14 won their 4th NBA title in 9 years, sweeping the Cleveland Cavaliers in 4 games. San Antonio was coached by Gregg Popovich. The Spurs' Tony Parker, a point guard and a native of France, was named the most valuable player of the final series.

Golfer Angel Cabrera Wins U.S. Open—Angel Cabrera of Argentina won the U.S. Open golf tournament June 17 in Oakmont, Pa. His 285 total, 5 over par on the challenging course, gave him a 1-stroke margin over Tiger Woods and Jim Furyk. Woods missed a chance to force a playoff when he failed to drop a birdie putt on the last hole.

Collapsing Roof Kills 9 Firefighters—Nine firefighters died in Charleston, SC, June 18, when the roof of a furniture warehouse collapsed during a fire. Thousands of firefighters from across the U.S. attended a memorial service June 22.

U.S. Economy at a Glance: June 2007	
Unemployment rate	4.5%
Consumer prices (change over 2006)	+2.3%
Trade deficit (12 months through June)	$731.5 bil
Dow Jones closing, 2nd quarter	13,408.62
Dow Jones highest close 2nd quarter (June 4)	13,676.32
Dow Jones lowest close 2nd quarter (Apr. 2)	12,050.41
2nd quarter GDP growth (annual rate)	+3.8

July 2007

National

Obama Leads in Fundraising for Presidential Campaign—Sen. Barack Obama (D, IL) reported July 1 that he had raised $32.5 mil for his presidential campaign during the 2nd quarter of 2007. Sen. Hillary Clinton (D, NY) reported raising $27 mil in the same period. Former New York City Mayor Rudy Giuliani led the Republican aspirants, raising $17 mil. Former Gov. Mitt Romney (MA) raised $14 mil and personally loaned his campaign an additional $6.5 mil. In all, the Democratic contenders raised $80 mil in the quarter, compared with $50 mil for those seeking the GOP nomination. With more than 258,000 donors so far in 2007, Obama had by far the broadest base of financial support. Lagging in fundraising and short on campaign cash, Sen. John McCain (R, AZ) was forced to dismiss two-thirds of his staff, including some top advisers.

Bush Commutes Sentence in CIA Leak Case—On July 2, Pres. George W. Bush commuted the 30-month prison sentence of I. Lewis "Scooter" Libby, the former chief of staff to Vice Pres. Dick Cheney. Libby had been convicted in March of obstructing a federal investigation into who leaked the identity of an undercover CIA agent. Bush took quick action after a U.S. Court of Appeals panel ruled that Libby must begin his prison sentence while appealing his conviction. Bush, in commuting the sentence, said he respected the jury's verdict but that the judge's 30-month sentence was "excessive." Bush let stand Libby's $250,000 fine.

Appeals Court Dismisses Challenge to Warrantless Wiretaps—A lawsuit challenging the legality of the National Security Agency's warrantless wiretap program was dismissed July 6 by a 3-judge panel of the U.S. Court of Appeals in Cincinnati. A district judge in 2006 had declared the program to be illegal and unconstitutional. The panel found, in a 2-1 ruling, that the plaintiffs had not demonstrated that they had suffered injury from the program.

Senator Admits His Number Was on List of "D.C. Madam"—Sen. David Vitter (R, LA) issued a statement July 9 confessing to a "very serious sin in my past for which I am, of course, completely responsible." He admitted that his phone number was on the list made public by Deborah Jeane Palfrey, the so-called D.C. Madam, who ran an escort service and was indicted on charges of racketeering and conspiracy to commit money laundering. Vitter, a conservative, was known for his advocacy of moral and pro-family values.

New Concerns Raised About an Attack on U.S.—Homeland Security Secretary Michael Chertoff told the *Chicago Tribune* July 10 that he had a "gut feeling" that the U.S. faced a rising chance of a terror attack during the summer. The U.S. government July 17 released a short, unclassified summary of the latest National Intelligence Estimate, representing a consensus of 16 intelligence agencies. It warned that the U.S. faced "a persistent and evolving terrorist threat over the next three years." It also reported that al-Qaeda "is and will remain the most serious terrorist threat" and that a 2006 cease-fire agreement between Pakistani Pres. Pervez Musharraf and tribal leaders in northwest Pakistan had allowed al-Qaeda to rebuild.

L.A. Archdiocese Agrees to $660 Mil Sexual Abuse Settlement—Cardinal Roger Mahony, archbishop of the Roman Catholic Archdiocese of Los Angeles, announced a settlement July 15 with 508 people who claimed they had been sexually abused by members of the clergy. The $660 mil payout was the highest made by any diocese that had been caught up in the nationwide abuse scandal. As of July 2007, the L.A. archdiocese, its insurers, and affiliated religious orders had already paid more than $114 mil to settle 86 previous abuse settlements.

Bush Sets Guidelines for Interrogation—Pres. Bush issued an executive order July 20 that set guidelines for CIA interrogations of terror suspects. The new order was a direct response to a June 2006 Supreme Court ruling that prisoners must be held in accordance with the Geneva Conventions. The order required that prisoners receive "the basic necessities of life." It barred cruel, inhuman, or degrading treatment or punishment, as well as sexual humiliation and the denigrating of a detainee's religion. It did not address specific interrogation techniques such as waterboarding or sleep deprivation.

Senators Rebuke Gonzales During His Testimony—Atty. Gen. Alberto Gonzales received withering criticism July 24 during an appearance before the Senate Judiciary Committee. In opening statements, chairman Pat Leahy (D, VT) bluntly told Gonzales, "I don't trust you." Gonzales denied that in March 2004, as White House counsel, he had pressured then-Atty. Gen. John Ashcroft to sign off on a controversial NSA warrantless wiretap program while Ashcroft was sedated and recovering from surgery. On many points, Gonzales' testimony appeared inconsistent with the recollections of other present and former Bush administration officials, including former deputy Atty. Gen. James Comey, who had testified in May about the Ashcroft meeting.

Federal Agents Investigate Alaska Senator's Home—On July 30 FBI and IRS agents photographed, videotaped, and removed items from the Girdwood, AK, home of Republican Sen. Ted Stevens, who was under investigation for his relationship with oil field contractor Bill Allen. The contractor, who was convicted earlier in 2007 of bribing state lawmakers, had overseen a renovation project on Stevens' home in 2000. On Sept. 20 the Associated Press reported that Allen had cooperated with the FBI in secretly taping phone calls with the Alaska senator.

Chief Justice Hospitalized After Seizure—Chief Justice John Roberts was hospitalized after suffering a seizure July 30, but had "fully recovered" within a day, according to a Supreme Court spokesperson. Roberts had experienced a similar seizure in 1993.

International

Doctors Arrested in British Terror Plot—On June 30 and July 1, British authorities arrested 6 male doctors in connection with botched bombings in London and at Glasgow Airport in late June. All of the men, who were from the Middle East or India, worked for Britain's National Health Service. Two were subsequently released. Kafeel Ahmed, who had driven an SUV into the Glasgow terminal, died Aug. 2 of burns suffered in the incident.

Violent Deaths Rising in Afghanistan—Afghan officials said July 1 that NATO air strikes killed 45 civilians and 62 Taliban in Helmand province June 29-30. The Associated Press reported July 1 that attacks in eastern Afghanistan rose 83% in 2007, while suicide bombings doubled.

Taliban militants seized 23 South Korean Presbyterians on a relief mission July 19 as they traveled from Kabul to Kandahar. The militants demanded the release of Taliban prisoners. When that did not happen, the Taliban killed one hostage July 25. A 2nd was killed later, but all the others were released, the last 7 on Aug. 30.

King Mohammad Zahir Shah, who ruled Afghanistan 1933-1973, died July 23 in Kabul at age 92. He had been the ceremonial "father of the nation" since 2002.

Israeli President Resigns—Moshe Katsav, Israel's president since 2000, stepped down July 1 after submitting his resignation June 29. His departure from the largely ceremonial office was accompanied by a plea bargain in which rape charges against him were dropped, in exchange for his agreement to plead guilty to charges of sexual harassment; no jail sentence was imposed. Former Prime Min. Shimon Peres became president July 15.

U.S. Concern Grows Over Iranian Role in Iraq—U.S. Brig. Gen. Kevin Bergner said July 2 that the Quds Force, a unit of the Iranian Revolutionary Guard, was training Iraqi Shiite militants at 3 camps near Tehran, the capital of Iran, and using Hezbollah as a proxy to train in Iraq. He stated that the Quds Force gave money and armor-piercing explosives to the fighters. U.S., Iraqi, and Iranian diplomats agreed to set up a security subcommittee for Iraq during a meeting in Baghdad July 24.

A truck bomb July 7 in Amerli, a Shiite Turkmen village in northern Iraq, killed about 150 and wounded 240. A truck bombing July 16 outside the headquarters of Pres. Jalal Talabani's Patriotic Union of Kurdistan and 2 smaller explosions killed more than 80 and wounded 180 in Kirkuk. The celebration of the Iraqi soccer team's victory in a semifinal match at the Asian Cup tournament was marred July 25 when explosions in Baghdad killed at least 50. Iraq defeated Saudi Arabia, 1-0, in Jakarta, Indonesia, to win the championship on July 29.

Iraq's parliament entered summer recess on July 30, leaving much important legislation unfinished. The U.S. military death toll in July dropped to 80; Iraqi civilian deaths during the month were estimated at 1,900. Representatives from Iraq, other Middle Eastern countries, and the U.S., UN, and European Union were among the delegates who gathered in Amman, Jordan, July 26, to discuss the growing problem of Iraqi refugees, including an estimated 1.5 mil in Syria and 750,000 in Jordan.

Bush, Putin Discuss U.S. Antimissile Facilities—Pres. George W. Bush and Pres. Vladimir Putin of Russia discussed missile defense July 1-2 at the Bush family compound in Kennebunkport, ME. Putin opposed Bush's plans to base U.S. antimissile facilities in the Czech Republic and Poland. He renewed his support for a Russian-U.S. joint system in Azerbaijan and southern Russia. On July 14, Russia suspended participation in the Conventional Armed Forces in Europe Treaty, which restricted deployment of such forces in Europe, calling it "hopelessly outmoded." Russia said that after 150 days it would no longer permit NATO to inspect its military installations as provided for by the treaty. Putin said July 25 that Russia would expand its spy network.

Musharraf Rule is Challenged, as Unrest Spreads in Pakistan—A 3-month standoff at the Lal Masjid, or Red Mosque, in Islamabad, the capital of Pakistan, ended July 10-11 in a bloody raid by Pakistan's army. Chief Cleric Maulana Muhammad Abdul Aziz had advocated that Islamabad adopt sharia, or Islamic law, and had set up a court there in April. On July 3, fighting between police and students killed 9 people. Aziz was arrested on July 4 while trying to escape, disguised in a woman's burqa. Government commandos stormed the mosque July 10, and more Islamists were killed the following day. In all, at least 100 died in the struggle, including 11 government soldiers. Violence increased across Pakistan after the mosque raid. On July 15, pro-Taliban chiefs in the North Waziristan region renounced an agreement with the government to keep out non-Pakistani militants.

Musharraf lost an important legal battle July 20 when Pakistan's Supreme Court reinstated Chief Justice Iftikhar Muhammad Chaudhry. Musharraf had suspended Chaudhry Mar. 9 after the jurist called for an investigation into the treatment of detainees. The suspension had sparked mass protests by lawyers and other pro-democracy advocates.

4 Convicted in 2005 London Bombing Attempts—Four African immigrants and would-be suicide bombers (Muktar Said Ibrahim, Yassin Hassin Omar, Hussein Osman, and Ramzi Mohammed) were convicted July 9 for conspiracy to murder. On July 21, 2005, in London, they had carried homemade bombs in backpacks onto trains and a bus, but the explosives failed to detonate. A judge July 11 sentenced them to life in prison.

North Korea Closes Nuclear Reactor—North Korea July 14 announced that it had closed its main nuclear reactor at Yongbyon and allowed international nuclear inspectors into the country in exchange for 50,000 metric tons of heavy fuel oil, the first step in implementing a February agreement with the U.S., China, Japan, Russia, and South Korea. International Atomic Energy Agency experts confirmed Yongbyon's shutdown and the closure of four other nuclear plants July 18.

Turkey's Ruling Party Increases Its Majority—The moderate Islamic party governing Turkey increased its majority in parliament in the July 22 national elections, receiving the largest share of votes (47%) for any party since 1965. Secular groups, including the military, remained suspicious that Prime Min. Recep Tayyip Erdogan's Justice and Development Party would try to move the country toward Islamic rule.

Historic Loss in Japan's Upper House—In elections July 29, the Liberal Democratic Party of Japanese Prime Min. Shinzo Abe lost its majority in the upper house for the first time since 1955. Many seats were lost in rural areas, the party's traditional base.

UN Authorizes Darfur Peacekeeping Force—The UN Security Council July 31 voted, 15-0, to authorize a force of up to 26,000 troops for the Darfur region of Sudan, where violence had killed at least 200,000 people and displaced more than 2 mil. The new joint UN-African Union mission would replace the 7,000-member AU force that had been unable to establish order and suppress the *janjaweed* militias.

General

Federer Takes 5th Straight Wimbledon Singles Crown—Roger Federer of Switzerland won his 5th straight Wimbledon men's tennis singles championship in England on July 8. He defeated Rafael Nadal of Spain, 7-6, 4-6, 7-6, 2-6, 6-2. In a big comeback, Venus Williams of the U.S. won the women's title July 7, defeating Marion Bartoli of France, 6-4, 6-1.

NFL Quarterback Michael Vick Involved in Dogfighting Ring—Michael Vick, quarterback for the Atlanta Falcons of the National Football League, was indicted July 17 on federal charges relating to an illegal dogfighting operation.

Dow Jones Average Closes Above 14,000—On Wall Street, the Dow Jones industrial average reached another milestone July 19 when it closed at 14,000.41, just 59 trading days after passing 13,000. Strong technology profits had propelled the recent surge in stock prices.

Last Harry Potter Book Sets 1-Day Sales Record—*Harry Potter and the Deathly Hallows*, the 7th and final novel in J.K. Rowling's phenomenally successful series about a student wizard, was released July 21. The U.S. publisher, Scholastic Inc., said that U.S. sales in the first 24 hours totaled 8.3 mil copies, an all-time single-day record.

Harrington Wins British Open—Golfer Padraig Harrington of Ireland won the British Open in Carnoustie, Scotland, July 22. After tying Spain's Sergio Garcia at 277, Harrington won by 1 stroke in a 4-hole playoff.

Tour de France Marred by More Drug Scandals—Spain's Alberto Contador, riding for the Discovery Channel team, won the Tour de France July 29, beating Australian rider Cadel Evans by only 23 seconds. Yet the tour continued to be plagued by drug scandals. After the close of the race, Contador's countryman Iban Mayo tested positive for a banned substance, the third rider of the 2007 Tour to do so. On July 26, Michael Rasmussen of the Netherlands, then leading the race, was removed from competition by his Rabobank team on suspicion of drug use.

2014 Winter Olympics in Russia—International Olympic Committee members voted July 4 to hold the 2014 Winter Olympics at Sochi, Russia. Pres. Putin lobbied hard for the Black Sea resort town, which beat Pyeongchang, South Korea, by 4 votes.

August 2007
National

Congress Approves Legal Framework for Warrantless Surveillance—The Senate, Aug. 3, and the House, Aug. 4, passed a bill that revised the rules covering the government's ability to monitor email and telephone communications between the U.S. and foreign countries. The bill gave the National Security Agency the right to monitor communications without court warrants, if it believed that the communications related to terrorism. Pres. George W. Bush had pressed Congress to make revisions in a 1978 law, the Foreign Intelligence Surveillance Act (FISA), to cope with new communications technologies. The new measure would allow the attorney general and the director of national intelligence, rather than the FISA court, to approve the surveillance. Many Democrats in Congress and civil liberties groups opposed the bill on the grounds that it breached Americans' expectation of privacy. Bush signed the bill Aug. 5.

Stock Prices Fluctuate Amid Worries Over Debt, Subprime Mortgage Crisis—After the Dow Jones Industrial Average reached 14,000 on July 19, the celebration on Wall Street proved to be short-lived. Rising consumer debt and tighter home-mortgage credit caused alarm, and home foreclosure rates were rising. Stock prices fluctuated wildly, but the overall trend for the month was down, with the Dow falling 281.42 points on Aug. 3 to close at 13,181.91. In the next trading week, ending Aug. 10, the market closed at about the same level, calmed with the help of the Federal Reserve's $62 bil infusion Aug. 9-10. Central banks in Asia and Europe also added liquidity as stock valuations declined. The Dow Aug. 27 plunged 280.28 points, closing at 13,041.85, but rallied to close the month at 13,357.74.

Fallout from the subprime mortgage crisis continued as Europe's largest publicly traded bank, BNP Paribas, Aug. 9, froze 3 of its funds which had been invested in subprime mortgage loans. American Home Mortgage Investment Corp., the nation's 10th-largest lender, filed for bankruptcy protection Aug. 6. Countrywide Financial, the largest U.S. mortgage provider, announced Aug. 16 that it would have to borrow from an $11.5 bil emergency line of credit after other short-term borrowing attempts failed.

Romney Wins Iowa Presidential Straw Poll—Former Gov. Mitt Romney (MA), a candidate for the Republican presidential nomination, won a straw poll in Ames, IA, Aug. 11, finishing with 32%. Former Gov. Mike Huckabee (AR) came in a surprising 2nd with 18%. Sen. Sam Brownback (KS) won 15%, Rep. Tom Tancredo (CO) 13%, and Rep. Ron Paul (TX) 9%. After winning only 7% of the vote, former Gov. Tommy Thompson (WI) announced Aug. 12 that he was withdrawing from the race. High-profile candidates Rudy Giuliani (NY) and Sen. John McCain (AZ) declined to participate in the poll. No delegates were at stake, but the poll was considered an early test of the GOP candidates' organizing strength and voter appeal.

With polls showing Democrats favored to keep control of Congress in 2008, several Republicans announced that they would not seek reelection. The most prominent was former House Speaker J. Dennis Hastert (IL), who formally announced Aug. 17 that he would not run again.

Rove, Gonzales, White House Press Secretary Resign—Karl Rove, who had been Bush's chief political strategist for for 13 years, Aug. 13 announced that he would resign at the end of the month. He had played a dominant role in Bush's successful campaigns for Texas governor and U.S. president,

pursuing a goal of insuring what he called "a permanent Republican majority." The extent of his involvement in the CIA leak case, the firing of U.S. prosecutors in 2006, and other controversial Bush administration activities and policies remained unclear.

Atty. Gen. Alberto Gonzales announced his resignation Aug. 27. At the Justice Dept. and, before that, as White House counsel, he had been at the center of several controversies, including the expansion of presidential powers, harsh treatment of detainees, extension of U.S. government surveillance activities, and U.S. attorney firings. A loyal Bush friend and ally since their Texas days, he was praised Aug. 27 by the president, who said Gonzales' "good name was dragged through the mud" for political reasons.

White House Press Sec. Tony Snow announced Aug. 31 that he too would resign his post. He had been diagnosed in March with a recurrence of colon cancer, but insisted he was leaving for financial rather than health reasons. Deputy Press Sec. Dana Perino assumed Snow's role.

U.S. Company Recalls Toys Shipped From China—Mattel, the world's largest toy company, said Aug. 14 that it was recalling nearly 19 mil toys made in China, about half of them distributed in the U.S. Most had been manufactured to Mattel's specifications and contained a small magnet that could be harmful if swallowed. The recall included some 436,000 toy cars coated with lead paint were also recalled. U.S. toymaker Fisher-Price, which is owned by Mattel, announced a recall Aug. 1 of 1 mil toys covered in lead paint, which were also manufactured in China. The year had already seen the recall of other imports from China, including contaminated pet food and toothpaste.

American Convicted of Conspiracy in Terror Plot—José Padilla, who had been the subject of legal controversy long before he went on trial, was convicted of conspiracy in a terrorism case; the verdict was returned by a federal jury in Miami, Aug. 16. Born in Brooklyn and a convert to Islam, Padilla had been arrested in Chicago in 2002 and held as an enemy combatant. He spent more than 3 years in a military prison in South Carolina. With a legal challenge to his case likely headed to the Supreme Court, the Bush administration abandoned its original explanation for his imprisonment and brought new charges in U.S. criminal court in 2006. Along with 2 other men, Adham Hassoun and Kifah Jayyousi, he was charged with conspiracy to murder, kidnap, and maim people in another country. They were accused of being in a terrorism support cell that aided Islamic extremists around the world. The chief evidence against Padilla was an application form, bearing his fingerprints, that he allegedly filled out to attend an al-Qaeda training camp in Afghanistan.

Senator Pleads Guilty After Incident in Men's Room—The Capitol Hill newspaper *Roll Call* revealed Aug. 27 that Sen. Larry Craig (R, ID) had pleaded guilty to disorderly conduct after being arrested by an undercover police officer June 11 in a men's bathroom at Minneapolis-St. Paul International Airport. The policeman said that Craig had made sexual advances to him. Craig was fined more than $500 and placed on 1 year of unsupervised probation.

Appearing with his wife at a press conference in Boise, the Idaho state capital, Aug. 28, Craig said he had pleaded guilty without consulting a lawyer in the hope that the case would just "go away." He denied doing anything wrong and said he had been viciously harassed by the *Idaho Statesman*, a daily newspaper that had been investigating reports of other alleged homosexual encounters by Craig. The senator also stated that he was not gay and never had been.

Poisonous Chemical Agent Discovered at UN—Phosgene, a potentially deadly chemical agent produced under the regime of Saddam Hussein in Iraq, was discovered at UN offices in New York, NY, and identified as a chemical agent Aug. 30. The nerve gas component, which was known to have been used in Iraqi attacks on Kurdish villages in the 1980s, was discovered in the UN Monitoring, Verification and Inspection Commission (UNMOVIC) office Aug. 24. The agent was contained in secure vials, and no one was injured. Records showed that it had been taken from an Iraqi chemical weapons facility near Samarra in 1996. Officials promised a full investigation into how the material had ended up in the UNMOVIC office.

Veteran GOP Senator Announces Retirement—Five-term Sen. John Warner (R, VA) announced Aug. 31 that he would not run for another term and would leave the Senate when his current term ended in Jan. 2009. Warner, 80, was considered one of the most authoritative legislators on military affairs.

International

U.S. Confidence in Iraqi Government Declines—The elected government of Iraq came under increasing criticism from the U.S., as the Iraqi prime minister and parliament made little progress toward reconciliation among the country's warring factions. Six Sunni members of the Iraqi cabinet, including a deputy prime minister, resigned Aug. 1, complaining that the government of Prime Min. Nouri al-Maliki was restricting their participation in deliberations on key issues. Pres. George W. Bush and U.S. Ambassador Ryan Crocker criticized the Maliki government Aug. 21, with Bush saying the "government's got to do more," and Crocker calling its attempts at reconciliation "very disappointing." Parliament was on summer break throughout the month.

In a speech to the Veterans of Foreign Wars, Aug. 22, Bush warned that a quick pullout from Iraq would result in a heavy loss of civilian life, which he said was the case when the U.S. left Vietnam in the 1970s. On Aug. 23, 16 U.S. intelligence agencies released a National Intelligence Estimate, which found that the current U.S. troop surge had brought some improvements in security. However, the agencies doubted that the Iraqi political leaders could resolve sectarian conflicts by the spring of 2008, when a shortage of troops would likely force a cutback in the U.S. force in Iraq. The report said that a U.S. pullout would make the situation in Iraq even worse. Speaking to an American Legion convention in Reno, NV, Aug. 28, Bush said that a pro-U.S. government must be established in Iraq to guard against the threat, posed by Iran, of a "nuclear holocaust" in the region.

Bombers in Iraq Kill Hundreds in 2 Kurdish Towns—The Kurdish region of Iraq, largely spared since 2003 from the lethal violence elsewhere in the country, came under attack Aug. 14, as 4 truck bombs exploded in 2 villages in a desert area near the Syrian border. Early estimates of the damage indicated that the bombs had killed at least 250 people, wounded 350 more, and destroyed many homes. On Aug. 21 the Iraqi Red Crescent Society raised the death toll to more than 500 and the number of wounded to 1,500.

On Aug. 28, rival Shiite factions battled on the streets of Karbala during a religious festival, and more than 50 people were killed and 200 wounded. The U.S. military reported 84 deaths among U.S. troops in Iraq in August.

Turkish Parliament Elects Candidate of Islamic Party as President—The Turkish Parliament Aug. 28 broke with tradition by electing an observant Muslim, Abdullah Gül, as the country's president. Gül, a former prime minister, was supported by the Justice and Development Party, which advocates a moderate Islamic program. In his address to parliament after taking the oath of office, Gül said, "Turkey is a secular democracy. ... These are basic values of our republic, and I will defend and strengthen these values." Gul said he would continue to seek Turkish membership in the European Union.

General

Bridge Collapse in Minneapolis Kills 13—A highway bridge across the Mississippi River in Minneapolis collapsed Aug. 1, causing the deaths of 13 people and injuring 79. The 8-lane bridge on Interstate Highway 35W fell during the evening rush hour, dropping about 50 vehicles into or near the water. Strong currents and shifting debris frustrated divers engaged in search and rescue operations. Remains of the last missing victim were found Aug. 20.

The bridge, which had been built in 1967, was under repair when it fell. It had been called "structurally deficient" in 1990. The bridge had passed annual inspections since 1993, though with low marks, and in 2006 its supporting structure was found to be in poor condition.

After the collapse, cities and towns across the country stepped up their inspections of local bridges. More than 70,000 U.S. bridges had been designated as structurally deficient according to 2006 Federal Highway Administration statistics.

Barry Bonds Breaks All-Time Home Run Record—Barry Bonds, an outfielder for the San Francisco Giants, tied Major League Baseball's all-time career home-run record at 755—set by Hank Aaron—on Aug. 4 in San Diego, homering off the Padres' Clay Hensley. Then, on Aug. 7, facing pitcher Mike Bacsik of the Washington Nationals in his home park, Bonds hit a ball over the right-center field fence for No. 756. The slugger's achievements were clouded by controversy over whether Bonds had used performance-enhancing steroids.

Long Effort to Save Trapped Miners Fails—Six coal miners were trapped 1,500 feet underground Aug. 6 near Huntington, UT, after a cave-in. They were also nearly 3 miles from the mine entrance. Without any evidence as to whether they were alive, rescuers worked for 2 weeks without success to rescue them. On Aug. 16, a 2nd cave-in killed 2 rescue workers and a mine inspector, and injured 6 other rescuers.

Extreme Weather Conditions Plague the U.S., Caribbean, and Britain—Extremely hot conditions, alternating with heavy rains, made life difficult for millions in North America in the last full month of summer. On Aug. 8, a tornado packing winds of up to 135 mph briefly touched down in the New York City borough of Brooklyn, damaging some houses; the tornado was the first ever recorded in the borough.

Hurricane Dean swept through the Caribbean Aug. 19, causing much damage and a few deaths. In the central U.S., heavy rainstorms claimed more than 20 lives, knocked out power, and caused widespread flooding. At the same time, wildfires were out of control in California, Idaho, and Montana. In the UK, rains drenched central England from June through August, causing flood damage estimated at more than $2 bil.

Tiger Woods Wins 13th Major Title—Tiger Woods shot an 8-under-par 272 to win the PGA championship in Tulsa, OK, Aug. 12. It was his 1st victory in one of golf's 4 major tournaments in 2007, and the 13th of his career.

Violent Earthquake Rocks Peru—More than 500 people were killed and 200,000 were left homeless by an 8.0-magnitude earthquake that devastated cities on the southern coast of Peru Aug. 15. Much of the damage was concentrated in Ica and Pisco, where the quake caused churches, hospitals, and a prison to collapse.

September 2007

National

Amid Controversy, Senator Wavers on Resignation—Under pressure from many of his Senate Republican colleagues and GOP party leaders, Larry Craig (R, ID) announced Sept. 1 that he intended to resign from the U.S. Senate. On Sept. 5, however, Craig launched a new effort to clear his name, saying he would remain in the Senate if he could withdraw his guilty plea to disorderly conduct for alleged improper advances to an undercover police officer in a Minneapolis airport men's room. Lawyers for Craig Sept. 10 filed court papers asking that the guilty plea be overturned, but a Minnesota judge Oct. 4 rejected the request. In a statement that same day, Craig declared his intention to remain in the Senate until his term expired in Jan. 2009.

Fred Thompson Joins Republican Presidential Field—Former Sen. Fred Thompson (R, TN) announced Sept. 5 on "The Tonight Show with Jay Leno" that he was seeking the Republican presidential nomination. Thompson, a film and television actor who had frequently appeared on the "Law & Order" TV series, had filed papers June 1 that had allowed him to set up a committee to raise money for a possible 2008 presidential bid. Even before formally announcing his candidacy, Thompson had been among the Republican front-runners in several national polls.

In the Democratic presidential race, Sen. Hillary Clinton (NY) was forced to deal with a scandal surrounding Norman Hsu, a Democratic fundraiser who had raised $850,000 for her presidential campaign. In a complaint unsealed in U.S. District Court in Manhattan Sept. 20, Hsu was accused of having swindled hundreds of investors out of $60 mil. Clinton's campaign had said Sept. 10 that it would return the funds to some 260 donors whose gifts had been funneled through Hsu.

Gen. Petraeus Reports Military Progress in Iraq—Gen. David Petraeus, the U.S. military commander in Iraq, told congressional committees that he saw progress on the ground as a result of the troop "surge," and said he supported a drawdown of 30,000 in U.S. troop levels in Iraq by mid-2008. Petraeus appeared before joint sessions of the House Foreign Affairs and

Armed Services committees Sept. 10 and the Senate Foreign Relations and Armed Services committees Sept. 11.

Ryan Crocker, the American ambassador to Iraq, appeared with Petraeus. Both officials faced tough questioning from members of both parties on the committees. Petraeus disagreed with several other recent official reports that were more pessimistic on the levels of sectarian violence and insurgent attacks and bombings. Asked by Sen. John Warner (R, VA) if U.S. strategy was "making America safer," Petraeus replied, "Sir, I don't know, actually."

In a televised address Sept. 13, Bush endorsed Petraeus's recommendations, and said that a drawdown in troops was possible because the surge strategy had worked. He warned that this "return on success" principle would not work if troop cutbacks were too deep or carried out too quickly. He advocated an "enduring relationship" with Iraq that would see U.S. forces remain in Iraq after his term ended.

Bush Chooses Former Federal Judge for Attorney General—Pres. Bush Sept. 17 nominated former U.S. District Court Judge Michael Mukasey to succeed Alberto Gonzales as U.S. attorney general. Mukasey, a Yale Law School graduate and a friend and adviser to Republican presidential candidate Rudy Giuliani, had presided over a number of terrorism cases from the bench of the Southern District Court in New York City. His nomination was subject to approval by the Senate.

Interest Rate Drops, and So Does the U.S. Dollar—On Sept. 18 the Federal Reserve cut the Federal Funds rate from 5.25% to 4.75%, bringing to some debtors the promise of lower borrowing costs for home mortgages and autos. The Dow Jones average gained over 335 points that day. But for 7 consecutive sessions Sept. 20-28, the dollar reached record lows against the euro and fell to parity with the Canadian dollar-for the first time in more than 30 years.

Interviewed Sept. 17 in connection with the publication of his book, *The Age of Turbulence*, former Fed chairman Alan Greenspan stated that odds of a recession were greater than one in three. In the book, Greenspan criticized Pres. Bush for not vetoing spending bills.

"Jena 6" Protest Draws Thousands—An estimated 20,000 people marched in Jena, LA, Sept. 20, to draw attention to the treatment of the so-called "Jena 6"—six African American high-school students who were accused of beating a white classmate in Dec. 2006 and were initially charged with attempted murder. Protesters focused on what they saw as unequal treatment in a series of earlier racially charged incidents at the school and in Jena, with a population that was 85% white. One incident, in Sept. 2006, occurred when several white students hung 3 nooses from a tree, known informally as "the white tree," where a black student had asked to sit. One of the Jena 6, Mychal Bell, was convicted of aggravated battery in the beating case. The conviction was overturned on appeal Sept. 14, 2007.

Auto Workers Strike—In the first large-scale auto industry strike since 1970, 73,000 workers for General Motors walked off the job Sept. 24. Contract negotiations with GM had faltered over the issue of funding health care for current and retired employees. The strike lasted less than 2 days, with a deal reached early Sept. 26.

International

Lebanese Troops Oust Palestinian Militants from Refugee Camp—Factional violence continued in Lebanon, as the Lebanese army Sept. 2 defeated militant Islamists based in the Nahr al-Bared Palestinian refugee camp in the northern part of the country. The army action climaxed a 3-month siege in which more than 400 people died. Most of the camp's 30,000 residents had fled in late May, when the conflict erupted. In the latest of a series of assassinations of anti-Syrian leaders, Lebanese legislator Antoine Ghanem of the Christian Phalange Party was killed by a car bomb Sept. 19 in Beirut.

Bush Visits Iraq—Pres. George W. Bush visited Iraq for the 3rd time Sept. 3, meeting with officials and U.S. troops at Al Asad Air Base in the predominantly Sunni province of Anbar. He conferred with Prime Min. Nouri al-Maliki and with local Sunni leaders who had joined with U.S. forces to fight the jihadist group al-Qaeda in Iraq. One of the Sunni Arab leaders with whom Bush met, Abdul Sattar Buzaigh al-Rishawi, was killed in a bomb attack on Sept. 13. A group calling itself the Islamic State of Iraq claimed responsibility

for a blast Sept. 24 that killed at least 18 people at a banquet intended to mark the reconciliation of provincial officials and former Sunni insurgents.

The British Army Sept. 2-3 carried out its planned withdrawal from its last base inside the southern Iraqi city of Basra, which was predominantly Shia and situated in an oil-rich region. The 550 soldiers joined Britain's other remaining 5,000 troops at a base at the Basra airport outside the city. About 170 UK troops have died in Iraq since the beginning of military operations in 2003. The U.S. death toll for Sept. was 63, the lowest monthly total since mid-2006.

Israeli Warplanes Attack Secret Target in Syria—Israeli warplanes struck one or more targets in northeastern Syria Sept. 6. Syria accused Israel of a "flagrant violation" of its airspace, but Israel made no official statement about the attack. The U.S. Defense Dept. confirmed the strike on Sept. 11. Press reports suggested that the target was what the Israelis believed to be a Syrian nuclear-related facility supported by North Korea.

Bombings in Algeria Kill More Than 50—Bombs at Batna in northeastern Algeria Sept. 6, and at a barracks in Dellys, 30 miles from Algiers, Sept. 8, killed a total of more than 50 people. Al Qaeda in the Islamic Maghreb claimed responsibility for both attacks Sept. 9.

Japanese Prime Minister Resigns—After just a year in office, Prime Min. Shinzo Abe of Japan resigned Sept. 12. His government had been embarrassed by financial scandals; 4 cabinet ministers had resigned and a 5th had committed suicide. The ruling Liberal Democratic Party Sept. 23 chose Yasuo Fukuda, the son of a former prime minister and a veteran party leader, to head the government.

Iraq Denounces U.S. Security Contractor After Baghdad Shootings—On Sept. 16, at least 8 Iraqi civilians died as a result of a shootout in Baghdad involving employees of Blackwater USA, a private security contractor. The company said that a convoy was ambushed before its employees returned defensive fire, but later investigations cast doubt on the claim. The Iraqi government cited a series of other incidents in which it accused Blackwater of using excessive force, and on Oct. 7 the prime minister's office labeled the Baghdad shootings "deliberate murder."

Ex-President Returns to Peru to Face Charges—Former Pres. Alberto Fujimori arrived in Peru Sept. 22 from Chile to face charges involving corruption and human rights abuses. He had been living in exile for nearly 7 years.

Government Suppresses Mass Protests in Myanmar—The Myanmar (Burma) military junta cracked down on the growing antigovernment movement, violently breaking up demonstrations and killing at least 9 people (according to the state-run media) Sept. 27. Protests had escalated throughout Sept., sparked by an Aug. cut in gas subsidies that more than doubled prices in the impoverished nation. Demonstrations had culminated Sept. 24 when an estimated 100,000 protesters, led by some 20,000 Buddhist monks and nuns, marched against the military junta in Yangon (Rangoon). The government imposed a curfew, raided monasteries, and made hundreds of arrests. The nation's government-controlled Internet access was shut down Sept. 28.

Pres. Bush had announced stricter sanctions against Myanmar at the opening of the UN General Assembly Sept. 25.

President of Iran Gets Frosty Welcome—In New York City to address the UN General Assembly, Iranian Pres. Mahmoud Ahmadinejad received a less than enthusiastic greeting from city officials, who turned down his request to lay a wreath at the World Trade Center memorial. Invited to speak to students at Columbia University Sept. 24, he was introduced by university Pres. Lee Bollinger, who said the Iranian leader had been behaving like "a petty and cruel dictator." At the UN General Assembly Sept. 25, Ahmadinejad said "arrogant powers" would not force Iran to give up its nuclear program.

General

Federer Wins 4th Straight U.S. Open Tennis Title—Roger Federer of Switzerland won his 4th straight U.S. Open men's tennis singles title in New York Sept. 9. He defeated Novak Djokovic of Serbia, 7-6, 7-6, 6-4. The win gave Federer 12 Grand Slam titles. Justine Henin of Belgium won her 2nd U.S. Open singles title Sept. 8, defeating Svetlana Kuznetsova of Russia, 6-1, 6-3. To reach the final, Henin had to beat Serena and Venus Williams.

O.J. Simpson Charged in Hotel Incident—Following a confrontation in a Las Vegas hotel room Sept. 13, O.J. Simpson was charged Sept. 16 with a number of felonies, including robbery and assault with a deadly weapon. He and 5 others allegedly took sports memorabilia that Simpson said had been stolen from him. Simpson, who was acquitted in 1995 of murdering his former wife and her friend, was released from jail Sept. 19 on $125,000 bail.

Leader of Polygamy Group Guilty of Aiding Rape—Warren Jeffs, the "prophet" of a splinter Mormon sect that practiced polygamy, was convicted Sept. 25 in St. George, UT, of being an accomplice to rape. He had forced a girl, 14, to marry her 19-year-old cousin against her will. Jeffs, the president of the Fundamentalist Church of Jesus Christ of Latter Day Saints, had officiated at the ceremony.

U.S. Economy at a Glance: September 2007	
Unemployment rate	4.7%
Dow Jones closing, 3rd quarter	13,895.63
Dow Jones highest close, 3rd quarter (July 19)	14,000.41
Dow Jones lowest close, 3rd quarter (Aug. 16)	12,845.78

October 1-12 Chronology
National

Dow Closes at Record High as Stocks Rebound—The Dow Jones closed at a record high of 14,164.53 on Oct. 9. Further boosting investor confidence, the Dept. of Labor had reported Oct. 5 that the economy had added 110,000 jobs in September; it also revised August employment numbers, which had showed the economy losing jobs, to show a gain of 89,000 jobs.

Bush Vetoes Health Insurance Plan for Children—Pres. George W. Bush Oct. 3 vetoed a bill passed by Congress that would have spent $35 bil, over 5 years, to expand a health insurance program to include children whose family income level disqualified them from Medicare coverage. He said he would support an alternative bill that would not expand coverage beyond children already covered. The bill had passed by a veto-proof margin, 67-29, in the Senate, but the House did not as of Oct. 11 have the two-thirds majority needed to override the veto.

Bush Denies That U.S. Resorts to Torture—The New York Times Oct. 4 reported that a classified Justice Dept. memorandum in Feb. 2005 had authorized the CIA to use psychological and physical techniques against captured terror suspects, including simulated drowning and climate manipulation. Some Democrats in Congress demanded to see the classified memoranda. "This government does not torture people," said Pres. Bush Oct. 5, adding, "You bet we're going to detain them, you bet we're going to question them because the American people expect us to find out information ... so we can help protect them."

International

FBI Investigates Killings of 17 Civilians in Iraq—The FBI Oct. 1 said it would send agents to Iraq to investigate a Sept. 16 incident in which 17 Iraqis were killed, apparently by employees of Blackwater USA, one of the largest private security contractors in Iraq. The Iraqi government had initially tried to expel the company, but later said they were reconsidering. Other investigations into the incident were being conducted by Iraqi authorities, the State Dept., and Congress. A report by the Democratic staff of the House Oversight and Government Reform Committee said Oct. 1 that Blackwater employees had been involved in 195 shootings in Iraq since 2005. The report also criticized the State Dept. for not properly supervising Blackwater's activities in Iraq.

A Decline in Violent Deaths Reported in Iraq—An Iraqi official said Oct. 1 that 884 Iraqi civilians and 78 Iraqi police and soldiers had died in violent incidents in September, down from more than double that figure in August. The U.S. military said Oct. 1 that 64 service members had been killed in September, a decline from 84 in August. On Oct. 5, U.S. air strikes on a majority-Shiite town killed at least 25 people. The U.S. military said that U.S. forces came under heavy fire as they approached the town, where they were investigating suspected arms smuggling. On Oct. 6, 2 Shiite factions—led

by the clerics Moqtada al-Sadr and Abdul Aziz Hakim—that had clashed in frequent gun battles in southern Iraq, announced a peace agreement. A U.S. air strike northwest of Baghdad Oct. 11 killed 19 alleged insurgents and 15 civilians.

British Prime Minister Gordon Brown announced Oct. 8 that he would withdraw half of the 5,000-member British force in Iraq by the spring of 2008, citing progress made in training Iraqi security forces.

Lt. Gen. Ricardo Sanchez (ret.), the former commander of U.S. forces in Iraq, attacked the Bush administration Oct. 12 for its "catastrophically flawed, unrealistically optimistic war plan." Sanchez had retired after the Abu Ghraib prison scandal, though he was cleared of wrongdoing by the Army's inspector-general. Speaking to military journalists in Arlington, VA, he said that the administration's leadership of the war was incompetent, that the current "surge" strategy would not work, and that the war was "a nightmare with no end in sight."

Putin Indicates Desire to Retain Power in Russia—On Oct. 1, Pres. Vladimir Putin of Russia, in an address to the congress of the United Russia party, said he would lead his party's list of candidates for parliament in the December election. After 8 years as president, Putin was not eligible under the constitution to seek another term in that office, but he introduced the possibility that he would become prime minister.

Pakistan President Wins Reelection—Pres. Pervez Musharraf of Pakistan was re-elected Oct. 6, but a legal challenge left his political fate in doubt. On Oct. 5 the Supreme Court had ruled that the election could go forward but stated that he could not constitutionally hold the offices of president and army chief. Musharraf had said that he would eventually give up the latter position. Musharraf was re-elected without formal opposition by national and provincial assemblies, winning 98% of the vote. Following the election, opposition parties continued to file challenges to its legality.

Meanwhile, fighters allied with the ousted Taliban government stepped up their attacks on the Pakistani military in a lawless area near Pakistan's border with Afghanistan. More than 60 Pakistani soldiers were killed Oct. 7-10. The Pakistani military said Oct. 11 that 200 militants had been killed in the fighting,

Turkey Weighs Entering Iraq to Raid Kurdish Rebel Camps—Turkish military and political leaders Oct. 9 authorized troops to enter Iraq to attack separatist Kurdish forces concentrated in rebel camps near the border. More than 2 dozen Turkish soldiers had been killed recently in clashes with the rebels, who favored creation of an independent Kurdistan. Ethnic Kurds occupied adjacent portions of Iraq, Iran, and Turkey. The United States sought to dissuade Turkey from any cross-border attacks.

At this critical juncture, the U.S. House Foreign Affairs Committee Oct. 10 approved, 27-21, a resolution that condemned the mass killings of Armenians by Turks in 1915-23 as an act of genocide. Some Turkish leaders warned that if the full House approved the resolution, it might cease its support for the U.S. endeavor in Iraq.

Russian President Warns U.S. on Missile Defense—Pres. Vladimir Putin met with Sec. of State Condoleezza Rice and Sec. of Defense Robert Gates near Moscow Oct. 12, and warned them not to proceed with plans for missile defense facilities in Poland and the Czech Republic. Putin threatened to pull out of a treaty that limits intermediate-range missiles if the U.S. plan continued.

General

Olympic Gold Medalist Admits She Used Steroids—Sprinter Marion Jones, who won 5 medals in the 2000 Olympic games, including 3 gold medals, admitted Oct. 5 that she had taken the designer steroid THG, a performance-enhancing drug. The admission came as Jones pled guilty to lying to federal investigators. Jones accepted a two-year ban from the sport and agreed to forfeit results dating back to 2000, including her Olympic medals.

Suicidal Gunman Wounds 4 at Ohio School—Two teachers and two teens were wounded by gunfire Oct. 10 at SuccessTech Academy in Cleveland, OH. The 14-year-old shooter, who had been suspended from the school for fighting, committed suicide.

OBITUARIES

A

Abbé Pierre (Henri-Antoine Grouès), 94, French priest who founded the worldwide Emmaus movement benefiting the homeless; Paris, France, Jan. 22, 2007.

Alexander, Lloyd, 83, author of fantasy novels for young adults, notably the five-volume *Prydain Chronicles*, inspired by Welsh mythology; Drexel Hill, PA, May 17, 2007.

Altman, Robert, 81, maverick Hollywood film director whose movies were known for their large ensemble casts and frequent use of overlapping dialogue; his films included *M*A*S*H* (1970) and *Nashville* (1975); Los Angeles, CA, Nov. 20, 2006.

Ando, Momofuku, 96, Japanese businessman who in 1958 invented instant ramen noodles; Ikeda, Japan, Jan. 5, 2007.

Antonioni, Michelangelo, 94, Italian film director who masterfully captured modern alienation in such works as *L'Avventura* (1960), *Blow-Up* (1966) and *The Passenger* (1975); Rome, Italy, July 30, 2007.

Astor, Brooke, 105, New York socialite, philanthropist, and author; Briarcliff Manor, NY, Aug. 13, 2007.

Auerbach, Red, 89, basketball coach who guided the Boston Celtics to a record eight consecutive NBA championships from 1959 to 1966; Washington, DC, Oct. 28, 2006.

Avis, Warren E., 91, founder (1946) of car rental company that became the U.S.'s second-largest in part by opening locations at airports; Ann Arbor, MI, April 24, 2007.

B

Barbera, Joseph, 95, animation pioneer who with his longtime partner, William Hanna, created iconic characters Tom and Jerry, the Flintstones, and Yogi Bear; Los Angeles, CA, Dec. 18, 2006.

Baudrillard, Jean, 77, French philosopher and social theorist who argued that the pervasiveness of the media in modern life had, in effect, turned all reality into "virtual reality"; Paris, France, March 6, 2007.

Bergman, Ingmar, 89, Swedish film director whose films explored the human condition; among his best-known works were *The Seventh Seal* (1957), *Persona* (1965), and *Fanny and Alexander* (1982); Fårö, Sweden, July 30, 2007.

Botha, P(ieter) W(illem), 90, leader of South Africa's white-minority government; as prime minister and, later, president (1978-89), he struggled vainly to preserve apartheid; Wilderness, South Africa, Oct. 31, 2006.

Bo Yibo, 98, last of China's "eight immortals," veteran Communist Party officials purged during the Cultural Revolution who regained power after Deng Xiaoping became China's leader (1978); Beijing, China, Jan. 15, 2007.

Boyle, Peter, 71, character actor known for his work in such films as *The Candidate* (1972) and *Young Frankenstein* (1974) and in the TV situation comedy *Everybody Loves Raymond* (1996-2005); New York, NY, Dec. 12, 2006.

Bradley, Ed, 65, TV journalist who in 1981 became the first black correspondent for CBS's long-running weekly newsmagazine *60 Minutes*; New York, NY, Nov. 9, 2006.

Brecker, Michael, 57, jazz saxophonist widely regarded as the leading such figure since John Coltrane, who died in 1967; New York, NY, Jan. 13, 2007.

Brown, James, 73, singer, songwriter, bandleader and dancer who sold millions of records in a five-decade career and came to be known as the "Godfather of Soul"; Atlanta, GA, Dec. 25, 2006.

Brown, Ruth, 78, rhythm-and-blues singer, who in the 1950s recorded a string of hits for Atlantic Records, which came to be known as the "house that Ruth built"; Henderson, NV, Nov. 17, 2006.

Browne, Roscoe Lee, 81, rich-voiced character actor in many TV shows and on Broadway; Los Angeles, CA, April 11, 2007.

Buchwald, Art, 81, Pulitzer Prize-winning journalist who poked fun at politicians, and at himself, in his long-running syndicated newspaper column; Washington, DC, Jan. 17, 2007.

C

Campbell, Bebe Moore, 56, author of best-selling novels exploring social issues from the standpoint of upwardly mobile African Americans; she also wrote for children, and wrote about mental illness in books aimed at both adults and children; Los Angeles, CA, Nov. 27, 2006.

Carlisle Hart, Kitty, 96, actress and singer who appeared on Broadway, starred in the Marx Brothers' film comedy *A Night at the Opera* (1935), and was a ubiquitous presence on TV game shows in the 1950s and 1960s; New York, NY, April 17, 2007.

Claiborne, Liz, 78, clothing designer who built a fashion empire by addressing the needs of working women; New York, NY, June 26, 2007.

Coltrane, Alice, 69, jazz pianist and composer, Hindu mystic, and manager of the estate of legendary saxophonist John Coltrane, to whom she was married for the last two years of his life; Los Angeles, CA, Jan. 12, 2007.

Comden, Betty, 89, lyricist and writer who, with longtime collaborator Adolph Green, helped create such hit Broadway musicals as *On the Town* (1944) and *Bells Are Ringing* (1956), as well as screenplays for a number of film musicals, most notably *Singin' in the Rain* (1952); New York, NY, Nov. 23, 2006.

Crespin, Régine, 80, French soprano who performed in major opera houses around the world; Paris, France, July 4, 2007.

D

Deaver, Michael, 69, deputy White House Chief of Staff for Ronald Reagan (1981-86), who shaped the presidential image with symbolic public appearances and later became an influential lobbyist. He was convicted of perjury for lying about his lobbyist activities (1987); Bethesda, MD, Aug. 18, 2007.

De Carlo, Yvonne, 84, actress whose roles included the wife of Moses in the film *The Ten Commandments* (1956) and the vampire-like Lily Munster in the TV series *The Munsters* (1964-66); Woodland Hills, CA, Jan. 8, 2007.

DeForest, Calvert G., 85, quirky character who was a regular on David Letterman's late-night TV shows for two decades, appearing as Larry (Bud) Melman; Babylon, NY, March 19, 2007.

De Gennes, Pierre-Gilles, 74, French scientist who won the 1991 Nobel Prize in Physics for research leading to the development of liquid-crystal-display (LCD) technology; Orsay, France, May 18, 2007.

Doherty, Dennis (Denny), 66, Canadian singer who was a member of the seminal 1960s folk-pop quartet The Mamas and the Papas; Mississauga, ON, Jan. 19, 2007.

Drinan, Robert, 86, five-term Democratic congressman from Massachusetts (1971-81) who was the first Catholic priest elected to Congress and who in 1973 filed the first impeachment resolution against then-President Richard Nixon; decided not to run for a sixth term after Pope John Paul II ordered him to get out of politics; Washington, DC, Jan. 28, 2007.

E

Eagleton, Thomas F., 77, senator from Missouri (1969-87) who in 1972 was the Democratic vice-presidential candidate for 18 days on the ticket headed by Sen. George McGovern (SD); he quit the race after it emerged that he had been hospitalized for depression and received electroshock treatments; Richmond Heights, MO, March 4, 2007.

Ecevit, Bulent, 81, leading Turkish politician since the 1970s who championed socialist democratic principles; also made his mark as a journalist, cultural commentator, poet, and translator; Ankara, Turkey, Nov. 5, 2006.

Ellis, Albert, 93, psychotherapist who in the 1950s developed rational emotive behavior therapy, which focused on directly confronting psychological problems rather than trying to link them to traumatic childhood experiences; New York, NY, July 24, 2007.

Ertegun, Ahmet, 83, Turkish-born founding chairman of Atlantic Records (1947) who made the label a dominant force in popular-music genres ranging from jazz to rhythm and blues to rock to soul; New York, NY, Dec. 14, 2006.

Evans, Bob, 89, founder of a national chain of sausage restaurants bearing his name, with nearly 600 locations in 18 states; Cleveland, OH, June 21, 2007.

Evans, Ray, 92, Hollywood lyricist who, with composer and lyricist Jay Livingston, won three best-song Oscars, including honors for "Que Sera, Sera (Whatever Will Be, Will Be)" in 1957; Los Angeles, CA, Feb. 15, 2007.

F

Falwell, Rev. Jerry, 73, Southern Baptist minister and televangelist whose Moral Majority organization played a key role in the emergence of the Christian conservative movement as a force in U.S. politics; Lynchburg, VA, May 15, 2007.

Fender, Freddy, 69, Tex-Mex vocalist who successfully crossed over to mainstream pop and country music; best-known for "Before the Next Teardrop"; Corpus Christi, TX, Oct. 14, 2006.

Ford, Gerald, 93, 38th president of the United States after the resignation of Richard Nixon in Aug. 1974, whom he pardoned in an effort to "heal" the nation. The nation's only non-elected president and vice president, Ford acted on the final withdrawal from Vietnam; Rancho Mirage, CA, Dec. 27, 2006.

France Jr., Bill, 74, sports executive who turned NASCAR (the National Association for Stock Car Racing) into a far-flung, multi-billion-dollar enterprise; Daytona Beach, FL, June 4, 2007.

Friedman, Milton, 94, Nobel-laureate and highly influential economist, who forcefully challenged government economic intervention in such landmark works as *Capitalism and Freedom* (1962); at the University of Chicago, where he taught for many years, he led the "Chicago School" of free-market economists; San Francisco, CA, Nov. 16, 2006.

G

Gallo, Ernest, 97, cofounder, with his brother Julio Gallo, of California's E&J Gallo Winery, which became one of the world's largest winemakers; Modesto, CA, March 6, 2007.

Geertz, Clifford, 80, cultural anthropologist who helped establish the field of interpretive, or symbolic, anthropology; Philadelphia, PA, Oct. 30, 2006.

Ghostly, Alice, 81, actress best known for her television roles including Bernice Clifton on *Designing Women*, and Esmerelda on *Bewitched*. She won a Best Actress Tony for *The Sign in Sidney Brustein's Window*; Studio City, CA, Sept. 21, 2007.

Goodman, Carolyn, 91, clinical psychologist who became a leading civil rights advocate after her son Andrew and two other civil rights workers were murdered by the Ku Klux Klan in Mississippi in 1964; New York, NY, Aug. 17, 2007.

Graham, Ruth, 87, wife of evangelist Billy Graham since 1943 and a major behind-the-scenes influence on his globetrotting Christian ministry; near Montreat, NC, June 14, 2007.

Griffin, Merv, 82, big band singer who went on to create and produce the long-running television game shows *Jeopardy!* and *Wheel of Fortune*; hosted the television talk show *The Merv Griffin Show* (1965-86); Los Angeles, CA, Aug. 12, 2007.

Grizzard, George, 79, film and stage actor who is best remembered for his performance in Edward Albee plays, including *Who's Afraid of Virginia Woolf?* and *A Delicate Balance*, for which he won a Best Actor Tony in 1996; New York, NY, Oct. 2, 2007.

H

Halberstam, David, 73, Pulitzer Prize-winning journalist and author of many books, on subjects ranging from the Vietnam War to civil rights to sports; Menlo Park, CA, April 23, 2007.

Hart, Johnny, 76, cartoonist who created the long-running comic strip "B.C." in 1958 and co-created another hugely successful newspaper cartoon, "The Wizard of Id," in 1964; Nineveh, NY, April 7, 2007.

Hazlewood, Lee, 78, singer, songwriter, and producer known best for writing the 1966 Nancy Sinatra hit, "These Boots Were Made for Walkin'"; Henderson, NV, Aug. 4, 2007.

Helmsley, Leona, 87, New York real estate magnate and hotel owner, she was tried and convicted of tax fraud in 1989, and served 18 months in prison; Greenwich, CT, Aug. 20, 2007.

Herbert, Don, 89, longtime champion of science for children as TV's Mr. Wizard; he originated the character on NBC in the early 1950s and revived it for the Nickelodeon cable network in the 1980s; Los Angeles, CA, June 12, 2007.

Hill, Arthur, 84, actor who created the role of George, the college professor trapped in a miserable marriage in Edward Albee's play *Who's Afraid of Virginia Woolf?* (1962); Pacific Palisades, CA, Oct. 22, 2006.

Hill, Oliver, 100, civil rights attorney who played a significant role in a Virginia case later incorporated into *Brown v. Board of Education*, the 1954 Supreme Court ruling that desegregated U.S. public schools; Richmond, VA, Aug. 5, 2007.

Ho, Don, 76, Hawaiian singer who frequently appeared on U.S. television in the 1960s and 1970s; his signature song was "Tiny Bubbles," which he recorded in 1966; Honolulu, HI, April 14, 2007.

Humbard, Rex, 88, pioneer televangelist whose preaching from the marble and glass "Cathedral of Tomorrow" reached worldwide audiences for over 40 years; Atlantis, FL, Sept. 21, 2007.

Hunt, E. Howard, 88, onetime Central Intelligence Agency operative who engineered the 1972 Watergate burglary that ultimately led to the collapse of Richard Nixon's presidency; he spent 33 months in prison for his Watergate role; Miami, FL, Jan. 23, 2007.

Hunt, Lamar, 74, Texas oil-fortune heir who was the founder and owner of the National Football League's Kansas City Chiefs and was credited with coining the term "Super Bowl;" Dallas, TX, Dec. 13, 2006.

Hutton, Betty, 86, actress and singer most popular in the 1940s and 1950s; one of her best-known roles was as sharpshooter Annie Oakley in the 1950 film version of the Irving Berlin musical *Annie Get Your Gun*; Palm Springs, CA, March 11, 2007.

I

Ivins, Molly, 62, syndicated columnist who poked fun at politicians, and the political and cultural climate of her adopted state, Texas; Austin TX, Jan. 31, 2007.

J

Jewell, Richard, 44, private security guard who discovered a pipe bomb at the 1996 Atlantic Olympics and alerted police, possibly saving lives by diverting visitors from the area; he was publicly considered a suspect in the crime but was cleared of charges; Woodbury, GA, Aug. 29, 2007.

Johnson, Claudia "Lady Bird," 94, widow of Lyndon B. Johnson, the 36th president of the U.S.; as first lady, she championed environmental causes, taking a particular interest in highway beautification; Austin, TX, July 11, 2007.

Johnson, Dennis, 52, five-time All-Star NBA guard who propelled the Seattle SuperSonics to their only NBA championship in 1979, and also played on Boston Celtics teams that won titles in 1984 and 1986; Austin, TX, Feb. 22, 2007.

K

King, Yolanda, 51, actress and social activist who was the oldest of the four children of civil rights leaders Rev. Martin Luther King Jr. and Coretta Scott King; Santa Monica, CA, May 15, 2007.

Kirkpatrick, Jeane J., 80, first female U.S. ambassador to the United Nations (1981-85) and a leading foreign policy influence during the Reagan administration; Bethesda, MD, Dec. 7, 2006.

Kollek, Teddy, 95, longtime mayor of Jerusalem (1965-93) who presided over the expansion of the city's infrastructure and its emergence as a cultural center; Jerusalem, Israel, Jan. 2, 2007.

Kuhn, Bowie, 80, lawyer, Major League Baseball's fifth commissioner (1969-84), during an era during which the league underwent many changes, including the introduction of free agency for players; Jacksonville, FL, March 15, 2007.

L

Laine, Frankie, 93, pop vocalist who sold millions of records in the pre-rock-and-roll era and was identified with the theme song of the TV western "Rawhide" (1959-66); San Diego, CA, Feb. 6, 2007.

L'Engle, Madeleine, 88, author best known for her children's novels, notably the Newbery-medal recipient *A Wrinkle in Time* (1962); Litchfield, CT, Sept 6, 2007.

LeWitt, Sol, 78, painter and sculptor who was a pioneer of both minimalism and conceptualism; his works included wall paintings and drawings executed by his assistants and eventually painted over; New York, NY, April 8, 2007.

Lockwood Jr., Robert, 91, Mississippi Delta blues singer and guitarist who became the torchbearer of blues legend Robert Johnson's legacy and a celebrated artist in his own right; Cleveland, Ohio, Nov. 21, 2006.

M

Makem, Tommy, 74, Irish baritone singer-songwriter who in the 1950s and 1960s helped popularize Irish folk music worldwide with the Clancy Brothers trio; Dover, NH, Aug. 1, 2007.

Marceau, Marcel, 84, well-known French mime-artist; Cahors, France, Sept 22, 2007.

Marlette, Doug, 57, Pulitzer Prize-winning editorial cartoonist who was also the creator of the syndicated comic strip "Kudzu," which satirized small-town Southern life; near Holly Springs, MS, July 10, 2007.

Maxwell, Lois, 80, actress and newspaper columnist best known for her role in 14 James Bond films as Miss Moneypenny; Freemantle, Australia, Sept. 29, 2007.

McNair, Barbara, 72, singer and actress who in the late 1960s and early 1970s was one of the first black entertainers to host a syndicated TV show; Los Angeles, CA, Feb. 4, 2007.

Menotti, Gian Carlo, 95, opera composer and organizer of music festivals; his most frequently performed work was *Amahl and the Night Visitors* (1951); Monte Carlo, Monaco, Feb. 1, 2007.

Messner, Tammy Faye, 65, televangelist and gospel singer, who with her first husband, evangelist Jim Bakker, hosted a TV show on the couple's PTL (Praise the Lord) network that reached millions of households; near Kansas City, MO, July 20, 2007.

N

Niekro, Joe, 61, right-handed knuckleball pitcher who won 221 MLB games in 22 seasons, and combined with his brother Phil, also a knuckleballer, for 539 wins, the most by any pair of brothers in MLB history; Tampa, FL, Oct. 27, 2006.

Niyazov, Saparmurat, 66, authoritarian leader of Turkmenistan since 1985; his reign began when his country was still the Turkmen Soviet Socialist Republic; Ashgabat, Turkmenistan, Dec. 21, 2006.

O

O'Day, Anita, 87, jazz singer, renowned for her scat-singing prowess; rose to fame with drummer Gene Krupa's band in the early 1940s and continued to perform well into her 80s; Los Angeles, CA, Nov. 23, 2006.

Oerter, Al, 71, discus thrower who was the first athlete to win four consecutive Olympic titles in one event (1956, 60, 64, & 68); Fort Meyers, FL, Oct. 1, 2007.

P

Papon, Maurice, 96, French official convicted of crimes against humanity in 1998 for his role in the deportation of hundreds of French Jews to Nazi concentration camps during World War II; Pontault-Combault, France, Feb. 17, 2007.

Palance, Jack, 87, memorably villainous actor known for such films as *Sudden Fear* (1952) and *Shane* (1953), who also had a flair for comedy, notably in *City Slickers*, for which he won a supporting-actor Oscar in 1992; Montecito, CA, Nov. 10, 2006.

Pavarotti, Luciano, 71, celebrated Italian tenor who often appeared on television and sold millions of recordings; as a member of the "Three Tenors", he recorded the best selling classical album of all time; Modena, Italy, Sept. 6, 2007.

Pep, Willie, 84, world featherweight champion for most of the period from 1942 to 1950, who had a career record of 230 wins and only 11 losses; Rocky Hill, CT, Nov. 23, 2006.

Pinochet, Augusto, 91, head of the military government that ruled Chile from the time the Marxist government of Salvador Allende was overthrown in 1973 until 1990; he was indicted for human rights abuses but never tried; Santiago, Chile, Dec. 10, 2006.

Ponti, Carlo, 94, prolific Italian film producer known for his long partnership with his wife Sophia Loren; he was the executive producer of many of her films, including *Two Women* (1960), for which she won a best-actress Oscar; Geneva, Switzerland, Jan. 9, 2007.

Pontecorvo, Gillo, 86, Italian film director best known for *The Battle of Algiers* (1965), a fictionalized account of the brutal realities of Algeria's war for independence from France; Rome, Italy, Oct. 12, 2006.

Poston, Tom, 85, comic actor best known for his work on TV, which included *Newhart* (1982-90) and an Emmy winning turn on *The Steve Allen Show*; Los Angeles, CA, April 30, 2007.

R

Reilly, Charles Nelson, 76, award-winning Broadway actor and director, and a ubiquitous presence on television game shows and talk shows in the 1970s and 1980s; Los Angeles, CA, May 25, 2007.

Rizzuto, Phil "Scooter", 89, shortstop for Major League Baseball's New York Yankees (1941-56), who went on to become a radio and television sports announcer for the Yankees (1956-96); West Orange, NJ, Aug. 13, 2007.

Roach, Max, 80, jazz percussionist and composer, known best for work in the bebop style with Charlie Parker, Charles Mingus, Dizzy Gillespie, and other jazz legends; New York, NY; Aug. 16, 2007.

Robinson, Eddie G., 88, legendary football coach at historically black Grambling State University in Louisiana for more than five decades (1941-97); Ruston, LA, April 3, 2007.

Rostropovich, Mstislav, 80, preeminent cellist of his era, whose vast repertoire included works written for him by leading 20th-cent. composers; served as the National Symphony Orchestra's music director (1977-94); Moscow, Russia, April 27, 2007.

Rothschild, Baron Guy de, 98, leader, for decades, of the French branch of Europe's banking dynasty and a leading figure in both thoroughbred racing and winemaking; Paris, France, June 12, 2007.

Russell, Anna, 94, singer and comedian who, in solo performances, TV shows and best-selling recordings, mocked various aspects of classical music; Batemans Bay, Australia, Oct. 18, 2006.

S

Sardi Jr., Vincent, 91, New York City restaurateur who for decades ran Sardi's, a legendary restaurant in the city's Broadway theater district; Berlin, VT, Jan. 4, 2007.

Schembechler, Bo, 77, one of the winningest coaches in college football history, who during his 21 seasons at the University of Michigan (1969-89) led the school to 13 Big Ten championships and

two Rose Bowl victories; Southfield, MI, Nov. 17, 2006.

Schirra, Wally, 84, one of the original "Mercury Seven" astronauts; the 5th American in space, he was the only astronaut to fly in the Mercury, Gemini and Apollo space programs; La Jolla, CA, May 3, 2007.

Schlesinger Jr., Arthur M. 89, Pulitzer Prize-winning historian, liberal political activist, and longtime Kennedy family confidant; New York, NY, Feb. 28, 2007.

Scott, Gordon, 80, actor who portrayed Tarzan in five films released between 1955 and 1960, including *Tarzan and the Lost Safari* (1957), the first Tarzan film in color; Baltimore, MD, April 30, 2007.

Servan-Schreiber, Jean-Jacques, 82, French journalist, author and politician; he co-founded (1953) what became France's first weekly newsmagazine, *L'Express*, wrote best-selling books on foreign relations, and was president of France's Radical Socialist Party during the 1970s; Fécamp, France, Nov. 7, 2006.

Sheldon, Sidney, 89, screenwriter and best-selling novelist whose books included *Rage of Angels* (1980) and *Memories of Midnight* (1990); Rancho Mirage, CA, Jan. 30, 2007.

Siegel, Joel, 63, film critic who had appeared regularly on ABC's *Good Morning America* daytime TV show since 1981; New York, NY, June 29, 2007.

Sills, Beverly, 78, one of the first exclusively U.S.-trained opera singers, she won acclaim with the New York City Opera; she was also an arts administrator, philanthropist, and TV personality; New York, NY, July 2, 2007.

Simmons, Silas, 111, pitcher in baseball's segregated Negro Leagues in the early decades of the 20th century; believed to have been the longest-living professional ballplayer ever; St. Petersburg, FL, Oct. 29, 2006.

Smathers, George A., 93, three-term Democratic senator from Florida (1951-69) who was a prominent anticommunist and opponent of civil rights legislation; Indian Creek Village, FL, Jan. 20, 2007.

Smith, Anna Nicole, 39, model and actress whose tumultuous life and death was endlessly covered by the media; Hollywood, FL, Feb. 8, 2007.

Snyder, Tom, 71, quirky TV interviewer who from 1973 to 1982 hosted a post-midnight talk show on NBC called *The Tomorrow Show*; Tiburon, CA, July 29, 2007.

Stafford, Robert T., 93, Vermont Republican politician, known for his efforts on behalf of education and the environment, who was his state's governor for 2 years (1959-61), before serving in the U.S. House of Representatives (1961-71) and the U.S. Senate (1971-89); millions of college students knew his name through a student loan program named after him in 1988; Rutland, Vt., Dec. 23, 2006.

Stanton, Frank, 98, president of the CBS network from 1946 to 1971; helped to guide the network into the television era and turn it into one of the world's most powerful media companies; Boston, MA., Dec. 24, 2006.

Studds, Gerry, 69, 12-term Democratic congressman from Massachusetts (1973-97) who in 1983 became the first member of Congress to openly declare his homosexuality; Boston, MA, Oct. 14, 2006.

Styron, William, 81, Pulitzer-winning author of a relatively small number of compelling novels, including *The Confessions of Nat Turner* (1967) and *Sophie's Choice* (1979); he chronicled his struggle with clinical depression in a nonfiction work, *Darkness Visible: A Memoir of Madness* (1990); Martha's Vineyard, MA, Nov. 1, 2006.

T

Thomas, Craig, 74, prominent conservative Republican from Wyoming who had served in the U.S. Senate since 1995; Bethesda, MD, June 4, 2007.

Troyat, Henri, 95, French novelist, short story writer and biographer; he had been the longest-standing member of the French Academy, to which he was elected in 1959; Paris, France, March 2, 2007.

U

Umeki, Miyoshi, 78, actress who was first Asian to win an Oscar, as supporting actress in *Sayonara* (1957); on television, played the housekeeper Mrs. Livingston on *The Courtship of Eddie's Father*, (1969-1972); Licking, MO, Aug. 28, 2007.

V

Valenti, Jack, 85, special assistant to President Lyndon Johnson who was President of the Motion Picture Association of America (1966-2004); Washington, DC, April 26, 2007.

Vander Jagt, Guy, 75, Michigan Republican who served in the U.S. House of Representatives from 1966 through 1992 and chaired the Republican National Committee for most of that time; Washington, DC, June 22, 2007.

Vonnegut Jr., Kurt, 84, author of the classic antiwar novel *Slaughterhouse-Five* (1969) and of such other well-known novels as *Cat's Cradle* (1963) and *Breakfast of Champions* (1973), which freely mixed satire with science-fiction elements; New York, NY, April 11, 2007.

W

Waldheim, Kurt, 88, U.N. secretary general (1972-82) and President of Austria (1986-92), he was largely shunned by the international community after being linked to World War II Nazi atrocities in the Balkans; Vienna, Austria, June 14,

Walsh, Bill, 75, football coach who led the San Francisco 49ers to three Super Bowl titles in the 1980s; Woodside, CA, July 30, 2007.

Walton, Helen, 87, matriarch of one of the world's richest families, whose fortune stemmed from the success of Wal-Mart Stores Inc., the retailing giant founded by her husband, Sam Walton, in the early 1960s; Bentonville, AR, April 19, 2007.

Wyatt, Jane, 96, actress best known for her role as an exemplary wife and mother in the 1950s TV situation comedy *Father Knows Best*; Bel Air, CA, Oct. 20, 2006.

Wyman, Jane, 90, Academy Award-winning actress best known for her roles in *Johnny Belinda* (1948) and *Magnificent Obsession (1957)*, as well as her marriage to Ronald Reagan; Palm Springs, CA, Sept 10, 2007.

Y

Yeltsin, Boris, 76, first freely elected leader of Russia in the post-Soviet era, from 1991 to 1999, he guided Russia through its turbulent economic transition; Moscow, Russia, April 23, 2007.

Z

Zahir Shah, Mohammad, 92, last king of Afghanistan; he ruled from 1933 until 1973; Kabul, Afghanistan, July 23, 2007.

Offbeat News Stories, 2007

Nation for Sale, $10 Million or Best Offer

One Belgian eBay listing attracted more attention than the usual video games, collectibles, and kitsch in Sept. 2007. Teacher and former journalist Gerrit Six, fed up with the partisan bickering that had kept the Belgian government at a standstill since elections June 10, decided to list the kingdom on eBay, in hopes of attracting attention to the need to resolve the crisis. The eBay listing advertised, "Belgium, a Kingdom in Three Parts…Free Premium: the King and his court (costs not included)." The listing also carried disclosure of the country's "secondhand" status and the warning that potential buyers would have to absorb over $300 billion in national debt.

Peter Burin, public relations manager of eBay Belgium, said the listing had received a $10 million bid and was removed to avoid confusion. "This person, in a very funny way, reminded the Belgians what a great country Belgium actually is and it would be a shame to sell it," Burin said.

I Fought the Law and the Law Won

If you thought U.S. congressional representatives, senators, and presidential candidates had the market cornered on political grandstanding, think again. Parliament members in Taiwan plan floor brawls in advance in order to show voters just how hard they fight—physically—for important issues. Political experts and some legislators believe that the fights are nothing more than staged media events, though they are not exactly the highly choreographed stunt fights seen in Hollywood films. Onlookers at a 4-hour-long melee in Jan. 2007 saw shoes thrown at the Speaker, a microphone ripped out and winged across the chamber, shoving, and tie-pulling—all in an attempt to keep the Speaker from his podium (successfully, it turned out). In 2005, one MP needed stitches after being struck by a flying cell phone; in 2006, another used tear gas on the parliament floor.

Can't Say We Didn't Warn You

Don't try to dry your cell phone in the microwave. Don't use a match to check the fuel level in your gas tank. Don't try to drive and read the phone book at the same time. In the real world, these gems of wisdom might elicit little more than a blank stare and a "Duh." But they're among the winning entries in the 2007 "Wacky Warning Labels" contest, which is run by a Michigan anti-lawsuit group.

Bob Wilkinson, the owner of a coin-operated laundry, submitted the contest's winning entry: a sticker affixed to a washing machine that read, "DO NOT put any person in this washer." A spokesperson for the washer's manufacturer said that the label was necessary because of lawsuits that had been filed in the past when children were injured while playing in laundry equipment.

Permanent Vacation

In a creative solution to their household drudgery and utility bills, a British couple has lived in a discount roadside Travelodge hotel room for more than a decade. David Davidson, a 79-year-old former Royal Navy sailor, and his wife Jean stayed at a Travelodge in 1985, while visiting a sick aunt, and got hooked on the ease of having a housekeeper around. They've spent most of their years since then in one room, near Grantham, England, that overlooks a parking lot and a busy road. The Davidsons eat their meals at the diner across the parking lot and exchange Christmas presents with the hotel staff. The couple estimated that they had spent 100,000 pounds, or about $200,000, paying rates as low as $30 a night, "because we book well in advance." They still return to their apartment, in Sheffield, England, once every two weeks to collect their mail. The Davidsons also leave the hotel to go on trips abroad, staying at—of course—Travelodge locations.

Accidental Invasion

Switzerland is famously neutral, so news reports in March that they had invaded a neighboring country seemed a little off-key. But on Mar. 1, a group of 170 Swiss soldiers on a routine training mission wandered off-track late one night and trooped past the unmarked border between Switzerland and its tiny neighbor, Liechtenstein. Armed with unloaded assault rifles (and, presumably, Swiss army knives), they drifted about 1.2 miles into the country before they realized their mistake and turned back.

Liechtenstein officials didn't seem overly concerned when asked about the accidental invasion. "It's not like they stormed over here with attack helicopters or something," said Interior Ministry spokesman Markus Amman. A good thing, too: Liechtenstein, which has a population of around 34,000 and is only about as big as Washington, DC, doesn't have a standing army.

Read It and Weep

Jane Austen's novels may have been the Harry Potter-style blockbuster best-sellers of their day, but an experiment by David Lassman, the director of the Jane Austen Festival in Bath, England, suggests that that Austen probably couldn't even get published today. Lassman sent chapters from three of Austen's novels, including *Pride and Prejudice*, to 18 of the biggest publishers in Britain in early 2007, changing only minor details such as character names and locations.

The manuscripts were rejected outright by every publisher, and only one person even acknowledged any resemblance to the original classics. One went so far as to compliment Lassman's *First Impressions* (an early working title for Austen's *Pride and Prejudice*) as seeming like "a really original and interesting read" even though it was rejected for publication.

A Rose By Any Other Name

Who's getting your vote in the presidential primaries? Virtue Soup? Oh Bus Horse? Sticky Rice? Massachusetts State Secretary William Galvin has pointed to these names as examples of how identities may be garbled when candidates' names are translated into Chinese characters on the state primary ballot as required by the federal justice department. Translators select characters that could be used to match the sound of each syllable, muddying the meaning of names. "Virtue Soup" is a potential transliteration of Fred Thompson. Barack Obama might be read as "Oh Bus Horse," and Mitt Romney could be either "Sticky Rice" or "Uncooked Rice."

Our Biggest Fan

The World Almanac is, for many readers, a traditional purchase made year after year. One reader, though, took his Almanac affinity to the next level. Rich Gruber, a self-proclaimed "trivia type," bought his first edition of *The World Almanac* in 1962, at the age of 8, from the neighborhood candy store, and has been buying one annually ever since. (Although the price has escalated from the $1.35 he originally paid.) Several years ago, Gruber began collecting the editions that preceded his original purchase. Now, through the magic of online auction sites, he has amassed a nearly complete collection. According to Gruber, he is missing only 4 editions—all of them more than 100 years old.

"As a kid I just sat there and read it for hours and hours. It's not like I was one-dimensional, I always had lots of interests, but the book always fascinated me. I guess, you know, once the idea of collecting it came, it just seemed like a natural thing to do," Gruber said.

Notable Quotes in 2007

Iraq and Global War on Terror

"The struggle in Iraq is winnable."

Gen. George W. Casey Jr., testifying during his Army chief-of-staff confirmation hearing Feb. 1.

"Odds are you're going to deal with tragedy."

Joyce Stahlschmidt, a Missouri mother of 11 children who had four sons deploying to Iraq in 2007.

"Our forces are stretched, there's no question about that."

Defense Sec. Robert Gates, on deciding Apr. 11 to extend the length of most combat tours from 12 to 15 months.

"We can categorically state that we have not released man-eating badgers into the area."

Maj. Mike Shearer, British military spokesman in Iraq, on rumors July 12 that forces had released carnivorous badgers in Basra.

"I have Sunni, I have Shi'ite, and I have no problems with that. They never talk politics."

Jorvan Vieira, the Brazilian coach of Iraq's national soccer team, which upset the Australian team July 14.

"I heard somebody say, 'Where's Mandela?' Well, Mandela's dead because Saddam Hussein killed all the Mandelas."

Pres. George W. Bush, referring Sept. 20 to the absence of symbolic figures of hope and reconciliation in Iraq.

"I was responsible for the 9/11 operation, from A to Z."

Khalid Sheikh Mohammed, in military tribunal transcripts released Mar. 14.

"America does not have any intention of being the world's jailer."

Deputy Press Sec. Dana Perino, June 22, on U.S. plans to release about 80 Guantanamo detainees.

"It's a serious issue that is going to outlast my presidency."

Pres. Bush, on al-Qaeda's lingering threat, July 12.

"This is about the best he can do. This is a man on the run, from a cave, who's virtually impotent other than these tapes."

Frances Fragos Townsend, White House aide, downplaying Osama bin Laden's taped messages Sept. 9.

Presidential Campaign

"These aren't debates—this is a cross between *The Bachelor*, *American Idol*, and *Who's Smarter Than a Fifth Grader?*"

Former Rep. Newt Gingrich (R, GA), who said Aug. 7 that the current presidential race was too long and "verging on insane."

"Well, you know, people can vote for whoever they want. That's true in my election, and it's true on *American Idol*."

Sen. Hillary Clinton (D, NY), Apr. 13, when asked what the U.S. could do about *Idol* contestant Sanjaya Malakar.

"If you like what I'm saying, I would like you to vote multiple times. If you don't like that, then stay home. Just kidding."

Former Gov. Mitt Romney, joking with prospective primary voters in New Hampshire July 25.

"You got the first mainstream African American who is articulate and bright and clean."

Sen. Joe Biden (D, CT), referring to Barack Obama's possible candidacy in a Feb. 7 article. Biden later apologized.

"I can't be hip anymore. I'm running for president."

Sen. Barack Obama (D, IL), commenting on wardrobe options—including high-top sneakers—offered at a photo shoot appearing in the Sept. issue of *Vibe* magazine.

"I'm probably one of the four or five best-known Americans in the world."

Former New York City Mayor Rudy Giuliani, Sept. 19, to reporters in London, on his foreign policy credentials.

"If he's dead, just prop him up and put some dark glasses on him like *Weekend at Bernie's.*"

Sen. John McCain (R, AZ), joking Oct. 4 about appointing retired Fed chairman Alan Greenspan to lead a review of the nation's tax codes.

National News

"I accept this gavel in the spirit of partnership, not partisanship."

Rep. Nancy Pelosi (D, CA), the first woman Speaker of the House, as Congress opened Jan. 3.

"I'm not going to get into a name-calling match with somebody who had a 9 percent approval rating."

Sen. Harry Reid (D, NV), responding Apr. 24 to Vice Pres. Dick Cheney's comment that Reid's remarks on the Iraq War represented "defeatism."

"At \$5.15 an hour, I get zero applicants—or maybe a guy with one leg who wouldn't pass a drug test."

Rob Elder, restaurant owner, commenting Jan. 9 on the task of finding people to work for the federal minimum wage.

"I'm a myth, I'm Beowulf, I'm Grendel."

Karl Rove, Aug. 19, on public perception of the power he wielded as Pres. Bush's adviser.

"If you can figure out how to make a schoolyard fight into an attempted murder charge, I'm sure you can figure out how to make stringing nooses into a hate crime."

Latese Brown, one of 10,000 marchers in Jena, LA, Sept. 20, who were protesting what they saw as racially-biased treatment of six black students.

Immigration

"We want your money whether you are here legally or not and whether you earned it legally or not."

Mark W. Everson, Internal Revenue Service commissioner, Mar. 27, on taxing illegal immigrants' income.

"People are at least as smart as goats . . . Now one of the ways I keep those goats in the fence is I electrified them. Once they got popped a couple of times, they quit trying to jump it."

Sen. Trent Lott (R, MS), June 21, on the proposal for a fence to keep out illegal immigrants.

Arts & Entertainment

"Could you double-check the envelope?"

Martin Scorsese, accepting his Academy Award for Best Director Feb. 25, after five fruitless nominations.

"In as few words as possible: no."

Bob Barker, departing host of *The Price is Right,* on whether his June 6 retirement included plans to watch the show.

Sports

"The most important thing for me is family, second is footba—soccer, sorry."

David Beckham, British soccer star, July 13, on joining the L.A. Galaxy major league soccer team.

"I hate baseball right now."

Moises Alou, veteran New York Mets outfielder, Oct. 1, after the team's record-setting late-season collapse.

Miscellaneous News

"This is a natural country. You should see it in its natural beauty. It's like putting a fifth leg on a horse."

Bob Simpson, Australian tourist, on his Mar. 28 visit to the glass-bottomed Arizona Grand Canyon Skywalk.

"Our education over here in the U.S. should help the U.S. or should help South Africa or should help the Iraq and Asian countries so we will be able to build up our future for us."

Miss South Carolina Lauren Caitlin Upton, at the Miss Teen USA pageant Aug. 24, responding to a question about why some Americans can't find the U.S. on a map.

"I am now a heavenly body."

George Takei, 70-year-old former *Star Trek* actor, Oct. 2, on having an asteroid renamed "7307 Takei" in his honor.

Historical Anniversaries, 2008

1908 – 100 Years Ago

176 children and teachers die in a fire at Lake View School in Collinwood, OH, March 4.

The Medical Reserve Corps, which later evolves into the **U.S. Army Reserve**, is created Apr. 23.

Large deposits of **oil** are discovered in Persia (Iran) May 26.

Attorney General Charles J. Bonaparte forms a task force of special agents July 26 to act as the investigative branch of the Dept. of Justice; the **FBI evolves** out of this group.

Anti-black **rioting** rocks Springfield, IL, Aug. 14-15.

Brutal ruler **King Leopold II** relinquishes control of the Belgian Congo Aug. 20 to Belgium's parliament.

General Motors Corp. is established Sept. 16 by William Durant.

Henry Ford begins selling the **Model T** automobile Oct. 1, for $850 (about $16,700 in today's dollars).

The Transvaal and the Orange Free State, both defeated in the Boer War, meet with Cape Colony and Natal Oct. 12 to draft the constitution that creates the Union of **South Africa**.

A 7.5-magnitude earthquake Dec. 28 in Messina, Sicily, kills more than 83,000 people and destroys 90% of Messina's buildings.

Art. Constantin Brancusi's *The Kiss*; Pierre Bonnard's *Nude Against the Light*. Henri Matisse publishes *Notes d'un peintre* in *Le Grande Révieu*. "The Eight," a group of modern painters led by Robert Henri, five of whom were members of what later was known as the "Ashcan school," hold a self-selected exhibition at the Macbeth Gallery in New York City.

Literature. Arnold Bennett's *The Old Wives' Tale*; E. M. Forster's *A Room With a View*; Kenneth Grahame's *The Wind in the Willows*; L. M. Montgomery's *Anne of Green Gables*.

Movies. *Tosca* starring Sarah Bernhardt; D.W. Griffith makes his directorial debut with *The Adventures of Dollie*. New York City Mayor George B. McClellan revokes the licenses of the city's 550 movie theaters, reinstating them only after managers pledge not to offer Sunday shows or screen "immoral" films.

Music. Béla Bartók's *String Quartet No. 1;* Edward Elgar's *Symphony No. 1*; Charles Ives' *The Unanswered Question*.

Nonfiction. Georges Sorel's *Reflections on Violence*; A. Lawrence Lowell's *The Government of England*; Mary Baker Eddy founds the *Christian Science Monitor*.

Pop Music. George M. Cohan's "The Small Town Gal"; Scott Joplin's "Fig Leaf Rag."

Science and Technology. Jacques Brandenberger invents cellophane; Ernest Rutherford and Hans Geiger invent the Geiger counter for detecting radioactive material. Orville Wright crashes his airplane, killing passenger Thomas Selfridge—the first person killed in an airplane accident.

Sports. The fourth Olympic Games were held in London. Boxer Jack Johnson becomes the first African American to win the Heavyweight title. The Chicago Cubs win their second consecutive World Series (over the Detroit Tigers, 4-1) and their last championship of the 20th century.

Theatre. *A Gentleman From Mississippi*, *The Man From Home*, and *Sporting Days* begin long runs on Broadway.

Miscellaneous. For the first time, revelers ring in the New Year with the descent of the New Year's Eve Ball on Jan. 1, 1908, in Times Square. Boer War veteran Robert Baden-Powell forms the first Boy Scout troop in Great Britain.

1958 – 50 Years Ago

Egypt and Syria proclaim themselves the **United Arab Republic** Feb. 1.

Nikita **Khrushchev** replaces Nikolai Bulganin as Soviet premier Mar. 27.

Pres. Eisenhower signs the Alaska statehood bill July 7, clearing the way for Alaska to become the **49th state** in the union following ratification by residents of the territory.

Iraqi King Faisal is killed in a military coup, and Iraq is declared a republic July 14.

U.S. Marines are sent to **Lebanon** to prevent an overthrow of the elected government July-Oct.

The *Nautilus* nuclear submarine makes the first undersea **crossing of the North Pole** Aug. 5.

Chinese leader Mao Zedong launches the economic program known as the **"Great Leap Forward"** Sept. 3.

U.S. presidential aide Sherman Adams resigns Sept. 22 over allegations of receiving improper gifts and favors.

A new constitution, approved by a wide margin in a referendum Sept. 28, sets the framework for **France's Fifth Republic**.

The Democratic Party wins a landslide victory in midterm elections Nov. 4, solidifying the **Democratic majority** in both chambers of the U.S. Congress.

Art. Bruce Connor's *A Movie*; in New York City, Jasper Johns opens his first solo exhibition at the Leo Castelli gallery.

Literature. Chinua Achebe's *Things Fall Apart*; Truman Capote's *Breakfast at Tiffany's*; Iris Murdoch's *The Bell*; Leon Uris's *Exodus*; Boris Pasternak declines the Nobel Prize in Literature.

Movies. *The Big Country* starring Carroll Baker, Charlton Heston, and Gregory Peck; *Cat on a Hot Tin Roof* starring Burl Ives, Paul Newman, and Elizabeth Taylor; *The Defiant Ones* starring Tony Curtis and Sidney Poitier; *Gigi*; *No Time for Sergeants* starring Andy Griffith; *Separate Tables* starring Rita Hayworth, Deborah Kerr, and David Niven; *South Pacific*; Orson Welles' *Touch of Evil* starring Charlton Heston and Janet Leigh; Alfred Hitchcock's *Vertigo* starring Jimmy Stewart and Kim Novak; *The Vikings*.

Music. A 23-year-old Texan, Van Cliburn, wins the prestigious International Tchaikovsky Competition; Samuel Barber's *Vanessa* debuts.

Nonfiction. Hannah Arendt's *The Human Condition*; John Kenneth Galbraith's *The Affluent Society*; Claude Lévi-Strauss's *Structural Anthropology*.

Pop Music. Chuck Berry's "Johnny B. Goode" and "Sweet Little Sixteen"; Danny and the Juniors' "At the Hop"; The Everly Brothers' "All I Have to Do Is Dream"; Peggy Lee's "Fever"; The Kingston Trio's "Tom Dooley"; Domenico Modugno's "Nel Blu Dipinto Di Blu (Volare)"; Richie Valens's "La Bamba"; Sheb Wooley's "Purple People Eater." Elvis Presley joins the U.S. Army. Perry Como is awarded the RIAA's first Gold certification for "Catch a Falling Star."

Science and Technology. The U.S. launches *Explorer I*, its first Earth satellite, Jan. 31; Congress creates NASA July 29.

Sports. Althea Gibson wins both Wimbledon and U.S. Open tournaments and is named Female Athlete of the Year by the AP; Sugar Ray Robinson reclaims the middleweight title for a record fifth time; the San Francisco Giants and Los Angeles Dodgers play the first Major League Baseball regular seasons on the West Coast.

Television. *Gunsmoke* is the highest-rated program; *The Donna Reed Show* debuts. Quiz show scandals mar the credibility of early TV as investigations into cheating on *Dotto* begin.

Theatre. *Flower Drum Song*, *Two for the Seesaw*, *Sunrise at Campobello*, and *J.B.* open on Broadway.

Miscellaneous. A hula hoop trend sweeps the U.S. The Bank of America launches the BankAmericard (later Visa), which is the first revolving credit charge card.

1983 – 25 Years Ago

The federal government offers Feb. 22 to use part of the $1.6 billion environmental **"Superfund"** to buy out business- and home-owners in Times Beach, MO, after the discovery of carcinogenic dioxin in its soil.

President Ronald Reagan announces plans for a Strategic Defense Initiative (SDI, later dubbed "Star Wars") to research and develop a **missile defense shield**.

A **truck bomb** at the U.S. embassy in Beirut, Lebanon, kills 63 people Apr. 18.

Harold Washington is sworn in Apr. 29 as the **first African American mayor** of Chicago.

A misidentified South Korean passenger jet is shot down Sept. 1 after infringing on Soviet airspace; 269 people (including 61 Americans) are killed.

Interior Sec. James G. **Watt resigns** Oct. 9 in the wake of criticism over controversial remarks he had made about his staff.

Two truck bombs explode Oct. 23 at French and U.S. Marine **bases in Beirut**, Lebanon, killing 62 French and 242 Americans.

U.S. troops and a Caribbean multinational force **invade Grenada** Oct. 25 to depose its Marxist regime.

Pres. Reagan signs legislation Nov. 2 designating **Martin Luther King Day** a federal holiday (as of 1986).

Drought plagues much of Africa, with nearly one-third of the **African population near famine** by year's end.

Art. Jean-Michel Basquiat's *In Italian*; Sandro Chia's *Three Boys on a Raft*; Nan Goldin's *Nan and Brian in Bed, NYC*; Keith Haring's "Subway Paintings"; Christo and Jeanne-Claude wrap Biscayne Bay, FL, islands in pink fabric for their *Surrounded Islands*.

Literature. William Kennedy's *Ironweed*; Mary Oliver's *American Primitive*; William Golding is awarded the Nobel Prize in Literature.

Movies. *The Big Chill*; *El Norte*; Ingmar Bergman's *Fanny and Alexander*; *Flashdance*; *Return of the Jedi*; *The Right Stuff*; *Risky Business*; *Scarface* starring Al Pacino and Michelle Pfeiffer; *Silkwood* starring Meryl Streep and Kurt Russell; *Tender Mercies* starring Robert Duvall; *Terms of Endearment* starring Shirley MacLaine and Jack Nicholson; *The Year of Living Dangerously*; *Yentl* starring Barbra Streisand.

Music. Leonard Bernstein's *A Quiet Place*; Bernard Rands' *Canti del Sole*.

Nonfiction. Louis R. Harlan's *Booker T. Washington: The Wizard of Tuskegee*; Paul Starr's *Social Transformation of American Medicine*.

Pop Music. Culture Club's "Karma Chameleon"; Eurythmics' *Sweet Dreams (Are Made of This)*; New Order's *Power, Corruption, & Lies*; The Police's *Synchronicity*, feat. "Every Breath You Take"; R.E.M.'s *Murmur*, feat. "Radio Free Europe"; Lionel Richie's "All Night Long"; Talking Heads' "Burning Down the House"; U2's "New Year's Day" and "Sunday Bloody Sunday." Singles from Michael Jackson's *Thriller*, released in 1982, continue to top charts worldwide.

Science and Technology. Astronaut Sally Ride becomes the first American woman to venture into space. Researchers at the U.S. National Cancer Institute and France's Pasteur Institute isolate the HIV virus.

Sports. The *Australia II* claims the America's Cup yachting prize in the contest's first non-U.S. victory in 131 years; Washington Redskins win the team's first Super Bowl title, over the Miami Dolphins.

Television. The *M*A*S*H* series finale airs and a record 50.1 million households tune in; *The A-Team* premieres.

Theatre. *Brighton Beach Memoirs*, *La Cage aux Folles*, *'night, Mother*, and *Noises Off* open in New York; David Mamet's *Glengarry Glen Ross* debuts in London.

Miscellaneous. CDs are sold in the U.S. for the first time. Cabbage Patch Kids dolls are the must-have holiday toy fad.

WORLD ALMANAC EDITORS' PICKS
2007 Time Capsule

The editors of *The World Almanac* have selected the following items as representative of the year 2007.

1. J. K. Rowling's *Harry Potter and the Deathly Hallows*, with a purchase receipt from its July 21 release date—on which it sold more than 10 mil copies in the U.S. and U.K.
2. The gavel used by Rep. Nancy Pelosi (D, CA), the first woman elected Speaker of the U.S. House of Representatives, to open the 110th Congress.
3. A pouch of contaminated pet food, one of the first of many tainted consumer products yanked from store shelves in 2007.
4. A candle from Virginia Tech's Apr. 17 nighttime vigil in memory of the victims of the Apr. 16 shootings.
5. Barry Bond's 756th home run ball, purchased at auction by designer Marc Ecko for $752,467. Ecko later sponsored an online vote which determined that the ball should be branded with an asterisk and donated to the Baseball Hall of Fame.
6. A copy of *Climate Change 2007*, a report by the Intergovernmental Panel on Climate Change, which called the global warming trend "unequivocal" and said that human behavior was "very likely" contributing to it.
7. A gallon of ethanol, which was produced in the U.S. in record amounts in 2007—13 mil barrels in July alone, a 33% increase over July 2006.
8. Florida Gators football and basketball jerseys, in honor of their unprecedented dual championship seasons.
9. One of the record number of foreclosure notices (nearly 250,000 in August alone) that were served upon home buyers in 2007 in the wake of the subprime mortgage crisis.
10. An iPhone, preloaded with an mp3 of Journey's "Don't Stop Believin'," in honor of the last scene in the final season of *The Sopranos*.

Notable Supreme Court Decisions, 2006-07

During the Supreme Court's 2006-07 term, which ended June 28, 72 decisions were announced (68 of which were signed), down from 82 the previous term. 24 of those decisions, or 33%, were decided by 5-4 votes, compared with 20% in 2005-06 and 21% in 2004-05. It was the first full term with Bush appointees Chief Justice John G. Roberts Jr. and Associate Justice Samuel A. Alito Jr. on the bench. Roberts, Alito, Antonin Scalia, and Clarence Thomas tended to vote as a conservative bloc, often at odds with members of the court's liberal wing—Justices Ruth Bader Ginsburg, Stephen G. Breyer, John Paul Stevens, and David H. Souter. The absence of Sandra Day O'Connor, who had been considered a swing vote, and who had voted in 20 cases in the previous term before retiring in Jan. 2006, was noticeable. The court's remaining moderate, Anthony M. Kennedy was in the majority in each of the 24 decisions decided by one vote.

Former Associate Justice O'Connor had announced her retirement July 1, 2005, pending confirmation of a successor, and Chief Justice Rehnquist died on Sept. 3, 2005. Federal appellate court judge John G. Roberts Jr., who had initially been nominated to take O'Connor's seat on the court, was confirmed by the Senate to replace Rehnquist as chief justice Sept. 29, 2005, and Samuel A. Alito Jr. was sworn in as associate justice on Jan. 31, 2006.

See also listings of justices on page 431.

Following are some of the major rulings of the 2006-07 term.

Abortion: The court Apr. 18 upheld, 5-4, the federal Partial Birth Abortion Ban Act, enacted in 2003, in *Gonzales v. Carhart.* The majority opinion emphasized abortion's "ethical and moral concerns" and went against a precedent set by the court in 2000, when it overturned a similar state ban.

Antitrust Rules: The court June 28 struck down, 5-4, a 96-year-old rule against manufacturers and retailers agreeing on minimum resale prices, ruling that it was not automatically a violation of the Sherman Antitrust Act, in *Leegin Creative Leather Products v. PSK Inc.*

Appellate Access: The court June 14 upheld, 5-4, an appellate court's decision to dismiss an appeal because it was filed after a federal filing deadline. The plaintiff had argued that because a federal judge had given incorrect instruction as to the time allowed for an appeal, the case should fall within the "unique circumstances" precedent established in the 1960s. The case was *Bowles v. Russell* and the decision overturned the "unique circumstances" precedents.

Campaign Finance: In *FEC v. Wisconsin Right to Life* and *McCain et. al. v. Wisconsin Right to Life,* the Supreme Court decided June 25, 5-4, that part of the 2002 campaign finance reform act—which prohibited issue-advocacy ads that use a specific candidate's name from airing within 30 days of a primary or 60 days of a general election—violated the First Amendment.

Capital Punishment: In *Uttecht v. Brown,* the court June 4 decided, 5-4, that appeals courts should defer to the trial judge's decision on whether potential jurors could overcome misgivings or ambivalence toward capital punishment and consider imposing the death sentence.

The court Apr. 25 decided, 5-4, to overturn the death sentence because of flawed jurisprudence regarding jury instruction, in 3 separate Texas cases: *Abdul-Kabir v. Quarterman, Brewer v. Quarterman,* and *Smith v. Texas.*

Criminal Sentencing: In *Cunningham v. California,* the justices Jan. 22 struck down, 6-3, a 30-year-old statute governing criminal sentencing, finding that it allowed judges to wield authority that the Constitution gives to juries alone.

The court June 21 ruled, 8-1, in *Rita v. United States,* that sentences falling within non-mandatory federal sentencing guidelines are to be presumed "reasonable" by appeals courts.

Employee Rights: The court May 29 ruled, 5-4, in *Ledbetter v. Goodyear Tire and Rubber Company,* that employees could not sue employers for discriminatory pay under Title VII of the 1964 Civil Rights Act if they had not made a formal complaint with a federal agency within 180 days of the first offense, regardless of whether the discrimination was immediately apparent or ongoing.

Environment: In *Commonwealth of Massachusetts v. U.S. Environmental Protection Agency,* the court Apr. 2 ruled, 5-4, that absent a scientific basis for refusing to take action, terms of the Clean Air Act both authorize and compel the EPA to regulate carbon dioxide and other "heat trapping" gases in auto emissions.

Free Speech: The court June 25 ruled, 6-3, in *Morse v. Frederick,* that a high-school principal had not violated a student's right to free speech when she took the student's large banner, which displayed a message she regarded as promoting illegal drug use, and suspended him.

School Desegregation: The Supreme Court June 28 ruled, 5-4, in *Meredith v. Jefferson County Board of Education* and *Parents Involved in Community Schools v. Seattle School District No. 1,* that school placement programs that used race explicitly in pursuing student body diversity violated the Constitution's equal protection guarantee.

Tobacco Industry: The court ruled Feb. 20, 5-4, in favor of overturning an Oregon jury's punitive award of $79.5 million against Philip Morris. The decision, in *Philip Morris USA v. Williams,* found that jurors may have been unduly influenced by desire to punish the cigarette maker for harm that was unrelated to the plaintiff, a smoker's widow.

The 2007 Nobel Prizes

The 2007 Nobel Prize winners were announced Oct. 8-15. Each prize is worth about $1.5 million.

Chemistry: Gerhard Ertl (Germany) was awarded the chemistry prize for his studies of chemical processes on solid surfaces. More specifically, Ertl's work focused on the interplay between gases and solid surfaces. His research has explained or improved processes in agriculture, climatology, manufacturing, and mechanics.

Literature: Doris Lessing (UK) was recognized as "that epicist of the female experience, who with scepticism, fire, and visionary power has subjected a divided civilisation to scrutiny." The Persian-born, southern Africa-raised Lessing's work was often feminist and autobiographical. Her novels included *The Golden Notebook* (1962), *The Grass is Singing* (1950), and *The Good Terrorist* (1985). She was the 11th woman to win the literature prize.

Economics: Americans Leonid Hurwicz, Eric S. Maskin, and Roger B. Myerson shared the economics prize for their development of mechanism design theory, which "has greatly enhanced our understanding of optimal allocation mechanisms in such situations, accounting for individuals' incentives and private information."

Peace: The Intergovernmental Panel on Climate Change (IPCC) and former Vice Pres. Al Gore shared the peace prize for their efforts to spread information about man-made climate change and the measures needed to counteract it. The IPCC, a group of 2,000 scientists, had been producing assessments of climate change since the panel was established in 1988. As vice president, Gore had played a major role in the Kyoto Protocol negotiations and, since leaving office, he had released the Academy Award-winning climate change documentary *An Inconvenient Truth.*

Physics: Albert Fert (France) and Peter Grünberg (Germany) shared the physics prize for separately discovering 'giant magnetoresistance' in 1988. The effect, in which small changes in a magnetic field produce huge changes in electrical resistance, ultimately became the basis for some methods of digital data storage—the iPod was noted as one of many gadgets made possible by the discovery.

Physiology or Medicine: Sir Martin J. Evans (UK) and Americans Mario R. Capecchi and Oliver Smithies shared the Nobel in physiology for their contributions to developing "knockout," or gene targeting, technology. The technology allows scientists to selectively introduce genetic modifications for researching anything from a specific gene's function to understanding and treating various human ailments.

Congressional Committees

Congress divides its tasks among some 225 committees and subcommittees. Standing committees generally have legislative jurisdiction and operate with subcommittees that handle work in specific areas. Select and joint committees are chiefly for oversight or housekeeping. The **chair of each House or Senate committee and a majority of its members come from the majority party** (Democratic Party as of Oct. 2007) in both the Senate and the House.

(as of Oct. 1, 2007)

Senate Standing Committees

Agriculture, Nutrition, and Forestry
Chair: Tom Harkin, D-IA
Ranking: Saxby Chambliss, R-GA

Appropriations
Chair: Robert C. Byrd, D-WV
Ranking: Thad Cochran, R-MS

Armed Services
Chair: Carl Levin, D-MI
Ranking: John McCain, R-AZ

Banking, Housing, and Urban Affairs
Chair: Christopher J. Dodd, D-UT
Ranking: Richard C. Shelby, R-AL

Budget
Chair: Kent Conrad, D-ND
Ranking: Judd Gregg, R-NH

Commerce, Science, and Transportation
Chair: Daniel K. Inouye, D-HI
Vice Chair: Ted Stevens, R-AK

Energy and Natural Resources
Chair: Jeff Bingaman, D-NM
Ranking: Pete V. Domenici, R-NM

Environment and Public Works
Chair: Barbara Boxer, D-CA
Ranking: James M. Inhofe, R-OK

Finance
Chair: Max Baucus, D-MT
Ranking: Chuck Grassley, R-IA

Foreign Relations
Chair: Joseph R. Biden Jr., D-DE
Ranking: Richard G. Lugar, R-IN

Health, Education, Labor, and Pensions
Chair: Edward M. Kennedy, D-MA
Ranking: Michael B. Enzi, R-WY

Homeland Security and Governmental Affairs
Chair: Joseph I. Lieberman, I-CT
Ranking: Susan M. Collins, R-ME

Judiciary
Chair: Patrick J. Leahy, D-VT
Ranking: Arlen Specter, R-PA

Rules and Administration
Chair: Dianne Feinstein, D-CA
Ranking: Robert Bennett, R-UT

Small Business and Entrepreneurship
Chair: John F. Kerry, D-MA
Ranking: Olympia J. Snowe, R-ME

Veterans' Affairs
Chair: Daniel K. Akaka, D-HI
Ranking: Richard M. Burr, R-NC

Senate Special, Select, and Other Committees

Special Committee on Aging
Chair: Herb Kohl, D-WI
Ranking: Gordon Smith, R-OR

Select Committee on Ethics
Chair: Barbara Boxer, D-CA
Vice Chair: John Cornyn, R-TX

Indian Affairs
Chair: Byron Dorgan, D-ND
Vice Chair: Lisa Murkowski, R-AK

Select Committee on Intelligence
Chair: John D. Rockefeller IV, D-WV
Vice Chair: Christopher S. Bond, R-MO

Joint Committees of Congress

Joint Committee on Printing
Chair: Rep. Robert A. Brady, D-PA
Ranking: Sen. Dianne Feinstein, D-CA

Joint Committee on Taxation
Chair: Rep. Charles B. Rangel, D-NY
Vice Chair: Sen. Max Baucus, D-MT

Joint Committee on the Library
Chair: Sen. Dianne Feinstein, D-CA
Vice Chair: Rep. Robert A. Brady, D-PA

Joint Economic Committee
Chair: Sen. Charles E. Schumer, D-NY
Vice Chair: Rep. Carolyn B. Maloney, D-NY

House Standing Committees

Agriculture
Chair: Collin C. Peterson, D-MN
Ranking: Bob Goodlatte, R-VA

Appropriations
Chair: David R. Obey, D-WI
Ranking: Jerry Lewis, R-CA

Armed Services
Chair: Ike Skelton, D-MO
Ranking: Duncan Hunter, R-CA

Budget
Chair: John M. Spratt Jr., D-SC
Ranking: Paul Ryan, R-WI

Education and Labor
Chair: George Miller, D-CA
Ranking: Howard P. "Buck" McKeon, R-CA

Energy and Commerce
Chair: John D. Dingell, D-MI
Ranking: Joe Barton, R-TX

Financial Services
Chair: Barney Frank, D-MA
Ranking: Spencer Bachus, R-AL

Homeland Security
Chair: Bennie G. Thompson, D-MS
Ranking: Peter T. King, R-NY

House Administration
Chair: Robert A. Brady, D-PA
Ranking: Vernon J. Ehlers, R-MI

Foreign Affairs
Chair: Tom Lantos, D-CA
Ranking: Ileana Ros-Lehtinen, R-FL

Judiciary
Chair: John Conyers Jr., D-MI
Ranking: Lamar Smith, R-TX

Natural Resources
Chair: Nick J. Rahall II, D-WV
Ranking: Don Young, R-AK

Oversight and Government Reform
Chair: Henry A. Waxman, D-CA
Ranking: Tom Davis, R-VA

Rules
Chair: Louise McIntosh Slaughter, D-NY
Ranking: David Dreier, R-CA

Science and Technology
Chair: Bart Gordon, D-TN
Ranking: Ralph M. Hall, R-TX

Small Business
Chair: Nydia M. Velázquez, D-NY
Ranking: Steve Chabot, R-OH

Standards of Official Conduct
Chair: Stephanie Tubbs Jones, D-OH
Ranking: Doc Hastings, R-WA

Transportation and Infrastructure
Chair: James L. Oberstar, D-MN
Ranking: John L. Mica, R-FL

Veterans' Affairs
Chair: Bob Filner, D-CA
Ranking: Steve Buyer, R-IN

Ways and Means
Chair: Charles B. Rangel, D-NY
Ranking: Jim McCrery, R-LA

House Select Committees

Permanent Committee on Intelligence
Chair: Silvestre Reyes, D-TX
Ranking: Peter Hoekstra, R-MI

Committee on Energy Independence & Global Warming
Chair: Edward J. Markey, D-MA
Ranking: James Sensenbrenner, R-WI

BUSINESS AND ECONOMICS

Money in America (pp. 42-43)

Amount of money that Americans put in savings . . . . in 1990: $299.4 bil . . . . in 2006: $38.8 bil
Average % of disposable income that Americans put in savings . . . . in 1990: 7.0% . . . . in 2006: 0.4%
Revolving consumer credit outstanding from commercial banks . . . . in 2006: $327.3 bil

Personal expenditures, by category, 2006 (p. 46)

Medical Care . . . . $1,587.7 bil
Housing . . . . $1,381.3 bil
Food. . . . . $1,259.3 bil
Clothing and shoes. . . . . $357.2 bil
Gasoline and oil . . . . $318.6 bil
New autos . . . . $107.1 bil
Tobacco products. . . . . $92.4 bil
Casino gambling . . . . $81.6 bil
Nursery, elementary, secondary schools . . . . $46.4 bil
Books and maps . . . . $43.4 bil

Spending on selected products, 2006 (p. 366)

Personal computers . . . . $19.3 bil
Cell phones . . . . $17.9 bil
Beer . . . . $9.2 bil
Cereal . . . . $6.3 bil
Ice cream . . . . $4.5 bil
Cookies . . . . $4.0 bil
Coffee . . . . $3.2 bil
Frozen pizza . . . . $2.8 bil
Chocolate candies (3.5 oz) . . . . $1.8 bil
Toothpaste. . . . . $1.5 bil

Top categories for ad spending (p. 245)

1. Automotive . . . . $19.8 bil
2. Retail . . . . $19.1 bil
3. Telecommunications/Internet. . . . . $11.0 bil
4. Medicine/remedies. . . . . $9.2 bil
5. General services . . . . $8.7 bil

Top advertisers (p. 245)

1. Procter & Gamble . . . . $4.9 bil
2. AT&T . . . . $3.3 bil
3. General Motors . . . . $3.3 bil
4. Time Warner . . . . $3.0 bil
5. Verizon Communications . . . . $2.8 bil

Wealth, Wages, and Poverty (pp. 44-48, 101)

Wealthiest American, 2007
Bill Gates, $59 billion net worth

Corporation with highest revenues, 2007
Wal-Mart Stores, $351 billion

	Median Weekly Earnings, 2007[1]		Percent below
	Men[2]	Women[2]	poverty level[3]
Asian	$959	$737	12.3%
White.	$846	$654	10.3%
Black	$623	$554	24.3%
Hispanic.	$559	$488	12.3%

Average weekly hours worked by U.S. production workers . . . . in 1969: 37.5 . . . . in 2006: 33.9
Average hourly earnings of U.S. production workers. . . . . in 1969: $3.22 . . . . in 2006: $16.76
% of Americans below poverty level . . . . in 1960: 22.2% . . . . in 2006: 12.3%
State with highest percentage of people living in poverty, 2005-06 . . . . Mississippi, 20.4%
State with lowest percentage of population living in poverty, 2005-06. . . . . New Hampshire, 5.5%

Housing (pp. 367-68)

Home ownership rates, by race/ethnicity

	1997	2007[1]	% change
White.	72.1%	75.4%	4.6%
Black	44.4%	46.3%	4.3%
Hispanic.	43.3%	50.0%	15.5%
Other.	52.7%	59.4%	12.7%

Median price for an existing home . . . . in 1997: $121,800 . . . . in 2007[1]: $223,800
Avg. monthly principal/interest payment . . . . in 1997: $693. . . . . in 2007[1]: $1,128
Monthly principal/interest payment as % of monthly income. . . . . in 1997: 18.7%. . . . . in 2007[1]: $22.9%
In 2nd quarter 2007, % of people who owned their own homes . . . . under age 35: 41.9% . . . . over age 65: 80.5%

International Trade (pp. 67-68)

(all figures in millions)

Top trade partners, 2006[4]

Canada. $533,094
China. $342,960
Mexico. $332,232
Japan $207,794
Germany $130,401

Top exports, 2006

Vehicles. $83,472
Electrical machinery $83,228
Gen. industrial machines. . . . $44,089
Power gen. machinery $44,036
Airplanes. $43,933

Top imports, 2006

Crude oil $225,156
Vehicles. $211,946
Televisions, VCRs, etc. $115,327
Electrical machinery $109,721
Data/office equip. $106,416

(1) 2nd quarter 2007. (2) Workers age 25 and older. (3) in 2006. (4) By total trade with U.S.

ECONOMICS

Index of Leading Economic Indicators

Source: The Conference Board

The index of leading economic indicators is used to project the U.S. economy's performance. The index is made up of 10 measurements of economic activity that tend to change direction in advance of the overall economy. The index has predicted economic downturns from 8 to 20 months in advance and recoveries from 1 to 10 months in advance; however, it can be inconsistent, and has occasionally shown "false signals" of recessions.

Components

Average weekly hours of production workers in manufacturing
Average weekly initial claims for unemployment insurance, state programs
Manufacturers' new orders for consumer goods and materials, adjusted for inflation
Vendor performance (slower deliveries diffusion index)

Manufacturers' new orders, nondefense capital goods industries, adjusted for inflation
New private housing units authorized by local building permits
Stock prices, 500 common stocks
Money supply: M-2, adjusted for inflation
Interest rate spread, 10-yr Treasury bonds less federal funds
Consumer expectations (researched by Univ. of Michigan)

U.S. Gross Domestic Product, Gross National Product, Net National Product, National Income, and Personal Income

Source: Bureau of Economic Analysis, U.S. Dept. of Commerce

(billions of current dollars; revised)

	1960	1970	1980	1990	2000	2003	2005	2006
Gross domestic product	526.4	1,038.5	2,789.5	5,803.1	9,817.0	10,960.8	12,433.9	13,194.7
Equals: Gross national product	529.5	1,044.9	2,823.7	5,837.9	9,855.9	11,017.6	12,502.4	13,252.7
Less: Consumption of fixed capital	55.6	106.7	343.0	682.5	1,187.8	1,336.5	1,609.5	1,615.2
Net national product	473.9	938.2	2,480.7	5,155.4	8,668.1	9,681.1	10,893.0	11,637.5
Less: Statistical discrepancy	−0.9	7.3	41.4	66.2	−127.2	48.8	5.4	−18.1
Equals: National income	474.9	930.9	2,439.3	5,089.1	8,795.2	9,632.3	10,887.6	11,655.6
Less: Corporate profits with inventory valuation and capital consumption adjustments	53.8	83.6	201.1	437.8	817.9	993.1	1,372.8	1,553.7
Taxes on production and imports less subsidies	43.4	86.7	190.9	398.7	664.6	759.3	863.1	917.6
Contributions for government social insurance	16.4	46.4	166.2	410.1	702.7	778.6	874.8	927.6
Net interest and miscellaneous payments on assets	10.6	39.1	181.8	442.2	559.0	524.7	558.0	598.5
Business current transfer payments (net)	1.9	4.5	14.4	39.4	87.1	83.8	66.5	90.2
Current surplus of government enterprises	0.9	0.0	−4.8	1.6	5.3	1.7	−15.1	−13.9
Wage accruals less disbursements	0.0	0.0	0.0	0.1	0.0	15.0	5.0	7.5
Plus: Personal income receipts on assets	37.9	93.5	338.7	924.0	1,387.0	1,336.6	1,617.8	1,796.5
Personal current transfer receipts	25.7	74.7	279.5	595.2	1,084.0	1,351.0	1,520.7	1,612.5
Equals: Personal income	411.5	838.8	2,307.9	4,878.6	8,429.7	9,163.6	10,301.1	10,983.4

U.S. Gross Domestic Product, 1996-2007

Source: Bureau of Economic Analysis, U.S. Dept. of Commerce

(billions of current dollars)

	1996	2006	2nd quarter 2007[1]		1996	2006	2nd quarter 2007[1]
Gross domestic product	7,816.9	13,194.7	13,768.8	**Net exports of goods and services**	−96.2	−762.0	−714.2
Personal consumption expenditures	5,256.8	9,224.5	9,674.0	Exports	868.6	1,467.6	1,598.7
Durable goods	652.6	1,048.9	1,074.7	Goods	618.3	1,030.5	1,115.2
Nondurable goods	1,555.5	2,688.0	2,822.7	Services	250.2	437.1	483.5
Services	3,048.7	5,487.6	5,776.5	Imports	964.8	2,229.6	2,312.9
				Goods	807.4	1,880.4	1,947.2
Gross private domestic investment	1,240.3	2,209.2	2,139.1	Services	157.4	349.2	365.7
Fixed investment	1,209.5	2,162.5	2,133.9	**Government consumption expenditures and gross investment**	1,416.0	2,523.0	2,670.0
Nonresidential	875.4	1,397.7	1,469.1	Federal	527.4	932.5	969.5
Structures	224.6	405.1	464.5	National defense	354.6	624.3	654.5
Equipment and software	650.8	992.6	1,004.5	Nondefense	172.8	308.2	315.0
Residential	334.1	764.8	664.8	State and local	888.6	1,590.5	1,700.5
Change in private inventories	30.8	46.7	5.1				

(1) Seasonally adjusted at annual rates; last revised Sept. 28, 2006

U.S. Gross Domestic Product, 1930-2006

Source: Bureau of Economic Analysis, U.S. Dept. of Commerce

(billions of 2000 dollars)

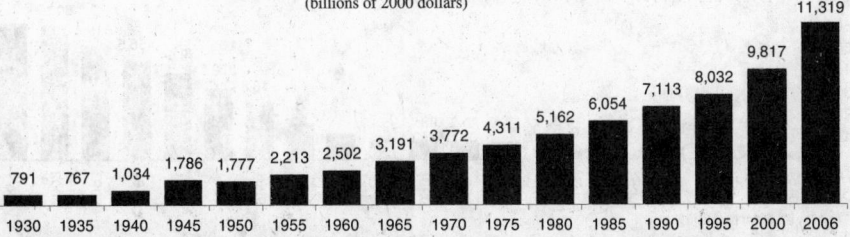

1930	1935	1940	1945	1950	1955	1960	1965	1970	1975	1980	1985	1990	1995	2000	2006
791	767	1,034	1,786	1,777	2,213	2,502	3,191	3,772	4,311	5,162	6,054	7,113	8,032	9,817	11,319

Consumer Price Index

The Consumer Price Index (CPI) is a measure of the change in prices over time of one or more kinds of basic consumer goods and services.

From Jan. 1978, the Bureau of Labor Statistics began publishing CPIs for 2 population groups: (1) a CPI for all urban consumers (CPI-U), which covers about 87% of the total population; and (2) a CPI for urban wage earners and clerical workers (CPI-W), which covers about 32% of the total population. The CPI-U includes, in addition to wage earners and clerical workers, groups such as professional, managerial, and technical workers, the self-employed, short-term workers, the unemployed, retirees, and others not in the labor force.

The CPI is based on prices of food, clothing, shelter, and fuels; transportation fares; charges for doctors' and dentists' services; drug prices; and prices of other goods and services bought for day-to-day living. The index currently measures price changes from a designated reference period, 1982-84, which equals 100.0. Use of this reference period began in Jan. 1988.

U.S. Consumer Price Indexes, 2006-2007

Source: Bureau of Labor Statistics, U.S. Dept. of Labor

(Data are semiannual averages of monthly figures. For all urban consumers; 1982-84 = 100; unless otherwise noted; % change not annualized)

	1st half 2006	% change 2nd half 2005 to 1st half 2006	2nd half 2006	% change 1st half 2006 to 2nd half 2006	1st half 2007	% change 2nd half 2006 to 1st half 2007
ALL ITEMS	200.6	1.6	202.6	1.0	205.7	1.5
Food, beverages	194.6	1.2	196.7	1.1	201.1	2.3
Housing	201.6	2.0	204.8	1.6	208.2	1.7
Apparel	119.7	0.9	119.2	−0.4	119.9	0.6
Transportation	181.4	1.6	180.4	−0.6	182.3	1.1
Medical care	333.6	2.4	338.8	1.6	347.3	2.5
Recreation[1]	100.7	1.0	111.2	0.5	111.4	0.1
Education and communication[1]	115.7	1.0	117.8	1.8	118.3	0.4
Other goods, services	319.8	1.4	323.6	1.2	331.5	2.4
Services	236.9	2.0	240.9	1.7	244.9	1.7
SPECIAL INDEXES						
All items less food	201.7	1.7	203.7	1.0	206.6	1.4
Commodities less food	148.4	1.1	147.5	−0.6	148.8	0.8
Nondurables	186.4	1.6	187.1	0.4	191.1	2.1
Energy	197.8	3.7	196.0	−0.9	202.1	3.1
All items less energy	202.5	1.5	204.9	1.2	207.8	1.4

(1) Dec. 1997 = 100.

U.S. Consumer Price Indexes (CPI-U),[1] Annual Percent Change, 1990-2006

Source: Bureau of Labor Statistics, U.S. Dept. of Labor

	1990	1991	1992	1993	1994	1995	1996	1997	1998	1999	2000	2001	2002	2003	2004	2005	2006
ALL ITEMS	5.4	4.2	3.0	3.0	2.6	2.8	3.0	2.3	1.6	2.2	3.4	2.8	1.6	2.3	2.7	3.4	3.2
Food	5.8	2.9	1.2	2.2	2.4	2.8	3.3	2.6	2.2	2.1	2.3	3.2	1.8	2.2	3.4	2.4	2.4
Shelter	5.4	4.5	3.3	3.0	3.1	3.2	3.2	3.1	3.3	2.9	3.3	3.7	3.7	2.4	2.7	2.6	3.4
Rent, residential	5.6	6.1	2.5	2.3	2.5	2.5	2.7	2.9	3.2	3.1	3.6	4.5	4.0	2.9	2.7	3.0	3.6
Fuel and other utilities	3.5	3.3	2.2	3.0	1.0	0.7	3.1	2.6	−1.8	0.2	7.1	8.9	−4.4	7.6	4.8	10.6	8.8
Apparel and upkeep	4.6	3.7	2.5	1.4	−0.2	−1.0	−0.2	0.9	0.1	−1.3	−1.3	−1.8	−2.6	−2.5	−0.4	−0.7	0.0
Private transportation	5.2	2.6	2.2	2.3	3.1	3.7	2.7	0.7	−2.2	1.9	6.1	0.6	−0.8	3.2	3.8	6.8	4.0
New cars	1.8	3.8	2.5	2.4	3.4	2.2	1.7	0.2	−0.6	−0.3	−0.1	−0.5	−1.2	−1.5	−0.6	0.6	−0.2
Gasoline	14.1	−1.8	−0.2	−1.3	0.5	1.6	6.1	−0.1	−13.4	9.3	28.5	−3.6	−6.5	16.5	18.2	21.9	12.9
Public transportation	10.1	4.4	1.7	10.3	3.0	2.3	3.4	2.6	1.9	3.9	6.0	0.5	−1.5	0.9	−0.1	3.9	4.3
Medical care	9.0	8.7	7.4	5.9	4.8	4.5	3.5	2.8	3.2	3.5	4.1	4.6	4.7	4.0	4.4	4.2	4.0
Entertainment, Recreation[2,3]	4.7	4.5	2.8	2.5	2.9	2.5	3.4	2.1	1.5	0.9	1.3	1.5	1.2	1.2	1.0	0.7	1.4
Education[3]	—	—	—	—	6.3	5.6	5.3	5.0	4.9	4.8	5.1	5.3	6.3	1.8	6.9	6.3	6.2
Commodities	5.2	4.2	2.0	1.9	1.7	1.9	2.6	1.4	0.1	1.8	3.3	1.0	−0.7	1.0	2.3	3.6	2.4

(1) The Consumer Price Index CPI-U measures average change in prices of goods and services purchased by all urban consumers. 1982-1984 = 100 unless otherwise noted. (2) The Bureau of Labor Statistics reclassified Entertainment as Recreation in 1997. (3) Dec. 1997 = 100.

Consumer Price Index, 1915-2007

Source: Bureau of Labor Statistics, U.S. Dept. of Labor

(1967 = 100. Annual averages of monthly figures, specified for all urban consumers.)

Prices as measured by the U.S. Consumer Price Index have risen steadily since World War II. What cost $1.00 in 1967 cost about 30 cents in 1915, 54 cents in 1945, and $6.16 by the first half of 2007.

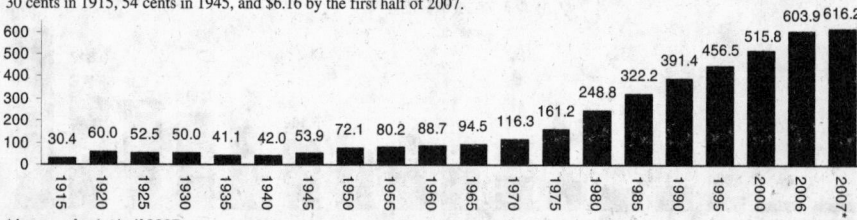

1915	1920	1925	1930	1935	1940	1945	1950	1955	1960	1965	1970	1975	1980	1985	1990	1995	2000	2006	2007*
30.4	60.0	52.5	50.0	41.1	42.0	53.9	72.1	80.2	88.7	94.5	116.3	161.2	248.8	322.2	391.4	456.5	515.8	603.9	616.2

*Average for 1st half 2007.

U.S. Consumer Price Indexes for Selected Items and Groups, 1970-2006

Source: Bureau of Labor Statistics, U.S. Dept. of Labor

(1982-84 = 100, unless otherwise noted. Annual averages of monthly figures. For all urban consumers.)

	1970	1975	1980	1985	1990	1995	2000	2001	2002	2003	2004	2005	2006
ALL ITEMS	38.8	53.8	82.4	107.6	130.7	152.4	172.2	177.1	179.9	184.0	188.9	195.3	201.6
Food and beverages	40.1	60.2	86.7	105.6	132.1	148.9	168.4	173.6	176.8	180.5	186.6	191.2	195.7
Food	39.2	59.8	86.8	105.6	132.4	148.4	167.8	173.1	176.2	180.0	186.2	190.7	195.2
Food at home	39.9	61.8	88.4	104.3	132.3	148.8	167.9	173.4	175.6	179.4	186.2	189.8	193.1
Cereals and bakery products	37.1	62.9	83.9	107.9	140.0	167.5	188.3	193.8	198.0	202.8	206.0	209.0	212.8
Meats, poultry, fish, and eggs	44.6	67.0	92.0	100.1	130.0	138.8	154.5	161.3	162.1	169.3	181.7	184.7	186.6
Dairy products	44.7	62.6	90.9	103.2	126.5	132.8	160.7	167.1	168.1	167.9	180.2	182.4	181.4
Fruits and vegetables	37.8	56.9	82.1	106.4	149.0	177.7	204.6	212.2	220.9	225.9	232.7	241.4	252.9
Sugar and sweets	30.5	65.3	90.5	105.8	124.7	137.5	154.0	155.7	159.0	162.0	163.2	165.2	171.5
Fats and oils	39.2	73.5	89.3	106.9	126.3	137.3	147.4	155.7	155.4	157.4	167.8	167.7	168.0
Nonalcoholic beverages	27.1	41.3	91.4	104.3	113.5	131.7	137.8	139.2	139.2	139.8	140.4	144.4	147.4
Other foods	39.6	58.9	83.6	106.4	131.2	151.1	172.2	176.0	177.1	178.8	179.7	182.5	185.0
Food away from home	37.5	54.5	83.4	108.3	133.4	149.0	169.0	173.9	178.3	182.1	187.5	193.4	199.4
Alcoholic beverages	52.1	65.9	86.4	106.4	129.3	153.9	174.7	179.3	183.6	187.2	192.1	195.9	200.7
Housing	36.4	50.7	81.1	107.7	128.5	148.5	169.6	176.4	180.3	184.8	189.5	195.7	203.2
Shelter	35.5	48.8	81.0	109.8	140.0	165.7	193.4	200.6	208.1	213.1	218.8	224.4	232.1
Rent of primary residence	46.5	58.0	80.9	111.8	138.4	157.8	183.9	192.1	199.7	205.5	211.0	217.3	225.1
Fuel and other utilities	29.1	45.4	75.4	106.5	111.6	123.7	137.9	150.2	143.6	154.5	161.9	179.0	194.7
Gas (piped) and electricity	25.4	40.1	71.4	107.1	109.3	119.2	128.0	142.4	134.4	145.0	150.6	166.5	182.1
Household furnishings & operations	46.8	63.4	86.3	103.8	113.3	123.0	128.2	129.1	128.3	126.1	125.5	126.1	127.0
Apparel	59.2	72.5	90.9	105.0	124.1	132.0	129.6	127.3	124.0	120.9	120.4	119.5	119.5
Men's and boys'	62.2	75.5	89.4	105.0	120.4	126.2	129.7	125.7	121.7	118.0	117.5	116.1	114.1
Women's and girls'	71.8	85.5	96.0	104.9	122.6	126.9	121.5	119.3	115.8	113.1	113.0	110.8	110.7
Footwear	56.8	69.6	91.8	102.3	117.4	125.4	123.8	123.0	121.4	119.6	119.3	122.6	123.5
Transportation	37.5	50.1	83.1	106.4	120.5	139.1	153.3	154.3	152.9	157.6	163.1	173.9	180.9
Private	37.5	50.6	84.2	106.2	118.8	136.3	149.1	150.0	148.8	153.6	159.4	170.2	177.0
New vehicles	53.0	62.9	88.4	106.1	121.4	139.0	142.8	142.1	140.0	137.9	137.1	137.9	137.6
Used cars and trucks	31.2	43.8	62.3	113.7	117.6	156.5	155.8	158.7	152.0	142.9	133.3	139.4	140.0
Gasoline	27.9	45.1	97.5	98.6	101.0	99.8	128.6	124.0	116.0	135.1	159.7	194.7	219.9
Public	35.2	43.5	69.0	110.5	142.6	175.9	209.6	210.6	207.4	209.3	209.1	217.3	226.6
Medical care	34.0	47.5	74.9	113.5	162.8	220.5	260.8	272.8	285.6	297.1	310.1	323.2	336.2
Entertainment/Recreation[1]	47.5	62.0	83.6	107.9	132.4	153.9	103.3	104.9	106.2	107.5	108.6	109.4	110.9
Other goods and services	40.9	54.9	75.2	114.5	159.0	206.9	271.1	282.6	293.2	298.7	304.7	313.4	321.7
Tobacco products	43.1	54.7	72.0	116.7	181.5	225.7	394.9	425.2	461.5	469.0	478.0	502.8	519.9
Personal care	43.5	57.9	81.9	106.3	130.4	147.1	165.6	170.5	154.7	153.5	181.7	185.6	190.2
Personal care products	42.7	58.0	79.6	107.6	128.2	143.1	153.7	155.1	174.7	178.0	153.9	154.4	155.8
Personal care services	44.2	57.7	83.7	108.9	132.8	151.5	178.1	184.3	188.4	193.2	197.6	203.9	209.7

(1) Dec. 1997 = 100; Entertainment was reclassified as Recreation in 1997.

Consumer Price Indexes by Region and Selected Cities, 2005-2007[1]

Source: Bureau of Labor Statistics, U.S. Dept. of Labor

(unless otherwise noted; % change not annualized)

	Semiannual averages				Percent change from preceding semiannual average		
	2nd half 2005	1st half 2006	2nd half 2006	1st half 2007	1st half 2006	2nd half 2006	1st half 2007
U.S. CITY AVERAGE	197.4	200.6	202.6	205.7	1.6	1.0	1.5
Northeast urban	209.7	213.8	216.2	218.7	2.0	1.1	1.2
Size A—More than 1,500,000	212.0	216.0	218.8	221.3	1.9	1.3	1.1
Size B/C—50,000 to 1,500,000[2]	123.9	126.4	127.3	129.1	2.0	0.7	1.4
Midwest urban	190.5	192.4	193.6	196.6	1.0	0.6	1.6
Size A—More than 1,500,000	192.1	194.0	195.4	198.5	1.0	0.7	1.6
Size B/C—50,000 to 1,500,000[2]	121.5	122.8	123.4	125.4	1.1	0.5	1.6
Size D—Nonmetro. (less than 50,000)	185.2	187.1	188.6	190.9	1.0	0.8	1.2
South urban	190.5	193.8	195.6	198.5	1.7	0.9	1.5
Size A—More than 1,500,000	192.4	195.7	197.9	200.9	1.7	1.1	1.5
Size B/C—50,000 to 1,500,000[2]	121.4	123.5	124.4	126.2	1.7	0.7	1.5
Size D—Nonmetro. (less than 50,000)	190.3	193.7	196.8	198.8	1.8	1.6	1.0
West urban	200.7	204.5	206.9	210.9	1.9	1.2	1.9
Size A—More than 1,500,000	203.5	207.6	210.3	214.4	2.0	1.3	1.9
Size B/C—50,000 to 1,500,000[2]	122.4	124.5	125.6	128.0	1.7	0.9	1.9
SELECTED AREAS							
Atlanta, GA.	190.8	192.6	195.0	198.1	0.9	1.2	1.6
Boston–Brockton–Nashua, MA–NH–ME–CT.	218.9	222.0	224.2	225.9	1.4	1.0	0.8
Chicago–Gary–Kenosha, IL–IN–WI	196.7	197.9	198.8	203.1	0.6	0.5	2.1
Cleveland–Akron, OH	190.0	191.4	190.9	194.5	0.7	-0.3	1.9
Dallas–Fort Worth, TX	187.4	189.7	190.5	191.1	1.2	0.4	0.3
Detroit–Ann Arbor–Flint, MI	193.0	195.9	197.2	199.6	1.5	0.7	1.2
Houston–Galveston–Brazoria, TX	177.0	180.3	181.0	182.9	1.9	0.4	1.0
L.A.–Riverside–Orange County, CA	204.5	209.3	211.6	216.3	2.3	1.1	2.2
Miami–Fort Lauderdale, FL	196.9	202.7	205.1	210.0	2.9	1.2	2.4
New York, NY–Northern NJ–Long Island, NY–NJ–CT–PA	214.8	219.2	222.3	225.1	2.0	1.4	1.3
Philadelphia–Wilmington–Atlantic City, PA–DE–NJ–MD	206.3	210.7	213.4	214.8	2.1	1.3	0.6
San Francisco–Oakland–San Jose, CA.	203.9	207.9	210.6	214.7	2.0	1.3	2.0
Seattle–Tacoma–Bremerton, WA	201.3	205.8	209.5	213.8	2.2	1.8	2.1
Washington–Baltimore, DC–MD–VA–WV[3].	125.8	127.7	130.0	132.0	1.5	1.8	1.5

(1) For all urban consumers. (2) Dec. 1996 = 100. (3) Nov. 1996 = 100.

U.S. National Income by Industry[1], 2000-2006

Source: Bureau of Economic Analysis, U.S. Dept. of Commerce; in billions of current dollars; revised Sept. 27, 2007.

	2000	2001	2002	2003	2004	2005	2006
National income without capital consumption adjustment	8,687.4	8,854.9	9,013.5	9,425.3	10,128.8	10,998.0	11,791.8
Domestic industries	8,648.5	8,811.2	8,982.9	9,368.5	10,052.6	10,929.5	11,733.8
Private industries	7,642.8	7,758.4	7,854.7	8,168.2	8,791.1	9,613.2	10,352.1
Agriculture, forestry, fishing, and hunting	70.1	69.3	65.9	80.7	95.7	85.7	87.0
Mining	93.8	101.0	81.4	104.0	124.1	158.8	199.2
Utilities	144.3	149.2	143.8	148.8	161.6	178.2	193.7
Construction	440.6	463.3	470.8	478.3	523.6	601.4	621.3
Manufacturing	1,228.5	1,094.1	1,071.6	1,112.3	1,214.2	1,351.2	1,421.6
Durable goods	744.0	617.8	613.8	630.4	678.6	747.7	777.6
Nondurable goods	484.5	476.2	457.8	481.9	535.7	603.5	644.0
Wholesale trade	563.8	557.7	553.4	576.0	631.9	682.2	721.6
Retail trade	665.3	689.0	710.1	737.4	764.3	822.8	864.9
Transportation and warehousing	261.2	251.9	250.3	258.8	290.7	318.3	348.2
Information	308.3	305.6	307.3	313.7	361.8	411.5	432.6
Finance, insurance, real estate, rental, leasing	1,529.3	1,643.7	1,644.7	1,690.7	1,780.4	1,939.3	2,127.6
Professional and business services	1,146.6	1,171.3	1,211.2	1,253.4	1,336.4	1,467.0	1,630.3
Educ. services, health care, social assistance	664.6	719.2	777.0	823.8	880.1	930.8	994.5
Arts, entert., recreation, accommodation, food service	310.5	316.8	330.3	343.4	369.4	395.3	425.8
Other services, except government	215.8	226.2	237.1	247.1	256.8	270.7	283.8
Government	1,005.7	1,052.8	1,128.2	1,200.2	1,261.5	1,316.3	1,381.6
Rest of the world	38.9	43.6	30.6	56.8	76.2	68.5	58.0

(1) Figures may not add because of rounding. Total national income also includes income from outside the U.S.

U.S. National Income by Type of Income[1], 1930-2006

Source: Bureau of Economic Analysis, U.S. Dept. of Commerce; in billions of current dollars; revised Sept. 27, 2007.

	1930	1940	1950	1960	1970	1980	1990	2000	2005	2006
National income[2]	83.1	91.2	264.4	474.9	930.9	2,439.3	5,089.1	8,795.2	10,887.6	11,655.6
Compensation of employees	46.9	52.2	155.3	296.4	617.2	1,651.8	3,338.2	5,782.7	7,029.6	7,448.3
Wage and salary accruals	46.2	49.9	147.3	272.9	551.6	1,377.6	2,754.0	4,829.2	5,672.9	6,025.7
Government	5.2	8.5	22.6	49.2	117.2	261.5	517.7	774.7	980.9	1,020.6
Supplements to wages and salaries	0.7	2.3	8.0	23.6	65.7	274.2	584.2	953.4	1,356.8	1,422.6
Employer contributions for employee pension and insurance funds	0.6	0.9	4.7	14.3	41.8	185.2	377.8	609.9	927.7	970.7
Employer contributions for government social insurance	0.0	1.4	3.4	9.3	23.8	88.9	206.5	343.5	429.1	451.8
Proprietors' income with inventory valuation and capital consumption adjustments	11.1	12.3	37.6	50.8	78.4	174.1	380.6	728.4	969.9	1,006.7
Farm	4.0	4.1	12.9	10.5	12.7	11.3	31.9	22.7	30.8	19.4
Nonfarm	7.0	8.2	24.7	40.3	65.7	162.8	348.7	705.7	939.1	987.4
Rental income of persons with capital consumption adjustments	5.5	3.9	9.2	17.1	21.4	30.0	50.7	150.3	42.9	54.5
Corporate profits with inventory valuation and capital consumption adjustment	7.5	9.8	36.0	53.8	83.6	201.1	437.8	817.9	1,372.8	1,553.7
Taxes on corporate income	0.8	2.8	17.9	22.8	34.8	87.2	145.4	265.2	392.9	453.9
Profits after tax with inventory valuation and capital consumption adjustments	6.6	7.0	18.1	31.0	48.9	113.9	292.4	552.7	979.9	1,099.8
Net dividends	5.5	4.0	8.8	13.4	24.3	64.1	169.1	377.9	601.4	698.9
Undistributed profits with inventory valuation and capital consumption adjustments	1.1	3.0	9.3	17.6	24.6	49.9	123.3	174.8	378.6	400.9
Net interest and miscellaneous payments	4.8	3.3	3.2	10.6	39.1	181.8	442.2	559.0	558.0	598.5

(1) Figures do not add, because of rounding and incomplete enumeration. (2) National income is the aggregate of labor and property earnings that arises in the production of goods and services. It is the sum of employee compensation, proprietors' income, rental income, adjusted corporate profits, and net interest. It measures the total factor costs of goods and services produced by the economy. Income is measured before deduction of taxes. Total national income figures include adjustments not itemized.

Distribution of U.S. Total Personal Income[1], 1930-2006

Source: Bureau of Economic Analysis, U.S. Dept. of Commerce; in billions of current dollars; revised Sept. 27, 2007.

Year	Personal income	Personal taxes and nontax payments	Disposable personal income	Personal outlays	Personal Savings Amount	Personal Savings As pct. of disposable income
1930	$76.3	$1.6	$74.7	$71.6	$3.1	4.1%
1940	78.5	1.7	76.8	72.4	4.4	5.7
1950	229.0	18.9	210.1	195.0	15.1	7.2
1960	411.5	46.1	365.4	338.8	26.7	7.3
1970	838.8	103.1	735.7	666.2	69.5	9.4
1980	2,307.9	298.9	2,009.0	1,807.5	201.4	10.0
1990	4,878.6	592.8	4,285.8	3,986.4	299.4	7.0
1995	6,152.3	744.1	5,408.2	5,157.3	250.9	4.6
2000	8,429.7	1,235.7	7,194.0	7,025.6	168.5	2.3
2001	8,724.1	1,237.3	7,486.8	7,354.5	132.3	1.8
2002	8,881.9	1,051.8	7,830.1	7,645.3	184.7	2.4
2003	9,163.6	1,001.1	8,162.5	7,987.7	174.9	2.1
2004	9,727.2	1,046.3	8,680.9	8,499.2	181.7	2.1
2005	10,301.1	1,209.1	9,092.0	9,047.4	44.6	0.5
2006	10,983.4	1,354.3	9,629.1	9,590.3	38.8	0.4

(1) Personal income minus taxes/nontax payments=disposable income; disposable income minus outlays=savings. Figures may not add because of rounding.

Median Income by Race, Hispanic Origin, and Sex, 1947-2005[1]

Source: Bureau of the Census, U.S. Dept. of Commerce

	Year	Male No. with income (thous.)	Male Median income Current dollars	Male Median income 2005 dollars	Female No. with income (thous.)	Female Median income Current dollars	Female Median income 2005 dollars
All Races	2005	102,986	$31,275	$31,275	104,245	$18,576	$18,576
	2004	101,772	30,516	31,537	103,384	17,667	18,258
	2003	100,769	29,931	31,763	102,713	17,259	18,316
	2002	99,788	29,238	31,739	102,487	16,812	18,250
	2001	98,873	29,101	32,092	101,941	16,614	18,322
	2000	98,504	28,343	32,129	101,704	16,063	18,209
	1990	88,220	20,293	29,390	92,245	10,070	14,584
	1980	78,661	12,530	28,116	80,826	4,920	11,040
	1970	65,008	6,670	29,040	51,647	2,237	9,739
	1960	55,172	4,080	22,789	36,526	1,261	7,043
	1950	47,585	2,570	17,649	24,651	953	6,544
	1947	46,813	2,230	16,553	21,479	1,017	7,549
White	2005	85,996	32,179	32,179	84,768	18,669	18,669
	2004	85,140	31,345	32,393	84,374	17,699	18,291
	2003	84,405	30,732	32,613	83,852	17,422	18,489
	2002	83,899	30,383	32,982	84,014	16,838	18,278
	2001	83,750	30,240	33,348	84,207	16,652	18,364
	2000	83,372	29,797	33,777	84,123	16,079	18,227
	1990	76,480	21,170	30,660	78,566	10,317	14,942
	1980	69,420	13,328	29,906	70,573	4,947	11,100
	1970	58,447	7,011	30,524	45,288	2,266	9,866
	1960	49,788	4,296	23,995	32,001	1,352	7,552
	1950	NA	2,709	18,603	NA	1,060	7,279
	1948	NA	2,510	17,237	NA	1,133	7,780
Black	2005	10,651	22,609	22,609	13,237	17,595	17,595
	2004	10,335	22,713	23,473	12,994	17,347	17,927
	2003	10,291	21,935	23,278	12,924	16,540	17,553
	2002	10,096	21,509	23,349	12,665	16,671	18,097
	2001	9,944	21,466	23,673	12,414	16,282	17,956
	2000	9,905	21,343	24,194	12,461	15,881	18,002
	1990	8,820	12,868	18,637	10,687	8,328	12,061
	1980	7,387	8,009	17,971	8,596	4,580	10,277
	1970	5,844	4,157	18,099	5,844	2,063	8,982
	1960	5,384	2,260	12,623	4,525	837	4,675
	1950	NA	1,471	10,102	NA	474	3,255
White not Hispanic	2005	73,219	35,345	35,345	75,014	19,451	19,451
	2004	72,797	33,678	34,804	74,813	18,435	19,052
	2003	72,535	32,331	34,310	74,486	18,301	19,421
	2002	72,146	32,034	34,774	74,814	17,389	18,876
	2001	72,649	31,791	35,059	75,117	17,229	19,000
	2000	72,530	31,508	35,717	75,206	16,665	18,891
	1990	69,987	21,958	31,802	72,939	10,581	15,324
	1980	65,564	13,681	30,699	67,084	4,980	11,175
Asian	2005	4,245	34,215	34,215	4,255	21,641	21,641
	2004	4,122	33,019	34,123	4,040	20,522	21,208
	2003	4,266	31,737	34,268	4,252	17,879	18,761
	2002	4,139	30,839	33,744	4,137	17,898	19,634
	2001	4,165	31,096	34,292	4,164	18,525	20,429
	2000	4,303	30,833	34,951	4,192	17,356	19,674
	1990	2,235	19,394	28,088	2,333	11,086	16,056
Hispanic	2005	13,714	22,089	22,089	10,638	15,036	15,036
	2004	13,256	21,556	22,277	10,396	14,452	14,935
	2003	12,753	21,053	22,342	10,175	13,642	14,477
	2002	12,624	20,702	22,473	10,018	13,364	14,507
	2001	11,766	20,189	22,264	9,691	12,583	13,876
	2000	11,343	19,498	22,102	9,431	12,248	13,884
	1990	6,767	13,470	19,509	5,903	7,532	10,909
	1980	3,996	9,659	21,674	3,617	4,405	9,884

NA = Not available. (1) People 15 years old and over beginning with March 1980, and people 14 years old and over as of March of the following year for previous years.

Consumer Credit Outstanding, 2004-2006

Source: Federal Reserve System
(in billions of dollars, revised)
Estimated amounts of credit outstanding as of end of year. Not seasonally adjusted.

	2004	2005	2006		2004	2005	2006
TOTAL	$2,231.7	$2,326.0	$2,430.8	Credit unions	$23.2	$24.7	$27.4
Major Holders				Fed. government and Sallie Mae	NA	NA	NA
Commercial banks	704.3	707.0	741.2	Savings institutions	27.9	40.8	42.5
Finance companies	492.3	516.5	534.4	Nonfinancial business	11.7	10.8	7.2
Credit unions	215.4	228.6	234.5	Pools of securitized assets[1]	395.8	396.0	419.1
Fed. govt. and Sallie Mae	98.4	102.1	103.2	**Nonrevolving[2]**	**1,408.0**	**1,476.2**	**1,527.4**
Savings institutions	91.3	109.1	95.5	Commercial banks	389.6	395.8	413.9
Nonfinancial business	59.7	58.1	56.2	Finance companies	442.0	450.2	454.5
Pools of securitized assets[1]	572.1	604.6	665.8	Credit unions	192.1	203.9	207.1
Major Types of Credit				Fed. government and Sallie Mae	98.4	102.1	103.2
Revolving[2]	**823.7**	**849.8**	**903.4**	Savings institutions	63.4	68.3	53.1
Commercial banks	314.6	311.2	327.3	Nonfinancial business	46.2	47.2	49.0
Finance companies	50.4	66.3	79.9	Pools of securitized assets[1]	176.3	208.6	246.7

NA = Not available. (1) Outstanding balances of pools upon which securities have been issued; these balances are no longer carried on the balance sheets of the loan originators. (2) Includes estimates for holders that do not separately report consumer credit holding by type.

Distribution of Financial Assets of U.S. Families[1]
Source: Federal Reserve System (by type of asset, in percent of family financial assets)

Type of financial asset	1989	1992	1995	1998	2001	2004
Transaction accounts	19.0	17.5	13.9	11.4	11.5	13.2
Certificates of deposit	10.2	8.0	5.6	4.3	3.1	3.7
Savings bonds	1.5	1.1	1.3	0.7	0.7	0.5
Bonds	10.2	8.4	6.3	4.3	4.6	5.3
Stocks	15.0	16.5	15.6	22.7	21.7	17.6
Mutual funds (excluding money market funds)	5.3	7.6	12.7	12.4	12.2	14.7
Retirement accounts	21.5	25.7	28.1	27.6	28.4	32.0
Cash value of life insurance	6.0	5.9	7.2	6.4	5.3	3.0
Other managed assets	6.6	5.4	5.9	8.6	10.6	8.0
Other	4.8	3.8	3.3	1.7	2.0	2.1
Financial assets as a percentage of total assets	30.5	31.6	36.7	40.7	42.0	35.7

(1) Data from the triennial *Survey of Consumer Finances.*

Stock Ownership of U.S. Families, by Income & Age, 1989, 1998, & 2001, 2004[1]
Source: Federal Reserve System
(in percent, except as noted)

		Families having direct or indirect stock holdings[2]				Median value of portfolios (thousands of 2004 dollars)				Stock holdings as share of financial assets[3]			
		1989	1998	2001	2004	1989	1998	2001	2004	1989	1998	2001	2004
All families		**31.7%**	**48.9%**	**52.2%**	**48.6%**	**$12.5**	**$29.0**	**$36.7**	**$24.4**	**27.8%**	**54.0%**	**56.1%**	**47.4%**
Percentile of income:	Less than 20	3.3	10.0	12.9	11.7	29.3	5.8	8.0	7.0	13.6	20.4	37.4	31.3
	20-39.9	15.2	30.8	34.1	28.8	8.8	11.6	8.3	8.8	10.0	29.8	35.6	29.6
	40-59.9	28.6	52.2	52.5	49.1	6.8	13.9	16.0	11.6	16.7	38.1	46.8	41.0
	60-79.9	44.0	69.3	75.7	66.5	8.5	22.0	30.5	20.0	21.8	45.8	52.0	37.5
	80-89.9	57.6	77.9	82.0	82.5	13.9	52.2	68.8	34.6	26.1	50.4	57.3	43.2
	90-100	76.9	90.4	89.7	91.0	57.9	156.5	263.8	169.9	34.3	62.5	60.5	53.6
By age of family head (years):	Under 35	22.4	40.8	49.0	38.8	4.4	8.1	7.5	5.2	20.2	44.9	52.5	30.0
	35-44	39.0	56.7	59.5	52.3	7.6	23.2	29.3	12.7	29.4	55.0	57.2	47.7
	45-54	41.8	58.6	59.3	54.4	19.3	44.1	53.3	30.6	33.5	55.7	59.1	46.8
	55-64	36.2	55.9	57.4	61.6	27.0	54.5	85.7	59.5	27.7	58.4	56.2	51.1
	65-74	26.7	42.7	40.0	45.7	29.8	64.9	160.1	75.0	26.0	51.3	55.4	51.1
	75 +	25.9	29.4	35.7	34.8	36.7	69.6	117.2	85.9	25.0	48.7	51.8	39.1

(1) Data from the triennial *Survey of Consumer Finances.* (2) Indirect holdings are those in mutual funds, retirement accounts, and other managed assets. (3) Among stock-holding families.

The Wealthiest Americans, 2007
Source: *Forbes* Magazine

Rank	Name	Net Worth ($bil)	Age	Residence	Source
1.	William Gates III	59.0	51	Medina, WA	Microsoft
2.	Warren Buffett	52.0	77	Omaha, NE	Berkshire Hathaway
3.	Sheldon Adelson	28.0	74	Las Vegas, NV	casinos, hotels
4.	Lawrence Ellison	26.0	63	Redwood City, CA	Oracle
5.	Sergey Brin	18.5	34	Palo Alto, CA	Google
5.	Larry Page	18.5	34	San Francisco, CA	Google
7.	Kirk Kerkorian	18.0	90	Los Angeles, CA	investments, casinos
8.	Michael Dell	17.2	42	Austin, TX.	Dell
9.	Charles Koch	17.0	71	Wichita, KS.	oil, commodities
	David Koch	17.0	67	New York, NY.	oil, commodities

Note: The total estimated net worth of all 400 came to $1.54 trillion, $290 billion more than in 2006 and $410 billion more than in 2005.

Poverty Rate
Source: Bureau of the Census, U.S. Dept. of Commerce

The poverty rate is the proportion of the population whose income falls below the government's official poverty level, and is adjusted each year for inflation. The national poverty rate was 12.3% in 2006, down from the 2005 rate of 12.6%, but above the 2000 rate of 11.3%. About 36.5 million people in the U.S. were in poverty in 2006, not statistically different from 2005. In 2006 17.4% of children and 9.4% of people aged 65 and older were defined as poor.

Persons Below Poverty Level, 1960-2006
Source: Bureau of the Census, U.S. Dept. of Commerce

YEAR	Number below poverty level (in millions)					Percentage below poverty level					Avg. income cut-offs for family of 4 at poverty level[4]
	All races[1]	Asian[2]	White	Black	Hispanic origin[3]	All races[1]	Asian[2]	White	Black	Hispanic origin[3]	
1960	39.9	NA	28.3	NA	NA	22.2	NA	17.8	NA	NA	$3,022
1970	25.4	NA	17.5	7.5	NA	12.6	NA	9.9	33.5	NA	3,968
1980	29.3	NA	19.7	8.6	3.5	13.0	NA	10.2	32.5	25.7	8,414
1990	33.6	0.9	22.3	9.8	6.0	13.5	12.2	10.7	31.9	28.1	13,359
1991	35.7	1.0	23.7	10.2	6.3	14.2	13.8	11.3	32.7	28.7	13,924
1992	38.0	1.0	25.3	10.8	7.6	14.8	12.7	11.9	33.4	29.6	14,335
1993	39.3	1.1	26.2	10.9	8.1	15.1	15.3	12.2	33.1	30.6	14,763
1994	38.1	1.0	25.4	10.2	8.4	14.5	14.6	11.7	30.6	30.7	15,141
1995	36.4	1.4	24.4	9.9	8.6	13.8	14.6	11.2	29.3	30.3	15,569
1996	36.5	1.5	24.7	9.7	8.7	13.7	14.5	11.2	28.4	29.4	16,036
1997	35.6	1.5	24.4	9.1	8.3	13.3	14.0	11.0	26.5	27.1	16,400
1998	34.5	1.4	23.5	9.1	8.1	12.7	12.5	10.5	26.1	25.6	16,660
1999	32.8	1.3	21.2	8.4	7.9	11.9	10.7	9.8	23.6	22.7	17,029
2000	31.6	1.3	21.6	8.0	7.7	11.3	9.9	9.5	22.5	21.5	17,063
2002	34.6	1.2	23.5	8.6	8.6	12.1	10.1	10.2	24.1	21.8	18,556
2003	35.9	1.4	24.3	8.8	9.1	12.5	11.8	10.5	24.4	22.5	18,979
2004	37.0	1.2	25.3	9.0	9.1	12.7	9.8	10.8	24.7	21.9	19,307
2005	37.0	1.4	24.9	9.2	9.4	12.6	11.1	10.6	24.9	21.8	19,971
2006	36.5	1.4	24.4	9.0	9.2	12.3	10.3	10.3	24.3	12.3	20,614

NA = Not available. **Note:** Because of a change in the definition of poverty, data prior to 1980 are not directly comparable to data since 1980. (1) Includes other races not shown separately. (2) Asian and Pacific Islander, 1990-2000. (3) Persons of Hispanic origin may be of any race. (4) Figures for 1960-80 represent only nonfarm families.

Poverty Thresholds by Family Size, 1980-2006[1]

Source: Bureau of the Census, U.S. Dept. of Commerce

Year	1980	1990	2000	2006	Year	1980	1990	2000	2006
1 person	$4,190	$6,652	$8,791	$10,294	4 people	$8,414	$13,359	$17,604	$20,614
Under age 65	4,290	6,800	8,959	10,488	5 people	9,966	15,792	20,815	24,382
Age 65 or older	3,949	6,268	8,259	9,669	6 people	11,269	17,839	23,533	27,560
2 people	5,363	8,509	11,235	13,167	7 people	12,761	20,241	26,750	31,205
Householder under age 65	5,537	8,794	11,589	13,569	8 people	14,199	22,582	29,701	34,774
Householder age 65 or older	4,983	7,905	10,418	12,201	9 people or more	16,896	26,848	35,150	41,499
3 people	6,565	10,419	13,740	16,079					

(1) Weighted average; not used for computing poverty data.

Poverty by Family Status, Sex, and Race, 1986-2006

Source: Bureau of the Census, U.S. Dept. of Commerce

(Number. in thousands)

	1986 No.	1986 %[1]	1990 No.	1990 %[1]	1995 No.	1995 %[1]	2000 No.	2000 %[1]	2006 No.	2006 %[1]
TOTAL POOR	32,370	13.6	33,585	13.5	36,425	13.8	31,581	11.3	36,460	12.3
In families	24,754	12.0	25,232	12.0	27,501	12.3	22,347	9.6	25,915	10.6
Head of household	7,023	10.9	7,098	10.7	7,532	10.8	6,400	8.7	7,668	9.8
Related children	12,257	19.8	12,715	19.9	13,999	20.2	11,005	15.6	12,299	16.9
Families, female householder, no husband present	11,944	38.3	12,578	37.2	14,205	36.5	10,926	28.5	13,199	30.5
Head of household	3,613	34.6	3,768	33.4	4,057	32.4	3,278	25.4	4,087	28.3
Related children	6,943	54.4	7,363	53.4	8,364	50.3	6,300	40.0	7,341	42.1
All other families	12,811	7.3	12,654	7.1	13,296	7.2	NA	NA	NA	NA
Head of household	3,410	6.3	3,330	6.0	3,475	6.1	NA	NA	NA	NA
Related children	5,313	10.8	5,352	10.7	5,635	10.7	NA	NA	NA	NA
Unrelated individuals	6,846	21.6	7,446	20.7	8,247	20.9	8,653	19.0	9,977	20.0
Unrelated female individuals	4,311	25.1	4,589	24.0	4,865	23.5	5,071	21.6	5,589	22.2
Unrelated male individuals	2,536	17.5	2,857	16.9	3,382	18.0	3,548	16.0	4,388	17.8
TOTAL WHITE POOR[2]	22,183	11.0	22,326	10.7	24,423	11.2	21,645	9.5	24,416	10.3
In families	16,393	9.4	15,916	9.0	17,593	9.6	14,692	7.8	16,644	8.5
Head of household	4,811	8.6	4,622	8.1	4,994	8.5	4,333	7.1	5,118	8.0
Related children	7,714	15.3	7,696	15.1	8,474	15.5	6,834	12.4	7,522	13.6
Families with female householder, no husband present	6,171	30.6	6,210	29.8	7,047	29.7	5,609	23.2	7,160	26.5
Unrelated individuals	5,198	19.2	5,739	18.6	6,336	19.0	6,454	17.1	7,334	18.1
TOTAL BLACK POOR[2]	8,983	31.1	9,837	31.9	9,872	29.3	7,982	22.5	9,048	24.3
In families	7,410	29.7	8,160	31.0	8,189	28.5	6,221	21.2	7,072	23.1
Head of household	1,987	28.0	2,193	29.3	2,127	26.4	1,686	19.3	2,007	21.6
Related children	4,037	42.7	4,412	44.2	4,644	41.5	3,495	30.9	3,690	33.0
Families with female householder, no husband present	5,473	53.8	6,005	50.6	6,553	48.2	4,774	36.5	5,180	39.1
Unrelated individuals	1,431	38.5	1,491	35.1	1,551	32.6	1,702	28.9	1,897	29.0

NA = Not available. (1) Percentage of total U.S. population in each category who fell below poverty level and are enumerated here. For example, of all persons in families in 2006, 10.6%, or 25,915,000, were poor. (2) Data are for one race only. The Census Bureau revised race categories in 2002; 2006 figures are not directly comparable with previous years.

Persons in Poverty, by State, 2004-2006

Source: Bureau of the Census, U.S. Dept. of Commerce

	2004-05[1]	2005-06[1]		2004-05[1]	2005-06[1]		2004-05[1]	2005-06[1]
Alabama	16.8%	15.5%	Louisiana	17.6%	17.6%	Ohio	11.9%	12.2%
Alaska	9.5	9.4	Maine	12.1	11.4	Oklahoma	13.2	15.4
Arizona	14.8	14.8	Maryland	9.8	9.1	Oregon	11.9	11.9
Arkansas	14.5	15.8	Massachusetts	9.7	11.1	Pennsylvania	11.3	11.3
California	13.2	12.7	Michigan	12.6	12.6	Rhode Island	11.8	11.3
Colorado	10.7	10.6	Minnesota	7.5	8.1	South Carolina	15.0	13.1
Connecticut	9.7	8.7	Mississippi	19.4	20.4	South Dakota	12.7	11.3
Delaware	9.1	9.3	Missouri	11.9	11.5	Tennessee	15.4	14.9
District of Columbia	19.1	19.8	Montana	14.0	13.7	Texas	16.3	16.3
Florida	11.4	11.3	Nebraska	9.5	9.9	Utah	9.6	9.2
Georgia	13.7	13.5	Nevada	10.8	10.1	Vermont	7.7	7.7
Hawaii	8.6	8.9	New Hampshire	5.5	5.5	Virginia	9.3	8.9
Idaho	9.9	9.7	New Jersey	7.4	7.8	Washington	10.8	9.1
Illinois	11.9	11.0	New Mexico	17.2	17.4	West Virginia	14.8	15.3
Indiana	12.1	11.6	New York	14.8	14.3	Wisconsin	11.3	10.2
Iowa	11.1	10.8	North Carolina	13.8	13.5	Wyoming	10.3	10.3
Kansas	12.0	12.7	North Dakota	10.4	11.3	U.S. Total	12.7	12.5
Kentucky	16.3	15.8						

(1) 2-year average.

Selected Personal Consumption Expenditures in the U.S., 1985-2006[1]

Source: Bureau of Economic Analysis, U.S. Dept. of Commerce
(billions of dollars)

	1985	1990	1995	2000	2004	2005	2006
Personal consumption expenditures	2,720.3	3,839.9	4,975.8	6,739.4	8,195.9	8,707.8	9,224.5
Durable goods	363.5	474.2	611.6	863.3	983.9	1,023.9	1,048.9
Motor vehicles and parts	175.9	212.8	266.7	386.5	436.8	444.9	434.2
New autos	86.3	89.7	82.1	103.6	97.7	104.0	107.1
Tires, tubes, accessories, and other parts	24.3	29.9	37.8	49.0	54.4	57.9	59.8
Furniture and household equipment	128.5	171.6	228.6	312.9	355.7	378.2	404.1
Furniture, including mattresses and bedsprings	29.3	38.4	48.5	67.6	75.3	79.9	84.5
Kitchen and other household appliances	19.8	23.7	26.5	30.4	34.7	36.8	38.6
China, glassware, tableware, and utensils	14.0	17.9	23.4	31.0	34.8	36.6	39.8
Video and audio goods, including musical instruments	33.0	44.1	57.2	72.8	81.7	85.8	90.1
Computers, peripherals, and software	2.9	8.9	24.3	43.8	51.6	56.5	61.4
Ophthalmic products and orthopedic appliances	6.2	13.7	15.0	22.1	23.4	24.3	26.1
Wheel goods, sports and photographic equipment, boats, and pleasure aircraft	21.2	29.7	39.7	57.6	71.3	76.2	78.9
Jewelry and watches	21.1	30.3	38.4	50.6	56.3	58.4	62.2
Books and maps	10.6	16.2	23.2	33.7	40.4	41.8	43.4
Nondurable goods	928.7	1,249.9	1,485.1	1,947.2	2,343.7	2,516.2	2,688.0
Food	467.6	636.8	740.9	925.2	1,113.1	1,183.8	1,259.3
Food purchased for off-premise consumption	271.1	352.7	404.1	495.5	591.1	627.7	661.6
Alcoholic beverages purchased for off-premise consumption	39.4	48.9	54.6	71.2	86.1	93.5	101.0
Purchased meals and beverages	150.0	227.7	274.0	348.8	424.5	450.2	482.4
Food furnished to employees (including military) and food produced and consumed on farms	7.1	7.4	8.3	9.7	11.4	12.4	14.3
Clothing and shoes	152.1	204.1	241.7	297.7	325.0	341.7	357.2
Shoes	22.9	31.5	37.6	47.0	51.9	55.1	58.2
Women's and children's clothing and accessories except shoes	85.3	113.0	129.5	156.7	171.2	179.8	187.7
Men's and boys' clothing and accessories except shoes	43.9	59.6	74.7	94.0	101.8	106.9	111.4
Gasoline, fuel oil, and other energy goods	110.8	124.1	133.3	191.5	249.7	301.8	340.1
Gasoline and oil	97.2	111.2	120.2	175.7	231.4	280.7	318.6
Fuel oil and coal	13.6	12.9	13.1	15.8	18.3	21.1	21.6
Other	198.2	285.0	369.2	532.9	655.9	688.8	731.4
Tobacco products	30.8	41.0	49.2	78.5	87.5	89.7	92.4
Toilet articles and preparations	25.7	36.0	45.9	55.0	58.3	61.1	63.8
Semidurable house furnishings	16.4	22.5	29.4	36.5	41.1	43.2	45.4
Cleaning and polishing preparations, misc. household supplies and paper products	30.6	38.9	48.8	61.6	72.8	77.1	81.3
Drug preparations and sundries	38.7	65.4	92.1	169.4	251.4	265.2	286.0
Nondurable toys and sport supplies	21.4	32.8	44.4	56.6	63.3	66.5	71.4
Stationery and writing supplies	8.5	13.2	16.3	19.0	18.8	19.6	21.0
Magazines, newspapers, and sheet music	15.9	21.6	27.5	35.0	39.4	42.1	45.0
Flowers, seeds, and potted plants	6.9	10.9	14.0	18.0	18.3	19.2	19.9
Services	1,428.1	2,115.9	2,879.1	3,928.8	4,868.3	5,167.8	5,487.6
Housing	412.7	597.9	764.4	1,006.5	1,226.8	1,298.7	1,381.3
Owner-occupied nonfarm dwellings—space rent	280.8	412.8	531.2	712.2	898.0	952.6	1,014.5
Tenant-occupied nonfarm dwellings—rent	108.3	150.7	186.6	227.5	251.8	262.7	277.0
Rental value of farm dwellings	5.1	6.3	9.4	10.7	13.0	13.8	14.8
Household operation	181.8	227.3	298.7	390.1	449.0	481.0	501.6
Electricity	61.2	74.2	91.0	102.3	120.1	133.4	146.3
Gas	29.5	26.8	31.2	41.0	55.3	65.3	63.5
Water and other sanitary services	17.0	27.1	39.3	50.8	60.6	63.3	66.4
Telephone and telegraph	46.0	60.5	85.0	125.1	133.0	134.3	137.6
Domestic service	7.7	10.4	13.8	17.4	19.5	19.9	20.7
Transportation	104.5	147.7	207.7	291.3	308.2	324.2	340.6
User-operated transportation	76.7	110.7	163.6	231.6	249.2	262.7	275.5
Purchased local transportation	6.8	8.4	10.1	12.2	13.8	14.6	15.7
Mass transit systems	4.2	5.8	7.1	9.1	10.2	10.7	11.5
Taxicab	2.6	2.6	3.0	3.1	3.6	3.9	4.2
Purchased intercity transportation	21.0	28.6	33.9	47.4	45.2	46.9	49.5
Railway	0.4	0.6	0.4	0.5	0.6	0.6	0.6
Bus	1.3	1.3	1.8	2.4	2.3	2.2	2.2
Airline	17.6	22.7	25.3	36.7	33.3	34.4	35.6
Medical care	331.5	556.0	797.9	1,026.8	1,395.5	1,492.6	1,587.7
Physicians	78.8	138.6	184.6	236.8	322.0	344.6	366.3
Dentists	22.6	32.4	45.4	61.8	80.2	85.2	90.3
Other professional services	31.8	70.7	126.6	161.6	217.1	230.9	246.1
Hospitals and nursing homes	169.9	270.9	380.5	482.6	646.8	690.7	735.8
Health insurance	28.4	43.4	60.7	84.0	129.5	141.3	149.2
Recreation	77.7	125.9	187.9	268.3	341.8	358.8	381.0
Admissions to specified spectator amusements	9.7	15.1	21.1	30.4	37.6	38.7	39.9
Casino gambling	6.8	11.5	28.5	49.0	70.9	75.5	81.6
Pets and pets services excluding veterinarians	1.9	2.4	3.6	4.5	4.9	5.1	5.3
Personal care	28.2	48.1	61.2	87.0	108.7	114.8	123.6
Cleaning, storage, and repair of clothing and shoes	7.3	11.3	12.3	15.7	15.5	16.1	16.9
Barbershops, beauty parlors, and health clubs	13.1	20.9	26.8	38.4	48.4	50.8	51.9
Personal business	177.5	250.9	349.6	539.1	610.9	651.5	691.9
Brokerage charges and investment counseling	15.2	23.2	43.5	100.6	86.4	92.7	104.2
Bank service charges, trust services, and safe deposit box rental	15.6	25.5	37.2	64.2	88.5	99.2	108.0
Expense of handling life insurance and pension plans	39.8	53.2	72.9	96.1	99.4	108.9	114.9
Legal services	24.5	40.9	47.4	63.9	82.0	86.0	91.8
Funeral and burial expenses	6.8	9.5	12.4	14.0	15.6	16.2	16.8
Education and research	53.9	83.7	114.3	163.8	212.8	225.9	239.6
Higher education	28.7	43.8	62.9	86.4	119.0	126.4	134.1
Nursery, elementary, and secondary schools	14.3	21.2	27.0	34.6	42.3	44.4	46.4
Religious and welfare activities	55.7	88.7	120.4	172.3	219.0	225.1	241.3
Net foreign travel	4.6	-10.3	-22.9	-16.2	-4.2	-4.9	-1.2
Foreign travel by U.S. residents	27.9	42.7	54.7	84.4	92.5	100.0	108.7
Less: Expenditures in the United States by nonresidents	23.3	53.0	77.6	100.7	96.8	104.9	109.9

(1) Subtotals may not add to total, due to rounding or incomplete enumeration.

Leading U.S. Businesses in 2006

Source: FORTUNE Magazine
(millions of dollars in revenues)

Advertising, Marketing
Omnicom $11,377
Interpublic Group 6,191

Aerospace
Boeing $61,530
United Technologies 47,829
Lockheed Martin. 39,620
Honeywell Intl. 31,367
Northrop Grumman 30,304
General Dynamics 24,212
Raytheon 23,274
Textron 12,591
L-3 Communications 12,477

Airlines
AMR $22,563
UAL 19,340
Delta Air Lines 17,171
Continental Airlines 13,128
Northwest Airlines 12,568
US Airways Group 11,557
Southwest Airlines 9,086

Apparel
Nike $14,955
VF. 7,034

Automotive Retailing, Services
AutoNation $19,314
United Auto Group 12,110
Sonic Automotive 8,706
Hertz Global Holdings 8,058

Beverages
Coca-Cola $24,088
Coca-Cola Enterprises. 19,804
Anheuser-Busch. 15,717
Pepsi Bottling 12,730

Chemicals
Dow Chemical $49,124
DuPont. 28,982
Lyondell Chemical 22,228
Huntsman. 13,148
PPG Industries. 11,037
Ashland 10,007
Air Products & Chem. 9,159
Praxair 8,324
Rohm & Haas. 8,308
Sherwin-Williams 7,810
Eastman Chemical 7,450
Monsanto 7,344
Celanese 6,668

Commercial Banks
Citigroup. $146,777
Bank of America Corp. 117,017
J.P. Morgan Chase &Co. 99,973
Wells Fargo 47,979
Wachovia Corp. 46,810
U.S. Bancorp. 19,109
Capital One Financial. 15,191
SunTrust Banks 13,260
National City Corp. 12,953
Bank of New York Co. 11,891
PNC Financial Services Group 10,939
State St. Corp. 9,525
BB&T Corp. 9,415
Fifth Third Bancorp. 8,108
Regions Financial. 7,756
KeyCorp 7,507

Computer Peripherals
EMC $11,155

Computer Software
Microsoft. $44,282
Oracle. 14,380

Computers, Office Equipment
Hewlett-Packard. $91,658
Intl. Business Machines 91,424
Dell. 57,095
Apple 19,315
Xerox 15,895
Sun Microsystems 13,068

Diversified Financials
General Electric $168,307
Freddie Mac. 44,002

American Express 27,145
Countrywide Financial 24,445
Marsh & McLennan 12,069
Aon. 10,311
SLM 8,751
Ameriprise Financial. 8,140
CIT Group 6,928

Diversified Outsourcing
Aramark $11,621

Electronics, Electrical Equipment
Emerson Electric $20,133
Whirlpool 18,080

Energy
Constellation Energy $19,446
American Electric Power 12,622
ONEOK 11,907
Williams 11,813
Reliant Energy 10,985
TXU 10,856
Energy Transfer Equity 7,859
Integrys Energy Group 6,979
Calpine. 6,706

Engineering, Construction
Fluor. $14,079
Jacobs Engineering Grp. 7,421

Entertainment
Time Warner $44,788
Walt Disney 34,285
News Corp. 25,327
CBS 14,479
Viacom 11,467
Clear Channel Communications 7,099

Financial Data Services
First Data $7,076

Food & Drug Stores
Kroger $66,111
Walgreen 47,409
CVS/Caremark. 43,814
Safeway 40,185
Publix Super Markets 21,820
Supervalu 19,864
Rite Aid. 17,271
Winn-Dixie Stores 7,878

Food
PepsiCo $35,137
Sara Lee. 18,539
ConAgra Foods 14,172
General Mills 11,640
Kellogg 10,907
Dean Foods 10,339
S&C Holdco 3. 9,350
H.J. Heinz. 9,331
Campbell Soup. 7,778
Land O'Lakes 7,102

Food Production
Archer Daniels Midland $36,596
Tyson Foods 25,559
Smithfield Foods 11,507

Food Services
McDonald's $21,586
Yum Brands 9,561
Starbucks 7,787

Forest & Paper Products
International Paper $24,186
Weyerhaeuser 22,250

General Merchandisers
Wal-Mart Stores $351,139
Target. 59,490
Sears Holdings 53,012
Federated Dept. Stores 28,711
J.C. Penney 19,903
Kohl's 15,544
Dollar General 9,170
Nordstrom 8,561
Dillard's 7,849

Health Care: Insurance & Managed Care
UnitedHealth Group $71,542
Wellpoint 56,953
Aetna 25,569

Humana 21,417
Cigna 16,547
Health Net 12,908
Coventry Health Care. 7,734

Health Care: Medical Facilities
HCA $25,477
Tenet Healthcare 9,622

Healthcare: Pharmacy and Other Services
Medco Health Solutions $42,544
Caremark Rx 36,750
Express Scripts 17,660

Home Equipment, Furnishings
Masco. $12,833
Fortune Brands 8,255
Newell Rubbermaid 6,710

Homebuilders
Lennar $16,267
Centex 15,465
D.R. Horton 15,051
Pulte Homes. 14,274
KB Home 11,004

Hotels, Casinos, Resorts
Marriott International $12,160
Harrah's Entertainment 9,781
Hilton Hotels. 8,162
MGM Mirage 7,588

Household & Personal Products
Procter & Gamble. $68,222
Kimberly-Clark 16,747
Colgate-Palmolive 12,238
Avon Products 8,764

Industrial & Farm Equipment
Caterpillar. $41,517
Deere 22,769
Illinois Tool Works 14,055
Eaton 12,370
Cummins 11,362
American Standard 11,208
Parker Hannifin 9,408
ITT 8,186
Terex 7,648
Dover 7,180

Information Technology Services
Electronic Data Systems $21,337
Computer Sciences 14,624
SAIC. 8,127

Insurance: Life, Health (Mutual)
New York Life Insurance $28,365
TIAA-CREF 26,757
Mass. Mutual Life Ins. 24,863
Northwestern Mutual 20,726
Guardian Life of America 9,694

Insurance: Life, Health (Stock)
MetLife $53,275
Prudential Financial 32,488
AFLAC 14,616
Genworth Financial 11,029
Unum Group. 10,719
Principal Financial 9,870
Lincoln National 9,063
Assurant. 8,071

Insurance: P & C (Mutual)
State Farm Insurance Cos $60,528

Insurance: P & C (Stock)
American Intl. Group $113,194
Berkshire Hathaway. 98,539
Allstate 35,796
Hartford Financial Services . . . 26,500
Travelers Cos. 25,090
Liberty Mutual Ins. Group. . . . 23,520
Nationwide 22,253
Loews. 17,228
Progressive 14,786
Chubb. 14,003
USAA 13,416
Fidelity National Financial . . . 9,436
First American Corp. 8,499
American Family Ins. Grp. 6,893

Internet Services and Retailing
Amazon.com	$10,711
Google	10,605
Liberty Media	8,948
IAC/InterActiveCorp	6,684

Mail, Package, Freight Delivery
United Parcel Service	$47,547
FedEx	32,294

Medical Products & Equipment
Medtronic	$11,292
Baxter International	10,378
Boston Scientific	7,821

Metals
Alcoa	$30,896
United States Steel	15,715
Nucor	14,751
Phelps Dodge	12,090
Commercial Metals	7,556

Mining, Crude-Oil Production
Occidental Petroleum	$19,029
Anadarko Petroleum	10,904
Devon Energy	10,696
Apache	8,289
Chesapeake Energy	7,326

Miscellaneous
3M	$22,923
Mohawk Industries	7,906

Motor Vehicles & Parts
General Motors	$207,349
Ford Motor	160,126
Johnson Controls	32,413
Delphi	26,392
Goodyear Tire & Rubber	20,258
Lear	17,839
Paccar	16,454
TRW Automotive Holdings	13,144
Visteon	11,418
ArvinMeritor	9,810
Dana	9,724

Network & Other Communications Equipment
Motorola	$43,739
Cisco Systems	28,484
Lucent Technologies	8,796
Qualcomm	7,526

Oil and Gas Equipment Services
Halliburton	$22,576
Baker Hughes	9,034
Smith Intl	7,334
National Oilwell Varco	7,026

Packaging, Containers
Smurfit-Stone Container	$7,944
Owens-Illinois	7,524
Crown Holdings	7,140
Ball	6,622
MeadWestvaco	6,530

Payroll Services
Automatic Data Proc	$9,263

Petroleum Refining
Exxon Mobil	$347,254
Chevron	200,567
ConocoPhillips	172,451

Valero Energy	91,051
Marathon Oil	60,643
Sunoco	36,081
Hess	28,720
Tesoro	18,002
Murphy Oil	14,307

Pharmaceuticals
Johnson & Johnson	$53,324
Pfizer	52,415
Merck	22,636
Abbott Laboratories	22,476
Wyeth	20,351
Bristol-Myers Squibb	17,914
Eli Lilly	15,691
Amgen	14,268
Schering-Plough	10,594

Pipelines
Plains All Amer. Pipeline	$22,444
Enterprise GP Holdings	13,991
Kinder Morgan	12,208
TEPPCO Partners	9,612

Publishing, Printing
R.R. Donnelley & Sons	$9,317
Gannett	8,033

Railroads
Union Pacific	$15,578
Burlington No. Santa Fe	14,985
CSX	9,566
Norfolk Southern	9,407

Savings Institutions
Washington Mutual	$26,561

Scientific, Photo, Control Equipment
Eastman Kodak	$13,274
Danaher	9,596

Securities
Morgan Stanley	$76,688
Merrill Lynch	70,591
Goldman Sachs Group	69,353
Lehman Brothers Hldgs.	46,709
Bear Stearns	16,551

Semiconductors and Other Electronic Components
Intel	$35,382
Texas Instruments	14,630
Sanmina-SCI	10,955
Solectron	10,561
Applied Materials	9,167

Specialty Retailers
Home Depot	$90,837
Costco Wholesale	60,151
Lowe's	46,927
Best Buy	30,848
Staples	18,161
TJX	17,516
Gap	15,943
Office Depot	15,011
Toys 'R' Us	12,206
Circuit City Stores	11,598
Limited Brands	10,671
OfficeMax	8,966
BJ's Wholesale Club	8,524

Telecommunications
Verizon Communications	$93,221
AT&T	63,055
Sprint Nextel	43,531
Comcast	25,700
DIRECTV Group	14,756
Qwest Communications	13,923
Echostar Communications	9,818
Alltell	9,723
Liberty Global	6,813
Virgin Media	6,637

Temporary Help
Manpower	$17,787

Tobacco
Altria Group	$70,324
Reynolds American	8,510

Transportation and Logistics
C.H. Robinson Worldwide	$6,556

Trucking, Truck Leasing
YRC Worldwide	$9,919

Utilities: Gas & Electric
Dominion Resources	$16,524
Duke Energy	15,967
FPL Group	15,710
Exelon	15,654
Southern	14,356
Edison International	12,622
PG&E Corp.	12,539
Public Service Enterprise Group	12,288
Consolidated Edison	12,137
Sempra Energy	11,850
FirstEnergy	11,726
Entergy	11,067
Progress Energy	10,702
Xcel Energy	9,848
CenterPoint Energy	9,319
DTE Energy	9,024
Pepco Holdings	8,363
NiSource	7,496
KeySpan	7,182
PPL	6,904
Northeast Utilities	6,897
Ameren	6,880
CMS Energy	6,810

Waste Management
Waste Management	$13,363

Wholesalers: Diversified
World Fuel Services	$10,785
Genuine Parts	10,458

Wholesalers: Electronics and Office Equiptment
Ingram Micro	$31,357
Tech Data	21,446
Avnet	14,254
Arrow Electronics	13,577
CDW	6,785

Wholesalers: Food and Grocery
Sysco	$32,628
CHS	14,384

Wholesalers: Health Care
McKesson	$88,050
Cardinal Health	81,895
AmerisourceBergen	61,203

25 U.S. Corporations with Largest Revenues in 2006
Source: *Fortune* Magazine
(millions of dollars)

Rank, Company (2005 rank)	Revenues	Profits
1. Wal-Mart Stores (2)	$351,139.0	$11,284.0
2. Exxon Mobil (1)	347,254.0	39,500.0
3. General Motors (3)	207,349.0	−1,978.0
4. Chevron (4)	200,567.0	17,138.0
5. ConocoPhillips (6)	172,451.0	15,550.0
6. General Electric (7)	168,307.0	20,829.0
7. Ford Motor (5)	160,126.0	−12,613.0
8. Citigroup (8)	146,777.0	21,538.0
9. Bank of America Corp. (12)	117,017.0	21,133.0
10. American Intl. Group (9)	113,194.0	14,048.0
11. J.P. Morgan Chase & Co. (17)	99,973.0	14,444.0
12. Berkshire Hathaway (13)	98,539.0	11,015.0
13. Verizon Communications (18)	93,221.0	6,197.0
14. Hewlett-Packard (11)	$91,658.0	$6,198.0
15. Intl. Business Machines (10)	91,424.0	9,492.0
16. Valero Energy (15)	91,051.0	5,463.0
17. Home Depot (14)	90,837.0	5,761.0
18. McKesson (16)	88,050.0	751.0
19. Cardinal Health (19)	81,895.1	1,000.1
20. Morgan Stanley (30)	76,688.0	7,472.0
21. UnitedHealth Group (37)	71,542.0	4,159.0
22. Merrill Lynch (34)	70,591.0	7,499.0
23. Altria Group (20)	70,324.0	12,022.0
24. Goldman Sachs Group (41)	69,353.0	9,537.0
25. Procter & Gamble (24)	68,222.0	8,684.0

Fastest-Growing U.S. Franchises in 2007[1]

Source: *Entrepreneur* Magazine

	Company	Type of Business	Minimum start-up cost[2]
1.	Subway	Submarine sandwiches & salads	$74.9K-222.8K
2.	Jan-Pro Franchising Int'l. Inc.	Commercial cleaning	$3.3K-49.9K
3.	Dunkin' Donuts	Donuts & baked goods	$179K-1.6M
4.	Coverall Cleaning Concepts	Commercial cleaning	$6.3K-35.9K
5.	Jazzercise Inc.	Dance/exercise classes	$2.99K-33.1K
6.	Jackson Hewitt Tax Service	Tax preparation services	$48.6K-91.8K
7.	RE/MAX Int'l. Inc.	Real estate	$25K-199K
8.	CleanNet USA Inc.	Commercial office cleaning	$3.9K-35.6K
9.	Bonus Building Care	Commercial cleaning	$7.2K-13.6K
10.	Jani-King	Commercial cleaning	$11.3K-34.1K+
11.	Liberty Tax Service	Income-tax preparation services	$33.4K-59.9K
12.	Cold Stone Creamery	Ice cream, Italian sorbet	$294.3K-438.9K
13.	Cartridge World	Printer/fax cartridge replacements & sales	$107.1K-175.1K
14.	Coffee News	Weekly newspaper distributed at restaurants	$7K
15.	Edible Arrangements	Floral-like designs from sculpted fresh fruit	$150.95K-291.2K
15.	Budget Blinds Inc.	Window coverings	$79.7K-153.1K
17.	Brooke Franchise Corp.	Insurance & financial services	$165.7K-385.8K
18.	Choice Hotels Int'l.	Hotels, inns, suites, resorts	$1.9M-11.8M
19.	UPS Store, The/Mail Boxes Etc.	Postal, business & communications services	$153.95K-266.8K
20.	Century 21 Real Estate LLC	Real estate	$11.8K-522.8K
20.	System4	Commercial cleaning	$5.5K-37.8K
22.	Home Helpers	Nonmedical care services	$41.7K-73.3K
23.	Great Clips Inc.	Family hair salon	$106.9K-197.7K
23.	Curves	Women's fitness & weight-loss center	$31.4K-53.5K
25.	Heaven's Best Carpet & Uphol. Cleaning	Carpet & upholstery cleaning	$33.9K-63.8K

(1) Ranked by number of new franchise units added. (2) In thousands; not including franchise fee, which varies.

Largest Corporate Mergers or Acquisitions in U.S.

Source: Securities Data Co.; World Almanac research
(as of Oct. 2007; * denotes an announced merger or acquisition not yet complete; year = year effective or announced)

Company	Acquirer	Dollars (in billions)	Year
Time Warner	America Online, Inc.	$181.6	2001
Warner-Lambert	Pfizer Inc.	88.8	2000
Mobil Corp.	Exxon Corp.	86.4	1999
BellSouth Corp.	AT&T Inc.	85.8	2006
Citicorp	Travelers Group Inc.	72.6	1998
Ameritech Corp	SBC Communic. Inc.	72.4	1999
GTE Corp.	Bell Atlantic Corp.	71.3	2000
Tele-Communications	AT&T	69.9	1999
AirTouch Communic.	Vodafone Group PLC	65.8	1999
Kraft Foods Inc.	shareholders	61.7	2007
BankAmerica Corp.	NationsBank Corp.	61.6	1998
Pharmacia Corp.	Pfizer, Inc	61.3	2003
Bank One Corp.	JP Morgan Chase	58.8	2004
US West	Qwest Communication	56.3	2000
Amoco Corp.	British Petroleum Co. PLC	55.0	1998
Gillette	Procter & Gamble	54.9	2005
MediaOne Group	AT&T	51.9	2000
FleetBoston Fin. Corp.	Bank of America	47.0	2004
Liberty Media Group (AT&T)	shareholders	46.0	2001
TXU Corp.	KKR & Texas Pacific.	44.4	2007
Texaco	Chevron	43.3	2001
MCI Communications	WorldCom Inc.	41.4	1998
AT&T Wireless Service	Cingular Wireless	41.0	2004
SDL Inc.	JDS Uniphase Corp.	41.0	2001
CBS Corp.	Viacom	40.9	2000
Chrysler Corp.	Daimler-Benz AG	40.5	1998
Equity Office Properties Trust	Blackstone Grp.	36.0	2006
MBNA	Bank of America	35.8	2005
Burlington Resources	Conoco Phillips	35.6	2005
Wells Fargo & Co.	Norwest Corp.	34.4	1998
VoiceStream Wireless Corp.	Deutsche Telekom AG	34.1	2001
ARCO	BP Amoco PLC	33.7	2000
J.P. Morgan & Co.	Chase Manhattan	33.6	2000
HCA Inc.	Bain Capital, KKR, Merrill Lynch, Bill Frist	32.7	2006
US West Media Grp.	shareholders	31.7	1998

Company	Acquirer	Dollars (in billions)	Year
Agilent Technologies	shareholders	$31.2	2000
Associates First Capital	Citigroup	31.0	2000
NYNEX	Bell Atlantic	30.8	1997
AT&T Broadband & Internet Services	Comcast Corp.	30.0	2001
Electronic Data Syst.	shareholders	29.7	1996
First Chicago NBD.	BANC ONE Corp.	29.6	1998
RJR Nabisco	Kohlberg Kravis Roberts	29.4	1989
*ALLTEL Corp.	TPG Capital & GS Capital	27.5	2007
Guidant Corp.	Boston Scientific.	27.2	2006
Pharmacia & Upjohn.	Monsanto Co.	26.9	2000
Associates First Capital	shareholders	26.6	1998
Caremark RX Inc.	CVS Corp.	26.3	2007
First Data Corp.	KKR	26.0	2007
Hilton Hotels Corp.	Blackstone Grp.	26.0	2007
Phelps Dodge Corp.	Freeport-McMoRan Copper & Gold Inc.	25.9	2007
Golden West Financial Corp.	Wachovia Corp.	25.0	2006
*Sallie Mae	J.P. Morgan, Chase & Co., & Bank of America Corp.	25.0	2007
Conoco	Phillips Petroleum	24.8	2002
Lucent Technologies (AT&T)	shareholders	24.1	1996
Bestfoods	Unilever PLC	23.7	2000
Compaq Computer	Hewlett-Packard.	23.5	2002
Amer. General Corp.	American Int'l. Group	23.4	2001
Kinder Morgan Inc.	shareholders led by Richard Kinder	23.0	2007
Tyco Healthcare (Covidien)	shareholders	22.8	2007
AMFM, Inc.	Clear Channel Communications	22.7	2000
Pacific Telesis Group	SBC Communications Inc.	22.4	1997
General Re Corp.	Berkshire Hathaway Inc.	22.3	1998

United States Mint
Source: United States Mint, U.S. Dept. of the Treasury

The United States Mint was created on Apr. 2, 1792, by an act of Congress, which established the U.S. national coinage system. In 1799 the mint became an independent agency reporting directly to the president. It was made a statutory bureau of the Treasury Department in 1873, with a director appointed by the president. The mint manufactures and ships all U.S. coins for circulation to Federal Reserve banks and branches, which in turn issue coins to the public and business community through depository institutions. The mint also safeguards the Treasury Department's stored gold and silver, as well as other monetary assets.

The composition of dimes, quarters, and half dollars, traditionally produced from silver, was changed by the Coinage Act of 1965, which mandated that these coins from then on be minted from a cupronickel-clad alloy and reduced the silver content of the half dollar to 40%. In 1970, legislative action mandated that the half dollar and a dollar coin be minted from the same alloy.

Mint headquarters are in Washington, DC. Mint production facilities are in Philadelphia, Denver, San Francisco, and West Point, NY. In addition, the mint is responsible for the U.S. Bullion Depository at Fort Knox, KY.

The mint offers free public tours and operates sales centers at the U.S. mints in Denver and Philadelphia. Further information is available from the U.S. Mint, Customer Care Center, 801 9th St., NW, Washington, DC 20220; (800) USA-MINT. **Website:** www.usmint.gov

History of the Dollar Coin: The Eisenhower dollar was minted 1971 through 1978, when legislation called for the minting of the smaller Susan B. Anthony dollar coin. The Anthony dollar, minted through 1981, marked the first time that a woman other than a mythical figure appeared on a generally circulated U.S. coin. It was replaced in 2000 by the Golden Dollar Coin. Golden in color, with a smooth edge and wide border, the obverse depicts Sacagawea (Shoshone woman who helped guide Lewis and Clark) and her infant son. The reverse shows an American eagle and 17 stars, one for each of the states at the time of the Lewis and Clark expedition. In 2007, the mint began issuing a series of Golden Dollar Coins featuring U.S. Presidents. Each includes the president's name, likeness, and years of service. Four will be issued each year in the order in which the presidents served. Presidents serving non-consecutive terms (Grover Cleveland) will be honored twice. In the current schedule, coins will be minted through 2016 as only presidents deceased more than two years will be honored. The reverse features the Statue of Liberty. The mint mark, "e Pluribus Unum," and "In God We Trust," are edge-incused.

New Circulating and Commemorative Coins
Source: United States Mint, U.S. Dept. of the Treasury

The 50 State Quarters program that began in 1999 ends in 2008 with the final 5 states to enter the union: Oklahoma, New Mexico, Arizona, Alaska, and Hawaii.

The 2004-06 Westward Journey Nickel Series commemorated the bicentennial of the Louisiana Purchase and Lewis and Clark expedition on redesigned, circulating 5-cent coins.

The mint produced congressionally authorized commemorative coins from 1892 to 1954, and again since 1982. Through 2007, Congress authorized 48 commemorative coin programs. Recent congressionally authorized coins are: the 2007 Jamestown 400th Anniversary gold $5 and silver $1; the 2007 Little Rock Central High School Desegregation silver $1; the 2008 American Bald Eagle Recovery and National Emblem gold $5, silver $1, and clad half dollar; the 2009 Louis Braille Bicentennial-Braille Literacy silver $1; and the 2009 Lincoln Penny Series.

Proof coin sets, silver proof coin sets, and uncirculated coin sets are available from the mint, which also produces medals in honor of significant persons, events, and sites.

Congressionally authorized American Eagle gold, platinum, and silver bullion coins are also available through dealers worldwide.

The Bureau of Engraving and Printing
Source: Bureau of Engraving and Printing, U.S. Dept. of the Treasury

The Bureau of Engraving and Printing manufactures the financial and other securities of the United States. It designs and prints a variety of products, including Federal Reserve notes (bills in various denominations), Treasury securities, identification cards, naturalization certificates, and other special security documents. Denominations of the various types of printings produced by the bureau range from a 1/5-cent wine stamp to a $100,000,000 International Monetary Fund special note. Among its products are all hand-engraved invitations issued by the White House.

The first general circulation of paper money by the federal government dates back to 1861, prior to the establishment of the bureau, when, to finance the Civil War, Congress authorized the U.S. Treasury to issue non-interest-bearing demand notes, nicknamed "greenbacks" because of their color. A portrait of Pres. Abraham Lincoln appeared on the face of the first $10 notes. By 1862, the design of U.S. currency incorporated fine-line engraving, intricate geometric lathework patterns, a Treasury seal, and engraved signatures, to aid in counterfeit deterrence. All U.S. currency issued since 1861 remains valid and redeemable at full face value.

The Bureau of Engraving and Printing began operations by 1862, originally separating and sealing bank notes that were printed by private companies. In 1877, the bureau became the sole producer of U.S. currency. In 1894, it also began producing Postage Stamps. On June 10, 2005, the bureau printed its last stamps, a roll of 37-cent flag stamps; stamps are now produced by private printers.

The Federal Reserve Act of 1913 created the Federal Reserve as the nation's central bank, and provided for currency called Federal Reserve notes. The first notes, issued the following year, were $10 notes bearing a portrait of Pres. Andrew Jackson. In 1929, the look of U.S. currency was standardized. The national motto, "In God We Trust," was added to paper money in 1957.

The Bureau of Engraving and Printing currently operates 2 facilities, one in Washington, DC, opened in 1914, and one in Forth Worth, TX, which began operations in 1991.

Website: www.moneyfactory.gov

Denominations of U.S. Currency

Since 1969 the largest denomination of U.S. currency that has been issued is the $100 bill. As larger-denomination bills reach the Federal Reserve Bank, they are removed from circulation. Because some discontinued currency is expected to be in the hands of holders for many years, the description of the various denominations below is continued.

Amt.	Portait	Embellishment on Back	Amt.	Portait	Embellishment on Back
$1	Washington.	Great Seal of U.S.	$500	McKinley	Ornate denominational marking
2	Jefferson.	Signers of Declaration	1,000	Cleveland.	Ornate denominational marking
5	Lincoln	Lincoln Memorial	5,000	Madison	Washington Resigning as Army
10	Hamilton	U.S. Treasury			Commander
20	Jackson	White House	10,000	Salmon Chase . . .	Embarkation of the Pilgrims
50	Grant.	U.S. Capitol	100,000*	Wilson	Ornate denominational marking
100	Franklin.	Independence Hall			

*For use only in transactions between Federal Reserve System and Treasury Department.

Portraits on U.S. Treasury Bills, Bonds, Notes, and Savings Bonds

Denomination	EE Savings bonds	Treasury bills*	Treasury bonds*	Treasury notes*
$50	Washington		Jefferson	
75	Adams			
100	Jefferson		Jackson	
200	Madison			
500	Hamilton		Washington	
1,000	B. Franklin	H. McCulloch	Lincoln	Lincoln
5,000	P. Revere	J. G. Carlisle	Monroe	Monroe
10,000	J. Wilson	J. Sherman	Cleveland	Cleveland
50,000	C. Glass			
100,000		A. Gallatin	Grant	Grant
1,000,000		O. Wolcott	T. Roosevelt	T. Roosevelt
100,000,000				Madison
500,000,000				McKinley

*The U.S. Treasury discontinued issuing treasury bill, bond, and note certificates in 1986. Since then, all issues of marketable treasury securities have been available only in book-entry form, although some certificates remain in circulation.

New U.S. Currency Designs

On Mar. 25, 1996, the U.S. Treasury issued a redesigned $100 note incorporating many new and modified anti-counterfeiting features. A new $50 note was issued Oct. 27, 1997, a new $20 bill was released into circulation Sept. 24, 1998, and new $10 and $5 notes were issued May 24, 2000. Old notes are being removed from circulation as they are returned to the Federal Reserve.

The new $100 bill has a larger portrait, moved off-center; a watermark (seen only when held up to the light) to the right of the portrait, depicting the same person (Benjamin Franklin); a security thread that glows red when exposed to ultraviolet light in a dark environment; color-shifting ink that changes from green to black when viewed at different angles, to appear in the numeral on the lower, front right-hand corner of the bill; microprinting in the numeral in the note's lower, front left-hand corner and on the portrait; and other features for security, machine authentication, and processing of the currency. The redesigned $5, $10, $20, and $50 bills incorporated the same features as the $100 bill,

with the notable addition of a low-vision feature, a large (14-mm high, as compared to 7.8-mm on the old design), dark numeral on a light background on the back of the note. (The security thread glows yellow in the $50, green in the $20, orange in the $10, and blue in the $5. There is no color-shifting ink on the $5 note.)

Beginning in 2003, the Treasury launched another major redesign of U.S. currency: on Oct. 9, 2003, the U.S. Treasury introduced a new $20 note, using background colors for the first time since 1905. The notes have a security thread running vertically up one side, with "USA TWENTY" and a small U.S. flag; the thread glows green under UV light. Other security features include color-shifting ink in the number "20" in the lower right corner on the note's face. A new $50 note with similar security features was released Sept. 28, 2004, followed by a new $10 note on March 2, 2006. A new $5 bill was scheduled for early 2008, followed by another redesign of the $100 note.

Website: www.moneyfactory.gov/newmoney

The U.S. $1 Bill

Plate position: Shows where on the 32-note plate this bill was printed.

Serial number Each bill has its own.

Federal Reserve District Number: Shows which district issued the bill.

Federal Reserve District Seal: The name of the Federal Reserve Bank that issued the bill is printed in the seal. The letter tells you quickly where the bill is from. Here are the letter codes for the 12 Federal Reserve Districts:

- **A:** Boston
- **B:** New York
- **C:** Philadelphia
- **D:** Cleveland
- **E:** Richmond
- **F:** Atlanta
- **G:** Chicago
- **H:** St. Louis
- **I:** Minneapolis
- **J:** Kansas City
- **K:** Dallas
- **L:** San Francisco

Treasurer of the U.S. signature

Series indicator (year note's design was first used)

Secretary of the Treasury signature

The Treasury Department seal: The balancing scales represent justice. The pointed stripe across the middle has 13 stars for the original 13 colonies. The key represents authority.

Plate serial number Shows which printing plate was used for the face of the bill.

Plate serial number Shows which plate was used for the back.

Front of the Great Seal of the United States: The bald eagle is the national bird. The shield has 13 stripes for the 13 original colonies. The eagle holds 13 arrows (symbol of war) and an olive branch (symbol of peace). Above the eagle is the motto "E Pluribus Unum," Latin for "out of many, one," and a constellation of 13 stars.

Reverse of the Great Seal of the United States: The pyramid symbolizes something that endures for ages. The eye, known as the "Eye of Providence," probably comes from an ancient Egyptian symbol. The pyramid has 13 levels; at its base are the Roman numerals for 1776, the year of American independence. "Annuit Coeptis" is Latin for "God has favored our undertaking." "Novus Ordo Seclorum" is Latin for "a new order of the ages." Both phrases are from the works of the Roman poet Virgil.

U.S. Currency and Coin
Source: Financial Management Service, U.S. Dept. of the Treasury (June 30, 2007)

Comparative Totals of Money in Circulation — Selected Dates

Date	Dollars (in millions)	Per capita[1]	Date	Dollars (in millions)	Per capita[1]	Date	Dollars (in millions)	Per capita[1]
June 30, 2007 ...	$812,760	$2,688	Sept. 30, 1995 ...	$409,272	$1,553	June 30, 1970 ...	$54,351	$265
May 31, 2007	813,989	2,694	Sept. 30, 1990 ...	278,903	1,105	June 30, 1965 ...	39,719	204
April 30, 2007....	807,015	2,673	Sept. 30, 1985 ...	187,337	782	June 30, 1960 ...	32,064	177
Sept. 30, 2005 ...	766,487	2,578	Sept. 30, 1980 ...	129,916	581	June 30, 1955 ...	30,229	183
Sept. 30, 2000 ...	568,614	2,061	June 30, 1975 ...	81,196	380			

(1) Based on Bureau of the Census estimates of population.

Amounts Outstanding and in Circulation

Currency	Total currency and coin	Total currency	Federal Reserve notes[1]	U.S. notes	Currency no longer issued
Amounts outstanding	$1,017,973,616,060	$979,949,564,157	$979,452,166,326	$250,981,466	$246,416,365
Less amounts held by:					
Treasury..............	335,742,065	25,261,521	25,050,505	7,505	203,511
Federal Reserve banks ...	204,877,418,625	203,919,045,589	203,919,042,063	—	3,526
Amounts in circulation	812,760,455,370	776,005,257,047	775,508,073,758	250,973,961	246,209,328

Coins[2]	Total	Dollars[3]	Fractional coins
Amounts outstanding	$38,024,051,903	$3,505,529,008	$34,518,522,895
Less amounts held by:			
Treasury.................................	310,480,544	270,190,544	40,290,000
Federal Reserve banks	958,373,036	212,409,714	745,963,322
Amounts in circulation	36,755,198,323	3,022,928,750	33,732,269,573

(1) Issued on or after July 1, 1929. (2) Excludes coins sold to collectors at premium prices. (3) Includes $481,781,898 in standard silver dollars.

Currency in Circulation by Denominations
(June 30, 2007)

Denomination	Total currency in circulation	Federal Reserve notes[1]	U.S. notes	Currency no longer issued
$1	$8,986,751,017	$8,843,228,887	$143,503	$143,378,627
$2	1,557,447,150	1,425,256,856	132,177,718	12,576
$5	10,192,114,700	10,055,601,525	108,985,410	27,527,765
$10	15,341,083,720	15,319,908,290	6,300	21,169,130
$20	115,646,649,760	115,626,547,800	3,840	20,098,120
$50	60,808,399,000	60,796,901,900	500	11,496,600
$100	563,159,562,100	563,127,938,500	9,646,100	21,977,500
$500	142,360,000	142,167,000	5,500	187,500
$1,000	165,664,000	165,453,000	5,000	206,000
$5,000	1,765,000	1,710,000	—	55,000
$10,000	3,460,000	3,360,000	—	100,000
Fractional notes[2]	600	—	90	510
TOTAL CURRENCY	$776,005,257,047	$775,508,073,758	$250,973,961	$246,209,328

(1) Issued on or after July 1, 1929. (2) Represents the value of certain partial denominations not presented for redemption.

U.S. Budget Receipts and Outlays, Fiscal Years 2002-2006
Source: Congressional Budget Office; Office of Management and Budget, Budget of the United States Government, Fiscal Year 2008

As of Oct. 2007, the estimate from the Congressional Budget Office of the total U.S. budget deficit for the fiscal year 2007 was $244 bil, or 1.8% of GDP, a $4 bil decrease from the $248 bil deficit in 2006.

(in millions of current dollars; many figures do not add to totals because of independent rounding or omitted subcategories, including some subcategories with negative values.)

Function and subfunction	2002	2003	2004	2005	2006
NET RECEIPTS.................	1,853,395	1,782,532	1,880,279	2,153,859	2,407,254
Individual Income Taxes	858,345	793,699	808,959	927,222	1,043,908
Corporation Income Taxes	148,044	131,778	189,371	278,282	353,915
Social Insurance and Retirement Receipts	700,760	712,978	733,407	794,125	837,821
Employment and general retirement	668,547	674,981	689,360	747,664	790,043
Old-age and survivors insurance	440,541	447,806	457,120	493,646	520,069
Disability insurance (Off-Budget)	74,780	76,036	77,625	83,830	88,313
Hospital insurance	149,049	147,186	150,589	166,068	177,429
Railroad retirement/pension fund:	2,525	2,333	2,297	2,284	2,338
Railroad social security equivalent account	1,652	1,620	1,729	1,836	1,894
Unemployment insurance	27,619	33,366	39,453	42,002	43,420
Other retirement	4,594	4,631	4,594	4,459	4,358
Excise Taxes..........	66,989	67,524	69,855	73,094	73,961
Federal funds	24,017	23,804	24,566	22,547	22,460
Alcohol	7,764	7,893	8,105	8,111	8,484
Tobacco	8,274	7,934	7,926	7,920	7,710
Telephone	5,829	5,788	5,997	6,047	4,897
Transportation fuels	814	920	1,381	−770	−2,386
Trust funds	42,972	43,720	45,289	50,547	51,501
Highway	32,603	33,726	34,711	37,892	38,378
Airport and airway	9,031	8,684	9,174	10,314	10,590
Black lung disability	567	506	566	610	607
Inland waterway	95	90	91	91	81
Oil spill liability	—	—	—	—	54
Aquatic resources	386	392	416	429	519
Leaking underground storage tank	181	184	189	189	197
Tobacco Assessments............................	—	—	—	899	891
Vaccine injury compensation	109	138	142	123	184
Other Receipts	79,257	76,553	78,687	81,136	97,649

Function and subfunction	2002	2003	2004	2005	2006
OUTLAYS	**2,011,153**	**2,160,117**	**2,293,006**	**2,472,205**	**2,655,435**
National defense	**348,482**	**404,778**	**455,847**	**495,326**	**521,840**
Department of Defense—Military:					
Military Personnel	86,799	106,744	113,576	127,463	127,543
Operation and Maintenance	130,005	151,408	174,045	188,118	203,789
Procurement	62,515	67,926	76,216	82,294	89,757
Research, Development, Test, and Evaluation	44,389	53,098	60,759	65,694	68,629
Military Construction	5,052	5,851	6,312	5,331	6,245
Family Housing	3,736	3,784	3,905	3,720	3,717
Subtotal, Department of Defense—Military	331,871	387,170	436,453	474,089	499,310
Atomic energy defense activities	14,795	16,029	16,625	18,042	17,468
Defense-related activities	1,816	1,579	2,769	3,195	5,062
International affairs	**22,351**	**21,209**	**26,891**	**34,595**	**29,549**
International development and humanitarian assistance	7,815	10,332	13,825	17,711	16,720
International security assistance	7,907	8,620	8,369	7,895	7,811
Conduct of foreign affairs	7,068	6,683	7,897	9,149	8,568
Foreign information and exchange activities	906	959	1,141	1,143	1,176
International financial programs	−1,345	−5,385	−4,341	−1,303	−4,726
General science, space and technology	**20,767**	**20,873**	**23,053**	**23,628**	**23,616**
General science and basic research	7,294	7,993	8,416	8,850	9,125
Space flight, research, and supporting activities	13,473	12,880	14,637	14,778	14,491
Energy	**475**	**−735**	**−166**	**429**	**782**
Energy supply	−803	−2,061	−1,555	−940	231
Energy conservation	878	897	926	883	747
Emergency energy preparedness	169	182	158	162	−441
Energy information, policy, and regulation	231	247	305	324	245
Natural resources and environment	**29,454**	**29,703**	**30,725**	**28,023**	**33,055**
Water resources	5,570	5,492	5,571	5,723	8,026
Conservation and land management	9,797	9,739	9,758	6,226	7,813
Recreational resources	2,750	2,872	2,963	3,018	3,069
Pollution control and abatement	7,615	8,208	8,485	8,079	8,572
Agriculture	**21,966**	**22,497**	**15,440**	**26,566**	**25,970**
Farm income stabilization	18,371	18,304	11,186	22,048	21,411
Agricultural research and services	3,595	4,193	4,254	4,518	4,559
Commerce and housing credit	**−406**	**728**	**5,266**	**7,567**	**6,188**
Mortgage credit	−7,015	−4,591	2,659	−862	−619
Postal Service	207	−5,169	−4,070	−1,223	−971
Deposit insurance	−1,026	−1,430	−1,976	−1,371	−1,110
Transportation	**61,833**	**67,069**	**64,627**	**67,894**	**70,244**
Ground transportation	40,158	37,491	40,744	42,317	45,209
Air transportation	16,538	23,343	16,743	18,807	18,005
Water transportation	5,041	5,907	6,898	6,439	6,688
Community and regional development	**12,981**	**18,850**	**15,822**	**26,264**	**54,531**
Community development	5,998	6,346	6,167	5,861	5,845
Area and regional development	2,633	2,397	2,351	2,745	2,580
Disaster relief and insurance	4,350	10,107	7,304	17,658	46,106
Education, training, employment, and social services	**70,581**	**82,603**	**87,990**	**97,567**	**118,560**
Elementary, secondary, and vocational education	25,879	31,473	34,360	38,271	39,710
Higher education	17,049	22,697	25,264	31,442	50,471
Research and general education aids	2,965	3,008	3,047	3,136	3,076
Training and employment	8,354	8,379	7,918	6,852	7,199
Social services	14,901	15,573	15,855	16,251	16,473
Health	**196,544**	**219,576**	**240,134**	**250,614**	**252,780**
Health care services	172,597	192,608	210,092	219,625	220,841
Health research and training	21,356	24,044	27,099	28,050	28,828
Consumer and occupational health and safety	2,591	2,924	2,943	2,939	3,111
Medicare	**230,855**	**249,433**	**269,360**	**298,638**	**329,868**
Income security	**312,720**	**334,632**	**333,059**	**345,847**	**352,477**
Retirement & disability insurance (excluding social security)	5,741	7,047	6,573	6,976	4,592
Federal employee retirement and disability	83,361	85,154	88,729	93,351	98,296
Unemployment compensation	53,267	57,054	44,994	35,435	33,814
Housing assistance	33,251	35,525	36,790	37,899	38,295
Food and nutrition assistance	38,150	42,526	46,012	50,833	53,928
Social security	**455,980**	**474,680**	**495,548**	**523,305**	**548,549**
Veterans benefits and services	**50,984**	**57,022**	**59,779**	**70,151**	**69,842**
Income security for veterans	26,720	29,091	30,849	35,767	35,771
Veterans education, training, and rehabilitation	1,726	2,106	2,562	2,790	2,638
Hospital and medical care for veterans	22,290	24,082	26,859	28,754	29,888
Veterans housing	−1,006	505	−1,982	860	−1,242
Administration of justice	**35,061**	**35,340**	**45,576**	**40,019**	**41,016**
Federal law enforcement activities	15,408	15,745	19,131	19,912	20,039
Federal litigative and judicial activities	9,137	9,085	9,685	9,641	10,051
Federal correctional activities	4,748	5,384	5,509	5,862	6,158
Criminal justice assistance	5,768	5,126	11,251	4,604	4,768
General government	**16,968**	**23,168**	**22,347**	**17,010**	**18,215**
Legislative functions	2,638	2,840	3,187	3,451	3,446
Executive direction and management	639	706	503	569	522
Central fiscal operations	10,216	11,455	9,302	9,516	10,165
General property and records management	−417	201	228	482	328
Central personnel management	47	203	217	101	151
General purpose fiscal assistance	2,403	7,464	7,675	3,333	3,798
Deductions for offsetting receipts	−812	−1,745	−1,068	−2,841	−1,359
Net interest	**170,949**	**153,073**	**160,245**	**183,986**	**226,603**
Undistributed offsetting receipts	**−47,392**	**−54,382**	**−58,537**	**−65,224**	**−68,250**
Employer share, employee retirement (on-budget)	−33,489	−39,751	−42,100	−47,977	−49,231
Total surplus/deficit	**−157,758**	**−377,585**	**−412,727**	**−318,346**	**−248,181**

Note: Fiscal year ends Sept. 30.

Summary of Receipts, Outlays, and Surpluses or Deficits, 1941-2007

Source: Financial Management Service, U.S. Dept. of the Treasury; Congressional Budget Office

(millions of current dollars)

Fiscal Year[1]	Receipts	Outlays	Surplus or Deficit (–)[2]	Fiscal Year[1]	Receipts	Outlays	Surplus or Deficit (–)[2]
1941	$8,712	$13,653	$–4,941	1975	$279,090	$332,332	$–53,242
1942	14,634	35,137	–20,503	1976	298,060	371,792	–73,732
1943	24,001	78,555	–54,554	Transition quarter[3]	81,232	95,975	–14,744
1944	43,747	91,304	–47,557	1977	355,559	409,218	–53,659
1945	45,159	92,712	–47,553	1978	399,561	458,746	–59,185
1946	39,296	55,232	–15,936	1979	463,302	504,028	–40,726
1947	38,514	34,496	4,018	1980	517,112	590,941	–73,830
1948	41,560	29,764	11,796	1981	599,272	678,241	–78,968
1949	39,415	38,835	580	1982	617,766	745,743	–127,977
1950	39,443	42,562	–3,119	1983	600,562	808,364	–207,802
1951	51,616	45,514	6,102	1984	666,486	851,853	–185,367
1952	66,167	67,686	–1,519	1985	734,088	946,396	–212,308
1953	69,608	76,101	–6,493	1986	769,215	990,441	–221,227
1954	69,701	70,855	–1,154	1987	854,353	1,004,083	–149,730
1955	65,451	68,444	–2,993	1988	909,303	1,064,481	–155,178
1956	74,587	70,640	3,947	1989	991,190	1,143,829	–152,639
1957	79,990	76,578	3,412	1990	1,032,094	1,253,130	–221,036
1958	79,636	82,405	–2,769	1991	1,055,093	1,324,331	–269,238
1959	79,249	92,098	–12,849	1992	1,091,328	1,381,649	–290,321
1960	92,492	92,191	301	1993	1,154,471	1,409,522	–255,051
1961	94,388	97,723	–3,335	1994	1,258,721	1,461,907	–203,186
1962	99,676	106,821	–7,146	1995	1,351,932	1,515,884	–163,952
1963	106,560	111,316	–4,756	1996	1,453,177	1,560,608	–107,431
1964	112,613	118,528	–5,915	1997	1,579,423	1,601,307	–21,884
1965	116,817	118,228	–1,411	1998	1,721,955	1,652,685	69,270
1966	130,835	134,532	–3,698	1999	1,827,645	1,702,035	125,610
1967	148,822	157,464	–8,643	2000	2,025,457	1,789,216	236,241
1968	152,973	178,134	–25,161	2001	1,991,426	1,863,190	128,236
1969	186,882	183,640	3,242	2002	1,853,395	2,011,153	–157,758
1970	192,807	195,649	–2,842	2003	1,782,532	2,160,117	–377,585
1971	187,139	210,172	–23,033	2004[R]	1,880,279	2,293,006	–412,727
1972	207,309	230,681	–23,373	2005[R]	2,153,859	2,472,205	–318,346
1973	230,799	245,707	–14,908	2006	2,407,254	2,655,435	–248,181
1974	263,224	269,359	–6,135	2007[P]	2,540,096	2,784,267	–244,171

R = Revised. P = Preliminary. (1) Fiscal years 1936 to 1976 end June 30; after 1976, fiscal years end Sept. 30. (2) May not equal difference between figures shown, because of rounding. (3) Transition quarter covers July 1, 1976-Sept. 30, 1976.

Budget Receipts and Outlays, 1789-1940

Source: U.S. Dept. of the Treasury; annual statements for years ending June 30 unless otherwise noted

(thousands of dollars)

Yearly Average	Receipts	Outlays	Yearly Average	Receipts	Outlays
1789-1800[1]	$5,717	$5,776	1886-1890	$375,448	$279,134
1801-1810[2]	13,056	9,086	1891-1895	352,891	363,599
1811-1820[2]	21,032	23,943	1896-1900	434,877	457,451
1821-1830[2]	21,928	16,162	1901-1905	559,481	535,559
1831-1840[2]	30,461	24,495	1906-1910	628,507	639,178
1841-1850[2]	28,545	34,097	1911-1915	710,227	720,252
1851-1860	60,237	60,163	1916-1920	3,483,652	8,065,333
1861-1865	160,907	683,785	1921-1925	4,306,673	3,578,989
1866-1870	447,301	377,642	1926-1930	4,069,138	3,182,807
1871-1875	336,830	287,460	1931-1935	2,770,973	5,214,874
1876-1880	288,124	255,598	1936-1940	4,960,614	10,192,367
1881-1885	366,961	257,691			

(1) Average for period March 4, 1789, to Dec. 31, 1800. (2) Years from 1801 to 1842 end Dec. 31; average for 1841-1850 is for the period Jan. 1, 1841, to June 30, 1850.

Budget Deficits as Percent of GDP, Selected Countries[1]

Source: Organization of Economic Cooperation and Development

	1990	1995	2000	2006		1990	1995	2000	2006
Australia	–2.0	–3.7	1.1	1.5	Korea	3.1	3.8	5.4	2.6
Austria	–2.5	–5.7	–1.6	–1.2	Luxembourg	4.3	2.4	6.0	0.1
Belgium	–6.7	–4.4	0.1	0.1	Netherlands	–5.7	–4.3	2.0	0.5
Canada	–5.8	–5.3	2.9	0.8	New Zealand	–4.6	2.9	1.6	3.9
Czech Republic	—	–13.4	–3.7	–2.9	Norway	2.2	3.2	15.4	19.3
Denmark	–1.3	–2.9	2.3	4.2	Poland	—	–4.4	–3.0	–3.9
Finland	5.4	–6.2	6.9	3.8	Portugal	–6.3	–5.2	–3.0	–3.9
France	–2.3	–5.5	–1.5	–2.6	Slovak Republic	—	–1.8	–11.8	–3.4
Germany	–1.9	–3.2	1.3	–1.7	Spain	–4.1	–6.5	–0.9	1.8
Greece	–12.2	–7.9	–3.3	–2.3	Sweden	3.4	–7.4	3.8	2.1
Hungary	—	–7.7	–3.0	–9.2	Switzerland	0.6	–1.2	2.4	1.1
Iceland	–3.3	–3.0	1.7	5.3	United Kingdom	–1.8	–5.8	4.0	–2.9
Ireland	–2.8	–2.0	4.6	2.9	United States	–4.2	–3.1	1.6	–2.3
Italy	–11.4	–7.4	–0.9	–4.5	Euro area	–4.3	–5.0	0.0	–1.6
Japan	2.1	–5.1	–7.6	–2.4	Total OECD	–2.9	–4.0	0.2	–1.6

(1) Financial balances include revenues from the sale of mobile telephone licenses.

Public Debt of the U.S.

Source: Bureau of Public Debt, U.S. Dept. of the Treasury; World Almanac research

Fiscal year	Debt (billions)	Debt per cap. (dollars)	Interest paid (billions)	% of federal outlays	Fiscal year	Debt (billions)	Debt per cap. (dollars)	Interest paid (billions)	% of federal outlays
1870	$2.4	$61.06	—	—	1987 ...	$2,350.3	$9,615	$195.4	19.5%
1880	2.0	41.60	—	—	1988 ...	2,602.3	10,534	214.1	20.1
1890	1.1	17.80	—	—	1989 ...	2,857.4	11,545	240.9	21.0
1900	1.2	16.60	—	—	1990 ...	3,233.3	13,000	264.8	21.1
1910	1.1	12.41	—	—	1991 ...	3,665.3	14,436	285.5	21.6
1920	24.2	228	—	—	1992 ...	4,064.6	15,846	292.3	21.2
1930	16.1	131	—	—	1993 ...	4,411.5	17,105	292.5	20.8
1940	43.0	325	$1.0	10.5%	1994 ...	4,692.8	18,025	296.3	20.3
1950	256.1	1,688	5.7	13.4	1996 ...	5,224.8	19,805	344.0	22.0
1960	284.1	1,572	9.2	10.0	1997 ...	5,413.1	20,026	355.8	22.2
1970	370.1	1,814	19.3	9.9	1998 ...	5,526.2	20,443	363.8	22.0
1976	620.4	2,852	37.1	10.0	1999 ...	5,656.3	20,746	353.5	20.7
1977	698.8	3,170	41.9	10.2	2000 ...	5,674.2	20,106[1]	362.0	20.2
1978	771.5	3,463	48.7	10.6	2001 ...	5,807.5	20,361[1]	359.5	19.3
1979	826.5	3,669	59.8	11.9	2002 ...	6,228.2	21,616[1]	332.5	16.5
1980	907.7	3,985	74.9	12.7	2003 ...	6,783.2	23,326[1]	318.1	14.7
1981	997.9	4,338	95.6	14.1	2004 ...	7,379.1	25,130[1]	321.6	14.0
1982	1,142.0	4,913	117.4	15.7	2005 ...	7,932.7	26,754[1]	352.4	14.3
1983	1,377.2	5,870	128.8	15.9	2006 ...	8,507.0	28,414[1]	405.9	15.3
1984	1,572.3	6,640	153.8	18.1	2007 ...	9,007.7	29,804[1]	430.0	15.4[1]
1986	2,125.3	8,774	190.2	19.2					

Note: As of end of fiscal year. Through 1976, the fiscal year ended June 30. From 1977 on, the fiscal year ends Sept. 30. (1) Estimated.

State Finances: Revenue, Expenditures, Debt, and Taxes

Source: Census Bureau, U.S. Dept. of Commerce

(fiscal year 2005)

STATE	Revenue (thousands)	Expenditures (thousands)	Debt (thousands)	Per capita debt	Per capita taxes	Per capita expenditures
Alabama	$22,538,186	$21,046,841	$6,261,529	$1,377	$1,715	$4,627
Alaska	9,115,808	8,055,975	5,766,931	8,695	2,802	12,146
Arizona	25,310,938	23,957,058	8,037,412	1,350	1,849	4,024
Arkansas	14,934,701	13,634,214	4,298,350	1,549	2,361	4,912
California	249,057,158	209,771,313	107,372,729	2,970	2,723	5,802
Colorado	22,473,929	18,769,570	12,409,574	2,661	1,640	4,025
Connecticut	20,550,806	20,203,170	23,046,930	6,584	3,309	5,771
Delaware	6,166,083	5,904,256	4,351,256	5,169	3,077	7,014
Florida	77,077,664	70,417,744	25,879,751	1,457	1,908	3,963
Georgia	36,111,681	33,806,582	8,188,637	897	1,716	3,702
Hawaii	9,091,681	8,405,444	5,844,308	4,590	3,483	6,601
Idaho	7,204,275	6,137,489	2,385,704	1,669	2,053	4,294
Illinois	60,061,672	55,666,989	48,257,297	3,780	2,069	4,361
Indiana	27,324,685	26,451,543	13,349,947	2,131	2,051	4,221
Iowa	15,677,109	14,142,676	4,930,582	1,663	1,939	4,769
Kansas	12,514,724	11,765,208	5,116,742	1,862	2,037	4,281
Kentucky	21,248,450	20,091,176	8,564,204	2,052	2,179	4,815
Louisiana	24,841,345	21,402,115	11,493,832	2,550	1,917	4,748
Maine	8,419,502	7,484,638	4,626,581	3,510	2,330	5,678
Maryland	28,889,827	26,803,282	13,722,618	2,455	2,415	4,795
Massachusetts	41,747,484	38,025,089	55,993,986	8,704	2,800	5,911
Michigan	55,726,406	51,408,421	26,167,479	2,591	2,329	5,090
Minnesota	31,723,566	30,169,448	7,265,044	1,417	3,098	5,885
Mississippi	15,518,347	14,704,763	4,328,368	1,488	1,868	5,056
Missouri	26,820,654	23,147,448	16,183,549	2,791	1,646	3,993
Montana	5,688,525	4,800,120	3,681,679	3,939	2,006	5,135
Nebraska	8,711,002	7,273,406	1,743,156	991	2,159	4,137
Nevada	11,535,175	9,158,273	3,910,573	1,621	2,351	3,796
New Hampshire	6,150,551	5,783,853	6,864,120	5,253	1,547	4,426
New Jersey	51,348,019	49,230,773	42,313,155	4,862	2,635	5,657
New Mexico	13,337,333	12,599,040	5,872,748	3,049	2,322	6,542
New York	140,222,453	136,786,401	101,992,376	5,280	2,598	7,082
North Carolina	44,892,190	39,482,250	15,773,058	1,819	2,149	4,553
North Dakota	3,877,194	3,490,904	1,683,444	2,653	2,211	5,501
Ohio	72,202,876	60,554,060	23,124,057	2,016	2,093	5,279
Oklahoma	17,873,970	15,710,022	7,468,710	2,108	1,936	4,434
Oregon	22,589,057	19,216,554	11,264,772	3,096	1,792	5,281
Pennsylvania	69,760,398	62,833,258	27,690,775	2,232	2,198	5,065
Rhode Island	7,252,620	6,753,641	6,829,330	6,361	2,449	6,291
South Carolina	22,990,747	22,708,996	13,369,988	3,148	1,723	5,347
South Dakota	4,059,264	3,261,813	2,572,928	3,320	1,433	4,209
Tennessee	24,660,867	23,989,642	3,574,196	600	1,680	4,028
Texas	96,134,134	81,368,646	18,153,032	792	1,430	3,549
Utah	13,122,463	11,148,591	5,267,269	2,115	1,882	4,477
Vermont	4,599,312	4,435,774	2,799,851	4,499	3,604	7,127
Virginia	37,294,045	32,790,458	16,894,239	2,233	2,104	4,335
Washington	36,831,190	33,059,244	17,023,263	2,706	2,359	5,254
West Virginia	12,170,191	9,826,128	5,014,053	2,764	2,371	5,417
Wisconsin	34,437,923	28,828,334	18,763,197	3,394	2,379	5,215
Wyoming	5,932,717	3,999,825	867,889	1,706	3,419	7,861
ALL STATES[1]	$1,637,820,897	$1,470,462,458	$798,355,198	$2,693	$2,186	$4,959

(1) Totals may not add because of rounding.

State and Local Government Receipts and Current Expenditures

Source: Bureau of Economic Analysis, U.S. Dept. of Commerce
(billions of current dollars; revised)

	2000	2001	2002	2003	2004	2005	2006
RECEIPTS	**$1,319.5**	**$1,373.0**	**$1,410.1**	**$1,494.2**	**$1,594.3**	**$1,706.9**	**$1,797.7**
Current tax receipts	893.2	915.8	929.0	979.4	1,061.2	1,156.0	1,232.3
Personal current taxes	236.6	242.7	221.3	226.6	249.0	276.7	301.2
Income taxes	217.3	223.1	200.8	204.5	225.0	251.8	275.1
Other.	19.4	19.6	20.5	22.2	23.9	24.9	26.1
Taxes on production and imports	621.1	642.8	675.5	717.5	769.2	822.6	868.8
Sales taxes	316.6	321.1	330.2	347.7	370.0	395.3	415.4
Property taxes	254.6	269.3	290.1	307.9	327.5	346.3	367.8
Other.	49.9	52.4	55.2	61.9	71.7	81.0	85.5
Taxes on corporate income	35.5	30.2	32.2	35.3	43.0	56.7	62.4
Contributions for government social insurance	11.0	13.6	15.8	19.8	23.6	25.5	26.0
Income receipts on assets	92.2	88.8	78.2	72.9	75.4	81.0	87.1
Interest receipts	84.0	80.3	69.6	62.9	64.3	69.0	73.8
Dividends	1.9	2.0	2.0	2.2	2.4	2.4	2.6
Rents and royalties	6.3	6.5	6.6	7.9	8.7	9.6	10.7
Current transfer receipts	315.4	350.8	384.7	422.7	437.2	454.8	462.9
Federal grants-in-aid	247.3	276.1	304.6	338.5	349.1	361.2	358.6
From business (net)	28.8	31.4	32.6	33.5	32.2	33.3	40.6
From persons	39.2	43.3	47.5	50.6	56.0	60.3	63.7
Current surplus of government enterprises	7.7	4.0	2.5	−0.6	−3.0	−10.3	−10.7
CURRENT EXPENDITURES.	**1,269.5**	**1,368.2**	**1,444.3**	**1,514.5**	**1,592.8**	**1,691.7**	**1,773.0**
Consumption expenditures	917.8	969.8	1,025.3	1,073.8	1,120.3	1,197.2	1,276.5
Government social benefit payments to persons	271.7	305.2	332.0	353.0	383.8	403.8	400.8
Interest payments.	79.5	85.5	86.0	87.7	88.4	90.4	95.4
Subsidies	0.5	7.7	0.9	0.1	0.4	0.4	0.4
Less: Wage accruals less disbursements	0.0	0.0	0.0	0.0	0.0	0.0	0.0
Net state and local government saving	50.0	4.8	−34.2	−20.4	1.5	15.2	24.6
Social insurance funds.	2.0	2.6	1.7	3.8	7.1	8.0	7.1
Other	47.9	2.2	−35.9	−24.1	−5.6	7.2	17.5
Addenda:							
Total receipts	1,363.2	1,421.6	1,462.2	1,545.8	1,646.4	1,761.1	1,854.5
Current receipts	1,319.5	1,373.0	1,410.1	1,494.2	1,594.3	1,706.9	1,797.7
Capital transfer receipts	43.7	48.6	52.1	51.6	52.1	54.1	56.9
Total expenditures	1,393.5	1,502.7	1,588.3	1,659.9	1,738.1	1,836.8	1,936.0
Current expenditures	1,269.5	1,368.2	1,444.3	1,514.5	1,592.8	1,691.7	1,773.0
Gross government investment	225.0	243.0	256.1	262.2	270.9	287.8	314.0
Net purchases of nonproduced assets	8.8	9.2	10.6	10.9	10.5	10.6	11.2
Less: Consumption of fixed capital	109.8	117.8	122.7	127.8	136.1	153.4	162.3
NET LENDING OR NET BORROWING (−).	**−30.4**	**−81.1**	**−126.1**	**−114.1**	**−91.7**	**−75.8**	**−81.5**

Federal Deposit Insurance Corporation (FDIC)

The Federal Deposit Insurance Corporation (FDIC) is the independent deposit insurance agency created by Congress to maintain stability and public confidence in the nation's banking system. In its unique role as deposit insurer of banks and savings associations, and in cooperation with other federal and state regulatory agencies, the FDIC seeks to promote the safety and soundness of insured depository institutions in the U.S. financial system by identifying, monitoring, and addressing risks to the deposit insurance funds. The FDIC aims at promoting public understanding and sound public policies by providing financial and economic information and analyses. It seeks to minimize disruptive effects from the failure of banks and savings associations, and to ensure fairness in the sale of financial products and the provision of financial services.

To maintain its insurance funds, the FDIC assesses depository institutions insurance premiums twice a year. The amount of the premium is based on the institution's balance of insured deposits for the preceding two quarters and the institution's risk to the insurance fund. The Corporation may borrow from the U.S. Treasury, not to exceed $30 bil outstanding, but the agency has made no such borrowings since it was organized in 1933. The FDIC's Bank Insurance Fund and the Savings Association Insurance Fund were merged March 31, 2006, to form the Deposit Insurance Fund, which stood at $51.2 bil as of June 30, 2007.

Banks in the U.S.–Number, Deposits

Source: Federal Deposit Insurance Corp. (as of June 30, 2007)
Comprises all FDIC-insured commercial and savings banks, including savings and loan institutions (S&Ls).

	TOTAL NUMBER OF BANKS				TOTAL DEPOSITS (millions of dollars)			
		Commercial banks[1]				Commercial banks[1]		
Year	ALL BANKS	Natl.	State	Non-members	All savings	ALL DEPOSITS	Natl.	State	Non-members	All savings
1935	15,295	5,386	1,001	7,735	1,173	$45,102[2]	$24,802	$13,653	$5,669	$978[2]
1940	15,772	5,144	1,342	6,956	2,330	67,494	35,787	20,642	7,040	4,025
1950	16,500	4,958	1,912	6,576	3,054	171,963	84,941	41,602	19,726	25,694
1960	17,549	4,530	1,641	6,955	4,423	310,262	120,242	65,487	34,369	90,164
1970	18,205	4,621	1,147	7,743	4,694	686,901	285,436	101,512	95,566	204,367
1980	18,763	4,425	997	9,013	4,328	1,832,716	656,752	191,183	344,311	640,470
1990	15,158	3,979	1,009	7,355	2,815	3,637,292	1,558,915	397,797	693,438	987,142
2000	9,905	2,230	991	5,094	1,590	4,914,808	2,250,464	1,032,110	894,000	738,234
2002	9,354	2,077	950	4,861	1,439	5,568,508	2,565,771	1,152,380	971,730	878,627
2003	9,182	2,001	935	4,833	1,413	5,954,288	2,786,756	1,195,914	1,046,195	925,423
2004	8,976	1,907	919	4,805	1,345	6,584,200	3,581,416	872,228	1,139,168	991,388
2005	8,832	1,818	907	4,802	1,305	7,141,178	3,850,051	936,299	1,286,983	1,067,845
2006[3]	8,755	1,780	903	4,796	1,276	6,439,714	3,190,482	818,565	1,311,720	1,118,948
2007[3]	8,605	1,677	888	4,785	1,244	6,702,212	3,273,777	831,080	1,425,361	1,165,118

(1) "Nonmembers" are banks that are not members of the Federal Reserve System; "National" and "State" institutions are members.
(2) Figures for 1935 do not include data for S&Ls (not available). (3) June 30.

U.S. Bank Failures, 1934-2007

Source: Federal Deposit Insurance Corp. (as of Oct. 4, 2007)

Covers all FDIC-insured commercial and savings banks, including savings and loan institutions (S&Ls) 1980 and after.

Year	Closed or assisted	Year	Closed or assisted	Year	Closed or assisted	Year	Closed or assisted	Year	Closed or assisted
1934	9	1963	2	1975	13	1986	204	1996	6
1935	26	1964	7	1976	17	1987	262	1997	1
1936	69	1965	5	1978	7	1988	465	1998	3
1937	77	1966	7	1979	10	1989	534	1999	8
1938	74	1967	4	1980	22	1990	382	2000	7
1939	60	1969	9	1981	40	1991	271	2001	4
1940	43	1970	7	1982	119	1992	181	2002	11
1955	5	1971	7	1983	99	1993	50	2003	3
1959	3	1972	2	1984	106	1994	15	2004	4
1960	1	1973	6	1985	180	1995	8	2007	3
1961	5								

Note: There were no bank failures in 2005, or in 2006.

World's 50 Largest Banking Companies[1]

Source: *American Banker* (as of Dec. 31, 2006)

Company Name	Total Assets (in millions)	Company Name	Total Assets (in millions)
UBS AG Zurich	$1,961,327	Groupe Caisse d'Epargne Paris	710,801
Barclays PLC London	1,949,167	Wachovia Corp. Charlotte	707,121
BNP Paribas Paris	1,898,186	China Construction Bank Corp. Beijing	697,445
Citigroup Inc. New York, N.Y.	1,884,318	Agricultural Bank of China Beijing	684,349
HSBC Holdings PLC London	1,857,520	Bank of China Ltd. Beijing	679,572
Royal Bank of Scotland Group PLC Edinburgh	1,705,044	Lloyds TSB Group PLC London	672,404
Credit Agricole SA Paris	1,662,600	HVB Group Munich	666,923
Mitsubishi UFJ Financial Group Tokyo	1,585,767	Dresdner Bank Frankfurt	654,928
Deutsche Bank AG Frankfurt	1,480,984	Credit Mutuel Paris	635,685
Bank of America Corp. Charlotte	1,459,737	Natixis Paris	604,366
JPMorgan Chase & Co. New York, N.Y.	1,351,520	Norinchukin Bank Tokyo	602,645
ABN Amro Holding NV Amsterdam	1,297,604	BBV Argentaria SA Bilbao, Spain	536,972
Mizuho Financial Group Inc. Tokyo	1,269,600	MetLife New York	527,715
Societe Generale Paris	1,261,478	Danske Bank A/S Copenhagen	484,515
ING Bank Amsterdam	1,178,697	Wells Fargo & Co. San Francisco	481,996
HBOS PLC Edinburgh	1,156,614	Royal Bank of Canada Toronto	477,432
Banco Santander Central Hispano SA Madrid	1,088,015	Nordea Bank AB Stockholm	457,134
Unicredito Italiano Spa Milan	1,077,209	KBC Groupe SA Brussells	428,485
Credit Suisse Group Zurich	1,025,111	Groupe Banques Populaires Paris	402,090
Fortis NV Brussells	1,020,098	Intesa Sanpaolo Milan	383,085
Industrial and Commercial Bank of China (ICBC) Beijing	962,969	SanPaolo IMI Turin, Italy	380,022
Sumitomo Mitsui Financial Group Tokyo	901,711	WestLB Dusseldorf	376,656
Commerzbank AG Frankfurt	795,900	National Australia Bank Ltd. Melbourne	360,563
Dexia Brussells	747,045	Toronto-Dominion Bank Toronto	349,714
Rabobank Utrecht	732,757	Washington Mutual Inc. Seattle	346,288

(1) Includes bank holding companies and commercial and savings banks. (2) Currency conversion based on Exchange rates on Dec. 31, 2006 or at end of latest fiscal year.

50 Largest U.S. Bank Holding Companies, 2006[1]

Source: *American Banker* (as of Dec. 31, 2006)

Company Name	Total Assets (in thousands)	Company Name	Total Assets (in thousands)
Citigroup Inc. New York	$1,884,318,000	Rabobank Utrecht, the Netherlands	75,245,500
Bank of America Corp. Charlotte	1,463,685,485	BNP Paribus Paris	67,313,365
JPMorgan Chase & Co. New York	1,351,520,000	ING USA Holding Corp Wilmington, Del.	62,692,937
Wachovia Corp. Charlotte	707,121,000	Northern Trust Corp. Chicago	60,712,241
MetLife Inc. New York	527,714,953	Harris Financial Corp. Wilmington, Del.	60,025,390
Wells Fargo & Co. San Francisco	481,996,000	Comerica Inc. Detroit	58,723,490
HSBC Holdings London	478,159,427	M&T Bank Corp. Buffalo	57,064,905
Deutsche Bank Frankfurt	430,398,000	Marshall & Ilsley Corp. Milwaukee	56,268,824
Washington Mutual Inc. Seattle	345,294,612	Mitsubishi Tokyo Financial Group	52,619,576
U.S. Bancorp Minneapolis	219,232,000	Charles Schwab Corp. San Francisco	48,992,466
Countrywide Financial Corp. Calabasas, Calif.	199,946,230	Popular Inc. Hato Rey, Puerto Rico	47,404,000
SunTrust Banks Inc. Atlanta	182,161,609	Zions Bancorp. Salt Lake City	46,970,226
Royal Bank of Scotland Group Edinburgh	160,900,923	Morgan Stanley New York	46,249,839
ABN Amro Amsterdam	156,293,592	Commerce Bancorp Inc. Cherry Hill, N.J.	45,316,383
Capital One Financial Corp. McLean, Va.	149,739,285	E-Trade Financial Corp. New York	42,203,037
Regions Financial Corp. Birmingham, Ala.	143,370,472	Mellon Financial Corp. Pittsburgh	41,584,506
National City Corp. Cleveland	140,203,110	American Express Co. New York	40,914,192
BB&T Corp. Winston-Salem, N.C.	121,351,065	Toronto-Dominion Bank Toronto	40,019,853
State Street Corp. Boston	107,385,095	First Horizon National Corp. Memphis	37,920,049
Bank of New York Co. Inc.	103,455,000	Hudson City Bancorp Inc. Paramus, N.J.	35,507,546
PNC Financial Services Group Inc. Pittsburgh	101,854,178	Huntington Bancshares Inc. Columbus, Ohio	35,330,726
Fifth Third Bancorp Cincinnati	100,669,263	Compass Bancshares Inc. Birmingham, Ala.	34,248,921
KeyCorp Cleveland	92,061,129	Synovus Financial Corp. Columbus, Ga.	31,885,290
Sovereign Bancorp Inc. Philadelphia	89,506,358	IndyMac Bancorp Inc. Pasadena, Calif.	28,740,902
Merrill Lynch & Co. Inc. New York	81,526,314	New York Community Bancorp Inc. Westbury	28,513,960

(1) Includes foreign-owned banks with a strong presence in the U.S.

Federal Reserve System

The Federal Reserve System is the central bank for the U.S. The system was established on Dec. 23, 1913, originally to give the country an elastic currency, provide facilities for discounting commercial paper, and improve the supervision of banking. Since then, the system's responsibilities have been broadened. Over the years, stability and growth of the economy, a high level of employment, stability in the purchasing power of the dollar, and reasonable balance in transactions with other countries have come to be recognized as primary objectives of governmental economic policy.

The Federal Reserve System consists of the Board of Governors, the 12 District Reserve Banks and their branch offices, and the Federal Open Market Committee. Several advisory councils help the board meet its varied responsibilities.

The hub of the system is the 7-member **Board of Governors** in Washington, DC. The members of the board are appointed by the president and confirmed by the Senate, to serve 14-year terms. The president also appoints the chairman and vice chairman of the board from among the board members for 4-year terms that may be renewed. As of Oct. 2007 the board members were: Ben Bernanke, chair; Donald Kohn, vice chair; Randall Kroszner; Kevin Warsh; and Frederic Mishkin.

The 12 **District Reserve Banks** and their branch offices serve as the decentralized portion of the system, carrying out day-to-day operations such as circulating currency and coin and providing fiscal agency functions and payments mechanism services. The 12 are in Boston, New York, Philadelphia, Cleveland, Richmond, Atlanta, Chicago, St. Louis, Minneapolis, Kansas City, Dallas, and San Francisco.

The system's principal function is monetary policy, which it controls using 3 tools: reserve requirements, the discount rate, and open market operations.

Uniform **reserve requirements**, set by the board, are applied to the transaction accounts and nonpersonal time deposits of all depository institutions. Responsibility for setting the **discount rate** (the interest rate at which depository institutions can borrow money from the Reserve Banks) is shared by the Board of Governors and the Reserve Banks. Changes in the discount rate are recommended by the individual boards of directors of the Reserve Banks and are subject to approval by the Board of Governors.

The most important tool of monetary policy is **open market operations** (the purchase and sale of government securities). Responsibility for influencing the cost and availability of money and credit through the purchase and sale of government securities lies with the **Federal Open Market Committee** (FOMC), which is composed of the 7 members of the Board of Governors, the president of the Federal Reserve Bank of New York, and 4 other Federal Reserve Bank presidents, who each serve 1-year terms on a rotating basis. The committee bases its decisions on economic and financial developments and outlook, setting yearly growth objectives for key measures of money supply and credit. The decisions of the committee are carried out by the Domestic Trading Desk of the Federal Reserve Bank of New York.

A Federal Advisory Council meets with the Federal Reserve Board 4 times a year to discuss business and financial conditions, as well as to make recommendations.

Website: www.federalreserve.gov

Federal Reserve Board Primary and Secondary Credit Rate

Prior to Jan. 9, 2003, the federal reserve set a single "discount rate," the interest rate that member banks were charged when borrowing money through the Federal Reserve System. The discount rate was replaced with two rates, the *primary credit rate* and *secondary credit rate*. The primary credit rate (listed first) is available to banks in generally sound financial condition. The secondary credit (listed second) rate is given to banks that do not qualify for the primary credit rate. Both are extended for very short terms, usually overnight. On Aug. 17, 2007, this term was temporarily extended to 30 days. Under the new system, financially sound institutions are not required to exhaust all funds before borrowing from the Fed.

Effective date Rates	Effective date Rates	Effective date Rates	Effective date Rates	Effective date Rates
1980:	Nov. 21 .... 8½%	Dec. 20 .... 3½%	**2001:**	Nov. 10 .... 3, 3½%
Feb. 15 .... 13%	Dec. 24 8	**1992:**	Jan. 3 .... 5¾%	Dec. 14 .... 3¼, 3¾
May 30 12	**1985:**	July 2 3	Jan. 31 5	**2005:**
June 13 11	May 20 .... 7½	**1994:**	Mar. 20 .... 4½	Feb. 2 .... 3½, 4
July 28 10	**1986:**	May 17 .... 3½	Apr. 18 4	Mar. 22 .... 3¾, 4¼
Sept. 26 11	March 7 7	Aug. 16 4	May 15 .... 3½	May 3 .... 4, 4½
Nov. 17 12	April 21 .... 6½	Nov. 15 .... 4¾	June 27 .... 3¼	June 30 .... 4¼, 4¾
Dec. 5 13	July 11 6	**1995:**	Aug. 21 3	Aug. 9 .... 4½, 5
1981:	Aug. 21 .... 5½	Feb. 1 5	Sept. 17 .... 2½	Sept. 20 .... 4¾, 5¼
May 5 14	**1987:**	**1996:**	Oct. 2 2	Nov. 1 .... 5, 5½
Nov. 2 13	Sept. 4 6	Jan. 31 5	Dec. 11 .... 1¼	Dec. 13 .... 5¼, 5¾
Dec. 4 12	**1988:**	**1998:**	**2002:**	**2006:**
1982:	Aug. 9 .... 6½	Oct. 15 .... 4¾	Nov. 6 .... ¾	Jan. 31 .... 5½, 6
July 20 .... 11½	**1989:**	Nov. 17 .... 4½	**2003:**	Mar. 28 .... 5¾, 6¼
Aug. 2 11	Feb. 24 7	**1999:**	Jan. 9 .... 2¼, 2¾	May 10 .... 6, 6½
Aug. 16 10	**1990:**	Aug. 24 .... 4¾	June 25 .... 2, 2½	Jun. 29 .... 6¼, 6¾
Aug. 27 10	Dec. 18 .... 6½	Nov. 16 5	**2004:**	Aug. 17 .... 5¾, 6¼
Oct. 12 .... 9½	**1991:**	**2000:**	Jun. 30 .... 2¼, 2¾	**2007[1]:**
Dec. 15 .... 8½	Apr. 30 .... 5½	Feb. 2 .... 5¼	Aug. 10 .... 2½, 3	Sept. 18 ... 5¼, 5¾
1984:	Sept. 13 ... 5	Mar. 21 .... 5½	Sept. 21 .... 2¾, 3¼	
April 9 9	Nov. 6 .... 4½	May 16 6		

(1) Through Oct. 1, 2007.

Standard & Poor's 500 Index, 1993-2007

Source: *Facts On File World News Digest;* monthly closing levels; record high daily closing was 1565.15, Oct. 9, 2007.

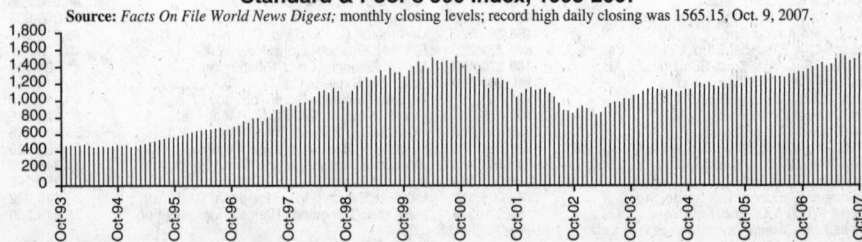

U.S. Holdings of Foreign Stocks[1]

Source: Bureau of Economic Analysis, U.S. Dept. of Commerce
(billions of dollars)

	2002	2004	2005	2006		2002	2004	2005	2006
Europe...........	$789.4	$1,356.2	$1,614.0	$2,069.4	Brazil...........	$19.7	$43.1	$68.6	$98.1
United Kingdom ...	289.5	461.8	544.5	734.2	Mexico...........	22.0	37.5	57.9	76.3
France	94.3	164.6	205.1	268.0					
Switzerland.......	75.6	138.2	191.9	236.9	Asia..............	258.7	565.8	849.9	1,114.9
Germany	66.5	123.7	158.0	196.1	Japan...........	148.1	330.4	493.3	603.9
Netherlands	88.1	136.5	132.8	158.8	Korea, Republic of..	27.8	66.6	110.3	146.1
Spain	29.9	63.0	63.5	77.7	Taiwan...........	8.5	34.6	57.1	80.2
Italy.............	28.2	57.5	63.9	77.1	Hong Kong	22.0	35.4	44.5	76.7
Finland..........	34.3	33.9	44.4	55.4					
Sweden	19.2	38.3	40.5	49.7	Africa	9.6	28.9	39.9	56.0
Canada	88.2	180.4	247.8	310.9	South Africa.......	7.9	21.6	31.6	44.5
Latin America and					Other countries	37.2	65.8	81.7	106.9
Caribbean	191.6	363.3	484.4	593.4	Australia	34.6	57.1	71.1	93.4
Bermuda........	88.6	153.5	173.8	214.2					
Cayman Islands ...	32.9	69.7	102.6	107.3	TOTAL HOLDINGS ..	1,374.7	2,560.4	3,317.7	4,251.5

(1) As of year end.

Global Stock Markets

Source: The Conference Board; not seasonally adjusted

Stock price indexes (1990=100):	June 1, 1960	June 1, 1970	June 1, 1980	June 1, 1990	June 1, 2000	June 1, 2003	June 1, 2004	June 1, 2005	June 1, 2006	June 1, 2007
United States	17.1	21.9	34.3	107.6	437.2	292.9	342.9	358.1	381.8	451.9
Japan........................	4.4	7.3	23.8	110.8	60.4	31.5	41.1	40.2	53.8	62.9
Germany	36.1	27.5	30.5	111.1	407.9	190.4	239.6	271.2	336.0	473.4
France	16.3	15.6	23.8	112.0	354.7	169.7	205.4	232.7	273.2	333.2
United Kingdom	8.2	11.6	24.9	108.2	279.9	182.1	205.9	236.5	274.1	314.5
Italy..........................	28.9	20.6	15.9	117.3	309.0	181.1	206.5	241.1	271.5	319.9
Canada.......................	14.8	25.0	60.3	103.6	298.0	204.1	249.8	289.5	339.4	406.5

(1) 12-month average.

Record One-Day Gains and Losses on the Dow Jones Industrial Average

Source: Dow Jones & Co., Inc.; as of Sept. 30, 2007

GREATEST POINT GAINS

Rank	Date	Close	Net Chg	% Chg
1.	3/16/2000	10630.60	499.19	4.93
2.	7/24/2002	8191.29	488.95	6.35
3.	7/29/2002	8711.88	447.49	5.41
4.	4/5/2001	9918.05	402.63	4.23
5.	4/18/2001	10615.83	399.10	3.91
6.	9/8/1998	8020.78	380.53	4.98
7.	10/15/2002	8255.68	378.28	4.80
8.	9/24/2001	8603.86	368.05	4.47
9.	10/1/2002	7938.79	346.86	4.57
10.	5/16/2001	11215.92	342.95	3.15

GREATEST POINT LOSSES

Rank	Date	Close	Net Chg	% Chg
1.	9/17/2001	8920.70	−684.81	−7.13
2.	4/14/2000	10305.77	−617.78	−5.66
3.	10/27/1997	7161.15	−554.26	−7.18
4.	8/31/1998	7539.07	−512.61	−6.37
5.	10/19/1987	1738.74	−508.00	−22.61
6.	3/12/2001	10208.25	−436.37	−4.10
7.	2/27/2007	12216.24	−416.02	−3.29
8.	7/19/2002	8019.26	−390.23	−4.63
9.	8/9/2007	13270.68	−387.18	−3.29
10.	9/20/2001	8376.21	−382.92	−4.37

GREATEST % GAINS

Rank	Date	Close	Net Chg	% Chg
1.	3/15/1933	62.10	8.26	15.34
2.	10/6/1931	99.34	12.86	14.87
3.	10/30/1929	258.47	28.40	12.34
4.	9/21/1932	75.16	7.67	11.36
5.	10/21/1987	2027.85	186.84	10.15
6.	8/3/1932	58.22	5.06	9.52
7.	2/11/1932	78.60	6.80	9.47
8.	11/14/1929	217.28	18.59	9.36
9.	12/18/1931	80.69	6.90	9.35
10.	2/13/1932	85.82	7.22	9.19

GREATEST % LOSSES

Rank	Date	Close	Net Chg	% Chg
1.	12/12/1914	54.00	−17.42	−24.39
2.	10/19/1987	1738.74	−508.00	−22.61
3.	10/28/1929	260.64	−38.33	−12.82
4.	10/29/1929	230.07	−30.57	−11.73
5.	11/6/1929	232.13	−25.55	−9.92
6.	12/18/1899	58.27	−5.57	−8.72
7.	8/12/1932	63.11	−5.79	−8.40
8.	3/14/1907	76.23	−6.89	−8.29
9.	10/26/1987	1793.93	−156.83	−8.04
10.	7/21/1933	88.71	−7.55	−7.84

Dow Jones Industrial Average, 1963-2007

High	YEAR	Low		High	YEAR	Low
Dec. 18 767.21	.....1963.....	Jan. 2 646.79	July 16	2999.75.....1990.....Oct. 11	2365.10
Dec. 31 969.26	.....1965.....	June 28 840.59	Dec. 31	3168.83.....1991.....Jan. 9	2470.30
Dec. 29 842.00	.....1970.....	May 6 631.16	June 1	3413.21.....1992.....Oct. 9	3136.58
July 15 881.81	.....1975.....	Jan. 2 632.04	Dec. 29	3794.33.....1993.....Jan. 20	3241.95
Sept. 21 1014.79	.....1976.....	Jan. 2 858.71	Jan. 31	3978.36.....1994.....Apr. 4	3593.35
Jan. 3 999.75	.....1977.....	Nov. 2 800.85	Dec. 13	5216.47.....1995.....Jan. 30	3832.08
Sept. 8 907.74	.....1978.....	Feb. 28 742.12	Dec. 27	6560.91.....1996.....Jan. 10	5032.94
Oct. 5 897.61	.....1979.....	Nov. 7 796.67	Aug. 6	8259.31.....1997.....Apr. 11	6391.69
Nov. 20 1000.17	.....1980.....	Apr. 21 759.13	Nov. 23	9374.27.....1998.....Aug. 31	7539.07
Apr. 27 1024.05	.....1981.....	Sept. 25 824.01	Dec. 31	11497.12.....1999.....Jan. 22	9120.67
Dec. 27 1070.55	.....1982.....	Aug. 12 776.92	Jan. 14	11722.98.....2000.....Mar. 7	9796.03
Nov. 29 1287.20	.....1983.....	Jan. 3 1027.04	May 21	11337.92.....2001.....Sept. 21	8235.81
Jan. 6 1286.64	.....1984.....	July 24 1086.57	Mar. 19	10635.25.....2002.....Oct. 9	7286.27
Dec. 16 1553.10	.....1985.....	Jan. 4 1184.96	Dec. 31	10453.90.....2003.....Mar. 11	7524.06
Dec. 2 1955.57	.....1986.....	Jan. 22 1502.29	Dec. 28	10854.54.....2004.....Oct. 25	9749.99
Aug. 25 2722.42	.....1987.....	Oct. 19 1738.74	Mar. 4	10940.50.....2005.....Apr. 20	10012.36
Oct. 21 2183.50	.....1988.....	Jan. 20 1879.14	Dec. 27	12510.57.....2006.....Jan. 20	10667.39
Oct. 9 2791.41	.....1989.....	Jan. 3 2144.64	Oct. 9	14164.53*.....2007.....Mar. 5	12050.41

* Record high closing as of Oct. 12, 2007.

Milestones of the Dow Jones Industrial Average
(as of Oct. 10, 2007)

First close over...		First close over...		First close over...		First close over...		First close over...	
100	Jan. 12, 1906	8000	July 16, 1997	9200	May 13, 1998	11100	May 13, 1999	12700	Feb. 14, 2007
500	Mar. 12, 1956	8100	July 24, 1997	9300	July 16, 1998	11200	July 12, 1999	12800	Apr. 18, 2007
1000	Nov. 14, 1972	8200	July 30, 1997	9500	Jan. 6, 1999*	11300	Aug. 25, 1999	12900	Apr. 20, 2007
1500	Dec. 11, 1985	8100	July 24, 1997	9600	Jan. 8, 1999	11400	Dec. 23, 1999	13000	Apr. 25, 2007
2000	Jan. 8, 1987	8200	July 30, 1997	9700	Mar. 5, 1999	11500	Jan. 7, 2000	13100	Apr. 26, 2007
2500	July 17, 1987	8300	Feb. 12, 1998	9800	Mar. 11, 1999	11700	Jan. 14, 2000*	13200	May 2, 2007
3000	April 17, 1991	8400	Feb. 18, 1998	9900	Mar. 15, 1999	11800	Oct. 4, 2006	13300	May 7, 2007
3500	May 19, 1993	8300	Feb. 12, 1998	10000	Mar. 29, 1999	11900	Oct. 12, 2006	13400	May 16, 2007
4000	Feb. 23, 1995	8400	Feb. 18, 1998	10100	Apr. 8, 1999	12000	Oct. 19, 2006	13500	May 18, 2007
4500	June 16, 1995	8500	Feb. 27, 1998	10300	Apr. 12, 1999*	12100	Oct 23, 2006	13600	May 30, 2007
5000	Nov. 21, 1995	8600	Mar. 10, 1998	10400	Apr. 14, 1999	12200	Nov. 14, 2006	13800	July 12, 2007
5500	Feb. 8, 1996	8700	Mar. 16, 1998	10500	Apr. 21, 1999	12300	Nov. 16, 2006	13900	July 13, 2007
6000	Oct. 14, 1996	8800	Mar. 19, 1998	10700	Apr. 22, 1999*	12400	Dec. 14, 2006	14000	July 19, 2007
6500	Nov. 25, 1996	8900	Mar. 20, 1998	10800	Apr. 21, 1999	12500	Dec. 27, 2006	14100	Oct. 9, 2007
7000	Feb. 13, 1997	9000	Apr. 6, 1998	11000	May 3, 1999*	12600	Jan. 24, 2007		
7500	June 10, 1997	9100	Apr. 14, 1998						

Note: 9400, 10200, 10600, 10900, 11600, and 13700 are not listed because the Dow had risen another 100 points or more by the time the market closed for the day.

Components of the Dow Jones Averages
(as of Oct. 10, 2007)

Dow Jones Industrial Average

Alcoa
Altria Group
American Express Co.
American International Group (AIG)
AT&T Inc.
Boeing Co.
Caterpillar Inc.
Citigroup Inc.
Coca-Cola Co.
E.I DuPont de Nemours & Co.

Exxon Mobil Corp.
General Electric Co.
General Motors Corp.
Hewlett-Packard Co.
Home Depot Inc.
Honeywell International Inc.
IBM
Intel Corp.
J.P. Morgan Chase & Co.
Johnson & Johnson

McDonald's Corp.
Merck & Co. Corp.
Microsoft Corp.
Pfizer Inc.
Procter & Gamble Co.
3M Co.
United Technologies Corp.
Verizon Communications Inc.
Wal-Mart Stores Inc.
Walt Disney Co.

Dow Jones Utility Average

AES Corp.
American Electric Power Co. Inc.
CenterPoint Energy
Consolidated Edison Inc.
Dominion Resources Inc. (Virginia)

Duke Energy Corp.
Edison International
Exelon Corp.
FirstEnergy Corp.
FPL Group Inc.

NiSource Inc.
PG&E Corp.
Public Service Enterprise Group Inc.
Southern Co.
Williams Cos.

Dow Jones Transportation Average

Alexander & Baldwin Inc.
AMR (American Airlines) Corp.
Burlington Northern Santa Fe Corp.
C.H. Robinson Worldwide Inc.
Con-way Inc.
Continental Airlines C.I.B.
CSX Corp.

Expeditors Int'l. of Washington Inc.
FedEx Corp.
GATX Corp.
J.B. Hunt Transportation Services Inc.
JetBlue Airways Corp.
Landstar System Inc.
Norfolk Southern Corp.

Overseas Shipholding Group Inc.
Ryder System Inc.
Southwest Airlines Co.
Union Pacific Corp.
United Parcel Service Inc. C.I.B.
YRC Worldwide Inc.

Record One-Day Gains and Losses on the Nasdaq Stock Market
Source: Nasdaq Stock Market; as of Sept. 30, 2007

	GREATEST POINT GAINS			GREATEST % GAINS			GREATEST POINT LOSSES			GREATEST % LOSSES	
Rank	**Date**	**Change**	**Rank**	**Date**	**% Change**	**Rank**	**Date**	**Change**	**Rank**	**Date**	**% Change**
1.	1/3/2001	324.83	1.	1/3/2001	14.17%	1.	4/14/2000	−355.49	1.	10/19/1987	−11.35%
2.	12/5/2000	274.05	2.	12/5/2000	10.48	2.	4/3/2000	−349.15	2.	4/14/2000	−9.67
3.	4/18/2000	254.41	3.	4/5/2001	8.92	3.	4/12/2000	−286.27	3.	10/20/1987	−9.00
4.	5/30/2000	254.37	4.	4/18/2001	8.12	4.	4/10/2000	−258.25	4.	10/26/1987	−9.00
5.	10/19/2000	247.04	5.	5/30/2000	7.94	5.	1/4/2000	−229.46	5.	8/31/1998	−8.56
6.	10/13/2000	242.09	6.	10/13/2000	7.87	6.	3/14/2000	−200.61	6.	4/3/2000	−7.64
7.	6/2/2000	230.88	7.	6/2/2000	7.79	7.	5/10/2000	−200.28	7.	1/2/2001	−7.23
8.	4/25/2000	228.75	8.	5/8/2002	7.78	8.	5/23/2000	−199.66	8.	12/20/2000	−7.12
9.	4/17/2000	217.87	9.	12/22/2000	7.56	9.	10/25/2000	−190.22	9.	4/12/2000	−7.06
10.	6/1/2000	181.59	10.	10/21/1987	7.34	10.	3/29/2000	−189.22	10.	10/27/1997	−7.02

Nasdaq Stock Market, 1971-2007

High	YEAR	Low	High	YEAR	Low	High	YEAR	Low	High	YEAR	Low
114.12	1971	99.68	223.96	1981	170.80	470.30	1990	322.93	4090.61	1999	2193.13
135.15	1972	113.65	241.63	1982	158.92	586.35	1991	352.85	5048.62*	2000	2332.78
136.84	1973	88.67	329.11	1983	229.88	676.95	1992	545.85	2892.36	2001	1387.06
96.53	1974	54.87	288.41	1984	223.91	790.56	1993	645.02	2059.38	2002	1114.11
88.00	1975	60.70	325.53	1985	245.82	803.93	1994	691.23	2009.88	2003	1271.47
97.88	1976	78.06	411.21	1986	322.14	1072.82	1995	740.53	2178.00	2004	1752.00
105.05	1977	93.66	456.27	1987	288.49	1328.45	1996	978.17	2273.37	2005	1904.18
139.25	1978	99.09	397.54	1988	329.00	1748.62	1997	1194.39	2465.98	2006	2020.39
152.29	1979	117.84	487.60	1989	376.87	2200.63	1998	1357.09	2811.61	2007	2340.68
208.29	1980	124.09									

* Record high closing, Mar. 10, 2000; as of Oct. 12, 2007.

Milestones of the Nasdaq Stock Market

Source: Nasdaq Stock Market; as of Sept. 30, 2007

First close over...	First close over...	First close over...	First close over...	First close over...
100.... Feb. 5, 1971	400 .... May 30, 1986	1,500 .. July 11, 1997	3,000 .. Nov. 3, 1999	4,500 .. Feb. 17, 2000
200.... Nov. 13, 1980	500 .... Apr. 12, 1991	2,000 .. July 16, 1998	3,500 .. Dec. 3, 1999	5,000 .. Mar. 9, 2000
300.... May 6, 1986	1,000 .. July 17, 1995	2,500 .. Jan. 29, 1999	4,000 .. Dec. 29, 1999	

Leading NYSE Stocks in Market Value, 2007

Source: New York Stock Exchange; in millions of dollars; as of June 2007.

Company	Market value	Company	Market value	Company	Market value
Exxon Mobil Corp.	$671,155	Altria Group, Inc.	$196,384	Berkshire Hathaway Inc.	$118,358
General Electric Co.	424,183	Johnson and Johnson	193,840	Pepsico Inc.	117,937
Citigroup.	289,982	JPMorgan Chase & Co.	182,423	Schlumberger Ltd.	112,756
AT&T Inc. Com.	260,239	Coca-Cola Co.	182,261	Merrill, Lynch & Co. Inc.	109,324
Procter & Gamble Co.	247,823	Merck & Co. Inc.	149,683	Morgan Stanley.	105,130
Pfizer Inc.	231,563	Goldman Sachs Group Inc.	136,979	Time Warner Inc.	102,496
Wal-Mart Stores Inc.	227,976	ConocoPhillips.	133,847	Wachovia Corp.	100,562
Bank Of America Corp.	221,212	Verizon Communications.	126,084	Boeing Co.	98,448
Intl. Business Machines Corp.	210,907	Wells Fargo & Co.	123,556	United Technologies Corp.	96,171
Chevron Corporation	201,303	Hewlett-Packard Co.	120,155	Home Depot Inc.	94,781
American Intl. Group Inc.	197,207				

Average Yields of Long-Term Treasury, Corporate, and Municipal Bonds

Source: Office of Market Finance, U.S. Dept. of the Treasury; Federal Reserve System

Period	Treasury 30-year bonds[1]	New Aa corporate bonds[2]	New Aa municipal bonds[3]	Period	Treasury 30-year bonds[1]	New Aa corporate bonds[2]	New Aa municipal bonds[3]	Period	Treasury 30-year bonds[1]	New Aa corporate bonds[2]	New Aa municipal bonds[3]
1986				**1993**				**2000**			
June	7.57	9.39	7.87	June	6.81	7.48	5.63	June	5.93	7.75	5.80
Dec.	7.37	8.87	6.87	Dec.	6.25	7.22	5.35	Dec.	5.49	7.21	5.22
1987				**1994**				**2001**			
June	8.57	9.64	7.79	June	7.40	8.16	6.11	June	5.67	7.11	5.20
Dec.	9.12	10.22	7.96	Dec.	7.87	8.66	6.80	Dec.	5.48	6.80	5.25
1988				**1995**				**2002**			
June	9.00	10.08	7.78	June	6.57	7.42	5.84	June	5.65	6.57	5.09
Dec.	9.01	10.05	7.61	Dec.	6.06	7.02	5.45	Dec.	5.01	5.93	4.85
1989				**1996**				**2003**			
June	8.27	9.24	7.02	June	7.06	8.00	6.02	June	4.34	4.97	4.33
Dec.	7.90	9.23	6.98	Dec.	6.55	7.45	5.64	Dec.	5.11	5.62	4.65
1990				**1997**				**2004**			
June	8.46	9.69	7.24	June	6.77	7.71	5.53	June	5.45	6.01	5.05
Dec.	8.24	9.55	7.09	Dec.	5.99	6.68	5.19	Dec.	4.88	5.47	4.49
1991				**1998**				**2005**			
June	8.47	9.37	7.13	Jun	5.70	6.43	5.12	June	4.35	4.96	4.23
Dec.	7.70	8.55	6.69	Dec.	5.06	6.13	4.98	Dec.	4.73	5.37	4.46
1992				**1999**				**2006**			
June	7.84	8.45	6.49	Jun.	6.04	7.21	5.37	June	5.15	5.89	4.60
Dec.	7.44	8.12	6.22	Dec.	6.35	7.55	5.95	Dec.	4.68	5.32	4.11
								2007			
								June	5.20	5.79	4.60

NA = Not available. (1) On Feb. 18, 2002, the U.S. treasury discontinued the 30-year constant maturity yield and reintroduced it on Feb. 9, 2006; rates in the interim are for 20-year yields. (2) Treasury series based on 3-week moving average of reoffering yields of new corporate bonds rated Aa by Moody's Investors Service with an original maturity of at least 20 years. Treasury discontinued yield index after Jan. 31, 2003. Rates thereafter are for Moody's seasoned Aaa corporate bonds as listed by Federal Reserve. (3) Index of new reoffering yields on 20-year general obligations rated Aa by Moody's Investors Service; discontinued by Treasury Jan. 31, 2003; rates thereafter are from Bond Buyer Index of general obligation, 20-year-to-maturity, mixed quality state and local bonds.

U.S. Capital Gains Tax, 1960-2007

Source: George W. Smith IV, CPA, Partner, George W. Smith & Company, P.C.

The following shows changes in the maximum tax rate on net long-term capital gains for individuals since 1960.

Year	Max %	Year	Max %	Year	Max %	Year	Max %	Year	Max %	Year	Max %
1960.... 25.0		1972.... 35.0[1]		1981.... 20.0		1988.... 33.0[2]		1997.... 20.0[4]		2001.... 20/18[6]	
1970.... 29.5		1978.... 28.0		1987.... 28.0		1990.... 28.0[3]		1999.... 20.0[5]		2003.... 20/15[7]	
1971.... 32.5											

(1) From 1972 to 1976, the interplay of minimum tax and maximum tax resulted in a marginal rate of 49.125%. (2) Statutory maximum of 28%, but "phase-out" notch increased marginal rate to 33%; interplay of all "phase-outs" could produce an effective marginal rate of 49.5%. (3) The Budget Act of 1990 increased the statutory rate to 31% and capped the marginal rate at 28%; effective marginal rates could exceed 34% because of the phase-out of personal exemptions and itemized deductions. (4) New rate was for those who, after July 28, 1997, sell capital assets held for more than 18 mos (12 mos for sales after Dec. 31, 1997). A 10% capital gains rate applied to individuals in the 15% income tax bracket. (Those who, after July 28, 1997, but before Jan. 1, 1998, sold capital assets held between 12 and 18 mos to be taxed at the old top rate of 28%. Those who sold capital assets after May 6, 1997, but before July 29, 1997, to be taxed at the 20% rate, so long as such assets were held for at least a year.) (5) The IRS Restructuring and Reform Act of 1998 repealed the more-than-18-month holding period for sales after Dec. 31, 1997. Beginning Jan. 1, 1998, capital assets needed only be held 12 months to have the 20%/10% capital gains rates apply. (6) For capital assets bought after Dec. 31, 2000, and held for more than 5 years, the 20% minimum capital gains rate was lowered to 18%. The 10% rate was lowered to 8%, regardless of when the assets were bought. This provision was repealed in 2003. (7) The maximum capital gains rate for capital assets held more than one year and sold on or after May 6, 2003, was decreased to 15%. The 10% bracket was reduced to 5%. The capital gains rate for the sale of collectibles such as antiques remained at 28%, and the sale of certain depreciable real estate was to be taxed at a maximum of 25%. A 0% rate will replace the 5% tax rate for tax years beginning after Dec. 31, 2007.

2007 Federal Corporate Tax Rates

Taxable Income Amount	Tax Rate	Taxable Income Amount	Tax Rate
Not more than $50,000	15%	$335,001 to $10,000,000	34%
$50,001 to $75,000	25%	$10,000,001 to $15,000,000	35%
$75,001 to $100,000	34%	$15,000,001 to $18,333,333	38%
$100,001 to $335,000	39%	More than $18,333,333	35%

Personal service corporations (used by incorporated professionals such as attorneys and doctors) pay a flat rate of 35%.

Performance of Mutual Funds by Type, 2007

Source: Thomson Financial, Rockville, MD, 800-232-2285

(data for periods ending Sept. 30; all figures are percents)

	AVERAGE ANNUAL RETURN		
Fund Type/Fund Objective	1-year	3-year	5-year
Diversified Stock			
Aggressive Growth	17.24	11.87	13.73
Equity Income	14.81	12.70	14.59
Growth–Domestic	17.80	12.95	14.71
Growth & Income	14.29	12.30	14.63
Mid Cap	20.10	15.39	17.73
S&P 500 Index	15.22	12.38	14.81
Small Cap	16.12	13.77	17.90
Specialty Stock			
Sector–Energy/Natural Res	38.18	27.65	29.00
Sector–Financial Services	3.93	10.05	14.43
Sector–Health/Biotechnology	12.56	10.54	13.28
Sector–Other	11.56	10.69	11.14
Sector–Precious Metals	36.05	26.79	27.28
Sector–Real Estate	6.50	18.27	21.30
Sector–Tech/Communications	25.64	16.22	20.74
Sector–Utilities	26.77	22.58	22.88
World Stock			
Emerging Market Equity	52.65	39.14	37.03
Global Equity	23.05	19.31	20.03
Non–US Equity	29.97	24.77	24.19
Emerging Market Income	8.51	11.04	16.43
Hybrid			
Asset Allocation–Domestic	13.14	10.38	11.58
Asset Allocation–Global	13.84	11.47	12.84
Balanced–Domestic	12.29	9.82	11.08
Balanced–Global	17.08	14.54	15.37
Bond			
Corporate–High Yield	6.60	6.27	10.60
Corporate–Investment Grade	3.81	3.31	4.54
Convertible	14.58	10.19	12.88
General Bd–Investment Grade	4.39	3.29	3.87
General Bd–Long	6.18	6.12	9.46
General Bd–Short & Interm	5.11	4.15	5.14
General Mortgage	4.99	4.39	3.16
Global Income	7.32	5.17	7.59
Loan Participation	5.02	4.92	5.64
Multi–Sector Bond	6.47	5.04	8.05
US Government/Agency	4.34	3.42	3.14
US Government–Long	3.53	2.67	2.79
US Government–Short & Interm	4.31	3.02	2.70
US Treasury	4.50	3.54	3.38
Municipal Bond			
Municipal–High Yield	1.44	4.36	4.53
Municipal–Insured	2.16	2.69	2.77
Municipal–National	2.18	2.87	3.02
Municipal–Single State	2.02	3.01	3.09

U.S. Mutual Fund Shareholders[1]

Source: The Investment Company Institute

Shareholder Characteristics, 2005

Median age[2]	48
Median annual household income	$68,700
Median household financial assets[4]	$125,000
Median mutual fund assets	$48,000
Median number of funds owned	4
Employed[2]	77%
Married or living with a partner[2]	71%
Spouse or partner employed	75%
Four-year college degree or more[2]	56%

Owning:

Equity funds	80%
Bond funds	44%
Hybrid funds	34%
Money market funds	49%

Households owning mutual funds

Year	(in mil)[3]	Year	(in mil)[3]	Year	(in mil)[3]
1980	4.6	1996	36.8	2003	53.3
1984	10.2	1999	48.4	2004	53.9
1988	22.2	2000	51.7	2005	53.7
1992	25.8	2001	56.3	2006	54.9
1994	30.2	2002	54.2		

(1) Except where noted, data include mutual funds both inside and outside employer-sponsored retirement plans. (2) Of persons responding to survey. (3) Data from 1980-88 exclude households owning mutual funds solely through employer-sponsored retirement plans. (4) Excluding primary residence.

Chicago Board of Trade, Contracts Traded 1996, 2006

Source: Chicago Board of Trade

	1996	2006	% change 1996-2006
FUTURES GROUP			
Agricultural	50,806,091	106,511,215	109.6%
Financial	120,268,387	530,790,549	341.3
Stock index	—	28,730,906	NA
Metals	59,707	12,203,057	20338.2
Total futures	**171,134,185**	**678,262,052**	**296.3**
OPTIONS GROUP			
Agricultural	14,563,288	21,665,875	48.8
Financial	36,725,763	105,209,831	65.1
Stock index	—	551,190	NA
Metals	515	195,465	37854.4%
Total options	**51,304,320**	**127,622,361**	**148.8**
COMBINED FUTURES AND OPTIONS			
Agricultural	65,369,379	128,177,090	96.1
Financial	156,994,150	636,000,380	305.1
Stock index[1]	—	29,282,096	NA
Metals	60,222	12,398,522	20488.0
GRAND TOTAL	**222,438,505**	**805,884,413**	**262.3**

(1) Now called the Equity Index, and composed of 6 Dow Jones Indexes; not comparable to Stock Index shown for 1996. A dash indicates item delisted from Board of Trade. NA = not applicable.

Economic and Financial Glossary

Source: Reviewed by William M. Gentry, Graduate School of Business, Columbia University

Annuity contract: An investment vehicle sold by insurance companies. Annuity buyers can elect to receive periodic payments for the rest of their lives. Annuities provide insurance against outliving one's wealth.

Arbitrage: A form of hedged investment meant to capture slight differences in the prices of 2 related securities—for example, buying gold in London and selling it at a higher price in New York.

Balanced budget: A budget is balanced when receipts equal expenditures. When receipts exceed expenditures, there is a **surplus;** when they fall short of expenditures, there is a **deficit.**

Balance of payments: The difference between all payments, for some categories of transactions, made to and from foreign countries over a set period of time. A *favorable* balance of payments exists when more payments are coming in than going out; an *unfavorable* balance of payments obtains when the reverse is true. Payments may include gold, the cost of merchandise and services, interest and dividend payments, money spent by travelers, and repayment of principal on loans.

Balance of trade (trade gap): The difference between exports and imports, in both actual funds and credit. A nation's balance of trade is *favorable* when exports exceed imports and *unfavorable* when the reverse is true.

Bear market: A market in which prices are falling.

Bearer bond: A bond issued in bearer form rather than being registered in a specific owner's name. Ownership is determined by possession.

Bond: A written promise, or IOU, by the issuer to repay a fixed amount of borrowed money on a specified date and generally to pay interest at regular intervals in the interim.

Bull market: A market in which prices are on the rise.

Capital gain (loss): An increase (decrease) in the market value of an asset over some period of time. For tax purposes, capital gains are typically calculated from when an asset is bought to when it is sold.

Commercial paper: An extremely short-term corporate IOU, generally due in 270 days or less.

Consumer price index (CPI): A statistical measure of the change in the price of consumer goods.

Convertible bond: A corporate bond (see below) that may be converted into a stated number of shares of common stock. Its price tends to fluctuate along with fluctuations in the price of the stock and with changes in interest rates.

Corporate bond: A bond issued by a corporation. The bond normally has a stated life and pays a fixed rate of interest. Considered safer than the common or preferred stock of the same company.

Cost of living: The cost of maintaining a standard of living measured in terms of purchased goods and services. Inflation typically measures changes in the cost of living.

Cost-of-living adjustments: Changes in promised payments, such as retirement benefits, to account for changes in the cost of living.

Credit crunch (liquidity crisis): A situation in which cash for lending is in short supply.

Debenture: An unsecured bond backed only by the general credit of the issuing corporation.

Deficit spending: Government spending in excess of revenues, generally financed with the sale of bonds. A deficit increases the government debt.

Deflation: A decrease in the level of prices.

Depression: A long period of economic decline marked by low prices, high unemployment, and many business failures.

Derivatives: Financial contracts, such as options, whose values are based on, or *derived* from, the price of an underlying financial asset or indicator such as a stock or an interest rate.

Devaluation: The official lowering of a nation's currency, decreasing its value in relation to other currencies.

Discount rate: The rate of interest set by the Federal Reserve that member banks are charged when borrowing money through the Federal Reserve System.

Disposable income: Income after taxes that is available to persons for spending and saving.

Diversification: Investing in more than one asset in order to reduce the riskiness of the overall asset portfolio. By holding more than one asset, losses on some assets may be offset by gains realized on other assets.

Dividend: Discretionary payment by a corporation to its shareholders, usually in the form of cash or stock shares.

Dow Jones Industrial Average: An index of stock market prices, based on the prices of 30 companies, 28 of which are on the New York Stock Exchange.

Econometrics: The use of statistical methods to study economic and financial data.

Federal Deposit Insurance Corp. (FDIC): A U.S. government-sponsored corporation that insures accounts in national banks and other qualified institutions against bank failures.

Federal Reserve System: The entire banking system of the U.S., incorporating 12 Federal Reserve banks (one in each of 12 Federal Reserve districts), 25 Federal Reserve branch banks, all national banks, and state-chartered commercial banks and trust companies that have been admitted to its membership. The governors of the system greatly influence the nation's monetary and credit policies.

Full employment: The economy is said to be at full employment when everyone who wishes to work at the going wage-rate for his or her type of labor is employed, save only for the small amount of unemployment due to the time it takes to switch from one job to another.

Futures: A futures contract is an agreement to buy or sell a specific amount of a commodity or financial instrument at a particular price at a set date in the future. For example, futures based on a stock index (such as the Dow Jones Industrial Average) are bets on the future price of that group of stocks.

Golden parachute: Provisions in contracts of some high-level executives guaranteeing substantial severance benefits if they lose their position in a corporate takeover.

Government bond: A bond issued by the U.S. Treasury, considered a safe investment. These are divided into 2 categories—marketable and not marketable. *Savings bonds* cannot be bought and sold once the original purchase is made. Marketable bonds fall into several categories. *Treasury bills* are short-term U.S. obligations, maturing in 3, 6, or 12 months. *Treasury notes* mature in up to 10 years. *Treasury bonds* mature in 10 to 30 years. *Indexed bonds* are adjusted for inflation.

Greenmail: A company buying back its own shares for more than the going market price to avoid a threatened hostile takeover.

Gross domestic product (GDP): The market value of all goods and services that have been bought for final use during a period of time. It became the official measure of the size of the U.S. economy in 1991, replacing *gross national product (GNP),* in use since 1941. GDP covers workers and capital employed within the nation's borders. GNP covers production by U.S. residents regardless of where it takes place. The switch aligned U.S. terminology with that of most other industrialized countries.

Hedge fund: A flexible investment fund for a limited number of large investors (the minimum investment is typically $1 million). Hedge funds use a variety of investment techniques, including those forbidden to mutual funds, such as short-selling and heavy leveraging.

Hedging: Taking 2 positions whose gains and losses will offset each other if prices change, in order to limit risk.

Individual retirement account (IRA): A self-funded tax-advantaged retirement plan that allows employed individuals to contribute up to a maximum yearly sum. With a *traditional* IRA, individuals contribute pre-tax earnings and defer income taxes until retirement. With a *Roth* IRA, individuals contribute after-tax earnings but do not pay taxes on future withdrawals (the interest is never taxed). *401(k) plans* are employer-sponsored plans similar to traditional IRAs, but having higher contribution limits.

Inflation: An increase in the level of prices.

Insider information: Important facts about the condition or plans of a corporation that have not been released to the general public.

Interest: The cost of borrowing money.

Investment bank: A financial institution that arranges the initial issuance of stocks and bonds and offers companies advice about acquisitions and divestitures.

Junk bonds: Bonds issued by companies with low credit ratings. They typically pay relatively high interest rates because of the fear of default.

Leading indicators: A series of 11 indicators from different segments of the economy used by the U.S. Commerce Department to predict when changes in the level of economic activity will occur.

Leverage: The extent to which a purchase was paid for with borrowed money. Amplifies the potential gain or loss for the purchaser.

Leveraged buyout (LBO): An acquisition of a company in which much of the purchase price is borrowed, with the debt to be repaid from future profits or by subsequently selling off company assets. A leveraged buyout is typically carried out by a small group of investors, often including incumbent management.

Liquid assets: Assets consisting of cash and/or items that are easily converted into cash.

Margin account: A brokerage account that allows a person to trade securities on credit. A **margin call** is a demand for more collateral on the account.

Money supply: The currency held by the public, plus checking accounts in commercial banks and savings institutions.

Mortgage-backed securities: Created when a bank, builder, or government agency gathers together a group of mortgages and then sells bonds to other institutions and the public. The investors receive their proportionate share of the interest payments on the loans as well as the principal payments. Usually, the mortgages in question are guaranteed by the government.

Municipal bond: Issued by governmental units such as states, cities, local taxing authorities, and other agencies. Interest is exempt from U.S.—and sometimes state and local—income tax. *Municipal bond unit investment trusts* offer a portfolio of many different municipal bonds chosen by professionals. The income is exempt from federal income taxes.

Mutual fund: A portfolio of professionally bought and managed financial assets in which you pool your money along with that of many other people. A share price is based on net asset value, or the value of all the investments owned by the funds, less any debt, and divided by the total number of shares. The major advantage, relative to investing individually in only a small number of stocks, is less risk—the holdings are spread out over many assets and if one or two do badly the remainder may shield you from the losses. *Bond funds* are mutual funds that deal in the bond market exclusively. *Money market mutual funds* buy in the so-called money market—institutions that need to borrow large sums of money for short terms. These funds often offer special checking account advantages.

National debt: The debt of the national government, as distinguished from the debts of political subdivisions of the nation and of private business and individuals.

National debt ceiling: Total borrowing limit set by Congress beyond which the U.S. national debt cannot rise. This limit is periodically raised by congressional vote.

Option: A type of contractual agreement between a buyer and a seller to buy or sell shares of a security. A **call** option contract gives the right to purchase shares of a specific stock at a stated price within a given period of time. A **put** option contract gives the buyer the right to sell shares of a specific stock at a stated price within a given period of time.

Per capita income: The total income of a group divided by the number of people in the group.

Prime interest rate: The rate charged by banks on short-term loans to large commercial customers with the highest credit rating.

Producer price index: A statistical measure of the change in the price of wholesale goods. It is reported for 3 different stages of the production chain: crude, intermediate, and finished goods.

Program trading: Trading techniques involving large numbers and large blocks of stocks, usually used in conjunction with computer programs. Techniques include *index arbitrage*, in which traders profit from price differences between stocks and futures contracts on stock indexes, and *portfolio insurance*, which is the use of stock-index futures to protect stock investors from potentially large losses when the market drops.

Public debt: The total of a nation's debts owed by state, local, and national government. Increases in this sum, reflected in public-sector deficits, indicate how much of the nation's spending is being financed by borrowing rather than by taxation.

Recession: A mild decrease in economic activity marked by a decline in real (inflation-adjusted) GDP, employment, and trade, usually lasting from 6 months to a year, and marked by widespread decline in many sectors of the economy.

Savings Association Insurance Fund (SAIF): Created in 1989 to insure accounts in savings and loan associations up to $100,000.

Seasonal adjustment: Statistical changes made to compensate for regular fluctuations in data that are so great they tend to distort the statistics and make comparisons meaningless. For instance, seasonal adjustments are made for a slowdown in housing construction in midwinter and for the rise in farm income in the fall after summer crops are harvested.

Short-selling: Borrowing shares of stock from a brokerage firm and selling them, hoping to buy the shares back at a lower price, return them, and realize a profit from the decline in prices.

Stagnation: Economic slowdown in which there is little growth in the GDP, capital investment, and real income.

Stock: *Common stocks* are shares of ownership in a corporation. For publicly held firms, the stock typically trades on an exchange, such as the New York Stock Exchange; for closely held firms, the founders and managers own most of the stock. There can be wide swings in the prices of this kind of stock. *Preferred stock* is a type of stock on which a fixed dividend must be paid before holders of common stock are issued their share of the issuing corporation's earnings. Preferred stock is less risky than common stock. *Convertible preferred stock* can be converted into the common stock of the company that issued the preferred. *Over-the-counter stock* is not traded on the major or regional exchanges, but rather through dealers from whom you buy directly. *Blue chip* stocks are so called because they have been leading stocks for a long time. *Growth stocks* are from companies that reinvest their earnings, rather than pay dividends, with the expectation of future stock price appreciation.

Supply-side economics: A school of thinking about economic policy holding that lowering income tax rates will inevitably lead to enhanced economic growth and general revitalization of the economy.

Takeover: Acquisition of one company by another company or group by sale or merger. A *friendly takeover* occurs when the acquired company's management is agreeable to the merger; when management is opposed to the merger, it is a *hostile takeover*.

Tender offer: A public offer to buy a company's stock; usually priced at a premium above the market.

Zero coupon bond: A corporate or government bond that is issued at a deep discount from the maturity value and pays no interest during the life of the bond. It is redeemable at face value.

Minerals

Source: U.S. Geological Survey, U.S. Dept. of the Interior, as of mid-2007; minerals.usgs.gov/minerals

Aluminum: the second most abundant metallic element in the earth's crust. Bauxite is the main source of aluminum. Guinea, Australia, and Jamaica have about 60% of the world's reserves. Main uses in the U.S. are transportation (37%), packaging (22%), and construction (16%).

Chromium: most of the world's production of chromite ore is in India, Kazakhstan, and South Africa. The metallurgical industry uses about 91% of the chromite consumed in the world; the chemical industry, 6%; and the refractory and foundry industry, 3%.

Cobalt: used in superalloys for jet engines; cemented carbides for cutting tools; batteries, catalysts, ceramics, and other chemical applications; permanent magnets, tool steels, and other alloys. Australia, Canada, Congo (Kinshasa), Cuba, Russia, and Zambia account for most of the world cobalt mine production.

Construction Aggregates: construction sand and gravel and crushed stone are two of the most accessible natural resources in the world. Construction sand and gravel is produced in every U.S. State, and crushed stone is mined in every State except Delaware. They are used in construction, agriculture, chemicals, and metallurgy and are produced worldwide.

Copper: main uses of copper and copper alloy products in the U.S. are in building construction (49%), electrical and electronic products (20%), consumer and general products (11%), industrial machinery and equipment (9%), and transportation (11%). The leading mine producers are Chile, the U.S. (mostly in Arizona, Utah, and New Mexico), Peru, Australia, China, Indonesia, Russia, and Canada.

Gold: used in the U.S. in jewelry and the arts (92%), electrical and electronics (4%), dentistry (3%), and other industrial (1%). South Africa has about half of the world's resources; significant quantities are also present in the U.S. (mined in most western States and Alaska), Australia, Russia, Uzbekistan, Canada, and Brazil.

Gypsum: used in wallboard and plaster products, cement production, and agriculture. Leading producers are the U.S., Iran, Canada, Spain, China, and Mexico.

Iron Ore: the source of primary iron for the world's iron and steel industries. Major iron ore producers include Brazil, Australia, China, India, Russia, Ukraine, and the U.S., listed in order of iron content of ore produced in 2005.

Lead: Australia, China, the U.S. (mostly in Alaska and Missouri), Peru, Canada, and Mexico are the world's largest producers of lead. The major end use in the U.S. is in lead acid storage batteries (88%). The U.S. produces and consumes about 20% of the world's lead metal. Most U.S. lead production (89%) is recycled material, and 97% of lead acid batteries (mostly automotive) are recycled.

Manganese: essential to iron and steel production. South Africa and Ukraine have over 80% and 10%, respectively, of the world's identified resources.

Nickel: vital to the stainless steel industry; and used to make superalloys. Leading producers are Russia, Canada, Australia, Indonesia, and New Caledonia.

Platinum-Group Metals: this group consists of 6 metals: platinum, palladium, rhodium, ruthenium, iridium, and osmium. They commonly occur together in nature and are among the scarcest of the metallic elements. In the U.S., the automotive and chemical industries use PGMs mainly as catalysts. They also are consumed in electrical and electronics, glass, dental, and medical industries. Russia and South Africa have most of the world's reserves.

Phosphate Rock: used in fertilizers, animal feed supplements, chemicals, and food. Phosphorus is an essential element for

Salt: used in chemicals, highway deicing, industry, agriculture, food, and water treatment. Leading producers are the U.S., China, Germany, India, and Canada.

Silver: used in industrial and decorative applications, coins, jewelry and silverware, and photography. Silver is mined in more than 50 countries, mainly as a byproduct from gold, copper, and lead-zinc mining. Alaska and Nevada produce more than 70% of U.S. silver, and Peru and Mexico lead the world in production.

Soda Ash: a raw material for glass, chemicals, and detergents, it can be mined or produced synthetically. The U.S. is the world's second leading producer of natural soda ash.

Sulfur: used in agricultural chemicals production, oil refining, metal mining, and many other industries. It is produced as a byproduct of oil refining, natural gas processing, and nonfer-rous metal smelting. Leading producers are the U.S., Canada, China, Russia, Japan, and Germany.

Titanium: ilmenite and rutile are the major mineral sources of titanium. Titanium minerals are used to produce TiO2 pigments (95%) and other uses (5%) including alloys, ceramics, chemicals, titanium metal, and welding rod coatings. Major mining operations are in Australia, Canada, China, Norway, and South Africa. U.S. mine production is in Florida and Virginia.

Zinc: used as a protective coating on steel, as diecastings, as an alloying metal with copper to make brass, and as a component of chemical compounds in rubber and paints. Leading producers of zinc ores and concentrates by zinc content are China, Australia, Peru, the U.S. (in Alaska, Missouri, and Washington), Canada, and Mexico.

U.S. Reliance on Foreign Supplies of Minerals
Source: U.S. Geological Survey, U.S. Dept. of the Interior

Mineral	% Imported in 2006	Major sources (2002-2005)	Major Uses
Arsenic (trioxide)	100%	China, Morocco, Mexico, Chile	Wood preservatives, nonferrous alloys
Asbestos	100	Canada	Roofing products, gaskets, friction products
Bauxite & alumina	100	Jamaica, Guinea, Australia, Brazil	Aluminum production, refractories, abrasives, chemicals
Cesium	100	Canada	Drilling fluids, atomic clocks, DNA separation, infrared detectors, night vision devices
Columbium (niobium)	100	Brazil, Canada, Estonia, Germany	Steelmaking, superalloys
Fluorspar	100	China, Mexico, South Africa, Mongolia	Hydrofluoric acid, aluminum fluoride, steelmaking
Graphite (natural)	100	China, Mexico, Canada, Brazil	Refractories, batteries, foundry operations, lubricants, brake linings, steelmaking
Indium	100	China, Canada, Japan, Russia	Coatings, electrical components, semiconductors, solders, alloys
Manganese	100	South Africa, Gabon, Australia, China	Iron & steelmaking, batteries, agricultural chemicals
Mica, sheet (natural)	100	India, Belgium, China, Brazil	Electronic and electrical equipment
Quartz crystal (industrial)	100	Brazil, Germany, Madagascar, Canada	Electronics, optical applications
Rare earths	100	China, France, Japan, Russia	Catalysts, metallurgy, glass polishing, ceramics, phosphors, magnets
Rubidium	100	Canada	DNA separation, fiber optics, inorganic chemicals, lamps, night vision devices
Strontium	100	Mexico, Germany	Television picture tubes, ferrite magnets, pyrotechnics
Thallium	100	Russia, Belgium	Medical imaging, radiation detection, superconductors, glass, alloys
Thorium	100	France	High-temperature ceramics, catalysts, welding electrodes
Vanadium	100	Czech Republic, Swaziland, Canada, Austria	Steelmaking, catalysts
Yttrium	100	China, Japan, France, Austria	Lamp & cathode ray tube phosphors, alloys
Gallium	99	China, Japan, Ukraine, Russia	Electronic components
Gemstones	99	Israel, India, Belgium, South Africa	Jewelry, carvings, gem & mineral collections
Bismuth	96	Belgium, Mexico, China, United Kingdom	Alloys, solder, ammunition, metallurgy, pharmaceuticals, chemicals
Platinum	95	South Africa, United Kingdom, Germany, Canada	Catalysts, jewelry, dental & medical alloys
Stone (dimension)	89	Italy, Turkey, China, Mexico	Construction, monuments
Antimony	88	China, Mexico, Belgium	Flame retardants, transportation, chemicals, ceramics & glass
Rhenium	87	Chile, Germany	Petroleum-reforming catalysts, superalloys
Tantalum	87	Australia, Canada, China, Japan	Capacitors, superalloys, cemented carbide tools
Barite	83	China, India	Oil & gas well drilling fluids, fillers & extenders, chemicals
Diamond (industrial stone)	82	Ireland, Botswana, Ghana, Belgium	Abrasives, stone cutting, highway repair & construction
Palladium	82	Russia, South Africa, United Kingdom, Belgium	Jewelry, catalysts, dental alloys, chemicals, electronics
Cobalt	81	Norway, Russia, Finland, Canada	Superalloys, cemented carbides, magnetic alloys, chemicals
Potash	80	Canada, Belarus, Russia, Germany	Fertilizers, chemicals
Tin	79	Peru, Bolivia, China, Indonesia	Chemicals, tinplate, solder, alloys
Chromium	75	South Africa, Kazakhstan, Zimbabwe, Russia	Steel, chemicals, refractories
Titanium (sponge)	72	Kazakhstan, Japan, Russia	High-strength alloys for aerospace and nonaerospace uses
Iodine	71	Chile, Japan	Biocides & disinfectants, catalysts, chemicals, nutrition, pharmaceuticals
Titanium mineral concentrates	71	South Africa, Australia, Canada, Ukraine	Pigment, metal, welding rod coatings, chemicals, ceramics
Tungsten	66	China, Canada, Germany, Portugal	Cemented carbides, electrical & electronic components, tool steels, alloys
Silver	65	Mexico, Canada, Peru, Chile	Coins & medals, industrial applications, jewelry & silverware, photography
Zinc	63	Canada, Mexico, Peru, Australia	Galvanizing, zinc-base alloys, brass & bronze
Nickel	60	Canada, Russia, Norway, Australia	Nonferrous alloys, superalloys, steel, electroplating
Silicon (ferrosilicon)	60	China, Venezuela, Russia, Norway	Iron & steel alloys, aluminum & aluminum alloys, specialty chemicals
Peat	59	Canada	Horticulture, absorbents, filter media
Magnesium metal	54	Canada, Russia, China, Israel	Castings & wrought products, aluminum alloys, desulfurization of iron & steel
Garnet (industrial)	53	Australia, India, China, Canada	Abrasive blasting media, water jet cutting, water filtration, abrasive powders
Magnesium compounds	53	China, Canada, Australia, Austria	Refractories, agriculture, chemicals, construction, environment, industry
Diamond (dust, grit, & powders)	51	China, Ireland, Ukraine, Russia	Abrasives, stone cutting, highway repair & construction

World Mineral Reserve Base, 2006
Source: U.S. Geological Survey, U.S. Dept. of the Interior; as of year-end 2006

Mineral	Reserve Base[1]	Mineral	Reserve Base[1]
Aluminum	32,000 mil metric tons[2]	Nickel	140 mil metric tons
Cobalt	.13 mil metric tons	Phosphate Rock	50,000 mil metric tons
Copper	.940 mil metric tons	Platinum-Group Metals	80,000 mil metric tons
Gold	.90,000 metric tons	Silver	570,000 metric tons
Iron Ore	370,000 mil metric tons	Soda Ash (Natural)	40,000 mil metric tons
Lead	140 mil metric tons	Titanium (ilmenite/rutile)	1,300 mil metric tons[3]
Manganese	5,200 mil metric tons	Zinc	460 mil metric tons

(1) Includes demonstrated resources that are currently economic or marginally economic, plus some that are currently subeconomic. (2) Bauxite. (3) Titanium dioxide (TiO$_2$) content of ilmenite and rutile.

World Gold Production, 1980-2006[1]
Source: U.S. Geological Survey, U.S. Dept. of the Interior
(thousands of troy ounces)

Year	World prod.	South Africa	Africa Ghana	Congo Dem. Rep.	North and South America United States	Canada	Mexico	Colombia	Australia	Other China	Philip- pines	Russia[2]
1980	39,197	21,669	353	96	970	1,627	196	510	548	NA	753	8,425
1985	49,284	21,565	299	257	2,427	2,815	266	1,142	1,881	1,950	1,063	8,700
1990	70,207	19,454	541	299	9,458	5,447	311	944	7,849	3,215	791	9,710
1991	70,423	19,326	846	283	9,454	5,676	326	1,120	7,530	3,858	833	8,359
1992	73,530	19,743	998	225	10,617	5,189	318	1,033	7,825	4,501	730	8,232
1993	73,300	19,908	1,250	280	10,642	4,917	357	883	7,948	5,144	509	8,228
1994	72,500	16,650	1,400	357	10,500	4,710	447	668	8,237	4,240	870	8,173
1995	71,800	16,800	1,710	322	10,200	4,890	652	680	8,150	4,500	873	4,250
1996	73,600	16,000	1,580	160	10,500	5,350	787	710	9,310	4,660	970	3,960
1997	78,900	15,800	1,760	220	11,600	5,510	836	605	10,100	5,630	1,050	3,990
1998	80,300	15,000	2,330	160	11,800	5,320	817	605	10,000	5,720	1,090	3,690
1999	82,600	14,500	2,570	180	11,000	5,070	764	1,410	9,680	5,560	1,000	4,050
2000	83,300	13,900	2,320	230	11,300	5,020	846	1,190	9,530	5,790	1,170	4,600
2001	82,300	12,700	2,200	196	10,800	5,110	757	701	9,010	5,950	1,090	4,900
2002	81,400	12,800	2,230	244	9,580	4,880	686	669	8,560	6,170	1,150	5,410
2003	82,200	12,000	2,270	132	8,910	4,530	656	1,500	9,070	6,590	1,220	5,470
2004	78,300	10,800	2,030	183	8,290	4,160	701	1,210	8,330	6,910	1,140	5,250
2005	79,300	9,470	2,150	135	8,394	3,840	976	1,150	8,420	7,230	1,210	5,280
2006E	79,200	8,750	2,130	135	8,100	3,340	1,290	1,290	7,840	7,880	1,210	5,120

(1) Figures are rounded. (2) Figures for 1980-94 are for USSR as constituted prior to Dec. 1991; after 1994, Russia only. E = Estimated. NA = Not available.

U.S. Nonfuel Minerals Production, 1998-2006
Source: U.S. Geological Survey, U.S. Dept. of the Interior
Production as measured by mine shipments, sales, or marketable production (including consumption by producers).

		1998	2000	2002	2003	2004	2005	2006
Beryllium (metal equivalent)	metric tons	243	180	80	85	90	110	155
Copper (recoverable content of ores, etc.)	thousand metric tons	1,860	1,450	1,140	1,120	1,160	1,140	1,200
Gold (recoverable content of ores, etc.)	metric tons	366	353	298	277	258	261E	251P
Iron ore, usable	million metric tons	62.9	63.1	51.6	48.6	54.7	54.3	52.9E
Lead (recoverable content of ores, etc.)	thousand metric tons	481	449	440	449	430	426	450
Magnesium metal (primary)	thousand metric tons	106	W	W	W	W	W	W
Molybdenum (content of ore and concentrates)	metric tons	53,300	40,900	32,300	33,500	41,500	58,000	59,800
Silver (recoverable content of ores, etc.)	metric tons	2,060	1,860	1,350	1,240	1,250	1,230	1,140
Zinc (recoverable content of ores, etc.)	thousand metric tons	722	805	700	738	715	720	696
Asbestos	thousand metric tons	6	5	3	—	—	—	—
Barite (sold or used)	thousand metric tons	476	392	420	468	532	489	540E
Boron minerals (B$_2$O$_3$ equivalent)	thousand metric tons	587	546	543	605	637	612	W
Bromine	thousand metric tons	230	228	222	216	222	224	213
Cement (portland, masonry; excludes Puerto Rico)	thousand metric tons	83,931	87,846	89,732	92,843	97,434	99,319	97,000E
Clays	thousand metric tons	41,900	40,800	39,300	40,000	41,200	41,700	41,300
Diatomite	thousand metric tons	725	677	599	625	620	653	799
Feldspar	thousand metric tons	820E	790E	790E	800E	770E	750E	760E
Garnet (industrial)	metric tons	74,000	60,200	38,500	29,200	28,400	40,100	34,100
Gemstones (natural)	million dollars	14	17	13	13	15	13	13E
Gypsum	thousand metric tons	19,000	19,500	15,700	16,700	17,200	21,100	21,100
Helium (extracted from natural gas)	million cubic meters	114	98	87	87	86	76	79
Helium (Grade A sold)	million cubic meters	114	127	127	122	130	133	137
Iodine	thousand kilograms	1,490	1,470	1,420	1,090	1,130	1,570	1,610
Lime	thousand metric tons	20,100	19,500	17,900	19,200	20,000	20,000	21,000
Mica (scrap & flake)	thousand metric tons	87	101	81	79	99	78	110
Peat	thousand metric tons	685	792	642	634	696	685	551
Perlite (sold & used by producers)	thousand metric tons	685	672	521	493	508	508	454
Phosphate rock (marketable product)	thousand metric tons	44,200	38,600	36,100	35,000	35,800	36,100	30,100
Potash (K$_2$O equivalent)	thousand metric tons	1,300	1,300	1,200	1,100	1,300	1,200	1,100
Pumice & pumicite	thousand metric tons	872	1,050	956	870	1,490	1,270	1,540
Salt	thousand metric tons	40,800	43,300	37,700	41,100	45,000	45,000	46,700
Sand & gravel (construction)	million metric tons	1,070	1,120	1,130	1,160	1,240	1,270	1,250E
Sand & gravel (industrial)	thousand metric tons	28,200	28,400	27,300	27,500	29,700	30,600	31,000E
Soda ash (sodium carbonate)	thousand metric tons	10,100	10,200	10,500	10,600	11,000	11,000	11,000
Stone (crushed)	million metric tons	1,510	1,550	1,510	1,530	1,630	1,700	1,720
Stone (dimension)	thousand metric tons	1,140	1,320	1,260	1,340	1,460	1,360	1,330
Sulfur (in all forms)	thousand metric tons	11,700	10,500	9,270	9,600	10,100	9,460	9,060
Talc	thousand metric tons	971	851	828	840	833	856	895
Titanium mineral concentrates (TiO$_2$ content)	thousand metric tons	400	300	300	300	300	300	300
Vermiculite concentrate	thousand metric tons	W	150E	100E	110E	100E	100E	100E

W= Withheld to avoid disclosing company proprietary data. —= No production. E= Estimated. NA= Not available. P=Preliminary.

TRADE

U.S. Trade With Selected Countries and Major Areas, 2006

Source: U.S. Bureau of Economic Analysis, U.S. Dept. of Commerce
(in millions of dollars; top 25 countries as ranked by amount of total trade with U.S.)

COUNTRY	Total trade with U.S.	U.S. exports to	Rank[1]	U.S. imports from	Rank[1]	U.S. trade balance with	Rank[2]
Canada	$533,093.9	$230,656.0	1	$302,437.9	1	–$71,781.8	3
China	342,960.1	55,185.7	4	287,774.4	2	–232,588.6	1
Mexico	332,232.0	133,978.8	2	198,253.2	3	–64,274.3	4
Japan	207,793.5	59,612.7	3	148,180.8	4	–88,568.1	2
Germany	130,401.1	41,319.1	6	89,082.0	5	–47,763.0	5
United Kingdom	98,923.1	45,410.1	5	53,513.0	6	–8,102.9	24
South Korea	78,245.2	32,441.6	7	45,803.6	7	–13,362.0	16
Taiwan	61,258.6	23,046.7	11	38,211.9	8	–15,165.2	12
France	61,257.0	24,217.4	10	37,039.6	10	–12,822.2	17
Malaysia	49,077.4	12,544.3	18	36,533.1	11	–23,988.9	9
Netherlands	48,471.5	31,129.2	8	17,342.3	22	13,787.0	230
Venezuela	46,136.1	9,002.3	22	37,133.8	9	–28,131.5	6
Brazil	45,597.7	19,231.0	13	26,366.7	16	–7,135.7	26
Italy	45,201.1	12,546.0	17	32,655.1	12	–20,109.0	10
Singapore	42,451.8	24,683.7	9	17,768.1	21	6,915.6	225
Saudi Arabia	39,328.5	7,639.5	25	31,689.0	13	–24,049.5	8
Ireland	37,041.9	8,516.0	23	28,525.9	14	–20,009.9	11
Belgium	35,745.4	21,340.0	12	14,405.4	24	6,934.6	226
India	31,887.0	10,056.2	21	21,830.8	18	–11,774.6	18
Thailand	30,613.0	8,146.7	24	22,466.3	17	–14,319.7	15
Israel	30,131.6	10,964.8	20	19,166.8	20	–8,201.9	23
Nigeria	30,096.6	2,233.5	50	27,863.1	15	–25,629.7	7
Switzerland	28,604.9	14,375.0	16	14,229.9	25	145.2	195
Australia	25,983.3	17,779.3	14	8,204.0	37	9,575.3	227
Hong Kong	25,722.3	17,775.6	15	7,946.7	38	9,828.9	228
MAJOR AREA/GROUP							
North America	865,325.8	364,634.8	NA	500,691.0	NA	–136,056.2	NA
Western Europe	629,543.5	245,536.0	NA	384,007.5	NA	–138,471.5	NA
Euro Area	402,401.5	155,734.8	NA	246,666.7	NA	–90,931.9	NA
EU	544,477.9	213,996.1	NA	330,481.8	NA	–116,485.8	NA
Africa	99,452.6	19,034.7	NA	80,417.9	NA	–61,383.2	NA
OECD	1,773,654.9	712,576.0	NA	1,061,078.9	NA	–348,502.9	NA
Pacific Rim Countries	875,507.3	256,985.6	NA	618,521.7	NA	–361,536.2	NA
Asia/Near East	110,458.4	38,558.1	NA	71,900.3	NA	–33,342.2	NA
Asia/NICS	207,677.8	97,947.6	NA	109,730.2	NA	–11,782.6	NA
Asia/South	44,113.6	13,048.9	NA	31,064.7	NA	–18,015.8	NA
ASEAN	168,507.8	57,307.3	NA	111,200.5	NA	–53,893.2	NA
APEC	1,829,370.7	645,081.0	NA	1,184,289.7	NA	–539,208.7	NA
South/Central America	222,645.4	88,969.6	NA	133,675.8	NA	–44,706.3	NA
Twenty Latin American Republics	529,113.4	211,188.9	NA	317,924.5	NA	–106,735.7	NA
Central American Common Market	28,281.2	14,234.5	NA	14,046.7	NA	187.8	NA
LAFTA	486,215.4	187,744.9	NA	298,470.5	NA	–110,725.5	NA
NATO	1,026,375.7	435,303.6	NA	591,072.1	NA	–155,768.6	NA
OPEC	185,450.9	40,081.0	NA	145,369.9	NA	–105,289.0	NA
WORLD TOTAL	**2,890,573.2**	**1,036,634.7**	**NA**	**1,853,938.5**	**NA**	**–817,303.8**	**NA**

NA = Not applicable. **Note:** Figures may not add to totals because of rounding or incomplete enumeration. (1) Rank shown is for column to the left. (2) Ranking includes territories as well as nations. Rank is by size of U.S. trade deficit. **Definitions of areas/groups used in table, as provided by the source: North America**—Canada, Mexico. **Western Europe**—Albania, Andorra, Armenia, Austria, Azerbaijan, Belarus, Belgium, Bosnia-Herzegovina, Bulgaria, Croatia, Cyprus, Czech Republic, Denmark, Estonia, Faroe Isls., Finland, France, Georgia, Germany, Gibraltar, Greece, Hungary, Iceland, Ireland, Italy, Liechtenstein, Kazakhstan, Kyrgyzstan, Latvia, Lithuania, Luxembourg, Macedonia, Malta and Gozo, Moldova, Monaco, Netherlands, Norway, Poland, Portugal, Romania, Russia, San Marino, Serbia and Montenegro, Slovakia, Slovenia, Spain, Svalbard, Jan Mayen Isl., Sweden, Switzerland, Tajikistan, Turkey, Turkmenistan, Ukraine, United Kingdom, Uzbekistan, Vatican City. **Euro Area**—Austria, Belgium, Finland, France, Germany, Greece, Ireland, Italy, Luxembourg, Netherlands, Portugal, Spain. **EU (European Union)**—Euro Area plus Cyprus, Czech Republic, Denmark, Estonia, Hungary, Latvia, Lithuania, Malta, Poland, Slovakia, Slovenia, Sweden, United Kingdom. **Africa**—Algeria, Angola, Benin, Botswana, British Indian Ocean Territories, Burkina, Burundi, Cameroon, Cape Verde, Central African Republic, Chad, Comoros, Congo (Brazzaville), Congo (Kinshasa), Djibouti, Egypt, Equatorial Guinea, Eritrea, Ethiopia, French Southern and Antarctic Lands, Gabon, Gambia, Ghana, Guinea, Guinea-Bissau, Ivory Coast, Kenya, Lesotho, Liberia, Libya, Madagascar, Malawi, Mali, Mauritania, Mauritius, Mayotte, Morocco, Mozambique, Namibia, Niger, Nigeria, Reunion, Rwanda, St. Helena, São Tomé and Príncipe, Senegal, Seychelles, Sierra Leone, Somalia, South Africa, Sudan, Swaziland, Tanzania, Togo, Tunisia, Uganda, Western Sahara, Zambia, Zimbabwe. **OECD (Org. for Econ. Cooperation and Development)**—Australia, Austria, Belgium, Canada, Czech Republic, Denmark, Finland, France, Germany, Greece, Hungary, Iceland, Ireland, Italy, Japan, Liechtenstein, Luxembourg, Mexico, Netherlands, New Zealand, Norway, Poland, Portugal, Slovakia, South Korea, Spain, Sweden, Switzerland, Turkey, United Kingdom. **Pacific Rim Countries**—Australia, Brunei, China, Hong Kong, Indonesia, Japan, Korea, Macao, Malaysia, New Zealand, Papua New Guinea, Philippines, Singapore, Taiwan. **Asia/Near East**—Bahrain, Iran, Iraq, Israel, Jordan, Kuwait, Lebanon, Oman, Qatar, Saudi Arabia, Syrian Arab Republic, United Arab Emirates, Yemen. **Asia/NICS (Newly Industrialized Countries)**—Hong Kong, Korea, Singapore, Taiwan. **Asia/South**—Afghanistan, Bangladesh, India, Nepal, Pakistan, Sri Lanka. **ASEAN (Assoc. of Southeast Asian Nations)**—Brunei, Cambodia, Indonesia, Laos, Malaysia, Myanmar, Philippines, Singapore, Thailand, Vietnam. **APEC (Asia-Pacific Economic Cooperation)**—Australia, Brunei, Canada, Chile, China, Hong Kong, Indonesia, Japan, Korea, Malaysia, Mexico, New Zealand, Papua New Guinea, Peru, Philippines, Russia, Singapore, Taiwan, Thailand, Vietnam. **South/Central America**—Anguilla, Antigua and Barbuda, Argentina, Aruba, Bahamas, Barbados, Belize, Bermuda, Bolivia, Brazil, British Virgin Isls., Cayman Isls., Chile, Colombia, Costa Rica, Cuba, Dominica, Dominican Republic, Ecuador, El Salvador, Falkland Isls., French Guiana, Grenada, Guadeloupe, Guatemala, Guyana, Haiti, Honduras, Jamaica, Martinique, Montserrat, Netherlands Antilles, Nicaragua, Panama, Paraguay, Peru, St. Kitts and Nevis, St. Lucia, St. Vincent and the Grenadines, Suriname, Trinidad and Tobago, Turks and Caicos Isls., Uruguay, Venezuela. **Twenty Latin American Republics**—Argentina, Bolivia, Brazil, Chile, Colombia, Costa Rica, Cuba, Dominican Republic, Ecuador, El Salvador, Guatemala, Haiti, Honduras, Mexico, Nicaragua, Panama, Paraguay, Peru, Uruguay, Venezuela. **Central American Common Market**—Costa Rica, El Salvador, Guatemala, Honduras, Nicaragua. **LAFTA (Latin American Free Trade Assoc.)**—Argentina, Bolivia, Brazil, Chile, Colombia, Ecuador, Mexico, Paraguay, Peru, Uruguay, Venezuela. **NATO (North Atlantic Treaty Org.)**—Belgium, Bulgaria, Canada, Czech Republic, Denmark, Estonia, France, Germany, Greece, Hungary, Iceland, Italy, Latvia, Lithuania, Luxembourg, Netherlands, Norway, Poland, Portugal, Romania, Slovakia, Slovenia, Spain, Turkey, United Kingdom. **OPEC (Org. of the Petroleum Exporting Countries)**—Algeria, Indonesia, Iran, Iraq, Kuwait, Libya, Nigeria, Qatar, Saudi Arabia, United Arab Emirates, Venezuela.

U.S. Exports and Imports by Principal Commodity Groupings, 2006
Source: U.S. Bureau of Economic Analysis, U.S. Dept. of Commerce
(in millions of dollars)

Items	Exports	Imports	Items	Exports	Imports
TOTAL[1]	$1,036,635	$1,853,938	Jewelry	$4,033	$11,222
Agricultural commodities	70,912	65,459	Lighting, plumbing	1,868	8,069
Animal feeds	4,534	828	Metal manufactures[3]	15,860	27,893
Cereal flour	2,339	3,357	Metalworking machinery	8,228	8,644
Coffee	4	2,829	Nickel	1,038	3,348
Corn	7,251	179	Optical goods	3,173	4,378
Cotton, raw and linters	4,514	15	Paper and paperboard	12,337	18,503
Hides and skins	1,834	62	Photographic equipment	3,590	4,506
Live animals	745	2,595	Plastic articles[3]	8,915	14,823
Meat and preparations	7,257	5,231	Platinum	1,739	5,833
Oils/fats, vegetable	1,166	2,500	Pottery	100	1,751
Rice	1,265	318	Power generating mach.	44,036	44,742
Soybeans	6,949	56	Printed materials	5,748	5,142
Sugar	30	862	Records/magnetic media	4,912	7,095
Tobacco, unmanufactured	1,141	714	Rubber articles[1]	1,787	3,039
Vegetables and fruits	11,071	15,455	Rubber tires and tubes	3,007	8,662
Wheat	4,205	311	Scientific instruments	39,278	32,297
Manufactured goods[2]	785,599	1,416,302	Ships, boats	2,575	1,548
ADP equipment; office machines	31,091	106,416	Silver and bullion	1,016	1,909
Airplane parts	20,515	6,771	Spacecraft	344	61
Airplanes	43,933	10,604	Specialized industrial machinery	37,469	33,010
Aluminum	5,596	14,919	Television, VCR, etc.	22,515	115,327
Artwork/antiques	3,250	6,633	Textile yarn, fabric	12,106	22,184
Basketware, etc.	6,200	9,093	Toys/games/sporting goods	4,172	26,547
Chemicals—cosmetics	9,100	8,333	Travel goods	461	6,882
Chemicals—dyeing	5,337	3,054	Vehicles	83,472	211,946
Chemicals—fertilizers	2,941	3,438	Watches/clocks/parts	304	4,082
Chemicals—inorganic	9,074	11,414	Wood manufactures	2,007	12,539
Chemicals—medicinal	28,431	45,746	Mineral fuels[2]	34,711	332,500
Chemicals—organic	29,839	42,212	Coal	3,663	2,639
Chemicals—plastics	32,617	18,813	Crude oil	853	225,156
Chemicals[3]	17,860	9,477	Liquefied propane/butane	805	4,419
Clothing	3,849	79,149	Mineral fuels[1]	4,435	3,942
Copper	3,266	12,888	Natural gas	2,226	28,268
Electrical machinery	83,228	109,721	Petroleum preparations	22,078	66,197
Footwear	572	19,160	Other commodities[2]		
Furniture and bedding	4,877	32,788	Alcoholic bev., distilled	844	4,912
Gem diamonds	3,884	17,285	Cigarettes	1,213	202
General industrial machinery	44,089	59,710	Cork, wood, lumber	4,273	10,386
Glass	3,041	2,956	Crude fertilizers	1,947	1,825
Glassware	891	2,362	Fish and preparations	4,012	13,176
Gold, nonmonetary	8,790	5,633	Metal ores; scrap	16,617	6,533
Iron and steel mill products	11,799	32,904	Pulp and waste paper	5,738	3,181

Note: Not all products are listed in each commodity group but are included in totals. (1) Includes both domestic and foreign exports (re-exports). (2) Includes domestic exports. (3) Not specified elsewhere.

Trends in U.S. Foreign Trade, 1790-2006
Source: U.S. Census Bureau and U.S. Bureau of Economic Analysis, U.S. Dept. of Commerce

In 1790, U.S. exports and imports combined came to $43 million, and there was a $3 million trade deficit. In 2006, U.S. exports and imports combined amounted to $2.9 trillion, and the trade deficit, which has steadily been climbing since the last recorded surplus in 1975, reached more than $817 billion, the highest dollar total to date.
(in millions of dollars)

Year	Exports	Imports	Trade balance	Year	Exports	Imports	Trade balance	Year	Exports	Imports	Trade balance
1790	$20	$23	–$3	1885	$742	$578	$165	1980	$220,626	$244,871	–$24,245
1795	48	70	–22	1890	858	789	69	1985	213,133	345,276	–132,143
1800	71	91	–20	1895	808	732	76	1990	394,030	495,042	–101,012
1805	96	121	–25	1900	1,394	850	545	1991	421,730	485,453	–63,723
1810	67	85	–19	1905	1,519	1,118	401	1992	448,164	532,665	–84,501
1815	53	113	–60	1910	1,745	1,557	188	1993	465,091	580,659	–115,568
1820	70	74	–5	1915	2,769	1,674	1,094	1994	512,626	683,256	–170,630
1825	91	90	1	1920	8,228	5,278	2,950	1995	584,742	743,445	–158,703
1830	72	63	9	1925	4,910	4,227	683	1996	625,075	795,289	–170,214
1835	115	137	–22	1930	3,843	3,061	782	1997	689,182	870,671	–181,489
1840	124	98	25	1935	2,283	2,047	235	1998	682,138	911,896	–229,758
1845	106	113	–7	1940	4,021	2,625	1,396	1999	695,797	1,024,618	–328,821
1850	144	174	–29	1945	9,806	4,159	5,646	2000	781,918	1,218,022	–436,104
1855	219	258	–39	1950	9,997	8,954	1,043	2001	729,100	1,140,999	–411,899
1860	334	354	–20	1955	14,298	11,566	2,732	2002	693,103	1,161,366	–468,263
1865	166	239	–73	1960	19,659	15,073	4,586	2003	724,771	1,257,121	–532,350
1870	393	436	–43	1965	26,742	21,520	5,222	2004	818,775	1,469,704	–650,930
1875	513	533	–20	1970	42,681	40,356	2,325	2005	905,978	1,673,455	–767,477
1880	836	668	168	1975	107,652	98,503	9,149	2006	1,036,635	1,853,939	–817,304

World Trade Organization (WTO)

The World Trade Organization is an international body that seeks to promote free trade by eliminating barriers to trade. Founded in 1995, the WTO had grown to 151 member countries as of mid-2007, with several others, including Russia, granted observer status.

In July 2006, the WTO formally suspended, for the first time, international negotiations in the Doha round of talks. The talks, launched in Doha, Qatar, in 2001, had sought to meet the demands of developing countries, who wanted to increase their agricultural and manufacturing exports to the markets of wealthy nations. Developing countries lobbied for the U.S. and the European Union to lower domestic subsidies and foreign import barriers on their agricultural products. At the same time, the U.S. and European nations pushed for those countries to further open their markets to foreign goods.

The major powers in the WTO agreed to resume free trade talks in Jan. 2007 and, as of early Oct. 2007, continued to negotiate.

Foreign Exchange Rates, 1970-2006

Source: Federal Reserve Board
(national currency units per U.S. dollar except as noted; annual average rates of exchange)

Year	Australia[1] (dollar)	Austria[1] (schilling)	Belgium[1] (franc)	Canada (dollar)	China (yuan)	Denmark (krone)	France[1] (franc)	Germany[1,2] (deutsche mark)	Greece[1] (drachma)
1970	1.1136	25.880	49.680	1.0103	NA	7.489	5.5200	3.6480	30.00
1975	1.3077	17.443	36.799	1.0175	NA	5.748	4.2876	2.4613	32.29
1980	1.1400	12.945	29.237	1.1693	NA	5.634	4.2250	1.8175	42.62
1985	0.7003	20.690	59.378	1.3655	NA	10.596	8.9852	2.9440	138.12
1990	0.7813	11.370	33.418	1.1668	NA	6.189	5.4453	1.6157	158.51
1995	0.7415	10.081	29.480	1.3724	8.3700	5.602	4.9915	1.4331	231.66
2000	0.5815	0.9232[3]	0.9232[3]	1.4855	8.2784	8.095	0.9232[3]	0.9232[3]	365.92
2003	0.6524	1.1321[3]	1.1321[3]	1.4008	8.2772	6.5774	1.1321[3]	1.1321[3]	1.1321[3]
2004	0.7365	1.2438[3]	1.2438[3]	1.3017	8.2768	5.9891	1.2438[3]	1.2438[3]	1.2438[3]
2005	0.7627	1.2449[3]	1.2449[3]	1.2115	8.1936	5.9953	1.2449[3]	1.2449[3]	1.2449[3]
2006	0.7535	1.2563[3]	1.2563[3]	1.1340	7.9723	5.9422	1.2563[3]	1.2563[3]	1.2563[3]

Year	Hong Kong (dollar)	India (rupee)	Ireland[1] (pound)	Italy[1] (lira)	Japan (yen)	Malaysia (ringgit)	Mexico (new peso)	Netherlands[1] (guilder)	Norway (krone)
1970	NA	7.576	2.3959	623.0	357.60	3.0900	NA	3.5970	7.1400
1975	NA	8.409	2.2216	653.0	296.78	2.4030	NA	2.5293	5.2282
1980	NA	7.887	2.0577	856.0	226.63	2.1767	NA	1.9875	4.9381
1985	NA	12.369	1.0656	1,909.0	238.54	2.4830	NA	3.3214	8.5972
1990	NA	17.504	1.6585	1,198.0	144.79	2.7049	2.8126	1.8209	6.2597
1995	7.7357	32.427	1.6038	1,628.9	94.06	2.5044	6.4194	1.6057	6.3352
2000	7.7925	45.000	0.9232[3]	0.9232[3]	107.80	3.8000	9.4590	0.9232[3]	8.8131
2003	7.7875	46.590	1.1321[3]	1.1321[3]	115.94	3.8000	10.7930	1.1321[3]	7.0803
2004	7.7891	45.260	1.2438[3]	1.2438[3]	108.15	3.8000	11.2900	1.2438[3]	6.7399
2005	7.7775	44.000	1.2449[3]	1.2449[3]	110.11	3.7869	10.8940	1.2449[3]	6.4412
2006	7.7681	45.190	1.2563[3]	1.2563[3]	116.31	3.6661	10.9060	1.2563[3]	6.4095

Year	Portugal[1] (escudo)	Singapore (dollar)	South Korea (won)	Spain[1] (peseta)	Sweden (krona)	Switzerland (franc)	Taiwan (dollar)	Thailand (baht)	UK[1] (pound)
1970	28.75	3.0800	310.57	69.72	5.1700	4.3160	NA	21.000	2.3959
1975	25.51	2.3713	484.00	57.43	4.1530	2.5839	NA	20.379	2.2216
1980	50.08	2.1412	607.43	71.76	4.2309	1.6772	NA	20.476	2.3243
1985	170.39	2.2002	870.02	170.04	8.6039	2.4571	NA	27.159	1.2963
1990	142.55	1.8125	707.76	101.93	5.9188	1.3892	NA	25.585	1.7847
1995	151.11	1.4174	771.27	124.69	7.1333	1.1825	26.495	24.915	1.5785
2000	0.9232[3]	1.7250	1,130.90	0.9232[3]	9.1735	1.6904	31.260	40.210	1.5156
2003	1.1321[3]	1.7429	1,192.08	1.1321[3]	8.0787	1.3450	34.405	41.556	1.6347
2004	1.2438[3]	1.6902	1,145.24	1.2438[3]	7.3480	1.2428	33.372	40.271	1.8330
2005	1.2449[3]	1.6639	1,023.75	1.2449[3]	7.4710	1.2459	32.131	40.262	1.8204
2006	1.2563[3]	1.5882	954.32	1.2563[3]	7.3718	1.2532	32.506	37.876	1.8434

NA = Not available. **Note:** As of 2007, the euro, the European Union's single currency, replaced the national currencies in the EU nations shown (Austria, Belgium, France, Germany, Greece, Ireland, Italy, Netherlands, Portugal, Spain) as well as in Andorra, Finland, Luxembourg, Monaco, Montenegro, San Marino, Slovenia, and Vatican City. (1) U.S. dollars per unit of national currency. (2) West Germany before 1991. (3) Euro area member, figures in euros per U.S. dollar.

The North American Free Trade Agreement (NAFTA)

NAFTA, a free trade pact between the U.S., Canada, and Mexico, took effect Jan. 1, 1994. Major provisions (all of which were to be implemented by Jan. 1, 2008) are as follows:

Agriculture—With limited exceptions, tariffs on all agricultural products to be eliminated over 15 years. Domestic price-support systems may continue provided they do not distort trade.

Automobiles—At least 62.5% of an automobile's value must have been produced in North America for it to qualify for duty-free status. Tariffs were phased out over 10 years.

Disputes—Special judges have jurisdiction to resolve disagreements within strict timetables.

Energy—Mexico continues to bar foreign ownership of its oil fields but, as of 2004, U.S. and Canadian companies could bid on contracts offered by Mexican oil and electricity monopolies.

Environment—The trade agreement cannot be used to override national and state environmental, health, or safety laws.

Finance—Limits on ownership of banks, insurance companies, and brokerages eliminated by Jan. 1, 2000.

Immigration—All 3 countries eased restrictions on the movement of business executives and professionals.

Jobs—Barriers to limit Mexican migration to U.S. remain unaffected by NAFTA.

Patent and copyright protection—Mexico strengthened its laws providing protection to intellectual property and agreed to honor pharmaceutical patents for 20 years.

Tariffs—Tariffs on 10,000 customs goods to be eliminated over 15 years. One-half of U.S. exports to Mexico were considered duty-free by 1999.

Textiles—A "rule of origin" provision requires most garments to be made from yarn and fabric that have been produced in North America. Most tariffs phased out by 1999.

Trucking—Trucks were to have free access on cross-border routes and throughout the 3 countries by 1999, but the U.S. continued to impose restrictions on Mexican trucks. In 2001, an arbitration panel ruled that the U.S. restrictions were in violation of NAFTA. Pres. George W. Bush in Nov. 2002 eased restrictions on Mexican trucks entering the U.S.

U.S. Trade With Mexico and Canada, 1996-2006

Source: U.S. Census Bureau and U.S. Bureau of Economic Analysis, U.S. Dept. of Commerce
(in millions of dollars)

	With MEXICO				With CANADA		
Year	Exports	Imports	U.S. trade balance[1]	Year	Exports	Imports	U.S. trade balance[1]
1996	$56,792	$74,297	−$17,506	1996	$134,210	$155,893	−$21,682
1997	71,388	85,938	−14,549	1997	151,767	167,234	−15,467
1998	78,773	94,629	−15,857	1998	156,603	173,256	−16,653
1999	86,909	109,721	−22,812	1999	166,600	198,711	−32,111
2000	111,349	135,926	−24,577	2000	178,941	230,838	−51,897
2001	101,297	131,338	−30,041	2001	163,424	216,268	−52,844
2002	97,470	134,616	−37,146	2002	160,923	209,088	−48,165
2003	97,412	138,060	−40,648	2003	169,924	221,595	−51,671
2004	110,835	155,902	−45,067	2004	189,880	256,360	−66,480
2005	120,365	170,109	−49,744	2005	211,899	290,384	−78,486
2006	133,979	198,253	−64,274	2006	230,656	302,438	−71,782

(1) Figures may not add to totals due to rounding.

The Central American Free Trade Agreement (CAFTA)

CAFTA (also known as CAFTA-DR)—a free trade agreement between the U.S. and Costa Rica, Dominican Republic, El Salvador, Guatemala, Honduras, and Nicaragua—was signed into law by the U.S. Aug. 2, 2005. It entered into force on Mar. 1, 2007, for the Dominican Republic. A referendum to decide ratification passed Oct. 7, 2007, in Costa Rica. El Salvador, Guatemala, Honduras, Nicaragua, and the U.S. had implemented the agreement's conditions by June 2006. Some highlights are as follows:

Agriculture: Tariffs on 50% of U.S. farm goods eliminated; other goods deemed "sensitive"—including corn, milk, and potatoes—to have tariffs reduced to zero over 20 years. Sugar imports to the U.S. allowed to rise to 1.2% of annual U.S. production, up to 1.7% over 15 years.

Automobiles: Tariffs on autos and auto parts to be phased out over 5 years.

Environment and labor: Party nations agree to enforce local labor and environmental protections (no mechanisms in place to monitor enforcement).

Manufacturing: Tariffs eliminated on 80% of U.S. goods.

Market barriers: Barriers for services such as telecommunications, insurance, and financial services eliminated or reduced.

Pharmaceuticals: U.S. pharmaceuticals given 5-year patent protection from their date of introduction to CAFTA markets, regardless of date introduced in U.S.

Textiles and clothing: Elimination of duties on nearly all textiles and clothing instituted, retroactive to Jan. 1, 2004.

Busiest U.S. Ports, 2005

Source: U.S. Army Corps of Engineers, Dept. of the Army, U.S. Dept. of Defense

(figures in tons; ranked by tonnage handled)

Rank	Port	Total	Domestic	Foreign	Imports	Exports
1.	South Louisiana, LA, Port of	212,245,241	117,671,578	94,573,663	43,489,700	51,083,963
2.	Houston, TX	211,665,685	66,615,112	145,050,573	103,189,879	41,860,694
3.	New York, NY and NJ	152,131,674	64,333,034	87,798,640	76,566,928	11,231,712
4.	Huntington, WV-KY-OH	83,888,903	83,888,903	0	0	0
5.	Long Beach, CA	79,857,710	16,556,717	63,300,993	44,492,991	18,808,002
6.	Beaumont, TX	78,886,680	18,784,402	60,102,278	55,505,173	4,597,105
7.	Corpus Christi, TX	77,646,945	23,838,680	53,808,265	45,418,170	8,390,095
8.	New Orleans, LA	65,875,811	32,797,181	33,078,630	21,251,947	11,826,683
9.	Baton Rouge, LA	59,293,661	36,888,876	22,404,785	17,585,231	4,819,554
10.	Texas City, TX	57,839,378	14,371,960	43,467,418	38,005,188	5,462,230
11.	Mobile, AL	57,664,833	26,288,742	31,376,091	21,224,217	10,151,874
12.	Los Angeles, CA	54,894,373	7,968,324	46,926,049	33,994,001	12,932,048
13.	Lake Charles, LA	52,724,998	20,618,903	32,106,095	27,083,364	5,022,731
14.	Tampa, FL	49,713,959	29,064,688	20,109,271	11,838,306	8,270,965
15.	Plaquemines, LA, Port of	47,871,813	31,918,401	15,953,412	8,039,242	7,914,170
16.	Duluth-Superior, MN and WI	44,721,871	30,208,593	14,513,278	561,486	13,951,792
17.	Valdez, AK	44,447,765	44,447,765	0	0	0
18.	Baltimore, MD	44,112,795	15,878,142	28,234,653	21,507,392	6,727,261
19.	Pittsburgh, PA	43,624,268	43,624,268	0	0	0
20.	Philadelphia, PA	39,364,692	13,127,246	26,237,446	25,914,744	322,702
21.	Norfolk Harbor, VA	35,281,008	8,837,249	26,443,759	8,567,591	17,876,168
22.	Freeport, TX	33,601,511	5,156,091	28,445,420	25,415,676	3,029,744
23.	Paulsboro, NJ	32,071,989	13,688,998	18,382,991	18,133,852	249,139
24.	St. Louis, MO and IL	30,346,537	30,346,537	0	0	0
25.	Savannah, GA	30,114,350	1,814,002	28,300,348	18,216,211	10,084,137
26.	Pascagoula, MS	29,323,586	9,429,381	19,894,205	16,542,106	3,352,099
27.	Portland, ME	29,285,943	1,092,817	28,193,126	28,038,852	154,274
28.	Tacoma, WA	28,288,564	7,614,911	20,673,653	7,658,776	13,014,877
29.	Portland, OR	28,126,716	11,770,760	16,355,956	4,410,840	11,945,116
30.	Seattle, WA	28,081,137	7,097,653	20,983,484	10,476,388	10,507,096
31.	Port Arthur, TX	26,384,712	8,331,907	18,052,805	12,992,497	5,060,308
32.	Chicago, IL	25,820,513	23,074,136	2,746,377	1,245,876	1,500,501
33.	Charleston, SC	25,438,931	3,564,377	21,874,554	15,560,101	6,314,453
34.	Port Everglades, FL	24,684,203	10,463,513	14,220,690	11,566,543	2,654,147
35.	Richmond, CA	24,513,396	12,776,943	11,736,453	9,991,591	1,744,862
36.	Boston, MA	22,377,751	7,218,887	15,158,864	14,090,568	1,068,296
37.	Jacksonville, FL	21,777,486	9,268,167	12,509,319	10,962,641	1,546,678
38.	Honolulu, HI	20,393,710	13,712,790	6,680,920	6,220,219	460,701
39.	Marcus Hook, PA	20,254,946	10,607,927	9,647,019	9,570,380	76,639
40.	Detroit, MI	17,447,534	13,061,538	4,385,996	4,120,212	265,784

U.S. Railroad Freight and Miles, 1890-2006

Source: Association of American Railroads

(in billion ton-miles)

Year	Class I[1] freight	All freight	Miles[2]	Year	Class I[1] freight	All freight	Miles[2]	Year	Class I[1] freight	All freight	Miles[2]
1890	NA	76	163,597	1940	373	375	233,670	1990	1,034	1,091	145,979
1900	NA	142	193,346	1950	589	592	223,779	2000	1,466	1,534	144,473
1910	NA	255	240,293	1960	572	575	217,552	2005	1,696	1,765	140,810
1920	410	414	252,845	1970	765	771	205,782	2006	1,772	NA	NA
1930	383	386	249,052	1980	919	932	178,056				

NA = Not available. **Note:** A ton-mile equals one ton of freight transported one statute mile. (1) Largest class of freight railroad companies, determined by annual operating revenue (in 2006, $346.8 mil and above). (2) Aggregate length of operating roadway in U.S., excluding yard tracks, sidings, and parallel tracks.

Merchant Fleets of the World, 2006

Source: Maritime Administration, U.S. Dept. of Transportation
(tonnage in thousands; self-propelled oceangoing vessels of 10,000 gross deadweight tons or more, ranked by total tons, all vessels)

Flag of registry	All vessels No.	All vessels Tons	Tanker No.	Tanker Tons	Dry bulk carrier No.	Dry bulk carrier Tons	Container No.	Container Tons	Other[1] No.	Other[1] Tons
Panama	3,668	221,216	616	59,016	1,851	122,519	588	25,324	613	14,357
Liberia	1,620	100,329	585	52,270	327	19,915	537	22,975	171	5,169
Greece	567	54,966	247	32,294	262	19,501	47	2,755	11	416
Hong Kong	777	51,850	88	11,839	512	33,244	112	5,168	65	1,599
Marshall Islands	738	51,315	341	32,511	185	11,098	148	4,890	64	2,816
Bahamas	772	49,755	235	26,085	310	16,028	70	2,561	157	5,081
Singapore	760	47,411	304	26,949	182	11,931	194	5,456	80	3,076
Malta	759	38,100	187	13,782	441	21,427	49	1,316	82	1,574
Cyprus	675	30,787	98	6,520	349	18,428	148	4,431	80	1,408
China[2]	812	28,862	133	7,143	375	14,926	89	3,374	215	3,418
Norway (NIS)[3]	389	20,189	158	8,869	86	5,409	4	165	141	5,747
Isle of Man	193	14,232	108	9,400	41	3,413	16	566	28	852
India	197	12,613	101	8,443	74	3,394	4	101	18	675
Germany	271	12,368	19	791	4	456	239	10,986	9	135
United States	286	12,269	94	5,494	60	2,314	70	2,922	62	1,538
South Korea	193	11,398	17	1,231	126	8,769	37	1,150	13	247
Italy	271	11,119	124	5,180	48	3,432	27	1,017	72	1,489
Japan	125	9,752	18	3,144	48	3,920	11	519	48	2,169
United Kingdom	226	9,526	43	1,575	24	1,785	112	5,105	47	1,061
Denmark (DIS)[4]	136	9,246	40	2,856	4	322	77	5,724	15	344
All others	3,314	132,577	726	49,156	1,155	48,555	583	15,955	850	18,911
Total	**16,749**	**929,880**	**4,282**	**364,549**	**6,464**	**370,785**	**3,162**	**122,462**	**2,841**	**72,083**
By country[5]										
Greece	2,506	171,099	795	76,865	1,347	82,124	174	7,499	190	4,611
Japan	2,259	150,308	428	44,368	1,150	85,121	225	10,118	456	10,701
China[2]	1,798	87,734	220	18,424	1,016	53,763	214	8,749	348	6,798
Germany	1,622	64,740	148	8,343	187	10,986	1,152	41,984	135	3,427
United States	684	39,632	301	23,931	203	10,157	52	1,736	128	3,808
Singapore	587	38,419	235	22,967	173	9,596	110	3,145	69	2,711
Norway	693	35,941	287	19,391	176	8,174	10	361	220	8,015
United Kingdom	500	35,583	167	18,184	158	11,246	68	2,636	107	3,517
South Korea	428	28,961	63	8,188	222	15,879	75	2,641	68	2,253
Taiwan	482	28,186	42	5,388	216	14,893	201	7,332	23	573
Denmark	385	20,655	102	6,651	41	1,822	191	11,274	51	908
Bermuda	97	19,277	79	17,620	5	153	2	47	11	1,458
India	239	14,740	103	8,795	105	5,007	3	87	28	851
Italy	334	14,551	153	7,035	79	5,023	19	728	83	1,766
Cyprus	259	11,972	86	6,729	90	3,404	50	1,247	33	591
Monaco	171	11,589	42	3,822	71	4,998	43	2,271	15	498
Saudi Arabia	72	11,136	64	10,888	—	—	—	—	8	248
Switzerland	242	10,198	13	352	26	1,195	173	8,080	30	571
Russia	222	10,061	102	7,506	73	1,633	21	419	26	503
Iran	126	9,792	35	6,272	52	2,534	11	409	28	578
All others	3,043	115,305	817	42,830	1,074	43,078	368	11,700	784	17,698
Total	**16,749**	**929,880**	**4,282**	**364,549**	**6,464**	**370,785**	**3,162**	**122,462**	**2,841**	**72,083**

— = Not available. (1) Includes roll-on/roll-off, gas carriers, general cargo carriers, partial container ships, refrigerated cargo ships, barge carriers, and specialized cargo ships. (2) Excludes Hong Kong. (3) NIS = Norwegian International Shipping Registry. (4) DIS = Danish International Shipping Registry. (5) Based on parent company nationality.

U.S. International Transactions, 1970-2006

Source: U.S. Bureau of Economic Analysis, U.S. Dept. of Commerce
(in millions of dollars; revised as of June 2007)

	1970	1975	1980	1985	1990	1995	2000	2006
Exports of goods and services and income receipts	$68,387	$157,936	$344,440	$387,612	$706,975	$1,004,631	$1,421,515	$2,096,165
Merchandise, bal. of payments basis[1]	42,469	107,088	224,250	215,915	387,401	575,204	771,994	1,023,109
Services	14,171	25,497	47,584	73,155	147,832	219,183	298,603	422,594
Income receipts on U.S.-owned assets abroad	11,748	25,351	72,606	98,542	170,570	208,065	348,083	647,582
Imports of goods and services and income payments	−59,901	−132,745	−333,774	−483,769	−759,290	−1,080,124	−1,780,296	−2,818,047
Merchandise, balance of payments basis[1]	−39,866	−98,185	−249,750	−338,088	−498,438	−749,374	−1,226,684	−1,861,380
Services	−14,520	−21,996	−41,491	−72,862	−117,659	−141,397	−223,748	−342,845
Income payments on foreign-owned assets in the U.S.	−5,515	−12,564	−42,532	−72,819	−139,728	−183,090	−322,345	−604,410
Unilateral current transfers, net	−6,156	−7,075	−8,349	−21,998	−26,654	−38,074	−58,645	−89,595
Capital acct. transactions, net	NA	NA	NA	315	−6,579	−927	−1,010	−3,913
U.S.-owned assets abroad, net (decrease/financial outflow [−])	−8,470	−39,703	−85,815	−44,752	−81,234	−352,264	−560,523	−1,055,176
U.S. official reserve assets, net	3,348	−849	−7,003	−3,858	−2,158	−9,742	−290	2,374
U.S. government assets, other than official reserve assets, net	−1,589	−3,474	−5,162	−2,821	2,317	−984	−941	5,346
U.S. private assets, net	−10,229	−35,380	−73,651	−38,074	−81,393	−341,538	−559,292	−1,062,896
Foreign-owned assets in the U.S., net (increase/financial inflow [+])	6,359	17,170	62,612	146,115	141,571	438,562	1,046,896	1,859,597
Stat. discrepancy (sum of above items with sign reversed)	−219	4,417	20,886	16,478	25,211	28,196	−67,937	−17,794
Memorandum: Balance on current account	2,331	18,116	2,317	−118,155	−78,968	−113,567	−417,426	−811,477

NA = Not available. (1) Excludes exports of goods under U.S. military agency sales contracts identified in Census export documents, excludes imports of goods under direct defense expenditures identified in Census import documents, and reflects various other adjustments.

Foreign Direct Investment[1] in the U.S. by Selected Countries and Territories, 1995-2006

Source: U.S. Bureau of Economic Analysis, U.S. Dept. of Commerce
(in millions of dollars)

	1995	2000	2006[4]		1995	2000	2006[4]
ALL COUNTRIES[2]	$560,850	$1,214,254	$1,789,087	Other Western Hemisphere[3]	$17,362	$40,782	$50,504
Canada	48,258	114,599	158,979	Bahamas	−1,780	1,268	664
Europe[3]	357,193	835,137	1,270,570	Bermuda	1,592	18,502	2,757
Austria	1,555	3,174	2,367	Netherlands Antilles	8,481	3,940	6,179
Belgium	3,676	14,585	12,590	UK islands, Caribbean	8,417	15,353	24,572
Denmark	2,990	4,428	7,209	Africa[3]	1,164	2,756	2,244
Finland	2,752	9,107	7,289	South Africa	−3	1,218	652
France	38,480	131,484	158,830	Middle East[3]	6,008	6,189	17,639
Germany	49,269	124,839	202,581	Israel	1,995	2,690	NA
Ireland	7,418	23,528	28,551	Kuwait	2,527	908	878
Italy	2,750	5,994	11,883	Lebanon	−9	1	−7
Liechtenstein	135	202	NA	Saudi Arabia	1,310	NA	NA
Luxembourg	5,957	53,794	130,925	United Arab Emirates	98	64	NA
Netherlands	65,806	146,493	189,293	Asia and Pacific[3]	122,986	201,110	259,810
Norway	2,089	2,241	7,835	Australia	7,833	20,701	25,727
Spain	2,452	5,459	14,942	China	NA	NA	554
Sweden	9,581	22,427	22,287	Hong Kong	1,557	1,544	3,524
Switzerland	35,593	69,240	140,259	India	NA	NA	2,002
United Kingdom	126,177	213,820	303,232	Japan	107,933	163,577	210,996
South and Central America[3]	7,878	13,682	29,341	Korea, South	626	3,287	8,609
Brazil	751	886	2,122	Singapore	1,548	7,751	2,412
Mexico	1,980	7,832	6,075	Taiwan	2,139	3,131	4,199
Panama	4,721	3,726	12,994	European Union[5]	318,995	760,017	1,113,507
Venezuela	−259	802	7,246	OPEC[6]	3,740	4,363	12,391

NA = Not available. (1) In all industries. Book value of foreign direct investors' equity in, and net outstanding loans to, their U.S. affiliates. A U.S. affiliate is a U.S. business enterprise in which a single foreign direct investor owns at least 10% of the voting securities, or the equivalent. (2) Total includes sources not reflected in regional subtotals. (3) Total includes countries or territories not shown. (4) Preliminary. (5) European Union members in 2006: Austria, Belgium, Cyprus, Czech Republic, Denmark, Estonia, Finland, France, Germany, Greece, Hungary, Ireland, Italy, Latvia, Lithuania, Luxembourg, Malta, Netherlands, Poland, Portugal, Slovakia, Slovenia, Spain, Sweden, and the United Kingdom. (6) Organization of Petroleum Exporting Countries: Algeria, Indonesia, Iran, Iraq, Kuwait, Libya, Nigeria, Qatar, Saudi Arabia, United Arab Emirates, and Venezuela.

U.S. Direct Investment Abroad in Selected Countries and Territories[1], 1995-2006

Source: U.S. Bureau of Economic Analysis, U.S. Dept. of Commerce
(in millions of dollars)

	1995	2000	2006[6]		1995	2000	2006[6]
ALL COUNTRIES[2]	$717,554	$1,293,431	$2,384,004	Central America[3]	$33,688	$70,474	$93,995
Canada	85,441	128,814	246,451	Costa Rica	870	1,655	1,573
Europe[3]	360,994	679,457	1,250,508	Honduras	191	257	517
Austria	2,777	2,686	17,405	Mexico	15,980	37,332	84,699
Belgium	17,969	19,527	52,054	Panama	16,216	29,316	5,728
Czech Republic	NA	NA	3,090	Other Western Hemisphere[3]	47,650	97,377	230,143
Denmark	2,123	5,363	5,753	Bahamas	1,806	2,317	NA
Finland	825	1,110	2,592	Barbados	755	1,170	4,756
France	32,950	38,752	65,933	Bermuda	29,980	56,594	108,462
Germany	44,226	50,963	99,253	Dominican Republic	394	813	896
Greece	424	637	2,073	UK islands, Caribbean	8,941	28,514	80,604
Hungary	NA	NA	4,014	Africa[3]	6,383	14,417	25,556
Ireland	8,400	33,816	83,615	Egypt	1,388	2,344	5,911
Italy	17,587	22,392	28,936	Nigeria	706	1,237	339
Luxembourg	5,857	25,571	82,588	South Africa	1,275	3,245	3,818
Netherlands	39,344	117,557	215,715	Middle East[3]	7,669	11,087	26,487
Norway	5,133	5,833	10,280	Israel	1,662	3,386	9,964
Poland	NA	NA	7,190	Saudi Arabia	3,245	4,225	4,346
Portugal	1,755	1,888	3,033	United Arab Emirates	660	737	4,547
Russia	NA	NA	10,064	Asia and Pacific[3]	125,834	205,317	431,718
Spain	10,770	19,846	49,413	Australia	25,003	35,364	122,587
Sweden	7,339	22,676	35,938	China	2,127	9,861	22,228
Switzerland	33,532	55,854	90,085	Hong Kong	14,206	26,621	38,118
Turkey	948	1,356	2,088	India	838	1,431	8,852
United Kingdom	122,767	241,663	364,084	Indonesia	6,607	8,514	10,585
European Union[4]	315,112	604,445	1,123,284	Japan	38,406	59,441	91,769
Eastern Europe[5]	4,739	11,149	NA	Korea, South	5,169	8,914	22,280
South America[3]	46,914	84,012	79,146	Malaysia	4,200	7,400	12,450
Argentina	7,496	15,646	13,086	New Zealand	4,845	3,854	5,721
Brazil	23,706	39,033	32,601	Philippines	2,531	2,735	7,034
Chile	5,878	9,451	10,243	Singapore	12,689	25,634	60,417
Colombia	3,352	4,606	4,897	Taiwan	4,210	7,821	16,126
Ecuador	833	763	461	Thailand	4,315	6,635	8,217
Peru	1,279	3,485	4,979	OPEC[7]	16,036	28,736	43,030
Venezuela	3,220	9,530	11,556				

NA = Not available. (1) In all industries. Book value of U.S. direct investors' equity in, and net outstanding loans to, their foreign affiliates. A foreign affiliate is a foreign business enterprise in which a single U.S. investor owns at least 10% of the voting securities, or the equivalent. (2) Total includes sources not reflected in regional subtotals. (3) Total includes countries or territories not shown. (4) European Union members in 2006: Austria, Belgium, Cyprus, Czech Republic, Denmark, Estonia, Finland, France, Germany, Greece, Hungary, Ireland, Italy, Latvia, Lithuania, Luxembourg, Malta, Netherlands, Poland, Portugal, Slovakia, Slovenia, Spain, Sweden, and the United Kingdom. (5) Eastern Europe: Albania, Armenia, Azerbaijan, Belarus, Bulgaria, Czech Republic, Estonia, Georgia, Hungary, Kazakhstan, Kyrgyzstan, Latvia, Lithuania, Moldova, Poland, Romania, Russia, Slovakia, Tajikistan, Turkmenistan, Ukraine, and Uzbekistan. (6) Preliminary. (7) Organization of Petroleum Exporting Countries: Algeria, Indonesia, Iran, Iraq, Kuwait, Libya, Nigeria, Qatar, Saudi Arabia, United Arab Emirates, and Venezuela.

TRANSPORTATION AND TRAVEL

Leading Motor Vehicle Producing Nations, 2006

Source: Automotive News Data Center and R.L. Polk Marketing Systems GmbH

(ranked by total production)

Country	Total	Cars	Trucks	Country	Total	Cars	Trucks
1. Japan	11,484,233	9,756,515	1,727,718	17. Turkey	991,621	545,682	445,939
2. United States	11,351,289	4,372,196	6,979,093	18. Belgium	910,614	881,930	28,684
3. China	7,271,814	4,315,290	2,956,524	19. Czech Republic.	851,504	846,128	5,376
4. Germany	5,818,171	5,398,508	419,663	20. Poland	711,648	607,579	104,069
5. South Korea	3,839,589	3,489,136	350,453	21. Sweden	701,066	555,945	145,121
6. France	3,164,368	2,722,168	442,200	22. South Africa	599,462	339,992	259,470
7. Spain	2,776,186	2,078,639	697,547	23. Malaysia	509,433	377,952	131,481
8. Brazil	2,597,382	2,092,029	505,353	24. Argentina	431,822	263,120	168,702
9. Canada	2,544,767	1,427,582	1,117,185	25. Indonesia	410,943	51,520	359,423
10. Mexico	2,043,602	1,371,323	672,279	26. Australia	344,435	274,225	70,210
11. India	1,876,188	1,411,717	464,471	27. Romania	315,018	303,084	11,934
12. United Kingdom	1,649,841	1,442,085	207,756	28. Taiwan	305,661	211,306	94,355
13. Russia	1,494,509	1,173,624	320,885	29. Slovakia	266,423	266,369	54
14. Italy	1,210,934	892,502	318,432	30. Ukraine	258,308	252,690	5,618
15. Thailand	1,184,339	297,539	886,800	31. Austria	252,945	226,558	26,387
16. Iran	1,032,880	880,880	152,000	World total[1]	70,927,676	50,353,978	20,573,698

(1) World total includes countries or territories not shown.

World Motor Vehicle Production, 1950-2006

Source: For 1950-97, American Automobile Manufacturers Assn.;
for 1998 and on, Automotive News Data Center and R.L. Polk Marketing Systems GmbH

(in thousands, unless otherwise noted)

Year	United States	Canada	Western Europe[1]	Japan	Other	World total	U.S. % of world total
1950	8,006	388	1,991	32	160	10,577	75.7
1960	7,905	398	6,837	482	866	16,488	47.9
1970	8,284	1,160	13,049	5,289	1,637	29,419	28.2
1980	8,010	1,324	15,496	11,043	2,692	38,565	20.8
1985	11,653	1,933	16,113	12,271	2,939	44,909	25.9
1990	9,783	1,928	18,866	13,487	4,496	48,554	20.1
1991	8,811	1,888	17,804	13,245	5,180	46,928	18.8
1992	9,729	1,961	17,628	12,499	6,269	48,088	20.2
1993	10,898	2,246	15,208	11,228	7,205	46,785	23.3
1994	12,263	2,321	16,195	10,554	8,167	49,500	24.8
1995	11,985	2,408	17,045	10,196	8,349	49,983	24.0
1996	11,799	2,397	17,550	10,346	9,241	51,332	23.0
1997	12,119	2,571	17,773	10,975	10,024	53,463	22.7
1998	12,047	2,568	16,332	10,050	12,844	53,841	22.4
1999	13,107	3,042	17,603	9,985	14,050	57,787	22.7
2000	12,832	2,952	17,678	10,145	16,098	59,704	21.5
2001	11,518	2,535	17,825	9,777	16,170	57,705	19.7
2002	12,328	2,624	17,419	10,240	16,975	59,587	20.7
2003	12,147	2,568	16,943	10,286	20,619	61,562	19.7
2004	12,021	2,698	16,982	10,512	22,175	64,388	18.7
2005	12,018	2,665	20,871	10,800	21,420	67,724	17.7
2006	11,351	2,545	22,396	11,484	23,151	70,928	16.0

Note: Data for 1998 and on not fully comparable with earlier years because derived from different source. (1) Data for 2005 and on includes all European countries.

New and Used Passenger Cars Imported Into the U.S., by Country of Origin[1], 1970-2006

Source: Foreign Trade Division, U.S. Census Bureau

(in number of units)

Year	Japan	Germany[2]	Italy	United Kingdom	Sweden	France	South Korea	Mexico	Canada	Total[3]
1970	381,338	674,945	42,523	76,257	57,844	37,114	NA	NA	692,783	2,013,420
1975	695,573	370,012	102,344	67,106	51,993	15,647	NA	0	733,766	2,074,653
1980	1,991,502	338,711	46,899	32,517	61,496	47,386	NA	1	594,770	3,116,448
1985	2,527,467	473,110	8,689	24,474	142,640	42,882	NA	13,647	1,144,805	4,397,679
1986	2,618,711	451,699	11,829	27,506	148,700	10,869	169,309	41,983	1,162,226	4,691,297
1987	2,417,500	377,542	8,648	50,059	138,565	26,707	399,856	126,266	926,927	4,589,010
1988	2,123,051	264,249	6,053	31,636	108,006	15,990	455,741	148,065	1,191,357	4,450,213
1989	2,051,525	216,881	9,319	29,378	101,571	4,885	270,609	133,049	1,151,122	4,042,728
1990	1,867,794	245,286	11,045	27,271	93,084	1,976	201,475	215,986	1,220,221	3,944,602
1991	1,762,347	171,097	2,886	14,862	62,905	1,727	186,740	249,498	1,109,248	3,612,665
1992	1,598,919	205,248	1,791	10,997	76,832	65	130,110	266,111	1,119,223	3,447,200
1993	1,501,953	180,383	1,178	20,029	58,742	23	122,943	299,634	1,371,856	3,604,361
1994	1,488,159	178,774	1,010	28,217	63,867	58	213,962	360,367	1,525,746	3,909,019
1995	1,114,360	204,932	1,031	42,450	82,593	14	131,718	462,800	1,552,691	3,624,428
1996	1,190,896	234,909	1,365	44,373	86,619	27	225,623	550,867	1,690,733	4,069,113
1997	1,387,812	300,489	1,912	43,691	79,780	67	222,568	544,075	1,731,209	4,378,295
1998	1,456,081	373,330	2,104	49,891	84,543	56	211,650	584,795	1,837,615	4,673,418
1999	1,707,277	461,061	1,697	68,394	83,399	186	372,965	639,878	2,170,427	5,639,616
2000	1,839,093	488,323	3,125	81,196	86,707	134	568,121	934,000	2,138,811	6,324,284
2001	1,790,346	494,131	2,580	82,487	92,439	92	633,769	861,853	1,855,789	6,065,138
2002	2,046,902	574,455	3,504	157,633	87,709	150	627,881	845,181	1,882,660	6,477,659
2003	1,770,355	561,482	2,943	207,158	119,773	298	692,863	680,214	1,811,892	6,127,485
2004	1,727,065	547,008	3,373	185,621	98,131	2,417	860,424	652,509	2,035,345	6,521,248
2005	1,832,534	547,191	5,377	184,716	93,736	412	730,500	693,149	1,967,985	6,564,844
2006	2,347,532	532,022	5,469	148,014	81,008	567	697,061	947,824	1,963,922	7,380,077

(1) Excludes cars assembled in U.S. foreign trade zones. (2) Figures prior to 1991 are for West Germany. (3) Includes countries not shown.

Passenger Car Production, U.S. Plants, 2005-06
Source: Ward's AutoInfoBank

	2005	2006		2005	2006
TOTAL CARS	4,321,272	4,366,996	Corvette	37,949	42,364
Ford Mustang	198,416	178,365	Malibu	212,049	190,482
Mazda6	74,216	71,495	Chevrolet total	572,058	465,759
AUTOALLIANCE TOTAL[1]	272,632	249,860	Bonneville	5,119	—
BMW Z4	19,830	38,756	G5	—	22,253
BMW TOTAL	19,830	38,756	G6	157,414	186,899
Neon	605	—	Grand Am	35,089	—
Sebring Convertible	34,439	17,551	Pursuit	21,448	23,010
Sebring Sedan	62,255	84,287	Solstice	9,382	23,679
Chrysler total	97,299	101,838	Pontiac total	228,452	255,841
Avenger	—	284	Aura	—	39,712
Caliber	—	168,088	Ion	110,073	123,776
Neon	125,791	—	Saturn L	5	—
Stratus Sedan	100,517	59,858	Sky	—	10,503
Viper	2,025	901	Saturn total	110,078	173,991
Dodge total	232,265	229,131	Opel	—	261
CHRYSLER GROUP TOTAL	325,632	330,969	GM TOTAL	1,153,358	1,156,809
Five Hundred	118,740	83,808	Acura TL	88,545	79,513
Focus	166,991	220,831	Honda Accord	358,794	350,393
Ford GT	1,898	1,640	Honda Civic	133,724	176,652
Taurus	180,494	174,124	HONDA TOTAL	581,063	606,558
Thunderbird	4,868	—	Sonata	91,218	175,155
Ford total	472,991	480,403	HYUNDAI TOTAL	91,218	175,155
LS	15,675	3,080	Chrysler Sebring Coupe	348	—
Town Car	50,284	37,099	Dodge Stratus Coupe	1,427	—
Lincoln total	65,959	40,179	Mitsubishi Eclipse	28,220	39,383
Montego	32,622	19,831	Mitsubishi Galant	34,939	35,429
Sable	13,065	—	MITSUBISHI TOTAL	64,934	74,812
Mercury total	45,687	19,831	Altima	306,479	269,440
FORD TOTAL	584,637	540,413	Maxima	76,773	78,204
LeSabre	51,673	—	NISSAN TOTAL	383,252	347,644
Lucerne	21,895	115,452	Pontiac Vibe	62,319	58,334
Buick total	73,568	115,452	Toyota Corolla	186,119	199,534
CTS	65,204	61,022	NUMMI TOTAL[2]	248,438	257,868
Deville	27,554	—	Legacy	87,151	84,267
DTS	36,360	56,682	SUBARU TOTAL	87,151	84,267
STS	36,559	24,747	Avalon	108,637	100,014
XLR	3,525	3,054	Camry	356,497	362,793
Cadillac total	169,202	145,505	Solara	43,993	41,078
Classic	42,349	—	TOYOTA TOTAL	509,127	503,885
Cobalt	279,711	232,913			

— = No production. (1) Company is a joint venture between Ford and Mazda. (2) NUMMI (New United Motor Manufacturing, Inc.) is a joint venture between GM and Toyota.

Domestic and Imported Retail Cars Sales in the U.S., 1980-2006
Source: Ward's AutoInfoBank

		Imports					Import (%)		
Year	Domestic[1]	Japan	Germany	Other countries	Total	Total U.S. sales	Total	Japan	Germany
1980	6,581,307	1,905,968	305,219	186,700	2,397,887	8,979,194	26.7	21.2	3.3
1981	6,208,760	1,858,896	282,881	185,502	2,327,279	8,536,039	27.3	21.8	3.3
1982	5,758,586	1,801,969	247,080	174,508	2,223,557	7,982,143	27.9	22.6	3.0
1983	6,795,295	1,915,621	279,748	191,403	2,386,772	9,182,067	26.0	20.9	3.0
1984	7,951,523	1,906,206	344,416	188,220	2,438,842	10,390,365	23.5	18.3	3.8
1985	8,204,542	2,217,837	423,983	195,925	2,837,745	11,042,287	25.7	20.1	3.8
1986	8,214,897	2,382,614	443,721	418,286	3,244,621	11,459,518	28.3	20.8	3.9
1987	7,080,858	2,190,405	347,881	657,465	3,195,751	10,276,609	31.1	21.3	3.4
1988	7,526,038	2,022,602	280,099	700,991	3,003,692	10,529,730	28.5	19.2	2.7
1989	7,072,902	1,897,143	248,561	553,660	2,699,364	9,772,266	27.6	19.4	2.5
1990	6,896,888	1,719,384	265,116	418,823	2,403,323	9,300,211	25.8	18.5	2.9
1991	6,136,757	1,500,309	192,776	344,814	2,037,899	8,174,656	24.9	18.4	2.4
1992	6,276,557	1,451,766	200,851	283,938	1,936,555	8,213,112	23.6	17.7	2.4
1993	6,741,667	1,328,445	186,177	261,570	1,776,192	8,517,859	20.9	15.6	2.2
1994	7,255,303	1,239,450	192,275	303,489	1,735,214	8,990,517	19.3	13.8	2.1
1995	7,128,707	981,506	207,482	317,269	1,506,257	8,634,964	17.4	11.4	2.4
1996	7,253,582	726,940	237,984	308,247	1,273,171	8,526,753	14.9	8.5	2.8
1997	6,916,769	726,104	297,028	332,173	1,355,305	8,272,074	16.4	8.8	3.6
1998	6,761,940	691,162	366,724	321,895	1,379,781	8,141,721	16.9	8.5	4.5
1999	6,979,357	757,568	466,870	494,489	1,718,927	8,698,284	19.8	8.7	5.4
2000	6,830,505	862,780	516,614	636,726	2,016,120	8,846,625	22.8	9.8	5.8
2001	6,324,996	836,685	522,659	738,285	2,097,629	8,422,625	24.9	9.9	6.2
2002	5,877,645	923,182	546,654	755,748	2,225,584	8,103,229	27.5	11.4	6.7
2003	5,527,430	817,038	543,823	722,190	2,083,051	7,610,481	27.4	10.7	7.1
2004	5,356,873	798,222	541,940	808,897	2,149,059	7,505,932	28.6	10.6	7.2
2005	5,480,533	922,934	534,286	729,313	2,186,533	7,667,066	28.5	12.0	7.0
2006	5,435,995	1,154,455	560,726	629,583	2,344,764	7,780,759	30.1	14.8	7.2

(1) Includes cars manufactured in Canada and Mexico.

U.S. Car Sales by Vehicle Size and Type, 1985-2006

Source: Ward's AutoInfoBank

(percent of total U.S. sales)

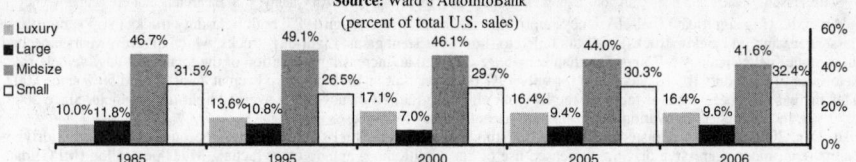

- Luxury
- Large
- Midsize
- Small

Top-Selling Passenger Cars in the U.S. by Calendar Year, 2003-06

Source: Ward's Automotive Group
(ranked by number of vehicles sold)

2006

1. Toyota Camry	448,445	8. Ford Focus	177,006
2. Toyota Corolla/Matrix	387,388	9. Ford Taurus	174,803
3. Honda Accord	354,441	10. Ford Mustang	166,530
4. Honda Civic	316,638	11. Chevrolet Malibu	163,853
5. Chevrolet Impala	289,868	12. Pontiac G6	157,644
6. Nissan Altima	232,457	13. Hyundai Sonata	149,513
7. Chevrolet Cobalt	211,449	14. Chrysler 300 Series	143,647

15. Ford Fusion	142,502
16. BMW 3 Series	120,180
17. Nissan Sentra	117,922
18. Dodge Charger	114,201
19. Pontiac Grand Prix	108,634
20. Toyota Prius	106,971

2005

1. Toyota Camry	431,703
2. Honda Accord	369,293
3. Toyota Corolla/Matrix	341,290
4. Honda Civic	308,415
5. Nissan Altima	255,371
6. Chevrolet Impala	246,481
7. Chevrolet Cobalt	212,667
8. Chevrolet Malibu	203,503
9. Ford Taurus	196,919
10. Ford Focus	184,825

2004

1. Toyota Camry	426,990
2. Honda Accord	386,770
3. Toyota Corolla/Matrix	333,161
4. Honda Civic	309,196
5. Chevrolet Impala	290,259
6. Chevrolet Malibu	268,017
7. Ford Taurus	248,148
8. Nissan Altima	235,889
9. Ford Focus	208,339
10. Chevrolet Cavalier	195,275

2003

1. Toyota Camry	413,296
2. Honda Accord	397,750
3. Toyota Corolla/Matrix	325,477
4. Ford Taurus	300,496
5. Honda Civic	299,672
6. Chevrolet Impala	267,882
7. Chevrolet Cavalier	256,550
8. Ford Focus	229,353
9. Nissan Altima	201,240
10. Chevrolet Malibu	173,263

Top-Selling Light Trucks in the U.S. by Calendar Year, 2004-06

2006

1. Ford F-Series	744,996
2. Chevrolet Silverado	636,069
3. Dodge Ram Pickup	364,177
4. Dodge Caravan	211,140
5. GMC Sierra	210,736
6. Ford Econoline	180,457
7. Ford Explorer	179,229
8. Toyota Tacoma	178,351
9. Honda Odyssey	177,919
10. Chevrolet TrailBlazer	174,797

2005

1. Ford F Series	854,878
2. Chevrolet Silverado	705,980
3. Dodge Ram Pickup	400,543
4. Chevrolet TrailBlazer	244,150
5. Ford Explorer	239,788
6. GMC Sierra	229,488
7. Dodge Caravan	226,771
8. Jeep Grand Cherokee	213,584
9. Chrysler Town & Country	180,759
10. Ford Econoline	179,543

2004

1. Ford F Series	891,482
2. Chevrolet Silverado	680,663
3. Dodge Ram Pickup	426,289
4. Ford Explorer	339,333
5. Chevrolet TrailBlazer	283,484
6. Dodge Caravan	242,307
7. GMC Sierra	213,736
8. Chevrolet Tahoe	186,161
9. Ford Escape	183,430
10. Jeep Grand Cherokee	182,313

Number of Sport Utility Vehicles Sold in the U.S., 1988-2006

Source: Ward's AutoInfoBank

In 1988, 960,852 sport utility vehicles (SUVs) were sold in the U.S. (The term SUV here includes lighter SUV models, known as crossover or cross utility vehicles, which are generally smaller and get better gas mileage.) That number accounted for almost 19% of all light truck sales and just over 6% of all light vehicles (cars, SUVs, minivans, vans, pickup trucks, and trucks under 14,000 lbs) sold that year. The percentage of SUVs among all light vehicles sold increased to 28% in 2004. But in 2006, the number of SUVs sold decreased 3.9% from its high in 2004, to 4,543,701, or 27.5% of all light vehicle sales.

Exluding cross utility vehicles, SUV sales declined 26.3%, from 2,974,466 in 2002 to 2,133,612 in 2006. But crossover vehicle sales dramatically increased to 2,410,089 in 2006, up 94.7% from 1,237,620 in 2002.

U.S. Sport Utility and Cross Utility Vehicle Sales

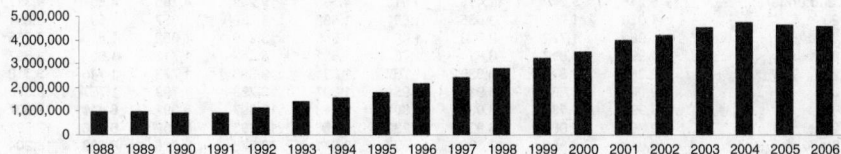

Most Popular Colors, by Type of Vehicle, 2006 Model Year

Source: Ward's Automotive Group; Du Pont Automotive Products

Luxury cars		Full size/intermediate cars		Compact/sports cars		Light trucks	
Color	Percent	Color	Percent	Color	Percent	Color	Percent
Black	22	Silver	25	Silver	18	White	25
Silver	16	Blue	13	Gray	15	Silver	16
White pearl	14	Gray	12	Black	15	Gray	13
Gray	12	White/white pearl	12	Red	15	Black	13
White	11	Black	10	Blue	13	Red	11
Blue	7	Red	10	White	10	Blue	10
Red	7	Light brown	10	Light brown	6	Light brown	6
Yellow/gold	6	Green	4	Yellow/gold	4	Green	4
Green	3	Yellow/gold	4	Green	2	Yellow/gold	1
Other	3	Other	1	Other	2	Other	2

U.S. Light-Duty Vehicle Fuel Efficiency, 1975-2007

Source: Natl. Vehicle and Fuel Emissions Laboratory, Office of Transportation and Air Quality, U.S. Environmental Protection Agency

After showing significant fuel-efficiency improvements from 1974 through 1987, both light-duty trucks (SUVs, minivans, passenger vans, and pickup trucks) and cars failed to show consistent gains. Light-duty trucks, which in recent years have had an average fuel efficiency 5-7 mpg less than cars, have captured an increasing proportion of the total light-duty vehicle market. Sales of light-duty trucks accounted for only 19% of the market in 1975 but have been at an estimated 50% since 2002. This increase has been a major factor in the leveling off in the fuel efficiency of the average light-duty vehicle. Since 2005, however, technological innovations have allowed fuel-efficiency to increase.

In Dec. 2006, the EPA adjusted its method of estimating real-world fuel economy values because of changes in driving habits (e.g., more aggressive driving, increased use of air conditioning) among other factors. Miles-per-gallon (MPG) data from 1986 on have been revised under this method.

Year[1]	Cars (MPG[2])	Light-duty trucks (MPG[2])	All light-duty vehicles (MPG[2])	Year[1]	Cars (MPG[2])	Light-duty trucks (MPG[2])	All light-duty vehicles (MPG[2])
1975....	13.5	11.6	13.1	2000 ...	22.9	16.9	19.8
1980....	20.0	15.8	19.2	2001 ...	23.0	16.7	19.6
1985....	23.0	17.5	21.3	2002 ...	23.1	16.7	19.4
1990....	23.3	17.4	21.2	2003 ...	23.2	16.9	19.6
1995....	23.4	17.0	20.5	2004 ...	23.1	16.7	19.3
1996....	23.3	17.2	20.4	2005 ...	23.5	17.2	19.9
1997....	23.4	17.0	20.1	2006 ...	23.3	17.6	20.2
1998....	23.4	17.1	20.1	2007 ...	23.4	17.7	20.2
1999....	23.0	16.7	19.7				

(1) Because of changes in methodology, MPG figures before 1986 are not entirely comparable with later values. (2) Adjusted composite (city and highway fuel efficiency combined in a 55%/45% ratio) values reflecting real-world use.

Cars Registered in the U.S., 1900-2005[1]

Source: Federal Highway Administration, U.S. Dept. of Transportation

(includes automobiles for public and private use)

Year	Cars reg.	Year	Cars reg.	Year	Cars reg.	Year	Cars reg.	Year	Cars reg.
1900....	8,000	1935 ...	22,567,827	1970 ...	89,243,557	1993....	127,327,189	2000....	133,621,420
1905....	77,400	1940 ...	27,465,826	1975 ...	106,705,934	1994....	127,883,469	2001....	137,633,467
1910....	458,377	1945 ...	25,796,985	1980 ...	121,600,843	1995....	128,386,775	2002....	135,920,677
1915....	2,332,426	1950 ...	40,339,077	1985 ...	127,885,193	1996....	129,728,311	2003....	135,669,897
1920....	8,131,522	1955 ...	52,144,739	1990 ...	133,700,497	1997....	129,748,704	2004....	136,430,651
1925....	17,481,001	1960 ...	61,671,390	1991 ...	128,299,601	1998....	131,838,538	2005....	136,568,083
1930....	23,034,753	1965 ...	75,257,588	1992 ...	126,581,148	1999....	132,432,044		

(1) There were no publicly owned vehicles before 1925; statistics also exclude military vehicles for all years. Alaska and Hawaii data included since 1960.

Licensed Drivers, by Age, 1980-2005

Source: Federal Highway Administration, U.S. Dept. of Transportation

(in thousands)

AGE	1980 Male	1980 Female	1980 Total[1]	1990 Male	1990 Female	1990 Total[1]	2005 Male	2005 Female	2005 Total[1]
Under 16	52	41	93	23	20	43	12	12	24
16.................	1,001	822	1,823	769	674	1,443	620	603	1,224
17.................	1,530	1,260	2,790	1,136	996	2,132	1,118	1,077	2,195
18.................	1,763	1,484	3,247	1,378	1,217	2,595	1,433	1,352	2,785
19.................	1,900	1,643	3,542	1,608	1,429	3,037	1,596	1,513	3,109
19 and under..........	6,246	5,249	11,496	4,913	4,336	9,249	4,780	4,557	9,337
20.................	1,930	1,706	3,636	1,691	1,538	3,229	1,657	1,594	3,251
21.................	1,961	1,772	3,733	1,694	1,555	3,249	1,652	1,613	3,265
22.................	1,998	1,813	3,811	1,701	1,561	3,262	1,717	1,681	3,397
23.................	2,062	1,876	3,938	1,767	1,631	3,398	1,773	1,745	3,518
24.................	2,047	1,868	3,915	1,951	1,807	3,758	1,799	1,777	3,576
20-24	9,998	9,034	19,032	8,804	8,093	16,897	8,597	8,410	17,007
25-29	9,865	9,060	18,925	10,239	9,656	19,895	8,852	8,676	17,527
30-34	9,010	8,359	17,369	10,507	10,071	20,578	9,216	8,988	18,204
35-39	7,113	6,583	13,696	9,684	9,371	19,055	9,820	9,579	19,399
40-44	5,828	5,306	11,134	8,610	8,295	16,905	10,586	10,484	21,071
45-49	5,311	4,765	10,076	6,642	6,378	13,020	10,478	10,493	20,971
50-54	5,351	4,739	10,090	5,376	5,108	10,484	9,420	9,491	18,911
55-59	5,198	4,572	9,770	4,855	4,583	9,438	8,231	8,286	16,516
60-64	4,439	3,793	8,232	4,738	4,497	9,235	6,109	6,155	12,264
65-69	3,631	2,949	6,580	4,266	4,109	8,375	4,576	4,646	9,222
70 and over	5,195	3,699	8,894	7,159	6,726	13,885	9,587	10,532	20,120
70-74	NA	NA	NA	NA	NA	NA	3,618	3,754	7,372
75-79	NA	NA	NA	NA	NA	NA	2,893	3,163	6,056
80-84	NA	NA	NA	NA	NA	NA	1,910	2,212	4,122
85 and over	NA	NA	NA	NA	NA	NA	1,166	1,403	2,570
TOTAL	77,187	68,108	145,295	85,792	81,223	167,015	100,252	100,297	200,549

NA = Not available. (1) Figures may not add to totals due to rounding.

Selected Motor Vehicle Statistics

Source: Federal Highway Admin.; U.S. Dept. of Transportation; Insurance Inst. for Highway Safety; American Petroleum Inst.

Driver's license age requirements, state gas tax, and safety belt laws (incl. laws passed, but not in effect) as of 2007; other figures for 2005.

STATE	Driver's license age requirements Regular[1]	Learner's permit	State gas tax (cents/gal.)	Safety belt use law[8]	Licensed drivers per 1,000 resident pop.	Licensed drivers per motor vehicle	Regist. motor vehicles per 1,000 pop.	Gals. of fuel used per reg. vehicle	Annual miles driven per gal.	Annual miles driven per reg. vehicle	Annual miles driven per lic. driver
Alabama	17	15	16	P	798	0.81	997	758	17.32	13,128	16,402
Alaska	16y, 6m	14	8	P	733	0.73	1,014	788	9.49	7,484	10,348
Arizona	16y, 6m[2]	15y, 6m[2]	18	S	664	1.00	669	929	16.21	15,057	15,165
Arkansas	16	14	21.5	S	728	1.06	698	1,072	15.38	16,484	15,793
California	17[3]	15y, 6m	18	P	634	0.72	899	585	17.31	10,135	14,381
Colorado	17	15	22	S	716	1.89	388	1,495	17.74	26,529	14,354
Connecticut	18[3]	16	25[7]	P	781	0.91	871	631	16.42	10,356	11,559
Delaware	17[3]	16	23	P	724	0.84	873	705	18.32	12,909	15,577
Dist. of Col.	18[4]	16	20	P	600	1.46	431	714	21.92	15,648	11,239
Florida	18	15	4[7]	S	752	0.87	882	664	19.34	12,843	15,069
Georgia	18	15	7.5	S	655	0.75	889	845	16.65	14,078	19,111
Hawaii	17[3]	15y, 6m	16	P	671	0.92	743	536	19.87	10,641	11,777
Idaho	16[3]	14y, 6m	25	S	685	0.72	961	636	17.01	10,819	15,193
Illinois	17[3]	15	19	P	617	0.84	741	710	16.04	11,388	13,684
Indiana	18	15	18	P	677	0.87	790	919	15.76	14,489	16,909
Iowa	17[3]	14	20.7	P	685	0.61	1,145	656	13.93	9,142	15,275
Kansas	16	14	24	S(a)	719	0.84	863	680	18.40	12,508	15,004
Kentucky	17[3]	16	17.1[7]	P	685	0.85	821	911	15.20	13,848	16,592
Louisiana	17[3]	15	20	P	682	0.82	844	803	14.67	11,777	14,587
Maine	16y, 6m	15	27.6	P	760	0.95	813	848	16.37	13,885	14,866
Maryland	17y, 9m	15y, 9m	23.5	P	662	0.87	772	756	17.23	13,031	15,182
Massachusetts	18[3]	16	21	S	721	0.86	847	603	16.96	10,232	12,023
Michigan	17[3]	14y, 9m	19	P	702	0.88	815	721	17.49	12,616	14,644
Minnesota	16[3]	15	20	S	601	0.67	905	726	16.87	12,246	18,453
Mississippi	16	15	18	P	673	1.01	677	1,148	18.58	21,326	21,464
Missouri	17y, 11m	15	17	S(a)	713	0.91	791	932	16.07	14,981	16,626
Montana	16	14y, 6m	27	S	765	0.73	1,078	734	15.03	11,028	15,550
Nebraska	17	15	27[7]	S	751	0.79	968	736	15.40	11,329	14,608
Nevada	18[3]	15y, 6m	23	S	661	1.21	559	1,133	13.59	15,397	13,015
New Hampshire	17y, 1m	15y, 6m	18	None	762	0.86	897	699	16.36	11,435	13,453
New Jersey	18	16	10.5	S	673	0.96	718	839	14.06	11,789	12,574
New Mexico	16y, 6m[3]	15	17	P	677	0.87	803	934	16.57	15,478	18,369
New York	18[3,5]	16	8	P	575	0.95	616	606	19.13	11,593	12,441
North Carolina	16y, 6m[3]	15	29.7[7]	P(b)	717	1.03	708	900	18.30	16,471	16,261
North Dakota	16	14	23	S	733	0.69	1,092	776	14.03	10,889	16,220
Ohio	18[3]	15y, 6m	28	S	672	0.74	928	642	16.18	10,390	14,335
Oklahoma	16y, 6m	15y, 6m	16	P	630	0.61	1,050	708	17.83	12,622	21,046
Oregon	17[3]	15	24	S	740	0.95	796	729	16.71	12,177	13,102
Pennsylvania	17[3]	16	12	S	681	0.87	794	685	16.00	10,953	12,770
Rhode Island	17y, 6m[3]	16	27	S(a)	694	0.93	754	547[9]	18.70	10,227	11,119
South Carolina	16y, 6m	15	16	P	702	0.91	785	952	15.56	14,803	16,546
South Dakota	16	14	22	S	730	0.68	1,100	723	13.60	9,838	14,829
Tennessee	17	15	20	P	730	0.89	835	836	17.00	14,220	16,272
Texas	16y, 6m[3]	15	20	S	641	0.86	764	877	15.34	13,462	16,042
Utah	17[6]	15	24.5	S(a)	648	0.73	895	647	17.60	11,385	15,729
Vermont	16y, 6m[3]	15	19	S	904	1.13	815	818	18.57	15,192	13,696
Virginia	18[3]	15y, 6m	17.5	S	684	0.80	871	772	15.80	12,188	15,515
Washington	17[3]	15	36	P	745	0.85	890	603	16.44	9,909	11,849
West Virginia	17	15	20.5	P	731	1.02	744	847	17.93	15,183	15,459
Wisconsin	16y, 9m[3]	15y, 6m	30.9[7]	S	721	0.86	854	692	18.34	12,701	15,029
Wyoming	16y, 6m[3]	15	13	S	752	0.61	1,269	1,083	12.94	14,017	23,667
U.S. average			18.2		677	0.85	814	743	16.69	12,396	14,908

Note: Most states have graduated licensing systems that phase in full driving privileges. During the learner's stage, driving generally is not permitted without adult supervision. In an intermediate stage, young licensees may be allowed to drive unsupervised only under certain conditions. (1) Min. age at which all restrictions may be lifted on private passenger car operation. (2) Goes into effect June 30, 2008. (3) Applicants under age 18 (17 in ID; 17y, 3m in IL; 17 in LA; 19 in VA, or 18 if applicant holds valid license from another state; 17 in WY) must complete driver education. (Exceptions: applicants may substitute home training in CT; state-sponsored traffic school in KY; or 50 hrs. of supervised driving in OR for driver ed. Driver ed. not required if none offered within 30-mi radius of applicant's residence in NV.) (4) Learner's stage mandatory for all license applicants regardless of age. (5) Unsupervised driving in New York City prohibited for all drivers under 18. (6) Driver ed. required regardless of age. (7) Variable tax. Price as of July 25, 2007. (8) P = officer may stop vehicle for violation (primary); S = officer may issue seat belt citation only when vehicle is stopped for another moving violation (secondary). (a) Primary enforcement for children under a specified age: KS-18; MO-16; RI-18; UT-19. (b) Secondary enforcement for rear seat occupants. (9) 2004 figure.

Highway Speed Limits, by State

Source: Insurance Institute for Highway Safety (IIHS)

Under the National Highway System Designation Act of 1995, states are allowed to set their own highway speed limits. Under federal legislation enacted in 1974 during the energy crisis, states had been, in effect, restricted to a National Maximum Speed Limit (NMSL) of 55 miles per hour (raised in 1987 to 65 mph on rural interstates).

Maximum posted speed limits, in miles per hour, are given by state in the table below. (Speeds shown in parentheses are for commercial use trucks.) Most data current as of Sept. 2007. For more information visit the IIHS website at www.hwysafety.org.

State	Rural interstate	Urban[1] interstate	Limited access roads[2]	Other roads	State	Rural interstate	Urban[1] interstate	Limited access roads[2]	Other roads
AL	70	65	65	65	MO	70	60	70	65
AK	65	55	65	55	MT	75 (65)	65	70[6]	70[6]
AZ	75	65	55	55	NE	75	65	65	60
AR	70 (65)	55	60[4]	55	NV	75	65	70	70
CA	70 (55)	65 (55)	70	65	NH	65	65	55	55
CO	75	65	65	65	NJ	65	55	65	55
CT	65	55	65	55	NM	75	75	65	55
DC	NA	55	NA	25	NY	65	65	65	55
DE	65	55	65	55	NC	70	70	70	55
FL	70	65	65	65	ND	75	75	70	65
GA	70	65	65	65	OH	65 (55)[5]	65	55	55
HI	60	50	45	45	OK	75	70	70	70
ID	75 (65)	75	65	65	OR	65 (55)	55	55	55
IL	65 (55)	55	65	55	PA	65	55	55	55
IN	70 (65)	55	60	55	RI	65	55	55	55
IA	70	55	70	55	SC	70	70	60	55
KS	70	70	70	65	SD	75	75	70	70
KY	65[3]	65	65	55	TN	70	70	70	65
LA	70	70	70	65	TX	75 (65)[6,7]	70[6]	75 (65)[6]	60[9]
ME	65	65	65	60	UT	75	65	75	65
MD	65	65	65	55	VT	65	55	50	50
MA	65	65	65	55	VA	65[8]	65[8]	65	55
MI	70 (60);	65	70	55	WA	70 (60)	60	60	60
	<70 (55)				WV	70	55	65	55
MN	70	65	65	55	WI	65	65	65	55
MS	70	70	70	65	WY	75	60	65	65

NA = Not applicable. (1) Urban interstates are determined by Census Bureau criteria, which may be adjusted by state and local governments to reflect planning and other issues. (2) Multiple-lane roads with restricted access via exit and entrance ramps rather than intersections. (3) 70 mph on specified road segments. (4) Might be raised to 65 mph on 2- and 4-lane highways based upon result of study to be completed by Sept. 2008. (5) For trucks on OH Turnpike, speed limit is 65 mph. (6) 65 mph at night (½ hour after sunset to ½ hour before sunrise). (7) 80 mph (70 mph for comm. use trucks) on certain sections of I-10, I-20 in rural western TX. (8) Posted speed limit may be as high as 70 mph on I-85. (9) 55 mph at night (½ hour after sunset to ½ hour before sunrise).

Tourism Trends

World tourist arrivals have grown steadily in recent years, increasing by 10.2% between 2003 and 2004 and 5.4% between 2004 and 2005, according to the World Tourism Organization, based in Madrid, Spain. Preliminary data for 2006 puts the number of international tourist arrivals at 842 mil, 40 mil more than in 2005, for an increase of 5%.

Worldwide tourism receipts, as measured in constant U.S. dollars, rose 8.4% between 2005 and 2006, to reach an estimated record value of $735 bil.

Europe again commanded the largest share of international arrivals in 2006 with an estimated 456.9 mil, or 54.3% of the world total. Asia and the Pacific posted the second-largest share of international tourist arrivals (19.9%), with an estimated 167.4 mil arrivals in 2006. With 136 mil arrivals, the Americas held a 16.2% share of the world total, with the greatest increase in arrivals between 2005 and 2006 happening in Central America (10.8%). Africa saw 40.9 mil arrivals, up 9.8% from 2005. The region that held the lowest share of international tourist arrivals was the Middle East at 4.8%, or 40.7 mil arrivals.

Preliminary data for the first six months of 2007 indicate that travel in most regions continued to climb, with South Asia and sub-Saharan Africa posting respective increases of 11.5% and 10% over the same period in 2006.

The International Air Transport Association (IATA) reported a 5.9% increase in actual international passenger traffic (as measured in revenue passenger kilometers) between 2005 and 2006. The Middle East region experienced the largest growth at 15.4%. The IATA forecasted the continued growth of the global airline industry in 2007, in both net profits and passenger volume, though the cost of fuel remained a challenge, having risen from 14% of airline operating costs in 2003 to an estimated 28% in 2007.

World Tourism Receipts, 1990-2006[1]

Source: World Tourism Organization

(in billions of dollars; figures rounded)

Year	Receipts	Year	Receipts	Year	Receipts	Year	Receipts	Year	Receipts	Year	Receipts
1990	$273	1993	$323	1996	$439	1999	$455	2002	$487	2005	$678
1991	278	1994	356	1997	443	2000	474	2003	533	2006	735*
1992	317	1995	405	1998	445	2001	472	2004	633		

*Preliminary. (1) Total of all expenditures made by or on behalf of visitors, for and during the trip and stay.

Top 10 Countries in Tourism Earnings, 2006

Source: World Tourism Organization

(in billions of dollars; ranked by receipts from most recent year)

Rank	Country	Receipts[1] 2006*	2005	% change	Rank	Country	Receipts[1] 2006*	2005	% change
1.	United States	$85.7	$81.8	4.8	6.	United Kingdom	$33.5	$30.7	9.1
2.	Spain	51.1	48.0	6.5	7.	Germany	32.8	29.2	12.3
3.	France	46.3	44.0	5.2	8.	Australia	17.8	16.9	5.3
4.	Italy	38.1	35.4	7.6	9.	Turkey	16.9	18.2	−7.1
5.	China[2]	33.9	29.3	15.7	10.	Austria	16.7	16.0	4.4

* Preliminary. (1) Excluding transportation. (2) Excluding Hong Kong.

World's Top 10 Tourist Destinations, 2006
Source: World Tourism Organization
(arrivals in millions, preliminary)

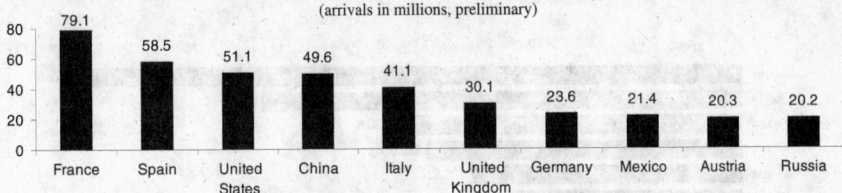

France	Spain	United States	China	Italy	United Kingdom	Germany	Mexico	Austria	Russia
79.1	58.5	51.1	49.6	41.1	30.1	23.6	21.4	20.3	20.2

International Travel to the U.S., 1986-2006
Source: Office of Travel and Tourism Industries, U.S. Dept. of Commerce; World Tourism Organization
(Visitors each year are in millions; some figures are revised and may differ from other sources.)

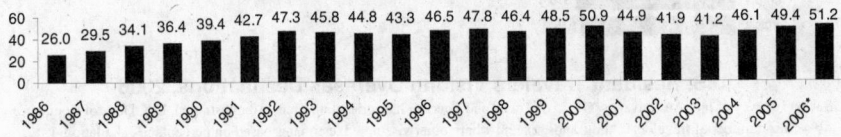

1986	1987	1988	1989	1990	1991	1992	1993	1994	1995	1996	1997	1998	1999	2000	2001	2002	2003	2004	2005	2006*
26.0	29.5	34.1	36.4	39.4	42.7	47.3	45.8	44.8	43.3	46.5	47.8	46.4	48.5	50.9	44.9	41.9	41.2	46.1	49.4	51.2

*Preliminary figure.

International Visitors to the U.S., 2006[1]
Source: Office of Travel and Tourism Industries, U.S. Dept. of Commerce
(ranked by number of visitors)

Country of origin	Visitors (thousands)	Expenditures (millions)[2]	Expenditures per visitor	Country of origin	Visitors (thousands)	Expenditures (millions)[2]	Expenditures per visitor
Canada[3]	15,995	$10,334	$646	Brazil	525	$1,947	$3,707
Mexico[3]	13,400	7,146	533	China[4]	458	2,115	2,428
United Kingdom	4,176	10,775	2,580	Netherlands	447	1,021	2,285
Japan	3,673	11,245	3,062	Spain	424	NA	NA
Germany	1,386	3,165	2,284	Ireland	414	NA	NA
France	790	2,289	2,898	India	407	1,865	4,584
South Korea	758	2,753	3,633	Venezuela	369	1,336	3,620
Australia	603	2,482	4,114	Colombia	348	NA	NA
Italy	533	1,564	2,935	All countries[3]	51,063	85,694	1,678

(1) Excludes cruise travel. (2) Does not include fares received by U.S. air carriers from international visitors for travel between the U.S. and foreign countries and between two foreign points. (3) Preliminary figure. (4) Data are for People's Republic of China and Hong Kong combined.

Traveler Spending in the U.S., 1987-2005
Source: Office of Travel and Tourism Industries, U.S. Dept. of Commerce
(in billions of dollars)

Year	Travelers Domestic	Travelers International	Year	Travelers Domestic	Travelers International	Year	Travelers Domestic	Travelers International
1987	$235	$31	1994	$340	$58	2000	$503	$82
1988	258	38	1995	360	63	2001	484	72
1989	273	47	1996	385	70	2002	478	67
1990	291	43	1997	406	73	2003	496	65
1991	296	48	1998	425	71	2004	532	75
1992	306	55	1999	458	75	2005	572	82
1993	323	58						

U.S. Domestic Leisure Travel Volume, 1995-2005[1]
Source: Travel Industry Association of America, TravelScope
(in millions of person-trips of 50 mi or more, one-way)

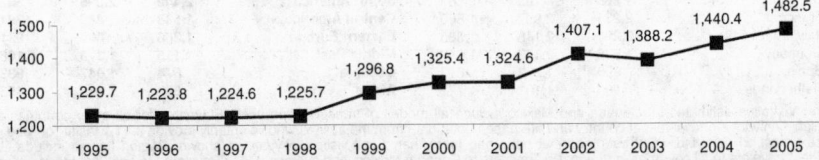

1995	1996	1997	1998	1999	2000	2001	2002	2003	2004	2005
1,229.7	1,223.8	1,224.6	1,225.7	1,296.8	1,325.4	1,324.6	1,407.1	1,388.2	1,440.4	1,482.5

(1) Method of collecting travel data has been revised; data for earlier years have been adjusted to maintain comparability.

Top U.S. States by Domestic Traveler Spending, 2004

Source: Travel Industry Association of America

(in billions of dollars)

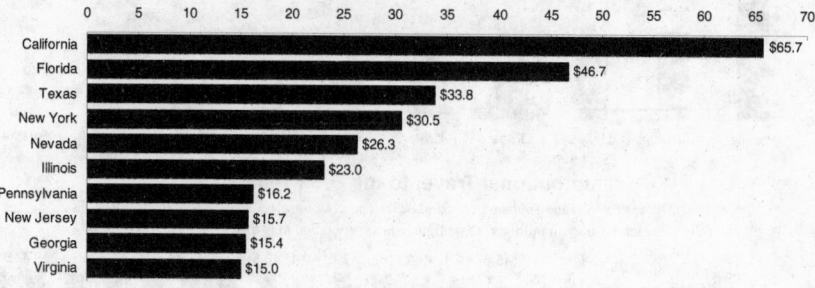

State	Spending
California	$65.7
Florida	$46.7
Texas	$33.8
New York	$30.5
Nevada	$26.3
Illinois	$23.0
Pennsylvania	$16.2
New Jersey	$15.7
Georgia	$15.4
Virginia	$15.0

U.S. Resident Travelers Visiting Overseas Destinations, 2006

Source: Survey of Intl. Air Travelers, Office of Travel and Tourism Industries, Intl. Trade Administration, U.S. Dept. of Commerce
(est. number of travelers in thousands, except where otherwise noted; estimates based on percentage calculations)

	U.S. resident travelers
Total	30,148
Male	16,883
Female	13,265
Avg. age of males (years)	46.7
Avg. age of females (years)	44.2
Avg. annual household income	$115,600
Median annual household income	$105,700
Avg. total trip expenditures per visitor	$3,111
Avg. expenditures outside the U.S. per visitor	$1,418
Avg. expenditures outside the U.S. per visitor per day	$87
Occupation	
Professional/technical	10,853
Manager/executive	8,441
Retired	3,618
Student	2,110
Homemaker	1,809
Clerical/sales	1,507
Craftsman/factory worker	904
Government/military	603
Main purpose of trip	
Leisure/recreation/holidays	12,662
Visit friends/relatives	9,346
Business	6,331
Study/teaching	603
Convention/conference	603

	U.S. resident travelers
Leisure/recreational activities	
Dining in restaurants	25,626
Shopping	22,310
Visit historical places	15,074
Sightseeing in cities	12,662
Visit small towns/villages	12,361
Touring the countryside	10,250
Cultural heritage sights	9,346
Water sports/sunbathing	7,537
Art gallery, museum	7,537
Nightclub/dancing	6,633
Guided tours	5,427
Ethnic heritage sites	3,919
Concert, play, musical	3,316
Amusement/theme parks	3,015
Casinos/gambling	3,015
Visit national parks	3,015
Cruises, one or more nights	1,809
Golf/tennis	1,507
Environmental/ecological sights	1,507
Camping, hiking	1,507
Attend sporting events	1,206
Hunting/fishing	904
Ranch vacations	603

U.S. Resident Travel Abroad[1], 1996-2006

Source: Office of Travel and Tourism Industries, Intl. Trade Administration, U.S. Dept. of Commerce
(in thousands)

Region/country[2]	2006	2000	1996	Region/country[2]	2006	2000	1996
Total outbound[3]	63,662	61,327	52,999	Asia	6,271	4,914	3,601
Mexico	19,659	19,285	20,304	Japan	1,538	1,262	871
Canada	13,855	15,189	12,909	China[5]	1,327	644	396
Overseas[4]	30,148	26,853	19,786	Caribbean	6,150	3,867	3,858
Europe	12,029	13,373	8,706	Jamaica	1,688	886	1,029
Western Europe	11,336	12,916	8,251	Bahamas	1,538	913	1,504
UK	3,286	4,189	2,869	South America	2,442	2,095	1,682
France	2,231	2,927	1,860	Central America	1,538	886	791
Italy	2,201	2,148	1,385	Eastern Europe	1,266	806	831
Germany	1,688	2,309	1,642	Middle East	1,115	1,370	1,108
Spain	995	1,262	613	Oceania	874	1,047	633
Netherlands	904	1,101	772	Africa	663	483	455

Note: Visitation estimates for Canada and Mexico include all modes of transportation used. Estimates for all other countries are available only for air travel to that country and are based upon data from the airlines who voluntarily provide it. (1) Visits of one or more nights. (2) Only individual countries that have had more than 1 mil visitors a year are shown. Region figures include U.S. resident travelers to all countries in region. (3) Travelers to Canada, Mexico, and overseas. (4) Travelers to all countries except Canada and Mexico. (5) Not including Hong Kong or Taiwan.

U.S. Airline Safety, Scheduled Commercial Carriers, 1985-2006

Source: National Transportation Safety Board; Federal Aviation Administration, U.S. Dept. of Transportation

Year	Departures (millions)	Fatal accidents	Fatalities	Accident rate[1]	Year	Departures (millions)	Fatal accidents	Fatalities	Accident rate[1]
1985	6.1	4	197	0.066	1998	10.5	1	1[3]	0.009
1990	7.8	6	39	0.077	1999	10.9	2	12	0.018
1991	7.5	4	62	0.053	2000	11.1	2	89	0.018
1992	7.5	4	33	0.053	2001[2]	10.6	6	531	0.019
1993	7.7	1	1	0.013	2002	10.3	0	0	0.000
1994[2]	7.8	4	239	0.051	2003	10.2	2	22	0.020
1995	8.1	1	160	0.012	2004	10.8	1	13	0.009
1996	7.9	3	342	0.038	2005	10.9	3	22	0.027
1997	9.9	3	3	0.030	2006*	11.2	2	50	0.018

*Preliminary. (1) Fatal accidents per 100,000 departures. (2) Suicide- and sabotage-caused accidents are included in the number of fatal accidents and fatalities but not in the calculation of accident rates. (3) On-ground employee fatality.

U.S. Scheduled Airline Traffic, 1995-2006

Source: Courtesy of Air Transport Association of America, Inc. Reprinted with permission.
Copyright © 2007 by Air Transport Association of America, Inc. All rights reserved.
(in millions, except where otherwise noted)

	1995	2000	2001[2]	2002[2]	2003[2]	2004	2005	2006
Revenue passengers enplaned	547.8	666.2	622.1	612.9	646.5	702.9	738.6	744.6
Revenue passenger miles	540,656	692,757	651,700	641,102	655,850	733,680	779,004	797,422
Available seat miles	807,078	956,950	930,511	892,554	893,902	971,466	1,003,312	1,006,391
% of seating utilized	67.0	72.4	70.0	71.8	73.4	75.5	77.6	79.2
Cargo traffic (ton miles)	16,921	23,888	22,003	23,243	24,608	27,978	28,036	29,283
Passenger revenue	$69,594	$93,622	$80,947	$73,577	$73,281	$85,646	$93,449	$101,208
Net profit	$2,314.0	$2,486.0	–$8,275.0	–$11,312.4	–$3,624.7	–$7,643.0	–$5,673.0	$3,045.0[3]
Avg. full-time employees[1]	546,987	679,967	671,969	601,355	570,868	569,498	552,857	544,540

(1) Not in millions. (2) Revenues and profit measures include aid payments from the U.S. government after the Sept. 2001 terrorist attacks. (3) Excludes bankruptcy-related charges (reorganization expenses and fresh-start accounting gains).

Leading U.S. Passenger Airlines, 2006

Source: Courtesy of Air Transport Association of America, Inc. Reprinted with permission.
Copyright © 2007 by Air Transport Association of America, Inc. All rights reserved.
(in thousands; ranked by number of passengers)

Airline	Passengers	Airline	Passengers	Airline	Passengers	Airline	Passengers
American	98,142	AirTran	20,033	Atlantic Southeast	11,814	Air Wisconsin	5,790
Southwest	96,276	SkyWest	19,496	Comair	10,590	PSA	5,153
Delta	73,524	American Eagle	18,765	Pinnacle	9,018	Spirit	4,477
United	69,265	JetBlue	18,507	Frontier	8,895	Midwest	3,870
US Airways	57,659	ExpressJet	17,962	Horizon	6,859	Mesaba	3,792
Northwest	54,837	Alaska	17,148	Chautauqua	6,780	Trans States	3,704
Continental	46,738	Mesa	13,316	Hawaiian	6,157	Shuttle America	3,646

Passenger Traffic at U.S. Airports, 2006

Source: Airports Council International-North America

City (airport code)	Passenger arrivals and departures[2]
1. Atlanta (ATL)	84,846,639
2. Chicago–O'Hare (ORD)	77,028,134
3. Los Angeles International (LAX)	61,041,066
4. Dallas/Fort Worth (DFW)	60,226,138
5. Denver (DEN)	47,325,016
6. Las Vegas-McCarran (LAS)	46,193,329
7. New York–Kennedy (JFK)	43,762,282
8. Houston–George Bush (IAH)	42,550,432
9. Phoenix–Sky Harbor (PHX)	41,436,737
10. Newark (EWR)	36,724,167
11. Detroit–Metropolitan Wayne Co. (DTW)	35,972,673
12. Minneapolis/St. Paul (MSP)	35,612,133
13. Orlando International (MCO)	34,640,451
14. San Francisco (SFO)	33,574,807
15. Miami International (MIA)	32,533,974
16. Philadelphia International (PHL)	31,768,272
17. Toronto (YYZ)	30,972,577
18. Seattle Tacoma (SEA)	29,979,949
19. Charlotte (CLT)	29,693,949
20. Boston–Logan (BOS)	27,725,443
21. New York–La Guardia (LGA)	26,571,146
22. Washington–Dulles (IAD)	22,813,067
23. Salt Lake City International (SLC)	21,557,656
24. Fort Lauderdale-Hollywood (FLL)	21,369,787
25. Baltimore/Washington International (BWI)	21,184,208
26. Honolulu International (HNL)	20,067,871
27. Tampa International (TPA)	18,867,541
28. Chicago–Midway (MDW)	18,680,663
29. Washington National (DCA)	18,545,557
30. San Diego (SAN)	17,481,942

Passenger Traffic at World Airports[1], 2006

Source: Airports Council International

Location (airport name)	Passenger arrivals and departures[2]
1. London, United Kingdom (Heathrow)	67,530,197
2. Tokyo, Japan (Haneda)	65,810,672
3. Paris, France (Charles de Gaulle)	56,849,567
4. Frankfurt, Germany (Frankfurt Intl.)	52,810,683
5. Beijing, China (Beijing Capital Intl.)	48,654,770
6. Amsterdam, Netherlands (Schiphol)	46,065,719
7. Madrid, Spain (Barajas)	45,501,168
8. Hong Kong, China (Hong Kong Intl.)	43,857,908
9. Bangkok, Thailand (Suvarnabhumi)	42,799,532
10. Singapore (Changi)	35,033,083
11. Tokyo, Japan (Narita Intl.)	34,975,225
12. London, UK (Gatwick)	34,172,492
13. Toronto, ON, Canada (Toronto Pearson Intl.)	30,972,577
14. Munich, Germany (Munich Intl.)	30,757,978
15. Jakarta, Indonesia (Soekarno-Hatta Intl.)	30,583,957
16. Sydney, Australia (Kingsford Smith)	30,375,799
17. Rome, Italy (Leonardo da Vinci Fiumicino)	30,102,097
18. Barcelona, Spain (Barcelona)	30,000,601
19. Dubai, United Arab Emirates (Dubai Intl.)	28,788,726
20. Seoul, South Korea (Incheon Intl.)	28,360,723
21. Shanghai, China (Pudong Intl.)	26,789,125
22. Guangzhou, China (Guangzhou Baiyun Intl.)	26,222,037
23. Paris, France (Orly)	25,622,152
24. Mexico City, Mexico (Benito Juárez Intl.)	24,727,296
25. Kuala Lumpur (KL Intl.)	24,129,748
26. London, United Kingdom (Stansted)	23,686,800
27. Istanbul, Turkey (Istanbul Atatürk Intl.)	23,261,878
28. Taipei, Taiwan (Taiwan Taoyuan Intl.)	22,857,445
29. Manchester, United Kingdom (Manchester)	22,776,337
30. Palma de Mallorca, Spain (Son Sant Joan)	22,402,257

(1) Excludes U.S. airports, and airports not participating in Airports Council Intl. Airport Traffic Statistics collection. (2) Arriving and departing passengers and direct transit passengers counted once.

Top 25 Travel Websites, July 2007

Source: comScore Media Metrix

(ranked by number of visitors)

Website	Visitors[1]	Website	Visitors[1]	Website	Visitors[1]
1. Expedia Inc	29,242,890	10. InterContinental Hotels Group	5,396,725	19. Disney Travel	3,645,257
2. Travelport	19,688,955			20. MSN Travel	3,530,692
3. Yahoo! Travel	12,943,448	11. Delta Airlines	5,239,313	21. US Airways Group, Inc.	3,503,332
4. Travelocity	12,068,651	12. American Airlines	5,143,741	22. JetBlue Airways	3,433,859
5. Southwest Airlines Co.	10,910,409	13. Wyndham Worldwide	5,007,046	23. Smarter Living Inc.	3,336,858
6. Priceline.com		14. Kayak.com Network	4,871,275	24. Enterprise.com	3,323,955
Incorporated	8,514,576	15. About.com Travel	4,746,559	25. Continental Airlines Sites	3,267,889
7. Marriott	5,898,883	16. United Airlines	4,483,773		
8. Hilton Hotels	5,775,197	17. Sidestep Network	4,439,159	**Travel**	**81,214,873**
9. Travel Ad Network	5,432,422	18. AOL Travel	3,701,067	**Total Internet audience**	**180,077,602**

(1) Number of users who visited at least once in July 2007.

Travel Websites

The following websites are among those that may be of use in planning trips and making arrangements. Websites listed under "Maps" enable the user to plot a route to a destination. Inclusion here does not represent endorsement by *The World Almanac*.

AIRLINES

American Airlines
www.aa.com
Continental Airlines
www.continental.com
Delta Air Lines
www.delta.com
Northwest Airlines
www.nwa.com
Southwest Airlines
www.southwest.com
United Airlines
www.united.com
USAirways
www.usairways.com

BUSES

Gray Line Worldwide
www.grayline.com
Greyhound Lines
www.greyhound.com
Peter Pan Bus Lines
www.peterpanbus.com

CAR RENTALS

Alamo Rent A Car
www.alamo.com
Avis Rent-A-Car
www.avis.com
Budget Rent A Car
www.budget.com
Dollar Rent A Car
www.dollar.com
Enterprise Rent-A-Car
www.enterprise.com
Hertz
www.hertz.com
National Car Rental
www.nationalcar.com
Rent-A-Wreck
www.rentawreck.com
Thrifty Rent-A-Car
www.thrifty.com

TRAINS

Amtrak
www.amtrak.com
BC Rail (Canada)
www.bcrco.com
Rail Europe
www.raileurope.com

CRUISE LINES

Carnival Cruise Lines
www.carnival.com
Celebrity Cruises
www.celebritycruises.com
Costa Cruise Lines
www.costacruise.com
Cunard Line
www.cunardline.com
Holland America Line
www.hollandamerica.com
Norwegian Cruise Line
www.ncl.com
Princess Cruises
www.princess.com
Royal Caribbean Intl.
www.royalcaribbean.com
Windjammer Barefoot Cruises
www.windjammer.com

HOTELS/RESORTS

Best Western Intl.
www.bestwestern.com
Choice Hotels Intl.,
Clarion Hotels & Resorts,
Comfort Inns,
Econo Lodges,
MainStay Suites,
Quality Inns,
Rodeway Inns,
Sleep Inns
www.hotelchoice.com
Days Inn of America
www.daysinn.com
Doubletree Hotels
www.doubletree.com

Embassy Suites
www.embassysuites.com
Four Seasons Hotels
www.fourseasons.com
Hilton Hotels
www.hilton.com
Holiday Inn Worldwide
www.holidayinn.com
Hyatt Hotels and Resorts
www.hyatt.com
Inter-Continental Hotels
www.ichotelsgroup.com
Loews Hotels
www.loewshotels.com
Marriott Intl.
www.marriott.com
Radisson Hotels Intl.
www.radisson.com
Sheraton Hotels & Resorts
www.starwood.com/sheraton
Westin Hotels & Resorts
www.starwood.com/westin
Wyndham Hotels & Resorts
www.wyndham.com

TRAVEL PLANNING

www.bestfares.com
www.cheaptickets.com
www.expedia.com
www.fodors.com
www.frommers.com
www.hotels.com
www.itn.net (American Express)
www.lowestfare.com
www.orbitz.com
www.priceline.com
www.travelocity.com

MAPS

maps.google.com
www.mapquest.com
maps.yahoo.com

Number of Paid Days Off per Year in Selected Countries

Source: *No-Vacation Nation* (2007) by Rebecca Ray and John Schmitt, Center for Economic and Policy Research

The figures below represent the amount of paid time off that workers in selected countries are entitled to each year by law. Individual employers may offer additional paid time off beyond the legal guaranteed minimum. Countries may refer to workdays, calendar days, or weeks in their legal mandates. For sake of comparison, table assumes a five-day workweek.

Country	Paid vacation days	Paid holidays	Total paid days off	Country	Paid vacation days	Paid holidays	Total paid days off
France	30	1	31	Ireland	20	9	29
Denmark	25	9	34	Australia	20	7	27
Finland[1]	25	9	34	New Zealand	20	7	27
Norway	25	2	27	Greece	20	6	26
Sweden	25	0	25	Netherlands	20	0	20
Germany[1]	24	10	34	Switzerland	20	0	20
Austria	22	13	35	United Kingdom	20	0	20
Portugal	22	13	35	Canada[1]	10	8	18
Spain	22	12	34	Japan	10	0	10
Italy	20	13	33	U.S.	0	0	0
Belgium	20	10	30				

(1) Number of paid vacation days and/or paid holidays varies by regional jurisdiction. Figures represent national average.

Passports, Health Regulations, and Travel Warnings for Foreign Travel

Source: Bureau of Consular Affairs, U.S. Dept. of State

Passports, Visas

Passports are issued by the Department of State to U.S. citizens and nationals to provide documentation for foreign travel. Passport applications should be submitted well in advance; it may take up to 6 weeks for applications to be processed. Fees for a new passport for persons age 16 and older total $97; provided certain criteria are met, passports can be renewed for $67.

For U.S. citizens traveling on business or as tourists, a U.S. passport is often sufficient to gain admission for a limited stay. Many countries, however, also require a visa before entering.

Each country has its own specific guidelines concerning length and purpose of visit, among other considerations. Some may require visitors to display proof that they have sufficient funds to stay for the intended time period, onward/return tickets, and/or at least 6-months remaining validity on their U.S. passports.

As of Jan. 23, 2007, all persons traveling by air between the U.S. and **Canada, Mexico, Bermuda,** and some **Caribbean** islands were required to show a passport or other valid document to enter or re-enter the U.S. Sometime in summer 2008, that requirement will be extended to persons traveling between the U.S. and those countries by land and sea.

For up-to-date passport and international travel information, visit the Consular Affairs website (travel.state.gov) or call the National Passport Information Center at (877) 487-2778.

Health Regulations

Under World Health Organization (WHO) regulations, first instituted in 1969 and revised in 2005, member countries agree to abide by resolutions meant to contain the spread of disease. For example, some countries may require travelers to provide proof of vaccination against yellow fever before being allowed to enter.

Detailed information and recommendations are included in *Health Information for International Travel,* also known as the "Yellow Book," published every two years by the Centers for Disease Control and Prevention (CDC). It can be ordered online through a link on the CDC website (www.cdc.gov/travel/) or by calling (800) 545-2522 for the price of $24.95. The book can also be viewed online at the CDC website.

Information may also be obtained by calling the CDC's Travelers' Health Automated Information Line at (877) FYI-TRIP (394-8747). WHO's more technical *International Travel and Health* can be ordered for $22.50 or downloaded for free from the WHO website at www.who.int/ith/.

Travel Warnings

The State Dept. issues travel warnings when it decides, based on relevant information, to recommend that Americans avoid travel to certain countries; these are subject to change. As of Oct. 5, 2007, travel warnings were in effect for the following countries: Afghanistan, Algeria, Burundi, Central African Republic, Chad, Colombia, Côte d'Ivoire, Democratic Republic of the Congo, Eritrea, Haiti, Indonesia, Iran, Iraq, Israel (incl. West Bank and Gaza), Kenya, Lebanon, Nepal, Nigeria, Pakistan, Philippines, Saudi Arabia, Somalia, Sri Lanka, Sudan, Syria, Timor-Leste, Uzbekistan, and Yemen. For the most current information, visit travel.state.gov.

Record-Breaking Roller Coasters

Source: Ultimate Rollercoaster.com

Steel-Tracked Roller Coasters

Fastest

	Roller coaster	Theme park, location
128 mph	Kingda Ka	Six Flags Great Adventure, Jackson, NJ
120 mph	Top Thrill Dragster	Cedar Point, Sandusky, OH
106.8 mph	Dodonpa	Fuji-Q High Land, Fujiyoshida-shi, Japan
100 mph	Tower of Terror	Dreamworld, Gold Coast, Australia
100 mph	Superman the Escape	Six Flags Magic Mountain, Valencia, CA

Tallest

456 ft	Kingda Ka	Six Flags Great Adventure, Jackson, NJ
420 ft	Top Thrill Dragster	Cedar Point, Sandusky, OH
415 ft	Superman the Escape	Six Flags Magic Mountain, Valencia, CA
377 ft	Tower of Terror	Dreamworld, Gold Coast, Australia
318 ft	Millennium Force	Cedar Point, Sandusky, OH

Largest drop

418 ft	Kingda Ka	Six Flags Great Adventure, Jackson, NJ
400 ft	Top Thrill Dragster	Cedar Point, Sandusky, OH
306 ft	Steel Dragon 2000	Nagashima Spa Land, Mie, Japan
300 ft	Millennium Force	Cedar Point, Sandusky, OH
255 ft	Goliath	Six Flags Magic Mountain, Valencia, CA

Longest

8,133 ft	Steel Dragon 2000	Nagashima Spa Land, Mie, Japan
7,677 ft	Daidarasaurus	Expoland, Suita, Japan
7,450 ft	The Ultimate	Lightwater Valley, United Kingdom
6,709 ft	Fujiyama	Fuji-Q High Land, Fujiyoshida-shi, Japan
6,595 ft	Millennium Force	Cedar Point, Sandusky, OH

Most inversions

10	Colossus	Thorpe Park, Surrey, UK

Wood-Tracked Roller Coasters

Fastest

	Roller coaster	Theme park, location
78.3 mph	Son of Beast	Kings Island, Cincinnati, OH
74.6 mph	Colossos	Heide Park, Soltau, Germany
70 mph	El Toro	Six Flags Great Adventure, Jackson, NJ
67.4 mph	The Voyage	Holiday World & Splashin' Safari, Santa Claus, IN
66.3 mph	The Boss	Six Flags St. Louis, Eureka, MO

Tallest

218 ft	Son of Beast	Kings Island, Cincinnati, OH
181 ft	El Toro	Six Flags Great Adventure, Jackson, NJ
179 ft	Rattler	Six Flags Fiesta Texas, San Antonio, TX
173 ft	The Voyage	Holiday World & Splashin' Safari, Santa Claus, IN
170 ft	Colossos	Heide Park, Soltau, Germany

Largest drop

214 ft	Son of Beast	Kings Island, Cincinnati, OH
176 ft	El Toro	Six Flags Great Adventure, Jackson, NJ
159 ft	Colossos	Heide Park, Soltau, Germany
155 ft	Mean Streak	Cedar Point, Sandusky, OH
154 ft	The Voyage	Holiday World & Splashin' Safari, Santa Claus, IN

Longest

7,400 ft	The Beast	Kings Island, Cincinnati, OH
7,032 ft	Son of Beast	Kings Island, Cincinnati, OH
6,442 ft	The Voyage	Holiday World & Splashin' Safari, Santa Claus, IN
5,427 ft	Mean Streak	Cedar Point, Sandusky, OH
5,384 ft	Shivering Timbers	Michigan's Adventure, Muskegon, MI

Road Mileage Between Selected U.S. Cities

	Atlanta	Boston	Chicago	Cincin- nati	Cleve- land	Dallas	Denver	Des Moines	Detroit	Houston
Atlanta, GA........	...	1,037	674	440	672	795	1,398	870	699	789
Boston, MA.......	1,037	...	963	840	628	1,748	1,949	1,280	695	1,804
Chicago, IL.......	674	963	...	287	335	917	996	327	266	1,067
Cincinnati, OH	440	840	287	...	244	920	1,164	571	259	1,029
Cleveland, OH	672	628	335	244	...	1,159	1,321	652	170	1,273
Dallas, TX........	795	1,748	917	920	1,159	...	781	684	1,143	243
Denver, CO	1,398	1,949	996	1,164	1,321	781	...	669	1,253	1,019
Detroit, MI........	699	695	266	259	170	1,143	1,253	584	...	1,265
Houston, TX.......	789	1,804	1,067	1,029	1,273	243	1,019	905	1,265	...
Indianapolis, IN ...	493	906	181	106	294	865	1,058	465	278	987
Kansas City, MO ...	798	1,391	499	591	779	489	600	195	743	710
Los Angeles, CA....	2,182	2,979	2,054	2,179	2,367	1,387	1,059	1,727	2,311	1,538
Memphis, TN	371	1,296	530	468	712	452	1,040	599	713	561
Milwaukee, WI	761	1,050	87	374	422	991	1,029	361	353	1,142
Minneapolis, MN ...	1,068	1,368	405	692	740	936	841	252	671	1,157
New Orleans, LA ...	479	1,507	912	786	1,030	496	1,273	978	1,045	356
New York, NY......	841	206	802	647	473	1,552	1,771	1,119	637	1,608
Omaha, NE	986	1,412	459	693	784	644	537	132	716	865
Philadelphia, PA....	741	296	738	567	413	1,452	1,691	1,051	573	1,508
Pittsburgh, PA	687	561	452	287	129	1,204	1,411	763	287	1,313
Portland, OR	2,601	3,046	2,083	2,333	2,418	2,009	1,238	1,786	2,349	2,205
St. Louis, MO	541	1,141	289	340	529	630	857	333	513	779
San Francisco, CA .	2,496	3,095	2,142	2,362	2,467	1,753	1,235	1,815	2,399	1,912
Seattle, WA	2,618	2,976	2,013	2,300	2,348	2,078	1,307	1,749	2,279	2,274
Tulsa, OK.........	772	1,537	683	736	925	257	681	443	909	478
Washington, DC....	608	429	671	481	346	1,319	1,616	984	506	1,375

	India- napolis	Kansas City	Los Angeles	Louis- ville	Memphis	Mil- waukee	Minne- apolis	New Orleans	New York	Omaha
Atlanta, GA.......	493	798	2,182	382	371	761	1,068	479	841	986
Boston, MA.......	906	1,391	2,979	941	1,296	1,050	1,368	1,507	206	1,412
Chicago, IL./.....	181	499	2,054	292	530	87	405	912	802	459
Cincinnati, OH	106	591	2,179	101	468	374	692	786	647	693
Cleveland, OH	294	779	2,367	345	712	422	740	1,030	473	784
Dallas, TX........	865	489	1,387	819	452	991	936	496	1,552	644
Denver, CO	1,058	600	1,059	1,120	1,040	1,029	841	1,273	1,771	537
Detroit, MI........	278	743	2,311	360	713	353	671	1,045	637	716
Houston, TX.......	987	710	1,538	928	561	1,142	1,157	356	1,608	865
Indianapolis, IN	...	485	2,073	111	435	268	586	796	713	587
Kansas City, MO ...	485	...	1,589	520	451	537	447	806	1,198	201
Los Angeles, CA....	2,073	1,589	...	2,108	1,817	2,087	1,889	1,883	2,786	1,595
Memphis, TN	435	451	1,817	367	...	612	826	390	1,100	652
Milwaukee, WI	268	537	2,087	379	612	...	332	994	889	493
Minneapolis, MN....	586	447	1,889	697	826	332	...	1,214	1,207	357
New Orleans, LA ...	796	806	1,883	685	390	994	1,214	...	1,311	1,007
New York, NY......	713	1,198	2,786	748	1,100	889	1,207	1,311	...	1,251
Omaha, NE	587	201	1,595	687	652	493	357	1,007	1,251	...
Philadelphia, PA....	633	1,118	2,706	668	1,000	825	1,143	1,211	100	1,183
Pittsburgh, PA	353	838	2,426	388	752	539	857	1,070	368	895
Portland, OR	2,272	1,809	959	2,320	2,259	2,010	1,678	2,505	2,885	1,654
St. Louis, MO	235	257	1,845	263	285	363	552	673	948	449
San Francisco, CA .	2,293	1,835	379	2,349	2,125	2,175	1,940	2,249	2,934	1,683
Seattle, WA	2,194	1,839	1,131	2,305	2,290	1,940	1,608	2,574	2,815	1,638
Tulsa, OK	631	248	1,452	659	401	757	695	647	1,344	387
Washington, DC....	558	1,043	2,631	582	867	758	1,076	1,078	233	1,116

	Phila- delphia	Pitts- burgh	Portland	St. Louis	Salt Lake City	San Francisco	Seattle	Toledo	Tulsa	Wash., DC
Atlanta, GA.......	741	687	2,601	541	1,878	2,496	2,618	640	772	608
Boston, MA........	296	561	3,046	1,141	2,343	3,095	2,976	739	1,537	429
Chicago, IL........	738	452	2,083	289	1,390	2,142	2,013	232	683	671
Cincinnati, OH	567	287	2,333	340	1,610	2,362	2,300	200	736	481
Cleveland, OH	413	129	2,418	529	1,715	2,467	2,348	111	925	346
Dallas, TX........	1,452	1,204	2,009	630	1,242	1,753	2,078	1,084	257	1,319
Denver, CO	1,691	1,411	1,238	857	504	1,235	1,307	1,218	681	1,616
Detroit, MI........	576	287	2,349	513	1,647	2,399	2,279	59	909	506
Houston, TX.......	1,508	1,313	2,205	779	1,438	1,912	2,274	1,206	478	1,375
Indianapolis, IN	633	353	2,272	235	1,504	2,293	2,194	219	631	558
Kansas City, MO ...	1,118	838	1,809	257	1,086	1,835	1,839	687	248	1,043
Los Angeles, CA....	2,706	2,426	959	1,845	715	379	1,131	2,276	1,452	2,631
Memphis, TN	1,000	752	2,259	285	1,535	2,125	2,290	654	401	867
Milwaukee, WI	825	539	2,010	363	1,423	2,175	1,940	319	757	758
Minneapolis, MN....	1,143	857	1,678	552	1,186	1,940	1,608	637	695	1,076
New Orleans, LA ...	1,211	1,070	2,505	673	1,738	2,249	2,574	986	647	1,078
New York, NY......	100	368	2,885	948	2,182	2,934	2,815	578	1,344	233
Omaha, NE	1,183	895	1,654	449	931	1,683	1,638	681	387	1,116
Philadelphia, PA....	...	288	2,821	868	2,114	2,866	2,751	514	1,264	133
Pittsburgh, PA	288	...	2,535	588	1,826	2,578	2,465	228	984	221
Portland, OR	2,821	2,535	...	2,060	767	636	172	2,315	1,913	2,754
St. Louis, MO	868	588	2,060	...	1,337	2,089	2,081	454	396	793
San Francisco, CA .	2,866	2,578	636	2,089	752	...	808	2,364	1,760	2,799
Seattle, WA	2,751	2,465	172	2,081	836	808	...	2,245	1,982	2,684
Tulsa, OK.........	1,264	984	1,913	396	1,172	1,760	1,982	850	...	1,189
Washington, DC....	133	221	2,754	793	2,047	2,799	2,684	447	1,189	...

Air Distances Between Selected World Cities in Statute Miles
Point-to-point measurements are usually from City Hall.

	Bangkok	Beijing	Berlin	Cairo	Cape Town	Caracas	Chicago	Hong Kong	Honolulu	Lima
Bangkok.........	...	2,046	5,352	4,523	6,300	10,555	8,570	1,077	6,609	12,244
Beijing	2,046	...	4,584	4,698	8,044	8,950	6,604	1,217	5,077	10,349
Berlin	5,352	4,584	...	1,797	5,961	5,238	4,414	5,443	7,320	6,896
Cairo............	4,523	4,698	1,797	...	4,480	6,342	6,141	5,066	8,848	7,726
Cape Town.......	6,300	8,044	5,961	4,480	...	6,366	8,491	7,376	11,535	6,072
Caracas	10,555	8,950	5,238	6,342	6,366	...	2,495	10,165	6,021	1,707
Chicago	8,570	6,604	4,414	6,141	8,491	2,495	...	7,797	4,256	3,775
Hong Kong.......	1,077	1,217	5,443	5,066	7,376	10,165	7,797	...	5,556	11,418
Honolulu.........	6,609	5,077	7,320	8,848	11,535	6,021	4,256	5,556	...	5,947
London	5,944	5,074	583	2,185	5,989	4,655	3,958	5,990	7,240	6,316
Los Angeles......	7,637	6,250	5,782	7,520	9,969	3,632	1,745	7,240	2,557	4,171
Madrid	6,337	5,745	1,165	2,087	5,308	4,346	4,189	6,558	7,872	5,907
Melbourne	4,568	5,643	9,918	8,675	6,425	9,717	9,673	4,595	5,505	8,059
Mexico City.......	9,793	7,753	6,056	7,700	8,519	2,234	1,690	8,788	3,789	2,639
Montreal.........	8,338	6,519	3,740	5,427	7,922	2,438	745	7,736	4,918	3,970
Moscow	4,389	3,607	1,006	1,803	6,279	6,177	4,987	4,437	7,047	7,862
New York	8,669	6,844	3,979	5,619	7,803	2,120	714	8,060	4,969	3,639
Paris............	5,877	5,120	548	1,998	5,786	4,732	4,143	5,990	7,449	6,370
Rio de Janeiro	9,994	10,768	6,209	6,143	3,781	2,804	5,282	11,009	8,288	2,342
Rome	5,494	5,063	737	1,326	5,231	5,195	4,824	5,774	8,040	6,750
San Francisco	7,931	5,918	5,672	7,466	10,248	3,902	1,859	6,905	2,398	4,518
Singapore........	883	2,771	6,164	5,137	6,008	11,402	9,372	1,605	6,726	11,689
Stockholm	5,089	4,133	528	2,096	6,423	5,471	4,331	5,063	6,875	7,166
Tokyo	2,865	1,307	5,557	5,958	9,154	8,808	6,314	1,791	3,859	9,631
Warsaw	5,033	4,325	322	1,619	5,935	5,559	4,679	5,147	7,366	7,215
Washington, DC....	8,807	6,942	4,181	5,822	7,895	2,047	596	8,155	4,838	3,509

	London	Los Angeles	Madrid	Melbourne	Mexico City	Montreal	Moscow	New Delhi	New York	Paris
Bangkok..........	5,944	7,637	6,337	4,568	9,793	8,338	4,389	1,813	8,669	5,877
Beijing	5,074	6,250	5,745	5,643	7,753	6,519	3,607	2,353	6,844	5,120
Berlin	583	5,782	1,165	9,918	6,056	3,740	1,006	3,598	3,979	548
Cairo............	2,185	7,520	2,087	8,675	7,700	5,427	1,803	2,758	5,619	1,998
Cape Town.......	5,989	9,969	5,308	6,425	8,519	7,922	6,279	5,769	7,803	5,786
Caracas	4,655	3,632	4,346	9,717	2,234	2,438	6,177	8,833	2,120	4,732
Chicago	3,958	1,745	4,189	9,673	1,690	745	4,987	7,486	714	4,143
Hong Kong.......	5,990	7,240	6,558	4,595	8,788	7,736	4,437	2,339	8,060	5,990
Honolulu.........	7,240	2,557	7,872	5,505	3,789	4,918	7,047	7,412	4,969	7,449
London	...	5,439	785	10,500	5,558	3,254	1,564	4,181	3,469	214
Los Angeles......	5,439	...	5,848	7,931	1,542	2,427	6,068	7,011	2,451	5,601
Madrid	785	5,848	...	10,758	5,643	3,448	2,147	4,530	3,593	655
Melbourne	10,500	7,931	10,758	...	8,426	10,395	8,950	6,329	10,359	10,430
Mexico City.......	5,558	1,542	5,643	8,426	...	2,317	6,676	9,120	2,090	5,725
Montreal.........	3,254	2,427	3,448	10,395	2,317	...	4,401	7,012	331	3,432
Moscow	1,564	6,068	2,147	8,950	6,676	4,401	...	2,698	4,683	1,554
New York	3,469	2,451	3,593	10,359	2,090	331	4,683	7,318	...	3,636
Paris............	214	5,601	655	10,430	5,725	3,432	1,554	4,102	3,636	...
Rio de Janeiro	5,750	6,330	5,045	8,226	4,764	5,078	7,170	8,753	4,801	5,684
Rome	895	6,326	851	9,929	6,377	4,104	1,483	3,684	4,293	690
San Francisco	5,367	347	5,803	7,856	1,887	2,543	5,885	7,691	2,572	5,577
Singapore........	6,747	8,767	7,080	3,759	10,327	9,203	5,228	2,571	9,534	6,673
Stockholm	942	5,454	1,653	9,630	6,012	3,714	716	3,414	3,986	1,003
Tokyo	5,959	5,470	6,706	5,062	7,035	6,471	4,660	3,638	6,757	6,053
Warsaw	905	5,922	1,427	9,598	6,337	4,022	721	3,277	4,270	852
Washington, DC....	3,674	2,300	3,792	10,180	1,885	489	4,876	7,500	205	3,840

	Rio de Janeiro	Rome	San Francisco	Singapore	Stockholm	Tehran	Tokyo	Vienna	Warsaw	Wash., DC
Bangkok..........	9,994	5,494	7,931	883	5,089	3,391	2,865	5,252	5,033	8,807
Beijing	10,768	5,063	5,918	2,771	4,133	3,490	1,307	4,648	4,325	6,942
Berlin	6,209	737	5,672	6,164	528	2,185	5,557	326	322	4,181
Cairo............	6,143	1,326	7,466	5,137	2,096	1,234	5,958	1,481	1,619	5,822
Cape Town.......	3,781	5,231	10,248	6,008	6,423	5,241	9,154	5,656	5,935	7,895
Caracas	2,804	5,195	3,902	11,402	5,471	7,320	8,808	5,372	5,559	2,047
Chicago	5,282	4,824	1,859	9,372	4,331	6,502	6,314	4,698	4,679	596
Hong Kong.......	11,009	5,774	6,905	1,605	5,063	3,843	1,791	5,431	5,147	8,155
Honolulu.........	8,288	8,040	2,398	6,726	6,875	8,070	3,859	7,632	7,366	4,838
London	5,750	895	5,367	6,747	942	2,743	5,959	771	905	3,674
Los Angeles......	6,330	6,326	347	8,767	5,454	7,682	5,470	6,108	5,922	2,300
Madrid	5,045	851	5,803	7,080	1,653	2,978	6,706	1,128	1,427	3,792
Melbourne	8,226	9,929	7,856	3,759	9,630	7,826	5,062	9,790	9,598	10,180
Mexico City.......	4,764	6,377	1,887	10,327	6,012	8,184	7,035	6,320	6,337	1,885
Montreal.........	5,078	4,104	2,543	9,203	3,714	5,880	6,471	4,009	4,022	489
Moscow	7,170	1,483	5,885	5,228	716	1,532	4,660	1,043	721	4,876
New York	4,801	4,293	2,572	9,534	3,986	6,141	6,757	4,234	4,270	205
Paris............	5,684	690	5,577	6,673	1,003	2,625	6,053	645	852	3,840
Rio de Janeiro	...	5,707	6,613	9,785	6,683	7,374	11,532	6,127	6,455	4,779
Rome	5,707	...	6,259	6,229	1,245	2,127	6,142	477	820	4,497
San Francisco	6,613	6,259	...	8,448	5,399	7,362	5,150	5,994	5,854	2,441
Singapore........	9,785	6,229	8,448	...	5,936	4,103	3,300	6,035	5,843	9,662
Stockholm	6,683	1,245	5,399	5,936	...	2,173	5,053	780	494	4,183
Tokyo	11,532	6,142	5,150	3,300	5,053	4,775	...	5,689	5,347	6,791
Warsaw	6,455	820	5,854	5,843	494	1,879	5,689	347	...	4,472
Washington, DC....	4,779	4,497	2,441	9,662	4,183	6,341	6,791	4,438	4,472	...

U.S. Farms—Number and Acreage by State, 2000, 2006

Source: National Agricultural Statistics Service, U.S. Dept. of Agriculture

STATE	No. of farms (1,000) 2006	2000[1]	Acreage in farms (mil.) 2006	2000	Acreage per farm 2006	2000	STATE	No. of farms (1,000) 2006	2000[1]	Acreage in farms (mil.) 2006	2000	Acreage per farm 2006	2000
AL....	43.0	47.0	8.6	9.0	200	191	NE	47.6	46.1	45.7	46.1	960	887
AK....	0.6	0.6	0.9	0.9	1,406	1,569	NV	3.0	3.1	6.3	6.4	2,100	2,065
AZ....	10.0	10.7	26.1	26.9	2,610	2,518	NH	3.4	3.3	0.5	0.4	132	133
AR....	46.5	48.0	14.3	14.6	308	304	NJ	9.8	9.7	0.8	0.8	81	86
CA....	76.0	83.1	26.3	28.0	346	337	NM	17.5	18.0	44.5	44.9	2,543	2,494
CO....	30.7	30.0	30.7	31.6	1,000	1,060	NY	35.0	37.5	7.5	7.7	214	205
CT....	4.2	4.2	0.4	0.4	86	86	NC	48.0	55.5	8.8	9.2	180	166
DE....	2.3	2.6	0.5	0.6	224	215	ND	30.3	30.8	39.4	39.4	1,300	1,279
FL....	41.0	44.0	10.0	10.4	244	238	OH	76.2	79.0	14.3	14.8	188	187
GA....	49.0	49.1	10.8	10.9	220	223	OK	83.0	84.5	33.7	33.8	406	401
HI	5.5	5.5	1.3	1.4	236	251	OR	39.3	40.0	17.1	17.3	435	433
ID	25.0	24.5	11.8	11.9	472	486	PA	58.2	59.0	7.7	7.7	131	130
IL	72.4	77.0	27.3	27.5	377	357	PR[2]	13.6	NA	0.6	NA	45	NA
IN	59.0	63.4	15.0	15.2	254	240	RI	0.9	0.8	0.1	0.1	71	75
IA	88.6	94.0	31.5	32.5	356	346	SC	24.6	24.2	4.9	4.9	198	203
KS	64.0	64.5	47.2	47.5	738	736	SD	31.3	32.4	43.7	44.0	1,396	1,358
KY	84.0	90.0	13.7	13.7	163	152	TN	82.0	88.0	11.4	11.8	139	134
LA	26.8	29.0	7.8	8.0	291	277	TX	230.0	228.3	129.7	130.9	564	573
ME	7.1	7.1	1.4	1.4	192	190	UT	15.1	15.5	11.6	11.6	768	747
MD	12.0	12.4	2.0	2.1	170	172	VT	6.3	6.6	1.2	1.3	198	192
MA	6.1	6.1	0.5	0.5	85	89	VA	46.8	48.5	8.5	8.7	182	180
MI	53.0	53.0	10.1	10.2	191	192	WA	34.0	37.0	15.1	15.6	444	420
MN	79.3	81.0	27.4	27.9	346	344	WV	21.2	20.8	3.6	3.6	170	173
MS	42.0	42.0	11.0	11.2	262	266	WI	76.0	77.5	15.3	16.0	201	206
MO	105.0	109.0	30.1	30.2	287	277	WY	9.1	9.2	34.4	34.5	3,780	3,750
MT	28.1	27.8	60.1	59.3	2,139	2,133	U.S.[3] ..	2,089.8	2,166.8	932.4	945.1	446	436

(1) Figs. for 2000 are revised. (2) Puerto Rico. Not included in U.S. total. (3) Totals may be different due to rounding.

U.S. Farms, Number and Average Size, 1940-2006

Source: National Agricultural Statistics Service, U.S. Dept. of Agriculture

The number of farms in the United States in 2006 was estimated at 2.09 million, 0.4% fewer than in 2005. Total land in farms decreased 780,000 acres from 2005, to 932.4 million acres. The average farm size in 2006 was 446 acres, an increase of one acre from the previous year. The continuing decline in the number of farms and land being farmed reflected consolidation in farming operations and the use of agricultural land for other purposes.

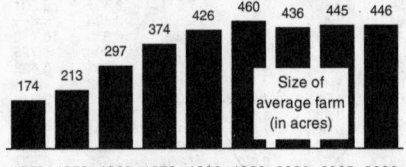

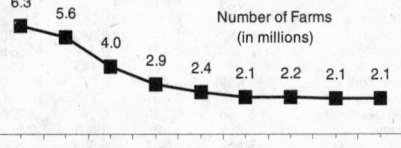

U.S. Federal Food Assistance Programs, 1990-2006[1]

Source: Food and Nutrition Service, U.S. Dept. of Agriculture

(in millions of dollars)

	1990	1995	2000	2001	2002	2003	2004	2005	2006
Food stamps[2].................	$15,491	$24,620	$17,054	$17,789	$20,637	$23,814	$27,099	$31,096	$32,921
Puerto Rico nutrition asst.[3]......	937	1,131	1,268	1,296	1,351	1,395	1,413	1,495	1,518
Natl. school lunch[4].........	3,834	5,160	6,149	6,475	6,853	7,189	7,626	8,031	8,191
School breakfast[4,5].............	596	1,048	1,393	1,450	1,567	1,652	1,776	1,927	2,043
WIC[6].........................	2,122	3,440	3,982	4,151	4,342	4,527	4,889	4,994	5,073
Summer food service[7]..........	164	237	267	270	263	257	263	267	276
Child/adult care[8]...............	813	1,464	1,683	1,737	1,853	1,926	2,020	2,111	2,154
Special milk[9]..................	19	17	15	16	16	14	14	17	15
Nutrition for the elderly (NSIP)[10] ...	142	148	137	152	150	3	4	4	3
Food distrib. to Indian reserv.[11]...	66	65	76	72	76	75	78	76	74
Commodity supp. food prog.[11]....	85	99	98	106	115	122	145	156	131
Food dist. to charitable inst.[12] ...	104	64	2	7	16	6	10	4	3
Emergency food assistance[13]	334	135	225	377	435	456	420	373	300
TOTAL[14].....................	$24,707	$37,628	$32,317	$33,905	$37,802	$41,566	$45,894	$50,695	$52,849

(1) Data are for fiscal years, ending Sept. 30. All 2005 data are preliminary; all data subject to revision by the FNS. (2) Includes benefits and admin. expenses. (3) Puerto Rico does not participate in the Food Stamp Program. (4) Data are 9-month averages (summer months excluded). (5) Costs are cash payments (federal reimbursements to states). (6) Includes food benefits, nutrition services and admin. funds, Farmers' Market Nutrition Program, infrastructure, program evaluation, and technical assistance. (7) Includes cash payments, commodity costs, and admin. expenditures. Similar services provided by Natl. School Lunch & Breakfast Program. (8) Includes cash payments, entitlement and bonus commodities, cash-in-lieu of commodities, sponsor admin. costs, start-up costs and audits. (9) Costs are cash payments. (10) For years 2003 and after, program was administered by the Agency on Aging; Food and Nutrition Service costs limited to value of commodities distributed. (11) Includes commodity distribution costs and admin. expenses. (12) Includes summer camps. (13) Food made available to hunger relief orgs. such as food banks and soup kitchens. (14) Totals may not add because of rounding and administrative costs not shown.

Eggs: U.S. Production, Price, and Value, 2005-06[1]

Source: National Agricultural Statistics Service, U.S. Dept. of Agriculture

STATE	Eggs produced (mil) 2005	2006	Price[2] per dozen (dollars) 2005	2006	Value of production (1,000 dollars) 2005	2006	STATE	Eggs produced (mil) 2005	2006	Price[2] per dozen (dollars) 2005	2006	Value of production (1,000 dollars) 2005	2006
AL....	2,071	2,002	1.630	1.650	281,595	274,490	NE....	3,217	3,129	0.310	0.370	82,989	96,358
AR....	3,416	3,267	1.240	1.220	352,645	331,932	NH....	39	36	0.736	0.794	2,391	2,381
CA....	5,082	4,962	0.429	0.515	181,655	212,889	NJ....	491	446	0.494	0.545	20,206	20,267
CO....	1,071	1,083	0.472	0.526	42,141	47,452	NY....	1,129	1,126	0.369	0.421	34,671	39,476
CT....	846	791	0.475	0.513	33,458	33,840	NC....	2,573	2,636	1.160	1.170	249,368	257,627
FL....	2,980	2,938	0.406	0.470	100,723	115,002	OH....	7,506	7,507	0.365	0.459	228,182	287,198
GA....	4,906	4,811	0.850	0.920	347,680	368,736	OK....	731	738	0.983	0.970	59,862	59,646
HI....	115	98	0.941	1.000	8,979	8,192	OR....	823	772	0.447	0.535	30,626	34,444
ID....	241	182	0.572	0.715	11,492	10,844	PA....	6,608	6,687	0.389	0.428	214,188	238,351
IL....	1,210	1,307	0.377	0.421	38,058	45,876	PR....	261	285	0.908	0.885	19,742	21,025
IN....	6,254	6,593	0.369	0.409	192,327	224,552	SC....	1,289	1,280	0.578	0.639	62,133	68,135
IA....	12,978	13,811	0.310	0.354	335,318	406,865	SD....	816	865	0.301	0.365	20,460	26,312
KY....	1,228	1,150	0.709	0.763	72,568	73,156	TN....	316	289	1.310	1.400	34,478	33,642
LA....	469	463	0.795	0.710	31,073	27,386	TX....	4,760	5,039	0.602	0.604	238,798	253,563
ME....	1,025	1,064	0.545	0.578	46,594	51,288	UT....	878	937	0.318	0.394	23,248	30,727
MD....	798	733	0.467	0.490	31,069	29,907	VT....	50	55	0.584	0.530	2,434	2,427
MA....	71	71	0.607	0.655	3,591	3,875	VA....	823	806	0.983	0.994	67,421	66,769
MI....	2,142	2,391	0.347	0.367	61,870	73,097	WA....	1,343	1,298	0.400	0.470	44,791	50,840
MN....	2,985	2,940	0.365	0.438	90,899	107,303	WV....	261	274	1.400	1.410	30,473	32,210
MS....	1,627	1,546	1.250	1.240	169,834	159,891	WI....	1,321	1,284	0.361	0.424	39,702	45,323
MO....	1,910	1,903	0.469	0.468	74,570	74,213	WY....	4	4	0.397	0.460	119	138
MT....	106	104	0.374	0.465	3,300	4,031	U.S.[3]..	90,027	90,877	0.540	0.579	4,049,293	4,387,528

(1) Estimates cover the 12-month period from Dec. 1 of the previous year through Nov. 30. (2) Average of all eggs sold by producers, including hatching eggs. (3) U.S. total includes other states not listed separately. Puerto Rico (PR) not included in total.

Livestock on Farms in the U.S., 1900-2007

Source: National Agricultural Statistics Service, U.S. Dept. of Agriculture
(in thousands)

Year (On Jan. 1)	All cattle[1]	Milk cows	Sheep and lambs	Hogs and pigs[2]	Year (On Jan. 1)	All cattle[1]	Milk cows	Sheep and lambs	Hogs and pigs[2]
1900........	59,739	16,544	48,105	51,055	1985........	109,582	10,777	10,716	54,073
1910........	58,993	19,450	50,239	48,072	1990........	95,816	10,015	11,358	53,788
1920........	70,400	21,455	40,743	60,159	1995........	102,755	9,487	8,886	57,150
1930........	61,003	23,032	51,565	55,705	2000........	98,199	9,183	7,036	59,335
1940........	68,309	24,940	52,107	61,165	2001........	97,298	9,172	6,908	59,110
1950........	77,963	23,853	29,826	58,937	2002........	96,723	9,106	6,623	59,722
1955........	96,592	23,462	31,582	50,474	2003........	96,100	9,142	6,321	59,554
1960........	96,236	19,527	33,170	59,026	2004........	94,888	8,990	6,105	60,444
1965........	109,000	16,981	25,127	56,106	2005........	95,838	9,005	6,135	60,975
1970........	112,369	12,091	20,423	57,046	2006........	96,702	9,063	6,230	61,449
1975........	132,028	11,220	14,515	54,693	2007[3]........	97,003	9,129	6,185	62,149
1980........	111,242	10,758	12,699	67,318					

(1) From 1970, includes milk cows and heifers that have calved. (2) As of Dec. 1 of preceding year. (3) Preliminary.

U.S. Meat Production and Consumption, 1940-2007

Source: Economic Research Service, U.S. Dept. of Agriculture
(in millions of pounds)

Year	Beef Prod.	Cons.	Veal Prod.	Cons.	Lamb and mutton Prod.	Cons.	Pork Prod.	Cons.	All red meats[1] Prod.	Cons.	All Poultry Prod.	Cons.
1940	7,175	7,257	981	981	876	873	10,044	9,701	19,076	18,812	NA	NA
1950	9,534	9,529	1,230	1,206	597	596	10,714	10,390	22,075	21,721	3,174	3,097
1960	14,728	15,465	1,109	1,118	769	857	13,905	14,057	30,511	31,497	6,310	6,168
1970	21,684	23,451	588	613	551	669	14,699	14,957	37,522	39,689	10,193	9,981
1980	21,643	23,560	400	420	318	351	16,617	16,838	38,978	41,170	14,173	13,525
1990	22,743	24,030	327	325	363	397	15,354	16,025	38,787	40,778	23,468	22,152
1995	25,222	25,534	319	319	285	346	17,849	17,768	43,675	43,967	30,393	25,944
2000	26,888	27,338	225	225	234	354	18,952	18,643	46,299	46,560	36,073	30,508
2001	26,212	27,026	205	204	227	368	19,160	18,492	45,804	46,089	38,942	30,823
2002	27,192	27,878	205	204	223	381	19,685	19,146	47,305	47,608	38,079	32,575
2003	24,650	27,750	176	177	200	372	20,529	19,437	45,555	47,735	39,585	34,139
2004	24,787	27,754	165	164	191	355	20,705	19,114	45,848	47,387	40,935	34,947
2005	26,258	28,131	156	155	190	356	21,075	19,047	47,679	47,689	41,485	35,732
2006	26,175	28,121	161	163	185	373	21,666	19,592	48,187	48,249	41,540	35,730
2007*	26,420	28,090	159	159	183	371	21,995	19,845	48,757	48,465	42,427	36,049

* Preliminary. (1) Meats may not add to total because of rounding. (2) Consumption (also called total disappearance) is estimated as: production plus beginning stocks, plus imports, minus exports, minus ending stocks. NA = Not available.

U.S. Annual Per Capita Consumption of Selected Foods, 1910-2005

Source: USDA/Economic Research Service

Year	Whole milk[1]	Low-fat & skim milk[1]	Butter[2]	Margarine[2]	Total fat[2, 3]	Red meat[2, 4]	Poultry[2, 5]	Fish & shellfish[2]
1910	25.2	7.1	18.4	1.6	37.7	96.0	11.8	11.2
1940	29.2	4.7	17.0	2.4	50.1	92.4	12.3	11.0
1970	25.5	5.8	5.4	10.8	55.7	131.9	33.8	11.7
2000	8.1	14.4	4.5	7.5	84.5	113.7	67.9	15.2
2005	6.9	14.1	4.6	4.0	85.5	110.0	73.6	16.1

(1) Gallons. (2) Pounds. (3) Includes edible rapeseed (canola) oil beginning in 1985. Includes specialty fats used mainly in confectionary products and non-dairy creamers. (4) Figures are calculated on the basis of raw and edible meat. Excludes edible offals, bones, and viscera. Excludes game consumption. (5) Figures are calculated on the basis of raw and edible meat. Includes skin, neck, and giblets. Excludes chicken for commercially prepared pet food.

U.S. Organic Cropland and Animals, 1995-2005

Source: USDA Economic Research Service

Organic acreage[1]	1995	2000	2001	2002	2003	2004	2005	%Change, 2000-05	Total U.S. farmland[2]
Grains									
Corn..........	32,650	77,912	93,551	96,270	105,574	99,111	130,672	67.7%	81,759,000
Wheat.........	96,100	181,262	194,640	217,611	234,221	214,244	277,487	53.1	57,229,000
Oats..........	13,250	29,771	33,254	53,459	46,074	42,616	46,465	56.1	4,246,000
Barley.........	17,150	41,904	31,478	34,031	30,265	26,629	39,271	-6.3	3,875,000
Rice	8,400	26,870	29,022	22,381	20,152	22,173	26,428	-1.6	3,384,000
Beans									
Soybeans.......	47,200	136,071	174,467	126,540	122,403	114,239	122,217	-10.2	72,142,000
Dry beans	NA	14,010	15,080	2,430	9,836	7,642	10,561	-24.6	1,659,300
Dry peas & lentils	5,900	10,144	9,362	7,476	16,188	15,893	17,757	75.1	571,000
Hay and silage	84,100	231,207	253,641	267,827	327,538	356,590	411,342	77.9	61,649,000
All Vegetables	NA	62,342	71,667	69,887	78,905	86,822	98,525	58.0	2,114,110
All Fruits..........	NA	43,481	55,675	60,693	77,989	80,707	97,277	123.7	3,911,200
Other cropland									
Cotton	32,850	15,027	11,456	10,551	9,875	9,213	9,537	-36.5	14,195,400
Peanuts	NA	2,085	4,653	5,134	5,698	9,514	11,940	472.8	1,657,000
Potatoes.......	NA	5,433	7,533	6,593	6,569	7,300	6,581	21.1	1,107,200
Trees for maple syrup	10,200	11,965	12,030	1,121	1,514	13,357	12,247	2.3	NA
Fallow land........	NA	57,688	72,595	64,668	83,003	116,582	165,040	186.1	16,559,229
Total cropland	638,500	1,218,905	1,302,392	1,299,632	1,451,601	1,452,353	1,723,271	41.4	340,650,083
Total pasture and									
rangeland	276,300	557,167	789,505	625,902	745,273	1,592,756	2,331,158	318.4	455,786,634
Total farmland ...	914,800	1,776,073	2,094,272	1,925,534	2,196,874	3,045,109	4,054,429	128.3	796,436,717

Organic animals[1]	1995	2000	2001	2002	2003	2004	2005	%Change, 2000-05	Total U.S. Animals
Total livestock	NA	56,028	72,209	108,362	124,346	157,253	196,506	250.7%	162,917,000
Beef cows	NA	13,829	15,197	23,384	27,285	36,662	36,113	161.1	32,915,000
Milk cows	NA	38,196	48,677	67,207	74,435	74,840	87,082	128.0	9,058,000
Other cows[3]........	NA	NA	993	10,103	11,501	36,598	58,822	NA	53,517,000
Hogs & pigs	NA	1,724	3,135	2,753	6,564	4,883	10,018	481.1	61,197,000
Sheep and lambs....	NA	2,279	4,207	4,915	4,561	4,270	4,471	96.2	6,230,000
Total poultry	NA	3,159,050	5,014,015	6,270,181	8,780,152	7,304,566	13,757,270	335.5	NA
Layer hens	NA	1,113,746	1,611,662	1,052,272	1,591,181	1,787,901	2,415,056	116.8	347,917,000
Broilers..........	NA	1,924,807	3,286,456	3,032,189	6,301,014	4,769,104	10,405,879	440.6	8,740,650,000
Turkeys	NA	9,138	98,653	305,605	217,353	164,292	144,086	1476.8	NA
Other/unclassified ...	NA	111,359	17,244	1,880,115	670,604	583,269	792,249	611.4	NA

NA = Not available. (1) Certified by USDA's National Organic Program. (2) Total organic and nonorganic land used for agricultural purposes. (3) Includes unclassified cows and some young stock.

Production of Principal U.S. Crops, 1990-2006

Source: National Agricultural Statistics Service, U.S. Dept. of Agriculture

Year	Corn for grain (1,000 bu)	Oats (1,000 bu)	Barley (1,000 bu)	Sorghum for grain (1,000 bu)	All wheat (1,000 bu)	Rye (1,000 bu)	Flaxseed (1,000 bu)	Upland Cotton (1,000 b)	Cottonseed (1,000 t)
1990	7,934,028	357,654	422,196	573,303	2,729,778	10,176	3,812	15,505.4	5,968.5
1991	7,474,765	243,851	464,326	584,860	1,980,139	9,734	6,200	17,614.3	6,925.5
1992	9,476,698	294,229	455,090	875,022	2,466,798	11,440	3,288	16,219.5	6,230.1
1993	6,336,470	206,770	398,041	534,172	2,396,440	10,340	3,480	16,134.6	6,343.2
1994	10,102,735	229,008	374,862	649,206	2,320,981	11,341	2,922	19,662.0	7,603.9
1995	7,373,876	162,027	359,562	460,373	2,182,591	10,064	2,211	17,532.2	6,848.7
1996	9,293,435	155,273	395,751	802,974	2,285,133	9,016	1,602	18,413.5	7,143.5
1997	9,206,832	167,246	359,878	633,545	2,481,466	8,132	2,420	18,245.0	6,934.6
1998	9,758,685	165,981	352,125	519,933	2,547,321	12,161	6,708	13,475.9	5,365.4
1999	9,430,612	146,193	280,292	595,166	2,299,010	11,038	7,864	16,293.7	6,354.0
2000	9,915,051	149,545	318,728	470,526	2,232,460	8,386	10,730	16,799.2	6,435.6
2001	9,506,840	117,024	249,420	514,524	1,957,043	6,971	11,455	19,602.4	7,452.2
2002	8,966,787	116,002	226,906	360,713	1,605,878	6,488	11,863	16,530.3	6,183.9
2003[1]	10,089,222	144,383	278,283	411,237	2,344,760	8,634	10,516	17,822.9	6,664.6
2004[1]	11,807,086	115,695	279,743	453,654	2,158,245	8,255	10,368	22,505.1	8,242.1
2005[1]	11,114,082	114,878	211,896	392,933	2,104,690	7,537	19,695	23,259.7	8,172.1
2006	10,534,868	93,764	180,051	277,538	1,812,036	7,193	11,019	20,973.0	7,632.0

Year	Tobacco (1,000 lb)	All hay (1,000 t)	Beans, dry edible (1,000 cwt)	Peas, dry edible (1,000 cwt)	Peanuts[2] (1,000 lb)	Soybeans[3] (1,000 bu)	Potatoes (1,000 cwt)	Sweet potatoes (1,000 cwt)
1990	1,626,380	146,212	32,379	2,372	3,602,770	1,925,947	402,110	12,594
1991	1,664,327	152,073	33,765	3,715	4,926,570	1,986,539	417,622	11,203
1992	1,721,671	146,903	22,615	2,535	4,284,416	2,190,354	425,367	12,005
1993	1,613,319	146,799	21,913	3,292	3,392,415	1,870,958	428,693	11,053
1994	1,582,896	150,060	29,028	2,255	4,247,455	2,516,694	467,054	13,395
1995	1,268,538	154,166	30,812	4,765	4,247,455	2,176,814	443,606	12,906
1996	1,517,334	149,457	27,960	2,671	3,661,205	2,382,364	498,633	13,456
1997	1,787,399	152,536	29,370	5,752	3,539,380	2,688,750	467,091	13,327
1998	1,479,867	151,780	30,418	5,934	3,963,440	2,741,014	475,771	12,382
1999	1,292,692	159,707	33,085	4,773	3,829,490	2,653,758	478,216	12,234
2000	1,052,999	151,921	26,409	3,474	3,265,505	2,757,810	513,621	13,794
2001	991,223	156,764	19,583	3,763	4,276,704	2,890,682	437,888	14,637
2002	871,122	149,467	30,312	4,727	3,321,040	2,756,147	458,171	12,799
2003[1]	802,560	157,585	22,492	5,202	4,144,150	2,453,665	457,814	15,891
2004[1]	881,973	158,247	17,788	11,419	4,288,200	3,123,686	456,041	16,112
2005[1]	645,015	151,017	26,772	14,003	4,869,860	3,063,237	423,926	15,730
2006	726,724	141,666	24,247	13,203	3,474,450	3,188,247	434,683	16,441

Year	Rice (1,000 cwt)	Sugarcane (1,000 t)	Sugar beets (1,000 t)	Pecans[4] (1,000 lb)	Apples (1,000 t)	Grapes (1,000 t)	Peaches (1,000 t)	Oranges[5] (1,000 bx)	Grapefruit[5] (1,000 bx)
1990	156,088	28,136	27,513	205,000	4,828	5,660	1,121	184,415	49,300
1991	159,367	30,252	28,203	299,000	4,853	5,556	1,348	178,950	55,500
1992	179,658	30,363	29,143	166,000	5,284	6,052	1,336	209,610	55,265
1993	156,110	31,101	26,249	365,000	5,342	6,023	1,330	255,760	68,375
1994	197,779	30,929	31,853	199,000	5,668	5,871	1,253	240,450	65,100
1995	173,871	30,944	27,954	268,000	5,293	5,922	1,150	263,605	71,050
1996	171,321	29,462	26,680	209,500	5,196	5,554	1,058	263,890	66,200
1997	182,992	31,709	29,886	335,000	5,162	7,291	1,312	292,620	70,200
1998	184,443	32,743	32,499	146,400	5,823	5,820	1,190	315,525	63,150
1999	206,027	35,299	33,420	406,100	5,316	6,236	1,252	224,580	61,200
2000	190,872	36,114	32,541	209,850	5,291	7,688	1,276	299,760	66,980
2001	215,270	34,587	25,764	338,500	4,712	6,569	1,204	280,935	59,750
2002	210,960	35,553	27,707	172,900	4,262	7,339	1,268	283,760	58,660
2003[1]	199,897	33,858	30,710	282,100	4,397	6,664	1,260	267,040	50,080
2004[1]	232,362	29,013	30,021	185,800	5,220	6,240	1,307	294,620	52,540
2005[1]	223,235	26,606	27,433	280,250	4,860	7,814	1,185	216,500	25,640
2006	193,736	29,489	33,765	188,900	5,036	6,346	1,010	210,750	30,600

(1) Some totals revised. (2) Harvested for nuts. (3) Harvested for beans. (4) Utilized production only. (5) Crop year ending in year cited.

Production of Principal U.S. Crops, by State, 2006

Source: National Agricultural Statistics Service, U.S. Dept. of Agriculture

STATE	Barley (1,000 bu)	Corn, grain (1,000 bu)	Upland Cotton (1,000 b)	All hay (1,000 t)	Oats (1,000 bu)	Potatoes (1,000 cwt)	Soybeans (1,000 bu)	Tobacco (1,000 lb)	All wheat (1,000 bu)
Alabama	—	11,880	680	1,440	400	240	3,000	—	2,610
Alaska	157,000	—	—	22,000	28,000	186,000	—	—	—
Arizona	2,530	3,060	570	2,251	—	1,170	—	—	7,580
Arkansas	—	26,280	2,560	2,519	—	—	107,450	—	18,605
California	3,575	18,150	770	9,048	1,720	15,152	—	—	20,935
Colorado	4,830	134,160	—	4,389	700	24,166	—	—	41,515
Connecticut	—	NE	—	120	—	—	—	4,046	—
Delaware	1,920	23,345	—	40	—	504	5,487	—	3,015
Florida	—	2,460	150	598	—	7,816	135	2,860	210
Georgia	—	25,200	2,330	1,170	1,590	—	3,500	30,090	5,880
Hawaii	—	—	—	—	—	—	—	—	—
Idaho	42,840	11,050	—	5,720	1,440	121,820	—	—	90,315
Illinois	—	1,817,450	—	2,508	3,080	2,489	482,400	—	60,970
Indiana	—	844,660	—	2,201	1,120	NE	284,000	NE	31,740
Iowa	—	2,050,100	—	5,306	8,360	—	510,050	—	1,188
Kansas	486	345,000	140	6,550	1,800	1,824	98,560	—	291,200
Kentucky	1,232	151,840	—	6,316	—	—	60,280	186,700	22,720
Louisiana	—	40,600	1,250	975	—	—	29,400	—	5,565
Maine	850	NE	—	253	1,650	18,270	—	—	—
Maryland	2,784	60,350	—	569	—	928	15,810	NE	8,500
Massachusetts	—	NE	—	170	—	806	—	1,923	—
Michigan	686	288,120	—	3,670	4,030	14,190	89,550	—	47,450
Minnesota	5,400	1,102,850	—	5,679	11,200	20,400	319,000	—	80,340
Mississippi	—	35,750	2,100	1,560	—	—	42,900	—	4,307
Missouri	—	362,940	985	6,944	1,820	2,394	194,180	3,375	49,140
Montana	31,000	2,628	—	4,320	1,104	3,518	—	—	153,075
Nebraska	NE	1,178,000	—	5,675	2,255	8,633	250,500	—	61,200
Nevada	200	NE	—	1,757	—	2,937	—	—	1,056
New Hampshire	—	NE	—	105	—	—	—	—	—
New Jersey	114	8,256	—	234	—	600	3,010	—	1,320
New Mexico	—	8,325	90	1,284	—	2,100	—	—	3,840
New York	660	61,920	—	2,790	4,958	5,700	9,108	—	5,795
North Carolina	1,360	97,680	1,300	1,663	1,586	3,255	43,520	330,410	24,780
North Dakota	48,755	155,400	—	3,137	4,920	25,480	119,970	—	251,770
Ohio	272	470,640	—	3,421	4,125	992	217,140	7,000	65,280
Oklahoma	—	23,100	190	3,598	240	—	3,655	—	81,600
Oregon	2,436	5,220	—	3,256	1,900	18,533	—	—	44,440
Pennsylvania	3,726	117,120	—	5,125	7,040	2,730	17,000	16,240	8,850
Rhode Island	—	NE	—	17	—	130	—	—	—
South Carolina	—	31,900	450	684	990	—	11,310	48,300	6,150
South Dakota	560	312,340	—	4,180	5,415	NE	130,900	—	84,090
Tennessee	—	62,500	1,350	4,251	—	—	44,070	49,135	12,160
Texas	—	175,450	6,000	8,675	3,700	7,124	3,720	—	33,600
Utah	2,280	2,669	—	2,540	539	NE	—	—	6,120
Vermont	—	NE	—	398	—	—	—	—	—
Virginia	3,234	41,400	158	2,882	220	1,512	15,810	46,642	10,540
Washington	11,970	15,750	—	3,113	688	89,900	—	—	140,050
West Virginia	—	3,120	—	1,046	—	—	—	672	366
Wisconsin	1,620	400,400	—	5,404	14,490	29,370	72,160	NE	18,290
Wyoming	4,731	5,805	—	2,115	684	—	—	—	3,879
UNITED STATES	180,051	10,534,868	20,973	141,666	193,764	434,683	3,188,247	726,724	1,812,036

NE = Not estimated; bu = bushels; b = bales (480-lbs); t = tons; cwt = hundredweight.

U.S. Farm Business Real Estate Debt Outstanding, by Lender Groups,[1] 1960-2006

Source: Economic Research Service, U.S. Dept. of Agriculture

Year	Real estate debt [2]	AMOUNTS HELD BY PRINCIPAL LENDER GROUPS				
		Farm Credit System [2]	Farm Service Agency [3]	Life insurance companies [4]	Commercial banks	Individuals and others [5]
1960	$11,309,593	$2,222,301	$623,895	$2,651,587	$1,355,733	$4,408,545
1970	27,238,348	6,368,922	2,168,992	5,038,804	3,333,945	10,181,409
1980	85,272,367	31,575,578	7,094,800	11,337,301	7,430,446	26,377,883
1985	94,089,977	39,638,435	9,231,655	10,596,325	10,087,966	24,228,530
1990	67,632,973	23,461,664	6,913,726	8,782,095	14,740,757	13,728,224
1991	67,449,880	22,774,771	6,336,758	8,591,225	15,674,874	14,068,465
1992	67,879,337	22,866,792	5,755,007	7,888,515	16,881,167	14,485,871
1993	68,432,731	22,409,618	5,253,647	8,086,943	17,635,101	15,047,423
1994	69,911,852	22,137,036	4,918,556	8,122,623	18,971,234	15,762,403
1995	71,722,937	22,480,484	4,572,770	8,224,581	20,151,323	16,293,778
1996	74,422,235	23,450,202	4,285,372	8,629,197	21,213,695	16,843,769
1997	78,513,555	24,924,671	4,021,975	8,920,956	23,215,498	17,430,456
1998	83,100,263	26,787,599	3,777,265	9,943,629	25,193,180	17,398,591
1999	87,206,087	28,044,751	3,583,694	10,633,978	27,578,839	17,364,826
2000	84,723,763	29,692,046	3,418,223	11,053,300	29,756,973	10,803,221
2001	88,541,011	32,854,687	3,347,374	11,205,391	31,082,102	10,051,456
2002	95,422,895	37,815,366	3,180,655	11,420,945	33,059,777	9,946,152
2003	94,138,446	37,661,508	2,484,643	11,371,377	32,936,809	9,684,109
2004	96,871,867	37,722,787	2,222,323	10,912,282	35,232,520	10,781,955
2005	101,517,822	40,125,202	2,050,287	11,019,099	36,938,827	11,384,407
2006[6]	109,038,260	43,850,504	2,259,711	11,019,099	40,521,098	11,387,848

(1) Excludes debt for non-farm purposes. (2) Includes data for joint stock land banks and real estate loans by Agricultural Credit Association. (3) Includes loans made directly by Farm Services Agency for farm ownership, soil, and water loans to individuals, Native American tribe land acquisition, grazing associations, and half of economic emergency loans. Also includes loans for rural housing on farm tracts and labor housing. (4) American Council of Life Insurance members. (5) Estimated by ERS, USDA. Includes Commodity Credit Corporation storage and drying facility loans. (6) Preliminary.

U.S. Farm Marketings by State, 2005-06

Source: Economic Research Service, U.S. Dept. of Agriculture; in thousands of dollars

STATE	2005 Farm Marketings			2006 Farm Marketings		
	Total	Crops	Livestock and products	Total	Crops	Livestock and products
Alabama	$4,174,340	$799,401	$3,374,939	$3,739,060	$695,921	$3,043,139
Alaska	50,068	25,879	24,189	64,218	24,850	39,368
Arizona	3,073,512	1,661,122	1,412,390	2,879,224	1,558,497	1,320,727
Arkansas	6,474,259	2,257,008	4,217,251	6,164,069	2,396,712	3,767,357
California	32,765,753	24,340,125	8,425,628	31,402,706	23,787,727	7,614,979
Colorado	5,394,782	1,440,317	3,954,465	5,614,394	1,552,540	4,061,854
Connecticut	523,951	363,308	160,643	523,611	372,322	151,289
Delaware	964,855	174,111	790,744	969,124	182,708	786,416
Florida	7,702,314	6,295,677	1,406,637	6,974,161	5,669,269	1,304,892
Georgia	6,212,167	2,200,016	4,012,151	6,005,101	2,240,211	3,764,890
Hawaii	576,031	487,195	88,836	554,580	466,875	87,705
Idaho	4,454,834	1,862,731	2,592,103	4,415,602	1,999,621	2,415,981
Illinois	8,843,905	6,848,776	1,995,129	8,635,700	6,840,840	1,794,860
Indiana	5,428,796	3,383,488	2,045,308	5,973,217	3,918,946	2,054,271
Iowa	14,522,964	6,617,644	7,905,320	15,108,261	7,229,148	7,879,113
Kansas	10,102,830	3,236,720	6,866,110	10,335,795	3,365,144	6,970,651
Kentucky	3,981,506	1,273,649	2,707,857	4,007,202	1,299,218	2,707,984
Louisiana	2,171,047	1,253,707	917,340	2,186,180	1,321,911	864,269
Maine	544,031	249,516	294,515	591,674	302,766	288,908
Maryland	1,704,426	703,786	1,000,640	1,597,699	725,556	872,143
Massachusetts	408,544	316,523	92,021	433,026	343,606	89,420
Michigan	4,224,000	2,496,123	1,727,877	4,487,765	2,833,395	1,654,370
Minnesota	9,306,710	4,344,606	4,962,104	9,769,512	5,127,587	4,641,925
Mississippi	4,171,916	1,268,427	2,903,489	3,788,510	1,244,984	2,543,526
Missouri	5,652,968	2,544,387	3,108,581	5,621,258	2,627,578	2,993,680
Montana	2,304,359	1,025,654	1,278,705	2,349,159	1,069,977	1,279,182
Nebraska	11,481,847	3,935,398	7,546,449	12,042,344	4,358,958	7,683,386
Nevada	464,961	157,383	307,578	446,550	166,179	280,371
New Hampshire	163,399	93,489	69,910	161,804	97,765	64,039
New Jersey	873,507	691,226	182,281	923,933	762,632	161,301
New Mexico	2,611,510	621,714	1,989,796	2,463,526	602,427	1,861,099
New York	3,660,517	1,333,285	2,327,232	3,509,003	1,527,292	1,981,711
North Carolina	8,264,179	2,668,237	5,595,942	8,199,349	2,925,338	5,274,011
North Dakota	3,846,636	2,858,549	988,087	3,980,728	3,088,353	892,375
Ohio	5,153,810	3,104,957	2,048,853	5,479,712	3,448,407	2,031,305
Oklahoma	5,390,362	1,169,882	4,220,480	5,093,622	974,121	4,119,501
Oregon	3,680,921	2,642,353	1,038,568	3,990,617	2,960,584	1,030,033
Pennsylvania	4,731,897	1,515,729	3,216,168	4,691,681	1,723,338	2,968,343
Rhode Island	63,741	53,823	9,918	65,640	55,550	10,090
South Carolina	1,827,412	737,087	1,090,325	1,890,661	788,075	1,102,586
South Dakota	4,837,448	2,237,460	2,599,988	4,716,173	2,064,550	2,651,623
Tennessee	2,564,829	1,297,971	1,266,858	2,564,931	1,373,292	1,191,639
Texas	16,592,506	5,949,888	10,642,618	16,026,756	5,703,021	10,323,735
Utah	1,354,103	307,138	1,046,965	1,243,673	312,849	930,824
Vermont	566,948	82,733	484,215	500,792	85,688	415,104
Virginia	2,705,193	824,088	1,881,105	2,688,669	834,053	1,854,616
Washington	5,913,275	4,083,812	1,829,463	6,138,973	4,524,433	1,614,540
West Virginia	455,884	76,190	379,694	449,551	79,749	369,802
Wisconsin	6,813,633	1,802,018	5,011,615	6,791,282	2,135,279	4,656,003
Wyoming	975,985	152,384	823,601	1,021,145	161,649	859,496
UNITED STATES	240,729,371	115,866,690	124,862,681	239,271,907	119,951,478	119,320,429

Total U.S. Government Agricultural Payments, by State, 1990-2006

Source: Economic Research Service, U.S. Dept. of Agriculture; in thousands of dollars

STATE	1990	1995	2000	2003	2004	2005	2006
Alabama	$82,226	$54,140	$170,852	$219,214	$128,668	$201,718	$183,353
Alaska	1,117	1,735	1,672	1,830	5,434	3,773	1,224
Arizona	43,349	9,456	107,066	135,261	82,256	116,230	103,059
Arkansas	312,696	383,783	900,648	819,994	404,890	441,349	426,619
California	252,333	239,809	667,466	645,272	381,353	443,509	374,216
Colorado	236,723	167,661	351,116	316,893	216,185	354,637	214,540
Connecticut	2,123	2,382	18,143	7,237	4,312	7,534	3,678
Delaware	3,213	3,150	25,028	17,096	13,067	21,837	13,515
Florida	37,155	55,778	56,741	109,824	206,157	392,588	153,195
Georgia	130,593	67,332	380,057	549,155	278,131	475,947	379,608
Hawaii	519	947	11,927	1,294	1,706	3,454	1,121
Idaho	133,431	89,482	261,297	151,620	150,504	176,191	118,197
Illinois	506,603	543,753	1,943,916	854,099	1,154,266	1,732,742	1,015,800
Indiana	244,170	246,026	938,464	438,053	521,365	860,064	515,864
Iowa	753,733	786,652	2,302,094	1,045,632	1,251,809	2,217,602	1,211,728
Kansas	834,746	422,226	1,231,923	807,415	640,189	1,049,611	623,295
Kentucky	81,610	67,382	448,473	145,219	140,215	211,983	142,598
Louisiana	154,631	164,251	451,831	422,076	230,532	294,438	309,508
Maine	6,982	14,114	13,851	11,494	9,485	16,777	6,088
Maryland	17,386	15,241	88,470	66,299	48,307	71,779	52,303
Massachusetts	3,023	2,490	10,973	11,439	4,099	7,878	3,734
Michigan	168,831	151,055	381,056	251,608	208,631	363,951	220,348
Minnesota	511,759	467,807	1,502,230	781,677	694,197	1,336,534	741,074
Mississippi	185,969	133,544	463,901	470,694	297,698	383,202	392,987
Missouri	299,065	256,629	869,390	506,049	426,638	638,428	450,934
Montana	299,599	189,809	490,002	353,350	276,013	353,820	248,108
Nebraska	624,646	507,302	1,406,971	722,620	720,919	1,367,729	777,678
Nevada	5,347	4,264	3,918	11,953	6,379	8,425	2,437
New Hampshire	1,856	1,216	4,768	4,762	2,619	2,394	2,307
New Jersey	15,744	5,491	22,481	12,041	8,371	15,005	7,785
New Mexico	63,840	55,134	79,495	92,390	76,908	99,156	64,444
New York	59,304	43,563	159,876	160,276	79,775	133,235	110,235
North Carolina	73,255	41,476	447,096	357,543	176,422	323,217	206,787
North Dakota	545,378	296,215	1,170,234	651,484	464,508	810,306	436,900
Ohio	197,006	167,351	678,104	395,322	326,313	570,082	398,074
Oklahoma	319,040	164,662	439,851	355,332	209,142	294,644	229,639
Oregon	89,137	52,145	137,401	106,595	73,414	86,460	72,383
Pennsylvania	41,414	41,096	147,848	182,426	87,143	128,844	119,948
Rhode Island	191	317	1,218	611	877	548	423
South Carolina	62,637	34,586	144,499	126,461	63,907	115,759	84,970
South Dakota	332,851	245,016	789,895	547,920	395,774	780,050	401,115
Tennessee	91,029	47,405	298,873	175,199	124,594	194,272	149,716
Texas	974,702	643,119	1,647,066	1,661,141	998,199	1,607,027	1,190,035
Utah	34,897	25,045	36,181	55,479	34,473	41,070	20,162
Vermont	5,793	4,334	26,093	28,479	14,991	17,054	16,613
Virginia	32,378	25,967	152,452	175,585	63,744	111,070	80,039
Washington	205,425	116,062	352,503	263,950	192,665	219,860	177,531
West Virginia	6,049	5,268	23,509	12,962	6,206	8,193	5,964
Wisconsin	181,243	184,350	603,213	475,696	291,465	549,187	382,643
Wyoming	31,283	31,432	34,302	51,042	33,867	63,413	24,668
UNITED STATES[1]	$9,298,030	$7,279,451	$22,896,433	$16,177,044	$12,581,287	$19,977,473	$12,928,824

(1) Total includes disbursements to territories not shown.

Animal Products: Average Prices Received by U.S. Farmers, 1940-2006

Source: National Agricultural Statistics Service, U.S. Dept. of Agriculture

Figures below represent dollars per 100 lb for hogs, beef cattle, veal calves, sheep, lamb, and milk (wholesale); dollars per head for milk cows; cents per lb for chickens, broilers, turkeys, and wool; cents per dozen for eggs; weighted calendar year prices for livestock and livestock products other than wool. For 1943-63, wool prices were weighted on marketing year basis. The marketing year was changed in 1964 from a calendar year to a Dec.-Nov. basis for hogs, chickens, broilers, and eggs.

Year	Broilers	Calves (veal)	Cattle (beef)	Chickens (excl. broilers)	Eggs	Hogs	Lambs	Milk cows	Milk	Sheep	Turkeys	Wool
1940	17.3	8.83	7.56	13.0	18.0	5.39	8.10	61	1.82	3.95	15.2	28.4
1950	27.4	26.30	23.30	22.2	36.3	18.00	25.10	198	3.89	11.60	32.8	62.1
1960	16.9	22.90	20.40	12.2	36.1	15.30	17.90	223	4.21	5.61	25.4	42.0
1970	13.6	34.50	27.10	9.1	39.1	22.70	26.40	332	5.71	7.51	22.6	35.4
1975	26.3	27.20	32.20	9.9	54.5	46.10	42.10	412	8.75	11.30	34.8	44.8
1980	27.7	76.80	62.40	11.0	56.3	38.00	63.00	1,190	13.05	21.30	41.3	88.1
1985	30.1	62.10	53.70	14.8	57.1	44.00	67.70	860	12.76	23.90	49.1	63.3
1990	32.6	95.60	74.60	9.3	70.9	53.70	55.50	1,160	13.74	23.20	39.4	80.0
1995	34.4	73.10	61.80	6.5	62.4	40.50	78.20	1,130	12.78	28.00	41.6	104.0
1996	38.1	58.40	58.70	6.6	74.9	51.90	82.20	1,090	14.75	29.90	43.3	70.0
1997	37.7	78.90	63.10	7.7	70.3	52.90	90.30	1,100	13.36	37.90	39.9	84.0
1998	39.3	78.80	59.60	8.0	65.5	34.40	72.30	1,120	15.41	30.60	38.0	60.0
1999	37.1	87.70	63.40	7.1	62.2	30.30	74.50	1,280	14.38	31.10	40.8	38.0
2000	33.6	104.00	68.60	5.7	61.8	42.30	79.80	1,340	12.40	34.30	-40.7	33.0
2001	39.3	106.00	71.30	4.5	62.2	44.30	66.90	1,500	15.04	34.60	39.0	36.0
2002	30.5	96.40	66.50	4.8	58.9	33.40	73.80	1,600	12.18	27.90	36.5	53.0
2003	34.6	102.00	79.70	4.9	73.2	37.20	94.40	1,340	12.55	34.90	36.1	73.0
2004[1]	44.6	119.00	85.80	5.8	71.4	49.30	101.00	1,580	16.13	38.80	42.0	80.0
2005[1]	43.6	135.00	89.70	6.5	54.0	50.20	110.00	1,770	15.19	45.10	44.9	71.0
2006	38.6	133.00	87.20	5.8	57.9	46.00	95.50	1,730	12.97	35.20	47.9	68.0

(1) Some prices revised.

Crops: Average Prices Received by U.S. Farmers, 1940-2006

Source: National Agricultural Statistics Service, U.S. Dept. of Agriculture

Figures below represent cents per lb for cotton, apples, and peanuts; dollars per bushel for oats, wheat, corn, barley, and soybeans; dollars per 100 lb for rice, sorghum, and potatoes; dollars per ton for cottonseed and baled hay; weighted crop year prices. The marketing year is described as follows: apples, June-May; wheat, oats, barley, hay, and potatoes, July-June; cotton, rice, peanuts, and cottonseed, Aug.-July; soybeans, Sept.-Aug.; and corn and sorghum grain, Oct.-Sept.

Year	Apples	Barley	Corn	Cotton- seed	Cotton (upland)*	Hay	Oats	Peanuts	Pota- toes	Rice	Sor- ghum	Soy- beans	Wheat
1940	NA	0.39	0.62	21.70	9.8	9.78	0.30	3.7	0.85	1.80	0.87	0.89	0.67
1950	NA	1.19	1.52	86.60	39.9	21.10	0.79	10.9	1.50	5.09	1.88	2.47	2.00
1960	2.7	0.84	1.00	42.50	30.1	21.70	0.60	10.0	2.00	4.55	1.49	2.13	1.74
1970	6.5	0.97	1.33	56.40	21.9	26.10	0.62	12.8	2.21	5.17	2.04	2.85	1.33
1975	8.8	2.42	2.54	97.00	51.1	52.10	1.45	19.0	4.48	8.35	4.21	4.92	3.55
1980	12.1	2.86	3.11	129.00	74.4	71.00	1.79	25.1	6.55	12.80	5.25	7.57	3.91
1985	17.3	1.98	2.23	66.00	56.8	67.60	1.23	24.4	3.92	6.53	3.45	5.05	3.08
1990	20.9	2.14	2.28	121.00	67.1	80.60	1.14	34.7	6.08	6.68	3.79	5.74	2.61
1991	25.1	2.10	2.37	71.00	56.8	71.20	1.21	28.3	4.96	7.58	4.01	5.58	3.00
1992	19.5	2.04	2.07	97.50	53.7	74.30	1.32	30.0	5.52	5.89	3.38	5.56	3.24
1993	18.4	1.99	2.50	113.00	58.1	84.70	1.36	30.4	6.18	7.98	4.13	6.40	3.26
1994	18.6	2.03	2.26	101.00	72.0	86.70	1.22	28.9	5.58	6.78	3.80	5.48	3.45
1995	24.0	2.89	3.24	106.00	75.4	82.20	1.67	29.3	6.77	9.15	5.69	6.72	4.55
1996	20.8	2.74	2.71	126.00	69.3	95.80	1.96	28.1	4.93	9.96	4.17	7.35	4.30
1997	22.1	2.38	2.43	121.00	65.2	100.00	1.60	28.3	5.62	9.70	3.95	6.47	3.38
1998	17.1	1.98	1.90	129.00	64.2	84.60	1.10	25.7	5.24	8.50	3.10	5.35	2.65
1999	21.3	2.13	1.82	89.00	45.0	76.90	1.12	25.4	5.77	5.93	2.80	4.63	2.48
2000	17.8	2.11	1.85	105.00	49.8	84.60	1.10	27.4	5.08	5.61	3.37	4.54	2.62
2001	22.9	2.22	1.97	90.50	29.8	96.50	1.59	23.4	6.99	4.25	4.25	4.38	2.78
2002	25.6	2.72	2.32	101.00	44.5	92.40	1.81	18.2	6.69	4.49	4.14	5.53	3.56
2003	29.4	2.83	2.42	117.00	61.8	85.50	1.48	19.3	5.89	8.08	4.26	7.34	3.40
2004[1]	21.8	2.48	2.06	107.00	41.6	92.00	1.48	18.9	5.67	7.33	3.19	5.74	3.40
2005[1]	24.4	2.53	2.00	96.00	47.7	98.20	1.63	17.3	7.06	7.65	3.33	5.66	3.42
2006	31.5	2.85	3.20	110.00	47.3	109.00	1.87	17.2	7.42	9.75	5.90	6.20	4.26

*Beginning in 1964, 480-lb net weight bales. NA = Not available. (1) Some prices revised.

World Wheat, Rice, and Corn Production, 2006

Source: UN Food and Agriculture Organization; in metric tons

Country	Corn	Rice[1]	Wheat	Country	Corn	Rice[1]	Wheat
Afghanistan	240,000	540,000	3,200,000	Kuwait	800	—	509
Albania	245,400	—	230,900	Laos	—	2,660,000	—
Algeria	1,000	20	2,687,930	Madagascar	293,464	3,485,000	10,285
Argentina	14,445,538	1,193,492	14,000,000	Malaysia	80,000	2,154,000	—
Australia	380,000	126,000	9,819,000	Mexico	21,764,652	338,891	3,335,617
Austria	1,471,668	—	1,396,300	Moldova	1,322,186	—	691,417
Bangladesh	479,000	43,729,000	772,000	Morocco	200,000	30,000	6,300,000
Belgium	575,898	—	1,583,427	Mozambique	1,300,000	174,000	1,103
Brazil	42,631,977	11,505,327	2,481,831	Myanmar	950,000	25,200,000	148,000
Bulgaria	1,587,805	20,008	3,301,882	Nepal	1,734,417	4,209,279	1,394,126
Cambodia	376,938	6,264,123	—	Netherlands	237,000	—	1,207,373
Cameroon	850,000	52,000	400	Nigeria	6,404,000	3,924,000	71,000
Canada	9,268,200	—	27,276,600	Pakistan	2,970,500	8,137,200	21,276,900
Chile	1,381,894	160,315	1,403,689	Paraguay	1,100,000	126,000	620,000
China	145,625,000	184,070,000	104,470,200	Peru	1,230,000	2,225,000	195,000
Colombia	1,340,000	2,250,000	32,000	Philippines	6,082,110	15,326,706	—
Congo, Dem Rep.	1,155,490	315,830	8,640	Poland	1,260,657	—	7,059,671
Côte d'Ivoire	600,000	700,000	—	Portugal	535,789	150,224	259,851
Croatia	1,934,517	—	804,601	Romania	8,984,729	18,420	5,526,190
Cuba	305,400	434,200	—	Russia	3,668,560	686,370	45,006,300
Cyprus	—	—	7,262	Saudi Arabia	90,634	—	2,400,000
Czech Republic	606,366	—	3,506,252	Serbia	6,016,765	—	1,875,335
Denmark	—	—	4,801,600	Slovakia	838,326	—	1,342,693
Ecuador	820,000	1,364,800	10,000	South Africa	6,935,056	3,158	2,105,000
Egypt	6,838,000	6,500,000	8,308,000	Spain	3,460,800	746,100	5,575,800
Ethiopia	4,029,630	16,000	2,779,058	Sri Lanka	47,530	3,342,000	—
France	12,901,769	94,782	35,366,784	Sweden	—	—	2,001,400
Germany	3,220,300	—	22,427,900	Syria	215,000	—	4,668,750
Ghana	1,189,000	250,000	—	Tanzania	3,373,000	784,000	110,000
Greece	1,710,000	200,660	1,379,750	Thailand	3,696,341	29,268,959	898
Guatemala	1,183,896	33,967	8,000	Turkey	3,811,000	696,000	20,010,000
Hungary	8,441,222	9,621	4,378,982	Turkmenistan	16,000	135,000	3,260,000
India	14,710,000	136,510,000	69,350,000	Uganda	1,258,000	154,000	18,000
Indonesia	11,610,646	54,400,000	—	Ukraine	6,320,000	72,000	14,000,000
Iran	1,700,000	3,600,000	14,500,000	United Kingdom	—	—	14,735,000
Iraq	—	230,000	—	U.S.	267,598,000	8,787,000	57,298,100
Israel	69,783	—	131,200	Uruguay	260,000	1,300,000	400,000
Italy	9,671,206	1,448,200	7,091,520	Uzbekistan	194,228	220,328	5,996,305
Japan	10	10,695,000	837,200	Venezuela	2,374,708	1,114,608	220
Kazakhstan	495,000	320,000	13,500,000	Vietnam	3,819,400	35,826,800	—
Kenya	3,247,200	64,840	358,061	Zambia	865,000	13,337	136,833
Korea, North	1,964,000	2,478,000	276,000	Zimbabwe	900,000	565	140,000
Korea, South	64,623	6,305,492	5,810	**World[2]**	**695,228,280**	**634,605,733**	**605,945,825**

— Production is small or nonexistent. (1) Paddy rice only. (2) Includes countries not listed.

Wheat, Rice, and Corn—Exports/Imports of 10 Leading Countries, 2005, 1995

Source: UN Food and Agriculture Organization; in metric tons

Wheat

TOP EXPORTERS 2005		1995		TOP IMPORTERS 2005		1995	
U.S.	27,235,050	U.S.	30,211,030	Egypt	7,477,500	China	12,678,230
France	15,779,250	Canada	16,908,240	Spain	7,388,270	Brazil	6,064,680
Australia	14,779,020	France	13,937,710	Italy	6,722,600	Japan	5,689,680
Canada	13,914,770	Argentina	6,754,040	Algeria	5,706,990	Egypt	5,246,770
Argentina	10,244,100	Australia	4,396,620	Japan	5,422,320	Italy	4,923,830
Russian	9,842,530	Kazakhstan	3,801,390	Brazil	5,039,150	Indonesia	3,418,100
Ukraine	5,878,690	Germany	3,375,340	China	4,501,330	Algeria	3,058,530
Germany	4,891,790	U.K.	2,586,650	Indonesia	4,275,920	Russian	2,961,000
U.K.	2,261,070	Hungary	1,996,620	Nigeria	3,793,900	Spain	2,737,980
Kazakhstan	2,210,190	Ukraine	1,935,750	Mexico	3,707,360	Morocco	2,577,060
World Total	**121,731,080**	**World Total**	**97,183,380**	**World Total**	**121,689,400**	**World Total**	**100,331,110**

Rice[1]

TOP EXPORTERS 2005		1995		TOP IMPORTERS 2005		1995	
U.S.	1,684,890	U.S.	627,390	Mexico	674,730	Brazil	248,060
Thailand	63,440	Uruguay	115,570	Turkey	212,800	Mexico	244,860
Paraguay	29,360	Greece	82,610	Costa Rica	157,470	Spain	128,830
India	29,180	Thailand	78,520	Nicaragua	155,610	Venezuela	80,930
France	27,850	Viet Nam	49,970	Honduras	152,300	Yemen	61,090
Spain	21,990	Argentina	40,000	El Salvador	93,960	Costa Rica	55,270
Uruguay	19,970	Australia	33,450	Guatemala	78,470	Cambodia	46,090
Pakistan	17,790	Italy	32,060	Panama	66,080	Portugal	44,230
Italy	17,290	France	30,360	Brazil	44,310	Italy	37,090
China	14,960	Switzerland	16,030	Jamaica	41,800	Honduras	36,740
World Total	**2,054,320**	**World Total**	**1,243,640**	**World Total**	**2,053,950**	**World Total**	**1,274,670**

Corn

TOP EXPORTERS 2005		1995		TOP IMPORTERS 2005		1995	
U.S.	45,320,920	U.S.	57,722,510	Japan	16,225,720	Japan	16,428,560
Argentina	13,849,370	Argentina	5,336,920	South Korea	8,571,220	China	11,705,550
China	8,493,680	France	5,169,020	Mexico	5,743,620	South Korea	9,045,010
France	7,389,150	South Africa	1,246,140	Egypt	5,428,870	Spain	2,932,620
Ukraine	2,447,120	Hungary	515,590	China	5,055,530	Mexico	2,749,300
Hungary	1,901,090	Canada	442,250	Spain	4,299,760	Malaysia	2,619,040
South Africa	1,897,550	Germany	406,620	Iran	2,746,360	Egypt	2,514,590
Brazil	1,131,650	Namibia	340,560	Malaysia	2,542,800	Netherlands	1,588,070
Germany	1,039,320	Greece	318,450	Colombia	2,529,200	U.K.	1,466,580
Paraguay	514,030	Zimbabwe	263,630	Netherlands	2,418,880	Colombia	1,411,850
World Total	**89,642,490**	**World Total**	**74,819,730**	**World Total**	**89,622,450**	**World Total**	**75,578,550**

(1) Paddy rice only.

Value of U.S. Agricultural Exports and Imports, 1978-2006

Source: Economic Research Service, U.S. Dept. of Agriculture

(in billions of dollars, except percent)

Year[1]	Agric. Trade surplus	Agric. exports	% of all exports	Agric. imports	% of all imports	Year[1]	Agric. Trade surplus	Agric. exports	% of all exports	Agric. imports	% of all imports
1978	$13.4	$27.3	21%	$13.9	8%	1993	$17.7	$42.9	10%	$25.1	4%
1979	15.8	32.0	19	16.2	8	1994	19.2	46.2	10	27.0	4
1980	23.2	40.5	19	17.3	8	1995	26.0	56.3	10	30.3	4
1981	26.4	43.8	19	17.3	7	1996	26.8	60.3	10	33.5	4
1982	23.6	39.1	18	15.5	6	1997	21.0	57.2	9	36.1	4
1983	18.5	34.8	18	16.3	7	1998	14.9	51.8	8	36.9	4
1984	19.1	38.0	18	18.9	6	1999	10.7	48.4	8	37.7	4
1985	11.5	31.2	15	19.7	6	2000	12.2	51.2	7	39.0	3
1986	5.4	26.3	13	20.9	6	2001	14.3	53.7	8	39.4	4
1987	7.2	27.9	12	20.7	5	2002	11.2	53.1	8	41.9	4
1988	14.3	35.3	12	21.0	5	2003	10.3	56.0	8	45.7	4
1989	18.1	39.7	12	21.6	5	2004[2]	9.7	62.4	9	52.7	4
1990	16.6	39.5	11	22.9	5	2005[2]	4.8	62.5	8	57.7	4
1991	16.4	39.3	10	22.9	5	2006[3]	4.7	68.7	8	64.0	3
1992	18.3	43.1	10	24.8	5						

(1) Fiscal year (Oct.-Sept.). (2) Revised. (3) Preliminary.

World Commercial Catch of Fish, Crustaceans, and Mollusks, by Major Fishing Areas, 1990-2005

Source: Food and Agriculture Organization of the United Nations (FAO)

(metric tons; live weight)

Area	1990	1995	2000	2001	2002	2003	2004	2005
Inland waters	14,500,761	21,238,974	29,943,818	31,191,822	32,527,015	34,078,197	36,355,624	38,508,981
Africa	1,937,935	2,086,571	2,486,764	2,482,018	2,568,836	2,698,810	2,840,817	3,022,426
North America	487,922	537,544	592,979	587,769	612,977	650,275	658,172	640,499
South America	330,177	444,754	554,631	587,598	644,544	651,503	693,148	699,362
Asia	10,426,648	17,310,417	25,398,077	26,682,940	27,850,845	29,218,233	31,351,598	33,305,115
Europe	1,293,972	837,973	887,043	826,947	828,004	840,560	791,878	820,543
Oceania	24,107	21,715	24,324	24,550	21,809	18,816	20,011	21,036
Marine waters	82,891,582	94,847,880	100,330,779	99,066,628	100,338,187	98,011,353	103,177,446	102,018,985
Atlantic Ocean	23,195,275	25,029,123	25,855,563	26,415,517	25,740,307	24,940,748	24,632,840	23,700,863
Indian Ocean	6,600,302	8,336,987	9,429,984	9,347,913	9,911,006	10,204,765	10,495,135	10,167,060
Pacific Ocean	52,590,922	61,333,822	64,908,218	63,182,645	64,540,372		67,910,597	68,004,136
World Total	97,392,342	116,086,854	130,274,597	130,258,450	132,865,203	132,089,550	139,533,070	140,527,966

Note: Data for marine mammals and aquatic plants are excluded. Totals include areas or territories not shown. Figures may be revised. Includes weight of clam, oyster, scallop and other mollusk shells.

World Capture of Fish, Crustaceans, and Mollusks, 1996-2005

Source: Food and Agriculture Organization of the United Nations (FAO)
(in thousands of metric tons)

	1996	2000	2003	2004	2005		1996	2000	2003	2004	2005
China	14,182	16,987	16,756	16,893	17,053	Vietnam	1,224	1,623	1,856	1,879	1,930
Peru	95,150	10,657	6,086	9,605	9,389	Myanmar	602	1,093	1,344	1,587	1,743
U.S.	5,001	4,718	4,939	4,960	4,889	Iceland	2,060	1,983	1,981	1,728	1,661
Indonesia	3,605	4,083	4,627	4,642	4,381	South Korea	2,414	1,825	1,643	1,575	1,639
Chile	6,693	4,300	3,613	4,919	4,330	Bangladesh	815	1,004	1,141	1,187	1,334
Japan	5,932	4,986	4,670	4,312	4,073	Mexico	1,464	1,316	1,357	1,259	1,305
India	3,448	3,666	3,712	3,391	3,481	Malaysia	1,130	1,289	1,287	1,336	1,214
Russia	4,676	3,974	3,281	2,942	3,191	Canada	902	998	1,111	1,176	1,081
Thailand	3,014	2,997	2,850	2,840	2,599	Taiwan	967	1,094	1,135	980	1,017
Norway	2,648	2,699	2,549	2,524	2,393						
Phillipines	1,784	1,897	2,166	2,216	2,246	**World Total**	**93,739**	**95,610**	**90,354**	**94,364**	**93,253**

World Aquaculture Production, 1996-2005

Source: Food and Agriculture Organization of the United Nations (FAO)

	Metric tons[1]					Value ($)[2]				
	1996	2000	2003	2004	2005	1996	2000	2003	2004	2005
China	17,715	24,581	28,884	30,613	32,414	$18,272	$24,317	$29,874	$30,867	$34,550
India	1,759	1,942	2,313	2,795	2,838	1,872	2,511	2,588	3,784	3,921
Vietnam	299	499	938	1,199	1,437	644	991	1,968	2,444	2,931
Indonesia	733	789	997	1,045	1,197	2,165	2,246	1,699	1,993	1,999
Thailand	556	738	1,064	1,260	1,144	1,903	2,514	1,463	1,705	1,689
Bangladesh	379	657	857	915	882	776	1,039	1,243	1,363	1,246
Japan	829	763	824	776	746	3,894	3,317	3,368	3,205	3,178
Chile	218	392	563	665	698	787	1,250	2,138	2,745	3,108
Norway	322	491	584	637	657	997	1,385	1,352	1,681	2,073
Philippines	350	394	460	512	557	1,206	681	601	701	794
Egypt	91	340	445	472	540	168	815	615	613	792
Myanmar	72	99	252	400	475	744	781	775	1,231	1,472
U.S.	393	456	544	607	472	736	843	805	907	850
South Korea	358	293	388	406	436	679	573	889	980	1,191
Taiwan	262	244	352	318	305	1,178	836	906	943	969
France	285	267	240	261	258	600	425	580	689	691
Brazil	78	172	278	270	258	298	684	979	966	916
Spain	232	312	273	299	222	250	378	375	406	349
Italy	184	214	192	118	181	385	446	519	365	593
Malaysia	109	152	167	171	176	184	254	300	324	339
World Total	**25,592**	**35,477**	**42,682**	**45,924**	**48,150**	**$41,789**	**$51,109**	**$59,104**	**$64,605**	**$70,929**

Note: Does not include aquatic plants or marine mammals. (1) In thousands. (2) In millions of dollars.

U.S. Commercial Landings of Fish and Shellfish, 1990-2006[1]

Source: U.S. Dept. of Commerce, Natl. Oceanic and Atmospheric Admin., Natl. Marine Fisheries Service
(in millions)

Year	Landings for human food		Landings for industrial purposes[2]		TOTAL	
	Weight (lbs)	Value	Weight (lbs)	Value	Weight (lbs)	Value
1990	7,041	$3,366	2,363	$156	9,404	$3,522
1991	7,031	3,169	2,453	139	9,484	3,308
1992	7,618	3,531	2,019	147	9,637	3,678
1993	8,214	3,317	2,253	154	10,467	3,471
1994	7,936	3,751	2,525	95	10,461	3,846
1995	7,667	3,625	2,121	145	9,788	3,770
1996	7,474	3,355	2,091	132	9,565	3,487
1997	7,244	3,285	2,598	163	9,842	3,448
1998	7,173	3,009	2,021	119	9,194	3,128
1999	6,832	3,265	2,507	202	9,339	3,467
2000	6,912	3,398	2,157	152	9,069	3,550
2001	7,314	3,074	2,178	154	9,492	3,228
2002	7,205	2,940	2,192	152	9,397	3,092
2003	7,521	3,185	1,986	157	9,507	3,347
2004	7,794	3,611	1,889	145	9,683	3,756
2005	7,997	3,825	1,710	117	9,707	3,942
2006	7,809	3,881	1,680	112	9,489	3,993

Note: Data do not include products of aquaculture, except oysters and clams. (1) Statistics on landings are shown in round (live) weight for all items except univale and bivalve mollusks such as clams, oysters, and scallops, which are shown in weight of meats (excluding the shell). (2) Processed into meal, oil, solubles, and shell products or used as bait or animal food.

U.S. Domestic Landings, by Region, 2005-06[1]

Source: U.S. Dept. of Commerce, Natl. Oceanic and Atmospheric Admin., Natl. Marine Fisheries Service

Region	2005[2]		2006[3]	
	Weight (1,000 lbs)	Value ($1,000)	Weight (1,000 lbs)	Value ($1,000)
New England	684,090	$971,663	752,387	$954,676
Middle Atlantic	199,937	221,505	212,960	209,198
Chesapeake	508,953	218,933	477,433	163,570
South Atlantic	122,422	125,117	113,842	149,878
Gulf	1,196,355	620,987	1,285,691	662,938
Pacific Coast incl. Alaska	6,950,647	1,700,927	6,602,297	1,772,753
Great Lakes	16,732	12,434	18,401	13,576
Hawaii	28,139	70,811	26,021	66,780
TOTAL	**9,707,275**	**$3,942,376**	**9,489,031**	**$3,993,370**

(1) Landings reported in round (live) weight items except for univale and bivalve mollusks (e.g., clams, oysters, scallops), which are reported in weight of meats (excluding shell). Landings for Mississippi River Drainage Area states not included (not available). (2) Revised. (3) Preliminary.

Employment and Unemployment in the U.S., 1900-2006

Source: Bureau of Labor Statistics, U.S. Dept. of Labor

(civilian labor force, persons 16 years of age and older; annual averages; in thousands)

Year[1]	Employed	Unemployed Number	Unemployed Rate	Year[1]	Employed	Unemployed Number	Unemployed Rate	Year[1]	Employed	Unemployed Number	Unemployed Rate
1900[2] ...	26,956	1,420	5.0%	1985....	107,150	8,312	7.2%	1996 ...	126,708	7,236	5.4%
1910[2] ...	34,599	2,150	5.9	1986....	109,597	8,237	7.0	1997[5]...	129,558	6,739	4.9
1920[2] ...	39,208	2,132	5.2	1987....	112,440	7,425	6.2	1998[5]...	131,463	6,210	4.5
1930[2] ...	44,183	4,340	8.9	1988....	114,968	6,701	5.5	1999[6]...	133,488	5,880	4.2
1940[2] ...	47,520	8,120	14.6	1989....	117,342	6,528	5.3	2000[7]...	136,891	5,692	4.0
1950	58,918	3,288	5.0	1990[3]...	118,793	7,047	5.6	2001 ...	136,933	6,801	4.7
1955	62,170	2,852	4.4	1991....	117,718	8,628	6.8	2002 ...	136,485	8,378	5.8
1960	65,778	3,852	5.5	1992....	118,492	9,613	7.5	2003 ...	137,736	8,774	6.0
1965	71,088	3,366	4.5	1993....	120,259	8,940	6.9	2004 ...	139,252	8,149	5.5
1970	78,678	4,093	4.9	1994[4]....	123,060	7,996	6.1	2005 ...	141,730	7,591	5.1
1975	85,846	7,929	8.5	1995....	124,900	7,404	5.6	2006 ...	144,427	7,001	4.6
1980	99,303	7,637	7.1								

(1) **Other unemployment rates (1905-1945):** 1905, 4.3; 1915, 8.5; 1925, 3.2; 1935, 20.3; 1936, 16.9; 1937, 14.3; 1938, 19.0; 1939, 17.2; 1945, 1.9; all for 14 years of age and older. (2) Persons 14 years of age and older. (3) Beginning in 1990, data incorporate 1990 census-based population controls, adjusted for estimated undercount. (4) Beginning in 1994, not strictly comparable with prior years, because of major redesign of the survey used. (5) From 1997 not strictly comparable with 1994-96 because of revisions in population controls used in household survey. (6) From 1999 not strictly comparable with 1998 and earlier years because of further revisions in population controls used in household survey. (7) From 2000, not strictly comparable with earlier years because of revisions to the controls used in the survey.

Unemployment Insurance Data, by State, 2006

Source: Employment and Training Admin., U.S. Dept. of Labor; state programs only

STATE	Monetarily eligible claimants	First payments	Final payments	Initial claims	Benefits paid	Average weekly benefit	Employers subject to state law
AL	130,509	104,538	27,112	243,099	$196,880,758	$183.76	88,022
AK	46,118	40,859	16,072	83,625	101,613,219	197.63	16,940
AZ	103,995	68,354	26,246	165,405	194,128,843	197.64	125,498
AR	114,201	80,412	28,685	201,223	229,182,522	243.98	64,986
CA	1,265,750	947,507	400,860	2,135,569	4,063,636,403	289.07	1,130,454
CO	95,962	69,203	30,003	115,982	288,162,526	312.33	154,188
CT	136,888	119,169	39,211	209,282	525,102,095	304.37	98,307
DE	29,999	22,545	7,009	57,075	91,078,019	251.08	26,449
FL	335,939	239,827	101,780	483,639	677,476,027	231.38	487,066
GA	264,731	197,792	74,547	455,638	515,790,621	255.57	210,902
HI	29,550	21,320	4,423	55,549	90,618,092	365.09	30,970
ID	47,662	39,749	10,439	89,289	96,346,218	241.02	48,518
IL	374,203	334,744	121,579	670,402	1,563,754,020	291.67	293,148
IN	240,786	186,602	70,455	406,428	693,377,510	286.32	126,981
IA	116,359	92,610	21,901	179,609	299,059,962	281.97	71,029
KS	74,255	54,376	18,921	127,294	167,077,162	286.83	70,476
KY	160,439	111,461	23,312	306,455	365,487,636	270.56	84,479
LA	91,153	59,614	95,223	137,384	255,557,486	191.12	99,415
ME	42,282	30,916	9,175	65,728	99,767,599	245.65	41,638
MD	135,473	95,915	29,671	202,999	365,147,862	273.68	141,628
MA	249,707	210,418	72,815	377,872	1,181,332,804	366.33	183,512
MI	571,375	475,596	159,310	946,815	1,877,440,565	293.66	217,835
MN	172,068	141,039	42,928	281,171	622,337,391	333.47	134,104
MS	79,487	53,135	27,641	134,861	151,834,276	185.84	55,030
MO	203,505	134,756	41,725	366,349	385,609,410	212.28	137,551
MT	29,574	20,422	6,318	47,395	60,182,199	203.74	36,222
NE	45,109	33,424	15,010	70,372	85,486,264	230.86	47,357
NV	82,074	63,614	18,727	136,019	237,575,767	274.02	56,615
NH	33,440	24,988	3,780	50,319	73,969,886	255.58	40,576
NJ	352,006	305,259	134,554	524,546	1,674,374,816	344.09	261,073
NM	42,037	27,170	9,405	49,286	105,061,150	237.70	44,505
NY	582,182	454,201	177,109	986,275	2,086,683,707	277.41	487,756
NC	321,626	238,656	96,747	612,050	692,345,999	265.08	191,507
ND	18,071	13,627	4,247	28,535	40,203,538	254.84	19,814
OH	338,706	275,431	79,243	627,903	1,049,617,947	287.03	229,209
OK	63,849	41,089	16,211	99,893	133,743,337	233.23	79,115
OR	164,578	125,609	38,641	314,968	434,855,851	269.63	109,871
PA	555,123	447,066	133,827	1,124,550	1,898,484,032	301.27	284,187
RI	46,334	37,588	13,867	75,165	195,161,641	341.76	33,793
SC	161,407	112,134	40,776	304,136	311,280,151	222.80	97,593
SD	11,109	7,872	963	18,107	20,761,431	218.51	24,566
TN	168,028	142,704	49,842	309,009	390,760,989	215.70	112,989
TX	454,859	297,478	115,584	661,795	1,011,728,946	271.04	421,248
UT	42,040	22,878	8,687	57,387	88,027,178	274.22	65,450
VT	26,870	22,143	4,115	40,027	77,531,516	275.27	21,581
VA	161,178	106,554	35,743	260,804	335,277,371	255.67	180,563
WA	236,292	171,137	38,575	410,968	665,373,458	322.13	194,306
WV	53,373	40,319	9,957	69,173	127,125,490	230.52	36,703
WI	302,126	258,845	64,761	601,807	749,652,726	258.79	128,808
WY	21,336	9,545	2,760	16,627	27,916,978	253.42	20,968
DC	17,233	16,185	8,839	16,185	87,170,195	282.70	28,241
PR	155,562	100,947	46,920	260,871	199,150,217	109.76	64,420
VI	1,956	1,392	478	2,244	4,968,141	269.94	3,505
U.S.	9,600,480	7,350,734	2,676,729	16,275,158	$27,962,269,944	$277.20	7,461,660

Unemployed Persons[1] by Industry and Duration of Unemployment, Sept. 2007

Source: Bureau of Labor Statistics, U.S. Dept. of Labor

OCCUPATION	Total	Less than 5 weeks	5 to 14 weeks	15 weeks and over Total	15 to 26 weeks	27 weeks and over	Average (mean) duration	Median duration
Management, professional, and related	1,098	363	372	362	173	190	17.2	9.6
Service	1,509	586	440	483	230	252	16.1	8.3
Sales and office	1,648	613	461	573	243	330	17	8.9
Natural resources, construction, and maintenance	885	372	257	256	106	150	15.4	7.5
Production, transportation, and material moving	1,135	391	355	389	172	217	17.5	9
INDUSTRY[2]								
Agriculture and related industries	54	32	15	7	3	4	[3]	[3]
Mining	25	12	4	9	3	5	[3]	[3]
Construction	602	244	183	176	78	98	14.9	7.8
Manufacturing	673	262	167	244	98	146	18.4	8.7
Wholesale and retail trade	1,037	319	340	378	180	199	17.4	10.1
Transportation and utilities	236	76	73	87	19	68	19.6	10.1
Information	127	21	34	72	21	51	32.5	17.7
Financial activities	321	116	100	105	62	44	14.8	8.5
Professional and business services	669	268	208	193	94	99	14.5	7.9
Education and health services	891	329	282	279	127	152	16	8.7
Leisure and hospitality	941	404	257	280	137	143	16.1	7.6
Other services	257	89	83	84	33	51	16.6	8.5
Public administration	136	40	45	51	29	22	17.4	9.9
No previous work experience	652	231	220	201	82	118	17.3	8.8

(1) Numbers are in thousands. (2) Includes wage and salary workers only. (3) Data not shown where base is less than 75,000.

Persons Not in the Labor Force, 2006

Source: Bureau of Labor Statistics, U.S. Dept. of Labor

The Labor Department's unemployment rate, based on its household survey, shows the number of people out of work as a percentage of U.S. adults in the labor force. Millions of other adults are considered not to be in the labor force.

(in thousands)

	Total	Age 16 to 24 years	Age 25 to 54 years	Age 55 years and over	Sex Men	Sex Women
Total not in the labor force	77,387	14,549	21,318	41,520	29,350	48,037
Do not want a job now[1]	72,602	12,867	19,221	40,514	27,248	45,354
Want a job[1]	4,786	1,682	2,097	1,006	2,102	2,684
Did not search for work in previous year	2,758	883	1,155	720	1,145	1,612
Searched for work in previous year[2]	2,028	800	942	286	956	1,071
Not available to work now	580	282	252	46	226	354
Available to work now	1,448	518	690	240	731	717
Reason not currently looking:						
Discouragement over job prospects[3]	381	118	195	68	229	152
Reasons other than discouragement	1,067	399	495	172	502	565
Family responsibilities	152	31	97	24	35	117
In school or training	207	177	28	2	111	96
Ill health or disability	130	18	76	36	63	68
Other[4]	578	174	294	110	292	285

(1) Includes some persons who are not asked if they want a job. (2) Persons who had a job in the prior 12 months must have searched since the end of that job. (3) Includes believes no work available, could not find work, lacks necessary schooling or training, employer thinks too young or old, and other types of discrimination. (4) Includes those who did not actively look for work in the prior 4 weeks for such reasons as child care and transportation problems, as well as a small number for which reason for nonparticipation was not ascertained.

Displaced Workers, Jan. 2006

Source: Bureau of Labor Statistics, U.S. Dept. of Labor

	Total (thousands)	Percent distribution by reason of job loss Plant or company closed down or moved	Insufficient work	Position or shift abolished
Total, 20 years and over	3,815	49.0	22.2	28.8
20 to 24 years	111	39.1	42.8	18.1
25 to 54 years	2,841	48.5	22.6	28.9
55 to 64 years	728	53.2	16.5	30.2
65 years and over	135	44.1	28.8	27.1
Men	2,076	48.8	24.8	26.5
Women	1,739	49.2	19.2	31.6
White	3,169	49.5	22.1	28.4
Black or African American	452	42.5	19.7	37.8
Asian	113	52.3	25.9	21.8
Hispanic or Latino ethnicity	416	59.6	26.1	14.3

Note: Displaced workers are persons 20 years or older who lost or left jobs they had held for at least 3 years. Workers in this table were displaced between Jan. 2003 and Dec. 2005.

U.S. Unemployment Rates by Selected Characteristics, 1995-2007[1]

Source: Bureau of Labor Statistics, U.S. Dept. of Labor

	1995	2000	2001	2002	2003	2004	2005	2006 Jan.	2006 June	2006 Annual	2007 Jan.	2007 June
Total (all civilian workers)	5.6	4.0	4.7	5.8	6.0	5.5	5.1	5.1	4.8	4.6	5.0	4.7
Men, 20 years and older	4.8	3.3	4.2	5.3	5.6	5.0	4.4	4.8	3.8	4.0	4.9	3.8
Women, 20 years and older	4.9	3.6	4.1	5.1	5.1	4.9	4.6	4.4	4.3	4.1	4.2	4.1
Both sexes, 16 to 19 years	17.3	13.1	14.7	16.5	17.5	17.0	16.6	15.5	18.4	15.4	15.1	18.9
White	4.9	3.5	4.2	5.1	5.2	4.8	4.4	4.6	4.2	4.0	4.6	4.2
Black	10.4	7.6	8.6	10.2	10.8	10.4	10.0	9.1	9.4	8.9	8.2	9.0
Hispanic origin	9.3	5.7	6.6	7.5	7.7	7.0	6.0	6.4	5.1	5.2	6.4	5.5
Asian	—	3.6	4.5	5.9	6.0	4.4	4.0	3.2	3.5	3.0	3.2	3.1
Married men, spouse present	3.3	—	—	—	—	—	—	2.4	2.5	—	2.5	2.4
Married women, spouse present	3.9	—	—	—	—	—	—	3.0	2.9	—	2.8	2.7
Women who maintain families	8.0	5.9	6.6	8.0	8.5	8.0	7.8	8.2	7.2	7.1	6.6	6.8
OCCUPATION												
Management, professional, and related occupations	2.4	1.8	2.3	3.0	3.1	2.7	2.3	2.1	2.4	2.1	2.0	2.3
Service occupations	7.5	5.2	5.8	6.6	7.1	6.6	6.4	6.4	5.8	5.9	6.4	5.9
Sales and office occupations	5.0	3.8	4.4	5.6	5.5	5.2	4.8	4.7	4.7	4.4	4.7	4.3
Nat. resources, constr., maint. occupations	—	5.3	6.4	7.8	8.1	7.3	6.5	7.8	4.8	6.0	8.0	5.2
Prod., trans., material moving occupations	—	5.1	6.4	7.6	7.9	7.2	6.5	7.1	5.2	5.8	6.8	5.3
INDUSTRY												
Nonagricultural, private wage, and salary workers	5.8	4.1	5.0	6.2	6.3	5.7	5.2	5.3	4.7	4.7	5.2	4.6
Mining	5.2	4.4	4.2	6.3	6.7	3.9	3.1	3.9	4.3	3.2	4.7	4.3
Construction	11.5	6.2	7.1	9.2	9.3	8.4	7.4	9.0	5.6	6.7	8.9	5.9
Manufacturing	4.9	3.5	5.2	6.7	6.6	5.7	4.9	4.6	3.8	4.2	4.6	4.0
Durable goods	4.4	3.2	5.2	6.9	6.9	5.5	4.6	4.1	3.6	3.9	5.1	3.9
Non durable goods	5.7	4.0	5.2	6.2	6.1	5.9	5.3	5.4	4.2	4.8	3.9	4.1
Wholesale and retail trade	6.5	4.3	4.9	6.1	6.0	5.8	5.4	5.7	5.1	4.9	5.5	4.6
Transportation and utilities	4.5	3.4	4.3	4.9	5.3	4.4	4.1	5.0	3.9	4.0	4.2	4.1
Information	—	3.2	4.9	6.9	6.8	5.7	5.0	3.3	3.4	3.7	4.0	3.4
Financial activities	3.3	2.4	2.9	3.5	3.5	3.6	2.9	2.4	3.1	2.7	2.4	3.1
Professional and business services	—	4.8	6.1	7.9	8.2	6.8	6.2	6.5	5.7	5.6	6.5	5.2
Education and health services	—	2.5	2.8	3.4	3.6	3.4	3.4	3.2	3.3	3.0	2.9	3.4
Leisure and hospitality	—	6.6	7.5	8.4	8.7	8.3	7.8	8.1	7.4	7.3	7.8	7.2
Other services	8.4	3.9	4.0	5.1	5.7	5.3	4.8	4.9	4.3	4.7	4.7	4.0
Agriculture and related	11.1	9.0	11.2	10.1	10.2	9.9	8.3	11.5	2.4	7.2	10.0	4.5
Government	2.9	2.1	2.2	2.5	2.8	2.7	2.6	2.2	2.8	2.3	2.2	2.7
Self-employed and unpaid family workers	—	2.1	2.1	2.6	2.7	2.8	2.7	3.2	2.2	2.7	3.5	2.3

(1) All monthly rates unadjusted, except for married men and women, which are seasonally adjusted. — = Not available.

Employed Persons in the U.S., by Occupation and Sex, 2005 and 2006

Source: Bureau of Labor Statistics, U.S. Dept. of Labor

(in thousands)

	Total 16 years and older 2005	2006	Men 16 years and older 2005	2006	Women 16 years and older 2005	2006
Total	141,730	144,427	75,973	77,502	65,757	66,925
Management, professional, and related	49,245	50,420	24,349	24,928	24,896	25,492
Management, business, and financial operations	20,450	21,233	11,761	12,347	8,689	8,886
Management	14,685	15,249	9,220	9,652	5,466	5,597
Business and financial operations	5,765	5,983	2,541	2,694	3,223	3,289
Professional and related	28,795	29,187	12,588	12,581	16,207	16,606
Computer and mathematical	3,246	3,209	2,371	2,354	875	855
Architecture and engineering	2,793	2,830	2,407	2,418	385	412
Life, physical, and social science	1,406	1,434	808	813	598	620
Community and social services	2,138	2,156	827	829	1,311	1,327
Legal	1,614	1,637	817	791	797	846
Education, training, and library	8,114	8,126	2,125	2,100	5,989	6,026
Arts, design, entertainment, sports, and media	2,736	2,735	1,427	1,401	1,309	1,334
Healthcare practitioner and technical	6,748	7,060	1,806	1,875	4,942	5,185
Service	23,133	23,811	9,882	10,159	13,251	13,653
Healthcare support	3,092	3,132	339	333	2,753	2,799
Protective service	2,894	2,939	2,246	2,284	648	654
Food preparation and serving related	7,374	7,606	3,202	3,297	4,173	4,309
Building and grounds cleaning and maintenance	5,241	5,381	3,111	3,230	2,130	2,151
Personal care and service	4,531	4,754	981	1,014	3,548	3,740
Sales and office	35,962	36,141	13,190	13,275	22,772	22,866
Sales and related	16,433	16,641	8,362	8,478	8,072	8,163
Office and administrative support	19,529	19,500	4,829	4,797	14,700	14,703
Natural resources, construction, and maintenance	15,348	15,830	14,635	15,079	713	752
Farming, fishing, and forestry	976	961	756	750	220	212
Construction and extraction	9,145	9,507	8,871	9,216	274	292
Installation, maintenance, and repair	5,226	5,362	5,008	5,114	219	248
Production, transportation, and material moving	18,041	18,224	13,917	14,061	4,124	4,163
Production	9,378	9,378	6,540	6,529	2,838	2,850
Transportation and material moving	8,664	8,846	7,377	7,533	1,286	1,313

Note: Beginning in Jan. 2005, data reflect revised population controls used in the household survey. Totals may not add because of independent rounding.

Projected Openings for Selected High-Paying Occupations, 2004-2014
Source: Bureau of Labor Statistics, U.S. Dept. of Labor

Job openings shown below represent the average number expected each year for workers in the U.S. who are entering these occupations for the first time.

Occupation	Annual avg. job openings[1]	Median annual earnings[2]	Occupation	Annual avg. job openings[1]	Median annual earnings[2]
Registered nurses	120,000	$52,330	Gen. maintenance & repair wkrs	46,000	$30,710
Postsecondary teachers	89,000	51,800	First-line office superv. or mgrs	44,000	41,030
Gen. & operations mgrs.	65,000	77,420	Secondary school teachers[4]	44,000	45,650
Elementary school teachers[4]	59,000	43,160	Carpenters	41,000	34,900
Sales representatives[3]	57,000	45,400	First-line retail superv. or mgrs	36,000	32,720
Truck drivers, heavy & tractor trailer	51,000	33,520	Auto mechanics/technicians	34,000	32,450
Exec. secretaries, admin. assists.	49,000	34,970	Lic. practical and voc. nurses	28,000	33,970
Accountants and auditors	49,000	50,770			

(1) As a result of growth and net replacement needs. (2) Median earnings are for 2004. (3) Wholesale and manufacturing, except technical and scientific products. (4) Except special and vocational education.

Top-Paying U.S. Counties by Average Weekly Wage, 4th Quarter 2006
Source: Bureau of Labor Statistics

County	Avg. weekly wage	% change 4th qtr. 2005-2006	County	Avg. weekly wage	% change 4th qtr. 2005-2006
New York, NY	$1,781	5.7	Somerset, NJ	$1,373	4.9
Santa Clara, CA	1,569	5.1	Fairfax, VA	1,297	4.0
Fairfield, CT	1,515	1.2	Morris, NJ	1,284	3.6
Suffolk, MA	1,481	4.9	Westchester, NY	1,211	2.9
San Francisco, CA	1,460	6.0	Middlesex, MA	1,209	4.3
Washington, DC	1,424	5.0	Marin, CA	1,148	0.5
Arlington, VA	1,419	4.2	Montgomery, MD	1,136	2.4
San Mateo, CA	1,402	2.9	United States	$861	4.2

Note: Cameron County, TX, recorded the lowest average weekly earnings among the 326 largest counties, with an average weekly wage of $527 in the fourth quarter of 2006. It was followed by: Hidalgo County, TX ($542); Yakima County, WA ($570); Webb County, TX ($571); San Juan, PR ($577); and Horry County, SC ($578). The top 15 were derived from a list of the 326 largest U.S. counties, which comprise 71% of the total covered workers. Data includes all workers covered by state and federal unemployment insurance programs.

Federal Minimum Hourly Wage Rates Since 1950
Source: Bureau of Labor Statistics, U.S. Dept. of Labor

EFFECTIVE DATE	NONFARM WORKERS Under laws prior to 1966[1]	Percent of avg. earnings[2]	Under 1966 and later provis.[3]	FARM WORKERS[4]	EFFECTIVE DATE	NONFARM WORKERS Under laws prior to 1966[1]	Percent of avg. earnings[2]	Under 1966 and later provis.[3]	FARM WORKERS[4]
Jan. 25, 1950	$0.75	54	NA	NA	Jan. 1, 1977	(5)	(5)	$2.30	$2.20
Mar. 1, 1956	1.00	52	NA	NA	Jan. 1, 1978	$2.65	44	2.65	2.65
Sept. 3, 1961	1.15	50	NA	NA	Jan. 1, 1979	2.90	45	2.90	2.90
Sept. 3, 1963	1.25	51	NA	NA	Jan. 1, 1980	3.10	43	3.10	3.10
Feb. 1, 1967	1.40	50	$1.00	$1.00	Jan. 1, 1981	3.35	42	3.35	3.35
Feb. 1, 1968	1.60	54	1.15	1.15	Apr. 1, 1990	3.80[6]	35	3.80	3.80[6]
Feb. 1, 1969	(5)	(5)	1.30	1.30	Apr. 1, 1991	4.25[6]	38	4.25	4.25[6]
Feb. 1, 1970	(5)	(5)	1.45	(5)	Oct. 1, 1996	4.75[7]	37	4.75	4.75[7]
Feb. 1, 1971	(5)	(5)	1.60	(5)	Sept. 1, 1997	5.15[7]	39[8]	5.15	5.15[7]
May 1, 1974	2.00	46	1.90	1.60	July 24, 2007	5.85[7]	NA	5.85	5.85[7]
Jan. 1, 1975	2.10	45	2.00	1.80	July 24, 2008	6.55[7]	NA	6.55	6.55[7]
Jan. 1, 1976	2.30	46	2.20	2.00	July 24, 2009	7.25[7]	NA	7.25	7.25[7]

NA = not applicable. (1) Applies to workers covered prior to 1961 Amendments and, after Sept. 1965, to workers covered by 1961 Amendments. Rates set by 1961 Amendments were: Sept. 1961, $1.00; Sept. 1964, $1.15; and Sept. 1965, $1.25. (2) Percent of gross average hourly earnings of production workers in manufacturing. (3) Applies to workers newly covered by Amendments of 1966, 1974, and 1977, and Title IX of Education Amendments of 1972. (4) Included in coverage as of 1966, 1974, and 1977 Amendments. (5) No change in rate. (6) Training wage for workers age 16-19 in first 6 months of first job: Apr. 1, 1990, $3.35; Apr. 1, 1991, $3.62. The training wage expired Mar. 31, 1993. (7) Under 1996 legislation, a subminimum training wage of $4.25 an hour was established for employees under 20 years of age during their first 90 consecutive calendar days of employment with an employer. For workers receiving gratuities, the minimum wage remained $2.13 per hour. (8) Minimum wage was 32-7% by this measure in 2003.

Fatal Occupational Injuries, 2006
Source: Bureau of Labor Statistics, U.S. Dept. of Labor

	FATALITIES Number	Percent		FATALITIES Number	Percent
TRANSPORTATION INCIDENTS	2,413	42	Caught in or compressed by equipment or objects	281	5
Highway	1,329	23	Caught in running equipment or machinery	148	3
Collision between vehicles, mobile equipment	644	11	Caught in or crushed in collapsing materials	107	2
Vehicle struck stationary object, equipment	337	6	FALLS	809	14
Worker struck by a vehicle	372	6	EXPOSURE TO HARMFUL SUBSTANCES OR ENVIRONMENTS	525	9
Water vehicle	89	2	Contact with electric current	247	4
Aircraft	215	4	Contact with overhead power lines	108	2
ASSAULTS AND VIOLENT ACTS	754	13	Contact with temperature extremes	53	1
Homicides	516	9	Exposure to caustic, noxious, or allergenic substances	153	3
Shooting	417	7	Inhalation of substance	58	1
Stabbing	38	1	Oxygen deficiency	64	1
Self-inflicted injuries	199	3	Drowning, submersion	50	1
CONTACT WITH OBJECTS & EQUIPMENT	983	17	FIRES AND EXPLOSIONS	201	4
Struck by object	583	10	TOTAL	5,703	100
Struck by falling object	378	6			
Struck by flying object	69	1			

Note: Totals for categories may include subcategories not shown separately. Percentages based on incidence rate per total fatalities.

U.S. Occupational Injuries or Illnesses, by Industry, 2005

Source: Bureau of Labor Statistics, U.S. Dept. of Labor
(percent distribution)

	Private Industry	Goods Producing			Service Providing					
		Natural Resources & Mining[2,3]	Construction	Manufacturing	Trade, Trans. & Utilities[4]	Info.	Financial	Prof. & Business	Edu & Health	Leisure and Hospitality
Total [1,234,680 cases]....	100.0	100.0	100.0	100.0	100.0	100.0	100.0	100.0	100.0	100.0
Nature of injury or illness										
Sprains, strains.........	40.8	30.8	34.7	35.5	45.3	39.4	35.9	37.9	52.0	32.5
Bruises, contusions......	8.7	12.7	7.2	8.0	9.5	8.4	7.1	8.1	9.4	9.0
Cuts, lacerations........	8.2	8.7	11.3	10.3	7.1	4.6	8.3	7.2	2.6	15.3
Fractures..............	7.8	12.9	11.5	8.2	7.1	5.9	6.4	8.0	5.2	7.3
Heat burns	1.4	0.9	0.8	1.7	0.7	0.3	1.3	0.5	0.9	6.5
Carpal tunnel syndrome ..	1.3	0.4	0.4	2.6	0.9	2.8	4.5	1.7	0.7	1.0
Tendonitis.............	0.5	0.2	0.4	0.9	0.3	0.9	0.3	0.5	0.3	0.3
Chemical burns........	0.5	0.8	0.5	0.9	0.5	0.1	1.2	0.3	0.3	0.5
Amputations	0.7	1.4	0.8	1.8	0.4	0.2	0.4	0.6	−5.0	0.5
Multiple traumatic injuries	4.1	5.0	4.3	3.7	4.0	5.4	5.2	4.1	4.0	4.1
Part of body affected by the injury or illness										
Head.................	6.6	8.7	8.2	7.7	6.4	4.8	7.8	6.1	4.7	5.1
Eye..................	2.8	4.2	4.1	4.6	2.2	1.5	3.1	2.3	1.3	1.7
Neck.................	1.5	1.1	1.5	1.1	1.6	1.9	1.9	1.8	1.9	0.7
Trunk................	34.7	31.1	30.8	32.7	37.4	31.5	28.8	31.9	42.0	29.1
Shoulder.............	6.3	5.8	5.1	7.2	7.1	5.5	3.9	5.5	6.4	5.2
Back	21.9	16.8	19.2	18.5	23.1	20.5	19.0	20.7	30.0	18.6
Upper extremities	23.1	22.8	23.9	32.6	19.5	20.6	19.9	21.4	15.6	31.9
Wrist	4.6	2.9	3.3	6.1	4.1	6.2	6.8	4.6	4.3	4.3
Hand, except finger......	3.8	3.0	4.6	5.2	3.0	2.6	2.4	3.6	2.2	6.6
Finger	9.0	11.5	10.0	14.7	7.1	4.9	5.9	7.7	4.2	14.1
Lower extremities	22.0	24.6	25.0	18.1	23.9	24.2	22.6	23.6	19.2	20.9
Knee................	8.1	8.5	8.0	6.4	9.0	8.7	8.8	8.1	8.3	8.2
Foot, except toe	3.6	3.4	4.5	3.6	4.0	4.5	3.3	3.5	2.3	2.7
Toe	1.0	0.9	1.0	1.0	1.3	1.0	0.8	1.2	0.7	0.7
Body systems.........	1.5	1.9	1.1	1.2	1.0	2.9	4.5	2.1	1.7	1.6
Multiple parts	9.8	8.9	8.7	6.2	9.5	13.6	13.6	11.4	14.2	8.7
Source of injury or illness										
Chemicals and chemical products	1.5	4.0	1.0	2.2	1.1	1.5	2.8	1.4	1.3	1.5
Containers	12.3	7.0	4.3	11.6	20.7	8.6	7.3	10.7	5.9	13.3
Furniture and fixtures	3.8	1.1	1.8	2.9	4.1	2.1	5.9	4.7	5.0	5.2
Machinery............	6.5	10.3	6.2	12.9	5.3	5.2	5.2	5.7	2.3	6.7
Parts and materials......	10.4	11.8	23.4	17.6	9.0	7.0	5.4	6.3	1.2	3.3
Worker motion or position	14.7	10.4	13.2	17.9	14.4	21.4	17.8	16.0	12.0	13.7
Floors, walkways, ground surfaces	19.0	17.4	20.4	11.7	17.8	27.2	24.6	21.1	22.6	25.1
Tools, instruments, and equipment...........	6.5	6.9	10.7	6.8	4.8	6.4	5.9	5.9	5.0	8.7
Vehicles	8.9	9.5	5.3	5.5	13.5	10.0	8.9	12.1	5.7	5.9
Health care patient	4.4	—	[5]	[5]	[5]	—	0.3	0.5	28.8	—
Event or exposure leading to injury or illness										
Contact with objects and equipment...........	27.4	40.2	35.4	36.8	26.0	18.8	21.4	24.0	13.2	29.8
Struck by object	13.6	20.5	19.5	15.2	13.6	7.0	11.9	11.0	6.6	15.5
Struck against object	6.9	8.2	8.0	7.8	6.8	7.7	5.5	6.7	3.9	10.1
Caught in equipment or object	4.4	8.7	3.8	10.3	3.7	2.8	1.5	3.3	1.7	2.4
Fall to lower level	6.4	8.0	13.8	3.7	6.3	9.8	8.6	6.5	3.6	4.4
Fall on same level.......	13.5	9.8	7.9	8.8	12.6	18.2	17.5	15.7	19.8	21.8
Slip, trip, loss of balance- without fall...........	2.9	2.2	3.1	2.6	2.9	3.5	3.1	2.6	2.9	3.8
Overexertion...........	24.1	16.0	18.2	22.9	27.6	16.6	17.3	18.6	35.8	13.9
Overexertion in lifting	13.0	7.0	10.0	11.8	15.7	8.2	10.0	11.1	16.9	7.8
Repetitive motion	3.5	1.0	1.6	7.3	2.7	6.9	7.6	3.8	2.0	2.7
Exposure to harmful substances	4.2	4.8	3.5	5.0	2.6	4.5	6.7	3.9	4.1	9.3
Transportation accidents	5.0	5.3	3.9	2.2	6.7	6.8	5.6	8.6	4.0	3.2
Fires and explosions.....	0.2	0.3	0.2	0.3	0.2	—	0.7	0.1	0.1	—
Assaults and violent acts by person	1.2	0.2	0.1	0.2	0.6	0.3	0.7	0.9	5.3	0.8

Note: Dashes (—) indicate data are not available. Because of rounding and classifications not shown, percentages may not add to 100. All injuries and illnesses reported involved days away from work. (1) Excludes farms with fewer than 11 employees. (2) Agriculture includes forestry and fishing, but excludes farms with fewer than 11 employees. (3) Data conforming to OSHA definitions for mining operators in coal, metal, and nonmetal mining are provided by the Mine Safety and Health Administration, U.S. Dept. of Labor. Independent mining contractors are excluded from the coal, metal, and nonmetal industries. Data for mining include establishments not governed by Mine Safety and Health Administration rules, such as those in oil and gas extraction. (4) Data for employers in railroad transportation are provided by the Federal Railroad Administration, U.S. Department of Transportation. (5) Less than 0.1%.

Civilian Employment of the Federal Government, January 2007

Source: Statistical Analysis and Services Division, U.S. Office of Personnel Management
(monthly payroll in thousands of dollars)

	ALL AREAS Employment	ALL AREAS Payroll	UNITED STATES Employment	UNITED STATES Payroll	WASH., D.C., MSA[1] Employment	WASH., D.C., MSA[1] Payroll	OVERSEAS Employment	OVERSEAS Payroll
TOTAL, all agencies[2,3]	2,670,857	12,994,722	2,583,277	12,572,791	329,618	2,057,051	87,580	421,931
Legislative Branch[2,3]	29,364	172,290	29,357	172,221	28,326	165,234	7	69
Congress	16,945	95,731	16,945	95,731	16,945	95,731	—	—
U.S. Senate	6,864	36,357	6,864	36,357	6,864	36,357	—	—
House of Representatives	10,081	59,374	10,081	59,374	10,081	59,374	—	—
Architect of the Capitol	2,150	10,549	2,150	10,549	2,149	10,540	—	—
Congressional Budget Ofc	235	1,878	235	1,878	235	1,878	—	—
Govt. Accountability Ofc	3,198	24,086	3,197	24,074	2,353	17,983	1	12
Govt. Printing Ofc[3]	2,359	12,314	2,359	12,314	2,207	11,578	—	—
Library of Congress	3,967	24,193	3,961	24,136	3,934	24,017	6	57
U.S. Tax Court	232	1,625	232	1,625	232	1,625	—	—
Judicial Branch	31,928	177,247	31,579	175,165	2,684	17,541	349	2,082
Supreme Court	478	1,323	478	1,323	478	1,323	—	—
U.S. Courts	31,450	175,924	31,101	173,842	2,206	16,218	349	2,082
Executive Branch[3]	2,609,565	12,645,185	2,522,341	12,225,405	298,608	1,874,276	87,224	419,780
Exec Ofc of the President	1,719	12,180	1,706	12,075	1,706	12,075	13	105
White House Office	413	2,076	413	2,076	413	2,076	—	—
Ofc of Vice President	18	147	18	147	18	147	—	—
Ofc of Mgmt & Budget	472	3,700	472	3,700	472	3,700	—	—
Ofc of Administration	225	1,403	225	1,403	225	1,403	—	—
Council Economic Advisors	24	160	24	160	24	160	—	—
Council Environmental Quality	18	125	18	125	18	125	—	—
Ofc of Policy Development	25	137	25	137	25	137	—	—
National Security Council	64	425	64	425	64	425	—	—
Ofc of Natl Drug Control Policy	108	897	108	897	108	897	—	—
Ofc of U.S. Trade Rep	233	2,242	220	2,137	220	2,137	13	105
Executive Departments	1,674,713	8,272,268	1,593,600	7,888,455	234,388	1,446,465	81,113	383,813
State	34,446	264,053	13,546	80,195	11,511	65,467	20,900	183,858
Treasury	110,078	559,142	109,395	556,478	14,499	107,985	683	2,664
Defense, Total	670,686	2,452,328	623,314	2,319,159	64,604	258,649	47,372	133,169
Defense, Mil Function	648,892	2,393,401	601,563	2,260,288	63,866	256,770	47,329	133,113
Defense, Civ Function	21,794	58,927	21,751	58,871	738	1,879	43	56
Dept of the Army	242,861	670,391	222,985	613,418	19,271	41,438	19,876	56,973
Army, Mil Function	221,068	611,465	201,235	554,548	18,533	39,559	19,833	56,917
Army, Civil Function	21,793	58,926	21,750	58,870	738	1,879	43	56
Corps of Engineers	21,722	58,746	21,679	58,690	667	1,699	43	56
Dept of the Navy	174,461	711,040	167,787	683,173	24,118	97,124	6,674	27,837
Dept of the Air Force	158,281	640,148	152,286	615,914	5,691	23,008	5,995	24,234
Defense Logist. Agency	20,831	93,931	20,287	89,381	1,694	11,452	544	4,550
Other Defense Activities	74,252	336,848	59,969	317,273	13,830	85,627	14,283	19,575
Justice	106,745	662,256	104,825	649,777	22,874	161,555	1,920	12,479
Interior	65,854	313,195	65,541	312,095	7,379	45,220	313	1,100
Agriculture	93,484	445,102	92,244	440,341	10,996	72,419	1,240	4,761
Commerce	39,381	228,229	38,601	224,430	21,228	145,091	780	3,799
Labor	16,126	100,325	16,091	100,134	5,938	41,019	35	191
Health & Human Services	60,512	385,660	60,256	383,794	27,804	198,715	256	1,866
Housing & Urban Dev.	9,720	65,964	9,648	65,497	3,304	24,125	72	467
Transportation	53,221	411,090	52,905	409,058	8,879	70,541	316	2,032
Energy	14,608	109,918	14,597	109,814	4,943	41,455	11	104
Education	4,157	29,179	4,148	29,132	3,033	21,794	9	47
Veterans Affairs	242,641	1,388,504	239,084	1,372,102	7,486	54,774	3,557	16,402
Homeland Security	153,054	857,323	149,405	836,449	19,910	137,656	3,649	20,874
Independent Agencies[3]	933,133	4,360,737	927,035	4,324,875	62,514	415,736	6,098	35,862
Bd of Govt, Fed Rsrv Sys[3]	1,873	13,535	1,873	13,535	1,873	13,535	—	—
Environmtl Protect Agcy	18,123	125,490	18,067	125,152	5,381	36,068	56	338
Equal Employ Opp Comm.	2,189	13,530	2,179	13,484	506	3,629	10	46
Federal Communic Comm	1,821	14,510	1,819	14,493	1,534	12,434	2	17
Federal Deposit Ins Corp	4,518	35,247	4,506	35,176	1,504	13,221	12	71
Federal Trade Comm	1,079	8,403	1,078	8,402	929	7,183	1	1
General Svcs Admin	12,031	78,058	11,964	77,692	4,211	30,252	67	366
Natl Aero & Space Admin	18,276	136,748	18,267	136,654	4,170	32,654	9	94
Natl Fnd Arts & Humanities[3]	379	2,577	379	2,577	377	2,569	—	—
Natl Science Foundation	1,347	10,087	1,341	10,039	1,335	9,999	6	48
Nuclear Regulatory Comm	3,532	27,527	3,531	27,512	2,497	20,136	1	15
Ofc Personnel Mangement	5,188	25,647	5,172	25,618	1,721	11,062	16	29
Peace Corps	1,059	5,721	693	3,924	573	3,405	366	1,797
Securities & Exch. Comm	3,513	33,816	3,513	33,816	2,082	19,507	—	—
Small Business Adm.[3]	6,045	45,721	6,010	45,449	874	9,070	35	272
Smithsonian Inst.	4,881	25,095	4,855	24,898	4,485	22,767	26	197
Social Security Admin	62,532	317,347	62,136	315,622	1,604	9,078	396	1,725
Tennessee Valley Authority	12,372	89,993	12,372	89,993	5	40	—	—
U.S. Postal Service	751,818	3,215,559	748,435	3,199,147	14,914	76,541	3,383	16,412

(1) Metropolitan Statistical Area. (2) Totals include agencies not listed. (3) Denotes figures that are preliminary or are based in whole or part on figures for the previous month.

U.S Median Weekly Earnings, 2nd Quarter 2007*
Source: Bureau of Labor Statistics, U.S. Dept. of Labor

Age, Race, Hispanic or Latino ethnicity	Total Number of workers (in thousands)	Total Median weekly earnings	Men Number of workers (in thousands)	Men Median weekly earnings	Women Number of workers (in thousands)	Women Median weekly earning
ALL WORKERS, BY AGE						
16 years and over	106,879	$690	60,507	$763	46,372	$607
16 to 24 years	11,170	421	6,537	436	4,633	404
16 to 19 years	1,659	317	1,003	338	657	302
20 to 24 years	9,510	445	5,535	464	3,976	426
25 years and over	95,709	735	53,970	819	41,739	635
25 to 54 years	79,296	730	45,052	804	34,244	632
25 to 34 years	25,854	635	15,025	683	10,829	588
35 to 44 years	26,991	770	15,539	871	11,453	657
45 to 54 years	26,451	788	14,489	905	11,962	668
55 years and over	16,413	761	8,918	917	7,495	648
55 to 64 years	14,049	790	7,514	950	6,535	664
65 years and over	2,364	611	1,404	664	960	548
WHITE[1]						
16 years and over	86,393	713	50,162	783	36,232	620
16 to 24 years	9,114	425	5,487	442	3,627	410
25 years and over	77,279	755	44,675	846	32,605	654
25 to 54 years	63,459	749	36,998	827	26,461	651
55 years and over	13,820	787	7,677	940	6,143	667
BLACK OR AFRICAN AMERICAN[1]						
16 years and over	13,048	562	6,190	597	6,858	521
16 to 24 years	1,352	389	681	401	671	368
25 years and over	11,696	591	5,509	623	6,187	554
25 to 54 years	10,065	589	4,772	616	5,293	560
55 years and over	1,630	602	737	681	894	533
ASIAN[1]						
16 years and over	5,025	827	2,766	942	2,258	709
16 to 24 years	314	535	135	677	179	502
25 years and over	4,711	862	2,631	959	2,080	737
25 to 54 years	3,997	872	2,265	969	1,732	742
55 years and over	714	803	366	894	348	697
HISPANIC AND LATINO[2]						
16 years and over	15,943	503	10,249	523	5,694	470
16 to 24 years	2,219	391	1,431	397	789	373
25 years and over	13,724	522	8,818	559	4,905	488
25 to 54 years	12,411	520	7,976	555	4,435	486
55 years and over	1,313	556	843	585	470	507
Occupation						
Managerial, professional, and related occupations	38,817	997	19,402	1,176	19,415	859
Management, business, and financial operations occupations	15,591	1,115	8,763	1,237	6,827	952
Professional and related occupations	23,226	945	10,639	1,142	12,587	823
Service occupations	14,811	459	7,526	521	7,285	404
Sales and office occupations	25,536	595	9,632	722	15,904	546
Sales and related occupations	10,477	640	5,831	802	4,646	489
Office and administrative support occupations	15,059	578	3,801	613	11,257	569
Natural resources, construction, and maintenance occupations	12,565	658	12,141	661	425	559
Farming, fishing, and forestry occupations	762	382	612	394	149	351
Construction and extraction occupations	7,322	634	7,192	635	130	566
Installation, maintenance, and repair occupations	4,482	744	4,336	741	146	782
Production, transportation, and material moving occupations	15,149	578	11,806	619	3,343	448
Production occupations	8,596	583	6,154	643	2,442	448
Transportation and material moving occupations	6,553	568	5,652	597	901	446

*Not seasonally adjusted; figures are for median usual weekly earnings of full-time wage and salary workers. (1) Persons who selected this race group only; persons who selected more than one race group are not included. (2) May be of any race.

Average Hours and Earnings of U.S. Production Workers, 1969-2006[1]
Source: Bureau of Labor Statistics, U.S. Dept. of Labor

(annual averages)

	Weekly hours	Hourly earnings	Weekly earnings		Weekly hours	Hourly earnings	Weekly earnings		Weekly hours	Hourly earnings	Weekly earnings
1969	37.5	$3.22	$120.75	1982	34.7	$7.87	$273.09	1995	34.3	$11.65	$400.07
1970	37.0	3.40	125.80	1983	34.9	8.20	286.18	1996	34.3	12.04	413.28
1971	36.8	3.63	133.58	1984	35.1	8.49	298.00	1997	34.5	12.51	431.86
1972	36.9	3.90	143.91	1985	34.9	8.74	305.03	1998	34.5	13.01	448.56
1973	36.9	4.14	152.77	1986	34.7	8.93	309.87	1999	34.3	13.49	463.15
1974	36.4	4.43	161.25	1987	34.7	9.14	317.16	2000	34.3	14.02	481.01
1975	36.0	4.73	170.28	1988	34.6	9.44	326.62	2001	34.0	14.54	493.79
1976	36.1	5.06	182.67	1989	34.5	9.80	338.10	2002	33.9	14.97	506.72
1977	35.9	5.44	195.30	1990	34.3	10.20	349.75	2003	33.7	15.37	518.06
1978	35.8	5.88	210.50	1991	34.1	10.52	358.51	2004	33.7	15.69	529.09
1979	35.6	6.34	225.70	1992	34.2	10.77	368.25	2005	33.8	16.13	544.33
1980	35.2	6.85	241.12	1993	34.3	11.05	378.89	2006	33.9	16.76	567.87
1981	35.2	7.44	261.89	1994	34.5	11.34	391.22				

(1) Data refer to production workers in natural resources, mining and manufacturing, construction workers, and non-supervisory workers in the service industries. Figures may be revised.

Elderly in U.S. Labor Force, 1890-2005
Source: Bureau of the Census, U.S. Dept. of Commerce

The percentage of men 65 years of age and older in the U.S. labor force steadily declined between 1890 and 1990, dropping 76% in 100 years, but since 1990 the rate has risen. The percentage of women 65 or older in the work force has always been much lower than that of men; after ranging from around 6% to 10% from 1890 to 1950, it has increased to 9%-12% in recent years.

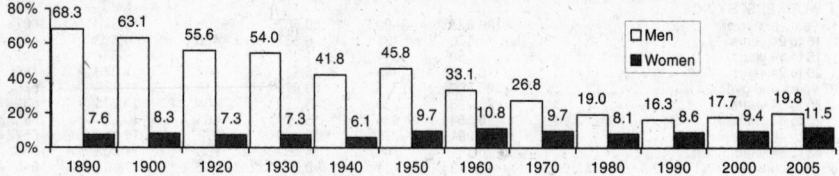

Union Affiliation and Median Weekly Earnings of Wage and Salary Workers in the U.S., 1996, 2006
Source: Bureau of Labor Statistics, U.S. Dept. of Labor

SEX AND AGE	1996 TOTAL	Members of unions[1]	Represented by unions[2]	Non-union	2006 TOTAL	Members of unions[1]	Represented by unions[2]	Non-union
Total, 16 years and older ..	$490	$615	$610	$462	$671	$833	$827	$642
16 to 24 years...........	298	371	362	294	409	526	523	404
25 years and older	520	625	621	498	718	850	845	691
25 to 34 years	463	554	548	447	621	773	766	606
35 to 44 years	559	636	632	530	748	853	849	728
45 to 54 years	594	687	686	552	773	888	884	750
55 to 64 years	535	620	616	505	765	882	883	741
65 years and older	384	510	510	367	583	675	667	573
Men, 16 years and older ..	557	653	651	520	743	887	885	717
16 to 24 years...........	307	375	369	303	418	526	521	413
25 years and older	599	669	668	580	797	904	902	771
25 to 34 years	499	591	587	485	661	831	822	640
35 to 44 years	632	683	683	617	836	918	914	816
45 to 54 years	698	718	721	682	897	936	939	883
55 to 64 years	643	667	664	633	902	928	930	893
65 years and older	477	589	593	424	658	650	653	659
Women, 16 years and older ..	418	549	543	398	600	758	753	579
16 to 24 years...........	284	358	339	280	395	527	529	391
25 years and older	444	560	555	420	627	768	763	607
25 to 34 years	415	497	495	405	583	727	716	565
35 to 44 years	463	561	556	439	645	759	755	626
45 to 54 years	481	620	616	445	659	807	798	628
55 to 64 years	420	524	523	395	658	819	822	627
65 years and older	334	417	413	321	510	690	678	495

Note: Data refer to the sole or principal job of full-time workers. Excluded are self-employed workers regardless of whether or not their businesses are incorporated. (1) Including members of an employee association similar to a union. (2) Including members of a labor union or employee association similar to a union, and others whose jobs are covered by a union or an employee-association contract.

Work Stoppages (Strikes and Lockouts) in the U.S., 1950-2006[1]
Source: Bureau of Labor Statistics, U.S. Dept. of Labor; involving 1,000 workers or more

Year	Number[1]	Workers (thous.)	Days idle (thous.)	Year	Number[1]	Workers (thous.)	Days idle (thous.)	Year	Number[1]	Workers (thous.)	Days idle (thous.)
1950....	424	1,698	30,390	1980....	187	795	20,844	1994	45	322	5,020
1955....	363	2,055	21,180	1981.....	145	729	16,908	1995	31	192	5,771
1960....	222	896	13,260	1982.....	96	656	9,061	1996	37	273	4,889
1965....	268	999	15,140	1983.....	81	909	17,461	1997	29	339	4,497
1970....	381	2,468	52,761	1984.....	62	376	8,499	1998	34	387	5,116
1971....	298	2,516	35,538	1985.....	54	324	7,079	1999	17	73	1,996
1972....	250	975	16,764	1986.....	69	533	11,861	2000	39	394	20,419
1973....	317	1,400	16,260	1987.....	46	174	4,481	2001....	29	99	1,151
1974....	424	1,796	31,809	1988.....	40	118	4,381	2002....	19	46	660
1975....	235	965	17,563	1989.....	51	452	16,996	2003	14	129	4,091
1976....	231	1,519	23,962	1990.....	44	185	5,926	2004	17	171	3,344
1977....	298	1,212	21,258	1991.....	40	392	4,584	2005	22	100	1,736
1978....	219	1,006	23,774	1992.....	35	364	3,989	2006	20	70	2,688
1979....	235	1,021	20,409	1993.....	35	182	3,981				

(1) Numbers cover stoppages that began in the year indicated. Workers are counted more than once if they are involved in more than 1 stoppage during the year. For work stoppages ongoing at the end of a calendar year, days idle include only the days for the calendar year.

Work Stoppages Involving 5,000 Workers or More Beginning in 2006

There were 20 major work stoppages in 2006, resulting in 2.7 mil workdays lost. There were 5 stoppages in which more than 5,000 workers participated. The largest work stoppage in terms of worker participation in 2006 involved the United Steelworkers Union and Goodyear Tire and Rubber. It began on October 6, and ended December 29, 2006. It involved 12,600 workers and accounted for about 718,000 days lost. The longest strike in 2006 was by the Armco Employees Independent Federation against the AK Steel Corporation. It began March 1, 2006, and ended exactly one year later.

U.S. Union Membership, 1930-2006[1]

Source: Bureau of Labor Statistics, U.S. Dept. of Labor; figures in thousands

Year	Total employed[1]	% in unions	Union members[2]	Year	Total employed[1]	% in unions	Union members[2]	Year	Total employed[1]	% in unions	Union members[2]
1930....	29,424	11.6	3,401	1980....	90,564	21.9	19,843	1998...	116,730	13.9	16,211
1935....	27,053	13.2	3,584	1985....	94,521	18.0	16,996	1999...	118,963	13.9	16,477
1940....	32,376	26.9	8,717	1990....	103,905	16.1	16,740	2000...	120,786	13.5	16,258
1945....	40,394	35.5	14,322	1991....	102,786	16.1	16,568	2001...	122,482	13.4	16,387
1950....	45,222	31.5	14,267	1992....	103,688	15.8	16,390	2002[3]...	121,826	13.3	16,145
1955....	50,675	33.2	16,802	1993....	105,067	15.8	16,598	2003[4]...	122,358	12.9	15,776
1960....	54,234	31.4	17,049	1994....	107,989	15.5	16,748	2004[4]...	123,554	12.5	15,472
1965....	60,815	28.4	17,299	1995....	110,038	14.9	16,360	2005[4]...	125,889	12.5	15,685
1970....	70,920	27.3	19,381	1996....	111,960	14.5	16,269	2006[4]...	128,237	12.0	15,359
1975....	76,945	25.5	19,611	1997....	114,533	14.1	16,110				

(1) Does not include agricultural employment; from 1985, does not include self-employed or unemployed persons. (2) From 1930 to 1980, includes dues-paying members of traditional trade unions, regardless of employment status; after that includes employed only. From 1985, includes members of employee associations that engage in collective bargaining with employers. (3) Revised to incorporate changes to the class of worker status associated with the introduction of the 2002 Census industry and occupational classification systems into the Current Population Survey. (4) Data reflect revised population controls used in the household survey.

Labor Union Directory

Source: Bureau of Labor Statistics, U.S. Dept. of Labor; AFL-CIO; World Almanac research.

(#) Member of Change to Win Coalition formed in 2005 by unions disaffiliated from AFL-CIO. (*) Independent union. All others are affiliated with AFL-CIO. Year established in parenthesis.

Air Line Pilots Association, (1931); 61,000+ members, 39 U.S. and Canadian airlines; www.alpa.org

American Federation of Labor & Congress of Industrial Organizations (AFL-CIO), (1955); 10 mil members; www.aflcio.org

Automobile, Aerospace & Agricultural Implement Workers of America, International Union, United (UAW), (1935); 640,000 active (500,000 ret.) members, 800 locals; www.uaw.org

Bakery, Confectionery, Tobacco Workers and Grain Millers International Union (BCTGM), (1881); 120,000 members; www.bctgm.org

Bricklayers and Allied Craftworkers, International Union of (BAC), (1865); 100,000 members, 50 locals; www.bacweb.org

#Carpenters and Joiners of America, United Brotherhood of, (1881); 520,000 members, 1,000 locals; www.carpenters.org

#Change to Win Coalition, (2005); 7 unions, 6 ex-affiliates unions of AFL-CIO, 1 independent; www.changetowin.org

*Communications Workers of America (IUE-CWA), (1938); 700,000+ members, 1,200 locals; www.cwa-union.org

*Education Association, National, (1857); 3.2 mil members, 14,000+ affiliates; www.nea.org

Electrical Workers, International Brotherhood of (IBEW), (1891); 750,000 members, 1,019 locals; www.ibew.org

Engineers, International Union of Operating (IUOE), (1896); 400,000 members, 170 locals; www.iuoe.org

#Farm Workers of America, United (UFW), (1962); 27,000+ members; www.ufw.org

*Federal Employees, Federal District 1, National Federation of (NFFE FD1, IAMAW, AFL-CIO), (1917); 90,000 members, 200 locals; www.nffe.org

Fire Fighters, International Association of, (1918); 281,000 members, 2,900 locals; www.iaff.org

Flight Attendants, Association of, (1945); 55,000 members, 20 carriers; merged with Communications Workers of America in 2004; www.afanet.org

#Food and Commercial Workers International Union, United (UFCW), (1979); 1.4 mil members, 500 locals; www.ufcw.org

Glass, Molders, Pottery, Plastics & Allied Workers Intl. Union (GMP), (1842); 51,000 members, 290+ locals; www.gmpiu.org

Government Employees, American Federation of (AFGE), (1932); 600,000 members, 1,100 locals; www.afge.org

Graphic Communications Conference (GCC), (1983); 150,000 members, 321 locals; merged with Teamsters in 2005; www.gciu.org

Iron Workers, International Association of Bridge, Structural, Ornamental and Reinforcing, (1896); 140,000 members, 213 locals; www.ironworkers.org

#Laborers' International Union of North America (LIUNA), (1903); more than 700,000 members, 500+ locals; www.liuna.org

Letter Carriers, National Association of (NALC), (1889); 300,000+ members, 2,500+ locals; www.nalc.org

#Locomotive Engineers and Trainmen, Brotherhood of (BLET), (1863); 53,386 members, 524 divisions; www.ble.org

Longshoremen's Association, International (ILA), (1892); 65,000 members; www.ilaunion.org

Machinists and Aerospace Workers, International Association of (IAMAW), (1888); 730,000 members (current and retired, 1,174 locals; merged with TCU in 2006; www.iamaw.org

Maintenance of Way Employees, Brotherhood of (BMWE), (1887); 35,000 members, 770 locals; merged with Teamsters in 2005; www.bmwe.org

Mine Workers of America, United (UMWA), (1890); 110,000 members, 600 locals; www.umwa.org

Musicians of the United States and Canada, American Federation of (AFM), (1896); 100,000 members, 249 locals; www.afm.org

Newspaper Guild-Communications Workers of America (CWA), The, (1933); 34,000 members, 90 locals; www.newsguild.org

*Nurses Association, American (ANA), (1897); 2.9 mil members, 54 constituent state & territorial assns; www.nursingworld.org

Office and Professional Employees International Union (OPEIU), (1945); 125,000 members, 200 locals; www.opeiu.org

Painters and Allied Trades, International Union of (IUPAT), (1887); 140,000 members, 425 locals; www.ibpat.org

Plumbing and Pipe Fitting Industry of the United States and Canada, United Association of Journeymen and Apprentices of the, (1889); 320,000 members, 317 locals; www.ua.org

*Police, National Fraternal Order of, 324,000 members, 2,100+ affiliates; www.grandlodgefop.org

Police Associations, International Union of, (1979); 80,000 members, 500 locals; www.iupa.org

Postal Workers Union, American (APWU), (1971); 333,000+ members, 1,600+ locals; www.apwu.org

Roofers, Waterproofers & Allied Workers, United Union of, (1906); 22,000 members; www.unionroofers.com

*Rural Letter Carriers' Association, National, (1903); 100,000+ members; 50 state org; www.nrlca.org

*Security, Police, and Fire Professionals of America (SPFPA), (1948); 27,000 members, 200 locals; www.spfpa.org

#Service Employees International Union (SEIU), (1921); 1.9 million members, 350 locals; www.seiu.org

Sheet Metal Workers' International Association (SMWIA), (1888); 150,000 members, 350 locals; www.smwia.org

State, County, and Municipal Employees, American Federation of (AFSCME), (1932); 1.4 mil members, 3,617 locals; www.afscme.org

Steelworkers of America, United (USWA), (1936); 850,000 active members, 2,700 locals; merged with PACE union in 2005; www.uswa.org

Teachers, American Federation of (AFT), (1916); 1.4 mil members, 3,000 locals; www.aft.org

#Teamsters, International Brotherhood of (IBT), (1903); 1.4 mil. members, 521 locals; www.teamsters.org

Theatrical Stage Employees, Moving Picture Technicians, Artists and Allied Crafts of the United States, Its Territories, and Canada, International Alliance of (IATSE), (1893); 109,000+ members, 555+ locals; www.iatse-intl.org

Transit Union, Amalgamated (ATU), (1892); 180,000+ members, 270 locals; www.atu.org

Transportation-Communications International Union (TCU), (1899); merged with IAMAW in 2006.

Transportation Union, United (UTU), (1969); 125,000 members, 620 locals; www.utu.org

Transport Workers Union of America, (1934); 126,000 members, 92 locals; www.twu.org

*Treasury Employees Union, National (NTEU), (1938); 150,000+ represented, 270+ chapters; www.nteu.org

#UNITE HERE, UNITE, (1900), HERE, (1891); unions merged 2004; 450,000 active members and 400,000 retirees, www.unitehere.org

ENERGY

U.S. Energy Overview, 1960-2006

Source: Energy Information Administration, U.S. Dept. of Energy, *Annual Energy Review 2006*; in quadrillion Btu

	1960	1965	1970	1975	1980	1985	1990	1995	2000	2005	2006P
Production	42.80	50.68	63.50	61.36	67.23	67.80	70.87	71.32	71.49	69.64	71.03
Fossil fuels	39.87	47.23	59.19	54.73	59.01	57.54	58.56	57.54	57.37	55.09	56.03
Coal	10.82	13.06	14.61	14.99	18.60	19.33	22.49	22.13	22.74	23.19	23.79
Natural gas (dry)	12.66	15.78	21.67	19.64	19.91	16.98	18.33	19.08	19.66	18.60	19.02
Crude oil[1]	14.93	16.52	20.40	17.73	18.25	18.99	15.57	13.89	12.36	10.96	10.87
Natural gas plant liquids (NGPL)	1.46	1.88	2.51	2.37	2.25	2.24	2.17	2.44	2.61	2.33	2.35
Nuclear electric power	0.01	0.04	0.24	1.90	2.74	4.08	6.10	7.08	7.86	8.16	8.21
Hydroelectric pumped storage[2]	(3)	(3)	(3)	(3)	(3)	(3)	-0.04	-0.03	-0.06	(3)	(3)
Renewable energy	2.93	3.40	4.08	4.72	5.49	6.18	6.21	6.70	6.26	6.39	6.79
Conventional hydroelectric power[4]	1.61	2.06	2.63	3.15	2.90	2.97	3.05	3.21	2.81	2.70	2.89
Biomass[5]	1.32	1.33	1.43	1.50	2.48	3.02	2.74	3.10	3.01	3.10	3.23
Geothermal energy	(*)	(*)	0.01	0.07	0.11	0.20	0.34	0.29	0.32	0.34	0.35
Solar	NA	NA	NA	NA	NA	(*)	0.06	0.07	0.07	0.07	0.07
Wind	NA	NA	NA	NA	NA	(*)	0.03	0.03	0.06	0.18	0.26
Imports	4.19	5.89	8.34	14.03	15.80	11.78	18.82	22.26	28.97	34.72	34.49
Coal	0.01	(*)	(*)	0.02	0.03	0.05	0.07	0.24	0.31	0.76	0.91
Natural gas	0.16	0.47	0.85	0.98	1.01	0.95	1.55	2.90	3.87	4.45	4.25
All crude oil and petroleum prods.[6]	4.00	5.40	7.47	12.95	14.66	10.61	17.12	18.88	24.53	29.26	29.03
Other[7]	0.02	0.01	0.02	0.08	0.10	0.17	0.08	0.24	0.26	0.24	0.25
Exports	1.48	1.83	2.63	2.32	3.69	4.20	4.75	4.51	4.01	4.56	4.93
Coal	1.02	1.38	1.94	1.76	2.42	2.44	2.77	2.32	1.53	1.27	1.26
Natural gas	0.01	0.03	0.07	0.07	0.05	0.06	0.09	0.16	0.25	0.74	0.76
All crude oil and petroleum prods.[6]	0.43	0.39	0.55	0.44	1.16	1.66	1.82	1.99	2.15	2.44	2.79
Other[7]	0.01	0.03	0.08	0.05	0.07	0.04	0.07	0.05	0.08	0.11	0.12
Consumption	45.09	54.02	67.84	72.00	78.12	76.49	84.65	91.17	98.98	100.69	99.87
Fossil fuels	42.14	50.58	63.52	65.35	69.83	66.09	72.33	77.26	84.73	86.04	84.76
Coal	9.84	11.58	12.26	12.66	15.42	17.48	19.17	20.09	22.58	22.79	22.51
Coal coke net imports	-0.01	-0.02	-0.06	0.01	-0.04	-0.01	0.00	0.06	0.07	0.04	0.06
Natural gas[8]	12.39	15.77	21.80	19.95	20.24	17.70	19.60	22.67	23.82	22.82	22.43
Petroleum[9]	19.92	23.25	29.52	32.73	34.20	30.92	33.55	34.44	38.26	40.39	39.76
Nuclear electric power	0.01	0.04	0.24	1.90	2.74	4.08	6.10	7.08	7.86	8.16	8.21
Hydroelectric pumped storage[2]	(3)	(3)	(3)	(3)	(3)	(3)	-0.04	-0.03	-0.06	(3)	(3)
Renewable energy	2.93	3.40	4.08	4.72	5.49	6.18	6.21	6.71	6.26	6.40	6.84
Conventional hydroelectric power[4]	1.61	2.06	2.63	3.15	2.90	2.97	3.05	3.21	2.81	2.70	2.89
Geothermal energy	(*)	(*)	0.01	0.07	0.11	0.20	0.34	0.29	0.32	0.34	0.35
Biomass[5]	1.32	1.33	1.43	1.50	2.48	3.02	2.74	3.10	3.01	3.11	3.28
Solar energy	NA	NA	NA	NA	NA	(*)	0.06	0.07	0.07	0.07	0.07
Wind energy	NA	NA	NA	NA	NA	(*)	0.03	0.03	0.06	0.18	0.26

(1) Incl. lease condensate. (2) Total pumped storage facility production minus energy used for pumping. (3) Included in conventional hydroelectric power. (4) Starting in 1990, pumped storage is removed and expanded coverage of industrial use of hydroelectric power is included. (5) Substituted in 2000 for former "Wood, waste, and alcohol" category. Includes wood, waste, and alcohol fuels (ethanol blended into motor gasoline). Ethanol is included in both "Petroleum" and "Biomass" categories, but is only counted once in totals. (6) Incl. imports of crude oil for the Strategic Petroleum Reserve, which began in 1977. (7) Coal coke and small amts. of electricity transmitted across borders with Canada and Mexico. (8) Incl. supplemental gaseous fuels. (9) Petroleum products supplied, incl. natural gas plant liquids and crude oil burned as fuel. NA = Not available. P = preliminary. (*) = Less than 0.005 quadrillion Btu. **Note:** Some figures have been revised. Some totals may not add because of rounding.

U.S. Energy Flow, 2006[1]

Source: Energy Information Administration, U.S. Dept. of Energy, *Annual Energy Review 2006*; in quadrillion Btu

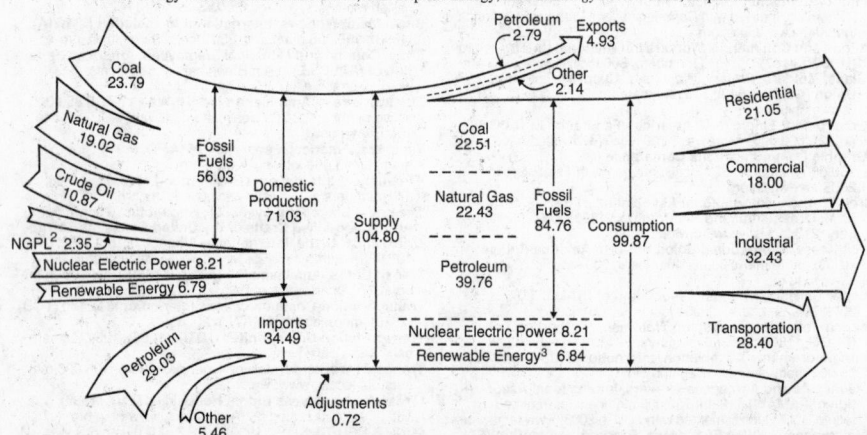

(1) Preliminary figures. (2) Natural Gas Plant Liquids. (3) Conventional hydroelectric power; wood, waste, and ethanol blended into gasoline; geothermal; solar; and wind power. Note: Some totals may not add because of rounding.

World Energy Consumption and Production Trends, 2005

Source: Energy Information Administration, U.S. Dept. of Energy, *International Energy Annual 2005*

The world's **consumption** of primary energy—petroleum, natural gas, coal, net hydroelectric, nuclear, geothermal, solar, wind, and wood and waste electric power increased to 463 quadrillion Btu in 2005, a 16 percent increase from 398 quadrillion Btu in 2000, and a 3 percent increase from 448 quadrillion Btu in 2004.

World **production** of primary energy increased to 460 quadrillion Btu in 2005 from 396 quadrillion Btu in 2000, a 16 percent rise. World production of petroleum, both the most consumed and most produced primary energy source,

was about 79.9 million barrels per day in 2004, rising 20% over 1994 production levels.

For the second consecutive year, the U.S. consumed over 100 quadrillion Btu, about 45 percent more primary energy than it produced in 2005. Five countries—U.S., China, Russia, Japan, and India—accounted for 51.2% of world energy consumption in 2005. Energy consumption in China increased from 38.8 quadrillion Btu in 2000 to 67.1 in 2005, a 72 percent increase, and a 249 percent increase over the 27.0 quadrillion Btu China consumed in 1990.

World's Major Consumers of Primary Energy, 2005

Source: Energy Information Administration, Dept. of Energy, *International Energy Annual 2005,* quadrillion Btu

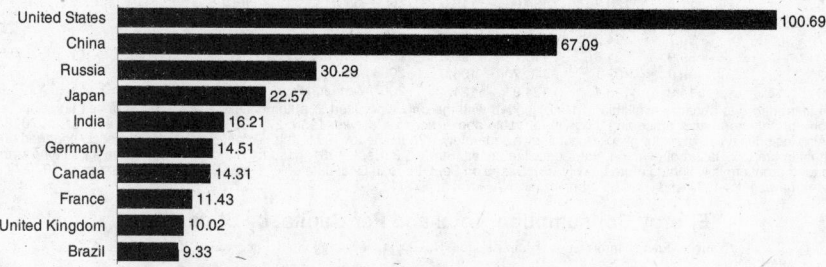

Country	quadrillion Btu
United States	100.69
China	67.09
Russia	30.29
Japan	22.57
India	16.21
Germany	14.51
Canada	14.31
France	11.43
United Kingdom	10.02
Brazil	9.33

World's Major Producers of Primary Energy, 2005

Source: Energy Information Administration, Dept. of Energy, *International Energy Annual 2005,* quadrillion Btu

Country	quadrillion Btu
United States	69.64
China	63.23
Russia	52.72
Saudi Arabia	25.51
Canada	19.09
Iran	13.01
India	11.73
Australia	11.23
Norway	10.66
Mexico	10.26

Gasoline Retail Prices in Selected Countries, 1990-2006

Source: Energy Information Administration, U.S. Dept. of Energy, *Annual Energy Review 2006*

(average price of unleaded regular gas unless otherwise noted; in dollars per gallon, including taxes)

Year	Australia	Brazil	Canada	China	Germany	Japan	Mexico	S. Korea	Taiwan	U.S.	France*	Italy*	S. Africa*	Spain*	Thailand*	UK*	U.S.*
1990	NA	$3.82	$1.87	NA	$2.65	$3.16	$1.00	$2.05	$2.49	$1.16	$3.63	$4.59	NA	NA	NA	$2.82	$1.35
1991	$1.96	2.91	1.92	NA	2.90	3.46	1.30	2.49	2.39	1.14	3.45	4.50	NA	NA	NA	3.01	1.32
1992	1.89	2.92	1.73	NA	3.27	3.59	1.50	2.65	2.42	1.13	3.57	4.53	NA	$3.50	$1.35	3.06	1.32
1993	1.73	2.40	1.57	NA	3.07	4.02	1.56	2.88	2.27	1.11	3.41	3.68	NA	3.01	1.26	2.84	1.30
1994	1.84	2.80	1.45	NA	3.52	4.39	1.48	2.87	2.14	1.11	3.59	3.70	NA	2.99	1.21	2.99	1.31
1995	1.95	2.16	1.53	NA	3.96	4.43	1.11	2.94	2.23	1.15	4.26	4.00	NA	3.24	1.25	3.21	1.34
1996	2.12	2.31	1.61	NA	3.94	3.65	1.25	3.18	2.15	1.23	4.41	4.39	NA	3.32	1.49	3.34	1.41
1997	2.05	2.61	1.62	NA	3.53	3.27	1.47	3.34	2.23	1.23	4.00	4.07	$1.72	3.01	1.27	3.83	1.42
1998	1.63	2.80	1.38	NA	3.34	2.83	1.49	3.04	1.86	1.06	3.87	3.84	1.51	2.80	1.09	4.06	1.25
1999	1.72	NA	1.52	NA	3.42	3.27	1.79	3.80	1.86	1.17	3.85	3.87	1.55	2.82	1.22	4.29	1.36
2000	1.94	NA	1.86	NA	3.45	3.65	2.01	4.18	2.15	1.51	3.80	3.77	1.78	2.86	1.38	4.58	1.69
2001	1.71	NA	1.72	$1.22	3.40	3.27	2.20	3.76	2.02	1.46	3.51	3.57	1.59	2.73	1.33	4.13	1.66
2002	1.76	NA	1.70	1.21	3.67	3.15	2.24	3.84	1.93	1.36	3.62	3.74	1.41	2.90	1.35	4.16	1.56
2003	2.19	NA	1.99	1.33	4.59	3.47	2.04	4.12	2.16	1.59	4.35	4.53	1.91	3.49	1.52	4.70	1.78
2004	2.72	NA	2.37	1.48	5.24	3.93	2.03	4.51	2.46	1.88	4.99	5.30	2.58	4.09	1.76	5.56	2.07
2005	3.23	NA	2.87	1.70	5.66	4.28	2.22	5.28	2.79	2.30	5.46	5.74	3.05	4.49	2.25	5.97	2.49
2006	3.54	NA	3.26	2.11	6.03	4.47	2.31	5.93	3.03	2.59	5.88	6.10	3.39	4.85	2.65	6.36	2.81

NA = Not available. *Premium unleaded gasoline. Note: Some countries report only premium averages and some do not sell unleaded regular gasoline.

Gasoline Retail Prices, U.S. City Average, 1974-2007

Source: Energy Information Administration, U.S. Dept. of Energy, *Monthly Energy Review*, Sept. 2007

(cents per gallon, including taxes)

Average	Leaded regular	Unleaded regular	Unleaded premium	All types[1]	Average	Leaded regular	Unleaded regular	Unleaded premium	All types[1]
1974	53.2	NA	NA	NA	1991	NA	114.0	132.1	119.6
1975	56.7	NA	NA	NA	1992	NA	112.7	131.6	119.0
1976	59.0	61.4	NA	NA	1993	NA	110.8	130.2	117.3
1977	62.2	65.6	NA	NA	1994	NA	111.2	130.5	117.4
1978	62.6	67.0	NA	65.2	1995	NA	114.7	133.6	120.5
1979	85.7	90.3	NA	88.2	1996	NA	123.1	141.3	128.8
1980	119.1	124.5	NA	122.1	1997	NA	123.4	141.6	129.1
1981[2]	131.1	137.8	147.0	135.3	1998	NA	105.9	125.0	111.5
1982	122.2	129.6	141.5	128.1	1999	NA	116.5	135.7	122.1
1983	115.7	124.1	138.3	122.5	2000	NA	151.0	169.3	156.3
1984	112.9	121.2	136.6	119.8	2001	NA	146.1	165.7	153.1
1985	111.5	120.2	134.0	119.6	2002	NA	135.8	157.8	144.1
1986	85.7	92.7	108.5	93.1	2003	NA	159.1	177.7	163.8
1987	89.7	94.8	109.3	95.7	2004	NA	188.0	206.8	192.3
1988	89.9	94.6	110.7	96.3	2005	NA	229.5	249.1	233.8
1989	99.8	102.1	119.7	106.0	2006	NA	258.9	280.5	263.5
1990	114.9	116.4	134.9	121.7	2007 (Jan.-June)	NA	269.9	292.5	274.6

Until unleaded gas became available in 1976, leaded was the only type used in automobiles. Average retail prices (in cents per gallon) for selected years preceding those in the table above were as follows: 1950: 27; 1955: 29; 1960: 31; 1965: 31; 1970: 36. (1) Also includes types of motor gasoline not shown separately. (2) In Sept. 1981, the Bureau of Labor Statistics changed the weights in the calculation of average motor gasoline prices. Starting in Sept. 1981, gasohol is included in average for all types, and unleaded premium is weighted more heavily. (3) Based on Sept. through Dec. data only. **Note:** Geographic coverage for 1974-77 is 56 urban areas; for 1978 and later, 85 urban areas. NA = Not applicable.

Energy Consumption, Total and Per Capita, by State, 2004

Source: Energy Information Administration, U.S. Dept. of Energy, State Energy Data Report 2004

Total Consumption

Rank/State	Trillion Btu	Rank/State	Trillion Btu
1. Texas	11,971.4	27. Colorado	1,383.9
2. California	8,364.6	28. Mississippi	1,214.3
3. Florida	4,452.5	29. Iowa	1,205.8
4. New York	4,254.0	30. Arkansas	1,135.9
5. Pennsylvania	4,049.4	31. Kansas	1,103.5
6. Ohio	4,022.8	32. Oregon	1,093.6
7. Illinois	3,960.5	33. Connecticut	923.8
8. Louisiana	3,816.3	34. West Virginia	821.3
9. Georgia	3,141.1	35. Alaska	779.1
10. Michigan	3,119.4	36. Utah	740.2
11. Indiana	2,945.7	37. Nevada	693.7
12. North Carolina	2,715.6	38. New Mexico	682.3
13. New Jersey	2,630.2	39. Nebraska	651.9
14. Virginia	2,558.2	40. Idaho	499.8
15. Tennessee	2,297.7	41. Maine	480.3
16. Alabama	2,159.7	42. Wyoming	454.4
17. Washington	2,004.8	43. Montana	402.9
18. Kentucky	1,956.4	44. North Dakota	402.3
19. Missouri	1,849.3	45. New Hampshire	340.7
20. Wisconsin	1,847.7	46. Hawaii	323.5
21. Minnesota	1,826.3	47. Delaware	304.8
22. South Carolina	1,717.5	48. South Dakota	263.6
23. Massachusetts	1,542.9	49. Rhode Island	226.4
24. Maryland	1,526.6	50. Wash., DC	190.3
25. Oklahoma	1,485.9	51. Vermont	169.3
26. Arizona	1,436.6	U.S.	100,278.6[1]

(1) Includes 137.8 tril Btu in coal coke imports not allocated to states.

Consumption Per Capita

Rank/State	Million Btu	Rank/State	Million Btu
1. Alaska	1,186.2	27. South Dakota	342.2
2. Wyoming	898.8	28. Wisconsin	336.0
3. Louisiana	848.9	29. Wash., DC	328.2
4. North Dakota	632.7	30. Pennsylvania	327.2
5. Texas	531.6	31. Washington	323.1
6. Alabama	478.1	32. Missouri	321.5
7. Indiana	473.3	33. North Carolina	318.3
8. Kentucky	472.5	34. Illinois	311.5
9. West Virginia	453.5	35. Michigan	309.1
10. Montana	435.0	36. Utah	305.7
11. Oklahoma	421.8	37. Oregon	304.7
12. Mississippi	419.8	38. New Jersey	303.2
13. Arkansas	413.5	39. Colorado	301.0
14. South Carolina	409.4	40. Nevada	297.4
15. Iowa	408.2	41. Maryland	274.9
16. Kansas	403.0	42. Vermont	272.8
17. Tennessee	390.4	43. Connecticut	264.4
18. Nebraska	373.1	44. New Hampshire	262.5
19. Delaware	367.7	45. Hawaii	256.9
20. Maine	365.6	46. Florida	256.4
21. New Mexico	359.0	47. Arizona	250.0
22. Minnesota	358.5	48. Massachusetts	239.7
23. Idaho	358.4	49. California	233.4
24. Georgia	351.5	50. New York	220.5
25. Ohio	351.0	51. Rhode Island	209.9
26. Virginia	342.4	U.S.	341.5

U.S. Production of Crude Oil by State, 2006

Source: Energy Information Administration, *Petroleum Supply Monthly*, April 2007

(thousand barrels)

State	Total	State	Total	State	Total	State	Total
1. Texas	385,060	10. Kansas	35,136	19. Arkansas	5,969	28. South Dakota	1,396
2. Alaska	270,492	11. Montana	35,021	20. Ohio	5,646	29. Texas	493
3. California	223,449	12. Colorado	20,336	21. Michigan	5,350	30. Nevada	426
4. Alaska	97,744	13. Utah	17,510	22. Pennsylvania	4,004	31. New York	298
5. Louisiana	74,570	14. Mississippi	17,412	23. Florida	2,360	32. Tennessee	192
6. Oklahoma	61,775	15. California	15,077	24. Kentucky	2,340	33. Missouri	65
7. New Mexico	57,930	16. Illinois	10,190	25. Nebraska	2,313	34. Arizona	55
8. Wyoming	50,907	17. Louisiana	8,819	26. Indiana	1,773	35. Virginia	7
9. North Dakota	39,942	18. Alabama	7,459	27. West Virginia	1,403	U.S. Total[1]	1,874,753

(1) Includes 411,173 thousand bbls offshore production.

U.S. Petroleum Trade, 1976-2007

Source: Energy Information Administration, U.S. Dept. of Energy, *Monthly Energy Review,* July 2007
(in thousands of barrels per day; average for the year)

Year	Imports from Persian Gulf[1]	Total imports	Total exports	Net imports[2]	Petroleum products supplied[3]	Year	Imports from Persian Gulf[1]	Total imports	Total exports	Net imports[2]	Petroleum products supplied[3]
1976	1,840	7,313	223	7,090	17,461	1992	1,778	7,888	950	6,938	17,033
1977	2,448	8,807	243	8,565	18,431	1993	1,782	8,620	1,003	7,618	17,237
1978	2,219	8,363	362	8,002	18,847	1994	1,728	8,996	942	8,054	17,718
1979	2,069	8,456	471	7,985	18,513	1995	1,573	8,835	949	7,886	17,725
1980	1,519	6,909	544	6,365	17,056	1996	1,604	9,478	981	8,498	18,309
1981	1,219	5,996	595	5,401	16,058	1997	1,755	10,162	1,003	9,158	18,620
1982	696	5,113	815	4,298	15,296	1998	2,136	10,708	945	9,764	18,917
1983	442	5,051	739	4,312	15,231	1999	2,464	10,852	940	9,912	19,519
1984	506	5,437	722	4,715	15,726	2000	2,488	11,459	1,040	10,419	19,701
1985	311	5,067	781	4,286	15,726	2001	2,761	11,871	971	10,900	19,649
1986	912	6,224	785	5,439	16,281	2002	2,269	11,530	984	10,546	19,761
1987	1,077	6,678	764	5,914	16,665	2003	2,501	12,264	1,027	11,238	20,034
1988	1,541	7,402	815	6,587	17,283	2004	2,493	13,145	1,048	12,097	20,731
1989	1,861	8,061	859	7,202	17,325	2005	2,334	13,714	1,165	12,549	20,802
1990	1,966	8,018	857	7,161	16,988	2006	2,209	13,612	1,333	12,278	20,588
1991	1,845	7,627	1,001	6,626	16,714	2007[4]	NA	13,711	1,314	12,397	20,779

(1) Bahrain, Iran, Iraq, Kuwait, Qatar, Saudi Arabia, and United Arab Emirates. (2) Net imports are total imports minus total exports. (3) Includes domestic production and imports minus change in stocks, refinery imports, and exports. (4) Annualized 6-month average, for Jan.-June 2007. **Notes:** Beginning in Oct. 1977, imports for the Strategic Petroleum Reserves are included. U.S. exports include shipments to U.S. territories; imports include receipts from U.S. territories. Totals may not add because of rounding. Some figures are revised. NA = Not available.

World Crude Oil and Natural Gas Reserves, Jan. 1, 2006

Sources: Energy Information Administration, U.S. Dept. of Energy, *U.S. Crude Oil, Natural Gas, and Natural Gas Liquids Reserves, Nov. 2006; Oil and Gas Journal (OGJ),* Dec. 2005; *World Oil (WO),* Sept. 2006

Region/Country	Crude oil (billion barrels) OGJ	WO	Natural gas (trillion cubic feet) OGJ	WO	Region/Country	Crude oil (billion barrels) OGJ	WO	Natural gas (trillion cubic feet) OGJ	WO
North America	213.4	46.1	276.9	278.0	Yemen	4.0	3.0	16.9	17.0
Canada	178.8[1]	12.0	56.6	53.7	Other	(2)	0.7	1.6	13.7
Mexico	12.9	12.4	16.0	20.0	Eurasia	77.8	123.2	1,952.6	2,040.7
United States	21.8	21.8	204.4	204.4	Azerbaijan	7.0	NA	30.0	NA
Central and South America	103.4	76.5	250.8	246.9	Kazakhstan	9.0	NA	65.0	NA
Argentina	2.3	2.4	18.9	21.4	Russia	60.0	74.4	1,680.0	1,688.7
Bolivia	0.4	0.5	24.0	26.7	Turkmenistan	0.5	NA	71.0	NA
Brazil	11.2	11.9	11.5	11.9	Ukraine	0.4	NA	39.6	NA
Chile	0.2	(2)	3.5	0.9	Uzbekistan	0.6	NA	66.2	NA
Colombia	1.5	1.5	4.0	6.7	Other	0.3	48.8	0.8	352.0
Cuba	0.8	0.6	2.5	0.6	Africa	102.6	109.8	485.8	490.9
Ecuador	4.6	5.1	0.3	0.4	Algeria	11.4	11.4	160.5	160.7
Peru	0.9	1.0	8.7	8.7	Angola	5.4	9.1	1.6	4.0
Trinidad and Tobago	1.0	0.6	25.9	18.8	Cameroon	0.4	NA	3.9	NA
Venezuela	79.7	52.7	151.4	150.9	Congo Republic	1.5	1.9	3.2	4.2
Other	0.6	0.2	0.1	(2)	Egypt	3.7	3.7	58.5	66.8
Europe	16.4	16.0	200.7	182.8	Equatorial Guinea	(2)	1.8	1.3	3.4
Austria	0.1	0.1	0.5	0.8	Gabon	2.5	2.1	1.2	1.5
Croatia	0.1	0.1	1.0	1.1	Libya	39.1	34.1	52.7	51.5
Denmark	1.3	1.3	2.8	2.5	Mozambique	0.0	0.0	4.5	0.0
Germany	0.4	0.2	9.1	6.6	Nigeria	35.9	37.2	184.7	182.0
Hungary	0.1	0.1	1.2	2.3	Sudan	0.6	6.4	3.0	4.0
Italy	0.6	0.8	8.0	6.0	Tunisia	0.3	0.7	2.8	3.9
Netherlands	0.1	0.2	62.0	50.5	Other	1.8	1.5	8.1	8.9
Norway	7.7	8.0	84.3	83.3	Asia and Oceania	35.9	36.4	391.6	455.7
Poland	0.1	0.3	5.8	5.1	Australia	1.4	4.0	27.6	119.5
Romania	1.0	0.4	3.6	4.5	Bangladesh	(2)	NA	5.0	NA
Serbia and Montenegro	0.1	NA	1.7	NA	Brunei	1.4	1.1	13.8	12.0
United Kingdom	4.0	3.8	18.8	17.8	China	18.3	16.2	53.3	55.6
Other	0.9	0.7	2.1	2.3	India	5.8	4.0	38.9	27.3
Middle East	743.4	711.6	2,565.4	2,531.6	Indonesia	4.3	5.0	97.8	91.5
Bahrain	0.1	NA	3.3	NA	Japan	0.1	NA	1.4	NA
Iran	132.5	131.5	971.2	965.0	Malaysia	3.0	2.9	75.0	58.0
Iraq	115.0	115.0	112.0	84.0	Myanmar (Burma)	0.1	0.2	10.0	12.7
Kuwait	104.0	100.9	56.0	57.0	New Zealand	0.1	0.1	0.9	2.0
Oman	5.5	4.8	29.3	27.1	Pakistan	0.3	0.3	28.2	30.1
Qatar	15.2	20.3	910.5	906.0	Papua New Guinea	0.2	0.2	12.2	13.7
Saudi Arabia	266.8	262.2	241.8	243.5	Thailand	0.3	0.9	14.8	22.9
Syria	2.5	3.0	8.5	12.8	Vietnam	0.6	1.3	6.8	8.2
United Arab Emirates	97.8	70.3	214.4	205.6	Other	0.1	0.1	6.0	2.3
					World	1,292.9	1,119.6	6,124.0	6,226.6

Note: NA = Not reported seperately, amounts included in totals. Totals may not add because of rounding. Some countries omitted for lack of appreciable reserves. Data for Kuwait and Saudi Arabia include one-half of the reserves in the Neutral Zone between Kuwait and Saudi Arabia. All reserve figures except those for the former USSR and natural gas reserves in Canada are *proved reserves.* Former USSR and Canadian natural gas figures include amounts understood as *proved,* and some *probable reserves.* Totals may include small amounts not listed. (1) Figure includes 4.7 bil barrels of conventional crude oil and 174.1 bil barrels contained in Alberta's oil sands. (2) Less than 50 mil barrels of crude oil or less than 50 mil cubic feet of natural gas.

U.S. Crude Oil Imports by Selected Country, 1990-2007

Source: Energy Information Administration, *Petroleum Supply Monthly*, Feb. & Aug. 2007; ranked by 2007 totals

(thousand barrels per day)

The United States has become increasingly dependent on foreign oil. From 1990 to 2007 (based on annualized Jan.-June data for the latter year), total U.S. oil imports went up about 67%. Over the same period, oil imports from OPEC countries increased 53%. The proportion of U.S. oil imports from OPEC nations has been declining; in 1990 they accounted for 60% of U.S. oil imports, while in 2007 they accounted for 54%, although OPEC imports were up over the 48% in 2006. Although OPEC countries, especially in the Persian Gulf region, have a significant production advantage because of the relatively low cost of developing their oil resources, non-OPEC oil production has been rising; North America dominated this growth in the early 1970s, the North Sea and Mexico became major producers in the 1980s, and more recent production increases have come from oil supplies in Latin America, West Africa, and the former Soviet Union. Sanctions do not permit the U.S. to import oil from Iran.

	2007[1]	2006	2005	2004	2003	2002	2001	2000	1995	1990
Canada.................	1,817	1,758	1,602	1,587	1,535	1,418	1,297	1,267	1,040	643
Mexico..................	1,456	1,576	1,550	1,597	1,589	1,490	1,379	1,301	1,027	689
Saudi Arabia#............	1,419	1,421	1,438	1,494	1,724	1,521	1,610	1,521	1,260	1,195
Venezuela#	1,109	1,139	1,231	1,294	1,193	1,195	1,281	1,223	1,151	666
Nigeria#	1,021	1,043	1,060	1,062	838	567	813	865	621	784
Angola#[2]	568	513	450	306	361	315	314	289	360	236
Algeria#	497	357	228	214	113	30	11	1	27	63
Iraq#....................	477	553	520	651	470	442	778	613	0	514
Kuwait#	196	179	215	241	205	212	233	261	213	79
Ecuador[3]	195	272	276	228	138	99	108	126	96	38
Brazil..................	162	133	94	51	48	57	13	5	0	0
Russia[4].................	135	108	193	150	149	86	0	7	14	1
United Kingdom	114	128	219	235	347	406	226	272	341	155
Colombia	108	141	156	138	163	233	245	308	207	140
Gabon[5].................	72	60	127	142	131	143	138	142	229	64
Norway.................	71	98	119	146	164	335	267	292	258	96
Libya#..................	66	65	44	18	0	0	0	0	0	0
Trinidad and Tobago	49	67	62	59	54	68	55	53	NA	NA
Argentina	27	29	56	49	67	68	51	56	62	76
Indonesia#	19	16	19	34	26	50	40	36	64	98
China	10	19	24	12	13	21	13	34	53	77
United Arab Emirates#......	8	5	9	5	10	16	21	1	5	9
Malaysia................	2	7	10	18	21	9	15	29	6	40
Australia................	0	5	10	21	26	51	36	42	16	47
Non-OPEC Imports........	**4,614**	**5,291**	**5,252**	**4,994**	**5,055**	**4,996**	**4,336**	**4,361**	**3,889**	**2,381**
OPEC Imports............	**5,380**	**4,780**	**4,762**	**5,018**	**4,579**	**4,042**	**4,787**	**4,520**	**3,341**	**3,514**
TOTAL................	**9,993**	**10,070**	**10,015**	**10,012**	**9,633**	**9,038**	**9,123**	**8,882**	**7,230**	**5,894**

# Denotes OPEC members. NA=Not available. (1) Jan.-June average annualized. (2) Angola was a member of OPEC as of Jan. 1, 2007, and is not included in OPEC totals from before that year. (3) Ecuador withdrew from OPEC Dec. 31, 1992. Imports after Jan. 1, 1993, appear in Non-OPEC totals. (4) May include oil from USSR states before 1992. (5) Gabon withdrew from OPEC Dec. 31, 1994. Imports after Jan. 1, 1995, appear in Non-OPEC totals.

U.S. Coal Production and Consumption, 1950-2006

Source: Energy Information Administration, U.S. Dept. of Energy, *Annual Energy Review 2006*

(in short tons)

	Coal Production			Coal Consumption				
	Surface mining	Underground mining	Total production	Residential	Commercial	Industrial	Electric power[1]	Total consumption
1950	139,388,000	421,000,000	560,388,000	51,562,350	63,020,650	224,637,000	91,870,770	494,101,770
1960	141,745,000	292,584,000	434,329,000	24,159,320	16,788,680	177,402,000	176,685,359	398,081,359
1970	272,131,000	340,530,000	612,661,000	9,023,840	7,090,160	186,637,000	320,181,708	523,230,708
1975	361,174,000	293,467,000	654,641,000	2,823,000	6,587,000	147,244,000	405,962,432	562,640,432
1980	492,192,000	337,508,000	829,700,000	1,354,920	5,097,080	127,004,000	569,273,735	702,729,735
1985	532,838,000	350,800,000	883,638,117	1,711,426	6,067,781	116,428,686	693,840,766	818,048,659
1990	604,529,000	424,546,000	1,029,075,527	1,344,774	5,379,096	115,207,053	782,566,645	904,497,568
1995	636,724,750	396,249,022	1,032,973,772	754,871	5,051,832	106,066,596	850,230,475	962,103,774
2000	699,952,835	373,658,726	1,073,611,561	453,949	3,672,864	94,147,215	985,820,847	1,084,094,875
2001	747,061,973	380,626,833	1,127,688,806	480,600	3,888,487	91,343,512	964,432,933	1,060,145,532
2002	736,898,094	357,384,967	1,094,283,061	533,410	3,911,676	84,402,776	977,506,711	1,066,354,573
2003	718,967,887	352,784,686	1,071,752,573	550,638	3,685,042	85,509,001	1,005,116,162	1,094,860,843
2004	744,541,615	367,557,255	1,112,098,870	563,394	4,558,370	85,864,763	1,016,268,012	1,107,254,539
2005	762,886,599	368,611,500	1,131,498,099	379,555	3,837,725	83,773,950	1,037,484,561	1,125,475,791
2006[P]	803,372,307	358,071,828	1,161,444,135	379,555	3,837,725	83,504,595	1,026,454,126	1,114,176,001

P=Preliminary. (1) Electricity-only and combined-heat-and-power (CHP) plants whose primary business is to sell electricity, or electicity and heat, to the public. Through 1988, data are for electric utilities only; beginning in 1989, data are for electric utilities and independent power producers.

World Nuclear Power Summary, 2007

Source: International Atomic Energy Agency, *Nuclear Technology Review 2007*, as of Jan. 1, 2007.

Country	Reactors in operation No. of units	Reactors in operation Total MW(e)	Reactors under construction No. of units	Reactors under construction Total MW(e)	Nuclear electricity supplied in 2006 TW(e).h[1]	Nuclear electricity supplied in 2006 % of nation's total	Total operating experience[2] Years	Total operating experience[2] Months
Argentina	2	935	1	692	7.2	6.9%	56	7
Armenia	1	376	—	—	2.4	42.0	32	8
Belgium	7	5,824	—	—	44.3	54.4	212	7
Brazil	2	1,901	—	—	13.0	3.3	31	3
Bulgaria	2	1,906	2	1,906	18.2	43.6	141	3
Canada	18	12,610	—	—	92.4	15.8	528	1
China	10	7,572	4	3,610	51.8	1.9	66	7
Czech Republic	6	3,323	—	—	24.5	31.5	92	10
Finland	4	2,696	1	1,600	22.0	28.0	111	4
France	59	63,260	—	—	429.8	78.1	1,523	2
Germany	17	20,339	—	—	158.7	31.8	700	5
Hungary	4	1,755	—	—	12.5	37.7	86	2
India	16	3,577	7	3,112	15.6	2.6	267	7
Iran	—	—	1	915	—	—	0	0
Japan	55	47,587	1	866	291.5	30.0	1,276	8
Korea, South	20	17,454	1	960	141.2	38.6	279	8
Lithuania	1	1,185	—	—	7.9	72.3	40	6
Mexico	2	1,360	—	—	10.4	4.9	29	11
Netherlands	1	482	—	—	3.3	3.5	62	0
Pakistan	2	425	1	300	2.6	2.7	41	10
Romania	1	655	1	655	5.3	9.0	10	6
Russia	31	21,743	5	4,525	144.6	15.9	901	4
Slovakia	5	2,034	—	—	16.6	57.2	118	7
Slovenia	1	666	—	—	5.3	40.3	25	3
South Africa	2	1,800	—	—	10.1	4.4	44	3
Spain	8	7,450	—	—	57.4	19.8	245	6
Sweden	10	9,097	—	—	65.1	48.0	342	6
Switzerland	5	3,220	—	—	26.4	37.4	158	10
Taiwan	6	4,921	2	2,600	38.3	19.5	152	1
Ukraine	15	13,107	2	1,900	84.9	47.5	323	6
United Kingdom	19	10,965	—	—	69.4	18.4	1,400	8
United States	103	99,257	—	—	788.3	19.4	3,188	2
TOTAL	**435**	**369,682**	**29**	**23,641**	**2,660.9**	**15.0%**	**12,599**	**1**

(1) 1 terawatt-hour [TW(e).h] = 10^6 megawatt-hour [MW(e).h]. For an average power plant, 1 TW(e).h = 0.39 megatons of coal equivalent (input) and 0.23 megatons of oil equivalent (input). (2) Through Dec. 31, 2006. Also includes shutdown plants.

Nations Most Reliant on Nuclear Energy, 2006

Source: International Atomic Energy Agency

(Nuclear electricity generation as % of total electricity generated)

Country	%	Country	%	Country	%
1. France	78.1	10. South Korea	38.6	19. United Kingdom	18.4
2. Lithuania	72.3	11. Hungary	37.7	20. Russia	15.9
3. Slovakia	57.2	12. Switzerland	37.4	21. Canada	15.8
4. Belgium	54.4	13. Germany	31.8	22. Romania	9.0
5. Sweden	48.0	14. Czech Republic	31.5	23. Argentina	6.9
6. Ukraine	47.5	15. Japan	30.0	24. Mexico	4.9
7. Bulgaria	43.6	16. Finland	28.0	25. South Africa	4.4
8. Armenia	42.0	17. Spain	19.8	26. Netherlands	3.5
9. Slovenia	40.3	18. United States	19.4	27. Brazil	3.3

U.S. Nuclear Reactors and Power Plant Operations, 1955-2006

Source: Energy Information Administration, U.S. Dept. of Energy, *Annual Energy Review 2006*

			Number of Reactor Units						Nuclear electricity generation (million net KW-hrs)[6]	Nuclear share of domestic electricity generation (percent)[6]
	Ordered[1]	Cancelled	Construction permits[2]	Low-power licensed[3]	Full-power licensed[4]	Shutdown[5]	Operable units[6]	Capacity factor[7] (percent)		
1955-59	14	0	8	2	2	0	2	NA	188.1	NA
1960-64	7	0	12	13	12	1	13	NA	3,342.7	0.3%
1965-69	81	0	50	8	9	5	17	NA	13,927.8	1.0
1970-74	143	16	59	41	41	3	55	47.8%	113,975.7	6.1
1975-79	13	43	48	17	17	3	69	58.4	255,154.6	11.3
1980-84	0	54	0	24	19	1	87	56.3	327,633.5	13.5
1985-89	0	7	0	24	28	4	111	62.2	529,354.7	17.8
1990-94	0	15	0	49	58	9	109	73.8	640,439.8	19.7
1995-99	0	2	0	1	1	6	104	85.3	728,254.1	19.7
2000-04	0	0	0	0	0	0	104	90.1	788,528.4	19.9
2005-06	0	0	0	0	0	0	104	89.9	787,218.6	19.4
Total	**259**	**124**	**177**	**132**	**132**	**28**				

Note: Revised permit/license procedures eliminate the historical categories shown. According to Senate testimony, the Nuclear Regulatory Commission anticipates 16 or more new "combined license applications" over the next few years—the first of which ws submitted Sept. 25, 2007—which may amount to 25 or more new reactor units. (1) Order placed by a utility or government agency for a nuclear steam supply system. (2) Numbers show permits issued in a given period, not extant permits. (3) Licenses granted to conduct testing. (4) Licenses granted for full power operation. (5) Permanently ceased operation. (6) As of the last year of designated period. (7) The ratio of electric energy produced to the amount that could be produced at continuous full power operation.

CRIME

Measuring Crime

The U.S. Dept. of Justice administers two statistical programs to measure trends in crime in the U.S. Because of differences in focus and methodology, their results are not strictly comparable.

The Federal Bureau of Investigation conducts the **Uniform Crime Report (UCR)** program, which aims to provide statistics for law enforcement administration, operation, and management. It collects actual counts on the crimes of homicide, forcible rape, robbery, aggravated assault, burglary, larceny-theft, motor vehicle theft, and arson as they are reported to law enforcement authorities. Each year, the program releases a preliminary report in the spring, followed by a more detailed, final report in the fall.

The **National Crime Victimization Survey (NCVS)** is conducted annually by the Bureau of Justice Statistics through interviews with members of a nationally representative sample of households about their experiences with crime. The survey complements the UCR by providing alternative and previously unavailable information, including information about the victims of crime and their offenders (e.g., age, sex, ethnicity, victim-offender relationship) and information on crimes not reported to law enforcement. In contrast to the UCR, the NCVS does not cover homicide, arson, commercial crimes, or crimes against children under age 12.

Further explanation of the UCR and NCVS is available at www.ojp.usdoj.gov/bjs/abstract/ntmc.htm.

Uniform Crime Report for 2006

Source: *Crime in the United States, 2006*, FBI, U.S. Dept. of Justice

For the second year in a row, the estimated number of violent crimes increased in the U.S. Between 2005 and 2006, violent crimes rose by 1.9%. The estimated number of property crimes in the country, however, fell by 1.9%, the fourth consecutive year to record a drop. The increase in violent crimes was only the third within the past 14 years. Between 1997 and 2006, the violent crime rate per 100,000 residents dropped 22.5%.

The estimated number of robberies rose by 7.2% and murder was up 1.8% from 2005 to 2006. Forcible rapes, however, decreased by 2% while aggravated assault declined 0.2%. Among property crimes, the number of larceny-thefts (e.g. pocket-picking, purse-snatching) decreased by 2.6% in 2005-06. Burglary increased by 1.3% over the same period. Motor vehicle theft numbers decreased 3.5%. Reports of arson, considered a property crime but not included in the property crime total, increased 2.1%. Victims of all property crimes except for arson lost an estimated $17.6 bil in 2006. An estimated average of $13,325 was lost for each arson offense the same year.

Violent crime numbers increased in all regions except the Northeast, where numbers dropped 0.4%.

The following are additional highlights from the 2006 report:
- Males accounted for 78.7% of all murder victims.
- Males made up 66.1% of all murder offenders.
- Firearms were used in 67.9% of all murders.
- Of the 14,990 murder victims, 6,335 (42.3%) were killed by a family member, friend, or other acquaintance; 1,905 (12.7%) were killed by strangers.
- The majority of robberies (44.5%) took place on the street or highway.
- Among all larceny-thefts (excluding motor vehicle thefts), 26.5% were from motor vehicles, 9.7% were of motor vehicle accessories, 13.2% were shoplifting, 12.6% were from buildings, 3.5% were of bikes.

More than 17,500 city, county, college and university, state, tribal, and federal agencies—representing about 94.2% of the U.S. population—participated in the UCR program in 2006.

National Crime Victimization Survey for 2005

Source: *Criminal Victimization, 2005*, Bureau of Justice Statistics, U.S. Dept. of Justice

The NCVS estimated that there were 23.4 mil victimizations of U.S. residents ages 12 and up in 2005 (the latest year for which figures were available), about the same as in 2004. Victimization rates—21.2 per 1,000 persons over age 12 for violent crime and 154 per 1,000 households for property crimes—continued their decline to record low levels since the NCVS began in 1973, when there were about 44 mil victimizations.

Based on the NCVS, the victimization rates for violent crimes decreased 57.7% between 1993 and 2005. During that same period, the percentage of crimes reported to the police increased (with the exception of rape/sexual assault and robbery)—from 42% to 47% for violent crimes and from 34% to 40% for property crimes.

Comparisons between the two-year average annual rates for 2002-03 and 2004-05 show drops in violent crime. Rates of violent crimes against women dropped 11.7% (to 17.6 per 1,000 persons in 2004-05), though violent crimes against men fell by only 2.6% (to 25.2 per 1,000). In suburban areas, the violent crime rate decreased by 11.7%, more than in urban areas (–3.9%) while violent crime rates went up in rural areas (0.7%).

Criminal Victimization, 2004-05

Source: *Criminal Victimization, 2005*, Bureau of Justice Statistics, U.S. Dept. of Justice

Type of crime	Number of victimizations		Victimization rates[1]	
	2004	2005	2004	2005
All crimes...................	24,061,140	23,440,720	NA	NA
Violent crimes[2]	5,182,670	5,173,720	21.4	21.2
Rape/sexual assault[3]	209,880	191,670	0.9	0.8
Robbery	501,820	624,850	2.1	2.6
Assault	4,470,960	4,357,190	18.5	17.8
Aggravated[4]	1,030,080	1,052,260	4.3	4.3
Simple[5]	3,440,880	227,070	14.2	13.5
Property crimes..................	18,654,400	18,039,930	161.1	154.0
Household burglary...............	3,427,690	3,456,220	29.6	29.5
Motor vehicle theft................	1,014,770	978,120	8.8	8.4
Theft[6]	14,211,940	13,605,590	122.8	116.2

NA = Not applicable. (1) Per 1,000 persons age 12 or older (est. 241,703,710 in 2004; est. 244,493,430 in 2005) or per 1,000 households (115,775,570 in 2004; 117,110,800 in 2005). (2) This survey does not measure murder. (3) Includes male as well as female victims and both heterosexual and homosexual rape. (4) Attack with a weapon or including serious injury. (5) Attack without a weapon resulting in no injury, minor injury, or undetermined injury requiring less than 2 days' hospitalization. (6) Purse snatching and pocket picking.

Crime in the U.S., 1986-2006

Source: *Crime in the United States, 2006,* Federal Bureau of Investigation (FBI), U.S. Dept. of Justice

Under the FBI's Uniform Crime Reporting (UCR) Program, the following offenses are classified as **violent crimes**, defined as offenses involving force or the threat of force: murder and nonnegligent manslaughter, forcible rape, robbery, and aggravated assault. The following offenses are considered **property crimes**: burglary, larceny-theft, motor vehicle theft, and arson. Motor vehicle theft and arson figures are available at www.fbi.gov/ucr/ucr.htm. Property crime totals exclude arson data because of variations in level of participation by reporting agencies.

Year	Population[2]	Crime Index[3]	Violent crime	Property crime	Murder & nonnegligent manslaughter	Forcible rape[5]	Robbery	Aggravated assault[6]	Burglary	Larceny-theft
1986	240,132,887	13,211,869	1,489,169	11,722,700	20,613	91,459	542,775	834,322	3,241,410	7,257,153
1990	249,464,396	14,475,613	1,820,127	12,655,486	23,438	102,555	639,271	1,054,863	3,073,909	7,945,670
1991	252,153,092	14,872,883	1,911,767	12,961,116	24,703	106,593	687,732	1,092,739	3,157,150	8,142,228
1992	255,029,699	14,438,191	1,932,274	12,505,917	23,760	109,062	672,478	1,126,974	2,979,884	7,915,199
1993	257,782,608	14,144,794	1,926,017	12,218,777	24,526	106,014	659,870	1,135,607	2,834,808	7,820,909
1994	260,327,021	13,989,543	1,857,670	12,131,873	23,326	102,216	618,949	1,113,179	2,712,774	7,879,812
1995	262,803,276	13,862,727	1,798,792	12,063,935	21,606	97,470	580,509	1,099,207	2,593,784	7,997,710
1996	265,228,572	13,493,863	1,688,540	11,805,323	19,645	96,252	535,594	1,037,049	2,506,400	7,904,685
1997	267,783,607	13,194,571	1,636,096	11,558,475	18,208	96,153	498,534	1,023,201	2,460,526	7,743,760
1998	270,248,003	12,485,714	1,533,887	10,951,827	16,974	93,144	447,186	976,583	2,332,735	7,376,311
1999	272,690,813	11,634,378	1,426,044	10,208,334	15,522	89,411	409,371	911,740	2,100,739	6,955,520
2000	281,421,906	11,608,070	1,425,486	10,182,584	15,586	90,178	408,016	911,706	2,050,992	6,971,590
2001	285,317,559	11,876,669	1,439,480	10,437,189	16,037[4]	90,863	423,557	909,023	2,116,531	7,092,267
2002	287,973,924	11,877,218	1,423,677	10,455,277	16,229	95,235	420,806	891,407	2,151,252	7,057,379
2003	290,788,976	—	1,383,676	10,442,862	16,528	93,883	414,235	859,030	2,154,834	7,026,802
2004	293,656,842	—	1,360,088	10,319,386	16,148	95,089	401,470	847,381	2,144,446	6,937,089
2005[1]	296,507,061	—	1,390,745	10,174,754	16,740	94,347	417,438	862,220	2,155,448	6,783,447
2006	299,398,484	—	1,417,745	9,983,568	17,034	92,455	447,403	860,853	2,183,746	6,607,013

PERCENT CHANGE: NUMBER OF OFFENSES

2006/2005	—		1.9	−1.9	1.8	−2.0	7.2	−0.2	1.3	−2.6
2006/2002	—		−0.4	−4.5	5.0	−2.9	6.3	−3.4	1.5	−6.4
2006/1997	—		−13.3	−13.6	−6.4	−3.8	−10.3	−15.9	−11.2	−14.7

RATE PER 100,000 INHABITANTS

1986		5,501.9	620.1	4,881.8	8.6	38.1	226.0	347.4	1,349.8	3,022.1
1990		5,802.7	729.6	5,073.1	9.4	41.1	256.3	422.9	1,232.2	3,185.1
1991		5,898.4	758.2	5,140.2	9.8	42.3	272.7	433.4	1,252.1	3,229.1
1992		5,661.4	757.7	4,903.7	9.3	42.8	263.7	441.9	1,168.4	3,103.6
1993		5,487.1	747.1	4,740.0	9.5	41.1	256.0	440.5	1,099.7	3,033.9
1994		5,373.8	713.6	4,660.2	9.0	39.3	237.8	427.6	1,042.1	3,026.9
1995		5,274.9	684.5	4,590.5	8.2	37.1	220.9	418.3	987.0	3,043.2
1996		5,087.6	636.6	4,451.0	7.4	36.3	201.9	391.0	945.0	2,980.3
1997		4,927.3	611.0	4,316.3	6.8	35.9	186.2	382.1	918.8	2,891.8
1998		4,620.1	567.6	4,052.5	6.3	34.5	165.5	361.4	863.2	2,729.5
1999		4,266.5	523.0	3,743.6	5.7	32.8	150.1	334.3	770.4	2,550.7
2000		4,124.8	506.5	3,618.3	5.5	32.0	145.0	324.0	728.8	2,477.3
2001		4,162.6	504.5	3,658.1	5.6[4]	31.8	148.5	318.6	741.8	2,485.7
2002		4,118.8	494.4	3,630.6	5.6	33.1	146.1	309.5	747.0	2,450.7
2003		—	475.8	3,591.2	5.7	32.3	142.5	295.4	741.0	2,416.5
2004		—	463.2	3,514.1	5.5	32.4	136.7	288.6	730.3	2,362.3
2005[1]		—	469.0	3,431.5	5.6	31.8	140.8	290.8	726.9	2,287.8
2006		—	473.5	3,334.5	5.7	30.9	149.4	287.5	729.4	2,206.8

PERCENT CHANGE: RATE PER 100,000 INHABITANTS

2006/2005	—		1.0	−2.8	0.8	−3.0	6.1	−1.1	0.3	−3.5
2006/2002			−4.2	−8.2	1.0	−6.6	2.3	−7.1	−2.4	−10.0
2006/1997			−22.5	−22.7	−16.3	−14.0	−19.7	−24.8	−20.6	−23.7

— = Not available or not applicable. (1) Figures have been adjusted since their original publication. (2) Populations are U.S. Census Bureau provisional estimates as of July 1 for each year except 1990 and 2000, which are decennial census counts. (3) Use of the UCR Crime Index—an annual aggregate of the offenses in this table as well as motor vehicle theft and arson numbers—was discontinued beginning with the 2003 report. (4) The murder and nonnegligent homicides that occurred as a result of the Sept. 11, 2001, terrorist attacks are not included. (5) Does not include statutory rape (rape not involving force) and other offenses of a sexual nature. Also does not include sexual attacks on males, which are considered aggravated assaults or sex offenses, depending on circumstances and extent of injuries. (6) Attack upon another with the intent of doing serious bodily harm; usually accompanied by use of a weapon. Does not include simple assaults.

Law Enforcement Officers, 2006

Source: *Crime in the United States, 2006,* FBI, U.S. Dept. of Justice
Later data may be available at www.fbi.gov/ucr/ucr.htm.

As of Oct. 31, 2006, 14,336 city, county, state, college and university, and tribal agencies around the country collectively employed 987,125 full-time law enforcement workers. About 69.2% of employees were officers, whom the FBI's Uniform Crime Report (UCR) program define as ordinarily carrying a firearm and badge and having full arrest powers. Civilians (e.g., clerks, radio dispatchers, correctional officers) made up the remaining 30.8% of law enforcement. Altogether, they provided service to an estimated 283.2 mil people, meaning that nationwide, there were 3.5 full-time law enforcement employees (civilian and sworn officers) and 2.4 sworn officers per 1,000 inhabitants. This rate varied only slightly between areas of different sizes in different parts of the country.

California employed the greatest number of full-time law enforcement workers (115,912) of any state. D.C., however, had the highest rate—8.4 full-time law enforcement employees per 1,000 in its population.

While in 2006, 61.6% of all full-time civilian law enforcement employees in the U.S. were female, males made up 88.2% of all sworn officers.

Nationwide, 55 law enforcement officers were slain in the line of duty in 2005, the latest year for which data was available. Another 67 were accidentally killed while performing official duties; over half (39) died in automobile accidents. In addition, 57,546 officers were assaulted while on duty. The majority of assaults (30.5%) occurred when officers responded to disturbance calls (e.g., bar fights). Personal weapons, such as hands and feet, were used in 80% of all assaults.

Federal Bureau of Investigation

The Federal Bureau of Investigation was created July 26, 1908, as the Office of Chief Examiner. It later became the Bureau of Investigation (Mar. 16, 1909), United States Bureau of Investigation (July 1, 1932), the Division of Investigation (Aug. 10, 1933), and finally, the Federal Bureau of Investigation (July 1, 1935).

Director	Assumed office	Director	Assumed office	Director	Assumed office
Stanley W. Finch	July 26, 1908	L. Patrick Gray, acting	May 3, 1972	John E. Otto, acting	May 26, 1987
A. Bruce Bielaski	Apr. 30, 1912	William D. Ruckelshaus,		William S. Sessions	Nov. 2, 1987
William E. Allen, acting.	Feb. 10, 1919	acting	Apr. 30, 1973	Floyd I. Clarke, acting	July 19, 1993
William J. Flynn	July 1, 1919	Clarence M. Kelley	July 9, 1973	Louis J. Freeh	Sept. 1, 1993
William J. Burns	Aug. 22, 1921	James B. Adams, acting	Feb. 15, 1978	Thomas J. Pickard, acting	June 25, 2001
J. Edgar Hoover, acting	May 10, 1924	William H. Webster	Feb. 23, 1978	Robert S. Mueller III	Sept. 4, 2001
J. Edgar Hoover	Dec. 10, 1924				

U.S. Crime Rates by Region, Geographic Division, and State, 2006

Source: *Crime in the United States, 2006*, FBI, U.S. Dept. of Justice
(per 100,000 population; calculated using U.S. Census Bureau midyear population estimates)

	Violent crime[1]	Murder & nonnegligent manslaughter	Forcible rape	Robbery	Aggravated assault	Property crime[2]	Burglary	Larceny-theft	Motor vehicle theft
U.S. TOTAL	473.5	5.7	30.9	149.4	287.5	3,334.5	729.4	2,206.8	398.4
Northeast	391.9	4.5	20.6	151.2	215.6	2,268.6	429.9	1,616.4	222.3
New England	317.1	2.6	24.5	97.7	192.3	2,393.8	488.6	1,658.0	247.2
Connecticut	280.8	3.1	18.1	121.0	138.6	2,504.1	419.3	1,788.4	296.4
Maine	115.5	1.7	25.7	29.1	59.0	2,518.7	512.9	1,904.3	101.4
Massachusetts	447.0	2.9	27.1	125.0	292.1	2,391.0	546.5	1,565.4	279.0
New Hampshire	138.7	1.0	26.2	32.2	79.4	1,874.1	331.4	1,434.5	108.1
Rhode Island	227.5	2.6	26.7	68.8	129.4	2,586.9	507.2	1,744.2	335.5
Vermont	136.6	1.9	24.0	17.6	93.0	2,304.7	528.9	1,681.8	93.9
Middle Atlantic	418.3	5.2	19.3	170.0	223.8	2,224.4	409.2	1,601.7	213.5
New Jersey	351.6	4.9	14.2	153.1	179.4	2,291.9	452.0	1,556.5	283.4
New York	434.9	4.8	16.4	178.6	235.1	2,052.7	355.1	1,531.1	166.4
Pennsylvania	439.4	5.9	27.3	168.6	237.6	2,443.5	463.2	1,742.9	237.4
Midwest	419.1	5.0	35.4	132.1	246.6	3,271.2	692.1	2,246.5	332.6
East North Central	436.8	5.5	36.4	151.2	243.7	3,266.9	715.2	2,203.8	347.9
Illinois	541.6	6.1	31.8	185.3	318.4	3,019.6	602.1	2,124.2	293.3
Indiana	314.8	5.8	29.1	114.7	165.2	3,502.4	731.3	2,424.8	346.3
Michigan	562.4	7.1	52.2	140.7	362.4	3,212.8	753.9	1,963.5	495.4
Ohio	350.3	4.7	39.6	166.8	139.2	3,678.6	909.8	2,442.8	326.1
Wisconsin	284.0	3.0	20.4	100.2	160.6	2,817.8	485.8	2,079.5	252.5
West North Central	377.8	3.7	32.9	87.8	253.4	3,281.4	638.5	2,345.6	297.3
Iowa	283.5	1.8	27.8	43.5	210.4	2,802.7	604.2	2,030.7	167.9
Kansas	425.0	4.6	44.8	67.9	307.7	3,750.2	723.3	2,712.0	314.9
Minnesota	312.0	2.4	31.8	105.1	172.6	3,079.5	583.9	2,236.6	258.9
Missouri	545.6	6.3	30.2	129.9	379.3	3,826.5	764.1	2,627.0	435.3
Nebraska	281.8	2.8	31.0	63.8	184.1	3,340.7	534.5	2,521.3	284.9
North Dakota	127.9	1.3	30.4	11.3	84.9	2,000.3	376.3	1,464.8	159.2
South Dakota	171.4	1.2	43.0	15.2	112.0	1,619.6	338.9	1,188.9	91.8
South	547.5	6.8	32.7	157.1	351.0	3,780.8	903.8	2,498.9	378.1
South Atlantic	573.0	6.8	29.5	170.8	366.0	3,714.0	869.9	2,449.5	394.7
Delaware	681.6	4.9	46.9	203.3	426.5	3,417.9	725.2	2,362.8	329.9
District of Columbia	1,508.4	29.1	31.8	658.4	789.1	4,653.8	659.5	2,735.4	1,258.9
Florida	712.0	6.2	35.8	188.8	481.2	3,986.1	944.6	2,619.0	422.5
Georgia	471.0	6.4	23.2	165.6	275.8	3,889.2	909.0	2,519.3	460.9
Maryland	678.6	9.7	21.0	256.0	392.0	3,480.9	667.0	2,270.4	543.5
North Carolina	475.6	6.1	28.2	152.2	289.1	4,120.8	1,212.7	2,567.9	340.2
South Carolina	765.5	8.3	40.8	136.5	579.9	4,242.3	989.8	2,873.0	379.6
Virginia	282.2	5.2	23.4	101.4	152.1	2,478.2	417.6	1,866.8	193.8
West Virginia	279.7	4.1	21.4	46.9	207.3	2,621.5	634.1	1,771.8	215.6
East South Central	480.0	6.7	34.3	140.4	298.6	3,552.5	911.3	2,331.4	309.9
Alabama	425.2	8.3	35.9	153.5	227.6	3,936.1	969.1	2,643.3	322.7
Kentucky	263.0	4.0	30.8	86.2	142.0	2,544.5	644.8	1,679.9	219.8
Mississippi	298.6	7.7	34.4	107.1	149.5	3,208.8	935.9	1,986.1	286.8
Tennessee	760.2	6.8	35.5	184.3	533.7	4,128.3	1,040.9	2,713.2	374.1
West South Central	540.0	6.8	37.2	143.0	353.0	4,011.1	956.7	2,668.6	385.8
Arkansas	551.6	7.3	46.5	98.4	399.4	3,967.5	1,139.9	2,562.1	265.5
Louisiana	697.8	12.4	36.4	133.6	515.4	3,993.7	1,049.2	2,579.7	364.8
Oklahoma	497.4	5.8	41.6	87.5	362.5	3,604.2	960.5	2,270.5	373.2
Texas	516.3	5.9	35.6	158.5	316.4	4,081.5	917.3	2,758.2	405.9
West	473.5	5.6	31.8	152.5	283.6	3,534.4	727.0	2,175.3	632.1
Mountain	449.0	5.2	38.6	115.0	290.1	3,810.3	780.4	2,429.8	600.0
Arizona	501.4	7.5	31.5	149.6	312.7	4,627.9	925.3	2,813.1	889.5
Colorado	391.6	3.3	43.7	80.7	264.0	3,451.3	682.1	2,331.8	437.5
Idaho	247.2	2.5	40.0	20.5	184.2	2,418.8	513.2	1,740.0	165.6
Montana	253.7	1.8	28.5	17.4	206.1	2,687.5	310.7	2,191.8	185.0
Nevada	741.6	9.0	43.2	281.6	407.8	4,088.8	994.6	2,013.8	1,080.4
New Mexico	643.2	6.8	56.0	107.7	472.8	3,937.2	1,069.7	2,395.5	472.0
Utah	224.4	1.8	34.1	48.8	139.7	3,516.4	576.5	2,614.5	325.4
Wyoming	239.6	1.7	27.2	14.0	196.7	2,980.6	450.5	2,379.4	150.7
Pacific	484.1	5.8	28.9	168.6	280.8	3,415.8	704.0	2,065.9	645.9
Alaska	688.0	5.4	76.0	90.3	516.4	3,604.9	617.3	2,610.2	377.4
California	532.5	6.8	25.3	194.7	305.7	3,170.9	676.0	1,829.1	665.7
Hawaii	281.2	1.6	27.6	88.9	163.0	4,230.4	677.5	2,949.1	603.9
Oregon	280.3	2.3	32.3	72.7	173.0	3,672.1	645.2	2,636.1	390.7
Washington	345.9	3.0	42.9	100.1	199.8	4,480.0	911.6	2,850.7	717.6
Puerto Rico	227.3	18.8	3.0	133.5	72.0	1,354.4	424.4	711.2	218.8

Note: Offense totals are based on all reporting agencies and estimates for unreported areas. Figures may not add to totals due to rounding. (1) Violent crimes are murder and nonnegligent manslaughter, forcible rape, robbery, and aggravated assault. (2) Property crimes are burglary, larceny-theft, and motor vehicle theft. Data for the property crime of arson are not included here.

State and Federal Prison Population, Death Penalty, 2005-06

Source: *Prison and Jail Inmates at Midyear 2006, Capital Punishment, 2005,* Bureau of Justice Statistics, U.S. Dept. of Justice

As of June 30, 2006, 1,556,518 prisoners—two-thirds of the nation's incarcerated population—were under the jurisdiction of federal or state adult correctional authorities. Jails, which are locally operated and typically hold persons awaiting trial and those with sentences of one year or less, held most of the remainder (766,010), not including those supervised in the community (60,222) through such means as weekender programs or electronic monitoring. The total prison population grew 2.8% over the previous year.

As of mid-2006, the incarceration rate in state and federal prisons for those with sentences over one year was 497 per 100,000 U.S. residents, up from 488 in mid-2005 and 411 at year-end 1995. The rate of incarceration was 67 out of every 100,000 women and 940 out of every 100,000 men. The change in the number of female prisoners continues to outpace the increase in male prisoners. The number of persons under sentence of death at the end of 2005 was 3,254, down from 3,320 the year before. In 2005, 60 prisoners were executed—one more than in the previous year. Also in 2005, 109 death sentences were overturned or removed.

	SENTENCED PRISONERS[5], 2005-06			DEATH PENALTY, 2005-06			
	Mid-2006	Mid-2005	% change 2005-06	Death penalty	Under sentence of death, year-end 2005	Executed, 2005	Total executed, 1977-2006[6]	Lethal injections, 1977-2006[6,7]
U.S. TOTAL	1,487,940	1,447,812	2.8	—	3,254	60	1,057	888
Federal institutions[1]	169,945	162,682	4.5	Yes	37	0	3	3
State institutions	1,317,995	1,285,130	2.6	38	3,217	60	1,054	885
Northeast	165,358	162,665	1.7		236	1	4	4
Connecticut[2]	13,388	13,181	1.6	Yes	7	1	1	1
Maine	1,861	2,017	−7.7	No	—	—	—	—
Massachusetts[3]	9,335	8,907	4.8	No	—	—	—	—
New Hampshire	2,625	2,561	2.5	Yes	0	0	0	0
New Jersey	28,436	28,124	1.1	Yes	10	0	0	0
New York	62,950	62,922	0.0	Yes	1	0	0	0
Pennsylvania	43,074	41,539	3.7	Yes	218	0	3	3
Rhode Island[2]	2,079	1,928	7.8	No	—	—	—	—
Vermont[2]	1,610	1,486	8.3	No	—	—	—	—
Midwest	259,772	252,116	3.0		286	14	122	116
Illinois	45,440	44,669	1.7	Yes	7	0	12	12
Indiana	27,472	24,476	12.2	Yes	20	5	17	14
Iowa	8,659	8,578	0.9	No	—	—	—	—
Kansas	8,936	9,042	−1.2	Yes	0	0	0	0
Michigan	50,701	49,014	3.4	No	—	—	—	—
Minnesota	9,776	9,187	6.4	No	—	—	—	—
Missouri	30,639	31,531	−2.8	Yes	46	5	66	66
Nebraska	4,362	4,173	4.5	Yes	10	0	3	0
North Dakota	1,342	1,265	6.1	No	—	—	—	—
Ohio	47,494	44,976	5.6	Yes	199	4	24	24
South Dakota	3,511	3,334	5.3	Yes	4	0	0	0
Wisconsin	21,440	21,871	−2.0	No	—	—	—	—
South	589,597	582,539	1.2		1,780	43	862	708
Alabama	27,003	26,758	0.9	Yes	189	4	35	11
Arkansas	13,450	13,330	0.9	Yes	38	1	27	26
Delaware[2]	4,102	4,030	1.8	Yes	16	1	14	13
Florida	89,082	87,544	1.8	Yes	372	1	64	20
Georgia[4]	51,536	47,677	8.1	Yes	107	3	39	16
Kentucky	19,516	18,014	8.3	Yes	36	0	2	1
Louisiana	35,795	37,254	−3.9	Yes	83	0	27	7
Maryland	22,447	22,654	−0.9	Yes	7	1	5	5
Mississippi	19,225	19,918	−3.5	Yes	68	1	8	4
North Carolina	32,007	31,335	2.1	Yes	174	5	43	41
Oklahoma	23,535	23,232	1.3	Yes	86	4	83	83
South Carolina	22,762	22,904	−0.6	Yes	68	3	36	30
Tennessee	26,119	26,208	−0.3	Yes	103	0	2	2
Texas	161,575	160,795	0.5	Yes	411	19	379	379
Virginia	36,074	35,667	1.1	Yes	22	0	98	70
West Virginia	5,369	5,219	2.9	No	—	—	—	—
West	303,268	287,810	5.4		915	2	66	57
Alaska[2]	2,680	2,479	8.1	No	—	—	—	—
Arizona[4]	32,644	29,829	9.4	Yes	109	0	22	20
California	173,453	164,847	5.2	Yes	646	2	13	11
Colorado	22,145	20,841	6.3	Yes	2	0	1	1
Hawaii[2]	4,440	4,259	4.2	No	—	—	—	—
Idaho	6,976	6,526	6.9	Yes	18	0	1	1
Montana	3,623	3,369	7.5	Yes	4	0	3	3
Nevada	12,328	11,551	6.7	Yes	82	0	12	11
New Mexico	6,521	6,308	3.4	Yes	2	0	1	1
Oregon	13,614	13,297	2.4	Yes	31	0	2	2
Utah	6,132	5,928	3.4	Yes	9	0	6	4
Washington	16,618	16,550	0.4	Yes	10	0	4	2
Wyoming	2,094	2,026	3.4	Yes	2	0	1	1

(1) District of Columbia inmates sentenced to more than 1 year are under the jurisdiction of the Federal Bureau of Prisons. Number of prisoners under sentence of death in federal institutions excludes persons held under Armed Forces jurisdiction with a military death sentence for murder. (2) Prisons and jails form one integrated system. Data include total inmate population. (3) Incarceration rate includes an estimated 6,200 inmates sentenced to more than 1 year but held in local jails or houses of corrections. (4) Population figures based on custody counts. (5) Number of prisoners with a sentence of more than 1 year per 100,000 residents. (6) Data on 2006 executions is preliminary. (7) Since the 1976 reinstatement of the death penalty by the U.S. Supreme Court, lethal injection has been used in 84% of total executions. 17 states—AL, AZ, AR, CA, DE, FL, GA, IN, KY, LA, MI, NV, NC, SC, UT, VA, and WA— have used 2 methods (i.e., lethal injection as well as electrocution, lethal gas, firing squad, or hanging).

Prison Situation Among the States and in the Federal System, Mid-2006

Source: *Prison and Jail Inmates at Midyear 2006*, Bureau of Justice Statistics, U.S. Dept. of Justice

10 largest prison populations	No. of inmates	10 highest incarceration rates	Prisoners per 100,000 residents[1]	10 largest % increases in prison population			
				Growth 2005-06[2]	% annual increase	Growth since 1995[2]	% increase
1. Federal	191,080	1. Louisiana.	835	1. Alaska.	9.4	1. North Dakota . . .	129.7
2. California	175,115	2. Texas	687	2. Vermont	8.3	2. West Virginia . . .	121.8
3. Texas	172,889	3. Mississippi.	661	3. Georgia.	8.1	3. Wisconsin.	116.6
4. Florida	91,001	4. Oklahoma	658	4. Nevada	7.8	4. Idaho	115.3
5. New York	63,295	5. Alabama	587	5. Rhode Island. . . .	7.6	5. Colorado	105.9
6. Georgia	51,536	6. Georgia	550	6. Montana	7.5	6. Minnesota	105.2
7. Michigan.	50,701	7. Arizona	529	7. Idaho.	6.9	7. Vermont	102.2
8. Ohio	47,494	8. South Carolina . .	527	8. Arizona	6.7	8. South Dakota . . .	93.8
9. Illinois.	45,440	9. Missouri.	524	9. Minnesota	6.4	9. Federal.	92.1
10. Pennsylvania . .	43,087	10. Michigan	502	10. Colorado	6.3	10. Montana	91.3

(1) Prisoners with a sentence of more than one year. (2) Comparisons are drawn from midyear figures.

Arrests by Race, 2006

Source: *Crime in the United States, 2006*, FBI, U.S. Dept. of Justice

Each instance in which a person is arrested, cited, and summoned for an offense is counted as one arrest. Some of the following figures might therefore represent multiple arrests of the same person. Table excludes arrest data from law enforcement agencies that did not report on race, so totals below may differ from those presented in other Uniform Crime Report tables.

Offense charged	Total arrests					% distribution among all races[1]			
	Total	White	Black	Amer. Indian or Alaskan Native	Asian or Pacific Islander	White	Black	Amer. Indian or Alaskan Native	Asian or Pacific Islander
Total.	10,437,620	7,270,214	2,924,724	130,589	112,093	69.7	28.0	1.3	1.1
Violent crime[2]	446,957	261,553	175,712	4,865	4,827	58.5	39.3	1.1	1.1
Murder and nonnegligent manslaughter.	9,801	4,595	4,990	110	106	46.9	50.9	1.1	1.1
Forcible rape	17,042	11,122	5,536	195	189	65.3	32.5	1.1	1.1
Robbery	93,393	39,419	52,541	611	822	42.2	56.3	0.7	0.9
Aggravated assault	326,721	206,417	112,645	3,949	3,710	63.2	34.5	1.2	1.1
Property crime[2]	1,133,299	773,213	333,342	12,594	14,150	68.2	29.4	1.1	1.2
Burglary	221,732	152,965	64,655	2,123	1,989	69.0	29.2	1.0	0.9
Larceny-theft (except motor vehicle theft)	798,983	548,057	230,980	9,377	10,569	68.6	28.9	1.2	1.3
Motor vehicle theft	100,612	63,090	35,116	978	1,428	62.7	34.9	1.0	1.4
Arson	11,972	9,101	2,591	116	164	76.0	21.6	1.0	1.4
Other assaults[3]	949,940	619,825	306,078	13,097	10,940	65.2	32.2	1.4	1.2
Forgery and counterfeiting .	79,258	55,562	22,337	433	926	70.1	28.2	0.5	1.2
Fraud	196,930	135,329	59,087	1,213	1,301	68.7	30.0	0.6	0.7
Embezzlement	14,705	9,668	4,741	82	214	65.7	32.2	0.6	1.5
Stolen property; buying, receiving, possessing . .	89,850	58,066	30,267	670	847	64.6	33.7	0.7	0.9
Vandalism	219,652	165,518	48,781	2,987	2,366	75.4	22.2	1.4	1.1
Weapons; carrying, possessing, etc.	147,312	84,929	59,863	1,134	1,386	57.7	40.6	0.8	0.9
Prostitution and commercialized vice . . .	59,616	33,827	23,612	569	1,608	56.7	39.6	1.0	2.7
Sex offenses (except forcible rape and prostitution)	63,048	46,194	15,465	640	749	73.3	24.5	1.0	1.2
Drug abuse violations.	1,376,792	875,101	483,886	8,198	9,607	63.6	35.1	0.6	0.7
Gambling	9,001	2,358	6,467	12	164	26.2	71.8	0.1	1.8
Offenses against the family and children.	91,618	61,278	28,086	1,678	576	66.9	30.7	1.8	0.6
Driving under the influence	1,034,651	914,226	95,260	13,484	11,681	88.4	9.2	1.3	1.1
Liquor laws.	466,523	398,068	50,035	12,831	5,389	85.4	10.7	2.8	1.2
Drunkenness	408,439	344,155	54,113	7,884	2,287	84.3	13.2	1.9	0.6
Disorderly conduct	517,264	325,991	179,733	7,606	3,934	63.0	34.7	1.5	0.8
Vagrancy	27,016	15,308	11,238	333	137	56.7	41.6	1.2	0.5
All other offenses (except traffic violations).	2,906,311	1,962,017	872,571	37,935	33,788	67.5	30.0	1.3	1.2
Suspicion[4]	1,723	1,011	658	41	13	58.7	38.2	2.4	0.8
Curfew and loitering law violations	114,166	69,624	42,496	814	1,232	61.0	37.2	0.7	1.1
Runaways	83,749	57,393	20,896	1,489	3,971	68.5	25.0	1.8	4.7

(1) Figures may not add to totals due to rounding. (2) Violent crimes are offenses of murder and nonnegligent manslaughter, forcible rape, robbery, and aggravated assault. Property crimes are offenses of burglary, larceny-theft, motor vehicle theft, and arson. (3) Simple assaults, where no weapons were used and where the victim did not sustain serious injury (e.g., stalking). (4) Arrested for no specific offense and released without formal charges being placed against a person.

Inmate Population by Gender, Race, Hispanic Origin, and Age, Mid-2006

Source: *Prison and Jail Inmates at Midyear 2006*, Bureau of Justice Statistics, U.S. Dept. of Justice

(number of inmates per 100,000 residents of each group)

	Males					Females			
Age	Total[1]	White[2]	Black[2]	Hispanic	Age	Total[1]	White[2]	Black[2]	Hispanic
18-19	1,766	935	5,336	2,112	18-19...	120	81	262	175
20-24	3,352	1,675	10,698	4,168	20-24...	290	221	637	346
25-29	3,395	1,685	11,695	3,912	25-29...	300	226	716	305
30-34	3,289	1,874	11,211	3,652	30-34...	370	292	924	333
35-39	2,805	1,641	9,804	3,094	35-39...	378	282	999	337
40-44	2,344	1,419	7,976	2,630	40-44...	284	200	798	279
45-54	1,209	677	4,421	1,813	45-54...	112	75	326	141
55 or older ..	256	170	869	543	55 or older..	12	9	28	26
Total......	1,384	736	4,789	1,862	Total......	134	94	358	152

Note: Based on U.S. resident population for July 1, 2006, by gender, race, Hispanic origin, and age. Detailed categories exclude persons identifying with two or more races. (1) Includes American Indians, Alaska Natives, Asians, Native Hawaiians, and other Pacific Islanders. (2) Not Hispanic.

Hate Crime Offenses by Bias Motivation, 2005

Source: *Hate Crime Statistics, 2005*, FBI, U.S. Dept. of Justice

Hate crimes are defined as crimes in which victims are chosen because of one or more of their personal characteristics, such as race, ethnicity, or religion. Congress enacted the Hate Crime Statistics Act of 1990, which led to the collection of hate crime data as part of the FBI's Uniform Crime Report (UCR) program beginning in 1992. Not all agencies that participate in the UCR program submitted hate crime data. For the 2005 report, only 71% of reporting agencies—covering 83% of the nation's population—collected hate crime data. The table below gives a breakdown of hate crimes reported through UCR.

The National Criminal Victimization Survey (NCVS) has also tracked bias crimes since 2000, and through their general-population survey, they estimate that an average of 210,000 hate crime victimizations occurred annually between July 2000 and Dec. 2003 (approximately 66% were unreported). Most hate crimes reported through NCVS (84%) were crimes against persons; the remaining 16% were property crimes.

	Total	Crimes against				Total	Crimes against		
Bias motivation	offenses	Persons[1]	Property[2]	Society[3]	Bias motivation	offenses	Persons[1]	Property[2]	Society[3]
Total...............	8,380	5,190	3,109	81	Anti-atheism/				
Single-bias incidents ..	8,373	5,188	3,104	81	agnosticism/etc.....	5	1	4	0
Race................	4,691	3,073	1,560	58	Sexual orientation	1,171	818	348	5
Anti-White	935	597	309	29	Anti-male homosexual	713	507	204	2
Anti-Black..........	3,200	2,165	1,011	24	Anti-female				
Anti-Amer. Indian/					homosexual	180	125	55	0
Alaskan Native	95	51	42	2	Anti-homosexual	228	158	69	1
Anti-Asian/Pacific					Anti-heterosexual	23	14	9	0
Islander............	231	151	78	2	Anti-bisexual	27	14	11	2
Anti-multiple races,					Ethnicity/national				
group..............	230	109	120	1	origin	1,144	810	322	12
Religion.............	1,314	454	855	5	Anti-Hispanic........	660	495	157	8
Anti-Jewish	900	290	610	0	Anti-other ethnicity/				
Anti-Catholic	61	12	47	2	national origin......	484	315	165	4
Anti-Protestant......	58	6	50	2	Disability	53	33	19	1
Anti-Islamic	146	99	47	0	Anti-physical	21	19	2	0
Anti-other religion.....	102	35	66	1	Anti-mental	32	14	17	1
Anti-mult. religions,					Multiple-bias				
group..............	42	11	31	0	incidents[4].........	7	2	5	0

(1) Includes the following offenses: murder and nonnegligent manslaughter, forcible rape, aggravated assault, simple assault, intimidation, and additional offenses collected in the National Incident-Based Reporting System (NIBRS). (2) Includes the following offenses: robbery, burglary, larceny-theft, motor vehicle theft, arson, destruction/damage/vandalism, and additional offenses collected in the NIBRS. (3) Includes drug or narcotic offenses, gambling and prostitution offenses, and weapon law violations where society as a whole is considered the victim. (4) More than one offense type must occur and at least two offense types must be motivated by different biases for an incident to be considered multiple-bias.

Notable Assassinations Since 1865

1865—Apr. 14: U.S. Pres. Abraham Lincoln shot by John Wilkes Booth, well-known actor with Confederate sympathies, at Ford's Theater in Washington, DC; died Apr. 15.

1881—Mar. 13: Alexander II of Russia. **July 2:** U.S. Pres. James A. Garfield shot by Charles J. Guiteau, disappointed office seeker, in Washington, DC; died Sept. 19.

1894—June 24: French Pres. Sadi Carnot, by Sante Caserio, Italian anarchist, in Lyon.

1898—Sept. 10: Empress Elizabeth of Austria stabbed by Luigi Luccheni, Italian anarchist.

1900—July 29: Umberto I, king of Italy.

1901—Sept. 6: U.S. Pres. William McKinley shot by Leon Czolgosz, anarchist, in Buffalo, NY; died Sept. 14.

1908—Feb. 1: King Carlos I of Portugal and his son Luis Felipe in Lisbon.

1913—Feb. 23: Mexican Pres. Francisco I. Madero and Vice Pres. Jose Pino Suarez. **Mar. 18:** King George of Greece.

1914—June 28: Archduke Francis Ferdinand of Austria-Hungary and his wife shot by Gavrilo Princip, Serb nationalist, in Sarajevo, Bosnia.

1916—Dec. 30: Grigory Rasputin, mystic and court figure, by group of aristocrats.

1918—July 12: Grand Duke Michael of Russia, at Perm. **July 16:** Nicholas II, former (abdicated) czar of Russia; his wife, Czarina Alexandra; their son, Czarevitch Alexis; their daughters, Grand Duchesses Olga, Tatiana, Marie, Anastasia; and 4 members of household, executed by Bolsheviks at Ekaterinburg.

1920—May 20: Mexican Pres. Gen. Venustiano Carranza in Tlaxcalantongo.

1922—Aug. 22: Michael Collins, Irish revolutionary, in ambush in West Cork. **Dec. 16:** Polish Pres. Gabriel Narutowicz in Warsaw.

1923—July 20: Gen. Francisco "Pancho" Villa, ex-rebel leader, in Parral, Mexico.

1928—July 17: Gen. Alvaro Obregon, president-elect of Mexico, in San Angel.

1932—May 6: French Pres. Paul Doumer shot by Russian émigré, Pavel Gorgulov, in Paris.

1934—July 25: Austrian Chancellor Engelbert Dollfuss by Nazis, in Vienna.

1935—Sept. 8: Sen. Huey P. Long, former Louisiana governor, shot by Dr. Carl Austin Weiss, son-in-law of political opponent, in Baton Rouge; died Sept. 10.

1940—Aug. 20: Leon Trotsky (Lev Bronstein), exiled Soviet commissar of war, fatally wounded with ice ax by Soviet agent near Mexico City.
1948—Jan. 30: Mohandas K. Gandhi (Mahatma) shot by Nathuram Godse, Hindu fanatic, in New Delhi. **Sept. 17:** Count Folke Bernadotte, UN mediator for Palestine, by Jewish extremists in Jerusalem.
1951—July 20: Jordanian King Abdullah ibn Hussein. **Oct. 16:** Prime Min. Liaquat Ali Khan of Pakistan shot, in Rawalpindi.
1956—Sept. 21: Pres. Anastasio Somoza of Nicaragua shot in Leon; died Sept. 29.
1957—July 26: Guatemalan Pres. Carlos Castillo Armas, in Guatemala City by one of own guards.
1958—July 14: King Faisal of Iraq, Crown Prince Abdullah, and **July 15,** Prem. Nuri as-Said, by rebels in Baghdad.
1959—Sept. 25: Prime Min. Solomon Bandaranaike of Ceylon, by Buddhist monk in Colombo.
1961—Jan. 17: Ex-Prem. Patrice Lumumba of the Congo, in Katanga Province. **May 30:** Dominican dictator Rafael Leonidas Trujillo Molina, near Ciudad Trujillo.
1963—June 12: Medgar Evers, NAACP's Mississippi field secretary, shot by Byron De La Beckwith in Jackson, MS. **Nov. 2:** Pres. Ngo Dinh Diem of South Vietnam and his brother, Ngo Dinh Nhu, in military coup. **Nov. 22:** U.S. Pres. John F. Kennedy shot while riding in motorcade through downtown Dallas, TX; accused gunman Lee Harvey Oswald murdered by nightclub owner Jack Ruby while awaiting trial.
1965—Jan. 21: Iranian Prem. Hassan Ali Mansour in Tehran; 4 executed. **Feb. 21:** Malcolm X, black nationalist leader, shot by three men linked to Nation of Islam, at New York City rally.
1966—Sept. 6: Prime Min. Hendrik F. Verwoerd of South Africa stabbed to death in parliament at Cape Town.
1968—Apr. 4: Rev. Martin Luther King Jr. fatally shot in Memphis, TN; James Earl Ray convicted of crime. **June 5:** Sen. Robert F. Kennedy (D-NY) shot in Los Angeles; died June 6. Sirhan Sirhan convicted of crime.
1971—Nov. 28: Jordanian Prime Min. Wasfi Tal by Palestinian guerrillas, in Cairo.
1973—Mar. 2: U.S. Amb. Cleo A. Noel Jr., U.S. Charge d'Affaires George C. Moore, and Belgian Charge d'Affaires Guy Eid, by Palestinian guerrillas in Khartoum, Sudan. **Dec. 20:** Spanish Prem. Luis Carrero Blanco in car bombing by Basque separatist group ETA, in Madrid.
1974—Aug. 19: U.S. Amb. to Cyprus, Rodger P. Davies, by sniper's bullet in Nicosia.
1975—Feb. 11: Pres. Richard Ratsimandrava of Madagascar shot in Tananarive. **Mar. 25:** Saudi Arabian King Faisal shot by nephew Prince Musad Abdel Aziz, in Riyadh. **Aug. 15:** Bangladesh Pres. Sheik Mujibur Rahman killed in coup.
1976—Feb. 13: Nigerian head of state, Gen. Murtala Ramat Mohammed, by self-styled "young revolutionaries."
1977—Mar. 16: Kamal Jumblat, Lebanese Druse chieftain, shot near Beirut. **Mar. 18:** Congo Pres. Marien Ngouabi shot in Brazzaville.
1978—May 9: Former Italian Prem. Aldo Moro killed by Red Brigades terrorists who abducted him Mar. 16 in Rome, held him hostage for several weeks. **July 9:** Former Iraqi Prem. Abdul Razak Al-Naif shot in London.
1979—Feb. 14: U.S. Amb. Adolph Dubs shot by Afghan Muslim extremists in Kabul. **Aug. 27:** Lord Mountbatten, WWII hero, and 2 others killed when a bomb exploded on his fishing boat off the coast of Co. Sligo, Ireland. IRA claimed responsibility. **Oct. 26:** S. Korean Pres. Park Chung Hee and 6 bodyguards fatally shot by Kim Jae Kyu, head of S. Korean CIA.
1980—Apr. 12: Liberian Pres. William R. Tolbert slain in military coup. **Sept. 17:** Former Nicaraguan Pres. Anastasio Somoza Debayle shot in Paraguay.
1981—Oct. 6: Egyptian Pres. Anwar al-Sadat shot by commandos while reviewing military parade in Cairo; 7 others killed, 28 wounded; 4 convicted as assassins and executed.
1982—Sept. 14: Lebanese Pres.-elect Bashir Gemayel killed by bomb in east Beirut.
1983—Aug. 21: Philippine opposition leader Benigno Aquino Jr. shot by gunman at Manila International Airport.
1984—Oct. 31: Indian Prime Min. Indira Gandhi shot and killed by 2 Sikh bodyguards, in New Delhi.
1986—Feb. 28: Swedish Prem. Olof Palme shot by gunman on Stockholm street.
1987—June 1: Lebanese Prem. Rashid Karami killed when bomb exploded aboard helicopter.
1988—Apr. 16: PLO military chief Khalil Wazir (Abu Jihad) gunned down by Israeli commandos in Tunisia.
1989—Aug. 18: Colombian pres. candidate Luis Carlos Galan killed by Medellín cartel drug traffickers at campaign rally in Bogotá. **Nov. 22:** Lebanese Pres. Rene Moawad killed when bomb exploded next to his motorcade.
1990—Mar. 22: Colombian pres. candidate Bernardo Jaramillo Ossa shot by gunman at airport in Bogotá.

1991—May 21: Former Indian Prime Min. Rajiv Gandhi, killed by bomb during election rally in Madras.
1992—June 29: Algerian Pres. Mohammed Boudiaf shot by gunman in Annaba.
1993—May 1: Sri Lankan Pres. Ranasinghe Premadasa killed by bomb in Colombo.
1994—Mar. 23: Mexican pres. candidate Luis Donaldo Colosio Murrieta shot by gunman Mario Aburto Martinez. **Apr. 6:** Burundian Pres. Cyprien Ntaryamira and Rwandan Pres. Juvenal Habyarimana killed with 8 others when their plane was apparently shot down.
1995—Nov. 4: Israeli Prime Min. Yitzhak Rabin shot by Yigal Amir, Jewish extremist, at peace rally in Tel Aviv.
1996—Oct. 2: Andrei Lukanov, former Bulgarian prime min., shot outside home by unidentified gunman.
1998—Feb. 6: Prefect of Corsica, Claude Erignac, shot in the back by 2 unidentified gunmen while walking to concert. **Apr. 26:** Guatemalan Roman Catholic Bishop Juan Gerardi Conedera, human rights champion, found beaten to death in Guatemala City; 4 persons convicted, June 8, 2001.
1999—Mar. 23: Paraguayan Vice-Pres. Luis Maria Argaña, ambushed and shot to death along with his driver, by 4 unidentified assailants, in Asunción. **Apr. 9:** Niger Pres. Ibrahim Bare Mainassara ambushed and killed by dissident soldiers. **Oct. 27:** Armenian Prime Min. Vazgen Sarkissian, along with 7 others, shot to death during session of parliament.
2000—Jan. 15: Serbian paramilitary leader Zeljko Raznjatovic (Arkan), with 2 others, shot and killed by unidentified gunman, in Belgrade; 4 suspects later charged with killing. **June 8:** Brig. Gen. Stephen Saunders, Britain's senior military representative in Greece, fatally shot by 2 men on motorcycle, while driving car in Athens suburb.
2001—Jan. 16: Dem. Rep. of the Congo Pres. Laurent Kabila shot to death by bodyguard at pres. palace in Kinshasa. **June 1:** Nepal's King Birendra, Queen Aiswarya, and 7 other royals fatally shot by Crown Prince Dipendra, who also fatally wounded himself. **Sept. 9:** Afghan Northern Alliance (anti-Taliban) guerrilla leader Ahmed Shah Massoud, injured in suicide-attack bombing by 2 Arabs posing as journalists, in N. Afghanistan; died Sept. 15. **Oct. 14:** Abdel Rahman Hamad, a leader of Palestinian militant group Hamas, shot by Israeli military snipers. **Oct. 17:** Israeli tourism min. Rehavam Zeevifatally shot; Popular Front for the Liberation of Palestine claimed responsibility.
2002—Mar. 16: Colombian cleric Isaias Duarte Cancino, critic of Colombian guerrillas and drug traffickers, shot by unidentified gunmen outside of church in Cali. **May 6:** Dutch rightwing politician Pim Fortuyn shot outside radio station in Hilversum. **July 6:** Afghan Vice-Pres. Haji Abdul Qadir shot outside his office in Kabul. **July 23:** Salah Sherhada, a founder of armed wing of Hamas, killed with 14 others in assassination air strike on Gaza City by Israeli fighter jet.
2003—Mar. 12: Serbian Prime Min. Zoran Djindjic shot by snipers (paramilitary) outside govt. headquarters in Belgrade. **Apr. 10:** Shiite Muslim cleric Abdul Majid al-Khoei attacked by crowd, hacked to death at Imam Ali mosque, Najaf, Iraq. **Apr. 17:** Sergei Yushenkov, former Russian legislator and Liberal Party head, shot outside apartment in Moscow. **Aug. 29:** Shiite Muslim cleric Bakir al-Hakim killed in car bombing at Imam Ali mosque in Najaf, Iraq. **Sept. 10:** Swedish Foreign Min. Anna Lindh stabbed in Stockholm dept. store; died Sept. 11.
2004—Feb. 13: Former Chechen Pres. Zelimkhan Yandarbiyev killed after car exploded in Qatar. **Mar. 22:** Sheik Ahmed Yassin, spiritual leader of Hamas, by Israeli missile attack in Gaza City. **Apr. 17:** Hamas leader Abdel Aziz Rantisi, by Israeli missile strike in Gaza City. **May 9:** Chechen Pres. Akhmad Kadyrov, by bomb explosion at WWII memorial service in Grozny. **May 17:** Iraqi Gov. Council Pres. Ezzedine Salim, by car bomb explosion at Green Zone checkpoint in Baghdad. **June 12:** Iraqi Dep. Foreign Min. Bassam Salih Kubba gunned down outside home in Baghdad. **Nov. 2:** Filmmaker Theo van Gogh, critic of Islam and great-grand-nephew of painter Vincent van Gogh, shot and stabbed by Muslim militant in Amsterdam.
2005—Jan. 4: Baghdad Gov. Ali al-Haidari gunned down by insurgents in Baghdad, Iraq. **Feb. 14:** Former Lebanese Prime Min. Rafik al-Hariri killed when motorcade bombed in Beirut. **Mar. 8:** Former Chechen pres. Aslan Maskhadov killed in raid by Russian special forces, in village outside Grozny. **June 21:** Lebanese Communist Party leader George Hawi killed after car bombed in Beirut. **July 1:** Sheik Kamaledding al-Ghuraifi, senior aide to Grand Ayatollah Ali Sistani, shot and killed on way to Friday prayers, in Baghdad. **July 7:** Egyptian Amb.-designate Ihab al-Sherif was killed in Iraq by kidnappers who abducted him July 2 in Baghdad. **Aug. 12:** Sri Lankan Foreign Min. Lakshman Kadirgamar, an ethnic Tamil, shot to death at his home in Colombo; Liberation Tigers of Tamil Eelam suspected.
2006—Feb. 11: Leading Kazakhstan opposition politician Altynbek Sarsenbayev (also known as Sarsenbaiuly) kidnapped,

found murdered outside Almaty. **Apr. 22:** Guyanese Agriculture Min. Satyadeow Sawh shot by unidentified gunmen, near Georgetown. **July 10:** Shamil Basayev, leader of Chechen separatist movement who claimed responsibility for many of Russia's worst terrorist attacks, killed in massive explosion near village of Ekazhevo. Chechen rebel website said explosion was accidental, but Russian security director said killing was result of special forces operation. **Jul. 14:** Prominent Shiite Muslim cleric Allama Hassan Turabi killed in suicide bombing at his home in Karachi, Pakistan. **Jul. 28:** Somali transitional government's Constitution and Federalism Min. Abdallah Deerow Isaq shot in Baidoa. **Sept. 10:** Hakim Taniwal, governor of eastern Afghan province, killed by suicide bomber outside of his office; Taliban claimed responsibility. **Sept. 14:** Andrei Kozlov, Russian central banker active in reforming industry, shot by unidentified gunmen in Moscow. **Sept. 25:** Safia Amajan, women's affairs official in Afghanistan, killed by gunmen in Kandahar; Taliban claimed responsibility. **Oct. 7:** Anna Politkovskaya, reporter critical of Kremlin's Chechnya policies, fatally shot by unidentified gunman in apartment building in Moscow. **Nov. 21:** Pierre Gemayel, Lebanese cabinet minister opposed to Syria, shot by unknown gunmen while driving through Beirut. **Nov. 23:** Aleksandr Litvinenko, former Russian intelligence agent and critic of Russia's government and security service, died after apparent poisoning with radioactive isotope; another former KGB agent suspected.

2007—June 13: Walid Eido, Lebanese parliament member who was part of anti-Syria coalition, killed by car bomb in Beirut. **Aug. 2:** *Oakland Post* editor Chauncey Bailey, who was investigating financial status of black Muslim organization, shot dead in downtown Oakland, CA. **Sept. 13:** Sunni Arab Sheik Abdul Sattar Buzaigh al-Rishawi (also known as Abu Risha), collaborator of U.S. military against extremists in Iraq's Anbar Province, killed in bombing in Ramadi. **Sept. 19:** Antoine Ghanem, member of ruling anti-Syria coalition in Lebanese parliament, killed by bomb in parked car near Beirut.

Notable Assassination Attempts Since 1912

1912—Oct. 14: Former U.S. Pres. Theodore Roosevelt shot and wounded by demented man in Milwaukee, WI.

1933—Feb. 15: In Miami, FL, Joseph Zangara, anarchist, shot at Pres.-elect Franklin D. Roosevelt, but a woman seized his arm; bullet fatally wounded Chicago Mayor Anton J. Cermak, who died Mar. 6.

1944—July 20: Adolf Hitler injured when a bomb, planted by a German officer, exploded in his headquarters; 1 aide killed and 12 injured.

1950—Nov. 1: In an attempt to assassinate Pres. Harry Truman, 2 members of a Puerto Rican nationalist movement—Griselio Torresola and Oscar Collazo—tried to shoot their way into Blair House, across the street from White House. Torresola killed. Pvt. Leslie Coffelt, White House policeman, fatally shot.

1970—Nov. 27: Pope Paul VI unharmed by knife-wielding assailant who attempted to attack him in airport in Manila, Philippines.

1972—May 15: Alabama Gov. George Wallace seriously wounded when shot in Laurel, MD, by Arthur Bremer.

1975—Sept. 5: Pres. Gerald R. Ford unharmed when Secret Service agent grabbed pistol aimed at him by Lynette (Squeaky) Fromme, a follower of cult leader Charles Manson, in Sacramento, CA. **Sept. 22:** Pres. Ford again unharmed when bystander grabbed arm of Sara Jane Moore as she fired handgun upon Ford in San Francisco.

1980—May 29: Civil rights leader Vernon E. Jordan Jr. shot and wounded in Ft. Wayne, IN.

1981—Jan. 16: Irish political activist Bernadette Devlin McAliskey and her husband shot and seriously wounded by 3 members of a Protestant paramilitary group in Co. Tyrone, Ireland. **Mar. 30:** Pres. Ronald Reagan, along with Press Sec. James Brady, Secret Service agent Timothy J. McCarthy, and Washington, DC, policeman Thomas Delahanty shot and seriously wounded by John W. Hinckley Jr. in Washington, DC. **May 13:** Pope John Paul II and 2 bystanders shot and wounded by Mehmet Ali Agca, an escaped Turkish prisoner, in St. Peter's Square, Rome.

1982—May 12: Pope John Paul II unharmed after guards overpowered a man with a knife, in Fatima, Portugal.

1984—Oct. 12: British Prime Min. Margaret Thatcher unharmed when a bomb, said to have been planted by the IRA, exploded at the Grand Hotel in Brighton, England, during a Party conference. Four died, including a member of Parliament.

1986—Sept. 7: Chilean Pres. Gen. Augusto Pinochet Ugarte unharmed after motorcade was attacked by rebels.

1995—June 26: Egyptian Pres. Hosni Mubarak unharmed when gunmen fired on his motorcade in Addis Ababa, Ethiopia. Four died, including 2 Ethiopian police officers.

1997—Feb. 12: Colombian Pres. Ernesto Samper Pizano unharmed when a bomb exploded on a runway in Barranquilla as his plane was preparing to land. **Apr. 30:** Tajik Pres. Imamali Rakhmanov injured when a grenade was thrown at him.

1998—Feb. 9: Georgian Pres. Eduard A. Shevardnadze unharmed when gunmen fired on his motorcade in Tbilisi. Three died, including 2 bodyguards and 1 assailant.

2000—Sept. 18: Armed men attempted to assassinate Côte d'Ivoire military leader Gen. Robert Guei in predawn raid.

2002—Apr. 14: Leading Colombian pres. candidate Alvaro Uribe Velez unharmed after bomb exploded under parked bus as his motorcade passed in Barranquilla; 3 bystanders killed. **July 14:** French Pres. Jacques Chirac unharmed after Maxime Brunerie, gunman with ties to neo-Nazi groups, fired at his open-top jeep during a Bastille Day parade in Paris. **Sept. 5:** Afghan Pres. Hamid Karzai unharmed after militant shot at car in Kandahar. **Nov. 25:** Turkmenistan Pres. Saparmurat Niyazov unharmed after gunmen opened fire on his motorcade in Ashgabat.

2003—Dec. 14: Pakistani Pres. Pervez Musharraf unharmed after bomb detonated on bridge in Rawalpindi seconds after his motorcade crossed over.

2004—Mar. 19: Taiwanese Pres. Chen Shui-bian shot while campaigning in motorcade; minor injuries. **July 13:** Separatists bombed motorcade of Sergei Abramov, Chechnya's acting pres. **Sept. 5:** Ukrainian opposition presidential candidate Viktor Yushchenko, who later won office, fell ill after meeting, diagnosed with dioxin poisoning. **Sept. 16:** Rocket fired at helicopter carrying Afghan Pres. Hamid Karzai, near Gardez.

2005—Mar. 15: Kosovo Pres. Ibrahim Rugova survived after a bomb damaged the vehicle he was in as his motorcade traveled through Pristina. **July 12:** Lebanon's pro-Syrian defense min. Elias Murr wounded by a car explosion in Beirut suburb.

2006—Apr. 12: Pro-democracy activist Edil Baisalov was beaten as he left his office in Bishkek, Kyrgyzstan. He had sought to block the parliamentary candidacy of a reputed crime boss. **Sept. 5:** Lt. Col. Samir Shehade, involved in investigation of 2005 assassination of former Lebanese Prime Min. Rafik al-Hariri, wounded by bomb as he drove in village near Sidon.

2007—June 29: Rockets hit a plane carrying former rebel chief and current Côte d'Ivoire Prime Min. Guillaume Soro, shortly after plane landed in Bouake; Soro unhurt.

Notable U.S. Kidnappings Since 1924

Robert Franks, 13, in Chicago, **May 22, 1924**, by 2 youths, Richard Loeb and Nathan Leopold, who killed boy. Demand for $10,000 ignored. Loeb died in prison; Leopold paroled 1958.

Charles A. Lindbergh Jr., 20 mos. old, in Hopewell, NJ, **Mar. 1, 1932**; found dead **May 12**. Ransom of $50,000 paid to man identified as Bruno Richard Hauptmann, 35, partially deaf German convict who entered U.S. illegally. Hauptmann convicted after spectacular trial at Flemington; electrocuted in Trenton, NJ, prison, **Apr. 3, 1936**.

William A. Hamm Jr., 39, in St. Paul, **June 15, 1933**. $100,000 paid. Alvin Karpis given life, paroled in 1969.

Charles F. Urschel, in Oklahoma City, **July 22, 1933**. Released **July 31** after $200,000 paid. George "Machine Gun" Kelly and 5 others sentenced to life.

Brooke L. Hart, 22, in San Jose, CA. Thomas Thurmond and John Holmes arrested after demanding $40,000. When Hart's body was found in San Francisco Bay, **Nov. 26, 1933**, a mob attacked the jail and lynched the 2 kidnappers.

June Robles, 6, abducted in Tucson, AZ, **Apr. 25, 1934**. Missing for 19 days after ransom note sent to parents. Found alive in iron cage buried in the desert. No arrests made.

George Weyerhaeuser, 9, in Tacoma, WA, **May 24, 1935**. Returned home **June 1** after $200,000 paid. Kidnappers given 20 to 60 years.

Charles Mattson, 10, in Tacoma, WA, **Dec. 27, 1936**. Found dead **Jan. 11, 1937**. Kidnapper asked $28,000 but failed to contact for delivery.

Arthur Fried, in White Plains, NY, **Dec. 4, 1937**. Body not found. Two kidnappers executed.

Robert C. Greenlease, 6, taken from Kansas City, MO, school **Sept. 28, 1953**, held for $600,000. Body was found **Oct. 7**. Bonnie Brown Heady and Carl A. Hall pleaded guilty, were executed.

Peter Weinberger, 32 days old, Westbury, NY, **July 4, 1956**, for $2,000 ransom, not paid. Child found dead. Angelo John LaMarca, 31, convicted, executed.

Lee Crary, 8, in Everett, WA, **Sept. 22, 1957**; $10,000 ransom, not paid. Escaped after 3 days, led police to George E. Collins, who was convicted.

Frank Sinatra Jr., 19, from hotel room in Lake Tahoe, CA, **Dec. 8, 1963**. Released **Dec. 11** after his father paid $240,000 ransom. Three men sentenced to prison.

Barbara Jane Mackle, 20, abducted **Dec. 17, 1968**, from Atlanta, GA, motel; found unharmed 3 days later, buried in a coffin-like box 18 in. underground, after her father had paid $500,000 ransom; Gary Steven Krist sentenced to life, Ruth Eisenmann-Schier to 7 years.

Mrs. Roy Fuchs, 35, and 3 children held hostage 2 hours, **May 14, 1969**, in Long Island, NY. Released after her husband, a bank manager, paid kidnappers $129,000 in bank funds; 4 men arrested, ransom recovered.

Virginia Piper, 49, abducted **July 27, 1972**, from her home in suburban Minneapolis; found unharmed near Duluth 2 days later after husband paid $1 mil ransom.

J. Paul Getty III, 17, grandson of the oil billionaire, disappeared **July 10, 1973**, in Italy. Reported payment of $2.8 mil ransom not made until after Getty's ear was sent to a newspaper with a warning that other parts of his body would be mutilated unless ransom was paid. Getty freed **Dec. 15**; 2 men sentenced to prison.

Patricia "Patty" Hearst, 19, taken from her Berkeley, CA, apartment **Feb. 4, 1974**, "Symbionese Liberation Army" captors demanded her father, publisher Randolph Hearst, give millions to the area's poor. Patricia implicated in a San Francisco bank holdup, **Apr. 15**. The FBI, **Sept. 18, 1975**, captured her and others; they were indicted on various charges. Patricia convicted of bank robbery, **Mar. 20, 1976**; released from prison under executive clemency, **Feb. 1, 1979**. In 1978, William and Emily Harris were sentenced to 10 years to life for the kidnapping; both were paroled in 1983.

J. Reginald Murphy, 40, an editor of *Atlanta* (GA) *Constitution*, kidnapped **Feb. 20, 1974**; freed **Feb. 22** after newspaper paid $700,000 ransom. William A. H. Williams arrested; most of the money recovered.

E. B. Reville, Hepzibah, GA, banker, and wife, Jean, kidnapped **Sept. 30, 1974**. $30,000 ransom paid. He was found alive; Jean Reville was found dead **Oct. 2**.

Jack Teich, Kings Point, NY, steel executive, seized **Nov. 12, 1974**; released **Nov. 19** after payment of $750,000.

Adam Walsh, 6, abducted from a Hollywood, FL, dept. store, **July 27, 1981**. Severed head found 2 weeks later. John Walsh, Adam's father, became active in raising awareness about missing children.

Sidney J. Reso, oil company executive, seized **Apr. 29, 1992**; died **May 3**. Arthur D. Seale and wife, Irene, arrested **June 19**.

Arthur pleaded guilty, sentenced to life in prison; Irene sentenced to 20-year prison term.

Polly Klaas, 12, Petaluma, CA, abducted at knife point, **Oct. 1, 1993**, during a slumber party at her home. Police arrested Richard Allen Davis on **Nov. 30**; he led them to her body, found **Dec. 4** in wooded area of Cloverdale, CA. Davis found guilty **June 18, 1996**, and sentenced to death **Sept. 26**.

Marshall I. Wais, 79, owner of 2 San Francisco steel companies, kidnapped **Nov. 19, 1996**, from his San Francisco home. Released unharmed the same day after $500,000 ransom paid; Thomas William Taylor and Michael K. Robinson arrested same day.

Tionda Z. Bradley, 10, and sister **Diamond Yvette Bradley**, 3, went missing **July 6, 2001**, in Chicago, IL. Note left by Tionda at home stated that the 2 girls were going to the store and the playground. Police believed girls kidnapped.

Daniel Pearl, 38, reporter for *Wall Street Journal*, disappeared **Jan. 23, 2002**, while researching story in Karachi, Pakistan. British-born militant Ahmad Omar Saeed Sheikh **Feb. 14** admitted to organizing the kidnapping and said Pearl was dead. Sheikh and 3 others convicted **July 15** of kidnapping and murder by a judge in Hyderabad.

Elizabeth Smart, 14, abducted from her home in Salt Lake City, UT, **June 5, 2002**, allegedly by Brian D. Mitchell, and forced to live with Mitchell and wife Wanda for 9 months in various U.S. cities; found walking down street with captors in Sandy, UT, 15 miles from Smart family home, **Mar. 12, 2003**.

Natalee Holloway, 18, of Birmingham, AL, vanished **May 30, 2005**, on high school graduation trip to Aruba. Officials believed she was kidnapped and murdered. Several suspects were detained but later released.

Jill Carroll, 28, freelance journalist, in Baghdad by group called the Revenge Brigade, **Jan. 7, 2006**. She was on assignment for the *Christian Science Monitor* when she was seized. She was released **Mar. 30**; 4 Iraqis arrested in connection with her kidnapping in Aug.

Steve Centanni, 60, a Fox News reporter released **Aug. 26, 2006** (along with a colleague), after being kidnapped and held hostage for 13 days by Palestinian militant group Holy Jihad Brigades. The group had demanded that the U.S. release all Muslims held in its prisons.

Notable Terrorist Incidents Worldwide, 1971-Sept. 2007

Note: Selected noteworthy incidents, excluding most assassinations, kidnappings, and military targets. Not including all 2005-07 incidents in Iraq; *see* Chronology of the Year's Events.

Source: U.S. Dept. of State; *Facts On File World News Digest @ Facts.com*; World Almanac research

1971—Mar. 1: Senate wing of U.S. Capitol Building in Wash., DC, bombed by Weather Underground; no deaths.

1972—July 21: "Bloody Friday." Provisional IRA exploded 20+ bombs across Belfast, N. Ireland; 9 killed, hundreds injured. **Sept. 5:** Members of Palestinian group Black September killed 2 Israeli athletes and seized 9 others at Olympic Village in Munich, W. Germany, during Summer Olympics. 9 hostages, 5 militants, 1 Ger. officer died in botched rescue.

1973—Dec. 17: Palestinian gunmen attacked Rome airport and bombed plane on tarmac; hijacked Lufthansa plane with 5 Italian hostages to Athens, then to Kuwait; 31 killed in all.

1974—June 17: Houses of Parliament in London, England, bombed by Provisional IRA; 11 injured.

1975—Jan. 27: Puerto Rican FALN nationalists bombed Fraunces Tavern in New York City; 4 killed, 53 injured. **Jan. 29:** U.S. State Dept. building in Wash., DC, bombed by Weather Underground; no deaths.

1976—June 27: Palestinian and Baader-Meinhof militants forced Air France jet to land at Entebbe, Uganda. Israeli army rescued 103 hostages from airport terminal in battle with terrorists and Ugandan troops, July 3-4; 32 killed in all.

1978—Mar. 11: Palestinian militants landed on beach near Haifa, Israel. Shot civilians and hijacked bus with hostages to Tel Aviv; exploded at roadblock; 43 killed.

1979—Nov. 4: Iranian radicals seized U.S. embassy in Tehran, taking 66 Americans hostage. 52 were held until Jan. 20, 1981. **Nov. 20:** 200 Islamic terrorists seized Grand Mosque in Mecca, Saudi Arabia, and held hundreds of pilgrims hostage. Saudi forces retook mosque Dec. 4; about 250 died.

1980—Feb. 27: Members of leftist guerrilla group April 19 Movement (M-19) seized Dominican Republic embassy in Bogota, Colombia; 80 hostages taken. 18 held until Apr. 27.

1983—April 18: Hezbollah suicide truck bomb at the U.S. embassy in Beirut, Lebanon, killed 63. **Oct. 9:** N. Korean agents ambushed a S. Korean govt. delegation in Rangoon, Burma, killing 21. **Oct. 23:** Hezbollah suicide truck bombings of U.S. and French military bases, Beirut, Lebanon; 242 Americans, 58 French killed.

1984—Sept. 20: U.S. embassy annex near Beirut, Lebanon, bombed, killing approx. 20.

1985—June 14: Hezbollah members hijacked TWA Flight 847 with 153 passengers and crew to Beirut, Lebanon; 39 held for 17 days; 1 U.S. Navy sailor killed. **June 23:** Air India Flight 182 destroyed by bomb off coast of Ireland; 329 killed. Blamed on Sikh terrorists. **Apr. 12:** 18 killed in bomb blast at restaurant near Air Force base in Torrejon, Spain. **Oct. 7:** 4 Palestinians hijacked Italian cruise ship *Achille Lauro*; 1 passenger killed. **Nov. 23:** EgyptAir Flight 648 from Athens to Cairo hijacked to Malta by Palestinian group Abu Nidal; 60 killed in rescue. **Dec. 27:** Palestinian militants opened fire at El-Al airline counters at Rome and Vienna airports; 19 killed.

1986—Apr. 5: Nightclub in Berlin, W. Germany, bombed; 3 killed, incl. 2 U.S. servicemen; 200+ hurt. 3 Libyan embassy workers in Germany convicted in bombing.

1987—Apr. 17: Bomb in Sri Lankan capital killed 100+; blamed on Tamil rebels who, 4 days later, attacked Sinhalese travelers on highway, killing 127. **June 19:** Basque group ETA bombed supermarket garage in Barcelona, Spain; 21 killed, 45 injured. **Nov. 29:** Bomb planted by N. Korean agents exploded on Korean Air Lines Flight 858 over Indian Ocean; 115 killed.

1988—Dec. 21: Pan Am Flight 103 exploded over Lockerbie, Scotland, killing all 259 aboard and 11 on the ground; Libya took responsibility for bombing in Aug. 2003.

1989—Sept. 19: French UTA Flight 722 from Congo to Paris destroyed by bomb in midair over Niger; 171 killed. Several Libyan officials convicted in absentia; no official admission.

1992—Mar. 17: Israeli embassy in Buenos Aires, Argentina, bombed; 28 killed, 200+ injured. Hezbollah suspected.

1993—Feb. 26: Truck bomb exploded in World Trade Center garage in New York City; 6 killed. Blast later linked to al-Qaeda. **Mar. 12-19:** At least 11 bombs ripped through Bombay and Calcutta, India; 300+ killed.

1994—Feb. 25: U.S.-born Israeli settler Baruch Goldstein opened fire in mosque in Hebron, West Bank; about 30 Muslim worshippers killed. **July 18:** Buenos Aires Jewish center bombed; 87 killed. Blamed on Hezbollah.

1995—Mar. 20: Twelve killed and over 5,000 injured when Japanese Aum Shinri-kyu cult members released Sarin nerve gas in several Tokyo subway cars. **Apr. 19:** Murrah Federal Building in Oklahoma City bombed, killing 168 and injuring 500+. Timothy McVeigh and Terry Nichols convicted in bombing. McVeigh executed, June 11, 2001; Nichols sentenced to life in prison, 1998 on state charges, 2004 on federal charges. **Nov. 13:** U.S. miltary compound in Riyadh, Saudi Arabia, bombed by Islamic Movement of Change; 7 killed. **Nov. 19:** Suicide bomber drove into Egyptian embassy in Islamabad, Pakistan; at least 16 killed, 60 injured.

1996—Jan. 31: Tamil Tigers drove explosives-laden truck into Central Bank in Colombo, Sri Lanka; 90 killed. **Feb. 25:** Hamas suicide bombers hit 2 buses in Jerusalem; 26 killed. **Mar. 4:** Bomb outside Tel Aviv shopping mall killed 14, injured 130. **June 25:** Bomb-laden fuel truck exploded outside Khobar Towers, a U.S. military complex in Dhahran, Saudi Arabia; killed 19. **June 27:** Bomb exploded at Centennial Olympic Park in Atlanta, GA, during Summer Games; killed 2, injured 100+. Suspect Eric Robert Rudolph arrested in 2003, pleaded guilty; sentenced to life in prison, Aug. 22, 2005. **Dec. 3:** Bomb exploded on subway train in Paris; 4 killed, 86 injured. Blamed on Algerian extremists.

1997—Nov. 17: Gamaa al-Islamiya gunmen killed 58 tourists and 4 Egyptians in Valley of the Kings near Luxor, Egypt.

1998—Aug. 7: U.S. embassies in Nairobi, Kenya, and Dar-es-Salaam, Tanzania, bombed; 257 people killed. Al-Qaeda blamed. **Aug. 15:** IRA car bomb exploded outside courthouse in Omagh, N. Ireland; killed 29, injured 300+. **Oct. 18:** National Liberation Army of Colombia blew up Ocensa oil pipeline; about 71 killed, 100+ injured.

1999—Sept. 9-16: Three apt. buildings bombed in Moscow and Volgodonsk, Russia; about 300 killed. Chechen rebels blamed.

2000—Oct. 12: Small boat assisting in docking of U.S.S. *Cole* exploded while alongside it in Aden, Yemen; 17 U.S. sailors killed, 39 injured. Blamed on al-Qaeda.

2001—Sept. 11: 19 al-Qaeda terrorists hijacked 4 U.S. domestic flights, including 2 planes that crashed into World Trade Center towers and 1 into Pentagon. Total dead minus hijackers: 2,973; deadliest attack of terrorism yet on U.S. soil. **Sept.-Nov. 7:** Letters tainted with deadly anthrax bacteria mailed through U.S. postal system killed 5; unsolved.

2002—Mar. 27: Suicide bombing at hotel in Netanya, Israel, during Passover celebration; 27 killed. **Oct 12:** Resort in Bali, Indonesia, bombed; 202 dead. Jemaah Islamiah blamed. **Oct. 23:** Chechen guerrillas seized theater in Moscow, held 700+ hostages. Russian authorities gassed theater; most guerrillas and about 128 hostages were killed. **Nov. 28:** Suicide bombers destroyed Israeli-owned hotel near Mombasa, Kenya; 13 killed. At the same time, 2 missiles narrowly missed Israeli plane taking off from Mombasa airport; blamed on al-Qaeda. **Dec. 27:** Chechen rebels plowed truck bomb into pro-Russian gov. headquarters in Grozny, Chechnya; 80 killed, 152 injured.

2003—May 12: Truck bombing near gov. buildings in Znamenskoye, Chechnya; 59 killed. **May 12-13:** Al-Qaeda militants detonated car bombs at 3 residential complexes used by Westerners in Riyadh, Saudi Arabia; 34 killed. **May 16:** 5 explosions in Casablanca, Morocco; 44 killed, 100+ wounded. Blamed on al-Qaeda. **May 17-19:** Five suicide bombings in Israel; 17 killed. Hamas and al-Aqsa Martyrs brigade blamed. **Aug. 1:** Truck bomb hit military hospital in Mozdok, Russia, near Chechnya; 50 killed. Blamed on Chechen

rebels. **Aug. 5:** Car bomb hit Marriott hotel in Jakarta, Indonesia; 12 killed, 150 injured. Blamed on Jemaah Islamiah. **Aug. 19:** UN headquarters in Baghdad bombed by truck; 22 killed, including UN envoy to Iraq. **Aug. 25:** Two bombs exploded in taxis in Mumbai (Bombay), India; 46 killed, 100+ injured. Islamic militants suspected. **Oct. 27:** Suicide bombings at Intl. Red Cross and police stations; 40 killed. **Nov. 15:** Two synagogues in Istanbul, Turkey, bombed; 25 killed. **Nov. 20:** British consulate and offices of British bank HSBC bombed in Istanbul, Turkey; 27 killed incl. Br. cons. gen. Blamed on al-Qaeda. **Dec. 5:** Suicide bombing on commuter train in Yessentuki, Russia; 44 killed, 150 injured. Blamed on Chechen rebels. **Dec. 9:** Chechen suicide bombing outside National Hotel in Red Square, Moscow; 5 killed.

2004—Feb. 6: Bomb exploded on Moscow subway; 39 killed, 130 injured. Chechen rebels blamed. **Mar. 11:** Al-Qaeda cell bombed 4 commuter trains during morning rush hour in Madrid, Spain; 191 killed, about 1,200 injured. **Mar. 28-29:** Suicide bombings by Muslim militants hit Tashkent, Uzbekistan; 19 killed. **Apr. 21:** Car bomb destroyed Saudi govt. security building in Riyadh; 4 killed, 148 injured. **May 29:** Al-Qaeda militants stormed foreigner compound in Khobar, Saudi Arabia, taking hostages; 22 killed. **July 30:** U.S. and Israeli embassies in Tashkent, Uzbekistan, bombed simultaneously; 2 killed. **Aug. 24:** Two Russian passenger planes crashed nearly simultaneously in diff. parts of Russia; 90 killed. Blamed on Chechen rebels. **Sept. 1:** Militants seized school in Beslan, in northern Ossetia, Russia; held 1,000+ hostage for 3 days before Russian troops stormed school. About 330 killed, incl. 27 hostage-takers. Blamed on Chechen militants. **Sept. 9:** Australian embassy in Jakarta, Indonesia, bombed; 9 killed. Blamed on Jemaah Islamiah.

2005—July 7: Four bombs exploded on 3 separate subways and a bus in central London, UK; 52 killed, incl. bombers, about 700 injured. **July 21:** Four bombs placed on 3 subways and a bus in London malfunction. **July 23:** Three car bombs explode near resorts at Sharm el Sheik, Egypt; about 90 killed. **Aug. 17:** More than 400 small bombs exploded in cities and towns across Bangladesh, killing 2 and injuring at least 125. Jamaat ul-Mujahedeen Bangladesh claimed responsibility. **Aug. 19:** Three rockets fired from Jordan hit cities of Eilat, Israel, and Aqaba, Jordan. One missile flies over a docked U.S. naval ship; 1 death. **Nov. 9:** Three suicide bombings targeting hotels in Amman, Jordan; killed 56+, injured about 100. Al-Qaeda in Iraq took responsibility.

2006—Apr. 24: Three deadly bombs within 5 minutes struck Egyptian Red Sea resort town of Dahab; 18 killed, 85 injured. Nasser Khamis el-Mallah, supposed "mastermind and leader" of Tawhid wal Jihad (Unity and Holy War), the terrorist cell that launched the attack, reported killed during gun battle in May. **July 11:** Eight explosions struck 7 different trains and 1 station of public commuter rail system in Mumbai, India; 207 killed, 700+ wounded. Lashkar-e-Qahhar (Army of Terror) claimed responsibility.

2007—Feb. 19: Train traveling between New Delhi and border with Pakistan caught fire, 68 killed; Indian ministers blamed Muslim militants for trying to disrupt peace talks between India and Pakistan. **June 30:** In apparent attempt at suicide attack, two men crashed their SUV into the main terminal of Scotland's Glasgow Airport; both also allegedly planted bombs on two cars parked in central London before attacking airport; driver later died of burns sustained in attack.

Homeland Security Advisories Timeline

Source: U.S. Dept of Homeland Security

Date	Event
Mar. 12, 2002	Homeland Security Advisory System established, with national threat level at Elevated, New York City at High.
Sept. 10-24, 2002	National threat level raised to High around the anniversary of Sept. 11.
Feb. 7-27, 2003	National threat level raised to High based on threats of attacks during the Hajj pilgrimage in Mecca.
Mar. 17-Apr. 16, 2003	National threat level raised to High during beginning of the Iraq War.
May 20-30, 2003	National threat level raised to High following terrorist bombings in Saudi Arabia and Morocco and as a precaution for Memorial Day.
Dec. 21, 2003-Jan. 9, 2004	National threat level raised to High based on threats specific to the holiday season.
Aug. 1-Nov. 10, 2004	Threat level raised to High for financial services sectors in New York City, northern New Jersey, and Washington, DC, based on gathered intelligence.
July 7-Aug. 12, 2005	Threat level raised to High for mass transit following London railway bombings.
Aug. 10-13, 2006	Threat level raised from Elevated to Severe for flights originating in UK bound for U.S. following arrest by British authorities of 21 individuals allegedly involved in plot to detonate liquid explosives on board U.S.-bound commercial aircraft. Threat level raised to High for all other commercial flights destined for or operating within U.S.
Aug. 13, 2006-present (as of Sept. 2007)	National threat level remains at Elevated; New York City threat level remains at High; threat level for all domestic and international flights at High.

MILITARY AFFAIRS

Chief Commanding Officers of the U.S. Military

Chairman, Joint Chiefs of Staff: Adm. Michael G. Mullen (USN)
Vice Chairman: Gen. James E. "Hoss" Cartwright (USMC)

The **Joint Chiefs of Staff** consists of the Chairman and Vice Chairman of the Joint Chiefs of Staff; the Chief of Staff, U.S. Army; the Chief of Naval Operations; the Chief of Staff, U.S. Air Force; and the Commandant of the Marine Corps. Date of rank is date when the individual achieved his or her current rank. While serving in any of these positions, or as Commander of a unified or specified combatant command, basic pay is $17,972.10 per month.

Army

Chief of Staff	Date of rank
Casey Jr., George W.	Apr. 10, 2007
Other Generals	
Bell, Burwell B.	Dec. 3, 2002
Campbell, Charles C.	Jan. 9, 2007
Cody, Richard	June 28, 2004
Craddock, Bantz John	Jan. 1, 2005
Griffin, Benjamin S.	Jan. 1, 2005
McKiernan, David.	Dec. 14, 2005
McNeill, Dan K.	July 1, 2004
Petraeus, David H.	Feb. 10, 2007
Wallace, William S.	Oct. 13, 2005
Ward, William E.	May 3, 2006

Air Force

Chief of Staff	Date of rank
Moseley, T. Michael	Oct. 1, 2003
Other Generals	
Carlson, Bruce	Sept. 1, 2005
Chilton, Kevin P.	June 26, 2006
Corley, John D.W.	Nov. 1, 2005
Hester, Paul V.	Aug. 1, 2004
Kehler, C. Robert	Oct. 12, 2007
Keys, Ronald E.	May 27, 2005
Looney III, William R.	Aug. 1, 2005
Renuart Jr., Victor E. "Gene"	Mar. 19, 2007
Schwartz, Norton	Oct. 1, 2005

Navy

Chief of Naval Operations	Date of rank
Roughead, Gary (surface warfare)	Sept. 29, 2007
Other Admirals	
Donald, Kirkland H. (submariner)	Jan. 1, 2005
Fallon, William J. (aviator)	Nov. 1, 2000
Fitzgerald, Mark P. (aviator)[1]	—
Greenert, Jonathan W. (submariner)	Sept. 29, 2007
Keating, Timothy J. (aviator)	Jan. 1, 2005
Olson, Eric T. (special operations)	July 9, 2007
Stavridis, James G. (surface warfare)	Oct. 19, 2006
Ulrich III, Henry G. (surface warfare)	July 22, 2005
Walsh, Patrick M. (aviator)	April, 2007
Willard, Robert F. (aviator)	Mar. 18, 2005

Marine Corps

Commandant of the Marine Corps (CMC)	Date of rank
Conway, James T.	Nov. 13, 2006
Other Generals	
Cartwright, James E.	July 9, 2004
Magnus, Robert	Sept. 8, 2005
Mattis, James N.[1]	—

Coast Guard

Commandant, with rank of Admiral	Date of rank
Allen, Thad W.	May 30, 2006
Vice Commandant, with rank of Vice Admiral	
Crea, Vivian S.	July 16, 2004

(1) As of Oct. 14, 2007, officer's promotion has been approved by the Senate but not yet bestowed.

Unified Combatant Commands Commanders-in-Chief

U.S. European Command, Stuttgart-Vaihingen, Germany
Gen. Bantz J. Craddock (U.S. Army)
U.S. Pacific Command, Honolulu, Hawaii
Adm. Timothy J. Keating (USN)
U.S. Joint Forces Command, Norfolk, Virginia
Gen. James N. Mattis (USMC)
U.S. Special Operations Command, MacDill AFB, Florida
Adm. Eric T. Olson (USN)
U.S. Transportation Command, Scott AFB, Illinois
Gen. Norton A. Schwartz (USAF)

U.S. Central Command, MacDill AFB, Florida
Adm. William J. Fallon (USN)
U.S. Southern Command, Miami, Florida
Admiral James G. Stavridis (USN)
U.S. Northern Command, Peterson AFB, Colorado
Gen. Victor E. "Gene" Renuart Jr. (USAF)
U.S. Strategic Command, Offutt AFB, Nebraska
Gen. Kevin P. Chilton (USAF)
U.S. Africa Command, Stuttgart, Germany
Gen. William "Kip" Ward (U.S. Army)

North Atlantic Treaty Organization (NATO) International Commands

NATO Headquarters: Chairman, NATO Military Committee—Gen. Raymond Henault (Canadian Forces)
Strategic Commands:
Allied Command Operations (ACO)—Gen. Bantz John Craddock (U.S. Army), Supreme Allied Commander, Europe
ACO Subordinate Commands:
Joint Force Command Brunssum (JFC Brunssum)—Gen. Egon Ramms (German Army), Commander
Joint Force Command Naples (JFC Naples)—Adm. H.G. Ulrich III (USN), Commander
Joint Headquarters Lisbon (JHQ Lisbon)—Vice Adm. James A. Winnefeld Jr. (USN), Commander
Allied Command Transformation (ACT)—Gen. James N. Mattis (USMC), Supreme Allied Commander Transformation

Chairmen of the Joint Chiefs of Staff, 1949-2007

Gen. of the Army Omar N. Bradley, USA	8/16/49–8/15/53	Gen. John W. Vessey Jr., USA	6/18/82–9/30/85
Adm. Arthur W. Radford, USN	8/15/53–8/15/57	Gen. William J. Crowe Jr., USN	10/1/85–9/30/89
Gen. Nathan F. Twining, USAF	8/15/57–9/30/60	Gen. Colin L. Powell, USA	10/1/89–9/30/93
Gen. Lyman L. Lemnitzer, USA	10/1/60–9/30/62	Gen. John M. Shalikashvili, USA	10/25/93–9/30/97
Gen. Maxwell D. Taylor, USA	10/1/62–7/1/64	Gen. Henry H. Shelton, USA	9/30/97–9/30/01
Gen. Earle G. Wheeler, USA	7/3/64–7/2/70	Gen. Richard B. Myers, USAF	10/1/01–9/30/05
Adm. Thomas H. Moorer, USN	7/2/70–7/1/74	Gen. Peter Pace, USMC	9/30/05–9/30/07
Gen. George S. Brown, USAF	7/1/74–6/20/78	Adm. Michael G. Mullen, USN	10/1/07–
Gen. David C. Jones, USAF	6/21/78–6/18/82		

Directors of the Central Intelligence Agency

In 1942, Pres. Franklin D. Roosevelt established the Office of Strategic Services (OSS); it was disbanded in 1945. In 1946, Pres. Harry Truman established the Central Intelligence Group (CIG) to operate under the National Security Authority (NIA). A 1947 law replaced the NIA with the National Security Council and the CIG with the Central Intelligence Agency.

Director	Served	Appointed by President	Director	Served	Appointed by President
Adm. Sidney W. Souers	1946	Truman	George H. W. Bush	1976-1977	Ford
Gen. Hoyt S. Vandenberg	1946-1947	Truman	Adm. Stansfield Turner	1977-1981	Carter
Adm. Roscoe H. Hillenkoetter	1947-1950	Truman	William J. Casey	1981-1987	Reagan
Gen. Walter Bedell Smith	1950-1953	Truman	William H. Webster	1987-1991	Reagan
Allen W. Dulles	1953-1961	Eisenhower	Robert M. Gates	1991-1993	Bush
John A. McCone	1961-1965	Kennedy	R. James Woolsey	1993-1995	Clinton
Adm. William F. Raborn Jr.	1965-1966	Johnson	John M. Deutch	1995-1997	Clinton
Richard Helms	1966-1973	Johnson	George J. Tenet	1997-2004	Clinton
James R. Schlesinger	1973	Nixon	Porter Goss	2004-2006	Bush
William E. Colby	1973-1976	Nixon	Gen. Michael V. Hayden	2006-	Bush

Military Units, U.S. Army and Air Force

ARMY UNITS. Squad: In infantry usually 8-16 enlisted personnel under a staff sergeant. **Platoon:** In infantry 2-4 squads under a lieutenant. **Company:** Headquarters section and 3-5 platoons under a captain. (Company-size unit in the artillery is a battery; in the cavalry, a troop.) **Battalion:** Hdqts. and 4-6 companies under a lieutenant colonel. (Battalion-size unit in the cavalry is a squadron.) **Brigade:** Hdqts. and 2-5 battalions under a colonel. (Brigade-size unit in the cavalry and rangers is a regiment; in the special forces, a group.) **Division:** Hdqts. and 3 brigades with artillery, combat support, and combat service support units under a major general. **Corps:** Two or more divisions with corps troops under a lieutenant general. **Army:** Hdqts. and 2 or more corps with operational and support responsibilities under a general.

AIR FORCE UNITS. Flight: Numerically designated flights are the lowest level unit in the Air Force. They are used primarily where there is a need for small mission elements to be incorporated into an organized unit. **Squadron:** The basic unit. Designates specific operational or support capability like mission units in operational commands. **Group:** A flexible unit composed of 2 or more squadrons whose functions may be operational, support, or administrative in nature. **Wing:** A primary group with supporting groups on a distinct mission with significant scope such as combat, flying training, or airlift. **Numbered Air Forces:** Normally an operationally oriented agency, the numbered air force is designed for the control of subordinate units with the same mission and/or geographical location. **Major Command:** A major subdivision of the Air Force with full staff that manages a major segment of the USAF mission. Major Command is composed of 3 or more numbered air forces.

Active Duty U.S. Military Personnel Strengths, Worldwide, 2007

Source: U.S. Dept. of Defense

(as of June 30, 2007)

TOTAL WORLDWIDE[1]	**1,372,905**	**EUROPE**		**EAST ASIA & PACIFIC**	
		Belgium	1,367	Australia	711
U.S. TERRITORIES		Bosnia and Herzegovina	207	Japan	33,068
& SPEC. LOCATIONS		Germany	58,894	Korea, South	27,114
U.S., 48 contiguous states	876,378	Greece	354	Philippines	111
Alaska	19,957	Italy	10,216	Singapore	116
Hawaii	35,874	Netherlands	562	Thailand	114
Guam	2,828	Portugal	865	Afloat	12,391
Puerto Rico	144	Serbia (incl. Kosovo)	1,395	**Regional Total[2]**	**73,799**
Transients	52,924	Spain	1,308	**NORTH AFRICA, NEAR EAST, &**	
Afloat	94,512	Turkey	1,668	**SOUTH ASIA***	
Regional Total[2]	**1,082,627**	United Kingdom	10,152	Afghanistan[3]	24,800
		Afloat	1,565	Bahrain	1,389
OTHER WESTERN HEMISPHERE		**Regional Total[2]**	**89,183**	Diego Garcia	240
Canada	143			Egypt	288
Cuba (Guantánamo)	903	**SUB-SAHARAN AFRICA**		Iraq[3]	202,100
Honduras	412	Djibouti	2,038	Qatar	512
Afloat	14	**Regional Total[2]**	**2,367**	Saudi Arabia	274
Regional Total[2]	**2,058**	**FORMER SOVIET UNION Total**	**155**	Afloat	362
				Regional Total[2,4]	**3,425**

*Special Forces personnel involved in Operation Enduring Freedom in Afghanistan not reported by Dept. of Defense. (1) Total worldwide also includes undistributed personnel. (2) Most countries and areas with fewer than 100 assigned U.S. military members not listed; regional totals include personnel stationed in those countries and areas not shown. (3) Rounded strengths for OEF/OIF deployment; includes troops in surrounding areas and deployed Reserve/National Guard. (4) Excludes troops deployed for OEF/OIF.

U.S. Army Personnel on Active Duty[1]

Source: Dept. of the Army, U.S. Dept. of Defense

(as of mid-year, except where noted)

Date	Total strength[2]	Commissioned officers			Warrant officers		Enlisted personnel		
		Total	Male	Female[3]	Male[4]	Female	Total	Male	Female
1940	267,767	17,563	16,624	939	763	—	249,441	249,441	—
1942	3,074,184	203,137	190,662	12,475	3,285	—	2,867,762	2,867,762	—
1943	6,993,102	557,657	521,435	36,222	21,919	—	6,413,526	6,358,200	55,325
1944	7,992,868	740,077	692,351	47,726	36,893	10	7,215,888	7,144,601	71,287
1945	8,266,373	835,403	772,511	62,892	56,216	44	7,374,710	7,283,930	90,780
1946	1,889,690	257,300	240,658	16,642	9,826	18	1,622,546	1,605,847	16,699
1950	591,487	67,784	63,375	4,409	4,760	22	518,921	512,370	6,551
1955	1,107,606	111,347	106,196	5,151	10,552	48	985,659	977,943	7,716
1960	871,348	91,056	86,832	4,224	10,141	39	770,112	761,833	8,279
1965	967,049	101,812	98,029	3,783	10,285	23	854,929	846,409	8,520
1970	1,319,735	143,704	138,469	5,235	23,005	13	1,153,013	1,141,537	11,476
1975	781,316	89,756	85,184	4,572	13,214	22	678,324	640,621	37,703
1980 (Sept. 30)	772,661	85,339	77,843	7,496	13,265	113	673,944	612,593	61,351
1985 (Sept. 30)	776,244	94,103	83,563	10,540	15,296	288	666,557	598,639	67,918
1990 (Mar. 31)	746,220	91,330	79,520	11,810	15,177	470	639,713	567,015	72,698
1995	521,036	72,646	62,250	10,396	12,053	599	435,807	377,832	57,975
2000	471,633	66,344	56,391	9,953	10,608	781	393,900	333,947	59,953
2001	478,918	64,809	54,570	10,239	10,575	795	398,983	336,264	62,719
2002	485,536	66,446	55,715	10,731	10,900	812	404,363	341,794	62,569
2003 (Sept. 30)	499,301	68,198	56,980	11,218	11,273	854	414,769	351,921	62,848
2004 (Sept. 30)	499,543	68,640	57,245	11,395	11,414	914	414,438	354,043	60,395
2005 (Sept. 30)	492,728	69,174	57,675	11,499	11,506	976	406,923	346,194	57,354
2006 (Sept. 30)	505,402	68,742	57,318	11,424	11,931	1,035	419,353	361,528	57,825
2007	510,024	70,893[5]	NA	NA	13,684[5]	NA	422,260[5]	NA	NA

NA = not available. (1) Represents strength of the active Army, including Philippine Scouts (1940-46), retired Regular Army personnel on extended active duty, and National Guard and Reserve personnel on extended active duty; excludes U.S. Military Academy cadets, contract surgeons, and National Guard and Reserve personnel not on extended active duty. (2) Includes categories not listed, e.g. West Point Cadets. Data for 1940 to 1946 include personnel in the Army Air Forces and its predecessors (Air Service and Air Corps). (3) Includes Army Nurse Corps for all years, Women's Army Corps (1942-78), Medical Specialists Corps (1949 and subsequent years). (4) Act of Congress approved Apr. 27, 1926, directed the appointment as warrant officers of field clerks still in active service. Includes flight officers as follows: 1943, 5,700; 1944, 13,615; 1945, 31,117; 1946, 2,580. (5) Total male and female.

U.S. Navy Personnel on Active Duty

Source: U.S. Dept. of Defense (as of mid-year, except where noted)

Date	Officers	Nurses	Enlisted	Officer Candidates	Total[1]	Date	Officers	Nurses	Enlisted	Officer Candidates	Total[1]
1940	13,162	442	144,824	2,569	160,997	1997	57,341	—	340,616	—	397,957
1945	320,293	11,086	2,988,207	61,231	3,380,817	1998 (Sept.)	55,007	—	326,196	—	381,203
1950	42,687	1,964	331,860	5,037	381,538	1999	55,726	—	322,372	—	378,098
1960	67,456	2,103	544,040	4,385	617,984	2000 (Oct.)	53,698	—	320,212	—	373,910
1970	78,488	2,273	605,899	6,000	692,660	2001 (Aug.)	54,177	—	317,100	—	375,618
1980[2]	63,100	—	464,100	—	527,200	2002	55,506	—	324,712	—	384,576
1990 (Sept.)	74,429	—	530,133	—	604,562	2003	55,852	—	324,927	—	380,779
1993 (Mar.)	66,787	—	445,409	—	512,196	2004	55,592	—	319,929	—	375,521
1994 (Apr.)	64,430	—	418,378	—	482,808	2005	54,039	—	305,368	—	363,858
1995 (May)	61,075	—	402,626	—	463,701	2006	53,209	—	295,773	—	353,496
1996	60,013	—	376,595	—	436,608	2007	52,405	—	283,873	—	340,744

(1) May include categories not shown, e.g. midshipmen. (2) Starting in 1980, "Nurses" are included with "Officers," and "Officer Candidates" are included with "Enlisted."

U.S. Air Force Personnel on Active Duty

Source: U.S. Dept. of Defense (as of mid-year)

Year[1]	Strength	Year[1]	Strength	Year[1]	Strength	Year[1]	Strength	Year[1]	Strength	Year[1]	Strength
1918	195,023	1943	2,197,114	1980	557,969	1993	444,351	1998	363,479	2003	373,116
1920	9,050	1944	2,372,292	1986	608,200	1994	426,327	1999	357,929	2004	379,887
1930	13,531	1945	2,282,259	1990	535,233	1995	400,051	2000	357,777	2005	358,705
1940	51,165	1950	411,277	1991	510,432	1996	389,400	2001	351,935	2006	352,620
1941	152,125	1960	814,213	1992	470,315	1997	378,681	2002	369,721	2007	340,596
1942	764,415	1970	791,078								

(1) Prior to 1947, data are for U.S. Army Air Corps and Air Service of the Signal Corps.

U.S. Marine Corps Personnel on Active Duty

Source: U.S. Dept. of Defense (as of mid-year)

Year	Officers	Enlisted	Total	Year	Officers	Enlisted	Total	Year	Officers	Enlisted	Total
1940	1,800	26,545	28,345	1992	19,132	165,397	184,529	2000	17,897	154,744	172,641
1945	37,067	437,613	474,680	1993	18,878	161,205	180,083	2001	18,072	152,559	170,631
1950	7,254	67,025	74,279	1994	18,430	159,949	178,379	2002	18,472	154,913	173,385
1960	16,203	154,418	170,621	1995	18,017	153,929	171,946	2003	18,908	160,814	179,722
1970	24,941	234,796	259,737	1996	18,146	154,141	172,287	2004	19,052	157,150	176,202
1980	18,198	170,271	188,469	1997	18,089	154,240	172,329	2005	19,118	159,113	178,231
1990	19,958	176,694	196,652	1998	17,984	154,648	172,632	2006	19,218	159,705	178,923
1991	19,753	174,287	194,040	1999	17,892	155,250	173,142	2007	19,456	162,085	181,541

U.S. Coast Guard Personnel on Active Duty

Source: U.S. Dept. of Defense (as of mid-year)

Year	Total	Officers	Cadets	Enlisted	Year	Total	Officers	Cadets	Enlisted	Year	Total	Officers	Cadets	Enlisted
1970	37,689	5,512	653	31,524	1995	36,731	7,489	841	28,401	2002	37,166	7,267	694	29,205
1980	39,381	6,463	877	32,041	1996	35,229	7,270	830	27,129	2003	39,000	7,532	983	30,859
1985	38,595	6,775	733	31,087	1997	34,717	7,079	868	26,770	2004	40,151	7,835	1,030	31,286
1990	37,308	6,475	820	29,860	1998	34,890	7,140	805	26,945	2005	40,814	7,908	1,006	31,900
1992	39,185	7,348	919	30,918	1999	35,266	7,135	880	27,251	2006	40,639	8,032	1,004	32,001
1993	38,832	7,724	691	30,417	2000	35,712	7,154	863	27,695	2007	41,265	8,231	720	32,314
1994	37,284	7,401	881	29,002	2001	35,328	7,112	631	27,585					

Women in the U.S. Armed Forces

Source: U.S. Dept. of Defense; U.S. Census Bureau; Women In Military Service For America Memorial Foundation

Women in the Army, Navy, Air Force, Marines, and Coast Guard are fully integrated with male personnel. All enlisted jobs were open to women when the draft ended June 30, 1973. Admission to service academies began in 1976. Under rules instituted in 1993, women were allowed to fly combat aircraft and serve aboard warships. By the mid-1990s, 80% of all jobs and more than 90% of all career fields had been opened to women. Women remained restricted from service in ground combat units.

Women Active Duty Troops in 2006

Service	% Women
Army	14.0
Navy	14.3
Marines	6.1
Air Force	19.7
Coast Guard	11.6

Note: (As of mid-year)

Women on Active Duty, All Services: 1973-2006

Year	% Women	Year	% Women
1973	2.5	1993	11.6
1975	4.6	1997	13.6
1981	8.9	2000	14.4
1987	10.2	2005	14.6
		2006	14.4

African American Service in U.S. Wars

Source: U.S. Dept. of Defense; U.S. Census Bureau

American Revolution. About 5,000 served in the Continental Army, mostly in integrated units, some in all-black regiments.

Civil War. Some 180,000 served in 163 units of the Union Army's U.S. Colored Troops, 200,000 worked in service units—10% of the Union Army in all; about 37,000 died, 31,000 wounded.

World War I. 350,000-400,000 served in the armed forces, 100,000 in France. Some 40,000 fought.

World War II. Some 1 mil served in the armed forces—8% of all troops—mostly in Army service units; all-black fighter and bomber AAF units and infantry divisions gave distinguished service.

Korean War. More than 600,000 served in the military; 3,075 lost their lives in combat. By 1954, armed forces were completely desegregated.

Vietnam War. 274,937 served in the armed forces (1965-74)—9.8% of all troops; 7,241 were killed in combat.

Persian Gulf War. About 104,000 served in the Kuwaiti theater—20% of all U.S. troops. 66 died in combat.

Iraq War. 350 military deaths and 2,274 wounded (as of Sept. 1, 2007).

Monthly Military Pay Scale[1]

Source: U.S. Dept. of Defense

(effective Apr. 1, 2007; Salaries rounded to nearest dollar.)

Grade	<2	2	3	4	6	8	10	12	14	16	18	20	22	24	26
Commissioned officers															
O-10...	NA	NA	NA	NA	NA	NA	NA	NA	NA	NA	NA	13,659	13,726	14,011	14,509
O-9....	NA	NA	NA	NA	NA	NA	NA	NA	NA	NA	NA	11,947	12,119	12,367	12,801
O-8....	8,453	8,730	8,914	8,965	9,194	9,577	9,666	10,030	10,134	10,448	10,901	11,319	11,598	11,598	11,598
O-7....	7,024	7,350	7,501	7,621	7,838	8,053	8,301	8,549	8,797	9,577	10,236	10,236	10,236	10,236	10,288
O-6....	5,206	5,719	6,095	6,095	6,118	6,380	6,415	6,415	6,779	7,424	7,802	8,180	8,395	8,613	9,036
O-5....	4,340	4,889	5,228	5,291	5,502	5,629	5,906	6,110	6,373	6,776	6,968	7,158	7,373	7,373	7,373
O-4....	3,745	4,335	4,624	4,688	4,957	5,245	5,603	5,882	6,076	6,188	6,252	6,252	6,252	6,252	6,252
O-3....	3,292	3,732	4,028	4,392	4,602	4,833	4,983	5,228	5,356	5,356	5,356	5,356	5,356	5,356	5,356
O-2....	2,844	3,240	3,731	3,857	3,937	3,937	3,937	3,937	3,937	3,937	3,937	3,937	3,937	3,937	3,937
O-1....	2,469	2,570	3,107	3,107	3,107	3,107	3,107	3,107	3,107	3,107	3,107	3,107	3,107	3,107	3,107
Commissioned officers with over 4 years' active duty service as enlisted member or warrant officer															
O-3E...	NA	NA	NA	4,392	4,602	4,833	4,983	5,228	5,435	5,554	5,716	5,716	5,716	5,716	5,716
O-2E...	NA	NA	NA	3,857	3,937	4,062	4,274	4,437	4,559	4,559	4,559	4,559	4,559	4,559	4,559
O-1E...	NA	NA	NA	3,107	3,318	3,440	3,566	3,689	3,857	3,857	3,857	3,857	3,857	3,857	3,857
Warrant officers															
W-5...	NA	NA	NA	NA	NA	NA	NA	NA	NA	NA	NA	6,050	6,356	6,585	6,838
W-4....	3,402	3,660	3,765	3,869	4,046	4,222	4,401	4,669	4,904	5,128	5,311	5,490	5,752	5,968	6,214
W-3....	3,107	3,236	3,369	3,413	3,552	3,826	4,111	4,245	4,400	4,560	4,848	5,042	5,159	5,282	5,450
W-2....	2,749	3,009	3,089	3,145	3,323	3,600	3,737	3,872	4,038	4,167	4,284	4,424	4,516	4,589	4,589
W-1....	2,413	2,672	2,743	2,891	3,065	3,322	3,442	3,610	3,776	3,905	4,025	4,170	4,170	4,170	4,170
Enlisted members															
E-9....	NA	NA	NA	NA	NA	NA	4,111	4,204	4,321	4,460	4,598	4,822	5,010	5,209	5,513
E-8....	NA	NA	NA	NA	NA	3,365	3,514	3,606	3,716	3,836	4,052	4,161	4,347	4,451	4,705
E-7....	2,339	2,553	2,651	2,781	2,882	3,055	3,153	3,327	3,471	3,570	3,674	3,716	3,852	3,925	4,204
E-6....	2,023	2,226	2,324	2,420	2,519	2,744	2,831	3,000	3,052	3,090	3,134	3,134	3,134	3,134	3,134
E-5....	1,854	1,978	2,073	2,171	2,324	2,484	2,614	2,630	2,630	2,630	2,630	2,630	2,630	2,630	2,630
E-4....	1,700	1,787	1,883	1,979	2,063	2,063	2,063	2,063	2,063	2,063	2,063	2,063	2,063	2,063	2,063
E-3....	1,534	1,631	1,729	1,729	1,729	1,729	1,729	1,729	1,729	1,729	1,729	1,729	1,729	1,729	1,729
E-2....	1,459	1,459	1,459	1,459	1,459	1,459	1,459	1,459	1,459	1,459	1,459	1,459	1,459	1,459	1,459
E-1[3]....	1,301	1,301	1,301	1,301	1,301	1,301	1,301	1,301	1,301	1,301	1,301	1,301	1,301	1,301	1,301

NA = not applicable. **Notes:** In 2007, the military pay scale was expanded to 40 years with the following raises: **Over 30 years**—O-10: $15,234.00; O-9: $13,441.50; O-8: $11,888.40; O-7: 10,493.70; O-6: $9,216.30; W-5: $7,180.20; W-4: $6,337.80; E-9: $5,788.50; E-8: $4,799.10. **Over 34 years**—O-10: $15,995.70; O-9: $14,113.50; O-8: $12,185.70; W-5: $7,539.30; E-9: $6,078.00. **Over 38 years**—O-10: $16,795.50; O-9: $14,819.10; W-5: $7,916.40; E-9: $6,381.90. (1) Basic pay is limited for O-7 to O-10 to $14,000.10. Basic pay for O-6 and below is limited to $11,349.90. (2) Basic Pay for the Master Chief Petty Officer of the Navy, Chief Master Sergeant of the AF, Sergeant Major of the Army or Marine Corps or Senior Enlisted Advisor of the JCS is $6,642.60. (3) E-1 with 4 months or more of active duty. Basic pay for an E-1 with less than 4 months of active duty is $1,203.90.

Outlays for Individual Payments to Veterans

Source: White House Office of Management and Budget

(in millions of dollars)

Year	Total	Compensation	Pensions	Hospital, medical	Education	Insurance & burial	Year	Total	Compensation	Pensions	Hospital, medical	Education	Insurance & burial
1940..	$578	$244	$185	$69	—	$80	2001..	$45,435	$18,579	$2,760	$20,966	$1,783	$1,347
1950..	8,827	1,533	476	764	$2,739	3,315	2002..	50,969	22,418	3,166	22,384	1,681	1,320
1960..	5,355	2,049	1,263	931	392	720	2003..	55,792	24,696	3,229	24,487	2,049	1,331
1970..	8,808	2,980	2,255	1,723	1,002	848	2004..	55,021	26,297	3,334	21,590	2,408	1,392
1980..	20,927	7,446	3,585	6,290	2,418	1,188	2005..	62,206	30,877	3,663	23,073	3,224	1,369
1990..	28,545	10,735	3,594	12,021	795	1,400	2006..	63,658	30,991	3,547	24,445	3,325	1,350
1995..	36,822	14,842	3,024	16,196	1,386	1,374	2007*..	66,970	32,267	3,382	26,113	3,794	1,414
2000..	46,086	20,775	2,969	19,343	1,636	1,363	2008*..	76,059	37,079	3,788	29,975	3,819	1,398

Note: Compensation is service-connected, pension is not. * Estimate.

U.S. Veteran Population, 2007

Source: U.S. Dept. of Veterans Affairs

(projection of population, as of Sept. 30, 2007)

TOTAL VETERANS IN CIVILIAN LIFE[1]	**23,531,672**
Total wartime veterans[2]	**17,484,129**
Total Gulf War[3]	4,877,396
Gulf War with no prior wartime service	4,530,766
Gulf War with service in Vietnam era	340,517
Gulf War, with service in Vietnam and Korea	5,359
Gulf War with service in Vietnam, Korea, and WWII	754
Total Vietnam era[3]	7,849,464
Vietnam era with no prior wartime service	7,202,602
Vietnam era with service in Korean conflict	210,451
Vietnam era with service in Korea and WWII	89,781

Total Korean conflict[3]	2,912,473
Korean conflict with no prior wartime service	2,399,558
Korean conflict with service in WWII	206,570
Total World War II[3]	2,794,876
WWII only	2,497,771
Total peacetime veterans[4]	**6,047,543**
Service between Vietnam era and Gulf War only	3,437,336
Service between Korean conflict and Vietnam era only	2,466,794
Pre-Korean conflict without service in WWII	143,413

Note: Figures are for U.S. veterans worldwide. (1) Includes those who served on active duty in Army, Navy, Air Force, Marines, Coast Guard, uniformed Public Health Service and NOAA, and reservists called to federal active duty. Excludes those dishonorably discharged, those whose only active duty was training, and those currently on active duty. (2) Veterans serving in more than one period are counted only once in total. (3) Total includes veterans who also served in previous periods. (4) Veterans with both wartime and peacetime service are counted only as "wartime veterans."

Nations with Largest Armed Forces, by Active-Duty Troop Strength[1]

Source: *The Military Balance. 2007* (International Institute for Strategic Studies, published by Routledge Journals, Taylor & Francis, UK)

	Active troops	Reserve troops	Defense expend. ($ bil)	Tanks (MBT) (army only)	Cruisers/ Frigates/ Destroyers	Sub-marines	FGA (air force only)	Fighters
	(thousands)							
1. China	2,255	800	122.0	7,580+	48F/28D	58	1,242	1,179
2. United States	1,507	974	535.0	7,620+	22C/31F/50D*	68	2,564 tactical	
3. India	1,316	1,155	22.3[2]	3,978	24F/8D*	16	674	137
4. N. Korea	1,106	4,700	2.3[2]	3,500+	3F	63	211	299
5. Russia	1,027	20,000	59.1[4]	22,831+	6C/19F/19D*	53	793	765
6. S. Korea	687	4,500	23.7[2]	2,330	9F/6D	20	295	210
7. Pakistan	619	—	4.0[4]	2,461+	6F	8	104	209
8. Iran	545	350	6.6[2]	1,613+	3F	3	168	118
9. Turkey	515	379	11.7[4]	4,205	26F	12	358	87
10. Egypt	469	479	4.2	3,855	10F/1D	4	235	165
11. Vietnam	455	5,000	3.4[2]	1,315	6F	2	64	140
12. Myanmar	375	—	6.2[3]	150	—	—	22	58
13. Syria	308	354	1.4[2]	4,950	2F	—	290	178
14. Thailand	307	200	2.1[2]	333	10F*	—	87 FGA/FTR	
15. Indonesia	302	400	10.3	—	12F	2	48	24
16. Taiwan	290	1,657	7.7[2]	926+	22F/11D	4	150	282
17. Brazil	288	1,340	16.4[2]	219	10F*	5	180	59
18. France	255	22	53.1[4]	926	20F/13D*	10	110	97
19. Germany	246	162	38.0[4]	2,035	15F	13	211	99
20. Japan	240	42	41.1[2]	980	9F/44D	16	—	260
21. Mexico	238	40	3.2[2]	—	6F/1D	—	8	10
22. Saudi Arabia	225	—	25.4[3]	910	7F	—	85	123
23. Colombia	209	62	5.3	—	—	4	24	—
24. Eritrea	202	120	65 mil[3]	150	—	—	—	13
25. Morocco	201	150	2.2	540	3F	—	—	66
26. Italy	191	57	31.3[4]	320	12F/5D*	7	154	48
27. United Kingdom	191	199	51.7[4]	386	17F/9D*	15	135	100
28. Ukraine	188	1,000	6.0[4]	3,784	1F	1	129	215
29. Israel	168	408	9.8[4]	3,657	—	3	177+	199
30. Ethiopia	153	—	345 mil[2]	250+	—	—	15	31

— = not available. MBT = main battle tank. FGA = fighter, ground attack. *Denotes navies with aircraft carriers, as follows: United States 12, United Kingdom 3, France 2, Italy 2, India 1, Russia 1, Brazil 1, Thailand 1. (1) All figures are for Aug. 2006, except Defense Expenditure, which is for 2006, unless otherwise noted. Iraq's security forces were estimated to be about 227,000 at this time but were not a fully developed military force. (2) 2006 budget. (3) 2005 budget. (4) 2005 defense expenditure.

Budget for Global War on Terror Operations: Fiscal Years 2001-2007

Source: Congressional Research Service

(Estimates in billions of dollars)

	2001/02[2]	2002	2003	2004	2005	2006	2007	Total
Total: All Missions	$16.3	$17.5	$81.1	$94.1	$107.6	$121.5	$173.0	$610.5
Dept. of Defense	16.0	17.0	77.4	72.4	102.6	116.8	165.8	568.0
State Dept. & USAID	0.3	0.5	3.7	21.7	4.8	4.3	6.3	41.0
Veterans Affairs Medical	0.0	0.0	0.0	0.0	0.2	0.4	1.0	1.6
Op. Iraqi Freedom[1]	0.0	0.0	53.0	75.9	84.7	101.7	135.2	450.4
Dept. of Defense	0.0	0.0	50.0	56.4	82.5	98.2	130.6	417.7
State Dept. & USAID[4]	0.0	0.0	3.0	19.5	2.0	3.2	3.7	31.3
Veterans Affairs Medical	0.0	0.0	0.0	0.0	0.2	0.4	0.9	1.6
Op. Enduring Freedom[3]	9.3	11.5	14.7	14.5	20.8	18.9	36.7	126.7
Dept. of Defense	9.0	11.0	14.0	12.4	18.0	17.9	34.7	116.9
State Dept. & USAID[4]	0.3	0.5	0.7	2.2	2.8	1.1	2.1	9.7
Veterans Affairs Medical	0.0	0.0	0.0	0.0	0.0	0.0	0.1	0.1
Op. Noble Eagle[5]	7.0	6.0	8.0	3.7	2.1	0.8	0.5	28.1
Dept. of Defense Unallocated	0.0	0.0	5.5	0.0	0.0	0.0	0.0	5.5

(1) Began in the fall of 2002 with the build up of troops for the March 2003 invasion of Iraq and continues with counter-insurgency and stability operations. (2) FY01 & FY02 funds combined because most were obligated in FY02 after the 9/11 attacks at the end of FY01. (3) Covering Afghanistan and other ongoing Global War on Terror (GWOT) operations, ranging from the Philippines to Djibouti, that began immediately after the 9/11 attacks. (4) Foreign operations figures include monies for reconstruction, development, and humanitarian aid, embassy operations, counter narcotics, initial training of the Afghan and Iraqi army, foreign military sales credits, and Economic Support Funds. (5) Dept. of Defense funds that rebuilt the Pentagon, provides higher security at U.S. military bases, and other homeland security, including combat air patrol.

Leading Purchasers of U.S. Defense Articles and Services

Source: Congressional Research Service

(in current U.S. dollars)

Worldwide Deliveries[1]

	1998-2001				2002-05	
1. Saudi Arabia	$12.6 billion	6. Turkey	$2.0 billion	1. Egypt	$5.8 billion	6. South Korea $2.2 billion
2. Taiwan	6.0 billion	7. Finland	1.9 billion	2. Israel	4.4 billion	7. Japan 1.8 billion
3. Israel	3.7 billion	8. Japan	1.8 billion	3. Saudi Arabia	4.4 billion	8. U.K. 1.6 billion
4. South Korea	3.6 billion	9. U.K.	1.7 billion	4. Taiwan	4.1 billion	9. Australia 1.3 billion
5. Egypt	3.3 billion	10. Greece	1.6 billion	5. Greece	3.2 billion	10. Turkey 1.0 billion

(1) Total dollar value of all U.S. defense articles and services actually delivered to top 10 purchasers worldwide. Figures include government-to-government sales through the Foreign Military Sales (FMS) system (which accounts for the overwhelming majority of U.S. conventional arms deliveries) concluded in calendar years listed, as well as commercially licensed exports concluded in pertinent fiscal years.

U.S. Foreign Military Financing Worldwide, Select Countries

Source: Defense Security Cooperation Agency, U.S. Dept. of Defense

(in thousands of U.S. dollars)

	2006	2002-05		2006	2002-05
Near East & S. Asia	**$4,139,399**	**$18,036,315**	**Europe**	**$146,708**	**$940,912**
Afghanistan	—	1,051,877	Bulgaria	9,900	42,894
Bahrain	15,593	162,029	Czech Rep.	3,957	49,721
Egypt	1,287,000	5,173,480	Georgia	11,880	86,304
Israel	2,257,200	9,475,846	Poland	29,700	149,370
Jordan	207,900	1,213,137	Romania	12,870	56,262
Lebanon	29,663	—	Turkey	14,850	134,078
Morocco	12,375	33,768	**Africa**	**$15,840**	**$109,715**
Oman	13,860	150,690	**Americas**	**$110,051**	**$274,909**
Pakistan	297,000	672,060	Colombia	89,100	214,750
Yemen	8,415	47,230			
E. Asia & Pacific	**$37,867**	**$165,203**			
Phillipines	29,700	143,510	**World Total**	**$4,449,864**	**$19,527,054**

Note: Grants extended to foreign governments in a fiscal year to pay for military equipment and services. May be from DOD or, for specific countries, negotiated directly with U.S. commercial suppliers with DOD approval.

Defense Contracts, 2006

Source: U.S. Dept. of Defense

Listed are the 50 companies or organizations receiving the largest dollar volume of prime contract awards from the U.S. Dept. of Defense during fiscal year 2006.

Rank	Company	TOTAL $[1]	Rank	Company	TOTAL $[1]
1.	Lockheed Martin	$26,619,693,002	27.	Bechtel Group, Inc	$1,264,475,040
2.	Boeing	20,293,350,668	28.	Booz Allen Hamilton, Inc.	1,245,215,183
3.	Northrop Grumman	16,627,067,499	29.	B P Plc	1,199,103,801
4.	General Dynamics	10,526,161,839	30.	Exxon Mobil	1,176,354,936
5.	Raytheon	10,068,657,019	31.	N.V. Koninklijke Nederlandsche	1,150,489,304
6.	Halliburton	6,059,726,743	32.	Alliant Techsystems, Inc	1,128,381,646
7.	L-3 Communications Holding, Inc	5,197,490,394	33.	Alliance Contractor Team	1,023,465,614
8.	Bae Systems Plc	4,734,920,429	34.	Kuwait Petroleum	1,011,270,194
9.	United Technologies	4,452,662,076	35.	Oshkosh Truck Corp	940,574,560
10.	Science Applications International	3,210,604,531	36.	Rockwell Collins, Inc.	823,753,676
11.	Computer Sciences	2,884,071,378	37.	Stewart & Stevenson Services, Inc.	822,214,021
12.	Humana, Inc	2,641,741,534	38.	Textron, Inc.	814,684,786
13.	ITT	2,522,008,179	39.	National Agricultural Coop	761,174,397
14.	General Electric	2,327,705,161	40.	Engineered Support Systems	729,901,370
15.	Health Net, Inc	2,119,413,915	41.	Phillips & Jordan	704,977,880
16.	Triwest Healthcare Alliance	2,021,511,222	42.	Caci International	680,525,055
17.	Electronic Data Systems	2,008,031,150	43.	General Atomic Technologies	669,885,080
18.	Renco Group	1,944,145,312	44.	Mckesson	669,833,959
19.	Public Warehousing	1,837,917,361	45.	Valero Energy	661,171,541
20.	Honeywell International	1,678,516,318	46.	Thales	656,886,890
21.	Bell Boeing Joint Project	1,427,698,881	47.	Aerospace	653,969,926
22.	Gm Gdls Defense Group	1,415,879,270	48.	Mitre	652,276,956
23.	URS	1,369,202,782	49.	Massachusetts Institute Of Tech	639,531,158
24.	Amerisourcebergen	1,346,208,758	50.	Dell	636,343,593
25.	Harris	1,339,125,502	Other		136,282,792,432
26.	Fedex Corp	1,303,032,027	**Total**		**294,975,795,948**

(1) Totals include subsidiaries of each company.

Arms Transfer Agreements with the World, by Supplier, 1998-2005

Source: Congressional Research Service

(in millions of current U.S. dollars)

Supplier	1998	1999	2000	2001	2002	2003	2004	2005	1998-2005
United States	$9,457	$11,673	$11,158	$11,573	$13,129	$14,576	$12,820	$12,758	$97,144
Russia	2,200	4,600	6,500	5,500	5,600	4,400	5,400	7,400	41,600
France	6,300	1,700	4,600	4,200	1,200	2,000	2,100	7,900	30,000
United Kingdom	2,000	1,500	600	600	700	300	6,400	2,800	14,900
China	700	3,100	500	1,100	400	500	700	2,100	9,100
Germany	5,000	4,000	1,200	1,200	1,000	1,500	1,600	1,500	17,000
Italy	600	700	200	1,200	300	600	600	1,400	5,600
All Other European	1,900	5,800	4,100	3,000	4,400	2,000	6,700	5,900	33,800
All Others	1,300	2,100	2,500	2,600	2,200	1,600	2,600	2,400	17,300
TOTAL	**$29,457**	**$35,173**	**$31,358**	**$30,973**	**$28,929**	**$27,476**	**$38,920**	**$44,158**	**$266,444**

Note: All data are for the calendar year given, except for U.S. MAP (Military Assistance Program) and IMET (International Military Education and Training), excess defense articles, which are included for the particular fiscal year. All amounts given include the values of all categories of weapons and ammunition, military spare parts, military construction, excess defense articles, military assistance and training programs, and all associated services. Statistics for foreign countries are based upon estimated selling prices. All foreign data are rounded to the nearest $100 mil. The U.S. total in 2000 includes a $6.432 bil licensed commercial agreement with the United Arab Emirates for 80 F-16 aircraft.

Personal Salutes and Honors, U.S.

The U.S. **national salute**, 21 guns, is also the salute to a national flag. U.S. independence is commemorated by the salute to the Union—one gun for each state—fired at noon July 4, at all military posts provided with suitable artillery.

A 21-gun salute on arrival and departure, with 4 ruffles and flourishes, is rendered to the **president** of the United States, to a former president, and to a president-elect. The national anthem or "Hail to the Chief," as appropriate, is played for the president, and the national anthem for the others. A 21-gun salute on arrival and departure, with 4 ruffles and flourishes, also is rendered to the **sovereign or chief of state of a foreign country** or a member of a reigning royal family, and the national anthem of his or her country is played. The music is considered an inseparable part of the salute and immediately follows the ruffles and flourishes without pause. For the Honors March, generals receive the "General's March," admirals receive the "Flag Officer's March," and all others receive the 32-bar medley of "The Stars and Stripes Forever."

GRADE, TITLE, OR OFFICE	SALUTE (IN GUNS) Arriving	Leaving	Ruffles and flourishes	Music
Vice President of U.S.	19	—	4	Hail, Columbia
Speaker of the House	19	—	4	Honors March
U.S. or foreign ambassador in country to which accredited	19	—	4	Nat. anthem of official
Premier or prime minister	19	—	4	Nat. anthem of official
Secretary of Defense, Army, Navy, or Air Force	19	19	4	Honors March
Other cabinet members, Senate president pro tempore, governor, or chief justice of U.S.	19	—	4	Honors March
Chairman, Joint Chiefs of Staff	19	19	4	Honors March
Army chief of staff, chief of naval operations, Air Force chief of staff, Marine commandant	19	19	4	Honors March
General of the Army, general of the Air Force, fleet admiral	19	19	4	Honors March
Generals, admirals	17	17	4	Honors March
Assistant secretaries of Defense, Army, Navy, or Air Force	17	17	4	Honors March
Chair of a committee of Congress	17	—	4	Honors March

OTHER SALUTES (on arrival only, with Honors March) include 17 guns, with 3 ruffles and flourishes, for U.S. ambassadors returning to the U.S. on official business; 15 guns, with 3 ruffles and flourishes, for U.S. envoys or ministers, foreign envoys or ministers accredited to the U.S., and lieutenant generals or vice admirals; 13 guns, with 2 ruffles and flourishes, for a major general or rear admiral (upper half) and for U.S. ministers resident and ministers resident accredited to the U.S.; 11 guns, with 1 ruffle and flourish, for a brigadier general or rear admiral (lower half) and for U.S. chargés d'affaires and like officials accredited to the U.S.; 11 guns, no ruffles and flourishes, for consuls general accredited to the U.S.

U.S. Military Awards
The Medal of Honor
Source: Congressional Medal of Honor Society; Army, U.S. Dept of Defense

The Medal of Honor is the highest military award for bravery that can be given to any individual in the United States. The first Army Medals were awarded on Mar. 25, 1863, and the first Navy Medals went to sailors and Marines on Apr. 3, 1863.

On Dec. 21, 1861, Pres. Abraham Lincoln signed into law a bill to create the Navy Medal of Honor. Lincoln, on July 14, 1862, approved a resolution providing for the presentation of Medals of Honor to enlisted men of the Army and Voluntary Forces, making it a law. The law was amended on March 3, 1863, to extend its provisions to include officers as well as enlisted men.

The Medal of Honor is awarded in the name of Congress to a person who, while a member of the armed forces, distinguishes himself or herself conspicuously by gallantry and intrepidity at the risk of life above and beyond the call of duty while engaged in an action against any enemy of the United States; while engaged in military operations involving conflict with an opposing foreign force; or while serving with friendly foreign forces engaged in an armed conflict against an opposing armed force in which the United States is not a belligerent party.

The deed performed must have been one of personal bravery or self-sacrifice so conspicuous as to clearly distinguish the individual above his or her comrades and must have involved risk of life. Incontestable proof of the performance of service is required, and each recommendation for award of this decoration is considered on the standard of extraordinary merit.

Prior to World War I, the 2,625 Army Medal of Honor awards up to that time were reviewed to determine which past awards met new stringent criteria. The Army removed

911 names from the list, most of them former members of a volunteer infantry group during the Civil War who had been induced to extend their enlistments when they were promised the medal. However, in 1977 a medal was restored to Dr. Mary Walker, and in 1989 medals were restored to Buffalo Bill Cody and 7 other Indian scouts.

Seven African-American soldiers were awarded Medals of Honor for service in World War II (6 of them posthumously) in Jan. 1997. Previously, no black soldier had received the medal for World War II service; an Army inquiry begun in 1993 concluded that the prevailing political climate and Army practices of the time had prevented proper recognition of heroism on the part of black soldiers in that war. In June 2002, 22 Asian Americans received the award for World War II service.

The most recent recipient was Navy Lt. Michael P. Murphy, whose posthumous award (the first for actions in Operation Enduring Freedom) was announced on Oct. 11, 2007. While serving in Afghanistan, on June 28, 2005, Lt. Murphy's Navy SEAL team came under attack by Taliban fighters. Heavily outnumbered and with all four team members wounded, Lt. Murphy left cover to radio for help and was shot in the back. One of his men survived the attack.

As of Sept. 30, 2007, two Medals of Honor had been awarded for actions in Operation Iraqi Freedom. On April 4, 2003, Army Sergeant First Class Paul R. Smith was mortally wounded while defending a prisoner of war holding area near Baghdad International Airport from an exposed position atop a damaged personnel carrier. On April 14, 2004, Marine Corporal Jason Dunham was mortally wounded at Karbala when he covered a live grenade with his helmet and body to protect his fellow Marines.

Other Selected Awards
Source: U.S. Army Institute of Heraldry; Navy Department Awards Web Service; Air Force Personnel Center

Distinguished Service Cross
Established in Congress July 9, 1918, on recommendation of Gen. John J. "Black Jack" Pershing, and awarded for extraordinary heroism not justifying the award of a Medal of Honor. The act or acts of heroism must have been so notable

and have involved risk of life so extraordinary as to set the individual apart from his or her comrades.

Silver Star
An earlier version of this award, the Citation Star, was established by Congress on July 19, 1918, and retroactively

awarded to soldiers for "gallantry in action," back to the Spanish-American War. The Silver Star medal replaced the Citation Star in 1932 and is awarded for gallantry in action which, while of a lesser degree than that required for award of the Distinguished Service Cross, must nevertheless have been performed with marked distinction.

Legion of Merit

Established by Congress on July 20, 1942, and awarded to individuals who have distinguished themselves by exceptionally meritorious conduct in the performance of outstanding services. There are different designs depending on the level of command of the award recipient.

Distinguished Flying Cross

Established by Congress July 2, 1926, and awarded for heroism or extraordinary achievement while participating in aerial flight. Awards are made only to recognize single acts of heroism or extraordinary achievement, not sustained operational activities against an armed enemy. Initial awards were given to persons who made record breaking long distance and endurance flights or who set altitude records. The first DFC was awarded to Cpt. Charles A. Lindbergh on May 31, 1927, and DFCs were awarded retroactively to Orville and Wilbur Wright.

Soldier's Medal

Established by Congress July 2, 1926, to recognize acts of heroism not involving actual conflict with an enemy. The same degree of heroism is required as for the award of the Distinguished Flying Cross. The performance must have involved personal hazard or danger and the voluntary risk of life under conditions not involving conflict with an armed enemy. Awards are not made solely on the basis of having saved a life.

Bronze Star

Established by Executive Order Feb. 4, 1944, largely to raise the morale of ground troops in WWII, on the recommendation of Gen. George C. Marshall. It is awarded to any person who, while serving in any capacity in or with the U.S. military, distinguishes himself or herself by heroic or meritorious achievement or service, not involving participation in aerial flight.

Purple Heart

The original Purple Heart, designated as the Badge of Military Merit, was established by Gen. George Washington on Aug. 7, 1782. Following the American Revolution, the badge fell into disuse until 1932, the 200th anniversary of Washington's birth. During WWII, the Order of the Purple Heart was awarded for both wounds received in action and for meritorious service; following the introduction of the Legion of Merit, it was awarded only for combat wounds. Today, the Purple Heart is awarded to any member of an armed force who, while serving with the U.S. Armed Services, has been wounded or killed, or who has died or may hereafter die after being wounded in action against an enemy of the U.S. or in an armed conflict in which the U.S. or friendly foreign forces are engaged; as the result of an act of any hostile foreign force; as a result of an international terrorist attack against the U.S. or a friendly foreign nation; as a result of military operations outside the U.S. as part of a peacekeeping force. Wounds must be inflicted by weapon fire while directly engaged in armed conflict, regardless of the fire causing the wound; or while held as a prisoner of war or while being taken captive.

Air Medal

Authorized by President Roosevelt on May 11, 1942, and awarded for heroism or meritorious achievement while participating in aerial flight. Awards may be made to recognize single acts of merit or heroism, or for meritorious service. Awards are not made to individuals who use air transportation solely for the purpose of moving from point to point in a combat zone.

Army Commendation

Established Dec. 18, 1945, and awarded for heroism, meritorious achievement or meritorious service. It may also be awarded to a member of the Armed Forces of a friendly foreign nation who distinguishes him or herself by an act of heroism, extraordinary achievement, or meritorious service which has been of mutual benefit to a friendly nation and the United States.

U.S. Military Awards in Selected Wars and Conflicts

Source: U.S. Army Human Resources Command, U.S. Dept. of Defense

AWARD	Civil War	WWI	WWII	Korea	Vietnam	Gulf War	OEF[1]	OIF[2]
Medal of Honor	1,522	124	464	131	246	0	1	2
Distinguished Service Cross	NA	6,430	4,434	723	846	0	1	5
Silver Star	NA	(3)	73,651	10,061	21,630	75	54	215
Legion of Merit	NA	NA	20,273	(3)	10,356	158	6	28
Distinguished Flying Cross	NA	NA	126,318	(3)	21,697	108	57	71
Soldier's Medal	NA	NA	12,485	581	5,402	43	22	79
Bronze Star (Total)[4]	NA	NA	395,379	30,358	719,960	27,967	13,488	46,458
Purple Heart	NA	NA	(3)	(3)	220,521	504	1,346	14,321
Air Medal (Total)[4]	NA	NA	1,166,471	0	1,039,124	6,399	3,658	10,522
Army Commendation (Total)[4]	NA	NA	0	0	837,036	81,979	19,766	126,978

(1) Operation Enduring Freedom (primarily Afghanistan). (2) Operation Iraqi Freedom. (3) Numbers for the individual decorations shown on these charts represent only those awards that were properly processed and reported to Headquarters, Department of the Army. The actual number of individual decorations awarded under combat conditions, when award approval authority is delegated to field commanders, cannot be stated with absolute certainty. These charts reflect the current statistics recorded by the Military Awards Branch, as of April 16, 2007. (4) Includes awards for valor/heroism and for meritorious service or achievement.

The Federal Service Academies

U.S. Military Academy, West Point, NY. Founded 1802. Awards BS degree and Army commission for a 5-year service obligation. For admissions information, write USMA Admissions, Bldg. 606, USMA, West Point, NY 10996. www.usma.edu

U.S. Naval Academy, Annapolis, MD. Founded 1845. Awards BS degree and Navy or Marine Corps commission for a 5-year service obligation. For admissions information, write Candidate Guidance Office, United States Naval Academy, 117 Decatur Rd., Annapolis, MD 21402-5018. www.usna.edu

U.S. Air Force Academy, Colorado Springs, CO. Founded 1954. Awards BS degree and Air Force commission for a 6-year service obligation. For admissions information, write HQ USAFA/RRS, 2304 Cadet Dr., Ste. 200, USAF Academy, CO 80840-5025. www.usafa.edu

U.S. Coast Guard Academy, New London, CT. Founded 1876. Awards BS degree and Coast Guard commission for a 5-year service obligation. For admissions information, write Director of Admissions, U.S. Coast Guard Academy, 31 Mohegan Ave., New London, CT 06320-8103. www.cga.edu

U.S. Merchant Marine Academy, Kings Point, NY. Founded 1943. Awards BS degree, a license as a deck, engineer, or dual officer, and a U.S. Naval Reserve commission. Service obligations vary according to options taken by the graduate. For admissions information, write Admissions Office, U.S. Merchant Marine Academy, 300 Steamboat Rd., Kings Point, NY 11024-1699. www.usmma.edu

Casualties in Principal Wars of the U.S.

Source: U.S. Dept. of Defense, U.S. Coast Guard

Data prior to World War I are based on incomplete records in many cases. Casualty data are confined to dead and wounded personnel and, therefore, exclude personnel captured or missing in action who were subsequently returned to military control. Dash (—) indicates information is not available. off. = officers.

WAR	Branch of service	Number serving	Battle deaths	Other deaths	Wounds not mortal[7]	Total[13]
				CASUALTIES		
Revolutionary War	Total	—	4,435	—	6,188	10,623
1775-83	Army	184,000	4,044	—	6,004	10,048
	Navy	to	342	—	114	456
	Marines	250,000	49	—	70	119
War of 1812	Total	286,730[8]	2,260	—	4,505	6,765
1812-15	Army	—	1,950	—	4,000	5,950
	Navy	—	265	—	439	704
	Marines	—	45	—	66	111
Mexican War	Total	78,718[8]	1,733	11,550	4,152	17,435
1846-48	Army	—	1,721	11,550	4,102	17,373
	Navy	—	1	—	3	4
	Marines	—	11	—	47	58
	Coast Guard[12]	71 off.	—	—	—	—
Civil War						
Union forces	Total	2,213,363	140,414	224,097	281,881	646,392
1861-65	Army	2,128,948[8]	138,154	221,374	280,040	639,568
	Navy	84,415	2,112	2,411	1,710	6,233
	Marines	(In Navy Total)	148	312	131	591
	Coast Guard[12]	219 off.	1	—	—	1
Confederate forces	Total	—	74,524	59,297	—	133,821
(estimate)[1]	Army	600,000	—	—	—	—
	Navy	to	—	—	—	—
	Marines	1,500,000	—	—	—	—
Spanish-American War	Total	306,760	385	2,061	1,662	4,108
1898	Army[3]	280,564	369	2,061	1,594	4,024
	Navy	22,875	10	—	47	57
	Marines	3,321	6	—	21	27
	Coast Guard[12]	660	0	—	—	—
World War I	Total	4,734,991	53,402	63,114	204,002	320,518
April 6, 1917 - Nov. 11, 1918	Army[4]	4,057,101	50,510	55,868	193,663	300,041
	Navy	599,051	431	6,856	819	8,106
	Marines	78,839	2,461	390	9,520	12,371
	Coast Guard	8,835	111	81	—	192
World War II	Total	16,112,566	291,557	113,842	671,846	1,077,245
Dec. 7, 1941 - Dec. 31, 1946[2]	Army[5]	11,260,000	234,874	83,400	565,861	884,135
	Navy[6]	4,183,466	36,950	25,664	37,778	100,392
	Marines	669,100	19,733	4,778	68,207	92,718
	Coast Guard	241,093	574	1,343	—	1,917
Korean War[9]	Total	5,720,000	33,574	2,833	103,284	139,691
June 25, 1950 - July 27, 1953	Army	2,834,000	27,731	2,125	77,596	107,452
	Navy	1,177,000	506	152	1,576	2,234
	Marines	424,000	4,266	242	23,744	28,252
	Air Force	1,285,000	1,238	314	368	1,920
	Coast Guard	44,143	—	—	—	—
Vietnam War[10]	Total	8,744,000	47,424	10,785	153,303	211,512
Aug. 4, 1964 - Jan. 27, 1973	Army	4,368,000	30,957	7,261	96,802	135,020
	Navy	1,842,000	1,631	934	4,178	6,743
	Marines	794,000	13,091	1,749	51,392	66,232
	Air Force	1,740,000	1,745	841	931	3,517
	Coast Guard	8,000	7	2	60	69
Persian Gulf War	Total	2,225,000	147	235	467	849
1991	Army	782,000	98	126	354	578
	Navy	669,000	5	50	12	67
	Marines	213,000	24	44	92	160
	Air Force	561,000	20	15	9	44
	Coast Guard	400	—	—	—	—
Iraq War[14]	Total	269,363[15]	3,098	699	28,093	31,890
Mar. 19, 2003-Sept. 29, 2007	Army	99,664[15]	2,195	511	18,835	21,541
	Navy	61,018[15]	58	25	595	678
	Marines	66,166[15]	821	147	8,338	9,306
	Air Force	42,515[15]	24	16	325	365
	Coast Guard	1,250[15]	1	—	—	1

(1) From the final report of the Provost Marshal General, 1863-1866. Authoritative statistics for the Confederate forces are not available. In addition, an estimated 26,000-31,000 Confederate personnel died in Union prisons. (2) Data are for Dec. 1, 1941, through Dec. 31, 1946, when hostilities were officially terminated by presidential proclamation; few battle deaths or wounds not mortal were incurred after Japanese acceptance of Allied peace terms on Aug. 14, 1945. Numbers serving Dec. 1, 1941-Aug. 31, 1945, were: Total—14,903,213; Army—10,420,000; Navy—3,883,520; Marine Corps—599,693. (3) Number serving covers the period April 21-Aug. 13, 1898, while dead and wounded data are for the period May 1-Aug. 31, 1898. Active hostilities ceased on Aug. 13, 1898, but ratifications of the treaty of peace were not exchanged between the U.S. and Spain until April 11, 1899. (4) Includes Army Air Forces battle deaths and wounds not mortal, as well as casualties suffered by American forces in northern Russia to Aug. 25, 1919, and in Siberia to April 1, 1920. Other deaths covered the period April 1, 1917-Dec. 31, 1918. (5) Includes Army Air Forces. (6) Battle deaths and wounds not mortal include casualties incurred in Oct. 1941 due to hostile action. (7) Marine Corps data for Iraq War, World War II, the Spanish-American War, and prior wars represent the number of individuals wounded, whereas all other data in this column represent the total number (incidence) of wounds. (8) As reported by Commissioner of Pensions in his Annual Report for Fiscal Year 1903. (9) As a result of an ongoing Dept. of Defense review of available Korean War casualty record information, updates to previously reported figures for battle deaths and other deaths are reflected in this table. (10) Number serving covers the period Aug. 4, 1964-Jan. 27, 1973 (date of ceasefire). Includes casualties incurred in Mayaguez incident. Wounds not mortal exclude 150,332 persons not requiring hospital care. (11) Estimated. (12) Actually the U.S. Revenue Cutter Services, predecessor to the U.S. Coast Guard. (13) Totals do not include categories for which no data are listed. (14) Military deaths through Apr. 30, 2003 only totaled 115 combat-related and 23 other. (15) Number serving figures for the Iraq War are current as of Mar. 31, 2003, and do not include numbers of troops deployed since then. **NOTE:** As of Sept. 29, 2007 there have been 256 battle deaths, 187 non-hostile deaths, and 1,627 wounded in Op. Enduring Freedom, mostly in Afghanistan and the Persian Gulf area.

U.S. Army, Navy, Air Force, Marine Corps, and Coast Guard Insignia

Source: Dept. of the Army, Dept. of the Navy, Dept. of the Air Force, U.S. Dept. of Defense, U.S. Coast Guard, U.S. Dept. of Homeland Security

Army

General of the Armies—Gen. John J. Pershing (1860-1948), the only person to have held this rank while living, was authorized to prescribe his own insignia but never wore in excess of four stars. The rank originally was established posthumously by Congress for George Washington in 1799, and he was promoted to the rank by joint resolution of Congress, approved by Pres. Gerald Ford, Oct. 19, 1976.

General of the Army—Five silver stars fastened together in a circle and the coat of arms of the United States in gold color metal with shield and crest enameled. Reserved for wartime use only.

Rank	Insignia
General	Four silver stars
Lieutenant General	Three silver stars
Major General	Two silver stars
Brigadier General	One silver star
Colonel	Silver eagle
Lieutenant Colonel	Silver oak leaf
Major	Gold oak leaf
Captain	Two silver bars
First Lieutenant	One silver bar
Second Lieutenant	One gold bar

Warrant Officers

Grade Five—Silver bar with enamel black line.
Grade Four—Silver bar with 4 enamel black squares.
Grade Three—Silver bar with 3 enamel black squares.
Grade Two—Silver bar with 2 enamel black squares.
Grade One—Silver bar with 1 enamel black square.

Noncommissioned Officers

Sergeant Major of the Army (E-9)—Three chevrons above 3 arcs, with a U.S. Coat of Arms centered on the chevrons, flanked by 2 stars—one star on each side of the eagle. Also wears distinctive red and white shield collar insignia.

Command Sergeant Major (E-9)—Three chevrons above 3 arcs with a 5-pointed star with a wreath around the star between the chevrons and arcs.

Sergeant Major (E-9)—Three chevrons above 3 arcs with a 5-pointed star between the chevrons and arcs.

First Sergeant (E-8)—Three chevrons above 3 arcs with a lozenge between the chevrons and arcs.

Master Sergeant (E-8)—Three chevrons above 3 arcs.
Sergeant First Class (E-7)—Three chevrons above 2 arcs.
Staff Sergeant (E-6)—Three chevrons above 1 arc.
Sergeant (E-5)—Three chevrons.
Corporal (E-4)—Two chevrons.

Specialists

Specialist (E-4)—Eagle device only.

Other Enlisted

Private First Class (E-3)—One chevron above one arc.
Private (E-2)—One chevron.
Private (E-1)—None.

Air Force

Insignia for Air Force officers are identical to those of the Army. Insignia for enlisted personnel are worn on both sleeves and consist of a star and an appropriate number of rockers. Chevrons appear above 5 rockers for the top 3 noncommissioned officer ranks, as follows (in ascending order): Master Sergeant, 1 chevron; Senior Master Sergeant, 2 chevrons; and Chief Master Sergeant, 3 chevrons. The insignia of the Chief Master Sergeant of the Air Force has 3 chevrons and a wreath around the star design. General of the Air Force is reserved for wartime use only.

Navy

The following stripes are worn on the lower sleeves of the Service Dress Blue uniform. They are of gold embroidery.

Rank	Insignia
Fleet Admiral*	1 two inch with 4 one-half inch
Admiral	1 two inch with 3 one-half inch
Vice Admiral	1 two inch with 2 one-half inch
Rear Admiral (upper half)	1 two inch with 1 one-half inch
Rear Admiral (lower half)	1 two inch
Captain	4 one-half inch
Commander	3 one-half inch
Lieutenant Commander	2 one-half inch with 1 one-quarter inch between
Lieutenant	2 one-half inch
Lieutenant (j.g.)	1 one-half inch with one-quarter inch above
Ensign	1 one-half inch
Warrant Officer-W-4	½"stripe with 1 break
Warrant Officer W-3	½"stripe with 2 breaks, 2"apart
Warrant Officer W-2	½"stripe with 3 breaks, 2"apart

Enlisted personnel (noncommissioned petty officers)—A rating badge worn on the upper left sleeve, consisting of a spread eagle, appropriate number of chevrons, and centered specialty mark.

*The rank of Fleet Admiral is reserved for wartime use only.

Marine Corps

Marine Corps' distinctive cap and collar ornament is the Marine Corps Emblem—a combination of the American eagle, a globe, and an anchor. Marine Corps and Army officer insignia are similar. Marine Corps enlisted insignia, although basically similar to the Army's, feature crossed rifles beneath the chevrons. Marine Corps enlisted rank insignia are as follows:

Sergeant Major of the Marine Corps (E-9)—Same as Sergeant Major (below) but with Marine Corps emblem in the center with a 5-pointed star on both sides of the emblem.

Sergeant Major (E-9)—Three chevrons above 4 rockers with a 5-pointed star in the center.

Master Gunnery Sergeant (E-9)—Three chevrons above 4 rockers with a bursting bomb insignia in the center.

First Sergeant (E-8)—Three chevrons above 3 rockers with a diamond in the middle.

Master Sergeant (E-8)—Three chevrons above 3 rockers with crossed rifles in the middle.

Gunnery Sergeant (E-7)—Three chevrons above 2 rockers with crossed rifles in the middle.

Staff Sergeant (E-6)—Three chevrons above 1 rocker with crossed rifles in the middle.

Sergeant (E-5)—Three chevrons above crossed rifles.
Corporal (E-4)—Two chevrons above crossed rifles.
Lance Corporal (E-3)—One chevron above crossed rifles.
Private First Class (E-2)—One chevron.
Private (E-1)—None.

Coast Guard

Coast Guard insignia follow Navy custom, with certain minor changes such as the officer cap insignia. The Coast Guard shield is worn on both sleeves of officers and on the right sleeve of all enlisted personnel.

For Further Information on the U.S. Armed Forces

Army—Office of the Chief of Public Affairs, Attn: Media Relations Division—MRD, 1500 Army Pentagon, Washington, DC 20310-1500. **Website:** www.army.mil

Navy—Chief of Information, 1200 Navy Pentagon, Washington, DC 20350-1200. **Website:** www.navy.mil

Air Force—Office of Public Affairs, 1690 Air Force Pentagon, Washington, DC 20330-1690. **Website:** www.af.mil

Marine Corps—Marine Corps Headquarters, Division of Public Affairs, U.S. Marine Corps, Washington, DC 20380-1775. **Website:** www.usmc.mil

Coast Guard—Commandant (G-IPA-2), U.S. Coast Guard Headquarters, 2100 Second St. SW, Washington, DC 20593. **Website:** www.uscg.mil

Additional information on all the U.S. Armed Forces branches, as well as many other related organizations, can be accessed through **DefenseLINK,** the official Internet site of the Dept. of Defense: www.defenselink.mil

Timeline of Major Wars Since 1066

Norman Conquest 1066-1071	William I, duke of Normandy, landed on the English coast near Hastings on Sept. 28, 1066, and defeated Harold II, Saxon king of England, at Battle of Hastings Oct. 14. William crowned king Dec. 25 in Westminster Abbey. Most revolts were suppressed by 1071. **Conquest linked England's interests with those of the continent and led to its rise as a powerful monarchy.**
Crusades 1095-1270/1291	Military expeditions undertaken by **Western European Christians** usually at the behest of the **papacy**, to recover **Jerusalem** and other Biblical places of pilgrimage from **Muslim** control; in the long term, stimulated trade and flow of ideas between East and West. Pope Urban II called Nov. 27, 1095 for the **First Crusade**; Crusaders took Jerusalem on July 15, 1099, massacred inhabitants, and founded four temporary states: Antioch, Edessa, Jerusalem, and Tripoli. The failed **Second Crusade** was prompted by Muslims' capture of Edessa in 1144. Jerusalem was captured by Ayyubid sultan Saladin on Oct. 2, 1187, launching the **Third Crusade,** which involved the Holy Roman emperor, Frederick I (Barbarossa); the French king, Philip II (Augustus); and the English king, Richard I (Lion-Heart), but did not lead to a Crusader victory. The **Fourth Crusade** sacked Constantinople on Apr. 13, 1204. The **Fifth Crusade** began with capture of Damietta in Egypt (1219) but failed at Cairo. A **Sixth Crusade** led to the Treaty of Jaffa in 1229, giving Jerusalem to the Crusaders until 1244, when it was taken by the Khwarizmians, launching a **Seventh Crusade.** The last crusade abruptly ended when its leader, French King Louis IX, died in 1270. The last major Crusader stronghold, Acre (now Akko, Israel), was lost on May 18, 1291.
Hundred Years War 1337-1453	Series of armed conflicts over rival claims to the French throne, broken by a number of truces and peace treaties. Edward III declared himself king of France in 1338 and invaded, with victories at Crécy in 1346 and Poitiers in 1356. **Treaty of Brétigny** signed May 8, 1360, but French King Charles V renewed fighting in 1369. Truce from 1396 until Henry V of England invaded in 1415 and **defeated French army at Agincourt,** capturing land north of Loire River including Paris. **Treaty of Troyes** in 1420 made Henry VI heir of both thrones. The siege of French stronghold Orléans, lifted in 1429 with help from **Joan of Arc,** turned the tide in favor of the French. **War ended English claims to France, paved the way for French absolute monarchy.**
Wars of the Roses 1455-1485	Series of dynastic civil wars in England fought by the **rival houses of Lancaster and York for the throne.** Richard, third duke of York, in conflict with the Lancastrian king **Henry VI**, won victories at St. Albans (1455) and Northampton (1460); Richard died at battle of Wakefield on Dec. 30, 1460, before coronation, leaving his son to become King Edward IV. Henry VI imprisoned in tower of London, 1465. Edward died in 1483; his brother became **Richard III** after usurping throne from Edward V. Henry Tudor defeated Richard III at the Battle of Bosworth Field (1485). As Henry VII, he married Edward's daughter Elizabeth, 1486, **finally uniting the houses.**
Thirty Years War 1618-1648	A series of religious and political conflicts involving **most countries of western Europe;** most fighting in Germany, devastating it. Protestants stormed Hapsburg palace in the "Defenestration of Prague" (May 23, 1618). Major conflicts included defeat of King Christian IV of Denmark and Norway by Catholic League (1626); victories by Lutheran King Gustav II Adolph of Sweden at Breitenfeld (1631) and Lützen (1632). France, under cardinal and statesman **Richelieu,** chief minister of King Louis XIII, declared war on the Hapsburgs in May 1635; defeated Austro-Bavarian army (Aug. 3, 1645), leading to Truce of Ulm. **Peace of Westphalia** signed at Münster on Oct. 24, 1648, bringing peace by recognizing the rulers' sovereignty within their lands and their right to determine the religious beliefs of their subjects.
English Civil Wars 1638-60	Series of conflicts between followers of King Charles (Cavaliers) and Parliament (Roundheads), over divine right of king versus Parliament's right to control national affairs. Presbyterian Scots, allied with Parliament, rioted and in 1640 occupied the northern counties of England. **Oliver Cromwell,** second in command of Parliament's New Model Army, destroyed the king's army at the Battle of Naseby (June 14, 1645); first civil war ended May 1646 when Charles surrendered to the Scots. Charles later allied with Scots, but was defeated by Cromwell at Preston Aug. 17-19, 1648, and executed Jan. 30, 1649. Parliament abolished monarchy and House of Lords. Cromwell suppressed Irish and Scottish rebellions, was briefly succeeded by son Richard after death (1658); **Charles II restored to the throne** by "The Long Parliament," May 1660.
War of the Spanish Succession 1701-1714	War fought by the Grand Alliance (originally England, Netherlands, Denmark, and Austria; later also Portugal), against a coalition of France, Spain, and a number of small Italian and German principalities to preserve balance of power after death of Spanish King Charles II. Opened with invasion of Italy, via Venice, by an Austrian army under Prince Eugène of Savoy in May 1701. French forced to withdraw from Netherlands and Italy in 1706, and finally defeated 1709 in bloodiest battle of the war at the French village of Malplaquet. Treaty of Rastatt and Baden signed in 1714; gave **Austria control of Spanish Netherlands and settled peace between Austria and France.**
War of the Austrian Succession 1740-48	Conflict over rival claims for the **hereditary dominions of the Habsburg family,** following death (1740) of Charles VI, Holy Roman emperor and archduke of Austria. An alliance of Bavaria, France, Spain, Sardinia, Prussia, and Saxony fought against Austria, allied with Holland and Great Britain. King Frederick the Great of Prussia captured Silesia from Austria in the First (1740-42) and Second Silesian Wars (1744-45). British King George II defeated French army at Battle of Dettingen am Main (June 27, 1743). French conquered Austrian Netherlands (1745-46). Treaty of Aix-la-Chapelle Oct. 18, 1748 **restored most original borders, and Prussia became a significant force.**
Seven Years War 1756-63	Worldwide conflicts fought for the **control of Germany** and for **supremacy in colonial N America and India.** French defeated British Gen. Edward Braddock on the Monongahela in 1754, leading to formal declaration of **French-Indian War,** May 1756. Frederick II of Prussia invaded Saxony on Aug. 29, 1756; defeated French at Rossbach (1757), Austrians at Leuthen (1757), Russians at Zorndorf (1758). By 1760, British conquered French Canada. Peter III signed armistice with Prussia, 1762. Treaty of Paris signed Feb. 10, 1763; Peace of Hubertusburg Feb. 15, 1763, between Prussia and Austria. **England emerged as leading world naval power.**
American Revolution 1775-83	Conflict between Great Britain and 13 British colonies on the eastern seaboard of North America. George Washington took command of the Continental Army, July 2, 1775 and King George III declared colonies traitors on Aug. 23. **Independence of colonies declared July 4, 1776.** France recognized the colonies' independence Feb. 6, 1778, followed by Spain on June 21, 1779; both pledged support. French fleet drove British fleet under Adm. Thomas Graves from the Chesapeake Bay on Sept. 5, 1781. French and Americans laid siege to Yorktown Sept. 28-Oct. 19, forcing British Gen. Cornwallis to surrender. **Treaty of Paris** (Sept. 3, 1783) recognized U.S. independence.
Wars of French Revolution & Napoleonic Wars 1792-1815	Large-scale wars fought between France and two multinational coalitions. France declared war on the Austrian part of the Holy Roman Empire for aiding King Louis XVI, Apr. 20, 1792. Newly created French Republic declared war on monarchs of Britain and Holland, Feb. 1, 1793, and Spain, Mar. 7. **Napoleon Bonaparte** defeated Austria in N Italy (1796-1797), captured Egypt from Britain (1798-1799; Battle of the Pyramids, July 21, 1798), and became First Consul after coup d'état of Nov. 9-10, 1799. French Grande Armée later swept through Europe using innovative and aggressive tactics. French navy defeated by British under Adm. Horatio Nelson at **Trafalgar** (Oct. 21, 1805), but Napoleon defeated Austro-Russian forces at Austerlitz (Dec. 2) and controlled most of Europe except Russia and Great Britain by 1808. France suffered its first major defeat by Austria at Aspern-Essling, May 21-22, 1809. **Napoleon invaded Russia,** captured Moscow Sept. 14, 1812, but was forced to flee the bitter Russian winter and abandoned Germany after defeat at Leipzig, Oct. 16-19, 1813. Paris captured by Allied armies Mar. 30-31, 1814. Napoleon exiled to Elba May 4 but returned for "Hundred Days" reign, Mar. 20-June 28, 1815; **final defeat at Waterloo** by British and Prussian troops (June 18). **The Bourbon monarchy was restored under Louis XVIII** and Britain, Prussia, Russia, and Austria maintained European peace.

Crimean War
1853-56

Conflict between **Russia** and a coalition of **Great Britain, France, Sardinia, and Turkey for influence over Balkans** and the straits between the Black Sea and the Mediterranean. Russia destroyed Turkish fleet at Sinope on Nov. 30, 1853. Britain and France declared war in Mar. 1854 and with Turkish troops defeated Russians at Battle of Alma River on Sept. 20. Lord Lucan of Britain prevented Russia from capturing Balaklava on Oct. 25 (the "Charge of the Light Brigade"). Siege of Sevastopol ended when Russia evacuated Sept. 8, 1855. Treaty of Paris signed Mar. 30, 1856; **curbed Russian expansion and loosened European power alignments.**

American Civil War
1861-65

Conflict between the United States (the Union) and 11 secessionist Southern states, organized as the Confederate States of America. Union garrison at Fort Sumter off Charleston, SC surrendered to Brig. Gen. Pierre Beauregard (Apr. 12-13, 1861). 22,000 Confederates under Beauregard repelled 35,000 Union troops under Gen. Irvin McDowell along Bull Run stream near Manassas, VA (July 21). The *Merrimack* (renamed the *Virginia*) battled the *Monitor* Mar. 9, 1862. In **Battle of Antietam** (Sept. 17), some 12,000 Northerners and 12,700 Southerners were killed or wounded. Pres. Abraham Lincoln announced **Emancipation Proclamation** on Sept. 22. Confederate Gen. Robert E. Lee's forces numbering 75,000 battled 88,000 Union troops under Gen. George Meade at **Gettysburg** July 1-3, 1863, forcing Lee's army back across the Potomac River. Lee surrendered to Ulysses S. Grant at **Appomattox Court House** (Apr. 9, 1865). **The Union was preserved and slavery abolished.**

Franco-Prussian War
1870-71

German states led by Prussia defeated France, seizing Alsace and part of Lorraine. French defeated in several major battles, culminating at **Sedan** Sept. 1, 1870 when Prussian forces decisively defeated the French army and captured emperor Napoleon III. Prussian king crowned William I, emperor of a unified Germany, Jan 18, 1871. **France surrendered** Jan. 28. Final treaty signed May 10; set the stage for later **German imperialistic expansion.**

Spanish-American War
1898

War waged by the U.S. to **liberate Cuba from Spanish rule**. A mysterious explosion, blamed on Spain by American newspapers, sank the U.S. battleship *Maine* in Havana's harbor (Feb. 15, 1898), killing 260. The U.S. called for Spain's withdrawal from Cuba, and Spain declared war (Apr. 24). Rufus Shafter led 17,000 U.S. troops from Daiquiri to Santiago de Cuba, taking **San Juan Hill** with help of the Rough Riders under Teddy Roosevelt. Santiago de Cuba surrendered July 17. The Treaty of Paris (Dec. 10, 1898) provided for the **independence of Cuba**; the cession by Spain to the U.S. of **Puerto Rico, Guam, and for a $20 mil payment, the Philippine Islands.**

World War I
1914-18

Local European war that grew into a global war involving 32 nations: the Allies and the Associated Powers—28 nations including Great Britain, France, Russia, Italy, and the U.S.—versus the Central Powers of Germany, Austria-Hungary, Turkey, and Bulgaria. Archduke Francis Ferdinand assassinated at Sarajevo, Bosnia (June 28, 1914). Germany invaded France through Belgium and the Netherlands; advance on Paris halted by the French under Gen. Joseph Jacques Césaire Joffre at the **First Battle of the Marne**, Sept. 5-12. Germany checked the Russian army at the Battle of Tannenberg, Aug. 26-30. The British suffered 57,470 casualties (19,240 dead) in the opening day of the **First Battle of the Somme** (July 1-Nov. 18, 1916), first of 12 battles that forced Germany back to the Hindenburg Line. **U.S. declared war on Germany Apr. 6, 1917.** Russian involvement ended when Bolshevik party seized power on Nov. 7; signed armistice Dec. 15. German offensive halted by U.S. and French troops at **Second Battle of the Marne** (July 15-Aug. 5, 1918), the turning point of the war. Allied counter-offensive broke the Hindenburg Line and an armistice was signed on Nov. 11.

World War II
1939-45

Global military conflict stemming from European unrest after World War I and Japan's aggressive expansion into Asia and the Pacific.
The War in Europe: The Nazi-Soviet nonaggression pact (Aug. 23, 1939) freed Germany and the Soviet Union to attack Poland in Sept. **Britain and France declared war on Germany** Sept. 3. German forces raced through Europe (Apr.-June, 1940), capturing Paris June 14. **Italy declared war on France and Britain** June 10; German-Italian campaigns won the Balkans and N Africa by June 1941. U.S. entered war Dec. 1941. Three million Axis troops invaded Russia June 22, 1941, but Russian counterthrusts stopped the German advance (**Stalingrad**, Aug. 20, 1942-Feb. 2, 1943), and Allies took N Africa (Nov. 8, 1942-May 13, 1943), Italy (July 10, 1943-May 2, 1945). Normandy invaded on **D-Day**, June 6, 1944; Paris liberated Aug. 25. Yalta Conference (Feb. 4-11, 1945) to defeat and split Germany into quarters. Adolf Hitler committed suicide Apr. 30. **Germany surrendered unconditionally** May 7.
The War in the Pacific: Japan invaded China (July 7, 1937), joined alliance with Germany and Italy (Sept. 27, 1940) and signed non-aggression pact with Russia (Apr. 13, 1941); attacked Hawaii's Pearl Harbor, Dec. 7, 1941; U.S. declared war on Japan Dec. 8. **Battle of Midway** (June 4-7, 1942) repulsed the Japanese advance. Marines landed on Guadalcanal Aug. 7. Navy defeated Japanese fleet at **Leyte Gulf**, Oct. 23-26, 1944. B-29 bombing raids on Japan began in Nov. Marines invaded Iwo Jima (Feb. 19-Mar. 16, 1945) with heavy casualties, then Okinawa (Apr. 1-June 21). **U.S. atom bombs dropped** on Hiroshima (Aug. 6) and Nagasaki (Aug. 9) and the Soviet invasion of Manchuria (Aug. 8) **forced Japan to agree, on Aug. 14, to surrender;** formal surrender was on Sept. 2.

Korean War
1950-53

Military struggle fought on the Korean Peninsula between the Democratic Peoples' Republic of Korea (N Korea) and the Republic of Korea (S Korea) that developed into an international war involving China allied with N Korea against the U.S. and other nations under the UN flag. DPRK army crossed the 38th parallel and invaded S Korea (June 25, 1950), entering Seoul (June 26). Amphibious assault launched at **Inchon** by Gen. Douglas MacArthur (Sept. 15) helped U.S. forces rout DPRK close to the Yalu River by Nov. 24. Chinese counterattack retook Seoul (Jan. 4, 1951), but forced back to the 38th parallel by Apr. 22. Armistice was signed (July 27, 1953) by the UN, DPRK, and China, but not ROK, **leaving the peninsula partitioned at 38th parallel.**

Vietnam War
1959-75

Struggle primarily in S Vietnam that widened into a war between S Vietnam supported mainly by the U.S. and N Vietnam supported by the USSR and China. Viet Minh, led by Communist leader Ho Chi Minh, formed the Democratic Republic of Vietnam (Sept. 2, 1945). Colonial power France withdrew after fortress at Dien Bien Phu fell (May 8, 1954). Pres. John F. Kennedy pledged U.S. commitment to S Vietnamese independence Dec. 14, 1961. USS *Maddox* destroyer damaged in **Gulf of Tonkin** (Aug. 2, 1964) prompted Congress to increase involvement. Regular bombing of N Vietnam began (Feb. 24, 1965) and the first U.S. combat ground-forces arrived (Mar. 6). North Vietnamese Army siege of **Khe Sanh** (Jan. 21-Apr. 7, 1968) and the "**Tet**" offensive (Jan. 30) aimed to cause insurrection in the south. **My Lai Massacre** by U.S. soldiers against civilians (Mar. 16, 1968) created scandal, fueled U.S. disaffection with war. U.S. forces peaked at 543,400 in Apr. 1969. NVA "**Easter Offensive**" (Mar. 30, 1972) rebuffed and U.S. responded with aerial bombings in May and Dec. U.S. withdrew after cease-fire, Jan. 1973. **NVA offensive captured Saigon, Apr. 30, 1975, and unified Vietnam under Communist rule.**

Persian Gulf Wars
1991, 2003

Conflicts fought principally between Iraq and the U.S. concerning Iraq's influence in the Middle East and its development of weapons of mass destruction. **First Gulf War:** Iraq under dictator Saddam Hussein invaded Kuwait Aug 2, 1990, and annexed it; UN Security Council ordered Iraqi forces to withdraw by Jan. 15, 1991. Beginning Jan. 17, a multinational force (**Operation Desert Storm**) led by the U.S. bombed military targets in Iraq and Kuwait. A coordinated air-land offensive (**Operation Desert Sabre**, begun Feb. 24) retook Kuwait City Feb. 26, and permanent cease-fire was signed on Apr. 6. Iraq was ordered to pay reparations to Kuwait, reveal locations of biological and chemical weapons, and eliminate weapons of mass destruction. **Second Gulf War:** The U.S. and U.K. mistakenly asserted that Iraq was still producing WMD, and posed an imminent threat. The UN passed Resolution 1441, Nov. 8, 2002, warning Iraq of "serious consequences" if it failed to cooperate fully and unconditionally with UN weapons inspectors. Iraq rejected a Mar. 17, 2003, U.S. ultimatum demanding Hussein and his sons leave Iraq; U.S. launched **Operation Iraqi Freedom** Mar. 19, 2003, with support from U.K. and other allies, but without full UN Security Council support. Baghdad fell Apr. 9, and major combat operations declared over May 1. Saddam Hussein was captured Dec. 13, but guerrilla opposition to U.S. troops and violence between Iraqi Shiites and Sunnis continued.

HEALTH

U.S. Health Expenditures, 1960-2004

Source: *Health, United States, 2006*, National Center for Health Statistics, U.S. Dept. of Health and Human Services

National health expenditures	1960	1970	1980	1990	1995	2000	2002	2003	2004
					Amount in billions				
National health expenditures	$27.6	$75.1	$254.9	$717.3	$1,020.4	$1,358.5	$1,607.9	$1,740.6	$1,877.6
					Percent distribution				
Health services and supplies	90.4	89.3	91.8	92.9	93.4	93.1	93.2	93.3	93.4
Personal health care	84.5	83.8	84.5	84.7	84.6	83.9	83.4	83.1	83.1
Hospital care	33.3	36.7	39.6	35.1	33.4	30.7	30.4	30.2	30.4
Professional services	30.2	27.5	26.4	30.2	31.0	31.4	31.3	31.2	31.3
Physician and clinical services......	19.4	18.6	18.5	22.0	21.6	21.2	21.0	21.1	21.3
Other professional services	1.4	1.0	1.4	2.5	2.8	2.9	2.8	2.8	2.8
Dental services.................	7.1	6.2	5.2	4.4	4.4	4.6	4.6	4.4	4.3
Other personal health care.........	2.2	1.7	1.3	1.3	2.3	2.7	2.9	2.9	2.8
Nursing home and home health.....	3.1	5.7	8.4	9.1	10.3	9.3	8.7	8.5	8.4
Home health care[1]	0.2	0.3	0.9	1.8	3.0	2.2	2.1	2.2	2.3
Nursing home care[1]	2.9	5.4	7.5	7.3	7.3	7.0	6.6	6.3	6.1
Retail outlet sales of medical products	17.9	13.9	10.1	10.3	10.0	12.5	13.0	13.1	13.0
Prescription drugs	9.7	7.3	4.7	5.6	6.0	8.9	9.8	10.0	10.0
Other medical products	8.2	6.6	5.3	4.7	4.0	3.6	3.2	3.1	2.9
Government administration and net cost of private health insurance	4.4	3.7	4.8	5.5	5.7	6.0	6.6	7.2	7.3
Government public health activities[2] ...	1.5	1.9	2.5	2.8	3.0	3.2	3.2	3.1	3.0
Investment	9.6	10.7	8.2	7.1	6.6	6.9	6.8	6.7	6.6
Research[3]	2.5	2.6	2.1	1.8	1.8	1.9	2.0	2.0	2.1
Structures and equipment	7.1	8.1	6.1	5.3	4.8	5.0	4.7	4.6	4.6
					Average annual percent change from previous year shown				
National health expenditures	—	10.5	13.0	10.9	7.3	5.9	8.8	8.2	7.9
Health services and supplies	—	10.4	13.3	11.0	7.4	5.8	8.9	8.4	7.9
Personal health care	—	10.4	13.1	10.9	7.3	5.7	8.5	7.8	7.9
Hospital care	—	11.6	13.9	9.6	6.3	4.1	8.2	7.5	8.6
Professional services	—	9.5	12.5	12.4	7.9	6.2	8.6	8.0	8.1
Physician and clinical services......	—	10.1	12.9	12.8	7.0	5.5	8.2	8.6	9.0
Other professional services	—	6.6	17.1	17.5	9.5	6.5	8.0	7.5	7.4
Dental services.................	—	7.3	11.1	9.0	7.1	6.9	8.8	4.8	6.1
Other personal health care.........	—	7.3	10.1	11.4	19.2	10.0	11.8	8.7	5.8
Nursing home and home health.....	—	17.2	17.5	11.8	9.9	3.8	5.5	6.1	6.6
Home health care[1]	—	14.5	26.9	18.1	19.4	0.0	5.9	11.1	13.3
Nursing home care[1]	—	17.4	16.8	10.7	7.1	5.2	5.3	4.5	4.3
Retail outlet sales of medical products	—	7.8	9.4	11.2	6.6	10.8	10.9	9.0	6.7
Prescription drugs	—	7.5	8.2	12.8	8.6	14.7	14.3	10.2	8.2
Other medical products	—	8.1	10.6	9.5	4.0	3.9	2.1	5.1	1.9
Government administration and net cost of private health insurance	—	8.6	16.0	12.4	8.3	6.8	14.3	17.7	9.4
Government public health activities[2] ...	—	12.8	16.5	12.0	9.2	7.0	9.2	4.4	4.0
Investment	—	11.7	10.1	9.3	5.9	6.9	7.6	6.7	7.3
Research[3]	—	10.9	10.8	8.9	7.7	6.9	12.8	9.5	9.3
Structures and equipment	—	12.0	9.8	9.4	5.2	6.9	5.6	5.5	6.5

Note: Numbers may not add to totals because of rounding. (1) Freestanding facilities only. (2) Includes personal care services delivered by government public health agencies. (3) Excludes R&D expenditures of drug companies and other manufacturers and suppliers of medical equip. and supplies

Health Coverage for Persons Under 65, by Characteristics, 1984-2004

Source: *Health, United States, 2006*, National Center for Health Statistics, U.S. Dept. of Health and Human Services

	PRIVATE INSURANCE				MEDICAID[1]				NOT COVERED[2]			
	1984	2000[3]	2002	2004	1984	2000[3]	2002	2004	1984	2000[3]	2002	2004
					Percent of each population group							
Total..................	76.8	71.5	69.4	68.8	6.8	9.5	11.8	12.5	14.5	17.0	16.8	16.4
Age												
Under 18 years	72.6	66.6	63.5	63.2	11.9	19.6	24.8	26.4	13.9	12.6	10.9	9.2
18-44 years.............	76.5	70.5	68.7	67.3	5.1	5.6	7.1	7.7	17.1	22.4	23.0	23.5
45-64 years	83.3	78.7	77.3	77.1	3.4	4.5	5.3	5.5	9.6	12.6	13.1	12.8
Race and Hispanic origin[4,5]												
White, non-Hispanic	82.3	79.5	77.9	77.9	3.7	6.1	7 .7	7.9	12.0	12.5	12.5	12.0
Black, non-Hispanic........	58.3	56.0	55.2	54.6	20.7	21.0	23.2	24.6	19.6	19.5	18.7	17.3
All Hispanic	55.7	47.8	44.4	41.7	13.3	15.5	20.8	22.5	29.5	35.6	33.9	34.4
Percent of poverty level[4]												
Below 100%.............	32.2	25.2	25.2	21.8	33.0	38.4	42.8	45.0	33.9	34.2	30.3	31.0
100-149%..............	62.2	41.7	38.4	39.0	7.7	20.7	27.6	27.1	27.2	34.9	32.2	30.8
150-199%	77.2	58.5	56.2	52.5	3.2	11.5	16.1	16.9	17.3	27.0	25.2	27.2
200% or more	91.5	85.7	83.9	84.2	0.6	2.3	3.1	3.5	6.0	10.1	11.1	10.2
Geographic region[4]												
Northeast................	80.5	76.3	73.9	74.0	8.6	10.6	12.5	13.0	10.2	12.2	12.8	11.8
Midwest.................	80.6	78.8	76.4	76.3	7.4	8.0	10.3	10.4	11.3	12.3	12.5	12.4
South...................	74.3	66.8	64.6	64.1	5.1	9.4	12.0	12.4	17.7	20.5	20.3	19.9
West...................	71.9	66.5	66.1	64.1	7.0	10.4	12.7	14.4	18.2	20.7	19.1	18.5

Note: Data based on household interviews of a sample of the civilian noninstitutionalized population. Percents do not add to 100 because other types of health insurance (e.g., Medicare, military) are not shown and persons with both private insurance and Medicaid appear in both sections. (1) Includes Medicaid or other public assistance. In 2002, the age-adjusted percent of the population under 65 covered by Medicaid was 9.2%; 1.2% were covered by state-sponsored health plans and 1.4% were covered by State Children's Health Insurance Program (SCHIP). (2) Includes persons not covered by private insurance, Medicaid or other public assistance, Medicare, or military plans. (3) In 1997 the questionnaire changed compared with previous years. (4) Age adjusted. (5) Changed reporting methods make percentages for race before 1999 not strictly comparable with those from 1999 on.

Spending on Health in the 50 Most Populous Countries

Source: *The World Health Report 2006*, The World Health Organization

Country	As % of GDP	Per capita[1]	Country	As % of GDP	Per capita[1]	Country	As % of GDP	Per capita[1]	Country	As % of GDP	Per capita[1]
Afghanistan	6.5	$11	Germany	11.1	$3,204	Nepal	5.3	$12	Sudan	4.3	$21
Algeria	4.1	89	Ghana	4.5	16	Nigeria	5.0	22	Tanzania	4.3	12
Argentina	8.9	305	India	4.8	27	North Korea	5.8	<1	Thailand	3.3	76
Bangladesh	3.4	14	Indonesia	3.1	30	Pakistan	2.4	13	Turkey	7.6	257
Brazil	7.6	212	Iran	6.5	131	Peru	4.4	98	Uganda	7.3	18
Canada	9.9	2,669	Iraq	2.7	23	Philippines	3.2	31	Ukraine	5.7	60
China	5.6	61	Italy	8.4	2,139	Poland	6.5	354	United Kingdom	8.0	2,428
Colombia	7.6	138	Japan	7.9	2,662	Romania	6.1	159	United States	15.2	5,711
Congo, Dem. Rep. of the	4.0	4	Kenya	4.3	20	Russia	5.6	167	Uzbekistan	5.5	21
Egypt	5.8	55	Malaysia	3.8	163	Saudi Arabia	4.0	366	Venezuela	4.5	146
Ethiopia	5.9	5	Mexico	6.2	372	South Africa	8.4	295	Vietnam	5.4	26
France	10.1	2,981	Morocco	5.1	72	South Korea	5.6	705	Yemen	5.5	32
			Myanmar	2.8	394	Spain	7.7	1,514			

(1) At average exchange rates.

Health Insurance Coverage,[1] by State, 1990-2006

Source: Bureau of the Census, U.S. Dept. of Commerce

	2004-06[2] Not covered[3]	2004-06[2] % not covered	2000 Not covered[3]	2000 % not covered	1990 Not covered[3]	1990 % not covered		2004-06[2] Not covered[3]	2004-06[2] % not covered	2000 Not covered[3]	2000 % not covered	1990 Not covered[3]	1990 % not covered
AL	636	14.1	582	13.3	710	17.4	MT	157	17.0	150	16.8	115	14.0
AK	110	16.7	117	18.7	77	15.4	NE	194	11.1	154	9.1	138	8.5
AZ	1,151	19.0	869	16.7	547	15.5	NV	451	18.3	344	16.8	201	16.5
AR	482	17.5	379	14.3	421	17.4	NH	136	10.4	103	8.4	107	9.9
CA	6,663	18.5	6,299	18.5	5,683	19.1	NJ	1,269	14.6	1,021	12.2	773	10.0
CO	772	16.6	620	14.3	495	14.7	NM	405	21.0	435	24.2	339	22.2
CT	362	10.4	330	9.8	226	6.9	NY	2,513	13.2	3,056	16.3	2,176	12.1
DE	106	12.5	72	9.3	96	13.9	NC	1,383	16.0	1,084	13.6	883	13.8
DC	68	12.4	78	14.0	109	19.2	ND	69	11.1	71	11.3	40	6.3
FL	3,609	20.3	2,829	17.7	2,376	18.0	OH	1,206	10.7	1,248	11.2	1,123	10.3
GA	1,594	17.6	1,166	14.3	971	15.3	OK	650	18.7	641	18.9	574	18.6
HI	108	8.6	113	9.4	81	7.3	OR	604	16.6	433	12.7	360	12.4
ID	213	14.9	199	15.4	159	15.2	PA	1,255	10.2	1,047	8.7	1,218	10.1
IL	1,715	13.6	1,704	13.9	1,272	10.9	RI	107	10.2	77	7.4	105	11.1
IN	809	13.1	674	11.2	587	10.7	SC	667	16.0	480	12.1	550	16.2
IA	271	9.3	253	8.8	225	8.1	SD	88	11.6	81	11.0	81	11.6
KS	300	11.1	289	10.9	272	10.8	TN	791	13.4	615	10.9	673	13.7
KY	564	13.8	545	13.6	480	13.2	TX	5,501	24.1	4,748	22.9	3,569	21.1
LA	784	18.5	789	18.1	797	19.7	UT	392	15.7	281	12.5	156	9.0
ME	124	9.5	138	10.9	139	11.2	VT	67	10.8	52	8.6	54	9.5
MD	755	13.5	547	10.4	601	12.7	VA	981	13.2	814	11.6	996	15.7
MA	653	10.3	549	8.7	530	9.1	WA	778	12.5	792	13.5	557	11.4
MI	1,061	10.6	901	9.2	865	9.4	WV	279	15.5	250	14.1	249	13.8
MN	439	8.5	399	8.1	389	8.9	WI	514	9.4	406	7.6	321	6.7
MS	520	18.1	380	13.6	531	19.9	WY	71	14.0	76	15.7	58	12.5
MO	703	12.3	524	9.5	665	12.7	U.S.	45,102	15.3	39,804	14.2	34,719	13.9

NA = Not available. (1) For population, all ages, including those 65 or over, an age group largely covered by Medicare. (2) 3-year average. (3) In thousands.

Persons Not Covered by Health Insurance, by Selected Characteristics, 2005

Source: Bureau of the Census, U.S. Dept. of Commerce

	Number[1]	% of specified population		Number[1]	% of specified population
Sex			**Age**		
Male	24,854	17.2	Under 18 years	8,310	11.2
Female	21,723	14.5	18 to 24 years	8,556	30.6
Race and Ethnicity			25 to 34 years	10,412	26.4
White	35,340	15.0	35 to 44 years	8,090	18.8
Non-Hispanic	21,144	11.3	45 to 64 years	10,740	14.6
Black	7,228	19.6	65 years and over	459	8.0
Asian and Pacific Islander	2,257	17.9	**Region**		
Hispanic[2]	14,122	32.7	Northeast	6,657	12.3
Education (18 years and older)			Midwest	7,777	11.9
No high school diploma	10,175	30.1	South	19,793	18.6
High school graduate only	14,113	20.3	West	12,352	18.1
Some college, no degree	7,006	16.5	**Household Income**		
Associate degree	2,312	12.7	Less than $25,000	14,561	24.4
Bachelor's degree or higher	4,661	8.3	$25,000 to $49,999	14,977	20.6
Nativity			$50,000 to $74,999	8,300	14.1
Native	34,608	13.4	$75,000 or more	8,740	8.5
Foreign born	11,969	33.6	TOTAL	46,577	15.9
Naturalized citizen	2,482	17.9			
Not a citizen	9,487	43.6			

(1) In thousands. (2) Persons of Hispanic origin may be of any race.

Enrollment in Health Maintenance Organizations (HMOs), 1976-2004

Source: *Health, United States, 2004*, National Center for Health Statistics, U.S. Dept. of Health and Human Services

	1976	1980	1990	1995	1997	1998	1999	2000	2001	2002	2003	2004
				Number of enrolled in millions								
TOTAL................	6.0	9.1	33.0	50.9	66.8	76.6	81.3	80.9	79.5	76.1	71.6	68.8
Model type[1]												
Individual practice assoc.[2]	0.4	1.7	13.7	20.1	26.7	32.6	32.8	33.4	33.1	31.6	27.9	24.6
Group[3]	5.6	7.4	19.3	13.3	11.0	13.8	15.9	15.2	15.6	15.0	16.1	15.3
Mixed	—	—	—	17.6	29.0	30.1	32.6	32.3	30.9	29.6	27.8	28.9
Federal program[4]												
Medicaid[5]	—	0.3	1.2	3.5	5.6	7.8	10.4	10.8	11.4	12.8	14.5	14.3
Medicare	—	0.4	1.8	2.9	4.8	5.7	6.5	6.6	6.1	5.4	4.9	4.9
				Percent of population enrolled in HMOs								
TOTAL................	2.8	4.0	13.4	19.4	25.2	28.6	30.1	30.0	28.3	26.4	24.6	23.4
Geographic region												
Northeast	2.0	3.1	14.6	24.4	32.4	37.8	36.7	36.5	35.1	33.4	31.8	30.1
Midwest.............	1.5	2.8	12.6	16.4	19.5	22.7	23.3	23.2	21.7	20.6	19.7	18.7
South...............	0.4	0.8	7.1	12.4	17.9	21.0	23.9	22.6	21.0	19.8	17.1	16.0
West...............	9.7	12.2	23.2	28.6	36.4	39.1	41.4	41.7	40.7	38.2	35.8	34.4

— = Not available. **Note:** Data as of June 30 in 1976-80, Jan. 1 from 1990 onwards. HMOs in Guam included starting in 1994; Puerto Rico, 1998; Guam HMO enrollment was 32,000 in 2003 and Puerto Rico enrollment was 1,726,000 in 2003. Open-ended enrollment in HMO plans, amounting to 7.6 mil on Jan. 1, 2003, included from 1994 onwards. (1) Enrollment may not equal total because some plans did not report these characteristics. (2) This type of HMO contracts with an association of physicians from various settings (a mixture of solo and group practices) to provide health services. (3) Group includes staff, group, and network model types. (4) Enrollment by Medicaid or Medicare beneficiaries, where the Medicaid or Medicare program contracts directly with the HMO to pay the premium. (5) Data for 1990 and later include enrollment in managed-care health insuring organizations.

Health Care Visits, by Selected Characteristics, 1997-2004

Source: Centers for Disease Control and Prevention, National Center for Health Statistics.
National Health Interview Survey, family core and sample adult questionnaires.

	No visits			1-3 visits			4-9 visits			10 or more visits		
	1997	2000	2004	1997	2000	2004	1997	2000	2004	1997	2000	2004
						Percent distribution						
All persons	16.5	16.7	16.1	46.2	45.4	45.8	23.6	24.6	24.6	13.7	13.3	13.5
Age												
Under 6 years	5.0	6.3	5.3	44.9	44.5	47.5	37.0	38.1	36.9	13.0	11.1	10.3
6–17 years............	15.3	15.2	13.1	58.7	58.2	59.0	19.3	20.6	21.1	6.8	6.0	6.8
18–24 years...........	22.0	24.8	25.7	46.8	45.3	45.0	20.0	18.7	19.2	11.2	11.2	10.1
25–44 years...........	21.6	23.1	23.1	46.7	45.1	45.8	18.7	19.2	19.2	13.0	12.5	12.0
45–54 years...........	17.9	16.4	16.9	43.9	45.2	45.0	23.4	23.7	22.9	14.8	14.7	15.2
55–64 years...........	15.3	12.8	12.3	41.3	40.6	40.9	26.7	28.8	28.9	16.7	17.8	18.0
65–74 years...........	9.8	9.0	6.8	36.9	34.5	36.0	31.6	34.5	34.5	21.6	22.1	22.6
75 years and over	7.7	5.8	4.1	31.8	29.3	26.4	33.8	39.3	39.5	26.6	25.6	30.0
Sex												
Male..................	21.3	21.7	20.9	47.1	45.9	46.6	20.6	22.3	21.6	11.0	10.1	10.9
Female...............	11.7	11.9	11.5	45.4	44.8	45.0	26.5	27.0	27.5	16.3	16.3	16.0
Race and Hispanic origin												
White, non-Hispanic	14.7	14.5	13.5	46.6	45.4	46.1	24.4	25.9	25.7	14.3	14.1	14.7
Black, non-Hispanic.......	16.9	17.1	15.6	46.1	46.8	47.3	23.1	23.5	24.6	13.8	12.6	12.5
Hispanic[1]	24.9	26.8	26.7	42.3	41.8	41.8	20.3	19.8	20.6	12.5	11.6	10.9
Health insurance status[2]												
Insured continuously ...	14.1	14.0	13.4	49.2	48.8	49.4	23.6	24.6	24.6	13.0	12.6	12.7
Uninsured for any period ...	18.9	20.6	20.0	46.0	44.5	45.7	20.8	20.8	21.9	14.4	14.1	12.3
Uninsured	39.0	43.2	43.9	41.4	39.6	41.3	13.2	12.1	10.0	6.4	5.1	4.8

Note: Covers visits to doctor's offices, emergency departments, and home visits in a 12-month period prior to interview. Estimates are age-adjusted to the year 2000 standard population. Includes all other races not shown separately and unknown health insurance status. (1) Persons of Hispanic origin may be of any race. (2) In 12 months prior to interview, for under-65 population only; persons with both Medicaid and private coverage are classified as having private coverage.

Top 20 Reasons Given by Patients for Physicians' Office Visits, 2005

Source: National Center for Health Statistics, U.S. Dept. of Health and Human Services

Rank		Number of visits (1,000)	Percent Distribution Total	Rank		Number of visits (1,000)	Percent Distribution Total
1.	General medical examination	71,392	7.4	12.	Back symptoms	14,643	1.5
2.	Progress visit, not otherwise specified	42,201	4.4	13.	Vision dysfunctions............	13,556	1.4
3.	Cough	32,482	3.4	14.	For other and unspecified test results.....................	13,211	1.4
4.	Postoperative visit..............	31,985	3.3	15.	Nasal congestion	13,164	1.4
5.	Medication, other and unspecified kinds	19,896	2.1	16.	Eye exam	12,528	1.3
6.	Gynecological examination	18,254	1.9	17.	Skin rash...................	12,527	1.3
7.	Hypertension	16,988	1.8	18.	Diabetes mellitus	12,192	1.3
8.	Prenatal examination, routine	16,759	1.7	19.	Depression	12,062	1.3
9.	Symptoms referable to throat	16,440	1.7	20.	Earache or ear infection	11,805	1.2
10.	Knee symptoms.................	16,076	1.7		All other reasons..................	550,190	57.1
11.	Well-baby examination	15,268	1.6		**ALL VISITS**	963,617[1]	100.0

(1) Based on 560,355,000 visits by women and 403,262,000 by men.

Top 20 Reasons Given by Patients for Emergency Room Visits, 2005

Source: National Center for Health Statistics, U.S. Dept. of Health and Human Services

Rank	Principal reason for visit	Number (thous.)	%
1.	Stomach and abdominal pain, cramps, and spasms	7,833	6.8
2.	Chest pain and related symptoms	5,812	5.0
3.	Fever	5,042	4.4
4.	Cough	3,359	2.9
5.	Headache, pain in head	3,104	2.7
6.	Back symptoms	2,918	2.5
7.	Shortness of breath	2,802	2.4
8.	Pain, site not referable to a specific body system	2,554	2.2
9.	Vomiting	2,535	2.2
10.	Symptoms referable to throat	2,178	1.9
11.	Lacerations and cuts—upper extremity	1,843	1.6
12.	Accident, not otherwise specified	1,808	1.6
13.	Earache or ear infection	1,707	1.5
14.	Leg symptoms	1,568	1.4
15.	Skin rash	1,548	1.3
16.	Injury, other and unspecified type—head, neck, and face	1,538	1.3
17.	Labored or difficult breathing (dyspnea)	1,530	1.3
18.	Nausea	1,525	1.3
19.	Vertigo-dizziness	1,524	1.3
20.	Motor vehicle accident, type of injury unspecified	1,494	1.3
	All other reasons	61,101	53.0
	ALL VISITS	115,323	100.0

Drugs Most Frequently Prescribed in Physicians' Offices, 2005

Source: National Center for Health Statistics, *Health, United States, 2006*

Rank	Therapeutic Classification[1]	Times prescribed (thous.)	% distrib.[2]
1.	Antidepressants	107,070	5.3
2.	Antihypertensive agents	105,295	5.2
3.	Hyperlipidemia	101,004	5.0
4.	Antiarthritics	85,511	4.2
5.	Antiasthmatics or bronchodilators	83,741	4.1
6.	Non-narcotic analgesics	83,560	4.1
7.	Antipyretics	75,381	3.7
8.	Acid or peptic disorders	75,346	3.7
9.	NSAIDs[3]	75,277	3.7
10.	Blood glucose regulators	72,535	3.6
11.	Vitamins or minerals	65,973	3.2
12.	Antihistamines	65,516	3.2
13.	Beta blockers	62,726	3.1
14.	Vaccines or antisera	61,155	3.0
15.	ACE inhibitors[4]	59,474	2.9
16.	Diuretics	58,671	2.9
17.	Narcotic analgesics	55,001	2.7
18.	Calcium channel blockers	49,135	2.4
19.	Adrenal corticosteroids	42,751	2.1
20.	Thyroid or antithyroid	41,745	2.1

(1) Based on the standard classification used in National Drug Code Directory. (2) Based on an estimated 2,030,804,000 drug prescriptions at office visits in 2005. (3) Nonsteroidal anti-inflammatory drugs. (4) Angiotensin-converting enzyme.

Transplant Waiting List, Sept. 2007*   Transplants Performed, 2006

Source: United Network for Organ Sharing

Type of transplant	Patients waiting
Kidney	73,181
Liver	16,737
Heart	2,635
Lung	2,336
Kidney-pancreas	2,316
Pancreas	1,643
Intestine	210
Heart-lung	115
Total[1]	**96,749**

Type of transplant	Number
Kidney	17,090
Liver	6,650
Heart	2,192
Lung	1,405
Kidney-pancreas	924
Pancreas	463
Intestine	175
Heart-lung	31
Total	**28,930**

* As of Sept. 27, 2007. (1) Some patients are waiting for more than one organ; therefore total number of patients waiting is less than the sum of patients waiting for each organ.

Physicians by Age, Sex, and Specialty, 2005

Source: American Medical Assn., as of Dec. 31, 2005

	Male	Female		Male	Female		Male	Female
All Specialties[1]	**649,347**	**235,627**	General Preventive Med.	1,297	751	Pediatrics	33,515	36,636
Aerospace Medicine	442	33	General Surgery	32,329	5,173	Physical Med./Rehab.	4,812	2,478
Allergy & Immunology	3,056	1,050	Internal Medicine	104,688	46,245	Plastic Surgery	6,075	777
Anaesthesiology	30,452	8,370	Medical Genetics	250	226	Psychiatry	27,213	13,079
Cardiovascular Disease	20,060	2,054	Neurological Surgery	4,976	312	Public Health	1,091	464
Child Psychiatry	3,829	3,019	Neurology	10,396	3,266	Pulmonary Diseases	8,385	1,422
Colon/Rectal Surgery	1,116	149	Nuclear Medicine	1,164	283	Radiation Oncology	3,271	1,017
Dermatology	6,535	3,906	Obstetrics/Gynecology	24,801	17,258	Radiology	7,465	1,270
Diagnostic Radiology	18,527	5,126	Occupational Medicine	2,172	502	Thoracic Surgery	4,750	166
Emergency Medicine	21,877	5,987	Ophthalmology	15,529	3,177	Transplantation Surgery	49	10
Family Practice	54,022	26,305	Orthopedic Surgery	22,775	1,021	Urology	10,060	508
Forensic Pathology	413	207	Otolaryngology	8,777	1,084	Vascular	17	5
Gastroenterology	10,473	1,255	Pathology-Anat./Clin.	12,523	6,037	Other Speciality	4,427	908
General Practice	9,544	2,120	Pediatric Cardiology	1,276	480	Unspecified	3,813	1,720

(1) Includes "Inactive," "Address Unknown," and certain specialties with very few practitioners.

Drug Use in the General U.S. Population, 2006

Source: Substance Abuse and Mental Health Services Administration (SAMHSA), U.S. Dept. of Health and Human Services

According to the Substance Abuse and Mental Health Services Administration's 2006 National Survey on Drug Use and Health, an estimated 111,774,000 Americans 12 years of age and older (45.4%) had used an illicit drug at least once during their lifetimes, 14.5% had used one during the previous year, and 8.3% had used one in the most recent month. The rate of current illicit drug use (in the past month) in 2006 was 10.5% for men; for women it was 6.2%. An estimated 29.6% of Americans 12 or older (72.9 mil) had used

an illicit drug other than marijuana at least once in their life. The overall rate of illicit drug use between 2005 and 2006 remained relatively steady. The Substance Abuse and Mental Health Services Administration's Drug Abuse Warning Network (DAWN) reported 1.45 mil drug abuse or misuse related episodes in hospital emergency departments in the coterminous U.S in 2005. Cocaine was a factor in 31% of these. Alcohol in combination with illegal drug use was a factor in 14%.

Illicit Drug Use Among Persons 12 or Older, 2002-2006

Source: *2006 National Survey on Drug Use & Health,* Substance Abuse and Mental Health Services Admin. (SAMHSA), U.S. Dept. of Health and Human Services.

(Numbers in thousands)

	2002		2003		2004		2005		2006	
Drug	No.	%	No.	%	No.	%	No.	%	No.	%
Used In Lifetime										
Illicit Drugs...............	108,255	46	110,205	46.4	110,057	45.8	112,085	46.1	111,774	45.4
Illicit Drugs Other Than Marijuana......	70,300	29.9	71,128	29.9	70,657	29.4	71,822	29.5	72,906	29.6
Used in Past Month										
Illicit Drugs...............	19,522	8.3	19,470	8.2	19,071	7.9	19,720	8.1	20,357	8.3
Illicit Drugs Other Than Marijuana......	8,777	3.7	8,849	3.7	8,247	3.4	8,963	3.7	9,615	3.9
Used In Past Year										
Illicit Drugs...............	35,132	14.9	34,993	14.7	34,807	14.5	35,041	14.4	35,775	14.5
Marijuana and Hashish...............	25,755	11.0	25,231	10.6	25,451	10.6	25,375	10.4	25,378	10.3
Illicit Drugs Other Than Marijuana......	20,423	8.7	20,305	8.5	19,658	8.2	20,109	8.3	21,254	8.6
Cocaine......................	5,902	2.5	5,908	2.5	5,658	2.4	5,523	2.3	6,069	2.5
Crack.......................	1,554	0.7	1,406	0.6	1,304	0.5	1,381	0.6	1,479	0.6
Heroin......................	404	0.2	314	0.1	398	0.2	379	0.2	560	0.2
Hallucinogens................	4,749	2.0	3,936	1.7	3,878	1.6	3,809	1.6	3,956	1.6
LSD.....................	999	0.4	558	0.2	592	0.2	563	0.2	666	0.3
PCP.....................	235	0.1	219	0.1	210	0.1	164	0.1	187	0.1
Ecstasy.................	3,167	1.3	2,119	0.9	1,915	0.8	1,960	0.8	2,130	0.9
Inhalants....................	2,084	0.9	2,075	0.9	2,255	0.9	2,187	0.9	2,218	0.9
Nonmedical Use of Psychotherapeutics..	14,680	6.2	14,986	6.3	14,643	6.1	15,172	6.2	16,287	6.6
Pain Relievers.............	10,992	4.7	11,671	4.9	11,256	4.7	11,815	4.9	12,649	5.1
OxyContin®...............	NA	NA	NA	NA	1,213	0.5	1,226	0.5	1,323	0.5
Tranquilizers..............	4,849	2.1	5,051	2.1	5,068	2.1	5,249	2.2	5,058	2.1
Stimulants................	3,181	1.4	2,751	1.2	2,918	1.2	2,771	1.1	3,394	1.4
Sedatives.................	981	0.4	831	0.3	737	0.3	750	0.3	926	0.4

Drug Use: America's High School Seniors, 1975-2006

Source: *Monitoring the Future,* Univ. of Michigan Inst. for Social Research and National Inst. on Drug Abuse

Class of:	1975	1980	1985	1990	1995	2000	2002	2003	2004	2005	2006	'05-'06 change[7]
Marijuana/hashish.....	47.3%	60.3%	54.2%	40.7%	41.7%	48.8%	47.8%	46.1%	45.7%	44.8%	42.3%	−2.5
Inhalants[1]............	—	17.3	18.1	18.5	17.8	14.2	11.7	11.2	10.9	11.4	11.1	−0.2
Amyl & butyl nitrites....	—	11.1	7.9	2.1	1.5	0.8	1.5	1.6	1.3	1.1	1.2	0.0
Hallucinogens[2]........	—	15.6	12.1	9.7	12.7	13.0	12.0	10.6	9.7	8.8	8.3	−0.5
LSD..............	11.3	9.3	7.5	8.7	11.7	11.1	8.4	5.9	4.6	3.5	3.3	−0.2
PCP.............	—	9.6	4.9	2.8	2.7	3.4	3.1	2.5	1.6	2.4	2.2	−0.2
Ecstasy............	—	—	—	—	—	11.0	10.5	8.3	7.5	5.4	6.5	1.1
Cocaine............	9.0	15.7	17.3	9.4	6.0	8.6	7.8	7.7	8.1	8.0	8.5	0.5
Crack.............	—	—	—	3.5	3.0	3.9	3.8	3.6	3.9	3.5	3.5	0.1
Heroin[3].............	2.2	1.1	1.2	1.3	1.6	2.4	1.7	1.5	1.5	1.5	1.4	−0.1
Other opiates[4]........	9.0	9.8	10.2	8.3	7.2	10.6	13.5	13.2	13.5	12.8	13.4	0.6
Amphetamines[4,5].......	22.3	26.4	26.2	17.5	15.3	15.6	16.8	14.4	15.0	13.1	12.4	−0.6
Methamphetamine...	—	—	—	—	—	7.9	6.7	6.2	6.2	4.5	4.4	−0.1
Crystal Meth........	—	—	—	2.7	3.9	4.0	4.7	3.9	4.0	4.0	3.4	−0.6
Barbiturates[4].......	16.9	11.0	9.2	6.8	7.4	9.2	9.5	8.8	9.9	10.5	10.2	−0.3
Methaqualone[4].....	8.1	9.5	6.7	2.3	1.2	0.8	1.5	1.0	1.3	1.3	1.2	−0.1
Tranquilizers[4].........	17.0	15.2	11.9	7.2	7.1	8.9	11.4	10.2	10.6	9.9	10.3	0.4
Alcohol[6].............	90.4	93.2	92.2	89.5	80.7	80.3	78.4	76.6	76.8	75.1	72.7	−2.4
Cigarettes.............	73.6	71.0	68.8	64.4	64.2	62.5	57.2	53.7	52.8	50.0	47.1	−2.9
Steroids..............	—	—	—	2.9	2.3	2.5	4.0	3.5	3.4	2.6	2.7	0.1

— Data not available. (1) Adjusted for underreporting of amyl and butyl nitrites. (2) Adjusted for underreporting of PCP. (3) Reflects use with or without injection. (4) Includes only drug use that was not under a doctor's orders. (5) Data for 1990-2005 are not directly comparable to prior years. (6) Data for 1995-2005 are not directly comparable to prior years. (7) In percentage points.

Cigarette Use in the U.S., 1985-2006

Source: Substance Abuse and Mental Health Services Administration (SAMHSA), U.S. Dept. of Health and Human Services
(percentage reporting use in the month prior to the survey; figures exclude persons under age 12)

	1985	2000	2003	2004	2005	2006
TOTAL	38.7	24.9	25.4	24.9	24.9	25.0
Sex						
Male	43.4	26.9	28.1	27.7	27.4	27.8
Female	34.5	23.1	23.0	22.3	22.5	22.4
Age group						
12-17	29.4	13.4	12.2	11.9	10.8	10.4
18 and older	47.4	38.3	40.2	39.5	39.0	38.4
26 and older	45.7[1]	24.2	24.7	24.1	24.3	24.7
Race/Ethnicity						
White	38.9	25.9	27.6	26.4	26.0	26.1
Black	38.0	23.3	26.2	23.5	24.5	24.4
Hispanic	40.0	20.7	23.2	21.3	22.1	22.4
Education[2]						
Non-high school graduate	37.3	32.4	35.3	34.8	34.8	35.6
High school graduate	37.0	31.1	31.5	30.4	31.8	31.9
Some college	32.6	27.7	28.9	29.0	28.1	27.7
College graduate	23.0	13.9	14.0	13.6	13.8	14.3

(1) Figures are for all persons aged 26 to 34 only. (2) Estimates for education are for persons aged 18 and older.

Trends in Daily Use of Cigarettes, for U.S. 8th, 10th, and 12th Graders[1]

Source: *Monitoring the Future*, Univ. of Michigan Inst. for Social Research and National Inst. on Drug Abuse
(percent who smoked daily in last 30 days; change 2005-2006 in percentage points)

	8th grade						10th grade						12th grade					
	1995	2000	2004	2005	2006	'05-'06 change	1995	2000	2004	2005	2006	'05-'06 change	1995	2000	2004	2005	2006	'05-'06 change
TOTAL	9.3	7.4	4.4	4.0	4.0	-0.1	16.3	14.0	8.3	7.5	7.6	0.0	21.6	20.6	15.6	13.6	12.2	-1.4
Sex																		
Male	9.2	7.0	4.3	3.9	4.0	0.1	16.3	13.7	8.2	7.2	6.9	-0.3	21.7	20.9	15.4	14.6	12.0	-2.6
Female	9.2	7.5	4.3	4.0	3.8	-0.3	16.1	14.1	8.2	7.7	8.1	0.4	20.8	19.7	15.0	11.9	11.8	-0.1
College plans																		
None or under 4 yrs.	22.5	21.7	15.4	14.4	13.2	-1.2	32.7	28.8	21.4	19.2	21.7	2.4	33.7	31.7	26.9	24.9	22.8	-2.1
Complete 4 yrs.	7.5	5.6	3.1	2.9	2.9	0.1	13.3	11.6	6.4	5.9	5.6	-0.2	17.4	16.6	12.2	10.5	9.4	-1.1
Region																		
Northeast	9.2	6.9	3.3	3.2	3.0	-0.2	15.8	14.1	8.5	7.6	6.2	-1.4	22.5	22.8	16.2	13.3	14.3	1.0
North central	11.0	9.0	5.7	4.8	4.7	-0.1	17.6	16.3	7.4	8.6	10.3	1.7	25.7	23.6	18.5	16.3	13.2	-3.1
South	9.4	7.8	4.7	5.0	5.3	0.4	19.3	15.7	11.0	8.8	8.4	-0.4	21.7	19.4	15.8	15.4	13.3	-2.1
West	7.0	4.9	3.3	2.4	1.8	-0.6	14.9	7.8	5.2	4.0	4.2	0.2	14.5	16.9	10.1	7.6	7.0	-0.5
Race/Ethnicity[2]																		
White	10.5	9.0	4.7	4.6	4.6	0.0	17.6	17.7	10.0	9.1	8.7	-0.4	23.9	25.7	18.3	17.1	15.3	-1.8
Black	2.8	3.2	2.7	2.1	1.9	-0.2	4.7	5.2	4.4	3.9	3.3	-0.6	6.1	8.0	5.2	5.6	5.7	0.0
Hispanic	9.2	7.1	3.5	3.1	2.8	-0.3	9.9	8.8	6.0	5.9	5.3	-0.6	11.6	15.7	8.2	7.7	7.0	-0.7

(1)Totals and percentage changes may not add up due to rounding. (2) For each of these groups, data for the specified year and previous year have been combined to increase sample size and thus provide a more reliable estimate.

Alcohol Use by 8th and 12th Graders, 1980-2006

Source: *Monitoring the Future*, Univ. of Michigan Inst. for Social Research and National Inst. on Drug Abuse

	1980	1990	1995	1996	1997	1998	1999	2000	2001	2002	2003	2004	2005	2006	'05-'06 change
ALCOHOL[1]						Percent using alcohol in the month before the survey									
All 12th graders	72.0	57.1	51.3	50.8	52.7	52.0	51.0	50.0	49.8	48.6	47.5	48.0	47.0	45.3	-1.7%
Male	77.4	61.3	55.7	54.8	56.2	57.3	55.3	54.0	54.7	52.3	51.7	51.1	50.7	47.3	-3.4
Female	66.8	52.3	47.0	46.9	48.9	46.9	46.8	46.1	45.1	45.1	43.8	45.1	43.3	43.0	-0.3
White	75.4	63.8	54.5	54.8	56.4	57.7	56.3	55.1	55.3	54.0	52.3	52.2	52.3	50.7	-1.7
Black	47.6	35.8	35.2	36.5	34.3	33.3	32.2	30.0	29.4	30.1	29.9	29.2	29.0	29.2	0.2
Hispanic	63.6	49.1	48.7	47.5	48.2	49.8	50.2	51.2	48.9	47.5	46.4	45.4	43.3	43.4	0.1
All 8th graders	—	—	24.6	26.2	24.5	23.0	24.0	22.4	21.5	19.6	19.7	18.6	17.1	17.2	0.1
Male	—	—	25.0	26.6	25.2	24.0	24.8	22.5	22.3	19.1	19.4	17.9	16.2	16.3	0.0
Female	—	—	24.0	25.8	23.9	21.9	23.3	22.0	20.6	20.0	19.8	19.0	17.9	17.6	-0.2
White	—	—	25.4	26.6	26.7	24.8	24.7	24.7	23.2	21.5	20.1	19.2	17.9	16.9	-1.0
Black	—	—	18.7	18.1	17.9	16.1	16.0	16.0	15.0	14.8	15.5	16.2	14.9	13.1	-1.8
Hispanic	—	—	32.4	29.7	29.8	29.5	29.0	26.7	25.7	26.5	25.3	23.5	20.6	21.2	0.6
HEAVY ALCOHOL[2]						Percent heavily using the 2 weeks before the survey									
All 12th graders	41.2	32.2	29.8	30.2	31.3	31.5	30.8	30.0	29.7	28.6	27.9	29.2	27.1	25.4	-1.6
Male	52.1	39.1	36.9	37.0	37.9	39.2	38.1	36.7	36.0	34.2	34.2	34.3	32.6	28.9	-3.7
Female	30.5	24.4	23.0	23.5	24.4	24.0	23.6	23.5	23.7	23.0	22.1	24.2	21.6	21.5	-0.1
White	44.3	36.6	32.3	33.4	35.1	36.4	35.7	34.6	34.5	33.7	32.4	32.5	32.5	30.4	-2.1
Black	17.7	14.4	14.9	15.3	13.4	12.3	12.3	11.5	11.8	11.5	10.8	11.4	11.3	11.4	0.1
Hispanic	33.1	25.6	26.6	27.1	27.6	28.1	29.3	31.0	28.4	26.4	25.9	26.0	23.9	23.3	-0.6
All 8th graders	—	—	14.5	15.6	14.5	13.7	15.2	14.1	13.2	12.4	11.9	11.4	10.5	10.9	0.4
Male	—	—	15.1	16.5	15.3	14.4	16.4	14.4	13.7	12.5	12.2	10.8	10.2	10.5	0.4
Female	—	—	13.9	14.5	13.5	12.7	13.9	13.6	12.4	12.1	11.6	11.8	10.6	10.8	0.3
White	—	—	13.9	15.1	15.1	14.1	14.3	14.9	13.8	12.7	11.8	11.3	10.8	10.2	-0.6
Black	—	—	10.8	10.4	9.8	9.0	9.9	10.0	9.0	9.4	10.4	9.8	8.2	8.0	-0.3
Hispanic	—	—	22.0	21.0	20.7	20.4	20.9	19.1	17.6	17.8	16.6	16.1	14.8	14.5	-0.3

— Data not available. **Note:** *Monitoring the Future* study excludes high school dropouts (about 3-6% of the class group, according to a 1996 report) and absentees (about 16-17% of 12th graders and about 9-10% of 8th graders). High school dropouts and absentees have higher alcohol usage than those included in the survey. (1) In 1993 the alcohol question was changed to indicate that a "drink" meant "more than a few sips." (2) Five or more drinks in a row at least once in the prior 2-week period.

Acquired Immune Deficiency Syndrome (AIDS)

Source: Centers for Disease Control and Prevention; www.cdc.gov

AIDS (Acquired Immune Deficiency Syndrome) is caused by the human immunodeficiency virus (**HIV**). HIV kills or disables crucial cells of the immune system, progressively destroying the body's ability to fight disease.

HIV is commonly spread through unprotected sexual contact with an infected partner. It is also spread through contact with infected blood. Where modern screening techniques are used it is rare to contract HIV from transfusion, but it can be contracted when intravenous drug users share syringes with others. Though HIV can be spread through semen, vaginal fluids, and breast milk, there is no evidence it can be spread through saliva. The rate of transmission from a pregnant woman to her infant is about 25% without treatment, but can be reduced to less than 2% with treatment. Studies have indicated no evidence of HIV transmission through casual contact such as the sharing of food utensils, towels and bedding, telephones, or toilet seats.

Some people experience flu-like symptoms a short time after infection with HIV, and scientists estimate that about half of those infected with HIV develop more serious, often chronic symptoms within ten years. Even when symptoms are not present, HIV is active in the body, multiplying, infecting, and killing CD4+ T cells, or "T-helper cells," the crucial immune cells that signal other cells in the immune system to perform their functions.

The term **AIDS** applies to the most advanced stages of HIV infection. According to the official definition set by the Centers for Disease Control and Prevention (CDC), an HIV–infected person with fewer than 200 CD4+ T cells can be said to have AIDS. (Healthy adults usually have 1,000 or more.) An HIV-infected person, regardless of T cell count, is diagnosed with AIDS if he or she develops one of 26 conditions that typically affect people with advanced HIV. Most of these conditions are "opportunistic infections" that occur when the immune system is so ravaged by HIV that the body cannot fight off certain bacteria, viruses and microbes.

Months or years prior to the onset of AIDS, many people experience such symptoms as swollen glands, lack of energy, fevers and sweats, and skin rashes. People with full-blown AIDS may develop infections of the intestinal tract, lungs, brain, eyes, and other organs, with a variety of symptoms, and may become severely debilitated. They also are prone to developing certain cancers, especially those caused by viruses, such as Kaposi's sarcoma, cervical cancer, and lymphoma. Children with AIDS may have delayed development or failure to thrive.

HIV is primarily **detected** by testing a person's blood for the presence of antibodies (disease-fighting proteins) to HIV. In about 5% of infected individuals, HIV antibodies may take more than 6 months after exposure to reach detectable levels, but in most cases the antibodies are detectable in about 6 weeks. HIV testing may also be performed on oral fluid and urine samples. New rapid HIV tests can provide preliminary results in about 20 minutes.

Patients are typically given a combination of different drugs, because HIV can much more easily become resistant to a single drug. While these drugs extend the period between HIV infection and serious illness, they do not prevent the spread of the disease to others, and can have severe side effects.

The **U.S. Food and Drug Administration** has approved a number of **drugs** that may slow down the growth of HIV in the body and treat the infections and cancers associated with AIDS. The first group of drugs used to treat HIV, called nucleoside analog reverse transcriptase inhibitors (NRTIs), include the drug zidovudine (commonly known as AZT). Nonnucleoside reverse transcriptase inhibitors (NNRTIs) have also been approved to treat HIV. A third class of drugs, called protease inhibitors, are also approved for HIV. In 2003 the FDA granted accelerated approval of Fuzeon for use with other anti-HIV drugs to treat advanced cases of infection. Fuzeon was the first among a new class of medications called fusion inhibitors; drugs in this class interfered with HIV's entry into cells by hindering the fusion of viral and cellular membranes. The FDA in July 2006 approved the first once-a-day, single-pill drug combination treatment for AIDS. The development was regarded as a significant milestone in treatment of the disease, which often required the daily administration of several drugs. Two drug companies, Bristol-Myers Squibb Co. and Gilead Sciences Inc., had cooperated to develop the drug, called Atripla. The pill combined three drugs—Sustiva, Viread and Emtriva—and would cost roughly $1,100 per month in the U.S. FDA officials said complicated AIDS drug regimens had often dissuaded patients from taking their pills as directed. They said the new drug would simplify drug regimens and help prevent HIV, the virus that caused AIDS, from gaining resistance to drugs. Health experts expect the drug to dramatically improve AIDS treatment in the developing world.

Since there is no vaccine or cure for AIDS, the only **protection** is to avoid activities that carry a risk. When it cannot be known with certainty whether a sexual partner has HIV, the CDC recommends abstinence (the only certain protection), mutual monogamy with an uninfected partner, or correct and consistent use of male latex condoms.

New AIDS Cases in the U.S., 1985-2003, by Transmission Category

Source: *HIV/AIDS Surveillance Report, 2003*, CDC, National Center for HIV, STD, and TB Prevention, Div. of HIV/AIDS Prevention

TRANSMISSION CATEGORY	Percent distribution	All years[1]	1985	1990	2000	2001	2002	2003
All males 13 years and older	100	729,478	7,504	36,193	30,251	31,901	32,513	33,250
Men who have sex with men	55	401,392	5,348	23,658	13,648	13,265	14,545	15,859
Injecting drug use	21	156,575	1,103	6,923	5,554	5,261	5,121	4,866
Men who have sex with men and injecting drug use	8	57,998	661	2,943	1,587	1,502	1,510	1,695
Hemophilia/coagulation disorder	1	5,130	68	332	93	97	79	74
Heterosexual contact[2]	6	40,947	32	715	2,537	2,762	3,213	3,371
Sex with injecting drug user	1	10,930	25	454	514	549	519	477
Transfusion[3]	1	5,219	102	440	146	105	147	111
Undetermined[4]	9	62,217	190	1,182	6,686	8,909	7,898	7,274
All females 13 years and older	100	163,396	524	4,547	9,979	11,082	11,279	11,561
Injecting drug use	38	61,621	287	2,347	2,545	2,212	2,381	2,262
Hemophilia/coagulation disorder	<1	318	3	15	5	9	11	11
Heterosexual contact[2]	43	70,200	119	1,538	4,025	4,142	4,740	5,234
Sex with injecting drug user	15	24,148	82	1,030	976	937	985	985
Transfusion[3]	2	4,076	63	330	151	113	118	108
Undetermined[4]	17	27,181	52	317	3,253	4,606	4,029	3,946

Note: The definition of AIDS cases for reporting purposes was expanded in 1985, 1987, and 1993, as more was learned about the spectrum of human immunodeficiency virus-associated diseases. Data exclude residents of U.S. territories. (1) Includes cases prior to 1985 and for years not shown. (2) Includes persons who have had heterosexual contact with a person with human immunodeficiency virus (HIV) infection or at risk of HIV infection. (3) Receipt of blood transfusion, blood components, or tissue. (4) Includes persons for whom risk information is incomplete, persons still under investigation, men reported only to have had heterosexual contact with prostitutes, and interviewed persons for whom no specific risk is identified.

AIDS Deaths and New AIDS Cases in the U.S., 1985-2003

Source: *Health, United States, 2004;* National Center for Health Statistics, U.S. Dept. of Health and Human Services

	Percent Distribu- tion	All Years[1]	1985	1990	1995	2000	2001	2002	2003	2003 rate[2]
TOTAL DEATHS	—	524,060	6,981	31,988	52,254	17,741	18,524	17,557	18,017	4.7
		NEW AIDS CASES								
All races	—	874,230	8,131	41,449	70,373	40,165	41,312	42,478	44,232	14.7
All males, 13 years and over	100.0	708,452	7,484	36,180	56,650	30,047	30,570	31,425	32,781	27.4
Race White, non-Hispanic	47.1	333,873	4,743	20,818	25,972	11,224	10,971	11,069	11,831	13.6
Black, non-Hispanic	35.7	253,078	1,695	10,244	20,812	13,041	13,720	14,214	13,820	109.2
Hispanic[3]	15.8	112,101	989	4,746	9,128	5,295	5,329	5,550	6,344	37.2
American Indian or Alaska Native[4]	0.3	2,353	9	81	196	135	145	146	169	16.0
Asian or Pacific Islander[4]	0.8	5,875	47	254	463	275	325	351	458	7.2
Age 13-19 years	0.4	2,861	27	106	223	142	179	197	249	1.3
20-29 years	15.2	107,651	1,497	6,917	8,387	3,327	3,280	3,418	3,570	17.1
30-39 years	44.4	314,224	3,575	16,670	25,680	12,510	12,041	12,011	12,214	55.8
40-49 years	28.1	199,248	1,632	8,832	16,120	9,614	10,234	10,593	11,257	48.4
50-59 years	8.9	62,905	596	2,645	4,691	3,372	3,629	3,926	4,239	23.9
60 years and over	3.0	21,563	157	1,010	1,549	1,082	1,207	1,280	1,252	6.3
All females, 13 years and over	100.0	156,837	519	4,544	12,978	9,932	10,572	10,914	11,297	9.0
Race White, non-Hispanic	21.5	33,766	143	1,230	3,031	1,841	1,977	1,893	1,923	2.2
Black, non-Hispanic	61.4	96,338	275	2,557	7,581	6,455	6,927	7,304	7,373	49.0
Hispanic[4]	15.9	24,997	98	724	2,244	1,476	1,547	1,579	1,776	11.3
American Indian or Alaska Native[4]	0.4	562	2	9	38	68	41	41	61	4.3
Asian or Pacific Islander[4]	0.6	905	1	20	69	71	64	67	105	1.3
Age 13-19 years	1.4	2,177	5	67	157	168	167	195	209	1.4
20-29 years	20.2	31,748	175	1,117	2,676	1,749	1,720	1,815	1,774	9.5
30-39 years	43.1	67,523	230	2,088	5,937	3,965	4,125	3,977	4,075	18.6
40-49 years	24.7	38,685	45	780	3,055	2,851	3,123	3,375	3,547	15.1
50-59 years	7.3	11,483	26	273	818	859	998	1,147	1,253	6.6
60 years and over	3.3	5,221	38	219	335	340	439	405	439	1.5
All children, under 13 years	100.0	8,939	128	725	745	186	170	139	153	0.7
Race White, non-Hispanic	18.0	1,613	26	156	117	30	29	21	23	0.2
Black, non-Hispanic	61.6	5,504	84	390	483	121	111	92	93	3.0
Hispanic[4]	19.2	1,714	18	169	135	30	27	22	34	0.6
American Indian or Alaska Native[4]	0.3	31	—	5	2	1	—	—	—	0.0
Asian or Pacific Islander[4]	0.6	57	—	4	5	3	3	4	1	0.5
Age Under 5 years	76.2	6,812	108	586	553	116	105	87	85	0.4
5-12 years	23.8	2,127	20	139	192	70	65	52	68	0.2

Note: The definition of AIDS cases for reporting purposes was expanded in 1985, 1987, and 1993, as more was learned about the spectrum of human immunodeficiency virus-associated diseases. Data exclude residents of U.S. territories. Figures were updated Dec. 31, 2002 to include delayed case reports and may differ from previous reports of *Health, United States.* (1) Revised figures; includes cases and deaths prior to 1985 and for years not shown. Through 2003. (2) Rate is per 100,000 pop. (3) Persons of Hispanic origin may be of any race. (4) Excludes persons of Hispanic origin.

Allergies and Asthma

Source: Asthma and Allergy Foundation of America, 1233 20th St., NW, Suite 402, Wash., DC 20036; phone: (800) 7-ASTHMA; www.aafa.org

One out of five Americans suffers from **allergies** of some kind. People with allergies have extra-sensitive immune systems that react to normally harmless substances. Common allergens that may produce this reaction include plant pollens, dust mites, or animal dander; plants such as poison ivy; certain drugs, such as penicillin; and certain foods such as eggs, milk, nuts, or seafood.

The **tendency to develop allergies** is usually inherited, and allergies usually begin to appear in childhood, but they can show up at any age. **Common allergies** for infants include food allergies and eczema (patches of dry skin). Older children and adults may often develop allergic rhinitis (hay fever), a reaction to an inhaled allergen; common symptoms include nasal congestion, runny nose, and sneezing.

It is best to avoid contact with the allergen, if feasible. In some cases, **medications** such as antihistamines are used to decrease the reaction, and there are treatments aimed at gradually desensitizing the patient to the allergen. Other effective allergy treatments include decongestants, eye drops, and ointments.

Some people with allergies also have **asthma**, and allergens are a common asthma trigger. Asthma is a disease of chronic inflammation affecting the passages that carry air into and out of the lungs. It can develop at any age.

People with asthma have inflamed, supersensitive airways that tighten and become filled with mucus during an asthma episode. Wheezing, difficulty in breathing, tightening of the chest, and coughing are common symptoms. Asthma can progress through stages to become life-threatening if not controlled. **Emergency symptoms** include: no improvement minutes after initial treatment; struggling to breathe, with patient hunched over and/or chest and neck pulled in; trouble walking or talking; stopping activity and not starting activity again; gray or blue lips or fingernails.

Besides common allergens, tobacco smoke, cold air, and pollution can trigger an asthma attack, as can viral infections or physical exercise. An accurate diagnosis by a physician is important. Although there is no cure for asthma or allergies, they can be controlled with medications and lifestyle changes.

Alzheimer's Disease

Source: Alzheimer's Association, 225 N Michigan Ave., 17th Fl., Chicago, IL 60601-7633; phone: (800) 272-3900; www.alz.org

Alzheimer's disease, the most common form of dementia, is a progressive, degenerative disease of the brain in which nerve cells deteriorate and die for unknown reasons. Its first symptoms usually involve impaired memory and confusion about recent events. As the disease advances, it results in greater impairment of memory, thinking, judgement, language, behavior, and physical health.

The **rate of progression** of Alzheimer's varies, ranging from 3 to 20 years; the average length of time from onset of symptoms until death is 8 years. Eventually, affected individuals lose their ability to care for themselves and become susceptible to infections of the lungs, urinary tract, or other organs as they grow progressively debilitated.

Alzheimer's disease affects an estimated 4.5 mil Americans, striking men and women of all ethnic groups. Although most people diagnosed with Alzheimer's are older than age 60, some cases occur in people in their 40s and 50s. An estimated 10% of the population over age 65 have Alzheimer's, and the disease affects almost half of those over 85. In the United States, annual costs of diagnosis, treatment, and long-term care are estimated at $100 billion.

Diagnosis involves a comprehensive evaluation that may include a complete health history, a physical examination, neurological and mental status assessments, and other testing as needed. Skilled health care professionals can generally diagnose Alzheimer's with about 90% accuracy. Other conditions that can cause similar symptoms include depression, drug interactions, nutritional imbalances, infections such as AIDS, meningitis, and syphilis, and other forms of dementia, such as those associated with stroke, Huntington's disease, Parkinson's disease, frontotemporal dementia, and vascular disease. Absolute confirmation of diagnosis requires a brain biopsy or autopsy.

Treatments for cognitive and behavioral symptoms are available, but no intervention has yet been developed that prevents Alzheimer's or reverses its course. Some research suggests that risk factors for heart disease, such as high blood pressure, elevated cholesterol, diabetes and excess body weight may also increase risk of developing Alzheimer's. Studies also suggest that staying physically and mentally active and socially connected may be associated with a lower risk for the disease.

Providing care for people with Alzheimer's is physically and psychologically demanding. Nearly 70% of affected individuals live at home, where family or friends care for them. In advanced stages of the disease, many individuals require long-term residential care. Nearly half of all nursing home residents in the U.S. have Alzheimer's.

People with Alzheimer's need a safe, stable environment and a regular daily schedule offering appropriate stimulation. Physical exercise and social interaction are important, as are proper nutritionand adequate pain management. Security is also a consideration, because many people with Alzheimer's tend to wander. An identification bracelet listing the person's name, address, and condition may help ensure the safe return of an individual who wanders.

Warning Signs of Alzheimer's Disease

- Forgetting recently learned information or inability to learn new information
- Difficulty with everyday tasks such as cooking or dressing
- Inability to remember simple words
- Use of inappropriate words when communicating
- Disorientation to time and place
- Poor or decreased judgment
- Problems with abstract thinking
- Putting objects in inappropriate places
- Rapid changes in mood or behavior
- Increased irritability, anxiety, depression, confusion, and restlessness
- Prolonged loss of initiative

Arthritis

Source: Arthritis Foundation, P.O. Box 7669, Atlanta, GA 30357-0669; phone: (800) 568-4045; www.arthritis.org

The term "arthritis" refers to more than 100 different diseases that cause pain, stiffness, swelling, and restricted movement in joints. The condition is usually chronic. The Centers for Disease Control and Prevention (CDC) estimates that nearly 70 million adults suffer from arthritis and/or chronic joint symptoms. Arthritis annually results in 39 mil doctor visits, 744,000 hospitalizations, and 2.2 mil visits to emergency rooms. The cause for most types of arthritis is unknown; scientists are studying the roles played by genetics, lifestyle, and the environment.

Symptoms of arthritis may develop either slowly or suddenly. A visit to the doctor is indicated when pain, stiffness, or swelling in a joint or difficulty in moving a joint persists for more than two weeks. To make a diagnosis of arthritis, the doctor records the patient's symptoms and examines joints, looking for any swelling or limited movement. In addition, the doctor checks for other signs often seen with arthritis, such as rashes, mouth sores, or eye involvement. Finally, the doctor may test the blood, urine, or joint fluid, or take X-rays of the joints.

Of the 3 most prevalent forms of arthritis, **osteoarthritis** is the most common, affecting more than 21 mil Americans; it usually occurs after age 45. In this type, which is also called degenerative arthritis, the protective cartilage of joints is lost and changes occur in the bone, leading to pain and stiffness. It usually occurs in the fingers, knees, feet, hips, and back.

Fibromyalgia, another common arthritis condition, affects more than 2 million Americans and affects more women than men. In this form, widespread pain and tenderness occur in muscles and their attachments to the bone. Common symptoms include fatigue, disturbed sleep, stiffness, and psychological distress.

Rheumatoid arthritis, which also affects more than 2 million people in the U.S., is one of the most serious and disabling forms of the disease. In this type, which is also more common and more degenerative in women, inflammation of the joints leads to damage of the cartilage and bone. The areas of the body that can be affected are the hands, wrists, feet, knees, ankles, shoulders, neck, jaw, and elbows.

Other forms of arthritis and related conditions include lupus, gout, ankylosing spondylitis, and scleroderma; also related are bursitis and tendinitis, which may result from injuring or overusing a joint.

Medications to treat arthritis include drugs that relieve pain and swelling such as analgesics, anti-inflammatory drugs, biologic response modifiers, glucocorticoids and antirheumatic drugs that also tend to slow the disease process. Most treatment programs call for exercise, use of heat or cold, and joint-protection techniques, such as avoiding excess stress on joints, using assistive devices, and controlling weight. In some cases, surgery can help.

Cancer Prevention

Source: American Cancer Society, 1599 Clifton Road NE, Atlanta, GA 30329-4251; phone: (800) 227-2345

PRIMARY PREVENTION: Modifiable determinants of cancer risk.

Smoking	Lung cancer mortality rates are about 23 times higher for current male smokers, and 13 times higher for current female smokers, than for those who have never smoked. Smoking accounts for about 30% of all cancer deaths in the U.S. Tobacco use is responsible for nearly 1 in 5 deaths in the U.S. Smoking is associated with cancer of the lung, mouth, nasal cavities, pharynx, larynx, esophagus, stomach, pancreas, uterine cervix, kidney, bladder, and myeloid leukemia.
Nutrition and Diet	Risk for colon, breast (among postmenopausal women), kidney, prostate, and endometrial cancers increases in obese people. While a diet high in fat may be a factor in the development of certain cancers, the link between obesity and cancer is more the result of an imbalance between caloric intake and energy expenditure than fat per se. Eating 5 or more servings of fruits and vegetables each day, and eating other foods from plant sources (especially grains and beans), may reduce risk for many cancers. Physical activity can help protect against some cancers.
Sunlight	Many of the 1 million skin cancers that are diagnosed annually in the U.S. could have been prevented by protection from the sun's rays. Epidemiological evidence shows that sun exposure is a major factor in the development of melanoma and that the incidence rates are increasing around the world.
Alcohol	Heavy drinking, especially when accompanied by cigarette smoking or smokeless tobacco use, increases risk of cancers of the mouth, larynx, pharynx, esophagus, and liver. Studies have also noted an association between regular alcohol consumption and an increased risk of breast cancer.
Smokeless Tobacco	Use of chewing tobacco or snuff increases risk of cancers of the mouth and pharynx. The excess risk of cancer of the cheek and gum may reach nearly 50-fold among long-term snuff users.
Estrogen	Estrogen replacement therapy (ERT) to control menopausal symptoms can increase the risk of endometrial cancer. However, adding progesterone to estrogen (hormone replacement therapy, or HRT) helps to minimize this risk. Most studies suggest that long-term use (5 years or more) of HRT after menopause increases the risk of breast cancer, and recent studies suggest that risks from taking HRT exceed benefits. The benefits and risks of the use of HRT or ERT by menopausal women should be discussed carefully by the woman and her doctor.
Radiation	Excessive exposure to ionizing radiation can increase cancer risk. Medical and dental X rays are adjusted to deliver the lowest dose possible without sacrificing image quality. Excessive radon exposure in the home may increase lung cancer risk, especially in cigarette smokers.
Environmental Hazards	Exposure to various chemicals (including benzene, asbestos, vinyl chloride, arsenic, and aflatoxin) increases risk of various cancers. Risk of lung cancer from asbestos is greatly increased when combined with smoking.

Cancer-Detection Guidelines

SECONDARY PREVENTION: Steps to diagnose a cancer or precursor as early as possible after it has developed.

In addition to indicated screening for cancers of the breast, colon, and rectum, prostate, and uterine cervix, a cancer-related checkup should include health counseling and, depending on a person's age, might include examinations for cancers of the thyroid, oral cavity, skin, lymph nodes, testes, and ovaries, as well as for some nonmalignant diseases. Special tests for certain cancer sites for individuals at average risk are recommended as outlined below:

Breast Cancer	Women should start getting annual mammograms beginning at age 40. Women who are at increased risk because of family history, genetic predisposition, or past breast cancer should discuss the benefits and limitations of initiating screening at an earlier age. Clinical breast exam should be part of a periodic health exam, about every 3 years for women in their 20's and 30's, and every year for women 40 and older. Women should be aware of any changes in their breasts and report these promptly to their health care provider.
Cervical Cancer	Women should begin cervical cancer screening about 3 years after they begin having vaginal intercourse, but no later than when they are 21 years old. Screening should be done every year with the regular Pap test or every 2 years using the newer liquid-based Pap test.
	Beginning at age 30, women who have had 3 normal Pap test results in a row may get screened every 2 to 3 years. Women who have certain risk factors such as diethylstilbestrol (DES) exposure before birth, HIV infection, or a weakened immune system due to organ transplant, chemotherapy, or chronic steroid use should continue to be screened annually.
	Another reasonable option for women over 30 is to get screened every 3 years (but no more frequently) with either the conventional or liquid-based Pap test, *plus* the HPV DNA test.
	Women 70 years of age or older who have had 3 or more normal Pap tests in a row and no abnormal Pap test results in the last 10 years may choose to stop having cervical cancer screening. Women with a history of cervical cancer, DES exposure before birth, HIV infection or a weakened immune system should continue to have screening as long as they are in good health. Women who have had a total hysterectomy (removal of the uterus and cervix) may also choose to stop having cervical cancer screening, unless the surgery was done as a treatment for cervical cancer or precancer. Women who have had a hysterectomy without removal of the cervix should continue to follow the guidelines above.
Colorectal Cancer	Beginning at age 50, both men and women should follow one of these testing schedules: • Yearly fecal occult blood test; or flexible sigmoidoscopy every five years; or • yearly fecal occult blood test plus flexible sigmoidoscopy every 5 years; or • colonoscopy every 10 years; or • double-contrast barium enema every 5-10 years. **Note:** Persons known to be at increased risk for colorectal cancer (due to inflammatory bowel disease, personal or family history, etc.) need to begin screening at an early age and may need more frequent screening.
Endometrial Cancer	For women with or at high risk of hereditary nonpolyposis colon cancer (HNPCC), annual screening including endometrial biopsy should be obtained beginning at age 35.
Prostate Cancer	The prostate specific antigen (PSA) test and the digital rectal examination should offered annually, beginning at age 50, by men who have a10-year life expectancy. Men at high risk such as African-American men and men with a strong family history of one or more first-degree relatives (father, brother, or son) diagnosed with prostate cancer at an early age, should start getting tested at age 45. For both men at average risk and high risk, information should be provided about what is known and what is uncertain about the benefits and limitations of early detection and treatment of prostate cancer so that they can make an informed decision about testing.
Skin Cancer	Adults should practice skin self-exam regularly. Suspicious lesions and moles should be evaluated promptly by a physician.

Expected New Cancer Cases and Deaths, by Sex, for Leading Sites, 2007

Source: American Cancer Society

The estimates of expected new cases are offered as a rough guide only. They exclude basal and squamous cell skin cancers and in situ carcinomas, except urinary bladder. Carcinoma in situ of the breast accounts for about 54,890 new cases annually, melanoma carcinoma in situ for about 46,170. More than 1 mil cases of basal cell and squamous cell cancer, which are highly curable forms of skin cancer, occur annually.

EXPECTED NEW CASES

Both sexes		Women		Men	
Lung	213,380	Breast	178,480	Prostate	218,890
Colorectal	153,760	Lung	98,620	Lung	114,760
Urinary bladder	67,160	Colorectal	74,630	Colorectal	79,130
Non-Hodgkin lymphoma	63,190	Uterine corpus	39,080	Urinary bladder	50,040
Melanoma	59,940	Non-Hodgkin lymphoma	28,990	Non-Hodgkins lymphoma	34,200
Kidney	51,190	Melanoma	26,030	Melanoma	33,910
Pancreas	37,170	Thyroid	25,480	Kidney	31,590
Thyroid	33,550	Ovary	22,430	Pancreas	18,830
Stomach	21,260	Kidney	19,600	Liver	13,650
Liver	19,160	Pancreas	18,340	Stomach	13,000
ALL SITES	1,444,920	ALL SITES	678,060	ALL SITES	766,860

EXPECTED DEATHS

Both sexes		Women		Men	
Lung	160,390	Lung	70,880	Lung	89,510
Colorectal	52,180	Breast	40,460	Colorectal	26,000
Pancreas	33,370	Colorectal	26,180	Prostate	27,050
Non-Hodgkin's lymphoma	18,660	Pancreas	16,530	Pancreas	16,840
Liver	16,780	Ovary	15,280	Liver	11,280
Esophagus	13,940	Non-Hodgkin lymphoma	9,060	Esophagus	10,900
Urinary bladder	13,750	Uterine corpus	7,400	Urinary bladder	9,630
Kidney	12,890	Liver	5,500	Non-Hodgkin lymphoma	9,600
Stomach	11,210	Kidney	4,810	Kidney	8,080
Acute myeloid Leukemia	8,990	Stomach	4,600	Stomach	6,610
ALL SITES	559,650	ALL SITES	270,100	ALL SITES	289,550

U.S. Cancer Incidence for Top 15 Sites

Source: Surveillance, Epidemiology, and End Results (SEER) Program, National Cancer Institute

	Rate[1]	Average yearly % change[2]		Rate[1]	Average yearly % change[2]
ALL SITES	470.1	−0.6	Kidney and renal pelvis	12.8	2.1
Prostate	73.9	0.3	Corpus and uterus, NOS	12.6	−1.0
Breast	69.6	−1.1	Leukemia	12.3	−1.0
Lung and bronchus	64.5	−1.4	Pancreas	11.4	0.0
Colon and rectum	51.6	−1.5	Oral cavity and pharynx	10.5	−1.5
Urinary bladder	21.1	0.0	Thyroid	8.5	5.3
Non-Hodgkin lymphoma	19.3	0.1	Stomach	8.1	−1.5
Melanoma of the skin	18.5	1.2	Ovary	7.4	−1.3

(1) For 2000-2004, per 100,000 population; rates for prostate, breast, corpus and uterus, and ovary are sex-specific; rates age-adjusted to the 2000 population, and so not comparable with previously published rates. (2) For 1995-2004.

U.S. Cancer Mortality for Top 15 Sites

Source: Surveillance, Epidemiology, and End Results (SEER) Program, National Cancer Institute

	Rate[1]	Average yearly % change[2]		Rate[1]	Average yearly % change[2]
ALL SITES	192.7	−1.2	Ovary	5.0	−0.3
Lung	54.7	−1.0	Liver and intrahepatic bile duct	4.9	1.7
Colon and rectum	19.4	−2.2	Brain and other nervous system	4.4	−1.0
Breast	14.5	−2.4	Esophagus	4.4	0.3
Pancreas	10.6	0.1	Urinary bladder	4.3	−0.2
Prostate	10.5	−3.6	Stomach	4.2	−3.2
Non-Hodgkin lymphoma	7.6	−2.5	Kidney and renal pelvis	4.2	−0.4
Leukemia	7.5	−0.8	Myeloma	3.7	−0.9

(1) For 2000-2004, per 100,000 population; rates age-adjusted to the 2000 population, and so not comparable with previously published rates; annual average for 8-year period; rates for prostate, breast, and ovary are sex-specific. (2) For 1995-2004.

Breast Cancer

Source: American Cancer Society, Inc., 1599 Clifton Road NE, Atlanta, GA 30329-4251; phone: (800) 227-2345

In 2007, an estimated 178,480 women and 2,030 men in the U.S. will have been diagnosed with breast cancer, and about 40,460 women and 450 men will have died from it. Currently, an estimated 2.4 mil women are living with a history of breast cancer, the 2nd biggest cause of cancer death for women in the U.S. (lung cancer ranks first). But mortality rates have been declining, especially among younger women, probably because of earlier detection and improved treatment.

The **risk** for breast cancer increases with age. It is higher for women with a personal or family history of cancer, a long menstrual history (menstrual periods that started early and ended late in life), recent use of birth control pills, long-term use of postmenopausal hormone replacement therapy, and no children or no live birth until age 30 or older. Other risk factors include alcohol consumption and obesity. Inherited mutations such as in the BRCA1 and BRCA2 genes greatly increase risk, but these probably account for 5% to 10% of all breast cancers. By far the majority of women who develop breast cancer have no family history of it.

Breast cancer is often **manifested** first as an abnormality on a mammogram, a type of X-ray. Physical symptoms that show up later, which may be detectable by a woman or her doctor, include a breast lump and, less commonly, breast thickening, swelling, distortion, or tenderness; skin irritation or dimpling; or pain, scaliness, or retraction of the nipple.

Breast pain is more commonly associated with benign (noncancerous) conditions.

Studies show that **early detection** increases survival and treatment options (*See* "Cancer Prevention" p. 141). Although most breast lumps that are detected are noncancerous, any suspicious lump needs to be biopsied.

Treatment for breast cancer may involve lumpectomy (local removal of a tumor), mastectomy (surgical removal of the breast), radiation therapy, chemotherapy, hormone therapy, immunotherapy, or some combination. For early-stage breast cancer, long-term survival rates following lumpectomy plus radiation therapy are similar to survival rates after mastectomy.

Prostate Cancer

Source: Prostate Cancer Foundation, 1250 Fourth Street Santa Monica, CA 90401

The **prostate** is a male gland located between the bladder and scrotum that secretes seminal fluid. Prostate cancer is the most common form of cancer among American men after skin cancer, and the most common cause of cancer death among American men after lung cancer. The American Cancer Society estimates that 218,890 men will be diagnosed with the disease in 2007, and over 27,050 will die from it. Over the course of a lifetime, 1 in 6 men will develop prostate cancer, but only 1 in 34 will die from it.

The exact **cause** of prostate cancer is unknown. The most identifiable risk factors are age, family history, and race. About 65% of all prostate cancers are diagnosed in men over the age of 65, and the chances of developing the disease rise dramatically with age. Men with a single relative with a history of prostate cancer are twice as likely to develop the disease, and those with two or more relatives are more than four times as likely to get it. African-American men are 65% more likely to get the disease than white men and are twice as likely to die from it. The cause for this disparity remains

unknown; it is likely that both socioeconomic and biologic differences are involved.

Usually, the disease has no **symptoms** in its early stages. If symptoms arise, they may include: a need to urinate frequently; difficulty starting urination; weak or interrupted flow; pain during urination; difficulty having an erection; painful ejaculation; blood in urine or semen; frequent pain or stiffness in lower back, hips or upper thighs.

White men over 50 with no family history of prostate cancer are typically encouraged to be screened annually for the disease with both a prostate specific antigen (**PSA**) **blood test** and a **digital rectal exam** (DRE). African-American men or those with a family history of the disease may be encouraged to undergo screening beginning at age 40 or 45. Men under 40 seldom get prostate cancer.

Treatment may include surgery, radiation, hormone deprivation therapy, chemotherapy, or a combination. If caught early, while tumor cells are localized within the prostate, the cure rate is over 90%.

Skin Cancer

Source: American Cancer Society

Skin cancer is generally divided into two main classes, nonmelanomas and melanomas, both types affecting different types of skin cells. Melanoma develops in skin cells called melanocytes, which are cells that produce melanin, a pigment that gives skin a tan or brown color and helps to protect the deeper layers of skin from the harmful effects of the sun. Melanoma is the most dangerous type of skin cancer because it can easily spread to other parts of the body.

Although skin cancer is the most common type of cancer diagnosed, Melanoma only accounts for about 4% of skin cancers. According to the American Cancer Society, in 2007 there will be 59,940 new cases of melanoma diagnosed in the U.S., and about 8,110 people will die from the disease.

The exact causes of melanoma are not clear, but there are several risk factors that have been associated with the disease, which include:

- Over-exposure to UV light (sunlight)
- Presence of moles; moles themselves are not harmful but they are associated with an increased risk for skin cancer
- Family history
- Taking immune suppression drugs
- Age; melanoma is more likely to happen in older people
- Gender; men get melanoma more often than women
- Past history with melanoma
- Xeroderma pigmentosum (XP), a rare, genetic condition in which people are less able to repair damage caused by sunlight.

Melanomas generally look like abnormal moles on the surface of the skin. Normal moles are most often an evenly colored brown, tan, or black spot on the skin that can either be flat or raised. They normally have a distinct border that separates them from normal skin cells. Moles can be present

at birth, form over time, or even disappear. Abnormal moles differ from regular skin cells and may be a sign of skin cancer. If you suspect you have an irregular mole, it is important to have it examined as soon as possible. Irregular moles generally have the following characteristics:

- Asymmetry—one half of the mole does not match the other half.
- Irregular border—the edge of the mole is jagged and doesn't have as distinct divide between it and regular skin.
- Color—it is not the same all over the mole; there may be shades of tan, brown, black, and sometimes patches of red, blue, or white.
- Diameter—moles wider than ¼ inch are abnormal (however, melanomas can be smaller).

After examination, if a melanoma is suspected, the doctor will perform a biopsy using either cells extracted from the suspected cancer or by removing the whole mass and examining it. If a melanoma is found, doctors will often check to see if the cancer has spread to other parts of the body. This is called staging and it is represented by Roman numerals I-IV (1-4). The lower the number, the less the cancer has spread. This will determine what course of treatment is necessary.

If caught early melanoma is highly curable. The 5-year survival rates for the various stages are as follows:

- **0.** 97%
- **I.** 90-95%
- **II.** 45-78%
- **III.** 28-70%
- **IV.** 18%

Treatment may include: simple removal of the melanoma; amputation if the cancer is found on the finger or toe; or treatment of cancer in other parts of the body if the melanoma spread, which may involve chemotherapy, immunotherapy, or radiation.

Depression

Source: National Institute of Mental Health (NIMH)

Depression is a serious illness that affects thoughts, feelings, and the ability to function in everyday life. It strikes across all age groups, and often goes unrecognized or inadequately treated. The National Institutes of Health estimates that about 19 million Americans suffer from depression in any given year and that more than 16% of all Americans will have had depression at some point in life. Young people are among those at risk; in a one-year period, 3 times as many persons with depression were 18 to 29 years old as were 60 or older.

Nearly twice as many women as men suffer from a depressive illness in a given year. Although conventional wisdom holds that depression is most closely associated with menopause, in fact, the childbearing years are marked by the highest rates of depression, followed by the years prior to menopause. The influence of hormones on depression in women has been an active area of NIMH research.

In a given year, 1-2% of people over age 65 living in the community (outside of institutions) suffer from major depression. Depression frequently occurs with other physical illnesses, including heart disease, stroke, cancer, and diabetes. It is not a normal part of aging.

The **treatments** that are now available can alleviate symptoms, and with awareness growing, more people with depression are seeking the help they need. But many depressed people—and those around them—still fail to realize that they have an illness or could benefit from medical help. According to the NIH, more than half of those seeking help do not get adequate treatment, often because they consult family practitioners who do not deal aggressively enough with the problem.

Symptoms and Types of Depression

- persistent sad mood
- loss of interest or pleasure in activities once enjoyed, including sex
- significant change in appetite or body weight
- difficulty sleeping or oversleeping
- lethargy or agitation
- loss of energy
- feelings of worthlessness or inappropriate guilt
- difficulty thinking or concentrating
- recurrent thoughts of death or suicide

A diagnosis of **major depressive disorder** (or **unipolar major depression**) is made if an individual has 5 or more of these symptoms during the same two-week period. Unipolar major depression typically comes to the fore in episodes that recur during a person's lifetime.

Bipolar disorder (or **manic-depressive illness**) is characterized by episodes of major depression as well as episodes of mania—abnormally and persistently elevated mood or irritability, accompanied by such symptoms as inflated self-esteem, less need for sleep, increased talkativeness, rac-

ing thoughts, distractibility, agitation, and excessive involvement in pleasurable activities that have a high potential for painful consequences. While sharing some of the features of major depression, bipolar disorder is a distinct illness.

Dysthymic disorder (or **dysthymia**), a less severe yet typically more chronic form of depression, is diagnosed when a depressed mood persists for at least two years in adults (one year in children or adolescents) and is accompanied by at least 2 other depressive symptoms. Many people with dysthymic disorder also experience major depressive episodes.

In contrast to the normal experiences of sadness, or passing moods, depression is extreme and persistent and can interfere significantly with an individual's ability to function. A recent study sponsored by the World Health Organization and the World Bank found unipolar major depression to be the leading cause of disability in the U.S. and worldwide.

Treatments for Depression

A variety of **medicines** are used to treat depression. These drugs influence the functioning of certain neurotransmitters in the brain, primarily serotonin and norepinephrine, known as monoamines. Older drugs—so-called tricyclic antidepressants (TCAs) and monoamine oxidase inhibitors (MAOIs)—affect the functioning of both of these neurotransmitters. But they can have strong side effects or, in the case of MAOIs, require dietary restrictions. Newer medications, such as the selective serotonin reuptake inhibitors (SSRIs), have fewer side effects. All of these medications can be effective, but some people respond to one type and not another.

NIMH research has shown that certain types of **psychotherapy**, particularly cognitive-behavioral therapy (CBT) and interpersonal therapy (IPT), can help relieve depression. CBT helps patients change the negative styles of thinking and behaving often associated with depression. IPT focuses on working through disturbed personal relationships that may contribute to depression. Studies of adults have shown that a combination of psychotherapy and antidepressant medication is most effective in treating moderate-to-severe depression.

Electroconvulsive therapy (ECT) has been found effective in treating 80-90% of cases of severe depression, particularly those that have not responded to other forms of treatment. ECT involves producing a seizure in the brain of a patient under general anesthesia by applying electrical stimulation through electrodes placed on the scalp. Memory loss and other cognitive problems are common, but typically short-lived, side effects.

For more information, start with the website www.nimh.nih.gov/healthinformation/depressionmenu.cfm

Diabetes

Source: American Diabetes Association, 1701 N Beauregard St., Alexandria, VA 22311; phone: (800) 342-2383

Diabetes is a chronic disease in which the body does not produce or properly use **insulin**, a hormone needed to convert sugar, starches, and other foods into energy necessary for daily life. Both genetics and environment appear to play roles in the onset of diabetes. This disease, which has no cure, is the 5th-leading cause of death by disease in the U.S. According to death certificate data, diabetes contributed to 224,092 deaths in 2002.

It is estimated that there are 20.8 mil Americans with diabetes, 6.2 mil of whom are undiagnosed.

The American Diabetes Association recommends the following **guidelines for diagnosing diabetes**: lowering the acceptable level of blood sugar in a fasting glucose test from 140 mg of glucose/deciliter of blood to 126 mg/deciliter; testing all adults 45 years and older, and then every 3 years

if normal; and testing at a younger age, or more frequently, in high-risk individuals. The American Diabetes Association supports studies that have proven that detection at an earlier stage and modest lifestyle changes, such as eating better and exercising more, will help prevent or delay complications.

There are 2 major types of diabetes:

Type 1 (formerly known as insulin dependent, or juvenile diabetes). The body produces very little or no insulin; disease most often begins in childhood or early adulthood. People with type 1 diabetes must take daily insulin injections to stay alive.

Type 2 (formerly known as non-insulin dependent, or adult-onset diabetes). The body does not produce enough or cannot properly use insulin. It is the most common form of the disease (90-95% of cases in people over age 20) and often begins later in life.

Pre-Diabetes

Among U.S. adults 40-74 years of age, 41 mil (40.1% of the population) have **pre-diabetes**, the state that occurs when a person's blood glucose levels are higher than normal but not high enough for a diagnosis of diabetes.

About 11% of people with pre-diabetes developed type 2 diabetes during each year of the study. Other studies show that most people with pre-diabetes develop type 2 diabetes in 10 years.

Complications of Diabetes

People often have diabetes many years before it is diagnosed. During that time, serious complications have a chance to develop. Potential complications include:

Blindness. Diabetes is the leading cause of blindness in people ages 20-74. Each year, from 12,000 to 24,000 people lose their sight because of diabetes.

Kidney disease. 10% to 21% of all people with diabetes develop kidney disease. In 2002, more than 44,400 people initiated treatment for end-stage renal disease (kidney failure) because of diabetes.

Amputations. Diabetes is the most frequent cause of nontraumatic lower limb amputations. The risk of a leg amputation is 15 to 40 times greater for a person with diabetes than for the average American. Each year, an estimated 80,000 people lose a foot or leg as a result of complications brought on by diabetes.

Heart disease and stroke. People with diabetes are 2 to 4 times more likely to have heart disease. And they are 2 to 4 times more likely to suffer a stroke. About 65% of deaths among people with diabetes are due to heart disease and stroke.

Warning Signs of Diabetes

Type 1 Diabetes (usually occurs suddenly):

frequent urination	unusual weight loss
unusual thirst	extreme fatigue
extreme hunger	irritability

Type 2 Diabetes (occurs less suddenly):

any type 1 symptoms	cuts/bruises slow to heal
frequent infections	tingling/numbness in hands or feet
blurred vision	recurring skin, gum, or bladder infections

Eating Disorders

Source: National Institute of Mental Health

Eating disorders involve serious disturbances in eating behavior, usually in the form of extreme and unhealthy reduction of food intake or severe overeating. They are not due to a failure of will; rather, they are real and treatable medical illnesses in which certain patterns of behavior get out of control. The **main types** are anorexia nervosa, bulimia nervosa, and binge-eating disorder. These disorders usually develop in adolescence or early adulthood and often occur with other illnesses such as depression, substance abuse, and anxiety disorders. They are much more common among females; only about 5% to 15% of anorexia or bulimia patients and 35% of binge eaters are male.

If not treated, eating disorders can lead serious complications, including heart conditions and kidney failure, which may lead to death.

Anorexia nervosa affects an estimated 0.5% to 3.7% of females during their lifetime. Symptoms include resistance to maintaining weight at even minimally normal levels, intense fear of gaining weight, exaggerated importance of body weight or shape in one's self image, and infrequent or absent menstrual periods. Anorexics see themselves as overweight even though they are dangerously thin. In response, they avoid food, and often takes other extreme measures to lose weight, such as compulsive exercise or purging by means of vomiting or laxatives and enemas. While some anorexics fully recover after a single episode, others may relapse frequently or experience chronic deterioration.

Bulimia nervosa affects an estimated 1.1% to 4.2% of females. It is characterized by recurrent uncontrolled binge-eating episodes followed by a compensatory behavior to prevent weight gain, such as self-induced vomiting, excessive exercise, or fasting. Persons with bulimia usually end up weighing within a normal range for their age and height, but they may fear gaining weight and feel intensely dissatisfied with their bodies. They often perform their behaviors in secret, feeling ashamed when they binge and relieved when they purge.

Binge-eating disorder (not officially approved as a psychiatric diagnosis) affects an estimated 2% to 5% of Americans in any given 6-month period. Like bulimia, a binge-eating disorder involves episodes of excessive eating during which the sufferer may lose all control, but individuals with this disorder do not compensate by purging, exercising, or fasting. Many are thus overweight, and the shame associated with the illness can lead to further bingeing.

Eating disorder sufferers may not admit they are ill and may resist treatment. Early diagnosis and a comprehensive treatment program are essential to recovery. Some patients may need immediate hospitalization. For anorexia, treatment usually follows 3 established steps: weight restoration (usually in an inpatient hospital setting), treatment of any accompanying psychological disturbances, and achieving long-term remission or recovery. Medications may be helpful in treating underlying depression or anxiety. Families are sometimes involved in the therapeutic process.

Heart and Blood Vessel Disease

Sources: American Heart Association, 7272 Greenville Ave., Dallas, TX 75231-4596; phone: (800) 242-8721; Centers for Disease Control and Prevention; National Center for Health Statistics; National Institutes of Health; National Heart, Blood, and Lung Institute

Warning Signs Of Heart Attack

- Chest discomfort. Most heart attacks involve discomfort in the center of the chest that lasts more than a few minutes, or that goes aways and comes back. It can feel like uncomfortable pressure, squeezing, fullness, or pain.
- Discomfort in other areas of the upper body. Symptoms can include pain or discomfort in one or both arms, the back, neck, jaw, or stomach.
- Shortness of breath. This feeling may occur with or without chest discomfort.
- Other signs: These may include breaking out in a cold sweat, nausea, or lightheadedness.
- The American Heart Assoc. advises immediate action at onset of symptoms, as more than half of heart attack victims die witin an hour of symptoms.

Of Stroke

- Sudden numbness or weakness of face, arm or leg, especially on one side of the body
- Sudden confusion, trouble speaking or understanding
- Sudden trouble seeing in one or both eyes
- Sudden trouble walking, dizziness, loss of balance or coordination
- Sudden severe headache with no known cause
- Prompt treatment of stroke can be a major factor in controlling the effects.

Some Major Modifiable Risk Factors

High Blood pressure—High blood pressure, or hypertension, increases the risk of stroke, heart attack, kidney failure, and heart failure. It affects people of all races, sexes, ethnic origins, and ages. Obesity, physical inactivity, and an unhealthy diet can contribute to this **often symptomless** disease, and it is recommended that individuals have a blood pressure reading at least once every 2 years (more often if advised by a physician).

A blood pressure reading is really two measurements in one, with one written over the other, such as 122/78. The **upper number (systolic pressure)** represents the amount of pressure in the blood vessels when the heart contracts (beats) and pushes blood through the circulatory system. The **lower number (diastolic pressure)** represents the pressure in the blood vessels between beats, when the heart is resting. According to recent National Institutes of Health guidelines, a blood pressure reading below 120/80 is considered normal, while readings from 120/80 to 139/89 are considered "prehypertension."

High blood pressure is divided into 2 stages:
Stage 1 is 140-159 (systolic) over 90-99 (diastolic);
Stage 2 is 160+ (systolic) over 100+ (diastolic).

Individuals with diabetes or chronic kidney disease are considered to have high blood pressure if they have a reading of 130/80 or higher. The diagnosis can be based on either the systolic or the diastolic reading.

High blood pressure usually cannot be cured, but it can be controlled in a variety of ways, including lifestyle modifications and medication. Treatment always should be at the direction and under the supervision of a physician.

High Blood Cholesterol—Cholesterol is a waxy fat-like substance found in all cells of the body. It is produced by the body and also comes in some foods. The body needs some cholesterol, but excess levels increase the risk of heart disease. High cholesterol itself **does not cause symptoms**, so many people are unaware that they have a problem.

There are 2 kinds of cholesterol: **LDL (low-density lipoprotein)**, often called "bad" cholesterol, leads to narrowing of the arteries; **HDL (high-density lipoprotein)**, known as "good" cholesterol, helps reduce this risk.

National Institutes of Health guidelines classify total cholesterol levels (determined by a blood test) of less than 200 mg/dl as desirable, 200-239 as borderline high, and 240 and above as high. About 37 mil Americans have a cholesterol level of 240 mg/dl or higher. LDL levels of less than 100 are considered optimal, 130-159 as borderline high, 160-189 as high, and 190 and over as very high. For HDL, levels of 60 mg/dl and above are considered protective against heart dis-

ease, while levels under 40 mg/dl are considered a risk factor for heart disease.

Like high-blood pressure, high cholestrol can be controlled by life-style modification and medication, and should be treated under supervision of a physician.

Triglycerides, another form of fat in the blood, can also raise the risk of heart disease. Levels that are borderline high (150-199) or high (200 or more) may need treatment.

Diabetes—Diabetes is a major risk factor for heart disease; at least 65% of people with diabetes mellitus die of some form of heart or blood vessel disease. *See also* "Diabetes" on page 144.

Smoking—Cigarette smokers are 2-4 times more likely to develop CHD. Smoking is also associated with the risk of sudden cardiac death.

Obesity—Using a body mass index (BMI) of 25 and higher for overweight and 30 and higher for obesity, an estimated 140 mil Americans age 20 and over are overweight and more than 66 mil are obese. *See also* "Weight Guidelines for Adults" on page 152.

Physical Inactivity—An infactive lifestyle is a risk factor for coronary heart disease (CHD). This increase in risk is comparable to that observed for high blood cholesterol, high blood pressure, or cigarette smoking.

Women and Cardiovascular Disease

The American Heart Association reports that diseases of the heart and stroke, respectively, are the No. 1 and No. 3 killers of women over the age of 25 (cancer is the 2nd); one in 2.6 women die of some form of cardiovascular disease. Because heart disease was long viewed as a "man's" disease, many of the major cardiovascular studies were conducted only on men. Much recent attention has been directed toward understanding the influence of gender on cardiovascular disease risk and prevention, but important gaps in knowledge remain.

Women often present some of the same "classic" symptoms of heart attack that men feel, such as chest pain that spreads to the shoulders and arms, but they may more often report atypical chest pain or complain of abdominal pain, difficulty breathing (dyspnea), and nausea. Another problem in diagnosis is that women tend to have heart attacks later in life than men, so symptoms may more often be masked by other age-related diseases such as arthritis or osteoporosis. Even certain diagnostic tests and procedures such as the exercise stress test may not be as accurate in women, with the result that the disease process that leads to heart attack or stroke may not be detected early on, with potentially serious consequences.

Irritable Bowel Syndrome

Source: National Institutes of Health, 9000 Rockville Pike Bethesda, MD 20892

Irritable Bowel Syndrome (IBS) is a functional disorder, not a disease, that occurs in the large intestine and is one of the most common disorders diagnosed by physicians. Nearly 1 in 5 Americans has symptoms of IBS, and it accounts for more than one out of every 10 doctor visits in the U.S. IBS occurs more frequently in women than in men and it usually begins before the age of 35 for about 50% those affected. Though IBS causes discomfort and may even be painful, it does not damage the bowel.

Most people are not comfortable discussing IBS because of its embarrassing symptoms. They include:
- bloating
- gas
- diarrhea
- constipation
- abdominal pain or cramping
- mucus in the stool
- feeling like you have not finished with a bowel movement

For most people, IBS is a chronic condition and there will likely be times where the symptoms are worse than during

other times, or they may disappear altogether only to reappear again in the future. Most complications are derived from the symptoms such as hemorrhoids, which may form as a result of the diarrhea and constipation. Often people with chronic IBS may feel discouraged and go through periods of depression partly because of the constant discomfort, but also because the symptoms can interfere with work and personal relationships.

The specific causes for IBS are unknown. The walls of the intestines are lined with layers of muscle that contract and relax in a coordinated manner as they move food through the digestive system. When a person has IBS, the contractions cause food to either speed up or slow down as it moves though the bowel, subsequently causing the gas, bloating, diarrhea, and/or constipation. Some researchers believe that people who suffer from IBS have a colon that is particularly sensitive to certain foods. In particular, milk products, alcohol, caffeine, carbonated drinks, chocolate, and fatty foods can trigger IBS symptoms. Another common factor is a low tolerance for stretching of the large intestine. Women tend to get IBS more often than men and they usually have more severe symptoms during menstrual periods, leading researchers to believe that IBS may have a hormonal trigger. Recent research has shown that serotonin, a neurotransmitter hormone, may be linked with gastrointestinal functioning.

IBS can sometimes be the result of infection or other problems in the body. Researchers have found that people who have had gastroenteritis have later developed IBS. But because symptoms of IBS can match those many serious diseases, it is important for chronic sufferers to consult their doctors. If symptoms began early in life and have been stable, a patient may require a colonoscopy to rule out any inflammatory bowel diseases, such as Crohn's, or even colon cancer. Patients over 50 should be regularly screened for colon cancer.

Despite the uncertainty over the cause of IBS, there are known precautionary measures that people with sensitive digestive systems can take. Having a well-balanced diet is the best possible prevention. High fiber foods such as bread and cereal reduce IBS symptoms, particularly constipation. In addition, vegetables, beans and bran can reduce symptoms if part of a daily diet. Eating large meals has been shown to worsen the condition, so eating smaller meals can also help reduce symptoms.

There is no particular cure for IBS, and treatment usually involves lessening the symptoms so that the sufferer may lead a more normal life.

Common Infectious Diseases

Sources: National Institutes of Health; Centers for Disease Control; World Health Organization

The following is a list of major infectious diseases. It is meant to be used for reference purposes only and not as a tool for diagnosis. If you think you may have a serious disease, you should see your doctor immediately. Statistics may appear uneven because of different methods of reporting by the various agencies, and because not all diseases are surveyed in the same year.

Chicken Pox

(Varicella simplex). Usually non-threatening viral disease commonly associated with children. In adults, the disease can be serious.**Transmission:** Highly contagious; transmitted by direct contact with rash, coughing, or sneezing of infected persons. **Symptoms:** blister-like rash, discomfort, high fever. Infected people may develop shingles later in life. **Vaccine:** became available 1995. **Treatment:** none; antibiotics in some severe cases. **Annual U.S. cases:** before 1995, about 4 mil, mostly children; in 2004, 32,931 reported cases.

Chlamydia

(Chlamydia trachomatis). One of the most widely spread sexually transmitted diseases. **Transmission:** Sexually transmitted. **Symptoms:** 70% of those infected have no symptoms. In women, vaginal discharge, infection of the cervix and urinary tract, can cause pelvic inflammatory disease; in men, infection of urinary tract and epididymitis (inflammation of testicular duct); can also infect the throat, rectum, and eye. **Treatment:** curable with antibiotics. **Annual U.S. cases:** 929,462 in 2004.

Common Cold

(more than 200 different viruses). An upper respiratory viral infection. **Transmission:** touching your nose, eyes, or mouth after touching something contaminated by the virus; inhalation of airborne virus. **Symptoms:** irritated nose or scratchy throat, sneezing and watery nasal discharge; green or yellow nasal discharge, cough, muscle aches, headache, postnasal drip, decreased appetite. **Treatment:** no cure, over-the-counter remedies can relieve symptoms; effectiveness of antiviral drugs is debated. **Annual U.S. cases:** about 1 billion.

Gonorrhea

(Neisseria Gonorhoeae). Common bacterial STD. **Transmission:** sexually transmitted. **Symptoms:** in men, discomfort in urethra, yellow or green discharge, burning during urination; in women, pelvic pain, bleeding associated with intercourse, burning during urination, yellow or bloody discharge. **Treatment:** highly curable with antibiotics. **Annual U.S. cases:** 330,132 (2004)

Hepatitis

A viral disease that causes inflammation of the liver. In the U.S., five forms are endemic: A, B, C, D, and E; A, B, and C are the most common. **Symptoms:** all forms have generally similar symptoms including jaundice, fatigue, abdominal pain, loss of appetite, nausea, mild flu like symptoms; many cases cause no symptoms; in extreme cases, liver transplants may be necessary.

Hepatitis A *(Hepatovirus Picornaviridae)*. **Transmission:** food or water contaminated with feces from infected persons. **Vaccine:** Effective; travelers are advised to not drink tap water in countries where disease is common.

Treatment: disease usually resolves itself on its own; alcohol consumption should be avoided. **Est. Annual U.S. cases:** 24,000; 5,683 acute lab-confirmed cases in 2004

Hepatitis B *(Orthohepadnavirus Hepadnaviridae)*. **Transmission:** unsterilized needle sharing; contaminated blood transfusions; sexual contact. **Vaccine:** highly effective **Treatment:** for chronic cases, drug treatment is necessary; for acute cases, disease usually resolves itself, severe cases treated with lamivudine. **Est. Annual U.S. cases:** 17,000; 6,212 lab-confirmed cases in 2004

Hepatitis C *(Hepacivirus Flaviviridae)*. **Transmission:** unsterilized needle sharing, contaminated blood transfusions; sexual contact. **Vaccine:** none. **Treatment:** chronic cases treated with drugs, eliminating virus in about 50% of patients; for acute cases, treatment recommended if disease present after 2-3 months. **Est. Annual U.S. cases:** 4,200

HPV Infection

(more than 100 strains of human papillomavirus). Common viral infection; leading cause of cervical cancer. **Transmission:** sexually transmitted. **Symptoms:** Most of those infected have no symptoms but can still transmit virus; in some cases, genital warts; pre-cancerous bumps on anus, cervix or vulva (women), or penis (men). **Treatment:** No cure for virus; warts may recur even with treatment; cervical cancer treated with surgery, chemotherapy, and/or radiation. Women with HPV should have pap smear and pelvic exam every 6 months. **Annual U.S. cases:** 6.8 million new cases of sexually transmitted HPV; approximately 20 million Americans currently infected with HPV.

Influenza

(various influenza viruses). Highly contagious viral respiratory infection. **Transmission:** Airborne transmission; contact with face after touching infected surface. **Symptoms:** chills, fatigue, fever, headache, sore throat, sinus congestion, coughing. "Stomach flu" is not influenza. **Vaccine:** Yearly vaccinations recommended. **Treatment:** Antiviral drugs; disease normally runs its course in a matter of days. **Annual U.S. Cases:** 5-20% of U.S. population; 200,000 hospitalized and 36,000 killed annually.

Lyme Disease

(borrelia burgdorferi). Bacterial inflammatory disease, first identified 1975 in Old Lyme, CT. Found across the U.S., usually in areas with large deer populations. **Transmission:** Bite of infected deer ticks. Mice and deer are most common hosts. **Symptoms:** Mimic those of other diseases: flu-like symptoms; fatigue; stiff neck, joint inflammation; skin rash may appear at site of tick bite. **Treatment:** Antibiotics in early stages; anti-inflammation drugs to relieve symptoms; without treatment, long-term complications (some fatal) involving joints, heart, and nervous system. **Annual U.S. cases:** about 19,804 in 2004.

Malaria

(*plasmodium* parasite). Infectious disease known from as early as 2700 BCE. Virtually eradicated in developed countries; still a major killer in tropical regions. **Transmission:** bite from an infected mosquito. **Symptoms:** high fever, shaking chills, heavy sweating, headache, fatigue, enlarged spleen; if left untreated, organ damage and death. **Treatment:** Antimalarial drugs, including chloroquine for treatment and prevention. **Annual U.S. Cases:** 1,458 (2004); worldwide, as many as 2.7 million people killed each year, 75% of them African children.

Measles

(*rubeola* virus). Once-common viral infection; today almost nonexistent in U.S. and Canada. **Transmission:** Airborne transmission by infected people. **Symptoms:** itchy and raised rash, sore throat, cough, pink-eye, high fever, high fever; in rare cases, encephalitis, seizures, permanent deafness, death. **Vaccine:** Highly effective. **Treatment:** no specific treatment; symptoms relieved with bed rest, acetaminophen, humidified air. **Annual U.S. cases:** 37 in 2004.

Mumps

(mumps virus). Acute and contagious viral infection. **Transmission:** direct contact with mucus or saliva of infected persons. **Symptoms:** Painful, visible swelling of the salivary or parotid glands in the face; chills, headache, fever, painful swallowing; in some cases, inflammation of testes, pancreas, ovaries; in severe cases, brain swelling and symptoms ranging from nausea and drowsiness to seizures and permanent deafness. **Vaccine:** MMR vaccine is effective. **Treatment:** No specific treatment; symptoms may be relieved by applying ice or heat to swollen glands. **Annual U.S. cases:** 258 in 2004

Peptic Ulcer

(most from *Helicobacter pylori* [*H. pylori*] bacteria; also overuse of aspirin or other anti-inflammatory drugs) Weakening of the stomach's protective mucous coating, allowing stomach acid and bacteria to irritate stomach lining. **Transmission:** *H. Pylori* may be transmitted through food and water. **Symptoms:** Indigestion; bloating; dull, transient abdominal pain or discomfort; nausea; vomiting. **Treatment:** antibiotics, acid-suppressing drugs. **Annual U.S. cases:** About 20% of Americans under 40 and half of those over 60 years may be infected with *H. pylori*. An estimated 500,000 to 850,000 develop peptic ulcers each year.

Pertssis or Whooping cough

(*Bordetella pertussis* or *B. parepertussis*). Upper respiratory bacterial infection. **Transmission:** Highly contagious; airborne transmission by infected people. **Symptoms:** initially, mild cold-like symptoms, fever, diarrhea, difficulty breathing; later, violent coughing with characteristic "whooping" heard when patient tries to breathe between coughs, vomiting; in severe cases, apnea, pneumonia, seizures, encephalopathy. **Vaccine:** TDaP vaccine or pertussis only vaccine. **Treatment:** Antibiotics in early cases, otherwise disease must run its course. **Annual U.S. Cases:** 25,827 in 2004; annual infections have been increasing since 1980s.

Salmonella or Salmonellosis

(*Salmonella enteritidis*). Bacterial infection. **Transmission:** Eating foods contaminated by feces carrying the bacteria; undercooked meats or raw eggs contaminated by bacteria; contact with feces of infected animal/pet. **Symptoms:** fever, diarrhea, abdominal cramps 12 to 72 hours after infection. **Treatment:** no standard treatment; runs its course in 4 to 7 days; antibiotics in severe cases. **Annual U.S. cases:** 42,197 in 2004.

Shigellosis

(Four species of *Shigella*: *boydii, dysenteriae, flexneri,* and *sonnei*). Bacterial infection and a form of dysentery (an intestinal disease). **Transmission:** Food contaminated by infected feces; vegetables grown in fields containing contaminated sewage; swimming in contaminated water. **Symptoms:** watery or bloody diarrhea 1 to 4 days after infection, high fever, vomiting, painful bowel movements, severe diarrhea; in extreme cases, seizures in children, intestinal perforation. **Treatment:** mild infection allowed to run its course; replacement of fluids and salts lost through excessive diarrhea; antibiotics in severe cases. Although severe diarrhea is symptomatic, antidiarrheal medicines may make illness worse. **Annual U.S. Cases:** 400,000 estimated; 14,627 reported in 2004.

Syphilis

(*Treponema pallidum*). Bacterial infection known since ancient times, and spread rampantly throughout Europe in the Middle Ages. **Transmission:** Sexually transmitted. **Symptoms:** Primary stage: painless ulcer where bacteria enters the body; usually heals in 3 to 12 weeks with or without treatment. Without treatment, disease enters secondary stage: skin rash 2-10 weeks after chancre. Without treatment, enters tertiary stage: mouth sores, fever, fatigue, loss of appetite, weight loss, hair loss, jaundice, syphilitic meningitis, aortal aneurysms, lesions, damage to nervous system, heart, and eyes. Most infected do not progress beyond primary or secondary stage. **Treatment:** Curable with antibiotics (mostly penicillin). **Annual U.S. Cases:** 33,401 total cases in 2004; 7,980 primary and secondary (2004)

Tetanus or Lockjaw

(*Clostridium tetani*). Bacterial infection. **Transmission:** Bacteria, found in soil, enters body through broken skin. **Symptoms:** muscle stiffness and spasm or "locking" of muscles of the jaw, neck, and limbs. **Vaccine:** 4 forms of tetanus immunization. **Treatment:** tetanus immune globulin can fight infection; with treatment, less than 10% of cases are fatal. **Annual U.S. Cases:** Approx. 100 cases per year, most due to lack of immunization.

Tuberculosis

(*Mycobacterium tuberculosis*). Bacterial infection that primarily affects the lungs. **Transmission:** Airborne transmission by people with active TB infection. **Symptoms:** weight loss, fever, cough with discharge (sometimes with bloody sputum), night sweats, growing shortness of breath over time, chest pains. **Vaccine:** BCG (Bacille Calmette Guerin) vaccine only effective in protecting young children and used where TB is common; not recommended by health experts in U.S. **Treatment:** Difficult to cure and fatal if untreated. Treated with cocktail of antibiotics given over 6-12 months or longer. **Annual U.S. Cases:** 14,093 (2005); worldwide, about 2 bil people are thought to be infected.

Yellow Fever

(Yellow fever virus, in *flavivirus* group). Viral infection that has caused large epidemics in S. America, the Caribbean and Africa. **Transmission:** bite from mosquitoes carrying the virus. **Symptoms:** headaches, muscle aches, fever, jaundice (yellowing skin), nausea and vomiting, kidney failure, severe generalized pain; in severe cases, shock, coma, and death. **Vaccine:** Available, safe and effective. **Treatment:** symptoms are treated until disease runs its course. **Annual U.S. cases:** 0; 200,000 estimated new cases worldwide per year, with 30,000 deaths.

MyPyramid.gov
STEPS TO A HEALTHIER YOU

Food Guide Pyramid

In 2005 the U.S. Dept. of Agriculture issued a revised food guide pyramid called My-Pyramid, along with new dietary guidelines for Americans. The new pyramid represents the latest findings in health and nutrition, with a focus on reducing calorie consumption and increasing physical activity. More specifically, the new system factors in weight, age, gender, physical activity in putting together a nutrition plan and distinguishes between necessary and unnecessary types of fats and sugars. In addition, the new pyramid allows for variation and personalization according to an individual's caloric needs. The guidelines below are general guidelines for better health and nutrition. To get a personalized nutrition and exercise assessment and for dietary recommendations visit MyPyramid.gov

2005 Dietary Guidelines for Americans—Some Key Recommendations:

• Choose nutrient-dense foods and beverages among the basic food groups, while limiting the intake of foods with saturated and trans fats, cholesterol, added sugars, salt, and alcohol.
• To maintain a healthy body weight, balance calories consumed with calories expended.
• To prevent gradual weight gain over time, make small decreases in calories and increase physical activity.
• Engage in regular physical activity and cut down on sedentary activities.
• Keep fit through cardiovascular conditioning, stretching exercises for flexibility, and resistance exercises or calisthenics for muscle strength and endurance.
• Eat a sufficient amount of fruits and vegetables each day.
• Choose from all 5 vegetable subgroups, dark greens, orange, legumes, starchy vegetables, and other vegetables.

• Consume 3 cups per day of fat-free or low-fat milk or equivalent milk products.
• Consume less than 10% of calories from saturated fatty acids and less than 300 mg/day of cholesterol, and keep trans fatty acid consumption as low as possible.
• Keep total fat intake between 20%-35% of calories, with most fats coming from sources of polyunsaturated and monounsaturated fatty acids, such as fish, nuts, and vegetable oils.
• Choose lean, low-fat, or fat-free meat, poultry, dry beans, and milk or milk products.
• Eat fiber-rich fruits, vegetables, and whole grains often.
• Consume less than 2,300 mg (approx. 1 teaspoon of salt) of sodium per day. Eat potassium-rich foods, such as fruits and vegetables.
• If you drink alcoholic beverages, do so in moderation: up to 1 drink per day for women and up to 2 drinks per day for men.

Estimated Calorie Requirements[1]

Estimated amounts of calories, rounded to the nearest 200, needed to maintain energy balance for various gender, age groups, and levels of physical activity.

	Age (years)	Sedentary[2]	Moderately[3] Active	Active[4]		Age (years)	Sedentary[2]	Moderately[3] Active	Active[4]
Child	2–3	1,000	1,000–1,400	1,000–1,400	Male	4–8	1,400	1,400–1,600	1,600–2,000
Female	4–8	1,200	1,400–1,600	1,400–1,800		9–13	1,800	1,800–2,200	2,000–2,600
	9–13	1,600	1,600–2,000	1,800–2,200		14–18	2,200	2,400–2,800	2,800–3,200
	14–18	1,800	2,000	2,400		19–30	2,400	2,600–2,800	3,000
	19–30	2,000	2,000–2,200	2,400		31–50	2,200	2,400–2,600	2,800–3,000
	31–50	1,800	2,000	2,200		51+	2,000	2,200–2,400	2,400–2,800
	51+	1,600	1,800	2,000–2,200					

(1) Based on median height and weight for ages up to age 18 years and Body Mass Index (BMI) of 21.5 for adult females and 22.5 for adult males. (2) Engaging only in minimal activities associated with ordinary day-to-day life. (3) Includes physical activity equivalent to walking 1.5 to 3 miles per day at 3-4 mph. (4) Includes physical activity equivalent to walking more than 3 miles per day at 3-4 mph.

Food Ingredients

PROTEIN

Proteins, composed of amino acids, are essential to good nutrition. They build, maintain, and repair the body. Best sources: eggs, milk, fish, meat, poultry, soybeans, nuts. High-quality proteins such as eggs, meat, or fish supply all 8 amino acids needed in the diet. Plant foods can be combined to meet protein needs as well: whole grain breads and cereals, rice, oats, soybeans, other beans, split peas, and nuts.

FATS

Fats provide energy by furnishing calories to the body, and they also carry vitamins A, D, E, and K. They are the most concentrated source of energy in the diet. Best sources of polyunsaturated and monounsaturated fats: margarine, vegetable/plant oils, nuts. Meats, cheeses, butter, cream, egg yolks, lard are concentrated sources of saturated fats.

CARBOHYDRATES

Carbohydrates provide energy for body function and activity by supplying immediate calories. The carbohydrate group includes sugars, starches, fiber, and starchy vegetables. Best sources: grains, legumes, potatoes, vegetables, fruits.

FIBER

The portion of plant foods that our bodies cannot digest is known as fiber. There are 2 basic types: *insoluble* ("roughage") and *soluble*. Insoluble fibers help move food materials through the digestive tract; soluble fibers tend to slow things down. Both types absorb water, thus prevent and treat constipation by softening and increasing the bulk of the undigested food components passing through the digestive tract. Soluble fibers have also been reported to be helpful in reducing blood cholesterol levels. Best sources: beans, bran, fruits, whole grains, vegetables.

WATER

Water dissolves and transports other nutrients throughout the body, aiding the processes of digestion, absorption, circulation, and excretion. It helps regulate body temperature.

VITAMINS

Vitamin A—promotes good eyesight and helps keep the skin and mucous membranes resistant to infection. Best sources: liver, sweet potatoes, carrots, kale, cantaloupe, turnip greens, collard greens, broccoli, fortified milk.

Vitamin B_1 (thiamine)—prevents beriberi. Essential to carbohydrate metabolism and health of nervous system. Best sources: pork, enriched cereals, grains, soybeans, nuts.

Vitamin B_2 (riboflavin)—protects the skin, mouth, eyes, eyelids, and mucous membranes. Essential to protein and energy metabolism. Best sources: milk, meat, poultry, cheese, broccoli, spinach.

Vitamin B_6 (pyridoxine)—important in the regulation of the central nervous system and in protein metabolism. Best sources: whole grains, meats, fish, poultry, nuts, brewers' yeast.

Vitamin B_{12} (cobalamin)—needed to form red blood cells. Best sources: meat, fish, poultry, eggs, dairy products.

Niacin—maintains health of skin, tongue, digestive system. Best sources: poultry, peanuts, fish, enriched flour and bread.

Folic acid (folacin)—required for normal blood cell formation, growth, and reproduction and for important chemical reactions in body cells. Best sources: yeast, orange juice, green leafy vegetables, wheat germ, asparagus, broccoli, nuts.

Other B vitamins—biotin, pantothenic acid.

Vitamin C (ascorbic acid)—maintains collagen, a protein necessary for the formation of skin, ligaments, and bones. It helps heal wounds and mend fractures and aids in resisting some types of viral and bacterial infections. Best sources: citrus fruits and juices, cantaloupe, broccoli, brussels sprouts, potatoes and sweet potatoes, tomatoes, cabbage.

Vitamin D—important for bone development. Best sources: sunlight, fortified milk and milk products, fish-liver oils, egg yolks.

Vitamin E (tocopherol)—helps protect red blood cells. Best sources: vegetable oils, wheat germ, whole grains, eggs, peanuts, margarine, green leafy vegetables.

Vitamin K—necessary for formation of prothrombin, which helps blood to clot. Also made by intestinal bacteria. Best dietary sources: green leafy vegetables, tomatoes.

MINERALS

Calcium—works with phosphorus in building and maintaining bones and teeth. Best sources: milk and milk products, cheese, blackstrap molasses, some types of tofu.

Phosphorus—performs more functions than any other mineral, and plays a part in nearly every chemical reaction in the body. Best sources: cheese, milk, meats, poultry, fish, tofu.

Iron—Necessary for the formation of myoglobin, which is a reservoir of oxygen for muscle tissue, and hemoglobin, which transports oxygen in the blood. Best sources: lean meats, beans, green leafy vegetables, shellfish, enriched breads and cereals, whole grains.

Other minerals—chromium, cobalt, copper, fluorine, iodine, magnesium, manganese, molybdenum, potassium, selenium, sodium, sulfur, and zinc.

Understanding Food Label Claims

Source: U.S. Food and Drug Admin., Center for Food Safety and Applied Nutrition

The federal Nutrition Labeling and Education Act of 1990 provides that manufacturers can make certain claims on processed food labels only if they meet the definitions specified here:

SUGAR

Sugar free: less than 0.5g per serving
No added sugar; Without added sugar; No sugar added: No sugars added during processing or packing, including ingredients that contain sugars (for example, fruit juices, applesauce, or dried fruit).
Processing does not increase sugar content above the amount naturally in the ingredients. (A functionally insignificant increase in sugars is acceptable from processes used for purposes other than increasing sugar content.)
Food for which it substitutes normally contains added sugars.
Reduced sugar: at least 25% less sugar than reference food

FAT

Fat free: less than 0.5g of fat per serving
Saturated fat free: less than 0.5g of saturated fat per serving, and the level of trans fatty acids does not exceed 1% of total fat
Low fat: 3g or less per serving and, if the serving is 30g or less or 2 tbs or less, per 50g of the food
Low saturated fat: 1g or less per serving and not more than 15% of calories from saturated fatty acids
Reduced or Less fat: at least 25% less per serving than reference food

FIBER

High fiber: 5g or more per serving. (Also, must meet low-fat definition, or must state level of total fat.)

Good source of fiber: 2.5g to 4.9g per serving
More or Added fiber: at least 2.5g more per serving than reference food

SODIUM

Sodium free: less than 5mg per serving
Low sodium: 140 mg or less per serving and, if the serving is 30g or less or 2 tbs or less, per 50g of the food
Very low sodium: 35 mg or less per serving and, if the serving is 30g or less or 2 tbs or less, per 50g of the food
Reduced or Less sodium: at least 25% less per serving than reference food

CALORIES

Low calorie: 40 calories per serving; if the serving is 30g or less or 2 tablespoons or less, 40 calories or less per 50g of food
Calorie free: under 5 calories per serving
Reduced or Fewer calories: at least 25% fewer calories than reference food

CHOLESTEROL

Cholesterol free: less than 2mg of cholesterol and 2g or less of saturated fat per serving
Low cholesterol: 20mg or less and 2g or less of saturated fat per serving and, if the serving is 30g or less or 2 tbs or less, per 50g of the food
Reduced or Less cholesterol: at least 25% less than reference food

Other Food Label Claims

Source: Food Safety and Inspection Service, U.S. Department of Agriculture

The FDA allows food producers and marketers to use language on their packaging that advertises the health benefits and production methods of their products. Products marked as "certified" have been formally evaluated for class, grade, or other quality characteristics by the USDA's Food Safety and Inspection Service. Below are some common packaging terms and their meanings.

Organic: Produced by farmers who use environmentally friendly methods to raise their crops or animals. Before a product can be labeled "organic," the farm where the food is grown must pass a special inspection by a USDA official. Organic foods must be produced without conventional pesticides; fertilizers made with synthetic ingredients, sewage or sludge; bioengineering; or ionizing radiation.

The official *USDA Organic* label may appear on vegetables, fruit, packages of meat, cartons of milk, eggs, cheese, and other single-ingredient foods. Foods with more than one ingredient can place the official seal on their packaging if at least 95% of the ingredients are organic. Products with at least 70% organic ingredients may advertise prominently on the front of the package that the item contains organic ingredients. Products with some organic ingredients, but less than 70%, may not make any organic claims on the front of the package, but may list organic ingredients on the side panel. Foods that contain 100% organic ingredients may advertise that fact on the front of the packaging along with the organic seal.

Natural: A product that does not contain any artificial ingredient or added color, and which has been minimally processed. The label must explain the specific use of the term natural with regard to the product, such as: no added colorings, no artificial ingredients, minimally processed.

Free-range: Generally means that the product comes from an animal that was given access to the outdoors to roam for an unspecified amount of time each day. Animals raised in slaughterhouses are not considered free range. Free range products do not necessarily mean healthier or more disease-free.

Halal and Zabiah Halal: Produced in federally inspected meat packing plants and handled in accordance with Islamic law and under Islamic authority.

Kosher: Only used on meat and poultry products prepared under Rabbinical supervision.

Minimal Processing: Produced using only traditional physical processes which do not fundamentally alter the raw products, in order to make food edible, to preserve it, or to make it safe for human consumption. Includes smoking, roasting, freezing, drying, and fermenting; applies mostly to meat and poultry.

No Hormones: Hormones are not allowed in raising hogs or poultry, so those products may not make this claim. If sufficient documentation is provided to the USDA to prove that hormones were not used, this term may be used on packages of beef.

No Antibiotics: This claim may be made on a package if sufficient documentation is provided to the USDA that shows the animals were raised without being administered antibiotics.

Recommended Levels for Elements (Minerals)

Source: Food and Nutrition Board, National Academy of Sciences—Institute of Medicine, 2005

in milligrams per day (mg/d) or in micrograms per day (µg/d); asterisks denote levels defined as "adequate intake" (AI).

		Calcium (mg/d)	Chromium (µg/d)	Copper (µg/d)	Fluoride (mg/d)	Iodine (µg/d)	Iron (mg/d)	Magnesium (mg/d)	Manganese (mg/d)	Molybdenum (µg/d)	Phosphorus (mg/d)	Selenium (µg/d)	Zinc (mg/d)
Infants	0-6 mos	210*	0.2*	200*	0.01*	110*	0.27*	30*	0.003*	2*	100*	15*	2*
	7-12 mos	270*	5.5*	220*	0.5*	130*	11	75*	0.6*	3*	275*	20*	3
	1-3 yrs	500*	11*	340	0.7*	90	7	80	1.2*	17	460	20	3
	4-8 yrs	800*	15*	440	1*	90	10	130	1.5*	22	500	30	5
Males	9-13 yrs	1,300*	25*	700	2*	120	8	240	1.9*	34	1,250	40	8
	14-18 yrs	1,300*	35*	890	3*	150	11	410	2.2*	43	1,250	55	11
	19-30 yrs	1,000*	35*	900	4*	150	8	400	2.3*	45	700	55	11
	31-50 yrs	1,000*	35*	900	4*	150	8	420	2.3*	45	700	55	11
	51-70 yrs	1,200*	30*	900	4*	150	8	420	2.3*	45	700	55	11
	over 70 yrs	1,200*	30*	900	4*	150	8	420	2.3*	45	700	55	11
Females	9-13 yrs	1,300*	21*	700	2*	120	8	240	1.6*	34	1,250	40	8
	14-18 yrs	1,300*	24*	890	3*	150	15	360	1.6*	43	1,250	55	9
	19-30 yrs	1,000*	25*	900	3*	150	18	310	1.8*	45	700	55	8
	31-50 yrs	1,000*	25*	900	3*	150	18	320	1.8*	45	700	55	8
	51-70 yrs	1,200*	20*	900	3*	150	8	320	1.8*	45	700	55	8
	over 70 yrs	1,200*	20*	900	3*	150	8	320	1.8*	45	700	55	8
Pregnancy	18 yrs. or less	1,300*	29*	1,000	3*	220	27	400	2.0*	50	1,250	60	12
	19-30 yrs.	1,000*	30*	1,000	3*	220	27	350	2.0*	50	700	60	11
	31-50 yrs.	1,000*	30*	1,000	3*	220	27	360	2.0*	50	700	60	11
Lactation	18 yrs. or less	1,300*	44*	1,300	3*	290	10	360	2.6*	50	1,250	70	13
	19-30 yrs.	1,000*	45*	1,300	3*	290	9	310	2.6*	50	700	70	12
	31-50 yrs.	1,000*	45*	1,300	3*	290	9	320	2.6*	50	700	70	12

Recommended Levels for Vitamins

Source: Food and Nutrition Board, National Academy of Sciences—Institute of Medicine, 2005

in milligrams per day (mg/d) or in micrograms per day (µg/d); asterisks denote levels defined as "adequate intake" (AI).

		Vitamin A (µg/d)[1]	Vitamin C (mg/d)	Vitamin D (µg/d)[2]	Vitamin E (mg/d)	Vitamin K (µg/d)	Thiamin (mg/d)	Riboflavin (mg/d)	Niacin (mg/d)[3]	Vitamin B6 (mg/d)	Folate (µg/d)[4]	Vitamin B12 (µg/d)	Pantothenic Acid (mg/d)	Biotin (µg/d)	Choline (mg/d)[5]
Infants	0-6 mos	400*	40*	5*	4*	2.0*	0.2*	0.3*	2*	0.1*	65*	0.4*	1.7*	5*	125*
	7-12 mos	500*	50*	5*	5*	2.5*	0.3*	0.4*	4*	0.3*	80*	0.5*	1.8*	6*	150*
Children	1-3 yrs	300	15	5*	6	30*	0.5	0.5	6	0.5	150	0.9	2*	8*	200*
	4-8 yrs	400	25	5*	7	55*	0.6	0.6	8	0.6	200	1.2	3*	12*	250*
Males	9-13 yrs	600	45	5*	11	60*	0.9	0.9	12	1.0	300	1.8	4*	20*	375*
	14-18 yrs	900	75	5*	15	75*	1.2	1.3	16	1.3	400	2.4	5*	25*	550*
	19-30 yrs	900	90	5*	15	120*	1.2	1.3	16	1.3	400	2.4	5*	30*	550*
	31-50 yrs	900	90	5*	15	120*	1.2	1.3	16	1.3	400	2.4	5*	30*	550*
	51-70 yrs	900	90	10*	15	120*	1.2	1.3	16	1.7	400	2.46	5*	30*	550*
	over 70 yrs	900	90	15*	15	120*	1.2	1.3	16	1.7	400	2.46	5*	30*	550*
Females	9-13 yrs	600	45	5*	11	60*	0.9	0.9	12	1.0	300	1.8	4*	20*	375*
	14-18 yrs	700	65	5*	15	75*	1.0	1.0	14	1.2	4007	2.4	5*	25*	400*
	19-30 yrs	700	75	5*	15	90*	1.1	1.1	14	1.3	4007	2.4	5*	30*	425*
	31-50 yrs	700	75	5*	15	90*	1.1	1.1	14	1.3	4007	2.4	5*	30*	425*
	51-70 yrs	700	75	10*	15	90*	1.1	1.1	14	1.5	400	2.46	5*	30*	425*
	over 70 yrs	700	75	15*	15	90*	1.1	1.1	14	1.5	400	2.46	5*	30*	425*
Pregnancy	18 yrs. or less	750	80	5*	15	75*	1.4	1.4	18	1.9	6008	2.6	6*	30*	450*
	19-30 yrs.	770	85	5*	15	90*	1.4	1.4	18	1.9	6008	2.6	6*	30*	450*
	31-50 yrs.	770	85	5*	15	90*	1.4	1.4	18	1.9	6008	2.6	6*	30*	450*
Lactation	18 yrs. or less	1,200	115	5*	19	75*	1.4	1.6	17	2.0	500	2.8	7*	35*	550*
	19-30 yrs.	1,300	120	5*	19	90*	1.4	1.6	17	2.0	500	2.8	7*	35*	550*
	31-50 yrs.	1,300	120	5*	19	90*	1.4	1.6	17	2.0	500	2.8	7*	35*	550*

NOTE: For healthy breastfed infants, the AI is the mean intake. The AI for other life stage and gender groups is believed to cover needs of all individuals in the group, but lack of data or uncertainty in the data prevent being able to specify with confidence the percentage of individuals covered by this intake. (1) As retinol activity equivalents. (2) In the absence of adequate exposure to sunlight. (3) As niacin equivalents (NE). 1 mg of niacin = 60 mg of tryptophan; 0-6 months = preformed niacin (not NE). (4) As dietary folate equivalents (DFE). 1 DFE = 1 µg food folate = 0.6 µg of folic acid from fortified food or as a supplement consumed with food = 0.5 µg of a supplement taken on an empty stomach. (5) Although AIs have been set for choline, there are few data to assess whether a dietary supply of choline is needed at all stages of the life cycle, and it may be that the choline requirement can be met by endogenous synthesis at some of these stages. (6) Because 10-30% of older people may malabsorb food-bound B12, it is advisable for those older than 50 years to meet their RDA mainly by consuming foods fortified with B12 or a supplement containing B12. (7) In view of evidence linking folate intake with neural tube defects in the fetus, it is recommended that all women capable of becoming pregnant consume 400 µg from supplements or fortified foods in addition to intake of food folate from a varied diet. (8) It is assumed that women will continue consuming 400 µg from supplements or fortified food until their pregnancy is confirmed and they enter prenatal care, which ordinarily occurs after the end of the periconceptional period—the critical time for formation of the neural tube.

Dietary Requirements

The Food and Nutrition Board of the National Academy of Sciences' Institute of Medicine, in reports published from 1997 to 2005, set **Dietary Reference Intakes (DRIs)** for vitamins and elements (often called minerals). The DRIs, based on recent scientific research, establish daily consumption values that aim to optimize health at all stages of life, not just to guard against nutritional deficiencies.

The DRIs include 4 categories of values. The **Recommended Dietary Allowance (RDA)** gives an intake that meets the nutrient requirements of almost all (97-98%) healthy individuals in a specified group. The **Estimated Average Requirement (EAR)** is the intake that meets the estimated nutrient need of half the individuals in a specified

group, while the **Adequate Intake (AI)** is the value given when adequate scientific evidence is not available to calculate an EAR. For healthy breastfed infants, the AI is the mean intake; for other life stage groups the AI is thought to cover the needs of all individuals in the group, but lack of data or uncertainty in the data prevents the percentage of individuals covered from being specified with confidence. The **Tolerable Upper Intake Level (UL)** designates the maximum intake that is unlikely to pose risks of adverse health effects in almost all healthy individuals in a specified group; taking the nutrient above that level could be bad for one's health. RDAs and AIs may both be used as goals for individual intake.

Weight Guidelines for Adults

Source: *Dietary Guidelines for Americans, 2005, U.S. Dept. of Agriculture.*

Guidelines on identification, evaluation, and treatment of overweight and obesity in adults were released in June 1998 by the National Heart, Lung, and Blood Institute (NHLBI), in cooperation with the National Institute of Diabetes and Digestive and Kidney Diseases. The guidelines, based on research into risk factors in heart disease, stroke, and other conditions, define degrees of overweight and obesity in terms of **body mass index (BMI)**, which is based on weight and height and is strongly correlated with total body fat content. A BMI of 25-29 is said to indicate **overweight**; a BMI of 30 or above is said to indicate **obesity**. Weight reduction is advised for persons with a BMI of 25 or higher. (Previous guidelines have been less stringent.) Factors such as large waist circumference, high blood pressure or cholesterol, and a family history of obesity-related disease may increase risk.

Despite growing awareness of the health problems associated, nearly 1/3 of Americans adults are obese (have a BMI of 30 or greater) and the number is growing, according to the National Center for Health Statistics. A high prevalence of overweight and obesity is a huge public health concern because excess body fat has been associated with type 2 diabetes, hypertension, dyslipidemia, cardiovascular disease, stroke, gall bladder disease, respiratory dysfunction, gout, osteoarthritis, and certain kinds of cancers. Over the last 2 decades, the prevalence of overweight children has doubled, and among adolescents it has tripled. It is estimated that, in 2005, as many as 16% of children and adolescents were overweight.

The table below shows the BMI for certain heights and weights. For weight reduction tips, contact the Weight-control Information Network, 1 WIN Way, Bethesda, MD 20892-3665. Phone: 1-877-946-4627. Website: win.niddk.nih.gov

Weight (lbs)

Height	HEALTHY						OVERWEIGHT						OBESE								
4'10"	91	96	100	105	110	115	119	124	129	134	138	143	148	153	158	162	167	172	177	181
4'11"	94	99	104	109	114	119	124	128	133	138	143	148	153	158	163	168	173	178	183	188
5'0"	97	102	107	112	118	123	128	133	138	143	148	153	158	163	168	174	179	184	189	194
5'1"	100	106	111	116	122	127	132	137	143	148	153	158	164	169	174	180	185	190	195	201
5'2"	104	109	115	120	126	131	136	142	147	153	158	164	169	175	180	186	191	196	202	207
5'3"	107	113	118	124	130	135	141	146	152	158	163	169	175	180	186	191	197	203	208	214
5'4"	110	116	122	128	134	140	145	151	157	163	169	174	180	186	192	197	204	209	215	221
5'5"	114	120	126	132	138	144	150	156	162	168	174	180	186	192	198	204	210	216	222	228
5'6"	118	124	130	136	142	148	155	161	167	173	179	186	192	198	204	210	216	223	229	235
5'7"	121	127	134	140	146	153	159	166	172	178	185	191	198	204	211	217	223	230	236	242
5'8"	125	131	138	144	151	158	164	171	177	184	190	197	203	210	216	223	230	236	243	249
5'9"	128	135	142	149	155	162	169	176	182	189	195	203	209	216	223	230	236	243	250	257
5'10"	132	139	146	153	160	167	174	181	188	195	202	209	216	222	229	236	243	250	257	264
5'11"	136	143	150	157	165	172	179	186	193	200	208	215	222	229	236	243	250	257	265	272
6'0"	140	147	154	162	169	177	184	191	199	206	213	221	228	235	242	250	258	265	272	279
6'1"	144	151	159	166	174	182	189	197	204	212	219	227	235	242	250	257	265	272	280	288
6'2"	148	155	163	171	179	186	194	202	210	218	225	233	241	249	256	264	272	280	287	295
6'3"	152	160	168	176	184	192	200	208	216	224	232	240	248	256	264	272	279	287	295	303
6'4"	156	164	172	180	189	197	205	213	221	230	238	246	254	263	271	279	287	295	304	312
BMI[1]	19	20	21	22	23	24	25	26	27	28	29	30	31	32	33	34	35	36	37	38

(1) The BMI numbers apply to both men and women. Some very muscular people may have a high BMI without health risks.

Calories Used During Physical Activity

Source: U.S. Dept. of Agriculture

Amounts of calories burned during physical activities are estimates for a 154-pound person. The more an individual weighs the more calories he or she will burn up with the same degree of exercise.

Moderate physical activities	In 1 hour	In 30 min.	Vigorous physical activities	In 1 hour	In 30 min.
Hiking	370	185	Running/jogging (5 miles per hour)	590	295
Light gardening/yard work	330	165	Bicycling (more than 10 miles per hour)	590	295
Dancing	330	165	Swimming (slow freestyle laps)	510	255
Golf (walking and carrying clubs)	330	165	Aerobics	480	240
Bicycling (less than 10 miles per hour)	290	145	Walking (4 ½ miles per hour)	460	230
Walking (3 ½ miles per hour)	280	140	Heavy yard work (e.g., chopping wood)	440	220
Weight training (general light workout)	220	110	Weight lifting (vigorous effort)	440	220
Stretching	180	90	Basketball (vigorous)	440	220

Finding Your Target Heart Rate

Source: Carole Casten, EdD, *Aerobics Today;* Peg Jordan, RN, Aerobics and Fitness Assoc. of America

The target heart rate is the heartbeat rate a person should have during aerobic exercise (such as running, fast walking, cycling, or cross-country skiing) to get the full benefit of the exercise for cardiovascular conditioning.

First, determine the intensity level at which one would like to exercise. A sedentary person may want to begin an exercise regimen at the 60% level and work up gradually to the 70% level. Athletes and highly fit individuals must work at an 85% or higher level to receive benefits. *Second,* calculate the target heart rate. One common way is by using the American College of Sports Medicine Method.

To obtain cardiovascular fitness benefits from aerobic exercise, it is recommended that an individual participate in an aerobic activity at least 3-5 times a week for 20-30 minutes per session, although cardiac patients and very sedentary individuals can obtain benefits with shorter periods (15-20 minutes). Generally, training changes occur in 4-6 weeks, but they can occur in as little as 2 weeks.

Using the American College of Sports Medicine Method to calculate one's target heart rate, an individual should subtract his or her age from 220, then multiply by the desired intensity level of the workout. Then divide the answer by 6 for a 10-second pulse count. (The 10-second pulse count is useful for checking whether the target heart rate is being achieved during the workout. One can easily check one's pulse—at the wrist or side of the neck—counting the number of beats in 10 seconds.)

For example, a 20-year-old wishing to exercise at 70% intensity would employ the following steps:

Maximum Heart Rate	220 − 20 = 200
Target Heart Rate	200 × .70 = 140
10-second Pulse Count	140/6 = 23

To work at the desired level of intensity, this 20-year-old would strive for a target heart rate of 140 beats per minute, or a 10-second pulse count of 23.

Overweight, Obesity, and Healthy Weight in the U.S.[1], 1960-2004

Source: National Center for Health Statistics, National Health and Nutrition Examination Survey

	1960-62	1971-74	1976-80	1988-94	1999-2002	2001-2004
			Percent of population			
Overweight[2]						
Both sexes[3,4]	44.8	47.7	47.4	56.0	65.2	66.0
Male	49.5	54.7	52.9	61.0	68.8	70.7
Female[3]	40.2	41.1	42.0	51.2	61.7	61.4
Obese[5]						
Both sexes[3,4]	13.3	14.6	15.1	23.3	31.1	32.1
Male	10.7	12.2	12.8	20.6	28.1	30.2
Female[3]	15.7	16.8	17.1	26.0	34.0	34.0
Healthy weight[6]						
Both sexes[3,4]	51.2	48.8	49.6	41.7	32.9	32.2
Male	48.3	43.0	45.4	37.9	30.2	28.1
Female[3]	54.1	54.3	53.7	45.3	35.6	36.2

NOTE: Percents do not sum to 100 because the percent of persons with BMI less than 18.5 is not shown and the percent of persons with obesity is a subset of the percent with overweight. Height was measured without shoes; two pounds were deducted from data for 1960-62 to allow for weight of clothing. (1) In persons aged 20-74, age-adjusted to 2000 standard population group; Data based on measured height and weight of a sample of the civilian noninstitutionalized population. (2) Body mass index (BMI) greater than or equal to 25. (3) Excludes pregnant women. (4) Includes persons of all races and Hispanic origins. (5) Body mass index (BMI) greater than or equal to 30. (6) BMI of 18.5 to less than 25. See pg. 153 for tables to calculate BMI.

Basic First Aid

Source: Courtesy of the American National Red Cross. All rights reserved in all countries.

NOTE: This information is not intended to be a substitute for formal training. It is recommended that you contact your local American Red Cross chapter (www.redcross.org) to sign up for a First Aid/CPR/AED course.

It is important to get medical assistance as soon as possible, but knowing what to do until a doctor or other trained person gets to the scene can save a life, especially in cases of severe bleeding, choking, poisoning, and shock.

People with special medical problems, such as diabetes, cardiovascular disease, epilepsy, or allergies, are urged to wear some sort of emblem identifying the problem, as a safeguard against receiving medication that might be harmful or even fatal. Emblems may be obtained from Medic Alert Foundation, 2323 Colorado Ave., Turlock, CA 95382; 888-633-4298.

Animal bite — Call 9-1-1 or the local emergency number if the wound is bleeding seriously or if you suspect the animal might have rabies. Control any bleeding. Wash minor wounds with soap under running water and apply triple antibiotic ointment and a dressing. When possible, proper authorities should test the animal for rabies.

Asphyxiation — Call 9-1-1, or the local emergency number. Give care for any life-threatening conditions.

Bleeding — Use a barrier between your hand and the wound to help prevent infection. Cover wound with a sterile compress. Apply direct pressure until bleeding stops. Cover compress with a bandage. Call 9-1-1, or the local emergency number if bleeding is severe.

Burn — Check for life-threatening conditions. If the burn is mild, with skin unbroken and no blisters, flush with cold running water until pain subsides. Apply a loose, sterile, dry dressing to prevent infection. If severe, call 9-1-1 or the local emergency number. Care for shock (see below). Keep the person from getting chilled or overheated until advanced medical assistance arrives. Do not try to clean a severe burn or break blisters.

Chemical in eye — Call 9-1-1 or the local emergency number. With the victim's head turned to the side with the affected eye lower than the unaffected eye, continuously flush the injured eye with water.

Choking — *See* **First Aid for Choking**, below.

Convulsions (seizures) — Remove nearby objects that might cause injury. Protect the person's head by placing a thin folded towel or clothing under it. If there is fluid in the person's mouth, roll him or her on one side so that the fluid may drain from the mouth. Do not place anything between the person's teeth. Stay with the person until he or she is fully conscious. If convulsions do not stop, get medical attention immediately.

Cut (minor) — Use a clean barrier between your hand and the wound to prevent infection. Apply direct pressure for a few minutes to control any bleeding. Wash the wound thoroughly with soap and water and apply triple-antibiotic ointment or cream. Cover the wound with a sterile compress and a bandage (or an adhesive bandage).

Fainting — If the victim feels faint, lower him or her to the ground. Lay the victim down on his or her back. If possible, elevate the victim's legs 8 to 12 inches. Care for any life-threatening conditions. Loosen any restrictive clothing and check for any other signs of injury. Call 9-1-1 or the local emergency number.

Foreign object in eye — If an object is embedded in someone's eye do not remove it. If not embedded, try to remove the object by having the victim blink several times. If the object doesn't come out, try gently flushing the eye with water. Do not rub the eye. If the object still doesn't come out, the victim should receive professional medical attention.

Frostbite — Handle frostbitten area gently. Do not rub., Soak affected area in warm water (not warmer than 105°F), if there is no danger of area refreezing. Do not allow frostbitten area to touch the container. Keep the frostbitten part in the water until normal color returns and it feels warm. Loosely bandage the area with dry, sterile dressings. If fingers or toes are frostbitten, put sterile gauze between them. Call 9-1-1 or seek emergency help as soon as possible.

Heat Stroke and Heat Exhaustion — Remove the victim from the heat. Loosen any tight clothing. Fan the person and apply cool, wet cloths to the skin. If the victim is conscious, give him or her cool water to drink slowly. Call 9-1-1 if the victim's condition does not improve or if you suspect heat stroke.

Heart Attack and Stroke — *See* page 145.

Hypothermia — Call 9-1-1 or the local emergency number. Move victim to a warm place. Remove wet clothing and dry victim, if necessary. Warm victim gradually by wrapping the person in warm blankets or clothing. Apply heat pads or other heat sources if available, but not directly to the body. If the person is alert, give the victim warm, non-alcoholic and decaffeinated liquids to drink.

Loss of Limb — Call 9-1-1 or the local emergency number and care for any life-threatening conditions. If a limb is severed, it is important to properly protect the limb so that it can possibly be reattached. After the victim is cared for, the limb should be wrapped in a sterile gauze or clean material and placed in a clean plastic bag, garbage can, or other suitable container. Pack ice around the limb on the OUTSIDE of the bag to keep the limb cold. Be sure the limb is taken to the hospital with the person.

Poisoning — Care for any life-threatening conditions. Call the National Poison Control Center (800-222-1222) , 9-1-1 or the local emergency number and follow their directions. Do not give the victim any food or drink or induce vomiting, unless specified by medical professionals.

Shock (injury-related) — Monitor breathing and consciousness. Have the victim lie down and keep him or her as comfortable as possible. Elevate legs 8 to 12 in. if you do not suspect a head, neck or back injury or broken bones in the hips or legs. Maintain normal body temperature; if the weather is cold or damp, place blankets or extra clothing over and under the victim; if weather is hot, provide shade. Do not attempt to move victim if spinal injury is suspected.

Snakebite — Call 9-1-1 or the local emergency number. Wash the injury. Keep the area still and at a lower level than the heart. Keep the victim calm. If the victim cannot get professional medical help within 30 minutes, consider using a snakebite kit if available. Care for a bite from an elapid snake, such as a coral snake, the same except that after washing the wound you should apply an elastic roller bandage.

Sprains and fractures — Apply ice to reduce swelling and pain. Do not try to straighten or move broken limbs. Apply a splint to immobilize the injured area only if you have to move or transport the victim to seek medical attention and if it does not cause more pain. If you suspect a serious injury, call 9-1-1 or the local emergency number.

Sting from insect — If possible, remove stinger by scraping it away with your finger, a plastic card (like a credit card) or using tweezers. If you use tweezers, grasp the stinger, not the venom sac. Wash the area with soap and water; cover it to keep it clean. Apply a cold pack to reduce pain and swelling. Call 9-1-1 or the local emergency number immediately if body swells, patient collapses, or you know that the victim is allergic to the sting.

Unconsciousness — Call 9-1-1 or the local emergency number immediately. Care for any life-threatening conditions. If the person shows signs of life (movement and breathing), place him or her in the recovery position (i.e., lying on a side, with head supported, so that the airway is open). Do not move the person if a spinal injury is suspected.

First Aid for Choking

The recommended first aid for a conscious choking victim who is unable to speak, cough or breathe, is to deliver a series of 5 back blows and 5 abdominal thrusts. Have someone call 9-1-1 or the local emergency number. Obtain consent. Lean the victim forward and give 5 back blows with the heel of your hand. Stand or kneel behind the victim and wrap your arms around his or her waist. Make a fist with one hand and place the thumb side against the middle of the person's abdomen, just above the navel and well below the lower tip of the breastbone. Grasp the fist with the other hand and give 5 quick, upward thrusts into the abdomen. Continue back blows and abdominal thrusts until the object is dislodged and the person can breathe or cough forcefully, or becomes unconscious.

Where to Get Help

Source: Based on *Health & Medical Year Book*. © by Collier Newfield, Inc.; additional data, World Almanac research

Listed here are some of the major U.S. and Canadian organizations providing information about good health practices generally, or about specific conditions and how to deal with them. (Canadian sources are identified as such.) Where a toll-free number is not available, an address is given when possible.

Some entries conclude with an e-mail address for the organization and/or an address for its Internet site, where you can also obtain useful information. In addition to these selected sites, there is a vast array of medical information on the Internet; however, it is very important to be certain that the source of information is reliable and accurate. Always check with a physician before embarking on any new health-related undertaking.

General Sources

Centers for Disease Control and Prevention Voice Information System
800-311-3435
Recorded information about public health topics, such as AIDS and Lyme disease. Also, you can request to talk with a CDC expert or have information faxed to you.
Website: www.cdc.gov

National Health Information Center
800-336-4797; in Maryland, 301-565-4167
Phone numbers for more than 1,000 health-related organizations in the United States. Printed materials offered.
E-mail: info@nhic.org
Website: www.health.gov/NHIC

National Institutes of Health
301-496-4000
Free information, including the latest research findings, on many diseases.
E-mail: NIHinfo@OD.NIH.GOV
Website: www.nih.gov

Aging

Administration on Aging's Eldercare Locator Line
800-677-1116
Information and assistance on a wide range of services and programs including adult day-care and respite services, consumer fraud, hospital and nursing home information, legal services, elder abuse/protective services, Medicaid/Medigap information, tax assistance, and transportation.
E-mail: eldercarelocator@spherix.com
Website: www.eldercare.gov

National Institute on Aging
800-222-2225
Information and publications about disabling conditions, support groups, and community resources.
Website: www.nia.nih.gov

AIDS

AIDSinfo
800-HIV-0440
Information on federally and privately sponsored clinical trials for patients with AIDS or HIV; treatment information for people with AIDS, their families and health care providers
E-mail: ContactUs@aidsinfo.nih.gov
Website: www.aidsinfo.nih.gov

Canadian AIDS Society
613-230-3580
Written materials and referrals.
Website: www.cdnaids.ca
E-mail: CASinfo@cdnaids.ca

CDC-INFO
1-800 CDC-INFO (232-4636);
TTY: 1-888-232-6348
Information on the prevention and spread of AIDS, along with referrals.
E-mail: cdcinfo@cdc.gov
Website: www.cdc.gov/hiv/

Alcoholism and Drug Abuse

Alcoholics Anonymous
212-870-3400
Worldwide support groups for alcoholics.
Check phone book for local chapters.
Websites: www.alcoholics-anonymous.org or www.AA.org

American Council on Alcoholism
800-527-5344
Treatment referrals and counseling for
recovering alcoholics.
E-mail: info@aca-usa.org
Website: www.aca-usa.org

Phoenix House
Answers questions on substance abuse
and provides referrals to treatment
centers.
Website: www.drughelp.org

**National Clearinghouse for Alcohol
and Drug Information**
800-729-6686
Provides written materials on alcohol and
drug-related subjects.
Website: www.ncadi.samhsa.gov

**National Council on Alcoholism and
Drug Dependence Hopeline**
800-622-2255
Advisory and referral service.
E-mail: national@ncadd.org
Website: www.ncadd.org

Wellplace
800-821-4357, 24 hours
Referrals to local facilities
Website: www.wellplace.com

Alzheimer's Disease

Alzheimer's Association
800-272-3900
Gives referrals to local chapters and
support groups; offers information on
publications available from the
association.
E-mail: info@alz.org
Website: www.alz.org

Alzheimer's Society of Canada
416-488-8772
Gives phone numbers for local support
chapters. Publishes support materials.
E-mail: info@alzheimer.ca
Website: www.alzheimer.ca

Amyotrophic Lateral Sclerosis (ALS)

ALS Association 818-880-9007
Information about ALS (Lou Gehrig's
Disease) and referrals to ALS specialists,
local chapters and support groups.
Website: www.alsa.org

Arthritis

Arthritis Foundation
800-283-7800
Information, publications, and referrals to
local groups.
Website: www.arthritis.org

Arthritis Society (Canada)
393 University Ave., Suite 1700
Toronto, ON M5G 1E6
416-979-7228; in Ontario only, 800-321-1433
Phone numbers for local chapters.
E-mail: info@arthritis.ca
Website: www.arthritis.ca

**National Institute of Arthritis and
Musculoskeletal and Skin Diseases**
877-226-4267 or 301-495-4484
Subject searches and resource referrals.
E-mail: niamsweb-l@mail.nih.gov
Website: www.niams.nih.gov

Asthma and Allergies

See also Lung Diseases

**Asthma and Allergy Foundation of
America**
800-7-ASTHMA
Information; education; links to support
groups.

E-mail: info@aafa.org
Website: www.aafa.org

**American Academy of Allergy,
Asthma, and Immunology Referral
Line**
800-822-ASMA, 24 hours; 414-272-6071
Patient information and referrals for
asthma and allergies.
E-mail: info@aaaai.org
Website: www.aaaai.org

Autism

Autism Society of America
301-657-0881 or 800-3AUTISM
Information about autism, referral to local
chapters.
E-mail: chapters@autism-society.org
Website: www.autism-society.org

Blindness and Eye Care

**Canadian National Institute for the
Blind**
416-486-2500
National office offers training and library
with braille books and audiotapes. Local
chapters provide core services:
orientation in mobility, sight enhancement,
counseling, referrals, career aid,
technology services.
E-mail: info@crib.ca
Website: www.cnib.ca

Foundation Fighting Blindness
888-394-3937; TDD 800-683-5555
Answers questions about retinal
degenerative diseases; has written
materials.
E-mail: info@blindness.org
Website: www.blindness.org

**Library of Congress National Library
Service for the Blind and Physically
Handicapped**
800-424-8567; in Washington, DC, 202-707-5100; for the hearing impaired, TDD
202-707-0744
Information on libraries that offer talking
books and books in **braille**.
E-mail: nls@loc.gov
Website: www.loc.gov/nls

**National Association for Parents of
Children with Visual Impairments**
800-562-6265 or 617-972-7441
Support and information for parents of
individuals who are visually impaired.
E-mail: napvi@perkins.org
Website: www.napvi.org

Blood Disorders

Cooley's Anemia Foundation
800-522-7222
Information on patient care and support
groups; makes referrals to local chapters.
E-mail: info@cooleysanemia.org
Website: www.thalassemia.org

**Sickle Cell Disease Association
of America**
800-421-8453
Referrals for genetic counseling and
information packet.
E-mail: scdaa@sicklecelldisease.org
Website: www.sicklecelldisease.org

Burns

Phoenix Society
800-888-2876; 616-458-2773
Counseling network for burn survivors and
information on self-help services for burn
survivors and their families.
E-mail: info@phoenix-society.org
Website: www.phoenix-society.org

Cancer

American Cancer Society
800-ACS-2345
Publications and information about cancer
and coping with cancer; makes referrals to
local chapters for support services.
Website: www.cancer.org

Canadian Cancer Information Service
888-939-3333 or 416-961-7223
Information on prevention, treatment,
drugs, clinical trails, local services.
E-mail: info@cis.cancer.ca
Website: www.cancer.ca

**National Cancer Institute's Cancer
Information Service**
800-4-CANCER
Information about clinical trials,
treatments, symptoms, prevention,
referrals to support groups, and
screening.
Website: cis.nci.nih.gov

Y-Me Breast Cancer Support Program
800-221-2141, 24 hours;
800-986-9505, Spanish, 24-hours
Information and literature on breast
cancer, counseling, and referrals.
Website: www.y-me.org

Cerebral Palsy

Ontario Federation for Cerebral Palsy
Ontario only: 877-244-9686; 416-244-9686
Canada does not have a national cerebral
palsy organization, but the provincial
organizations offer information on
housing, services, and coping with life,
and each one will provide contact
numbers for the others.
E-mail: info@ofcp.on.ca
Website: www.ofcp.on.ca

United Cerebral Palsy Associations
800-872-5827, (TTY) 202-973-7197; in
Washington, DC, 202-776-0406
Written materials.
Website: www.ucp.org

Child Abuse

See Domestic Violence

Children

American Academy of Pediatrics
847-434-4000
Child-care publications and materials;
referrals to pediatricians.
E-mail: kidsdocs@aap.org
Website: www.aap.org

**National Center for Missing and
Exploited Children**
800-843-5678; 703-274-3900. Operates
24 hours.
Hotline for reporting missing children and
sightings of missing children.
Website: www.missingkids.com

National Runaway Switchboard
800-786-2929 (Runaway)
Crisis intervention and referrals for
runaways. Runaways can leave
messages for parents, and vice versa.
Operates 24 hours.
E-mail: info@nrscrisisline.org
Website: www.nrscrisisline.org

Chronic Fatigue Syndrome

CFIDS Association of America
704-365-2343
Literature and a list of support groups.
E-mail: cfids@cfids.org
Website: www.cfids.org

Cystic Fibrosis

Canadian Cystic Fibrosis Foundation
416-485-9149;
800-378-2233 in Canada only,
Information and brochures; makes
referrals to local chapters.
E-mail: info@cysticfibrosis.ca
Website: www.cysticfibrosis.ca

Cystic Fibrosis Foundation
800-FIGHT-CF or 301-951-4422
Answers questions and offers literature
and referrals to local clinics.
E-mail: info@cff.org
Website: www.cff.org

Diabetes

American Diabetes Association
800-342-2383
Information about diabetes, nutrition, exercise, and treatment; offers referrals.
E-mail: askADA@diabetes.org
Website: www.diabetes.org

Canadian Diabetes Association
416-363-0177;
800-226-8464 in Canada only.
Information about diabetes and its management.
E-mail: info@diabetes.ca
Website: www.diabetes.ca

Juvenile Diabetes Research Foundation Hotline
800-533-2873
Answers questions, provides literature (some in Spanish). Offers referrals to local chapters, physicians, and clinics.
E-mail: info@jdrf.org
Website: www.jdrf.org

Digestive Diseases

Crohn's and Colitis Foundation of America
800-932-2423
Educational materials; offers referrals to local chapters, which can provide referrals to support groups and physicians.
E-mail: info@ccfa.org
Website: www.ccfa.org

Crohn's and Colitis Foundation of Canada
416-920-5035;
in Canada only, 800-387-1479
Will send out educational materials upon request.
E-mail: ccfc@ccfc.ca
Website: www.ccfc.ca

Domestic Violence

Childhelp's USA National Child Abuse Hotline
800-4-A-CHILD
Crisis intervention, professional counseling, referrals to local groups and shelters for runaways, and literature. Operates 24 hours.
Website: www.childhelpusa.org

National Council on Child Abuse and Family Violence
800-422-4453, (TTY) 800-787-3244
Information and referrals.
Website: www.nccafv.org

National Domestic Violence Hotline
800-799-7233; (TTY) 800-787-3224

Down Syndrome

National Down Syndrome Congress
800-232-6372; in Georgia, 770-604-9500
Answers questions on all aspects of Down syndrome. Provides referrals.
E-mail: info@ndsccenter.org
Website: www.ndsccenter.org

National Down Syndrome Society
800-221-4602; 212-460-9330 (NYC)
E-mail: info@ndss.org
Website: www.ndss.org

Drug Abuse

See Alcoholism and Drug Abuse

Dyslexia

International Dyslexia Association
800-ABCD-123; in Maryland, 410-296-0232
Information on testing, tutoring, and computers used to aid people with dyslexia and related disorders.
E-mail: info@interdys.org
Website: www.interdys.org

Eating Disorders

National Association of Anorexia Nervosa and Associated Disorders
847-831-3438
Written materials, referrals to health professionals treating eating disorders, telephone counseling, offers self-help groups and information on how to set up a self-help group.
E-mail: anad20@aol.com
Website: www.anad.org

Endometriosis

Endometriosis Association
800-992-ENDO, an answering machine for callers to request information; 414-355-2200
Website: www.endometriosisassn.org

Epilepsy

Epilepsy Foundation's Answer Place
800-332-1000, Mon. through Thurs.
Information and referrals to local chapters.
Website: www.epilepsyfoundation.org

Erectile Dysfunction

American Urological Association
866-746-4282.
Information on various urological disorders and referrals.
E-mail: aua@auanet.org
Website: www.auanet.org

Food Safety and Nutrition

Meat and Poultry Hotline of the U.S. Department of Agriculture's Food, Safety, and Inspection Service
888-674-6854; TTY 800-256-7072
Information on prevention of food-borne illness and the proper handling, preparation, storage, labeling, and cooking of meat, poultry, and eggs.
E-mail: MPHotline.fsis@usda.gov
Website: www.foodsafety.gov

FDA Center for Food Safety and Applied Nutrition Outreach & Information Center
888-SAFE-FOOD
Information on how to buy and use food products and on their proper handling and storage, women's health, and cosmetics & colors. Callers may speak to food specialists, Mon. through Fri., 10 am to 4 PM (EST).
Website: www.cfsan.fda.gov

Headaches

National Headache Foundation
888-NHF-5552
Literature on headaches and treatment.
E-mail: info@headaches.org
Website: www.headaches.org

Heart Disease and Stroke

American Heart Association
800-242-8721
Information, publications, and referrals to organizations.
Website: www.americanheart.org

National Institute of Neurological Disorders and Stroke
800-352-9424, 301-496-5751;
TTY 301-468-5981
Literature and information.
Website: www.ninds.nih.gov

National Stroke Association
800-787-6537; in Colorado, 303-649-9299
Information on support networks for stroke victims and their families; referrals to local support groups.
Website: www.stroke.org

Hospices

Children's Hospice International
800-242-4453, in Virginia, 703-684-0330
Information, referrals to children's hospices.
E-mail: info@chionline.org
Website: www.chionline.org

Hospice Education Institute Hospicelink
800-331-1620; in Maine, 207-255-8800
Information, referrals to local programs.
E-mail: info@hospiceworld.org
Website: www.hospiceworld.org

Huntington's Disease

Huntington's Disease Society of America
800-345-4372; in New York, 212-242-1968
Information and referrals to physicians and support groups.
E-mail: hdsainfo@hdsa.org
Website: www.hdsa.org

Kidney Diseases

Kidney Foundation of Canada
514-369-4806; in Canada only, 800-361-7494
Educational materials and general information.
Website: www.kidney.ca

National Kidney and Urologic Diseases Information Clearinghouse
800-891-5390
Information, referrals to organizations.
Website: www.kidney.niddk.nih.gov

National Kidney Foundation
800-622-9010, 212-889-2210
Information and referrals.
E-mail: info@kidney.org
Website: www.kidney.org

Lead Exposure

National Lead Information Center
800-424-LEAD
Recommendations (in English and Spanish) for reducing a child's exposure to lead. Referrals to state and local agencies.
Website: www.epa.gov/lead

Liver Diseases

American Liver Foundation
800-465-4837
Information on hepatitis, liver, and gallbladder diseases.
E-mail: info@liverfoundation.org
Website: www.liverfoundation.org

Lung Diseases

See also Asthma and Allergies
American Lung Association
Check the phone book for local listings or call the national office at 800-LUNG-USA for automatic connection to the office nearest you. Answers questions about asthma and lung diseases; publications and referrals.
Website: www.lungusa.org

Lung Line Information Service at the National Jewish Medical and Research Center
800-222-LUNG; outside the U.S.: 303-388-4461
Answers questions on asthma, emphysema, allergies, smoking, and other respiratory and immune system disorders.
E-mail: lungline@njc.org
Website: www.njc.org

Lupus

Lupus Foundation of America
800-558-0121; 202-349-1155
Sends information to those who leave name and address on answering machine.
E-mail: info@lupus.org
Website: www.lupus.org

Lyme Disease

Lyme Disease Foundation
860-870-0070
Written information; doctor referrals.
E-mail: info@lyme.org
Website: www.lyme.org

Mental Health

Depression and Bipolar Support Alliance
800-826-3632
Support for patients and families, provides publications, and makes referrals to affiliated organizations.
E-mail: questions@dbsalliance.org
Website: www.dbsalliance.org

Mental Health America
800-969-6642
Referrals to mental health groups.
Website:
www.mentalhealthamerica.net.org

National Institute of Mental Health
301-443-4513, toll free 866-615-6464; TTY 301-443-8431
Information on a range of topics, from children's mental disorders to schizophrenia, depression, eating disorders, and others.
E-mail: nimhinfo@nih.gov
Website: www.nimh.nih.gov

Multiple Sclerosis

Multiple Sclerosis Society of Canada
416-922-6065, 800-268-7582 in Canada only.
Counseling, literature, and referrals to local chapters.
E-mail: info@mssociety.ca
Website: www.mssociety.ca

National Multiple Sclerosis Society
800-344-4867
Information about local chapters.
Website: www.nationalmssociety.org

Muscular Dystrophy

Muscular Dystrophy Association
800-FIGHT-MD
Written materials on 40 neuromuscular diseases, including muscular dystrophy. Will give information over the phone about such matters as MDA clinics, support groups, summer camps, and wheelchair purchase assistance.
E-mail: mda@mdausa.org
Website: www.mdausa.org

Nutrition

See Food Safety and Nutrition

Organ Donation

Living Bank
800-528-2971, 24 hours
A registry and referral service for people wanting to commit organs to transplantation or research.
E-mail: info@livingbank.org
Website: www.livingbank.org

Osteoporosis

National Osteoporosis Foundation
800-223-9994; in Washington, DC, 202-223-2226
Information packet available on request.
Website: www.nof.org

Pain

National Chronic Pain Outreach Association
Information packet available on request.
Website: www.chronicpain.org

Parkinson's Disease

National Parkinson Foundation
800-327-4545; in Miami, 305-547-6666
Answers questions, makes physician referrals, and provides written information in English and Spanish.
E-mail: contact@parkinson.org
Website: www.parkinson.org

Parkinson Society Canada
800-565-3000, Canada only; 416-227-9700
Information; referrals to support groups.
E-mail: General.info@parkinson.ca
Website: www.parkinson.ca

Plastic Surgery

Plastic Surgery Referral Service
888-475-2784
Referrals to board-certified plastic surgeons in the U.S. and Canada; general information.
Website: www.plasticsurgery.org

Polio

Post-Polio Health International
314-534-0475
Information on coping with the late effects of polio; referrals to other organizations.
E-mail: info@post-polio.org
Website: www.post-polio.org

Prostate Problems

American Urological Association Foundation
800-828-7866, 410-689-3990
Information and publications.
Website: www.urologyhealth.org

Rare Disorders

National Organization for Rare Disorders
800-999-6673, 203-744-0100
Information on diseases and networking programs; referrals to organizations for specific disorders.
E-mail: orphan@rarediseases.org
Website: www.rarediseases.org

Rehabilitation

National Rehabilitation Information Center
800-34-NARIC; in Maryland, 301-459-5900; TTY 301-459-5984
Research referrals and information on rehabilitation issues.
E-mail: naricinfo@heitechservices.com
Website: www.naric.com

Scleroderma

United Scleroderma Foundation
800-722-4673
Referrals to local support groups and treatment centers, as well as information on scleroderma and related skin disorders.
E-mail: sfinfo@scleroderma.org
Website: www.scleroderma.org

Sexually Transmitted Diseases

See also AIDS
National STD Hotline
800-227-8922
Information; confidential referrals.
E-mail: info@ashastd.org
Website: www.ashastd.org

Sjogren's Syndrome

Sjogren's Syndrome Foundation
800-475-6473;
Provides an answering machine for callers to request treatment literature.
Website: www.sjogrens.org

Skin Problems

National Psoriasis Foundation
800-723-9166
Information and referrals.
E-mail: getinfo@psoriasis.org
Website: www.psoriasis.org

Speech and Hearing

American Speech-Language-Hearing Association Action Center
800-638-8255 (also TTY)
Materials on speech and language disorders and hearing impairment; referrals.
E-mail: actioncenter@asha.org
Website: www.asha.org

Canadian Hard of Hearing Association
800-263-8068, Canada only; TTY 613-526-2692; 613-526-1584
Publications; answers general questions.
E-mail: chhanational@chha.ca
Website: www.chha.ca

Dial a Hearing Screening Test
800-222-EARS
Answers questions on hearing problems. Makes referrals to local telephone numbers for a two-minute hearing test. Also to ear, nose, and throat specialists and to organizations that can provide specialized ear and hearing aid information. 9 AM-5 PM EST

Hearing Aid Helpline
800-521-5247, ext. 333
Information and distributes a directory of hearing aid specialists certified by the International Hearing Society.
Website: www.ihsinfo.org

National Center for Stuttering
800-221-2483; 212-532-1460
Information on stuttering in all age groups.
E-mail: executivedirector@stuttering.com
Website: www.stuttering.com

Stuttering Foundation of America
800-992-9392
Referrals to speech pathologists; resource lists, publications.
E-mail: info@stutteringhelp.org
Website: www.stutteringhelp.org

Spinal Injuries

National Spinal Cord Injury Association
800-962-9629; 301-214-4006
Peer counseling; referrals to local chapters and other organizations.
E-mail: info@spinalcord.org
Website: www.spinalcord.org

Stroke

See Heart Disease and Stroke

Sudden Infant Death Syndrome

American Sudden Infant Death Syndrome Institute
800-232-SIDS; in Georgia, 770-426-8746
Answers questions; literature; referrals to other organizations.
E-mail: prevent@sids.org
Website: www.sids.org

Tourette Syndrome

Tourette Syndrome Association
718-224-2999
Printed information.
E-mail: ts@tsa-usa.org
Website: tsa-usa.org

Urinary Incontinence

National Association for Continence
800-BLADDER, 843-377-0900
Information on bladder control, services available for incontinence, and assistive devices.
E-mail: memberservices@nafc.org
Website: www.nafc.org

Simon Foundation for Continence
800-23-SIMON
Support and literature on incontinence.
E-mail: Simoninfo@simonfoundation.org
Website: www.simonfoundation.org

Women's Health

National Women's Health Network
202-347-1140; 202-628-7814
Information and referrals on more than 70 women's health concerns.
E-mail: nwhn@nwhn.org
Website: www.nwhn.org

National Women's Health Resource Center
877-986-9472
A national clearinghouse for women's health information.
E-mail: snelson@healthywomen.org
Website: www.healthywomen.org

VITAL STATISTICS

Recent Trends in Vital Statistics

Source: National Center for Health Statistics, U.S. Dept. of Health and Human Services; latest years available

Births

An estimated 4,269,000 babies were born in the U.S. in 2006, a rise from 4,143,000 births in 2005. The birth rate increased to 14.3 per 1,000 total population, up from the record low of 13.9 in 2002.

The fertility rate (number of live births per 1,000 women aged 15-44 years) rose to an estimated 68.7 for 2006, up from the 2005 rate of 66.7; this marked the highest rate since 1993, but was still low by historical standards.

Deaths

The number of deaths during 2006 was estimated at 2,416,000 according to provisional data, down from 2,432,000 in 2005. The death rate in 2006 decreased to 8.1 per 1,000 population from 8.2 in 2005. The infant death rate was 6.6 deaths under 1 year per 1,000 live births in 2006, down from 6.8 in 2005.

Natural Increase

As a result of natural increase (the excess of births over deaths), an estimated 1,853,000 persons were added to the population in 2006. The rate of increase jumped to 6.2 per 1,000 population from 5.8 for 2005.

Marriages

An estimated 2,160,000 marriages were performed in 2006, compared to 2,249,000 in 2005. The provisional marriage rate for 2006 (7.3 per 1,000 population) was down from the 2005 rate of 7.6. Louisiana has suspended its marriage count since Hurricane Katrina.

Divorces

The divorce rate in 2006 stayed at 3.6 per 1,000 population according to provisional data. Data are incomplete, however. The NCHS no longer includes divorce data for California, Georgia, Hawaii, Indiana, Louisiana, and Minnesota.

Births and Deaths in the U.S.

Source: National Center for Health Statistics, U.S. Dept. of Health and Human Services

Year	BIRTHS Total number	Rate	DEATHS Total number	Rate	Year	BIRTHS Total number	Rate	DEATHS Total number	Rate
1960	4,257,850	23.7	1,711,982	9.5	1997	3,880,894	14.2	2,314,245	8.5
1970	3,731,386	18.4	1,921,031	9.5	1998	3,941,553	14.3	2,337,256	8.5
1980	3,612,258	15.9	1,989,841	8.8	1999	3,959,417	14.2	2,391,399	8.6
1990	4,092,994	16.7	2,148,463	8.6	2000	4,058,814	14.4	2,403,351	8.5
1991	4,094,566	16.2	2,169,518	8.6	2001	4,025,933	14.1	2,416,425	8.5
1992	4,049,024	15.8	2,175,613	8.5	2002	4,021,726	13.9	2,443,387	8.5
1993	4,000,240	15.4	2,268,553	8.7	2003	4,089,950	14.1	2,448,288	8.4
1994	3,952,767	15.0	2,278,994	8.7	2004	4,112,052	14.0	2,397,615	8.2
1995	3,899,589	14.6	2,312,132	8.7	2005	4,143,000(P)	14.0(P)	2,432,000(P)	8.2(P)
1996	3,891,494	14.4	2,314,690	8.6	2006	4,269,000(P)	14.3(P)	2,416,000(P)	8.1(P)

(P) = provisional data. **NOTE:** Statistics cover only events occurring within the U.S. and exclude fetal deaths. Rates per 1,000 population; enumerated as of Apr. 1 for census years; estimated as of July 1 for all other years. Beginning 1970 statistics exclude births and deaths occurring among nonresidents of the U.S. Data include revisions. Birth and death rates for years in the 1990s revised on basis of the 2000 Census.

Marriage and Divorce Rates, 1920-2006

Source: National Center for Health Statistics, U.S. Dept. of Health and Human Services

The U.S. marriage rate dipped during the Depression and peaked sharply just after World War II; the trend after that has been more gradual. The divorce rate generally rose from the 1920s through 1981, when it peaked at 5.3 per 1,000 population, before declining somewhat. The graph below shows marriage and divorce rates since 1920. (2005-06 divorce rates were calculated excluding data and populations from the non-reporting states California, Georgia, Hawaii, Indiana, Louisiana, and Minnesota; Louisiana marriage rate and population excluded in 2006. Some data are provisional.)

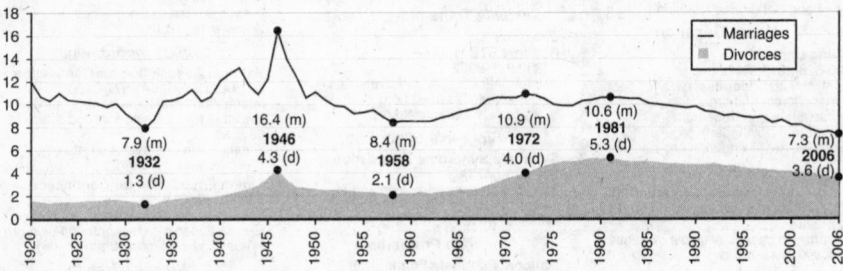

U.S. Median Age at First Marriage, 1890-2006

Source: Bureau of the Census, U.S. Dept. of Commerce

Year[1]	Men	Women	Year[1]	Men	Women	Year[1]	Men	Women	Year[1]	Men	Women	Year[1]	Men	Women
1890	26.1	22.0	1950	22.8	20.3	1985	25.5	23.3	1995	26.9	24.5	2001	26.9	25.1
1900	25.9	21.9	1960	22.8	20.3	1990	26.1	23.9	1996	27.1	24.8	2002	26.9	25.3
1910	25.1	21.6	1965	22.8	20.6	1991	26.3	24.1	1997	26.8	25.0	2003	27.1	25.3
1920	24.6	21.2	1970	23.2	20.8	1992	26.5	24.4	1998	26.7	25.0	2004	27.4	25.3
1930	24.3	21.3	1975	23.5	21.1	1993	26.5	24.5	1999	26.9	25.1	2005	27.1	25.3
1940	24.3	21.5	1980	24.7	22.0	1994	26.7	24.5	2000	26.8	25.1	2006	27.5	25.9

(1) Figures after 1940 based on pop. 15 to 54 years in Current Population Survey data; earlier figures based on decennial censuses.

Birth Rates; Fertility Rates by Age of Mother, 1950-2005

Source: National Center for Health Statistics, U.S. Dept. of Health and Human Services

				AGE OF MOTHER							
			10-14 years	15-19 years			20-24 years	25-29 years	30-34 years	35-39 years	40-44 years	45-49 years
Year	Birth rate[1]	Fertility rate[2]		Total	15-17	18-19						
					Live births per 1,000 women by age group							
1950	24.1	106.2	1.0	81.6	40.7	132.7	196.6	166.1	103.7	52.9	15.1	1.2
1960	23.7	118.0	0.8	89.1	43.9	166.7	258.1	197.4	112.7	56.2	15.5	0.9
1970	18.4	87.9	1.2	68.3	38.8	114.7	167.8	145.1	73.3	31.7	8.1	0.5
1980	15.9	68.4	1.1	53.0	32.5	82.1	115.1	112.9	61.9	19.8	3.9	0.2
1990	16.7	70.9	1.4	59.9	37.5	88.6	116.5	120.2	80.8	31.7	5.5	0.2
1991	16.2	69.3	1.4	61.8	38.6	94.0	115.3	117.2	79.2	31.9	5.5	0.2
1992	15.8	68.4	1.4	60.3	37.6	93.6	113.7	115.7	79.6	32.3	5.9	0.3
1993	15.4	67.0	1.4	59.0	37.5	91.1	111.3	113.2	79.9	32.7	6.1	0.3
1994	15.0	65.9	1.4	58.2	37.2	90.2	109.2	111.0	80.4	33.4	6.4	0.3
1995	14.6	64.6	1.3	56.0	35.5	87.7	107.5	108.8	81.1	34.0	6.6	0.3
1996	14.4	64.1	1.2	53.5	33.3	84.7	107.8	108.6	82.1	34.9	6.8	0.3
1997	14.2	63.6	1.1	51.3	31.4	82.1	107.3	108.3	83.0	35.7	7.1	0.4
1998	14.3	64.3	1.0	50.3	29.9	80.9	108.4	110.2	85.2	36.9	7.4	0.4
1999	14.2	64.4	0.9	48.8	28.2	79.1	107.9	111.2	87.1	37.8	7.4	0.4
2000	14.4	65.9	0.9	47.7	26.9	78.1	109.7	113.5	91.2	39.7	8.0	0.5
2001	14.1	65.3	0.8	45.3	24.7	76.1	106.2	113.4	91.9	40.6	8.1	0.5
2002	13.9	64.8	0.7	43.0	23.2	72.8	103.6	113.6	91.5	41.4	8.3	0.5
2003	14.1	66.1	0.6	41.6	22.4	70.7	102.6	115.6	95.1	43.8	8.7	0.5
2004	14.0	66.3	0.7	41.1	22.1	70.0	101.7	115.5	95.3	45.4	8.9	0.5
2005[3]	14.0	66.7	0.7	40.4	21.4	69.9	102.2	115.6	95.9	46.3	9.1	0.6

(1) Live births per 1,000 population. (2) Live births per 1,000 women 15-44 years of age. (3) Preliminary.

Numbers of Multiple Births in the U.S., 1990-2004

Source: National Center for Health Statistics, U.S. Dept. of Health and Human Services
The general upward trend in multiple births reflects greater numbers of births to older women and increased use of fertility drugs.

Year	Twins	Triplets	Quadruplets	Quintuplets and higher	Year	Twins	Triplets	Quadruplets	Quintuplets and higher
1990	93,865	2,830	185	13	1998	110,670	6,919	627	79
1992	95,372	3,547	310	26	1999	114,307	6,742	512	67
1993	96,445	3,834	277	57	2000	118,916	6,742	506	77
1994	97,064	4,233	315	46	2001	121,246	6,885	501	85
1995	96,736	4,551	365	57	2002	125,134	6,898	434	69
1996	100,750	5,298	560	81	2003	128,665	7,110	468	85
1997	104,137	6,148	510	79	2004	132,219	6,750	439	86

Top 15 Countries for U.S. Foreign Adoptions, Fiscal Years 1998-2006[1]

Source: Dept. of Homeland Security, Office of Immigration Statistics

Country	2006	2005	2004	2003	2002	2001	2000	1999	1998
China	6,520	7,939	7,033	6,638	6,062	4,629	4,943	4,009	3,988
Guatemala	4,093	3,748	3,252	2,327	2,361	1,601	1,504	987	938
Russia	3,710	4,652	5,878	5,134	4,904	4,210	4,210	4,250	4,320
South Korea	1,381	1,604	1,708	1,793	1,713	1,863	1,711	1,956	1,705
Ethiopia	711	430	277	166	102	160	103	100	88
Kazakhstan	580	755	824	819	801	664	392	108	54
Ukraine	463	841	772	691	1,093	1,227	645	307	168
Colombia	349	302	279	275	329	261	246	226	221
Liberia	338	166	88	22	23	50	20	20	9
Haiti	313	226	355	246	192	187	136	93	113
India	307	324	394	466	459	540	491	486	462
Philippines	252	259	188	218	208	220	176	185	189
Taiwan	188	133	89	104	41	44	24	26	18
Vietnam	162	NA	25	393	736	730	709	704	576
Mexico	76	94	98	67	71	105	115	145	170
Total[2]	20,705	22,710	22,911	21,320	21,100	19,087	18,120	16,037	14,867

NA = Not available. (1) Ranked by 2006 totals. (2) Total includes countries not shown.

10 Leading Causes of Infant Death in the U.S., 2004

Source: National Center for Health Statistics, U.S. Dept. of Health and Human Services

Cause	Number	Percent of total deaths	Mortality rate[1]
Congenital malformations, deformations, and chromosomal abnormalities	5,622	20.1	136.7
Disorders related to short gestation, and low birth weight, not elsewhere classified	4,642	16.6	112.9
Sudden infant death syndrome	2,246	8.0	54.6
Newborn affected by maternal complications of pregnancy	1,715	6.1	41.7
Accidents (unintentional injuries)	1,052	3.8	25.6
Newborn affected by complications of placenta, cord, and membranes	1,042	3.7	25.3
Respiratory distress of newborn	875	3.1	21.3
Bacterial sepsis[2] of newborn	827	3.0	20.1
Neonatal hemorrhage	616	2.2	15.0
Diseases of the circulatory system	593	2.1	14.4
All other causes	8,706	31.2	211.7
All causes	**27,936**	**100.0**	**679.4**

(1) Infant deaths per 100,000 live births. (2) Toxic condition resulting from the spread of bacteria.

Nonmarital Childbearing in the U.S., 1970-2004

Source: National Center for Health Statistics, U.S. Dept. of Health and Human Services

	1970	1975	1980	1985	1990	1995	1998	1999	2000	2001	2002	2003	2004
Births to unmarried mothers (1,000s)..	399	448	666	828	1,165	1,254	1,294	1,309	1,347	1,349	1,366	1,416	1,470
Race of Mother	*Percent of live births to unmarried mothers*												
All races.........................	10.7	14.3	18.4	22.0	28.0	32.2	32.8	33.0	33.2	33.5	34.0	34.6	35.8
White	5.5	7.1	11.2	14.7	20.4	25.3	26.3	26.8	27.1	27.7	28.5	29.4	30.5
Black..........................	37.5	49.5	56.1	61.2	66.5	69.9	69.1	68.9	68.5	68.4	68.2	68.2	68.8
American Indian or Alaska Native	22.4	32.7	39.2	46.8	53.6	57.2	59.3	58.9	58.4	59.7	59.7	61.3	62.3
Asian or Pacific Islander............	—	—	7.3	9.5	13.2	16.3	15.6	15.4	14.8	14.9	14.9	15.0	15.5
Hispanic origin (selected states)[1,2]....	—	—	23.6	29.5	36.7	40.8	41.6	42.2	42.7	42.5	43.5	45.0	46.4
White, non-Hispanic (selected states)[1]	—	—	9.5	12.4	16.9	21.2	21.9	22.1	22.1	22.5	23.0	23.6	24.5
Black, non-Hispanic (selected states)[1].	—	—	57.2	62.0	66.7	70.0	69.3	69.1	68.7	68.6	68.4	68.5	69.3
Maternal age	*Percent distribution of live births to unmarried mothers*												
Under 20 years....................	50.1	52.1	40.8	33.8	30.9	30.9	30.1	29.3	28.0	26.6	25.4	24.3	23.7
20–24 years......................	31.8	29.9	35.6	36.3	34.7	34.5	35.6	36.4	37.4	38.2	38.6	38.8	38.5
25 years and over	18.1	18.0	23.5	29.9	34.4	34.7	34.3	34.3	34.6	35.2	35.9	36.9	37.8
	Live births per 1,000 unmarried women 15–44 years of age[3]												
All races and origins...............	26.4	24.5	29.4	32.8	43.8	44.3	43.3	43.3	44.0	43.8	43.7	44.9	46.1
White[4].........................	13.9	12.4	18.1	22.5	32.9	37.0	36.9	37.4	38.2	38.5	38.9	40.4	41.6
Black[4].........................	95.5	84.2	81.1	77.0	90.5	74.5	71.6	69.7	70.5	68.2	66.2	66.3	67.2
Hispanic origin (selected states)[1,2]....	—	—	—	—	89.6	88.7	82.8	84.9	87.2	87.8	87.9	92.2	95.7
White, non-Hispanic................	—	—	—	—	—	28.1	27.9	27.9	28.0	27.8	27.8	28.6	29.4

— Data not available. (1) Data for Hispanics and non-Hispanics are affected by expansion of the reporting area for an Hispanic-origin item on the birth certificate and by immigration. The states in the reporting area increased from 22 in 1980, to 23 and the District of Columbia in 1983, 48 and DC by 1990, and 50 and DC by 1993. (2) Includes mothers of all races. (3) Rates computed by relating births to unmarried mothers, regardless of mother's age, to unmarried women 15–44 years of age. (4) For 1970 and 1975, birth rates are by race of child.

Number, Ratio, and Rate of Legal Abortions in U.S., 1970-2003

Source: Centers for Disease Control, *Abortion Surveillance, U.S., 2003*

Year	Legal Abortions	Ratio[1]	Rate[2]	Year	Legal Abortions	Ratio[1]	Rate[2]	Year	Legal Abortions	Ratio[1]	Rate[2]
1970....	193,491	52	5	1982....	1,303,980	354	24	1994....	1,267,415	321	21
1971....	485,816	137	11	1983....	1,268,987	349	23	1995....	1,210,883	311	20
1972....	586,760	180	13	1984....	1,333,521	364	24	1996....	1,225,937	315	21
1973....	615,831	196	14	1985....	1,328,570	354	24	1997....	1,186,039	306	20
1974....	763,476	242	17	1986....	1,328,112	354	23	1998[3]....	884,273	264	17
1975....	854,853	272	18	1987....	1,353,671	356	24	1999[3]....	861,789	256	17
1976....	988,267	312	21	1988....	1,371,285	352	24	2000[3]....	857,475	245	16
1977....	1,079,430	325	22	1989....	1,396,658	346	24	2001[4]....	853,485	246	16
1978....	1,157,776	347	23	1990....	1,429,247	344	24	2002[4]....	854,122	246	16
1979....	1,251,921	358	24	1991....	1,388,937	338	24	2003[5]....	848,163	241	16
1980....	1,297,606	359	25	1992....	1,359,146	334	23				
1981....	1,300,760	358	24	1993....	1,330,414	333	23				

(1) Number of abortions per 1,000 live births. (2) Number of abortions per 1,000 women aged 15-44 years. (3) Without estimates for AK, CA, NH, and OK. (4) Without estimates for AK, CA, and NH. (5) Without estimates for CA, NH, and WV.

Sexual Behavior in the U.S.

Data released by the National Center for Health Statistics in 2005 show that about 90% of U.S. men and women 18-44 years of age think of themselves as heterosexual; 2.3% of men and 1.3% of women as homosexual; and 1.8% of men and 2.8% of women as bisexual. However, 6.2% of men 18-44 years of age reported ever having had sex with another male as of 2002 (up from 2.3% in 1991) and 11.5% of women reported ever having had a sexual experience with another woman (up from 4.1% in 1992).

Ten percent of males age 15-44 had never had sex with a female, but this percentage varied greatly with age: more than half (52%) of males age 15-17 had never had sex with a female, but only 1.8% of males age 40-44 had not done so.

Percentages were slightly lower for women, with only 8.4% of females age 15-44 having never had sex with a male, with specific percentages ranging from 50.2% for females age 15-17 to only 1.3% for females age 40-44.

Among men age 15-44 who had sex with at least one partner in the previous year, 39% reported using a condom in their most recent sexual encounter (24% of married men and 65% of never-married men). Among women, only 22% reported using a condom (13% of married and 42% of never-married women). Condom use was also more frequent among younger men and women: in the 15-19 age group, 66% of males and 44% of females used a condom in their most recent sexual encounter.

Median Number of Opposite-Sex Partners in Past Year

Source: National Center for Health Statistics, *Sexual Behavior and Selected Health Measures, 2002*
Note: U.S. males and females 15-44 years of age

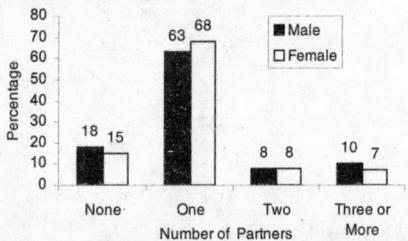

Median Number of Opposite-Sex Partners in Lifetime

Source: National Center for Health Statistics, *Sexual Behavior and Selected Health Measures, 2002*

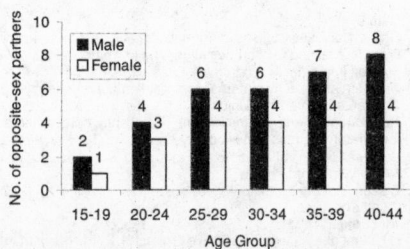

Lifetime and Median Number of Sexual Partners, by Age and Race, 2002
Source: National Center for Health Statistics, Sexual Behavior and Selected Health Measures, 2002

Number of opposite-sex partners in lifetime, percent distribution	0	1	2	3-6	7-14	15+	Median[1]
Males 15-44 years[2]	9.6	12.5	8.0	27.2	19.5	23.2	5.6
Age							
15-19..............	43.5	23.4	9.0	17.0	4.9	2.3	1.6
20-24..............	9.9	15.7	11.6	33.1	13.9	15.8	3.8
25-44..............	2.9	9.5	6.9	27.7	23.7	29.2	6.7
Race							
White, non-Hispanic..	9.8	13.4	8.3	27.0	19.2	22.3	5.3
Black, non-Hispanic ..	8.6	5.8	5.9	24.0	22.1	33.7	8.3
Hispanic or Latino....	9.1	13.5	8.5	32.5	18.4	17.9	4.5

Number of opposite-sex partners in lifetime, percent distribution	0	1	2	3-6	7-14	15+	Median[1]
Females 15-44 years[2]..	8.6	22.5	10.8	32.6	16.3	9.2	3.3
Age							
15-19	37.8	27.2	9.0	19.1	5.0	1.9	1.4
20-24	8.9	24.6	13.0	32.2	14.4	6.9	2.8
25-44	1.7	20.9	10.7	36.0	19.4	11.4	3.8
Race							
White, non-Hispanic..	7.8	21.0	10.6	32.1	18.2	10.2	3.6
Black, non-Hispanic ..	7.7	12.4	8.4	44.8	18.0	8.8	4.1
Hispanic or Latina ...	10.5	34.6	14.9	27.2	8.2	4.6	1.7

(1) Excludes people who have never had intercourse with an opposite-sex partner. (2) Includes people of other or multiple race and origin groups, not shown separately.

Sexual Activity of High School Students, 2005
Source: CDC, *Youth Risk Behavior Surveillance—United States, 2005*

		Ever had sexual intercourse			First sexual intercourse before age 13			Currently sexually active[1]			Condom Use[2]		
		Female	Male	Total	Female	Male	Total	Female	Male	Total	Female	Male	Total
Race/ Ethnicity	White[3] ...	43.7	42.2	43.0	2.9	5.0	4.0	33.5	30.6	32.0	55.6	70.1	62.6
	Black[3] ...	61.2	74.6	67.6	7.1	26.8	16.5	43.8	51.3	47.4	62.1	75.5	68.9
	Hispanic..	44.4	57.6	51.0	3.6	11.1	7.3	33.7	36.3	35.0	49.8	65.3	57.7
Grade	9.......	29.3	39.3	34.3	5.4	12.0	8.7	19.5	24.5	21.9	71.5	77.1	74.5
	10......	44.0	41.5	42.8	4.1	7.7	5.9	31.1	27.2	29.2	57.1	74.4	65.3
	11......	52.1	50.6	51.4	2.6	8.0	5.2	40.8	37.9	39.4	57.8	66.0	61.7
	12......	62.4	63.8	63.1	2.0	6.2	4.1	51.7	47.0	49.4	46.1	65.8	55.4
Total..............		45.7	47.9	46.8	3.7	8.8	6.2	34.6	33.3	33.9	55.9	70.0	62.8

(1) Sexual intercourse during the 3 months preceding the survey. (2) Among the 33.9% who were sexually active. (3) Non-Hispanic.

Sexual Activity of Older Adults
Source: National Social Life, Health, and Aging Project at the Univ. of Chicago

		% sexually active with a partner		% reporting sexual behavior			% reporting sexual problem[1]				
Sex	Age	In prev. 12 mo.	2-3+ times per mo.[1]	Inter-course[1]	Oral sex[1]	Mastur-bation[2]	Lack of interest	Stimulation problems	No Pleasure	Anxiety	Pain
Men	57-64	83.7	67.5	91.1	62.1	63.4	28.2	30.7	3.8	25.1	3.0
	65-74	67.0	65.4	78.5	47.9	53.0	28.5	44.6	7.0	28.9	3.2
	75-85	38.5	54.2	83.5	28.3	27.9	24.2	43.5	5.1	29.3	1.0
Women	57-64	61.6	62.6	86.8	52.7	31.6	44.2	35.9	24.0	10.4	17.8
	65-74	39.5	65.4	85.4	46.5	21.9	38.4	43.2	22.0	12.5	18.6
	75-85	16.7	54.1	74.4	35.0	16.4	49.3	43.6	24.9	9.9	11.8

Note: Based on in-home interviews of 3,005 U.S. adults (1,550 women and 1,455 men) between July 2005 and March 2006. (1) If reported having sex in prev. 12 months. (2) In prev. 12 months asked of all respondents by questionnaire.

U.S. Fires, 2006
Source: National Fire Protection Assn.

Fires
• Public fire departments responded to 1,642,500 fires in 2006, an increase of 2.5% from 2005. Every 19 seconds, a fire department responds to a fire somewhere in the United States.
• There were 524,000 structure fires in 2006, an increase of 2.5% from 2005. 78.7% of all structure fires, or 412,500 fires, occurred in homes.
• Fires in vehicles dropped 4.1% from the previous year, totaling 278,000 in 2006.
• There were 840,500 fires in outside properties, an increase of 4.9% from 2005.

Civilian deaths
• There were an estimated 3,245 civilian fire deaths in 2006. This was a decrease of 11.7% from the year before.
• The number of civilian fire deaths that occurred in home structure fires decreased by 14.2%, to 2,620, but fires in the home still caused 80.7% of all fire deaths.
• Home fires caused an average of one civilian death every 162 minutes.

Civilian injuries
• There were an estimated 16,400 civilian fire injuries reported in 2006, a decrease of 8.5% from 2005. Nationwide, a civilian was injured in a fire every 32 minutes.

• Home structure fires were the site of 12,925 civilian fire injuries in 2006, and non-home structure fires accounted for 1,425 civilian injuries.

Property damage
• Direct property damage from fires amounted to an estimated $11.3 billion in 2006, an increase of 6.0% from 2005. Structure fires accounted for $9.6 billion of property damage.
• Property loss associated with home fires came to $6.99 billion for 2006.

Intentionally set fires
• There were an estimated 31,000 intentionally set structure fires in 2006, a slight decrease of 1.6% from 2005.
• Intentionally set structure fires are believed to have resulted in 305 civilian deaths in 2006, a decrease of 3.2% from the year before. Property damage from intentionally set structure fires totaled $755 million, a significant increase of 13.7% from the 2005 figure.
• The number of intentionally set vehicle fires in 2006 was 20,500, a decrease of 2.4% from 2005. Intentionally set vehicle fires caused an estimated $134 million in property damage, an increase of 18.6% from 2005.

U.S. Motor Vehicle Accidents, 2005

Sources: National Safety Council; Natl. Highway Traffic Safety Admin.

About 45,800 people in the U.S. were killed in motor vehicle accidents in 2005, according to preliminary figures from the National Safety Council, up 1% from the revised total for 2004. As the number of drivers (201.5 million) and vehicle miles driven (3 trillion) increased in 2005, the death rate per 100 million vehicle miles increased 1% to 1.54.

Motor-vehicle deaths per 10,000 registered vehicles held steady from 2004 to 2005 at 2.09, but dropped from 2.11 in 1995, a decrease of 12% over 10 years. This rate has declined in most years since the introduction of the automobile. The rate of fatalities per 100,000 population declined 6% from 1995 to 2005, but increased slightly[1] from 2004 to 2005.

The split between male and female licensed drivers was basically 50-50. Male drivers were involved in about 6.2 mil accidents while female drivers were in 4.5 mil. Male drivers were also involved in 73% of fatal accidents, about 43,000 compared to 15,000 female drivers.

In 2005, 13,582 traffic fatalities, or 31%, involved an intoxicated (blood alcohol concentration of 0.08 or greater) driver or

Note: NSC numbers are rounded. NHTSA intoxication data is final.

motorcycle operator, the highest since 13,739 people were killed in 1993. In cases where a driver or nonoccupant drank at all, traffic fatalities totaled 17,590 people or 40%. Alcohol factored in about 7% of all traffic accidents.

Seat belt use reached a record high of 82% in 2005. Safety belts and child restraints saved an estimated 16,052 lives. Another 2,741 lives were saved by air bags. Women used safety belts more often, 84%, than men, 80%. The least likely safety belt users were rural drivers, 79%, and drivers of pickup trucks, 73%.

	Deaths 2005	% change from 2004	Rate 2005[2]
All motor vehicle accidents	45,800	+1	15.5
Collision between motor vehicles . .	19,200	-1	6.5
Collision with fixed object.	13,700	+1	4.6
Pedestrian accidents	6,200	+3	2.1
Noncollision accidents	5,300	+4	1.8
Collision with pedal cycle	1,000	+11	0.3
Collision with railroad train.	300	0	0.1
Other collision (animal, animal-drawn vehicles)	100	0	(1)

(1) Less than 0.05. (2) Deaths per 100,000 population.

Improper Driving Reported in Accidents, 2000, 2002, 2005

Source: National Safety Council

Type	Percentage of fatal accidents 2005	2002	2000	Percentage of injury accidents 2005	2002	2000	Percentage of all accidents 2005	2002	2000
Improper driving	62.7	59.5	61.6	62.7	54.7	60.3	58.5	50.3	57.8
Speed too fast or unsafe.	18.1	21.9	18.6	15.0	12.6	16.3	12.7	10.1	13.6
Right of way	12.2	17.4	10.1	17.5	18.9	19.9	14.3	16.4	20.1
Failed to yield	8.0	10.1	4.6	12.5	14.3	15.0	10.8	11.4	12.7
Disregarded signal	1.4	4.0	8.2	2.5	3.3	1.3	1.7	3.4	2.2
Passed stop sign	2.8	3.3	3.8	2.5	1.3	3.6	1.8	1.6	5.3
Drove left of center	8.0	5.7	0.7	2.2	0.9	1.1	1.6	0.7	1.0
Improper overtaking	1.4	1.0	0.9	0.6	0.5	2.0	0.8	0.8	2.4
Made improper turn.	4.5	0.5	0.7	4.2	1.2	0.6	4.5	1.7	0.9
Followed too closely	1.0	0.4	0.9	6.8	2.8	4.3	8.7	3.8	5.7
Other improper driving	17.5	12.5	9.0	16.4	17.9	16.1	15.9	16.8	14.1
No improper driving stated	37.3	40.5	38.4	37.3	45.3	39.7	41.5	49.7	42.2

Note: Based on reports from state traffic authorities. When a driver was under the influence of alcohol or drugs, the accident was considered a result of the driver's physical condition—not a driving error. For this reason, accidents in which the driver was reported to be under the influence are included under "no improper driving stated."

Risk Behaviors in High School Students, 2005

Source: CDC, *Youth Risk Behavior Surveillance—United States, 2005*

		Percent rarely or never wear seatbelts[1] Female	Male	Total	Percent rarely or never wear bicycle helmets[2] Female	Male	Total	Percent who rode with a driver who had been drinking alcohol[3] Female	Male	Total
Race	Non-Hispanic White	7.2	11.5	9.4	77.9	84.4	81.5	30.4	26.2	28.3
	Non-Hispanic Black	9.4	17.7	13.4	90.1	93.5	92.0	24.0	24.3	24.1
	Hispanic	8.7	12.5	10.6	83.4	88.6	86.5	34.7	37.4	36.1
Grade	9	8.7	13.0	10.9	78.6	86.7	83.0	30.1	25.8	27.9
	10	7.7	9.5	8.6	80.4	87.1	84.3	29.5	26.2	27.8
	11	7.1	13.2	10.1	78.4	85.1	82.2	28.1	27.7	28.0
	12	7.5	14.1	10.8	83.3	84.5	84.0	30.7	29.5	30.1
Total	. . . .	7.8	12.5	10.2	79.9	86.1	83.4	29.6	27.2	28.5

(1) When riding in a car or truck driven by someone else. (2) Among the 62.3% of students who rode bicycles during the 12 months preceding the survey. (3) In a car or truck one or more times during the 30 days preceding the survey.

Death Rates[1] for Suicide at Selected Ages, 1960, 1980, 2000, 2004

Source: *Health, United States, 2006*, National Center for Health Statistics, U.S. Dept. of Health and Human Services

Age	2004 Both sexes	Male	Female	2000 Both sexes	Male	Female	1980 Both sexes	Male	Female	1960 Both sexes	Male	Female
15-24	10.3	16.8	3.6	10.2	17.1	3.0	12.3	20.2	4.3	5.2	8.2	2.2
25-44	13.9	21.7	6.0	13.4	21.3	5.4	15.6	24.0	7.7	12.2	17.9	6.6
45-64	15.4	23.7	7.6	13.5	21.3	6.2	15.9	23.7	8.9	22.0	34.4	10.2
65 and older . .	14.3	29.0	3.8	15.2	31.1	4.0	17.6	35.0	6.1	24.5	44.0	8.4
All ages	10.9	18.0	4.5	10.4	17.7	4.0	12.2	19.9	5.7	12.5	20.0	5.6

(1) Per 100,000 population.

The Leading Causes of Death in the U.S., 2004

Source: National Center for Health Statistics, U.S. Dept. of Health and Human Services

	Number	Death rate[1]	% of deaths		Number	Death rate[1]	% of deaths
ALL CAUSES	2,397,615	816.5	100.0	9. Kidney disease	42,480	14.5	1.8
1. Heart disease	652,486	222.2	27.2	10. Blood poisoning	33,373	11.4	1.4
2. Cancer	553,888	188.6	23.1	11. Intentional self-harm	32,439	11.0	1.4
3. Stroke	150,074	51.1	6.3	12. Chronic liver disease and			
4. Chronic lower respiratory				cirrhosis	27,013	9.2	1.1
diseases	121,987	41.5	5.1	13. Hypertension and			
5. Accidents	112,012	38.1	4.7	hypertensive renal disease.	23,076	7.9	1.0
6. Diabetes mellitus	73,138	24.9	3.1	14. Parkinson's disease	17,989	6.1	0.8
7. Alzheimer's disease	65,965	22.5	2.8	15. Assault homicide	17,357	5.9	0.7
8. Influenza and pneumonia . . .	59,664	20.3	2.5	All other causes	414,674	141.2	17.3

(1) Per 100,000 population.

Principal Types of Accidental Deaths in the U.S., 1970-2005
Source: National Safety Council

Year	Total	Motor vehicle	Falls	Poisoning	Drowning	Fires, flames, smoke	Suffocation: Ingestion of food, object	Firearms	Mechanical Suffocation
1970	NA	54,633	16,926	5,299	7,860	6,718	2,753	2,406	NA
1980	105,718	53,172	13,294	4,331	7,257	5,822	3,249	1,955	NA
1985	93,457	45,901	12,001	5,170	5,316	4,938	3,551	1,649	NA
1990	91,983	46,814	12,313	5,803	4,685	4,175	3,303	1,416	NA
1991	89,347	43,536	12,662	6,434	4,818	4,120	3,240	1,441	NA
1992	86,777	40,982	12,646	7,082	3,542	3,958	3,182	1,409	NA
1993	90,437	41,893	13,141	8,537	3,807	3,900	3,160	1,521	NA
1994	91,437	42,524	13,450	8,994	3,942	3,986	3,065	1,356	NA
1995	93,320	43,363	13,986	9,072	4,350	3,761	3,185	1,225	NA
1996	94,948	43,649	14,986	9,510	3,959	3,741	3,206	1,134	NA
1997	95,644	43,458	15,447	10,163	4,051	3,490	3,275	981	NA
1998	97,835	43,501	16,274	10,801	4,406	3,255	3,515	866	NA
1999[1]	97,860	42,401	13,162	12,186	3,529	3,348	3,885	824	1,618
2000	97,900	43,354	13,322	12,757	3,482	3,377	4,313	776	1,335
2001	101,537	43,788	15,019	14,078	3,281	3,309	4,185	802	1,370
2002	106,742	45,380	16,257	18,550	3,447	3,159	4,128	762	1,389
2003[2]	109,277	44,757	17,229	19,457	3,306	3,369	4,272	730	1,309
2004[2]	112,000	45,300	17,500	20,000	3,600	3,600	4,500	750	1,400
2005[3]	113,000	45,800	17,700	20,900	3,600	3,100	4,600	730	1,400
Death rates per 100,000 population									
1970	NA	26.8	8.3	2.6	3.9	3.3	1.4	1.2	NA
1980	47.8	23.4	5.9	1.9	3.2	2.6	1.4	0.9	NA
1985	39.3	19.3	5.0	2.2	2.2	2.1	1.5	0.7	NA
1990	36.9	18.8	4.9	2.3	1.9	1.7	1.3	0.6	NA
1991	35.4	17.3	5.0	2.6	1.8	1.6	1.3	0.6	NA
1992	34.0	16.1	5.0	2.7	1.4	1.6	1.2	0.6	NA
1993	35.1	16.3	5.1	3.4	1.5	1.5	1.2	0.6	NA
1994	35.1	16.3	5.2	3.5	1.5	1.5	1.2	0.5	NA
1995	35.5	16.5	5.3	3.4	1.7	1.4	1.2	0.5	NA
1996	35.8	16.5	5.6	3.5	1.5	1.4	1.2	0.4	NA
1997	35.7	16.2	5.8	3.8	1.5	1.3	1.2	0.4	NA
1998	36.2	16.1	6.0	4.0	1.6	1.2	1.3	0.3	NA
1999[1]	35.9	15.5	4.8	4.5	1.3	1.2	1.4	0.3	0.6
2000	35.6	15.7	4.8	4.6	1.3	1.2	1.6	0.3	0.5
2001	35.6	15.4	5.3	4.9	1.2	1.2	1.5	0.3	0.5
2002	37.1	15.8	5.6	6.4	1.2	1.1	1.4	0.3	0.5
2003[2]	37.6	15.4	5.9	6.7	1.1	1.2	1.5	0.3	0.4
2004[2]	38.1	15.4	6.0	6.8	1.2	1.2	1.5	0.3	0.5
2005[3]	38.1	15.5	6.0	7.1	1.2	1.0	1.6	0.2	0.5

NA = Not available. **Note:** There were 15,170 other accidental deaths in 2005. All figures include on-the-job deaths. (1) Data for 1999 and later not comparable with earlier data because of classification changes. (2) Revised data. (3) Preliminary data.

Worldwide Airline Fatalities, 1986-2005
Source: National Safety Council

Year	Aircraft accidents[1]	Passenger deaths	Death rate[2]	Year	Aircraft accidents[1]	Passenger deaths	Death rate[2]
1986	24	641	0.04	1996	24	1,146	0.05
1987	25	900	0.06	1997	25	921	0.04
1988	29	742	0.04	1998	20	904	0.03
1989	29	879	0.05	1999	21	499	0.02
1990	27	544	0.03	2000	18	757	0.03
1991	29	638	0.03	2001[3]	13	577	0.02
1992	28	1,070	0.06	2002	13	791	0.03
1993	33	864	0.04	2003	7	466	0.02
1994	27	1,170	0.05	2004	9	203	0.01
1995	25	711	0.03	2005[4]	18	713	0.02

(1) Involving 1 or more passenger fatalities and an aircraft with a maximum take-off mass greater than 2,250 kg. (2) Passenger deaths per 100 mil passenger kilometers. (3) Excluding accidents caused by terrorism or sabotage. (4) Preliminary.

Deaths in the U.S. Involving Firearms, by Age and Sex, 2003
Source: National Safety Council

	All ages	Under 5	5-14	15-19	20-24	25-44	45-64	65-74	75 & over
Total firearms deaths	30,136	56	324	2,469	4,377	11,306	7,354	1,912	2,338
Male	26,124	35	256	2,231	3,955	9,694	6,139	1,694	2,120
Female	4,012	21	68	238	422	1,612	1,215	218	218
Unintentional	730	7	49	95	105	238	154	39	43
Male	656	7	46	88	94	215	137	30	39
Female	74	0	3	7	11	23	17	9	4
Suicide	16,907	—	74	736	1,339	5,308	5,596	1,700	2,154
Male	14,827	—	63	659	1,220	4,569	4,769	1,538	2,009
Female	2,080	—	11	77	119	739	827	162	145
Homicide	11,920	48	187	1,587	2,823	5,481	1,504	161	129
Male	10,126	27	134	1,436	2,541	4,660	1,152	115	61
Female	1,794	21	53	151	282	821	352	46	68
Legal Intervention	347	0	2	20	72	198	49	4	2
Male	329	0	1	19	69	191	43	4	2
Female	18	0	1	1	3	7	6	0	0
Undetermined[1]	232	1	12	31	38	81	51	8	10
Male	186	1	12	29	31	59	38	7	9
Female	46	0	0	2	7	22	13	1	1

Note: There were 28,663 firearms deaths in 2000. (1) "Undetermined" means that the intention involved (whether accident, suicide, or homicide) could not be determined.

U.S. Infant Mortality Rates, by Race and Sex, 1960-2005[1]

Source: National Center for Health Statistics, U.S. Dept. of Health and Human Services

Year	ALL RACES			WHITE			BLACK		
	Total	Male	Female	Total	Male	Female	Total	Male	Female
1960	26.0	29.3	22.6	22.9	26.0	19.6	44.3	49.1	39.4
1970	20.0	22.4	17.5	17.8	20.0	15.4	32.6	36.2	29.0
1980	12.6	13.9	11.2	11.0	12.3	9.6	21.4	23.3	19.4
1985	10.6	11.9	9.3	9.3	10.6	8.0	18.2	19.9	16.5
1988	10.0	11.0	8.9	8.5	9.5	7.4	17.6	19.0	16.1
1989	9.8	10.8	8.8	8.1	9.0	7.1	18.6	20.0	17.2
1990	9.2	10.3	8.1	7.6	8.5	6.6	18.0	19.6	16.2
1991	8.9	10.0	7.8	7.3	8.3	6.3	17.6	19.4	15.7
1992	8.5	9.4	7.6	6.9	7.7	6.1	16.8	18.4	15.3
1993	8.4	9.3	7.4	6.8	7.6	6.0	16.5	18.3	14.7
1994	8.0	8.8	7.2	6.6	7.2	5.9	15.8	17.5	14.1
1995	7.6	8.3	6.8	6.3	7.0	5.6	15.1	16.3	13.9
1996	7.3	8.0	6.6	6.1	6.7	5.4	14.7	16.0	13.3
1997	7.2	8.0	6.5	6.0	6.7	5.4	14.2	15.5	12.8
1998	7.2	7.8	6.5	6.0	6.5	5.4	14.3	15.7	12.8
1999	7.1	7.7	6.4	5.8	6.4	5.2	14.6	15.9	13.2
2000	6.9	7.6	6.2	5.7	6.2	5.1	14.1	15.5	12.6
2001	6.8	7.5	6.1	5.7	6.2	5.1	14.0	15.5	12.5
2002	7.0	7.6	6.3	5.8	6.4	5.1	14.4	15.4	13.3
2003	6.9	7.6	6.1	5.7	6.3	5.0	14.0	15.5	12.4
2004	6.8	7.5	6.1	5.7	6.2	5.1	13.8	15.2	12.3
2005[2]	6.9	NA	NA	5.8	NA	NA	13.7	NA	NA

NA = Not available. (1) Rates per 1,000 live births in specified group. (2) Preliminary.

Years of Life Expected at Birth in U.S., 1900-2004

Source: National Center for Health Statistics, U.S. Dept. of Health and Human Services

Year[1]	ALL RACES			WHITE			BLACK		
	Total	Male	Female	Total	Male	Female	Total	Male	Female
1900	47.3	46.3	48.3	47.6	46.6	48.7	NA	NA	NA
1910	50.0	48.4	51.8	50.3	48.6	52.0	NA	NA	NA
1920	54.1	53.6	54.6	54.9	54.4	55.6	NA	NA	NA
1930	59.7	58.1	61.6	61.4	59.7	63.5	NA	NA	NA
1940	62.9	60.8	65.2	64.2	62.1	66.6	NA	NA	NA
1950	68.2	65.6	71.1	69.1	66.5	72.2	NA	NA	NA
1960	69.7	66.6	73.1	70.6	67.4	74.1	NA	NA	NA
1970	70.8	67.1	74.7	71.7	68.0	75.6	64.1	60.0	68.3
1975	72.6	68.8	76.6	73.4	69.5	77.3	68.8	62.4	71.3
1980	73.7	70.0	77.5	74.4	70.7	78.1	68.1	63.8	72.5
1985	74.7	71.2	78.2	75.3	71.9	78.7	69.3	65.0	73.4
1990	75.4	71.8	78.8	76.1	72.7	79.4	69.1	64.5	73.6
1991	75.5	72.0	78.9	76.3	72.9	79.2	69.3	64.6	73.8
1992	75.5	72.1	78.9	76.4	73.0	79.5	69.6	65.0	73.9
1993	75.5	72.1	78.9	76.3	73.0	79.5	69.2	64.6	73.7
1994	75.7	72.4	79.0	76.5	73.3	79.6	69.5	64.9	73.9
1995	75.8	72.5	78.9	76.5	73.4	79.6	69.6	65.2	73.9
1996	76.1	73.1	79.1	76.8	73.9	79.7	70.2	66.1	74.2
1997	76.5	73.6	79.4	77.1	74.3	79.9	71.1	67.2	74.7
1998	76.7	73.8	79.5	77.3	74.5	80.0	71.3	67.6	74.8
1999	76.7	73.9	79.4	77.3	74.6	79.9	71.4	67.8	74.7
2000	77.0	74.3	79.7	77.6	74.9	80.1	71.9	68.3	75.2
2001	77.2	74.4	79.8	77.7	75.0	80.2	72.2	68.6	75.5
2002	77.3	74.5	79.9	77.7	75.1	80.3	72.3	68.8	75.6
2003[2]	77.4	74.7	80.0	77.9	75.3	80.4	72.6	68.9	75.9
2004	77.8	75.2	80.4	78.3	75.7	80.8	73.1	69.5	76.3

NA = Not available. (1) Data prior to 1940 for death-registration states only. (2) Revised.

U.S. Life Expectancy at Selected Ages, 2004

Source: National Center for Health Statistics, U.S. Dept. of Health and Human Services

Exact age in years	ALL RACES[1]			WHITE			BLACK		
	Both sexes	Male	Female	Both sexes	Male	Female	Both sexes	Male	Female
0	77.8	75.2	80.4	78.3	75.7	80.8	73.1	69.5	76.3
1	77.4	74.7	79.9	77.7	75.2	80.2	73.1	69.6	76.3
5	73.5	70.8	76.0	73.8	71.3	76.3	69.2	65.7	72.4
10	68.5	65.9	71.0	68.9	66.3	71.3	64.3	60.8	67.5
15	63.6	61.0	66.1	63.9	61.4	66.4	59.4	55.9	62.5
20	58.8	56.2	61.2	59.1	56.6	61.5	54.6	51.2	57.7
25	54.0	51.6	56.3	54.4	52.0	56.6	50.0	46.7	52.8
30	49.3	46.9	51.5	49.6	47.3	51.8	45.4	42.3	48.1
35	44.5	42.2	46.6	44.8	42.6	46.9	40.8	37.8	43.4
40	39.9	37.6	41.9	40.1	37.9	42.1	36.3	33.4	38.8
45	35.3	33.1	37.2	35.5	33.4	37.4	31.9	29.1	34.3
50	30.9	28.8	32.7	31.1	29.1	32.9	27.8	25.1	30.1
55	26.6	24.7	28.3	26.7	24.9	28.4	24.0	21.5	26.0
60	22.5	20.8	24.0	22.6	20.9	24.1	20.4	18.2	22.2
65	18.7	17.1	20.0	18.7	17.2	20.0	17.1	15.2	18.6
70	15.1	13.7	16.2	15.1	13.7	16.2	14.1	12.4	15.3
75	11.9	10.7	12.8	11.9	10.7	12.8	11.4	9.9	12.2
80	9.1	8.2	9.8	9.1	8.1	9.7	9.1	8.0	9.6
85	6.8	6.1	7.2	6.7	6.0	7.1	7.1	6.3	7.5
90	5.0	4.4	5.2	4.9	4.3	5.1	5.5	4.9	5.7
95	3.6	3.2	3.7	3.5	3.1	3.6	4.2	3.8	4.3
100	2.6	2.3	2.6	2.5	2.2	2.5	3.2	2.9	3.2

(1) Includes races other than white and black.

NOTED PERSONALITIES

Widely Known Americans of the Present

Political leaders, journalists, other prominent living persons. As of Sept. 2007. Excludes most who fall in categories listed elsewhere in Noted Personalities, such as Writers of the Present and Entertainment Personalities of the Present, or in Sports Personalities. Includes some figures active in American life but not U.S. citizens.

Jack Abramoff, b 2/28/58 (Atlantic City, NJ), former lobbyist; convicted in 2006 of crimes including bribing public officials.

Roger Ailes, b 5/15/40 (Warren, OH), TV exec.

Madeleine K. Albright, b 5/15/37 (Prague, Czech.), former sec. of state.

Edwin "Buzz" Aldrin, b 1/20/30 (Montclair, NJ), former astronaut; 2nd person to walk on the Moon.

Samuel A. Alito Jr., b 4/1/50 (Trenton, NJ), Supreme Court justice.

Paul Allen, b 1/21/53 (Mercer Is., WA), co-founder of Microsoft.

Christiane Amanpour, b 1/12/58 (London, Eng.), TV journalist.

Richard K. Armey, b 7/7/40 (Cando, ND), former U.S. rep., House majority leader.

Neil Armstrong, b 8/5/30 (Wapakoneta, OH), former astronaut, 1st person to walk on the Moon.

John Ashcroft, b 5/9/42 (Chicago, IL), former MO gov., attorney gen.

F. Lee Bailey, b 6/10/33 (Waltham, MA), attorney.

Russell Baker, b 8/14/25 (Loudoun Co., VA), columnist.

Haley Barbour, b 10/22/47 (Yazoo City, MS), MS governor.

Dave Barry, b 7/3/47 (Armonk, NY), humorist.

Marion Barry, b 3/6/36 (Itta Bena, MS), former Wash., DC, mayor; DC city council member.

William Bennett, b 7/31/43 (Brooklyn, NY), author, former education secretary.

Chris Berman, b 5/10/55 (Greenwich, CT), sportscaster.

Ben Bernanke, b 12/13/53 (Augusta, GA), Federal Reserve Chairman, appointed in 2006.

Carl Bernstein, b 2/14/44 (Washington, DC), journalist; with Woodward cracked Watergate scandal.

Jeff Bezos, b 1/12/64 (Albuquerque, NM), founder and CEO of Amazon.com.

Joseph R. Biden Jr., b 11/20/42 (Scranton, PA), senator (DE), 2008 pres. contender.

James H. Billington b 6/1/29 (Bryn Mawr, PA), librarian of Congress.

Kathleen Babineaux Blanco, b 12/15/42 (Coteau, LA), LA governor.

Wolf Blitzer, b 3/22/48 (Buffalo, NY), TV journalist.

Harold Bloom, b 7/11/30 (New York City), literary critic.

Michael R. Bloomberg, b 2/14/42 (Medford, MA), NYC mayor; financial information/media entrepreneur.

Roy Blunt, b 1/10/50 (Niangua, MO), House minority whip (MO).

Samuel W. Bodman, b 11/26/38 (Chicago, IL), sec. of energy.

John Boehner, b. 11/17/49 (Cincinnati, OH), House minority leader

Joshua Bolten, b. 8/16/54 (Washington, D.C.), White House chief of staff

John Bolton, b 11/20/48 (Baltimore), former U.S. amb. to UN.

Julian Bond, b 1/14/40 (Nashville), civil rights leader; NAACP chairman

Barbara Boxer, b 11/11/40 (Brooklyn, NY), senator (CA).

Bill Bradley, b 7/28/43 (Crystal City, MO), former senator (NJ), basketball player, presid. candidate.

James Brady, b 8/29/40 (Centralia, IL), former presid. press sec.; gun control advocate.

L. Paul Bremer III, b 9/30/41 (Hartford, CT), diplomat, former top U.S. civilian administrator in Iraq.

Jimmy Breslin, b 10/17/30 (Queens, NY), columnist, author.

Stephen Breyer, b 8/15/38 (San Francisco), Sup. Ct. justice.

Sergey Brin, b 3/26/73 (Moscow, Russia), co-founder of Google.

David Broder, b 9/11/29 (Chicago Heights, IL), journalist.

Tom Brokaw, b 2/6/40 (Webster, SD), TV journalist, retired NBC anchor.

David Brooks, b 8/11/61 (NYC), columnist, political commentator.

Joyce Brothers, b 10/20/28 (NYC), psychologist.

Aaron Brown, b 11/10/48 (Hopkins, MN), CNN anchor.

Jerry (Edmund G.) Brown Jr., b 4/7/38 (San Francisco), Oakland mayor; former CA gov., pres. candidate.

Michael Brown, b 11/11/54 (Guymon, OK), former FEMA head, resigned under fire after Hurricane Katrina.

Sam Brownback, b. 9/12/56 (Parker, KS), senator (KS), 2008 pres. contender

Pat Buchanan, b 11/2/38 (Washington, DC), journalist, former presid. candidate.

William F. Buckley Jr., b 11/24/25 (NYC), columnist, author.

Warren Buffett, b 8/30/30 (Omaha), investor, leading philanthropist.

Barbara Bush, b 6/8/25 (Rye, NY), former first lady.

Barbara Bush, b 11/25/81 (Dallas, TX), daughter of Pres. George W. Bush.

George H. W. Bush, b 6/12/24 (Milton, MA), former president.

George W. Bush, b 7/6/46 (New Haven, CT), U.S. president.

Jeb Bush, b 2/11/53 (Midland, TX), FL governor.

Jenna Bush, b 11/25/81(Dallas, TX), daughter of Pres. George W. Bush.

Laura Bush, b 11/4/46 (Midland, TX), first lady.

Robert Byrd, b 11/20/17 (N. Wilkesboro, NC), senator (WV), former majority leader, President pro tempore.

Andrew Card, b 5/10/47 (Brockton, MA), former White House chief of staff.

Tucker Carlson, b 5/16/69 (San Francisco), journalist, TV commentator.

Jimmy Carter, b 10/1/24 (Plains, GA), former president; won 2002 Nobel Peace Prize.

James Carville Jr., b 10/25/44 (Fort Benning, GA), TV political commentator.

Steve Case, b 8/21/58 (Honolulu, HI), former AOL Time Warner chairman.

Elaine Chao, b 3/26/53 (Taipei, Taiwan), sec. of Labor.

Julie Chen, b. 1/6/70 (New York, NY), co-host of *The Early Show* and *Big Brother*.

Dick Cheney, b 1/30/41 (Lincoln, NE), U.S. vice president.

Lynne Cheney, b 8/14/41 (Casper, WY), political commentator, wife of Dick Cheney.

Michael Chertoff, b 11/28/53 (Elizabeth, NJ), sec. of homeland security.

Noam Chomsky, b 12/7/28 (Philadelphia), linguist; activist.

Connie Chung, b 8/20/46 (Washington, DC), TV journalist.

Wesley Clark, b 12/23/44 (Chicago), retired general, former NATO commander in Europe; 2004 presid. contender.

Bill Clinton, b 8/19/46 (Hope, AR), former U.S. president.

Chelsea Clinton, b 2/27/80 (Little Rock, AR), daughter of Pres. Clinton and Sen. Hillary Rodham Clinton.

Hillary Rodham Clinton, b 10/26/47 (Chicago), senator (NY), former first lady, 2008 pres. contender.

James Clyburn, b. 7/21/40 (Sumter, SC), House majority whip (SC).

Anderson Cooper, b 6/3/67 (NYC), CNN anchor.

Jon Corzine, b. 1/1/47 (Willey's Station, IL), NJ gov.

Bob Costas, b 3/22/52 (Queens, NY), TV sports journalist.

Ann Coulter, b 12/8/61 (New Canaan, CT), political commentator, author.

Katie Couric, b 1/7/57 (Arlington, VA), TV journalist; former NBC morning anchor; anchor of *CBS Evening News.*

Walter Cronkite, b 11/4/16 (St. Joseph, MO), former CBS news anchor.

Mario Cuomo, b 6/15/32 (Queens, NY), former NY gov.

Ann Curry, b. 11/19/56 (Guam), news anchor on *Today* show

Richard M. Daley, b 4/24/42 (Chicago), Chicago mayor.

John Danforth, b 9/5/36 (St. Louis, MO), former senator (MO); former ambassador to the UN.

Thomas Daschle, b 12/9/47 (Aberdeen, SD), former senator (SD) and Senate minority leader.

Howard Dean, b 11/17/48 (NYC), former VT gov., 2004 pres. contender; Democratic National Committee chair.

Oscar de la Renta, b 7/22/36 (Santo Domingo, Dominican Rep.), fashion designer.

Tom DeLay, b 4/8/47 (Laredo, TX), former House Majority leader.

Michael Dell, b 2/23/65 (Houston, TX), founder, chairman, and CEO of Dell computers.

Alan Dershowitz, b 9/1/38 (Brooklyn, NY), attorney.

Barry Diller, b 2/2/42 (San Francisco), TV exec.

Lou Dobbs, b 9/24/45 (Childress, TX), TV journalist.

Christopher Dodd, b 5/27/44 (Willimantic, CT), senator (CT), 2008 pres. contender.

Elizabeth Hanford Dole, b 7/29/36 (Salisbury, NC), senator (CT); former Red Cross pres., cabinet member.

Robert Dole, b 7/22/23 (Russell, KS), former Senate majority leader (NC), presid. nominee.

Sam Donaldson, b 3/11/34 (El Paso, TX), TV journalist.

Elizabeth Drew, b 11/16/35 (Cincinnati), journalist.

Matt Drudge, b 10/27/66 (Tacoma Park, MD), internet journalist.

Michael S. Dukakis, b 11/3/33 (Brookline, MA), former MA gov., presid. nominee.

Dick Durbin, b 11/21/44 (East. St. Louis, IL), Senate majority whip (IL).

Bernard Ebbers, b 8/27/41 (Edmonton, Alberta, Can.), former WorldCom CEO, jailed for fraud.

Roger Ebert, b 6/18/42 (Urbana, IL), film critic.

Marian Wright Edelman, b 6/6/39 (Bennettsville, SC), pres. and founder of the Children's Defense Fund.

John Edwards, b 6/10/53 (Seneca, SC), former senator (NC); 2004 vice-presid. candidate; 2008 pres. contender.

Edward Egan, b 4/2/32 (Oak Park, IL), Rom. Cath. cardinal, archbishop of New York.

Michael Eisner, b 3/7/42 (Mt. Kisco, NY), former Disney Co. CEO.

Lawrence J. Ellison, b 8/17/44 (NYC), Oracle Corp. founder, CEO.

Louis Farrakhan, b 5/11/33 (Roxbury, MA), Nation of Islam leader.

Russell Feingold, b 3/2/53 (Janesville, WI), senator (WI).

Dianne Feinstein, b 6/22/33 (San Francisco), senator (CA).

W. Mark Felt, b 8/17/13 (Twin Falls, ID), former No. 2 at FBI, revealed (2005) as "Deep Throat" Watergate informant.

Geraldine Ferraro, b 8/26/35 (Newburgh, NY), former U.S. rep., vice-presid. nominee.

Bobby Fischer, b 3/9/43 (Chicago, IL), former chess champion.

Larry Flynt, b 11/1/42 (Salyersville, KY), publisher.

Steve (Malcolm) Forbes Jr., b 7/18/47 (Morristown, NJ), publisher, former presid. contender.

Betty Ford, b 4/8/18 (Chicago), former first lady.

Al Franken, b 5/21/51 (NYC), humorist, political writer, radio host.

Tommy R. Franks, b 6/17/45 (Wynnewood, OK), gen., former commander in chief U.S. Central Command.

Thomas Friedman, b 7/20/53 (Minneapolis), columnist, author.

Bill Frist, b 8/19/42 (Nashville, TN), fmr. Senate majority leader (TN); physician.

Bill Gates, b 10/28/55 (Seattle), software pioneer; Microsoft exec.

Henry Louis Gates Jr., b 9/16/50 (Keyser, WV), African American studies scholar.

Robert M. Gates, b 9/25/43 (Wichita, KS), sec. of Defense

David Geffen, b 2/21/43 (Brooklyn, NY), entertainment exec.

Richard Gephardt, b 1/31/41 (St. Louis, MO), former House party leader; 2004 presid. contender.

Louis Gerstner, b 3/1/42 (Mineola, NY), retired IBM exec.

Charles Gibson, b 3/4/43 (Evanston, IL), TV journalist; host of ABC's *World News*.

Newt Gingrich, b 6/17/43 (Harrisburg, PA), former House Speaker.

Ruth Bader Ginsburg, b 3/15/33 (Brooklyn, NY), Sup. Ct. justice.

Rudolph Giuliani, b 5/28/44 (Brooklyn, NY), Republican presidential contender; former NYC mayor.

John Glenn, b 7/18/21 (Cambridge, OH), former senator, astronaut.

Alberto Gonzales, b 8/4/55 (San Antonio, TX), fmr. Attorney general.

Roger Goodell, b 2/19/59 (Jamestown, NY), NFL commissioner.

Ellen Goodman, b 4/11/41 (Newton, MA), columnist.

Doris Kearns Goodwin, b 1/4/43 (Rockville Centre, NY), historian, TV commentator.

Berry Gordy, b 11/28/29 (Detroit), Motown record label founder.

Al Gore Jr., b 3/31/48 (Washington, DC), former senator, U.S. vice president, presid. candidate.

Tipper Gore, b 8/19/48 (Washington, DC), wife of Al Gore.

Porter Goss, b 11/26/38 (Waterbury, CT), former CIA director; former U.S. rep. (FL).

Rev. Billy Graham, b 11/7/18 (Charlotte, NC), evangelist.

Bob Graham, b 4/9/36 (Coral Gables, FL), former U.S. senator, FL gov; 2004 pres. contender.

(William) Franklin Graham III, b 7/14/52 (Asheville, NC), evangelist, son of Billy Graham.

Mike Gravel, b 5/13/30 (Springfield, MA), fmr. Senator (AK), 2008 pres. contender

Andrew Greeley, b 2/5/28 (Oak Park, IL), Rom. Cath. priest, sociologist, writer.

Jeff Greenfield, b 6/10/43 (NYC), TV journalist.

Alan Greenspan, b 3/6/26 (NYC), former Fed chairman.

Michael Griffin, b 11/1/99 (Aberdeen, MD), NASA head.

Andrew Grove, b 9/2/36 (Budapest, Hungary), Intel chairman.

Bryant Gumbel, b 9/29/48 (New Orleans), TV journalist.

Greg Gumbel, b 5/3/46 (New Orleans), sportscaster.

Carlos Gutierrez, b 11/4/52 (Havana, Cuba), sec. of commerce.

Chuck Hagel, b 10/4/46 (North Platte, NE), U.S. senator.

Pete Hamill, b 6/24/35 (Brooklyn, NY), journalist, author.

Lee Hamilton, b 4/20/31 (Daytona Beach, FL), 9-11 commission vice-chair; former U.S. rep. from Indiana.

Paul Harvey, b 9/4/18 (Tulsa, OK), radio journalist.

J. Dennis Hastert, b 1/2/42 (Aurora, IL), fmr. Speaker of the House (IL).

Orrin Hatch, b 3/22/34 (Homestead Park, PA), senator (UT).

Gen. Michael V. Hayden, b. 3/17/45 (Pittsburgh, PA), CIA Director

Hugh Hefner, b 4/9/26 (Chicago), publisher.

Jesse Helms, b 10/18/21 (Monroe, NC), former senator.

Tommy Hilfiger, b 3/24/51 (Elmira, NY), fashion designer.

Anita Hill, b 7/30/56 (Morris, OK), legal scholar, complainant against Clarence Thomas.

Paris Hilton, b. 2/17/81 (New York, NY), heiress, actress.

Christopher Hitchens, b 4/13/49 (Portsmouth, England), journalist, author.

James P. Hoffa, b 5/19/41, (Detroit), Teamsters Union head.

Richard Holbrooke, b 4/24/41 (Scarsdale, NY), former U.S. rep. to UN.

David Horowitz, b 1/10/39 (NYC), consumer advocate, columnist, author.

Steny H. Hoyer, b 6/14/39 (NYC), U.S. House majority leader (MD).

Mike Huckabee, b. 8/24/55 (Hope, AR), fmr. Gov (AR), minister, 2008 pres. contender

Arianna Huffington, b 7/15/50 (Athens, Greece), political commentator.

H. Wayne Huizenga, b 12/29/39 (Evergreen Park, IL), entrepreneur, sports exec.

Brit Hume, b 6/22/43 (Washington DC), TV journalist (FOX).

Duncan Hunter, b. 5/31/48 (Riverside, CA), congressman (CA), 2008 pres. contender

Kay Bailey Hutchison, b 7/22/43 (Galveston, TX), senator (TX).

Lee Iacocca, b 10/15/24 (Allentown, PA), former auto exec.

Carl Icahn, b 1936 (Queens, NY), financier.

Gwen Ifill, b 9/29/55 (Queens, NY), TV journalist, moderator (PBS).

Jeffrey Immelt, b 2/19/56 (Cincinnati, OH), General Electric CEO.

Don Imus, b 7/23/40 (Riverside, CA), fmr. talk-show host.

Patricia Ireland, b 10/19/45 (Oak Park, IL), feminist leader.

Alphonso Jackson, b 1947 (Marshall, TX), sec. of housing and urban development.

Rev. Jesse Jackson, b 10/8/41 (Greenville, SC), civil rights leader, former presid. contender.

Steve Jobs, b 2/24/55 (San Francisco), Apple Computer exec.; Pixar exec.

Mike Johanns, b 6/18/50 (Osage, IA), sec. of agriculture.

Jasper Johns, b 5/15/30 (Augusta, GA), artist.

Vernon E. Jordan Jr., b 8/15/35 (Atlanta), attorney, former presid. adviser, civil rights leader.

Donna Karan, b 10/2/48 (Queens, NY), fashion designer.

Jeffrey Katzenberg, b 12/21/50 (NYC), entertainment exec.

Thomas Kean, b 4/21/35 (NYC), 9/11 commission chair, Drew Univ. pres., former NJ gov.

Garrison Keillor, b 8/7/42 (Anoka, MN), author, broadcaster.

Jack Kemp, b 7/13/35 (Los Angeles), former vice-presid. nominee, HUD sec., pro football quarterback.

Anthony M. Kennedy, b 7/23/36 (Sacramento, CA), Sup. Ct. justice.

Edward M. Kennedy, b 2/22/32 (Brookline, MA), senator (MA).

Robert ("Bob") Kerrey, b 8/27/43 (Lincoln, NE), former senator (NE).

Teresa Heinz Kerry, b 10/5/38 (Mozambique), heiress, philanthropist; wife of John Kerry.

John Kerry, b 12/11/43 (Aurora, CO), senator (MA), 2004 presid. candidate.

Jack Kevorkian, b 5/26/28 (Pontiac, MI), physican, assisted-suicide activist.

Larry King, b 11/19/33 (Brooklyn, NY), TV talk show host.

Michael Kinsley, b 3/9/51 (Detroit), editor, pol. commenator.

Henry Kissinger, b 5/27/23 (Fuerth, Germany), former sec. of state, nat. security adviser; won 1973 Nobel Peace Prize.

Calvin Klein, b 11/19/42 (Bronx, NY), fashion designer.

Philip H. Knight, b 2/24/38 (Portland, OR), founder and chairman of the board of Nike.

Edward I. Koch, b 12/12/24 (NYC), former NYC mayor.

Ted Koppel, b 2/8/40 (Lancashire, England), former ABC network TV journalist; former anchor of *Nightline*.

Larry Kramer, b 6/25/35 (Bridgeport, CT), AIDS activist, writer.

William Kristol, b 12/23/52 (NYC), editor, columnist.
Steve Kroft, b 8/22/45 (Kokomo, IN), TV journalist.
Dennis Kucinich, b 10/8/46 (Cleveland, OH), U.S. repr., 2004 pres. contender; 2008 pres. contender.
Brian Lamb, b 10/9/41 (Lafayette, IN), cable TV exec., journalist.
Matt Lauer, b 12/30/57 (NYC), TV journalist; NBC morning anchor.
Ralph Lauren, b 10/14/39 (Bronx, NY), fashion designer.
Bernard F. Law, b 11/4/31 (Torreon, Mexico), cardinal, former Rom. Cath. archbishop of Boston, figure in church scandal.
Patrick Leahy, b 3/31/40 (Montpelier, VT), senator (VT).
Norman Lear, b 7/27/22 (New Haven, CT), TV producer, political activist.
Michael O. Leavitt, b 2/11/51 (Cedar City, UT), sec. of health and human services.
Jim Lehrer, b 5/19/34 (Wichita, KS), TV journalist, author.
Carl Levin, b 6/28/34 (Detroit), senator (MI).
Monica Lewinsky, b 7/23/73 (San Francisco), former White House intern, key figure in Clinton White House scandal.
Joseph Lieberman, b 2/24/42 (Stamford, CT), senator (CT); former vice presid. candidate; 2004 presid. contender.
Rush Limbaugh, b 1/12/51 (Cape Girardeau, MO), radio talk-show host.
Trent Lott, b 10/9/41 (Grenada, MS), senator (MS), Senate minority whip.
Shannon Lucid, b 1/14/43 (Shanghai, China), NASA scientist, astronaut.
Richard Lugar, b 4/4/32 (Indianapolis), senator (IN).
Roger Mahony, b 2/27/36 (Hollywood, CA), Rom. Cath. cardinal, archbishop of Los Angeles.
Mary Matalin, b 8/19/53 (Chicago), political commentator.
Chris Matthews, b 12/18/45 (Philadelphia), TV journalist.
John McCain, b 8/29/36 (Panama Canal Zone), senator (AZ); 2008 pres. contender.
Scott McClellan, b 2/14/68 (Austin, TX), former White House press sec.
Mitch McConnell, b 2/20/42 (Tuscumbia, AL), senator (KY), Senate minority leader.
David McCullough, b 7/7/33 (Pittsburgh, PA), historian, biographer.
George McGovern, b 7/19/22 (Avon, SD), former senator (SD), presid. nominee.
Dr. Phil McGraw, b 9/1/50 (Vinita, OK), talk-show host, motivational speaker, author.
James McGreevey, b 8/6/57 (Jersey City, NY), former NJ governor; resigned amid allegations of sexual harassment and admitted he was gay.
John McLaughlin, b 3/29/27 (Providence, RI), TV journalist.
Robert S. McNamara, b 6/9/16 (San Francisco), former defense sec., World Bank head.
Russell Means, b 11/10/39 (Pine Ridge Indian Reserv., SD), Native American activist.
Kate Michelman, b 8/4/42 (NJ), abortion-rights activist.
Ken Mehlman, b. 1967 (Baltimore, MD), fmr. Republican National Committee chair.
Kate Millett, b 9/14/34 (St. Paul, MN), author, feminist.
Norman Mineta, b 11/12/31 (San Jose, CA), former transportation sec.
George Mitchell, b 8/20/33, (Waterville, ME), former Senate majority leader (ME); diplomat, Disney Co. chairman.
Walter Mondale, b 1/5/28 (Ceylon, MN), former vice pres., senator (MN), presid. nominee.
Michael Moore, b 4/23/54 (Davison, MI), activist, documentary filmmaker; author.
Bill Moyers, b 6/5/34 (Hugo, OK), TV journalist, author.
Robert S. Mueller III, b 8/7/44 (NYC), FBI director.
Michael Mullen, b 10/4/46 (Los Angeles, CA), chairman of Joint Chiefs of Staff (as of Oct. 1, 2007).
Rupert Murdoch, b 3/11/31 (Melbourne, Aust.), media exec.
John Murtha, b 6/17/32 (New Martinsville, WV), Congressman (PA); Vietnam War hero; outspoken critic of Iraq War.
Richard B. Myers, b 3/1/42 (Kansas City, MO), former chairman of Joint Chiefs of Staff.
Ralph Nader, b 2/27/34 (Winsted, CT), consumer advocate, 2000, 2004 independent presid. cand.
(Clarence) Ray Nagin, b 6/11/56 (New Orleans, LA), New Orleans mayor.
John Negroponte, b 7/21/39 (London, Eng.), director of National Intelligence; former U.S. rep. to UN.
Craig Newmark, b 12/6/52 (Morristown, NY), founder of Craigslist.com.
Peggy Noonan, b 9/7/50 (Brooklyn, NY), columnist, speechwriter.
Oliver North, b 10/7/43 (San Antonio, TX), talk-show host, former Nat. Sec. Council aide, fig. in Iran-contra scandal.
Eleanor Holmes Norton, b 6/13/37 (Washington, DC), U.S. House delegate for Washington, DC.
Robert Novak, b 2/26/31 (Joliet, IL), journalist.
Sam Nunn, b 9/8/38 (Perry, GA), former senator (GA).
Barack Obama, b 8/4/61 (Hawaii), senator (IL); 2004 Dem. convention keynote speaker; 2008 pres. contender.

Soledad O'Brien, b 9/19/66 (Smithtown, NY), anchor and special correspondent for CNN: Special Investigations Unit.
Sandra Day O'Connor, b 3/26/30 (El Paso, TX), former Sup. Ct. justice.
Joel Osteen, b 3/5/63 (Houston, TX), televangelist, author.
Paul O'Neill, b 12/4/35 (St. Louis, MO), former treasury sec.
Bill O'Reilly, b 9/10/49 (NYC), TV commentator, host.
Michael Ovitz, b 12/14/46 (Encino, CA), entertainment exec.
Clarence Page, b 6/2/47 (Dayton, OH), journalist, TV commentator.
Lawrence Page, b 9/26/73 (East Lansing, MI), co-founder of Google.
Camille Paglia, b 4/2/47 (Endicott, NY), scholar, author.
Leon F. Panetta, b 6/28/38 (Monterey, CA), former White House chief of staff, U.S. rep.
Richard Parsons, b 4/4/48 (NYC), Time Warner CEO.
George Pataki, b 6/24/45 (Peekskill, NY), fmr. NY gov.
Jane Pauley, b 10/31/50 (Indianapolis), TV journalist.
Nancy Pelosi, b 3/26/40 (Baltimore, MD), U.S. rep. (CA); Speaker of the House.
Dana Perino, b 5/9/72 (Evanston, WY), White House press sec.
Ross Perot, b 6/27/30 (Texarkana, TX), entrepreneur, former presid. nominee.
David Petraeus, b. 11/7/52 (Cornwall on Hudson, NY), Cmdr. Mutli-National Force-Iraq
Colin Powell, b 4/5/37 (NYC), former sec. of state, nat. security adviser, Joint Chiefs of Staff chairman.
Dan Quayle, b 2/4/47 (Indianapolis), former U.S. vice pres., senator (IN), presid. contender.
Anna Quindlen, b 7/8/53 (Philadelphia), author, columnist.
Dan Rather, b 10/31/31 (Wharton, TX), TV journalist, retired CBS anchor.
Nancy Reagan, b 7/6/21 (NYC), former first lady.
Sumner Redstone, b 5/27/23 (Boston), Viacom/CBS chairman.
Ralph Reed, Jr., b 6/24/61 (Portsmouth, VA), political adviser.
Robert B. Reich, b 6/24/46 (Scranton, PA), economist, author, former labor sec.
Harry Reid, b 12/2/39 (Searchlight, NV), Senate majority leader (NV).
Janet Reno, b 7/21/38 (Miami, FL), former attorney gen.
Condoleezza Rice, b 11/14/54 (Birmingham, AL), sec. of state, former nat. security adviser.
Bill Richardson, b 11/15/47 (Pasadena, CA), NM gov.; former energy sec., UN ambassador, U.S. rep; 2008 presid. contender.
Sally K. Ride, b 5/26/51 (Encino, CA), former astronaut, 1st U.S. woman in space.
Tom (Thomas Joseph) Ridge, b 8/26/45 (Munhall, PA) former sec. of homeland security; former PA gov.
Geraldo Rivera, b 7/4/43 (NYC), TV journalist.
Cokie Roberts, b 12/27/43 (New Orleans), TV journalist.
John G. Roberts, b 1/27/55 (Buffalo, NY), Sup. Ct. chief justice.
Rev. Oral Roberts, b 1/24/18 (nr. Ada, OK), TV evangelist, educator.
Robin Roberts, b. 11/23/60 (Tuskegee, AL), co-anchor Good Morning America
Rev. Pat Robertson, b 3/22/30 (Lexington, VA), religious broadcasting exec, former presid. contender.
V. Gene Robinson, b 5/29/47 (Lexington, KY), first openly gay Episcopal bishop.
David Rockefeller, b 6/12/15 (NYC), banker.
John D. "Jay" Rockefeller 4th, b 6/18/37 (NYC), senator (WV), former WV Gov.
Al Roker, b 8/20/54 (Queens, NY), TV weather person.
Mitt Romney, b 3/12/47 (Detroit), fmr. MA gov, former Olympics organizer; 2008 pres. contender.
Andy Rooney, b 1/14/19 (Albany, NY), TV commentator.
Charlie Rose, b 1/5/42 (Henderson, NC), TV journalist.
Karl Rove, b 12/25/50 (Denver, CO) fmr. White House senior domestic policy advisor.
Donald Rumsfeld, b 7/9/32 (Chicago), fmr. Sec of Defense.
Tim Russert, b 5/7/50 (Buffalo, NY), TV journalist, moderator Meet the Press (NBC).
Morley Safer, b 11/8/31 (Toronto, Can.), TV journalist.
Diane Sawyer, b 12/22/45 (Glasgow, KY), TV journalist; ABC morning anchor.
Antonin Scalia, b 3/11/36 (Trenton, NJ), Sup. Ct. justice.
Bob Schieffer, b 2/25/37 (Austin, TX), CBS TV news anchor.
Phyllis Schlafly, b 8/15/24 (St. Louis, MO), political activist.
Caroline Kennedy Schlossberg, b 11/27/57 (NYC), author, daughter of Pres. Kennedy.
Patricia Schroeder, b 7/30/40 (Portland, OR), former U.S. rep (CO).
Rev. Robert Schuller, b 9/16/26 (Alton, IA), TV evangelist.
Charles Schumer, b 11/23/50 (Brooklyn, NY), senator (NY).
Arnold Schwarzenegger, b 7/30/47 (Thal, Styria, Austria), CA governor; former actor.
H. Norman Schwarzkopf, b 8/22/34 (Trenton, NJ), former military leader.
Willard Scott, b 3/7/34 (Alexandria, VA), fmr. TV weather person.
Allan H. ("Bud") Selig, b 7/30/34 (Milwaukee), MLB comm.
Richard Serra, b 11/2/39 (San Francisco), sculptor.

Rev. Al Sharpton, b 10/3/54 (Brooklyn, NYC), activist, civil rights leader; 2004 presid. contender.

Cindy Sheehan, b 7/10/57 (Bellflower, CA), anti-Iraq-War activist.

Maria Shriver, b 11/6/55 (Chicago), TV journalist; CA first lady.

George P. Shultz, b 12/13/20 (NYC), former sec. of state; other cabinet posts.

Russell Simmons, b 10/4/57 (Queens, NY), music producer.

O. J. Simpson, b 7/9/47 (San Francisco), former football star, murder defendant.

Harry Smith, b 8/21/51 (Lansing, IL), TV journalist; CBS morning anchor.

Liz Smith, b 2/2/23 (Ft. Worth, TX), gossip columnist.

John Snow, b 8/2/39 (Toledo, OH), former treasury sec, former CSX CEO.

Tony Snow, b 6/1/55 (Berea, KY), fmr. White House press sec.

George Soros, b 8/12/30 (Budapest, Hungary), financier, philanthropist.

David H. Souter, b 9/17/39 (Melrose, MA), Sup. Ct. justice.

Arlen Specter, b 2/12/30 (Wichita, KS), senator (PA); Judiciary Committee chair.

Margaret Spellings, b 11/30/57 (Michigan), sec of education.

Steven Spielberg, b 12/18/46 (Cincinnati, OH), movie director, producer.

Eliot Spitzer, b. 6/10/59 (New York, NY), NY gov.

Lesley Stahl, b 12/16/41 (Swampscott, MA), TV journalist.

Kenneth Starr, b 7/21/46 (Vernon, TX), former Whitewater indep. counsel.

Shelby Steele, b 1/1/46 (Chicago), scholar, critic.

George Steinbrenner, b 7/4/30 (Rocky River, OH), NY Yankees owner.

Gloria Steinem, b 3/25/34 (Toledo, OH), author, feminist.

Frank Stella, b 5/12/36 (Malden, MA), painter.

George Stephanopoulos, b 2/10/61 (Fall River, MA), TV journalist, former presid. adviser.

David J. Stern, b 9/22/42 (NYC), NBA comm.

Howard Stern, b 1/12/54 (Roosevelt, NY), radio talk show host.

John Paul Stevens, b 4/20/20 (Chicago), Sup. Ct. justice.

Ted Stevens, b 11/18/23 (Indianapolis, IN), senator (AK), Senate pres. pro tempore.

Martha Stewart, b 8/3/41 (Nutley, NJ), homemaking adviser, entrepreneur; TV personality.

Arthur Ochs Sulzberger Jr., b 9/22/51 (Mt. Kisco, NY), newspaper publisher.

Lawrence H. Summers, b 11/30/54 (New Haven, CT), former Harvard Univ. pres.

John J. Sweeney, b 5/5/34 (NYC), AFL-CIO pres.

Paul Tagliabue, b 11/24/40 (Jersey City, NJ), former NFL comm.

Tom Tancredo, b 12/20/45 (North Denver, CO), congressman (CO), 2008 pres. contender.

George Tenet, b 1/5/53 (Queens, NY), former CIA director.

Clarence Thomas, b 6/23/48 (Savannah, GA), Sup. Ct. justice.

Helen Thomas, b 8/4/20 (Winchester, KY), journalist.

Fred Thompson, b 8/19/42 (Sheffield, AL), former senator (TN); actor; 2008 pres. contender.

Tommy G. Thompson, b 11/19/41 (Elroy, WI), former sec. of health and human services, former WI gov.

Margaret Truman (Daniel), b 2/17/24 (Independence, MO), author, daughter of Pres. Truman.

Donald Trump, b 6/14/46 (NYC), real estate exec.; TV personality.

Ted Turner, b 11/19/38 (Cincinnati), TV exec, philanthropist.

Peter Ueberroth, b 9/2/37 (Evanston, IL), sports & travel exec.; former MLB comm.

Abigail Van Buren, b 7/4/18 (Sioux City, IA), retired advice columnist.

Gloria Vanderbilt, 2/20/24 (NYC), fashion designer, heiress.

Jesse Ventura, b 7/15/51 (Minneapolis), former wrestler, former MN governor; radio talk show host.

Meredith Vieira, b. 12/30/53 (Providence, RI), co-host *Today* show

Antonio Villaraigosa, b 1/23/53 (East LA), 1st Hispanic mayor of LA since 1870s.

Paul Volcker, b 9/5/27 (Cape May, NJ), economist, former Fed chairman; chair of inquiry into UN Oil for Food scandal.

Mike Wallace, b 5/9/18 (Brookline, MA), TV journalist.

Barbara Walters, b 9/25/31 (Boston), TV journalist.

James Watson, b 4/6/28 (Chicago), biochemist, DNA pioneer, co-winner 1962 Nobel Prize.

Dr. Andrew Weil, b 6/8/42 (Philadelphia), health adviser.

Harvey Weinstein, b 3/19/52 (NYC), movie exec.

Jack Welch, b 11/19/35 (Peabody, MA), former General Electric CEO.

Jann Wenner, b 1/7/46 (NYC), publisher, founder *Rolling Stone*.

Cornel West, b 6/23/53 (Tulsa, OK), African American scholar, critic.

Ruth Westheimer, b 6/4/28 (Frankfurt am Main, Germany), human sexuality expert.

Christine Todd Whitman, b 9/26/46 (NYC), former EPA head, NJ gov.

Meg Whitman, b 8/4/56 (Cold Spring Harbor, NY), eBay pres. and CEO.

Elie Wiesel, b 9/30/28 (Sighet, Romania), scholar, author, 1986 Nobel Peace Prize winner.

George Will, b 5/4/41 (Champaign, IL), journalist, author.

Brian Williams, b 5/5/59 (Elmira, NY), NBC TV news anchor.

Oprah Winfrey, b 1/29/54 (Kosciusko, MS), TV and media personality, businesswoman, actress.

Paul Wolfowitz, b 12/22/43 (NYC), fmr. World Bank head.

Bob Woodward, b 3/26/43 (Geneva, IL), journalist; with Bernstein cracked Watergate scandal.

Steve Wynn, b 1/27/42 (New Haven, CT), casino developer.

Paula Zahn, b 2/24/56 (Omaha, NE), TV journalist.

Mortimer Zuckerman, b 6/4/37 (Montreal, Quebec, Can.), publisher, columnist.

Widely Known World Personalities of the Present

Living Non-Americans only. Generally excludes current heads of state or government (see Nations chapter) and excludes most others covered elsewhere, such as in Widely Known Americans, Entertainers and Writers lists or Sports Personalities.

Mahmoud Abbas (Abu Mazen), b 3/26/35 (Safed, Palestine [now Israel]), president of the Palestinian National Authority.

Gerry Adams, b 10/6/48 (Belfast, N. Ireland), Sinn Fein leader.

Theo Albrecht, b 3/28/22 (Schonebeck, Ger.), German billionaire, CEO of Aldi.

Giulio Andreotti, b 1/14/19 (Rome, Italy), former Italian premier.

Prince Andrew, b 2/19/60 (London, Eng.), Duke of York (2nd son of Queen Elizabeth II).

Kofi Annan, b 4/8/38 (Kumasi, Ghana), former. UN sec.-gen.; 2001 Nobel laureate.

Princess Anne, b 8/15/50 (London, Eng.), Princess Royal (daughter of Queen Elizabeth II).

Corazon Aquino, b 1/25/33 (Manila, Philip.), former pres. of Philippines.

Oscar Arias Sánchez, b 9/13/41 (Heredia, Costa Rica), former Costa Rican pres., peace negotiator, 1987 Nobel laureate.

Giorgio Armani, b 7/30/34 (Piacenza, Italy), fashion designer.

Ban Ki-Moon, b. 6/13/44 (Umsong, [now] South Korea), UN sec-gen.

Ehud Barak, b 2/12/42 (Mishmar Ha-Sharon Kibbutz, Israel), former Israeli prime min.

Ahmed Ben Bella, b 12/25/18 (Marnia, Algeria), 1st Algerian prime min.; revolutionary leader.

Benedict XVI (Joseph Ratzinger), b 4/16/27 (Marktl am Inn, Germany), pope of Rom. Cath. Church, elected 2005.

Boris Berezovsky, b 1/23/46 (Moscow, USSR), businessman, politician.

Tim Berners-Lee, b 6/8/55 (London, Eng.), World Wide Web inventor.

Benazir Bhutto, b 6/21/53 (Karachi, Pak.), former prime min. of Pakistan.

Osama bin Laden, b 3/10/57 (Riyadh, Saudi Ar.), leader of al-Qaeda terrorist organization.

Tony Blair, b. 5/6/53 (Edinburgh, Scot.). former British Prime minister.

Hans Blix, b 6/28/28 (Uppsala, Sweden), former UN weapons inspector.

Fernando Botero, b 4/19/32 (Medellín, Col.), Colombian artist.

Boutros Boutros-Ghali, b 11/14/22 (Cairo, Egypt), former UN sec.-gen.

Richard Branson, b 7/18/50 (S. London, Eng.), British Virgin Records and Airways founder.

Mark Burnett, b 7/17/60 (Myland, England), reality TV producer.

Kim Campbell, b 3/10/47 (Port Alberni, British Columbia, Can.), former Canadian prime min.

Pierre Cardin, b 7/7/22 (Venice, Italy), fashion designer.

Princess Caroline, b 1/23/57 (Monte Carlo, Monaco), Monaco royal (eldest daughter of Prince Rainier and Princess Grace).

Prince Charles, b 11/14/48 (London, Eng.), Prince of Wales (eldest son of Queen Elizabeth II); heir to British throne.

Jean Chrétien, b 1/11/34 (Shawinigan, Que., Can.), former Canadian prime min.

Christo (Javacheff), b 6/13/35 (Gabrovo, Bulg.), artist.

Joe (Charles Joseph) Clark, b 6/5/39 (High River, Alberta, Can.), former Canadian prime min.

King Constantine II, b 6/2/40 (Psychiko, Greece), former king of Greece.

Dalai Lama (Tenzin Gyatso), b 7/6/35 (Taktser, Amdo, Tibet), Buddhist leader; 1989 Nobel laureate.

Jean Claude Duvalier ("Baby Doc"), b 7/3/51 (Port-au-Prince, Haiti), former Haitian dictator.

Shirin Ebadi, b 6/21/47 (Hamadan, Iran), human rights activist, 2003 Nobel laureate.

Prince Edward, b 3/10/64 (London, Eng.), Earl of Essex (3rd son of Queen Elizabeth II).

Mohammed ElBaradei, b 6/17/42 (Cairo, Egypt), Director general of the International Atomic Energy Agency (IAEA).

Prince Felipe, b 1/30/68 (Madrid, Spain), heir to Spanish throne.

Sarah Ferguson, b 10/15/58 (London, Eng.), Duchess of York; ex-wife of Prince Andrew.

John Galliano, b 11/28/60 (Gibraltar), fashion designer.

Valery Giscard d'Estaing, b 2/2/26 (Koblenz, Ger.), former French pres.

Jane Goodall, b 4/3/34 (London, Eng.), British anthropologist and primatologist.

Mikhail Gorbachev, b 3/2/31 (Privolnoye, USSR), former Soviet pres.; 1990 Nobel laureate.

Jurgen Habermas, b 6/18/29 (Dusseldorf, Ger.), philosopher.

Prince Henry ("Harry") of Wales, b 9/15/84 (London, Eng.), son of Prince Charles; 3rd in line to British throne.

Vaclav Havel, b 10/5/36 (Prague, Czech.), former Czech pres.; playwright.

Stephen Hawking, b 1/8/42 (Oxford, Eng.), physicist; author.

Sir Edmund Hillary, b 7/20/19 (Auckland, New Zeal.), 1st to reach summit of Mt. Everest, with Tenzing Norgay, 1953.

David Hockney, b 7/9/37 (Bradford, Eng.), artist.

Jiang Zemin, b 8/17/26 (Yangzhou, Jiangsu Prov., China), former pres. of China.

Kim Dae Jung, b 12/3/25 (near Mokpo, S. Korea), former S. Korean dissident, opposition leader, pres.; 2000 Nobelist.

Garry Kasparov, b 4/13/63 (Baku, Azerbaijan, USSR), former world chess champion; Russian pro-democracy leader.

Mikhail Khodorkovsky, b 6/26/63 (Moscow, Russia), oil oligarch, jailed for tax evasion (2005).

F.W. (Frederik Willem) de Klerk, b 3/18/36 (Johannesburg, S. Africa), former S. African pres.; 1993 Nobel laureate.

Helmut Kohl, b 4/3/30 (Ludwigshafen, Ger.), former German chancellor.

Vladimir Kramnik, b 7/25/75 (Tuapse, Russia, USSR), world chess champion.

Hans Kung, b 3/19/28 (Sursee, Switz.), Rom. Cath. theologian.

Richard Leakey, b 12/19/44 (Nairobi, Kenya), anthropologist, paleontologist, conservationist.

Claude Lévi-Strauss, b 11/28/08 (Brussels, Belg.), French anthropologist, developed structuralism.

John Major, b 3/29/43 (Wimbledon, Eng.), former British prime min.

Nelson Mandela, b 7/18/18 (Transkei, S. Africa), former pres. of S. Africa; 1993 Nobel laureate.

Imelda Marcos, b 7/2/29 (Manila, Philip.), former first lady of Philippines.

Paul Martin, b 8/28/38 (Windsor, Ont., Can.), former Canadian Prime Min.

Peter Max, b 10/19/37 (Berlin, Ger.), artist, designer.

Angela Merkel, b 7/17/54 (Hamburg, Ger.), Chancellor of Germany; 1st woman to hold the office.

Jean-Marie Messier, b 12/13/56 (Grenoble, Fr.), former CEO of Vivendi Universal.

Empress Michiko, b 10/20/34 (Tokyo, Jap.), empress of Japan.

Rev. Sun Myung Moon, b 1/6/20 (Kwangju Sangsa Ri, N. Korea), Unification Church founder.

Brian Mulroney, b 3/20/39 (Baie-Corneau, Quebec, Can.), former Canadian prime min.

Prince Naruhito, b 2/23/60 (Tokyo, Jap.), crown prince of Japan.

Hassan Nasrallah, b 1960 (Beirut, Lebanon), leader of the Hezbollah in Lebanon.

Benjamin Netanyahu, b 10/21/49 (Tel-Aviv, Israel), former Israeli prime min. 1996-1999.

Queen Noor (Lisa Halaby), b 8/23/51 (Washington, DC), American-born widow of Jordan's King Hussein.

Manuel Noriega, b 2/11/34 (Panama City, Pan.), ousted Panamanian pres., jailed in Miami.

Daniel Ortega Saavedra, b 11/11/45 (La Libertad, Nicar.), former Nicaraguan pres., Sandinista leader.

Camilla Parker-Bowles, Duchess of Cornwall, b 7/17/47 (London, Eng.) wife of Prince Charles.

Jean-Marie le Pen, b 6/20/28 (La Trinite-sur-Mer, Fr.), French right-wing politician

Javier Perez de Cuellar, b 1/19/20 (Lima, Peru), former UN sec. gen.

Prince Philip, b 6/10/21 (Corfu, Greece), Duke of Edinburgh (husband of Queen Elizabeth II).

Gerhard Richter, b 2/9/32 (Dresden, Ger.), artist.

Mary Robinson, b 5/21/44 (Ballina, Co. Mayo, Ireland), former Irish pres., UN High Commissioner for Human Rights.

Moqtada al-Sadr, b 1974 (Iraq), extremist Shiite cleric.

Yves Saint Laurent, b 8/1/36 (Oran, Algeria), fashion designer.

Carlos Salinas de Gortari, b 4/3/48 (Mexico City, Mex.), former Mexican pres.

Ariel Sharon, b 2/26/28 (Kfar Malal, Palestine), former Israeli prime min. 2000-2006.

Eduard Shevardnadze, b 1/25/28 (Mamati, Georgia, USSR), former Georgian pres.

Ayatollah Ali al-Sistani, b 8/4/30(Mashhad, Iran), major Iraqi Shiite religious leader.

Princess Stephanie, b 2/1/65 (Monte Carlo, Monaco), youngest daughter and child of Prince Rainier and Princess Grace.

Suharto, b 6/8/21 (Kemusa Argamulja, Java), former longtime Indonesian ruler.

Aung San Suu Kyi, b 6/19/45 (Rangoon, Myanmar), political activist, 1991 Nobel laureate, under effective house arrest.

Valentina Tereshkova, b 3/6/37 (Maslennikovo, Russia, USSR), 1st woman in space.

Margaret Thatcher, b 10/13/25 (Grantham, Eng.), former British prime min.

John Napier Turner, b 6/7/29 (Richmond, Surrey, Eng.), former Canadian prime min.

Desmond Tutu, b 10/7/31 (Klerksdorp, Transvaal, S. Africa), former S. African archbishop; 1984 Nobel laureate.

Lech Walesa, b 9/29/43 (Popowo, Pol.), Solidarity leader; 1983 Nobel laureate; former president of Poland.

Prince William (of Wales), b 6/21/82 (London, Eng.), son of Prince Charles; 2nd in line to British throne.

Rowan Williams, b 6/14/50 (Ystradgynlais, Wales), Archbishop of Canterbury.

Ayman al-Zawahri, b 6/19/51 (Cairo, Egypt), reputed high-ranking al-Qaeda leader.

Architects and Some of Their Projects

Max Abramovitz, 1908-2004, Avery Fisher Hall, NYC; U.S. Steel Bldg. (now USX Towers), Pittsburgh, PA.

Henry Bacon, 1866-1924, Lincoln Memorial, Washington, DC.

Benjamin Banneker, 1731-1806, African American inventor, astronomer, mathematician; helped design and lay out Washington, D.C.

Pietro Belluschi, 1899-1994, Juilliard School, Lincoln Center, Pan Am, now MetLife, Bldg. (with Walter Gropius), NYC.

Marcel Breuer, 1902-81, Whitney Museum of American Art (with Hamilton Smith), NYC.

Charles Bulfinch, 1763-1844, State House, Boston; Capitol (part), Washington, DC.

Gordon Bunshaft, 1909-90, Lever House, Park Ave, NYC; Hirshhorn Museum, Washington, DC.

Daniel H. Burnham, 1846-1912, Union Station, Washington DC; Flatiron Bldg., NYC.

Irwin Chanin, 1892-1988, theaters, skyscrapers, NYC.

David Childs, b 1941, Washington Mall Master Plan/Constitution Gardens, Washington, DC; WTC Freedom Tower, NYC.

Lucio Costa, 1902-98, master plan for city of Brasilia, with Oscar Niemeyer.

Ralph Adams Cram, 1863-1942, Cath. of St. John the Divine, NYC; U.S. Military Acad. (part), West Point, NY.

Norman Foster, b 1935, Commerzbank Headquarters, Frankfurt-am-Main, Ger.; London Millennium Bridge, London.

James Ingo Freed, 1930-2005, Holocaust Memorial Museum, Washington, DC; Jacob K. Javits Center, NYC.

R. Buckminster Fuller, 1895-1983, U.S. Pavilion (geodesic domes), Expo 67, Montreal.

Frank O. Gehry, b 1929, Guggenheim Museum, Bilbao, Spain; Experience Music Project, Seattle, WA.

Cass Gilbert, 1859-1934, Custom House, Woolworth Bldg., NYC; Supreme Court Bldg., Washington, DC.

Bertram G. Goodhue, 1869-1924, Capitol, Lincoln, NE; St. Thomas's Church, St. Bartholomew's Church, NYC.

Michael Graves, b 1934, Portland Bldg., Portland, OR; Humana Bldg., Louisville, KY.

Walter Gropius, 1883-1969, Pan Am Bldg. (now MetLife Bldg.) (with Pietro Belluschi), NYC.

Lawrence Halprin, b 1916, Ghirardelli Sq., San Francisco; Nicollet Mall, Minneapolis; FDR Memorial, Washington, DC.

Peter Harrison, 1716-75, Touro Synagogue, Redwood Library, Newport, RI.

Wallace K. Harrison, 1895-1981, Metropolitan Opera House, Lincoln Center, NYC.

Thomas Hastings, 1860-1929, NY Public Library (with John Carrère), Frick Mansion, NYC.

James Hoban, 1762-1831, White House, Washington, DC.

Raymond Hood, 1881-1934, Rockefeller Center (part), Daily News, NYC; Tribune, Chicago, IL.

Richard M. Hunt, 1827-95, Metropolitan Museum (part), NYC; National Observatory, Washington, DC.

Helmut Jahn, b 1940, United Airlines Terminal, O'Hare Airport, Chicago.

William Le Baron Jenney, 1832-1907, Home Insurance (demolished 1931), Chicago, IL.

Philip C. Johnson, 1906-2005, AT&T headquarters (now 550 Madison Ave.), NYC; Transco Tower, Houston, TX.

Albert Kahn, 1869-1942, General Motors Bldg., Detroit, MI.

Louis Kahn, 1901-74, Salk Laboratory, La Jolla, CA; Yale Art Gallery, New Haven, CT.

Christopher Grant LaFarge, 1862-1938, Roman Catholic Chapel, West Point, NY.

Benjamin H. Latrobe, 1764-1820, Capitol (part), Washington, DC; State Capitol Bldg., Richmond, VA.

Le Corbusier, (Charles-Edouard Jeanneret), 1887-1965, Salvation Army Hostel and Swiss Dormitory, both Paris; master plan for cities of Algiers and Buenos Aires.

William Lescaze, 1896-1969, Philadelphia Savings Fund Society; Borg-Warner Bldg., Chicago.

Maya Lin, b 1959, Vietnam Veterans Mem., Washington, DC.

Charles Rennie Mackintosh, 1868-1928, Glasgow School of Art; Hill House, Helensburgh.

Bernard R. Maybeck, 1862-1957, Hearst Hall, Univ. of CA, Berkeley; First Church of Christ Scientist, Berkeley, CA.

Charles F. McKim, 1847-1909, Public Library, Boston; Columbia Univ. (part), NYC.

Charles M. McKim, b 1920, KUHT-TV Transmitter Bldg., Lutheran Church of the Redeemer, Houston, TX.

Richard Meier, b 1934, Getty Center Museum, Los Angeles, CA; High Museum of Art, Atlanta, GA.

Ludwig Mies van der Rohe, 1886-1969, Seagram Bldg. (with Philip C. Johnson), NYC; National Gallery, Berlin.

Robert Mills, 1781-1855, Washington Monument, Wash., DC.

Charles Moore, 1925-93, Sea Ranch, near San Francisco; Piazza d'Italia, New Orleans, LA.

Richard J. Neutra, 1892-1970, Mathematics Park, Princeton, NJ; Orange Co. Courthouse, Santa Ana, CA.

Oscar Niemeyer, b 1907, government buildings, Brasilia Palace Hotel, all Brasilia.

Gyo Obata, b 1923, Natl. Air & Space Museum, Smithsonian Inst., Washington, DC; Dallas-Ft. Worth Airport.

Frederick L. Olmsted, 1822-1903, Central Park, NYC; Fairmount Park, Philadelphia, PA.

I(eoh) M(ing) Pei, b 1917, East Wing, Natl. Gallery of Art, Washington, DC; Pyramid, The Louvre, Paris; Rock & Roll Hall of Fame and Museum, Cleveland, OH.

Cesar Pelli, b 1926, World Financial Center, Carnegie Hall Tower, NYC; Petronas Twin Towers, Malaysia.

William Pereira, 1909-85, Cape Canaveral; Transamerica Bldg., San Francisco, CA.

John Russell Pope, 1874-1937, National Gallery, Wash., DC.

John Portman, b 1924, Peachtree Center, Atlanta, GA.

George Browne Post, 1837-1913, NY Stock Exchange; Capitol, Madison, WI.

James Renwick Jr., 1818-95, Grace Church, St. Patrick's Cath., NYC.; Corcoran (Renwick) Gallery, Washington, DC.

Henry H. Richardson, 1838-86, Trinity Church, Boston, MA.

Kevin Roche, b 1922, Oakland Museum, Oakland, CA; Fine Arts Center, University of Massachusetts, Amherst.

James Gamble Rogers, 1867-1947, Columbia-Presbyterian Medical Center, NYC; Northwestern Univ., Evanston, IL.

John Wellborn Root, 1887-1963, Palmolive Bldg., Chicago; Hotel Statler, Washington, DC.

Paul Rudolph, 1918-97, Jewitt Art Center, Wellesley Colllege, MA; Art & Architecture Bldg., Yale Univ., New Haven, CT.

Eero Saarinen, 1910-61, Gateway to the West Arch, St. Louis, MO; Trans World Airlines Flight Center, NYC.

Louis Skidmore, 1897-1962, Atomic Energy Commission town site, Oak Ridge, TN; Terrace Plaza Hotel, Cincinnati, OH.

Clarence S. Stein, 1882-1975, Temple Emanu-El, NYC.

Edward Durell Stone, 1902-78, U.S. Embassy, New Delhi, India; (H. Hartford) Gallery of Modern Art, NYC.

Louis H. Sullivan, 1856-1924, Auditorium Bldg., Chicago, IL.

Kenzo Tange, 1913-2005, Hiroshima Peace Park, 1964 Tokyo Olympics twin stadiums.

Richard Upjohn, 1802-78, Trinity Church, NYC.

Max O. Urbahn, 1912-95, Vehicle Assembly Bldg., Cape Canaveral, FL.

Robert Venturi, b 1925, Gordon Wu Hall, Princeton, NJ; Mielparque Nikko Kirifuri Resort, Japan.

Ralph T. Walker, 1889-1973, NY Telephone Bldg. (now NYNEX); IBM Research Lab, Poughkeepsie, NY.

Roland A. Wank, 1898-1970, Cincinnati Union Terminal, OH; head architect (1933-44), Tennessee Valley Authority.

Stanford White, 1853-1906, Washington Arch in Washington Square Park, first Madison Square Garden, NYC.

Frank Lloyd Wright, 1867-1959, Imperial Hotel, Tokyo; Guggenheim Museum, NYC; Marin County Civic Center, San Rafael; Kaufmann "Fallingwater" house, Bear Run, PA.; Taliesin West, Scottsdale, AZ.

William Wurster, 1895-1973, Ghirardelli Sq., San Francisco.

Minoru Yamasaki, 1912-86, World Trade Center, NYC.

Artists, Photographers, and Sculptors of the Past

Artists are painters unless otherwise indicated.

Berenice Abbott, 1898-1991, (U.S.) photographer. Documentary of New York City, *Changing New York* (1939).

Ansel Easton Adams, 1902-84, (U.S.) photographer. Landscapes of the American Southwest.

Washington Allston, 1779-1843, (U.S.) landscapist. *Belshazzar's Feast.*

Albrecht Altdorfer, 1480-1538, (Ger.) landscapist.

Andrea del Sarto, 1486-1530, (It.) frescoes. *Madonna of the Harpies.*

Fra Angelico, c1400-55, (It.) Renaissance muralist. *Madonna of the Linen Drapers' Guild.*

Diane Arbus, 1923-71, (U.S.) photographer. Disturbing images.

Alexsandr Archipenko, 1887-1964, (U.S.) sculptor. *Boxing Match, Medranos.*

Jean Arp, 1887-1966, (Fr.) sculptor and painter, founder of Dada movement.

Eugène Atget, 1856-1927, (Fr.) photographer. Paris life.

John James Audubon, 1785-1851, (U.S.) *Birds of America.*

Hans Baldung-Grien, 1484-1545, (Ger.) *Todentanz.*

Ernst Barlach, 1870-1938, (Ger.) Expressionist sculptor. *Man Drawing a Sword.*

Frederic-Auguste Bartholdi, 1834-1904, (Fr.) *Liberty Enlightening the World, Lion of Belfort.*

Fra Bartolommeo, 1472-1517, (It.) *Vision of St. Bernard.*

Romare Bearden, 1911-88, (U.S.) collage and other media. *The Visitation.*

Aubrey Beardsley, 1872-98, (Br.) illustrator. *Salome, Lysistrata, Morte d'Arthur, Volpone.*

Max Beckmann, 1884-1950, (Ger.) Expressionist. *The Descent From the Cross.*

Gentile Bellini, 1426-1507, (It.) Renaissance. *Procession in St. Mark's Square.*

Giovanni Bellini, 1428-1516, (It.) *St. Francis in Ecstasy.*

Jacopo Bellini, 1400-70, (It.) *Crucifixion.*

George Wesley Bellows, 1882-1925, (U.S.) sports artist, portraitist, landscapist. *Stag at Sharkey's, Edith Clavell.*

Thomas Hart Benton, 1889-1975, (U.S.) American regionalist. *Threshing Wheat, Arts of the West.*

Gianlorenzo Bernini, 1598-1680, (It.) Baroque sculpture. *The Assumption.*

Ruth Bernhard, 1905-2006, (Ger.-U.S.) photographer, black and white studies of female nudes.

Albert Bierstadt, 1830-1902, (U.S.) landscapist. *The Rocky Mountains, Mount Corcoran.*

George Caleb Bingham, 1811-79, (U.S.) *Fur Traders Descending the Missouri.*

William Blake, 1752-1827, (Br.) engraver. *Book of Job, Songs of Innocence, Songs of Experience.*

Rosa Bonheur, 1822-99, (Fr.) *The Horse Fair.*

Pierre Bonnard, 1867-1947, (Fr.) Intimist. *The Breakfast Room, Girl in a Straw Hat.*

Gutzon Borglum, 1871-1941, (U.S.) sculptor. Mt. Rushmore Memorial.

Hieronymus Bosch, 1450-1516, (Flem.) religious allegories. *The Crowning With Thorns.*

Sandro Botticelli, 1444-1510, (It.) Renaissance. *Birth of Venus, Adoration of the Magi, Guliano de'Medici.*

Margaret Bourke-White, 1906-71, (U.S.) photographer, photojournalist. WW2, USSR, rural South during the Depression.

Mathew Brady, c1823-96, (U.S.) photographer. Official photographer of the Civil War.

Constantin Brancusi, 1876-1957, (Romanian-Fr.) Nonobjective sculptor. *Flying Turtle, The Kiss.*

Georges Braque, 1882-1963, (Fr.) Cubist. *Violin and Palette.*

Pieter Bruegel the Elder, c1525-69, (Flem.) *The Peasant Dance, Hunters in the Snow, Magpie on the Gallows.*

Pieter Bruegel the Younger, 1564-1638, (Flem.) *Village Fair, The Crucifixion.*

Edward Burne-Jones, 1833-98, (Br.) Pre-Raphaelite artist-craftsman. *The Mirror of Venus.*

Alexander Calder, 1898-1976, (U.S.) sculptor. *Lobster Trap and Fish Tail.*

Julia Cameron, 1815-79, (Br.) photographer. Considered one of the most important portraitists of the 19th cent.

Robert Capa (Andrei Friedmann), 1913-54, (Hung.-U.S.) photographer. War photojournalist; invasion of Normandy.

Michelangelo Merisi da Caravaggio, 1573-1610, (It.) Baroque. *The Supper at Emmaus.*

Emily Carr, 1871-1945, (Can.) landscapist. *Blunden Harbour, Big Raven, Rushing Sea of Undergrowth.*

Carlo Carrà, 1881-1966, (It.) Metaphysical school. *Lot's Daughters, The Enchanted Room.*

Henri Cartier-Bresson, 1908-2004, (Fr.) photographer. *Imagenes à la sauvette.*

Mary Cassatt, 1844-1926, (U.S.) Impressionist. *The Cup of Tea, Woman Bathing, The Boating Party.*

Oleg Cassini, 1913-2006, (Fr.-U.S.) fashion designer.

George Catlin, 1796-1872, (U.S.) American Indian life. *Gallery of Indians, Buffalo Dance.*

Benvenuto Cellini, 1500-71, (It.) Mannerist sculptor, goldsmith. *Perseus and Medusa.*

Paul Cézanne, 1839-1906, (Fr.) *Card Players, Mont-Sainte-Victoire With Large Pine Trees.*

Marc Chagall, 1887-1985, (Russ.) Jewish life and folklore. *I and the Village, The Praying Jew.*

Jean Simeon Chardin, 1699-1779, (Fr.) still lifes. *The Kiss, The Grace.*

Giorgio de Chirico, 1888-1978, (It.) painter, founded the metaphysical school. *Enigma of an Autumn Night.*

Frederick Church, 1826-1900, (U.S.) Hudson River school. *Niagara, Andes of Ecuador.*

Giovanni Cimabue, 1240-1302, (It.) Byzantine mosaicist. *Madonna Enthroned With St. Francis.*

Claude Lorrain (Claude Gellée), 1600-82, (Fr.) ideal-landscapist. *The Enchanted Castle.*

Thomas Cole, 1801-48, (U.S.) Hudson River school. *The Ox-Bow, In the Catskills.*

John Constable, 1776-1837, (Br.) landscapist. *Salisbury Cathedral From the Bishop's Grounds.*

John Singleton Copley, 1738-1815, (U.S.) portraitist. *Samuel Adams, Watson and the Shark.*

Lovis Corinth, 1858-1925, (Ger.) Expressionist. *Apocalypse.*

Jean-Baptiste-Camille Corot, 1796-1875, (Fr.) landscapist. *Souvenir de Mortefontaine, Pastorale.*

Correggio, 1494-1534, (It.) Renaissance muralist. *Mystic Marriages of St. Catherine.*

Gustave Courbet, 1819-77, (Fr.) Realist. *The Artist's Studio.*

Lucas Cranach the Elder, 1472-1553, (Ger.) Protestant Reformation portraitist. *Luther.*

Imogen Cunningham, 1883-1976, (U.S.) photographer, portraitist. Plant photography.

Nathaniel Currier, 1813-88, and **James M. Ives**, 1824-95, (both U.S.) lithographers. *A Midnight Race on the Mississippi, American Forest Scene—Maple Sugaring.*

John Steuart Curry, 1897-1946, (U.S.) Americana, murals. *Baptism in Kansas.*

Salvador Dalí, 1904-89, (Sp.) Surrealist. *Persistence of Memory, The Crucifixion.*

Honoré Daumier, 1808-79, (Fr.) caricaturist. *The Third-Class Carriage.*

Jacques-Louis David, 1748-1825, (Fr.) Neoclassicist. *The Oath of the Horatii.*

Arthur Davies, 1862-1928, (U.S.) Romantic landscapist. *Unicorns, Leda and the Dioscuri.*

Aaron Douglas, 1900-79, Harlem Renaissance artist.

Willem de Kooning, 1904-1997, (Dutch-U.S.) abstract expressionist. *Excavation, Woman I, Door to the River.*

Edgar Degas, 1834-1917, (Fr.) *The Ballet Class.*

Eugène Delacroix, 1798-1863, (Fr.) Romantic. *Massacre at Chios, Liberty Leading the People.*

Paul Delaroche, 1797-1856, (Fr.) historical themes. *Children of Edward IV.*

Luca Della Robbia, 1400-82, (It.) Renaissance terracotta artist. *Cantoria* (singing gallery), Florence cathedral.

Donatello, 1386-1466, (It.) Renaissance sculptor. *David, Gattamelata.*

Jean Dubuffet, 1902-85, (Fr.) painter, sculptor, printmaker. *Group of Four Trees.*

Marcel Duchamp, 1887-1968, (Fr.) Dada artist. *Nude Descending a Staircase, No. 2.*

Raoul Dufy, 1877-1953, (Fr.) Fauvist. *Chateau and Horses.*

Asher Brown Durand, 1796-1886, (U.S.) Hudson River school. *Kindred Spirits.*

Albrecht Dürer, 1471-1528, (Ger.) Renaissance painter, engraver, woodcuts. *St. Jerome in His Study, Melencolia I.*

Anthony van Dyck, 1599-1641, (Flem.) Baroque portraitist. *Portrait of Charles I Hunting.*

Thomas Eakins, 1844-1916, (U.S.) Realist. *The Gross Clinic.*

Alfred Eisenstaedt, 1898-1995, (Ger.-U.S.) photographer, photojournalist. Famous photo, V-J Day, Aug. 14, 1945.

Peter Henry Emerson, 1856-1936, (Br.) photographer. Promoted photography as an independent art form.

Jacob Epstein, 1880-1959, (Br.) religious and allegorical sculptor. *Genesis, Ecce Homo.*

Erté, 1892-1990, (Fr.) b. Romain de Tiertoff; painter, fashion and stage designer.

Jan van Eyck, c1390-1441, (Flem.) naturalistic panels. *Adoration of the Lamb.*

Roger Fenton, 1819-68, (Br.) photographer. Crimean War.

Anselm Feuerbach, 1829-80, (Ger.) Romantic Classicist. *Judgment of Paris, Iphigenia.*

John Bernard Flannagan, 1895-1942, (U.S.) animal sculptor. *Triumph of the Egg.*

Jean-Honoré Fragonard, 1732-1806, (Fr.) Rococo. *The Swing.*

Daniel Chester French, 1850-1931, (U.S.) *The Minute Man of Concord;* seated *Lincoln,* Lincoln Memorial, Washington, DC.

Caspar David Friedrich, 1774-1840, (Ger.) Romantic landscapes. *Man and Woman Gazing at the Moon.*

Thomas Gainsborough, 1727-88, (Br.) portraitist. *The Blue Boy, The Watering Place, Orpin the Parish Clerk.*

Alexander Gardner, 1821-82, (U.S.) photographer. Civil War; railroad construction; Great Plains Indians.

Paul Gauguin, 1848-1903, (Fr.) Post-impressionist. *The Tahitians, Spirit of the Dead Watching.*

Lorenzo Ghiberti, 1378-1455, (It.) Renaissance sculptor. Gates of Paradise baptistery doors, Florence.

Alberto Giacometti, 1901-66, (Swiss) attenuated sculptures of solitary figures. *Man Pointing.*

Giorgione, c1477-1510, (It.) Renaissance. *The Tempest.*

Giotto di Bondone, 1267-1337, (It.) Renaissance. *Presentation of Christ in the Temple.*

François Girardon, 1628-1715, (Fr.) Baroque sculptor of classical themes. *Apollo Tended by the Nymphs.*

Vincent van Gogh, 1853-90, (Dutch) *The Starry Night, L'Arlesienne, Bedroom at Arles, Self-Portrait.*

Edward Gorey, 1925-2000, (U.S.) artist, illustrator. *The Doubtful Guest.*

Arshile Gorky, 1905-48, (U.S.) Surrealist. *The Liver Is the Cock's Comb.*

Francisco de Goya y Lucientes, 1746-1828, (Sp.) *The Naked Maja, The Disasters of War* (etchings).

El Greco, 1541-1614, (Sp.) *View of Toledo, Assumption of the Virgin.*

Horatio Greenough, 1805-52, (U.S.) Neo-classical sculptor.

Matthias Grünewald, 1480-1528, (Ger.) mystical religious themes. *The Resurrection.*

Frans Hals, c1580-1666, (Dutch) portraitist. *Laughing Cavalier, Gypsy Girl.*

Austin Hansen, 1910-96, (U.S.) photographer. Harlem, NY, life.

Childe Hassam, 1859-1935, (U.S.) Impressionist. *Southwest Wind, July 14 Rue Daunon.*

Edward Hicks, 1780-1849, (U.S.) folk painter. *The Peaceable Kingdom.*

Lewis Wickes Hine, 1874-1940, (U.S.) photographer. Studies of immigrants, children in industry.

Hans Hofmann, 1880-1966, (U.S.) early abstract Expressionist. *Spring, The Gate.*

William Hogarth, 1697-1764, (Br.) caricaturist. *The Rake's Progress.*

Katsushika Hokusai, 1760-1849, (Jpn.) printmaker. *Crabs.*

Hans Holbein the Elder, 1460-1524, (Ger.) late Gothic. *Presentation of Christ in the Temple.*

Hans Holbein the Younger, 1497-1543, (Ger.) portraitist. *Henry VIII, The French Ambassadors.*

Winslow Homer, 1836-1910, (U.S.) naturalist painter, marine themes. *Marine Coast, High Cliff.*

Edward Hopper, 1882-1967, (U.S.) realistic urban scenes. *Nighthawks, House by the Railroad.*

Horst P. Horst, 1906-99, (Ger.) fashion, celebrity photographer.

Jean-Auguste-Dominique Ingres, 1780-1867, (Fr.) Classicist. *Valpincon Bather.*

George Inness, 1825-94, (U.S.) luminous landscapist. *Delaware Water Gap.*

William Henry Jackson, 1843-1942, (U.S.) photographer. American West, building of Union Pacific Railroad.

Donald Judd, 1928-94, (U.S.) sculptor, major Minimalist.

Frida Kahlo, 1907-54, (Mex.) painter; *Self-Portrait With Monkey.*

Vasily Kandinsky, 1866-1944, (Russ.) Abstractionist. *Capricious Forms, Improvisation 38 (second version).*

Paul Klee, 1879-1940, (Swiss) Abstractionist. *Twittering Machine, Pastoral, Death and Fire.*

Gustav Klimt, 1862-1918, (Austrian) cofounder of Vienna Secession Movement, *The Kiss.*

Oscar Kokoschka, 1886-1980, (Austrian) Expressionist. *View of Prague, Harbor of Marseilles.*

Kathe Kollwitz, 1867-1945, (Ger.) printmaker, social justice themes. *The Peasant War.*

Gaston Lachaise, 1882-1935, (U.S.) figurative sculptor. *Standing Woman.*

John La Farge, 1835-1910, (U.S.) muralist. *Red and White Peonies, The Ascension.*

Sir Edwin (Henry) Landseer, 1802-73, (Br.) painter, sculptor. *Shoeing, Rout of Comus.*

Dorothea Lange, 1895-1965, (U.S.) photographer. Depression photographs, migrant farm workers.

Fernand Léger, 1881-1955, (Fr.) machine art. *The Cyclists.*

Leonardo da Vinci, 1452-1519, (It.) *Mona Lisa, Last Supper, The Annunciation.*

Emanuel Leutze, 1816-68, (U.S.) historical themes. *Washington Crossing the Delaware.*

Roy Lichtenstein, 1923-97, (U.S.) pop artist.

Jacques Lipchitz, 1891-1973, (Fr.) Cubist sculptor. *Harpist.*

Filippino Lippi, 1457-1504, (It.) Renaissance.

Fra Filippo Lippi, 1406-69, (It.) Renaissance. *Coronation of the Virgin, Madonna and Child With Angels.*

Morris Louis, 1912-62, (U.S.) abstract Expressionist. *Signa, Stripes, Alpha-Phi.*

René Magritte, 1898-1967, (Belgian) Surrealist. *The Descent of Man, The Betrayal of Images.*

Aristide Maillol, 1861-1944, (Fr.) sculptor. *L'Harmonie.*

Édouard Manet, 1832-83, (Fr.) forerunner of Impressionism. *Luncheon on the Grass, Olympia.*

Andrea Mantegna, 1431-1506, (It.) Renaissance frescoes. *Triumph of Caesar.*

Franz Marc, 1880-1916, (Ger.) Expressionist. *Blue Horses.*

John Marin, 1870-1953, (U.S.) Expressionist seascapes. *Maine Island.*

Reginald Marsh, 1898-1954, (U.S.) satirical artist. *Tattoo and Haircut.*

Agnes Martin, 1912-2004, (U.S.) abstract artist. *Night Sea.*

Masaccio, 1401-28, (It.) Renaissance. *The Tribute Money.*

Henri Matisse, 1869-1954, (Fr.) Fauvist. *Woman With the Hat.*

Michelangelo Buonarroti, 1475-1564, (It.) *Pietà, David, Moses, The Last Judgment,* Sistine Chapel ceiling.

Jean-Francois Millet, 1814-75, (Fr.) painter of peasant subjects. *The Gleaners, The Man With a Hoe.*

Joan Miró, 1893-1983, (Sp.) Exuberant colors, playful images. Catalan landscape, *Dutch Interior.*

Amedeo Modigliani, 1884-1920, (It.) *Reclining Nude.*

Piet Mondrian, 1872-1944, (Dutch) Abstractionist. *Composition With Red, Yellow and Blue.*

Claude Monet, 1840-1926, (Fr.) Impressionist. *The Bridge at Argenteuil, Haystacks.*

Henry Moore, 1898-1986, (Br.) sculptor of large-scale, abstract works. *Reclining Figure* (several).

Gustave Moreau, 1826-98, (Fr.) Symbolist. *The Apparition, Dance of Salome.*

James Wilson Morrice, 1865-1924, (Can.) landscapist. *The Ferry, Quebec, Venice, Looking Over the Lagoon.*

William Morris, 1834-1896, (Br.) decorative artist, leader of the Arts and Crafts movement.

Grandma Moses, 1860-1961, (U.S.) folk painter. *Out for the Christmas Trees, Thanksgiving Turkey.*

Edvard Munch, 1863-1944, (Nor.) Expressionist. *The Cry.*

Bartolome Murillo, 1618-82, (Sp.) Baroque religious artist. *Vision of St. Anthony, The Two Trinities.*

Elizabeth Murray, 1940-2007, (U.S.) abstract color painter.

Eadweard Muybridge, 1830-1904, (Br.-U.S.) photographer. Studies of motion, *Animal Locomotion.*

Nadar (Gaspar-Félix Tournachon), 1820-1910, (Fr.) photographer, caricaturist, portraitist. Invented photo-essay.

Arnold Newman, 1918-2006, (U.S.) portrait photographer.

Barnett Newman, 1905-70, (U.S.) abstract Expressionist. *Stations of the Cross.*

Isamu Noguchi, 1904-88, (U.S.) abstract sculptor, designer. *Kouros, BirdC(MU),* sculptural gardens.

Georgia O'Keeffe, 1887-1986, (U.S.) Southwest motifs. *Cow's Skull: Red, White, and Blue, The Shelton With Sunspots.*

José Clemente Orozco, 1883-1949, (Mex.) frescoes. *House of Tears, Pre-Columbian Golden Age.*

Timothy H. O'Sullivan, 1840-82, (U.S.) Civil War photographer.

Gordon Parks, 1912-2006, (U.S.) African American photographer and film maker. *Life* photographer 1948-68.

Charles Willson Peale, 1741-1827, (U.S.) Amer. Revolutionary portraitist. *The Staircase Group,* U.S. presidents.

Rembrandt Peale, 1778-1860, (U.S.) portraitist. Thomas Jefferson.

Pietro Perugino, 1446-1523, (It.) Renaissance. *Delivery of the Keys to St. Peter.*

Pablo Picasso, 1881-1973, (Sp.) painter, sculptor. *Guernica; Dove; Head of a Woman; Head of a Bull, Metamorphosis.*

Piero della Francesca, c1415-92, (It.) Renaissance. *Duke of Urbino, Flagellation of Christ.*

Camille Pissarro, 1830-1903, (Fr.) Impressionist. *Boulevard des Italiens, Morning, Sunlight; Bather in the Woods.*

Jackson Pollock, 1912-56, (U.S.) abstract Expressionist. *Autumn Rhythm.*

Nicolas Poussin, 1594-1665, (Fr.) Baroque pictorial classicism. *St. John on Patmos.*

Maurice B. Prendergast, c1860-1924, (U.S.) Post-impressionist water colorist. *Umbrellas in the Rain.*

Pierre-Paul Prud'hon, 1758-1823, (Fr.) Romanticist. *Crime Pursued by Vengeance and Justice.*

Pierre Cecile Puvis de Chavannes, 1824-98, (Fr.) muralist. *The Poor Fisherman.*

Niki de Saint Phalle, 1930-2002, (Fr.) creator of paintings, sculptures, prints and large public installations.

Raphael Sanzio, 1483-1520, (It.) Renaissance. *Disputa, School of Athens, Sistine Madonna.*

Man Ray, 1890-1976, (U.S.) Dada artist. *Observing Time, The Lovers, Marquis de Sade.*

Odilon Redon, 1840-1916, (Fr.) Symbolist painter, lithographer. *In the Dream, Vase of Flowers.*

Rembrandt van Rijn, 1606-69, (Dutch) *The Bridal Couple, The Night Watch.*

Frederic Remington, 1861-1909, (U.S.) painter, sculptor. Portrayer of the American West, *Bronco Buster.*

Pierre-Auguste Renoir, 1841-1919, (Fr.) Impressionist. *The Luncheon of the Boating Party, Dance in the Country.*

Joshua Reynolds, 1723-92, (Br.) portraitist. *Mrs. Siddons as the Tragic Muse.*

Herb Ritts, 1952-2002, (U.S.) photographer. Nudes, celebrities.

Diego Rivera, 1886-1957, (Mex.) frescoes. *The Fecund Earth.*

Larry Rivers, 1923-2002, (U.S.) painter, sculptor, often realistic; Dutch Masters series.

Henry Peach Robinson, 1830-1901 (Br.) photographer. A leader of "high art" photography.

Norman Rockwell, 1894-1978, (U.S.) painter, illustrator. *Saturday Evening Post* covers.

Auguste Rodin, 1840-1917, (Fr.) sculptor. *The Thinker.*

Mark Rothko, 1903-70, (U.S.) abstract Expressionist. *Light, Earth and Blue.*

Georges Rouault, 1871-1958, (Fr.) Expressionist. *Three Judges.*

Henri Rousseau, 1844-1910, (Fr.) primitive exotic themes. *The Snake Charmer.*

Theodore Rousseau, 1812-67, (Swiss-Fr.) landscapist. *Under the Birches, Evening.*

Peter Paul Rubens, 1577-1640, (Flem.) Baroque. *Mystic Marriage of St. Catherine.*

Jacob van Ruisdael, c1628-82, (Dutch) landscapist. *Jewish Cemetery.*

Charles M. Russell, 1866-1926, (U.S.) Western life.

Salomon van Ruysdael, c1600-70, (Dutch) landscapist. *River With Ferry-Boat.*

Albert Pinkham Ryder, 1847-1917, (U.S.) seascapes and allegories. *Toilers of the Sea.*

Augustus Saint-Gaudens, 1848-1907, (U.S.) memorial statues. *Farragut, Mrs. Henry Adams (Grief).*

Andrea Sansovino, 1460-1529, (It.) Renaissance sculptor. *Baptism of Christ.*

Jacopo Sansovino, 1486-1570, (It.) Renaissance sculptor. *St. John the Baptist.*

John Singer Sargent, 1856-1925, (U.S.) Edwardian society portraitist. The Wyndham Sisters, Madam X.

George Segal, 1924-2000, (U.S.) sculptor of life-sized figures realistically depicting daily life.

Georges Seurat, 1859-91, (Fr.) Pointillist. *Sunday Afternoon on the Island of La Grande Jatte.*

Gino Severini, 1883-1966, (It.) Futurist and Cubist. *Dynamic Hieroglyph of the Bal Tabarin.*

Ben Shahn, 1898-1969, (U.S.) social and political themes. Sacco and Vanzetti series, *Seurat's Lunch, Handball.*

Charles Sheeler, 1883-1965, (U.S.) abstractionist.

David Alfaro Siqueiros, 1896-1974, (Mex.) political muralist. *March of Humanity.*

David Smith, 1906-65, (U.S.) welded metal sculpture. *Hudson River Landscape, Zig, Cubi* series.

Edward Steichen, 1879-1973, (U.S.) photographer. Credited with transforming photography into an art form.

Alfred Stieglitz, 1864-1946, (U.S.) photographer, editor; helped create acceptance of photography as art.

Paul Strand, 1890-1976, (U.S.) photographer. People, nature, landscapes.

Gilbert Stuart, 1755-1828, (U.S.) portraitist. George Washington, Thomas Jefferson, James Madison.

Thomas Sully, 1783-1872, (U.S.) portraitist. *Col. Thomas Handasyd Perkins, The Passage of the Delaware.*

William Henry Fox Talbot, 1800-77, (Br.) photographer. *Pencil of Nature,* early photographically illustrated book.

George Tames, 1919-94, (U.S.) photographer. Chronicled presidents, political leaders.

Yves Tanguy, 1900-55, (Fr.) Surrealist. *Rose of the Four Winds, Mama, Papa Is Wounded!*

Giovanni Battista Tiepolo, 1696-1770, (It.) Rococo frescoes. *The Crucifixion.*

Jacopo Tintoretto, 1518-94, (It.) Mannerist. *The Last Supper.*

Titian, c1485-1576, (It.) Renaissance. *Venus and the Lute Player, The Bacchanal.*

Jose Rey Toledo, 1916-94, (U.S.) Native American artist. Captured the essence of tribal dances on canvas.

Henri de Toulouse-Lautrec, 1864-1901, (Fr.) *At the Moulin Rouge.*

John Trumbull, 1756-1843, (U.S.) historical themes. *The Declaration of Independence.*

J(oseph) M(allord) W(illiam) Turner, 1775-1851, (Br.) Romantic landscapist. *Snow Storm.*

Paolo Uccello, 1397-1475, (It.) Gothic-Renaissance. *The Rout of San Romano.*

Maurice Utrillo, 1883-1955, (Fr.) Impressionist. *Sacre-Coeur de Montmartre.*

John Vanderlyn, 1775-1852, (U.S.) Neo-classicist. *Ariadne Asleep on the Island of Naxos.*

Diego Velázquez, 1599-1660, (Sp.) Baroque. *Las Meninas, Portrait of Juan de Pareja.*

Jan Vermeer, 1632-75, (Dutch) interior genre subjects. *Young Woman With a Water Jug.*

Paolo Veronese, 1528-88, (It.) devotional themes, vastly peopled canvases. *The Temptation of St. Anthony.*

Andrea del Verrocchio, 1435-88, (It.) Floren. sculptor. *Colleoni.*

Maurice de Vlaminck, 1876-1958, (Fr.) Fauvist landscapist. *Red Trees.*

Andy Warhol, 1928-87, (U.S.) Pop Art. *Campbell's Soup Cans, Marilyn Diptych.*

Antoine Watteau, 1684-1721, (Fr.) Rococo painter of "scenes of gallantry." *The Embarkation for Cythera.*

George Frederic Watts, 1817-1904, (Br.) painter and sculptor of grandiose allegorical themes. *Hope.*

Benjamin West, 1738-1820, (U.S.) realistic historical themes. *Death of General Wolfe.*

Edward Weston, 1886-1958, (U.S.) photographer. Landscapes of American West.

James Abbott McNeill Whistler, 1834-1903, (U.S.) *Arrangement in Grey and Black, No. 1: The Artist's Mother.*

Archibald M. Willard, 1836-1918, (U.S.) *The Spirit of '76.*

Grant Wood, 1891-1942, (U.S.) Midwestern regionalist. *American Gothic, Daughters of Revolution.*

Ossip Zadkine, 1890-1967, (Russ.) School of Paris sculptor. *The Destroyed City, Musicians, Christ.*

Business Leaders and Philanthropists of the Past

Giovanni Agnelli, 1921-2003, (It.) industrialist, principal shareholder of Fiat.

Walter Annenberg, 1908-2002, (U.S.) publisher, founder *TV Guide*, philanthropist.

Elizabeth Arden (F. N. Graham), 1884-1966, (U.S.) Canadian-born founder of cosmetics empire.

Philip D. Armour, 1832-1901, (U.S.) industrialist; streamlined meatpacking.

Brooke Astor, 1902-2007, philanthropist; president of Vincent Astor Foundation.

John Jacob Astor, 1763-1848, (U.S.) German-born fur trader, banker, real estate magnate; at death, richest in U.S.

Francis W. Ayer, 1848-1923, (U.S.) ad industry pioneer.

August Belmont, 1816-90, (U.S.) German-born financier.

James B. (Diamond Jim) Brady, 1856-1917, (U.S.) financier, philanthropist, legendary bon vivant.

Adolphus Busch, 1839-1913, (U.S.) German-born businessman; established brewery empire.

Asa Candler, 1851-1929, (U.S.) founded Coca-Cola Co.

Andrew Carnegie, 1835-1919, (U.S.) Scottish-born industrialist; philanthropist; founded Carnegie Steel Co.

Tom Carvel, 1908-89, (Gr.-U.S.) founded ice cream chain.

William Colgate, 1783-1857, (Br.-U.S.) Br.-born businessman, philanthropist; founded soap-making empire.

Jay Cooke, 1821-1905, (U.S.) financier; sold $1 billion in Union bonds during Civil War.

Peter Cooper, 1791-1883, (U.S.) industrialist, inventor, philanthropist; founded Cooper Union (1859).

Ezra Cornell, 1807-74, (U.S.) businessman, philanthropist; headed Western Union, established university.

Erastus Corning, 1794-1872, (U.S.) financier; headed N.Y. Central.

Charles Crocker, 1822-88, (U.S.) railroad builder, financier.

Samuel Cunard, 1787-1865, (Can.) pioneered trans-Atlantic steam navigation.

Marcus Daly, 1841-1900, (U.S.) Irish-born copper magnate.

W. Edwards Deming, 1900-93, (U.S.) quality-control expert who revolutionized Japanese manufacturing.

Walt Disney, 1901-66, (U.S.) pioneer in cinema animation; built entertainment empire.

Herbert H. Dow, 1866-1930, (U.S.) founder of chemical co.

James Duke, 1856-1925, (U.S.) founded American Tobacco, Duke Univ.

Eleuthere I. du Pont, 1771-1834, (Fr.-U.S.) gunpowder manufacturer; founded one of the largest business empires.

Thomas C. Durant, 1820-85, (U.S.) railroad official, financier.

William C. Durant, 1861-1947, (U.S.) industrialist; formed General Motors.

George Eastman, 1854-1932, (U.S.) inventor; manufacturer of photographic equipment.

Marshall Field, 1834-1906, (U.S.) merchant; founded Chicago's largest department store.

Harvey Firestone, 1868-1938, (U.S.) founded tire company.

Avery Fisher, 1906-94, (U.S.) industrialist, philanthropist, founded Fisher electronics.

Henry M. Flagler, 1830-1913, (U.S.) financier; helped form Standard Oil; developed Florida as resort state.

Malcolm Forbes, 1919-90, (U.S.) magazine publisher.

Henry Ford, 1863-1947, (U.S.) auto maker; developed first popular low-priced car.

Henry Ford 2nd, 1917-87, (U.S.) headed auto company founded by grandfather.

Henry C. Frick, 1849-1919, (U.S.) steel and coke magnate; had prominent role in development of U.S. Steel.

Jakob Fugger (Jakob the Rich), 1459-1525, (Ger.) headed leading banking, trading house, in 16th-cent. Europe.

Alfred C. Fuller, 1885-1973, (U.S.) Canadian-born businessman; founded brush company.

Elbert H. Gary, 1846-1927, (U.S.) one of the organizers of U.S. Steel; chaired board of directors, 1903-27.

Jean Paul Getty, 1892-1976, (U.S.) founded oil empire.

Amadeo Giannini, 1870-1949, (U.S.) founded Bank of America.

Stephen Girard, 1750-1831, (U.S.) French-born financier, philanthropist; richest man in U.S. at his death.

Leonard H. Goldenson, 1905-99, (U.S.) turned ABC into major TV network.

Jay Gould, 1836-92, (U.S.) railroad magnate, financier.

Hetty Green, 1834-1916, (U.S.) financier, the "witch of Wall St."; richest woman in U.S. in her day.

William Gregg, 1800-67, (U.S.) launched textile industry in S.

Meyer Guggenheim, 1828-1905, (U.S.) Swiss-born merchant, philanthropist; built merchandising, mining empires.

Armand Hammer, 1898-1990, (U.S.) headed Occidental Petroleum; promoted U.S.-Soviet ties.

Edward H. Harriman, 1848-1909, (U.S.) railroad financier, administrator; headed Union Pacific.

Henry J. Heinz, 1844-1919, (U.S.) founded food empire.

Leona Helmsley, 1920-2007, real estate, philanthropist.

Milton Snavely Hershey, 1857-1945, (U.S.) chocolate co. founder, philanthropist.

James J. Hill, 1838-1916, (U.S.) Canadian-born railroad magnate, financier; founded Great Northern Railway.

Conrad N. Hilton, 1888-1979, (U.S.) hotel chain founder.

Howard Hughes, 1905-76, (U.S.) industrialist, aviator, movie maker.

H. L. Hunt, 1889-1974, (U.S.) oil magnate.

Collis P. Huntington, 1821-1900, (U.S.) railroad magnate.

Henry E. Huntington, 1850-1927, (U.S.) railroad builder, philanthropist.

Walter L. Jacobs, 1898-1985, (U.S.) founder of the first rental car agency, which later became Hertz.

Howard Johnson, 1896-1972, (U.S.) founded restaurants.

John H. Johnson, 1918-2005; built publishing empire based on *Ebony* and *Jet.*

Samuel Curtis Johnson, 1928-2004, (U.S.) headed S.C. Johnson & Sons.

Henry J. Kaiser, 1882-1967, (U.S.) industrialist; built empire in steel, aluminum.

Minor C. Keith, 1848-1929, (U.S.) railroad magnate; founded United Fruit Co.

Will K. Kellogg, 1860-1951, (U.S.) businessman, philanthropist; founded breakfast food co.

Richard King, 1825-85, (U.S.) cattleman; founded half-million-acre King Ranch in Texas.

William S. Knudsen, 1879-1948, (U.S.) Danish-born auto industry executive.

Samuel H. Kress, 1863-1955, (U.S.) businessman, art collector, philanthropist; founded "dime store" chain.

Ray A. Kroc, 1902-84, (U.S.) original CEO of McDonald's Corp.; oversaw company's vast expansion.

Alfred Krupp, 1812-87, (Ger.) armaments magnate.

Kenneth L. Lay, 1942-2006, (U.S.), former CEO of Enron, indicted on fraud charges.

William Levitt, 1907-94, (U.S.) industrialist, "suburb maker".

Thomas Lipton, 1850-1931, (Scot.) merchant, tea empire.

James McGill, 1744-1813, (Scot.-Can.) founded university.

Andrew W. Mellon, 1855-1937, (U.S.) financier, industrialist; benefactor of National Gallery of Art.

Charles E. Merrill, 1885-1956, (U.S.) financier; developed firm of Merrill Lynch.

John Pierpont Morgan, 1837-1913, (U.S.) most powerful figure in finance and industry at the turn of the cent.

Akio Morita, 1921-99, (Japan) co-founded Sony Corp.

Malcolm Muir, 1885-1979, (U.S.) created *Business Week* magazine; headed *Newsweek*, 1937-61.

Samuel Newhouse, 1895-1979, (U.S.) publishing and broadcasting magnate; built communications empire.

Aristotle Onassis, 1906-75, (Gr.) shipping magnate.

William S. Paley, 1901-90, (U.S.) built CBS communic. empire.

Frederick D. Patterson, 1901-88, founder of United Negro College Fund, 1944.

George Peabody, 1795-1869, (U.S.) merchant, financier, philanthropist.

James C. Penney, 1875-1971, (U.S.) businessman; developed department store chain.

William C. Procter, 1862-1934, (U.S.) headed soap co.

Frank Perdue, 1920-2005, (U.S.) founder of Perdue Farms, chicken-processing company.

John D. Rockefeller, 1839-1937, (U.S.) industrialist; established Standard Oil.

John D. Rockefeller Jr., 1874-1960, (U.S.) philanthropist; established foundation; provided land for UN.

Laurance S. Rockefeller, 1910-2004, (U.S.) philanthropist, conservationist.

Meyer A. Rothschild, 1743-1812, (Ger.) founded international banking house.
Thomas Fortune Ryan, 1851-1928, (U.S.) financier; a founder of American Tobacco.
Edmond J. Safra, 1932-99, (U.S.), banker.
David Sarnoff, 1891-1971, (U.S.) broadcasting pioneer; established first radio network, NBC.
Richard Sears, 1863-1914, (U.S.) founded mail-order co.
Werner von Siemens, 1816-92, (Ger.) industrialist; inventor.
Alfred P. Sloan, 1875-1966, (U.S.) industrialist, philanthropist; headed General Motors.
A. Leland Stanford, 1824-93, (U.S.) railroad official, philanthropist; founded university.
Frank Stanton, 1908-2006, (U.S.) president of CBS network, 1946-71.
Larry Stewart, 1948-2007, "Kansas City's Secret Santa."
Nathan Straus, 1848-1931, (U.S.) German-born merchant, philanthropist; headed Macy's.
Levi Strauss, c1829-1902, (U.S.) pants manufacturer.
Clement Studebaker, 1831-1901, (U.S.) wagon, carriage maker.
Gustavus Swift, 1839-1903, (U.S.) pioneer meatpacker.
Gerard Swope, 1872-1957, (U.S.) industrialist, economist; headed General Electric.
Dave Thomas, 1932-2002, (U.S.) Wendy's founder.
James Walter Thompson, 1847-1928, (U.S.) ad executive.

Alice Tully, 1902-93, (U.S.) philanthropist, arts patron.
Theodore N. Vail, 1845-1920, (U.S.) organized Bell Telephone system; headed AT&T.
Cornelius Vanderbilt, 1794-1877, (U.S.) financier; established steamship, railroad empires.
Henry Villard, 1835-1900, (U.S.) German-born railroad executive, financier.
George Westinghouse, 1846-1914, (U.S) inventor, manufacturer; organized Westinghouse Electric Co., 1886.
Charles R. Walgreen, 1873-1939, (U.S.) founded drugstore chain.
DeWitt Wallace, 1889-1981, (U.S.) and **Lila Wallace**, 1889-1984, (U.S.) cofounders of *Reader's Digest* magazine.
Sam Walton, 1918-92, (U.S.) founder of Wal-Mart stores.
John Wanamaker, 1838-1922, (U.S.) pioneered department-store merchandising.
Aaron Montgomery Ward, 1843-1913, (U.S.) established first mail-order firm.
Thomas J. Watson, 1874-1956, (U.S.) IBM head, 1914-56.
John Hay Whitney, 1905-82, (U.S.) publisher, sportsman, philanthropist.
Charles E. Wilson, 1890-1961, (U.S.) auto exec., public official.
Frank W. Woolworth, 1852-1919, (U.S.) created 5 & 10 chain.
William Wrigley Jr., 1861-1932, (U.S.) founded Wrigley chewing gum company.

American Cartoonists

Reviewed by Lucy Shelton Caswell, Professor and Curator, Cartoon Research Library, Ohio State University

Scott Adams, b 1957, Dilbert.
Charles Addams, 1912-88, macabre cartoons.
Brad Anderson, b 1924, Marmaduke.
Sergio Aragones, b 1937, *MAD Magazine*.
Peter Arno, 1904-68, *The New Yorker*.
Tex Avery, 1908-80, animator, Bugs Bunny, Porky Pig.
George Baker, 1915-75, The Sad Sack.
Carl Barks, 1901-2000, Donald Duck comic books.
C. C. Beck, 1910-89, Captain Marvel.
Dave Berg, 1920-2002, *MAD Magazine*.
Jim Berry, b 1932, Berry's World.
Herb Block (Herblock), 1909-2001, political cartoonist.
George Booth, b 1926, *The New Yorker*.
Berkeley Breathed, b 1957, Bloom County.
Dik Browne, 1917-89, Hi & Lois, Hagar the Horrible.
Marjorie Buell, 1904-93, Little Lulu.
Ernie Bushmiller, 1905-82, Nancy.
Milton Caniff, 1907-88, Terry & the Pirates, Steve Canyon.
Al Capp, 1909-79, Li'l Abner.
Roz Chast, b 1954, *The New Yorker*.
Paul Conrad, 1924, political cartoonist.
Roy Crane, 1901-77, Captain Easy, Buz Sawyer.
Robert Crumb, b 1943, underground cartoonist.
Shamus Culhane, 1908-96, animator.
Jay N. Darling (Ding), 1876-1962, political cartoonist.
Jack Davis, b 1926, *MAD Magazine*.
Jim Davis, b 1945, Garfield.
Billy DeBeck, 1890-1942, Barney Google.
Rudolph Dirks, 1877-1968, The Katzenjammer Kids.
Walt Disney, 1901-66, produced animated cartoons, created Mickey Mouse, Donald Duck.
Steve Ditko, b 1927, Spider-Man.
Mort Drucker, b 1929, *MAD Magazine*.
Will Eisner, 1917-2005, The Spirit.
Jules Feiffer, b 1929, political cartoonist.
Bud Fisher, 1884-1954, Mutt & Jeff.
Ham Fisher, 1900-55, Joe Palooka.
Max Fleischer, 1883-1972, Betty Boop.
Hal Foster, 1892-1982, Tarzan, Prince Valiant.
Fontaine Fox, 1884-1964, Toonerville Folks.
Isadore "Friz" Freleng, 1905-95, animator, Yosemite Sam, Porky Pig, Sylvester and Tweety Bird.
Rube Goldberg, 1883-1970, Boob McNutt.
Chester Gould, 1900-85, Dick Tracy.
Harold Gray, 1894-1968, Little Orphan Annie.
Matt Groening, b 1954, Life in Hell, The Simpsons.
Cathy Guisewite, b 1950, Cathy.
Bill Hanna, 1910-2001, & **Joe Barbera**, b 1911-2006, animators, Tom & Jerry, Yogi Bear, Flintstones.
Oliver Harrington, 1912-95, Bootsie.
Johnny Hart, 1931-2007, BC, Wizard of Id.
Alfred Harvey, 1913-94, created Casper the Friendly Ghost.
Jimmy Hatlo, 1898-1963, Little Iodine.
John Held Jr., 1889-1958, Jazz Age.
George Herriman, 1881-1944, Krazy Kat.
Harry Hershfield, 1885-1974, Abie the Agent.
Al Hirschfeld, 1903-2003, *N.Y. Times* theater caricaturist.
Burne Hogarth, 1911-96, Tarzan.
Helen Hokinson, 1900-49, *The New Yorker*.
Nicole Hollander, b 1939, Sylvia.
Chuck Jones, 1912-2002, animator, Bugs Bunny, Porky Pig.

Mike Judge, b. 1962, Beavis and Butt-head, King of the Hill.
Bob Kane, b 1916-98, Batman.
Bil Keane, b 1922, The Family Circus.
Walt Kelly, 1913-73, Pogo.
Hank Ketcham, 1920-2001, Dennis the Menace.
Ted Key, b 1912, Hazel.
Frank King, 1883-1969, Gasoline Alley.
Jack Kirby, 1917-94, Fantastic Four, The Incredible Hulk.
Rollin Kirby, 1875-1952, political cartoonist.
B(ernard) Kliban, 1935-91, cat books.
Edward Koren, b 1935, *The New Yorker*.
Harvey Kurtzman, 1924-1993, *MAD Magazine*.
Walter Lantz, 1900-94, Woody Woodpecker.
Gary Larson, b 1950, The Far Side.
Mell Lazarus, b 1929, Momma, Miss Peach.
Stan Lee, b 1922, Marvel Comics.
David Levine, b 1926, *N.Y. Review of Books* caricatures.
Doug Marlette, 1949-2007, political cartoonist, Kudzu.
Don Martin, 1931-2000, *MAD Magazine*.
Bill Mauldin, 1921-2003, political cartoonist.
Jeff MacNelly, 1947-2000, political cartoonist, Shoe.
Winsor McCay, 1872-1934, Little Nemo.
John T. McCutcheon, 1870-1949, political cartoonist.
Aaron McGruder, b 1974, The Boondocks.
George McManus, 1884-1954, Bringing Up Father.
Dale Messick, 1906-2005, Brenda Starr.
Norman Mingo, 1896-1980, Alfred E. Neuman.
Bob Montana, 1920-75, Archie.
Dick Moores, 1909-86, Gasoline Alley.
Willard Mullin, 1902-78, sports cartoonist; Dodgers "Bum," Mets "Kid."
Russell Myers, b 1938, Broom Hilda.
Thomas Nast, 1840-1902, political cartoonist; Republican elephant and Democratic donkey.
Pat Oliphant, b 1935, political cartoonist.
Frederick Burr Opper, 1857-1937, Happy Hooligan.
Richard Outcault, 1863-1928, Yellow Kid, Buster Brown.
Brant Parker, 1949-2007, Wizard of Id.
Trey Parker, b 1969, animator, co-creator of *South Park*.
Mike Peters, b 1943, cartoonist, Mother Goose & Grimm.
George Price, 1901-95, *The New Yorker*.
Antonio Prohias, 1921-98, Spy vs. Spy.
Alex Raymond, 1909-56, Flash Gordon, Jungle Jim.
Forrest (Bud) Sagendorf, 1915-94, Popeye.
Art Sansom, 1920-91, The Born Loser.
Charles Schulz, 1922-2000, Peanuts.
Elzie C. Segar, 1894-1938, Popeye.
Joe Shuster, 1914-92, & **Jerry Siegel**, 1914-96, Superman.
Sidney Smith, 1887-1935, The Gumps.
Otto Soglow, 1900-75, Little King.
Art Spiegelman, b 1948, Raw, Maus.
William Steig, b 1907-2003, *The New Yorker*.
Matt Stone, b 1971, animator, co-creator of South Park.
Paul Szep, b 1941, political cartoonist.
James Swinnerton, 1875-1974, Little Jimmy, Canyon Kiddies.
Paul Terry, 1887-1971, animator of Mighty Mouse.
Bob Thaves, 1949-2006, Frank and Ernest.
James Thurber, 1894-61, *The New Yorker*.
Garry Trudeau, b 1948, Doonesbury.
Mort Walker, b 1923, Beetle Bailey.
Bill Watterson, b 1958, Calvin and Hobbes.

Russ Westover, 1887-1966, Tillie the Toiler.
Signe Wilkinson, b 1950, political cartoonist.
Frank Willard, 1893-1958, Moon Mullins.
J. R. Williams, 1888-1957, The Willets Family, Out Our Way.

Gahan Wilson, b 1930, The New Yorker.
Tom Wilson, b 1931, Ziggy.
Art Young, 1866-1943, political cartoonist.
Chic Young, 1901-73, Blondie.

Economists, Educators, Historians, and Social Scientists of the Past

For Psychologists see Scientists of the Past.

Brooks Adams, 1848-1927, (U.S.) historian, political theoretician; The Law of Civilization and Decay.
Henry Adams, 1838-1918, (U.S.) historian, autobiographer; The Education of Henry Adams.
Francis Bacon, 1561-1626, (Eng.) philosopher, essayist, and statesman; championed observation and induction.
George Bancroft, 1800-91, (U.S.) historian; wrote 10-volume History of the United States.
Jack Barbash, 1911-94, (U.S.) labor economist who helped create the AFL-CIO.
Henry Barnard, 1811-1900, (U.S.) public school reformer.
Charles A. Beard, 1874-1948, (U.S.) historian; The Economic Basis of Politics.
(St.) Bede (the Venerable), c673-735, (Br.) scholar, historian; Ecclesiastical History of the English People.
Ruth Benedict, 1887-1948, (U.S.) anthropologist; studied Indian tribes of the Southwest.
Sir Isaiah Berlin, 1909-97, (Br.) philosopher, historian; The Age of Enlightenment.
Leonard Bloomfield, 1887-1949, (U.S.) linguist; Language.
Franz Boas, 1858-1942, (U.S.) German-born anthropologist; studied American Indians.
Van Wyck Brooks, 1886-1963, (U.S.) historian; critic of New England culture, especially literature.
William Edward Burghardt (W.E.B.) Du Bois, 1868-1963, (U.S.) historian, sociologist; and NAACP founder, 1909.
Edmund Burke, 1729-97, (Ir.) British parliamentarian and political philosopher; Reflections on the Revolution in France.
Nicholas Murray Butler, 1862-1947, (U.S.) educator; headed Columbia Univ., 1902-45; Nobel Peace Prize, 1931.
Joseph Campbell, 1904-87, (U.S.) author, editor, teacher; wrote books on mythology, folklore.
Thomas Carlyle, 1795-1881, (Sc.) historian, critic; Sartor Resartus, Past and Present, The French Revolution.
Edward Channing, 1856-1931, (U.S.) historian; wrote 6-volume History of the United States.
Henry Steele Commager, 1902-98, (U.S.) historian, educator; wrote The Growth of the American Republic.
John R. Commons, 1862-1945, (U.S.) economist, labor historian; Legal Foundations of Capitalism.
James B. Conant, 1893-1978, (U.S.) educator, diplomat; The American High School Today.
Benedetto Croce, 1866-1952, (It.) philosopher, statesman, and historian; Philosophy of the Spirit.
Bernard A. De Voto, 1897-1955, (U.S.) historian; wrote trilogy on American West; edited Mark Twain manuscripts.
Melvil Dewey, 1851-1931, (U.S.) devised decimal system of library-book classification.
St. Clair Drake, 1911-90, (U.S.) Sociologist, black studies pioneer, Black Metropolis (1945), with Horace R. Cayton.
Emile Durkheim, 1858-1917, (Fr.) a founder of modern sociology; The Rules of Sociological Method.
Jean Baptiste Point du Sable, c1750-1818, (U.S.) pioneer trader and first settler of Chicago, 1779.
Charles Eliot, 1834-1926, (U.S.) educator, Harvard president.
Friedrich Engels, 1820-95, (Ger.) political writer; with Marx wrote the Communist Manifesto.
Irving Fisher, 1867-1947, (U.S.) economist; contributed to the development of modern monetary theory.
John Fiske, 1842-1901, (U.S.) historian and lecturer; popularized Darwinian theory of evolution.
Charles Fourier, 1772-1837, (Fr.) utopian socialist.
Milton Friedman, 1912-2006, (U.S.) economist.
John Kenneth Galbraith, 1908-2006, (Can.-U.S.) economist, author, professor, former amb. to India.
Giovanni Gentile, 1875-1944, (It.) philosopher, educator; reformed Italian educational system.
Sir James George Frazer, 1854-1941, (Br.) anthropologist; studied myth in religion; The Golden Bough.
Henry George, 1839-97, (U.S.) economist, reformer; led single-tax movement.
Edward Gibbon, 1737-94, (Br.) historian; The History of the Decline and Fall of the Roman Empire.
Francesco Guicciardini, 1483-1540, (It.) historian; Storia d'Italia, principal historical work of the 16th cent.
Thomas Hobbes, 1588-1679, (Eng.) philosopher, political theorist; Leviathan.
Richard Hofstadter, 1916-70, (U.S.) historian; The Age of Reform.

Charles Hamilton Houston, 1895-1950, (U.S.) African American lawyer, Howard University instructor, champion of minority rights,
George F. Kennan, 1904-2005, (U.S.) diplomat, historian; main architect of the U.S. Cold War "containment" strategy.
John Maynard Keynes, 1883-1946, (Br.) economist; principal advocate of deficit spending.
Alfred Kinsey, 1894-1956, (U.S.) zoologist; pioneering human sex researcher.
Russell Kirk, 1918-94, (U.S.), social philosopher; The Conservative Mind.
Alfred L. Kroeber, 1876-1960, (U.S.) cultural anthropologist; studied tribes of North and South America.
Elisabeth Kubler-Ross, 1926-2004, (Swiss) psychiatrist, author. On Death and Dying.
Christopher Lasch, 1932-94, (U.S.) social critic, historian; The Culture of Narcissism.
James L. Laughlin, 1850-1933, (U.S.) economist; helped establish Federal Reserve System.
Lucien Lévy-Bruhl, 1857-1939, (Fr.) philosopher; studied the psychology of primitive societies; Primitive Mentality.
John Locke, 1632-1704, (Eng.) philosopher and political theorist; Two Treatises of Government.
Thomas B. Macaulay, 1800-59, (Br.) historian, statesman.
Niccolò Machiavelli, 1469-1527, (It.) writer, statesman. The Prince.
Bronislaw Malinowski, 1884-1942, (Pol.) considered the father of social anthropology.
Thomas R. Malthus, 1766-1834, (Br.) economist; famed for Essay on the Principle of Population.
Horace Mann, 1796-1859, (U.S.) pioneered modern public school system.
Karl Mannheim, 1893-1947, (Hung.) sociologist, historian; Ideology and Utopia.
Harriet Martineau, 1802-76, (Eng.) writer, feminist; Society in America
Karl Marx, 1818-83, (Ger.) political theorist, proponent of Communism; Communist Manifesto, Das Kapital.
Benjamin Mays, 1895-1984, (U.S.) minister, educator, civil rights leader; headed Morehouse College, 1940-67.
Giuseppe Mazzini, 1805-72, (It.) political philosopher.
William H. McGuffey, 1800-73, (U.S.) whose Reader was a mainstay of 19th-cent. U.S. public education.
George H. Mead, 1863-1931, (U.S.) philosopher, social psychologist.
Margaret Mead, 1901-78, (U.S.) cultural anthropologist; popularized field; Coming of Age in Samoa.
Alexander Meiklejohn, 1872-1964, (U.S.) Br.-born educator; championed academic freedom and experimental curricula.
James Mill, 1773-1836, (Sc.) philosopher, historian, economist; a proponent of utilitarianism.
John Stuart Mill, 1806-73, (Eng.) philosopher, economist, Utilitarianism; eldest son of James Mill.
Perry G. Miller, 1905-63, (U.S.) historian; interpreted 17th-cent. New England.
Theodor Mommsen, 1817-1903, (Ger.) historian; The History of Rome.
Ashley Montagu, 1905-99, (Eng.) anthropologist; The Natural Superiority of Women.
Charles-Louis Montesquieu, 1689-1755, (Fr.) social philosopher; The Spirit of Laws.
Maria Montessori, 1870-1952, (It.) educator, physician; started Montessori method of student self-motivation.
Samuel Eliot Morison, 1887-1976, (U.S.) historian; chronicled voyages of early explorers.
Lewis Mumford, 1895-1990, (U.S.) sociologist, critic; The Culture of Cities.
Gunnar Myrdal, 1898-1987, (Swed.) economist, social scientist; Asian Drama: An Inquiry Into the Poverty of Nations.
Allan Nevins, 1890-1971, (U.S.) historian, biographer; The Ordeal of the Union.
José Ortega y Gasset, 1883-1955, (Sp.) philosopher; advocated control by elite, The Revolt of the Masses.
Robert Owen, 1771-1858, (Br.) political philosopher, reformer; pioneer in cooperative movement.
Thomas (Tom) Paine, 1737-1809, (U.S.) political theorist, writer. Common Sense.
Vilfredo Pareto, 1848-1923, (It.) economist, sociologist.
Francis Parkman, 1823-93, (U.S.) historian; France and England in North America.

Elizabeth P. Peabody, 1804-94, (U.S.) education pioneer; founded 1st kindergarten in U.S., 1860.

William Prescott, 1796-1859, (U.S.) early American historian; *The Conquest of Peru.*

Pierre Joseph Proudhon, 1809-65, (Fr.) social theorist; father of anarchism; *The Philosophy of Property.*

François Quesnay, 1694-1774, (Fr.) economic theorist.

David Ricardo, 1772-1823, (Br.) economic theorist; advocated free international trade.

David Riesman, 1909-2002, (U.S.) sociologist, coauthor *The Lonely Crowd.*

Jean-Jacques Rousseau, 1712-78, (Fr.) social philosopher; the father of romantic sensibility; *Confessions.*

Edward Sapir, 1884-1939, (Ger.-U.S.) anthropologist; studied ethnology and linguistics of U.S. Indian groups.

Ferdinand de Saussure, 1857-1913, (Swiss) a founder of modern linguistics.

Arthur Schlesinger Jr., 1917-2007, (U.S.) historian, author; *The Imperial Presidency.*

Joseph Schumpeter, 1883-1950, (Czech.-U.S.) economist, sociologist.

Elizabeth Seton, 1774-1821, (U.S.) nun; est. parochial school education in U.S.; first native-born American saint.

George Simmel, 1858-1918, (Ger.) sociologist, philosopher; helped establish German sociology.

Adam Smith, 1723-90, (Br.) economist; advocated laissez-faire economy, free trade; *The Wealth of Nations.*

Jared Sparks, 1789-1866, (U.S.) historian, educator, editor; *The Library of American Biography.*

Oswald Spengler, 1880-1936, (Ger.) philosopher and historian; *The Decline of the West.*

William G. Sumner, 1840-1910, (U.S.) social scientist, economist; laissez-faire economy, Social Darwinism.

Hippolyte Taine, 1828-93, (Fr.) historian; basis of naturalistic school; *The Origins of Contemporary France.*

A(lan) J(ohn) P(ercivale) Taylor, 1906-89, (Br.) historian; *The Origins of the Second World War.*

Nikolaas Tinbergen, 1907-88, (Dutch-Br.) ethologist; pioneer in study of animal behavior.

Alexis de Tocqueville, 1805-59, (Fr.) political scientist, historian; *Democracy in America.*

Francis E. Townsend, 1867-1960, (U.S.) led old-age pension movement, 1933.

Arnold Toynbee, 1889-1975, (Br.) historian; *A Study of History*, sweeping analysis of hist. of civilizations.

George Trevelyan, 1838-1928, (Br.) historian, statesman; favored "literary" over "scientific" history; *History of England.*

Henri Troyat, 1911-2007 (Rus.-Fr.), biographies of major figures in Russian history.

Frederick J. Turner, 1861-1932, (U.S.) historian, educator; *The Frontier in American History.*

Thorstein B. Veblen, 1857-1929, (U.S.) economist, social philosopher; *The Theory of the Leisure Class.*

Giovanni Vico, 1668-1744, (It.) historian, philosopher; regarded by many as first modern historian; *New Science.*

Izaak Walton, 1593-1683, (Eng.) wrote biographies; political-philosophical study of fishing, *The Compleat Angler.*

Booker T. Washington, 1856-1915, (U.S.) founder, 1881, and first pres. of Tuskegee Institute; *Up From Slavery.*

Sidney J., 1859-1947, and **Beatrice**, 1858-1943, **Webb**, (Br.) leading figures in Fabian Society and Labor Party.

Max Weber, 1864-1920, (Ger.) sociologist; *The Protestant Ethic and the Spirit of Capitalism.*

Walter White, 1893-1955, (U.S.) exec. sec., NAACP, 1931-55.

Roy Wilkins, 1901-81, (U.S.) exec. director, NAACP, 1955-77.

Emma Hart Willard, 1787-1870, (U.S.) pioneered higher education for women.

Carter G. Woodson, 1875-1950, (U.S.) historian; founded Assn. for the Study of Negro Life and History.

C. Vann Woodward, 1908-99, (U.S.) historian; *The Strange Career of Jim Crow.*

American Journalists of the Past

Reviewed by Dean Mills, Dean, Missouri School of Journalism
See also Business Leaders, Cartoonists, Writers of the Past.

Franklin P. Adams (F.P.A.), 1881-1960, humorist; wrote column "The Conning Tower."

Joseph W. Alsop, 1910-89, and **Stewart Alsop**, 1914-74, Washington-based political analysts, columnists.

Jack Anderson, 1922-2006, muckraking Washington, DC, syndicated columnist.

Brooks Atkinson, 1894-1984, theater critic.

Bartley, Robert L., 1937-2003, editorial-page editor for *Wall Street Journal.*

James Gordon Bennett, 1795-1872, editor and publisher; founded *NY Herald.*

James Gordon Bennett, 1841-1918, succeeded father, financed expeditions, founded afternoon paper.

Elias Boudinot, d 1839, founding editor of first Native American newspaper in U.S., *Cherokee Phoenix* (1828-34).

Margaret Bourke-White, 1904-71, photojournalist.

Ed Bradley, 1941-2006, TV journalist known mostly for his 25 years reporting on *60 Minutes*; one of the first African-American journalists to report on the Vietnam War.

David Brinkley, 1920-2003, co-anchor of NBC's *Huntley-Brinkley Report*, host of ABC's *This Week With David Brinkley.*

Arthur Brisbane, 1864-1936, editor; helped introduce "yellow journalism" with sensational, simply written articles.

Heywood Broun, 1888-1939, author, columnist; founded American Newspaper Guild.

Art Buchwald, 1925-2007, journalist, humorist, syndicated columnist.

Herb Caen, 1916-97, longtime columnist for *San Francisco Chronicle* and *Examiner.*

John Campbell, 1653-1728, published *Boston News-Letter*, first continuing newspaper in the American colonies.

Jimmy Cannon, 1909-73, syndicated sports columnist.

John Chancellor, 1927-96, NBC TV reporter, anchor.

Harry Chandler, 1864-1944, *Los Angeles Times* publisher, 1917-41; made it a dominant force.

Otis Chandler, 1928-2006, *Los Angeles Times* publisher, 1960-80.

Marquis Childs, 1903-90, reporter and columnist for *St. Louis Post-Dispatch* and United Feature syndicate.

Craig Claiborne, 1920-2000, *NY Times* food editor and critic; key in internationalizing American taste.

Elizabeth Cochrane (Nellie Bly), 1867-1922, pioneer woman journalist, investig. reporter, noted for races on trip around the world.

Charles Collingwood, 1917-85, CBS news correspondent.

Alistair Cooke, 1908-2004, journalist, TV narrator, naturalized American citizen, "Letter from America" series.

Howard Cosell, 1920-95, TV and radio sportscaster.

Gardner Cowles, 1861-1946, founded newspaper chain.

Cyrus Curtis, 1850-1933, publisher of *Saturday Evening Post, Ladies' Home Journal, Country Gentleman.*

John Charles Daly, 1914-91, war correspondent; TV journalist; Voice of America head.

Charles Anderson Dana, 1819-97, editor, publisher; made *NY Sun* famous for its news reporting.

Elmer (Holmes) Davis, 1890-1958, *NY Times* editorial writer; radio commentator.

Richard Harding Davis, 1864-1916, war correspondent, travel writer, fiction writer.

Benjamin Day, 1810-89, published *NY Sun* beginning in 1833, introducing penny press to the U.S.

Finley Peter Dunne, 1867-1936, humorist, social critic, wrote "Mr. Dooley" columns.

Mary Baker Eddy, 1821-1910, founded Christian Science movement and *Christian Science Monitor.*

Rowland Evans Jr., 1921-2001, Washington columnist.

Fanny Fern (Sarah Willis Parton), 1811-1872, newspaper columnist, author.

Marshall Field III, 1893-1956, retail magnate, *Chicago Sun* founder.

Doris Fleeson, 1901-70, war correspondent, columnist.

James Franklin, 1697-1735, printer, pioneer journalist, publisher of *New England Courant* and *Rhode Island Gazette.*

Fred W. Friendly, 1915-98, radio, TV reporter, producer, executive, collaborator with Edward R. Murrow.

Margaret Fuller, 1810-50, social reformer, transcendentalist, critic and foreign correspondent for *NY Tribune.*

Frank E. Gannett, 1876-1957, founded newspaper chain.

William Lloyd Garrison, 1805-79, abolitionist; publisher of *The Liberator.*

Elizabeth Meriwether Gilmer (Dorothy Dix), 1861-1951, reporter, pioneer of the advice column genre.

Edwin Lawrence Godkin, 1831-1902, founder of *The Nation*, editor of *N.Y. Evening Post.*

Katharine Graham, 1917-2001, *Washington Post* publisher.

Sheilah Graham, 1904-89, Hollywood gossip columnist.

Horace Greeley, 1811-72, editor and politician; founded *NY Tribune.*

Meg Greenfield, 1930-1999, *Newsweek* columnist, editorial page editor *Washington Post.*

Gilbert Hovey Grosvenor, 1875-1966, longtime editor of *National Geographic* magazine.

John Gunther, 1901-70, *Chicago Daily News* foreign correspondent, author.

David Halberstam, 1934-2007, journalist, sports reporter, author; *The Best and the Brightest, Summer of '49.*

Sarah Josepha Buell Hale, 1788-1879, first female magazine editor, (Ladies' Magazine, later Godey's Lady's Book)

William Randolph Hearst, 1863-1951, founder of Hearst newspaper chain and one of the pioneer yellow journalists.

Gabriel Heatter, 1890-1972, radio commentator.

John Hersey, 1914-98, foreign correspondent for *Time*, *Life*, and *The New Yorker*; author.

Marguerite Higgins, 1920-66, reporter, war correspondent.

Hedda Hopper, 1885-1966, Hollywood gossip columnist.

Roy Howard, 1883-1964, editor, executive, Scripps-Howard papers and United Press (later United Press International).

Chet (Chester Robert) Huntley, 1911-74, co-anchor of NBC's *Huntley-Brinkley Report*.

Ralph Ingersoll, 1900-85, editor, *Fortune*, *Time*, *Life* exec.

Molly Ivins, 1944-2007, author, syndicated political columnist.

Peter Jennings, 1938-2005, ABC TV correspondent, anchor.

H. V. (Hans von) Kaltenborn, 1878-1965, radio commentator, reporter.

Murray Kempton, 1917-97, reporter, columnist for magazines and newspapers, including *NY Post*.

Dorothy Kilgallen, 1913-65, crime reporter; columnist.

John S. Knight, 1894-1981, editor, publisher; founded Knight newspaper group, which merged into Knight-Ridder.

Joseph Kraft, 1942-86, foreign policy columnist.

Arthur Krock, 1886-1974, *NY Times* political writer, Washington bureau chief.

Charles Kuralt, 1934-97, TV anchor and host of CBS "On the Road" featuring stories about life in the U.S.

Ann Landers (Eppie Lederer), 1918-2002, advice columnist.

David Lawrence, 1888-1973, reporter, columnist, publisher; founded *U.S. News & World Report*.

Frank Leslie, 1821-80, engraver and publisher of newspapers and magazines, notably *Leslie's Illustrated Newspaper*.

Alexander Liberman, 1912-99, editorial director for Conde Nast magazines.

A(bbott) J(oseph) Liebling, 1904-63, foreign correspondent, critic, principally with *The New Yorker*.

Walter Lippmann, 1889-1974, political analyst, social critic, columnist, author.

Peter Lisagor, 1915-76, Washington bureau chief, *Chicago Daily News*; broadcast commentator.

David Ross Locke, 1833-88, humorist, satirist under pseudonym P.V. Nasby; owned *Toledo (Ohio) Blade*.

Elijah Parish Lovejoy, 1802-37, abolitionist editor in St. Louis and in Alton, IL; killed by proslavery mob.

Clare Booth Luce, 1903-87, war correspondent for *Life;* diplomat, playwright.

Henry R. Luce, 1898-1967, founded *Time*, *Fortune*, *Life*, *Sports Illustrated*.

C(harles) K(enny) McClatchy, 1858-1936 founder of McClatchy newspaper chain.

Sarah McClendon, 1910-2003, veteran White House correspondent.

Samuel McClure, 1857-1949, founder (1893) of *McClure's Magazine*, famous for its investigative reporting.

Anne O'Hare McCormick, 1889-1954, foreign correspondent, first woman on *NY Times* editorial board.

Robert R. McCormick, 1880-1955, editor, publisher, executive of *Chicago Tribune* and *NY Daily News*.

Dwight Macdonald, 1906-1982, reporter, social critic.

Ralph McGill, 1893-1969, crusading editor and publisher of *Atlanta Constitution*.

Mary McGrory, 1918-2004, Washington, DC, columnist.

O(scar) O(dd) McIntyre, 1884-1938, feature writer, syndicated columnist on everyday life in New York City.

Don Marquis, 1878-1937, humor columnist for *NY Sun* and *N.Y. Tribune;* wrote "archy and mehitabel" stories.

Robert Maynard, 1937-97, first African American editor and then owner of major U.S. paper, the *Oakland Tribune*.

Joseph Medill, 1823-99, longtime *editor of Chicago Tribune*.

H(enry) L(ouis) Mencken, 1880-1956, reporter, editor, columnist with *Baltimore Sun* papers; anti-establishment viewpoint.

Edwin Meredith, 1876-1928, founder of magazine company.

Frank A. Munsey, 1854-1925, owner, editor, and publisher of newspapers and magazines, including *Munsey's Magazine*.

Edward R. Murrow, 1908-65, broadcast reporter, executive; reported from Britain in WW2; hosted *See It Now*, *Person to Person*.

Louella Parsons, 1881-1972, Hollywood gossip columnist.

Daniel Pearl, 1963-2002, American journalist, kidnapped and murdered in Pakistan.

Drew (Andrew Russell) Pearson, 1897-1969, investigative reporter and columnist.

(James) Westbrook Pegler, 1894-1969, reporter, columnist.

Shirley Povich, 1905-98, sports columnist.

Joseph Pulitzer, 1847-1911, *NY World* publisher; founded Columbia Journalism School, Pulitzer Prizes.

Joseph Pulitzer II, 1885-1955, longtime *St. Louis Post-Dispatch* editor, publisher; built it into major paper.

Ernie (Ernest Taylor) Pyle, 1900-45, reporter, war correspondent; killed in WW2.

Henry Raymond, 1820-69, cofounder, editor, *NY Times*.

Harry Reasoner, 1923-91, ABC and CBS news reporter, anchor.

John Reed, 1887-1920, reporter, foreign correspondent famous for coverage of Bolshevik Revolution; buried at the Kremlin.

Whitelaw Reid, 1837-1912, longtime editor, *NY Tribune*.

James Reston, 1909-95 *NY Times* political reporter, columnist.

Frank Reynolds, 1923-83, ABC reporter, anchor.

(Henry) Grantland Rice, 1880-1954, sportswriter.

Jacob Riis, 1849-1914, reporter, photographer; exposed slum conditions in *How the Other Half Lives*.

Max Robinson, 1939-88, first African American to anchor network news (ABC), 1978.

Harold Ross, 1892-1951, founder, editor, The *New Yorker*.

Carl T. Rowan, 1925-2000, reporter, columnist, author.

Mike Royko, 1932-97, Chicago newspaper columnist; wrote *Boss*, biography of Mayor Richard Daley.

(Alfred) Damon Runyon, 1884-1946, sportswriter, columnist; stories collected in *Guys and Dolls*.

John B. Russwurm, 1799-1851, cofounded (1827) nation's first black newspaper, *Freedom's Journal*, in NYC.

Adela Rogers St. Johns, 1894-1988, reporter, sportswriter for Hearst newspapers.

Joe Rosenthal, 1911-2006, (U.S.) photojournalist; photographed six marines raising the U.S. flag over Iwo Jima in WWII.

A. M. Rosenthal, 1922-2006, reporter and editor for the *New York Times* (1943-99).

Louis Rukeyser, 1933-2006, TV journalist, financial analyst, hosted "Wall Street Week" on public television.

Pierre Salinger, 1925-2004, press secretary under Pres. Kennedy and Johnson; foreign correspondent.

Harrison Salisbury, 1908-93, reporter, foreign correspondent; a Soviet specialist.

E(dward) W(yllis) Scripps, 1854-1926, founded first large U.S. newspaper chain, pioneered syndication.

Eric Sevareid, 1912-92, war correspondent, radio newscaster, CBS commentator.

William L. Shirer, 1904-93, broadcaster, foreign correspondent; wrote *The Rise and Fall of the Third Reich*.

Howard K. Smith, 1914-2002, ABC TV reporter, anchor.

Red (Walter) Smith, 1905-82, sportswriter.

Edgar P. Snow, 1905-71, correspondent, expert on Chinese Communist movement.

Tom Snyder, 1936-2007, television journalist.

Lawrence Spivak, 1900-94, co-creator, moderator, producer of *Meet the Press*.

(Joseph) Lincoln Steffens, 1866-1936, muckraking journalist.

I(sidor) F(einstein) Stone, 1907-89, one-man editor of *I.F. Stone's Weekly*.

Arthur Hays Sulzberger, 1891-1968, longtime publisher of *N.Y. Times*.

C(yrus) L(eo) Sulzberger, 1912-93, *N.Y. Times* foreign correspondent and columnist.

David Susskind, 1920-87, TV producer, public affairs talk-show host (*Open End*).

John Cameron Swayze, 1906-95, early TV newscaster (NBC).

Herbert Bayard Swope, 1882-1958, war correspondent and editor of *N.Y. World*.

Ida Tarbell, 1857-1944, muckraking journalist.

Isaiah Thomas, 1750-1831, printer, publisher, cofounder of revolutionary journal, *Massachusetts Spy*.

Lowell Thomas, 1892-1981, radio newscaster, world traveler.

Dorothy Thompson, 1894-1961, foreign correspondent, columnist, radio commentator.

Hunter S. Thompson, 1937-2005, political journalist, author *Fear and Loathing* on the Campaign Trail (1972).

Kenneth Thomson, 1923-2006, Canadian media magnate; owned Toronto *Globe and Mail* newspaper.

Ida Bell Wells-Barnett, 1862-1931, African American reporter, editor, anti-lynching crusader.

William Allen White, 1868-1944, newspaper editor, publisher.

Walter Winchell, 1897-1972, reporter, columnist, broadcaster of celebrity news.

John Peter Zenger, 1697-1746, printer and journalist; acquitted in precedent-setting libel suit (1735).

Military and Naval Leaders of the Past

Reviewed by Alan C. Aimone, USMA Library

Alexander the Great, 356-323 BCE, (Maced.) conquered Persia and much of the world known to Europeans.

Harold Alexander, 1891-1969, (Br.) led Allied invasion of Italy, 1943, WW2.

Ethan Allen, 1738-89, (U.S.) headed Green Mountain Boys; captured Ft. Ticonderoga, 1775, Amer. Rev.

Edmund Allenby, 1861-1936, (Br.) in Boer War, WW1; led Egyptian expeditionary force, 1917-18.

Benedict Arnold, 1741-1801, (U.S.) victorious at Saratoga; tried to betray West Point to British, Amer. Rev.

Henry "Hap" Arnold, 1886-1950, (U.S.) commanded Army Air Force in WW2.

Ashurnasirpal II, 884-859 BCE, (Assyria) king, began Assyrian conquest of Middle East.

John Barry, 1745-1803, (U.S.) won numerous sea battles during Amer. Rev.

Belisarius, c505-565, (Byzant.) won remarkable victories for Byzantine Emperor Justinian I.

Pierre Beauregard, 1818-93, (U.S.) Confed. general, ordered bombardment of Ft. Sumter that began Civil War.

Gebhard von Blücher, 1742-1819, (Ger.) helped defeat Napoleon at Waterloo.

Simón Bolívar, 1783-1830, (Venez.) S. Amer. Revolutionary who liberated much of the continent from Spanish rule.

Napoleon Bonaparte, 1769-1821, (Fr.) defeated Russia and Austria at Austerlitz, 1805; invaded Russia, 1812; defeated at Waterloo, 1815.

Edward Braddock, 1695-1755, (Br.) commanded forces in French and Indian War.

Omar N. Bradley, 1893-1981, (U.S.) headed U.S. ground troops in Normandy invasion, 1944, WW2.

John Burgoyne, 1722-92, (Br.) general, defeated at Saratoga, Amer. Rev.

Julius Caesar, 100-44 BCE, (Rom.) general and politician; conquered northern Gaul; overthrew Roman Republic.

Charlemagne, 742-814, (Fr.) king of the Franks, Holy Roman Emperor, conquered most of Western Europe.

El Cid (Rodrigo Díaz de Vivar), 1040-99, (Sp.) renowned knight, captured Valencia (1094); hero of "Song of Cid" epic.

Claire Lee Chennault, 1893-1958, (U.S.) headed Flying Tigers in WW2.

Mark W. Clark, 1896-1984, (U.S.) helped plan N. African invasion in WW2; commander of UN forces in Korean War.

Karl von Clausewitz, 1780-1831, (Pruss.) military theorist.

Lucius D. Clay, 1897-1978, (U.S.) led Berlin airlift, 1948-49.

Henry Clinton, 1738-95, (Br.) commander of forces in Amer. Rev., 1778-81.

Cochise, c1815-74, (Nat. Am.) chief of Chiricahua band of Apache Indians in Southwest.

Charles Cornwallis, 1738-1805, (Br.) victorious at Brandywine, 1777; surrendered at Yorktown, Amer. Rev.

Hernán Cortés, 1485-1547, (Sp.) led Spanish conquistadors in the defeat of the Aztec empire, 1519-28.

Crazy Horse, 1849-77, (Nat. Am.) Sioux war chief victorious at battle of Little Bighorn.

George Armstrong Custer, 1839-76, (U.S.) U.S. army officer defeated and killed at battle of Little Bighorn.

Moshe Dayan, 1915-81, (Isr.) directed campaigns in the 1967, 1973 Arab-Israeli wars.

Benjamin O. Davis Jr., 1912-2002, leader of World War II black aviators, first African American general in U.S. Air Force.

Benjamin O. Davis Sr., 1877-1970, first African American general, 1940, in U.S. Army.

Stephen Decatur, 1779-1820, (U.S.) naval hero of Barbary wars, War of 1812.

Anton Denikin, 1872-1947, (Russ.) led White forces in Russian civil war.

George Dewey, 1837-1917, (U.S.) destroyed Spanish fleet at Manila, 1898, Span.-Amer. War.

Karl Doenitz, 1891-1980, (Ger.) submarine com. in chief and naval commander, WW2.

Jimmy Doolittle, 1896-1993, (U.S.) led 1942 air raid on Tokyo and other Japanese cities in WW2.

Hugh C. Dowding, 1883-1970, (Br.) headed RAF, 1936-40, WW2.

Jubal Early, 1816-94, (U.S.) Confed. general, led raid on Washington, 1864, Civil War.

Dwight D. Eisenhower, 1890-1969, (U.S.) commanded Allied forces in Europe, WW2.

Erich von Falkenhayn, 1861-1922, (Ger.) minister of war, general, commander at Verdun in WW1.

David Farragut, 1801-70, (U.S.) Union admiral, captured New Orleans, Mobile Bay, Civil War.

John Arbuthnot Fisher, 1841-1920, (Br.) WW1 admiral, naval reformer.

Ferdinand Foch, 1851-1929, (Fr.) headed victorious Allied armies, 1918, WW1.

Nathan Bedford Forrest, 1821-77, (U.S.) Confed. general, led raids against Union supply lines, Civil War.

Frederick the Great, 1712-86, (Pruss.) led Prussia in Seven Years War.

Horatio Gates, 1728-1806, (U.S.) commanded army at Saratoga, Amer. Rev.

Daniel James Jr., 1920-78, first black 4-star general, 1975; commander, North American Air Defense Command.

Genghis Khan, 1162-1227, (Mongol) unified Mongol tribes and subjugated much of Asia, 1206-21.

Geronimo, 1829-1909, (Nat. Am.) leader of Chiricahua band of Apache Indians.

Charles G. Gordon, 1833-85, (Br.) led forces in China, Crimean War; killed at Khartoum.

Ulysses S. Grant, 1822-85, (U.S.) headed Union army, Civil War, 1864-65; forced Lee's surrender, 1865.

Nathanael Greene, 1742-86, (U.S.) defeated British in Southern campaign, 1780-81, Amer. Rev.

Heinz Guderian, 1888-1953, (Ger.) tank theorist, led panzer forces in Poland, France, Russia, WW2.

Gustavus Adolphus, 1594-1632, (Swed.) King; military tactician; reformer; led forces in Thirty Years' War.

Douglas Haig, 1861-1928, (Br.) led British armies in France, 1915-18, WW1.

William F. Halsey, 1882-1959, (U.S.) defeated Japanese fleet at Leyte Gulf, 1944, WW2.

Hannibal, 247-183 BCE, (Carthage) invaded Rome, crossing Alps, in Second Punic War, 218-201 BCE

Sir Arthur Travers Harris, 1895-1984, (Br.) led Britain's WW2 bomber command.

Paul von Hindenburg, 1847-1934, (Ger.) chief of general staff, WW1; 2nd pres. of Weimar Republic.

Richard Howe, 1726-99, (Br.) commanded navy in Amer. Rev., 1776-78; June 1 victory against French, 1794.

William Howe, 1729-1814, (Br.) commanded forces in Amer. Rev., 1776-78.

Isaac Hull, 1773-1843, (U.S.) sunk British frigate *Guerriere*, War of 1812.

Thomas (Stonewall) Jackson, 1824-63, (U.S.) Confed. general, led Shenandoah Valley campaign, Civil War.

Joseph Joffre, 1852-1931, (Fr.) headed Allied armies, won Battle of the Marne, 1914, WW1.

Chief Joseph, c1840-1904, (Nat. Am.) chief of the Nez Percé, forced by army to retreat and surrender.

John Paul Jones, 1747-92, (U.S.) commanded *Bonhomme Richard* in victory over *Serapis*, Amer. Rev., 1779.

Stephen Kearny, 1794-1848, (U.S.) headed Army of the West in Mexican War.

Albert Kesselring, 1885-1960 (Ger.) field marshal who led the defense of Italy in WW2.

Ernest J. King, 1878-1956, (U.S.) key WW2 naval strategist.

Horatio H. Kitchener, 1850-1916, (Br.) led forces in Boer War; victorious at Khartoum; organized army in WW1.

Henry Knox, 1750-1806, (U.S.) general in Amer. Rev.; first sec. of war under U.S. Constitution.

Lavrenti Kornilov, 1870-1918, (Russ.) commander-in-chief, 1917; led counter-revolutionary march on Petrograd.

Thaddeus Kosciusko, 1746-1817, (Pol.) aided Amer. Rev.

Walter Krueger, 1881-1967, (U.S.) led Sixth Army in WW2 in Southwest Pacific.

Mikhail Kutuzov, 1745-1813, (Russ.) fought at Borodino, Napol. Wars, 1812; abandoned Moscow; forced French retreat.

Marquis de Lafayette, 1757-1834, (Fr.) fought in, secured French aid for Amer. Rev.

T(homas) E. Lawrence (of Arabia), 1888-1935, (Br.) organized revolt of Arabs against Turks in WW1.

William Daniel Leahy, 1875-1959, (U.S.) chief of staff to Pres. Roosevelt in WWII, Fleet Admiral.

Henry (Light-Horse Harry) Lee, 1756-1818, (U.S.) cavalry officer in Amer. Rev.

Robert E. Lee, 1807-70, (U.S.) Confed. general defeated at Gettysburg, Civil War; surrendered to Grant, 1865.

Curtis LeMay, 1906-90, (U.S.) Air Force commander in WW2, Korean War, and Vietnam War.

Lyman Lemnitzer, 1899-1988, (U.S.) WW2 hero, later general, chairman of Joint Chiefs of Staff.

James Longstreet, 1821-1904, (U.S.) aided Lee at Gettysburg, Civil War.

Erich Ludendorff, 1865-1937, (Ger.) general, victor at Tannenberg, WW1.

Maurice, Count of Nassau, 1567-1625, (Dutch) military innovator; led forces in Thirty Years' War.

Douglas MacArthur, 1880-1964, (U.S.) commanded forces in SW Pacific in WW2; headed occupation forces in Japan, 1945-51; UN commander in Korean War.

Erich von Manstein, 1887-1973, (Ger.) served WW1-2, planned inv. of France (1940), convicted of war crimes.

Carl Gustaf Mannerheim, 1867-1951, (Finn.) army officer and pres. of Finland 1944-46.

Francis Marion, 1733-95, (U.S.) led guerrilla actions in South Carolina during Amer. Rev.

Duke of Marlborough, 1650-1722, (Br.) led forces against Louis XIV in War of the Spanish Succession.

George C. Marshall, 1880-1959, (U.S.) chief of staff in WW2; authored Marshall Plan.

George B. McClellan, 1826-85, (U.S.) Union general, commanded Army of the Potomac, 1861-62, Civil War.

George Meade, 1815-72, (U.S.) commanded Union forces at Gettysburg, Civil War.

Dorie Miller, 1919-43, Navy hero of Pearl Harbor attack.

Billy Mitchell, 1879-1936, (U.S.) WW1 air-power advocate; court-martialed for insubordination, later vindicated.

Helmuth von Moltke, 1800-91, (Ger.) victorious in Austro-Prussian, Franco-Prussian wars.

Louis de Montcalm, 1712-59, (Fr.) headed troops in Canada, French and Indian War; defeated at Quebec, 1759.

Bernard Law Montgomery, 1887-1976, (Br.) stopped German offensive at Alamein, 1942, WW2; helped plan Normandy.

Daniel Morgan, 1736-1802, (U.S.) victorious at Cowpens, 1781, Amer. Rev.

Louis Mountbatten, 1900-79, (Br.) Supreme Allied Commander of SE Asia, 1943-46, WW2.

Joachim Murat, 1767-1815, (Fr.) led cavalry at Marengo, Austerlitz, and Jena, Napoleonic Wars.

Horatio Nelson, 1758-1805, (Br.) naval commander, destroyed French fleet at Trafalgar.

Michel Ney, 1769-1815, (Fr.) commanded forces in Switz., Aust., Russ., Napoleonic Wars; defeated at Waterloo.

Chester Nimitz, 1885-1966, (U.S.) commander of naval forces in Pacific in WW2.

George S. Patton, 1885-1945, (U.S.) led assault on Sicily, 1943, Third Army invasion of Europe, WW2.

Oliver Perry, 1785-1819, (U.S.) won Battle of Lake Erie in War of 1812.

John Pershing, 1860-1948, (U.S.) commanded Mexican border campaign, 1916, Amer. Expeditionary Force, WW1.

Henri Philippe Pétain, 1856-1951, (Fr.) defended Verdun, 1916; headed Vichy government in WW2.

George E. Pickett, 1825-75, (U.S.) Confed. general famed for "charge" at Gettysburg, Civil War.

Charles Portal, 1893-1971, (Br.) chief of staff, Royal Air Force, 1940-45, led in Battle of Britain.

Manfred Frieherr von Richthofen (Red Baron), 1892-1918, (Ger.) WW1 flying ace, led elite fighter squadron.

Hyman Rickover, 1900-86, (U.S.) father of nuclear navy.

Matthew Bunker Ridgway, 1895-1993, (U.S.) commanded Allied ground forces in Korean War.

Erwin Rommel, 1891-1944, (Ger.) headed Afrika Korps, WW2.

Gerd von Rundstedt, 1875-1953, (Ger.) supreme commander in West, 1942-45, WW2.

Saladin, 1138-93, (Kurdish Muslim) recaptured Jerusalem from Crusaders.

Aleksandr Samsonov, 1859-1914, (Russ.) led invasion of E Prussia, WW1, defeated at Tannenberg, 1914.

Antonio Lopez de Santa Anna, 1794-1876, (Mex.) defeated Texans at the Alamo; defeated in Mexican War.

Maurice, Count of Saxe, 1696-1750, (Fr.) general, War of Aust. Succession, War of Pol. Succession; noted tactician.

Scipio Africanus the Elder, 234?-183, (Rom.) hero of 2nd Punic War, defeated Hannibal, invaded N. Africa.

Winfield Scott, 1786-1866, (U.S.) hero of War of 1812; headed forces in Mexican War, took Mexico City.

Philip Sheridan, 1831-88, (U.S.) Union cavalry officer, headed Army of the Shenandoah, 1864-65, Civil War.

William T. Sherman, 1820-91, (U.S.) Union general, sacked Atlanta during "march to the sea," 1864, Civil War.

Carl Spaatz, 1891-1974, (U.S.) directed strategic bombing against Germany, later Japan, in WW2.

Raymond Spruance, 1886-1969, (U.S.) victorious at Midway Island, 1942, WW2.

Joseph W. Stilwell, 1883-1946, (U.S.) headed forces in the China, Burma, India theater in WW2.

J.E.B. Stuart, 1833-64, (U.S.) Confed. cavalry commander, Civil War.

Sun Tzu, 6th? cent. BCE, (Chin.) general, author of *The Art of War.*

Aleksandr Suvorov, 1729-1800, (Russ.) commanded Allied Russian and Austrian armies, Russo-Turkish War.

Tamerlane, 1336-1405, (Turkoman Mongol) conqueror, established empire from India to Mediterranean Sea.

George H. Thomas, 1816-70, (U.S.) saved Union army at Chattanooga, 1863; won at Nashville, 1864, Civil War.

Semyon Timoshenko, 1895-1970, (USSR) defended Moscow, Stalingrad, WW2; led winter offensive, 1942-43.

Alfred von Tirpitz, 1849-1930, (Ger.) responsible for submarine blockade in WW1.

Henri de la Tour d'Auvergne, Viscount of Turenne, 1611-75, (Fr.) marshal, Thirty Years' War, Fronde, War of Devolution.

Sebastien Le Prestre de Vauban, 1633-1707, (Fr.) innovative military engineer and theorist.

Jonathan M. Wainwright, 1883-1953, (U.S.) forced to surrender on Corregidor, 1942, WW2.

George Washington, 1732-99, (U.S.) led Continental army, 1775-83, Amer. Rev.

Archibald Wavell, 1883-1950, (Br.) commanded forces in N and E Africa, and SE Asia in WW2.

Anthony Wayne, 1745-96, (U.S.) captured Stony Point, 1779, Amer. Rev.

Duke of Wellington, 1769-1852, (Br.) defeated Napoleon at Waterloo, 1815.

William Westmoreland, 1914-2005, (U.S.) commanded forces in Vietnam 1964-68.

William I (The Conqueror), 1027-87, (Br.) victor Battle of Hastings 1066, became first Norman king of England.

James Wolfe, 1727-59, (Br.) captured Quebec from French, 1759, French and Indian War.

Isoroku Yamamoto, 1884-1943, (Jpn.) com. in chief of Japanese fleet and naval planner before and during WW2.

Georgi Zhukov, 1895-1974, (Russ.) defended Moscow, 1941, led assault on Berlin, 1945, WW2.

Philosophers and Religious Figures of the Past

Excludes most biblical figures and popes (see Religion). For Greeks and Romans, see also Historical Figures chapter.

Lyman Abbott, 1835-1922, (U.S.) clergyman, reformer; advocate of Christian Socialism.

Pierre Abelard, 1079-1142, (Fr.) philosopher, theologian, teacher; used dialectic method to support Christian beliefs.

Mortimer Adler, 1902-2001, (U.S.) philosopher, helped create "Great Books" program.

Felix Adler, 1851-1933, (U.S.) German-born founder of the Ethical Culture Society.

(St.) Anselm, c1033-1109, (It.) philosopher-theologian, church leader; "ontological argument" for God's existence.

(St.) Thomas Aquinas, 1225-74, (It.) preeminent medieval philosopher-theologian; *Summa Theologica.*

Aristotle, 384-322 BCE, (Gr.) pioneering wide-ranging philosopher, logician, ethician, naturalist.

(St.) Augustine, 354-430, (N Africa) philosopher, theologian, bishop; *Confessions, City of God, On the Trinity.*

J. L. Austin, 1911-60, (Br.) ordinary-language philosopher.

Averroes (Ibn Rushd), 1126-98, (Sp.) Islamic philosopher, physician.

Avicenna (Ibn Sina), 980-1037, (Iran.) Islamic philosopher, scientist.

A(lfred) J(ules) Ayer, 1910-89, (Br.) philosopher; logical positivist; *Language, Truth, and Logic.*

Roger Bacon, c1214-94, (Eng.) philosopher and scientist.

Bahaullah (Mirza Husayn Ali), 1817-92, (Pers.) founder of Bahá'í faith.

Karl Barth, 1886-1968, (Swiss) theologian; a leading force in 20th-cent. Protestantism.

Thomas à Becket, 1118-70, (Eng.) archbishop of Canterbury; opposed Henry II; murdered by King's men.

(St.) Benedict, c480-547, (It.) founded the Benedictines.

Jeremy Bentham, 1748-1832, (Br.) philosopher, reformer; enunciated utilitarianism.

Henri Bergson, 1859-1941, (Fr.) philosopher of evolution.

George Berkeley, 1685-1753, (Ir.) idealist philosopher, bishop.

John Biddle, 1615-62, (Eng.) founder of English Unitarianism.

Jakob Boehme, 1575-1624, (Ger.) theosophist and mystic.

Dietrich Bonhoeffer, 1906-1945 (Ger.) Lutheran theologian, pastor; executed as opponent of Nazis.

William Brewster, 1567-1644, (Eng.) headed Pilgrims.

Emil Brunner, 1889-1966, (Swiss) Protestant theologian.

Giordano Bruno, 1548-1600, (It.) philosopher, pantheist.

Martin Buber, 1878-1965, (Ger.) Jewish philosopher, theologian; *I and Thou.*

Buddha (Siddhartha Gautama), c563-c483 BCE, (Indian) philosopher; founded Buddhism.

John Calvin, 1509-64, (Fr.) theologian; a key figure in the Protestant Reformation.

Rudolph Carnap, 1891-1970, (U.S.) German-born analytic philosopher; a founder of logical positivism.

William Ellery Channing, 1780-1842, (U.S.) clergyman; early spokesman for Unitarianism.

Auguste Comte, 1798-1857, (Fr.) philosopher; originated positivism.

Confucius, 551-479 BCE, (Chin.) founder of Confucianism.

John Cotton, 1584-1652, (Eng.) Puritan theologian.

Thomas Cranmer, 1489-1556, (Eng.) Anglican churchman; wrote much of *Book of Common Prayer.*

Jacques Derrida, 1930-2004 (Fr.), deconstructionist philosopher.

René Descartes, 1596-1650, (Fr.) philosopher, mathematician; "father of modern philosophy." *Discourse on Method, Meditations on First Philosophy.*

John Dewey, 1859-1952, (U.S.) philosopher, educator; instrumentalist theory of knowledge; progressive education.

Denis Diderot, 1713-84, (Fr.) philosopher, encyclopedist.

John Duns Scotus, c1266-1308, (Sc.) Franciscan philosopher and theologian.

Mary Baker Eddy, 1821-1910, (U.S.) founder of Christian Science; *Science and Health.*

Jonathan Edwards, 1703-58, (U.S.) preacher, theologian; "Sinners in the Hands of an Angry God."

(Desiderius) Erasmus, c1466-1536, (Dutch) Renaissance humanist; *On the Freedom of the Will.*

Rev. Jerry Falwell, 1933-2007, (U.S.) TV evangelist, religious commentator.

Johann Fichte, 1762-1814, (Ger.) idealist philosopher.

Michel Foucault, 1926-84, (Fr.) structuralist philosopher, historian.

George Fox, 1624-91, (Br.) founder of Society of Friends.

(St.) Francis of Assisi, 1182-1226, (It.) espoused voluntary poverty; founded Franciscans.

al-Ghazali, 1058-1111, Islamic philosopher.

Billy James Hargis, 1925-2004, (U.S.) anti-Communist televangelist; founder of the Church of the Christian Crusade.

Georg W. F. Hegel, 1770-1831, (Ger.) idealist philosopher; *Phenomenology of Mind.*

Martin Heidegger, 1889-1976, (Ger.) existentialist philosopher; affected many fields; *Being and Time.*

Johann G. Herder, 1744-1803, (Ger.) philosopher, cultural historian; a founder of German Romanticism.

Thomas Hobbes, 1588-1679, (Eng.) philosopher, political theorist; *Leviathan.*

David Hume, 1711-76, (Br.) empiricist philosopher; *Enquiry Concerning Human Understanding.*

Jan Hus, 1369-1415, (Czech.) religious reformer.

Edmund Husserl, 1859-1938, (Ger.) philosopher; founded the phenomenological movement.

Thomas Huxley, 1825-95, (Br.) philosopher, educator.

William Inge, 1860-1954, (Br.) theologian; explored mystic aspects of Christianity.

William James, 1842-1910, (U.S.) philosopher, psychologist; pragmatist; studied religious experience.

Karl Jaspers, 1883-1969, (Ger.) existentialist philosopher.

Joan of Arc, 1412-1431, (Fr.) national heroine and a patron saint of France; key figure in the Hundred Years' War.

Immanuel Kant, 1724-1804, (Ger.) philosopher; founder of modern critical philosophy; *Critique of Pure Reason.*

Thomas à Kempis, c1380-1471, (Ger.) monk, devotional writer; *Imitation of Christ* attributed to him.

Soren Kierkegaard, 1813-55, (Dan.) religious philosopher; pre-existentialist; *Either/Or, The Sickness Unto Death.*

John Knox, 1505-72, (Sc.) leader of the Protestant Reformation in Scotland.

Lao-Tzu, 604-531 BCE, (Chin.) philosopher; considered the founder of the Taoist religion.

Gottfried von Leibniz, 1646-1716, (Ger.) rationalistic philosopher, logician, mathematician.

John Locke, 1632-1704, (Eng.) political theorist, empiricist philosopher; *Essay Concerning Human Understanding.*

(St.) Ignatius Loyola, 1491-1556, (Sp.) founder of the Jesuits; *Spiritual Exercises.*

Martin Luther, 1483-1546, (Ger.) leader of the Protestant Reformation, founded Lutheran church.

Jean-Francois Lyotard, 1924-98, (Fr.) postmodern philosopher, lecturer; *The Post-Modern Condition.*

Maimonides, 1135-1204, (Sp.) major Jewish philosopher.

Gabriel Marcel, 1889-1973, (Fr.) Rom. Cath. existentialist philosopher, dramatist.

Jacques Maritain, 1882-1973, (Fr.) Neo-Thomist philosopher.

Cotton Mather, 1663-1728, (U.S.) defender of orthodox Puritanism; founded Yale, 1701.

Philipp Melanchthon, 1497-1560, (Ger.) theologian, humanist; an important voice in the Reformation.

Maurice Merleau-Ponty, 1908-61, (Fr.) existentialist philosopher; *Phenomenology of Perception.*

Thomas Merton, 1915-68, (U.S.) Trappist monk, spiritual writer; *The Seven Storey Mountain.*

Dwight Moody, 1837-99, (U.S.) evangelist.

G(eorge) E(dward) Moore, 1873-1958, (Br.) philosopher; *Principia Ethica,* "A Defense of Common Sense."

Muhammad, c570-632, (Arab) the prophet of Islam.

Elijah Muhammad, 1897-1975, (U.S.) Black Muslim sect leader.

Heinrich Muhlenberg, 1711-87, (Ger.) organized the Lutheran Church in America.

John H. Newman, 1801-90, (Br.) Rom. Cath. convert, cardinal; led Oxford Movement; *Apologia pro Vita Sua.*

Reinhold Niebuhr, 1892-1971, (U.S.) Protestant theologian.

Richard Niebuhr, 1894-1962 (U.S.) Protestant theologian.

Friedrich Nietzsche, 1844-1900, (Ger.) philosopher; *The Birth of Tragedy, Beyond Good and Evil, Thus Spake Zarathustra.*

Robert Nozick, 1938-2002, (U.S.) political philosopher; *Anarchy, State, and Utopia.*

Blaise Pascal, 1623-62, (Fr.) philosopher, mathematician; *Pensées.*

(St.) Patrick, c389-c461, (Br.) brought Christianity to Ireland.

Norman Vincent Peale, 1898-1993, (U.S.) minister, author; *The Power of Positive Thinking.*

C(harles) S. Peirce, 1839-1914, (U.S.) philosopher, logician; originated concept of pragmatism, 1878.

Plato, c428-347 BCE, (Gr.) philosopher; wrote Socratic dialogues; argued for immortality of soul, indep. reality of ideas or forms; *Republic, Meno, Phaedo, Apology.*

Plotinus, 205-70, (Rom.) a founder of neo-Platonism; *Enneads.*

W(illard) V(an) O(rman) Quine, 1908-2001, (U.S.) philosopher, logician; "On What There Is."

John Rawls, 1922-2002, (U.S.) political philosopher; *A Theory of Justice* (1971).

Josiah Royce, 1855-1916, (U.S.) idealist philosopher

Bertrand Russell, 1872-1970, (Br.) philosopher, logician; one of the founders of modern logic; a prolific popular writer.

Charles T. Russell, 1852-1916, (U.S.) founder of Jehovah's Witnesses.

Gilbert Ryle, 1900-76, (Br.) analytic philosopher; *The Concept of Mind.*

George Santayana, 1863-1952, (U.S.) philosopher, writer, critic; *The Sense of Beauty, The Realms of Being.*

Jean-Paul Sartre, 1905-80, (Fr.) philosopher, novelist, playwright. *Nausea, No Exit, Being and Nothingness.*

Friedrich von Schelling, 1775-1854, (Ger.) philosopher of romantic movement.

Friedrich Schleiermacher, 1768-1834, (Ger.) theologian; a founder of modern Protestant theology.

Arthur Schopenhauer, 1788-1860, (Ger.) philosopher; *The World as Will and Idea.*

Albert Schweitzer, 1875-1965, (Ger.) theologian, social philosopher, medical missionary.

Joseph Smith, 1805-44, (U.S.) founded Latter-Day Saints (Mormon) movement, 1830.

Socrates, 469-399 BCE, (Gr.) philosopher immortalized by Plato.

Herbert Spencer, 1820-1903, (Br.) philosopher of evolution.

Baruch de Spinoza, 1632-77, (Dutch) rationalist philosopher; *Ethics.*

Billy Sunday, 1862-1935, (U.S.) evangelist.

Emanuel Swedenborg, 1688-1772, (Swed.) philosopher, mystic; *Principia.*

Pierre Teilhard de Chardin, 1881-1955, (Fr.) Jesuit priest, paleontologist, philosopher-theologian; *The Divine Milieu.*

Daisetz Teitaro Suzuki, 1870-1966, (Jpn.) Buddhist scholar.

(St.) Therese of Lisieux, 1873-97, (Fr.) Carmelite nun ("Little Flower"), revered for everyday sanctity; *The Story of a Soul.*

Paul Tillich, 1886-1965, (U.S.) German-born philosopher and theologian; brought depth psychology to Protestantism.

John Wesley, 1703-91, (Br.) theologian, evangelist; founded Methodism.

Alfred North Whitehead, 1861-1947, (Br.) philosopher, mathematician; *Process and Reality.*

William of Occam, c1285-c1349 (Eng.) medieval scholastic philosopher; nominalist.

Roger Williams, c1603-83, (U.S.) clergyman; championed religious freedom and separation of church and state.

Ludwig Wittgenstein, 1889-1951, (Austrian) philosopher; major influence on contemporary language philosophy; *Tractatus Logico-Philosophicus, Philosophical Investigations.*

John Woolman, 1720-72, (U.S.) Quaker social reformer, abolitionist, writer; *The Journal.*

John Wycliffe, 1320-84, (Eng.) theologian, reformer.

(St.) Francis Xavier, 1506-52, (Sp.) Jesuit missionary, "Apostle of the Indies."

Brigham Young, 1801-77, (U.S.) Mormon leader after Smith's assassination; colonized Utah.

Huldrych Zwingli, 1484-1531, (Swiss) theologian; led Swiss Protestant Reformation.

Political Leaders of the Past

(U.S. presidents, vice presidents, Supreme Ct. justices, signers of Decl. of Indep. listed elsewhere.)

Abu Bakr, 573-634, Muslim leader, first caliph, chosen successor to Muhammad.

Dean Acheson, 1893-1971, (U.S.) sec. of state; architect of cold war foreign policy.

Samuel Adams, 1722-1803, (U.S.) patriot, Boston Tea Party firebrand.

Konrad Adenauer, 1876-1967, (Ger.) first West German chancellor.

Emilio Aguinaldo, 1869-1964, (Philip.) revolutionary; fought against Spain and the U.S.

Akbar, 1542-1605, greatest Mogul emperor of India.

Carl Albert, 1908-2000 (U.S.) House rep. from OK, Speaker, 1971-76.

Salvador Allende Gossens, 1908-1973, (Chilean) Marxist pres. 1970-73; ousted and died in coup.

Idi Amin, 1925-2003 (Uganda), Ugandan ruler from 1971 to 1979, blamed for hundreds of thousands of deaths.

Hafez al Assad, 1930-2000 (Syr.), Syrian ruler from 1970.

Herbert H. Asquith, 1852-1928, (Br.) liberal prime min.; instituted major social reform.

Atahualpa, ?-1533, Inca (ruling chief) of Peru.

Kemal Ataturk, 1881-1938, (Turk.) founded modern Turkey.

Clement Attlee, 1883-1967, (Br.) Labour party leader, prime min.; enacted natl. health, nationalized many industries.

Stephen F. Austin, 1793-1836, (U.S.) led Texas colonization.

Mikhail Bakunin, 1814-76, (Rus.) revolutionary; leading exponent of anarchism.

Arthur J. Balfour, 1848-1930, (Br.) foreign sec. under Lloyd George; issued Balfour Declaration backing Zionism.

Bernard M. Baruch, 1870-1965, (U.S.) financier, govt. adviser.

Fulgencio Batista y Zaldívar, 1901-73, (Cub.) Cuban pres. (1940-44, 1952-59), overthrown by Castro.

Lord Beaverbrook, 1879-1964, (Br.) financier, statesman, newspaper owner.

Menachem Begin, 1913-92, (Isr.) Israeli prime min., shared 1978 Nobel Peace Prize.

Eduard Benes, 1884-1948, (Czech.) pres. during interwar and post-WW2 eras.

David Ben-Gurion, 1886-1973, (Isr.) first prime min. of Israel, 1948-53, 1955-63.

Thomas Hart Benton, 1782-1858, (U.S.) Missouri senator; championed agrarian interests and westward expansion.

Lloyd Bentsen, 1921-2006 (U.S.), former senator, treasury sec., vice-pres. nominee.

Aneurin Bevan, 1897-1960, (Br.) Labour party leader.

Ernest Bevin, 1881-1951, (Br.) Labour party leader, foreign minister; helped lay foundation for NATO.

Otto von Bismarck, 1815-98, (Ger.) statesman known as the Iron Chancellor; uniter of Germany, 1870.

James G. Blaine, 1830-93, (U.S.) Republican politician, diplomat; influential in Pan-American movement.

Léon Blum, 1872-1950, (Fr.) socialist leader, writer; headed first Popular Front government.

William E. Borah, 1865-1940, (U.S.) isolationist senator; helped block U.S. membership in League of Nations.

Cesare Borgia, 1476-1507, (It.) soldier, politician; an outstanding figure of the Italian Renaissance.

P.W. Botha, 1916-2006, (So. Africa) So. African president, prime minister

Tom Bradley, 1917-98, (U.S.) first African American LA mayor.

Willy Brandt, 1913-92, (Ger.) statesman, chancellor of West Germany, 1969-74; promoted East/West peace, *Ostpolitik.*

Leonid Brezhnev, 1906-82, (USSR) Soviet leader, 1964-82.

Aristide Briand, 1862-1932, (Fr.) foreign min.; chief architect of Locarno Pact and anti-war Kellogg-Briand Pact.

William Jennings Bryan, 1860-1925, (U.S.) Democratic, populist leader, orator; 3 times lost race for presidency.

Ralph Bunche, 1904-71, (U.S.) first black person to win the Nobel Peace Prize, 1950; undersecretary of the UN, 1950.

John C. Calhoun, 1782-1850, (U.S.) political leader; champion of states' rights and a symbol of the Old South.

James Callaghan (Baron Callaghan), 1912-2005 (Br.) Labour Party politician, prime min. 1976-79.

Robert Castlereagh, 1769-1822, (Br.) foreign sec.; guided Grand Alliance against Napoleon.

Camillo Benso Cavour, 1810-61, (It.) statesman; largely responsible for uniting Italy under the House of Savoy.

Nicolae Ceausescu, 1918-89, (Roman.) Communist leader, head of state 1967-89; executed.

Austen Chamberlain, 1863-1937, (Br.) statesman; helped finalize Locarno Treaties, both 1925.

Neville Chamberlain, 1869-1940, (Br.) Conservative prime min. whose appeasement of Hitler led to Munich Pact.

Chiang Kai-shek, 1887-1975, (Chin.) Nationalist Chinese pres. whose government was driven from mainland to Taiwan.

Chiang Kai-shek, Madame, 1898-2003, (Chin.) highly influential wife of Nationalist Chinese leader Chiang Kai-shek.

Shirley Chisholm, 1924-2005, first black woman elected to U.S. House (1968); pres. contender, 1972.

Winston Churchill, 1874-1965, (Br.) prime min., soldier, author; guided Britain through WW2.

Galeazzo Ciano, 1903-44, (It.) fascist foreign minister; helped create Rome-Berlin Axis, executed by Mussolini.

Henry Clay, 1777-1852, (U.S.) "The Great Compromiser," one of the most influential pre-Civil War political leaders.

Georges Clemenceau, 1841-1929, (Fr.) twice prem., Wilson's antagonist at Paris Peace Conference after WW1.

DeWitt Clinton, 1769-1828, (U.S.) political leader; responsible for promoting the Erie Canal.

Robert Clive, 1725-74, (Br.) first administrator of Bengal; laid foundation for British Empire in India.

Jean Baptiste Colbert, 1619-83, (Fr.) statesman; influential under Louis XIV, created the French navy.

Bettino Craxi, 1934-2000, (It.) Italy's first post-WWII Socialist premier.

David Crockett, 1786-1836, (U.S.) frontiersman, congressman, died defending the Alamo.

Oliver Cromwell, 1599-1658, (Br.) Lord Protector of England, led parliamentary forces during Civil War.

Curzon of Kedleston, 1859-1925, (Br.) viceroy of India, foreign sec.; major force in post-WW1 world.

Édouard Daladier, 1884-1970, (Fr.) Radical Socialist politician, arrested by Vichy, interned by Germans until 1945.

Richard J. Daley, 1902-1976, (U.S.) Chicago mayor.

Georges Danton, 1759-94, (Fr.) leading French Rev. figure.

Jefferson Davis, 1808-89, (U.S.) pres. of the Confederacy.

Charles G. Dawes, 1865-1951, (U.S.) statesman, banker; advanced plan to stabilize post-WW1 German finances.

William L. Dawson, 1886-1970, Illinois congressman, first black chairman of a major U.S. House committee.

Alcide De Gasperi, 1881-1954, (It.) prime min.; founder of Christian Democratic party.

Charles De Gaulle, 1890-1970, (Fr.) general, statesman; first pres. of the Fifth Republic.

Deng Xiaoping, 1904-97, (Chin.) "paramount leader" of China; backed economic modernization.

Eamon De Valera, 1882-1975, (Ir.-U.S.) statesman; led fight for Irish independence.

Thomas E. Dewey, 1902-71, (U.S.) NY governor; twice loser in try for presidency.

Ngo Dinh Diem, 1901-63, (Viet.) South Vietnamese pres.; assassinated in government takeover.

Everett M. Dirksen, 1896-1969, (U.S.) Senate Republican minority leader, orator.

Benjamin Disraeli, 1804-81, (Br.) prime min.; considered founder of modern Conservative party.

Engelbert Dollfuss, 1892-1934, (Austrian) chancellor; assassinated by Austrian Nazis.

Andrea Doria, 1466-1560, (It.) Genoese admiral, statesman; called "Father of Peace" and "Liberator of Genoa."

Stephen A. Douglas, 1813-61, (U.S.) Democratic leader, orator; opposed Lincoln for the presidency.

Alexander Dubcek, 1921-92, (Czech.) statesman whose attempted liberalization was crushed, 1968.

John Foster Dulles, 1888-1959, (U.S.) sec. of state under Eisenhower, cold war policy-maker.

Abba Eban, 1915-2002, (Isr.) diplomat, foreign min. 1966-74.

Friedrich Ebert, 1871-1925, (Ger.) Social Democratic movement leader; 1st pres., Weimar Republic, 1919-25.

Sir Anthony Eden, 1897-1977, (Br.) foreign sec., prime min. during Suez invasion of 1956.

Ludwig Erhard, 1897-1977, (Ger.) economist, West German chancellor; led nation's economic rise after WW2.

King Fahid, 1921-2005, (Saudi Arab.) monarch since 1982, but inactive since 1995 stroke; encouraged U.S. relations.

Joao Baptista de Figueiredo, 1918-99, (Braz.) president of Brazil, restored the nation's democracy.

Hamilton Fish, 1808-93, (U.S.) sec. of state, successfully mediated disputes with Great Britain, Latin America.

James V. Forrestal, 1892-1949, (U.S.) sec. of navy, first sec. of defense.

Francisco Franco, 1892-1975, (Sp.) leader of rebel forces during Spanish Civil War and longtime ruler of Spain.

Benjamin Franklin, 1706-90, (U.S.) printer, publisher, author, inventor, scientist, diplomat.

Louis de Frontenac, 1620-98, (Fr.) governor of New France (Canada); encouraged explorations, fought Iroquois.

J. William Fulbright, 1905-95, (U.S.) U.S. senator; leading figure in U.S. foreign policy during cold war years.

Hugh Gaitskell, 1906-63, (Br.) Labour party leader; major force in reversing its stand for unilateral disarmament.

Albert Gallatin, 1761-1849, (U.S.) sec. of treasury; instrumental in negotiating end of War of 1812.

Léon Gambetta, 1838-82, (Fr.) statesman, politician; one of the founders of the Third Republic.

Indira Gandhi, 1917-84, (In.) daughter of Jawaharlal Nehru, prime min. of India, 1966-77, 1980-84; assassinated.

Mohandas K. Gandhi, 1869-1948, (In.) political leader, ascetic; led movement against British rule; assassinated.

Giuseppe Garibaldi, 1807-82, (It.) patriot, soldier; a leader in the Risorgimento, Italian unification movement.

William E. Gladstone, 1809-98, (Br.) prime min. 4 times; dominant force of Liberal party from 1868 to 1894.

Paul Joseph Goebbels, 1897-1945, (Ger.) Nazi propagandist, master of mass psychology.

Barry Goldwater, 1909-98 (U.S.) conservative U.S. senator and 1964 Republican presid. nominee.

Klement Gottwald, 1896-1953, (Czech.) Communist leader; ushered Communism into his country.

Alexander Hamilton, 1755-1804, (U.S.) first treasury sec.; champion of strong central government.

Dag Hammarskjold, 1905-61, (Swed.) statesman; UN sec.-general.

Hassan II, King, 1929-99, (Moroc.), ruler of Morocco,1962-99.

John Hay, 1838-1905, (U.S.) sec. of state; primarily associated with Open Door Policy toward China.

Sir Edward Heath, 1916-205, (Br.) Conserative prime min., 1970-74; promoted European unity.

Patrick Henry, 1736-99, (U.S.) major Revolutionary War figure, remarkable orator.

Édouard Herriot, 1872-1957, (Fr.) Radical Socialist leader; twice prem., pres. of National Assembly.

Theodor Herzl, 1860-1904, (Hung.) founded modern Zionism.

Heinrich Himmler, 1900-45, (Ger.) head of Nazi SS and Gestapo.

Paul von Hindenburg, 1847-1934, (Ger.) field marshal, WW1; 2nd pres. of Weimar Republic, 1925-34.

Adolf Hitler, 1889-1945, (Ger.) dictator; built Nazism, launched WW2, presided over the Holocaust.

Ho Chi Minh, 1890-1969, (Viet.) N Vietnamese pres., Vietnamese Communist leader.

Harry L. Hopkins, 1890-1946, (U.S.) New Deal administrator; closest adviser to FDR during WW2.

Edward M. House, 1858-1938, (U.S.) diplomat; confidential adviser to Woodrow Wilson.

Samuel Houston, 1793-1863, (U.S.) leader of struggle for Texas independence.

Cordell Hull, 1871-1955, (U.S.) sec. of state, 1933-44; initiated reciprocal trade to lower tariffs, helped organize UN.

Hubert H. Humphrey, 1911-78, (U.S.) MN Democrat; senator; vice pres., pres. candidate.

Hussein, King, 1935-99 (Jordan), peacemaker; ruler of Jordan, 1952-99.

Saddam Hussein, 1937-2006, (Iraq) Iraqi ruler, put to death for crimes against humanity.

Jinnah, Muhammad Ali, 1876-1948, (Pak.) founder, first governor-general of Pakistan.

Barbara Jordan, 1936-96, (U.S.) congresswoman, orator, educator; first black woman to win a seat in the Texas senate, 1966.

Benito Juarez, 1806-72, (Mex.) rallied his country against foreign threats, sought to create democratic, federal republic.

Constantine Karamanlis, 1907-98, (Gr.) Greek prime min., restored democracy; later president.

Frank B. Kellogg, 1856-1937, (U.S.) sec. of state; negotiated Kellogg-Briand Pact to outlaw war.

Robert F. Kennedy, 1925-68, (U.S.) attorney general, senator; assassinated while seeking presidency.

Aleksandr Kerensky, 1881-1970, (Russ.) headed provisional government after Feb. 1917 revolution.

Ayatollah Ruhollah Khomeini, 1900-89, (Iranian) religious-political leader, spearheaded overthrow of shah, 1979.

Nikita Khrushchev, 1894-1971, (USSR) prem., first sec. of Communist party; initiated de-Stalinization.

Kim Il Sung, 1912-94, (Korean) N Korean dictator, 1948-94.

Lajos Kossuth, 1802-94, (Hung.) principal figure in 1848 Hungarian revolution.

Pyotr Kropotkin, 1842-1921, (Russ.) anarchist; championed the peasants but opposed Bolshevism.

Kublai Khan, c1215-94, (Mongol) emperor; founder of Yüan dynasty in China.

Béla Kun, 1886-c1939, (Hung.) member of 3rd Communist Internat.; tried to foment worldwide revolution.

Robert M. LaFollette, 1855-1925, (U.S.) Wisconsin public official; leader of progressive movement.

Fiorello La Guardia, 1882-1947, (U.S.) colorful NYC reform mayor.

Pierre Laval, 1883-1945, (Fr.) politician, Vichy foreign min.; executed for treason.

Andrew Bonar Law, 1858-1923, (Br.) Conservative party politician; led opposition to Irish home rule.

Vladimir Ilyich Lenin (Ulyanov), 1870-1924, (Russ.) revolutionary; founded Bolshevism; Soviet leader 1917-24.

Ferdinand de Lesseps, 1805-94, (Fr.) diplomat, engineer; conceived idea of Suez Canal.

Rene Levesque, 1922-87, (Can.) prem. of Quebec, 1976-85; led unsuccessful separartist campaign.

Maxim Litvinov, 1876-1951, (Pol.-Russ.) revolutionary, commissar of foreign affairs; favored cooperation with West.

Liu Shaoqi, c1898-1974, (Chin.) Communist leader; fell from grace during Cultural Revolution.

David Lloyd George, 1863-1945, (Br.) Liberal party prime min.; laid foundations for modern welfare state.

Henry Cabot Lodge, 1850-1924, (U.S.) Republican senator; led opposition to participation in League of Nations.

Huey P. Long, 1893-1935, (U.S.) Louisiana political demagogue, governor, U.S. senator; assassinated.

Rosa Luxemburg, 1871-1919, (Ger.) revolutionary; leader of the German Social Democratic party and Spartacus party.

J. Ramsay MacDonald, 1866-1937, (Br.) first Labour party prime min. of Great Britain.

Harold Macmillan, 1895-1986, (Br.) prime min. of Great Britain, 1957-63.

Eugene McCarthy, 1916-2005, (U.S.) political leader and author; 1968 presidential contender.

Joseph R. McCarthy, 1908-57, (U.S.) senator, extremist in searching out alleged Communists and pro-Communists.

Makarios III, 1913-77, (Cypriot) Greek Orthodox archbishop; first pres. of Cyprus.

Mao Zedong, 1893-1976, (Chin.) chief Chinese Marxist theorist, revolutionary, political leader; led Chinese revolution establishing his nation as Communist state.

Jean Paul Marat, 1743-93, (Fr.) revolutionary, politician; identified with radical Jacobins; assassinated.

Thurgood Marshall, 1908-93, (U.S.) first black U.S. solicitor general, 1965; first black justice of U.S. Sup. Ct., 1967-91.

José Martí, 1853-95, (Cub.) patriot, poet; leader of Cuban struggle for independence.

Jan Masaryk, 1886-1948, (Czech.) foreign min.; died by mysterious alleged suicide following Communist coup.

Thomas G. Masaryk, 1850-1937, (Czech.) statesman, philosopher; first pres. of Czechoslovak Republic.

Jules Mazarin, 1602-61, (Fr.) cardinal, statesman; prime min. under Louis XIII and queen-regent Anne of Austria.

Giuseppe Mazzini, 1805-72, (It.) reformer dedicated to Risorgimento movement for renewal of Italy.

Tom Mboya, 1930-69, (Kenyan) political leader; instrumental in securing independence for Kenya.

Cosimo I de' Medici, 1519-74, (It.) Duke of Florence, grand duke of Tuscany.

Lorenzo de' Medici, the Magnificent, 1449-92, (It.) merchant prince; a towering figure in Italian Renaissance.

Catherine de Médicis, 1519-89, (Fr.) queen consort of Henry II, regent of France; influential in Catholic-Huguenot wars.

Golda Meir, 1898-1978, (Isr.) a founder of the state of Israel and prime min., 1969-74.

Klemens W. N. L. Metternich, 1773-1859, (Austrian) statesman; arbiter of post-Napoleonic Europe.

Slobodan Milosevic, 1941-2006, (Serbian/Yugoslavian), former Yugoslav pres.; tried for war crimes.

François Mitterrand, 1916-96, (Fr.) pres. of France, 1981-95.

Mobutu Sese Seko, 1930-97, (Zaire) longtime ruler of Zaire (now Congo) (1965-97); exiled after rebellion.

Guy Mollet, 1905-75, (Fr.) socialist politician, resistance leader.

Henry Morgenthau Jr., 1891-1967, (U.S.) sec. of treasury; fundraiser for New Deal and U.S. WW2 activities.

Gouverneur Morris, 1752-1816, (U.S.) statesman, diplomat. financial expert, helped plan decimal coinage.

Daniel Patrick Moynihan 1927-2003, (U.S.) senator, diplomat, social scientist and author.

Benito Mussolini, 1883-1945, (It.) leader of the Italian fascist state; assassinated.

Imre Nagy, 1896-1958, (Hung.) Communist min.; assassinated after Soviets crushed 1956 uprising.

Gamal Abdel Nasser, 1918-70, (Egypt.) leader of Arab unification, 2nd Egyptian pres.

Jawaharlal Nehru, 1889-1964, (In.) prime min.; guided India through its early years of independence.

Kwame Nkrumah, 1909-72, (Ghan.) 1st prime min., 1957-60, and pres., 1960-66, of Ghana.

Frederick North, 1732-92, (Br.) prime min.; his inept policies led to loss of American colonies.

Julius K. Nyerere, 1923?-99, (Tanz.) founding father, 1st pres., 1962-85, of Tanzania.

Daniel O'Connell, 1775-1847, (Ir.) nationalist political leader; known as The Liberator.

Omar, c581-644, Muslim leader; 2nd caliph, led Islam to become an imperial power.

Thomas P. (Tip) O'Neill Jr., 1912-94, (U.S.) U.S. congressman, Speaker of the House, 1977-86.

Ignace Paderewski, 1860-1941, (Pol.) statesman, pianist; composer, briefly prime min., an ardent patriot.

Viscount Palmerston, 1784-1865, (Br.) Whig-Liberal prime min., foreign min.; embodied British nationalism.

Andreas George Papandreou, 1919-1996, (Gk.) leftist politician, served 2 times as prem. (1981-89, 1993-96).

Georgios Papandreou, 1888-1968, (Gk.) Republican politician; served 3 times as prime min.

Franz von Papen, 1879-1969, (Ger.) politician; major role in overthrow of Weimar Republic and rise of Hitler.

Charles Stewart Parnell, 1846-1891, (Ir.) nationalist leader; "uncrowned king of Ireland."

Lester Pearson, 1897-1972, (Can.) diplomat, Liberal party leader, prime min.

Robert Peel, 1788-1850, (Br.) reformist prime min., founder of Conservative party.

Eva (Evita) Perón, 1919-52 (Arg.) highly influential 2nd wife of Juan Perón.

Juan Perón, 1895-1974, (Arg.) dynamic pres. of Argentina (1946-55, 1973-74).

Joseph Pilsudski, 1867-1935, (Pol.) statesman; instrumental in reestablishing Polish state in the 20th cent.

Charles Pinckney, 1757-1824, (U.S.) founding father; his Pinckney plan largely incorporated into Constitution.

Christian Pineau, 1905-95, (Fr.) leader of French Resistance during WW2; French foreign min., 1956-58.

Augusto Pinochet (Ugarte), 1915-2006, (Chile) former Chilean ruler; indicted for human rights abuses while in office.

William Pitt, the Elder, 1708-78, (Br.) statesman; the "Great Commoner," transformed Britain into imperial power.

William Pitt, the Younger, 1759-1806, (Br.) prime min. during French Revolutionary wars.

Georgi Plekhanov, 1857-1918, (Russ.) revolutionary, social philosopher; called "father of Russian Marxism."

Raymond Poincaré, 1860-1934, (Fr.) 9th pres. of the Republic; advocated harsh punishment of Germany after WW1.

Pol Pot, 1925-98, (Camb.) leader of Khmer Rouge; ruled Cambodia, 1975-79; responsible for mass deaths.

Georges Pompidou, 1911-74, (Fr.) Gaullist political leader; pres. 1969-74.

Grigori Potemkin, 1739-91, (Russ.) field marshal; favorite of Catherine II.

Adam Clayton Powell Jr., 1908-72, (U.S.) civil rights leader, congressman, 1945-69.

Yitzhak Rabin, 1922-95, (Isr.) military, political leader; prime min. of Israel, 1974-77, 1992-95; assassinated.

Joseph H. Rainey, 1832-87, (U.S.) first black person elected to U.S. House, 1869, from South Carolina.

Edmund Randolph, 1753-1813, (U.S.) attorney; prominent in drafting, ratification of constitution.

John Randolph, 1773-1833, (U.S.) Southern planter; strong advocate of states' rights.

Jeannette Rankin, 1880-1973, (U.S.) pacifist; first woman member of U.S. Congress.

Walter Rathenau, 1867-1922, (Ger.) industrialist, statesman.

Sam Rayburn, 1882-1961, (U.S.) Democratic leader; representative for 47 years, House Speaker for 17.

Hiram R. Revels, 1822-1901, (U.S.) first African American U.S. senator, elected in Mississippi, served 1870-71.

Paul Reynaud, 1878-1966, (Fr.) statesman; prem. in 1940 at the time of France's defeat by Germany.

Syngman Rhee, 1875-1965, (Korean) first pres. of S Korea.

Cecil Rhodes, 1853-1902, (Br.) imperialist, industrial magnate; established Rhodes scholarships in his will.

Ann Richards, 1933-2006, (U.S.) former TX gov.

Cardinal de Richelieu, 1585-1642, (Fr.) statesman, known as "red eminence;" chief minister to Louis XIII.

Maximilien Robespierre, 1758-94, (Fr.) leading figure in French Revolution and Reign of Terror.

Nelson Rockefeller, 1908-79, (U.S.) Republican governor of NY, 1959-73; U.S. vice pres., 1974-77.

George W. Romney, 1907-95, (U.S.) auto exec.; 3-term Republican governor of Michigan.

Eleanor Roosevelt, 1884-1962, (U.S.) influential First Lady, humanitarian, UN diplomat.

Elihu Root, 1845-1937, (U.S.) lawyer, statesman, diplomat; leading Republican supporter of the League of Nations.

Dean Rusk, 1909-95, (U.S.) statesman; sec. of state, 1961-69.

John Russell, 1792-1878, (Br.) Liberal prime min. during the Irish potato famine.

Anwar al-Sadat, 1918-81, (Egypt.) pres., 1970-1981, promoted peace with Israel; Nobel laureate; assassinated.

António de Oliveira Salazar, 1889-1970, (Port.) longtime dictator.

José de San Martin, 1778-1850, S Amer. revolutionary; protector of Peru.

Eisaku Sato, 1901-75, (Jpn.) prime min.; presided over Japan's post-WW2 emergence as major world power.

Abdul Aziz Ibn Saud, c1880-1953, (Saudi Arabia) king of Saudi Arabia, 1932-53.

Robert Schuman, 1886-1963, (Fr.) statesman; founded European Coal and Steel Community.

Carl Schurz, 1829-1906, (U.S.) German-American political leader, journalist, orator, dedicated reformer.

Kurt Schuschnigg, 1897-1977, (Austrian) chancellor; unsuccessful in stopping Austria's annexation by Germany.

William H. Seward, 1801-72, (U.S.) anti-slavery activist; as U.S. sec. of state purchased Alaska.

Carlo Sforza, 1872-1952, (It.) foreign min., anti-fascist.

Sitting Bull, c1831-90, (Nat. Am.) Sioux leader in Battle of Little Bighorn over George A. Custer, 1876.

Alfred E. Smith, 1873-1944, (U.S.) NY Democratic governor; first Roman Catholic to run for presidency.

Margaret Chase Smith, 1897-1995, (U.S.) congresswoman, senator; 1st woman elected to both houses of Congress.

Jan C. Smuts, 1870-1950, (S. African) statesman, philosopher, soldier, prime min.

Paul Henri Spaak, 1899-1972, (Belg.) statesman, socialist leader.

Joseph Stalin, 1879-1953, (USSR) Soviet dictator, 1924-53; instituted forced collectivization, massive purges, and labor camps, causing millions of deaths.

Edwin M. Stanton, 1814-69, (U.S.) sec. of war, 1862-68.

Edward R. Stettinius Jr., 1900-49, (U.S.) industrialist, sec. of state who coordinated aid to WW2 allies.

Adlai E. Stevenson, 1900-65, (U.S.) Democratic leader, diplomat, Illinois governor, presidenial candidate.

Henry L. Stimson, 1867-1950, (U.S.) statesman; served in 5 administrations, foreign policy adviser in 30s and 40s.

Carl Stokes, 1927-1996, (U.S.) first black mayor of a major American city (Cleveland), 1967-72.

Sukarno, 1901-70, (Indon.) dictatorial first pres. of the Indonesian republic.

Sun Yat-sen, 1866-1925, (Chin.) revolutionary; leader of Kuomintang, regarded as the father of modern China.

Robert A. Taft, 1889-1953, (U.S.) conservative Senate leader, called "Mr. Republican."

Charles de Talleyrand, 1754-1838, (Fr.) statesman, diplomat; the major force of the Congress of Vienna of 1814-15.

U Thant, 1909-74 (Bur.) statesman, UN sec.-general.

Norman M. Thomas, 1884-1968, (U.S.) social reformer; 6 times Socialist party presidential candidate.

Josip Broz Tito, 1892-1980, (Yug.) pres. of Yugoslavia from 1953, WW2 guerrilla chief, postwar rival of Stalin.

Palmiro Togliatti, 1893-1964, (It.) major Italian Communist leader.

Hideki Tojo, 1885-1948, (Jpn.) statesman, soldier; prime min. during most of WW2.

François Toussaint L'Ouverture, c1744-1803, (Haitian) patriot, martyr; thwarted French colonial aims.

Leon Trotsky, 1879-1940, (Russ.) revolutionary, founded Red Army, expelled from party in conflict with Stalin; assassinated.

Pierre Elliott Trudeau, 1919-2000, (Can.) longtime liberal prime minister of Canada, 1968-79, 1980-84; achieved native Canadian constitution.

Rafael L. Trujillo Molina, 1891-1961, (Dom.) dictator of Dominican Republic, 1930-61; assassinated.

Moise K. Tshombe, 1919-69, (Cong.) pres. of secessionist Katanga, prem. of Congo.

William M. Tweed, 1823-78, (U.S.) politicial boss of Tammany Hall, NYC's Democratic political machine.

Walter Ulbricht, 1893-1973, (Ger.) Communist leader of German Democratic Republic.

Arthur H. Vandenberg, 1884-1951, (U.S.) senator; proponent of bipartisan anti-Communist foreign policy.

Eleutherios Venizelos, 1864-1936, (Gk.) most prominent Greek statesman of early 20th cent.

Hendrik F. Verwoerd, 1901-66, (S. African) prime min.; rigorously applied apartheid policy despite protest.

Kurt Waldheim, 1918-2007, (Austria) UN sec.-gen, and Austrian pres.

George Wallace, 1919-98, (U.S.) former segregationist governor of Alabama and presid. candidate.

Robert Walpole, 1676-1745, (Br.) statesman; generally considered Britain's first prime min.

Harold Washington, 1922-87, (U.S.) first black mayor of Chicago.

Robert C. Weaver, 1907-97, (U.S.) first African American appointed to cabinet; secretary of HUD.

Daniel Webster, 1782-1852, (U.S.) orator, politician; advocate of business interests during Jacksonian agrarianism.

Caspar Weinberger, 1917-2006 (U.S.), business exec, former defense sec., other cabinet posts.

Chaim Weizmann, 1874-1952, (Russ.-Isr.) Zionist leader, scientist; first Israeli pres.

Wendell L. Willkie, 1892-1944, (U.S.) Republican who tried to unseat FDR when he ran for his 3d term.

Harold Wilson, 1916-95, (Br.) Labour party leader; prime min., 1964-70, 1974-76.

Boris Yeltsin, 1931-2007, (USSR-Russia) first freely elected president of post-Soviet Russia.

Coleman A. Young, 1918-97, (U.S.) first Afr.-Amer. mayor of Detroit, 1974-93.

Emiliano Zapata, c1879-1919, (Mex.) revolutionary; major influence on modern Mexico.

Todor Zhivkov, 1911-98, (Bulg.) Communist ruler of Bulgaria from 1954 until ousted in a 1989 coup.

Zhou Enlai, 1898-1976, (Chin.) diplomat, prime min.; a leading figure of the Chinese Communist party.

Scientists of the Past
Revised by Peter Barker, Prof. & Chair, Dept. of the Hist. of Science, Univ. of Oklahoma

For pre-modern scientists see also Philosophers and Religious Figures of the Past and Historical Figures chapter.

Albertus Magnus, c1200-1280, (Ger.) theologian, philosopher; helped found medieval study of natural science.

Alhazen (Ibn al-Haytham), c965-c1040, mathematician, astronomer; optical theorist.

Andre-Marie Ampère, 1775-1836, (Fr.) mathematician, chemist; founder of electrodynamics.

John V. Atanasoff, 1903-95, (U.S.) physicist; co-invented Atanasoff-Berry Computer (1939-41).

Amedeo Avogadro, 1776-1856, (It.) chemist, physicist; proposed that equal volumes of gas contain equal numbers of molecules, permitting determination of molecular weights.

John Bardeen, 1908-91, (U.S.) double Nobel laureate in physics (transistor, 1956; superconductivity, 1972).

A. H. Becquerel, 1852-1908, (Fr.) physicist; discovered radioactivity in uranium (1896).

Alexander Graham Bell, 1847-1922, (U.S.) inventor; first to patent and commercially exploit the telephone (1876).

Daniel Bernoulli, 1700-82, (Swiss) mathematician; developed fluid dynamics and kinetic theory of gases.

Clifford Berry, 1918-1963, (U.S.) collaborated with Atanasoff on the ABC computer (1939-41).

Jöns Jakob Berzelius, 1779-1848, (Swed.) chemist; developed modern chemical symbols and formulas.

Henry Bessemer, 1813-98, (Br.) engineer; invented Bessemer steel-making process.

Hans Bethe, 1906-2005, (Ger.-U.S.) physicist; won Nobel Prize in 1967 for describing how stars generate energy.

Bruno Bettelheim, 1903-90, (Austrian-U.S.) psychoanalyst; studied disturbed children; *Uses of Enchantment* (1976).

Louis Blériot, 1872-1936, (Fr.) engineer; monoplane pioneer, first Channel flight (1909).

Franz Boas, 1858-1942, (Ger.-U.S.) founded modern anthropology; studied Pacific Coast tribes.

Niels Bohr, 1885-1962, (Dan.) atomic and nuclear physicist; founded quantum mechanics.

Max Born, 1882-1970, (Ger.) atomic and nuclear physicist; helped develop quantum mechanics.

Satyendranath Bose, 1894-1974, (Indian) physicist; forerunner of modern quantum theory for integral-spin particles.

Louis de Broglie, 1892-1987, (Fr.) physicist; proposed quantum wave-particle duality.

Robert Bunsen, 1811-99, (Ger.) chemist; pioneered spectroscopic analysis; discovered rubidium, caesium.

Luther Burbank, 1849-1926, (U.S.) naturalist; developed plant breeding into a modern science.

Vannevar Bush, 1890-1974, (U.S.) electrical engineer; developed differential analyzer, an early analogue computer; headed WWII Office of Scientific Res. and Dev.

Marvin Camras, 1916-95, (U.S.) inventor, electrical engineer; invented magnetic tape recording.

Alexis Carrel, 1873-1944, (Fr.) surgeon, biologist; developed methods of suturing blood vessels and transplanting organs.

Rachel Carson, 1907-64, (U.S.) marine biologist, environmentalist; *Silent Spring* (1962).

James Chadwick, 1891-1974, (Br.) physicist; discovered the neutron (1932); led Brit. Manhattan Project group in U.S..

Albert Claude, 1898-1983, (Belg.-U.S.) a founder of modern cell biology; determined role of mitochondria.

Nicolaus Copernicus, 1473-1543, (Pol.) first modern astronomer to propose sun as center of the planets' motions.

Jacques Yves Cousteau, 1910-1997, (Fr.) oceanographer; co-inventor, with E. Gagnan, of the Aqualung (1943).

Seymour Cray, 1925-96, (U.S.) computer industry pioneer; developed supercomputers.

Francis Crick, (1916-2004), (Br.) biophysicist; co-discoverer of genetic code; shared 1962 Nobel Prize.

Marie, 1867-1934 (Pol.-Fr.) and **Pierre Curie**, 1859-1906, (Fr.) physical chemists; pioneer investigators of radioactivity, discovered radium and polonium (1898).

Gottlieb Daimler, 1834-1900, (Ger.) engineer, inventor; pioneer automobile manufacturer.

John Dalton, 1766-1844, (Br.) chemist, physicist; formulated atomic theory, made first table of atomic weights.

Charles Darwin, 1809-82, (Br.) naturalist; established theory of organic evolution; *Origin of Species* (1859).

Lee De Forest, 1873-1961, (U.S.) inventor of triode, pioneer in wireless telegraphy, sound pictures, television.

Pierre-Gilles de Gennes, 1932-2007, (Fr.) physicist whose research furthered the development of liquid-crystal-display (LCD) technology; awarded Nobel Prize for Physics in 1991.

Max Delbruck, 1906-81, (Ger.-U.S.) founded molecular biology.

Rudolf Diesel, 1858-1913, (Ger.) mechanical engineer; patented Diesel engine (1892).

Theodosius Dobzhansky, 1900-75, (Russ.-U.S.) biologist; reconciled genetics and natural selection.

Christian Doppler, 1803-53, (Austrian) physicist; showed change in wave frequency caused by motion of source, now known as Doppler effect.

J. Presper Eckert Jr., 1919-95, (U.S.) co-inventor, with Mauchly, of the ENIAC computer (1943-45).

Thomas A. Edison, 1847-1931, (U.S.) inventor; held more than 1,000 patents, including incandescent electric lamp.

Paul Ehrlich, 1854-1915, (Ger.) medical researcher in immunology and bacteriology; pioneered antitoxin production.

Albert Einstein, 1879-1955, (Ger.-U.S.) theoretical physicist; founded relativity theory.

John F. Enders, 1897-1985, (U.S.) virologist; helped discover vaccines against polio, measles, mumps and chicken pox.

Erik Erikson, 1902-94, (U.S.) psychoanalyst, author; theory of developmental stages of life, *Childhood and Society* (1950).

Leonhard Euler, 1707-83, (Swiss) mathematician, physicist; pioneer of calculus, revived ideas of Fermat.

Gabriel Fahrenheit, 1686-1736, (Ger.) physicist; improved thermometers and introduced Fahrenheit temperature scale.

Michael Faraday, 1791-1867, (Br.) chemist, physicist; discovered electrical induction and invented dynamo (1831).

Philo T. Farnsworth, 1906-71, (U.S.) inventor; built first television system (San Francisco, 1928).

Pierre de Fermat, 1601-65, (Fr.) mathematician; founded modern theory of numbers.

Enrico Fermi, 1901-54, (It.-U.S.) nuclear physicist; demonstrated first controlled chain reaction (Chicago, 1942).

Richard Feynman, 1918-88, (U.S.) theoretical physicist, author; founder of Quantum Electrodynamics (QED).

Alexander Fleming, 1881-1955, (Br.) bacteriologist; discovered penicillin (1928).

Jean B. J. Fourier, 1768-1830, (fr.) introduced method of analysis in math and physics known as Fourier Series.

Sigmund Freud, 1856-1939, (Austrian) psychiatrist; founder of psychoanalysis. *Interpretation of Dreams* (1901).

Erich Fromm, 1900-1980, (U.S.) psychoanalyst. *Man for Himself* (1947).

Galileo Galilei, 1564-1642, (It.) physicist; used telescope to vindicate Copernicus, founded modern science of motion.

Carl Friedrich Gauss, 1777-1855, (Ger.) math. physicist; completed work of Fermat and Euler in number theory.

Josiah W. Gibbs, 1839-1903, (U.S.) theoretical physicist, chemist; founded chemical thermodynamics.

Robert H. Goddard, 1882-1945, (U.S.) physicist; invented liquid fuel rocket (1926).

George W. Goethals, 1858-1928, (U.S.) chief engineer who completed Panama Canal (1907-14).

William C. Gorgas, 1854-1920, (U.S.) physician; pioneer in prevention of yellow fever and malaria.

Stephen Jay Gould, 1941-2002, (U.S.) paleontologist, evolutionary biologist, writer.

Ernest Haeckel, 1834-1919, (Ger.) zoologist, evolutionist; early Darwinist, introduced concept of "ecology."

Otto Hahn, 1879-1968, (Ger.) chemist; with Meitner discovered nuclear fission (1938).

Edmund Halley, 1656-1742, (Br.) astronomer; predicted return of 1682 comet ("Halley's Comet") in 1759.

William Harvey, 1578-1657, (Br.) physician, anatomist; discovered circulation of the blood (1628).

Werner Heisenberg, 1901-76, (Ger.) physicist; developed matrix mechanics and uncertainty principle (1927).

Hermann von Helmholtz, 1821-94, (Ger.) physicist, physiologist; formulated principle of conservation of energy.

William Herschel, 1738-1822, (Ger.-Br.) astronomer; discovered Uranus (1781).

Heinrich Hertz, 1857-94, (Ger.) physicist; discovered radio waves and photo-electric effect (1886-7).

David Hilbert, 1862-1943, (Ger.) mathematician; contributed to algebra, calculus and foundational studies (formalism).

Edwin P. Hubble, 1889-1953, (U.S.) astronomer; discovered observational evidence of expanding universe.

Alexander von Humboldt, 1769-1859, (Ger.) naturalist, author; explored S America, created ecology.

Edward Jenner, 1749-1823, (Br.) physician; pioneered vaccination, introduced term "virus."

James Joule, 1818-89, (Br.) physicist; found relation between heat and mechanical energy (conservation of energy).

Carl Jung, 1875-1961, (Swiss) psychiatrist; founder of analytical psychology.

Ernest Everett Just, 1883-1941, (U.S.) marine biologist; studied egg development; author, *Biology of Cell Surfaces*, 1941.

Johannes Kepler, 1571-1630, (Ger.) astronomer; discovered laws of planetary motion.

Al-Khawarizmi, early 9th cent., (Arab.), mathematician; regarded as founder of algebra.

Robert Koch, 1843-1910 (Ger.) bacteriologist; isolated bacterial causes of tuberculosis and other diseases.

Georges Köhler, 1946-95, (Ger.) immunologist; with Cesar Milstein he developed monoclonal antibody technique.

Jacques Lacan, 1901-81, (Fr.) influential psychoanalyst.

Joseph Lagrange, 1736-1813, (Fr.) geometer, astronomer; showed that gravity of earth and moon cancels creating stable points in space around them.

Jean B. Lamarck, 1744-1829, (Fr.) naturalist; forerunner of Darwin in evolutionary theory.

Pierre Simon de Laplace, 1749-1827, (Fr.) astronomer, physicist; proposed nebular origin for solar system.

Lewis H. Latimer, 1848-1928, (U.S.) African American scientist; associate of Edison; supervised installation of first electric street lighting in NYC.

Antoine Lavoisier, 1743-94, (Fr.) a founder of mod. chemistry.

Ernest O. Lawrence, 1901-58, (U.S.) physicist; invented the cyclotron.

Jerome Lejeune, 1927-94, (Fr.) geneticist; discovered chromosomal cause of Down syndrome (1959).

Louis 1903-72, and **Mary Leakey**, 1913-96, (Br.) early hominid paleoanthropologists; discovered remains in Africa.

Anton van Leeuwenhoek, 1632-1723, (Dutch) founder of microscopy.

Kurt Lewin, 1890-1947, (Ger.-U.S.) social psychologist; studied human motivation and group dynamics.

Justus von Liebig, 1803-73, (Ger.) founded quantitative organic chemistry.

Joseph Lister, 1827-1912, (Br.) physician; pioneered antiseptic surgery.

Hendrik Lorentz, 1853-1928 (Neth.), physicist, developed electron theory of matter, contrib. to relativity theory.

Konrad Lorenz, 1903-89, (Austrian) ethologist; pioneer in study of animal behavior.

Percival Lowell, 1855-1916, (U.S.) astronomer; predicted the existence of Pluto.

Louis, 1864-1948, and **Auguste Lumière**, 1862-1954, (Fr.) invented cinematograph and made first motion picture (1895).

Theodore H. Maiman, 1927-2007, (U.S.) physicist who invented the first workable laser, which he displayed in 1960.

Guglielmo Marconi, 1874-1937, (It.) physicist; developed wireless telegraphy.

John W. Mauchly, 1907-80, (U.S.) co-inventor, with Eckert, of computer ENIAC (1943-45).

James Clerk Maxwell, 1831-79, (Br.) physicist; unified electricity and magnetism; electromagnetic theory of light.

Maria Goeppert Mayer, 1906-72, (Ger.-U.S.) physicist; developed shell model of atomic nuclei.

Barbara McClintock, 1902-92, (U.S.) geneticist; showed that some genetic elements are mobile.

Lise Meitner, 1878-1968, (Austrian) co-discoverer, with Hahn, of nuclear fission (1938).

Gregor J. Mendel, 1822-84, (Austrian) botanist, monk; his experiments became the foundation of modern genetics.

Dmitri Mendeleyev, 1834-1907, (Russ.) chemist; established Periodic Table of the Elements.

Bruce R. Merrifield, 1921-2006, (U.S.) chemist; discovered how to synthesize proteins quickly and efficiently.

Franz Mesmer, 1734-1815, (Ger.) physician; introduced hypnotherapy.

Albert A. Michelson, 1852-1931, (U.S.) physicist; invented interferometer.

Robert A. Millikan, 1868-1953, (U.S.) physicist; measured electronic charge.

Thomas Hunt Morgan, 1866-1945, (U.S.) geneticist, embryologist; established role of chromosomes in heredity.

Isaac Newton, 1642-1727, (Br.) natural philosopher; discovered laws of gravitation, motion; with Leibniz, founded calculus.

Robert N. Noyce, 1927-90, (U.S.) invented microchip.

J. Robert Oppenheimer, 1904-67, (U.S.) physicist; scientific director of Manhattan project.

Wilhelm Ostwald, 1853-1932, (Ger.) chemist, philosopher; main founder of modern physical chemistry.

Louis Pasteur, 1822-95, (Fr.) chemist; showed that germs cause disease and fermentation, originated pasteurization.

Linus C. Pauling, 1901-94, (U.S.) chemist; studied chemical bonds; campaigned for nuclear disarmament.

Jean Piaget, 1896-1980, (Swiss) psychologist; four-stage theory of intellectual development in children.

Max Planck, 1858-1947, (Ger.) physicist; introduced quantum hypothesis (1900).

Jules Henri Poincaré, 1854-1912 (Fr.), mathematician, founded algebraic topology, many other discoveries.

Walter S. Reed, 1851-1902, (U.S.) army physician; proved mosquitoes transmit yellow fever.

Theodor Reik, 1888-1969, (Austrian-U.S.) psychoanalyst, major Freudian disciple.

Bernhard Riemann, 1826-66, (Ger.) mathematician; developed non-Euclidean geometry used by Einstein.

Norbert Rillieux, 1806-94, (U.S.) African American inventor of a vacuum pan evaporator, 1846, revolutionized sugar-refining industry.

Wilhelm Roentgen, 1845-1923, (Ger.) physicist; discovered X-rays (1895).

Carl Rogers, 1902-87, (U.S.) psychotherapist, author; originated nondirective therapy.

Ernest Rutherford, 1871-1937, (Br.) physicist; pioneer investigator of radioactivity, identified the atomic nucleus.

Albert B. Sabin, 1906-93, (Russ.-U.S.), developed oral polio live-virus vaccine.

Carl Sagan, 1934-96, (U.S.) astronomer, author.

Jonas Salk, 1914-95, (U.S.) developed first successful polio vaccine, widely used in U.S. after 1955.

Giovanni Schiaparelli, 1835-1910, (It.) astronomer; reported canals on Mars.

Erwin Schrödinger, 1887-1961, (Austrian) physicist; developed wave equation for quantum systems.

Glenn T. Seaborg, 1912-99, (U.S.) chemist, Nobel Prize winner (1951); codiscoverer of plutonium.

Harlow Shapley, 1885-1972, (U.S.) astronomer; mapped galactic clusters and position of Sun in our own galaxy.

Norman E. Shumway, 1923-2006, (U.S.) surgeon; performed the world's first successful heart-lung transplant.

B(urrhus) F(rederick) Skinner, 1904-89, (U.S.) psychologist; leading advocate of behaviorism.

Richard E. Smalley, 1943-2006, (U.S.) chemist; along with three other scientists, discovered "buckminsterfullerenes," a previously unknown class of carbon molecules.

Roger W. Sperry, 1913-94, (U.S.) neurobiologist; established different functions of right and left sides of brain.

Benjamin Spock, 1903-98, (U.S.) pediatrician, child care expert; *Common Sense Book of Baby and Child Care*.

Charles P. Steinmetz, 1865-1923, (Ger.-U.S.) electrical engineer; developed basic ideas on alternating current.

Leo Szilard, 1898-1964, (Hung.-U.S.) physicist; helped on Manhattan project, later opposed nuclear weapons.

Edward Teller, 1908-2003, (Hung.-U.S.) physicist, aided on Manhattan project, had key role in development of H-bomb.

Nikola Tesla, 1856-1943, (Serb.-U.S.) invented electrical devices including a.c. dynamos, transformers and motors.

William Thomson (Lord Kelvin), 1824-1907, (Br.) physicist; aided in success of transatlantic telegraph cable (1865); proposed Kelvin absolute temperature scale.

Alan Turing, 1912-54, (Br.) mathematician; helped develop basis for computers.

Rudolf Virchow, 1821-1902, (Ger.) pathologist; pioneered the modern theory that diseases affect the body through cells.

James Van Allen, 1914-2006, (U.S.) physicist; discovered the presence of radiation belts around Earth (Van Allen belts).

Alessandro Volta, 1745-1827, (It.) physicist; electricity pioneer.

Werner von Braun, 1912-77, (Ger.-U.S.) developed rockets for warfare and space exploration.

John Von Neumann, 1903-57, (Hung.-U.S.) mathematician; originated game theory; basic design for modern computers.

Alfred Russell Wallace, 1823-1913, (Br.) naturalist; proposed concept of evolution independently of Darwin.

John B. Watson, 1878-1958, (U.S.) psychologist; a founder of behaviorism.

James C. Watt, 1736-1819, (Br.) mechanical engineer, inventor; invented modern steam engine (1765).

Alfred L. Wegener, 1880-1930, (Ger.) meteorologist, geophysicist; postulated continental drift.

Norbert Wiener, 1894-1964, (U.S.) mathematician; founder of cybernetics.

Daniel Hale Williams, 1858-1931, (U.S.) African American surgeon; performed one of first two open-heart operations, 1893.

Sewall Wright, 1889-1988, (U.S.) evolutionary theorist; helped found population genetics.

Wilhelm Wundt, 1832-1920, (Ger.) founder of experimental psychology.

Ferdinand von Zeppelin, 1838-1917, (Ger.) soldier, aeronaut, airship designer.

Social Reformers, Activists, and Humanitarians of the Past

Ralph David Abernathy, 1926-90, (U.S.) black civil rights activist; pres., 1968, Southern Christian Leadership Conf.

Jane Addams, 1860-1935, (U.S.) cofounder of Hull House; won Nobel Peace Prize, 1931.

Susan B. Anthony, 1820-1906, (U.S.) a leader in temperance, anti-slavery, and woman suffrage movements.

Thomas Barnardo, 1845-1905, (Br.) social reformer; pioneered in care of destitute children.

Clara Barton, 1821-1912, (U.S.) organized American Red Cross.

Daisy Bates, 1914-99, (U.S.) black civil rights leader who fought for school integration; leading advocate for the "Little Rock 9" during the Arkansas desegregation crisis in 1957.

Henry Ward Beecher, 1813-87, (U.S.) clergyman, abolitionist.

Peter Benenson, 1921-2005, (Br.) activist, founded Amnesty International in 1961.

Mary McCleod Bethune, 1875-1955, (U.S.) black educator and civil rights activist; adviser to FDR and Truman; founder, pres., Bethune-Cookman College.

Amelia Bloomer, 1818-94, (U.S.) suffragette, social reformer.

William Booth, 1829-1912, (Br.) founded Salvation Army.

John Brown, 1800-59, (U.S.) abolitionist who led murder of 5 pro-slavery men, was hanged.

Stokely Carmichael (Kwame Toure), 1941-98, (U.S.) black power activist, major proponent of Pan-Africanism. Prime Min. Black Panthers.

Frances Xavier (Mother) Cabrini, 1850-1917, (It.-U.S.) Italian-born nun; founded charitable institutions; first American canonized as a saint, 1946.

Carrie Chapman Catt, 1859-1947, (U.S.) suffragette.

Eldridge Cleaver, 1935-98, (U.S.) revolutionary social critic; former "minister of information" for Black Panthers; *Soul on Ice.*

Cesar Chavez, 1927-93, (U.S.) labor leader; helped establish United Farm Workers of America.

Clarence Darrow, 1857-1938, (U.S.) lawyer; defender of "underdog," opponent of capital punishment.

Ossie Davis, 1917-2005, (U.S.) black civil rights activist, actor, director.

Dorothy Day, 1897-1980, (U.S.) founder of Catholic Worker movement.

Eugene V. Debs, 1855-1926, (U.S.) labor leader; led Pullman strike, 1894; 4-time Socialist presidential candidate.

Vine Deloria, Jr., 1933-2005, (U.S) Native American activist and author; wrote *Custer Died for Your Sins.*

Dorothea Dix, 1802-87, (U.S.) crusader for mentally ill.

Thomas Dooley, 1927-61, (U.S.) "jungle doctor," noted for efforts to supply medical aid to developing countries.

Frederick Douglass, 1817-95, (U.S.) slave, author, editor, orator, diplomat; edited abolitionist weekly *The North Star.*

Marjory Stoneman Douglas, 1890-1998, (U.S.) writer and environmentalist; campaigned to save Florida Everglades.

Andrea Dworkin, 1946-2005, (U.S.) radical feminist and anti-pornography crusader.

Betty Friedan, 1921-2006 (U.S.), author, feminist; wrote *The Feminine Mystique.*

Medgar Evers, 1925-63, (U.S.) black civil rights leader; campaigned to register black voters; assassinated.

James Farmer, 1920-99, (U.S.) black civil rights leader; founded Congress of Racial Equality (CORE).

William Lloyd Garrison, 1805-79, (U.S.) abolitionist.

Emma Goldman, 1869-1940, (Russ.-U.S.) published anarchist *Mother Earth,* birth-control advocate.

Samuel Gompers, 1850-1924, (U.S.) labor leader. First president of the American Federation of Labor (AFL).

Prince Hall, 1735-1807, (U.S.) activist; founded black Freemasonry; served in American Revolutionary war.

Michael Harrington, 1928-89, (U.S.) exposed poverty in affluent U.S. in *The Other America,* 1963.

Sidney Hillman, 1887-1946, (U.S.) labor leader; helped organize CIO.

Samuel G. Howe, 1801-76, (U.S.) social reformer; changed public attitudes toward the handicapped.

Helen Keller, 1880-1968, (U.S.) crusader for better treatment for the handicapped; deaf and blind herself.

Coretta Scott King, 1927-2006, (U.S.) black civil rights leader; wife of Rev. Martin Luther King Jr.

Rev. Martin Luther King Jr., 1929-68, (U.S.) civil rights leader; led 1955-56 Montgomery, AL, boycott; founder, pres., Southern Christian Leadership Conference, 1957; Nobel laureate (1964); assassinated.

Malcolm X (Little), 1925-65, (U.S.) Black Muslim, black nationalist leader; promoted black pride; assassinated.

Maggie Kuhn, 1905-95, (U.S.) founded Gray Panthers, 1970.

William Kunstler, 1919-95, (U.S.) civil liberties attorney.

John L. Lewis, 1880-1969, (U.S.) labor leader; headed United Mine Workers, 1920-60.

Karl Menninger, 1893-1990, (U.S.) with brother William founded Menninger Clinic and Menninger Foundation.

Lucretia Mott, 1793-1880, (U.S.) reformer, pioneer feminist.

Philip Murray, 1886-1952, (U.S.) Scottish-born labor leader.

Huey P. Newton, 1942-89, (U.S.) co-founded Black Panther Party, 1966.

Florence Nightingale, 1820-1910, (Br.) founder of modern nursing.

Rosa Parks,1913-2005, (U.S.), black civil rights activist; her actions sparked 1955-56 Montgomery bus boycott.

Emmeline Pankhurst, 1858-1928, (Br.) woman suffragist.

A. Philip Randolph, 1889-1979, (U.S.) organized Brotherhood of Sleeping Car Porters, 1925; an organizer of 1941 and 1963 March on Washington movements.

Walter Reuther, 1907-70, (U.S.) labor leader; headed UAW.

Jacob Riis, 1849-1914, (U.S.) crusader for urban reforms.

Paul Robeson, 1898-1976, (U.S.) actor, singer, black civil rights activist.

Bayard Rustin, 1910-87, (U.S.) an organizer of the 1963 March on Washington; exec. director, A. Philip Randolph Institute.

Margaret Sanger, 1883-1966, (U.S.) social reformer; pioneered the birth-control movement.

Earl of Shaftesbury (A. A. Cooper), 1801-85, (Br.) social reformer.

Elizabeth Cady Stanton, 1815-1902, (U.S.) woman suffrage pioneer.

Lucy Stone, 1818-93, (U.S.) feminist, abolitionist.

Mother Teresa of Calcutta, 1910-97, (Alban.) nun; founded order to care for sick, dying poor; 1979 Nobel Peace Prize.

Willard Townsend, 1895-1957, (U.S.) organized the United Transport Service Employees (redcaps), 1935.

Sojourner Truth (Isabella Baumfree), 1797-1883, (U.S.) preacher, abolitionist; worked for black educ. opportunity.

Harriet Tubman, 1823-1913, (U.S.) prominent figure in the Underground Railroad, which helped runaway slaves in the south reach safety in the north; nurse and spy for Union Army in the Civil War.

Nat Turner, 1800-31, (U.S.) slave who led the most significant of more than 200 slave revolts in U.S., in Southampton, VA; hanged.

Philip Vera Cruz, 1905-94, (Filipino-U.S.) helped to found the United Farm Workers Union.

William Wilberforce, 1759-1833, (Br.) social reformer; prominent in struggle to abolish the slave trade.

Frances E. Willard, 1839-98, (U.S.) temperance, women's rights leader.

Mary Wollstonecraft, 1759-97, (Br.) wrote *Vindication of the Rights of Women.*

Writers of the Present

Name (Birthplace)	Birthdate
Chinua Achebe (Ogidi, Nigeria)	11/16/30
Richard Adams (Newbury, Eng.)	5/9/20
Edward Albee (Wash., DC)	3/12/28
Mitch Albom (Passaic, NJ)	5/23/58
Isabel Allende (Lima, Peru)	8/2/42
Dorothy Allison (Greenville, SC)	4/11/49
Martin Amis (Oxford, Eng.)	8/25/49
Maya Angelou (St. Louis, MO)	4/4/28
Piers Anthony (Oxford, Eng.)	8/6/34
Jeffrey Archer (Somerset, Eng.)	4/15/40
Oscar Arias Sanchez (Heredia, Costa Rica)	9/13/41
John Ashbery (Rochester, NY)	7/28/27
Margaret Atwood (Ottawa, Ont.)	11/18/39
David Auburn (Chicago)	1969
Louis Auchincloss (Lawrence, NY)	9/27/17
Jean Auel (Chicago)	2/18/36

Name (Birthplace)	Birthdate
Paul Auster (Newark, NJ)	2/3/47
Alan Ayckbourn (Hampstead, Eng.)	4/12/39
Nicholson Baker (Rochester, NY)	1/7/57
David Baldacci (Richmond, VA)	1960
Russell Banks (Newton, MA)	3/28/40
John Barth (Cambridge, MD)	5/27/30
Ann Beattie (Wash., DC)	9/8/47
John Berendt (Syracuse, NY)	12/5/39
Thomas Berger (Cincinnati, OH)	7/20/24
Maeve Binchy (Dalkey, Ireland)	3/28/40
Judy Blume (Elizabeth, NJ)	2/12/38
T. Coraghessan Boyle (Peekskill, NY)	12/2/48
Ray Bradbury (Waukegan, IL)	8/22/20
Barbara Taylor Bradford (Leeds, Eng.)	5/10/33
Christopher Bram (Buffalo, NY)	2/22/52
Dan Brown (Exeter, NH)	6/22/64

Name (Birthplace)	Birthdate
Rita Mae Brown (Hanover, PA)	11/28/44
Christopher Buckley (NYC)	9/28/52
James Lee Burke (Houston, TX)	12/5/36
Augusten Burroughs (Pittsburgh, PA)	1965
Robert Olen Butler (Granite City, IL)	1/20/45
A. S. Byatt (Sheffield, England)	8/24/36
Hortense Calisher (NYC)	12/20/11
Ethan Canin (Ann Arbor, MI)	7/19/60
Peter Carey (Bacchus-Marsh, Victoria, Australia)	5/7/43
Caleb Carr (NYC)	5/19/63
Michael Chabon (Wash., DC)	5/19/63
Tracy Chevalier (Wash., DC)	10/62
Sandra Cisneros (Chicago)	12/20/54
Tom Clancy (Baltimore, MD)	4/12/47
Mary Higgins Clark (NYC)	12/24/29
Arthur C. Clarke (Minehead, Eng.)	12/16/29
Beverly Cleary (McMinnville, OR)	4/12/16
Paulo Coelho (Rio de Janeiro, Brazil)	8/24/47
J(ohn) M(axwell) Coetzee (Capetown, S. Africa)	2/9/40
Billy Collins (NYC)	3/22/41
Jackie Collins (London, Eng.)	10/4/41
Evan S. Connell (Kansas City, MO)	8/17/24
Pat Conroy (Atlanta, GA)	10/26/45
Robin Cook (NYC)	5/4/40
Patricia Cornwell (Miami, FL)	6/9/56
Harry Crews (Alma, GA)	6/6/35
Michael Crichton (Chicago)	10/23/42
Michael Cunningham (Cincinnati, Ohio)	11/6/52
Don DeLillo (NYC)	11/20/36
Nelson DeMille (NYC)	8/23/43
Joan Didion (Sacramento, CA)	12/5/34
E. L. Doctorow (NYC)	1/6/31
Takako Doi (Hyogo, Jap.)	11/30/28
Rita Dove (Akron, OH)	8/28/52
Roddy Doyle (Dublin, Ireland)	5/5/58
Umberto Eco (Alessandria, Italy)	1/5/32
Bret Easton Ellis (Los Angeles,)	3/7/64
Dave Eggers (Chicago)	3/12/70
James Ellroy (Los Angeles)	3/4/48
Louise Erdrich (Little Falls, MN)	7/6/54
Laura Esquivel (Mexico City, Mexico)	9/30/51
Jeffrey Eugenides (Detroit, MI)	1960
Lawrence Ferlinghetti (Yonkers, NY)	3/24/19
Helen Fielding (Morley, Yorkshire, Eng.)	2/19/58
Ken Follet (Cardiff, Wales)	6/5/49
Dario Fo (San Giano, Italy)	3/26/26
Horton Foote (Wharton, TX)	3/14/16
Richard Ford (Jackson, MS)	2/16/44
Frederick Forsyth (Ashford, Eng.)	8/25/38
Paula Fox (NYC)	4/22/23
Dick Francis (Tenby, Pembrokeshire, Wales)	10/31/20
Jonathan Franzen (Western Springs, IL)	8/17/59
Michael Frayn (London, Eng.)	9/8/33
Charles Frazier (Asheville, NC)	11/4/50
Marilyn French (NYC)	11/21/29
Brian Friel (Omagh, County Tyrone, N. Ireland)	1/9/29
Carlos Fuentes (Panama City, Panama)	11/11/28
Ernest J. Gaines (Oscar, LA)	1/15/33
Gabriel Garcia Marquez (Aracataca, Colombia)	3/6/28
Frank Gilroy (Bronx, NY)	10/13/25
Gail Godwin (Birmingham, AL)	6/18/37
William Goldman (Highland Park, IL)	8/12/31
Nadine Gordimer (Springs, S. Africa)	11/20/23
Mary Gordon (Far Rockaway, Long Island, NY)	12/8/49
Sue Grafton (Louisville, KY)	4/24/40
Günter Grass (Danzig, now Gdansk, Poland)	10/16/27
Shirley Ann Grau (New Orleans, LA)	7/8/29
John Grisham (Jonesboro, AR)	2/8/55
John Guare (NYC)	2/5/38
David Handler (Los Angeles)	9/14/52
David Hare (St. Leonards, Sussex, Eng.)	6/5/47
Jim Harrison (Grayling, MI)	12/11/37
Robert Hass (San Francisco, CA)	3/1/41
Vaclav Havel (Prague, Czech.)	10/5/36
Seamus Heaney (Mossbaum, Cty. Derry, N. Ire.)	4/13/39
Mark Helprin (NYC)	6/28/47
Carl Hiaasen (S. Florida)	3/12/53
Oscar Hijuelos (NYC)	8/24/51
Tony Hillerman (Sacred Heart, OK)	5/27/25
S. E. Hinton (Tulsa, OK)	7/22/50

Name (Birthplace)	Birthdate
Alice Hoffman (NYC)	3/16/52
Khaled Hosseini (Afghanistan)	1965
John Irving (Exeter, NH)	3/2/42
Kazuo Ishiguro (Nagasaki, Japan)	11/8/54
John Jakes (Chicago)	3/31/32
P. D. James (Oxford, Eng.)	8/3/20
Ha Jin (Liaoning, China)	2/21/56
Erica Jong (NYC)	3/26/42
Garrison Keillor (Anoka, MN)	8/7/42
Thomas Keneally (Sydney, Austral.)	10/7/35
William Kennedy (Albany, NY)	1/16/28
Sue Monk Kidd (Sylvester, GA)	8/12/48
Jamaica Kincaid (St. Johns, Antigua)	5/25/49
Stephen King (Portland, ME)	9/21/47
Barbara Kingsolver (Annapolis, MD)	4/8/55
Maxine Hong Kingston (Stockton, CA)	10/27/40
Galway Kinnell (Providence, RI)	2/1/27
Dean Koontz (Everett, PA)	7/9/45
Ted Kooser (Ames, IA)	4/25/39
Jon Krakauer (Brookline, MA)	4/12/54
Judith Krantz (NYC)	1/9/28
Maxine Kumin (Philadelphia, PA)	6/6/25
Milan Kundera (Brno, Czechoslovakia)	4/1/29
Tony Kushner (NYC)	7/16/56
David Leavitt (Pittsburgh, PA)	6/23/61
John Le Carré (Poole, Eng.)	10/19/31
Harper Lee (Monroeville, AL)	4/28/26
Ursula K. Le Guin (Berkeley, CA)	10/21/29
Elmore Leonard (New Orleans, LA)	10/11/25
Doris Lessing (Kermanshah, Persia)	10/22/19
Jonathan Lethem (Bklyn, NY)	2/19/64
Ira Levin (NYC)	8/27/29
David Lodge (South London, Eng.)	1/28/35
Alison Lurie (Chicago)	9/3/26
Gregory Maguire (Albany, NY)	6/9/54
Norman Mailer (Long Branch, NJ)	1/31/23
Thomas Mallon (Glen Cove, Long Island, NY)	11/2/51
David Mamet (Chicago)	11/30/47
Yann Martel (Salamanca, Spain)	6/25/63
Bobbie Ann Mason (nr. Mayfield, KY)	5/1/40
Peter Matthiessen (NYC)	5/22/27
Armistead Maupin (Wash., DC)	4/13/44
Cormac McCarthy (Providence, RI)	7/20/33
Frank McCourt (Bklyn, NY)	8/19/30
Colleen McCullough (Wellington, N.S.W., Austral.)	6/1/37
Alice McDermott (Bklyn, NY)	6/27/53
Ian McEwan (Aldershot, England)	6/21/48
Thomas McGuane (Wyandotte, MI)	12/11/39
Terry McMillan (Port Huron, MI)	10/18/51
Larry McMurtry (Wichita Falls, TX)	6/3/36
Terrence McNally (St. Petersburg, FL)	11/3/39
John McPhee (Princeton, NJ)	3/8/31
W(illiam) S(tanley) Merwin (NYC)	9/30/27
Toni Morrison (Lorain, OH)	2/18/31
Walter Mosley (Los Angeles, CA)	1/12/52
Andrew Motion (London)	10/26/52
Bharati Mukherjee (Calcutta, India)	7/27/40
Alice Munro (Wingham, Ont.)	7/10/31
Haruki Murakami (Kyoto, Japan)	1/12/49
V. S. Naipaul (Chaguanas, Trinidad)	8/17/32
Joyce Carol Oates (Lockport, NY)	6/16/38
Edna O'Brien (Tuamgraney, Ir.)	12/15/32
Tim O'Brien (Austin, MN)	10/1/46
Kenzaburo Oe (Uchiko, Japan)	1/31/35
Michael Ondaatje (Colombo, Sri Lanka)	9/12/43
Cynthia Ozick (NYC)	4/17/28
Orhan Pamuk (Istanbul, Turk.)	6/7/52
Robert B. Parker (Springfield, MA)	9/17/32
Suzan-Lori Parks (Fort Knox, KY)	5/10/63
James Patterson (Newburgh, NY)	3/22/47
Jodi Picoult (NYC)	5/19/66
Marge Piercy (Detroit, MI)	3/31/36
Robert Pinsky (Long Branch, NJ)	10/20/40
Harold Pinter (Hackney, East London, Eng.)	10/10/30
Richard Powers (Evanston, IL)	6/18/57
Reynolds Price (Macon, NC)	2/1/33
Richard Price (Bronx, NY)	10/12/49
E. Annie Proulx (Norwich, CT)	8/22/35
Philip Pullman (Norwich, Eng.)	10/19/46
Thomas Pynchon (Glen Cove, Long Island, NY)	5/8/37

Name (Birthplace)	Birthdate
David Rabe (Dubuque, IA)	3/10/40
Ishmael Reed (Chattanooga, TN)	2/22/38
Ruth Rendell (London, England)	2/17/30
Anne Rice (New Orleans, LA)	10/4/41
Adrienne Rich (Baltimore, MD)	5/16/29
Nora Roberts (Wash., DC)	10/10/50
Marilyn Robinson (Sandpoint, IL)	1944
Philip Roth (Newark, NJ)	3/19/33
J.K. Rowling (Chipping Sodbury, Eng.)	7/31/65
Norman Rush (Oakland, CA)	10/24/33
Salman Rushdie (Bombay, India)	6/19/47
Richard Russo (Johnstown, NY)	7/15/49
J. D. Salinger (NYC)	1/1/19
Jose Saramago (Azinhaga, Portugal)	11/16/22
Alice Sebold (Madison, WI)	1963
David Sedaris (Johnson City, NY)	12/26/56
Vikram Seth (Calcutta, India)	6/20/52
Sam Shepard (Ft. Sheridan, IL)	11/5/43
Neil Simon (Bronx, NY)	7/4/27
Jane Smiley (Los Angeles, CA)	9/26/49
Aleksandr Solzhenitsyn (Kislovodsk, Russia)	12/11/18
Wole Soyinka (Abeokuta, Nigeria)	7/13/34
Nicholas Sparks (Omaha, NE)	12/31/65
Danielle Steel (NYC)	8/14/47
Richard Stern (NYC)	2/25/28
Mary Stewart (Sunderland, Eng.)	9/17/16

Name (Birthplace)	Birthdate
R(obert) L(awrence) Stine (Columbus, OH)	10/8/43
Tom Stoppard (Zlin, Czech.)	7/3/37
Mark Strand (P.E.I., Can.)	4/11/34
Wislawa Szymborska (Kornik, Pol.)	7/2/23
Amy Tan (Oakland, CA)	2/19/52
Donna Tartt (Greenwood, MS)	12/23/63
Paul Theroux (Medford, MA)	4/10/41
Calvin Trillin (Kansas City, MO)	12/5/35
Scott F. Turow (Chicago)	4/12/49
Anne Tyler (Minneapolis, MN)	10/25/41
John Updike (Shillington, PA)	3/18/32
Mario Vargas Llosa (Arequipa, Peru)	3/28/36
Gore Vidal (West Point, NY)	10/3/25
Paula Vogel (Wash., DC)	11/16/51
Derek Walcott (Castries, Saint Lucia)	1/23/30
Alice Walker (Eatonton, GA)	2/9/44
Robert James Waller (Rockford, IA)	8/1/39
Joseph Wambaugh (East Pittsburgh, PA)	1/22/37
Eli Wiesel (Sighet, Romania)	9/30/28
Edmund White (Cincinnati, OH)	1/19/40
Lanford Wilson (Lebanon, MO)	4/13/37
Tom Wolfe (Richmond, VA)	3/2/31
Tobias Wolff (Birmingham, AL)	6/19/45
Herman Wouk (NYC)	5/27/15
Yevgeny Yevtushenko (Irkutsk, Russia)	7/18/33

Writers of the Past

See also Journalists of the Past, and Greeks and Romans in Historical Figures chapter.

Alice Adams, 1926-99, (U.S.) novelist, short-story writer. *Superior Woman.*

James Agee, 1909-55, (U.S.) novelist. *A Death in the Family.*

S(hmuel) Y(osef)Agnon, 1888-1970, (Is.) Hebrew novelist. *Only Yesterday.*

Conrad Aiken, 1889-1973, (U.S.) poet, critic. *Ushant.*

Anna Akhmatova, 1889-1966, (Russ.) poet. *Requiem.*

Louisa May Alcott, 1832-88, (U.S.) novelist. *Little Women.*

Sholom Aleichem, 1859-1916, (Russ.) Yiddish writer. *Tevye's Daughters, The Old Country.*

Vicente Aleixandre, 1898-1984, (Sp.) poet. *La destrucción o el amor, Dialogolos del conocimiento.*

Horatio Alger, 1832-1899, (U.S.) "rags-to-riches" books.

Jorge Amado, 1912-2001, (Brazil) novelist. *Dona Flor and Her Two Husbands, The Violent Land.*

Eric Ambler, 1909-98, (Br.) suspense novelist. *A Coffin for Dimitrios.*

Kingsley Amis, 1922-95, (Br.) novelist, critic. *Lucky Jim.*

Hans Christian Andersen, 1805-75, (Dan.) author of fairy tales. *The Ugly Duckling.*

Maxwell Anderson, 1888-1959, (U.S.) playwright. *What Price Glory?, High Tor, Winterset, Key Largo.*

Sherwood Anderson, 1876-1941, (U.S.) short-story writer. "Death in the Woods;" *Winesburg, Ohio.*

Reinaldo Arenas, 1943-1990, (Cuba) short-story writer, novelist. *Before Night Falls.*

Ludovico Ariosto, 1474-1533, (It.) poet. *Orlando Furioso.*

Matthew Arnold, 1822-88, (Br.) poet, critic. "Thrysis," "Dover Beach," "Culture and Anarchy."

Isaac Asimov, 1920-92, (U.S.) versatile writer, espec. of science-fiction. *I Robot.*

Miguel Angel Asturias, 1899-1974, (Guatemala) novelist. *El Señor Presidente.*

W(ystan) H(ugh) Auden, 1907-73, (Br.) poet, playwright, literary critic. "The Age of Anxiety."

Jane Austen, 1775-1817, (Br.) novelist. *Pride and Prejudice, Sense and Sensibility, Emma, Mansfield Park.*

Isaac Babel, 1894-1941, (Russ.) short-story writer, playwright. *Odessa Tales, Red Cavalry.*

James Baldwin, 1924-87, (U.S.) author, playwright. *The Fire Next Time, Blues for Mister Charlie.*

Honoré de Balzac, 1799-1850, (Fr.) novelist. *Le Père Goriot, Cousine Bette, Eugénie Grandet.*

James M. Barrie, 1860-1937, (Br.) playwright, novelist. *Peter Pan, Dear Brutus, What Every Woman Knows.*

Charles Baudelaire, 1821-67, (Fr.) poet. *Les Fleurs du Mal.*

L(yman) Frank Baum, 1856-1919, (U.S.) *Wizard of Oz* series.

Simone de Beauvoir, 1908-86, (Fr.) novelist, essayist. *The Second Sex, Memoirs of a Dutiful Daughter.*

Samuel Beckett, 1906-89, (Ir.) novelist, playwright. *Waiting for Godot, Endgame* (plays); *Murphy, Watt, Molloy* (novels).

Brendan Behan, 1923-64, (Ir.) playwright. *The Quare Fellow, The Hostage, Borstal Boy.*

Saul Bellow, 1915-2005, (U.S.) novelist. *The Adventures of Augie March, Humboldt's Gift.*

Robert Benchley, 1889-1945, (U.S.) humorist.

Stephen Vincent Benét, 1898-1943, (U.S.) poet, novelist. *John Brown's Body.*

Stan Berenstain 1923-2005, (U.S.) co-writer and illustrator of *Berenstain Bears* series of children's books.

John Berryman, 1914-72, (U.S.) poet. *Homage to Mistress Bradstreet.*

Ambrose Bierce, 1842-1914, (U.S.) short-story writer, journalist. *In the Midst of Life, The Devil's Dictionary.*

Elizabeth Bishop, 1911-79, (U.S.) poet. *North and South—A Cold Spring.*

William Blake, 1757-1827, (Br.) poet, artist. *Songs of Innocence, Songs of Experience.*

Aleksandr Blok, 1880-1921, (Russ.) poet. "The Twelve", "The Scythians."

Giovanni Boccaccio, 1313-75, (It.) poet. *Decameron.*

Heinrich Böll, 1917-85, (Ger.) novelist, short-story writer. *Group Portrait With Lady.*

Jorge Luis Borges, 1900-86, (Arg.) short-story writer, poet, essayist. *Labyrinths.*

James Boswell, 1740-95, (Sc.) biographer. *The Life of Samuel Johnson.*

Pierre Boulle, 1913-94, (Fr.) novelist. *The Bridge Over the River Kwai, Planet of the Apes.*

Paul Bowles, 1910-99, (U.S.) novelist, short-story writer. *The Sheltering Sky*

Anne Bradstreet, c1612-72, (U.S.) poet. *The Tenth Muse Lately Sprung Up in America.*

Bertolt Brecht, 1898-1956, (Ger.) dramatist, poet. *The Threepenny Opera, Mother Courage and Her Children.*

Charlotte Brontë, 1816-55, (Br.) novelist. *Jane Eyre.*

Emily Brontë, 1818-48, (Br.) novelist. *Wuthering Heights.*

Elizabeth Barrett Browning, 1806-61, (Br.) poet. *Sonnets From the Portuguese, Aurora Leigh.*

Joseph Brodsky, 1940-96, (Russ.-U.S.) poet. *A Part of Speech, Less Than One, To Urania.*

Sterling A. Brown, 1901-89, (U.S.) poet, literature professor. *Southern Road.*

William Wells Brown, 1815-84, (U.S.) writer, memoirist, first African American to publish a novel, *Clotel,* 1853.

Robert Browning, 1812-89, (Br.) poet. "My Last Duchess," "Fra Lippo Lippi," *The Ring and The Book.*

Pearl S. Buck, 1892-1973, (U.S.) novelist. *The Good Earth.*

Mikhail Bulgakov, 1891-1940, (Russ.) novelist, playwright. *The Heart of a Dog, The Master and Margarita.*

John Bunyan, 1628-88, (Br.) writer. *Pilgrim's Progress.*

Anthony Burgess, 1917-93, (Br.) author. *A Clockwork Orange.*

Frances Hodgson Burnett, 1849-1924, (Br.-U.S.) novelist. *The Secret Garden.*

Robert Burns, 1759-96, (Sc.) poet. "Flow Gently, Sweet Afton," "My Heart's in the Highlands," "Auld Lang Syne."

Edgar Rice Burroughs, 1875-1950, (U.S.) "Tarzan" books.

William S. Burroughs, 1914-97, (U.S.) novelist. *Naked Lunch.*

George Gordon, Lord Byron, 1788-1824, (Br.) poet. *Don Juan, Childe Harold, Manfred, Cain.*

Pedro Calderon de la Barca, 1600-81, (Sp.) playwright. *Life Is a Dream.*

Italo Calvino, 1923-85, (It.) novelist, short-story writer. *If on a Winter's Night a Traveler.*

Luis Vaz de Camoes, 1524?-80 (Port.) poet. *The Lusiads.*

Albert Camus, 1913-60, (Fr.) writer. *The Stranger, The Fall.*

Elias Canetti, 1905-94, (Bulg.) novelist, essayist. *Auto-Da-Fe.*

Karel Capek, 1890-1938, (Czech.) playwright, novelist, essayist. *R.U.R. (Rossum's Universal Robots).*

Truman Capote, 1924-84, (U.S.) author. *Other Voices, Other Rooms, Breakfast at Tiffany's, In Cold Blood.*

Lewis Carroll (Charles Dodgson), 1832-98, (Br.) mathematician. *Alice's Adventures in Wonderland.*

Giacomo Casanova, 1725-98, (It.) adventurer, memoirist.

Willa Cather, 1873-1947, (U.S.) novelist. *O Pioneers!, My Ántonia, Death Comes for the Archbishop.*

Constantine Cavafy, 1863-1933, (Gr.) poet. "Ithaka," "Sensual Pleasures."

Camilo Jose Cela, 1916-2001, (Sp.) novelist. *The Family of Pascual Duarte, The Hive.*

Miguel de Cervantes Saavedra, 1547-1616, (Sp.) novelist, dramatist, poet. *Don Quixote.*

Raymond Chandler, 1888-1959, (U.S.) writer of detective fiction. Philip Marlowe series.

Geoffrey Chaucer, c1340-1400, (Br.) poet. *The Canterbury Tales, Troilus and Criseyde.*

John Cheever, 1912-82, (U.S.) novelist, short-story writer. *The Wapshot Scandal,* "The Country Husband."

Anton Chekhov, 1860-1904, (Russ.) short-story writer, dramatist. *Uncle Vanya, The Cherry Orchard, The Three Sisters.*

Charles Waddell Chesnutt, 1858-1932, (U.S.) author known for his short stories, such as in *The Conjure Woman* (1899).

G(ilbert) K(eith) Chesterton, 1874-1936, (Br.) critic, novelist, relig. apologist. Father Brown series of mysteries.

Kate Chopin, 1851-1904, (U.S.) writer. *The Awakening.*

Agatha Christie, 1890-1976, (Br.) mystery writer; created Miss Marple, Hercule Poirot; *And Then There Were None, Murder on the Orient Express, Murder of Roger Ackroyd.*

James Clavell, 1924-94, (Br.-U.S.) novelist. *Shogun, King Rat.*

Jean Cocteau, 1889-1963, (Fr.) writer, visual artist, filmmaker. *The Beauty and the Beast, Les Enfants Terribles.*

Samuel Taylor Coleridge, 1772-1834, (Br.) poet, critic. "Kubla Khan," "The Rime of the Ancient Mariner."

(Sidonie) Colette, 1873-1954, (Fr.) novelist. *Claudine, Gigi.*

Wilkie Collins, 1824-89, (Br.) novelist. *The Moonstone.*

Joseph Conrad, 1857-1924, (Br.) novelist. *Lord Jim, Heart of Darkness, The Secret Agent.*

James Fenimore Cooper, 1789-1851, (U.S.) novelist. *Leatherstocking Tales, The Last of the Mohicans.*

Pierre Corneille, 1606-84, (Fr.) dramatist. *Medeé, Le Cid.*

Hart Crane, 1899-1932, (U.S.) poet. "The Bridge."

Stephen Crane, 1871-1900, (U.S.) novelist, short-story writer. *The Red Badge of Courage,* "The Open Boat."

Countee Cullen, 1903-46, (U.S.) poet, prominent in the Harlem Renaissance of the 1920s; *The Black Christ.*

E. E. Cummings, 1894-1962, (U.S.) poet. *Tulips and Chimneys.*

Roald Dahl, 1916-90, (Br.-U.S.) writer. *Charlie and the Chocolate Factory, James and the Giant Peach.*

Gabriele D'Annunzio, 1863-1938, (It.) poet, novelist, dramatist. *The Child of Pleasure, The Intruder, The Victim.*

Dante Alighieri, 1265-1321, (It.) poet. *The Divine Comedy.*

Robertson Davies, 1913-95, (Can.) novelist, playwright, essayist. Salterton, Deptford, and Cornish trilogies.

Daniel Defoe, 1660-1731, (Br.) writer. *Robinson Crusoe, Moll Flanders, Journal of the Plague Year.*

Charles Dickens, 1812-70, (Br.) novelist. *David Copperfield, Oliver Twist, Great Expectations, A Tale of Two Cities.*

Philip K. Dick, 1928-82, (U.S.) science fiction writer. *Do Androids Dream of Electric Sheep?*

James Dickey, 1923-1997, (U.S.) poet, novelist. *Deliverance.*

Emily Dickinson, 1830-86, (U.S.) lyric poet. "Because I could not stop for Death . . .," "Success is counted sweetest . . ."

Isak Dinesen (Karen Blixen), 1885-1962, (Dan.) author. *Out of Africa, Seven Gothic Tales, Winter's Tales.*

John Donne, 1573-1631, (Br.) poet. *Songs and Sonnets.*

José Donoso, 1924-96, (Chil.) surreal novelist and short-story writer. *The Obscene Bird of Night.*

John Dos Passos, 1896-1970, (U.S.) novelist. *U.S.A.*

Fyodor Dostoyevsky, 1821-81, (Russ.) novelist. *Crime and Punishment, The Brothers Karamazov, The Possessed.*

Arthur Conan Doyle, 1859-1930, (Br.) novelist. Sherlock Holmes mystery stories.

Theodore Dreiser, 1871-1945, (U.S.) novelist. *An American Tragedy, Sister Carrie.*

John Dryden, 1631-1700, (Br.) poet, dramatist, critic. *All for Love, Mac Flecknoe, Absalom and Achitophel.*

Alexandre Dumas, 1802-70, (Fr.) novelist, dramatist. *The Three Musketeers, The Count of Monte Cristo.*

Alexandre Dumas (fils), 1824-95, (Fr.) dramatist, novelist. *La Dame aux Camélias, Le Demi-Monde.*

Paul Laurence Dunbar, 1872-1906, (U.S.) poet, novelist; won fame with *Lyrics of Lowly Life,* 1896.

Lawrence Durrell, 1912-90, (Br.) novelist, poet. *Alexandria Quartet.*

Ilya G. Ehrenburg, 1891-1967, (Russ.) writer. *The Thaw.*

George Eliot (Mary Ann Evans or Marian Evans), 1819-80, (Br.) novelist. *Silas Marner, Middlemarch.*

T(homas) S(tearns) Eliot, 1888-1965, (Br.) poet, critic. *The Waste Land,* "The Love Song of J. Alfred Prufrock."

Stanley Elkin, 1930-95, (U.S.) novelist, short story writer. *George Mills.*

Ralph Ellison, 1914-94, (U.S.) writer. *Invisible Man.*

Ralph Waldo Emerson, 1803-82, (U.S.) poet, essayist. "Brahma," "Nature," "The Over-Soul," "Self-Reliance."

James T. Farrell, 1904-79, (U.S.) novelist. *Studs Lonigan.*

William Faulkner, 1897-1962, (U.S.) novelist. *Sanctuary, Light in August, The Sound and the Fury, Absalom, Absalom!*

Edna Ferber, 1887-1968, (U.S.) novelist, short-story writer, playwright. *So Big, Cimarron, Show Boat.*

Henry Fielding, 1707-54, (Br.) novelist. *Tom Jones.*

F(rancis) Scott Fitzgerald, 1896-1940, (U.S.) short-story writer, novelist. *The Great Gatsby, Tender Is the Night.*

Gustave Flaubert, 1821-80, (Fr.) novelist. *Madame Bovary.*

Ian Fleming, 1908-64, (Br.) novelist; James Bond spy thrillers. *Dr. No, Goldfinger.*

Ford Madox Ford, 1873-1939, (Br.) novelist, critic, poet. *The Good Soldier.*

C(ecil) S(cott) Forester, 1899-1966, (Br.) writer. Horatio Hornblower books.

E(dward) M(organ) Forster, 1879-1970, (Br.) novelist. *A Passage to India, Howards End.*

Anatole France, 1844-1924, (Fr.) writer. *Penguin Island, My Friend's Book, The Crime of Sylvestre Bonnard.*

Robert Frost, 1874-1963, (U.S.) poet. "Birches," "Fire and Ice," "Stopping by Woods on a Snowy Evening."

William Gaddis, 1922-98, (U.S.) novelist. *The Recognitions.*

John Galsworthy, 1867-1933, (Br.) novelist, dramatist. *The Forsyte Saga.*

Federico Garcia Lorca, 1898-1936, (Sp.) poet, dramatist. *Blood Wedding.*

Erle Stanley Gardner, 1889-1970, (U.S.) mystery writer; created Perry Mason.

Jean Genet, 1911-86, (Fr.) playwright, novelist. *The Maids.*

Kahlil Gibran, 1883-1931, (Lebanese-U.S.) mystical novelist, essayist, poet. *The Prophet.*

André Gide, 1869-1951, (Fr.) writer. *The Immoralist, The Pastoral Symphony, Strait Is the Gate.*

Allen Ginsberg, 1926-1997, (U.S.) Beat poet. "Howl."

Jean Giraudoux, 1882-1944, (Fr.) novelist, dramatist. *Electra, The Madwoman of Chaillot, Ondine, Tiger at the Gate.*

Johann Wolfgang von Goethe, 1749-1832, (Ger.) poet, dramatist, novelist. *Faust, Sorrows of Young Werther.*

Nikolai Gogol, 1809-52, (Russ.) short-story writer, dramatist, novelist. *Dead Souls, The Inspector General.*

William Golding, 1911-93, (Br.) novelist. *Lord of the Flies.*

Oliver Goldsmith, 1728-74, (Br.-Ir.) dramatist, novelist. *The Vicar of Wakefield, She Stoops to Conquer.*

Maxim Gorky, 1868-1936, (Russ.) dramatist, novelist. *The Lower Depths.*

Robert Graves, 1895-1985, (Br.) poet, classical scholar, novelist. *I, Claudius; The White Goddess.*

Thomas Gray, 1716-71, (Br.) poet. "Elegy Written in a Country Churchyard," "The Progress of Poesy."

Julien Green, 1900-98, (U.S.-Fr.) expatriate American, French novelist. *Moira, Each Man in His Darkness.*

Graham Greene, 1904-91, (Br.) novelist. *The Power and the Glory, The Heart of the Matter, The Ministry of Fear.*

Zane Grey, 1872-1939, (U.S.) writer of Western stories.

Jakob Grimm, 1785-1863, (Ger.) philologist, folklorist; with brother **Wilhelm,** 1786-1859, collected *Grimm's Fairy Tales.*

Alex Haley, 1921-92, (U.S.) author. *Roots.*

Dashiell Hammett, 1894-1961, (U.S.) detective-story writer; created Sam Spade. *The Maltese Falcon, The Thin Man.*

Jupiter Hammon, c1720-1800, (U.S.) poet; first African American to have his works published, 1761.

Knut Hamsun, 1859-1952 (Nor.) novelist. *Hunger.*

Lorraine Hansberry, 1930-65, (U.S.) playwright; won New York Drama Critics Circle Award, 1959; *A Raisin in the Sun.*

Thomas Hardy, 1840-1928, (Br.) novelist, poet. *The Return of the Native, Tess of the D'Urbervilles, Jude the Obscure.*

Joel Chandler Harris, 1848-1908, (U.S.) Uncle Remus stories.

Moss Hart, 1904-61, (U.S.) playwright. *Once in a Lifetime, You Can't Take It With You, The Man Who Came to Dinner.*

Bret Harte, 1836-1902, (U.S.) short-story writer, poet. *The Luck of Roaring Camp.*

Jaroslav Hasek, 1883-1923, (Czech.) writer, playwright. *The Good Soldier Schweik.*

John Hawkes, 1925-98, (U.S.) experimental fiction writer. *The Goose on the Grave, Blood Oranges.*

Nathaniel Hawthorne, 1804-64, (U.S.) novelist, short-story writer. *The Scarlet Letter,* "Young Goodman Brown."

Heinrich Heine, 1797-1856, (Ger.) poet. *Book of Songs.*

Robert Heinlein, 1907-88, (U.S.) science fiction writer. *Stranger in a Strange Land.*

Joseph Heller, 1923-99, (U.S.) novelist. *Catch-22.*

Lillian Hellman, 1905-84, (U.S.) playwright, author of memoirs. *The Little Foxes, An Unfinished Woman, Pentimento.*

Ernest Hemingway, 1899-1961, (U.S.) novelist, short-story writer. *A Farewell to Arms, For Whom the Bell Tolls.*

O. Henry (W. S. Porter), 1862-1910, (U.S.) short-story writer. "The Gift of the Magi."

George Herbert, 1593-1633, (Br.) poet. "The Altar," "Easter Wings."

Zbigniew Herbert, 1924-98, (Pol.) poet. "Apollo and Marsyas."

Robert Herrick, 1591-1674, (Br.) poet. "To the Virgins to Make Much of Time."

John Hersey, 1914-93, (U.S.) novelist, journalist. *Hiroshima, A Bell for Adano.*

Hermann Hesse, 1877-1962, (Ger.) novelist, poet. *Death and the Lover, Steppenwolf, Siddhartha.*

James Hilton, 1900-54, (Br.) novelist. *Lost Horizon.*

Chester Himes, 1909-84, (U.S.) novelist; *Cotton Comes to Harlem.*

Oliver Wendell Holmes, 1809-94, (U.S.) poet, novelist. *The Autocrat of the Breakfast-Table.*

Gerard Manley Hopkins, 1844-89, (Br.) poet. "Pied Beauty," "God's Grandeur."

A(lfred) E. Housman, 1859-1936, (Br.) poet. *A Shropshire Lad.*

William Dean Howells, 1837-1920, (U.S.) novelist, critic. *The Rise of Silas Lapham.*

Langston Hughes, 1902-67, (U.S.) poet, lyric writer, author; a major influence in 1920s Harlem Renaissance.

Ted Hughes, 1930-98, (Br.) British poet laureate, 1984-98. *Crow, The Hawk in the Rain.*

Victor Hugo, 1802-85, (Fr.) poet, dramatist, novelist. *Notre Dame de Paris, Les Misérables.*

Zora Neale Hurston, 1903-60, (U.S.) novelist, folklorist. *Their Eyes Were Watching God, Mules and Men.*

Aldous Huxley, 1894-1963, (Br.) writer. *Brave New World.*

Henrik Ibsen, 1828-1906, (Nor.) dramatist, poet. *A Doll's House, Ghosts, The Wild Duck, Hedda Gabler.*

William Inge, 1913-73, (U.S.) playwright. *Picnic; Come Back, Little Sheba; Bus Stop.*

Eugene Ionesco, 1910-94, (Fr.) surrealist dramatist. *The Bald Soprano, The Chairs.*

Washington Irving, 1783-1859, (U.S.) writer. "Rip Van Winkle," "The Legend of Sleepy Hollow."

Christopher Isherwood, 1904-1986, (Br.) novelist, playwright. *The Berlin Stories.*

Shirley Jackson, 1919-65, (U.S.) short-story writer. "The Lottery."

Henry James, 1843-1916, (U.S.) novelist, short-story writer, critic. *The Portrait of a Lady, The Ambassadors, Daisy Miller.*

Robinson Jeffers, 1887-1962, (U.S.) poet, dramatist. *Tamar and Other Poems, Medea.*

Samuel Johnson, 1709-84, (Br.) author, scholar, critic. *Dictionary of the English Language, Vanity of Human Wishes.*

Ben Jonson, 1572-1637, (Br.) dramatist, poet. *Volpone.*

James Weldon Johnson, 1871-1938, (U.S.) poet, novelist, diplomat; lyricist for *Lift Every Voice and Sing.*

James Joyce, 1882-1941, (Ir.) writer. *Ulysses, Dubliners, A Portrait of the Artist as a Young Man, Finnegans Wake.*

Ernst Junger, 1895-1998, (Ger.) novelist, essayist. *The Peace, On the Marble Cliff.*

Franz Kafka, 1883-1924, (Austro-Hung./Czech) novelist, short-story writer. *The Trial, The Castle,* "The Metamorphosis."

George S. Kaufman, 1889-1961, (U.S.) playwright. *The Man Who Came to Dinner, You Can't Take It With You.*

Yasunari Kawabata, 1899-1972, (Japan) novelist. *The Sound of the Mountains.*

Nikos Kazantzakis, 1883-1957, (Gk.) novelist. *Zorba the Greek, A Greek Passion.*

Alfred Kazin, 1915-98 (U.S.) author, critic, teacher. *On Native Grounds.*

John Keats, 1795-1821, (Br.) poet. "Ode on a Grecian Urn," "Ode to a Nightingale," "La Belle Dame Sans Merci."

Jack Kerouac, 1922-1969, (U.S.) author, Beat poet. *On the Road, The Dharma Bums,* "Mexico City Blues."

Joyce Kilmer, 1886-1918, (U.S.) poet. "Trees."

Rudyard Kipling, 1865-1936, (Br.) author, poet. "The White Man's Burden," "Gunga Din," *The Jungle Book.*

Jean de la Fontaine, 1621-95, (Fr.) poet. *Fables choisies.*

Pär Lagerkvist, 1891-1974, (Swed.) poet, dramatist, novelist. *Barabbas, The Sybil.*

Selma Lagerlöf, 1858-1940, (Swed.) novelist. *Jerusalem, The Ring of the Lowenskolds.*

Alphonse de Lamartine, 1790-1869, (Fr.) poet, novelist, statesman. *Méditations poétiques.*

Charles Lamb, 1775-1834, (Br.) essayist. *Specimens of English Dramatic Poets, Essays of Elia.*

Giuseppe di Lampedusa, 1896-1957, (It.) novelist. *The Leopard.*

William Langland, c1332-1400, (Eng.) poet. *Piers Plowman.*

Ring Lardner, 1885-1933, (U.S.) short-story writer, humorist.

Louis L'Amour, 1908-88, (U.S.) western author, screenwriter. *Hondo, The Cherokee Trail.*

D(avid) H(erbert) Lawrence, 1885-1930, (Br.) novelist. *Sons and Lovers, Women in Love, Lady Chatterley's Lover.*

Halldor Laxness, 1902-98, (Icelandic) novelist. *Iceland's Bell.*

Madeleine L'Engle, 1918-2007, (U.S.) novelist of young adult fiction. *A Wrinkle in Time.*

Mikhail Lermontov, 1814-41, (Russ.) novelist, poet. "Demon," *Hero of Our Time.*

Alain-René Lesage, 1668-1747, (Fr.) novelist. *Gil Blas de Santillane.*

Gotthold Lessing, 1729-81, (Ger.) dramatist, philosopher, critic. *Miss Sara Sampson, Minna von Barnhelm.*

C(live) S(taples) Lewis, 1898-1963, (Br.) critic, novelist, religious writer. *Allegory of Love; The Lion, the Witch and the Wardrobe; Out of the Silent Planet.*

Sinclair Lewis, 1885-1951, (U.S.) novelist. *Babbitt, Main Street, Arrowsmith, Dodsworth.*

Li Po, 701-762, (China) poet. "Song Before Drinking," "She Spins Silk."

Vachel Lindsay, 1879-1931, (U.S.) poet. *General William Booth Enters Into Heaven, The Congo.*

Hugh Lofting, 1886-1947, (Br.) writer. Dr. Doolittle series.

Jack London, 1876-1916, (U.S.) novelist, journalist. *Call of the Wild, The Sea-Wolf, White Fang.*

Henry Wadsworth Longfellow, 1807-82, (U.S.) poet. *Evangeline, The Song of Hiawatha.*

Lope de Vega, 1562-1635, (Sp.) playwright. *Noche de San Juan, Maestro de Danzar.*

H(oward) P(hillips) Lovecraft, 1890-1937, (U.S.), novelist, short-story writer. "At the Mountains of Madness."

Amy Lowell, 1874-1925, (U.S.) poet, critic. "Lilacs."

James Russell Lowell, 1819-91, (U.S.) poet, editor. *Poems, The Biglow Papers.*

Robert Lowell, 1917-77, (U.S.) poet. "Lord Weary's Castle."

Joaquim Maria Machado de Assis, 1839-1908, (Brazil) novelist, poet. *The Posthumous Memoirs of Bras Cubas.*

Archibald MacLeish, 1892-1982, (U.S.) poet. *Conquistador.*

Naguib Mahfouz, 1911-2006, (Egypt) novelist; first Arabic-language writer to win the Nobel Prize for Literature. *Cairo Trilogy.*

Bernard Malamud, 1914-86, (U.S.) short-story writer, novelist. "The Magic Barrel," *The Assistant, The Fixer.*

Stéphane Mallarmé, 1842-98, (Fr.) poet. *Poésies.*

Sir Thomas Malory, ?-1471, (Br.) writer. *Morte d'Arthur.*

Andre Malraux, 1901-76, (Fr.) novelist. *Man's Fate.*

Osip Mandelstam, 1891-1938, (Russ.) poet. *Stone, Tristia.*

Thomas Mann, 1875-1955, (Ger.) novelist, essayist. *Buddenbrooks, The Magic Mountain,* "Death in Venice."

Katherine Mansfield, 1888-1923, (Br.) short-story writer. "Bliss."

Christopher Marlowe, 1564-93, (Br.) dramatist, poet. *Tamburlaine the Great,* Dr. *Faustus, The Jew of Malta.*

Andrew Marvell, 1621-78, (Br.) poet. "To His Coy Mistress."

John Masefield, 1878-1967, (Br.) poet. "Sea Fever," "Cargoes," *Salt Water Ballads.*

Edgar Lee Masters, 1869-1950, (U.S.) poet, biographer. *Spoon River Anthology.*

W(illiam) Somerset Maugham, 1874-1965, (Br.) author. *Of Human Bondage, The Moon and Sixpence.*

Guy de Maupassant, 1850-93, (Fr.) novelist, short-story writer. "A Life," "Bel-Ami," "The Necklace."

François Mauriac, 1885-1970, (Fr.) novelist, dramatist. *Viper's Tangle, The Kiss to the Leper.*

Vladimir Mayakovsky, 1893-1930, (Russ.) poet, dramatist. *The Cloud in Trousers.*

Mary McCarthy, 1912-89, (U.S.) critic, novelist, memoirist. *Memories of a Catholic Girlhood.*

Carson McCullers, 1917-67, (U.S.) novelist. *The Heart Is a Lonely Hunter, Member of the Wedding.*

Herman Melville, 1819-91, (U.S.) novelist, poet. *Moby-Dick, Typee, Billy Budd, Omoo.*

George Meredith, 1828-1909, (Br.) novelist, poet. *The Ordeal of Richard Feverel, The Egoist.*

Prosper Mérimée, 1803-70, (Fr.) author. *Carmen.*

James Merrill, 1926-95, (U.S.) poet. *Divine Comedies.*

James Michener, 1907-97, (U.S.) novelist. *Tales of the South Pacific.*

Edna St. Vincent Millay, 1892-1950, (U.S.) poet. *The Harp Weaver and Other Poems.*

Arthur Miller, 1915-2005, (U.S.) playwright. *The Crucible, After the Fall, Death of a Salesman.*

Henry Miller, 1891-1980, (U.S.) erotic novelist. *Tropic of Cancer.*

A(lan) A(lexander) Milne, 1882-1956, (Br.) author. *Winnie-the-Pooh.*

Czeslaw Milosz, 1911-2004, (Pol.) essayist, poet. "Esse," "Encounter."

John Milton, 1608-74, (Br.) poet, writer. *Paradise Lost, Comus, Lycidas, Areopagitica.*

Mishima Yukio (Hiraoka Kimitake), 1925-70, (Jpn.) writer. *Confessions of a Mask.*

Gabriela Mistral, 1889-1957, (Chil.) poet. *Sonnets of Death.*

Margaret Mitchell, 1900-49, (U.S.) novelist. *Gone With the Wind.*

Jean Baptiste Molière, 1622-73, (Fr.) dramatist. *Tartuffe, Le Misanthrope, Le Bourgeois Gentilhomme.*

Ferenc Molnár, 1878-1952, (Hung.) dramatist, novelist. *Liliom, The Guardsman, The Swan.*

Michel de Montaigne, 1533-92, (Fr.) essayist. *Essais.*

Eugenio Montale, 1896-1981, (It.) poet.

Brian Moore, 1921-99, (Ir.-U.S.) novelist. *The Lonely Passion of Judith Hearne.*

Clement C. Moore, 1779-1863, (U.S.) poet, educator. "A Visit From Saint Nicholas."

Marianne Moore, 1887-1972, (U.S.) poet.

Alberto Moravia, 1907-90, (It.) novelist, short-story writer. *The Time of Indifference.*

Sir Thomas More, 1478-1535, (Br.) writer, statesman, saint. *Utopia.*

Wright Morris, 1910-98 (U.S.) novelist. *My Uncle Dudley.*

Murasaki Shikibu, c978-1026, (Jpn.) novelist. *The Tale of Genji.*

Iris Murdoch, 1919-99 (Br.), novelist, philosopher. *The Sea, The Sea.*

Alfred de Musset, 1810-57, (Fr.) poet, dramatist. *La Confession d'un Enfant du Siècle.*

Vladimir Nabokov, 1899-1977, (Russ.-U.S.) novelist. *Lolita, Pale Fire.*

R.K. Narayan, 1906-2001, (India), novelist, *The Guide.*

Ogden Nash, 1902-71, (U.S.) poet of light verse.

Irène Némirovsky, 1903-1942, (Ukraine) novelist. *David Golder, Suite Française.*

Pablo Neruda, 1904-73, (Chil.) poet. *Twenty Love Poems and One Song of Despair, Toward the Splendid City.*

Patrick O'Brian, 1914-2000, (Br.) historical novelist. *Master and Commander, Blue at the Mizzen.*

Sean O'Casey, 1884-1964, (Ir.) dramatist. *Juno and the Paycock, The Plough and the Stars.*

Frank O'Connor (Michael Donovan), 1903-66, (Ir.) short-story writer. "Guests of a Nation."

Flannery O'Connor, 1925-64, (U.S.) novelist, short-story writer. *Wise Blood,* "A Good Man Is Hard to Find."

Clifford Odets, 1906-63, (U.S.) playwright. *Waiting for Lefty, Awake and Sing, Golden Boy, The Country Girl.*

John O'Hara, 1905-70, (U.S.) novelist, short-story writer. *From the Terrace, Appointment in Samarra, Pal Joey.*

Omar Khayyam, c1028-1122, (Per.) poet. *Rubaiyat.*

Eugene O'Neill, 1888-1953, (U.S.) playwright. *Emperor Jones, Anna Christie, Long Day's Journey Into Night.*

George Orwell (Eric Arthur Blair), 1903-50, (Br.) novelist, essayist. *Animal Farm, Nineteen Eighty-Four.*

John Osborne, 1929-95, (Br.) dramatist, novelist. *Look Back in Anger, The Entertainer.*

Wilfred Owen, 1893-1918 (Br.) poet. "Dulce et Decorum Est."

Grace Paley, 1922-2007, (U.S.) short-story writer, poet. *The Little Disturbances of Man.*

Dorothy Parker, 1893-1967, (U.S.) poet, short-story writer. *Enough Rope, Laments for the Living.*

Boris Pasternak, 1890-1960, (Russ.) poet, novelist. *Doctor Zhivago.*

Alan Paton, 1903-88, (S. Africa) novelist. *Cry, the Beloved Country.*

Octavio Paz, 1914-98, (Mex.) poet, essayist. *The Labyrinth of Solitude, They Shall Not Pass!, The Sun Stone.*

Samuel Pepys, 1633-1703, (Br.) public official, diarist.

S(idney) J(oseph) Perelman, 1904-79, (U.S.) humorist. *The Road to Miltown, Under the Spreading Atrophy.*

Charles Perrault, 1628-1703, (Fr.) writer. *Tales From Mother Goose* (*Sleeping Beauty, Cinderella*).

Petrarch (Francesco Petrarca), 1304-74, (It.) poet. *Africa, Trionfi, Canzoniere.*

Luigi Pirandello, 1867-1936, (It.) novelist, dramatist. *Six Characters in Search of an Author.*

Sylvia Plath, 1932-63, (U.S.) author, poet. *The Bell Jar.*

Edgar Allan Poe, 1809-49, (U.S.) poet, short-story writer, critic. "Annabel Lee," "The Raven," "The Purloined Letter."

Alexander Pope, 1688-1744, (Br.) poet. *The Rape of the Lock, The Dunciad, An Essay on Man.*

Katherine Anne Porter, 1890-1980, (U.S.) novelist, short-story writer. *Ship of Fools.*

Chaim Potok, 1929-2002, (U.S.) novelist. *The Chosen.*

Ezra Pound, 1885-1972, (U.S.) poet. *Cantos.*

Anthony Powell, 1905-2000, (Br.) novelist. *A Dance to the Music of Time* series.

J(ohn) B. Priestley, 1894-1984, (Br.) novelist, dramatist. *The Good Companions.*

Marcel Proust, 1871-1922, (Fr.) novelist. *Remembrance of Things Past.*

Aleksandr Pushkin, 1799-1837, (Russ.) poet, novelist. *Boris Godunov, Eugene Onegin.*

Mario Puzo, 1920-99, (U.S.) novelist. *The Godfather.*

François Rabelais, 1495-1553, (Fr.) writer. *Gargantua.*

Jean Racine, 1639-99, (Fr.) dramatist. *Andromaque, Phèdre, Bérénice, Britannicus.*

Ayn Rand, 1905-82, (Russ.-U.S.) novelist, moral theorist. *The Fountainhead, Atlas Shrugged.*

Terence Rattigan, 1911-77, (Br.) playwright. *Separate Tables, The Browning Version.*

Erich Maria Remarque, 1898-1970, (Ger.-U.S.) novelist. *All Quiet on the Western Front.*

Samuel Richardson, 1689-1761, (Br.) novelist. *Pamela; or Virtue Rewarded.*

Rainer Maria Rilke, 1875-1926, (Ger.) poet. *Life and Songs, Duino Elegies, Poems From the Book of Hours.*

Arthur Rimbaud, 1854-91, (Fr.) poet. *A Season in Hell.*

Edwin Arlington Robinson, 1869-1935, (U.S.) poet. "Richard Cory," "Miniver Cheevy," *Merlin.*

Theodore Roethke, 1908-63, (U.S.) poet. *Open House, The Waking, The Far Field.*

Romain Rolland, 1866-1944, (Fr.) novelist, biographer. *Jean-Christophe.*

Pierre de Ronsard, 1524-85, (Fr.) poet. *Sonnets pour Hélène, La Franciade.*

Christina Rossetti, 1830-94, (Br.) poet. "When I Am Dead, My Dearest."

Dante Gabriel Rossetti, 1828-82, (Br.) poet, painter. "The Blessed Damozel."

Edmond Rostand, 1868-1918, (Fr.) poet, dramatist. *Cyrano de Bergerac.*

Damon Runyon, 1880-1946, (U.S.) short-story writer, journalist. *Guys and Dolls, Blue Plate Special.*

John Ruskin, 1819-1900, (Br.) critic, social theorist. *Modern Painters, The Seven Lamps of Architecture.*

François Sagan, (Françoise quoirez) 1935-2004, (Fr.) novelist *Bonjour Tristesse.*

Antoine de Saint-Exupéry, 1900-44, (Fr.) writer. *Wind, Sand and Stars, The Little Prince.*

Saki, or H(ector) H(ugh) Munro, 1870-1916, (Br.) writer. *The Chronicles of Clovis.*

George Sand (Amandine Lucie Aurore Dupin), 1804-76, (Fr.) novelist. *Indiana, Consuelo.*

Carl Sandburg, 1878-1967, (U.S.) poet. *The People, Yes; Chicago Poems, Smoke and Steel, Harvest Poems.*

William Saroyan, 1908-81, (U.S.) playwright, novelist. *The Time of Your Life, The Human Comedy.*

Nathalie Sarraute, 1900-99, (Fr.) Nouveau Roman novelist. *Tropisms.*

May Sarton, 1914-95, (Belg.-U.S.) poet, novelist. *Encounter in April, Anger.*

Dorothy L. Sayers, 1893-1957, (Br.) mystery writer; created Lord Peter Wimsey.

Richard Scarry, 1920-94, (U.S.) author of children's books. *Richard Scarry's Best Story Book Ever.*

Friedrich von Schiller, 1759-1805, (Ger.) dramatist, poet, historian. *Don Carlos, Maria Stuart, Wilhelm Tell.*

Sir Walter Scott, 1771-1832, (Sc.) novelist, poet. *Ivanhoe.*

Jaroslav Seifert, 1902-86, (Czech.) poet.

Dr. Seuss (Theodor Seuss Geisel), 1904-91, (U.S.) children's book author and illustrator. *The Cat in the Hat.*

William Shakespeare, 1564-1616, (Br.) dramatist, poet. *Romeo and Juliet, Hamlet, King Lear, Julius Caesar,* sonnets.

Karl Shapiro, 1913-2000, (U.S.) poet. "Elegy for a Dead Soldier."

George Bernard Shaw, 1856-1950, (Ir.-Br.) playwright, critic. *St. Joan, Pygmalion, Major Barbara, Man and Superman.*

Sidney Sheldon, 1917-2007, (U.S.) screenwriter; novelist. *Rage of Angels, Memories of Midnight.*

Mary Wollstonecraft Shelley, 1797-1851, (Br.) novelist, feminist. *Frankenstein. The Last Man.*

Percy Bysshe Shelley, 1792-1822, (Br.) poet. *Prometheus Unbound, Adonais,* "Ode to the West Wind," "To a Skylark."

Richard B. Sheridan, 1751-1816, (Br.) dramatist. *The Rivals, School for Scandal.*

Robert Sherwood, 1896-1955, (U.S.) playwright, biographer. *The Petrified Forest, Abe Lincoln in Illinois.*

Mikhail Sholokhov, 1906-84, (Russ.) writer. *The Silent Don.*

Georges Simenon (Georges Sims), 1903-89, (Belg.-Fr.) mystery writer; created inspector Maigret.

Upton Sinclair, 1878-1968, (U.S.) novelist. *The Jungle.*

Isaac Bashevis Singer, 1904-91, (Pol.-U.S.) novelist, short-story writer, in Yiddish. *The Magician of Lublin.*

C(harles) P(ercy) Snow, 1905-80, (Br.) novelist, scientist. *Strangers and Brothers, Corridors of Power.*

Susan Sontag, 1933-2004, (U.S.) critic, essayist, novelist. *Notes on Camp, The Volcano Lover, In America.*

Stephen Spender, 1909-95, (Br.) poet, critic, novelist. *Twenty Poems,* "Elegy for Margaret."

Edmund Spenser, 1552-99, (Br.) poet. *The Faerie Queen.*

Mickey Spillane, 1918-2006, (U.S.) novelist; series of novels with the character detective Mike Hammer. *The Killing Man.*

Johanna Spyri, 1827-1901, (Swiss) children's author. *Heidi.*

Christina Stead, 1903-83, (Austral.) novelist, short-story writer. *The Man Who Loved Children.*

Richard Steele, 1672-1729, (Br.) essayist, playwright, began the *Tatler* and *Spectator. The Conscious Lovers.*

Gertrude Stein, 1874-1946, (U.S.) writer. *Three Lives.*

John Steinbeck, 1902-68, (U.S.) novelist. *The Grapes of Wrath, Of Mice and Men, The Winter of Our Discontent.*

Stendhal (Marie Henri Beyle), 1783-1842, (Fr.) novelist. *The Red and the Black, The Charterhouse of Parma.*

Laurence Sterne, 1713-68, (Br.) novelist. *Tristram Shandy.*

Wallace Stevens, 1879-1955, (U.S.) poet. *Harmonium, The Man With the Blue Guitar, Notes Toward a Supreme Fiction.*

Robert Louis Stevenson, 1850-94, (Br.) novelist, poet, essayist. *Treasure Island, A Child's Garden of Verses.*

Bram Stoker, 1845-1910, (Br.) writer. *Dracula.*

Rex Stout, 1886-1975, (U.S.) mystery writer; created Nero Wolfe.

Harriet Beecher Stowe, 1811-96, (U.S.) novelist. *Uncle Tom's Cabin.*

Lytton Strachey, 1880-1932, (Br.) biographer, critic. *Eminent Victorians. Queen Victoria, Elizabeth and Essex.*

August Strindberg, 1849-1912, (Swed.) dramatist, novelist. *The Father, Miss Julie, The Creditors.*

William Styron, 1925-2006, (U.S.) novelist, essayist. *The Confessions of Nat Turner, Sophie's Choice, Darkness Visible: A Memoir of Madness.*

Jonathan Swift, 1667-1745, (Br.) satirist, poet. *Gulliver's Travels,* "A Modest Proposal."

Algernon C. Swinburne, 1837-1909, (Br.) poet, dramatist. *Atalanta in Calydon.*

John M. Synge, 1871-1909, (Ir.) poet, dramatist. *Riders to the Sea, The Playboy of the Western World.*

Rabindranath Tagore, 1861-1941, (In.) author, poet. *Sadhana, The Realization of Life, Gitanjali.*

Booth Tarkington, 1869-1946, (U.S.) novelist. *Seventeen.*

Peter Taylor, 1917-94, (U.S.) novelist. *A Summons to Memphis.*

Sara Teasdale, 1884-1933, (U.S.) poet. *Helen of Troy and Other Poems, Rivers to the Sea.*

Alfred, Lord Tennyson, 1809-92, (Br.) poet. *Idylls of the King, In Memoriam,* "The Charge of the Light Brigade."

William Makepeace Thackeray, 1811-63, (Br.) novelist. *Vanity Fair, Henry Esmond, Pendennis.*

Dylan Thomas, 1914-53, (Welsh) poet. *Under Milk Wood, A Child's Christmas in Wales.*

Hunter S. Thompson, 1937-2005, (U.S.) author, journalist. *Hell's Angels, Fear and Loathing in Las Vegas.*

Henry David Thoreau, 1817-62, (U.S.) writer, philosopher, naturalist. *Walden,* "Civil Disobedience."

James Thurber, 1894-1961, (U.S.) humorist; "The Secret Life of Walter Mitty," *My Life and Hard Times.*

J(ohn) R(onald) R(euel) Tolkien, 1892-1973, (Br.) writer. *The Hobbit, Lord of the Rings* trilogy.

Leo Tolstoy, 1828-1910, (Russ.) novelist, short-story writer. *War and Peace, Anna Karenina,* "The Death of Ivan Ilyich."

Lionel Trilling, 1905-75 (U.S.) critic, author, teacher. *The Liberal Imagination.*

Anthony Trollope, 1815-82, (Br.) novelist. *The Warden, Barchester Towers,* the Palliser novels.

Ivan Turgenev, 1818-83, (Russ.) novelist, short-story writer. *Fathers and Sons, First Love, A Month in the Country.*

Amos Tutuola, 1920-97, (Nigerian) novelist. *The Palm-Wine Drunkard, My Life in the Bush of Ghosts.*

Mark Twain (Samuel Clemens), 1835-1910, (U.S.) novelist, humorist. *The Adventures of Huckleberry Finn.*

Sigrid Undset, 1881-1949, (Nor.) novelist, *Kristin Lavransdatter.*

Paul Valéry, 1871-1945, (Fr.) poet, critic. *La Jeune Parque, The Graveyard by the Sea.*

Paul Verlaine, 1844-96, (Fr.) Symbolist poet. *Songs Without Words.*

Jules Verne, 1828-1905, (Fr.) novelist. *Twenty Thousand Leagues Under the Sea.*

François Villon, 1431-63?, (Fr.) poet. *The Lays, The Grand Testament.*

Voltaire (F.M. Arouet), 1694-1778, (Fr.) writer of "philosophical romances"; philosopher, historian; *Candide.*

Kurt Vonnegut, Jr., 1922-2007, (U.S.) novelist, essayist; *Cat's Cradle, Slaughterhouse-Five,* and *Breakfast of Champions.*

Robert Penn Warren, 1905-89, (U.S.) novelist, poet, critic. *All the King's Men.*

Wendy Wasserstein, 1950-2006, (U.S.) playwright; *The Heidi Chronicles.*

Evelyn Waugh, 1903-66, (Br.) novelist. *The Loved One, Brideshead Revisited, A Handful of Dust.*

H(erbert) G(eorge) Wells, 1866-1946, (Br.) novelist. *The Time Machine, The Invisible Man, The War of the Worlds.*

Eudora Welty, 1909-2001, (U.S.) Southern short story writer, novelist. "Why I Live at the P.O.," "The Ponder Heart."

Rebecca West, 1893-1983, (Br.) novelist, critic, journalist. *Black Lamb and Grey Falcon.*

Edith Wharton, 1862-1937, (U.S.) novelist. *The Age of Innocence, The House of Mirth, Ethan Frome.*

Phillis Wheatley, c1753-84, (U.S.) poet; 2nd American woman and first black woman to be published, 1770.

E(lwyn) B(rooks) White, 1899-1985, (U.S.) essayist, novelist. *Charlotte's Web, Stuart Little.*

Patrick White, 1912-90, (Austral.) novelist. *The Tree of Man.*

T(erence) H(anbury) White, 1906-64, (Br.) author. *The Once and Future King, A Book of Beasts.*

Walt Whitman, 1819-92, (U.S.) poet. *Leaves of Grass.*

John Greenleaf Whittier, 1807-92, (U.S.) poet, journalist. *Snow-Bound.*

Oscar Wilde, 1854-1900, (Ir.) novelist, playwright. *The Picture of Dorian Gray, The Importance of Being Earnest.*

Laura Ingalls Wilder, 1867-1957, (U.S.) novelist. Little House on the Prairie series of children's books.

Thornton Wilder, 1897-1975, (U.S.) playwright. *Our Town, The Skin of Our Teeth, The Matchmaker.*

Tennessee Williams, 1911-83, (U.S.) playwright. *A Streetcar Named Desire, Cat on a Hot Tin Roof, The Glass Menagerie.*

William Carlos Williams, 1883-1963, (U.S.) poet, physician. *Tempers, Al Que Quiere! Paterson,* "This Is Just to Say."

Edmund Wilson, 1895-1972, (U.S.) critic, novelist. *Axel's Castle, To the Finland Station.*

P(elham) G(renville) Wodehouse, 1881-1975, (Br.-U.S.) humorist. The "Jeeves" novels, *Anything Goes.*

Thomas Wolfe, 1900-38, (U.S.) novelist. *Look Homeward, Angel; You Can't Go Home Again.*

Virginia Woolf, 1882-1941, (Br.) novelist, essayist. *Mrs. Dalloway, To the Lighthouse, A Room of One's Own.*

William Wordsworth, 1770-1850, (Br.) poet. "Tintern Abbey," "Ode: Intimations of Immortality," *The Prelude.*

Richard Wright, 1908-60, (U.S.) novelist, short-story writer. *Native Son, Black Boy, Uncle Tom's Children.*

Elinor Wylie, 1885-1928, (U.S.) poet. *Nets to Catch the Wind.*

William Butler Yeats, 1865-1939, (Ir.) poet, playwright. "The Second Coming," *The Wild Swans at Coole.*

Frank Yerby, 1916-91, (U.S.) first best-selling African American novelist; *The Foxes of Harrow.*

Émile Zola, 1840-1902, (Fr.) novelist. *Nana, Thérèse Raquin.*

Poets Laureate

There is no record of the origin of the office of Poet Laureate of England. Henry III (1216-72) reportedly had a Versificator Regis, or King's Poet, paid 100 shillings per year. Other poets said to have filled the role include Geoffrey Chaucer (d 1400), Edmund Spenser (d 1599), Ben Jonson (d 1637), and Sir William d'Avenant (d 1668). The first official English poet laureate was John Dryden, appointed 1668, for life (as was customary). Then came Thomas Shadwell, in 1689; Nahum Tate, 1692; Nicholas Rowe, 1715; Rev. Laurence Eusden, 1718; Colley Cibber, 1730; William Whitehead, 1757; Rev. Thomas Warton, 1785; Henry James Pye, 1790; Robert Southey, 1813; William Wordsworth, 1843; Alfred, Lord Tennyson, 1850; Alfred Austin, 1896; Robert Bridges, 1913; John Masefield, 1930; C. Day Lewis, 1968; Sir John Betjeman, 1972; Ted Hughes, 1984; Andrew Motion, 1999.

In U.S., appointment is by Librarian of Congress and is not for life: Robert Penn Warren, appointed 1986; Richard Wilbur, 1987; Howard Nemerov, 1988; Mark Strand, 1990; Joseph Brodsky, 1991; Mona Van Duyn, 1992; Rita Dove, 1993; Robert Hass, 1995; Robert Pinsky, 1997; Stanley Kunitz, 2000; Billy Collins, 2001; Louise Gluck, 2003; Ted Kooser, 2004; Donald Hall, 2006; Charles Simic, 2007.

YEAR IN PICTURES

SIGNS OF DECLINE
Signs like this one in Glendale, CA, popped up with increasing frequency in 2007, as the U.S. housing market tumbled and foreclosures soared over previous years' rates.

SCHOOL INTEGRATION ON TRIAL
Kentucky citizens registered opposition to a June 28, 2007, Supreme Court decision that invalidated voluntary school desegregation plans.

MINIMUM WAGE INCREASE
Representative Dave Loebsack (D, IA) bagged groceries in Burlington, IA, on July 21, 2007, calling attention to an impending increase in the federal minimum wage, which rose the following week from $5.15 to $5.85 an hour.

LADY SPEAKER
Representative Nancy Pelosi (D, CA), the first woman elected Speaker of the House, held up her gavel in the U.S. Capitol, Jan. 4, 2007.

THE RACE IS ON

The race for the 2008 Democratic and Republican presidential nominations heated up in 2007, as challengers struggled to stake out clear positions on the U.S. economy and the war in Iraq. Democratic hopefuls (above) met at a debate sponsored by CNN, YouTube, and Google in Charleston, SC, on July 23, 2007 (left to right: former Sen. Mike Gravel, Sen. Christopher Dodd, former Sen. John Edwards, Sen. Hillary Clinton, and Sen. Barack Obama). Republican hopeful and former New York City mayor Rudy Giuliani (below) answered a question about Iraq at a debate in Manchester, NH, June 5, 2007 (seated, left to right: Sen. Sam Brownback, former Massachusetts Gov. Mitt Romney, and Sen. John McCain).

GONZALES UNDER FIRE

Atty. Gen. Alberto Gonzales, a focal point of several Bush administration controversies, announced his resignation on August 27, 2007.

LIBBY WALKS FREE

In June 2007, former White House aide I. Lewis "Scooter" Libby, left, was sentenced to 30 months in prison and fined $250,000 for his role in leaking the identity of undercover CIA agent Valerie Plame. Pres. Bush commuted the "excessive" sentence in July.

GERALD R. FORD, 1913-2006

Former President Gerald R. Ford, remembered for efforts to "heal" the nation after Vietnam and Watergate, died Dec. 26, 2006, at age 93. He was the longest living president in history.

DOD

MINNESOTA BRIDGE DISASTER

Thirteen people died and at least 100 were injured in the Aug. 1, 2007, collapse of the I-35W bridge, which crossed the Mississippi River between St. Paul and Minneapolis, MN. The bridge had been rated "structurally deficient" and in possible need of replacement by the federal government in 2005.

AP Images
The Minnesota Daily, Stacy Bengs

AP Images/The Potomac News, Jason Hornick

TRAGEDY AT VIRGINIA TECH

Students and others honored the victims of an April 16, 2007 shooting massacre on the university's Blacksburg, VA campus. Cho Seung Hui killed 32 fellow students and teachers before fatally shooting himself.

GIRLS GONE WILD
Nicole Richie, Lindsay Lohan, and Paris Hilton made tabloid headlines in 2006 and 2007 when they were arrested, in separate incidents, for driving under the influence.

IMUS IS OUT
Controversial radio personality Don Imus was fired, April 12, 2007, from his syndicated CBS radio show, after making racist-tinged comments about members of the Rutgers women's basketball team.

CANCER SURVIVOR ON THE CAMPAIGN TRAIL
Elizabeth Edwards, wife of Democratic presidential hopeful John Edwards, played a prominent role in his campaign in 2007, despite her ongoing battle with breast cancer.

EVERYDAY HERO
"Subway Superhero" Wesley Autrey, a New York City construction worker (shown with daughters Syshe and Shuqui), made headlines Jan. 2, 2007, when he saved the life of a young man who had fallen in front of an oncoming subway train.

197

ASTRONAUT UNDER PRESSURE

NASA Astronaut Lisa Nowak was charged with attempted murder, Feb. 6, 2007, after attempting to carry out a bizarre plot to kidnap a woman she believed to be romantically involved with a fellow astronaut (Nowak shown at left in a 2005 NASA photo, at right in a Feb. 2007 photo from Orange County, FL Sheriff).

"TB GUY" COMES HOME

Andrew Speaker, a U.S. lawyer infected with a dangerous strain of tuberculosis, went to Europe in May 2007 for his wedding, defied federal warnings not to return by plane, and became the first person to be quarantined by the government since 1963.

REUTERS/STR/Landov

WOLFOWITZ RESIGNS

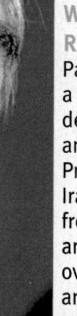

Paul Wolfowitz, a former deputy defense secretary and close adviser to Pres. Bush on the Iraq War, resigned from the World Bank amid controversy over a promotion and pay increase awarded to a close female friend.

A QUEEN IN THE COLONIES

Britain's Queen Elizabeth II (with Vice Pres. Dick Cheney, at left), paid a visit to Jamestown, Virginia. 2007 marked the 400th anniversary of the settlement, the first permanent English colony in the U.S.

BIG DEBUT FOR iPHONE
Huge crowds lined up outside of Apple Stores nationwide as Apple released its much-anticipated iPhone on June 29, 2007. Apple announced Sept. 10 that it had sold 1 million iPhones in just over two months.

iPhone: Courtesy of Apple

OVERDUE WIN FOR SCORSESE
Martin Scorsese won the 2007 Academy Award for Best Director for *The Departed*, after five previous Directing nominations had left him empty-handed.

A FINAL SPIN OF THE WHEEL
Bob Barker bade a final farewell to game show fans, ending a 35-year tenure as host of *The Price Is Right*. Comedian Drew Carey was to take over hosting duties.

DIXIE CHICKS WIN BIG
Country trio Dixie Chicks scooped up 5 Grammy Awards, including Album of the Year for *Taking the Long Way*, and Record of the Year and Song of the Year for "Not Ready to Make Nice."

ROCKING THE PLANET
Live Earth, a series of concerts held in 11 cities around the world to raise awareness about global warming, featured U.S. performances by Garth Brooks, Kelly Clarkson, Ludacris, John Mayer, Sting (pictured) and The Police, and Kanye West.

POTTER MANIA HITS NEW HEIGHTS
Eager Harry Potter fans bought more than 11 million copies of *Harry Potter and the Deathly Hallows*, J. K. Rowling's seventh and final book in the series, in its first 24 hours on sale.

SIMPSONS MAKE BIG BOX OFFICE "D'OH!"
The Simpsons Movie (characters pictured with creator Matt Groening, center) made its long-anticipated debut at a theater in Springfield, VT, which won the honor of hosting the premiere over 13 other Springfields across the U.S.

FAREWELL TO THE FAMILY
Viewers said goodbye to *The Sopranos* after six seasons as one of premium cable's highest-rated and most critically acclaimed shows.

HBO/Photofest

Composers of Classical and Avant Garde Music

John Adams, b 1947, (U.S.) *Nixon in China, The Death of Klinghoffer.*

Carl Philipp Emanuel Bach, 1714-88, (Ger.) Cantatas, passions, numerous keyboard and instrumental works.

Johann Christian Bach, 1735-82, (Ger.) Concertos, operas, sonatas. Known as the "English" Bach.

Johann Sebastian Bach, 1685-1750, (Ger.) *St. Matthew Passion, The Well-Tempered Clavier.*

Samuel Barber, 1910-81, (U.S.) *Adagio for Strings, Vanessa.*

Béla Bartók, 1881-1945, (Hung.) *Concerto for Orchestra, The Miraculous Mandarin.*

Amy Beach (Mrs. H. H. A. Beach), 1867-1944, (U.S.) *The Year's at the Spring, Fireflies, The Chambered Nautilus.*

Ludwig van Beethoven, 1770-1827, (Ger.) Concertos (*Emperor*), sonatas (*Moonlight, Pathetique*), 9 symphonies.

Vincenzo Bellini, 1801-35, (It.) *I Puritani, La Sonnambula, Norma.*

Alban Berg, 1885-1935, (Austrian) *Wozzeck, Lulu.*

Hector Berlioz, 1803-69, (Fr.) *Damnation of Faust, Symphonie Fantastique, Requiem.*

Leonard Bernstein, 1918-90, (U.S.) *Chichester Psalms, Jeremiah Symphony, Mass.*

Georges Bizet, 1838-75, (Fr.) *Carmen, Pearl Fishers.*

Ernest Bloch, 1880-1959, (Swiss-U.S.) *Macbeth* (opera), *Schelomo, Voice in the Wilderness.*

Luigi Boccherini, 1743-1805, (It.) Chamber music and guitar pieces.

Alexander Borodin, 1833-87, (Russ.) *Prince Igor, In the Steppes of Central Asia, Polovtzian Dances.*

Pierre Boulez, b 1925, (Fr.) *Le Visage nuptial, Edats/Multiple, Domaines.*

Johannes Brahms, 1833-97, (Ger.) *Liebeslieder Waltzes, Acad. Festival Overture,* chamber music, 4 symphonies.

Benjamin Britten, 1913-76, (Br.) *Peter Grimes, Turn of the Screw, A Ceremony of Carols, War Requiem.*

Anton Bruckner, 1824-96, (Austrian) 9 symphonies.

Dietrich Buxtehude, 1637-1707, (Dan.) Organ works, vocal music.

William Byrd, 1543-1623, (Br.) Masses, motets.

John Cage, 1912-92, (U.S.) *Winter Music, Fontana Mix.*

Emmanuel Chabrier, 1841-94, (Fr.) *Le Roi Malgré Lui, España.*

Gustave Charpentier, 1860-1956, (Fr.) *Louise.*

Frédéric Chopin, 1810-49, (Pol.) Mazurkas, waltzes, etudes, nocturnes, polonaises, sonatas.

Aaron Copland, 1900-90, (U.S.) *Appalachian Spring, Fanfare for the Common Man, Lincoln Portrait.*

Claude Debussy, 1862-1918, (Fr.) *Pelleas et Melisande, La Mer, Prelude to the Afternoon of a Faun.*

Gaetano Donizetti, 1797-1848, (It.) *Elixir of Love, Lucia di Lammermoor, Daughter of the Regiment.*

Paul Dukas, 1865-1935, (Fr.) *Sorcerer's Apprentice.*

Antonin Dvorak, 1841-1904, (Czech.) *Songs My Mother Taught Me, Symphony in E Minor (From the New World).*

Edward Elgar, 1857-1934, (Br.) *Enigma Variations, Pomp and Circumstance.*

Manuel de Falla, 1876-1946, (Sp.) *El Amor Brujo, La Vida Breve, The Three-Cornered Hat.*

Gabriel Faurè, 1845-1924, (Fr.) *Requiem, Elègie for Cello and Piano.*

Cesar Franck, 1822-90, (Belg.) *Symphony in D minor, Violin Sonata.*

George Gershwin, 1898-1937, (U.S.) *Rhapsody in Blue, An American in Paris, Porgy and Bess.*

Philip Glass, b 1937, (U.S.) *Einstein on the Beach, The Voyage.*

Mikhail Glinka, 1804-57, (Russ.) *A Life for the Tsar, Ruslan and Ludmilla.*

Christoph W. Gluck, 1714-87, (Ger.) *Alceste, Iphigènie en Tauride.*

Charles Gounod, 1818-93, (Fr.) *Faust, Romeo and Juliet.*

Edvard Grieg, 1843-1907, (Nor.) *Peer Gynt Suite, Concerto in A minor for piano.*

George Frideric Handel, 1685-1759, (Ger.-Br.) *Messiah, Water Music.*

Howard Hanson, 1896-1981, (U.S.) Symphonies No. 1 (Nordic) and No. 2 (Romantic).

Roy Harris, 1898-1979, (U.S.) Symphonies.

(Franz) Joseph Haydn, 1732-1809, (Austrian) Symphonies (*Clock, London, Toy*), chamber music, oratorios.

Paul Hindemith, 1895-1963, (U.S.) *Mathis der Maler.*

Gustav Holst, 1874-1934, (Br.) *The Planets.*

Arthur Honegger, 1892-1955, (Fr.) *Judith, Le Roi David, Pacific 231.*

Alan Hovhaness, 1911-2000, (U.S.) Symphonies, *Magnificat.*

Engelbert Humperdinck, 1854-1921, (Ger.) *Hansel and Gretel.*

Charles Ives, 1874-1954, (U.S.) *Concord Sonata,* symphonies.

Aram Khachaturian, 1903-78, (Russ.) Ballets, piano pieces, *Sabre Dance.*

Zoltán Kodaly, 1882-1967, (Hung.) *Háry János, Psalmus Hungaricus.*

Fritz Kreisler, 1875-1962, (Austrian) *Caprice Viennois, Tambourin Chinois.*

Edouard Lalo, 1823-92, (Fr.) *Symphonie Espagnole.*

Ruggero Leoncavallo, 1857-1919, (It.) *Pagliacci.*

Franz Liszt, 1811-86, (Hung.) 20 Hungarian rhapsodies, symphonic poems.

Edward MacDowell, 1861-1908, (U.S.) *To a Wild Rose.*

Gustav Mahler, 1860-1911, (Austrian) *Das Lied von der Erde;* 9 complete symphonies.

Pietro Mascagni, 1863-1945, (It.) *Cavalleria Rusticana.*

Jules Massenet, 1842-1912, (Fr.) *Manon, Le Cid, Thaïs.*

Felix Mendelssohn, 1809-47, (Ger.) *A Midsummer Night's Dream, Songs Without Words,* violin concerto.

Gian Carlo Menotti, 1911-2007, (It.-U.S.) *The Medium, The Consul, Amahl and the Night Visitors.*

Claudio Monteverdi, 1567-1643, (It.) Opera, masses, madrigals.

Modest Mussorgsky, 1839-81, (Russ.) *Boris Godunov, Pictures at an Exhibition.*

Wolfgang Amadeus Mozart, 1756-91, (Austrian) Chamber music, concertos, operas (*Magic Flute, Marriage of Figaro*), 41 symphonies.

Jacques Offenbach, 1819-80, (Fr.) *Tales of Hoffmann.*

Carl Orff, 1895-1982, (Ger.) *Carmina Burana.*

Johann Pachelbel, 1653-1706, (Ger.) *Canon and Fugue in D major.*

Ignacy Paderewski, 1860-1941, (Pol.) *Minuet in G.*

Niccolò Paganini, 1782-1840, (It.) *Caprices for violin solo.*

Giovanni Palestrina, c1525-94, (It.) Masses, madrigals.

Krzysztof Penderecki, b 1933, (Pol.) *Psalmus, Polymorphia, De natura sonoris.*

Francis Poulenc, 1899-1963, (Fr.) *Dialogues des Carmélites.*

Mel Powell, 1923-98, (U.S.) *Duplicates: A Concerto for Two Pianos and Orchestra, Cantilena Concertante.*

Sergei Prokofiev, 1891-1953, (Russ.) *Classical Symphony, Love for Three Oranges, Peter and the Wolf.*

Giacomo Puccini, 1858-1924, (It.) *La Boheme, Manon Lescaut, Tosca, Madama Butterfly.*

Henry Purcell, 1659-95, (Eng.) *Dido and Aeneas.*

Sergei Rachmaninoff, 1873-1943, (Russ.) Concertos, preludes (Prelude in C sharp minor), symphonies.

Maurice Ravel, 1875-1937, (Fr.) *Bolèro, Daphnis et Chloè, Piano Concerto in D for Left Hand Alone.*

Nikolai Rimsky-Korsakov, 1844-1908, (Russ.) *Golden Cockerel, Scheherazade, Flight of the Bumblebee.*

Gioacchino Rossini, 1792-1868, (It.) *Barber of Seville, Otello, William Tell.*

John Rutter, b 1945, (Br.) *Magnificat, Requiem.*

Camille Saint-Saëns, 1835-1921, (Fr.) *Carnival of Animals (The Swan), Samson and Delilah, Danse Macabre.*

Alessandro Scarlatti, 1660-1725, (It.) Cantatas, oratorios, operas.

Domenico Scarlatti, 1685-1757, (It.) Harpsichord works.

Alfred Schnittke, 1934-98 (Sov.-Ger.) *Life With an Idiot.*

Arnold Schoenberg, 1874-1951, (Austrian) *Pelleas and Melisande, Pierrot Lunaire, Verklärte Nacht.*

Franz Schubert, 1797-1828, (Austrian) Chamber music (*Trout Quintet*), lieder, symphonies (Unfinished).

Robert Schumann, 1810-56, (Ger.) *Die Frauenliebe und Leben, Träumerei.*

Dimitri Shostakovich, 1906-75, (Russ.) Symphonies, *Lady Macbeth of the District Mzensk.*

Jean Sibelius, 1865-1957, (Finn.) *Finlandia.*

Bedrich Smetana, 1824-84, (Czech.) *The Bartered Bride.*

Karlheinz Stockhausen, b 1928, (Ger.) *Kontra-Punkte, Kontakte for Electronic Instruments.*

Richard Strauss, 1864-1949, (Ger.) *Salome, Elektra, Der Rosenkavalier, Thus Spake Zarathustra.*

Igor Stravinsky, 1882-1971, (Russ.) *Noah and the Flood, The Rake's Progress, The Rite of Spring.*

Toru Takemitsu, 1930-96, (Jpn.) *Requiem for Strings, Dorian Horizon.*

Peter I. Tchaikovsky, 1840-93, (Russ.) *Nutcracker, Swan Lake, The Sleeping Beauty.*

Georg Philipp Telemann, 1681-1767, (Ger.) church music, orchestral suites, chamber music.

Virgil Thomson, 1896-1989, (U.S.) Opera, film music, *Four Saints in Three Acts.*

Dmitri Tiomkin, 1894-1979, (Russ.-U.S.) film scores, including *High Noon.*

Sir Michael Tippett, 1905-98, (Br.) *A Child of Our Time, The Midsummer Marriage, The Knot Garden.*

Ralph Vaughan Williams, 1872-1958, (Eng.) *Fantasiz on a Theme by Thomas Tallis,* symphonies, vocal music.

Giuseppe Verdi, 1813-1901, (It.) *Aida, Rigoletto, Don Carlo, Il Trovatore, La Traviata, Falstaff, Macbeth.*

Heitor Villa-Lobos, 1887-1959, (Brazil) *Bachianas Brasileiras.*

Antonio Vivaldi, 1678-1741, (It.) *Concerto grossos (The Four Seasons).*

Richard Wagner, 1813-83, (Ger.) *Rienzi, Tannhäuser, Lohengrin, Tristan and Isolde.*

Carl Maria von Weber, 1786-1826, (Ger.) *Der Freischutz.*

Composers of Operettas, Musicals, and Popular Music

Richard Adler, b 1921, (U.S.) *Pajama Game; Damn Yankees.*

Milton Ager, 1893-1979, (U.S.) I Wonder What's Become of Sally; Hard-Hearted Hannah; Ain't She Sweet?

Arthur Altman, 1910-94, (U.S.) All or Nothing at All.

Leroy Anderson, 1908-75, (U.S.) Sleigh Ride, Blue Tango, Syncopated Clock.

Paul Anka, b 1941, (Can.) My Way; *Tonight Show* theme.

Harold Arlen, 1905-86, (U.S.) Stormy Weather; Over the Rainbow; Blues in the Night; That Old Black Magic.

Burt Bacharach, b 1928, (U.S.) Raindrops Keep Fallin' on My Head; Walk on By; What the World Needs Now Is Love.

Ernest Ball, 1878-1927, (U.S.) Mother Machree; When Irish Eyes Are Smiling.

Irving Berlin, 1888-1989, (U.S.) *Annie Get Your Gun; Call Me Madam;* God Bless America; White Christmas.

Leonard Bernstein, 1918-90, (U.S.) *On the Town; Wonderful Town; Candide; West Side Story.*

Eubie Blake, 1883-1983, (U.S.) *Shuffle Along;* I'm Just Wild About Harry.

Jerry Bock, b 1928, (U.S.) *Mr. Wonderful; Fiorello; Fiddler on the Roof; The Rothschilds.*

Carrie Jacobs Bond, 1862-1946, (U.S.) I Love You Truly.

Nacio Herb Brown, 1896-1964, (U.S.) Singing in the Rain; You Were Meant for Me; All I Do Is Dream of You.

Hoagy Carmichael, 1899-1981, (U.S.) Stardust; Georgia on My Mind; Old Buttermilk Sky.

James Cleveland, 1931-91, (U.S.) composer, musician, singer; first black gospel artist to appear at Carnegie Hall.

George M. Cohan, 1878-1942, (U.S.) Give My Regards to Broadway; You're a Grand Old Flag; Over There.

Cy Coleman, 1929-2004, (U.S.) *Sweet Charity;* Witchcraft.

John Frederick Coots, 1895-1985, (U.S.) Santa Claus Is Coming to Town; You Go to My Head; For All We Know.

Noel Coward, 1899-1973, (Br.) *Bitter Sweet;* Mad Dogs and Englishmen; Mad About the Boy.

Neil Diamond, b 1941, (U.S.) I'm a Believer; Sweet Caroline.

Walter Donaldson, 1893-1947, (U.S.) My Buddy; Carolina in the Morning; Makin' Whoopee.

Vernon Duke, 1903-69, (U.S.) April in Paris.

Bob Dylan, b 1941, (U.S.) Blowin' in the Wind.

Gus Edwards, 1879-1945, (U.S.) School Days; By the Light of the Silvery Moon; In My Merry Oldsmobile.

Sherman Edwards, 1919-81, (U.S.) See You in September; Wonderful! Wonderful!

Duke Ellington, 1899-1974, (U.S.) Sophisticated Lady; Satin Doll; It Don't Mean a Thing; Solitude.

Sammy Fain, 1902-89, (U.S.) I'll Be Seeing You; Love Is a Many-Splendored Thing.

Fred Fisher, 1875-1942, (U.S.) Peg O' My Heart; Chicago.

Stephen Collins Foster, 1826-64, (U.S.) My Old Kentucky Home; Old Folks at Home, Beautiful Dreamer.

Rudolf Friml, 1879-1972, (Czech-U.S.) *The Firefly; Rose Marie; Vagabond King; Bird of Paradise.*

John Gay, 1685-1732, (Br.) *The Beggar's Opera.*

George Gershwin, 1898-1937, (U.S.) Someone to Watch Over Me; I've Got a Crush on You; Embraceable You.

Morton Gould, 1913-96, (U.S.) Fall River Suite, Holocaust Suite, Spirituals for Orchestra, Stringmusic.

Ferde Grofe, 1892-1972, (U.S.) Grand Canyon Suite.

Marvin Hamlisch, b 1944, (U.S.) The Way We Were; Nobody Does It Better; *A Chorus Line.*

Ray Henderson, 1896-1970, (U.S.) *George White's Scandals;* That Old Gang of Mine; Five Foot Two, Eyes of Blue.

Victor Herbert, 1859-1924, (Ir.-U.S.) *Mlle. Modiste; Babes in Toyland; The Red Mill; Naughty Marietta; Sweethearts.*

Jerry Herman, b 1931, (U.S.) *Hello Dolly; Mame.*

Brian Holland, b 1941, **Lamont Dozier,** b 1941, **Eddie Holland,** b 1939, (all U.S.) Heat Wave; Stop! In the Name of Love; Baby, I Need Your Loving.

Antonio Carlos Jobim, 1927-94, (Brazil) *The Girl From Ipanema; Desafinado; One Note Samba.*

Billy (William Martin) Joel, b 1949, (U.S.) Just the Way You Are; Honesty; Piano Man.

Elton John, b 1947 (Br.) *The Lion King;* Candle in the Wind; Your Song.

Scott Joplin, 1868-1917, (U.S.) Maple Leaf Rag; *Treemonisha.*

John Kander, b 1927, (U.S.) *Cabaret; Chicago; Funny Lady.*

Jerome Kern, 1885-1945, (U.S.) *Sally; Sunny; Show Boat.*

Carole King, b 1942, (U.S.) Will You Love Me Tomorrow?; Natural Woman; One Fine Day; Up on the Roof.

Burton Lane, 1912-1997, (U.S.) *Finian's Rainbow.*

Franz Lehar, 1870-1948, (Hung.) *Merry Widow.*

Jerry Leiber, & **Mike Stoller,** both b 1933, (both U.S.) Hound Dog; Searchin'; Yakety Yak; Love Me Tender.

Mitch Leigh, b 1928, (U.S.) *Man of La Mancha.*

John Lennon, 1940-80, & **Paul McCartney,** b 1942, (both Br.) I Want to Hold Your Hand; She Loves You.

Jay Livingston, 1915-2001 (U.S.) Mona Lisa; Que Sera, Sera.

Andrew Lloyd Webber, b 1948, (Br.) *Jesus Christ Superstar; Evita; Cats; The Phantom of the Opera.*

Frank Loesser, 1910-69, (U.S.) *Guys and Dolls; Where's Charley?; The Most Happy Fella; How to Succeed....*

Frederick Loewe, 1901-88, (Austrian-U.S.) *Brigadoon; Paint Your Wagon; My Fair Lady; Camelot.*

Henry Mancini, 1924-94, (U.S.) Moon River; Days of Wine and Roses; Pink Panther Theme.

Barry Mann, b 1939, & **Cynthia Weil,** b 1937, (both U.S.) You've Lost That Loving Feeling.

Jimmy McHugh, 1894-1969, (U.S.) Don't Blame Me; I'm in the Mood for Love; I Feel a Song Coming On.

Alan Menken, b 1949, (U.S.) *Little Shop of Horrors, Beauty and the Beast.*

Joseph Meyer, 1894-1987, (U.S.) If You Knew Susie; California, Here I Come; Crazy Rhythm.

Chauncey Olcott, 1858-1932, (U.S.) Mother Machree.

Jerome "Doc" Pomus, 1925-91, (U.S.) Save the Last Dance for Me; A Teenager in Love.

Cole Porter, 1893-1964, (U.S.) *Anything Goes; Kiss Me Kate; Can Can; Silk Stockings.*

Smokey Robinson, b 1940, (U.S.) Shop Around; My Guy; My Girl; Get Ready.

Richard Rodgers, 1902-79, (U.S.) *Oklahoma!; Carousel; South Pacific; The King and I; The Sound of Music.*

Sigmund Romberg, 1887-1951, (Hung.) *Maytime; The Student Prince; Desert Song; Blossom Time.*

Harold Rome, 1908-93, (U.S.) *Pins and Needles; Call Me Mister; Wish You Were Here; Fanny; Destry Rides Again.*

Vincent Rose, b 1880-1944, (U.S.) Avalon; Whispering; Blueberry Hill.

Harry Ruby, 1895-1974, (U.S.) Three Little Words; Who's Sorry Now?

Arthur Schwartz, 1900-84, (U.S.) *The Band Wagon;* Dancing in the Dark; By Myself; That's Entertainment.

Neil Sedaka, b 1939, (U.S.) Breaking Up Is Hard to Do.

Paul Simon, b 1942, (U.S.) Sounds of Silence; I Am a Rock; Mrs. Robinson; Bridge Over Troubled Waters.

Stephen Sondheim, b 1930, (U.S.) *A Little Night Music; Company; Sweeney Todd; Sunday in the Park With George.*

John Philip Sousa, 1854-1932, (U.S.) *El Capitan;* Stars and Stripes Forever.

Oskar Straus, 1870-1954, (Austrian) *Chocolate Soldier.*

Johann Strauss, 1825-99, (Austrian) *Gypsy Baron; Die Fledermaus;* waltzes: Blue Danube; Artist's Life.

Charles Strouse, b 1928, (U.S.) *Bye Bye, Birdie; Annie.*

Jule Styne, 1905-94, (Br.-U.S.) *Gentlemen Prefer Blondes; Bells Are Ringing; Gypsy; Funny Girl.*

Arthur S. Sullivan, 1842-1900, (Br.) *H.M.S. Pinafore; Pirates of Penzance; The Mikado.*

Deems Taylor, 1885-1966, (U.S.) *Peter Ibbetson.*

Harry Tobias, 1895-1994, (U.S.) I'll Keep the Lovelight Burning.

Egbert van Alstyne, 1882-1951, (U.S.) In the Shade of the Old Apple Tree; Memories; Pretty Baby.

Jimmy Van Heusen, 1913-90, (U.S.) Moonlight Becomes You; Swinging on a Star; All the Way; Love and Marriage.

Albert von Tilzer, 1878-1956, (U.S.) I'll Be With You in Apple Blossom Time; Take Me Out to the Ball Game.

Harry von Tilzer, 1872-1946, (U.S.) Only a Bird in a Gilded Cage; On a Sunday Afternoon.

Fats Waller, 1904-43, (U.S.) Honeysuckle Rose; Ain't Misbehavin'.

Harry Warren, 1893-1981, (U.S.) You're My Everything; We're in the Money; I Only Have Eyes for You.

Jimmy Webb, b 1946, (U.S.) Up, Up and Away; By the Time I Get to Phoenix; Didn't We?; Wichita Lineman.

Kurt Weill, 1900-50, (Ger.-U.S.) *Threepenny Opera; Lady in the Dark; Knickerbocker Holiday; One Touch of Venus.*

Percy Wenrich, 1887-1950, (U.S.) When You Wore a Tulip; Moonlight Bay; Put On Your Old Gray Bonnet.

Richard A. Whiting, 1891-1938, (U.S.) Till We Meet Again; Sleepytime Gal; Beyond the Blue Horizon; My Ideal.

John Williams, b 1932, (U.S.) *Jaws; E.T.; Star Wars* series; *Raiders of the Lost Ark* series.

Meredith Willson, 1902-84, (U.S.) *The Music Man.*

Stevie Wonder, b 1950, (U.S.) You Are the Sunshine of My Life; Signed, Sealed, Delivered, I'm Yours.

Vincent Youmans, 1898-1946, (U.S.) Two Little Girls in Blue; Wildflower; No, No, Nanette; Hit the Deck; Rainbow; Smiles.

Lyricists

Howard Ashman, 1950-91, (U.S.) *Little Shop of Horrors; The Little Mermaid.*

Johnny Burke, 1908-84, (U.S.) Misty; Imagination.

Irving Caesar, 1895-1996, (U.S.) Swanee; Tea for Two; Just a Gigolo.

Sammy Cahn, 1913-93, (U.S.) High Hopes; Love and Marriage; The Second Time Around; It's Magic.

Leonard Cohen, b 1934, (Can.) Suzanne; Stranger Song.

Betty Comden, 1917-2006, (U.S.) and **Adolph Green,** 1915-2002, (U.S.) The Party's Over; Just in Time; New York, New York.

Hal David, b 1921, (U.S.) What the World Needs Now Is Love.

Buddy De Sylva, 1895-1950, (U.S.) When Day Is Done; Look for the Silver Lining; April Showers.

Howard Dietz, 1896-1983, (U.S.) Dancing in the Dark; You and the Night and the Music; That's Entertainment.

Al Dubin, 1891-1945, (U.S.) Tiptoe Through the Tulips; Anniversary Waltz; Lullaby of Broadway.

Fred Ebb, b 1936-2004, (U.S.) *Cabaret; Zorba; Woman of the Year; Chicago.*

Ray Evans, 1915-2007, (U.S.) Mona Lisa; Que Sera, Sera.

Dorothy Fields, 1905-74, (U.S.) On the Sunny Side of the Street; Don't Blame Me; The Way You Look Tonight.

Ira Gershwin, 1896-1983, (U.S.) The Man I Love; Fascinating Rhythm; S'Wonderful; Embraceable You.

William S. Gilbert, 1836-1911, (Br.) *The Mikado; H.M.S. Pinafore; Pirates of Penzance.*

Gerry Goffin, b 1939, (U.S.) Will You Love Me Tomorrow; Take Good Care of My Baby; Up on the Roof.

Mack Gordon, 1905-59, (Pol.-U.S.) You'll Never Know; The More I See You; Chattanooga Choo-Choo.

Oscar Hammerstein II, 1895-1960, (U.S.) *Ol' Man River; Oklahoma!; Carousel.*

E. Y. (Yip) Harburg, 1898-1981, (U.S.) Brother, Can You Spare a Dime; April in Paris; Over the Rainbow.

Sheldon Harnick, b 1924, (U.S.) *Fiddler on the Roof; She Loves Me.*

Lorenz Hart, 1895-1943, (U.S.) .) Isn't It Romantic; Blue Moon; Lover; Manhattan; My Funny Valentine.

DuBose Heyward, 1885-1940, (U.S.) Summertime.

Gus Kahn, 1886-1941, (U.S.) Memories; Ain't We Got Fun.

Alan J. Lerner, 1918-86, (U.S.) *Brigadoon; My Fair Lady; Camelot; Gigi; On a Clear Day You Can See Forever.*

Johnny Mercer, 1909-76, (U.S.) Blues in the Night; Come Rain or Come Shine; Laura; That Old Black Magic.

Bob Merrill, 1921-98, (U.S.) People; (How Much Is That) Doggie in the Window.

Jack Norworth, 1879-1959, (U.S.) Take Me Out to the Ball Game; Shine On Harvest Moon.

Mitchell Parish, 1901-93, (U.S.) Stardust; Stairway to the Stars.

Andy Razaf, 1895-1973, (U.S.) Honeysuckle Rose; Ain't Misbehavin'; S'posin'.

Leo Robin, 1900-84, (U.S.) Thanks for the Memory; Hooray for Love; Diamonds Are a Girl's Best Friend.

Bernie Taupin, b 1947 (Br.) Rocket Man; Your Song.

Paul Francis Webster, 1907-84, (U.S.) Secret Love; The Shadow of Your Smile; Love Is a Many-Splendored Thing.

Jack Yellen, 1892-1991, (U.S.) Down by the O-Hi-O; Ain't She Sweet; Happy Days Are Here Again.

Blues and Jazz Artists of the Past

Julian "Cannonball" Adderley, 1928-75, alto sax
Nat Adderley, 1931-2000, cornet
Henry "Red" Allen, 1908-67, trumpet
Louis "Satchmo" Armstrong, 1901-71, trumpet, singer, bandleader
Albert Ayler, 1936-70, tenor sax, alto sax
Mildred Bailey, 1907-51, singer
Chet Baker, 1929-88, trumpet, singer
Ray Barretto, 1930-2006, conga drummer
Count Basie, 1904-84, bandleader, piano, composer
Sidney Bechet, 1897-1959, soprano sax, clarinet
Bix Beiderbecke, 1903-31, cornet, composer, piano
Bunny Berigan, 1908-42, trumpet
Barney Bigard, 1906-80, clarinet
Eubie Blake, 1883-1983, composer, piano
Art Blakey, 1919-90, drums, bandleader
Jimmy Blanton, 1921-42, bass
Charles "Buddy" Bolden, 1877-1931, cornet, pioneer bandleader
Lester Bowie, 1941-99, trumpet, composer, bandleader
Brecker, Michael, 1949-2007, saxophone
Big Bill Broonzy, 1893-1958, blues singer, guitar
Clarence "Gatemouth" Brown, 1924-2006, guitar, singer
Clifford Brown, 1930-56, trumpet
Ray Brown, 1926-2002, bass
Don Byas, 1912-72, tenor sax
Charlie Byrd, 1925-99, guitarist; popularized bossa nova
Cab Calloway, 1907-94, bandleader, singer
Harry Carney, 1910-74, baritone sax, clarinet
Betty Carter, 1930-98, jazz singer
Sidney "Big Sid" Catlett, 1910-51, drums
Doc Cheatham, 1905-97, trumpet
Don Cherry, 1936-95, trumpet
Charlie Christian, 1916-42, guitar
Kenny "Klook" Clarke, 1914-85, drums
Buck Clayton, 1911-91, trumpet
Al Cohn, 1925-88, tenor sax
Cozy Cole, 1909-81, drums
Alice Coltrane, 1937-2007, pianist, composer
John Coltrane, 1926-67, tenor sax, soprano sax, composer
Eddie Condon, 1905-73, guitar, bandleader
Tadd Dameron, 1917-65, piano, composer
Eddie "Lockjaw" Davis, 1921-86, tenor sax
Miles Davis, 1926-91, trumpet, composer
Wild Bill Davison, 1906-89, cornet
Paul Desmond, 1924-77, alto sax
Vic Dickenson, 1906-84, trombone
Willie Dixon, 1915-92, blues composer, bass
Johnny Dodds, 1892-1940, clarinet
Warren "Baby" Dodds, 1898-1959, drums
Eric Dolphy, 1928-64, alto sax, bass clarinet, flute
Jimmy Dorsey, 1904-57, alto sax, bandleader
Tommy Dorsey, 1905-56, trombone, bandleader
Billy Eckstine, 1914-93, singer, bandleader
Harry "Sweets" Edison, 1915-99, trumpet
Roy Eldridge, 1911-89, trumpet, singer

Duke Ellington, 1899-1974, piano, bandleader, composer
Bill Evans, 1929-80, piano
Gil Evans, 1912-88, composer, arranger, piano
Art Farmer, 1928-99, trumpet, flugelhorn
Maynard Ferguson, 1926-2006, trumpeter, bandleader
Ella Fitzgerald, 1917-96, singer
Tommy Flanagan, 1930-2001, piano
Erroll Garner, 1921-77, piano, composer
Stan Getz, 1927-91, tenor sax
Dizzy Gillespie, 1917-93, trumpet, composer, singer
Benny Goodman, 1909-86, clarinet, bandleader
Dexter Gordon, 1923-90, tenor sax
Stéphane Grappelli, 1908-97, violin
Bobby Hackett, 1915-76, trumpet, cornet
Lionel Hampton, 1908-2002, vibraphone, bandleader
W. C. Handy, 1873-1958, composer
Jimmy Harrison, 1900-31, trombone
Coleman Hawkins, 1904-69, tenor sax
Percy Heath, 1923-2005, bass
Fletcher Henderson, 1898-1952, bandleader, arranger
Woody Herman, 1913-87, clarinet, alto sax, bandleader
Jay C. Higginbotham, 1906-73, trombone
Ruiz Hilton, 1952-2006, piano, composer
Earl "Fatha" Hines, 1903-83, piano
Milt Hinton, 1910-2000, bass
Al Hirt, 1922-99, trumpet
Johnny Hodges, 1906-70, alto sax
Billie Holiday, 1915-59, singer
John Lee Hooker, 1917-2001, blues guitar, singer
Sam "Lightnin'" Hopkins, 1912-82, blues singer, guitar
Shirley Horn, 1934-2005, piano, singer
Howlin' Wolf, 1910-1976, blues singer, harmonica, guitar
Alberta Hunter, 1895-1984, singer
Mahalia Jackson, 1911-72, gospel singer
Milt Jackson, 1923-99, vibraphone
Elmore James, 1918-63, blues singer, guitar
Blind Lemon Jefferson, 1897-1930, blues singer, guitar
Bunk Johnson, 1879-1949, trumpet
J.J. Johnson, 1924-2001, trombone
James P. Johnson, 1891-1955, piano, composer
Robert Johnson, 1912-38, blues singer, guitar
Elvin Jones, 1927-2004, drums
Jo Jones, 1911-85, drums
Philly Joe Jones, 1923-85, drums
Thad Jones, 1923-86, cornet, bandleader, composer
Scott Joplin, 1868-1917, ragtime composer
Louis Jordan, 1908-75, singer, alto sax
Stan Kenton, 1911-79, bandleader, composer, piano
Barney Kessel, 1923-2004, guitar
Albert King, 1923-92, blues guitar
John Kirby, 1908-52, bandleader, bass
Rahsaan Roland Kirk, 1936-77, saxophones, composer
Gene Krupa, 1909-73, drums, bandleader
Scott LaFaro, 1936-61, bass
Huddie Ledbetter (Lead Belly), 1888-1949, folk and blues singer, guitar

John Lewis, 1920-2001, piano, Modern Jazz Quartet founder
Mel Lewis, 1929-90, drums, bandleader
Jimmie Lunceford, 1902-47, bandleader
Machito (Frank Grillo), 1912-84, Latin percussion, singer, bandleader
Shelly Manne, 1920-84, drums, bandleader
Jackie McLean, 1931-2006, saxophone, composer
Jimmy McPartland, 1907-91, trumpet
Carmen McRae, 1920-94, singer
Glenn Miller, 1904-44, trombone, bandleader
Charles Mingus, 1922-79, bass, composer, bandleader
Thelonious Monk, 1917-82, piano, composer
Wes Montgomery, 1925-68, guitar
"Jelly Roll" Morton, 1885-1941, composer, piano
Bennie Moten, 1894-1935, piano, bandleader
Gerry Mulligan, 1927-96, baritone sax, composer
"Fats" Navarro, 1923-50, trumpet
Red Nichols, 1905-65, cornet, bandleader
Red Norvo, 1908-99, vibraphone, xylophone, bandleader
Anita O'Day, 1919-2006, singer
Arturo "Chico" O'Farrill, 1921-2001, Latin composer, arranger
King Oliver, 1885-1938, cornet, band leader
Sy Oliver, 1910-88, arranger, composer
Kid Ory, 1886-1973, trombone, bandleader
Oran "Hot Lips" Page, 1908-54, trumpet, singer
Charlie "Bird" Parker, 1920-55, alto sax, composer
Joe Pass, 1929-94, guitar
Art Pepper, 1925-82, alto sax
Oscar Pettiford, 1922-60, bass
Bud Powell, 1924-66, piano
Chano Pozo, 1915-48, Cuban percussion, singer
Louis Prima, 1911-78, singer, bandleader
Tito Puente, 1923-2000, Latin percussion, bandleader
Gertrude "Ma" Rainey, 1886-1939, blues singer
Lou Rawls, 1933- 2006, singer
Dewey Redman, 1931-2006, tenor saxophone
Don Redman, 1900-64, composer, arranger
Django Reinhardt, 1910-53, guitar
Buddy Rich, 1917-87, drums
Max Roach, 1924-2007, drummer, composer
Red Rodney, 1928-94, trumpet
Jimmy Rowles, 1918-96, piano
Jimmy Rushing, 1903-72, blues and jazz singer
Pee Wee Russell, 1906-69, clarinet

Artie Shaw, 1910-2004, swing-era bandleader, clarinet
Zoot Sims, 1925-85, tenor sax
Zutty Singleton, 1898-1975, drums
Bessie Smith, 1894-1937, blues singer
Clarence "Pinetop" Smith, 1904-29, piano, singer; boogie woogie pioneer
Willie "The Lion" Smith, 1897-1973, piano, composer
Muggsy Spanier, 1906-67, cornet
Sonny Stitt, 1924-82, tenor sax, alto sax
Billy Strayhorn, 1915-67, composer, piano; Duke Ellington collaborator
Sun Ra, 1915?-93, bandleader, piano, composer
Art Tatum, 1910-56, piano
Art Taylor, 1929-95, drums
Jack Teagarden, 1905-64, trombone, singer
Mel Tormé, 1925-99, singer ("the Velvet Fog")
Dave Tough, 1908-48, drums
Lennie Tristano, 1919-78, piano, composer
Joe Turner, 1911-85, blues singer
Sarah Vaughan, 1924-90, singer
Joe Venuti, 1904-78, violin
T-Bone Walker, 1910-75, blues guitar
Thomas "Fats" Waller, 1904-43, piano, singer, composer
Dinah Washington, 1924-63, singer
Grover Washington Jr., 1943-99, pop-jazz sax, composer
Ethel Waters, 1896-1977, jazz and blues singer
Muddy Waters, 1915-83, blues singer, songwriter
Julius Watkins, 1921-77, French horn
Chick Webb, 1902-39, bandleader, drums
Ben Webster, 1909-73, tenor sax
Junior Wells, 1934-98, blues singer, harmonica
Paul Whiteman, 1890-1967, bandleader
Charles "Cootie" Williams, 1910-85, trumpet, bandleader
Joe Williams, 1918-99, singer
Mary Lou Williams, 1910-81, piano, composer
Tony Williams, 1945-97, drums
John Lee "Sonny Boy" Williamson, 1914-48, blues singer, harmonica
Sonny Boy Williamson (Aleck "Rice" Miller), 1900?-65, blues singer, harmonica
Teddy Wilson, 1912-86, piano
Kai Winding, 1922-83, trombone
Jimmy Yancey, 1894-1951, piano
Lester "Pres" Young, 1909-59, tenor sax

Noted Country Music Artists of the Past and Present

Roy Acuff, 1903-92, fiddler, singer, songwriter; "Wabash Cannon Ball"
Alabama (Randy Owen, b 1949; Jeff Cook, b 1949; Teddy Gentry, b 1952 ; Mark Herndon, b 1955) "Feels So Right"
Eddy Arnold, b 1918, singer, guitarist, the "Tennessee Plowboy"
Chet Atkins, 1924-2001, guitarist, composer, producer, helped create the "Nashville sound"
Gene Autry, 1907-98, first great singing movie cowboy; "Back in the Saddle Again"
Garth Brooks, b 1962, singer, songwriter; "Friends in Low Places"
Brooks & Dunn (Kix Brooks, b 1955; Ronnie Dunn, b 1953) "Hard Workin' Man"
Boudleaux and Felice Bryant (Boudleaux, 1920-87; Felice, 1925-2003), songwriting team; "Hey Joe"
Mary Chapin Carpenter, b 1958, singer, songwriter; "I Feel Lucky"
Carter Family (original members,"Mother" Maybelle 1909-78; A.P., 1891-1960, Sara, 1898-1979) "Wildwood Flower"
Johnny Cash, 1932-2003, singer, songwriter; "I Walk the Line," "Ring of Fire," "Folsom Prison Blues"
Kenny Chesney, b 1968, guitar, singer, songwriter; "You Had Me from Hello"
Patsy Cline, 1932-63, singer; "Walkin' After Midnight," "Crazy," "Sweet Dreams"
John Denver, 1943-97, singer, songwriter; "Rocky Mountain High"
Dixie Chicks (Natalie Maines, b 1974; Martie Seidel, b 1969; Emily Erwin Robison, b 1972) "Wide Open Spaces," "Fly"
Dale Evans (Lucille Wood Smith), 1912-2001, singer, actress, married Roy Rogers
Flatt & Scruggs (Lester Flatt, 1914-79; Earl Scruggs, b 1924), guitar-banjo duo and soloists; "Foggy Mountain Breakdown"
Red Foley, 1910-68, singer; "Chattanoogie Shoe Shine Boy"
Tennessee Ernie Ford, 1919-91, singer, TV host; "Sixteen Tons"
Lefty Frizzell, 1928-75, singer, guitarist; "Long Black Veil"
Vince Gill, b 1957, singer, songwriter; "When I Call Your Name"
Merle Haggard, b 1937, singer, songwriter; "Okie from Muskogee"
Emmylou Harris, b 1947, singer, songwriter, folk-country crossover artist; "If I Could Only Win Your Love"
Faith Hill, b 1967, singer, songwriter, married Tim McGraw; "Wild One," "This Kiss," "Breathe"
Alan Jackson, b 1958, singer, songwriter, "Where Were You (When the World Stopped Turning)"

Waylon Jennings, 1937–2002, singer, songwriter, "outlaw country" pioneer; "Luckenbach, Texas"
George Jones, b 1931, singer, "He Stopped Loving Her Today"
The Judds (Naomi, 1946- ; Wynonna, 1964-), mother-daughter duo; Wynonna also a solo act
Alison Krauss, b 1971, bluegrass fiddler, singer, bandleader; "When You Say Nothing at All"
Kris Kristofferson, b 1936, singer, songwriter, actor; "Me and Bobby McGee"
Patty Loveless, b 1957, singer, songwriter; "How Can I Help You Say Goodbye"
Lyle Lovett, b 1957, singer, songwriter, bandleader, actor; "Cowboy Man"
Loretta Lynn, b 1935, singer, songwriter; "Coal Miner's Daughter"
Kathy Mattea, b 1959, singer, songwriter; "Eighteen Wheels and a Dozen Roses"
Martina McBride, b 1966, singer, songwriter; "Independence Day"
Reba McEntire, b 1955, singer, songwriter, actress; "Whoever's in New England"
Tim McGraw, b 1967, singer; "It's Your Love," with wife, Faith Hill
Roger Miller, 1936-92, singer, songwriter; "King of the Road"
Ronnie Milsap, b 1944, singer, songwriter; "There's No Gettin' Over Me"
Bill Monroe, 1911-96, singer, songwriter, mandolin player, "father of bluegrass music"; "Mule Skinner Blues"
Willie Nelson, b 1933, singer, songwriter, actor; "On the Road Again"
Mark O'Connor, b 1961, fiddler, country-classical crossover composer
Brad Paisley, b 1972, singer, songwriter; "Whiskey Lullaby," "When I Get Where I'm Going"
Dolly Parton, b 1946, singer, songwriter, actress; "Dollywood" theme park; "Here You Come Again," "9 to 5"
Minnie Pearl, 1912-96, comedienne, Grand Ole Opry star
Charley Pride, b 1938, singer, 1st African American country star; "Kiss an Angel Good Mornin'"
Rascal Flatts, (Jay DeMarcus, b 1971; Gary LeVox, b 1970; Joe Don Rooney, b 1975) "Life Is A Highway"
Jim Reeves, 1923-64, singer, songwriter; "Four Walls"
Charlie Rich, 1932-95, singer, songwriter called the "Silver Fox"; "The Most Beautiful Girl"
LeAnn Rimes, b 1982, singer; "Blue"

Tex Ritter, 1905-74, singer, songwriter; "Jingle, Jangle, Jingle"

Marty Robbins, 1925-82, singer, songwriter; "A White Sport Coat and a Pink Carnation"

Jimmie Rodgers, 1897-1933, singer, songwriter; "T for Texas"

Kenny Rogers, b 1938, singer, songwriter; "The Gambler"

Roy Rogers (Leonard Slye), 1911-98, singer, actor; "King of the Cowboys," sang with Sons of the Pioneers.

Fred Rose, 1898-1954, songwriter, singer, producer; "Blue Eyes Cryin' in the Rain"

Ricky Skaggs, b 1954, singer, songwriter, bandleader; "Don't Cheat in Our Hometown"

Ralph Stanley, b 1927, singer, banjo player; "Man of Constant Sorrow"

George Strait, b 1952, singer, bandleader; "Ace in the Hole"

Merle Travis, 1917-83, singer, guitarist, songwriter; "Divorce Me C.O.D."

Randy Travis, b 1959, singer, songwriter; "Forever and Ever, Amen"

Ernest Tubb, 1914-84, singer, songwriter, guitarist; "Walking the Floor Over You"

Shania Twain, b 1965, singer, songwriter; "You're Still the One"

Conway Twitty, 1933-93, singer, songwriter; "Hello Darlin' "

Carrie Underwood, b 1983, singer, American Idol winner

Keith Urban, b 1967, guitar, singer, songwriter; "It's a Love Thing"

Dottie West, 1932-91, singer, songwriter; "Here Comes My Baby"

Hank Williams Jr., b 1949, singer, songwriter; "Bocephus"; "All My Rowdy Friends (Have Settled Down)"

Hank Williams Sr., 1923-53, singer, songwriter; "Your Cheatin' Heart"

Bob Wills, 1905-75, Western Swing fiddler, singer, bandleader, songwriter; "New San Antonio Rose"

Tammy Wynette, 1942-98, singer; "Stand By Your Man"

Trisha Yearwood, b 1964, singer, songwriter; "How Do I Live"

Dwight Yoakam, b 1957, singer, songwriter, actor; "Ain't That Lonely Yet"

Dance Figures of the Past

Alvin Ailey, 1931-89, (U.S.) modern dancer, choreographer; melded modern dance and Afro-Caribbean techniques.

Frederick Ashton, 1904-88, (Br.) ballet choreographer; director of Great Britain's Royal Ballet, 1963-70.

Fred Astaire, 1899-1987, (U.S.) dancer, actor; teamed with dancer/actress **Ginger Rogers** 1911-95, (U.S.) in movie musicals.

George Balanchine, 1904-83, (Russ.-U.S.) ballet choreographer, teacher; most influential exponent of the neoclassical style; founded, with Lincoln Kirstein, School of American Ballet and New York City Ballet.

Carlo Blasis, 1803-78, (It.) ballet dancer, choreographer, writer; his teaching methods are standards of classical dance.

August Bournonville, 1805-79, (Dan.) ballet dancer, choreographer, teacher; exuberant, light style.

Fernando Bujones, 1955-2005, (Cuba-U.S.) ballet dancer.

Gisella Caccialanza, 1914-97, (U.S.) ballerina, charter member of Balanchine's American Ballet.

Enrico Cecchetti, 1850-1928, (It.) ballet dancer, leading dancer of Russia's Imperial Ballet; his technique was basis for Britain's Imperial Soc. of Teachers of Dancing.

Gower Champion, 1921-80, (U.S.) dancer, choreographer, director; with his wife **Marge,** b 1923, (U.S.) choreographed, danced in Broadway musicals and films.

John Cranko, 1927-73, (S. African) choreographer; created narrative ballets based on literary works.

Agnes de Mille, 1909-93, (U.S.) dancer, choreographer; known for using American themes, she choreographed the ballet *Rodeo* and the musical *Oklahoma!*

Alexandra Danilova, 1903-97, (Russ.) ballerina; noted teacher at the School of American Ballet.

Dame Ninette DeValois, 1898-2001, (Br.) choreographer, founding director London's Royal Ballet; *The Rake's Progress.*

Sergei Diaghilev, 1872-1929, (Russ.) impresario; founded Les Ballet Russes; saw ballet as an art unifying dance, drama, music, and decor.

Isadora Duncan, 1877-1927, (U.S.) expressive dancer who united free movement with serious music; one of the founders of modern dance.

Katherine Dunham, 1910-2006, (U.S.) dancer, choreographer; internationally known for African, Caribbean, and African American dance forms.

Fanny Elssler, 1810-84, (Austrian) ballerina of the Romantic era; known for dramatic skill, sensual style.

Michel Fokine, 1880-1942, (Russ.) ballet dancer, choreographer, teacher; rejected strict classicism in favor of dramatically expressive style.

Margot Fonteyn, 1919-91, (Br.) prima ballerina, Royal Ballet of Great Britain; famed performance partner of Rudolf Nureyev.

Bob Fosse, 1927-87, (U.S.) jazz dancer, choreographer, director; Broadway musicals and film.

Serge Golovine, 1924-98, (Fr.) ballet dancer with Grand Ballet du Marquis de Cuevas; choreographer.

Martha Graham, 1893-1991, (U.S.) modern dancer, choreographer; created and codified her own dramatic technique.

Melissa Hayden, 1923-2006, (Canada) ballet dancer.

Martha Hill, 1901-95, (U.S.) educator; leading figure in modern dance; founded American Dance Festival.

Gregory Hines, 1946-2003, (U.S.) tap-dance innovator and master of improvisation.

Doris Humphrey, 1895-1958, (U.S.) modern dancer, choreographer, writer, teacher.

Robert Joffrey, 1930-88, (U.S.) ballet dancer, choreographer; cofounded with **Gerald Arpino,** b 1928, (U.S.), the Joffrey Ballet.

Kurt Jooss, 1901-79, (Ger.) choreographer, teacher; created expressionist works using modern and classical techniques.

Tamara Karsavina, 1885-1978, (Russ.) prima ballerina of Russia's Imperial Ballet and Diaghilev's Ballets Russes; partner of Nijinsky.

Nora Kaye, 1920-87, (U.S.) ballerina with Metropolitan Opera Ballet and Ballet Theater (now American Ballet Theatre).

Lincoln Kirstein, 1907-96 (U.S.) brought ballet as an art form to U.S.; founded, with George Balanchine, School of American Ballet and New York City Ballet.

Serge Lifar, 1905-86, (Russ.-Fr.) prem. danseur, choreographer; director of dance at Paris Opera, 1930-45, 1947-58.

José Limón, 1908-72, (Mex.-U.S.) modern dancer, choreographer, teacher; developed technique based on Humphrey.

Catherine Littlefield, 1908-51, (U.S.) ballerina, choreographer, teacher; pioneer of American ballet.

Alicia Markova, 1910-2004, (Br.) ballet dancer.

Léonide Massine, 1896-1979, (Russ.-U.S.) ballet dancer, choreographer; known for his "symphonic ballet."

Kenneth MacMillan, 1929-92, (Br.) dancer, choreographer; directed Royal Ballet of Great Britain 1970-77.

Dame Alicia Markova, 1910-2004, (Br.) ballerina; helped popularize ballet in U.S. and Britain; known for title role in *Giselle.*

Fayard Nicholas, 1914-2006, (U.S.) tap dancer, choreographer, actor; together with brother **Harold Nicholas,** 1921-2000, (U.S.) formed the "Nicholas Brothers."

Vaslav Nijinsky, 1890-50, (Russ.) prem. danseur, choreographer; leading member of Diaghilev's Ballets Russes; his ballets were revolutionary for their time.

Alwin Nikolais, 1910-93, (U.S.) modern choreographer; created dance theater utilizing mixed media effects.

Jean-George Noverre, 1727-1810, (Fr.) ballet choreographer, teacher, writer; "Shakespeare of the Dance."

Rudolf Nureyev, 1938-93, (Russ.) prem. danseur, choreographer; leading male dancer of his generation; director of dance at Paris Opera, 1983-89.

Ruth Page, 1903-91, (U.S.) ballerina, choreographer; danced and directed ballet at Chicago Lyric Opera.

Anna Pavlova, 1881-1931, (Russ.) prima ballerina; toured with her own company to world acclaim.

Marius Petipa, 1818-1910, (Fr.) ballet dancer, choreographer; ballet master of the Imperial Ballet; established Russian classicism as leading style of late 19th cent.

Pearl Primus, 1919-95, (Trinidad-U.S.) modern dancer, choreographer, scholar; combined African, Caribbean, and African American styles.

Jerome Robbins, 1918-98, (U.S.) choreographer, director, dancer; *The King and I, West Side Story, Fiddler on the Roof.*

Bill (Bojangles) Robinson, 1878-1949, (U.S.) famed tap dancer; called King of Tapology on stage and screen.

Ruth St. Denis, 1877-1968, (U.S.) influential interpretive dancer, choreographer, teacher.

Ted Shawn, 1891-1972, (U.S.) modern dancer, choreographer; formed dance company and school with Ruth St. Denis; established Jacob's Pillow Dance Festival.

Marie Taglioni, 1804-84, (It.) ballerina, teacher; in title role of *La Sylphide* established image of the ethereal ballerina.

Glen Tetley, 1926-2007, (U.S.) dancer, choreographer, ballet director; fused elements of modern cance with ballet.

Antony Tudor, 1908-87, (Br.) choreographer, teacher; exponent of the "psychological ballet."

Galina Ulanova, 1910-98, (Russ.) revered ballerina with Bolshoi Ballet.

Agrippina Vaganova, 1879-1951, (Russ.) ballet teacher, director; codified Soviet ballet technique that developed virtuosity; called "queen of variations."

Mary Wigman, 1886-1973, (Ger.) modern dancer, choreographer, teacher; influenced European expressionist dance.

Opera Singers of the Past

Frances Alda, 1883-1952, (N.Z.) soprano
Pasquale Amato, 1878-1942, (It.) baritone
Marian Anderson, 1897-1993, (U.S.) contralto
Jussi Björling, 1911-60, (Swed.) tenor
Lucrezia Bori, 1887-1960, (It.) soprano
Maria Callas, 1923-77, (U.S.) soprano
Emma Calvé, 1858-1942, (Fr.) soprano
Enrico Caruso, 1873-1921, (It.) tenor
Feodor Chaliapin, 1873-1938, (Russ.) bass
Boris Christoff, 1914-93, (Bulg.) bass
Franco Corelli, 1921-2003, (It.) tenor
Victoria De Los Angeles, 1923-2005, (Sp.) soprano
Giuseppe De Luca, 1876-1950, (It.) baritone
Fernando De Lucia, 1860-1925, (It.) tenor
Edouard De Reszke, 1853-1917, (Pol.) bass
Jean De Reszke, 1850-1925, (Pol.) tenor
Emmy Destinn, 1878-1930, (Czech.) soprano
Emma Eames, 1865-1952, (U.S.) soprano
(Carlo Broschi) Farinelli, 1705-82, (It.) castrato
Geraldine Farrar, 1882-1967, (U.S.) soprano
Eileen Farrell, 1920-2002, (U.S.) soprano
Kathleen Ferrier, 1912-53, (Eng.) contralto
Kirsten Flagstad, 1895-1962, (Nor.) soprano
Olive Fremstad, 1871-1951, (Swed.-U.S.) soprano
Amelita Galli-Curci, 1882-1963, (It.) soprano
Mary Garden, 1874-1967, (Br.) soprano
Nicolai Ghiaurov, 1929-2004, (Bulg.) bass
Beniamino Gigli, 1890-1957, (It.) tenor
Tito Gobbi, 1913-84, (It.) baritone
Giulia Grisi, 1811-69, (It.) soprano
Frieda Hempel, 1885-1955, (Ger.) soprano
Jerome Hines, 1921-2003, (U.S.) bass
Hans Hotter, 1909-2003, (Ger.) bass-baritone
Maria Jeritza, 1887-1982, (Czech.) soprano
Alexander Kipnis, 1891-1978, (Russ.-U.S.) bass
Dorothy Kirsten, 1910-1992, (U.S.) soprano
Alfredo Kraus, 1927-99, (Sp.) tenor
Luigi Lablache, 1794-1858, (It.) bass
Lilli Lehmann, 1848-1929, (Ger.) soprano
Lotte Lehmann, 1888-1976, (Ger.-U.S.) soprano

Jenny Lind, 1820-87, (Swed.) soprano
Maria Malibran, 1808-36, (Sp.) mezzo-soprano
Giovanni Martinelli, 1885-1969, (It.) tenor
John McCormack, 1884-1945, (Ir.) tenor
Nellie Melba, 1861-1931, (Austral.) soprano.
Lauritz Melchior, 1890-1973, (Dan.) tenor
Robert Merrill, 1919-2004, (U.S.) baritone
Zinka Milanov, 1906-89, (Yugo.) soprano
Birgit Nilsson, 1918-2005, (Swed.) soprano
Lillian Nordica, 1857-1914, (U.S.) soprano
Giuditta Pasta, 1797-1865, (It.) soprano
Adelina Patti, 1843-1919, (It.) soprano
Luciano Pavarotti, 1934-2007, (It.) tenor
Peter Pears, 1910-86, (Eng.) tenor
Jan Peerce, 1904-84, (U.S.) tenor
Ezio Pinza, 1892-1957, (It.) bass
Lily Pons, 1898-1976, (Fr.) soprano
Rosa Ponselle, 1897-1981, (U.S.) soprano
Hermann Prey, 1929-98, (Ger.) baritone.
Elisabeth Rethberg, 1894-1976, (Ger.) soprano
Giovanni Battista Rubini, 1794-1854, (It.) tenor
Leonie Rysanek, 1926-1998, (Austrian) soprano
Bidú Sayão, 1902-99, (Braz.) soprano
Friedrich Schorr, 1888-1953, (Hung.) bass-baritone
Elisabeth Schwarzkopf, 1915-2006, (Ger.) soprano
Marcella Sembrich, 1858-1935, (Pol.) soprano
Beverly Sills, 1929-2007 (U.S.) soprano
Eleanor Steber, 1916-90, (U.S.) soprano
Ferrucio Tagliavini, 1913-95, (It.) tenor
Renata Tebaldi, 1922-2004 (It.) soprano
Luisa Tetrazzini, 1871-1940, (It.) soprano
Lawrence Tibbett, 1896-1960, (U.S.) baritone
Tatiana Troyanos, 1938-93, (U.S.) mezzo-soprano
Richard Tucker, 1913-75, (U.S.) tenor
Pauline Viardot, 1821-1910, (Fr.) mezzo-soprano
William Warfield, 1920-2002, (U.S.) bass-baritone
Leonard Warren, 1911-60, (U.S.) baritone
Ljuba Welitsch, 1913-96, (Bulg.) soprano
Wolfgang Windgassen, 1914-74, (Ger.) tenor

Selected Rock and Roll, Rhythm and Blues, Rap Artists

Titles in quotation marks are singles; others are albums. * Inducted into Rock and Roll Hall of Fame as performer between 1986 and 2007; year is in parentheses.

Aaliyah: "More than a Woman"
Paula Abdul: "Straight Up"
*AC/DC (2003): "Back in Black"
Bryan Adams: "Cuts Like a Knife"
*Aerosmith (2001): "Sweet Emotion"
Christina Aguilera: "What a Girl Wants"
Alice In Chains: "Heaven Beside You"
*The Allman Brothers Band (1995): "Ramblin' Man"
Paul Anka: "Lonely Boy"
Fiona Apple: "Criminal"
Ashanti: "Foolish"
Frankie Avalon: "Venus"
The B-52s: "Love Shack"
Bachman Turner Overdrive: "Takin' Care of Business"
Backstreet Boys: "I Want it That Way"
Bad Company: "Can't Get Enough"
Erykah Badu: "On and On"
*La Vern Baker (1991): "I Cried a Tear"
*Hank Ballard[1] and the Midnighters (1990): "Work With Me, Annie"
*The Band (1994): "The Weight"
Barenaked Ladies: "One Week"
*The Beach Boys (1988): "Good Vibrations"
Beastie Boys: "(You Gotta) Fight for Your Right (to Party)"
*The Beatles (1988): Sgt. Pepper's Lonely Hearts Club Band
Beck: "Loser"
*The Bee Gees (1997): "Stayin' Alive"
Pat Benatar: "Hit Me With Your Best Shot"
Beyoncé: "Crazy in Love"
Ben Folds Five: "Brick"
*Chuck Berry (1986): "Johnny B. Goode"
The Big Bopper: "Chantilly Lace"
Björk: "Human Behavior"
The Black Crowes: "Hard to Handle"
Black Eyed Peas: Elephunk
*Black Sabbath (2006): "Paranoid"
*Bobby "Blue" Bland (1992): "Turn On Your Love Light"
Mary J. Blige: My Life
Blind Faith: "Can't Find My Way Home"
Blink-182: "All the Small Things"
*Blondie (2006): "Heart of Glass"
Blood, Sweat, and Tears: "Spinning Wheel"
Blues Traveler: "Run-Around"

Gary "U.S." Bonds: "Quarter to Three"
Bon Jovi: "Livin' on a Prayer"
*Booker T. and the M.G.'s (1992): "Green Onions"
Earl Bostic: "Flamingo"
Boston: "More Than A Feeling"
*David Bowie (1996): "Space Oddity"
Boyz II Men: "I'll Make Love to You"
Toni Braxton: "Un-Break My Heart"
*James Brown (1986): "Papa's Got a Brand New Bag"
*Ruth Brown (1993): "Lucky Lips"
*Jackson Browne (2004): "Doctor My Eyes"
*Buffalo Springfield (1997): "For What It's Worth"
*Jimmy Buffett: "Margaritaville"
*Solomon Burke (2001): "Over and Over (Huggin' and Lovin')"
Bush: "Glycerine"
*The Byrds (1991): "Turn! Turn! Turn!"
Mariah Carey: "Vision of Love"
The Carpenters: "(They Long to Be) Close to You"
The Cars: "Shake It Up"
*Johnny Cash (1992): "I Walk the Line"
*Ray Charles (1986): "Georgia on My Mind"
Cheap Trick: "Surrender"
Chicago: "Saturday in the Park"
Chubby Checker: "The Twist"
*Eric Clapton (2000): "Layla"
Kelly Clarkson: "Since U Been Gone"
*The Clash (2003): "Rock the Casbah"
*The Coasters (1987): "Yakety Yak"
*Eddie Cochran (1987): "Summertime Blues"
Joe Cocker: "With a Little Help From My Friends"
Coldplay: "Clocks"
Collective Soul: "The World I Know"
Phil Collins: "Against All Odds"
*Sam Cooke (1986): "You Send Me"
Coolio: "Gangsta's Paradise"
Alice Cooper: "School's Out"
*Elvis Costello and the Attractions (2003): "Alison"
Counting Crows: "Mr. Jones"
*Cream (1993): "Sunshine of Your Love"
Creed: "Arms Wide Open"
*Creedence Clearwater Revival (1993): "Proud Mary"
*Crosby, Stills, and Nash (1997): "Suite: Judy Blue Eyes"
Sheryl Crow: "All I Want to Do"
The Cure: "Boys Don't Cry"

The Crystals: "Da Doo Ron Ron"
Cypress Hill: "Insane in the Brain"
Danny and the Juniors: "At the Hop"
*Bobby Darin (1990): "Splish Splash"
*Miles Davis (2006): *Bitches Brew*
Spencer Davis Group: "Gimme Some Lovin' "
Deep Purple: "Smoke on the Water"
Def Leppard: "Photograph"
*The Dells (2004): "Oh, What a Night"
Depeche Mode: "Strange Love"
Destiny's Child: "Survivor"
*Bo Diddley (1987): "Who Do You Love?"
*Dion[1] and the Belmonts (1989): "A Teenager in Love"
Celine Dion: "Because You Loved Me"
Dire Straits: "Money for Nothing"
DMX: "What's My Name"
*Fats Domino (1986): "Blueberry Hill"
Donovan: "Mellow Yellow"
The Doobie Brothers: "What a Fool Believes"
*The Doors (1993): "Light My Fire"
Dr. Dre: "Nothin' But a 'G' Thang"
*The Drifters (1988): "Save the Last Dance for Me"
Duran Duran: "Hungry Like the Wolf"
*Bob Dylan (1988): "Like a Rolling Stone"
*The Eagles (1998): "Hotel California"
*Earth, Wind, and Fire (2000): "Shining Star"
*Duane Eddy (1994): "Rebel-Rouser"
Missy Elliott: "Sock It 2 Me"
Eminem: "The Real Slim Shady"
En Vogue: "Hold On"
The Eurythmics: "Sweet Dreams (Are Made of This)"
Everclear: "Father Of Mine"
*The Everly Brothers (1986): "Wake Up, Little Susie"
50 Cent (Curtis Jackson): *Get Rich Or Die Tryin'*
The Five Satins: "In the Still of the Night"
*The Flamingos (2001): "I Only Have Eyes for You"
*Fleetwood Mac (1998): *Rumours*
The Foo Fighters: "I'll Stick Around"
Foreigner: "Double Vision"
*The Four Seasons (1990): "Sherry"
*The Four Tops (1990): "I Can't Help Myself (Sugar Pie, Honey Bunch)"
*Aretha Franklin (1987): "Respect"
Nelly Furtado: "I'm Like a Bird"
Peter Gabriel: "Shock the Monkey"
*Marvin Gaye (1987): "I Heard It Through the Grapevine"
Genesis: "No Reply at All"
Goo Goo Dolls: "Iris"
Grand Funk Railroad: "We're an American Band"
*Grandmaster Flash and the Furious Five (2007): "The Message"
*The Grateful Dead (1994): "Uncle John's Band"
*Al Green (1995): "Let's Stay Together"
Green Day: "Boulevard of Broken Dreams"
The Guess Who: "American Woman"
Guns N' Roses: "Sweet Child o' Mine"
*Buddy Guy (2005): *A Man and His Blues*
*Bill Haley[1] and His Comets (1987): "Rock Around the Clock"
Hall and Oates: "Kiss on My List"
Hanson: "MMMBop"
*Isaac Hayes (2002): "Theme from 'Shaft'"
Heart: "Barracuda"
*Jimi Hendrix (1992): "Purple Haze"
Lauryn Hill: "Doo-Wop (That Thing)"
Hole: "Doll Parts"
The Hollies: "Long Cool Woman (In a Black Dress)"
*Buddy Holly (1986): "Peggy Sue"
*John Lee Hooker (1991): "Boogie Chillen"
Hootie and the Blowfish: *Cracked Rear View*
Whitney Houston: "I Will Always Love You"
*The Impressions (1991): "For Your Precious Love"
Indigo Girls: "Closer to Fine"
INXS: "Need You Tonight"
*The Isley Brothers (1992): "It's Your Thing"
*The Jackson Five (1997): "ABC"
Janet Jackson: *Rhythm Nation*
*Michael Jackson (2001): *Thriller*
*Etta James (1993): "At Last"
Tommy James & The Shondells: "Crimson and Clover"
Jane's Addiction: "Jane Says"
Ja Rule: *Venni, Vetti, Vecci*
Jay and the Americans: "This Magic Moment"
Jay-Z: "Can I Live"
*Jefferson Airplane (1996): "White Rabbit"
Jethro Tull: *Aqualung*
Joan Jett: "I Love Rock 'n' Roll"
Jewel: "You Were Meant for Me"
*Billy Joel (1999): "Piano Man"
*Elton John (1994): "Candle in the Wind"
*Little Willie John (1996): "Sleep"
Norah Jones: *Come Away With Me*

*Janis Joplin (1995): "Me and Bobby McGee"
Journey: "Don't Stop Believin'"
K.C. and the Sunshine Band: "Get Down Tonight"
R. Kelly: "I Can't Sleep Baby (If I)"
Alicia Keys: "Fallin'"
Kid Rock: "Cowboy"
*B.B. King (1987): "The Thrill Is Gone"
Carole King: *Tapestry*
*The Kinks (1990): "You Really Got Me"
Kiss: "Rock 'n' Roll All Night"
*Gladys Knight and the Pips (1996): "Midnight Train to Georgia"
Korn: "Blind"
Lenny Kravitz: "Are You Gonna Go My Way?"
*Led Zeppelin (1995): "Stairway to Heaven"
*Brenda Lee (2002): "I'm Sorry"
John Legend: "Ordinary People"
*Jerry Lee Lewis (1986): "Whole Lotta Shakin' Going On"
Lil' Kim: "No Matter What They Say"
Limp Bizkit: "Break Stuff"
Linkin Park: "One Step Closer"
Little Anthony and the Imperials: "Tears on My Pillow"
*Little Richard (1986): "Tutti Frutti"
Live: "Lightning Crashes"
L. L. Cool J: "Mama Said Knock You Out"
Jennifer Lopez: "Love Don't Cost a Thing"
*The Lovin' Spoonful (2000): "Summer in the City"
Ludacris: "Money Maker"
*Frankie Lymon and the Teenagers (1993): "Why Do Fools Fall in Love?"
*Lynyrd Skynyrd (2006): "Free Bird"
Madonna: "Material Girl"
Taj Mahal: "Going up to the Country, Paint My Mailbox Blue"
*The Mamas and the Papas (1998): "Monday, Monday"
Aimee Mann: "Save Me"
Marilyn Manson: "Beautiful People"
*Bob Marley (1994): *Exodus*
Maroon 5: *Songs About Jane*
*Martha and the Vandellas (1995): "Dancin' in the Streets"
The Marvelettes: "Please, Mr. Postman"
Matchbox 20: "Push"
Dave Matthews Band: "Don't Drink the Water"
John Mayer: "Daughters"
*Curtis Mayfield (1999): "Superfly"
*Paul McCartney (1999): "Band on the Run"
Don McLean: "American Pie"
*Clyde McPhatter (1987): "A Lover's Question"
Meat Loaf: "Paradise by the Dashboard Light"
John (Cougar) Mellencamp: "Jack and Diane"
Men at Work: "Who Can It Be Now?"
Metallica: "Enter Sandman"
George Michael: "Faith"
*Joni Mitchell (1997): "Both Sides Now"
Moby: "Bodyrock"
The Monkees: "I'm a Believer"
Moody Blues: "Nights in White Satin"
*The Moonglows (2000): "Blue Velvet"
Alanis Morissette: "Ironic"
*Van Morrison (1993): "Brown-Eyed Girl"
Nelly: *Country Grammar*
*Ricky Nelson (1987): "Hello, Mary Lou"
Nine Inch Nails: "Closer"
Nirvana: *Nevermind*
No Doubt: *Rock Steady*
The Notorious B.I.G.: "Mo Money Mo Problems"
'N Sync: "Bye, Bye, Bye"
Oasis: "Wonderwall"
The Offspring: "Pretty Fly (for a White Guy)"
*The O'Jays (2005): "Back Stabbers"
*Roy Orbison (1987): "Oh, Pretty Woman"
OutKast: *Speakerboxxx/The Love Below*
Ozzy Osbourne: "Crazy Train"
*Parliament/Funkadelic (1997): "One Nation Under a Groove"
Pearl Jam: "Jeremy"
*Carl Perkins (1987): "Blue Suede Shoes"
Peter, Paul, and Mary: "Leaving on a Jet Plane"
*Tom Petty and the Heartbreakers (2002): "Refugee"
Liz Phair: *Exile in Guyville*
Phish: "Sample in a Jar"
*Wilson Pickett (1991): "Land of 1,000 Dances"
Pink: *Missundaztood!*
*Pink Floyd (1996): *The Wall*
*Gene Pitney (2002): "Only Love Can Break a Heart"
*The Platters (1990): "The Great Pretender"
*The Police (2003): "Every Breath You Take"
Iggy Pop: "Lust for Life"
*Elvis Presley (1986): "Love Me Tender"
*The Pretenders (2005): "Back on the Chain Gang"
*Lloyd Price (1998): "Stagger Lee"
*Prince (The Artist) (2004): "Purple Rain"
Public Enemy: "Fight the Power"

Puff Daddy and the Family: *No Way Out*
*Queen (2001): "Bohemian Rhapsody"
Radiohead: *OK Computer*
Rage Against the Machine: "Bulls on Parade"
*Bonnie Raitt (2000): "Something to Talk About"
*The Ramones (2002): "I Wanna Be Sedated"
*Otis Redding (1989): "(Sittin' on) the Dock of the Bay"
Red Hot Chili Peppers: "Under the Bridge"
*Jimmy Reed (1991): "Ain't That Loving You, Baby?"
Lou Reed: "Walk on the Wild Side"
*R.E.M. (2007): "Losing My Religion"
REO Speedwagon: "Can't Fight This Feeling"
Busta Rhymes: "What's It Gonna Be?"
*The Righteous Brothers (2003): "You've Lost That Lovin' Feelin'"
Johnny Rivers: "Poor Side of Town"
*Smokey Robinson[1] and the Miracles (1987): "Shop Around"
*The Rolling Stones (1989): "Satisfaction"
*The Ronettes (2007): "Be My Baby"
Linda Ronstadt: "You're No Good"
Run-D.M.C.: "Raisin' Hell"
Rush: "Tom Sawyer"
Sade: "Smooth Operator"
Salt-N-Pepa: "Shoop"
*Sam and Dave (1992): "Soul Man"
*Santana (1998): "Black Magic Woman"
Seal: "Kiss From a Rose"
Neil Sedaka: "Breaking Up Is Hard to Do"
*Bob Seger (2004): "Old Time Rock & Roll"
*Sex Pistols (2006): "Anarchy in the U.K."
Shaggy: "It Wasn't Me"
Shakira: "Whenever, Wherever"
Tupac Shakur: "How Do U Want It"
*Del Shannon (1999): "Runaway"
*The Shirelles (1996): "Soldier Boy"
Carly Simon: "You're So Vain"
*Paul Simon (2001): "50 Ways to Leave Your Lover"
*Simon and Garfunkel (1990): "Bridge Over Troubled Water"
*Percy Sledge (2005): "When a Man Loves a Woman"
*Sly and the Family Stone (1993): "Everyday People"
Smashing Pumpkins: "Today"
*Patti Smith (2007): "Because the Night"
Will Smith: "Gettin' Jiggy With It"
The Smiths: "This Charming Man"
Snoop Dogg: "Gin and Juice"
Sonic Youth: "Bull in the Heather"
Soundgarden: "Black Hole Sun"
Britney Spears: "Hit Me Baby One More Time"
Spice Girls: "Wannabe"
*Dusty Springfield (1999): "I Only Want to Be With You"
*Bruce Springsteen (1999): "Born to Run"
*Staple Singers (1999): "I'll Take You There"

*Steely Dan (2001): "Rikki Don't Lose That Number"
Gwen Stefani: "Hollaback Girl"
Steppenwolf: "Born to Be Wild"
*Rod Stewart (1994): "Maggie Mae"
Sting: "If You Love Somebody, Set Them Free"
Stone Temple Pilots: "Plush"
Styx: "Come Sail Away"
Sublime: "What I Got"
The Sugar Hill Gang: "Rapper's Delight"
Donna Summer: "Bad Girls"
*The Supremes (1988): "Stop! In the Name of Love"
*Talking Heads (2002): "Once in a Lifetime"
*James Taylor (2001): "You've Got a Friend"
*The Temptations (1989): "My Girl"
Three Dog Night: "Joy to the World"
Justin Timberlake: "SexyBack"
TLC: "Waterfalls"
T. Rex: "Bang a Gong (Get It On)"
*Traffic (2004): *Traffic*
*Big Joe Turner (1987): "Shake, Rattle & Roll"
*Ike and Tina Turner (1991): "Proud Mary"
*Tina Turner: "What's Love Got to Do With It?"
The Turtles: "Happy Together"
*U2 (2005): "With or Without You"
Usher: "You Make Me Wanna"
*Ritchie Valens (2001): "La Bamba"
*Van Halen (2007): "Running With the Devil"
Stevie Ray Vaughan: "Crossfire"
*The Velvet Underground (1996): "Sweet Jane"
*Gene Vincent (1998): "Be-Bop-A-Lula"
Tom Waits: "Downtown Train"
The Wallflowers: "One Headlight"
Dionne Warwick: "I Say a Little Prayer"
*Muddy Waters (1987): "I Can't Be Satisfied"
Mary Wells: "My Guy"
Kanye West: "Gold Digger"
The White Stripes: "Seven Nation Army"
*The Who (1990): *Tommy*
Lucinda Williams: *Car Wheels on a Gravel Road*
*Jackie Wilson (1987): "That's Why"
*Stevie Wonder (1989): "You Are the Sunshine of My Life"
Wu-Tang Clan: "Protect Ya Neck"
Weird Al Yankovic: *Dare to Be Stupid*
*The Yardbirds (1992): "For Your Love"
Yes: "Roundabout"
*Neil Young (1995): "Down by the River"
*The Young Rascals/The Rascals (1997): "Good Lovin' "
*Frank Zappa[1]/Mothers of Invention (1995): *Hot Rats*
John Zorn: *News for Lulu*
*ZZ Top (2004): "Legs"

(1) Only individual performer is in Rock and Roll Hall of Fame.

Entertainment Personalities of the Present
Living actors, musicians, dancers, singers, producers, directors, radio-TV performers.

Name	Birthplace	Birthdate	Name	Birthplace	Birthdate
Abbado, Claudio	Milan, Italy	6/26/33	Ambrose, Lauren	New Haven, CT	2/20/78
Abdul, Paula	San Fernando, CA	6/19/62	Ames, Ed	Malden, Boston, MA	7/9/27
Abraham, F. Murray	Pittsburgh, PA	10/24/39	Amos, John	Newark, NJ	12/27/41
Adams, Bryan	Kingston, Ontario	11/5/59	Amos, Tori	Newton, NC	8/22/63
Adams, Edie	Kingston, PA	4/16/29	André 3000	Atlanta, GA	5/27/75
Adjani, Isabelle	Paris, France	6/27/55	Anderson, Gillian	Chicago, IL	8/9/68
Ad-Rock	South Orange, NJ	10/31/66	Anderson, Harry	Newport, RI	10/14/52
Affleck, Ben	Berkeley, CA	8/15/72	Anderson, Ian	Dunfermline, Scotland	8/10/47
Aghdashloo, Shohreh	Tehran, Iran	1952	Anderson, Kevin	Gurnee, IL	1/13/60
Aguilera, Christina	Staten Is., New York, NY	12/18/80	Anderson, Loni	St. Paul, MN	8/5/46
Agutter, Jenny	Taunton, Somerset, Eng.	12/20/52	Anderson, Lynn	Grand Forks, ND	9/26/47
Aiello, Danny	New York, NY	6/20/33	Anderson, Melissa Sue	Berkeley, CA	9/26/62
Aiken, Clay	Raleigh, NC	11/30/78	Anderson, Pamela	Comox, Vancouver Isl., BC	7/1/67
Aimee, Anouk	Paris, France	4/27/32	Anderson, Richard	Long Branch, NJ	8/8/26
Alba, Jessica	Pomona, CA	4/28/81	Anderson, Richard Dean	Minneapolis, MN	1/23/50
Albanese, Licia	Bari, Italy	7/22/13	Anderson, Wes	Houston, TX	5/1/69
Alberghetti, Anna Maria	Pesaro, Italy	5/15/36	Andersson, Bibi	Stockholm, Sweden	11/11/35
Albert, Marv	Brooklyn, New York, NY	6/12/41	Andress, Ursula	Bern, Switzerland	3/19/36
Alda, Alan	New York, NY	1/28/36	Andrews, Julie	Walton-on-Thames,	
Alexander, Jane	Boston, MA	10/28/39		Surrey, England	10/1/35
Alexander, Jason	Newark, NJ	9/23/59	Andrews, Patty	Minneapolis, MN	2/16/18
Allen, Debbie	Houston, TX	1/16/50	Angel, Criss	Long Island, NY	12/19/67
Allen, Joan	Rochelle, IL	8/20/56	Aniston, Jennifer	Sherman Oaks, CA	2/11/69
Allen, Karen	Carrollton, IL	10/5/51	Anka, Paul	Ottawa, Ontario	7/30/41
Allen, Krista	Ventura, CA	04/5/71	Ann-Margret	Stockholm, Sweden	4/28/41
Allen, Ted	Carmel, IN	5/20/65	Anthony, Marc	New York, NY	9/16/68
Allen, Tim	Denver, CO	6/13/53	Apatow, Judd	Syosset, NY	12/6/67
Allen, Woody	Brooklyn, NY	12/1/35	Apple, Fiona	New York, NY	9/13/77
Alley, Kirstie	Wichita, KS	1/12/51	Applegate, Christina	Los Angeles, CA	11/25/71
Allman, Gregg	Nashville, TN	12/8/47	Archer, Anne	Los Angeles, CA	8/25/47
Alonso, Maria Conchita	Cienfuegos, Cuba	6/29/57	Arkin, Adam	Brooklyn, NY	8/19/56
Alpert, Herb	Los Angeles, CA	3/31/35	Arkin, Alan	New York, NY	3/26/34
Almodóvar, Pedro	Calzada de Calatrava, Spain	9/25/51	Arnaz, Desi, Jr.	Hollywood, CA	1/19/53

Name	Birthplace	Birthdate
Arnaz, Lucie	Hollywood, CA	7/17/51
Arness, James	Minneapolis, MN.	5/26/23
Arnold, Eddy	Henderson, TN.	5/15/18
Arnold, Tom	Ottumwa, IA	3/6/59
Arquette, David	Winchester, VA.	9/8/71
Arquette, Patricia	Chicago, IL	4/8/68
Arquette, Rosanna	New York, NY.	8/10/59
Arroyo, Martina	Harlem, New York, NY	2/2/37
Arthur, Beatrice	New York, NY.	5/13/23
Ashanti (Douglas)	Glen Cove, NY	10/13/80
Ashley, Elizabeth	Ocala, FL	8/30/39
Asner, Ed	Kansas City, KS	11/15/29
Assante, Armand	New York, NY.	10/4/49
Astin, John	Baltimore, MD.	3/30/30
Astin, Sean	Santa Monica, CA	2/25/71
Atkins, Eileen	London, England	6/16/34
Atkins, Sharif	Pittsburgh, PA	1/29/75
Atkinson, Rowan	Newcastle-Upon-Tyne, Eng.	1/6/55
Attenborough, Richard.	Cambridge, England.	8/29/23
Auberjonois, Rene	New York, NY.	6/1/40
Austin, Patti	New York, NY.	8/10/48
Autry, Alan	Shreveport, LA	7/31/52
Avalon, Frankie	Philadelphia, PA.	9/18/39
Aykroyd, Dan	Ottawa, Ontario	7/1/52
Azaria, Hank	Forest Hills, Queens, NY	4/25/64
Aznavour, Charles	Paris, France	5/22/24
Babyface (Kenneth Edmonds)	Indianapolis, IN.	4/10/59
Bacall, Lauren	Bronx, New York, NY	9/16/24
Bacon, Kevin	Philadelphia, PA.	7/8/58
Badalucco, Michael	Brooklyn, NY	12/20/54
Bader, Diedrich	Alexandria, VA	12/24/66
Badu, Erykah	Dallas, TX.	2/26/71
Baez, Joan	Staten Island, NY	1/9/41
Bain, Conrad	Lethbridge, Alberta.	2/4/23
Baio, Scott	Brooklyn, NY	9/22/61
Baker, Anita	Toledo, OH.	1/26/58
Baker, Carroll	Johnstown, PA	5/28/31
Baker, Diane	Hollywood, CA	2/25/38
Baker, Joe Don	Groesbeck, TX	2/12/36
Baker, Kathy	Midland, TX	6/8/50
Bakula, Scott	St. Louis, MO	10/9/54
Baldwin, Alec	Massapequa, NY	4/3/58
Baldwin, Daniel	Massapequa, NY	10/5/60
Baldwin, Stephen	Massapequa, NY	5/12/66
Baldwin, William	Massapequa, NY	2/21/63
Bale, Christian	Pembrokeshire, Wales	1/30/74
Ballard, Kaye	Cleveland, OH	11/20/26
Bana, Eric	Melbourne, Australia	8/9/68
Banderas, Antonio	Málaga, Spain	8/10/60
Banks, Elizabeth	Pittsfield, MA	2/10/75
Banks, Tyra	Los Angeles, CA.	12/4/73
Bannon, Jack	Los Angeles, CA.	6/14/40
Baranski, Christine	Buffalo, NY	5/2/52
Barbeau, Adrienne	Sacramento, CA.	6/11/45
Bardem, Javier	Las Palmas, Canary Isl.	3/1/69
Bardot, Brigitte	Paris, France	9/28/34
Barker, Bob	Darrington, WA.	12/12/23
Barkin, Ellen	Bronx, New York, NY	4/16/55
Barrie, Barbara	Chicago, IL	5/23/31
Barrino, Fantasia	High Point, NC	6/30/84
Barry, Gene	New York, NY.	6/14/19
Barrymore, Drew	Los Angeles, CA.	2/22/75
Bartoli, Cecilia	Rome, Italy	6/4/66
Barton, Misha	London, Eng.	1/24/86
Baryshnikov, Mikhail	Riga, Latvia	1/28/48
Basinger, Kim	Athens, GA.	12/8/53
Bass, Lance	Laurel, MS	5/4/79
Bassett, Angela	Harlem, New York, NY.	8/16/58
Bassey, Shirley	Cardiff, Wales.	1/8/37
Bateman, Jason	Rye, NY	1/14/69
Bateman, Justine	Rye, NY	2/19/66
Bates, Kathy	Memphis, TN	6/28/48
Battle, Kathleen	Portsmouth, OH	8/13/48
Baxter, Meredith	Los Angeles, CA.	6/21/47
Bean, Orson	Burlington, VT.	7/22/28
Bean, Sean	Sheffield, England	4/17/59
Beatty, Ned	Louisville, KY	7/6/37
Beatty, Warren	Richmond, VA	3/30/37
Beauvais, Garcelle	St. Marc, Haiti.	11/26/66
Beck (Hansen)	Los Angeles, CA.	7/8/70
Beck, Jeff	Wallington, Surrey, Eng.	6/24/44
Beckinsale, Kate	London, England	7/26/73
Bedelia, Bonnie	New York, NY.	3/25/48
Begley, Ed, Jr.	Los Angeles, CA.	9/16/49
Behar, Joy	Brooklyn, NY	10/7/43
Belafonte, Harry	Harlem, New York, NY.	3/1/27
Bell, Art	Camp Lejeune, NC.	6/17/45
Bell, Catherine	London, England	8/14/68
Bello, Maria	Norristown, PA.	4/18/67
Belmondo, Jean-Paul	Neuilly-sur-Seine, France.	4/9/33
Belushi, James	Chicago, IL.	6/15/54
Belzer, Richard	Bridgeport, CT	8/4/44
Benatar, Pat.	Brooklyn, NY	1/10/53
Benedict, Dirk	Helena, MT.	3/1/45
Benigni, Roberto	Misericordia, Italy	10/27/52
Bening, Annette	Topeka, KS.	5/29/58
Benjamin, Richard	New York, NY.	5/22/38
Bennett, Alan	Leeds, England	5/9/34
Bennett, Tony	Astoria, Queens, NY.	8/3/26
Benson, George	Pittsburgh, PA	3/22/43
Benson, Robby	Dallas, TX.	1/21/56
Berenger, Tom	Chicago, IL.	5/31/50
Berfield, Justin	Ventura County, CA	2/25/86
Bergen, Candice	Beverly Hills, CA.	5/9/46
Bergen, Polly	Knoxville, TN	7/14/30
Bergeron, Tom	Haverhill, MA	5/6/55
Berlinger, Warren	Brooklyn, NY	8/31/37
Berman, Shelley	Chicago, IL.	2/3/26
Bernard, Crystal	Dallas, TX.	9/30/64
Bernhard, Sandra	Flint, MI.	6/6/55
Bernsen, Corbin	N. Hollywood, CA	9/7/54
Berry, Chuck	St. Louis, MO	10/18/26
Berry, Halle	Cleveland, OH	8/14/66
Berry, Ken	Moline, IL	11/3/33
Bertinelli, Valerie	Wilmington, DE.	4/23/60
Bertolucci, Bernardo	Parma, Italy	3/16/40
Bettany, Paul	London, England	5/27/71
Biafra, Jello	Boulder, CO	6/17/58
Bialik, Mayim	San Diego, CA	12/12/75
Big Boi	Savanah, GA	2/1/75
Biggs, Jason	Pompton Plains, NJ	5/12/78
Bikel, Theodore	Vienna, Austria	5/2/24
Billingsley, Barbara	Los Angeles, CA.	12/22/22
Bilson, Rachel	Los Angeles, CA.	8/25/81
Binoche, Juliette	Paris, France	3/9/64
Birch, Thora	Beverly Hills, CA.	3/11/82
Birney, David	Washington, DC	4/23/39
Bishop, Joey	Bronx, NY	2/3/18
Bisset, Jacqueline	Weybridge, England.	9/13/44
Bissett, Josie	Seattle, WA	10/5/70
Björk (Gudmundsdottir)	Reykjavik, Iceland	11/21/65
Black, Clint	Long Branch, NJ.	2/4/62
Black, Jack	Los Angeles, CA.	4/7/69
Black, Karen	Park Ridge, IL.	7/1/42
Blades, Ruben	Panama City, Panama	7/16/48
Blair, Linda	St. Louis, MO	1/22/59
Blair, Selma	Southfield, MI	6/23/72
Blake, Robert	Nutley, NJ.	9/18/33
Blanchett, Cate	Melbourne, Australia	5/14/69
Bledsoe, Tempestt	Chicago, IL.	8/1/73
Bleeth, Yasmine	New York, NY.	6/14/68
Blethyn, Brenda	Ramsgate, Kent, England	2/20/46
Blige, Mary J.	Bronx, NY	1/11/71
Bloom, Claire	London, England	2/15/31
Bloom, Orlando	Canterbury, England	1/13/77
Blyth, Ann	Mt. Kisco, NY	8/16/28
Bochco, Steven	New York, NY.	12/16/43
Bocelli, Andrea	Lajatico, Italy	9/22/58
Bogdanovich, Peter	Kingston, NY	7/30/39
Bogosian, Eric	Woburn, MA	4/24/53
Bologna, Joseph	Brooklyn, NY	12/30/38
Bolton, Michael	New Haven, CT	2/26/53
Bonet, Lisa	San Francisco, CA	11/16/67
Bonham Carter, Helena	London, England	5/26/66
Bon Jovi, Jon	Sayreville, NJ	3/2/62
Bono (Vox)	Dublin, Ireland	5/10/60
Boone, Debby	Hackensack, NJ	9/22/56
Boone, Pat	Jacksonville, FL	6/1/34
Boreanaz, David	Buffalo, NY.	5/16/71
Borgnine, Ernest	Hamden, CT.	1/24/17
Bosco, Philip	Jersey City, NJ	9/26/30
Bosley, Tom	Chicago, IL.	10/1/27
Bosson, Barbara	Charleroi, PA	11/1/39
Bostwick, Barry	San Mateo, CA.	2/24/45
Bosworth, Kate	Los Angeles, CA.	1/2/83
Bottoms, Timothy	Santa Barbara, CA.	8/30/51
Bow Wow	Columbus, OH	3/9/87
Bowen, Julie	Baltimore, MD.	3/3/70
Bowie, David	London, England	1/8/47
Bowles, Peter	London, England	10/16/36
Boxleitner, Bruce	Elgin, IL	5/12/50
Boy George	Bexleyheath, England	6/14/61
Boyle, Lara Flynn	Davenport, IA	3/24/70
Bracco, Lorraine	Brooklyn, NY	10/2/55
Brady, Wayne	Orlando, FL	6/2/72
Braff, Zach	S. Orange, NJ	4/6/75
Branagh, Kenneth	Belfast, N. Ireland.	12/10/60
Brandauer, Klaus Maria	Steiermark, Austria.	6/22/44
Brandy (Norwood)	McComb, MS	2/11/79

Name	Birthplace	Birthdate
Braschi, Nicoletta	Cesena, Italy	8/10/60
Bratt, Benjamin	San Francisco, CA	12/16/63
Braugher, Andre	Chicago, Il	7/1/62
Braxton, Toni	Severn, MD	10/7/66
Bremner, Ewen	Edinburgh, Scotland	1971
Brendon, Nicholas	Los Angeles, CA	4/12/71
Brennan, Eileen	Los Angeles, CA	9/3/35
Brenneman, Amy	Glastonbury, CT	6/22/64
Brenner, David	Philadelphia, PA	2/4/45
Brewer, Teresa	Toledo, OH	5/7/31
Bridges, Beau	Hollywood, CA	12/9/41
Bridges, Jeff	Los Angeles, CA	12/4/49
Brightman, Sarah	Berkhamstead, England	8/14/60
Brimley, Wilford	Salt Lake City, UT	9/27/34
Brinkley, Christie	Malibu, CA	2/2/54
Broadbent, Jim	Lincolnshire, England	5/24/49
Brochtrup, Bill	Inglewood, CA	3/7/63
Broderick, Matthew	New York, NY	3/21/62
Brody, Adam	San Diego, CA	12/15/79
Brody, Adrien	New York, NY	4/14/73
Brolin, James	Los Angeles, CA	7/18/40
Brooks, Albert	Beverly Hills, CA	7/22/47
Brooks, Garth	Tulsa, OK	2/7/62
Brooks, James L	North Bergen, NJ	5/9/40
Brooks, Mel	Brooklyn, NY	6/28/26
Brosnan, Pierce	Navan, Co. Meath, Ireland	5/16/53
Brown, Blair	Washington, DC	4/23/46
Brown, Bobby	Roxbury, Boston, MA	2/5/69
Brown, Bryan	Panania, Australia	6/23/47
Brown, Foxy	Brooklyn, NY	9/6/79
Browne, Jackson	Heidelberg, Germany	10/9/48
Brubeck, Dave	Concord, CA	12/6/20
Bryant, Paul (Cubby)	Virginia Beach, VA	6/1/71
Bryson, Peabo	Greenville, SC	4/13/51
Buckley, Betty	Ft. Worth, TX	7/3/47
Buffett, Jimmy	Pascagoula, MS	12/25/46
Bujold, Genevieve	Montreal, Quebec	7/1/42
Bullock, Sandra	Arlington, VA	7/26/64
Bumbry, Grace	St. Louis, MO	1/4/37
Bundchen, Gisele	Horizontina, Brazil	7/20/80
Burghoff, Gary	Bristol, CT.	5/24/43
Burke, Delta	Orlando, FL	7/30/56
Burnett, Carol	San Antonio, TX	4/26/33
Burns, Edward	Woodside, Queens, NY	1/29/68
Burrows, Darren E.	Winfield, KS	9/12/66
Burstyn, Ellen	Detroit, MI.	12/7/32
Burton, LeVar	Landstuhl, W Germany	2/16/57
Burton, Tim	Burbank, CA	8/25/58
Buscemi, Steve	Brooklyn, NY	12/13/57
Busey, Gary	Goose Creek, TX	6/29/44
Busfield, Timothy	Lansing, MI.	6/12/57
Butler, Brett	Montgomery, AL.	1/30/58
Buzzi, Ruth	Westerly, RI	7/24/36
Bynes, Amanda	Thousand Oaks, CA	4/3/86
Byrne, David	Dumbarton, Scotland	5/14/52
Byrne, Gabriel	Dublin, Ireland	5/12/50
Caan, James	Bronx, NY	3/26/40
Caballe, Montserrat	Barcelona, Spain	4/12/33
Caesar, Sid	Yonkers, NY	9/8/22
Cage, Nicolas	Long Beach, CA	1/7/64
Cain, Dean	Mt. Clemens, MI	7/31/66
Caine, Michael	London, England	3/14/33
Caldwell, Zoe	Hawthorne, Australia	9/14/33
Cameron, James	Kapuskasing, Ontario	8/16/54
Cameron, Kirk	Panorama City, CA.	10/12/70
Campanella, Joseph	New York, NY.	11/21/27
Campbell, Bruce	Royal Oak, MI.	6/22/58
Campbell, Glen	Delight, AR	4/22/36
Campbell, Naomi	South London, England	5/22/70
Campbell, Neve	Guelph, Ontario	10/3/73
Campion, Jane	Waikanae, New Zealand	4/30/54
Cannell, Stephen J.	Pasadena, CA	5/2/41
Cannon, Dyan	Tacoma, WA.	1/4/37
Capshaw, Kate	Ft. Worth, TX	11/3/53
Cara, Irene	New York, NY.	3/18/64
Carell, Steve	Concord, MA	8/16/62
Cardellini, Linda	Redwood City, CA	6/25/75
Cardinale, Claudia	Tunis, Tunisia	4/15/39
Carey, Drew	Cleveland, OH	5/23/58
Carey Jr., Harry	Saugus, CA	5/16/21
Carey, Mariah	Huntington, NY	3/27/70
Cariou, Len	Winnipeg, Canada	9/30/39
Carlin, George	Bronx, New York, NY	5/12/37
Carlton, Vanessa	Milford, PA	8/16/80
Carlyle, Robert	Glasgow, Scotland	4/14/61
Carmen, Eric	Cleveland, OH	8/11/49
Caron, Leslie	Boulogne, France	7/1/31
Carpenter, John	Carthage, NY	1/16/48
Carpenter, Mary Chapin	Princeton, NJ	2/21/58
Carr, Vikki	El Paso, TX	7/19/41

Name	Birthplace	Birthdate
Carradine, David	Hollywood, CA	12/8/36
Carradine, Keith	San Mateo, CA	8/8/49
Carreras, Jose	Barcelona, Spain	12/5/46
Carrere, Tia	Honolulu, HI	1/2/67
Carrey, Jim	Newmarket, Ontario	1/17/62
Carroll, Diahann	Bronx, NY	7/17/35
Carroll, Pat	Shreveport, LA	5/5/27
Carson, Lisa Nicole	Brooklyn, NY	7/12/69
Carter, Dixie	McLemoresville, TN	5/25/39
Carter, Jack	Brooklyn, New York, NY	6/24/23
Carter, Lynda	Phoenix, AZ	7/24/51
Carter, Nick	Jamestown, NY	1/28/80
Carter, Ron	Ferndale, MI	5/4/37
Cartwright, Nancy	Kettering, OH	10/25/59
Caruso, David	Forest Hills, Queens, NY	1/17/56
Carvey, Dana	Missoula, MT	6/2/55
Case, Sharon	Detroit, MI	2/9/71
Cash, Rosanne	Memphis, TN	5/24/55
Cassidy, David	New York, NY	4/12/50
Castellaneta, Dan	Chicago, IL	9/10/58
Castle-Hughes, Keisha	Donnybrook, W. Australia, Australia	3/24/90
Cates, Phoebe	New York, NY	7/16/63
Cattrall, Kim	Liverpool, England	8/21/56
Cavanagh, Tom	Ottawa, Canada	10/26/68
Cavett, Dick	Gibbon, NE	11/19/36
Cedric the Entertainer	Jefferson City, MO	4/24/64
Cera, Michael	Brampton, Ont, Can.	6/7/88
Chabert, Lacey	Purvis, MS	9/30/82
Chalke, Sarah	Ottawa, Ontario	8/27/76
Chamberlain, Richard	Beverly Hills, CA.	3/31/34
Chan, Jackie	Hong Kong	4/7/54
Channing, Carol	Seattle, WA	1/31/21
Channing, Stockard	New York, NY	2/13/44
Chaplin, Geraldine	Santa Monica, CA	7/31/44
Chapman, Tracy	Cleveland, OH	3/30/64
Chappelle, Dave	Washington, DC	8/24/73
Charisse, Cyd	Amarillo, TX	3/8/21
Charo	Murcia, Spain	1/15/41
Chase, Chevy	New York, NY	10/8/43
Chasez, Joshua (J.C.)	Washington, DC	8/8/76
Cheadle, Don	Kansas City, MO	11/29/64
Checker, Chubby	Spring Gulley, SC	10/3/41
Chenoweth, Kristin	Broken Arrow, OK	7/24/68
Cher	El Centro, CA	5/20/46
Chesney, Kenny	Knoxville, TN	3/26/68
Chianese, Dominic	Bronx, NY	2/24/31
Chiba, Sonny	Fukuoka, Kyushu, Japan	1/23/39
Chiklis, Michael	Lowell, MA	8/30/63
Cho, Margaret	San Francisco	12/5/68
Chong, Rae Dawn	Vancouver, B. C, Can.	2/28/61
Chong, Thomas	Edmonton, Alberta, Can.	5/24/38
Chow Yun-Fat	Hong Kong	5/18/55
Christensen, Hayden	Vancouver, B. C. Can.	4/19/81
Christensen, Helena	Copenhagen, Denmark	12/25/68
Christie, Julie	Chukua, Assam, India	4/14/40
Christopher, William	Evanston, IL	10/20/32
Chuck D	New York, NY.	8/1/60
Church, Charlotte	Llandaff, Cardiff, Wales	2/21/86
Church, Thomas Haden	El Paso, TX	6/17/61
Clapp, Gordon	North Conway, NH	9/24/48
Clapton, Eric	Surrey, England	3/30/45
Clark, Anthony	Lynchburg, VA	4/4/64
Clark, Dick	Mt. Vernon, NY	11/30/29
Clark, Petula	Ewell, Surrey, England	11/15/32
Clark, Roy	Meherrin, VA	4/15/33
Clarkson, Kelly	Burleson, TX.	4/24/82
Clarkson, Patricia	New Orleans, LA	12/29/59
Clay, Andrew Dice	Brooklyn, NY	9/29/58
Clayburgh, Jill	New York, NY	4/30/44
Cleese, John	Weston-super-Mare, Eng.	10/27/39
Cliburn, Van	Shreveport, LA	7/12/34
Clooney, George	Lexington, KY	5/6/61
Close, Glenn	Greenwich, CT	3/19/47
Coen, Ethan	St. Louis Park, MN	9/21/57
Coen, Joel	St. Louis Park, MN	11/29/54
Cohen, Leonard	Montreal, Canada	9/21/34
Cohen, Sacha Baron	London, England	10/13/71
Colbert, Stephen	Charleston, SC	5/13/64
Cole, Gary	Park Ridge, IL.	9/20/57
Cole, Natalie	Los Angeles, CA.	2/6/50
Cole, Olivia	Memphis, TN	11/26/42
Cole, Paula	Manchester, CT	4/5/68
Coleman, Dabney	Austin, TX.	1/3/32
Coleman, Gary	Zion, IL.	2/8/68
Coleman, Ornette	Fort Worth, TX	3/19/30
Collette, Toni	Blacktown, Australia	11/1/72
Collins, Joan	London, England	5/23/33
Collins, Judy	Seattle, WA	5/1/39
Collins, Pauline	Exmouth, England	9/3/40

Name	Birthplace	Birthdate
Collins, Phil	London, England	1/30/51
Collins, Stephen	Des Moines, IA	10/1/47
Colvin, Shawn	Vermillion, SD	1/10/56
Combs, Sean "Diddy"	Harlem, NY	11/4/69
Connelly, Jennifer	Catskill Mountains, NY	12/12/70
Connery, Sean	Edinburgh, Scotland	8/25/30
Connick, Harry, Jr.	New Orleans, LA	9/11/67
Connolly, Kevin	New York, NY	3/5/74
Connors, Mike	Fresno, CA	8/15/25
Conrad, Robert	Chicago, IL	3/1/35
Conroy, Frances	Monroe, GA	11/13/53
Constantine, Michael	Reading, PA	5/22/27
Conti, Tom	Paisley, Scotland	11/22/41
Conway, Tim	Willoughby, OH	12/15/33
Cook, Barbara	Atlanta, GA	10/25/27
Coolidge, Rita	Nashville, TN	5/1/45
Coolio	Los Angeles, CA.	8/1/63
Cooper, Alice	Detroit, MI.	2/4/48
Cooper, Chris	Kansas City, MO	7/9/51
Cooper, Jackie	Los Angeles, CA.	9/15/21
Copperfield, David	Metuchen, NJ	9/16/56
Coppola, Francis Ford	Detroit, MI.	4/7/39
Coppola, Sofia	New York, NY.	5/12/71
Corbett, John	Wheeling, WV.	5/9/61
Corbin, Barry	Lamesa, TX	10/16/40
Cord, Alex	Floral Park, NY	5/3/33
Corea, Chick	Chelsea, MA.	6/12/41
Corgan, Billy	Elk Grove, IL.	3/17/67
Corley, Pat	Dallas, TX.	6/1/30
Cornell, Chris	Seattle, WA	7/20/64
Corwin, Jeff	Halifax, Nova Scotia	7/11/67
Cosby, Bill	Philadelphia, PA.	7/12/37
Costas, Bob	Queens, New York, NY	3/22/52
Costello, Elvis	London, England	8/25/54
Costner, Kevin	Compton, CA	1/18/55
Courtenay, Tom	Hull, England	2/25/37
Cowell, Simon	London, England	10/7/59
Cox, Brian	Dundee, Scotland	6/1/46
Cox, Nikki	Los Angeles, CA.	6/2/78
Cox, Ronny	Cloudcroft, NM	7/23/38
Cox Arquette, Courteney	Birmingham, AL	6/15/64
Coyote, Peter	New York, NY.	10/10/42
Craig, Daniel	Chester, England	3/2/68
Cranston, Bryan	San Fernando Valley, CA	3/7/56
Crawford, Cindy	DeKalb, IL	2/20/66
Crawford, Michael	Salisbury, England	1/19/42
Cromwell, James	Los Angeles, CA.	1/27/40
Crosby, David	Los Angeles, CA.	8/14/41
Cross, Ben.	London, England	12/16/47
Cross, Marcia	Marlborough, MA	3/25/62
Crouse, Lindsay	New York, NY.	5/12/48
Crow, Sheryl	Kennett, MO	2/11/62
Crowe, Cameron	Palm Springs, CA	7/13/57
Crowe, Russell	Wellington, New Zealand	4/7/64
Crowell, Rodney	Houston, TX	8/17/50
Crudup, Billy	Manhasset, NY.	7/8/68
Cruise, Tom	Syracuse, NY	7/3/62
Cruz, Penelope	Madrid, Spain	4/28/74
Cryer, Jon	New York, NY.	4/16/65
Crystal, Billy	Long Beach, NY	3/14/47
Culkin, Kieran	New York, NY.	9/30/82
Culkin, Macaulay	New York, NY.	8/26/80
Culkin, Rory	New York, NY.	7/21/89
Cullum, John	Knoxville, TN	3/2/30
Culp, Robert	Oakland, CA.	8/16/30
Cumming, Alan	Perthshire, Scotland	1/27/65
Curry, Tim	Cheshire, England	4/19/46
Curtin, Jane	Cambridge, MA	9/6/47
Curtis, Jamie Lee	Los Angeles, CA.	11/22/58
Curtis, Tony	New York, NY.	6/3/25
Cusack, Joan	New York, NY.	10/11/62
Cusack, John	Evanston, IL	6/28/66
Cyrus, Billy Ray	Flatwoods, KY	8/25/61
Cyrus, Miley	Nashville, TN	11/23/92
Dafoe, Willem	Appleton, WI.	7/22/55
Dahl, Arlene	Minneapolis, MN.	8/11/28
Dale, Jim	Rothwell, England	8/15/35
Dalton, Abby	Las Vegas, NV	8/15/32
Dalton, Timothy	Colwyn Bay, Wales	3/21/46
Daltrey, Roger	London, England	3/1/44
Daly, Carson	Santa Monica, CA	6/22/73
Daly, Timothy	New York, NY.	3/1/56
Daly, Tyne	Madison, WI	2/21/46
Damon, Matt	Cambridge, MA	10/8/70
Damone, Vic	Brooklyn, NY	6/12/28
Danes, Claire	New York, NY.	4/12/79
D'Angelo	Richmond, VA	2/11/74
D'Angelo, Beverly	Columbus, OH	11/15/54
Daniels, Anthony	Salisbury, England	2/21/46
Daniels, Charlie	Wilmington, NC	10/28/36
Daniels, Jeff	Athens, GA	2/19/55
Daniels, William	Brooklyn, NY	3/31/27
Danner, Blythe	Rosemont, PA	2/3/43
Danson, Ted	San Diego, CA	12/29/47
Danza, Tony	Brooklyn, New York, NY.	4/21/51
Darby, Kim	Hollywood, CA	7/8/48
David, Larry	Brooklyn, NY	7/2/47
Davidson, John	Pittsburgh, PA	12/13/41
Davis, Ann B.	Schenectady, NY	5/5/26
Davis, Clifton	Chicago, IL	10/4/45
Davis, Geena	Wareham, MA	1/21/56
Davis, Hope	Englewood, NJ	3/23/64
Davis, Judy	Perth, Australia.	4/23/55
Davis, Kristin	Boulder, CO	2/24/65
Davis, Mac	Lubbock, TX	1/21/42
Dawber, Pam	Farmington Hills, MI	10/18/51
Dawson, Richard	Gosport, Hampshire, Eng.	11/20/32
Dawson, Rosario	Bronx, New York, NY	5/9/79
Day, Doris	Cincinnati, OH	4/3/24
Day, Laraine	Roosevelt, UT.	10/13/17
Day-Lewis, Daniel	London, England	4/29/57
Dean, Jimmy	Plainview, TX	8/10/28
Dearie, Blossom	E. Durham, NY	4/28/26
Dee, Ruby	Cleveland, OH	10/27/24
DeFranco, Buddy	Camden, NJ	2/17/23
DeGeneres, Ellen	Metairie, LA	1/26/58
DeHaven, Gloria	Los Angeles, CA.	7/23/25
De Havilland, Olivia	Tokyo, Japan	7/1/16
Delaney, Kim	Philadelphia, PA.	11/29/61
Delany, Dana	New York, NY.	3/13/56
De la Rocha, Zack	Long Beach, CA	1/12/70
DeLaurentiis, Dino	Torre Annunziata, Italy	8/8/19
Delon, Alain	Sceaux, France	11/8/35
Del Toro, Benicio	Santurce, Puerto Rico	2/19/67
DeLuise, Dom	Brooklyn, NY	8/1/33
Demme, Jonathan	Baldwin, NY	2/22/44
De Mornay, Rebecca	Santa Rosa, CA	8/29/62
Dempsey, Patrick	Lewiston, ME	1/13/66
Dench, Judi	York, England.	12/9/34
Deneuve, Catherine	Paris, France	10/22/43
De Niro, Robert	New York, NY.	8/17/43
Dennehy, Brian	Bridgeport, CT	7/9/38
DePalma, Brian	Newark, NJ.	9/11/40
Depardieu, Gerard	Chateauroux, France	12/27/48
Depp, Johnny	Owensboro, KY	6/9/63
Derek, Bo	Long Beach, CA.	11/20/56
De Rossi, Portia	Melbourne, Victoria, Aust.	1/31/73
Dern, Bruce	Winnetka, IL	6/4/36
Dern, Laura	Santa Monica, CA	2/10/67
DeVito, Danny	Neptune, NJ	11/17/44
DeWitt, Joyce	Wheeling, WV.	4/23/49
Dey, Susan	Pekin, IL.	12/10/52
Diamond, Neil	Brooklyn, NY	1/24/41
Diaz, Cameron	San Diego, CA	8/30/72
DiCaprio, Leonardo	Hollywood, CA	11/11/74
Dick, Andy	Charleston, SC	12/21/65
Dickinson, Angie	Kulm, ND	9/30/31
Diddley, Bo	McComb, MS	12/30/28
Diesel, Vin	New York, NY.	7/18/67
Diggs, Taye	Essex Co., NJ.	1/2/72
Diller, Phyllis	Lima, OH	7/17/17
Dillman, Bradford	San Francisco, CA	4/14/30
Dillon, Kevin	Mamaroneck, NY	8/16/65
Dillon, Matt	New Rochelle, NY	2/18/64
Dinklage, Peter	Mendham, NJ.	6/11/69
Dion, Céline	Charlemagne, Quebec	3/30/68
Djalili, Omid	London, England	9/30/65
Dobson, Kevin	Queens, New York, NY	3/18/43
Dogg, Snoop	Long Beach, CA	10/20/71
Doherty, Shannen	Memphis, TN	4/12/71
Dolenz, Mickey	Los Angeles, CA.	3/8/45
Domingo, Placido	Madrid, Spain	1/21/41
Domino, Fats	New Orleans, LA	2/26/28
Donahue, Phil	Cleveland, OH	12/21/35
D'Onofrio, Vincent	Brooklyn, NY	6/30/59
Donovan (Leitch)	Glasgow, Scotland	5/10/46
Donovan, Tate	Tenafly, NJ	9/25/63
Dorn, Michael	Luling, TX	12/9/52
Dorough, Howie	Orlando, FL	8/22/73
Dotrice, Roy	Guernsey, England.	5/26/23
Douglas, Kirk	Amsterdam, NY	12/9/16
Douglas, Michael	New Brunswick, NJ	9/25/44
Dourdan, Gary	Philadelphia, PA.	12/11/66
Dow, Tony	Hollywood, CA	4/13/45
Down, Lesley-Ann	London, England	3/17/54
Downey, Robert, Jr.	New York, NY.	4/4/65
Downey, Roma	Derry, Northern Ireland.	5/6/60
Downs, Hugh	Akron, OH.	2/14/21
Drescher, Fran	Flushing, Queens, NY	9/30/57
Dreyfuss, Richard	Brooklyn, NY	10/29/47

Name	Birthplace	Birthdate
Driver, Minnie	London, England	1/31/70
Dryer, Fred	Hawthorne, CA	7/6/46
Duchovny, David	New York, NY	8/7/60
Duff, Haylie	Houston, TX	2/19/85
Duff, Hilary	Houston, TX	9/28/87
Duffy, Julia	Minneapolis, MN	6/27/51
Duffy, Patrick	Townsend, MT	3/17/49
Duhamel, Josh	Minot, ND	11/14/72
Dukakis, Olympia	Lowell, MA	6/20/31
Duke, Patty	Elmhurst, NY	12/14/46
Dullea, Keir	Cleveland, OH	5/30/36
Dunaway, Faye	Bascom, FL	1/14/41
Duncan, Lindsay	Edinburgh, Scotland	11/7/50
Duncan, Sandy	Henderson, TX	2/20/46
Dunne, Griffin	New York, NY	6/8/55
Dunst, Kirsten	Point Pleasant, NJ	4/30/82
Durbin, Deanna	Winnipeg, Manitoba	12/4/21
Durning, Charles	Highland Falls, NY	2/28/23
Dussault, Nancy	Pensacola, FL	6/30/36
Dutton, Charles S.	Baltimore, MD	1/30/51
Duvall, Robert	San Diego, CA	1/5/31
Duvall, Shelley	Houston, TX	7/7/49
Dylan, Bob	Duluth, MN	5/24/41
Dylan, Jakob	New York, NY	12/9/69
Dysart, Richard	Brighton, MA	3/30/29
Dzundza, George	Rosenheim, Germany	7/19/45
Eads, George	Fort Worth, TX	3/1/67
Easton, Sheena	Bellshill, Scotland	4/27/59
Eastwood, Clint	San Francisco, CA	5/31/30
Ebert, Roger	Urbana, IL	6/18/42
Eden, Barbara	Tucson, AZ	8/23/34
Edwards, Anthony	Santa Barbara, CA	7/19/62
Edwards, Blake	Tulsa, OK	7/26/22
Efron, Zac	San Luis Obispo, CA	10/18/87
Ehle, Jennifer	Winston-Salem, NC	12/29/69
Eichhorn, Lisa	Reading, PA	2/4/52
Eikenberry, Jill	New Haven, CT	1/21/47
Ekberg, Anita	Malmo, Sweden	9/29/31
Ekland, Britt	Stockholm, Sweden	10/6/42
Electra, Carmen	Cincinnati, OH	4/20/72
Elfman, Jenna	Los Angeles, CA.	9/30/71
Elizabeth, Shannon	Houston, TX	9/7/73
Elizondo, Hector	New York, NY	12/22/36
Elliott, Bob	Boston, MA.	3/26/23
Elliott, Chris	New York, NY.	5/31/60
Elliott, Sam	Sacramento, CA.	8/9/44
Elvira	Manhattan, KS	9/17/51
Emerson, Michael	Cedar Rapids, IA	9/7/1954
Eminem	St. Joseph, MO.	10/17/72
Enberg, Dick	Mt. Clemens, MI	1/9/35
Englund, Robert.	Glendale, CA	6/6/49
Enya	Gweedore, Ireland	5/17/61
Ephron, Nora	New York, NY	5/19/41
Ermey, R. Lee	Emporia, KS	3/24/44
Estefan, Gloria	Havana, Cuba	9/1/57
Estevez, Emilio	New York, NY	5/12/62
Estrada, Erik	New York, NY.	3/16/49
Etheridge, Melissa	Leavenworth, KS	5/29/61
Evans, Linda	Hartford, CT	11/18/42
Evans, Robert	New York, NY.	6/29/30
Everett, Chad	South Bend, IN.	6/11/36
Everett, Rupert	Norfolk, England.	5/29/59
Everly, Don	Brownie, KY	2/1/37
Everly, Phil.	Chicago, IL.	1/19/39
Evigan, Greg	South Amboy, NJ	10/14/53
Fabares, Shelley	Santa Monica, CA	1/19/44
Fabian (Forte)	Philadelphia, PA.	2/6/43
Fabio	Milan, Italy	3/15/61
Fabolous	Brooklyn, NU	11/18/77
Fairchild, Morgan	Dallas, TX.	2/3/50
Faison, Donald	New York, NY.	6/22/74
Falana, Lola	Philadelphia, PA.	9/11/43
Falco, Edie	Brooklyn, NY	7/5/63
Falk, Peter	New York, NY.	9/16/27
Fallon, Jimmy	Brooklyn, NY	9/19/74
Farentino, James	Brooklyn, NY	2/24/38
Fargo, Donna	Mt. Airy, NC	11/10/49
Farina, Dennis	Chicago, IL.	2/29/44
Farr, Jamie	Toledo, OH.	7/1/34
Farrell, Colin	Dublin, Ireland	5/31/76
Farrell, Mike	St. Paul, MN	2/6/39
Farrell, Perry	Queens, NY	3/29/59
Farrelly, Bob	Cumberland, RI	6/17/58
Farrelly, Peter	Phoenixville, PA	12/17/56
Farrow, Mia	Los Angeles, CA.	2/9/45
Fatone, Joey	Brooklyn, New York, NY	1/28/77
Fawcett, Farrah	Corpus Christi, TX	2/2/47
Feinstein, Michael	Columbus, OH	9/7/56
Feldon, Barbara	Pittsburgh, PA	3/12/41
Feldshuh, Tovah	New York, NY	12/27/52
Feliciano, Jose	Lares, Puerto Rico	9/10/45
Fenn, Sherilyn	Detroit, MI	2/1/65
Fergie	Hacienda Heights, CA	3/27/75
Ferrara, Jerry	Brooklyn, NY	11/29/79
Ferrell, Conchata	Charleston, WV	3/28/43
Ferrell, Will	Irvine, CA	7/16/67
Ferrer, Mel	Elberon, NJ.	8/25/17
Ferrera, America	Los Angeles, CA.	4/18/84
Feuerstein, Mark	New York, NY.	6/8/71
Fey, Tina	Upper Darby, PA	5/18/70
Field, Sally	Pasadena, CA	11/6/46
Fiennes, Joseph	Salisbury, England	5/27/70
Fiennes, Ralph	Suffolk, England.	12/22/62
Fierstein, Harvey	Brooklyn, NY	6/6/54
50 Cent	Queens, NY	7/6/76
Filicia, Thom	Syracuse, NY	5/17/69
Fincher, David	Denver, CO	5/10/62
Finney, Albert.	Salford, England.	5/9/36
Fiorentino, Linda	Philadelphia, PA.	3/9/60
Firth, Colin	Grayshott, England.	9/10/60
Firth, Peter	Bradford, Yorkshire, Eng.	10/27/53
Fischer-Dieskau, Dietrich	Berlin, Germany	5/28/25
Fischer, Jenna	Ft. Wayne, IN	3/7/74
Fishburne, Laurence	Augusta, GA	7/30/61
Fisher, Carrie	Beverly Hills, CA	10/21/56
Fisher, Eddie	Philadelphia, PA.	8/10/28
Flack, Roberta	Black Mountain, NC	2/10/39
Flanagan, Fionnula	Dublin, Ireland	12/10/41
Flavor Flav	New York, NY.	3/16/59
Fleetwood, Mick	Redruth, Cornwall, Eng.	6/24/42
Fleming, Rhonda	Hollywood, CA.	8/10/23
Fletcher, Louise	Birmingham, AL	7/22/34
Flockhart, Calista	Freeport, IL.	11/11/64
Florek, Dann	Flat Rock, MI	5/1/50
Foch, Nina	Leyden, Netherlands	4/20/24
Fogelberg, Dan	Peoria, IL	8/13/51
Fogerty, John	Berkeley, CA.	5/28/45
Foley, Dave	Etobicoke, Ontario	1/4/63
Fonda, Bridget	Los Angeles, CA.	1/27/64
Fonda, Jane	New York, NY.	12/21/37
Fonda, Peter	New York, NY.	2/23/40
Fontaine, Joan	Tokyo, Japan	10/22/17
Ford, Faith	Alexandria, LA	9/14/64
Ford, Harrison	Des Plaines, IL	7/13/42
Forman, Milos	Caslav, Czechoslovakia	2/18/32
Forsythe, John	Penns Grove, NJ	1/29/18
Foster, Jodie	Los Angeles, CA.	11/19/62
Foster, Sutton	Statesboro, Georgia	3/18/75
Fox, James	London, England	5/19/39
Fox, Jorja	New York, NY.	7/7/68
Fox, Matthew	Crowheart, WY.	7/14/66
Fox, Michael J.	Edmonton, Alberta	6/9/61
Fox, Vivica A.	Indianapolis, IN.	7/30/64
Foxworth, Robert	Houston, TX.	11/1/41
Foxworthy, Jeff	Atlanta, GA.	9/6/58
Foxx, Jamie	Terrell, TX.	12/13/67
Frampton, Peter	Kent, England.	4/22/50
Francis, Anne	Ossining, NY	9/16/30
Francis, Connie	Newark, NJ.	12/12/38
Franco, James	Palo Alto, CA.	4/19/78
Franken, Al	New York, NY.	5/21/51
Franklin, Aretha	Memphis, TN	3/25/42
Franklin, Bonnie	Santa Monica, CA	1/6/44
Franz, Dennis	Maywood, IL.	10/28/44
Fraser, Brendan	Indianapolis, IN.	12/3/68
Freeman, Al, Jr.	San Antonio, TX	3/21/34
Freeman, Mona	Baltimore, MD.	6/9/26
Freeman, Morgan	Memphis, TN	6/1/37
French, Dawn	Holyhead, Wales	10/11/57
Fricker, Brenda	Dublin, Ireland	2/17/45
Friedkin, William	Chicago, IL.	8/29/39
Frost, David	Tenterden, England	4/7/39
Fry, Stephen	London, England	8/24/57
Fuentes, Daisy	Havana, Cuba	11/17/66
Fuller, Robert.	Troy, NY.	7/29/34
Funicello, Annette	Utica, NY	10/22/42
Furlong, Edward	Pasadena, CA	8/2/77
Furtado, Nelly	Victoria, British Columbia	12/2/78
Gabor, Zsa Zsa	Budapest, Hungary.	2/6/17
Gabriel, John	Niagara Falls, NY	5/25/31
Gabriel, Peter	Surrey, England	2/13/50
Gaines, Boyd	Atlanta, GA.	5/11/53
Gallagher, Peter.	Armonk, NY	8/19/55
Gallo, Vincent	Buffalo, NY.	4/11/62
Galway, James	Belfast, N. Ireland.	12/8/39
Gandolfini, James	Westwood, NJ	9/18/61
Garagiola, Joe	St. Louis, MO	2/12/26
Garber, Victor	London, Ont.	3/16/49
Garcia, Andy	Havana, Cuba	4/12/56
Garfunkel, Art.	Queens, New York, NY	11/5/41

Name	Birthplace	Birthdate
Garland, Beverly	Santa Cruz, CA	10/17/26
Garlin, Jeff	Chicago, IL	6/5/62
Garner, James	Norman, OK	4/7/28
Garner, Jennifer	Houston, TX	4/17/72
Garofalo, Janeane	Newton, NJ	9/28/64
Garr, Teri	Lakewood, OH	12/11/49
Garrett, Betty	St. Joseph, MO	5/23/19
Garrett, Brad	Woodland Hills, CA	4/14/60
Garth, Jennie	Urbana, IL	4/3/72
Gatlin, Larry	Seminole, TX	5/2/48
Gavin, John	Los Angeles, CA	4/8/31
Gayle, Crystal	Paintsville, KY	1/9/51
Gaynor, Mitzi	Chicago, IL	9/4/31
Gazzara, Ben	New York, NY	8/28/30
Geary, Anthony	Coalville, UT	5/29/47
Geary, Cynthia	Jackson, MS	3/21/65
Gedda, Nicolai	Stockholm, Sweden	7/11/25
Gellar, Sarah Michelle	New York, NY	4/14/77
Gere, Richard	Philadelphia, PA	8/31/49
Gervais, Ricky	Reading, England	6/25/61
Getty, Estelle	New York, NY	7/25/23
Giannini, Giancarlo	La Spezia, Italy	8/1/42
Gibb, Barry	Isle of Man, England	9/1/46
Gibb, Robin	Isle of Man, England	12/22/49
Gibbons, Leeza	Irmo, SC	3/26/57
Gibbs, Marla	Chicago, IL	6/14/31
Gibson, Deborah	Brooklyn, New York, NY	8/31/70
Gibson, Henry	Germantown, PA	9/21/35
Gibson, Mel	Peekskill, NY	1/3/56
Gibson, Thomas	Charleston, SC	7/3/62
Gifford, Frank	Santa Monica, CA	8/16/30
Gifford, Kathie Lee	Neuilly-sur-Seine, France	8/16/53
Gilbert, Sara	Santa Monica, CA	1/29/75
Gilbert, Melissa	Los Angeles, CA	5/8/64
Gilberto, Astrud	Salvador, Brazil	3/30/40
Gill, Vince	Norman, OK	4/12/57
Gillette, Anita	Baltimore, MD	8/16/36
Gilley, Mickey	Natchez, MS	3/9/36
Gilliam, Terry	Minneapolis, MN	11/22/40
Gilmour, David	Cambridge, England	3/6/44
Gilpin, Peri	Waco, TX	5/27/61
Ginty, Robert	New York, NY	11/14/48
Givens, Robin	New York, NY	11/27/64
Glaser, Paul Michael	Cambridge, MA	3/25/43
Gleeson, Brendan	Belfast, N. Ireland	11/9/55
Glenn, Scott	Pittsburgh, PA	1/26/42
Gless, Sharon	Los Angeles, CA	5/31/43
Glover, Crispin	New York, NY	9/20/64
Glover, Danny	San Francisco, CA	7/22/47
Glover, John	Kingston, NY	8/7/44
Glover, Julian	London, England	3/27/35
Glover, Savion	Newark, NJ	11/19/73
Godard, Jean Luc	Paris, France	12/3/30
Goldberg, Whoopi	New York, NY	11/13/55
Goldblum, Jeff	Pittsburgh, PA	10/22/52
Goldthwait, Bobcat	Syracuse, NY	5/26/62
Goldwyn, Tony	Los Angeles, CA	5/20/60
Gooding, Cuba, Jr.	Bronx, NY	1/2/68
Goodman, John	Affton, MO	6/20/52
Gordon-Levitt, Joseph	Los Angeles, CA	2/17/81
Gorme, Eydie	Bronx, NY	8/16/32
Gosselaar, Mark-Paul	Panorama City, CA	3/1/74
Gossett, Louis, Jr.	Brooklyn, NY	5/27/36
Gould, Elliott	Brooklyn, NY	8/29/38
Gould, Harold	Schenectady, NY	12/10/23
Goulet, Robert	Lawrence, MA	11/26/33
Grace, Topher	New York, NY	7/19/78
Graham, Heather	Milwaukee, WI	1/29/70
Grammer, Kelsey	St. Thomas, Virgin Isl.	2/21/55
Granger, Farley	San Jose, CA	7/1/25
Grant, Amy	Augusta, GA	11/25/60
Grant, Hugh	London, England	9/9/60
Grant, Lee	New York, NY	10/31/27
Graves, Peter	Minneapolis, MN	3/18/26
Gray, Linda	Santa Monica, CA	9/12/40
Gray, Macy	Canton, OH	9/9/70
Grayson, Kathryn	Winston-Salem, NC	2/9/22
Green, Al	Forrest City, AR	4/13/46
Green, Seth	Overbrook Park, PA	2/8/74
Green, Tom	Pembroke, Ontario	7/30/71
Greene, Shecky	Chicago, IL	4/8/26
Greenwood, Bruce	Noranda, Quebec	8/12/56
Gregory, Cynthia	Los Angeles, CA	7/8/46
Gregory, Dick	St. Louis, MO	10/12/32
Grenier, Adrian	Brooklyn, NY	7/10/76
Grey, Jennifer	New York, NY	3/26/60
Grey, Joel	Cleveland, OH	4/11/32
Grier, David Alan	Detroit, MI	6/30/55
Grier, Pam	Winston-Salem, NC	5/26/49
Gries, Jon	Glendale, CA	6/17/57
Griffith, Andy	Mount Airy, NC	6/1/26
Griffith, Melanie	New York, NY	8/9/57
Griffiths, Rachel	New Castle, Australia	2/20/68
Griffiths, Richard	Stockton-on-Tees, Cleveland, United Kingdom	7/31/47
Grimes, Tammy	Lynn, MA	1/30/34
Grint, Rupert	Hertfordshire, England	8/24/88
Grizzard, George	Roanoke Rapids, NC	4/1/28
Groban, Josh	Los Angeles, CA	2/27/81
Grodin, Charles	Pittsburgh, PA	4/21/35
Grohl, David	Warren, OH	1/14/69
Grosbard, Ulu	Antwerp, Belgium	1/9/29
Gross, Michael	Chicago, IL	6/21/47
Guest, Christopher	New York, NY	2/5/48
Guillaume, Robert	St. Louis, MO	11/30/37
Gumbel, Greg	New Orleans, LA	5/3/46
Guthrie, Arlo	Brooklyn, New York, NY	7/10/47
Guttenberg, Steve	Brooklyn, New York, NY	8/24/58
Guy, Buddy	Lettsworth, LA	7/30/36
Guy, Jasmine	Boston, MA	3/10/64
Gyllenhaal, Jake	Los Angeles, CA	12/19/80
Gyllenhaal, Maggie	New York, NY	11/16/77
Hackman, Gene	San Bernardino, CA	1/30/30
Hagerty, Julie	Cincinnati, OH	6/15/55
Haggard, Merle	Bakersfield, CA	4/6/37
Hagman, Larry	Fort Worth, TX	9/21/31
Haid, Charles	San Francisco, CA	6/2/43
Haines, Connie	Savannah, GA	1/20/22
Hale, Barbara	DeKalb, IL	4/18/22
Hall, Anthony Michael	West Roxbury, MA	4/14/68
Hall, Arsenio	Cleveland, OH	2/12/55
Hall, Daryl	Pottstown, PA	10/11/49
Hall, Deidre	Milwaukee, WI	10/31/47
Hall, Michael C.	Raleigh, NC	2/1/71
Hall, Monty	Winnipeg, Manitoba	8/25/21
Hall, Tom T.	Olive Hill, KY	5/25/36
Halliwell, Geri	Watford, England	8/6/72
Hamill, Mark	Oakland, CA	9/25/51
Hamilton, George	Memphis, TN	8/12/39
Hamilton, Linda	Salisbury, MD	9/26/56
Hamlin, Harry	Pasadena, CA	10/30/51
Hammer	Oakland, CA	3/29/63
Hammond, Darrell	Melbourne, FL	10/8/60
Hampshire, Susan	London, England	5/12/37
Hancock, Herbie	Chicago, IL	4/12/40
Hanks, Tom	Concord, CA	7/9/56
Hannah, Daryl	Chicago, IL	12/3/60
Hannigan, Alyson	Washington, DC	3/24/74
Hanson, Curtis	Reno, NV	3/24/45
Hanson, Isaac	Tulsa, OK	11/17/80
Hanson, Taylor	Tulsa, OK	3/14/83
Hanson, Zac	Tulsa, OK	10/22/85
Harden, Marcia Gay	La Jolla, CA	8/14/59
Hardison, Kadeem	New York, NY	7/24/66
Harewood, Dorian	Dayton, OH	8/6/50
Hargitay, Mariska	Los Angeles, CA	1/23/64
Harmon, Angie	Highland Park, TX	8/10/72
Harmon, Mark	Burbank, CA	9/2/51
Harper, Ben	Claremont, CA	10/28/69
Harper, Jessica	Chicago, IL	10/10/49
Harper, Tess	Mammoth Springs, AR	8/15/50
Harper, Valerie	Suffern, NY	8/22/40
Harrelson, Woody	Midland, TX	7/23/61
Harrington, Pat.	New York, NY	8/13/29
Harris, Barbara	Evanston, IL	7/25/35
Harris, Ed.	Tenafly, NJ	11/28/50
Harris, Emmylou	Birmingham, AL	4/2/47
Harris, Julie	Grosse Pte. Park, MI	12/2/25
Harris, Neil Patrick	Albuquerque, NM	6/15/73
Harris, Rosemary	Ashby, England	9/19/30
Harris, Steve	Chicago, IL	12/3/65
Harrison, Gregory	Avalon, CA	5/31/50
Harry, Deborah	Miami, FL	7/1/45
Hart, Mary	Madison, SD	11/8/50
Hart, Melissa Joan	Sayville, NY	4/18/76
Hartley, Hal	Lindenhurst, NY	11/3/59
Hartley, Mariette	New York, NY	6/21/40
Hartman, David	Pawtucket, RI	5/19/35
Hartman Black, Lisa.	Houston, TX	6/1/56
Hartnett, Josh	San Francisco, CA	7/21/78
Harvey, P.J.	Yeovil, Somerset, England	10/9/69
Harvey, Steve	Welch, WV	11/23/56
Hasselbeck, Elisabeth	Cranston, RI	5/28/77
Hasselhoff, David	Baltimore, MD	7/17/52
Hatcher, Teri	Sunnyvale, CA	12/8/64
Hatfield, Juliana	Wiscasset, ME	7/27/67
Hathaway, Anne	Brooklyn, NY	11/12/82
Hauer, Rutger	Breukelen, Netherlands	1/23/44
Havoc, June	Seattle, WA	11/8/16
Hawke, Ethan	Austin, TX	11/6/70

Name	Birthplace	Birthdate
Hawk, Goldie	Washington, DC	11/21/45
Hayek, Salma	Coatzacoalcos, Mexico	9/2/66
Hayes, Isaac	Covington, TN	8/20/42
Hayes, Sean	Glen Ellyn, IL	6/26/70
Haynes, Roy	Roxbury, Boston, MA	3/13/26
Hays, Robert	Bethesda, MD	7/24/47
Head, Anthony Stewart	North London, England	2/20/54
Heard, John	Washington, DC	3/7/46
Hearn, George	St. Louis, MO	6/18/34
Heaton, Patricia	Bay Village, OH	3/4/58
Heche, Anne	Aurora, OH	5/25/69
Heder, Jon	Fort Collins, CO	10/26/77
Hedren, Tippi	Lafayette, MN	1/19/31
Heigl, Katherine	Washington, DC	11/24/78
Helfgott, David	Melbourne, Australia	5/19/47
Helgenberger, Marg.	Fremont, NE	11/16/58
Helmond, Katherine	Galveston, TX	7/5/34
Hemingway, Mariel	Mill Valley, CA	11/22/61
Hemsley, Sherman	Philadelphia, PA	2/1/38
Henderson, Florence	Dale, IN	2/14/34
Henley, Don	Gilmer, TX	7/22/47
Henner, Marilu	Chicago, IL	4/6/52
Hennessy, Jill	Edmonton, Alberta	11/25/68
Henry, Buck	New York, NY	12/9/30
Herman, Pee-Wee	Peekskill, NY	8/27/52
Herrmann, Edward	Washington, DC	7/21/43
Hershey, Barbara	Hollywood, CA	2/5/48
Hesseman, Howard	Lebanon, OR	2/27/40
Heston, Charlton	Evanston, IL	10/4/24
Hetfield, James	Downey, CA	8/3/63
Hewitt, Jennifer Love	Waco, TX	2/21/79
Hicks, Catherine	Scottsdale, AZ	8/6/51
Hill, Dulé	Orange, NJ.	5/3/74
Hill, Faith	Jackson, MS	9/21/67
Hill, Lauryn	South Orange, NJ.	5/25/75
Hill, Steven	Seattle, WA	2/24/22
Hillerman, John	Denison, TX	12/20/32
Hilton, Paris	New York, NY	2/17/81
Hines, Cheryl	Miami Beach, FL	9/21/65
Hingle, Pat	Denver, CO	7/19/24
Hirsch, Judd	New York, NY	3/15/35
Hodgman, John	Cambridge, MA	6/3/71
Hoffman, Dustin	Los Angeles, CA.	8/8/37
Hoffman, Philip Seymour	Fairport, NY	7/23/67
Hogan, Hulk	Augusta, GA	8/11/53
Hogan, Paul	Lightning Ridge, New South Wales, Australia	10/8/39
Holbrook, Hal	Cleveland, OH	2/17/25
Holder, Geoffrey	Port of Spain, Trinidad	8/1/30
Holliday, Polly	Jasper, AL	7/2/37
Holliman, Earl	Delhi, LA.	9/11/28
Holly, Lauren	Bristol, PA.	10/28/63
Holm, Celeste	New York, NY.	4/29/19
Holm, Ian	Ilford, England	9/12/31
Holmes, Katie	Toledo, OH	12/18/78
Hooks, Jan	Decatur, GA	4/23/57
Hopkins, Anthony	Port Talbot, South Wales	12/31/37
Hopkins, Bo	Greenville, SC	2/2/42
Hopkins, Telma	Louisville, KY	10/28/48
Hopper, Dennis	Dodge City, KS.	5/17/36
Horne, Lena	Brooklyn, NY	6/30/17
Horne, Marilyn	Bradford, PA.	1/16/34
Hornsby, Bruce	Williamsburg, VA	11/23/54
Horsley, Lee	Muleshoe, TX	5/15/55
Horton, Robert	Los Angeles, CA.	7/29/24
Hoskins, Bob	Suffolk, England	10/26/42
Hounsou, Djimon	Benin	4/24/64
Houston, Whitney	Newark, NJ.	8/9/63
Howard, Ken	El Centro, CA	3/28/44
Howard, Ron	Duncan, OK	3/1/54
Howell, C. Thomas	Van Nuys, CA	12/7/66
Howes, Sally Ann	London, England	7/20/30
Hudson, Kate	Los Angeles, CA.	4/19/79
Hudson, Jennifer	Chicago, IL	9/12/81
Huffman, Felicity	Bedford, NY	12/6/62
Hughley, D.L.	Los Angeles, CA.	3/6/63
Hulce, Tom	Whitewater, WI	12/6/53
Humperdinck, Engelbert	Madras, India	5/2/36
Humphries, Barry.	Melbourne, Australia	2/17/34
Hunt, Bonnie	Chicago, IL	9/22/64
Hunt, Helen	Culver City, CA.	6/15/63
Hunt, Linda	Morristown, NJ.	4/2/45
Hunter, Holly	Conyers, GA.	3/20/58
Hunter, Tab	New York, NY.	7/11/31
Hurley, Elizabeth	Hampshire, England.	6/10/65
Hurt, John	Chesterfield, England.	1/22/40
Hurt, Mary Beth	Marshalltown, IA.	9/26/48
Hurt, William	Washington, DC	3/20/50
Huston, Anjelica	Santa Monica, CA	7/8/51
Hutton, Lauren	Charleston, SC.	11/17/43

Name	Birthplace	Birthdate
Hutton, Timothy	Malibu, CA	8/16/60
Hyman, Earle	Rocky Mount, NC	10/11/26
Ian, Janis	New York, NY.	4/7/51
Ice Cube	Los Angeles, CA.	6/15/69
Ice-T.	Newark, NJ.	2/16/58
Idle, Eric.	S. Shields, England	3/29/43
Idol, Billy	Middlesex, England	11/30/55
Iglesias, Enrique	Madrid, Spain	5/8/75
Iglesias, Julio	Madrid, Spain	9/23/43
Iler, Robert	New York, NY	3/2/85
Iman	Mogadishu, Somalia	7/25/55
Imbruglia, Natalie	Sydney, Australia	2/4/75
Imperioli, Michael	Mount Vernon, NY	1/1/66
Imus, Don	Riverside, CA	7/23/40
Ingram, James	Akron, OH.	2/16/56
Innes, Laura	Pontiac, MI	8/16/59
Ireland, Kathy.	Glendale, CA	3/20/63
Irons, Jeremy	Isle of Wight, England	9/19/48
Irving, Amy.	Palo Alto, CA	9/10/53
Irving, George S.	Springfield, MA.	11/1/22
Irwin, Bill	Santa Monica, CA	4/11/50
Irwin, Steve	Beerwah, Queensl., Aust.	2/22/62
Ivey, Judith	El Paso, TX	9/4/51
Ivory, James	Berkeley, CA	6/7/28
Jackee (Harry)	Winston-Salem, NC	8/14/56
Jackman, Hugh	Sydney, Australia	10/12/68
Jackson, Anne	Allegheny, PA.	9/3/26
Jackson, Glenda	Birkenhead, England	5/9/36
Jackson, Janet.	Gary, IN	5/16/66
Jackson, Jermaine	Gary, IN	12/11/54
Jackson, Jonathan	Orlando, FL	5/11/82
Jackson, Joshua	Vancouver, Brit. Columbia	6/11/78
Jackson, Kate	Birmingham, AL	10/29/48
Jackson, La Toya	Gary, IN	5/29/56
Jackson, Michael	Gary, IN	8/29/58
Jackson, Peter	Wellington, New Zealand	10/31/61
Jackson, Samuel L.	Chattanooga, TN	12/21/48
Jacobi, Derek	London, England	10/22/38
Jagger, Mick	Dartford, England	7/26/43
James, Etta	Los Angeles, CA.	1/25/38
James, Kevin	Mineola, NY	4/26/65
Janis, Conrad	New York, NY.	2/11/28
Janney, Allison	Boston, MA.	11/19/60
Janssen, Famke	Amsterdam, Netherlands	11/5/65
Jardine, Al	Lima, OH	9/3/42
Jarmusch, Jim	Akron, OH.	1/22/53
Jarreau, Al	Milwaukee, WI	3/12/40
Jarrette, Keith	Allentown, PA.	5/8/45
Ja Rule	Queens, NY	2/29/76
Jay Z	Brooklyn, NY	12/4/69
Jeffreys, Anne	Goldsboro, NC	1/26/23
Jett, Joan	Philadelphia, PA.	9/22/60
Jewel (Kilcher)	Payson, UT.	5/23/74
Jewison, Norman	Toronto, Ontario	7/21/26
Jillian, Ann	Cambridge, MA	1/29/50
Jillette, Penn	Greenfield, MA	3/5/55
Joel, Billy	Bronx, NY.	5/9/49
Johansson, Scarlett	New York, NY.	11/22/84
John, Elton	Pinner, Middlesex, Eng.	3/25/47
Johns, Glynis	Durban, S Africa.	10/5/23
Johnson, Arte	Benton Harbor, MI	1/20/34
Johnson, Beverly	Buffalo, NY.	10/13/52
Johnson, Don	Flatt Creek, MO	12/15/49
Johnson, Van	Newport, RI	8/25/16
Johnston, Bruce	Chicago, IL	6/24/44
Johnston, Kristen	Washington, DC	9/20/67
Jolie, Angelina	Los Angeles, CA.	6/4/75
Jones, Charlie	Ft. Smith, AR	11/9/30
Jones, Cherry	Paris, TN	11/21/56
Jones, Davy	Manchester, England	12/30/45
Jones, Dean	Morgan City, AL	1/25/31
Jones, Elvin	Pontiac, MI	9/9/27
Jones, Gemma	London, England	12/4/42
Jones, George	Saratoga, TX	9/12/31
Jones, Grace	Spanishtown, Jamaica	5/19/52
Jones, Jack	Hollywood, CA	1/14/38
Jones, James Earl	Arkabutla, MS.	1/17/31
Jones, Jennifer	Tulsa, OK.	3/2/19
Jones, Mick	London, England	6/26/55
Jones, Norah	New York, NY.	3/30/79
Jones, Quincy	Chicago, IL.	3/14/33
Jones, Shirley	Smithton, PA	3/31/34
Jones, Star.	Badin, NC	3/24/62
Jones, Tom	Pontypridd, Wales	6/7/40
Jones, Tommy Lee	San Saba, TX	9/15/46
Jonze, Spike	Rockville, MD	10/22/69
Jourdan, Louis	Marseilles, France	6/19/19
Jovovich, Milla	Kiev, Ukraine	12/17/75
Judd, Ashley	Granada Hills, CA.	4/19/68
Judd, Naomi	Ashland, KY	1/11/46

Name	Birthplace	Birthdate
Judd, Wynonna	Ashland, KY	5/30/64
Kaczmarek, Jane	Milwaukee, WI	12/21/55
Kanaly, Steve	Burbank, CA	3/14/46
Kane, Carol	Cleveland, OH	6/18/52
Kaplan, Gabe	Brooklyn, NY	3/31/45
Karlen, John	Brooklyn, NY	5/28/33
Karn, Richard	Seattle, WA	2/17/56
Karras, Alex	Gary, IN	7/15/35
Kasem, Casey	Detroit, MI	4/27/32
Kattan, Chris	Sherman Oaks, CA	10/19/70
Kavner, Julie	Burbank, CA	9/7/51
Kazan, Lainie	New York, NY	5/15/42
Keach, Stacy	Savannah, GA	6/2/41
Keaton, Diane	Santa Ana, CA	1/5/46
Keaton, Michael	Pittsburgh, PA	9/9/51
Keener, Catherine	Miami FL	3/23/59
Keillor, Garrison	Anoka, MN	8/7/42
Keitel, Harvey	Brooklyn, NY	5/13/39
Keith, David	Knoxville, TN	5/8/54
Keith, Penelope	Sutton, Surrey, England	4/2/40
Kellerman, Sally	Long Beach, CA	6/2/37
Kelly, Jean Louisa	Worcester, MA	3/9/72
Kelly, R(obert)	Chicago, IL	1/8/67
Kennedy, George	New York, NY	2/18/25
Kennedy, Jamie	Upper Darby, PA	5/25/70
Kennedy, Jayne	Washington, DC	10/27/51
Kenny G.	Seattle, WA	6/5/56
Kent, Allegra	Santa Monica, CA	8/11/37
Kercheval, Ken	Wolcottville, IN	7/15/35
Kerns, Joanna	San Francisco, CA	2/12/53
Kerr, Deborah	Helensburgh, Scotland	9/30/21
Keys, Alicia	New York, NY	1/25/81
Khan, Chaka	Great Lakes, IL	3/23/53
Kidder, Margot	Yellowknife, N.W.T.	10/17/48
Kidman, Nicole	Honolulu, HI	6/20/67
Kiel, Richard	Detroit, MI	9/13/39
Kilborn, Craig	Kansas City, KS	8/24/62
Kilmer, Val	Los Angeles, CA	12/31/59
Kimmel, Jimmy	Brooklyn, NY	11/13/67
King, B. B.	Itta Bena, MS	9/16/25
King, Carole	Brooklyn, NY	2/9/42
King, Larry	Brooklyn, NY	11/19/33
King, Perry	Alliance, OH	4/30/48
Kingsley, Ben	Scarborough, England	12/31/43
Kingston, Alex	London, England	3/11/63
Kinnear, Greg	Logansport, IN	6/17/63
Kinney, Kathy	Stevens Point, WI.	11/3/53
Kinski, Nastassja	Berlin, W. Germany	1/24/60
Kirkland, Gelsey	Bethlehem, PA	12/29/52
Kirkpatrick, Chris	Clarion, PA	10/17/71
Kirshner, Mia	Toronto, Canada	1/25/75
Kitt, Eartha	North, SC	1/17/27
Klein, Robert	Bronx, New York, NY	2/8/42
Kline, Kevin	St. Louis, MO	10/24/47
Klugman, Jack	Philadelphia, PA.	4/27/22
Knight, Gladys	Atlanta, GA.	5/28/44
Knight, Shirley	Goessel, KS	7/5/36
Knight, T.R.	Minneapolis, MN.	3/26/73
Knight, Wayne	New York, NY.	8/7/55
Knightley, Keira	Teddington, England	3/26/85
Knopfler, Mark	Glasgow, Scotland	8/12/49
Knowles, Beyoncé	Houston, TX	9/4/81
Knoxville, Johnny	Knoxville, TN	3/11/71
Konitz, Lee	Chicago, IL	10/13/27
Kopell, Bernie	New York, NY	6/21/33
Korman, Harvey	Chicago, IL	2/15/27
Kotto, Yaphet	New York, NY.	11/15/37
Krakowski, Jane	Parsippany, NJ	10/11/68
Krasinski, John	Newton, MA	10/20/79
Krause, Peter	Alexandria, MN	8/12/65
Kressley, Carson	Allentown, PA	11/11/69
Kretschmann, Thomas	Dessau, E. Germany	9/8/62
Kristofferson, Kris	Brownsville, TX.	6/22/36
Kudrow, Lisa	Encino, CA	7/30/63
Kunis, Mila	Kiev, Ukraine, Soviet Union	8/14/83
Kuriyama, Chiaki	Tsuchiura, Ibaraki, Japan	10/10/84
Kurtz, Swoosie	Omaha, NE.	9/6/44
Kutcher, Ashton	Cedar Rapids, IA	2/7/78
Kwan, Nancy	Hong Kong	5/19/39
LaBelle, Patti	Philadelphia, PA.	5/24/44
LaBeouf, Shia	Los Angeles, CA.	6/11/86
Ladd, Cheryl	Huron, SD.	7/12/51
Ladd, Diane	Meridian, MS	11/29/32
Lagasse, Emeril	Fall River, MA.	10/15/59
Lahti, Christine	Royal Oak, MI.	4/4/50
Laine, Cleo	Southall, England	10/28/27
Lake, Ricki	Hastings-on-Hudson, NY	9/21/68
Lamas, Lorenzo	Santa Monica, CA	1/20/58
Lambert, Christopher	Great Neck, NY	3/29/57
Landau, Martin	Brooklyn, NY	6/20/28

Name	Birthplace	Birthdate
Landis, John	Chicago, IL	8/3/50
Lane, Diane	New York, NY.	1/22/65
Lane, Nathan	Jersey City, NJ	2/3/56
lang, k.d.	Consort, Alberta	11/2/61
Lang, Stephen	Queens, New York, NY	7/11/52
Lange, Jessica	Cloquet, MN	4/20/49
Langella, Frank	Bayonne, NJ.	1/1/40
Lansbury, Angela	London, England	10/16/25
LaPaglia, Anthony	Adelaide, Australia	1/31/59
Larroquette, John	New Orleans, LA	11/25/47
LaSalle, Eriq	Hartford, CT	6/23/62
Lauper, Cyndi	Brooklyn, NY	6/20/53
Laurie, Hugh	Oxford, England	6/11/59
Laurie, Piper	Detroit, MI.	1/22/32
Lavigne, Avril	Napanee, Ontario	9/27/84
Lavin, Linda	Portland, ME.	10/15/37
Law, Jude	London, England	12/29/72
Lawless, Lucy	Mount Albert, New Zealand	3/29/68
Lawrence, Carol	Melrose Park, IL	9/5/34
Lawrence, Joey	Montgomery, PA.	4/20/76
Lawrence, Martin	Frankfurt, Germany	4/16/65
Lawrence, Steve	Brooklyn, NY	7/8/35
Lawrence, Vicki	Inglewood, CA	3/26/49
Leach, Robin	London, England	8/29/41
Leachman, Cloris	Des Moines, IA.	4/30/26
Lear, Norman	New Haven, CT	7/27/22
Learned, Michael	Washington, DC	4/9/39
Leary, Denis.	Worcester, MA	8/18/57
LeBlanc, Matt.	Newton, MA	7/25/67
LeBon, Simon	Bushey, England	10/27/58
Ledger, Heath	Perth, Australia.	4/4/79
Lee, Ang	Pingtung, Taiwan	10/23/54
Lee, Brenda	Lithonia, GA	12/11/44
Lee, Christopher	London, England	5/27/22
Lee, Jason	Huntington Beach, CA	4/25/70
Lee, Michele	Los Angeles, CA.	6/24/42
Lee, Spike	Atlanta, GA.	3/20/57
Leeves, Jane	London, England	4/18/61
Legrand, Michel	Paris, France	2/24/32
Leguizamo, John	Bogotá, Colombia	7/22/64
Leibman, Ron	New York, NY.	10/11/37
Leigh, Jennifer Jason	Hollywood, CA	2/5/62
Leighton, Laura	Iowa City, IA	7/24/68
Lennox, Annie	Aberdeen, Scotland	12/25/54
Leno, Jay	New Rochelle, NY	4/28/50
Leonard, Robert Sean	Westwood, NJ	2/28/69
Leoni, Tea	New York, NY.	2/25/66
Leslie, Joan	Detroit, MI.	1/26/25
Leto, Jared	Bossier City, LA	12/26/71
Letterman, David	Indianapolis, IN.	4/12/47
Levine, James	Cincinnati, OH	6/23/43
Levine, Ted	Parma, OH	5/29/58
Levinson, Barry	Baltimore, MD.	4/6/42
Levy, Eugene.	Hamilton, Ontario	12/17/46
Lewis, Huey	New York, NY.	7/5/50
Lewis, Jason	Newport Beach, CA	6/25/71
Lewis, Jerry	Newark, NJ.	3/16/26
Lewis, Jerry Lee.	Ferriday, LA	9/29/35
Lewis, Juliette	San Fernando Valley, CA.	6/21/73
Lewis, Richard	Brooklyn, NY	6/29/47
Li, Jet	Beijing, China	4/26/63
Light, Judith	Trenton, NJ.	2/9/49
Lightfoot, Gordon	Orillia, Ontario	11/17/38
Lil' Kim	Brooklyn, NY	7/11/75
Lil' Romeo	New Orleans, LA	8/19/89
Linden, Hal.	Bronx, New York, NY	3/20/31
Ling, Lisa	Sacramento, CA.	8/30/73
Linkletter, Art	Moose Jaw, Sask., Can	7/17/12
Linn-Baker, Mark	St. Louis, MO	6/17/54
Linney, Laura	New York, NY.	2/5/64
Liotta, Ray	Newark, NJ.	12/18/55
Lithgow, John	Rochester, NY	10/19/45
Little, Rich	Ottawa, Ontario	11/26/38
Little Richard	Macon, GA	12/5/32
Littrell, Brian.	Lexington, KY	2/20/75
Liu, Lucy	Queens, NY	12/2/68
L. L. Cool J.	St. Albans, Queens, NY	1/14/68
Lloyd, Christopher	Stamford, CT	10/22/38
Lloyd, Emily	North London, England	9/29/70
Lloyd Webber, Andrew	London, England	3/22/48
Locke, Sondra	Shelbyville, TN	5/28/47
Lockhart, June	New York, NY.	6/25/25
Locklear, Heather	Westwood, CA	9/25/61
Loggia, Robert	Staten Island, NY	1/3/30
Loggins, Kenny	Everett, WA	1/7/48
Logue, Donal	Ottawa, Canada	2/27/66
Lohan, Lindsay	New York, NY	7/2/86
Lollobrigida, Gina	Subiaco, Italy	7/4/27
Lom, Herbert	Prague, Czechoslovakia.	1/9/17
Lonergan, Kenneth	New York, NY.	10/16/62

Name	Birthplace	Birthdate
Long, Nia	Brooklyn, NY	10/30/70
Long, Shelley	Ft. Wayne, IN	8/23/49
Longoria, Eva	Corpus Christi, TX	3/15/75
Lopez, George	Mission Hills, CA	4/23/61
Lopez, Jennifer	Bronx, NY	7/24/70
Lopez, Mario	San Diego, CA	10/10/73
Loren, Sophia	Rome, Italy	9/20/34
Loring, Gloria	New York, NY	12/10/46
Louis-Dreyfus, Julia	New York, NY	1/13/61
Love, Courtney	San Francisco, CA	7/9/64
Love, Mike	Baldwin Hills, CA	3/15/41
Lovett, Lyle	Klein, TX	11/1/57
Lovitz, Jon	Tarzana, CA	7/21/57
Loveless, Patty	Pikeville, KY	1/4/57
Lowe, Rob	Charlottesville, VA	3/17/64
Lowell, Carey	Huntington, NY	2/11/61
Lucas, George	Modesto, CA	5/14/44
Lucci, Susan	Scarsdale, NY	12/23/46
Luckinbill, Laurence	Ft. Smith, AR	11/21/34
Ludacris	Champaign, IL	9/11/77
Ludwig, Christa	Berlin, Germany	3/16/24
Luhrmann, Baz	Sydney, Australia	9/17/62
Lumet, Sidney	Philadelphia, PA	6/25/24
LuPone, Patti	Northport, NY	4/21/49
Lynch, David	Missoula, MT	1/20/46
Lynch, Susan	Corrinshego, N. Ireland,UK	6/5/71
Lynley, Carol	New York, NY	2/13/42
Lynn, Loretta	Butcher Hollow, KY	4/14/35
Lynn, Vera	London, England	3/20/17
Lynne, Shelby	Quantico, VA	10/22/68
Lyonne, Natasha	Great Neck, NY	4/4/79
Ma, Yo-Yo	Paris, France	10/7/55
Maazel, Lorin	Neuilly-sur-Seine, France	3/6/30
Mac, Bernie	Chicago, IL	10/5/58
MacArthur, James	Los Angeles, CA	12/8/37
Macchio, Ralph	Huntington, NY	11/4/62
MacCorkindale, Simon	Ely, England	2/12/52
MacDonald, Kelly	Glasgow, Scotland	2/23/76
MacDowell, Andie	Gaffney, SC	4/21/58
MacFarlane, Seth	Kent, CT	11/26/73
MacGraw, Ali	Pound Ridge, NY	4/1/38
MacGowan, Shane	Tunbridge, Kent, England	12/25/57
MacLachlan, Kyle	Yakima, WA	2/22/59
MacLaine, Shirley	Richmond, VA	4/24/34
MacLeod, Gavin	Mt. Kisco, NY	2/28/31
MacNee, Patrick	London, England	2/6/22
MacNeil, Cornell	Minneapolis, MN	9/24/22
MacNicol, Peter	Dallas, TX	4/10/54
MacPherson, Elle	Sydney, Australia	3/29/64
Macy, Bill	Revere, MA	5/18/22
Macy, William H.	Miami, FL	3/13/50
Madden, John	Austin, MN	4/10/36
Madigan, Amy	Chicago, IL	9/11/50
Madonna (Ciccone)	Bay City, MI	8/16/58
Madsen, Michael	Chicago, IL	9/25/58
Maguire, Tobey	Santa Monica, CA	6/27/75
Maher, Bill	New York, NY	1/20/56
Mahoney, John	Manchester, England	6/20/40
Majors, Lee	Wyandotte, MI	4/23/39
Malden, Karl	Gary, IN	3/22/12
Malick, Terrence	Ottawa, IL	11/30/43
Malick, Wendie	Buffalo, NY	12/13/50
Malina, Joshua	New York, NY	1/17/66
Malkovich, John	Christopher, IL	12/9/53
Malone, Dorothy	Chicago, IL	1/30/25
Mamet, David	Chicago, IL	11/30/47
Manchester, Melissa	Bronx, NY	2/15/51
Mandel, Howie	Toronto, Ontario	11/29/55
Mandrell, Barbara	Houston, TX	12/25/48
Mangione, Chuck	Rochester, NY	11/29/40
Manheim, Camryn	Caldwell, NJ	3/8/61
Manilow, Barry	Brooklyn, NY	6/17/46
Mann, Aimee	Richmond, VA	8/9/60
Manoff, Dinah	New York, NY	1/25/58
Manson, Marilyn	Canton, OH	1/5/69
Mantegna, Joe	Chicago, IL	11/13/47
Marcil, Vanessa	Indio, CA	10/15/69
Margulies, Julianna	Spring Valley, NY	6/8/66
Marie, Constance	Hollywood, CA	9/9/69
Marin, Cheech	Los Angeles, CA	7/13/46
Marinaro, Ed	New York, NY	3/31/50
Marriner, Neville	Lincoln, England	4/15/24
Marsalis, Branford	New Orleans, LA	8/26/60
Marsalis, Wynton	New Orleans, LA	10/18/61
Marsh, Jean	London, England	7/1/34
Marshall, Garry	Bronx, New York, NY	11/13/34
Marshall, Penny	Bronx, New York, NY	10/15/42
Marshall, Peter	Huntington, WV	3/30/27
Martin, Chris	Devon, England	3/22/77
Martin, Dick	Detroit, MI	1/30/22

Name	Birthplace	Birthdate
Martin, Jesse L.	Rocky Mount, VA	1/18/69
Martin, Kellie	Riverside, CA	10/16/75
Martin, Ricky	San Juan, Puerto Rico	12/24/71
Martin, Steve	Waco, TX	8/14/45
Martin, Tony	Oakland, CA	12/25/13
Martins, Peter	Copenhagen, Denmark	10/27/46
Mason, Jackie	Sheboygan, WI	6/9/34
Mason, Marsha	St. Louis, MO	4/3/42
Masterson, Christopher	Long Island, NY	1/22/80
Masterson, Mary Stuart	New York, NY	6/28/66
Mastrantonio, Mary Elizabeth	Lombard, IL	11/17/58
Masur, Kurt	Brieg, Germany	7/18/27
Masur, Richard	New York, NY	11/20/48
Mathers, Jerry	Sioux City, IA	6/2/48
Matheson, Tim	Glendale, CA	12/31/47
Mathis, Johnny	Gilmer, TX	9/30/35
Matlin, Marlee	Morton Grove, IL	8/24/65
Matthews, Dave	Johannesburg, S. Africa	1/9/67
May, Elaine	Philadelphia, PA	4/21/32
Mayer, John	Bridgeport, CT	10/16/77
Mazar, Debi	Queens, NY	8/15/64
Mazursky, Paul	Brooklyn, NY	4/25/30
MCA	Brooklyn, NY	11/20/65
McAdams, Rachel	London, Ontario, Canada	10/7/86
McArdle, Andrea	Abington, PA	11/5/63
McBride, Patricia	Teaneck, NJ	8/23/42
McCallum, David	Glasgow, Scotland	9/19/33
McCarthy, Andrew	Westfield, NJ	11/29/62
McCarthy, Jenny	Chicago, IL	11/1/72
McCarthy, Kevin	Seattle, WA	2/15/14
McCartney, Paul	Liverpool, England	6/18/42
McCarver, Tim	Memphis, TN	10/16/41
McClanahan, Rue	Healdton, OK	2/21/34
McConaughey, Matthew	Uvalde, Texas	11/4/69
McCoo, Marilyn	Jersey City, NJ	9/30/43
McCormack, Eric	Toronto, Canada	4/18/63
McCormack, Mary	Plainsfield, NJ	2/8/69
McCrane, Paul	Philadelphia, PA	1/19/61
McDaniel, James	Washington, DC	3/25/58
McDermott, Dylan	Waterbury, CT	10/26/61
McDiarmid, Ian	Carnoustie, Tayside, Scotland	4/17/47
McDonald, Audra	Berlin, Germany	7/3/70
McDonnell, Mary	Wilkes-Barre, PA	4/28/52
McDormand, Frances	Chicago, Illinois	6/23/57
McDowell, Malcolm	Leeds, England	6/13/43
McEntire, Reba	McAlester, OK	3/28/55
McFerrin, Bobby	New York, NY	3/11/50
McGillis, Kelly	Newport Beach, CA	7/9/57
McGoohan, Patrick	Astoria, Queens, NY	3/19/28
McGovern, Elizabeth	Evanston, IL	7/18/61
McGovern, Maureen	Youngstown, OH	7/27/49
McGraw, Tim	Delhi, LA	5/1/67
McGregor, Ewan	Crieff, Scotland	3/31/71
McGuire, Al	New York, NY	9/7/31
McKean, Michael	New York, NY	10/17/47
McKechnie, Donna	Pontiac, MI	11/16/42
McKellen, Ian	Burnley, England	5/25/39
McKenzie, Benjamin	Austin, TX	9/12/78
McLachlan, Sarah	Halifax, Nova Scotia	1/28/68
McLean, A.J.	West Palm Beach, FL	1/9/78
McMahon, Ed	Detroit, MI	3/6/23
McNichol, Kristy	Los Angeles, CA	9/11/62
McPartland, Marian	Stough, England	3/20/20
McRaney, Gerald	Collins, MS	8/19/47
McShane, Ian	Blackburn, England	9/29/42
Meadows, Jayne	Wu Chang, China	9/27/20
Meara, Anne	Brooklyn, NY	9/20/29
Meat Loaf	Dallas, TX	9/27/51
Mehta, Zubin	Bombay, India	4/29/36
Mellencamp, John	Seymour, IN	10/7/51
Meloni, Christopher	Washington, DC	4/2/61
Mendes, Sam	Redding, England	8/1/65
Mendes, Sergio	Niteroi, Brazil	2/11/41
Menzel, Idina	Syosset, NY	5/30/71
Mercer, Marian	Akron, OH	11/26/35
Merchant, Natalie	Jamestown, NY	10/26/63
Merkerson, S. Epatha	Saginaw, MI	11/28/52
Merrill, Dina	New York, NY	12/9/25
Messing, Debra	Brooklyn, NY	8/15/68
Metcalf, Laurie	Carbondale, IL	6/16/55
Michael, George	London, England	6/25/63
Michaels, Al	Brooklyn, NY	11/12/44
Michaels, Lorne	Toronto, Canada	11/17/44
Midler, Bette	Honolulu, HI	12/1/45
Midori	Osaka, Japan	10/25/71
Mike D	Brooklyn, NY	11/20/65
Milano, Alyssa	Brooklyn, NY	12/19/72
Miles, Sarah	Ingatestone, England	12/31/41
Miles, Vera	near Boise City, OK	8/23/29

Name	Birthplace	Birthdate
Miller, Dennis	Pittsburgh, PA	11/3/53
Miller, Mitch	Rochester, NY	7/4/11
Miller, Penelope Ann	Santa Monica, CA	1/13/64
Mills, Donna	Chicago, IL	12/11/43
Mills, Hayley	London, England	4/18/46
Milner, Martin	Detroit, MI	12/28/27
Milnes, Sherrill	Downers Grove, IL	1/10/35
Milsap, Ronnie	Robinsville, NC	1/16/44
Mimieux, Yvette	Hollywood, CA	1/8/42
Minghella, Anthony	Isle of Wight, England	1/6/54
Ming-Na	Macao	11/20/63
Minnelli, Liza	Los Angeles, CA	3/12/46
Minogue, Kylie	Melbourne, Australia	5/28/68
Mirren, Helen	London, England	7/26/45
Mitchell, Brian Stokes	Seattle, WA	10/31/57
Mitchell, Elizabeth	Los Angeles, CA	3/27/70
Mitchell, Joni	Fort McLeod, Alberta	11/7/43
Moby	Harlem, New York, NY	9/11/65
Modine, Matthew	Loma Linda, CA	3/22/59
Moffat, Donald	Plymouth, England	12/26/30
Molina, Alfred	London, England	5/24/53
Molinaro, Al	Kenosha, WI	6/24/19
Moll, Richard	Pasadena, CA	1/13/43
Moloney, Janel	Woodland Hills, CA	10/3/69
Monica (Arnold)	College Park, GA	10/24/80
Mo'Nique	Woodlawn, MD	12/11/67
Montalban, Ricardo	Mexico City, Mexico	11/25/20
Moody, Ron	London, England	1/8/24
Moore, Demi	Roswell, NM	11/11/62
Moore, Julianne	Fort Bragg, NC	12/3/60
Moore, Mandy	Nashua, NH	4/10/84
Moore, Mary Tyler	Brooklyn, NY	12/29/36
Moore, Melba	New York, NY	10/29/45
Moore, Michael	Flint, MI	4/23/54
Moore, Roger	London, England	10/14/27
Moore, Terry	Los Angeles, CA	1/7/29
Morales, Esai	Brooklyn, NY	10/1/62
Moranis, Rick	Toronto, Ontario	4/18/54
Moreau, Jeanne	Paris, France	1/23/28
Moreno, Rita	Humacao, PR	12/11/31
Morgan, Harry	Detroit, MI	4/10/15
Moriarty, Michael	Detroit, MI	4/5/41
Morissette, Alanis	Ottawa, Ontario	6/1/74
Morris, Garrett	New Orleans, LA	2/1/37
Morrison, Van	Belfast, N. Ireland	8/31/45
Morrissey	Manchester, England	5/22/59
Morrow, Rob	New Rochelle, NY	9/21/62
Morse, David	Beverly, MA	10/11/53
Morse, Robert	Newton, MA	5/18/31
Mortensen, Viggo	New York, NY	10/20/58
Mortimer, Emily	London, England	12/1/71
Morton, Joe	Brooklyn, NY	10/18/47
Morton, Samantha	Nottingham, Enlgand	5/13/77
Moses, William	Los Angeles, CA	11/17/59
Moss, Carrie-Anne	Vancouver, B.C., Can.	8/21/67
Moss, Kate	Croydon, Surrey, England	1/16/74
Mueller-Stahl, Armin	Tilsit, E. Prussia	12/17/30
Muldaur, Diana	Brooklyn, NY	8/19/38
Mulgrew, Kate	Dubuque, IA	4/29/55
Mull, Martin	Chicago, IL	8/18/43
Mullally, Megan	Los Angeles, CA	11/12/58
Mullan, Peter	Peterhead, Scotland	1960
Mulroney, Dermot	Alexandria, VA	10/31/63
Muniz, Frankie	Ridgewood, NJ	12/5/85
Munsel, Patrice	Spokane, WA	5/14/25
Murphy, Ben	Jonesboro, AR	3/6/42
Murphy, Brittany	Atlanta, GA	11/10/77
Murphy, Donna	Queens, NY	3/7/58
Murphy, Eddie	Brooklyn, NY	4/3/61
Murphy, Michael	Los Angeles, CA	5/5/38
Murray, Anne	Springhill, Nova Scotia	6/20/45
Murray, Bill	Wilmette, IL	9/21/50
Murray, Don	Hollywood, CA	7/31/29
Musburger, Brent	Portland, OR	5/26/39
Muti, Riccardo	Naples, Italy	7/28/41
Myers, Mike	Scarborough, Ontario	5/25/63
Nabors, Jim	Sylacauga, AL	6/12/30
Nagra, Parminder	Leicester, England	10/5/75
Nash, Graham	Blackpool, England	2/2/42
Naughton, James	Middletown, CT	12/6/45
Navarro, Dave	Santa Monica, CA	6/7/67
Neal, Patricia	Packard, KY	1/20/26
Nealon, Kevin	Bridgeport, CT	11/18/53
Neeson, Liam	Ballymena, N. Ireland	6/7/52
Neill, Sam	Ulster, N. Ireland	9/14/47
Nelligan, Kate	London, Ontario	3/16/51
Nelly	Austin, TX	11/2/74
Nelson, Craig T.	Spokane, WA	4/4/46
Nelson, Ed	New Orleans, LA	12/21/28
Nelson, Judd	Portland, ME	11/28/59

Name	Birthplace	Birthdate
Nelson, Tracy	Santa Monica, CA	10/25/63
Nelson, Willie	Abbott, TX	4/30/33
Nero, Peter	Brooklyn, NY	5/22/34
Nesmith, Mike	Houston, TX	12/30/42
Nettleton, Lois	Oak Park, IL	8/16/29
Neuwirth, Bebe	Newark, NJ	12/31/58
Neville, Aaron	New Orleans, LA	1/24/41
Newhart, Bob	Oak Park, IL	9/5/29
Newman, Paul	Cleveland, OH	1/26/25
Newman, Randy	New Orleans, LA	11/28/43
Newton, Wayne	Norfolk, VA	4/3/42
Newton-John, Olivia	Cambridge, England	9/26/48
Nicholas, Denise	Detroit, MI	7/12/44
Nichols, Mike	Berlin, Germany	11/6/31
Nicholson, Jack	Neptune, NJ	4/22/37
Nicks, Stevie	Phoenix, AZ	5/26/48
Nielsen, Connie	Copenhagen, Denmark	7/3/65
Nielsen, Leslie	Regina, Sask	2/11/26
Nighy, Bill	Caterham, Surrey, Eng.	12/12/49
Nimoy, Leonard	Boston, MA	3/26/31
Nixon, Cynthia	New York, NY	4/9/66
Nolte, Nick	Omaha, NE	2/8/41
Noone, Peter	Manchester, England	11/5/47
Norman, Jessye	Augusta, GA	9/15/45
Norris, Chuck	Ryan, OK	3/10/40
Northam, Jeremy	Cambridge, Enlgand	12/1/61
Norton, Edward	Columbia, MD	8/18/69
Noth, Christopher	Madison, WI	11/13/54
Novak, Kim	Chicago, IL	2/13/33
Nuyen, France	Marseilles, France	7/31/39
Oates, John	New York, NY	4/7/49
Obradors, Jacqueline	San Fernando Valley, CA	10/6/66
O'Brian, Hugh	Rochester, NY	4/19/25
O'Brien, Conan	Brookline, MA	4/18/63
O'Brien, Margaret	Los Angeles, CA	1/15/37
Ocean, Billy	Fyzabad, Trinidad	1/21/50
O'Connor, Frances	Oxford, England	6/12/69
O'Connor, Sinead	Glenageary, Ireland	12/8/66
Odetta	Birmingham, AL	12/31/30
O'Donnell, Chris	Winnetka, IL	6/26/70
O'Donnell, Rosie	Commack, NY	3/21/62
O'Grady, Gail	Detroit, MI	1/23/63
Oh, Sandra	Nepean, Ontario	7/20/71
O'Hara, Catherine	Toronto, Canada	3/4/54
O'Hara, Maureen	Dublin, Ireland	8/17/20
Oka, Masi	Tokyo, Japan	12/27/74
Oldman, Gary	South London, England	3/21/58
Olin, Ken	Chicago, IL	7/30/54
Olin, Lena	Stockholm, Sweden	3/22/55
Olmos, Edward James	E. Los Angeles, CA	2/24/47
Olsen, Ashley	Sherman Oaks, CA	6/13/86
Olsen, Mary-Kate	Sherman Oaks, CA	6/13/86
Olsen, Merlin	Logan, UT	9/15/40
Olson, Nancy	Milwaukee, WI	7/14/28
O'Malley, Mike	Boston, MA	10/31/69
O'Neal, Ryan	Los Angeles, CA	4/20/41
O'Neal, Tatum	Los Angeles, CA	11/5/63
O'Neill, Ed	Youngstown, OH	4/12/46
Ontkean, Michael	Vancouver, B.C.	1/24/46
O'Quinn, Terry	Newbury, MI	7/15/52
Orlando, Tony	New York, NY	4/3/44
Ormond, Julia	Epsom, England	1/4/65
Osbourne, Jack	London, England	11/8/85
Osbourne, Kelly	London, England	10/27/84
Osbourne, Ozzy	Birmingham, England	12/3/48
Osbourne, Sharon	London, England	10/10/52
O'Shea, Milo	Dublin, Ireland	6/2/26
Oslin, K.T.	Crossett, AR	5/15/42
Osment, Haley Joel	Los Angeles, CA	4/10/88
Osmond, Donny	Ogden, UT	12/9/57
Osmond, Marie	Ogden, UT	10/13/59
O'Toole, Annette	Houston, TX	4/1/53
O'Toole, Peter	Connemara, Ireland	8/2/32
Otto, Miranda	Brisbane, Australia	12/16/67
Owen, Clive	Keresley, England	10/3/64
Oz, Frank	Herford, England	5/25/44
Ozawa, Seiji	Shenyang, China	9/1/35
Pacino, Al	East Harlem, NY	4/25/40
Packer, Billy	Wellsville, NY	2/25/40
Page, Bettie	Nashville, TN	4/22/23
Page, Jimmy	Heston, England	1/9/44
Page, Patti	Claremore, OK	11/8/27
Paget, Debra	Denver, CO	8/19/33
Paige, Janis	Tacoma, WA	9/16/22
Palin, Michael	Sheffield, England	5/5/43
Palmer, Betsy	East Chicago, IN	11/1/29
Palmer, Geoffrey	London, England	6/4/27
Palminteri, Chazz	Bronx, NY	5/15/51
Paltrow, Gwyneth	Los Angeles, CA	9/28/72
Panettiere, Hayden	Palisades, NY	8/21/89

Name	Birthplace	Birthdate
Pantoliano, Joe	Hoboken, NJ.	9/12/51
Papas, Irene	Chiliomodion, Greece	9/3/26
Paquin, Anna	Wellington, New Zealand	7/24/82
Parker, Alan	London, England	2/14/44
Parker, Eleanor	Cedarville, OH	6/26/22
Parker, Fess	Ft. Worth, TX	8/16/25
Parker, Jameson	Baltimore, MD.	11/18/47
Parker, Mary-Louise	Fort Jackson, SC	8/2/64
Parker, Sarah Jessica	Nelsonville, OH.	3/25/65
Parsons, Estelle	Marblehead, MA.	11/20/27
Parton, Dolly	Sevierville, TN	1/19/46
Pasdar, Adrian	Pittsfield, MA	4/30/65
Patinkin, Mandy	Chicago, IL	11/30/52
Patric, Jason	Queens, NY	6/17/66
Patton, Will	Charleston, SC.	6/14/54
Paul, Adrian	London, England	5/29/59
Paul, Les	Waukesha, WI	1/9/15
Paulson, Sarah	Tampa, FL	12/17/75
Paxton, Bill	Fort Worth, TX	5/17/55
Pearce, Guy	Ely, England	10/5/67
Peet, Amanda	New York, NY.	1/11/72
Pendergrass, Teddy	Philadelphia, PA.	3/26/50
Penn, Arthur	Philadelphia, PA.	9/27/22
Penn, Sean	Burbank, CA.	8/17/60
Perez, Rosie	Brooklyn, NY	9/6/64
Perkins, Elizabeth	Queens, NY	11/18/60
Perlman, Itzhak	Tel Aviv, Israel	8/31/45
Perlman, Rhea	Brooklyn, NY	3/31/48
Perlman, Ron	New York, NY.	4/13/50
Perrine, Valerie	Galveston, TX.	9/3/43
Perry, Luke	Fredericktown, OH	10/11/66
Perry, Mathew	Williamstown, MA	8/19/69
Persoff, Nehemiah	Jerusalem, Israel	8/2/20
Pesci, Joe	Newark, NJ.	2/9/43
Peters, Bernadette	Queens, NY	2/28/48
Peters, Roberta	Bronx, NY	5/4/30
Petersen, Wolfgang	Emden, Germany	3/14/41
Peterson, Oscar	Montreal, Quebec.	8/15/25
Petty, Lori	Chattanooga, TN	3/23/63
Petty, Tom	Gainesville, FL	10/20/50
Pfeiffer, Michelle	Santa Ana, CA	4/29/58
Philbin, Regis	New York, NY.	8/25/31
Phair, Liz	New Haven, CT	4/17/67
Phillippe, Ryan	New Castle, DE	9/10/74
Phillips, Lou Diamond	Subic Bay, Philippines	2/17/62
Phillips, Mackenzie	Alexandria, VA	11/10/59
Phillips, Michelle	Long Beach, CA.	6/4/44
Phillips, Sian	Bettws, Wales, UK	5/14/34
Phoenix, Joaquin	San Juan, Puerto Rico	10/28/74
Pierce, David Hyde	Albany, NY	4/3/59
Pinchot, Bronson	New York, NY.	5/20/59
Pink (Alecia Moore)	Doylestown, PA	9/8/79
Pinkett Smith, Jada	Baltimore, MD.	9/18/71
Pirner, David	Green Bay, WI	4/16/64
Piscopo, Joe	Passaic, NJ	6/17/51
Pitt, Brad	Shawnee, OK.	12/18/63
Piven, Jeremy	New York, NY.	7/26/65
Plant, Robert	W. Bromwich, England.	8/20/48
Pleshette, Suzanne	New York, NY.	1/31/37
Plowright, Joan	Brigg, England	10/28/29
Plummer, Amanda	New York, NY.	3/23/57
Plummer, Christopher	Toronto, Ontario.	12/13/27
Poitier, Sidney	Miami, FL	2/20/27
Polanski, Roman	Paris, France	8/18/33
Pollack, Sydney	Lafayette, IN.	7/1/34
Pompeo, Ellen	Everett, MA.	11/10/69
Pop, Iggy	Muskegon, MI.	4/21/47
Portman, Natalie	Jerusalem, Israel	6/9/81
Posey, Parker	Baltimore, MD.	11/8/68
Post, Markie	Palo Alto, CA	11/4/50
Potente, Franka	Dulmen, Germany	7/22/74
Potts, Annie	Nashville, TN.	10/28/52
Povich, Maury	Bethesda, MD.	1/17/39
Powell, Jane	Portland, OR.	4/1/28
Powers, Stefanie	Hollywood, CA	11/2/42
Prentiss, Paula	San Antonio, TX.	3/4/39
Prepon, Laura	Watchung, NJ.	3/7/80
Presley, Priscilla	Brooklyn, NY	5/24/45
Pressly, Jaime	Kinston, NC	7/30/77
Previn, Andre	Berlin, Germany	4/6/29
Price, Leontyne	Laurel, MS	2/10/27
Price, Molly	North Plainfield, NJ.	12/15/66
Price, Ray	Perryville, TX	1/12/26
Pride, Charley	Sledge, MS.	3/18/38
Priestley, Jason	Vancouver, Brit. Columbia	8/28/69
Prince (The Artist)	Minneapolis, MN.	6/7/58
Prince, Faith	Augusta, GA.	8/5/57
Principal, Victoria	Fukuoka, Japan	1/3/50
Prinze, Freddie, Jr.	Albuquerque, NM	3/8/76
Probst, Jeff	Wichita, KS.	11/1/61

Name	Birthplace	Birthdate
Proctor, Emily	Raleigh, NC	10/18/68
Prosky, Robert	Philadelphia, PA.	12/13/30
Provine, Dorothy	Deadwood, SD	1/20/37
Pryce, Jonathan	Holywell, N. Wales	6/1/47
Puck, Wolfgang	St. Veit, Austria.	1/8/49
Pulliam, Keshia Knight.	Newark, NJ.	4/9/79
Pullman, Bill	Hornell, NY.	12/17/53
Purcell, Sarah	Richmond, IN	10/8/48
Quaid, Dennis	Houston, TX.	4/9/54
Quaid, Randy	Houston, TX.	10/1/50
Queen Latifah	Newark, NJ.	3/18/70
Quinn, Aidan	Chicago, IL	3/8/59
Quinn, Colin	Brooklyn, NY	8/15/59
Quinn, Martha	Albany, NY.	5/11/59
Rachins, Alan.	Cambridge, MA	10/3/42
Radcliffe, Daniel	London, England	7/23/89
Rae, Charlotte	Milwaukee, WI	4/22/26
Raffi	Cairo, Egypt	7/8/48
Rainer, Luise	Vienna, Austria	1/12/10
Raitt, Bonnie	Burbank, CA.	11/8/49
Ramey, Samuel	Colby, KS	3/28/42
Ramirez, Efren	Los Angeles, CA.	10/2/83
Ramirez, Sara	Mazatlan, Mexico	09/31/76
Ramone, Tommy	Budapest, Hungary.	1/29/52
Randolph, Joyce	Detroit, MI.	10/21/25
Raphael, Sally Jessy	Easton, PA	2/25/35
Rashad, Phylicia	Houston, TX	6/19/48
Ratzenberger, John	Bridgeport, CT	4/6/47
Raver, Kim	New York, NY.	3/15/69
Reddy, Helen	Melbourne, Australia	10/25/41
Redford, Robert	Santa Monica, CA	8/18/37
Redgrave, Lynn	London, England	3/8/43
Redgrave, Vanessa	London, England	1/30/37
Reed, Jerry	Atlanta, GA.	3/20/37
Reed, Lou	Brooklyn, NY	3/2/42
Reed, Rex	Ft. Worth, TX	10/2/38
Reese, Della	Detroit, MI.	7/6/31
Reeves, Keanu	Beirut, Lebanon	9/2/64
Reeves, Martha	Eufaula, AL.	7/18/41
Regalbuto, Joe.	Brooklyn, NY	8/24/49
Reid, Tara	Wyckoff, NJ	11/8/75
Reid, Tim	Norfolk, VA.	12/19/44
Reid, Vernon	London, England	8/22/58
Reilly, John C.	Chicago, IL	5/24/65
Reiner, Carl	Bronx, NY.	3/20/22
Reiner, Rob	Bronx, NY.	3/6/47
Reinhold, Judge	Wilmington, DE.	5/21/57
Reinking, Ann	Seattle, WA	11/10/49
Reiser, Paul	New York, NY.	3/30/57
Reitman, Ivan.	Komarno, Czechoslovakia	10/26/46
Remini, Leah	Brooklyn, NY	6/15/70
Resnik, Regina	New York, NY.	8/30/22
Reynolds, Burt.	Waycross, GA	2/11/36
Reynolds, Debbie	El Paso, TX	4/1/32
Reznor, Trent.	Mercer, PA	5/17/65
Rhames, Ving	Harlem, New York, NY	5/12/59
Rhymes, Busta	Brooklyn, NY	5/20/72
Ribisi, Giovanni	Los Angeles, CA.	12/17/74
Ricci, Christina	Santa Monica, CA	2/12/80
Richards, Denise	Downers Grove, IL	2/17/71
Richards, Keith	Dartford, Kent, England	12/18/43
Richards, Michael	Culver City, CA.	7/24/49
Richardson, Kevin	Lexington, KY	10/3/71
Richardson, Miranda	Lancashire, England.	3/3/58
Richardson, Natasha	London, England	5/11/63
Richardson, Patricia.	Bethesda, MD.	2/23/51
Richie, Lionel	Tuskegee, AL.	6/20/49
Richter, Andy	Grand Rapids, MI	8/28/66
Rickles, Don.	Queens, NY	5/8/26
Rickman, Alan	Hammersmith, England	2/21/46
Riegert, Peter.	New York, NY.	4/11/47
Rigg, Diana	Doncaster, England	7/20/38
Rimes, LeAnn	Flowood, MS	8/28/82
Ringwald, Molly	Roseville, CA	2/18/68
Ripa, Kelly	Stratford, NJ	10/2/70
Rivera, Chita	Washington, DC	1/23/33
Rivera, Geraldo	New York, NY.	7/4/43
Rivers, Joan	Brooklyn, NY	6/8/33
Robbins, Tim	W. Covina, CA	10/16/58
Roberts, Doris	St. Louis, MO	11/4/29
Roberts, Eric	Biloxi, MS	4/18/56
Roberts, Julia	Smyrna, GA	10/28/67
Roberts, Pernell	Waycross, GA	5/18/28
Roberts, Tony	New York, NY.	10/22/39
Robertson, Cliff	La Jolla, CA	9/9/25
Robertson, Dale	Harrah, OK.	7/14/23
Robinson, Smokey	Detroit, MI.	2/19/40
Rochon, Lela	Torrance, CA	4/17/64
Rock, Chris	South Carolina	2/7/66
Rock, The	Hayward, CA	5/2/72

Name	Birthplace	Birthdate
Rodgers, Jimmy	Camas, WA	9/18/33
Rodriguez, Jai	Brentwood, NY	6/22/77
Rodriguez, Johnny	Sabinal, TX	12/10/51
Rogan, Joe	Newark, NJ	8/11/67
Rogen, Seth	Vancouver, BC	4/15/82
Rogers, Kenny	Houston, TX	8/21/38
Rogers, Mimi	Coral Gables, FL	1/27/56
Rogers, Wayne	Birmingham, AL	4/7/33
Rohm, Elisabeth	Dusseldorf, Germany	4/28/73
Rollins, Henry	Washington, DC	2/13/61
Rollins, Sonny	Harlem, NY	9/7/30
Romano, Ray	Queens, NY	12/21/57
Romijn, Rebecca	Berkeley, CA	11/6/72
Ronstadt, Linda	Tucson, AZ	7/15/46
Rooney, Mickey	Brooklyn, NY	9/23/20
Root, Stephen	Sarasota, FL	11/17/51
Rose, Axl	Lafayette, IN	2/6/62
Rose Marie	New York, NY	8/15/23
Roseanne	Salt Lake City, UT	11/3/52
Ross, Charlotte	Winnetka, IL	1/21/68
Ross, Diana	Detroit, MI	3/26/44
Ross, Katharine	Hollywood, CA	1/29/40
Rossdale, Gavin	London, England	10/30/67
Ross, Marion	Albert Lea, MN	10/25/28
Rossellini, Isabella	Rome, Italy	6/18/52
Rossum, Emmy	New York, NY	9/12/86
Roth, David Lee	Bloomington, IN	10/10/55
Roth, Tim	London, England	5/14/61
Rotten, Johnny	London, England	1/31/56
Rourke, Mickey	Schenectady, NY	9/16/56
Routh, Brandon	Des Moines, IA	10/9/79
Routledge, Patricia	Birkenhead, England	2/17/29
Rowan, Kelly	Ottawa, Canada	1967
Rowlands, Gena	Cambria, WI	6/19/36
Rubinstein, John	Beverly Hills, CA	12/8/46
Rudd, Paul	Passaic, NJ	4/6/1969
Rudner, Rita	Miami, FL	9/17/56
Ruehl, Mercedes	Queens, NY	2/28/48
Ruffalo, Mark	Kenosha, WI	11/22/67
Rupp, Debra Jo	Glendale, CA	2/24/51
Rush, Barbara	Denver, CO	1/4/27
Rush, Geoffrey	Toowoomba, Australia	7/6/51
Russell, Jane	Bemidji, MN	6/21/21
Russell, Ken	Southampton, England	7/3/27
Russell, Keri	Fountain Valley, CA	3/23/76
Russell, Kurt	Springfield, MA	3/17/51
Russell, Leon	Lawton, OK	4/2/41
Russell, Mark	Buffalo, NY	8/23/32
Russell, Theresa	San Diego, CA	3/20/57
Russo, Rene	Burbank, CA	2/17/54
Rutherford, Ann	Toronto, Ontario	11/2/20
Ruttan, Susan	Oregon City, OR	9/16/50
Ryan, Meg	Fairfield, CT	11/19/61
Ryan, Roz	Detroit, MI	7/7/51
Rydell, Bobby	Philadelphia, PA	4/26/42
Ryder, Winona	Winona, MN	10/29/71
Sabato, Antonio, Jr.	Rome, Italy	2/29/72
Sade	Ibadan, Nigeria	1/16/59
Sagal, Katey	Hollywood, CA	1/19/53
Saget, Bob	Philadelphia, PA	5/17/56
Sagnier, Ludivine	La Celle-St.-Cloud, France	7/3/79
Sahl, Mort	Montreal, Quebec	5/11/27
Saint, Eva Marie	Newark, NJ	7/4/24
St. James, Susan	Hollywood, CA	8/14/46
St. John, Jill	Los Angeles, CA	8/19/40
St. Patrick, Mathew	Philadelphia, PA	3/17/69
Sajak, Pat	Chicago, IL	10/26/46
Saks, Gene	New York, NY	11/8/21
Sales, Soupy	Franklinton, NC	1/8/26
Salonga, Lea	Manila, Philippines	2/22/71
Samms, Emma	London, England	8/28/60
Sandler, Adam	Brooklyn, NY	9/9/66
Sands, Julian	West Yorkshire, England	1/15/58
San Giacomo, Laura	West Orange, NJ	11/14/61
Santana, Carlos	Autlan, Mexico	7/20/47
Sara, Mia	Brooklyn, NY	6/19/67
Sarandon, Susan	New York, NY	10/4/46
Sarnoff, Dorothy	New York, NY	5/25/17
Sartain, Gailard	Tulsa, OK	9/18/46
Savage, Ben	Highland Park, IL	9/13/80
Savage, Fred	Highland Park, IL	7/9/76
Sawa, Devon	Vancouver, B.C., Can.	9/7/78
Saxon, John	Brooklyn, NY	8/5/35
Sayles, John	Schenectady, NY	9/28/50
Scacchi, Greta	Milan, Italy	2/18/60
Scaggs, Boz	Canton, OH	6/8/44
Scales, Prunella	Sutton Abinger, England	6/22/32
Scalia, Jack	Brooklyn, NY	11/10/51
Schallert, William	Los Angeles, CA	7/6/22
Scheider, Roy	Orange, NJ	11/10/35
Schell, Maximilian	Vienna, Austria	12/8/30
Schiff, Richard	Bethesda, MD	5/27/55
Schiffer, Claudia	Rheinbach, Germany	8/25/70
Schneider, John	Mt. Kisco, NY	4/8/54
Schneider, Rob	San Francisco, CA	10/31/63
Schram, Bitty	New York, NY	7/17/68
Schreiber, Liev	San Francisco, CA	10/4/67
Schroder, Rick	Staten Island, NY	4/13/70
Schwarzenegger, Arnold	Thal, Austria	7/30/47
Schwimmer, David	Astoria, Queens, NY	11/2/66
Sciorra, Annabella	New York, NY	3/24/64
Scofield, Paul	Hurstpierpoint, England	1/21/22
Scolari, Peter	New Rochelle, NY	9/12/54
Scorsese, Martin	Flushing, Queens, NY	11/17/42
Scott, Lizabeth	Scranton, PA	9/29/22
Scott, Ridley	South Shields, England	11/30/37
Scott, Seann William	Cottage Grove, MN	10/3/76
Scott-Heron, Gil	Chicago, IL	4/1/49
Scott Thomas, Kristin	Redruth, England	5/24/60
Scotto, Renata	Savona, Italy	2/24/35
Scram, Bitty	New York, NY	7/17/68
Scully, Vin	Bronx, NY	11/29/27
Seacrest, Ryan	Atlanta, GA	12/24/74
Seagal, Steven	Lansing, MI	4/10/51
Secor, Kyle	Tacoma, WA	5/31/58
Sedaka, Neil	Brooklyn, NY	3/13/39
Sedgwick, Kyra	New York, NY	8/19/65
Seeger, Pete	New York, NY	5/3/19
Segal, George	Great Neck, NY	2/13/34
Seidelman, Susan	Abington, PA	12/11/52
Seinfeld, Jerry	Brooklyn, NY	4/29/54
Sellecca, Connie	Bronx, NY	5/25/55
Selleck, Tom	Detroit, MI	1/29/45
Severinsen, Doc	Arlington, OR	7/7/27
Sevigny, Chloë	Springfield, MA	11/18/74
Sewell, Rufus	London, England	10/29/67
Seymour, Jane	Hillingdon, England	2/15/51
Shackelford, Ted	Oklahoma City, OK	6/23/46
Shaffer, Paul	Thunder Bay, Ontario	11/28/49
Shakira	Barranquilla, Colombia	2/2/77
Shalhoub, Tony	Green Bay, WI	10/9/53
Shandling, Garry	Chicago, IL	11/29/49
Shankar, Ravi	Benares, India	4/7/20
Shannon, Molly	Shaker Heights, OH	9/16/64
Sharif, Omar	Alexandria, Egypt	4/10/32
Shatner, William	Montreal, Quebec	3/22/31
Shaughnessy, Charles	London, England	2/9/55
Shaver, Helen	St. Thomas, Ontario	2/24/51
Shea, John	N. Conway, NH	4/14/49
Shearer, Harry	Los Angeles, CA	12/23/43
Shearing, George	London, England	8/13/19
Sheedy, Ally	New York, NY	6/13/62
Sheen, Charlie	Los Angeles, CA	9/3/65
Sheen, Martin	Dayton, OH	8/3/40
Sheindlin, Judge Judy	Brooklyn, NY	10/21/42
Shelley, Carole	London, England	8/16/39
Shepard, Sam	Ft. Sheridan, IL	11/5/43
Shepherd, Cybill	Memphis, TN	2/18/50
Shepherd, Sherri	Chicago, IL	4/22/67
Sheridan, Nicollette	Worthing, England	11/21/63
Shields, Brooke	New York, NY	5/31/65
Shire, Talia	Lake Success, NY	4/25/46
Short, Martin	Hamilton, Ontario	3/26/50
Shortz, Will	Crawfordsville, IN	8/26/52
Show, Grant	Detroit, MI	2/27/62
Shue, Andrew	Washington, DE	2/20/67
Shue, Elisabeth	Wilmington, DE	10/6/63
Shyamalan, M. Night	Pondicherry, India	8/6/70
Siepi, Cesare	Milan, Italy	2/14/23
Sigler, Jamie-Lynn	Jericho, NY	5/15/81
Sikking, James B.	Los Angeles, CA	3/5/34
Silver, Ron	New York, NY	7/2/46
Silverman, Jonathan	Beverly Hills, CA	8/5/66
Silverman, Sarah	Bedford, NH	12/1/70
Silverstone, Alicia	Hillsborough, CA	10/4/76
Simmons, Gene	Haifa, Israel	8/25/49
Simmons, Henry	Stamford, CT	7/1/70
Simmons, Jean	London, England	1/31/29
Simmons, Richard	New Orleans, LA	7/12/48
Simon, Carly	Riverdale, NY	6/25/45
Simon, Paul	Newark, NJ	10/13/41
Simpson, Ashlee	Waco, TX	10/3/84
Simpson, Jessica	Abilene, TX	7/10/80
Sinatra, Nancy	Jersey City, NJ	6/8/40
Sinbad	Benton Harbor, MI	11/10/56
Singleton, John	Los Angeles, CA	1/6/68
Sinise, Gary	Blue Island, IL	3/17/55
Sirico, Tony	Brooklyn, NY	7/29/42
Sisto, Jeremy	Grass Valley, CA	10/6/74
Sizemore, Tom	Detroit, MI	9/29/64

Name	Birthplace	Birthdate
Skerritt, Tom	Detroit, MI	8/25/33
Skye, Ione	Hertfordshire, England	9/4/70
Slater, Christian	New York, NY	8/18/69
Slater, Helen	Massapequa, NY	12/15/63
Slezak, Erika	Hollywood, CA	8/5/46
Slick, Grace	Evanston, IL	10/30/39
Smirnoff, Yakov	Odessa, Ukraine	1/24/51
Smith, Allison	Bronx, NY	12/9/69
Smith, Jaclyn	Houston, TX	10/26/47
Smith, Keely	Norfolk, VA	3/9/32
Smith, Kevin	Red Bank, NJ	8/2/70
Smith, Maggie	Ilford, England	12/28/34
Smith, Patti	Chicago, IL	12/30/46
Smith, Robert	Blackpool, England	4/21/59
Smith, Will	West Philadelphia, PA	9/25/68
Smits, Jimmy	New York, NY	7/9/55
Smothers, Dick	Governor's Island, NY	11/20/38
Smothers, Tom	Governor's Island, NY	2/2/37
Snipes, Wesley	Orlando, FL	7/31/62
Snoop Dogg	Long Beach, CA	10/20/72
Soderbergh, Steven	Atlanta, GA	1/14/63
Somers, Suzanne	San Bruno, CA	10/16/46
Sommer, Elke	Berlin, Germany	11/5/40
Sorbo, Kevin	Mound, MN	9/24/58
Sorvino, Mira	Tenafly, NJ	9/28/67
Sorvino, Paul	Brooklyn, NY	4/13/39
Soul, David	Chicago, IL	8/28/43
Spacek, Sissy	Quitman, TX	12/25/49
Spacey, Kevin	S. Orange, NJ	7/26/59
Spade, David	Birmingham, MI	7/22/64
Spader, James	Boston, MA	2/7/60
Spano, Joe	San Francisco, CA	7/7/46
Sparks, Jordin	Phoenix, AZ	12/22/89
Spears, Britney	Kentwood, LA	12/2/81
Spector, Phil	Bronx, NY	12/26/40
Spelling, Tori	Los Angeles, CA	5/16/73
Spielberg, Steven	Cincinnati, OH	12/18/46
Spiner, Brent	Houston, TX	2/2/49
Springer, Jerry	London, England	2/13/44
Springfield, Rick	Sydney, Australia	8/23/49
Springsteen, Bruce	Freehold, NJ	9/23/49
Spurlock, Morgan	Parksburg, WV	11/7/70
Stafford, Jo	Coalinga, CA	11/12/17
Stahl, Nick	Harlingen, TX	12/5/79
Stallone, Sylvester	New York, NY	7/6/46
Stamos, John	Cypress, CA	8/19/63
Stamp, Terence	Stepney, England	7/22/39
Stang, Arnold	Chelsea, MA	9/28/25
Stanton, Harry Dean	West Irvine, KY	7/14/26
Stapleton, Jean	New York, NY	1/19/23
Starr, Ringo	Liverpool, England	7/7/40
Steenburgen, Mary	Newport, AR	2/8/53
Stefani, Gwen	Anaheim, CA	10/3/69
Stein, Ben	Washington, DC	11/25/44
Stephens, James	Mt. Kisco, NY	5/18/51
Stern, Daniel	Bethesda, MD	8/28/57
Stern, Howard	Roosevelt, NY	1/12/54
Sternhagen, Frances	Washington, DC	1/13/30
Stevens, Andrew	Memphis, TN	6/10/55
Stevens, Cat	London, England	7/21/48
Stevens, Connie	Brooklyn, NY	8/8/38
Stevens, Rise	Bronx, NY	6/11/13
Stevens, Stella	Hot Coffee, MS	10/1/36
Stevenson, Parker	Philadelphia, PA	6/4/52
Stewart, French	Albuquerque, NM	2/20/64
Stewart, Jon	Trenton, NY	11/28/62
Stewart, Patrick	Mirfield, England	7/13/40
Stewart, Rod	London, England	1/10/45
Stiers, David Ogden	Peoria, IL	10/31/42
Stiles, Julia	New York, NY	3/28/81
Stiller, Ben	New York, NY	11/30/65
Stiller, Jerry	Brooklyn, NY	6/8/27
Stills, Stephen	Dallas, TX	1/3/45
Sting	Newcastle, England	10/2/51
Stipe, Michael	Decatur, GA	1/4/60
Stockwell, Dean	North Hollywood, CA	3/5/36
Stoltz, Eric	Whittier, CA	9/30/61
Stone, Dee Wallace	Kansas City, KS	12/14/48
Stone, Oliver	New York, NY	9/15/46
Stone, Sharon	Meadville, PA	3/10/58
Stookey, Paul	Baltimore, MD	12/30/37
Storch, Larry	New York, NY	1/8/23
Storm, Gale	Bloomington, TX	4/5/22
Stowe, Madeleine	Eagle Rock, CA	8/18/58
Strait, George	Pearsall, TX	5/18/52
Strasser, Robin	New York, NY	5/7/45
Stratas, Teresa	Toronto, Ontario	5/26/38
Strathairn, David	San Francisco, CA	1/26/49
Strauss, Peter	Croton-on-Hudson, NY	2/20/47
Streep, Meryl	Summit, NJ	6/22/49
Streisand, Barbra	Brooklyn, NY	4/24/42
Stringfield, Sherry	Colorado Springs, CO	6/24/67
Stritch, Elaine	Detroit, MI	2/2/26
Stroman, Susan	Wilmington, DE	10/17/54
Struthers, Sally	Portland, OR	7/28/48
Stuart, Gloria	Santa Monica, CA	7/4/10
Studdard, Ruben	Birmingham, AL	9/12/78
Suchet, David	London, England	5/2/46
Sullivan, Erik Per	Worcester, MA	7/12/91
Sullivan, Susan	New York, NY	11/18/42
Sumac, Yma	Ichocan, Peru	9/10/27
Summer, Donna	Dorchester, MA	12/31/48
Sutherland, Donald	St. John, New Brunswick	7/17/34
Sutherland, Joan	Sydney, Australia	11/7/26
Sutherland, Kiefer	London, England	12/21/66
Suvari, Mena	Newport, RI	2/9/79
Swank, Hilary	Bellingham, WA	7/30/74
Swayze, Patrick	Houston, TX	8/18/52
Swinton, Tilda	London, England	11/5/60
Swit, Loretta	Passaic, NJ	11/4/37
Sykes, Wanda	Portsmouth, VA	3/7/64
Szmanda, Eric	Milwaukee, WI	7/24/75
T, Mr.	Chicago, IL	5/21/52
Takei, George	Los Angeles, CA	4/20/37
Tallchief, Maria	Fairfax, OK	1/24/25
Tamblyn, Amber	Santa Monica, CA	5/14/83
Tamblyn, Russ	Los Angeles, CA	12/30/34
Tarantino, Quentin	Knoxville, TN	3/27/63
Tautou, Audrey	Beaumont, France	8/9/78
Taylor, Billy	Greenville, NC	7/21/21
Taylor, Buck	Hollywood, CA	5/13/38
Taylor, Elizabeth	London, England	2/27/32
Taylor, James	Boston, MA	3/12/48
Taylor, Rip	Washington, DC	1/13/34
Taylor, Rod	Sydney, Australia	1/11/30
Taymor, Julie	Newton, MA	12/15/52
Te Kanawa, Kiri	Gisborne, New Zealand	3/6/44
Teller	Philadelphia, PA	2/14/48
Temple Black, Shirley	Santa Monica, CA	4/23/28
Tennant, Victoria	London, England	9/30/50
Tennille, Toni	Montgomery, AL	5/8/43
Tesh, John	Garden City, NY	7/9/52
Tharp, Twyla	Portland, IN	7/1/41
Thaxter, Phyllis	Portland, ME	11/20/21
Theron, Charlize	South Africa	8/7/75
Thicke, Alan	Kirkland Lake, Ontario	3/1/47
Thiessen, Tiffani	Long Beach, CA	1/23/74
Thomas, Jay	Kermit, TX	7/12/48
Thomas, Jonathan Taylor	Bethlehem, PA	9/8/81
Thomas, Marlo	Deerfield, MI	11/21/38
Thomas, Michael Tilson	Hollywood, CA	12/21/44
Thomas, Philip Michael	Columbus, OH	5/26/49
Thomas, Richard	New York, NY	6/13/51
Thomas, Sean Patrick	Wilmington, DE	12/17/70
Thompson, Emma	London, England	4/15/59
Thompson, Jack	Sydney, Australia	8/31/40
Thompson, Lea	Rochester, MN	5/31/61
Thompson, Sada	Des Moines, IA	9/27/29
Thorne-Smith, Courtney	San Francisco, CA	11/8/67
Thornton, Billy Bob	Hot Springs, AR	8/4/55
Thurman, Uma	Boston, MA	4/29/70
Tiegs, Cheryl	Breckenridge, MN	9/25/47
Tierney, Maura	Boston, MA	2/3/65
Tillis, Mel	Tampa, FL	8/8/32
Tilly, Jennifer	Harbor City, CA	9/16/58
Tilly, Meg	Long Beach, CA	2/14/60
Timberlake, Justin	Memphis, TN	1/31/81
Todd, Richard	Dublin, Ireland	6/11/19
Tomei, Marisa	Brooklyn, NY	12/4/64
Tomlin, Lily	Detroit, MI	9/1/39
Tork, Peter	Washington, DC	2/13/42
Torn, Rip	Temple, TX	2/6/31
Townsend, Robert	Chicago, IL	2/6/57
Townshend, Peter	Chiswick, England	5/19/45
Travanti, Daniel J.	Kenosha, WI	3/7/40
Travers, Mary	Louisville, KY	11/7/37
Travis, Nancy	Astoria, Queens, NY	9/21/61
Travis, Randy	Marshville, NC	5/4/59
Travolta, John	Englewood, NJ	2/18/54
Trebek, Alex	Sudbury, Ontario	7/22/40
Tripplehorn, Jean	Tulsa, OK	6/10/63
Tritt, Travis	Marietta, GA	2/9/63
Tucci, Stanley	Katonah, NY	1/11/60
Tucker, Chris	Decatur, GA	8/31/72
Tucker, Michael	Baltimore, MD	2/6/44
Tucker, Tanya	Seminole, TX	10/10/58
Tune, Tommy	Wichita Falls, TX	2/28/39
Turlington, Christy	Walnut Creek, CA	1/2/69
Turner, Ike	Clarksdale, MS	11/5/31
Turner, Janine	Lincoln, NE	12/6/62

Name	Birthplace	Birthdate
Turner, Kathleen	Springfield, MO.	6/19/54
Turner, Tina	Brownsville, TN	11/26/39
Turturro, John	Brooklyn, NY	2/28/57
Twain, Shania	Windsor, Ontario	8/28/65
Twiggy (Lawson)	London, England	9/19/49
Tyler, Liv	New York, NY	7/1/77
Tyler, Steven	Yonkers, NY	3/26/48
Tyson, Cicely	Harlem, NY.	12/19/33
Uecker, Bob	Milwaukee, WI	1/26/35
Uggams, Leslie	New York, NY.	5/25/43
Ullman, Tracey	Slough, England	12/30/59
Ullmann, Liv.	Tokyo, Japan	12/16/39
Ulrich, Skeet	New York, NY.	1/20/69
Underwood, Carrie	Checotah, OK.	3/10/83
Underwood, Blair	Tacoma, WA.	8/25/64
Urban, Keith.	Whangarei, North Island, New Zealand	10/26/67
Usher (Raymond IV)	Chattanooga,TN.	10/14/78
Vaccaro, Brenda	Brooklyn, NY	11/18/39
Vale, Jerry	Bronx, NY.	7/8/32
Valente, Caterina	Paris, France	1/14/31
Valley, Mark.	Ogdensburg, NY.	12/24/64
Valli, Frankie	Newark, NJ.	5/3/37
Van Ark, Joan	New York, NY.	6/16/43
Vance, Courtney B.	Birmingham, MI	3/12/60
Van Damme, Jean-Claude	Brussels, Belgium.	10/18/60
Van Der Beek, James	Chesire, CT	3/8/77
Van Doren, Mamie.	Rowena, SD.	2/6/31
Van Dyke, Dick	West Plains, MO.	12/13/25
Van Dyke, Jerry	Danville, IL.	7/27/31
Van Halen, Eddie.	Nijmegen, Netherlands.	1/26/55
Van Patten, Dick	Queens, NY	12/9/28
Van Peebles, Mario	Mexico City, Mexico	1/15/57
Van Sant, Gus	Louisville, KY	7/24/52
Van Zandt, Steven.	Boston, MA.	11/22/50
Vardalos, Nia	Winnipeg, Manit. Can.	9/24/62
Vaughn, Robert	New York, NY.	11/22/32
Vaughn, Vince	Minneapolis, MN.	3/28/70
Vedder, Eddie	Evanston, IL.	12/23/64
Vega, Alexa	Miami, FL	8/27/88
Vereen, Ben.	Miami, FL	10/10/46
Verrett, Shirley	New Orleans, LA	5/31/31
Vickers, Jon.	Prince Albert, Sask.	10/29/26
Vieira, Meredith	Providence, RI	12/30/53
Vigoda, Abe.	New York, NY.	2/24/21
Vincent, Jan-Michael	Denver, CO	7/15/44
Vinton, Bobby	Canonsburg, PA.	4/16/35
Visnjic, Goran	Sibenik, Yugo. (Croatia)	9/9/72
Vitale, Dick.	East Rutherford, NJ	6/9/39
Voight, Jon.	Yonkers, NY.	12/29/38
Von Stade, Frederica.	Somerville, NJ	6/1/45
Von Sydow, Max	Lund, Sweden	4/10/29
Von Trier, Lars	Copenhagen, Denmark	4/30/56
Wagner, Jack.	Washington, MO.	10/3/59
Wagner, Lindsay	Los Angeles, CA.	6/22/49
Wagner, Robert	Detroit, MI.	2/10/30
Wahl, Ken	Chicago, IL.	2/14/56
Wahlberg, Mark	Dorchester, MA	6/5/71
Wain, Bea.	Bronx, NY.	4/30/17
Waite, Ralph	White Plains, NY	6/22/28
Waits, Tom	Pomona, CA.	12/7/49
Walden, Robert	New York, NY.	9/25/43
Walken, Christopher	Astoria, Queens, NY.	3/31/43
Wallace, Marcia.	Creston, IA.	11/1/42
Wallach, Eli	Brooklyn, NY	12/7/15
Walsh, Kate	San Jose, CA	10/13/67
Walter, Jessica	Brooklyn, NY	1/31/40
Ward, Fred.	San Diego, CA	12/30/42
Ward, Sela.	Meridian, MS	7/11/56
Ward, Simon	Kent, London, England.	10/19/41
Warfield, Marsha	Chicago, IL.	3/5/54
Warner, Malcolm-Jamal.	Jersey City, NJ	8/18/70
Warren, Lesley Ann	New York, NY.	8/16/46
Warwick, Dionne	East Orange, NJ.	12/12/40
Washington, Denzel	Mt. Vernon, NY.	12/28/54
Washington, Isaiah	Houston, TX.	8/3/63
Watanabe, Ken	Koide, Niigata, Japan.	10/21/59
Waters, John	Baltimore, MD.	4/22/46
Waters, Roger	Great Bookham, England.	9/6/44
Waterston, Sam.	Cambridge, MA	11/15/40
Watson, Emily	London, England	1/14/67
Watson, Emma	Oxford, England.	4/15/90
Watts, Andre	Nuremberg, Germany.	6/20/46
Watts, Naomi	Shoreham, England	9/28/68
Wayans, Damon	New York, NY.	9/4/60
Wayans, Keenen Ivory	Brooklyn, NY	6/8/58
Wayans, Marlon.	New York, NY.	723/72
Wayans, Shawn.	New York, NY.	1/19/71
Weathers, Carl.	New Orleans, LA	1/14/48
Weaver, Fritz.	Pittsburgh, PA	1/19/26
Weaver, Sigourney	New York, NY.	10/8/49
Weiland, Scott	Santa Cruz, CA	10/27/67
Weir, Peter.	Sydney, Australia	8/8/44
Weisz, Rachel	London, England	3/7/71
Weitz, Bruce	Norwalk, CT	5/27/43
Welch, Raquel	Chicago, IL.	9/5/40
Weld, Tuesday.	New York, NY.	8/27/43
Weller, Peter	Stevens Point, WI.	6/24/47
Welling, Tom	PutnamValley, NY	4/26/77
Wells, Kitty.	Nashville, TN	8/30/19
Wendt, George	Chicago, IL.	10/17/48
West, Adam	Walla Walla, WA.	9/19/28
West, Kayne	Atlanta, GA.	6/8/77
West, Shane	Baton Rouge, LA	6/10/78
Wettig, Patricia.	Cincinnati, OH	12/4/51
Whalley, Joanne	Manchester, England.	8/25/64
Wheaton, Wil.	Burbank, CA	7/29/72
Whitaker, Forest	Longview, TX	7/15/61
White, Betty	Oak Park, IL	1/17/22
White, Jack	Detroit, MI.	7/9/75
White, Jaleel	Pasadena, CA	11/27/76
White, Vanna	N. Myrtle Beach, SC.	2/18/57
Whitford, Bradley	Madison, WI.	10/10/59
Whiting, Margaret	Detroit, MI.	7/22/24
Whitman, Stuart.	San Francisco, CA	2/1/26
Whitmore, James.	White Plains, NY	10/1/21
Widmark, Richard	Sunrise, MN	12/26/14
Wiest, Dianne	Kansas City, MO	3/28/48
Wilder, Gene	Milwaukee, WI	6/11/33
Wilkinson, Tom	Leeds, England	12/12/48
Williams, Andy	Wall Lake, IA	12/3/27
Williams, Armstong	Marion, SC	2/5/59
Williams, Barry	Santa Monica, CA	9/30/54
Williams, Billy Dee	Harlem, NY.	4/6/37
Williams, Cindy	Van Nuys, CA.	8/22/47
Williams, Esther	Los Angeles, CA.	8/8/23
Williams, Hal	Columbus, OH	12/14/38
Williams, Hank, Jr.	Shreveport, LA	5/26/49
Williams, JoBeth	Houston, TX	12/6/48
Williams, Kimberly	Rye, NY	9/14/71
Williams, Lucinda	Lake Charles, LA	1/26/53
Williams, Michelle	Kalispell, MT.	9/9/80
Williams, Montel	Baltimore, MD.	7/3/56
Williams, Paul	Omaha, NE.	9/19/40
Williams, Robin	Chicago, IL.	7/21/51
Williams, Treat	Rowayton, CT.	12/1/51
Williams, Vanessa	Tarrytown, NY	3/18/63
Williamson, Kevin	New Bern, NC	3/14/65
Williamson, Nicol	Hamilton, Scotland	9/14/38
Willis, Bruce	Idar-Oberstein, W. Germ.	3/19/55
Wilson, Brian	Hawthorne, CA	6/20/42
Wilson, Cassandra.	Jackson, MS	12/4/55
Wilson, Chandra	Houston, TX	8/27/69
Wilson, Demond	Valdosta, GA	10/13/46
Wilson, Elizabeth	Grand Rapids, MI	4/4/21
Wilson, Luke	Dallas, TX.	9/21/71
Wilson, Nancy	Chillicothe, OH	2/20/37
Wilson, Owen.	Dallas, TX.	11/18/68
Wilson, Rainn.	Seattle, WA	1/20/66
Windom, William	New York, NY.	9/28/23
Winfrey, Oprah.	Kosciusko, MS	1/29/54
Winger, Debra	Cleveland, OH	5/16/55
Winkler, Henry.	New York, NY.	10/30/45
Winningham, Mare.	Phoenix, AZ	5/16/59
Winokur, Marissa Jaret	New York, NY.	2/2/73
Winslet, Kate.	Reading, England.	10/5/75
Winter, Johnny.	Beaumont,TX	2/23/44
Winters, Jonathan	Dayton, OH.	11/11/25
Winwood, Steve.	Birmingham, England.	5/12/48
Wiseman, Joseph	Montreal, Quebec.	5/15/18
Withers, Jane.	Atlanta, GA.	4/12/26
Witherspoon, Reese	New Orleans, LA	3/22/76
Witt, Alicia	Worcester, MA.	8/21/75
Wolf, Scott	Boston, MA.	6/4/68
Wonder, Stevie	Saginaw, MI	5/13/50
Wong, Faye	Beijing, China.	8/8/69
Woo, John	Guangzhou, China	5/1/46
Wood, Elijah.	Cedar Rapids, IA	1/28/81
Woodard, Alfre.	Tulsa, OK.	11/8/53
Woods, James	Vernal, UT	4/18/47
Woodward, Edward	Croyden, England.	6/1/30
Woodward, Joanne	Thomasville, GA.	2/27/30
Wopat, Tom.	Lodi, WI	9/9/51
Wright, Jeffrey	Washington, DC	12/7/65
Wright, Max	Detroit, MI.	8/2/43
Wright, Steven	New York, NY.	12/6/55
Wright Penn, Robin	Dallas, TX.	4/8/66
Wyle, Noah	Hollywood, CA.	6/4/71
Wyman, Bill	London, England	10/24/36
Yankovic, Weird Al.	Lynwood, CA	10/23/59

Name	Birthplace	Birthdate
Yanni	Kalamata, Greece	11/14/54
Yarrow, Peter	New York, NY	5/31/38
Yearwood, Trisha	Monticello, GA	9/19/64
Yoakam, Dwight	Pikesville, KY	10/23/56
York, Michael	Fulmer, England	3/27/42
York, Susannah	London, England	1/9/41
Young, Alan	North Shields, England	11/19/19
Young, Burt	New York, NY	4/30/40
Young, Neil	Toronto, Ontario	11/12/45
Young, Sean	Louisville, KY	11/20/59
Zane, Billy	Chicago, IL	2/24/66

Name	Birthplace	Birthdate
Zeffirelli, Franco	Florence, Italy	2/12/23
Zellweger, Renee	Katy, TX	4/25/69
Zemeckis, Robert	Chicago, IL	5/14/52
Zerbe, Anthony	Long Beach, CA	5/20/36
Zeta-Jones, Catherine	Swansea, Wales	9/25/69
Zimbalist, Efrem, Jr.	New York, NY	11/30/18
Zimbalist, Stephanie	New York, NY	10/8/56
Zimmer, Kim	Grand Rapids, MI	2/2/55
Zhang, Ziyi	Beijing, China	2/9/79
Zukerman, Pinchas	Tel Aviv, Israel	7/16/48
Zuniga, Daphne	San Francisco, CA	10/28/62

Entertainment Personalities of the Past

See also other lists for some deceased entertainers not included here.

Name	Born	Died
Aaliyah	1979	2001
Abbott, Bud	1895	1974
Abbott, George	1887	1995
Acuff, Roy	1903	1992
Adams, Don	1923	2005
Adams, Joey	1911	1999
Adams, Maude	1872	1953
Adams, Mason	1919	2005
Adler, Jacob P	1855	1926
Adoree, Renee	1898	1933
Agar, John	1921	2002
Aherne, Brian	1902	1986
Ailey, Alvin	1931	1989
Akins, Claude	1918	1994
Albert, Eddie	1908	2005
Albertson, Frank	1909	1964
Albertson, Jack	1907	1981
Alda, Robert	1914	1986
Allen, Fred	1894	1956
Allen, Gracie	1906	1964
Allen, Mel	1913	1996
Allen, Peter	1944	1992
Allen, Steve	1921	2000
Allgood, Sara	1883	1950
Allyson, June	1917	2006
Altman, Robert	1926	2006
Ameche, Don	1908	1993
Ames, Leon	1903	1993
Amsterdam, Morey	1908	1996
Anderson, G.M. "Bronco Billy"	1882	1971
Anderson, Judith	1897	1992
Anderson, Marian	1897	1993
Andre the Giant	1946	1993
Andrews, Dana	1909	1992
Andrews, Laverne	1913	1967
Andrews, Maxine	1918	1995
Angeli, Pier	1933	1971
Anita Louise	1915	1970
Antonioni, Michelangelo	1912	2007
Arbuckle, Fatty (Roscoe)	1887	1933
Arden, Eve	1908	1990
Arlen, Richard	1900	1976
Arliss, George	1868	1946
Armstrong, Louis	1901	1971
Arnaz, Desi	1917	1986
Arnold, Edward	1890	1956
Arquette, Cliff	1905	1974
Arthur, Jean	1900	1991
Ashcroft, Peggy	1907	1991
Astaire, Fred	1899	1987
Astor, Mary	1906	1987
Atkins, Chet	1924	2001
Atwill, Lionel	1885	1946
Auer, Mischa	1905	1967
Aumont, Jean-Pierre	1911	2001
Austin, Gene	1900	1972
Autry, Gene	1907	1998
Axton, Hoyt	1938	1999
Ayres, Lew	1908	1996
Backus, Jim	1913	1989
Bailey, Pearl	1918	1990
Bainter, Fay	1892	1968
Baker, Josephine	1906	1975
Balanchine, George	1904	1983
Ball, Lucille	1911	1989
Balsam, Martin	1919	1996
Bancroft, Anne	1931	2005
Bancroft, George	1882	1956
Bankhead, Tallulah	1903	1968
Bara, Theda	1890	1955
Barnett, Etta Moten	1902	2004
Barnum, Phineas T.	1810	1891
Barrett, Syd	1946	2006

Name	Born	Died
Barrymore, Ethel	1879	1959
Barrymore, John	1882	1942
Barrymore, Lionel	1878	1954
Barrymore, Maurice	1848	1905
Bartel, Paul	1938	2000
Barthelmess, Richard	1897	1963
Bartholomew, Freddie	1924	1992
Bartok, Eva	1926	1998
Barty, Billy	1924	2000
Basehart, Richard	1914	1984
Basie, Count	1904	1984
Bates, Alan	1934	2003
Bates, Clayton (Peg Leg)	1907	1998
Bavier, Francis	1902	1989
Baxter, Anne	1923	1985
Baxter, Warner	1889	1951
Beaumont, Hugh	1909	1982
Beavers, Louise	1902	1962
Beery, Noah, Sr.	1884	1946
Beery, Noah, Jr.	1913	1994
Beery, Wallace	1889	1949
Begley, Ed	1901	1970
Bel Geddes, Barbara	1922	2005
Bellamy, Ralph	1904	1991
Belushi, John	1949	1982
Benaderet, Bea	1906	1968
Bendix, William	1906	1964
Bennett, Constance	1904	1965
Bennett, Joan	1910	1990
Bennett, Michael	1943	1987
Benny, Jack	1894	1974
Berg, Gertrude	1899	1966
Bergen, Edgar	1903	1978
Bergman, Ingmar	1918	2007
Bergman, Ingrid	1915	1982
Berkeley, Busby	1895	1976
Berle, Milton	1908	2002
Berlin, Irving	1888	1989
Bernardi, Herschel	1923	1986
Berman, Lazar	1930	2005
Bernhardt, Sarah	1844	1923
Bernstein, Leonard	1918	1990
Berry, Jan	1941	2004
Bessell, Ted	1939	1996
Bickford, Charles	1889	1967
Big Bopper, The	1930	1959
Bing, Rudolf	1902	1997
Bissell, Whit	1909	1996
Bixby, Bill	1934	1993
Bjoerling, Jussi	1911	1960
Blackmer, Sidney	1895	1973
Blackstone, Harry	1885	1965
Blake, Amanda	1931	1989
Blake, Eubie	1883	1983
Blaine, Vivian	1921	1995
Blanc, Mel	1908	1989
Blocker, Dan	1928	1972
Blondell, Joan	1909	1979
Blondin, Charles	1824	1897
Blore, Eric	1888	1959
Blue, Ben	1901	1975
Blyden, Larry	1925	1975
Bogarde, Dirk	1920	1999
Bogart, Humphrey	1899	1957
Boland, Mary	1880	1965
Boles, John	1895	1969
Bolger, Ray	1904	1987
Bond, Ward	1903	1960
Bondi, Beulah	1892	1981
Bono, Sonny	1935	1998
Boone, Richard	1917	1981
Booth, Edwin	1833	1893
Booth, Junius Brutus	1796	1852
Booth, Shirley	1898	1992

Name	Born	Died
Borge, Victor	1909	2000
Bow, Clara	1905	1965
Bowes, Maj. Edward	1874	1946
Bowman, Lee	1914	1979
Brown, Les	1912	2001
Boxcar Willie	1931	1999
Boyd, Stephen	1928	1977
Boyd, William	1898	1972
Boyer, Charles	1899	1978
Boyle, Peter	1933	2006
Bracken, Eddie	1915	2002
Brady, Alice	1893	1939
Brand, Neville	1921	1992
Brando, Marlon	1924	2004
Branigan, Laura	1957	2004
Brazzi, Rossano	1916	1994
Brennan, Walter	1894	1974
Brent, George	1904	1979
Brett, Jeremy	1935	1995
Brice, Fanny	1891	1951
Bridges, Lloyd	1913	1998
Broderick, Helen	1891	1959
Bronson, Charles	1921	2003
Brooks, Foster	1912	2001
Brooks, Louise	1906	1985
Brown, James	1933	2006
Brown, Joe E.	1892	1973
Brown, Les	1912	2001
Browne, Roscoe Lee	1925	2007
Bruce, Lenny	1925	1966
Bruce, Nigel	1895	1953
Bruce, Virginia	1910	1982
Brynner, Yul	1915	1985
Buchanan, Edgar	1903	1979
Buchholz, Horst	1933	2003
Buñuel, Luis	1900	1983
Buono, Victor	1938	1982
Burke, Billie	1885	1970
Burnette, Smiley	1911	1967
Burns, George	1896	1996
Burr, Raymond	1917	1993
Burton, Richard	1925	1984
Busch, Mae	1897	1946
Bushman, Francis X.	1883	1966
Buttons, Red	1919	2006
Byington, Spring	1893	1971
Cabot, Bruce	1904	1972
Cabot, Sebastian	1918	1977
Cagney, James	1899	1986
Caldwell, Sarah	1924	2006
Calhern, Louis	1895	1956
Calhoun, Rory	1923	1999
Callas, Maria	1923	1977
Calloway, Cab	1907	1994
Cambridge, Godfrey	1933	1976
Camp, Hamilton	1934	2005
Campbell, Mrs. Patrick	1865	1940
Candy, John	1950	1994
Cantinflas	1911	1993
Cantor, Eddie	1892	1964
Capra, Frank	1897	1991
Carey, Harry	1878	1947
Carey, Macdonald	1913	1994
Carle, Frankie	1903	2001
Carlisle Hart, Kitty	1910	2007
Carney, Art	1918	2003
Carpenter, Karen	1950	1983
Carradine, John	1906	1988
Carrillo, Leo	1880	1961
Carroll, Leo G.	1892	1972
Carroll, Madeleine	1906	1987
Carson, Jack	1910	1963
Carson, Jean	1923	2005
Carson, Johnny	1925	2005

Name	Born	Died	Name	Born	Died	Name	Born	Died
Carter, Benny	1907	2003	Cukor, George	1899	1983	Edwards, Ralph	1913	2005
Carter, Nell	1948	2003	Cullen, Bill	1920	1990	Edwards, Vince	1928	1996
Caruso, Enrico	1873	1921	Cummings, Constance	1910	2005	Egan, Richard	1923	1987
Casals, Pablo	1876	1973	Cummings, Robert	1908	1990	Eisenstein, Sergei	1898	1948
Cash, Johnny	1932	2003	Currie, Finlay	1878	1968	Elam, Jack	1916	2003
Cash, June Carter	1929	2003	Curtis, Keene	1923	2002	Ellington, Duke	1899	1974
Cass, Peggy	1924	1999	Curtis, Ken	1916	1991	Elliot, Cass	1941	1974
Cassidy, Jack	1927	1976	Cushing, Peter	1913	1994	Elliott, Denholm	1922	1992
Cassavetes, John	1929	1989	Dailey, Dan	1914	1978	Ellis, Mary	1897	2003
Castle, Irene	1893	1969	Dandridge, Dorothy	1923	1965	Elman, Mischa	1891	1967
Castle, Vernon	1887	1918	Dangerfield, Rodney	1921	2004	Errol, Leon	1881	1951
Caulfield, Joan	1922	1991	Daniell, Henry	1894	1963	Evans, Dale	1912	2001
Chaliapin, Feodor	1873	1938	Daniels, Bebe	1901	1971	Evans, Edith	1888	1976
Champion, Gower	1919	1980	Darin, Bobby	1936	1973	Evans, Maurice	1901	1989
Chandler, Jeff	1918	1961	Darnell, Linda	1921	1965	Ewell, Tom	1909	1994
Chaney, Lon	1883	1930	Darwell, Jane	1879	1967	Fadiman, Clifton	1904	1999
Chaney, Lon, Jr.	1905	1973	Da Silva, Howard	1909	1986	Fairbanks, Douglas	1883	1939
Chapin, Harry	1942	1981	Davenport, Harry	1866	1949	Fairbanks, Douglas, Jr.	1909	2000
Chaplin, Charles	1889	1977	Davies, Marion	1897	1961	Falkenburg, Jinx	1919	2003
Chapman, Graham	1941	1989	Davis, Bette	1908	1989	Farley, Chris	1964	1997
Charles, Ray	1930	2004	Davis, Joan	1907	1961	Farmer, Frances	1914	1970
Chase, Ilka	1905	1978	Davis, Sammy Jr.	1925	1990	Farnsworth, Richard	1920	2000
Chatterton, Ruth	1893	1961	Davis, Ossie	1917	2005	Farnum, Dustin	1870	1929
Cherrill, Virginia	1908	1996	Day, Dennis	1917	1988	Farnum, William	1876	1953
Chevalier, Maurice	1888	1972	De Carlo, Yvonne	1922	2007	Farrar, Geraldine	1882	1967
Child, Julia	1912	2004	De Wilde, Brandon	1942	1972	Farrell, Charles	1901	1990
Clair, René	1898	1981	De Wolfe, Billy	1907	1974	Farrell, Eileen	1920	2002
Clayton, Jan.	1917	1983	Dean, James	1931	1955	Fassbinder, Rainer Werner.	1946	1982
Clift, Montgomery	1920	1966	Dee, Frances	1907	2004	Fay, Frank	1897	1961
Cline, Patsy	1932	1963	Dee, Sandra	1942	2005	Faye, Alice	1912	1998
Clooney, Rosemary	1928	2002	Defore, Don	1917	1993	Fazenda, Louise	1895	1962
Clyde, Andy	1892	1967	Dekker, Albert	1905	1968	Feld, Fritz	1900	1993
Cobain, Kurt	1967	1994	Del Rio, Dolores	1908	1983	Feldman, Marty	1933	1982
Cobb, Lee J.	1911	1976	Demarest, William	1892	1983	Fell, Norman	1924	1998
Coburn, Charles	1877	1961	DeMille, Agnes	1905	1993	Fellini, Federico	1920	1993
Coburn, James	1928	2002	DeMille, Cecil B.	1881	1959	Fenneman, George	1919	1997
Coca, Imogene	1908	2001	Denison, Michael	1915	1998	Ferrer, Jose	1912	1992
Cochran, Steve	1917?	1965	Denning, Richard	1914	1998	Fetchit, Stepin	1898	1985
Coco, James	1930	1987	Dennis, Sandy	1937	1992	Fiedler, Arthur	1894	1979
Cody, Buffalo Bill	1846	1917	Denny, Reginald	1891	1967	Fiedler, John	1925	2005
Cody, Iron Eyes	1907	1999	Denver, Bob	1935	2005	Field, Betty	1918	1973
Cohan, George M.	1878	1942	Denver, John	1943	1997	Fields, Gracie	1898	1979
Cohen, Myron	1902	1986	Derek, John	1926	1998	Fields, W.C.	1879	1946
Colbert, Claudette	1903	1996	DeSica, Vittorio	1901	1974	Fields, Totie	1931	1978
Cole, Nat "King"	1919	1965	Devine, Andy	1905	1977	Finch, Peter	1916	1977
Collins, Ray	1890	1965	Dewhurst, Colleen	1924	1991	Fine, Larry	1902	1975
Colman, Ronald	1891	1958	Diamond, Selma	1920	1985	Firkusny, Rudolf	1912	1994
Columbo, Russ	1908	1934	Dietrich, Marlene	1901	1992	Fiske, Minnie Maddern	1865	1932
Comden, Betty	1917	2006	Digges, Dudley	1879	1947	Fitzgerald, Barry	1888	1961
Como, Perry	1912	2001	Disney, Walt	1901	1966	Fitzgerald, Ella	1917	1996
Coniff, Ray	1916	2002	Dix, Richard	1894	1949	Fitzgerald, Geraldine	1913	2005
Connors, Chuck	1921	1992	Dmytryk, Edward	1908	1999	Flagstad, Kirsten	1895	1962
Conrad, William	1920	1994	Donahue, Troy	1936	2001	Fleischer, Richard	1916	2006
Conried, Hans	1917	1982	Donat, Robert	1905	1958	Fleming, Art.	1924	1995
Conte, Richard	1911	1975	Donlevy, Brian	1901?	1972	Flynn, Errol	1909	1959
Convy, Bert	1933	1991	Dors, Diana	1931	1984	Flynn, Joe	1925	1974
Conway, Tom	1904	1967	Dorsey, Tommy	1905	1956	Foley, Red	1910	1968
Coogan, Jackie	1914	1984	Douglas, Melvyn	1901	1981	Fonda, Henry	1905	1982
Cook, Elisha, Jr.	1904	1995	Douglas, Paul	1907	1959	Fontaine, Frank	1920	1978
Cooke, Alistair	1908	2004	Dove, Billie	1900	1998	Fontanne, Lynn	1887	1983
Cooke, Sam	1935	1964	Downey, Morton, Jr.	1933	2001	Fonteyn, Margot	1919	1991
Cooper, Gary	1901	1961	Doyle, David	1929	1997	Ford, Glenn	1916	2006
Cooper, Gladys	1888	1971	Drake, Alfred	1914	1992	Ford, John	1895	1973
Cooper, Melville	1896	1973	Draper, Ruth	1889	1956	Ford, Paul	1901	1976
Copland, Aaron	1900	1990	Dresser, Louise	1881	1965	Ford, Tennessee Ernie	1919	1991
Corby, Ellen	1913	1999	Dressler, Marie	1869	1934	Forrest, Helen	1918	1999
Corelli, Franco	1923	2003	Drew, Ellen	1915	2003	Fosse, Bob	1927	1987
Corey, Jeff	1914	2002	Drew, Mrs. John	1820	1897	Foster, Phil	1914	1985
Corio, Ann	1914	1999	Dru, Joanne	1923	1996	Foster, Preston	1901	1970
Cornell, Katharine	1893	1974	Duchin, Eddy	1909	1951	Foxx, Redd	1922	1991
Correll, Charles ("Andy")	1890	1972	Duff, Howard	1917	1990	Foy, Eddie	1857	1928
Costello, Dolores	1905	1979	Duggan, Andrew	1923	1988	Franchi, Sergio	1933?	1990
Costello, Lou	1906	1959	Dumbrille, Douglass	1890	1974	Franciosa, Anthony	1929	2006
Cotten, Joseph	1905	1994	Dumont, Margaret	1889	1965	Francis, Arlene	1908	2001
Coward, Noel	1899	1973	Duncan, Isadora	1878	1927	Francis, Kay	1903	1968
Cox, Wally	1924	1973	Dunham, Katherine	1910	2006	Franciscus, James	1934	1991
Crabbe, Buster	1908	1983	Dunn, James	1905	1967	Frankenheimer, John	1930	2002
Crain, Jeanne	1925	2003	Dunne, Irene	1898	1990	Frann, Mary	1943	1998
Crane, Bob	1928	1978	Dunnock, Mildred	1904	1991	Frawley, William	1887	1966
Crawford, Broderick	1911	1986	Durante, Jimmy	1893	1980	Freed, Alan	1921	1965
Crawford, Joan	1904	1977	Duryea, Dan	1907	1968	Frederick, Pauline	1885	1938
Crenna, Richard	1926	2003	Duse, Eleanora	1858	1924	French, Victor	1934	1989
Crews, Laura Hope	1880	1942	Dvorak, Ann	1912	1979	Friganza, Trixie	1870	1955
Crisp, Donald	1880	1974	Eagels, Jeanne	1894	1929	Frisco, Joe	1890	1958
Croce, Jim	1942	1973	Ebsen, Buddy	1908	2003	Froman, Jane	1907	1980
Cronyn, Hume	1911	2003	Eckstine, Billy	1914	1993	Fuller, Samuel	1912	1997
Crosby, Bing	1903	1977	Eddington, Paul	1927	1995	Funt, Allen	1914	1999
Crothers, Scatman	1910	1986	Eddy, Nelson	1901	1967	Furness, Betty	1916	1994
Cruz, Celia	1925	2003	Edelman, Herb	1933	1996	Gabin, Jean	1904	1976
Cugat, Xavier	1900	1990	Edwards, Cliff	1897	1971	Gable, Clark	1901	1960

Name	Born	Died
Gabor, Eva	1920	1995
Garbo, Greta	1905	1990
Garcia, Jerry	1942	1995
Gardenia, Vincent	1922	1992
Gardner, Ava	1922	1990
Garfield, John	1913	1952
Garland, Judy	1922	1969
Garson, Greer	1904	1996
Gassman, Vittorio	1922	2000
Gaye, Marvin	1939	1984
Gaynor, Janet	1906	1984
Gebel-Williams, Gunther	1934	2001
Geer, Will	1902	1978
George, Gladys	1900	1954
Gershwin, George	1898	1937
Ghostley, Alice	1926	2007
Gibb, Andy	1958	1988
Gibb, Maurice	1949	2003
Gibson, Hoot	1892	1962
Gielgud, John	1904	2000
Gilbert, Billy	1894	1971
Gilbert, John	1895	1936
Gilford, Jack	1907	1990
Gillespie, Dizzy	1917	1993
Gillette, William	1855	1937
Gingold, Hermione	1897	1987
Gish, Dorothy	1898	1968
Gish, Lillian	1893	1993
Giulini, Carlos Maria	1914	2005
Gleason, Jackie	1916	1987
Gleason, James	1886	1959
Gluck, Alma	1884	1938
Gobel, George	1919	1991
Goddard, Paulette	1905	1990
Godfrey, Arthur	1903	1983
Godunov, Alexander	1949	1995
Goldwyn, Samuel	1882	1974
Goodman, Benny	1909	1986
Gorcey, Leo	1915	1969
Gordon, Gale	1906	1995
Gordon, Ruth	1896	1985
Gorshin, Frank	1934	2005
Gosden, Freeman ("Amos")	1899	1982
Gottschalk, Ferdinand	1869	1944
Gottschalk, Louis	1829	1869
Gould, Glenn	1932	1982
Gould, Morton	1913	1996
Grable, Betty	1916	1973
Graham, Martha	1894	1991
Graham, Virginia	1912	1998
Grahame, Gloria	1925	1981
Granger, Stewart	1913	1993
Grant, Cary	1904	1986
Granville, Bonita	1923	1988
Gray, Dolores	1924	2002
Gray, Spalding	1941	2004
Greco, Jose	1918	2001
Green, Adolph	1915	2002
Greene, Lorne	1915	1987
Greenstreet, Sydney	1879	1954
Greenwood, Charlotte	1890	1978
Gregory, James	1911	2002
Griffin, Merv	1925	2007
Griffith, David Wark	1874	1948
Griffith, Hugh	1912	1980
Guardino, Harry	1925	1995
Guinness, Sir Alec	1914	2000
Guthrie, Woody	1912	1967
Gwenn, Edmund	1875	1959
Gwynne, Fred	1926	1993
Hackett, Buddy	1924	2003
Hackett, Joan	1934	1983
Hagen, Uta	1919	2004
Hale, Alan	1892	1950
Hale, Alan, Jr.	1918	1990
Haley, Bill	1925	1981
Haley, Jack	1899	1979
Hall, Huntz	1919	1999
Hall, Jon	1915	1979
Hamilton, Margaret	1902	1985
Hammerstein, Oscar	1847	1919
Hammerstein II, Oscar	1895	1960
Hampton, Lionel	1908	2002
Hardwicke, Cedric	1893	1964
Hardy, Oliver	1892	1957
Harlow, Jean	1911	1937
Harris, Phil	1904	1995
Harris, Richard	1930	2002
Harrison, George	1943	2001
Harrison, Rex	1908	1990

Name	Born	Died
Hart, William S.	1870	1946
Hartman, Phil	1948	1998
Harvey, Laurence	1928	1973
Hatfield, Bobby	1940	2003
Haver, June	1926	2005
Hawkins, Jack	1910	1973
Hawkins, Screamin' Jay	1929	2000
Hawthorne, Nigel	1929	2001
Hayakawa, Sessue	1890	1973
Hayden, Sterling	1916	1986
Hayes, Gabby	1885	1969
Hayes, Helen	1900	1993
Hayward, Leland	1902	1971
Hayward, Louis	1909	1985
Hayward, Susan	1917	1975
Hayworth, Rita	1918	1987
Head, Edith	1907	1981
Healy, Ted	1896	1937
Heckart, Eileen	1919	2001
Heflin, Van	1910	1971
Heifetz, Jascha	1901	1987
Held, Anna	1873	1918
Hemingway, Margaux	1955	1996
Hemmings, David	1941	2003
Henderson, Skitch	1918	2005
Hendrix, Jimi	1942	1970
Henie, Sonja	1912	1969
Henreid, Paul	1908	1992
Henson, Jim	1936	1990
Hepburn, Audrey	1929	1993
Hepburn, Katharine	1907	2003
Hersholt, Jean	1886	1956
Hewett, Christopher	1922	2001
Hickey, William	1928	1997
Hickson, Joan	1906	1998
Hildegarde	1906	2005
Hill, Arthur	1922	2006
Hill, Benny	1925	1992
Hill, George Roy	1921	2002
Hiller, Wendy	1912	2003
Hines, Gregory	1946	2003
Hines, Jerome	1921	2003
Hirt, Al	1922	1999
Hitchcock, Alfred	1899	1980
Ho, Don	1930	2007
Hobson, Valerie	1917	1998
Hodiak, John	1914	1955
Holden, William	1918	1981
Holiday, Billie	1915	1959
Holliday, Judy	1922	1965
Holloway, Sterling	1905	1992
Holly, Buddy	1936	1959
Holt, Jack	1888	1951
Holt, Tim	1918	1973
Homolka, Oscar	1898	1978
Hooker, John Lee	1917	2001
Hoon, Shannon	1967	1995
Hope, Bob	1903	2003
Hopkins, Miriam	1902	1972
Hopper, DeWolf	1858	1935
Hopper, Hedda	1885	1966
Hopper, William	1915	1970
Horowitz, Vladimir	1904	1989
Horton, Edward Everett	1886	1970
Houdini, Harry	1874	1926
Houseman, John	1902	1988
Hovis, Larry	1936	2003
Howard (Horwitz), Curly	1903	1952
Howard, Leslie	1890	1943
Howard (Horwitz), Moe	1897	1975
Howard (Horwitz), Shemp	1895	1955
Howard, Trevor	1916	1988
Hudson, Rock	1925	1985
Hughes, Bernard	1915	2006
Hull, Henry	1890	1977
Hull, Josephine	1886	1957
Humphrey, Doris	1895	1958
Hunter, Jeffrey	1925	1969
Hunter, Kim	1922	2002
Hunter, Ross	1921	1996
Husing, Ted	1901	1962
Hussey, Ruth	1911	2005
Huston, John	1906	1987
Huston, Walter	1884	1950
Hutchence, Michael	1960	1997
Hutton, Betty	1921	2007
Hutton, Jim	1934	1979
Hutton, Robert	1920	1994
Hyde-White, Wilfrid	1903	1991
Ingram, Rex	1895	1969

Name	Born	Died
Iturbi, Jose	1895	1980
Ireland, Jill	1936	1990
Ireland, John	1915	1992
Irving, Henry	1838	1905
Ives, Burl	1909	1995
Jack, Wolfman	1938	1995
Jackson, Joe	1875	1942
Jackson, Mahalia	1911	1972
Jackson, Milt	1922	1999
Jaeckel, Richard	1926	1997
Jaffe, Sam	1891	1984
Jagger, Dean	1903	1991
Jam Master Jay	1965	2003
James, Dennis	1917	1997
James, Harry	1916	1983
James, Rick	1948	2004
Janis, Elsie	1889	1956
Jannings, Emil	1886	1950
Janssen, David	1930	1980
Jenkins, Allen	1900	1974
Jennings, Waylon	1937	2002
Jessel, George	1898	1981
Jeter, Michael	1952	2003
Johnson, Ben	1918	1996
Johnson, Celia	1908	1982
Johnson, Chic	1892	1962
Johnson, J.J.	1924	2001
Johnson, Robert	1911	1938
Jolson, Al	1886	1950
Jones, Brian	1942	1969
Jones, Buck	1889	1942
Jones, Carolyn	1933	1983
Jones, Elvin	1927	2004
Jones, Henry	1912	1999
Jones, Spike	1911	1965
Joplin, Janis	1943	1970
Joplin, Scott	1868	1917
Jordan, Richard	1938	1993
Jory, Victor	1902	1982
Joslyn, Allyn	1905	1981
Julia, Raul	1940	1994
Jump, Gordon	1932	2003
Jurado, Katy	1924	2002
Jurgens, Curt	1915	1982
Kahn, Madeline	1942	1999
Kane, Helen	1910	1966
Kanin, Garson	1912	1999
Karloff, Boris	1887	1969
Karns, Roscoe	1893	1970
Kaufman, Andy	1949	1984
Kaye, Danny	1913	1987
Kaye, Stubby	1918	1997
Kazan, Elia	1909	2003
Kean, Charles	1811	1868
Kean, Mrs. Charles	1806	1880
Kean, Edmund	1787	1833
Keaton, Buster	1895	1966
Keeler, Ruby	1910	1993
Keeshan, Bob (Captain Kangaroo)	1927	2004
Keel, Howard	1919	2005
Keith, Brian	1921	1997
Kellaway, Cecil	1894	1973
Kelley, DeForest	1920	1999
Kelly, Emmett	1898	1979
Kelly, Gene	1912	1996
Kelly, Grace	1929	1982
Kelly, Jack	1927	1992
Kelly, Nancy	1921	1985
Kelly, Patsy	1910	1981
Kelton, Pert	1907	1968
Kendall, Kay	1926	1959
Kennedy, Arthur	1914	1990
Kennedy, Edgar	1890	1948
Kibbee, Guy	1886	1956
Kilbride, Percy	1888	1964
Kiley, Richard	1922	1999
King, Alan	1927	2004
Kinski, Klaus	1926	1991
Kirby, Bruno	1949	2006
Kirby, George	1923	1995
Kirby, Durward	1912	2000
Kirsten, Dorothy	1910	1992
Klemperer, Werner	1919	2000
Knight, Ted	1923	1986
Knotts, Don	1924	2006
Kostelanetz, Andre	1901	1980
Kovacs, Ernie	1919	1962
Kramer, Stanley	1913	2001
Kruger, Otto	1885	1974

Name	Born	Died
Kubrick, Stanley	1928	1999
Kulp, Nancy	1921	1991
Kurosawa, Akira	1910	1998
Kyser, Kay	1906	1985
Ladd, Alan	1913	1964
Lahr, Bert	1895	1967
Laine, Frankie	1913	2007
Lake, Arthur	1905	1987
Lake, Veronica	1919	1973
Lamarr, Hedy	1913	2000
Lamas, Fernando	1915	1982
Lamour, Dorothy	1914	1996
Lancaster, Burt	1913	1994
Lanchester, Elsa	1902	1986
Lane, Pricilla	1917	1995
Landis, Carole	1919	1948
Landis, Jessie Royce	1904	1972
Landon, Michael	1936	1991
Lang, Fritz	1890	1976
Langdon, Harry	1884	1944
Lange, Hope	1931	2003
Langford, Frances	1914	2005
Langtry, Lillie	1853	1929
Lanza, Mario	1921	1959
LaRue, Lash (Alfred)	1917	1996
Lauder, Harry	1870	1950
Laughton, Charles	1899	1962
Laurel, Stan	1890	1965
Lawford, Peter	1923	1984
Lawrence, Florence	1886	1938
Lawrence, Gertrude	1898	1952
Lean, David	1908	1991
Lee, Bernard	1908	1981
Lee, Bruce	1940	1973
Lee, Canada	1907	1952
Lee, Gypsy Rose	1914	1970
Lee, Anna	1913	2004
Lee, Peggy	1920	2002
LeGallienne, Eva	1899	1991
Lehmann, Lotte	1888	1976
Leigh, Janet	1927	2004
Leigh, Vivien	1913	1967
Leighton, Margaret	1922	1976
Lemmon, Jack	1925	2001
Lennon, John	1940	1980
Lenya, Lotte	1898	1981
Leonard, Eddie	1870	1941
Leonard, Sheldon	1907	1997
LeRoy, Mervyn	1900	1987
Levant, Oscar	1906	1972
Levene, Sam	1905	1980
Levenson, Sam	1911	1980
Lewis, Al	1923	2006
Lewis, Joe E.	1902	1971
Lewis, Shari	1934	1998
Lewis, Ted	1892	1971
Liberace	1919	1987
Lillie, Beatrice	1894	1989
Lind, Jenny	1820	1887
Lindfors, Viveca	1920	1995
Lindley, Audra	1918	1997
Linville, Larry	1939	2000
Little, Cleavon	1939	1992
Llewelyn, Desmond	1914	1999
Lloyd, Harold	1893	1971
Lloyd, Marie	1870	1922
Lockhart, Gene	1891	1957
Logan, Ella	1913	1969
Lombard, Carole	1909	1942
Lombardo, Guy	1902	1977
Long, Richard	1927	1974
Lopes, Lisa	1971	2002
Lopez, Vincent	1895	1975
Lord, Jack	1920?	1998
Lorne, Marion	1888	1968
Lorre, Peter	1904	1964
Loudon, Dorothy	1933	2003
Lovejoy, Frank	1912	1962
Lowe, Edmund	1890	1971
Loy, Myrna	1905	1993
Lubitsch, Ernst	1892	1947
Ludden, Allen	1918	1981
Lugosi, Bela	1882	1956
Lukas, Paul	1894	1971
Lunt, Alfred	1892	1977
Lupino, Ida	1918	1995
Lymon, Frankie	1942	1968
Lynde, Paul	1926	1982
Lynn, Diana	1926	1971
MacDonald, Jeanette	1903	1965
Mack, Ted	1904	1976
MacKenzie, Gisele	1927	2003
MacLane, Barton	1902	1969
MacMurray, Fred	1908	1991
MacRae, Gordon	1921	1986
Macready, George	1909	1973
Madison, Guy	1922	1996
Magnani, Anna	1908	1973
Mancini, Henry	1924	1994
Main, Marjorie	1890	1975
Malle, Louis	1932	1995
Mann, Herbie	1930	2003
Mansfield, Jayne	1932	1967
Mantovani, Annunzio	1905	1980
Marais, Jean	1913	1998
March, Fredric	1897	1975
March, Hal	1920	1970
Marchand, Nancy	1928	2000
Markova, Alicia	1910	2004
Marley, Bob	1945	1981
Marshall, E.G.	1910	1998
Marshall, Herbert	1890	1966
Martin, Barney	1923	2005
Martin, Dean	1917	1995
Martin, Mary	1913	1990
Martin, Ross	1920	1981
Marvin, Lee	1924	1987
Marx, Arthur (Harpo)	1888	1964
Marx, Herbert (Zeppo)	1901	1979
Marx, Julius (Groucho)	1890	1977
Marx, Leonard (Chico)	1886	1961
Marx, Milton (Gummo)	1893	1977
Mason, James	1909	1984
Massey, Daniel	1933	1998
Massey, Raymond	1896	1983
Mastroianni, Marcello	1924	1996
Matthau, Walter	1920	2000
Mature, Victor	1916	1999
Maxwell, Marilyn	1921	1972
Mayer, Louis B.	1885	1957
Mayfield, Curtis	1942	1999
Maynard, Ken	1895	1973
Mayo, Virginia	1920	2005
Mazurki, Mike	1909	1990
McCambridge, Mercedes	1916	2004
McCartney, Linda	1941	1998
McClure, Doug	1935	1995
McCormack, John	1884	1945
McCrary, Tex	1910	2003
McCrea, Joel	1905	1990
McDaniel, Hattie	1895	1952
McDowall, Roddy	1928	1998
McFarland, George "Spanky"	1928	1993
McGavin, Darren	1922	2006
McGuire, Dorothy	1916	2001
McHugh, Frank	1899	1981
McIntire, John	1907	1991
McKay, Gardner	1932	2001
McKern, Leo	1920	2002
McLaglen, Victor	1883	1959
McNally, Stephen	1913	1994
McNeill, Don	1907	1996
McQueen, Butterfly	1911	1995
McQueen, Steve	1930	1980
Meader, Vaughn	1936	2004
Meadows, Audrey	1924	1996
Medford, Kay	1920	1980
Meek, Donald	1880	1946
Meeker, Ralph	1920	1988
Melba, Nellie	1861	1931
Melchior, Lauritz	1890	1973
Menjou, Adolphe	1890	1963
Menken, Helen	1902	1966
Menuhin, Yehudi	1916	1999
Mercouri, Melina	1925	1994
Mercury, Freddie	1946	1991
Meredith, Burgess	1909	1997
Merman, Ethel	1908	1984
Merrick, David	1911	2000
Merrill, Gary	1915	1990
Mifune, Toshiro	1920	1997
Milland, Ray	1905	1986
Miller, Ann	1923	2004
Miller, Glenn	1904	1944
Miller, Marilyn	1898	1936
Miller, Roger	1936	1992
Mills, Harry	1913	1982
Mills, Sir John	1908	2005
Mineo, Sal	1939	1976
Miner, Jan	1917	2004
Mingus, Charles	1922	1979
Miranda, Carmen	1913	1955
Mitchell, Cameron	1918	1994
Mitchell, Thomas	1892	1962
Mitchum, Robert	1917	1997
Mix, Tom	1880	1940
Monica, Corbett	1930	1998
Moffo, Anna	1934	2006
Monroe, Marilyn	1926	1962
Monroe, Vaughn	1911	1973
Montand, Yves	1921	1991
Montez, Maria	1917	1951
Montgomery, Elizabeth	1933	1995
Montgomery, George	1916	2000
Montgomery, Robert	1904	1981
Moore, Clayton	1914	1999
Moore, Colleen	1900	1988
Moore, Dudley	1935	2002
Moore, Grace	1901	1947
Moore, Garry	1914	1993
Moore, Victor	1876	1962
Moorehead, Agnes	1906	1974
Moreland, Mantan	1902	1973
Morgan, Dennis	1910	1994
Morgan, Frank	1890	1949
Morgan, Helen	1900	1941
Morgan, Henry	1915	1994
Morita, Pat	1932	2005
Morley, Robert	1908	1992
Morris, Chester	1901	1970
Morris, Greg	1934	1996
Morris, Howard	1919	2005
Morris, Wayne	1914	1959
Morrison, Jim	1943	1971
Morrow, Vic	1932	1982
Morton, Jelly Roll	1885	1941
Mostel, Zero	1915	1977
Mowbray, Alan	1897	1969
Mulhare, Edward	1923	1997
Mulligan, Gerry	1927	1996
Mulligan, Richard	1932	2000
Muni, Paul	1895	1967
Munshin, Jules	1915	1970
Murphy, Audie	1924	1971
Murphy, George	1902	1992
Murray, Arthur	1895	1991
Murray, Kathryn	1906	1999
Murray, Mae	1885	1965
Nagel, Conrad	1896	1970
Naish, J. Carroll	1900	1973
Naldi, Nita	1898	1961
Nance, Jack	1943	1997
Natwick, Mildred	1908	1994
Nazimova, Alla	1879	1945
Negri, Pola	1897	1987
Nelson, Harriet (Hilliard)	1909	1994
Nelson, Ozzie	1906	1975
Nelson, Rick	1940	1985
Nesbit, Evelyn	1885	1967
Newley, Anthony	1931	1999
Newton, Robert	1905	1956
Nicholas, Harold	1924	2000
Nijinsky, Vaslav	1890	1950
Nilsson, Anna Q.	1893	1974
Niven, David	1910	1983
Nolan, Lloyd	1902	1985
Normand, Mabel	1894	1930
North, Sheree	1933	2005
Notorious B.I.G.	1972	1997
Novarro, Ramon	1899	1968
Nureyev, Rudolf	1938	1993
Oakie, Jack	1903	1978
Oakley, Annie	1860	1926
Oates, Warren	1928	1982
Oberon, Merle	1911	1979
O'Brien, Edmond	1915	1985
O'Brien, Pat	1899	1983
O'Connell, Arthur	1908	1981
O'Connell, Helen	1921	1993
O'Connor, Carroll	1924	2001
O'Connor, Donald	1925	2003
O'Connor, Una	1880	1959
O'Keefe, Dennis	1908	1968
O'Herlihy, Daniel	1919	2005
Oland, Warner	1880	1938
Olcott, Chauncey	1860	1932
Oliver, Edna May	1883	1942
Olivier, Laurence	1907	1989
Olsen, Ole	1892	1963
O'Neill, James	1849	1920

Name	Born	Died	Name	Born	Died	Name	Born	Died
O'Neal, Ron	1937	2004	Ramone, Joey	1951	2001	Schell, Maria	1926	2005
Orbach, Jerry	1935	2004	Ramone, Johnny	1951	2004	Schenkel, Chris	1923	2005
Orbison, Roy	1936	1988	Rampal, Jean-Pierre	1922	2000	Schiavelli, Vincent	1948	2005
Ormandy, Eugene	1899	1985	Randall, Tony	1920	2004	Schildkraut, Joseph	1895	1964
O'Sullivan, Maureen	1911	1998	Randolph, John	1915	2004	Schipa, Tito	1889	1965
Ouspenskaya, Maria	1876	1949	Rathbone, Basil	1892	1967	Schlesinger, John	1926	2003
Owen, Reginald	1887	1972	Ratoff, Gregory	1897	1960	Schnabel, Artur	1882	1951
Owens, Buck	1929	2006	Rawls, Lou	1933	2006	Schneider, Romy	1938	1982
Paar, Jack	1918	2004	Ray, Aldo	1926	1991	Schwartzkopf, Elizabeth	1915	2006
Paderewski, Ignace	1860	1941	Ray, Johnnie	1927	1990	Scott, George C.	1927	1999
Page, Geraldine	1924	1987	Rayburn, Gene	1917	1999	Scott, Gordon	1926	2007
Pakula, Alan	1928	1998	Raye, Martha	1916	1994	Scott, Hazel	1920	1981
Palance, Jack	1919	2006	Raymond, Gene	1908	1998	Scott, Martha	1914	2003
Pallette, Eugene	1889	1954	Reagan, Ronald	1911	2004	Scott, Randolph	1898	1987
Palmer, Lilli	1914	1986	Redding, Otis	1941	1967	Scott, Zachary	1914	1965
Palmer, Robert	1949	2003	Redgrave, Michael	1908	1985	Scott-Siddons, Mrs.	1843	1896
Pangborn, Franklin	1894	1958	Reed, Donna	1921	1986	Seberg, Jean	1938	1979
Parker, Jean	1915	2005	Reed, Oliver	1938	1999	Seeley, Blossom	1892	1974
Parks, Bert	1914	1992	Reed, Robert	1932	1992	Segovia, Andres	1893	1987
Parks, Larry	1914	1975	Reeve, Christopher	1952	2004	Selena	1971	1995
Pasternack, Josef A.	1881	1940	Reeves, George	1914	1959	Sellers, Peter	1925	1980
Pastor, Tony (vaudevillian)	1837	1908	Reeves, Steve	1926	2000	Selznick, David O.	1902	1965
Pastor, Tony (bandleader)	1907	1969	Reid, Wallace	1891	1923	Sennett, Mack	1884	1960
Patti, Adelina	1843	1919	Reilly, Charles Nelson	1931	2007	Senor Wences	1896	1999
Patti, Carlotta	1840	1889	Reinhardt, Max	1873	1943	Serling, Rod	1924	1975
Patrick, Gail	1911	1980	Remick, Lee	1935	1991	Shakur, Tupac	1971	1996
Pavlova, Anna	1885	1931	Renaldo, Duncan	1904	1980	Shaw, Robert (actor)	1927	1978
Pavarotti, Luciano	1935	2007	Rennie, Michael	1909	1971	Shaw, Robert (conductor)	1916	1999
Paycheck, Johnny	1938	2003	Renoir, Jean	1894	1979	Shawn, Ted	1891	1972
Payne, John	1912	1989	Rettig, Tommy	1941	1996	Shean, Al	1868	1949
Pearl, Minnie	1912	1996	Reynolds, Marjorie	1923	1997	Shearer, Moira	1926	2006
Peck, Gregory	1916	2003	Rich, Charlie	1932	1995	Shearer, Norma	1902	1983
Peckinpah, Sam	1925	1984	Richardson, Ian	1934	2007	Sheridan, Ann	1915	1967
Peerce, Jan	1904	1984	Richardson, Ralph	1902	1983	Shore, Dinah	1917	1994
Penn, Chris	1965	2006	Riddle, Nelson	1921	1985	Short, Bobby	1924	2005
Penner, Joe	1905	1941	Riefenstahl, Leni	1902	2003	Shubert, Lee	1875	1953
Peppard, George	1928	1994	Ripperton, Minnie	1947	1979	Shull, Richard B.	1929	1999
Perkins, Anthony	1932	1992	Ritchard, Cyril	1898	1977	Siddons, Mrs. Sarah	1755	1831
Perkins, Carl	1932	1998	Ritter, John	1948	2003	Sidney, Sylvia	1910	1999
Perkins, Marlin	1905	1986	Ritter, Tex	1907	1974	Signoret, Simone	1921	1985
Peters, Brock	1927	2005	Ritter, Thelma	1905	1969	Sills, Beverly	1929	2007
Peters, Jean	1926	2000	Ritz, Al	1901	1965	Silverheels, Jay	1912	1980
Peters, Susan	1921	1952	Ritz, Harry	1906	1986	Silvers, Phil	1912	1985
Phillips, John	1935	2001	Ritz, Jimmy	1903	1985	Sim, Alastair	1900	1976
Phoenix, River	1970	1993	Roach, Max	1924	2007	Simmons, Richard	1913	2003
Piaf, Edith	1915	1963	Robards, Jason	1922	2000	Simone, Nina	1933	2003
Pickens, Slim	1919	1983	Robbins, Jerome	1918	1998	Sims, Irene	1930	2001
Pickett, Wilson	1941	2006	Robbins, Marty	1925	1982	Sinatra, Frank	1915	1998
Pickford, Mary	1893	1979	Roberts, Rachel	1927	1980	Sinclair, Madge	1938	1995
Picon, Molly	1898	1992	Robeson, Paul	1898	1976	Singleton, Penny	1908	2003
Pidgeon, Walter	1897	1984	Robinson, Bill	1878	1949	Siskel, Gene	1946	1999
Pinza, Ezio	1892	1957	Robinson, Edward G.	1893	1973	Sitka, Emil	1914	1998
Pitney, Gene	1941	2006	Robson, Flora	1902	1984	Sjostrom, Victor	1879	1960
Pitts, Zasu	1898	1963	Roche, Eugene	1928	2004	Skelton, Red	1913	1997
Plato, Dana	1964	1999	Rochester (E. Anderson)	1905	1977	Skinner, Otis	1858	1942
Pleasence, Donald	1919	1995	Roddenberry, Gene	1921	1991	Smith, Alexis	1921	1993
Pons, Lily	1904	1976	Rodgers, Jimmie	1897	1933	Smith, Bessie	1894?	1937
Ponselle, Rosa	1897	1981	Rogers, Buddy	1904	1999	Smith, Buffalo Bob	1917	1998
Ponti, Carlo	1922	2007	Rogers, Fred	1928	2003	Smith, C. Aubrey	1863	1948
Porter, Eric	1928	1995	Rogers, Ginger	1911	1995	Smith, Elliott	1969	2003
Porter, Edwin S.	1870	1941	Rogers, Roy	1911	1998	Smith, Jeff	1939	2004
Porter, Nyree Dawn	1940	2001	Rogers, Will	1879	1935	Smith, Kate	1907	1986
Poston, Tom	1921	2007	Roland, Gilbert	1905	1994	Smith, Kent	1907	1985
Powell, Dick	1904	1963	Rolle, Esther	1920?	1998	Snodgress, Carrie	1946	2004
Powell, Eleanor	1912	1982	Rollins, Howard	1950	1996	Snow, Hank	1914	1999
Powell, William	1892	1984	Roman, Ruth	1924	1999	Snyder, Tom	1936	2007
Power, Tyrone	1913	1958	Romero, Cesar	1907	1994	Solti, George	1912	1997
Preminger, Otto	1905	1986	Rooney, Pat	1880	1962	Sondergaard, Gale	1899	1985
Presley, Elvis	1935	1977	Rose, Billy	1899	1966	Sothern, Ann	1909	2001
Preston, Billy	1946	2006	Rossellini, Roberto	1906	1977	Sousa, John Philip	1854	1932
Preston, Robert	1918	1987	Rostropovich, Mstislav	1927	2007	Sparks, Ned	1884	1957
Price, Vincent	1911	1993	Rowan, Dan	1922	1987	Spelling, Aaron	1928	2006
Prima, Louis	1911	1978	Rubinstein, Artur	1887	1982	Spencer, John	1946	2005
Prinze, Freddie	1954	1977	Ruggles, Charles	1886	1970	Sperber, Wendy Jo	1958	2005
Prowse, Juliet	1936	1996	Russell, Harold	1914	2002	Springfield, Dusty	1939	1999
Pryor, Richard	1940	2005	Russell, Lillian	1861	1922	Stack, Robert	1919	2003
Puente, Tito	1923	2000	Russell, Nipsey	1923	2005	Stander, Lionel	1908	1994
Pyle, Denver	1920	1997	Russell, Rosalind	1911	1976	Stanley, Kim	1925	2001
Quayle, Anthony	1913	1989	Rutherford, Margaret	1892	1972	Stanwyck, Barbara	1907	1990
Questel, Mae	1908	1998	Ryan, Irene	1903	1973	Stapleton, Maureen	1925	2006
Quinn, Anthony	1915	2001	Ryan, Robert	1909	1973	Steiger, Rod	1925	2002
Quintero, José	1924	1999	Sabu	1924	1963	Sterling, Jan	1921	2004
Rabb, Ellis	1930	1998	Sanford, Isabel	1917	2004	Stern, Isaac	1920	2001
Rabbit, Eddie	1941	1998	Sargent, Dick	1933	1994	Stevens, Craig	1918	2000
Radner, Gilda	1946	1989	St. Cyr, Lili	1917	1999	Stevens, Inger	1934	1970
Raft, George	1895	1980	St. Denis, Ruth	1877	1968	Stevens, Mark	1916	1994
Rains, Claude	1890	1967	Sakall, S.Z.	1884	1955	Stevenson, McLean	1929	1996
Ralston, Esther	1902	1994	Sale (Chic), Charles	1885	1936	Stewart, James	1908	1997
Raitt, John	1917	2005	Sanders, George	1906	1972	Stickney, Dorothy	1896	1998
Ramone, Dee Dee	1952	2002	Savalas, Telly	1924	1994	Stokowski, Leopold	1882	1977

Name	Born	Died	Name	Born	Died	Name	Born	Died
Stone, Lewis	1879	1953	Tucker, Sophie	1884	1966	Weston, Jack	1924	1996
Stone, Milburn	1904	1980	Turner, Lana	1920	1995	Whale, James	1889	1957
Straight, Beatrice	1918	2001	Turpin, Ben	1874	1940	Wheeler, Bert	1895	1968
Strasberg, Lee	1901	1982	Twelvetrees, Helen	1908	1958	White, Barry	1944	2003
Strasberg, Susan	1938	1999	Twitty, Conway	1933	1993	White, Jesse	1919	1997
Strode, Woody	1914	1994	Urich, Robert	1947	2002	White, Pearl	1889	1938
Strummer, Joe	1952	2002	Ustinov, Peter	1921	2004	Whiteman, Paul	1891	1967
Stuarti, Enzo	1919	2005	Valens, Ritchie	1941	1959	Whitty, May	1865	1948
Sturges, Preston	1898	1959	Valentino, Rudolph	1895	1926	Wickes, Mary	1910	1995
Sullavan, Margaret	1911	1960	Vallee, Rudy	1901	1986	Wilde, Cornel	1918	1989
Sullivan, Barry	1912	1994	Van, Bobby	1928	1980	Wilder, Billy	1906	2002
Sullivan, Ed	1902	1974	Vance, Vivian	1912	1979	Wilding, Michael	1912	1979
Sullivan, Francis L.	1903	1956	Van Cleef, Lee	1925	1989	Williams, Bert	1877	1922
Summerville, Slim	1892	1946	Vandross, Luther	1951	2005	Williams, Guy	1924	1989
Swanson, Gloria	1899	1983	Van Fleet, Jo	1922	1996	Williams, Hank Sr.	1923	1953
Swarthout, Gladys	1904	1969	Varney, Jim	1949	2000	Wills, Bob	1905	1975
Sweet, Blanche	1896	1986	Vaughan, Sarah	1924	1990	Wills, Chill	1903	1978
Switzer, Carl "Alfalfa"	1926	1959	Veidt, Conrad	1893	1943	Wilson, Carl	1946	1998
Talbot, Lyle	1904	1996	Velez, Lupe	1908	1944	Wilson, Dennis	1944	1983
Talmadge, Norma	1893	1957	Vera-Ellen	1926	1981	Wilson, Dooley	1894	1953
Tamiroff, Akim	1899	1972	Verdon, Gwen	1925	2000	Wilson, Flip	1933	1998
Tandy, Jessica	1909	1994	Vernon, Jackie	1925	1987	Wilson, Jackie	1934	1984
Tanguay, Eva	1878	1947	Vernon, John	1932	2005	Wilson, Marie	1917	1972
Tati, Jacques	1908	1982	Villechaize, Herve	1943	1993	Windsor, Marie	1919	2000
Taylor, Deems	1885	1966	Vincent, Gene	1935	1971	Winfield, Paul	1941	2004
Taylor, Dub	1907	1994	Vicious, Sid	1957	1979	Winninger, Charles	1884	1969
Taylor, Estelle	1899	1958	Vinson, Helen	1907	1999	Winters, Shelley	1920	2006
Taylor, Laurette	1887	1946	Von Stroheim, Erich	1885	1957	Wise, Robert	1914	2005
Taylor, Robert	1911	1969	Von Zell, Harry	1906	1981	Withers, Grant	1904	1959
Tebaldi, Renata	1922	2004	Walker, Junior	1942	1995	Wong, Anna May	1907	1961
Terry, Ellen	1847	1928	Walker, Nancy	1922	1992	Wood, Natalie	1938	1981
Thalberg, Irving	1899	1936	Walker, Robert	1918	1951	Wood, Peggy	1892	1978
Thaw, John	1942	2002	Wallenda, Karl	1905	1978	Wooley, Sheb	1921	2003
Thigpen, Lynne	1948	2003	Walsh, J. T.	1943	1998	Woolley, Monty	1888	1963
Thomas, Danny	1912	1991	Walsh, Raoul	1887	1980	Worth, Irene	1916	2002
Thomas, John Charles	1892	1960	Walston, Ray	1914	2001	Wray, Fay	1907	2004
Thorndike, Sybil	1882	1976	Walter, Bruno	1876	1962	Wright, Teresa	1918	2005
Thulin, Ingrid	1926	2004	Ward, Helen	1916	1998	Wyatt, Jane	1910?	2006
Tibbett, Lawrence	1896	1960	Warden, Jack	1914	2006	Wyler, William	1902	1981
Tierney, Gene	1920	1991	Waring, Fred	1900	1984	Wyman, Jane	1914?	2007
Tiny Tim	1923	1996	Warner, H. B.	1876	1958	Wynette, Tammy	1942	1998
Tippett, Sir Michael	1905	1998	Warrick, Ruth	1915	2005	Wynn, Ed.	1886	1966
Todd, Michael	1909	1958	Washington, Dinah	1924	1963	Wynn, Keenan	1916	1986
Tomlinson, David	1917	2000	Waters, Ethel	1896	1977	Yankovic, Frank	1915	1998
Tone, Franchot	1903	1968	Waters, Muddy	1915	1983	York, Dick	1929	1992
Torme, Mel	1925	1999	Waxman, Al	1935	2001	Young, Clara Kimball	1890	1960
Toscanini, Arturo	1867	1957	Wayne, David	1914	1995	Young, Gig	1913	1978
Tracy, Lee	1898	1968	Wayne, John	1907	1979	Young, Loretta	1913	2000
Tracy, Spencer	1900	1967	Weaver, Dennis	1924	2006	Young, Robert	1907	1998
Traubel, Helen	1903	1972	Webb, Clifton	1891	1966	Young, Roland	1887	1953
Travers, Henry	1874	1965	Webb, Jack	1920	1982	Youngman, Henny	1906	1998
Treacher, Arthur	1894	1975	Weems, Ted	1901	1963	Zanuck, Darryl F.	1902	1979
Tree, Herbert Beerbohm	1853	1917	Weissmuller, Johnny	1904	1984	Zappa, Frank	1940	1993
Trevor, Claire	1909	2000	Welk, Lawrence	1903	1992	Zevon, Warren	1947	2003
Truex, Ernest	1890	1973	Welles, Orson	1915	1985	Zinneman, Fred.	1907	1997
Truffaut, Francois	1932	1984	Wellman, William	1896	1975	Ziegfeld, Florenz	1869	1932
Tucker, Forrest	1919	1986	Werner, Oskar	1922	1984	Zukor, Adolph	1873	1976
Tucker, Richard	1913	1975	West, Mae	1893	1980			

Original Names of Selected Entertainers

ALI G: Sacha Baron Cohen
EDDIE ALBERT: Edward Albert Heimberger
ALAN ALDA: Alphonso D'Abruzzo
JASON ALEXANDER: Jay Greenspan
FRED ALLEN: John Sullivan
WOODY ALLEN: Allen Konigsberg
JUNE ALLYSON: Ella Geisman
ANDRÉ 3000: Andre Benjamin
JULIE ANDREWS: Julia Wells
CRISS ANGEL: Christopher Sarantakos
EVE ARDEN: Eunice Quedens
BEATRICE ARTHUR: Bernice Frankel
JEAN ARTHUR: Gladys Greene
ASHANTI: Ashanti Douglas
FRED ASTAIRE: Frederick Austerlitz
BABYFACE: Kenneth Edmonds
LAUREN BACALL: Betty Joan Perske
ERYKAH BADU: Erica Wright
ANNE BANCROFT: Anna Maria Italiano
THEDA BARA: Theodosia Goodman
PAT BENATAR: Patricia Andrejewski
TONY BENNETT: Anthony Benedetto
IRVING BERLIN: Israel Baline
JACK BENNY: Benjamin Kubelsky
SARAH BERNHARDT: Henriette-Rosine Bernard

MILTON BERLE: Mendel Berlinger
JELLO BIAFRA: Eric Reed Boucher
ROBERT BLAKE: Michael James Vijencio Gubitosi
BIG BOI: Antwan Patton
JON BON JOVI: John Francis Bongiovi
JOEY BISHOP: Joseph Gottlieb
THE BIG BOPPER: Jiles Perry "J.P." Richardson
BONO (VOX): Paul Hewson
BOW WOW: Shad Gregory Moss
DAVID BOWIE: David Robert Jones
BOY GEORGE: George Alan O'Dowd
FANNY BRICE: Fanny Borach
CHARLES BRONSON: Charles Buchinski
ALBERT BROOKS: Albert Einstein
MEL BROOKS: Melvin Kaminsky
FOXY BROWN: Inga Marchand
GEORGE BURNS: Nathan Birnbaum
ELLEN BURSTYN: Edna Gilhooley
RICHARD BURTON: Richard Jenkins
RED BUTTONS: Aaron Chwatt
NICOLAS CAGE: Nicholas Coppola
MICHAEL CAINE: Maurice Micklewhite
MARIA CALLAS: Maria Kalogeropoulos
CEDRIC THE ENTERTAINER: Cedric Kyles

JACKIE CHAN: Chan Kwong-Sung
CYD CHARISSE: Tula Finklea
RAY CHARLES: Ray Charles Robinson
CHARO: Maria Rosario Pilar Martinez Molina Baeza
CHUBBY CHECKER: Ernest Evans
CHUCK D: Carlton Ridenhour
CHER: Cherilyn Sarkisian
PATSY CLINE: Virginia Patterson Hensley
CLAUDETTE COLBERT: Lily Chauchoin
COOLIO: Artis Leon Ivey, Jr.
ALICE COOPER: Vincent Furnier
DAVID COPPERFIELD: David Kotkin
HOWARD COSELL: Howard Cohen
ELVIS COSTELLO: Declan McManus
LOU COSTELLO: Louis Cristillo
PETER COYOTE: Peter Cohon
TOM CRUISE: Thomas Mapother IV
TONY CURTIS: Bernard Schwartz
VIC DAMONE: Vito Farinola
RODNEY DANGERFIELD: Jacob Cohen
BOBBY DARIN: Walden Robert Cassotto
DORIS DAY: Doris von Kappelhoff
YVONNE DE CARLO: Peggy Middleton
SANDRA DEE: Alexandra Zuck

JOHN DENVER: Henry John Deutschendorf Jr.
BO DEREK: Mary Cathleen Collins
DIVINE: Harris Glenn Milstead
DANNY DEVITO: Daniel Michaeli
ANGIE DICKINSON: Angeline Brown
BO DIDDLEY: Elias Bates
PHYLLIS DILLER: Phyllis Driver
DMX: Earl Simmons
EARL TROY DONAHUE: Merle Johnson Jr.
KIRK DOUGLAS: Issur Danielovitch
MELVYN DOUGLAS: Melvyn Hesselberg
BOB DYLAN: Robert Zimmerman
BARBARA EDEN: Barbara Huffman
CARMEN ELECTRA: Tara Leigh Patrick
ELVIRA: Cassandra Peterson
EMINEM: Marshall Mathers
ENYA: Eithne Ni Bhraonian
DALE EVANS: Frances Smith
CHAD EVERETT: Raymond Cramton
FABOLOUS: Skylar Jackson
DOUGLAS FAIRBANKS: Douglas Ullman
MORGAN FAIRCHILD: Patsy McClenny
JAMIE FARR: Jameel Farah
ALICE FAYE: Alice Jeanne Leppert
STEPIN FETCHIT: Lincoln Perry
W.C. FIELDS: William Claude Dukenfield
50 CENT: Curtis Jackson
BARRY FITZGERALD: William Shields
FLAVOR FLAV: William Drayton
JOAN FONTAINE: Joane de Havilland
JODIE FOSTER: Alicia Christian Foster
REDD FOXX: John Sanford
ARLENE FRANCIS: Arlene Kazanjian
CONNIE FRANCIS: Concetta Franconero
KENNY G: Kenneth Gorelick
GRETA GARBO: Greta Gustafsson
VINCENT GARDENIA: Vincent Scognamiglio
JOHN GARFIELD: Julius Garfinkle
JUDY GARLAND: Frances Gumm
JAMES GARNER: James Bumgarner
CRYSTAL GAYLE: Brenda Gayle Webb
GEORGE GERSHWIN: Jacob Gershowitz
KATHIE LEE GIFFORD: Kathie Epstein
WHOOPI GOLDBERG: Caryn Johnson
EYDIE GORME: Edith Gormezano
STEWART GRANGER: James Stewart
CARY GRANT: Archibald Leach
LEE GRANT: Lyova Rosenthal
ROBERT GUILLAUME: Robert Williams
BUDDY HACKETT: Leonard Hacker
HAMMER: Stanley Kirk Burrell
JEAN HARLOW: Harlean Carpentier
REX HARRISON: Reginald Carey
LAURENCE HARVEY: Larushka Skikne
HELEN HAYES: Helen Brown
SUSAN HAYWARD: Edythe Marriner
RITA HAYWORTH: Margarita Cansino
PEE-WEE HERMAN: Paul Reubenfeld
CHARLTON HESTON: John Charlton Carter
HULK HOGAN: Terry Gene Bollea
WILLIAM HOLDEN: William Beedle
BILLIE HOLIDAY: Eleanora Fagan
BUDDY HOLLY: Charles Hardin Holley
JUDY HOLLIDAY: Judith Tuvim
BOB HOPE: Leslie Townes Hope
HARRY HOUDINI: Ehrich Weiss
LESLIE HOWARD: Leslie Stainer
HOWLIN' WOLF: Chester Burnett
ROCK HUDSON: Roy Scherer Jr. (later Fitzgerald)
ENGELBERT HUMPERDINCK: Arnold Dorsey
KIM HUNTER: Janet Cole
ICE CUBE: O'Shea Jackson
ICE-T: Tracy Morrow
BILLY IDOL: William Broad
JA RULE: Jeffrey Atkins
ETTA JAMES: Jamesetta Hawkins
JAY-Z: Shawn Carter
JEWEL: Jewel Kilcher
ELTON JOHN: Reginald Dwight

DON JOHNSON: Donald Wayne
AL JOLSON: Asa Yoelson
JENNIFER JONES: Phylis Isley
TOM JONES: Thomas Woodward
SPIKE JONZE: Adam Spiegel
LOUIS JOURDAN: Louis Gendre
WYNONNA JUDD: Christina Ciminella
BORIS KARLOFF: William Henry Pratt
DANNY KAYE: David Kaminsky
DIANE KEATON: Diane Hall
MICHAEL KEATON: Michael Douglas
CHAKA KHAN: Yvette Stevens
CAROLE KING: Carole Klein
LARRY KING: Larry Zeiger
BEN KINGSLEY: Krishna Banji
TED KNIGHT: Tadeus Wladyslaw Konopka
CHERYL LADD: Cheryl Stoppelmoor
VERONICA LAKE: Constance Ockleman
HEDY LAMARR: Hedwig Kiesler
DOROTHY LAMOUR: Mary Leta Dorothy Slaton
MICHAEL LANDON: Eugene Orowitz
MARIO LANZA: Alfredo Cocozza
QUEEN LATIFAH: Dana Owens
STAN LAUREL: Arthur Jefferson
STEVE LAWRENCE: Sidney Leibowitz
BRENDA LEE: Brenda Mae Tarpley
GYPSY ROSE LEE: Rose Louise Hovick
MICHELLE LEE: Michelle Dusiak
PEGGY LEE: Norma Egstrom
JANET LEIGH: Jeanette Morrison
VIVIEN LEIGH: Vivian Hartley
HUEY LEWIS: Hugh Cregg
JERRY LEWIS: Joseph Levitch
LIL' KIM: Kimberly Denise Jones
LIL' ROMEO: Percy Romeo Miller, Jr.
CAROLE LOMBARD: Jane Peters
SOPHIA LOREN: Sophia Scicolone
PETER LORRE: Laszio Lowenstein
MYRNA LOY: Myrna Williams
BELA LUGOSI: Bela Ferenc Blasko
MOMS MABLEY: Loretta Mary Aitken
SHIRLEY MACLAINE: Shirley Beaty
ELLE MACPHERSON: Eleanor Gow
MADONNA: Madonna Louise Veronica Ciccone
LEE MAJORS: Harvey Lee Yeary
KARL MALDEN: Mladen Sekulovich
BARRY MANILOW: Barry Alan Pincus
JAYNE MANSFIELD: Vera Jane Palmer
MARILYN MANSON: Brian Warner
FREDRIC MARCH: Frederick Bickel
GROUCHO MARX: Julius Henry Marx
WALTER MATTHAU: Walter Matuschanskayasky
DEAN MARTIN: Dino Crocetti
MEAT LOAF: Marvin Lee Aday
FREDDIE MERCURY: Frederick Bulsara
ETHEL MERMAN: Ethel Zimmerman
GEORGE MICHAEL: Georgios Panayiotou
RAY MILLAND: Reginald Truscott-Jones
ANN MILLER: Lucille Collier
HELEN MIRREN: Ilynea Lydia Mironoff
JONI MITCHELL: Roberta Joan Anderson
MOBY: Richard Melville Hall
MARILYN MONROE: Norma Jean Mortenson (later Baker)
YVES MONTAND: Ivo Livi
DEMI MOORE: Demetria Guynes
RITA MORENO: Rosita Alverio
HARRY MORGAN: Harry Bratsburg
MR. T: Lawrence Tero
PAUL MUNI: Muni Weisenfreund
MIKE NICHOLS: Michael Igor Peschowsky
CHUCK NORRIS: Carlos Ray
NOTORIOUS B.I.G.: Christopher Wallace
HUGH O'BRIAN: Hugh Krampke
MAUREEN O'HARA: Maureen Fitzsimons
OZZY OSBOURNE: John Michael Osbourne
JACK PALANCE: Walter Palanuik
MINNIE PEARL: Sarah Ophelia Cannon

BERNADETTE PETERS: Bernadette Lazzaro
EDITH PIAF: Edith Gassion
SLIM PICKENS: Louis Lindley
MARY PICKFORD: Gladys Smith
PINK: Alecia Moore
ROBERT PRESTON: Robert Preston Meservey
PRINCE: Prince Rogers Nelson
DEE DEE RAMONE: Douglas Colvin
JOEY RAMONE: Jeffrey Hyman
JOHNNY RAMONE: John Cummings
TOMMY RAMONE: Tom Erdelyi
TONY RANDALL: Leonard Rosenberg
MARTHA RAYE: Margaret O'Reed
DELLA REESE: Delloreese Patricia Early
BUSTA RHYMES: Trevor Smith Jr.
JOAN RIVERS: Joan Sandra Molinsky
EDWARD G. ROBINSON: Emmanuel Goldenberg
THE ROCK: Dwayne Johnson
GINGER ROGERS: Virginia McMath
ROY ROGERS: Leonard Franklin Slye
MICKEY ROONEY: Joe Yule Jr.
JOHNNY ROTTEN: John Lydon
LILLIAN RUSSELL: Helen Leonard
MEG RYAN: Margaret Hyra
WINONA RYDER: Winona Horowitz
SADE: Helen Folsad Abu
SOUPY SALES: Milton Hines
SUSAN SARANDON: Susan Tomaling
SEAL: Samuel Sealhenry
RANDOLPH SCOTT: George Randolph Crane
JANE SEYMOUR: Joyce Frankenberg
SHAKIRA: Shakira Isabel Mebarak Ripoll
OMAR SHARIF: Michael Shalhoub
CHARLIE SHEEN: Carlos Irwin Estevez
MARTIN SHEEN: Ramon Estevez
TALIA SHIRE: Talia Coppola
BEVERLY SILLS: Belle Silverman
GENE SIMMONS: Haim Witz
PHIL SILVERS: Philip Silversmith
SINBAD: David Atkins
SNOOP DOGGY DOG: Calvin Broadus
ANNA NICOLE SMITH: Vickie Lynn Hogan
ANN SOTHERN: Harriette Lake
ROBERT STACK: Robert Modini
BARBARA STANWYCK: Ruby Stevens
JEAN STAPLETON: Jeanne Murray
RINGO STARR: Richard Starkey
CAT STEVENS: Stephen Demetre Georgiou
CONNIE STEVENS: Concetta Ingolia
STING: Gordon Sumner
JOE STRUMMER: John Graham Mellor
DONNA SUMMER: La Donna Gaines
RIP TAYLOR: Charles Elmer Jr.
ROBERT TAYLOR: Spangler Brugh
DANNY THOMAS: Muzyad Yakhoob, later Amos Jacobs
TINY TIM: Herbert Khaury
RIP TORN: Elmore Rual Torn Jr.
RANDY TRAVIS: Randy Traywick
SOPHIE TUCKER: Sophia Kalish
TINA TURNER: Annie Mae Bullock
SHANIA TWAIN: Eileen Regina Edwards
TWIGGY: Leslie Hornby
CONWAY TWITTY: Harold Lloyd Jenkins
USHER: Usher Raymond IV
RUDOLPH VALENTINO: Rudolpho D'Antonguolla
FRANKIE VALLI: Frank Castelluccio
SID VICIOUS: John Simon Ritchie
JOHN WAYNE: Marion Morrison
RAQUEL WELCH: Raquel Tejada
GENE WILDER: Jerome Silberman
SHELLEY WINTERS: Shirley Schrift
STEVIE WONDER: Stevland Morris
JANE WYMAN: Sarah Jane Fulks
LORETTA YOUNG: Gretchen Michaels
BUCKWHEAT ZYDECO: Stanley Dural, Jr.

ARTS, MEDIA, AND PERSONALITIES

Award Winners, Then and Now (pp. 246-63)

	1957	2007
Highest-rated TV show	*I Love Lucy* (1956-57)	*American Idol* (2006-07)
Best Picture Oscar[1]	*Around the World in 80 Days*	*The Departed*
Emmy Awards		
Comedy	*The Phil Silvers Show*	*30 Rock*
Drama	*Requiem for a Heavyweight*	*The Sopranos*
Album of the Year Grammy[1]	No award[2]	*Taking the Long Way*, Dixie Chicks
Tony Awards		
Drama	*A Long Day's Journey Into Night*	*The Coast of Utopia*
Musical	*My Fair Lady*	*Spring Awakening*
Pulitzer Prizes		
Fiction	No award[3]	*The Road*, Cormac McCarthy
Drama	*A Long Day's Journey Into Night*, Eugene O'Neill	*Rabbit Hole*, David Lindsay-Abaire

Thespians of the Year, 2006-07 (pp. 246-63)

	Best Actor	Best Actress
Academy Awards	Forest Whitaker, *The Last King of Scotland*	Helen Mirren, *The Queen*
Golden Globes		
Drama (Film)	Forest Whitaker, *The Last King of Scotland*	Helen Mirren, *The Queen*
Comedy/Musical (Film)	Sacha Baron Cohen, *Borat*	Meryl Streep, *The Devil Wears Prada*
Drama (TV)	Hugh Laurie, *House*	Kyra Sedgwick, *The Closer*
Comedy (TV)	Alec Baldwin, *30 Rock*	America Ferrera, *Ugly Betty*
Emmy Awards (Prime-Time)		
Drama	James Spader, *Boston Legal*	Sally Field, *Brothers & Sisters*
Comedy	Ricky Gervais, *Extras*	America Ferrera, *Ugly Betty*
Tony Awards		
Play	Frank Langella, *Frost/Nixon*	Julie White, *The Little Dog Laughed*
Musical	David Hyde Pierce, *Curtains*	Christine Ebersole, *Grey Gardens*

Best-Sellers, 2006 (pp. 230-45)

DVD	*Pirates of the Caribbean: Dead Man's Chest*
Video game	*Madden '07*
PC game	*World of Warcraft: The Burning Crusade*
PC software	*TurboTax 2006 Deluxe*
Newspaper	*USA Today*
Magazine	*AARP the Magazine*
Fiction book	*For One More Day*, Mitch Albom
Nonfiction book	*The Innocent Man*, John Grisham

TV Nation (pp. 242-43)

82% of American households have 2 or more TVs
52% have 3 or more TVs
84% have a DVD player
86% receive basic cable
32% receive premium cable
Average weekly TV viewing time: over 30 hours
Teens watched less than any other age group, viewing about 21 hours, 20 minutes each week.

Number Ones (pp. 230-45)

Top-grossing U.S. movie, 2006	*Pirates of the Caribbean: Dead Man's Chest*, $423.3 mil
All-time top-grossing U.S. movie	*Titanic* (1997), $600.8 mil
#1 syndicated TV program, 2006-07	*ESPN NFL Regular Season*, 8.7% of TV households
All-time most watched TV program	*M*A*S*H* finale, Feb. 28, 1983, 50.2 mil households
#1 commercial radio format in U.S., 2007	Country, 2,034 stations
#1 recorded music genre in U.S., 2006	Rock, 34% of all music sold
All-time top-selling U.S. album	*Eagles/Their Greatest Hits 1971-75*, Eagles, 29 mil copies
Longest-running Broadway play	*The Phantom of the Opera* (1988-), 8,181 performances[4]

Milestone Birthdays in 2008 (pp. 165-228)

100
Michael DeBakey, Sep. 7
Claude Lévi-Strauss, Nov. 2

90
John Forsythe, Jan. 29
Patty Andrews, Feb. 16
Betty Ford, April 8
Mike Wallace, May 9
Eddy Arnold, May 15
Abigail Van Buren, July 4
Nelson Mandela, July 18
Billy Graham, Nov. 7

80
Fats Domino, Feb. 26
Edward Albee, March 12
Maya Angelou, April 4
Shirley Temple Black, April 23
Burt Bacharach, May 12
Jack Kevorkian, May 26
Eli Wiesel, Sept. 30

70
Joyce Carol Oates, June 16
Stephen Breyer, Aug. 15
Kenny Rogers, Aug. 21
Connie Francis, Dec. 12

60
Mikhail Baryshnikov, Jan. 28
Alice Cooper, Feb. 4
Al Gore Jr., March 31
Clarence Thomas, June 23

50
Ellen DeGeneres, Jan. 26
Mitch Albom, May 23
Prince, June 7
Kevin Bacon, July 8
Michael Jackson, Aug. 29
Andrea Bocelli, Sept. 22
Madonna, Aug. 16

40
LL Cool J, Jan. 14
Gary Coleman, Feb. 8
Celine Dion, March 30
Rachael Ray, Aug. 25
Mike Piazza, Sept. 4

30
Ashton Kutcher, Feb. 7
Nelly Furtado, Dec. 2

21
Maria Sharapova, April 19
Hilary Duff, Sept. 28
Zac Efron, Oct. 18

(1) Awards for 1956 (Then) and 2006 (Now). (2) The first Grammy Awards weren't awarded until February 1958—the same year that the first Gold Records were certified. (3) No prize for Fiction awarded in 1957. (4) As of Sept. 9, 2007.

ARTS AND MEDIA

Some Notable Movies, Sept. 2006–Aug. 2007

Film	Stars	Director
300	Gerard Butler, Lena Headey, David Wenham, Dominic West	Jack Snyder
1408	John Cusack, Samuel L. Jackson, Mary McCormack	Mikael Hofström
49 Up	Documentary	Michael Apted
All the King's Men	James Gandolfini, Anthony Hopkins, Jude Law, Sean Penn, Kate Winslet	Steven Zaillian
Apocalypto	Dalia Hernández, Rudy Youngblood	Mel Gibson
Babel	Gael García Bernal, Cate Blanchett, Rinko Kikuchi, Brad Pitt	Alejandro González Iñárritu
The Black Dahlia	Aaron Eckhart, Josh Hartnett, Scarlett Johanssen, Hilary Swank	Brian DePalma
Blades of Glory	Will Arnett, Will Ferrell, Jenna Fischer, Jon Heder, Amy Poehler	Josh Gordon, Will Speck
Blood Diamond	Jennifer Connelly, Leonardo DiCaprio, Djimon Hounsou	Edward Zwick
Borat	Sacha Baron Cohen	Larry Charles
The Bourne Ultimatum	Joan Allen, Matt Damon, Albert Finney, Julia Stiles, David Strathairn	Paul Greengrass
Casino Royale	Daniel Craig, Judi Dench, Eva Green, Jeffrey Wright	Martin Campbell
Children of Men	Michael Caine, Julianne Moore, Clive Owen	Alfonso Cuarón
The Departed	Matt Damon, Leonardo DiCaprio, Jack Nicholson, Mark Wahlberg	Martin Scorsese
Dreamgirls	Jamie Foxx, Jennifer Hudson, Beyoncé Knowles, Eddie Murphy	Bill Condon
Eragon	Robert Carlyle, Garrett Hedlund, Jeremy Irons, John Malkovich, Edward Speelers	Stefen Fangmeier
Evan Almighty	Steve Carell, Morgan Freeman, John Goodman, Lauren Graham	Tom Shadyac
Fearless	Jet Li	Ronny Yu
Flags of Our Fathers	Adam Beach, Jesse Bradford, Ryan Phillippe	Clint Eastwood
Flushed Away	Hugh Jackman, Ian McKellen, Bill Nighy, Kate Winslet	David Bowers, Sam Fell
For Your Consideration	Bob Balaban, Ed Begley Jr., Ricky Gervais, Christopher Guest, Eugene Levy, Catherine O'Hara, Parker Posey, Fred Willard	Christopher Guest
The Good Shepherd	Alec Baldwin, Matt Damon, Robert De Niro, Angelina Jolie	Robert De Niro
Gridiron Gang	The Rock, Xzibit	Phil Joanou
Grindhouse (Planet Terror/Death Proof)	Rosario Dawson, Rose McGowan, Kurt Russell, Bruce Willis	Robert Rodriguez/ Quentin Tarantino
The Guardian	Kevin Costner, Ashton Kutcher, Sela Ward	Andrew Davis
Hairspray	Nikki Blonsky, Queen Latifah, Brittany Snow, Michelle Pfeiffer, John Travolta, Christopher Walken	Adam Shankman
Halloween	Tyler Mane, Malcolm McDowell, Sheri Moon Zombie	Rob Zombie
Happy Feet	Nicole Kidman, Brittany Murphy, Robin Williams, Elijah Wood	George Miller
Harry Potter: Order of the Phoenix	Rupert Grint, Daniel Radcliffe, Emma Watson	David Yates
The Holiday	Jack Black, Cameron Diaz, Jude Law, Kate Winslet	Nancy Meyers
Hollywoodland	Ben Affleck, Adrien Brody, Bob Hoskins, Diane Lane	Allen Coulter
Hot Fuzz	Jim Broadbent, Nick Frost, Simon Pegg	Edgar Wright
I Now Pronounce You Chuck and Larry	Dan Aykroyd, Jessica Biel, Kevin James, Adam Sandler	Dennis Dugan
Inland Empire	Laura Dern, Jeremy Irons, Harry Dean Stanton, Justin Theroux	David Lynch
Knocked Up	Katherine Heigl, Leslie Mann, Seth Rogen, Paul Rudd	Judd Apatow
La Vie en Rose	Marion Cotillard, Gérard Depardieu, Sylvie Testud	Olivier Dahan
The Last King of Scotland	Gillian Anderson, James McAvoy, Kerry Washington, Forest Whitaker	Kevin Macdonald
Letters From Iwo Jima	Ken Watanabe, Kazunari Ninomiya	Clint Eastwood
Little Children	Jennifer Connelly, Jackie Earle Haley, Patrick Wilson, Kate Winslet	Todd Field
Live Free or Die Hard	Justin Long, Timothy Olyphant, Bruce Willis	Len Wiseman
The Lives of Others	Martina Gedeck, Sebastian Koch, Ulrich Mühe	Florian Henckel von Donnersmarck
Marie Antoinette	Judy Davis, Kirsten Dunst, Jason Schwartzman, Rip Torn	Sofia Coppola
The Nativity Story	Shohreh Aghdashloo, Keisha Castle-Hughes, Oscar Isaac	Catherine Hardwicke
Night at the Museum	Dick Van Dyke, Ricky Gervais, Mickey Rooney, Ben Stiller	Shawn Levy
Notes on a Scandal	Cate Blanchett, Judi Dench	Richard Eyre
Open Season	Ashton Kutcher, Martin Lawrence, Debra Messing, Gary Sinise	Roger Allers, Jill Culton
Pan's Labyrinth	Ivana Baquero, Maribel Verdú	Guillermo del Toro
Pirates of the Caribbean: At World's End	Orlando Bloom, Johnny Depp, Keira Knightley, Geoffrey Rush	Gore Verbinski
The Prestige	Christian Bale, Michael Caine, Hugh Jackman	Christopher Nolan
The Pursuit of Happyness	Thandie Newton, Jaden Smith, Will Smith	Gabriele Muccino
The Queen	James Cromwell, Helen Mirren	Stephen Frears
Ratatouille	Brian Dennehy, Janeane Garofalo, Brad Garrett, Peter O'Toole, Patton Oswalt	Brad Bird
Rescue Dawn	Christian Bale, Jeremy Davies, Steve Zahn	Werner Herzog
Rocky Balboa	Sylvester Stallone, Antonio Tarver, Burt Young	Sylvester Stallone
Rush Hour 3	Jackie Chan, Chris Tucker	Brett Ratner
Shrek the Third	Julie Andrews, Antonio Banderas, John Cleese, Cameron Diaz, Eddie Murphy, Mike Myers, Justin Timberlake	Chris Miller
Sicko	Documentary	Michael Moore
The Simpsons Movie	Hank Azaria, Nancy Cartwright, Dan Castellaneta, Julie Kavner, Harry Shearer, Yeardley Smith	David Silverman
Spider-Man 3	Thomas Haden Church, Kirsten Dunst, James Franco, Topher Grace, Tobey Maguire	Sam Raimi
Stranger Than Fiction	Will Ferrell, Maggie Gyllenhaal, Dustin Hoffman, Queen Latifah, Emma Thompson	Marc Forster
Superbad	Michael Cera, Jonah Hill, Christopher Mintz-Plasse, Seth Rogen	Greg Mottola
This Film Is Not Yet Rated	Documentary	Kirby Dick
TMNT	Laurence Fishburne, Sarah Michelle Gellar, Mako, Patrick Stewart	Kevin Munroe
Volver	Penélope Cruz	Pedro Almodóvar
We Are Marshall	Matthew Fox, Matthew McConaughey, Ian McShane, David Strathairn	McG
Wild Hogs	Tim Allen, Martin Lawrence, Ray Liotta, William H. Macy, Marisa Tomei, John Travolta	Walt Becker
Zodiac	Brian Cox, Robert Downey Jr., Jake Gyllenhaal, Mark Ruffalo	David Fincher

50 Top-Grossing Movies, 2006
Source: *Variety*, box-office grosses in the U.S. and Canada during calendar year 2006

Rank	Title	Gross (mil)	Rank	Title	Gross (mil)
1.	Pirates of the Caribbean: Dead Man's Chest	$423.3	26.	Saw III	$80.2
2.	Cars	244.1	27.	Nacho Libre	80.2
3.	X-Men: The Last Stand	234.4	28.	You, Me and Dupree	75.6
4.	The Da Vinci Code	217.5	29.	Monster House	73.7
5.	Superman Returns	200.1	30.	Jackass: Number Two	72.8
6.	Ice Age: The Meltdown	195.3	31.	Barnyard	72.6
7.	Happy Feet	181.4	32.	RV	71.5
8.	Casino Royale	156.8	33.	V for Vendetta	70.5
9.	Over the Hedge	155.0	34.	World Trade Center	70.3
10.	Talladega Nights: The Ballad of Ricky Bobby	148.2	35.	Big Momma's House 2	70.2
11.	Night at the Museum	140.1	36.	Brokeback Mountain	66.3
12.	Click	137.3	37.	Step Up	65.3
13.	Mission: Impossible 3	133.5	38.	Miami Vice	63.5
14.	Borat	126.1	39.	Medea's Family Reunion	63.3
15.	The Devil Wears Prada	124.7	40.	Fast & the Furious: Tokyo Drift	62.5
16.	The Departed	120.6	41.	Underworld: Evolution	62.3
17.	The Break-Up	118.7	42.	Eragon	62.2
18.	The Pursuit of Happyness	111.2	43.	Deja Vu	62.2
19.	Scary Movie 4	90.7	44.	Flushed Away	61.7
20.	Failure to Launch	88.7	45.	The Shaggy Dog	61.1
21.	Inside Man	88.5	46.	Poseidon	60.7
22.	Open Season	84.3	47.	Charlotte's Web	60.4
23.	The Santa Clause 3: The Escape	83.9	48.	The Chronicles of Narnia: The Lion, the Witch and the Wardrobe	59.6
24.	The Pink Panther	82.2	49.	Little Miss Sunshine	59.5
25.	Eight Below	81.6	50.	Curious George	58.4

All-Time Top-Grossing American Movies[1]
Source: *Variety* magazine

Rank	Title (original release)	Gross[2]	Rank	Title (original release)	Gross[2]
1.	Titanic (1997)	$600.8	26.	Pirates of the Caribbean: The Curse of the Black Pearl (2003)	$305.4
2.	Star Wars: Episode IV—A New Hope (1977)	461.0	27.	The Sixth Sense (1999)	293.5
3.	Shrek 2 (2004)	436.7	28.	The Chronicles of Narnia: The Lion, the Witch and the Wardrobe (2005)	291.7
4.	E.T.: The Extra-Terrestrial (1982)	435.0	29.	Star Wars: Episode V—The Empire Strikes Back (1980)	290.3
5.	Star Wars: Episode I—The Phantom Menace (1999)	431.1	30.	Harry Potter and the Goblet of Fire (2005)	290.0
6.	Pirates of the Caribbean: Dead Man's Chest (2006)	423.3	31.	Home Alone (1990)	285.8
7.	Spider-Man (2002)	403.7	32.	Harry Potter and the Order of the Phoenix (2007)	284.3
8.	Star Wars: Episode III—Revenge of the Sith (2005)	380.3	33.	The Matrix: Reloaded (2003)	281.5
9.	The Lord of the Rings: The Return of the King (2003)	377.0	34.	Meet the Fockers (2004)	279.2
10.	Spider-Man 2 (2004)	373.4	35.	Shrek (2001)	267.7
11.	The Passion of the Christ (2004)	370.3	36.	Harry Potter and the Chamber of Secrets (2002)	262.0
12.	Jurassic Park (1993)	357.1	37.	The Incredibles (2004)	261.4
13.	The Lord of the Rings: The Two Towers (2002)	341.8	38.	Dr. Seuss' How the Grinch Stole Christmas (2000)	260.0
14.	Finding Nemo (2003)	339.7	39.	Jaws (1975)	260.0
15.	Spider-Man 3 (2007)	336.5	40.	Monsters, Inc. (2001)	255.9
16.	Forrest Gump (1994)	329.7	41.	Batman (1989)	251.2
17.	The Lion King (1994)	328.5	42.	Night at the Museum (2006)	250.9
18.	Shrek the Third (2007)	321.0	43.	Men in Black (1997)	250.7
19.	Harry Potter and the Sorcerer's Stone (2001)	317.6	44.	Harry Potter and the Prisoner of Azkaban (2004)	249.5
20.	The Lord of the Rings: The Fellowship of the Ring (2001)	314.8	45.	Toy Story 2 (1999)	245.9
21.	Star Wars: Episode II—Attack of the Clones (2002)	310.7	46.	Raiders of the Lost Ark (1981)	245.0
22.	Star Wars: Episode VI—Return of the Jedi (1983)	309.2	47.	Cars (2006)	244.1
23.	Transformers (2007)	309.0	48.	Bruce Almighty (2003)	242.7
24.	Pirates of the Caribbean: At World's End (2007)	308.3	49.	Twister (1996)	241.7
25.	Independence Day (1996)	306.2	50.	My Big Fat Greek Wedding (2002)	241.4

(1) Through Sept. 1, 2007. (2) Gross is in millions of absolute dollars based on box office sales in the U.S. and Canada. Rising ticket prices favor newer films. Revenues from re-releases are included.

100 Best American Movies of All Time
Source: American Film Institute

First unveiled in 1998 based on ballots sent to 1,500 individuals, mostly from the film world, in 1997. Updated in 2007 (the version shown here) to include newly eligible films and reflect shifting cultural perspectives. Criteria for judging included historical significance, cultural impact, critical recognition and awards, and popularity. The year each film was first released is in parentheses.

1. Citizen Kane (1941)
2. The Godfather (1972)
3. Casablanca (1942)
4. Raging Bull (1980)
5. Singin' in the Rain (1952)
6. Gone With the Wind (1939)
7. Lawrence of Arabia (1962)
8. Schindler's List (1993)
9. Vertigo (1958)
10. The Wizard of Oz (1939)
11. City Lights (1931)
12. The Searchers (1956)
13. Star Wars (1977)
14. Psycho (1960)
15. 2001: A Space Odyssey (1968)
16. Sunset Boulevard (1950)
17. The Graduate (1967)
18. The General (1927)
19. On the Waterfront (1954)
20. It's a Wonderful Life (1946)
21. Chinatown (1974)
22. Some Like It Hot (1959)
23. The Grapes of Wrath (1940)
24. E.T.: The Extra-Terrestrial (1982)
25. To Kill a Mockingbird (1962)
26. Mr. Smith Goes to Washington (1939)
27. High Noon (1952)
28. All About Eve (1950)
29. Double Indemnity (1944)
30. Apocalypse Now (1979)
31. The Maltese Falcon (1941)
32. The Godfather Part II (1974)
33. One Flew Over the Cuckoo's Nest (1975)
34. Snow White and the Seven Dwarfs (1937)
35. Annie Hall (1977)
36. The Bridge on the River Kwai (1957)
37. The Best Years of Our Lives (1946)
38. The Treasure of the Sierra Madre (1948)
39. Dr. Strangelove (1964)

40. The Sound of Music (1965)
41. King Kong (1933)
42. Bonnie and Clyde (1967)
43. Midnight Cowboy (1969)
44. The Philadelphia Story (1940)
45. Shane (1953)
46. It Happened One Night (1934)
47. A Streetcar Named Desire (1951)
48. Rear Window (1954)
49. Intolerance (1916)
50. The Lord of the Rings: The Fellowship of the Ring (2001)
51. West Side Story (1961)
52. Taxi Driver (1976)
53. The Deer Hunter (1978)
54. M*A*S*H (1970)
55. North By Northwest (1959)
56. Jaws (1975)
57. Rocky (1976)
58. The Gold Rush (1925)
59. Nashville (1975)

60. Duck Soup (1933)
61. Sullivan's Travels (1941)
62. American Graffiti (1973)
63. Cabaret (1972)
64. Network (1976)
65. The African Queen (1951)
66. Raiders of the Lost Ark (1981)
67. Who's Afraid of Virginia Woolf? (1966)
68. Unforgiven (1992)
69. Tootsie (1982)
70. A Clockwork Orange (1971)
71. Saving Private Ryan (1998)
72. The Shawshank Redemption (1994)
73. Butch Cassidy and the Sundance Kid (1969)
74. The Silence of the Lambs (1991)
75. In the Heat of the Night (1967)
76. Forrest Gump (1994)
77. All the President's Men (1976)
78. Modern Times (1936)
79. The Wild Bunch (1969)

80. The Apartment (1960)
81. Spartacus (1960)
82. Sunrise (1927)
83. Titanic (1997)
84. Easy Rider (1969)
85. A Night at the Opera (1935)
86. Platoon (1986)
87. 12 Angry Men (1957)
88. Bringing Up Baby (1938)
89. The Sixth Sense (1999)
90. Swing Time (1936)
91. Sophie's Choice (1982)
92. Goodfellas (1990)
93. The French Connection (1971)
94. Pulp Fiction (1994)
95. The Last Picture Show (1971)
96. Do the Right Thing (1989)
97. Blade Runner (1982)
98. Yankee Doodle Dandy (1942)
99. Toy Story (1995)
100. Ben-Hur (1959)

National Film Registry, 1989-2006

Source: National Film Registry, Library of Congress
"Culturally, historically, or aesthetically significant" American films. * = selected in 2006.

Abbott and Costello Meet Frankenstein (1948)
Adam's Rib (1949)
The Adventures of Robin Hood (1938)
The African Queen (1951)
Alien (1979)
All About Eve (1950)
All My Babies (1953)
All That Heaven Allows (1955)
All That Jazz (1979)
All Quiet on the Western Front (1930)
All the King's Men (1949)
An American in Paris (1951)
America, America (1963)
American Graffiti (1973)
A Movie (1958)
Annie Hall (1977)
Antonia: A Portrait of the Woman (1974)
The Apartment (1960)
Apocalypse Now (1979)
Applause (1929)*
Atlantic City (1980)
The Awful Truth (1937)
Baby Face (1933)
The Bad and the Beautiful (1952)
Badlands (1973)
The Band Wagon (1953)
The Bank Dick (1940)
The Battle of San Pietro (1945)
Beauty and the Beast (1991)
Ben-Hur (1926)
Ben-Hur (1959)
The Best Years of Our Lives (1946)
Big Business (1929)
The Big Parade (1925)
The Big Sleep (1946)
The Big Trail (1930)*
The Birth of a Nation (1915)
The Black Pirate (1926)
Blacksmith Scene (1893)
The Black Stallion (1979)
Blade Runner (1982)
Blazing Saddles (1974)*
The Blood of Jesus (1941)
The Blue Bird (1918)
Bonnie and Clyde (1967)
Boyz N the Hood (1991)
Bride of Frankenstein (1935)
The Bridge on the River Kwai (1957)
Bringing Up Baby (1938)
Broken Blossoms (1919)
A Bronx Morning (1931)
The Buffalo Creek Flood: An Act of Man (1975)
Butch Cassidy and the Sundance Kid (1969)
Cabaret (1972)
The Cameraman (1928)
Carmen Jones (1954)
Casablanca (1942)
Castro Street (1966)
Cat People (1942)
Chan Is Missing (1982)
The Cheat (1915)
The Chechahcos (1924)
Chinatown (1974)
Chulas Fronteras (1976)

Citizen Kane (1941)
The City (1939)
City Lights (1931)
Civilization (1916)
Clash of the Wolves (1925)
Cologne: From the Diary of Ray and Esther (1939)
Commandment Keeper Church, Beaufort South Carolina, May 1940 (1940)
The Conversation (1974)
Cool Hand Luke (1967)
The Cool World (1963)
Cops (1922)
A Corner in Wheat (1909)
The Court Jester (1956)
The Crowd (1928)
The Curse of Quon Gwon (1916-17)*
Czechoslovakia 1968 (1968)
Daughter of Shanghai (1937)*
Daughters of the Dust (1991)
David Holzman's Diary (1968)
The Day the Earth Stood Still (1951)
Dead Birds (1964)
The Deer Hunter (1978)
Destry Rides Again (1939)
Detour (1946)
Dickson Experimental Sound Film (1894-95)
D.O.A. (1950)
Dodsworth (1936)
The Docks of New York (1928)
Dog Star Man (1964)
Don't Look Back (1967)
Do the Right Thing (1989)
Double Indemnity (1944)
Dracula (1931)
Dr. Strangelove (or, How I Learned to Stop Worrying and Love the Bomb) (1964)
Drums of Winter (1988)*
Duck Amuck (1953)
Duck and Cover (1951)
Duck Soup (1933)
Early Abstractions, #1-5,7,10 (1939-56)*
Easy Rider (1969)
Eaux D'Artifice (1953)
El Norte (1983)
The Emperor Jones (1933)
Empire (1964)
The Endless Summer (1966)
Enter the Dragon (1973)
Eraserhead (1978)
E.T.: The Extra-Terrestrial (1982)
Evidence of the Film (1913)
The Exploits of Elaine (1914)
The Fall of the House of Usher (1928)
Fantasia (1940)
Fargo (1996)*
Fast Times at Ridgemont High (1982)
Fatty's Tintype Tangle (1915)
Film Portrait (1970)
Five Easy Pieces (1970)
Flash Gordon serial (1936)
Flesh and the Devil (1927)*
Footlight Parade (1933)
Force of Evil (1948)
The Forgotten Frontier (1931)
42nd Street (1933)

The Four Horsemen of the Apocalypse (1921)
Fox Movietone News: Jenkins Orphanage Band (1928)
Frankenstein (1931)
Frank Film (1973)
Freaks (1932)
The French Connection (1971)
The Freshman (1925)
From Here to Eternity (1953)
From the Manger to the Cross (1912)
From Stump to Ship (1930)
Fuji (1974)
Fury (1936)
Garlic is as Good as Ten Mothers (1980)
The General (1927)
Gerald McBoing Boing (1951)
Gertie the Dinosaur (1914)
Giant (1956)
Gigi (1958)
The Godfather (1972)
The Godfather, Part II (1974)
Going My Way (1944)
Gold Diggers of 1933 (1933)
The Gold Rush (1925)
Gone With the Wind (1939)
GoodFellas (1990)
The Graduate (1967)
The Grapes of Wrath (1940)
Grass (1925)
The Great Dictator (1940)
The Great Train Robbery (1903)
Greed (1924)
Groundhog Day (1993)*
Gun Crazy (1949)
Gunga Din (1939)
H2O (1929)
Halloween (1978)*
Hands Up (1926)
Harlan County, U.S.A. (1976)
Harold and Maude (1972)
The Heiress (1949)
Hell's Hinges (1916)
High Noon (1952)
High School (1968)
Hindenburg Disaster Newsreel Footage (1937)
His Girl Friday (1940)
The Hitch-Hiker (1953)
Hoop Dreams (1994)
Hoosiers (1986)
Hospital (1970)
The Hospital (1971)
The House in the Middle (1954)
House of Usher (1960)
How Green Was My Valley (1941)
How the West Was Won (1962)
The Hunters (1957)
The Hustler (1961)
I Am a Fugitive from a Chain Gang (1932)
Imitation of Life (1934)
The Immigrant (1917)
In the Heat of the Night (1967)
In the Land of the Head-Hunters aka In the Land of the War Canoes (1914)
In the Street (1948/1952)*

Intolerance (1916)
Invasion of the Body Snatchers (1956)
It (1927)
It Happened One Night (1934)
It's a Wonderful Life (1946)
The Italian (1915)
Jailhouse Rock (1957)
Jammin' the Blues (1944)
Jam Session (1942)
Jaws (1975)
Jazz on a Summer's Day (1959)
The Jazz Singer (1927)
Jeffries-Johnson World's Championship
    Boxing Contest (1910)
Kannapolis, NC (1941)
Killer of Sheep (1977)
King: A Filmed Record . . . Montgomery to
    Memphis (1970)
King Kong (1933)
The Kiss (1896)
Kiss Me Deadly (1955)
Knute Rockne, All American (1940)
Koyaanisqatsi (1983)
The Lady Eve (1941)
Lady Helen's Escapade (1909)
Lady Windermere's Fan (1925)
Lambchops (1929)
The Land Beyond the Sunset (1912)
Lassie Come Home (1943)
The Last Command (1928)*
The Last of the Mohicans (1920)
The Last Picture Show (1972)
Laura (1944)
Lawrence of Arabia (1962)
The Learning Tree (1969)
Let's All Go to the Lobby (1957)
Letter From an Unknown Woman (1948)
The Life and Death of 9413—A Hollywood
    Extra (1928)
Life and Times of Rosie the Riveter (1980)
The Life of Emile Zola (1937)
Little Caesar (1930)
The Little Fugitive (1953)
Little Miss Marker (1934)
The Living Desert (1953)
The Lost World (1925)
Louisiana Story (1948)
Love Finds Andy Hardy (1938)
Love Me Tonight (1932)
Magical Maestro (1952)
The Magnificent Ambersons (1942)
Making of an American (1920)
The Maltese Falcon (1941)
The Manchurian Candidate (1962)
Manhattan (1921)
Manhattan (1979)
March of Time: Inside Nazi Germany—1938
    (1938)
Marian Anderson: The Lincoln Memorial
    Concert (1939)
Marty (1955)
M*A*S*H (1970)
Master Hands (1936)
Matrimony's Speed Limit (1913)
Mean Streets (1973)
Medium Cool (1969)
Meet Me in St. Louis (1944)
Melody Ranch (1940)
Memphis Belle (1944)
Meshes of the Afternoon (1943)
Midnight Cowboy (1969)
Mildred Pierce (1945)
The Miracle of Morgan's Creek (1944)
Miracle on 34th Street (1947)
Miss Lulu Bett (1921)
Modern Times (1936)
Modesta (1956)
Mom and Dad (1944)
Morocco (1930)
Motion Painting No. 1 (1947)
Mr. Smith Goes to Washington (1939)
Multiple Sidosis (1970)
The Music Box (1932)
The Music Man (1962)
My Darling Clementine (1946)
My Man Godfrey (1936)
The Naked Spur (1953)
Nanook of the North (1922)
Nashville (1975)
National Lampoon's Animal House (1978)
National Velvet (1944)

Naughty Marietta (1935)
Network (1976)
A Night at the Opera (1935)
The Night of the Hunter (1955)
Night of the Living Dead (1968)
Ninotchka (1939)
North by Northwest (1959)
Nostalgia (1971)
Nothing but a Man (1964)
Notorious (1946)*
The Nutty Professor (1963)
OffOn (1968)
One Flew Over the Cuckoo's Nest (1975)
One Froggy Evening (1956)
On the Waterfront (1954)
The Outlaw Josey Wales (1976)
Out of the Past (1947)
The Ox-Bow Incident (1943)
Pass the Gravy (1928)
Paths of Glory (1957)
Patton (1970)
The Pearl (1948)
Peter Pan (1924)
Phantom of the Opera (1925)
The Philadelphia Story (1940)
Pinocchio (1940)
A Place in the Sun (1951)
Planet of the Apes (1968)
The Plow That Broke the Plains (1936)
Point of Order (1964)
The Poor Little Rich Girl (1917)
Popeye the Sailor Meets Sindbad the Sailor
    (1936)
Porky in Wackyland (1938)
Power of the Press (1928)
Powers of Ten (1978)
President McKinley Inauguration Footage
    (1901)
Primary (1960)
Princess Nicotine; or The Smoke Fairy
    (1909)
The Prisoner of Zenda (1937)
The Producers (1968)
Psycho (1960)
The Public Enemy (1931)
Pull My Daisy (1959)
Punch Drunks (1934)
Pups is Pups (Our Gang) (1930)
Raging Bull (1980)
Raiders of the Lost Ark (1981)
A Raisin in the Sun (1961)
Rear Window (1954)
Rebel Without a Cause (1955)
Red Dust (1932)*
Red River (1948)
Regeneration (1915)
Reminiscences of a Journey to Lithuania
    (1971-72)*
Republic Steel Strike Riots Newsreel
    Footage (1937)
Return of the Secaucus 7 (1980)
Ride the High Country (1962)
Rip Van Winkle (1896)
The River (1937)
Road to Morocco (1942)
Rocky (1976)*
The Rocky Horror Picture Show (1975)
Roman Holiday (1953)
Rose Hobart (1936)
Sabrina (1954)
Safety Last (1923)
St. Louis Blues (1929)*
Salesman (1969)
Salomé (1922)
Salt of the Earth (1954)
San Francisco Earthquake and Fire, April
    18,1906 (1906)
Scarface (1932)
Schindler's List (1993)
The Searchers (1956)
Serene Velocity (1970)
Seven Brides for Seven Brothers (1954)
Seventh Heaven (1927)
Sex, Lies and Videotape (1989)*
Shadow of a Doubt (1943)
Shadows (1959)
Shaft (1971)
Shane (1953)
She Done Him Wrong (1933)
Sherlock, Jr. (1924)
Sherman's March (1986)

Shock Corridor (1963)
The Shop Around the Corner (1940)
Show Boat (1936)
Show People (1928)
Siege (1940)*
Singin' in the Rain (1952)
Sky High (1922)
Snow White (1933)
Snow White and the Seven Dwarfs (1937)
Some Like It Hot (1959)
The Son of the Sheik (1926)
The Sound of Music (1965)
Stagecoach (1939)
A Star Is Born (1954)
Star Theatre (1901)
Star Wars (1977)
Steamboat Willie (1928)
Stranger Than Paradise (1984)
A Streetcar Named Desire (1951)
The Sting (1973)
Stormy Weather (1943)
Sullivan's Travels (1941)
Sunrise (1927)
Sunset Boulevard (1950)
Sweet Smell of Success (1957)
Swing Time (1936)
Tabu (1931)
Tacoma Narrows Bridge Collapse (1940)
The Tall T (1957)
The T.A.M.I. Show (1964)*
Tarzan and His Mate (1934)
Taxi Driver (1976)
The Ten Commandments (1956)
The Tell-Tale Heart (1953)
Tess of the Storm Country (1914)*
Tevye (1939)
Theodore Case Sound Tests: Gus Visser
    and His Singing Duck (1925)
There It Is (1928)
The Thief of Bagdad (1924)
The Thin Blue Line (1988)
The Thing From Another World (1951)
The Thin Man (1934)
Think of Me First As a Person (1960-75)*
This Is Cinerama (1952)
This Is Spinal Tap (1984)
Through Navajo Eyes (series) (1966)
A Time for Burning (1966)
A Time Out of War (1954)*
Tin Toy (1988)
To Be or Not To Be (1942)
To Fly (1976)
To Kill a Mockingbird (1962)
Tootsie (1982)
Topaz (1943-45)
Top Hat (1935)
Touch of Evil (1958)
Toy Story (1995)
Traffic in Souls (1913)*
Trance and Dance in Bali (1936-39)
The Treasure of the Sierra Madre (1948)
Trouble in Paradise (1932)
Tulips Shall Grow (1942)
Twelve O'Clock High (1949)
2001: A Space Odyssey (1968)
Unforgiven (1992)
Verbena Tragica (1939)
Vertigo (1958)
The Wedding March (1928)
Westinghouse Works 1904 (1904)
West Side Story (1961)
What's Opera, Doc? (1957)
Where Are My Children? (1916)
White Heat (1949)
Why Man Creates (1968)
Why We Fight (Series/1943-45)
Wild and Wooly (1917)
The Wild Bunch (1969)
Wild River (1960)
Will Success Spoil Rock Hunter? (1957)
The Wind (1928)
Wings (1927)
Within Our Gates (1920)
The Wizard of Oz (1939)
Woman of the Year (1942)
A Woman Under the Influence (1974)
Woodstock (1970)
Yankee Doodle Dandy (1942)
Young Frankenstein (1974)
Young Mr. Lincoln (1939)
Zapruder Film (1963)

Most Popular DVDs, 2006
Source: Rentrak Home Video Essentials

Top Rentals, 2006

Rank	Title
1.	Flightplan
2.	Wedding Crashers
3.	Walk the Line
4.	Failure to Launch
5.	Fun With Dick and Jane
6.	Click
7.	Inside Man
8.	King Kong (2005)
9.	RV
10.	Lord of War
11.	The Benchwarmers
12.	Rumor Has It...
13.	The Break-Up
14.	The Family Stone
15.	The Chronicles of Narnia: The Lion, the Witch and the Wardrobe

Top Selling DVDs, 2006

Rank	Title
1.	Pirates of the Caribbean: Dead Man's Chest
2.	Cars
3.	The Chronicles of Narnia: The Lion, the Witch, and the Wardrobe
4.	Harry Potter and the Goblet of Fire
5.	Over the Hedge
6.	King Kong (2005)
7.	Ice Age: The Meltdown
8.	Wedding Crashers
9.	Walk the Line
10.	The Little Mermaid
11.	Chicken Little
12.	The Da Vinci Code
13.	Lady and the Tramp
14.	X-Men: The Last Stand
15.	Talladega Nights: The Ballad of Ricky Bobby

Top-Selling Video Games, 2006
Source: The NPD Group / NPD Funworld / Point-of-Sale; ranked by units sold.

The video game industry (which also includes consoles and accessories) generated record retail sales in 2006 totaling nearly $12.5 billion—a 19% increase over 2005. More than half of the revenue (about $7.4 billion) was from game (software) sales.

Rank	Title	Platforms[1]
1.	Madden NFL '07	360, Wii, PS3, PSP, NDS, XBX, PS2, GCN, GBA
2.	Cars	360, Wii, PSP, NDS, XBX, PS2, GCN, GBA
3.	Lego Star Wars II: The Original Trilogy	360, PSP, NDS, XBX, PS2, GCN, GBA
4.	NCAA Football '07	360, PSP, XBX, PS2
5.	New Super Mario Brothers NDS	
6.	Need for Speed: Most Wanted	360, PSP, NDS, XBX, PS2, GCN, GBA
7.	Gears of War	360
8.	Call of Duty 3	360, Wii, PS3, XBX, PS2, GCN, GBA
9.	Lego Star Wars	XBX, PS2, GCN, GBA
10.	Fight Night: Round 3	360, PS3, PSP, XBX, PS2

(1) 360 = Microsoft Xbox 360; GBA = Nintendo Game Boy Advance; GCN = Nintendo GameCube; NDS = Nintendo DS; PS2 = Sony PlayStation 2; PS3 = Sony PlayStation 3; PSP = Sony PlayStation Portable; Wii = Nintendo Wii; Xbox = Microsoft Xbox.

Broadway Season Statistics, 1959-2007
Source: The League of American Theatres and Producers, Inc., New York, NY

Season	Gross (mil $)	Attendance (mil)	Playing Weeks	New Productions	Season	Gross (mil $)	Attendance (mil)	Playing Weeks	New Productions
1959-1960	46	7.9	1,156	58	1983-1984	227	7.9	1,097	36
1960-1961	44	7.7	1,210	48	1984-1985	209	7.3	1,078	33
1961-1962	44	6.8	1,166	53	1985-1986	190	6.5	1,041	34
1962-1963	44	7.4	1,134	54	1986-1987	208	7.1	1,039	41
1963-1964	40	6.8	1,107	63	1987-1988	253	8.1	1,113	30
1964-1965	50	8.2	1,250	67	1988-1989	262	8.1	1,108	33
1965-1966	54	9.6	1,295	68	1989-1990	282	8.0	1,070	40
1966-1967	55	9.3	1,269	69	1990-1991	267	7.3	971	28
1967-1968	59	9.5	1,259	74	1991-1992	293	7.4	905	37
1968-1969	58	8.6	1,209	67	1992-1993	328	7.9	1,019	34
1969-1970	53	7.1	1,047	62	1993-1994	356	8.1	1,066	39
1970-1971	55	7.4	1,107	49	1994-1995	406	9.0	1,120	33
1971-1972	52	6.5	1,157	55	1995-1996	436	9.5	1,146	38
1972-1973	45	5.4	889	55	1996-1997	499	10.6	1,349	37
1973-1974	46	5.7	907	43	1997-1998	558	11.5	1,442	33
1974-1975	57	6.6	1,101	54	1998-1999	588	11.7	1,441	39
1975-1976	71	7.3	1,136	55	1999-2000	603	11.4	1,464	37
1976-1977	93	8.8	1,349	54	2000-2001	666	11.9	1,484	28
1977-1978	114	9.6	1,433	42	2001-2002	643	11.0	1,434	28
1978-1979	134	9.6	1,542	50	2002-2003	721	11.4	1,544	36
1979-1980	146	9.6	1,540	61	2003-2004	771	11.6	1,451	39
1980-1981	197	11.0	1,544	60	2004-2005	769	11.5	1,494	39
1981-1982	223	10.1	1,455	48	2005-2006	862	12.0	1,501	39
1982-1983	209	8.4	1,258	50	2006-2007	939	12.3	1,509	35

Longest-Running Broadway Plays[1]
Source: The League of American Theatres and Producers, Inc., New York, NY

Title (Run)	Performances[2]
1. *The Phantom of the Opera (1988-)	8,181
2. Cats (1982-2000)	7,485
3. Les Misérables (1987-2003)	6,680
4. A Chorus Line (1975-90)	6,137
5. Oh! Calcutta! (revival, 1976-89)	5,959
6. Beauty and the Beast (1994-2007)	5,461
7. *Rent (1996-)	4,729
8. *Chicago (revival, 1996-)	4,506
9. Miss Saigon (1991-2001)	4,092
10. *The Lion King (1997-)	4,091
11. 42nd Street (1980-89)	3,486
12. Grease (1972-80)	3,388
13. Fiddler on the Roof (1964-72)	3,242
14. Life With Father (1939-47)	3,224
15. Tobacco Road (1933-41)	3,182
16. Hello, Dolly! (1964-70)	2,844
17. My Fair Lady (1956-62)	2,717
18. The Producers (2001-07)	2,502
19. *Mamma Mia! (2001-)	2,454
20. Annie (1977-83)	2,377
Cabaret (revival, 1998-2004)	2,377
22. Man of La Mancha (1965-71)	2,328
23. Abie's Irish Rose (1922-27)	2,327
24. Oklahoma! (1943-48)	2,212
25. *Hairspray (2002-)	2,112
26. Smokey Joe's Cafe (1995-2000)	2,036
27. Pippin (1972-77)	1,944
28. South Pacific (1949-54)	1,925
29. The Magic Show (1974-78)	1,920
30. Aida (2000-04)	1,852
31. Gemini (1977-81)	1,819
32. Deathtrap (1978-82)	1,793
33. Harvey (1944-49)	1,775
34. Dancin' (1978-82)	1,774
35. La Cage aux Folles (1983-87)	1,761
36. Hair (1968-72)	1,750
37. *Avenue Q (2003-)	1,716
38. The Wiz (1975-79)	1,672
39. Born Yesterday (1946-49)	1,642
40. Crazy For You (1992-96)	1,622
41. *Wicked (2003-)	1,612
42. Ain't Misbehavin' (1978-82)	1,604
43. The Best Little Whorehouse in Texas (1978-82)	1,584
44. Mary, Mary (1961-64)	1,572
45. Evita (1979-83)	1,567
46. The Voice of the Turtle (1943-48)	1,557
47. Jekyll & Hyde (1997-2001)	1,543
48. Barefoot in the Park (1963-67)	1,530
49. 42nd Street (revival, 2001-05)	1,524
50. Dreamgirls (1981-85)	1,521

*Still running Sept. 9, 2007. (1) Unless noted, listings reflect a play's first run on Broadway. (2) Number of performances through Sept. 9, 2007.

Notable U.S. Museums

This unofficial list of some of the largest (by budget) museums in the U.S. was compiled with the assistance of the American Association of Museums, a national association representing the concerns of the museum community. Association members also include zoos, aquariums, arboretums, botanical gardens, and planetariums, but these are not included in *The World Almanac* listing.

Museum	City	State
American Museum of Natural History	New York	NY
Amon Carter Museum of Western Art	Ft. Worth	TX
The Art Institute of Chicago	Chicago	IL
Brooklyn Museum of Art	Brooklyn	NY
Busch-Reisinger Museum	Cambridge	MA
California Academy of Sciences	San Francisco	CA
California Science Center	Los Angeles	CA
Carnegie Museums of Pittsburgh	Pittsburgh	PA
Chicago Historical Society	Chicago	IL
Children's Museum of Indianapolis	Indianapolis	IN
Cincinnati Art Museum	Cincinnati	OH
Cincinnati Museum Center	Cincinnati	OH
Cleveland Museum of Art	Cleveland	OH
Colonial Williamsburg	Williamsburg	VA
Corning Museum of Glass	Corning	NY
Dallas Museum of Art	Dallas	TX
Denver Art Museum	Denver	CO
Denver Museum of Nature and Science	Denver	CO
Detroit Institute of Arts	Detroit	MI
Exploratorium	San Francisco	CA
The Field Museum	Chicago	IL
Fine Arts Museums of San Francisco	San Francisco	CA
Franklin Institute	Philadelphia	PA
The Frick Collection	New York	NY
J. Paul Getty Museum	Los Angeles	CA
Harvard University Art Museums	Cambridge	MA
Henry F. Dupont Winterthur Museum	Winterthur	DE
Henry Ford Museum/Greenfield Village	Dearborn	MI
High Museum of Art	Atlanta	GA
Houston Museum of Natural Science	Houston	TX
Jamestown-Yorktown Foundation	Williamsburg	VA
Jewish Museum	New York	NY
L.A. County Museum of Art	Los Angeles	CA
Liberty Science Center, Liberty State Park	Jersey City	NJ
Maryland Science Center	Baltimore	MD
Mashantucket Pequot Museum and Research Center	Mashantucket	CT
Metropolitan Museum of Art	New York	NY
Milwaukee Public Museum	Milwaukee	WI
Minneapolis Institute of Art	Minneapolis	MN
Museum of African American History	Detroit	MI
Museum of the American West	Los Angeles	CA
Museum of Contemporary Art	Los Angeles	CA
Museum of Fine Arts	Boston	MA
Museum of Fine Arts	Houston	TX
Museum of Modern Art	New York	NY
Museum of New Mexico	Santa Fe	NM
Museum of Science	Boston	MA
Mystic Seaport Museum	Mystic	CT
National Air & Space Museum	Washington	DC
National Baseball Hall of Fame and Museum, Inc.	Cooperstown	NY
National Gallery of Art	Washington	DC
National Museum of American History	Washington	DC
National Museum of the American Indian	Washington	DC
National Museum of Natural History	Washington	DC
Nelson-Atkins Museum of Art	Kansas City	MO
New York Historical Society	New York	NY
New York State Museum	Albany	NY
Peabody Essex Museum	Salem	MA
Pennsylvania Historical & Museum Commission	Harrisburg	PA
Philadelphia Museum of Art	Philadelphia	PA
Public Museum of Grand Rapids	Grand Rapids	MI
Rock & Roll Hall of Fame and Museum, Inc.	Cleveland	OH
San Diego Museum of Art	San Diego	CA
San Francisco Museum of Modern Art	San Francisco	CA
Science Museum of Minnesota	Saint Paul	MN
Scottsdale Museum of Contemp. Art	Scottsdale	AZ
St. Louis Science Center	St. Louis	MO
Toledo Museum of Art	Toledo	OH
U.S. Holocaust Memorial Museum	Washington	DC
Univ. of Pennsylvania Museum of Archaeology and Anthropology	Philadelphia	PA
Virginia Museum of Fine Arts	Richmond	VA
Wadsworth Atheneum	Hartford	CT
Walker Art Center	Minneapolis	MN
Whitney Museum of American Art	New York	NY

Best-Selling U.S. Magazines, 2006

Source: Audit Bureau of Circulations, Schaumburg, IL

General magazines, exclusive of comics; also excluding magazines that failed to file reports to ABC by press time. Based on total average paid circulation during the 6 months ending Dec. 31, 2006.

Publication	Paid circ.
1. AARP The Magazine	23,434,052
2. AARP Bulletin	22,840,177
3. Reader's Digest	10,094,281
4. Better Homes and Gardens	7,638,912
5. National Geographic	5,071,134
6. Good Housekeeping	4,741,353
7. Ladies' Home Journal	4,169,444
8. Time	4,066,545
9. Woman's Day	4,027,113
10. Family Circle	3,953,651
11. People	3,750,548
12. AAA Westways	3,735,510
13. Prevention	3,346,530
14. TV Guide	3,281,316
15. Sports Illustrated	3,204,699
16. Newsweek	3,118,432
17. Playboy	3,001,723
18. Cosmopolitan	2,947,220
19. Via Magazine	2,826,638
20. Southern Living	2,824,105
21. AAA Going Places	2,540,873
22. American Legion	2,519,021
23. Maxim	2,501,175
24. AAA Living	2,433,553
25. Redbook	2,408,206
26. O, The Oprah Magazine	2,382,917
27. Guideposts	2,362,700
28. Glamour	2,301,687
29. Game Informer	2,286,270
30. Parents	2,213,583
31. Parenting	2,176,843
32. Remedy	2,046,654
33. U.S. News & World Report	2,036,261
34. Seventeen	2,034,856
35. ESPN The Magazine	2,034,694
36. Smithsonian	2,028,001
37. FamilyFun	2,008,429
38. Martha Stewart Living	2,000,036
39. Real Simple	1,959,990
40. Money	1,945,757
41. Men's Health	1,804,921
42. Entertainment Weekly	1,776,932
43. In Style	1,760,542
44. US Weekly	1,751,709
45. Cooking Light	1,716,636
46. Shape	1,700,232
47. Country Living	1,651,057
48. Golf Digest	1,647,715
49. Fitness	1,553,545
50. Teen People	1,546,108
51. Star Magazine	1,542,218
52. Field & Stream	1,532,107
53. Woman's World	1,514,630
54. Self	1,488,868
55. Sunset	1,483,199
56. Home & Away	1,475,583
57. First for Women	1,473,953
58. Rolling Stone	1,462,095
59. Cosmo Girl!	1,443,482
60. Golf Magazine	1,419,907
61. Ebony	1,409,178
62. Health	1,356,227
63. Bon Appetit	1,353,049
64. Popular Science	1,340,052
65. American Rifleman	1,339,358
66. Car and Driver	1,304,239
67. Vogue	1,282,589
68. Country Home	1,272,745
69. In Touch Weekly	1,268,579
70. Weight Watchers	1,259,398
71. Stuff	1,247,825
72. Vanity Fair	1,239,850
73. Popular Mechanics	1,219,086
74. More	1,188,932
75. Family Handyman	1,184,847
76. Lucky	1,161,278
77. Nick Jr. Family	1,159,571
78. National Enquirer	1,149,106
79. Allure	1,131,262
80. Boys' Life	1,122,116
81. Motor Trend	1,107,784
82. Essence	1,075,622
83. New Yorker	1,067,202
84. WebMD The Magazine	1,061,839
85. Elle	1,060,634
86. National Geographic International	1,024,416
87. Scouting	1,010,677
88. Teen Vogue	1,005,437
89. GQ	1,005,303
90. Home	1,002,585
91. Every Day with Rachael Ray	994,567
92. Gourmet	987,918
93. Handy	984,330
94. Traditional Home	983,664
95. Travel + Leisure	967,215
96. Food & Wine	964,890
97. Marie Claire	962,025
98. This Old House	959,130
99. Midwest Living	948,035
100. Outdoor Life	944,766

Some Notable New Books, 2006

Source: Reference and User Services Assn. and Young Adult Library Services Assn., divisions of the American Library Association, for books published in 2006

Fiction

Beautiful Dreamer, Christopher Bigsby
The Madonnas of Leningrad, Debra Dean
The Inheritance of Loss, Kiran Desai
The Whistling Season, Ivan Doig
The Secret River, Kate Grenville
The Attack, Yasmina Khadra
The Girls, Lori Lansens
The Road, Cormac McCarthy
The People's Act of Love, James Meek
Black Swan Green, David Mitchell
Blind Willow, Sleeping Woman, Haruki Murakami
Firman: Adventures of a Metropolitan Lowlife, Sam Savage

Nonfiction

Fun Home: A Family Tragicomic, Alison Bechdel
The Worst Hard Time: The Untold Story of Those Who Survived the Great American Dust Bowl, Timothy Egan
The Weather Makers: How Man Is Changing the Climate and What It Means for Life on Earth, Tim Flannery

There Is No Me Without You: One Woman's Odyssey to Rescue Africa's Children, Melissa Fay Greene
Oracle Bones: A Journey Between China's Past and Present, Peter Hessler
Breach of Faith: Hurricane Katrina and the Near Death of a Great American City, Jed Horne
The Judgment of Paris: The Revolutionary Decade That Gave the World Impressionism, Ross King
Field Notes From a Catastrophe: Man, Nature, and Climate Change, Elizabeth Kolbert
Mayflower: A Story of Courage, Community, and War, Nathaniel Philbrick
James Tiptree, Jr.: The Double Life of Alice B. Sheldon, Julie Phillips
The Heartless Stone: A Journey Through the World of Diamonds, Deceit, and Desire, Tom Zoellner

Poetry

Famous, Kathleen Flenniken
Burning Wyclif, Thom Satterlee
William Henry Harrison and Other Poems, David R. Slavitt

Some Notable New Books for Children, 2006

Source: Association for Library Service to Children, a division of the American Library Association, for books published in 2006.

Younger Readers

Once Upon a Banana, Jennifer Armstrong
My Cat, the Silliest in the World, Gilles Bachelet
Keeper of Soles, Teresa Bateman
Move Over, Rover!, Karen Beaumont
Cork & Fuzz: Short and Tall, Dori Chaconas
Best Best Friends, Margaret Chodos-Irvine
Below, Nina Crews
I Lost My Tooth in Africa, Penda Diakité
Mercy Watson Goes For a Ride, Kate DiCamillo
Wolves, Emily Gravett
The Adventures of the Dish and the Spoon, Mini Grey
Lilly's Big Day, Kevin Henkes
Duck & Goose, Tad Hills
Sky Boys: How They Built the Empire State Building, Deborah Hopkinson
Houndsley and Catina, James Howe
Zelda and Ivy: The Runaways, Laura McGee Kvasnosky
Uncle Peter's Amazing Chinese Wedding, Lenore Look
Tunjur! Tunjur! Tunjur! A Palestinian Folktale, Margaret Read MacDonald
Once I Ate a Pie, Patricia MacLachlan and Emily MacLachlan Charest
Adèle & Simon, Barbara McClintock
Gone Wild: An Endangered Animal Alphabet, David McLimans
Los Gatos Black on Halloween, Marisa Montes
Hippo! No, Rhino!, Jeff Newman
The Little Red Hen, Jerry Pinkney
Not a Box, Antoinette Portis
Black? White! Day? Night! A Book of Opposites, Laura Vaccaro Seeger
Good Boy, Fergus!, David Shannon
Thelonius Monster's Sky-High Fly Pie, Judy Sierra
Scaredy Squirrel, Mélanie Watt
Mammoths on the Move, Lisa Wheeler
Dizzy, Jonah Winter

Middle Readers

Gregor Mendel: The Friar Who Grew Peas, Cheryl Bardoe
Ivy and Bean, Annie Barrows
Hugging the Rock, Susan Taylor Brown
Su Dongpo: Chinese Genius, Demi
The Miraculous Journey of Edward Tulane, Kate DiCamillo
The Adventures of Polo, Régis Faller
All in Just One Cookie, Susan E. Goodman
Owen & Mzee: The True Story of a Remarkable Friendship, Isabella Hatkoff and others
Lugalbanda: The Boy Who Got Caught Up in a War, Kathy Henderson
Toys Go Out: Being the Adventures of a Knowledgeable Stingray, a Toughy Little Buffalo, and Someone Called Plastic, Emily Jenkins
Families, Susan Kuklin
The Story of Salt, Mark Kurlansky

The Year of the Dog, Grace Lin
Ruby Lu, Empress of Everything, Lenore Look
Rules, Cynthia Lord
Oh, Rats! The Story of Rats and People, Albert Marrin
Aliens Are Coming! The True Account of the 1938 War of the Worlds Radio Broadcast, Meghan McCarthy
Quest for the Tree Kangaroo: An Expedition to the Cloud Forest of New Guinea, Sy Montgomery
Jazz, Walter Dean Myers
The Higher Power of Lucky, Susan Patron
Clementine, Sara Pennypacker
Here's Looking at Me: How Artists See Themselves, Bob Raczka
The Cat With the Yellow Star: Coming of Age in Terezin, Susan Goldman Rubin and Ela Weissberger
She's All That! Poems About Girls, ed. Belinda Hollyer
Butterfly Eyes and Other Secrets of the Meadow, Joyce Sidman
To Dance: A Ballerina's Graphic Novel, Siena Cherson Siegel
Younguncle Comes to Town, Vandana Singh
Team Moon: How 400,000 People Landed Apollo 11 on the Moon, Catherine Thimmesh
Crossing Bok Chitto: A Choctaw Tale of Friendship and Freedom, Tim Tingle
Moses: When Harriet Tubman Led Her People to Freedom, Carole Boston Weatherford

Older Readers

Crispin: At the Edge of the World, Avi
Freedom Riders: John Lewis and Jim Zwerg on the Front Lines of the Civil Rights Movement, Ann Bausum
The Killer's Tears, Anne-Laure Bondoux
Ask Me No Questions, Marina Budhos
The Runaway Princess, Kate Coombs
Framed, Frank Cottrell Boyce
The Last Dragon, Silvana DeMari
Odd Man Out, Sarah Ellis
Escape! The Story of the Great Houdini, Sid Fleischman
Jane Addams: Champion of Democracy, Judith Bloom Fradin and Dennis Brindell Fradin
The Adventures of Marco Polo, Russell Freedman
Freedom Walkers: The Story of the Montgomery Bus Boycott, Russell Freedman
Penny From Heaven, Jennifer L. Holm
Up Before Daybreak: Cotton and People in America, Deborah Hopkinson
Isaac Newton, Kathleen Krull
Sigmund Freud, Kathleen Krull
Hattie Big Sky, Kirby Larson
Gossamer, Lois Lowry
Heat, Mike Lupica
The Pull of the Ocean, Jean-Claude Mourlevat
The Legend of Bass Reeves: Being the True and Fictional Account of the Most Famous Marshal in the West, Gary Paulsen

Wintersmith, Terry Pratchett

Larklight: A Rousing Tale of Dauntless Pluck in the Farthest Reaches of Space, Philip Reeve

Yellow Star, Jennifer Roy

Andy Warhol: Pop Art Painter, Susan Goldman Rubin

House of the Red Fish, Graham Salisbury

Whatcha Mean, What's a Zine? The Art of Making Zines and Mini-Comics, Mark Todd and Esther Pearl Watson

Remember Little Bighorn: Indians, Soldiers, and Scouts Tell Their Stories, Paul Robert Walker

Counting on Grace, Elizabeth Winthrop

All Ages

Tales Our Abuelitas Told: A Hispanic Folktale Collection, F. Isabel Campoy and Alma Flor Ada

It's Not the Stork!: A Book About Girls, Boys, Babies, Bodies, Families, and Friends, Robie H. Harris

Porch Lies: Tales of Slicksters, Tricksters, and Other Wily Characters, Patricia C. McKissack

Solomon and the Ant and Other Jewish Folktales, Sheldon Oberman

Flotsam, David Wiesner

Best-Selling Books, 2006
Source: Publishers Weekly

Hardcover Fiction
1. For One More Day, Mitch Albom
2. Cross, James Patterson
3. Dear John, Nicholas Sparks
4. Next, Michael Crichton
5. Hannibal Rising, Thomas Harris
6. Lisey's Story, Stephen King
7. Twelve Sharp, Janet Evanovich
8. Cell, Stephen King
9. Beach Road, James Patterson & Peter de Jonge
10. The 5th Horseman, James Patterson & Maxine Paetro

Hardcover Nonfiction
1. The Innocent Man, John Grisham
2. You: On a Diet—The Owner's Manual for Waist Management, Mehmet C. Oz & Michael F. Roizen
3. Marley & Me, John Grogan
4. The Audacity of Hope, Barack Obama
5. Culture Warrior, Bill O'Reilly
6. Guinness World Records 2007, Craig Glenday
7. The Best Life Diet, Bob Greene
8. Cesar's Way: The Natural Everyday Guide to Understanding and Correcting Common Dog Problems, Cesar Millan & Melissa Jo Peltier
9. The World is Flat, Thomas L. Friedman
10. State of Denial: Bush at War, Part III, Bob Woodward

Trade Paperback
1. The Da Vinci Code, Dan Brown
2. The Memory Keeper's Daughter, Kim Edwards
3. Night, Elie Wiesel
4. Rachael Ray Express Lane Meals, Rachael Ray
5. The Kite Runner, Khaled Hosseini
6. The Mermaid Chair, Sue Monk Kidd
7. The Five People You Meet in Heaven, Mitch Albom
8. Cameras in Narnia, Ian Brodie
9. 90 Minutes in Heaven, Don Piper
10. The Glass Castle, Jeannette Walls

Mass Market
1. Morrigan's Cross, Nora Roberts
2. Dance of the Gods, Nora Roberts
3. Valley of Silence, Nora Roberts
4. Blue Smoke, Nora Roberts
5. 4th of July, James Patterson
6. Lifeguard, James Patterson
7. Mary, Mary, James Patterson
8. Predator, Patricia Cornwell
9. Eleven on Top, Janet Evanovich
10. Angels and Demons, Dan Brown

Children's Hardcover
1. The End (A Series of Unfortunate Events #13), Lemony Snicket
2. Pirateology, Dugald A. Steer
3. Cars, Ben Smiley
4. Artemis Fowl: The Lost Colony, Eoin Colfer
5. Panda Bear, Panda Bear, What Do You See?, Bill Martin Jr., illus. by Eric Carle
6. Pirates, John Matthews
7. Guess How Much I Love You, Sam McBratney, illus. by Anita Jeram
8. Maximum Ride #2: School's Out Forever, James Patterson
9. Is There Really a Human Race?, Jamie Lee Curtis, illus. by Laura Cornell
10. A Series of Unfortunate Events: The Beatrice Letters, Lemony Snicket

Almanacs, Atlases, & Annuals
1. The World Almanac and Book of Facts 2007, ed. Ken Park
2. The Old Farmer's Almanac 2007
3. J.K. Lasser's Your Income Tax 2007, J.K. Lasser
4. The World Almanac and Book of Facts 2006, ed. Ken Park
5. What Color Is Your Parachute? 2007, Richard Nelson Bolles
6. 2006 Europe TravelBook, AAA
7. AAA Road Atlas, AAA

Note: Bestseller calculations are based on shipped-and-billed figures supplied by publishers and reflect 2006 sales only.

Leading U.S. Daily Newspapers, 2006
Source: 2007 Editor & Publisher International Yearbook

(Circulation as of Sept. 30, 2006; m = morning, e = evening, d=all day)

As of Feb. 1, 2007, the number of U.S. daily newspapers had fallen to 1,437, for a net loss of 15 since Feb. 1, 2006. Average daily circulation fell by 1.0 mil, from 53.3 mil in 2006 to 52.3 mil in 2007. The overall number of Sunday papers dipped by 7, to 907. Average Sunday circulation as of Feb. 1, 2007, fell 2.1 mil, from 55.3 mil to 53.2 mil.

Newspaper	Circulation	Newspaper	Circulation
1. Arlington (VA) USA Today	(m) 2,269,509	19. Detroit (MI) Free Press	(m) 345,861
2. New York (NY) Wall Street Journal	(m) 2,043,235	20. Cleveland (OH) Plain Dealer	(m) 336,939
3. New York (NY) Times	(m) 1,086,798	21. Philadelphia (PA) Inquirer	(m) 330,622
4. Los Angeles (CA) Times	(m) 775,766	22. Portland (OR) Oregonian	(d) 310,803
5. New York (NY) Post	(m) 704,011	23. St. Petersburg (FL) Times	(m) 305,854
6. New York (NY) Daily News	(m) 693,382	24. San Diego (CA) Union-Tribune	(m) 304,334
7. Washington (DC) Post	(m) 656,297	25. Orange County (CA) Register	(m) 287,204
8. Chicago (IL) Tribune	(m) 576,132	26. Miami (FL) Herald	(m) 279,878
9. Houston (TX) Chronicle	(m) 508,097	27. St. Louis (MO) Post-Dispatch	(m) 276,588
10. Long Island (NY) Newsday	(m) 410,579	28. Sacramento (CA) Bee	(m) 273,609
11. Dallas (TX) Morning News	(m) 404,653	29. New York (NY) am New York	(m) 266,852
12. Phoenix (AZ) Republic	(m) 397,294	30. New Orleans (LA) Times-Picayune	(m) 261,573
13. Boston (MA) Globe	(m) 386,415	31. Washington (DC) Examiner	(m) 260,950
14. Chicago (IL) Sun-Times	(m) 382,796	32. Indianapolis (IN) Star	(m) 258,696
15. Newark (NJ) Star-Ledger	(m) 378,100	33. Denver (CO) Post	(m) 255,935
16. San Francisco (CA) Chronicle	(d) 373,805	34. Denver (CO) Rocky Mountain News	(m) 255,675
17. Minneapolis (MN) Star Tribune	(m) 358,887	35. Kansas City (MO) Star	(m) 254,793
18. Atlanta (GA) Journal-Constitution	(m) 350,157	36. Baltimore (MD) Sun	(m) 236,172

Newspaper		Circulation	Newspaper		Circulation
37. Fort Lauderdale *South Florida Sun-Sentinel*	(m)	235,154	68. San Francisco (CA) *Examiner*	(m)	165,163
38. Milwaukee (WI) *Journal Sentinel*	(m)	230,781	69. Nashville (TN) *Tennessean*	(m)	165,131
39. San Jose (CA) *Mercury News*	(m)	228,880	70. Rochester (NY) *Democrat and Chronicle*	(m)	156,128
40. San Antonio (TX) *Express-News*	(m)	223,846	71. Jacksonville (FL) *Times-Union*	(m)	154,700
41. Orlando (FL) *Sentinel*	(d)	221,826	72. Memphis (TN) *Commercial Appeal*	(m)	154,403
42. Tampa (FL) *Tribune*	(m)	220,277	73. Providence (RI) *Journal*	(m)	152,736
43. Columbus (OH) *Dispatch*	(m)	217,291	74. Los Angeles (CA) *Daily News*	(m)	151,215
44. Seattle (WA) *Times*	(m)	212,691	75. Chicago (IL) *Daily Herald*	(m)	151,200
45. Pittsburgh (PA) *Post-Gazette*	(m)	212,075	76. Fresno (CA) *Bee*	(m)	149,491
46. Louisville (KY) *Courier-Journal*	(m)	210,081	77. Neptune (NJ) *Asbury Park Press*	(m)	148,690
47. Fort Worth (TX) *Star-Telegram*	(m)	206,991	78. Des Moines (IA) *Register*	(m)	147,701
48. Charlotte (NC) *Observer*	(m)	206,497	79. Birmingham (AL) *News*	(m)	143,781
49. Boston (MA) *Herald*	(m)	203,552	80. Honolulu (HI) *Advertiser*	(d)	139,312
50. Oklahoma City (OK) *Oklahoman*	(m)	201,947	81. Grand Rapids (MI) *Press*	(e)	132,214
51. Detroit (MI) *News*	(m)	201,482	82. Salt Lake City (UT) *Tribune*	(m)	131,361
52. Cincinnati (OH) *Enquirer*	(m)	197,962	83. Seattle (WA) *Post-Intelligencer*	(m)	126,225
53. St. Paul (MN) *Pioneer Press*	(m)	184,371	84. Dayton (OH) *Daily News*	(m)	123,181
54. Buffalo (NY) *News*	(d)	183,856	85. Toledo (OH) *Blade*	(m)	123,095
55. Norfolk (VA) *Virginian-Pilot*	(m)	183,210	86. Westchester Co. (NY) *Journal News*	(m)	122,356
56. Richmond (VA) *Times-Dispatch*	(m)	181,369	87. Los Angeles (CA) *La Opinion*	(m)	121,572
57. Hartford (CT) *Courant*	(m)	179,066	88. Akron (OH) *Beacon Journal*	(m)	118,771
58. Omaha (NE) *World-Herald*	(d)	177,919	89. Tulsa (OK) *World*	(m)	117,844
59. Little Rock (AR) *Democrat-Gazette*	(m)	176,172	90. Tacoma (WA) *News Tribune*	(m)	116,150
60. Los Angeles (CA) *Investor's Business Daily*	(m)	173,169	91. Knoxville (TN) *News Sentinel*	(m)	115,608
			92. Syracuse (NY) *Post-Standard*	(m)	114,179
61. Riverside (CA) *Press-Enterprise*	(m)	170,965	93. Philadelphia (PA) *Daily News*	(m)	112,540
62. Walnut Creek (CA) *Contra Costa Times*	(m)	168,689	94. Wilmington (DE) *News Journal*	(d)	112,492
63. Las Vegas (NV) *Review-Journal*	(m)	168,653	95. Lexington (KY) *Herald-Leader*	(m)	108,442
64. Austin (TX) *American-Statesman*	(m)	168,569	96. Allentown (PA) *Morning Call*	(m)	108,200
65. West Palm Beach (FL) *Post*	(m)	167,605	97. Sarasota (FL) *Herald-Tribune*	(m)	107,755
66. Bergen County (NJ) *Record*	(m)	166,392	98. Columbia (SC) *State*	(m)	104,880
67. Raleigh (NC) *News & Observer*	(m)	165,483	99. Tucson (AZ) *Daily Star*	(m)	104,731
			100. Albuquerque (NM) *Journal*	(m)	103,889

Leading Canadian Daily Newspapers, 2006

Source: 2007 *Editor & Publisher International Yearbook*

(Circulation as of Sept. 30, 2006; all morning papers)

Rank	Circulation	Rank	Circulation
1. Toronto (ON) *Star*	446,493	6. Montreal (QC) *La Presse*	196,970
2. Toronto (ON) *Globe and Mail*	330,145	7. Vancouver (BC) *Sun*	162,835
3. Montreal (QC) *Le Journal*	260,394	8. Vancouver (BC) *Province*	141,506
4. Toronto (ON) *National Post*	209,211	9. Montreal (QC) *Gazette*	129,153
5. Toronto (ON) *Sun*	197,453	10. Ottawa (ON) *Citizen*	124,822

Top News/Information Websites, July 2007

Source: comScore Media Metrix, Inc.

Rank	Visitors[1]	Rank	Visitors[1]	Rank	Visitors[1]
1. New York Times Digital	42,710,000	9. WorldNow Sites	11,184,000	18. Lee Enterprises, Inc.	5,546,000
2. The Weather Channel	38,534,000	10. Tribune Newspapers	8,983,000	19. Discovery.com	5,532,000
3. Yahoo! News	33,757,000	11. ABCNews Digital	7,834,000	20. WashingtonPost.com	5,291,000
4. MSNBC	24,544,000	12. CBS News Digital	7,344,000	21. MediaNews Group, Inc.	5,172,000
5. AOL News	23,949,000	13. Military.com	6,866,000	22. MSN News & Weather	5,136,000
6. CNN	22,494,000	14. FoxNews.com	6,660,000	23. Belo	4,875,000
7. Gannett Sites	20,089,000	15. Legacy.com	6,308,000	24. Slate.com	4,718,000
8. Weatherbug Property	16,289,000	16. McClatchey Corp.	5,910,000	25. AP.org	4,370,000
		17. Topix.com	5,825,000		

(1) Number of unique visitors who visited Website at least once in July 2007.

Symphony Orchestras: Most Performed Composers, 2006-07

Source: American Symphony Orchestra League

Composer	Scheduled performances	Composer	Scheduled performances
Wolfgang Amadeus Mozart	425	Franz Joseph Haydn	111
Ludwig Van Beethoven	391	Sergei Rachmaninoff	109
Johannes Brahms	270	Jean Sibelius	103
Piotr Ilyich Tchaikovsky	242	Gustav Mahler	101
Dmitri Shostakovich	188	Johann Sebastian Bach	98
Richard Strauss	155	Aaron Copland	97
Antonin Dvorak	150	Richard Wagner	89
Sergei Prokofiev	130	Robert Schumann	88
Igor Stravinsky	126	George Frederic Handel	71
Maurice Ravel	124	Leonard Bernstein	71
Felix Mendelssohn	117		

Note: Number of performances of a given composer's work(s) scheduled during the 2006-07 season (generally Oct.-Sept.) by a member of the American Symphony Orchestra League.

Opera: Most Produced Works, 2006-07
Source: Opera America

Work, Composer	Productions	Work, Composer	Productions
Madama Butterfly, Giacomo Puccini	21	Rigoletto, Giuseppe Verdi	10
The Barber of Seville, Gioachino Rossini	16	The Magic Flute, Wolfgang Amadeus Mozart	9
La traviata, Giuseppe Verdi	15	The Marriage of Figaro, Wolfgang Amadeus Mozart	9
Carmen, Georges Bizet	14	The Merry Widow, Franz Lehár	9
La bohème, Giacomo Puccini	12	Tosca, Giacomo Puccini	9
Don Giovanni, Wolfgang Amadeus Mozart	12		

Note: Number of productions (not individual performances) of a given opera by professional member companies of OPERA America and Opera.ca during the 2006-07 Opera season (roughly Oct.-Sept.).

U.S. Commercial Radio Stations, by Format, 1998-2007[1]
Source: The M Street Radio Directory, M Street Corporation, Littleton, NH © 2007; counts are for June of each year

Primary format	2007	2006	2005	2004	2003	2002	2001	1999	1998
1. Country	2,034	2,035	2,019	2,047	2,088	2,131	2,190	2,306	2,368
2. News/Talk	1,370	1,336	1,324	1,282	1,224	1,179	1,139	1,159	1,131
3. Spanish	777	705	703	665	628	603	574	536	493
4. Oldies	711	727	773	816	807	813	786	766	799
5. Adult Contemporary (AC)	661	660	684	703	692	713	709	775	844
6. Sports	557	530	497	469	429	388	338	256	251
7. Top 40	473	485	502	497	491	474	468	401	379
8. Classic Rock	456	454	461	450	425	384	338	314	282
9. Hot AC	377	375	380	416	399	395	369	325	281
10. Adult Standards	370	366	405	460	497	547	569	595	561
11. Classic Hits	296	276	262	229	237	258	265	222	192
12. Religion (Teaching, Variety)	290	312	318	336	347	332	356	363	356
13. Rock	282	278	270	280	273	278	282	280	266
14. Black Gospel	255	266	286	273	253	254	264	257	238
15. Soft AC	243	302	324	322	336	340	375	382	368
16. Southern Gospel	206	208	207	208	207	240	255	269	273
17. Adult Hits	171	149	54	0	0	0	0	0	0
17. Urban AC	162	166	153	136	128	121	118	112	127
18. Contemporary Christian	151	150	174	159	167	164	164	167	164
19. R&B	134	138	150	159	189	193	183	166	171
20. Off Air	88	93	70	79	123	110	113	96	102
TOTAL OPERATING STATIONS[2]	**10,755**	**10,696**	**10,661**	**10,648**	**10,605**	**10,569**	**10,516**	**10,444**	**10,292**

(1) Data for 2000 unavailable. (2) Totals include stations that are changing or did not report format.

Top-Grossing North American Concert Tours, 1985-2006
Source: Pollstar, Fresno, CA

Rank	Artist (Year)	Total gross[1]	Cities/Shows	Rank	Artist (Year)	Total gross[1]	Cities/Shows
1.	The Rolling Stones (2005)	$162.0	38/42	13.	The Rolling Stones (2002)	$87.9	33/34
2.	U2 (2005)	138.9	43/78	14.	Prince (2004)	87.4	69/96
3.	The Rolling Stones (2006)	138.5	35/39	15.	'N Sync (2001)	86.8	36/43
4.	The Rolling Stones (1994)	121.2	43/60	16.	Madonna (2006)	85.9	14/34
5.	Bruce Springsteen & The E Street Band (2003)	115.9	30/47	17.	Backstreet Boys (2001)	82.1	73/98
					Cirque du Soleil: Delirium (2006)	82.1	61/156
6.	U2 (2001)	109.7	56/80	19.	Celine Dion (2005)	81.3	1/155
7.	Pink Floyd (1994)	103.5	39/59	20.	Celine Dion (2003)	80.5	1/145
8.	Paul McCartney (2002)	103.3	43/53	21.	Celine Dion (2004)	80.4	1/154
9.	The Rolling Stones (1989)	98.0	33/60	22.	Tina Turner (2000)	80.2	88/95
10.	Barbra Streisand (2006)	92.5	16/20	23.	U2 (1997)	79.9	37/46
11.	The Rolling Stones (1997)	89.3	26/33	24.	Madonna (2004)	79.5	14/39
12.	Tim McGraw/Faith Hill (2006)	88.8	55/73	25.	The Eagles (1994)	79.4	32/54

(1) In millions. Not adjusted for inflation.

Top-Selling Albums of All-Time[1]
Source: Recording Industry Assn. of America, Washington, DC

Rank	Title, Artist	Sales (in millions)	Rank	Title, Artist	Sales (in millions)
1.	Eagles/Their Greatest Hits 1971-1975, Eagles	29.0	13.	The Beatles 1967-1970, The Beatles	16.0
2.	Thriller, Michael Jackson	27.0		No Fences, Garth Brooks	16.0
3.	Led Zeppelin IV, Led Zeppelin	23.0		Hotel California, Eagles	16.0
	The Wall, Pink Floyd	23.0		Cracked Rear View, Hootie & the Blowfish	16.0
5.	Back in Black, AC/DC	21.0		Greatest Hits, Elton John	16.0
	Greatest Hits Volume I & Volume II, Billy Joel	21.0		Physical Graffiti, Led Zeppelin	16.0
7.	Double Live, Garth Brooks	20.0		Jagged Little Pill, Alanis Morissette	16.0
	Come on Over, Shania Twain	20.0	20.	The Beatles 1962-1966, The Beatles	15.0
9.	The Beatles, The Beatles	19.0		Saturday Night Fever (soundtrack), Bee Gees	15.0
	Rumours, Fleetwood Mac	19.0		Appetite for Destruction, Guns N' Roses	15.0
11.	Boston, Boston	17.0		Dark Side of the Moon, Pink Floyd	15.0
	The Bodyguard (soundtrack), Whitney Houston	17.0		Supernatural, Santana	15.0
				Born in the U.S.A., Bruce Springsteen	15.0

(1) As of Sept. 2007; sales figures represent RIAA multi-platinum certifications, albums ranked by latest sales certification.

Multi-Platinum and Platinum Awards for Recorded Music and Music Videos, 2006-07

Source: Recording Industry Assn. of America, Washington, DC

To achieve platinum status, an **album** must reach a minimum sale of 1 mil units in LPs, tapes, and CDs, with a manufacturer's dollar volume of at least $2 mil based on one-third of the suggested retail list price for each record, tape, or CD sold. To achieve multi-platinum status, an album must reach a minimum sale of at least 2 mil units in LPs, tapes, and CDs, with a manufacturer's dollar volume of at least $4 mil based on one-third of the list price.

Singles must sell 1 mil units to achieve a platinum award (created in 1976) and 2 mil to achieve a multi-platinum award (created in 1984). In 1999, the Diamond Award, honoring sales of 10 mil or more copies of an album or single, was introduced. EP singles count as 2 units. Double-CD sets count as 2 units. **Music videos** (long form) must sell 100,000 units to qualify for a platinum award, more than 200,000 units for a multi-platinum award, and are recertified with each additional 100,000 sold. **Video singles**, which must have a maximum running time of 15 minutes and no more than 2 songs per title, must sell 50,000 units to qualify for a platinum award, at least 100,000 units to qualify for a multi-platinum award, and are recertified with each additional 50,000 sold. In Oct. 2004, digital gold (100,000 sold), platinum (200,000 sold), and multi-platinum (400,000 sold) awards were introduced.

Awards listed here are for albums and digital singles (released Sept. 2005-Aug. 2007) and for music videos (released at any time) that were certified Sept. 2006-Aug. 2007. Numbers in parentheses = millions sold. For digital singles, ** = multi-platinum. Alphabetized by artist's name.

Albums, Multi-Platinum

Konvicted, Akon
B'day, Beyoncé (2)
The Breakthrough, Mary J. Blige (2)
Chris Brown, Chris Brown
The Road and the Radio, Kenny Chesney (2)
Daughtry, Daughtry
Taking the Long Way, Dixie Chicks
Extreme Behavior, Hinder
Kingdom Come, Jay-Z
Not Too Late, Norah Jones
All the Right Reasons, Nickelback (5)
Me and My Gang, Rascal Flatts (3)
Stadium Arcadium, Red Hot Chili Peppers
FutureSex/LoveSounds, Justin Timberlake (2)
Some Hearts, Carrie Underwood (5)
Hannah Montana soundtrack, Various Artists
High School Musical soundtrack, Various Artists (3)
Now That's What I Call Music! Vol. 23, Various Artists

Corinne Bailey Rae, Corinne Bailey Rae
Face the Promise, Bob Seger and the Silver Bullet Band
Fresh Cut Christmas, George Strait
It Just Comes Natural, George Strait
Enjoy the Ride, Sugarland
Taylor Swift, Taylor Swift
The Evolution of Robin Thicke, Robin Thicke
Eye to the Telescope, KT Tunstall
Love, Pain & the Whole Crazy Thing, Keith Urban
Dreamgirls soundtrack, Various Artists
Eminem Presents: The Re-Up, Various Artists
Now That's What I Call Christmas! Vol. 3, Various Artists
Now That's What I Call Music! Vol. 21, Various Artists
Now That's What I Call Music! Vol. 22, Various Artists
The Inspiration, Young Jeezy

Music Videos, Multi-Platinum

Family Jewels, AC/DC
One Night Only, Bee Gees
Live at Montreux, 1994, Johnny Cash
A New Journey: Live at Slaine Castle, Celtic Woman
Farewell I Tour: Live From Melbourne, Eagles
Live at the Greek, Josh Groban
Kissology Volume 1: 1974-1977, Kiss
Kiss: Rock the Nation Live!, Kiss
Dark Side of the Moon, Pink Floyd
Eric Clapton Crossroads Guitar Festival, Various Artists

Albums, Platinum

Back to Basics, Christina Aguilera
If You're Going Through Hell, Rodney Atkins
Love, The Beatles
Duets: An American Classic, Tony Bennett
Foiled, Blue October
Cheetah Girls 2 soundtrack, The Cheetah Girls
The Evolution, Ciara
Doin' Somethin' Right, Billy Currington
Danity Kane, Danity Kane
Modern Times, Bob Dylan
The Open Door, Evanescence
Infinity on High, Fall Out Boy
The Dutchess, Fergie
Hero, Kirk Franklin
Loose, Nelly Furtado
These Days, Vince Gill
Awake, Josh Groban
Taylor Hicks, Taylor Hicks
The Christmas Collection, Il Divo
Siempre, Il Divo
20 Y.O., Janet Jackson
Sam's Town, The Killers
Once Again, John Legend
LeToya, LeToya
The Road to Here, Little Big Town
Release Therapy, Ludacris
Continuum, John Mayer
Let It Go, Tim McGraw
The Black Parade, My Chemical Romance
Idlewild, OutKast
I'm Not Dead, Pink

Digital Singles, Platinum

"Ain't No Other Man," Christina Aguilera
"Unwritten," Natasha Bedingfield
"Run It!," Chris Brown
"Everytime We Touch," Cascada
"One, Two Step," Ciara featuring Missy Elliot
"It's Not Over," Daughtry
"Dance, Dance," Fall Out Boy
"Over My Head (Cable Car)," The Fray
**"How to Save a Life," The Fray
"Promiscuous," Nelly Furtado
"Crazy," Gnarls Barkley
"Girlfriend," Avril Lavigne
"Waiting on the World to Change," John Mayer
"Hey Ya!," OutKast
"I Write Sins Not Tragedies," Panic! At The Disco
"Temperature," Sean Paul
"SOS," Rihanna
"Hips Don't Lie," Shakira
**"SexyBack," Justin Timberlake
"My Love," Justin Timberlake
"What Goes Around... Comes Around," Justin Timberlake
"Before He Cheats," Carrie Underwood
"Yeah!," Usher
"Gold Digger," Kanye West

Sales of Recorded Music and Music Videos, by Genre and Format, 2000-06

Source: Recording Industry Assn. of America, Washington, DC

Breakdown is by percentage of sales revenue for all recorded music sold, ranked for 2005.

GENRE	2006	2005	2004	2003	2000	GENRE	2006	2005	2004	2003	2000
Rock	34.0%	31.5%	23.9%	25.2%	24.8%	New Age	0.3%	0.4%	1.0%	0.5%	0.5%
Rap/Hip-Hop	11.4	13.3	12.1	13.3	12.9	Other[3]	7.3	8.5	8.9	7.6	8.3
R&B/Urban[1]	11.0	10.2	11.3	10.6	9.7						
Country	13.0	12.5	13.0	10.4	10.7	**FORMAT**	**2006**	**2005**	**2004**	**2003**	**2000**
Pop	7.1	8.1	10.0	8.9	11.0	Compact disc (CD)	85.6%	87.0%	90.3%	87.8%	89.3%
Religious[2]	5.5	5.3	6.0	5.8	4.8	Digital download[4]	6.7	5.7	0.9	1.3	NA
Children's	2.9	2.3	2.8	0.6	0.6	Singles (all types)	3.4	2.7	2.4	2.4	2.5
Jazz	2.0	1.8	2.7	2.9	2.9	DVD audio	1.3	0.8	1.7	2.7	NA
Classical	1.9	2.4	2.0	3.0	2.7	Music Videos/DVDs[4]	1.1	0.7	1.0	0.6	0.8
Oldies	1.1	1.1	1.4	1.3	0.9	Cassette	0.8	1.1	1.7	2.2	4.9
Soundtracks	0.8	0.9	1.1	1.4	0.7	Vinyl LPs	0.6	0.7	0.9	0.5	0.5

(1) Includes R&B, blues, dance, disco, funk, fusion, Motown, reggae, soul. (2) Includes Christian, gospel, inspirational, religious, and spiritual. (3) "Other" includes big band, Broadway, comedy, contemporary, electronic, emo, ethnic, exercise, folk, gothic, grunge, holiday music, house music, humor, instrumental, language, latin, love songs, mix, mellow, modern, ska, spoken-word, standards, swing, Top-40, trip-hop. (4) 2001 is the first year that data were collected on digital download purchases, and that music video/DVD was recorded separately from audio DVD.

Sales of Recorded Music and Music Videos, by Units Shipped and Value, 1996-2006

Source: Recording Industry Assn. of America, Washington, DC

(in millions, net after returns)

	1996	1998	2000	2001	2002	2003	2004	2005	2006	% Change 2005-06
Physical units shipped ..	1,137.2	1,123.9	1,079.2	968.5	859.7	798.4	814.1	748.7	642.6	−14.2%
Dollar value............	12,533.8	13,711.2	14,323.7	13,740.9	12,614.2	11,854.4	12,154.7	11,195.0	9,651.4	−13.8
Compact discs (CD)[1] ...	778.9	847.0	942.5	881.9	803.3	746.0	767.0	705.4	614.9	−12.8
Dollar value	9,934.7	11,416.0	13,214.5	12,909.4	12,044.1	11,232.9	11,446.5	10,520.2	9,162.9	−12.9
Other albums[2]........	228.2	161.9	78.2	47.6	33.3	20.5	7.7	4.4	1.7	−61.6
Dollar value	1,942.1	1,453.9	653.7	396.8	238.8	164.2	66.1	48.5	22.1	−54.5
Cassettes	225.3	158.5	76.0	45.0	31.1	17.2	5.2	2.5	(9)	(9)
Dollar value.....	1,905.3	1,419.9	626.0	363.4	209.8	108.1	23.7	13.1	(9)	(9)
LP/EP	2.9	3.4	2.2	2.3	1.7	1.5	1.4	1.0	(9)	(9)
Dollar value.....	36.8	34.0	27.7	27.4	20.5	21.7	19.3	14.2	(9)	(9)
All singles[3]	113.2	87.8	40.3	21.3	8.4	12.1	6.6	5.0	2.9	−41.4
Dollar value	420.9	333.3	173.6	105.5	42.9	57.4	34.9	24.2	15.4	−36.3
CD singles	43.2	56.0	34.2	17.3	4.5	8.3	3.1	2.8	(9)	(9)
Dollar value.....	184.1	213.2	142.7	79.4	19.6	36.0	15.0	10.9	(9)	(9)
Cassette singles ...	59.9	26.4	1.3	−1.5	−0.5	—	—	—	(9)	(9)
Dollar value.....	189.3	94.4	4.6	−5.3	−1.6	—	—	—	(9)	(9)
Vinyl singles	10.1	5.4	4.8	5.5	4.4	3.8	3.5	2.3	(9)	(9)
Dollar value.....	47.5	25.7	26.3	31.4	24.9	21.5	19.9	13.2	(9)	(9)
Music videos[4]........	16.9	27.2	18.2	17.7	14.7	19.9	32.8	33.8	23.1	31.8
Dollar value	236.1	508.0	281.9	329.2	288.4	399.9	607.2	602.2	451.0	25.1
Digital formats[5]........	—	—	—	—	—	—	143.9	383.1	625.3	63.2
Dollar value............	—	—	—	—	—	—	183.4	503.6	878.0	74.4
Download albums......	—	—	—	—	—	—	4.6	13.6	27.6	103.3
Dollar value	—	—	—	—	—	—	45.5	135.7	275.9	103.3
Download singles.....	—	—	—	—	—	—	139.4	366.9	586.4	59.8
Dollar value	—	—	—	—	—	—	138.0	363.3	580.6	59.8
Music videos	—	—	—	—	—	—	—	1.9	9.9	434.3
Dollar value	—	—	—	—	—	—	—	3.7	19.7	434.2
Mobile formats[6]	—	—	—	—	—	—	—	170.0	315.3	85.5
Dollar value	—	—	—	—	—	—	—	421.6	774.5	83.7
Subscription formats[7]...	—	—	—	—	—	—	—	1.3	1.7	27.6
Dollar value	—	—	—	—	—	—	—	149.2	206.2	38.2
TOTAL UNITS[8].........	1,137.2	1,123.9	1,079.2	968.5	859.7	798.4	958.0	1,301.8	1,583.2	21.6
TOTAL VALUE	12,533.8	13,711.2	14,323.7	13,740.9	12,614.2	11,854.4	12,338.1	12,269.5	11,510.2	−6.2

(1) Includes DualDisc. (2) Includes Cassette, LP/EP, DVD Audio, and SACD. (3) Includes CD, Cassette, and Vinyl. (4) Includes DVD Videos. (5) Includes kiosk singles and albums. (6) Includes Master ringtunes, ringbacks, music videos, full-length downloads, and other mobile music. (7) Weighted annual average. (8) Includes albums and singles, excludes subscriptions. If digital singles were counted as 1/10 of an album, units in 2006 were 8.6% greater than 2005. (9) The RIAA stopped breaking out sales in these formats separately in 2006, but they are included in other categories.

U.S. Households With Cable Television, 1977-2007

Source: Nielsen Media Research

Year	Subscribers[1] (mil)	As % of house-holds with TVs	Year	Subscribers[1] (mil)	As % of house-holds with TVs	Year	Subscribers[1] (mil)	As % of house-holds with TVs
1977	12.2	16.6%	1988	46.3	52.0%	1998	65.9	67.2%
1978	13.4	17.9	1989	50.2	55.6	1999[2]	76.4	76.9
1979	14.9	19.4	1990	53.9	58.6	2000[2]	78.6	77.9
1980	17.7	22.6	1991	56.1	60.3	2001[2]	81.5	79.8
1981	23.2	28.3	1992	56.2	61.1	2002[2]	87.8	83.8
1982	27.4	33.4	1993	57.6	61.9	2003[2]	88.4	82.9
1983	31.8	37.9	1994	59.7	63.4	2004[2]	92.4	85.3
1984	35.8	42.5	1995	62.1	65.1	2005[2]	94.0	85.7
1985	38.7	45.3	1996	63.6	66.3	2006[2]	95.0	86.2
1986	40.9	47.4	1997	65.1	67.2	2007[2]	94.5	83.8
1987	43.3	49.2						

(1) Households that subscribe to basic cable service. (2) After 1998, figures include wired-cable households as well as households that receive TV programming via an alternate delivery systems (including satellite receivers, SMATV, MMDS).

Number of Cable TV Systems, 1975-2007

Source: *2005 Television and Cable Factbook*, Warren Communications News, Inc., Washington, DC; estimates as of Jan. 1

Year	Systems[1]	Year	Systems[1]	Year	Systems[1]	Year	Systems[1]	Year	Systems[1]	Year	Systems[1]
1975	3,506	1984	6,200	1989	9,050	1994	11,214	1999	10,700	2004	8,869*
1980	4,225	1985	6,600	1990	9,575	1995	11,218	2000	10,400	2005	8,409*
1981	4,375	1986	7,500	1991	10,704	1996	11,119	2001	9,924	2006	7,926*
1982	4,825	1987	7,900	1992	11,035	1997	10,950	2002	9,947	2007	7,090*
1983	5,600	1988	8,500	1993	11,108	1998	10,845	2003	9,339*		

(1) The satellite-signal-receiving hardware, cable lines, and cable boxes that provide cable programming to homes within a geographic area. *Figures as of March of the year noted.

Top Cable TV Networks, 2006
Source: Natl. Cable Television Assn., Dec. 2006; ranked by number of subscribers

1. Discovery Channel (1985)	92.5	12. TBS (Superstation) (1976)	91.7
2. ESPN (1979)	92.3	TLC (The Learning Channel) (1980)	91.7
CNN (Cable News Network) (1980)	92.3	Spike TV² (2003)	91.7
4. TNT (Turner Network Television) (1988)	92.1	15. CNN Headline News (1982)	91.5
Lifetime Television (LIFE) (1984)	92.1	16. ABC Family Channel (2001)	91.3
USA Network (1980)	92.1	MTV (1981)	91.3
7. Weather Channel (1982)	92.0	18. Home and Garden Television (HGTV) (1994)	91.2
8. Nickelodeon (1979)	91.9	19. Food Network (1993)	91.1
History Channel (1995)	91.9	Cartoon Network (1992)	91.1
10. ESPN2 (1993)	91.8		
A&E Networks (1984)	91.8		

Note: Data include noncable affiliates. (1) Date in parentheses is year service began. (2) Formerly The Nashville Network (1983-2000); The National Network (2000-2003); The New TNN (2003).

Average U.S. Television Viewing Time, May 2007
Source: Nielsen Media Research (hours: minutes per week)

Group	Age	Total per week	M-F 7-10 AM	M-F 10 AM-4:00 PM	M-Sun. 8-11 PM	Sat. 7 AM-1 PM	M-F 11:30 PM-1 AM	Sunday 1-7:00 PM
Men	18+	29:44	1:43	3:36	7:50	0:50	1:34	1:27
	18-24	21:40	0:56	2:51	4:57	0:32	1:26	0:58
	25-54	28:13	1:35	3:07	7:29	0:50	1:36	1:23
	55+	36:48	2:20	4:53	9:53	0:58	1:32	1:51
Women	18+	35:07	2:28	5:15	8:57	0:56	1:43	1:21
	18-24	26:53	1:31	4:16	6:12	0:41	1:34	1:04
	25-54	32:05	2:16	4:25	8:19	0:53	1:43	1:13
	55+	43:21	3:08	7:01	11:02	1:06	1:46	1:42
Children	2-11	21:40	1:51	3:11	4:45	1:07	0:40	0:58
Teens	12-17	21:20	0:50	1:35	5:39	0:46	1:08	1:02
ALL VIEWERS		30:04	1:57	4:01	7:39	0:54	1:27	1:18

TV Viewing Shares, Broadcast Years 1990-2006[1]
Source: Cable TV Facts, Cable Advertising Bureau, New York, NY

	All Television Households[2]						All Cable Households[2]						Pay Cable Households[2]					
	'90	'95	'00	'04	'05	'06	'90	'95	'00	'04	'05	'06	'90	'95	'00	'04	'05	'06
Network Affiliates[3]	55	48	44	37	30	29	46	41	40	33	27	26	43	38	37	30	24	23
Indep. TV Stations[4]	20	22	12	10	9	7	16	17	9	8	7	5	16	17	9	8	6	5
Public TV Stations	3	3	3	2	2	2	3	3	2	2	1	1	2	2	1	1	1	1
Basic Cable[5]	21	30	46	53	48	49	32	42	55	60	54	55	30	41	55	60	52	53
Pay Cable	6	6	6	6	5	4	10	8	7	5	5	4	18	15	11	13	10	9

(1) Broadcast years represent the 12-month period October-September. (2) Share figures refer to percentage of the viewing audience for all television viewing, 24 hours/day. As a result of multiset use and rounding, share figures add to more than 100. (3) Includes CBS, NBC, ABC, and FOX after 1998. (4) Includes WB, UPN, and PAX. (5) Includes ad-supported cable and all other cable (non-pay and non-ad-supported channels).

Selected Reality TV Show Winners
Numbers in parentheses represent the season/edition of the show.

Age of Love. Debuted June 2007 on NBC. Mark Philippoussis chose Amanda Salinas.

The Amazing Race. Debuted Aug. 2001 on CBS. (1) Rob Frisbee & Brennan Swain; (2) Chris Luca & Alex Boylan; (3) Flo Pesenti & Zach Behr; (4) Reichen Lehmkuhl & Chip Arndt; (5) Chip & Kim McAllister; (7) Freddy Holliday & Kendra Bentley; (7) Uchenna & Joyce Agu; (8) The Linz Family; (9) B.J. Averell & Tyler MacNiven; (10) Tyler Denk & James Branaman; (11-All-Stars) Eric Sanchez & Danielle Turner.

American Idol. Debuted July 2002 on Fox. (1) Kelly Clarkson; (2) Ruben Studdard; (3) Fantasia Barrino; (4) Carrie Underwood; (5) Taylor Hicks; (6) Jordin Sparks.

America's Got Talent. Debuted June 2006 on NBC. (1) Bianca Ryan; (2) Terry Fator.

America's Next Top Model. Debuted May 2003. (1) Adrianne Curry; (2) Yoanna House; (3) Eva Pigford; (4) Naima Mora; (5) Nicole Linkletter; (6) Danielle Evans; (7) CariDee English; (8) Jaslene Gonzalez.

The Apprentice. Debuted Jan. 2004 on NBC. (1) Bill Rancic; (2) Kelly Perdew; (3) Kendra Todd; (4) Randal Pinkett; (5) Sean Yazbeck; (6) Stefani Schaeffer.

The Bachelor. Debuted Mar. 2002 on ABC. (1) Alex Michel chose Amanda Marsh; (2) Aaron Buerge chose Helene Eksterowicz; (3) Andrew Firestone chose Jen Schefft; (4) Bob Guiney chose Estella Gardinier; (5) Jesse Palmer chose Jessica Bowlin; (6) Byron Velvick chose Mary Delgado; (7) Charlie O'Connell chose Sarah Brice; (8) Travis Stork chose Sarah Stone; (9) Lorenzo Borghese chose Jennifer Wilson; (10) Andy Baldwin chose Tessa Horst.

The Bachelorette. Debuted Jan. 2003 on ABC. (1) Trista Rehn chose Ryan Sutter; (2) Meredith Phillips chose Ian McKee; (3) Jen Schefft chose Jerry Ferris.

The Biggest Loser. Debuted October 2004 on NBC. (1) Ryan Benson; (2) Matt Hoover; (3) Erik Chopin.

Big Brother. Debuted July 2000 on CBS. (1) Eddie McGee; (2) Will Kirby; (3) Lisa Donahue; (4) Jun Song; (5) Drew Daniel; (6) Maggie Ausburn; (7) Mike Malinto; (8) Dick Donato.

The Contender. Debuted Mar. 2005 on NBC; 2nd season aired on ESPN. (1) Sergio Mora; (2) Grady Brewer.

Dancing With the Stars. Debuted June 2005 on ABC. (1) John O'Hurley & Charlotte Jorgensen; (2) Drew Lachey & Cheryl Burke; (3) Emmitt Smith & Cheryl Burke; (4) Apolo Anton Ohno & Julianne Hough.

Hell's Kitchen. Debuted Mar. 2005 on FOX. (1) Michael Wray; (2) Heather West; (3) Rock Harper.

Last Comic Standing. Debuted June 2003 on NBC. (1) Dat Phan; (2) John Heffron; (3) Alonzo Bodden; (4) Josh Blue; (5) Jon Reep.

Nashville Star. Debuted Mar. 2003 on USA Network. (1) Buddy Jewell; (2) Brad Cotter; (3) Erika Jo Heriges; (4) Chris Young; (5) Angela Hacker.

Project Runway. Debuted Dec. 2004 on Bravo. (1) Jay McCarroll; (2) Chloe Dao; (3) Jeffrey Sebelia.

Rock Star. Debuted July 2005 on CBS. INXS (1) J.D. Fortune; Supernova (2) Lukas Rossi.

So You Think You Can Dance. Debuted July 2005 on Bravo. (1) Nick Lazzarini; (2) Benji Schwimmer; (3) Sabra Johnson.

Survivor. Debuted May 2000 on CBS. Borneo (1), Richard Hatch; Outback (2), Tina Wesson; Africa (3), Ethan Zohn; Marquesas (4), Vecepia Towery; Thailand (5), Brian Heidik; The Amazon (6), Jenna Morasca; Pearl Islands (7), Sandra Diaz-Twine; All-Stars (Panama) (8), Amber Brkich; Vanuatu (9), Chris Daugherty; Palau (10), Tom Westman; Guatemala (11), Danni Boatwright; Panama (12), Aras Baskauskas; Cook Islands (13), Yul Kwon; Fiji (14), Earl Cole.

Top Chef. Debuted Mar. 2006 on Bravo. (1) Harold Dieterle; (2) Ilan Hall; (3) Hung Huynh.

U.S. Television Set Owners, 2006
Source: Nielsen Media Research; Aug. 2006

Of the 111.4 million U.S. households that owned at least one TV set in 2006:

82% had 2 or more TV sets   85% had a VCR   86% received basic cable
52% had 3 or more TV sets   84% had a DVD player   32% received premium cable

Favorite Prime-Time Television Programs, 2006-07
Source: Nielsen Media Research

Data are for regularly scheduled network programs in the 2006-07 season through May 23; ranked by average audience percentage. Average audience percentages, or ratings, are estimates of the percentage of all TV-owning households that are watching a particular program. Audience share percentages are estimates of the percentage of those watching TV that are tuned into a particular program. Tied programs are given the same rank.

Rank Program	Avg. audience	Audience share	Rank Program	Avg. audience	Audience share
1. American Idol-Wednesday	17.3	26	27. Law and Order: SVU	7.9	13
2. American Idol-Tuesday	16.8	26	28. Rules of Engagement	7.8	12
3. Dancing With the Stars	13.3	20	29. Extreme Makeover: Home Edition...	7.7	12
4. Dancing With the Stars-Monday	12.7	20	The OT	7.7	13
5. Dancing With the Stars-Results	12.6	20	31. 24	7.4	11
6. CSI	12.2	19	E.R.	7.4	12
7. Grey's Anatomy	12.1	18	Ugly Betty	7.4	12
8. Dancing With the Stars-Tuesday	11.8	18	34. Brothers and Sisters	7.3	12
9. House	11.0	17	King of Queens	7.3	11
10. Desperate Housewives	10.8	16	Are You Smarter than a Fifth Grader?	7.3	12
NBC Sunday Night Football	10.8	17	37. Sunday Night NFL Pre-Kick	7.2	12
12. CSI: Miami	10.7	18	38. Deal or No Deal-Friday	7.1	13
13. FOX NFL Sunday	9.5	17	39. The Bachelor: An Officer & a Gentleman	7.0	11
14. Without a Trace	9.4	16	40. Amazing Race	6.9	10
15. Deal or No Deal-Monday	9.2	14	41. October Road	6.8	12
16. Survivor: Cook Islands	9.1	14	The Unit	6.8	10
Two and a Half Men	9.1	13	43. Close to Home	6.7	12
18. NCIS	9.0	14	Deal or No Deal-Thursday	6.7	10
19. Cold Case	8.9	13	The New Adventures of Old Christine	6.7	10
CSI: NY	8.9	15	46. NUMB3RS	6.6	12
21. Criminal Minds	8.8	13	47. Deal or No Deal-Sunday	6.4	10
22. 60 Minutes	8.7	15	48. Deal or No Deal-Wednesday	6.3	9
Shark	8.7	15	49. Ghost Whisperer	6.2	11
24. Survivor: Fiji	8.4	14	50. Boston Legal	6.1	10
25. Lost	8.3	13			
26. Heroes	8.0	12			

Favorite Syndicated Programs, 2006-07
Source: Nielsen Media Research, Sept. 25, 2006-Aug. 19, 2007

Average audience percentages, or ratings, are estimates of the percentage of TV-owning households watching a program.

Rank Program	Avg. audience	Rank Program	Avg. audience
1. ESPN NFL Regular Season	8.7	12. Seinfeld (weekend)	3.4
2. Wheel of Fortune	7.8	16. Live with Regis and Kelly	3.2
3. ESPN NFL Regular Season	7.2	16. Who Wants to be a Millionaire	3.2
4. Jeopardy	6.2	18. King of Queens	3.2
5. Oprah Winfrey Show	5.8	19. That 70s Show	3.1
6. Entertainment Tonight	5.1	20. Everybody Loves Raymond (weekend)	2.9
7. Everybody Loves Raymond	4.9	21. Judge Joe Brown	2.9
8. Dr. Phil Show	4.6	22. King of Queens (weekend)	2.9
8. Judge Judy	4.6	23. Century	2.8
10. CSI Miami	4.5	24. Entertainment Tonight (weekend)	2.8
11. Seinfeld	4.3	25. People's Court	2.6
12. Friends	3.4	25. NFL Regular Season	2.6
12. Wheel of Fortune (weekend)	3.4	25. Access Hollywood	2.6
12. Inside Edition	3.4	25. Without a Trace	2.6

Highest-Rated TV Shows of Each Season, 1950-51 to 2006-07
Source: Nielsen Media Research; regular series programs, Sept.-May season

Season	Program	Rating[1]	TV-owning households (in thousands)	Season	Program	Rating[1]	TV-owning households (in thousands)
1950-51	Texaco Star Theatre	61.6	10,320	1961-62	Wagon Train	32.1	48,555
1951-52	Godfrey's Talent Scouts	53.8	15,300	1962-63	Beverly Hillbillies	36.0	50,300
1952-53	I Love Lucy	67.3	20,400	1963-64	Beverly Hillbillies	39.1	51,600
1953-54	I Love Lucy	58.8	26,000	1964-65	Bonanza	36.3	52,700
1954-55	I Love Lucy	49.3	30,700	1965-66	Bonanza	31.8	53,850
1955-56	$64,000 Question	47.5	34,900	1966-67	Bonanza	29.1	55,130
1956-57	I Love Lucy	43.7	38,900	1967-68	Andy Griffith	27.6	56,670
1957-58	Gunsmoke	43.1	41,920	1968-69	Rowan & Martin's Laugh-In	31.8	58,250
1958-59	Gunsmoke	39.6	43,950	1969-70	Rowan & Martin's Laugh-In	26.3	58,500
1959-60	Gunsmoke	40.3	45,750	1970-71	Marcus Welby, MD	29.6	60,100
1960-61	Gunsmoke	37.3	47,200	1971-72	All in the Family	34.0	62,100

Season	Program	Rating[1]	TV-owning households (in thousands)	Season	Program	Rating[1]	TV-owning households (in thousands)
1972-73	All in the Family	33.3	64,800	1990-91	Cheers	21.6	93,100
1973-74	All in the Family	31.2	66,200	1991-92	60 Minutes	21.7	92,100
1974-75	All in the Family	30.2	68,500	1992-93	60 Minutes	21.6	93,100
1975-76	All in the Family	30.1	69,600	1993-94	Home Improvement	21.9	94,200
1976-77	Happy Days	31.5	71,200	1994-95	Seinfeld	20.5	95,400
1977-78	Laverne & Shirley	31.6	72,900	1995-96	E.R.	22.0	95,900
1978-79	Laverne & Shirley	30.5	74,500	1996-97	E.R.	21.2	97,000
1979-80	60 Minutes	28.2	76,300	1997-98	Seinfeld	22.0	98,000
1980-81	Dallas	31.2	79,900	1998-99	E.R.	17.8	99,400
1981-82	Dallas	28.4	81,500	1999-			
1982-83	60 Minutes	25.5	83,300	2000	Who Wants to Be a Millionaire	18.6	100,800
1983-84	Dallas	25.7	83,800	2000-01	Survivor II	17.4	102,200
1984-85	Dynasty	25.0	84,900	2001-02	Friends	15.3	105,500
1985-86	Cosby Show	33.8	85,900	2002-03	CSI	16.1	106,700
1986-87	Cosby Show	34.9	87,400	2003-04	CSI	15.9	108,400
1987-88	Cosby Show	27.8	88,600	2004-05	CSI	16.3	106,900
1988-89	Roseanne	25.5	90,400	2005-06	American Idol-Tuesday	17.6	110,200
1989-90	Roseanne	23.4	92,100	2006-07	American Idol- Wednesday	17.3	112,800

(1) Rating is percent of TV-owning households tuned in to the program. Data prior to 1988-89 exclude Alaska and Hawaii.

All-Time Highest-Rated Television Programs
Source: Nielsen Media Research, Jan. 1961-May 2007

Estimates exclude unsponsored or joint network telecasts (e.g., presidential addresses) or programs under 30 minutes long. Ranked by rating (**percentage** of TV-owning households tuned in to the program).

Rank	Program	Telecast date	Network	Rating (%)	Avg. households (in thousands)
1.	M*A*S*H (last episode)	2/28/83	CBS	60.2	50,150
2.	Dallas (Who Shot J.R.?)	11/21/80	CBS	53.3	41,470
3.	Roots-Pt. 8	1/30/77	ABC	51.1	36,380
4.	Super Bowl XVI	1/24/82	CBS	49.1	40,020
5.	Super Bowl XVII	1/30/83	NBC	48.6	40,480
6.	XVII Winter Olympics (Women's figure skating)	2/23/94	CBS	48.5	45,690
7.	Super Bowl XX	1/26/86	NBC	48.3	41,490
8.	Gone With the Wind-Pt. 1	11/7/76	NBC	47.7	33,960
9.	Gone With the Wind-Pt. 2	11/8/76	NBC	47.4	33,750
10.	Super Bowl XII	1/15/78	CBS	47.2	34,410
11.	Super Bowl XIII	1/21/79	NBC	47.1	35,090
12.	Bob Hope Christmas Show	1/15/70	NBC	46.6	27,260
13.	Super Bowl XIX	1/20/85	ABC	46.4	39,390
	Super Bowl XVIII	1/22/84	CBS	46.4	38,800
15.	Super Bowl XIV	1/20/80	CBS	46.3	35,330
16.	Super Bowl XXX	1/28/96	NBC	46.0	44,150
	ABC Theater (The Day After)	11/20/83	ABC	46.0	38,550
18.	Roots-Pt. 6	1/28/77	ABC	45.9	32,680
	The Fugitive	8/29/67	ABC	45.9	25,700
20.	Super Bowl XXI	1/25/87	CBS	45.8	40,030
21.	Roots-Pt. 5	1/27/77	ABC	45.7	32,540
22.	Super Bowl XXVIII	1/30/94	NBC	45.5	42,860
	Cheers (last episode)	5/20/93	NBC	45.5	42,360
24.	Ed Sullivan	2/9/64	CBS	45.3	23,240
25.	Super Bowl XXVII	1/31/93	NBC	45.1	41,990

All-Time Most Watched Television Programs
Source: Nielsen Media Research, Jan. 1961-May 2007

Estimates exclude unsponsored or joint network telecasts (e.g., presidential addresses) or programs under 30 minutes long. Ranked by **number** of TV-owning households tuned in to the program.

Rank	Program	Telecast date	Network	Rating (%)	Avg. households (in thousands)
1.	M*A*S*H (last episode)	2/28/83	CBS	60.2	50,150
2.	Super Bowl XLI	2/4/07	CBS	42.7	47,535
3.	Super Bowl XL	2/5/06	ABC	41.6	45,869
4.	XVII Winter Olympics (Women's figure skating)	2/23/94	CBS	48.5	45,690
5.	Super Bowl XXXIX	2/6/05	FOX	41.1	45,080
6.	Super Bowl XXXVIII	2/1/04	CBS	41.4	44,910
7.	Super Bowl XXX	1/28/96	NBC	46.0	44,150
8.	Super Bowl XXXII	1/25/98	NBC	44.5	43,630
9.	Super Bowl XXXIV	1/30/00	ABC	43.3	43,620
10.	Super Bowl XXXVII	1/26/03	ABC	40.7	43,430
11.	Super Bowl XXVIII	1/30/94	NBC	45.5	42,860
12.	Super Bowl XXXVI	2/3/02	FOX	40.4	42,660
13.	Cheers	5/20/93	NBC	45.5	42,360
14.	Super Bowl XXXI	1/26/97	FOX	43.3	42,000
15.	Super Bowl XXVII	1/31/93	NBC	45.1	41,990
16.	XVII Winter Olympics (Women's figure skating)	2/25/94	CBS	44.1	41,540
17.	Super Bowl XX	1/26/86	NBC	48.3	41,490
18.	Dallas	11/21/80	CBS	53.3	41,470
19.	Super Bowl XXXV	1/28/01	CBS	40.4	41,270
20.	Seinfeld	5/14/98	NBC	41.3	40,510

100 Leading U.S. Advertisers, 2006

Source: Reprinted with permission from Ad Age (www.adage.com). © 2007, Crain Communications Inc.

(in millions of dollars)

Rank	Advertiser	Ad Spending
1.	Procter & Gamble Co.	$4,898
2.	AT&T	3,345
3.	General Motors Corp.	3,296
4.	Time Warner	3,089
5.	Verizon Communications	2,822
6.	Ford Motor Co.	2,577
7.	GlaxoSmithKline.	2,444
8.	Walt Disney Co.	2,320
9.	Johnson & Johnson	2,291
10.	Unilever	2,098
11.	Toyota Motor Corp.	1,995
12.	Sony Corp.	1,994
13.	DaimlerChrysler	1,952
14.	General Electric Co.	1,860
15.	Sprint Nextel Corp.	1,775
16.	McDonald's Corp.	1,748
17.	Sears Holdings Corp.	1,653
18.	L'Oreal	1,456
19.	Kraft Foods.	1,423
20.	Macy's	1,361
21.	Honda Motor Co.	1,351
22.	Bank of America Corp.	1,334
23.	Nissan Motor Co.	1,329
24.	PepsiCo	1,323
25.	Nestle	1,315
26.	News Corp.	1,245
27.	J.C. Penney Co.	1,162
28.	Target Corp.	1,157
29.	U.S. Government	1,133
30.	Home Depot	1,118
31.	Pfizer	1,105
32.	Berkshire Hathaway	1,093
33.	Wyeth	1,077
34.	Wal-Mart Stores	1,073
35.	JPMorgan Chase & Co.	1,063
36.	Novartis	1,052
37.	Estee Lauder Cos.	1,031
38.	Merck & Co.	1,024
39.	Citigroup	1,012
40.	AstraZeneca	1,005
41.	Viacom.	934
42.	Schering-Plough Corp.	932
43.	American Express Co.	929
44.	General Mills	921
45.	Microsoft Corp.	912
46.	Yum Brands.	902
47.	Dell	883
48.	Best Buy Co.	879
49.	Capital One Financial Corp.	864
50.	Lowe's Cos.	839
51.	Hewlett-Packard Co.	829
52.	Deutsche Telekom.	815
53.	Anheuser-Busch Cos.	813
54.	Hyundai Motor Co.	786
55.	Kohl's Corp.	766
56.	Kellogg Co.	765
57.	IAC/InterActiveCorp	744
58.	Coca-Cola Co.	741
59.	Bristol-Myers Squibb Co.	691
60.	Nike	678
61.	Mars Inc.	658
62.	Cadbury Schweppes	644
63.	Limited Brands.	601
64.	Visa International.	597
65.	SC Johnson	597
66.	Clorox Co.	584
67.	Comcast Corp.	569
68.	Campbell Soup Co.	564
69.	Eli Lilly & Co.	561
70.	Bayer.	554
71.	Doctor's Associates.	540
72.	Safeway	534
73.	Kroger Co.	528
74.	IBM Corp.	517
75.	Circuit City Stores	498
76.	Gap Inc.	489
77.	MasterCard International.	486
78.	Allstate Corp.	477
79.	Vonage Holdings Corp.	465
80.	Sanofi-Aventis.	463
81.	Staples	457
82.	Wells Fargo & Co.	456
83.	eBay	453
84.	Washington Mutual.	443
85.	Wendy's International	435
86.	Volkswagen.	419
87.	Diageo.	419
88.	Mattel	394
89.	Apple.	384
90.	Burger King Holdings	380
91.	Abbott Laboratories.	374
92.	SABMiller	371
93.	Molson Coors Brewing Co.	370
94.	CBS Corp.	369
95.	Reckitt Benckiser	367
96.	ConAgra Foods.	366
97.	Qwest Communications International	362
98.	Philips Electronics	351
99.	Office Depot	343
100.	State Farm Mutual Auto Insurance Co.	338

U.S. Ad Spending Categories, 2006

Source: Reprinted with permission from Ad Age (www.adage.com). © 2007, Crain Communications Inc.

(in millions of dollars)

Category	Total	Mag.	Bus. Pub.	News-paper	Out door	Television Net-work	Spot	Cable	Spanish Lang.	Syndi-cated	Radio	Inter-net
Automotive	19,799	2,089	86	5,025	344	2,956	5,217	1,348	301	164	1,544	727
Retail	19,114	1,993	105	6,763	387	2,096	2,668	1,040	330	326	2,148	1,258
Telecommunications, internet services	10,950	682	217	2,173	278	2,093	1,355	1,270	305	309	775	1,495
Medicine & remedies	9,193	2,730	56	280	23	2,799	353	1,382	136	752	304	379
General services	8,702	698	335	2,271	584	215	1,960	454	13	114	1,320	738
Financial services	8,689	928	261	1,891	245	1,445	573	932	63	144	725	1,482
Food, beverages & candy	7,225	1,892	105	50	77	1,939	476	1,451	258	517	326	134
Personal care	5,732	2,348	40	29	14	1,534	141	797	172	499	54	106
Airlines, hotels, car rental, travel	5,416	1,234	251	1,413	332	422	398	515	27	29	343	452
Movies, recorded video & music	5,380	239	78	1,028	92	1,510	486	1,047	257	194	259	190
Restaurants	5,292	133	2	184	240	1,542	1,418	811	151	228	534	49
Media	5,051	1,527	217	1,269	247	42	198	67	10	16	741	716
Government, politics, religion	3,511	343	44	530	149	180	1,322	239	42	42	465	156
Insurance	3,446	220	57	386	113	613	639	635	54	194	384	151
Real estate	3,132	363	18	1,894	258	88	125	77	14	25	138	132
Apparel	2,912	2,105	81	60	29	271	23	223	17	42	21	39
Computers, software	2,510	451	715	226	49	335	44	168	0	3	63	456
Home furnishings, appliances & electronics	2,214	882	187	114	17	374	101	308	17	61	69	85
Beer, wine & liquor	2,100	505	15	54	164	491	115	341	105	23	226	61
Education	1,942	153	229	342	75	2	505	167	9	29	158	274
Home supplies & cleaners	1,938	358	10	6	3	614	106	526	102	157	28	30
Toys & games	1,253	97	83	8	3	221	10	608	12	44	8	160
Hardware & home building supplies	1,028	368	152	104	9	78	79	169	4	8	32	26
Sporting goods	562	374	2	28	5	72	7	48	7	0	6	14
Gas & oil	524	104	8	70	35	102	39	74	1	6	73	12
Pet food & pet care	490	150	2	3	0	142	31	98	0	37	7	21
Office equipment	334	102	43	25	2	66	3	36	0	24	21	10
Shipping & freight	327	33	33	14	3	143	3	42	0	1	43	11
Cigarettes & tobacco	156	105	5	2	1	19	2	6	6	5	1	6
Direct response advertising	6,462	2,347	139	494	2	258	187	2,121	494	216	70	135
Miscellaneous	4,306	952	944	1,285	54	217	106	275	6	27	172	267
Total	149,689	26,507	4,518	28,021	3,831	22,879	18,688	17,274	2,911	4,235	11,055	9,770

AWARDS — MEDALS — PRIZES

The Alfred B. Nobel Prize Winners, 1901-2006

Alfred B. Nobel (1833-96) bequeathed $9 mil, the interest on which was to be distributed yearly to those judged to have most benefited humankind in physics, chemistry, medicine-physiology, literature, and promotion of peace. Prizes were first awarded in 1901. The 1st prize in economics was awarded in 1969, funded by Sweden's central bank. Each prize is now worth 10 mil Swedish kroner (about $1.5 mil). If year is omitted, no award was given. For 2007 winners, see page 36.

Physics

1901 Wilhelm C. Röntgen, Ger.
1902 Hendrik A. Lorentz,
 Pieter Zeeman, Neth.
1903 Antoine Henri Becquerel, Pierre Curie,
 Fr.; Marie Curie, Pol.-Fr.
1904 Lord Rayleigh (John W. Strutt), UK
1905 Philipp E. A. von Lenard, Ger.
1906 Sir Joseph J. Thomson, UK
1907 Albert A. Michelson, U.S.
1908 Gabriel Lippmann, Fr.
1909 Carl F. Braun, Ger.;
 Guglielmo Marconi, It.
1910 Johannes D. van der Waals, Neth.
1911 Wilhelm Wien, Ger.
1912 Nils G. Dalén, Swed.
1913 Heike Kamerlingh Onnes, Neth.
1914 Max von Laue, Ger.
1915 Sir William H. Bragg,
 Sir William L. Bragg, UK
1917 Charles G. Barkla, UK
1918 Max K. E. L. Planck, Ger.
1919 Johannes Stark, Ger.
1920 Charles E. Guillaume, Fr.-Switz.
1921 Albert Einstein, Ger.-U.S.
1922 Niels Bohr, Den.
1923 Robert A. Millikan, U.S.
1924 Karl M. G. Siegbahn, Swed.
1925 James Franck, Gustav Hertz, Ger.
1926 Jean B. Perrin, Fr.
1927 Arthur H. Compton, U.S.;
 Charles T. R. Wilson, UK
1928 Owen W. Richardson, UK
1929 Prince Louis-Victor de Broglie, Fr.
1930 Sir Chandrasekhara V. Raman, India
1932 Werner Heisenberg, Ger.
1933 Paul A. M. Dirac, UK;
 Erwin Schrödinger, Austria
1935 Sir James Chadwick, UK
1936 Carl D. Anderson, U.S.;
 Victor F. Hess, Austria
1937 Clinton J. Davisson, U.S.;
 Sir George P. Thomson, UK
1938 Enrico Fermi, It.-U.S.
1939 Ernest O. Lawrence, U.S.
1943 Otto Stern, U.S.
1944 Isidor Isaac Rabi, U.S.
1945 Wolfgang Pauli, U.S.-Austria
1946 Percy W. Bridgman, U.S.
1947 Sir Edward V. Appleton, UK
1948 Patrick M. S. Blackett, UK
1949 Hideki Yukawa, Jpn.

1950 Cecil F. Powell, UK
1951 Sir John D. Cockcroft, UK;
 Ernest T. S. Walton, Ire.
1952 Felix Bloch, Edward M. Purcell, U.S.
1953 Frits Zernike, Neth.
1954 Max Born, UK; Walter Bothe, Ger.
1955 Polykarp Kusch, Willis E. Lamb, U.S.
1956 John Bardeen, Walter H. Brattain,
 William Shockley, U.S.
1957 Tsung-dao Lee, Chen Ning Yang,
 U.S.-China
1958 Pavel Cherenkov, Il'ja Frank,
 Igor Y. Tamm, USSR
1959 Owen Chamberlain,
 Emilio G. Segre, U.S.
1960 Donald A. Glaser, U.S.
1961 Robert Hofstadter, U.S.;
 Rudolf L. Mossbauer, Ger.
1962 Lev D. Landau, USSR
1963 Maria Goeppert-Mayer, Eugene P.
 Wigner, U.S.; J. Hans D. Jensen, Ger.
1964 Nicolay G. Basov,
 Aleksandr M. Prokhorov, USSR;
 Charles H. Townes, U.S.
1965 Richard P. Feynman,
 Julian S. Schwinger, U.S.;
 Sin-Itiro Tomonaga, Jpn.
1966 Alfred Kastler, Fr.
1967 Hans A. Bethe, U.S.
1968 Luis W. Alvarez, U.S.
1969 Murray Gell-Mann, U.S.
1970 Louis Néel, Fr.; Hannes Alfvén, Swed.
1971 Dennis Gabor, UK
1972 John Bardeen, Leon N. Cooper,
 John R. Schrieffer, U.S.
1973 Ivar Giaever, U.S.; Leo Esaki, Jpn.;
 Brian D. Josephson, UK
1974 Sir Martin Ryle, Antony Hewish, UK
1975 Leo James Rainwater, U.S.;
 Ben Mottelson, U.S.-Den.;
 Aage Bohr, Den.
1976 Burton Richter,
 Samuel C.C. Ting, U.S.
1977 John H. van Vleck, Philip W.
 Anderson, U.S.; Sir Nevill F. Mott, UK
1978 Pyotr Kapitsa, USSR; Arno Penzias,
 Robert Wilson, U.S.
1979 Steven Weinberg,
 Sheldon L. Glashow, U.S.;
 Abdus Salam, Pakistan
1980 James W. Cronin, Val L. Fitch, U.S.

1981 Nicolaas Bloembergen,
 Arthur Schawlow, U.S.;
 Kai M. Siegbahn, Swed.
1982 Kenneth G. Wilson, U.S.
1983 Subramanyan Chandrasekhar,
 William A. Fowler, U.S.
1984 Carlo Rubbia, It.; Simon van der Meer,
 Neth.
1985 Klaus von Klitzing, Ger.
1986 Ernest Ruska, Ger.; Gerd Binnig, Ger.;
 Heinrich Rohrer, Switz.
1987 K. Alex Müller, Switz.;
 J. Georg Bednorz, Ger.
1988 Leon M. Lederman, Melvin Schwartz,
 Jack Steinberger, U.S.
1989 Norman F. Ramsey, U.S.;
 Hans G. Dehmelt, Ger.-U.S.;
 Wolfgang Paul, Ger.
1990 Richard E. Taylor, Can.; Jerome I.
 Friedman, Henry W. Kendall, U.S.
1991 Pierre-Gilles de Gennes, Fr.
1992 Georges Charpak, Pol.-Fr.
1993 Joseph H. Taylor,
 Russell A. Hulse, U.S.
1994 Bertram N. Brockhouse, Can.;
 Clifford G. Shull, U.S.
1995 Martin Perl, Frederick Reines, U.S.
1996 David M. Lee, Douglas D. Osheroff,
 Robert C. Richardson, U.S.
1997 Steven Chu, William D. Phillips, U.S.;
 Claude Cohen-Tannoudji, Fr.
1998 Robert B. Laughlin, U.S.;
 Horst L. Störmer, Ger.-U.S;
 Daniel C. Tsui, China-U.S.
1999 Gerardus't Hooft and Martinus J. G.
 Veltman, Netherlands
2000 Jack S. Kilby, U.S.; Herbert Kroemer,
 Ger.-U.S.; Zhores I. Alferov, Russ.
2001 Eric A. Cornell, Carl E. Wieman, U.S.;
 Wolfgang Ketterle, Ger.
2002 Raymond Davis Jr.,
 Riccardo Giacconi, U.S.;
 Masatoshi Koshiba, Jpn.
2003 Vitaly L. Ginzburg,
 Alexei A. Abrikosov, Russ.,
 Anthony J. Leggett, UK
2004 David J. Gross, H. David Politzer,
 Frank Wilczek, U.S.
2005 Roy J. Glauber, John L. Hall, U.S.;
 Theodor W. Hänsch, Ger.
2006 John C. Mather,
 George F. Smoot, U.S.

Chemistry

1901 Jacobus H. van't Hoff, Neth.
1902 Emil Fischer, Ger.
1903 Svante A. Arrhenius, Swed.
1904 Sir William Ramsay, UK
1905 Adolf von Baeyer, Ger.
1906 Henri Moissan, Fr.
1907 Eduard Buchner, Ger.
1908 Ernest Rutherford, UK
1909 Wilhelm Ostwald, Ger.
1910 Otto Wallach, Ger.
1911 Marie Curie, Pol.-Fr.
1912 Victor Grignard, Paul Sabatier, Fr.
1913 Alfred Werner, Switz.
1914 Theodore W. Richards, U.S.
1915 Richard M. Willstätter, Ger.
1918 Fritz Haber, Ger.
1920 Walther H. Nernst, Ger.
1921 Frederick Soddy, UK
1922 Francis W. Aston, UK
1923 Fritz Pregl, Austria
1925 Richard A. Zsigmondy, Ger.
1926 Theodor Svedberg, Swed.
1927 Heinrich O. Wieland, Ger.
1928 Adolf O. R. Windaus, Ger.

1929 Sir Arthur Harden, UK;
 Hans von Euler-Chelpin, Swed.
1930 Hans Fischer, Ger.
1931 Friedrich Bergius, Carl Bosch, Ger.
1932 Irving Langmuir, U.S.
1934 Harold C. Urey, U.S.
1935 Frédéric & Irène Joliot-Curie, Fr.
1936 Peter J. W. Debye, Neth.
1937 Walter N. Haworth, UK;
 Paul Karrer, Switz.
1938 Richard Kuhn, Ger.
1939 Adolf F. J. Butenandt, Ger.;
 Leopold Ruzicka, Switz.
1943 George de Hevesy, Hung.
1944 Otto Hahn, Ger.
1945 Artturi I. Virtanen, Fin.
1946 James B. Sumner, John H. Northrop,
 Wendell M. Stanley, U.S.
1947 Sir Robert Robinson, UK
1948 Arne W. K. Tiselius, Swed.
1949 William F. Giauque, U.S.
1950 Kurt Alder, Otto P. H. Diels, Ger.
1951 Edwin M. McMillan,
 Glenn T. Seaborg, U.S.

1952 Archer J. P. Martin,
 Richard L. M. Synge, UK
1953 Hermann Staudinger, Ger.
1954 Linus C. Pauling, U.S.
1955 Vincent du Vigneaud, U.S.
1956 Sir Cyril N. Hinshelwood, UK;
 Nikolay N. Semenov, USSR
1957 Lord (Alexander R.) Todd, UK
1958 Frederick Sanger, UK
1959 Jaroslav Heyrovsky, Czech.
1960 Willard F. Libby, U.S.
1961 Melvin Calvin, U.S.
1962 John C. Kendrew, Max F. Perutz, UK
1963 Giulio Natta, It.; Karl Ziegler, Ger.
1964 Dorothy C. Hodgkin, UK
1965 Robert B. Woodward, U.S.
1966 Robert S. Mulliken, U.S.
1967 Manfred Eigen, Ger.; Ronald G. W.
 Norrish, George Porter, UK
1968 Lars Onsager, U.S.
1969 Derek H. R. Barton, UK;
 Odd Hassel, Nor.
1970 Luis F. Leloir, Arg.
1971 Gerhard Herzberg, Can.

1972 Christian B. Anfinsen, Stanford Moore, William H. Stein, U.S.
1973 Ernst Otto Fischer, Ger.; Geoffrey Wilkinson, UK
1974 Paul J. Flory, U.S.
1975 John Cornforth, Austral.-UK; Vladimir Prelog, Bosnia-Switz.
1976 William N. Lipscomb, U.S.
1977 Ilya Prigogine, Belg.
1978 Peter Mitchell, UK
1979 Herbert C. Brown, U.S.; Georg Wittig, Ger.
1980 Paul Berg, Walter Gilbert, U.S.; Frederick Sanger, UK
1981 Kenichi Fukui, Jpn.; Roald Hoffmann, U.S.
1982 Aaron Klug, UK-Lith.
1983 Henry Taube, Can.
1984 Robert Bruce Merrifield, U.S.
1985 Herbert A. Hauptman, Jerome Karle, U.S.

1986 Dudley Herschbach, Yuan T. Lee, U.S.; John C. Polanyi, Can.
1987 Donald J. Cram, Charles J. Pedersen, U.S.; Jean-Marie Lehn, Fr.
1988 Johann Deisenhofer, Robert Huber, Hartmut Michel, Ger.
1989 Thomas R. Cech, Sidney Altman, U.S.
1990 Elias James Corey, U.S.
1991 Richard R. Ernst, Switz.
1992 Rudolph A. Marcus, Can.-U.S.
1993 Kary B. Mullis, U.S.; Michael Smith, UK-Can.
1994 George A. Olah, U.S.
1995 Paul Crutzen, Neth.; Mario Molina, Mex.-U.S.; Sherwood Rowland, U.S.
1996 Sir Harold W. Kroto; Robert F. Curl Jr., Richard E. Smalley, U.S.
1997 Paul D. Boyer, U.S., & John E. Walker, UK; Jens C. Skou, Den.

1998 Walter Kohn, U.S.; John A. Pople, UK
1999 Ahmed H. Zewail, U.S.
2000 Alan J. Heeger, U.S.; Alan G. MacDiarmid, N. Zea.-U.S.; Hideki Shirakawa, Jpn.
2001 K. Barry Sharpless, U.S.; William S. Knowles, U.S., Ryoji Noyori, Jpn.
2002 John B. Fenn, U.S.; Koichi Tanaka, Jpn.; Kurt Wüthrich, Switz.
2003 Peter Agre, Roderick MacKinnon, U.S.
2004 Aaron Ciechanover, Avram Hershko, Isr.; Irwin Rose, U.S.
2005 Yves Chauvin, Fr.; Robert H. Grubbs, Richard R. Schrock, U.S.
2006 Roger D. Kornberg, U.S.

Physiology or Medicine

1901 Emil A. von Behring, Ger.
1902 Sir Ronald Ross, UK
1903 Niels R. Finsen, Den.
1904 Ivan P. Pavlov, Russ.
1905 Robert Koch, Ger.
1906 Camillo Golgi, It.; Santiago Ramon y Cajal, Spain
1907 Charles L. A. Laveran, Fr.
1908 Paul Ehrlich, Ger.; Ilya Mechnikov, Fr.
1909 Emil T. Kocher, Switz.
1910 Albrecht Kossel, Ger.
1911 Allvar Gullstrand, Swed.
1912 Alexis Carrel, Fr.
1913 Charles R. Richet, Fr.
1914 Robert Bárány, Austria
1919 Jules Bordet, Belg.
1920 Schack A. S. Krogh, Den.
1922 Archibald V. Hill, UK; Otto F. Meyerhof, Ger.
1923 Frederick G. Banting, Can.; John J. R. Macleod, Scot.
1924 Willem Einthoven, Neth.
1926 Johannes A. G. Fibiger, Den.
1927 Julius Wagner-Jauregg, Austrian
1928 Charles J. H. Nicolle, Fr.
1929 Christiaan Eijkman, Neth.; Sir Frederick G. Hopkins, UK
1930 Karl Landsteiner, U.S.
1931 Otto H. Warburg, Ger.
1932 Edgar D. Adrian, Sir Charles S. Sherrington, UK
1933 Thomas H. Morgan, U.S.
1934 George R. Minot, William P. Murphy, G. H. Whipple, U.S.
1935 Hans Spemann, Ger.
1936 Sir Henry H. Dale, UK; Otto Loewi, U.S.
1937 Albert Szent-Gyorgyi, Hung.-U.S.
1938 Corneille J. F. Heymans, Belg.
1939 Gerhard Domagk, Ger.
1943 Henrik C. P. Dam, Den.; Edward A. Doisy, U.S.
1944 Joseph Erlanger, Herbert S. Gasser, U.S.
1945 Ernst B. Chain, Sir Alexander Fleming, Sir Howard W. Florey, UK
1946 Hermann J. Muller, U.S.
1947 Carl F. Cori, Gerty T. Cori, U.S.; Bernardo A. Houssay, Arg.
1948 Paul H. Müller, Switz.
1949 Walter R. Hess, Switz.; Antonio Moniz, Port.
1950 Philip S. Hench, Edward C. Kendall, U.S.; Tadeus Reichstein, Switz.

1951 Max Theiler, U.S.
1952 Selman A. Waksman, U.S.
1953 Hans A. Krebs, UK; Fritz A. Lipmann, U.S.
1954 John F. Enders, Frederick C. Robbins, Thomas H. Weller, U.S.
1955 Alex H. T. Theorell, Swed.
1956 André F. Cournand, Dickinson W. Richards, U.S.; Werner Forssmann, Ger.
1957 Daniel Bovet, It.
1958 George W. Beadle, Edward L. Tatum, Joshua Lederberg, U.S.
1959 Arthur Kornberg, Severo Ochoa, U.S.
1960 Sir F. MacFarlane Burnet, Austral.; Peter B. Medawar, UK
1961 Georg von Békésy, U.S.
1962 Francis H. C. Crick, Maurice H. F. Wilkins, UK; James D. Watson, U.S.
1963 Sir John C. Eccles, Austral.; Alan L. Hodgkin, Andrew F. Huxley, UK
1964 Konrad E. Bloch, U.S.; Feodor Lynen, Ger.
1965 François Jacob, André Lwoff, Jacques Monod, Fr.
1966 Charles B. Huggins, Peyton Rous, U.S.
1967 Ragnar Granit, Swed.; Haldan Keffer Hartline, George Wald, U.S.
1968 Robert W. Holley, H. Gobind Khorana, Marshall W. Nirenberg, U.S.
1969 Max Delbrück, Alfred D. Hershey, Salvador Luria, U.S.
1970 Julius Axelrod, U.S.; Sir Bernard Katz, UK; Ulf von Euler, Swed.
1971 Earl W. Sutherland Jr., U.S.
1972 Gerald M. Edelman, U.S.; Rodney R. Porter, UK
1973 Karl von Frisch, Ger.; Konrad Lorenz, Austria; Nikolaas Tinbergen, UK
1974 Albert Claude, Lux.-U.S.; George Emil Palade, Rom.-U.S.; Christian de Duve, Belg.
1975 David Baltimore, Howard Temin, U.S.; Renato Dulbecco, It.-U.S.
1976 Baruch S. Blumberg, Daniel Carleton Gajdusek, U.S.
1977 Rosalyn S. Yalow, Roger C.L. Guillemin, Andrew V. Schally, U.S.

1978 Daniel Nathans, Hamilton O. Smith, U.S.; Werner Arber, Switz.
1979 Allan M. Cormack, U.S.; Godfrey N. Hounsfield, UK
1980 Baruj Benacerraf, George Snell, U.S.; Jean Dausset, Fr.
1981 Roger W. Sperry, David H. Hubel, Torsten N. Wiesel, U.S.
1982 Sune Bergström, Bengt Samuelsson, Swed.; John R. Vane, UK
1983 Barbara McClintock, U.S.
1984 César Milstein, UK-Arg.; Georges J. F. Köhler, Ger.; Niels K. Jerne, UK-Den.
1985 Michael S. Brown, Joseph L. Goldstein, U.S.
1986 Rita Levi-Montalcini, It.-U.S.; Stanley Cohen, U.S.
1987 Susumu Tonegawa, Jpn.
1988 Gertrude B. Elion, George H. Hitchings, U.S; Sir James Black, UK
1989 J. Michael Bishop, Harold E. Varmus, U.S.
1990 Joseph E. Murray, E. Donnall Thomas, U.S.
1991 Edwin Neher, Bert Sakmann, Ger.
1992 Edmond H. Fisher, Edwin G. Krebs, U.S.
1993 Phillip A. Sharp, U.S.; Richard J. Roberts, UK
1994 Alfred G. Gilman, Martin Rodbell, U.S.
1995 Edward B. Lewis, Eric F. Wieschaus, U.S.; Christiane Nüsslein-Volhard, Ger.
1996 Peter C. Doherty, Austral.; Rolf M. Zinkernagel, Switz.
1997 Stanley B. Prusiner, U.S.
1998 Robert F. Furchgott, Louis J. Ignarro, Ferid Murad, U.S.
1999 Günter Blobel, U.S.
2000 Arvid Carlsson, Swed.; Paul Greengard, U.S.; Eric R. Kandel, Austria-U.S.
2001 Leland H. Hartwell, U.S.; R. Timothy (Tim) Hunt, Sir Paul M. Nurse, UK
2002 Sydney Brenner, John E. Sulston, UK; H. Robert Horvitz, U.S.
2003 Paul C. Lauterbur, U.S.; Sir Peter Mansfield, UK
2004 Richard Axel, Linda B. Buck, U.S.
2005 Barry J. Marshall, J. Robin Warren, Australia
2006 Andrew Z. Fire, Craig C. Mello, U.S.

Literature

1901 Rene F. A. Sully Prudhomme, Fr.
1902 Theodor Mommsen, Ger.
1903 Bjørnstjerne Bjørnson, Nor.
1904 Fréderic Mistral, Fr.; José Echegaray y Eizaguirre, Spain
1905 Henryk Sienkiewicz, Pol.
1906 Giosuè Carducci, It.

1907 Rudyard Kipling, UK
1908 Rudolf C. Eucken, Ger.
1909 Selma Lagerlöf, Swed.
1910 Paul J. L. Heyse, Ger.
1911 Maurice Maeterlinck, Belg.
1912 Gerhart Hauptmann, Ger.
1913 Rabindranath Tagore, India

1915 Romain Rolland, Fr.
1916 Verner von Heidenstam, Swed.
1917 Karl A. Gjellerup, Henrik Pontoppidan, Den.
1919 Carl F. G. Spitteler, Switz.
1920 Knut Hamsun, Nor.
1921 Anatole France, Fr.

1922 Jacinto Benavente, Spain	1955 Halldór K. Laxness, Ice.	1980 Czeslaw Milosz, Pol.-U.S.
1923 William Butler Yeats, Ire.	1956 Juan Ramón Jiménez, Spain	1981 Elias Canetti, Bulg.-UK
1924 Wladyslaw S. Reymont, Pol.	1957 Albert Camus, Fr.	1982 Gabriel García Márquez,
1925 George Bernard Shaw, Ire.-UK	1958 Boris L. Pasternak, USSR (declined)	Colombia-Mex.
1926 Grazia Deledda, It.	1959 Salvatore Quasimodo, It.	1983 William Golding, UK
1927 Henri Bergson, Fr.	1960 Saint-John Perse, Fr.	1984 Jaroslav Siefert, Czech.
1928 Sigrid Undset, Nor.	1961 Ivo Andric, Yugo.	1985 Claude Simon, Fr.
1929 Thomas Mann, Ger.	1962 John Steinbeck, U.S.	1986 Wole Soyinka, Nigeria
1930 Sinclair Lewis, U.S.	1963 Giorgos Seferis, Greece	1987 Joseph Brodsky, USSR-U.S.
1931 Erik A. Karlfeldt, Swed.	1964 Jean-Paul Sartre, Fr. (declined)	1988 Naguib Mahfouz, Egypt
1932 John Galsworthy, UK	1965 Mikhail Sholokhov, USSR	1989 Camilo José Cela, Spain
1933 Ivan A. Bunin, USSR	1966 Shmuel Yosef Agnon, Isr.;	1990 Octavio Paz, Mex.
1934 Luigi Pirandello, It.	Nelly Sachs, Swed.	1991 Nadine Gordimer, S. Afr.
1936 Eugene O'Neill, U.S.	1967 Miguel Angel Asturias, Guat.	1992 Derek Walcott, W. Ind.
1937 Roger Martin du Gard, Fr.	1968 Yasunari Kawabata, Jpn.	1993 Toni Morrison, U.S.
1938 Pearl S. Buck, U.S.	1969 Samuel Beckett, Ire.	1994 Kenzaburo Oe, Jpn.
1939 Frans E. Sillanpää, Fin.	1970 Aleksandr I. Solzhenitsyn, USSR	1995 Seamus Heaney, Ire.
1944 Johannes V. Jensen, Den.	1971 Pablo Neruda, Chile	1996 Wislawa Szymborska, Pol.
1945 Gabriela Mistral, Chile	1972 Heinrich Böll, Ger.	1997 Dario Fo, It.
1946 Hermann Hesse, Ger.-Switz.	1973 Patrick White, Austral.	1998 Jose Saramago, Por.
1947 André Gide, Fr.	1974 Eyvind Johnson, Harry Edmund	1999 Günter Grass, Ger.
1948 T.S. Eliot, UK	Martinson, Swed.	2000 Gao Xingjian, China-Fr.
1949 William Faulkner, U.S.	1975 Eugenio Montale, It.	2001 Sir V.S. Naipaul, UK
1950 Bertrand Russell, UK	1976 Saul Bellow, U.S.	2002 Imre Kertész, Hung.
1951 Pär F. Lagerkvist, Swed.	1977 Vicente Aleixandre, Spain	2003 J.M. Coetzee, S. Afr.
1952 François Mauriac, Fr.	1978 Isaac Bashevis Singer, U.S.	2004 Elfriede Jelinek, Austria
1953 Sir Winston Churchill, UK	1979 Odysseus Elytis, Greece	2005 Harold Pinter, UK
1954 Ernest Hemingway, U.S.		2006 Orhan Pamuk, Turk.

Peace

1901 Jean H. Dunant, Switz.;	1936 Carlos Saavedra Lamas, Arg.	1980 Adolfo Pérez Esquivel, Arg.
Frédéric Passy, Fr.	1937 Viscount Cecil of Chelwood, UK	1981 Office of UN High Com. for Refugees
1902 Élie Ducommun,	1938 Nansen International Office for	1982 Alva Myrdal, Swed.;
Charles A. Gobat, Switz.	Refugees	Alfonso García Robles, Mex.
1903 Sir William R. Cremer, UK	1944 International Red Cross	1983 Lech Walesa, Pol.
1904 Institute of International Law	1945 Cordell Hull, U.S.	1984 Bishop Desmond Tutu, S. Afr.
1905 Baroness Bertha von Suttner, Austria	1946 Emily G. Balch, John R. Mott, U.S.	1985 Intl. Physicians for the Prevention
1906 Theodore Roosevelt, U.S.	1947 Friends Service Council, UK; Amer.	of Nuclear War, U.S.
1907 Ernesto T. Moneta, It.;	Friends Service Committee, U.S.	1986 Elie Wiesel, Rom.-U.S.
Louis Renault, Fr.	1949 Lord John Boyd Orr of Brechin, UK	1987 Oscar Arias Sánchez, Costa Rica
1908 Klas P. Arnoldson, Swed.;	1950 Ralph J. Bunche, U.S.	1988 UN Peacekeeping Forces
Fredrik Bajer, Den.	1951 Léon Jouhaux, Fr.	1989 Dalai Lama (Tenzin Gyatso), Tibet
1909 Auguste M. F. Beernaert, Belg.;	1952 Albert Schweitzer, Fr.	1990 Mikhail S. Gorbachev, USSR
Paul H. B. B. d'Estournelles	1953 George C. Marshall, U.S.	1991 Aung San Suu Kyi, Burm.
de Constant, Fr.	1954 Office of UN High Com. for Refugees	1992 Rigoberta Menchú Tum, Guat.
1910 Permanent Intl. Peace Bureau	1957 Lester B. Pearson, Can.	1993 Frederik W. de Klerk,
1911 Tobias M.C. Asser, Neth.;	1958 Georges Pire, Belg.	Nelson Mandela, S. Afr.
Alfred H. Fried, Austria	1959 Philip J. Noel-Baker, UK	1994 Yasser Arafat, Pal.; Shimon Peres,
1912 Elihu Root, U.S.	1960 Albert J. Lutuli, S. Afr.	Yitzhak Rabin, Isr.
1913 Henri La Fontaine, Belg.	1961 Dag Hammarskjöld, Swed.	1995 Joseph Rotblat, Pol.-UK;
1917 International Red Cross	1962 Linus C. Pauling, U.S.	Pugwash Conference
1919 Woodrow Wilson, U.S.	1963 International Red Cross, League of	1996 Bishop Carlos Ximenes Belo,
1920 Léon V.A. Bourgeois, Fr.	Red Cross Societies	José Ramos-Horta, Timor-Leste
1921 Karl H. Branting, Swed.;	1964 Martin Luther King Jr., U.S.	1997 Jody Williams, U.S.; International
Christian L. Lange, Nor.	1965 UN Children's Fund (UNICEF)	Campaign to Ban Landmines
1922 Fridtjof Nansen, Nor.	1968 René Cassin, Fr.	1998 John Hume, David Trimble, N. Ire.
1925 Sir J. Austen Chamberlain, UK;	1969 Intl. Labor Organization	1999 Doctors Without Borders
Charles G. Dawes, U.S.	1970 Norman E. Borlaug, U.S.	(Médecins Sans Frontières), Fr.
1926 Aristide Briand, Fr.;	1971 Willy Brandt, Ger.	2000 Kim Dae-Jung, S. Kor.
Gustav Stresemann, Ger.	1973 Henry Kissinger, U.S.; Le Duc Tho,	2001 UN; Kofi Annan, Ghana
1927 Ferdinand E. Buisson, Fr.;	N. Viet. (Tho declined)	2002 Jimmy Carter, U.S.
Ludwig Quidde, Ger.	1974 Eisaku Sato, Jpn.; Seán MacBride, Ire.	2003 Shirin Ebadi, Iran
1929 Frank B. Kellogg, U.S.	1975 Andrei Sakharov, USSR	2004 Wangari Maathai, Kenya
1930 Nathan Söderblom, Swed.	1976 Mairead Corrigan, Betty Williams,	2005 Mohamed ElBaradei, Egypt;
1931 Jane Addams,	N. Ire.	International Atomic Energy Agency,
Nicholas Murray Butler, U.S.	1977 Amnesty International	Austria
1933 Sir Norman Angell, UK	1978 Anwar al-Sadat, Egypt;	2006 Muhammad Yunus, Grameen Bank,
1934 Arthur Henderson, UK	Menachem Begin, Isr.	Bang.
1935 Carl von Ossietzky, Ger.	1979 Mother Teresa of Calcutta, Alb.-Ind.	

Nobel Memorial Prize in Economic Science

1969 Ragnar Frisch, Nor.;	1981 James Tobin, U.S.	1996 James A. Mirrlees, UK; William
Jan Tinbergen, Neth.	1982 George J. Stigler, U.S.	Vickrey, Can.-U.S.
1970 Paul A. Samuelson, U.S.	1983 Gerard Debreu, Fr.-U.S.	1997 Robert C. Merton, U.S.;
1971 Simon Kuznets, U.S.	1984 Richard Stone, UK	Myron S. Scholes, Can.-U.S.
1972 Kenneth J. Arrow, U.S.;	1985 Franco Modigliani, It.-U.S.	1998 Amartya Sen, India
John R. Hicks, UK	1986 James M. Buchanan, U.S.	1999 Robert A. Mundell, Can.
1973 Wassily Leontief, U.S.	1987 Robert M. Solow, U.S.	2000 James J. Heckman,
1974 Gunnar Myrdal, Swed.;	1988 Maurice Allais, Fr.	Daniel L. McFadden, U.S.
Friedrich A. von Hayek, Austria	1989 Trygve Haavelmo, Nor.	2001 George A. Akerlof, A. Michael Spence,
1975 Tjalling Koopmans, Neth.-U.S.;	1990 Harry M. Markowitz, William F.	Joseph E. Stiglitz, U.S.
Leonid Kantorovich, USSR	Sharpe, Merton H. Miller, U.S.	2002 Daniel Kahneman, U.S.-Isr.;
1976 Milton Friedman, U.S.	1991 Ronald H. Coase, UK-U.S.	Vernon L. Smith, U.S.
1977 Bertil Ohlin, Swed.;	1992 Gary S. Becker, U.S.	2003 Robert F. Engle, U.S.;
James E. Meade, UK	1993 Robert W. Fogel,	Clive W.J. Granger, UK
1978 Herbert A. Simon, U.S.	Douglass C. North, U.S.	2004 Finn E. Kydland, Nor.;
1979 Theodore W. Schultz, U.S.;	1994 John C. Harsanyi, John F. Nash, U.S.;	Edward C. Prescott, U.S.
Sir Arthur Lewis, UK	Reinhard Selten, Ger.	2005 Robert J. Aumann, Israel-U.S.;
1980 Lawrence R. Klein, U.S.	1995 Robert E. Lucas Jr., U.S.	Thomas C. Schelling, U.S.
		2006 Edmund S. Phelps, U.S.

Pulitzer Prizes in Journalism, Letters, and Music

Endowed by Joseph Pulitzer (1847-1911), publisher of the *New York World*, in a bequest to Columbia Univ. and awarded annually, in years shown, for work the previous year. Prizes are now $10,000 in each category, except Public Service (in Journalism), for which a medal is given. For letters and music, prizes in past years are listed; if a year is omitted, no award was given that year.

Journalism, 2007

Public Service: *Wall Street Journal* for probing into backdated stock options for executives, triggering investigations and change in corporate America.

Breaking News Reporting: *Oregonian* (Portland, OR) staff for coverage of a family missing in the Oregon mountains.

Investigative Reporting: Brett Blackledge, *The Birmingham* (AL), for exposure of corruption in the state's two-year college system.

Explanatory Reporting: Kenneth R. Weiss, Usha Lee McFarling, and Rick Loomis, *LA Times*, for reporting the world's distressed oceans.

Local Reporting: Debbie Cenziper, *Miami Herald*, for reports on waste, favoritism, and lack of oversight at the Miami housing agency.

National Reporting: Charlie Savage, *Boston Globe*, for revelations on Pres. Bush's use of controversial "signing statements," to assert his right to bypass new laws' provisions.

International Reporting: *Wall Street Journal* staff, for reports on the adverse impacts of China's booming capitalism.

Feature Writing: Andrea Elliott, *NY Times*, for an intimate portrait of an immigrant imam striving to serve people and find his way in the U.S.

Commentary: Cynthia Tucker, *Atlanta Journal-Constitution*, for courageous columns that evince a strong sense of morality and community knowledge.

Criticism: Jonathan Gold, *LA Weekly*, for wide-ranging restaurant reviews, expressing the delight of an erudite eater.

Editorial Writing: Arthur Browne, Beverly Weintraub, and Heidi Evans, *NY Daily News*, for compassionate and compelling editorials on Ground Zero workers with health problems neglected by the city and nation.

Editorial Cartooning: Walt Handelsman, *Newsday* (Long Island, NY).

Breaking News Photog.: Oded Balilty, *Associated Press*, for photograph of a lone woman defying Israeli security forces as they removed illegal Jewish settlers from the West Bank.

Feature Photog.: Renée C. Byer, *Sacramento Bee* (CA), for portrayal of a single mother and her young son as he lost his battle with cancer.

Letters

Fiction

1918 Ernest Poole, *His Family*
1919 Booth Tarkington, *The Magnificent Ambersons*
1921 Edith Wharton, *The Age of Innocence*
1922 Booth Tarkington, *Alice Adams*
1923 Willa Cather, *One of Ours*
1924 Margaret Wilson, *The Able McLaughlins*
1925 Edna Ferber, *So Big*
1926 Sinclair Lewis, *Arrowsmith* (refused prize)
1927 Louis Bromfield, *Early Autumn*
1928 Thornton Wilder, *Bridge of San Luis Rey*
1929 Julia M. Peterkin, *Scarlet Sister Mary*
1930 Oliver LaFarge, *Laughing Boy*
1931 Margaret Ayer Barnes, *Years of Grace*
1932 Pearl S. Buck, *The Good Earth*
1933 T. S. Stribling, *The Store*
1934 Caroline Miller, *Lamb in His Bosom*
1935 Josephine W. Johnson, *Now in November*
1936 Harold L. Davis, *Honey in the Horn*
1937 Margaret Mitchell, *Gone With the Wind*
1938 John P. Marquand, *The Late George Apley*
1939 Marjorie Kinnan Rawlings, *The Yearling*
1940 John Steinbeck, *The Grapes of Wrath*
1942 Ellen Glasgow, *In This Our Life*
1943 Upton Sinclair, *Dragon's Teeth*
1944 Martin Flavin, *Journey in the Dark*
1945 John Hersey, *A Bell for Adano*
1947 Robert Penn Warren, *All the King's Men*
1948 James A. Michener, *Tales of the South Pacific*
1949 James Gould Cozzens, *Guard of Honor*
1950 A. B. Guthrie Jr., *The Way West*
1951 Conrad Richter, *The Town*
1952 Herman Wouk, *The Caine Mutiny*
1953 Ernest Hemingway, *The Old Man and the Sea*
1955 William Faulkner, *A Fable*
1956 MacKinlay Kantor, *Andersonville*
1958 James Agee, *A Death in the Family*
1959 Robert Lewis Taylor, *The Travels of Jaimie McPheeters*
1960 Allen Drury, *Advise and Consent*
1961 Harper Lee, *To Kill a Mockingbird*
1962 Edwin O'Connor, *The Edge of Sadness*
1963 William Faulkner, *The Reivers*
1965 Shirley Ann Grau, *The Keepers of the House*
1966 Katherine Anne Porter, *Collected Stories*
1967 Bernard Malamud, *The Fixer*
1968 William Styron, *The Confessions of Nat Turner*
1969 N. Scott Momaday, *House Made of Dawn*
1970 Jean Stafford, *Collected Stories*
1972 Wallace Stegner, *Angle of Repose*
1973 Eudora Welty, *The Optimist's Daughter*
1975 Michael Shaara, *The Killer Angels*
1976 Saul Bellow, *Humboldt's Gift*
1978 James Alan McPherson, *Elbow Room*
1979 John Cheever, *The Stories of John Cheever*
1980 Norman Mailer, *The Executioner's Song*
1981 John Kennedy Toole, *A Confederacy of Dunces*
1982 John Updike, *Rabbit Is Rich*
1983 Alice Walker, *The Color Purple*
1984 William Kennedy, *Ironweed*

1985 Alison Lurie, *Foreign Affairs*
1986 Larry McMurtry, *Lonesome Dove*
1987 Peter Taylor, *A Summons to Memphis*
1988 Toni Morrison, *Beloved*
1989 Anne Tyler, *Breathing Lessons*
1990 Oscar Hijuelos, *The Mambo Kings Play Songs of Love*
1991 John Updike, *Rabbit at Rest*
1992 Jane Smiley, *A Thousand Acres*
1993 Robert Olen Butler, *A Good Scent From a Strange Mountain*
1994 E. Annie Proulx, *The Shipping News*
1995 Carol Shields, *The Stone Diaries*
1996 Richard Ford, *Independence Day*
1997 Steven Millhauser, *Martin Dressler: The Tale of an American Dreamer*
1998 Philip Roth, *American Pastoral*
1999 Michael Cunningham, *The Hours*
2000 Jhumpa Lahiri, *Interpreter of Maladies*
2001 Michael Chabon, *The Amazing Adventures of Kavalier & Clay*
2002 Richard Russo, *Empire Falls*
2003 Jeffrey Eugenides, *Middlesex*
2004 Edward P. Jones, *The Known World*
2005 Marilynne Robinson, *Gilead*
2006 Geraldine Brooks, *March*
2007 Cormac McCarthy, *The Road*

Drama

1918 Jesse Lynch Williams, *Why Marry?*
1920 Eugene O'Neill, *Beyond the Horizon*
1921 Zona Gale, *Miss Lulu Bett*
1922 Eugene O'Neill, *Anna Christie*
1923 Owen Davis, *Icebound*
1924 Hatcher Hughes, *Hell-Bent for Heaven*
1925 Sidney Howard, *They Knew What They Wanted*
1926 George Kelly, *Craig's Wife*
1927 Paul Green, *In Abraham's Bosom*
1928 Eugene O'Neill, *Strange Interlude*
1929 Elmer Rice, *Street Scene*
1930 Marc Connelly, *The Green Pastures*
1931 Susan Glaspell, *Alison's House*
1932 George S. Kaufman, Morrie Ryskind, and Ira Gershwin, *Of Thee I Sing*
1933 Maxwell Anderson, *Both Your Houses*
1934 Sidney Kingsley, *Men in White*
1935 Zoe Akins, *The Old Maid*
1936 Robert E. Sherwood, *Idiot's Delight*
1937 George S. Kaufman and Moss Hart, *You Can't Take It With You*
1938 Thornton Wilder, *Our Town*
1939 Robert E. Sherwood, *Abe Lincoln in Illinois*
1940 William Saroyan, *The Time of Your Life*
1941 Robert E. Sherwood, *There Shall Be No Night*
1943 Thornton Wilder, *The Skin of Our Teeth*
1945 Mary Chase, *Harvey*
1946 Russel Crouse and Howard Lindsay, *State of the Union*
1948 Tennessee Williams, *A Streetcar Named Desire*
1949 Arthur Miller, *Death of a Salesman*
1950 Richard Rodgers, Oscar Hammerstein II and Joshua Logan, *South Pacific*
1952 Joseph Kramm, *The Shrike*

1953 William Inge, *Picnic*
1954 John Patrick, *Teahouse of the August Moon*
1955 Tennessee Williams, *Cat on a Hot Tin Roof*
1956 Frances Goodrich and Albert Hackett, *The Diary of Anne Frank*
1957 Eugene O'Neill, *Long Day's Journey Into Night*
1958 Ketti Frings, *Look Homeward, Angel*
1959 Archibald MacLeish, *J. B.*
1960 George Abbott, Jerome Weidman, Sheldon Harnick, and Jerry Bock, *Fiorello!*
1961 Tad Mosel, *All the Way Home*
1962 Frank Loesser and Abe Burrows, *How to Succeed in Business Without Really Trying*
1965 Frank D. Gilroy, *The Subject Was Roses*
1967 Edward Albee, *A Delicate Balance*
1969 Howard Sackler, *The Great White Hope*
1970 Charles Gordone, *No Place to Be Somebody*
1971 Paul Zindel, *The Effect of Gamma Rays on Man-in-the-Moon Marigolds*
1973 Jason Miller, *That Championship Season*
1975 Edward Albee, *Seascape*
1976 Michael Bennett, James Kirkwood, Nicholas Dante, Marvin Hamlisch, and Edward Kleban, *A Chorus Line*
1977 Michael Cristofer, *The Shadow Box*
1978 Donald L. Coburn, *The Gin Game*
1979 Sam Shepard, *Buried Child*
1980 Lanford Wilson, *Talley's Folly*
1981 Beth Henley, *Crimes of the Heart*
1982 Charles Fuller, *A Soldier's Play*
1983 Marsha Norman, *'night, Mother*
1984 David Mamet, *Glengarry Glen Ross*
1985 Stephen Sondheim and James Lapine, *Sunday in the Park With George*
1987 August Wilson, *Fences*
1988 Alfred Uhry, *Driving Miss Daisy*
1989 Wendy Wasserstein, *The Heidi Chronicles*
1990 August Wilson, *The Piano Lesson*
1991 Neil Simon, *Lost in Yonkers*
1992 Robert Schenkkan, *The Kentucky Cycle*
1993 Tony Kushner, *Angels in America: Millennium Approaches*
1994 Edward Albee, *Three Tall Women*
1995 Horton Foote, *The Young Man From Atlanta*
1996 Jonathan Larson, *Rent*
1998 Paula Vogel, *How I Learned to Drive*
1999 Margaret Edson, *Wit*
2000 Donald Margulies, *Dinner With Friends*
2001 David Auburn, *Proof*
2002 Suzan-Lori Parks, *Topdog/Underdog*
2003 Nilo Cruz, *Anna in the Tropics*
2004 Doug Wright, *I Am My Own Wife*
2005 John Patrick Shanley, *Doubt, a parable*
2007 David Lindsay-Abaire, *Rabbit Hole*

History (U.S.)

1917 J. J. Jusserand, *With Americans of Past and Present Days*
1918 James Ford Rhodes, *History of the Civil War*
1920 Justin H. Smith, *The War With Mexico*
1921 William Sowden Sims, *The Victory at Sea*
1922 James Truslow Adams, *The Founding of New England*
1923 Charles Warren, *The Supreme Court in United States History*
1924 Charles Howard McIlwain, *The American Revolution: A Constitutional Interpretation*
1925 Frederick L. Paxton, *A History of the American Frontier*
1926 Edward Channing, *A History of the U.S.*
1927 Samuel Flagg Bemis, *Pinckney's Treaty*
1928 V. L Parrington, *Main Currents in American Thought*
1929 Fred A. Shannon, *The Organization and Administration of the Union Army, 1861-65*
1930 Claude H. Van Tyne, *The War of Independence*
1931 Bernadotte E. Schmitt, *The Coming of the War, 1914*
1932 Gen. John J. Pershing, *My Experiences in the World War*
1933 Frederick J. Turner, *The Significance of Sections in American History*
1934 Herbert Agar, *The People's Choice*
1935 Charles McLean Andrews, *The Colonial Period of American History*
1936 Andrew C. McLaughlin, *The Constitutional History of the United States*
1937 Van Wyck Brooks, *The Flowering of New England*
1938 Paul Herman Buck, *The Road to Reunion, 1865-1900*
1939 Frank Luther Mott, *A History of American Magazines*
1940 Carl Sandburg, *Abraham Lincoln: The War Years*
1941 Marcus Lee Hansen, *The Atlantic Migration, 1607-1860*
1942 Margaret Leech, *Reveille in Washington*
1943 Esther Forbes, *Paul Revere and the World He Lived In*
1944 Merle Curti, *The Growth of American Thought*
1945 Stephen Bonsal, *Unfinished Business*
1946 Arthur M. Schlesinger Jr., *The Age of Jackson*
1947 James Phinney Baxter III, *Scientists Against Time*

1948 Bernard De Voto, *Across the Wide Missouri*
1949 Roy F. Nichols, *The Disruption of American Democracy*
1950 O. W. Larkin, *Art and Life in America*
1951 R. Carlyle Buley, *The Old Northwest: Pioneer Period 1815-1840*
1952 Oscar Handlin, *The Uprooted*
1953 George Dangerfield, *The Era of Good Feelings*
1954 Bruce Catton, *A Stillness at Appomattox*
1955 Paul Horgan, *Great River: The Rio Grande in North American History*
1956 Richard Hofstadter, *The Age of Reform*
1957 George F. Kennan, *Russia Leaves the War*
1958 Bray Hammond, *Banks and Politics in America—From the Revolution to the Civil War*
1959 Leonard D. White and Jean Schneider, *The Republican Era; 1869-1901*
1960 Margaret Leech, *In the Days of McKinley*
1961 Herbert Feis, *Between War and Peace: The Potsdam Conference*
1962 Lawrence H. Gibson, *The Triumphant Empire: Thunderclouds Gather in the West*
1963 Constance McLaughlin Green, *Washington: Village and Capital, 1800-1878*
1964 Sumner Chilton Powell, *Puritan Village: The Formation of a New England Town*
1965 Irwin Unger, *The Greenback Era*
1966 Perry Miller, *Life of the Mind in America*
1967 William H. Goetzmann, *Exploration and Empire: The Explorer and Scientist in the Winning of the American West*
1968 Bernard Bailyn, *The Ideological Origins of the American Revolution*
1969 Leonard W. Levy, *Origin of the Fifth Amendment*
1970 Dean Acheson, *Present at the Creation: My Years in the State Department*
1971 James McGregor Burns, *Roosevelt: The Soldier of Freedom*
1972 Carl N. Degler, *Neither Black nor White*
1973 Michael Kammen, *People of Paradox: An Inquiry Concerning the Origins of American Civilization*
1974 Daniel J. Boorstin, *The Americans: The Democratic Experience*
1975 Dumas Malone, *Jefferson and His Time*
1976 Paul Horgan, *Lamy of Santa Fe*
1977 David M. Potter, *The Impending Crisis*
1978 Alfred D. Chandler Jr., *The Visible Hand: The Managerial Revolution in American Business*
1979 Don E. Fehrenbacher, *The Dred Scott Case: Its Significance in American Law and Politics*
1980 Leon F. Litwack, *Been in the Storm So Long*
1981 Lawrence A. Cremin, *American Education: The National Experience, 1783-1876*
1982 C. Vann Woodward, ed., *Mary Chesnut's Civil War*
1983 Rhys L. Issac, *The Transformation of Virginia, 1740-1790*
1985 Thomas K. McCraw, *Prophets of Regulation*
1986 Walter A. McDougall, *The Heavens and the Earth*
1987 Bernard Bailyn, *Voyagers to the West*
1988 Robert V. Bruce, *The Launching of Modern American Science, 1846-1876*
1989 Taylor Branch, *Parting the Waters: America in the King Years, 1954-63*; and James M. McPherson, *Battle Cry of Freedom: The Civil War Era*
1990 Stanley Karnow, *In Our Image: America's Empire in the Philippines*
1991 Laurel Thatcher Ulrich, *A Midwife's Tale: The Life of Martha Ballard*, based on her diary, 1785-1812
1992 Mark E. Neely Jr., *The Fate of Liberty: Abraham Lincoln and Civil Liberties*
1993 Gordon S. Wood, *The Radicalism of the American Revolution*
1995 Doris Kearns Goodwin, *No Ordinary Time: Franklin and Eleanor Roosevelt: The Home Front in World War II*
1996 Alan Taylor, *William Cooper's Town: Power and Persuasion on the Frontier of the Early American Republic*
1997 Jack N. Rakove, *Original Meanings: Politics and Ideas in the Making of the Constitution*
1998 Edward J. Larson, *Summer for the Gods: The Scopes Trial and America's Continuing Debate Over Science and Religion*
1999 Edwin G. Burrows and Mike Wallace, *Gotham: A History of New York City to 1898*
2000 David M. Kennedy, *Freedom From Fear: The American People in Depression and War, 1929-1945*
2001 Joseph J. Ellis, *Founding Brothers: The Revolutionary Generation*
2002 Louis Menand, *The Metaphysical Club: A Story of Ideas in America*
2003 Rick Atkinson, *An Army at Dawn: The War in North Africa, 1942-1943*
2004 Steven Hahn, *A Nation Under Our Feet: Black Political Struggles in the Rural South from Slavery to the Great Migration*

2005 David Hackett Fischer, *Washington's Crossing*
2006 David M. Oshinsky, *Polio: An American Story*
2007 Gene Roberts and Hank Klibanoff, *The Race Beat: The Press, the Civil Rights Struggle, and the Awakening of a Nation*

Biography or Autobiography

1917 Laura E. Richards and Maude Howe Elliott, assisted by Florence Howe Hall, *Julia Ward Howe*
1918 William Cabell Bruce, *Benjamin Franklin, Self-Revealed*
1919 Henry Adams, *The Education of Henry Adams*
1920 Albert J. Beveridge, *The Life of John Marshall*
1921 Edward Bok, *The Americanization of Edward Bok*
1922 Hamlin Garland, *A Daughter of the Middle Border*
1923 Burton J. Hendrick, *The Life and Letters of Walter H. Page*
1924 Michael Pupin, *From Immigrant to Inventor*
1925 M. A. DeWolfe Howe, *Barrett Wendell and His Letters*
1926 Harvey Cushing, *Life of Sir William Osler*
1927 Emory Holloway, *Whitman: An Interpretation in Narrative*
1928 Charles Edward Russell, *The American Orchestra and Theodore Thomas*
1929 Burton J. Hendrick, *The Training of an American: The Earlier Life and Letters of Walter H. Page*
1930 Marquis James, *The Raven (Sam Houston)*
1931 Henry James, *Charles W. Eliot*
1932 Henry F. Pringle, *Theodore Roosevelt*
1933 Allan Nevins, *Grover Cleveland*
1934 Tyler Dennett, *John Hay*
1935 Douglas Southall Freeman, *R. E. Lee*
1936 Ralph Barton Perry, *The Thought and Character of William James*
1937 Allan Nevins, *Hamilton Fish: The Inner History of the Grant Administration*
1938 Divided between Odell Shepard, *Pedlar's Progress* (Bronson Alcott) and Marquis James, *Andrew Jackson*
1939 Carl Van Doren, *Benjamin Franklin*
1940 Ray Stannard Baker, *Woodrow Wilson, Life and Letters*
1941 Ola Elizabeth Winslow, *Jonathan Edwards*
1942 Forrest Wilson, *Crusader in Crinoline* (Harriet Beecher Stowe)
1943 Samuel Eliot Morison, *Admiral of the Ocean Sea* (Christopher Columbus)
1944 Carleton Mabee, *The American Leonardo: The Life of Samuel F. B. Morse*
1945 Russell Blaine Nye, *George Bancroft: Brahmin Rebel.*
1946 Linny Marsh Wolfe, *Son of the Wilderness* (John Muir)
1947 William Allen White, *Autobiography of William Allen White*
1948 Margaret Clapp, *Forgotten First Citizen: John Bigelow*
1949 Robert E. Sherwood, *Roosevelt and Hopkins*
1950 Samuel Flagg Bemis, *John Quincy Adams and the Foundations of American Foreign Policy*
1951 Margaret Louise Coit, *John C. Calhoun: American Portrait*
1952 Merlo J. Pusey, *Charles Evans Hughes*
1953 David J. Mays, *Edmund Pendleton, 1721-1803*
1954 Charles A. Lindbergh, *The Spirit of St. Louis*
1955 William S. White, *The Taft Story*
1956 Talbot F. Hamlin, *Benjamin Henry Latrobe*
1957 John F. Kennedy, *Profiles in Courage*
1958 Douglas Southall Freeman (I-VI), John Alexander Carroll and Mary Wells Ashworth (VII), *George Washington*
1959 Arthur Walworth, *Woodrow Wilson: American Prophet*
1960 Samuel Eliot Morison, *John Paul Jones*
1961 David Donald, *Charles Sumner and the Coming of the Civil War*
1963 Leon Edel, *Henry James: Vols. 2-3*
1964 Walter Jackson Bate, *John Keats*
1965 Ernest Samuels, *Henry Adams*
1966 Arthur M. Schlesinger Jr., *A Thousand Days*
1967 Justin Kaplan, *Mr. Clemens and Mark Twain*
1968 George F. Kennan, *Memoirs (1925-1950)*
1969 B. L. Reid, *The Man From New York: John Quinn and His Friends*
1970 T. Harry Williams, *Huey Long*
1971 Lawrence Thompson, *Robert Frost: The Years of Triumph, 1915-1938*
1972 Joseph P. Lash, *Eleanor and Franklin*
1973 W. A. Swanberg, *Luce and His Empire*
1974 Louis Sheaffer, *O'Neill, Son and Artist*
1975 Robert A. Caro, *The Power Broker: Robert Moses and the Fall of New York*
1976 R.W.B. Lewis, *Edith Wharton: A Biography*
1977 John E. Mack, *A Prince of Our Disorder: The Life of T. E. Lawrence*
1978 Walter Jackson Bate, *Samuel Johnson*
1979 Leonard Baker, *Days of Sorrow and Pain: Leo Baeck and the Berlin Jews*
1980 Edmund Morris, *The Rise of Theodore Roosevelt*
1981 Robert K. Massie, *Peter the Great: His Life and World*
1982 William S. McFeely, *Grant: A Biography*
1983 Russell Baker, *Growing Up*

1984 Louis R. Harlan, *Booker T. Washington*
1985 Kenneth Silverman, *The Life and Times of Cotton Mather*
1986 Elizabeth Frank, *Louise Bogan: A Portrait*
1987 David J. Garrow, *Bearing the Cross: Martin Luther King Jr. and the Southern Christian Leadership Conference*
1988 David Herbert Donald, *Look Homeward: A Life of Thomas Wolfe*
1989 Richard Ellmann, *Oscar Wilde*
1990 Sebastian de Grazia, *Machiavelli in Hell*
1991 Steven Naifeh and Gregory White Smith, *Jackson Pollock: An American Saga*
1992 Lewis B. Puller Jr., *Fortunate Son: The Healing of a Vietnam Vet*
1993 David McCullough, *Truman*
1994 David Levering Lewis, *W.E.B. DuBois: Biography of a Race, 1868-1919*
1995 Joan D. Hedrick, *Harriet Beecher Stowe: A Life*
1996 Jack Miles, *God: A Biography*
1997 Frank McCourt, *Angela's Ashes: A Memoir*
1998 Katharine Graham, *Personal History*
1999 A. Scott Berg, *Lindbergh*
2000 Stacy Schiff, *Véra (Mrs. Vladimir Nabokov)*
2001 David Levering Lewis, *W.E.B. Du Bois: The Fight for Equality and the American Century, 1919-1963*
2002 David McCullough, *John Adams*
2003 Robert Caro, *The Years of Lyndon Johnson: Master of the Senate*
2004 William Taubman, *Khrushchev: The Man and His Era*
2005 Mark Stevens and Annalyn Swan, *de Kooning: An American Master*
2006 Kai Bird and Martin J. Sherwin, *American Prometheus: The Triumph and Tragedy of J. Robert Oppenheimer*
2007 Debby Applegate, *The Most Famous Man in America: The Biography of Henry Ward Beecher*

American Poetry

Before 1922, awards were funded by the Poetry Society.

1918 Sara Teasdale, *Love Songs*
1919 Margaret Widdemer, *Old Road to Paradise*; Carl Sandburg, *Corn Huskers.*
1922 Edwin Arlington Robinson, *Collected Poems*
1923 Edna St. Vincent Millay, *The Ballad of the Harp-Weaver; A Few Figs From Thistles; other works*
1924 Robert Frost, *New Hampshire: A Poem With Notes and Grace Notes*
1925 Edwin Arlington Robinson, *The Man Who Died Twice*
1926 Amy Lowell, *What's O'Clock*
1927 Leonora Speyer, *Fiddler's Farewell*
1928 Edwin Arlington Robinson, *Tristram*
1929 Stephen Vincent Benet, *John Brown's Body*
1930 Conrad Aiken, *Selected Poems*
1931 Robert Frost, *Collected Poems*
1932 George Dillon, *The Flowering Stone*
1933 Archibald MacLeish, *Conquistador*
1934 Robert Hillyer, *Collected Verse*
1935 Audrey Wurdemann, *Bright Ambush*
1936 Robert P. Tristram Coffin, *Strange Holiness*
1937 Robert Frost, *A Further Range*
1938 Marya Zaturenska, *Cold Morning Sky*
1939 John Gould Fletcher, *Selected Poems*
1940 Mark Van Doren, *Collected Poems*
1941 Leonard Bacon, *Sunderland Capture*
1942 William Rose Benet, *The Dust Which Is God*
1943 Robert Frost, *A Witness Tree*
1944 Stephen Vincent Benet, *Western Star*
1945 Karl Shapiro, *V-Letter and Other Poems*
1947 Robert Lowell, *Lord Weary's Castle*
1948 W. H. Auden, *The Age of Anxiety*
1949 Peter Viereck, *Terror and Decorum*
1950 Gwendolyn Brooks, *Annie Allen*
1951 Carl Sandburg, *Complete Poems*
1952 Marianne Moore, *Collected Poems*
1953 Archibald MacLeish, *Collected Poems*
1954 Theodore Roethke, *The Waking*
1955 Wallace Stevens, *Collected Poems*
1956 Elizabeth Bishop, *Poems, North and South*
1957 Richard Wilbur, *Things of This World*
1958 Robert Penn Warren, *Promises: Poems 1954-1956*
1959 Stanley Kunitz, *Selected Poems 1928-1958*
1960 W. D. Snodgrass, *Heart's Needle*
1961 Phyllis McGinley, *Times Three: Selected Verse From Three Decades*
1962 Alan Dugan, *Poems*
1963 William Carlos Williams, *Pictures From Breughel*
1964 Louis Simpson, *At the End of the Open Road*
1965 John Berryman, *77 Dream Songs*
1966 Richard Eberhart, *Selected Poems*
1967 Anne Sexton, *Live or Die*
1968 Anthony Hecht, *The Hard Hours*
1969 George Oppen, *Of Being Numerous*

1970 Richard Howard, *Untitled Subjects*
1971 William S. Merwin, *The Carrier of Ladders*
1972 James Wright, *Collected Poems*
1973 Maxine Winokur Kumin, *Up Country*
1974 Robert Lowell, *The Dolphin*
1975 Gary Snyder, *Turtle Island*
1976 John Ashbery, *Self-Portrait in a Convex Mirror*
1977 James Merrill, *Divine Comedies*
1978 Howard Nemerov, *Collected Poems*
1979 Robert Penn Warren, *Now and Then: Poems 1976-1978*
1980 Donald Justice, *Selected Poems*
1981 James Schuyler, *The Morning of the Poem*
1982 Sylvia Plath, *The Collected Poems*
1983 Galway Kinnell, *Selected Poems*
1984 Mary Oliver, *American Primitive*
1985 Carolyn Kizer, *Yin*
1986 Henry Taylor, *The Flying Change*
1987 Rita Dove, *Thomas and Beulah*
1988 William Meredith, *Partial Accounts*
1989 Richard Wilbur, *New and Collected Poems*
1990 Charles Simic, *The World Doesn't End*
1991 Mona Van Duyn, *Near Changes*
1992 James Tate, *Selected Poems*
1993 Louise Glück, *The Wild Iris*
1994 Yusef Komunyakaa, *Neon Vernacular*
1995 Philip Levine, *The Simple Truth*
1996 Jorie Graham, *The Dream of the Unified Field*
1997 Lisel Mueller, *Alive Together: New and Selected Poems*
1998 Charles Wright, *Black Zodiac*
1999 Mark Strand, *Blizzard of One*
2000 C. K. Williams, *Repair*
2001 Stephen Dunn, *Different Hours*
2002 Carl Dennis, *Practical Gods*
2003 Paul Muldoon, *Moy Sand and Gravel*
2004 Franz Wright, *Walking to Martha's Vineyard*
2005 Ted Kooser, *Delights & Shadows*
2006 Claudia Emerson, *Late Wife*
2007 Natasha Trethewey, *Native Guard*

General Nonfiction

1962 Theodore H. White, *The Making of the President 1960*
1963 Barbara W. Tuchman, *The Guns of August*
1964 Richard Hofstadter, *Anti-Intellectualism in American Life*
1965 Howard Mumford Jones, *O Strange New World*
1966 Edwin Way Teale, *Wandering Through Winter*
1967 David Brion Davis, *The Problem of Slavery in Western Culture*
1968 Will and Ariel Durant, *Rousseau and Revolution*
1969 Norman Mailer, *The Armies of the Night*; Rene Jules Dubos, *So Human an Animal: How We Are Shaped by Surroundings and Events*
1970 Eric H. Erikson, *Gandhi's Truth*
1971 John Toland, *The Rising Sun*
1972 Barbara W. Tuchman, *Stilwell and the American Experience in China, 1911-1945*
1973 Frances FitzGerald, *Fire in the Lake: The Vietnamese and the Americans in Vietnam*; Robert Coles, *Children of Crisis, Volumes II & III*
1974 Ernest Becker, *The Denial of Death*
1975 Annie Dillard, *Pilgrim at Tinker Creek*

1976 Robert N. Butler, *Why Survive? Being Old in America*
1977 William W. Warner, *Beautiful Swimmers*
1978 Carl Sagan, *The Dragons of Eden*
1979 Edward O. Wilson, *On Human Nature*
1980 Douglas R. Hofstadter, *Gödel, Escher, Bach: An Eternal Golden Braid*
1981 Carl E. Schorske, *Fin-de-Siecle Vienna: Politics and Culture*
1982 Tracy Kidder, *The Soul of a New Machine*
1983 Susan Sheehan, *Is There No Place on Earth for Me?*
1984 Paul Starr, *Social Transformation of American Medicine*
1985 Studs Terkel, *The Good War*
1986 Joseph Lelyveld, *Move Your Shadow*; J. Anthony Lukas, *Common Ground*
1987 David K. Shipler, *Arab and Jew*
1988 Richard Rhodes, *The Making of the Atomic Bomb*
1989 Neil Sheehan, *A Bright Shining Lie: John Paul Vann and America in Vietnam*
1990 Dale Maharidge and Michael Williamson, *And Their Children After Them*
1991 Bert Holldobler and Edward O. Wilson, *The Ants*
1992 Daniel Yergin, *The Prize: The Epic Quest for Oil*
1993 Garry Wills, *Lincoln at Gettysburg*
1994 David Remnick, *Lenin's Tomb: The Last Days of the Soviet Empire*
1995 Jonathan Weiner, *The Beak of the Finch: A Story of Evolution in Our Time*
1996 Tina Rosenberg, *The Haunted Land: Facing Europe's Ghosts After Communism*
1997 Richard Kluger, *Ashes to Ashes: America's Hundred-Year Cigarette War, the Public Health, and the Unabashed Triumph of Philip Morris*
1998 Jared Diamond, *Guns, Germs, and Steel: The Fates of Human Societies*
1999 John McPhee, *Annals of the Former World*
2000 John W. Dower, *Embracing Defeat: Japan in the Wake of World War II*
2001 Herbert P. Bix, *Hirohito and the Making of Modern Japan*
2002 Diane McWhorter, *Carry Me Home: Birmingham, Alabama, the Climactic Battle of the Civil Rights Revolution*
2003 Samantha Power, *A Problem From Hell: America and the Age of Genocide*
2004 Anne Applebaum, *Gulag: A History*
2005 Steve Coll, *Ghost Wars*
2006 Caroline Elkins, *Imperial Reckoning: The Untold Story of Britain's Gulag in Kenya*
2007 Lawrence Wright, *The Looming Tower: Al-Qaeda and the Road to 9/11*

Special Citation in Letters

1944 Richard Rodgers and Oscar Hammerstein II, for *Oklahoma!*
1957 Kenneth Roberts, for his historical novels
1960 *The Armada*, by Garrett Mattingly
1961 *American Heritage Picture History of the Civil War*
1973 *George Washington, Vols. I-IV*, by James Thomas Flexner
1977 Alex Haley, for *Roots*
1978 E.B. White
1984 Theodore Seuss Geisel (Dr. Seuss)
1992 Art Spiegelman, for *Maus*
2006 Edmund S. Morgan
2007 Ray Bradbury

Music

1943 William Schuman, *Secular Cantata No. 2, A Free Song*
1944 Howard Hanson, *Symphony No. 4, Op. 34*
1945 Aaron Copland, *Appalachian Spring*
1946 Leo Sowerby, *The Canticle of the Sun*
1947 Charles E. Ives, *Symphony No. 3*
1948 Walter Piston, *Symphony No. 3*
1949 Virgil Thomson, *Louisiana Story*
1950 Gian-Carlo Menotti, *The Consul*
1951 Douglas Moore, *Giants in the Earth*
1952 Gail Kubik, *Symphony Concertante*
1954 Quincy Porter, *Concerto for Two Pianos and Orchestra*
1955 Gian-Carlo Menotti, *The Saint of Bleecker Street*
1956 Ernest Toch, *Symphony No. 3*
1957 Norman Dello Joio, *Meditations on Ecclesiastes*
1958 Samuel Barber, *Vanessa*
1959 John La Montaine, *Concerto for Piano and Orchestra*
1960 Elliott Carter, *Second String Quartet*
1961 Walter Piston, *Symphony No. 7*
1962 Robert Ward, *The Crucible*
1963 Samuel Barber, *Piano Concerto No. 1*
1966 Leslie Bassett, *Variations for Orchestra*
1967 Leon Kirchner, *Quartet No. 3*
1968 George Crumb, *Echoes of Time and The River*
1969 Karel Husa, *String Quartet No. 3*
1970 Charles W. Wuorinen, *Time's Encomium*
1971 Mario Davidovsky, *Synchronisms No. 6*
1972 Jacob Druckman, *Windows*
1973 Elliott Carter, *String Quartet No. 3*

1974 Donald Martino, *Notturno*
1975 Dominick Argento, *From the Diary of Virginia Woolf*
1976 Ned Rorem, *Air Music*
1977 Richard Wernick, *Visions of Terror and Wonder*
1978 Michael Colgrass, *Deja Vu for Percussion and Orchestra*
1979 Joseph Schwantner, *Aftertones of Infinity*
1980 David Del Tredici, *In Memory of a Summer Day*
1982 Roger Sessions, *Concerto for Orchestra*
1983 Ellen T. Zwilich, *Three Movements for Orchestra*
1984 Bernard Rands, *Canti del Sole*
1985 Stephen Albert, *Symphony, RiverRun*
1986 George Perle, *Wind Quintet IV*
1987 John Harbison, *The Flight Into Egypt*
1988 William Bolcom, *12 New Etudes for Piano*
1989 Roger Reynolds, *Whispers Out of Time*
1990 Mel Powell, *Duplicates: A Concerto for Two Pianos and Orchestra*
1991 Shulamit Ran, *Symphony*
1992 Wayne Peterson, *The Face of the Night, The Heart of the Dark*
1993 Christopher Rouse, *Trombone Concerto*
1994 Gunther Schuller, *Of Reminiscences and Reflections*
1995 Morton Gould, *Stringmusic*
1996 George Walker, *Lilacs*
1997 Wynton Marsalis, *Blood on the Fields*
1998 Aaron Jay Kernis, *String Quartet No. 2*
1999 Melinda Wagner, *Concerto for Flute, Strings and Percussion*

2000	Lewis Spratlan, *Life is a Dream, Opera in Three Acts: Act II, Concert Version*		**Special Citation in Music**
2001	John Corigliano, *Symphony No. 2 for String Orchestra*	**1974**	Roger Sessions
2002	Henry Brant, *Ice Field*	**1976**	Scott Joplin
2003	John Adams, *On the Transmigration of Souls*	**1982**	Milton Babbitt
2004	Paul Moravec, *Tempest Fantasy*	**1985**	William Schuman
2005	Steven Stucky, *Second Concerto for Orchestra*	**1998**	George Gershwin
2006	Yehudi Wyner, *Piano Concerto: 'Chiavi in Mano'*	**1999**	Edward Kennedy "Duke" Ellington
2007	Ornette Coleman, *Sound Grammar*	**2006**	Thelonious Monk
		2007	John Coltrane

The Man Booker Prize for Fiction, 1969–2006

The Booker Prize for fiction, established in 1968, is awarded annually in October for what is judged the best full-length novel written in English by a citizen of the UK, the Commonwealth, or the Irish Republic. In 2002 sponsorship of the award was taken over by Man Group PLC, the name was changed to the Man Booker Prize, and the amount was increased from £20,000 to £50,000.

Year	Author, Book	Year	Author, Book
1969	P. H. Newby, *Something to Answer For*	1988	Peter Carey, *Oscar and Lucinda*
1970	Bernice Rubens, *The Elected Member*	1989	Kazuo Ishiguro, *The Remains of the Day*
1971	V. S. Naipaul, *In a Free State*	1990	A. S. Byatt, *Possession*
1972	John Berger, *G*	1991	Ben Okri, *The Famished Road*
1973	J. G. Farrell, *The Siege of Krishnapur*	1992	Michael Ondaatje, *The English Patient*;
1974	Nadine Gordimer, *The Conservationist*;		Barry Unsworth, *Sacred Hunger*
	Stanley Middleton, *Holiday*	1993	Roddy Doyle, *Paddy Clarke Ha Ha Ha*
1975	Ruth Prawer Jhabvala, *Heat & Dust*	1994	James Kelman, *How Late It Was, How Late*
1976	David Storey, *Saville*	1995	Pat Barker, *The Ghost Road*
1977	Paul Scott, *Staying On*	1996	Graham Swift, *Last Orders*
1978	Iris Murdoch, *The Sea, The Sea*	1997	Arundhati Roy, *The God of Small Things*
1979	Penelope Fitzgerald, *Offshore*	1998	Ian McEwan, *Amsterdam*
1980	William Golding, *Rites of Passage*	1999	J. M. Coetzee, *Disgrace*
1981	Salman Rushdie, *Midnight's Children*	2000	Margaret Atwood, *The Blind Assassin*
1982	Thomas Keneally, *Schindler's Ark*	2001	Peter Carey, *True History of the Kelly Gang*
1983	J. M. Coetzee, *Life and Times of Michael K*	2002	Yann Martel, *Life of Pi*
1984	Anita Brookner, *Hotel du Lac*	2003	DBC Pierre, *Vernon God Little*
1985	Keri Hulme, *The Bone People*	2004	Alan Hollinghurst, *The Line of Beauty*
1986	Kingsley Amis, *The Old Devils*	2005	John Banville, *The Sea*
1987	Penelope Lively, *Moon Tiger*	2006	Kiran Desai, *The Inheritance of Loss*

Newbery Medal Books, 1922–2007

The Newbery Medal was awarded annually in the years shown, by the Association for Library Service to Children, a division of the American Library Association, to the author of the most distinguished contribution to American literature for children.

Year	Book, Author	Year	Book, Author
1922	*The Story of Mankind*, Hendrik Willem van Loon	1967	*Up a Road Slowly*, Irene Hunt
1923	*The Voyages of Dr. Dolittle*, Hugh Lofting	1968	*From the Mixed-Up Files of Mrs. Basil E. Frankweiler*, E. L. Konigsburg
1924	*The Dark Frigate*, Charles Boardman Hawes		
1925	*Tales From Silver Lands*, Charles Joseph Finger	1969	*The High King*, Lloyd Alexander
1926	*Shen of the Sea*, Arthur Bowie Chrisman	1970	*Sounder*, William H. Armstrong
1927	*Smoky, the Cowhorse*, Will James	1971	*The Summer of the Swans*, Betsy Byars
1928	*Gay-Neck*, Dhan Gopal Mukerji	1972	*Mrs. Frisby and the Rats of NIMH*, Robert C. O'Brien
1929	*The Trumpeter of Krakow*, Eric P. Kelly	1973	*Julie of the Wolves*, Jean George
1930	*Hitty, Her First Hundred Years*, Rachel Field	1974	*The Slave Dancer*, Paula Fox
1931	*The Cat Who Went to Heaven*, Elizabeth Coatsworth	1975	*M. C. Higgins the Great*, Virginia Hamilton
1932	*Waterless Mountain*, Laura Adams Armer	1976	*Grey King*, Susan Cooper
1933	*Young Fu of the Upper Yangtze*, Elizabeth Foreman Lewis	1977	*Roll of Thunder, Hear My Cry*, Mildred D. Taylor
1934	*Invincible Louisa*, Cornelia Lynde Meigs	1978	*Bridge to Terabithia*, Katherine Paterson
1935	*Dobry*, Monica Shannon	1979	*The Westing Game*, Ellen Raskin
1936	*Caddie Woodlawn*, Carol Ryrie Brink	1980	*A Gathering of Days*, Joan Blos
1937	*Roller Skates*, Ruth Sawyer	1981	*Jacob Have I Loved*, Katherine Paterson
1938	*The White Stag*, Kate Seredy	1982	*A Visit to William Blake's Inn: Poems for Innocent and Experienced Travelers*, Nancy Willard
1939	*Thimble Summer*, Elizabeth Enright		
1940	*Daniel Boone*, James Daugherty	1983	*Dicey's Song*, Cynthia Voigt
1941	*Call It Courage*, Armstrong Sperry	1984	*Dear Mr. Henshaw*, Beverly Cleary
1942	*The Matchlock Gun*, Walter D. Edmonds	1985	*The Hero and the Crown*, Robin McKinley
1943	*Adam of the Road*, Elizabeth Janet Gray	1986	*Sarah, Plain and Tall*, Patricia MacLachlan
1944	*Johnny Tremain*, Esther Forbes	1987	*The Whipping Boy*, Sid Fleischman
1945	*Rabbit Hill*, Robert Lawson	1988	*Lincoln: A Photobiography*, Russell Freedman
1946	*Strawberry Girl*, Lois Lenski	1989	*Joyful Noise: Poems for Two Voices*, Paul Fleischman
1947	*Miss Hickory*, Carolyn S. Bailey	1990	*Number the Stars*, Lois Lowry
1948	*Twenty-One Balloons*, William Pène Du Bois	1991	*Maniac Magee*, Jerry Spinelli
1949	*King of the Wind*, Marguerite Henry	1992	*Shiloh*, Phyllis Reynolds Naylor
1950	*The Door in the Wall*, Marguerite de Angeli	1993	*Missing May*, Cynthia Rylant
1951	*Amos Fortune, Free Man*, Elizabeth Yates	1994	*The Giver*, Lois Lowry
1952	*Ginger Pye*, Eleanor Estes	1995	*Walk Two Moons*, Sharon Creech
1953	*Secret of the Andes*, Ann Nolan Clark	1996	*The Midwife's Apprentice*, Karen Cushman
1954	*. . . And Now Miguel*, Joseph Krumgold	1997	*The View From Saturday*, E. L. Konigsburg
1955	*The Wheel on the School*, Meindert DeJong	1998	*Out of the Dust*, Karen Hesse
1956	*Carry On, Mr. Bowditch*, Jean Lee Latham	1999	*Holes*, Louis Sachar
1957	*Miracles on Maple Hill*, Virginia Sorensen	2000	*Bud, Not Buddy*, Christopher Paul Curtis
1958	*Rifles for Watie*, Harold Keith	2001	*A Year Down Yonder*, Richard Peck
1959	*The Witch of Blackbird Pond*, Elizabeth George Speare	2002	*A Single Shard*, Linda Sue Park
1960	*Onion John*, Joseph Krumgold	2003	*Crispin: The Cross of Lead*, Avi
1961	*Island of the Blue Dolphins*, Scott O'Dell	2004	*The Tale of Despereaux: Being the Story of a Mouse, a Princess, Some Soup, and a Spool of Thread*, by Kate DiCamillo, illustrated by Timothy Basil Ering
1962	*The Bronze Bow*, Elizabeth George Speare		
1963	*A Wrinkle in Time*, Madeleine L'Engle		
1964	*It's Like This, Cat*, Emily Cheney Neville	2005	*Kira-Kira*, Cynthia Kadohata
1965	*Shadow of a Bull*, Maja Wojciechowska	2006	*Criss Cross*, Lynne Rae Perkins
1966	*I, Juan de Pareja*, Elizabeth Borton de Trevino	2007	*The Higher Power of Lucky*, Susan Patron

Caldecott Medal Books, 1938-2007

The Caldecott Medal was awarded annually in the years shown, by the Association for Library Service to Children, a division of the American Library Association, to the illustrator of the most distinguished American picture book for children.

Year	Book, Illustrator	Year	Book, Illustrator
1938	*Animals of the Bible*, Dorothy P. Lathrop	1974	*Duffy and the Devil*, Margot Zemach
1939	*Mei Li*, Thomas Handforth	1975	*Arrow to the Sun*, Gerald McDermott
1940	*Abraham Lincoln*, Ingri & Edgar Parin d'Aulaire	1976	*Why Mosquitoes Buzz in People's Ears*, Leo & Diane Dillon
1941	*They Were Strong and Good*, Robert Lawson	1977	*Ashanti to Zulu: African Traditions*, Leo & Diane Dillon
1942	*Make Way for Ducklings*, Robert McCloskey	1978	*Noah's Ark*, Peter Spier
1943	*The Little House*, Virginia Lee Burton	1979	*The Girl Who Loved Wild Horses*, Paul Goble
1944	*Many Moons*, Louis Slobodkin	1980	*Ox-Cart Man*, Barbara Cooney
1945	*Prayer for a Child*, Elizabeth Orton Jones	1981	*Fables*, Arnold Lobel
1946	*The Rooster Crows*, Maude & Miska Petersham	1982	*Jumanji*, Chris Van Allsburg
1947	*The Little Island*, Leonard Weisgard	1983	*Shadow*, Marcia Brown
1948	*White Snow, Bright Snow*, Roger Duvoisin	1984	*The Glorious Flight: Across the Channel with Louis Bleriot*, Alice and Martin Provensen
1949	*The Big Snow*, Berta & Elmer Hader	1985	*Saint George and the Dragon*, Trina Schart Hyman
1950	*Song of the Swallows*, Leo Politi	1986	*The Polar Express*, Chris Van Allsburg
1951	*The Egg Tree*, Katherine Milhous	1987	*Hey, Al*, Richard Egielski
1952	*Finders Keepers*, Nicolas, pseud. (Nicholas Mordvinoff)	1988	*Owl Moon*, John Schoenherr
1953	*The Biggest Bear*, Lynd Ward	1989	*Song and Dance Man*, Stephen Grammell
1954	*Madeline's Rescue*, Ludwig Bemelmans	1990	*Lon Po Po: A Red-Riding Hood Story From China*, Ed Young
1955	*Cinderella, or the Little Glass Slipper*, Marcia Brown	1991	*Black and White*, David Macaulay
1956	*Frog Went A-Courtin'*, Feodor Rojankovsky	1992	*Tuesday*, David Wiesner
1957	*A Tree Is Nice*, Marc Simont	1993	*Mirette on the High Wire*, Emily Arnold McCully
1958	*Time of Wonder*, Robert McCloskey	1994	*Grandfather's Journey*, Allen Say
1959	*Chanticleer and the Fox*, Barbara Cooney	1995	*Smoky Night*, David Diaz
1960	*Nine Days to Christmas*, Marie Hall Ets	1996	*Officer Buckle and Gloria*, Peggy Rathmann
1961	*Baboushka and the Three Kings*, Nicolas Sidjakov	1997	*Golem*, David Wisniewski
1962	*Once a Mouse*, Marcia Brown	1998	*Rapunzel*, Paul O. Zelinsky
1963	*The Snowy Day*, Ezra Jack Keats	1999	*Snowflake Bentley*, Mary Azarian
1964	*Where the Wild Things Are*, Maurice Sendak	2000	*Joseph Had a Little Overcoat*, Simms Taback
1965	*May I Bring a Friend?*, Beni Montressor	2001	*So You Want to be President?*, David Small
1966	*Always Room for One More*, Nonny Hogrogian	2002	*The Three Pigs*, David Wiesner
1967	*Sam, Bang, and Moonshine*, Evaline Ness	2003	*My Friend Rabbit*, Eric Rohmann
1968	*Drummer Hoff*, Ed Emberley	2004	*The Man Who Walked Between the Towers*, Mordicai Gerstein
1969	*The Fool of the World and the Flying Ship*, Uri Shulevitz	2005	*Kitten's First Full Moon*, Kevin Henkes
1970	*Sylvester and the Magic Pebble*, William Steig	2006	*The Hello, Goodbye Window*, Chris Raschka
1971	*A Story A Story*, Gail E. Haley	2007	*Flotsam*, David Wiesner
1972	*One Fine Day*, Nonny Hogrogian		
1973	*The Funny Little Woman*, Blair Lent		

National Book Awards, 1950-2006

The National Book Awards (known as American Book Awards 1980-86) are administered by the National Book Foundation and have been given annually in the years shown, since 1950. The prizes, each valued at $10,000, are awarded to U.S. citizens for works published in the U.S. In some years, multiple awards were given for nonfiction in various categories; in such cases, the history and biography (if any) or biography winner is listed. Selected additional awards in nonfiction are listed in footnotes.

Other National Book Awards, 2006: Poetry: Nathaniel Mackey, *Splay Anthem*; Young People's Literature: M. T. Anderson, *The Astonishing Life of Octavian Nothing, Traitor to the Nation, Vol. 1: The Pox Party*. Medal for Distinguished Contribution to American Letters: Adrienne Rich.

Fiction

Year	Author, Book	Year	Author, Book
1950	Nelson Algren, *The Man With the Golden Arm*	1978	Mary Lee Settle, *Blood Ties*
1951	William Faulkner, *The Collected Stories*	1979	Tim O'Brien, *Going After Cacciato*
1952	James Jones, *From Here to Eternity*	1980	William Styron, *Sophie's Choice*
1953	Ralph Ellison, *Invisible Man*	1981	Wright Morris, *Plains Song*
1954	Saul Bellow, *The Adventures of Augie March*	1982	John Updike, *Rabbit Is Rich*
1955	William Faulkner, *A Fable*	1983	Alice Walker, *The Color Purple*
1956	John O'Hara, *Ten North Frederick*	1984	Ellen Gilchrist, *Victory Over Japan*
1957	Wright Morris, *The Field of Vision*	1985	Don DeLillo, *White Noise*
1958	John Cheever, *The Wapshot Chronicle*	1986	E.L. Doctorow, *World's Fair*
1959	Bernard Malamud, *The Magic Barrel*	1987	Larry Heinemann, *Paco's Story*
1960	Philip Roth, *Goodbye, Columbus*	1988	Pete Dexter, *Paris Trout*
1961	Conrad Richter, *The Waters of Kronos*	1989	John Casey, *Spartina*
1962	Walker Percy, *The Moviegoer*	1990	Charles Johnson, *Middle Passage*
1963	J. F. Powers, *Morte d'Urban*	1991	Norman Rush, *Mating*
1964	John Updike, *The Centaur*	1992	Cormac McCarthy, *All the Pretty Horses*
1965	Saul Bellow, *Herzog*	1993	E. Annie Proulx, *The Shipping News*
1966	Katherine Anne Porter, *The Collected Stories*	1994	William Gaddis, *A Frolic of His Own*
1967	Bernard Malamud, *The Fixer*	1995	Philip Roth, *Sabbath's Theater*
1968	Thornton Wilder, *The Eighth Day*	1996	Andrea Barrett, *Ship Fever and Other Stories*
1969	Jerzy Kosinski, *Steps*	1997	Charles Frazier, *Cold Mounatin*
1970	Joyce Carol Oates, *Them*	1998	Alice McDermott, *Charming Billy*
1971	Saul Bellow, *Mr. Sammler's Planet*	1999	Ha Jin, *Waiting*
1972	Flannery O'Connor, *The Complete Stories*	2000	Susan Sontag, *In America*
1973	John Barth, *Chimera*	2001	Jonathan Franzen, *The Corrections*
1974	Thomas Pynchon, *Gravity's Rainbow*	2002	Julia Glass, *Three Junes*
1974	Isaac Bashevis Singer, *A Crown of Feathers*	2003	Shirley Hazzard, *The Great Fire*
1975	Robert Stone, *Dog Soldiers*	2004	Lily Tuck, *The News from Paraguay*
1976	William Gaddis, *JR*	2005	William T. Vollmann, *Europe Central*
1977	Wallace Stegner, *The Spectator Bird*	2006	Richard Powers, *The Echo Maker*

Nonfiction

Year	Author, Title
1950	Ralph L. Rusk, *Ralph Waldo Emerson*
1951	Newton Arvin, *Herman Melville*
1952	Rachel Carson, *The Sea Around Us*
1953	Bernard A. De Voto, *The Course of an Empire*
1954	Bruce Catton, *A Stillness at Appomattox*
1955	Joseph Wood Krutch, *The Measure of Man*
1956	Herbert Kubly, *An American in Italy*
1957	George F. Kennan, *Russia Leaves the War*
1958	Catherine Drinker Bowen, *The Lion and the Throne*
1959	J. Christopher Herold, *Mistress to an Age: A Life of Madame De Stael*
1960	Richard Ellman, *James Joyce*
1961	William L. Shirer, *The Rise and Fall of the Third Reich*
1962	Lewis Mumford, *The City in History: Its Origins, Its Transformations, and Its Prospects*
1963	Leon Edel, *Henry James: Vol. II: The Conquest of London; Vol. III: The Middle Years*
1964	William H. McNeill, *The Rise of the West: A History of the Human Community*
1965	Louis Fisher, *The Life of Lenin*
1966	Arthur M. Schlesinger, Jr., *A Thousand Days: John F. Kennedy in the White House*
1967	Peter Gay, *The Enlightenment, An Interpretation Vol I: The Rise of Modern Paganism*
1968	George F. Kennan, *Memoirs: 1925–1950*[1]
1969	Winthrop D. Jordan, *White Over Black: American Attitudes Toward the Negro, 1550-1812*[2]
1970	T. Harry Williams, *Huey Long*[3]
1971	James MacGregor Burns, *Roosevelt: The Soldier of Freedom*
1972	Joseph P. Lash, *Eleanor and Franklin: The Story of Their Relationship, Based on Eleanor Roosevelt's Private Papers*
1973	James Thomas Flexner, *George Washington, Vol. IV: Anguish and Farewell, 1793-1799*[4]
1974	John Clive, *Macaulay, The Shaping of the Historian*; Douglas Day, *Malcolm Lowry: A Biography*[5]
1975	Richard B. Sewall, *The Life of Emily Dickinson*[6]
1976	David Brion Davis, *The Problem of Slavery in the Age of Revolution, 1770-1823*
1977	W.A. Swanberg, *Norman Thomas: The Last Idealist*[7]
1978	W. Jackson Bate, *Samuel Johnson*
1979	Arthur M. Schlesinger, Jr., *Robert Kennedy and His Times*

Year	Author, Title
1980	Tom Wolfe, *The Right Stuff*
1981	Maxine Hong Kingston, *China Men*
1982	Tracy Kidder, *The Soul of a New Machine*
1983	Fox Butterfield, *China: Alive in the Bitter Sea*
1984	Robert V. Remini, *Andrew Jackson and the Course of American Democracy, 1833-1845*
1985	J. Anthony Lukas, *Common Ground: A Turbulent Decade in the Lives of Three American Families*
1986	Barry Lopez, *Arctic Dreams*
1987	Richard Rhodes, *The Making of the Atom Bomb*
1988	Neil Sheehan, *A Bright Shining Lie: John Paul Vann and America in Vietnam*
1989	Thomas L. Friedman, *From Beirut to Jerusalem*
1990	Ron Chernow, *The House of Morgan: An American Banking Dynasty and the Rise of Modern Finance*
1991	Orlando Patterson, *Freedom*
1992	Paul Monette, *Becoming a Man: Half a Life Story*
1993	Gore Vidal, *United States: Essays 1952-1992*
1994	Sherwin B. Nuland, *How We Die: Reflections on Life's Final Chapter*
1995	Tina Rosenberg, *The Haunted Land: Facing Europe's Ghosts After Communism*
1996	James Carroll, *An American Requiem: God, My Father, and the War That Came Between Us*
1997	Joseph J. Ellis, *American Sphinx: The Character of Thomas Jefferson*
1998	Edward Ball, *Slaves in the Family*
1999	John W. Dower, *Embracing Defeat: Japan in the Wake of World War II*
2000	Nathaniel Philbrick, *In the Heart of the Sea: The Tragedy of the Whaleship Essex*
2001	Andrew Solomon, *The Noonday Demon: An Atlas of Depression*
2002	Robert A. Caro, *Master of the Senate: The Years of Lyndon Johnson*
2003	Carlos Eire, *Waiting for Snow in Havana: Confessions of a Cuban Boy*
2004	Kevin Boyle, *Arc of Justice: A Saga of Race, Civil Rights, and Murder in the Jazz Age*
2005	Joan Didion, *The Year of Magical Thinking*
2006	Timothy Egan, *The Worst Hard Time: The Untold Story of Those Who Survived the Great American Dust Bowl*

(1) Science, Philosophy, and Religion: Jonathan Kozol, *Death at an Early Age*. (2) Arts & Letters: Norman Mailer, *The Armies of the Night: History as a Novel, The Novel as History.* (3) Arts & Letters: Lillian Hellman, *An Unfinished Woman: A Memoir.* (4) Contemp. Affairs: Frances FitzGerald, *Fire in the Lake: The Vietnamese and the Americans in Vietnam.* (5) Arts & Letters: Pauline Kael, *Deeper Into the Movies.* (6) Arts & Letters: Roger Shattuck, *Marcel Proust*; Lewis Thomas, *The Lives of a Cell: Notes of a Biology Watcher.* (7) Contemp. Thought: Bruno Bettelheim, *The Uses of Enchantment: The Meaning and Importance of Fairy Tales.*

Journalism Awards, 2007

National Journalism Awards, by Scripps Howard Foundation. Investigative Reporting: Charles Forelle, James Bandler, Mark Maremont, and Steve Stecklow, *Wall Street Journal.* Public Service Reporting: Michael Smith and David Voreacos, Bloomberg News. Editorial Writing: John Diaz, Pati Poblete, and Caille Millner, *San Francisco Chronicle.* Commentary: Chris Rose, *Times-Picayune* (New Orleans). Human Interest Writing: Lane DeGregory, *St. Petersburg Times.* Web Reporting: Washingtonpost.com. Environmental Reporting: Kenneth R. Weiss and Usha Lee McFarling, *LA Times.* Washington Reporting: Wes Allison, *St. Petersburg Times.* Editorial Cartooning: Stephen Benson, *Arizona Republic.* Distinguished Service to the 1st Amendment: Mark Fainaru-Wada and Lance Williams, *San Francisco Chronicle.* Photojournalism: Rick Loomis, *LA Times.* Business/Economics Reporting: Steve Everly, *Kansas City Star* (MO). Excellence in Electronic Media/TV-Cable: WTHR-TV, Indianapolis. College Cartooning: Erin Russell, *Michigan Daily*, Univ. of Michigan. Journalism Teacher of the Year: Robert Richards, Penn. State. Journalism Administrator of the Year: Dr. Shirley Staples Carter, Univ. of South Carolina.

National Magazine Awards, by American Society of Magazine Editors and Columbia Univ. Graduate School of Journalism. Gen. excel., circ. over 2 mil: *National Geographic*; 1 mil-2 mil: *Rolling Stone*; 500,000 to 1 mil: *Wired*; 250,000-500,000: *New York*; 100,000-250,000: *Foreign Policy*; under 100,000: *Bulletin of the Atomic Scientists.* Personal Service: *Glamour.* Leisure Interests: *O, The Oprah Magazine.* Reporting: *Esquire.* Public Interest: *Vanity Fair.* Feature Writing: *GQ.* Profile Writing: *New York.* Essays: *The Georgia Review.* Columns and Commentary: *Vanity Fair.* Reviews and Criticism: *The Nation.* Magazine Section: *New York.* Single-Topic Issue: *Departures.* Design: *New York.* Photography: *National Geographic.* Photojournalism: The

Paris Review. Photo Portfolio: *City.* Fiction: *McSweeney's.* General Excellence Online: Beliefnet.com. Interactive Service: B-School Channel, Businessweek.com. Interactive Feature: "Show & Talk" blog, NYmag.com.

George Foster Peabody Awards, by Univ. of Georgia. "Mental Anguish and the Military," NPR. "Crossing East: Our History, Our Stories, Our America," PRI. "Crossing Borders," KUNM-FM (Albuquerque, NM). "This American Life: Habeas Schmabeas," WBEZ (Chicago). "StoryCorps," NPR. "Defective Parts on Blackhawk Helicopters," WTNH-TV (New Haven, CT). "Left Behind: The Failure of East St. Louis Schools," KMOV-TV (St. Louis, MO). "The Education of Ms. Groves," *Dateline*, NBC. "The Duke Rape Case," *60 Minutes*, CBS. "Prescription Privacy"/"Cause for Alarm," WTHR-TV (Indianapolis, IN). "Conduct Unbecoming," ABC News: Brian Ross Investigates. "Command Mistake," WISH-TV (Indianapolis, IN). "Galapagos: Born of Fire," BBC2. "Andy Warhol," *American Masters*, PBS. "For My Country? Latinos in the Military," mun2. *Baghdad ER*, HBO. *Braindamadj'd...Take II*, CBC. *When the Levees Broke: A Requiem in Four Acts*, HBO. "Out of Control: AIDS in Black America," ABC. *Why We Fight*, CBC. *Brotherhood*, Showtime. *Billy Jean: Portrait of a Pioneer*, HBO. *Elizabeth I*, HBO. "Return of the King," *Boondocks*, Cartoon Network. *Scrubs*, NBC. *Ugly Betty*, ABC. *Gideon's Daughter*, BBC America. *The Office*, NBC. *Friday Night Lights*, NBC. *Good Eats*, Food Network. *The Music in Me*, HBO. *Beyond Borders: Personal Stories From a Small Planet*, IFC. "The Three Amigos HIV/AIDS Prevention Programme," SABC (South Africa), OMNI (Canada), SBS 6 (Holland), TVM (Mozambique). "Being a Black Man," www.washingtonpost.com. "Four Docs," Channel 4.

Reuben Award, by National Cartoonists Society. For Outstanding Cartoonist of the Year, 2006: Bill Amend.

Miscellaneous Book Awards

(Awarded in 2007 unless otherwise noted.)

Academy of American Poets Awards. Wallace Stevens Award, for poetry mastery, $100,000 (2006): Michael Palmer. Academy Fellowship, $25,000 (2006): Carl Phillips. Lenore Marshall Poetry Prize, $25,000 (2006): Eleanor Lerman, *Our Post-Soviet History Unfolds.* James Laughlin Award, $5,000 (2006): Tracy K. Smith, *Duende.* Walt Whitman Award, $5,000: Sally Van Doren, *Sex at Noon Taxes.* Harold Morton Landon Trans. Award, $1,000 (tie): Robert Fagles, for Virgil's *The Aeneid;* Susanna Nied, for Inger Christensen's *it.* Raiziss/de Palchi Trans. Fellowship (2006): Adria Bernardi, for Rafaello Baldini's *Small Talk.*

American Academy of Arts and Letters. Academy Awards in Literature ($7,500 each): Joan Acocella, Charles D'Ambrosio, Barbara Ehrenreich, David Markson, Robert Morgan, Joan Silber, William T. Vollmann, Dean Young. Benjamin H. Danks Award, $20,000: Adam Rapp. E. M. Forster Award, $15,000: Jez Butterworth. Sue Kaufman Prize for First Fiction, $5,000: Tony D'Souza, *Whiteman.* Award of Merit for the Short Story, $10,000: Charles Baxter. Addison M. Metcalf Award, $10,000: Suji Kwock Kim. Rome Fellowships in Literature: Junot Diaz, Sarah Manguso. Richard and Hinda Rosenthal Foundation Award, $5,000: Dana Spiotta, *Eat the Document.* Harold D. Vursell Memorial Award, $10,000: Amy Hempel.

Bollingen Prize in Poetry, $100,000, by the Yale Univ. Library: Frank Bidart.

Edgar Awards, by the Mystery Writers of America: Best Novel: *The Janissary Tree,* Jason Goodwin. Best First Novel by an American Author: *The Faithful Spy,* Alex Berenson. Best Paperback Original: *Snakeskin Shamisen,* Naomi Hirahara. Best Fact Crime: *Manhunt: The 12-Day Chase for Lincoln's Killer,* James L. Swanson. Best Critical/Biographical: *The Science of Sherlock Holmes: From Baskerville Hall to the Valley of Fear,* E. J. Wagner. Best Short Story: "The Home Front," Charles Ardai. Best Juvenile: *Room One: A Mystery or Two,* Andrew Clements. Best Young Adult: *Buried,* Robin Merrow MacCready. Best Play: *Sherlock Holmes: The Final Adventure,* Steven Dietz. Best Television Episode Teleplay: *Life on Mars—Episode 1,* Matthew Graham. Best Television Feature/Mini-Series Teleplay: *The Wire: Season 4.* Best Motion Picture Screenplay: *The Departed,* William Monahan.

Golden Kite Awards, by Society of Children's Book Writers and Illustrators. Fiction: *Firegirl,* Tony Abbott. Nonfiction: *The Ad-*

ventures of Marco Polo, Russell Freedman. Picture Book Text: *Jazz,* Walter Dean Myers. Picture Book Illustration: *Not Afraid of Dogs,* Larry Day.

Le Prix Goncourt, by Académie Goncourt (2006): Jonathan Littell, *Les Bienveillantes (The Furies).*

Hugo Awards, by the World Science Fiction Convention. Novel: *Rainbows End,* Vernor Vinge. Novella: *A Billion Eves,* Robert Reed. Novelette: *The Djinn's Wife,* Ian McDonald. Short story: "Impossible Dreams," Tim Pratt. John W. Campbell Award for Best New Writer (not a Hugo): Naomi Novik.

Coretta Scott King Award, by American Library Assn., for African American authors and illustrators of outstanding books for children and young adults. Author: Sharon Draper, *Copper Sun.* Illustrator: Kadir Nelson, *Moses: When Harriet Tubman Led Her People to Freedom.* John Steptoe New Talent Award (Author): Traci L. Jones, *Standing Against the Wind.*

Lincoln Prize, by Lincoln and Soldiers Institute at Gettysburg College, for contribution to Civil War studies, $50,000 and a bust of Lincoln: Douglas L. Wilson, *Lincoln's Sword: The Presidency and the Power of Words.*

National Book Critics Circle Awards. Fiction: Kiran Desai, *The Inheritance of Loss.* Nonfiction: Simon Schama, *Rough Crossings: Britain, the Slaves and the American Revolution.* Biography: Julie Phillips, *James Tiptree, Jr.: The Double Life of Alice B. Sheldon.* Autobiography: Daniel Mendelsohn, *The Lost: A Search for Six of Six Million.* Criticism: Lawrence Weschler, *Everything That Rises: A Book of Convergences.* Poetry: Troy Jollimore, *Tom Thomson in Purgatory.* Ivan Sandrof Lifetime Achievement Award: John Leonard. Nona Balakian Citation for Excellence in Reviewing: Steven G. Kellman.

Nebula Awards, by the Science Fiction Writers of America. Novel: *Seeker,* Jack McDevitt. Novella: "Burn," James Patrick Kelly. Novelette: "Two Hearts," Peter S. Beagle. Short Story: "Echo," Elizabeth Hand. Script: *Howl's Moving Castle,* Hayao Miyazaki, Cindy Davis Hewitt, and Donald H. Hewitt. Andre Norton Award: *Magic or Madness,* Justine Larbalestier.

PEN/Faulkner Award, for fiction, $15,000: Philip Roth, *Everyman.*

Costa Book of the Year (formerly Whitbread Award): £25,000: *The Tenderness of Wolves,* Stef Penney.

The Spingarn Medal, 1915-2007

The Spingarn Medal has been awarded annually since 1915 (except in 1938) by the National Assoc. for the Advancement of Colored People for outstanding achievement by an African American.

1915	Ernest E. Just	1947	Dr. Percy L. Julian	1977	Alex Haley
1916	Charles Young	1948	Channing H. Tobias	1978	Andrew Young
1917	Harry T. Burleigh	1949	Ralph J. Bunche	1979	Rosa L. Parks
1918	William S. Braithwaite	1950	Charles H. Houston	1980	Dr. Rayford W. Logan
1919	Archibald H. Grimké	1951	Mabel K. Staupers	1981	Coleman Young
1920	W. E. B. Du Bois	1952	Harry T. Moore	1982	Dr. Benjamin E. Mays
1921	Charles S. Gilpin	1953	Paul R. Williams	1983	Lena Horne
1922	Mary B. Talbert	1954	Theodore K. Lawless	1984	Thomas Bradley
1923	George W.Carver	1955	Carl Murphy	1985	Bill Cosby
1924	Roland Hayes	1956	Jack R. Robinson	1986	Dr. Benjamin L. Hooks
1925	James W. Johnson	1957	Martin Luther King Jr.	1987	Percy E. Sutton
1926	Carter G. Woodson	1958	Daisy Bates and the	1988	Frederick D. Patterson
1927	Anthony Overton		Little Rock Nine	1989	Jesse Jackson
1928	Charles W. Chesnutt	1959	Duke Ellington	1990	L. Douglas Wilder
1929	Mordecai W. Johnson	1960	Langston Hughes	1991	Gen. Colin L. Powell
1930	Henry A. Hunt	1961	Kenneth B. Clark	1992	Barbara Jordan
1931	Richard B. Harrison	1962	Robert C. Weaver	1993	Dorothy I. Height
1932	Robert R. Moton	1963	Medgar W. Evers	1994	Maya Angelou
1933	Max Yergan	1964	Roy Wilkins	1995	John Hope Franklin
1934	William T. B. Williams	1965	Leontyne Price	1996	A. Leon Higginbotham
1935	Mary McLeod Bethune	1966	John H. Johnson	1997	Carl T. Rowan
1936	John Hope	1967	Edward W. Brooke	1998	Myrlie Evers-Williams
1937	Walter White	1968	Sammy Davis Jr.	1999	Earl G. Graves Sr.
1939	Marian Anderson	1969	Clarence M. Mitchell Jr.	2000	Oprah Winfrey
1940	Louis T. Wright	1970	Jacob Lawrence	2001	Vernon E. Jordan Jr.
1941	Richard Wright	1971	Leon H. Sullivan	2002	John Lewis
1942	A. Philip Randolph	1972	Gordon Parks	2003	Constance Baker Motley
1943	William H. Hastie	1973	Wilson C. Riles	2004	Robert L. Carter
1944	Charles Drew	1974	Damon Keith	2005	Oliver W. Hill
1945	Paul Robeson	1975	Henry (Hank) Aaron	2006	Dr. Benjamin S. Carson
1946	Thurgood Marshall	1976	Alvin Ailey	2007	John Conyers Jr.

Miscellaneous Awards, 2007

(Awarded in 2007, unless otherwise noted.)

American Academy of Arts and Letters. Architecture Awards: Arthur W. Brunner Memorial Prize, $5,000: Eric Owen Moss. Academy Awards, $7,500 each: Wes Jones, Tom Kundig, Lebbeus Woods. **Art Awards:** Academy Awards, $7,500 each: Bryan Hunt, Jackie Gendel, Dana Schutz, Julian Hatton, Sarah Oppenheimer. Jimmy Ernst Award, $5,000: Sally Hazelet Drummond. Rosenthal Foundation Award in Painting, $5,000: Juan Gomez. **Music Awards:** Academy Awards, $7,500 each: Leonardo Balada, Mason Bates, Chester Biscardi, Ben Johnston. Goddard Lieberson Fellowships, $15,000 each: Shih-Hui Chen, Seung-Ah Oh. Walter Hinrichsen Award: Jeffrey Cotton. Charles Ives Fellowships, $15,000 each: Arlene Sierra, Aleksandra Vrebalov. Charles Ives Scholarships, $7,500 each: David Fulmer, Trevor Gureckis, Dan Visconti, Jay Wadley, Zachary Wadsworth, Orianna Webb. Charles Ives Living, $75,000 annually for 3 years: George Tsontakis. Richard Rodgers Awards for Musical Theater: *Calvin Berger* by Barry Wyner, *Main-Travelled Roads* by Paul Libman and Dave Hudson.

Congressional Gold Medal, by Congress: Tuskegee Airmen, Apr. 11, 2006; Dr. Norman E. Borlaug, Dec. 14, 2006.

Intel Science Talent Search (formerly given by Westinghouse): First place ($100,000 scholarship): Mary Masterman, Oklahoma City, OK; second place ($75,000 scholarship): John Vincent Pardon, Chapel Hill, NC; third place ($50,000 scholarship): Dmitry Vaintrob.

John F. Kennedy Center Honors (Dec. 2006): Zubin Mehta, Dolly Parton, William "Smokey" Robinson, Stephen Spielberg, Andrew Lloyd Webber.

John W. Kluge Prize, by Library of Congress, $500,000 each (2006): John Hope Franklin, Yu Ying-shih.

Library of the Year Award, by Thomson Gale and *Library Journal*, $10,000: Worthington Libraries, Worthington, OH.

National Humanities Medal (Charles Frankel Prize), by National Endowment for the Humanities. $5,000 each (2006): Fouad Ajami, James Buchanan, Nickolas Davatzes, Robert Fagles, Mary Lefkowitz, Bernard Lewis, Mark Noll, John Raisian, Meryle Secrest, Kevin Starr.

National Inventor of the Year Awards, by Intellectual Property Owners Education Foundation. Dr. Raymond V. Damadian, for developing Upright™ MRI technology.

National Medal of the Arts, by the National Endowment for the Arts and the White House (2006): William Bolcom, Cyd Charisse, Roy R. DeCarava, Wilhelmina Holladay, Interlochen Center for the Arts, Erich Kunzel, Preservation Hall Jazz Band, Gregory Rabassa, Viktor Schreckengost, Dr. Ralph Stanley.

Presidential Medal of Freedom, by the White House (Dec. 2006): Ruth Johnson Colvin, Norman Francis, Paul Johnson, Riley "B.B." King, Joshua Lederberg, David McCullough, Norman Mineta, John "Buck" O'Neil, William Safire, Natan Sharansky.

Pritzker Architecture Prize, by the Hyatt Foundation, $100,000: Richard Rogers, UK.

Teacher of the Year, by Council of Chief State School Officers and ING: Andrea Peterson, Monte Cristo Elementary School, Granite Falls, WA.

Templeton Prize for Progress Toward Research or Discoveries about Spiritual Realities, by Templeton Foundation, £800,000 (about $1.6 million): Charles Taylor.

Miss America Winners, 1921-2007

1921	Margaret Gorman, Washington, DC	1969	Judith Anne Ford, Belvidere, Illinois
1922-23	Mary Campbell, Columbus, Ohio	1970	Pamela Anne Eldred, Birmingham, Michigan
1924	Ruth Malcolmson, Philadelphia, Pennsylvania	1971	Phyllis Ann George, Denton, Texas
1925	Fay Lamphier, Oakland, California	1972	Laurie Lea Schaefer, Columbus, Ohio
1926	Norma Smallwood, Tulsa, Oklahoma	1973	Terry Anne Meeuwsen, DePere, Wisconsin
1927	Lois Delander, Joliet, Illinois	1974	Rebecca Ann King, Denver, Colorado
1933	Marion Bergeron, West Haven, Connecticut	1975	Shirley Cothran, Fort Worth, Texas
1935	Henrietta Leaver, Pittsburgh, Pennsylvania	1976	Tawney Elaine Godin, Yonkers, New York
1936	Rose Coyle, Philadelphia, Pennsylvania	1977	Dorothy Kathleen Benham, Edina, Minnesota
1937	Bette Cooper, Bertrand Island, New Jersey	1978	Susan Perkins, Columbus, Ohio
1938	Marilyn Meseke, Marion, Ohio	1979	Kylene Barker, Galax, Virginia
1939	Patricia Donnelly, Detroit, Michigan	1980	Cheryl Prewitt, Ackerman, Mississippi
1940	Frances Marie Burke, Philadelphia, Pennsylvania	1981	Susan Powell, Elk City, Oklahoma
1941	Rosemary LaPlanche, Los Angeles, California	1982	Elizabeth Ward, Russellville, Arkansas
1942	Jo-Caroll Dennison, Tyler, Texas	1983	Debra Maffett, Anaheim, California
1943	Jean Bartel, Los Angeles, California	1984	Vanessa Williams[1], Milwood, New York
1944	Venus Ramey, Washington, D.C.		Suzette Charles, Mays Landing, New Jersey
1945	Bess Myerson, New York City, New York	1985	Sharlene Wells, Salt Lake City, Utah
1946	Marilyn Buferd, Los Angeles, California	1986	Susan Akin, Meridian, Mississippi
1947	Barbara Walker, Memphis, Tennessee	1987	Kellye Cash, Memphis, Tennessee
1948	BeBe Shopp, Hopkins, Minnesota	1988	Kaye Lani Rae Rafko, Monroe, Michigan
1949	Jacque Mercer, Litchfield, Arizona	1989	Gretchen Carlson, Anoka, Minnesota
1951	Yolande Betbeze, Mobile, Alabama	1990	Debbye Turner, Columbia, Missouri
1952	Coleen Kay Hutchins, Salt Lake City, Utah	1991	Marjorie Vincent, Oak Park, Illinois
1953	Neva Jane Langley, Macon, Georgia	1992	Carolyn Suzanne Sapp, Honolulu, Hawaii
1954	Evelyn Margaret Ay, Ephrata, Pennsylvania	1993	Leanza Cornett, Jacksonville, Florida
1955	Lee Meriwether, San Francisco, California	1994	Kimberly Aiken, Columbia, South Carolina
1956	Sharon Ritchie, Denver, Colorado	1995	Heather Whitestone, Birmingham, Alabama
1957	Marian McKnight, Manning, South Carolina	1996	Shawntel Smith, Muldrow, Oklahoma
1958	Marilyn Van Derbur, Denver, Colorado	1997	Tara Dawn Holland, Overland Park, Kansas
1959	Mary Ann Mobley, Brandon, Mississippi	1998	Kate Shindle, Evanston, Illinois
1960	Lynda Lee Mead, Natchez, Mississippi	1999	Nicole Johnson, Roanoke, Virginia
1961	Nancy Fleming, Montague, Michigan	2000	Heather Renee French, Maysville, Kentucky
1962	Maria Fletcher, Asheville, North Carolina	2001	Angela Perez Baraquio, Honolulu, Hawaii
1963	Jacquelyn Mayer, Sandusky, Ohio	2002	Katie Harman, Gresham, Oregon
1964	Donna Axum, El Dorado, Arkansas	2003	Erika Harold, Urbana, Illinois
1965	Vonda Kay Van Dyke, Phoenix, Arizona	2004	Ericka Dunlap, Orlando, Florida
1966	Deborah Irene Bryant, Overland Park, Kansas	2005[2]	Deidre Downs, Birmingham, Alabama
1967	Jane Anne Jayroe, Laverne, Oklahoma	2006	Jennifer Berry, Tulsa, Oklahoma
1968	Debra Dene Barnes, Moran, Kansas	2007	Lauren Nelson, Lawton, Oklahoma

(1) Resigned July 23, 1984. (2) The Sept. 2005 Miss America Pageant and award were postponed until Jan. 2006, when the pageant was broadcast from Las Vegas, NV, by Country Music Television (CMT) (rather than from Atlantic City by ABC).

Entertainment Awards
Tony (Antoinette Perry) Awards, 2007

Play: The Coast of Utopia, Tom Stoppard
Musical: Spring Awakening
Book of a Musical: Steven Sater, Spring Awakening
Original Score: Duncan Sheik and Steven Sater, Spring Awakening
Play Revival: Journey's End
Musical Revival: Company
Special Theatrical Event: Jay Johnson: The Two and Only
Actor, Play: Frank Langella, Frost/Nixon
Actress, Play: Julie White, The Little Dog Laughed
Actor, Musical: David Hyde Pierce, Curtains
Actress, Musical: Christine Ebersole, Grey Gardens
Featured Actor, Play: Billy Crudup, The Coast of Utopia
Featured Actress, Play: Jennifer Ehle, The Coast of Utopia
Featured Actor, Musical: John Gallagher Jr., Spring Awakening

Featured Actress, Musical: Mary Louise Wilson, Grey Gardens
Director, Play: Jack O'Brien, The Coast of Utopia
Director, Musical: Michael Mayer, Spring Awakening
Choreography: Bill T. Jones, Spring Awakening
Orchestrations: Duncan Sheik, Spring Awakening
Scenic Design, Play: Bob Crowley & Scott Pask, The Coast of Utopia
Scenic Design, Musical: Bob Crowley, Mary Poppins
Costume Design, Play: Catherine Zuber, The Coast of Utopia
Costume Design, Musical: William Ivey Long, Grey Gardens
Lighting Design, Play: Brian MacDevitt, Kenneth Posner, Natasha Katz; The Coast of Utopia
Lighting Design, Musical: Kevin Adams, Spring Awakening
Regional Theater: Alliance Theatre, Atlanta, GA

Tony Awards, 1948-2007

Year	Play	Musical	Year	Play	Musical
1948	Mister Roberts	No Award	1977	The Shadow Box	Annie
1949	Death of a Salesman	Kiss Me Kate	1978	Da	Ain't Misbehavin'
1950	The Cocktail Party	South Pacific	1979	The Elephant Man	Sweeney Todd
1951	The Rose Tattoo	Guys and Dolls	1980	Children of a Lesser God	Evita
1952	The Fourposter	The King and I	1981	Amadeus	42nd Street
1953	The Crucible	Wonderful Town	1982	The Life and Adventures of Nicholas Nickelby	Nine
1954	The Teahouse of the August Moon	Kismet	1983	Torch Song Trilogy	Cats
1955	The Desperate Hours	The Pajama Game	1984	The Real Thing	La Cage aux Folles
1956	The Diary of Anne Frank	Damn Yankees	1985	Biloxi Blues	Big River
1957	Long Day's Journey Into Night	My Fair Lady	1986	I'm Not Rappaport	The Mystery of Edwin Drood
1958	Sunrise at Campobello	The Music Man	1987	Fences	Les Miserables
1959	J.B.	Redhead	1988	M. Butterfly	Phantom of the Opera
1960	The Miracle Worker	(tie) Fiorello!, The Sound of Music	1989	The Heidi Chronicles	Jerome Robbins' Broadway
1961	Becket	Bye, Bye Birdie	1990	The Grapes of Wrath	City of Angels
1962	A Man for All Seasons	How to Succeed in Business Without Really Trying	1991	Lost in Yonkers	The Will Rogers Follies
1963	Who's Afraid of Virginia Woolf?	A Funny Thing Happened on the Way to the Forum	1992	Dancing at Lughnasa	Crazy for You
1964	Luther	Hello, Dolly!	1993	Angels in America: Millennium Approaches	Kiss of the Spider Woman
1965	The Subject Was Roses	Fiddler on the Roof	1994	Angels in America: Perestroika	Passion
1966	Marat/Sade	Man of La Mancha	1995	Love! Valour! Compassion!	Sunset Boulevard
1967	The Homecoming	Cabaret	1996	Master Class	Rent
1968	Rosencrantz and Guildenstern Are Dead	Hallelujah, Baby!	1997	The Last Night of Ballyhoo	Titanic
1969	The Great White Hope	1776	1998	Art	The Lion King
1970	Borstal Boy	Applause	1999	Side Man	Fosse
1971	Sleuth	Company	2000	Copenhagen	Contact
1972	Sticks and Bones	Two Gentleman of Verona	2001	Proof	The Producers
1973	That Championship Season	A Little Night Music	2002	Edward Albee's The Goat or Who Is Sylvia?	Thoroughly Modern Millie
1974	The River Niger	Raisin	2003	Take Me Out	Hairspray
1975	Equus	The Wiz	2004	I Am My Own Wife	Avenue Q
1976	Travesties	A Chorus Line	2005	Doubt	Monty Python's Spamalot
			2006	The History Boys	Jersey Boys
			2007	The Coast of Utopia	Spring Awakening

Selected 2007 Daytime Emmy Awards

Drama series: (tie) Guiding Light, CBS; The Young and the Restless, CBS
Actress: Maura West, As the World Turns, CBS
Actor: Christian LeBlanc, The Young and the Restless, CBS
Sup. actress: Genie Francis, General Hospital, ABC
Sup. actor: Rick Hearst, General Hospital, ABC
Younger actress: Jennifer Landon, As the World Turns, CBS
Younger actor: Bryton McClure, The Young and the Restless, CBS

Game show host: Bob Barker, The Price Is Right, CBS
Talk show host: Ellen DeGeneres, The Ellen DeGeneres Show, synd.
Talk show: The Ellen DeGeneres Show, synd.
Children's series performer: (tie) Caroll Spinney (Oscar the Grouch) and Kevin Clash (Elmo), Sesame Street, PBS
Drama series directing team: As the World Turns, CBS
Drama series writing team: Guiding Light, CBS
Lifetime achievement awards: Lee Phillip Bell, James Lipton

Selected 2007 Prime-Time Emmy Awards (for 2006-07 TV season)

Drama series: The Sopranos, HBO
Comedy series: 30 Rock, NBC
Miniseries: Broken Trail, AMC
Variety, music, or comedy series: The Daily Show With John Stewart, Comedy Central
Made-for-television movie: Bury My Heart at Wounded Knee, HBO
Lead actor, drama: James Spader, Boston Legal, ABC
Lead actress, drama: Sally Field, Brothers & Sisters, ABC
Lead actor, comedy: Ricky Gervais, Extras, HBO
Lead actress, comedy: America Ferrera, Ugly Betty, ABC
Lead actor, miniseries/movie: Robert Duvall, Broken Trail, AMC
Lead actress, miniseries/movie: Helen Mirren, Prime Suspect: The Final Act, PBS
Sup. actor, drama: Terry O'Quinn, Lost, ABC

Sup. actress, drama: Katherine Heigl, Grey's Anatomy, ABC
Sup. actor, comedy: Jeremy Piven, Entourage, HBO
Sup. actress, comedy: Jaime Pressly, My Name is Earl, NBC
Sup. actor, miniseries/movie: Thomas Haden Church, Broken Trail, AMC
Sup. actress, miniseries/movie: Judy Davis, The Starter Wife, USA
Individual performance, variety series/music program: Tony Bennett, Tony Bennett: An American Classic, NBC
Reality/competition program: The Amazing Race, CBS
Director, drama: Alan Taylor, "Kennedy and Heidi," The Sopranos, HBO
Director, comedy: Richard Shepard, "Pilot," Ugly Betty, ABC
Director, variety, music or comedy: Rob Marshall, Tony Bennett: An American Classic, NBC

Prime-Time Emmy Awards, 1952-2007

The Academy of Television Arts and Sciences presented the first Emmy Awards in 1949. Through the years, award categories have changed, but since 1952, the Academy has given out an outstanding comedy and drama award each year.

Year	Comedy	Drama	Year	Comedy	Drama
1952	*Red Skelton Show*, NBC	*Studio One*, CBS	1977	*Mary Tyler Moore Show*, CBS	*Masterpiece Theatre: Upstairs, Downstairs*; PBS
1953	*I Love Lucy*, CBS	*Robert Montgomery Presents*, NBC	1978	*All in the Family*, CBS	*The Rockford Files*, NBC
1954	*I Love Lucy*, CBS	*The U.S. Steel Hour*, ABC	1979	*Taxi*, ABC	*Lou Grant*, CBS
1955	*Make Room for Daddy*, ABC	*The U.S. Steel Hour*, ABC	1980	*Taxi*, ABC	*Lou Grant*, CBS
1956	*Phil Silvers Show*, CBS	*Producer's Showcase*, NBC	1981	*Taxi*, ABC	*Hill Street Blues*, NBC
1957	*Phil Silvers Show*, CBS	*Requiem for a Heavyweight*, CBS[1]	1982	*Barney Miller*, ABC	*Hill Street Blues*, NBC
			1983	*Cheers*, NBC	*Hill Street Blues*, NBC
1958	*Phil Silvers Show*, CBS	*Gunsmoke*, CBS	1984	*Cheers*, NBC	*Hill Street Blues*, NBC
1959[2]	*Jack Benny Show*, CBS	·	1985	*The Cosby Show*, NBC	*Cagney & Lacey*, CBS
1960	*Art Carney Special*, NBC	*Playhouse 90*, CBS	1986	*Golden Girls*, NBC	*Cagney & Lacey*, CBS
1961	*Jack Benny Show*, CBS	*Hallmark Hall of Fame: Macbeth*, NBC	1987	*Golden Girls*, NBC	*L.A. Law*, NBC
			1988	*The Wonder Years*, ABC	*thirtysomething*, ABC
1962	*Bob Newhart Show*, CBS	*The Defenders*, CBS	1989	*Cheers*, NBC	*L.A. Law*, NBC
1963	*Dick Van Dyke Show*, CBS	*The Defenders*, CBS	1990	*Murphy Brown*, CBS	*L.A. Law*, NBC
1964	*Dick Van Dyke Show*, CBS	*The Defenders*, CBS	1991	*Cheers*, NBC	*L.A. Law*, NBC
1965	*Dick Van Dyke Show*, CBS	*Hallmark Hall of Fame: The Magnificent Yankee*, NBC	1992	*Murphy Brown*, CBS	*Northern Exposure*, CBS
			1993	*Seinfeld*, NBC	*Picket Fences*, CBS
1966	*Dick Van Dyke Show*, CBS	*The Fugitive*, ABC	1994	*Frasier*, NBC	*Picket Fences*, CBS
1967	*The Monkees*, NBC	*Mission: Impossible*, CBS	1995	*Frasier*, NBC	*NYPD Blue*, ABC
1968	*Get Smart*, NBC	*Mission: Impossible*, CBS	1996	*Frasier*, NBC	*ER*, NBC
1969	*Get Smart*, NBC	*NET Playhouse*, NET	1997	*Frasier*, NBC	*Law & Order*, NBC
1970	*My World and Welcome to It*, NBC	*Marcus Welby, M.D.*, ABC	1998	*Frasier*, NBC	*The Practice*, ABC
			1999	*Ally McBeal*, Fox	*The Practice*, ABC
1971	*All in the Family*, CBS	*The Bold Ones: "The Senator,"* NBC	2000	*Will & Grace*, NBC	*The West Wing*, NBC
			2001	*Sex and the City*, HBO	*The West Wing*, NBC
1972	*All in the Family*, CBS	*Masterpiece Theatre: Elizabeth R*, PBS	2002	*Friends*, NBC	*The West Wing*, NBC
			2003	*Everybody Loves Raymond*, CBS	*The West Wing*, NBC
1973	*All in the Family*, CBS	*The Waltons*, CBS			
1974	*M*A*S*H*, CBS	*Masterpiece Theatre: Upstairs, Downstairs*; PBS	2004	*Arrested Development*, Fox	*The Sopranos*, HBO
			2005	*Everybody Loves Raymond*, CBS	*Lost*, ABC
1975	*Mary Tyler Moore Show*, CBS	*Masterpiece Theatre: Upstairs, Downstairs*; PBS	2006	*The Office*, NBC	*24*, Fox
1976	*Mary Tyler Moore Show*, CBS	*Police Story*, NBC	2007	*30 Rock*, NBC	*The Sopranos*, HBO

(1) "Best Single Program of the Year," shown on *Playhouse 90*, which was named "Best New Series." (2) Beginning in 1959, Emmys awarded for work in the season encompassing the previous and current year. (*) *Playhouse 90* (CBS) was best drama of 1 hour or longer; *Alcoa-Goodyear Theatre* (NBC) was best drama of less than 1 hour.

2007 Golden Globe Awards

Film

Drama: *Babel*
Comedy/Musical: *Dreamgirls*
Actress, Drama: Helen Mirren, *The Queen*
Actor, Drama: Forest Whitaker, *The Last King of Scotland*
Actress, Comedy/Musical: Meryl Streep, *The Devil Wears Prada*
Actor, Comedy/Musical: Sacha Baron Cohen, *Borat: Cultural Learnings of America for Make Benefit Glorious Nation of Kazakhstan*
Sup. Actress: Jennifer Hudson, *Dreamgirls*
Sup. Actor: Eddie Murphy, *Dreamgirls*
Director: Martin Scorsese, *The Departed*
Screenplay: Peter Morgan, *The Queen*
Animated Film: *Cars*
Foreign-Language Film: *Letters From Iwo Jima*
Original Score: Alexandre Desplat, *The Painted Veil*

Original Song: "The Song of the Heart," *Happy Feet* (w/m by Prince Rogers Nelson)
Cecil B. DeMille Award for lifetime achievement: Warren Beatty

Television

Series, Drama: *Grey's Anatomy*, ABC
Series, Comedy/Musical: *Ugly Betty*, ABC
Actress, Drama: Kyra Sedgwick, *The Closer*, TNT
Actor, Drama: Hugh Laurie, *House*, FOX
Actress, Comedy/Musical: America Ferrera, *Ugly Betty*, ABC
Actor, Comedy/Musical: Alec Baldwin, *30 Rock*, NBC
Miniseries or Movie Made for TV: *Elizabeth I*, HBO
Actress, Miniseries/Movie: Helen Mirren, *Elizabeth I*, HBO
Actor, Miniseries/Movie: Bill Nighy, *Gideon's Daughter*, BBC America
Sup. Actress: Emily Blunt, *Gideon's Daughter*, BBC America
Sup. Actor: Jeremy Irons, *Elizabeth I*, HBO

2007 People's Choice Awards

Film

Picture: *Pirates of the Caribbean: Dead Man's Chest*
Drama: *Pirates of the Caribbean: Dead Man's Chest*
Comedy: *Click*
Family Movie: *Cars*
Movie Stars: Jennifer Aniston, Johnny Depp
Leading Lady/Man: Cameron Diaz, Vince Vaughn
Action Movie Stars: Halle Berry, Johnny Depp
On-Screen Matchup: Johnny Depp & Keira Knightley

Music

Male Singer: Kenny Chesney
Female Singer: Carrie Underwood
Group or Band: Nickelback
R&B Song: "SexyBack," Justin Timberlake
Hip-Hop Song: "Shake That," Eminem

Pop Song: "Hips Don't Lie," Shakira
Country Song: "Before He Cheats," Carrie Underwood
Rock Song: "Who Says You Can't Go Home," Bon Jovi
Remake: "Life Is a Highway," Rascal Flatts

Television

Drama: *Grey's Anatomy*
Comedy: *Two and a Half Men*
Animated Comedy: *The Simpsons*
Male TV Star: Patrick Dempsey
Female TV Star: Eva Longoria
New Comedy: *The Class*
New Drama: *Heroes*
Talk Show Host: Ellen DeGeneres
Competition/Reality Program: *American Idol*

Academy Awards (Oscars), 1927-2006

Year Picture	Actor	Actress	Sup. Actor[1]	Sup. Actress[1]	Director
1927-Wings 28	Emil Jannings, *The Way of All Flesh*	Janet Gaynor, *Seventh Heaven*			Frank Borzage, *Seventh Heaven;* Lewis Milestone, *Two Arabian Knights*
1928-Broadway Melody 29	Warner Baxter, *In Old Arizona*	Mary Pickford, *Coquette*			Frank Lloyd, *The Divine Lady*
1929-All Quiet on the 30 Western Front	George Arliss *Disraeli*	Norma Shearer *The Divorcee*			Lewis Milestone *All Quiet on the Western Front*
1930-Cimarron 31	Lionel Barrymore *Free Soul*	Marie Dressler *Min and Bill*			Norman Taurog *Skippy*
1931-Grand Hotel 32	Fredric March *Dr. Jekyll and Mr. Hyde;* Wallace Beery *The Champ* (tie)	Helen Hayes *The Sin of Madelon Claudet*			Frank Borzage *Bad Girl*
1932-Cavalcade 33	Charles Laughton *The Private Life of Henry VIII*	Katharine Hepburn *Morning Glory*			Frank Lloyd *Cavalcade*
1934 It Happened One Night	Clark Gable *It Happened One Night*	Claudette Colbert *It Happened One Night*			Frank Capra *It Happened One Night*
1935 Mutiny on the Bounty	Victor McLaglen *The Informer*	Bette Davis *Dangerous*			John Ford *The Informer*
1936 The Great Ziegfeld	Paul Muni *Story of Louis Pasteur*	Luise Rainer *The Great Ziegfeld*	Walter Brennan *Come and Get It*	Gale Sondergaard *Anthony Adverse*	Frank Capra *Mr. Deeds Goes to Town*
1937 Life of Emile Zola	Spencer Tracy *Captains Courageous*	Luise Rainer *The Good Earth*	Joseph Schildkraut *Life of Emile Zola*	Alice Brady *In Old Chicago*	Leo McCarey *The Awful Truth*
1938 You Can't Take It With You	Spencer Tracy *Boys Town*	Bette Davis *Jezebel*	Walter Brennan *Kentucky*	Fay Bainter *Jezebel*	Frank Capra *You Can't Take It With You*
1939 Gone With the Wind	Robert Donat *Goodbye Mr. Chips*	Vivien Leigh *Gone With the Wind*	Thomas Mitchell *Stage Coach*	Hattie McDaniel *Gone With the Wind*	Victor Fleming *Gone With the Wind*
1940 Rebecca	James Stewart *The Philadelphia Story*	Ginger Rogers *Kitty Foyle*	Walter Brennan *The Westerner*	Jane Darwell *The Grapes of Wrath*	John Ford *The Grapes of Wrath*
1941 How Green Was My Valley	Gary Cooper *Sergeant York*	Joan Fontaine *Suspicion*	Donald Crisp *How Green Was My Valley*	Mary Astor *The Great Lie*	John Ford *How Green Was My Valley*
1942 Mrs. Miniver	James Cagney *Yankee Doodle Dandy*	Greer Garson *Mrs. Miniver*	Van Heflin *Johnny Eager*	Teresa Wright *Mrs. Miniver*	William Wyler *Mrs. Miniver*
1943 Casablanca	Paul Lukas *Watch on the Rhine*	Jennifer Jones *The Song of Bernadette*	Charles Coburn *The More the Merrier*	Katina Paxinou *For Whom the Bell Tolls*	Michael Curtiz *Casablanca*
1944 Going My Way	Bing Crosby *Going My Way*	Ingrid Bergman *Gaslight*	Barry Fitzgerald *Going My Way*	Ethel Barrymore *None But the Lonely Heart*	Leo McCarey *Going My Way*
1945 The Lost Weekend	Ray Milland *The Lost Weekend*	Joan Crawford *Mildred Pierce*	James Dunn *A Tree Grows in Brooklyn*	Anne Revere *National Velvet*	Billy Wilder *The Lost Weekend*
1946 The Best Years of Our Lives	Fredric March *The Best Years of Our Lives*	Olivia de Havilland *To Each His Own*	Harold Russell *The Best Years of Our Lives*	Anne Baxter *The Razor's Edge*	William Wyler *The Best Years of Our Lives*
1947 Gentleman's Agreement	Ronald Colman *A Double Life*	Loretta Young *The Farmer's Daughter*	Edmund Gwenn *Miracle on 34th Street*	Celeste Holm *Gentleman's Agreement*	Elia Kazan *Gentleman's Agreement*
1948 Hamlet	Laurence Olivier *Hamlet*	Jane Wyman *Johnny Belinda*	Walter Huston *Treasure of Sierra Madre*	Claire Trevor *Key Largo*	John Huston *Treasure of Sierra Madre*
1949 All the King's Men	Broderick Crawford *All the King's Men*	Olivia de Havilland *The Heiress*	Dean Jagger *Twelve O'Clock High*	Mercedes McCambridge *All the King's Men*	Joseph L. Mankiewicz *Letter to Three Wives*
1950 All About Eve	Jose Ferrer *Cyrano de Bergerac*	Judy Holliday *Born Yesterday*	George Sanders *All About Eve*	Josephine Hull *Harvey*	Joseph L. Mankiewicz *All About Eve*
1951 An American in Paris	Humphrey Bogart *The African Queen*	Vivien Leigh *A Streetcar Named Desire*	Karl Malden *A Streetcar Named Desire*	Kim Hunter *A Streetcar Named Desire*	George Stevens *A Place in the Sun*
1952 The Greatest Show on Earth	Gary Cooper *High Noon*	Shirley Booth *Come Back Little Sheba*	Anthony Quinn *Viva Zapata!*	Gloria Grahame *The Bad and the Beautiful*	John Ford *The Quiet Man*
1953 From Here to Eternity	William Holden *Stalag 17*	Audrey Hepburn *Roman Holiday*	Frank Sinatra *From Here to Eternity*	Donna Reed *From Here to Eternity*	Fred Zinnemann *From Here to Eternity*
1954 On the Waterfront	Marlon Brando *On the Waterfront*	Grace Kelly *The Country Girl*	Edmond O'Brien *The Barefoot Contessa*	Eva Marie Saint *On the Waterfront*	Elia Kazan *On the Waterfront*
1955 Marty	Ernest Borgnine *Marty*	Anna Magnani *The Rose Tattoo*	Jack Lemmon *Mister Roberts*	Jo Van Fleet *East of Eden*	Delbert Mann *Marty*
1956 Around the World in 80 Days	Yul Brynner *The King and I*	Ingrid Bergman *Anastasia*	Anthony Quinn *Lust for Life*	Dorothy Malone *Written on the Wind*	George Stevens *Giant*
1957 The Bridge on the River Kwai	Alec Guinness *The Bridge on the River Kwai*	Joanne Woodward *The Three Faces of Eve*	Red Buttons *Sayonara*	Miyoshi Umeki *Sayonara*	David Lean *The Bridge on the River Kwai*

Year	Picture	Actor	Actress	Sup. Actor[1]	Sup. Actress[1]	Director
1958	Gigi	David Niven *Separate Tables*	Susan Hayward *I Want to Live*	Burl Ives *The Big Country*	Wendy Hiller *Separate Tables*	Vincente Minnelli *Gigi*
1959	Ben-Hur	Charlton Heston *Ben-Hur*	Simone Signoret *Room at the Top*	Hugh Griffith *Ben-Hur*	Shelley Winters *Diary of Anne Frank*	William Wyler *Ben-Hur*
1960	The Apartment	Burt Lancaster *Elmer Gantry*	Elizabeth Taylor *Butterfield 8*	Peter Ustinov *Spartacus*	Shirley Jones *Elmer Gantry*	Billy Wilder *The Apartment*
1961	West Side Story	Maximilian Schell *Judgment at Nuremberg*	Sophia Loren *Two Women*	George Chakiris *West Side Story*	Rita Moreno *West Side Story*	Jerome Robbins, Robert Wise *West Side Story*
1962	Lawrence of Arabia	Gregory Peck *To Kill a Mockingbird*	Anne Bancroft *The Miracle Worker*	Ed Begley *Sweet Bird of Youth*	Patty Duke *The Miracle Worker*	David Lean *Lawrence of Arabia*
1963	Tom Jones	Sidney Poitier *Lilies of the Field*	Patricia Neal *Hud*	Melvyn Douglas *Hud*	Margaret Rutherford *The V.I.P.s*	Tony Richardson *Tom Jones*
1964	My Fair Lady	Rex Harrison *My Fair Lady*	Julie Andrews *Mary Poppins*	Peter Ustinov *Topkapi*	Lila Kedrova *Zorba the Greek*	George Cukor *My Fair Lady*
1965	The Sound of Music	Lee Marvin *Cat Ballou*	Julie Christie *Darling*	Martin Balsam *A Thousand Clowns*	Shelley Winters *A Patch of Blue*	Robert Wise *The Sound of Music*
1966	A Man for All Seasons	Paul Scofield *A Man for All Seasons*	Elizabeth Taylor *Who's Afraid of Virginia Woolf?*	Walter Matthau *The Fortune Cookie*	Sandy Dennis *Who's Afraid of Virginia Woolf?*	Fred Zinnemann *A Man for All Seasons*
1967	In the Heat of the Night	Rod Steiger *In the Heat of the Night*	Katharine Hepburn *Guess Who's Coming to Dinner*	George Kennedy *Cool Hand Luke*	Estelle Parsons *Bonnie and Clyde*	Mike Nichols *The Graduate*
1968	Oliver!	Cliff Robertson *Charly*	Katharine Hepburn *The Lion in Winter*; Barbra Streisand *Funny Girl* (tie)	Jack Albertson *The Subject Was Roses*	Ruth Gordon *Rosemary's Baby*	Sir Carol Reed *Oliver!*
1969	Midnight Cowboy	John Wayne *True Grit*	Maggie Smith *The Prime of Miss Jean Brodie*	Gig Young *They Shoot Horses, Don't They?*	Goldie Hawn *Cactus Flower*	John Schlesinger *Midnight Cowboy*
1970	Patton	George C. Scott *Patton* (refused)	Glenda Jackson *Women in Love*	John Mills *Ryan's Daughter*	Helen Hayes *Airport*	Franklin Schaffner *Patton*
1971	The French Connection	Gene Hackman *The French Connection*	Jane Fonda *Klute*	Ben Johnson *The Last Picture Show*	Cloris Leachman *The Last Picture Show*	William Friedkin *The French Connection*
1972	The Godfather	Marlon Brando *The Godfather* (refused)	Liza Minnelli *Cabaret*	Joel Grey *Cabaret*	Eileen Heckart *Butterflies Are Free*	Bob Fosse *Cabaret*
1973	The Sting	Jack Lemmon *Save the Tiger*	Glenda Jackson *A Touch of Class*	John Houseman *The Paper Chase*	Tatum O'Neal *Paper Moon*	George Roy Hill *The Sting*
1974	The Godfather Part II	Art Carney *Harry and Tonto*	Ellen Burstyn *Alice Doesn't Live Here Anymore*	Robert DeNiro *The Godfather Part II*	Ingrid Bergman *Murder on the Orient Express*	Francis Ford Coppola *The Godfather Part II*
1975	One Flew Over the Cuckoo's Nest	Jack Nicholson *One Flew Over the Cuckoo's Nest*	Louise Fletcher *One Flew Over the Cuckoo's Nest*	George Burns *The Sunshine Boys*	Lee Grant *Shampoo*	Milos Forman *One Flew Over the Cuckoo's Nest*
1976	Rocky	Peter Finch *Network*	Faye Dunaway *Network*	Jason Robards *All the President's Men*	Beatrice Straight *Network*	John G. Avildsen *Rocky*
1977	Annie Hall	Richard Dreyfuss *The Goodbye Girl*	Diane Keaton *Annie Hall*	Jason Robards *Julia*	Vanessa Redgrave *Julia*	Woody Allen *Annie Hall*
1978	The Deer Hunter	Jon Voight *Coming Home*	Jane Fonda *Coming Home*	Christopher Walken *The Deer Hunter*	Maggie Smith *California Suite*	Michael Cimino *The Deer Hunter*
1979	Kramer vs. Kramer	Dustin Hoffman *Kramer vs. Kramer*	Sally Field *Norma Rae*	Melvyn Douglas *Being There*	Meryl Streep *Kramer vs. Kramer*	Robert Benton *Kramer vs. Kramer*
1980	Ordinary People	Robert DeNiro *Raging Bull*	Sissy Spacek *Coal Miner's Daughter*	Timothy Hutton *Ordinary People*	Mary Steenburgen *Melvin & Howard*	Robert Redford *Ordinary People*
1981	Chariots of Fire	Henry Fonda *On Golden Pond*	Katharine Hepburn *On Golden Pond*	John Gielgud *Arthur*	Maureen Stapleton *Reds*	Warren Beatty *Reds*
1982	Gandhi	Ben Kingsley *Gandhi*	Meryl Streep *Sophie's Choice*	Louis Gossett Jr. *An Officer and a Gentleman*	Jessica Lange *Tootsie*	Richard Attenborough *Gandhi*
1983	Terms of Endearment	Robert Duvall *Tender Mercies*	Shirley MacLaine *Terms of Endearment*	Jack Nicholson *Terms of Endearment*	Linda Hunt *The Year of Living Dangerously*	James L. Brooks *Terms of Endearment*
1984	Amadeus	F. Murray Abraham *Amadeus*	Sally Field *Places in the Heart*	Haing S. Ngor *The Killing Fields*	Peggy Ashcroft *A Passage to India*	Milos Forman *Amadeus*
1985	Out of Africa	William Hurt *Kiss of the Spider Woman*	Geraldine Page *The Trip to Bountiful*	Don Ameche *Cocoon*	Anjelica Huston *Prizzi's Honor*	Sydney Pollack *Out of Africa*
1986	Platoon	Paul Newman *The Color of Money*	Marlee Matlin *Children of a Lesser God*	Michael Caine *Hannah and Her Sisters*	Dianne Wiest *Hannah and Her Sisters*	Oliver Stone *Platoon*
1987	The Last Emperor	Michael Douglas *Wall Street*	Cher *Moonstruck*	Sean Connery *The Untouchables*	Olympia Dukakis *Moonstruck*	Bernardo Bertolucci *The Last Emperor*
1988	Rain Man	Dustin Hoffman *Rain Man*	Jodie Foster *The Accused*	Kevin Kline *A Fish Called Wanda*	Geena Davis *The Accidental Tourist*	Barry Levinson *Rain Man*
1989	Driving Miss Daisy	Daniel Day-Lewis *My Left Foot*	Jessica Tandy *Driving Miss Daisy*	Denzel Washington *Glory*	Brenda Fricker *My Left Foot*	Oliver Stone *Born on the Fourth of July*
1990	Dances With Wolves	Jeremy Irons *Reversal of Fortune*	Kathy Bates *Misery*	Joe Pesci *Goodfellas*	Whoopi Goldberg *Ghost*	Kevin Costner *Dances With Wolves*
1991	The Silence of the Lambs	Anthony Hopkins *The Silence of the Lambs*	Jodie Foster *The Silence of the Lambs*	Jack Palance *City Slickers*	Mercedes Ruehl *The Fisher King*	Jonathan Demme *The Silence of the Lambs*

Year	Picture	Actor	Actress	Sup. Actor[1]	Sup. Actress[1]	Director
1992	Unforgiven	Al Pacino, Scent of a Woman	Emma Thompson, Howards End	Gene Hackman, Unforgiven	Marisa Tomei, My Cousin Vinny	Clint Eastwood, Unforgiven
1993	Schindler's List	Tom Hanks, Philadelphia	Holly Hunter, The Piano	Tommy Lee Jones, The Fugitive	Anna Paquin, The Piano	Steven Spielberg, Schindler's List
1994	Forrest Gump	Tom Hanks, Forrest Gump	Jessica Lange, Blue Sky	Martin Landau, Ed Wood	Dianne Wiest, Bullets Over Broadway	Robert Zemeckis, Forrest Gump
1995	Braveheart	Nicolas Cage, Leaving Las Vegas	Susan Sarandon, Dead Man Walking	Kevin Spacey, The Usual Suspects	Mira Sorvino, Mighty Aphrodite	Mel Gibson, Braveheart
1996	The English Patient	Geoffrey Rush, Shine	Frances McDormand, Fargo	Cuba Gooding Jr., Jerry Maguire	Juliette Binoche, The English Patient	Anthony Minghella, The English Patient
1997	Titanic	Jack Nicholson, As Good As It Gets	Helen Hunt, As Good As It Gets	Robin Williams, Good Will Hunting	Kim Basinger, L.A. Confidential	James Cameron, Titanic
1998	Shakespeare in Love	Roberto Benigni, Life Is Beautiful	Gwyneth Paltrow, Shakespeare in Love	James Coburn, Affliction	Judi Dench, Shakespeare in Love	Steven Spielberg, Saving Private Ryan
1999	American Beauty	Kevin Spacey, American Beauty	Hilary Swank, Boys Don't Cry	Michael Caine, The Cider House Rules	Angelina Jolie, Girl, Interrupted	Sam Mendes, American Beauty
2000	Gladiator	Russell Crowe, Gladiator	Julia Roberts, Erin Brockovich	Benicio Del Toro, Traffic	Marcia Gay Harden, Pollock	Steven Soderbergh, Traffic
2001	A Beautiful Mind	Denzel Washington, Training Day	Halle Berry, Monster's Ball	Jim Broadbent, Iris	Jennifer Connelly, A Beautiful Mind	Ron Howard, A Beautiful Mind
2002	Chicago	Adrien Brody, The Pianist	Nicole Kidman, The Hours	Chris Cooper, Adaptation	Catherine Zeta-Jones, Chicago	Roman Polanski, The Pianist
2003	The Lord of the Rings: The Return of the King	Sean Penn, Mystic River	Charlize Theron, Monster	Tim Robbins, Mystic River	Renée Zellweger, Cold Mountain	Peter Jackson, The Lord of the Rings: The Return of the King
2004	Million Dollar Baby	Jamie Foxx, Ray	Hilary Swank, Million Dollar Baby	Morgan Freeman, Million Dollar Baby	Cate Blanchett, The Aviator	Clint Eastwood, Million Dollar Baby
2005	Crash	Philip Seymour Hoffman, Capote	Reese Witherspoon, Walk the Line	George Clooney, Syriana	Rachel Weisz, The Constant Gardener	Ang Lee, Brokeback Mountain
2006	The Departed	Forest Whitaker, The Last King of Scotland	Helen Mirren, The Queen	Alan Arkin, Little Miss Sunshine	Jennifer Hudson, Dreamgirls	Martin Scorsese, The Departed

(1) These awards not given until 1936.

Other 2006 Oscar Winners: Original Screenplay: *Little Miss Sunshine*. Adapted Screenplay: *The Departed*. Animated Feature: *Happy Feet*. Art Direction: *Pan's Labyrinth*. Foreign Language Film: *The Lives of Others*. Cinematography: *Pan's Labyrinth*. Documentary Short: *The Blood of Yingzhou District*. Short Films: *The Danish Poet* (animated), *West Bank Story* (live-action). Visual Effects: *Pirates of the Caribbean: Dead Man's* Chest. Costume Design: *Marie Antoinette*. Documentary Feature: *An Inconvenient Truth*. Film Editing: *The Departed*. Sound Mixing: *Dreamgirls*. Sound Editing: *Letters From Iwo Jima*. Original Score: *Babel*, Gustavo Santaolalla. Original Song: "I Need to Wake Up," *An Inconvenient Truth* (w/m by Melissa Etheridge). Makeup: *Pan's Labyrinth*.

Other 2007 Film Awards

Cannes Film Festival Awards: Feature Films—Palme d'Or (Golden Palm): *4 Luni, 3 Saptamini si 2 Zile* (*4 Months, 3 Weeks, and 2 Days*), Cristian Mungiu, Romania. 60th Anniversary Award: *Paranoid Park*, Gus Van Sant, U.S./France. Grand Prix: *Mogari No Mori*, Naomi Kawase, Japan/France. Best Actress: Jeon Do Yeon, *Secret Sunshine*, South Korea. Best Actor: Konstantin Lavronenko, *Izgnanie*, Russia. Best Director: Julian Schnabel, *Le Scaphandre et le papillon*, France. Best Screenplay: Fatih Akin, *Auf der anderen seite*, Germany/Turkey. Jury Prize: *Persepolis*, Marjane Satrapi/Vincent Paronnaud, France; *Stellet Licht*, Carlos Reygadas, Mexico/France. Prize "Vulcain de l'Artiste-Technicien": Janusz Kaminski, *Le Scaphandre et le papillon*, France. Caméra d'Or: *Meduzot*, Etgar Keret/Shira Geffen, Israel; Mention spéciale: *Control*, Anton Corbijn, U.K./U.S.

Short Films—Palme d'Or: *Ver Llover*, Elisa Miller, Mexico. Mention spéciale: *Ah Ma*, Anthony Chen, Singapore; *Run*, Mark Albiston, New Zealand.

Director's Guild of America Awards: Feature film: Martin Scorsese, *The Departed*; Documentary: Arunas Matelis, *Before Flying Back to the Earth*.

Sundance Film Festival Awards: Grand Jury Prize: *Padre Nuestro*, Christopher Zalla (drama); *Manda Bala* (*Send a Bullet*), Jason Kohn (doc.). World Cinema Jury Prize: *Enemies of Happiness* (*Vores Lykkes Fjender*), Eva Mulvad/Anja Al Erhayem, Denmark (doc.); *Sweet Mud* (*Adama Meshugaat*), Dror Shaul, Israel (drama). Audience Awards: *Hear and Now*, Irene Taylor Brodsky (doc.); *Grace is Gone*, James C. Strouse, (drama). World Cinema Audience Award: *In the Shadow of the Moon*, David Sington, U.K. (doc.); *Once*, John Carney, Ireland (drama). Directing Award: *War/Dance*, Sean Fine/Andrea Nix Fine (doc.); *Rocket Science*, Jeffrey Blitz (drama). Cinematography: Heloisa Passos, *Manda Bala* (doc.); Benoit Debie, *Joshua* (drama). Documentary Editing Award: Hibah Sherif Frisina/Charlton McMillan/Michael Schweitzer, *Nanking*. Waldo Salt Screenwriting Award: James C. Strouse, *Grace is Gone*. Special Jury Prize: *No End in Sight*, Charles Ferguson (doc.). Special Jury Prize for Acting: Jess Weixler, *Teeth*; Tamara Podemski, *Four Sheets to the Wind*. Special Jury Prize for Singularity of Vision: Chris Smith, *The Pool*.

2007 MTV Video Music Awards

Monster Single of the Year: "Umbrella," Rihanna feat. Jay-Z
Quadruple Threat of the Year: Justin Timberlake
Best Collaboration: "Beautiful Liar," Beyoncé feat. Shakira
Male Artist of the Year: Justin Timberlake
Female Artist of the Year: Fergie
Best Group: Fall Out Boy
Best New Artist: Gym Class Heroes

Video of the Year: "Umbrella," Rihanna feat. Jay-Z
Best Choreography: "My Love," Justin Timberlake; Marty Kudelka, choreographer
Best Direction: "What Goes Around...Comes Around," Justin Timberlake; Samuel Bayer, director
Best Editing: "Smiley Faces," Gnarls Barkley; Ken Mowe, editor

2007 Academy of Country Music Awards

Entertainer of the Year: Kenny Chesney
Album of the Year: *Some Hearts*, Carrie Underwood; prod. Mark Bright, Dann Huff
Record of the Year (single): "Give It Away," George Strait; prod. Tony Brown, George Strait
Song of the Year: "Give It Away," George Strait; written by Bill Anderson, Buddy Cannon, Jamey Johnson
Vocal Event of the Year: "Building Bridges," Brooks & Dunn, Vince Gill, Sheryl Crow; prod. Tony Brown, Ronnie Dunn, Kix Brooks

Female Vocalist: Carrie Underwood
Male Vocalist: Brad Paisley
Vocal Duo: Brooks & Dunn
Vocal Group: Rascal Flatts
New Female Vocalist: Miranda Lambert
New Male Vocalist: Rodney Atkins
New Duo/Group: Little Big Town
Video of the Year: "Before He Cheats," Carrie Underwood; dir. Roman White
Humanitarian Award: Brooks & Dunn

Grammy Awards

Source: National Academy of Recording Arts & Sciences
2006 Grammy Awards are for albums released Oct. 1, 2005–Sept. 30, 2006, and were presented in Feb. 2007.

Selected Grammy Awards for 2006

Record of the Year (single): "Not Ready to Make Nice," Dixie Chicks
Album of the Year: *Taking the Long Way*, Dixie Chicks
Song of the Year: "Not Ready to Make Nice," Dixie Chicks
New Artist: Carrie Underwood
Short Form Music Video: "Here It Goes Again," OK Go
Pop Vocal Perf., Female: "Ain't No Other Man," Christina Aguilera
Pop Vocal Perf., Male: "Waiting on the World to Change," John Mayer
Pop Vocal Perf., Duo/Group: "My Humps," The Black Eyed Peas
Pop Vocal Perf., Collaboration: "For Once in My Life," Tony Bennett & Stevie Wonder
Pop Instrumental Album: *Fingerprints*, Peter Frampton
Pop Vocal Album: *Continuum*, John Mayer
Pop Vocal Album, Traditional: *Duets: An American Classic*, Tony Bennett
Dance Recording: "SexyBack," Justin Timberlake
Electronic/Dance Album: *Confessions on a Dance Floor*, Madonna
Rock Vocal Perf., Solo: "Someday Baby," Bob Dylan
Rock Vocal Perf., Duo/Group: "Dani California," Red Hot Chili Peppers
Rock Instrumental Perf.: "The Wizard Turns on...," The Flaming Lips
Hard Rock Perf.: "Woman," Wolfmother
Metal Perf.: "Eyes of the Insane," Slayer
Rock Song: "Dani California," Red Hot Chili Peppers
Rock Album: *Stadium Arcadium*, Red Hot Chili Peppers
Alternative Album: *St. Elsewhere*, Gnarls Barkley
R&B Vocal Perf., Female: "Be Without You," Mary J. Blige
R&B Vocal Perf., Male: "Heaven," John Legend
R&B Vocal Perf., Duo/Group: "Family Affair," Sly & the Family Stone, John Legend, Joss Stone, with Van Hunt
R&B Vocal Performance, Traditional: "God Bless the Child," George Benson & Al Jarreau feat. Jill Scott

Urban/Alternative Perf.: "Crazy," Gnarls Barkley
R&B Song: "Be Without You," Mary J. Blige
R&B Album: *The Breakthrough*, Mary J. Blige
R&B Album, Contemporary: *B'Day*, Beyoncé
Rap Perf., Solo: "What You Know," T.I.
Rap Perf., Duo/Group: "Ridin," Chamillionaire feat. Krayzie Bone
Rap Song: "Money Maker," Ludacris feat. Pharrell
Rap Album: *Release Therapy*, Ludacris
Country Vocal Perf., Female: "Jesus, Take the Wheel," Carrie Underwood
Country Vocal Perf., Male: "The Reason Why," Vince Gill
Country Vocal Perf., Duo/Group: "Not Ready to Make Nice," Dixie Chicks
Country Song: "Jesus, Take the Wheel," Carrie Underwood
Country Album: *Taking the Long Way*, Dixie Chicks
Bluegrass Album: *Instrumentals*, Ricky Skaggs and Kentucky Thunder
Jazz Album, Contemporary: *The Hidden Land*, Béla Fleck & the Flecktones
Jazz Album, Instr.: *The Ultimate Adventure*, Chick Corea
Jazz Album, Vocal: *Turned to Blue*, Nancy Wilson
Blues Album, Contemporary: *After the Rain*, Irma Thomas
Blues Album, Traditional: *Risin' With the Blues*, Ike Turner
Folk/Americana Album, Contemporary: *Modern Times*, Bob Dylan
Folk Album, Traditional: *We Shall Overcome–The Seeger Sessions*, Bruce Springsteen
Latin Pop Album: *Adentro*, Arjona
Producer, Non-Classical: Rick Rubin
Classical Album: *Mahler: Symphony No. 7*, Michael Tilson Thomas, San Francisco Symphony
Classical Vocal Perf.: *Rilke Songs*, Lorraine Hunt Lieberson (Peter Serkin)

Grammy Awards for 1958-2006

Record of the Year (single)	Year	Album of the Year
Domenico Modugno, "Nel Blu Dipinto Di Blu (Volare)"	1958	Henry Mancini, *The Music From Peter Gunn*
Bobby Darin, "Mack the Knife"	1959	Frank Sinatra, *Come Dance With Me*
Percy Faith, "Theme From a Summer Place"	1960	Bob Newhart, *Button Down Mind*
Henry Mancini, "Moon River"	1961	Judy Garland, *Judy at Carnegie Hall*
Tony Bennett, "I Left My Heart in San Francisco"	1962	Vaughn Meader, *The First Family*
Henry Mancini, "The Days of Wine and Roses"	1963	Barbra Streisand, *The Barbra Streisand Album*
Stan Getz, Astrud Gilberto, "The Girl From Ipanema"	1964	Stan Getz, Astrud Gilberto, *Getz/Gilberto*
Herb Alpert, "A Taste of Honey"	1965	Frank Sinatra, *September of My Years*
Frank Sinatra, "Strangers in the Night"	1966	Frank Sinatra, *A Man and His Music*
5th Dimension, "Up, Up and Away"	1967	The Beatles, *Sgt. Pepper's Lonely Hearts Club Band*
Simon & Garfunkel, "Mrs. Robinson"	1968	Glen Campbell, *By the Time I Get to Phoenix*
5th Dimension, "Aquarius/Let the Sunshine In"	1969	Blood Sweat and Tears, *Blood, Sweat and Tears*
Simon & Garfunkel, "Bridge Over Troubled Water"	1970	Simon & Garfunkel, *Bridge Over Troubled Water*
Carole King, "It's Too Late"	1971	Carole King, *Tapestry*
Roberta Flack, "The First Time Ever I Saw Your Face"	1972	George Harrison and friends, *The Concert for Bangla Desh*
Roberta Flack, "Killing Me Softly With His Song"	1973	Stevie Wonder, *Innervisions*
Olivia Newton-John, "I Honestly Love You"	1974	Stevie Wonder, *Fulfillingness' First Finale*
Captain & Tennille, "Love Will Keep Us Together"	1975	Paul Simon, *Still Crazy After All These Years*
George Benson, "This Masquerade"	1976	Stevie Wonder, *Songs in the Key of Life*
Eagles, "Hotel California"	1977	Fleetwood Mac, *Rumours*
Billy Joel, "Just the Way You Are"	1978	Bee Gees, *Saturday Night Fever*
The Doobie Brothers, "What a Fool Believes"	1979	Billy Joel, *52nd Street*
Christopher Cross, "Sailing"	1980	Christopher Cross, *Christopher Cross*
Kim Carnes, "Bette Davis Eyes"	1981	John Lennon, Yoko Ono, *Double Fantasy*
Toto, "Rosanna"	1982	Toto, *Toto IV*
Michael Jackson, "Beat It"	1983	Michael Jackson, *Thriller*
Tina Turner, "What's Love Got to Do With It"	1984	Lionel Richie, *Can't Slow Down*
USA for Africa, "We Are the World"	1985	Phil Collins, *No Jacket Required*
Steve Winwood, "Higher Love"	1986	Paul Simon, *Graceland*
Paul Simon, "Graceland"	1987	U2, *The Joshua Tree*
Bobby McFerrin, "Don't Worry, Be Happy"	1988	George Michael, *Faith*
Bette Midler, "Wind Beneath My Wings"	1989	Bonnie Raitt, *Nick of Time*
Phil Collins, "Another Day in Paradise"	1990	Quincy Jones, *Back on the Block*
Natalie Cole, with Nat "King" Cole, "Unforgettable"	1991	Natalie Cole, with Nat "King" Cole, *Unforgettable*
Eric Clapton, "Tears in Heaven"	1992	Eric Clapton, *Unplugged*
Whitney Houston, "I Will Always Love You"	1993	Whitney Houston, *The Bodyguard*
Sheryl Crow, "All I Wanna Do"	1994	Tony Bennett, *MTV Unplugged*
Seal, "Kiss From a Rose"	1995	Alanis Morissette, *Jagged Little Pill*
Eric Clapton, "Change the World"	1996	Celine Dion, *Falling Into You*
Shawn Colvin, "Sunny Came Home"	1997	Bob Dylan, *Time Out of Mind*
Celine Dion, "My Heart Will Go On"	1998	Lauryn Hill, *The Miseducation of Lauryn Hill*
Santana featuring Rob Thomas, "Smooth"	1999	Santana, *Supernatural*
U2, "Beautiful Day"	2000	Steely Dan, *Two Against Nature*
U2, "Walk On"	2001	Various Artists, *O Brother, Where Art Thou?*
Norah Jones, "Don't Know Why"	2002	Norah Jones, *Come Away With Me*
Coldplay, "Clocks"	2003	OutKast, *Speakerboxxx/The Love Below*
Ray Charles & Norah Jones, "Here We Go Again"	2004	Ray Charles & Various Artists, *Genius Loves Company*
Green Day, "Boulevard of Broken Dreams"	2005	U2, *How to Dismantle an Atomic Bomb*
Dixie Chicks, "Not Ready to Make Nice"	2006	Dixie Chicks, *Taking the Long Way*

Top Nations: Wired and Wireless (pp. 350-56)

Internet users	Personal computers in use	Cell phone subscriptions
1. U.S. . . . . 210.2 mil	1. U.S. . . . . .240.5 mil	1. China . . . . 461.1 mil
2. China . . . . 131.1 mil	2. Japan . . . . .78.0 mil	2. U.S. . . . . 233.0 mil
3. Japan. . . . . 90.9 mil	3. China. . . . . .74.1 mil	3. India. . . . . 166.1 mil
4. India . . . . 67.6 mil	4. Germany . . . . .54.5 mil	4. Russia . . . . 120.0 mil
5. Germany. . . . . 50.3 mil	5. UK . . . . .41.5 mil	5. Japan . . . . 101.7 mil

Number of wireless phone subscribers in U.S. . . . . in 1987: 1.2 mil. . . . . in 2006: 233.0 mil
Number of cell phone antennas in U.S. . . . . in 1987: 2,305. . . . . in 2006: 195,613
Average local monthly wireless bill in U.S. . . . . in 1987: $96.83. . . . . in 2006: $50.56

Computers and Internet (pp. 350-55)

Avg. weekly time spent online in U.S., 2006	Desktop & notebook computers in U.S., 2006
E-mail . . . . 4.3 hours	Number of units sold. $24.4 mil[1]
Online entertainment . . . . 2.3 hours	Number of units disposed of . . . . 38.5 mil
Online newspapers . . . . 0.8 hours	Weight of all disposed of . . . . 346,800 tons
E-commerce retail sales in U.S., 2000 . . . . $28.0 bil	E-commerce retail sales in U.S., 2005 . . . . $93.3 bil

Inventions and Patents (pp. 272-76)

Foreign country that received the most U.S. patents, 2006 . . . . Japan, 39,411 patents
Company that received the most U.S. patents, 2006. . . . . I.B.M., 3,621 patents

Timeline of notable inventions, discoveries, and innovations

105	Paper	1853	Aspirin	1928	Bubble gum	1954	Birth-control pill
1589	Flush toilet	1860	Cocaine	1928	Penicillin	1959	Seat belt
1670	Calculus	1866	Dynamite	1937	Nylon	1963	Coffeemaker, auto drip
1709	Piano	1888	Ballpoint pen	1943	LSD	1963	Measles vaccine
1774	Oxygen	1891	Submarine	1945	Tupperware®	1972	Compact disc
1780	Bifocal lens	1902	Air conditioning	1951	Liquid Paper®	1972	Pong (video game)
1836	Pistol (revolver)	1922	Insulin	1953	DNA	1980	Post-it® notes

Environment (pp. 281-87)

Emissions of CO^2 from burning fossil fuels, China (in metric tons). . . . . in 1990: 2.24 bil. . . . . .in 2004: 4.71 bil
Emissions of CO^2 from burning fossil fuels, U.S. (in metric tons) . . . . in 1990: 5.01 bil . . . . .in 2004: 5.91 bil
Emissions of CO^2 from burning fossil fuels, U.K. (in metric tons) . . . . in 1990: 0.60 bil . . . . .in 2004: 0.58 bil

Change in CO^2 Emissions, 1990-2004

China . . . . 110%   U.S. . . . . 18%   U.K. . . . . –3%
Country with most renewable water resources per capita . . . . Greenland, 10.6 million m³ per capita
Country with least renewable water resources per capita. . . . . Kuwait, 7.5 m³ per capita
Country with largest total forest area. . . . . Russia, 3.1 mil sq mi

Meteorology (pp. 288-96)

All-time temperature records

Highest worldwide: El Azizia, Libya: 136°F, Sept. 13, 1922
Highest U.S.: Furnace Creek Ranch, CA: 134°F, July 10, 1913
Lowest worldwide: Vostok Station (Russia), Antarctica: –129°F, July 21, 1983
Lowest U.S.: Prospect Creek Camp, AK: –80°F, Jan. 23, 1971

Weather fatalities and injuries in U.S., 2006	Worst U.S. storms since 1980	Deaths/damages
Extreme heat. . . . . 253 fatalities, 1,513 injuries	Hurricane Katrina	1,833/$125.0 bil[1]
Floods. . . . . 76 fatalities, 23 injuries	1988 drought/heat wave	7,500[1]/$61.6 bil[1]
Tornadoes. . . . . 67 fatalities, 989 injuries	1980 drought/heat wave	10,000[1]/$48.4 bil[1]
Lightning . . . . 47 fatalities, 246 injuries	Hurricane Andrew.	61/$35.6 bil[1]

Noteworthy Astronomical and Space Exploration Events in 2008 (pp. 309-335)

Feb. 5: Gamma-Ray Large Area Space Telescope (NASA). Scheduled launch. Designed to study celestial gamma-ray sources.

Feb. 21: Total lunar eclipse. Beginning visible across central Asia, Africa, North and South America (excluding Alaska); end visible in Europe, western Africa, North and South America.

May 25: *Phoenix Mars Lander*. Scheduled arrival at Mars to study northern polar region.

Aug. 1: Total solar eclipse. Totality across northern Canada and Greenland, central Russia, western and central China.

Aug. 7: Space Shuttle *Atlantis*. Fifth and final servicing mission to Hubble Space Telescope.

Aug. 13: Perseid meteor shower. Viewing favorable from 10 PM to sunrise; best shower of the year, due to waxing gibbous Moon.

Oct. 21: Orionid meteor shower. Viewing favorable from 10 PM until moonrise, after midnight.

(1) Estimated.

SCIENCE AND TECHNOLOGY

Science News 2007

The following were some of the more newsworthy developments in Science in the past year. (See also Astronomy, Computers and Telecommunications, and the Chronology of the Year's Events on pp. 12-28.)

Earth and Life Science

New Light Shed on Prehistoric Impact

A joint U.S.-Czech research team from the Southwest Research Institute and Charles University in Prague announced new findings about the massive impact believed to have killed the dinosaurs and most other forms of life on Earth 65 million years ago. The researchers believe that the asteroid fragments that created the Chicxulub crater on the Yucatan peninsula and the Tycho crater on the Moon were both spawned from a 160-million-year-old collision between the parent object of asteroid Baptistina and another large asteroid, an estimated 60 km in diameter. The collision produced the group of asteroids known today as the Baptistina family. (*Nature*, Sept. 6)

Climate Not a Factor in Neanderthal Extinction

Researchers led by Professor Chronis Tzedakis at the University of Leeds announced that they had ruled out climate change as the cause of the extinction of Neanderthals. After comparing three possible sets of radiocarbon dates for the Neanderthal's extinction with a known paleoclimatic record, the team found that none of the possible dates coincided with massive environmental changes. The team's methods may be applicable to other studies, helping to unravel the role of climate in other significant events in the fossil record. (*Nature*, Sept. 13)

New Primate Ancestor Identified

Researchers led by University of Florida paleontologist Jonathan Bloch found evidence that the most primitive primates are plesiadapiforms, mammals previously thought to be more closely related to flying lemurs. The mammals have some, but not all of the major characteristics of modern primates, but researchers note that the missing features could have been acquired over millions of years. Plesiadapiforms are believed to have originated in the Paleocene era, after the extinction of dinosaurs and before the arrival of known ancestors of today's mammals. (*Proceedings of the National Academy of Sciences*, Jan. 23).

Scientists Replace DNA of One Organism With Another

Researchers for the first time transformed one species of bacteria into another by replacing its DNA. The scientists (at the J. Craig Venter Institute in Maryland) reported that DNA of the bacteria *M. mycoides*, when inserted into a closely related bacterium, took over the host cell and caused it to produce new proteins. The team says that their work suggests that a cell can be "booted up" with the DNA of another species, and that it may be possible to insert a man-made genome into a cell and bring it to life. Possible benefits include microbes that could be used to clean up toxic environments, but critics assert that synthetic organisms could pose a threat to the natural environment, if released into the wild. (*Science*, June 28, 2007)

Influenza in the Off-Season

Researchers at Penn State University and the National Institutes of Health reported that the influenza A virus migrates and mixes with other viruses during the summer, then returns to the Northern Hemisphere before winter as a genetically different virus. The scientists analyzed the genomes of influenza A samples from New Zealand, Australia, and New York state between 1998 and 2005, and discovered that the New York viruses were related to viruses circulating during the winter in the Southern Hemisphere—implying a significant amount of traffic in both directions each season. The teams noted that the best protection against emerging, evolving viruses was the development of universal vaccines to protect against multiple strains of influenza. (*PLoS Pathogens*, Sept. 2007)

Bones Join the Endocrine System

Researchers at Columbia University Medical Center discovered a surprising new role for the human skeleton in controlling body weight and metabolism. Bones secrete a protein called osteocalcin, which travels through the bloodstream to the pancreas and stimulates the production of insulin; it also causes fat cells to release a hormone that increases the body's insulin sensitivity. This discovery means that the skeleton is a member of the endocrine system, along with glands like the pancreas and thyroid; it may also open the door to new treatments for diabetes in humans. (*Cell*, August 10, 2007)

Oldest Known Protein Found in T. Rex Bones

Paleontologist Mary Schweitzer of North Carolina State University made a startling discovery in a set of Tyrannosaurus Rex bones that had been unearthed in Montana: fragments of tissue, including blood vessels, bone cells, and collagen. Mass spectrometry analysis confirmed the presence of collagen, as well as a new world record for the oldest known protein: roughly 68 million years old, far older than the previous oldest known proteins, a mere 100,000-300,000 years old. The protein sequences do not contain complete DNA samples, but they have provided new evidence to support the theory that modern birds are descended from dinosaurs. (*Science*, April 13, 2007)

Resuscitating Million-Year-Old Microbes

Researchers at Rutgers University, led by Kay Bidle, successfully grew ancient microbes, harvested from Antarctic ice, in a laboratory. The microbes were the oldest ever to have been cultivated in a lab from a frozen state, providing insight into how long cells can remain viable in that state. The scientists used ice samples that ranged from 100,000 to 8 million years old; younger microbes grew more quickly, but even the 8 million year old samples were successfully "resuscitated" and made to grow. (*Proceedings of the National Academy of Sciences*, August 14, 2007)

Thousands of Species Found in Deep Antarctic Sea

A team of scientists, led by Angelika Brandt of the University of Hamburg in Germany, dredged up thousands of deep-sea creatures—many of them previously unknown to science—from the Weddell Sea in Antarctica's Southern Ocean. The study team reported on May 17 that more than 700 species had never been seen before, and that the final count could reach 1,500. Among the unusual life forms discovered was a carnivorous sponge, a red octopus that steers itself with wings on its head, and an enormous spider crab. Preliminary genetic analyses suggest many of the deep ocean species are similar to species found in other oceans. According to Brandt, "The Antarctic deep sea is potentially the cradle of life of the global marine species." (*Nature*, May 17)

New Proof for Common Origin of Humanity

Andrea Manica and his University of Cambridge research team claimed that they had conclusively proven the "Out of Africa" theory of a common point of origin for humans. The team examined samples of 6,245 skulls from 105 populations around the world, factored out the influence of climate on skull development, and measured 37 different skull characteristics. They found that skulls from central and Southern Africa showed the largest variety, followed by Europe, Asia, North America, and South America. After comparing their results with genetic data, which has long demonstrated a similar decline in genetic diversity as distance from Africa increased, the researchers concluded that humans do share a common ancestral home in sub-Saharan Africa. (*Nature*, July 2007)

Physical Science

"Spooky Action" in Another Step Towards Quantum Computer

University of Michigan physicists used light to "entangle" two atoms trapped one meter away from each other, which allowed them to communicate with each other through a phenomenon described by Albert Einstein as "spooky action-at-a-distance." The technique could one day be the basis of a new type of super-fast computer architecture. The atoms were used as "qubits," or quantum bits, whose electron configuration represented a piece of information. Scientists excited each atom, causing electrons within them to emit photons which indicated the particular state of the atom. The photons were then guided to interact along a fiber optic thread, allowing the researchers to "entangle" the atoms. The thread could then be severed, but the atoms would remain entangled, no matter how far they were removed from each other. When entangled atoms are subsequently measured, they will always show some correlation—a phenomenon that scientists hope to exploit to create quantum computers that perform tasks impossible for conventional computers, with greater security and higher levels of encryption. (*Nature*, Sept. 6)

New Model for the Neutron

Physicists have believed for dozens of years that neutrons carried a positive charge at their centers and a negative charge at their outside edge. The basic theorem was first described by Enrico Fermi in 1947. University of Washington physicist Gerald A. Miller discovered in 2007 that although the neutron is still electrically neutral, its precise composition is a negative charge in its core *and* its outer edge, with a positive charge in between. The discovery may have an impact on scientists' understanding of the strong force, one of the four fundamental forces of nature, which holds atomic nuclei together and makes it possible for them to exist at all. (*Physical Review Letters*, Sept. 13)

"Solving" Checkers, Once and for All

A team led by University of Alberta prof. Jonathan Schaeffer announced it had "solved" the game of checkers, which has approximately 500 billion billion (5×10^{20}) possible positions; they found that a perfectly-played game will always end in a draw. Schaeffer's team spent more than two decades studying this problem, utilizing dozens of computers that played the game virtually non-stop, applying artificial intelligence techniques to the process. (*Science*, July 19, 2007)

"Le Gran K" Loses Some Weight

The International Bureau of Weights and Measures, keepers of the International Prototype Kilogram (or "Le Gran K"), announced that the official kilogram, a platinum-iridium cylinder cast 118 years ago, has lost approximately 50 micrograms in that time. U.S. professors at the Georgia Institute of Technology have launched a campaign to redefine the kilogram as the mass of an object made from a specific number of carbon-12 atoms. This would bring the kilogram in line with other major standard measurements, all of which have been defined in terms of fundamental physical properties instead of actual, physical objects.

Breakthroughs in Transistor Manufacturing

Intel Corp. announced in January 2007 a new breakthrough in transistor construction, utilizing a material called hafnium (a transition element in the periodic table) which would allow transistors to be made much smaller than ever before. Previously, the smallest transistors were 65 nm (65 nanometers, or about 0.000003 inches) wide; the new transistors are 45 nm wide, allowing roughly twice as many to be packed into the same space and resulting in greater processing power and energy efficiency. New Intel desktop processors utilizing the 45-nm process were scheduled to be available by the end of 2007. IBM was using similar technology to focus on larger-scale servers and supercomputers, and also to prepare for a future shift from 45-nm to 32-nm transistor production.

New Nanowire Production Techniques

Researchers developed a new technique to create tiny light-emitting diodes (LEDs) from nanowires. The new LEDs are highly efficient and emit light in the ultraviolet range, which could make them useful in a number of applications, including optical communications and data storage. The research team, led by scientists at the National Institute of Standards and Technology (NIST), used a variety of fabrication techniques to produce the nanowires, including photolithography (using light to print a pattern into a material) and metal deposition. The wires were then aligned with an electric field, an advance over previous methods which required manual placement of each wire. The resulting LEDs were stable at high temperatures and also after heavy use at room temperature. The researchers suggested that the new production techniques could be applied to other nanoscale structures and applications. (*Applied Physics Letters*, April 30, 2007).

Large Hadron Collider to "Switch On" in 2008

In 2008, the European Organization for Nuclear Research (known as CERN), plans to switch on the Large Hadron Collider (LHC), the largest and highest-energy particle accelerator ever built. When it becomes fully operational, the LHC will accelerate streams of protons to just below (99.9999991%) the speed of light, completing 11,245 laps around the collider's 27 km (17 mi) "track" each second. Superconducting magnets produce the powerful magnetic fields needed to keep the particles traveling in a circle; they are cooled with 128 tons of liquid helium and designed to operate at −456.25°F (−271.25°C), colder than temperatures in deep space.

The most powerful accelerator in operation in 2007 was Fermilab's Tevatron, near Chicago. The Tevatron accelerates particles to nearly one trillion electron volts, known as one TeV; the LHC will accelerate two beams of protons to seven TeV each, traveling in opposite directions. The beams will cross an estimated forty million times each second, each crossing producing about twenty collisions. (A hadron is a collection of quarks, or quarks and antiquarks; protons and neutrons are types of hadrons, hence the name of the collider.) Detectors spaced around the track will record data from the collisions with a massive amount of detail—an estimated four million megabytes of data per hour, or 3 million DVDs of data every year.

The primary goal of the LHC is to discover the Higgs particle, which was predicted more than forty years ago but has never been observed. Physicists have observed sixteen fundamental particles, including electrons, quarks, and neutrinos. Confirmed observations of the Higgs may help to answer—or invalidate—a number of theories that comprise the Standard Model of physics, including why fundamental particles have mass, and why gravity is weak compared with the other three fundamental forces (electromagnetism, the strong force, and the weak force). Because the Higgs, if it exists, is emitted so rarely from these collisions, scientists expect it may take a year or more for the first to be discovered. But the immense power of the LHC may produce other phenomena, including mini black holes or extra dimensions, and may help physicists determine the source of the "dark matter" that makes up an estimated 20-25% of the universe.

In March 2007, a magnet assembly provided by the U.S. failed a pressure test, pushing back the LHC's start-up date. Parts of the collider were scheduled to be cooled and powered up throughout late 2007 and early 2008, before commencing high-energy operations in May 2008.

Science Glossary

This glossary covers some concepts that come up frequently in the news, in biology, chemistry, geology, and physics. See also Astronomy, Computers and Telecommunications, Environment, Health, Meteorology, Weights and Measures.

Biology

Note: For classification terms such as *kingdom, phylum*, etc., see Environment chapter.

Amino acid: one of about 20 similar small molecules that are the building blocks of proteins.

Antibiotic: a drug made from a substance produced by a bacterium, fungus, or other organism that battles bacterial infections and diseases, killing the bacteria or halting their growth.

Autoimmunity: a condition in which an individual's immune system reacts against his or her own tissues; leads to diseases such as lupus, diabetes, inflammatory bowel disease, rheumatoid arthritis.

Bacteriophage: a virus that infects or lyses bacteria. Also called "phage."

Bacterium (plural, bacteria): one of a large, varied class of microscopic and simple, single-celled organisms; bacteria live almost everywhere—some forms cause disease, while others are useful in digestion and other natural processes.

Biodiversity—variety of life forms—both plant and animal—in a given environment.

Cell: the smallest unit of life capable of living independently, or with other cells; usually bounded by a membrane; may include a nucleus and other specialized parts.

Cholesterol: a fatty substance in animal tissues; it is produced by the liver in humans, and is found in foods such as butter, eggs, and meat, and is an essential body constituent.

Chromosome: one of the rod-like structures in the nuclei of cells that carry genetic material (DNA).

Cloning: the process of copying a particular piece of DNA to allow it to be sequenced, studied, or used in some other way; can also refer to producing a genetic copy of an organism.

DNA (deoxyribonucleic acid): the chemical substance that carries genetic information, which determines the form and functioning of all living things.

Ecosystem: an interdependent community of living organisms and their climatic and geographical habitat.

Enzyme: a protein that promotes a particular chemical reaction in the body.

Estrogen: one of a group of hormones that promote development of female secondary sex characteristics and the growth and health of the female reproductive system; males also produce small amounts of estrogen.

Eukaryote: single- or multi-celled organisms whose cells have distinct nuclei.

Evolution: the process of gradual change that may occur as a species adapts to its environment; natural selection is the process by which evolution occurs.

Gene: a portion of a DNA molecule that provides the blueprint for the assembly of a protein.

Gene pool: the collection and total diversity of genes in an interbreeding population.

Gene therapy: a treatment in which scientists try to implant functioning genes into a person's cells so the genes can produce proteins that the person lacks or that help the person fight disease.

Genetic sequencing: the process of determining the order of subunits within a gene or even the order of all genes for an organism.

Genome: the complete set of an organism's genetic material.

Hormone: a substance secreted in one part of an organism that regulates the functioning of other tissues or organs.

Meiosis: the process of cell division that results in gametes (sperm or egg cells), all of which contain half the number of chromosomes as their precursor.

Metabolism: the sum total of the body's chemical processes providing energy for vital functions, and enabling new material to be synthesized.

Mitosis: the process by which a cell divides its nucleus and other cell materials into two duplicate daughter cells with the same DNA.

Neuron: a nerve cell, of the type found in the brain or spinal cord, that sends electrical and chemical messages to other cells.

Nucleus (plural: nuclei): the center of an atom; or the portion of a cell containing the chemical directions for functioning.

Organism: a living being.

Phenotype: the observable properties and characteristics of an organism arising at least in part from its genetic makeup.

Pheromone: a chemical secreted by an animal to influence the behavior of other members of its own species.

Placebo effect: a phenomenon in which patients show improvements even though they have taken a medically inactive substance, called a placebo.

Prokaryote: a single-celled organism that does not have a distinct nucleus, such as bacteria, cyanobacteria, and blue-green algae.

Protein: a complex molecule made up of one or more chains of amino acids; essential to the structure and function of all cells.

RNA (ribonucleic acid): a complex molecule similar to the genetic material DNA, but usually single-stranded; several forms of RNA translate the genetic code of DNA and use that code to assemble proteins for structural and biological functions in the body.

Species: a population of organisms that breed with each other in nature and produce fertile offspring; other definitions of species exist to accommodate the diversity of life on Earth.

Stem cell: a cell that can give rise to other types of cells; for instance, bone marrow stem cells divide and produce different types of blood cells.

Steroid: type of hormone that freely enters cells (other hormones bind to cell surfaces); different varieties can suppress immune response or influence stress reaction, blood pressure, or sexual development; includes testosterone- and estrogen-related compounds.

Testosterone: a hormone that stimulates the development and maintenance of male sexual characteristics and the production of sperm; women also produce small amounts of testosterone.

Virus: a microscopic, often disease-causing, organism made of genetic material surrounded by a protein shell; can only reproduce inside a living cell.

Chemistry

Acid: a class of compound that contrasts with bases. Acids taste sour, turn litmus red/pink, and often produce hydrogen gas in contact with some metals. Acids donate protons (hydrogen atoms minus the electron) in chemical reactions.

Base: a substance that yields hydroxyl ions (OH-) when dissolved in water; any of a class of compounds whose aqueous solutions taste bitter, feel slippery, turn litmus blue, and react with acids to form salts; also known as **alkaline**.

Carbon fiber: an extremely strong, thin fiber made by pyrolyzing (decomposing by heat) synthetic fibers, such as rayon, until charred; used to make high-strength composites

Chlorofluorocarbon (CFC): one of a group of industrial chemicals that contain chlorine, fluorine, and carbon and have been found to damage Earth's ozone layer.

Element: a substance that cannot be chemically decomposed into simpler substances; the atoms of an element all have the same number of protons and electrons.

Isotope: an atom of a chemical element with the same number of protons in its nucleus as other atoms of that element, but with a different number of neutrons.

Molecule: the basic unit of a chemical compound, composed of two or more atoms bound together.

Noble gases: a group of gasses including helium, neon, argon, krypton, xenon, and radon that are not reactive except in rare and limited instances. Also called "inert gases."

Osmosis: the transfer of a fluid from an area of higher concentration to an area of lower concentration, usually through a membrane.

Phase: any of the possible states of matter—solid, liquid, gas, or plasma—that change according to temperature and pressure.

Polymer: a huge molecule containing hundreds or thousands of smaller molecules arranged in repeating units.

Salt: a neutral compound produced by the reaction of an acid and a base.

Geology

Fault, tectonic: a crack or break in Earth's crust, often due to the slippage of tectonic plates past or over one another; usually geologically unstable.

Igneous: a type of rock formed by solidification from a molten state, especially from molten magma.

Magma: hot liquid rock material under Earth's crust, from which igneous rock is formed by cooling.

Metamorphic: in geology, the name given to sedimentary rocks or minerals that have recrystallized under the influence of heat and pressure since their original deposition.

Pangaea: a single super-continent that scientists believe broke apart about 170 mil years ago to form the current continents.

Plate tectonics: theory that Earth's crust is made up of many separate rigid plates of rock that float on top of hot semi-liquid rock.

Sedimentary rock: rock formed by the buildup of material at the bottoms of bodies of water.

Physics

Absolute zero: the theoretical temperature at which all motion within a molecule stops, corresponding to −273.15° C (−459.67° F).

Antimatter: matter that consists of antiparticles, such as antiprotons, that have an opposite charge from normal particles; when matter meets antimatter, both are destroyed and their combined mass is converted to energy. Antimatter is created in certain radioactive decay processes, but appears to be present in only small amounts in the universe.

Atom: the basic unit of a chemical element.

Atomic mass: the total mass of an atom of a given element; atoms of the same element with different atomic masses (different numbers of neutrons, not protons) are called isotopes.

Atomic number: the number of protons in an atom of a given element of the periodic table; the characteristic that sets atoms of different elements apart.

Axion: a hypothetical subatomic particle with low mass and energy that is thought to exist because of the properties of the strong nuclear force.

Bose-Einstein condensate: a "super-atom" comprised of thousands of atoms super-cooled to within a few billionths of a degree of absolute zero and thus condensed into the lowest energy state; atoms bound in the BEC behave synchronously, giving the BEC wavelike properties.

Boson: force-carrying particles including photons, gluons, and the W and Z particles; one of the two primary categories of particles in the Standard Model, the other being fermions.

Dark energy: a mysterious, undefined energy leading to a repulsive force pervading all of space-time; proposed by cosmologists as counteracting gravity and accelerating the expansion of the universe; predicted to make up 65% of the universe's composition.

Dark matter: hypothetical, invisible matter that some scientists believe makes up 90% of the matter in the universe; its existence was proposed to account for otherwise inexplicable gravitational forces observed in space.

Doppler effect: a change in the frequency of sound, light, or radio waves caused by the motion of the source emitting the waves or the motion of the person or instrument perceiving the waves.

Electron: negatively charged particle that is the least massive electrically charged fundamental particle; the most common charged lepton in the Standard Model.

Energy: capacity to perform work. Energy can take various forms, such as potential energy, kinetic energy, chemical energy, etc.

Entropy: A measure of disorder in a system.

Fermion: any one of a number of matter particles including electrons, protons, neutrons, and quarks; one of the two primary categories of particles in the Standard Model, the other being bosons.

Field: the effects of forces (gravitational, electric, etc.) are visualized and described mathematically by physicists in terms of fields, which show the strength and direction of a force at a given position.

Fission: a nuclear reaction that occurs when the nuclei of large, unstable atoms break apart, releasing large amounts of energy.

Fluorescence: luminescence that is caused by the absorption of radiation at one wavelength followed by an immediate reradiation, usually at a different wavelength, that stops almost immediately when the radiation stops.

Force: In classical physics, a force is something that causes acceleration in a body, and can be thought of as a push or pull.

Fusion: a nuclear reaction occurring when atomic nuclei collide at high temperatures and combine to form one heavier atomic nucleus, releasing enormous energy in the process.

Gravity: an attractive force between any 2 objects or particles, proportional to the mass (or energy) of the objects; strength of the force decreases with greater distance; the only fundamental force still unaccounted for by the Standard Model.

Half-life: the time it takes for half of a given amount of a radioactive element to decay.

Hertz: a measure of frequency, or how many times a given event occurs per second; applied to sound waves, electrical current, microchip clock speeds; abbreviated as Hz.

Laser: light consisting of a cascade of photons all having the same wavelength; *laser* stands for Light Amplification by Stimulated Emission of Radiation.

Light-emitting diode (LED): A semiconductor that emits light when an electrical current is passed through it. The color of the light depends on the material used in making the diode.

Neutrino: a tiny fundamental particle with no electrical charge and very small mass that moves very quickly through the universe; comes in three varieties, or flavors, called electron, muon, and tau.

Neutron: a neutral particle found in the nuclei of atoms.

Particle accelerator: a large machine with a long tunnel in which atoms smash into each other at high speeds; physicists use these machines to study subatomic particles.

Phosphorescence: luminescence that is caused by the absorption of radiation at one wavelength followed by a delayed reradiation, usually at a different wavelength, that continues for a noticeable time after the radiation stops.

Photon: the elementary unit, or quantum, of light or electromagnetic radiation, having no mass or electrical charge; one of the fundamental force-carrying particles, or bosons, described by the Standard Model.

Plasma: a high-energy state of matter different from solid, liquid or gas in which atomic nuclei and the electrons orbiting them separate from each other.

Proton: a positively charged subatomic particle found in the nuclei of atoms.

Quantum: a natural unit of some physically measurable property, such as energy or electrical charge.

Quark: a fermion and a fundamental matter particle that makes up protons and neutrons, forming atomic nuclei; there are 6 different "flavors" of quarks grouped in pairs; up and down, charm and strange, top and bottom.

Radiation: energy emitted as rays or particles; radiation includes heat, light, ultraviolet rays, gamma rays, X rays, cosmic rays, alpha particles, beta particles, and the protons, neutrons, and electrons of radioactive atoms.

Relativity, general theory of: a theory of space-time proposed by Albert Einstein in 1915; gravitational and other forces are transmitted through the effects of the curvature of space-time.

Relativity, special theory of: Einstein's theory of space and time: all laws of physics are valid in all uniformly moving frames of reference and the speed of light in a vacuum is always the same, so long as the source and the observer are moving uniformly (not accelerating).

Standard Model: prevailing theory of fundamental particles and forces of matter; matter particles are fermions: either leptons or quarks; force-carrying particles are bosons: either gluons, W or Z bosons or photons; gravity has not yet been worked into the model.

String theory: a theory that seeks to unify quantum mechanics and general relativity, positing that the basic constituents of matter can best be understood not as point objects but as tiny closed loops ("strings").

Subatomic particle: one of the small particles, such as electrons, neutrons, and protons, which make up an atom.

Superconductivity: the property of certain materials, usually metals and chemically complex ceramics, to conduct electricity without resistance, generally at very cold temperatures.

Thermodynamics: the branch of physics that describes how energy, heat, and temperature flow in physical systems.

Ultraviolet radiation: a form of light, invisible to the human eye, that has a shorter wavelength and greater energy than visible light but a longer wavelength and less energy than X rays.

Virtual particle: subatomic particles that rapidly pop into and out of existence and can exert real forces; usually occur in particle-antiparticle pairs and are rapidly annihilated.

Mohs Scale of Hardness

Hardness is the ability of a solid substance to resist abrasion or deformation on the surface. Soft minerals scratch easier than hard ones. For example, a diamond will scratch graphite because the graphite is softer. In 1812, German mineralogist Frederich Mohs (1773-1839) created the arbitrary scale shown below to measure relative hardness using ten minerals that were readily available at that time. The numbers in the Mohs scale are arranged in order of increasing hardness. A mineral's hardness is obtained by determining which mineral in the Mohs scale will scratch the specimen.

Mohs Scale		Selected items and their relative hardness include:	
1. Talc	6. Orthoclase Feldspar	2.5 . . . . . . Fingernails	5.5 . . . . . . Knife Blade
2. Gypsum	7. Quartz	2.5-3 . . . . Gold, Silver	6-7 . . . . . Glass
3. Calcite	8. Topaz	3 . . . . Copper Penny	6.5 . . . . . . Iron pyrite
4. Fluorite	9. Corundum	4-4.5 . . . . Platinum	7+ . . . . . . Hardened steel file
5. Apatite	10. Diamond	4-5 . . . . . . Iron	

Chemical Elements, Atomic Numbers, Year Discovered

Reviewed by Darleane C. Hoffman, Ph.D., Lawrence Berkeley National Laboratory and Department of Chemistry, Univ. of California, Berkeley.

See Periodic Table of the Elements on page 277 for atomic weights.

Element	Symbol	Atomic number	Year discov.	Element	Symbol	Atomic number	Year discov.	Element	Symbol	Atomic number	Year discov.
Actinium	Ac	89	1899	Gold	Au	79	BCE	Promethium	Pm	61	1945
Aluminum	Al	13	1825	Hafnium	Hf	72	1923	Protactinium	Pa	91	1917
Americium	Am	95	1944	Hassium	Hs	108	1984	Radium	Ra	88	1898
Antimony	Sb	51	1450	Helium	He	2	1868	Radon	Rn	86	1900
Argon	Ar	18	1894	Holmium	Ho	67	1878	Rhenium	Re	75	1925
Arsenic	As	33	c. 13th	Hydrogen	H	1	1766	Rhodium	Rh	45	1803
Astatine	At	85	1940	Indium	In	49	1863	Roentgenium	Rg	111	1995
Barium	Ba	56	1808	Iodine	I	53	1811	Rubidium	Rb	37	1861
Berkelium	Bk	97	1949	Iridium	Ir	77	1804	Ruthenium	Ru	44	1845
Beryllium	Be	4	1798	Iron	Fe	26	BCE	Rutherfordium	Rf	104	1969
Bismuth	Bi	83	c. 15th	Krypton	Kr	36	1898	Samarium	Sm	62	1879
Bohrium	Bh	107	1981	Lanthanum	La	57	1839	Scandium	Sc	21	1879
Boron	B	5	1808	Lawrencium	Lr	103	1961	Seaborgium	Sg	106	1974
Bromine	Br	35	1826	Lead	Pb	82	BCE	Selenium	Se	34	1817
Cadmium	Cd	48	1817	Lithium	Li	3	1817	Silicon	Si	14	1823
Calcium	Ca	20	1808	Lutetium	Lu	71	1907	Silver	Ag	47	BCE
Californium	Cf	98	1950	Magnesium	Mg	12	1829	Sodium	Na	11	1807
Carbon	C	6	BCE	Manganese	Mn	25	1774	Strontium	Sr	38	1790
Cerium	Ce	58	1803	Meitnerium	Mt	109	1982	Sulfur	S	16	BCE
Cesium	Cs	55	1860	Mendelevium	Md	101	1955	Tantalum	Ta	73	1802
Chlorine	Cl	17	1774	Mercury	Hg	80	BCE	Technetium	Tc	43	1937
Chromium	Cr	24	1797	Molybdenum	Mo	42	1782	Tellurium	Te	52	1782
Cobalt	Co	27	1735	Neodymium	Nd	60	1885	Terbium	Tb	65	1843
Copper	Cu	29	BCE	Neon	Ne	10	1898	Thallium	Tl	81	1861
Curium	Cm	96	1944	Neptunium	Np	93	1940	Thorium	Th	90	1828
Darmstadtium	Ds	110	1995	Nickel	Ni	28	1751	Thulium	Tm	69	1879
Dubnium (Hahnium)[1]	Db (Ha)	105	1970	Niobium[2]	Nb	41	1801	Tin	Sn	50	BCE
Dysprosium	Dy	66	1886	Nitrogen	N	7	1772	Titanium	Ti	22	1791
Einsteinium	Es	99	1952	Nobelium	No	102	1958	Tungsten (Wolfram)	W	74	1783
Erbium	Er	68	1843	Osmium	Os	76	1804	Uranium	U	92	1789
Europium	Eu	63	1901	Oxygen	O	8	1774	Vanadium	V	23	1830
Fermium	Fm	100	1953	Palladium	Pd	46	1803	Xenon	Xe	54	1898
Fluorine	F	9	1771	Phosphorus	P	15	1669	Ytterbium	Yb	70	1878
Francium	Fr	87	1939	Platinum	Pt	78	1735	Yttrium	Y	39	1794
Gadolinium	Gd	64	1886	Plutonium	Pu	94	1941	Zinc	Zn	30	BCE
Gallium	Ga	31	1875	Polonium	Po	84	1898	Zirconium	Zr	40	1789
Germanium	Ge	32	1886	Potassium	K	19	1807				
				Praseodymium	Pr	59	1885				

Note: 111 elements are listed here. The discovery of element 111 with a mass number of 272 was reported by S. Hofmann et al. in 1995 and was approved by a Joint Working Party of the International Unions of Pure & Applied Chemistry (IUPAC) and Pure and Applied Physics (IUPAP) in 2003. The discoverers proposed the name Roentgenium with symbol Rg in early 2004 and it was confirmed by IUPAC in Nov. 2004. The discovery of element 112 by S. Hofmann et al. in 1996 still awaits confirmation. Between 1999 and 2006, a multinational group and a Dubna/Lawrence Livermore National Laboratory group working in Dubna, Russia, have published evidence in refereed journals for observation of many isotopes of elements 112 through 116 and 118 has been reported. These reports all await confirmation and are shown in Italics in the periodic table. Evidence for Element 117 has not been published in refereed journals and is shown in parentheses. (1) The name Dubnium (Db) has been approved by IUPAC for element 105, but the name Hahnium (Ha) is used in most of the scientific literature before 1998 and is still sometimes used in the U.S. (2) Formerly Columbium.

Periodic Table of the Elements

Source: © 1996 Lawrence Berkeley National Laboratory

Parentheses indicate undiscovered elements.

Legend:
- atomic number — 14
- symbol — Si
- atomic weight — 28.09
- name — Silicon

Groups: alkali metals · alkaline earth metals · transitional metals · other metals · nonmetals · noble gases

alkali metals	alkaline earth metals																noble gases
1 1.01 **H** Hydrogen																	2 4.003 **He** Helium
3 6.94 **Li** Lithium	4 9.01 **Be** Beryllium											5 10.81 **B** Boron	6 12.01 **C** Carbon	7 14.01 **N** Nitrogen	8 15.999 **O** Oxygen	9 18.998 **F** Fluorine	10 20.18 **Ne** Neon
11 22.99 **Na** Sodium	12 24.31 **Mg** Magnesium											13 26.98 **Al** Aluminum	14 28.09 **Si** Silicon	15 30.97 **P** Phosphorus	16 32.06 **S** Sulfur	17 35.45 **Cl** Chlorine	18 39.95 **Ar** Argon
19 39.10 **K** Potassium	20 40.08 **Ca** Calcium	21 44.96 **Sc** Scandium	22 47.90 **Ti** Titanium	23 50.94 **V** Vanadium	24 51.996 **Cr** Chromium	25 54.94 **Mn** Manganese	26 55.85 **Fe** Iron	27 58.93 **Co** Cobalt	28 58.70 **Ni** Nickel	29 63.55 **Cu** Copper	30 65.37 **Zn** Zinc	31 69.72 **Ga** Gallium	32 72.59 **Ge** Germanium	33 74.92 **As** Arsenic	34 78.96 **Se** Selenium	35 79.90 **Br** Bromine	36 83.80 **Kr** Krypton
37 85.47 **Rb** Rubidium	38 87.62 **Sr** Strontium	39 88.91 **Y** Yttrium	40 91.22 **Zr** Zirconium	41 92.91 **Nb** Niobium	42 95.94 **Mo** Molybdenum	43 98 **Tc** Technetium	44 101.07 **Ru** Ruthenium	45 102.91 **Rh** Rhodium	46 106.40 **Pd** Palladium	47 107.87 **Ag** Silver	48 112.41 **Cd** Cadmium	49 114.82 **In** Indium	50 118.69 **Sn** Tin	51 121.75 **Sb** Antimony	52 127.60 **Te** Tellurium	53 126.90 **I** Iodine	54 131.30 **Xe** Xenon
55 132.91 **Cs** Cesium	56 137.33 **Ba** Barium	57 138.91 **La** Lanthanum	72 178.49 **Hf** Hafnium	73 180.95 **Ta** Tantalum	74 183.85 **W** Tungsten	75 186.21 **Re** Rhenium	76 190.20 **Os** Osmium	77 192.22 **Ir** Iridium	78 195.09 **Pt** Platinum	79 196.97 **Au** Gold	80 200.59 **Hg** Mercury	81 204.37 **Tl** Thallium	82 207.19 **Pb** Lead	83 208.98 **Bi** Bismuth	84 209 **Po** Polonium	85 210 **At** Astatine	86 222 **Rn** Radon
87 223 **Fr** Francium	88 226.03 **Ra** Radium	89 227.03 **Ac** Actinium	104 261 **Rf** Rutherfordium	105 262 **Db (Ha)** Dubnium (Hahnium)	106 266 **Sg** Seaborgium	107 267 **Bh** Bohrium	108 269 **Hs** Hassium	109 268 **Mt** Meitnerium	110 271 **Ds** Darmstadtium	111 272 **Rg** Roentgenium	112 **112**	113 **113**	114 **114**	115 **115**	116 **116**	(117) **(117)**	118 **118**

Lanthanide series

58 140.12 **Ce** Cerium	59 140.91 **Pr** Praseodymium	60 144.24 **Nd** Neodymium	61 145 **Pm** Promethium	62 150.35 **Sm** Samarium	63 151.96 **Eu** Europium	64 157.25 **Gd** Gadolinium	65 158.93 **Tb** Terbium	66 162.50 **Dy** Dysprosium	67 164.93 **Ho** Holmium	68 167.26 **Er** Erbium	69 168.93 **Tm** Thulium	70 173.04 **Yb** Ytterbium	71 174.97 **Lu** Lutetium

Actinide series

90 232.04 **Th** Thorium	91 231.04 **Pa** Protactinium	92 238.03 **U** Uranium	93 237.05 **Np** Neptunium	94 244 **Pu** Plutonium	95 243 **Am** Americium	96 247 **Cm** Curium	97 247 **Bk** Berkelium	98 251 **Cf** Californium	99 252 **Es** Einsteinium	100 257 **Fm** Fermium	101 258 **Md** Mendelevium	102 259 **No** Nobelium	103 262 **Lr** Lawrencium

Basic Laws of Physics

Isaac Newton's Laws of Motion

1. An object in motion moves at a constant velocity in a straight line unless acted upon by a force. Likewise, an object at rest will stay at rest. This is known as inertia.

2. The acceleration of an object is proportional to the force acting on it and inversely proportional to the mass of an object.

Force (F) equals mass (m) times acceleration (a)

$$F = ma$$

3. For every action, there is an equal and opposite reaction.

Law of Gravity

In common usage, gravity only refers to the gravitational force between the Earth and objects on or near it. More specifically, gravitation is one of four basic forces controlling the interactions of matter, the others being strong and weak nuclear forces and electromagnetic force. The gravitational force (F) between objects is proportional to the product of their masses ($m1$ and $m2$) and inversely proportional to the square of the distance (d) between them. G represents the "gravitational constant" in Newton's law of gravity, a fixed ratio measured in metric terms as, $G = 6.67390$ x 10^{-11} newton m^2/kg^2.

The basic law of gravity is:

$$F = G\,\frac{m_1\,m_2}{d^2}$$

Excluding factors such as high winds and wind resistance, objects close to the Earth's surface will fall at constant acceleration of 32.174 ft/sec^2 (9.8 m/sec^2), which is usually written as g. Using g will yield the velocity (v) and the distance travelled by a falling object (d) after any amount of time, (t) in seconds. (Positive numbers represent up, negative numbers down.)

$$v = -g\,t$$
$$d = -{}^1/_2\,g(t^2)$$

If an object has an initial velocity of v_0 and an initial height above ground called a, the equations become:

$$v = v_0 - g\,t$$
$$d = -{}^1/_2\,g(t^2) + v_0 t + a$$

Assuming that height is measured in feet and speeds in feet per second, the maximum height (H) reached by an object with a positive initial velocity ($v0$) and a known initial height (a) is expressed as:

$$H = a + \frac{v_0^{\,2}}{64}$$

The force of gravity on Earth is lessened by the centrifugal force caused by the Earth's rotation. This counteracts the gravitational effect to a small degree. At the poles, where technically there is no centrifugal force, acceleration due to gravity is greater.

The force of gravity decreases slightly with an increase in distance from the Earth's center; gravity is weaker on a mountaintop than it is at sea level.

Conservation Laws

In physics, laws of conservation state that in a closed system certain measurable quantities remain constant. Anything added from outside the system could affect the quantity of the entity being conserved.

Conservation of Mass: Mass is neither created nor destroyed within a closed system except when converted to energy.

Conservation of Momentum: All moving objects have momentum, and in a closed system, momentum is always conserved. Linear momentum is the product of the mass of an object and its velocity. In the following equation, M and V represent the initial total mass and velocity of objects within a closed system. After a collision between those objects, the mass and velocity of individual objects may change (for example, one object could break into smaller pieces, each traveling at a different velocity) but the product of the total mass and velocity in the system after the collision (mv) will remain the same.

$$MV = mv$$

Any object moving in a circle has *angular momentum*. Motion in a circle requires acceleration which is directed to-

wards the center of the circle and which depends on the speed of the object and the square of the radius of the circle. [Angular momentum is the product of this speed, the mass of the object and the square of the radius.]

Conservation of Energy: The amount of energy of a closed system will not change except when converted to mass.

Conservation of Mass-energy: According to Einstein, as part of his special theory of relativity, mass and energy are related. Because they can be converted into one another, mass and energy alone cannot be conserved. However, the total amount of mass and energy together must be conserved. This is reflected in the following equation where m is mass, E is energy, and c is the speed of light in a vacuum (which is constant):

$$E = mc^2$$

Einstein also discovered that mass increases with velocity. The following equation—where m is the mass of a moving object, m_0 is the object's mass when not moving, v is its velocity in relation to a stationary observer, and c is the speed of light—shows how mass is related to velocity in this context.

$$m = \frac{m_0}{\sqrt{1 - \dfrac{v^2}{c^2}}}$$

This equation accounts for the theory that no object can travel faster than the speed of light. As an object approaches c, so much energy is converted to mass that it no longer accelerates.

Laws of Thermodynamics

1. Heat is a form of energy. Within a closed system energy must be conserved except in nuclear reactions or other extreme conditions. It is neither created nor destroyed.

2. Within a self-sustaining system, heat can never go from an area of low temperature to an area of high temperature. Disorder, or entropy, can only increase in closed system.

3. Absolute zero cannot be attained by any procedure in a finite number of steps. Absolute zero can be approached arbitrarily closely, but it can never be reached.

Laws of Current Electricity

Electricity is the result of electrons flowing through a conductor. When electrons flow through a conductor, the amount of current generated, measured in amperes, is defined in terms of the coulomb (an amount of electric charge equal to about 6.25 quintillion or 6.25×10^{18} electrons) and the time it takes for electrons to pass through the conductor. One ampere is equal to 1 coulomb of charge moving past a point in 1 second. As an electric current moves through a conductor, energy can vary depending on varying charges within the conductor. This variation is known as the *potential difference* and is measured in volts.

Certain substances are more prone to conductivity. The resistance to conductivity is measured in ohms.

Ohm's law: Electric current is directly proportional to the potential difference and inversely proportional to the total resistance of the circuit. I is electric current (measured in amperes), and V is the potential difference (measured in volts), and R is resistance (measured in ohms):

$$I = \frac{V}{R}$$

Law of electric power: The rate at which electricity is used is electric power. If electric power (P) is measured in watts, then P is the product of current and potential difference.

$$P = IV$$

Two Basic Laws of Quantum Physics

1. Heisenberg's uncertainty principle: Certain pairs of observable quantities like energy and time, or position and momentum cannot be measured with complete accuracy simultaneously. Also known as indeterminacy principle.

2. Pauli's exclusion principle: Two electrons in an atom cannot simultaneously occupy the same quantum or energy state. This has since been shown to be true for many subatomic particles.

Breaking the Sound Barrier; Speed of Sound

The prefix **Mach** is used to describe supersonic speed. It was named for Ernst Mach (1838-1916), a Czech-born Austrian physicist. When a plane moves at the speed of sound, it is Mach 1. When the plane is moving at twice the speed of sound, it is Mach 2. Mach may be defined as the ratio of the velocity of a rocket or a jet to the velocity of sound in the medium being considered.

When a plane passes the sound barrier—flying faster than sound travels—listeners in the area hear thunderclaps, but the pilot of the plane does not hear them.

Sound is produced by vibrations of an object and is transmitted by alternate increase and decrease in pressures that radiate outward through a material media of molecules—somewhat like waves spreading out on a pond after a rock has been tossed into it.

The **frequency of sound** is determined by the number of times the vibrating waves undulate per second and is measured in cycles per second. The slower the cycle of waves, the lower the frequency. As frequencies increase, the sound is higher in pitch. The human ear is usually not sensitive to frequencies of fewer than 20 vibrations per second or greater than about 20,000 vibrations per second—although this range varies among individuals.

Intensity, or loudness, is the strength of the pressure of these radiating waves and is measured in decibels. (See Weights and Measures.)

The **speed of sound** is generally defined as 1,088 feet per second at sea level at 32° F. It varies in other temperatures and in different media. Sound travels faster in water than in air, and even faster in iron and steel.

Light; Colors of the Spectrum

Light, a form of electromagnetic radiation similar to radiant heat, radio waves, and X rays, is emitted from a source in straight lines and spreads out over larger areas as it travels; light per unit area diminishes as the square of the distance.

The English mathematician and physicist Sir Isaac Newton (1642-1727) described light as an **emission of particles**; the Dutch astronomer, mathematician, and physicist Christiaan Huygens (1629-95) developed the theory that light travels by a **wave motion**. It is now believed that these 2 theories are essentially complementary, and the development of quantum theory has led to results where light acts like a series of particles in some experiments and like a wave in others.

The **speed of light** was first measured in a laboratory experiment by the French physicist Armand Hippolyte Louis Fizeau (1819-96). Today the speed of light is known very precisely as 299,792.458 km per sec (or 186,282.396 mi per sec) in a vacuum; in water the speed of light is about 25% less, and in glass, 33% less.

Color sensations are produced through the excitation of the retina of the eye by light vibrating at different frequencies. The different colors of the spectrum may be produced by viewing a light beam that is refracted by passage through a prism, which breaks the light into its wavelengths.

Customarily, the **primary colors** are taken to be the 6 monochromatic colors that occupy relatively large areas of the spectrum: red, orange, yellow, green, blue, and violet. Scientists have differed, however, in how many and which primary colors they recognized. The color sensation of **black** is due to complete lack of stimulation of the retina, that of **white** to complete stimulation.

The **infrared and ultraviolet rays**, below the red (long) end of the spectrum and above the violet (short) end of the spectrum, respectively, are invisible to the naked eye. Heat is the principal effect of the infrared rays, and chemical action that of the ultraviolet rays.

Discoveries and Innovations: Chemistry, Physics, Biology, Medicine

	Date	Discoverer	Nationality		Date	Discoverer	Nationality
Acetylene gas	1862	Berthelot	French	Classification of plants			
ACTH	1927	Evans, Long	U.S.	and animals	1735	Linnaeus	Swedish
Adrenaline	1901	Takamine	Japan	Cloning, DNA	1973	Boyer, et al.	U.S.
Aluminum, electrolytic				Cloning, mammal	1996	Wilmut, et al.	Scottish
process	1886	Hall	U.S.	Cocaine	1860	Niemann	German
Aluminum, isolated	1825	Oersted	Danish	Combustion explained	1777	Lavoisier	French
Anesthesia, ether	1842	Long	U.S.	Conditioned reflex	1914	Pavlov	Russian
Anesthesia, local	1885	Koller	Austrian	Cortisone	1936	Kendall	U.S.
Anesthesia, spinal	1898	Bier	German	Cortisone, synthesis	1946	Sarett	U.S.
Aniline dye	1856	Perkin	English	Cosmic rays	1910	Gockel	Swiss
Anti-rabies	1885	Pasteur	French	Cyanamide	1905	Frank, Caro	German
Antiseptic surgery	1867	Lister	English	Cyclotron	1930	Lawrence	U.S.
Antitoxin, diphtheria	1891	Von Behring	German	DDT (not applied as			
Argyrol	1897	Bayer	German	insecticide until 1939)	1874	Zeidler	German
Arsphenamine	1910	Ehrlich	German	Deuterium	1932	Urey, Brickwedde,	
Aspirin	1853	Gerhardt	French			Murphy	U.S.
Atabrine	1932	Mietzsch, et al.	German	DNA (structure)	1953	Crick	English
Atomic numbers	1913	Moseley	English			Watson	U.S.
Atomic theory	1803	Dalton	English			Wilkins	English
Atomic time clock	1948	Lyons	U.S.	Electric resistance, law of	1827	Ohm	German
Atomic time clock,				Electric waves	1888	Hertz	German
cesium beam	1948	Essen	English	Electrolysis	1852	Faraday	English
Atom-smashing theory	1919	Rutherford	English	Electromagnetism	1819	Oersted	Danish
Bacitracin	1943	Johnson, Meleneyl	U.S.	Electron	1897	Thomson, J.	English
Bacteria, description	1676	Leeuwenhoek	Dutch	Electron diffraction	1936	Thomson	English
Bleaching powder	1798	Tennant	English			Davisson, G.	U.S.
Blood, circulation	1628	Harvey	English	Electroshock treatment	1938	Cerletti, Bini	Italian
Blood plasma storage				Erythromycin	1952	McGuire	U.S.
(blood banks)	1940	Drew	U.S.	Evolution, natural			
Bordeaux mixture	1885	Millardet	French	selection	1858	Darwin	English
Bromine from the sea	1826	Balard	French	Falling bodies, law of	1590	Galileo	Italian
Calcium carbide	1888	Wilson	U.S.	Gases, law of combining			
Calculus	1670	Newton	English	volumes	1808	Gay-Lussac	French
Camphor synthetic	1896	Haller	French	Geometry, analytic	1619	Descartes	French
Canning (food)	1804	Appert	French	Gold, cyanide process			
Carbon oxides	1925	Fisher	German	for extraction	1887	MacArthur, Forest	British
Chemotherapy	1909	Ehrlich	German	Gravitation, law	1687	Newton	English
Chloamphenicol	1947	Burkholder	U.S.	HIV (human immuno-			
Chlorine	1774	Scheele	Swedish	deficiency virus)	1984	Montagnier	French
Chloroform	1831	Guthrie, S.	U.S.			Gallo	U.S.
Chlortetracycline	1948	Duggen	U.S.	Holograph	1948	Gabor	British
				Human heart transplant	1967	Barnard	S. African

Discovery	Date	Discoverer	Nationality
Indigo, synthesis of	1880	Baeyer	German
Induction, electric	1830	Henry	U.S.
Insulin	1922	Banting, Best	Canadian
		Macleod	Scottish
Intelligence testing	1905	Binet, Simon	French
In vitro fertilization	1978	Steptoe, Edwards	English
Isotopes, theory	1912	Soddy	English
Laser	1957	Gould	U.S.
Light, velocity	1675	Roemer	Danish
Light, wave theory	1690	Huygens	Dutch
Lithography	1796	Senefelder	Bohemian
Logarithms	1614	Napier	Scottish
LSD-25	1943	Hoffman	Swiss
Mendelian laws	1866	Mendel	Austrian
Mercator projection (map)	1568	Mercator (Kremer)	Flemish
Methanol	1661	Boyle	Irish
Milk condensation	1853	Borden	U.S.
Molecular hypothesis	1811	Avogadro	Italian
Motion, laws of	1687	Newton	English
Neomycin	1949	Waksman, Lechevalier	U.S.
Neutron	1932	Chadwick	English
Nitric acid	1648	Glauber	German
Nitric oxide	1772	Priestley	English
Nitroglycerin	1846	Sobrero	Italian
Oil cracking process	1891	Dewar	U.S.
Oxygen	1774	Priestley	English
Oxytetracycline	1950	Finlay, et al.	U.S.
Ozone	1840	Schonbein	German
Paper, sulfite process	1867	Tilghman	U.S.
Paper, wood pulp, sulfate process	1884	Dahl	German
Penicillin	1928	Fleming	Scottish
practical use	1941	Florey, Chain	English
Periodic law and table of elements	1869	Mendeleyev	Russian
Physostigmine synthesis	1935	Julian	U.S.
Pill, birth-control	1954	Pincus, Rock	U.S.
Planetary motion, laws	1609	Kepler	German
Plutonium fission	1940	Kennedy, Wahl, Seaborg, Segre	U.S.
Polymyxin	1947	Ainsworth	English
Positron	1932	Anderson	U.S.
Proton	1919	Rutherford	N. Zealand
Psychoanalysis	1900	Freud	Austrian
Quantum theory	1900	Planck	German
Quasars	1963	Matthews, Sandage	U.S.
Quinine synthetic	1946	Woodward, Doering	U.S.
Radioactivity	1896	Becquerel	French
Radiocarbon dating	1947	Libby	U.S.
Radium	1898	Curie, Pierre	French
		Curie, Marie	Pol.-Fr.
Relativity theory	1905	Einstein	German
Reserpine	1949	Jal Vaikl	Indian
Schick test	1913	Schick	U.S.
Silicon	1823	Berzelius	Swedish
Smallpox eradication	1979	World Health Org.	UN
Streptomycin	1944	Waksman, et al	U.S.
Sulfanilamide	1935	Bovet, Trefouel	French
Sulfanilamide theory	1908	Gelmo	German
Sulfapyridine	1938	Ewins, Phelps	English
Sulfathiazole	1939	Fosbinder, Walter	U.S.
Sulfuric acid	1831	Phillips	English
Sulfuric acid, lead	1746	Roebuck	English
Syphilis test	1906	Wassermann	German
Tuberculin	1890	Koch	German
Uranium fission theory	1939	Hahn, Meitner, Strassmann	German
		Bohr	Danish
		Fermi	Italian
		Einstein, Pegram, Wheeler	U.S.
Uranium fission, atomic reactor	1942	Fermi, Szilard	U.S.
Vaccine, measles	1963	Enders	U.S.
Vaccine, meningitis (first conjugate)	1987	Gordon, et al., Connaught Lab.	U.S.
Vaccine, polio	1954	Salk	U.S.
Vaccine, polio, oral	1960	Sabin	U.S.
Vaccine, rabies	1885	Pasteur	French
Vaccine, smallpox	1796	Jenner	English
Vaccine, typhus	1909	Nicolle	French
Vaccine, varicella	1974	Takahashi	Japan
Van Allen belts, radiation	1958	Van Allen	U.S.
Vitamin A	1913	McCollum, Davis	U.S.
Vitamin B	1916	McCollum	U.S.
Vitamin C	1928	Szent-Gyorgyi	Hungarian
		King	U.S.
Vitamin D	1922	McCollum	U.S.
Vitamin K	1935	Dam, Doisy	U.S.
Xerography	1938	Carlson	U.S.
X ray	1895	Roentgen	German

Inventions

Invention	Date	Inventor	Nationality
Adding machine	1642	Pascal	French
Adding machine	1885	Burroughs	U.S.
Aerosol spray	1926	Rotheim	Norwegian
Airbag	1952	Hetrick	U.S.
Air brake	1868	Westinghouse	U.S.
Air conditioning	1902	Carrier	U.S.
Air pump	1654	Guericke	German
Airplane, automatic pilot	1912	Sperry	U.S.
Airplane, experimental	1896	Langley	U.S.
Airplane, hydro	1911	Curtiss	U.S.
Airplane jet engine	1939	Ohain	German
Airplane with motor	1903	Wright Bros.	U.S.
Airship	1852	Giffard	French
Arc welder	1919	Thomson	U.S.
Aspartame	1965	Schlatter	U.S.
Autogyro	1920	de la Cierva	Spanish
Automobile, differential gear	1885	Benz	German
Automobile, electric	1892	Morrison	U.S.
Automobile, exp'mtl	1864	Marcus	Austrian
Automobile, gasoline	1889	Daimler	German
Automobile, gasoline	1892	Duryea	U.S.
Automobile magneto	1897	Bosch	German
Automobile muffler	1904	Pope	U.S.
Automobile self-starter	1911	Kettering	U.S.
Bakelite	1907	Baekeland	Belgian, U.S.
Balloon	1783	Montgolfier	French
Barometer	1643	Torricelli	Italian
Bicycle, modern	1885	Starley	English
Bifocal lens	1780	Franklin	U.S.
Bottle machine	1895	Owens	U.S.
Braille printing	1829	Braille	French
Bubble gum	1928	Diemer	U.S.
Burner, gas	1855	Bunsen	German
Calculating machine	1833	Babbage	English
Calculator, electronic pocket	1972	Merryman, Van Tassel	U.S.
Camera, Kodak	1888	Eastman, Walker	U.S
Camera, Polaroid Land	1948	Land	U.S.
Car coupler	1873	Janney	U.S.
Carburetor, gasoline	1893	Maybach	German
Carding machine	1797	Whittemore	U.S.
Carpet sweeper	1876	Bissell	U.S.
Cash register	1879	Ritty	U.S.
Cassette, audio	1963	Philips Co.	Dutch
Cassette, videotape	1969	Sony	Japanese
Cathode-ray tube	1897	Braun	German
CAT, or CT, scan	1973	Hounsfield	English
Cellophane	1908	Brandenberger	Swiss
Celluloid	1870	Hyatt	U.S.
Cement, Portland	1824	Aspdin	English
Chronometer	1735	Harrison	English
Circuit breaker	1925	Hilliard	U.S.
Circuit, integrated	1959	Kilby, Noyce, Texas Instr.	U.S.
Clock, pendulum	1657	Huygens	Dutch
Coaxial cable system	1929	Affel, Espensched	U.S.
Coffeemaker, automatic drip	1963	Bunn Corp.	U.S.
Compressed air rock drill	1871	Ingersoll	U.S.
Comptometer	1887	Felt	U.S.
Computer, automatic sequence	1944	Aiken, et al.	U.S.
Computer, electronic	1942	Atanasoff, Berry	U.S.
Computer, laptop	1987	Sinclair	English
Computer, mini	1960	Digital Corp	U.S.
Condenser microphone (telephone)	1916	Wente	U.S.
Contact lens, corneal	1948	Tuohy	U.S.
Contraceptive, oral	1954	Pincus, Rock	U.S.

Invention	Date	Inventor	Nationality
Corn, hybrid	1917	Jones	U.S.
Cotton gin	1793	Whitney	U.S.
Cream separator	1878	DeLaval	Swedish
Cultivator, disc	1878	Mallon	U.S.
Cystoscope	1878	Nitze	German
Diapers, disposable	1950	Donovan	U.S.
Diesel engine	1895	Diesel	German
Disc, compact	1972	RCA	U.S.
Disc player, compact	1979	Sony, Philips Co.	Japan, Dutch
Dishwasher	1893	Cochrane	U.S.
Disk, floppy	1970	IBM	U.S.
Disk, video	1972	Philips Co.	Dutch
Dynamite	1866	Nobel	Swedish
Dynamo, contin. current	1871	Gramme	Belgian
Electric battery	1800	Volta	Italian
Electric fan	1882	Wheeler	U.S.
Electrocardiograph	1903	Einthoven	Dutch
Electroencephalograph	1929	Berger	German
Electromagnet	1824	Sturgeon	English
Electron spectrometer	1944	Deutsch, Elliott, Evans	U.S.
Electron tube multigrid	1913	Langmuir	U.S.
Electroplating	1805	Brugnatelli	Italian
Electrostatic generator	1929	Van de Graaff	U.S.
Elevator brake	1852	Otis	U.S.
Elevator, push button	1922	Larson	U.S.
Engine, automatic transmission	1910	Fottinger	German
Engine, coal-gas 4-cycle	1876	Otto	German
Engine, compression ignition	1883	Daimler	German
Engine, electric ignition	1883	Benz	German
Engine, gas, compound	1926	Eickemeyer	U.S.
Engine, gasoline	1872	Brayton, Geo.	U.S.
Engine, gasoline	1889	Daimler	German
Engine, jet	1930	Whittle	English
Engine, steam, piston	1705	Newcomen	English
Engine, steam, piston	1769	Watt	Scottish
Engraving, half-tone	1852	Talbot	U.S.
Fiberglass	1938	Owens-Corning	U.S.
Fiber optics	1955	Kapany	English
Fiber optic wire	1970	Keck, Maurer Schulz	U.S.
Filament, tungsten	1913	Coolidge	U.S.
Flanged rail	1831	Stevens	U.S.
Flatiron, electric	1882	Seely	U.S.
Food, frozen	1923	Birdseye	U.S.
Freon	1930	Midgley, et al.	U.S.
Furnace (for steel)	1858	Siemens	German
Galvanometer	1820	Sweigger	German
Garbage bag, polyethylene	1950	Wasylyk	Canadian
Gas discharge tube	1922	Hull	U.S.
Gas lighting	1792	Murdoch	Scottish
Gas mantle	1885	Welsbach	Austrian
Gasoline (lead ethyl)	1922	Midgley	U.S.
Gasoline, cracked	1913	Burton	U.S.
Gasoline, high octane	1930	Ipatieff	Russian
Geiger counter	1913	Geiger	German
Glass, laminated safety	1909	Benedictus	French
Glider	1853	Cayley	English
Gun, breechloader	1811	Thornton	U.S.
Gun, Browning	1897	Browning	U.S.
Gun, magazine	1875	Hotchkiss	U.S.
Gun, silencer	1908	Maxim, H.P.	U.S.
Guncotton	1847	Schoenbein	German
Gyrocompass	1911	Sperry	U.S.
Gyroscope	1852	Foucault	French
Harvester-thresher	1818	Lane	U.S.
Heart, artificial	1982	Jarvik	U.S.
Helicopter	1939	Sikorsky	U.S.
Hydrometer	1768	Baume	French
Iron lung	1928	Drinker, Slaw.	U.S.
Kaleidoscope	1817	Brewster	Scottish
Kevlar	1965	Kwolek, Blades	U.S.
Kinetoscope	1889	Edison	U.S.
Lamp, arc	1847	Staite	English
Lamp, fluorescent	1938	General Electric, Westinghouse	U.S.
Lamp, incandescent	1879	Edison	U.S.
Lamp, incand., gas	1885	Langmuir	U.S.
Lamp, klieg	1911	Kliegl, A. & J.	U.S.
Lamp, mercury vapor	1912	Hewitt	U.S.
Lamp, miner's safety	1816	Davy	English
Lamp, neon	1909	Claude	French
Lathe, turret	1845	Fitch	U.S.
Launderette	1934	Cantrell	U.S.
Lens, achromatic	1758	Dollond	English
Lens, fused bifocal	1908	Borsch	U.S.
Leyden jar (condenser)	1745	von Kleist	German
Lightning rod	1752	Franklin	U.S.
Linoleum	1860	Walton	English
Linotype	1884	Mergenthaler	U.S.
Liquid Paper	c.1951	Graham	U.S.
Lock, cylinder	1851	Yale	U.S.
Locomotive, electric	1851	Vail	U.S.
Locomotive, exp'mtl	1802	Trevithick	English
Locomotive, exp'mtl	1812	Fenton, et al.	English
Locomotive, exp'mtl	1814	Stephenson	English
Locomotive, practical	1829	Stephenson	English
Locomotive, 1st U.S.	1830	Cooper, P.	U.S.
Loom, power	1785	Cartwright	English
Loudspeaker, dynamic	1924	Rice, Kellogg	U.S.
Machine gun	1862	Gatling	U.S.
Machine gun, improved	1872	Hotchkiss	U.S.
Machine gun (Maxim)	1883	Maxim, H.S.	U.S., Eng.
Magnet, electro	1828	Henry	U.S.
Magnetic Resonance Imaging (MRI)	1971	Damadian	U.S.
Mason jar	1858	Mason, J.	U.S.
Match, friction	1827	Walker, J.	English
Mercerized textiles	1843	Mercer, J.	English
Meter, induction	1888	Shallenberger	U.S.
Metronome	1816	Malezel	German
Microcomputer	1973	Truong, et al.	French
Micrometer	1636	Gascoigne	English
Microphone	1877	Berliner	U.S.
Microprocessor	1971	Intel Corp.	U.S.
Microscope, compound	1590	Janssen	Dutch
Microscope, electronic	1931	Knoll, Ruska	German
Microscope, field ion	1951	Mueller	German
Microwave oven	1947	Spencer	U.S.
Monitor, warship	1861	Ericsson	U.S.
Monotype	1887	Lanston	U.S.
Motor, AC	1892	Tesla	U.S.
Motor, DC	1837	Davenport	U.S.
Motor, induction	1887	Tesla	U.S.
Motorcycle	1885	Daimler	German
Movie machine	1894	Jenkins	U.S.
Movie, panoramic	1952	Waller	U.S.
Movie, talking	1927	Warner Bros.	U.S.
Mower, lawn	1831	Budding, Ferrabee	English
Mowing machine	1822	Bailey	U.S.
Neoprene	1930	Carothers	U.S.
Nylon	1937	Du Pont lab	U.S.
Nylon synthetic	1930	Carothers	U.S.
Oil cracking furnace	1891	Gavrilov	Russian
Oil filled power cable	1921	Emanueli	Italian
Oleomargarine	1869	Mege-Mouries	French
Ophthalmoscope	1851	Helmholtz	German
Pacemaker	1952	Zoll	U.S.
Paper	105	Ts'ai	Chinese
Paper clip	1900	Waaler	Norwegian
Paper machine	1809	Dickinson	U.S.
Parachute	1785	Blanchard	French
Pen, ballpoint	1888	Loud	U.S.
Pen, fountain	1884	Waterman	U.S.
Pen, steel	1780	Harrison	English
Pendulum	1583	Galileo	Italian
Percussion cap	1807	Forsythe	Scottish
Phonograph	1877	Edison	U.S.
Photo, color	1892	Ives	U.S.
Photo film, celluloid	1893	Reichenbach	U.S.
Photo film, transparent	1884	Eastman, Goodwin	U.S.
Photoelectric cell	1895	Elster	German
Photocopier	1938	Carlson	U.S.
Photographic paper	1835	Talbot	English
Photography	1816	Niepce	French
Photography	1835	Talbot	English
Photography	1835	Daguerre	French
Photophone	1880	Bell	U.S.-Scot.
Phototelegraphy	1925	Bell Labs	U.S.
Piano	1709	Cristofori	Italian
Piano, player	1863	Fourneaux	French
Pin, safety	1849	Hunt	U.S.
Pistol (revolver)	1836	Colt	U.S.
Plow, cast iron	1785	Ransome	English
Plow, disc	1896	Hardy	U.S.
Pneumatic hammer	1890	King	U.S.

Invention	Date	Inventor	Nationality
Post-it note	1980	Spencer Silver, 3M	U.S.
Powder, smokeless	1884	Vieille	French
Printing press, rotary	1845	Hoe	U.S.
Printing press, web	1865	Bullock	U.S.
Propeller, screw	1804	Stevens	U.S.
Propeller, screw	1837	Ericsson	Swedish
Pulsars	1967	Bell	English
Punch card accounting	1889	Hollerith	U.S.
Radar	1940	Watson-Watt	Scottish
Radio, magnetic detector	1902	Marconi	Italian
Radio, signals	1895	Marconi	Italian
Radio amplifier	1906	De Forest	U.S.
Radio beacon	1928	Donovan	U.S.
Radio crystal oscillator	1918	Nicolson	U.S.
Radio receiver, cascade tuning	1913	Alexanderson	U.S.
Radio receiver, heterodyne	1913	Fessenden	Canadian
Radio transmitter triode modulation	1914	Alexanderson	U.S.
Radio tube diode	1904	Fleming	English
Radio tube oscillator	1915	De Forest	U.S.
Radio tube triode	1906	De Forest	U.S.
Radio FM, 2-path	1933	Armstrong	U.S.
Rayon (acetate)	1895	Cross	English
Rayon (cuprammonium)	1890	Despeissis	French
Rayon (nitrocellulose)	1884	Chardonnet	French
Razor, electric	1917	Schick	U.S.
Razor, safety	1895	Gillette	U.S.
Reaper	1834	McCormick	U.S.
Record, cylinder	1887	Bell, Tainter	U.S.
Record, disc	1887	Berliner	U.S.
Record, long playing	1947	Goldmark	U.S.
Record, wax cylinder	1888	Edison	U.S.
Refrigerator car	1868	David	U.S.
Remote Control	1898	Tesla	U.S.
Resin, synthetic	1931	Hill	English
Richter scale	1935	Richter	U.S.
Rifle, repeating	1860	Henry	U.S.
Rocket, liquid fuel	1926	Goddard	U.S.
Rollerblades	1980	Olson	U.S.
Rubber, vulcanized	1839	Goodyear	U.S.
Saccharin	1879	Remsen, Fahlberg	U.S.
Saw, circular	1777	Miller	English
Scotch tape	1930	Drew	U.S.
Seat belt	1959	Volvo	Swedish
Sewing machine	1846	Howe	U.S.
Shoe-lasting machine	1883	Matzeliger	U.S.
Shoe-sewing machine	1860	McKay	U.S.
Shrapnel shell	1784	Shrapnel	English
Shuttle, flying	1733	Kay	English
Sleeping-car	1865	Pullman	U.S.
Slide rule	1620	Oughtred	English
Smoke detector	1969	Smith, House	U.S.
Soap, hardwater	1928	Bertsch	German
Spectroscope	1859	Kirchoff, Bunsen	German
Spectroscope (mass)	1918	Dempster	U.S.
Spinning jenny	c.1764	Hargreaves	English
Spinning mule	1779	Crompton	English
Steamboat, exp'mtl	1778	Jouffroy	French
Steamboat, exp'mtl	1785	Fitch	U.S.
Steamboat, exp'mtl	1787	Rumsey	U.S.
Steamboat, exp'mtl	1803	Fulton	U.S.
Steamboat, exp'mtl	1804	Stevens	U.S.
Steamboat, practical	1802	Symington	Scottish
Steamboat, practical	1807	Fulton	U.S.
Steam car	1770	Cugnot	French
Steam turbine	1884	Parsons	English
Steel (converter)	1856	Bessemer	English
Steel alloy	1891	Harvey	U.S.
Steel alloy, high-speed	1901	Taylor, White	U.S.
Steel, manganese	1884	Hadfield	English
Steel, stainless	1916	Brearley	English
Stereoscope	1838	Wheatstone	English
Stethoscope	1819	Laennec	French
Stethoscope, binaural	1840	Cammann	U.S.
Stock ticker	1870	Edison	U.S.
Storage battery, rechargeable	1859	Plante	French
Stove, electric	1896	Hadaway	U.S.
Submarine	1891	Holland	U.S.
Submarine, even keel	1894	Lake	U.S.
Submarine, torpedo	1776	Bushnell	U.S.
Superconductivity	1957	Bardeen, Cooper, Schreiffer	U.S.
Superconductivity in ceramics at high temp	1986	Bednorz, Muller	German, Swiss
Synthesizer	1964	Moog	U.S.
Tank, military	1914	Swinton	English
Tape recorder, magnetic	1899	Poulsen	Danish
Teflon	1938	Du Pont	U.S.
Telegraph, magnetic	1837	Morse	U.S.
Telegraph, quadruplex	1864	Edison	U.S.
Telegraph, railroad	1887	Woods	U.S.
Telegraph, wireless high frequency	1895	Marconi	Italian
Telephone[1]	1871	Meucci	U.S.-Italian
Telephone[1]	1876	Bell	U.S.-Scot.
Telephone answering machine (1st practical)	1954	Hashimoto	Japanese
Telephone, automatic	1891	Strowger	U.S.
Telephone, cellular	1947	Bell Labs	U.S.
Telephone, cordless[2]	1950	Gross	U.S.
Telephone, radio	1900	Poulsen, Fessenden	Danish, Canadian
Telephone, radio	1906	De Forest	U.S.
Telephone, radio, long dist.	1915	AT&T	U.S.
Telephone, recording	1898	Poulsen	Danish
Telephone amplifier	1912	De Forest	U.S.
Telescope	1608	Lippershey	Neth.
Telescope	1609	Galileo	Italian
Telescope, astronomical	1611	Kepler	German
Teletype	1928	Morkrum, Kleinschmidt	U.S.
Television, color	1928	Baird	Scottish
Television, electronic	1927	Farnsworth	U.S.
Television, iconoscope	1923	Zworykin	U.S.
Television, mech. scanner	1923	Baird	Scottish
Tesla Coil	1891	Tesla	U.S.
Thermometer	1593	Galileo	Italian
Thermometer	1730	Reaumur	French
Thermometer, mercury	1714	Fahrenheit	German
Time recorder	1890	Bundy	U.S.
Tire, double-tube	1845	Thomson	Scottish
Tire, pneumatic	1888	Dunlop	Scottish
Toaster, automatic	1918	Strite	U.S.
Toilet, flush	1589	Harington	English
Tool, pneumatic	1865	Law	English
Torpedo, marine	1804	Fulton	U.S.
Tractor, crawler	1904	Holt	U.S.
Transformer, AC	1885	Stanley	U.S.
Transistor	1947	Shockley, Brattain, Bardeen	U.S.
Trolley car, electric	1884-87	Van DePoele, Sprague	U.S.
Tungsten, ductile	1912	Coolidge	U.S.
Tupperware®	1945	Tupper	U.S.
Turbine, gas	1849	Bourdin	French
Turbine, hydraulic	1849	Francis	U.S.
Turbine, steam	1884	Parsons	English
Type, movable	1447	Gutenberg	German
Typewriter	1867	Sholes, Soule, Glidden	U.S.
Vacuum cleaner, electric	1907	Spangler	U.S.
Vacuum evaporating pan	1846	Rillieux	U.S.
Velcro	1948	de Mestral	Swiss
Video game ("Pong")	1972	Bushnell	U.S.
Video home system (VHS)	1975	Matsushita, JVC	Japanese
Washer, electric	1901	Fisher	U.S.
Welding, atomic hydrogen	1924	Langmuir, Palmer	U.S.
Welding, electric	1877	Thomson	U.S.
Windshield wiper	1903	Anderson	U.S.
Wind tunnel	1912	Eiffel	French
Wire, barbed	1874	Glidden	U.S.
Wrench, double-acting	1913	Owen	U.S.
X-ray tube	1913	Coolidge	U.S.
Zeppelin	1900	Zeppelin	German
Zipper, early model	1893	Judson	U.S.
Zipper, improved	1913	Sundback	Canadian

(1) While Alexander Graham Bell has traditionally been credited with invention of the telephone, which he patented, Antonio Meucci developed a working model before Bell. (2) Al Gross held a number of important early patents in the field of wireless communication; other people were also involved in the development of practical cordless telephones.

Top 20 Corporations Receiving U.S. Patents in 2006

Source: U.S. Patent and Trademark Office, U.S. Department of Commerce

Rank	Company	No. of patents	Rank	Company	No. of patents
1.	International Business Machines Corporation	3,621	12.	Microsoft Corporation	1,463
2.	Samsung Electronics Co., Ltd.	2,451	13.	Seiko Epson Corporation	1,200
3.	Canon Kabushiki Kaisha	2,366	14.	General Electric Company	1,051
4.	Matsushita Electric Industrial Co., Ltd.	2,229	15.	Fuji Photo Film Co., Ltd.	906
5.	Hewlett-Packard Development Company, L.P.	2,099	16.	Koninklijke Philips Electronics N.V.	896
6.	Intel Corporation	1,959	17.	Infineon Technologies Ag	890
7.	Sony Corporation	1,771	18.	Texas Instruments, Incorporated	880
8.	Hitachi, Ltd.	1,732	19.	Siemens Aktiengesellschaft	854
9.	Toshiba Corporation	1,672	20.	Honda Giken Kogyo Kabushiki Kaisha (Honda	
10.	Micron Technology, Inc.	1,610		Motor Co., Ltd.).	778
11.	Fujitsu Limited	1,487			

Note: Reflects patent ownership at time of patent grant. Changes may occur after patent grant. Where more than one assignee exists, patents are attributed to first-named assignee.

Foreign Countries Receiving Most U.S. Patents, 2006

Source: U.S. Patent and Trademark Office

2006 Rank	Country (2005 Rank)	2006 Patents	Share of total issued	Change, 2005–06	2006 Rank	Country (2005 Rank)	2006 Patents	Share of total issued	Change, 2005–06
1.	Japan (1)	39,411	20.1%	23.8%	7.	France (7)	3,856	2.0%	24.1%
2.	Germany (2)	10,889	5.5	13.7	8.	Italy (8)	1,899	1.0	19.4
3.	Taiwan (3)	7,919	4.0	32.1	9.	Netherlands (9)	1,647	0.8	37.3
4.	South Korea (4)	6,509	3.3	41.8	10.	Australia (12)	1,538	0.8	49.0
5.	United Kingdom (5)	4,329	2.2	21.6		**United States**	102,267	52.1	23.8
6.	Canada (6)	4,094	2.1	28.9		**All Countries**	196,436	100.0	24.5

Note: Country of origin is determined by residence of first–named inventor.

Top 20 U.S. Patent Categories, 1985–2005

Source: U.S. Patent and Trademark Office
(ranked by number of patents issued in 2005)

Rank	Category	Pre-1985	1985	1995	2005	Change, 1985–2005
1.	Semiconductor Device Manufacturing Processes	2,296	430	1,482	4,467	938.8%
2.	Active Solid-State Devices (Transistors, Solid-State Diodes)	2,100	321	1,365	4,287	1,235.5
3.	Drug, Bio-Affecting and Body Treating Compositions	11,965	1,667	2,553	2,784	67.0
4.	Multiplex Communications	1,207	312	866	2,754	782.7
5.	Chemistry: Molecular Biology and Microbiology	3,105	425	1,503	2,423	470.1
6.	Telecommunications	1,532	187	581	2,271	1,114.4
7.	Stock Material or Miscellaneous Articles	7,541	1,397	1,980	2,263	62.0
8.	Static Information Storage and Retrieval	1,738	234	922	2,019	762.8
9.	Optical: Systems and Elements	3,219	499	753	2,013	303.4
10.	Computer Graphics Processing and Selective Visual Display Systems	1,147	190	760	2,004	954.7
11.	Optical Waveguides	1,247	196	563	1,915	877.0
12.	Electrical Connectors	3,248	574	934	1,806	214.6
13.	Measuring and Testing	7,740	1,211	1,356	1,779	46.9
14.	Drug, Bio-Affecting and Body Treating Compositions	3,199	494	1,341	1,711	246.4
15.	Electricity: Measuring and Testing	3,077	514	1,023	1,698	230.4
16.	Internal-Combustion Engines	7,089	1,273	864	1,624	27.6
17.	Multicomputer Data Transferring (Computers and Digital Processing)	98	27	162	1,586	5,774.1
18.	Pulse or Digital Communications	1,073	218	717	1,567	618.8
19.	Radiant Energy	4,148	651	1,143	1,554	138.7
20.	Electricity: Communications	3,490	490	844	1,491	204.3

Bottom 20 U.S. Patent Categories, 1985–2005

Source: U.S. Patent and Trademark Office
(ranked by number of patents issued in 2005)

Rank	Category	Pre-1985	1985	1995	2005	Change, 1985–2005
1.	Wood Turning	16	5	1	0	−100.0%
2.	Coopering	1	0	1	0	NA
3.	Needle and Pin Making	2	5	0	0	−100.0
4.	Mineral Oils: Apparatus	53	6	2	0	−100.0
5.	Type Casting	0	0	0	0	NA
6.	Whips and Whip Apparatus	5	2	0	0	−100.0
7.	Railway Mail Delivery	1	1	0	0	−100.0
8.	Typesetting	0	0	0	0	NA
9.	Electric Lamp and Discharge Devices: Consumable Electrodes	4	0	0	0	NA
10.	Books, Strips, and Leaves for Manifolding	59	4	12	0	−100.0
11.	Button Making	1	0	0	1	NA
12.	Wire Fabrics and Structure	12	0	0	1	NA
13.	Land Vehicles: Animal Draft Appliances	1	0	0	1	NA
14.	Railway Wheels and Axles	24	2	0	1	−50.0
15.	Textiles: Braiding, Netting, and Lace Making	49	12	11	2	−83.3
16.	Motors: Spring, Weight, or Animal Powered	34	2	5	2	0.0
17.	Wooden Receptacles	28	1	2	2	100.0
18.	Selective Cutting (e.g., Punching)	19	1	0	2	100.0
19.	Chemistry of Carbon Compounds	21	1	3	2	100.0
20.	Merchandising	48	5	9	3	−40.0

Note: Excludes patents for which design classification could not be determined

Geologic Time Scale

Our understanding of Earth's ancient history is largely a result of geoscientists' study of climate, rock strata, ice samples, mineral deposits, and fossils from around the world; clues to the planet's origin have also been found through the study of extraterrestrial bodies. Geologists divide Earth's history into the following units (MYA = million years ago):

PRECAMBRIAN TIME (4,600-542 MYA)

HADEAN EON (4,600-3,800 MYA) Earth has no continents, oceans, or life; surface conditions are defined by intense volcanic activity and widespread meteorite impact. Oldest known minerals and rocks, many of meteoric origin, date to this era.

ARCHEAN EON (3,800-2,500 MYA) Earth's surface cools and water vapor in atmosphere condenses to form early oceans, which define small protocontinents; the first single-celled organisms, primarily bacteria, appear in these oceans.

PROTEROZOIC EON (2,500-542 MYA) Protocontinents merge into larger landmasses as Earth's crust continues to shift. Atmospheric oxygen levels increase, and first known multicellular life (a form of algae) appears. Later, soft-bodied marine animals emerge.

PHANEROZOIC EON

Paleozoic Era (542-251 MYA)

Cambrian Period (542-488 MYA) Collisions between Earth's plates create a supercontinent of the southern hemisphere known as Gondwanaland. Seas experience an explosion of invertebrate animal life, including thousands of species of trilobites; there is no life on land.

Ordovician Period (488-443 MYA) Gondwanaland extends from South Pole to tropic regions; northern hemisphere is mostly open ocean. Average global temperatures are warmer than present era. First primitive land plants, early ancestors of starfish and mollusks, and first known vertebrates (armored, jawless fishes) appear. The period ends in extinction of a majority of species, possibly a result of a global drop in sea level due to glaciation.

Silurian Period (443-416 MYA) South Pole remains covered by supercontinent, but precursors of present-day N America, Europe, and Asia coalesce around the equator and middle latitudes. Appearance of first known vascular land plants, first freshwater fish, first jawed fish, first coral reefs, and first air-breathing animals (*eurypterids*, a scorpion-like creature).

Devonian Period (416-359 MYA) Collisions between Gondwanaland and ancestral landmasses of N America and Eurasia produce mountains visible today as northern Appalachians. Newly-formed ozone layer offers protection from sun's rays, allowing first air-breathing spiders and mites to appear on dry land; emergence of first jawed fish, fish with fins and scales, and first amphibians.

Carboniferous Period (359-299 MYA) Precursors of modern N America and Northern Europe lie in tropical latitudes north of the Equator; warm and humid conditions there facilitate spread of lush forests and peat swamps that later form most of the world's coal and limestone. Later period sees emergence of first true conifers, *lepidodendrales* ("scale trees") as tall as 100 ft, and first true reptiles.

Permian Period (299-251 MYA) All major landmasses collide to form the supercontinent Pangaea, surrounded by the world ocean Panthalassa. Gradual warming throughout the Permian allows for initial flourishing of species—including dinosaur precursors (up to 10 ft in length) and marine species in shallow inland seas—but later precipitates mass extinction of as much as 95% of all species.

Mesozoic Era (251-65.5 MYA)

Triassic Period (251-199 MYA) Pangea separates into supercontinents of Laurasia and Gondwana; subtropical conditions extend as far north as present-day Wyoming and New England. Emergence of *icthyosaurs* and *plesiosaurs* (large marine reptiles), several species of dinosaurs (up to 15 ft long), first true mammals, and first insects to undergo metamorphosis from larva to pupa to adult.

Jurassic Period (199-145 MYA) North American continent drifts westward, opening Gulf of Mexico; rift forms between South America and Africa. Warm, moist climate contributes to flourishing of coral reefs and temperate and subtropical forests. Appearance of first *angiosperms* (flowering plants), *pterosaurs* (winged reptiles), earliest known bird (*Archaeopteryx*), and huge dinosaurs such as the carnivorous *Allosaurus* and herbivorous *Apatosaurus*.

Cretaceous Period (145-65.5 MYA) African continental plate drifts north, creating roots of European Alps; gap between S America and Africa broadens; western movement of N America drives formation of Sierra Nevada and Rocky Mountains, turning the western interior of continent into a vast swamp. Later, sea levels rise and cover about one-third of Earth's present land area; global climate is warm and mild. The period ends in a mass extinction of plant and animal species (including dinosaurs), possibly caused by volcanic activity or impact of one or more asteroids or comet fragments.

Cenozoic Era (65.5 MYA-present)

Paleogene Period (65.5-23 MYA)

• Paleocene Epoch (65.5-55.8 MYA) Australia separates from Antarctica; N America and Greenland spread apart. Mammalian life predominates, including early marsupials, insectivores, creodonts (carnivorous ancestors to both cats and dogs), and primitive hoofed mammals.

• Eocene Epoch (55.8-33.9 MYA) Australia drifts farther from Antarctica; the Indian subcontinent becomes welded to Asia, and tectonic forces drive the upheaval of the Alpine-Himalayan system. Climate in N America and Europe is subtropical and moist, with temperate forests as far north as Greenland and Siberia. Ancestors of modern horse, rhinoceros, camel, bats, primates, and squirrel-like rodents emerge; earliest known marine mammals appear in later Eocene.

• Oligocene Epoch (33.9-23 MYA) San Andreas fault develops between N American and Pacific plates. Mammalian species continue to diversify, producing the first elephants, modern horses, multiple rodent, camel, and rhinoceros-like species, as well as first known species of great ape. Long-term cooling trend begins that would later cause Pleistocene ice ages.

Neogene Period (23 MYA-present)

• Miocene Epoch (23-5.3 MYA) Crustal plate collisions continue to drive uplift of Alps, Himalayas, and Cordilleran Ranges in Americas; eroded sediment is deposited in shallow marine basins, forming reservoirs for oil fields of California, Romania, and Caspian Sea. Ocean currents prevent Antarctica from receiving warmer waters, fostering growth of Antarctic ice sheet; northern forests become grassy prairies. Elephants give rise to first mastodons, and large apes related to the orangutan live in Asia and southern Europe; oldest hominid fossils from Africa date to this epoch.

• Pliocene Epoch (5.3-1.8 MYA) Alps continue to rise in Europe, and subduction of the Pacific tectonic plate elevates the Sierra Nevada and volcanic Cascade Range. Climate becomes cooler and drier, driving formation of permanent Arctic ice cap. Rapid primate evolution produces *Australopithecus*, earliest direct ancestor of *Homo sapiens*.

• Pleistocene Epoch (1.8 MYA-11,800 years ago) Glacier ice covers as much as 25% of more of Earth's land surface, carving numerous present-day features including the Great Lakes; increased rainfall in lower latitudes allows plant and animal life to flourish in northern and eastern Africa. Late Pleistocene brings worldwide extinction of many large mammals, including the mastodon, saber-toothed tiger, and ground sloth.

• Holocene Epoch (11,800 years ago to the present) Melting ice caused sea levels to rise 100 ft or more in early Holocene, covering large areas of land and extending continental shelf of North America. Humans proliferate, and civilization begins.

Classification

Source: *Funk & Wagnalls New Encyclopedia*

In biology, classification is the identification, naming, and grouping of organisms into a formal system. The 2 fields that are most directly concerned with classification are taxonomy and systematics. Although the 2 disciplines overlap considerably, taxonomy is more concerned with nomenclature (naming) and with constructing hierarchical systems, and systematics with uncovering evolutionary relationships. Two kingdoms of living forms, Plantae and Animalia, have been recognized since Aristotle established the first taxonomy in the 4th century BC. In addition, there are the following 3 kingdoms: Protista (one-celled organisms), Monera (bacteria and blue-green algae; also known as the kingdom Procaryotae), and Fungi. The 7 basic categories of classification (from most general to most specific) are: kingdom, phylum (or division), class, order, family, genus, and species. Below are 2 examples:

ZOOLOGICAL HIERARCHY

Kingdom	Phylum	Class	Order	Family	Genus	Species name	Common name
Animalia	Chordata	Mammalia	Primates	Hominidae	Homo	Homo sapiens	Human

BOTANICAL HIERARCHY

Kingdom	Division*	Class	Order	Family	Genus	Species name	Common name
Plantae	Magnoliophyta	Magnoliopsida	Magnoliales	Magnoliaceae	Magnolia	M. virginiana	Sweet Bay

* In botany, the division is generally used in place of the phylum.

Gestation, Longevity, and Incubation of Selected Animals

Information reviewed by Ronald M. Nowak, author *Walker's Mammals of the World* (6th ed., Johns Hopkins University Press, 1999). Average longevity figures supplied by Ronald T. Reuther. These apply to animals in captivity; the potential life span of animals is rarely attained in nature. Figures on gestation and incubation are averages based on estimates.

ANIMAL	Gestation (days)	Average longevity (years)	Maximum longevity (yr-mo)	ANIMAL	Gestation (days)	Average longevity (years)	Maximum longevity (yr-mo)
Ass	365	12	47	Leopard	98	12	23
Baboon	187	20	45	Lion	100	15	30
Bear: Black	219	18	36-10	Monkey (rhesus)	166	15	37
Grizzly	225	25	50	Moose	240	12	27
Polar	240	20	45	Mouse (meadow)	21	3	4
Beaver	105	5	50	Mouse (dom. white)	19	3	6
Bison	285	15	40	Opossum (American)	13	1	5
Camel	406	12	50	Pig (domestic)	112	10	27
Cat (domestic)	63	12	28	Puma	90	12	20
Chimpanzee	230	20	60	Rabbit (domestic)	31	5	13
Chipmunk	31	6	10	Rhinoceros (black)	450	15	45-10
Cow	284	15	30	Rhinoceros (white)	480	20	50
Deer (white-tailed)	201	8	20	Sea lion (California)	350	12	34
Dog (domestic)	61	12	20	Sheep (domestic)	154	12	20
Elephant (African)	660	35	70	Squirrel (gray)	44	10	23-6
Elephant (Asian)	645	40	77	Tiger	105	16	26-3
Elk	250	15	26-8	Wolf (maned)	63	5	15-8
Fox (red)	52	7	14	Zebra (Grant's)	365	15	50
Giraffe	457	10	36-2				
Goat (domestic)	151	8	18				Incubation time (days)
Gorilla	258	20	54	Chicken			21
Guinea pig	68	4	8	Duck			30
Hippopotamus	238	41	61	Goose			30
Horse	330	20	50	Pigeon			18
Kangaroo (gray)	36	7	24	Turkey			26

Major Venomous Animals

Snakes

Asian pit viper — from 2 ft to 5 ft long; throughout Asia; reactions vary, but most bites cause tissue damage, and mortality is generally low.

Australian brown snake — 4 ft to 7 ft long; very slow onset of cardiac or respiratory distress; moderate mortality, but because death can be sudden and unexpected, it is the most dangerous of the Australian snakes; antivenom.

Barba Amarilla or fer-de-lance — up to 7 ft long; from tropical Mexico to Brazil; severe tissue damage common; moderate mortality; antivenom.

Black mamba — up to 14 ft long, fast-moving; S and C Africa; rapid onset of dizziness, difficulty breathing, erratic heartbeat; mortality high, nears 100% without antivenom.

Boomslang — less than 6 ft long; in African savannahs; rapid onset of nausea and dizziness, often followed by slight recovery and then sudden death from internal hemorrhaging; bites rare, mortality high; antivenom.

Bushmaster — up to 12 ft long; wet tropical forests of C and S America; few bites occur, but mortality rate is high.

Common or Asian cobra — 4 ft to 8 ft long; throughout southern Asia; considerable tissue damage, sometimes paralysis; mortality probably not more than 10%; antivenom.

Copperhead — less than 4 ft long; from New England to Texas; pain and swelling; very seldom fatal; antivenom seldom needed.

Coral snake — 2 ft to 5 ft long; in Americas south of Canada; bite may be painless; slow onset of paralysis, impaired breathing; mortalities rare, but high without antivenom and mechanical respiration.

Cottonmouth water moccasin — up to 5 ft long; wetlands of southern U.S. from Virginia to Texas. Rapid onset of severe pain, swelling; mortality low, but tissue destruction can be extensive; antivenom.

Death adder — less than 3 ft long; Australia; rapid onset of faintness, cardiac and respiratory distress; at least 50% mortality without antivenom.

Desert horned viper — in dry areas of Africa and western Asia; swelling and tissue damage; low mortality; antivenom.

European viper — 1 ft to 3 ft long; bleeding and tissue damage; mortality low; antivenom.

Gaboon viper — more than 6 ft long; fat; 2-in. fangs; south of the Sahara; massive tissue damage, internal bleeding; few recorded bites.

King cobra — up to 16 ft long; throughout southern Asia; rapid swelling, dizziness, loss of consciousness, difficulty breathing, erratic heartbeat; mortality varies sharply with amount of venom involved, but most bites involve nonfatal amounts; antivenom.

Krait — up to 5 ft long; in SE Asia; rapid onset of sleepiness; numbness; up to 50% mortality even with use of antivenom.

Puff adder — up to 5 ft long; fat; south of the Sahara and throughout the Middle East; rapid large swelling, great pain, dizziness; moderate mortality, often from internal bleeding; antivenom.

Rattlesnake — 2 ft to 6 ft long; throughout W Hemisphere; rapid onset of severe pain, swelling; mortality low, but amputation of affected digits is sometimes necessary; antivenom. Mojave rattler may produce temporary paralysis.

Ringhals, or spitting, cobra — 5 ft to 7 ft long; southern Africa; squirts venom through holes in front of fangs as a defense; venom is severely irritating, can cause blindness.

Russell's viper or tic-polonga — more than 5 ft long; throughout Asia; internal bleeding; bite reports common; moderate mortality rate; antivenom.

Saw-scaled or carpet viper — as much as 2 ft long; in dry areas from India to Africa; severe bleeding, fever; high mortality, causes more human fatalities than any other snake; antivenom.

Sea snakes — throughout Pacific, Indian oceans except NE Pacific; almost painless bite, variety of muscle pain, paralysis; mortality rate low, many bites not envenomed; some antivenoms.

Sharp-nosed pit viper or one hundred pace snake — up to 5 ft long; in S Vietnam, Taiwan, and China; the most toxic of Asian pit vipers; very rapid onset of swelling and tissue damage, internal bleeding; moderate mortality; antivenom.

Taipan — up to 11 ft long; in Australia and New Guinea; rapid paralysis with severe breathing difficulty; mortality nears 100% without antivenom.

Tiger snake — 2 ft to 6 ft long; S Australia; pain, numbness, mental disturbances with rapid paralysis; may be deadliest of all land snakes, but antivenom is quite effective.

Yellow or Cape cobra — 7 ft long; in S Africa; most toxic venom of any cobra; rapid onset of swelling, breathing and cardiac difficulties; mortality is high without treatment; antivenom.

Note: Not all bites by venomous snakes are actually envenomed. Any animal bite, however, carries the danger of tetanus, and anyone suffering a venomous snake bite should seek medical attention. Antivenoms do not cure; they are only an aid in the treatment of bites. Mortality rates above are for envenomed bites; low mortality, c. 2% or less; moderate, 2%-5%; high, 5%-15%.

Lizards

Gila monster — as much as 24 in. long, with heavy body and tail; in high desert in SW U.S. and N Mexico; immediate severe pain and transient low blood pressure; no recent mortality.

Mexican beaded lizard — similar to Gila monster; Mexican west coast; reaction and mortality rate similar to Gila monster.

Insects

Ants, bees, wasps, hornets, etc. Global distribution. Usual reaction is piercing pain in area of sting. Not directly fatal, except in cases of massive multiple stings. However, many people suffer allergic reactions — swelling and rashes — and a few may die within minutes from severe sensitivity to the venom (anaphylactic shock).

Spiders, Scorpions

Atrax spider — also known as funnel web spider; several varieties, often large; in Australia; slow onset of breathing, circulation difficulties; low mortality; antivenom.

Black widow — small, round-bodied with red hourglass marking; the widow and its relatives are found in tropical and temperate zones; severe musculoskeletal pain, weakness, breathing difficulty, convulsions; may be more serious in small children; low mortality; antivenom. The **redback** spider of Australia has the hourglass marking on its back, rather than on its front, but is otherwise identical to the black widow.

Brown recluse, or fiddleback, spider — small, oblong body; throughout U.S.; pain with later ulceration at place of bite; in severe cases fever, nausea, and stomach cramps; ulceration may last months; very low mortality.

Scorpion — crablike body with stinger in tail, various sizes, many varieties throughout tropical and subtropical areas; various symptoms may include severe pain spreading from the wound, numbness, severe agitation, cramps; severe reaction may include respiratory failure; low mortality, usually in children; antivenoms.

Tarantula — large, hairy spider found around the world; the American tarantula, and probably all other tarantulas, are harmless to humans, though their bite may cause some pain and swelling.

Sea Life

Cone-shell — mollusk in small, beautiful shell; in the S Pacific and Indian oceans; shoots barbs into victims; paralysis; low mortality.

Octopus — global distribution, usually in warm waters; all varieties produce venom, but only a few can cause death; rapid onset of paralysis with breathing difficulty.

Portuguese man-of-war — jellyfishlike, with tentacles up to 100 ft long; in most warm water areas; immediate severe pain; not directly fatal, though shock may cause death in rare cases.

Sea wasp — jellyfish, with tentacles up to 30 ft long, in the S Pacific; very rapid onset of circulatory problems; high mortality because of speed of toxic reaction; antivenom.

Stingray — several varieties of differing sizes; found in tropical and temperate seas and some fresh water; severe pain, rapid onset of nausea, vomiting, breathing difficulties; wound area may ulcerate, gangrene may appear; seldom fatal.

Stonefish — brownish fish that lies motionless as a rock on bottom in shallow water; throughout S Pacific and Indian oceans; extraordinary pain, rapid paralysis; low mortality; antivenom available, amount determined by number of puncture wounds; warm water relieves pain.

Speeds of Selected Animals

Source: Natural History magazine. © American Museum of Natural History

ANIMAL	mph	ANIMAL	mph	ANIMAL	mph
Cheetah	70	Greyhound	39.35	Black mamba snake	20
Pronghorn antelope	61	Whippet	35.50	Six-lined race runner (lizard)	18
Wildebeest	50	Rabbit (domestic)	35	Wild turkey	15
Lion	50	Mule deer	35	Squirrel	12
Thomson's gazelle	50	Jackal	35	Pig (domestic)	11
Quarterhorse	47.5	Reindeer	32	Chicken	9
Elk	45	Giraffe	32	Spider (Tegenaria atrica)	1.17
Cape hunting dog	45	White-tailed deer	30	Giant tortoise	0.17
Coyote	43	Wart hog	30	Three-toed sloth	0.15
Gray fox	42	Grizzly bear	30	Garden snail	0.03
Hyena	40	Cat (domestic)	30		
Zebra	40	Human	27.89		
Mongolian wild ass	40	Elephant	25		

Note: Most of these measurements are for maximum speeds over approximate quarter-mile distances. Exceptions are the lion and elephant, whose speeds were clocked in the act of charging; the whippet, which was timed over a 200-yd course; the cheetah, timed over a 100-yd distance; humans timed over a 15-yard segment of a 100-yard run; and the black mamba, six-lined race runner, spider, giant tortoise, three-toed sloth, and garden snail, which were measured over various small distances.

Top 50 American Kennel Club Registrations

Source: American Kennel Club, New York, NY; covers (new) dogs registered during calendar year shown

Breed	2006 Rank	2006 Number registered	2005 Rank	2005 Number registered	Breed	2006 Rank	2006 Number registered	2005 Rank	2005 Number registered
Retrievers (Labrador)	1.	123,760	1.	137,867	Cavalier King Charles Spaniels	27.	8,124	31.	7,678
Yorkshire Terriers	2.	48,346	3.	47,238	Basset Hounds	28.	7,844	27.	8,890
German Shepherd Dogs	3.	43,575	4.	45,014	Bichons Frises	29.	7,839	26.	9,184
Retrievers (Golden)	4.	42,962	2.	48,509	Weimaraners	30.	7,720	29.	8,623
Beagles	5.	39,484	5.	42,592	Brittanys	31.	7,560	30.	7,853
Dachshunds	6.	36,033	6.	38,566	Mastiffs	32.	6,913	33.	6,799
Boxers	7.	35,388	7.	37,268	West Highland White Terriers	33.	6,572	32.	7,597
Poodles	8.	29,939	8.	31,638	Australian Shepherds	34.	6,533	34.	6,221
Shih Tzu	9.	27,282	9.	28,087	Papillons	35.	5,673	35.	6,005
Miniature Schnauzers	10.	22,920	10.	24,144	French Bulldogs	36.	5,509	38.	4,210
Chihuahuas	11.	22,562	11.	23,575	Collies	37.	4,711	36.	5,098
Bulldogs	12.	21,037	13.	20,556	Havanese	38.	4,038	43.	3,595
Pugs	13.	20,008	12.	22,064	St. Bernards	39.	3,828	37.	4,352
Pomeranians	14.	18,218	14.	19,511	Bullmastiffs	40.	3,760	42.	3,668
Boston Terriers	15.	14,955	17.	15,852	Bernese Mountain Dogs	41.	3,714	47.	3,479
Spaniels (Cocker)	16.	14,790	15.	16,343	Scottish Terriers	42.	3,545	40.	3,795
Rottweilers	17.	14,709	16.	15,916	Vizslas	43.	3,509	44.	3,559
Maltese	18.	13,312	19.	13,676	Newfoundlands	44.	3,415	46.	3,493
Shetland Sheepdogs	19.	12,822	18.	14,278	Bloodhounds	45.	3,343	50.	3,112
Pointers (German Shorthaired)	20.	12,822	20.	13,273	Lhasa Apsos	46.	3,326	39.	3,921
Doberman Pinschers	21.	11,546	21.	11,662	Chinese Shar-Pei	47.	3,261	45.	3,544
Pembroke Welsh Corgis	22.	10,250	23.	10,648	Cairn Terriers	48.	3,224	41.	3,739
Miniature Pinschers	23.	9,615	22.	11,454	Pekingese	49.	3,155	48.	3,441
Great Danes	24.	9,438	24.	9,640	Retrievers (Chesapeake Bay)	50.	3,120	49.	3,332
Siberian Huskies	25.	9,342	25.	9,452					
Spaniels (English Springer)	26.	8,205	28.	8,749					

Breed Registration for Top 10 Pedigreed Cats, 1979-2005[1]

Source: The Cat Fanciers' Association, Manasquan, NJ; ranked by new registrations, 2005.

Breed	2005	2004	2000	1995	1990	1979	Breed	2005	2004	2000	1995	1990	1979
Persian	16,657	18,176	25,524	44,735	60,661	25,819	Birman	991	945	998	990	969	258
Maine Coon	3,932	4,162	4,539	4,332	2,727	401	American Shorthair	802	846	885	1,050	1,176	738
Exotic	3,006	2,838	2,094	1,610	1,311	289	Oriental	764	854	1,085	1,237	1,288	260
Siamese	1,445	1,621	2,131	3,025	3,860	3,607	Tonkinese	704	717	803	780	618	—
Abyssinian	1,344	1,462	1,683	2,469	2,702	1,524	TOTAL	NA	41,606	49,551	70,288	84,729	37,630
Ragdoll	1,215	981	—	—	—	—							

(1) Figures were not available for 2006. Rankings were identical to 2005, except the 10th most popular breed was the Sphynx.

Trees of the U.S.

Source: American Forests, Washington, DC

Approximately 826 native and naturalized species of trees are grown in the U.S. The oldest living tree is believed to be a bristlecone pine tree in California named Methuselah, estimated to be 4,700 years old. The world's largest known living tree*, the General Sherman giant sequoia in California, weighs more than 6,167 tons—as much as 41 blue whales or 740 elephants. California naturalists in Septemberare reported finding three redwood trees topping 370 feet in height, including "Hyperion," estimated at 378.1 feet.

Listed here are 10 largest National Champion trees as listed by American Forests.

10 Largest National Champion Trees

Tree Type	Girth at 4.5 ft. (in.)	Height (ft.)	Crown Spread (ft.)	Total Points*	Location
Giant sequoia (Gen. Sherman tree)	1,020	274	107	1,321	Sequoia National Park, CA
Coast redwood	950	321	75	1,290	Jedidiah Smith State Park, CA
Coast redwood	895	307	83	1,223	Jedidiah Smith State Park, CA
Coast redwood	867	311	101	1,203	Prairie Creek State Park, CA
Western red cedar	761	159	45	931	Olympic National Park, WA
Sitka spruce	668	191	96	883	Olympic National Forest, WA
Sitka spruce	629	204	93	856	Kloochy Creek Park, OR
Douglas-fir	512	301	65	829	Jedidiah Smith State Park, CA
Douglas-fir	505	281	71	804	Olympic National Forest, WA
Common Baldcypress	644	83	85	762	Cat Island, LA

* American Forests uses a point system to determine the largest trees. The following calculation to determine a tree's total points: Trunk Circumference (in inches) + Height (in feet) + ¼ Average Crown Spread (in feet) = Total Points

ENVIRONMENT
Notable Environment News in 2007

IPCC Warns Of 21st Century Warming

The UN Intergovernmental Panel on Climate Change (IPCC) released the report "Climate Change 2007: Impacts, Adaptation and Vulnerability" on April 6, 2007. The study described several likely scenarios for climate change in the future, including an expected global warming of 3°C over the course of the 21st century, with largely negative effects on plant and animal life and on human water and food supplies. The IPCC noted that at this rate of temperature change, 20-30% of plant and animal species could be at increased risk of extinction. In addition, by mid-century, river runoff and water availability could increase by 10-40% in high latitudes and wet tropical areas, but decrease 10-30% in mid-latitude dry regions and in dry tropics, increasing the number of areas affected by drought. The strongest impact is likely to be felt in the Arctic, sub-Saharan Africa, small island states, and low-lying coasts. UN Secretary-General Ban Ki-moon called on nations to make new efforts to ameliorate climate change, asking members of the UN Framework Convention on Climate Change (UNFCCC) to create a new plan to replace the Kyoto Protocol, which expires in 2012.

Fabled Northwest Passage Opens

Scientists at the University of Colorado's National Snow and Ice Data Centre (www.nsidc.com) announced that Arctic ice set a new record low on Sept. 16, 2007, reaching its lowest minimum extent in the thirty years that measurements have been taken and beating the previous low, set Sept. 20, 2005, by 460,000 sq mi, or approximately the area of Texas and California combined. Satellite tracking of sea ice has only been performed since 1979, but Russian and Alaskan records indicate that the ice retreat in 2007 was probably more dramatic than any other time in the 20th century. The most dramatic effect was the opening of the fabled Northwest

Passage route around the top of North America, which was fully navigable for about five weeks of the summer. Scientists at the NSIDC said that the Arctic could experience ice-free summers by 2030, but they also noted that it was difficult to sort out the relative influence of natural processes and human activity on the extent of sea ice. Sea ice around Antarctica, in fact, approached record highs around the same period. However, a new NASA study confirmed in 2007 that Antarctic snow was melting farther inland (up to 500 miles from the coast) and at higher altitudes (up to 1.2 miles above sea level) than in the past, and that more snow was melting on the Ross Ice Shelf, which normally serves to insulate glaciers against warmer marine air.

New Species Join the "Red List"

The International Union for Conservation of Nature and Natural Resources (IUCN) announced Sept. 13 that there were 41,415 species on its "Red List." 16,306 of them were threatened with extinction, up from 16,118 in 2006. According to the IUCN, 1 in 4 mammals, 1 in 8 birds, one-third of amphibians, and 70% of assessed plants on the 2007 Red List were "in jeopardy." Notable among species joining the Critically Endangered group was the Western Gorilla (*gorilla gorilla*) which has lost a large percentage of one subspecies to the bushmeat trade and to Ebola. The IUCN also placed corals on the list for the first time, including two Critically Endangered species from the Galapagos which have been damaged by El Nino and the effects of global climate change. In 2007, scientists also declared that the Yangtze River Dolphin, or Baiji, was possibly extinct, due primarily to fishing, pollution, and degradation of its habitat—the first cetacean to be driven to extinction by man. A possible sighting in August 2007 was under investigation.

U.S. Greenhouse Gas Emissions from Human Activities, 1990-2005
Source: U.S. Environmental Protection Agency

GAS AND MAJOR SOURCE(S)	1990	1995	2000	2002	2003	2004	2005	Percent Change
Carbon dioxide (CO$_2$)	5,061.6	5,384.6	5,940.0	5,892.7	5,952.5	6,064.3	6,089.5	20.3%
Fossil fuel combustion	4,724.1	5,030.0	5,584.9	5,557.2	5,624.5	5,713.0	5,751.2	21.7
Methane (CH$_4$)	609.1	598.7	563.7	549.7	549.2	540.3	539.3	−11.5
Landfills	161.0	157.1	131.9	130.4	134.9	132.1	132.0	−18.0
Enteric fermentation[1]	115.7	120.6	113.5	112.6	113.0	110.5	112.1	−3.1
Natural gas systems	124.5	128.1	126.6	125.0	123.7	119.0	111.1	−10.7
Coal mining	81.9	66.5	55.9	52.0	52.1	54.5	52.4	−36.0
Nitrous oxide (N$_2$O)	482.0	484.2	499.8	479.2	459.8	445.2	468.6	−2.8
Agricultural soil management	366.9	353.4	376.8	366.1	350.2	338.8	365.1	−0.5
Hydrofluorocarbons (HFCs), perfluorocarbons (PFCs), and sulfur hexafluoride (SF$_6$)	89.3	103.5	143.8	143.0	142.7	153.9	163.0	82.5
TOTAL U.S. EMISSIONS	6,242.0	6,571.0	7,147.2	7,064.6	7,104.2	7,203.7	7,260.4	16.3
NET U.S. EMISSIONS[2]	5,529.2	5,742.2	6,390.5	6,252.7	6,292.3	6,378.9	6,431.9	16.3

Note: Emissions given in terms of equivalent emissions of carbon dioxide (CO$_2$), using units of teragrams of carbon dioxide equivalents (Tg CO$_2$ Eq.). (1) Digestive process of ruminant animals, such as cattle and sheep, producing methane as a by-product. (2) Total emissions minus carbon dioxide absorbed by forests or other means.

Top 15 Nations Producing Carbon Dioxide Emissions, Ranked by 2004 Totals, 1980-2004
Source: U.S. Department of Energy
(million metric tons of carbon dioxide emitted from fossil fuel consumption)

Region/Country	1980	1985	1990	1995	2000	2004	Percent Change 1980-2004	Percent Change 1990-2004
United States	4,754.52	4,585.20	5,013.45	5,292.67	5,815.50	5,912.21	24%	18%
China	1,454.65	1,838.47	2,241.17	2,873.10	3,030.88	4,707.28	224	110
Russia[1]	3,027.53	3,496.77	3,792.16	1,590.82	1,556.27	1,684.84	NA	NA
Japan	937.50	892.96	1,014.85	1,075.84	1,190.06	1,262.10	35	24
India	299.76	439.34	588.24	867.08	1,000.69	1,112.84	271	89
Germany[2]	751.02	689.20	693.90	875.85	847.08	862.23	NA	NA
Canada	452.51	434.73	478.57	504.93	568.23	587.98	30	23
United Kingdom	608.30	588.25	598.48	555.00	551.02	579.68	−5	−3
Korea, South	126.48	165.05	237.87	393.35	442.51	496.76	293	109
Italy	366.75	374.00	413.38	427.52	443.95	484.98	32	17
South Africa	234.19	298.81	295.48	344.04	378.59	429.56	83	45
France	487.89	394.61	368.64	372.65	399.79	405.66	−17	10
Iran	119.52	164.72	201.79	260.13	318.27	401.91	236	99
Australia	198.31	224.59	262.77	284.84	353.20	386.18	95	47
Mexico	231.43	270.46	300.09	318.70	379.99	385.46	67	28
World Total[3]	18,333.26	19,412.76	21,426.12	22,033.53	23,851.46	27,043.57	48	26

(1) Numbers for 1980-90 are for the former Soviet Union. (2) Numbers for 1980-90 are for the former West Germany. (3) Includes nations not listed

Air Pollution in Selected World Cities

Source: World Bank, *World Development Indicators 2006*

Particulate matter in the following table refers to smoke, soot, dust, and liquid droplets from combustion that are in the air—specifically, to particulates less than 10 microns in diameter capable of reaching deep into the respiratory tract. The level of particulates, an important indicator of air quality, is significantly affected by the state of technology and pollution controls. Particulate pollution causes an estimated 500,000 premature deaths each year. **Sulfur dioxide** is a pollutant formed when fossil fuels containing sulfur are burned. **Nitrogen dioxide** is a poisonous, pungent gas formed when nitric oxide combines with hydrocarbons and sunlight, producing a photochemical reaction. Nitrogen oxides are emitted by bacteria, nitrogenous fertilizers, aerobic decomposition of organic matter, biomass combustion, and, especially, burning fuel for vehicles and industrial activities. Emissions of sulfur dioxide and nitrogen oxides lead to **acid rain**.

Data in the following table are average concentrations based on reports from urban monitoring sites, measured in micrograms per cubic meter, mpcm; the figures give a general indication of air quality, but results should be interpreted with caution. World Health Organization standards for acceptable air quality are 50 mpcm for sulfur dioxide and 40 mpcm for nitrogen dioxide; the WHO has set no guidelines for acceptable levels of suspended particulate matter.

City and Country	Particulate matter[1]	Sulfur dioxide[2]	Nitrogen dioxide[2]
Accra, Ghana	40	NA	NA
Amsterdam, Netherlands	40	10	58
Athens, Greece	51	34	64
Bangkok, Thailand	83	11	23
Barcelona, Spain	43	11	43
Beijing, China	99	90	122
Berlin, Germany	25	18	26
Cairo, Egypt, Arab Rep.	159	69	NA
Calcutta, India	145	49	34
Capetown, South Africa	15	21	72
Caracas, Venezuela, RB	17	33	57
Chicago, United States	26	14	57
Delhi, India	177	24	41
Jakarta, Indonesia	115	NA	NA
London, England	23	25	77
Los Angeles, U.S.	36	9	74
Manila, Philippines	42	33	NA
Mexico City, Mexico	55	74	130
Milan, Italy	36	31	248
Montreal, Canada	20	10	42
Moscow, Russia	25	109	NA
Mumbai, India	74	33	39
Nairobi, Kenya	42	NA	NA
New York City, U.S.	22	26	79
Oslo, Norway	19	8	43
Paris, France	12	14	57
Prague, Czech Republic	25	14	33
Quito, Ecuador	33	22	NA
Rio de Janeiro, Brazil	42	129	NA
Rome	35	NA	NA
Sao Paulo, Brazil	49	43	83
Seoul, South Korea	46	44	60
Shanghai, China	81	53	73
Sofia, Bulgaria	76	39	122
Tokyo, Japan	42	18	68
Toronto, Canada	24	17	43
Warsaw, Poland	43	16	32

NA = Not available. (1) Data was collected in 2002. (2) Average of data collected between 1995 and 2001.

Air Quality of Selected U.S. Metropolitan Areas, 1990-2005

Source: U.S. Environmental Protection Agency, Office of Air Quality Planning and Standards

Data indicate the number of days metropolitan statistical areas failed to meet acceptable air-quality standards.

Metropolitan Statistical Area	1990	1995	2000	2001	2002	2003	2004	2005
Atlanta, GA	42	35	39	24	20	12	11	11
Bakersfield, CA	99	105	132	124	150	141	133	87
Baltimore, MD	28	36	23	33	42	20	16	27
Baton Rouge, LA	28	15	29	5	5	15	11	12
Boston, MA–NH	0	0	0	3	7	6	1	1
Chicago, IL	5	23	13	33	23	10	9	23
Cincinnati, OH–KY–IN	12	19	15	15	31	10	4	14
Cleveland-Lorain–Elyria,OH	10	24	21	29	30	17	18	25
Dallas, TX	0	20	20	14	7	5	9	10
Denver, CO	9	3	2	8	7	16	0	1
Detroit, MI	11	14	16	31	28	19	9	23
Fresno, CA	62	61	131	139	152	127	48	64
Greensboro-Winston Salem-High Point, NC	12	6	14	11	24	4	2	2
Houston, TX	51	65	42	27	21	31	22	28
Indianapolis, IN	9	19	8	14	24	11	1	18
Las Vegas, NV–AZ	4	0	0	1	2	3	1	2
Los Angeles–Long Beach, CA	161	103	63	81	81	88	65	45
Miami, FL	1	2	2	1	1	1	3	1
Minneapolis-St. Paul, MN–WI	4	3	4	6	1	1	0	2
New Haven-Meriden, CT	15	14	9	15	25	16	3	13
New York, NY	15	17	19	21	26	14	6	15
Orange County, CA	42	8	5	6	4	5	3	0
Philadelphia, PA-NJ	39	30	21	35	35	20	14	26
Phoenix-Mesa, AZ	12	16	11	7	8	8	1	4
Riverside-San Bernardino, CA	158	124	144	156	146	138	118	103
Sacramento, CA	56	41	41	46	57	35	26	39
St. Louis, MO-IL	22	34	20	20	34	13	2	29
Salt Lake City-Ogden, UT	5	4	20	27	33	10	37	26
San Diego, CA	96	48	31	30	20	20	16	7
San Francisco, CA	0	2	3	5	1	0	0	0
Seattle–Bellevue-Everett, WA	2	0	7	6	6	2	1	1
Washington, DC-MD-VA-WV	25	32	22	28	34	13	10	19

U.S. Greenhouse Gas Emissions, 2005

Source: U.S. Environmental Protection Agency

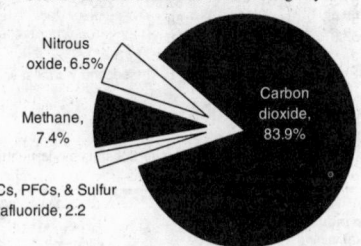

Nitrous oxide, 6.5%
Methane, 7.4%
HFCs, PFCs, & Sulfur hexafluoride, 2.2
Carbon dioxide, 83.9%

World Carbon Dioxide Emissions from the Use of Fossil Fuels, 2005

Source: U.S. Energy Information Administration

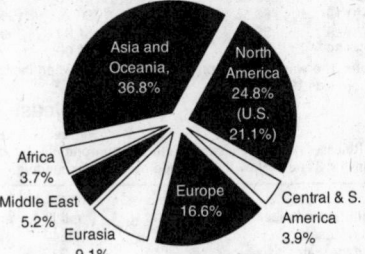

Asia and Oceania, 36.8%
North America 24.8% (U.S. 21.1%)
Africa 3.7%
Middle East 5.2%
Eurasia 9.1%
Europe 16.6%
Central & S. America 3.9%

Atmospheric Concentration of Carbon Dioxide, 1744-2006

Sources: Carbon Dioxide Information Analysis Center, Dept. of Energy

Year[1]	CO_2 in ppm[2]	Year[1]	CO_2 in ppm[2]	Year[1]	CO_2 in ppm[2]	Year[1]	CO_2 in ppm[2]	Year[1]	CO_2 in ppm[2]	Year[1]	CO_2 in ppm[2]
1744	277	1843	287	1903	295	1943	308	1980	339	2004	377
1791	280	1869	289	1915	301	1960	317	1990	354	2005	377
1816	284	1878	290	1927	306	1970	326	2000	369	2006	379

(1) Measurements for the years 1744-1943 were derived from a 200m ice core sample drilled near Siple Station in Antarctica between 1983-84. Measurements from 1960-2004 were taken directly from the atmosphere at Mauna Loa Observatory in Hawaii. Measurements for 2005-2006 were taken directly from the atmosphere at Jubany Station, Antarctica. (2) parts per million.

Emissions of Principal Air Pollutants in the U.S., 1970-2006

Source: U.S. Environmental Protection Agency, Office of Air Quality Planning and Standards; in million tons; estimated

Pollutant Emitted	1970	1975	1980	1985	1990	1995	2000	2005	2006
Carbon monoxide	197.3	184.0	177.8	169.6	143.6	120.0	102.4	91	88
Nitrogen oxides[1]	26.9	26.4	27.1	25.8	25.2	24.7	22.3	19	18
Particulate matter[2]									
PM 10	12.2	7.0	6.2	3.6	3.2	3.1	2.3	2	2
PM 2.5	NA	NA	NA	NA	2.3	2.2	1.8	2	1
Sulfur dioxide	32.1	28.0	25.9	23.3	23.1	18.6	16.3	15	14
Volatile org. compounds[1]	3.7	30.2	30.1	26.9	23.1	21.6	16.9	15	15
Lead	0.221	0.16	0.074	0.022	0.005	0.004	0.003	0.003	0.002
TOTAL[3]	301.5	275.8	267.2	249.2	218.2	188.0	160.2	142	137

(1) Ozone, a major air pollutant and the primary constituent of smog, is not emitted directly to the air but is formed by sunlight acting on emissions of nitrogen oxides and volatile organic compounds. (2) PM_{10}, particulates 10 microns or smaller in diameter. $PM_{2.5}$, particulates 2.5 microns or smaller diameter. (3) Totals are rounded, as are components of totals.

Carbon Monoxide Emission Estimates, 1970-2006

(in thousand tons)

Source	1970	1975	1980	1985	1990	1995	2000	2002	2004	2006
Fuel combustion, elec. util.	237	276	322	291	363	372	484	656	666	677
Industrial processes[1]	10,610	8,304	7,700	5,894	5,572	5,631	3,628	3,346	3,402	3,460
Transportation[2]	174,602	167,884	160,512	153,216	131,702	107,755	92,239	85,352	81,691	78,031
TOTAL[3]	204,042	188,398	185,408	176,845	154,188	126,778	114,465	109,235	104,892	100,552

(1) Industrial fuel combustion, chemical and allied manufacturing, metals processing, and petroleum and other industrial sectors. (2) Highway and off-highway vehicles. (3) Totals may not add because of rounding or because all categories are not listed.

Nitrogen Oxides Emission Estimates, 1970-2006

(in thousand tons)

Source	1970	1975	1980	1985	1990	1995	2000	2002	2004	2006
Fuel combustion, elec. util.	4,900	5,694	7,024	6,127	6,663	6,384	5,330	4,709	3,961	3,585
Industrial processes[1]	5,100	4,546	4,110	4,009	3,831	3,909	3,518	2,904	2,942	2,981
Transportation[2]	15,276	15,029	14,846	14,508	13,373	12,989	12,561	12,645	11,633	10,622
TOTAL[3]	26,882	26,378	27,080	25,757	25,527	24,955	22,599	21,277	19,564	18,226

(1) Industrial fuel combustion, chemical and allied manufacturing, metals processing, and petroleum and other industrial sectors. (2) Highway and off-highway vehicles. (3) Totals may not add because of rounding or because all categories are not listed.

Sulfur Dioxide Emissions Estimates, 1970-2006

(in thousand tons)

Source	1970	1975	1980	1985	1990	1995	2000	2002	2004	2006
Fuel combustion, elec. util.	17,398	18,268	17,469	16,272	15,909	12,080	11,396	10,436	10,500	9,613
Industrial processes[1]	11,661	7,993	6,725	5,597	5,402	4,945	3,516	2,745	2,802	2,859
Transportation[2]	551	635	717	809	874	741	697	773	695	616
TOTAL[3]	31,218	28,044	25,926	23,307	23,077	18,619	16,348	14,623	14,672	13,770

(1) Industrial fuel combustion, chemical and allied manufacturing, metals processing, and petroleum and other industrial sectors. (2) Highway and off-highway vehicles. (3) Totals include miscellaneous sources not determined.

Average Global Temperatures, 1900-2006

Source: National Oceanic and Atmospheric Administration; in degrees Fahrenheit

1900-09 . . . . . . 56.58	1940-49 . . . . . 57.13	1980-89 . . . . . . .57.35	2001 . . . . 57.90	2004 . . . . 57.98
1910-19 . . . . . . 56.56	1950-59 . . . . . 56.98	1990-99 . . . . . . .57.64	2002 . . . . 58.02	2005 . . . . 58.11
1920-29 . . . . . . 56.76	1960-69 . . . . . 57.04	2000 . . . . .57.67	2003 . . . . 58.02	2006 . . . . 57.99
1930-39 . . . . . . 57.01	1970-79 . . . . . 57.06			

Note: The warmest year on record was 2005, when the average global temperature reached 58.1°F. The second warmest year on record was 1998.

Toxics Release Inventory, U.S., 2004-2005

Source: U.S. Environmental Protection Agency

Releases of toxic chemicals into the environment, by manner of release and industry sector; pollutant transfers by destination of transfer. Totals below may not add because of rounding.

Pollutant releases	2004 mil lb	2005 mil lb	Top industries, total releases	2004 %	2005 %
Air releases	1,540	1,512	Metal mining	25	27
Surface water discharges	235	240	Electric utilities.	25	25
Underground injection	238	231	Chemicals	13	11
On-site land releases.	1,701	1,824	Primary metals	12	12
Off-site releases.	508	533	Hazardous waste/solvent recovery	5	5
TOTAL on- and off-site releases.	4,223	4,339	All others	15	20

Pollutant transfers			Top carcinogens, air/water/land releases	mil lb	mil lb
To recycling	2,036	2,014	Lead compounds.	451	426
To energy recovery	650	608	Arsenic compounds.	184	119
To treatment.	326	337	Chromium compounds	52	56
To publicly owned treatment works	260	265	Styrene	55	55
Other transfers.	71	<1	Nickel compounds.	32	33
Off-site to disposal	606	637	Formaldehyde	22	25
TOTAL.	3,950	3,862			

Note: This information does not indicate whether (or to what degree) the public has been exposed to toxic chemicals.

Top 10 States, Total Toxics Releases, 2005

Source: U.S. Environmental Protection Agency

State	Total lb	State	Total lb	State	Total lb	State	Total lb
Alaska	548,412,055	Ohio	220,202,286	Tennessee . . .	128,341,708	Florida	125,801,560
Nevada.	324,883,916	Utah	170,830,842	Georgia	126,949,564		
Texas	235,781,204	Indiana	135,045,234	North Carolina	126,369,585	U.S. Total* . . .	4,339,463,751

*Total includes District of Columbia, Puerto Rico, American Samoa, Guam, Northern Marianas, and the Virgin Islands.

Hazardous Waste Sites in the U.S., 2007

Source: U.S. Environmental Protection Agency, National Priorities List, Aug. 2007

State/Territory	Proposed Gen	Proposed Fed	Final Gen	Final Fed	Total Number	State/Territory	Proposed Gen	Proposed Fed	Final Gen	Final Fed	Total Number
Alabama.	2	0	10	3	15	Nevada	0	0	1	0	1
Alaska	0	0	0	5	5	New Hampshire. . . .	1	0	19	1	21
Arizona	0	0	6	2	8	New Jersey	3	0	106	8	117
Arkansas	0	0	10	0	10	New Mexico.	2	0	11	1	14
California	3	0	69	24	96	New York.	1	0	82	4	87
Colorado.	2	0	14	3	19	North Carolina	0	0	29	2	31
Connecticut	1	0	13	1	15	North Dakota	0	0	0	0	0
Delaware	0	0	13	1	14	Ohio.	5	2	27	3	37
District of Columbia .	0	0	0	1	1	Oklahoma	1	0	9	1	11
Florida	1	0	43	6	50	Oregon	1	0	9	2	12
Georgia	1	0	13	2	16	Pennsylvania	2	0	87	6	95
Hawaii	0	0	1	2	3	Rhode Island	0	0	10	2	12
Idaho	3	0	4	2	9	South Carolina.	0	0	24	2	26
Illinois.	6	1	38	4	49	South Dakota	0	0	1	1	2
Indiana	1	0	30	0	31	Tennessee.	0	1	10	3	14
Iowa	1	0	10	1	12	Texas.	2	0	39	4	45
Kansas	1	0	9	1	11	Utah.	5	0	10	4	19
Kentucky	0	0	13	1	14	Vermont	0	0	11	0	11
Louisiana	3	0	10	1	14	Virginia	0	0	18	11	29
Maine	0	0	9	3	12	Washington	0	0	33	13	46
Maryland	1	0	8	9	18	West Virginia	0	0	7	2	9
Massachusetts.	1	0	25	6	32	Wisconsin	1	0	37	0	38
Michigan.	1	1	65	0	67	Wyoming	0	0	1	1	2
Minnesota.	1	0	22	2	25	Guam.	0	0	1	1	2
Mississippi	2	0	4	0	6	Puerto Rico	0	0	11	1	12
Missouri	0	0	23	3	26	Virgin Islands	0	0	2	0	2
Montana	1	0	14	0	15						
Nebraska	0	0	12	1	13	Total	56	5	1,083	157	1,301

Note: Fed. = for hazardous waste produced by federal agency; Gen. = non-Fed./ sites. Proposed = proposed for federal Superfund financing; Final = qualified for Superfund financing.

Renewable Energy Sources

Source: U.S. Department of Energy

Concern over the environmental impact of burning fossil fuels has helped spur interest in alternative fuels that are less polluting. And since the supply of fossil fuels is finite and diminishing, there is interest in "renewable" sources that do not deplete existing supplies. However, renewable energy sources still make up only a small share of U.S. domestic energy production (about 6.8%, or excluding hydropower about 4%). The major reason for this is their relatively higher cost (in some cases 2 to 4 times that of power obtained from traditional fuels). The following are the major renewable energy sources available.

Biomass is plant-derived material usable as a renewable energy source, including wood energy crops such as hybrid poplars and willow trees, agricultural crops including soybeans and corn, and animal and other wastes. Biomass is one of the two most common energy sources in the U.S. today along with hydropower. Forms of biomass such as wood can be burned to produce heat and generate electricity. Agricultural crops can be chemically converted into fuels such as ethanol and biodiesel; these are the only known renewable liquid energy sources, and may one day replace petroleum and fossil-fuel produced diesel. But bringing ethanol and biodiesel into wide use would require more energy-efficient methods of production and transportation. Overall, biomass fuels are much cleaner-burning than fossil fuels, though biomass fuels do produce carbon dioxide and other pollutants.

Geothermal energy is generated from heat from inside Earth. This form of energy is both clean and renewable. The technology has caught on in countries with substantial geothermal activity such as Iceland, where it accounts for 16% of electricity output and 86% of all energy used for home heating. In the U.S. the best sources for geothermal power are in the west, where there are many underground lakes of heated water; however, large-scale access would require drilling. A major goal in this field is to find a way to harness energy directly from magma (molten rock material), which has great potential because of its high temperature.

Hydrogen is the 3rd most abundant element on Earth. It does not naturally occur on Earth as a pure gas or liquid, but is always combined with other elements (such as with oxygen to form water or carbon to form methane). For energy use it is produced from hydrocarbons using heat, bacteria or algae through photosynthesis, or by using sunlight or electricity to split water into hydrogen and oxygen. Hydrogen batteries or "fuel cells" are already used by NASA on the space shuttle. In a fuel cell, electrons are released from the hydrogen atoms in a chemical reaction and flow through an external circuit as electricity. The protons then combine with oxygen (and some of the electrons in the electric current) to make heat and water suitable for drinking. Fuel cells do not run down, but work as long as hydro-gen is supplied. Some experts think hydrogen will be the power source of the future. However, an infrastructure would need to be created for safe and cost-effective transportation and storage of hydrogen.

Hydropower, or hydroelectric power, is generated by water flowing through turbines. With biomass fuels, it is one of the two most common renewable energy sources in the U.S. today. A dam on a river is a common hydropower producer. No harmful greenhouse gases are produced, but the dams needed to generate the power can harm river ecosystems. Researchers are working on turbine technologies that may maximize use of hydropower and reduce adverse environmental effects.

Ocean energy is generated in two ways. Thermal ocean energy uses the heat that the ocean absorbs from the sun to power generators, and sometimes drinkable desalinated water is a by-product. Mechanical ocean energy is generated by the movement of tides and waves through a turbine. In both cases, power generation is not very efficient with current technology. Much more research is needed to make thermal ocean energy generation a reality. Mechanical ocean energy requires large dams or breakwater-type structures called "tidal barrages" to be built, which could cause harm to coastal ecosystems.

Solar energy is generated using heat and light from the sun. Solar energy is an increasingly common source of electricity. Photovoltaic (PV) solar cells are made of semiconducting materials that can directly convert sunlight to electricity without any harmful waste product. Solar collectors are made more efficient by using arrays of mirrors to concentrate the sun's rays onto PV panels. Another way of using sunlight is to heat water directly. According to the DOE, homes incorporating solar heating designs can save as much as 50% on heating bills. The downside to solar energy is that it depends heavily on a range of factors including location, time of year, and weather.

Wind energy uses wind turbines to produce energy. They are perched on high towers, usually 100 feet or higher, and often placed in large groups ("farms") to generate electricity for towns and cities. On a much smaller scale, stand-alone turbines are sometimes used by farmers and homeowners to generate supplemental electricity. In the past 20 years, government incentives in the form of tax credits to producers and incentives for homeowners have helped lower the price of wind power by 85%, making it a more feasible option. Some people object to wind farms because of their appearance or the noise the turbines make. Wind power raises few other environmental problems; but the turbines can pose a danger to birds. In addition, because weather is involved, consistent generation is a challenge.

Alternative-Fueled Vehicles in Use in the U.S., by Fuel, 1995-2004

Source: Energy Information Administration, U.S. Dept. of Energy

Fuel	1995	2000	2001	2002	2003[1]	2004[2]	Growth Rate
Liquefied Petroleum Gases (LPG) . .	172,806	181,994	185,053	187,680	190,43	194,389	1.3
Compressed Natural Gas (CNG) . . .	50,218	100,750	111,851	120,839	132,988	143,742	12.4
Liquefied Natural Gas (LNG)	603	2,090	2,576	2,708	3,030	3,134	20.1
Methanol, 85 Percent (M85)[3]	18,319	10,426	7,827	5,873	4,917	4,592	−14.3
Methanol, Neat (M100)	386	0	0	0	0	0	0.0
Ethanol, 85 Percent (E85)[3,4]	1,527	87,570	100,303	120,951	133,776	146,195	78.8
Ethanol, 95 Percent (E95)[3]	136	4	0	0	0	0	0.0
Electricity[5]	2,860	11,830	17,847	33,047	45,656	55,852	39.1
Total.	246,855	394,664	425,457	471,098	510,805	547,904	9.3

(1) Estimated. (2) Projected. (3) The remaining portion of 85-percent methanol and both ethanol fuels is gasoline. (4) In 1997, some vehicle manufacturers began including E85-fueling capability in certain model lines of vehicles. For 2002, the EIA estimated that the number of E-85 vehicles that are capable of operating on E85, gasoline, or both, is about 4.1 million. Many are sold and used as traditional gasoline-powered vehicles. In this table, AFVs in use include only those E85 vehicles believed to be intended for use as AFVs (primarily fleet-operated vehicles). (5) Excludes gasoline-electric hybrids.

Renewable Water Resources

Source: Food and Agriculture Organization, United Nations, 2007

Globally, water supplies are abundant, but they are unevenly distributed among and within countries. In some areas, water withdrawals are so high, relative to supply, that surface water supplies are shrinking and groundwater reserves are being depleted faster than they can be replenished by precipitation. The U.S. (including Alaska and Hawaii) has a total of 2,818 cubic kilometers of internal renewable water resources, an actual total (which takes into account incoming water flow from outside the country) of 3,069 cubic kilometers, and 10,333 cubic meters per capita. Totals for all countries are 43,219 cubic kilometers of internal resources, 55,273 cubic kilometers of actual resources, and 8,549 cubic meters per capita.

These numbers, and those in the tables below, were published by the Food and Agriculture Organization in 2007; the tables draw upon studies done over a number of years and use 2005 population data.

Countries With Most Resources Per Capita
(ranked by per capita resources)

Country	Cubic meters per capita	Total cubic km
Greenland	10,578,947.4	603.0
French Guiana	716,577.5	134.0
Iceland	578,231.3	170.0
Guyana	313,802.1	241.0
Suriname	276,018.1	122.0
Congo, Republic of	212,190.8	832.0
Papua New Guinea	134,418.5	801.0
Gabon	119,272.7	164.0
Canada	90,766.9	2,902.0
Solomon Islands	88,690.5	44.7

Note: *Data not available from all nations.

Countries With Least Resources Per Capita*
(ranked by per capita resources, starting with the lowest)

Country/Territory	Cubic meters per capita	Total cubic km
Kuwait	7.5	0.02
United Arab Emirates	48.3	0.15
Bahamas	62.3	0.02
Qatar	84.4	0.05
Maldives	88.8	0.03
Saudi Arabia	93.7	2.40
Libya	104.0	0.60
Malta	125.9	0.05
Singapore	137.2	0.60
Jordan	153.0	0.88

Forest Area Top 50 Countries, 1990–2005*

Source: World Resources Institute; United Nations

Units: Thousand hectares

Country	Total Forest Area (thousand hectares)			Percent change in forest area 1990–2005	Country	Total Forest Area (thousand hectares)			Percent change in forest area 1990–2005
	2005	2000	1990			2005	2000	1990	
Russian Federation	808,790	809,268	808,950	0	Congo	22,471	22,556	22,726	−1
Brazil	477,698	493,213	520,027	−8	Gabon	21,775	21,826	21,927	−1
Canada	310,134	310,134	310,134	0	Cameroon	21,245	22,345	24,545	−13
United States	303,089	302,294	298,648	1	Malaysia	20,890	21,591	22,376	−7
China	197,290	177,001	157,141	26	Mozambique	19,262	19,512	20,012	−4
Australia	163,678	164,645	167,904	−3	Paraguay	18,475	19,368	21,157	−13
Congo, Dem Rep	133,610	135,207	140,531	−5	Spain	17,915	16,436	13,479	33
Indonesia	88,495	97,852	116,567	−24	Zimbabwe	17,540	19,105	22,234	−21
Peru	68,742	69,213	70,156	−2	Lao People's Dem Rep	16,142	16,532	17,314	−7
India	67,701	67,554	63,939	6	Chile	16,121	15,834	15,263	6
Sudan	67,546	70,491	76,381	−12	France	15,554	15,351	14,538	7
Mexico	64,238	65,540	69,016	−7	Guyana	15,104	15,104	15,104	0
Colombia	60,728	60,963	61,439	−1	Suriname	14,776	14,776	14,776	0
Angola	59,104	59,728	60,976	−3	Thailand	14,520	14,814	15,965	−9
Bolivia	58,740	60,091	62,795	−6	Ethiopia	13,000	13,705	15,114	−14
Venezuela	47,713	49,151	52,026	−8	Viet Nam	12,931	11,725	9,363	38
Zambia	42,452	44,676	49,124	−14	Madagascar	12,838	13,023	13,692	−6
Tanzania	35,257	37,318	41,441	−15	Mali	12,572	13,072	14,072	−11
Argentina	33,021	33,770	35,262	−6	Botswana	11,943	12,535	13,718	−13
Myanmar	32,222	34,554	39,219	−18	Chad	11,921	12,317	13,110	−9
Papua New Guinea	29,437	30,132	31,523	−7	Nigeria	11,089	13,137	17,234	−36
Sweden	27,528	27,474	27,367	−1	Germany	11,076	11,076	10,741	3
Japan	24,868	24,876	24,950	0	Iran, Islamic Rep	11,075	11,075	11,075	0
Central African Rep.	22,755	22,903	23,203	−2	Ecuador	10,853	11,841	13,817	−21
Finland	22,500	22,475	22,194	1	Cambodia	10,447	11,541	12,946	−19
					World	**3,952,025**	**3,988,610**	**4,077,291**	**−3**

Note: *Ranked by hectares of forest

Some Endangered Animal Species

Source: Fish and Wildlife Service, U.S. Dept. of the Interior

Common name	Scientific name	Range
Albatross, Amsterdam	Diomedia amsterdamensis	Amsterdam Island, Indian Ocean
Antelope, giant sable	Hippotragus niger variani	Angola
Armadillo, giant	Pridontes maximus	Venezuela, Guyana to Argentina
Babirusa	Babyrousa babyrussa	Indonesia
Bandicoot, desert	Perameles eremiana	Australia
Bat, gray	Myotis grisescens	Central, southeastern U.S.
Bear, Mexican grizzly	Ursus aretos	Mexico
Bison, wood	Bison bison athabascae	Canada, northwestern U.S.
Bobcat, Mexican	Felis rufus escuinapae	Central Mexico
Caiman, black	Melanosuchus niger	Amazon basin

Common name	Scientific name	Range
Camel, Bactrian	Camelus bactrianus	Mongolia, China
Caribou, woodland	Rangifer tarandus caribou	Canada, Northwestern U.S.
Cheetah	Acinonyx jubatus	Africa to India
Chimpanzee, pygmy	Pan paniscus	Congo (formerly Zaire)
Condor, California	Gymnogyps californianus	U.S. (AZ, CA, OR), Mexico (Baja California)
Crane, whooping	Grus americana	Canada, Mexico, U.S. (Rocky Mts. to Carolinas)
Crocodile, American	Crocodylus acutus	U.S. (FL), Mexico, Caribbean Sea, Central and S America
Deer, Columbian white-tailed	Odocoileus virginianus leucurus	U.S. (OR, WA)
Dolphin, Chinese river	Lipotes vexillifer	China
Dugong	Dugong dugon	East Africa to southern Japan
Elephant, Asian	Elephas maximus	S central and southeastern Asia
Fox, northern swift	Vulpes velox hebes	Canada
Frog, mountain yellow-legged	Rano capito sevosa	Western U.S. (CA, NV)
Gorilla	Gorilla gorilla	Central and W Africa
Hartebeest, Tora	Alcelaphus buselaphus tora	Egypt, Ethiopia, Sudan
Hawk, Hawaiian	Buteo solitarius	U.S. (HI)
Hyena, brown	Hyaena brunnea	Southern Africa
Impala, black-faced	Aepyceros melampus petersi	Angola, Namibia
Kangaroo, Tasmanian forester	Macropus giganteus tasmaniensis	Australia (Tasmania)
Leopard	Panthera pardus	Africa and Asia
Lion, Asiatic	Panthera leo persica	Turkey to India
Manatee, West Indian	Trichechus manatus	Southeastern U.S., Caribbean Sea, Mexico
Monkey, spider	Ateles geoffroyi frontatus	Costa Rica, Nicaragua
Ocelot	Felis pardalis	U.S. (AZ, TX) to Central and S America
Orangutan	Pongo pygmaeus	Borneo, Sumatra
Ostrich, West African	Struthio camelus spatzi	W Sahara
Otter, marine	Lutra felina	Peru south to Straits of Magellan
Panda, giant	Ailuropoda melanoleuca	China
Panther, Florida	Felis concolor coryi	U.S. (FL)
Parakeet, golden	Aratinga guarouba	Brazil
Parrot, imperial	Amazona imperialis	West Indies (Dominica)
Penguin, Galapagos	Spheniscus mendiculus	Ecuador (Galapagos Islands)
Puma, eastern	Felis concolor couguar	Eastern N America (presumed extinct in wild)
Python, Indian	Python molurus molurus	Sri Lanka, India
Rat-kangaroo, brush-tailed	Bettongia penicillata	Australia
Rhinoceros, black	Diceros bicornis	Sub-Saharan Africa
Rhinoceros, northern white	Ceratotherium simum cottoni	Congo, Sudan, Uganda, Central African Rep.
Salamander, Chinese giant	Andrias davidianus	Western China
Sea-lion, Steller	Eumetopias jubatus	Alaska, Russia
Sheep, bighorn	Ovis canadensis	California
Squirrel, Carolina northern flying	Glaucomys sabrinus coloratus	U.S. (NC, TN)
Tiger	Panthera tigris	Asia
Tortoise, Galapagos	Geochelone elephantopus	Ecuador (Galapagos Islands)
Turtle, Plymouth red-bellied	Pseudemys rubriventris bangsi	U.S. (MA)
Whale, gray	Eschrichtius robustus	N Pacific Ocean
Whale, humpback	Megaptera novaeangliae	Oceania
Wolf, red	Canis rufus	U.S. (FL, NC, SC)
Woodpecker, ivory-billed	Campephilus principalis	Cuba
Yak, wild	Bos grunniens mutus	China (Tibet), India
Zebra, mountain	Equus zebra zebra	South Africa

U.S. List of Endangered and Threatened Species, 2007

Source: Fish and Wildlife Service, U.S. Dept. of Interior; as of Sept. 2007

Group	Endangered		Threatened		Total species[1]	Species with recovery plans
	U.S.	Foreign	U.S.	Foreign		
Mammals	69	256	12	20	357	54
Birds	75	176	14	6	271	79
Reptiles	13	65	24	16	118	35
Amphibians	13	8	10	1	32	17
Fishes	74	11	65	1	151	99
Clams	62	2	8	0	72	69
Snails	64	1	11	0	76	28
Insects	47	4	10	0	61	33
Arachnids	12	0	0	0	12	6
Crustaceans	19	0	3	0	22	18
Corals	0	0	2	0	2	0
Animal subtotal	**448**	**523**	**159**	**44**	**1,174**	**438**
Flowering plants	570	1	143	0	714	607
Conifers & cycads	2	0	1	2	5	3
Ferns and allies	24	0	2	0	26	26
Lichens	2	0	0	0	2	2
Plant subtotal	**598**	**1**	**146**	**2**	**747**	**638**
GRAND TOTAL	**1,046**	**524**	**305**	**46**	**1,921**	**1,076**

(1) Some species are classified as both endangered and threatened. The table tallies these "dual status" species only once, as endangered, except for the olive ridley sea turtle, which is dual status but tallied as a U.S. threatened species. The other dual status species, all tallied as endangered, are: (U.S.) California tiger salamander, chinook salmon, gray wolf, green sea turtle, piping plover, roseate tern, sockeye salmon, steelhead, Steller sea lion; (non-U.S.) argali, chimpanzee, leopard, saltwater crocodile.

METEOROLOGY

National Weather Service Watches and Warnings

Source: National Weather Service, National Oceanic and Atmospheric Admin. (NOAA),
U.S. Dept. of Commerce; *Glossary of Meteorology*, American Meteorological Society

The **National Weather Service** issues watches, warnings, and advisories for specific geographic areas to alert people to the possibility or imminent arrival of various forms of severe weather. A severe thunderstorm or tornado watch is issued when a severe convective storm that usually covers a relatively small geographic area or moves in a narrow path is sufficiently intense to threaten life and/or property. Examples include thunderstorms with large hail, damaging winds, and tornadoes. Excessive localized convective rains are not classified as severe storms but are often the product of severe local storms. Such rainfall may result in phenomena that threaten life and property, such as flash floods. Lightning occurs with all thunderstorms and, along with flash floods, is a leading cause of storm deaths and injuries.

Severe thunderstorm—a thunderstorm that produces a tornado, winds greater than 50 knots (58 mph), and/or hail at least ¾ inch in diameter. A *severe thunderstorm watch* is issued for an area where such storms are most likely to develop within a 3- to 6-hr period. A *severe thunderstorm warning* indicates that a severe thunderstorm has been sighted or indicated by radar.

Tornado—a violent rotating column of air that extends from the base of a thunderstorm to the ground. On a local scale, it is the most destructive of all atmospheric phenomena. Tornado paths range from a few feet to more than 100 mi long (avg. 5 mi) and from a few feet to more than 1 mi in diameter (avg. 220 yds). The average forward speed is 30 mph. Tornado watches and warnings follow the same criteria as those for thunderstorms.

Cyclone—an atmospheric circulation of winds rotating counterclockwise in the Northern Hemisphere and clockwise in the Southern Hemisphere. Tornadoes, hurricanes, and the lows shown on weather maps are all examples of cyclones of various size and intensity. Cyclones are usually accompanied by precipitation or stormy weather.

Subtropical storm—a cyclone that develops over subtropical waters (N of 20° lat.) with 1-min. sustained surface winds of 34 knots (39 mph) or more. It may form over warm or cold water and can develop into a tropical storm or a hurricane.

Tropical storm—a cyclone that develops over tropical waters (23.5° N-23.5° S lat.), with 1-min. sustained surface winds between 34 and 63 knots (39-72 mph). A *tropical storm watch* is issued when tropical storm conditions pose a threat to specified coastal areas within 36 hours. A *tropical storm warning* is issued when tropical storm conditions are expected in a specified coastal area within 24 hours.

Hurricane—a severe cyclone originating over tropical ocean waters and having 1-min. sustained surface winds of 64 knots (74 mph) or higher. (West of the international date line, north of the equator, such storms are known as **typhoons**.) The hurricane-force winds form a circle or oval, sometimes as wide as 300 mi in diameter. In the lower latitudes, hurricanes usually move west or northwest at 10-15 mph. When the center approaches 25° to 30° N lat., the direction of motion often changes to the northeast, with increased forward speed. In the Atlantic, hurricane season is June 1-Nov. 30. Hurricane season is May 15-Nov. 30 in the eastern Pacific. Hurricane watches and warnings follow the same criteria as those for tropical storms.

Winter storm and blizzard—A *winter storm watch* is issued when conditions are favorable for hazardous winter weather, such as heavy snow, sleet, or freezing rain. A *winter storm warning* is issued when such hazardous conditions are imminent. A *blizzard warning* is issued for winter storm conditions with winds of 35 mph or higher and sufficient falling and/or blowing snow to frequently reduce visibility to less than ¼ mi for at least 3 hours.

Flood—Flooding takes many forms. *River flooding:* Occurs when rains, sometimes coupled with melting snow, quickly fill river basins with an excess of water. Torrential rains from decaying hurricanes or tropical systems can also be a major cause of river flooding. *Coastal flooding:* Tropical storm and hurricane winds or intense offshore low pressure systems can drive ocean water inland. Coastal floods can also be produced by sea waves called tsunamis, sometimes referred to as tidal waves, produced by earthquakes or volcanic activity. *Flash flooding:* Usually due to copious amounts of rain falling in a short time, flash flooding typically occurs within 6 hours of a rain event. Flash floods account for the majority of flood deaths in the U.S. and are the leading cause of deaths associated with thunderstorms. Urbanization significantly increases runoff over what would occur on natural terrain, making flash flooding in urban areas extremely dangerous. Streets can become swift-moving rivers, and basements can fill with water. Ice can also cause flash flooding. When ice accumulates at natural or artificial obstructions, stopping the flow of water, the water buildup can lead to flooding upstream. If the jam suddenly gives way, the gush of ice and water can cause flash flooding downstream.

A *flood watch* or *flash flood watch* means that flooding or flash flooding is possible within a designated area. A *flood warning* or *flash flood warning* means that flooding or flash flooding has been reported or is imminent.

National Weather Service Marine Warnings and Advisories

Small craft advisory—alerts mariners to sustained (more than 2 hours) weather and/or sea conditions, present or forecast, potentially hazardous to small boats, including winds 18-33 knots (21-38 mph) and/or dangerous wave conditions. The advisory is also issued for lower wind speeds that may affect small craft. Criteria vary depending on region and type of marine environment.

Gale warning—indicates that winds of 34-47 knots (39-54 mph), not directly associated with a tropical storm, are forecast for the area.

Tropical storm warning—indicates that winds 34-63 knots (39-72 mph) associated with a tropical storm are forecast to occur within 24 hours.

Storm warning—indicates that winds 48 knots (55 mph) or more, not directly associated with a tropical storm, are forecast for the area.

Hurricane warning—indicates that winds 64 knots (74 mph) or greater associated with a hurricane are forecast for the area within 24 hours.

Special marine warning—indicates potentially hazardous weather conditions, usually of short duration (2 hours or less) and producing wind speeds of 34 knots (39 mph) or more, not adequately covered by existing marine warnings.

Primary sources of dissemination are commercial radio, TV, U.S. Coast Guard radio stations, and NOAA VHF-FM broadcasts. These NOAA broadcasts on a group of frequencies, the most common being 162.40 to 162.55 MHz. They can usually be received within 50 mi of the transmission site.

Monthly Normal Mean Temperatures, Normal Precipitation, U.S. Cities

Source: National Climatic Data Center, NESDIS, NOAA, U.S. Dept. of Commerce

Normals are averages covering a 30-year period. The temperature and precipitation normals given here are based on records for 1971-2000. Temperatures listed below represent means of the normal daily maximum and normal daily minimum temperatures for each month. For stations that did not have continuous records from the same site for the entire 30 years, the means have been adjusted to the record at the present site. (*) = city station. Other figures are for airport stations. T = Temperature in Fahrenheit; P = Precipitation in inches.

	Jan.		Feb.		Mar.		Apr.		May		June		July		Aug.		Sept.		Oct.		Nov.		Dec.	
Station	T	P	T	P	T	P	T	P	T	P	T	P	T	P	T	P	T	P	T	P	T	P	T	P
Albany, NY	22	2.7	25	2.3	35	3.2	47	3.3	58	3.7	66	3.7	71	3.5	69	3.7	61	3.3	49	3.2	39	3.3	28	2.8
Albuquerque, NM	36	0.5	41	0.4	48	0.6	56	0.5	65	0.6	75	0.7	79	1.3	76	1.7	69	1.1	57	1.0	44	0.6	36	0.5
Anchorage, AK	16	0.7	19	0.7	26	0.7	36	0.5	47	0.7	55	1.1	58	1.7	56	2.9	48	2.9	34	2.1	22	1.1	18	1.1
Asheville, NC	36	3.1	39	3.2	46	3.9	54	3.2	62	3.5	69	3.2	73	3.0	72	3.3	66	3.0	55	2.4	46	2.9	39	2.6
Atlanta, GA	43	5.0	47	4.7	54	5.4	62	3.6	70	4.0	77	3.6	80	5.1	79	3.7	73	4.1	63	3.1	53	4.1	45	3.8
Atlantic City, NJ	32	3.6	34	2.9	42	4.1	51	3.5	61	3.4	70	2.7	75	3.9	74	4.3	66	3.1	55	2.9	46	3.3	37	3.2
Baltimore, MD	32	3.5	36	3.0	44	3.9	53	3.0	63	3.9	72	3.4	77	3.9	75	3.7	67	4.0	55	3.2	46	3.1	37	3.4
Barrow, AK	–14	0.1	–16	0.1	–14	0.1	–1	0.1	20	0.1	35	0.3	40	0.9	39	1.0	31	0.7	15	0.4	–1	0.2	–11	0.1
Birmingham, AL	43	5.5	47	4.2	55	6.1	61	4.7	69	4.8	76	3.8	80	5.1	80	3.5	74	4.1	63	3.2	53	4.6	46	4.5
Bismarck, ND	10	0.5	18	0.5	30	0.9	43	1.5	56	2.2	65	2.6	70	2.6	69	2.2	58	1.6	45	1.3	28	0.7	15	0.4
Boise, ID	30	1.4	37	1.1	44	1.4	51	1.3	59	1.3	67	0.7	75	0.4	74	0.3	64	0.8	53	0.8	40	1.4	31	1.4
Boston, MA	29	3.9	32	3.3	39	3.9	48	3.6	59	3.2	68	3.2	74	3.1	72	3.4	65	3.5	54	3.8	45	4.0	35	3.7
Buffalo, NY	25	3.2	26	2.4	34	3.0	45	3.0	57	3.4	66	3.8	71	3.1	69	3.9	62	3.8	51	3.2	40	3.9	30	3.8
Burlington, VT	18	2.2	20	1.7	31	2.3	44	2.9	57	3.3	66	3.4	71	4.0	68	4.0	59	3.8	48	3.1	37	3.1	25	2.2
Caribou, ME	10	3.0	13	2.1	25	2.6	38	2.6	52	3.3	61	3.3	66	3.9	63	4.2	54	3.3	43	3.0	31	3.1	16	3.2
Charleston, SC	48	4.1	51	3.1	58	4.0	64	2.8	72	3.7	78	5.9	82	6.1	81	6.9	76	6.0	66	3.1	58	2.7	51	3.2
Charleston, WV	33	3.3	37	3.2	45	3.9	54	3.3	62	4.3	70	4.1	74	4.9	73	4.1	66	3.5	55	2.7	46	3.7	38	3.3
Chicago, IL	22	1.8	27	1.6	37	2.7	48	3.7	59	3.4	68	3.6	73	3.5	72	4.6	64	3.3	52	2.7	39	3.0	27	2.4
Cleveland, OH	26	2.5	28	2.3	38	2.9	48	3.4	59	3.5	68	3.9	72	3.5	70	3.7	63	3.8	52	2.7	42	3.4	31	3.1
Columbus, OH	28	2.5	32	2.2	42	2.9	52	3.3	63	3.9	71	4.1	75	4.6	74	3.7	67	2.9	55	2.3	44	3.2	34	2.9
Dallas–Ft. Worth, TX	44	1.9	49	2.4	57	3.1	65	3.2	73	5.2	81	3.2	85	2.1	84	2.0	78	2.4	67	4.1	55	2.6	47	2.6
Denver, CO	29	0.5	33	0.5	40	1.3	48	1.9	57	2.3	68	1.6	73	2.2	72	1.8	62	1.1	51	1.0	38	1.0	30	0.6
Des Moines, IA	20	1.0	27	1.2	38	2.2	51	3.6	62	4.3	71	4.6	76	4.2	74	4.5	65	3.2	53	2.6	38	2.1	25	1.3
Detroit, MI	25	1.9	27	1.9	37	2.5	48	3.1	60	3.1	69	3.6	74	3.2	72	3.1	64	3.3	52	2.2	41	2.7	30	2.5
Dodge City, KS	30	0.6	36	0.7	44	1.8	54	2.3	64	3.0	74	3.2	80	3.2	78	2.7	69	1.7	57	1.5	42	1.0	33	0.8
Duluth, MN	8	1.1	15	0.8	25	1.7	39	2.1	52	3.0	60	4.3	66	4.2	64	4.2	55	4.1	44	2.5	28	2.1	14	0.9
Fairbanks, AK	–10	0.6	–4	0.4	11	0.3	32	0.2	49	0.6	60	1.4	62	1.7	56	1.7	45	1.1	24	1.0	2	0.7	–6	0.7
Fresno, CA	46	2.2	51	2.1	56	2.2	61	0.8	69	0.4	76	0.2	81	0.0	80	0.0	75	0.3	65	0.7	53	1.1	45	1.3
Galveston, TX*	56	4.1	58	2.6	64	2.8	70	2.6	77	3.7	82	4.0	84	3.5	84	4.2	81	5.8	74	3.5	65	3.6	58	3.5
Grand Rapids, MI	22	2.0	25	1.5	35	2.6	46	3.5	58	3.4	67	3.7	71	3.6	69	3.8	61	4.3	50	2.8	38	3.4	28	2.7
Hartford, CT	26	3.8	29	3.0	38	3.9	49	3.9	60	4.4	69	3.9	74	3.7	72	4.0	63	4.1	52	3.9	42	4.1	31	3.6
Helena, MT	20	0.5	26	0.4	35	0.6	44	0.9	53	1.8	61	1.8	68	1.3	67	1.3	56	1.1	45	0.7	31	0.5	21	0.5
Honolulu, HI	73	2.7	73	2.4	74	1.9	76	1.1	77	0.8	80	0.4	81	0.5	82	0.5	82	0.7	80	2.2	78	2.3	75	2.9
Houston, TX	52	3.7	55	3.0	62	3.4	69	3.6	76	5.2	81	5.4	84	3.2	83	3.8	79	4.3	70	4.5	61	4.2	54	3.7
Huron, SD	14	0.5	21	0.6	33	1.7	46	2.3	58	3.0	68	3.3	73	2.9	72	2.1	61	1.8	48	1.6	31	0.9	19	0.4
Indianapolis, IN	27	2.5	31	2.4	42	3.4	52	3.6	63	4.4	72	4.1	75	4.4	74	3.8	66	2.9	55	2.8	43	3.6	32	3.0
Jackson, MS	45	5.7	49	4.5	57	5.7	63	6.0	72	4.9	79	3.8	81	4.7	81	3.7	76	3.2	64	3.4	55	5.0	48	5.3
Jacksonville, FL	53	3.7	56	3.2	62	3.9	67	3.1	73	3.5	79	5.4	82	6.0	81	6.9	78	7.9	69	3.9	62	2.3	55	2.6
Juneau, AK	26	4.8	29	4.0	34	3.5	41	3.0	48	3.5	54	3.4	57	4.1	56	5.4	50	7.6	42	8.3	33	5.4	29	5.4
Kansas City, MO	27	1.2	33	1.3	44	2.4	54	3.4	64	5.4	74	4.4	79	4.4	77	3.5	68	4.6	57	3.3	43	2.3	31	1.6
Knoxville, TN	38	4.6	42	4.0	50	5.2	58	4.0	66	4.7	74	4.0	78	4.7	77	2.9	71	3.0	59	2.7	49	4.0	41	4.5
Lander, WY	20	0.5	26	0.5	36	1.2	44	2.1	53	2.4	64	1.2	71	0.8	69	0.6	59	1.1	46	1.4	30	1.0	21	0.6
Lexington, KY	32	3.3	36	3.3	46	4.4	55	3.7	64	4.8	72	4.6	76	4.8	75	3.8	68	3.1	57	2.7	46	3.4	36	4.0
Little Rock, AR	40	3.6	45	3.3	53	4.9	61	5.5	70	5.1	78	4.0	82	3.3	81	2.9	74	3.7	63	4.3	52	5.7	43	4.7
Los Angeles, CA*	57	3.0	58	3.1	58	2.4	61	0.6	63	0.2	66	0.1	69	0.0	71	0.1	70	0.3	67	0.4	62	1.1	58	1.8
Louisville, KY	33	3.3	38	3.3	47	4.4	56	3.9	66	4.9	74	3.8	78	4.3	77	3.4	70	3.1	59	2.8	48	3.8	38	3.7
Marquette, MI*	12	2.6	15	1.9	24	3.1	36	2.8	50	3.1	59	3.2	64	3.0	62	3.6	54	3.7	43	3.7	29	3.3	17	2.4
Memphis, TN	40	4.2	45	4.3	54	5.6	62	5.8	71	5.2	79	4.3	83	4.2	81	3.0	75	3.3	64	3.3	52	5.8	43	5.7
Miami, FL	68	1.9	69	2.1	72	2.6	76	3.4	80	5.5	82	8.5	84	5.8	84	8.6	82	8.4	79	6.2	74	3.4	70	2.2
Milwaukee, WI	21	1.9	25	1.7	35	2.6	45	3.8	56	3.1	66	3.6	72	3.6	71	4.0	63	3.3	51	2.5	38	2.7	26	2.2
Minneapolis, MN	13	1.0	20	0.8	32	1.9	47	2.3	59	3.2	68	4.3	73	4.0	71	4.1	61	2.7	49	2.1	33	1.9	19	1.0
Mobile, AL	61	5.8	65	5.1	71	7.2	77	5.1	84	6.1	89	5.0	91	6.5	91	6.2	87	6.0	79	3.3	70	5.4	63	4.7
Moline, IL	21	1.6	27	1.5	39	2.9	51	3.8	62	4.3	71	4.6	75	4.0	73	4.4	65	3.2	53	2.8	39	2.7	26	2.2
Nashua, NH	23	3.9	26	3.1	35	4.1	46	3.9	57	3.7	66	3.9	71	3.7	69	3.8	61	3.6	49	3.9	39	4.2	28	3.7
Nashville, TN	37	4.0	41	3.7	50	4.9	59	3.9	67	5.1	75	4.1	79	3.8	78	3.3	71	3.6	60	2.9	49	4.5	41	4.5
Newark, NJ	31	4.0	34	3.0	42	4.2	52	3.9	63	4.5	72	3.4	77	4.7	76	4.0	68	4.0	56	3.2	46	3.9	36	3.6
New Orleans, LA	53	5.9	56	5.5	62	5.2	68	5.0	76	4.6	81	6.8	83	6.2	83	6.2	79	5.6	70	3.1	61	5.1	55	5.1
New York, NY*	33	3.6	35	2.8	42	3.9	52	3.7	62	4.2	72	3.6	77	4.4	76	4.1	69	3.8	58	3.3	48	3.7	38	3.5
Norfolk, VA	40	3.9	42	3.3	49	4.1	57	3.4	66	3.7	75	3.8	79	5.2	77	4.8	72	4.1	61	3.5	52	3.0	44	3.0
Oklahoma City, OK	37	1.3	42	1.6	51	2.9	60	3.0	68	5.4	77	4.6	82	2.9	81	2.5	73	4.0	62	3.6	49	2.1	40	1.9
Omaha, NE	22	0.8	28	0.8	39	2.1	51	2.9	62	4.4	72	4.0	77	3.9	75	3.2	65	3.2	53	2.2	38	1.8	26	0.9
Philadelphia, PA	32	3.5	35	2.7	43	3.8	53	3.5	64	3.9	72	3.3	78	4.4	76	3.8	69	3.9	57	2.8	47	3.2	37	3.3
Phoenix, AZ	54	0.8	58	0.8	63	1.1	70	0.3	79	0.2	89	0.1	93	1.0	91	0.9	86	0.8	75	0.8	62	0.7	54	0.9
Pittsburgh, PA	28	2.7	31	2.4	40	3.2	50	3.0	60	3.8	68	4.1	73	4.0	71	3.4	64	3.2	53	2.3	42	3.0	33	2.9
Portland, ME	22	4.1	25	3.1	34	4.1	44	4.3	54	3.8	63	3.3	69	3.3	67	3.1	59	3.4	48	4.4	38	4.7	28	4.2
Portland, OR	40	5.1	43	4.2	47	3.7	51	2.6	57	2.4	63	1.6	68	0.7	69	0.9	64	1.7	54	2.9	46	5.6	40	5.7
Providence, RI	29	4.4	31	3.5	39	4.4	49	4.2	59	3.7	68	3.4	73	3.2	72	3.9	64	3.7	53	3.7	44	4.4	34	4.1
Raleigh, NC	40	4.0	43	3.5	51	4.0	59	2.8	67	3.8	75	3.4	79	4.3	77	3.8	71	4.3	60	3.2	51	3.0	43	3.0
Rapid City, SD	22	0.4	27	0.5	35	1.0	45	1.9	55	3.0	65	2.8	72	2.0	71	1.6	61	1.1	48	1.4	33	0.6	25	0.4
Reno, NV	34	1.1	39	1.1	43	0.9	49	0.4	56	0.6	65	0.5	71	0.2	70	0.3	62	0.5	52	0.4	41	0.8	34	0.9
Richmond, VA	36	3.6	40	3.0	48	4.1	57	3.2	65	4.0	74	3.5	78	4.7	76	4.2	70	4.0	58	3.6	49	3.1	40	3.1
St. Louis, MO	30	2.1	35	2.3	46	3.6	57	3.7	67	4.1	77	3.8	80	3.9	78	3.0	70	3.0	58	2.8	45	3.7	34	2.9
Salt Lake City, UT	29	1.4	35	1.3	43	1.9	50	2.0	59	2.1	69	0.8	77	0.7	76	0.8	65	1.3	53	1.6	40	1.4	30	1.2
San Antonio, TX	51	1.7	55	1.8	63	1.9	69	2.6	76	4.7	81	4.3	84	2.0	84	2.6	79	3.0	71	3.9	60	2.6	53	2.0
San Diego, CA	58	2.3	59	2.0	60	2.3	63	0.8	65	0.2	67	0.1	71	0.0	73	0.1	72	0.2	68	0.4	62	1.1	58	1.3
San Francisco, CA	49	4.5	52	4.0	54	3.3	56	1.2	59	0.4	61	0.1	63	0.0	64	0.1	64	0.2	61	1.0	55	2.5	50	2.9
San Juan, PR	77	3.0	77	2.3	78	2.1	79	3.7	81	5.3	82	3.5	82	4.2	82	5.2	82	5.6	82	5.1	80	6.2	78	4.6
Santa Fe, NM	29	0.6	35	0.5	41	0.8	48	0.7	57	1.3	66	1.2	70	2.3	68	2.1	62	1.7	51	1.3	38	1.1	30	0.7
Savannah, GA	49	4.0	53	2.9	59	3.6	65	3.3	73	3.6	79	5.5	82	6.0	81	7.2	77	5.1	67	3.1	59	2.4	51	2.8
Seattle, WA	41	5.1	43	4.2	46	3.8	50	2.6	56	1.8	61	1.5	65	0.8	66	1.0	61	1.6	53	3.2	45	5.9	41	5.6
Spokane, WA	27	1.8	33	1.5	40	1.5	47	1.3	54	1.6	62	1.2	69	0.8	69	0.7	59	0.8	47	1.1	35	2.2	27	2.3
Springfield, MO	32	2.1	37	2.3	46	3.8	56	4.3	65	4.6	73	5.0	79	3.6	78	3.4	69	4.8	58	3.5	46	4.5	36	3.2
Tampa, FL	61	2.3	63	2.7	67	2.9	72	1.8	78	2.9	82	5.5	83	6.5	83	7.6	82	6.5	76	2.3	69	1.6	63	2.3
Washington, DC	34	3.6	36	2.8	44	3.9	54	3.3	64	4.3	73	3.6	78	4.2	76	3.9	69	4.1	57	3.4	47	3.3	38	3.2
Wilmington, DE	32	3.4	34	2.8	43	4.0	52	3.4	63	4.1	72	4.0	77	4.3	75	3.5	68	4.0	56	3.0	46	3.2	36	3.4

Normal High and Low Temperatures, Precipitation, U.S. Cities

Source: National Climatic Data Center, NESDIS, NOAA, U.S. Dept. of Commerce

The normal temperatures and precipitation data given here are based on records for the period 1971-2000. The extreme temperatures are based on records from the time of each station's installation. (*) = city station. Other figures are for airport stations.

State	Station	NORMAL TEMPERATURE (°F) January Max.	January Min.	July Max.	July Min.	EXTREME TEMPERATURE (°F) Highest	Lowest	AVG. ANNUAL PRECIPITATION (in.)
Alabama	Mobile	61	40	91	72	105	3	66.29
Alaska	Anchorage	22	9	65	52	85	−34	16.08
Alaska	Barrow	−8	−20	47	34	79	−56	4.16
Alaska	Juneau	31	21	64	49	90	−22	58.33
Arizona	Phoenix	65	43	104	81	122	17	8.29
Arkansas	North Little Rock	49	31	94	73	111	−6	49.19
California	Los Angeles*	66	49	75	63	110	23	13.15
California	San Francisco	56	43	71	55	106	20	20.11
Colorado	Denver	43	15	88	59	101	−19	15.81
Connecticut	Hartford	34	17	85	62	102	−26	46.16
Delaware	Wilmington	39	24	86	67	102	−14	42.81
District of Columbia	Washington–National	43	27	89	67	105	−5	39.35
Florida	Jacksonville	64	42	91	72	105	7	52.34
Florida	Miami	77	60	91	77	98	30	58.53
Georgia	Atlanta	52	34	89	71	105	−8	50.20
Georgia	Savannah	60	38	92	72	105	3	49.58
Hawaii	Honolulu	80	66	88	74	95	53	18.29
Idaho	Boise	37	24	89	60	111	−25	12.19
Illinois	Chicago	30	14	84	63	104	−27	36.27
Indiana	Indianapolis	35	19	86	65	104	−27	40.95
Iowa	Des Moines	29	12	86	66	108	−26	34.72
Kansas	Dodge City	41	19	93	67	110	−21	22.35
Kentucky	Lexington	40	24	86	66	103	−21	45.91
Kentucky	Louisville	41	25	87	70	106	−22	44.54
Louisiana	New Orleans	62	43	91	74	102	11	64.16
Maine	Caribou	19	0	76	55	96	−41	37.44
Maine	Portland	31	13	79	59	103	−39	45.83
Maryland	Baltimore	41	24	87	66	105	−7	41.94
Massachusetts	Boston	37	22	82	66	102	−12	42.53
Michigan	Detroit	31	18	83	64	104	−21	32.89
Michigan	Grand Rapids	29	16	82	61	100	−22	37.13
Michigan	Sault Ste. Marie*	22	5	76	52	98	−36	34.67
Minnesota	Duluth	18	−1	76	55	97	−39	31.00
Minnesota	Minneapolis-St. Paul	22	4	83	63	105	−34	29.41
Mississippi	Jackson	55	35	91	71	107	2	55.95
Missouri	Kansas City	36	18	89	68	109	−23	37.98
Missouri	St. Louis	38	21	90	71	107	−18	38.75
Montana	Helena	31	10	83	52	105	−42	11.32
Nebraska	Omaha	32	12	87	66	114	−23	30.22
Nevada	Reno	46	22	91	51	108	−16	7.48
New Hampshire	Concord	31	10	83	57	102	−37	37.60
New Jersey	Atlantic City	41	23	85	65	106	−11	40.59
New Mexico	Albuquerque	48	24	92	65	107	−17	9.47
New York	Albany	31	13	82	60	100	−28	38.60
New York	Buffalo	31	18	80	62	99	−20	40.54
New York	New York–Central Park*	38	26	84	69	106	−15	49.69
North Carolina	Raleigh	50	30	89	69	105	−9	43.05
North Dakota	Bismarck	21	−1	85	56	111	−44	16.84
Ohio	Cleveland	33	19	81	62	104	−20	38.71
Ohio	Columbus	36	20	85	65	102	−22	38.52
Oklahoma	Oklahoma City	47	26	93	71	110	−8	35.85
Oregon	Portland	46	34	79	57	107	−3	37.07
Pennsylvania	Philadelphia	39	26	86	70	104	−7	42.05
Pennsylvania	Pittsburgh	35	20	83	62	103	−22	37.85
Puerto Rico	San Juan	82	71	87	77	98	46	50.76
Rhode Island	Providence	37	20	83	64	104	−13	46.45
South Carolina	Charleston	59	37	91	73	105	6	51.53
South Dakota	Huron	25	4	86	61	112	−41	20.90
South Dakota	Rapid City	34	11	86	58	110	−31	16.64
Tennessee	Memphis	49	31	92	73	108	−13	54.65
Tennessee	Nashville	46	28	89	70	107	−17	48.11
Texas	Dallas-Fort Worth	54	34	95	75	109	17	34.73
Texas	Houston	62	41	94	74	109	17	47.84
Utah	Salt Lake City	37	21	91	63	107	−30	16.50
Vermont	Burlington	27	9	81	60	101	−30	36.05
Virginia	Norfolk	48	32	87	71	104	−3	45.74
Virginia	Richmond	45	28	88	68	105	−12	43.91
Washington	Seattle-Tacoma	46	36	75	55	100	0	37.07
Washington	Spokane	33	22	83	55	108	−25	16.67
West Virginia	Charleston	43	24	85	63	104	−16	44.05
Wisconsin	Milwaukee	28	13	81	63	103	−26	34.81
Wyoming	Lander	32	9	86	55	101	−37	13.42

Mean annual snowfall (in.): Based on climate normals 1971-2000: Boston, MA, 41.8; Sault Ste. Marie, MI, 132.6; Albany, NY, 62.7; Burlington, VT, 83.1; Lander, WY, 102.9; Anchorage, AK, 69.5.

Wettest spot: Mount Waialeale, HI, on the island of Kauai, is the rainiest place in the world. It has an average annual rainfall of 460 in.

Temperature extremes: A temperature of 136°F observed at El Azizia (Al Aziziyah), near Tripoli, Libya, on Sept. 13, 1922, is generally accepted as the world's highest temperature recorded under standard conditions. The record high in the U.S. was 134°F in Death Valley, CA, July 10, 1913. The world record low of −129°F was recorded at the Soviet station of Vostok in Antarctica on July 21, 1983. The record low in the U.S. was −80°F at Prospect Creek, AK, Jan. 23, 1971.

Annual Climatological Data for U.S. Cities, 2006

Source: National Climatic Data Center, NESDIS, NOAA, U.S. Dept. of Commerce

Station	Elev. (ft)	TEMPERATURE (°F)				PRECIPITATION[1]			Snowfall[3]			FASTEST[2] WIND		NO. OF DAYS	
		Highest	Date	Lowest	Date	Total (in.)	Greatest in 24 hrs. (in.)	Date	Total snowfall (in.)	Greatest in 24 hrs. (in.)	Date	MPH	Date	Prec. 0.01 in. or more	Snow, sleet 1 in. or more
Albany, NY	281	96	8/01	2	1/16	46.58	2.66	6/25-26	19.8	5.2	1/23	46	2/17	150	6
Albuquerque, NM	5,308	98	7/14	8	12/31	13.06	1.47	10/09	22.9	11.3	12/29	32	10/09	131	20
Anchorage, AK	222	76	5/27	-11	1/26+	20.33	1.21	8/18	83.5	10	12/23	32	12/23	125	1
Asheville, NC	2,174	93	8/02	13	12/09	48.29	4.29	8/11-12	1.4	1	2/12	40	1/14	125	1
Atlanta, GA	974	98	8/04	19	12/08	48.46	4.29	8/30-31	T	T	2/19+	38	6/12	107	0
Atlantic City, NJ	117	99	7/18	11	1/15	50.67	3.12	6/24-25	8.9	4.2	2/12	41	7/28	106	0
Baltimore, MD	196	100	8/03+	12	2/19	43.24	3.56	9/1-2	13.1	9.6	2/12	39	4/05	101	2
Barrow, AK	38	64	6/24	-55	2/03	4.17	0.44	7/23	48.7	2.6	11/13	58	2/24	96	18
Birmingham, AL	630	100	8/08	17	12/08	56.56	3.83	4/19-20	T	T	6/23	41	3/09	111	0
Bismarck, ND	1,654	112	7/30	-19	2/17	11.10	0.82	9/21-22	29.7	10.2	12/30	47	7/18	88	8
Boise, ID	2,861	107	7/22	10	12/1	12.14	1.09	4/4-5	6.6	1	12/22	45	8/10	98	3
Boston, MA	180	98	8/02	7	2/27	52.84	4.73	5/13-14	28.4	17.5	2/12	49	1/18	129	0
Buffalo, NY	717	92	8/01	8	2/19	44.41	1.79	7/12	72.2	14	10/13	48	12/01	161	17
Burlington, VT	348	94	8/01	-4	2/26	46.99	2.36	5/18-19	57.6	13.8	3/04	36	6/20	165	17
Caribou, ME	626	86	7/14	-14	1/04	40.54	2.22	11/14	42.5	3.6	12/26	39	4/02	167	14
Charleston, SC	48	98	8/04	19	12/09	49.29	4.69	8/24-25	T	T	11/21	47	5/14	102	0
Chicago, IL	658	99	8/01	-7	2/18	41.96	2.37	9/22-23	20.1	5.8	12/01	40	7/17	132	6
Cleveland, OH	805	92	8/02+	5	2/19	40.64	2.57	6/1-2	5.2	1.5	1/18	46	5/25	144	1
Columbus, OH	812	95	8/01	7	2/19	43.63	2.08	6/1-2	T	T	11/30	52	5/02	61	0
Dallas-Ft. Worth, TX	562	107	7/18	20	12/8	29.75	3.44	3/19	T	T	11/30	52	9/16	71	13
Denver, CO	5,382	103	7/16	-13	2/18	8.64	0.84	12/20	59.3	17.4	12/20	45	9/16	99	5
Des Moines, IA	971	100	7/19	-7	2/18	33.39	2.11	11/27-28	11.0	4.3	3/21	43	4/11	123	6
Detroit, MI	631	97	8/01	4	2/18	39.24	1.65	6/3-4	14.9	3.9	1/18	39	10/12	121	22
Duluth, MN	1,429	97	7/28	-22	2/18	24.55	1.97	9/22-23	61.4	11.1	2/24	39	2/21	105	13
Fairbanks, AK	464	81	7/10	-51	1/27	8.58	1.06	7/5-6	39.4	4.4	2/25	30	3/03	58	—
Fresno, CA	375	113	7/30	30	12/30+	13.94	2.74	1/1-2	—	—	—	45	4/29	58	—
Grand Rapids, MI	788	95	7/31+	1	2/18	44.39	2.96	7/27	37.0	4.4	12/04	44	1/18	147	15
Hartford, CT	165	100	8/02	4	2/13	51.81	2.97	5/12-13	50.0	21.9	2/12	44	6/29	77	7
Helena, MT	3,867	97	7/23	-15	2/17	12.53	1.57	4/5-6	16.6	3.6	3/18	31	12/15	97	—
Honolulu, HI	18	90	8/02	60	5/02	29.45	3.56	3/30-31	—	—	—	47	5/06	100	0
Houston, TX	107	100	6/13	30	12/05	57.86	6.52	10/15-16	T	T	3/20	47	8/24	72	7
Huron, SD	1,284	109	7/15	-10	2/18+	17.53	2.43	9/01	21.9	4.4	12/30	49	8/24	139	6
Indianapolis, IN	797	93	8/02+	4	2/18	51.04	2.49	7/11	13.0	5.4	3/21	52	4/14	139	4
Jackson, MS	296	101	8/09+	20	12/09	51.21	3.72	10/16-17	—	—	—	45	4/29	87	—
Jacksonville, FL	34	98	6/11+	26	2/14	38.07	4.41	8/24	—	—	—	33	5/15	84	—
Kansas City, MO	1,008	104	8/06+	4	2/18	30.87	3.33	8/27	2.7	1	3/20-21	39	8/02	88	0
Knoxville, TN	982	99	6/23	14	12/09	47.79	3.71	4/21-22	2.7	1	2/18+	44	12/01	125	2
Lander, WY	5,560	101	7/29+	-25	2/18	7.42	0.76	10/25	69.1	8.8	2/15	49	5/22	50	4
Lexington, KY	984	95	8/03+	4	2/19	52.79	6.16	9/22-23	11.4	3.1	2/11	38	12/01	132	4
Los Angeles, CA	326	94	6/27	37	12/19	9.18	1.77	3/27-28	—	—	—	41	12/27	39	—
Louisville, KY	484	95	8/10+	9	2/19	56.85	4.95	9/22-23	5.0	1.4	2/18	54	5/25	130	3
Marquette, MI	1,415	96	7/31+	-17	2/18	32.28	3.77	5/11-12	170.0	16.8	2/16-17	—	—	158	45
Memphis, TN	286	102	8/10	16	12/08	42.20	2.64	1/22	—	—	—	35	4/29	106	—
Miami, FL	29	96	8/13	44	2/14	64.17	5.30	5/15-16	—	—	—	32	7/28	118	—
Milwaukee, WI	680	98	7/31	-12	2/18	37.93	2.76	7/9	31.9	10.1	12/01	41	4/24	132	9
Minn.-St. Paul, MN	874	101	7/31	-13	2/18+	27.57	3.47	8/1-2	29.3	9.9	3/13	41	11/15	98	7
Mobile, AL	212	97	8/15	23	1/07	49.35	5.71	11/14-15	T	T	6/02	36	3/12	115	0
Moline, IL	607	100	7/17	-8	2/18	37.34	1.86	4/29-30	16.9	8.3	12/01	53	3/12	115	0
Nashville, TN	574	100	7/19	12	2/19	45.72	2.96	9/23-24	1.7	0.7	2/18	37	3/09	128	0
Newark, NJ	28	97	8/03	14	2/19	50.16	4.35	11/7-8	26.9	18.8	2/12	48	7/18	107	5
New Orleans, LA	7	97	8/15	29	12/08	45.88	4.37	12/20-21	—	—	—	39	3/09	101	—
New York, NY	161	97	8/02	15	2/19+	59.89	3.62	11/7-8	30.3	24.1	2/12	47	11/22	109	0
Norfolk, VA	69	102	8/03	21	12/09	49.16	8.93	9/01	0.8	0.5	1/14	45	2/10	94	1
North Little Rock, AR	565	104	7/20+	16	12/08	49.78	4.43	4/29	1.8	1.5	11/30	45	1/01	69	2
Oklahoma City, OK	1,284	107	8/10	11	2/18	27.84	2.49	9/17	6.4	4.1	11/30	44	1/14	111	2
Philadelphia, PA	62	98	8/03+	15	2/19	48.20	2.71	6/2-3	12.5	10.6	2/12	51	7/23	25	—
Phoenix, AZ	1,106	118	7/21	35	12/23	5.45	1.44	3/11-12	—	—	—	44	2/17	143	4
Pittsburgh, PA	1,175	91	8/03+	3	2/19	34.90	1.68	10/16-17	17.3	4	1/25	44	2/17	138	8
Portland, ME	72	95	8/02	1	2/27	60.84	3.57	5/2-3	9.1	5.8	2/12	43	12/14	160	—
Portland, OR	223	104	7/21	22	2/20	43.00	3.01	11/6-7	—	—	—	44	11/23	115	0
Providence, RI	53	100	8/02	8	1/16	54.30	3.65	10/27-28	23.9	9.4	2/12	44	11/23	133	4
Raleigh, NC	430	99	8/29+	16	12/09	53.69	5.65	6/13-14	T	T	11/21	38	11/16	107	0
Rapid City, SD	3,153	111	7/15	-23	2/18	11.72	1.04	9/22-23	43.5	6	3/12	52	5/02	74	16
Reno, NV	4,407	104	8/12	18	12/18	7.17	1.24	1/1-2	20.2	4.2	2/18	51	12/26	53	7
Richmond, VA	167	102	8/03	14	2/19	52.12	3.62	9/01	4.1	1.7	2/12	37	4/03	101	1
St. Louis, MO	710	101	8/02+	5	2/18	29.93	3.00	12/30-1/1	11.1	4.2	12/30-1/1	53	4/02	91	6
Salt Lake City, UT	4,224	104	7/22+	4	11/29	16.14	1.10	4/06	56.2	9.5	2/15-16	45	5/19	98	19
San Antonio, TX	821	99	7/22	42	2/18	6.15	0.77	5/22	—	—	—	32	12/27	42	—
San Diego, CA	89	97	7/22	35	12/19+	20.60	1.42	3/5-6	—	—	—	60	2/27	84	—
San Francisco, CA	10	94	6/09+	66	1/24+	65.88	3.59	11/27-28	—	—	—	31	12/01	193	0
San Juan, PR	10	94	6/09+	66	1/24+	65.88	3.59	11/27-28	—	—	—	31	12/01	193	0
Sault Ste. Marie, MI	722	92	7/15+	-4	2/18	28.82	1.51	9/23-24	95.9	8.7	1/29	35	7/16	148	31
Savannah, GA	143	100	7/15	21	12/09	34.45	3.29	6/13-14	T	T	11/21	35	8/09	97	0
Scottsbluff, NE	3,949	108	7/16	-23	2/18	12.03	1.79	6/22	55.7	11.3	2/15	49	5/28	70	13
Seattle, WA	434	97	7/21	18	11/29	48.42	3.78	11/5-6	T	T	12/15	52	12/15	152	0
Spokane, WA	2,384	102	7/23	1	11/29	21.13	0.99	1/9-10	31.0	3	11/26	52	11/13	117	15
Springfield, MO	1,280	103	7/20	5	12/08	38.87	3.62	11/29-30	13.5	7.0	11/30	33	5/03	89	2
Tampa, FL	40	96	5/29	37	2/14	56.66	8.54	2/3-4	T	T	8/29	33	6/13	90	0
Washington, DC	3	101	8/03	14	2/19	47.77	7.94	6/25-26	8.8	6.7	2/12	43	2/25	113	2
Wilmington, DE	40	97	7/17	14	2/19	49.41	3.30	6/25-26	14.8	11.3	2/12	43	2/25	113	2

(+) Indicates value for extreme also occurred on an earlier date(s). (T) Trace amount. (—) Data not available or unreported. (1) Where one date is shown, it is the starting date of the storm. (2) Sustained for at least 2 mins., not peak gust. (3) Comprises all forms of frozen precipitation, including hail and sleet.

Record Temperatures by State

Source: National Climatic Data Center, NESDIS, NOAA, U.S. Dept. of Commerce
(through Aug. 2006)

State	LOWEST TEMPERATURE °F	Latest date	Station	Approx. elevation (ft)	HIGHEST TEMPERATURE °F	Latest date	Station	Approx. elevation (ft)
Alabama	−27	Jan. 30, 1966	New Market	760	112	Sept. 5, 1925	Centerville	345
Alaska	−80	Jan. 23, 1971	Prospect Creek Camp	1,100	100	June 27, 1915	Fort Yukon	c. 420
Arizona	−40	Jan. 7, 1971	Hawley Lake	8,180	128	June 29, 1994	Lake Havasu City	505
Arkansas	−29	Feb. 13, 1905	Pond	1,250	120	Aug. 10, 1936	Ozark	396
California	−45	Jan. 20, 1937	Boca	5,532	134	July 10, 1913	Furnace Creek Ranch	−178
Colorado	−61	Feb. 1, 1985	Maybell	5,920	118	July 11, 1888	Bennett	5,484
Connecticut	−32	Jan. 22, 1961[1]	Coventry	480	106	July 15, 1995	Danbury	450
Delaware	−17	Jan. 17, 1893	Millsboro	20	110	July 21, 1930	Millsboro	20
Florida	−2	Feb. 13, 1899	Tallahassee	193	109	June 29, 1931	Monticello	207
Georgia	−17	Jan. 27, 1940	CCC Camp F-16	1,000	112	Aug. 20, 1983[1]	Greenville	860
Hawaii	12	May 17, 1979	Mauna Kea Obs.	13,770	100	Apr. 27, 1931	Pahala	850
Idaho	−60	Jan. 18, 1943	Island Park Dam	6,285	118	July 28, 1934	Orofino	1,027
Illinois	−36	Jan. 5, 1999	Congerville	635	117	July 14, 1954	East St. Louis	410
Indiana	−36	Jan. 19, 1994	New Whiteland	785	116	July 14, 1936	Collegeville	672
Iowa	−47	Feb. 3, 1996[1]	Elkader	770	118	July 20, 1934	Keokuk	614
Kansas	−40	Feb. 13, 1905	Lebanon	1,812	121	July 24, 1936[1]	Alton (near)	1,651
Kentucky	−37	Jan. 19, 1994	Shelbyville	730	114	July 28, 1930	Greensburg	581
Louisiana	−16	Feb. 13, 1899	Minden	194	114	Aug. 10, 1936	Plain Dealing	268
Maine	−48	Jan. 19, 1925	Van Buren	510	105	July 10, 1911[1]	North Bridgton	450
Maryland	−40	Jan. 13, 1912	Oakland	2,461	109	July 10, 1936[1]	Cumberland Frederick	623 325
Massachusetts	−35	Jan. 12, 1981	Chester	640	107	Aug. 2, 1975	Chester New Bedford	640 120
Michigan	−51	Feb. 9, 1934	Vanderbilt	785	112	July 13, 1936	Mio	963
Minnesota	−60	Feb. 2, 1996	Tower	1,460	114	July 6, 1936[1]	Moorhead	904
Mississippi	−19	Jan. 30, 1966	Corinth	420	115	July 29, 1930	Holly Springs	600
Missouri	−40	Feb. 13, 1905	Warsaw	700	118	July 14, 1954[1]	Warsaw Union	705 560
Montana	−70	Jan. 20, 1954	Rogers Pass	5,470	117	July 5, 1937	Medicine Lake	1,950
Nebraska	−47	Dec. 22, 1989[1]	Oshkosh	3,379	118	July 24, 1936[1]	Minden	2,169
Nevada	−50	Jan. 8, 1937	San Jacinto	5,200	125	June 29, 1994[1]	Laughlin	605
New Hampshire	−47	Jan. 29, 1934	Mt. Washington	6,262	106	July 4, 1911	Nashua	125
New Jersey	−34	Jan. 5, 1904	River Vale	70	110	July 10, 1936	Runyon	18
New Mexico	−50	Feb. 1, 1951	Gavilan	7,350	122	June 27, 1994	Waste Isolat. Pilot Plt.	3,418
New York	−52	Feb. 18, 1979	Old Forge	1,720	108	July 22, 1926	Troy	35
North Carolina	−34	Jan. 21, 1985	Mt. Mitchell	6,525	110	Aug. 21, 1983	Fayetteville	213
North Dakota	−60	Feb. 15, 1936	Parshall	1,929	121	July 6, 1936	Steele	1,857
Ohio	−39	Feb. 10, 1899	Milligan	800	113	July 21, 1934[1]	Gallipolis (near)	673
Oklahoma	−27	Jan. 18, 1930[1]	Watts	958	120	June 27, 1994[1]	Tipton	1,350
Oregon	−54	Feb. 10, 1933[1]	Seneca	4,700	119	Aug. 10, 1898[1]	Pendleton	1,074
Pennsylvania	−42	Jan. 5, 1904	Smethport	1,500	111	July 10, 1936[1]	Phoenixville	100
Rhode Island	−25	Feb. 5, 1996	Greene	425	104	Aug. 2, 1975	Providence	51
South Carolina	−19	Jan. 21, 1985	Caesars Head	3,115	111	June 28, 1954[1]	Camden	170
South Dakota	−58	Feb. 17, 1936	McIntosh	2,277	120	July 15, 2006[1]	Kelly Ranch/Usta	2,339
Tennessee	−32	Dec. 30, 1917	Mountain City	2,471	113	Aug. 9, 1930[1]	Perryville	377
Texas	−23	Feb. 8, 1933[1]	Seminole	3,275	120	June 28, 1994[1]	Monahans	2,660
Utah	−69	Feb. 1, 1985	Peter's Sink	8,092	117	July 5, 1985	Saint George	2,880
Vermont	−50	Dec. 30, 1933	Bloomfield	915	105	July 4, 1911	Vernon	310
Virginia	−30	Jan. 22, 1985	Mountain Lake Bio. Station	3,870	110	July 15, 1954	Balcony Falls	725
Washington	−48	Dec. 30, 1968	Mazama Winthrop	2,120 1,755	118	Aug. 5, 1961[1]	Ice Harbor Dam	475
West Virginia	−37	Dec. 30, 1917	Lewisburg	2,200	112	July 10, 1936[1]	Martinsburg	435
Wisconsin	−55	Feb. 4, 1996	Couderay	1,300	114	July 13, 1936	Wisconsin Dells	900
Wyoming	−66	Feb. 9, 1933	Riverside R.S.	6,500	115	Aug. 8, 1983	Basin	3,500

(1) Also on earlier dates at the same or other places.

Hurricane and Tornado Classifications

Source: National Weather Service, NOAA, U.S. Dept. of Commerce

The Saffir-Simpson Hurricane Scale rates a hurricane's intensity from 1 to 5. The scale is used to give an estimate of the potential property damage and flooding expected along the coast from a hurricane landfall. Wind speed is the determining factor in the scale. The Fujita (or F) Scale, created by T. Theodore Fujita, is used to classify tornadoes. The F Scale uses a 0-5 rating system, based on the amount and type of wind damage. The Enhanced Fujita Scale, an update to the original, was implemented in the U.S. in Feb. 2007.

Saffir-Simpson Scale (Hurricanes)				Enhanced Fujita Scale (Tornadoes)			
Category	Wind speed	Severity	Storm surge[1]	Rank	3-sec. gust	Damage	Strength
1	74-95 mph	Weak	4-5 ft	EF-0	65-85 mph	Light	Weak
2	96-110 mph	Moderate	6-8 ft	EF-1	86-110 mph	Moderate	Weak
3	111-130 mph	Strong	9-12 ft	EF-2	111-135 mph	Considerable	Strong
4	131-155 mph	Very Strong	13-18 ft	EF-3	136-165 mph	Severe	Strong
5	Over 155 mph	Devastating	above 18 ft	EF-4	166-200 mph	Devastating	Violent
				EF-5	Over 200 mph	Incredible	Violent

(1) Above normal tides.

Atlantic Tropical Storm Names in 2008
Source: National Weather Service, NOAA, U.S. Dept. of Commerce

Names for Atlantic tropical storms in 2008 are Arthur, Bertha, Cristobal, Dolly, Edouard, Fay, Gustav, Hanna, Ike, Josephine, Kyle, Laura, Marco, Nana, Omar, Paloma, Rene, Sally, Teddy, Vicky, and Wilfred. If there are more than 21 named Atlantic storms in one season, remaining storms take names from the Greek alphabet, starting with Alpha.

World Temperature and Precipitation
Source: World Meteorological Organization

Average daily maximum and minimum temperatures and annual precipitation based on records for the period 1961-90. Records of extreme temperatures include all available years of data for a given location and are usually for a longer period. Surface elevations are supplied by the WMO and may differ from figures in other sections of *The World Almanac*. NA = Not available.

		Temperature (°F)						Average annual precipitation (in.)
		AVERAGE DAILY				EXTREME		
		January		July				
Station	Surface elevation (ft)	Max.	Min.	Max.	Min.	Max.	Min.	
Algiers, Algeria	82	61.7	42.6	87.1	65.3	NA	NA	27.0
Athens, Greece	49	56.1	44.6	88.9	73.0	NA	NA	14.6
Auckland, New Zealand	20	74.8	61.2	58.5	46.4	NA	NA	49.4
Bangkok, Thailand	66	89.6	69.8	90.9	77.0	104	51	59.0
Berlin, Germany	190	35.2	26.8	73.6	55.2	107	−4	23.3
Bogotá, Colombia	8,357	67.3	41.7	64.6	45.5	75	21	32.4
Bombay (Mumbai), India	36	85.3	66.7	86.2	77.5	110	46	85.4
Bucharest, Romania	298	34.7	22.1	83.8	60.1	105	−18	23.4
Budapest, Hungary	456	34.2	24.8	79.7	59.7	103	−10	20.3
Buenos Aires, Argentina	82	85.8	67.3	59.7	45.7	104	22	45.2
Cairo, Egypt	243	65.8	48.2	93.9	71.1	118	34	1.0
Cape Town, South Africa	138	79.0	60.3	63.3	44.6	105	28	20.5
Caracas, Venezuela	2,739	79.9	60.8	81.3	66.0	96	45	36.1
Casablanca, Morocco	203	62.8	47.1	77.7	66.7	NA	NA	16.8
Copenhagen, Denmark	16	35.6	28.4	68.9	55.0	NA	NA	NA
Damascus, Syria	2,004	54.3	32.9	97.2	61.9	NA	NA	5.6
Dublin, Ireland	279	45.7	36.5	66.0	52.5	86	8	28.8
Geneva, Switzerland	1,364	38.3	27.9	76.3	53.2	101	−3	35.6
Havana, Cuba	164	78.4	65.5	88.3	74.8	NA	NA	46.9
Hong Kong, China	203	65.5	56.5	88.7	79.9	97	32	87.2
Istanbul, Turkey	108	47.8	37.2	82.8	65.3	105	7	27.4
Jerusalem, Israel	2,483	53.4	39.4	83.8	63.0	107	26	23.2
Lagos, Nigeria	125	90.0	72.3	82.8	72.1	NA	NA	59.3
Lima, Peru	43	79.0	66.9	66.4	59.4	NA	NA	0.2
London, England	203	44.1	32.7	71.1	52.3	99	2	29.7
Manila, Philippines	79	85.8	74.8	87.1	76.8	NA	NA	49.6
Mexico City, Mexico	7,570	70.3	43.7	73.8	53.2	NA	NA	33.4
Montreal, Canada	118	21.6	5.2	79.2	59.7	100	−36	37.0
Nairobi, Kenya	5,897	77.9	50.9	71.6	48.6	NA	NA	41.9
Paris, France	213	42.8	33.6	75.2	55.2	105	−1	25.6
Prague, Czech Republic	1,197	32.7	22.5	73.9	53.2	98	−16	20.7
Reykjavik, Iceland	200	35.4	26.6	55.9	46.9	76	−3	31.5
Rome, Italy	79	53.8	35.4	88.2	62.1	NA	NA	33.0
San Salvador, El Salvador	2,037	86.5	61.3	86.2	66.4	105	45	68.3
São Paulo, Brazil	2,598	81.1	65.7	71.2	53.1	NA	NA	57.4
Shanghai, China	23	45.9	32.9	88.9	76.6	104	10	43.8
Singapore	52	85.8	73.6	87.4	75.6	NA	NA	84.6
Stockholm, Sweden	171	30.7	23.0	71.4	56.1	97	−26	21.2
Sydney, Australia	10	79.5	65.5	62.4	43.9	114	32	46.4
Tehran, Iran	3,906	45.0	30.0	98.2	75.2	109	−5	9.1
Tokyo, Japan	118	49.1	34.2	83.8	72.1	NA	NA	55.4
Toronto, Canada	567	27.5	12.0	80.2	57.6	105	−26	30.8

Speed of Winds in the U.S.
Source: National Climatic Data Center, NESDIS, NOAA, U.S. Dept. of Commerce

In miles per hour. Based on available records through 2006. Average and max. speeds are annual. Max. speeds are highest 1-min. average values, except where noted.

Station	Avg.	Max.	Station	Avg.	Max.	Station	Avg.	Max.
Albuquerque, NM	8.9	52	Helena, MT[2]	7.7	73	Oklahoma City, OK	12.2	74
Anchorage, AK[1]	7.1	64	Honolulu, HI	11.3	46	Omaha (Eppley Airfield), NE	10.5	58
Atlanta, GA	9.1	60	Houston, TX	7.6	46	Philadelphia, PA[2]	9.5	73
Baltimore, MD[2]	8.8	80	Indianapolis, IN	9.6	54	Phoenix, AZ	6.2	51
Bismarck, ND	10.2	64	Jackson, MS	6.9	55	Pittsburgh, PA	9.0	58
Boise, ID[2]	8.7	61	Jacksonville, FL	7.8	57	Portland, ME	8.7	57
Boston, MA	12.4	54	Las Vegas, NV	9.2	56	Portland, OR	7.9	70
Buffalo, NY[2]	11.8	91	Little Rock, AR[2]	7.7	65	Providence, RI	10.4	90
Burlington, VT	9.0	39	Los Angeles, CA[2]	5.4	49	Richmond, VA	7.7	46
Cape Hatteras, NC	10.9	66	Louisville, KY	8.3	56	St. Louis, MO	9.6	52
Charleston (Intl. Airport), SC	8.6	52	Miami, FL	9.2	80	Salt Lake City, UT[2]	8.8	71
Charleston, WV	5.8	55	Milwaukee, WI	11.5	54	San Francisco, CA[2]	8.7	47
Cheyenne, WY	12.9	71	Minn.-St. Paul, MN	10.5	51	Seattle (Sea-Tac Intl. Airport), WA[2]	8.8	66
Chicago, IL	10.3	58	Mobile, AL	8.8	63	Sioux Falls, SD	11.0	70
Cleveland, OH	10.5	53	Mt. Washington, NH[1]	35.1	231	Washington (Natl. Airport), DC	9.4	49
Denver, CO	8.7	54	Nashville, TN	8.0	58	Wichita, KS	12.2	70
Des Moines, IA[2]	10.7	76	Newark, NJ	10.2	54	Wilmington, DE	9.0	58
Detroit, MI	10.2	61	New Orleans, LA	8.2	69			
Hartford, CT	8.4	46	New York (Central Park), NY	9.3	40			

(1) Max. speed based on short gusts. (2) Max. speed calculated from minimum time during which one mile of wind passed station.

Tides and Their Causes

Source: National Ocean Service, NOAA, U.S. Dept. of Commerce

The tides are a natural phenomenon involving the movement of waves in the Earth's large fluid bodies as a result of the combined gravitational attraction of the Sun and Moon. These 2 variable influences combined produce the complex recurrent cycle of the tides. Tides may occur in both oceans and seas; to a limited extent in large lakes and in the atmosphere; and, to a very minute degree, in the Earth itself. The length of time between succeeding tides can vary.

The tide-generating force represents the difference between (1) the centrifugal force produced by Earth's revolution around the common center-of-gravity of the Earth-Moon system and (2) the gravitational attraction of the Moon acting upon the Earth's overlying waters. The Moon is about 400 times closer than the Sun. So despite its smaller mass, the Moon's tide-raising force is 2.5 times greater.

The tide-generating forces of the Moon and Sun acting tangentially to the Earth's surface tend to cause a maximum accumulation of waters at 2 diametrically opposite points on the Earth's surface and to withdraw compensating amounts of water from all points 90° removed from these tidal bulges. As the Earth rotates beneath the maxima and minima of these tide-generating forces, a sequence of 2 high tides, separated by 2 low tides, is produced each day in what is called a **semidiurnal tide**. Each ocean basin reacts differently to this tidal forces.

Twice each month, when the Sun, Moon, and Earth are directly aligned, with the Moon between the Earth and Sun (at New Moon) or on the opposite side of the Earth from the Sun (at Full Moon), the Sun and Moon exert gravitational forces in a mutual or additive fashion. The highest high tides and lowest low tides, called **spring tides**, are produced at these times. At 2 positions 90° in between, the Moon and Sun's gravitational forces—imposed at right angles—counteract each other to the greatest extent, and the range between high and low tides is reduced, resulting in **neap tides**.

The inclination of the Moon's monthly orbit to the equator and the inclination of the Sun to the equator during the Earth's yearly orbit produce a difference in the height of succeeding high tides and in the depression of succeeding low tides that is known as the diurnal inequality. In most cases, this produces a so-called **mixed tide**. In extreme cases, these phenomena may result in a **diurnal tide**, with only one high tide and one low tide each day. There are other monthly and yearly variations in the tides because of the elliptical shape of the orbits.

U.S. convention distinguishes between mean higher high water (MHHW), mean high water (MHW), mean tide level (MTL), mean sea level (MSL), mean low water (MLW), and mean lower low water (MLLW). Diurnal range of tide is the difference in height between MHHW and MLLW. Mean range of tide is the difference between MHW and MLW.

The range of tides in the open ocean is generally less than in the coastal regions, where the incoming tide can be augmented by the continental shelves, as well as by bays and estuaries. In some shallow inlets and bays, though, the range may be diminished. The range of tide, or difference between high and low waters, may reach 43½ ft or more under spring tide conditions in Nova Scotia's Bay of Funday.

In New Orleans, the periodic rise and fall of the diurnal tide is affected by the seasonal stages of the Mississippi River, being about 10 in. at low stage and 0 at high. The Canadian Tide Tables for 1972 gave a maximum range of nearly 50 ft at Leaf Basin, Ungava Bay, Quebec.

In every case, actual high or low tide can vary considerably from the average, as a result of weather conditions such as strong winds, abrupt barometric pressure changes, or prolonged periods of extreme high or low pressure.

Average Rise and Fall of Tides[1]

Place	Ft	In.	Place	Ft	In.	Place	Ft	In.
Baltimore, MD	1	8	Hampton Roads, VA	2	10	St. John's, NL, Canada	2	7
Boston, MA.	10	4	Key West, FL	1	10	St. Petersburg, FL	2	3[2]
Charleston, SC.	5	10	Mobile, AL	1	6[2]	San Diego, CA	5	9
Cristobal, Panama	1	1	New London, CT	3	1	Sandy Hook, NJ	5	2
Eastport, ME	19	4	Newport, RI	3	11	San Francisco, CA	5	10
Ft. Pulaski, GA.	7	6	New York, NY.	5	1	Seattle, WA	11	4
Galveston, TX	1	5[2]	Philadelphia, PA.	6	9	Vancouver, BC, Canada	10	6
Halifax, NS, Canada	4	5[2]	Portland, ME	9	11	Washington, DC	3	2

(1) Mean ranges, except where noted. (2) Diurnal range.

El Niño and La Niña

Source: National Weather Service, NOAA, U.S. Dept. of Commerce

El Niño is a climatically significant disruption of the ocean-atmosphere system characterized by large-scale weakening of trade winds and warming of the surface layers in the central and eastern equatorial Pacific. The term *El Niño*, Spanish for "the Christ Child," was originally used by fishermen to refer to a warm ocean current that appeared around Christmas off the west coasts of Ecuador and Peru and lasted several months. The term has come to be reserved for exceptionally strong, warm currents that bring heavy rains.

El Niño events generally occur at irregular intervals of 2 to 7 years, at an average of once every 3 to 4 years. They typically last 12 to 18 months. The intensity of El Niño events varies depending on the intensity of and area encompassed by the abnormally warm ocean temperatures. Some are strong, such as in 1982-83 and 1997-98. Others are considerably weaker, such as the 2004-05 event. The eastward extent of warmer than normal water varies from episode to episode.

El Niño influences weather around the globe, and its impacts are most clearly seen in the winter. During El Niño years, winter temperatures in the continental U.S. tend to be warmer than normal in the the North and West Coast states and cooler than normal in the Southeast. Conditions tend to be wetter than normal over central and southern California, the Southwest states and across much of the South, and drier than normal over the northern portions of the Rocky Mountains and in the Ohio valley. Globally, El Niño brings wetter than normal conditions to Peru and Chile and dry conditions to Australia and Indonesia. It should be noted that El Niño is only one of a number of factors influencing seasonal variations of climate.

La Niña ("The Little Girl") is characterized by colder than normal sea surface temperatures in the equatorial Pacific. La Niña typically brings wetter, cooler conditions to the Pacific Northwest and drier, warmer conditions to much of the southern U.S. El Niño and La Niña are opposite phases of the El Niño-Southern Oscillation (ENSO) cycle, a shift in tropical sea-level pressure between the Eastern and Western hemispheres.

The National Weather Service's Climate Prediction Center, using satellites and buoys in the Pacific Ocean, monitors these events. Highly sophisticated numerical computer models of the ocean and atmosphere use these data to predict the onset and evolution of El Niño and La Niña. In early Sept. 2007, the NOAA predicted that La Niña conditions would build up within the next few months.

Wind Chill Table

Source: National Weather Service, NOAA, U.S. Dept. of Commerce

Temperature and wind combine to cause heat loss from body surfaces. For example, a temperature of 5°F, plus a 10-mph wind, causes body heat loss equal to that which would occur in –10°F with no wind. In other words, a 10-mph wind makes 5°F feel like –10°F. Wind speeds greater than 45 mph have little additional chilling effect. Direct sunlight can increase the wind chill temperature 10° to 15°F. When the wind chill temperature falls within the shaded area, frostbite can occur in 30 mins. or less.

Wind speed (mph)	Calm	Temperature (°F)																	
		40	35	30	25	20	15	10	5	0	–5	–10	–15	–20	–25	–30	–35	–40	–45
		Wind chill temperature (°F)																	
5		36	31	25	19	13	7	1	–5	–11	–16	–22	–28	–34	–40	–46	–52	–57	–63
10		34	27	21	15	9	3	–4	–10	–16	–22	–28	–35	–41	–47	–53	–59	–66	–72
15		32	25	19	13	6	0	–7	–13	–19	–26	–32	–39	–45	–51	–58	–64	–71	–77
20		30	24	17	11	4	–2	–9	–15	–22	–29	–35	–42	–48	–55	–61	–68	–74	–81
25		29	23	16	9	3	–4	–11	–17	–24	–31	–37	–44	–51	–58	–64	–71	–78	–84
30		28	22	15	8	1	–5	–12	–19	–26	–33	–39	–46	–53	–60	–67	–73	–80	–87
35		28	21	14	7	0	–7	–14	–21	–27	–34	–41	–48	–55	–62	–69	–76	–82	–89
40		27	20	13	6	–1	–8	–15	–22	–29	–36	–43	–50	–57	–64	–71	–78	–84	–91
45		26	29	12	5	–2	–9	–16	–23	–30	–37	–44	–51	–58	–65	–72	–79	–86	–93

Heat Index

Source: National Weather Service, NOAA, U.S. Dept. of Commerce

The heat index is a measure of the impact humidity, in combination with abnormally high temperatures, has on the body's ability to cool itself. In other words, it measures what hot weather feels like to the average person. For example, when the air temperature is 100°F, and the relative humidity is 50%, it will feel as if it's 120°F (with no humidity). Full sunlight can make one feel even hotter. Sunstroke and heat exhaustion are likely when the heat index reaches 105°F, within the shaded area.

Relative humidity	Air temperature (°F)										
	70	75	80	85	90	95	100	105	110	115	120
	Apparent temperature (°F)										
0%	64	69	73	78	83	87	91	95	99	103	107
10%	65	70	75	80	85	90	95	100	105	111	116
20%	66	72	77	82	87	93	99	105	112	120	130
30%	67	73	78	84	90	96	104	113	123	135	148
40%	68	74	79	86	93	101	110	123	137	151	
50%	69	75	81	88	96	107	120	135	150		
60%	70	76	82	90	100	114	132	149			
70%	70	77	85	93	106	124	144				
80%	71	78	86	97	113	136					
90%	71	79	88	102	122						
100%	72	80	91	108							

Ultraviolet (UV) Index Forecast

Source: National Weather Service, NOAA, U.S. Dept. of Commerce; U.S. Environmental Protection Agency

The National Weather Service (NWS), Environmental Protection Agency (EPA), and Centers for Disease Control and Prevention (CDC) developed and began offering a UV index on June 28, 1994, in response to increasing incidences of skin cancer, cataracts, and other effects from exposure to the sun's harmful rays. In 2004, the Global Solar UV Index was released. The UV index is now a regular element of NWS atmospheric forecasts.

The UV index, ranging from 0 to 11+, is an indication of the expected intensity of UV radiation reaching the Earth's surface during the solar noon hour (11:30 AM-2:30 PM standard time). The lower the UV index value, the less the radiation. The UV index forecast is produced daily for 58 cities by the NWS Climate Prediction Center and uses the following scale.

UV index	Exposure	Minimum precautions
0-2	Low	Sunscreen with an SPF of at least 15
3-5	Moderate	Sunscreen, covering up
6-7	High	Sunscreen, hat, UV-blocking sunglasses, avoid sun 10 AM-4 PM
8-10	Very High	Same as above
11+	Extreme	Same as above

The index value is valid for a radius of about 30 miles around a listed city and is based on several factors:

Ozone. Ozone, a form of oxygen, the molecules of which consist of three atoms rather than two, blocks UV radiation. The more ozone, the lower the UV radiation at the surface.

Cloudiness. Clear skies allow 100% UV transmission to the surface, broken clouds allow about 73%, and overcast conditions allow 32%.

Reflectivity. Reflective surfaces intensify UV exposure. Grass reflects 2.5% to 3% of UV radiation reaching the surface; sand, 20% to 30%; snow and ice, 80% to 90%; water, up to 100% (depending on reflection angle).

Elevation. At higher elevations, UV radiation travels a shorter distance to reach Earth's surface since there is less atmosphere to absorb the rays. For every 4,000 ft one travels above sea level, the UV index value increases by 1 unit. Snow and lack of pollutants intensify UV exposure at higher altitudes.

Latitude. The closer a location is to the equator, the higher the UV radiation level.

SPF number. The UV index is not linked in any way to the SPF number on suntan lotions and sunscreens. For an explanation of the SPF factor, contact the product's manufacturer or the Food and Drug Administration.

Further information. For precautions to take after learning the UV index value, call the EPA's stratospheric ozone protection hotline (800-296-1996) or your doctor. For questions on scientific aspects, call the NWS's Climate Prediction Center at 301-763-8000.

Lightning

Source: National Weather Service, NOAA, U.S. Dept. of Commerce

Lightning is a result of ice in storm clouds. As ice particles rise and sink in a cloud, numerous collisions between them cause a separation of electrical charge. Positively charged crystals rise to the top, while negatively charged crystals drop. As the storm travels, a pool of positive charges gathers in the ground below and follows along, traveling up objects like trees and telephone poles. In a common form of lightning, the negatively charged area in a storm sends charges downward, which are attracted to positively charged objects. A channel develops and the electrical transfer that you see is lightning. Lightning can travel miles away from the area of a storm.

The transfer of charges in lightning generates a huge amount of heat, sending the temperature in the channel to 50,000°F and causing the air within it to expand rapidly. The sound of that expansion is thunder. Sound travels more slowly than light, so you usually see lightning before you hear thunder.

To (very roughly) gauge one's danger, use the 30-30 rule. In good visibility, count the time between a lightning flash and the crack of thunder. If it's less than 30 secs., the storm is within 6 miles of you. Find shelter immediately. The threat of more lightning does not stop right away; you need to wait about 30 mins. after the last flash of the storm to be sure.

There are an estimated 25 mil cloud-to-ground lightning bolts in the U.S. each year, killing an average of 62 people annually. This is a small number compared to U.S. deaths from fire (about 4,000 a year) and motor vehicle accidents (about 40,000-50,000), but it is still significant. In comparison, tornadoes cause an average of 54 deaths a year and hurricanes an average of 49. Documented injuries from lightning numbered 246 in 2006; probably many more injuries occurred.

Most lightning deaths and injuries occur in the summer months when people are outdoors. When a storm threatens people need to move to a safe place promptly. Even while indoors, people are advised to stay away from windows and avoid contact with anything conducting electricity.

More information about lightning can be found at the website www.lightningsafety.noaa.gov/overview.htm.

Global Measured Extremes of Temperature and Precipitation Records

Source: World Weather/Climate Extremes Archive, World Meteorological Organization Commission for Climatology

(each category ranked from most to least extreme)

Highest Temperature Extremes

Continent	Highest temp. (°F)	Place	Elevation (ft)	Date
Africa	136	El Azizia, Libya	367	Sept. 13, 1922
North America	134	Death Valley, CA, U.S. (Furnace Creek Ranch)	−179	July 10, 1913
Asia	129	Tirat Tsvi, Israel	−722	June 21, 1942
Australia	123	Oodnadatta, South Australia	367	Jan. 2, 1960
South America	120	Rivadavia, Argentina	2,192	Dec. 11, 1905
Europe	117	Murcia, Spain	150	July 4, 1994
Oceania	108	Tuguegarao, Philippines	676	Dec. 11, 1912
Antarctica	59	Vanda Station (New Zeland), Wright Valley	49	Jan. 5, 1974

Lowest Temperature Extremes

Continent	Lowest temp. (°F)	Place	Elevation (ft)	Date
Antarctica	−129	Vostok Station (Russia)	11,220	July 21, 1983
Asia	−90	Verkhoyansk, Russia	350	Feb. 5 & 7, 1892
	−90	Oimekon, Russia	2,625	Feb. 6, 1933
North America	−81.4	Snag, Yukon Territory, Canada	2,120	Feb. 3, 1947
Europe	−72.6	Ust'Shchugor, Russia	279	Dec. 31, 1978
South America	−27	Sarmiento, Argentina	879	June 1, 1907
Africa	−11	Ifrane, Morocco	5,364	Feb. 11, 1935
Australia	−9.4	Charlotte Pass, New South Wales	5,758	June 29, 1994

Highest Measured Average Annual Precipitation Extremes

Continent	Highest avg. (in.)[1]	Place	Elevation (ft)	Years in averaging period
Asia	467.4	Mawsynram, India	4,695	38
Africa	405	Debundscha, Cameroon	30	32
South America	354	Quibdo, Colombia	230	29
Australia	316.3	Bellenden Ker, Queensland	5,102	34
North America	276	Henderson Lake, British Columbia, Canada	115	16
Europe	183	Crkvica, Bosnia-Herzegovina	4,298	22

(1) Official greatest average annual precipitation. The average annual precipitation record of 523.6 in., set in Lloro, Colombia (14 mi SE and at a higher elevation than Quibdo), is an estimated amount.

Lowest Measured Average Annual Precipitation Extremes

Continent	Lowest avg. (in.)	Place	Elevation (ft)	Years in averaging period
South America	0.03	Arica, Chile	213	59
Africa	<0.1	Wadi Halfa, Sudan	590	39
Antarctica	0.8	Amundsen-Scott South Pole Station (U.S.)	9,301	10
North America	1.2	Batagues, Mexico	69	14
Asia	1.8	Aden, Yemen	63	50
Australia	4.1	Astrakhan, Russia	46	42
Europe	6.4	Mulka (Troudaninna), South Australia	66	25

DISASTERS

Some Notable Aircraft Disasters Since 1937

Source: National Transportation Safety Board; World Almanac research

(most notable in bold)

Date	Aircraft	Site of accident	Deaths
1937, May 6	**German zeppelin Hindenburg**	**Burned at mooring, Lakehurst, NJ**	**36***[*]
1944, Aug. 23	U.S. Air Force B-24 Liberator bomber	Hit school, Freckleton, England	61*[*]
1945, July 28	U.S. Army B-25	Hit Empire State Building after getting lost in fog, New York, NY	14*[*]
1952, Dec. 20	U.S. Air Force C-124	Fell, burned, Moses Lake, WA	87
1953, Mar. 3	**Canadian Pacific DH-106 Comet**	**Crashed on takeoff from Karachi, Pakistan**	**111**[1]
1953, June 18	U.S. Air Force C-124	Crashed, burned near Tokyo	129
1955, Oct. 6	United Airlines DC-4	Crashed in Medicine Bow Peak, WY	66
1955, Nov. 1	United Airlines DC-6	Exploded, crashed near Longmont, CO	44[2]
1956, June 20	Venezuelan Super Constellation	Crashed into Atlantic off Asbury Park, NJ	74
1956, June 30	TWA Super Const., United DC-7	Collided over Grand Canyon, AZ	128
1960, Dec. 16	United DC-8, TWA Super Const.	Collided over New York, NY	134[3]
1962, Mar. 16	Flying Tiger Super Constellation	Vanished in W Pacific en route to Philippines from Guam	107
1962, June 3	Air France Boeing 707	Crashed on takeoff from Paris	130
1962, June 22	Air France Boeing 707	Crashed in storm, Guadeloupe, French West Indies	113
1963, Feb. 1	Lebanese Middle East Airlines Vickers Viscount 754, Turkish Mil. Douglas C-47	Collided over Ankara, Turkey, killing all 17 on planes, 87 on ground	104
1963, June 3	Northwest Airlines DC-7	Crashed into Pacific off British Columbia, Canada	101
1963, Nov. 29	Trans-Canada Air Lines DC-8	Crashed after takeoff from Montreal, Quebec, Canada	118
1965, May 20	Pakistani Boeing 720	Crashed at airport in Cairo, Egypt	121
1966, Jan. 24	Air India Boeing 707	Crashed on Mont Blanc, France-Italy	117
1966, Feb. 4	All-Nippon Boeing 727	Plunged into Tokyo Bay	133
1966, Mar. 5	BOAC Boeing 707	Crashed into Mt. Fuji, Japan, after encountering severe turbulence	124
1966, Dec. 24	U.S. military-chartered CL-44	Crashed into village in S Vietnam	129*[*]
1967, Apr. 20	Globe Air Bristol Britannia	Crashed on approach to airport, Nicosia, Cyprus	126
1967, July 19	Piedmont Boeing 727, Cessna 310	Collided in air, Hendersonville, NC	82
1968, Apr. 20	S. African Airways Boeing 707	Crashed on takeoff from Windhoek, South-West Africa	122
1968, May 3	Braniff International Electra	Crashed in storm near Dawson, TX	85
1969, Mar. 16	Venezuelan DC-9	Crashed after takeoff from Maracaibo, Venezuela	155[4]
1969, Dec. 8	Olympic Airways DC-6B	Crashed in storm, near Athens, Greece	93
1970, Feb. 15	Dominicana DC-9	Crashed into sea on takeoff from Santo Domingo, Dominican Rep.	102
1970, July 3	British-chartered DH-106 Comet	Crashed near Barcelona, Spain	112
1970, July 5	Air Canada DC-8	Crashed near Toronto International Airport	108
1970, Aug. 9	LANSA Lockheed L-188A Electra	Crashed after takeoff from Cuzco, Peru	101*[*]
1970, Nov. 14	Southern Airways DC-9	Crashed in mountains near Huntington, WV	75[5]
1971, July 30	All-Nippon Boeing 727, Jap. AF F-86	Collided over Morioka, Japan	162[6]
1971, Sept. 4	Alaska Airlines Boeing 727	Crashed into mountain near Juneau, AK	111
1972, Aug. 14	East German IL-62	Crashed on takeoff, East Berlin	156
1972, Oct. 13	Aeroflot IL-62	Crashed near Moscow	176
1972, Dec. 3	Spanish-chartered Convair CV-990	Crashed on takeoff from Canary Islands, Spain	155
1972, Dec. 29	Eastern Airlines Lockheed Tristar	Crashed on approach to Miami Intl. Airport, FL	101
1973, Jan. 22	Nigerian-chartered Boeing 707	Burst into flames upon landing, Kano Airport, Nigeria	176
1973, Feb. 21	**Libyan Arab Boeing 727**	**Shot down by Israeli fighter planes over Sinai**	**108**
1973, Apr. 10	British Vickers Vanguard	Crashed during snowstorm on approach to Basel, Switzerland	104
1973, June 3	Soviet Supersonic Tu-144	Crashed near Goussainville, France	147
1973, July 11	Brazilian Boeing 707	Crashed on approach to Orly Airport, Paris	122
1973, July 31	Delta Airlines DC-9	Crashed landing in fog at Logan Airport, Boston	89
1973, Dec. 23	French Caravelle jet	Crashed in Morocco	106
1974, Mar. 3	Turkish DC-10	Crashed at Ermenonville, near Paris	346
1974, Apr. 22	Pan American Boeing 707	Crashed in Bali, Indonesia	107
1974, Dec. 1	TWA Boeing 727	Crashed on approach in storm, Upperville, VA	92
1974, Dec. 4	Dutch-chartered DC-8	Crashed in storm near Colombo, Sri Lanka	191
1975, Apr. 4	Air Force Galaxy C-5A	Crashed near Saigon, S Viet., after takeoff; carried orphans	172
1975, June 24	Eastern Airlines 727	Crashed in storm, JFK Airport, New York, NY	113
1975, Aug. 3	Alia Royal Jordanian Boeing 707	Hit mountainside in heavy fog near Agadir, Morocco	188
1976, Sept. 10	Brit. Airways Trident, Yug. DC-9	Collided near Zagreb, Yugoslavia	176
1976, Sept. 19	Turkish 727	Hit mountain, S Turkey	155
1976, Oct. 13	LAB Boeing 707	Crashed after takeoff from Santa Cruz, Bolivia	100[8]
1977, Mar. 27	**KLM 747, Pan American 747**	**Collided on runway, Tenerife, Canary Islands, Spain**	**583**[9]
1977, Nov. 19	TAP Portugal Boeing 727	Crashed on Madeira, Portugal	130
1977, Dec. 4	Malaysian Airlines Boeing 737	Hijacked and forced to fly to Singapore, crashed near Strait of Johore	100
1977, Dec. 13	National Jet Service DC-3	Crashed after takeoff from Evansville, IN; passengers included Univ. of Evansville men's basketball team	29
1978, Jan. 1	Air India 747	Exploded, crashed into sea off Bombay	213
1978, Sept. 25	Boeing 727, Cessna 172	Collided in air, San Diego, CA	150
1978, Nov. 15	Indonesian-chartered DC-8	Crashed on approach to airport, Colombo, Sri Lanka	183
1979, May 25	**American Airlines DC-10**	**Crashed after takeoff from O'Hare Airport, Chicago**	**275**[10]
1979, Aug. 11	Aeroflot/Moldova Tu-134, Aeroflot Tu-134	Collided over Ukraine	178
1979, Nov. 26	Pakistani Boeing 707	Crashed near Jidda, Saudi Arabia	156
1979, Nov. 28	Air New Zealand DC-10	Crashed into mountain after takeoff from Antarctica	257
1980, Mar. 14	PLL LOT IL-62	Crashed making emergency landing, Warsaw, Poland	87[11]
1980, Aug. 19	Saudi Arabian Tristar	Burned after emergency landing, Riyadh	301
1981, Dec. 1	Inex Adria DC-9	Crashed into mountain on Corsica, France	180
1982, Jan. 13	Air Florida Boeing 737	Crashed into Potomac R. after takeoff from Washington, DC	78
1982, July 9	Pan Am Boeing 727	Crashed after takeoff from Kenner, LA	153*[*]
1983, Sept. 1	**S. Korean Boeing 747**	**Shot down after violating Soviet airspace; plane apparently misidentified**	**269**
1983, Nov. 27	Avianca Boeing 747	Crashed near Barajas Airport, Madrid, Spain	183
1984, Oct. 11	Aeroflot/East Siberia Tu-154	Crashed into vehicles on runway while landing in poor weather, Omsk, Russia	178*[*]
1985, Feb. 19	Spanish Boeing 727	Crashed into Mt. Oiz, Spain	148
1985, June 23	Air-India Boeing 747	Crashed into Atlantic S of Ireland	329

Date	Aircraft	Site of accident	Deaths
1985, Aug. 2	Delta Air Lines L-1011	Crashed at Dallas-Ft. Worth Airport, TX	137
1985, Aug. 12	**Japan Air Lines Boeing 747**	**Crashed into Mt. Ogura, Japan**	**520[12]**
1985, Dec. 12	Arrow Air DC-8	Crashed after takeoff from Gander, Newfoundland, Canada	256[13]
1986, Mar. 31	Mexican Boeing 727	Crashed NW of Mexico City	166
1986, Aug. 31	Aeromexico DC-9	Collided with Piper PA-28 over Cerritos, CA	82[14]
1987, May 9	Polish IL-62M	Crashed after takeoff from Warsaw, Poland	183
1987, Aug. 16	Northwest Airlines MD-82	Crashed after takeoff from Romulus, MI	156
1987, Nov. 28	S. African Boeing 747	Crashed into Indian Ocean near Mauritius	159
1987, Nov. 29	S. Korean Boeing 707	Exploded over Thai-Burmese border	155
1988, Mar. 17	Colombian Boeing 707	Crashed into mountainside near Venezuela border	137
1988, July 3	**Iran Air Airbus A300**	**Shot down by U.S. Navy warship *Vincennes* over Pers. Gulf**	**290**
1988, Dec. 21	**Pan Am Boeing 747**	**Bomb on board; exploded over Lockerbie, Scotland**	**270[15]**
1989, Feb. 8	U.S.-chartered Boeing 707	Crashed into mountain on Azores Islands, off Portugal	144
1989, June 7	Suriname DC-8	Crashed near Paramaribo Airport, Suriname	168
1989, July 19	United Airlines DC-10	Crashed while landing in Sioux City, IA	111
1989, Sept. 19	**UTA DC-10**	**Bomb exploded on board over desert in Niger**	**171**
1989, Nov. 27	Avianca Boeing 727	Bomb exploded on flight from Bogotá, Colombia	107
1990, Jan. 25	Avianca Air Boeing 707	Crashed on landing, JFK Airport, New York, NY	73
1990, Feb. 14	Indian Airlines Airbus 320	Crashed and burned landing in Bangalore, India	91
1990, Oct. 2	Xiamen Airlines Boeing 737	737 hijacked after takeoff from Xiamen; struck empty 707, then China Southern 757 on runway at Guangzhou, China	132
1991, May 26	Lauda-Air Boeing 767-300	Exploded over rural Thailand	223
1991, July 11	Nigerian DC-8	Crashed while landing at Jidda, Saudi Arabia	261
1991, Oct. 5	Air Force Lockheed C-130 Hercules	Crashed after takeoff from Jakarta, Indonesia	137*
1992, July 31	Thai Airbus A300-310	Crashed into mountain N of Kathmandu, Nepal	113
1992, Oct. 4	**El Al Boeing 747-200F**	**Crashed into 2 apartment bldgs., Amsterdam, Netherlands**	**120***
1993, Feb. 8	Iran Air Tu-154, Iranian Air Force jet	Collided with military jet after takeoff from Tehran, Iran	133
1993, Mar. 5	Macedonian Pal Air Fokker 100	Crashed after takeoff in snowstorm from Skopje, Macedonia	83
1994, Jan. 3	Aeroflot Tu-154	Crashed and exploded after takeoff from Irkutsk, Russia	125*
1994, Apr. 26	China Airlines Airbus A300	Crashed on approach to Nagoya Airport, Japan	264
1994, June 6	China Northwest Airlines Tu-154	Crashed near Xian, China	160
1994, Sept. 8	USAir Boeing 737-300	Crashed near Pittsburgh Intl. Airport, in Aliquippa, PA	132
1994, Oct. 31	American Eagle ATR-72-210	Crashed in field near Roselawn, IN	68
1995, Aug. 11	Aviateca Boeing 737	Crashed into Chichontepec volcano, El Salvador	65
1995, Dec. 20	American Airlines Boeing 757	Crashed into mountain 50 mi N of Cali, Colombia	160
1996, Jan. 8	Antonova 32 cargo jet	Crashed into central market, Kinshasa, Zaire	350+*
1996, Feb. 6	Turkish Boeing 757	Crashed into Atlantic off Dominican Republic	189
1996, Apr. 3	U.S. Air Force Boeing T-43A	Crashed into mountain near Dubrovnik, Croatia	35[16]
1996, May 11	ValuJet DC-9	Crashed into Florida Everglades after takeoff	110
1996, July 17	Trans World Airlines Boeing 747	Exploded and crashed into Atlantic, off Long Isl., NY	230
1996, Aug. 29	Vnukovo Tu-154	Crashed into mountain on Arctic island of Spitsbergen	141
1996, Oct. 2	Aeroperu Boeing 757	Crashed into Pacific after takeoff from Lima, Peru	70
1996, Oct. 31	Brazilian TAM Fokker-100	Crashed shortly after takeoff from São Paulo, Brazil	97*
1996, Nov. 7	ADG Boeing 727	Crashed into lagoon 40 mi SE of Lagos, Nigeria	143
1996, Nov. 12	**Saudi Arabian Boeing 747, Kazakh IL-76 cargo plane**	**Collided in midair near New Delhi, India**	**349[17]**
1996, Nov. 23	Ethiopian Airlines Boeing 767	Hijacked, then crashed into Indian Ocean off the Comoros	127
1997, Jan. 9	Comair Embraer 120	Crashed on approach to Detroit Metro. Airport, MI	29
1997, May 8	China Southern Airlines Boeing 737	Crashed on approach to Shenzhen's Huangtian Airport	35
1997, July 11	Cubana de Aviación Antonov-24	Crashed into the Caribbean off SE Cuba	44
1997, Aug. 6	Korean Air Boeing 747-300	Crashed into jungle on Guam on approach to airport	228
1997, Sept. 3	Vietnamese Airlines Tu-134	Crashed on approach to Phnom Penh airport	64
1997, Sept. 14	U.S. C-141 cargo plane, Ger. Tu-154	Collided in midair off SW Africa	33
1997, Sept. 26	Indonesian Airbus A300	Crashed near airport, Medan, Indonesia	234
1997, Oct. 10	Austral Boeing DC-9-32	Crashed and exploded near Neuvo Berlin, Uruguay	74
1997, Dec. 6	Russian AN-124 transport cargo plane	Crashed into apartment complex near Irkutsk, Siberia	67*
1997, Dec. 15	Tajik Air Tu-154	Crashed in desert near airport, Sharja, UAE	85
1997, Dec. 17	AeroSvit Airlines Yakovlev-42	Crashed in mountains near Katerini, Greece	70
1997, Dec. 19	SilkAir Boeing 737-300	Crashed into Musi River, Sumatra, Indonesia	104
1998, Feb. 2	Cebu Pacific Air DC-9-32	Crashed into mountain near Cagayan de Oro, Philippines	104
1998, Feb. 16	China Airlines Airbus A300	Crashed on approach to airport, Taipei, Taiwan	203[18]
1998, Apr. 20	Air France Boeing 727-200	Crashed into mountain after takeoff from Bogotá, Colombia	53
1998, Sept. 2	Swissair MD-11	Crashed into Atlantic off Nova Scotia	229
1998, Sept. 25	Pauknair BAE146	Crashed into hillside in Morocco	38
1998, Oct. 11	Congo Our Lines Boeing 727	Shot down by rebels in Kindu, Congo	40
1998, Dec. 11	Thai Airways Airbus A310	Crashed on third attempt to land at Surat Thani airport, Thailand	101
1999, Feb. 24	China Southwest Airlines Tu-154	Crashed on approach to Wenzhou airport, E China	61
1999, Sept. 1	LAPA Boeing 737-200	Crashed on takeoff from Jorge Newbery Airport, Buenos Aires, Argentina	74[19]
1999, Oct. 31	EgyptAir Boeing 767	Crashed off Nantucket, MA; result of deliberate actions by copilot	217
2000, Jan. 30	Kenya Airways Airbus A310	Crashed into Atlantic after takeoff from Abidjan, Ivory Coast	169
2000, Jan. 31	Alaska Airlines MD-83	Crashed into Pacific off coast of Southern CA	88
2000, Apr. 19	Air Philippines Boeing 737-200	Crashed on approach to airport, Davao, S Philippines	131
2000, May 21	U.S.-chartered Jetstream 31	Crashed near Wilkes-Barre, PA	19
2000, July 25	Air France Concorde	Crashed into hotel after takeoff from Paris; world's first Concorde crash	113*
2000, Aug. 23	Gulf Air Airbus A320	Crashed into Persian Gulf on approach to airport in Bahrain	143
2000, Oct. 31	Singapore Airlines Boeing 747	Crashed immediately after takeoff from Taipei, Taiwan	81
2000, Oct. 31	Chartered Antonov 26	Exploded after takeoff from northern Angola	50
2000, Nov. 15	Chartered Antonov 24	Crashed after takeoff from Luanda, Angola	40+
2001, Mar. 3	C23 Sherpa military transport	Crashed in storm, central GA	21
2001, Apr. 7	M-17 helicopter	Crashed into mountain S of Hanoi, Vietnam	16[20]
2001, July 3	Vladivostokavia Tu-154	Crashed on approach to airport, Irkutsk, Russia	145
2001, Sept. 11	**2 Boeing 767s, 2 Boeing 757s**	**September 11 terrorist attacks.[21]**	**265[21]**
2001, Oct. 4	Sibir Airlines Tu-154	Crashed into Black Sea after being struck by errant Ukrainian missile	78
2001, Oct. 8	Cessna 525A Citation, Scandinavian Airlines System (SAS) MD-87	Collided in heavy fog during takeoff from Milan, Italy	118*

Date	Aircraft	Site of accident	Deaths
2001, Nov. 12	American Airlines Airbus A300	Crashed after takeoff from JFK Airport, New York, NY	265*
2002, Jan. 28	TAME Ecuador Boeing 727	Crashed into Andes mountains, S Colombia	92
2002, Feb. 12	Iran Air Tours Tu-154	Crashed in Khorramabad, Iran	119
2002, Apr. 15	Air China Boeing 767	Crashed into mountainside amid rain and fog on approach to airport, Pusan, S. Korea	129
2002, May 4	EAS Airlines BAC 1-11	Crashed shortly after takeoff from Kano, Nigeria	149
2002, May 7	China Northern Airlines MD-82	Plunged into Yellow Sea after cabin fire, approaching Dalian, China	112
2002, May 25	China Airlines Boeing 747	Broke apart in midair, plunged into Taiwan Strait en route to Hong Kong airport	225
2002, July 1	Bashkirian Airlines Tu-154, DHL Boeing 757 cargo	Collided over S Germany	71
2002, July 4	Prestige Airlines Cargo Boeing B-707	Crashed short of runway in Bangui, Central African Rep.	25
2002, July 27	Ukraine Air Force Sukhoi Su-27	Crashed amid spectators at air show in Lviv, Ukraine	83
2002, Aug. 19	Russian MI-26 helicopter	Troop-carrier hit by Chechen missile near Grozny, Chechnya	127
2002, Dec. 23	Aeromist Kharkiv An-140	Crashed into mountain in fog near Baghrabad, Iran	46
2003, Jan. 8	Turkish Airlines British Aerospace RJ-100	Crashed on approach to airport in Diyarbakir, Turkey	75
2003, Jan. 9	TANS Airlines Fokker 28 Fellowship	Crashed into mountain near Chachopoyas, Peru	46
2003, Feb. 19	Iranian Revolutionary Guard Il-76	Crashed into mountain near Kerman, Iran; passengers were Revolutionary Guard members	275
2003, Mar. 6	Air Algérie Boeing 737-200	Crashed on takeoff from Tamanrasset, Algeria	102
2003, May 8	Congolese Air Force Il-76	On flight from Kinshasa, Dem. Rep. of Congo, cargo door opened, passengers sucked out	7+[22]
2003, May 26	Ukrain.-Medit. Airlines Yak-42	Crashed into mountain in fog approaching Trabzon, Turkey; passengers incl. Spanish peacekeepers returning from Afghan.	75
2003, July 8	Sudan Airways Boeing 737-200	Crashed after takeoff, return to Port Sudan Airport	116
2003, Aug. 24	Tropical Airways Let 410UVP-E	Overloading caused crash on takeoff from Haiti	21
2003, Nov. 29	Congolese Air Force Antonov 26	Crashed on takeoff attempt from Boendo, Dem. Rep. of Congo	33
2003, Dec. 25	Union Transp. Africains Boeing 727	Overloading caused crash on takeoff from Cotonou, Benin	138
2004, Jan. 3	Flash Airlines Boeing 737-300	Crashed into Red Sea after takeoff from Sharm el-Sheik, Egypt	148
2004, Jan. 13	Uzbekistan Airways Yakovlev YAK-40	Crashed on landing attempt in fog at Tashkent, Uzbekistan	37
2004, Feb. 10	Iranian Kish Airline Fokker-50	Crashed on approach to Sharjah, UAE	43
2004, May 15	Rico Linhas Aereas Embraer 120ER Brasilia	Crashed in Amazon jungle near Manaus, Brazil	33
2004, June 8	Gabon Express Hawker Siddeley HS-748	Crashed into sea after takeoff from Libreville, Gabon	19
2004, Aug. 24	Volga-Aviaexpress Tu-134, Sibir Airlines Tu-154	2 planes that had taken off from Moscow crashed within minutes of each other; brought down by Chechen suicide bombers	90
2005, Feb. 3	Kam Air Boeing 737-200	Crashed on approach to airport in Kabul, Afghan.	104
2005, Mar. 16	Russian Antonov-24	Crashed near Barents Sea, in Varandei, Russia	29
2005, Apr. 7	Russian AN-24 turboprop	Crashed into hill near Barents Sea port	28+
2005, Aug. 14	Helios Airways Boeing 737-300	Crashed after air pressure failure on board, near Athens, Greece	121
2005, Aug. 16	West Caribbean Airways MD-82	Crashed after engine failure, near Machiques, Venezuela	160
2005, Aug. 23	TANS Boeing 737-200	Crashed during severe storm on approach to airport, Pucallpa, Peru	40
2005, Sept. 5	Mandala Airlines Boeing 737-200	Crashed shortly after takeoff from Medan, Sumatra, Indonesia	145[23]
2005, Oct. 22	Bellview Airlines Boeing 737-200	Crashed in heavy electrical storm near Lagos, Nigeria	117
2005, Dec. 6	Islamic Rep. of Iran Air Force Lockheed C-130	Crashed into apartment building after reportedly attempting emergency landing back at airport, Tehran, Iran	116+[24]
2005, Dec. 10	Sosoliso Airlines DC-9-30	Crashed during severe storm on approach to Port Harcourt, Nigeria	107
2006, May 3	Armavia Airbus A-320	Crashed into Black Sea on approach to airport, Sochi, Russia	113
2006, July 9	S7 Airlines Airbus A-310	Skidded off runway, crashed into concrete barrier after landing, Irkutsk, Russia	125
2006, Aug. 22	Pulkovo Aviation Tu-154	Crashed after encountering storm, near Donetsk, Ukraine	170
2006, Aug. 27	Comair Bombardier CRJ-100	Crashed after takeoff from Lexington, KY	49
2006, Sept. 29	Gol Airlines Boeing 737	Crashed into Amazon jungle after collision with Embraer Legacy jet in midair, Brazil	154
2006, Oct. 29	ADC Airlines Boeing 737-200	Crashed in stormy weather shortly after takeoff from Abuja, Nigeria	96
2007, Jan. 1	Adam Air Boeing 737-400	Crashed into sea off coast, Makassar, Indonesia	102
2007, May 5	Kenya Airways Boeing 737-800	Crashed shortly after takeoff from Douala, Cameroon	114
2007, July 17	TAM Airlines Airbus 320	Crashed into cargo depot, gas station after skidding off airport runway, São Paulo, Brazil	199*

*Including those on ground and in buildings. (1) First fatal crash of commercial passenger jet. (2) Caused by bomb planted by Jack G. Graham in insurance plot to kill his mother, Daisie E. King, a passenger. (3) Incl. all 128 aboard planes and 6 on ground. (4) Killed 84 on plane and 71 on ground. (5) Incl. 43 Marshall Univ. football players and coaches. (6) Airliner-fighter crash; pilot of fighter parachuted to safety. (7) First supersonic plane crash; killed 8 on ground. (8) Crew of 3 killed; 97 killed on the ground. (9) World's worst airline disaster. (10) Incl. 2 on ground. Highest death toll in U.S. aviation history. (11) Incl. 22 members of U.S. amateur boxing team. (12) Worst single-plane disaster. (13) Incl. 248 members of U.S. 101st Airborne Division. (14) Incl. 15 on ground. (15) Incl. 11 on ground. (16) Incl. U.S. Sec. of Commerce Ron Brown. (17) World's worst midair collision. (18) Incl. 7 on ground. (19) Incl. 10 on ground. (20) Carried U.S. mil. personnel, searching for MIAs from Vietnam War. (21) 4 planes were hijacked and crashed, with all on board (265, incl. 19 hijackers) killed. American Airlines Flight 11, a Boeing 767-200, with 81 passengers, 11 crew, crashed into Tower 1 of World Trade Center; United Airlines Flight 175, a Boeing 767-200, with 56 passengers, 9 crew, crashed into Tower 2 of World Trade Center; American Airlines Flight 77, a Boeing 757-200, with 58 passengers, 6 crew, crashed into Pentagon outside Washington, DC; United Air Lines Flight 93, a Boeing 757-200, with 37 passengers, 7 crew, crashed near Shanksville, PA. In May 2007, for first time, the New York City medical examiner linked a death to exposure to dust from collapsed towers on Sept. 11. The woman, who died in Feb. 2002, brought number of ground victims of attacks on twin towers to 2,750. About 125 died on ground in the Pentagon. (22) 7 confirmed dead. Actual number might be 60-100+. (23) Incl. 44 on ground. (24) 94 on plane plus 22+ on ground.

German Airship Hindenburg

Date: May 6, 1937. **Location:** Lakehurst, NJ. **Fatalities:** 36.

The largest rigid airship ever built was preparing to land when a fire appeared on board. Flames quickly consumed the 804-ft structure before it crashed to the ground. It was originally believed that the hydrogen used to keep the *Hindenburg* aloft had ignited. A more recent theory proposes that the combination of electricity in the atmosphere and the zeppelin's highly flammable fabric cover led to the catastrophe. Yet others believe the disaster was an act of sabotage. Prior to its destruction, the *Hindenburg* had completed 10 commercial transatlantic crossings; its loss signaled the end of the use of airships in commercial aviation.

Some Notable Shipwrecks Since 1854

(Figures indicate estimated lives lost. Does not include most wartime disasters.)

1854, Mar. 1—City of Glasgow; Brit. steamer left Liverpool for Philadelphia, never heard from again; 480.

1854, Sept. 27—Arctic and Vesta; U.S. (Collins Line) steamer sunk in collision with French steamer nr. Cape Race, Canada; 285-351.

1856, Jan. 23—Pacific; U.S. (Collins Line) steamer went missing in N Atlantic; 186-286.

1858, Sept. 23—Austria; German steamer destroyed by fire in N Atlantic; 471.

1863, Apr. 27—Anglo-Saxon; Brit. steamer wrecked at Cape Race, Canada; 238.

1865, Apr. 27—Sultana; Mississippi R. steamer blew up nr. Memphis, TN; 1,450.

1869, Oct. 27—Stonewall; steamer burned, Mississippi R. below Cairo, IL; 200.

1870, Jan. 25—City of Boston; Brit. (Inman Line) steamer vanished between New York and Liverpool; 177.

1870, Oct. 19—Cambria; Brit. steamer off N Ireland; 196.

1872, Nov. 7—Mary Celeste; U.S. half-brig sailing from New York to Genoa, Italy, found abandoned; loss of life unknown.

1873, Jan. 22—Northfleet; Brit. steamer foundered off Dungeness, England; 300.

1873, Apr. 1—Atlantic; Brit. (White Star) steamer off Nova Scotia, Can.; 585.

1873, Nov. 23—Ville du Havre and Loch Earn; French steamer sank after collision with Brit. sailing ship; 226.

1875, May 7—Schiller; German steamer off Scilly Isles, UK; 312.

1875, Nov. 4—Pacific; U.S. steamer sank after collision off Cape Flattery, WA; 236.

1878, Sept. 3—Princess Alice; Brit. steamer sank after collision with *Bywell Castle* in Thames R.; 700.

1878, Dec. 18—Byzantin; French steamer sank after collision in Dardanelles, off Turkey; 210.

1881, May 24—Victoria; steamer capsized in Thames R., ON, Canada; 200.

1883, Jan. 19—Cimbria and Sultan; German steamer sank in collision with Brit. steamer in North Sea; 389.

1890, Feb. 1—Duburg; Brit. steamer wrecked, China Sea; 400.

1890, Sept. 19—Ertogrul; Turkish frigate off Japan; 540.

1891, Mar. 17—Utopia and Anson; Brit. steamer sank in collision with Brit. ironclad off Gibraltar; 562.

1895, Jan. 30—Elbe and Craithie; German steamer sank in collision with Brit. steamer in North Sea; 332.

1895, Mar. 11—Reina Regenta; Spanish cruiser foundered nr. Gibraltar; 400.

1898, Feb. 15—USS Maine; battleship blown up in Havana Harbor, Cuba; 260.

1898, July 4—La Bourgogne and Cromartyshire; French steamer sank in collision with Brit. sailing ship off Nova Scotia, Can.; 549.

1898, Nov. 26—Portland; U.S. steamer, off Cape Cod, MA; 157.

1904, June 15—General Slocum; excursion steamer burned in East R., New York, NY; 1,021.

1904, June 28—Norge; Danish steamer wrecked on Rockall Isl., Scotland; 620.

1906, Aug. 4—Sirio; Italian steamer wrecked off Cape Palos, Spain; 350.

1908, Mar. 23—Matsu Maru; Japanese steamer sank in collision nr. Hakodate, Japan; 300.

1909, Aug. 1—Waratah; Brit. steamer, Sydney to London, vanished; 300.

1910, Feb. 9—General Chanzy; French steamer wrecked off Minorca, Spain; 200.

1911, Sept. 25—Liberté; French battleship exploded at Toulon; 285.

1912, Mar. 5—Principe de Asturias; Spanish steamer wrecked off Spanish coast; 500.

1912, Apr. 14-15—Titanic; Brit. (White Star) steamer hit iceberg in N Atlantic; 1,503.

1912, Sept. 28—Kichemaru; Japanese steamer sank off Japan coast; 1,000.

1914, May 29—Empress of Ireland; Brit. (Canadian Pacific) steamer collided with Norwegian *Storstad* in St. Lawrence R., Can.; 1,014.

1915, May 7—Lusitania; Brit. (Cunard Line) steamer torpedoed and sunk by German submarine off Ireland; 1,198.

1915, July 24—Eastland; steamer capsized, Chicago R., IL; 844.

1916, Feb. 26—Provence; French cruiser sank in Medit.; 3,100.

1916, Mar. 2—Principe de Asturias; Spanish steamer wrecked nr. Santos, Brazil; 558.

1917, Dec. 6—Mont Blanc and Imo; French ammunition ship and Belgian steamer collided in Halifax Harbor, Can.; 1,600.

1918, Apr. 25—Kiang-Kwan; Chinese steamer sank in collision off Hankow; 500.

1918, July 12—Kawachi; Japanese battleship blew up in Tokayama Bay; 500.

1918, Oct. 25—Princess Sophia; Canadian steamer sank off Alaskan coast; 398.

1919, Jan. 17—Chaonia; French steamer lost in Straits of Messina, Italy; 460.

1919, Sept. 9—Valbanera; Spanish steamer lost off FL coast; 500.

1921, Mar. 18—Hong Kong; steamer wrecked, S China Sea; 1,000.

1922, Aug. 26—Niitaka; Japanese cruiser sank in storm off Kamchatka, USSR; 300.

1924, June 12—USS Mississippi; explosions in battleship's gun turret, off San Pedro, CA; 48.

1927, Oct. 25—Principessa Mafalda; Italian steamer blew up, sank off Porto Seguro, Brazil; 314.

1928, Nov. 12—Vestris; Brit. steamer sank off VA coast; 113.

1934, Sept. 8—Morro Castle; U.S. steamer, Havana to New York, burned off Asbury Park, NJ; 134.

1939, May 23—Squalus; U.S. submarine sank off Portsmouth, NH; 26.

1939, June 1—Thetis; submarine sank, Liverpool Bay; 99.

1942, Feb. 18—USS Truxtun and Pollux; destroyer and cargo ship ran aground, sank off Newfoundland, Can.; 204.

1942, Oct. 2—Curacao and Queen Mary; Brit. cruiser sank after collision with liner; 338.

**1944, Dec. 17-18—3 U.S. Third Fleet destroyers sank during typhoon, Philippine Sea; 790.

1945, Jan. 30—Wilhelm Gustloff; liner with German refugees, soldiers sunk by Soviet submarine in Baltic; 5,000-9,000.

1945, Apr. 16—Goya; cargo ship carrying German refugees, soldiers sunk by Soviet submarine in Baltic; 6,000-7,000.

1945, May 3—Cap Arcona and Thielbek; German liners carrying concentration camp inmates sunk by British warplanes in Lubeck Bay, Ger.; 7,000-8,000.

1947, Jan. 19—Himera; Greek steamer hit mine off Athens, Greece; 392.

1947, Apr. 16—Grandcamp; French freighter exploded, Texas City, TX, harbor, started fires; 576+.

1948, Dec. 3—Kiangya; Chinese refugee ship wrecked in explosion S of Shanghai; 1,100+.

1949, Sept. 17—Noronic; Canadian Great Lakes Cruiser burned at Toronto, Can.; dock; 130.

1952, Apr. 26—USS Hobson and USS Wasp; destroyer and aircraft carrier collided in Atlantic; 176.

1954, Sept. 26—Toya Maru; Japanese ferry sank, Tsugaru Strait, Japan; 1,172.

1956, July 26—Andrea Doria and Stockholm; Italian liner and Swedish liner collided off Nantucket Isl., MA; 51.

1957, July 14—Eshghabad; Soviet ship ran aground in Caspian Sea; 270.

1961, Apr. 8—Dara; British liner exploded in Persian Gulf; 236.

1961, July 8—Save; Portuguese ship ran aground off Mozambique; 259.

1963, Apr. 10—Thresher; U.S. Navy atomic submarine sank in N Atlantic; 129.

1964, Feb. 10—Voyager; Australian destroyer sank after collision with aircraft carrier *Melbourne* off New South Wales; 82.

1965, Nov. 13—Yarmouth Castle; Panamanian-registered cruise ship burned, sank off Nassau, Bahamas; 89.

1968, Jan. 25—Dakar; Israeli submarine vanished in Medit.; 69.

1968, missing May 27—Scorpion; U.S. nuclear submarine sank in Atlantic nr. Azores; 99 (located Oct. 31).

1969, June 2—Evans and Melbourne; U.S. destroyer cut in half by Australian carrier, S China Sea; 74.

1970, Mar. 4—Eurydice; French submarine sank in Medit. nr. Toulon; 57.

1970, Dec. 15—Namyong-Ho; S. Korean ferry sank in Korea Strait; 308.

**1974, Sept. 26—Soviet destroyer sank in Black Sea; 200+.

1975, Nov. 10—Edmund Fitzgerald; U.S. cargo ship sank during storm on Lake Superior; 29.

1976, Oct. 20—George Prince and Frosta; ferryboat and Norwegian tanker collided, Mississippi R., at Luling, LA; 77.

1976, Dec. 25—Patria; Egyptian liner caught fire and sank in Red Sea; 100.

**1979, Aug. 14—23 yachts competing in Fastnet yacht race sank or abandoned during storm in S Irish Sea; 18.

1980, Apr. 22—Don Juan; sank off Mindoro Isl., Philippines, after colliding with barge; 1,000+.

1981, Jan. 27—Tamponas II; Indonesian passenger ship caught fire and sank in Java Sea; 580.

1983, Feb. 12—Marine Electric; coal freighter sank during storm off Chincoteague, VA; 33.

1983, May 25—10th of Ramadan; Nile steamer caught fire and sank in Lake Nasser, Egypt; 357.

1986, Apr. 20—Atlas Star; ferry sank in storm, Dhaleswari R. nr. Dhaka, Bangladesh; 300+.

1986, May 25—Shamia; ferry capsized in storm, Meghna R., Bangladesh; 500+.

1986, Sept. 1—Admiral Nakhimov and Pyotr Vasev; Soviet cruise ship collided with Soviet freighter in Black Sea; 425.

1987, Mar. 6—The Herald of Free Enterprise; British ferry capsized off Zeebrugge, Belgium; 189.

1987, Dec. 20—Dona Paz and Victor; Philippine ferry and oil tanker collided in Tablas Strait; 4,341.

1988, Aug. 6—Indian ferry capsized on Ganges R.; 400+.

1989, Apr. 19—USS Iowa; explosion in gun turret while ship in Atlantic but did not sink; 47.

1989, Apr. 7—Komsolets; Soviet submarine sank after fire off Norwegian coast; 42.

1989, Aug. 20—Bowbelle and Marchioness; Brit. barge struck Brit. pleasure cruiser on Thames R. in central London; 56.

1989, Sept. 10—Romanian pleasure boat and Bulgarian barge collided on Danube R.; 161.

1991, Apr. 10—Moby Prince and Agip Abruzzo; auto ferry and oil tanker collided outside Livorno Harbor, Italy; 140.

1991, Dec. 14—Salem Express; ferry rammed coral reef nr. Safaga, Egypt; 462.

1993, Feb. 17—Neptune; ferry capsized off Port-au-Prince, Haiti; 500+.

1993, Oct. 10—Seohae; capsized in Yellow Sea nr. W S. Korea during storm; 285.

1994, Sept. 28—Estonia; ferry sank in Baltic Sea; 1,049.

1996, May 21—Bukoba; overcrowded Tanzanian ferry sank in Lake Victoria; 500+.

1997, Feb. 20—Tamil refugee boat sank off Sri Lanka; 165.

1997, Mar. 28—Albanian refugee boat sank in Adriatic after being rammed by Italian navy warship *Sibilla*; 83.

1997, Sept. 8—Pride of la Gonâve; Haitian ferry sank off Montrouis, Haiti; 200+.

1998, Apr. 4—Passenger boat capsized off coast nr. Ibaka beach, Nigeria; 280.

1998, Sept. 2—2 passenger boats capsized on Lake Kivu, nr. Bukavu, Congo; 200+.

1998, Sept. 18—Ferry sank south of Manila, Philippines; 97.

1999, Feb. 6—Harta Rimba; cargo ship sank off Indonesia; 280+.

1999, Mar. 26—Passenger boat overturned off Sierra Leone; 150+.

1999, Apr. 2—Passenger ferry sank off Nigeria; 100+.

1999, May 1—Excursion "duck" boat sank, Lake Hamilton, AR; 13.

1999, May 8—Passenger ferry capsized off Bangladesh; 200+.

1999, Nov. 24—Dashun; passenger ferry capsized nr. Yantai, China; 280.

2000, May 3—2 ferries capsized in Meghna R., Bangladesh; 72+.

2000, June 29—Cahaya Bahari; overloaded ferry carrying refugees from religious strife capsized in storm off Sulawesi Isl., Indonesia; 500+.

2000, Aug. 12—Kursk; Russian sub sank in Barents Sea; 118.

2000, Sept. 26—Express Samina; Greek ferry sank off Paros, Greece; 81+.

2001, Feb. 9—Ehime Maru; Japanese trawler sunk by surfacing U.S. submarine *Greeneville*, nr. Hawaii; 9.

2001, Oct. 19—Fishing boat overloaded with refugees, mainly from Middle East, sank off Indonesia; 350+.

2001, Dec. 22—Suspected N. Korean spy ship sank after exchanging fire with Japanese coast guard; 15.

2002, May 4—Salahuddin-2; overloaded Bangladesh ferry sank in Meghna R.; 300+.

2002, Sept. 26—Joola; overloaded Senegalese ferry capsized in ocean off The Gambia; 1,863.

2003, Mar. 23—Kashowgwe; overloaded ferry capsized in Lake Tanganyika, off Burundi; 111+.

2003, Apr. 21—2 ferries capsized in storms in Meghna and Buriganga rivers, Bangladesh; 180+.

2003, July 8—MV-Nasrin 1; overcrowded ferry sank nr. Chandpur in Bangladesh R.; 400.

2003, Oct. 15—Andrew J. Barberi; NYC ferry crashed into dock on approach to Staten Isl.; 11.

2003, Nov. 25—Dieu Merci; overloaded ferry sank on Lake Mayi Ndombe, Dem. Rep. of Congo; 130-200.

2004, Jan. 26—Convoi Lengi; ferry caught fire on Congo R., Dem. Rep. of Congo; 200.

2004, Feb. 28—Bow Mariner; tanker carrying ethariol caught fire, exploded off VA coast; 21.

2004, Mar 6—Lady D; water taxi capsized in storm, Inner Harbor, Baltimore, MD; 5.

2004, Mar. 11—Samson; ferry sank off Madagascar during cyclone; 113.

2004, May 24—Lightning Sun; ferry sank in Meghna R., Bangladesh; 60+

2005, July 7—KMP Digul; ferry capsized in rough waters nr. Merauke, Indonesia; 150+.

2005, Aug. 12—Fishing boat overloaded with Ecuadorans attempting to migrate to U.S. sank off Colombia; 94.

2005, Oct. 2—Ethan Allen; glass boat carrying senior citizens capsized on tour, Lake George, NY; 20.

2006, Feb. 3—Al-Salam Boccaccio 98; ferry caught fire, sank in Red Sea off Egypt; 1,000+.

2006, Dec. 30—Senopati Nusantara; high waves capsized ferry en route to Java, Indonesia; 400+.

2007, May 4—Boat overloaded with Haitian illegal immigrants capsized in storm nr. Turks and Caicos Islands; 61+.

Some Notable Railroad Disasters Since 1925

Date	Location	Deaths	Date	Location	Deaths
1925, June 16	Hackettstown, NJ	50	1958, Sept. 15	Elizabethport, NJ	48
1925, Oct. 27	Victoria, MS	21	1960, Nov. 14	Pardubice, Czechoslovakia	110
1926, Sept. 5	Waco, CO	30	1962, Jan. 8	Woerden, Netherlands	91
1937, July 16	Bhita, India	107	1962, May 3	Tokyo, Japan	163
1938, June 19	Saugus, MT	47	1963, Nov. 9	Yokohama, Japan	120+
1939, Aug. 12	Harney, NV	24	1964, July 26	Porto, Portugal	94
1939, Dec. 22	Near Magdeburg, Germany	132	1967, July 6	Madgeburg, Germany	94
1939, Dec. 22	Near Friedrichshafen, Germany	99	1970, Feb. 1	Buenos Aires, Argentina	236
1940, Apr. 19	Little Falls, NY	31	1972, June 16	Vierzy, France	107
1940, July 31	Cuyahoga Falls, OH	43	1972, July 21	Seville, Spain	76
1943, Aug. 29	Wayland, NY	27	1972, Oct. 6	Saltillo, Mexico	208
1943, Sept. 6	Frankford Junction, Philad., PA	79	1972, Oct. 30	Chicago, IL	45
1943, Dec. 16	Between Rennert and Buie, NC	72	1974, Aug. 30	Zagreb, Yugoslavia	153
1944, Jan. 16	León Province, Spain	500	1975, Feb. 28	Subway train, London, England	41
1944, Mar. 2	Salerno, Italy	521	1977, Jan. 18	Granville, Australia	83
1944, July 6	High Bluff, TN	35	1981, June 6	Bihar, India	800+
1944, Aug. 4	Near Stockton, GA	47	1982, Jan. 27	El Asnam, Algeria	130
1944, Sept. 14	Dewey, IN	29	1982, July 11	Tepic, Mexico	120
1944, Dec. 31	Bagley, UT	50	1983, Feb. 19	Empalme, Mexico	100
1945, Aug. 9	Michigan, MI	34	1985, Feb. 23	Madhya Pradesh state, India	50
1946, Mar. 20	Aracaju, Mexico	185	1987, July 2	Kasumbalesha Shaba, Zaire	125
1946, Apr. 25	Naperville, IL	45	1988, June 27	Gare de Lyon train station, Paris	57
1947, Feb. 18	Gallitzin, PA	24	1988, Dec. 12	London, England	35
1949, Oct. 22	Near Dwor, Poland	200+	1989, Jan. 15	Maizdi Khan, Bangladesh	110+
1950, Feb. 17	Rockville Centre, NY	31	1989, June 9	Train collision with bus, S Russia	31
1950, Sept. 11	Coshocton, OH	33	1990, Jan. 4	Sindh Province, Pakistan	210+
1950, Nov. 22	Richmond Hill, NY	79	1991, May 14	Shigaraki, Japan	42
1951, Feb. 6	Woodbridge, NJ	84	1993, Sept. 22	Big Bayou Conot, AL	47
1952, Mar. 4	Near Rio de Janeiro, Brazil	119	1994, Mar. 8	Near Durban, South Africa	63
1952, July 9	Rzepin, Poland	160	1994, Sept. 22	Tolunda, Angola	300
1952, Oct. 8	Harrow, England	112	1995, Aug. 20	Firozabad, India	358
1953, Mar. 27	Conneaut, OH	21	1997, Mar. 3	Punjab prov., Pakistan	125
1955, Apr. 3	Guadalajara, Mexico	300	1997, Apr. 29	Rongjiawan, China	58
1956, Jan. 22	Los Angeles, CA	30	1997, May 4	Rwandan refugees crushed or suffocated on overcrowded trains, Kisangani, Zaire	109+
1957, Sept. 1	Kendal, Jamaica	178			
1957, Sept. 29	Montgomery, W Pakistan	250	1997, Sept. 14	Madhya Pradesh state, India	77
1957, Dec. 4	London, England	90	1998, June 3	Eschede, Germany	102
1958, May 8	Rio de Janeiro, Brazil	128	1998, Feb. 19	Yaounde, Cameroon	100+

Date	Location	Deaths	Date	Location	Deaths
1998, Nov. 26	Khanna, India	200+	2003, Jan. 3	Maharashtra, India	18
1998, Mar. 15	Bourbonnais, IL.	11	2003, Feb. 1	NW Zimbabwe	46
1999, Mar. 24	Nairobi, Kenya	32+	2003, May 8	Near Lake Balaton, Hungary	33
1999, Aug. 2	Gauhati, India	285+	2003, May 15	Ludhiana, India.	36
1999, Oct. 5	London, England.	31	2003, June 3	Albacete province, Spain	19
2000, Jan. 4	Rena, Norway.	35	2003, June 22	Rajapur, India.	33
2000, July 28	São Paulo, Brazil	12	2003, July 2	Andhra Pradesh state, India.	22
2000, Nov. 11	Kaprun, Austria	155	2004, Feb. 18	Neyshabur, NE Iran	300+
2001, Feb. 28	Great Heck, England	13	2004, Apr. 22	Ryongchon, North Korea	161
2001, June 22	Cochin, India.	64	2004, July 22	Mekece, NW Turkey.	36
2002, Feb. 20	S of Cairo, Egypt.	373	2005, Jan. 6	Graniteville, SC	8
2002, Apr. 18	Seville, FL.	4	2005, Jan. 26	Glendale, CA	11
2002, Apr. 23	Placentia, CA	2	2005, Apr. 25	Near Amagasaki, Japan.	107+
2002, May 25	Muamba, Mozambique	196+	2005, July 13	Ghotki, Pakistan	133
2002, June 24	Igandu, Tanzania	281+	2005, Oct. 29	Near Veligonda, India	114+
2002, Sept. 10	Bihar, India	118	2006, Jan. 26	Podgorica, Montenegro	46
2002, Nov. 6	Nancy, France	12	2007, Aug. 2	Nr. Benaleka, Dem. Rep. of Congo	70+

Some Notable U.S. Tornadoes Since 1925

Date	Location	Deaths	Date	Location	Deaths
1925, Mar. 18	MO, IL, IN	689	1969, Jan. 23	MS	32
1927, Apr. 12	Rocksprings, TX	74	1970, May 11	Lubbock, TX	23
1927, May 9	AR; Poplar Bluff, MO	92	1971, Feb. 21	Mississippi Delta: MS, LA, AR, TN.	110
1927, Sept. 29	St. Louis, MO	90	1973, May 26-27	South, Midwest.	47
1930, May 6	Hill, Navarro, Ellis Cos., TX	41	1974, Apr. 3-4	AL; GA; KY; Xenia, OH; other states	315
1932, Mar. 21	AL	268	1977, Apr. 4	AL, MS, GA	22
1936, Apr. 5-6	Tupelo, MS; Gainesville, GA.	454	1979, Apr. 10	TX, OK	60
1938, Sept. 29	Charleston, SC	32	1984, Mar. 28	NC, SC	57
1942, Mar. 16	Central to NE Mississippi	75	1985, May 31	NY, PA, OH, Ont.	75
1942, Apr. 27	Rogers and Mayes Cos., OK	52	1987, May 22	Saragosa, TX	30
1944, June 23	OH, PA, WV, MD	150	1989, Nov. 15	Huntsville, AL	18
1945, Apr. 12	OK, AR	102	1990, Aug. 28	Northern IL	25
1947, Apr. 9	TX; Woodward, OK; KS	181	1991, Apr. 26	KS, OK	23
1948, Mar. 19	Bunker Hill and Gillespie, IL	33	1992, Nov. 21-23	South, Midwest	26
1949, Jan. 3	LA, AR	58	1994, Mar. 27-28	AL, TN, GA, NC, SC.	52
1952, Mar. 21-22	AR, MO, TN	208	1995, May 6-7	S Oklahoma, N Texas	23
1953, May 11	Waco, TX	114	1997, Mar. 1	Central AR	26
1953, June 8	Flint-Beecher, MI; OH.	142	1997, May 27	Jarrell, TX.	27
1953, June 9	Worcester and vicinity, MA	90	1998, Feb. 22-23	Central FL	42
1953, Dec. 5	Vicksburg, MS.	38	1998, Apr. 8	AL, GA, MS	39
1955, May 25	Udall, KS; MO; Blackwell, OK; TX	115	1999, May 3	OK, KS	54
1957, May 20	KS, MO.	48	2000, Feb. 14	SW Georgia	22+
1958, June, 4	NW Wisconsin	30	2000, Dec. 16	AL.	12
1959, Feb. 10	St. Louis, MO	21	2001, Nov. 23-24	AL, AR, MS	13
1960, May 5, 6	Southeastern OK, AR	30	2002, Nov. 10-11	AL, MS, TN, IN, OH, PA.	36
1962, Mar. 31	Milton, FL	17	2003, May 4-11	TN, MO, KS, IL, OK, WV, AL	48
1965, Apr. 11	IA, IN, IL, OH, MI, WI	271	2004, Apr. 20-21	IL, IN	8
1966, Mar. 3	Jackson, MS.	57	2005, Nov. 6	KY, IN.	22
1966, Mar. 3	MS, AL	61	2006, Apr. 7-8	Central U.S., TX to WV	12
1967, Apr. 21	IL, MO, IA, MI	33	2007, Mar. 1	AL, GA, MO, Midwest U.S.	20
1968, May 15	Midwest	71	2007, May 4	Greensburg, KS	11

Principal U.S. Mine Disasters Since 1900

Source: Bureau of Mines, U.S. Dept. of the Interior; Mine Safety and Health Admin., U.S. Dept. of Labor; World Almanac research
(All are bituminous-coal mines unless otherwise noted.)

Date	Location	Deaths	Date	Location	Deaths	Date	Location	Deaths
1900, May 1	Scofield, UT	200	1913, Oct. 22	Dawson, NM	263	1940, Jan. 10	Bartley, WV	91
1902, May 19	Coal Creek, TN	184	1914, Apr. 28	Eccles, WV	181	1940, Mar. 16	St. Clairesville, OH.	72
1902, July 10	Johnstown, PA.	112	1915, Mar. 2	Layland, WV	115	1942, Mar. 26	Allentown, PA[3]	31
1903, June 30	Hanna, WY	169	1917, Apr. 27	Hastings, CO	121	1943, Feb. 27	Washoe, MT.	74
1904, Jan. 25	Cheswick, PA	179	1917, June 8	Butte, MT[1]	163	1947, Mar. 25	Centralia, IL	111
1905, Feb. 20	Virginia City, AL.	112	1919, June 5	Wilkes-Barre, PA[2]	92	1951, Dec. 21	West Frankfort, IL.	119
1907, Jan. 29	Stuart, WV	84	1922, Nov. 6	Spangler, PA	77	1968, Mar. 6	Belle Isle, LA[4]	21
1907, Dec. 6	Monongah, WV	362	1922, Nov. 22	Dolomite, AL	90	1968, Nov. 20	Farmington, WV	78
1907, Dec. 19	Jacobs Creek, PA	239	1923, Feb. 8	Dawson, NM	120	1972, May 2	Kellogg, ID[1]	91
1908, Nov. 28	Marianna, PA.	154	1923, Aug. 14	Kemmerer, WY	99	1976, Mar. 9	Oven Fork, KY	15
1909, Nov. 13	Cherry, IL.	259	1924, Mar. 8	Castle Gate, UT	172	1981, Apr. 15	Redstone, CO	15
1910, Jan. 31	Primero, CO.	75	1924, Apr. 28	Benwood, WV	119	1981, Dec. 8	Whitwell, TN.	13
1910, May 5	Palos, AL.	84	1926, Jan. 13	Wilburton, OK	91	1984, Dec. 19	Orangeville, UT	27
1910, Nov. 8	Delagua, CO	79	1926, Nov. 3	Ishpeming, MI[1]	51	1989, Sept. 13	Wheatcroft, KY.	10
1911, Apr. 8	Littleton, AL.	128	1927, Apr. 30	Everettville, WV	97	2001, Sept. 23	Brookwood, AL.	13
1911, Dec. 9	Briceville, TN	84	1928, May 19	Mather, PA.	195	2006, Jan. 2	Sago, WV	12
1912, Mar. 26	Jed, WV	83	1930, Nov. 5	Millfield, OH.	82	2007, Aug. 6	Huntington, UT.	6[5]
1913, Apr. 23	Finleyville, PA	98						

Note: World's worst mine disaster killed 1,549 workers in Manchuria, Apr. 25, 1942. (1) Metal mine. (2) Anthracite mine. (3) Limestone mine. (4) Salt mine. (5) Trapped after mine collapse, believed to be dead. Does not incl. deaths of 3 rescue workers in tunnel collapse.

Sinking of the *General Slocum*

Date: June 15, 1904. **Location:** New York, NY. **Fatalities:** 1,021.

The highest death toll of any incident in New York City prior to the Sept. 11, 2001, terrorist attacks. The *General Slocum* caught fire while on the East River. Most of its 1,300-1,500 passengers were women and children, German immigrants on a daylong church outing. Shortly after the ship launched, a fire erupted on board. The inexperienced crew didn't know how to respond, and the ship, which was in poor condition, lacked adequate safety measures. Those who didn't know how to swim died in the fire or drowned when they jumped into the water.

Some Notable Hurricanes, Typhoons, Blizzards, Other Storms

(As of mid-Sept. 2007)

H.—hurricane; T.—typhoon; TS.—tropical storm

Date	Location	Deaths
1881, Aug. 24-29	H., GA, SC	700
1888, Mar. 11-14	Blizzard, eastern U.S.	400
1893, Aug. 15-Sept. 2	H., GA, SC	1,000+
1893, Oct. 1	H., LA	1,100+
1900, Sept. 8	H., Galveston, TX	8,000+
1906, Sept. 19-24	H., LA, MS	350
1906, Sept. 18	T., Hong Kong	10,000+
1909, Sept. 20	H., LA	350+
1915, Aug. 16	H., Galveston, TX	275
1915, Sept. 29	H., LA	275
1919, Sept. 6-14	H., Carib., Florida Keys, Gulf, TX	600+[1]
1926, Sept. 11-22	H., FL, AL, MS	370+
1926, Oct. 20	H., Cuba	600
1928, Sept. 6-20	H., southern FL	2,500+
1930, Sept. 3	H., Dominican Republic	2,000
1935, Aug. 29-Sept. 10	H., Caribbean, SE U.S.	400+
1937, Sept. 2	T., "The Great Typhoon," Hong Kong	10,000+
1938, Sept. 21	H., Long Isl., NY; New England	287[2]
1940, Nov. 11-12	Blizzard, NE, Midwest U.S.	144
1942, Oct. 15-16	H., Bengal, India	40,000
1947, Dec. 26	Blizzard, NYC, N Atlan. states	55
1952, Oct. 22	T., Philippines	440
1954, Aug. 30	H. Carol, northeastern U.S.	68
1954, Oct. 5-18	H. Hazel, E Canada, U.S., Haiti	347
1955, Aug. 12-13	H. Connie, NC, SC, VA, MD	43
1955, Aug. 7-21	H. Diane, eastern U.S.	400
1955, Sept. 19	H. Hilda, Mexico	200
1956, Feb. 1-29	Blizzard, W Europe	1,000
1957, June 25-30	H. Audrey, TX to AL	390
1958, Feb. 15-16	Blizzard, NE U.S.	171
1959, Sept. 17-19	T. Sarah, Japan, S. Korea	2,000
1959, Sept. 26-27	T. Vera, Honshu, Japan	4,466
1960, Sept. 4-12	H. Donna, Caribbean, E U.S.	148
1961, Oct. 31	H. Hattie, Br. Honduras	400
1962, Sept. 1	T. Wanda, Hong Kong	130-200
1963, May 28-29	Windstorm, Bangladesh	22,000
1963, Oct. 4-8	H. Flora, Caribbean	6,000
1964, June 30	T. Winnie, N Philippines	107
1964, Sept. 5	T. Ruby, Hong Kong and China	735
1965, May 11-12	Windstorm, Bangladesh	17,000
1965, June 1-2	Windstorm, Bangladesh	30,000
1965, Sept. 7-12	H. Betsy, FL, MS, LA	74
1965, Dec. 15	Windstorm, Bangladesh	10,000
1966, June 4-10	H. Alma, Honduras, SE U.S.	51
1966, Sept. 24-30	H. Inez, Carib., FL, Mexico	293
1967, July 9	T. Billie, SW Japan	347
1967, Sept. 5-23	H. Beulah, Carib., Mex., TX	54
1967, Dec. 12-20	Blizzard, SW U.S.	51
1968, Nov. 18-28	T. Nina, Philippines	63
1969, Aug. 17-18	H. Camille, MS, LA	256
1970, Sept. 15	T. Georgia, Philippines	300
1970, Oct. 14	T. Sening, Philippines	583
1970, Oct. 15	T. Titang, Philippines	526
1970, Nov. 13	Cyclone, Bangladesh	300,000
1971, Aug. 1	T. Rose, Hong Kong	130
1972, June 19-29	H. Agnes, FL to NY	118
1972, Dec. 3	T. Theresa, Philippines	169
1973, June-Aug.	Monsoon rains, India	1,217
1974, June 11	TS. Dinah, Luzon Isl., Philippines	71
1974, July 11	T. Gilda, Japan, S. Korea	108
1974, Sept. 19-20	H. Fifi, Honduras	2,000
1974, Dec. 25	Cyclone, Darwin, Australia	50
1975, Sept. 13-27	H. Eloise, Caribbean, NE U.S.	71
1976, May 20	T. Olga, floods, Philippines	215
1976, Sept. 25-Oct. 2	H. Liza, W Mexico	630
1978, Oct. 27	T. Rita, Philippines	400
1979, Aug. 30-Sept. 7	H. David, Caribbean, E U.S.	1,100
1980, Aug. 4-11	H. Allen, Caribbean, TX	272
1981, Nov. 25	T. Irma, Luzon Isl., Philippines	176
1983, June	Monsoon, India	900
1984, Sept. 2	T. Ike, S Philippines	1,363
1985, May 25	Cyclone, Bangladesh	10,000
1985, Oct. 26-Nov. 6	H. Juan, SE U.S.	97
1987, Nov. 25	T. Nina, Philippines	650
1988, Sept. 10-17	H. Gilbert, Carib., Gulf of Mex.	260
1989, Sept. 16-22	H. Hugo, Caribbean, SE U.S.	86
1990, May 6-11	Cyclones, SE India	450
1991, Apr. 30	Cyclone, Bangladesh	139,000
1991, Nov. 5	TS. Thelma, flash floods, central Philippines	7,000+
1992, Aug. 24-26	H. Andrew, southern FL, LA	65
1993, Mar. 12-14	Blizzard, E U.S.	270+
1993, June	Monsoon, Bangladesh	2,000
1994, Nov. 8-18	TS. Gordon, Caribbean, FL	830
1995, Oct. 2-4	H. Opal, S Mexico, FL, AL	59
1995, Nov. 2-3	T. Angela, Philippines	600+
1996, Jan. 7-8	Blizzard, NE U.S.	100
1996, Aug. 22	Blizzard, Himalayas, N India	239
1996, Aug. 29-Sept. 6	H. Fran, Carib., NC, VA, WV	30
1996, Sept. 9	T. Sally, S China	114
1996, Nov. 6	Cyclone, Andhra Pradesh, India	1,000+
1996, Nov. 24-25	Ice storms, TX to MO	26
1996, Dec. 25	TS. Greg, E Malaysia	100+
1997, May 19	Cyclone, Bangladesh	108
1997, Aug. 18-21	T. Winnie, Taiwan, E China.	140+
1997, Oct. 8-10	H. Pauline, SW Mexico	230
1998, June 9	Cyclone, Gujarat, India	1,320
1998, Aug.	Monsoon, Bangladesh.	326
1998, Sept. 21-23	H. Georges, Carib., FL, U.S. Gulf	600+
1998, Oct. 27-29	H. Mitch, Honduras, Nicaragua, Guatemala, El Salvador	10,866+
1999, Sept. 4-17	H. Floyd, Baha., E seaboard U.S	56
1999, Oct. 29	Cyclone, E India	9,392
1999, Dec. 26-29	Gales, France, Switz., Germany	120
2000, Dec. 27	Winter storm, TX, OK, AR	40+
2001, July 30	T. Toraji, Taiwan	200
2001, Nov. 2-5	H. Michelle, Cuba, Jamaica.	17
2001, Nov. 6-12	T. Lingling, S Philip., Vietnam	220+
2002, July 1-11	T. Chata'an, Micron., Philip., Jap.	70+
2002, Aug.-Sept.	T. Rusa, N. & S. Korea	115+
2003, Feb. 16-17	Blizzard, E seaboard U.S.	59
2003, Sept. 12	T. Maemi, S. Korea	130
2003, Sept. 7-19	H. Isabel, NC, VA E seaboard.	40+
2003, Dec. 17	Cyclone, southern India	50
2004, Jan. 26-Feb. 4	Cyclone Elita, Madagascar	29
2004, Mar. 7-19	Cyclone Gafilo, Madagascar	198
2004, May 19	Cyclone, Myanmar	220
2004, Aug. 12-15	T. Rananim, E China	164
2004, Aug. 13-14	H. Charley, FL, SC	36
2004, Aug. 24-Sept. 10	T. Aere, China, Taiwan, Philip.	67
2004, Sept. 5-6	H. Frances, Bahamas, Florida.	35
2004, Sept. 7-16	H. Ivan, Barbados, Grenada, U.S. Gulf Coast	115
2004, Sept. 16-26	H. Jeanne, Dom. Rep., Haiti, FL	1,500+
2005, July 7-11	H. Dennis, Jamaica, Haiti, Cuba, FL	50
2005, Aug. 25-29	H. Katrina, LA, MS, FL, AL, GA.	1,833+[3]
2005, Aug. 31-Sept. 1	T. Talim, Taiwan; E China	129+
2005, Sept. 21-24	H. Rita, TX, LA	62[4]
2005, Sept. 21-28	T. Damrey, SE Asia; Philippines; Hainan, China	145
2005, Oct. 4	H. Stan, Central Amer., Mex.	1,000+[5]
2006, Jul. 14	TS. Bilis, SE China	612
2006, Aug. 10	T. Saomai, SE China	295
2006, Nov. 30	T. Durian, landslides, Philippines	450-1,000+
2007, June 6-7	Cyclone Gonu, Oman, Iran	54[6]

(1) Incl. about 500 lost on ships at sea. (2) 600 incl. offshore deaths and deaths from flooding that started Sept. 12. (3) Official toll as of Aug. 2006 was 1,577 in LA, 238 in MS, 14 in FL, and 2 each in AL and GA. (4) Incl. 35 indirect deaths, among them 20 people, mostly elderly evacuees froma nursing home, whose bus exploded and caught fire oustide Dallas. (5) Incl. deaths from floods and landslides generated by heavy rainstorms. (6) First documented super cyclone in Arabian Sea.

The "Storm of the Century"

Dates: Mar. 12-14, 1993. **Location:** East Coast, U.S. **Fatalities:** 270+. **Damages:** $5-6 bil.

One of the worst winter storms to strike the eastern U.S. About 90 mil people were subjected to high wind gusts (max. 71-144 mph) and record low temperatures, from 31° in FL to –12°F in VT and ME. Snowfall totals ranged from 4 in. to 56 in. A reported 15 tornadoes struck FL, causing deadly storm surges. For the first time, every major airport on the East Coast experienced closings because of the storm. The National Weather Service estimated that 44 mil acre-ft of water fell as snow during the storm—comparable to the volume of water in the Mississippi R. that flows past New Orleans in 40 days.

Some Notable Floods, Tidal Waves

Date	Location	Deaths	Date	Location	Deaths
1703	Awa, Japan	100,000+	1995, Dec. 25	KwaZulu Natal, South Africa	166
1889, May 31	Johnstown, PA	2,200+	1996, Feb. 17	Biak Isl., Indonesia	105
1903, June 15	Heppner, OR	325	1996, April	Afghanistan	100+
1911	Chang Jiang R., China	100,000	1996, June-July	S China	950+
1913, Mar. 25-27	OH, IN	732	1996, Aug. 7	Pyrenees Mts., Spain	71
1915, Aug. 17	Galveston, TX	275	1997, Mar.	Ohio R. Valley	35
1927, Jan.-July	Mississippi Valley	246+	1997, July	Poland, Czech Republic	98
1928, Mar. 13	Dam collapse, Saugus, CA	450	1997, Nov.	Spanish-Portuguese border	31+
1928, Sept. 16	Lake Okeechobee, FL	1,770+	1997, Nov.	Bardera, Somalia	1,300+
1931, Aug.	Huang He R., China	3,700,000	1998, Jan.	Kenya	86
1937, Jan. 22	OH, MS valleys	250	1998, Feb.	CA to Tijuana, Mexico	30+
1939	N China	200,000	1998, Mar.	SW Pakistan	300+
1946, Apr. 1	HI, AK	159	1998, July-Aug.	China	4,150
1947, Sept. 20	Honshu Isl., Japan	1,900	1998, July-Sept.	Bangladesh	1,441
1951, Aug.	Manchuria	1,800	1998, July 17	Papua New Guinea	3,000
1953, Jan. 31	W Europe	2,000	1999, Aug. 1-4	Philippines, SE Asia	188+
1954, Aug. 17	Farahzad, Iran	2,000	1999, Sept.-Oct.	NE Mexico	350+
1955, Oct. 7-12	India, Pakistan	1,700	1999, Oct.-Dec.	Central Vietnam	700+
1959, Nov. 1	W Mexico	2,000	1999, Feb. 6-11	Botswana	70+
1959, Dec. 2	Frejus, France	412	1999, Dec. 15-17	NW Venezuela	9,000+
1960, Oct. 10	Bangladesh	6,000	2000, Feb.-Mar.	Madagascar	150+
1960, Oct. 31	Bangladesh	4,000	2000, Feb.-Mar.	Mozambique	700
1962, Feb. 17	North Sea coast, Germany	343	2000, May 17	Timor Island	50+
1962, Sept. 27	Barcelona, Spain	445	2000, Aug. 2	Himachal Pradesh, India	120+
1963, Oct. 9	Dam collapse, Vaiont, Italy	1,800	2000, Aug. 2	Bhutan	200+
1966, Nov. 3-4	Florence, Venice, Italy	113	2000, Sept. 19-30	India, Bangladesh	1,000+
1967, Jan. 18-24	E Brazil	894	2000, Oct. 12-17	France, Brit., Italy, Switz.	35
1967, Mar. 19	Rio de Janeiro, Brazil	436	2001, Jan.-Feb.	Mozambique	84+
1967, Nov. 26	Lisbon, Portugal	464	2001, Aug.-Nov.	S Vietnam, Cambodia	360+
1968, Aug. 7-14	Gujarat state, India	1,000	2001, Aug. 1-6	Taiwan	100+
1968, Oct. 7	NE India	780	2001, Aug. 10-12	NE Iran	247
1969, Jan. 18-26	Southern CA	100	2001, Aug.	N Thailand	170
1969, Mar. 17	Mundau Valley, Alagoas, Brazil	218	2001, Nov. 9-10	N Algeria	711+
1969, Aug. 20-22	Western VA	189	2001, Dec. 23-31	Rio de Janeiro	66
1969, Sept. 15	South Korea	250	2002, Jan. 30-Feb. 15	Java Isl., Indonesia	147
1969, Oct. 1-8	Tunisia	500	2002, Feb. 19	La Paz, Bolivia	65
1970, May 20	Central Romania	160	2002, Apr.-May	E Africa	150+
1970, July 22	Himalayas, India	500	2002, early May	MO, IL, IN, WV, VA KY	20
1971, Feb. 26	Rio de Janeiro, Brazil	130	2002, Apr.-Aug.	China	800+
1972, Feb. 26	Buffalo Creek, WV	118	2002, July-Aug.	India, Nepal, Bangladesh	1,100+
1972, June 9	Rapid City, SD	238	2002, Aug.	Russia	110
1972, Aug. 7	Luzon Isl., Philippines	454	2002, Aug.	Germany, Hungary, Austria, Czech Rep.	100+
1972, Aug. 19-31	Pakistan	1,500	2003, May 17-27	Sri Lanka	250
1974, Mar. 29	Tubarao, Brazil	1,000	2003, Aug.-mid-Sept.	E India	200+
1974, Aug. 12	Monty-Long, Bangladesh	2,500	2003, early Nov.	Sumatra, Indonesia	65+
1976, June 5	Teton Dam collapse, ID	11	2003, Dec. 10-Jan. 23, 2004	Sumatra, Indonesia	148
1976, July 31	Big Thompson Canyon, CO	140	2003, Dec. 19-Jan. 7, 2004	Central Philippines	200
1976, Nov. 17	East Java, Indonesia	136	2004, Jan. 10-Mar. 8	Brazil	161
1977, July 19-20	Johnstown, PA	68	2004, Apr. 4-6	Coahuila, N Mexico	37
1977, Nov. 6	Toccoa, GA	39	2004, Apr. 9-May 11	W Kenya	50
1978, June-Sept.	N India	1,200	2004, Apr. 12-16	Djibouti City, Djibouti	53
1979, Jan.-Feb.	Brazil	204	2004, May 23-25	Dom. Republic, Haiti	2,000
1979, July 17	Lomblem Isl., Indonesia	539	2004, June-Sept.	Banglad., India, Myan., Nepal	2,000+
1979, Aug. 11	Morvi, India	15,000	2004, June-Sept.	China	500
1981, Apr.	N China	550	2004, Aug. 8-12	NE Nigeria	65
1981, July	Sichuan, Hubei Prov., China	1,300	2004, Nov-Dec.	Philippines	1,060+
1982, Jan. 23	Near Lima, Peru	600	2004, Dec. 26	12 Indian Ocean nations, espec. Indonesia, Sri Lanka, India, Thailand	226,328[1]
1982, May 12	Guangdong, China	430			
1982, Sept. 17-21	El Salvador, Guatemala	1,300+	2005, July 26-Aug. 2	W Maharashtra state, India	1,000+
1984, Aug-Sept.	South Korea	200+	2005, Aug. 21-23	Central Eur., espec. Romania	67
1985, July 19	Dam collapse, N Italy	361	2006, Feb. 17	Landslides fr. heavy rain, Leyte Isl., Philippines	137+
1987, Aug.-Sept.	N Bangladesh	1,000+			
1988, Sept.	N India	1,000+	2006, July 17	S of Java, Indonesia	530+
1990, June 14	Shadyside, OH	26	2007, Aug. 19-27	MN, WI, OH, Midwest U.S.	25
1993, July-Aug.	ND, SD, NE, KS, MN, IA, MO, WI, IL	47			
1995, Jan. 30-Feb. 9	NW Europe	40			
1995, July	NE China	1,200			
1995, Aug. 19	SW Morocco	136			

(1) Based on official estimates assembled by the Intl. Fed. of Red Cross and Red Crescent Societies, including 50,773 missing; as reported Dec. 15, 2005. The nearly 176,300 listed as dead include 128,645 from Indonesia; 31,147 from Sri Lanka; 10,749 from India; and 5,395 from Thailand.

Hurricane Katrina

Dates: Aug. 25-29, 2005. **Location:** FL, LA, MS, AL, other inland states. **Fatalities:** 1,833+. **Damages:** $125 bil.

The costliest storm to date in U.S. history first made landfall in SE Florida, Aug. 25, as a Category 1 hurricane. Katrina brought heavy rains that led to flooding in the FL peninsula. Katrina then weakened slightly, strengthened over the Gulf of Mexico, but was downgraded again to Category 3 status before hitting land south of Buras, LA, on Aug. 29. Despite weakening, Katrina caused massive storm surges measuring up to 25-28 ft. throughout SE Louisiana, S Mississippi, and SW Alabama. These storm surges, combined with strong winds and heavy rainfall, contributed to the failure of New Orleans' levee system Aug. 30. About 80% of the city eventually flooded. Approximately 1 mil were displaced from their homes.

Some Major Earthquakes

Source: Global Volcanism Network, Smithsonian Institution; U.S. Geological Survey, U.S. Dept. of the Interior; World Almanac research
Magnitude of earthquakes (mag.) is measured on the Richter scale; an increase of one whole point represents a release of about 30 times more energy. Adopted in 1935, the scale is applied to earthquakes as far back as reliable seismograms are available, but earlier figures should be considered estimates.

Date	Location	Deaths	Mag.	Date	Location	Deaths	Mag.
526, May 20	Antioch, Syria	250,000	NA	1978, Sept. 16	NE Iran	15,000	7.8
856	Corinth, Greece	45,000	NA	1979, Sept. 12	Indonesia	100	8.1
856, Dec. 22	Damghan, Iran	200,000	NA	1979, Dec. 12	Colombia, Ecuador	800	7.9
893, Mar. 23	Ardabil, Iran	150,000	NA	1980, Oct. 10	NW Algeria	3,500	7.7
1057	Chihli, China	25,000	NA	1980, Nov. 23	S Italy	3,000	7.2
1138, Aug. 9	Aleppo, Syria	230,000	NA	1981, June 11	S Iran	3,000	6.9
1169, Feb. 11	Nr. Mt. Etna, Sicily	15,000	NA1	1981, July 28	S Iran	1,500	7.3
1268	Cilicia, Asia Minor	60,000	NA	1982, Dec. 13	W Arabian Peninsula	2,800	6.0
1290, Sept. 27	Chihli, China	100,000	NA	1983, Oct. 30	E Turkey	1,342	6.9
1293, May 20	Kamakura, Japan	30,000	NA	1985, Mar. 3	Chile	146	7.8
1531, Jan. 26	Lisbon, Portugal	30,000	NA	1985, Sept. 19	Michoacan, Mexico	9,500	8.1
1556, Jan. 24	Shaanxi, China	830,000	NA	1986, Oct. 10	El Salvador	1,000+	5.5
1667, Nov.	Shemakha, Caucasia	80,000	NA	1987, Mar. 6	Colombia-Ecuador	4,000+	7.0
1693, Jan. 11	Catania, Italy	60,000	NA	1988, Aug. 20	India-Nepal border	1,450	6.6
1737, Oct. 11	India, Calcutta	300,000	NA	1988, Nov. 6	China-Burma border	1,000	7.3
1755, June 7	N Persia	40,000	NA	1988, Dec. 7	Soviet Armenia	55,000	7.0
1755, Nov. 1	Lisbon, Portugal	60,000	8.75²	1989, Oct. 17	San Francisco Bay area	63	6.9
1783, Feb. 4	Calabria, Italy	30,000	NA	1990, May 30	N Peru	115	6.3
1797, Feb. 4	Quito, Ecuador	41,000	NA	1990, June 20	W Iran	40,000+	7.7
1822, Sept. 5	Asia Minor, Aleppo	22,000	NA	1990, July 16	Luzon, Philippines	1,621	7.8
1828, Dec. 28	Echigo, Japan	30,000	NA	1991, Feb. 1	Pakistan-Afgh. border	1,200	6.8
1868, Aug. 13-15	Peru, Ecuador	40,000	NA	1991, Oct. 19	N India	2,000	7.0
1875, May 16	Venezuela, Colombia	16,000	NA	1992, Mar. 13, 15	E Turkey	4,000	6.2/6.0
1886, Aug. 31	Charleston, SC	60	6.6	1992, June 28	S California	1	7.5/6.6
1896, June 15	Sea wave, Japan	27,120	NA	1992, Sept. 1	SW Nicaragua	116	7.0
1905, Apr. 4	Kangra, India	19,000	8.6	1992, Oct. 12	Cairo, Egypt	450	5.9
1906, Apr. 18-19	San Francisco, CA	3,000+	7.7³	1992, Dec. 12	Flores Isl., Indonesia	2,500	7.5
1906, Aug. 17	Valparaiso, Chile	20,000	8.6	1993, July 12	Nr. Hokkaido, Japan	200+	7.7
1907, Oct. 21	Central Asia	12,000	8.1	1993, Sept. 30	Maharashtra, S India	9,748	6.3⁶
1908, Dec. 28	Messina, Italy	83,000	7.5	1994, Jan. 17	Northridge, CA	61	6.8
1915, Jan. 13	Avezzano, Italy	29,980	7.5	1994, Feb. 15	S Sumatra, Indonesia	215	7.0
1918, Oct. 11	Mona Passage, PR	116	7.5	1994, June 6	Cauca, SW Colombia	1,000	6.8
1920, Dec. 16	Gansu, China	200,000	8.6	1994, Aug. 19	N Algeria	164	6.0
1923, Sept. 1	Yokohama, Japan	143,000	8.3	1995, Jan. 16	Kobe, Japan	5,502	6.9
1925, Mar. 16	Yunnan, China	5,000	7.1	1995, May 27	Sakhalin Isl., Russia	1,989	7.5
1927, May 22	Tsinghai, China	200,000	8.3	1996, Feb. 3	SW China	200+	7.0
1932, Dec. 25	Gansu, China	70,000	7.6	1997, Feb. 27	W Pakistan	100+	7.3
1933, Mar. 2	Japan	2,990	8.9	1997, Feb. 28	NW Iran	1,000+	6.1
1933, Mar. 10	Long Beach, CA	115	6.2	1997, May 10	N Iran	1,560	7.5
1934, Jan. 15	India, Bihar-Nepal	10,700	8.4	1998, Feb. 4, 8	Takhar Prov., NE Afghan.	2,323	6.1
1935, Apr. 21	Taiwan	3,276	7.4	1998, May 22	Central Bolivia	105	6.5
1935, May 30	Quetta, Pakistan	50,000	7.5	1998, May 30	NE Afghanistan	4,700+	6.9
1939, Jan. 25	Chillan, Chile	28,000	8.3	1998, June 27	Adana, Turkey	144	6.3
1939, Dec. 26	Erzincan, Turkey	30,000	8.0	1999, Jan. 25	Armenia, Colombia	1,185+	6.0
1946, Dec. 20	Honshu, Japan	1,330	8.4	1999, Aug. 17	Western Turkey	17,200+	7.4
1948, June 28	Fukui, Japan	5,390	7.3	1999, Sept. 7	Athens, Greece	143	5.9
1948, Oct. 5	Ashgabat, Turkmenistan	110,000	7.3	1999, Sept. 21	Taichung, Taiwan	2,474	7.6
1949, Aug. 5	Pelileo, Ecuador	6,000	6.8	1999, Nov. 12	Duzce, Turkey	675+	7.2
1950, Aug. 15	Assam, India	1,530	8.7	2000, June 4	Sumatra, Indonesia	103	7.9
1953, Mar. 18	NW Turkey	1,200	7.2	2001, Jan. 13	San Vicente, El Salvador	800+	7.6
1956, June 10-17	N Afghanistan	2,000	7.7	2001, Jan. 26	Gujarat, India	20,000+	7.9
1957, July 2	N Iran	1,200	7.4	2001, Feb. 13	San Vicente, El Salvador	255	6.6
1957, Dec. 13	W Iran	1,130	7.3	2001, June 23	Arequipa, Peru	102	8.1
1960, Feb. 29	Agadir, Morocco	12,000	5.9	2002, Feb. 3	Central Turkey	44+	6.5
1960, May 21-30	S Chile	5,000	9.5⁴	2002, Mar. 3	N Afghanistan	166	7.4
1962, Sept. 1	NW Iran	12,230	7.3	2002, Mar. 25-26	Nahrin, N Afghanistan	1,000+	6.1
1963, July 26	Skopje, Yugoslavia	1,100	6.0	2002, Apr. 12	Hindu Kush, Afghanistan	50+	5.9
1964, Mar. 27	Alaska	131	9.2⁵	2002, June 22	W Iran	261+	6.5
1966, Aug. 19	E Turkey	2,520	7.1	2003, Jan. 22	Colima, Mexico	29	7.6
1968, Aug. 31	NE Iran	12,000	7.3	2003, Feb. 24	S Xinjiang Prov., China	261	6.4
1970, Jan. 5	Yunnan Prov., China	15,621	7.7	2003, May 1	E Turkey	177	6.4
1970, Mar. 28	W Turkey	1,100	7.3	2003, May 21	N Algeria	2,200+	6.8
1970, May 31	N Peru	66,000	7.8	2003, Dec. 26	Bam, SE Iran	26,271	6.6
1971, Feb. 9	San Fernando Val., CA	65	6.6	2004, Feb. 4	Papua, Indonesia	37	7.0
1972, Apr. 10	S Iran	5,054	7.1	2004, Feb. 14	NW Pakistan	24	5.5
1972, Dec. 23	Managua, Nicaragua	5,000	6.2	2004, Feb. 24	Al Hoceima, NE Morocco	629	6.4
1974, Dec. 28	Pakistan	5,200	6.3	2004, May 28	N Iran	35	6.3
1975, Sept. 6	Turkey	2,300	6.7	2004, Dec. 26	Nr. Sumatra, Indonesia	226,328	9.3⁷
1976, Feb. 4	Guatemala	23,000	7.5	2005, Feb. 22	Central Iran	549	6.4
1976, May 6	NE Italy	1,000	6.5	2005, Mar. 28	Isls. off Sumatra, Indon.	1,000+	8.7
1976, June 25	Irian Jaya, New Guinea	422	7.1	2005, Oct. 8	Kashmir, Pakistan, India	80,000+	7.6
1976, July 27	Tangshan, China	255,000	8.0	2006, Mar. 31	W Iran	70+	6.1
1976, Aug. 16	Mindanao, Philippines	8,000	7.8	2006, May 27	Java, Indonesia	6,200+	6.3
1976, Nov. 24	NW Iran-USSR border	5,000	7.3	2006, July 17	S of Java, Indonesia	530+	7.7
1977, Mar. 4	Romania	1,500	7.2	2007, Mar. 6	S Sumatra, Indonesia	70	6.4
1977, Aug. 19	Indonesia	200	8.0	2007, Aug. 15	Nr. coast of central Peru	519	8.0

*Estimated from earthquake intensity. NA = Not available. (1) Once thought to have been a volcanic eruption; evidence indicates a destructive earthquake and tsunami occurred on this date. (2) This earthquake caused the most deadly tsunami to have occurred to date in the Atlantic Ocean. (3) Total estimate includes deaths from resulting fires; revised estimates of magnitude range from 7.7 to 7.9. (4) This, the largest recorded earthquake ever, caused a deadly tsunami that spread across the Pacific Ocean as far as Japan. (5) The "Good Friday" earthquake sent a tsunami that hit British Columbia, Canada, and the U.S. Pacific coast. (6) Official death toll from Indian government. Other sources reported estimates of about 30,000 deaths. (7) This undersea earthquake triggered devastating tsunamis that hit 12 Indian Ocean nations. See listing above under Floods; see also Nations of the World.

Some Notable Fires Since 1930

(See also Some Notable Explosions Since 1920.)

Date	Location	Deaths	Date	Location	Deaths
1930, Apr. 21	Penitentiary, Columbus, OH	320	1982, Sept. 4	Apt. house, Los Angeles, CA	24
1931, July 24	Home for aged, Pittsburgh, PA	48	1982, Nov. 8	County jail, Biloxi, MS	29
1934, Dec. 11	Hotel Kerns, Lansing, MI	34	1983, Feb. 13	Movie theater, Turin, Italy	64
1938, May 16	Terminal Hotel, Atlanta, GA	35	1983, Dec. 17	Discotheque, Madrid, Spain	83
1940, Apr. 23	Nightclub, Natchez, MS	198	1984, May 11	Great Adventure Amusement Pk., NJ	8
1942, Nov. 28	Cocoanut Grove Nightclub, Boston, MA	492	1985, Apr. 21	Movie theaters, Tabaco, Philippines	44
1942, Dec. 12	Hostel, St. John's, NL, Canada	100	1985, Apr. 26	Hospital, Buenos Aires, Argentina	79
1943, Sept. 7	Gulf Hotel, Houston, TX	55	1985, May 11	Soccer stadium, Bradford, England	53
1944, July 6	Ringling Circus, Hartford, CT	168	1985, May 13	MOVE headquarters, row houses,	
1946, June 5	LaSalle Hotel, Chicago, IL	61		Philadelphia, PA	11
1946, Dec. 7	Winecoff Hotel, Atlanta, GA	119	1986, Dec. 31	Dupont Plaza Hotel, Puerto Rico	96
1946, Dec. 12	Ice plant, tenement, New York, NY	37	1987, May 6-	
1949, Apr. 5	Hospital, Effingham, IL	77	June 2	Forest fire, N China	193
1950, Jan. 7	Mercy Hospital, Davenport, IA	41	1987, Nov. 17	Subway, London, England	30
1953, Mar. 29	Nursing home, Largo, FL	35	1988, Mar. 20	2000 buildings, Lashio, Burma	134
1953, Apr. 16	Metalworking plant, Chicago, IL	35	1990, Mar. 25	Social club, Bronx, NY	87
1957, Feb. 17	Home for aged, Warrenton, MO	72	1991, Mar. 3	Munitions dump, Addis Ababa, Ethiopia	260+
1958, Mar. 19	Loft building, New York, NY	24	1991, Sept. 3	Processing plant, Hamlet, NC	25
1958, Dec. 1	Parochial school, Chicago, IL	95	1991, Oct. 20-21	Wildfire, Oakland, Berkeley, CA	24
1958, Dec. 16	Store, Bogotá, Colombia	83	1993, Apr. 19	Cult compound, Waco, TX	72
1959, June 23	Resort hotel, Stalheim, Norway	34	1994, May 10	Toy factory, Bangkok, Thailand	213
1960, Mar. 12	Chemical plant, Pusan, Korea	68	1994, July 4-10	(Firefighters) Glenwood Springs, CO	14
1960, July 14	Mental hospital, Guatemala City	225	1994, Nov. 2	Burning fuel flood, Durunka, Egypt	500
1960, Nov. 13	Movie theater, Amude, Syria	152	1994, Dec. 10	Theater, Karamay, China	300
1960, Dec. 19	USS *Constellation*, Brooklyn, NY	49	1995, Oct. 28	Subway train, Baku, Azerbaijan	300
1961, Jan. 6	Thomas Hotel, San Francisco, CA	20	1995, Dec. 23	School, Mandi Dabwali, India	500+
1961, Dec. 8	Hospital, Hartford, CT	16	1996, Mar. 19	Nightclub, Quezon City, Philippines	150+
1961, Dec. 17	Circus, Niteroi, Brazil	323	1996, Mar. 28	Shopping mall, Bogor, Indonesia	78
1963, May 4	Theater, Diourbel, Senegal	64	1996, Oct. 22	Jail, Caracas, Venezuela	25
1963, Nov. 18	Surfside Hotel, Atlantic City, NJ	25	1996, Nov. 20	Building, Hong Kong	39
1963, Nov. 23	Rest home, Fitchville, OH	63	1997, Feb. 23	Worship site, Baripada, India	164
1963, Dec. 29	Roosevelt Hotel, Jacksonville, FL	22	1997, Apr. 15	Encampment, Mina, Saudi Arabia	343
1964, May 8	Apt. bldg., Manila, Philippines	30	1997, June 7	Temple, Thanjavur, India	60+
1964, Dec. 18	Nursing home, Fountaintown, IN.	20	1997, June 13	Movie theater, New Delhi, India	60+
1965, Mar. 1	Apartment, LaSalle, Quebec	28	1997, July 11	Hotel, Pattaya, Thailand	90
1965, Aug. 11-16	Watts riot fires, Los Angeles, CA	30+	1997, Sept. 29	Children's home, nr. Colina, Chile	30
1966, Mar. 11	2 ski resorts, Numata, Japan	31	1998, Dec. 3	Orphanage, Manila, Philippines	28
1966, Oct. 17	Bldg. (firefighters), New York, NY	12	1999, Mar. 24	Mt. Blanc Tunnel, France and Italy	40
1966, Dec. 7	Barracks, Erzurum, Turkey	68	1999, Oct. 30	Karaoke salon, Inchon, S. Korea	55+
1967, Feb. 7	Restaurant, Montgomery, AL	25	2000, Mar. 17	Church, Kanungu, Uganda	530
1967, May 22	Store, Brussels, Belgium	322	2000, Oct. 20	Nightclub, Mexico City, Mexico	20
1967, July 16	State prison, Jay, FL	37	2000, Nov. 11	Cable car, Kaprun, Austria	155
1967, July 29	USS *Forrestal*, off N Vietnam	134	2000, Dec. 25	Shopping center, Luoyang, China	309
1968, May 11	Wedding hall, Vijayawada, India	58	2001, Jan. 1	Cafe, Volendam, Netherlands	10
1969, Dec. 2	Nursing home, Notre Dame, Can.	54	2001, Mar. 6	School, Central China	41
1970, Jan. 9	Nursing home, Marietta, OH	27	2001, Mar. 26	School, Machakos, Kenya	64
1970, Nov. 1	Dance hall, Grenoble, France	145	2001, Aug. 6	Home for mentally ill, Madras, India	27
1970, Dec. 20	Hotel, Tucson, AZ	28	2001, Aug. 18	Hotel, Quezon City, Philippines	73
1971, Dec., 25	Hotel, Seoul, South Korea	162	2001, Sept. 1	Nightclub, Tokyo, Japan	44
1972, May 13	Nightclub, Osaka, Japan	116	2001, Oct. 24	St. Gotthard Tunnel, Swiss Alps	11
1972, July 5	Hospital, Sherborne, England	30	2001, Dec. 29	Fireworks accident, Lima, Peru	291
1973, June 24	Bar, New Orleans, LA	32	2002, Mar. 11	Girls' school, Mecca, Saudi Arabia	15
1973, Aug. 3	Amusement park, Isle of Man, Eng.	51	2002, June 16	Internet cafe, Beijing, China	24
1973, Sept. 1	Hotel, Copenhagen, Denmark	35	2002, July 7	Coal mine, Donetsk region, Ukraine	34+
1973, Nov. 29	Dept. store, Kumamoto, Japan	107	2002, July 20	Disco, Lima, Peru	25+
1973, Dec. 2	Theater, Seoul, South Korea	50	2002, July 31	Coal mine, Donetsk region, Ukraine	20
1974, Feb. 1	Bank building, São Paulo, Brazil	189	2003, Feb. 18	Subway train, Taegu, S. Korea	198
1974, June 30	Discotheque, Port Chester, NY	24	2003, Feb. 20	Nightclub (pyrotechnics), Warwick, RI	100
1974, Nov. 3	Hotel, disco, Seoul, S. Korea	88	2003, Sept. 15	Prison, Riyadh, Saudi Arabia	94
1975, Dec. 12	Tent city, Mina, Saudi Arabia	138	2003, late Oct.-	
1976, Oct. 24	Social club, Bronx, NY	25	early Nov.	Wildfires, southern CA	22
1977, Feb. 25	Rossiya hotel, Moscow, Russia	45	2003, Nov. 24	Students' hostel, Moscow, Russia	36
1977, May 28	Nightclub, Southgate, KY	164	2004, May 17	Prison, San Pedro Sula, Honduras	104
1977, June 9	Nightclub, Abidjan, Ivory Coast	41	2004, July 16	Pvt. school, Kumbakonam, India	80+
1977, June 26	Jail, Columbia, TN	42	2004, Aug. 1	Market, Asunción, Paraguay	400+
1977, Nov. 14	Hotel, Manila, Philippines	47	2004, Dec. 30	Club, Buenos Aires, Argentina	194
1978, Jan. 28	Coates House Hotel, Kansas City, MO	16	2005, Feb. 14	Mosque, Tehran, Iran	59
1978, Aug. 19	Movie theater, Abadan, Iran	425+	2005, Mar. 7	Prison, Higuey, Dom. Republic	159
1979, July 14	Hotel, Saragossa, Spain	80	2005, Apr. 15	Hotel, Paris, France	22
1979, Dec. 31	Social club, Chapais, Quebec, Can.	42	2005, Sept. 5	Theater, Beni Suef, Egypt	32
1980, May 20	Nursing home, Kingston, Jamaica	157	2006, Jan. 8	Orphanage, Dushanbe, Tajikistan	13
1980, Nov. 21	MGM Grand Hotel, Las Vegas, NV	84	2006, Dec. 9	Drug treatment center, Moscow, Russia	45
1980, Dec. 4	Stouffer Inn, Harrison, NY	26	2007, Mar. 20	Nursing home for elderly and disabled,	
1981, Jan. 9	Boarding home, Keansburg, NJ	30		Kamyshevatskaya, Russia	62
1981, Feb. 10	Las Vegas Hilton, Las Vegas, NV	8	2007, Aug. 24-29	Wildfires (possible arson), Greece	60+
1981, Feb. 14	Discotheque, Dublin, Ireland	44			

Cocoanut Grove Nightclub Fire

Date: Nov. 28, 1942. **Location:** Boston, MA. **Fatalities:** 492.

More than 1,000 people were packed into the popular Cocoanut Grove nightclub one Saturday night when a lit match accidentally set an artificial palm tree ablaze. The fire quickly spread from a downstairs lounge through the rest of the nightclub, which was furnished with highly flammable material. The crowds—larger than should have been allowed in the club—panicked and mobbed the exits that weren't locked. Hundreds were trampled or were consumed by the conflagration. The survivors suffered burns, smoke inhalation, and other injuries.

Some Notable Explosions Since 1920

(See also Principal U.S. Mine Disasters Since 1900. Some bombings related to political conflicts and terrorism are not included.)

Date	Location	Deaths
1920, Sept. 16	Wall Street, New York, NY	30
1921, Sept. 21	Chem. storage facility, Oppau, Ger.	561
1924, Jan. 3	Food plant, Pekin, IL	42
1927, May 18	Bath school, Lansing, MI	38
1928, April 13	Dance hall, West Plains, MO	40
1937, Mar. 18	School, New London, TX	311
1940, Sept. 12	Hercules Powder factory, Kenvil, NJ	55
1942, June 5	Ordnance plant, Elwood, IL	49
1944, Apr. 14	Harbor, Bombay, India	700
1944, July 17	Munitions ships, depot, Port Chicago, CA	322
1944, Oct. 21	Liquid gas tank, Cleveland, OH	135
1947, Apr. 16	Freighter, chemical co. plant, Texas City, TX	576
1948, July 28	Farben works, Ludwigshafen, Ger.	184
1950, May 19	Munitions barges, S. Amboy, NJ	30
1954, May 26	USS *Bennington*, off RI	103
1956, Aug. 7	Dynamite trucks, Cali, Colombia	1,100
1958, Apr. 18	Sunken munitions ship, Okinawa, Japan	40
1958, May 22	Nike missiles, Leonardo, NJ	10
1959, Apr. 10	WWII bomb, Philippines	38
1959, June 28	Rail tank cars, Meldrin, GA	25
1959, Aug. 7	Dynamite truck, Roseburg, OR	13
1959, Nov. 2	Explosives, Jamuri Bazar, India	46
1959, Dec. 13	2 apt. bldgs., Dortmund, Ger.	26
1960, Mar. 4	Belgian munitions ship, Havana, Cuba	100
1962, Oct. 3	Telephone Co. office, New York, NY	23
1963, Jan. 2	Packing plant, Terre Haute, IN	17
1963, Mar. 9	Dynamite plant, S. Africa	45
1963, Aug. 13	Explosives dump, Gauhaiti, India	32
1963, Oct. 31	State Fair Coliseum, Indianapolis, IN	73
1964, July 23	Harbor munitions, Bone, Algeria	100
1965, Aug. 9	Missile silo, Searcy, AR	53
1965, Oct. 21	Bridge, Tila Bund, Pakistan	80
1965, Nov. 24	Armory, Keokuk, IA	20
1967, Dec. 25	Apartment bldg., Moscow, USSR	20
1968, Apr. 6	Sports store, Richmond, IN	43
1969, Mar. 31	Coal mine, nr. Barroteran, Mexico	180
1970, Apr. 8	Subway construction, Osaka, Japan	73
1971, June 24	Tunnel, Sylmar, CA	17
1973, Feb., 10	Liquid gas tank, Staten Island, NY	40
1975, Dec. 27	Coal mine, Chasnala, India	431
1976, Apr. 13	Munitions works, Lapua, Finland	40
1977, Nov. 11	Freight train, Iri, S. Korea	57
1977, Dec. 22	Grain elevator, Westwego, LA	35
1978, Feb. 24	Derailed tank car, Waverly, TN	12
1978, July 11	Propylene tank truck, Tarragona, Spain	150
1980, Oct. 23	School, Ortuella, Spain	64
1982, Apr. 25	Antiques exhibition, Todi, Italy	33
1982, Nov. 2	Salang Tunnel, Afghanistan	1,000+
1984, Feb. 25	Oil pipeline, Cubatao, Brazil	508
1984, June 21	Naval supply depot, Severomorsk, USSR	200+
1984, Nov. 19	Gas storage area, NE Mexico City	334
1984, Dec. 3	Chemical plant, Bhopal, India	3,849
1984, Dec. 5	Coal mine, Taipei, Taiwan	94
1985, June 25	Fireworks factory, Hallett, OK	21
1988, Apr. 10	Army ammunitions dump nr. Rawalpindi and Islamabad, Pakistan	100
1988, July 6	Oil rig, North Sea off NE Scotland	167
1989, June 3	Gas pipeline, between Ufa, Asha, USSR	650+
1992, Mar. 3	Coal mine, Kozlu, Turkey	270+
1992, Apr. 22	Sewer, Guadalajara, Mexico	190
1992, May 9	Coal mine, Plymouth, Nova Scotia	26
1993, Feb. 26	World Trade Center, New York, NY	6
1994, July 18	Jewish com. center, Buenos Aires, Arg.	100
1995, Apr. 19	Fed. office building, Oklahoma City, OK	168
1995, Apr. 29	Subway construction, S. Korea	110
1995, Nov. 13	Military facility, Riyadh, Saudi Arabia	7
1996, Jan. 31	Bank, Colombo, Sri Lanka	53
1996, Feb. 25	Jerusalem and Ashkelon, Israel	27
1996, Mar. 3-4	Jerusalem and Tel Aviv, Israel	33
1996, June 25	U.S. military housing complex, nr. Dhahran, Saudi Arabia	19
1996, July 24	Train, Colombo, Sri Lanka	86
1996, Nov. 16	Military apt., Dagestan region, Russia	68
1996, Nov. 21	Building, San Juan, Puerto Rico	29
1996, Nov. 27	Coal mine, Shanxi Prov., China	91+
1996, Dec. 30	Train, Assam, India	59+
1997, Jan. 18	Nr. courthouse, Lahore, Pakistan	25
1997, Mar. 19	Ammunition depot, Jalalabad, Afgh.	16
1997, July 8	Train, Punjab, India	36
1997, Nov. 19	Car, Hyderabad, India	23
1997, Dec. 2	Coal mine, Novokuznetsk, Siberia.	68
1998, Jan. 17	Coal mine, Sokobanja, Serbia	29
1998, Feb. 14	2 oil tankers, Yaounde, Cameroon	120
1998, Feb. 14	17 bombs, Coimbatore, India	50
1998, Mar. 5	Bus, Colombo, Sri Lanka	32
1998, Apr. 4	Coal mine, Donetsk, Ukraine	63
1998, Aug. 7	Bomb, U.S. emb., Nairobi, Kenya	213
	Bomb, U.S. emb., Dar-es-Salaam, Tanz.	11
1998, Aug. 15	Car bomb, Omagh, Ireland	29
1998, Sept. 8	Two buses, São Paulo, Brazil	59
1998, Oct. 17	Oil pipeline, Jesse, Nigeria	700+
1999, May 16	Fuel truck, Punjab Prov., Pakistan	75
1999, Sept. 10	Apartment building, Moscow, Russia	94
1999, Sept. 13	Apartment building, Moscow, Russia	118
1999, Sept. 16	Apartment building, Moscow, Russia	18
1999, Sept. 26	Fireworks factory, Celaya, Mexico	56
2000, Feb. 25	Bombs on 2 buses, Ozamis, Philippines	41
2000, Mar. 11	Coal mine, Krasnodon, Ukraine	80
2000, Apr. 16	Airport hangar, Dem. Rep. of Congo	100+
2000, July 16	Oil pipeline, Warri, Nigeria	30
2000, Aug. 19	Train derailment, Nairobi, Kenya	25
2000, Sept. 9	Truck explosion, Urumqi, China.	60
2000, Sept. 13	Bomb, Jakarta, Indonesia	15
2000, Sept. 19	Bomb, Islamabad, Pakistan	16
2000, Oct. 12	U.S. destroyer, Yemen	17
2001, Mar. 6	School, Wanzai Co., China	41
2001, Apr. 21	Coal mine, Shaanxi, China	51
2001, June 1	Dance club, Tel Aviv, Israel	21
2001, July 17	Coal mine, Guanxi, China	76+
2001, Aug. 19	Coal mine, Donetsk region, Ukraine	52
2001, Sept. 21	Chem. plant, Toulouse, France	29
2002, Jan. 21	Volcanic lava caused gas station blast, Goma, Dem. Rep. of Congo	50+
2002, Jan. 27	Munitions dump, Lagos, Nigeria	1,000+
2002, Mar. 21	Car bomb nr. U.S. embassy, Lima, Peru	9
2002, Apr. 11	Truck nr. synagogue, Djerba, Tunisia	17
2002, Apr. 21	Bomb, dept. store, Mindanao, Philip.	14
2002, Apr. 26	Bomb at mosque, central Pakistan	12
2002, May 8	Bomb on bus outside hotel, Karachi, Pak.	14
2002, May 9	Land mine at parade, Kaspiisk, Russia	34+
2002, June 14	Car bomb outside U.S. consulate, Karachi, Pakistan	12
2002, June 18	Bomb on bus, Jerusalem, Israel	20
2002, July 5	Bomb in market, Larba, Algeria	35+
2002, Aug. 9	Explosion, Jalalabad, Afghanistan	25+
2002, Sept. 5	Car bomb, Kabul, Afghanistan	30
2002, Oct. 12	Nightclub bombings, Bali, Indonesia	202
2003, Aug. 5	Car bomb at hotel, Jakarta, Indon.	12
2003, Aug. 19	Truck bomb, UN HQ, Baghdad, Iraq	22
2003, Aug. 25	Bombs in 2 taxis, Mumbai, India	52
2003, Dec. 5	Bomb on train, Yessentuki, Russia	45
2003, Dec. 23	Gas well explosion, Chongqing, China	233
2004, Jan. 19	Natural gas facility, Skikda, Algeria	27
2004, Feb. 6	Bomb on subway car, Moscow, Russia	39
2004, Mar. 11	Bombs on commuter trains, Madrid, Spain	191
2004, July 19	Coal mine, Ukraine	31
2005, Feb. 14	Coal mine, NE China	214
2005, Mar. 23	Oil refinery, Texas City, TX	15
2005, May 2	Arms cache, Baghlan Prov., Afghan.	34+
2005, July 7	Bombs in mass transit, London, Eng.	56
2005, Oct. 1	Bombings of restaurants, Bali, Indonesia	26
2005, Nov. 27	Coal mine, NE China	161+
2006, May 12	Oil pipeline, nr. Lagos, Nigeria	200
2006, July 1	Bombings of trains, station, Mumbai, India	207
2007, Mar. 19	Coal mine, Siberia, Russia	108

Bhopal Industrial Disaster

Date: Dec. 3, 1984. **Location:** Bhopal, India. **Fatalities:** 16,000 (est.). **Damages:** $470 mil+.
Tons of toxic methyl isocyanate gas leaked from a defective storage tank at a Union Carbide pesticide plant in Bhopal, central India. Between 2,000 and 3,000—many of them residents of slums adjacent to the plant—died shortly thereafter. About 50,000 were treated for severe injuries to their eyes, lungs, and kidneys. An estimated 15,000-20,000 may have subsequently died from exposure to the lethal gas. In 1989, Union Carbide settled a lawsuit by agreeing to provide $470 mil in compensation. Bhopal residents still contend with the effects of the disaster, including health problems and contaminated groundwater.

Notable Nuclear Accidents

Oct. 7, 1957—Fire in the Windscale plutonium production reactor N of Liverpool, England, released radioactive material; later blamed for 39 cancer deaths.

Jan. 3, 1961—Reactor explosion at a federal installation near Idaho Falls, ID, killed 3 workers. Radiation contained.

Oct. 5, 1966—Sodium cooling system malfunction caused a partial core meltdown at the Enrico Fermi demonstration breeder reactor, near Detroit, MI. Radiation contained.

Jan. 21, 1969—Coolant malfunction from an experimental underground reactor at Lucens Vad, Switzerland, released radiation into a cavern, which was then sealed.

Mar. 22, 1975—Fire at the Brown's Ferry reactor in Decatur, AL, caused dangerous lowering of cooling water levels.

Mar. 28, 1979—Worst commercial nuclear accident in the U.S. occurred as equipment failures and human mistakes led to a loss of coolant and a partial core meltdown at the Three Mile Island reactor in Middletown, PA.

Feb. 11, 1981—8 workers were contaminated when 100,000 gallons of radioactive coolant fluid leaked into containment building of TVA's Sequoyah 1 plant near Chattanooga, TN.

Apr. 25, 1981—Some 100 workers were exposed to radiation during repairs of a nuclear plant at Tsuruga, Japan.

Jan. 6, 1986—Cylinder of nuclear material burst after being improperly heated at a Kerr-McGee plant at Gore, OK. One worker died; 100 were hospitalized.

Apr. 26, 1986—In the worst nuclear accident in the history of nuclear power, fires and explosions resulting from an unauthorized experiment at the Chernobyl nuclear power plant near Kiev, USSR (now in Ukraine), left at least 31 dead in the immediate aftermath and spread radioactive material over much of Europe. An estimated 135,000 people were evacuated from the region, some of which was uninhabitable for years. As a result of the radiation released, tens of thousands of excess cancer deaths (as well as increased birth defects) were expected.

Sept. 30, 1999—Japan's worst nuclear accident ever occurred at a uranium-reprocessing facility in Tokaimura, NE of Tokyo, when workers accidentally overloaded a container with uranium, thereby exposing workers and area residents to extremely high radiation levels.

Record Oil Spills

The number of tons can be multiplied by 7 to estimate roughly the number of barrels spilled; the exact number of barrels in a ton varies with the type of oil. Each barrel contains 42 gallons.

Name, place	Date	Cause	Tons
Ixtoc I oil well, S Gulf of Mexico	June 3, 1979	Blowout	600,000
Nowruz oil field, Persian Gulf	Feb. 1983	Blowout	600,000 (est.)
Atlantic Empress and *Aegean Captain*, off Trinidad and Tobago	July 19, 1979	Collision	300,000
Castillo de Bellver, off Cape Town, South Africa	Aug. 6, 1983	Fire	250,000
Amoco Cadiz, near Portsall, France	Mar. 16, 1978	Grounding	223,000
Torrey Canyon, off Land's End, England	Mar. 18, 1967	Grounding	119,000
Sea Star, Gulf of Oman	Dec. 19, 1972	Collision	115,000
Urquiola, La Coruna, Spain	May 12, 1976	Grounding	100,000

Other Notable Oil Spills

Name, place	Date	Cause	Gallons
Persian Gulf	Began Jan. 23, 1991	Spillage by Iraq	130,000,000[1]
Braer, off Shetland Islands	Jan. 5, 1993	Grounding	26,000,000
Prestige, off N Spain	Nov. 13-19, 2002	Ship broke in half	22,600,000
Aegean Sea, off N Spain	Dec. 3, 1992	Unknown	21,500,000
Sea Empress, off SW Wales	Feb. 15, 1996	Grounding	18,000,000
World Glory, off South Africa	June 13, 1968	Hull failure	13,524,000
Newtown Creek, Greenpoint, Brooklyn, NY	Oct. 5, 1950-present	Industrial explosion, preceded by leaks in 1940s-50s	17,000,000
Exxon Valdez, Prince William Sound, AK	Mar. 24, 1989	Grounding	10,080,000

(1) Est. by Saudi Arabia. Some estimates as low as 25 mil gal.

Some Notable Miscellaneous Disasters Since 1950

Date	Event	Location	Details	Est. deaths
1952, Dec.	Pollution	London, England	Heavy smog blanketed city; caused difficulty breathing	4,000
1973-74	Drought and famine	Ethiopia	Caused by 6-year drought	200,000
1974	Famine	Bangladesh	Caused by flooding	26,000+
1974-75	Famine	Sub-Saharan Africa	Drought in some regions, torrential rains in others, compounded by government mismanagement	40,000+
1980, summer	Heat wave	United States	June through Sept.	1,265
1984, Dec. 3	Industrial accident	Bhopal, India	Toxic gas leaked from a Union Carbide factory	16,000
1984	Famine	Africa, chiefly Ethiopia	Several years of drought compounded by government mismanagement	800,000-1 mil
1986, Aug. 21	Gas	Nr. Lake Nyos, Cameroon	Volcanic lake released toxic gas	1,700
1990, July 2	Stampede	Mecca, Saudi Arabia	Pilgrims panicked in tunnel leading to the holy city	1,426
2003, summer	Heat wave	Europe	Abnormally high temperatures from Russia to Britain; France suffered most, with 14,800 dead	35,000
2005, Aug. 31	Stampede	Baghdad, Iraq	Fear of suicide bomber caused bridge stampede	1,000

The 1918 Flu Pandemic
Dates: 1918-19. **Location:** Worldwide. **Fatalities:** 50-100 mil.

One of the most devastating known epidemics in history, also known as the Spanish flu, in which approximately one-third of the world's population, or 500 mil, were infected by the flu virus. In spring of 1918, a deadly new strain of influenza appeared within the army training grounds of Camp Funston, KS. American soldiers are believed to have carried the virus to W Europe, where they had been shipped to fight in World War I. The pandemic peaked in fall 1918: many of those infected with the flu also developed complications from pneumonia and died within days of the first appearance of their symptoms.

AEROSPACE

Memorable Moments in Human Spaceflight

Sources: National Aeronautics and Space Administration; Congressional Research Service; World Almanac research

The spaceflights listed are a selection of notable U.S. missions by the National Aeronautics and Space Administration (NASA), unless otherwise noted, plus non-U.S. missions (shown with an asterisk). The non-U.S missions were sponsored by the USSR (later, the Commonwealth of Independent States and, from 1997, Russia) or by China. Dates are Eastern standard time. EVA = extravehicular activity. ASTP = Apollo-Soyuz Test Project. STS = Space Transportation System, NASA's name for the overall Shuttle program. Number of total flights by each crew member is given in parentheses when flight listed is not the first.

Launch Date	Mission[1]	Crew (no. of flights)	Duration (hr:min)	Remarks
4/12/61	*Vostok 1	Yuri A. Gagarin	1:48	**1st human orbital flight**
5/5/61	Mercury-Redstone 3	Alan B. Shepard Jr.	0:15	**1st American in space**
7/21/61	Mercury-Redstone 4	Virgil I. Grissom	0:15	Spacecraft sank, Grissom rescued
8/6/61	*Vostok 2	Gherman S. Titov	25:18	1st spaceflight of more than 24 hrs
2/20/62	Mercury-Atlas 6	John H. Glenn Jr.	4:55	**1st American in orbit;** 3 orbits
5/24/62	Mercury-Atlas 7	M. Scott Carpenter	4:56	Manual retrofire error caused 250-mi landing overshoot
8/11/62	*Vostok 3	Andrian G. Nikolayev	94:22	Vostok 3 and 4 made 1st group flight
8/12/62	*Vostok 4	Pavel R. Popovich	70:57	On 1st orbit, it came within 3 mi of Vostok 3
10/3/62	Mercury-Atlas 8	Walter M. Schirra Jr.	9:13	Landed 5 mi from target
5/15/63	Mercury-Atlas 9	L. Gordon Cooper	34:19	1st U.S. evaluation of effects of one day in space on a person; 22 orbits
6/14/63	*Vostok 5	Valery F. Bykovsky	119:06	Vostok 5 and 6 made 2nd group flight
6/16/63	*Vostok 6	Valentina V. Tereshkova	70:50	**1st woman in space;** passed within 3 mi of Vostok 5
10/12/64	*Voskhod 1	Vladimir M. Komarov, Konstantin P. Feoktistov, Boris B. Yegorov	24:17	1st 3-person orbital flight; 1st without space suits
3/18/65	*Voskhod 2	Pavel I. Belyayev, Aleksei A. Leonov	26:02	Leonov made **1st "space walk"** (10 min)
3/23/65	Gemini-Titan 3	Grissom (2), John W. Young	4:53	1st piloted spacecraft to change its orbital path
6/3/65	Gemini-Titan 4	James A. McDivitt, Edward H. White 2nd	97:56	White was 1st American to "walk in space" (36 min)
8/21/65	Gemini-Titan 5	Cooper (2), Charles Conrad Jr.	190:55	Longest-duration human flight to date
12/15/65	Gemini-Titan 6A	Schirra (2), Thomas P. Stafford	25:51	Completed 1st U.S. space rendezvous, with Gemini 7
12/4/65	Gemini-Titan 7	Frank Borman, James A. Lovell	330:35	Longest-duration Gemini flight
3/16/66	Gemini-Titan 8	Neil A. Armstrong, David R. Scott	10:41	**1st docking of one space vehicle with another;** mission aborted, control malfunction; 1st Pacific landing
6/3/66	Gemini-Titan 9A	Stafford (2), Eugene A. Cernan	72:21	Performed simulation of lunar module rendezvous
7/18/66	Gemini-Titan 10	Young (2), Michael Collins	70:47	1st use of Agena target vehicle's propulsion systems; 1st orbital docking
9/12/66	Gemini-Titan 11	Conrad (2), Richard F. Gordon Jr.	71:17	1st tethered flight; highest Earth-orbit altitude (850 mi)
11/11/66	Gemini-Titan 12	Lovell (2), Edwin E. "Buzz" Aldrin Jr.	94:34	Final Gemini mission; 5-hr EVA
4/23/67	*Soyuz 1	Komarov (2)	26:40	Crashed on reentry, killing Komarov
10/11/68	Apollo-Saturn 7	Schirra (3), Donn F. Eisele, R. Walter Cunningham	260:09	1st piloted flight of Apollo spacecraft command-service module only; 1st live TV footage of crew
12/21/68	Apollo-Saturn 8	Borman, Lovell (3), William A. Anders	147:00	**1st lunar orbit** and piloted lunar return reentry (command-service module only); views of lunar surface televised to Earth
1/14/69	*Soyuz 4	Vladimir A. Shatalov	71:21	Docked with Soyuz 5
1/15/69	*Soyuz 5	Boris V. Volyanov, Aleksei S. Yeliseyev, Yevgeny V. Khrunov	72:54	Docked with 4; Yeliseyev and Khrunov transferred to Soyuz 4 via a spacewalk
3/3/69	Apollo-Saturn 9	McDivitt (2), D. Scott (2), Russell L. Schweickart	241:00	1st piloted flight of lunar module
5/18/69	Apollo-Saturn 10	Stafford (3), Young (3), Cernan (2)	192:03	1st lunar module orbit of Moon, 50,000 ft from Moon surface
7/16/69	Apollo-Saturn 11	Armstrong (2), Collins (2), Aldrin (2)	195:18	**1st lunar landing** made by Armstrong and Aldrin (7/20); collected 48.5 lb of soil, rock samples; lunar stay time 21:36:21
10/11/69	*Soyuz 6	Georgi S. Shonin, Valery N. Kubasov	118:43	1st welding of metals in space
10/12/69	*Soyuz 7	Anatoly V. Flipchenko, Vladislav N. Volkov, Viktor V. Gorbatko	118:40	Space lab construction test made; Soyuz 6, 7, and 8: 1st time 3 spacecraft, 7 crew members orbited the Earth at once
10/13/69	*Soyuz 8	Shatalov (2), Yeliseyev (2)	118:51	Part of space lab construction team
11/14/69	Apollo-Saturn 12	Conrad (3), Richard F. Gordon Jr. (2), Alan L. Bean	244:36	Conrad and Bean made **2nd Moon landing** (11/18); collected 74.7 lb of samples, lunar stay time 31:31
4/11/70	Apollo-Saturn 13	Lovell (4), Fred W. Haise Jr., John L. Swigert Jr.	142:54	Aborted after service module oxygen tank ruptured; crew returned in lunar module
6/1/70	*Soyuz 9	Nikolayev (2), Vitaliy I. Sevastyanov	424:59	Longest human spaceflight to date
1/31/71	Apollo-Saturn 14	A. Shepard (2), Stuart A. Roosa, Edgar D. Mitchell	216:01	Shepard and Mitchell made **3rd Moon landing** (2/3); collected 96 lb of lunar samples; lunar stay 33:31
4/19/71	*Salyut 12	(Occupied by Soyuz 11 crew)	—	**1st space station**
4/22/71	*Soyuz 10	Shatalov (3), Yeliseyev (3), Nikolay N. Rukavishnikov	47:46	**1st successful docking with a space station;** failed to enter space station
6/6/71	*Soyuz 11	Georgi T. Dobrovolskiy, V. Volkov (2), Viktor I. Patsayev	570:22	Docked and entered Salyut 1 space station; **crew died** during reentry from loss of pressurization
7/26/71	Apollo-Saturn 15	D. Scott (3), James B. Irwin, Alfred M. Worden	295:12	Scott and Irwin made **4th Moon landing** (7/30); 1st lunar rover use; 1st deep space walk; 170 lb of samples; 66:55 stay
4/16/72	Apollo-Saturn 16	Young (4), Charles M. Duke Jr., Thomas K. Mattingly 2nd	265:51	Young and Duke made **5th Moon landing** (4/20); collected 213 lb of lunar samples; lunar stay 71:2
12/7/72	Apollo-Saturn 17	Cernan (3), Ronald E. Evans, Harrison H. Schmitt	301:51	Cernan and Schmitt made 6th and **last lunar landing** (12/11); collected 243 lb of samples; record lunar stay over 75 hrs

Launch Date	Mission[1]	Crew (no. of flights)	Duration (hr:min) Remarks
5/14/73[2]	Skylab 1	(Occupied by Skylab 2, 3, and 4 crews)	— **1st U.S. space station**; fell out of orbit 7/11/79
5/25/73	Skylab 2	Conrad (4), Joseph P. Kerwin, Paul J. Weitz	672:49 1st Amer. piloted orbiting space station; crew repaired damage caused in boost
7/28/73	Skylab 3	Bean (2), Owen K. Garriott, Jack R. Lousma	1,427:09 Crew systems and operational tests; scientific activities; 3 EVAs, 13:44
11/16/73	Skylab 4	Gerald P. Carr, Edward G. Gibson, William Pogue	2,017:15 Final Skylab mission
7/15/75	*Soyuz 19 (ASTP)	Leonov (2), Kubasov (2)	143:31 U.S.-USSR joint flight; crews linked up in space (7/17), conducted experiments, shared meals, held a joint news conf.
7/15/75	Apollo (ASTP)	Vance Brand, Stafford (4), Donald K. Slayton	217:28 Joint flight with Soyuz 19
12/10/77	*Soyuz 26	Yuri V. Romanenko, Georgiy M. Grechko (2)	2,314:00 1st multiple docking to a space station (Soyuz 26 and 27 docked at Salyut 6)
1/10/78	*Soyuz 27	Vladimir A. Dzhanibekov	142:59 See Soyuz 26
3/2/78	*Soyuz 28	Aleksei A. Gubarev (2), Vladimir Remek	190:16 1st international crew launch; Remek was 1st Czech in space
4/12/81	Columbia (STS-1)	Young (5), Robert L. Crippen	54:21 **1st space shuttle** to fly into Earth's orbit
11/12/81	Columbia (STS-2)	Joe H. Engle, Richard H. Truly	54:13 1st scientific payload; 1st reuse of space shuttle
11/11/82	Columbia (STS-5)	Brand (2), Robert Overmyer, William Lenoir, Joseph Allen	122:14 1st 4-person crew
6/18/83	Challenger (STS-7)	Crippen (2), Frederick Hauck, Sally K. Ride, John M. Fabian, Norman Thagard	146:24 Ride was **1st U.S. woman in space**; 1st 5-person crew
6/27/83	*Soyuz T-9	Vladimir A. Lyakhov (2), Aleksandr Pavlovich	3,585:46 Docked at Salyut 7; 1st construction in space
8/30/83	Challenger (STS-8)	Truly (2), Daniel Brandenstein, William Thornton, Guion Bluford, Dale Gardner	145:09 Bluford was **1st African-American in space**
11/28/83	Columbia (STS-9)	Young (6), Brewster Shaw Jr., Robert Parker, Garriott (2), Byron Lichtenberg, Ulf Merbold	247:47 1st 6-person crew; 1st Spacelab mission
2/3/84	Challenger (41-B)	Brand (3), Robert Gibson, Ronald McNair, Bruce McCandless, Robert Stewart	191:16 1st untethered EVA
2/8/84	*Soyuz T-10B	Leonid Kizim, Vladimir Solovyov, Oleg Atkov	1,510:43 Docked with Salyut 7; crew set space duration record of 237 days
4/3/84	*Soyuz T-11	Yury Malyshev (2), Gennady Strekalov (3), Rakesh Sharma	4,365:48 Docked with Salyut 7; Sharma 1st Indian in space
4/6/84	Challenger (41-C)	Crippen (3), Francis R. Scobee, George D. Nelson, Terry J. Hart, James D. van Hoften	167:40 1st in-orbit satellite repair
7/17/84	*Soyuz T-12	Dzhanibekov (4), Svetlana Y. Savitskaya (2), Igor P. Volk	283:14 Docked at Salyut 7; Savitskaya was 1st woman to perform EVA
8/30/84	Discovery (41-D)	Henry W. Hartsfield, Michael L. Coats, Richard M. Mullane, Steven A. Hawley, Judith A. Resnik, Charles D. Walker	144:56 1st flight of U.S. nonastronaut (Walker)
10/5/84	Challenger (41-G)	Crippen (5), Jon A. McBride, Kathryn D. Sullivan, Ride (2), Marc Garneau, David C. Leestma, Paul D. Scully-Power	197:24 1st 7-person crew
11/8/84	Discovery (51-A)	Hauck (2); David M. Walker, Dr. Anna L. Fisher, J. Allen (2), D. Gardner (2)	191:45 1st satellite retrieval/repair
4/12/85	Discovery (51-D)	Karol J. Bobko, Donald E. Williams, Jake Garn, C. Walker (2), Jeffrey A. Hoffman, S. David Griggs, M. Rhea Seddon	167:55 Garn (R, UT) was **1st U.S. senator in space**
6/17/85	Discovery (51-G)	Brandenstein (2), John O. Creighton, Shannon W. Lucid, Steven R. Nagel, Fabian (2), Prince Sultan Salman al-Saud, Patrick Baudry	169:39 Launched 3 satellites; Salman al-Saud was 1st Arab in space; Baudry was 1st French person on U.S. mission
10/3/85	Atlantis (51-J)	Bobko (3), Ronald J. Grabe, David C. Hilmers, Stewart (2), William A. Pailes	97:47 1st Atlantis flight
10/30/85	Challenger (61-A)	Hartsfield (3), Nagel (2), Buchli (2), Bluford (2), Bonnie J. Dunbar, Wubbo J. Ockels, Richard Furrer, Ernst Messerschmid	168:45 1st 8-person crew; 1st German Spacelab mission
1/12/86	Columbia (61-C)	R. Gibson (2), Charles F. Bolden Jr., Hawley (2), G. Nelson (2), Franklin R. Chang-Diaz, Robert J. Cenker, Bill Nelson	146:04 B. Nelson was 1st U.S. representative in space; material and astronomy experiments conducted
1/28/86	Challenger (51-L)	Scobee (2), Michael J. Smith, Resnik (2), Ellison S. Onizuka (2), Ronald E. McNair (2), Gregory B. Jarvis, Christa McAuliffe	— **Exploded 73 sec after liftoff**; all aboard were killed
2/20/86	*Mir[2]	—	— **Mir** space station with 6 docking ports launched
3/13/86	*Soyuz T-15	Kizim (3), Solovyov (2)	3,000:01 Ferry between stations; docked at Mir
2/5/87	*Soyuz TM-2	Romanenko (3), Aleksandr I. Laveikin	7,835:38 Romanenko set endurance record, since broken
7/22/87	*Soyuz TM-3	Aleksandr Viktorenko, Aleksandr Pavlovich Aleksandrov (2), Mohammed Faris	3,847:16 Docked with Mir; Faris 1st Syrian in space
9/29/88	Discovery (STS-26)	Hauck (3), Richard O. Covey (2), Hilmers (2), G. Nelson (2), John M. Lounge (2)	97:00 **1st shuttle flight since Challenger explosion** 1/28/86
5/4/89	Atlantis (STS-30)	D. Walker (2), Grabe (2), Thagard (2), Mary L. Cleave (2), Mark C. Lee	96:56 Launched Venus orbiter Magellan
10/18/89	Atlantis (STS-34)	Donald E. Williams (2), Michael J. McCulley, Lucid (2), Chang-Diaz (2), Ellen S. Baker	119:39 Launched Jupiter probe and orbiter Galileo
4/24/90	Discovery (STS-31)	McCandless (2), Sullivan (2), Loren J. Shriver (2), Bolden (2), Hawley (3)	121:16 **Launched Hubble Space Telescope**
10/6/90	Discovery (STS-41)	Richard N. Richards (2), Robert D. Cabana, Bruce E. Melnick, William M. Shepherd (2), Thomas D. Akers	98:10 Launched Ulysses spacecraft to investigate interstellar space and the Sun
5/18/91	*Soyuz TM-12	Anatoly Artsebarskiy, Sergei Krikalev (2) (to Mir), Helen Sharman	3,471:22 Docked with Mir; Sharman 1st from United Kingdom in space
3/17/92	*Soyuz TM-14	Viktorenko (3) (to Mir), Alexandr Kaleri (to Mir), Klaus-Dietrich Flade, Aleksandr Volkov (3) (from Mir), Krikalev (2) (from Mir)	3,495:11 First human CIS space mission; docked with Mir 3/19; Viktorenko and Kaleri to Mir; Volkov and Krikalev from Mir; Krikalev was in space 313 days

Launch Date	Mission[1]	Crew (no. of flights)	Duration (hr:min)	Remarks
5/7/92	Endeavour (STS-49)	Brandenstein (4), Kevin C. Chilton, Melnick (2), Pierre J. Thuot (2), Richard J. Hieb (2), Kathryn Thornton (2), Akers (2)	213:30	1st 3-person EVA; satellite recovery and redeployment
9/12/92	Endeavour (STS-47)	R. Gibson (4), Curtis L. Brown Jr., Lee (2), Jay Apt (2), N. Jan Davis, Mae Carol Jemison, Mamoru Mohri	190:30	**Jemison was 1st black woman in space; Lee and Davis 1st married couple to travel together in space;** 1st Japanese Spacelab
6/21/93	Endeavour (STS-57)	Grabe (4), Brian J. Duffy (2), G. David Low (3), Nancy J. Sherlock, Peter J. K. Wisoff, Janice E. Voss	239:46	Carried Spacelab commercial payload module
12/2/93	Endeavour (STS-61)	Covey (3), Kenneth D. Bowersox (2), Claude Nicollier (2), Story Musgrave (5), Akers (3), K. Thornton (3), Hoffman (4)	259:58	Hubble Space Telescope repaired; Akers set new U.S. EVA duration record (29 hr, 40 min)
2/3/94	Discovery (STS-60)	Bolden (3), Kenneth S. Reightler Jr. (2), Davis (2), Chang-Diaz (3), Ronald M. Sega, Krikalev (3)	199:10	Krikalev was 1st Russian on U.S. shuttle
7/1/94	*Soyuz TM-19	Yuri I. Malenchenko, Talgat A. Musabayev, Merbold (2) (from Mir)	3,022:53	Docked with Mir; Merbold from Mir
9/9/94	Discovery (STS-64)	Richards (4), L. Blaine Hammond Jr. (2), Jerry M. Linenger, Susan J. Helms (2), Carl J. Meade (3), Lee (3)	262:50	Performed atmospheric research; 1st untethered EVA in over 10 years
2/3/95	Discovery (STS-63)	James D. Wetherbee (3), Eileen M. Collins, Bernard A. Harris (2), C. Michael Foale (3), Janice E. Voss (2), V. Titov (4)	198:29	Discovery and Russian space station rendezvous
3/2/95	Endeavour (STS-67)	Stephen S. Oswald (3), William G. Gregory, Samuel T. Durrance (2), Ronald Parise (2), Wendy B. Lawrence, Tamara E. Jernigan (3), John M. Grunsfeld	399:09	Shuttle data made available on the Internet; astronomy research conducted
3/14/95	*Soyuz TM-21	Thagard (3), Vladimir Dezhurov, Strekalov (5)	2,688[3]	Docked with Mir 3/16/95; Thagard was 1st Amer. on the Russ. spacecraft; Valery Polyakov returned to Earth, 3/22/95, after record stay in space (439 days)
6/27/95	Atlantis (STS-71)	R. Gibson (5), Charles J. Precourt (2), E. Baker (3), Gregory J. Harbaugh (3), Dunbar (4), Anatoly Solovyev (4) (to Mir), Nikolai M. Budarin (to Mir), Thagard (5) (from Mir), Strekalov (from Mir), Dezhurov (from Mir)	269:47	**1st shuttle-Mir docking**; exchanged crew members with Mir; Thagard, with his stay on Mir, had spent 115 days in space
11/12/95	Atlantis (STS-74)	Kenneth D. Cameron (3), James D. Halsell Jr. (2), Chris Hadfield (3), Jerry L. Ross (5), William S. McArthur (2)	196:30	2nd shuttle-Mir docking (11/15-11/18); erected a 15-ft permanent docking tunnel to Mir for future use by U.S. orbiters
2/22/96	Columbia (STS-75)	Andrew M. Allen (3), Scott J. Horowitz, Chang-Diaz (5), Umberto Guidoni, Hoffman (5), Maurizio Cheli, Nicollier (3)	377:40	Lost an Italian satellite when its tether was severed; microgravity experiments performed; singe marks found on 2 O-rings
3/22/96	Atlantis (STS-76)	Chilton (2), Richard A. Searfoss (2), Sega (2), Michael R. Clifford (3), Linda Godwin (3), Lucid (5) (to Mir)	221:15	3rd shuttle-Mir docking (5 days); Lucid to Mir, 2-person EVA
9/16/96	Atlantis (STS-79)	Apt (4), Terry Wilcutt (2), WilliamReaddy (3), Akers (4), Carl E. Walz (3), Lucid (5) (from Mir), John E. Blaha (5) (to Mir)	243:19	Docked with Mir 9/18/96; exchanged crew members; **Lucid set U.S. and women's duration in space record (188 days)**
11/19/96	Columbia (STS-80)	Kenneth D. Cockrell (3), Kent V. Rominger (2), Jernigan (4), Thomas D. Jones (3), Musgrave (6)	423:53	Longest-duration shuttle flight; Musgrave 61, oldest thus far to fly in space; 2 science satellites deployed, retrieved
1/12/97	Atlantis (STS-81)	Michael A. Baker (4), Brent W. Jett (2), Wisoff (3), Grunsfeld (2), Marsha Ivins (4), Linenger (2) (to Mir), Blaha (5) (from Mir)	243:30	Docked with Mir 1/14-1/19/97; Linenger to Mir; Blaha from Mir, spent 128 days in space
2/11/97	Discovery (STS-82)	Bowersox (4), Horowitz (2), Joe Tanner (2), Hawley (4), Harbaugh (4), Lee (4), Steve Smith (2)	238:47	Increased capabilities of Hubble Space Telescope; 5 EVAs used to service it
5/15/97	Atlantis (STS-84)	Precourt (3), E. Collins (2), Jean-François Clervoy (2), Carlos Noriega, Ed Lu, Elena Kondakova (2), Foale (4) (to Mir), Linenger (2) (from Mir)	221:20	Docked with Mir 5/16-5/21; Foale to Mir; Linenger from Mir, 132 days in space, 2nd-longest time for an American; stay on Mir marked by troubles incl. fire 2/23
8/5/97	*Soyuz TM-26	Solovyev (5), Pavel Vinogradov	4,743:35	Docked with Mir 8/7/97; repaired damaged space station
8/7/97	Discovery (STS-85)	Brown (4), Rominger (3), Davis (3), Robert L. Curbeam Jr., Stephen K. Robinson, Bjarni V. Tryggvason	284:27	Deployed and retrieved satellite designed to study Earth's middle atmosphere; demonstrated robotic arm
9/25/97	Atlantis (STS-86)	Wetherbee (4), Michael J. Bloomfield, V. Titov (4), Scott Parazynski (2), Jean-Loup Chrétien (3), Lawrence (2), David A. Wolf (2) (to Mir), Foale (4) (from Mir)	236:24	Docked with Mir 9/27-10/3/97; delivered new computer to Mir; Wolf to Mir; Foale from Mir; stay on Mir marked by major collision with cargo ship 6/25
4/17/98	Columbia (STS-90)	Searfoss, Scott D. Altman, Richard M. Linnehan (2), Dafydd Rhys Williams, Kathryn P. Hire, Jay C. Buckey, James A. Pawelczyk	381:50	Studied effects of microgravity on the nervous systems of the crew and over 2,000 live animals; 1st surgery in space on animals meant to survive
6/2/98	Discovery (STS-91)	Precourt (4), Dominic L. Gorie, Lawrence (3), Chang-Diaz (6), Janet L. Kavandi, Valery Ryumin (4), A. Thomas (2) (from Mir)	235:53	Final docking mission with Mir; Thomas from Mir, 141 days in space
10/29/98	Discovery (STS-95)	Brown (4), Steven W. Lindsey (2), Parazynski (3), Robinson (2), Pedro Duque, Chiaki Mukai (2), Glenn (2)	213:44	Sen. John Glenn (D, OH), 77, was **oldest person to fly in space**; Duque was 1st Spaniard in space; experiments to study aging performed on Glenn
12/4/98	Endeavour (STS-88)	Cabana (4), Frederick W. Sturckow, Nancy J. Currie (3), Ross (6), James H. Newman (3), Krikalev (4)	283:18	**1st assembly of International Space Station (ISS)**; attached U.S.-built Unity connecting module to Russian-built Zarya control module; 1st crew to enter ISS
7/23/99	Columbia (STS-93)	E. Collins (3), Jeffrey S. Ashby, Hawley (5), Catherine G. Coleman (2), Michel Tognini (2)	118:50	Collins was **1st woman to command a space shuttle**; deployed Chandra X-ray Observatory telescope

Launch Date	Mission[1]	Crew (no. of flights)	Duration (hr:min)	Remarks
2/11/00	Endeavour (STS-99)	Kevin Kregel (4), Gorie (2), Kavandi (2), Janice E. Voss (5), Mohri (2), Gerhard P.J. Thiele	269:38	Used radar to make most complete topographic map of Earth's surface ever produced
5/19/00	Atlantis (STS-101)	Halsell (5), Horowitz (3), Helms (4), Yury Usachev (3), James S. Voss (4), Mary Ellen Weber (2), Jeffrey N. Williams	236:09	Serviced and resupplied ISS; boosted orbit of ISS to an altitude of about 238 mi; 1 EVA
9/8/00	Atlantis (STS-106)	Wilcutt (4), Altman (2), Lu (2), Richard A. Mastracchio, Daniel C. Burbank, Malenchenko (2), Boris V. Morukov	283:10	Prepared ISS for 1st permanent crew; 1 EVA by all 7 crew members
10/11/00	Discovery (STS-92)	Duffy (4), Pamela A. Melroy (2), Koichi Wakata (2), Leroy Chiao (3), Wisoff (4), Michael Lopez-Alegria (2), McArthur (3)	309:43	Installed framework structure on ISS, setting the stage for future additions; 4 EVAs
10/31/00	*Soyuz TM-204	Shepherd (4), Yuri Gidzenko (2), Krikalev (5)	—	Established 1st permanent manning of ISS with 3-person crew for a 4-month stay
2/7/01	Atlantis (STS-98)	Cockrell (4), Ivins (5), Jones (4), Curbeam (2), Mark L. Polansky	309:20	Installed U.S. Destiny Laboratory Module on the ISS; 3 EVAs
3/8/01	Discovery (STS-102)	Wetherbee (5), James M. Kelly, Helms (4 to ISS), James S. Voss (4 to ISS), Paul Richards, Andrew S.W. Thomas (2), Usachev (4) (to ISS), Shepherd (4 from ISS), Gidzenko (2 from ISS), Krikalev (5) (from ISS)	307:49	Transported 2nd permanent crew (Voss, Helms, Usachev) to ISS and returned 1st crew to Earth; 2 EVAs
7/12/01	Atlantis (STS-104)	Lindsey (3), Charles O. Hobaugh, Michael L. Gernhardt (4), Kavandi (3), James F. Reilly II(2)	259:58	Installed a Joint Airlock, with nitrogen and oxygen tanks to permit future spacewalks from the ISS; 3 EVAs
8/10/01	Discovery (STS-105)	Horowitz (4), Sturckow (2), Daniel Barry (3), Patrick G. Forrester, Culbertson (3) to ISS, Dezhurov (2) (to ISS), Mikhail Tyurin (to ISS), Usachev, (4), Voss (5) (from ISS), Helms (5) (from ISS)	285:13	Transported Expedition 3 crew to ISS (Culbertson, Tyurin, Dezhurov) and returned Expedition 2 crew to Earth; 2 EVAs
12/5/01	Endeavour (STS-108)	Gorie (3), Mark Kelly, Godwin (4), Daniel Tani, Yury Onufrienko (2) (to ISS), Daniel Bursch (4) (to ISS), Walz (4) (to ISS), Culbertson (3) (from ISS), Dezhurov (2) (from ISS), Tyurin (from ISS)	283:36	Transported Expedition 4 crew to ISS (Onufrienko, Bursch, Walz) and returned Expedition 3 crew to Earth; deployed STARSHINE 2 satellite; 1 EVA
3/1/02	Columbia (STS-109)	Altman (3), Duane G. Carey, Grunsfeld (4), Currie (4), Linnehan (3), Newman (4), Michael J. Massimino	262:10	Installed powerful new camera and upgraded other equipment on Hubble Space Telescope; 5 EVAs
4/8/02	Atlantis (STS-110)	Bloomfield (3), Stephen N. Frick, Rex J. Walheim, Ellen Ochoa (4), Lee M.E. Morin, Ross (7), S. Smith (4)	259:42	Installed S0 Truss, backbone for expansion of ISS; Ross set records with 7th spaceflight, 9th spacewalk; 4 EVAs
6/5/02	Endeavour (STS-111)	Cockrell (5), Paul Lockhart, Chang-Diaz (7), Philippe Perrin, Valery Korzun (2) (to ISS), Peggy Whitson (to ISS), Sergei Treschev (to ISS), Onufrienko (2) (from ISS), Bursch (4) (from ISS), Walz (4) (from ISS)	332:35	Transported Expedition 5 crew to ISS (Korzun, Whitson, Treschev) and returned Expedition 4 crew to Earth; brought platform for ISS robot arm; 3 EVAs
10/30/02	*Soyuz TMA-1	Sergei Zalyotin (2), Frank De Winne, Yuri Lonchakov (2)	—	1st launch of Soyuz TMA (Crew returned 11/10/02 on Soyuz TM-34 already docked at ISS)
11/23/02	Endeavour (STS-113)	Wetherbee (6), Lockhart (2), Lopez-Alegria (3), John Herrington, Bowersox (5) (to ISS), Budarin (3) (to ISS), Don Pettit (to ISS), Korzun (2) (from ISS), Whitson (from ISS), Treschev (from ISS)	330:47	Delivered Expedition 6 crew to ISS (Bowersox, Budarin, Pettit) and returned Expedition 5 crew to Earth; installed P1 Truss to ISS; 3 EVAs
1/16/03	Columbia (STS 107)	Rick Husband (2), William McCool, Michael Anderson (2), David Brown, Kalpana Chawla (2), Laurel Clark, Ilan Ramon	382:20	Entire crew lost when Columbia burned up during reentry, 2/1/03; Ramon first Israeli astronaut
10/15/03	*Shenzhou 5	Yang Liwei	21:00	1st Chinese manned spacecraft
6/21/04	SpaceShipOne	Mike Melvill	0:90	1st privately funded manned spaceflight[4]
7/26/05	Discovery (STS-114)	Charles Camarda, E. Collins (4), J. Kelly (2), Lawrence (4), Soichi Noguchi, Robinson (3), A.Thomas (3)		1st manned shuttle flight since Columbia disaster; tested new safety modifications to craft; delivered supplies to ISS
7/4/06	Discovery (STS-121)	Lindsey (4), J. Kelly (2), Michael E. Fossum, Sellers (2), Lisa M. Nowak, Thomas Reiter (to ISS), Stephanie D. Wilson	306:36	1st shuttle to launch on Independence Day. Conducted more safety tests to craft; brought supplies to and performed maintenance on ISS.
9/9/06	Atlantis (STS-115)	Burbank (2), Christopher J. Ferguson, Jett (4), Steven G. MacLean (3), Heidemarie M. Stefanyshyn-Piper, Tanner (4)	283:07	Continued ISS construction; installed a new truss segment, two solar arrays, and a solar alpha rotary joint (used to orient the solar arrays).
12/9/06	Discovery (STS-116)	Robert L. Curbeam (3), Christer Fuglesang, Joan E. Higginbotham, William A. Oefelein, Nicholas J.M. Patrick, Mark L. Polansky (2), Sunita L. Williams (from ISS), T. Reiter (from ISS)	308:45	First nighttime launch in more than 4 years. Rewired ISS power system, delivered supplies, prepared station for European and Japanese lab modules.
4/7/07	*Soyuz TMA-10	Oleg Kotov (to ISS), Charles Simonyi (US), Fyodor Yurchikhin (to ISS)	—	Kotov and Yurchikhin joined ISS expedition 15; Simonyi became fifth space tourist.
6/8/07	Atlantis (STS-117)	Clayton Anderson (to ISS), Lee Archambault, Patrick Forrester (2), John "Danny" Olivas, Jim Reilly (3), Frederick Sturckow (3), Steven Swanson, S.L. Williams (from ISS)	332:11	Delivered truss segments and solar arrays to ISS. Williams set record for longest spaceflight by a woman.
8/8/07	Endeavour (STS-118)	Alvin Drew, Barbara R. Morgan, Scott Kelly (2), Charlie Hobaugh (2), Tracy Caldwell, Rick Mastracchio (2), Dave Williams (2)	305:55	Brought Teacher in Space Project participant Morgan to ISS. Attached new truss segment, repaired faulty gyroscope.

Note: As of Sept. 2007, there have been 119 space shuttle flights, 93 since the 1986 Challenger explosion, 6 since the 2003 loss of Columbia. Totals include the final (28th) Columbia flight. There are 3 remaining shuttles: Discovery (33 flights), Atlantis (28), and Endeavour (20); the Challenger completed 9 missions in all. Four Soviets have died in spaceflight: Vladimir Komarov was killed on Soyuz 1 (1967) when parachute lines tangled during descent; the 3-person Soyuz 11 crew (1971) was asphyxiated. Six Americans and an Israeli astronaut died aboard the Columbia; 7 Americans died in the Challenger explosion, and 3 astronauts—Virgil I. Grissom, Edward H. White, and Roger B. Chaffee—died in the Jan. 27, 1967, Apollo 1 fire on the ground at Cape Canaveral, Fla.

(1) For shuttle flights, mission name is in parentheses following name of orbiter. (2) Space stations, such as the Salyuts and Mir, were used to house crews starting in 1971. (3) Approx. crew duration for Thgard's stay. Crew did not return together. (4) Date of first successful flight; later, SpaceShipOne flew at least 100 km (62 mi) into space, 9/29/04, piloted by Mike Melvill, and 10/4/04, piloted by Brian Binnie, winning the $10 mil Ansari Prize for 1st private venture to accomplish this feat twice within 2 weeks.

U.S. Manned Space Program

Following the Feb. 1, 2003, *Columbia* disaster, when the craft broke up on re-entry, all space shuttle flights were grounded. Improvements to future spacecrafts were made, including a redesigned external tank, new sensors to register impact, and a boom with a camera to allow astronauts to inspect the shuttle in flight for potential damage. On July 26, 2005, a modified *Discovery* made it into orbit, but onboard cameras showed that foam insulation broke off from the external fuel tank during launch—the same problem that caused the *Columbia* disaster. Despite a successful return, the shuttle program was grounded again until July 4, 2006, when *Discovery* lifted off with new safety features in place. The crew visited the *International Space Station* and returned to Earth without incident. Following *Discovery*'s flight, there have been four more successful shuttle missions as of Sept. 2007.

Even before the *Columbia* disaster it was clear that that a new vehicle was needed to replace the space shuttle, which is due to be retired in 2010. President George W. Bush in 2004 outlined his vision for future space exploration: Following the retirement of the space shuttle fleet, NASA will employ a new space vessel to aid not only in finishing the ISS, but also in sending astronauts to the moon and eventually to Mars. In August 2006, NASA unveiled plans for the new spacecraft, a multi-purpose orbital capsule called *Orion*, developed by Lockheed Martin. *Orion* will be designed to carry astronauts into orbit, ferry personnel and equipment to the ISS, serve as the orbital vehicle for missions to the Moon, and eventually to help with the construction of a vehicle to carry the first astronauts to Mars.

The reusable *Orion* craft abandons the 25-year old space shuttle design and returns to an *Apollo*-style design which will launch with the aid of new type of expendable rocket called *Ares* (also currently under development). *Orion*, costing $3.9 bil, will incorporate the latest technology in electronics, life support, computers, propulsion and heat protection systems. At 16.5 ft in diameter, *Orion* will have 2.5 times the interior volume of the original *Apollo* capsules, and like the Russian *Soyuz* capsules, *Orion* will use parachutes to touch down on land (the *Apollo* capsules landed in water). Like the *Apollo* craft, *Orion* will launch on top of its booster rocket, which will prevent ice or insulating foam from the booster rocket from hitting the capsule. In addition, the capsule will be able to jettison from its booster in the event of launch failure—a safety mechanism unavailable to space shuttle crews.

The earliest *Orion* flight is scheduled for 2014, with a manned Moon mission expected by 2020.

International Space Station

The International Space Station (ISS) is considered the largest cooperative scientific project in history.

16 cooperating nations: U.S., Russia, Canada, Belgium, Denmark, France, Germany, Italy, Netherlands, Norway, Spain, Sweden, Switzerland, United Kingdom, Japan, and Brazil.

Impact of *Columbia* disaster: The grounding of U.S. space shuttles after the *Columbia* disaster and then after complications with *Discovery* in 2005 interrupted further assembly of the station. Since lower-capacity Russian *Soyuz* and *Progress* craft were the usual means of ferrying provisions and crew to and from Earth, the size of the crew aboard the ISS was reduced to 2.

In 2006, the flights resumed, allowing operations on the station to move forward and bringing the ISS crew back up to 3. Over the course of the year, the crew tested new equipment and safety procedures and performed maintenance on the station, notably the station's mobile transporter (a device that moves along exterior rails and facilitates repair, maintenance, and module additions). New and updated research equipment was installed inside the Leonardo Multi-Purpose Logistics Module. In September, the space shuttle *Atlantis* arrived with a new truss segment, two solar arrays, and a rotary joint that is used to position the solar panels so that they face the sun as the ISS moves through its orbit.

The station when completed:
- mass of 1,040,000 lb
- 356' x 290', with almost an acre of solar panels
- internal volume roughly equivalent to passenger cabin of a 747 jumbo jet
- 6 laboratories; living space for up to 7 people

Examples of research conducted or planned:
- growing living cells in a gravity-free environment
- studying the effects on humans of long-term exposure to reduced gravity
- studying large-scale long-term changes in Earth's environment by observing Earth from orbit

Summary of Worldwide Successful Launches, 1957-2007

Source: National Aeronautics and Space Administration

Year	Total[1]	Russia[2]	U.S.	ESA[3]	China	Japan	France	India	U.K.	Germany	Canada	Israel
1957-59	24	6	18	—	—	—	—	—	—	—	—	—
1960-69	1,035	399	614	2	—	—	4	—	1	—	—	—
1970-79	1,366	1,028	247	5	8	18	14	1	6	3	4	—
1980-89	1,431	1,132	191	14	16	26	5	9	4	7	5	—
1990-99	1,045	542	300	55	33	23	16	11	7	6	4	—
2000-07[4]	466	189	160	49	41	15	0	9	0	0	0	3
Total	5,367	3,296	1,530	125	98	82	39	30	18	16	13	3

(1) Includes launches sponsored by countries not shown. (2) Data for 1957-91 apply to the Soviet Union, for 1992-96 to the Commonwealth of Independent States, after 1996 to Russia. (3) European Space Agency. Member States are Austria, Belgium, Denmark, Finland, France, Germany, Greece, Ireland, Italy, Luxembourg, the Netherlands, Norway, Portugal, Spain, Sweden, Switzerland and the United Kingdom. Canada, Hungary and the Czech Republic also participate in some projects under cooperation agreements. (4) As of Sept. 19, 2007.

Notable Proposed U.S. Space Missions in 2008

Source: National Aeronautics and Space Administration

Planned Launch	Mission	Purpose
Feb. 5	Gamma-ray Large Area Space Telescope (GLAST)	Observatory designed to study celestial gamma-ray sources, the most energetic objects and phenomena in the universe.
Feb. 14	Endeavour (STS-123)	Space shuttle mission to ISS.
Apr. 24	Discovery (STS-124)	Space shuttle mission to ISS.
June 15	Interstellar Boundary Explorer (IBEX)	Map the boundary between the Solar System and interstellar space.
Aug. 7	Atlantis (STS-125)	Space shuttle mission; fifth and final servicing mission to Hubble Space Telescope, improving its capabilities through 2013.
Sept. 18	Endeavour (STS-126)	Space shuttle mission to ISS.
Oct. 31	Lunar Crater Observation and Sensing Satellite	Confirm presence or absence of water ice in a permanently shadowed crater at Moon's North or South Pole.
Nov. 1	Kepler	Survey our region of the Milky Way to detect Earth-size and smaller planets.

Notable Lunar and Planetary Science Missions

Source: National Aeronautics and Space Administration

Spacecraft	Launch date[1]	Mission	Remarks
Mariner 2	Aug. 27, 1962	Venus	Passed within 22,000 mi of Venus 12/14/62; confirmed high surface temperature on planet; contact lost 1/3/63 at 54 million mi
Ranger 7	July 28, 1964	Moon	Yielded over 4,000 photos of lunar surface
Mariner 4	Nov. 28, 1964	Mars	1st probe to fly by mars; passed behind planet 7/14/65; took 22 photos from 6,000 mi above surface
Ranger 8	Feb. 17, 1965	Moon	Yielded over 7,000 photos of lunar surface
Surveyor 3	Apr. 17, 1967	Moon	Scooped and tested lunar soil
Venera 3	Nov. 16, 1965	Venus	Soviet probe; first artificial probe to impact on the surface of another planet 3/1/66; probe failed to send back data.
Mariner 5	June 14, 1967	Venus	In solar orbit; closest Venus flyby 10/19/67; allowed scientists to obtain accurate readings on the composition of the Venusian atmosphere.
Mariner 6	Feb. 24, 1969	Mars	Came within 2,000 mi of Mars 7/31/69; collected data, photos
Mariner 7	Mar. 27, 1969	Mars	Came within 2,000 mi of Mars 8/5/69
Venera 7	Aug. 17, 1970	Venus	Soviet probe; first probe to land safely on the surface of another planet; because of high atmospheric temperatures, probe is thought to have melted.
Mariner 9	May 30, 1971	Mars	First craft to orbit Mars 11/13/71; sent back over 7,000 photos
Pioneer 10	Mar. 2, 1972	Jupiter	Passed Jupiter 12/4/73; took readings on Jupiter's composition, found that the planet is composed mostly of hydrogen; exited the planetary system 6/13/83; transmission ended 3/31/97 at 6.39 bil mi
Pioneer 11	Apr. 5, 1973	Jupiter, Saturn	Passed Jupiter 12/3/74, Saturn 9/1/79; discovered an additional ring and 2 moons around Saturn; operating in outer solar system; transmission ended 9/95
Mariner 10	Nov. 3, 1973	Venus, Mercury	Passed Venus 2/5/74; arrived Mercury 3/29/74. 1st time gravity of 1 planet (Venus) used to whip spacecraft toward another (Mercury). 1st probe to visit 2 planets. Took readings of cloud and wind patterns in Venusian atmosphere.
Viking 1	Aug. 20, 1975	Mars	Landed on Mars 7/20/76; 1st probe to land safely on Mars; performed chemical analysis of soil; functioned 6 years
Viking 2	Sept. 9, 1975	Mars	Sister probe of *Viking 1*; landed on Mars 9/3/76; functioned 3 years
Voyager 1	Sept. 5, 1977	Jupiter, Saturn	Encountered Jupiter 3/5/79, provided evidence of rings around Jupiter; passed near Saturn 11/12/80; passed *Pioneer 10* to become most distant human-made object 2/17/98; 8/15/06 reached a distance of 100 AUs from sun
Voyager 2	Aug. 20, 1977	Jupiter, Saturn, Uranus, Neptune	Encountered Jupiter 7/9/79; Saturn 8/25/81; Uranus 1/24/86; Neptune 8/25/89; confirmed existence of rings around Neptune; observed Neptune's "great dark spot," which has since dissipated
Pioneer Venus 1	May 20, 1978	Venus	Entered Venus orbit 12/4/78; spent 14 years studying atmosphere, magnetic field, weather and surface; fuel ran out and probe was destroyed in atmospheric entry, 8/92
Pioneer Venus 2 (multiprobe)	Aug. 8, 1978	Venus	Consisted of a "bus" which carried 1 large and 3 small atmospheric probes. All four probes entered the Venus atmosphere 12/9, followed by the bus; took readings of Venusian atompshere; probes impacted on surface
Magellan	May 4, 1989	Venus	Landed on Venus 8/10/90; monitored geological activity; mapped more than 99% of planet surface, observed more than 1,600 volcanoes and volcanic features, enabling creation of a 3 dimensional map; showed that about 85% of the surface is covered by volcanic flows; ceased operating 10/11/94
Galileo	Oct. 18, 1989	Jupiter	Used Earth's gravity to propel it toward Jupiter; encountered Venus Feb. 1990; encountered Jupiter 12/7/95; encountered moons; released probe into Jovian atmosphere; intentionally flown into Jupiter 9/21/03 to prevent accidental contamination of Jupiter's moon Europa.
Mars Global Surveyor	Nov. 7, 1996	Mars	Began orbiting Mars 9/11/97; began mapping survey of entire surface 3/9/99; discovered a weak magnetic field on planet; observed Martian moon Phobos; found evidence of liquid water in past 6/22/00
Mars Pathfinder	Dec. 4, 1996	Mars	Landed on Mars 7/4/97; rover *Sojourner* made measurements of climate and soil composition, sending thousands of surface images; ceased operating 9/27/97
Cassini-Huygens	Oct. 15, 1997	Saturn	Began orbiting Saturn 6/30/04; 4-year mission to study planet's atmosphere, rings, and moons; spotted a 270-mi-wide crater and 300-mi-wide hot spot region on Titan; and detected an atmosphere on Saturn's moon Enceladus. *Huygens* probe landed on Titan 1/14/05; found a muddy surface, possible deposits of water ice, channels carved by liquid methane springs, possible evidence of a coastline.
Lunar Prospector	Jan. 6, 1998	Moon	Began orbiting Moon 1/11/98; mapped abundance of 11 elements on Moon's surface; discovered evidence of water-ice at both lunar poles; made 1st precise gravity map of entire lunar surface; crashed into crater near Moon's south pole 7/31/99 to end mission
Deep Space 1	Oct. 24, 1998	Comet Borrelly	Flew within 1,500 mi of comet, sent back photos showing a 6 mi long nucleus.
Stardust	Feb. 7, 1999	Comet Wild-2	Reached comet 1/2/04; gathered dust samples; returned samples to Earth Jan. 15, 2006.
2001 Mars Odyssey	Apr. 7, 2001	Mars	Reached Mars 10/24/01; detected evidence of water ice near South Pole; primary mission to study climate and geologic history completed 8/04; began extended mission
Genesis	Aug. 8, 2001	Sun	Orbited Sun, collected particles from solar wind. Capsule containing specimens crashed to Earth 9/8/04; some samples survived.
Mars Express/ Beagle 2 lander	June 3, 2003	Mars	First European Space Agency probe to another planet; arrived at Mars 12/03; performing remote sensing including high-resolution photography in a search for subsurface water; *Beagle 2* lander was deployed 12/19/03 but contact was lost soon after.
Mars Exploration Rovers	June 7 & July 10, 2003	Mars	Rovers *Spirit* and *Opportunity* landed on Mars Jan. 2004, found further evidence that water existed on surface; *Spirit* took first photo of a Martian meteor; survived severe dust storms in 2007; *Opportunity* entered massive Victoria Crater Sept. 11.

Spacecraft	Launch date[1]	Mission	Remarks
MESSENGER	Mar. 2, 2004	Mercury	Due to fly by Mercury in 2008, enter orbit in 2011. Probe will map and study Mercury's surface. Reached two-billion-mile mark in Sept. 2007.
Deep Impact	Jan. 12, 2005	Comet Tempel 1	Reached Tempel 1; deployed an impact probe which slammed into the comet on 7/4/05, impacting with a force equivalent to roughly 5 tons of TNT; orbiter probe will pass Earth Dec. 2007 en route to Comet Boethin (in 2008).
Mars Reconnaissance Orbiter	Aug. 12, 2005	Mars	Reached Mars March 10, 2006 and began taking detailed images of the Martian surface. In Sept. 2007, identified vertical shaft cutting through Arsia Mars volcano.
New Horizons (Pluto)	Jan. 19, 2006	Pluto & Charon	Will fly by Jupiter between Feb. and March 2007. Due to reach Pluto and Charon in July 2015; may examine other Kuiper Belt Objects.
Phoenix Mars Lander	Aug. 4, 2007	Mars	Aiming for May 25, 2008 arrival and examination of northern polar region. Will dig for subsurface ice and monitor weather.

(1) Coordinated Universal Time

General Aviation and Air Taxi Active Aircraft, 2005

Source: Federal Aviation Administration; Aircraft not associated with major airlines or the military.

	Total Active	Personal	Business	Corporate	Instructional	Aerial Apps	External Load	Other Work	Sight Seeing	Air Medical	Other	On Demand Operations
Fixed Wing	185,373	123,315	24,072	9,893	11,479	6,346	5	482	340	222	2,763	6,457
Piston	167,608	121,295	21,371	2,012	11,384	5,625	5	408	333	185	2,063	2,927
Turboprop	7,942	1,300	1,868	2,372	70	718	0	69	7	21	96	1,421
Turbojet	9,823	720	834	5,508	25	4	0	5	0	15	604	2,107
Rotorcraft	8,728	1,368	529	522	1,246	2,498	218	46	121	197	144	1,840
Piston	3,039	1,006	251	35	1,166	419	21	10	48	3	46	35
Turbine	5,689	362	278	487	79	2,079	197	36	73	194	98	1,805
Other Aircraft	6,454	5,458	19	0	244	0	0	156	432	0	9	136
Gliders	2,074	1,806	7	0	208	0	0	0	47	0	5	0
Lighter-than-air	4,380	3,652	11	0	36	0	0	156	386	0	3	136
Experimental	23,627	21,151	899	139	394	178	3	49	52	0	683	80
Amateur	19,817	18,367	700	0	343	14	0	0	37	0	357	0
Exhibition	2,120	1,914	28	0	41	0	0	24	2	0	112	0
Other	1,691	871	171	139	11	165	3	25	13	0	214	80
Light Sport	170	115	5	0	36	0	0	0	0	0	14	0
Total All Aircraft	224,352	151,408	25,524	10,553	13,399	9,022	226	732	945	418	3,612	8,515

Note: Columns may not add to totals due to rounding. **Personal**—Flying for personal reasons; **Business**—Individual or group use for business transportation without a paid, professional crew; **Corporate**—Individual or group business transportation with a paid, professional crew (includes fractional ownership); **Instructional**—Flying under the supervision of a flight instructor; **Aerial Applications**—Includes observation (Aerial mapping/photography, patrol, search and rescue, hunting, traffic advisory, ranching, surveillance, oil and mineral exploration, etc.), agriculture, forestry, public health, fire fighting, and other applications; **External Load**—Operations such as helicopter hoists, hauling logs, etc.; **Other Work Use**—Construction work, parachuting, aerial advertising, towing gliders, etc.; **Sight-seeing**—Commercial sight-seeing; **Air Medical Services**—Air ambulance services, rescue, human organ transportation, emergency medical services; **Other**—Positioning flights, proficiency flights, training, ferrying, sales demos; **On Demand Operations**—On-demand air taxi, air tours, commuter, and air medical services.

Estimated Active Airmen Certificates Held, 2005

Source: U.S. Dept. of Transportation, Federal Aviation Administration

CATEGORY		CATEGORY		CATEGORY	
Pilot Total	609,737	Airline Transport	141,992	Parachute Rigger	8,150
Student	87,213	Rotorcraft only (helicopters)	9,518	Ground Instructor	74,378
Recreational	278	Glider	21,369	Dispatcher	18,079
Sport	134	**CATEGORY**		Flight Navigator	298
Airplane[1]		**Nonpilot—Total**	644,016	Flight Attendant	125,032
Private	228,619	Mechanic	320,293	Flight Engineer	57,756
Commercial	120,614	Repairmen	40,030		

Note: The term airmen includes men and women certified as pilots, mechanics or other aviation technicians. (1) Includes pilots with an airplane only certificate as well as those with an airplane and a helicopter and/or glider certificate.

Aircraft Operating Statistics

Source: Courtesy of Air Transport Association of America, Inc. Reprinted with permission. © 2003 by Air Transport Association of America, Inc. All rights reserved. Figures are averages for most commonly used models.

	No. of seats	Speed airborne (mph)	Flight length (mi)	Fuel (gal per hr)	Operating cost per hr		No. of seats	Speed airborne (mph)	Flight length (mi)	Fuel (gal per hr)	Operating cost per hr
B747-200/300*	370	520	3,148	3,625	$9,153	B727-200*	148	430	644	1,289	$4,075
B747-400	367	534	3,960	3,411	8,443	B727-100*	—	417	468	989	13,667
B747-100*	—	503	2,022	1,762	3,852	A320	146	454	1,065	767	2,359
B747-F*	—	506	2,512	3,593	7,138	B737-400	141	409	646	703	2,595
L-1011	325	494	2,023	1,981	8,042	MD-80	134	432	791	953	2,718
DC-10*	286	497	1,637	2,405	7,374	B737-700LR	132	441	879	740	1,692
B767-400	265	495	1,682	1,711	3,124	B737-300/700	132	403	542	723	2,388
B-777	263	525	3,515	2,165	5,105	A319	122	442	904	666	1,913
A330	261	509	3,559	1,407	3,076	A310-200*	—	455	847	1,561	8,066
MD-11*	261	515	2,485	2,473	7,695	B737-100/200	119	396	465	824	2,377
A300-600*	235	460	947	1,638	6,518	B717-200	112	339	175	573	3,355
B757-300	235	472	1,309	985	2,345	B737-500	110	407	576	756	2,347
B767-300ER*	207	497	2,122	1,579	4,217	DC-9	101	387	496	826	2,071
DC-8*	—	437	686	1,712	8,065	F-100	87	398	587	662	2,303
B757-200*	181	464	1,175	1,045	3,312	B737-200C	55	387	313	924	3,421
B767-200ER	175	487	1,987	1,404	3,873	ERJ-145	50	360	343	280	1,142
A321	169	454	1,094	673	1,347	CRJ-145	49	397	486	369	1,433
B737-800/900	151	454	1,035	770	2,248	ERJ-135	37	357	382	267	969
MD-90	150	446	886	825	2,716	SD 340B	33	230	202	84	644

* Data include cargo operations.

Some Notable Aviation Firsts[1]

1903: On Dec. 17, near Kitty Hawk, NC, brothers Wilbur and Orville Wright made the 1st human-carrying, powered flight. Each made 2 flights; the longest, about 852 ft, lasted 59 sec.

1907: U.S. airplane manufacturing company formed by Glenn H. Curtiss.

1908: 1st airplane passenger, Lt. Frank P. Lahm, rode with Wilbur Wright in a brief (6 min, 24 sec) flight.

1911: 1st transportation of mail by airplane officially approved by the U.S. Postal Service began on Sept. 23. It lasted one week. In 1918, limited scheduled airmail service began. In 1921, scheduled transcontinental airmail service began between New York City and San Francisco.

1914: 1st scheduled passenger airline service began. It operated between St. Petersburg and Tampa, FL.

1919: 1st airline food, a basket lunch, was served as part of a commercial airline service.

1930: Ellen Church became 1st flight attendant.

1939: On Aug. 27, the German Heinkel He 178 made the 1st successful flight powered by a jet engine.

1947: Mach 1, the sound barrier was broken by Amer. Chuck Yeager in a Bell X-1 rocket-powered aircraft.

1947: Largest airplane ever flown, Howard Hughes's "Spruce Goose," flew 1 mi at an altitude of 80 ft.

(1) Excludes notable around-the-world and international trips.

1953: Jacqueline Cochran became 1st woman to fly faster than sound.

1960: Convair B-58, 1st supersonic bomber, was introduced.

1969: Tupolev Tu-144 became first passenger airliner to reach Mach 2. The plane had an approximate maximum speed of 1,200 mph.

1970: The Tupolev Tu-144, during commercial transport, reached about 1,335 mph at 53,475 ft.

1976: The Concorde began 1st scheduled supersonic commercial service.

1977: The Gossamer Condor successfully demonstrated human-powered flight, completing figure-8 course of 1.15 miles.

1979: The human-powered Gossamer Albatross crossed the English Channel in 2 hr, 49 min.

1981: Solar Challenger became the 1st solar-powered airplane to cross the English Channel.

2001: Solar powered, propeller-driven plane *Helios* (NASA) reached 96,863 ft, breaking altitude record for non-rocket-powered aircraft.

2005: The Airbus 380, the biggest-ever commercial jet, was unveiled. It was 240 ft. long, had a wingspan of 262 ft., and could seat a maximum of 840 passengers. Scheduled to begin comercial flights Oct. 25, 2007.

Some Notable Around-the-World and Intercontinental Trips

Aviator or Craft	From/To	Miles	Time	Date
J. Alcock-A.W. Brown[1]	Newfoundland/Ireland	1,960	16h 12m	June 14-15, 1919
2 U.S. Army airplanes	Seattle/Seattle	26,103	35d 01h 11m	1924
Richard E. Byrd, Floyd Bennett[2]	Spitsbergen (Nor.)/N. Pole	1,545	15h 30m	May 9, 1926
Amundsen-Ellsworth-Nobile Polar Expedition (in a dirigible)	Spitsbergen (Nor.)/over N. Pole to Teller, Alaska		80h	May 11-14,1926
E.S. Evans and L. Wells (*New York World*)	New York/ New York	18,410[3]	28d 14h 36m 05s	June-July 14, 1926
Charles Lindbergh[4]	New York/Paris	3,610	33h 29m 30s	May 20-21, 1927
Amelia Earhart, W. Stultz, L. Gordon	Newfoundland/Wales	20h 40m		June 17-18, 1928
Graf Zeppelin	Friedrichshafen, Ger./Lakehurst, NJ	6,630	4d 15h 46m	Oct. 11-15, 1928
Graf Zeppelin	Lakehurst, NJ/Lakehurst, NJ.	20,373	21d 05h 31m	Aug. 8-Aug. 29, 1929
Wiley Post and Harold Gatty (Monoplane Winnie Mae)	New York/New York	15,474	8d 15h 51m	July 1, 1931
C. Pangborn-H. Herndon Jr.[5]	Misawa, Japan/Wenatchee, WA	4,458	41h 34m	Oct. 3-5, 1931
Amelia Earhart [6]	Newfoundland/Ireland	2,026	14h 56m	May 20-21, 1932
Wiley Post (Monoplane Winnie Mae)[7]	New York/New York	15,596	115h 36m 30s	July 15-22, 1933
Hindenburg Zeppelin	Lakehurst, NJ/Frankfort, Ger.		42h 53m	May 9-11, 1936
Howard Hughes and 4 assistants	New York/New York	14,824	3d 19h 08m 10s	July 10-13, 1938
America, Pan American 4-engine Lockheed Constellation[8]	New York/New York	22,219	101h 32m	June 17-30, 1947
Col. Edward Eagan	New York/New York	20,559	147h 15m	Dec. 13, 1948
USAF B-50 Lucky Lady II (Capt. James Gallagher)[9]	Ft. Worth, TX/Ft. Worth, TX	23,452	94h 01m	Mar. 2, 1949
Col. D. Schilling, USAF [10]	England/Limestone, ME	3,300	10h 01m	Sept. 22, 1950
C.F. Blair Jr.	Norway/Alaska	3,300	10h 29m	May 29, 1951
Canberra Bomber[11]	N. Ireland/Newfoundland	2,073	04h 34m	Aug. 26, 1952
	Newfoundland/N. Ireland	2,073	03h 25m	Aug. 26, 1952
3 USAF B-52 Strato-fortresses[12]	Merced, CA/CA	24,325	45h 19m	Jan. 15-18, 1957
USSR TU-114[13]	Moscow/New York	5,092	11h 06m	June 28, 1959
Peter Gluckmann (solo)	San Francisco/San Francisco	22,800	29d	Aug. 22-Sept. 20, 1959
Robert & Joan Wallick	Manila/Manila	23,129	5d 06h 17m 10s	June 2-7, 1966
Trevor K. Brougham	Darwin, Australia/Darwin	24,800	5d 05h 57m	Aug. 5-10, 1972
Arnold Palmer	Denver/Denver	22,985	57h 7m 12s	May 17-19, 1976
Boeing 747[14]	San Francisco/San Francisco	26,382	57h 25m 42s	Oct. 28-31, 1977
Richard Rutan & Jeana Yeager[15]	Edwards AFB, CA	24,986	09d 03m 44s	Dec. 14-23, 1986
Concorde	New York/New York	1,114 mph	31h 27m 49s	Aug. 15-16, 1995
Col. Douglas L. Raaberg and crew, B1 bomber[16]	Dyess AFB, Abilene, TX/ Dyess AFB	6,250	36h 13m 36s	June 3, 1995
Linda Finch[17]	Oakland, CA/Oakland, CA	26,000	73d	Mar. 17-May 28, 1997
Bertrand Piccard, Brian Jones[18]	Switzerland/Egypt	29,054.6	19d 21h 55m	Mar. 1-21, 1999
Steve Fossett[19]	Australia/Australia	21,109.6	14d 20h 01m	June 19-July 4, 2002
Steve Fossett[20]	Salina, KS/Salina, KS	26,366	67h 2m 38s	Mar. 1-Mar. 3, 2005
Steve Fossett[21]	Cape Canaveral, FL/Bournemouth, UK	26,389.3	76h 45m	Feb. 8-11, 2006

(1) Nonstop transatlantic flight. (2) Claim of reaching N. Pole in dispute; if claim is untrue, then Amundsen-Ellsworth-Nobile were the first to fly over N. Pole. (3) Includes mileage by train and auto, 4,110; by plane, 6,300; by steamship, 8,000. (4) Solo transatlantic flight in the Ryan monoplane "Spirit of St. Louis." (5) Nonstop transpacific flight. (6) First woman to complete a transoceanic solo flight. Earhart disappeared in the Pacific in 1937 while attempting an around-the-world flight. (7) First to fly solo around N circumference of the world and first to fly twice around the world. (8) Inception of regular commercial global air service. (9) First nonstop round-the-world flight, refueled 4 times in flight. (10) Nonstop jet transatlantic flight. (11) Transatlantic round trip on same day. (12) First nonstop global flight by jet planes; refueled in flight by KC-97 aerial tankers; average speed approx. 525 mph. (13) Nonstop between Moscow and New York. (14) Speed record around the world over both Earth's poles. (15) Circled Earth nonstop without refueling. (16) Refueled in flight 6 times. Tested B-1B bomber by bombing 3 pre-arranged target sites on 3 continents. (17) Followed the intended around-the-world flight route (1937) of Amelia Earhart. (18) First to circumnavigate the globe nonstop in a balloon. (19) First solo circumnavigation of globe nonstop in a balloon; time, dates, and distance are for complete flight, which exceeded circumnavigation because winds prevented landing. (20) First non-stop solo circumnavigation in an airplane without refueling. (21) Longest non-stop, non-refueled solo flight.

ASTRONOMY

Edited by Michael J. Kaufman, Dept. of Physics and Astronomy, San Jose State University

Celestial Events Summary, 2008

There are 4 **eclipses** in 2008: one total solar eclipse, one annular solar eclipse, one total lunar eclipse and one partial lunar eclipse. However, in N America, the annular solar eclipse is not viewable, and the total solar eclipse will only be visible from extreme northern Canada. The total lunar eclipse will be visible across N America while the partial lunar eclipse will not be visible in N America. *See* page 326..

The most likely viewing successes for **meteor showers** will be the Perseids in August and the Orionids in October. All of the other usual meteor showers will be badly affected by bright Moon phases this year. *See* page 320.

At the start of the year Mars and Saturn are up most of the night. Jupiter rises a couple hours before dawn, and Venus is low in the southeast before sunrise. Venus gradually gets closer to the Sun through March, emerging in the evening sky in June for the remainder of the year. Jupiter gradually extends in visibility from just the morning sky until June when it is up all night. In July, it continues moving into the evening sky, eventually disappearing from view after November. Mars begins the year as an evening object, gradu-

ally approaching the Sun at the end of August, and is difficult to see the rest of the year. Saturn is up all night long in February, then begins its move into the evening sky; by August it is lost in the glare of the Sun, reappearing in the morning sky in mid-September. By December, Saturn is visible more than half the night. The best opportunities for seeing Mercury occur in late January, mid-May and early September in the evening sky and early March, early July and late October in the morning sky.

The crescent **Moon**, with its subdued light, regularly makes pretty pairings with the 2 brightest planets, Venus and Jupiter. Waxing crescent **pairings** are visible in the early evening soon after sunset, while waning crescent pairings are visible in the early morning before sunrise. The waning crescent Moon pairs with Venus in each of the months from January through March and then with Jupiter during January and February. The waxing crescent Moon pairs with Jupiter in the evening in October, November and December, and with Venus each month from August through December.

Astronomical Positions and Constants

Two celestial bodies are in **conjunction** when they are due North and South of each other, either in **right ascension** (with respect to the North celestial pole) or in **celestial longitude** (with respect to the North ecliptic pole). Celestial bodies in conjunction will rise and set at nearly the same time. For the inner planets—Mercury and Venus—**inferior conjunction** occurs when either planet passes between Earth and the Sun, while **superior conjunction** occurs when either Mercury or Venus is on the far side of the Sun. Celestial bodies are in **opposition** when their Right Ascensions differ by exactly 12 hours, or when their Celestial Longitudes differ by exactly 180°. In this case one of the 2 objects in opposition will rise while the other is setting. **Quadrature** refers to the arrangement where the coordinates of 2 bodies differ by exactly 90°. These terms may refer to the relative positions of any 2 bodies as seen from Earth, but one of the bodies is so frequently the Sun that mention of the Sun is omitted in that case.

When objects are in conjunction, the alignment is not perfect, and one is usually passing above or below the other.

The geocentric angular separation between the Sun and an object is termed **elongation**. Elongation is limited only for Mercury and Venus; the greatest elongation for each of these bodies is approximately the time for longest observation. **Perihelion** is the point in an orbit that is nearest to the Sun, and **aphelion** is the point farthest from the Sun. **Perigee** is the point in an orbit that is nearest Earth, and **apogee** is the point that is farthest from Earth. An **occultation** of a planet or a star is an eclipse of it by some other body, usually the Moon. A **transit** of the Sun occurs when Mercury or Venus passes directly between Earth and the Sun, appearing to cross the disk of the Sun.

The following were adopted as part of the International Astronomical Union System of Astronomical Constants (1976): **Speed of light**, 299,792.458 km per sec., or about 186,282 statute mi per sec.; **solar parallax**, 8".794148; **Astronomical Unit** (the mean distance between the Earth and the Sun), 149,597,870 km, or 92,955,807 mi; **constant of nutation**, 9".2025; and **constant of aberration**, 20".49552.

Celestial Events Highlights, 2008

(Coordinated Universal Time, or UTC—the standard time of the prime meridian)

January

Mercury is visible low in the SW near the end of the month.

Venus is a very bright early morning object all month.

Mars rises mid-afternoon and is up most of the night.

Jupiter is low in the SE before sunrise.

Saturn, rising a couple of hours after sunset, is up most of the night.

Moon passes Venus on the 5th, Jupiter on the 7th, Mercury on the 9th, Uranus on the 13th, Mars on the 20th, and Saturn on the 25th.

Jan. 1— Jupiter in Sagittarius, Saturn in Leo, Uranus in Aquarius and Neptune in Capricornus all year. Mercury, Sun in Sagittarius. Venus in Libra, Mars in Taurus. Moon passes 2.4° S of Spica.

Jan. 2— Venus enters Scorpius.

Jan. 3—Earth at perihelion, closest approach to the Sun.

Jan. 5—Moon passes 0.5° S of Antares, occults Antares (like all occultations, this one is only visible from some parts of the Earth).

Jan. 6—Venus enters Ophiuchus.

Jan. 7—Moon passes 4.3° S of Jupiter, Venus passes 6.5° N of Antares.

Jan. 9—Moon passes 0.3° S of Mercury, occults Mercury.

Jan. 11—Moon passes 0.4° S of Neptune, occults Neptune.

Jan. 13—Moon passes 2.6° N of Uranus.

Jan. 19—Moon passes 10.6° N of Aldebaran.

Jan. 20—Moon passes 1.1° N of Mars, occults Mars Sun enters Capricornus.

Jan. 22—Moon passes 3.8° S of Pollux, Mercury at greatest elongation 18° (E of the Sun and sets after the Sun). Venus enters Sagittarius.

Jan. 23—Mercury passes 0.3° N of Neptune.

Jan. 24—Moon passes 0.7° S of Regulus, occults Regulus.

Jan. 25—Moon passes 2.9° S of Saturn.

Jan. 28—Moon passes 2.5° S of Spica.

February

Mercury is visible in the SE before sunrise during the second half of the month.

Venus is visible in the SE before sunrise all month, pairing with Jupiter on the 1st and Mercury on the 26th.

Mars rises midday and is visible until several hours before sunrise.

Jupiter is visible in the SE before sunrise.

Saturn rises in the early evening and is up most of the night.

Moon, passes Jupiter and Venus on the 4th; passes Mars on the 16th and Saturn on the 21st. Watch for the waning crescent Moon passing close to the pairing of Venus and Jupiter on the 4th. Eclipsed Moon will be visible near Saturn on the 21st (beginning before midnight on the 20th from the U.S.).

Feb. 1—Venus passes 0.6° N of Jupiter, Neptune passes 3.2° S of Mercury, Moon passes 0.6° S of Antares, occults Antares.

Feb. 4—Moon passes 4.02° S of Jupiter, Moon passes 4.3° S of Venus.

Feb. 6—Mercury in inferior conjunction 4° N of Sun.

Feb. 7—Moon passes 4.9° S of Mercury, 0.3° S of Neptune, occults Neptune. Annular eclipse of the Sun, *see* details under Eclipses.

Feb. 9—Moon passes 2.8° N of Uranus.

Feb. 11—Neptune passes 0.3° S of Sun.

Feb. 15—Moon passes 10.7° N of Aldebaran.

Feb. 16—Moon passes 1.6° N of Mars. Sun enters Aquarius.

Feb. 18—Moon passes 3.8° S of Pollux. Venus enters Capricornus.

Feb. 21—Moon passes 0.7° S of Regulus, 2.8° S of Saturn, occults Regulus. Total lunar eclipse, *see* details under Eclipses.

Feb. 24—Saturn at opposition.

Feb. 25—Moon passes 2.6° S of Spica

Feb. 26—Venus passes 1.3° S of Mercury.

Feb. 29—Moon passes 0.6° S of Antares, occults Antares.

March

Mercury is visible in SE just before sunrise early in the month, reaching greatest elongation on the 3rd.

Venus is visible in SE just before sunrise early in the month but rapidly approaches the Sun as the month proceeds

Mars is visible high in the sky at sunset all month, setting after midnight.

Jupiter rises several hours before sunrise and is in the SE at sunrise all month.

Saturn rises before sunset all month and is visible for much of the night.

Moon passes Mercury, Venus and Neptune on the 5th, Mars on the 15th, Saturn on the 19th, Jupiter on the 30th.

Mar. 3—Moon passes 3.7° S of Jupiter, Mercury at greatest elongation 27° (W of the Sun and rises before the Sun).

Mar. 5—Moon passes 0.3° S of Mercury, 0.2° S of Neptune, 0.2° N of Venus, occults Mercury, Neptune and Venus.

Mar. 6—Venus passes 0.6° S of Neptune. Mars enters Gemini.

Mar. 7—Moon passes 2.9° N of Uranus.

Mar. 8—Uranus passes 0.7° S of Sun.

Mar. 9—Mercury passes 0.9° S of Neptune.

Mar. 11—Venus enters Aquarius. Sun enters Pisces.

Mar. 13—Moon passes 10.6° N of Aldebaran.

Mar. 15—Moon passes 1.7° N of Mars.

Mar. 16—Moon passes 3.9° S of Pollux.

Mar. 19—Moon passes 0.8° S of Regulus, 2.7° S of Saturn, occults Regulus.

Mar. 23—Venus passes 1.1° N of Mercury, Moon passes 2.5° S of Spica.

Mar. 27—Moon passes 0.5° S of Antares, occults Antares. Mercury passes 1.8° S of Uranus.

Mar. 28—Venus passes 0.7° S of Uranus.

Mar. 30—Moon passes 3.2° S of Jupiter.

April

Mercury will be too close to the Sun to see all month.

Venus is rapidly approaching the rising Sun and will be difficult to see all month.

Mars is high in the sky at sunset and sets around midnight.

Jupiter rises around midnight and is high in the S at sunrise.

Saturn is high in the S/SE at sunset all month and sets after midnight.

Moon passes Mercury and Venus on the 5th, Mars on the 12th, Jupiter on the 27th.

Apr. 2—Moon passes 0.1° N of Neptune, occults Neptune.

Apr. 3—Venus enters Pisces.

Apr. 4—Moon passes 3.1° N of Uranus.

Apr. 5—Moon passes 5.8° N of Mercury, 4.7° N of Venus.

Apr. 9—Moon passes 10.5° N of Aldebaran.

Apr. 12—Moon passes 1.2° N of Mars, 4° S of Pollux, occults Mars. Venus enters Cetus.

Apr. 15—Moon passes 0.9° S of Regulus, 2.6° S of Saturn, occults Regulus. Venus enters Pisces.

Apr. 16—Mercury in superior conjunction. Sun enters Aries.

Apr. 19—Moon passes 2.4° S of Spica.

Apr. 22—Lyrid meteor shower, but with bright full Moon.

Apr. 23—Moon passes 0.3° S of Antares, occults Antares.

Apr. 27—Moon passes 2.8° S of Jupiter.

Apr. 28—Pollux passes 4.9° N of Mars.

Apr. 29—Moon passes 0.3° N of Neptune, occults Neptune.

May

Mercury is at greatest elongation on the 14th, visible after sunset.

Venus is very low in the E at sunset and difficult to spot.

Mars is in the SW at sunset, setting before midnight.

Jupiter rises before midnight and is in the SW at sunrise.

Saturn is high in the sky at sunset and sets after midnight

Moon passes Venus on the 5th, Mercury on the 6th , Mars on the 10th, Saturn on the 13th, Jupiter on the 24th, Neptune on the 27th, Uranus on the 29th.

May 1—Moon passes 3.41° N of Uranus.

May 2—Venus enters Aries.

May 5—Moon passes 6.3° N of Venus.

May 6—Moon passes 2.5° N of Mercury. Mars enters Cancer.

May 7—Moon passes 10.3° N of Aldebaran.

May 10—Mercury passes 8° N of Aldebaran, Moon passes 0.3° N of Mars, occults.

May 12—Moon passes 1.1° S of Regulus, occults Regulus.

May 13—Moon passes 2.8° S of Saturn.

May 14—Mercury at greatest elongation 22° (E of the Sun and sets after the Sun). Sun enters Taurus.

May 17—Moon passes 2.5° S of Spica.

May 20—Moon passes 0.2° S of Antares, occults Antares. Venus enters Taurus.

May 24—Moon passes 2.5° S of Jupiter.

May 27—Moon passes 0.6° N of Neptune, occults Neptune.

May 29—Moon passes 3.8° N of Uranus.

June

Mercury is visible in the E just before sunrise late in the month.

Venus is very close to the Sun all month and very difficult to spot.

Mars is in the SW at sunset and sets a few hours later.

Jupiter is in the SE after sunset and in the SW at sunrise, up most of the night.

Saturn is in the SW at sunset and sets before midnight.

Moon passes Venus on the 2nd, Mercury on the 4th, Mars on the 8th, Saturn on the 9th , Jupiter on the 20th, Neptune on the 23rd and Uranus on the 25th. Look for the waxing crescent Moon between Mars and Saturn after sunset on the 8th.

June 2—Venus passes 5.3° N of Aldebran.

June 3—Moon passes 4.9° N of Venus, 10.3° N of Aldebaran.

June 4—Moon passes 6.4° N of Mercury.

June 6—Moon passes 4.5° S of Pollux.

June 7—Mercury at inferior conjunction.

June 8—Moon passes 1.1° S of Mars, occults Mars. Mercury passes 3° S of Venus.

June 9—Moon passes 1.4° S of Regulus, 3.1° S of Saturn, Venus at superior conjunction.

June 11—Mars enters Leo.

June 13—Moon passes 2.7° S of Spica.

June 17—Moon passes 0.2° S of Antares, occults Antares.

June 19—Venus enters Gemini.

June 20—Moon passes 2.4° S of Jupiter. Northern Solstice at 23:59 UTC (19:59 EDT).

June 21—Sun enters Gemini.

June 23—Moon passes 0.8° N of Neptune, occults Neptune.

June 25—Moon passes 4° N of Uranus.

June 28—Ceres at conjunction.

July

Mercury is visible low in the E at sunrise early in the month.

Venus is visible very low in the W at sunset by the end of the month.

Mars is low in the W at sunset and sets a few hours later, makes a nice paring with Saturn for a few days around the 11th.

Jupiter rises around sunset and is visible most of the night.

Saturn is low in the SW at sunset and sets several hours later.

Moon passes Venus on the 3rd, Mars and Saturn on the 6th, Jupiter on the 17th, Neptune on the 20th, Uranus on the 22nd. Look for a nice grouping of the young crescent Moon with Saturn, Mars, and Regulus after sunset on the 6th.

July 1—Mars passes 0.7° N of Regulus, Moon passes 7.7° N of Mercury, 10° N of Aldebaran, Mercury at greatest elongation 22° (W of the Sun and rises before the Sun).

July 3—Moon passes 1.7° N of Venus, 4.6° S of Pollux.

July 4—Earth at aphelion, largest distance from the Sun.

July 6—Moon passes 1.6° S of Regulus, 2.6° S of Mars, 3.5° S of Saturn.

July 8—Pollux passes 5.7° N of Venus.

July 9—Jupiter at opposition.

July 10—Moon passes 2.9° S of Spica.

July 11—Mars passes 0.7° S of Saturn.

July 12—Venus enters Cancer.

July 14—Moon passes 0.3° S of Antares, occults Antares.

July 17—Moon passes 2.6° S of Jupiter.

July 20—Moon passes 0.9° N of Neptune, occults Neptune. Sun enters Cancer.

July 22—Moon passes 4.2° N of Uranus.

July 23—Pollux passes 5.6° N of Mercury.

July 28—Moon passes 10° N of Aldebaran. Venus enters Leo.

July 29—Mercury at superior conjunction.

July 31—Moon passes 4.6° S of Pollux.

August

Mercury is visible low in the W after sunset the second half of the month. Look for a nice pairing of Mercury with Venus low in the W after sunset on the 23rd and for several nights afterwards. Look for Mercury between Venus and Mars at sunset on the 30th.

Venus is low in the W at sunset all month.

Mars is low in W at sunset and sets several hours later.

Jupiter rises before sunset and is visible most of the night all month.

Saturn is very low in the W all month. Look for Saturn in a very close pairing with Venus on the 13th just after sunset.

Moon passes Mercury on 1st, Venus on 2nd, Saturn on 3rd, Mars on 4th, Jupiter on 13th, Neptune on 16th, Uranus on 19th, Saturn on 31st. Moon is partially eclipsed on the 16th but not visible from N. America.

Aug. 1—Moon passes 1.3° S of Mercury, occults Mercury. Total solar eclipse, *see* details under Eclipses.

Aug. 2—Moon passes 1.7° S of Regulus, 2.34° S of Venus.

Aug. 3—Moon passes 3.8° S of Saturn.

Aug. 4—Moon passes 4° S of Mars.

Aug. 5—Regulus passes 1.1° S of Venus.

Aug. 7—Moon passes 3° S of Spica.

Aug. 10—Moon passes 0.4° S of Antares, occults Antares. Mercury passes 1.1° N of Regulus. Mars enters Virgo. Sun enters Leo

Aug. 12—Perseid meteor shower, 10 PM until sunrise.

Aug. 13—Moon passes 2.8° S of Jupiter, Venus passes 0.2° S of Saturn.

Aug. 15—Neptune at opposition.

Aug. 16—Moon passes 0.8° N of Neptune, occults Neptune. Mercury passes 0.7° S of Saturn. Partial lunar eclipse, *see* details under Eclipses.

Aug. 19—Moon passes 4.1° N of Uranus.

Aug. 23—Mercury passes 1.3° S of Venus.

Aug. 24—Moon passes 10° N of Aldebaran.

Aug. 26—Venus enters Virgo.

Aug. 27—Moon passes 4.6° S of Pollux.

Aug. 30—Moon passes 1.7° S of Regulus.

Aug. 31—Moon passes 4.2° S of Saturn.

September

Mercury is low in the W at sunset all month, more easily visible later in the month. Look for grouping with Mars and Venus on the 11th.

Venus is low in the W at sunset early in the month and in the SW at sunset later in the month.

Mars is low in the W at sunset all month.

Jupiter is visible in the S/SE at sunset all month and is visible the first half of the night.

Saturn is visible low in the E before sunrise the second half of the month.

Moon passes Mercury and Venus on the 1st, Mars on the 2nd, Jupiter on the 9th, Neptune on the 13th, Uranus on the 15th , Saturn on the 22nd, Mercury on the 30th.

Sep. 1—Moon passes 2.9° S of Mercury, Moon passes 5.28° S of Venus.

Sep. 2—Moon passes 5° S of Mars.

Sep. 3—Moon passes 2.9° S of Spica.

Sep. 4—Saturn passes 1.7° N of Sun.

Sep. 7—Moon passes 0.3° S of Antares, occults Antares.

Sep. 9—Moon passes 2.8° S of Jupiter.

Sep. 11—Venus passes 0.3° N of Mars, 3.57° N of Mercury, Mercury at greatest elongation 27° (E of the Sun and sets after the Sun).

Sep. 12—Mercury passes 3.4° S of Mars.

Sep. 13—Moon passes 0.8° N of Neptune, occults Neptune. Uranus at opposition.

Sep. 15—Moon passes 4° N of Uranus.

Sep. 16—Sun enters Virgo.

Sep. 18—Spica passes 2.7° S of Venus.

Sep. 19—Mercury passes 4.1° S of Mars.

Sep. 20—Moon passes 10° N of Aldebaran

Sep. 22—Autumnal Equinox at 15:44 UTC (11:44 EDT)

Sep. 23—Spica passes 2.5° S of Mars, Moon passes 4.68° S of Pollux.

Sep. 26—Moon passes 1.7° S of Regulus.

Sep. 27—Moon passes 4.5° S of Saturn.

Sep. 30—Moon passes 1.1° S of Mercury, 2.87° S of Spica, occults Mercury.

October

Mercury is visible low in the E before sunrise late in the month.

Venus is low in the SW at sunset all month.

Mars is very near the setting Sun all month and difficult to see.

Jupiter is high in the S at sunset and visible the first half of the night.

Saturn is visible in the E several hours before sunrise all month.

Moon passes Mars on the 1st, Venus on the 2nd, Jupiter on the 7th, Neptune on the 10th, Uranus on the 12th, Saturn on the 25th, Mercury on the 27th, Mars on the 30th.

Oct. 1—Moon passes 5.4° S of Mars. Venus enters Libra.

Oct. 2—Moon passes 5.1° S of Venus.

Oct. 4—Moon passes 0.1° S of Antares, occults Antares.

Oct. 6—Mercury at inferior conjunction.

Oct. 7—Moon passes 2.5° S of Jupiter.

Oct. 10—Moon passes 0.9° N of Neptune, occults Neptune.

Oct. 12—Moon passes 4° N of Uranus.

Oct. 16—Mars enters Libra.

Oct. 18—Moon passes 10° N of Aldebaran.

Oct. 19—Venus enters Scorpius.

Oct. 21—Moon passes 4.9° S of Pollux; Orionid meteor shower from 10 PM until moonrise after midnight.

Oct. 22—Mercury at greatest elongation 18° (W of the Sun and rises before the Sun).

Oct. 23—Moon passes 1.9° S of Regulus.

Oct. 25—Moon passes 5° S of Saturn.

Oct. 26—Antares passes 3.2° S of Venus. Venus enters Ophiuchus.

Oct. 27—Moon passes 7.2° S of Mercury.

Oct. 28—Moon passes 2.8° S of Spica.

Oct. 30—Spica passes 4.4° S of Mercury, Moon passes 5.08° S of Venus.

Oct. 31—Moon passes 0.1° N of Antares, occults Antares. Sun enters Libra.

November

Mercury is too close to the Sun to be seen this month.

Venus is low visible in the SW after sunset all month.

Mars is very near the setting Sun all month and difficult to see.

Jupiter is in the S/SW at sunset and sets mid-evening.

Saturn rises after midnight and is high in the S at sunrise.

Moon passes Venus on the 1st, Jupiter on the 3rd, Neptune on the 6th, Uranus on the 9th, Saturn on the 21st, Mercury and Mars on the 27th. Look for the crescent Moon between Venus and Jupiter on the 2nd.

Nov. 1—Moon passes 2.6° S of Venus.

Nov. 3—Moon passes 1.9° S of Jupiter.

Nov. 6—Moon passes 1.1° N of Neptune, occults Neptune.

Nov. 9—Moon passes 4.1° N of Uranus.

Nov. 10—Venus enters Sagittarius.

Nov. 14—Moon passes 10° N of Aldebaran.

Nov. 17—Moon passes 5.2° S of Pollux. Mars enters Scorpius. Leonid meteor shower, poor because of bright Moon nearby.

Nov. 20—Moon passes 2.2° S of Regulus.

Nov. 21—Moon passes 5.6° S of Saturn.

Nov. 23—Sun enters Scorpius.

Nov. 24—Moon passes 3° S of Spica.

Nov. 25—Mercury in superior conjunction.

Nov. 27—Moon passes 3.7° S of Mercury, 4.1° S of Mars.

Nov. 28—Moon passes 0.1° N of Antares, occults Antares. Mars enters Ophiuchus.

Nov. 29—Mercury passes 0.6° S of Mars, 3.7° N of Antares. Sun enters Ophiuchus.

December

Mercury is visible low in the SW after sunset the second half of the month. Look for Mercury, Jupiter and the crescent Moon after sunset on the 29th.

Venus is visible in the SW after sunset all month. Look for Venus, Jupiter and the several day old Moon on the 1st.

Mars is very close to the Sun and difficult to see all month.

Jupiter is low in the SW at sunset and sets several hours later.

Saturn rises around midnight and is high in the S at sunrise.

Moon passes Venus and Jupiter on the 1st, Neptune on the 4th, Uranus on the 6th, Saturn on the 19th, Mars on the 26th, Jupiter and Mercury on the 29th, Neptune and Venus on the 31st. Look for the several day old Moon with Jupiter and Venus on the 1st.

Dec. 1—Moon passes 0.8° N of Venus, 1.29° S of Jupiter, occults Venus.

Dec. 4—Moon passes 1.4° N of Neptune.

Dec. 5—Mars passes 0.5° S of Sun.

Dec. 6—Moon passes 4.4° N of Uranus.

Dec. 8—Venus enters Capricornus.

Dec. 12—Moon passes 10° N of Aldebaran.

Dec. 13—Geminid meteor shower, obscured by bright full moon.

Dec. 14—Moon passes 5.4° S of Pollux.

Dec. 17—Moon passes 2.4° S of Regulus.

Dec. 18—Sun enters Sagittarius.

Dec. 19—Moon passes 6.1° S of Saturn.

Dec. 21—Moon passes 3.2° S of Spica. Southern Solstice at 12:04 UTC (07:04 EST).

Dec. 23—Mars enters Sagittarius.

Dec. 25—Moon passes 0.1° N of Antares, occults Antares.

Dec. 26—Moon passes 2.7° S of Mars.

Dec. 27—Venus passes 1.5° S of Neptune.

Dec. 29—Moon passes 0.6° S of Jupiter, 0.7° N of Mercury, occults Jupiter and Mercury.

Dec. 31—Mercury passes 1.3° S of Jupiter, Moon passes 1.7° N of Neptune, 3.4° N of Venus.

Meteorites and Meteor Showers

When a chunk of material, ice or rock, plunges into Earth's atmosphere and burns up in a fiery display, the event is a **meteor**. While the chunk of material is still in space, it is a **meteoroid**. If a portion of the material survives passage through the atmosphere and reaches the ground, the remnant on the ground is a **meteorite**.

Meteorites found on Earth are classified into types, depending on their composition: **irons**, those composed chiefly of iron, a small percentage of nickel, and traces of other metals such as cobalt; **stones**, stony meteors consisting of silicates; and **stony irons**, containing varying proportions of both iron and stone.

Serious study of meteorites as non-earth objects began in the 20th century. Scientists use sophisticated chemical analysis, X rays, and mass spectrography in determining their origin and composition. Although most meteorites are now believed to be fragments of asteroids or comets, geochemical studies have shown that a few Antarctic stones came from the Moon or from Mars, presumably ejected by the explosive impact of asteroids.

The **largest known meteorite**, estimated to weigh about 55 metric tons, is situated at Hoba West near Grootfontein, Namibia. The Manicouagan impact crater in Quebec, Canada, with an estimated diameter of 60 mi, is one of the largest crater structures still visible on the surface of the Earth. Although not visible to the eye, other still larger impact craters identified include the Vredefort crater in South Africa at 185 mi across and the Sudbury crater in Ontario, Canada, es-

timated at 125 mi across. The Bedout impact site off the NW coast of Australia gained attention in 2004, when scientists identified further evidence in support of the idea that it may be linked to the Permian extinction event 250 million years ago.

Meteor showers vary in strength, but usually the 3 best meteor showers of the year are the **Perseids**, around Aug. 13, the **Orionids**, around Oct. 21, and the **Geminids**, around Dec. 14. These showers feature meteors at the rate of about 60 per hour. Best observing conditions occur with the absence of moonlight, usually when the Moon's phase is between waning crescent Moon and waxing quarter Moon.

For most meteor showers the cometary debris is relatively uniformly scattered along the comet's orbit. However, in the case of the **Leonid** meteor shower, which occurs every year around Nov. 17-18, the cometary debris, from Comet Temple-Tuttle, seems to be bunched up in one stretch. Hence, most years when Earth crosses the orbit of this comet, the meteor shower produced is relatively weak. However, about every 33 years, Earth encounters the bunched-up debris. Sometimes the storm is a disappointment, as it was in 1899 and 1933; at other times it is a roaring success, as in 1833 and 1866. The Leonids stormed again more recently, producing rates of 1,000-3,000 meteors per hour in 2001. Best showers in 2008 are the Perseids in mid-August with a waxing gibbous Moon, and to a lesser extent the Orionids in October. All other major meteor showers are badly affected this year by bright Moon phases.

Rising and Setting of Planets, 2008

In Coordinated Universal Time (0 in the *h* col. designates 12 AM).

Venus, 2008

Date	20° N Latitude Rise h m	20° N Latitude Set h m	30° N Latitude Rise h m	30° N Latitude Set h m	40° N Latitude Rise h m	40° N Latitude Set h m	50° N Latitude Rise h m	50° N Latitude Set h m	60° N Latitude Rise h m	60° N Latitude Set h m
Jan. 1	3 45	14 54	4 01	14 38	4 21	14 17	4 50	13 49	5 36	13 03
11	4 00	15 02	4 18	14 43	4 42	14 20	5 14	13 47	6 09	12 52
21	4 15	15 13	4 35	14 53	5 00	14 28	5 35	13 52	6 36	12 52
31	4 29	15 26	4 50	15 06	5 15	14 40	5 51	14 05	6 53	13 03
Feb. 10	4 41	15 41	5 01	15 22	5 25	14 58	5 59	14 24	6 57	13 26
20	4 51	15 57	5 09	15 40	5 30	15 18	6 00	14 48	6 51	13 58
Mar. 1	4 58	16 13	5 12	15 59	5 31	15 41	5 56	15 16	6 36	14 36
11	5 02	16 28	5 13	16 17	5 27	16 03	5 46	15 45	6 15	15 16
21	5 03	16 43	5 11	16 35	5 20	16 26	5 32	16 14	5 51	15 56
31	5 03	16 56	5 06	16 53	5 11	16 49	5 16	16 44	5 24	16 36
Apr. 10	5 02	17 09	5 01	17 10	5 00	17 11	4 59	17 13	4 57	17 16
20	5 01	17 22	4 56	17 27	4 50	17 34	4 42	17 42	4 29	17 56
30	5 00	17 36	4 51	17 45	4 40	17 56	4 25	18 12	4 01	18 37
May 10	5 02	17 50	4 49	18 03	4 33	18 20	4 10	18 42	3 35	19 19
20	5 05	18 06	4 49	18 22	4 28	18 43	3 59	19 13	3 11	20 02
30	5 12	18 22	4 52	18 42	4 28	19 06	3 53	19 41	2 53	20 43
Jun. 9	5 21	18 38	5 00	19 00	4 32	19 27	3 53	20 07	2 42	21 18
19	5 34	18 54	5 11	19 16	4 43	19 45	4 01	20 26	2 45	21 43
29	5 48	19 08	5 26	19 30	4 58	19 58	4 18	20 38	3 03	21 52
Jul. 9	6 05	19 18	5 44	19 39	5 18	20 05	4 41	20 41	3 35	21 46
19	6 21	19 26	6 03	19 44	5 41	20 06	5 09	20 37	4 15	21 30
29	6 37	19 30	6 22	19 45	6 04	20 02	5 39	20 27	4 58	21 08
Aug. 8	6 52	19 32	6 41	19 42	6 28	19 55	6 10	20 13	5 41	20 41
18	7 05	19 31	6 59	19 38	6 51	19 45	6 40	19 56	6 23	20 12
28	7 18	19 29	7 16	19 31	7 14	19 34	7 10	19 37	7 04	19 42
Sept. 7	7 31	19 27	7 33	19 25	7 36	19 22	7 40	19 18	7 45	19 12
17	7 44	19 25	7 50	19 18	7 59	19 10	8 10	18 59	8 26	18 41
27	7 57	19 24	8 08	19 13	8 22	18 59	8 40	18 41	9 09	18 12
Oct. 7	8 12	19 25	8 27	19 10	8 45	18 52	9 11	18 26	9 52	17 44
17	8 27	19 29	8 46	19 11	9 09	18 47	9 42	18 15	10 36	17 20
27	8 44	19 37	9 05	19 15	9 32	18 48	10 10	18 10	11 18	17 02
Nov. 6	9 00	19 47	9 23	19 24	9 52	18 54	10 34	18 12	11 52	16 54
16	9 14	20 00	9 38	19 36	10 08	19 06	10 51	18 23	12 12	17 02
26	9 26	20 14	9 48	19 51	10 17	19 23	10 59	18 42	12 14	17 26
Dec. 6	9 34	20 29	9 54	20 08	10 20	19 42	10 57	19 06	12 01	18 02
16	9 37	20 42	9 55	20 25	10 17	20 03	10 48	19 32	11 39	18 42
26	9 37	20 54	9 51	20 40	10 08	20 23	10 32	19 59	11 10	19 21

Mars, 2008

Date	20° N Latitude Rise h m	20° N Latitude Set h m	30° N Latitude Rise h m	30° N Latitude Set h m	40° N Latitude Rise h m	40° N Latitude Set h m	50° N Latitude Rise h m	50° N Latitude Set h m	60° N Latitude Rise h m	60° N Latitude Set h m
Jan. 1	16 30	6 03	16 04	6 29	15 31	7 02	14 42	7 52	12 58	9 35
11	15 37	5 10	15 11	5 36	14 38	6 09	13 48	6 59	12 05	8 42
21	14 49	4 22	14 24	4 48	13 51	5 21	13 02	6 10	11 19	7 52
31	14 08	3 39	13 42	4 05	13 10	4 38	12 21	5 26	10 41	7 07
Feb. 10	13 32	3 03	13 07	3 28	12 34	4 01	11 46	4 49	10 07	6 28
20	13 01	2 31	12 35	2 56	12 03	3 28	11 15	4 16	9 38	5 53
Mar. 1	12 33	2 03	12 08	2 28	11 36	3 00	10 49	3 47	9 13	5 23
11	12 09	1 37	11 44	2 02	11 12	2 34	10 25	3 21	8 52	4 55
21	11 47	1 14	11 23	1 39	10 51	2 10	10 05	2 56	8 34	4 27
31	11 27	0 53	11 03	1 17	10 33	1 48	9 48	2 32	8 21	4 00
Apr. 10	11 09	0 32	10 46	0 56	10 16	1 26	9 33	2 09	8 10	3 31
20	10 52	0 13	10 30	0 35	10 01	1 04	9 20	1 45	8 03	3 02
30	10 36	23 51	10 15	0 15	9 48	0 42	9 09	1 21	7 58	2 32
May 10	10 21	23 32	10 01	23 52	9 36	0 20	8 59	0 56	7 55	2 00
20	10 07	23 13	9 48	23 32	9 24	23 55	8 51	0 31	7 54	1 28
30	9 53	22 54	9 35	23 11	9 14	23 32	8 44	0 05	7 53	0 56
Jun. 9	9 39	22 34	9 23	22 49	9 04	23 08	8 37	23 35	7 53	0 22
19	9 25	22 14	9 12	22 28	8 55	22 44	8 31	23 08	7 53	23 45
29	9 12	21 54	9 00	22 06	8 46	22 20	8 26	22 40	7 54	23 11
Jul. 9	8 58	21 34	8 49	21 44	8 37	21 55	8 20	22 11	7 55	22 37
19	8 45	21 14	8 38	21 21	8 28	21 30	8 16	21 43	7 56	22 02
29	8 32	20 53	8 27	20 59	8 20	21 05	8 11	21 14	7 57	21 28
Aug. 8	8 19	20 33	8 16	20 36	8 12	20 40	8 07	20 45	7 58	20 53
18	8 07	20 13	8 06	20 14	8 04	20 15	8 03	20 16	8 00	20 19
28	7 54	19 53	7 56	19 52	7 57	19 50	7 59	19 48	8 02	19 45
Sept. 7	7 42	19 33	7 46	19 30	7 50	19 25	7 56	19 19	8 05	19 11
17	7 31	19 14	7 37	19 08	7 44	19 01	7 53	18 52	8 08	18 37
27	7 20	18 56	7 28	18 48	7 38	18 38	7 51	18 24	8 12	18 04
Oct. 7	7 10	18 38	7 20	18 28	7 33	18 15	7 50	17 58	8 17	17 31
17	7 01	18 22	7 13	18 09	7 28	17 54	7 49	17 33	8 22	16 59
27	6 52	18 06	7 06	17 52	7 24	17 34	7 49	17 09	8 29	16 29
Nov. 6	6 44	17 52	7 00	17 35	7 21	17 15	7 49	16 46	8 36	16 00
16	6 37	17 39	6 55	17 21	7 17	16 58	7 49	16 26	8 42	15 33
26	6 30	17 27	6 49	17 07	7 14	16 43	7 49	16 08	8 48	15 08
Dec. 6	6 23	17 17	6 44	16 56	7 10	16 30	7 48	15 53	8 53	14 48
16	6 17	17 08	6 39	16 47	7 06	16 19	7 45	15 41	8 54	14 31
26	6 11	17 01	6 33	16 39	7 01	16 11	7 40	15 32	8 51	14 20

Jupiter, 2008

Date	20° N Latitude Rise h m	Set h m	30° N Latitude Rise h m	Set h m	40° N Latitude Rise h m	Set h m	50° N Latitude Rise h m	Set h m	60° N Latitude Rise h m	Set h m
Jan. 1	6 06	16 58	6 27	16 37	6 53	16 10	7 31	15 32	8 37	14 26
11	5 36	16 28	5 57	16 07	6 23	15 41	7 01	15 03	8 07	13 58
21	5 06	15 59	5 27	15 38	5 53	15 12	6 31	14 34	7 36	13 29
31	4 36	15 29	4 57	15 08	5 23	14 42	6 00	14 05	7 04	13 01
Feb. 10	4 05	14 59	4 26	14 38	4 52	14 12	5 29	13 36	6 32	12 32
20	3 34	14 28	3 55	14 08	4 20	13 42	4 57	13 06	6 00	12 03
Mar. 1	3 03	13 57	3 23	13 37	3 48	13 12	4 24	12 36	5 26	11 34
11	2 30	13 25	2 50	13 05	3 15	12 40	3 51	12 05	4 52	11 04
21	1 57	12 53	2 17	12 33	2 41	12 08	3 16	11 33	4 17	10 33
31	1 22	12 19	1 42	11 59	2 07	11 34	2 42	11 00	3 41	10 00
Apr. 10	0 47	11 44	1 07	11 24	1 31	11 00	2 06	10 26	3 05	9 27
20	0 11	11 08	0 30	10 48	0 55	10 24	1 29	9 50	2 27	8 52
30	23 30	10 31	23 49	10 11	0 17	9 47	0 51	9 13	1 49	8 15
May 10	22 51	9 52	23 10	9 32	23 34	9 08	0 12	8 34	1 11	7 36
20	22 11	9 12	22 30	8 52	22 55	8 28	23 29	7 54	0 31	6 55
30	21 29	8 30	21 49	8 11	22 14	7 46	22 48	7 12	23 47	6 13
Jun. 9	20 47	7 47	21 07	7 28	21 31	7 03	22 06	6 28	23 06	5 29
19	20 04	7 03	20 24	6 44	20 49	6 19	21 24	5 44	22 24	4 43
29	19 20	6 19	19 40	5 59	20 05	5 34	20 41	4 58	21 42	3 57
Jul. 9	18 35	5 34	18 56	5 13	19 21	4 48	19 57	4 12	20 59	3 10
19	17 51	4 49	18 11	4 28	18 37	4 03	19 13	3 26	20 17	2 23
29	17 07	4 04	17 28	3 43	17 53	3 17	18 30	2 41	19 34	1 37
Aug. 8	16 23	3 20	16 44	2 59	17 10	2 33	17 47	1 56	18 52	0 52
18	15 41	2 37	16 02	2 16	16 28	1 50	17 05	1 13	18 10	0 08
28	15 00	1 56	15 21	1 35	15 47	1 08	16 24	0 31	17 30	23 22
Sept. 7	14 20	1 15	14 41	0 55	15 07	0 28	15 44	23 47	16 50	22 41
17	13 41	0 37	14 02	0 16	14 28	23 46	15 06	23 08	16 11	22 03
27	13 03	23 56	13 24	23 35	13 51	23 08	14 28	22 31	15 33	21 26
Oct. 7	12 27	23 20	12 48	22 59	13 14	22 33	13 52	21 56	14 57	20 51
17	11 52	22 45	12 13	22 24	12 39	21 58	13 16	21 21	14 21	20 17
27	11 18	22 12	11 39	21 51	12 05	21 25	12 41	20 49	13 45	19 45
Nov. 6	10 45	21 39	11 05	21 19	11 31	20 53	12 07	20 17	13 10	19 14
16	10 13	21 07	10 33	20 47	10 58	20 22	11 34	19 46	12 36	18 45
26	9 41	20 37	10 01	20 17	10 26	19 52	11 01	19 17	12 01	18 16
Dec. 6	9 10	20 06	9 29	19 47	9 54	19 22	10 28	18 48	11 27	17 49
16	8 39	19 37	8 58	19 18	9 22	18 54	9 56	18 20	10 53	17 23
26	8 08	19 07	8 27	18 49	8 50	18 25	9 23	17 52	10 19	16 57

Saturn, 2008

Date	20° N Latitude Rise h m	Set h m	30° N Latitude Rise h m	Set h m	40° N Latitude Rise h m	Set h m	50° N Latitude Rise h m	Set h m	60° N Latitude Rise h m	Set h m
Jan. 1	21 42	10 18	21 33	10 27	21 22	10 38	21 07	10 53	20 43	11 17
11	21 01	9 38	20 52	9 47	20 41	9 58	20 26	10 13	20 02	10 37
21	20 20	8 57	20 11	9 06	19 59	9 18	19 44	9 33	19 19	9 58
31	19 38	8 16	19 28	8 25	19 17	8 37	19 01	8 53	18 35	9 18
Feb. 10	18 55	7 34	18 46	7 44	18 34	7 56	18 17	8 12	17 51	8 39
20	18 13	6 53	18 03	7 03	17 50	7 15	17 33	7 32	17 06	7 59
Mar. 1	17 30	6 11	17 20	6 21	17 07	6 34	16 49	6 51	16 22	7 19
11	16 47	5 29	16 37	5 39	16 24	5 52	16 06	6 10	15 37	6 39
21	16 05	4 47	15 54	4 58	15 41	5 11	15 22	5 30	14 53	5 59
31	15 23	4 06	15 12	4 17	14 58	4 30	14 40	4 49	14 10	5 19
Apr. 10	14 41	3 25	14 30	3 36	14 17	3 50	13 58	4 09	13 28	4 39
20	14 01	2 45	13 50	2 56	13 36	3 10	13 17	3 29	12 46	3 59
30	13 21	2 05	13 10	2 16	12 56	2 30	12 37	2 49	12 06	3 19
May 10	12 42	1 26	12 31	1 37	12 17	1 51	11 58	2 10	11 27	2 40
20	12 03	0 47	11 52	0 58	11 39	1 12	11 20	1 31	10 50	2 01
30	11 26	0 09	11 15	0 20	11 01	0 33	10 43	0 52	10 13	1 22
Jun. 9	10 49	23 27	10 38	23 38	10 25	23 51	10 06	0 14	9 37	0 43
19	10 12	22 50	10 02	23 01	9 49	23 14	9 31	23 32	9 03	0 04
29	9 37	22 14	9 27	22 24	9 14	22 36	8 56	22 54	8 29	23 21
Jul. 9	9 01	21 37	8 52	21 47	8 39	21 59	8 22	22 16	7 56	22 43
19	8 27	21 01	8 17	21 11	8 05	21 23	7 49	21 39	7 23	22 04
29	7 52	20 25	7 43	20 35	7 31	20 46	7 16	21 01	6 51	21 26
Aug. 8	7 18	19 50	7 09	19 59	6 58	20 09	6 43	20 24	6 20	20 48
18	6 44	19 14	6 35	19 23	6 25	19 33	6 11	19 47	5 48	20 09
28	6 10	18 39	6 02	18 47	5 52	18 57	5 38	19 10	5 17	19 31
Sept. 7	5 36	18 04	5 28	18 11	5 19	18 21	5 06	18 33	4 46	18 53
17	5 02	17 28	4 55	17 35	4 46	17 44	4 34	17 56	4 15	18 15
27	4 28	16 53	4 21	17 00	4 13	17 08	4 01	17 19	3 44	17 37
Oct. 7	3 54	16 17	3 47	16 24	3 39	16 32	3 29	16 42	3 12	16 59
17	3 19	15 42	3 13	15 48	3 06	15 55	2 56	16 05	2 40	16 21
27	2 44	15 06	2 39	15 11	2 32	15 18	2 22	15 28	2 07	15 43
Nov. 6	2 09	14 29	2 04	14 35	1 57	14 41	1 48	14 50	1 34	15 05
16	1 33	13 53	1 28	13 58	1 22	14 04	1 13	14 13	1 00	14 26
26	0 57	13 16	0 52	13 21	0 46	13 27	0 38	13 35	0 25	13 48
Dec. 6	0 20	12 38	0 15	12 43	0 09	12 49	0 01	12 57	23 45	13 09
16	23 38	12 00	23 34	12 05	23 28	12 10	23 20	12 18	23 08	12 31
26	23 00	11 21	22 55	11 26	22 49	11 32	22 42	11 40	22 29	11 52

Morning and Evening "Stars," 2008

(Coordinated Universal Time)

	Morning	Evening		Morning	Evening
Jan.	Venus Jupiter Saturn	Mercury Mars Uranus Neptune	Aug.	Uranus Neptune to Aug. 15	Mercury Venus Mars Jupiter Saturn Neptune from Aug. 16
Feb.	Mercury from Feb 7 Venus Jupiter Saturn to Feb. 25 Neptune from Feb. 12	Mercury to Feb. 6 Venus Mars Saturn from Feb. 26 Uranus Neptune to Feb. 11	Sept.	Saturn from Sept. 5 Uranus to Sept. 13	Mercury Venus Mars Jupiter Saturn to Sept. 4 Uranus from Sept. 14
Mar.	Mercury Venus Jupiter Uranus from Mar. 9 Neptune	Venus Mars Saturn Uranus to Mar. 8	Oct.	Mercury from Oct. 7 Saturn	Mercury to Oct. 6 Venus Mars Jupiter Uranus Neptune
Apr.	Mercury to Apr. 16 Venus Jupiter Uranus Neptune	Mercury from Apr. 17 Mars Saturn	Nov.	Mercury to Nov. 25 Saturn	Mercury from Nov. 26 Venus Mars Jupiter Uranus Neptune
May	Venus Jupiter Uranus Neptune	Mercury Mars Saturn	Dec.	Mars from Dec. 6 Saturn	Mercury Venus Mars to Dec. 5 Jupiter Uranus Neptune
June	Mercury from June 8 Venus to June 9 Jupiter Uranus Neptune	Mercury to June 7 Venus from June 10 Mars Saturn			
July	Mercury to July 29 Jupiter to July 9 Uranus Neptune	Mercury from July 30 Venus Jupiter from July 8 Mars Saturn			

Greenwich Sidereal Time for 0h UTC*, 2008

(Add 12 hours to obtain Right Ascension of Mean Sun)

Date	d	h	m	Date	d	h	m	Date	d	h	m	Date	d	h	m
Jan.	1	6	40.1	Apr.	10	13	14.4	July	9	19	9.2	Oct.	7	1	4.0
	11	7	19.5		20	13	53.8		19	19	48.6		17	1	43.5
	21	7	59.0		30	14	33.2		29	20	28.1		27	2	22.9
	31	8	38.4	May	10	15	12.7	Aug.	8	21	7.5	Nov.	6	3	2.3
Feb.	10	9	17.8		20	15	52.1		18	21	46.9		16	3	41.7
	20	9	57.2		30	16	31.5		28	22	26.3		26	4	21.2
Mar.	1	10	36.7	June	9	17	10.9	Sept.	7	23	5.8	Dec.	6	5	0.6
	11	11	16.1		19	17	50.4		17	23	45.2		16	5	40.0
	21	11	55.5		29	18	29.8		27	0	24.6		26	6	19.4
	31	12	35.0												

* Universal coordinated Time.

Largest Telescopes

Astronomers indicate the size of telescopes not by length or magnification, but by the diameter of the primary light-gathering component of the system—such as the lens or mirror. This measurement is a direct indication of the telescope's light-gathering power. The bigger the diameter, the fainter the objects you are able to detect. The Earth's atmosphere limits the resolution of what you see. That is why the Hubble Space Telescope, which is outside the atmosphere, can have better resolution than larger telescopes on the Earth.

Refracting (lens) telescopes are currently not made with lens diameters of more than 40 in. Mirror telescopes can be made less expensively than lens telescopes, so all modern large optical telescopes are made with mirrors. **Radio telescopes**, also reflecting telescopes, view at wavelengths not visible to optical telescopes or to the human eye. Radio telescopes are made larger than optical telescopes because larger diameters are required at longer wavelengths to obtain equivalent resolution. Arrays of telescopes are used to achieve even better resolution through a technique called interferometry. Originally developed for radio telescopes, the technique is now also used with optical and infrared telescopes.

Largest Refracting (lens) Optical Telescope: Yerkes Observatory—1 m (40 in), at Williams Bay, WI

Largest Reflecting (mirror) Optical/Infrared Telescope: Keck—9.8 m (32 ft), on Mauna Kea in Hawaii (segmented mirror; 2 equal-size telescopes)

Largest Infrared Interferometer: Four 8.2 m (27 ft) telescopes of the Very Large Telescope Interferometer (VLTI) with a 200 m (656 ft) baseline on Cerro Paranal in Chile

Largest Fully Steerable Radio Dish: 100 m (328 ft) telescope at Max Planck Inst. for Radio Astronomy, Effelsberg, Germany

Largest Single Radio Dish: Arecibo Observatory—305 m (1,000 ft), in Puerto Rico

Largest Radio Interferometer: Ten 25 m (82 ft) diameter telescopes of the Very Long Baseline Array (VLBA), dispersed from Hawaii to the Virgin Islands with a resolution equal to a radio dish of 8,600 km (5,000 mi), making it the highest resolution telescope in the solar system

Constellations

Culturally, constellations are imagined patterns among the stars that, in some cases, have been recognized through millennia. Knowledge of constellations was once necessary in order to function as an astronomer. For today's astronomers, constellations are simply areas on the entire sky in which interesting objects await observation and interpretation.

Because Western culture has prevailed in establishing modern science, equally viable and interesting constellations and celestial traditions of other cultures are not well known outside their regions of origin. Even the patterns with which we are most familiar today have undergone considerable change over the centuries.

Today, **88 constellations** are officially recognized. Although many have ancient origins, some are "modern," devised out of unclaimed stars by astronomers a few centuries ago. Unclaimed stars were those too faint or inconveniently placed to be included in the more prominent constellations. Stars in a constellation are not necessarily near each other; they are just located in the same direction on the celestial sphere.

When astronomers began to travel to South Africa in the 16th and 17th centuries, they found an unfamiliar sky that showed numerous brilliant stars. Thus, we find constellations in the southern hemisphere that depict technological marvels of the time, as well as some arguably traditional forms, such as the "fly."

Many of the commonly recognized constellations had their **origins** in ancient Asia Minor. These were adopted by the Greeks and Romans, who translated their names and stories into their own languages, modifying some details in the process. After the declines of these cultures, most such knowledge entered oral tradition or remained hidden in monastic libraries. From the 8th century, the Muslim explosion spread through the Mediterranean world. Wherever possible, everything was translated into Arabic to be taught in the universities the Muslims established all over their new-found world.

In the 13th century, Alfonso X of Castile, an avid student of astronomy, had Ptolemy's *Almagest* translated into Latin. It thus became widely available to European scholars. In the process, the constellation names were translated, but the star names were retained in their Arabic forms. Thus the names of many stars—e.g., Altair, Alnitak, Mirfak—have Arabic roots, although linguistic adaptation and the inaccuracies of transliteration have wrought changes.

Until the 1920s, astronomers used curved boundaries for the constellation areas. As these were rather arbitrary at best, the International Astronomical Union adopted new constellation boundaries that ran due north-south and east-west, filling the sky much as the contiguous states fill up the area of the "lower 48" United States.

Common names of stars often referred to parts of the traditional figures they represented: Deneb, the tail of the swan; Betelgeuse, the armpit of the giant. Avoiding traditional names, astronomers may label stars by using Greek letters, generally to denote order of brightness. Thus, the "alpha star" would generally be the brightest star of that constellation. The "of" implies possession, so the genitive (possessive) form of the constellation name is used, as in Alpha Orionis, the first star of Orion (Betelgeuse). Astronomers usually use a 3-letter abbreviation for the constellation name, as indicated here.

Within these boundaries, and occasionally crossing them, popular "asterisms" are recognized: the so-called Big Dipper is a small part of the constellation Ursa Major, the big bear; the Sickle is the traditional head and mane of Leo, the lion; the three stars of the Summer Triangle are each in a different constellation, with Vega in Lyra the lyre, Deneb in Cygnus the swan, and Altair in Aquila the eagle; the northeast star of the Great Square of Pegasus is Alpha Andromedae.

Name	Genitive Case	Abbr.	Meaning
Andromeda	Andromedae	And	Chained Maiden
Antlia	Antliae	Ant	Air Pump
Apus	Apodis	Aps	Bird of Paradise
Aquarius	Aquarii	Aqr	Water Bearer
Aquila	Aquilae	Aql	Eagle
Ara	Arae	Ara	Altar
Aries	Arietis	Ari	Ram
Auriga	Aurigae	Aur	Charioteer
Boötes	Boötis	Boo	Herdsmen
Caelum	Caeli	Cae	Chisel
Camelopardalis	Camelopardalis	Cam	Giraffe
Cancer	Cancri	Cnc	Crab
Canes Venatici	Canum Venaticorum	CVn	Hunting Dogs
Canis Major	Canis Majoris	CMa	Greater Dog
Canis Minor	Canis Minoris	CMi	Littler Dog
Capricornus	Capricorni	Cap	Sea-goat
Carina	Carinae	Car	Keel
Cassiopeia	Cassiopeiae	Cas	Queen
Centaurus	Centauri	Cen	Centaur
Cepheus	Cephei	Cep	King
Cetus	Ceti	Cet	Whale
Chamaeleon	Chamaeleontis	Cha	Chameleon
Circinus	Circini	Cir	Compasses (art)
Columba	Columbae	Col	Dove
Coma Berenices	Comae Berenices	Com	Berenice's Hair
Corona Australis	Coronae Australis	CrA	Southern Crown
Corona Borealis	Coronae Borealis	CrB	Northern Crown
Corvus	Corvi	Crv	Crow
Crater	Crateris	Crt	Cup
Crux	Crucis	Cru	Cross (southern)
Cygnus	Cygni	Cyg	Swan
Delphinus	Delphini	Del	Dolphin
Dorado	Doradus	Dor	Goldfish
Draco	Draconis	Dra	Dragon
Equuleus	Equulei	Equ	Little Horse
Eridanus	Eridani	Eri	River
Fornax	Fornacis	For	Furnace
Gemini	Geminorum	Gem	Twins
Grus	Gruis	Gru	Crane (bird)
Hercules	Herculis	Her	Hercules
Horologium	Horologii	Hor	Clock
Hydra	Hydrae	Hya	Water Snake (female)
Hydrus	Hydri	Hyi	Water Snake (male)
Indus	Indi	Ind	Indian
Lacerta	Lacertae	Lac	Lizard
Leo	Leonis	Leo	Lion
Leo Minor	Leonis Minoris	LMi	Littler Lion
Lepus	Leporis	Lep	Hare
Libra	Librae	Lib	Balance
Lupus	Lupi	Lup	Wolf
Lynx	Lyncis	Lyn	Lynx
Lyra	Lyrae	Lyr	Lyre
Mensa	Mensae	Men	Table Mountain
Microscopium	Microscopii	Mic	Microscope
Monoceros	Monocerotis	Mon	Unicorn
Musca	Muscae	Mus	Fly
Norma	Normae	Nor	Square (rule)
Octans	Octantis	Oct	Octant
Ophiuchus	Ophiuchi	Oph	Serpent Bearer
Orion	Orionis	Ori	Hunter
Pavo	Pavonis	Pav	Peacock
Pegasus	Pegasi	Peg	Flying Horse
Perseus	Persei	Per	Hero
Phoenix	Phoenicis	Phe	Phoenix
Pictor	Pictoris	Pic	Painter
Pisces	Piscium	Psc	Fishes
Piscis Austrinus	Piscis Austrini	PsA	Southern Fish
Puppis	Puppis	Pup	Stern (deck)
Pyxis	Pyxidis	Pyx	Compass (sea)
Reticulum	Reticuli	Ret	Reticle
Sagitta	Sagittae	Sge	Arrow
Sagittarius	Sagittarii	Sgr	Archer
Scorpius	Scorpii	Sco	Scorpion
Sculptor	Sculptoris	Scl	Sculptor
Scutum	Scuti	Sct	Shield
Serpens	Serpentis	Ser	Serpent
Sextans	Sextantis	Sex	Sextant
Taurus	Tauri	Tau	Bull
Telescopium	Telescopii	Tel	Telescope
Triangulum	Trianguli	Tri	Triangle
Triangulum Australe	Trianguli Australis	TrA	Southern Triangle
Tucana	Tucanae	Tuc	Toucan
Ursa Major	Ursae Majoris	UMa	Greater Bear
Ursa Minor	Ursae Minoris	UMi	Littler Bear
Vela	Velorum	Vel	Sail
Virgo	Virginis	Vir	Maiden
Volans	Volantis	Vol	Flying Fish
Vulpecula	Vulpeculae	Vul	Fox

Eclipses, 2008
(in Coordinated Universal Time, standard time of the prime meridian)

There are 4 eclipses in 2008: an annular eclipse of the Sun, a total eclipse of the Moon, a total eclipse of the Sun, and a partial eclipse of the Moon. During an annular eclipse of the Sun, the Moon's angular diameter is not large enough to block the entire disk of the Sun, and the Sun appears as a bright ring about the dark disk of the Moon.

I. Annular eclipse of the Sun, February 7

The path of the annular eclipse will begin over Western Antarctica, and move mainly northward over the far south Pacific. A partial eclipse will be visible over a wider area including New Zealand and southeastern Australia.

Event	Date	h	m
Penumbral Eclipse Begins	Feb. 7	1	38.5
Annular Eclipse Begins	7	3	20.0
Greatest eclipse	7	3	55.1
Annular Eclipse Ends	7	4	30.9
Penumbral Eclipse Ends	7	6	11.9

II. Total eclipse of the Moon, February 21

The beginning of the eclipse will be visible over a wide area extending across Central Asia, Africa, the Atlantic Ocean, North and South America (excluding Alaska), and the Arctic. The end will be visible in much of Europe, West Africa, the Atlantic, North and South America, the Arctic, and the eastern Pacific.

Event	Date	h	m
Penumbral Eclipse Begins	Feb. 21	0	34.9
Partial eclipse begins	21	1	42.9
Total eclipse begins	21	3	00.5
Greatest eclipse	21	3	26.0
Total eclipse ends	21	3	51.5
Partial eclipse ends	21	5	09.1
Penumbral; Eclipse Ends	21	6	17.2

III. Total eclipse of the Sun, August 1

The path of totality begins over far northern Canada, crosses the very northern tip of Greenland, then continues southward through central Russia, then across western China, and ending over central China. Theh Sun will be partially obscured as seen from a wide region including northeastern Canada, Greenland, and most of Europe and Asia.

Event	Date	h	m
Penumbral Eclipse Begins	Aug. 1	8	4.1
Total eclipse begins	1	9	21.0
Greatest eclipse	1	10	21.1
Total eclipse ends	1	11	21.5
Penumbral Eclipse Ends	1	12	38.5

IV. Partial eclipse of the Moon, August 16

The partial eclipse will be visible across Australia, and most of Asia, Africa, Europe and the Antarctic. The end of the eclipse will be visible from western China, across Europe, Africa, the Antarctic, and most of South America.

Event	Date	h	m
Partial eclipse begins	Aug. 16	19	35.6
Greatest eclipse	16	21	10.1
Partial eclipse ends	16	22	44.7

Total Solar Eclipses, 2000-2030

Total solar eclipses actually take place nearly as often as total lunar eclipses. Total lunar eclipses are visible over at least half of the Earth, while total solar eclipses can be seen only along a very narrow path up to a few hundred miles wide and a few thousand miles long. Observing a total solar eclipse is thus a rarity for most people.

Solar eclipses can be dangerous to observe. This is not because the Sun emits more potent rays, but because the Sun is always dangerous to observe directly and people are particularly likely to stare at it during a solar eclipse.

Date	Duration[1] m	s	Width (mi)	Path of Totality
2001, June 21	4	56	125	Atlantic Ocean, Africa, Madagascar
2002, Dec. 4	2	4	54	S Africa, Indian Ocean, Australia
2003, Nov. 23	1	57	338	Antarctica
2005, Apr. 8[h]	0	42	17	Pacific Ocean, northwestern S America
2006, Mar. 29	4	7	118	Atlantic Ocean, Africa, Asia
2008, Aug. 1	2	27	157	Arctic Ocean, Asia
2009, July 22	6	39	160	Asia, Pacific Ocean
2010, July 11	5	20	164	Pacific Ocean, southern S America
2012, Nov. 13	4	2	112	N Australia, Pacific Ocean
2013, Nov. 3[h]	1	40	36	Atlantic Ocean, Africa
2015, Mar. 20	2	47	304	N Atlantic Ocean, Arctic Ocean
2016, Mar. 9	4	10	96	Indonesia, Pacific Ocean
2017, Aug. 21	2	40	71	Pacific Ocean, U.S., Atlantic Ocean
2019, July 2	4	33	125	S Pacific Ocean, S America
2020, Dec. 14	2	10	56	S Pacific Ocean, S America, S Atlantic Ocean
2021, Dec. 4	1	55	282	Antarctica, S Atlantic Ocean
2023, Apr. 20[h]	1	16	31	Indian Ocean, New Guinea, Pacific Ocean
2024, Apr. 8	4	28	127	Pacific Ocean, Mexico, N America, Atlantic Ocean
2026, Aug. 12	2	18	198	Arctic Ocean, Greenland, N Atlantic Ocean, Indian Ocean, Australia, New Zealand
2027, Aug. 2	6	23	161	N Atlantic Ocean, N Africa, Middle East, Indian Ocean
2028, July 22	5	9	145	Indian Ocean, Australia, New Zealand
2030, Nov. 25	3	44	105	S Pacific Ocean, S Africa, Indian Ocean, Australia

h = indicates annular-total hybrid eclipse. (1) Duration refers to length of time at optimal viewing area.

Total Solar Eclipses in the U.S. in the 21st Century

During the 21st century there will be 8 total solar eclipses visible somewhere in the continental U.S. The first comes after a long gap; the last total solar eclipse was on Feb. 26, 1979, in the northwestern U.S.

Date	Path of Totality	Date	Path of Totality
Aug. 21, 2017	Oregon to South Carolina	Mar. 30, 2052	Florida to Georgia
Apr. 8, 2024	Mexico to Texas and up through Maine	May 11, 2078	Louisiana to North Carolina
Aug. 23, 2044	Montana to North Dakota	May 1, 2079	New Jersey to the lower edge of New England
Aug. 12, 2045	N California to Florida	Sept. 14, 2099	North Dakota to Virginia

Beginnings of the Universe

One of the dominating astronomical discoveries of the 20th century was that the galaxies of the universe all seem to be moving away from us. Doppler redshifts were observed for the spiral nebulae around 1920, even though they were not yet known to be galaxies. By the early 1930s, Edwin Hubble and M.L. Humason had established that the more distant a galaxy, the faster it was receding. It turned out that they are moving away not just from us but from one another—that is, the universe is expanding. Scientists conclude that the universe must once, very long ago, have been extremely compact and dense, until an explosion or a similar event caused the matter to spread out. The explosion that gave birth to the universe is called the **Big Bang**.

On the subatomic level, according to this theory, there were vast changes of energy and matter and the way physical laws operated during the first few minutes. After those early minutes the percentages of the basic matter of the universe—hydrogen, helium, and lithium—were set. Everything was so compact and so hot that **radiation dominated the early universe** and there were no stable, un-ionized atoms. At first, the universe was opaque, in the sense that any energy emitted was quickly absorbed and then re-emitted by free electrons. **As the universe expanded, density and temperature continued to drop.** A few hundred thousand years after the Big Bang, the temperature dropped far enough that electrons and nuclei could combine to form stable atoms as the universe became transparent. Once that occurred, the radiation that had been trapped was free to escape.

In the 1940s, George Gamov and others predicted that astronomers should be able to see remnants of this escaped radiation. They were starting to search for this background radiation when physicists Arno Penzias and Robert Wilson, using a radio telescope, inadvertently beat them to the punch (the 2 were later awarded a Nobel Prize).

In 2003, NASA's Wilkinson Microwave Anisotropy Probe made measurements of the temperature of this **cosmic microwave background** radiation to within millionths of a degree. From these measurements, scientists were able to deduce that our universe is **13.7 bil years old** and that first-generation stars began to form a mere 200 mil years after the Big Bang.

A related mystery is that evidence suggests there is hidden matter and hidden energy that cannot be directly observed. This **dark matter** may be composed of gas, large numbers of cool, small objects, or even sub-atomic particles. The presence of dark matter is indicated by the rotation curves of galaxies and the dynamics of clusters of galaxies. Evidence for **dark energy** is derived from studies of distant Type Ia supernovae in far galaxies indicating that the expansion of the universe is accelerating, rather than slowing. The visible matter we see seems to constitute only about 4% of the total mass of the universe, while the rest of the mass of the universe is in the form of dark matter (23%) and dark energy (73%). Dark energy is a mysterious force that seems to work on the very fabric of the universe, spreading it apart.

Galaxies

The 20th century might be called the century of the galaxy. By the start of the century, more than 10,000 **nebulae**—cloud-like luminous objects in the sky—had been discovered. Some were correctly identified as star clusters and others as clouds of gas and dust. Those nebulae which were spiral or elliptical in shape were found in regions of the sky far from the glowing band that is our own Milky Way Galaxy. Immanuel Kant had written in 1775 that some of these fuzzy objects might be **"island universes"** apart from our own. But the idea remained speculative until 1923-24, when Edwin Hubble discovered the existence of variable stars in some of these nebulae. This provided conclusive evidence that these systems were outside our own "island universe," the Milky Way Galaxy.

Galaxies range in **size** from small dwarf elliptical ones, with perhaps 1 mil stars, to spiral galaxies containing 300 billion stars, to giant elliptical galaxies that may be home to more than 10 tril stars. The diameters of galaxies range from 3,000 light-years in dwarf elliptical galaxies to over 500,000 light-years in giant elliptical galaxies. It is estimated that the Milky Way galaxy is about 100,000 light-years in diameter with about 400 bil stars.

Galaxies also congregate into **clusters**. The smallest are poor clusters of only a few dozen galaxies, while the largest rich clusters may contain thousands of galaxies. The Milky Way is part of a poor cluster of about 3 dozen galaxies called the **Local Group**. The largest member of the Local Group is the Andromeda Galaxy, a spiral galaxy visible to the unaided eye in the constellation of Andromeda on a very dark night away from lights. The Milky Way is the second largest galaxy in this group; most other galaxies in our Local Group are small.

The Solar System

The major planets of the solar system, in order of mean distance from the Sun, are **Mercury, Venus, Earth, Mars, Jupiter, Saturn, Uranus,** and **Neptune.** The dwarf planets in order of distance from the Sun are **Ceres** (located between Mars and Jupiter), **Pluto,** and **Eris.** All planets orbit counterclockwise around the Sun.

Because **Mercury and Venus** are nearer to the Sun than is Earth, their motions about the Sun appear from Earth as wide swings first to one side of the Sun then to the other, though both planets move continuously around the Sun in almost circular orbits. When their passage takes them either between Earth and the Sun or beyond the Sun as seen from Earth, they cannot be seen.

The **planets that lie farther from the Sun** than does Earth may be seen for longer periods and are invisible only when so located in our sky so that they rise and set at about the same time as the Sun—and thus become overwhelmed by the Sun's light.

The giant planets emit their own energy. On occasion, radio emissions from Jupiter exceed even those emitted by the Sun in intensity.

Mercury and Venus, because they are between Earth and the Sun, show phases much as the Moon does. The planets farther from the Sun are always seen as full, although Mars does occasionally present a slightly gibbous phase—like the Moon when not quite full.

The **planets appear to move rapidly among the stars** because they are relatively closer to Earth than the stars. The stars are also in motion, some at tremendous speeds, but they are so far away that their motion does not change their apparent positions in the heavens enough to be perceived. The nearest star is about 9,000 times farther away than Neptune. The count for identified **moons** in the solar system orbiting planets and dwarf planets stood at 170 in Fall 2007.

Planet Superlatives			
Largest, most massive planet	Jupiter	Smallest, least massive planet	Mercury
Fastest orbiting planet	Mercury	Slowest orbiting planet	Neptune
Fastest sidereal rotation	Jupiter	Slowest sidereal rotation	Venus
Longest (synodic) day	Mercury	Shortest (synodic) day	Jupiter
Rotational pole closest to ecliptic	Uranus	Hottest planet	Venus
Most moons	Jupiter	No moons	Mercury, Venus
Planet with largest moon	Jupiter	Planet with moon with most eccentric orbit	Neptune
Greatest average density	Earth	Lowest average density	Saturn
Tallest mountain	Mars	Deepest oceans	Jupiter
Strongest magnetic fields	Jupiter	Greatest amount of liquid, surface water	Earth
Most circular orbit	Venus		

Planets and the Sun, by Selected Characteristics

Sun and Planets	Radius: at unit distance[1] "	at mean least distance[2] "	in mi mean radius	Volume[3]	Mass[3]	Density[3]	Sidereal period d	h	m	s	Gravity at surface[3]	Reflecting power Pct°	Daytime surface temp. °F
Sun	959.5	976.0	432,500	1,304,000	333,000	0.26	25	9	7		28.0		+9,941
Mercury	3.36	6.5	1,516	0.0562	0.0553	0.98	58	15	36		0.38	0.11	845
Venus	8.34	33.0	3,760	0.857	0.815	0.95	243		30R		0.91	0.65	867
Earth	8.78	—	3,959	1.000	1.000	1.00		23	56	4.2	1.00	0.37	59
Moon	2.40	986.2	1,079	0.0203	0.0123	0.61	27	7	43	40	0.16	0.12	260
Mars	4.67	12.8	2,106	0.151	0.107	0.71		24	37	22	0.38	0.15	−24
Jupiter	96.40	24.5	43,441	1,321	317.8	0.24		9	55	30	2.53	0.52	−162
Saturn	80.29	10.05	36,184	764	95.16	0.12		10	39	20	1.06	0.47	−218
Uranus	34.97	2.05	15,759	63.1	14.54	0.23		17	14	20R	0.90	0.51	−323
Neptune	33.95	1.2	15,301	57.7	17.15	0.30		16	6	40	1.14	0.41	−330

(1) Angular radius, in seconds of arc, if object were seen at a distance of 1 astronomical unit. (2) Angular radius, in seconds of arc, when object is closest to Earth. (3) Earth = 1. R = Retrograde rotation.

The Planets: Motion, Distance, and Brightness

Planet	Mean daily motion[1]	Orbital velocity mi per sec.[2]	Sidereal revolution days[3]	Synodic revolution days[4]	Distance from Sun in millions of mi Max.	Min.	Distance from Earth in millions of mi Max.	Min.	Light at[5] perihelion	aphelion
Mercury	14,732	29.75	87.97	115.9	43.4	28.6	137.9	48.0	10.56	4.59
Venus	5,768	21.76	224.7	583.9	67.7	66.8	162.2	23.7	1.94	1.89
Earth	3,548	18.50	365.256	—	94.5	91.4	—	—	1.03	0.97
Mars	1,887	15.00	686.98	779.9	154.9	128.4	249.4	33.9	0.52	0.36
Jupiter	299	8.12	4,332.6	398.9	507.4	460.1	602	366	0.041	0.034
Saturn	120	6.02	10,759.2	378.1	941.1	840.4	1,031	743	0.012	0.0098
Uranus	42	4.23	30,685.4	369.7	1,866	1,703	1,962	1,605	0.0030	0.0025
Neptune	22	3.37	60,189.0	367.5	2,824	2,762	2,913	2,676	0.0011	0.0011

(1) Average angular motion measured in seconds of arc per day. (2) Speed of revolution around Sun. (3) Number of Earth days to orbit Sun with respect to background stars. (4) Number of Earth days to get back to the same position in its orbit around Sun, relative to Earth. (5) Light at perihelion and aphelion is solar illumination measured in units of mean illumination at Earth.

Planets of the Solar System

Note: AU = astronomical unit (92.96 mil mi, mean distance of Earth from the Sun); **d** = 1 Earth synodic (solar) day (24 hrs); **synodic day** = rotation period of a planet measured with respect to the Sun (the "true" day, i.e. the time from midday to midday, or from sunrise to sunrise); **sidereal day** = the rotation period of a planet with respect to the stars

The International Astronomical Union (IAU) on August 24, 2006, at their General Assembly in Prague, agreed on a new definition for "planet," and in the process effectively removed Pluto's planet status. The ruling came after years of debate as to whether Pluto, discovered in 1930, should still be considered the ninth planet in our Solar System because of its size, orbit, and other characteristics. New discoveries of other Pluto-like objects in the Solar System, such as the 2003 discovery of Eris, a Kuiper Belt object (KBO) bigger than Pluto, also contributed to the debate.

Under the IAU's new definition, Mercury, Venus, Earth, Mars, Jupiter, Saturn, Uranus, and Neptune are regarded as "classical" planets. A planet is now defined as a celestial body that (a) is in orbit around the Sun, (b) has sufficient mass for its self-gravity to overcome rigid body forces so that it assumes a hydrostatic equilibrium (nearly round) shape, and (c) has cleared the neighborhood around its orbit.

Pluto, Eris, and Ceres are now regarded as "dwarf planets," with the status of Pluto's moon, Charon, to be determined at a later date. A **dwarf planet** is a celestial body that (a) is in orbit around the Sun, (b) has sufficient mass for its self-gravity to overcome rigid body forces so that is assumed a hydrostatic equilibrium (nearly round) shape, (c) has not cleared the neighborhood around its orbit, and (d) is not a satellite.

The IAU also created a new category, **Small Solar System Bodies,** for all other objects orbiting the Sun, including comets, asteroids, KBOs, and other small objects, although it has not yet established a process by which other Solar System objects will be classified.

Mercury

Distance from the Sun	
Perihelion	28.6 mil mi
Aphelion	43.4 mil mi
Semi-major axis (mean distance)	36.0 mil mi (0.387 AU)
Period of revolution around Sun	87.97 d
Orbital eccentricity	0.2056
Orbital inclination	7.00°
Synodic day (midday to midday)	175.94 d
Sidereal day	58.65 d
Rotational inclination	0.01°
Mass (Earth = 1)	0.0553
Mean radius	1,516 mi
Mean density (Earth = 1)	0.984
Natural satellites	0
Average surface temperature	333°F

Mercury, named for the Roman gods' messenger, is the closest planet to the Sun and the smallest in the Solar System. Mercury is too much in line with the Sun to be observed against a dark sky; therefore it is always seen during morning or evening twilight.

Orbit and Rotation. Mercury moves with great speed around the Sun, averaging about 30 mi per second to complete its orbit, which takes about 88 Earth days. Mercury takes nearly 59 days to rotate on its axis. Because its orbital period is only about 50% longer than its sidereal rotation, the time from one sunrise to the next on Mercury is about 176 days—twice as long as a Mercurial year. Oddly, Mercury has a magnetic field, albeit very weak. It has been held that both a fluid core and rapid rotation—neither of which Mercury is believed to have—are necessary for the generation of a planetary magnetic field. Mercury may demonstrate the contrary.

Atmosphere. Mercury's atmosphere is almost non-existent. What very little it has is composed of 42% oxygen, 29% sodium, 22% hydrogen, 6% helium, 0.5% potassium, and 0.5% other particles. Because of Mercury's lack of atmosphere to regulate temperatures between day and night, the surface during the day may reach a temperature of about 845°F, while the temperature at night may fall as low as −300°F. Earth-based observation has provided evidence of water ice near the poles.

Surface and Composition. Mercury's surface is rocky and cratered similar to that of the Earth's Moon. The most imposing feature on Mercury, the Caloris Basin, is a huge impact crater more than 800 mi in diameter. Mercury has a huge iron core that takes up about 75% of the planet's radius; it has higher percentage of iron than any other planet.

Venus

Distance from the Sun
Perihelion . . . . .66.8 mil mi
Semi-major axis (mean distance) . 67.2 mil mi (0.723 AU)
Aphelion . . . . .67.7 mil mi
Period of revolution around Sun . . . . 224.70 d
Orbital eccentricity 0.0067
Orbital inclination . . . . 3.39°
Synodic day (midday to midday) . . . . . 116.75 d (retrograde)
Sidereal day. . . . . 243.02 d (retrograde)
Rotational inclination . . . . 177.4°
Mass (Earth = 1) 0.815
Mean radius. . . . . 3,760 mi
Mean density (Earth = 1) 0.951
Natural satellites 0
Average surface temperature . . . . .867°F

Venus, named for the Roman goddess of love, is the second planet out from the Sun. Almost the same size as Earth, it is believed that the two planets were formed at the same time by the same general process and from the same mixture of chemical elements. Venus can easily be seen from Earth with the naked eye; it is the 3rd-brightest object in the sky, exceeded only by the Sun and the Moon.

Orbit and Rotation. It takes Venus 225 Earth days to complete its orbit around the sun. Its synodic revolution—its return to the same relationship with Earth and the Sun, which is a result of the combination of its own motion with that of Earth—is 584 days. Because of this, every 19 months Venus is closer to Earth than any other planet. The rotation period of Venus appears to be 243 days clockwise—in other words, contrary to the spin of the other planets and contrary to its own motion around the Sun. This rate and sense of rotation makes for a solar day (sunrise to sunrise) on Venus of 116.8 Earth days; nighttime lasts 58 days and daytime lasts 58 days. Venus has no detectible magnetic field.

Atmosphere. The Venusian atmosphere is very thick and toxic. It is composed primarily of 96.5% carbon dioxide, 3.5% nitrogen, trace concentrations of sulfur dioxide, argon, water, carbon monoxide, helium, and neon. In addition, it exerts an atmospheric pressure at the surface more than 90 times Earth's normal sea-level pressure. The planet is covered with a dense, white, cloudy atmosphere that conceals whatever is below it. These clouds are believed to contain sulfuric acid, meaning that when it rains on Venus, it may rain sulfuric acid. Due to the thickness of the atmosphere and resulting extreme greenhouse effect, the temperature is essentially the same day and night; the planet has an average surface temperature of about 867°F making it the hottest planet in the solar system. Winds of about 200 mph in the clouds may account for the transfer of heat into the night side despite the low rotation speed of the planet. However, at the surface, the winds are very slow.

Surface and Composition. Radar-produced maps of the entire planet show large craters, continent-sized highlands, and extensive dry lowlands. No tectonic activity has been found similar to Earth's moving tectonic plates, but a system of global rift zones and numerous broad, low, dome-like structures, called coronae, may have been produced by the upwelling and subsidence of magma from the mantle. Volcanic surface features, such as vast lava plains, fields of small lava domes, and large shield volcanoes, are common. About 1,600 volcanoes and volcanic features appear on the Venusian surface; more than 85% of the surface is covered by volcanic flows. Theia Mons, a huge shield volcano, has a diameter of over 600 mi and a height of over 3.5 mi. (The largest Hawaiian volcano is only about 125 mi in diameter, but rises nearly 5.5 mi from the ocean floor.) Aside from volcanoes, there are highly deformed mountain belts across Venus along with a few meteor-impact craters more than 20 mi wide. Erosion is a very slow process on Venus due to the lack of water. There are indications of some wind movement of dust and sand. The few impact craters on Venus suggest that the surface is generally geologically young—less than 800 million years old. Despite the fact that probes have landed on Venus, there are very few pictures because the probes themselves couldn't survive the high temperature and atmospheric pressure.

Mars

Distance from the Sun
Perihelion . . . . 128.4 mil mi
Semi-major axis (mean distance) . 141.6 mil mi (1.524 AU)
Aphelion . . . . 154.9 mil mi
Period of revolution around Sun . . . . 686.98 d (1.88 y)
Orbital eccentricity 0.0935
Orbital inclination . . . . .1.85°
Synodic day (midday to midday). 24h 39m 35s
Sidereal day 24h 37m 22s
Rotational inclination. . . . . .25.19°
Mass (Earth = 1). 0.107
Mean radius . . . . 2,106 mi
Mean density (Earth = 1) 0.713
Natural satellites 2
Average surface temperature . . . . −81° F

Named for the Roman god of war, the "Red Planet" has some features much like Earth. Mars has climate, seasons, volcanoes, and possibly once had liquid water flowing across its surface. Mars can easily be seen with the naked eye on most clear nights, which is why it was one of the first planets to be studied by ancient astronomers. Later, when telescopes came into use, many observers claimed that canals made by Martians existed on the planet's surface, which led to speculation as to whether there was intelligent life there. Unmanned probes have since put all those theories to rest; the canals turned out to be topographic patterns and dust storms.

Orbit and Rotation. Although Mars' orbital path is nearly circular, it is somewhat more eccentric than that of most other planets; Mars is more than 26 mil mi farther from the Sun at its most distant point compared to its closest approach. Its orbit and speed in relation to Earth's bring it fairly close to Earth about every 2 years. Every 15-17 years the close approaches are especially favorable for observation.

Mars rotates in 24 hours and 37 minutes, almost the same period of time as Earth. Mars' mean distance from the Sun is 142 mil mi. Because Mars' axis of rotation is inclined by about 25° from the vertical to the plane of its solar orbit about the Sun, the planet has seasons.

Unlike Earth's global magnetic field, the Martian magnetic field is small, weak, and localized and may be the remnant of a stronger field from the planet's past.

Atmosphere. The Martian atmosphere is composed primarily of 95.32% carbon dioxide, 2.7% nitrogen, 1.6% argon, 0.13% oxygen, 0.08% carbon monoxide, and in very minor quantities, water, hydrogen oxide, and neon. The atmosphere on Mars is very thin; it has an atmospheric pressure between 1% and 2% of Earth's (if Earth's atmosphere were that thin, we would not have enough oxygen to breathe). Because the Martian atmosphere is so thin and because of the planet's weak magnetic field, its surface is bombarded by cosmic radiation about 100 times as intense as on Earth.

Martian weather systems consist mainly of huge dust storms. On the poles, white caps (believed to be both water ice and carbon dioxide ice) grow in winter and shrink in summer. It is mainly the carbon dioxide that comes and goes with the seasons. The water ice is apparently in many layers with dust between them, indicating climatic cycles.

Surface and Composition. Mars is an alien world with rust-red sand and pink skies. In the planet's beginning stages when it was much hotter, Mars' surface melted to a sufficient extent to separate into dense and lighter layers. At some point later, Mars cooled enough to allow liquid water to possibly flow across its surface. Today, Mars is very dry.

Natural Satellites. Mars has 2 satellites called Phobos and Deimos, each discovered in 1877 by Asaph Hall. (Phobos measures about 11 by 17 mi and Deimos about 7 by 9 mi.) Deimos, the outer satellite, revolves around the planet in about 31 hours. Phobos, the inner satellite, whips around Mars in a little more than 7 hours, making 3 trips each Martian day. Since it orbits Mars faster than the planet rotates, Phobos rises in the west and sets in the east, opposite to what other bodies appear to do in the Martian sky. Both moons are irregularly shaped and pitted with numerous craters. Their origins are not known; however, some astronomers consider them to be asteroid-like objects that were captured by Mars very early in its history.

Jupiter

Distance from the Sun	
Perihelion	460.1 mil mi
Semi-major axis (mean distance)	483.8 mil mi (5.204 AU)
Aphelion	507.4 mil mi
Period of revolution around Sun	11.862 y
Orbital eccentricity	0.0489
Orbital inclination	1.304°
Synodic day (midday to midday)	9h 55m 33s
Sidereal day	9h 55m 30s
Rotational inclination	3.13°
Mass (Earth = 1)	317.8
Mean radius	43,441 mi
Mean density (Earth = 1)	0.24
Natural satellites	63
Average temperature*	−162°F

*i.e., temperature where atmosphere pressure equals 1 Earth atmosphere.

Jupiter, named for the Roman ruler of the gods, is the largest planet in the solar system (11 times the diameter of Earth). Its mass is more than twice the mass of all the other planets, moons, and asteroids put together. Visible to the naked eye and known to the ancients, it was a focus of the Italian scientist Galileo Galilei who viewed the planet and its 4 largest moons through a homemade telescope.

Orbit and Rotation. Jupiter is at an average distance of 484 mil mi from the Sun and takes almost 12 Earth years to make a complete revolution. The largest of the planets, Jupiter has an equatorial diameter of 88,846 mi; however, its polar diameter is more than 5,700 mi shorter. This noticeable oblateness is a result of the liquidity of the planet and its extremely rapid rotation rate—a Jupiter day is less than 10 Earth hours long. For a planet this size, this rotational speed is amazing. A point on Jupiter's equator moves at a speed of 22,000 mph, as compared with 1,000 mph for a point on Earth's equator. Jupiter's magnetic field is by far the strongest of any planet. Electrical activity caused by this field is so strong that it discharges billions of watts into Earth's magnetic field daily.

Atmosphere. Jupiter's atmosphere is primarily composed of 90% molecular hydrogen and 10% helium. Minor constituents include methane, ammonia, hydrogen deuteride, ethane, and water. Jupiter has a turbulent atmosphere characterized by thick clouds, high winds, and huge lightning storms many times larger than those on Earth. The atmospheric temperature varies but the temperature at the tops of clouds may be about −280°F. The Great Red Spot seen prominently on Jupiter is a huge hurricane-like storm that is three times the diameter of Earth. In 2006, the Hubble Space Telescope detected the appearance of a second, smaller red spot.

Surface and Composition. Gas giant planets like Jupiter, Saturn, and Neptune do not have a surface like Earth or any of the other rocky planets. The gases become denser with depth, until they may turn into a slush or slurry. Jupiter has a liquid hydrogen ocean more than 35,000 mi deep. It likely has a rocky core about the size of Earth, but 13 times more massive. There is no sharp interface between the gaseous atmosphere and the hydrogen ocean that accounts for most of Jupiter's volume. At lower depths, under enormous pressure, the liquid hydrogen takes on the properties of a metal. It is likely that this liquid metallic hydrogen is the source for both Jupiter's persistent radio noise and for its improbably strong magnetic field.

Natural Satellites. Jupiter has 63 known satellites, 23 of which were found as recently as 2003. Four of the moons—in order from Jupiter, Io, Europa, Ganymede, and Callisto—all discovered by Galileo in 1610—are large and bright and are close in diameter to Earth's Moon and Mercury. Because they move so rapidly around Jupiter, their change in position from night to night can be seen from Earth using binoculars.

Io is one of the most intriguing moons because it is the most volcanically active body in the Solar System. A gaseous, doughnut-shaped ring, or torus, enveloping Io's orbit around Jupiter may have been formed by material ejected from Io's active volcanoes. (This is not to be confused with Jupiter's rings.) These volcanoes, hotter than Earth's volcanoes, erupt mainly molten sulfur.

Europa may have a 30-mi-deep salty, liquid ocean beneath its icy crust, perhaps a small metallic core, and a very tenuous atmosphere. Ganymede is the biggest moon in the Solar System. With a diameter of 3,120 mi, it is bigger than both Mercury and Pluto. Ganymede also has it own magnetic field produced by a molten core perhaps of iron sulfide. Callisto has the oldest, most heavily cratered surface in the solar system, a very thin atmosphere of carbon dioxide, and possibly a subsurface liquid ocean.

The other satellites are much smaller, with 4 closer to Jupiter than Io, 5 between Ganymede and Callisto, and the rest farther out. Most of Jupiter's moons revolve around Jupiter clockwise as seen from the north, contrary to the motions of most satellites in the solar system and to the direction of revolution of planets around the Sun. These moons may be captured asteroids.

Jupiter has a set of rings that cannot be seen from Earth without powerful telescopes. They are composed of small dust grains possibly blasted off the 4 innermost moons by meteoroid impacts.

Saturn

Distance from the Sun	
Perihelion	840.44 mil mi
Semi-major axis (mean distance)	890.8 mil mi (9.582 AU)
Aphelion	941.07 mil mi
Period of revolution around Sun	29.458 y
Orbital eccentricity	0.0565
Orbital inclination	2.485°
Synodic day (midday to midday)	10h 39m 23s
Sidereal day	10h 39m 22s
Rotational Inclination	26.73°
Mass (Earth = 1)	95.159
Mean radius	36,184 mi
Mean density (Earth = 1)	0.125
Natural satellites	60
Average temperature*	−218° F

*i.e., temperature where atmosphere pressure equals 1 Earth atmosphere.

Saturn, named for the Roman ruler of the Titans, is the 6th planet from the sun and most distant of the planets visible to the unaided eye. Saturn is 2nd in size to Jupiter, but its mass is much smaller. Saturn is the only planet less dense than water, meaning that Saturn would float if there were a pool of water gigantic enough to hold it.

Orbit and Rotation. Saturn's diameter is almost 74,900 mi at the equator, while its polar diameter is more than 7,300 mi shorter. Like Jupiter, its noticeable oblateness is a result of the liquidity of the planet and its extremely rapid rate of rotation; a day is little more than 10 Earth hours long.

Atmosphere. Saturn's atmosphere is composed primarily of 96.3% hydrogen, 3.3% helium, and traces of methane, ammonia, hydrogen deuteride, ethane, and water. Saturn's atmosphere is much like that of Jupiter, except that the temperature at the top of its cloud layer is at least 50°F colder.

Surface and Composition. Saturn's atmosphere resembles Jupiter's; it likely has a small dense center surrounded by a deep ocean of hydrogen.

Natural Satellites. Saturn has many natural satellites, most of which were not discovered until space probes reached the planet. Saturn's moon Mimas has an impact crater 81 miles across (the moon itself is only 249 miles across). Enceladus has an atmosphere and shows evidence of geysers that spit water ice and vapor. Two tiny moons orbit within the rings, plowing through and making gaps in the rings along their orbits. Pan, the innermost satellite creates the Encke Gap of Saturn's A-ring. 2005 S1 creates the Keeler Gap. The most intriguing Saturnian moon is Titan. The second biggest moon in the Solar System, Titan is bigger than Mercury. Its atmosphere is similar to Earth's atmosphere of long ago; it is made up of approximately 95% nitrogen with traces of methane. Titan's atmosphere extends about 360 mi into space whereas Earth's atmosphere extends about 37 mi. Photographs from the surface show a muddy terrain, with possible deposits of water ice, channels carved by liquid methane springs, and an interesting boundary between light and dark material on the surface.

In addition, in 2006, scientists found sand dunes on Titan's surface. The "sand" is believed to be tiny water ice crystals or organic compounds. Surface phenomena such as sand dunes are signs of erosion and wind. However, unlike on Earth or Mars, Titan's winds are not the result of uneven solar heating on the moon's surface, but rather the strong gravitational pull from Saturn that creates atmospheric "tides" almost in the same way Earth's moon does to its oceans.

Rings. Saturn's ring system is the planet's most recognizable feature. It begins about 4,000 mi above the visible disk of Saturn lying above its equator and extends about 260,000 mi into space. The diameter of the ring system visible from Earth is about 170,000 mi; the rings are estimated to be about 700 feet thick. The rings are composed of rock and ice and range in size from tiny particles to large chunks of material the size of a bus. There are several divisions in the rings. The 2,920 mi Cassini division, the gap between the A and B rings, is the largest division.

Uranus

Distance from the Sun	
Perihelion	1,703.4 mil mi
Semi-major axis (mean distance)	1,784.8 mil mi (19.201 AU)
Aphelion	1,866.4 mil mi
Period of revolution around Sun	84.01 y
Orbital eccentricity	0.0457
Orbital inclination	0.772°
Synodic day (midday to midday)	17h 14m 23s (retrograde)
Sidereal day	17h 14m 24s (retrograde)
Rotational inclination	97.77°
Mass (Earth = 1)	14.536
Mean radius	15,759mi
Mean density (Earth = 1)	0.230
Natural satellites	27
Average temperature*	–323° F

*i.e., temperature where atmosphere pressure equals 1 Earth atmosphere.

Uranus, discovered by Sir William Herschel in 1781, was the first planet discovered using a telescope. It was named for the father of the Titans in Roman mythology.

Rotation and Orbit. Uranus has a diameter of over 31,000 mi and spins once in approximately 17.23 hours, according to flyby magnetic data. One of the most fascinating features of Uranus is how far over it is tipped. Its north pole lies 98° from being directly up and down to its orbit plane. Thus, its seasons are extreme. Over its 84 year orbit, when the Sun rises at the north pole, it shines there for about 42 Earth years; then it sets, and the north pole is in darkness for 42 Earth years. In addition to its rotational tilt, Uranus's magnetic field axis is tipped an incredible 58.6° from its rotational axis and is displaced about 30% of its radius away from the planet's center.

Atmosphere. The atmosphere is composed primarily of 82.5% hydrogen, 15.2 % helium, 2.3% methane, with small amounts of hydrogen deuteride, ammonia ice, water ice, ammonia hydrosulfide, and methane ice.

Surface and Composition. Uranus has no solid surface, and likely no rocky core but rather a mixture of rocks and assorted ices with about 15% hydrogen and some helium.

Natural Satellites. Uranus has 27 known moons, which have orbits lying in the plane of the planet's equator. Five moons are relatively large, while 22 are very small and were only discovered with the *Voyager 2* mission or in later observations. Miranda has grooved markings, reminiscent of Jupiter's Ganymede, but often arranged in a chevron pattern. Rifts and channels on Ariel provide evidence of liquid flowing over its surface in the past. Umbriel is extremely dark, prompting some observers to regard its surface as among the oldest in the system. Titania has rifts and fractures, but not the evidence of flow found on Ariel. Oberon's main feature is its surface saturated with craters, unrelieved by other formations.

In the equatorial plane there is also a complex of 11 rings, 9 of which were discovered in 1978 by observers watching Uranus pass before a star.

Neptune

Distance from the Sun	
Perihelion	2,761.7 mil mi
Semi-major axis (mean distance)	2,793.1 (30.047 AU)
Aphelion	2,824.5 mil mi
Period of revolution around Sun	164.79 y
Orbital eccentricity	0.0113
Orbital inclination	1.769°
Synodic day (midday to midday)	16h 6m 37s
Sidereal day	16h 6m 36s
Rotational inclination	28.32°
Mass (Earth = 1)	17.147
Mean radius	15,301 mi
Mean density (Earth = 1)	0.297
Natural satellites	13
Average temperature*	–330° F

*i.e., temperature where atmosphere pressure equals 1 Earth atmosphere.

Named for the Roman god of the sea, Neptune was the first planet discovered through mathematical calculations and not observation. Its approximate orbit and position was first calculated independently by John Couch Adams and Urbain Le Verrier in 1845. In 1846, Johann Galle first observed Neptune through a telescope.

Orbit and Rotation. Neptune orbits the Sun in 164.8 years in a nearly circular orbit. It's magnetic field is considerably asymmetric to the planet's structure, similar to, but not so extreme as, that found at Uranus. Neptune's magnetic field axis is tipped 46.9° from its rotational axis and is displaced more than 55% of its radius away from the planet's center.

Atmosphere. The Neptunian atmosphere is composed primarily of 80% hydrogen, 19% helium, 1.5% methane, and small amounts of hydrogen deuteride, ethane, ammonia ice, water ice, ammonia hydrosulfide, and methane ice. Neptune's atmosphere is quite blue, with quickly changing white clouds often suspended high above an apparent surface. A Great Dark Spot was discovered in 1989 when *Voyager 2* visited the planet, reminiscent of the Great Red Spot of Jupiter. Observations with the *Hubble Space Telescope* have shown that the Great Dark Spot originally seen by *Voyager* has apparently dissipated, but a new dark spot has since appeared. Lightning and auroras have been found on other giant planets, but only the aurora phenomenon has been seen on Neptune. As with the other giant planets, Neptune is emitting more energy than it receives from the Sun. The excess has been found to be 2.7 times the solar contribution.

Surface and Composition. As with other giant planets, Neptune may have no solid surface, or exact diameter. However, a mean value of 30,600 mi may be assigned to a diameter between atmosphere levels where the pressure is about the same as sea level on Earth.

Natural Satellites. Largest of Neptune's 13 satellites is Triton. It is the only large moon in a retrograde orbit, which suggests that it was captured rather than having been there from the beginning. Triton's large size, sufficient to raise significant tides on the planet, may one day, billions of years from now, cause Triton to come close enough to Neptune for it to be torn apart. Triton has a tenuous atmosphere of nitrogen with a trace of hydrocarbons and evidence of active geysers injecting material into it. Triton is the coldest object yet measured in the Solar System with a surface temperature of –391° F. Only about half of Triton has been observed, but its terrain shows cratering and a strange regional feature described as resembling the skin of a cantaloupe. Nereid has the highest orbital eccentricity (0.75) of any moon. Its long looping orbit suggests that it was also captured. In 2003, 2 more moons, which orbit farther from their parent planet than any other moons, were discovered. The *Voyager 2* probe in 1989 confirmed the existence of 6 rings around Neptune composed of very fine particles. There may be some clumpiness in the rings' structure. It is not known whether Neptune's satellites influence the formation or maintenance of the rings.

Dwarf Planets

Note: See page 327 for the definition of a dwarf planet.

Ceres

Distance from the Sun	
Perihelion	237 mil mi (2.55 AU)
Semi-major axis (mean distance)	257 mil mi (2.77 AU)
Period of revolution around Sun	4.6 y
Orbital eccentricity	0.0789
Orbital inclination	10.58°
Sidereal day	9.075 hours
Mean radius	300 mi

Ceres was the first asteroid ever discovered, on January 1, 1801, by Guiseppe Piazzi. In the 1800s, it was considered a planet, but as more asteroids were discovered, it lost that designation. In August of 2006, it was designated a "dwarf planet" by the International Astronomical Union.

No probe has ever visited Ceres. NASA's DAWN space probe, scheduled to launch in September 2007, may become the first. The DAWN probe's mission is to Vesta and Ceres, the solar system's two largest asteroids. When DAWN arrives at Ceres in February 2015, months before the New Horizons probe arrives at Pluto, it will be the first mission to study a dwarf planet.

Orbit and rotation. Ceres orbits the sun in the asteroid belt region between Mars and Jupiter.

Atmosphere. It is not known if Ceres has an atmosphere. However, it may be similar to the atmosphere on Mercury or the Earth's moon.

Surface and Composition. Ceres is in a class of stony meteorites known as carbonaceous chondrites. These are considered to be the oldest materials in the solar system, with a composition reflecting that of the primitive solar nebula. Extremely dark in color, probably because of their hydrocarbon content, they show evidence of having absorbed water of hydration. Thus, unlike the earth and the moon, they have never either melted or been reheated since they first formed.

Pluto

Distance from the Sun	
Perihelion	2,756.9 mil mi
Semi-major axis (mean distance)	3,647.2 (39.482 AU)
Aphelion	4,583.2 mil mi
Period of revolution around Sun	247.68 y
Orbital eccentricity	0.2488
Orbital inclination	17.16°
Synodic day (midday to midday)	6d 9h 17m (retrograde)
Sidereal day	6d 9h 18m (retrograde)
Rotational inclination	122.53°
Mass (Earth = 1)	0.0021
Mean radius	742.5 mi
Mean density (Earth = 1)	0.317
Natural satellites	3
Average surface temperature	–369°

Pluto, named for the Roman god of the underworld, is the second largest known KBO (Kuiper Belt Object) in the Solar System. It was first discovered in 1930 by Clyde Tombaugh, and was classified as a planet until 2006 when the International Astronomical Union changed its designation to dwarf planet. The New Horizons spacecraft was launched on a voyage to Pluto and beyond in 2006; the spacecraft will make its closest approach to Pluto in July of 2015.

Orbit and Rotation. Pluto's orbit is highly irregular. Although Pluto on the average stays about 3.6 bil mi from the Sun, it may get as close as 2.76 bil mi, and for about 20 years of its orbit, it is closer to the Sun than Neptune. Currently, it is beyond Neptune's orbit.

Atmosphere and Surface. Because no probes have visited Pluto, it is difficult for astronomers to accurately take readings of the planet's atmospheric composition. It is believed that an atmosphere of methane, nitrogen, and carbon monoxide exists when the planet is closer to the Sun. When Pluto is farther away from the sun during its orbit, the atmosphere freezes and becomes part of the surface. Large regions on Pluto are dark, others light; Pluto has spots and perhaps polar caps. There is also evidence of temperature fluctuations on the planet that may indicate primitive weather. Its core may be rocky with a mantle of water ice surrounding it.

Natural Satellites. Pluto has 3 natural satellites. Charon, the biggest, has a diameter of 737 mi—about half of Pluto's diameter of 1,485 mi. No other planet of any kind has a moon so close to its size. Discovered in 1978, Charon orbits Pluto at a distance of 12,200 mi and takes 6.39 days to move around the planet. In this same length of time, Pluto and Charon both rotate once around their axes, meaning that a person standing on Pluto would always see the same face of Charon in the same part of the sky, every day and night. The Pluto-Charon system thus appears to rotate as virtually a rigid body. Both worlds are roughly spherical and have comparable densities. Because of these similarities and their peculiar relationship, there is a debate as to whether Charon should one day be designated a dwarf planet.

The 2 other moons were discovered in 2005 and in 2006 were officially named Nix and Hydra.

Eris (formerly known as UB313)

Distance from the Sun	
Semi-major axis (mean distance)	67.6681 AU
Period of revolution around Sun	560 years
Mean radius	925 mi
Orbital eccentricity	0.44177
Orbital inclination	44.177°
Natural satellites	1

Eris is the largest dwarf planet. Discovered in 2003 by astronomers at the California Institute of Technology, it is the most distant object ever seen in orbit around the sun. Little is known about Eris.

Orbit and Rotation. Eris has a highly elliptical orbit and takes about 560 years to go around the sun—more than twice the time it takes Pluto. Its inclination is steep, tilted at 44° to the planetary plane. It also has an extremely eccentric orbit. It will be at its closest, actually coming inside part of Pluto's orbit, in about 280 years.

Atmosphere. As of yet, nothing is known about Eris's atmosphere, however, it may be similar to Pluto's.

Surface and Composition. Eris, with a surface covered in frozen methane, may be similar to Pluto and the Neptunian moon Triton. Observations made by the Hubble Space Telescope show that Eris's surface is almost white and uniform, reflecting 86% of the light that hits it. This makes it the most reflective body in the Solar System. The dwarf planet's interior is likely a mixture of rock and ice.

Natural Satellites. Eris has one moon. It is officially called S/2005 (2003 UB313) 1. Unofficially, it is referred to as Gabrielle. Little is known about this object.

Small Solar System Bodies: Asteroids, Comets, Kuiper Belt, and the Oort Cloud

Asteroids

Besides planets and moons, there are many smaller objects that orbit the sun. In 2006, the IAU officially designated these objects "small Solar System bodies." **Asteroids** or minor planets are found mainly in a belt between the orbits of Mars and Jupiter, but some may be found outside this region. Within this belt there may be millions of asteroids of varying sizes. Most of asteroids are very small, however, some such as Ceres, which can be classified both as an aster-

oid and a dwarf planet, is 588 mi in diameter is about one-quarter the diameter of our Moon.

Some of these objects, or asteroids, are gravitationally locked with Jupiter and the Sun so that they have roughly the same orbit as Jupiter but either 60° ahead or behind the planet. These are the **Trojan asteroids**. Many of the smaller moons of the solar system, especially those in retrograde orbits, may be captured asteroids. Asteroids whose orbits either cross or come close to the Earth's orbit are labeled **Near Earth Asteroids** or NEAs. A handful of asteroids have actually been imaged by the Arecibo and Goldstone radio telescopes, and by the NEAR Shoemaker space probe, while the *Galileo* spacecraft imaged the asteroids Gaspra and Ida (including its moon Dactyl) on its way to Jupiter.

Comets

Comets are small icy bodies that orbit the Sun. When they approach the Sun, the energy from the Sun boils off material from the comet's icy nucleus, producing an enlarged head (or **coma**), and in many cases an extended tail. Because of the proximity to the Sun and the expanded head and tail, comets are brighter when near the Sun. For large comets, the head may be a 100,000 mi across and the tail more than a million mi long, though both are mainly empty space.

Comets have been known since ancient times; ultimately, British astronomer Edmund Halley (1656-1742) realized that a group of historical reports were just repeated visits of the same object. Comets are the only astronomical objects named after their discoverers. In 1986, the European spacecraft *Giotto* took the first close-up images of a comet's nucleus, specifically of Comet Halley, showing it had a peanut-shaped nucleus whose longest dimension was about 10 mi.

In 1995, Alan Hale and Thomas Bopp independently discovered a comet that was then beyond the orbit of Jupiter. It was the farthest comet ever discovered by amateurs and one of the brightest of all time. It also holds the record for length of naked-eye visibility—19 months—and is the most photographed comet in history.

Kuiper Belt

The **Kuiper Belt** is a donut-shaped region that extends to about 50 AU from the Sun and is thought to be the source for short-period comets such as Comet Halley or Comet Swift-Tuttle. It is filled with icy bodies that are in solar orbit. The more than 800 objects found in this region in recent years are called Kuiper Belt Objects (KBOs). It is estimated that there are more than 70,000 objects 60 mi in diameter or larger within the Kuiper Belt. Dwarf planets Pluto and UB313 are considered KBOs. There are at least 6 KBOs larger than 500 mi in diameter.

Oort Cloud

The Oort Cloud is a vast spherical shell hypothesized to exist around the Sun. Astronomer Jan Oort proposed its existence as the origin for long-period comets that enter the inner part of the solar system where the planets orbit. As of yet, our technology is not sufficient to detect any members of the Oort Cloud, other than those comets that have been observed that indicate the most distant parts of their orbits may reach out to 50,000 AU. Recent examples of such long-period comets are Comet Hale-Bopp and Comet Hyakutake.

The Sun

Distance from Earth, mean	92.96 mil mi (1 AU)
Sidereal day	25.38 d
Mass (Earth=1)	332,900
Mean Radius	432,200 mi
Mean Density (Earth=1)	0.255
Average surface temperature	9,941°F

The Sun is the Earth's primary source of light and heat, and its closest star. The biggest object in the solar system, the Sun is 332,900 times more massive than Earth and contains 99.86% of the mass of the entire solar system. On the whole, the Sun is made up of about 92.1% hydrogen and 7.8S% helium, with trace amounts of other elements. It has a mass and luminosity greater than that of 90% of the stars in the Milky Way galaxy. Although most of the stars that can be easily seen on a clear night are bigger and brighter than the Sun, its proximity to Earth that makes it appear tremendously large and bright. The Sun is 400,000 times as bright as the full moon and it gives Earth 6 mil times as much light as do all other stars put together. Because of the great distance between the Sun and Earth, it takes about 499 seconds, or slightly more than 8 minutes, for light from the Sun to reach Earth.

Composition. The Sun has six regions. The first three from the inside out are the core, the radiative zone, and the convective zone. Together they form the interior. The others, which comprise the visible surface, are the photosphere, the chromosphere, and the outermost region, the corona.

The Sun's core is where its heat and energy are produced. Through a series of nuclear fusion reactions, hydrogen nuclei are converted to helium nuclei. Temperatures in the core are theorized to be 28 mil° F. From the core, photons transport the energy outward through the radiative zone. It can take photons several millions of years to pass through this area. In the convective zone, gases move energy outward at a faster rate. Like a boiling pot, bubbles of gas bring energy to the surface.

The photosphere is the visible surface of the sun, that is, the light from here is what we see as sunlight. When sunlight is analyzed with a spectroscope, it is found to consist of a continuous spectrum composed of all the colors of the rainbow in order, crossed by many dark lines. The dark "absorption lines" are produced by gaseous materials in the outer layers of the Sun. More than 60 of the natural terrestrial elements have been identified in the Sun, all in gaseous form because of the Sun's intense heat.

Just above the photosphere is the chromosphere, which is visible to the naked eye only at total solar eclipses, appearing then to be a pinkish-violet layer with occasional great prominences projecting above its general level. With proper instruments, the chromosphere can be seen or photographed whenever the Sun is visible. Above the chromosphere is the corona, also visible to the naked eye only at times of total eclipse or with instruments that permit the brighter portions of the corona to be seen. The light of the corona surges millions of miles from the Sun, where atoms of which it is composed are all in a state of extreme attenuation and high ionization that indicates temperatures nearly 2 mil° F.

Sunspots. These dark, irregularly shaped regions may reach diameters of thousands of miles. There is an intimate connection between sunspots and the corona. At times of low sunspot activity, the fine streamers of the corona are longer above the Sun's equator than over the polar regions of the Sun; during periods of high sunspot activity, the corona extends fairly evenly outward from all regions of the Sun, but to a much greater distance in space. The average life of a sunspot group is 2 months, but some have lasted for more than a year.

Sunspots reach a low point, on average, every 11.3 years, with a maximum peak of activity occurring irregularly between 2 successive periods of minimal activity. Currently, the number of sunspots is declining. Solar minimum occurred late in 2006.

Solar Wind and Magnetic Field. Magnetic arches, called prominences, may extend tens of thousands of miles into the corona, and may release enormous amounts of energy heating the corona. Coronal mass ejections are enormous releases of solar energy. Coronal holes are regions where the corona appears dark in X–rays, and are associated with open magnetic field lines, where the magnetic field lines project out into space instead of back towards the Sun. It is in these regions where the high-speed solar wind originates.

The solar wind carries the Sun's magnetic field, which extends beyond the planets. This is called the Interplanetary Magnetic Field (IMF). Far past Pluto and the Kuiper Belt, the solar wind and the IMF lose their influence, and the boundary between them and interstellar space is called the heliopause.

Searching for Extrasolar Planets

During the last 10 years of the 20th century, astronomers began to detect the presence of planets orbiting stars other than the Sun. Except for a few possible instances, they have not seen those objects, but merely inferred their existence by their effect on their parent star. The Sun is a typical star in many respects. With over 200 billion stars in the Milky Way, it seems plausible that many other stars might have planets.

As of Fall 2007, astronomers had found a total of 252 planets in 204 star systems. Of those, about 160 were more massive than Jupiter, which is about 318 times more massive than the Earth. About 79 star systems may have planets less massive than Jupiter. In June 2005, astronomers reported detecting a planet that is only about 6 times the mass of the Earth. The planet orbits much closer to its parent star; Gliese 876 takes less than 2 days to complete one orbit.

Using the Doppler Effect to detect radial velocity changes in the motions of individual stars, astronomers are more likely to find high-mass planets in close and eccentric orbits around stars, because that situation produces larger and more noticeable changes.

In addition to the radial velocity method, astronomers are now using an optical gravitational lensing means of detecting extrasolar planets. Using this technique, Southern hemisphere astronomers found the most distant planet yet detected, about halfway to the center of our own Milky Way galaxy. Astronomers have also found planets by looking for the periodic dimming of starlight as orbiting planets pass in front of their host stars. About 25 planets have been discovered this way.

In 2005, astronomers obtained the first direct photograph of an extra-solar planet. The unnamed planet orbits a star called GQ Lupi, which is a star like our Sun but younger. The planet is about 100 AUs away from its star, and it is estimated to be about twice as massive as Jupiter.

In 2006, astronomers discovered what they call a "super Earth" orbiting a red dwarf star 9,000 light-years away. The planet appears to have about 13 times the mass of Earth and may be composed of rock and ice. Although the planet is similar in structure to the Earth, it is believed to orbit too far from its star for there to be any liquid on the surface. In 2007, astronomers for the first time detected water in the atmosphere of an extra-solar planet.

Earth: Size, Computation of Time, Seasons

Distance from the Sun	
Perihelion	91.4 mil mi
Semi-major axis	93.0 mil mi (1.0000 AU)
Aphelion	94.5 mil mi
Period of revolution	365.256 d
Orbital eccentricity	0.0167
Orbital inclination	0.0°
Sidereal day (rotation period)	23h 56m 4.2s
Synodic day (midday to midday)	24h 0m 0s
Rotational inclination	23.45°
Mass (Earth = 1)	1.00
Mean radius	3,958.8 mi
Mean density (Earth = 1)	1.00
Natural satellites	1
Average surface temperature	59° F

Earth is the 5th-largest planet and the 3rd from the Sun. Its mass is 5.9736×10^{24} kg. Earth's equatorial diameter is 7,926 miles while its polar diameter is only 7,900 mi.

Size and Dimensions. Earth is considered a solid mass, yet it has a large, liquid iron, **magnetic core** with a radius of about 2,160 mi. Surprisingly, it has a solid **inner core** that may be a large iron crystal, with a radius of 760 mi. Around the core is a thick shell, or **mantle**, of dense rock. This mantle is composed of materials rich in iron and magnesium. It is somewhat plastic-like, and under slow steady pressure, it can flow like a liquid. The mantle, in turn, is covered by a thin **crust** forming the solid granite and basalt base of the continents and ocean basins. Over broad areas of Earth's surface, the crust has a thin cover of sedimentary rock such as sandstone, shale, and limestone formed by weathering and by deposits of sands, clays, and plant and animal remains.

The **temperature** inside the Earth increases about 1° F with every 100 to 200 feet in depth, in the upper 100 km of Earth, and reaches nearly 8,000-9,000° F at the center. The heat is believed to come from radioactivity in rocks, pressures within Earth, and the original heat of formation.

Atmosphere of Earth. Earth's atmosphere is a blanket composed of 78% nitrogen, 21% oxygen, and 1% argon. Present in minute quantities are carbon dioxide, hydrogen, neon, helium, krypton, and xenon. Water vapor displaces other gases and varies from nearly zero to about 4% by volume. The atmosphere rests on Earth's surface with a weight equivalent to a layer of water 34 ft deep. For about 300,000 ft upward, the gases remain in the proportions stated. Gravity holds the gases to Earth. The weight of the air compresses it at the bottom so that the greatest density is at Earth's surface. Pressure and density decrease as height increases.

The lowest layer of the atmosphere extending up about 7.5 mi is the **troposphere**, which contains 90% of the air and the tallest mountains. This is also where most weather phenomena occur. The temperature drops with increasing height throughout this layer. The atmosphere for about 23 mi above the troposphere is the **stratosphere**, where the temperature generally increases with height. The stratosphere contains **ozone**, which prevents ultraviolet rays from reaching Earth's surface. Since there is very little convection in the stratosphere, jets regularly cruise in the lower parts to provide a smoother ride for passengers.

Above the stratosphere is the **mesosphere**, where the temperature again decreases with height for another 19 mi. Extending above the mesosphere to the outer fringes of the atmosphere is the **thermosphere**, a region where temperature once more increases with height to a value measured in thousands of degrees Fahrenheit. The lower portion of this region, extending from 50 to about 400 mi in altitude, is characterized by a high ion density and is thus called the **ionosphere**. Most meteors are in the lower thermosphere or the mesosphere at the time they are observed.

Longitude, Latitude. Position on the globe is measured by meridians and parallels. Meridians, which are imaginary lines drawn around Earth through the poles, determine **longitude**. The meridian running through Greenwich, England, is the **prime meridian** of longitude, and all others are either E or W. Parallels, which are imaginary circles parallel with the equator, determine **latitude**. The length of a degree of longitude varies as the cosine of the latitude. At the equator a degree of longitude is 69.171 statute mi; this is gradually reduced toward the poles. Value of a longitude degree at the poles is zero.

Latitude is reckoned by the number of degrees N or S of the **equator**, an imaginary circle on Earth's surface everywhere equidistant between the two poles. According to the International Astronomical Union, the length of a degree of latitude is 68.708 statute mi at the equator and varies slightly N and S because of the oblate form of the globe; at the poles it is 69.403 statute mi.

Definitions of Time. Earth rotates on its axis and follows an elliptical orbit around the Sun. The rotation makes the Sun appear to move across the sky from E to W. This rotation determines day and night, and the complete rotation, in relation to the Sun, is called the **apparent** or **true solar day**. A sundial thus measures **apparent solar time**. This length of time varies, but an average determines the mean solar day of 24 hours.

The mean solar day and **mean solar time** are in universal use for civil purposes. Mean solar time may be obtained from apparent solar time by correcting observations of the Sun for the **equation of time**. Mean solar time may be up to 16 minutes different from apparent solar time.

Sidereal time is the measure of time defined by the diurnal motion of the vernal equinox and is determined from observation of the meridian transits of stars. One complete rotation of Earth relative to the equinox is called the **sidereal day**. The **mean sidereal day** is 23 hours, 56 minutes, 4.091 seconds of mean solar time.

The interval required for Earth to make one absolute revolution around the Sun is a **sidereal** year; it consisted of 365 days, 6 hours, 9 minutes, and 9.5 seconds of mean solar time (approximately 24 hours per day) in 1900 and has been increasing at the rate of 0.0001 second annually.

The **tropical year**, upon which our calendar is based, is the interval between 2 consecutive returns of the Sun to the vernal equinox. The tropical year consisted of 365 days, 5 hours, 48 minutes, and 46 seconds in 1900. It has been decreasing at the rate of 0.530 second per century. The **calendar year** begins at 12 o'clock midnight precisely, local clock time, on the night of Dec. 31-Jan. 1. The day and the calendar month also begin at midnight by the clock.

On Jan. 1, 1972, the Bureau International des Poids et Mesures in Paris introduced **International Atomic Time** (TAI) as the most precisely determined time scale for astronomical usage. The fundamental unit of TAI in the international system of units is the second, defined as the duration of 9,192,631,770 periods of the radiation corresponding to the transition between 2 hyperfine levels of the ground state of the cesium–133 atom. **Coordinated Universal Time** (UTC), which serves as the basis for civil timekeeping and is the standard time of the prime meridian, is officially defined by a formula which relates UTC to mean sidereal time in Greenwich, England. (UTC has replaced GMT as the basis for standard time for the world.)

The Zones and Seasons. The 5 zones of Earth's surface are the Torrid, lying between the Tropics of Cancer and Capricorn; the N Temperate, between Cancer and the Arctic Circle; the S Temperate, between Capricorn and the Antarctic Circle; and the 2 Frigid Zones, between the Polar Circles and the Poles.

The inclination, or **tilt**, of Earth's axis, 23° 27′ away from a perpendicular to Earth's orbit of the Sun, determines the seasons. These are commonly marked in the N Temperate Zone, where spring begins at the vernal equinox, summer at the summer solstice, autumn at the autumnal equinox, and winter at the winter solstice. In the S Temperate Zone, the seasons are reversed. Spring begins at the autumnal equinox, summer at the winter solstice, etc.

The points at which the Sun crosses the equator are the **equinoxes**, when day and night are most nearly equal. The points at which the Sun is at a maximum distance from the equator are the **solstices**. Days and nights are then most unequal. However, at the equator, day and night are equal throughout the year.

In June, the North Pole is tilted 23°27′ toward the Sun, and the days in the northern hemisphere are longer than the nights, while the days in the southern hemisphere are shorter than the nights. In Dec., the North Pole is tilted 23°27′ away from the Sun, and the situation is reversed.

The Seasons in 2008. In 2008, the 4 seasons begin in the northern hemisphere as shown. (Add 1 hour to Eastern Standard Time for Atlantic Time; subtract 1 hour for Central, 2 for Mountain, 3 for Pacific, 4 for Alaska, 5 for Hawaii-Aleutian. Also shown is Coordinated Universal Time.)

Seasons	Date	UTC	EST/EDT
Vernal Equinox (spring)	Mar. 20	05:48	01:48
Northern Solstice (summer)	June 20	23:59	19:59
Autumnal Equinox (autumn)	Sept. 22	15:44	11:44
Southern Solstice (winter)	Dec. 21	12:04	07:04

Poles of Earth. The geographic (rotation) poles, or points where Earth's axis of rotation cuts the surface, are not absolutely fixed in the body of Earth. The pole of rotation describes an irregular curve about its mean position.

Two periods have been detected in this motion: (1) an annual period due to seasonal changes in barometric pressure, to load of ice and snow on the surface, and to other seasonal phenomena; (2) a period of about 14 months due to the shape and constitution of Earth. In addition, there are small but as yet unpredictable irregularities. The whole motion is so small that the actual pole at any time remains within a circle of 30 or 40 feet in radius centered at the mean position of the pole.

The pole of rotation for the time being is of course the pole having a latitude of 90° and an indeterminate longitude.

Magnetic Poles. Although Earth's magnetic field resembles that of an ordinary bar magnet, this magnetic field is probably produced by electric currents in the liquid currents of the Earth's outer core. The **north magnetic pole** of Earth is that region where the magnetic force is vertically downward, and the **south magnetic pole** is that region where the magnetic force is vertically upward. A compass placed at the magnetic poles experiences no directive force in azimuth (i.e., direction).

There are slow changes in the distribution of Earth's magnetic field. This slow temporal change is referred to as the secular change of the main magnetic field, and the magnetic poles shift due to this. The location of the N magnetic pole was first measured in 1831 at Cape Adelaide on the west coast of Boothia Peninsula in Canada's Northwest Territories (about latitude 70° N and longitude 96° W). Since then it has moved over 500 mi. It is now estimated to be at 82.7° N and 114.4°W, northwest of Ellef Ringnes Island in N Canada. Measurement for several decades by Canadian scientists indicates the motion of the pole has accelerated, now averaging about 25 mi per year.

The direction of the horizontal components of the magnetic field at any point is known as magnetic N at that point, and the angle by which it deviates E or W of true N is known as the magnetic declination.

A compass without error points in the direction of magnetic north. (In general, this is not the direction of the true rotational north pole.) If you follow the direction indicated by the N end of the compass, you will go along an irregular curve that eventually reaches the north magnetic pole (though not usually by a great-circle route). However, the action of the compass should not be thought of as due to any influence of the distant pole, but simply as an indication of the distribution of Earth's magnetism at the place of observation.

Rotation of Earth. The speed of rotation of Earth about its axis is slightly variable. The variations may be classified as:

(A) **Secular.** Tidal friction acts as a brake on the rotation and causes a slow secular increase in the length of the day, about 1 millisecond per century.

(B) **Irregular.** The speed of rotation may increase for a number of years, about 5 to 10, and then start decreasing. The maximum difference from the mean in the length of the day during a century is about 5 milliseconds. The accumulated difference in time has amounted to approximately 44 seconds since 1900. The cause is probably motion in the interior of Earth.

(C) **Periodic.** Seasonal variations exist with periods of 1 year and 6 months. The cumulative effect is such that each year, Earth is late about 30 milliseconds near June 1 and is ahead about 30 milliseconds near Oct. 1. The maximum seasonal variation in the length of the day is about 0.5 millisecond. It is believed that the principal cause of the annual variation is the seasonal change in the wind patterns of the northern and southern hemispheres. The semiannual variation is due chiefly to tidal action of the Sun, which distorts the shape of Earth slightly.

The Moon

Distance from Earth	
Perigee	225,744 mi
Semi-major axis	238,855 mi
Apogee	251,966 mi
Period of revolution	27.322 d
Synodic orbital period (period of phases)	29.53 d
Orbital eccentricity	0.0549
Orbital inclination	5.145°
Sidereal day (rotation period)	27.322 d
Rotational inclination	6.68°
Mass (Earth = 1)	0.0123
Mean radius	1,079 mi
Mean density (Earth = 1)	0.607
Average surface temperature	−100° F

The Moon is the second brightest object in the sky (the sun is the first). Earth's only natural satellite, the Moon is the force behind the rising and falling of tides, and it helps to regulate the Earth's orbit around the sun. Many probes have been sent to the moon and between 1969 and 1972, 12 U.S. astronauts walked on its surface.

Orbit and Rotation. The Moon completes a circuit around Earth in a period that averages 27 days, 7 hours, 43.2 minutes. This is the Moon's sidereal period. Because of the motion of the Moon in common with Earth around the Sun, the mean duration of the lunar month—the period from one New Moon to the next New Moon—is 29 days, 12 hours, 44.05 minutes. This is the Moon's synodic period.

The mean distance of the Moon from Earth is 238,855 mi, but its orbit about Earth is elliptical, and thus the actual distance varies considerably. The maximum distance from Earth that the Moon may reach is 251,966 mi and the least distance is 225,744 mi.

The Moon rotates on its axis in a period of time that is exactly equal to its sidereal revolution about Earth—27.322 days. Thus the backside or farside of the Moon always faces away from Earth. But this does not mean that the backside is always dark. The farside of the Moon gets just as much direct sunlight as the nearside; at New Moon phase, the farside of the Moon is fully lit, but not visible from Earth.

The Moon's revolution about Earth is irregular because of its elliptical orbit. The Moon's rotation, however, is regular, and this, together with the irregular revolution, produces what is called "libration in longitude," which permits an observer on Earth to see first farther around the E side and then farther around the western side of the Moon. The Moon's variation north or south of the ecliptic permits one to see farther over first one pole and then the other of the Moon; this is called "libration in latitude." These two libration effects permit observers on Earth to see a total of about 60% of the Moon's surface over a period of time.

Atmosphere and Surface. The Moon, like the planet Mercury, has no real atmosphere to speak of. What little exists is variable and tenuous. With its long day and night, the daytime temperature can reach 260°F, while the coldest nighttime temperature may reach −280°F. This day-to-night contrast is exceeded only by that on Mercury.

The lunar surface has not changed much since humans have been observing it. The side visible from Earth has large craters and vast dark areas called maria that were once lava. The farside has almost no maria but is pockmarked with craters.

Recent findings show that up to 300 mil metric tons of water ice may exist in craters at the lunar poles. In its interior, the Moon may have a small core, which supports the idea that most of the mass of the Moon was ripped away from the early Earth when a Mars-size object collided with Earth. The hidden side of the Moon was first photographed in 1959 by the Soviet space probe *Lunik III*.

Harvest Moon and Hunter's Moon. The Harvest Moon, the full Moon nearest the autumnal equinox, ushers in a period of several successive days when the Moon rises soon after sunset. This phenomenon gives farmers in temperate latitudes extra hours of light in which to harvest their crops before frost and winter. The 2008 Harvest Moon falls on Sept. 15. Harvest Moon in the southern hemisphere temperate latitudes falls on Mar. 21.

The next full Moon after Harvest Moon is called the Hunter's Moon; it is accompanied by a similar but less marked phenomenon. In 2008, the Hunter's Moon occurs on Oct. 14 in the northern hemisphere and on Apr. 20 in the southern hemisphere.

Moon's Perigee and Apogee, 2008

Perigee is the point in the moon's orbit where it is closest to the Earth. Apogee is the point where it is farthest.

(Coordinated Universal Time, standard time of the prime meridian)

Perigee Date	Hour	Perigee Date	Hour	Apogee Date	Hour	Apogee Date	Hour
Jan. 19	9	July 1	21	Jan. 3	8	July 14	4
Feb. 14	1	July 29	23	Jan. 31	4	Aug. 10	20
Mar. 10	22	Aug. 26	3	Feb. 28	1	Sep. 7	15
Apr. 7	19	Sept. 20	3	Mar. 26	20	Oct. 5	11
May 6	3	Oct. 17	6	Apr. 23	9	Nov. 2	5
June 3	13	Nov. 14	10	May 20	14	Nov. 29	17
		Dec. 12	22	June 16	18	Dec. 26	18

Moon Phases, 2008

(Coordinated Universal Time, standard time of the prime meridian)

New Moon Month	d	h	m	Waxing Quarter Month	d	h	m	Full Moon Month	d	h	m	Waning Quarter Month	d	h	m
Jan.	8	11	37	Jan.	15	19	46	Jan.	22	13	35	Jan.	30	5	3
Feb.	7	3	44	Feb.	14	3	33	Feb.	21	3	30	Feb.	29	2	18
Mar.	7	17	14	Mar.	14	10	46	Mar.	21	18	40	Mar.	29	21	47
Apr.	6	3	55	Apr.	12	18	32	Apr.	20	10	25	Apr.	28	14	12
May	5	12	18	May	12	3	47	May	20	2	11	May	28	2	57
June	3	19	23	June	10	15	4	June	18	17	30	June	26	12	10
July	3	2	19	July	10	4	35	July	18	7	59	July	25	18	42
Aug.	1	10	13	Aug.	8	20	20	Aug.	16	21	16	Aug.	23	23	50
Aug.	30	19	58	Sept.	7	14	4	Sept.	15	9	13	Sept.	22	5	4
Sept.	29	8	12	Oct.	7	9	4	Oct.	14	20	2	Oct.	21	11	55
Oct.	28	23	14	Nov.	6	4	3	Nov.	13	6	17	Nov.	19	21	31
Nov.	27	16	55	Dec.	5	21	26	Dec.	12	16	37	Dec.	19	10	29
Dec.	27	12	22												

CALENDAR

Julian and Gregorian Calendars; Leap Year; Century

The **Julian calendar**, under which all Western nations measured time until 1582 CE, was authorized by Julius Caesar in 46 BCE. It called for a year of 365¼ days, starting in January, with every 4th year being a **leap year** of 366 days. St. Bede, an Anglo-Saxon monk also known as the Venerable Bede, announced in 730 CE that the Julian year was 11 min, 14 sec too long, a cumulative error of about a day every 128 years, but nothing was done about this for centuries.

By 1582 the accumulated error was estimated at 10 days. In that year Pope Gregory XIII decreed that the day following Oct. 4, 1582, should be called Oct. 15, thus dropping 10 days and initiating the **Gregorian calendar**.

The Gregorian calendar continued a system devised by the monk Dionysius Exiguus (6th century), starting from the first year following the birth of Jesus Christ, which was inaccurately taken to be year 753 in the Roman calendar. Leap years were continued but, to prevent further displacements, centesimal years (years ending in 00) were made common years, not leap years, unless divisible by 400. Under this plan, **1600** and **2000** were leap years (as was **2004**); 1700, 1800, and 1900 were not.

The Gregorian calendar was adopted at once by France, Italy, Spain, Portugal, and Luxembourg. Within 2 years most German Catholic states, Belgium, and parts of Switzerland and the Netherlands were brought under the new calendar, and Hungary followed in 1587. The rest of the Netherlands, along with Denmark and the German Protestant states, made the change in 1699-1700.

The British government adopted the Gregorian calendar and imposed it on all its possessions, including the American colonies, in 1752, decreeing that the day following Sept. 2, 1752, should be called Sept. 14, a loss of 11 days. All dates preceding were marked OS, for Old Style. In addition, New Year's Day was moved to Jan. 1 from Mar. 25 (under the old reckoning, for example, Mar. 24, 1700, had been followed by Mar. 25, 1701). Thus George Washington's birthdate, which was Feb. 11, 1731, OS, became Feb. 22, 1732, NS (New Style). In 1753 Sweden also went Gregorian.

In 1793 the French revolutionary government adopted a calendar of 12 months of 30 days with 5 extra days in September of each common year and a 6th every 4th year. Napoleon reinstated the Gregorian calendar in 1806.

The Gregorian system later spread to non-European regions, replacing traditional calendars at least for official purposes. Japan in 1873, Egypt in 1875, China in 1912, and Turkey in 1925 made the change, usually in conjunction with political upheaval. In China, the republican government began reckoning years from its 1911 founding. After 1949, the People's Republic adopted the Common, or Christian Era, year count, even for the traditional lunar calendar, which is also retained. In 1918 the Soviet Union decreed that the day after Jan. 31, 1918, OS, would be Feb. 14, 1918, NS. Greece changed over in 1923. For the first time in history, all major nations had one calendar. The Russian Orthodox church and some other Christian sects retained the Julian calendar.

To convert from the Julian to the Gregorian calendar, add 10 days to dates Oct. 5, 1582, through Feb. 28, 1700; after that date add 11 days through Feb. 28, 1800; 12 days through Feb. 28, 1900; and 13 days through Feb. 28, 2100.

A **century** consists of 100 consecutive years. The 1st century CE may be said to have run from the years 1 through 100. The 20th century by this reckoning consisted of the years 1901 through 2000 and technically ended Dec. 31, 2000, as did the 2nd millennium CE. The 21st century thus technically began Jan. 1, 2001.

For a **Perpetual Calendar,** see pages 342-43.

Gregorian Calendar

Choose the desired year from the table below or from the Perpetual Calendar (for years 1803 to 2080). The number after each year designates which calendar to use for that year, as shown in the Perpetual Calendar. (The Gregorian calendar was inaugurated Oct. 15, 1582. From that date to Dec. 31, 1582, use calendar 6.)

1583-1802

1583	7	1603	4	1623	1	1643	5	1663	2	1683	6	1703	2	1723	6	1743	3	1763	7	1783	4
1584	1	1604	12	1624	9	1644	13	1664	10	1684	14	1704	10	1724	14	1744	11	1764	8	1784	12
1585	3	1605	7	1625	4	1645	1	1665	5	1685	2	1705	5	1725	2	1745	6	1765	3	1785	7
1586	4	1606	1	1626	5	1646	2	1666	6	1686	3	1706	6	1726	3	1746	7	1766	4	1786	1
1587	5	1607	2	1627	6	1647	3	1667	7	1687	4	1707	7	1727	4	1747	1	1767	5	1787	2
1588	13	1608	10	1628	14	1648	11	1668	8	1688	12	1708	8	1728	12	1748	9	1768	13	1788	10
1589	1	1609	5	1629	2	1649	6	1669	3	1689	7	1709	3	1729	7	1749	4	1769	1	1789	5
1590	2	1610	6	1630	3	1650	7	1670	4	1690	1	1710	4	1730	1	1750	5	1770	2	1790	6
1591	3	1611	7	1631	4	1651	1	1671	5	1691	2	1711	5	1731	2	1751	6	1771	3	1791	7
1592	11	1612	8	1632	12	1652	9	1672	13	1692	10	1712	13	1732	10	1752	14	1772	11	1792	8
1593	6	1613	3	1633	7	1653	4	1673	1	1693	5	1713	1	1733	5	1753	2	1773	6	1793	3
1594	7	1614	4	1634	1	1654	5	1674	2	1694	6	1714	2	1734	6	1754	3	1774	7	1794	4
1595	1	1615	5	1635	2	1655	6	1675	3	1695	7	1715	3	1735	7	1755	4	1775	1	1795	5
1596	9	1616	13	1636	10	1656	14	1676	11	1696	8	1716	11	1736	8	1756	12	1776	9	1796	13
1597	4	1617	1	1637	5	1657	2	1677	6	1697	3	1717	6	1737	3	1757	7	1777	4	1797	1
1598	5	1618	2	1638	6	1658	3	1678	7	1698	4	1718	7	1738	4	1758	1	1778	5	1798	2
1599	6	1619	3	1639	7	1659	4	1679	1	1699	5	1719	1	1739	5	1759	2	1779	6	1799	3
1600	14	1620	11	1640	8	1660	12	1680	9	1700	6	1720	9	1740	13	1760	10	1780	14	1800	4
1601	2	1621	6	1641	1	1661	7	1681	4	1701	7	1721	4	1741	1	1761	5	1781	2	1801	5
1602	3	1622	7	1642	4	1662	1	1682	5	1702	1	1722	5	1742	2	1762	6	1782	3	1802	6

The Julian Period

How many days have you lived? To determine this, multiply your age by 365, add the number of days since your last birthday, and account for all leap years. Chances are your calculations will go wrong somewhere. Astronomers, however, find it convenient to express dates and time intervals in days rather than in years, months, and days. This is done by placing events within the Julian period.

The Julian period was devised in 1582 by the French classical scholar Joseph Scaliger (1540-1609), and it was named after his father, Julius Caesar Scaliger, not after the Julian calendar as might be supposed.

Scaliger began with a zero hour, or starting time, of noon on Jan. 1, 4713 BCE (on the Julian calendar). This was the most recent time that 3 major chronological cycles began on the same day: (1) the 28-year solar cycle, after which dates in the Julian calendar (e.g., Feb. 11) return to the same days of the week (e.g., Monday); (2) the 19-year lunar cycle, after which the phases of the moon return to the same dates of the year; and (3) the 15-year indiction cycle, used in ancient Rome to regulate taxes.

It will take 7,980 years to complete the period, the product of 28, 19, and 15.

Noon of Dec. 31, 2007 will be Julian Date (JD) 2,454,466; that many days will have passed since the start of the Julian period. The JD at noon of any date in 2008 may be found by adding to this figure the day of the year for that date, which can be obtained from the left half of the "How Far Apart Are Two Dates?" chart on the next page.

Julian Calendar

To find which of the 14 calendars of the Perpetual Calendar (pages 362-63) applies to any year under the Julian system, find the century for the desired year in the 3 leftmost columns below. Read across and find the year in the 4 top rows. Then read down. The number in the intersection is the calendar designation for that year. For some years and countries the Julian new year did not start Jan. 1; to find the correct Perpetual Calendar for Britain and its possessions, you can generally add one year for dates from Jan. 1-Mar. 24. For example, to look up Feb. 2, 1705, Old Style, use the year 1706.

Year (last 2 figures of desired year)

		01 02 03 04 05 06 07 08 09 10 11 12 13 14 15 16 17 18 19 20 21 22 23 24 25 26 27 28
		29 30 31 32 33 34 35 36 37 38 39 40 41 42 43 44 45 46 47 48 49 50 51 52 53 54 55 56
		57 58 59 60 61 62 63 64 65 66 67 68 69 70 71 72 73 74 75 76 77 78 79 80 81 82 83 84
Century	00	85 86 87 88 89 90 91 92 93 94 95 96 97 98 99
0	700 1400	12 7 1 2 10 5 6 7 8 3 4 5 13 1 2 3 11 6 7 1 9 4 5 6 14 2 3 4 12
100	800 1500	11 6 7 1 9 4 5 6 14 2 3 4 12 7 1 2 10 5 6 7 8 3 4 5 13 1 2 3 11
200	900 1600	10 5 6 7 8 3 4 5 13 1 2 3 11 6 7 1 9 4 5 6 14 2 3 4 12 7 1 2 10
300	1000 1700	9 4 5 6 14 2 3 4 12 7 1 2 10 5 6 7 8 3 4 5 13 1 2 3 11 6 7 1 9
400	1100 1800	8 3 4 5 13 1 2 3 11 6 7 1 9 4 5 6 14 2 3 4 12 7 1 2 10 5 6 7 8
500	1200 1900	14 2 3 4 12 7 1 2 10 5 6 7 8 3 4 5 13 1 2 3 11 6 7 1 9 4 5 6 14
600	1300 2000	13 1 2 3 11 6 7 1 9 4 5 6 14 2 3 4 12 7 1 2 10 5 6 7 8 3 4 5 13

How Far Apart Are Two Dates?

This table covers a range of 2 years. To use, **find the numbers in the tables for each date and subtract** the smaller from the larger. Example—to find the number of days from Mar. 15, 2007, to Sept. 22, 2008, subtract 74 from 630; the result is 556. For leap years, such as 2008, where Feb. 29 intervenes, one day must be then added; thus Feb. 4, 2008, and Mar. 13, 2009, are 403 days apart.

First Year

Date	Jan.	Feb.	Mar.	April	May	June	July	Aug.	Sept.	Oct.	Nov.	Dec.
1	1	32	60	91	121	152	182	213	244	274	305	335
2	2	33	61	92	122	153	183	214	245	275	306	336
3	3	34	62	93	123	154	184	215	246	276	307	337
4	4	35	63	94	124	155	185	216	247	277	308	338
5	5	36	64	95	125	156	186	217	248	278	309	339
6	6	37	65	96	126	157	187	218	249	279	310	340
7	7	38	66	97	127	158	188	219	250	280	311	341
8	8	39	67	98	128	159	189	220	251	281	312	342
9	9	40	68	99	129	160	190	221	252	282	313	343
10	10	41	69	100	130	161	191	222	253	283	314	344
11	11	42	70	101	131	162	192	223	254	284	315	345
12	12	43	71	102	132	163	193	224	255	285	316	346
13	13	44	72	103	133	164	194	225	256	286	317	347
14	14	45	73	104	134	165	195	226	257	287	318	348
15	15	46	74	105	135	166	196	227	258	288	319	349
16	16	47	75	106	136	167	197	228	259	289	320	350
17	17	48	76	107	137	168	198	229	260	290	321	351
18	18	49	77	108	138	169	199	230	261	291	322	352
19	19	50	78	109	139	170	200	231	262	292	323	353
20	20	51	79	110	140	171	201	232	263	293	324	354
21	21	52	80	111	141	172	202	233	264	294	325	355
22	22	53	81	112	142	173	203	234	265	295	326	356
23	23	54	82	113	143	174	204	235	266	296	327	357
24	24	55	83	114	144	175	205	236	267	297	328	358
25	25	56	84	115	145	176	206	237	268	298	329	359
26	26	57	85	116	146	177	207	238	269	299	330	360
27	27	58	86	117	147	178	208	239	270	300	331	361
28	28	59	87	118	148	179	209	240	271	301	332	362
29	29	—	88	119	149	180	210	241	272	302	333	363
30	30	—	89	120	150	181	211	242	273	303	334	364
31	31	—	90	—	151	—	212	243	—	304	—	365

Second Year

Date	Jan.	Feb.	Mar.	April	May	June	July	Aug.	Sept.	Oct.	Nov.	Dec.
1	366	397	425	456	486	517	547	578	609	639	670	700
2	367	398	426	457	487	518	548	579	610	640	671	701
3	368	399	427	458	488	519	549	580	611	641	672	702
4	369	400	428	459	489	520	550	581	612	642	673	703
5	370	401	429	460	490	521	551	582	613	643	674	704
6	371	402	430	461	491	522	552	583	614	644	675	705
7	372	403	431	462	492	523	553	584	615	645	676	706
8	373	404	432	463	493	524	554	585	616	646	677	707
9	374	405	433	464	494	525	555	586	617	647	678	708
10	375	406	434	465	495	526	556	587	618	648	679	709
11	376	407	435	466	496	527	557	588	619	649	680	710
12	377	408	436	467	497	528	558	589	620	650	681	711
13	378	409	437	468	498	529	559	590	621	651	682	712
14	379	410	438	469	499	530	560	591	622	652	683	713
15	380	411	439	470	500	531	561	592	623	653	684	714
16	381	412	440	471	501	532	562	593	624	654	685	715
17	382	413	441	472	502	533	563	594	625	655	686	716
18	383	414	442	473	503	534	564	595	626	656	687	717
19	384	415	443	474	504	535	565	596	627	657	688	718
20	385	416	444	475	505	536	566	597	628	658	689	719
21	386	417	445	476	506	537	567	598	629	659	690	720
22	387	418	446	477	507	538	568	599	630	660	691	721
23	388	419	447	478	508	539	569	600	631	661	692	722
24	389	420	448	479	509	540	570	601	632	662	693	723
25	390	421	449	480	510	541	571	602	633	663	694	724
26	391	422	450	481	511	542	572	603	634	664	695	725
27	392	423	451	482	512	543	573	604	635	665	696	726
28	393	424	452	483	513	544	574	605	636	666	697	727
29	394	—	453	484	514	545	575	606	637	667	698	728
30	395	—	454	485	515	546	576	607	638	668	699	729
31	396	—	455	—	516	—	577	608	—	669	—	730

Signs of the Zodiac

The **zodiac** is the apparent yearly path of the sun among the stars as viewed from earth, and was divided by the ancients into 12 equal sections or signs, each named for the constellation situated within its limits in ancient times. Astrologers claim that the temperament and destiny of each individual depend on the zodiac sign under which the person was born and the relationships between the planets at that time and throughout life.

Below are the 12 traditional signs and the traditional range of dates pertaining to each:

♈ **Aries** (Ram), March 21– April 19

♉ **Taurus** (Bull), April 20– May 20

♊ **Gemini** (Twins), May 21– June 21

♋ **Cancer** (Crab), June 22– July 22

♌ **Leo** (Lion), July 23– August 22

♍ **Virgo** (Maiden), August 23– September 22

♎ **Libra** (Balance), September 23– October 23

♏ **Scorpio** (Scorpion), October 24– November 21

♐ **Sagittarius** (Archer), November 22– December 21

♑ **Capricorn** (Goat), December 22– January 19

♒ **Aquarius** (Water Bearer), January 20– February 18

♓ **Pisces** (Fishes), February 19– March 20

Calendar for the Year 2008

JANUARY	FEBRUARY	MARCH	APRIL
S M T W T F S	S M T W T F S	S M T W T F S	S M T W T F S
1 2 3 4 5	1 2	1	1 2 3 4 5
6 7 8 9 10 11 12	3 4 5 6 7 8 9	2 3 4 5 6 7 8	6 7 8 9 10 11 12
13 14 15 16 17 18 19	10 11 12 13 14 15 16	9 10 11 12 13 14 15	13 14 15 16 17 18 19
20 21 22 23 24 25 26	17 18 19 20 21 22 23	16 17 18 19 20 21 22	20 21 22 23 24 25 26
27 28 29 30 31	24 25 26 27 28 29	23 24 25 26 27 28 29	27 28 29 30
		30 31	

MAY	JUNE	JULY	AUGUST
S M T W T F S	S M T W T F S	S M T W T F S	S M T W T F S
1 2 3	1 2 3 4 5 6 7	1 2 3 4 5	1 2
4 5 6 7 8 9 10	8 9 10 11 12 13 14	6 7 8 9 10 11 12	3 4 5 6 7 8 9
11 12 13 14 15 16 17	15 16 17 18 19 20 21	13 14 15 16 17 18 19	10 11 12 13 14 15 16
18 19 20 21 22 23 24	22 23 24 25 26 27 28	20 21 22 23 24 25 26	17 18 19 20 21 22 23
25 26 27 28 29 30 31	29 30	27 28 29 30 31	24 25 26 27 28 29 30
			31

SEPTEMBER	OCTOBER	NOVEMBER	DECEMBER
S M T W T F S	S M T W T F S	S M T W T F S	S M T W T F S
1 2 3 4 5 6	1 2 3 4	1	1 2 3 4 5 6
7 8 9 10 11 12 13	5 6 7 8 9 10 11	2 3 4 5 6 7 8	7 8 9 10 11 12 13
14 15 16 17 18 19 20	12 13 14 15 16 17 18	9 10 11 12 13 14 15	14 15 16 17 18 19 20
21 22 23 24 25 26 27	19 20 21 22 23 24 25	16 17 18 19 20 21 22	21 22 23 24 25 26 27
28 29 30	26 27 28 29 30 31	23 24 25 26 27 28 29	28 29 30 31
		30	

Federal Holidays and Other Notable Dates, 2008
Some dates may be subject to change.

The days marked on the calendar above and shown below in *italics* are U.S. federal holidays, designated by the president or Congress and applicable to federal employees and the District of Columbia. Most U.S. states also observe these holidays, and many states observe others; practices vary from state to state. In most states the secretary of state's office can provide details.

January
1   *New Year's Day*; Sugar Bowl; Rose Bowl
2   Fiesta Bowl
3   Orange Bowl
7   BCS Football Championship Game (New Orleans, LA)
10   Muharram 1 (Islamic New Year), 1st full day
14-27   Australian Open tennis tournament
21   *Martin Luther King Jr. Day* (3rd Mon. in Jan.)
26   Australia Day, Australia

February
2   Groundhog Day
4   Super Bowl XLII (Phoenix, AZ)
2-5   Carnival, Brazil
5   Mardi Gras
6   Ash Wednesday
7   Chinese New Year
10   NFL Pro Bowl (Honolulu, HI)
11-12   Westminster Dog Show
12   Lincoln's Birthday
14   Valentine's Day
17   Daytona 500; NBA All-Star Game
18   *Washington's Birthday* (observed), *Presidents' Day*, or *Washington-Lincoln Day* (3rd Mon. in Feb.)
24   Academy Awards

March
1   Iditarod Trail Sled Dog Race begins
9   Daylight Saving Time begins in U.S.
10   Commonwealth Day, Canada
17   St. Patrick's Day
20   First day of spring (Northern Hemisphere)
21   Benito Juárez's Birthday, Mexico; Purim (Feast of Lots), 1st full day; Good Friday
23   Easter

April
1   April Fool's Day
5-7   NCAA men's basketball championship
6-8   NCAA women's basketball championship
10-13   Masters golf tournament
20   First full day of Passover; Earth Day
21   Patriots' Day; Boston Marathon
23   Administrative Professionals Day
24   Take Our Daughters and Sons to Work Day
25   Arbor Day, U.S.

May
1   May Day
3   Kentucky Derby
5   Cinco de Mayo (Battle of Puebla Day), Mexico
6   National Teacher Day, U.S.
11   Mother's Day
12   Buddha's Birthday, Korea, Hong Kong
17   Armed Forces Day; Preakness Stakes
19   Victoria Day, Canada
25-June 8   French Open tennis tournament
26   *Memorial Day*, or *Decoration Day* (last Mon. in May)

June
7   Belmont Stakes
14   Flag Day, U.S.
9-15   U.S. Open golf tournament
15   Father's Day
8   Dragon Boat Festival, China
21   First day of summer (Northern Hemisphere)
23-July 6   Wimbledon tennis tournament

July
1   Canada Day
4   *Independence Day*
6-14   Running of the Bulls (Pamplona, Spain)
14   Bastille Day, France
17-20   British Open golf tournament

August
9-12   PGA Championship

September
1   *Labor Day*, U.S. (1st Monday in Sept.); Labor Day, Canada
2   Ramadan (Islamic month of fasting), 1st full day
7   Grandparents' Day, U.S.
16   Independence Day, Mexico
17   Citizenship Day, U.S.
19   San Gennaro, Italy
23   First day of autumn (Northern Hemisphere)

October
1   Rosh Hashanah (New Year), 1st full day; U.S. Supreme Court session begins
3   German Unification Day, Germany
9   Yom Kippur (Day of Atonement), 1st full day
12   Día de la Raza, Spain, Mexico
13   *Columbus Day* (2nd Mon. in Oct.); Thanksgiving Day, Canada
24   United Nations Day
31   Halloween

November
1   All Saints' Day
1-2   Día de los Muertos, Mexico
2   Daylight Saving Time ends in U.S.; New York City Marathon
4   Election Day (1st Tues. after 1st Mon. in Nov.)
5   Guy Fawkes Day, UK
9   Remembrance Sunday, UK
11   *Veterans Day*; Remembrance Day, Canada, UK
15   Shichi-Go-San (Seven-Five-Three), Japan
27   *Thanksgiving Day*, (4th Thurs. in Nov.)

December
10   Nobel Prizes awarded (winners announced in Oct.)
12   Día de la Virgen de Guadalupe, Mexico
22-29   Hanukkah (Festival of Lights)
22   First day of winter (Northern Hemisphere)
25   *Christmas Day*
26   Boxing Day, Australia, Canada, New Zealand, UK
26-Jan. 1   Kwanzaa

Chinese Calendar, Asian Festivals

Source: Chinese Information and Culture Center, New York, NY

The Chinese calendar, like the Jewish and Islamic calendars (see the Religion chapter), is a lunar calendar. It is divided into 12 months of 29 or 30 days (compensating for the lunar month's mean duration of 29 days, 12 hr, 44.05 min). This calendar is synchronized with the solar year by the addition of extra months at fixed intervals.

The Chinese calendar runs on a 60-year cycle. The cycles 1876-1935 and 1936-95, with the years grouped under their 12 animal designations, are printed below, along with the first 24 years of the current cycle. This cycle began in 1996 and will last until 2055. Feb. 17, 2008, marks the beginning of the year 4706 in the Chinese calendar, and is designated the Year of the Rat. Readers can find the animal name for the year of their birth in the chart below. (Note: The first 3-7 weeks of each Western year belong to the previous Chinese year and animal designation.)

Both the Western (Gregorian) and traditional lunar calendars are used publicly in China and in North and South Korea, and 2 New Year's celebrations are held. In Taiwan, in overseas Chinese communities, and in Vietnam, the lunar calendar is used only to set the dates for traditional festivals, with the Gregorian system in general use.

The 4-day Chinese New Year, Hsin Nien, the 3-day Vietnamese New Year festival, Tet, and the 3-to-4-day Korean festival, Suhl, begin at the 2nd new moon after the winter solstice. The new moon in the Far East, which is west of the International Date Line, may be a day later than the new moon in the U.S. The festivals may start, therefore, anywhere between Jan. 21 and Feb. 19 of the Gregorian calendar.

Rat	Ox	Tiger	Hare (Rabbit)	Dragon	Snake	Horse	Sheep (Goat)	Monkey	Rooster	Dog	Pig (Boar)
1876	1877	1878	1879	1880	1881	1882	1883	1884	1885	1886	1887
1888	1889	1890	1891	1892	1893	1894	1895	1896	1897	1898	1899
1900	1901	1902	1903	1904	1905	1906	1907	1908	1909	1910	1911
1912	1913	1914	1915	1916	1917	1918	1919	1920	1921	1922	1923
1924	1925	1926	1927	1928	1929	1930	1931	1932	1933	1934	1935
1936	1937	1938	1939	1940	1941	1942	1943	1944	1945	1946	1947
1948	1949	1950	1951	1952	1953	1954	1955	1956	1957	1958	1959
1960	1961	1962	1963	1964	1965	1966	1967	1968	1969	1970	1971
1972	1973	1974	1975	1976	1977	1978	1979	1980	1981	1982	1983
1984	1985	1986	1987	1988	1989	1990	1991	1992	1993	1994	1995
1996	1997	1998	1999	2000	2001	2002	2003	2004	2005	2006	2007
2008	2009	2010	2011	2012	2013	2014	2015	2016	2017	2018	2019

Other Calendars: Year and New Year's in 2008

Era	Year	Begins in 2007	Era	Year	Begins in 2007
Byzantine	7517	Sept. 14	Grecian (Seleucidae)	2320	Sept. 14 or Oct.14
Jewish	5769	Sept. 19[1]	Diocletian	1725	Sept. 11
Roman (Ab Urbe Condita)	2761	Jan. 14	Indian (Saka)	1930	Mar. 21
Nabonassar (Babylonian)	2757	Apr. 23	Islamic/Muslim (Hijra)	1429	Jan. 9/10[2]
Japanese (starts at 0 with new emperor)	20	Jan. 1	Chinese (Year of the Rat)	4706	Feb. 7

(1) Year begins at sunset. (2) Year begins with moon crescent.

Chronological Cycles, 2008

Dominical Letter	FE	Roman Indiction	1	Solar Cycle	1
Golden Number (Lunar Cycle)	14	Epact	22	Julian Period (year of)	6721

Dominical Letter .... FE
Golden Number (Lunar Cycle) 14
Roman Indiction 1
Epact 22
Solar Cycle 1
Julian Period (year of) 6721

Special Months

Every year there are many thousands of special months, days, and weeks as a result of anniversaries, official proclamations, and promotional events, both trivial and serious. Here are a few of the special months:

January: Jump Out of Bed Month, National Mentoring Month, National Poverty in America Awareness Month

February: Black History Month, American Heart Month, Library Lovers Month, Youth Leadership Month, Return Shopping Carts to the Supermarket Month

March: Irish-American Heritage Month, Women's History Month, American Red Cross Month, National Frozen Foods Month, National Talk With Your Teen About Sex Month

April: National Child Abuse Prevention Month, National Humor Month, Stress Awareness Month, Grange Month

May: Clean Air Month, Get Caught Reading Month, National Barbecue Month, Asian Pacific American Heritage Month, National Mental Health Month

June: National Candy Month, Gay and Lesbian Pride Month, Potty Training Awareness Month, National Safety Month

July: Cell Phone Courtesy Month, National Hot Dog Month, Women's Motorcycle Month

August: Black Business Month, National Inventors' Month, Happiness Happens Month, National Toddler Month

September: Library Card Sign-Up Month, National Hispanic Heritage Month (Sept. 15-Oct. 15), National Biscuit Month

October: National Domestic Violence Awareness Month, National Breast Cancer Awareness Month, Diversity Awareness Month, National Popcorn Poppin' Month

November: National AIDS Awareness Month, National American Indian Heritage Month, National Adoption Month, American Diabetes Month, Peanut Butter Lovers' Month

December: Universal Human Rights Month, National Drunk and Drugged Driving Prevention Month, National Tie Month, Colorectal Cancer Education and Awareness Month

Wedding Anniversaries

The traditional names for wedding anniversaries go back many years in social usage and have been used to suggest types of appropriate anniversary gifts. Traditional products for gifts are listed here in capital letters, with a few allowable revisions in parentheses, followed by common modern gifts in each category.

1st	PAPER, clocks	13th	LACE, textiles, furs
2nd	COTTON, china	14th	IVORY, gold jewelry
3rd	LEATHER, crystal, glass	15th	CRYSTAL, watches
4th	LINEN (SILK), appliances	20th	CHINA, platinum
5th	WOOD, silverware	25th	SILVER, sterling silver
6th	IRON, wood objects	30th	PEARL, diamond
7th	WOOL (COPPER), desk sets	35th	CORAL (JADE), jade
8th	BRONZE, linens, lace	40th	RUBY, ruby
9th	POTTERY (CHINA), leather goods	45th	SAPPHIRE, sapphire
10th	TIN, ALUMINUM, diamond	50th	GOLD, gold
11th	STEEL, fashion jewelry	55th	EMERALD, emerald
12th	SILK, pearls, colored gems	60th	DIAMOND, diamond

Birthstones

Source: Jewelry Industry Council

MONTH	Ancient	Modern	MONTH	Ancient	Modern
January	Garnet	Garnet	July	Onyx	Ruby
February	Amethyst	Amethyst	August	Carnelian	Sardonyx or Peridot
March	Jasper	Bloodstone or Aquamarine	September	Chrysolite	Sapphire
April	Sapphire	Diamond	October	Aquamarine	Opal or Tourmaline
May	Agate	Emerald	November	Topaz	Topaz
June	Emerald	Pearl, Moonstone, or Alexandrite	December	Ruby	Turquoise or Zircon

Standard Time, Daylight Saving Time, and Others

Source: National Imagery and Mapping Agency; U.S. Dept. of Transportation

See also Time Zone map, page 460.

Standard Time

Standard Time is reckoned from the Prime Meridian of Longitude in Greenwich, England. The world is divided into 24 zones, each 15 deg of arc, or one hour in time apart. The Greenwich meridian (0 deg) extends through the center of the initial zone, and the zones to the east are numbered from 1 to 12, with the prefix "minus" indicating the number of hours to be subtracted to obtain Greenwich Time. Each zone extends 7.5 deg on either side of its central meridian.

Westward zones are similarly numbered, but prefixed "plus," showing the number of hours that must be added to get Greenwich Time. Although these zones apply generally to sea areas, the Standard Time maintained in many countries does not coincide with zone time. A graphical representation of the zones is shown on the Standard Time Zone Chart of the World (WOBZC76) published by the National Imagery and Mapping Agency. This chart is available by calling (800) 638-8972.

The U.S. and possessions are divided into 10 Standard Time zones. Each zone is approximately 15 deg of longitude in width. All places in each zone use, instead of their own local time, the time counted from the transit of the "mean sun" across the Standard Time meridian that passes near the middle of that zone. These time zones are designated as Atlantic, Eastern, Central, Mountain, Pacific, Alaska, Hawaii-Aleutian, Samoa, Wake Island, and Guam; the time in these zones is reckoned from the 60th, 75th, 90th, 105th, 120th, 135th, 150th, and 165th meridians west of Greenwich and the 165th and 150th meridians east of Greenwich. The time zone line wanders to conform to local geographical regions. The time in the various zones in the U.S. and U.S. territories west of Greenwich is earlier than Greenwich Time by 4, 5, 6, 7, 8, 9, 10, and 11 hours, respectively. However, Wake Island and Guam cross the International Date Line and are 12 and 10 hours later than Greenwich Time, respectively.

24-Hour Time

Twenty-four-hour time is widely used in scientific work throughout the world. In the U.S. it is also used in operations of the armed forces. In Europe it is frequently used by the transportation networks in preference to the 12-hour AM and PM system. With the 24-hour system the day begins at midnight, and times are designated 00:00 through 23:59.

International Date Line

The Date Line, approximately coinciding with the 180th meridian, separates the calendar dates. The date must be advanced one day when crossing in a westerly direction and set back one day when crossing in an easterly direction. The Date Line frequently deviates from the 180th meridian because of decisions made by individual nations affected. The line is deflected eastward through the Bering Strait and westward of the Aleutians to prevent separating these areas by date. The line is deflected eastward of the Tonga and New Zealand Islands in the South Pacific for the same reason. In 1995, Kiribati announced that all of its islands east of the Date Line would observe the same date as islands to the west, though most maps and atlases do not depict this as a deviation in the Date Line. The line is established by international custom; there is no international authority prescribing its exact course.

Daylight Saving Time

Daylight Saving Time is achieved by advancing the clock one hour. As of 2007, Daylight Saving Time begins at 2 AM on the 2nd Sunday in Mar. and ends at 2 AM on the first Sunday in Nov. **In 2008, Daylight Saving Time begins at 2 AM on Mar. 9 and ends at 2 AM on Nov. 2.** Prior to 2007, Daylight Saving Time traditionally ran from the first Sunday in Apr. to the last Sunday in Oct.

Daylight Saving Time was first observed in the U.S. during World War I, and then again during World War II. In the intervening years, some states and communities observed Daylight Saving Time, using whatever beginning and ending dates they chose. In 1966, Congress passed the Uniform Time Act, which provided that any state or territory that chooses to observe Daylight Saving Time must begin and end on the federal dates. Any state could, by law, exempt itself; a 1972 amendment to the act authorized states split by time zones to observe Daylight Saving Time in one time zone and standard time in the other time zone. Currently, Arizona, Hawaii, Puerto Rico, the U.S. Virgin Islands, Guam, and American Samoa do not observe Daylight Saving Time. On Apr. 2, 2006, all of Indiana observed Daylight Saving Time for the first time.

Congress and the secretary of transportation both have authority to change time zone boundaries. Since 1966 there have been a number of changes to U.S. time zone boundaries. In addition, efforts to conserve energy have prompted various changes in the times that Daylight Saving Time is observed.

Daylight Saving Time: International Usage

Adjusting clock time so as to gain the added daylight on summer evenings is common throughout the world.

Canada, which extends over 6 time zones, generally observes Daylight Saving Time during the same period as the U.S. Most provincial governments—with the exceptions of Newfoundland, Nunavut, and Yukon Territory—pledged to observe the 4 week extension to Daylight Saving Time that went into effect in 2007. Most of Saskatchewan remains on standard time all year. Communities elsewhere in Canada also may exempt themselves from Daylight Saving Time. Except for the state of Sonora, which shares a border with Arizona, most of Mexico observes Daylight Saving Time.

Member nations of the European Union (EU) observe a "summer-time period," a version of Daylight Saving Time, from the last Sunday of Mar. until the last Sunday in Oct.

Russia, which extends over 11 time zones, maintains its Standard Time 1 hour fast for its zone designation. Additionally, it proclaims Daylight Saving Time from the last Sunday in Mar. until the 4th Sunday in Oct.

China, which extends across 5 time zones, has decreed that the entire country be placed on Greenwich Time plus 8 hours. Daylight Saving Time is not observed. Japan, which lies within one time zone, also does not modify its legal time during the summer months.

Many countries in the Southern Hemisphere maintain Daylight Saving Time, generally from Oct. to Mar.; however, most countries near the equator do not deviate from Standard Time.

Standard Time Differences—World Cities

The time indicated in the table is fixed by law and is called the legal time or, more generally, Standard Time. Use of Daylight Saving Time varies widely. *Indicates morning of the following day. At 12:00 noon, Eastern Standard Time, the Standard Time (in 24-hour time) in selected cities is as follows:

City	Time		City	Time		City	Time	
Addis Ababa	20	00	Helsinki	19	00	Paris	18	00
Amsterdam	18	00	Ho Chi Minh City	0	00*	Prague	18	00
Ankara	19	00	Hong Kong	1	00*	Quito	12	00
Athens	19	00	Islamabad	22	00	Rio de Janeiro	14	00
Auckland	5	00*	Istanbul	19	00	Riyadh	20	00
Baghdad	20	00	Jakarta	0	00*	Rome	18	00
Bangkok	0	00*	Jerusalem	19	00	St. Petersburg	20	00
Beijing	1	00*	Johannesburg	19	00	Santiago	13	00
Belfast	17	00	Kabul	21	50	Sarajevo	18	00
Belgrade	18	00	Karachi	22	00	Seoul	2	00*
Berlin	18	00	Kathmandu	22	45	Shanghai	1	00*
Bogotá	12	00	Kiev	19	00	Singapore	1	00*
Bombay (Mumbai)	22	30	Lagos	18	00	Stockholm	18	00
Brussels	18	00	Lima	12	00	Sydney	3	00*
Bucharest	19	00	Lisbon	17	00	Taipei	1	00*
Budapest	18	00	London	17	00	Tashkent	22	00
Buenos Aires	14	00	Madrid	18	00	Tehran	20	30
Cairo	19	00	Manila	1	00*	Tel Aviv	19	00
Calcutta (Kolkata)	22	30	Mecca	20	00	Tokyo	2	00*
Cape Town	19	00	Melbourne	3	00*	Vladivostok	3	00*
Caracas	13	00	Montevideo	14	00	Vienna	18	00
Casablanca	17	00	Moscow	20	00	Warsaw	18	00
Copenhagen	18	00	Munich	18	00	Wellington	5	00*
Dhaka	23	00	Nagasaki	2	00*	Yangon (Rangoon)	23	30
Dublin	17	00	Nairobi	20	00	Yokohama	2	00*
Edinburgh	17	00	New Delhi	22	30	Zurich	18	00
Geneva	18	00	Oslo	18	00			

Standard Time Differences—North American Cities

At 12:00 noon, Eastern Standard Time, the Standard Time in selected North American cities is as follows:

City	Time			City	Time			City	Time		
Akron, OH	12	00	Noon	Fort Wayne, IN[1]	12	00	Noon	Ottawa, Ont.	12	00	Noon
Albuquerque, NM	10	00	AM	Frankfort, KY	12	00	Noon	*Panama City, Panama	12	00	Noon
Anchorage, AK	8	00	AM	Havana, Cuba	12	00	Noon	Peoria, IL	11	00	AM
Atlanta, GA	12	00	Noon	Helena, MT	10	00	AM	*Phoenix, AZ	10	00	AM
Austin, TX	11	00	AM	*Honolulu, HI	7	00	AM	Pierre, SD	11	00	AM
Baltimore, MD	12	00	Noon	Houston, TX	11	00	AM	Pittsburgh, PA	12	00	Noon
Birmingham, AL	11	00	AM	Indianapolis, IN[1]	12	00	Noon	*Regina, Sask.	11	00	AM
Bismarck, ND	11	00	AM	Jackson, MS	11	00	am	Reno, NV	9	00	AM
Boise, ID	10	00	AM	Jacksonville, FL	12	00	Noon	Richmond, VA	12	00	Noon
Boston, MA	12	00	Noon	Juneau, AK	8	00	AM	Rochester, NY	12	00	Noon
Buffalo, NY	12	00	Noon	Kansas City, MO	11	00	AM	Sacramento, CA	9	00	AM
Butte, MT	10	00	AM	*Kingston, Jamaica	12	00	Noon	St. John's, Nfld.	1	30	PM
Calgary, Alta.	10	00	AM	Knoxville, TN	12	00	Noon	St. Louis, MO	11	00	AM
Charleston, SC	12	00	Noon	Las Vegas, NV	9	00	AM	St. Paul, MN	11	00	AM
Charleston, WV	12	00	Noon	Lexington, KY	12	00	Noon	Salt Lake City, UT	10	00	AM
Charlotte, NC	12	00	Noon	Lincoln, NE	11	00	AM	San Antonio, TX	11	00	AM
Charlottetown, PEI	1	00	PM	Little Rock, AR	11	00	AM	San Diego, CA	9	00	AM
Chattanooga, TN	12	00	Noon	Los Angeles, CA	9	00	AM	San Francisco, CA	9	00	AM
Cheyenne, WY	10	00	AM	Louisville, KY	12	00	Noon	San Jose, CA	9	00	AM
Chicago, IL	11	00	AM	Madison, WI	11	00	am	*San Juan, PR	1	00	PM
Cincinnati, OH	12	00	Noon	Mexico City, Mexico	11	00	AM	Santa Fe, NM	10	00	AM
Cleveland, OH	12	00	Noon	Memphis, TN	11	00	AM	Savannah, GA	12	00	Noon
Colorado Spr., CO	10	00	AM	Miami, FL	12	00	Noon	Seattle, WA	9	00	AM
Columbus, OH	12	00	Noon	Milwaukee, WI	11	00	AM	Shreveport, LA	11	00	AM
Dallas, TX	11	00	AM	Minneapolis, MN	11	00	AM	Sioux Falls, SD	11	00	AM
*Dawson, Yuk.	9	00	AM	Mobile, AL	11	00	AM	Spokane, WA	9	00	AM
Dayton, OH	12	00	Noon	Montreal, Que	12	00	Noon	Tampa, FL	12	00	Noon
Denver, CO	10	00	AM	Nashville, TN	11	00	AM	Toledo, OH	12	00	Noon
Des Moines, IA	11	00	AM	Nassau, Bahamas	12	00	Noon	Topeka, KS	11	00	AM
Detroit, MI	12	00	Noon	New Haven, CT	12	00	Noon	Toronto, Ont.	12	00	Noon
Duluth, MN	11	00	AM	New Orleans, LA	11	00	AM	*Tucson, AZ	10	00	AM
Edmonton, Alta.	10	00	AM	New York, NY	12	00	Noon	Tulsa, OK	11	00	AM
El Paso, TX	10	00	AM	Nome, AK	8	00	AM	Vancouver, BC	9	00	AM
Erie, PA	12	00	Noon	Norfolk, VA	12	00	Noon	Washington, DC	12	00	Noon
Evansville, IN[1]	11	00	AM	Oklahoma City, OK	11	00	AM	Wichita, KS	11	00	AM
Fairbanks, AK	8	00	AM	Omaha, NE	11	00	AM	Wilmington, DE	12	00	Noon
Flint, MI	12	00	Noon	Orlando, FL	12	00	Noon	Winnipeg, Man.	11	00	AM

(1) While most of Indiana is in the Eastern Time Zone, as of Mar. 11, 2007, 17 counties in the southwestern and northwestern parts of the state observe Central Time. **Note:** This same table can be used for Daylight Saving Time when it is in effect, but allowance must be made for cities that do not observe it; they are marked with an asterisk (*). Daylight Saving Time is one hour later than Standard Time.

Perpetual Calendar

The number shown for each year indicates which Gregorian calendar to use. For 1583-1802, see "Gregorian Calendar" on page 336. For 1803-20, use numbers for 1983-2000, respectively. For Julian Calendar, see "Julian Calendar" on page 337.

1821 ... 2	1847 ... 6	1873 ... 4	1899 ... 1	1925 ... 5	1951 ... 2	1977 ... 7	2003 ... 4	2029 ... 2	2055 ... 6
1822 ... 3	1848 ... 14	1874 ... 5	1900 ... 2	1926 ... 6	1952 ... 10	1978 ... 1	2004 ... 12	2030 ... 3	2056 ... 14
1823 ... 4	1849 ... 2	1875 ... 6	1901 ... 3	1927 ... 7	1953 ... 5	1979 ... 2	2005 ... 7	2031 ... 4	2057 ... 2
1824 ... 12	1850 ... 3	1876 ... 14	1902 ... 4	1928 ... 8	1954 ... 6	1980 ... 10	2006 ... 1	2032 ... 12	2058 ... 3
1825 ... 7	1851 ... 4	1877 ... 2	1903 ... 5	1929 ... 3	1955 ... 7	1981 ... 5	2007 ... 2	2033 ... 7	2059 ... 4
1826 ... 1	1852 ... 12	1878 ... 3	1904 ... 13	1930 ... 4	1956 ... 8	1982 ... 6	2008 ... 10	2034 ... 1	2060 ... 12
1827 ... 2	1853 ... 7	1879 ... 4	1905 ... 1	1931 ... 5	1957 ... 3	1983 ... 7	2009 ... 5	2035 ... 2	2061 ... 7
1828 ... 10	1854 ... 1	1880 ... 12	1906 ... 2	1932 ... 13	1958 ... 4	1984 ... 8	2010 ... 6	2036 ... 10	2062 ... 1
1829 ... 5	1855 ... 2	1881 ... 7	1907 ... 3	1933 ... 1	1959 ... 5	1985 ... 3	2011 ... 7	2037 ... 5	2063 ... 2
1830 ... 6	1856 ... 10	1882 ... 1	1908 ... 11	1934 ... 2	1960 ... 13	1986 ... 4	2012 ... 8	2038 ... 6	2064 ... 10
1831 ... 7	1857 ... 5	1883 ... 2	1909 ... 6	1935 ... 3	1961 ... 1	1987 ... 5	2013 ... 3	2039 ... 7	2065 ... 5
1832 ... 8	1858 ... 6	1884 ... 10	1910 ... 7	1936 ... 11	1962 ... 2	1988 ... 13	2014 ... 4	2040 ... 8	2066 ... 6
1833 ... 3	1859 ... 7	1885 ... 5	1911 ... 1	1937 ... 6	1963 ... 3	1989 ... 1	2015 ... 5	2041 ... 3	2067 ... 7
1834 ... 4	1860 ... 8	1886 ... 6	1912 ... 9	1938 ... 7	1964 ... 11	1990 ... 2	2016 ... 13	2042 ... 4	2068 ... 8
1835 ... 5	1861 ... 3	1887 ... 7	1913 ... 4	1939 ... 1	1965 ... 6	1991 ... 3	2017 ... 1	2043 ... 5	2069 ... 3
1836 ... 13	1862 ... 4	1888 ... 8	1914 ... 5	1940 ... 9	1966 ... 7	1992 ... 11	2018 ... 2	2044 ... 13	2070 ... 4
1837 ... 1	1863 ... 5	1889 ... 3	1915 ... 6	1941 ... 4	1967 ... 1	1993 ... 6	2019 ... 3	2045 ... 1	2071 ... 5
1838 ... 2	1864 ... 13	1890 ... 4	1916 ... 14	1942 ... 5	1968 ... 9	1994 ... 7	2020 ... 11	2046 ... 2	2072 ... 13
1839 ... 3	1865 ... 1	1891 ... 5	1917 ... 2	1943 ... 6	1969 ... 4	1995 ... 1	2021 ... 6	2047 ... 3	2073 ... 1
1840 ... 11	1866 ... 2	1892 ... 13	1918 ... 3	1944 ... 14	1970 ... 5	1996 ... 9	2022 ... 7	2048 ... 11	2074 ... 2
1841 ... 6	1867 ... 3	1893 ... 1	1919 ... 4	1945 ... 2	1971 ... 6	1997 ... 4	2023 ... 1	2049 ... 6	2075 ... 3
1842 ... 7	1868 ... 11	1894 ... 2	1920 ... 12	1946 ... 3	1972 ... 14	1998 ... 5	2024 ... 9	2050 ... 7	2076 ... 11
1843 ... 1	1869 ... 6	1895 ... 3	1921 ... 7	1947 ... 4	1973 ... 2	1999 ... 6	2025 ... 4	2051 ... 1	2077 ... 6
1844 ... 9	1870 ... 7	1896 ... 11	1922 ... 1	1948 ... 12	1974 ... 3	2000 ... 14	2026 ... 5	2052 ... 9	2078 ... 7
1845 ... 4	1871 ... 1	1897 ... 6	1923 ... 2	1949 ... 7	1975 ... 4	2001 ... 2	2027 ... 6	2053 ... 4	2079 ... 1
1846 ... 5	1872 ... 9	1898 ... 7	1924 ... 10	1950 ... 1	1976 ... 12	2002 ... 3	2028 ... 14	2054 ... 5	2080 ... 9

1 2006

JANUARY

S	M	T	W	T	F	S
1	2	3	4	5	6	7
8	9	10	11	12	13	14
15	16	17	18	19	20	21
22	23	24	25	26	27	28
29	30	31				

FEBRUARY

S	M	T	W	T	F	S
			1	2	3	4
5	6	7	8	9	10	11
12	13	14	15	16	17	18
19	20	21	22	23	24	25
26	27	28				

MARCH

S	M	T	W	T	F	S
			1	2	3	4
5	6	7	8	9	10	11
12	13	14	15	16	17	18
19	20	21	22	23	24	25
26	27	28	29	30	31	

APRIL

S	M	T	W	T	F	S
						1
2	3	4	5	6	7	8
9	10	11	12	13	14	15
16	17	18	19	20	21	22
23	24	25	26	27	28	29
30						

MAY

S	M	T	W	T	F	S
	1	2	3	4	5	6
7	8	9	10	11	12	13
14	15	16	17	18	19	20
21	22	23	24	25	26	27
28	29	30	31			

JUNE

S	M	T	W	T	F	S
				1	2	3
4	5	6	7	8	9	10
11	12	13	14	15	16	17
18	19	20	21	22	23	24
25	26	27	28	29	30	

JULY

S	M	T	W	T	F	S
						1
2	3	4	5	6	7	8
9	10	11	12	13	14	15
16	17	18	19	20	21	22
23	24	25	26	27	28	29
30	31					

AUGUST

S	M	T	W	T	F	S
		1	2	3	4	5
6	7	8	9	10	11	12
13	14	15	16	17	18	19
20	21	22	23	24	25	26
27	28	29	30	31		

SEPTEMBER

S	M	T	W	T	F	S
					1	2
3	4	5	6	7	8	9
10	11	12	13	14	15	16
17	18	19	20	21	22	23
24	25	26	27	28	29	30

OCTOBER

S	M	T	W	T	F	S
1	2	3	4	5	6	7
8	9	10	11	12	13	14
15	16	17	18	19	20	21
22	23	24	25	26	27	28
29	30	31				

NOVEMBER

S	M	T	W	T	F	S
			1	2	3	4
5	6	7	8	9	10	11
12	13	14	15	16	17	18
19	20	21	22	23	24	25
26	27	28	29	30		

DECEMBER

S	M	T	W	T	F	S
					1	2
3	4	5	6	7	8	9
10	11	12	13	14	15	16
17	18	19	20	21	22	23
24	25	26	27	28	29	30
31						

2 2001/2007

JANUARY

S	M	T	W	T	F	S
	1	2	3	4	5	6
7	8	9	10	11	12	13
14	15	16	17	18	19	20
21	22	23	24	25	26	27
28	29	30	31			

FEBRUARY

S	M	T	W	T	F	S
				1	2	3
4	5	6	7	8	9	10
11	12	13	14	15	16	17
18	19	20	21	22	23	24
25	26	27	28			

MARCH

S	M	T	W	T	F	S
				1	2	3
4	5	6	7	8	9	10
11	12	13	14	15	16	17
18	19	20	21	22	23	24
25	26	27	28	29	30	31

APRIL

S	M	T	W	T	F	S
1	2	3	4	5	6	7
8	9	10	11	12	13	14
15	16	17	18	19	20	21
22	23	24	25	26	27	28
29	30					

MAY

S	M	T	W	T	F	S
		1	2	3	4	5
6	7	8	9	10	11	12
13	14	15	16	17	18	19
20	21	22	23	24	25	26
27	28	29	30	31		

JUNE

S	M	T	W	T	F	S
					1	2
3	4	5	6	7	8	9
10	11	12	13	14	15	16
17	18	19	20	21	22	23
24	25	26	27	28	29	30

JULY

S	M	T	W	T	F	S
1	2	3	4	5	6	7
8	9	10	11	12	13	14
15	16	17	18	19	20	21
22	23	24	25	26	27	28
29	30	31				

AUGUST

S	M	T	W	T	F	S
			1	2	3	4
5	6	7	8	9	10	11
12	13	14	15	16	17	18
19	20	21	22	23	24	25
26	27	28	29	30	31	

SEPTEMBER

S	M	T	W	T	F	S
						1
2	3	4	5	6	7	8
9	10	11	12	13	14	15
16	17	18	19	20	21	22
23	24	25	26	27	28	29
30						

OCTOBER

S	M	T	W	T	F	S
	1	2	3	4	5	6
7	8	9	10	11	12	13
14	15	16	17	18	19	20
21	22	23	24	25	26	27
28	29	30	31			

NOVEMBER

S	M	T	W	T	F	S
				1	2	3
4	5	6	7	8	9	10
11	12	13	14	15	16	17
18	19	20	21	22	23	24
25	26	27	28	29	30	

DECEMBER

S	M	T	W	T	F	S
						1
2	3	4	5	6	7	8
9	10	11	12	13	14	15
16	17	18	19	20	21	22
23	24	25	26	27	28	29
30	31					

3 2002

JANUARY

S	M	T	W	T	F	S
		1	2	3	4	5
6	7	8	9	10	11	12
13	14	15	16	17	18	19
20	21	22	23	24	25	26
27	28	29	30	31		

FEBRUARY

S	M	T	W	T	F	S
					1	2
3	4	5	6	7	8	9
10	11	12	13	14	15	16
17	18	19	20	21	22	23
24	25	26	27	28		

MARCH

S	M	T	W	T	F	S
					1	2
3	4	5	6	7	8	9
10	11	12	13	14	15	16
17	18	19	20	21	22	23
24	25	26	27	28	29	30
31						

APRIL

S	M	T	W	T	F	S
	1	2	3	4	5	6
7	8	9	10	11	12	13
14	15	16	17	18	19	20
21	22	23	24	25	26	27
28	29	30				

MAY

S	M	T	W	T	F	S
			1	2	3	4
5	6	7	8	9	10	11
12	13	14	15	16	17	18
19	20	21	22	23	24	25
26	27	28	29	30	31	

JUNE

S	M	T	W	T	F	S
						1
2	3	4	5	6	7	8
9	10	11	12	13	14	15
16	17	18	19	20	21	22
23	24	25	26	27	28	29
30						

JULY

S	M	T	W	T	F	S
	1	2	3	4	5	6
7	8	9	10	11	12	13
14	15	16	17	18	19	20
21	22	23	24	25	26	27
28	29	30	31			

AUGUST

S	M	T	W	T	F	S
				1	2	3
4	5	6	7	8	9	10
11	12	13	14	15	16	17
18	19	20	21	22	23	24
25	26	27	28	29	30	31

SEPTEMBER

S	M	T	W	T	F	S
1	2	3	4	5	6	7
8	9	10	11	12	13	14
15	16	17	18	19	20	21
22	23	24	25	26	27	28
29	30					

OCTOBER

S	M	T	W	T	F	S
		1	2	3	4	5
6	7	8	9	10	11	12
13	14	15	16	17	18	19
20	21	22	23	24	25	26
27	28	29	30	31		

NOVEMBER

S	M	T	W	T	F	S
					1	2
3	4	5	6	7	8	9
10	11	12	13	14	15	16
17	18	19	20	21	22	23
24	25	26	27	28	29	30

DECEMBER

S	M	T	W	T	F	S
1	2	3	4	5	6	7
8	9	10	11	12	13	14
15	16	17	18	19	20	21
22	23	24	25	26	27	28
29	30	31				

4 2003

JANUARY

S	M	T	W	T	F	S
			1	2	3	4
5	6	7	8	9	10	11
12	13	14	15	16	17	18
19	20	21	22	23	24	25
26	27	28	29	30	31	

FEBRUARY

S	M	T	W	T	F	S
						1
2	3	4	5	6	7	8
9	10	11	12	13	14	15
16	17	18	19	20	21	22
23	24	25	26	27	28	

MARCH

S	M	T	W	T	F	S
						1
2	3	4	5	6	7	8
9	10	11	12	13	14	15
16	17	18	19	20	21	22
23	24	25	26	27	28	29
30	31					

APRIL

S	M	T	W	T	F	S
		1	2	3	4	5
6	7	8	9	10	11	12
13	14	15	16	17	18	19
20	21	22	23	24	25	26
27	28	29	30			

MAY

S	M	T	W	T	F	S
				1	2	3
4	5	6	7	8	9	10
11	12	13	14	15	16	17
18	19	20	21	22	23	24
25	26	27	28	29	30	31

JUNE

S	M	T	W	T	F	S
1	2	3	4	5	6	7
8	9	10	11	12	13	14
15	16	17	18	19	20	21
22	23	24	25	26	27	28
29	30					

JULY

S	M	T	W	T	F	S
		1	2	3	4	5
6	7	8	9	10	11	12
13	14	15	16	17	18	19
20	21	22	23	24	25	26
27	28	29	30	31		

AUGUST

S	M	T	W	T	F	S
					1	2
3	4	5	6	7	8	9
10	11	12	13	14	15	16
17	18	19	20	21	22	23
24	25	26	27	28	29	30
31						

SEPTEMBER

S	M	T	W	T	F	S
	1	2	3	4	5	6
7	8	9	10	11	12	13
14	15	16	17	18	19	20
21	22	23	24	25	26	27
28	29	30				

OCTOBER

S	M	T	W	T	F	S
			1	2	3	4
5	6	7	8	9	10	11
12	13	14	15	16	17	18
19	20	21	22	23	24	25
26	27	28	29	30	31	

NOVEMBER

S	M	T	W	T	F	S
						1
2	3	4	5	6	7	8
9	10	11	12	13	14	15
16	17	18	19	20	21	22
23	24	25	26	27	28	29
30						

DECEMBER

S	M	T	W	T	F	S
	1	2	3	4	5	6
7	8	9	10	11	12	13
14	15	16	17	18	19	20
21	22	23	24	25	26	27
28	29	30	31			

5 2009

JANUARY

S	M	T	W	T	F	S
				1	2	3
4	5	6	7	8	9	10
11	12	13	14	15	16	17
18	19	20	21	22	23	24
25	26	27	28	29	30	31

FEBRUARY

S	M	T	W	T	F	S
1	2	3	4	5	6	7
8	9	10	11	12	13	14
15	16	17	18	19	20	21
22	23	24	25	26	27	28

MARCH

S	M	T	W	T	F	S
1	2	3	4	5	6	7
8	9	10	11	12	13	14
15	16	17	18	19	20	21
22	23	24	25	26	27	28
29	30	31				

APRIL

S	M	T	W	T	F	S
			1	2	3	4
5	6	7	8	9	10	11
12	13	14	15	16	17	18
19	20	21	22	23	24	25
26	27	28	29	30		

MAY

S	M	T	W	T	F	S
					1	2
3	4	5	6	7	8	9
10	11	12	13	14	15	16
17	18	19	20	21	22	23
24	25	26	27	28	29	30
31						

JUNE

S	M	T	W	T	F	S
	1	2	3	4	5	6
7	8	9	10	11	12	13
14	15	16	17	18	19	20
21	22	23	24	25	26	27
28	29	30				

JULY

S	M	T	W	T	F	S
			1	2	3	4
5	6	7	8	9	10	11
12	13	14	15	16	17	18
19	20	21	22	23	24	25
26	27	28	29	30	31	

AUGUST

S	M	T	W	T	F	S
						1
2	3	4	5	6	7	8
9	10	11	12	13	14	15
16	17	18	19	20	21	22
23	24	25	26	27	28	29
30	31					

SEPTEMBER

S	M	T	W	T	F	S
		1	2	3	4	5
6	7	8	9	10	11	12
13	14	15	16	17	18	19
20	21	22	23	24	25	26
27	28	29	30			

OCTOBER

S	M	T	W	T	F	S
				1	2	3
4	5	6	7	8	9	10
11	12	13	14	15	16	17
18	19	20	21	22	23	24
25	26	27	28	29	30	31

NOVEMBER

S	M	T	W	T	F	S
1	2	3	4	5	6	7
8	9	10	11	12	13	14
15	16	17	18	19	20	21
22	23	24	25	26	27	28
29	30					

DECEMBER

S	M	T	W	T	F	S
		1	2	3	4	5
6	7	8	9	10	11	12
13	14	15	16	17	18	19
20	21	22	23	24	25	26
27	28	29	30	31		

6 2010

JANUARY

S	M	T	W	T	F	S
					1	2
3	4	5	6	7	8	9
10	11	12	13	14	15	16
17	18	19	20	21	22	23
24	25	26	27	28	29	30
31						

FEBRUARY

S	M	T	W	T	F	S
	1	2	3	4	5	6
7	8	9	10	11	12	13
14	15	16	17	18	19	20
21	22	23	24	25	26	27
28						

MARCH

S	M	T	W	T	F	S
	1	2	3	4	5	6
7	8	9	10	11	12	13
14	15	16	17	18	19	20
21	22	23	24	25	26	27
28	29	30	31			

APRIL

S	M	T	W	T	F	S
				1	2	3
4	5	6	7	8	9	10
11	12	13	14	15	16	17
18	19	20	21	22	23	24
25	26	27	28	29	30	

MAY

S	M	T	W	T	F	S
						1
2	3	4	5	6	7	8
9	10	11	12	13	14	15
16	17	18	19	20	21	22
23	24	25	26	27	28	29
30	31					

JUNE

S	M	T	W	T	F	S
		1	2	3	4	5
6	7	8	9	10	11	12
13	14	15	16	17	18	19
20	21	22	23	24	25	26
27	28	29	30			

JULY

S	M	T	W	T	F	S
				1	2	3
4	5	6	7	8	9	10
11	12	13	14	15	16	17
18	19	20	21	22	23	24
25	26	27	28	29	30	31

AUGUST

S	M	T	W	T	F	S
1	2	3	4	5	6	7
8	9	10	11	12	13	14
15	16	17	18	19	20	21
22	23	24	25	26	27	28
29	30	31				

SEPTEMBER

S	M	T	W	T	F	S
			1	2	3	4
5	6	7	8	9	10	11
12	13	14	15	16	17	18
19	20	21	22	23	24	25
26	27	28	29	30		

OCTOBER

S	M	T	W	T	F	S
					1	2
3	4	5	6	7	8	9
10	11	12	13	14	15	16
17	18	19	20	21	22	23
24	25	26	27	28	29	30
31						

NOVEMBER

S	M	T	W	T	F	S
	1	2	3	4	5	6
7	8	9	10	11	12	13
14	15	16	17	18	19	20
21	22	23	24	25	26	27
28	29	30				

DECEMBER

S	M	T	W	T	F	S
			1	2	3	4
5	6	7	8	9	10	11
12	13	14	15	16	17	18
19	20	21	22	23	24	25
26	27	28	29	30	31	

Perpetual calendar reference tables. Each numbered block (7–14) contains twelve monthly calendars (JANUARY through DECEMBER) with columns S M T W T F S.

Block	Year
7	2005
8	
9	
10	2008
11	
12	2004
13	
14	2000

WEIGHTS AND MEASURES

Source: National Institute of Standards and Technology, U.S. Dept. of Commerce

The International System of Units (SI)

Two systems of weights and measures coexist in the U.S. today: the **U.S. Customary System** and the **International System of Units** (SI, after the initials of Système International). SI, **commonly identified with the metric system**, is actually a more complete, coherent version of it. Throughout U.S. history, the Customary System (inherited from, but now different from, the British Imperial System) has been generally used; federal and state legislation has given it, through implication, standing as the primary weights and measures system. The metric system, however, is the only system that Congress has ever specifically sanctioned. An 1866 law reads:

"It shall be lawful throughout the United States of America to employ the weights and measures of the metric system; and no contract or dealing, or pleading in any court, shall be deemed invalid or liable to objection because the weights or measures expressed or referred to therein are weights or measures of the metric system."

Since that time, use of the metric system in the U.S. has slowly and steadily increased, particularly in the scientific community, the pharmaceutical industry, and the manufacturing sector—the last motivated by the practice in international commerce, in which the metric system is now predominantly used.

On Feb. 10, 1964, the National Bureau of Standards (now known as the National Institute of Standards and Technology) issued the following statement:

"Henceforth it shall be the policy of the National Bureau of Standards to use the units of the International System (SI), as adopted by the 11th General Conference on Weights and Measures (October 1960), except when the use of these units would obviously impair communication or reduce the usefulness of a report."

On Dec. 23, 1975, Pres. Gerald R. Ford signed the Metric Conversion Act of 1975. It defines the metric system as being the International System of Units as interpreted in the U.S. by the secretary of commerce. The Trade Act of 1988 and other legislation declare the metric system the preferred system of weights and measures for U.S. trade and commerce, call for the federal government to adopt metric specifications, and mandate the Commerce Dept. to oversee the program. However, the metric system has still not become the system of choice for most Americans' daily use.

The following 7 units serve as the base units for the system: **length**—meter; **mass**—kilogram; **time**—second; **electric current**—ampere; **thermodynamic temperature**—kelvin; **amount of substance**—mole; and **luminous intensity**—candela.

Frequently Used Conversions

Boldface indicates exact values. For greater accuracy, use the "multiply by" number in parentheses. For weights, *avdp* is an abbreviation for avoirdupois weight, the system of weights applied to all goods except medicines, precious metals, and precious stones (see p. 347). For more detailed tables, see pp. 346-349.

U.S. Customary to Metric

	If you have:	Multiply by:	To get:
Length	inches	25.4	millimeters
	inches	2.54	centimeters
	inches	0.0254	meters
	feet	0.3 **(0.3048)**	meters
	yards	0.9 **(0.9144)**	meters
	miles[1]	1.6 **(1.609344)** ...	kilometers
Area	sq. inches ...	6.5 **(6.4516)**	sq. cm.
	sq. feet	0.09 (0.09290341) ...	sq. meters
	sq. yards	0.84 (0.83612736) ...	sq. meters
	acres	0.4 (0.4046873)	hectares
	sq. miles	2.6 (2.58998811) ...	sq. kilometers
Weight	ounces (avdp)	28 **(28.349523125)** ..	grams
	pounds (avdp)	454 **(453.59237)**	grams
	pounds (avdp)	0.45 **(0.45359237)** ...	kilograms
	short tons[2]	0.91 **(0.90718474)** ...	metric tons
	long tons[3]	1 **(1.0160469088)** ...	metric tons
Liquid meas.	ounces	0.03 (0.02957353) ...	liters
	cups	0.24 (0.23658824) ...	liters
	pints	0.47 (0.473176473) ..	liters
	quarts	0.95 (0.946352946) ..	liters
	gallons	3.79 (3.785411784) ..	liters

Metric to U.S. Customary

	If you have:	Multiply by:	To get:
Length	millimeters ..	0.04 (0.03937)	inches
	centimeters ..	0.4 (0.3937)	inches
	meters	39 (39.37)	inches
	meters	3.3 (3.280840)	feet
	meters	1.1 (1.093613) ...	yards
	kilometers ...	0.6 (0.621371) ...	miles
Area	sq. cm.	0.16 (0.15500)	sq. inches
	sq. meters	10.8 (10.76391) ...	sq. feet
	sq. meters	1.2 (1.195990) ...	sq. yards
	hectares	2.5 (2.471044) ...	acres
	sq. kilometers ..	0.39 (0.386102) ...	sq. miles
Weight	grams	0.035 (0.03527396)	ounces (avdp)
	grams	0.002 (0.00220462)	pounds (avdp)
	kilograms	2.2 (2.204623) ...	pounds (avdp)
	metric tons	1.1 (1.102311) ...	short tons
	metric tons	0.98 (0.9842065) ..	long tons
Liquid meas.	liters	33.8 (33.81402) ...	ounces
	liters	4.2 (4.226752) ...	cups
	liters	2.1 (2.113376) ...	pints
	liters	1.1 (1.056688) ...	quarts
	liters	0.26 (0.264172) ...	gallons

(1) Statute mile. (2) A short ton is 2,000 pounds. (3) A long ton is 2,240 pounds.

Temperature Conversions

The left-hand column below gives a temperature according to the **Celsius** scale, and the right-hand gives the same temperature according to the **Fahrenheit** scale. The lowest number on each scale is equivalent to absolute zero, the temperature at which all motion within a molecule would stop.

For temperatures not shown: To convert Fahrenheit to Celsius by formula, subtract 32 degrees and divide by 1.8; to convert Celsius to Fahrenheit, multiply by 1.8 and add 32 degrees.

Note: Although the term *centigrade* is still frequently used, the International Committee on Weights and Measures and the National Institute of Standards and Technology have recommended since 1948 that this scale be called *Celsius*.

Celsius	Fahrenheit	Celsius	Fahrenheit	Celsius	Fahrenheit	Celsius	Fahrenheit	Celsius	Fahrenheit
−273.15	−459.67	−45.6	−50	−1.1	30	30	86	66	150
−250	−418	**−40**	**−40**	**0**	**32**	32.2	90	70	158
−200	−328	−34.4	−30	4.4	40	35	95	80	176
−184	−300	−30	−22	10	50	37	98.6	90	194
−157	−250	−28.9	−20	15.6	60	37.8	100	93	200
−150	−238	−23.3	−10	**20**	**68**	40	104	**100**	**212**
−129	−200	−20	−4	21.1	70	43	110	121	250
−101	−150	−17.8	0	23.9	75	49	120	149	300
−100	−148	−12.2	10	25	77	50	122	150	302
−73.3	−100	−10	14	26.7	80	54	130	200	392
−50	−58	−6.7	20	29.4	85	60	140	300	572

Boiling and Freezing Points

Water boils at 212° F (100° C) at sea level. For every 550 feet above sea level, boiling point of water is lower by about 1° F. Methyl alcohol boils at 148° F. Average human oral temperature, 98.6° F. **Water freezes** at 32° F (0° C).

Mathematical Formulas

Note: The value of π (the Greek letter pi) is approximately 3.14159265 (equal to the ratio of the circumference of a circle to the diameter). The equivalence is typically rounded further to 3.1416 or 3.14.

To find the Circumference of a:
Circle — Multiply the diameter by π.

To find the Area of a:
Circle — Multiply the square of the radius (equal to ½ the diameter) by π.
Rectangle — Multiply the length of the base by the height.
Sphere (surface) — Multiply the square of the radius by π and multiply by 4.
Square — Square the length of one side.
Trapezoid — Add the 2 parallel sides, multiply by the height, and divide by 2.
Triangle — Multiply the base by the height, divide by 2.

To find the Volume of a:
Cone — Multiply the square of the radius of the base by π, multiply by the height, and divide by 3.
Cube — Cube the length of one edge.
Cylinder — Multiply the square of the radius of the base by π and multiply by the height.
Pyramid — Multiply the area of the base by the height and divide by 3.
Rectangular Prism — Multiply the length by the width by the height.
Sphere — Multiply the cube of the radius by π, multiply by 4, and divide by 3.

Playing Cards and Dice Chances

5-Card Poker Hands

Hand	Number possible	Odds against
Royal flush	4	649,739 to 1
Other straight flush	36	72,192 to 1
Four of a kind	624	4,164 to 1
Full house	3,744	693 to 1
Flush	5,108	508 to 1
Straight	10,200	254 to 1
Three of a kind	54,912	46 to 1
Two pairs	123,552	20 to 1
One pair	1,098,240	4 to 3 (1.37 to 1)
Nothing	1,302,540	1 to 1
TOTAL	**2,598,960**	

Bridge

The odds—against suit distribution in a hand of 4-4-3-2 are about 4 to 1, against 5-4-2-2 about 8 to 1, against 6-4-2-1 about 20 to 1, against 7-4-1-1 about 254 to 1, against 8-4-1-0 about 2,211 to 1, and against 13-0-0-0 about 158,753,389,899 to 1.

Dice
(probabilities on 2 dice)

Total	Odds against (single toss)	Total	Odds against (single toss)
2	35 to 1	8	31 to 5
3	17 to 1	9	8 to 1
4	11 to 1	10	11 to 1
5	8 to 1	11	17 to 1
6	31 to 5	12	35 to 1
7	5 to 1		

Large Numbers

No. of zeros	U.S.	British[1], French, German	No. of zeros	U.S.	British[1], French, German
6	million	million	42	tredecillion	septillion
9	billion	milliard	45	quattuordecillion	1,000 septillion
12	trillion	billion	48	quindecillion	octillion
15	quadrillion	1,000 billion	51	sexdecillion	1,000 octillion
18	quintillion	trillion	54	septendecillion	nonillion
21	sextillion	1,000 trillion	57	octodecillion	1,000 nonillion
24	septillion	quadrillion	60	novemdecillion	decillion
27	octillion	1,000 quadrillion	63	vigintillion	1,000 decillion
30	nonillion	quintillion	100	googol	googol
33	decillion	1,000 quintillion	303	centillion	—
36	undecillion	sextillion	600	—	centillion
39	duodecillion	1,000 sextillion	googol	googolplex	googolplex

(1) In recent years, it has become more common in Britain to use U.S. terminology for large numbers.

Prime Numbers

A prime number is a positive integer that is divisible only by two positive integers, 1 and itself.

Prime Numbers to 1,009

	2	3	5	7	11	13	17	19	23
29	31	37	41	43	47	53	59	61	67
71	73	79	83	89	97	101	103	107	109
113	127	131	137	139	149	151	157	163	167
173	179	181	191	193	197	199	211	223	227
229	233	239	241	251	257	263	269	271	277
281	283	293	307	311	313	317	331	337	347
349	353	359	367	373	379	383	389	397	401
409	419	421	431	433	439	443	449	457	461
463	467	479	487	491	499	503	509	521	523
541	547	557	563	569	571	577	587	593	599
601	607	613	617	619	631	641	643	647	653
659	661	673	677	683	691	701	709	719	727
733	739	743	751	757	761	769	773	787	797
809	811	821	823	827	829	839	853	857	859
863	877	881	883	887	907	911	919	929	937
941	947	953	967	971	977	983	991	997	1,009

Common Fractions Converted to Decimals

8ths	16ths	32nds	64ths	Decimal	8ths	16ths	32nds	64ths	Decimal	8ths	16ths	32nds	64ths	Decimal	8ths	16ths	32nds	64ths	Decimal
			1	= 0.015625				17	= 0.265625				33	= 0.515625				49	= 0.765625
		1	2	= 0.03125			9	18	= 0.28125			17	34	= 0.53125			25	50	= 0.78125
			3	= 0.046875				19	= 0.296875				35	= 0.546875				51	= 0.796875
	1	2	4	= 0.0625		5	10	20	= 0.3125			18	36	= 0.5625		13	26	52	= 0.8125
			5	= 0.078125				21	= 0.328125				37	= 0.578125				53	= 0.828125
		3	6	= 0.09375			11	22	= 0.34375			19	38	= 0.59375			27	54	= 0.84375
			7	= 0.109375				23	= 0.359375				39	= 0.609375				55	= 0.859375
1	2	4	8	= 0.125	3	6	12	24	= 0.375	5	10	20	40	= 0.625	7	14	28	56	= 0.875
			9	= 0.140625				25	= 0.390625				41	= 0.640625				57	= 0.890625
		5	10	= 0.15625			13	26	= 0.40625			21	42	= 0.65625			29	58	= 0.90625
			11	= 0.171875				27	= 0.421875				43	= 0.671875				59	= 0.921875
	3	6	12	= 0.1875		7	14	28	= 0.4375		11	22	44	= 0.6875		15	30	60	= 0.9375
			13	= 0.203125				29	= 0.453125				45	= 0.703125				61	= 0.953125
		7	14	= 0.21875			15	30	= 0.46875			23	46	= 0.71875			31	62	= 0.96875
			15	= 0.234375				31	= 0.484375				47	= 0.734375				63	= 0.984375
2	4	8	16	= 0.25	4	8	16	32	= 0.5	6	12	24	48	= 0.75	8	16	32	64	= 1.0

Roman Numerals

I — 1	IV — 4	VII — 7	X — 10	XX — 20	L — 50	C — 100	D — 500
II — 2	V — 5	VIII — 8	XI — 11	XXX — 30	LX — 60	CC — 200	CM — 900
III — 3	VI — 6	IX — 9	XIX — 19	XL — 40	XC — 90	CD — 400	M — 1,000

Note: The numerals V, X, L, C, D, or M shown with a horizontal line on top denote 1,000 times the original value.

Ancient Measures

Biblical
Cubit . . . . = 21.8 inches
Omer . . . . = 0.45 peck
= 3.964 liters
Ephah . . . . = 10 omers
Shekel . . . . = 0.497 ounce
= 14.1 grams

Greek
Cubit . . . . = 18.3 inches
Stadion . . . . = 607.2 or 622 feet
Obolos . . . . = 715.38 milligrams
Drachma . . . . = 4.2923 grams
Mina . . . . = 0.9463 pound
Talent . . . . = 60 mina

Roman
Cubit . . . . = 17.5 inches
Stadium . . . . = 202 yards
As, libra,
pondus . . . . = 325.971 grams
= 0.71864 pound

Metric System Prefixes

The following prefixes, in combination with the basic unit names, provide the multiples and submultiples in the metric system. For example, the unit name *meter*, with the prefix *kilo* added, produces *kilometer*, meaning "1,000 meters."

Prefix	Symbol	Multiples	Equivalent	Prefix	Symbol	Multiples	Equivalent
yotta	Y	10^{24}	septillionfold	deci	d	10^{-1}	tenth part
zetta	Z	10^{21}	sextillionfold	centi	c	10^{-2}	hundredth part
exa	E	10^{18}	quintillionfold	milli	m	10^{-3}	thousandth part
peta	P	10^{15}	quadrillionfold	micro	µ	10^{-6}	millionth part
tera	T	10^{12}	trillionfold	nano	n	10^{-9}	billionth part
giga	G	10^{9}	billionfold	pico	p	10^{-12}	trillionth part
mega	M	10^{6}	millionfold	femto	f	10^{-15}	quadrillionth part
kilo	k	10^{3}	thousandfold	atto	a	10^{-18}	quintillionth part
hecto	h	10^{2}	hundredfold	zepto	z	10^{-21}	sextillionth part
deka	da	10	tenfold	yocto	y	10^{-24}	septillionth part

Metric Weights and Measures

(**Note:** The metric system generally uses the term *mass* instead of *weight*. Mass is a measure of an object's inertial property, or the amount of matter it contains. Weight is a measure of the force exerted on an object by gravity or the force needed to support it. Also, the metric system does not make a distinction between "dry volume" and "liquid volume.")

Length
10 millimeters (mm) . . . . = 1 centimeter (cm)
10 centimeters . . . . = 1 decimeter (dm)
= 100 millimeters
10 decimeters . . . . = 1 meter (m)
= 1,000 millimeters
10 meters . . . . = 1 dekameter (dam)
10 dekameters . . . . = 1 hectometer (hm)
= 100 meters
10 hectometers . . . . = 1 kilometer (km)
= 1,000 meters

Area
100 square millimeters (mm²) = 1 square centimeter (cm²)
10,000 square centimeters . . . . = 1 square meter (m²)
= 1,000,000 square millimeters
100 square meters . . . . = 1 are (a)
100 ares . . . . = 1 hectare (ha)
= 10,000 square meters
100 hectares . . . . = 1 square kilometer (km²)
= 1,000,000 square meters

Volume
10 milliliters (mL) . . . . = 1 centiliter (cL)
10 centiliters . . . . = 1 deciliter (dL)
= 100 milliliters
10 deciliters . . . . = 1 liter (L)
= 1,000 milliliters
10 liters . . . . = 1 dekaliter (daL)
10 dekaliters . . . . = 1 hectoliter (hL)
= 100 liters
10 hectoliters . . . . = 1 kiloliter (kL)
= 1,000 liters

Volume (Cubic Measure)
1,000 cubic millimeters (mm³) = 1 cubic centimeter (cm³)
1,000 cubic centimeters . . . . . = 1 cubic decimeter (dm³)
= 1,000,000 cubic millimeters
1,000 cubic decimeters . . . . . . = 1 cubic meter (m³)
= 1 stere
= 1,000,000 cubic centimeters
= 1,000,000,000 cubic millimeters

Weight (Mass)
10 milligrams (mg) . . . . = 1 centigram (cg)
10 centigrams . . . . = 1 decigram (dg)
= 100 milligrams
10 decigrams . . . . = 1 gram (g)
= 1,000 milligrams
10 grams . . . . = 1 dekagram (dag)
10 dekagrams . . . . = 1 hectogram (hg)
= 100 grams
10 hectograms . . . . = 1 kilogram (kg)
= 1,000 grams
1,000 kilograms . . . . = 1 metric ton (t)

U.S. Customary Weights and Measures

Length

12 inches (in) . . . . = 1 foot (ft)
3 feet . . . . = 1 yard (yd)
5½ yards . . . . = 1 rod (rd), pole, or perch (16½ feet)
40 rods . . . . = 1 furlong (fur)
                                = 220 yards
                                = 660 feet
8 furlongs . . . . = 1 statute mile (mi)
                                = 1,760 yards
                                = 5,280 feet
3 miles . . . . = 1 league (land)
                                = 5,280 yards
                                = 15,840 feet
6076.11549 feet . . . . = 1 international nautical mile

Volume (Liquid Measure)

When necessary to distinguish the liquid pint or quart from the dry pint or quart, the word *liquid* or the abbreviation *liq* is used in combination with the name or abbreviation of the liquid unit.

4 gills (gi) . . . . = 1 pint (pt)
                                = 28.875 cubic inches
2 pints . . . . = 1 quart (qt)
                                = 57.75 cubic inches
4 quarts . . . . = 1 gallon (gal)
                                = 231 cubic inches
                                = 8 pints
                                = 32 gills

Volume (Dry Measure)

When necessary to distinguish the dry pint or quart from the liquid pint or quart, the word *dry* is used in combination with the name or abbreviation of the dry unit.

2 pints (pt) . . . . = 1 quart (qt)
                                = 67.2006 cubic inches
8 quarts . . . . = 1 peck (pk)
                                = 537.605 cubic inches
                                = 16 pints
4 pecks . . . . = 1 bushel (bu)
                                = 2,150.42 cubic inches
                                = 32 quarts

Area

Squares and cubes of units are sometimes abbreviated by using superscripts. For example, ft^2 means square foot, and ft^3 means cubic foot.

144 square inches . . . . = 1 square foot (ft^2)
9 square feet . . . . = 1 square yard (yd^2)
                                = 1,296 square inches
30 ¼ square yards . . . . = 1 square rod (rd^2)
                                = 272¼ square feet
160 square rods . . . . = 1 acre
                                = 4,840 square yards
                                = 43,560 square feet

640 acres . . . . = 1 square mile (mi^2)
1 mile square . . . . = 1 section (of land)
6 miles square . . . . = 1 township
                                = 36 sections
                                = 36 square miles

Cubic Measure

1 cubic foot (ft^3) . . . . = 1,728 cubic inches (in^3)
27 cubic feet . . . . = 1 cubic yard (yd^3)

Gunter's, or Surveyor's, Chain Measure

7.92 inches (in) . . . . = 1 link
100 links . . . . = 1 chain (ch)
                                = 4 rods
                                = 66 feet
80 chains . . . . = 1 statute mile (mi)
                                = 320 rods
                                = 5,280 feet

Avoirdupois Weight

When necessary to distinguish the avoirdupois ounce or pound from the troy ounce or pound, the word *avoirdupois* or the abbreviation *avdp* is used in combination with the name or abbreviation of the avoirdupois unit. The *grain* is the same in avoirdupois and troy weight.

27 $^{11}/_{32}$ grains . . . . = 1 dram (dr)
16 drams . . . . = 1 ounce (oz)
                                = 437 ½ grains
16 ounces . . . . = 1 pound (ib)
                                = 256 drams
                                = 7,000 grains
100 pounds . . . . = 1 hundredweight (cwt)*
20 hundredweights . . . . = 1 ton
                                = 2,000 pounds*

In *gross* or *long* measure, the following values are recognized.

112 pounds . . . . = 1 gross or long hundredweight*
20 gross or long hundredweights . . . . = 1 gross or long ton
                                = 2,240 pounds*

*When the terms *hundredweight* and *ton* are used unmodified, they are commonly understood to mean the 100-pound hundredweight and the 2,000-pound ton, respectively; these units may be designated *net* or *short* when necessary to distinguish them from the corresponding units in gross or long measure.

Troy Weight

24 grains . . . . = 1 pennyweight (dwt)
20 pennyweights . . . . = 1 ounce troy (oz t)
                                = 480 grains
12 ounces troy . . . . = 1 pound troy (lb t)
                                = 240 pennyweights
                                = 5,760 grains

Weight and Measurement Equivalents

In this table it is necessary to distinguish between the *international* and the *survey* foot. The international foot, defined in 1959 as exactly equal to 0.3048 meter, is shorter than the old survey foot by exactly 2 parts in 1 million. The survey foot is still used in data expressed in feet in geodetic surveys within the U.S. In this table the survey foot is indicated with capital letters.

When the name of a unit is enclosed in brackets, e.g., [1 hand], either (1) the unit is not in general current use in the U.S. or (2) the unit is believed to be based on custom and usage rather than on formal definition.

Equivalents involving decimals are, in most instances, rounded to the 3rd decimal place; exact equivalents are so designated.

Lengths

1 angstrom (Å) . . . . = 0.1 nanometer (exactly)
                                = 0.000 1 micrometer (exactly)
                                = 0.000 000 1 millimeter (exactly)
                                = 0.000 000 004 inch
1 cable's length . . . . = 120 fathoms (exactly)
                                = 720 FEET (exactly)
                                = 219 meters
1 centimeter (cm) . . . . = 0.3937 inch
1 chain (ch) (Gunter's or surveyor's) . . . . = 66 FEET (exactly)
                                = 20.1168 meters
1 chain (engineer's) . . . . = 30.48 meters (exactly)
                                = 100 feet
1 decimeter (dm) . . . . = 3.937 inches
1 degree (geographical) . . . . . . = 364,566.929 feet
                                = 69.047 miles (avg.)
                                = 111.123 kilometers (avg.)
    of latitude . . . . = 68.708 miles at equator
                                = 69.403 miles at poles
    of longitude . . . . = 69.171 miles at equator

1 dekameter (dam) . . . . = 32.808 feet
1 fathom . . . . = 6 FEET (exactly)
                                = 1.8288 meters
1 foot (ft) . . . . = 0.3048 meters (exactly)
                                = 0.015 chains (surveyors)
1 furlong (fur) . . . . = 660 FEET (exactly)
                                = ⅛ statute mile (exactly)
                                = 201.168 meters
[1 hand] (height measure for horses from ground to top of shoulders) . . . . = 4 inches
1 inch (in) . . . . = 2.54 centimeters (exactly)
1 kilometer (km) . . . . = 0.621371 mile
                                = 3,280.8 feet
1 league (land) . . . . = 3 statute miles (exactly)
                                = 4.828 kilometers
1 link (Gunter's or surveyor's) . = 7.92 inches (exactly)
                                = 0.201 meter
1 link (engineer's) . . . . = 1 foot
                                = 0.305 meter

1 meter (m). . . . . = 39.37 inches
= 1.09361 yards
1 micrometer (µm) . . . . = 0.001 millimeter (exactly)
= 0.00003937 inch
1 mil . . . . = 0.001 inch (exactly)
= 0.0254 millimeter (exactly)
1 mile (mi) (statute or land) . . . = 5,280 FEET (exactly)
= 1.609344 kilometers (exactly)
1 international nautical mile (nmi) = 1.852 kilometers (exactly)
= 1.150779 statute miles
= 6,076.11549 feet
1 millimeter (mm) . . . . = 0.03937 inch
1 nanometer (nm) . . . . = 0.001 micrometer (exactly)
= 0.00000003937 inch
1 pica (typography) . . . . = 12 points
1 point (typography) . . . . = 0.013837 inch (exactly)
= 0.351 millimeter
1 rod (rd), pole, or perch . . . . . = 16½ FEET (exactly)
= 5.029 meters
1 yard (yd) . . . . = 0.9144 meter (exactly)

Areas or Surfaces

1 acre . . . . = 43,560 square FEET (exactly)
= 4,840 square yards
= 0.405 hectare
1 are (a) . . . . = 119.599 square yards
= 0.025 acre
1 bolt (cloth measure):
length . . . . = 100 yards (on modern looms)
width . . . . = 45 or 60 inches
1 hectare (ha) . . . . = 2.471 acres
[1 square (building)] . . . . = 100 square feet
1 square centimeter (cm²) . . . . = 0.155 square inch
1 square decimeter (dm²). . . . . = 15.500 square inches
1 square foot (ft²) . . . . = 929.030 square centimeters
1 square inch (in²) . . . . = 6.4516 square centimeters
(exactly)
1 square kilometer (km²) . . . . . = 247.104 acres
= 0.386102 square mile
1 square meter (m²) . . . . = 1.196 square yards
= 10.764 square feet
1 square mile (mi²) . . . . = 258.999 hectares
1 square millimeter (mm²) . . . . = 0.002 square inch
1 square rod (rd²), sq. pole,
or sq. perch . . . . = 25.293 square meters
1 square yard (yd²) . . . . = 0.836127 square meter

Capacities or Volumes

1 barrel (bbl), liquid   = 31 to 42 gallons*
*There are a variety of "barrels" established by law or usage. For example: federal taxes on fermented liquors are based on a barrel of 31 gallons; many state laws fix the "barrel for liquids" as 31½ gallons; one state fixes a 36-gallon barrel for cistern measurement; federal law recognizes a 40-gallon barrel for "proof spirits"; by custom, 42 gallons constitute a barrel of crude oil or petroleum products for statistical purposes, and this equivalent is recognized "for liquids" by 4 states.

1 barrel (bbl), standard for
fruits, vegetables, and other
dry commodities except dry
cranberries . . . . = 7,056 cubic inches
= 1 barrel (bbl), standard for
fruits
1 barrel (bbl), standard,
cranberry . . . . = 86⁴⁵/₆₄ dry quarts
= 2.709 bushels, struck measure
= 5,826 cubic inches
1 board foot (lumber measure) = a foot-square board 1 inch
thick
1 bushel (bu) (U.S.) (struck
measure) . . . . = 2,150.42 cu in (exactly)
= 35.239 liters
[1 bushel, heaped (U.S.)] . . . . = 2,747.715 cubic inches
= 1.278 bushels, struck
measure*
*Frequently recognized as 1¼ bushels, struck measure.
[1 bushel (bu) (British Imperial)
(struck measure)] . . . . = 1.032 U.S. bushels, struck
measure
= 2,219.36 cubic inches
1 cord (cd) firewood . . . . = 128 cubic feet (exactly)
1 cubic centimeter (cm³) . . . . . = 0.061 cubic inch
1 cubic decimeter (dm³) . . . . . . = 61.024 cubic inches

1 cubic inch (in³) . . . . = 0.554 fluid ounce
= 4.433 fluid drams
= 16.387 cubic centimeters
1 cubic foot (ft³) . . . . = 7.481 gallons
= 28.317 cubic decimeters
1 cubic meter (m³) . . . . = 1.308 cubic yards
1 cubic yard (yd³) . . . . = 0.765 cubic meter
1 cup, measuring . . . . = 8 fluid ounces (exactly)
= ½ liquid pint (exactly)
[1 dram, fluid (fl dr) (British)] . . = 0.961 U.S. fluid dram
= 0.217 cubic inch
= 3.552 milliliters
1 dekaliter (daL) . . . . = 2.642 gallons
= 1.135 pecks
1 gallon (gal) (U.S.) . . . . = 231 cubic inches (exactly)
= 3.785 liters
= 0.833 British gallon
= 128 U.S. fluid ounces (exactly)
[1 gallon (gal) British Imperial] = 277.42 cubic inches
= 1.201 U.S. gallons
= 4.546 liters
= 160 British fluid ounces
(exactly)
1 gill (gi) . . . . = 7.219 cubic inches
= 4 fluid ounces (exactly)
= 0.118 liter
1 hectoliter (hL) . . . . = 26.418 gallons
= 2.838 bushels
1 liter (L) (1 cubic decimeter
exactly) . . . . = 1.057 liquid quarts
= 0.908 dry quart
= 61.024 cubic inches
1 milliliter (mL) (1 cu cm
exactly) . . . . = 0.271 fluid dram
= 16.231 minims
= 0.061 cubic inch
1 ounce, liquid (U.S.) . . . . = 1.805 cubic inches
= 29.574 milliliters
= 1.041 British fluid ounces
[1 ounce, fluid (fl oz) (British)] . . = 0.961 U.S. fluid ounce
= 1.734 cubic inches
= 28.412 milliliters
1 peck (pk). . . . . = 8.810 liters
1 pint (pt), dry . . . . = 33.600 cubic inches
= 0.551 liter
1 pint (pt), liquid. . . . . = 28.875 cubic inches (exactly)
= 0.473 liter
1 quart (qt), dry (U.S.) . . . . . . = 67.201 cubic inches
= 1.101 liters
= 0.969 British quart
1 quart (qt), liquid (U.S.) . . . . . = 57.75 cubic in (exactly)
= 0.946 liter
= 0.833 British quart
[1 quart (qt) (British)] . . . . . . = 69.354 cubic inches
= 1.032 U.S. dry quarts
= 1.201 U.S. liquid quarts
1 tablespoon . . . . = 3 teaspoons*(exactly)
= 4 fluid drams
= ½ fluid ounce (exactly)
1 teaspoon. . . . . = ⅓ tablespoon*(exactly)
= 1⅓ fluid drams*
*The equivalent "1 teaspoon = 1⅓ fluid drams" has been found to correspond more closely with the actual capacities of teaspoons in use than the equivalent "1 teaspoon = 1 fluid dram" which is given by many dictionaries.

Weights or Masses

1 assay ton** (AT) . . . . = 29.167 grams
**Used in assaying. The assay ton bears the same relation to the milligram that a ton of 2,000 pounds avoirdupois bears to the ounce troy; hence, the weight in milligrams of precious metal obtained from one assay ton of ore gives directly the number of troy ounces to the net ton.

1 bale (cotton measure) . . . . . = 500 pounds in U.S.
= 750 pounds in Egypt
1 carat (c) . . . . = 200 milligrams (exactly)
= 3.086 grains
1 dram avoirdupois (dr avdp) . . = 27¹¹/₃₂ (= 27.344) grains
= 1.772 grams
1 gamma (g) . . . . = 1 microgram (exactly),
see below
1 grain . . . . = 64.7989 milligrams
1 gram. . . . . = 15.432 grains
= 0.035 ounce, avoirdupois

1 hundredweight, gross or long*** (gross cwt)	= 112 pounds (exactly)	
	= 50.802 kilograms	
1 hundredweight, net or short (cwt or net cwt)	= 100 pounds (exactly)	
	= 45.359 kilograms	
1 kilogram (kg)	= 2.20462 pounds	
1 microgram (µg)	= 0.000001 gram (exactly)	
1 milligram (mg)	= 0.015 grain	
1 ounce, avoirdupois (oz avdp)	= 437.5 grains (exactly)	
	= 0.911 troy ounce	
	= 28.3495 grams	
1 ounce, troy (oz t)	= 480 grains (exactly)	
	= 1.097 avoirdupois ounces	
	= 31.103 grams	
1 pennyweight (dwt)	= 1.555 grams	
1 pound, avoirdupois (lb avdp)	= 7,000 grains (exactly)	
	= 1.215 troy pounds	
	= 453.59237 grams (exactly)	

1 pound, troy (lb t) . . . . = 5,760 grains (exactly)
= 0.823 pound, avoirdupois
= 373.242 grams
1 stone, (avdp) . . . . = 14 pounds avdp (exactly)
= 6.350 kilograms
1 ton, gross or long***(gross ton) . . . . = 2,240 pounds (exactly)
= 1.12 net tons (exactly)
= 1.016 metric tons

***The gross or long ton and hundredweight are used commercially in the U.S. to only a limited extent, usually in restricted industrial fields. These units are the same as the British ton and hundredweight.

1 ton, metric (t) . . . . = 2,204.623 pounds
= 0.984 gross ton
= 1.102 net tons
1 ton, net or short (sh ton) . . . . = 2,000 pounds (exactly)
= 0.893 gross ton
= 0.907 metric ton

Electrical Units

The **watt** is the unit of power (electrical, mechanical, thermal, etc.). Electrical power is given by the product of the voltage and the current.

Energy is sold by the **joule**, but in common practice the billing of electrical energy is expressed in terms of the **kilowatt-hour**, which is 3,600,000 joules or 3.6 megajoules.

The **horsepower** is a nonmetric unit sometimes used in mechanics. It is equal to 746 watts.

The **ohm** is the unit of electrical resistance and represents the physical property of a conductor that offers a resistance to the flow of electricity, permitting just 1 ampere to flow at 1 volt of pressure.

Measures of Force and Pressure

Dyne = force necessary to accelerate a 1-gram mass 1 centimeter per second squared = 0.000072 poundal

Poundal = force necessary to accelerate a 1-pound mass 1 foot per second squared = 13,825.5 dynes = 0.138255 newtons

Newton = force needed to accelerate a 1-kilogram mass 1 meter per second squared

Pascal (pressure) = 1 newton per square meter = 0.020885 pound per square foot

Atmosphere (air pressure at sea level) = 2,116.102 pounds per square foot = 14.6952 pounds per square inch = 1.0332 kilograms per square centimeter = 101,323 newtons per square meter

Spirits Measures

Pony	= 0.5 jigger	Quart	= 32 shots
Shot	= 0.667 jigger		= 1.25 fifths
	= 1.0 ounce	Magnum	= 2 quarts
Jigger	= 1.5 shots		= 2.49797 bottles (wine)
Pint	= 16 shots		
	= 0.625 fifth	For champagne and brandy only:	
Fifth	= 25.6 shots	Jeroboam	= 6.4 pints
	= 1.6 pints		= 1.6 magnum
	= 0.8 quart		= 0.8 gallon
	= 0.75706 liter		

For champagne only:

Rehoboam	= 3 magnums
Methuselah	= 4 magnums
Salmanazar	= 6 magnums
Balthazar	= 8 magnums
Nebuchadnezzar	= 10 magnums
Wine bottle (standard)	= 0.800633 quart
	= 0.7576778 liter

Miscellaneous Modern Measures

Caliber—the diameter of a gun bore. In the U.S., caliber is traditionally expressed in hundredths of inches, e.g., .22. In Britain, caliber is often expressed in thousandths of inches, e.g., .270. Now it is commonly expressed in millimeters, e.g., the 5.56 mm M16 rifle. Heavier weapons' caliber has long been expressed in millimeters, e.g., the 155 mm howitzer. Naval guns' caliber refers to the barrel length as a multiple of the bore diameter. A 5-inch, 50-caliber naval gun has a 5-inch bore and a barrel length of 250 inches.

Decibel (dB)—a measure of the relative loudness or intensity of sound. A 20-decibel sound is 10 times louder than a 10-decibel sound; 30 decibels is 100 times louder; 40 decibels is 1,000 times louder, etc.

One decibel is the smallest difference between sounds detectable by the human ear. A 120-decibel sound is painful.

10 decibels	– a light whisper
20	– quiet conversation
30	– normal conversation
40	– light traffic
50	– typewriter, loud conversation
60	– noisy office
70	– normal traffic, quiet train
80	– rock music, subway
90	– heavy traffic, thunder
100	– jet plane at takeoff

Em—a printer's measure designating the square width of any given type size. Thus, an em of 10-point type is 10 points. An en is half an em.

Gauge—a measure of shotgun bore diameter. Gauge numbers originally referred to the number of lead balls just fitting the gun barrel diameter required to make a pound. Thus, a 16-gauge shotgun's bore was smaller than a 12-gauge shotgun's. Today, an international agreement assigns millimeter measures to each gauge, e.g.:

Gauge	Bore diameter (in mm)	Gauge	Bore diameter (in mm)
6 ..	23.34	14	17.60
10 ..	19.67	16	16.81
12 ..	18.52	20	15.90

Horsepower—the power needed to lift 550 pounds 1 foot in 1 second or to lift 33,000 pounds 1 foot in 1 minute. Equivalent to 746 watts or 2,546.0756 Btu/hr.

Karat or carat—a measure of fineness for gold equal to ¹⁄₂₄ part of pure gold in an alloy. Thus 24-karat gold is pure; 18-karat gold is ¼ alloy. The *carat* is also used as a unit of weight for precious stones; it is equal to 200 milligrams or 3.086 grains.

Knot—a measure of the speed of ships. A knot equals 1 nautical mile per hour.

Quire—25 sheets of paper

Ream—500 sheets of paper

━━ COMPUTERS AND TELECOMMUNICATIONS ━━

Computer Milestones

1623: German mathematician Wilhelm Schickard developed the **1st mechanical calculator**, capable of adding, subtracting, multiplying, and dividing.

1642: French mathematician Blaise Pascal built the 1st of more than 4 dozen copies of an **adding and subtracting machine** that he invented.

1801: French inventor Joseph Marie Jacquard demonstrated a new control system for looms. He **"programmed"** the loom, communicating desired weaving operations to the machine via patterns of holes in paper cards.

1833-71: British mathematician and scientist Charles Babbage used the Jacquard punch-card system in his design for a sophisticated, programmable **"Analytical Engine"** that foreshadowed basic features of today's computers. Babbage's conception was beyond the capabilities of the technology of his time, and the machine remained unfinished at his death in 1871.

1889: American engineer Herman Hollerith patented an electromechanical **punch-card tabulating system** that facilitated the handling of large amounts of statistical data and quickly found use in censuses in the U.S. and other countries.

1911: Hollerith's Tabulating Machine Company merged with 2 other enterprises to form the Computing-Tabulating-Recording Company, renamed in 1924 the International Business Machines Corporation (**IBM**).

1941: German engineer Konrad Züse completed the Z3, the **1st fully functional digital computer** to be **controlled by a program;** the Z3 was not electronic—it was based on electrical switches called relays.

1942: Iowa State College physicist John Vincent Atanasoff and his assistant Clifford Berry completed a working model of the **1st fully electronic computer**, using vacuum tubes, which could operate much more quickly than relays; the rudimentary machine was not programmable.

1943: IBM and Harvard Professor Howard Aiken completed the **1st large-scale automatic digital computer**, the Mark I, a relay-based machine 55 ft long and 8 ft high.

1943: British scientists built the **Colossus**, an electronic computer designed specifically for breaking German codes.

1946: **ENIAC** (for Electronic Numerical Integrator and Computer), a 30-ton room-sized electronic computer with over 18,000 vacuum tubes, was completed by physicist John Mauchly and engineer J. Presper Eckert at the University of Pennsylvania for the U.S. Army. ENIAC could be programmed to do different tasks, although programming could take a couple of days, since cables had to be plugged in and switches set by hand.

1951: Eckert and Mauchly's **UNIVAC** ("Universal Automatic Computer") became the 1st computer commercially available in the U.S.; the 1st customer: the Census Bureau. CBS-TV used a UNIVAC in 1952 to predict election results.

1969-71: The powerful **Unix operating system** was developed at Bell Laboratories; later versions became widely used on large computers and formed the basis for the popular Linux and Macintosh OS X operating systems for personal computers.

1971: Intel released the 4004, the 1st commerical **microprocessor** (an entire computer processing unit on a chip).

1973: The Alto computer, developed at Xerox's Palo Alto Research Center, became operational, implementing many features used years later in commerical personal computers, including a **graphical user interface** (GUI) featuring windows, icons, a mouse, and pointers.

1975: The **1st widely marketed personal computer**, the MITS Altair 8800, was introduced in kit form, with no keyboard, video display, or printer, for under $400.

1975: **Microsoft** was founded by college dropouts Bill Gates and Paul Allen.

1976: The **1st word-processing program** for personal computers, the Electric Pencil, was written.

1976: **Apple** Computer Company was founded by Steven Jobs and Stephen Wozniak.

1977: Apple introduced the **Apple II;** capable of displaying text and graphics in color, the machine enjoyed phenomenal success.

1981: **IBM** unveiled its **"Personal Computer,"** which used Microsoft's DOS (disk operating system).

1984: Apple introduced the 1st **Macintosh**. The easy-to-use Macintosh came with a proprietary operating system and was the 1st popular computer to have a GUI and a mouse.

1990: Microsoft released **Windows** 3.0, the 1st workable version of its own GUI.

1991: **Linux** was invented for the personal computer by Helsinki University student Linus Torvalds and made available for free.

1996: The **Palm Pilot**, the 1st widely successful handheld computer and personal information manager, arrived.

1997: The IBM computer **Deep Blue** beat world chess champion Garry Kasparov in a 6-game match, 3.5-2.5.

2000: **Microsoft** was found guilty of **antitrust violations** by a a federal district judge. Microsoft settled in 2001 by accepting certain restrictions on its competitive practices and creating an antitrust compliance committee.

2001: Apple introduced the **Unix-based operating system** OS X for the **Macintosh**.

2002: The total number of **personal computers** (PCs), including desktop and laptop machines of all types, shipped by manufacturers since 1975 reached 1 bil, according to computer industry research firm Gartner Dataquest.

2004: The European Union (EU) found **Microsoft** guilty of **anticompetitive practices** and fined the company $613 mil. In mid-2006 the EU levied an additional penalty of $357 mil for noncompliance.

2006: **Apple** began using **Intel microprocessors** in its Macintosh computers instead of the IBM PowerPC.

Nations With the Most Personal Computers in Use, 2006

Source: Computer Industry Almanac at www.c-i-a.com for year end 2006

Rank	PCs in Use[1]	% of Worldwide Total	Rank	PCs in Use[1]	% of Worldwide Total
1. U.S.	240.5	24.15	10. Brazil	25.99	2.61
2. Japan	77.95	7.83	11. Canada	25.10	2.52
3. China	74.11	7.44	12. India	21.17	2.13
4. Germany	54.48	5.47	13. Australia	15.47	1.55
5. UK	41.53	4.17	14. Mexico	14.77	1.48
6. France	35.99	3.61	15. Spain	13.42	1.35
7. South Korea	30.62	3.07			
8. Italy	29.31	2.94	Top 15 Countries	727.4	73.0
9. Russia	26.97	2.71	Worldwide Total	996.1	100.0

(1) In millions.

Status of Electronics Sold 1980-2004

Source: U.S. Environmental Protection Agency.
(millions of units)

	Disposed or Recycled		In Storage		Still in Use		Total
	Units	%	Units	%	Units	%	Units
Desktop PCs............	188.1	42.6	43.3	9.8	210.0	47.6	441.0
PC monitors...........	250.4	46.1	28.0	5.1	265.3	48.8	543.7
Portable PCs...........	36.4	37.6	1.4	1.4	59.0	60.9	96.9
Hard copy peripherals[1]	137.1	45.1	13.8	4.6	152.9	50.3	303.8
Televisions.............	229.7	37.5	93.9	15.3	288.3	47.1	611.9
Total.................	841.8	42.1	180.3	9.0	975.7	48.8	1997.8

Note: Estimates as of 2005. (1) Printers, scanners, fax machines.

Computer Products Disposal, 1999-2006

Source: U.S. Environmental Protection Agency.
(Millions of Units and Thousands of Tons)

	Desktops		Portables		Peripherals*		CRT Monitors		Flat Panel Monitors		Total		Total Recycled	
Year	Units	Tons	Units	Tons	Units	Tons	Units	Tons	Units	Tons	Units	Tons	Units	Tons
1999	12.6	138.3	3.2	13.5	90.4	141.7	15.7	238.3	1.8	21.7	123.7	553.5	18.4	82.4
2000	15.4	174.3	3.9	16.0	77.6	162.7	18.9	314.8	1.9	23.4	117.8	691.1	17.5	102.6
2001	18.4	204.4	4.8	19.0	89.7	190.9	21.1	386.6	1.9	23.6	136.0	824.5	19.8	120.0
2002	21.9	244.8	5.8	22.0	96.7	217.8	23.9	480.7	3.6	44.2	151.9	1,009.5	23.0	153.1
2003	24.7	275.0	6.9	25.4	112.5	263.6	27.7	597.8	4.6	56.4	176.3	1,218.2	26.1	180.3
2004	26.6	293.6	7.8	28.2	124.5	278.0	27.8	627.8	7.8	96.2	194.6	1,323.8	29.9	203.2
2005	28.4	322.6	9.0	31.8	130.8	278.9	28.5	673.1	10.0	122.6	206.6	1,429.1	32.1	221.8
2006	28.3	311.6	10.2	35.2	120.8	267.9	23.8	550.3	12.1	148.5	195.2	1,313.4	NA	NA

Note: Estimated figures. * Includes printers, scanners, fax machines, mice, & keyboards

Top-Selling Software, 2006-2007

Source: The NPD Group/Retail Tracking Service
(based on unit U.S. sales, June 2006-2007[1])

All Software
1. TurboTax 2006 Deluxe w/State
2. Spy Sweeper
3. World Of Warcraft: Burning Crusade Expansion Pack
4. Norton Internet Security 2007
5. Norton Antivirus 2007
6. PC-Cillin AntiVirus 11.0
7. MS Office 2003 Student/Teacher Ed
8. MS Office 2007 Home & Student
9. World Of Warcraft
10. PC-Cillin AntiVirus 2007

Business
1. MS Office 2003 Student/Teacher Ed
2. MS Office 2007 Home & Student
3. MS Office 2004 Student/Teacher Ed
4. .Mac 4.0
5. Quicktime 7.0 Pro (PC)
6. Quicktime 7.0 Pro (Mac)
7. iWork 2006
8. MS Campus Agreement 3.1 License
9. MS Office 2007 Pro Upgrade
10. MS Office 2007 Upgrade

Education
1. I Spy Mystery
2. Mavis Beacon Teaches Typing 17.0
3. Brain Play Preschool-1st Grade
4. Jumpstart Advanced Preschool 2.0
5. Adventure Workshop Preschool-1st Grade 7.0
6. Jumpstart Advanced Kindergarten 2.0
7. Brain Play 1st-3rd Grade
8. Instant Immersion Spanish 2.0 Deluxe
9. Jumpstart Advanced First Grade 2.0
10. Typing Instructor For Kids 2

Finance
1. TurboTax 2006 Deluxe w/State
2. Taxcut 2006 Premium w/State
3. TurboTax 2006 Deluxe
4. TurboTax 2006 Basic
5. QuickBooks 2007 Pro
6. TurboTax 2006 Premier w/State
7. Quicken 2007 Basic
8. TurboTax 2006 Home & Business w/State
9. Taxcut 2006 Premium
10. Quicken 2007 Deluxe

Imaging/Graphics
1. Adobe Photoshop Elements 5.0
2. Print Shop 22.0 Deluxe
3. iLife 2006
4. Print Shop 20.0 (Jewel case)
5. Adobe Photoshop Elements 5.0/
   Premiere Elements 3.0 Bundle

6. Printmaster 17.0 Platinum
7. Hallmark Card Studio Special Ed (Jewel case)
8. Photo Explosion 3.0 Deluxe
9. Art Explosion Scrapbook Factory 3.0 Deluxe
10. Printmaster 17.0 Gold

Operating Systems
1. MS Windows XP Home Ed Upgrade
2. MS Windows Vista Home Premium Upgrade
3. MS Windows XP Home Ed
4. MS Windows XP Pro Upgrade
5. Mac OS X 10.4 Tiger
6. MS Windows Vista Ultimate Upgrade
7. MS Windows XP Pro
8. MS Windows Vista Home Basic Upgrade
9. MS Windows Vista Home Premium
10. MS Plus Super Pack

PC Games
1. World Of Warcraft: Burning Crusade Expansion Pack
2. World Of Warcraft
3. The Sims 2
4. The Sims 2 Pets Expansion Pack
5. Battlefield 2142
6. The Sims 2 Glamour Life Stuff Expansion Pack
7. MS Age Of Empires III
8. The Sims 2 Seasons Expansion Pack
9. Paws & Claws Pet Vet
10. The Sims 2 Nightlife Expansion Pack

Personal Productivity
1. MS Streets & Trips 2007
2. Easy CD & DVD Burning
3. MS Streets & Trips 2007 w/GPS Locator
4. Tune Tools For iPod
5. PSP Media Manager 2
6. Easy Media Creator 9.0 Suite
7. PSP Max Media Manager w/USB Link Cable
8. Nero 7.0 Ultra Edition Enhanced
9. MS Works 8.0
10. MS Streets & Trips 2006

System Utilities
1. Spy Sweeper
2. Norton Internet Security 2007
3. Norton Antivirus 2007
4. PC-Cillin AntiVirus 11.0
5. PC-Cillin AntiVirus 2007
6. Norton Internet Security 2007 Upgrade
7. Norton Internet Security 2007/
   System Works 2007 Upgrade Bundle
8. Norton Antivirus 2007 Upgrade
9. Norton Antivirus 2006
10. Norton 360 Upgrade

(1) Some widely used software is often bundled with computers when sold; these are not included in sales figures above.

U.S. Sales of Selected Hardware, 1997-2008

Source: Consumer Electronics Association
(Factory sales to dealers in millions of dollars and millions of units)

	1997 $	2000 $	2001 $	2001 units	2003 $	2003 units	2006 $	2006 units	2007 (est.) $	2007 (est.) units
Computers	$15,950[1]	$16,400[1]	$12,960[1]	14.4[1]	$15,584	18.1	$19,276	24.4	$21,569	27.3
Desktop					7,212	10.9	7,340	10.7	7,888	11.1
Notebook					8,372	7.2	11,936	13.7	13,681	16.3
Wireless Telephones & PDAs	5,940[2]	10,260[3]	9,728[3]	59.9[3]	8,997	74.6	13,153	113.4	13,498	117.5
Smartphones	—	(3)	(3)	(3)	925	2.3	4,781	14.0	6,821	20.7
Electronic Gaming Hardware	1,650	2,700	3,250	—	3,188	—	4,425	—	6,615	—
Digital Video Recorders	—	77	144	—	848	3.3	975	5.0	1,580	8.9
Digital Cameras	483	1,823	1,972	5.6	3,921	14.8	7,149	32.9	6,619	33.5
Digital Camcorder	—	2,838	2,236	5.3	2,002	5.3	1,828	5.3	1,998	6.4
Portable Media/MP3 Players	—	107	100	0.7	424	3.0	5,559	38.1	5,400	41.5

(1) Desktop & notebook computers were not separated. (2) No PDAs. (3) All wireless telephones.

About the Internet

Internet Milestones

The **Internet** is a vast and rapidly growing computer network of computer networks. In 1994, a total of 3 mil people (most of them in the U.S.) made use of it; by the end of 2005 the number of users worldwide exceeded 1 bil (Computer Industry Almanac Inc.).

The Internet is not owned or funded by any one institution, organization, or government. It has no CEO and is not a commercial service. Its development is guided by the Internet Society (ISOC), composed of volunteers. The ISOC appoints the Internet Architecture Board (IAB), which oversees issues of standards, network resources, etc.

Major historical highlights:

1969: ARPANET, an experimental 4-computer network, was established by the Advanced Research Projects Agency (ARPA) of the U.S. Defense Dept. Two years later, ARPANET linked about 2 dozen computers ("hosts") at 15 sites, including MIT and Harvard.

1978: The 1st **spam**, or junk e-mail, message was sent over ARPANET.

1983: The protocol, or set of communications rules, known as **TCP/IP**, became the main networking protocol of ARPANET. TCP/IP facilitates connection between networks, and its adoption was tantamount to the birth of the Internet.

1983: The military portion of ARPANET was moved onto the **MILNET**.

1986: The U.S. National Science Foundation (NSF) launched **NSFNET**, the 1st large-scale network using Internet technology.

1988: Internet Relay Chat (IRC) was developed by Finnish student Jarkko Oikarinen, enabling people to communicate via the Internet in "real time."

1988: A **"worm"** crafted by Cornell Univ. graduate student Robert Morris, Jr., infected thousands of computers, shutting many down and causing millions of dollars of damage—the 1st known case of large-scale damage caused by a computer virus spread via the Internet.

1989: The World—the **1st commercial Internet service** provider supplying dial-up access—appeared.

1989-90: Tim Berners-Lee invented the **World Wide Web.** Begun as an environment in which scientists at the European Center for Nuclear Research in Switzerland could share information, it gradually evolved into a medium with text, graphics, audio, animation, and video.

1990: ARPANET was disbanded.

1991: The NSFNET was opened to commercial traffic.

1991: Berners-Lee introduced the **1st browser**, or software for accessing the Web.

1993: The U.S. National Center for Supercomputing Applications released versions of **Mosaic**, the 1st Web browser able to present both text and images in a single page, for Microsoft Windows, Unix systems running the X Window GUI, and the Apple Macintosh.

1994: Netscape Communications released the **Netscape Navigator** browser.

1995: Microsoft released its **Internet Explorer** browser. It initially failed to make a dent in Netscape's dominance of the browser market but surpassed it by 1999.

1996: A group of universities launched **Internet2**, an advanced, high-performance network for the research community and a test bed for development of new capabilities that might find use in the commercial Internet.

1998: Under a contract with the U.S. Dept. of Commerce, the nonprofit Internet Corporation for Assigned Numbers and Names (ICANN) took over the management of such basic Internet functions as assignment of **domain names** and Internet (IP) addresses.

1999: Release of the free **Napster** file-sharing service enabled users to easily exchange files containing music or other content without regard to copyright restrictions.

2003: Niue, a self-governing Pacific island associated with New Zealand, became the 1st "country" to offer free **nationwide wireless access** to the Internet (using Wi-Fi technology).

2004: The Mozilla Foundation released the first official version of the open-source browser **Mozilla Firefox**.

2006: Websites with rich user interfaces that encourage collective participation and personalization through online applications and scripts, known as **Web 2.0**, became prevalent.

Safety and Security on the Internet

Common sense dictates some basic security rules:

- Pick passwords that are difficult to guess, preferably consisting of both letters and numbers, and perhaps also other symbols (if permitted). It's a bad idea to use the same password at multiple websites.
- Do not give out your phone number, address, credit card number, or other personal information, unless needed for a transaction at a site you trust.
- If you feel someone is being threatening or dangerous, inform your Internet service provider.
- Use protective "firewall," antivirus, and antispyware software to guard your system against attacks by hackers. Be sure to keep the software up to date.
- Be careful about opening e-mail and file attachments from unknown correspondents.
- If you have programs that can make use of macros—bits of auxiliary coding that are meant to play a helpful role but can be taken advantage of by some viruses—make sure the programs' macro virus protection (if any) is turned on. Keep macros disabled if you do not know what you might want to use them for.
- Users of so-called **peer-to-peer** (P2P) file-sharing networks or protocols should open up only part of their computer system to sharing—not the entire hard drive.
- Security flaws turn up from time to time in operating systems, Web browsers, and other software, and when the manufacturers provide **patches** to solve the problem, it is usually advisable to install these fixes. If a fix is not available for a serious security problem, you may want to consider switching to an alternative program.

Malware. Software designed to harm a computer system—such as a virus (malicious code carried within a program) or a worm (a self-contained malicious program)—may be picked up from the Internet or elsewhere, received on a disk, or communicated via e-mail.

Some malicious software may install a "back door" on an infected system, giving access to a hacker; may attempt to turn off any antivirus program on the system; or may try to log the user's keystrokes.

A **Trojan horse** is computer code concealed within harmless code or data that is capable of taking control and causing damage. It can be used to mount a massive **"denial-of-service"** attack, which overwhelms targeted computers by inundating them with messages. The infected computers, acting under hacker control without their owners' knowledge, are called **zombies**, and the network of zombie computers that carry out the attack is called a **botnet**.

Spyware. Software that observes your computer activity without your knowledge—is often regarded as a type of malware. Spyware programs may gain entry to your machine via a Trojan horse. They may record your keystrokes and report passwords or other personal information to a hacker. Some may flood your screen with ads.

Phishing. A popular scam is **phishing**—the use of a forged e-mail message purportedly from a respectable organization, such as a bank, to elicit such personal data. The e-mail typically contains a hyperlink that leads to a fabricated website resembling the site of the ostensible sender. A simple way to avoid falling victim to a phishing scam is to refuse to click on links in e-mails from companies where you have an account. If you want to visit such a company's website, open your browser and manually enter the site's normal address.

Spam. Junk e-mail, or **spam**, can be a time-wasting annoyance or worse—spam may hawk pornography or products dangerous to health; seek to defraud the recipient; may carry a destructive virus; or turn the recipient's machine into a zombie that stores illicit material, takes part in a denial-of-service attack, or distributes spam. Net administrators worry that the flood of spam may cause delays or even a breakdown in the flow of Internet traffic.

In 2003 Congress enacted a law that attempted to restrict spam, but it had little effect on the ever-increasing volume of spam received on e-mail accounts.

While filtering software can help reduce the deluge of spam—some e-mail programs include filters—it is not completely accurate. Experts recommend that you be wary of revealing your e-mail address as you surf the Web. When leaving an e-mail address on a public website, spell out "at" instead of using the @ symbol.

Internet Addresses

The fundamental part of an address on the Internet is called the domain. The final part of a domain name, known as the **top-level domain (TLD)**, is its most basic part. For example, in *The World Almanac*'s web address (www.worldalmanac.com) .com is the top-level domain.

So-called generic top-level domains (gTLDs), consisting of 3 or more letters, include:

Domain	What It Is
.aero	an organization in the air-transport industry
.asia	Legal entities within the Pan-Asia and Asia-Pacific region
.biz	a business
.cat	a site associated with Catalan language and culture
.com	generally a commercial organization, business, or company
.coop	a nonprofit business cooperative, such as a rural electric coop
.edu	a 4-year higher-educational institution
.gov	a nonmilitary U.S. governmental entity, usually federal
.info	an informational site for an individual or organization, without restriction
.int	an international organization
.jobs	information about employment, such as job openings
.mil	a U.S. military organization
.mobi	a site providing content for mobile devices
.museum	a museum
.name	an individual
.net	suggested for a network administration, but actually used by a wide variety of sites
.org	suggested for a nonprofit organization, but actually used by a wide variety of sites
.pro	a professional, such as an accountant, lawyer, or physician
.tel	Internet communications identifier for an individual or organization
.travel	information about travel

Domain names with 2 letters are generally for countries or regions. The **top-level domain** .us, for instance, is available to persons, organizations, and entities in the U.S. More examples: .eu (European Union), .jp (Japan), .ru (Russia), .uk (United Kingdom).

Internet Lingo

The following abbreviations are sometimes used on the Internet and in e-mail.

BTW	By the way	GOK	God only knows	LOL	Laughing out loud
CBLO	See below	GTG	Got to go	PLS	Please
F2F	Face to face; a personal meeting	HHOK	Ha, ha—only kidding	ROTFL	Rolling on the floor laughing
FCOL	For crying out loud	IMHO	In my humble opinion	TAFN	That's all for now
FWIW	For what it's worth	IMO	In my opinion	TTFN	Ta-ta for now

Emoticons, or **smileys**, are a series of typed characters that, when turned sideways, resemble a face and express an emotion. Here are some smileys often encountered on the Internet.

:-)	Smile	:-D	Laugh	:-(	Unhappy	:-b..	Drooling
;-)	Wink	:-*	Kiss	:-o	Surprised	{*}	A hug and a kiss

Nations With the Most Internet Users, 2006

Source: Computer Industry Almanac at www.c-i-a.com for year end 2006

Rank	Country	Internet Users[1]	% of Worldwide Users	Rank	Country	Internet Users[1]	% of Worldwide Users	Rank	Country	Internet Users[1]	% of Worldwide Users
1.	U.S.	210.2	17.29	7.	South Korea	35.0	2.88	13.	Indonesia	22.7	1.87
2.	China	131.1	10.78	8.	France	32.0	2.63	14.	Mexico	20.6	1.70
3.	Japan	90.9	7.47	9.	Italy	31.6	2.60	15.	Spain	17.8	1.47
4.	India	67.6	5.56	10.	Brazil	29.5	2.42	**Top 15 Total**		**829.9**	**68.25**
5.	Germany	50.3	4.14	11.	Russia	27.6	2.27				
6.	UK	39.7	3.27	12.	Canada	23.3	1.91	**Worldwide Total**		**1,216.0**	**100.0**

(1) In millions.

U.S. Broadband Internet Access

Changes in the percentage of each group who have broadband connections at home

Source: Horrigan, John B., Home Broadband Adoption 2007, Pew Internet & American Life Project, July 3, 2007

	% with broadband at home		Percentage increase,		% with broadband at home		Percentage increase,
	2006	2007	2006-07		2006	2007	2006-07
Total.................	42	47	12	**Educational attainment**			
Gender				Less than High School ...	17	21	24
Male................	45	50	11	High School grad	31	34	10
Female	38	44	16	Some college	47	58	23
Age				College + ...	62	70	13
18-29................	55	63	15	**Annual household income**			
30-49................	50	59	18	Under $30K	21	30	43
50-64................	38	40	5	$30K-$50K	43	46	7
65+	13	15	15	$50K-$75K	48	58	21
Race/ethnicity				Over $75K	68	76	12
White (not hispanic).....	42	48	14	**Community type**			
Black (not hispanic).....	31	40	29	Urban	44	52	18
Hispanic	29[1]	—	NA	Suburban	46	49	7
				Rural.................	25	31	24

NA = Not Applicable. (1) From the Pew Internet Project's and Pew Hispanic Center's Latinos Online survey June-October 2006 of 6,016 Hispanic adults. **Note:** 2006 data comes from the Pew Internet Project's February 15-April 6 survey of 4,001 adults; 1,562 were home broadband users. 2007 data comes from the Pew Internet Project's February-March survey of 2,200 adults; 966 were home broadband users.

Most-Visited Websites, July 2007

Source: comScore Media Metrix, Inc.

Rank	Website*	Visitors[1]	Rank	Website*	Visitors[1]
1.	Yahoo! Sites (Flickr; del.icio.us)	133,428	12.	Apple Inc. (iTunes)......................	42,561
2.	Google Sites (YouTube; Blogger)	123,892	13.	Weather Channel, The....................	38,534
3.	Time Warner Network (AOL; Mapquest)......	123,702	14.	Adobe Sites	33,361
4.	Microsoft Sites...........................	118,154	15.	Gorilla Nation	32,560
5.	Fox Interactive Media (Myspace; Photobucket) .	81,233	16.	CNET Networks (TV.com; GameSpot; MP3.com; ZDNet; Chow)...........................	32,182
6.	eBay (PayPal; Shopping.com; Skype)	79,787	17.	FACEBOOK.COM	30,557
7.	Amazon Sites (IMDb)	52,702	18.	Target Corporation	30,391
8.	Ask Network (Bloglines; Excite; iWon)	51,885	19.	AT&T, Inc (Yellowpages.com)...............	29,692
9.	Wikipedia Sites	46,372	20.	Expedia Inc (Hotels.com; Hotwire)	29,243
10.	Viacom Digital (MTV; BET; Paramount)	43,056			
11.	New York Times Digital (About.com)	42,710			

*In some cases, represents an aggregation of commonly owned domain names. Popular domains within a group added in parenthesis by World Almanac editors. (1) Number of visitors, in thousands, who visited Website at least once in July 2007.

Internet Access in the U.S., 2000-2006

Source: 2007 Digital Future Report, USC Annenberg School Center for the Digital Future

	% of Americans Accessing Internet[1]						Avg. Hours Per Week Spent Online[1]					
Type of Internet Access	2000	2001	2002	2003	2005	2006	2000	2001	2002	2003	2005	2006
All access	66.9	72.3	71.1	75.9	78.6	77.6	9.4	9.8	11.1	12.5	13.3	14.0
at home	46.9	58.4	59.3	65.1	66.2	68.1	3.3	5.9	6.8	6.9	7.8	8.9
at school[2]	55.3	61.0	59.4	58.7	74.6	68.7	NA	NA	NA	NA	NA	NA
at work[3]	42.3	37.5	40.2	49.6	55.1	55.8	NA	4.6	5.5	4.9	5.6	7.8
by cell phone/mobile devices.......	NA	NA	5.2	8.1	9.0	11.1	NA	0.3[4]	NA	1.5	2.0	1.8
by wireless computer	NA	NA	2.8	4.7	6.5	10.7	NA	(4)	NA	5.3	5.7	8.6

NA = Not Available. (1) Internet users age 12 and older who connect from all locations. (2) Students only. (3) Work outside the home. (4) Via Wireless Device.

Hours Spent Weekly on Internet Activities in the U.S., 2006

Source: 2007 Digital Future Report, USC Annenberg School Center for the Digital Future

Online Activities	All Users[1]	New Users[2]	Very Experienced Users[3]	Online Activities	All Users[1]	New Users[2]	Very Experienced Users[3]
Actively using the Internet at home	8.9	3.1	10.3	Entertainment	2.3	2.8	2.7
Actively using the Internet at work	7.8	1.4	9.7	Playing video/computer games..	1.4	1.9	1.0
				Listening to the radio..........	1.1	1.2	1.6
E-mail	4.3	1.7	6.0	Transactions	0.9	0.1	1.3
Information for work/school	4.1	0.9	5.7	Discussion/chat group.........	0.8	0.5	0.9
Information for personal or other reasons	2.7	1.4	3.3	Reading newspapers..........	0.8	0.3	1.1
				Reading magazines...........	0.2	0.1	0.3
				Reading books	0.1	0.1	0.1

(1) Internet users age 12 and older who connect from all locations. (2) People who have been using the Internet less than one year. (3) People who have been using the Internet more than 9 years.

U.S. Retail Trade E-Commerce Sales, 2000-2005

Year	E-Commerce Retail Sales (millions $)	% of Total Commerce	% Change from prior year	E-Shopping & Mail Order Houses (millions $)	% of Total E-Commerce
2000	$27,968	0.94	NA	$21,397	77
2001	35,296	1.15	26	26,429	75
2002	46,819	1.49	33	34,833	74
2003	60,015	1.84	28	42,784	71
2004	76,344	2.20	27	53,420	70
2005	93,280	2.53	22	65,387	70

NA = Not available.

Electronic Shopping, Percent of All Mail-Order and Online Shopping

(Sales in Millions of Dollars)

	2005 Sales	%	2004[R] Sales	%	2003[R] Sales	%	2002[R] Sales	%	2001[R] Sales	%	2000[R] Sales	%
Books & magazines	$3,225	54	$2,816	49	$2,417	48	$2,110	44	$1,843	42	$1,837	42
Clothing, footware, accessories	7,921	50	6,101	44	5,004	37	4,361	31	3,256	21	2,252	15
Computer hardware	9,079	46	7,765	40	6,531	36	6,162	33	5,475	26	6,070	22
Computer software	1,850	50	1,563	48	1,288	42	1,328	35	1,207	30	1,126	30
Drugs, health aids, & beauty aids	6,450	15	5,993	15	3,877	12	2,436	9	1,323	7	732	5
Electronics & appliances	5,997	67	4,583	61	3,311	55	2,370	48	1,715	41	1,100	31
Food, beer, & wine	1,369	45	829	35	701	34	650	33	484	24	587	30
Furniture & home furnishings	5,075	52	3,890	47	3,245	41	2,435	33	1,664	25	1,008	15
Music & videos	2,164	59	2,055	49	1,814	46	1,662	38	1,380	31	1,205	26
Office equipment & supplies	4,288	61	3,658	56	3,264	53	2,507	42	1,920	30	1,393	20
Sporting Goods	1,568	48	1,013	39	914	38	925	34	479	27	410	23
Toys, hobby goods, & games	1,809	50	1,440	43	1,412	41	1,171	34	856	29	798	26
Other merchandise[1]	9,930	39	7,340	33	5,722	29	4,210	23	3,045	17	1,869	12
Nonmerchandise receipts[2]	4,662	56	4,374	55	3,284	49	2,506	46	1,782	42	1,010	32
Total	65,387	40	53,420	36	42,784	33	34,833	28	26,429	23	21,397	19

R = Revised. (1) Includes other merchandise such as collectibles, souvenirs, auto parts & accessories, hardware, lawn & garden equipment and supplies, and jewelry. (2) Includes nonmerchandise receipts such as auction commissions, customer training, customer support, advertising, and shipping & handling.

Informative and Useful Websites[1]

Name	URL	Description
Daily Data		
MetaFilter	www.metafilter.com	A community weblog where users share and discuss interesting links.
ResourceShelf	www.resourceshelf.com	Librarians and researchers share the websites they find.
Shorpy	www.shorpy.com	"The 100-Year-Old Photo Blog" provides a continuous supply of historical photos.
Today's Front Pages	www.newseum.org/todaysfrontpages	Today's front page from more than 500 newspapers worldwide.
Education & Exhibits		
American Memory	memory.loc.gov	More than 5 million items from the Library including audio, maps, movies, photos, prints, and sheet music.
British Library	www.bl.uk/onlinegallery/homepage.html	Scanned rarities from (among others) Gutenberg, Shakespeare, Leonardo as well as audio, maps, music, and photos.
Internet Archive	www.archive.org	Digital library of free cultural artifacts and Internet sites.
Library of Congress	www.loc.gov/exhibits	Online counterparts to LOC exhibits since 1992.
MIT OpenCourseWare	ocw.mit.edu	Free and open educational course material from Massachusetts Institute of Technology.
National Archives	www.archives.gov/exhibits	Documents from defining events and personalities in America's history.
New York Public Library Digital Gallery	digitalgallery.nypl.org	More than 550,000 images digitized from primary sources and printed rarities in the library's collections.
Our Documents	www.ourdocuments.gov	Digitized images and text of 100 milestone documents from America's history.
Statistics		
FedStats	www.fedstats.gov	Find statistics by topic or program from more than 100 Federal agencies.
Swivel	www.swivel.com	Community for users to visually map out and share statistics.
United Nations Statistics Division	unstats.un.org	International datasets and country profiles with demographics and stats on society, industry, and the environment.
U.S. Economy at a Glance	stats.bls.gov/eag	Quick reference tables on employment and wages from the Bureau of Labor Statistics.
Online Tools		
Kayak	www.kayak.com	One stop search of multiple travel-booking sites for the lowest fares and price trends.
LibraryThing	www.librarything.com	Track the books you've read, receive suggestions for new books, and compare lists with similar readers.
Open Congress	www.opencongress.org	Easily follow Congress and find news about specific members, bills, committees, and issues. Receive updates by RSS feed.
Downloadable Tools		
Google Earth	earth.google.com	Free downloadable interactive world atlas and mapping software.
Stellarium	www.stellarium.org	Free downloadable planetarium that visualizes astronomical phenomena in real time from any point on Earth.

(1) Websites are subject to change. *The World Almanac* cannot take responsibility for contents.

www.WorldAlmanac.com

The World Almanac Blog: Daily facts, informative links, and offbeat news from the editors of *The World Almanac*.
The World Almanac e-Newsletter: Current and historical events, celebrity birthdays and obituaries, and more. E-mail newsletter@waegroup.com to subscribe.
Bonus Content: Classic covers, essays, and facts from previous editions, plus additional coverage of U.S. presidential elections and historical World Series stats. See inside front cover for your password.

TELECOMMUNICATIONS

Worldwide Telecommunications: Market Data (1990-2004)

Source: © International Telecommunication Union

	1990	1999	2000	2001	2002	2003	2004[3]
Total market revenue (billions of U.S. $)[1]	$508	$1,123	$1,210	$1,232	$1,314	$1,426	NA
Intl. phone traffic (billions of minutes)[2]	33	100	118	127	131	142	$145
Main telephone lines (millions)...................	520	905	983	1,053	1,086	1,140	1,207
Mobile cellular subscriptions (millions).............	11	490	740	955	1,166	1,414	1,758

NA=not available. (1) Revenue from installation, subscription, and local, trunk, and international call charges. (2) From 1994 including traffic between countries of the former Soviet Union. (3) Preliminary.

Top 50 Nations for Use of Cellular Telephones, Year-End 2006

Source: © International Telecommunication Union, estimated; top countries or regions ranked by subscriptions.

Country/Region	Subscriptions (thousands)	per 100 pop.	Country/Region	Subscriptions (thousands)	per 100 pop.
China.............	461,058.0	34.8	Australia	19,760.0	97.0
United States........	233,000.0	77.4	Saudi Arabia........	19,662.6	78.1
India	166,050.0	14.8	Malaysia...........	19,463.7	75.5
Russia	120,000.0	83.6	Bangladesh	19,131.0	13.3
Japan	101,698.0	79.3	Venezuela	18,789.5	69.0
Brazil..............	99,918.6	52.9	Egypt	18,001.1	23.9
Germany...........	84,300.0	101.9	Canada............	17,017.0	52.5
Italy	71,500.0	123.1	Morocco	16,004.7	52.1
United Kingdom......	69,656.6	116.4	Netherlands	15,834.0	97.2
Indonesia...........	63,803.0	28.3	Viet Nam..........	15,505.4	18.2
Mexico............	57,016.4	52.6	Iran (I.R.)	13,659.1	19.4
France............	51,662.0	85.1	Romania	13,354.1	61.8
Ukraine	49,076.2	106.7	Chile..............	12,450.8	75.6
Spain	46,152.0	106.4	Portugal	12,226.4	116.0
Turkey............	43,609.0	59.6	Czech Republic	12,149.9	119.0
Philippines.........	41,000.0	49.2	Greece	11,097.5	99.6
Thailand	40,815.5	63.0	Hungary	9,965.0	99.0
Korea (Rep.)........	40,197.1	83.8	Belgium	9,659.8	92.6
Poland.............	36,745.5	95.5	Hong Kong, China	9,356.4	131.5
Pakistan	34,506.6	22.0	Austria	9,255.0	112.8
South Africa........	33,960.0	71.6	Sweden	9,087.0	100.5
Nigeria............	32,322.2	24.1	Peru	8,500.0	30.0
Argentina..........	31,510.4	80.5	Ecuador	8,485.0	63.2
Colombia...........	29,762.7	64.3	Israel.............	8,403.8	122.7
Taiwan, China......	23,249.3	102.0			
Algeria............	20,998.0	63.0	**World**	**2,661,075.2**	**40.8**

U.S. Wireless Industry, 1985-2006[1]

Source: The CTIA Semi-Annual Industry Survey, used with permission of CTIA.

Date	Est. Total Subscribers	Twelve-Month Total Service Revenues (in $000s)	Cell Phone Antennas	Avg. Local Monthly Bill	Avg. Local Call Length (min.)
1985	340,213	$482,428	913	NA	NA
1986	681,825	$823,052	1,531	NA	NA
1987	1,230,855	$1,151,519	2,305	$96.83	2.33
1988	2,069,441	$1,959,548	3,209	$98.02	2.26
1989	3,508,944	$3,340,595	4,169	$89.30	2.48
1990	5,283,055	$4,548,820	5,616	$80.90	2.20
1991	7,557,148	$5,708,522	7,847	$72.74	2.38
1992	11,032,753	$7,822,726	10,307	$68.68	2.58
1993	16,009,461	$10,892,175	12,824	$61.49	2.41
1994	24,134,421	$14,229,922	17,920	$56.21	2.24
1995	33,785,661	$19,081,239	22,663	$51.00	2.15
1996	44,042,992	$23,634,971	30,045	$47.70	2.32
1997	55,312,293	$27,485,633	51,600	$42.78	2.31
1998	69,209,321	$33,133,175	65,887	$39.43	2.39
1999	86,047,003	$40,018,489	81,698	$41.24	2.38
2000	109,478,031	$52,466,020	104,288	$45.27	2.56
2001	128,374,512	$65,316,235	127,540	$47.37	2.74
2002	140,766,842	$76,508,187	139,338	$48.40	2.73
2003	158,721,981	$87,624,093	162,986	$49.91	3.07
2004	182,140,362	$102,121,210	175,725	$50.64	3.05
2005	207,896,198	$113,538,221	183,689	$49.98	3.00
2006	233,040,781	$125,456,825	195,613	$50.56	3.03

(1) In December

U.S. Sales and Household Penetration, Selected Products[1], 1985-2006

Source: Consumer Electronics Association

	1985		1990		1995		2000		2005		2006 (est.)	
	Sales[2]	% of all house-holds	Sales[2]	% of all house-holds	Sales[2]	% of all house-holds	Sales[2]	% of all house-holds	Sales[2]	% of all house-holds	Sales[2]	% of all house-holds
Cordless telephones	$280	11	$842	28	$1,141	55	$1,307	80	$943	88	$778	88
Pagers	—	—	118	1	300	11	750	23	525	11	400	7
Modems/Fax modems	10	0	191	2.7	770	16	1,564	55	1,525	70	1,455	75
Telephone answering devices	325	7	827	35	1,077	57	984	75	1,279	76	1,085	74
Cellular phones	116	0.1	1,098	5	2,574	29	8,995	60	14,265	—	17,934	—

(1) Data may differ slightly from other sources. (2) In millions of dollars.

Telephone Area Codes, by Number

As of 2007. For area codes listed by place, see pages 605-638.

Area Code	Location or Service	Area Code	Location or Service	Area Code	Location or Service	Area Code	Location or Service
201	New Jersey	403	Alberta	613	Ontario	809	Dominican Republic
202	District of Columbia	404	Georgia	614	Ohio	810	Michigan
203	Connecticut	405	Oklahoma	615	Tennessee	811	*Pipeline excavation damage prevention*
204	Manitoba	406	Montana	616	Michigan		
205	Alabama	407	Florida	617	Massachusetts	812	Indiana
206	Washington	408	California	618	Illinois	813	Florida
207	Maine	409	Texas	619	California	814	Pennsylvania
208	Idaho	410	Maryland	620	Kansas	815	Illinois
209	California	411	*Directory Assistance*	623	Arizona	816	Missouri
210	Texas	412	Pennsylvania	626	California	817	Texas
211	*Community Info.*	413	Massachusetts	630	Illinois	818	California
212	New York	414	Wisconsin	631	New York	819	Quebec
213	California	415	California	636	Missouri	828	North Carolina
214	Texas	416	Ontario	641	Iowa	829	Dominican Republic
215	Pennsylvania	417	Missouri	646	New York	830	Texas
216	Ohio	418	Quebec	647	Ontario	831	California
217	Illinois	419	Ohio	649	Turks & Caicos Isl.	832	Texas
218	Minnesota	423	Tennessee	650	California	843	South Carolina
219	Indiana	424	California	651	Minnesota	845	New York
224	Illinois	425	Washington	660	Missouri	847	Illinois
225	Louisiana	430	Texas	661	California	848	New Jersey
226	Ontario	432	Texas	662	Mississippi	850	Florida
228	Mississippi	434	Virginia	664	Montserrat	856	New Jersey
229	Georgia	435	Utah	670	N. Mariana Islands	857	Massachusetts
231	Michigan	438	Quebec	671	Guam	858	California
234	Ohio	440	Ohio	678	Georgia	859	Kentucky
239	Florida	441	Bermuda	682	Texas	860	Connecticut
240	Maryland	443	Maryland	684	American Samoa	862	New Jersey
242	Bahamas	450	Quebec	700	*IC Services*	863	Florida
246	Barbados	456	Inbound Intl.	701	North Dakota	864	South Carolina
248	Michigan	469	Texas	702	Nevada	865	Tennessee
250	British Columbia	473	Grenada	703	Virginia	866	*Toll-Free Service*
251	Alabama	478	Georgia	704	North Carolina	867	Yukon, NW Terr., Nunavut
252	North Carolina	479	Arkansas	705	Ontario	868	Trinidad & Tobago
253	Washington	480	Arizona	706	Georgia	869	St. Kitts & Nevis
254	Texas	484	Pennsylvania	707	California	870	Arkansas
256	Alabama	500	*Personal Comm. Serv.*	708	Illinois	876	Jamaica
260	Indiana	501	Arkansas	709	Newfoundland	877	*Toll-Free Service*
262	Wisconsin	502	Kentucky	710	U.S. Government	878	Pennsylvania
264	Anguilla	503	Oregon	711	*Telecommunications Relay Service (TRS)*	880	*Paid Toll-Free Serv.*
267	Pennsylvania	504	Louisiana			881	*Paid Toll-Free Serv.*
268	Antigua/Barbuda	505	New Mexico	712	Iowa	882	*Paid Toll-Free Serv.*
269	Michigan	506	New Brunswick	713	Texas	888	*Toll-Free Service*
270	Kentucky	507	Minnesota	714	California	900	*Premium Service*
276	Virginia	508	Massachusetts	715	Wisconsin	901	Tennessee
281	Texas	509	Washington	716	New York	902	Nova Scotia, Prince Ed. Isl.
284	British Virgin Islands	510	California	717	Pennsylvania	903	Texas
289	Ontario	511	*Traffic Info.*	718	New York	904	Florida
301	Maryland	512	Texas	719	Colorado	905	Ontario
302	Delaware	513	Ohio	720	Colorado	906	Michigan
303	Colorado	514	Quebec	724	Pennsylvania	907	Alaska
304	West Virginia	515	Iowa	727	Florida	908	New Jersey
305	Florida	516	New York	731	Tennessee	909	California
306	Saskatchewan	517	Michigan	732	New Jersey	910	North Carolina
307	Wyoming	518	New York	734	Michigan	911	*Emergency*
308	Nebraska	519	Ontario	740	Ohio	912	Georgia
309	Illinois	520	Arizona	754	Florida	913	Kansas
310	California	530	California	757	Virginia	914	New York
311	*Non-Emergency Access*	540	Virginia	758	St. Lucia	915	Texas
312	Illinois	541	Oregon	760	California	916	California
313	Michigan	551	New Jersey	762	Georgia	917	New York
314	Missouri	559	California	763	Minnesota	918	Oklahoma
315	New York	561	Florida	765	Indiana	919	North Carolina
316	Kansas	562	California	767	Dominica	920	Wisconsin
317	Indiana	563	Iowa	769	Mississippi	925	California
318	Louisiana	567	Ohio	770	Georgia	928	Arizona
319	Iowa	570	Pennsylvania	772	Florida	931	Tennessee
320	Minnesota	571	Virginia	773	Illinois	936	Texas
321	Florida	573	Missouri	774	Massachusetts	937	Ohio
323	California	574	Indiana	775	Nevada	939	Puerto Rico
325	Texas	575	New Mexico	778	British Columbia	940	Texas
330	Ohio	580	Oklahoma	779	Illinois	941	Florida
331	Illinois	585	New York	780	Alberta	947	Michigan
334	Alabama	586	Michigan	781	Massachusetts	949	California
336	North Carolina	600	*(Canadian Services)*	784	St. Vincent & Gren.	951	California
337	Louisiana	601	Mississippi	785	Kansas	952	Minnesota
339	Massachusetts	602	Arizona	786	Florida	954	Florida
340	U.S. Virgin Islands	603	New Hampshire	787	Puerto Rico	956	Texas
345	Cayman Islands	604	British Columbia	800	*Toll-Free Service*	970	Colorado
347	New York	605	South Dakota	801	Utah	971	Oregon
351	Massachusetts	606	Kentucky	802	Vermont	972	Texas
352	Florida	607	New York	803	South Carolina	973	New Jersey
360	Washington	608	Wisconsin	804	Virginia	978	Massachusetts
361	Texas	609	New Jersey	805	California	979	Texas
386	Florida	610	Pennsylvania	806	Texas	980	North Carolina
401	Rhode Island	611	*Repair Service*	807	Ontario	985	Louisiana
402	Nebraska	612	Minnesota	808	Hawaii	989	Michigan

CONSUMER INFORMATION

Business Directory

Listed below are major corporations offering products and services to U.S. consumers. Information as of Sept. 2007. Alphabetization is by first key word. Listings generally include examples of products offered.

Company Name (NYSE/NASDAQ symbol): Address; Telephone Number; Website; Top Executive; Business, Products, or Services.

A&P: *see* Great Atlantic & Pacific Tea Co.

Abbott Laboratories (ABT): 100 Abbott Park Rd., Abbott Park, IL 60064; (847) 937-6100; www.abbott.com; Miles D. White; develops and manuf. pharmaceutical, nutritional, and hospital prods.

Advance Publications, Inc.: 950 Fingerboard Rd., Staten Island, NY, 10305; (212) 286-2860; www.advance.net; Samuel I. Newhouse Jr.; newspaper and magazine (*Parade, New Yorker, Vanity Fair, Vogue*) publisher.

Aetna, Inc. (AET): 151 Farmington Ave., Hartford, CT 06156; (860) 273-0123; www.aetna.com; Ronald A. Williams; health insurance, financial services.

AFLAC, Inc. (AFL): 1932 Wynnton Rd., Columbus, GA 31999; (706) 323-3431; www.aflac.com; Daniel P. Amos; supplemental health and life insurance.

Alaska Air Group (ALK): 19300 International Blvd., Seattle, WA 98188; (206) 392-5040; www.alaskaair.com; William S. Ayer; air travel (Alaska Air, Horizon Air).

Alberto-Culver (ACV): 2525 Armitage Ave., Melrose Park, IL 60160; (708) 450-3000; www.alberto.com; Carol Lavin Bernick; hair care (Nexxus, VO5), consumer prods. (Mrs. Dash, Sugar Twin), personal care prods. (St. Ives).

Alcatel-Lucent (ALU): 54, rue La Boétie, 75008 Paris, France; +33-1-40-76-10-10; www.alcatel-lucent.com; Patricia F. Russo; telecommunications equip.; wireless networks. France-based Alcatel acquired Lucent Technologies, 11/30/06.

Albertsons LLC: 250 Parkcenter Blvd., Boise, ID 83706; (208) 395-6200; www.albertsons.com; Robert Miller; supermarkets.

Alcoa Inc. (AA): 390 Park Ave., NY, NY 10022; (212) 553-4545; www.alcoa.com; Alain J.P. Belda; aluminum products; aerospace & automotive components; industrial materials/ tools.

Allegheny Technologies, Inc. (ATI): 1000 Six PPG Place, Pittsburgh, PA 15222; (412) 394-2800; www.allegheny techologies.com; L. Patrick Hassey; metals (steel, titanium, alloys) mfgr.

Allied Waste Industries (AW): 18500 N. Allied Way, Phoenix, AZ 85054; (480) 627-2700; www.alliedwaste.com; John J. Zillmer; 2nd-largest U.S. waste management co.

Allstate Corp. (ALL): 2775 Sanders Rd., Northbrook, IL 60062; (847) 402-5000; www.allstate.com; Edward M. Liddy; property/casualty, life insurance; financial services.

Altria Group, Inc. (MO): 120 Park Ave., NY, NY 10017; (917) 663-4000; www.altria.com. Louis C. Camilleri; largest U.S. tobacco company (Marlboro, Merit, Parliament, Virginia Slims). Philip Morris Companies, Inc., changed its name to Altria, 1/27/03. Altria spun off its Kraft Foods division, 3/16/07.

Amazon.com, Inc. (AMZN): 1200 12th Ave. S., Suite 1200, Seattle, WA 98144; (206) 266-1000; www.amazon.com; Jeff Bezos; online retailer of books, music, electronics, photo, and home and garden products.

American Electric Power Co., Inc. (AEP): 1 Riverside Plaza, Columbus, OH 43215; (614) 716-1000; www.aep.com; Michael G. Morris; utilities.

American Express Co. (AXP): 200 Vesey St., NY, NY 10285; (212) 640-2000; www.americanexpress.com; Kenneth I. Chenault; credit cards, travel and financial services.

American Greetings Corp. (AM): 1 American Rd., Cleveland, OH 44144; (216) 252-7300; www.americangreetings.com; Morry Weiss; greeting cards, stationery, party goods, gift items.

American Intl. Group (AIG): 70 Pine St., NY, NY 10270; (212) 770-7000; www.aig.com; Bob Willumstad; insurance, financial services.

American Standard (ASD): One Centennial Ave., Piscataway, NJ 08855; (732) 980-6000; www.americanstandard.com; Frederic M. Poses; plumbing fixtures, air conditioning systems, vehicle control systems.

AMR Corp. (AMR): 4333 Amon Carter Blvd., Ft. Worth, TX 76155; (817) 963-1234; www.aa.com; Gerard J. Arpey; world's largest air carrier (American Airlines, American Eagle); acquired assets of Trans World Air Lines Inc. in 2001.

Anheuser-Busch Cos., Inc. (BUD): 1 Busch Pl., St. Louis, MO 63118; (314) 577-2000; www.anheuser-busch.com; Patrick T. Stokes; world's largest brewer (Budweiser, Michelob, Busch, O'Doul's), aluminum can manuf. and recycling, theme parks.

AOL Time Warner Inc.: *see* Time Warner, Inc.

Apple Inc. (AAPL): 1 Infinite Loop, Cupertino, CA 95014; (408) 996-1010; www.apple.com; Steve Jobs; manuf. of computers (Mac), software, digital media players (iPod, iPhone); distrib. digital media (iTunes store).

Aramark Corp. (RMK): Aramark Tower, 1101 Market St., Philadelphia, PA 19107; (215) 238-3000; www.aramark.com; Joseph Neubauer; food and support services, uniforms and career apparel, child care and early education.

Archer Daniels Midland Co. (ADM): 4666 Faries Pkwy., Decatur, IL 62525; (217) 424-5200; www.admworld.com; Patricia A. Woertz; agricultural commodities and prods.

Armstrong World Industries, Inc. (AWI): 2500 Columbia Ave., Lancaster, PA 17603; (717) 397-0611; www.armstrong.com; Michael D. Lockhart; carpeting, flooring, interior furnishings, specialty prods.; emerged from Chapt. 11, 10/2/06.

ArvinMeritor Inc. (ARM): 2135 W. Maple Road, Troy, MI 48084; (248) 435-1000; www.arvinmeritor.com; Charles G. McClure Jr.; auto control systems; vehicle components.

Ashland Inc. (ASH): 50 E. RiverCenter Blvd., Covington, KY 41012; (859) 815-3333; www.ashland.com; James J. O'Brien Jr.; petroleum producer and refiner (Valvoline, plastics), chemicals, road construction.

AT&T Inc. (T): 175 E. Houston, San Antonio, TX 78205; (210) 821-4105; www.att.com; Randall L. Stephenson.; telecommunications, global information management. Created by merger of SBC Communications and AT&T Corp., finalized 11/19/05; completed acquisition of BellSouth, 12/29/06.

AutoNation (AN): 110 SE 6th St., Ft. Lauderdale, FL 33301; (954) 769-6000; www.autonation.com; Michael J. Jackson; new and used auto vehicles; auto parts, maintenance, and repair; auto protection products.

Avon Products, Inc. (AVP): 1345 Ave. of Americas, NY, NY 10105; (212) 282-5000; www.avon.com; Andrea Jung; cosmetics, fragrances, toiletries, jewelry, apparel.

Bank of America Corp. (BAC): Bank of America Corporate Center, 100 N. Tryon St., Charlotte, NC 28255; (704) 386-5681; www.bankofamerica.com; Kenneth D. Lewis; 2nd-largest U.S. bank; acquired FleetBoston, 4/1/2004; acquired credit card co. MBNA, 1/1/06.

Barnes & Noble, Inc. (BKS): 122 Fifth Ave., NY, NY 10011; (212) 633-3300; www.barnesandnoble.com; Steve Riggio; leading U.S. bookstore chain (Barnes & Noble, B. Dalton stores), publishing (Sterling Pub. Co.).

Bausch & Lomb Inc. (BOL): One Bausch & Lomb Place, Rochester, NY 14604; (585) 338-6000; www.bausch.com; Ronald L. Zarrella; vision and health-care prods., surgical equip. Agreed to merge with Warburg Pincus, 5/16/07.

Baxter International Inc. (BAX): 1 Baxter Pkwy., Deerfield, IL 60015; (847) 948-2000; www.baxter.com; Robert Parkinson Jr.; health care prods. & services.

Bear Stearns Cos. (BSC): 383 Madison Ave., NY, NY 10179; (212) 272-2000; www.bearstearns.com; James E. Cayne; investment banking, securities trading, brokerage.

Becton, Dickinson & Co. (BDX): 1 Becton Dr., Franklin Lakes, NJ 07417; (201) 847-6800; www.bd.com; Edward J. Ludwig; medical, laboratory, diagnostic prods.

BellSouth Corp.: see AT&T Inc.

Berkshire Hathaway Inc. (BRK.A): 1440 Kiewit Plaza, Omaha, NE 68131; (402) 346-1400; www.berkshirehathaway.com; Warren E. Buffett; subsidiaries include GEICO Direct insurance, Johns Manville building materials, Fruit of the Loom apparel, Dairy Queen restaurants/desserts, Benjamin Moore paints, Shaw carpeting.

Bertelsmann AG: Carl-Bertelsmann-Strasse 270, D-33311 Gütersloh, Germany; +49-5241-80-0; www.bertelsmann.de; Gunter Thielen; largest trade book publisher (Random House: Knopf, Ballantine, Bantam, Crown, Doubleday), 2nd-largest music company (Sony BMG).

Best Buy Co., Inc. (BBY): 7601 Penn Ave. S., Richfield, MN 55423; (612) 291-1000; www.bestbuy.com; Bradbury H. Anderson; retailer of software, appliances, consumer electronics, cameras, music, DVDs.

Black & Decker Corp. (BDK): 701 E. Joppa Rd., Towson, MD 21286; (410) 716-3900; www.bdk.com; Nolan D. Archibald; #1 U.S. manuf. of power tools (DeWalt, Black & Decker), household prods. (Kwikset locks, Price Pfister faucets, Black & Decker small appliances).

H&R Block, Inc. (HRB): 1 H&R Block Way., Kansas City, MO 64105; (816) 753-6900; www.hrblock.com; Mark A. Ernst; tax return preparation, software; residential mortgages.

Blockbuster Inc. (BBI): 1201 Elm St., Dallas, TX 75270; (214) 854-3000; www.blockbuster.com; Larry J. Zine; DVD and video game rental.

Boeing Co. (BA): 100 N. Riverside Plaza, Chicago, IL 60606; (312) 544-2000; www.boeing.com; W. James McNerney Jr.; world's 2nd-largest mfgr. of commercial jet aircraft; 2nd-largest U.S. defense contractor.

The Brink's Co. (BCO): 1801 Bayberry Ct., Richmond, VA 23226; (804) 289-9600; www.brinkscompany.com; Michael T. Dan; security (alarm systems, armored cars).

Bristol-Myers Squibb Co. (BMY): 345 Park Ave., NY, NY 10154; (212) 546-4000; www.bms.com; James D. Robinson; drugs (Bufferin, Avapro, Abilify), nutritionals (Enfamil infant formula, Boost energy drink).

Brown-Forman Corp. (BFB): 850 Dixie Hwy., Louisville, KY 40210; (502) 585-1100; www.brown-forman.com; Owsley Brown II; distilled spirits (Jack Daniel's, Southern Comfort), wines (Bolla, Fetzer, Korbel).

Brown Shoe Co., Inc. (BWS): 8300 Maryland Ave., St. Louis, MO 63105; (314) 854-4000; www.brownshoe.com; Ronald A. Fromm; mfgr. and retailer (Famous Footwear) of women's, men's, and children's shoes (Buster Brown, Naturalizer, Dr. Scholl's).

Brunswick Corp. (BC): 1 N. Field Ct., Lake Forest, IL 60045; (847) 735-4700; www.brunswick.com; Dustan McCoy; largest U.S. maker of leisure and recreation prods., incl. marine, camping, billiards, fitness, and fishing equip.; bowling centers and equip.

Burger King Holdings, Inc. (BKC): 5505 Blue Lagoon Dr., Miami, FL 33126; (305) 378-3000; www.burgerking.com; Brian Thomas Swette; fast-food restaurants.

Burlington Northern Santa Fe Inc. (BNI): 2650 Lou Menk Dr., Ft. Worth, TX 76131; (800) 795-2673; www.bnsf.com; Matthew K. Rose; 2nd-largest U.S. rail transportation co.

Cablevision Systems Corp. (CVC): 1111 Stewart Ave., Bethpage, NY 11714; (516) 803-2300; www.cablevision.com; James L. Dolan; cable & VoIP provider; cable channels (AMC, Fuse, IFC, WE); sports teams (NY Knicks, NY Rangers); arenas.

Cadbury Schweppes plc (CSG): 25 Berkeley Sq., London, W1J 6HB, UK; +44 20 7409 1313; www.cadburyschweppes.com; Sir John M. Sunderland; world's 3rd-largest beverage producer (A&W, Canada Dry, Dr. Pepper); candies, gum.

Campbell Soup Co. (CPB): One Campbell Pl., Camden, NJ 08103; (856) 342-4800; www.campbellsoup.com; Douglas R. Conant; soups, sauces (Pace, Prego), V8 juice, Pepperidge Farm baked goods.

Caterpillar Inc. (CAT): 100 NE Adams St., Peoria, IL 61629; (309) 675-1000; www.cat.com; James W. Owens; world's largest producer of earth moving equip.

CBS Corp. (CBS): 51 W. 52nd St., NY, NY 10019; www.cbscorporation.com; Summer Redstone; TV stations, networks (CBS, Showtime); distrib. TV shows (Paramount, King World); radio stations; book publishing (Simon & Schuster). Split from parent co. Viacom, 1/1/06.

Chevron Corp. (CVX): 6001 Bollinger Canyon Rd., San Ramon, CA 94583; (925) 842-1000; www.chevron.com; David J. O'Reilly; 2nd-largest U.S.-based oil co; acquired Unocal, 8/10/05.

Chiquita Brands International, Inc. (CQB): 250 E. 5th St., Cincinnati, OH 45202; (513) 784-8000; www.chiquita.com; Fernando Aguirre; bananas; other fruits and vegetables.

Church & Dwight Co., Inc. (CHD): 469 N. Harrison St., Princeton, NJ 08543; (609) 683-5900; www.churchdwight.com; James R. Craigie; world's largest producer of sodium bicarbonate (Arm & Hammer baking soda); household products (Brillo, SpinBrush); personal care products (Arrid antiperspirant, Trojan condoms, First Response pregnancy tests).

CIGNA Corp. (CI): 2 Liberty Pl., Philadelphia, PA 19192; (215) 761-1000; www.cigna.com; H. Edward Hanway; accident, health, life insurance provider.

Cintas Corp. (CTAS): 6800 Cintas Blvd., Cincinnati, OH 45262; (513) 459-1200; www.cintas.com; Scott D. Farmer; largest U.S. uniform supplier; laundry services.

Circuit City Stores, Inc. (CC): 9950 Mayland Dr., Richmond, VA 23233; (804) 486-4000; www.circuitcity.com; Philip J. Schoonover; retailer of electronics, audio/video equip., consumer appliances.

Cisco Systems (CSCO): 170 West Tasman Dr., Bldg. 10, San Jose, CA 95134; (408) 526-4000; www.cisco.com; John Chambers; networking and communication products.

Citigroup (C): 399 Park Ave., NY, NY 10043; (212) 559-1000; www.citigroup.com; Charles O. Prince III; diversified financial services.

Clear Channel Communications, Inc. (CCU): 200 E. Basse Rd., San Antonio, TX 78209; (210) 822-2828; www.clearchannel.com; Mark P. Mays; largest radio station owner in U.S. (1,200 stations); outdoor advertising (billboards, mass transit ads); TV stations.

Clorox Co. (CLX): 1221 Broadway, Oakland, CA 94612; (510) 271-7000; www.clorox.com; Donald R. Knauss; retail consumer prods. (Clorox, Formula 409, Pine-Sol, S.O.S., Soft Scrub cleansers; Armor All, STP, automotive prods.; Scoop Away, Fresh Step cat litters; Kingsford charcoal; Hidden Valley dressing; Glad plastic bags; Brita water systems)

Coca-Cola Co. (KO): 1 Coca-Cola Plaza, Atlanta, GA 30313; (404) 676-2121; www.cocacola.com; E. Neville Isdell; world's largest soft drink co. (Coca-Cola, Sprite, Dasani water, POWERade), world's largest dist. of juice prods. (Minute Maid).

Colgate-Palmolive Co. (CL): 300 Park Ave., NY, NY 10022; (212) 310-2000; www.colgate.com; Reuben Mark; soap (Palmolive, Irish Spring), detergent (Ajax), toothpaste (Colgate, Tom's of Maine), pet food (Hill's Science Diet).

Collective Brands, Inc. (PSS): 3231 SE 6th Ave., Topeka, KS 66607; (785) 233-5171; www.paylessshoesource.com; Matthew E. Rubel; shoe mfgr./retailer. Formed by merger of StrideRite and Payless Shoe Source, 8/17/07.

Comcast Corp.: 1500 Market St., Philadelphia, PA 19102; 215-665-1700; www.comcast.com; Brian L. Roberts; largest U.S. cable company; broadband cable, internet, and voice services. Some programming, incl. E!, Golf Channel, et al.

Compaq Computer Corp.: *see* Hewlett-Packard Co.

CompUSA Inc.: 14951 N. Dallas Pkwy., Dallas, TX 75254; (972) 982-4000; www.compusa.com; Carlos Slim Domit; retailer of computers and peripherals.

Computer Sciences Corp. (CSC): 2100 E. Grand Ave., El Segundo, CA 90245; (310) 615-0311; www.csc.com; Van B. Honeycutt; technology services.

ConAgra Foods, Inc. (CAG): 1 ConAgra Dr., Omaha, NE 68102; (402) 595-4000; www.conagra.com; Gary M. Rodkin; 2nd-largest U.S. food processor (Chef Boyardee, Healthy Choice frozen dinners, Egg Beaters, Reddi-Wip); food service supplier.

ConocoPhillips Co. (COP): 600 N. Dairy Ashford Rd., P.O. Box 2197, Houston, TX 77079; (281) 293-1000; www.conocophillips.com; James J. Mulva; 3rd-largest U.S. oil and gas company. Formed by merger of Conoco and Phillips Petroleum, 8/30/02.

Consolidated Edison (ED): 4 Irving Pl., NY, NY 10003; (212) 460-4600; www.conedison.com; Kevin Burke; electric utility.

Continental Airlines, Inc. (CAL): 1600 Smith St., Dept. HQSEO, Houston, TX 77002; (713) 324-2950; www.continental.com; Larry Kellner; air transportation.

Corning Inc. (GLW): 1 Riverfront Plaza, Corning, NY 14831; (607) 974-9000; www.corning.com; Wendell P. Weeks; telecommunications, specialty equipment, fiber optics.

Costco Wholesale Corp. (COST): 999 Lake Dr., Issaquah, WA 98027; (425) 313-8100; www.costco.com; James D. Sinegal; wholesale warehouse stores.

Crane Co. (CR): 100 First Stamford Place, Stamford, CT 06902; (203) 363-7300; www.craneco.com; Eric C. Fast; manuf. fluid control devices, vending machines, aircraft components.

A. T. Cross Co. (ATX): 1 Albion Rd., Lincoln, RI 02865; (401) 333-1200; www.cross.com; David Whalen; writing instruments.

Crown Holdings, Inc. (CCK): 1 Crown Way, Philadelphia, PA 19154; (215) 698-5100; www.crowncork.com; John W. Conway; leading producer of packaging prods.

CSX Corp. (CSX): 500 Water St., 15th Fl., Jacksonville, FL 32202; (904) 359-3200; www.csx.com; Michael J. Ward; rail and road freight transport.

CVS/Caremark Corp. (CVS): 1 CVS Dr., Woonsocket, RI 02895; (401) 765-1500; www.cvs.com; Thomas M. Ryan; acquired Eckerd Corp. in August 2004, to become nation's largest drugstore chain; prescription benefits mgmt.

Dana Corp.: 4500 Dorr St., Toledo, OH 43615; (419) 535-4500; www.dana.com; Michael Burns; truck and auto parts, supplies; began Chapt. 11 reorganization, 3/3/06.

Darden Restaurants, Inc. (DRI): 5900 Lake Ellenor Dr., Orlando, FL 32809; (407) 245-4000; www.dardenrestaurants.com; Clarence Otis Jr.; casual-dining restaurants (Red Lobster, Olive Garden, Bahama Breeze).

Dean Foods Co. (DF): 2515 McKinney Ave., Ste. 1200, Dallas, TX 75201; (214) 303-3400; www.deanfoods.com; Gregg L. Engles; milk and specialty dairy products (Land O'Lakes, Horizon Organic, Silk soymilk), salad dressings (Marie's), pickles.

Deere & Co. (DE): One John Deere Pl., Moline, IL 61265; (309) 765-8000; www.deere.com; Robert W. Lane; world's largest manuf. of farm equip.; also makes industrial equip., and lawn and garden tractors.

Dell Inc. (DELL): 1 Dell Way, Round Rock, TX 78682; (512) 338-4400; www.dell.com; Michael S. Dell; laptop and desktop computers, network accessories, peripherals.

Del Monte Foods Co. (DLM): One Market @ The Landmark, San Francisco, CA 94105; (415) 247-3000; www.delmonte. com; Richard G. Wolford; canned food (College Inn, Del Monte, StarKist); pet food (9Lives, Gravy Train, Milk-Bone, Meow Mix).

Delphi Corp.: 5725 Delphi Dr., Troy, MI 48098; (248) 813-2000; www.delphi.com; Robert S. Miller Jr.; automotive systems, audio systems, mobile electronics; began Chapt. 11 reorganization, 10/8/05.

Delta Air Lines, Inc.: 1030 Delta Blvd., Atlanta, GA 30320; (404) 715-2600; www.delta.com; Gerald Grinstein; air transportation; emerged from Chapt. 11, 4/30/07.

Dial Corp.: 15501 N. Dial Blvd., Scottsdale, AZ 85260; (480) 754-3425; www.dialcorp.com; Bradley A. Casper; consumer prods. (Dial soap, Purex detergent, Renuzit air fresheners); U.S. subsidiary of Germany's Henkel company.

Diebold, Inc. (DBD): 5995 Mayfair Rd., North Canton, OH 44720; (330) 490-4000; www.diebold.com; Thomas W. Swidarski; manuf. ATMs, security systems and prods.

Dillard's, Inc. (DDS): 1600 Cantrell Rd., Little Rock, AR 72201; (501) 376-5200; www.dillards.com; William Dillard II; 2nd-largest dept. store chain in U.S.

The Walt Disney Co. (DIS): 500 S. Buena Vista St., Burbank, CA 91521; (818) 560-1000; www.disney.com; Robert A. Iger; motion pictures (Touchstone, Pixar, Miramax); television (ESPN, ABC, Disney Channel); radio stations; theme parks (Walt Disney World, Disneyland); resorts; publishing; recordings.

Doctor's Associates Inc.: 325 Bic Dr., Milford, CT 06460; (203) 877-4281; www.subway.com; Frederick A. DeLuca; restaurants (Subway).

Dole Food Co., Inc.: One Dole Drive, Westlake Village, CA 91362; (818) 879-6600; www.dole.com; David H. Murdock; food prods., fresh fruits and vegetables.

R. R. Donnelley & Sons Co. (RRD): 111 S. Wacker Dr., Chicago, IL 60606; (312) 326-8000; www.rrdonnelley.com; Thomas J. Quinian III; commercial printing; photos/graphics, translation; printer of *The World Almanac.*

Dow Chemical Co. (DOW): 2030 Dow Center, Midland, MI 48674; (989) 636-1463; www.dow.com; Andrew N. Liveris; chemicals, plastics (world's 2nd-largest chemical co.).

Dow Jones & Co., Inc. (DJ): 200 Liberty St., NY, NY 10281; (212) 416-2000; www.dj.com; Richard F. Zannino; financial news service, publishing (*Wall Street Journal, Barron's,* Ottaway Newspapers). Agreed to merge with News Corp., 8/1/07.

Duke Energy Corp. (DUK): 526 S. Church St., Charlotte, NC 28202; (704) 594-6200; www.duke-energy.com; James E. Rogers; utilities, fiber optics.

Dun & Bradstreet Corp. (DNB): 103 JFK Parkway, Short Hills, NJ 07078; (973) 921-5500; www.dnb.com; Steven Alesio; business information, supplies, research.

Duracell: *see* Gillette.

E. I. du Pont de Nemours & Co. (Dupont) (DD): 1007 Market St., Wilmington, DE 19898; (302) 774-1000; www.dupont. com; Charles Holliday Jr.; 3rd-largest U.S. chemical co.; petroleum, consumer prods.

Eastman Kodak Co. (EK): 343 State St., Rochester, NY 14650; (800) 698-3324; www.kodak.com; Antonio Perez; film; digital cameras; printers.

Eaton Corp. (ETN): 1111 Superior Ave., Cleveland, OH 44114; (216) 523-5000; www.eaton.com; Alexander Cutler; manuf. of vehicle components, controls.

eBay Inc. (EBAY): 2145 Hamilton Ave., San Jose, CA 95125; (408) 376-7400; www.ebay.com; Meg C. Whitman; online auctions.

Eckerd Corp.: *see* CVS Corp.

Edison Intl. (EIX): 2244 Walnut Grove Ave., Rosemead, CA 91770; (626) 302-2222; www.edison.com; John Bryson; electric utilities.

Electronic Arts Inc. (ERTS): 209 Redwood Shores Pkwy., Redwood City, CA 94065; (650) 628-1500; www.ea.com; Larry Probst III; leading U.S. video game publisher (*Madden NFL, The Sims*).

Electronic Data Systems (EDS): 5400 Legacy Dr., Plano, TX 75024; (972) 604-6000; www.eds.com; Michael H. Jordan; systems management and services; software.

Eli Lilly and Co. (LLY): Lilly Corporate Center, Indianapolis, IN 46285; 317-276-2000; www.lilly.com; Sidney Taurel; pharmaceutical research, development, and manufacturing (Prozac, Stratera, Cialis).

El Paso Corp. (EP): 1001 Louisiana Street, Houston, TX 77002; (713) 420-2600; www.elpaso.com; Ronald L. Kuehn Jr.; natural gas/oil transportation, storage, exploration, production.

EMC Corp. (EMC): 176 South St., Hopkinton, MA 01748; (877) 362-6973; www.emc.com; Joseph M. Tucci; data storage and protection.

Emerson Electric Co. (EMR): 8000 W. Florissant Avenue, St. Louis, MO 63136; (314) 553-2000; www.gotoemerson.com; David Farr; electrical, electronics prods. & systems.

Energizer Holdings Inc. (ENR): 533 Maryville Univ. Dr., St. Louis, MO 63141; (314) 985-2000; www.energizer.com; Ward M. Klein; batteries, flashlights, razors (Schick).

Estée Lauder Cos. Inc. (EL): 767 5th Ave., NY, NY 10153; (212) 572-4200; www.elcompanies.com; William P. Lauder; cosmetics (Clinique, Bobbi Brown), fragrance prods.

Exelon Corp. (EXC): 10 S. Dearborn St., 37th Fl., Chicago, IL 60680; (312) 394-7398; www.exeloncorp.com; John W. Rowe; electricity generation and distribution; nat. gas.

Exxon Mobil Corp. (XOM): 5959 Las Colinas Blvd., Irving, TX 75039; (972) 444-1000; www.exxon.mobil.com; Rex W. Tillerson; world's largest integrated oil co.

Fannie Mae (FNM): 3900 Wisconsin Ave. NW, Washington, DC 20016; (202) 752-7000; www.fanniemae.com; Daniel H. Mudd; largest U.S. provider of residential mortgage funds.

Fedders Corp.: 505 Martinsville Road, Liberty Corner, NJ 07938; (908) 604-8686; www.fedders.com; Salvatore Giordano Jr.; manuf. air conditioners (Fedders, Airtemp), dehumidifiers.

Federated Department Stores: *see* Macy's.

FedEx Corp. (FDX): 942 S. Shady Grove Rd., Memphis, TN 38120; (901) 818-7500; www.fedex.com; Frederick W. Smith; world's largest express delivery service.

First Data Corp. (FDC): 6200 S. Quebec St., Greenwood Village, CO, 80111; (303) 967-8000; www.firstdatacorp.com; Henry C. Duques; financial transaction processing.

FirstEnergy Corp. (FE): 76 S. Main St., Akron, OH 44308; (800) 633-4766; www.firstenergycorp.com; Anthony J. Alexander; public electricity and natural gas utility.

Fleetwood Enterprises, Inc. (FLE): 3125 Myers St., Riverside, CA 92503; (951) 351-3500; www.fleetwood.com; Elden L. Smith; manufactured homes, recreational vehicles.

Fluor Corp. (FLR): 6700 Las Colinas Blvd., Irving, TX 75039; (469) 398-7000; www.fluor.com; Alan L. Boeckmann; international engineering and construction co.

Foot Locker, Inc. (FL): 112 West 34th St., NY, NY 10120; (212) 720-3700; www.footlocker-inc.com; Matthew D. Serra; retail athletic stores: Footaction, Foot Locker, Champs.

Ford Motor Co. (F): 1 American Rd., Dearborn, MI 48126; (313) 322-3000; www.ford.com; William Clay Ford Jr.; 2nd-largest auto manufacturer; motor vehicle sales (Ford, Lincoln, Jaguar, Mercury, Volvo); largest U.S. auto. finance co. (Ford Motor Credit).

Fortune Brands, Inc. (FO): 520 Lake Cook Rd., Deerfield, IL 60015; (847) 484-4400; www.fortunebrands.com; Norman H. Wesley; spirits and wine (Jim Beam, Absolut, Sauza); hardware (Moen); golf and leisure prods. (Titleist, Cobra, FootJoy).

Freddie Mac (Federal Home Loan Mortgage Corp.) (FRE): 8200 Jones Branch Dr., McLean, VA 22102; (703) 903-2000; www.freddiemac.com; Richard F. Syron; residential mortgage provider.

Fruit of the Loom, Inc.: *see* Berkshire Hathaway.

Gannett Co., Inc. (GCI): 7950 Jones Branch Dr., McLean, VA 22107; (703) 854-6000; www.gannett.com; Craig A. Dubow; largest U.S. newspaper publisher (*USA Today*); network and cable TV.

Gap Inc. (GPS): Two Folsom St., San Francisco, CA 94105; (650) 952-4400; www.gap.com; Glenn K. Murphy; casual apparel retailer (Gap, Banana Republic, Old Navy).

Gateway, Inc. (GTW): 7565 Irvine Ctr. Dr., Irvine, CA 92618; (949) 471-7000; www.gateway.com; Richard D. Snyder; personal computers, network servers, peripherals.

General Dynamics (GD): 2941 Fairview Park Dr., Ste. 100, Falls Church, VA 22042; (703) 876-3000; www.gendyn.com; Nicholas D. Chabraja; defense contractor: nuclear submarines, armored vehicles, combat systems, computing devices.

General Electric Co. (GE): 3135 Easton Tpke., Fairfield, CT 06828; (203) 373-2211; www.ge.com; Jeffrey Immelt; electrical, electronic equip., radio and TV broadcasting (NBC, Bravo, USA, Telemundo); aircraft engines, power generation, appliances.

General Mills, Inc. (GIS): One General Mills Blvd., Minneapolis, MN 55426; (763) 764-7600; www.generalmills.com; Stephen W. Sanger; food mfgr. (Betty Crocker, Bisquick, Cheerios, Chex, Hamburger Helper, Pillsbury, Total, Wheaties).

General Motors Corp. (GM): 300 Renaissance Center, Detroit, MI 48265; (313) 556-5000; www.gm.com; G. Richard Wagoner Jr.; world's largest auto manuf. (Chevrolet, Pontiac, Cadillac, Buick, Saab, Saturn); auto financing (GMAC).

Genuine Parts Co. (GPC): 2999 Circle 75 Pkwy., Atlanta, GA 30339; (770) 953-1700; www.genpt.com; Thomas C. Gallagher; auto replacement parts distributor (NAPA).

Georgia-Pacific Corp.: *see* Koch Industries.

Gillette: *see* Proctor & Gamble.

Goldman Sachs Group, Inc. (GS): 85 Broad St., NY, NY 10004; (212) 902-1000; www.goldmansachs.com; Lloyd C. Blankfein; investment banking, asset management, securities services.

Goodyear Tire & Rubber Co. (GT): 1144 E. Market St., Akron, OH 44316; (330) 796-2121; www.goodyear.com; Robert Keegan; world's largest rubber manuf.; tires and other auto prods.

Google, Inc. (GOOG): 1600 Amphitheatre Pkwy., Mountain View, CA 94043; (650) 253-0000; www.google.com; Eric E. Schmidt; leading internet search engine.

W. R. Grace & Co. (GRA): 7500 Grace Dr., Columbia, MD 21044; (410) 531-4000; www.grace.com; Alfred E. Festa; chemicals, construction prods.

Great Atlantic & Pacific Tea Co., Inc. (GAP): 2 Paragon Dr., Montvale, NJ 07645; (201) 573-9700; www.aptea.com; Christian Haub; supermarkets (A&P, Farmer Jack, Super Fresh, Waldbaum's).

Halliburton Co. (HAL): 5 Houston Center, 1401 McKinney, Ste. 2400, Houston, TX 77010; (713) 759-2600; www.halliburton.com; David J. Lesar; oilfield mgmt and other energy services; split off subsidiary KBR, Inc., 4/5/07.

Hanesbrands Inc. (HBI): 1000 E. Hanes Mill Rd., Winston-Salem, NC 27105; (336) 519-4400; www.hanesbrands.com; Brenda Barnes; apparel mfgr. (Hanes, L'eggs, Just My Size, Playtex, Wonderbra). Spun off from fmr. parent co. Sara Lee Corp., 9/5/06.

Harley-Davidson, Inc. (HOG): 3700 W. Juneau Ave., Milwaukee, WI 53208; (414) 342-4680; www.harley-davidson.com; James L. Ziemer; manuf. of motorcycles, parts, and accessories.

Harrah's Entertainment, Inc. (HET): One Caesar's Palace Dr., Las Vegas, NV 89109; (702) 407-6000; www.harrahs.com; Gary W. Loveman; casino-hotels (Bally's, Caesars) and riverboats (Showboat); agreed to be acquired by Apollo Mgmt. and Texas Pacific Group, 4/5/07.

Hartford Financial Services Group, Inc. (HIG): One Hartford Plaza, 690 Asylum Ave., Hartford, CT 06115; (860) 547-5000; www.thehartford.com; Ramani Ayer; insurance, financial services.

Hartmarx (HMX): 101 N. Wacker Dr., Chicago, IL 60606; (312) 372-6300; www.hartmarx.com; Homi B. Patel; apparel manuf. (Hart Schaffner & Marx, Hickey-Freeman, Tommy Hilfiger, Perry Ellis).

Hasbro, Inc. (HAS): 1027 Newport Ave., Pawtucket, RI 02862; (401) 431-8697; www.hasbro.com; Alfred J Verrecchia; toy and game manuf. (Milton Bradley, Playskool, G.I. Joe, Parker Bros., Nerf, Play-Doh).

HCA Inc.: 1 Park Plaza, Nashville, TN 37203; (615) 344-9551; www.hcahealthcare.com; Jack O. Bovender Jr.; largest hospital mgmt. co. in the U.S.

H. J. Heinz Co. (HNZ): 600 Grant St., Pittsburgh, PA 15219; (412) 456-5700; www.heinz.com; William R. Johnson; food mfgr. (Ore-Ida, 57 Varieties ketchup), pet food (Kibbles 'n Bits, 9 Lives), Weight Watchers foods.

Hershey Co. (HSY): 100 Crystal A Dr., Hershey, PA 17033; (717) 534-4200; www.hersheys.com; Richard H. Lenny; largest U.S. producer of chocolate and confectionery prods. (Reese's, Kit Kat, Mounds, Almond Joy, Cadbury, Jolly Rancher, Twizzlers, Milk Duds, Good & Plenty).

Hertz Global Holdings, Inc. (HTZ): 225 Brae Blvd., Park Ridge, NJ 07656; (201) 307-2000; www.hertz.com; Mark P. Frissora; car rentals.

Hess Corp. (HES): 1185 Ave. of the Americas, NY, NY 10036; (212) 997-8500; www.hess.com; John B. Hess; integrated oil co.

Hewlett-Packard Co. (HPQ): 3000 Hanover St., Palo Alto, CA 94304; (650) 857-1501; www.hp.com; Mark V. Hurd; manuf. computers, electronic prods. and systems.

Hillenbrand Industries, Inc. (HB): 700 State Rte. 46 E., Batesville, IN 47006; (812) 934-7000; www.hillenbrand.com; Peter H. Soderberg; manuf. caskets, other memorial prods.; adjustable hospital beds.

Hilton Hotels Corp. (HLT): 9336 Civic Center Dr., Beverly Hills, CA 90210; (310) 278-4321; www.hiltonworldwide.com; Stephen F. Bollenbach; hotels, resorts.

Home Depot, Inc. (HD): 2455 Paces Ferry Rd. NW, Atlanta, GA 30339; (770) 433-8211; www.homedepot.com; Francis S. Blake; 2nd-largest U.S. retailer; home improvement warehouse stores.

Honeywell Intl. Inc. (HON): 101 Columbia Road, Morristown, NJ 07962; (973) 455-2000; www.honeywell.com; David Cote; industrial and home control systems, aerospace guidance systems.

Hormel Foods Corp. (HRL): 1 Hormel Pl., Austin, MN 55912; (507) 437-5611; www.hormel.com; Jeffrey M. Ettinger; meat processor; pork, turkey, and beef prods. (SPAM, Dinty Moore, Jennie-O).

Houghton Mifflin Co.: 222 Berkeley St., Boston, MA 02116; (617) 351-5000; www.hmco.com; Anthony Lucki; publisher of textbooks, reference, general interest books.

Humana, Inc. (HUM): 500 W. Main Street, Louisville, KY 40202; (502) 580-1000; www.humana.com; Michael B. McCallister; managed healthcare service provider, related specialty products.

IAC/InterActive Corp (IACI): 152 W. 57th St., New York, NY 10019; (212) 314-7300; www.iac.com; Barry Diller; media conglomerate (HSN, Ticketmaster, Match.com, LendingTree).

Illinois Tool Works Inc. (ITW): 3600 West Lake Ave., Glenview, IL 60026; (847) 724-7500; www.itw.com; David B. Speer; consumer & industrial tools; food equip. (Hobart), home appliances and cookware (West Bend).

Ingersoll-Rand Co. Ltd. (IR): 155 Chestnut Ridge Road, Montvale, NJ 07645; (201) 573-0123; www.irco.com; Herbert L. Henkel; industrial and construction equip.; locks and security systems (Schlage, Kryptonite).

Intel Corp. (INTC): 2200 Mission College Blvd., Santa Clara, CA 95054; (408) 765-8080; www.intel.com; Paul S. Otellini; manuf. semiconductors, microprocessors (Core, Centrino).

International Business Machines Corp. (IBM): One New Orchard Rd., Armonk, NY 10504; (914) 499-1900; www.ibm.com; Samuel Palmisano; world's largest supplier of advanced information processing technology equip., services.

International Paper Co. (IP): 6400 Poplar Ave., Memphis, TN 38197; (901) 419-7000; www.paper.com; John V. Faraci Jr.; world's largest paper/forest prods. co.; packaging.

Interstate Bakeries Corp.: 12 E. Armour Blvd., Kansas City, MO 64111; (816) 502-4000; www.interstatebakeriescorp.com; Michael D. Kafoure; baked goods wholesaler, distributor (Wonder, Hostess, Dolly Madison, Drake's, Home Pride); began Chapter 11 reorganization, 9/22/04.

J. Crew Group, Inc. (JCG): 770 Broadway, NY, NY 10003; (212) 209-2500; www.jcrew.com; Millard S. Drexler; retail and mail order apparel and accessories.

JetBlue Airways (JBLU): 118-29 Queens Blvd., Forest Hills, NY 11375; (718) 286-7900; www.jetblue.com; David Neeleman; air transportation.

Jo-Ann Stores, Inc. (JAS): 5555 Darrow Rd., Hudson, OH 44236; (330) 656-2600; www.joann.com; Darrell D. Webb; nation's largest specialty fabric and craft stores.

Johnson & Johnson (JNJ): 1 Johnson & Johnson Plaza, New Brunswick, NJ 08933; (732) 524-0400; www.jnj.com; William Weldon; health care prods. (Band-Aid), pharmaceuticals (Tylenol, Motrin), toiletries (Neutrogena); acquired Pfizer's consumer prods. division (Nasoporin, Listerine, Sudafed), 12/20/06.

S.C. Johnson & Son, Inc.: 1525 Howe St., Racine, WI 53403; (262) 260-2000; www.scjohnson.com; H. Fisk Johnson; cleaning and other household prods. (Johnson's Wax, Windex, Pledge, Fantastik, Raid, Off!, Shout, Glade, Scrubbing Bubbles, Ziploc bags).

Johnson Controls, Inc. (JCI): 5757 N. Green Bay Ave., Milwaukee, WI 53209; (414) 524-1200; www.johnsoncontrols.com; John Barth; fire protection services, auto interiors, batteries.

Jones Apparel Group, Inc. (JNY): 250 Rittenhouse Circle, Bristol, PA 19007; (215) 785-4000; www.jny.com; Wesley R. Card; apparel (Jones New York, Gloria Vanderbilt), shoes (Nine West, Anne Klein); luxury (Barney's New York), retail, and outlet stores.

JPMorgan Chase & Co. (JPM): 270 Park Ave., NY, NY 10017; (212) 270-6000; www.jpmorganchase.com; James Dimon; financial services; merged with Bank One Corp., 7/1/04.

KBR, Inc. (KBR): 601 Jefferson St., Ste. 3400, Houston, TX 77002; (713) 753-3011; www.kbr.com; William P. Utt; engineering; construction mgmt. services. Separated from parent company Halliburton, 4/5/07.

Kellogg Co. (K): One Kellogg Sq., Battle Creek, MI 49016; (269) 961-2000; www.kelloggcompany.com; James M. Jenness; world's largest mfgr. of ready-to-eat cereals, other food prods. (Frosted Flakes, Rice Krispies, Froot Loops, Pop-Tarts, Nutri-Grain, Keebler, Eggo).

Kelly Services, Inc.: 999 West Big Beaver Rd., Troy, MI 48084; (248) 362-4444; www.kellyservices.com; Carl T. Camden; temporary staffing services.

Kimberly-Clark Corp. (KMB): 351 Phelps Dr., Irving, TX 75038; (972) 281-1200; www.kimberly-clark.com; Thomas Falk; personal care prods. (Kleenex, Scott, Cottonelle, Huggies, Kotex).

Kmart Corp.: see Sears Holdings.

Knight Ridder: see McClatchy Co.

Koch Industries, Inc.: 4111 E. 37th St. N., Wichita, KS 67220; (316) 828-5500; www.kochind.com; Charles G. Koch; 2nd-largest U.S. forest prod. mfgr.; oil refineries/pipeline/ranching. Acquired Georgia Pacific, 12/23/05.

Kraft Foods, Inc. (KFT): 3 Lakes Dr., Northfield, IL 60093; (847) 646-2000; www.kraft.com; Irene B. Rosenfeld; world's largest cheese brand; Nabisco (world's largest cookie and cracker prod.); other food brands (Jell-O, Oscar Mayer, Tombstone Pizza, Post cereals). Spinoff from Altria completed 3/16/07.

Kroger Co. (KR): 1014 Vine St., Cincinnati, OH 45202; (513) 762-4000; www.kroger.com; David Dillon; largest U.S. retail grocery chain, convenience stores, mall jewelry stores.

La-Z-Boy Inc. (LZB): 1284 N. Telegraph Rd., Monroe, MI 48162; (734) 242-1444; www.lazboy.com; Kurt L. Darrow; reclining chairs, other furniture.

Leggett & Platt, Inc. (LEG): No. 1 Leggett Rd., Carthage, MO 64836; (417) 358-8131; www.leggett.com; David S. Haffner; furniture and furniture components, industrial materials, automotive seating suspension, train and cable control systems.

Lehman Bros. Holdings, Inc. (LEH): 745 7th Ave., NY, NY 10019; (212) 526-7000; www.lehman.com; Richard S. Fuld Jr.; investment bank.

Levi Strauss & Co: 1155 Battery St., San Francisco, CA 94111; (415) 501-6000; www.levistrauss.com; R. John Anderson; blue jeans, casual sportswear (Dockers).

Lexmark Intl., Inc. (LXK): 740 W. New Circle Rd., Lexington, KY 40550; (859) 232-2000; www.lexmark.com; Paul J. Curlander; computer printers and peripherals.

Liberty Mutual Holding Co. Inc.: 175 Berkeley St., Boston, MA 02116; (617) 357-9500; www.libertymutual.com; Edmund F. Kelly; auto, home, and life insurance.

Limited Brands Inc. (LTD): 3 Limited Pkwy., Columbus, OH 43230; (614) 415-7000; www.limitedbrands.com; Leslie H. Wexner; apparel stores (Lane Bryant, Lerner, Limited, Express, Victoria's Secret, Henri Bendel), home decor (White Barn Candle Co.), personal care (Bath & Body Works).

Liz Claiborne, Inc. (LIZ): 1441 Bway., NY, NY 10018; (212) 354-4900; www.lizclaiborne.com; Kay Koplovitz; women's apparel (Ellen Tracy, Kate Spade, Laundry, Crazy Horse, Dana Buchman).

L.L. Bean, Inc.: 3 Campus Dr., Freeport, ME 04033; (207) 552-3028; www.llbean.com; Chris McCormick; catalog and retail outdoor apparel and footwear.

Lockheed Martin Corp. (LMT): 6801 Rockledge Dr., Bethesda, MD 20817; (301) 897-6000; www.lockheedmartin.com; Robert J. Stevens; leading U.S. defense contractor; commercial and military aircraft, electronics, missiles, information tech., and communications.

Loews Corp. (LTR): 667 Madison Ave., NY, NY 10021; (212) 521-2000; www.loews.com; Andrew H. Tisch; tobacco prods. (Kent, True, Newport), watches (Bulova), hotels, insurance (CNA Financial), offshore drilling (Diamond).

Longs Drug Stores Corp. (LDG): 141 N. Civic Dr., Walnut Creek, CA 94596; (925) 937-1170; www.longs.com; Warren Bryant; drug store chain.

Lowe's Cos., Inc. (LOW): 1000 Lowe's Blvd. Mooresville, NC 28117; (704) 758-1000; www.lowes.com; Robert A. Niblock; building material and home improvement superstores.

Lucent Technologies, Inc.: *see* Alcatel-Lucent.

Macy's, Inc. (M): 7 W. 7th St., Cincinnati, OH 45202; (513) 579-7000; www.Federated-fds.com; Terry J. Lundgren; dept. stores (Macy's, Bloomingdale's); acquired May Dept. Stores (Lord & Taylor, Marshall Field's), 2/28/05. Federated Dept. Stores changed its name to Macy's, 6/1/07.

Manpower Inc. (MAN): 5301 N. Ironwood Rd., Milwaukee, WI 53217; (414) 961-1000; www.manpower.com; Jeffrey A. Joerres; 2nd-largest non-govt. employment services co. in the world.

Marathon Oil Corp. (MRO): 5555 San Felipe Rd., Houston, TX 77056; (713) 629-6600; www.marathon.com; Clarence P. Cazalot Jr.; integrated oil co.

Marriott International, Inc. (MAR): 10400 Fernwood Rd., Bethesda, MD 20817; (301) 380-3000; www.marriott.com; J. W. Marriott Jr; hotels (Renaissance, Courtyard, Fairfield, Ritz-Carlton.

Masco Corp. (MAS): 21001 Van Born Rd., Taylor, MI 48180; (313) 274-7400; www.masco.com; Richard A. Manoogian; manuf. kitchen, bathroom prods. (Delta, Peerless faucets; Fieldstone, Merillat cabinets); paints (Behr).

MassMutual Financial Group: 1295 State St., Springfield, MA 01111; (413) 744-1000; www.massmutual.com; James R. Birle; financial planning and investment, life insurance.

Mattel, Inc. (MAT): 333 Continental Blvd., El Segundo, CA 90245; (310) 252-2000; www.mattel.com; Robert A. Eckert; largest U.S. toymaker (Barbie, Fisher-Price, Hot Wheels, Matchbox, American Girls).

MBNA Corp.: *see* Bank of America.

McClatchy Co. (MNI): 2100 Q St., Sacramento, CA 95816; (916) 321-1846; www.mcclatchy.com; Gary B. Pruitt; 3rd-largest newspaper publisher; acquired Knight Ridder papers, 6/27/06.

McDonald's Corp. (MCD): McDonald's Plaza, Oak Brook, IL 60523; (630) 623-3000; www.mcdonalds.com; James A. Skinner; world's largest fast food co.

McGraw-Hill Cos., Inc. (MHP): 1221 Ave. of the Americas, NY, NY 10020; (212) 512-2000; www.mcgraw-hill.com; Harold (Terry) McGraw III; book, textbook, magazine publishing (*Business Week*); information and financial services (Standard & Poor's); TV stations.

McKesson Corp. (MCK): 1 Post St., San Francisco, CA 94104; (415) 983-8300; www.mckesson.com; John Hammergren; distributor of drugs and toiletries; provides mgmt. software and services.

MeadWestvaco Corp. (MWV): 11013 W. Broad St., Glen Allen, VA 23060; (804) 327-5200; www.meadwestvaco.com; John A. Luke Jr., packaging, shipping containers, chemicals.

Medco Health Solutions, Inc. (MHS): 100 Parsons Pond Dr., Franklin Lakes, NJ 07417; (201) 269-3400; www.medco.com; David B. Snow Jr.; pharmacy benefits management.

Medtronic, Inc. (MDT): 710 Medtronic Pkwy. Minneapolis, MN 55432; (763) 514-4000; www.medtronic.com; Arthur D. Collins Jr.; world's largest manuf. of implantable biomedical devices.

Merck & Co., Inc. (MRK): 1 Merck Dr., Whitehouse Station, NJ 08889; (908) 423-1000; www.merck.com; Richard T. Clark; pharmaceuticals (Gardasil, Propecia, Singulair, Vytorin, Zocor).

Meredith Corp. (MDP): 1716 Locust St., Des Moines, IA 50309; (515) 284-3000; www.meredith.com; Steven M. Lacy; magazine publishing (*Better Homes and Gardens, Ladies' Home Journal, Parents, Family Circle*), book publishing, broadcasting.

Merrill Lynch & Co., Inc. (MER): 4 World Financial Ctr., NY, NY 10080; (212) 449-1000; www.merrilllynch.com; E. Stanley O'Neal; securities broker, financial services.

MetLife, Inc. (MET): 200 Park Ave., NY, NY 10166; (212) 578-2211; www.metlife.com; C. Robert Henrikson; insurance, financial services.

MGM MIRAGE (MGM): 3600 Las Vegas Blvd. S., Las Vegas, NV 89109; (702) 693-7111; www.mgmmirage.com; J. Terrence Lanni; hotel-casino operator (Mirage, Treasure Island, Golden Nugget, Monte Carlo); acquired Mandalay Resort Group, 4/25/05.

Microsoft Corp. (MSFT): One Microsoft Way, Redmond, WA 98052; (425) 882-8080; www.microsoft.com; William H. Gates; world's largest independent software maker (Windows, Word, Excel); video game consoles (Xbox).

Miller Brewing Co.: 3939 W. Highland Blvd. Milwaukee, WI 53208; (414) 931-2000; www.millerbrewing.com; Tom Long; 2nd-largest U.S. brewer (Miller, Sharp's); subsidiary of SABMiller plc.

Mittal Steel USA: 1 S. Dearborn St., Chicago, IL 60603; (312) 899-3440; www.mittalsteel.com; Michael G. Rippey; U.S. subsidiary of Netherlands-based Arcelor Mittal, world's largest steel co.

Molson Coors Brewing Co. (TAP): 1225 17th St., Denver CO 80202; (303) 279-6565; www.molsoncoors.com; W. Leo Kiely III; brewer (Coors, Killian's, Molson, Zima). Formed by merger of Adolph Coors and Molson, 2/9/05.

Morgan Stanley (MS): 1585 Broadway, NY, NY 10036; (212) 761-4000; www.morganstanley.com; John J. Mack; diversified financial services.

Motorola, Inc. (MOT): 1303 E. Algonquin Rd., Schaumburg, IL 60196; (847) 576-5000; www.motorola.com; Edward Zander; electronic equipment and components; communication devices.

Nabisco: *see* Altria Group., Inc.

National Semiconductor Corp. (NSM): 2900 Semiconductor Dr., Santa Clara, CA 95052; (408) 721-5000; www.national.com; Brian L. Halla; manuf. semiconductors, integrated circuits.

Nationwide Mutual Insurance Co.: One Nationwide Plaza, Columbus, OH 43215; (800) 882-2822; www.nationwide.com; William G. Jurgensen; life insurance and financial services.

Navistar Intl. Corp.: 4201 Winfield Rd., Warrenville, IL 60555; (630) 753-5000; www.navistar.com; Daniel Ustian; manuf. heavy-duty trucks, parts, school buses.

NCR Corp. (NCR): 1700 S. Patterson Blvd., Dayton, OH 45479; (937) 445-5000; www.ncr.com; William R. Nuti; manuf ATMs, retail technology, hardware and software; computer services and supplies.

Nestlé USA, Inc.: 800 North Brand Blvd., Glendale, CA 91203; (818) 549-6000; www.nestleusa.com; Brad Alford; candy (Baby Ruth, Raisinets), beverages (Nestea, Juicy Juice, Perrier), frozen foods (Stouffer's), pet foods (Purina, Alpo, Friskies). Subsidiary of Nestlé SA in Switzerland, world's largest food co.

Netflix, Inc. (NFLX): 100 Winchester Cir., Los Gatos, CA 95032; (408) 540-3700; www.netflix.com; Reed Hastings; online DVD rentals.

New York Life Insurance Co.: 51 Madison Ave., NY, NY 10010; (212) 576-7000; www.newyorklife.com; Seymour Sternberg; life insurance, annuities, mutual funds.

New York Times Co. (NYT): 620 8th Ave., NY, NY 10018; (212) 556-1234; www.nytco.com; A. O. Sulzberger Jr.; newspapers (New York Times, Boston Globe), radio and TV stations.

Newell Rubbermaid Inc. (NWL): 10 B Glenlake Pkwy, Ste. 300, Atlanta, GA 30328; (770) 407-3800; www.newell rubbermaid.com; Mark D. Ketchum; housewares (Anchor Hocking, Rubbermaid); hair accessories (Goody); writing utensils (Eberhard Faber, Sharpie); childrens' prods. (Little Tikes, Graco).

News Corp. (NWS): 1211 Ave. of the Americas, 8th Fl., NY, NY 10036; (212) 852-7000; www.newscorp.com; K. Rupert Murdoch; newspaper, magazine, book publishing (Harper Collins); TV and CATV stations (FOX, Fox News Channel, FX); film (20th Century Fox, Fox Searchlight); websites (MySpace.com, RottenTomatoes.com). Agreed to acquire Dow Jones, 8/1/07.

NIKE, Inc. (NKE): 1 Bowerman Dr., Beaverton, OR 97005; (503) 671-6453; www.nikebiz.com; Mark G. Parker; world's largest footwear mfgr.

Nordstrom, Inc. (JWN): 1617 6th Ave., Seattle, WA 98101; (206) 628-2111; www.nordstrom.com; Enrique Hernandez Jr.; upscale dept. store chain.

Norfolk Southern Corp. (NSC): Three Commercial Pl., Norfolk, VA 23510; (757) 629-2600; www.nscorp.com; Charles W. Moorman IV; railway operator; freight carrier.

Northrop Grumman Corp (NOC): 1840 Century Park East, Los Angeles, CA 90067; (310) 553-6262; www.northgrum.com; Ronald D. Sugar; world's largest shipbuilder; defense contractor: aircraft, electronics, data systems, information systems, missiles.

Northwest Airlines Corp. (NWA): 2700 Lone Oak Pkwy., Eagan, MN 55121; (612) 726-2111; www.nwa.com; Gary L. Wilson; air transportation; emerged from Chapt. 11 reorganization, 5/31/07.

Northwestern Mutual Life Insurance Co.: 720 E. Wisconsin Ave., Milwaukee, WI 53202; (414) 271-1444; www.nmfn.com; Edward J. Zore; life insurance, investment products and services, annuities.

Occidental Petroleum Corp. (OXY): 10889 Wilshire Blvd., Los Angeles, CA 90024; (310) 208-8800; www.oxy.com; Ray R. Irani; oil, natural gas, chemicals, plastics, fertilizers.

Office Depot, Inc. (ODP): 2200 Old Germantown Rd., Delray Beach, FL 33445; (561) 438-4800; www.officedepot.com; Steve Odland; office supply retail stores.

Omnicom Group Inc. (OMC): 437 Madison Ave., NY, NY 10022; (212) 415-3600; www.omnicomgroup.com; John D. Wren; advertising, marketing, interactive/digital media.

Oracle Corp. (ORCL): 500 Oracle Pkwy., Redwood Shores, CA 94065; (650) 506-7000; www.oracle.com; Lawrence J. Ellison; database and file management software.

Owens Corning (OC): 1 Owens Corning Parkway, Toledo, OH 43659; (419) 248-8000; www.owenscorning.com; Michael H. Thaman; world leader in advanced glass, composite materials. Emerged from Chapt. 11 protection, 10/31/06.

Owens-Illinois (OI): 1 Michael Owens Way, Perrysburg, OH 43551; (567) 336-5000; Albert Stroucken; www.o-i.com; one of the world's largest producers of glass and plastic packaging.

J.C. Penney Co., Inc. (JCP): 6501 Legacy Dr., Plano, TX 75024; (972) 431-1000; www.jcpenney.com; Myron E. Ulman III; dept. stores, catalog sales, insurance.

Pepsi Bottling Group, Inc. (PBG): 1 Pepsi Way; Somers, NY 10589; (914) 767-6000; www.pbg.com; Eric J. Foss; world's #1 mfgr. & distrib. of PepsiCo prods.

PepsiCo, Inc. (PEP): 700 Anderson Hill Rd., Purchase, NY 10577; (914) 253-2000; www.pepsico.com; Indra K. Nooyi; soft drinks (Pepsi-Cola, Mountain Dew), fruit juice (Tropicana), sports drinks (Gatorade), FritoLay snacks (Ruffles, Lay's, Fritos, Doritos, Rold Gold), Quaker Oats.

Petters Group Worldwide LLC: 4400 Baker Rd., Minnetonka, MN 55343; (952) 934-9918; www.pettersgroup.com; Thomas J. Petters; conglomeration of consumer prod. mfgrs (Polaroid), retailers (Fingerhut, uBid.com), and air transportation cos. (Sun Country).

Pfizer, Inc. (PFE): 235 E. 42nd St., NY, NY 10017; (212) 573-2323; www.pfizer.com; Jeffrey B. Kindler; pharmaceuticals (Celebrex, Lipitor, Viagra, Zoloft); hospital, agricultural, chemical prods.

PG&E Corp. (PCG): One Market, Spear Tower, Ste. 2400, San Francisco, CA 94105; (415) 267-7000; www.pgecorp.com; Peter A. Darbee; energy supplier.

Philip Morris Cos. Inc.: see Altria Group, Inc.

Phillips-Van Heusen Corp. (PVH): 200 Madison Ave., NY, NY 10016; (212) 381-3500; www.pvh.com; Emanuel Chirico; mfgr. of licensed apparel (Calvin Klein, IZOD, Geoffrey Beene, DKNY, Kenneth Cole).

Pitney Bowes, Inc. (PBI): 1 Elmcroft Rd., Stamford, CT 06926; (203) 356-5000; www.pb.com; Michael J. Critelli; world's largest mfgr. of postage meters and mailing equip.

Plains All American Pipeline, L.P. (PAA): 333 Clay St., Ste. 1600, Houston, TX 77002; (713) 646-4100; www.plainsall american.com; Greg L. Armstrong; oil transportation, storage.

Polaroid Corp.: see Petters Group Worldwide

Polo Ralph Lauren Corp. (RL): 650 Madison Ave., NY, NY 10022; (212) 318-7000; www.polo.com; Ralph Lauren; men's and women's apparel.

PPG Industries, Inc. (PPG): 1 PPG Place, Pittsburgh, PA 15272; (412) 434-3131; www.ppg.com; Charles E. Bunch; glass prods., silicas, fiberglass, chemicals, sealants; world's leading supplier of automobile/industrial coatings.

Procter & Gamble Co. (PG): 1 Procter & Gamble Plaza, Cincinnati, OH 45202; (513) 983-1100; www.pg.com; Alan Lafley; soaps and detergents (Ivory, Cheer, Tide, Mr. Clean, Comet, Zest); toiletries (Crest, Scope, Head & Shoulders, Noxzema, Oil of Olay, Old Spice); pharmaceuticals (NyQuil, Pepto-Bismol, Vicks cough medicines); foods (Folgers coffee, Pringles); paper prods. (Charmin toilet tissues, Bounty towels, Tampax tampons, Pampers & Luvs disposable diapers); Cover Girl and Max Factor cosmetics, Clairol haircare. Acquired Gillette (razors, batteries), 10/1/06.

Prudential Financial, Inc. (PRU): 751 Broad St., Newark, NJ 07102; (973) 802-6000; www.prudential.com; Arthur F. Ryan; insurance, financial services.

Publix Super Markets Inc. (PUSH): 3300 Publix Corporate Pkwy., Lakeland, FL 33811; (863) 688-1188; www.publix. com; Charles H. Jenkins Jr.; chain of supermarkets.

Quest Diagnostics Inc. (DGX): 1290 Wall St. W., Lyndhurst, NJ 07071; (201) 393-5000; www.questdiagnostics.com; Surya N. Mohapatra; leading clinical laboratory.

Qwest Communications, Inc. (Q): 1801 California St., Denver, CO 80202; (303) 992-1400; www.qwest.com; Edward A. Mueller; telecommunications, wireless, and directory services.

RadioShack Corp (RSH): 300 RadioShack Circle, Fort Worth, TX 76102; (817) 415-3011; www.radioshack.com; Julian C. Day; consumer electronics retailer.

Ralcorp Holdings, Inc. (RAH): 800 Market St., St. Louis, MO 63101; (314) 877-7000; www.ralcorp.com; William Stiritz; private-label breakfast cereals, snack foods; baby food (Beech-Nut).

Raytheon Co. (RTN): 870 Winter St., Waltham, MA 02451; (781) 522-3000; www.raytheon.com; William Swanson; defense systems, electronics.

Reader's Digest Assn., Inc. (RDA): Reader's Digest Road, Pleasantville, NY 10570; (914) 238-1000; www.rd.com; Mary G. Berner; world's best-selling gen. interest magazines; direct-mail marketer of magazines, books. Acquired by Ripplewood Holdings, 3/02/07.

Reebok Intl. Ltd.: 1895 J.W. Foster Blvd., Canton, MA 02021; (781) 401-5000; www.reebok.com; Paul Harrington; athletic and leisure footwear, apparel; acquired by Germany's adidas AG, 1/31/06.

Revlon, Inc. (REV): 237 Park Ave., NY, NY 10017; (212) 527-4000; www.revlon.com; David L. Kennedy; cosmetics, skin care.

Reynolds American Inc. (RAI): 401 N. Main St., Winston-Salem, NC 27102; (336) 741-2000; www.reynoldsamerican. com; Susan M. Ivey; 2nd-largest U.S. producer of cigarettes (Winston, Salem, Camel, Lucky Strike).

Rite Aid Corp. (RAD): 30 Hunter Lane, Camp Hill, PA 17011; (717) 761-2633; www.riteaid.com; Mary F. Sammons; 3rd-largest U.S. drugstore chain.

Rockwell Automation, Inc. (ROK): 1201 S. 2nd St., Milwaukee, WI 53204; (414) 382-2000; www.rockwell.com; Keith D. Nosbusch; diversified industrial automation co.

Rohm & Haas Co. (ROH): 100 Independence Mall West, Philadelphia, PA 19106; (215) 592-3000; www.rohmhaas. com; Rajiv Gupta; adhesives and sealants, performance chemicals, automotive coatings; salt (Morton).

Ryder System, Inc. (R): 11690 NW 105th St., Miami, FL 33178; (305) 500-3726; www.ryder.com; Gregory T. Swienton; truck-leasing service.

Safeway Inc. (SWY): 5918 Stoneridge Mall Rd., Pleasanton, CA 94588; (925) 467-3000; www.safeway.com; Steven A. Burd; supermarkets.

Sara Lee Corp. (SLE): 3500 Lacey Rd., Downers Grove, IL 60515; (630) 598-8100; www.saralee.com; Brenda Barnes; baked goods, fresh and processed meats (Ball Park, Jimmy Dean, Hillshire Farms, Kahn's). Spun off apparel business as Hanesbrands Inc., 9/5/06.

SBC Communications, Inc.: see AT&T, Inc.

Schering-Plough Corp. (SGP): 2000 Galloping Hill Rd., Kenilworth, NJ 07033; (908) 298-4000; www.sch-plough.com; Fred Hassan; pharmaceuticals (Clarinex, Levitra, Nasonex, Proventil), consumer prods. (Afrin, Claritin, Coppertone), animal health prods.

Sears Holdings Corp. (SHLD): 3333 Beverly Rd., Hoffman Estates, IL 60179; (847) 286-2500; www.searshc.com; Eddie Lampert; 3rd largest U.S. retailer; formed by merger of Kmart and Sears, 3/24/05.

Shell Oil Co.: 1 Shell Plaza, 910 Louisiana St., Houston, TX 77002; (713) 241-6161; www.shellus.com; John D. Hofmeister; integrated oil co; subsidiary of Royal Dutch Shell, world's 2nd-largest oil co.

Sherwin-Williams Co. (SHW): 101 Prospect Ave. NW, Cleveland, OH 44115; (216) 566-2000; www.sherwin-williams.com; Christopher Connor; largest North American paint and varnish producer (Dutch Boy, Pratt & Lambert, Martha Stewart, Minwax).

Smithfield Foods, Inc. (SFD): 200 Commerce St., Smithfield, VA 23430; (757) 365-3000; www.smithfieldfoods.com; C. Larry Pope; world's largest producer of pork and processed meat products.

J. M. Smucker Co. (SJM): One Strawberry Lane, Orrville, OH 44667; (330) 682-3000; www.smucker.com; Timothy P. Smucker; largest U.S. producer of preserves, jams, jellies; toppings (Magic Shell), Jif peanut butter; Crisco oil.

Smurfit-Stone Container Corp. (SSCC): 150 N. Michigan Ave., Chicago, IL 60601; (312) 346-6600; www.smurfit.com; Patrick J. Moore; industry leader for corrugated containers, paper bags and sacks.

Southwest Airlines Co. (LUV): 2702 Love Field Dr., Dallas, TX 75235; (214) 792-4000; www.southwest.com; Gary Kelly; air transportation.

Sprint Nextel Corp. (S): 2001 Edmund Halley Dr., Reston, VA 20191; (703) 433-4000; www.sprint.com; Gary D. Forsee; wireless and long-distance telecommunications; merged with Nextel, 8/12/05.

Staples, Inc. (SPLS): 500 Staples Dr., Framingham, MA 01702; (508) 253-5000; www.staples.com; Ron Sargent; largest U.S. office-supply retailer.

Starbucks Corp. (SBUX): 2401 Utah Ave. S., Seattle, WA 98134; (206) 447-1575; www.starbucks.com; James L. Donald; coffee producer; world's leading coffee retailer.

Starwood Hotels & Resorts Worldwide, Inc. (HOT): 1111 Westchester Ave., White Plains, NY 10604; (914) 640-8100; www.starwoodhotels.com; Bruce W. Duncan; hotel and resort co. (Westin, Sheraton, W Hotels).

State Farm Mutual Automobile Ins. Co.: 1 State Farm Plaza, Bloomington, IL 61710; (309) 766-2311; www.statefarm.com; Edward B. Rust Jr.; largest U.S. provider of auto/homeowners insurance.

Sun Microsystems, Inc. (SUNW): 4150 Network Circle, Santa Clara, CA 95054; (800) 555-9SUN; www.sun.com; Jonathan I. Schwartz; supplier of network computer systems.

Sunoco, Inc. (SUN):1735 Market St., Ste. LL, Philadelphia, PA 19103; (215) 977-3000; www.sunocoinc.com; John G. Drosdick; energy resources co., gasoline retailer.

SUPERVALU Inc. (SVU): 11840 Valley View Rd., Eden Prairie, MN 55344; (952) 828-4000; www.supervalu.com; Jeffrey Noddle; food wholesaler, retailer.

Sysco Corp. (SYY): 1390 Enclave Pkwy., Houston, TX 77077; (281) 584-1390; www.sysco.com; Richard J. Schnieders; leading U.S. food-service distributor.

Target Corp. (TGT): 1000 Nicollet Mall, Minneapolis, MN 55403; (612) 304-6073; www.target.com; Robert J. Ulrich; 2nd-largest U.S. discount retailer.

Tenneco Inc. (TEN): 500 N. Field Drive, Lake Forest, IL 60045; (847) 482-5000; www.tenneco.com; Gregg M. Sherrill; automotive parts (Monroe, Walker).

Texas Instruments Inc. (TXN): 12500 TI Blvd., Dallas, TX 75266; (972) 995-2011; www.ti.com; Thomas Engibous; processors, semiconductors, software, handheld calculators.

Intl. Textile Group (ITXN): 804 Green Valley Rd., Ste. 300, Greensboro, NC 29605; (336) 379-6220; www.itg-global.com; Joseph L. Gorga; apparel and home textiles/fabrics.

Textron Inc. (TXT): 40 Westminster St., Providence, RI 02903; (401) 421-2800; www.textron.com; Lewis B. Campbell; aerospace (Cessna), industrial, automotive prods.; financial services.

3M Company (MMM): 3M Center, St. Paul, MN 55144; (612) 733-1110; www.mmm.com; George W. Buckley; abrasives, adhesives, electrical, health care, cleaning (Scotch-Brite, O-Cel-O sponges, Scotchgard), printing, consumer prods. (Scotch Tape, Post-it).

TIAA-CREF: 730 Third Ave., NY, NY 10017; (212) 490-9000; www.tiaa-cref.org; Herb Allison; financial services provider.

Timberland Company (TBL): 200 Domain Dr., Stratham, NH 03885; (603) 772-9500; www.timberland.com; Jeffrey Swartz; footwear, apparel, accessories.

Time Warner Inc. (TWX): One Time Warner Ctr., NY, NY 10019; (212) 484-8000; www.timewarner.com; Richard D. Parsons; Internet service provider (AOL); magazine publishing (Time, Sports Illustrated, Fortune, Money, People, DC Comics), TV and CATV (Cartoon Network, HBO, CNN, TBS, TNT), book publishing (Little, Brown; Warner Books), motion pictures (Warner Bros., New Line Cinema), recordings. America Online and Time Warner completed the largest corporate merger in history in 2001, becoming the largest media company in the U.S. Dropped "AOL" from name, 9/18/03.

TJX Cos., Inc. (TJX): 770 Cochituate Rd., Framingham, MA 01701; (508) 390-1000; www.tjx.com; Bernard Cammarata; world's largest off-price apparel retailer (T.J. Maxx, Marshalls).

Toro Co. (TTC): 8111 Lyndale Ave. S, Bloomington, MN 55420; (952) 888-8801; www.thetorocompany.com; Michael J. Hoffman; lawn and turf maintenance prods. (Lawn-Boy), snow removal equip., lighting and irrigation systems.

Toys "R" Us, Inc.: 1 Geoffrey Way, Wayne, NJ 07470; (973) 617-3500; www.toysrus.com; Gerald L. Storch; children's specialty retailer (Toys "R" Us, Babies "R" Us).

Triarc Cos., Inc. (TRY): 280 Park Ave., NY, NY 10017; (212) 451-3000; www.triarc.com; Nelson Peltz; fast-food restaurants (Arby's).

Tribune Co. (TRB): 435 N. Michigan Ave., Chicago, IL 60611; (312) 222-9100; www.tribune.com; Dennis J. FitzSimons; newspapers (Los Angeles Times, Chicago Tribune, Newsday), broadcasting (incl. WGN and 23 other stations), Chicago Cubs baseball team.

Trinity Industries, Inc. (TRN): 2525 Stemmons Fwy., Dallas, TX 75207; (214) 631-4420; www.trin.net; Timothy R. Wallace; manufactures metal prods., rail and freight equip.

Tyco Intl. Ltd. (TYC): 9 Roszel Rd., Princeton, NJ 08540; (609) 720-4200; www.tyco.com; Edward D. Breen Jr.; security and engineered prods. Separated its health care and electronics divisions, 6/29/07, to form 3 separate cos.

Tyson Foods, Inc. (TSN): 2210 West Oaklawn Dr., Springdale, AR 72762; (479) 290-4000 www.tysonfoodsinc.com; Richard L. Bond; fresh and processed poultry; beef, pork, and seafood prods.

UAL Corp. (UAUA): 77 W. Wacker Dr., Chicago IL 60601; (312) 997-8000; www.united.com; Glenn Tilton; air transportation (United Airlines).

UBS Financial Services Inc.: 1285 Ave. of the Americas, NY, NY 10019; (212) 713-2000; www.ubs.com; Marten Hoekstra; financial services; subsidiary of Switzerland's UBS AG.

Unilever US (UN/UL): 800 Sylvan Ave., Englewood Cliffs, NJ 07632; (877) 995-4483; www.unilever.com; Patrick Cescau; food (Hellmann's mayonnaise, Knorr soups, Ragu pasta sauce, Wish-Bone salad dressing, Lipton Tea, Skippy Peanut Butter, Slim-Fast), hygiene prods. (Dove, Q-Tips, Vaseline). Subsidiary of Unilever NV (Neth.) and Unilever PLC (UK).

Union Pacific Corp. (UNP): 1400 Douglas St., Omaha, NE, 68179; (402) 544-5000; www.up.com; James R. Young; largest railroad freight co. in U.S.

Unisys Corp. (UIS): Unisys Way, Blue Bell, PA 19424; (215) 986-4011; www.unisys.com; Joseph W. McGrath; designs, manuf. computer information systems and related prods..

UnitedHealth Group Inc. (UNH): UHG Center, 9900 Bren Rd. E., Minnetonka, MN 55343; (952) 936-1300; www.unitedhealth group.com; Stephen J. Hemsley; 2nd-largest U.S. health insurer.

United Parcel Service, Inc. (UPS): 55 Glenlake Pkwy. NE, Atlanta, GA 30328; (404) 828-6000; www.ups.com; Michael L. Eskew; world's largest package delivery co.

United States Steel Corp. (X): 600 Grant St., Pittsburgh, PA 15219; (412) 433-1121; www.ussteel.com; John P. Surma Jr.; steel, tin prods.

United Technologies Corp. (UTX): One Financial Plaza, Hartford, CT 06103; (860) 728-7000; www.utc.com; George David; aerospace, industrial prods. and services (Carrier, Otis Elevator, Pratt & Whitney, Sikorsky Aircraft).

Unocal Corp.: see Chevron Corp.

US Airways Group, Inc. (LCC): 111 W. Rio Salado Pkwy., Tempe, AZ 85281; (480) 693-0800; www.usairways.com; William Douglas Parker; air transportation.

Verizon Communications Inc. (VZ): 140 West St., NY, NY 10036; (212) 395-1000; www.verizon.com; Ivan Seidenberg; telecommunications; largest U.S. wireline and 2nd-largest wireless provider. Acquired MCI, Inc., 1/6/06.

VF Corp. (VFC): 105 Corporate Center Blvd., Greensboro, NC 27408; (336) 424-6000; www.vfc.com; Mackey J. McDonald; apparel (Lee, Wrangler, Jantzen, North Face).

Viacom, Inc. (VIA): 1515 Broadway, NY, NY 10036; (212) 258-6000; www.viacom.com; Philippe Dauman; CATV (BET, Comedy Central, MTV, VH1, Nickelodeon); produces, distributes movies (Paramount); theme parks. (Co. split into 2 separately traded entities, 1/1/06. See CBS Corp.)

Visteon Corp. (VC): One Village Ctr. Dr., Van Buren Twp., MI 48111; (734) 710-2020; www.visteon.com; Mike Johnston; automotive parts manufacturing, architectural glass.

Wachovia Corp. (WB): One Wachovia Center, Charlotte, NC 28288; (704) 374-6565; www.wachovia.com; G. Kennedy Thompson; financial services provider.

Walgreen Co. (WAG): 200 Wilmot Rd., Deerfield, IL 60015; (847) 914-2500; www.walgreens.com; Jeffrey A. Rein; 2nd-largest U.S. drugstore chain.

Wal-Mart Stores, Inc. (WMT): 702 SW 8th St., Bentonville, AR 72716; (479) 273-4000; www.walmartstores.com; H. Lee Scott Jr.; world's largest retailer; discount stores, wholesale clubs (Sam's).

Washington Post Co. (WPO): 1150 15th St. NW, Washington, DC 20071; (202) 334-6000; www.washpostco.com; Donald E. Graham; newspapers, *Newsweek* magazine, Salon.com, TV and CATV stations, Kaplan educational services.

Waste Management, Inc. (WMI): 1001 Fannin St., Suite 4000, Houston, TX 77002; (713) 512-6200; www.wm.com; David P. Steiner; N. America's largest solid waste collection and disposal co.

WellPoint Inc. (WLP): 120 Monument Circle, Indianapolis, IN 46204; (317) 532-6000; www.wellpoint.com; Larry C. Glass-cock; largest U.S. health insurer; HMOs and PPOs, incl. Blue Cross Blue Shield (licensed in some states), HealthLink, Unicare, WellChoice.

Wells Fargo & Co. (WFC): 420 Montgomery St., San Francisco, CA 94163; (866) 878-5865; www.wellsfargo.com; Dick Kovacevich; financial services.

Wendy's Intl., Inc. (WEN): 288 W. Dublin-Granville Rd., Dublin, OH 43017; (614) 764-3100; www.wendys.com; Kerrii B. Anderson; fast food restaurants (Tim Horton's, Baja Fresh, Wendy's).

Western Union Co. (WU): 12500 E. Belford Ave., Englewood, CO 80112; (720) 332-1000; www.westernunion.com; Christina A. Gold; money transfers, financial services.

Weyerhaeuser Co. (WY): 33663 Weyerhaeuser Way S., Federal Way, WA 98003; (253) 924-2345; www.weyerhaeuser.com; Steven R. Rogel; produces and distributes paper and wood prods.

Whirlpool Corp. (WHR): 2000 N. M-63, Benton Harbor, MI 49022; (269) 923-5000; www.whirlpoolcorp.com; Jeff M. Fettig; largest U.S. manuf. of major home appliances (KitchenAid, Kenmore, Roper). Acquired Maytag Corp. appliances, 3/31/06.

Whole Foods Market, Inc. (WFMI): 550 Bowie St., Austin, TX 78703; (512) 477-4455; www.wholefoodsmarket.com; John P. Mackey; world's largest natural food market chain.

Winn-Dixie Stores, Inc.: 5050 Edgewood Ct., Jacksonville, FL 32254; (904) 783-5000; www.winn-dixie.com; Peter Lynch; supermarkets (Winn Dixie, Save Rite); emerged from Chapt. 11, 11/21/06.

Winnebago Industries, Inc. (WGO): 605 W. Crystal Lake Rd., Forest City, IA 50436; (641) 585-3535; www.winnebago ind.com; Bruce D. Hertzke; manuf. of motor homes, recreational vehicles.

Wm. Wrigley Jr. Co. (WWY): 410 N. Michigan Ave., Chicago, IL 60611; (312) 644-2121; www.wrigley.com; William Wrigley Jr.; world's largest mfgr. of chewing gum.

Wyeth (WYE): 5 Giralda Farms, Madison, NJ 07940; (973) 660-5000; www.wyeth.com; Robert Essner; manuf. prescription (Alavert, Effexor) and over-the-counter drugs (Advil, Centrum, Chap Stick, Robitussin).

Xerox Corp. (XRX): 800 Long Ridge Road, Stamford, CT 06904; (203) 968-3000; www.xerox.com; Anne Mulcahy; copiers, printers, document publishing equip.

Yahoo! Inc. (YHOO): 701 First Ave. Sunnyvale, CA 94089; (408) 349-3300; www.yahoo.com; Terry Semel; internet media company.

Yum! Brands, Inc. (YUM): 1441 Gardiner Lane, Louisville, KY 40213; (502) 874-8300; www.yum.com; David C. Novak; fast food restaurants (Pizza Hut, KFC, Taco Bell).

Who Owns What: Familiar Consumer Products and Services

The following is a partial list of well-known consumer brands with their (U.S.) parent companies. Among brands not listed are many brands whose parent companies have the same or a similar name (e.g., Colgate is product of Colgate-Palmolive Co.). For company contact information, see Business Directory on previous pages.

A&W Rootbeer: Cadbury Schweppes
ABC broadcasting: Walt Disney
Admiral appliances: Maytag
Advil: Wyeth
Ajax cleanser: Colgate-Palmolive
Almond Joy candy bar: Hershey
American Girl: Mattel
Arm & Hammer: Church & Dwight
Arrid antiperspirant: Church & Dwight
Aunt Jemima Pancake mix: PepsiCo
Banana Republic stores: Gap Inc.
Band-Aids: Johnson & Johnson
Barbie dolls: Mattel
BENGAY: Pfizer
Betty Crocker prods.: General Mills
Bounty paper towels: Procter & Gamble
Brillo soap pads: Church & Dwight
Brita water systems: Clorox
Budweiser beer: Anheuser-Busch
Bulova watches: Loews
Business Week magazine: McGraw-Hill
Cap'n Crunch cereal: PepsiCo
Calphalon cookware: Newell Rubbermaid
Camel cigarettes: Reynolds American
Charmin toilet tissue: Procter & Gamble
Cheer detergent: Procter & Gamble
Cheerios cereal: General Mills
Cheez Whiz: Kraft
Chef Boyardee: ConAgra
Chips Ahoy!: Kraft (Nabisco)
Clairol hair prods.: Procter & Gamble
Clinique: Estée Lauder
CNN: Time Warner
Combat insecticides: Henkel
Coppertone sun care prods.: Schering-Plough
Crest toothpaste: Procter & Gamble
Crisco shortening: J.M. Smucker
DC Comics: Time Warner
Dr. Pepper: Cadbury Schweppes
Doritos chips: PepsiCo
Dove soaps: Unilever
Duracell batteries: Procter & Gamble
Dutch Boy paints: Sherwin-Williams

Efferdent dental cleanser: Pfizer
ESPN: Walt Disney
Fantastik: S.C. Johnson
Febreeze: Proctor & Gamble
Fisher Price Toys: Mattel
Folger's coffee: Procter & Gamble
Formula 409 spray cleaner: Clorox
Fox News Channel: News Corp.
Fortune magazine: Time Warner
Friskies Cat Food: Nestlé
Frito-Lays snacks: PepsiCo
Fruit of the Loom apparel: Berkshire Hathaway
Gatorade: PepsiCo
Gilette razors: Procter & Gamble
Glade air fresheners: SC Johnson
Glad Prods.: Clorox
Haagen-Dazs: General Mills
Halcion: Pfizer
Halls cough drops: Cadbury Schweppes
Hamburger Helper: General Mills
HBO: Time Warner
Head and Shoulders shampoo: Procter & Gamble
Hellmann's mayonnaise: Unilever
Hi-C fruit drinks: Coca-Cola
Hidden Valley prods.: Clorox
Hillshire Farm meats: Sara Lee
Hot Wheels/Matchbox cars: Mattel
Hostess cupcakes: Interstate Bakeries
Huggies diapers: Kimberly-Clark
Irish Spring: Colgate-Palmolive
Ivory soap: Procter & Gamble
Jack Daniel's whiskey: Brown-Forman
Jell-O: Kraft
Jennie-O turkey: Hormel
Jif peanut butter: J.M. Smucker
Jim Beam bourbon: Fortune Brands
Keds footwear: Collective Brands
Kent cigarettes: Loews
KFC restaurants: Yum! Brands
Kibbles 'n Bits pet foods: Del Monte
KitchenAid appliances: Whirlpool
Kit Kat candy: Hershey

Kleenex: Kimberly-Clark
Kmart: Sears Holdings Co.
Knorr soups: Unilever
Kool-Aid: Kraft
Ladies Home Journal magazine: Meredith
Lee jeans: V.F. Corp.
L'eggs hosiery: Hanesbrands
LifeSavers candy: Wm. Wrigley Jr. Co.
Lipton tea: Unilever
Listerine mouthwash: Pfizer
Marlboro cigarettes: Altria (Philip Morris)
Max Factor beauty products: Procter & Gamble
Maxwell House coffee: Kraft
Maytag appliances: Whirlpool
Metamucil: Procter & Gamble
Michelob beer: Anheuser-Busch
Miller beer: Miller Brewing (SABMiller)
Milton Bradley games: Hasbro
Minute Maid juices: Coca-Cola
Mr. Clean: Procter & Gamble
Monroe automotive parts: Tenneco Automotive
Mountain Dew soda: PepsiCo
MTV: Viacom
Nature Valley granola bars: General Mills
NBC broadcasting: General Electric
Neosporin: Johnson & Johnson
Neutrogena soap: Johnson & Johnson
Newport cigarettes: Loews
Newsweek magazine: Washington Post
Nickelodeon TV: Viacom
9 Lives cat food: Del Monte
Olay: Procter & Gamble
Old Navy clothing: Gap Inc.
Oreo cookies: Kraft (Nabisco)
Oscar Mayer meats: Kraft
Pampers: Procter & Gamble
Pantene Shampoos: Procter & Gamble
Parker Bros. games: Hasbro
People magazine: Time Warner
Pepperidge Farm prods.: Campbell Soup
Pepto-Bismol: Procter & Gamble
Philadelphia Cream Cheese: Kraft

Pillsbury: General Mills
Pine-Sol cleaner: Clorox
Pizza Hut restaurants: Yum! Brands
Planters nuts: Kraft
Playskool toys: Hasbro
PlayStation: Sony
Playtex apparel: Hanesbrands
Post cereals: Kraft
Post-it notes: 3M
Prego pasta sauce: Campbell Soup
Prozac: Eli Lilly
Purina pet foods: Nestlé
Q-Tips: Unilever
Ragu sauce: Unilever
Reese's candy: Hershey
Rice-A-Roni: PepsiCo
Rice Krispies: Kellogg Co.
Right Guard deodorant: Henkel
Ritz crackers: Kraft (Nabisco)
Robitussin: Wyeth
Rogaine hair growth aide: Pfizer
Ruffles chips: PepsiCo
Schick razors: Energizer

Scope mouthwash: Procter & Gamble
Scotch tape: 3M
Scott tissue: Kimberly-Clark
Simon & Schuster publishing: CBS Corp.
Skippy peanut butter: Unilever
Slimfast: Unilever
SnackWell's cookies: Kraft (Nabisco)
S.O.S. cleanser: Clorox
Southern Comfort liquor: Brown-Forman
SPAM meat: Hormel Foods
Sports Illustrated magazine: Time Warner
Sprite soda: Coca-Cola
StarKist tuna: Del Monte
Sudafed: Johnson & Johnson
Swanson broth: Campbell Soup
Swiffer: Procter & Gamble
Taco Bell restaurants: Yum! Brands
Tampax tampons: Procter & Gamble
Tide detergent: Procter & Gamble
Time magazine: Time Warner
Titleist: Fortune Brands
Tombstone pizza: Kraft
Triscuits: Kraft (Nabisco)

Trojan condoms: Church & Dwight
Tropicana juice: PepsiCo
Tylenol: Johnson & Johnson
USA Today newspaper: Gannett
V8 vegetable juice: Campbell Soup
Vanity Fair apparel: V.F. Corp.
Vaseline: Unilever
Velveeta cheese prods.: Kraft
VH-1: Viacom
Viagra: Pfizer
Vicks cold medicines: Procter & Gamble
Victoria's Secret stores: Limited Brands
Visine eye drops: Pfizer
Weight Watchers: H.J. Heinz
Wheaties cereal: General Mills
Windex: S.C. Johnson
Windows software applications: Microsoft
Wonderbra: Hanesbrands
Wonder bread: Interstate Bakeries
Xbox: Microsoft
Zest soap: Procter & Gamble
Ziploc storage bags: S.C. Johnson

Top Brands in Selected Categories, 2006-07

Source: Information Resources, Inc., a Chicago-based marketing research company; figures for 12-month period ending 8/12/07.

Beer	Sales	Market Share (%)
Bud Light	$1,428,247,000	15.5%
Budweiser	751,068,100	8.1
Miller Lite	732,490,400	7.9
Coors Light	638,101,200	6.9
Corona Extra	470,582,000	5.1
Total Category Sales	$9,224,054,000	

Chocolate Candies	Sales	Market Share (%)
M&Ms	$238,425,500	13.2%
Hershey's	209,924,900	11.6
Hershey's Kisses	130,838,400	7.2
Dove Chocolate	82,927,990	4.6
Reese's	66,916,390	3.7
Total Category Sales	1,809,636,000	

Ready-to-Eat Cold Cereals	Sales	Market Share (%)
Private Label	$585,497,700	9.2%
General Mills Cheerios	296,630,700	4.7
Post Honey Bunches of Oats	288,605,500	4.6
General Mills Honey Nut Cheerios	263,937,600	4.2
Kellogg's Frosted Flakes	238,097,400	3.8
Total Category Sales	6,333,710,000	

Ground Coffee (excluding Decaf)	Sales	Market Share (%)
Folgers	$447,863,400	21.5%
Maxwell House	344,135,700	16.5
Starbucks	216,858,400	10.4
Folgers Coffee House	185,570,800	8.9
Private Label	165,046,700	7.9
Total Category Sales	3,188,918,000	

Cookies	Sales	Market Share (%)
Private Label	$481,154,100	12.0%
Nabisco Chips Ahoy	294,572,300	7.4
Nabisco Oreo	256,434,000	6.4
Nabisco Oreo Double Stuf	133,403,500	3.3
Nabisco Newtons	113,198,800	2.8
Total Category Sales	4,006,705,000	

Ice Cream	Sales	Market Share (%)
Private Label	$846,152,600	18.9%
Breyers	618,797,200	13.9
Dreyers Edy's Grand	426,366,100	9.5
Dreyers Edy's Slow-Churned	342,514,200	7.7
Haagen Dazs	290,367,400	6.5
Total Category Sales	4,466,491,000	

Paper Towels	Sales	Market Share (%)
Bounty	$912,732,200	39.2%
Private Label	477,119,100	20.5
Brawny	240,858,800	10.3
Kleenex Viva	211,691,300	9.1
Scott	174,454,200	7.5
Total Category Sales	2,328,505,000	

Frozen Pizza	Sales	Market Share (%)
Di Giorno	$478,299,600	16.9%
Red Baron	291,972,600	10.3
Tombstone	247,074,100	8.7
Freschetta	200,962,700	7.1
Private Label	197,471,300	7.0
Total Category Sales	2,844,804,000	

Salad Dressing	Sales	Market Share (%)
Kraft	$229,479,200	16.0%
Wishbone	148,972,600	10.4
Ken's Steak House	138,857,900	9.7
Private Label	138,110,700	9.6
Hidden Valley Ranch	118,845,800	8.3
Total Category Sales	1,436,676,000	

Toothpaste	Sales	Market Share (%)
Crest	$129,166,300	8.7%
Crest Whitening Plus Scope	101,963,700	6.9
Colgate Total	101,067,900	6.8
Colgate	89,492,740	6.0
Crest Pro Health	65,222,850	4.4
Total Category Sales	1,480,602,000	

Note: For all categories brands are ranked by dollar sales at supermarkets, drugstores, and mass merchandisers, excluding Wal-Mart. "Private Label" represents the aggregated sales figures for store-branded products in that category. Total category sales include other brands not listed here.

Most Visited Shopping Websites, July 2007

Source: comScore Media Metrix, Inc.

Rank	Website[1]	Visitors[2]	Rank	Website[1]	Visitors[2]
1.	eBay	79,787,000	11.	Moviefone	13,652,000
2.	Amazon Sites	52,702,000	12.	Dell	13,106,000
3.	Apple Inc.	42,561,000	13.	Hewlett Packard	12,608,000
4.	Target Corp.	30,391,000	14.	JCPenney Sites	11,097,000
5.	Wal-Mart	29,213,000	15.	Blockbuster Inc.	10,563,000
6.	Shopzilla.com Sites	21,983,000	16.	Fandango.com	10,210,000
7.	Yahoo! Shopping	18,027,000	17.	Circuit City Stores, Inc.	10,000,000
8.	Ticketmaster	15,170,000	18.	The Home Depot, Inc.	9,940,000
9.	Best Buy Sites	15,041,000	19.	Yahoo! Stores	9,485,000
10.	Mezi Media Sites	13,771,000	20.	Netflix.com	9,314,000

(1) May include affiliated websites not shown; e.g. Apple Inc. sites include the iTunes digital media store. (2) Unique visitors (visited website at least once in July 2007).

Median Price of Existing Single-Family Homes, by Metropolitan Area, 2005-2007

Source: National Association of REALTORS®
Median prices are in thousands and based on all transactions within the time period shown.

Metropolitan Area	2005	2006	2nd Qtr. 2007	Metropolitan Area	2005	2006	2nd Qtr. 2007
Akron, OH	120.5	114.6	125.3	Little Rock, AR	119.0	127.0	132.6
Albany-Schenectady-Troy, NY	183.5	195.4	191.6	Los Angeles-Long Beach-Santa Ana, CA	529.0	584.8	593.0
Albuquerque, NM	169.2	184.2	199.6	Louisville, KY/IN	135.8	137.6	139.3
Allentown-Bethlehem-Easton, PA/NJ	243.4	248.1	274.5	Madison, WI	218.3	223.2	223.5
Amarillo, TX	107.1	114.9	115.0	Memphis, TN/MS/AR	141.2	142.3	144.3
Anaheim-Santa Ana, CA (Orange Co.)	691.9	709.0	727.0	Miami-Ft. Lauderdale-Miami Beach, FL	363.9	371.2	384.4
Atlanta-Sandy Springs-Marietta, GA	167.2	171.8	175.5	Milwaukee-Waukesha-West Allis, WI	215.7	220.9	229.3
Atlantic City, NJ	256.1	254.8	NA	Minneapolis-St. Paul-Bloomington, MN/WI	234.8	232.3	227.1
Austin-Round Rock, TX	163.8	173.7	186.6	Mobile, AL	130.5	137.0	140.4
Baltimore-Towson, MD	265.3	279.9	293.7	Montgomery, AL	133.3	144.2	150.1
Baton Rouge, LA	146.2	169.5	174.7	Nashville-Davidson-Murfreesboro, TN	161.8	NA	186.4
Beaumont-Port Arthur, TX	98.5	112.7	127.7	New Haven-Milford, CT	279.1	287.7	296.5
Birmingham-Hoover, AL	157.0	165.1	164.9	New Orleans-Metairie-Kenner, LA	159.2	173.1	166.0
Bismarck, ND	124.9	134.9	151.4	New York-N. New Jersey-Long Island, NY/NJ/PA	445.2	469.3	482.3
Bloomington-Normal, IL	159.2	152.2	161.5	New York-Wayne-White Plains, NY/NJ	495.2	539.4	557.5
Boise City-Nampa, ID	147.0	NA	212.8	NY: Newark-Union, NJ/PA	416.8	433.0	416.0
Boston-Cambridge, MA	413.2	402.2	413.3	Norwich-New London, CT	255.9	264.0	276.6
Boulder, CO	348.4	366.4	383.7	Oklahoma City, OK	114.7	125.0	129.3
Bridgeport-Stamford-Norwalk, CT	482.4	473.7	515.3	Omaha, NE/IA	136.2	138.4	136.8
Buffalo-Niagara Falls, NY	99.0	97.9	103.3	Orlando, FL	243.6	270.4	265.1
Canton-Massillon, OH	102.2	109.3	114.6	Pensacola-Ferry Pass-Brent, FL	162.1	166.0	168.7
Cedar Rapids, IA	131.8	133.8	NA	Philadelphia-Camden-Wilmington, PA/NJ/DE/MD	215.3	230.2	243.0
Champaign-Urbana, IL	137.7	143.0	144.9	Phoenix-Mesa-Scottsdale, AZ	247.4	268.2	264.8
Charleston-North Charleston, SC	197.0	212.4	223.2	Pittsburgh, PA	116.1	116.1	123.5
Charleston, WV	118.4	119.4	127.6	Portland-South Portland-Biddeford, ME	246.6	243.8	244.9
Charlotte-Gastonia-Concord, NC/SC	180.9	190.6	207.3	Portland-Vancouver-Beaverton, OR/WA	244.9	280.8	298.3
Chattanooga, TN/GA	131.9	136.0	135.3	Providence-New Bedford-Fall River, RI/MA	293.4	289.6	291.0
Chicago-Naperville-Joliet, IL	264.2	273.5	283.2	Raleigh-Cary, NC	194.9	213.8	225.1
Cincinnati-Middletown, OH/KY/IN	145.9	143.2	146.2	Reno-Sparks, NV	349.9	347.2	331.9
Cleveland-Elyria-Mentor, OH	138.9	134.4	128.7	Richmond, VA	201.9	225.5	236.8
Colorado Springs, CO	205.9	218.2	221.3	Riverside-San Bernardino-Ontario, CA	374.2	400.1	396.8
Columbia, SC	135.0	141.6	148.3	Rochester, NY	113.5	114.8	117.2
Columbus, OH	152.0	148.1	153.9	Rockford, IL	118.2	119.3	122.2
Corpus Christi, TX	125.2	131.8	136.0	Sacramento-Arden-Arcade-Roseville, CA	375.9	374.8	356.5
Cumberland, MD/WV	87.4	95.7	109.3	Saint Louis, MO/IL	141.0	148.4	157.2
Dallas-Fort Worth-Arlington, TX	147.6	149.5	156.5	Salem, OR	177.7	212.9	227.9
Davenport-Moline-Rock Island, IA/IL	117.9	119.7	103.3	Salt Lake City, UT	173.9	203.0	233.1
Dayton, OH	119.7	116.7	120.3	San Antonio, TX	133.9	141.7	154.3
Denver-Aurora, CO	145.5	145.1	147.7	San Diego-Carlsbad-San Marcos, CA	604.3	601.8	614.1
Des Moines, IA	163.8	151.7	144.6	San Francisco-Oakland-Fremont, CA	715.7	736.8	846.8
Detroit-Warren-Livonia, MI	180.4	208.0	209.8	San Jose-Sunnyvale-Santa Clara, CA	744.5	775.0	865.0
Dover, DE	NA	172.8	180.1	Sarasota-Bradenton-Venice, FL	354.2	334.3	311.4
Durham, NC	111.8	127.6	132.3	Seattle-Tacoma-Bellevue, WA	316.8	361.2	395.3
El Paso, TX	100.0	101.3	99.9	Shreveport-Bossier City, LA	124.3	132.2	137.1
Erie, PA	197.6	230.6	240.9	Sioux Falls, SD	135.8	138.0	142.3
Eugene-Springfield, OR	132.8	136.5	139.0	South Bend-Mishawaka, IN	96.6	92.7	93.6
Fargo-Moorhead, ND/MN	155.0	172.0	201.9	Spartanburg, SC	121.2	126.7	133.2
Farmington, NM	269.2	268.2	266.2	Spokane, WA	156.4	184.1	197.7
Fort Myers-Cape Coral, FL	102.3	99.7	101.6	Springfield, IL	106.4	105.4	111.2
Ft. Wayne, IN	184.0	213.2	216.2	Springfield, MA	201.8	209.6	216.8
Gainesville, FL	129.8	128.1	137.8	Springfield, MO	121.1	124.8	123.7
Gary-Hammond, IN	137.8	134.5	132.3	Syracuse, NY	110.6	116.8	122.6
Grand Rapids, MI	154.8	151.3	153.1	Tallahassee, FL	167.6	177.5	180.9
Green Bay, WI	147.8	149.4	156.3	Tampa-St. Petersburg-Clearwater, FL	205.3	228.9	222.7
Greensboro-High Point, NC	145.4	152.0	152.5	Toledo, OH	117.3	110.0	109.8
Greenville, SC	131.4	145.8	154.2	Topeka, KS	105.7	106.1	111.7
Gulfport-Biloxi, MS	208.7	223.1	218.7	Trenton-Ewing, NJ	261.1	289.6	313.9
Hagerstown-Martinsburg, MD/WV	253.3	258.1	242.7	Tucson, AZ	231.6	244.9	250.1
Hartford, CT	590.0	630.0	665.0	Virginia Beach-Norfolk-Newport News, VA/NC	197.2	235.5	250.8
Honolulu, HI	143.0	149.1	154.9	Washington-Arlington-Alexandria, DC/VA/MD/WV	425.8	431.0	445.3
Houston-Baytown-Sugar Land, TX	123.8	119.3	125.3	Waterloo-Cedar Falls, IA	102.2	108.9	113.5
Indianapolis, IN	133.8	147.1	145.1	Wichita, KS	108.0	114.9	110.7
Jackson, MS	175.2	193.0	198.7	Worcester, MA	290.7	281.7	278.9
Jacksonville, FL	156.7	155.8	157.7	Yakima, WA	85.6	81.5	76.7
Kansas City, MO/KS	143.7	151.2	160.2	Youngstown-Warren-Boardman, OH/PA	133.9	136.5	NA
Knoxville, TN	142.2	137.7	133.9	**United States**	**219.0**	**221.9**	**223.8**
Lansing-E.Lansing, MI	304.7	317.4	307.9				
Las Vegas-Paradise, NV	146.9	147.8	148.3				
Lexington-Fayette, KY	137.2	137.5	138.0				
Lincoln, NE							

U.S. Home Ownership Rates, by Selected Characteristics, 1997, 2007[1]

Source: Bureau of the Census, U.S. Dept. of Commerce

Region	1997	2007	Age	1997	2007	Race/Ethnicity[2]	1997	2007	Income	1997	2007
Northeast	62.4%	65.4%	Under 35	38.6%	41.9%	White, non-Hispanic	72.1%	75.4%	Median family income or more	80.8%	83.4%
Midwest	70.3	71.8	35-44	66.3	67.6	Black	44.4	46.3	Below median family income	.50.0	52.0
South	68.1	69.9	45-54	75.6	75.5	Hispanic	43.3	50.0	**TOTAL U.S.**	**65.7%**	**68.2%**
West	59.9	64.1	55-64	80.3	80.6	Other	52.7	59.4			
			65+	79.1	80.5						

(1) In 2007, figures are for 2nd quarter of the year. Not seasonally-adjusted. (2) Hispanic householders may be of any race. "Other" includes householders reporting Asian, Native Hawaiian/Pacific Islander, and Native American/AK Native, as well as combinations of two or more races/ethnicities.

Housing Affordability, U.S., 1990-2007

Source: National Association of REALTORS®

Year	Median priced existing home	Average mortgage rate[1]	Monthly principal & interest payment	Payment as percentage of median monthly income	Year	Median priced existing home	Average mortgage rate[1]	Monthly principal & interest payment	Payment as percentage of median monthly income
1990	$92,000	10.04%	$648	22.0%	1999	$133,300	7.33%	$733	18.0%
1991	97,100	9.30	642	21.4	2000	139,000	8.03	818	19.3
1992	99,700	8.11	591	19.3	2001	147,800	7.03	789	18.4
1993	103,100	7.16	558	18.1	2002	158,100	6.55	804	18.3
1994	107,200	7.47	598	18.5	2003	180,200	5.74	840	19.1
1995	110,500	7.85	639	18.9	2004	195,200	5.73	909	20.2
1996	115,800	7.71	661	18.8	2005	219,000	5.91	1,040	21.8
1997	121,800	7.68	693	18.7	2006	221,900	6.58	1,131	23.6
1998	128,400	7.10	690	17.4	2007[2]	223,800	6.47	1,128	22.9

(1) All figures assume a down payment of 20% of the home price. Based on effective rate on loans closed on existing homes for the period shown. (2) Preliminary, as of the 2nd quarter of fiscal year 2007.

Average Insurance Costs by State, 2004

Source: National Association of Insurance Commissioners

	Automobile Insurance			Homeowners Insurance		
	Avg. annual expenditure[1]	Rank	% Change, 2003-04	Avg. annual premium	Rank	% Change, 2003-04
Alabama	$677	39	3.1%	$793	11	16.4%
Alaska	974	11	3.8	810	10	10.8
Arizona	931	14	1.0	642	29	4.6
Arkansas	708	32	1.3	768	15	6.5
California	833	20	0.6	835	7	10.9
Colorado	850	16	-7.9	811	9	6.4
Connecticut	991	9	0.3	777	13	8.8
Delaware	1,022	8	4.6	488	48	10.4
District of Columbia[2]	1,185	2	4.4	894	6	10.9
Florida	1,062	6	4.4	929	4	14.7
Georgia	779	24	2.5	635	32	11.4
Hawaii	817	22	5.3	726	20	5.7
Idaho	590	48	0.7	448	51	3.5
Illinois	760	26	-0.3	659	26	8.0
Indiana	671	40	0.0	636	31	7.1
Iowa	580	50	-0.1	575	44	6.1
Kansas	603	46	-1.2	833	8	7.9
Kentucky	758	27	2.6	615	37	10.0
Louisiana	1,062	5	4.7	1,074	2	10.2
Maine	650	42	2.7	513	46	11.0
Maryland	947	12	6.1	652	27	11.6
Massachusetts[3]	1,113	4	5.8	759	18	13.1
Michigan	980	10	3.2	726	21	7.9
Minnesota	829	21	-0.9	767	17	4.6
Mississippi	749	29	5.4	907	5	14.4
Missouri	702	33	0.0	689	23	6.0
Montana	683	37	1.3	661	25	5.3
Nebraska	637	43	2.2	730	19	5.8
Nevada	939	13	2.7	632	33	8.6
New Hampshire	798	23	2.5	599	40	11.1
New Jersey[2,4]	1,221	1	2.3	641	30	9.6
New Mexico	728	30	-0.7	585	43	6.2
New York	1,172	3	0.3	785	12	8.9
North Carolina	597	47	-1.3	623	34	8.2
North Dakota	562	51	4.8	704	22	12.6
Ohio	680	38	1.2	523	45	9.9
Oklahoma	690	36	0.1	991	3	7.1
Oregon	753	28	2.4	492	47	6.7
Pennsylvania	843	18	3.7	593	41	9.2
Rhode Island	1,034	7	3.7	769	14	14.3
South Carolina	763	25	2.4	768	16	14.3
South Dakota	587	49	4.1	601	39	7.9
Tennessee	666	41	2.4	681	24	9.5
Texas[5]	847	17	1.1	1,362	1	2.6
Utah	722	31	-1.5	473	50	2.2
Vermont	693	35	1.4	608	38	10.1
Virginia	702	34	6.7	616	35	10.0
Washington	839	19	1.6	590	42	7.5
West Virginia	875	15	3.6	616	36	15.4
Wisconsin	636	44	2.4	483	49	11.3
Wyoming	629	45	1.8	650	28	4.7
United States	**$838**		**1.8%**	**$729**		**9.1%**

(1) Average expenditure is equal to the total written premium for combined liability, collision and comprehensive coverages divided by the liability written car-years (a car-year is equal to 365 days of insured coverage for a single vehicle) in that state. This assumes that all insured vehicles carry liability coverage but do not necessarily carry the physical damage coverages—collision and/or comprehensive. (2) The District of Columbia is entirely urban and New Jersey is predominately urban. Their results cannot be directly compared with states with large rural areas. (3) Data incorporates Safe Driver Plan credits and surcharges. (4) Historically, New Jersey insurers have paid 2 to 4 times the national average in dividends to policyholders, and at times as high as 6 times the national average, which reduces New Jersey's average expenditure. (5) Due to the exclusion of county mutuals, which had 45 percent of the market in 2004, Texas results are not comparable with results from other states.

Auto Insurance Premiums by City, 2006[1]

Source: Insurance Information Institute; Runzheimer International

	Most expensive cities			Least expensive cities	
Rank	City	Avg. annual premium	Rank	City	Avg. annual premium
1.	Detroit, MI	$5,894	1.	Roanoke, VA	$912
2.	Philadelphia, PA	4,440	2.	Chattanooga, TN	980
3.	Newark, NJ	3,977	3.	Nashville, TN	1,040
4.	New York City, NY	3,430	4.	Green Bay, WI	1,042
5.	Los Angeles, CA	3,303	5.	Raleigh, NC	1,057

(1) Assumes $100/$300/$50 liability limits, collision and comprehensive with $500 deductibles, and $100/$300 uninsured coverage.

Leading Auto Insurers, 2005[1]

Source: National Association of Insurance Commissioners

Rank Company/Group	Direct premiums written[2]	% Market Share
1. State Farm Mutual Group	$29,471,232	18.0%
2. Allstate Insurance Co. Group	18,131,607	11.1
3. Progressive Casualty Group	12,052,274	7.4
4. National Indemnity Co. Group (Berkshire Hathaway)	10,101,325	6.2
5. Farmers Insurance Group	8,022,571	4.9

(1) By direct premiums written. (2) After reinsurance transactions, excluding state funds, as of 2005.

Leading Home Insurers, 2005[1]

Source: National Association of Insurance Commissioners

Rank Company/Group	Direct premiums written[2]	% Market Share
1. State Farm Mutual Group	$12,835,980	22.2%
2. Allstate Insurance Co. Group	7,054,405	12.2
3. Farmers Insurance Group	3,936,087	6.8
4. Nationwide Group	2,703,828	4.7
5. St. Paul Travelers Companies and Affiliates	2,416,817	4.2

(1) By direct premiums. (2) Before reinsurance transactions, excluding state funds.

Top U.S. Charities by Donations[1]

Source: The Chronicle of Philanthropy, 2006

(ranked by private support; in millions of dollars)

Rank Organization	Private Support[2]	Total Income[3]
1. United Way of America (Alexandria, VA)	$4,036.2	$4,175.5
2. Salvation Army (Alexandria, VA)	3,595.5	4,559.3
3. AmeriCares Foundation (Stamford, CT)	1,315.1	1,316.5
4. American National Red Cross (Washington, DC)	1,278.8	3,888.2
5. American Cancer Society (Atlanta, GA)	929.6	977.9
6. Fidelity Charitable Gift Fund (Boston, MA)	891.4	989.3
7. Gifts In Kind International (Alexandria, VA)	838.4	842.5
8. YMCA (Chicago, IL)	826.0	5,130.9
9. Feed the Children (Oklahoma City, OK)	803.4	852.0
10. Tulsa Community Foundation (OK)	791.3	1,052.8
11. Food for the Poor (Deerfield Beach, FL)	732.5	781.8
12. Lutheran Services in America (Baltimore, MD)	723.3	9,500.0
13. World Vision (Federal Way, WA)	647.9	905.1
14. Catholic Charities USA (Alexandria, VA)	646.2	3,385.1
15. Boys & Girls Clubs of America (Atlanta, GA)	630.4	1,335.4
16. Stanford University (CA)	603.6	NA
17. University of Wisconsin at Madison	600.1	2,489.9
18. Harvard University (Cambridge, MA)	589.9	4,994.1
19. America's Second Harvest (Chicago, IL)	542.7	550.5
20. Nature Conservancy (Arlington, VA)	475.1	919.1
21. United States Fund for UNICEF (New York, NY)	450.8	462.2
22. Habitat for Humanity International (Americus, GA)	449.6	940.5
23. American Heart Association (Dallas, TX)	447.1	589.9
24. Vanguard Charitable Endowment Program (Southeastern, PA)	435.1	457.3
25. American Lebanese Syrian Associated Charities/St. Jude Children's Research Hospital (Memphis, TN)	434.4	498.2
26. Campus Crusade for Christ International (Orlando, FL)	413.8	454.5
27. Goodwill Industries International (Bethesda, MD)	413.7	2,592.6
28. University of Pennsylvania (Philadelphia, PA)	394.3	3,786.0
29. National Christian Foundation (Atlanta, GA)	363.1	404.5
30. Cornell University (Ithaca, NY)	353.9	NA

(1) Fiscal year 2005 data used, except: 2004 data used for organizations with fiscal years ending in Jan.–March; 2004 data used for organizations with incomplete 2005 data. (2) Private support consists of donations from individuals, foundations, and corporations. (3) Total income includes private support as well as government funding, fees charged, and revenue or losses from investments made by the charity. NA = not available.

How to Obtain Birth, Death, Marriage, Divorce Records

The pamphlet "Where to Write for Vital Records: Births, Deaths, Marriages, and Divorces" (Stock # 017-022-01597-8) is available from the U.S. Government Printing Office (GPO) at a cost of $4.25. Orders can also be placed by calling (866) 512-1800 or (202) 512-1800; by mail at Superintendent of Documents, P.O. Box 371954, Pittsburgh, PA 15250; or on the Website bookstore.gpo.gov.

The complete pamphlet and other vital records information can also be accessed online at www.cdc.gov/nchs/howto/w2w/w2welcom.htm

Annual Cost of Raising a Child Born in 2006

Source: Center for Nutrition Policy and Promotion, U.S. Dept. of Agriculture

Estimated annual expenditures in 2006 dollars for a child born in 2006, by income group, for each year to age 17, assuming an average inflation rate of 3.1%. Estimates are for the younger child in a 2-parent family with 2 children, for the overall U.S.

Year (Age)	Income group[1]			Year (Age)	Income group[1]		
	Lowest	Middle	Highest		Lowest	Middle	Highest
2006 (<1)	$7,580	$10,600	$15,760	2016 (10)	$10,460	$14,400	$21,020
2007 (1)	7,810	10,930	16,250	2017 (11)	10,790	14,840	21,670
2008 (2)	8,060	11,270	16,750	2018 (12)	12,360	16,360	23,530
2009 (3)	8,490	11,960	17,690	2019 (13)	12,750	16,860	24,260
2010 (4)	8,760	12,330	18,240	2020 (14)	13,140	17,390	25,010
2011 (5)	9,030	12,710	18,800	2021 (15)	13,500	18,430	26,830
2012 (6)	9,340	12,950	18,960	2022 (16)	13,920	19,000	27,660
2013 (7)	9,630	13,350	19,550	2023 (17)	14,350	19,590	28,520
2014 (8)	9,930	13,760	20,160	TOTAL	$190,050	$260,700	$381,050
2015 (9)	10,150	13,970	20,390				

(1) In 2006, the lowest annual income group included those households earning less than $44,500 (average in this range = $27,800); middle income covered those earning $43,200-72,600 (average = $57,400); highest income group had earnings of more than $74,900 (average = $112,200).

Identity Theft

Source: Federal Trade Commission; Dept. of Justice

Identity theft and fraud are crimes in which a person wrongfully obtains and uses deception or fraud to take advantage of another person's personal data, usually for financial gain. Identifying information—such as Social Security, bank account, and credit card numbers—can be used without permission to remove funds from bank and other financial accounts. In the worst-case scenario, an identity thief could mirror a person's identity altogether, creating new accounts and vast debts, and even committing other crimes in the victim's name.

In 2006, the Federal Trade Commission (FTC) received 246,035 identity theft complaints from U.S. law enforcement and consumers, down 4% from 2005. The U.S. Dept. of Justice made identity theft and identity fraud federal offenses in 1998.

Identity Theft Prevention

You can take these simple steps (acronym, **SCAM**) to reduce your vulnerability to identity theft.

Be stingy about revealing personal information to others unless you have a reason to trust them. Adopt a "need to know" basis for revealing personal data. Keep information printed on personal bank checks to a minimum. If someone contacts you via telephone or the Internet and offers a prize but asks for personal data, ask them to mail you a form, and check the company with the Better Business Bureau (www.bbb.org). When traveling, have mail held at the post office or have a trusted person collect your mail. Be careful when throwing out documents; shredding documents containing personal or financial information is advised. Never click on links in unsolicited emails; type addresses into web browsers. Use firewalls, anti-spyware, and anti-virus software to protect your computer and the information it stores.

Check financial information often for irregular activity, and review statements for any charges or transactions that should not be there. Statements for your bank and credit card accounts should arrive monthly; if not, contact the company or financial institution.

Ask for a copy of your credit report periodically, and review it to confirm that no unknown accounts have been opened in your name. Free annual credit reports are now available by visiting www.annualcreditreport.com, calling (877) 322-8228, or writing Annual Credit Report Request Service, P.O. Box 105283, Atlanta, GA 30348. Note: Do not contact the credit bureaus directly for this.

Maintain careful records. Keep monthly statements and cancelled checks or their copies for at least a year. These can be useful if you need to dispute a transaction.

Identity Theft Recovery

If you think you have become a victim of identity theft or fraud, take action immediately.

Contact one of the three major credit bureaus to have them place a fraud alert in your file. This will require that creditors contact you before opening new accounts in your name or changing information on existing accounts. Once the alert is activated, the other two credit bureaus will be notified.

Get a copy of your credit report and review it closely. Close any accounts that have been tampered with or opened fraudulently. Speak with someone in the fraud/security department of each creditor, and follow up in writing, with copies of supporting documents. Victims of identity theft have the right to request that those debts incurred through fraud are blocked from future credit reports. An ID Theft affidavit, accepted by most credit companies, is available online at www.consumer.gov/idtheft/pdf/affidavit.pdf

Report the crime to local police or police in the community where the theft took place. Report the theft to the FTC at www.consumer.gov/idtheft or (877) IDTHEFT. You can also report to the FTC in writing at the Identity Theft Clearinghouse, Federal Trade Commission, 600 Pennsylvania Ave. NW, H-130, Washington, DC 20580.

Obtain copies of fraudulent credit and account applications from the three major credit bureaus and give copies to the police.

Contact the Social Security Administration (www.ssa.gov) if you suspect your social security number is being used.

Credit Bureau Contacts

If you think you have become a victim of identity theft or fraud, take action immediately.

Equifax. Reports: (800) 685-1111; fraud alerts: (888) 766-0008. P.O. Box 740241, Atlanta, GA 30374-0241. www.equifax.com

Experian (formerly TRW). Reports and fraud alerts: (888) 397-3742. P.O. Box 2002, Allen, TX 9530. www.experian.com

Trans Union. Reports: (877) 322-8228; P.O. Box 105281, Atlanta, GA 30348-5281. Fraud alerts: (800) 680-7289; P.O. Box 6790, Fullerton, CA 92834. www.transunion.com

POSTAL INFORMATION

Basic U.S. Postal Service

The Postal Reorganization Act, creating a government-owned postal service under the executive branch and replacing the old Post Office Department, was signed into law by Pres. Richard Nixon, Aug. 12, 1970. The service officially came into being on July 1, 1971. The U.S. Postal Service is governed by an 11-person Board of Governors. Nine of the members are appointed by the president, with Senate approval. These 9 choose a postmaster general. The board and the postmaster general choose the 11th member, who serves as deputy postmaster general. An independent Postal Rate Commission of 5 members, appointed by the president, reviews and rules on proposed postal rate increases submitted by the Board of Governors.

Congress passed the Postal Accountability and Enhancement Act, which overhauled postal service operations for the first time since 1971, on Dec. 8, 2006. New operating provisions—including the ability to adjust rates annually, negotiate for contracts with big mailers, and invest profits in internal improvements—are expected to be in place by June 2008.

U.S. Domestic Rates

(Domestic rates apply to the U.S., to its territories and possessions, and to APOs and FPOs. Many changes in domestic postal rates, fees, and services took effect May 14, 2007.)

First-Class Mail

First-Class Mail includes written matter such as letters, postal cards, and postcards (private mailing cards), plus all other matter wholly or partly in writing, whether sealed or unsealed, except book manuscripts, periodical articles and music, manuscript copy accompanying proofsheets or corrected proofsheets of the same, and the writing authorized by law on matter of other classes. Also included: matter sealed or closed against inspection, bills, and statements of accounts.

Written letters and matter sealed against inspection cost 41¢ for first ounce or fraction, 17¢ for each additional ounce or fraction thereof. Postcard postage is 26¢. U.S. Postal Service cards cost 26¢ for postage, with a 2¢ fee for the card. Presort and automation-compatible mail can qualify for lower rates if certain price minimums, mailing permits, and other requirements are met.

Express Mail

Express Mail provides guaranteed expedited service for any mailable article (up to 70 lbs and not over 108 in. in combined length and girth). Offers next day delivery by noon to most destinations; no extra charge for Saturday, Sunday, or holiday delivery. Second-day service is available to locations not on the Next Day Delivery Network. The basic rate for Express Mail weighing up to 8 oz is **$16.25**. All rates include insurance up to $100, shipment receipt, record of delivery at the destination post office, and free tracking on the USPS Web site (www.usps.com).

Express Mail Flat Rate: $16.25, regardless of weight, if matter fits into a special Postal Service flat-rate envelope.

Pickup on Demand service is available for $14.25 per stop, regardless of the number of pieces or service used (e.g., Express Mail, Priority Mail, or Parcel Post can be picked up together). Carrier pickup is complimentary.

Contact your local post office for further information.

Standard Mail

Standard Mail is limited to items less than 16 ounces such as solicitations, newsletters, advertising materials, books, cassettes, and other merchandise. It may not be used for personal correspondence. A minimum volume of 200 pieces or 50 lbs of such items is necessary, and specific bulk mail preparation and sortation requirements apply.

The minimum rate per piece for pieces 3.3 ounces or less is $0.328 for basic nonmachinable letters. Contact your post office for the discounts offered for automation, presorted, carrier route, destination entry, and other discounts. Separate rates are available for some nonprofit organizations.

Any mailer who uses standard mail is required to pay an annual (calendar year) fee of $160. Additional standards apply to mailings of nonidentical-weight pieces.

Priority Mail

Due to expeditious handling and transportation, Priority Mail is delivered in 1-3 days, on average. Priority Mail may include any mailable article up to 70 lbs and not over 108 in. in length and girth combined, including written and other First Class material.

Packages weighing less than 20 lbs and measuring over 84 in. (but less than 108 in.) in length and girth combined cost the same as the zoned rate for a 20-lb parcel. Pickup-on-demand service costs an additional $14.25 per stop, regardless of the number of pieces or service used (e.g. Express Mail, Priority Mail, or Parcel Post can be picked up together).

Priority Mail Flat Rate: $4.60, regardless of weight, if matter fits into a special Postal Service flat-rate envelope. **$8.95**, regardless of weight (under 70 lbs), if matter fits into a special Postal Service flat-rate box.

Priority Mail Rates

Weight not over (lbs)	ZONES						
	1-2	3	4	5	6	7	8
1	$4.60	$4.60	$4.60	$4.60	$4.60	$4.60	$4.60
2	4.60	4.90	5.30	6.20	6.55	7.00	7.50
3	5.05	5.70	6.40	8.25	9.10	9.65	10.55
4	5.70	6.65	7.70	10.20	11.10	12.20	13.45
5	6.30	7.55	8.90	11.90	12.90	14.35	15.85
6	6.85	8.25	10.00	12.95	13.10	14.75	16.05
7	7.35	8.85	11.00	13.95	14.35	16.40	18.30
8	7.75	9.60	11.95	14.90	15.60	18.00	20.55
9	8.15	10.25	12.50	15.90	16.85	19.60	22.85
10	8.50	10.75	13.10	16.95	18.25	21.30	25.05
11	8.80	11.20	13.65	17.95	19.75	22.90	26.35
12	9.15	11.70	14.20	18.95	21.30	24.10	27.50
13	9.50	12.20	14.75	20.00	22.85	25.05	28.45
14	9.80	12.70	15.35	20.90	24.10	26.50	29.85
15[1]	10.15	13.20	15.90	21.55	24.65	26.75	30.50

(1) See postmaster for pieces over 15 lbs.

Periodicals

Periodicals include newspapers and magazines.

For the general public, the applicable Package Services or First-Class postage is paid for periodicals.

For publishers, rates vary according to:
(1) whether item is sent to same county,
(2) percentage of editorial and advertising matter,
(3) whether the publishing org. is nonprofit or produces educational material for use in classrooms,
(4) weight,
(5) distance,
(6) level of presort,
(7) automation compatibility.

Historical Postage Rates

Postage cost for a prepaid, one-ounce letter (the first-class standard after July 1, 1885).

Effective Date	Rate	2007 Dollars	Effective Date	Rate	2007 Dollars	Effective Date	Rate	2007 Dollars
July 1, 1851	$0.06[1]	$1.48	Jan. 7, 1963	$0.05	$0.34	Feb. 17, 1985	$0.22	$0.42
July 1, 1863	0.06	1.00	Jan. 7, 1968	0.06	0.35	Apr. 3, 1988	0.25	0.43
Oct. 1, 1883	0.04	0.88	May 16, 1971	0.08	0.41	Feb. 3, 1991	0.29	0.44
July 1, 1885	0.02	0.46	Mar. 2, 1974	0.10	0.42	Jan. 1, 1995	0.32	0.43
Nov. 2, 1917[2]	0.03	0.48	Dec. 31, 1975	0.13	0.50	Jan. 10, 1999	0.33	0.41
July 1, 1919	0.02	0.24	May 29, 1978	0.15	0.47	Jan. 7, 2001	0.34	0.39
July 6, 1932	0.03	0.45	Mar. 22, 1981	0.18	0.41	June 30, 2002	0.37	0.39
Aug. 1, 1958	0.04	0.28	Nov. 1, 1981	0.20	0.45	Jan. 8, 2006	0.39	0.40

(1) For domestic letters traveling under 3,000 miles. (2) The price increased one cent during World War I; Congress restored its prewar-rate in 1919.

Package Services

Package Services, formerly "Standard Mail (B)," is any mailable matter that is not included in First-Class or Periodicals (unless permitted or required by regulations). There are currently five subclasses of Package Services: Parcel Post, Parcel Select, Bound Printed Matter, Media Mail (formerly "Special Standard Mail"), and Library Mail.

The post office determines charges for Package Services according to the weight of the package in pounds and the zone distance shipped (Media Mail and Library Mail rates are determined by weight alone). There is no minimum weight; see separate headings for maximum weight. Presort and automation-compatible mail for all Package Services can qualify for lower rates if certain piece minimums, mailing permits, and other requirements are met. Contact your local post office for further information. Package Services is not sealed against postal inspection.

Parcel Post

Parcel Post is any Package Services not mailed as Bound Print Matter, Media Mail, or Library Mail. (Parcel Select, a separate service, is used for medium-to-large volumes of packages.) Any Package Services matter may be mailed at the Parcel Post rates, subject to these basic standards: not to exceed 70 lbs. or 130 in. in combined length and girth (packages over 84 in., but not more than 108 in. in combined length and girth and under 20 lbs. are subject to the 20 lb. "balloon rate"). All fractions of a pound are counted as a full pound. Parcel Post subclass consists of two basic retail rate categories and three drop-shipped categories, the latter collectively known as Parcel Select.

Parcel Post Basic Rate Schedule

(Inter BMC/ASF ZIP codes only, machinable[1] parcels, no discount, no surcharge)

Weight not over	ZONES						
	1 & 2	3	4	5	6	7	8
1 lb.	$4.38	$4.50	$4.50	$4.50	$4.50	$4.50	$4.50
2	4.50	4.80	5.20	5.67	6.00	6.15	6.15
3	4.95	5.60	6.30	7.02	7.05	7.33	7.93
4	5.60	6.55	7.47	7.78	8.04	8.45	9.25
5	6.20	7.45	8.23	8.59	8.98	9.50	10.50
6	6.75	8.15	8.97	9.36	9.83	10.48	11.77
7	7.25	8.61	9.67	10.09	10.64	11.44	12.88
8	7.65	8.94	10.36	10.79	11.41	12.31	14.08
9	8.05	9.27	10.99	11.47	12.14	13.14	15.21
10	8.40	10.37	11.62	12.12	12.84	13.92	16.17
11	8.70	10.69	12.22	12.75	13.52	14.68	17.08
12	8.96	10.97	12.80	13.36	14.17	15.40	17.96
13	9.14	11.22	13.37	13.95	14.80	16.10	18.80
14	9.32	11.53	13.91	14.53	15.41	16.77	19.61
15	9.48	11.79	14.44	15.09	15.99	17.43	20.40
16	9.62	12.04	14.96	15.64	16.56	18.06	21.16
17	9.80	12.25	15.46	16.18	17.12	18.67	21.89
18	9.93	12.48	15.78	16.70	17.66	19.27	22.61
19	10.10	12.71	16.11	17.21	18.18	19.85	23.30
20[2]	10.22	12.92	16.42	17.71	18.70	20.41	23.98

(1) Machinable parcels must be: not less than 6 in. long, 3 in. high, and .25 in. thick or more than 34 in. long, 17 in. high, and 17 in. thick; at least 6 oz. but not more than 35 lbs. (2) Consult postmaster for pieces greater than 20 lbs.

Library Mail

(minimum weight: none; maximum weight: 70 lbs)

Applies to books, printed music, bound academic theses, periodicals, sound recordings, museum materials, and other library materials mailed between schools, colleges, universities, public libraries, museums, veteran and fraternal organizations, and nonprofit religious, educational, scientific, and labor organizations or associations (or to or from these organizations). Advertising restrictions apply. All packages must be marked "Library Mail," and may not exceed 108 in. in combined length and girth. Contact your local post office for further information.

Rates are calculated by weight only. Single-piece rates are: $2.02, up to 1 lb; 32¢ for each additional pound or fraction thereof.

Media Mail

(minimum weight: none; maximum weight: 70 lbs)

Formerly "Special Standard Mail." Applies to books of at least 8 printed pages; 16-mm or narrower-width films; printed music; printed test materials; sound recordings, playscripts, and manuscripts for books; printed educational charts; loose-leaf pages and binders consisting of medical information; computer-readable media. Advertising restrictions apply. Packages must be marked "Media Mail" and may not exceed 108 in. in combined length and girth. Contact your local post office for further information.

Rates are calculated by weight only. Single-piece rates are: $2.13, up to 1 lb; additional pounds thereafter, 34¢ each.

Bound Printed Matter

(minimum weight: none; maximum weight: 15 lbs)

Applies to advertising, promotional, directory, or editorial material that is bound by permanent fastening and consists of sheets of which at least 90% are imprinted by any process other than handwriting or typewriting. Does not include stationery (or pads of blank forms) or personal correspondence. Packages may not exceed 108 in. in combined length and girth, and must be marked "Bound Printed Matter" or "BPM."

Bound Printed Matter Rates

(zone rate for parcels; flat single pieces pay 16¢ less)

Weight not over	ZONES						
	1 & 2	3	4	5	6	7	8
1.0 lb.	$2.12	$2.17	$2.23	$2.30	$2.38	$2.45	$2.62
1.5	2.12	2.17	2.23	2.30	2.38	2.45	2.62
2.0	2.21	2.27	2.35	2.45	2.55	2.65	2.87
2.5	2.30	2.38	2.48	2.60	2.73	2.85	3.13
3.0	2.39	2.48	2.60	2.75	2.90	3.05	3.38
3.5	2.48	2.59	2.73	2.90	3.08	3.25	3.64
4.0	2.57	2.69	2.85	3.05	3.25	3.45	3.89
4.5	2.66	2.80	2.98	3.20	3.43	3.65	4.15
5.0	2.75	2.90	3.10	3.35	3.60	3.85	4.40
6.0	2.93	3.11	3.35	3.65	3.95	4.25	4.91
7.0	3.11	3.32	3.60	3.95	4.30	4.65	5.42
8.0	3.29	3.53	3.85	4.25	4.65	5.05	5.93
9.0	3.47	3.74	4.10	4.55	5.00	5.45	6.44
10.0	3.65	3.95	4.35	4.85	5.35	5.85	6.95
11.0	3.83	4.16	4.60	5.15	5.70	6.25	7.46
12.0	4.01	4.37	4.85	5.45	6.05	6.65	7.97
13.0	4.19	4.58	5.10	5.75	6.40	7.05	8.48
14.0	4.37	4.79	5.35	6.05	6.75	7.45	8.99
15.0	4.55	5.00	5.60	6.35	7.10	7.85	9.50

Domestic Mail Special Services

Delivery Confirmation

Applies to First-Class Mail parcels, Priority Mail, and Package services. Available for purchase at the time of mailing only. Provides mailer with the date and time an article was delivered and, if delivery was attempted but not successful, the date and time of the attempt. Electronic confirmation is available for barcoded matter.

Manual confirmation is available for retail purchasers on the Internet (www.usps.com) or toll-free by phone (800-222-1811).

Priority Mail fees: retail, 65¢; electronic, free. First-Class Mail parcels and Package Services fees: retail, 75¢; electronic, 18¢. Standard Mail fee: retail, 75¢; electronic, 18¢.

Change of Address

The USPS will forward mail to another address provided a Change of Address (COA) card has been filed, either in person (free), on www.usps.com ($1 fee), or by phone at 1-800-ASK-USPS ($1). The COA card, which can be picked up at any post office or printed off the Internet, can also be dropped in any mailbox for filing.

Special Handling

Provides preferential handling, but not preferential delivery, to the extent practicable in dispatch and transportation. Available for First-Class Mail, Priority Mail, and Package Services for the following surcharge: up to 10 lb, $6.90; over 10 lb, $9.60. Pieces must be marked "Special Handling."

The U.S.P.S. introduced the "Forever" stamp Apr. 12, 2007. The "Forever" stamp cost 41¢ and would always be valid as First-Class postage on standard envelopes weighing one ounce or less, even if rates change.

Registered Mail

Provides sender with mailing receipt, and a delivery record is maintained. Only matter prepaid with postage at First Class or priority mail rates may be registered. Stamps or meter stamps must be attached. The face of the article must be at least 5" long, 3½" high.

Declared Value	Fee
$0.00	$9.50
$0.01 to $100.00	10.15
$100.01 to $500.00	11.25
$500.01 to $1,000.00	12.35
$1,000.01 to $2,000.00	13.45
$2,000.01 to $3,000.00	14.55
$3,000.01 to $4,000.00	15.65
$4,000.01 to $5,000.00	16.75
$5,000.01 to $6,000.00	17.85
$6,000.01 to $7,000.00	18.95
$7,000.01 to $8,000.00	20.05
$8,000.01 to $9,000.00	21.15
$9,000.01 to $10,000.00	22.25
$10,000.01 to $25,000.00	22.25 plus $1.10 for each $1,000 or fraction thereof over $10,000
$25,000.01 to $15 million	38.75 plus $1.10 for each $1,000 or fraction thereof over $25,000
Over $15 million	16,511.25 plus any additional amount determined by the Postal Service

Note: The mailer is required to declare the value of mail presented for registration. Fee for articles with declared value over $0.00 up to $25,000.00 includes insurance; fee is in addition to postage.

Collect on Delivery (C.O.D.): Fee: $4.55 in addition to other C.O.D. charges; items must be sent as bona fide orders or be in conformity with agreements between senders and addressees. Maximum amount collectible is $1,000. For details, consult postmaster.

Certified mail: Available for any matter having no intrinsic value on which First Class or Priority Mail postage is paid. A receipt is furnished at the time of mailing, and evidence of delivery is obtained. Basic fee is $2.65 in addition to regular postage. Return receipt and restricted delivery available upon payment of additional fees. No indemnity.

Insured Mail

Applicable to Standard Mail, Package Services, and First-Class or Priority Mail items eligible to be mailed as Package Services. Matter for sale addressed to prospective purchasers who have not ordered it or authorized its sending cannot be insured. **Note:** for Express Mail, insurance is included up to $100, and additional insurance can be purchased for slightly higher fees than those on this table.

Declared Value	Insured Mail Fee[1]
$0.01 to $50.00	$1.65
$50.01 to $100.00	2.05
$100.01 to $200.00	2.45
$200.01 to $300.00	4.60
$300.01 to $400.00	5.50
$400.01 to $500.00	6.40
$500.01 to $600.00	7.30
$600.01 to $5,000.00	7.30 plus $0.90 per each $100 or fraction thereof over $600 in desired coverage

(1) In addition to postage. (Maximum liability is $5,000.) See postmaster for details on bulk discounts.

International Mail Special Services

Registration: Available, for letter-post items only, to most countries. Fee $10.15. The maximum indemnity payable is $43.7. Additional insurance may be purchased for most destinations.

Return Receipt: Shows to whom and when delivered; Fee: $2.15 (must be purchased at time of mailing).

First Class Mail International: Letter-post items weighing under 1 oz can be sent airmail for **90¢** to most countries daily; **69¢** to Canada or Mexico.

International postcards (single): 69¢ to Canada and Mexico; 90¢ to all other countries.

International Reply Coupons (IRC): Provide foreign addressees with a prepaid means of responding to communications initiated by a U.S. sender. Each IRC is equivalent to the destination country's minimum postage rate for an unregistered airmail letter. Fee: $2.00 per coupon.

Restricted Delivery: Places restrictions on who receives an item. Available to many countries for registered mail; some limitations. Fee: $4.10.

Insurance: Available to many countries for loss of or damage to items paid at parcel post rate. Consult postmaster for indemnity limits for individual countries.

Limit of indemnity not over	Fees	
	Canada[1]	Other countries[1]
$50	$1.65	$2.40
100	2.05	3.30
200	2.45	4.20
300	4.60	5.10
400	5.50	6.00
500	6.40	6.90
600	7.30	7.80
675	8.20	

(1) Not all countries insure items up to the amounts listed in the table. Canada does not insure items for more than $675.

Post Office-Authorized 2-Letter State Abbreviations

The abbreviations below are approved by the U.S. Postal Service for use in addresses.

Alabama	AL	Hawaii	HI	Missouri	MO	Pennsylvania	PA
Alaska	AK	Idaho	ID	Montana	MT	Puerto Rico	PR
American Samoa	AS	Illinois	IL	Nebraska	NE	Rhode Island	RI
Arizona	AZ	Indiana	IN	Nevada	NV	South Carolina	SC
Arkansas	AR	Iowa	IA	New Hampshire	NH	South Dakota	SD
California	CA	Kansas	KS	New Jersey	NJ	Tennessee	TN
Colorado	CO	Kentucky	KY	New Mexico	NM	Texas	TX
Connecticut	CT	Louisiana	LA	New York	NY	Utah	UT
Delaware	DE	Maine	ME	North Carolina	NC	Vermont	VT
District of Columbia	DC	Marshall Islands[1]	MH	North Dakota	ND	Virgin Islands	VI
Federated States of		Maryland	MD	Northern Mariana Is.	MP	Virginia	VA
Micronesia[1]	FM	Massachusetts	MA	Ohio	OH	Washington	WA
Florida	FL	Michigan	MI	Oklahoma	OK	West Virginia	WV
Georgia	GA	Minnesota	MN	Oregon	OR	Wisconsin	WI
Guam	GU	Mississippi	MS	Palau[1]	PW	Wyoming	WY

(1) Although an independent nation, this country is currently subject to domestic rates and fees.

Canadian Province and Territory Postal Abbreviations

Source: Canada Post

Alberta	AB	Newfoundland and		Nunavut	NU	Quebec	QC[1]
British Columbia	BC	Labrador	NL	Ontario	ON	Saskatchewan	SK
Manitoba	MB	Northwest Territories	NT	Prince Edward		Yukon Territory	YT
New Brunswick	NB	Nova Scotia	NS	Island	PE		

(1) PQ is also acceptable.

Old-Age, Survivors, and Disability Insurance; Medicare; Supplemental Security Income; Temporary Assistance to Needy Families

Source: Social Security Administration; World Almanac research; provisions shown are as under current law, Sept. 2007

Social Security Benefits

Social Security benefits are based on a worker's **primary insurance amount (PIA)**, which is related by law to the average indexed monthly earnings (AIME) on which Social Security contributions have been paid. The full PIA is payable to a worker retiring at age 65 (plus a certain number of months after the 65th birthday, depending on birth year), and to an entitled disabled worker at any age. Spouses and children of retired or disabled workers and survivors of deceased workers receive set proportions of the PIA subject to a family maximum amount.

The PIA is calculated by applying varying percentages to succeeding parts of the AIME. The formula is adjusted annually to reflect changes in average annual wages.

Automatic increases in Social Security benefits are initiated for December of each year, assuming the Consumer Price Index (CPI) for the 3rd calendar quarter of the year increased relative to the base quarter, which is either the 3rd calendar quarter of the preceding year or the quarter in which an increase legislated by Congress became effective. The size of the benefit increase is determined by the percentage rise of the CPI between the quarters measured.

The **average monthly benefit** payable to all retired workers amounted to $1,044 in Dec. 2006. The average benefit for disabled workers in that month amounted to $978.

Minimum and maximum monthly retired-worker benefits payable for individuals who retired at age 65[1]

Year attaining age 65	Minimum benefit[2] Paid at retirement	Minimum benefit[2] Payable as of Dec. 2005	Maximum benefit[2] Payable at retirement	Maximum benefit[2] Payable effective Dec. 2006
1970....	$64.00	$360.90	(3)	(4)
1980....	133.90	360.90	$572.00	$1,597.90
1990....	(5)	(5)	975.00	1,572.20
1995....	(5)	(5)	1,199.10	1,628.80
1996....	(5)	(5)	1,248.90	1,653.50
1997....	(5)	(5)	1,326.60	1,707.10
1998....	(5)	(5)	1,342.80	1,692.85
1999....	(5)	(5)	1,373.10	1,708.40
2000....	(5)	(5)	1,434.80	1,742.40
2001....	(5)	(5)	1,536.70	1,804.20
2002....	(5)	(5)	1,660.50	1,898.30
2003....	(5)	(5)	1,741.10	1,941.20
2004....	(5)	(5)	1,825.40	1,970.90
2005....	(5)	(5)	1,847.30	2,015.40
2006....	(5)	(5)	1,961.90	2,026.60

(1) Assumes retirement at beginning of year. (2) The final benefit amount payable is rounded to next lower $1 (if not already a multiple of $1). (3) Benefits $196.40 for women and $189.80 for men. (4) Benefits $1,110.43 for women and $1,072.20 for men. (5) Minimum eliminated for workers who reached age 62 after 1981.

Amount of Work Required

To qualify for benefits, the worker generally must have worked a certain length of time in covered employment. Just how long depends on when the worker reaches age 62 or, if earlier, when he or she dies or becomes disabled. A person born after 1929 who dies, becomes disabled, or reaches age 62 after 1991 must generally have had at least 10 years work credit to qualify for benefits.

A person is **fully insured** who has 1 quarter of coverage for every year after 1950 (or year age 21 is reached, if later) up to but not including the year the worker reaches 62, dies, or becomes disabled. In 2007, a person earns 1 quarter of coverage for each $1,000 of annual earnings in covered employment, up to 4 quarters per year.

To receive **disability benefits**, the worker, in addition to being fully insured, must generally have credit for 20 quarters of coverage out of the 40 calendar quarters before he or she became disabled. A disabled blind worker need meet only the fully insured requirement. Persons disabled before age 31 can qualify with a briefer period of coverage. Certain survivor benefits are payable if the deceased worker had 6 quarters of coverage in the 13 quarters preceding death.

Contribution and benefit base

Calendar year	OASDI[1]	Calendar year	OASDI[1]	Calendar year	OASDI[1]
1994	$60,600	1999	$72,600	2004	$87,900
1995	61,200	2000	76,200	2005	90,000
1996	62,700	2001	80,400	2006	94,200
1997	65,400	2002	84,900	2007	97,500
1998	68,400	2003	87,000	2008	102,300[2]

(1) Old-Age, Survivors, and Disability Ins. (2) Estimate. **Note:** There is no base limit for Hospital Ins.

Tax Rate Schedule

(percentage of covered earnings)

Year	Total (for employees and employers, each)	OASDI	HI
1979-80	6.13	5.08	1.05
1981	6.65	5.35	1.30
1982-83	6.70	5.40	1.30
1984	7.00	5.70	1.30
1985	7.05	5.70	1.35
1986-87	7.15	5.70	1.45
1988-89	7.51	6.06	1.45
1990 and after	7.65	6.20	1.45
	(for self-employed)		
1979-80	8.10	7.05	1.05
1981	9.30	8.00	1.30
1982-83	9.35	8.05	1.30
1984	14.00	11.40	2.60
1985	14.10	11.40	2.70
1986-87	14.30	11.40	2.90
1988-89	15.02	12.12	2.90
1990 and after	15.30	12.40	2.90

What Aged Workers Receive

A person may receive monthly old-age benefits when he or she has enough work in covered employment and has reached retirement age—age 62 for reduced benefits, the age below for full benefits.

Full-Benefit Retirement Age (FRA) by Birth Year

Year of Birth	FRA	Year of Birth	FRA
1937 or earlier	65	1943-1954	66
1938	65 and 2 months	1955	66 and 2 months
1939	65 and 4 months	1956	66 and 4 months
1940	65 and 6 months	1957	66 and 6 months
1941	65 and 8 months	1958	66 and 8 months
1942	65 and 10 months	1959	66 and 10 months
		1960	67

Note: If born on Jan. 1, refer to the previous birth year.

In 2000, the retirement **earnings test** was eliminated beginning with the month when the beneficiary reaches **full-benefit retirement age (FRA)**. A person at and above FRA no longer has benefits reduced because of earnings. However, in the calendar year a beneficiary reaches FRA, benefits are reduced $1 for every $3 of earnings above the limit allowed by law ($34,440 in 2007) for the months prior to FRA. For years before the beneficiary attains FRA, the reduction is $1 for every $2 of earnings over the exempt amount ($12,960 for year 2007).

For workers who reached age 65 between 1982 and 1989, Social Security benefits are raised by 3% for each year for which the worker between FRA and 70 (72 before 1984) failed to receive benefits, whether because of earnings from work, because the worker had not applied for benefits, or because the worker declined benefits after entitlement. The **delayed retirement credit** is 1% per year for workers who reached age 65 before 1982. The delayed retirement credit is scheduled to rise to 8% per year for 2008 and years after. The rate for workers who reached age 65 in 1998-99 is 5.5%; 2000-01, 6.0%; 2002-03, 6.5%; 2004-05, 7.0%. For 2006-07 it is 7.5%.

For workers retiring early, before full retirement age, benefits are **permanently reduced** ⁵⁄₉ of 1% for each month before FRA, up to 36 months. If the number of months exceeds 36, then the benefit is further reduced ⁵⁄₁₂ of 1% per month.

For example, when FRA reaches 67, for workers who retire at exactly age 62, there are a total of 60 months of reduction. The reduction for the first 36 months is ⅗ of 36%, or

20%. The reduction for the remaining 24 months is $5/12$ of 24%, or 10%. Thus, when the FRA reaches 67, the amount of reduction at age 62 will be 30%. The nearer to FRA the worker is when he or she begins collecting a benefit, the larger the monthly benefit will be.

Benefits for Worker's Spouse

The spouse of a worker who is getting Social Security retirement or disability payments may become entitled to an insurance benefit of **one-half of the worker's PIA** if he or she claims benefits at full retirement age. Reduced spouse's benefits are available at age 62 and are permanently reduced $25/36$ of 1% for each month before FRA, up to 36 months. If the number of months exceeds 36, then the benefit is further reduced $5/12$ of 1% per month. Benefits are also payable to the aged divorced spouse of an insured worker if he or she was married to the worker for at least 10 years. To qualify for divorced spouse benefits, the insured worker does not have to be receiving benefits if the divorce occurred at least 2 years earlier. Benefits received as a spouse are reduced by the amount of one's own PIA based on their own earnings.

Benefits for Children of Workers

If a retired or disabled worker has a child under age 18, the **child** will usually get a benefit equal to half of the worker's unreduced benefit. So will the worker's spouse, even if under age 62, if he or she is **caring for an entitled child** of the worker who is under 16 or became disabled before age 22. However, total benefits paid on a worker's earnings record are subject to a family maximum. Total monthly benefits paid to the family of a worker who retired in 2007 at 65 and 10 months and always had the maximum earnings creditable under Social Security cannot exceed $3,704.10.

When entitled children reach age 18, their benefits generally stop, but a child disabled before age 22 may get a benefit as long as the disability meets the definition in the law. Benefits will be paid until age 19 to a child attending elementary or secondary school full-time.

Benefits may also be paid to a grandchild or step-grandchild of a worker or of his or her spouse, in special circumstances.

OASDI Beneficiaries

Beneficiaries	May 2004	May 2005	May 2006	May 2007
Total (in thousands)[1]	47,378	48,068	48,877	49,614
Aged 65 and over, total . . .	33,400	33,811	34,232	34,752
Retired workers	27,014	27,413	27,898	28,448
Survivors/dependents . .	6,386	6,286	6,192	6,304
Under age 65, total.	13,978	14,257	14,645	14,862
Retired workers	2,668	2,809	2,883	2,874
Disabled workers	6,035	6,239	6,465	6,702
Survivors/dependents . .	5,275	5,209	5,297	5,286
Total monthly benefits (in millions)	$39,960	$42,074	$44,956	$47,592

(1) Totals may not add because of rounding or incomplete enumeration.

What Disabled Workers Receive

A worker who becomes unable to work may be eligible for a monthly **disability benefit**. Benefits continue until it is determined that the individual is no longer disabled. When a disabled-worker beneficiary reaches FRA (65 years, 10 months in 2007 for workers born in 1942), the disability benefit becomes a retired-worker benefit. In June 2007, there were 200,204 disabled worker beneficiaries aged 65 and older who had not reached FRA.

Benefits generally like those for dependents of retired-worker beneficiaries may be paid to dependents of disabled beneficiaries. However, the maximum family benefit in disability cases is generally lower than in retirement cases.

Survivor Benefits

If an insured worker should die, one or more types of benefits may be payable to survivors, again subject to a maximum family benefit as described above.

1. If claiming benefits at FRA, the **surviving spouse** will receive a benefit equal to 100% of the deceased worker's benefit. Benefits claimed before FRA are reduced for age with a maximum reduction of 28.5% at age 60. However, if the deceased worker claimed benefits before FRA, the sur-

viving spouse's benefits are limited to the reduced amount the worker would be getting if alive, but not less than 82.5% of the worker's PIA. Remarriage after the worker's death ends the surviving spouse's benefit rights. However, if the widow(er) marries and the marriage is ended, he or she regains benefit rights. (A marriage after age 60, age 50 if disabled, is deemed not to have occurred for benefit purposes.) Survivor benefits may also be paid to a divorced spouse if the marriage lasted for at least 10 years.

Disabled widows and widowers may under certain circumstances qualify for benefits after attaining age 50 at the rate of 71.5% of the deceased worker's PIA. The widow or widower must have become totally disabled before or within 7 years after the spouse's death or the last month in which he or she received mother's or father's insurance benefits.

2. There is a benefit for each **child under age 18**. The monthly benefit for a child of a deceased worker is $3/4$ of the PIA, subject to the family maximum. A child with a disability that began before age 22 may also receive benefits. Also, a child may receive benefits until reaching age 19 if he or she is in full-time attendance at an elementary or secondary school.

3. There is a **mother's or father's benefit** for the widow(er) if children of the worker under age 16 are in his or her care. The benefit is 75% of the PIA (subject to the family maximum), and it continues until the youngest child reaches age 16, at which time payments stop even if the child's benefit continues. However, if the widow(er) has a disabled child beneficiary age 16 or over in care, benefits may continue.

4. **Dependent parents** may be eligible for benefits if they have been receiving at least half their support from the worker before his or her death, have reached age 62, and (except in certain circumstances) have not remarried since the worker's death. Each parent gets 75% of the worker's PIA; if only one parent survives, the benefit is 82%, but could be reduced for the family maximum.

5. A **lump sum** cash payment of **$255** is made when there is a spouse who was living with the worker or a spouse or child eligible for immediate monthly survivor benefits.

Self-Employed Workers

A self-employed person who has **net earnings of $400** or more in a year must report such earnings for Social Security tax and credit purposes. The person reports net returns from the business. Income from real estate, savings, dividends, loans, pensions, or insurance policies are not included unless it is part of the business.

A self-employed person receives 1 quarter of coverage for each $1,000 (for 2007), up to a maximum of 4 quarters per year.

The nonfarm self-employed have the option of reporting their earnings as $2/3$ of their gross income from self-employment. This option can be used only if actual net earnings from self-employment income are less than $1,600 and less than $2/3$ of their gross income. The option may be used only 5 times. Also, the self-employed person must have actual net earnings of $400 or more in 2 of the 3 taxable years immediately preceding the year in which he or she uses the option.

When a person has both taxable wages and earnings from self-employment, wages are credited for Social Security purposes first; only as much self-employment income as brings total earnings up to the current taxable maximum becomes subject to the self-employment tax.

Farm Owners and Workers

Self-employed farmers whose gross annual earnings from farming are from **$600-$2,400** may report $2/3$ of their gross earnings instead of net earnings for Social Security purposes. (Farmers whose gross annual earnings are under $600 cannot use the optional method.) Farmers whose gross income is over $2,400 and whose net earnings are less than $1,600 can report $1,600. Cash or crop shares received from a tenant or share farmer count if the owner participated materially in production or management. The self-employed farmer pays contributions at the same rate as other self-employed persons.

Agricultural employees. A worker's earnings from farm work count toward benefits (1) if the employer pays the worker $150 or more in cash during the year; or (2) if the employer spends $2,500 or more in the year for agricultural labor. Under these rules, a person gets credit for 1 calendar quarter for each $1,000 in cash pay in 2007.

Foreign farm workers admitted to the U.S. on a temporary basis are not covered.

Household Workers

If an employer pays a household worker (e.g. maid, cook, laundry worker, nurse, babysitter, chauffeur, gardener, or other worker), who is age 18 or older, $1,500 or more in wages in 2007, the wages are covered under Social Security. This includes transportation costs paid for in cash. The job need not be regular or full-time. The employee should get a Social Security card at the Social Security office and show it to the employer.

The employer deducts the amount of the employee's Social Security tax from the worker's pay, adds an identical amount as the employer's Social Security tax, and sends the total amount to the federal government.

Medicare Coverage

The Medicare health insurance program provides acute-care coverage for Social Security and Railroad Retirement beneficiaries age 65 and over, for persons entitled to 24 months to receive Social Security or Railroad Retirement disability benefits, and for certain persons with end-stage kidney disease. What follows is a basic description and may not cover all circumstances.

The **basic Medicare plan**, available nationwide, is a fee-for-service arrangement, where the beneficiary may use any provider accepting Medicare; some services are not covered and there are some out-of-pocket costs.

Hospital insurance (Part A). The basic hospital insurance program pays covered services for hospital and posthospital care including the following:

- All necessary inpatient hospital care for the first 60 days of each benefit period, except for a deductible ($992 in 2007). For days 61-90, Medicare pays for services over and above a coinsurance amount ($248 per day in 2007). After 90 days, the beneficiary has 60 lifetime reserve days for which Medicare helps pay. The coinsurance amount for reserve days was $496 in 2007.
- Up to 100 days of care in a skilled-nursing facility in each benefit period. Hospital insurance pays for all covered services for the first 20 days; for the 21-100th day, the beneficiary pays coinsurance ($124 per day in 2007).
- Part-time home health care provided by nurses or other health workers.
- Limited coverage of hospice care for individuals certified to be terminally ill.

There is a premium for this insurance in certain cases.

Medical insurance (Part B). Elderly persons can receive benefits under this supplementary program only if they sign up for them and agree to a monthly premium. As of 2007, the monthly premium is tied to annual income. Individuals with income less than $80,000 and couples with income under $160,000 pay $93.50 per person if signing up upon becoming eligible in 2007. The federal government pays the covered costs of treatment. The Part B deductible was $131 in 2007; as of 2006, the deductible rose annually in proportion to the increase in average cost of Part B services to beneficiaries. After the deductible, the medical insurance program usually pays 80% of the approved amount for the following services:

- Covered services received from a doctor in his or her office, in a hospital, in a skilled-nursing facility, at home, or in other locations.
- Medical and surgical services, including anesthesia.
- Diagnostic tests and procedures that are part of the patient's treatment.
- Radiology and pathology services by doctors while the individual is a hospital inpatient or outpatient.
- Other services such as X rays, services of a doctor's office nurse, drugs and biologicals that cannot be self-administered, transfusions of blood and blood components, medical supplies, physical/occupational therapy and speech pathology services.

In addition to the above, certain other tests or preventive measures are now covered without an additional premium. These include a "Welcome to Medicare" physical exam and related services, mammograms, bone mass measurement, colo-rectal cancer screening, and flu shots. Routine physical exams, dental care, hearing aids, and routine eye care are generally not covered under the basic plan. There is limited coverage for nonhospital treatment of mental illness.

To get medical insurance (Part B), persons approaching age 65 may enroll in the **Initial Enrollment Period** that lasts from 3 months before to 3 months after the 65th birthday, and the month of their birthday. If new enrollers desire coverage to begin in the month they reach age 65, they must enroll in the 3 months before their birthday. Persons not enrolling within their first enrollment period may enroll later, but late-enrollment premiums may apply.

The monthly premium is deducted from the cash benefit for persons receiving Social Security, Railroad Retirement, or Civil Service retirement benefits. Income from the medical premiums and the federal matching payments are put in a Supplementary Medical Insurance Trust Fund, from which benefits and administrative expenses are paid.

Under **Medicare Advantage (Part C)** (formerly Medicare + Choice), persons eligible for Medicare may have the option of getting services through a health maintenance organization (HMO) or other **managed care** plan. Any such plan must provide at least the same benefits, except for hospice services, and may provide added benefits—such as lower or no deductibles and coverage for some prescription drugs—but is usually subject to restrictions in choice of health care providers. In some plans services by outside providers are still covered for an extra out-of-pocket cost. Also available as options in some areas are Medicare-approved private fee-for-service plans and Medicare medical savings accounts.

Prescription Drug Coverage (Part D). Effective Jan. 1, 2006, a Medicare prescription drug plan provides insurance coverage for prescription drugs. Medicare recipients pay a monthly premium (averaging about $22 in 2007, depending on the provider) and a portion of drug costs. **Enrollment is scheduled to take place Nov. 15-Dec. 31 each year**, and is optional. Coverage varies depending on the drug plan selected.

Further details are available on the Internet at www.medicare.gov or by calling 1-800-MEDICARE (1-800-633-4227).

Medicare card. Persons qualifying for hospital insurance under Social Security receive a health insurance card similar to cards used by other health insurers. The card indicates whether the individual has taken out medical insurance protection. It is to be shown to the hospital, skilled-nursing facility, home health agency, doctor, or whoever provides the covered services.

Payments are generally made only in the 50 states, Puerto Rico, Virgin Islands, Guam, and American Samoa.

Social Security Financing

Social Security is paid for by a tax on certain earnings (for 2007, on earnings up to $97,500) for **Old Age, Survivors, and Disability Insurance** and on all earnings (no upper limit) for Hospital Insurance with the **Medicare** Program; the taxable earnings base for OASDI has been adjusted annually to reflect increases in average wages. The employed worker and his or her employer share Social Security taxes equally.

Employers remit amounts withheld from employee wages for Social Security and income taxes to the Internal Revenue Service; employer Social Security taxes are also payable at the same time. (Self-employed workers pay Social Security taxes when filing their regular income tax forms.) The Social Security taxes (along with revenues arising from partial taxation of the Social Security benefits of certain high-income people) are transferred to the Social Security Trust Funds—the Federal Old-Age and Survivors Insurance (OASI) Trust Fund, the Federal Disability Insurance (DI) Trust Fund, and the Federal Hospital Insurance (HI) Trust Fund; they can be used only to pay benefits, the cost of rehabilitation services, and administrative expenses. Money not immediately needed for these purposes is by law invested in obligations of the federal government, which must pay interest on the money borrowed and repay the principal when the obligations are redeemed or mature.

Supplemental Security Income

On Jan. 1, 1974, the **Supplemental Security Income** (**SSI**) program established by the 1972 Social Security Act amendments replaced the former federal grants to states for aid to the needy aged, blind, and disabled in the 50 states and the District of Columbia. The program provides both for federal payments, based on uniform national standards and eligibility requirements, and for state supplementary payments varying from state to state. The Social Security Administration administers the federal payments financed from general funds of the Treasury—and the state supplements as well, if the state elects to have its supplementary program federally administered. States may supplement the federal payment for all recipients and must supplement it for per-

sons otherwise adversely affected by the transition from the former public assistance programs. In May 2007, the number of persons receiving federally administered SSI payments was 7,312,686 and the payments totaled approximately $3.6 billion.

The **maximum** monthly federal SSI payment for individuals with no other countable income, living in their own household, was $623 in 2007. For couples the maximum payment was $934.

Social Security Statement

On Oct. 1, 1999, the Social Security Administration initiated regular mailings of an annual *Social Security Statement* to all workers age 25 and older not already receiving benefits. Workers will automatically receive statements about 3 months before their birth month. The statement provides estimates of potential monthly Social Security retirement, disability, and survivor benefits as well as a record of lifetime earnings. The statement also gives workers an easy way to determine whether their earnings are accurately posted in Social Security records.

For further information contact the Social Security Administration toll-free at 1-800-772-1213 or visit its website at www.socialsecurity.gov

Examples of Monthly Benefits Available

Description of benefit or beneficiary	For low earnings ($17,400 in 2007)[1]	For med. earnings ($38,700 in 2007)[2]	For max. earnings ($86,000 in 2007)
Primary insurance amount (worker retiring at 65 years, 10 months...	$833.20	$1,372.80	$2,116.30
Maximum family benefit (worker retiring at 65 years, 10 months)	1,249.90	2,506.50	3,704.10
Maximum family disability benefit (worker disabled at 55; in 2007)* ..	1,203.60	2,102.10	3,289.00
Disabled worker (worker disabled at 55)			
Worker alone[2]	847.00	1,401.00	2,192.00
Worker, spouse, and 1 child.	1,203.00	2,102.00	3,289.00
Retired worker claiming benefits at age 62:			
Worker alone[2]	628.00	1,035.00	1,589.00
Worker with spouse claiming benefits at—			
FRA or over	1,047.00	1,725.00	2,648.00
Age 62[3]	921.00	1,518.00	2,330.00
Widow or widower claiming benefits at—			
Age 65 and 10 months or over[3]	833.00	1,372.00	2,116.00
Age 60[3]	595.00	981.00	1,513.00
Disabled widow or widower claiming benefits at age 50-59[4]	595.00	981.00	1,513.00
1 surviving child[3]	624.00	1,029.00	1,587.00
Widow or widower NRA or over and 1 child[3]	1,249.00	2,401.00	3,703.00
Widowed mother or father and 1 child[3]	1,248.00	2,058.00	3,174.00
Widowed mother or father and 2 children[3]...................	1,249.00	2,506.00	3,704.00

Effective Jan. 2007. *Assumes work beginning at age 22. (1) Career average earnings: an average of lifetime earnings indexed to the year prior to entitlement (2006 in this case). (2) Assumes maximum reduction. (3) Assumes worker lived and worked until NRA without receiving reduced benefits. (4) Effective Jan. 1984, disabled widow(er) claiming a benefit at ages 50-59 receive a benefit equal to 71.5% of the PIA.

Social Security Recipients[1], by Age, Sex, and Race, 2006

Source: Social Security Administration

	Total[2]	White	Black	American Indian, Alaska Native	Asian
Social Security beneficiaries (thousands)					
Total	41,364	36,087	4,154	564	976
Sex					
Male	17,781	15,662	1,671	263	386
Female	23,584	20,425	2,482	301	589
Age					
15–54	4,912	3,794	984	125	113
55–64	5,272	4,483	651	110	107
65–74	15,743	13,867	1,373	195	437
75 or older...............................	15,437	13,943	1,146	134	318
Supplemental Security Income recipients (thousands)					
Total......................................	5,215	3,617	1,324	156	222
Sex					
Male	2,132	1,525	501	59	91
Female	3,083	2,092	823	97	131
Age					
15–54	3,074	2,114	859	102	74
55–64	965	713	200	26	42
65–74	602	412	146	15	34
75 or older................................	574	379	119	13	71
Average annual benefit in 2005					
Social Security	$10,732	$10,902	$9,402	$9,726	$10,365
Supplemental Security Income.......................	5,973	5,966	5,826	5,543	7,289

Note: Race categories include people who reported themselves as that race alone or in combination with one or more other races. (1) Persons 15 or older receiving Social Security benefits or Supplemental Security Income in March 2006. (2) The sum of the individual categories may not equal the total because of independent rounding.

OASDI Recipients and Monthly Payments, 1940-2005

Source: Social Security Administration

Year	Total recipients	Monthly Benefits Total (thousands)	Avg.[1]	Avg. (2005 dollars[2])	Year	Total recipients	Monthly Benefits Total (thousands)	Avg.[1]	Avg. (2005 dollars[2])
1940	222,488	$4,070	$18.29	$255.19	1985	37,058,317	$15,901,579	$429.10	$778.83
1945	1,288,107	23,801	18.48	200.48	1990	39,832,125	21,686,763	544.45	813.56
1950	3,477,243	126,857	36.48	295.64	1995	43,387,259	28,148,078	648.76	831.39
1955	7,960,616	411,613	51.71	376.80	2000	45,414,794	34,848,920	767.35	870.28
1960	14,844,589	936,321	63.07	416.17	2001	45,877,506	36,504,206	795.69	846.68
1965	20,866,767	1,516,802	72.69	450.68	2002	46,444,317	37,854,453	815.05	884.82
1970	26,228,629	2,628,326	100.21	504.40	2003	47,038,486	39,541,528	840.62	892.25
1975	32,084,511	5,727,758	178.52	648.05	2004	47,687,693	41,574,348	871.80	901.34
1980	35,584,955	10,682,791	300.21	1089.78	2005	48,434,281	44,351,668	915.71	915.71

Note: OASDI = Old Age, Survivors, and Disability Insurance. Disability insurance payments began in 1957. (1) Avg. monthly benefit does not necessarily reflect individual payments to OASDI recipients. (2) Monthly benefit adjusted for inflation.

Social Security Trust Funds

Old-Age and Survivors Insurance Trust Fund, 1940-2006

(in millions)

Fiscal year[1]	INCOME Total	Net contribs.[2]	Income from taxing benefits	Payments from the Treasury fund[3]	Net interest[4]	DISBURSEMENTS Total	Benefit payments[5]	Admin. expenses	Transfers to Railroad Retirement program	Net increase in fund[6]	Fund at end of period
1940	$592	$550	—	—	$42	$28	$16	$12	—	$564	$1,745
1950	2,367	2,106	—	$4	257	784	727	57	—	1,583	12,893
1960	10,360	9,843	—	—	517	11,073	10,270	202	$600	–713	20,829
1970	31,746	29,955	—	442	1,350	27,321	26,268	474	579	4,425	32,616
1980	100,051	97,608	—	557	1,886	103,228	100,626	1,160	1,442	–3,177	24,566
1990	278,607	261,506	2,924	34	14,143	223,481	218,948	1,564	2,969	55,126	203,445
1995	326,067	289,529	5,114	7	31,417	294,456	288,607	1,797	4,052	31,611	447,946
2000	484,228	418,219	12,476	—	53,532	353,396	347,868	1,990	3,538	130,832	893,003
2001	513,834	440,819	11,771	—	61,243	372,996	367,654	2,069	3,273	140,837	1,033,840
2002	529,257	448,133	12,597	414	68,113	389,546	383,942	2,111	3,493	139,711	1,173,551
2003	542,343	456,014	12,340	—	73,990	402,814	396,710	2,522	3,580	139,530	1,313,080
2004	556,523	466,807	13,269	1	76,446	417,053	411,148	2,274	3,628	139,470	1,452,550
2005	599,992	502,998	15,332	—	81,662	436,919	430,439	2,900	3,579	163,073	1,615,623
2006	632,157	530,006	15,176	–350	87,324	455,560	449,191	2,911	3,458	176,597	1,792,220

(1) Fiscal years 1980 and later consist of the 12 months ending on Sept. 30 of each year. Fiscal years prior to 1977 consisted of the 12 months ending on June 30 of each year. (2) Beginning in 1983, includes transfers from general fund of Treasury representing contributions that would have been paid on deemed wage credits for military service in 1957 and later, if such credits were considered covered wages. (3) Includes payments (a) in 1947-52 and in 1967 and later, for costs of noncontributory wage credits for military service performed before 1957; (b) in 1972-83, for costs of deemed wage credits for military service performed after 1956; and (c) in 1969 and later, for costs of benefits to certain uninsured persons who attained age 72 before 1968. (4) Net interest includes net profits or losses on marketable investments. Beginning in 1967, administrative expenses were charged currently to the trust fund on an estimated basis, with a final adjustment, including interest, made in the next fiscal year. The amounts of these interest adjustments are included in net interest. For years prior to 1967, the method of accounting for administrative expenses is described in the 1970 Annual Report. Beginning in Oct. 1973, the figures shown include relatively small amounts of gifts to the fund. During 1983-91, interest paid from the trust fund to the general fund on advance tax transfers is reflected. (5) Beginning in 1967, includes payments for vocational rehabilitation services furnished to disabled persons receiving benefits because of their disabilities. Beginning in 1983, amounts are reduced by amount of reimbursement for unnegotiated benefit checks. (6) Net change in assets during fiscal year, including amounts borrowed or repaid by other funds.

Disability Insurance Trust Fund, 1960-2006

(in millions)

Fiscal year[1]	INCOME Total	Net contribs.[2]	Income from taxing benefits	Payments from the Treasury fund[3]	Net interest[4]	DISBURSEMENTS Total	Benefit pymts.[5]	Admin. expenses	Transfers to Railroad Retirement program	Net increase in fund[6]	Fund at end of period
1960	$1,034	$987	—	—	$47	$533	$528	$32	$–27	$501	$2,167
1970	4,380	4,141	—	$16	223	2,954	2,795	149	10	1,426	5,104
1980	17,376	16,805	—	118	453	15,320	14,998	334	–12	2,056	7,680
1990	28,215	27,291	$158	—	766	25,124	24,327	717	80	3,091	11,455
1995	70,209	67,987	335	—	1,888	41,374	40,234	1,072	68	28,835	35,206
2000	77,023	70,001	756	—	6,266	56,008	54,244	1,608	159	21,014	113,752
2001	82,079	74,611	732	–836	7,573	59,930	58,098	1,762	10	22,149	135,901
2002	85,720	76,067	936	—	8,717	66,364	64,138	2,005	154	19,356	155,258
2003	87,909	77,431	919	—	9,559	71,907	69,716	1,968	167	16,002	171,260
2004	90,105	79,269	1,047	—	9,789	78,471	76,139	2,070	215	11,634	182,893
2005	96,765	85,418	1,164	—	10,183	86,360	83,721	2,301	338	10,405	193,298
2006	101,571	90,001	1,174	—	10,396	92,932	90,064	2,480	388	8,640	201,938

(1) Fiscal years 1977 and later consist of the 12 months ending Sept. 30 of each year. Fiscal years prior to 1977 consisted of the 12 months ending June 30 of each year. (2) Beginning in 1983, includes transfers from general fund of Treasury representing contributions that would have been paid on deemed wage credits for military service in 1957 and later, if such credits were considered to be covered wages. (3) Includes payments (a) for costs of noncontributory wage credits for military service performed before 1957; and (b) in 1972-83, for costs of deemed wage credits for military service performed after 1956. (4) Net interest includes net profits or losses on marketable investments. Administrative expenses are charged currently to the trust fund on an estimated basis, with a final adjustment, including interest, made in the following fiscal year. Figures shown include relatively small amounts of gifts to the fund. During the years 1983-91, interest paid from the trust fund to the general fund on advance tax transfers is reflected. (5) Includes payments for vocational rehabilitation services. Beginning in 1983, amounts are reduced by amount of reimbursement for unnegotiated benefit checks. (6) Net change in assets during fiscal year, including amounts borrowed or repaid by other funds. **NOTE:** Totals may not add because of rounding.

Supplementary Medical Insurance Trust Fund (Medicare SMI), 1975-2006

(in millions)

Fiscal year[1]	Total	INCOME Premium from participants[2]	INCOME Government contribs.[3]	INCOME Transfers from states[4]	INCOME Interest and other income[5,6]	Total	DISBURSEMENTS Benefit payments[6,7,8]	DISBURSEMENTS Admin. expenses	Net change	Balance in fund at end of year[9]
1975	$4,322	$1,887	$2,330	—	$106	$4,170	$3,765	$404	$152	$1,424
1980	10,275	2,928	6,932	—	416	10,737	10,144	593	-462	4,532
1990	46,138[10]	11,494[10]	33,210	—	1,434[10]	43,022[10]	41,498	1,524[10]	3,115[10]	14,527[10]
1995	58,169	19,244	36,988	—	1,937	65,213	63,491	1,722	-7,045	13,874
1996	82,025	18,931	61,702	—	1,392	68,946	67,176	1,771	26,953	1,392
1997	80,806	19,141	59,471	—	2,193	72,553	71,133	1,420	35,206	2,193
1998	81,955	19,427	59,919	—	2,608	76,272	74,837[7]	1,435	40,889	2,608
1999	85,278	20,160	62,185	—	2,933	80,518	79,008[7]	1,510	45,649	2,933
2000	89,239	20,515	65,561	—	3,164	88,992	87,212[11]	1,780	247	45,896
2001	95,336	22,307	69,838	—	3,191	99,452	97,466[11]	1,986	-4,116	41,780
2002	105,705	24,427	78,318	—	2,960	108,825	106,995[11]	1,830	-3,121	38,659
2003	110,194	26,834	80,905	—	2,455	124,055	121,699[11]	2,356	-13,861	24,799
2004	126,805	30,341	94,734	—	1,730	134,490	131,673	2,817	-7,684	17,114
2005	152,505	35,939	115,200	—	1,366	152,735	149,820	2,914	-230	16,885
2006	211,926	44,216[12]	162,601	3,630	1,478	195,531	192,058[12]	3,474	16,394	33,279

(1) Fiscal year 1975 consists of the 12 months ending on June 30, 1975; fiscal years 1980 and later consist of the 12 months ending on Sept. 30 of each year. (2) For Part D, premiums include both amounts withheld from Social Security benefit checks (and other certain federal benefit payments) and amounts paid directly to Part D plans (estimated). (3) For Part B, includes matching payments from the general fund, plus certain interest-adjustment items. For Part D, includes all federal govt. transfers. Includes amounts for the transitional assistance benefits in 2004-06. (4) As of 2006, Medicaid is no longer the primary payer for full-benefit dual eligibles. States must pay a portion of their estimated forgone drug costs for this population. In 2006, states pay 90% of estimated costs, with the percentage phasing down, to 75% in 2015 and later. (5) "Other income" includes recoveries of amounts reimbursed from the trust fund—that are not obligations of the trust fund—and other miscellaneous income. (6) Values after 2005 include additional premiums for Medicare Advantage (MA) plans that are deducted from beneficiaries' Social Security checks, transferred to the HI and SMI trust funds, and then transferred to the plans. (These additional premiums are incurred when an MA plan is chosen with a monthly payment exceeding the benchmark amount. Enrollees may pay plans directly or have the amounts deducted from their Social Security checks. (7) Includes costs of Peer Review Organizations from 1983-2001 and costs of Quality Review Organizations beginning in 2002. (8) For Part D, includes payments to plans, subsidies to employer-sponsored retiree drug plans, payments to states for low-income eligibility determinations, and Part D plan premiums (the amount collected from beneficiaries and transferred to plans and an estimated amount for premiums paid directly by enrollees to plans). (9) The financial status of SMI depends on the assets and liabilities of the trust fund. (10) Includes the impact of the Medicare Catastrophic Coverage Act of 1988. (11) Benefit payments less monies transferred from the HI trust fund for home health agency costs. (12) Includes an estimated 1.779 bil for premiums paid directly to Part D plans. NOTE: Totals do not necessarily equal sums of rounded components.

Hospital Insurance Trust Fund (Medicare HI), 1975-2006

(in millions)

Fisc. year[1]	Total	INCOME Payroll taxes	INCOME Taxation of benefits	INCOME Transfers from Railroad Retirement acct.	INCOME Rmbrs. for uninsured persons	INCOME Premiums from voluntary enrollees	INCOME Pymts. for military wage credits	INCOME Interest and other income[2,3]	Total	DISBURSEMENTS Benefit pymts.[3,4]	DISBURSEMENTS Admin. expenses[5]	Net change	Balance
1975	$12,568	$11,291	—	$132	$481	$6	$48	$609	$10,612	$10,353	$259	$1,956	$9,870
1980	25,415	23,244	—	244	697	17	141	1,072	24,288	23,790	497	1,127	14,490
1990	79,563	70,655	—	367	413	113	107	7,908	66,687	65,912	774	12,876	95,631
1995	114,847	98,053	$3,913	396	462	998	61	10,963	114,883	113,583	1,300	-36	129,520
1996	121,135	106,934	4,069	401	419	1,107	-2,293[5]	10,496	125,317	124,088	1,229	-4,182	125,338
1997	128,548	112,725	3,558	419	481	1,279	70	10,017	137,836	136,175	1,661	-9,287	116,050
1998	138,203	121,913	5,067	419	34	1,320	67	9,382	137,140	135,487[6]	1,653	1,063	117,113
1999	153,015	134,385	6,552	430	652	1,401	71	9,523	131,441	129,463[6]	1,978	21,574	138,687
2000	159,681	137,738	8,787	465	470	1,392	2	10,827	130,284	127,934[6]	2,350	29,397	168,084
2001	171,014	151,931	4,903	470	453	1,440	-1,175[7]	12,993	141,723	139,356[6]	2,368	29,290	197,374
2002	179,762	151,573	10,946	425	442	1,525	0	14,850	148,031	145,566[6]	2,464	31,731	229,105
2003	175,813	149,839	8,318	426	393	1,598	0	15,239	153,792	151,250[6]	2,541	22,021	251,127
2004	180,815	153,448	8,577	419	365	1,799	173	16,034	166,998	164,079	2,920	13,816	264,943
2005	196,921	168,954	8,765	445	286	2,303	0	16,168	184,142	181,292	2,850	12,779	277,723
2006	210,309	180,392	10,319	471	408	2,632	0	16,086	184,901	181,815	3,086	25,408	303,130

(1) Fiscal year 1975 consists of the 12 months ending on June 30, 1975; fiscal years 1980 and later consist of the 12 months ending Sept. 30 of each year. (2) Other income includes recoveries of amounts reimbursed from the trust fund that are not obligations of the trust fund, receipts from the fraud and abuse control program, and a small amount of miscellaneous income. (3) Values after 2005 include additional premiums for Medicare Advantage (MA) plans that are deducted from beneficiaries' Social Security checks, transferred to the HI and SMI trust funds, and then transferred to the plans. (These additional premiums are incurred when an MA plan is chosen with a monthly payment exceeding the benchmark amount. Enrollees may pay plans directly or have the amounts deducted from their Social Security checks. (4) Includes costs of Peer Review Organizations from 1983 through 2001 (beginning with the implementation of the Prospective Payment System on Oct. 1, 1983), and costs of Quality Improvement Organizations beginning in 2002. (5) Includes costs of experiments and demonstration projects. Beginning in 1997, includes fraud and abuse control expenses, as provided for by PL 104-191. (6) Includes monies transferred to the SMI trust fund for home health agency costs, as provided for by PL 105-33. (7) Includes the lump-sum general review adjustment of -$1,117 million, as provided for by sec. 151 of PL 98-21. NOTE: Totals do not necessarily equal sums of rounded components.

Block Grants for Welfare (Temporary Assistance for Needy Families), 2005[1]

Source: Office of Family Assistance, Admin. for Children and Families, U.S. Dept. of Health and Human Services

State	Total Federal and State TANF Expenditures, 2005[2]	2005 Average Monthly Expenditure per		2005 Average Monthly Number of		
		Family	Recipient	Families	Recipients	Children
Alabama	$123,378	$513.06	$216.97	20,040	47,388	36,791
Alaska	74,253	1,412.28	513.58	4,381	12,048	8,191
Arizona	298,582	568.88	250.59	43,738	99,294	73,758
Arkansas	66,627	642.51	295.97	8,642	18,759	14,407
California	5,882,428	1,057.45	450.61	463,569	1,087,862	895,382
Colorado	213,740	1,166.63	464.90	15,268	38,313	27,509
Connecticut	458,790	1,928.00	953.23	19,830	40,109	28,712
Delaware	61,310	911.43	407.77	5,606	12,530	9,504
Dist. of Columbia	155,938	770.14	309.55	16,873	41,980	31,723
Florida	868,327	1,208.98	677.44	59,853	106,815	88,069
Georgia	520,067	1,038.13	480.89	41,747	90,123	73,905
Hawaii	128,385	1,337.94	526.86	7,996	20,307	14,438
Idaho	39,785	1,782.95	1,001.58	1,860	3,310	2,744
Illinois	998,429	2,167.25	863.67	38,391	96,336	77,308
Indiana	306,732	580.38	204.85	44,042	124,777	96,273
Iowa	161,535	760.23	313.90	17,707	42,884	30,087
Kansas	154,302	729.70	279.38	17,622	46,026	31,449
Kentucky	216,277	519.38	240.29	34,701	75,005	56,076
Louisiana	186,382	964.53	414.65	16,103	37,458	31,472
Maine	126,905	1,108.20	414.58	9,543	25,509	17,460
Maryland	348,939	1,256.94	530.13	23,134	54,851	40,662
Massachusetts	688,520	1,175.18	552.20	48,824	103,906	72,049
Michigan	1,175,293	1,215.30	456.50	80,590	214,547	157,103
Minnesota	392,354	1,127.62	449.05	28,996	72,812	53,421
Mississippi	78,871	409.25	189.44	16,060	34,695	26,026
Missouri	298,938	621.84	257.85	40,061	96,611	68,069
Montana	43,921	793.23	299.41	4,614	12,224	8,321
Nebraska	78,064	649.43	258.81	10,017	25,136	17,717
Nevada	69,950	858.81	373.64	6,788	15,601	12,490
New Hampshire	62,766	851.30	370.58	6,144	14,114	9,766
New Jersey	993,845	1,922.90	787.75	43,071	105,135	76,863
New Mexico	127,398	604.37	234.29	17,566	45,314	32,390
New York	3,969,869	2,337.77	1,023.79	141,512	323,134	233,764
North Carolina	447,863	1,105.08	551.74	33,773	67,644	53,686
North Dakota	33,632	981.21	382.16	2,856	7,334	5,177
Ohio	990,071	998.90	459.84	82,597	179,422	136,228
Oklahoma	174,381	1,203.67	521.30	12,073	27,876	22,138
Oregon	268,823	1,149.53	504.19	19,488	44,432	32,914
Pennsylvania	1,190,363	1,026.51	391.54	96,635	253,352	178,567
Rhode Island	168,053	1,306.96	518.35	10,715	27,017	18,866
South Carolina	229,540	1,206.52	530.32	15,854	36,069	27,666
South Dakota	30,398	914.30	418.07	2,771	6,059	5,066
Tennessee	233,268	275.45	104.50	70,572	186,025	133,280
Texas	850,593	817.20	352.01	86,739	201,365	165,090
Utah	107,836	995.12	394.86	9,030	22,758	16,437
Vermont	67,501	1,230.87	492.90	4,570	11,412	7,347
Virginia	289,746	2,434.90	854.99	9,916	28,241	18,068
Washington	524,958	769.88	319.59	56,823	136,882	96,372
West Virginia	123,977	860.71	379.59	12,003	27,218	19,943
Wisconsin	445,942	1,839.79	797.32	20,199	46,609	37,662
Wyoming	32,267	8,673.85	4,906.74	310	548	482
2005 Totals	25,580,110	1,109.96	468.61	1,920,504	4,548,903	3,459,239
2004 Totals	25,821,230	1,082.66	449.78	1,987,476	4,784,042	3,617,569
2003 Totals	26,339,994	1,092.33	447.99	2,009,468	4,899,677	3,691,479
2002 Totals	25,414,383	1,039.38	418.01	2,037,618	5,066,574	3,790,207
2001 Totals	25,667,381	1,024.57	400.86	2,087,646	5,335,891	3,968,499
2000 Totals	24,780,711	926.32	353.72	2,229,315	5,838,043	4,303,943
1999 Totals	23,114,572	720.45	267.99	2,673,610	7,187,658	NA
1998 Totals	22,036,420	573.92	208.91	3,199,700	8,790,149	NA
1997 Totals	19,010,190	402.42	144.87	3,936,610	10,935,125	NA

NOTE: Under 1996 legislation, the Aid to Families with Dependent Children (AFDC) program was converted to this state block-grant program. (1) Fiscal year 2005; covers period from Oct. 2004 to Sept. 2005. (2) In thousands.

Adults Receiving TANF[1] (Welfare) Funds, by Employment Status, 2006[2]

Source: Office of Family Assistance, Admin. for Children and Families, U.S. Dept. of Health and Human Services

State	Adults	Employed	State	Adults	Employed	State	Adults	Employed	State	Adults	Employed
AL	9,869	32.8%	IL	18,409	14.8%	NE	6,555	39.3%	SC	7,622	38.9%
AK	3,011	32.4	IN	24,017	27.8	NV	2,157	39.6	SD	996	21.1
AZ	21,424	20.1	IA	11,774	36.4	NH	4,238	20.3	TN	51,444	19.4
AR	4,191	16.0	KS	14,039	10.0	NJ	29,203	15.8	TX	26,049	36.4
CA	187,313	25.1	KY	17,441	25.9	NM	12,368	26.9	UT	4,900	29.4
CO	10,402	32.1	LA	3,585	29.2	NY	87,067	21.6	VT	3,785	13.7
CT	9,886	25.8	ME	7,017	30.2	NC	12,121	20.0	Virgin Isls.	305	5.2
DE	2,962	22.5	MD	10,395	7.4	ND	2,008	33.6	VA	9,349	63.4
DC	9,447	20.3	MA	28,646	16.5	OH	40,267	4.4	WA	38,691	18.9
FL	15,654	17.6	MI	60,657	27.1	OK	3,944	7.8	WV	5,978	13.1
GA	7,431	20.6	MN	18,191	29.0	OR	10,664	13.1	WI	6,853	13.7
Guam	NA	NA	MS	6,546	18.8	PA	72,058	9.7	WY	54	8.4
HI	4,773	28.8	MO	27,823	22.0	Puerto Rico	11,842	2.4	**U.S.**	**996,312**	**21.6**
ID	439	36.9	MT	3,082	29.4	RI	7,430	23.0			

NA = Not available. (1) TANF = The state block grant program known as Temporary Assistance for Needy Families. (2) Fiscal year 2006; covers period from Oct. 2005 to Sept. 2006.

TAXES

Federal Income Tax

Source: George W. Smith III, CPA, Managing Partner, George W. Smith & Company, P.C.

HIGHLIGHTS OF RECENT LEGISLATION

Simplification. A simplified version of the income tax Form 1040 will be available to taxpayers in 2008. The new, less-cluttered form, called the Schedule O, will be ready for filing in 2009.

Small Business and Work Opportunity Tax Act of 2007

This business tax incentives bill (which included an increase in the federal minimum wage) was signed into law by Pres. George W. Bush on May 25, 2007. For more on the minimum wage increase, see the Employment Chapter.

Kiddie Tax. Children with investment income such as interest, dividends, and capital gains, will be subject to tax at the parents' higher rate, not the child's. This now will include all children under age 19 (previously 18) and students under age 24, each with unearned income over $1,700. Changes go into effect after May 25, 2007.

Section 179. In lieu of depreciation, taxpayers can expense the cost of qualifying business equipment and machinery. The new law increases the dollar limitation to $125,000 for tax years beginning in 2007. The investment limitation increases to $500,000, up from $400,000, and is indexed for inflation from 2008 through 2010.

Tax Preparers. Depending upon the understatement of tax caused by the preparer, the amount of penalty for "willful or reckless conduct," such as taking obviously improper deductions, was increased to the greater of $5,000 or 50% of the income derived by the tax return preparer. Lesser amounts apply to an "unreasonable position."

Tax Relief and Health Care Act

On December 20, 2006, Pres. Bush signed this legislation into law. The bill added several deductions for 2006 and 2007 tax years at an estimated cost of approximately $45 bil. Unfortunately, this law was enacted after the IRS printed millions of 2006 tax forms and instructions that had not included the changes in this package.

Higher Education. The deduction for qualified tuition and related expenses was extended for 2006 and 2007. The maximum amount deductible for each year remains at $4,000 depending on the taxpayer's adjusted gross income.

Classroom Expenses. Teachers can claim the $250 classroom expense deduction through December 31, 2007.

Whistle-Blowers. This provision of the legislation changes the amounts of collected proceeds to 15%-30% for whistle-blowers who provide information to the government regarding violations of federal laws.

Frivolous Returns. This law increases the penalty for filing a frivolous tax return from $500 to $5,000. The penalty applies to all taxpayers and all types of federal taxes.

Tax Increase Prevention and Reconciliation Act

This $70 billion tax-cut package was signed into law by Pres. Bush on May 18, 2006.

Dividend Income/Capital Gains. The maximum tax rate for qualified dividends or capital gains will remain at 15%. For taxpayers in the 10 or 15% bracket, the rate will remain at 5% through December 31, 2007, and then fall to 0% starting in 2008. The new rates will remain until Dec. 31, 2010.

Roth IRA. The $100,000 adjusted gross income ceiling for the conversion of a traditional IRA to a Roth IRA is eliminated effective for tax years beginning after December 31, 2009.

Other Tax Legislation and Laws

Energy Policy Act (2005)

Hybrid Vehicles. Hybrid car buyers can claim a tax credit for certain vehicles including autos, pickups, and SUVs. Depending on their fuel economy, the tax credit can go as high as $3,400. This credit starts to phase out once a manufacturer's line of hybrids sells its 60,000th vehicle. Thereafter, taxpayers can claim a partial credit for the remainder of the year.

Home Improvements. Congress encouraged homeowners to use energy saving technology with a 10% credit that applies for the purchase of skylights, outside doors, windows, pigmented roofs and high-efficiency furnaces, water heaters, and central air conditioners. The credit has a lifetime limitation of $500 ($200 max for windows) and is available only for expenditures made in 2006 and 2007.

Solar Energy. Homeowners can take a credit of 30% of the cost of solar water heaters or solar electricity-generating equipment. The maximum credit is $2,000 for each category of solar equipment installed. Swimming pools and hot tubs don't qualify. The Tax Relief & Health Care Act of 2006 extended this credit through 2008.

Working Families Tax Relief Act and American Jobs Creation Act (2004)

Child Tax Credit. Congress extended the $1,000 child tax credit through 2010, canceling a provision that would have cut it to $700.

Filing Jointly. The standard deduction for married taxpayers filing jointly was increased to double the standard deduction amount for single taxpayers through 2010. The 15% tax bracket amount that applies to married taxpayers will be double the 15% tax bracket amount for single taxpayers through 2010.

Donated Vehicles. Individuals who donate their vehicles to charity can no longer deduct the "Blue Book" value unless the charity retains the vehicle for its own use or makes material improvements to it. Otherwise, taxpayers can deduct only the amount of gross proceeds received by the charity from the sale of the donor's vehicle if the claimed deduction is greater than $500.

U.S. Citizenship. Congress closed a tax loophole that allowed wealthy individuals to relinquish their U.S. citizenship and claim they were moving to a foreign tax haven, even though they still spent most of their time in residence in the U.S. The law in effect states that if the individual is not really going to leave the country to live somewhere else, then the U.S. is going to tax the person.

Jobs and Growth Tax Relief Act (2003)

This 10-year, $350 billion package was the 3rd-largest tax cut in U.S. history.

Lower Rates. This legislation reduced individual tax rates above 15% to 25%, 28%, 33%, with a maximum rate of 35%.

Dividend Income/Capital Gains. Congress reduced the tax rate for dividends and capital gains to a maximum of 15%. In 2006 Congress extended these cuts through 2010.

Collectibles. Depending on the taxpayer's income there are additional capital gain rates for collectibles. Collectibles include works of art, antiques, gold and silver, gems, stamps, and coins. The rates are 5%, 15%, 25%, and 28%.

A New Ballgame. Unless Congress decides otherwise, after 2010 almost all the income and estate tax rules and regulations will revert back to previous higher tax rates.

IRS Rulings and Other Tax Matters

Combat Pay. For purposes of taking an IRA deduction, earned income includes any nontaxable combat pay received by a member of the U.S. Armed Forces.

Same Sex Marriage. The IRS ruled that it is unlawful for same-sex couples to file federal tax returns under any married status, even if the jurisdiction in which the couple lives recognizes such marriages.

Day Camps. The cost of computer camps, soccer camps and other specialty day camps (not overnight) for children may qualify for the child care credit. The child must be under 13 and the expenses must be incurred so the parent or parents can work.

Weight Loss. The IRS allows a medical deduction for costs of certain weight loss programs. Participation must be for treatment of a physician-diagnosed disease, including obesity. No deduction is allowed for purely cosmetic reasons or special diet foods.

Auto Damage. Damage to your car may be a deductible casualty loss unless it was caused by your willful conduct, such as drunken driving.

Smoking. Taxpayers can deduct two types of aids for quitting cigarette smoking as a medical expense: (1) the cost of participation in a smoking-cessation program; (2) prescription drugs to alleviate the effects of nicotine withdrawal. Over-the-counter products such as nicotine patches and chewing gum remain nondeductible.

Alimony. Payments to an individual under a written separation agreement constitute alimony for federal tax purposes even if the separation agreement is not enforceable under state law.

Penalties. Penalties and fines paid to a governmental agency or department are not deductible. This includes parking and speeding tickets as well as penalties for the late filing of a tax return.

Death Benefits. Qualified accelerated death benefits paid under a life insurance contract to terminally ill persons (certified as expected to die within 24 months) are excludable from gross income.

Sale of Residence. Married couples filing jointly who have lived in their principal residence for at least 2 years out of the last 5-year period can exclude from income up to $500,000 of the gain on the sale of their residence. Single taxpayers can exclude up to $250,000.

Domestic Workers. The annual threshold dollar amount for reporting and paying Social Security and federal unemployment taxes on domestic employees including nannies and housekeepers is $1,500 for 2007. Household workers under 18 are exempt unless household work is their principal occupation.

Student Loans. Starting in 2007, the income phase-out range for the $2,500 student loan interest deduction increased to $55,000-$70,000 for single taxpayers and $110,000-$140,000 for married taxpayers filing jointly.

Rate Change. The mileage allowance deduction for driving to obtain medical treatment, prescriptions, or dental care increased to 20 cents per mile starting in 2007. For cars used in volunteer work for charity, the rate remains at 14 cents per mile.

Investment Expenses. Investors may take a miscellaneous deduction on Schedule A for financial newspapers and reports, and other expenses incurred in managing their investment portfolio. However, investors cannot deduct expenses for attending a convention, seminar or similar meeting.

Garage Sale. Revenues received from a garage sale usually do not result in taxable income. In most cases, the item sold cost more than the revenue received. Also, losses are considered personal and not deductible.

"Hands Off." In a unanimous decision, the U.S. Supreme Court held that individual retirement accounts (IRAs) are beyond the reach of creditors. This includes IRA assets of taxpayers who have filed for bankruptcy.

Full-Time Student. A taxpayer may not claim a dependency exemption in 2007 for an individual who qualifies as a full-time student and is over age 23 at the end of the year, unless the student's gross income is less than $3,400.

First Job. Graduates may not deduct the expenses of seeking their first job.

Income Tax Filing and Payment Due Dates

Facts. The IRS received nearly 128 mil individual income tax returns in April 2007. This was a 2.9% increase in returns filed over the previous year. The I.R.S. also approved 96.3 mil refunds, up 3.9% also from the previous year. Total refunds: $217.1 bil, 6.6% higher than last year. The average refund was $2,255.

Filing Dates. The due date for filing a 2007 Form 1040, 1040A or 1040EZ U.S. Individual Income Tax Return includ-ing partnership tax returns is Tue, Apr. 15, 2008. Calendar-year-ending corporate returns are due March 17, 2008 (the 15th falls on a Saturday).

Estimated Taxes. Due dates for filing individual quarterly federal estimated tax payments, Form 1040-ES, are: 1st quarter, Tue., Apr. 15, 2008; 2nd quarter, Mon., June 16; 3rd quarter, Mon., Sept. 15; and 4th quarter, Thu., Jan. 15, 2009. Different filing dates may apply for state and local tax payments.

Refunds. Individuals can call the IRS's toll-free number at 1-800-829-4477 for a recorded message to check on the status of the expected refund. Or, visit the IRS Web site at www.irs.gov.

Filing Penalties. The IRS can levy 2 potential penalties when a return is filed after the due date with a balance owing: one penalty is for failing to file a timely tax return, the other is for failure to pay the tax when due. In addition, interest will be charged on any unpaid tax balance.

Installment Payments. Depending on the amount of tax owed, taxpayers may apply for monthly installment payments by attaching Form 9465 to their tax return. There is an IRS filing fee if the request is approved.

Need More Time to File? Individuals who cannot file their 2007 tax return by the due date may apply for an automatic 6-month extension to Wed, Oct. 15, 2008. Form 4868 must be filed no later than Apr. 15, 2008 to qualify. Approximately nine mil extensions were filed by April 17, 2007 for 2006 tax returns.

Statute of Limitations. If you have not yet filed your 2004 federal tax return, you have until Apr. 15, 2008 to file and claim your refund. After that date any tax or withholding refund for the year 2004, including the refundable earned income tax credit, will be lost.

Electronic Filing. Setting new records for e-filing, 77% of income tax returns were filed electronically through the middle of May 2007. Roughly 22 mil returns were filed by self-preparers and 55 mil by tax professionals.

Tax Tip. For security purposes, taxpayers should request that tax refunds be deposited directly into their bank accounts. If you choose, you may be able to split the refund and have it deposited among two or three accounts.

IRS Services and Information

For Tax Questions: Call 1-800-829-1040

Website: www.irs.gov Fax: 1-703-368-9694

For Forms/Publications: 1-800-829-3676

For English And Spanish. The IRS provides videotaped instructions both in English and Spanish at participating libraries. Many IRS publications and tax forms, including instructions, are also printed in Spanish. For more information, call 1-800-TAX-FORM and ask for the free IRS Publication 1SP, Derechos del Contribuyente.

For Hearing Impaired. The IRS telephone service for hearing impaired persons is available for taxpayers with access to TDD equipment. The toll-free number is 1-800-829-4059.

Top Five List. Periodically, the IRS issues a list of the most commonly made income tax errors. The top five in 2006 were:
1. Incorrect or missing Social Security numbers.
2. Incorrect tax entered from tax tables.
3. Mathematical errors or wrong ID numbers listed for tax credits.
4. Entering withholding and estimated tax payments on the wrong line.
5. General math mistakes.

Meeting With Your Tax Preparer

More than 60% of all individual income tax returns are signed by paid tax professionals. Here are some ideas to keep in mind when visiting your tax preparer:

- Review last year's tax return. Make notes of any changes since then such as marriage, divorce, number of dependents, retirement, job changes, additional income, new deductions, etc.
- Organize your records with income items first, followed by itemized deductions in sequence (medical, taxes, interest, charitable, and other miscellaneous deductions), then any other questionable items.
- Time spent with your preparer may affect your bill. If you bring in jumbled records and deductions, there may be an additional cost to have your tax preparer organize your records.
- Prepare a list of questions in advance. Bring with you any bills that you are not sure of.
- Alert your preparer if you're waiting to receive additional information. He or she can begin preparation of your tax return and include the missing data later to finalize your return.
- Don't hesitate to call the preparer if you receive additional information at a later time. However, if you call after the return is completed, changes may cost you additional fees.
- Review your tax return before signing it. Ask questions about any item you don't understand. Remember, even though your preparer is required to sign the return, you are responsible for its contents.

Additional Help: For more information about choosing tax preparers, call the IRS Tele-Tax information at 800-829-4477. Follow the prompts and select Topic 254. This information is also available online at www.irs.gov/taxtopics/tc254.html.

Individual Income Tax Rates and Tax Brackets

Taxable Income And Rates For 2007

Tax Rate	Single	Married Filing Separately	Married Filing Jointly or Qualifying Widow(er)	Head of Household	Estates and Trusts
10%	$1 to $7,825	$1 to $7,825	$1 to $15,650	$1 to $11,200	$0
15%	$7,826 to $31,850	$7,826 to $31,850	$15,651 to $63,700	$11,201 to $42,650	$1 to $2,150
25%	$31,851 to $77,100	$31,851 to $64,250	$63,701 to $128,500	$42,651 to $110,100	$2,151 to $5,000
28%	$77,101 to $160,850	$64,251 to $97,925	$128,501 to $195,850	$110,101 to $178,350	$5,001 to $7,650
33%	$160,851 to $349,700	$97,926 to $174,850	$195,851 to $349,700	$178,351 to $349,700	$7,651 to $10,450
35%	Over $349,700	Over $174,850	Over $349,700	Over $349,700	Over $10,450

Exemptions

Dollar Amounts. The personal exemption amount for each taxpayer, spouse, and dependent for 2007 is $3,400, a $100 increase over 2006. These exemption amounts are adjusted each year for the cost of living.

Exemption Phase-Out. The exemption deduction for higher-income taxpayers begins to be phased out when their income exceeds certain threshold dollar amounts, adjusted annually for the cost of living. Each exemption is reduced by 2% for each $2,500 ($1,250 for married persons filing separately) or fraction thereof by which adjusted gross income for year 2007 exceeds the following:

Married filing jointly	$234,600
Qualifying widow(er)	$234,600
Head of household	$195,500
Single	$156,400
Married filing separately	$117,300

Standard Deduction

The standard deduction is a flat dollar amount that is subtracted from the adjusted gross income of taxpayers who do not itemize deductions.

2007 Standard Deduction Amount

Single	$5,350
Married filing jointly or qualifying widow(er)	$10,700
Married filing separately	$5,350
Head of household	$7,850

These figures are not applicable if an individual can be claimed as a dependent on another person's tax return.

Standard Deduction for Dependents. An individual reported as a dependent on another person's 2007 income tax return generally may claim on his or her own tax return only the greater of $850 or the sum of $300 plus earned income not to exceed the regular standard deduction.

Dependents Standard Deduction

Taxpayers in 2007 who are 65 or older and/or blind may claim an additional standard deduction:

Single or head of household, 65 or older OR blind	$1,300
Single or head of household, 65 or older AND blind	$2,600
Married filing jointly or qualifying widow(er), 65 or older OR blind (per person)	$1,050
Married filing jointly or qualifying widow(er), 65 or older AND blind (per person)	$2,100
Married filing separately, 65 or older OR blind	$1,050
Married filing separately, 65 or older AND blind	$2,100

Savings Plans For Traditional and Roth IRAs

Traditional IRA. The maximum tax-deferred Individual Retirement Arrangement (IRA) deduction for a 2007 married couple filing jointly is $8,000 ($4,000 for singles). Each spouse can contribute up to $4,000 annually even if one spouse has little or no income. Individuals age 50 or older can fund an additional "catch-up" amount of $1,000. However, there are income limitations and phase-outs.

Withdrawals. There is a 10% penalty for IRA distributions before age 59½. Distributions paid to the beneficiary due to a disability or death of the owner are not subject to this penalty, nor are payments used for certain unreimbursed medical expenses, higher-education expenses, or first-time home buyer acquisition costs (up to $10,000).

Caution. Contributions for a 2007 IRA or Roth IRA made after the due date, April 15, 2008, automatically will be considered deposits for 2008.

Roth IRA. Although contributions paid into a Roth IRA are not deductible, distributions of funds including investment earnings held in the account for 5 years or longer and distributed after age 59½ are both free of income tax and the 10% early withdrawal penalty at the time of distribution. Withdrawals in less than 5 years can be subject to income tax and the 10% withdrawal penalty regardless of age. There are income limitations on contributions.

Distributions. The owner of a traditional IRA (or a SIMPLE,

pension, or profit sharing plan account) must begin receiving distributions by Apr. 1 of the calendar year following the year in which he or she reaches age 70½. Any employee who works beyond 70½ and is not a 5% or more owner of the business can continue to defer profit sharing and pension plan distributions.

IRA Publication. For more information on IRAs call the IRS at 1-800-829-3676 for a free copy of Publication 590, Individual Retirement Arrangements (IRAs).

Itemized Deductions

If the total amount of itemized deductions is more than the standard deduction, taxpayers generally should itemize their deductions on Schedule A, Form 1040. The following examples are just a few of the deductions that may be itemized. Some are subject to income limitations.

Medical expenses that exceed 7.5% of the taxpayer's adjusted gross income are deductible. Medicines, birth control pills, and insulin qualify if prescribed by a physician. Cosmetic surgery for congenital abnormality, for personal injury from an accident or trauma, or for a disfiguring disease also is allowed as a medical deduction.

Tax Tip. A mother-to-be may deduct the cost of classes taken in Lamaze breathing and relaxation techniques, stages of labor, and delivery procedures as a medical expense.

Long-Term Care. Based on various annual limits, long-term care insurance premiums are deductible as medical expenses. Taxpayers age 71 and older can claim as much as $3,680 per person. There are lesser amounts for taxpayers between ages 41 and 70. People age 40 and younger can deduct $290.

Mortgage interest paid on a primary residence or a second home is deductible. However, there are limitations on mortgages in excess of $1 mil. Interest on home equity loans also is deductible, but only covering the first $100,000 of equity debt. Credit card interest is not deductible.

Taxes. State and local income taxes including real estate taxes are deductible. Sales taxes may be deductible if taken in lieu of income taxes. You may not deduct an auto license fee based on weight, model, year, or horsepower. A tax based on the car's value qualifies as a personal property tax.

Personal losses. Casualty and theft losses are deductible, but subject to the $100 reduction. Losses are further reduced 10% for each occurrence. Unreimbursed automobile accident damage may be a deductible casualty loss.

Charitable contributions. Taxpayers deducting individual contributions of $250 or more must obtain written substantiation from the charity. You may not deduct the value of volunteer work you perform for charities.

Miscellaneous Deductions. Certain miscellaneous expenses are deductible, but only the amount that exceeds 2% of adjusted gross income. These include investment expenses, union and professional dues, cost of tax preparation, safe deposit box rental fees and most (not all) expenses for a job search.

Employee Business Expenses. Deductible miscellaneous expenses include unreimbursed employee business expenses such as travel, automobile, telephone, and gifts. However, only 50% of the cost of customer meals and entertainment is deductible. The 2007 standard mileage rate for business use of autos, including leased cars, is 48½ cents per mile.

Moving Expenses. Taxpayers who change jobs or are transferred, usually can deduct part of their moving expenses, including travel and the cost of the moving of household goods, but not meals. The mileage rate for automobiles used in the move increased to 20 cents per mile for 2007.

Medical Traveling. Taxpayers may deduct part of the expense of having to travel to seek health care. The mileage rate for automobiles used for medical traveling has increased to 20 cents per mile for 2007.

Gambling. Lottery, slots, Texas Hold 'em, bingo or other gambling expenses are deductible if the taxpayer itemizes. However, expenses are limited to gambling winnings reported on page one. If there are no winnings, there are no deductions!

Tax Credits

A tax deduction reduces a taxpayer's taxable income. Tax credits reduce, dollar-for-dollar, the amount of tax owed.

Earned Income Credit. Lower-income workers who maintain a household may be eligible for an earned income credit (EIC). This credit is based on total earned income such as wages, commissions and tips. Military personnel can include tax-free combat pay in income to compute the credit.

The phase-out range of the earned income credit for joint filers increases to a maximum of $3,000 in 2008. Starting in 2009 the credit will be adjusted annually for the cost of living. After 2010 all these credits will expire.

Hope Scholarship Credit applies to qualified tuition and expenses for the first 2 years of postsecondary education in a degree or certificate program at an eligible institution. However, it does not apply to room and board or cost of books. The credit can be as high as $1,650.

Lifetime Learning Credit is available for taxpayers whose post-secondary education expenses are not eligible for the Hope credit. The credit is 20% of tuition and other qualifying expenses paid for by the taxpayer, spouse, or dependents up to a total credit of $2,000 (20% of $10,000 in expenses) for all entitled students who are enrolled in an eligible educational institution. The credit begins to phase out for higher income levels.

Adoption Credit. The adoption credit for qualified expenses increased to $11,390 in 2007. The credit limit is per person, not per year, and is adjusted annually for inflation. The exclusion phases out for taxpayers whose income is between $170,820 and $210,820.

Alternative Minimum Tax

The Alternative Minimum Tax (AMT) was established in 1969 to prevent people with very high incomes from using special tax breaks to pay little or no tax. It was never indexed or adjusted for inflation. Because of changes in the tax law, this tax now affects more and more middle-income taxpayers every year. It is estimated that an additional 15 mil taxpayers will be hit with this tax in 2007.

The instructions included with tax forms 1040 and 1040A provide help for individuals to determine whether they are subject to the AMT. Form 6251, Alternative Minimum Tax, is used to figure how much additional tax is owed.

Estate and Gift Taxes

Exclusion. The Tax Relief Reconciliation Act of 2001 increased the estate tax exclusion from $675,000 in 2001 to $1 mil in 2002 and 2003, and $1.5 in 2004 and 2005. In 2006, the exclusion increased to $2 mil through 2008 and $3.5 mil starting in 2009.

Estate Tax Rates. The maximum tax rate on the value of an estate was 55% in 2001, reduced to 50% in 2002, 47% in 2005 and 46% for 2006. The tax rate decreases once more for 2007 through 2009 to a maximum of 45%.

Good News/Bad News. All estate taxes are repealed for the year 2010. However, unless Congress passes new legislation prior to 2011, the estate laws revert to a lower exclusion of $1 mil and a higher maximum tax rate of 55%.

Resident Aliens. The estate of a resident alien is subject to the same rules as that of an American citizen. All property owned worldwide is subject to the U.S. estate tax rules and regulations.

Gifting. Citizens, resident and non-resident aliens can make tax-free gifts of up to $12,000 each year to as many individuals as he or she chooses. For married couples, the gift is twice that amount even if only one spouse does all the gifting.

Lifetime Gifting. A $1 mil gift tax exclusion is the total limit an individual is allowed to give to other individuals (other than charities and the annual $12,000 gifting) during his or her lifetime before having to pay gift taxes.

Taxable Social Security Benefits

Earnings Limitations. Social Security recipients who have not reached full retirement age lose $1 of their benefits for every $2 of earned income over $12,960, an increase of $480 over 2006. That means they have to pay back into the system for income over that amount.

Taxable Benefits. Up to 50% of Social Security benefits may be taxable if the person's total income is: over $25,000 but less than $34,000 for a single individual, head of household, qualifying widow(er), or a married person who is filing separately if spouses lived apart all year; or over $32,000 but less than $44,000 for married individuals filing jointly. For higher incomes, 85% of Social Security benefits may become taxable.

Tax-Free! If the only income you received during 2007 was Social Security, these benefits are not taxable and you probably do not have to file a tax return.

Retention Of Income Tax Records

How long to keep your records is a combination of judgment and the statutes of limitations. Since federal tax returns generally can be audited for up to three years after filing, or six years if the IRS suspects underreported income, it's wise to keep income tax records at least seven years after a return is filed.

IRS Tax Audits

The IRS conducted more than 1.28 mil audits of individual taxpayers in 2006, less than 1% of all the tax returns filed. The audit selection process is not random. It is based on a set of formulas that are designed to spot questionable returns.

If the IRS concludes that you owe more and you disagree with the findings, you can meet with a supervisor. If you still do not agree, you can appeal to a separate Appeals Office.

For more information about audits, call the IRS at 1-800-829-3676 for its free Publication 556, Examination of Returns, Appeal Rights, and Claims for Refund. Or visit www.irs.gov.

U.S. Tax Court

The U.S. Tax Court is a Federal court where taxpayers can dispute tax deficiencies as determined by the Commissioner of Internal Revenue *before payment* of the disputed amounts. The Tax Court is composed of presidentially appointed members. Trial sessions and other work are performed by these judges along with senior judges serving on recall, and by special trial judges. If you're not satisfied with the outcome of your tax audit, you can take it to the U.S. Tax Court, Federal District Court or the U.S. Court of Federal Claims. Many people choose the Tax Court because they are not required to pay the contested tax up front.

Your Rights as a Taxpayer

Congress has enacted "taxpayer bill of rights" legislation and created an Office of the Taxpayer Advocate within the IRS, with authority to order IRS personnel to issue refund checks and meet deadlines for resolving disputes. Taxpayer advocates can be contacted at 1-877-777-4778 (1-800-829-4059 for TTY/TDD). The IRS must pay legal fees if the taxpayer wins the case and the IRS cannot show it was "substantially justified" in pursuing it.

To confidentially report misconduct, waste, fraud or abuse by an IRS employee, call 1-800-366-4484.

For more information ask for IRS Publication 1, *Your Rights as a Taxpayer*, by calling 1-800-TAX-FORM for a free copy.

To find out what other services are available, ask for Publication 910, *IRS Guide to Free Tax Services*. It contains a list of free tax publications and describes other free tax information services including tax education and assistance programs and a list of Tele-Tax topics.

Federal Outlays to States Per Dollar of Tax Revenue Received

Source: The Tax Foundation
(figures for fiscal year 2004; ranked highest to lowest)

State	Outlay	State	Outlay	State	Outlay	State	Outlay	State	Outlay
District of Columbia	6.64	South Dakota	1.49	Idaho	1.28	Rhode Island	1.02	Colorado	0.79
New Mexico	2.00	Oklahoma	1.48	Utah	1.14	Ohio	1.01	New York	0.79
Alaska	1.87	Arkansas	1.47	Kansas	1.12	Indiana	0.97	California	0.79
West Virginia	1.83	Louisiana	1.45	Vermont	1.12	Oregon	0.97	Massachusetts	0.77
Mississippi	1.77	Kentucky	1.45	Iowa	1.11	Georgia	0.96	Nevada	0.73
North Dakota	1.73	Maryland	1.44	Wyoming	1.11	Texas	0.94	Illinois	0.73
Alabama	1.71	Maine	1.40	North Carolina	1.10	Washington	0.80	Minnesota	0.69
Virginia	1.66	South Carolina	1.38	Nebraska	1.07	Michigan	0.85	New Hampshire	0.67
Hawaii	1.60	Tennessee	1.30	Pennsylvania	1.06	Wisconsin	0.82	Connecticut	0.66
Montana	1.58	Arizona	1.30	Florida	1.02	Delaware	0.79	New Jersey	0.55
		Missouri	1.29						

State Government Personal Income Tax Rates, 2007

Source: Reproduced with permission from *CCH State Tax Guide,* published and copyrighted by CCH Inc., 2700 Lake Cook Road, Riverwoods, IL 60015
Alaska, Florida, Nevada, South Dakota, Texas, Washington, and Wyoming did not have state income taxes and are thus not listed. Tax rates apply in stages—for example, a single person in Arizona making $60,000 in taxable income would pay 2.59% on the first $10,000 of income, 2.88% on the next $15,000, etc. For further details, see notes at end of table.

Alabama
Single, Head of household, or Married filing separately
$0 to $500	2%
$501 to $3,000	4%
$3,001 and over	5%

Married filing jointly
$0 to $1,000	2%
$1,001 to $6,000	4%
$6,001 and over	5%

Arizona[1]
Single or Married filing separately
$0 to $10,000	2.59%
$10,001 to $25,000	2.88%
$25,001 to $50,000	3.36%
$50,001 to $150,000	4.24%
$150,001 and over	4.54%

Married filing jointly, Head of household
$0 to $20,000	2.59%
$20,001 to $50,000	2.88%
$50,001 to $100,000	3.36%
$100,001 to $300,000	4.24%
$300,001 and over	4.54%

Arkansas[2,3]
Single, Head of household, Married filing jointly, or Married filing separately
$0 to $3,599	1%
$3,600 to $7,199	2.5%
$7,200 to $10,799	3.5%
$10,800 to $17,999	4.5%
$18,000 to $30,099	6%
$30,100 and over	7%

California[1,2]
Single or Married filing separately
$0 to $6,827	1%
$6,828 to $16,185	2%
$16,186 to $25,544	4%
$25,545 to $35,460	6%
$35,461 to $44,814	8%
$44,815 and over	9.3%

Head of household
$0 to $13,662	1%
$13,663 to $32,370	2%
$32,371 to $41,728	4%
$41,729 to $51,643	6%
$51,644 to $61,000	8%
$61,001 and over	9.3%

Married filing jointly or Surviving spouse
$0 to $13,654	1%
$13,655 to $32,370	2%
$32,371 to $51,088	4%
$51,089 to $70,920	6%
$70,921 to $89,628	8%
$89,629 and over	9.3%

Colorado
4.63% of federal taxable income

Connecticut
Single & Married filing separately
$0 to $10,000	3%
$10,001 and over	5%

Head of household
$0 to $16,000	3%
$16,001 and over	5%

Married filing jointly or Surviving spouse
$0 to $20,000	3%
$20,001 and over	5%

Delaware
Single, Head of household, Married filing jointly, or Married filing separately
$2,000 to $5,000	2.2%
$5,001 to $10,000	3.9%
$10,001 to $20,000	4.8%
$20,001 to $25,000	5.2%
$25,001 to $60,000	5.55%
$60,001 and over	5.95%

District of Columbia
Single, Head of household, Married filing jointly, or Married filing separately
$0 to $10,000	4%
$10,001 to $40,000	6%
$40,001 and over	8.5%

Georgia
Single
$0 to $750	1%
$751 to $2,250	2%
$2,251 to $3,750	3%
$3,751 to $5,250	4%
$5,251 to $7,000	5%
$7,001 and over	6%

Head of household, Married filing jointly, or Surviving spouse
$0 to $1,000	1%
$1,001 to $3,000	2%
$3,001 to $5,000	3%
$5,001 to $7,000	4%
$7,001 to $10,000	5%
$10,001 and over	6%

Married filing separately
$0 to $500	1%
$501 to $1,500	2%
$1,501 to $2,500	3%
$2,501 to $3,500	4%
$3,501 to $5,000	5%
$5,001 and over	6%

Hawaii
Single or Married filing separately
$0 to $2,400	1.4%
$2,401 to $4,800	3.2%
$4,801 to $9,600	5.5%
$9,601 to $14,400	6.4%
$14,401 to $19,200	6.8%
$19,201 to $24,000	7.2%
$24,001 to $36,000	7.6%
$36,001 to $48,000	7.9%
$48,001 and over	8.25%

Head of household
$0 to $3,600	1.4%
$3,601 to $7,200	3.2%
$7,201 to $14,400	5.5%
$14,401 to $21,600	6.4%
$21,601 to $28,800	6.8%
$28,801 to $36,000	7.2%
$36,001 to $54,000	7.6%
$54,001 to $72,000	7.9%
$72,001 and over	8.25%

Married filing jointly or Surviving spouse
$0 to $4,800	1.4%
$4,801 to $9,600	3.2%
$9,601 to $19,200	5.5%
$19,201 to $28,800	6.4%
$28,801 to $38,400	6.8%
$38,401 to $48,000	7.2%
$48,001 to $72,000	7.6%
$72,001 to $96,000	7.9%
$96,001 and over	8.25%

Idaho[1,2,3]
Single or Married filing separately
$0 to $1,198	1.6%
$1,199 to $2,396	3.6%
$2,397 to $3,594	4.1%
$3,595 to $4,793	5.1%
$4,794 to $5,991	6.1%
$5,992 to $8,986	7.1%
$8,987 to $23,963	7.4%
$23,964 and over	7.8%

Head of household, Married filing jointly, or Surviving spouse
$0 to $2,396	1.6%
$2,397 to $4,792	3.6%
$4,793 to $7,188	4.1%
$7,189 to $9,586	5.1%
$9,587 to $11,982	6.1%
$11,983 to $17,972	7.1%
$17,973 to $47,926	7.4%
$47,927 and over	7.8%

Illinois
3% of taxable net income

Indiana
3.4% of adjusted gross income

Iowa[2]
Single, Head of household, Married filing jointly, or Married filing separately
$0 to $1,343	0.36%
$1,344 to $2,686	0.72%
$2,687 to $5,372	2.43%
$5,373 to $12,087	4.5%
$12,088 to $20,145	6.12%
$20,146 to $26,860	6.48%
$26,861 to $40,290	6.8%
$40,291 to $60,435	7.92%
$60,436 and over	8.98%

Kansas
Single, Head of household, or Married filing separately
$0 to $15,000	3.5%
$15,001 to $30,000	6.25%
$30,001 and over	6.45%

Married filing jointly
$0 to $30,000	3.5%
$30,001 to $60,000	6.25%
$60,001 and over	6.45%

Kentucky
Single, Head of household, Married filing jointly, or Married filing separately
$0 to $3,000	2%
$3,001 to $4,000	3%
$4,001 to $5,000	4%
$5,001 to $8,000	5%
$8,001 to $75,000	5.8%
75,001 and over	6%

Louisiana[1]
Single, Head of household, or Married filing separately
$0 to $12,500	2%
$12,501 to $25,000	4%
$25,001 and over	6%

Married filing jointly
$0 to $25,000	2%
$25,001 to $50,000	4%
$50,001 and over	6%

Maine[2]
Single or Married filing separately
$0 to $4,749	2%
$4,750 to $9,449	4.5%
$9,450 to $18,949	7%
$18,950 and over	8.5%

Head of household
$0 to $7,149	2%
$7,150 to $14,199	4.5%
$14,200 to $28,449	7%
$28,450 and over	8.5%

Married filing jointly
$0 to $9,499	2%
$9,500 to $18,949	4.5%
$18,950 to $37,949	7%
$37,950 and over	8.5%

Maryland
Single, Head of household, Married filing jointly, or Married filing separately
$0 to $1,000	2%
$1,001 to $2,000	3%
$2,001 to $3,000	4%
$3,001 and over	4.75%

Massachusetts
Short-term capital gains	12%
All other income	5.3%

Michigan
3.9% of taxable income

Minnesota[2]
Single
$0 to $21,310	5.35%
$21,311 to $69,990	7.05%
$69,991 and over	7.85%

Head of household
$0 to $26,230	5.35%
$26,231 to $105,410	7.05%
$105,411 and over	7.85%

Married filing jointly
$0 to $31,150	5.35%
$31,151 to $123,750	7.05%
$123,751 and over	7.85%

Married filing separately
$0 to $15,580	5.35%
$15,581 to $61,880	7.05%
$61,881 and over	7.85%

Mississippi
Single, Head of household, Married filing jointly, or Married filing separately
$0 to $5,000	3%
$5,001 to $10,000	4%
$10,001 and over	5%

Missouri
Single, Head of household, Married filing jointly, or Married filing separately
$0 to $1,000	1.5%
$1,001 to $2,000	2%
$2,001 to $3,000	2.5%
$3,001 to $4,000	3%
$4,001 to $5,000	3.5%
$5,001 to $6,000	4%
$6,001 to $7,000	4.5%
$7,001 to $8,000	5%
$8,001 to $9,000	5.5%
$9,001 and over	6%

Montana[2]
Single, Head of household, Married filing jointly, or Married filing separately
$0 to $2,499	1%
$2,500 to $4,399	2%
$4,400 to $6,599	3%
$6,600 to $8,999	4%
$9,000 to $11,599	5%
$11,600 to $14,899	6%
$14,900 and over	6.9%

Nebraska
Single
$0 to $2,400	2.56%
$2,401 to $17,500	3.57%
$17,501 to $27,000	5.12%
$27,001 and over	6.84%

Head of household
$0 to $3,800	2.56%
$3,801 to $25,000	3.57%
$25,001 to $35,000	5.12%
$35,001 and over	6.84%

Married filing jointly
$0 to $4,000	2.56%
$4,001 to $31,000	3.57%
$31,001 to $50,000	5.12%
$50,001 and over	6.84%

Married filing separately
$0 to $2,000	2.56%
$2,001 to $15,500	3.57%
$15,501 to $25,000	5.12%
$25,001 and over	6.84%

New Hampshire
5% on interest and dividends only

New Jersey
Single or Married filing separately
$0 to $20,000	1.4%
$20,001 to $35,000	1.75%
$35,001 to $40,000	3.5%
$40,001 to $75,000	5.525%
$75,001 to $500,000	6.37%
$500,001 and over	8.97%

Head of household, Married filing jointly, or Surviving spouse
$0 to $20,000	1.4%
$20,001 to $50,000	1.75%
$50,001 to $70,000	2.45%
$70,001 to $80,000	3.5%
$80,001 to $150,000	5.525%
$150,001 to $500,000	6.37%
$500,001 and over	8.97%

New Mexico[1]
Single
$0 to $5,500	1.7%
$5,501 to $11,000	3.2%
$11,001 to $16,000	4.7%
$16,001 and over	5.3%

Head of household
$0 to $8,000	1.7%
$8,001 to $16,000	3.2%
$16,001 to $24,000	4.7%
$24,001 and over	5.3%

Married filing jointly
$0 to $8,000	1.7%
$8,001 to $16,000	3.2%
$16,001 to $24,000	4.7%
$24,001 and over	5.3%

Married filing separately
$0 to $4,000	1.7%
$4,001 to $8,000	3.2%
$8,001 to $12,000	4.7%
$12,001 and over	5.3%

New York

Single & Married filing separately

$0 to $8,000	4%
$8,001 to $11,000	4.5%
$11,001 to $13,000	5.25%
$13,001 to $20,000	5.9%
$20,001 and over	6.85%

Head of household

$0 to $11,000	4%
$11,001 to $15,000	4.5%
$15,001 to $17,000	5.25%
$17,001 to $30,000	5.9%
$30,001 and over	6.85%

Married filing jointly

$0 to $16,000	4%
$16,001 to $22,000	4.5%
$22,001 to $26,000	5.25%
$26,001 to $40,000	5.9%
$40,001 and over	6.85%

North Carolina

Single

$0 to $12,750	6%
$12,751 to $60,000	7%
$60,001 to $120,000	7.75%
$120,001 and over	8%

Head of household

$0 to $17,000	6%
$17,001 to $80,000	7%
$80,001 to $160,000	7.75%
$160,001 and over	8%

Married filing jointly, or Surviving spouse

$0 to $21,250	6%
$21,251 to $100,000	7%
$100,001 to $200,000	7.75%
$200,001 and over	8%

Married filing separately

$0 to $10,625	6%
$10,626 to $50,000	7%
$50,001 to $100,000	7.75%
$100,001 and over	8%

North Dakota[2]

Single

$0 to $31,850	2.1%
$31,851 to $77,100	3.92%
$77,101 to $160,850	4.34%
$160,851 to $349,700	5.04%
$349,701 and over	5.54%

Head of household

$0 to $42,650	2.1%
$42,651 to $110,100	3.92%
$110,101 to $178,350	4.34%
$178,351 to $349,700	5.04%
$349,701 and over	5.54%

Married filing jointly, Surviving spouse

$0 to $53,200	2.1%
$53,201 to $128,500	3.92%
$128,501 to $195,850	4.34%
$195,851 to $349,700	5.04%
$349,701 and over	5.54%

Married filing separately

$0 to $26,600	2.1%
$26,601 to $64,250	3.92%
$64,251 to $97,925	4.34%
$97,926 to $174,850	5.04%
$174,851 and over	5.54%

Ohio

Single, Head of household, Married filing jointly, or Married filing separately

$0 to $5,000	0.649%
$5,001 to $10,000	1.299%
$10,001 to $15,000	2.598%
$15,001 to $20,000	3.247%
$20,001 to $40,000	3.895%
$40,001 to $80,000	4.546%
$80,001 to $100,000	5.194%
$100,001 to $200,000	6.031%
$200,001 and over	6.555%

Oklahoma

Single or Married filing separately

$0 to $1,000	0.5%
$1,001 to $2,500	1%
$2,501 to $3,750	2%
$3,751 to $4,900	3%
$4,901 to $7,200	4%
$7,201 to $8,700	5%
$8,701 and over	5.65%

Head of household or Married filing jointly

$0 to $2,000	0.5%
$2,001 to $5,000	1%
$5,001 to $7,500	2%
$7,501 to $9,800	3%
$9,801 to $12,200	4%
$12,201 to $15,000	5%
$15,001 and over	5.65%

Oregon[2]

Single or Married filing separately

$0 to $2,850	5%
$2,851 to $7,150	7%
$7,151 and over	9%

Married filing jointly or Head of household

$0 to $5,700	5%
$5,701 to $14,300	7%
$14,301 and over	9%

Pennsylvania

3.07% of taxable compensation, net profits, net gains from the sale of property, rent, royalties, patents or copyrights, income from estates or trusts, dividends, interest and winnings

Rhode Island

25% of the federal income tax rates, including capital gains rates and any other special rates for other types of income, that were in effect prior to enactment of the Economic Growth and Tax Relief Reconciliation Act of 2001. Effective for the 2007 tax year, taxpayers may elect to compute income tax liability based on the graduated rate schedule or an alternative flat rate equal to 7.5%.

South Carolina[2]

Single, Head of household, Married filing jointly, or Married filing separately

$0 to $2,630	0%
$2,631 to $5,260	3%
$5,261 to $7,890	4%
$7,891 to $10,520	5%
$10,521 to $13,150	6%
$13,151 and over	7%

Tennessee

6% of interest and dividends

Utah

Single & Married filing separately

$0 to $1,000	2.3%
$1,001 to $2,000	3.3%
$2,001 to $3,000	4.2%
$3,001 to $4,000	5.2%
$4,001 to $5,500	6%
$5,501 and over	6.98%

Head of household or Married filing jointly

$0 to $2,000	2.3%
$2,001 to $4,000	3.3%
$4,001 to $6,000	4.2%
$6,001 to $8,000	5.2%
$8,001 to $11,000	6%
$11,001 and over	6.98%

Vermont[2]

Single

$0 to $31,850	3.6%
$31,851 to $77,100	7.2%
$77,101 to $160,850	8.5%
$160,851 to $349,700	9.0%
$349,701 and over	9.5%

Head of household

$0 to $42,650	3.6%
$42,651 to $110,100	7.2%
$110,101 to $178,350	8.5%
$178,351 to $349,700	9.0%
$349,701 and over	9.5%

Married filing jointly, Surviving spouse, Civil Union filing jointly

$0 to $53,150	3.6%
$53,151 to $128,500	7.2%
$128,501 to $195,850	8.5%
$195,851 to $349,700	9.0%
$349,701 and over	9.5%

Married or Civil Union filing separately

$0 to $26,575	3.6%
$26,576 to $64,250	7.2%
$64,251 to $97,925	8.5%
$97,926 to $174,850	9.0%
$174,851 and over	9.5%

Virginia

Single, Head of household, Married filing jointly, or Married filing separately

$0 to $3,000	2%
$3,001 to $5,000	3%
$5,001 to $17,000	5%
$17,001 and over	5.75%

West Virginia

Single, Head of household, or Married filing jointly

$0 to $10,000	3%
$10,001 to $25,000	4%
$25,001 to $40,000	4.5%
$40,001 to $60,000	6%
$60,001 and over	6.5%

Married filing separately

$0 to $5,000	3%
$5,001 to $12,500	4%
$12,501 to $20,000	4.5%
$20,001 to $30,000	6%
$30,001 and over	6.5%

Wisconsin[1, 2]

Single or Head of household

$0 to $9,510	4.6%
$9,511 to $19,020	6.15%
$19,021 to $142,650	6.5%
$142,651 and over	6.75%

Married filing jointly

$0 to $12,680	4.6%
$12,681 to $25,360	6.15%
$25,361 to $190,210	6.5%
$190,211 and over	6.75%

Married filing separately

$0 to $6,340	4.6%
$6,341 to $12,680	6.15%
$12,681 to $95,100	6.5%
$95,101 and over	6.75%

(1) Community property state in which, in general, one-half of the community income is taxable to each spouse. (2) Brackets indexed for inflation annually. (3) 2007 adjusted brackets were not available. Bracketed rates listed are for 2006. **Arkansas:** Tax liability is associated with a 3% tax surcharge based on existing rates. Married filing separately combined-status couples calculate taxes separately and add the results. **California:** An additional 1% tax is imposed on taxable income in excess of $1 million. **Colorado:** Alternative minimum tax imposed. Individual taxpayers are subject to an alternative minimum tax equal to the amount by which 3.47% of their Colorado alternative minimum taxable income exceeds their Colorado normal tax. **Connecticut:** Resident estates and trusts are subject to the 5% income tax rate on all of their income. Additional state minimum tax imposed on resident individuals, trusts, and estates that are subject to the federal alternative minimum tax, equal to the amount by which the Connecticut minimum tax exceeds the Connecticut basic income tax (the lesser of [a] 19% of adjusted federal tentative minimum tax, or [b] 5.5% of adjusted federal alternative minimum taxable income). Separate provisions apply for non- and part-year resident individuals, trusts, and estates. **Illinois:** Additional personal property replacement tax of 1.5% of net income is imposed on partnerships, trusts, and S corporations. **Indiana:** Counties may impose an adjusted gross income tax on residents or on nonresidents, or a county option income tax. (Note: Rates have apparently changed.) **Iowa:** An alternative minimum tax of 6.7% of alternative minimum income is imposed if the minimum tax exceeds the taxpayer's regular income tax liability. The minimum tax is 75% of the maximum regular tax rate. **Maine:** Additional state minimum tax is imposed equal to the amount by which the tentative minimum tax exceeds regular income tax liability. **Massachusetts:** Part A income represents either interest and dividends or short-term capital gains. Part B income represents wages, salaries, tips, pensions, state bank interest, partnership income, business income, rents, alimony, winnings, and certain other items of income. Part C income represents gains from the sale of capital assets held for more than one year. **Michigan:** Persons with business activity allocated or apportioned to Michigan are also subject to a single business tax on an adjusted tax base. **Minnesota:** A 6.4% alternative minimum tax is imposed. **Montana:** Minimum tax, $1. **Nebraska:** The tax rates in the schedules are determined by multiplying the primary rate set by the legislature by the following factors for the brackets, from lowest to highest bracket. For tax years beginning on or after January 1, 2003, the respective factors are: 0.6932, 0.9646, 1.3846, and 1.848. For tax years beginning before January 1, 2003, the respective factors are: 0.6784, 0.9432, 1.3541, and 1.8054. The figure obtained for each bracket is rounded to the nearest hundredth of 1%. One rate schedule is to be established for each federal filing status (Sec. 77-2715.02). **New Mexico:** Qualified nonresident taxpayers may pay alternative tax of 0.75% of gross receipts from New Mexico sales. **New York:** A supplemental tax is imposed to recapture the tax table benefit. The supplemental tax is calculated in accordance with N.Y. Tax Law Sec. 601(d). **Oklahoma:** Rates given are for taxpayers not deducting federal income tax. Rates for married individuals filing jointly, surviving spouses and heads of households deducting federal income tax range from .50% of the first $2,000 to 10% of income over $24,000. For single individuals and married individuals filing separately that are deducting federal income tax, rates range from .50% of the first $1,000 to 10% of income over $16,000. **Vermont:** The tax amount in the schedules is increased by 24% of a taxpayer's federal tax liability for: additional taxes assessed due to early withdrawals from qualified retirement plans, individual retirement accounts, and medical savings accounts; recapture of the federal investment tax credit; or tax on qualified lump-sum distributions of pension income not included in federal taxable income. The amount of tax is decreased by 24% of the reduction in the taxpayer's federal liability due to farm income averaging. **West Virginia:** Minimum tax equal to the excess by which 25% of any federal minimum tax or alternative minimum tax for the taxable year exceeds the sum of the primary tax for West Virginia personal income tax purposes for the taxable year. **Wisconsin:** A permanent recycling surcharge is imposed on individuals, estates, trusts, and partnerships with at least $4 million in gross receipts at the rate of the greater of $25 or 0.2% of net business income as allocated or apportioned to Wisconsin. The maximum surcharge is $9,800. Farming is no longer treated preferentially.

ASSOCIATIONS AND SOCIETIES

Source: World Almanac research

Selected list, generally by first distinctive **key word** in each title; e.g., Retired Persons, American Association of. Listed by acronym when that is the official name. Founding year in parentheses; figure after ZIP code = membership as reported. Information, especially website addresses, subject to change. For other organizations, see Directory of Sports Organizations; Where to Get Help in Health chapter; Membership of Religious Groups in Religion chapter; Major International Organizations in Nations chapter; Labor Union Directory in Employment chapter.

AAA (American Automobile Assn.) (1902): 1000 AAA Dr., Box 28, Heathrow, FL 32746; www.aaa.com

AARP. See Retired Persons, American Assn. of

Abortion Federation, National (1977): 1755 Massachusetts Ave. NW, Ste. 600, Washington, DC 20036; 400 institutions; www.prochoice.org

Academies, Natl. (1863): 500 Fifth St. NW, Washington, DC 20001; approx. 6,000; www.nationalacademies.org

Accountants, American Institute of Certified Public (1887): 1211 Ave. of the Americas, New York, NY 10036; 336,000+; www.aicpa.org

Actuaries, Society of (1949): 475 N. Martingale Rd., Ste. 600, Schaumburg, IL 60173; 18,000; www.soa.org

Administrative Professionals, Intl. Assn. of (1942): 10502 NW Ambassador Dr., Kansas City, MO 64195-0404; 40,000; www.iaap-hq.org

Advancement and Support of Education, Council for (1974): 1307 New York Ave. NW, Ste. 1000, Washington, DC 20005; 3,300 schools; www.case.org

Aeronautic Assn., Natl. (1922): 1737 King St., Ste. 220, Alexandria, VA 22314; 3,000; www.naa-usa.org

Aerospace Industries Assn. of America Inc. (1919): 1000 Wilson Blvd., Ste. 1700, Arlington, VA 22209; 105 cos.; www.aia-aerospace.org

Aerospace Medical Assn. (1929): 320 S. Henry St., Alexandria, VA 22314; 3,200+; www.asma.org

AFCEA (Armed Forces Communications and Electronics Assn.) (1946): 4400 Fair Lakes Ct., Fairfax, VA 22033; 20,000 indiv., 11,000 corp.; www.afcea.org

African-American Life and History, Assn. for the Study of (1915): C.B. Powell Building, 525 Bryant St., Ste. C142, Washington, DC 20059; 3,500; www.asalh.org

AFS Intercultural Programs USA (1947): One Whitehall St., 2nd Fl., New York, NY 10004; 11,000 exchange students annually; www.afs.org/usa

Agricultural and Biological Engineers, American Soc. of (ASABE) (1907): 2950 Niles Road, St. Joseph, MI 49085; 9,000; www.asabe.org

Air & Waste Management Assn. (1907): One Gateway Center, 3rd Fl., 420 Fort Duquesne Blvd., Pittsburgh, PA 15222; 9,000+; www.awma.org

Aircraft Owners and Pilots Assn. (1939): 421 Aviation Way, Frederick, MD 21701; 412,000+; www.aopa.org

Air Force Assn. (1946): 1501 Lee Hwy., Arlington, VA 22209; 230+ chapt.; www.afa.org

Al-Anon/Alateen (1951): 1600 Corporate Landing Pkwy., Virginia Beach, VA 23454; 26,000+ grps.; www.al-anon.alateen.org

Alcoholics Anonymous (AA) (1935): Box 459, Grand Central Station, New York, NY 10163; 2 mil+; www.aa.org

Alcoholism and Drug Dependence, Inc., Natl. Council on (1944): 244 E. 58th St., 4th Fl., New York, NY 10022; 100 affil.; www.ncadd.org

Allergy, Asthma, and Immunology, American Academy of (1943): 555 E. Wells St., Ste. 1100, Milwaukee, WI 53202; 6,500; www.aaaai.org

Alpha Delta Kappa (1947): 1615 W. 92nd St., Kansas City, MO 64114; 46,563; www.alphadeltakappa.org

Alzheimer's Assn. (1980): 225 N. Michigan Ave., 17th Fl., Chicago, IL 60601; 81 chapt.; www.alz.org

American. See also other entries under next major word in title.

American Indians, Natl. Congress of (1944): 1301 Connecticut Ave. NW, Ste. 200, Washington, DC 20036; 250 member tribes; www.ncai.org

American-Islamic Relations, Council on (1994): 453 New Jersey Ave. SE, Washington, DC 20003; www.cair.com

American Legion (1919): P.O. Box 1055, 700 N. Pennsylvania St., Indianapolis, IN 46206; 3 mil.; www.legion.org

American Legion Auxiliary (1919): 777 N. Meridian St., 3rd Floor, Indianapolis, IN 46204; 1 mil; www.legion-aux.org

AmeriCares Foundation (1982): 88 Hamilton Ave., Stamford, CT 06902; www.americares.org

AMIDEAST (formerly American Mideast Educational & Training Services) (1951): 1730 M St. NW, Ste. 1100, Washington, DC 20036; www.amideast.org

Amnesty Intl. USA (1961): 5 Penn Plaza, 14th Fl., New York, NY 10001; 320,000+; www.amnestyusa.org

AMSUS (Society of the Federal Health Agencies) (1891): 9320 Old Georgetown Road, Bethesda, MD 20814; 9,000+; www.amsus.org

AMVETS (American Veterans) (1944): 4647 Forbes Blvd., Lanham, MD 20706; 176,000; www.amvets.org

Amusement Parks and Attractions, Intl. Assn. of (IAAPA) (1918): 1448 Duke St., Alexandria, VA 22314; 4,500+; www.iaapa.org

Animals, American Society for Prevention of Cruelty to (ASPCA) (1866): 424 E. 92nd St., New York, NY 10128; 1 mil+; www.aspca.org

Animals, People for the Ethical Treatment of (PETA) (1980): 501 Front St., Norfolk, VA 23510; 1.6 mil+; www.peta.org

Animal Welfare Institute (1951): P.O. Box 3650, Washington, DC 20027; 22,000; www.awionline.org

Anthropological Assn., American (1902): 2200 Wilson Blvd., Ste. 600, Arlington, VA 22201; 11,500; www.aaanet.org

Antiquarian Society, American (1812): 185 Salisbury St., Worcester, MA 01609; 800; www.americanantiquarian.org

Anti-Vivisection Soc., Natl. (1929): 53 W. Jackson Blvd., Ste. 1552, Chicago, IL 60604; www.navs.org

APICS (Assn. for Operations Mgmt.) (1957): 5301 Shawnee Rd., Alexandria, VA 22312- 2317; 42,000; www.apics.org

Appalachian Mountain Club (1876): 5 Joy St., Boston, MA 02108; 90,000+; www.outdoors.org

Appalachian Trail Conservancy (1925): 799 Washington St., P.O. Box 807, Harpers Ferry, WV 25425; 125,000; www.appalachiantrail.org

Arc of the United States, The (1950): 1010 Wayne Avenue, Ste. 650, Silver Spring, MD 20910; 140,000; www.thearc.org

Archaeological Institute of America (1879): 656 Beacon St., 6th Fl., Boston, MA 02215; 8,500; www.archaeological.org

Architects, American Institute of (1857): 1735 New York Ave. NW, Washington, DC 20006; 80,000+; www.aia.org

Army, Assn. of the United States (1950): 2425 Wilson Blvd., Arlington, VA 22201; 130 chapt.; www.ausa.org

Arthritis Foundation (1948): P.O. Box 7669, Atlanta, GA 30357; www.arthritis.org

Arts, Americans for the (1996): 1000 Vermont Ave. NW, 6th Fl., Washington, DC 20005; 5,000; www.artsusa.org

Arts and Sciences, American Academy of (1780): 136 Irving St., Cambridge, MA 02138; 4,000 fellows; www.amacad.org

ASPCA. See Animals, Amer. Soc. for Prev. of Cruelty to.

Associated Press (1846): 450 W. 33rd St., New York, NY 10001; 4,100 staff, 1,700+ newspapers, 5,000+ U.S. TV/radio stations; www.ap.org

Astrologers, Inc., American Federation of (AFA, Inc.) (1938): 6535 South Rural Road, Tempe, AZ 85283; 4,000; www.astrologers.com

Astronautical Society, American (1954): 6352 Rolling Mill Pl., Ste. #102, Springfield, VA 22152; 1,500; www.astronautical.org

Astronomical Society, American (1899): 2000 Florida Ave. NW, Ste. 400, Washington, DC 20009; 6,400+; www.aas.org

Atheists, American (1963): P.O. Box 5733, Parsippany, NJ 07054; 2,300; www.atheists.org

Audubon Soc., Natl. (1905): 700 Broadway, New York, NY 10003; 500,000; www.audubon.org

Authors Guild, The (1912): 31 E. 32nd St., 7th Fl., New York, NY 10016; 8,200; www.authorsguild.org

Authors Registry, The (1995): 31 E. 32nd St., 7th Fl., New York, NY 10016; 30,000; www.authorsregistry.org

Autism Soc. of America (1965): 7910 Woodmont Ave., Ste. 300, Bethesda, MD 20814; 120,000; www.autism-society.org

Autograph Collectors Club, Universal (1965): P.O. Box 1392, Mount Dora, FL 32756; 2,000; www.uacc.org

Automobile Club of America, Antique (1935): 501 W. Governor Road, P.O. Box 417, Hershey, PA 17033; 60,000; www.aaca.org

Automobile License Plate Collectors Assn. (1954): 508 Coastal Dr., Virginia Beach, VA 23451; 3,025; www.alpca.org

Badminton Assn., USA (1938): One Olympic Plaza, Colorado Springs, CO 80909; 3,000; www.usabadminton.org

Bald-Headed Men of America (1973): 102 Bald Dr., Morehead City, NC 28557; approx. 22,000; baldusa.org

Bankers of America, Independent Community (1930): 1615 L St. NW, Ste. 900, Washington, DC 20036; 5,000; www.icba.org

Bar Assn., American (1878): 321 N. Clark St., Chicago, IL 60610; 400,000+; www.abanet.org

Bar Assn., Federal (1920): 2011 Crystal Dr., Ste. 400, Arlington, VA 22202; 16,000; www.fedbar.org

Barbershop Harmony Society (1938): 7930 Sheridan Rd., Kenosha, WI 53143; 30,000; www.barbershop.org

Baseball Congress, American Amateur (1935): 100 W. Broadway, Farmington, NM 87401; 14,500 teams; www.aabc.us

Baseball Congress, Natl. (1934): P.O. Box 1420, Wichita, KS 67201; www.nbcbaseball.com

Baseball Research, Inc., Society for American (1971): 812 Huron Road E, Ste. #719, Cleveland, OH 44115; 6,800; www.sabr.org

Beta Gamma Sigma Honor Society (1913): 125 Weldon Pkwy., Maryland Heights, MO 63043; 400,000; www.betagammasigma.org

Beta Sigma Phi (1931): 1800 W. 91st Pl., Kansas City, MO 64114; 200,000; www.betasigmaphi.org

Better Business Bureaus, Council of (1912): 4200 Wilson Blvd., Suite 800, Arlington, VA 22203; 150 bureaus; www.bbb.org

Bible Society, American (1816): 1865 Broadway, New York, NY 10023; 136 societies; www.bibles.com

Biblical Literature, Society of (1880): 825 Houston Mill Rd., Atlanta, GA 30329; 8,000; www.sbl-site.org

Big Brothers/Big Sisters of America (1904): 230 N. 13th St., Philadelphia, PA 19107; 470 agencies; bbbsa.org

Biochemistry and Molecular Biology, American Society for (1906): 9650 Rockville Pike, Bethesda, MD 20814; 11,900; www.asbmb.org

Biological Sciences, American Institute of (1947): 1444 I St. NW, Ste. 200, Washington, DC 20005; 250,000; www.aibs.org

Blind, American Council of the (1961): 1155 15th St. NW, Ste. 1004, Washington, DC 20005; 71 orgs.; www.acb.org

Blind, Natl. Federation of the (1940): 1800 Johnson St., Baltimore, MD 21230; 50,000+; www.nfb.org

Blinded Veterans Assn. (1958): 477 H St. NW, Washington, DC 20001; 10,035; www.bva.org

Blindness America, Prevent (1908): 211 W. Wacker Dr., Ste. 1700, Chicago, IL 60606; 50,000; www.preventblindness.org

B'nai B'rith Intl. (1843): 2020 K St. NW, 7th Fl., Washington, DC 20006; 180,000; www.bnaibrith.org

Boat Owners Assn. of the U.S. (1966): 880 S. Pickett St., Alexandria, VA 22304; 650,000; www.boatUS.com

Bookplate Collectors & Designers, Amer. Soc. of (1922): P.O. Box 14964, Tuscon, AZ 85732; 150+; www.bookplate.org

Boy Scouts of America (1910): P.O. Box 152079, Irving, TX 75015; 4 mil+; www.scouting.org

Boys & Girls Clubs of America (1906): 1275 Peachtree St. NE, Atlanta, GA 30309; 4.4 mil; www.bgca.org

Bread for the World (1974): 50 F St. NW, Ste. 500, Washington, DC 20001; 58,000; www.bread.org

Brewery Collectibles Club of America (1970): 747 Merus Ct., Fenton, MO 63026; 4,000; www.bcca.com

Brewing Chemists, American Society of (1934): 3340 Pilot Knob Road, St. Paul, MN 55121; 800+; www.asbcnet.org

Broadcasters, Natl. Assn. of (1923): 1771 N St. NW, Washington, DC 20036; www.nab.org

Business Women's Assn., American (1949): 9100 Ward Pkwy., P.O. Box 8728, Kansas City, MO 64114; 55,000; www.abwa.org

Button Society, Natl. (1938): 2733 Juno Pl., Akron, OH 44333-4137; 3,000+; www.nationalbuttonsociety.org

Camp Fire USA (formerly Camp Fire Boys & Girls) (1910): 1100 Walnut St., Ste. 1900, Kansas City, MO 64106; 750,000; www.campfireusa.org

Camping Assn., American (1910): 5000 State Rd. 67 N., Martinsville, IN 46151; 7,300+; www.acacamps.org

Cancer Society, American (1913): 1599 Clifton Rd. NE, Atlanta, GA 30329; 3,400 local offices; www.cancer.org

Cartoonists Society, Natl. (1948): 341 N. Maitland Ave., Ste. 130, Maitland, FL 32751; 500; www.reuben.org

Cat Fanciers' Assn., The (1906): P.O. Box 1005, Manasquan, NJ 08736; 653 clubs; www.cfa.org

Catholic Bishops, United States Conference of (1966): 3211 4th St. NE, Washington, DC 20017; 402 members, 350 staff; www.nccbuscc.org

Catholic Church Extension Society of the USA (1905): 150 S. Wacker Dr., 20th Fl., Chicago, IL 60606; 38 dioceses; www.catholic-extension.org

Catholic Daughters of the Americas (1903): 10 West 71st St., New York, NY 10023; 95,000; www.catholicdaughters.org

Catholic Educational Assn., Natl. (1904): 1077 30th St. NW, Ste. 100, Washington, DC 20007; 200,000; www.ncea.org

Catholic Library Association (1921): 100 North St., Ste. 224, Pittsfield, MA 01201-5109; 1,000; www.cathla.org

Catholic War Veterans, USA Inc. (1935): 441 N. Lee St., Alexandria, VA 22314-2301; 20,000; cwv.org

Ceramic Society, The American (1899): 735 Ceramic Pl., Ste. 100, Westerville, OH 43081; 7,500; www.ceramics.org

Cerebral Palsy, Inc., United (1949): 1660 L St. NW, Ste. 700, Washington, DC 20036; 100 affiliates; www.ucp.org

Chamber of Commerce of the U.S.A. (1912): 1615 H St. NW, Washington, DC 20062; 215,000; www.uschamber.com

Chamber Music Players Inc., Amateur (1969): 1123 Broadway, Ste. 904, New York, NY 10010; 5,400; www.acmp.net

Chemical Society, American (1876): 1155 16th St. NW, Washington, DC 20036; 160,000+; www.chemistry.org

Chemistry Council, American (1872): 1300 Wilson Blvd., Arlington, VA 22209; 170 cos.; www.americanchemistry.com

Chess Federation, U.S. (1939): P.O. Box 3967, Crossville, TN 38557; 90,000+; www.uschess.org

Chiefs of Police, Intl. Assn. of (1893): 515 N. Washington St., Alexandria, VA 22314; 20,000+; www.theiacp.org

Children's Aid Society (1912): 181 West Valley Ave., Ste. 300, Homewood, AL 35209; www.childrensaid.org

Children's Book Council, The (1945): 12 W. 37th St., 2nd Fl., New York, NY 10018; 75 publishers; www.cbcbooks.org

Children's Tumor Foundation (1978): 95 Pine St., 16th Fl., New York, NY 10005; 6,050; www.ctf.org

Child Welfare League of America (1920): 2345 Crystal Dr., Ste. 250, Arlington, VA 22202; 800 orgs.; www.cwla.org

Chiropractic Assn., American (1963): 1701 Clarendon Blvd., Arlington, VA 22209; 18,000; www.amerchiro.org

Chris-Craft Antique Boat Club (1973): 112 14th St. SE, Cedar Rapids, IA 52403; 3,000; www.chris-craft.org

Christian Children's Fund (1938): 2821 Emerywood Pkwy., Richmond, VA 23294; 159 staff; www.christianchildrensfund.org

Cities, Natl. League of (1924): 1301 Pennsylvania Ave. NW, Ste. 550, Washington, DC 20004; 1,600+; www.nlc.org

Civil Air Patrol (1941): 105 S. Hansell St., Bldg. 714, Maxwell AFB, AL 36112; 64,000; www.cap.gov

Civil Engineers, American Society of (1852): 1801 Alexander Bell Dr., Reston, VA 20191; 140,000+; www.asce.org

Civil Liberties Union, American (ACLU) (1920): 125 Broad St., 18th Fl., New York, NY 10004; 500,000+; www.aclu.org

Coaster Enthusiasts, American (1978): 1100-H Brandywine Blvd., Zanesville, OH 43701; 8,000; www.aceonline.org

Coast Guard Combat Veterans Assn. (1985): P.O. Box 544, Westfield Center, OH 44251; 1,800; www.aug.edu/~libwrw/cgcva/cgcva.htm

Collectors, Natl. Assn. of (1996): 18222 Flower Hill Way, #299, Gaithersburg, MD 20879; 30,000; collectors.org

Co-dependents Anonymous (1986): P.O. Box 33577; Phoenix, AZ 85030; www.codependents.org

College Admission Counseling, Natl. Assn. for (1937): 1631 Prince Street, Alexandria, VA 22314; 9,800; www.nacac.com

College Board, The (1900): 45 Columbus Ave., New York, NY 10023; 5,200 inst.; www.collegeboard.com

Colleges and Universities, Assn. of American (1915): 1818 R St. NW, Washington, DC 20009; 1,000+ institutions; www.aacu.org

Colonial Dames XVII Century, Natl. Soc. (1915): 1300 New Hampshire Ave. NW, Washington, DC 20036; 13,000+; www.colonialdames17c.net

Commercial Law League of America (1895): 70 E. Lake St., Ste. 630, Chicago, IL 60601; 4,000; www.clla.org

Common Cause (1970): 1133 19th St. NW, 9th Fl., Washington, DC 20036; 300,000+; www.commoncause.org

Communication Assn., Natl. (1914): 1765 N St. NW, Washington, DC 20036; 7,700; www.natcom.org

Community & Justice, National Conference for (1927): 760 N. Frontage Rd., Ste. 105, Willowbrook, IL 60527; 55 offices; www.nccj.org

Community Colleges, American Assn. of (1920): One Dupont Circle NW, Ste. 410, Washington, DC 20036; 1,100 inst; www.aacc.nche.edu

Composers, Authors & Publishers, American Soc. of (ASCAP) (1914): One Lincoln Plaza, New York, NY 10023; 295,000; www.ascap.com

Computing Machinery, Assn. for (1947): 2 Penn Plaza, Ste. 701, New York, NY 10121; 78,000+; www.acm.org

Computing Professionals, Institute for Certification of (1973): 2350 E. Devon Ave., Ste. 115, Des Plaines, IL 60018-4610; 50,000; www.iccp.org

Concerned Women for America (1979): 1015 Fifteenth St. NW, Ste. 1100, Washington, DC 20005; 500,000; www.cwfa.org

Congress of Racial Equality (CORE) (1942): 817 Broadway, 3rd Floor, New York, NY 10003; 82,000; www.core-online.org

Conscientious Objectors, Central Committee for (1948): 405 14th St., #205, Oakland, CA 94612; www.objector.org

Construction Inspectors, Assn. of (1974): 1224 N. Nokomis NE, Alexandria, MN 56308; 1,000; www.iami.org/aci/home.cfm

Construction Specifications Institute (1948): 99 Canal Center Plaza, Ste. 300, Alexandria, VA 22314; 15,000+; www.csinet.org

Consumer Federation of America (1968): 1620 I St. NW, Ste. 200, Washington, DC 20006; 300 member organizations; www.consumerfed.org

Consumer Interests, American Council on (ACCI) (1953): 555 E. Wells St., Ste. 1100, Milwaukee, WI 53202; 750; www.consumerinterests.org

Consumers Union of the U.S. (1936): 101 Truman Ave., Yonkers, NY 10703; 405,990; www.consumersunion.org

Contract Bridge League, American (1937): 2990 Airways Blvd., Memphis, TN 38116; 160,000; www.acbl.org

Co-op America (1982): 1612 K St. NW, Ste. 600, Washington, DC 20006; 65,000 indiv., 2,500 cos.; www.coopamerica.org

Correctional Assn., American (1870): 206 N. Washington St., Ste. 200, Alexandria, VA 22314; 20,000; www.aca.org

Cosmetology Assn., Natl. (1921): 401 N. Michigan Ave., Chicago, IL 60611; 25,000; www.ncacares.org

Counseling Assn., American (1952): 5999 Stevenson Ave., Alexandria, VA 22304; 45,000; www.counseling.org

Country Music Assn. (1958): One Music Circle S., Nashville, TN 37203; 6,000+; www.CMAworld.com

Craft & Hobby Assn. (2004): 319 E. 54th St., Elmwood Park, NJ 07407; 5,500; www.hobby.org

Crime and Delinquency, Natl. Council on (1907): 1970 Broadway, Ste. 500, Oakland, CA 94612; 300+; www.nccd-crc.org

Croplife America (1933): 1156 15th St. NW, Ste. 400, Washington, DC 20005; 80 cos.; www.croplifeamerica.org

Cryogenic Soc. of America, Inc. (1964): 218 Lake St., Oak Park, IL 60302; 500; www.cryogenicsociety.org

Customs Brokers and Forwarders Assn. of America, Inc., Natl. (1897): 1200 18th St. NW, Ste. 901, Washington, DC 20036; 800 cos.; www.ncbfaa.org

Cystic Fibrosis Foundation (1955): 6931 Arlington Rd., Bethesda, MD 20814; 30,000; www.cff.org

Dark-Sky Association, Intl. (1988): 3225 N. First Ave., Tucson, AZ 85719-2103; 11,289+; www.darksky.org

Daughters of the American Revolution Natl. Society (1890): 1776 D Street NW, Washington, DC 20006; 168,000; www.dar.org

Daughters of the Confederacy, United (1894): 328 North Blvd., Richmond, VA 23220; 25,000; www.hqudc.org

Deaf, Natl. Assn. of the (1880): 8630 Fenton St., Ste. 820, Silver Spring, MD 20910; 16,500; www.nad.org

Defenders of Wildlife (1947): 1130 17th St. NW, Washington, DC 20036; 500,000; www.defenders.org

Delta Kappa Gamma Society Intl. (1929): P.O. Box 1589, Austin, TX 78767; 136,000; www.deltakappagamma.net

Democratic Natl. Committee (1848): 430 S. Capitol St. SE, Wash., DC 20003; 447 elected mem.; www.democrats.org

Dental Assn., American (1859): 211 E. Chicago Ave., Chicago, IL 60611; 155,000; www.ada.org

Diabetes Assn., American (1940): 1701 North Beauregard St., Alexandria, VA 22311; 416,967; www.diabetes.org

Directors Guild of America (1936): 7920 Sunset Blvd., Los Angeles 90046; 12,700+; www.dga.org

Disabled American Veterans (1932): 3725 Alexandria Pike, Cold Spring, KY 41076; 1.2 mil; www.dav.org

Disabled Sports USA (1967): 451 Hungerford Dr., Ste. 100, Rockville, MD 20850; 60,000+; www.dsusa.org

Doctors Without Borders/Médecins Sans Frontières (1971): 333 Seventh Ave., 2nd Fl., New York, NY 10001; 4,700+ missions; www.doctorswithoutborders.org

Down Syndrome Society, Natl. (1979): 666 Broadway, 8th Fl., New York, NY 10012; 30,000; www.ndss.org

Ducks Unlimited (1937): One Waterfowl Way, Memphis, TN 38120; 774,022; www.ducks.org

Eagles, Fraternal Order of (1898): 1623 Gateway Circle South, Grove City, OH 43123; 700 chapt.; www.foe.com

Easter Seals (1919): 230 W. Monroe St., Ste. 1800, Chicago, IL 60606; www.easterseals.com

Eastern Star, General Grand Chapter, Order of the (1876): 1618 New Hampshire Ave. NW, Washington, DC 20009; 1 mil.; www.easternstar.org

Edsel Club (1967): 19296 Tuckaway Ct., N. Fort Myers, FL 33903; 300; www.edselworld.com

Education, American Council on (1918): One Dupont Circle NW, Ste. 800, Washington, DC 20036; 1,800 org.; www.acenet.edu

Education, Council for Advancement & Support of (1974): 1307 New York Ave. NW, Ste 1000, Washington, DC 20005; 3,300+ schools; www.case.org

Education of Young Children, Natl. Assn. for the (1926): 1313 L St. NW, Ste. 500, Washington, DC 20005; 100,000; www.naeyc.org

Educators for World Peace, Intl. Assn. of (1973): P.O. Box 3282, Mastin Lake Station, Huntsville, AL 35810; 35,000; www.iaewp.org

Egalitarian Communities, Federation of (1976): 2 Dancing Rabbit Ln., Rutledge, MO 63563; 14 comm.; www.thefec.org

88th Infantry Division Assn. (1946): 11 Lovett Ave., Brockton, MA 02301-1750; 4,200; www.88infdiv.org

82nd Airborne Division Assn., Inc. (1946): P.O. Box 9308, Fayetteville, NC 28311; 27,000+; www.82ndassociation.org

Electrical and Electronics Engineers, Institute of (1963): 445 Hoes Lane, Piscataway, NJ 08854; 370,000; www.ieee.org

Electrical Manufacturers Assn., Natl. (1926): 1300 N. 17th St., Ste. 1752, Rosslyn, VA 22209; 400 cos.; www.nema.org

Electrochemical Society, Inc., The (ECS, Inc.) (1902): 65 South Main St., Bldg. D, Pennington, NJ 08534-2839; 8,000+; www.electrochem.org

Electronics Technicians, Intl. Soc. of Certified (1980): 3608 Pershing Ave., Ft. Worth, TX 76107; 50,000; www.iscet.org

Elks of the U.S.A., Benevolent and Protective Order of (1868): 2750 N. Lakeview Ave., Chicago, IL 60614; 1 mil+ mem., 2,100 chapt.; www.elks.org

Energy Engineers, Assn. of (1977): 4025 Pleasantdale Rd., Ste. 420, Atlanta, GA 30340; 9,000; www.aeecenter.org

Engineers, Natl. Society of Professional (1934): 1420 King St., Alexandria, VA 22314; 50,000; www.nspe.org

English Inc., U.S. (1983): 1747 Pennsylvania Ave. NW, Ste. 1050, Washington, DC 20006; 1.8 mil; www.usenglish.org

English-Speaking Union of the U.S. (1920): 144 E. 39th St., New York, NY 10016; 10,000; www.esuus.org

Entomological Society of America (1889): 10001 Derekwood Ln., Ste 100, Lanham, MD 20706-4876; 5,700; www.entsoc.org

Environmental Assessment Association (1972): 1224 North Nokomis NE, Alexandria, MN 56308; 5,000; www.iami.org/eaa/home.cfm

Environmental Health Assn., Natl. (1937): 720 S. Colorado Blvd., Ste. 1000-N, Denver, CO 80246; approx. 4,500; www.neha.org

Esperanto League for North America Inc. (1953): P.O. Box 1129, El Cerrito, CA 94530; 700; www.esperanto-usa.org

Experimental Aircraft Assn. (1953): P.O. Box 3086, Oshkosh, WI 54903; 170,000+; www.eaa.org

Ex-Prisoners of War, American (1942): 3201 E. Pioneer Pkwy., #40, Arlington, TX 76010; 27,000; www.axpow.org

Fairs & Expositions, Intl. Assn. of (1885): P.O. Box 985, Springfield, MO 65801; 2,600; www.fairsandexpos.com

Family, Career and Com. Leaders of Am. (1945): 1910 Association Dr., Reston, VA 20191; 225,000; www.fcclainc.org

Family Physicians, American Academy of (1947): P.O. Box 11210, Shawnee Mission, KS 66207; 94,000; www.aafp.org

Family Relations, Natl. Council on (1938): 3989 Central Avenue NE, Suite 550, Minneapolis, MN 55421; 4,000; www.ncfr.org

Farm Bureau, American (1919): 600 Maryland Ave. SW, Ste. 1000W, Washington, DC 20024; 5 mil+ families; www.fb.org

Farmers of America Org., Natl. Future (1928): P.O. Box 68960, Indianapolis, IN 46268; 495,046; www.ffa.org

Farmers Union, Natl. (1902): 5619 DTC Pkwy., Ste. 300, Greenwood Village, CO 80111; 250,000; www.nfu.org

Fat Acceptance, Natl. Assn. to Advance (NAAFA) (1969): P.O. Box 22510, Oakland, CA 94609; 50 chapt.; www.naafa.org

Feminists for Life of America (1972): P.O. Box 20685, Alexandria, VA 22320; c. 5,000; www.feministsforlife.org

Financial Professionals, Assn. for (1979): 4520 East West Hwy., Ste. 750, Bethesda, MD 20814; 14,000; www.AFPonline.org

Financial Service Professionals, Soc. of (1928): 17 Campus Blvd, Newtown Square, PA 19073; 20,000; www.financialpro.org

Financial Women Intl. (1921 as Natl. Assoc. of Bank Women): 1027 W. Roselawn Ave., Roseville, MN 55113; 1,000+; www.fwi.org

Fire Chiefs, Intl. Assn. of (1873): 4025 Fair Ridge Dr., Ste. 300, Fairfax, VA 22033; 12,000; www.iafc.org

Fire Protection Assn., Natl. (NFPA) (1896): 1 Batterymarch Park, Quincy, MA 02169; 81,000; www.nfpa.org

Fire Protection Engineers, Soc. of (1950): 7315 Wisconsin Avenue, Ste. 620E, Bethesda, MD 20814; 4,500; www.sfpe.org

First Candle/SIDSAlliance (1987): 1314 Bedford Ave., Ste. 210, Baltimore, MD 21208; www.sidsalliance.org

Fisheries Soc., American (1870): 5410 Grosvenor Ln., Ste. 110, Bethesda, MD 20814; 300 chapt.; www.fisheries.org

Fleet Reserve Association (1924): 125 N. West St., Alexandria, VA 22314-2754; 122,000; www.fra.org

Food Technologists, Institute of (1939): 525 W. Van Buren, Ste. 1000, Chicago, IL 60607; 22,000; www.ift.org

Foreign Study, The American Institute for (1964): River Plaza, 9 W. Broad St., Stamford, CT 06902; 1 mil+; www.aifs.com

Foreign Trade Council, Inc., Natl. (1914): 1625 K St. NW, Ste. 200, Washington, DC 20006; 300 companies.; www.nftc.org

Forensic Sciences, American Academy of (1948): 410 N. 21st St., Colorado Springs, CO 80904; 6,000; www.aafs.org

Foresters, Society of American (1900): 5400 Grosvenor La., Bethesda, MD 20814; 14,997; www.safnet.org

Forest History Society (1946): 701 Wm. Vickers Ave., Durham, NC 27701-3162; 1,500; www.foresthistory.org

4-H Clubs (1914): CSREES/USDA, 1400 Independence Ave. SW, Washington, DC 20250; 7 mil; www.4h-usa.org

Freedom From Religion Foundation (1978): P.O. Box 750, Madison, WI 53701; 6,000; www.ffrf.org

Freedom of Information Center (1958): Missouri School of Journalism, 133 Neff Annex, Columbia, MO 65211-0012; foi.missouri.edu

Freemasonry, Scottish Rite of, Supreme Council Ancient and Accepted Scottish Rite of, Northern Masonic Jurisdiction (1813): P.O. Box 519, Lexington, MA 02420; 270,000; www.supremecouncil.org

Freemasonry, Scottish Rite of, Supreme Council Ancient and Accepted Scottish Rite of, Southern Jurisdiction (1802): 1733 16th St. NW, Washington, DC 20009-3103; 350,000; www.srmason-sj.org

Free Men, Natl. Coalition of (1977): P.O. Box 582023, Minneapolis, MN 55458; 2,000; www.ncfm.org

Free Press Readership Council, American (2001): 645 Pennsylvania Ave., S.E., Washington, DC 20003; 4,500; www.americanfreepress.net

French Institute/Alliance Française (1971): 22 E. 60th St., New York, NY 10022; 6,000; www.fiaf.org

Friends of the Earth (1969): 1717 Massachusetts Ave. NW, Ste. 600, Washington, DC 20036; 1.5 mil; www.foe.org

Funeral Consumers Alliance (1963): 33 Patchen Rd., S. Burlington, VT 05403; 115 soc.; www.funerals.org

Funeral Directors Assn., Natl. (1882): 13625 Bishop's Dr., Brookfield, WI 53005; 20,300; www.nfda.org

Future Business Leaders of America/Phi Beta Lambda, Inc. (1942): 1912 Association Dr., Reston, VA 20191; 240,000; www.fbla-pbl.org

Gamblers Anonymous (1957): P.O. Box 17173, Los Angeles, CA 90017; approx. 30,000; www.gamblersanonymous.org

Garden Club of America (1913): 14 E. 60th St., New York, NY 10022; 18,000; www.gcamerica.org

Garden Clubs, Inc., National Council of State (1929): 4401 Magnolia Ave., St. Louis, MO 63110; 204,143; www.gardenclub.org

Gay and Lesbian Alliance Against Defamation (1985): 248 W. 35th St., 8th Fl., New York, NY 10001; www.glaad.org

Gay and Lesbian Task Force, Natl. (1973): 1325 Massachusetts Ave. NW, Ste. 600, Washington, DC 20005; 20,000; www.thetaskforce.org

Genealogical Society, Natl. (1903): 3108 Columbia Pike, Ste. 300, Arlington, VA 22204; 11,000; www.ngsgenealogy.org

General Contractors of America, The Associated (1918): 2300 Wilson Blvd., Ste. 400, Arlington, VA 22201; 33,000+ cos.; www.agc.org

Genetic Association, American (1903): P.O. Box 257, Buckeystown, MD 21717; www.theaga.org

Geographers, Assn. of American (1904): 1710 16th St. NW, Washington, DC 20009; 7,500+; www.aag.org

Geographic Society, Natl. (1888): 1145 17th St. NW, Washington, DC 20036; 8.5 mil.; www.nationalgeographic.com

Geological Society of America (1888): P.O. Box 9140, Boulder, CO 80301; 20,500+; www.geosociety.org

Geriatrics Society, American (1942): 350 5th Ave., Ste. 801, New York, NY 10118; 6,800+; www.americangeriatrics.org

Gideons Intl. (1899): P.O. Box 140800, Nashville, TN 37214; 250,000+; www.gideons.org

Gifted Children, Natl. Assn. for (1954): 1707 L Street NW, Suite 550, Washington, DC 20036; 8,000; www.nagc.org

Girl Scouts of the U.S.A. (1912): 420 5th Ave., New York, NY 10018; 3.7 mil; www.girlscouts.org

Golf Assn., U.S. (1894): P.O. Box 708, Far Hills, NJ 07931; 900,000; www.usga.org

Gospel Music Assn. (1964): 1205 Division St., Nashville, TN 37203; 4,000; www.gospelmusic.org

Governors' Assn., Natl. (1908): Hall of the States, 444 N. Capitol, Ste. 267, Washington, DC 20001; 55 govs.; www.nga.org

Grange Patrons of Husbandry, Natl. (1867): 1616 H Street NW, Washington, DC 20006; 300,000; www.nationalgrange.org

Graphic Arts, American Institute of (1914): 164 5th Ave., New York, NY 10010; 19,000; www.aiga.org

Gray Panthers (1970): 1612 K St. NW, Ste. 300, Washington, DC 20006; approx. 20,000; www.graypanthers.org

Green Mountain Club, The (1910): 4711 Waterbury-Stowe Rd., Waterbury Center, VT 05677; 9,000+; www.greenmountainclub.org

Green Party (1984): P.O. Box 408316, Chicago, IL 60640; www.greenparty.org

Greenpeace, Inc. (1971): 702 H St. NW, Suite 300, Washington, DC 20001; 2.5 mil; www.greenpeaceusa.org

Ground Water Assn., Natl. (1948): 601 Dempsey Rd., Westerville, OH 43081; 14,000; www.ngwa.org

Guide Dog Foundation for the Blind, Inc. (1946): 371 E. Jericho Turnpike, Smithtown, NY 11787; www.guidedog.org

Hadassah, the Women's Zionist Organization of America (1912): 50 W. 58th St., New York, NY 10019; 300,000+; www.hadassah.org

Handball Assn., U.S. (1951): 2333 N. Tucson Blvd., Tucson, AZ 85716; 8,500; www.ushandball.org

Health Council, Natl. (1920): 1730 M St. NW, Ste. 500, Washington, DC 20036; 115 org.; www.nationalhealthcouncil.org

Hearing Society, Intl. (1951): 16880 Middlebelt Rd., Ste. 4, Livonia, MI 48154; 3,000; www.ihsinfo.org

Heart Assn., American (1924): 7272 Greenville Ave., Dallas, TX 75231; 22.5 mil.; www.americanheart.org

Heating, Refrigerating & Air-Conditioning Engineers, Inc., American Soc. of (1894): 1791 Tullie Cir. NE, Atlanta, GA 30329; 50,000; www.ashrae.org

Helicopter Society, American (1944): 271 N. Washington St., Alexandria, VA 22314, 6,000; www.vtol.org

Hemispheric Affairs, Council on (1975): 1250 Connecticut Ave. NW, Ste. 1C, Washington, DC 20036; 4,000; www.coha.org

Highpointers Club (1986): P.O. Box 1496, Golden, CO 80402; 2,600; www.highpointers.org

Hiking Society, American (1976): 1422 Fenwick Lane, Silver Spring, MD 20910; 170 clubs; www.americanhiking.org

Historic Preservation, Natl. Trust for (1949): 1785 Massachusetts Avenue NW, Washington, DC 20036; 270,000; www.nationaltrust.org

Historical Assn., American (1884): 400 A St. SE, Washington, DC 20003; 14,000; www.historians.org

Historical Society, United States (1971): 7433 Whitepine Rd., Richmond, VA 23237; 250,000; www.ushs.org

Hockey, U.S.A. (1936): 1775 Bob Johnson Dr., Colorado Springs, CO 80906; 561,721; www.usahockey.com

Home Builders, Natl. Assn. of (1942): 1201 15th St. NW, Washington, DC 20005; 235,000; www.nahb.org

Homeless, Natl. Coalition for the (1984): 2201 P St. NW, Ste. 600, Washington, DC 20037; 2,500; www.nationalhomeless.org

Honor Society, Natl. (1921): 1904 Association Dr., Reston, VA 20191; 1 mil+; www.nhs.us

Horse Council, American (1969): 1616 H St. NW, 7th Fl., Washington, DC 20006; 160 org., 1,200 ind.; www.horsecouncil.org

Hospital Assn., American (1899): 1 N. Franklin, Chicago, IL 60606; 5,000 hosp., 37,000 indiv. members; www.aha.org

Hostelling Intl. USA (1934): 8401 Colesville Rd, Ste. 600, Silver Spring, MD 20910; 100 affil.; www.hiayh.org

Hotel & Lodging Assn., American (1910): 1201 New York Ave. NW, #600, Washington, DC 20005; 10,000+; www.ahla.com

Hot Rod Assn., Natl. (1951): 2035 Financial Way, Glendora, CA 91741; 80,000; www.nhra.com

Housing Inspection Foundation (1979): 1224 N. Nokomis NE, Alexandria, MN 56308; 1,800; www.iami.org/hif/home.cfm

Humane Society of the U.S. (1954): 2100 L St. NW, Washington, DC 20037; approx. 9.98 mil; www.hsus.org

Human Resource Management, Society for (SHRM) (1948): 1800 Duke St., Alexandria, VA 22314; 210,000; www.shrm.org

Human Rights Campaign (1980): 1640 Rhode Island Ave. NW, Washington, DC 20036; 700,000; www.hrc.org

Human Rights Watch (1978): 350 Fifth Ave. 34th Fl., New York, NY 10118; www.hrw.org

Illustrators, Inc., Society of (1901): 128 E. 63rd St., New York, NY 10021-7303; 900; www.societyillustrators.org

Industrial and Applied Mathematics, Society for (1952): 3600 Market St., Philadelphia, PA 19104; 10,000; www.siam.org

Industrial Designers Society of America (1965): 45195 Business Ct., Ste. 250, Dulles, VA 20166; 3,300; www.idsa.org

Industrial Security, American Soc. for (1955): 1625 Prince St., Alexandria, VA 22314; 35,000+; www.asisonline.org

Insurance Assn., American (1866): 1130 Connecticut Avenue NW, Suite 1000, Washington, DC 20036; 350 companies; www.aiadc.org

Intelligence Officers, Assn. of Former (1975): 6723 Whittier Ave., Ste. 303A, McLean, VA 22101; 24 chapt.; www.afio.com

Intercollegiate Athletics, Natl. Assn. of (1937): 23500 W. 105th St., Olathe, KS 66061; 300 member coll./univ.; www.naia.org

Interfaith Alliance, The (1994): 1331 H St., 11th Floor, Washington, DC 20005-4706; 185,000; www.interfaithalliance.org

Interior Designers, American Society of (1975): 608 Massachusetts Avenue NE, Washington, DC 20002; 38,000; www.asid.org

International. See organizations under next major word in title.

Intl. Education, Institute of (1919): 809 United Nations Plaza, 7th Fl., New York, NY 10017; 18,000; www.iie.org

Intl. Educational Exchange, Council on (1947): 7 Custom House St., 3rd Fl., Portland, ME 04101; 240 member groups; www.ciee.org

Intl. Law, American Society of (1906): 2223 Massachusetts Ave. NW, Washington, DC 20008; 4,000; www.asil.org

Inventors, American Soc. of (1953): P.O. Box 58426, Philadelphia, PA 19102; 150; www.asoi.org

Investigative Pathology, American Soc. for (1900): 9650 Rockville Pike, Bethesda, MD 20814; 1,718; www.asip.org

Investors Corp., Natl. Assn. of (1951): P.O. Box 220, Royal Oak, MI 48068; 132,000; www.better-investing.org

Irish American Cultural Inst. (1962): 1 Lackawanna Pl., Morristown, NJ 07960; 20 chapt.; www.irishaci.org

Jail Assn., American (1981): 1135 Professional Ct., Hagerstown, MD 21740; 5,000; www.aja.org

Japanese-American Citizens League (1929): 1765 Sutter St., San Francisco, CA 94115; 24,000; www.jacl.org

Jewish Committee, American (1906): P.O. Box 705, New York, NY 10150; 125,000; www.ajc.org

Jewish Community Centers Assn. of North America (1917): 520 8th Ave., New York, NY 10018; 1,000,000+; www.jcca.org

Jewish Congress, American (1918): 825 Third Ave., New York, NY 10022; 50,000; www.ajcongress.org

Jewish War Veterans of the U.S.A. (1896): 1811 R St. NW, Washington, DC 20009; 37,000; jwv.org

Jewish Women, Natl. Council of (1893): 53 W. 23rd St., 6th Fl., New York, NY 10010; 90,000; www.ncjw.org

John Birch Society (1958): P.O. Box 8040, Appleton, WI 54912; www.jbs.org

Journalists, Society of Professional (1909): 3909 N. Meridian St., Indianapolis, IN 46208; 10,000; spj.org

Journalists and Authors, American Society of (1948): 1501 Broadway, Ste. 302, New York, NY 10036; 1,100+; www.asja.org

Judicature Society, American (1913): Opperman Ctr., 2700 University Ave., Des Moines, IA 50311; 5,500; www.ajs.org

Jugglers Assn., Intl. (1947): P.O. Box 7307, Austin, TX 78713; 2,500; www.juggle.org

Junior Achievement, Inc. (1919): One Education Way, Colorado Springs, CO 80906; www.ja.org

Junior Auxiliaries, Natl. Assn. of (1941): P.O. Box 1873, Greenville, MS 38701; 13,809; www.najanet.org

Junior Chamber of Commerce, U.S. (1920): P.O. Box 7, Tulsa, OK 74102; 200,000; www.usjaycees.org

Junior Honor Society, Natl. (1929): 1904 Association Dr., Reston, VA 20191; 1 mil+; www.njhs.us

Junior Leagues, Assn. of (1921): 80 Maiden Ln., Ste. 305, New York, NY 10038; 293 leagues; www.ajli.org

Kidney Fund, The American (1971): 6110 Executive Blvd., Ste. 1010, Rockville, MD 20852; www.kidneyfund.org

Kiwanis International (1915): 3636 Woodview Trace, Indianapolis, IN 46268; 600,000+; www.kiwanis.org

Knights of Columbus (1882): One Columbus Plaza, New Haven, CT 06510-4000; 1.7 mil; www.kofc.org

Knights of Pythias, (1864): 59 Coddington Street, #202, Quincy, MA 02169; www.pythias.org

La Leche League Intl. (1957): P.O. Box 4079, Schaumburg, IL 60168; 26,000; www.lalecheleague.org

Lady Bird Johnson Wildflower Center (1982): 4801 La Crosse Avenue, Austin, TX 78739; 22,000; www.wildflower.org

Landscape Architects, American Society of (1899): 636 Eye St. NW, Washington, DC 20001; 17,000+; www.asla.org

Law Libraries, American Assn. of (1906): 53 W. Jackson Blvd., #940, Chicago, IL 60604; 5,000; www.aallnet.org

Lawn Mower Racing Association, U.S. (1992): 1812 Glenview Rd., Glenview, IL 60025; www.letsmow.com

Learned Societies, American Council of (1919): 633 Third Ave., New York, NY 10017; 69 societies; www.acls.org

Legal Administrators, Assn. of (1971): 75 Tri-State Intl., Ste. 222, Lincolnshire, IL 60069-4435; 10,000+; www.alanet.org

Legal Secretaries, Natl. Assn. of (NALS) (1929): 8159 E. 41st St., Tulsa, OK 74145; 8,500; www.nals.org

Legion of Valor Museum (1991): 2425 Fresno St., Ste. 103, Fresno, CA 93721; 700+; www.legionofvalormuseum.org

Leukemia and Lymphoma Society (1949): 1311 Mamaroneck Ave., White Plains, NY 10605; www.lls.org

Lewis and Clark Trail Heritage Foundation (1969): 4201 Giant Springs Rd., Great Falls, MT 59405; 3,600; www.lewisandclark.org

Libertarian Party (1971): 2600 Virginia Ave. NW, Ste. 200, Washington, DC 20037; 224,000; www.lp.org

Libraries Assn., Special (1909): 331 S. Patrick St., Alexandria, VA 22314; 12,000+; www.sla.org

Library Assn., American (1876): 50 E. Huron St., Chicago, IL 60611; 66,700+; www.ala.org

Lifesaving Assn., U.S. (1964): P.O. Box 366, Huntington Beach, CA 92648; 12,500; www.usla.org

Lighter-Than-Air Society (1952): 526 S. Main St., Akron, OH 44311; 1,000; www.blimpinfo.com

Linguistic Society of America (1924): 1325 18th St. NW, Ste. 211, Washington, DC 20036; 5,000 indiv.; www.lsadc.org

Lions Clubs, Intl., Assn. of (1917): 300 W. 22nd St., Oak Brook, IL 60523; 1.4 mil; www.lionsclubs.org

Little League Baseball, Inc. (1939): 539 U.S. Rte. 15 Hwy., P.O. Box 3485, Williamsport, PA 17701; 4 mil; www.littleleague.org

Little People of America, Inc. (1957): 5289 NE Elam Young Pkwy, Ste. F100, Hillsboro, OR 97124; 5,000+; www.lpaonline.org

Logistics, Intl. Society of (SOLE) (1966): 8100 Professional Pl., Ste. 111, Hyattsville, MD 20785; 3,500; www.sole.org

Lung Assn., American (1904): 61 Broadway, 6th Fl., New York, NY 10006; www.lungusa.org

Magazine Publishers of America (1919): 810 Seventh Ave., 24th Fl., New York, NY 10019; 1,400 titles; www.magazine.org

Magicians, Intl. Brotherhood of (1922): 11155 S Towne Sq., Ste. C, St. Louis, MO 63123; 13,000; www.magician.com

Management Accountants, Institute of (1919): 10 Paragon Dr., Montvale, NJ 07645; 65,000; www.imanet.org

Management Assn., American (1923): 1601 Broadway, New York, NY 10019; 700,000; www.amanet.org

Manufacturers, Natl. Assn. of (1895): 1331 Pennsylvania Ave. NW, Washington, DC 20004; 14,000 cos.; www.nam.org

March of Dimes Birth Defects Foundation (1938): 1275 Mamaroneck Avenue, White Plains, NY 10605; 3 mil; www.marchofdimes.com

Marine Corps League (1937): P.O. Box 3070, Merrifield, VA 22116-3070; 61,000+; www.mcleague.org

Marketing Assn., American. (1915): 311 S. Wacker Dr., Ste. 5800, Chicago, IL 60606; 38,000; www.marketingpower.com

Masons. see Freemasonry.

Master Brewers Association of the Americas (1887): 3340 Pilot Knob Rd., St. Paul, MN 55121; 3,500; www.mbaa.com

Materials and Process Engineering, Soc. for the Advancement of (1944): 1161 Park View Dr., Ste. 200, Covina, CA 91724; 12,000+; www.sampe.org

Mathematical Society, American (1888): 201 Charles St., Providence, RI 02904; 30,000; www.ams.org

Mayflower Descendants, General Society of (1897): P.O. Box 3297, Plymouth, MA 02361; 26,000; www.themayflowersociety.com

Mayors, U.S. Conference of (1932): 1620 Eye St. NW, Washington, DC 20006; 1,139; www.usmayors.org

Mechanical Engineers, American Soc. of (1880): 3 Park Ave., New York, NY 10016; 120,000; www.asme.org

Medical Assn., American (1847): 515 N. State St., Chicago, IL 60601; 300,000; www.ama-assn.org

Medical Library Assn. (1898): 65 E. Wacker Pl., Ste. 1900, Chicago, IL 60601; 3,600; www.mlanet.org

MENC: The Natl. Assn. for Music Education (formerly Music Educators Natl. Conference) (1907): 1806 Robert Fulton Dr., Reston, VA 20191; 130,000; www.menc.org

Mended Hearts, Inc. (1950): 7272 Greenville Ave., Dallas, TX 75231; 460 hospitals; www.mendedhearts.org

Mensa, Ltd., American (1960): 1229 Corporate Dr. W, Arlington, TX 76006; 50,000; www.us.mensa.org

Mental Health Assn., Natl. (1909): 2000 N. Beauregard St., 6th Fl., Alexandria, VA 22311; 320 affiliates; www.nmha.org

Mentally Ill, Natl. Alliance for the (1979): Colonial Place Three, 2107 Wilson Blvd. Ste. 300, Arlington, VA 22201; 1,200 affiliates; www.nami.org

Meteorological Society, American (1919): 45 Beacon St., Boston, MA 02108; 11,000+; www.ametsoc.org

Metric Assn., Inc., U.S. (1916): 10245 Andasol Ave., Northridge, CA 91325-1504; 1,200; www.metric.org

Microbiology, American Society for (1899): 1752 N. St. NW, Washington, DC 20036; 43,000; www.asm.org

Military Officers Assn. (1929): 201 N. Washington St., Alexandria, VA 22314; 360,000; www.moaa.org

Military Order of the Purple Heart of the USA (1932): 5413-B Backlick Road, Springfield, VA 22151; 36,765; www.purpleheart.org

Military Order of the World Wars (1919): 435 N. Lee St., Alexandria, VA 22314; 143+ chapters; www.militaryorder.net

Military Surgeons of the U.S., Assn. of. see AMSUS

Missing and Exploited Children, Natl. Center for (1984): The Charles B. Wang International Children's Building, 699 Prince St., Alexandria, VA 22314; www.missingkids.com

Model Railroad Assn., Natl. (1935): 4121 Cromwell Rd., Chattanooga, TN 37421-2119; 20,500; www.nmra.org

Modern Language Assn. of America (1883): 26 Broadway, 3rd Fl., New York, NY 10004; 30,000+; www.mla.org

Moose Intl., Inc. (1888): 155 S. International Dr., Mooseheart, IL 60539; 1 mil; www.mooseintl.org

Mothers of Twins Clubs, Natl. Organization of (1960): P.O. Box 700860, Plymouth, MI 48170; 25,000; www.nomotc.org

Motion Picture Arts & Sciences, Academy of (1927): 8949 Wilshire Blvd., Beverly Hills, CA 90211; 6,000+; www.oscars.org

Motion Picture & Television Engineers, Soc. of (1916): 3 Barker Ave., White Plains, NY 10601; 10,000; www.smpte.org

Motorcyclist Assn., American (1924): 13515 Yarmouth Dr., Pickerington, OH 43147; 260,000+; www.amadirectlink.com

Multiple Sclerosis Society, Natl. (1946): 733 3rd Ave,. 6th Fl., New York, NY 10017; 500,000; www.nationalmssociety.org

Muscular Dystrophy Assn., Inc. (1950): 3300 E. Sunrise Dr., Tucson, AZ 85718; 2 mil. volunteers; www.mdausa.org

Museums, American Assn. of (1906): 1575 Eye St. NW, Ste. 400, Washington, DC 20005; 15,000 indiv., 3,000 institutions; www.aam-us.org

Musicological Society, American (1934): Bowdoin Coll. 6010 College Station, Brunswick, ME 04011; 3,300; www.ams-net.org

Muzzle Loading Rifle Assn., Natl. (1933): P.O. Box 67, Friendship, IN 47021; 22,000; www.nmlra.org

Mystery Writers of America, Inc. (1945): 17 E. 47th St., 6th Fl., New York, NY 10017; 2,235; www.mysterywriters.org

NA'AMAT USA (1921): 350 Fifth Ave., Ste. 4700, New York, NY 10118; 25,000; www.naamat.org

Name Society, American (1951): c/o Michael McGoff, Vice Provost, Provost's Office, SUNY Binghamton, Binghamton, NY 13902; 200+; www.wtsn.binghamton.edu/ANS

Narcotics Anonymous World Services (1953): P.O Box 9999, Van Nuys, CA 94109; 20,000 groups; www.na.org

National. See other organizations under next major word in title.

Natl. Assn. for the Advancement of Colored People (NAACP) (1909): 4805 Mt. Hope Dr., Baltimore, MD 21215; www.naacp.org

National Guard Assn. of the U.S. (1878): One Massachusetts Ave. NW, Washington, DC 20001; 45,000; www.ngaus.org

Nature Conservancy, The (1951): 4245 N. Fairfax Drive, Ste. 100, Arlington, VA 22203; 1 mil; nature.org

Naval Institute, U.S. (1873): 291 Wood Rd., Annapolis, MD 21402; 100,000; www.usni.org

Naval Reserve Assn. (1954): 1619 King St., Alexandria, VA 22314; 23,000; www.navy-reserve.org

Navy League of the United States (1902): 2300 Wilson Blvd., Arlington,VA 22201-3308; 65,000+; www.navyleague.org

Negro College Fund, United (1944): 8260 Willow Oaks Corporate Dr., Fairfax, VA 22031; 39 institutions; www.uncf.org

Newspaper Assn. of America (NAA) (1992): 4401 Wilson Blvd., Arlington, VA 22203; 2,000+; www.naa.org

Ninety-Nines (Intl. Organization of Women Pilots) (1929): 4300 Amelia Earhart Rd., Oklahoma City, OK 73159; 6,000; www.ninety-nines.org

Non-Commissioned Officers Assn. (1960): P.O. Box 427, Alexandria, VA 22314; 160,000; www.ncoausa.org

Notaries, American Society of (1965): P.O. Box 5707, Tallahassee, FL 32314; approx. 20,000; www.notaries.org

Nuclear Society, American (1954): 555 N. Kensington Ave., La Grange Park, IL 60526; 10,500; www.ans.org

Nude Recreation, American Assn. for (1931): 1703 N. Main St., Kissimmee, FL 34744; almost 50,000; www.aanr.com

Numismatic Assn., American (1891): 818 N. Cascade Ave., Colorado Springs, CO 80903; 33,000; www.money.org

Nursing, Natl. League for (1893): 61 Broadway, 33rd Fl., New York, NY 10006; 20,000; www.nln.org

Ocean Conservancy (1972): 2029 K St. NW, Wash., DC 20006; 500,000; www.oceanconservancy.org

Odd Fellows, Independent Order of (1819): 422 Trade St., Winston-Salem, NC 27101; 250,000; www.ioof.org

Optimist Intl. (1919): 4494 Lindell Blvd., St. Louis, MO 63108; 105,000; www.optimist.org

Optometric Assn., American (1898): 243 N. Lindbergh Blvd., St. Louis, MO 63141; 35,000; www.aoa.org

Organ Sharing, United Network for (1984): P.O. Box 2484, Richmond, VA 23218; 405; www.unos.org

Organists, American Guild of (1896): 475 Riverside Dr., Ste. 1260, New York, NY 10115; 20,000; www.agohq.org

Oriental Society, American (1842): Univ. of Michigan, Hatcher Graduate Library, 110D, Ann Arbor, MI 48109; 1,350; www.umich.edu/~aos

ORT Inc., American (Org. for Rehabilitation Through Training) (1922): 75 Maiden Ln., 10th Fl., New York, NY 10038; 10,000; www.ortamerica.org

Ornithologists' Union, American (1883): 1313 Dolley Madison Blvd., Ste. 402, McLean, VA 22101; 4,000; www.aou.org

Overeaters Anonymous (1960): P.O. Box 44020, Rio Rancho, NM 87174; www.oa.org

Oxfam America (1970): 226 Causeway St., 5th Fl., Boston, MA 02114; 150,000; www.oxfamamerica.org

Paralyzed Veterans of America (1946): 801 18th St. NW, Washington, DC 20006; 19,000; www.pva.org

Parents Without Partners, Inc. (1957): 1650 South Dixie Hwy, Ste. 510, Boca Raton, FL 33432; 200 chapt.; www.parentswithoutpartners.org

Parkinson's Disease Foundation, Inc. (1957): 1359 Broadway, Ste. 1509, New York, NY 10018; 100,000; www.pdf.org

Parliamentarians, Natl. Assn. of (1930): 213 S. Main St., Independence, MO 64050; 4,000; www.parliamentarians.org

Peace Corps (1961): 1111 20th St., NW, Washington, DC 20526; 187,000; www.peacecorps.gov

PEN American Center, Inc. (1922): 588 Broadway, Ste. 303, New York, NY 10012; 3,000+; www.pen.org

Pen Women, Natl. League of American (1897): 1300 17th St. NW, Washington, DC 20036; 3,569; www.americanpenwomen.org

People for the Ethical Treatment of Animals. See Animals.

Performance Improvement, Intl. Society for (1962): 1400 Spring St., Ste. 260, Silver Spring, MD 20910; 10,000; www.ispi.org

Petroleum Institute, American (1919): 1220 L St. NW, Washington, DC 20005; 400 companies; www.api.org

Pharmacists Assn., American (1852): 1100 15th St. NW, Ste. 400, Washington, DC 20005; 60,000; www.aphanet.org, www.pharmacist.com

Phi Beta Kappa Society (1776): 1606 New Hampshire Ave. NW, Washington, DC 20009; 276 inst.; www.pbk.org

Phi Kappa Phi, Honor Society of (1897): P.O. Box 16000, LSU Baton Rouge, Baton Rouge, LA 70893; 120,000+; www.phikappaphi.org

Phi Theta Kappa Int'l. Honor Society (1918): 1625 Eastover Drive, Jackson, MS 39211; 2 mil+; www.ptk.org

Philatelic Society, American (1886): 100 Match Factory Place, Bellefonte, PA 16823; 44,000+; www.stamps.org

Philological Association, American (1869): Univ. of Penn., 292 Logan Hall, 249 S. 36th St., Philadelphia, PA, 19104-6304; 3,100; www.apaclassics.org

Philosophical Assn., American (1900): 31 Amstel Ave., Univ. of Delaware, Newark, DE 19716; 11,097; www.apa.udel.edu/apa

Physical Therapy Assn., American (1921): 1111 N. Fairfax St., Alexandria, VA 22314; 66,000; www.apta.org

Physically Handicapped, Inc., Natl. Assn. of the (1958): 754 Staeger St., Akron, OH 44306; approx. 400; www.naph.net

Physics, American Inst. of (1931): One Physics Ellipse, College Park, MD 20740; 125,000; www.aip.org

Physiological Society, American (1887): 9650 Rockville Pike, Bethesda, MD 20814-3991; 10,500; www.the-aps.org

Pilgrims Natl. Soc., Sons and Daughters of (1908): 3917 Heritage Dr., #104, Bloomington, MN 55437-2633; 1,400; www.nssdp.com

Pilot Intl. & Pilot Intl. Foundation (1921): P.O. Box 4844, Macon, GA 31208; 25,000; www.pilotinternational.org

Planetary Society (1980): 65 N. Catalina Ave., Pasadena, CA 91106; approx. 70,000; www.planetary.org

Planned Parenthood Federation of America, Inc. (1916): 434 West 33rd Street, New York, NY 10001; www.plannedparenthood.org

Plastics Engineers, Society of (1942): 14 Fairfield Dr., P.O. Box 403, Brookfield, CT 06804; 20,000+; www.4spe.org

Poetry Society of America (1910): 15 Gramercy Park, New York, NY 10003; approx. 3,000; www.poetrysociety.org

Poets, The Academy of American (1934): 584 Broadway, Ste. 604, New York, NY 10012; 8,000; www.poets.org

Police Assn., Intl. (1950 in UK, 1962 in U.S.): 100 Chase Ave., Yonkers, NY 10703; 291,000+; www.ipa-usa.org

Political Items Collectors, American (1945): P.O. Box 55, Avon, NY 14414; 3,000; apic.us

Political Science, Academy of (1880): 475 Riverside Drive, Ste. 1274, New York, NY 10115; 5,825; www.psqonline.org

Polo Assn., U.S. (1890): 4037 Ironworks Pkwy., Ste. 110, Lexington, KY 40511; 3,737; www.uspolo.org

Population Assn. of America (1931): 8630 Fenton St., Ste. 722, Silver Spring, MD 20910; 3,000; www.popassoc.org

Population Connection (1968): 2120 L St. NW, Ste. 500, Washington, DC 20037; www.populationconnection.org

Postal Stationery Society, United (1945): P.O. Box 3982, Chester, VA 23831; 1,100; www.upss.org

Postcard Dealers, Inc., International Federation of (1979): P.O. Box 1765, Manassas, VA 20108; 205; www.playle.com/IFPD

Postmasters of the U.S., Natl. Assn. of (1898): 8 Herbert St., Arlington, VA 22305; 42,000 mem., 95 clubs; www.napus.org

Power Boat Assn., American (1903): 17640 Nine Mile Rd., Eastpointe, MI 48021; 6,000; www.apba-racing.com

Press Club, National (1908): 529 14th St. NW, Washington, DC 20045; 4,000; www.press.org

Printing Industries of America, Inc. (1887): 200 Deer Run Rd., Sewickley, PA 15143; 12,000 cos.; www.gain.net

Procrastinators Club of America (1956): P.O. Box 712, Bryn Athyn, PA 19009; 14,500; www.geocities.com/procrastinators_club_of_america

Professional Ball Players of America, Assn. of (1924): 1820 W. Orangewood Ave., Ste. 206, Orange, CA 92868; 11,000; www.apbpa.org

ProLiteracy Worldwide (2002): 1320 Jamesville Ave., Syracuse, NY 13210; 1,200 affiliates; www.proliteracy.org

Psoriasis Foundation, Natl. (1968): 6600 SW 92nd Ave., Ste. 300, Portland, OR 97223; 33,000; www.psoriasis.org

Psychiatric Assn., American (1844): 1000 Wilson Blvd., Suite 1825, Arlington, VA 22209-3901; 37,000; www.psych.org

Psychological Assn., American (1892): 750 1st St. NE, Washington, DC 20002; 148,000; www.apa.org

PTA, Natl. (1897): 541 N. Fairbanks Ct., Ste. 1300, Chicago, IL 60611; 5,896,672; www.pta.org

Public Administration, American Soc. for (1939): 1301 Pennsylvania Ave. NW, Ste. 840, Washington, DC 20004; 9,000+; www.aspanet.org

Public Health Assn., American (1872): 800 I St. NW, Washington, DC 20001; 50,000+; www.apha.org

Public Relations Soc. of America (1947): 33 Maiden Ln., 11th Fl., New York, NY 10038; 21,000; www.prsa.org

Publishers, Assn. of American (1970): 71 5th Ave., 2nd Fl., New York, NY 10003; 300+; www.publishers.org

Quota International, Inc. (1919): 1420 21st St. NW, Washington, DC 20036; 7,000+; www.quota.org

Rabbis, Central Conference of American (1889): 355 Lexington Ave., New York, NY 10017; 1,800; ccarnet.org

Radio and Television Society Foundation, Intl. (1939): 420 Lexington Ave., Ste. 1601, New York, NY 10170; 1,787; www.irts.org

Radio Relay League, American (1914): 225 Main St., Newington, CT 06111; 152,000; www.arrl.org

Railway Historical Society, Natl. (1935): 100 N. 17th St., Ste. 1203, Philadelphia, PA 19103; app. 17,000+; www.nrhs.com

Range Management, Society for (1948): 10030 W. 27th Ave., Wheat Ridge, CO 80215; 4,000; www.rangelands.org/srm.shtml

Reading Assn., Intl. (1956): 800 Barksdale Rd., P.O. Box 8139, Newark, DE 19714; 350,000; www.reading.org

Real Estate Appraisers, Natl. Assn. of (1966): 1224 N. Nokomis NE, Alexandria, MN 56308; 3,000; www.iami.org/narea.html

Recreation and Park Assn., Natl. (1965): 22377 Belmont Ridge Rd., Ashburn, VA 20148; 21,000; www.nrpa.org

Recycling Coalition, Natl. (1978): 805 15th St. NW, Ste. 425, Washington, DC 20005; 4,000; www.nrc-recycle.org

Red Cross, American Natl. (1881): 2025 E St. NW, Washington, DC 20006; 1 mil volunteers; www.redcross.org

Reform Party of the U.S.A. (1995): P.O. Box 3236, Abilene, TX 79604; 500,000; www.reformparty.org

Refugee Committee, American (1979): 430 Oak Grove St., Ste. 204, Minneapolis, MN 55403; www.archq.org

Rehabilitation Assn., Natl. (1925): 633 S. Washington St., Alexandria, VA 22314; approx. 11,000; www.nationalrehab.org

Religion, American Academy of (1909): 825 Houston Mill Rd. NE, Ste. 300, Atlanta, GA 30329; 10,000; www.aarweb.org

Renaissance Society of America (1954): (CUNY) 365 5th. Ave., Rm. 5400, New York, NY 10016; 3,000; www.rsa.org

Republican National Committee (1856): 310 1st St. SE, Washington, DC 20003; www.rnc.org

Reserve Officers Assn. of the U.S. (1922): One Constitution Ave. NE, Washington, DC 20002; 75,000; www.roa.org

Retail Federation, Natl. (1908): 325 7th St. NW, Ste. 1100, Washington, DC 20004; 50,000; www.nrf.com

Retired Persons, American Assn. of (1958): 601 E St. NW, Washington, DC 20049; 35 mil+; www.aarp.org

Reye's Syndrome Foundation, Natl. (1974): 426 N. Lewis St., Bryan, OH 43506-0829; 5,000+; www.reyessyndrome.org

Rifle Assn., Natl. (1871): 11250 Waples Mill Rd., Fairfax, VA 22030; approx 3 mil; www.nra.org

Road & Transportation Builders Assn., American (1902): The ARTBA Building, 1219 28th St. NW, Washington, DC 20007; 5,000+; www.artba.org

Roller Sports, U.S.A. (1937): 4730 South St., Lincoln, NE 68506; 30,000; www.usarollersports.org

Rose Society, American (1892): P.O. Box 30000, Shreveport, LA 71130; 15,000; www.ars.org

Rotary Intl. (1905): One Rotary Center, 1560 Sherman Ave., Evanston, IL 60201; 1.2 mil; www.rotary.org

Running Assn., American (1968): 4405 East West Hwy, Ste. 405, Bethesda, MD 20814; 15,000; www.americanrunning.org

Safety Council, Natl. (1913): 1121 Spring Lake Dr., Itasca, IL 60143; 48,000 member facilities; www.nsc.org

Safety Engineers, American Soc. of (1911): 1800 E. Oakton St., Des Plaines, IL 60018; 31,000; www.asse.org

Save-the-Redwoods League (1918): 114 Sansome St., Ste. 1200, San Francisco, CA 94104; 50,000; www.savethered woods.org

School Administrators, American Assn. of (1865): 801 N. Quincy St., Ste 700, Arlington, VA 22203; 13,000+; www.aasa.org

Science, American Assn. for the Advancement of (1848): 1200 New York Ave. NW, Washington, DC 20005; approx. 10 mil.; www.aaas.org

Science Fiction Society, World (1939): P.O. Box 426159, Kendall Square Station, Cambridge, MA 02142; 10,000; www.wsfs.org

Sciences, Natl. Academy of (1863): 500 5th St. NW, Washington, DC 20001; 2,000+; www.nas.edu

Science Teachers Assn., Natl. (1944): 1840 Wilson Blvd., Arlington, VA 22201; 55,000; www.nsta.org

Science Writers, Natl. Assn. of (1955): P.O. Box 890, Hedgesville, WV 25427; 2,400; www.nasw.org

Scrabble® Assn., Natl. (1978): P.O. Box 700, 403 Front St., Greenport, NY 11944; 10,000+; www.scrabble-assoc.com

Screen Actors Guild (1933): 5757 Wilshire Blvd., Los Angeles, CA 90036; 120,000; www.sag.com

Secular Humanism, Council for (1980): P.O. Box 664, Amherst, NY 14226; 24,000; www.secularhumanism.org

Separation of Church & State, Americans United for (1947): 518 C St. NE, Washington, DC 20002; 75,000+; www.au.org

Sharkhunters Intl. (1983): P.O. Box 1539-WS, Hernando, FL 34442; 6,900; www.sharkhunters.com

Shipbuilders Council of America (1920): 1455 F St., NW, Ste. 225, Washington, DC 20005; 36 member cos.; www.ship builders.org

Ships in Bottles Assn. of America (1982): P.O. Box 180550, Coronado, CA 92178; 250; www.shipsinbottles.org

Shriners of North America, The (1872): 2900 Rocky Point Dr., Tampa, FL 33607; approx 411,000+; www.shrinershq.org

Sierra Club (1892): 85 2nd St., 2nd Fl., San Francisco, CA 94105; 750,000+; www.sierraclub.org

Sigma Beta Delta (1994): P.O. Box 210570, St. Louis, MO 63121-0570; 20,000; www.sigmabetadelta.org

Skeet Shooting Assn., Natl. (1934): 5931 Roft Rd., San Antonio, TX 78253; 20,000; www.mynssa.com

Small Business Assn., Natl. (1937): 1156 15th St. NW, Ste. 1100, Washington, DC 20005; 150,000+; www.nsba.biz

Sociological Assn., American (1905): 1307 New York Avenue NW, Suite 700, Washington, DC 20005; 14,000; www.asanet.org

Softball Assn., Amateur (1933): 2801 NE 50th St., Oklahoma City, OK 73111; 250,000+ teams; www.softball.org

Software and Information Industry Assn. (1999): 1090 Vermont Ave. NW, 6th Fl., Wash. DC 20005; 750 cos.; www.siia.net

Songwriters Guild of America (1931): 209 10th Ave. S., Ste. 321, Nashville, TN 37203; 5,000+; www.songwritersguild.com

Sons of the American Legion (1932): P.O. Box 1055, Indianapolis, IN 46206; 300,000; www.sal.legion.org

Sons of the American Revolution, Natl. Society of (1889): 1000 S. 4th St., Louisville, KY 40203; 26,000; www.sar.org

Sons of Confederate Veterans (1896): P.O. Box 59, Columbia, TN 38402; 35,000; www.scv.org

Sons of Italy in America, Order (1905): 219 E St. NE, Washington, DC 20002; 600,000; www.osia.org

Sons of Norway (1895): 1455 W. Lake St., Minneapolis, MN 55408; 69,298; www.sofn.com

Southern Christian Leadership Conference (1957): P.O. Box 89128, Atlanta, GA 30312; 1 mil; sclcnational.org

Space Society, Natl. (1974): 1620 Eye St. NW, Ste. 615, Washington, DC 20006; 20,000+; www.nss.org

Speech-Language-Hearing Assn., American (1925): 10801 Rockville Pike, Rockville, MD 20852; 127,000; www.asha.org

Speedskating, U.S. (1966): P.O. Box 18370, Kearns, UT 84118; 1,800; www.usspeedskating.org

Speleological Society, Natl. (1941): 2813 Cave Ave., Huntsville, AL 35810; 12,000; www.caves.org

Sports Car Club of America (1944): P.O. Box 19400, Topeka, KS 66619; 60,000; www.scca.org

Sportscasters Assn., The American (1980): 225 Broadway, Ste. 2030, New York, NY 10007; 500+; www.american sportscastersonline.com

State & Local History, American Assn. for (1940): 1717 Church St., Nashville, TN 37203; 6,100; www.aaslh.org

State Governments, Council of (1933): 2760 Research Park Drive, P.O. Box 11910, Lexington, KY 40578; 50 states, 4 territories; www.csg.org

Steamship Historical Society of America, Inc. (1935): 1029 Waterman Ave., E. Providence, RI 02916; 3,400; www.sshsa.org

Student Councils, Natl. Assn. of (1931): 1904 Association Dr., Reston, VA 20191; 17,000 councils; www.nasc.us

Stuttering Assn., Natl. (1977): 119 W. 40th St., 14th Fl, New York, NY 10018; 2,800; www.nsastutter.org

Supreme Court Historical Society (1974): Opperman House, 224 East Capitol St. NE, Washington, DC 20003; 5,700; www.supremecourthistory.org

Surgeons, American College of (1913): 633 N. Saint Clair St., Chicago, IL 60611; 70,000; www.facs.org

Symphony Orchestra League, American (1942): 33 W. 60th St., 5th Fl., New York, NY 10023; 1,000; www.symphony.org

Table Tennis Assn., U.S. (1933): One Olympic Plaza, Colorado Springs, CO 80909; 8,000+; www.usatt.org

Tall Buildings and Urban Habitat, Council on (1969): Illinois Inst. of Tech., S.R. Crown Hall, 3360 S. State St., Chicago, IL 60616; 1,400; www.ctbuh.org

Tau Beta Pi Association (1885): P.O. Box 2697, Knoxville, TN 37901; 493,019; www.tbp.org

Tax Administrators, Federation of (1937): 444 N. Capitol St. NW, Ste. 348, Washington, DC 20001; www.taxadmin.org

Tax Foundation (1937): 2001 L St. NW, Ste. 1050, Washington, DC 20036; 50 U.S. states; www.taxfoundation.org

Taxpayers Union, Natl. (1969): 108 N. Alfred St., Alexandria, VA 22314; 335,000; www.ntu.org

Teachers of English, Natl. Council of (1911): 1111 W. Kenyon Rd., Urbana, IL 61801; 60,000; www.ncte.org

Teachers of English to Speakers of Other Languages (1966): 700 S. Washington St., Ste. 200, Alexandria, VA 22314; 13,500+; www.tesol.org

Teachers of French, American Assn. of (1927): Southern Illinois University, Mailcode 4510, Carbondale, IL 62901; 9,500; www.frenchteachers.org

Teachers of German, American Assn. of (1926): 112 Haddontowne Ct. #104, Cherry Hill, NJ 08034; 5,500; www.aatg.org

Teachers of Mathematics, Natl. Council of (1920): 1906 Association Dr., Reston, VA 20191; 100,000; www.nctm.org

Teachers of Spanish & Portuguese, American Assn. of (1917): 900 Ladd Rd., Walled Lake, MI 48390; 12,500; www.aatsp.org

TelecomPioneers (1911): P.O. Box 13888, Denver, CO 80201; 620,000; www.telecompioneers.com

Television Academy, Natl. (1955): 111 W. 57th St., Ste. 600, New York, NY 10019; www.emmyonline.org

Term Limits, U.S. (1992): 9900 Main St., Ste. 303, Fairfax, VA 22031; www.termlimits.org

Theodore Roosevelt Assn. (1920): P.O. Box 719, Oyster Bay, NY 11771; 2,500; www.theodoreroosevelt.org

Theological Library Assn., American (1946): 300 S. Wacker Dr., Ste. 2100, Chicago, IL 60606; 1,000+; www.atla.com

Theological Schools in the U.S. and Canada, Assn. of (1918): 10 Summit Park Dr., Pittsburgh, PA 15275; 251; www.ats.edu

Theosophical Society in America (1875): P.O. Box 270, Wheaton, IL 60189; 5,000; www.theosophical.org

Therapy Dogs Intl., Inc. (1976): 88 Bartley Rd., Flanders, NJ 07836; 13,000; www.tdi-dog.org

Thoreau Society (1941): 55 Old Bedford Rd., Concord, MA 01742; 1,700+; www.thoreausociety.org

Thoroughbred Racing Assns. (1942): 420 Fair Hill Dr., Ste. 1, Elkton, MD 21921; 49 racing assoc.; www.tra-online.com

Tin Can Sailors (1976): P.O. Box 100, Somerset, MA 02726; 23,000; www.destroyers.org

Titanic Historical Society & Museum (1963): 208 Main St., Indian Orchard, MA 01151-0053; 4,328; www.titanichistorical society.org

Toastmasters Intl. (1924): P.O. Box 9052, Mission Viejo, CA 92690; 211,000++; www.toastmasters.org

Topical Assn., American (1949): P.O. Box 57, Arlington, TX, 76004-0057; 3,300; americantopicalassn.org

Toy Industry Assn., Inc. (1916): 1115 Broadway, Suite 400, New York, NY 10010; 500+ cos.; www.toy-tma.org

Transportation Alternatives (1973): 127 W. 26th St., Ste. 1002, New York, NY 10001; 5,000; www.transalt.org

Transportation Engineers, Inst. of (1930): 1099 14th St. NW, Suite 300-W, Washington, DC 20005; 17,000; www.ite.org

Trapshooting Assn. of America, Amateur (1900): 601 W. National Road, Vandalia, OH 45377; 54,208; www.shoot ata.com

Travel Agents, American Soc. of (1931): 1101 King St., Ste. 200, Alexandria, VA 22314; 20,000+; www.astanet.com

Travelers Protective Assn. of America (1890): 3755 Lindell Blvd., St. Louis, MO 63108; 91,008; www.tpahq.org

Truck Historical Soc., American (1971): P.O. Box 901611, Kansas City, MO 64190; 23,000+; www.aths.org

Tuberous Sclerosis Alliance (1974): 801 Roeder Rd., Ste. 750, Silver Spring, MD 20910; approx. 2,000; www.tsalliance.org

UFOs, Natl. Investigations Committee on (1967): 21601 Devonshire St., #217, Chatsworth, CA 91311; 250; www.nicufo.org

Underwriters (CPCU): Soc. of Chartered Property and Casualty (1944): 720 Providence Rd., Malvern, PA 19355; 28,000; www.cpcusociety.org

UNICEF, U.S. Fund for (1947): 333 E. 38th St., New York, NY 10016; www.unicefusa.org

United. See also other entries under next major word in title.

Uniformed Services, Natl. Assn. for (1968): 5535 Hempstead Way, Springfield, VA 22151; 200,000; www.naus.org

United Nations Assn. of the U.S.A. (1943): 801 2nd Ave., 2nd Fl., New York, NY 10017; 20,000; www.unausa.org

United Press Intl. (1907): 1510 H St. NW, Washington, DC 20005; www.upi.com

United Way of America (1918): 701 N. Fairfax St., Alexandria, VA 22314; approx. 1,350 org.; national.unitedway.org

Universities, Assn. of American (1900): 1200 New York Ave. NW, Ste. 550, Washington, DC 20005; 62 coll/univ.; www.aau.edu

University Women, American Assn. of (1881): 1111 16th St. NW, Washington, DC 20036; 100,000+; www.aauw.org

Urban League, Natl. (1910): 120 Wall St., New York, NY 10005; 105 local affiliates; www.nul.org

USO World Headquarters (1941): 2111 Wilson Blvd., Ste. 1200, Arlington, VA 22201; www.uso.org

USS Forrestal CVA/CV/AVT-59 Assn., Inc. (1990): P.O. Box 225, Ft. Loramie, OH 45845; 2,700; www.lancehatfield.com/cv59.htm

USS Missouri Memorial Assn., Inc. (1994): P.O. Box 879, Aiea, HI 96701; 1,500; www.ussmissouri.org

Ventriloquists' Assn., International (1944): P.O. Box 17153, Las Vegas, NV 89114; 1,450; www.ventriloquists.net

Veterans of Foreign Wars of the U.S. (1899): 406 W. 34th St., Kansas City, MO 64111; 1.7 mil+.; www.vfw.org

Veterans of Foreign Wars of the U.S., Ladies Auxiliary to the (1914): 406 W. 34th St.,10th Fl., Kansas City, MO 64111; 616,439; www.ladiesauxvfw.org

Veterans of the Vietnam War, Inc. (1978): 805 S. Township Blvd., Pittston, PA 18640-3327; 15,000; www.vvnw.org

Veterinary Medical Assn., American (1863): 1931 N. Meacham Rd., Schaumburg, IL 60173; 75,000; www.avma.org

Victorian Society in America (1966): 205 S. Camac St., Philadelphia, PA 19107; 3,000; www.victoriansociety.org

Volleyball, USA (1928): 715 S. Circle Dr., Colorado Springs, CO 80910; 191,000; www.usavolleyball.org

Volunteers of America (1896): 1660 Duke St., Alexandria, VA 22314; 15,000 staff, 95,000 volunteers; www.voa.org

War Mothers, American (1917): 5415 Connecticut Ave. NW, Ste. L-30, Washington, DC 20015; 500; www.american warmoms.org

Watch & Clock Collectors, Inc., Natl. Assn. of (NAWCC) (1943): 514 Poplar St., Columbia, PA 17512; 23,000; www.nawcc.org

Water Environment Federation (1928): 601 Wythe St., Alexandria, VA 22314; 32,000 indiv. members; 80 assns.; www.wef.org

Water Works Assn., American (1881): 6666 W. Quincy Ave., Denver, CO 80235; 60,000; www.awwa.org

Wheelchair Sports, USA (1956): P.O. Box 5266, Kendall Park, NJ 08824; 4,000; www.wsusa.org

Wildlife Federation, Natl. (1936): 11100 Wildlife Center Dr., Reston, VA, 20190; 4 mil; www.nwf.org

Wizard of Oz Club, Intl. (1957): P.O. Box 2657, Alameda, CA 94501; 1,300+; www.ozclub.org

Women, Natl. Organization for (NOW) (1966): 1100 H St. NW, 3rd Fl., Washington, DC 20005; 500,000; www.now.org

Women and Families, Natl. Partnership for (1971): 1875 Connecticut Ave. NW, Ste. 650, Washington, DC 20009; 2,000; www.nationalpartnership.org

Women in Communications, The Association for (1909 as Theta Sigma Phi): 3337 Duke St., Alexandria, VA 22314; 4,000+; www.womcom.org

Women Engineers, Society of (1950): 230 E. Ohio St., Ste. 400, Chicago, IL 60611; 17,000; www.swe.org

Women in Radio and Television Inc., Amer. (1951): 8405 Greensboro Dr., Ste. 800, McLean, VA 22102; www.awrt.org

Women's Army Corps Veterans Assn. (1946): P.O. Box 5577, Ft. McClellan, AL 36205; 4,500; www.armywomen.org

Women's Christian Temperance Union, Natl. (1874): 1730 Chicago Ave., Evanston, IL 60201; www.wctu.org

Women's Clubs, General Federation of (1890): 1734 N St. NW, Washington, DC, 20036; 180,000 U.S.; www.gfwc.org

Women Voters of the U.S., League of (1920): 1730 M St. NW, Ste. 1000, Washington, DC 20036; 130,000; www.lwv.org

Woodmen of America, Modern (1883): 1701 1st Ave., Rock Island, IL 61201; 750,000; www.modern-woodmen.org

Workmen's Circle (1900): 45 E. 33rd St., New York, NY 10016; 35,000; www.circle.org

World Council of Churches, U.S. Office (1948): 475 Riverside Drive, Rm. 1371, New York, NY 10115; 330+ denominations; www.wcc-usa.org

World Federalist Assn. (1947): 418 7th St. SE, Washington, DC 20003; 11,000; www.wfa.org

World Future Society (1966): 7910 Woodmont Ave., Ste. 450, Bethesda, MD 20814; 25,000; www.wfs.org

World Learning (1954): Kipling Rd., P.O. Box 676, Brattleboro, VT 05302-0676; 100,000; www.worldlearning.org

World Wildlife Fund (1961): 1250 24th St. NW, Washington, DC 20037; 1.2 mil+; www.worldwildlife.org

Writers Guild of America, West (1933): 7000 W. Third St., Los Angeles, CA 90048; 10,500; www.wga.org

YMCA (Young Men's Christian Assn.) of the U.S.A. (1851): 101 N. Wacker Dr., Chicago, IL 60606; 20.2 mil; www.ymca.net

YWCA (Young Women's Christian Assn.) of the U.S.A. (1858): 1015 18th St. NW, Ste. 1100, Washington, DC 20036; 2.6 mil; www.ywca.org

Zionist Organization of America (1897): 4 E. 34th St., New York, NY 10016; 30,000; www.zoa.org

Zoo and Aquarium Assn., American (1924): 8403 Colesville Road, Suite 710, Silver Spring, MD 20910; 212 institutions, 5,500 individuals; www.aza.org

EDUCATION

U.S. Public Schools: Students, Staff, Spending, 1899-2005
Source: National Center for Education Statistics, U.S. Dept. of Education

	1899-1900	1919-20	1939-40	1959-60	1969-70	1979-80	1989-90	1999-2000	2004-05
Population statistics (thousands)									
Total U.S. population[1]	75,995	104,514	131,028	177,830	203,302	226,546	248,765	282,193	296,410
Population 5-17 years of age. . . .	21,573	27,571	30,151	43,881	52,540	47,407	45,178	53,173	53,166
Percentage 5-17 years of age . . .	28.4%	26.4%	23.0%	24.7%	25.8%	20.9%	18.2%	18.8%	17.9%
Enrollment (thousands)									
Elementary and secondary[2]	15,503	21,578	25,434	35,182	45,550	41,651	40,543	46,857	48,795
Pre-kindergarten to grade 1-8 . . .	14,984	19,378	18,833	27,602	32,513	28,034	29,152	33,488	34,178
Grades 9-12.	519	2,200	6,601	8,485	13,037	13,616	11,390	13,369	14,614
Percentage pop. 5-17 enrolled.	71.9%	78.3%	84.4%	82.2%	87.0%	86.7%	90.2%	88.7%	91.6%
Percentage in high schools	3.3%	10.2%	26.0%	23.5%	28.6%	32.7%	28.1%	28.5%	30.0%
High school graduates (thousands) .	62	231	1,143	1,627	2,589	2,748	2,320	2,554	2,801
Instructional staff									
Total instructional staff (thousands) .	*	678	912	1,457	2,286	2,406	2,986	3,820	4,119
Teachers, librarians, and other non-supervisory instructional staff (thousands)	423	657	875	1,393	2,195	2,300	2,860	3,683	3,954
Revenue and expenditures (millions)									
Total revenue	$220	$970	$2,261	$14,747	$40,267	$96,881	$208,548	$372,944	$487,761
Total expenditures[3,5]	215	1,036	2,344	15,613	40,683	95,962	212,770	381,838	499,069
Current expenditures[3,5]	180	861	1,942	12,329	34,218	86,984	188,229	323,889	424,562
Capital outlay.	35	154	258	2,662	4,659	6,506	17,781	43,357	53,541
Interest on school debt	*	18	131	490	1,171	1,874	3,776	9,135	13,301
Others	*	3	13	133	636	598	2,983	5,457	7,665
Salaries and pupil cost									
Avg. annual salary of instruct. staff[4].	$325	$871	$1,441	$3,010	$8,626	$15,970	$31,367	$41,807	$47,950
Expenditure per capita total pop. . . .	2.83	9.91	17.89	88	202	427	862	1,368	1,646
Current expenditure[5] per pupil ADA[6]	16.67	53.32	88.09	375	816	2,272	4,980	7,394	9,995

NOTE: Because of rounding, details may not add to totals. Prior to 1959-60, data do not include Alaska and Hawaii. * = Data not collected. (1) Population data for 1899-1900 are based on total population from the decennial census. From 1919-20 to 1959-60, population data are total population, including armed forces overseas, as of July 1 preceding the school year. Data for later years are for resident population that excludes armed forces overseas. (2) Data for 1899 through 1960 are school year enrollment; data for later years are fall enrollment. (3) In 1899-1900, includes interest on school debt. (4) Data prior to 1959-60 include supervisors, principals, teachers, and nonsupervisory instructional staff. (5) Because of changes in the definition of "current expenditures," data for 1959-60 and later years are not entirely comparable with prior years. (6) ADA means average daily attendance.

U.S. Public High School Graduation Rates, 2003-2004
Source: National Center for Education Statistics, U.S. Dept. of Education

	Rate (%)[1]	Rank		Rate (%)[1]	Rank		Rate (%)[1]	Rank		Rate (%)[1]	Rank
Alabama	65.0	46	Illinois	80.3	16	Montana	80.4	14	Rhode Island	75.9	29
Alaska	67.2	41	Indiana	73.5	33	Nebraska	87.6	1	South Carolina	60.6	50
Arizona	66.8	43	Iowa	85.8	5	Nevada	57.4	51	South Dakota	83.7	8
Arkansas	76.8	26	Kansas	77.9	22	New Hampshire	78.7	20	Tennessee	66.1	45
California	73.9	32	Kentucky	73.0	34	New Jersey	86.3	2	Texas	76.7	27
Colorado	78.7	21	Louisiana	69.4	39	New Mexico	67.0	42	Utah	83.0	9
Connecticut	80.7	13	Maine	77.6	23	New York	60.9	49	Vermont	85.4	6
Delaware	72.9	35	Maryland	79.5	17	North Carolina	71.4	38	Virginia	79.3	18
District of Columbia	68.2	40	Massachusetts	79.3	19	North Dakota	86.1	3	Washington	74.6	30
Florida	66.4	44	Michigan	72.5	37	Ohio	81.3	12	West Virginia	76.9	25
Georgia	61.2	48	Minnesota	84.7	7	Oklahoma	77.0	24	Wisconsin	85.8	4
Hawaii	72.6	36	Mississippi	62.7	47	Oregon	74.2	31	Wyoming	76.0	28
Idaho	81.5	11	Missouri	80.4	15	Pennsylvania	82.2	10	**TOTAL U.S.**	74.3	

NOTE: The averaged freshman graduation rate provides an estimate of the percentage of high school students who graduate. The rate uses aggregate student enrollment data to estimate the size of an incoming freshman class and aggregate counts of the number of diplomas awarded 4 years later. (1) Includes estimates for New York and Wisconsin. Without estimates for these two states, the averaged freshman graduation rate for the remaining 48 states and the District of Columbia is 75.0 percent.

Technology in U.S. Public Schools*
Source: Quality Education Data, Inc., Denver, CO

Number and percentage of schools in each category that have the technology indicated.

	Total		Elementary[1]		Middle/ Jr. High[2]		Senior High[3]		K-12[4]		Special Ed./ Adult Ed.	
TOTAL SCHOOLS	93,189	100%	56,232	100%	14,475	100%	20,161	100%	2,530	100%	2,310	100%
Schools with computers . .	83,057	89	51,418	91	12,911	89	17,100	85	2,026	80	1,625	70
By number of computers:												
1-10	3,170	3	1,990	4	194	1	597	3	59	2	389	17
11-20 . . . .: . . .	4,590	5	3,123	6	345	2	829	4	129	5	293	13
21-50	16,741	18	11,934	21	1,728	12	2,628	13	493	19	449	19
51-100	23,753	25	16,940	30	3,372	23	3,178	16	607	24	262	11
100+	34,803	37	17,431	31	7,272	50	9,868	49	738	29	232	10
Schools with LANs[5] . . .	61,104	66	36,791	66	10,652	74	14,030	72	1,614	65	707	30
By enrollment:												
100-299	13,607	15	8,610	15	1,212	8	3,309	17	774	31	476	20
300-499	18,256	20	13,802	25	2,098	15	2,294	12	403	16	62	3
500+	29,241	32	14,379	26	7,342	51	8,427	43	437	18	169	7
Schools with WANs[6] . .	45,933	50	27,549	49	8,011	56	9,932	51	996	40	441	19
By enrollment:												
100-299	8,816	10	5,701	10	769	5	2,032	10	434	18	314	13
300-499	14,574	16	11,100	20	1,735	12	1,707	9	289	12	32	1
500+	22,543	24	10,748	19	5,507	38	6,193	32	273	11	95	4

*Data for schools with computers as of 2005. All other data from 2004. (1) Includes preschool and schools with grade spans of Preschool-3, K-6, K-8, and K-12. (2) Includes schools with grade spans of 4-8, 7-8, and 7-9. (3) Includes vocational, technical, and alternative high schools and schools with grade spans of 7-12, 9-12, and 10-12. (4) K-12 also included under Elementary schools. (5) LAN=Local area computer network. (6) WAN=Wide area computer network.

Overview of U.S. Public Schools, Fall 2005*

Source: National Center for Education Statistics, U.S. Dept. of Education; National Education Association

	Local school districts	Elementary schools[1]	Secondary schools[2]	Classroom teachers	Total enrollment	Pupils per teacher	Teacher's avg. pay	Expend. per pupil
Alabama	132	944	413	49,692	738,450	14.9	$40,347	$7,585
Alaska	53	188	84	8,004	133,437	16.7	53,553	11,726
Arizona	628	1,279	563	46,358	1,010,094	21.8	44,672	5,791
Arkansas	254	728	422	33,477	453,209	13.5	42,093	7,197
California	1,053	6,645	2,360	321,237	6,423,824	20.0	59,345	8,607
Colorado	178	1,208	409	47,128	780,738	16.6	45,616	8,925
Connecticut	192	820	244	44,127	576,780	13.1	59,499	12,936
Delaware	32	139	47	7,731	120,938	15.6	54,264	12,363
Dist. of Columbia	41	144	43	4,955	61,484	12.4	61,195	17,545
Florida	67	2,420	475	162,849	2,669,565	16.4	43,302	8,105
Georgia	184	1,665	365	107,807	1,598,461	14.8	48,300	9,836
Hawaii	1	207	55	11,409	182,767	16.0	51,599	9,805
Idaho	114	415	223	14,292	251,270	17.6	43,390	7,408
Illinois	874	3,157	1,001	132,142	2,033,248	15.4	57,819	10,959
Indiana	333	1,449	464	60,485	1,034,399	17.1	47,255	9,757
Iowa	365	1,034	455	35,175	483,482	13.7	40,877	8,325
Kansas	300	975	422	32,363	467,201	14.4	41,369	9,126
Kentucky	176	1,002	319	39,475	638,450	16.2	41,903	9,012
Louisiana	89	1,027	308	44,153	654,146	14.8	40,253	8,633
Maine	288	509	155	15,962	199,118	12.5	40,737	12,223
Maryland	24	1,083	265	57,846	873,342	15.1	54,486	10,174
Massachusetts	498	1,473	348	68,069	971,909	14.3	56,587	13,091
Michigan	752	2,727	848	97,921	1,741,737	17.8	58,482	10,646
Minnesota	473	1,263	850	51,372	835,588	16.3	48,489	10,361
Mississippi	152	600	326	30,665	482,475	15.7	37,924	7,240
Missouri	524	1,551	654	65,891	897,982	13.6	39,922	8,357
Montana	439	491	363	10,329	145,416	14.1	39,832	9,620
Nebraska	460	857	334	20,929	285,549	13.6	41,026	8,781
Nevada	17	412	136	21,714	413,252	19.0	44,426	7,551
New Hampshire	179	379	98	15,489	205,567	13.3	45,263	11,110
New Jersey	615	1,892	464	110,905	1,394,779	12.6	57,707	13,626
New Mexico	89	587	224	21,983	326,859	14.9	41,637	9,588
New York	699	3,223	1,034	228,903	2,815,504	12.3	57,354	13,216
North Carolina	115	1,786	412	94,129	1,382,651	14.7	43,922	7,976
North Dakota	204	319	198	7,607	97,120	12.8	37,773	8,401
Ohio	891	2,727	1,019	119,587	1,862,880	15.6	50,314	11,316
Oklahoma	540	1,201	581	41,616	634,468	15.2	38,722	7,236
Oregon	199	854	300	28,382	553,314	19.5	48,981	9,191
Pennsylvania	501	2,369	812	123,264	1,813,250	14.7	54,027	10,714
Rhode Island	36	265	72	14,512	161,237	11.1	54,730	11,693
South Carolina	87	847	277	46,406	685,919	14.8	43,242	9,073
South Dakota	168	434	263	8,963	120,682	13.5	34,709	8,334
Tennessee	136	1,257	361	59,596	934,968	15.7	42,537	7,625
Texas	1,228	5,312	2,095	302,402	4,505,572	14.9	41,744	7,913
Utah	40	552	327	21,070	484,623	23.0	40,316	5,815
Vermont	353	276	70	9,009	94,600	10.5	46,662	14,659
Virginia	136	1,485	403	91,783	1,214,737	13.2	43,823	10,011
Washington	296	1,424	586	53,570	1,033,489	19.3	46,326	8,787
West Virginia	55	583	185	19,791	279,788	14.1	38,284	10,005
Wisconsin	426	1,551	604	59,552	875,174	14.7	46,390	11,063
Wyoming	48	249	109	6,841	83,705	12.6	43,255	12,888
TOTAL U.S.	**15,734**	**65,984**	**23,445**	**3,128,716**	**48,719,196**	**15.6**	**49,109**	**9,576**

*Full-time elementary and secondary day schools only. (1) Includes schools with grade 6 and below and those with no grade higher than 8. (2) Includes schools with no grade lower than 7.

Programs for the Disabled, 1993-2004

Source: Office of Special Education Programs, U.S. Dept. of Education

Number of children from 6 to 21 years old served annually in educational programs for the disabled; in thousands.

Type of Disability	1993	1994	1995	1996	1997	1998	1999	2000	2001	2002	2003	2004[1]
Learning disabilities	2,366	2,428	2,510	2,602	2,674	2,754	2,817	2,834	2,848	2,846	2,834	2,790
Speech impairments	998	1,018	1,020	1,027	1,049	1,064	1,075	1,081	1,085	1,084	1,102	1,138
Mental retardation	532	554	571	586	594	603	611	600	599	592	580	556
Emotional disturbance	402	415	428	439	446	454	463	469	472	476	480	483
Multiple disabilities	103	110	90	95	99	107	108	111	121	127	130	132
Hearing impairments	61	65	65	68	69	70	71	71	70	70	71	72
Orthopedic impairments	53	57	60	63	66	67	69	71	73	73	74	65
Other health impairments	66	83	107	134	161	191	221	253	290	337	390	508
Visual impairments	24	25	25	25	26	26	26	65	25	25	25	26
Autism	16	19	23	29	34	43	54	65	78	97	118	166
Deaf-blindness	1	1	1	1	1	1	2	2	1	2	2	2
Traumatic brain injury	4	5	7	10	10	12	13	14	15	21	21	23
Developmental delay[2]	—	—	—	—	—	—	—	—	—	45	59	74
ALL DISABILITIES	**4,626**	**4,779**	**4,908**	**5,079**	**5,231**	**5,397**	**5,541**	**5,614**	**5,705**	**5,795**	**5,885**	**6,033**

NOTE: Counts based on reports from states and District of Columbia. Details may not add to totals because of rounding and/or incomplete enumeration. — = not available or not reliable data. (1) Data for 2004 includes Bureau of Indian Affairs programs. (2) Applicable only to ages 3-9.

Trends in International Mathematics and Science Study (TIMSS), 2003

Source: National Center for Education Statistics

The TIMSS is an international assessment test that was administered to 4th and 8th graders in 1995, and again in 2003, to measure the degree to which students have learned concepts of mathematics and science that they studied in school. Listed below are the average scaled scores for each country. Only countries with data for 2003 are listed.

	Mathematics		Science	
	2003	Change 1995-2003	2003	Change 1995-2003
4th Grade				
International Avg..	495	NA	489	NA
Australia	499	4	521	-1
Cyprus	510	35	480	30
England	531	47	540	13
Hong Kong	575	18	542	35
Hungary	529	7	530	22
Iran	389	2	414	34
Japan	565	-3	543	-10
Latvia	533	34	530	43
Netherlands	540	-9	525	-5
New Zealand	496	26	523	18
Norway	451	-25	466	-38
Scotland	490	-3	502	-12
Singapore	594	4	565	42
Slovenia	479	17	490	26
United States	518	0	536	-6
8th Grade				
International Avg..	466	NA	473	NA
Australia	505	-4	527	13
Belgium-Flemish	537	-13	516	-17
Bulgaria	476	-51	479	-66
Chile	387	NA	413	NA
Chinese Taipei	585	NA	571	NA
Cyprus	459	-8	441	-11
Hong Kong	586	17	556	46
Hungary	529	3	543	6
Indonesia	411	NA	420	NA
Iran	411	-7	453	-9
Israel*	496	NA	488	NA
Italy*	484	NA	491	NA
Japan	570	-11	552	-2
Jordan	424	NA	475	NA
Korea, Republic of	589	8	558	13
Latvia	505	17	513	37
Lithuania	502	30	519	56
Macedonia	435	NA	449	NA
Malaysia	508	NA	510	NA
Moldova	460	NA	472	NA
Netherlands	536	7	536	-6
New Zealand	494	-7	520	9
Norway	461	-37	494	-21
Philippines	378	NA	377	NA
Romania	475	2	470	-1
Russian Federation	508	-16	514	-9
Scotland	498	4	512	10
Singapore	605	-3	578	-3
Slovak Republic	508	-26	517	-15
Slovenia	493	-2	520	7
South Africa	264	NA	244	NA
Sweden	499	-41	524	-28
Tunisia	410	NA	404	NA
United States	504	12	527	15

* Because of changes in the population tested, 1995 data for Israel and Italy are not shown.

Mathematics, Reading, and Science Achievement of U.S. Students

Source: National Assessment of Educational Progress, National Center for Education Statistics, U.S. Dept. of Education

Percent of public school students who scored at or above basic level in national tests.*

	GRADE 4				GRADE 8					
	Math		Reading		Math		Reading		Science	
State	2000	2007	1998	2007	2000	2007	1998	2007	2000	2005
AL	55	70	56	62	52	55	67	62	53	48
AK	NA	79	NA	62	NA	73	NA	71	NA	NA
AZ	57	74	51	56	62	66	72	65	55	49
AR	55	81	54	64	52	65	68	70	53	56
CA	50	70	48	53	52	59	63	62	38	44
CO	NA	82	69	70	NA	75	77	79	NA	66
CT	76	84	76	73	72	73	81	77	64	63
DE	NA	87	53	78	NA	74	64	77	NA	63
DC	24	49	27	39	23	34	44	48	NA	NA
FL	NA	86	53	70	NA	68	67	71	NA	51
GA	57	79	54	66	55	64	68	70	52	53
HI	55	77	45	59	52	59	59	62	40	44
ID	68	85	NA	70	71	75	NA	78	71	71
IL	63	79	NA	65	68	70	NA	75	59	58
IN	77	89	NA	68	76	76	NA	76	66	62
IA	75	87	67	74	NA	77	NA	80	NA	NA
KS	76	89	70	72	77	81	81	81	NA	NA
KY	59	79	62	68	63	69	74	73	60	63
LA	57	73	44	52	48	64	63	64	44	47
ME	73	85	72	73	76	78	83	83	72	72
MD	60	80	58	69	65	74	70	76	57	54
MA	77	93	70	81	76	85	79	84	70	72
MI	71	80	62	66	70	66	NA	72	68	66
MN	76	87	69	73	80	81	78	80	72	71
MS	45	70	47	51	41	54	62	60	41	40
MO	71	82	61	67	67	72	75	75	66	66
MT	72	88	72	75	80	79	83	85	79	76
NE	65	80	NA	71	74	74	NA	79	52	48
NV	60	74	51	57	58	60	70	63	NA	56
NH	NA	91	75	76	NA	78	NA	82	NA	76
NJ	NA	90	NA	77	NA	77	NA	81	NA	65
NM	50	70	51	58	50	57	71	62	48	46
NY	66	85	62	69	68	70	76	75	NA	NA
NC	73	85	58	64	70	73	74	71	54	53
ND	73	91	NA	75	77	86	NA	84	72	77
OH	73	87	NA	73	75	76	NA	79	72	67
OK	67	82	66	65	64	66	80	72	60	57
OR	65	79	58	62	71	73	78	77	68	66
PA	NA	85	NA	73	NA	77	NA	79	NA	66
RI	65	80	64	65	64	65	76	69	58	58
SC	59	80	53	59	55	71	66	69	48	54
SD	NA	86	NA	71	NA	81	NA	83	NA	76
TN	59	76	57	61	53	64	71	71	55	55
TX	76	87	59	66	68	78	74	73	52	53
UT	69	83	62	69	68	72	77	75	67	65
VT	73	89	NA	74	75	81	NA	84	71	76
VA	71	87	62	74	67	77	78	79	61	66
WA	71	84	64	70	74	75	76	77	NA	66
WV	65	81	60	63	62	61	75	68	57	57
WI	NA	85	72	70	NA	76	78	76	NA	70
WY	71	88	64	73	70	80	76	80	69	74
U.S.	64	81	58	66	65	70	71	73	57	57

NA = Not administered. * "Basic level" denotes a partial mastery of prerequisite knowledge and skills fundamental for proficient work at each grade.

Revenues[1] for Public Elementary and Secondary Schools, by State, 2005-2006

Source: National Education Association; in thousands

STATE	Total	Federal		State		Local and intermediate	
		Amount	%	Amount	%	Amount	%
Alabama*	6,027,248	720,672	12.0	3,322,430	55.1	1,984,146	32.9
Alaska*	1,325,067	165,975	12.5	841,855	63.5	317,237	23.9
Arizona*	7,979,468	630,777	7.9	4,113,926	51.6	3,234,765	40.5
Arkansas*	3,915,342	461,943	11.8	1,968,685	50.3	1,484,714	37.9
California	64,054,472	7,256,296	11.3	39,302,232	61.4	17,495,944	27.3
Colorado	6,762,506	470,781	7.0	2,929,771	43.3	3,361,954	49.7
Connecticut*	8,014,885	493,769	6.2	3,126,618	39.0	4,394,498	54.8
Delaware*	1,490,287	154,728	10.4	932,373	62.6	403,186	27.1
District of Columbia*	900,846	126,846	14.1	0	0.0	774,000	85.9
Florida	24,967,922	2,596,757	10.4	10,231,993	41.0	12,139,172	48.6
Georgia*	15,337,449	1,550,725	10.1	6,584,302	42.9	7,202,422	47.0
Hawaii	2,184,981	241,221	11.0	1,891,808	86.6	51,952	2.4
Idaho*	1,721,085	170,968	9.9	1,029,758	59.8	520,359	30.2
Illinois	20,735,556	1,746,088	8.4	5,827,242	28.1	13,162,226	63.5
Indiana*	10,487,474	740,641	7.1	5,279,099	50.3	4,467,734	42.6
Iowa	4,632,469	316,311	6.8	2,140,500	46.2	2,175,658	47.0
Kansas	4,480,322	357,500	8.0	2,637,933	58.9	1,484,889	33.1
Kentucky*	5,687,252	693,800	12.2	3,303,060	58.1	1,690,392	29.7
Louisiana	6,325,490	908,673	14.4	2,983,943	47.2	2,432,874	38.5
Maine	2,309,974	221,601	9.6	941,399	40.8	1,146,974	49.7
Maryland*	9,732,002	729,137	7.5	3,998,316	41.1	5,004,550	51.4
Massachusetts	13,455,151	757,255	5.6	5,776,444	42.9	6,921,452	51.4
Michigan*	21,250,527	1,570,772	7.4	13,526,957	63.7	6,152,797	29.0
Minnesota*	9,084,783	645,304	7.1	6,529,270	71.9	1,910,209	21.0
Mississippi*	3,768,462	571,554	15.2	2,038,039	54.1	1,158,869	30.8
Missouri*	8,688,352	816,697	9.4	2,880,368	33.2	4,991,287	57.4
Montana*	1,331,410	163,098	12.3	631,764	47.5	536,548	40.3
Nebraska	2,479,683	221,577	8.9	898,126	36.2	1,359,980	54.8
Nevada	3,602,479	278,421	7.7	975,122	27.1	2,348,936	65.2
New Hampshire*	2,276,558	140,220	6.2	956,224	42.0	1,180,114	51.8
New Jersey	20,023,212	654,526	3.3	7,361,402	36.8	12,007,284	60.0
New Mexico	3,176,148	600,857	18.9	2,199,960	69.3	375,331	11.8
New York*	41,346,057	2,843,612	6.9	18,860,995	45.6	19,641,450	47.5
North Carolina	10,333,356	1,147,052	11.1	6,588,327	63.8	2,597,977	25.1
North Dakota	920,203	142,520	15.5	314,489	34.2	463,194	50.3
Ohio*	20,636,385	1,310,588	6.4	9,580,162	46.4	9,745,635	47.2
Oklahoma*	4,789,409	688,020	14.4	2,510,138	52.4	1,591,251	33.2
Oregon*	5,330,328	549,009	10.3	2,646,000	49.6	2,135,319	40.1
Pennsylvania*	20,759,648	1,802,931	8.7	7,230,274	34.8	11,726,443	56.5
Rhode Island*	1,588,108	53,270	3.4	579,425	36.5	955,413	60.2
South Carolina	6,587,609	688,409	10.5	2,922,998	44.4	2,976,202	45.2
South Dakota*	1,101,547	196,439	17.8	365,218	33.2	539,890	49.0
Tennessee*	6,972,142	885,224	12.7	3,143,715	45.1	2,943,203	42.2
Texas	38,512,169	4,370,671	11.3	13,727,188	35.6	20,414,310	53.0
Utah*	3,338,752	351,643	10.5	1,807,041	54.1	1,180,068	35.3
Vermont	1,318,274	99,803	7.6	1,145,064	86.9	73,407	5.6
Virginia*	12,789,820	924,815	7.2	5,064,693	39.6	6,800,311	53.2
Washington	9,628,722	947,607	9.8	6,002,917	62.3	2,678,198	27.8
West Virginia	2,936,823	360,050	12.3	1,756,492	59.8	820,281	27.9
Wisconsin*	9,799,241	696,169	7.1	5,075,782	51.8	4,027,290	41.1
Wyoming	1,169,165	113,450	9.7	535,605	45.8	520,110	44.5
50 States and DC	498,066,621	45,346,771	9.1	237,017,445	47.6	215,702,404	43.3

*Indicates NEA estimate. (1) Included as revenue receipts are all appropriations from general funds of federal, state, county, and local governments; receipts from taxes levied for school purposes; income from permanent school funds and endowments; and income from leases of school lands and miscellaneous sources (interest on bank deposits, tuition, gifts, school lunch charges, etc.).

Enrollment in U.S. Public and Private Schools*, 1899-2016

Source: National Center for Education Statistics, U.S. Dept. of Education

School year[1]	Public school[2]	Private school[2]	% Private	School year[1]	Public school[2]	Private school[2]	% Private
1899-1900	15,503	1,352	8.7	1979-80	41,651	5,000[3]	12.0
1909-10	17,814	1,558	8.7	1989-90	40,543	5,599[3]	13.8
1919-20	21,578	1,699	7.9	1999-2000	46,857	6,018	11.4
1929-30	25,678	2,651	10.3	2004-05	48,795	6,151[4]	12.6
1939-40	25,434	2,611	10.3	2005-06[4]	48,710	6,062	12.4
1949-50	25,111	3,380	13.5	2006-07[4]	48,948	6,127	12.5
1959-60	35,182	5,675	16.1	2007-08[4]	49,091	6,147	12.5
1969-70	45,550	5,500[3]	12.1	2015-16[4]	51,220	6,461	12.6

*Private includes all nonpublic schools. (1) Fall enrollment. (2) In thousands. (3) Estimated. (4) Projected.

Enrollment in U.S. Religious and Nonsectarian Private Schools, 2003-2004

Source: U.S. Department of Education, National Center for Education Statistics, *Private School Universe Survey, 2003–2004.*

Number and percentage distribution of private school students, by school level and religious or nonsectarian orientation of school. Religious groups listed only if at least some data met reporting standards.

	Total		Elementary		Secondary		Combined	
	Number	Percent	Number	Percent	Number	Percent	Number	Percent
Total....................	5,122,772	100.0%	2,694,494	100.0%	845,083	100.0%	1,583,194	100.0%
Nonsectarian	921,993	18.0	301,318	11.2	118,497	14.0	502,179	31.7
Religious orientation	4,200,778	82.0	2,393,176	88.8	726,587	86.0	1,081,016	68.3
Roman Catholic	2,365,220	46.2	1,658,769	61.6	609,601	72.1	96,850	6.1
Amish..........................	22,287	0.4	21,408	0.8	0	0.0	880	0.1
Assembly of God	62,360	1.2	23,780	0.9	(2)	(2)	37,948	2.4
Baptist	272,556	5.3	59,191	2.2	6,553	0.8	206,811	13.1
Brethren........................	10,898	0.2	2,599	0.1	(2)	(2)	7,855	0.5
Calvinist........................	41,809	0.8	19,452	0.7	7,065	0.8	15,292	1.0
Christian (unspecified)	584,415	11.4	168,385	6.2	26,898	3.2	389,132	24.6
Church of Christ	40,515	0.8	6,661	0.2	(2)	(2)	33,557	2.1
Church of God	10,576	0.2	4,197	0.2	(2)	(2)	6,167	0.4
Church of God in Christ	1,799	(1)	1,276	(1)	0	0.0	(2)	(2)
Episcopal	99,675	1.9	43,163	1.6	10,845	1.3	45,667	2.9
Friends.........................	17,970	0.4	5,658	0.2	(2)	(2)	11,331	0.7
Greek Orthodox	4,014	0.1	3,057	0.1	(2)	(2)	(2)	(2)
Islamic	22,958	0.4	10,080	0.4	(2)	(2)	12,830	0.8
Jewish	201,901	3.9	99,699	3.7	25,744	3.0	76,458	4.8
Lutheran Church—Missouri Synod	148,824	2.9	127,136	4.7	15,579	1.8	6,109	0.4
Evangelical Lutheran Church In America.	17,415	0.3	15,722	0.6	0	0.0	(2)	(2)
Wisconsin Evangelical Lutheran Synod..	32,477	0.6	25,710	1.0	6,513	0.8	(2)	(2)
Other Lutheran..................	9,626	0.2	5,719	0.2	(2)	(2)	12,618	0.8
Mennonite	25,977	0.5	12,211	0.5	(2)	(2)	9,068	0.6
Methodist	18,613	0.4	8,304	0.3	(2)	(2)	20,093	1.3
Pentecostal	26,039	0.5	5,905	0.2	(2)	(2)	19,717	1.2
Presbyterian....................	40,177	0.8	18,362	0.7	(2)	(2)	23,027	1.5
Seventh-Day Adventist.............	57,891	1.1	26,096	1.0	8,769	1.0	23,027	1.5
Other	62,984	1.2	19,481	0.7	1,649	0.2	41,854	2.6

Note: Details may not add up to totals because of rounding and/or missing data. (1) Rounds to zero. (2) Reporting standards not met.

Homeschooled Students

A total of 1,096,000 U.S. students in grades K-12 were being homeschooled in 2003, 82% of them full-time, according to the latest available statistics from the U.S. Dept. of Education.

In a 2003 U.S. Dept. of Education survey of parents who homeschool their children the reasons given as *most important* included concern over the school environment, including such factors as safety, drugs, or negative peer pressure (31.2%); desire to provide religious or moral instruction (29.8%); dissatisfaction with academic instruction in schools (16.5%); and a physical or mental health problem or other special need (13.7%). In all, 85.4% cited concern over school environment as one of their reasons, while 72.3% cited religious or moral instruction and 68.2% cited dissatisfaction with academic instruction.

Below is a breakdown of homeschooled students by categories for 1999 and 2003.

	1999			2003		
Characteristic	Number	Percentage distribution	Home-schooling rate[1]	Number	Percentage distribution	Home-schooling rate[1]
Total..........................	850,000	100.0	1.7	1,096,000	100.0	2.2
Homeschooled entirely....................	697,000	82.0	—	898,000	82.0	—
Homeschooled and enrolled in school part time ..	153,000	18.0	—	198,000	18.0	—
Race/ethnicity[2]						
Black	84,000	9.9	1.0	103,000	9.4	1.3
White	640,000	75.3	2.0	843,000	77.0	2.7
Other	49,000	5.8	1.9	91,000	8.3	3.0
Hispanic........................	77,000	9.1	1.1	59,000	5.3	0.7
Number of children in the household						
One child	120,000	14.1	1.5	110,000	10.1	1.4
Two children.....................	207,000	24.4	1.0	306,000	28.0	1.5
Three or more children...................	523,000	61.6	2.4	679,000	62.0	3.1
Household income						
$25,000 or less..................	262,000	30.9	1.6	283,000	25.8	2.3
$25,001–50,000..................	278,000	32.7	1.8	311,000	28.4	2.4
$50,001–75,000..................	162,000	19.1	1.9	264,000	24.1	2.4
$75,001 or more.................	148,000	17.4	1.5	238,000	21.7	1.7
Parents' education						
High school diploma or less...........	160,000	18.9	0.9	269,000	24.5	1.7
Some college or vocational/technical...........	287,000	33.7	1.9	338,000	30.8	2.1
Bachelor's degree	213,000	25.1	2.6	274,000	25.0	2.8
Graduate/professional degree	190,000	22.3	2.3	215,000	19.6	2.5

(1) The homeschooling rate is the percentage of the total group or subgroup that is homeschooled. For example, in 2003, 0.7% of all Hispanic students K-12 were homeschooled. (2) Race categories exclude Hispanic.

Teachers' Salaries in Upper Secondary Education, Selected Countries, 2004
Source: Organization for Economic Cooperation and Development

Annual statutory teachers' salaries in public institutions in upper secondary (senior high school) education, general programs, in equivalent U.S. dollars converted using PPPs[1]; ranked by starting salaries.

	Starting salary	Salary with 15 years' experience	Salary at top of scale		Starting salary	Salary with 15 years' experience	Salary at top of scale
Luxembourg	$66,712	$83,390	$115,899	Sweden	$26,991	$31,772	$36,575
Switzerland	53,340	69,061	81,462	Austria	26,801	37,035	56,307
Germany	42,321	51,883	54,211	France	25,928	33,906	48,845
Spain	35,792	41,552	51,225	Italy	25,595	32,168	40,113
Belgium (Fl.)	34,959	50,476	60,679	Iceland	24,948	30,605	32,153
Finland	34,825	43,526	43,526	Japan	24,469	45,761	60,104
Denmark	33,092	46,500	46,500	Greece	23,700	28,646	34,540
Belgium (Fr.)	33,084	48,200	58,140	Portugal	19,189	31,635	49,644
Netherlands	32,703	59,762	65,910	New Zealand	18,641	36,063	36,063
United States	31,578	40,043	NA	Turkey	15,683	17,421	19,773
Australia	30,062	44,139	44,139	Czech Republic	15,259	20,800	26,356
Norway	29,618	35,420	36,679	Israel	13,608	16,695	23,235
England	28,769	42,046	42,046	Hungary	12,789	17,913	23,930
Scotland	28,603	45,616	45,616	Chile	10,922	13,579	18,321
S. Korea	28,449	48,754	78,351	Poland	6,394	10,263	10,652
Ireland	27,587	44,185	50,071				

Percent of Population with Upper Secondary Education, Selected Countries, 2004
Source: Organization for Economic Cooperation and Development

Percentage of the population ages 25-64 that have received at least some upper secondary (senior high school) education

Czech Republic	89%	Canada	84	Finland	78	Australia	64	Poland	50
Russian Federation[1]	89	Germany	84	New Zealand	78	Belgium	64	Italy	48
Norway	88	Japan[1]	84	Hungary	75	Ireland	63	Spain	45
United States	88	Sweden	83	S. Korea	74	Luxembourg	62	Brazil	30
Slovak Republic	85	Denmark	81	Netherlands	71	Iceland	60	Turkey	26
Switzerland	85	Austria	80	France	65	Greece	56	Portugal	25
		Israel	79	United Kingdom	65	Chile	50	Mexico	23

(1) Year of reference 2003.

Charges at U.S. Institutions of Higher Education, 1969-70 to 2005-2006
Source: National Center for Education Statistics, U.S. Dept. of Education

Figures for 1969-70 are average charges for full-time resident degree-credit students; figures for later years are average charges per full-time equivalent student. Room and board are based on full-time students. These figures are enrollment-weighted, according to the number of full-time-equivalent undergraduates, and thus may vary from averages given elsewhere.

	TUITION AND FEES			BOARD RATES			DORMITORY CHARGES		
	All institutions	2-yr	4-yr	All institutions	2-yr	4-yr	All institutions	2-yr	4-yr
PUBLIC (in-state)									
1969-70	$323	$178	NA	$511	$465	NA	$369	$308	NA
1979-80	583	355	$738	867	893	$865	715	574	$725
1989-90	1,356	756	1,780	1,635	1,581	1,638	1,513	962	1,557
1990-91	1,454	824	1,888	1,691	1,594	1,698	1,612	1,050	1,657
1995-96	2,179	1,239	2,848	2,020	1,681	2,045	2,057	1,297	2,121
1996-97	2,271	1,276	2,987	2,111	1,789	2,133	2,148	1,339	2,214
1997-98	2,360	1,314	3,110	2,228	1,795	2,263	2,225	1,401	2,301
1998-99	2,430	1,327	3,229	2,347	1,828	2,389	2,330	1,450	2,409
1999-2000	2,506	1,338	3,349	2,364	1,834	2,406	2,440	1,549	2,519
2000-2001	2,562	1,333	3,501	2,455	1,906	2,499	2,569	1,600	2,654
2001-2002	2,700	1,380	3,735	2,598	2,036	2,645	2,723	1,722	2,816
2002-2003	2,903	1,483	4,046	2,669	2,164	2,712	2,930	1,954	3,029
2003-2004	3,319	1,702	4,587	2,823	2,233	2,875	3,107	2,086	3,212
2004-2005	3,629	1,849	5,027	2,931	2,353	2,981	3,304	2,174	3,418
2005-2006	3,874	1,935	5,351	3,035	2,306	3,093	3,545	2,251	3,664
PRIVATE									
1969-70	1,533	1,034	NA	561	546	NA	436	413	NA
1979-80	3,130	2,062	3,225	955	923	957	827	766	831
1989-90	8,147	5,196	8,396	1,948	1,811	1,953	1,923	1,663	1,935
1990-91	8,772	5,570	9,083	2,074	1,989	2,077	2,063	1,744	2,077
1995-96	11,864	7,094	12,243	2,606	2,098	2,617	2,738	2,371	2,751
1996-97	12,498	7,236	12,881	2,663	2,181	2,672	2,878	2,537	2,889
1997-98	12,801	7,464	13,344	2,762	2,785	2,761	2,954	2,672	2,964
1998-99	13,428	7,854	13,973	2,865	2,884	2,865	3,075	2,581	3,091
1999-2000	14,081	8,235	14,588	2,882	2,922	2,881	3,224	2,808	3,237
2000-2001	15,000	9,067	15,470	2,993	3,000	2,993	3,374	2,722	3,392
2001-2002	15,742	10,076	16,211	3,104	2,633	3,109	3,567	3,116	3,576
2002-2003	16,383	10,651	16,826	3,206	3,870	3,197	3,752	3,232	3,764
2003-2004	17,327	11,546	17,777	3,364	4,432	3,354	3,945	3,581	3,952
2004-2005	18,154	12,122	18,604	3,485	3,728	3,483	4,171	4,243	4,170
2005-2006	18,862	12,450	19,292	3,647	4,726	3,639	4,380	3,994	4,386

NA = Not Available

Top 20 Colleges and Universities in Endowment Assets, 2006[1]

Source: *2006 NACUBO Endowment Study*, National Association of College and University Business Officers (NACUBO)

College/University	Endowment assets[2]	% Change, 2005-06	College/University	Endowment assets[2]	% Change, 2005-06
1. Harvard University	$28,915,706	13.5	11. University of Pennsylvania	5,313,268	21.6
2. Yale University	18,030,600	18.4	12. Northwestern University	5,140,668	22.0
3. Stanford University	14,084,676	15.4	13. Emory University	4,870,019	11.3
4. University of Texas System	13,234,848	14.0	14. University of Chicago	4,867,003	17.6
5. Princeton University	13,044,900	16.4	15. Washington University	4,684,737	9.8
6. Massachusetts Institute of Technology	8,368,066	24.7	16. Duke University	4,497,718	17.6
7. Columbia University	5,937,814	14.4	17. University of Notre Dame	4,436,624	21.5
8. University of California	5,733,621	9.8	18. Cornell University	4,321,199	14.4
9. University of Michigan	5,652,262	14.6	19. Rice University	3,986,664	10.4
10. The Texas A&M University System and Foundations	5,642,978	13.7	20. University of Virginia	3,618,172	12.4

NOTE: Market value of endowment assets, excluding pledges and working capital. (1) Fiscal year 2006. (2) In thousands.

U.S. Higher Education Trends: Bachelor's Degrees Conferred

Figures for and 2013-2014 are projected.

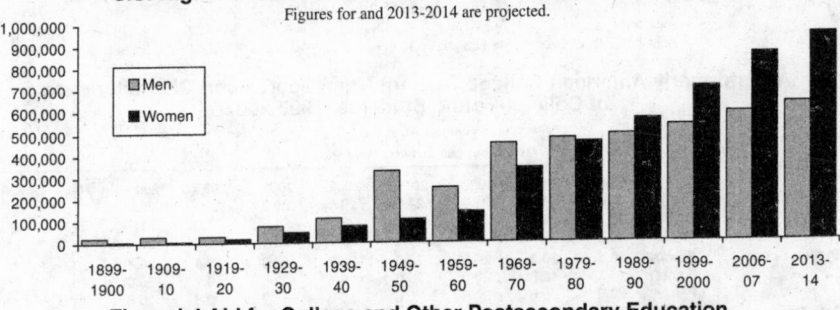

Financial Aid for College and Other Postsecondary Education

As of July 2007. Reviewed by National Assoc. of Student Financial Aid Administrators

The cost of postsecondary education in the U.S. has increased in recent years, but financial aid, which may be in the form of **grants** (no repayment needed), **loans**, and/or **work-study** programs, is widely available to help families meet these expenses. Most aid is limited to family financial need as determined by standard formulas. Students interested in receiving aid are advised to apply, without making prior assumptions. Financial aid personnel at each school can provide information about programs available to students, steps to apply for them, and deadlines, all of which may vary.

All applicants for federal aid must file a Free Application for Federal Student Aid (**FAFSA**), generally as soon as possible after Jan. 1 for the academic year starting the following September. Figures provided should agree with federal income tax forms filed for the previous year. Other possible sources of aid include state governments, employers and unions, civic organizations, and the institutions themselves. There are also special federal programs that pay for postsecondary education in return for service: AmeriCorps (phone: 1-800-942-2677) and ROTC (phone: 1-800-USA-ROTC). Additional forms and certain fees may be required if a student is to be considered for institutional aid. Aid must be reapplied for annually.

A **federal formula**, based on information provided on the FAFSA, takes into account such factors as family income in the preceding calendar year, parental and student assets (excluding the parents' home or farm), length of time to parents' retirement, and unusual expenses (such as very high medical expenses).

The resulting **Expected Family Contribution**, or EFC (which is divided among the family members—excluding parents—in college), is subtracted from the total cost of attendance for each person (including tuition and fee charges, room and board or allowance for living costs, books and supplies, transportation to and from school, and other miscellaneous costs) to determine financial need, and thus the maximum federal aid for which the family may be eligible. (Some institutions use a separate formula for need-based institutional aid.) Some schools guarantee to meet the full financial need of each admitted student; however, most others try to do so but may fall short, depending on the availability of funds. Outside scholarships (even if non-need-based) are taken into account in determining the amount of aid eligibility for federal, institutional, and state financial aid programs.

The **aid package** offered by each school may include one or more of the following resources: Federal Pell Grants, for those with greatest financial need; Federal Supplemental Educational Opportunity Grants, for those with great financial need who are also eligible for Pell Grants; grants from the school; Federal Work-Study or other work programs; low-interest Perkins loans; and subsidized and unsubsidized Stafford loans. Parents of undergraduates may also apply for a Federal PLUS loan. For unsubsidized Stafford loans and all PLUS loans to parents, need is not a requirement, but students and parents must still complete the FAFSA before eligibility for unsubsidized Stafford loans is determined.

Loans have varying interest rates and other requirements. Repayment of Perkins and Stafford loans does not begin until after graduation; deferments are available under certain circumstances. For PLUS loans, parents must pass a credit check and begin repayment of both principal and interest while the student is still in school.

Certain federal income **tax credits**—dollar for dollar reductions of the amount of tax due—are available to families who meet income and other requirements; see the chapter on Taxes.

Rules for financial aid are complex and changeable. *The Student Guide*, a comprehensive resource on financial aid from the U.S. Dept. of Education, can be found at the website www.studentaid.ed.gov/students/publications/student_guide/index.html

Further information and FAFSA forms are available from the school or from the Federal Student Aid Information Center, PO Box 84, Washington, DC 20044; phone: 1-800-4-FED-AID, Mon.-Fri., 8 AM - 12 midnight Eastern Time. The Information Center also has a free booklet called *The EFC Formula Book*. FAFSA forms can be obtained online at www.fafsa.ed.gov

Average Salaries of U.S. College Professors, 2006-2007

Source: American Association of University Professors. NA = Not available.

		MEN Type of institution			WOMEN Type of institution		
TEACHING LEVEL		Public	Private/ Independent	Church-related	Public	Private/ Independent	Church-related
Doctoral level	Professor...........	$108,481	$138,921	$121,312	$98,552	$127,542	$109,720
	Associate	76,030	89,936	82,941	70,764	83,148	76,814
	Assistant...........	65,498	78,079	70,227	60,155	71,207	65,882
Master's level	Professor...........	82,834	93,020	84,493	79,493	86,476	78,355
	Associate	66,102	71,130	66,448	63,630	66,881	63,338
	Assistant...........	56,225	57,610	55,107	53,907	55,065	52,467
General 4-year	Professor...........	78,390	91,563	69,969	73,372	87,570	66,427
	Associate	63,658	67,210	56,752	61,363	66,444	55,315
	Assistant...........	52,960	55,180	47,853	50,714	54,011	47,085
2-year	Professor...........	69,884	60,557	NA	66,804	51,616	NA
	Associate	56,331	48,209	NA	54,493	43,199	NA
	Assistant...........	49,505	36,378	NA	48,409	35,635	NA

ACT (formerly American College Testing) Mean Scores and Characteristics of College-Bound Students, 1990-2007

Source: ACT, Inc.

(for school year ending in year shown)

SCORES[1]	Unit[1]	1990	1995	2000	2001	2002	2003	2004	2005	2006	2007
Composite Scores ..	Points	20.6	20.8	21.0	21.0	20.8	20.8	20.9	20.9	21.1	21.2
Male..............	Points	21.0	21.0	21.2	21.1	20.9	21.0	21.0	21.1	21.2	21.2
Female..........	Points	20.3	20.7	20.9	20.9	20.7	20.8	20.9	20.9	21.0	21.0
English Score......	Points	20.5	20.2	20.5	20.5	20.2	20.3	20.4	20.4	20.6	20.7
Male..............	Points	20.1	19.8	20.0	20.0	19.7	19.8	19.9	20.0	20.1	20.2
Female..........	Points	20.9	20.6	20.9	20.8	20.6	20.7	20.8	20.8	21.0	21.0
Math Score........	Points	19.9	20.2	20.7	20.7	20.6	20.6	20.7	20.7	20.8	21.0
Male..............	Points	20.7	20.9	21.4	21.4	21.2	21.2	21.3	21.3	21.5	21.6
Female..........	Points	19.3	19.7	20.2	20.2	20.1	20.1	20.2	20.2	20.3	20.4
PARTICIPANTS											
Total Number	(1000s)	817	945	1,065	1,070	1,116	1,175	1,171	1,186	1,206	1,301
Male..............	Percent	46	44	43	43	44	44	43	44	44	42
White............	Percent	79	80	72	71	69	68	67	66	63	60
Black	Percent	9	9	10	11	11	11	11	12	12	12
Hispanic	Percent	4	5	5	6	6	6	7	7	7	7
Composite Scores											
27 or above	Percent	12	13	14	14	13	14	14	14	14	15
18 or below......	Percent	35	34	32	33	35	35	34	34	34	32

(1) Minimum point score, 1; maximum score, 36. Test scores and characteristics of college-bound students are based on the performance of all ACT-tested students who graduated in the spring of a given school year and took the ACT Assessment during junior or senior year of high school.

ACT Average Composite Scores by State, 2006-2007

Source: ACT, Inc.

STATE	Avg. Comp. Score	% Grads Taking ACT[1]	STATE	Avg. Comp. Score	% Grads Taking ACT[1]	STATE	Avg. Comp. Score	% Grads Taking ACT[1]
Alabama..........	20.3	81	Kentucky	20.7	77	Ohio.............	21.6	68
Alaska	21.2	27	Louisiana.........	20.1	79	Oklahoma	20.7	71
Arizona..........	21.8	18	Maine............	22.5	11	Oregon	22.0	18
Arkansas	20.5	75	Maryland	21.6	14	Pennsylvania.....	22.0	11
California	22.1	15	Masschusetts......	23.5	15	Rhode Island......	21.8	9
Colorado.........	20.4	100	Michigan	21.5	70	South Carolina ...	19.6	43
Connecticut	23.2	16	Minnesota	22.5	70	South Dakota	21.9	76
Delaware	21.7	9	Mississippi........	18.9	96	Tennessee	20.7	96
District of			Missouri..........	21.6	74	Texas	20.5	30
Columbia	18.7	31	Montana..........	21.9	59	Utah.............	21.7	70
Florida	19.9	54	Nebraska.........	22.1	77	Vermont..........	22.8	22
Georgia	20.3	34	Nevada	21.5	29	Virginia	21.4	18
Hawaii	22.3	59	New Hampshire ...	22.9	15	Washington.......	23.1	16
Idaho	21.4	59	New Jersey	22.2	11	West Virginia......	20.6	66
Illinois...........	20.5	100	New Mexico.......	20.2	60	Wisconsin	22.3	70
Indiana..........	22.0	21	New York	23.0	21	Wyoming.........	21.5	78
Iowa.............	22.3	66	North Carolina	21.0	16			
Kansas...........	21.9	76	North Dakota	21.6	82	U.S. AVG.	21.2	42

(1) Based on number of high school graduates in 2006, as projected by the Western Interstate Commission for Higher Education, and number of students in the class of 2006 who took the ACT.

The New SAT

The College Board administered a brand-new SAT in March 2005, to the graduating high school class of 2006. The new SAT, the first revision to the test since 1995, adds a new writing section in which test takers are asked to write an essay in 25 minutes, and changes other aspects of the two traditional sections: the critical reading section (formerly the verbal section) places more emphasis on reading comprehension, and the math section includes more concepts learned in Algebra II and Geometry. Each section is still scored on an 800 point scale, making a perfect score 2400. The new test has a time limit of three hours and 45 minutes, up from three hours for the old test.

Results for the graduating high school class of 2006 showed the sharpest drop in SAT scores in 31 years: composite reading and math scores fell by about 7 points. At the same time, the ACT reported its largest composite score increase on its competing test in 20 years. Some critics have charged that the drop in SAT scores may be attributed to the increased length, which leaves many test-takers feeling more tired. However, a College Board study of some 700,000 tests found no evidence to support this claim; College Board officials suggest that the drop may be due to a decrease in repeat test-taking.

SAT Mean Verbal and Math Scores of College-Bound Seniors, 1975-2007

Source: The College Board

(recentered scale; for school year ending in year shown)

	1975	1980	1985	1990	1995	1998	1999	2000	2001	2002	2003	2004	2005	2006	2007
Critical Reading Scores	512	502	509	500	504	505	505	505	506	504	507	508	508	503	502
Male	515	506	514	505	505	509	509	507	509	507	512	512	513	505	504
Female	509	498	503	496	502	502	502	504	502	502	503	504	505	502	502
Math Scores	498	492	500	501	506	512	511	514	514	516	518	518	520	518	515
Male	518	515	522	521	525	531	531	533	533	534	537	537	538	536	533
Female	479	473	480	483	490	496	495	498	498	500	503	501	504	502	499
Writing Scores														497	494
Male														491	489
Female														502	500

NOTE: In 1995, the College Board recentered the scoring scale for the SAT by reestablishing the original mean score of 500 on the 200-800 scale. Earlier scores have been adjusted to account for this recentering. The Writing test was first given in March 2005, however, only the scores of the first graduating class to take them are given.

SAT Mean Scores by State, 1990, 2000, and 2005-2007

Source: The College Board

(recentered scale; for school year ending in year shown)

STATE	1990		2000		2005		2006[1]			2007[1]			% Grads Taking SAT[2]
	V	M	V	M	V	M	CR	M	W	CR	M	W	
Alabama	545	534	559	555	567	559	565	561	565	563	556	554	9
Alaska	514	501	519	515	523	519	517	517	493	519	519	491	48
Arizona	521	520	521	523	526	530	521	528	507	519	525	502	32
Arkansas	545	532	563	554	563	552	574	568	567	578	566	565	5
California	494	508	497	518	504	522	501	518	501	499	516	498	49
Colorado	533	534	534	537	560	560	558	564	548	560	565	549	24
Connecticut	506	496	508	509	517	517	512	516	511	510	512	511	84
Delaware	510	496	502	496	503	502	495	500	484	497	496	486	72
District of Columbia	483	467	494	486	490	478	487	472	482	478	462	471	78
Florida	495	493	498	500	498	498	496	497	480	494	495	483	65
Georgia	478	473	488	486	497	496	494	496	487	494	496	483	69
Hawaii	480	505	488	519	490	516	482	509	472	484	506	473	61
Idaho	542	524	540	541	544	542	543	545	525	541	539	519	19
Illinois	542	547	568	586	594	606	591	609	586	594	611	588	8
Indiana	486	486	498	501	504	508	498	509	486	497	507	483	62
Iowa	584	588	589	600	596	608	602	613	591	608	613	586	4
Kansas	566	563	574	580	585	588	582	590	566	583	590	569	8
Kentucky	548	541	548	550	561	559	562	562	555	567	565	553	10
Louisiana	551	537	562	558	565	562	570	571	571	569	567	563	7
Maine	501	490	504	500	509	505	501	501	491	466	465	457	100
Maryland	506	502	507	509	511	515	503	509	499	500	502	496	70
Massachusetts	503	498	511	513	520	527	513	524	510	513	522	511	85
Michigan	529	534	557	569	568	579	568	583	555	568	579	553	85
Minnesota	552	558	581	594	592	597	591	600	574	596	603	577	9
Mississippi	552	538	562	549	564	554	556	541	562	568	549	560	9
Missouri	548	541	572	577	588	588	587	591	582	594	594	587	4
Montana	540	542	543	546	540	540	538	545	524	538	543	522	6
Nebraska	559	562	560	571	574	579	576	583	566	579	585	562	28
Nevada	511	511	510	517	508	513	498	508	481	500	506	480	6
New Hampshire	518	510	520	519	525	525	520	524	509	521	521	512	41
New Jersey	495	498	498	513	503	517	496	515	496	495	510	494	83
New Mexico	554	546	549	543	558	547	557	549	543	555	546	540	82
New York	489	496	494	506	497	511	493	510	483	491	505	482	12
North Carolina	478	470	492	496	499	511	495	513	485	495	509	482	89
North Dakota	579	578	588	609	590	605	610	617	588	584	596	562	71
Ohio	526	522	533	539	539	543	535	544	521	536	542	522	4
Oklahoma	553	542	563	560	570	563	576	574	563	578	571	559	27
Oregon	515	509	527	527	526	528	523	529	503	522	526	502	6
Pennsylvania	497	490	498	497	501	503	493	500	483	493	499	482	54
Rhode Island	498	488	505	500	503	505	495	502	490	496	498	492	75
South Carolina	475	467	484	482	494	499	487	498	480	488	496	475	68
South Dakota	580	570	587	588	589	589	590	604	578	589	602	567	62
Tennessee	558	544	563	553	572	563	573	569	572	574	569	568	3
Texas	490	489	493	500	493	502	491	506	487	492	507	482	13
Utah	566	555	570	569	566	557	560	557	550	558	556	544	52
Vermont	507	493	513	508	521	517	513	519	502	516	518	508	6
Virginia	501	496	509	500	516	514	512	513	500	511	511	498	67
Washington	513	511	526	528	532	534	527	532	511	526	531	510	73

STATE	1990 V	1990 M	2000 V	2000 M	2005 V	2005 M	2006[1] CR	2006[1] M	2006[1] W	2007[1] CR	2007[1] M	2007[1] W	% Grads Taking SAT[2]
West Virginia	520	514	526	511	523	511	519	510	515	516	507	505	53
Wisconsin	552	559	584	597	592	599	588	600	577	587	598	575	20
Wyoming	534	538	545	545	544	543	548	555	537	565	571	544	6
NATIONAL AVG.	500	501	505	514	508	520	503	518	497	502	515	494	48

NOTE: In 1995, the College Board recentered the scoring scale for the SAT by reestablishing the original mean score of 500 on the 200-800 scale. The College Board states that comparing states or ranking them on the basis of SAT scores alone is invalid, and the College Board discourages doing so. (1) In 2005, the SAT was changed. The Verbal portion became Critical Reading, and a new Writing test was added. The 2006 graduating class was the first to take the new test. (2) Based on number of high school graduates in 2006, as projected by the Western Interstate Commission for Higher Education, and number of students in the class of 2006 who took the SAT.

Top 100 Libraries in U.S. by Volumes Held, 2006

Source: American Library Association, *ALA Library Fact Sheet 22*

Institution	Volumes Held*	Institution	Volumes Held*
1. Library of Congress	30,011,748	51. University of Southern California	3,921,704
2. Harvard University	15,555,533	52. Washington University - St. Louis	3,694,504
3. Boston Public Library	15,458,022	53. Johns Hopkins University	3,648,821
4. Yale University	12,025,695	54. Brigham Young University	3,621,577
5. University of Illinois - Urbana-Champaign	10,370,777	55. University of Rochester	3,564,683
6. County of Los Angeles Public Library	10,117,319	56. University of Colorado	3,554,826
7. University of California - Berkeley	9,985,905	57. North Carolina State University	3,530,949
8. Columbia University	9,277,042	58. Brown University	3,509,710
9. Public Library of Cincinnati & Hamilton County	9,148,846	59. University of California - Davis	3,490,356
10. University of Texas - Austin	8,937,002	60. University of South Carolina	3,478,256
11. Stanford University	8,200,000	61. Hawaii State Public Library System	3,452,240
12. University of Michigan	8,133,917	62. Mid-Continent Public Library	3,448,146
13. University of California - Los Angeles	8,064,896	63. Texas A&M University Libraries	3,437,376
14. University of Wisconsin - Madison	7,911,834	64. University of Hawaii	3,410,468
15. Cornell University	7,644,371	65. Louisiana State University	3,406,434
16. Detroit Public Library	7,572,562	66. State University of New York - Buffalo	3,390,583
17. University of Chicago	7,363,549	67. Wayne State University	3,383,826
18. Indiana University	7,241,929	68. King County Library System	3,372,574
19. University of Washington	6,639,850	69. St. Louis Public Library	3,364,996
20. University of Minnesota	6,587,430	70. Broward County Libraries Division	3,351,668
21. Queens Borough Public Library	6,557,823	71. Cuyahoga County Public Library	3,316,816
22. Princeton University	6,495,597	72. University of Kentucky	3,286,731
23. Los Angeles Public Library	6,393,429	73. University of Maryland	3,259,600
24. Free Library of Philadelphia	6,307,978	74. University of Missouri - Columbia	3,249,783
25. Ohio State University	5,936,434	75. University of Connecticut	3,247,976
26. Chicago Public Library	5,891,661	76. Buffalo & Erie County Public Library	3,236,363
27. New York Public Library	5,879,441	77. University of Utah	3,230,854
28. University of Pennsylvania	5,760,065	78. University of Massachusetts	3,204,025
29. University of North Carolina - Chapel Hill	5,710,686	79. University of Notre Dame	3,185,926
30. Duke University	5,560,966	80. Syracuse University	3,161,075
31. University of Arizona	5,340,726	81. University of California - San Diego	3,149,836
32. University of Virginia	5,053,162	82. University of Cincinnati Libraries	3,123,318
33. Pennsylvania State University Libraries	5,031,196	83. Emory University	3,107,525
34. New York University	4,939,724	84. Vanderbilt University	3,056,707
35. Brooklyn Public Library	4,630,323	85. Temple University	3,016,007
36. Michigan State University	4,830,861	86. Southern Illinois University - Carbondale	2,999,736
37. University of Oklahoma	4,796,089	87. Minneapolis Public Library	2,986,326
38. University of Pittsburgh	4,786,175	88. University of Tennessee - Knoxville	2,971,837
39. Northwestern University Library	4,603,824	89. Milwaukee Public Library	2,960,818
40. University of Iowa	4,551,217	90. University of Nebraska - Lincoln	2,942,946
41. San Diego Public Library	4,514,228	91. Auburn University	2,918,859
42. Dallas Public Library	4,199,655	92. Toledo-Lucas County Public Library	2,917,835
43. University of Georgia	4,179,316	93. Enoch Pratt Free Library	2,903,223
44. Rutgers University	4,169,347	94. Florida State University Library	2,889,810
45. Arizona State University Libraries	4,156,732	95. St. Louis County Library District	2,846,307
46. Miami-Dade Public Library System	4,142,711	96. University of California - Santa Barbara	2,837,752
47. University of Florida	4,137,528	97. Tampa-Hillsborough County Public Library	2,819,837
48. University of Kansas	4,121,573	98. Massachusetts Institute of Technology	2,782,406
49. Cleveland Public Library	4,107,112	99. Columbus Metropolitan Library	2,719,477
50. Houston Public Library	4,060,443	100. Kent State University Libraries	2,715,986

*Figures for public libraries include holdings by branches and include circulating books only.

Number of Public Libraries and Operating Income, by State, FY 2004

Source: Public Libraries Survey, National Center for Education Statistics, U.S. Dept. of Education

STATE	No.[1]	Income[2] (thous.)	STATE	No.[1]	Income[2] (thous.)	STATE	No.[1]	Income[2] (thous.)	STATE	No.[1]	Income[2] (thous.)
AL	284	$77,114	IL	789	$603,712	MT	108	$17,985	RI	72	$42,878
AK	105	25,198	IN	438	257,252	NE	292	41,146	SC	183	88,942
AZ	187	134,368	IA	564	81,006	NV	84	72,015	SD	144	17,170
AR	211	46,967	KS	374	91,025	NH	238	42,595	TN	286	93,020
CA	1,087	1,016,281	KY	190	102,947	NJ	454	378,385	TX	847	356,157
CO	241	193,005	LA	335	125,506	NM	120	36,724	UT	113	68,538
CT	244	157,124	ME	276	31,711	NY	1,081	970,962	VT	191	15,083
DE	33	20,752	MD	179	204,474	NC	381	163,353	VA	341	216,024
DC	27	28,952	MA	485	213,265	ND	91	9,937	WA	330	271,414
FL	498	474,698	MI	658	362,953	OH	717	650,503	WV	174	28,008
GA	369	165,056	MN	355	162,585	OK	206	70,931	WI	456	185,208
HI	51	26,430	MS	241	39,956	OR	210	133,658	WY	74	19,633
ID	143	31,407	MO	360	175,444	PA	632	290,127	U.S. Total.	16,549	9,129,588

(1) Includes central libraries and branches. (2) Some totals may be underestimated because of nonresponse.

Four-Year Colleges and Universities

General Information for the 2005-2006 Academic Year

Source: © Thomson Peterson's, a part of The Thomson Corporation. All Rights Reserved.

Note: These listings **include only accredited degree-granting institutions** in the U.S. and the U.S. territories with a total enrollment of 1,000 or more. Only **four-year** colleges and universities (which award a bachelor's degree as their highest undergraduate degree) are included. Data reported **only for institutions that provided updated information** on Peterson's Annual Survey of Undergraduate Institutions for the 2005-2006 academic year.

All institutions are coeducational except those where the ZIP code is followed directly by a number in parentheses. (1) = men only, (2) = primarily men, (3) = women only, (4) = primarily women.

The **Tuition & Fees** column shows the annual tuition and required fees for full-time students, or, where indicated, the tuition and standard fees per unit for part-time students. Where tuition varies according to residence, the figure is given for the most local resident and is coded: (A) = area residents, (S) = state residents; all other figures apply to all students regardless of residence. Where annual expenses are expressed as a lump sum (including full-time tuition, mandatory fees, and room and board), the figure is entered under Tuition & Fees and coded: (C) = comprehensive fee. Rm. & Board is the average cost for one academic year. * indicates fee only.

Control: 1 = independent (nonprofit), 2 = independent-religious, 3 = proprietary (profit-making), 4 = federal, 5 = state, 6 = commonwealth (Puerto Rico), 7 = territory (U.S. territories), 8 = county, 9 = district, 10 = city, 11 = state and local, 12 = state-related, 13 = private (unspecified). **Degree** means the highest degree offered (B = bachelor's, M = master's, F = first professional, D = doctorate).

Enrollment is the total number of matriculated undergraduate and (if applicable) graduate students.

Faculty is the total number of faculty members teaching undergraduate courses and (if available) graduate courses.

NA or a dash indicates category is inapplicable or data not available.

Name, address	Year Founded	Tuition & Fees	Rm. & Board	Control/Degree	Enrollment	Faculty
Abilene Christian Univ, Abilene, TX 79699-9100	1906	$17,410	$6,350	2-D	4,777	378
Acad of Art Univ, San Francisco, CA 94105-3410	1929	$14,680	$12,600	3-M	9,483	1,047
Adams State Coll, Alamosa, CO 81102	1921	$2,925 (S)	$6,160	5-M	4,899	217
Adelphi Univ, Garden City, NY 11530-0701	1896	$20,900	$9,500	1-D	8,053	908
Adrian Coll, Adrian, MI 49221-2575	1859	$19,900	$6,780	2-B	1,051	139
Alabama Agr & Mech Univ, Huntsville, AL 35811	1875	$3,900 (S)	$4,770	5-D	6,076	391
Alabama State Univ, Montgomery, AL 36101-0271	1867	$4,008 (S)	$3,400	5-D	5,565	409
Albany Coll of Pharmacy of Union Univ, Albany, NY 12208-3425	1881	$19,820	$6,900	1-F	1,230	84
Albany State Univ, Albany, GA 31705-2717	1903	$3,142 (S)	$2,460	5-M	3,927	249
Albertus Magnus Coll, New Haven, CT 06511-1189	1925	$19,390	$8,403	2-M	2,186	217
Albion Coll, Albion, MI 49224-1831	1835	$26,122	$7,406	2-B	1,941	170
Albright Coll, Reading, PA 19612-5234	1856	$27,420	$8,158	2-M	2,222	156
Alcorn State Univ, Alcorn State, MS 39096-7500	1871	$4,156 (S)	$4,616	5-M	3,584	203
Alfred Univ, Alfred, NY 14802-1205	1836	$23,162	$10,384	1-D	2,310	220
Allegheny Coll, Meadville, PA 16335	1815	$30,000	$7,500	1-B	2,095	167
Alliant Intl Univ, San Diego, CA 92131-1799	1952	$14,770	NA	1-D	3,521	288
Alma Coll, Alma, MI 48801-1599	1886	$22,380	$7,774	2-B	1,215	117
Alvernia Coll, Reading, PA 19607-1799	1958	$20,422	$8,193	2-M	2,735	235
Alverno Coll, Milwaukee, WI 53234-3922	1887	$17,296	$6,106	2-M	2,480	226
Amberton Univ, Garland, TX 75041-5595	1971	$6,000	NA	3-M	1,648	39
American InterContinental Univ, Atlanta, GA 30326-1016	1977	NA	NA	3-M	1,152	69
American InterContinental Univ, Atlanta, GA 30328	1970	NA	NA	3-M	1,150	119
American InterContinental Univ, Los Angeles, CA 90066	1982	NA	NA	3-M	1,405	133
American InterContinental Univ, Weston, FL 33326	1998	$21,272	NA	3-M	1,844	83
American Intl Coll, Springfield, MA 01109-3189	1885	$20,990	$9,270	1-D	1,815	159
American Public Univ System, Charles Town, WV 25414	1991	$250/cr. hr.	NA	3-M	16,718	420
American Univ of Puerto Rico, Bayamón, PR 00960-2037	1963	$2,105	NA	1-M	3,399	221
American Univ, Washington, DC 20016-8001	1893	$29,673	$11,570	2-D	11,279	941
Amherst Coll, Amherst, MA 01002-5000	1821	$34,916	$9,080	1-B	1,648	212
Anderson Univ, Anderson, IN 46012-3495	1917	$19,990	$6,460	2-D	2,730	250
Anderson Univ, Anderson, SC 29621-4035	1911	$17,850	$7,000	2-M	1,706	136
Andrews Univ, Berrien Springs, MI 49104	1874	$19,528	$6,750	2-D	3,195	266
Angelo State Univ, San Angelo, TX 76909	1928	$3,804 (S)	$5,314	5-M	6,265	344
Anna Maria Coll, Paxton, MA 01612	1946	$23,234	$8,410	2-M	1,200	181
Appalachian State Univ, Boone, NC 28608	1899	$4,187 (S)	$5,760	5-M	15,117	1,042
Aquinas Coll, Grand Rapids, MI 49506-1799	1886	$20,048	$6,422	2-M	2,098	151
Arcadia Univ, Glenside, PA 19038-3295	1853	$25,990	$9,660	2-D	3,595	396
Argosy Univ, Twin Cities, Eagan, MN 55121	1961	$425/credit	NA	3-D	1,700	140
Arizona State Univ at the Polytechnic Campus, Mesa, AZ 85212	1995	$4,448 (S)	$5,100	5-M	6,545	158
Arizona State Univ at the West campus, Phoenix, AZ 85069-7100	1984	$4,444 (S)	$4,200	5-M	8,211	462
Arizona State Univ, Tempe, AZ 85287	1885	$4,688 (S)	$6,900	5-D	51,234	1,974
Arkansas State Univ, State University, AR 72467	1909	$5,710 (S)	$4,440	5-D	10,727	619
Arkansas Tech Univ, Russellville, AR 72801	1909	$4,880 (S)	$4,422	5-M	7,038	372
Armstrong Atlantic State Univ, Savannah, GA 31419-1997	1935	$3,074 (S)	$6,000	5-M	6,728	372
Art Ctr Coll of Design, Pasadena, CA 91103-1999	1930	$27,910	NA	1-M	1,631	407
Art Inst of Atlanta, Atlanta, GA 30328	1949	$20,064	$8,250	3-B	2,694	164
Art Inst of Boston at Lesley Univ, Boston, MA 02215-2598	1912	$23,450	$12,100	1-M	6,539	185
Art Inst of California–Los Angeles, Santa Monica, CA 90405-3035	NA	$21,840	$10,652	3-B	2,068	120
Art Inst of California–Orange County, Santa Ana, CA 92704-9888	2000	$22,704	$10,600	3-B	1,637	100
Art Inst of California–San Diego, San Diego, CA 92121	1981	$21,024	$9,200	3-B	2,386	126
Art Inst of California–San Francisco, San Francisco, CA 94102-4908	1939	$20,640	$7,851	3-B	1,624	108
Art Inst of Colorado, Denver, CO 80203	1952	$419/credit	NA	3-B	2,765	137
Art Inst of Dallas, Dallas, TX 75231-9959	1978	$20,600	$8,504	3-B	1,354	98
Art Inst of Fort Lauderdale, Fort Lauderdale, FL 33316-3000	1968	$19,940	$5,385	3-B	3,058	148
Art Inst of Houston, Houston, TX 77056-4115	1978	$25,400	$6,996	3-B	1,619	86
Art Inst of Las Vegas, Henderson, NV 89074	2002	$20,872	$5,850	3-B	1,046	79
Art Inst of Phoenix, Phoenix, AZ 85021-2859	1995	$18,576	$6,028	3-B	1,055	83
Art Inst of Pittsburgh, Pittsburgh, PA 15219	1921	$24,320	$5,640	3-B	7,856	914
Art Inst of Portland, Portland, OR 97209	1963	$18,630	$8,250	3-B	1,614	104
Art Inst of Seattle, Seattle, WA 98121-1642	1982	$19,968	$9,156	3-B	2,352	144
Art Inst of Washington, Arlington, VA 22209	2000	$19,968	NA	3-B	1,400	82
Art Institutes Intl Minnesota, Minneapolis, MN 55402-3137	1964	$18,336	NA	3-B	1,594	111
Asbury Coll, Wilmore, KY 40390-1198	1890	$21,286	$5,152	2-M	1,220	144
Ashford Univ, Clinton, IA 52733-2967	1918	$15,340	$5,800	3-M	3,836	268
Ashland Univ, Ashland, OH 44805-3702	1878	$22,990	$8,374	2-D	6,648	589
Assumption Coll, Worcester, MA 01609-1296	1904	$26,060	$5,775	2-M	2,498	226
Athens State Univ, Athens, AL 35611	1822	$3,870 (S)	$900	5-B	2,777	177
Auburn Univ Montgomery, Montgomery, AL 36124-4023	1967	$5,020 (S)	$3,050	5-D	5,079	346
Auburn Univ, Auburn University, AL 36849	1856	$5,496 (S)	$7,564	5-D	23,547	1,292

Name, address	Year Founded	Tuition & Fees		Rm. & Board	Control, Degree	Enrollment	Faculty
Augsburg Coll, Minneapolis, MN 55454-1351	1869	$23,422		$6,604	2-M	3,732	355
Augusta State Univ, Augusta, GA 30904-2200	1925	$3,066	(S)	$4,920	5-M	6,552	359
Augustana Coll, Rock Island, IL 61201-2296	1860	$24,924		$6,807	2-B	2,463	235
Augustana Coll, Sioux Falls, SD 57197	1860	$19,986		$5,664	2-M	1,768	186
Aurora Univ, Aurora, IL 60506-4892	1893	$16,850		$7,034	1-D	3,791	293
Austin Coll, Sherman, TX 75090-4400	1849	$24,945		$8,234	2-M	1,354	134
Austin Peay State Univ, Clarksville, TN 37044	1927	$4,837	(S)	$5,190	5-M	9,207	494
Avila Univ, Kansas City, MO 64145-1698	1916	$18,850		$5,750	2-M	1,683	203
Azusa Pacific Univ, Azusa, CA 91702-7000	1899	$23,750		$7,328	2-D	8,128	334
Babson Coll, Babson Park, MA 02457-0310	1919	$34,112		$11,670	1-M	3,359	242
Baker Coll of Allen Park, Allen Park, MI 48101 (4)	2003	$6,660		NA	1-B	1,923	88
Baker Coll of Auburn Hills, Auburn Hills, MI 48326-1586	1911	$6,660		NA	1-B	3,740	155
Baker Coll of Cadillac, Cadillac, MI 49601	1986	$6,660		NA	1-B	1,640	105
Baker Coll of Clinton Township, Clinton Township, MI 48035-4701	1990	$6,660		NA	1-B	5,281	208
Baker Coll of Flint, Flint, MI 48507-5508	1911	$6,660		$2,600	1-B	5,776	315
Baker Coll of Jackson, Jackson, MI 49202	1994	$6,660		NA	1-B	1,730	85
Baker Coll of Muskegon, Muskegon, MI 49442-3497	1888	$6,660		$2,500	1-B	5,022	177
Baker Coll of Owosso, Owosso, MI 48867-4400	1984	$6,660		$2,400	1-B	2,875	144
Baker Coll of Port Huron, Port Huron, MI 48060-2597	1990	$6,660		NA	1-B	1,598	126
Baldwin-Wallace Coll, Berea, OH 44017-2088	1845	$21,236		$6,974	2-M	4,365	382
Ball State Univ, Muncie, IN 47306-1099	1918	$6,810	(S)	$6,898	5-D	17,082	1,148
Bard Coll, Annandale-on-Hudson, NY 12504	1860	$34,080		$9,850	1-D	2,012	237
Barnard Coll, New York, NY 10027-6598 (3)	1889	$33,078		$11,392	1-B	2,350	324
Barry Univ, Miami Shores, FL 33161-6695	1940	$24,000		$7,850	2-D	8,885	845
Barton Coll, Wilson, NC 27893-7000	1902	$17,654		$6,264	2-B	1,136	111
Bastyr Univ, Kenmore, WA 98028-4966	1978	$16,365		$3,650	1-F	1,126	151
Bates Coll, Lewiston, ME 04240-6028	1855	$44,350	(C)	NA	1-B	1,744	193
Bay Path Coll, Longmeadow, MA 01106-2292	1897	$22,073		$9,200	1-M	1,479	128
Bayamón Central Univ, Bayamón, PR 00960-1725	1970	$4,440		NA	2-M	2,913	218
Baylor Univ, Waco, TX 76798	1845	$24,490		$7,526	2-D	14,040	928
Becker Coll, Worcester, MA 01609	1784	$21,460		$8,500	1-B	1,660	103
Belhaven Coll, Jackson, MS 39202-1789	1883	$15,580		$6,000	2-M	2,575	287
Bellarmine Univ, Louisville, KY 40205-0671	1950	$24,150		$6,880	2-D	2,627	300
Bellevue Univ, Bellevue, NE 68005-3098	1965	$5,795		NA	1-M	6,808	370
Belmont Abbey Coll, Belmont, NC 28012-1802	1876	$17,302		$9,430	2-B	1,110	90
Belmont Univ, Nashville, TN 37212-3757	1951	$19,780		$9,529	2-D	4,481	466
Beloit Coll, Beloit, WI 53511-5596	1846	$28,350		$6,162	1-B	1,432	136
Bemidji State Univ, Bemidji, MN 56601-2699	1919	$6,690	(S)	$5,860	5-M	4,918	362
Benedict Coll, Columbia, SC 29204	1870	$13,602		$6,256	2-B	3,005	168
Benedictine Coll, Atchison, KS 66002-1499	1859	$16,710		$6,208	2-M	1,553	112
Benedictine Univ, Lisle, IL 60532-0900	1887	$20,310		$6,700	2-D	3,900	353
Bentley Coll, Waltham, MA 02452-4705	1917	$30,044		$10,530	1-M	5,497	473
Berea Coll, Berea, KY 40404	1855	$775		$5,230	1-B	1,576	173
Berklee Coll of Music, Boston, MA 02215-3693	1945	$29,331		$12,550	1-B	3,894	484
Bernard M. Baruch Coll of the City Univ of New York, New York, NY 10010-5585	1919	$4,320	(S)	NA	11-D	15,730	1,021
Berry Coll, Mount Berry, GA 30149-0159	1902	$18,950		$7,164	2-M	1,842	193
Bethel Coll, McKenzie, TN 38201	1842	NA		NA	2-F	1,297	74
Bethel Coll, Mishawaka, IN 46545-5591	1947	$17,450		$5,380	2-M	2,093	184
Bethel Univ, St. Paul, MN 55112-6999	1871	$24,510		$7,380	2-M	5,185	284
Bethune-Cookman Coll, Daytona Beach, FL 32114-3099	1904	$11,792		$7,206	2-B	3,112	189
Biola Univ, La Mirada, CA 90639-0001	1908	$25,143		$7,370	2-D	5,752	444
Birmingham-Southern Coll, Birmingham, AL 35254	1856	$24,300		$8,062	2-M	1,256	131
Black Hills State Univ, Spearfish, SD 57799	1883	$5,335	(S)	$3,988	5-M	3,896	190
Bloomfield Coll, Bloomfield, NJ 07003-9981	1868	$16,400		$8,100	2-B	2,084	244
Bloomsburg Univ of Pennsylvania, Bloomsburg, PA 17815-1301	1839	$6,412	(S)	$5,616	5-D	8,723	410
Bluefield State Coll, Bluefield, WV 24701-2198	1895	$3,648	(S)	NA	5-B	1,788	124
Bluffton Univ, Bluffton, OH 45817	1899	$20,570		$7,082	2-M	1,155	113
Bob Jones Univ, Greenville, SC 29614	1927	$9,770		$4,980	2-D	4,096	309
Boise State Univ, Boise, ID 83725-0399	1932	$4,154	(S)	$5,778	5-D	18,826	1,073
Boricua Coll, New York, NY 10032-1560	1974	$9,050		NA	1-M	1,520	116
Boston Architectural Coll, Boston, MA 02115-2795	1889	$9,276		NA	1-M	1,019	226
Boston Univ, Boston, MA 02215	1839	$33,506		$11,438	2-D	13,652	1,221
Bowdoin Coll, Brunswick, ME 04011	1794	$33,792		$10,480	1-D	31,574	2,489
Bowie State Univ, Bowie, MD 20715-9465	1865	$5,730	(S)	$5,992	5-D	1,734	193
Bowling Green State Univ, Bowling Green, OH 43403	1910	$9,060	(S)	$6,684	5-D	19,108	1,032
Bradley Univ, Peoria, IL 61625-0002	1897	$20,060		$6,750	1-F	6,126	547
Brandeis Univ, Waltham, MA 02454-9110	1948	$34,035		$9,463	1-D	5,313	458
Brewton-Parker Coll, Mt. Vernon, GA 30445-0197	1904	$13,360		$4,750	2-B	1,119	189
Briar Cliff Univ, Sioux City, IA 51104-0100	1930	$19,239		$5,709	2-M	1,146	64
Briarcliffe Coll, Bethpage, NY 11714	1966	$15,892		$7,938	3-B	2,343	247
Bridgewater Coll, Bridgewater, VA 22812-1599	1880	$21,490		$9,310	2-B	1,514	129
Bridgewater State Coll, Bridgewater, MA 02325-0001	1840	$5,866	(S)	$6,852	5-M	9,655	567
Brigham Young Univ, Provo, UT 84602-1001	1875	$7,680		$6,460	2-D	34,185	1,759
Brigham Young Univ—Hawai'i, Laie, HI 96762-1294	1955	$3,040		$5,170	2-B	2,473	184
Brooklyn Coll of the City Univ of New York, Brooklyn, NY 11210-2889	1930	$4,375	(S)	NA	11-M	15,947	1,256
Brown Univ, Providence, RI 02912	1764	$34,620		$9,134	1-D	8,125	824
Bryant Univ, Smithfield, RI 02917-1284	1863	$27,639		$10,715	1-M	3,651	283
Bryn Mawr Coll, Bryn Mawr, PA 19010-2899	1885	$33,010		$10,550	1-D	1,799	182
Bucknell Univ, Lewisburg, PA 17837	1846	$38,134		$8,052	1-M	3,706	321
Buena Vista Univ, Storm Lake, IA 50588	1891	$22,556		$6,296	2-M	1,229	114
Buffalo State Coll, State Univ of New York, Buffalo, NY 14222-1095	1867	$5,285	(S)	$7,482	5-M	11,220	755
Butler Univ, Indianapolis, IN 46208-3485	1855	$25,414		$8,530	1-F	4,437	454
Cabrini Coll, Radnor, PA 19087-3698	1957	$25,950		$9,900	2-M	2,389	224
Caldwell Coll, Caldwell, NJ 07006-6195	1939	$22,120		$9,220	2-M	2,291	184
California Baptist Univ, Riverside, CA 92504-3206	1950	$18,900		$6,810	2-M	3,409	285
California Coll of the Arts, San Francisco, CA 94107	1907	$27,914		$8,615	1-M	1,622	375
California Inst of Integral Studies, San Francisco, CA 94103	1968	$16,610		NA	1-D	1,005	61
California Inst of Tech, Pasadena, CA 91125-0001	1891	$32,835		$9,540	1-D	2,086	311
California Inst of the Arts, Valencia, CA 91355-2340	1961	$31,855		$8,000	1-M	1,349	287
California Lutheran Univ, Thousand Oaks, CA 91360-2787	1959	$25,990		$9,230	2-D	3,298	283
California Polytechnic State Univ, San Luis Obispo, San Luis Obispo, CA 93407	1901	$4,350	(S)	$8,453	5-M	18,722	1,170
California State Polytechnic Univ, Pomona, Pomona, CA 91768-2557	1938	$3,015	(S)	$7,908	5-M	20,510	1,289
California State Univ Channel Islands, Camarillo, CA 93012	2002	$2,980	(S)	$9,800	5-M	3,123	227
California State Univ, Bakersfield, Bakersfield, CA 93311-1022	1970	$2,959	(S)	$5,946	5-M	7,549	515

Name, address	Year Founded	Tuition & Fees		Rm. & Board	Control, Degree	Enroll-ment	Faculty
California State Univ, Chico, Chico, CA 95929-0722	1887	$3,412	(S)	$8,314	5-M	16,250	965
California State Univ, Dominguez Hills, Carson, CA 90747-0001	1960	$3,051	(S)	$8,690	5-M	12,068	687
California State Univ, East Bay, Hayward, CA 94542-3000	1957	$2,916	(S)	$8,939	5-M	12,706	738
California State Univ, Fresno, Fresno, CA 93740-8027	1911	$3,039	(S)	$6,880	5-D	22,098	1,251
California State Univ, Fullerton, Fullerton, CA 92834-9480	1957	$3,030	(S)	$4,408	5-M	35,921	2,031
California State Univ, Long Beach, Long Beach, CA	1949	$3,116	(S)	$7,536	5-M	35,574	2,227
California State Univ, Los Angeles, Los Angeles, CA 90032-8530	1947	$3,080	(S)	$7,866	5-D	20,565	1,184
California State Univ, Monterey Bay, Seaside, CA 93955-8001	1994	$3,035	(S)	$7,696	5-M	3,577	291
California State Univ, Northridge, Northridge, CA 91330	1958	$3,042	(S)	$9,328	5-M	34,560	1,941
California State Univ, Sacramento, Sacramento, CA 95819-6048	1947	$3,284	(S)	$7,966	5-D	28,529	1,719
California State Univ, San Bernardino, San Bernardino, CA 92407-2397	1965	$3,398	(S)	$5,886	5-M	16,479	633
California State Univ, San Marcos, San Marcos, CA 92096-0001	1990	$3,092	(S)	$5,600	5-M	6,956	501
California State Univ, Stanislaus, Turlock, CA 95382	1957	$3,043	(S)	$7,178	5-M	8,374	511
California Univ of Pennsylvania, California, PA 15419-1394	1852	$6,586	(S)	$8,144	5-M	7,720	402
Calumet Coll of Saint Joseph, Whiting, IN 46394-2195	1951	$10,650		NA	2-M	1,252	142
Calvin Coll, Grand Rapids, MI 49546-4388	1876	$20,470		$7,040	2-M	4,187	411
Cambridge Coll, Cambridge, MA 02138-5304	1971	$8,890		NA	1-D	4,670	945
Cameron Univ, Lawton, OK 73505-6377	1908	$3,432	(S)	$3,282	5-M	5,734	313
Campbell Univ, Buies Creek, NC 27506	1887	$18,598		$6,160	2-D	6,033	336
Campbellsville Univ, Campbellsville, KY 42718-2799	1906	$17,260		$6,230	2-M	2,376	223
Canisius Coll, Buffalo, NY 14208-1098	1870	$24,937		$9,480	2-M	4,850	532
Capella Univ, Minneapolis, MN 55402	1993	$10,440		NA	3-D	17,203	796
Capital Univ, Columbus, OH 43209-2394	1830	$25,100		$6,552	2-F	3,825	419
Cardinal Stritch Univ, Milwaukee, WI 53217-3985	1937	$18,000		$5,590	2-D	6,000	449
Caribbean Univ, Bayamón, PR 00960-0493	1969	$3,750		NA	1-M	1,603	158
Carleton Coll, Northfield, MN 55057-4001	1866	$34,272		$8,592	1-M	1,980	225
Carlos Albizu Univ, Miami Campus, Miami, FL 33172-2209 (4)	1980	$11,724		NA	1-D	1,038	58
Carlow Univ, Pittsburgh, PA 15213-3165 (4)	1929	$19,514		$7,684	2-M	2,154	224
Carnegie Mellon Univ, Pittsburgh, PA 15213-3891	1900	$34,578		$9,280	1-D	10,120	1,028
Carroll Coll, Helena, MT 59625-0002	1909	$18,410		$6,350	2-B	1,452	134
Carroll Coll, Waukesha, WI 53186-5593	1846	$20,830		$6,350	2-M	3,292	283
Carson-Newman Coll, Jefferson City, TN 37760	1851	$16,000		$5,200	2-M	1,949	189
Carthage Coll, Kenosha, WI 53140	1847	$23,650		$6,800	2-M	2,699	210
Case Western Reserve Univ, Cleveland, OH 44106	1826	$31,738		$9,280	1-D	9,592	863
Castleton State Coll, Castleton, VT 05735	1787	$7,244	(S)	$7,220	5-M	2,130	202
Catawba Coll, Salisbury, NC 28144-2488	1851	$19,690		$6,570	2-M	1,269	100
Catholic Univ of America, Washington, DC 20064	1887	$28,990		$10,808	2-D	6,148	691
Cazenovia Coll, Cazenovia, NY 13035-1084	1824	$21,490		$8,940	1-B	1,006	141
Cedar Crest Coll, Allentown, PA 18104-6196 (3)	1867	$25,340		$8,624	2-M	1,943	173
Cedarville Univ, Cedarville, OH 45314-0601	1887	$19,800		$5,010	2-M	3,112	262
Centenary Coll of Louisiana, Shreveport, LA 71104	1825	$18,900		$6,780	2-M	1,044	122
Centenary Coll, Hackettstown, NJ 07840-2100	1867	$22,415		$8,400	2-M	2,662	323
Central Coll, Pella, IA 50219-1999	1853	$21,222		$7,224	2-B	1,606	141
Central Connecticut State Univ, New Britain, CT 06050-4010	1849	$6,734	(S)	$8,348	5-M	12,144	850
Central Michigan Univ, Mount Pleasant, MI 48859	1892	$6,753	(S)	$6,824	5-D	26,710	1,119
Central Pennsylvania Coll, Summerdale, PA 17093-0309	1881	$12,165		$5,925	3-B	1,017	109
Central State Univ, Wilberforce, OH 45384	1887	$5,294	(S)	$7,402	5-M	1,766	179
Central Washington Univ, Ellensburg, WA 98926	1891	$5,238	(S)	$7,140	5-M	10,688	579
Centre Coll, Danville, KY 40422-1394	1819	$33,000	(C)	NA	2-B	1,147	133
Chadron State Coll, Chadron, NE 69337	1911	$3,662	(S)	$4,074	5-M	2,636	110
Chaminade Univ of Honolulu, Honolulu, HI 96816-1578	1955	$14,960		$9,380	2-M	1,810	131
Champlain Coll, Burlington, VT 05402-0670	1878	$22,550		$10,910	1-M	2,741	256
Chapman Univ, Orange, CA 92866	1861	$30,748		$10,500	2-F	5,908	538
Charleston Southern Univ, Charleston, SC 29423-8087	1964	$16,780		$6,450	2-M	3,224	178
Charter Oak State Coll, New Britain, CT 06053-2142	1973	$985	(S)	NA	5-B	1,711	97
Chatham Univ, Pittsburgh, PA 15232-2826	1869	$24,808		$7,586	1-D	1,590	207
Chestnut Hill Coll, Philadelphia, PA 19118-2693 (4)	1924	$22,750		$7,950	2-D	1,918	265
Cheyney Univ of Pennsylvania, Cheyney, PA 19319-0200	1837	$6,118	(S)	$6,006	5-M	1,667	113
Chicago State Univ, Chicago, IL 60628	1867	$7,138	(S)	$6,492	5-D	7,035	453
Christian Brothers Univ, Memphis, TN 38104-5581	1871	$20,080		$5,650	2-M	1,776	144
Christopher Newport Univ, Newport News, VA 23606-2998	1960	$9,106	(S)	$8,100	5-M	4,793	334
Cincinnati Christian Univ, Cincinnati, OH 45204-3200	1924	$11,420		$5,960	2-F	1,125	68
Citadel, The Military Coll of South Carolina, Charleston, SC 29409	1842	$8,168	(S)	$5,090	5-M	3,386	157
City Coll of the City Univ of New York, New York, NY 10031-9198	1847	$4,359	(S)	$9,135	11-F	13,244	1,012
City Univ, Bellevue, WA 98005	1973	$8,160		NA	1-M	4,020	1,241
Claflin Univ, Orangeburg, SC 29115	1869	$11,764		$6,322	2-M	1,758	148
Claremont McKenna Coll, Claremont, CA 91711	1946	$34,850		$10,740	1-B	1,153	146
Clarion Univ of Pennsylvania, Clarion, PA 16214	1867	$6,616	(S)	$5,546	5-M	6,591	286
Clark Atlanta Univ, Atlanta, GA 30314	1865	$16,100		$7,014	2-D	4,514	324
Clark Univ, Worcester, MA 01610-1477	1887	$31,465		$5,900	1-D	3,071	278
Clarke Coll, Dubuque, IA 52001-3198	1843	$20,297		$6,574	2-M	1,201	135
Clarkson Univ, Potsdam, NY 13699	1896	$27,090		$9,648	1-D	2,964	198
Clayton State Univ, Morrow, GA 30260-0285	1969	$3,688	(S)	NA	5-B	6,081	353
Clemson Univ, Clemson, SC 29634	1889	$9,868	(S)	$5,874	5-D	17,165	1,178
Cleveland State Univ, Cleveland, OH 44115	1964	$7,920	(S)	$7,800	5-D	15,483	963
Coastal Carolina Univ, Conway, SC 29528-6054	1954	$7,500	(S)	$6,690	5-M	8,049	443
Coe Coll, Cedar Rapids, IA 52402-5092	1851	$26,390		$6,600	2-M	1,300	142
Colby Coll, Waterville, ME 04901-8840	1813	$44,080	(C)	NA	1-B	1,865	226
Colgate Univ, Hamilton, NY 13346-1386	1819	$35,030		$8,530	1-M	2,788	322
Coll for Creative Studies, Detroit, MI 48202-4034	1926	$26,375		$3,900	1-B	1,302	246
Coll Misericordia, Dallas, PA 18612-1098	1924	$20,860		$8,640	2-D	2,358	257
Coll of Biblical Studies–Houston, Houston, TX 77036	1979	$4,310		NA	2-B	1,492	50
Coll of Charleston, Charleston, SC 29424-0001	1770	$7,234	(S)	$7,596	5-M	11,218	895
Coll of Mount Saint Vincent, Riverdale, NY 10471-1093	1911	$22,750		$8,925	1-M	1,812	156
Coll of Mount St. Joseph, Cincinnati, OH 45233-1670	1920	$20,050		$6,300	2-D	2,259	238
Coll of New Jersey, Ewing, NJ 08628	1855	$10,553	(S)	$8,843	5-M	6,934	703
Coll of New Rochelle, New Rochelle, NY 10805-2308 (4)	1904	$21,910		$8,200	1-M	2,341	207
Coll of Notre Dame of Maryland, Baltimore, MD 21210-2476	1873	$21,600		$8,000	2-D	3,307	88
Coll of Saint Benedict, Saint Joseph, MN 56374 (4)	1887	$24,924		$6,898	2-B	2,059	178
Coll of Saint Elizabeth, Morristown, NJ 07960-6989	1899	$21,150		$9,424	2-D	1,982	197
Coll of Saint Rose, Albany, NY 12203-1419	1920	$19,258		$8,116	1-M	5,062	464
Coll of Santa Fe, Santa Fe, NM 87505-7634	1947	$26,072		$7,585	1-M	2,004	267
Coll of St. Catherine, St. Paul, MN 55105-1789	1905	$22,880		$6,432	2-D	5,246	483
Coll of St. Catherine–Minneapolis, Minneapolis, MN 55454-1494 (4)	1964	$14,750		$6,120	2	4,807	519
Coll of St. Scholastica, Duluth, MN 55811-4199	1912	$23,574		$6,514	2-F	3,304	260

Name, address	Year Founded	Tuition & Fees	Rm. & Board	Control, Degree	Enrollment	Faculty
Coll of Staten Island of the City Univ of New York, Staten Island, NY 10314-6600	1955	$4,328 (S)	NA	11-M	12,313	851
Coll of the Holy Cross, Worcester, MA 01610-2395	1843	$33,313	$9,580	2-B	2,821	299
Coll of the Ozarks, Point Lookout, MO 65726	1906	$295/cr. hr.	NA	2-B	1,345	133
Coll of William & Mary, Williamsburg, VA 23187-8795	1693	$8,490 (S)	$6,932	5-D	7,709	758
Coll of Wooster, Wooster, OH 44691-2363	1866	$30,060	$7,520	2-B	1,819	202
Collins Coll: A School of Design & Tech, Tempe, AZ 85281-5206	1978	$24,250	$4,600	3-B	1,690	102
Colorado Christian Univ, Lakewood, CO 80226	1914	$18,350	$7,625	2-M	2,221	46
Colorado Coll, Colorado Springs, CO 80903-3294	1874	$32,124	$8,052	1-M	1,998	195
Colorado School of Mines, Golden, CO 80401-1887	1874	$9,010 (S)	$6,880	5-D	4,056	299
Colorado State Univ, Fort Collins, CO 80523-0015	1870	$4,717 (S)	$6,602	5-D	26,723	892
Colorado State Univ-Pueblo, Pueblo, CO 81001-4901	1933	$4,190 (S)	$5,810	5-M	6,205	315
Colorado Tech Univ Sioux Falls Campus, Sioux Falls, SD 57108	1965	NA	NA	3-M	1,036	61
Colorado Tech Univ, Colorado Springs, CO 80907-3896	1965	NA	NA	3-D	1,684	137
Columbia Coll Chicago, Chicago, IL 60605-1996	1890	$16,788	$9,765	1-M	11,499	1,477
Columbia Coll, Columbia, MO 65216-0002	1851	$12,414	$5,164	2-M	1,186	89
Columbia Coll, Columbia, SC 29203-5998	1854	$20,302	$6,022	2-M	1,446	165
Columbia Coll, New York, NY 10027	1754	$35,164	$9,648	1-B	4,184	1,057
Columbia Southern Univ, Orange Beach, AL 36561	1993	$4,460	NA	3-M	7,128	82
Columbia Union Coll, Takoma Park, MD 20912-7796	1904	$18,439	$6,247	2-M	1,092	53
Columbia Univ, School of General Studies, New York, NY 10027-6939	1754	$33,906	$8,913	1-B	1,260	784
Columbia Univ, The Fu Foundation School of Engineering & Applied Sci, New York, NY 10027	1864	$35,164	$9,648	1-D	1,409	137
Columbus Coll of Art & Design, Columbus, OH 43215-1758	1879	$21,346	$6,600	1-B	1,581	170
Columbus State Univ, Columbus, GA 31907-5645	1958	$3,188 (S)	$6,284	5-M	7,597	449
Concord Univ, Athens, WV 24712-1000	1872	$4,084 (S)	$6,070	5-M	2,928	197
Concordia Coll, Moorhead, MN 56562	1891	$20,980	$5,090	2-M	2,764	238
Concordia Univ at Austin, Austin, TX 78705-2799	1926	$18,910	$7,300	2-M	1,254	172
Concordia Univ Wisconsin, Mequon, WI 53097-2402	1881	$18,140	$6,860	2-D	5,574	204
Concordia Univ, Irvine, CA 92612-3299	1972	$21,130	$7,060	2-M	2,317	199
Concordia Univ, Portland, OR 97211-6099	1905	$21,090	$6,270	2-M	1,598	114
Concordia Univ, River Forest, IL 60305-1499	1864	$21,320	$6,992	2-D	3,710	349
Concordia Univ, Seward, NE 68434-1599	1894	$19,790	$5,070	2-M	1,251	133
Concordia Univ, St. Paul, St. Paul, MN 55104-5494	1893	$23,496	$6,776	2-M	2,046	437
Connecticut Coll, New London, CT 06320-4196	1911	$44,240 (C)	NA	1-M	1,886	248
Converse Coll, Spartanburg, SC 29302-0006	1889	$22,234	$6,848	1-M	1,977	174
Coppin State Univ, Baltimore, MD 21216-3698	1900	$4,910 (S)	$6,511	5-M	4,003	202
Cornell Coll, Mount Vernon, IA 52314-1098	1853	$24,800	$6,660	2-B	1,121	100
Cornell Univ, Ithaca, NY 14853-0001	1865	$32,981	$10,776	1-D	19,639	1,869
Cornerstone Univ, Grand Rapids, MI 49525-5897	1941	$17,080	$5,860	2-F	2,509	136
Creighton Univ, Omaha, NE 68178-0001	1878	$25,126	$7,842	2-D	6,981	654
Crichton Coll, Memphis, TN 38111	1941	$10,536	$6,084	1-B	1,090	79
Crown Coll, St. Bonifacius, MN 55375-9001	1916	$18,588	$6,922	2-M	1,344	155
Culinary Inst of America, Hyde Park, NY 12538-1499	1946	$21,280	$7,170	1-B	2,742	178
Cumberland Univ, Lebanon, TN 37087-3408	1842	$15,510	$5,313	1-M	1,345	90
Curry Coll, Milton, MA 02186-9984	1879	$24,300	$9,640	1-M	3,073	372
Daemen Coll, Amherst, NY 14226-3592	1947	$17,690	$8,190	1-F	2,414	269
Dakota State Univ, Madison, SD 57042-1799	1881	$5,699 (S)	$3,927	5-M	2,392	105
Dallas Baptist Univ, Dallas, TX 75211-9299	1965	$13,650	$4,959	2-M	5,153	488
Dalton State Coll, Dalton, GA 30720-3797	1963	$1,742 (S)	NA	5-B	4,349	199
Dartmouth Coll, Hanover, NH 03755	1769	$33,297	$9,840	1-D	5,753	647
Davenport Univ, Dearborn, MI 48126-3799	1985	$9,956	$4,450	1-M	12,617	1,157
Davidson Coll, Davidson, NC 28035	1837	$30,194	$8,590	2-B	1,667	172
Delaware State Univ, Dover, DE 19901-2277	1891	$5,746 (S)	$8,658	5-D	3,657	328
Delaware Valley Coll, Doylestown, PA 18901-2697	1896	$23,110	$8,965	1-M	2,035	190
Delta State Univ, Cleveland, MS 38733-0001	1924	$4,498 (S)	$4,499	5-D	4,217	277
Denison Univ, Granville, OH 43023	1831	$30,660	$8,560	1-B	2,263	207
DePaul Univ, Chicago, IL 60604-2287	1898	$22,575	$10,392	2-D	23,149	1,697
DePauw Univ, Greencastle, IN 46135-0037	1837	$27,780	$7,800	2-B	2,326	265
DeSales Univ, Center Valley, PA 18034-9568	1964	$22,000	$8,250	2-M	2,936	172
DeVry Inst of Tech, Long Island City, NY 11101	1998	$14,640	NA	3-M	1,254	110
DeVry Univ Online, Oakbrook Terrace, IL 60181	2000	$12,650	$9,598	3-M	6,569	791
DeVry Univ, Addison, IL 60101-6106	1982	$13,220	NA	3-B	1,440	106
DeVry Univ, Chicago, IL 60618-5994	1931	$13,220	NA	3-B	2,055	103
DeVry Univ, Columbus, OH 43209-2705	1952	$13,220	NA	3-M	2,546	106
DeVry Univ, Decatur, GA 30030-2198	1969	$12,900	NA	3-M	2,279	160
DeVry Univ, Fremont, CA 94555	1998	$14,640	NA	3-M	1,581	124
DeVry Univ, Irving, TX 75063-2439	1969	$13,220	NA	3-M	1,717	103
DeVry Univ, Kansas City, MO 64131-3698	1931	$13,220	NA	3-M	1,148	95
DeVry Univ, Long Beach, CA 90806	1984	$14,020	NA	3-M	1,098	94
DeVry Univ, Naperville, IL 60563-2361	NA	$14,440	NA	3-M	8,828	2,248
DeVry Univ, North Brunswick, NJ 08902-3362	1969	$13,220	NA	3-B	1,417	152
DeVry Univ, Orlando, FL 32839	2000	$14,020	NA	3-M	1,295	101
DeVry Univ, Phoenix, AZ 85021-2995	1967	$13,220	NA	3-M	1,185	70
DeVry Univ, Pomona, CA 91768-2642	1983	$14,020	NA	3-M	1,706	93
DeVry Univ, Tinley Park, IL 60477	2000	$13,220	NA	3-M	1,261	120
Dickinson Coll, Carlisle, PA 17013-2896	1773	$35,784	$8,980	1-B	2,400	208
Dickinson State Univ, Dickinson, ND 58601-4896	1918	$5,295 (S)	$3,882	5-B	2,572	217
Dillard Univ, New Orleans, LA 70122-3097	1869	$12,240	$5,364	2-B	1,124	116
Dominican Coll, Orangeburg, NY 10962-1210	1952	$18,610	$8,980	1-D	1,856	192
Dominican Univ of California, San Rafael, CA 94901-2298	1890	$30,780	$12,000	2-M	2,045	306
Dominican Univ, River Forest, IL 60305-1099	1901	$21,250	$6,620	2-M	3,292	315
Dordt Coll, Sioux Center, IA 51250-1697	1955	$18,660	$5,160	2-M	1,261	98
Dowling Coll, Oakdale, NY 11769-1999	1955	$18,430	$8,988	1-D	5,546	407
Drake Univ, Des Moines, IA 50311-4516	1881	$22,682	$6,500	1-D	5,366	391
Drew Univ, Madison, NJ 07940-1493	1867	$33,068	$9,000	2-D	2,647	241
Drexel Univ, Philadelphia, PA 19104-2875	1891	$27,650	$11,010	1-D	19,882	NA
Drury Univ, Springfield, MO 65802	1873	$15,512	$5,790	1-M	2,053	167
Duke Univ, Durham, NC 27708-0586	1838	$33,963	$9,152	2-D	13,373	NA
Duquesne Univ, Pittsburgh, PA 15282-0001	1878	$22,665	$8,296	2-D	10,110	880
D'Youville Coll, Buffalo, NY 14201-1084	1908	$17,000	$8,300	1-D	3,024	NA
Earlham Coll, Richmond, IN 47374-4095	1847	$29,320	$6,200	2-F	1,410	111
East Carolina Univ, Greenville, NC 27858-4353	1907	$4,003 (S)	$6,940	5-D	24,351	1,894
East Central Univ, Ada, OK 74820-6899	1909	$3,497 (S)	$3,190	5-M	4,506	246
East Stroudsburg Univ of Pennsylvania, East Stroudsburg, PA 18301-2999	1893	$6,640 (S)	$5,302	5-M	7,013	332
East Tennessee State Univ, Johnson City, TN 37614	1911	$4,637 (S)	$5,024	5-D	12,390	784

Name, address	Year Founded	Tuition & Fees	Rm. & Board	Control, Degree	Enrollment	Faculty
East Texas Baptist Univ, Marshall, TX 75670-1498	1912	$13,700	$4,190	2-B	1,365	102
Eastern Connecticut State Univ, Willimantic, CT 06226-2295.	1889	$6,442 (S)	$8,020	5-M	5,239	404
Eastern Illinois Univ, Charleston, IL 61920-3099	1895	$7,069	$6,660	5-M	12,349	770
Eastern Kentucky Univ, Richmond, KY 40475-3102	1906	$5,192 (S)	$5,392	5-M	15,763	948
Eastern Mennonite Univ, Harrisonburg, VA 22802-2462.	1917	$20,712	$6,550	2-F	1,324	163
Eastern Michigan Univ, Ypsilanti, MI 48197	1849	$6,935 (S)	$6,610	5-D	22,821	1,242
Eastern Nazarene Coll, Quincy, MA 02170-2999	1918	$20,574	$7,395	2-M	1,212	48
Eastern New Mexico Univ, Portales, NM 88130	1934	$2,964 (S)	$4,568	5-M	4,033	263
Eastern Oregon Univ, La Grande, OR 97850-2899	1929	$5,829 (S)	$7,776	5-M	3,425	117
Eastern Univ, St. Davids, PA 19087-3696.	1952	$21,350	$8,350	2-M	3,918	343
Eastern Washington Univ, Cheney, WA 99004-2431	1882	$4,565 (S)	$6,182	5-D	11,161	NA
East-West Univ, Chicago, IL 60605-2103	1978	$12,645	NA	1-B	1,040	70
Eckerd Coll, St. Petersburg, FL 33711	1958	$27,618	$7,868	2-B	1,845	167
Edgewood Coll, Madison, WI 53711-1997	1927	$19,080	$6,535	2-D	2,565	270
Edinboro Univ of Pennsylvania, Edinboro, PA 16444	1857	$6,484 (S)	$5,718	5-M	7,579	403
Elizabeth City State Univ, Elizabeth City, NC 27909-7806	1891	$3,223 (S)	$4,709	5-M	2,470	216
Elizabethtown Coll, Elizabethtown, PA 17022-2298	1899	$29,000	$7,600	2-M	2,366	215
Elmhurst Coll, Elmhurst, IL 60126-3296	1871	$24,660	$7,164	2-M	3,107	313
Elmira Coll, Elmira, NY 14901	1855	$30,050	$9,100	1-M	1,853	99
Elms Coll, Chicopee, MA 01013-2839 (4)	1928	$21,520	$8,400	2-M	1,234	146
Elon Univ, Elon, NC 27244-2010.	1889	$20,441	$6,850	2-D	5,230	400
Embry-Riddle Aeronautical Univ Worldwide, Daytona Beach, FL 32114-3900.	1970	$4,584	NA	1-M	16,826	2,496
Embry-Riddle Aeronautical Univ, Daytona Beach, FL 32114-3900.	1926	$26,496	$9,150	1-M	4,863	328
Embry-Riddle Aeronautical Univ, Prescott, AZ 86301-3720	1978	$26,130	$7,214	1-M	1,674	124
Emerson Coll, Boston, MA 02116-4624	1880	$25,894	$10,870	1-D	4,324	378
Emmanuel Coll, Boston, MA 02115.	1919	$24,200	$10,400	2-M	2,340	271
Emory & Henry Coll, Emory, VA 24327-0947	1836	$20,860	$7,360	2-M	1,051	120
Emory Univ, Atlanta, GA 30322-1100	1836	$34,336	$11,020	2-D	12,338	1,459
Emporia State Univ, Emporia, KS 66801-5087	1863	$3,586 (S)	$5,170	5-D	6,473	284
Endicott Coll, Beverly, MA 01915-2096.	1939	$21,374	$10,254	1-M	1,721	150
Eugene Lang Coll The New School for Liberal Arts, New York, NY 10011-8601	1978	$29,210	$11,750	1-B	1,164	122
Evangel Univ, Springfield, MO 65802-2191	1955	$14,300	$5,120	2-M	1,721	156
Evergreen State Coll, Olympia, WA 98505	1967	$4,861 (S)	$7,140	5-M	4,416	232
Excelsior Coll, Albany, NY 12203-5159.	1970	$275/cr. hr.	NA	1-M	30,680	232
Fairfield Univ, Fairfield, CT 06824-5195	1942	$31,955	$9,980	2-M	5,091	450
Fairleigh Dickinson Univ, Coll at Florham, Madison, NJ 07940-1099	1942	$26,518	$9,472	1-M	3,562	304
Fairleigh Dickinson Univ, Metro Campus, Teaneck, NJ 07666-1914	1942	$24,644	$9,974	1-D	8,491	625
Fairmont State Univ, Fairmont, WV 26554	1865	$4,538 (S)	$6,052	5-M	7,417	666
Farmingdale State Coll, Farmingdale, NY 11735	1912	$5,300 (S)	$11,190	5-B	6,256	469
Fashion Inst of Tech, New York, NY 10001-5992 (4)	1944	$4,770 (S)	$11,213	11-M	10,010	908
Faulkner Univ, Montgomery, AL 36109-3398	1942	$11,565	$5,400	2-F	2,625	147
Fayetteville State Univ, Fayetteville, NC 28301-4298	1867	$3,382 (S)	$4,870	5-D	6,301	331
Felician Coll, Lodi, NJ 07644-2117	1942	$19,950	$7,432	2-M	1,992	321
Ferris State Univ, Big Rapids, MI 49307	1884	$7,342 (S)	$7,220	5-F	12,575	864
Ferrum Coll, Ferrum, VA 24088-9001	1913	$20,885	$6,900	2-B	1,060	94
Fitchburg State Coll, Fitchburg, MA 01420-2697	1894	$5,542 (S)	$6,486	5-M	5,508	259
Five Towns Coll, Dix Hills, NY 11746-6055.	1972	$17,085	$16,800	1-D	1,254	128
Flagler Coll, St. Augustine, FL 32085-1027.	1968	$11,200	$6,800	1-B	2,253	170
Florida Agr & Mech Univ, Tallahassee, FL 32307-3200	1887	$3,274 (S)	$5,956	5-D	13,064	621
Florida Atlantic Univ, Boca Raton, FL 33431-0991	1961	$3,327 (S)	$8,280	5-D	25,385	1,260
Florida Gulf Coast Univ, Fort Myers, FL 33965-6565	1991	$3,730 (S)	$7,740	5-M	8,292	490
Florida Inst of Tech, Melbourne, FL 32901-6975	1958	$27,540	$7,400	1-D	4,741	416
Florida Intl Univ, Miami, FL 33199	1965	$3,130 (S)	$9,740	5-D	37,997	1,495
Florida Metro Univ–North Orlando Campus, Orlando, FL 32810-5674	1953	$10,440	NA	3-M	1,498	96
Florida Metro Univ–Pinellas Campus, Clearwater, FL 33759	1890	$15,120	NA	3-M	1,201	44
Florida Metro Univ–Pompano Beach Campus, Pompano Beach, FL 33062	1940	$28,884	NA	3-M	1,377	61
Florida Metro Univ–South Orlando Campus, Orlando, FL 32819	1987	$9,900	NA	3-M	1,964	77
Florida Metro Univ–Tampa Campus, Tampa, FL 33614-5899	1890	$9,900	NA	3-M	1,390	83
Florida Southern Coll, Lakeland, FL 33801-5698	1885	$21,190	$7,500	2-M	1,873	180
Florida State Univ, Tallahassee, FL 32306	1851	$3,307 (S)	$7,078	5-D	39,973	1,654
Fontbonne Univ, St. Louis, MO 63105-3098	1917	$17,440	$6,357	2-M	2,924	339
Fordham Univ, New York, NY 10458	1841	$30,655	$11,630	2-D	14,732	NA
Fort Hays State Univ, Hays, KS 67601-4099	1902	$3,192 (S)	$5,553	5-M	7,403	291
Fort Lewis Coll, Durango, CO 81301-3999	1911	$5,973 (S)	$6,468	5-B	3,907	240
Fort Valley State Univ, Fort Valley, GA 31030-4313	1895	$3,856 (S)	$4,720	5-M	2,174	121
Framingham State Coll, Framingham, MA 01701-9101	1839	$5,449 (S)	$6,699	5-M	5,861	230
Francis Marion Univ, Florence, SC 29501-0547	1970	$7,038 (S)	$5,860	5-M	4,075	272
Franciscan Univ of Steubenville, Steubenville, OH 43952-1763	1946	$18,250	$6,300	2-M	2,387	189
Franklin & Marshall Coll, Lancaster, PA 17604-3003	1787	$34,450	$8,540	1-B	2,028	228
Franklin Coll, Franklin, IN 46131-2623	1834	$20,325	$5,970	2-B	1,013	115
Franklin Pierce Univ, Rindge, NH 03461-0060	1962	$25,300	$8,200	1-B	1,704	150
Franklin Univ, Columbus, OH 43215-5399	1902	$7,620	NA	1-M	6,823	599
Freed-Hardeman Univ, Henderson, TN 38340-2399.	1869	$13,192	$6,560	2-M	1,969	148
Fresno Pacific Univ, Fresno, CA 93702-4709	1944	$20,790	$5,990	2-M	2,324	238
Friends Univ, Wichita, KS 67213.	1898	NA	NA	1-M	3,190	225
Frostburg State Univ, Frostburg, MD 21532-1099.	1898	$6,550 (S)	$6,746	5-M	4,910	352
Furman Univ, Greenville, SC 29613	1826	$28,840	$7,552	1-M	3,010	274
Gallaudet Univ, Washington, DC 20002-3625.	1864	$10,250	$8,500	1-D	1,834	230
Gannon Univ, Erie, PA 16541-0001	1925	$19,996	$7,880	2-D	3,815	312
Gardner-Webb Univ, Boiling Springs, NC 28017.	1905	$17,590	$5,740	2-D	3,840	339
Geneva Coll, Beaver Falls, PA 15010-3599	1848	$19,430	$7,200	2-M	1,952	210
George Fox Univ, Newberg, OR 97132-2697	1891	$23,790	$7,600	2-D	3,252	324
George Mason Univ, Fairfax, VA 22030	1957	$6,408 (S)	$6,750	5-D	29,889	2,038
George Washington Univ, Washington, DC 20052	1821	$39,240	$11,520	1-D	24,531	2,062
Georgetown Coll, Georgetown, KY 40324-1696	1829	$22,360	$6,380	2-M	1,910	160
Georgetown Univ, Washington, DC 20057	1789	$35,568	$12,146	2-D	14,148	1,215
Georgia Coll & State Univ, Milledgeville, GA 31061	1889	$4,424 (S)	$7,116	5-M	6,041	405
Georgia Inst of Tech, Atlanta, GA 30332-0001	1885	$4,926 (S)	$7,094	5-D	17,936	859
Georgia Southern Univ, Statesboro, GA 30460	1906	$4,082 (S)	$6,860	5-D	16,425	738
Georgia Southwestern State Univ, Americus, GA 31709-4693.	1906	$3,162 (S)	$4,956	5-M	2,457	143
Georgia State Univ, Atlanta, GA 30303-3083	1913	$4,746 (S)	$7,264	5-D	26,134	1,514
Georgian Court Univ, Lakewood, NJ 08701-2697.	1908	$20,632	$7,800	2-M	3,047	294
Gettysburg Coll, Gettysburg, PA 17325-1483	1832	$34,050	$8,260	2-B	2,689	284
Glenville State Coll, Glenville, WV 26351-1200.	1872	$4,042 (S)	$5,370	5-B	1,381	79
Global Univ of the Assemblies of God, Springfield, MO 65804	1948	$2,376	NA	2-F	5,033	605

Name, address	Year Founded	Tuition & Fees	Rm. & Board	Control, Degree	Enrollment	Faculty
Globe Inst of Tech, New York, NY 10007	NA	$9,086	$3,600	3-B	1,671	113
Golden Gate Univ, San Francisco, CA 94105-2968	1901	$11,520	NA	1-D	3,891	489
Goldey-Beacom Coll, Wilmington, DE 19808-1999	1886	$17,510	$4,600	1-M	1,223	44
Gonzaga Univ, Spokane, WA 99258	1887	$25,012	$7,220	2-D	6,610	639
Gordon Coll, Wenham, MA 01984-1899	1889	$24,278	$6,640	2-M	1,660	145
Goucher Coll, Baltimore, MD 21204-2794	1885	$29,325	$8,925	1-M	2,310	226
Governors State Univ, University Park, IL 60466-0975	1969	$4,492 (S)	NA	5-M	5,405	212
Grace Coll, Winona Lake, IN 46590-1294	1948	$17,350	$6,360	2-D	1,291	53
Graceland Univ, Lamoni, IA 50140	1895	$17,900	$6,000	2-M	2,116	111
Grambling State Univ, Grambling, LA 71245	1901	$3,606 (S)	$4,718	5-D	5,065	284
Grand Canyon Univ, Phoenix, AZ 85017-1097	1949	$14,420	$7,500	2-M	10,297	1,683
Grand Valley State Univ, Allendale, MI 49401-9403	1960	$6,588 (S)	$6,600	5-M	23,295	1,414
Grand View Coll, Des Moines, IA 50316-1599	1896	$16,940	$5,596	2-B	1,707	174
Granite State Coll, Concord, NH 03301	1972	$5,187 (S)	NA	11-B	1,553	398
Grantham Univ, Kansas City, MO 64153	1951	$6,360	NA	3-M	9,500	NA
Greensboro Coll, Greensboro, NC 27401-1875	1838	$19,470	$7,400	2-M	1,226	125
Greenville Coll, Greenville, IL 62246-0159	1892	$17,932	$6,136	2-M	1,451	152
Grinnell Coll, Grinnell, IA 50112-1690	1846	$29,030	$7,700	1-B	1,589	201
Grove City Coll, Grove City, PA 16127-2104	1876	$10,962	$5,766	2-B	2,489	189
Guilford Coll, Greensboro, NC 27410-4173	1837	$23,020	$6,690	2-B	2,687	210
Gustavus Adolphus Coll, St. Peter, MN 56082-1498	1862	$28,515	$4,275	2-B	2,618	267
Gwynedd-Mercy Coll, Gwynedd Valley, PA 19437-0901	1948	$21,000	$8,600	2-M	2,727	259
Hamilton Coll, Clinton, NY 13323-1296	1812	$34,980	$8,910	1-B	1,821	213
Hamline Univ, St. Paul, MN 55104-1284	1854	$25,040	$7,280	2-D	4,575	481
Hampden-Sydney Coll, Hampden-Sydney, VA 23943 (1)	1776	$27,732	$8,671	2-B	1,106	112
Hampshire Coll, Amherst, MA 01002	1965	$34,605	$9,030	1-B	1,448	149
Hampton Univ, Hampton, VA 23668	1868	$14,818	$6,746	1-D	6,152	447
Hannibal-LaGrange Coll, Hannibal, MO 63401-1999	1858	$12,608	$4,930	2-B	1,091	99
Harding Univ, Searcy, AR 72149-0001	1924	$11,650	$5,442	2-M	6,085	391
Hardin-Simmons Univ, Abilene, TX 79698-0001	1891	$16,946	$4,950	2-D	2,372	184
Harrington Coll of Design, Chicago, IL 60606 (4)	1931	$20,520	$2,600	3-B	1,563	142
Harris-Stowe State Univ, St. Louis, MO 63103-2136	1857	$5,210 (S)	$4,950	5-B	1,868	107
Hartwick Coll, Oneonta, NY 13820-4020	1797	$28,030	$7,910	1-B	1,519	169
Harvard Univ, Cambridge, MA 02138	1636	$33,709	$9,946	1-D	19,538	2,035
Haskell Indian Nations Univ, Lawrence, KS 66046-4800	1884	$420 (S)	NA	4-B	1,028	48
Hastings Coll, Hastings, NE 68901-7696	1882	$18,302	$5,148	2-M	1,137	128
Haverford Coll, Haverford, PA 19041-1392	1833	$33,710	$10,390	1-B	1,168	128
Hawai`i Pacific Univ, Honolulu, HI 96813-2785	1965	$13,080	$10,560	1-M	8,080	618
Heidelberg Coll, Tiffin, OH 44883-2462	1850	$18,618	$7,902	2-M	1,569	159
Henderson State Univ, Arkadelphia, AR 71999-0001	1890	$4,230 (S)	$4,176	5-M	3,664	229
Hendrix Coll, Conway, AR 72032-3080	1876	$22,916	$6,738	2-M	1,095	126
Heritage Univ, Toppenish, WA 98948-9599	1982	$9,645	NA	1-M	1,311	187
High Point Univ, High Point, NC 27262-3598	1924	$19,850	$7,960	2-M	2,811	267
Hilbert Coll, Hamburg, NY 14075-1597	1957	$15,700	$5,900	1-B	1,064	119
Hillsdale Coll, Hillsdale, MI 49242-1298	1844	$18,260	$7,030	1-B	1,346	149
Hiram Coll, Hiram, OH 44234-0067	1850	$24,885	$7,781	2-M	1,239	103
Hobart & William Smith Colleges, Geneva, NY 14456-3397	1822	$34,688	$8,828	1-B	1,883	185
Hodges Univ, Naples, FL 34119	1990	$13,130	NA	1-M	1,640	111
Hofstra Univ, Hempstead, NY 11549	1935	$24,830	$9,800	1-D	12,550	1,206
Hollins Univ, Roanoke, VA 24020-1603	1842	$24,325	$8,650	1-M	1,061	101
Holy Family Univ, Philadelphia, PA 19114-2094	1954	$18,850	$8,300	2-M	2,670	258
Holy Names Univ, Oakland, CA 94619-1699 (4)	1868	$22,710	$8,000	2-M	1,048	136
Hood Coll, Frederick, MD 21701-8575	1893	$23,655	$8,135	1-M	2,248	238
Hope Coll, Holland, MI 49422-9000	1866	$22,570	$6,982	2-B	3,203	322
Houghton Coll, Houghton, NY 14744	1883	$20,400	$6,680	2-M	1,432	126
Houston Baptist Univ, Houston, TX 77074-3298	1960	$17,716	$4,995	2-M	2,143	177
Howard Payne Univ, Brownwood, TX 76801-2715	1889	$15,515	$2,256	2-B	1,328	146
Howard Univ, Washington, DC 20059-0002	1867	$12,295	$6,186	1-D	10,623	1,576
Humboldt State Univ, Arcata, CA 95521-8299	1913	NA	NA	5-M	7,435	551
Hunter Coll of the City Univ of New York, New York, NY 10021-5085	1870	$4,349 (S)	$5,083	11-M	20,899	1,497
Huntington Univ, Huntington, IN 46750-1299	1897	$19,430	$6,730	2-M	1,084	84
Husson Coll, Bangor, ME 04401-2999	1898	$11,770	$6,240	1-M	2,242	58
Idaho State Univ, Pocatello, ID 83209	1901	$4,190 (S)	$4,950	5-D	12,679	908
Illinois Coll, Jacksonville, IL 62650-2299	1829	$17,100	$6,730	2-B	1,023	90
Illinois Inst of Art–Chicago, Chicago, IL 60654	1916	$20,284	$11,512	3-B	2,680	175
Illinois Inst of Art–Schaumburg, Schaumburg, IL 60173	NA	$18,675	NA	3-B	1,213	72
Illinois Inst of Tech, Chicago, IL 60616-3793	1890	$24,113	$8,049	1-D	6,795	631
Illinois State Univ, Normal, IL 61790-2200	1857	$8,040 (S)	$6,148	5-D	20,521	1,113
Illinois Wesleyan Univ, Bloomington, IL 61702-2900	1850	$30,750	$7,030	1-B	2,144	224
Immaculata Univ, Immaculata, PA 19345 (4)	1920	$22,650	$9,800	2-D	4,067	397
Indiana State Univ, Terre Haute, IN 47809-1401	1865	$6,436 (S)	$6,294	5-D	10,568	641
Indiana Tech, Fort Wayne, IN 46803-1297	1930	$19,460	$7,300	1-M	3,405	251
Indiana Univ Bloomington, Bloomington, IN 47405-7000	1820	$7,460 (S)	$6,352	5-D	38,247	2,233
Indiana Univ East, Richmond, IN 47374-1289	1971	$5,040 (S)	NA	5-B	2,246	186
Indiana Univ Kokomo, Kokomo, IN 46904-9003	1945	$5,072 (S)	NA	5-M	2,734	174
Indiana Univ Northwest, Gary, IN 46408-1197	1959	$5,142 (S)	NA	5-M	4,819	367
Indiana Univ of Pennsylvania, Indiana, PA 15705-1087	1875	$6,390 (S)	$5,162	5-D	14,248	733
Indiana Univ South Bend, South Bend, IN 46634-7111	1922	$5,232 (S)	NA	5-M	7,420	523
Indiana Univ Southeast, New Albany, IN 47150-6405	1941	$5,118 (S)	NA	5-M	6,183	425
Indiana Univ–Purdue Univ Fort Wayne, Fort Wayne, IN 46805-1499	1917	$5,437 (S)	$4,940	5-M	11,672	798
Indiana Univ–Purdue Univ Indianapolis, Indianapolis, IN 46202-2896	1969	$6,524 (S)	$4,834	5-D	29,764	3,091
Indiana Wesleyan Univ, Marion, IN 46953-4974	1920	$18,284	$6,368	2-D	2,935	265
Inter American Univ of Puerto Rico, Aguadilla Campus, Aguadilla, PR 00605	1957	$3,784	NA	1-M	4,297	254
Inter American Univ of Puerto Rico, Arecibo Campus, Arecibo, PR 00614-4050	1957	$4,636	NA	1-M	4,761	234
Inter American Univ of Puerto Rico, Barranquitas Campus, Barranquitas, PR 00794	1957	$4,770	NA	1-B	2,399	134
Inter American Univ of Puerto Rico, Bayamón Campus, Bayamón, PR 00957	1912	$3,772	NA	1-M	5,045	320
Inter American Univ of Puerto Rico, Fajardo Campus, Fajardo, PR 00738-7003	1965	$4,624	NA	1-M	2,234	193
Inter American Univ of Puerto Rico, Guayama Campus, Guayama, PR 00785	1958	$3,896	NA	1-M	2,270	139
Inter American Univ of Puerto Rico, Metro Campus, San Juan, PR 00919-1293	1960	$3,836	NA	1-D	10,451	599
Inter American Univ of Puerto Rico, Ponce Campus, Mercedita, PR 00715-1602	1962	$4,756	NA	1-M	5,327	257
Inter American Univ of Puerto Rico, San Germán Campus, San Germán, PR 00683-5008	1912	$4,638	$2,400	1-D	5,960	325
Intl Acad of Design & Tech, Chicago, IL 60602-9736	1977	$23,000	NA	3-B	2,341	166
Intl Acad of Design & Tech, Tampa, FL 33634-7350	1984	$385/cr. hr.	NA	3	2,405	167
Iona Coll, New Rochelle, NY 10801-1890	1940	$23,218	$9,998	2-M	4,242	382
Iowa State Univ of Sci & Tech, Ames, IA 50011	1858	$6,161 (S)	NA	5-D	25,462	1,622

Name, address	Year Founded	Tuition & Fees		Rm. & Board	Control, Degree	Enrollment	Faculty
Ithaca Coll, Ithaca, NY 14850-7020.	1892	$26,832		$10,314	1-D	6,409	670
Jackson State Univ, Jackson, MS 39217	1877	$4,224	(S)	$5,212	5-D	8,256	474
Jacksonville State Univ, Jacksonville, AL 36265-1602	1883	$5,070	(S)	$3,764	5-M	8,957	450
Jacksonville Univ, Jacksonville, FL 32211-3394	1934	$21,200		$6,780	1-M	3,093	232
James Madison Univ, Harrisonburg, VA 22807	1908	$6,290	(S)	$6,756	5-D	17,393	1,131
John Brown Univ, Siloam Springs, AR 72761-2121	1919	$16,158		$5,956	2-M	1,882	145
John Carroll Univ, University Heights, OH 44118-4581.	1886	$25,072		$7,790	2-M	4,101	409
John F. Kennedy Univ, Pleasant Hill, CA 94523-4817	1964	NA		NA	1-D	1,653	728
John Jay Coll of Criminal Justice of the City Univ of New York, New York, NY 10019-1093	1964	$4,259	(S)	NA	11-D	14,051	913
Johns Hopkins Univ, Baltimore, MD 21218-2699	1876	$33,900		$10,622	1-D	6,124	NA
Johnson & Wales Univ, Charlotte, NC 28202	2004	$21,462		$8,550	1-B	2,493	108
Johnson & Wales Univ, Denver, CO 80220	1993	$21,462		$8,550	1-B	1,543	78
Johnson & Wales Univ, North Miami, FL 33181	1992	$21,460		$9,600	1-B	2,215	86
Johnson & Wales Univ, Providence, RI 02903-3703.	1914	$21,462		$7,650	1-D	10,310	417
Johnson C. Smith Univ, Charlotte, NC 28216-5398	1867	$15,004		$5,840	1-B	1,470	131
Johnson State Coll, Johnson, VT 05656-9405	1828	$7,625	(S)	$7,745	5-M	1,866	143
Jones Intl Univ, Centennial, CO 80112	1995	$10,200		NA	3-M	1,411	60
Judson Coll, Elgin, IL 60123-1498.	1963	$20,420		$7,200	2-M	1,243	133
Juniata Coll, Huntingdon, PA 16652-2119	1876	$28,920		$8,040	2-B	1,460	130
Kalamazoo Coll, Kalamazoo, MI 49006-3295	1833	$27,054		$6,915	2-B	1,345	113
Kansas State Univ, Manhattan, KS 66506	1863	$5,434	(S)	$5,912	5-D	23,141	1,047
Kean Univ, Union, NJ 07083	1855	$8,036	(S)	$8,880	5-M	13,050	1,222
Keene State Coll, Keene, NH 03435	1909	$7,822	(S)	$7,026	5-M	4,940	405
Keiser Univ, Fort Lauderdale, FL 33309	1977	NA		NA	3-B	6,121	495
Kennesaw State Univ, Kennesaw, GA 30144-5591	1963	$3,266	(S)	$4,620	5-M	19,854	1,003
Kent State Univ, Kent, OH 44242-0001.	1910	$8,430	(S)	$6,880	5-D	22,697	1,449
Kentucky State Univ, Frankfort, KY 40601	1886	$5,378	(S)	$6,272	12-M	2,500	192
Kenyon Coll, Gambier, OH 43022-9623	1824	$36,050		$5,900	1-B	1,661	186
Kettering Univ, Flint, MI 48504-4898.	1919	$24,908		$5,690	1-M	2,809	146
Keuka Coll, Keuka Park, NY 14478-0098	1890	$19,120		$8,210	2-M	1,521	91
King Coll, Bristol, TN 37620-2699	1867	$19,262		$6,508	2-M	1,271	122
King's Coll, Wilkes-Barre, PA 18711-0801	1946	$22,280		$8,590	2-M	2,386	197
Knox Coll, Galesburg, IL 61401.	1837	$27,900		$5,925	1-B	1,351	127
Kutztown Univ of Pennsylvania, Kutztown, PA 19530-0730	1866	$6,619	(S)	$6,208	5-M	10,193	501
La Roche Coll, Pittsburgh, PA 15237-5898.	1963	$18,220		$7,564	2-M	1,533	191
La Salle Univ, Philadelphia, PA 19141-1199.	1863	$27,810		$10,300	2-D	6,191	371
La Sierra Univ, Riverside, CA 92515.	1922	$21,846		$6,330	2-D	1,896	178
Lafayette Coll, Easton, PA 18042-1798	1826	$33,811		$10,377	2-B	2,381	236
LaGrange Coll, LaGrange, GA 30240-2999	1831	$18,575		$7,598	2-M	1,136	126
Lake Forest Coll, Lake Forest, IL 60045-2399	1857	$29,164		$6,960	1-M	1,448	155
Lake Superior State Univ, Sault Sainte Marie, MI 49783	1946	$6,698	(S)	$6,836	5-M	2,919	202
Lakeland Coll, Sheboygan, WI 53082-0359	1862	$17,595		$6,145	2-M	4,047	71
Lamar Univ, Beaumont, TX 77710	1923	$4,080	(S)	$5,888	5-D	10,595	542
Lander Univ, Greenwood, SC 29649-2099	1872	$7,472	(S)	$5,554	5-M	2,682	190
Lane Coll, Jackson, TN 38301-4598	1882	$7,620		$5,000	2-B	1,370	58
Lasell Coll, Newton, MA 02466-2709	1851	$20,900		$9,200	1-M	1,253	162
Lawrence Tech Univ, Southfield, MI 48075-1058	1932	$19,443		$7,266	1-D	4,049	375
Lawrence Univ, Appleton, WI 54912-0599	1847	$29,598		$6,882	1-B	1,480	182
Le Moyne Coll, Syracuse, NY 13214.	1946	$22,580		$8,620	2-M	3,536	338
Lebanon Valley Coll, Annville, PA 17003-1400.	1866	$26,385		$7,115	2-F	1,961	187
Lee Univ, Cleveland, TN 37320-3450	1918	$10,258		$5,024	2-M	4,012	320
Lehigh Univ, Bethlehem, PA 18015-3094	1865	$33,770		$8,920	1-D	6,858	614
Lehman Coll of the City Univ of New York, Bronx, NY 10468-1589	1931	$4,290	(S)	NA	11-M	10,814	881
Lenoir-Rhyne Coll, Hickory, NC 28603	1891	$20,180		$7,230	2-M	1,579	146
Lesley Univ, Cambridge, MA 02138-2790.	1909	$25,850		$12,100	1-D	6,539	212
LeTourneau Univ, Longview, TX 75607-7001.	1946	$16,920		$6,570	2-M	3,975	352
Lewis & Clark Coll, Portland, OR 97219-7899.	1867	$29,772		$8,048	1-D	3,641	376
Lewis Univ, Romeoville, IL 60446	1932	$20,450		$7,800	2-D	5,289	499
Lewis-Clark State Coll, Lewiston, ID 83501-2698	1893	$3,897	(S)	$4,670	5-B	3,394	NA
Liberty Univ, Lynchburg, VA 24502.	1971	$15,800		$5,400	2-D	17,606	701
Life Univ, Marietta, GA 30060-2903	1974	$5,823		$12,000	1-F	1,662	128
Lincoln Memorial Univ, Harrogate, TN 37752-1901	1897	$14,400		NA	1-M	2,981	162
Lincoln Univ, Jefferson City, MO 65102	1866	$5,123	(S)	$3,990	5-M	3,224	199
Lincoln Univ, Lincoln University, PA 19352	1854	$7,892	(S)	$7,142	12-M	2,423	193
Lindenwood Univ, St. Charles, MO 63301-1695	1827	$12,700		$6,200	2-M	9,525	453
Lindsey Wilson Coll, Columbia, KY 42728-1298.	1903	$15,806		$6,540	2-M	1,832	120
Linfield Coll, McMinnville, OR 97128-6894	1849	$24,174		$7,080	2-B	1,754	181
Lipscomb Univ, Nashville, TN 37204-3951.	1891	$15,566		$6,730	2-F	2,563	260
Lock Haven Univ of Pennsylvania, Lock Haven, PA 17745-2390	1870	$6,445	(S)	$6,060	5-M	5,175	256
Logan Univ-Coll of Chiropractic, Chesterfield, MO 63006-1065	1935	$3,750		NA	1-F	1,098	85
Loma Linda Univ, Loma Linda, CA 92350.	1905	$27,320		$2,460	2-D	3,972	155
Long Island Univ, Brentwood Campus, Brentwood, NY 11717.	1959	$651/credit		NA	1-M	1,115	110
Long Island Univ, Brooklyn Campus, Brooklyn, NY 11201-8423	1926	$24,328		$7,810	1-D	8,144	954
Long Island Univ, C.W. Post Campus, Brookville, NY 11548-1300.	1954	$25,770		$9,430	1-D	8,494	834
Longwood Univ, Farmville, VA 23909	1839	$7,589	(S)	$6,058	5-M	4,479	242
Loras Coll, Dubuque, IA 52004-0178	1839	$22,053		$6,305	2-M	1,673	162
Louisiana Coll, Pineville, LA 71359-0001	1906	$10,840		$4,112	2-B	1,085	92
Louisiana State Univ & Agr & Mech Coll, Baton Rouge, LA 70803	1860	$4,449	(S)	$6,498	5-D	29,925	1,422
Louisiana State Univ Health Sci Ctr, New Orleans, LA 70112-2223	1931	NA		NA	5-D	2,240	1,380
Louisiana State Univ in Shreveport, Shreveport, LA 71115-2399	1965	$3,595	(S)	NA	5-M	4,023	227
Louisiana Tech Univ, Ruston, LA 71272	1894	$4,502	(S)	$4,365	5-D	11,203	492
Lourdes Coll, Sylvania, OH 43560-2898	1958	$13,200		NA	2-M	1,881	178
Loyola Coll in Maryland, Baltimore, MD 21210-2699	1852	$31,715		$9,578	2-D	6,035	552
Loyola Marymount Univ, Los Angeles, CA 90045-2659	1911	$29,834		$11,290	2-D	8,903	1,154
Loyola Univ Chicago, Chicago, IL 60611-2196	1870	$27,966		$9,930	2-D	15,194	1,143
Loyola Univ New Orleans, New Orleans, LA 70118-6195.	1912	$26,508		$9,150	2-F	4,604	396
Lubbock Christian Univ, Lubbock, TX 79407-2099.	1957	$14,290		$4,750	2-F	2,076	154
Luther Coll, Decorah, IA 52101-1045	1861	$26,380		$4,290	2-B	2,504	246
Luther Rice Univ, Lithonia, GA 30038-2454	1962	$4,800		NA	2-D	1,600	33
Lycoming Coll, Williamsport, PA 17701-5192	1812	$25,605		$6,826	2-B	1,430	131
Lynchburg Coll, Lynchburg, VA 24501-3199.	1903	$25,265		$7,000	2-M	2,398	229
Lyndon State Coll, Lyndonville, VT 05851-0919	1911	$6,828	(S)	$6,942	5-M	1,412	162
Lynn Univ, Boca Raton, FL 33431-5598	1962	$28,850		$9,650	1-D	2,715	238
Macalester Coll, St. Paul, MN 55105-1899	1874	$33,694		$8,220	2-B	1,918	215
Macon State Coll, Macon, GA 31206	1968	$1,792	(S)	NA	5-B	6,244	293

Name, address	Year Founded	Tuition & Fees		Rm. & Board	Control, Degree	Enrollment	Faculty
Madonna Univ, Livonia, MI 48150-1173	1947	$10,960		$5,946	2-M	4,156	368
Malone Coll, Canton, OH 44709-3897	1892	$17,790		$6,400	2-M	2,296	209
Manchester Coll, North Manchester, IN 46962-1225	1889	$21,700		$7,450	2-M	1,056	90
Manhattan Coll, Riverdale, NY 10471	1853	$21,550		$9,325	2-M	3,357	331
Manhattanville Coll, Purchase, NY 10577-2132	1841	$30,776		$12,240	1-M	2,974	288
Mansfield Univ of Pennsylvania, Mansfield, PA 16933	1857	$6,676	(S)	$5,934	5-M	3,360	227
Marian Coll of Fond du Lac, Fond du Lac, WI 54935-4699	1936	$17,625		$5,200	2-D	3,040	278
Marian Coll, Indianapolis, IN 46222-1997	1851	$20,800		$7,100	2-M	1,796	138
Marietta Coll, Marietta, OH 45750-4000	1835	$23,815		$7,030	1-M	1,530	139
Marist Coll, Poughkeepsie, NY 12601-1387	1929	$22,576		$9,790	1-M	5,877	610
Marquette Univ, Milwaukee, WI 53201-1881	1881	$25,074		$8,120	2-D	11,548	1,054
Mars Hill Coll, Mars Hill, NC 28754	1856	$17,950		$6,206	2-B	1,378	144
Marshall Univ, Huntington, WV 25755	1837	$4,150	(S)	$6,492	5-D	13,936	749
Mary Baldwin Coll, Staunton, VA 24401-3610 (4)	1842	$21,450		$6,100	1-M	1,755	137
Marygrove Coll, Detroit, MI 48221-2599 (4)	1905	$13,960		$6,400	2-M	2,953	64
Maryland Inst Coll of Art, Baltimore, MD 21217	1826	$28,670		$7,910	4-M	1,866	294
Marylhurst Univ, Marylhurst, OR 97036-0261	1893	$14,220		NA	2-M	1,249	228
Marymount Manhattan Coll, New York, NY 10021-4597	1936	$19,638		$12,090	1-B	1,938	308
Marymount Univ, Arlington, VA 22207-4299	1950	$19,199		$8,212	2-D	3,604	350
Maryville Coll, Maryville, TN 37804-5907	1819	$23,800		$7,400	2-B	1,155	113
Maryville Univ of Saint Louis, St. Louis, MO 63141-7299	1872	$18,120		$7,720	1-D	3,333	355
Marywood Univ, Scranton, PA 18509-1598	1915	$24,090		$10,410	2-D	3,180	307
Massachusetts Coll of Art, Boston, MA 02115-5882	1873	$7,200	(S)	$11,090	5-M	2,286	209
Massachusetts Coll of Liberal Arts, North Adams, MA 01247-4100	1894	$6,326	(S)	$6,542	5-M	1,805	178
Massachusetts Coll of Pharmacy & Health Sci, Boston, MA 02115-5896	1823	$21,880		$11,300	1-D	3,298	176
Massachusetts Inst of Tech, Cambridge, MA 02139-4307	1861	$33,600		$9,950	1-D	10,253	1,613
Massachusetts Maritime Acad, Buzzards Bay, MA 02532-1803 (2)	1891	$5,466	(A)	$6,935	5-M	1,008	70
Master's Coll & Seminary, Santa Clarita, CA 91321-1200	1927	$20,770		$6,900	2-D	1,521	188
McDaniel Coll, Westminster, MD 21157-4390	1867	$27,280		$5,900	1-M	3,671	201
McKendree Coll, Lebanon, IL 62254-1299	1828	$18,900		$7,380	2-M	3,212	215
McMurry Univ, Abilene, TX 79697	1923	$16,300		$6,425	2-B	1,385	132
McNeese State Univ, Lake Charles, LA 70609	1939	$3,246	(S)	$4,450	5-M	8,343	392
Medaille Coll, Buffalo, NY 14214-2695	1875	$15,780		$8,024	1-M	2,971	411
Medgar Evers Coll of the City Univ of New York, Brooklyn, NY 11225-2298	1969	$4,230	(S)	NA	11-B	5,562	416
Medical Coll of Georgia, Augusta, GA 30912	1828	$4,288	(S)	$2,556	5-D	2,227	790
Medical Univ of South Carolina, Charleston, SC 29425-0002	1824	NA		NA	5-D	2,428	1,281
Mercer Univ, Macon, GA 31207-0003	1833	$25,256		$7,710	2-D	5,090	591
Mercy Coll, Dobbs Ferry, NY 10522-1189	1951	$14,170		NA	1-M	9,120	800
Mercyhurst Coll, Erie, PA 16546	1926	$20,364		$7,458	2-M	4,155	296
Meredith Coll, Raleigh, NC 27607-5298	1891	$21,200		$5,940	1-M	2,139	281
Merrimack Coll, North Andover, MA 01845-5800	1947	$27,070		$10,755	2-M	2,251	208
Mesa State Coll, Grand Junction, CO 81501-3122	1925	$3,840	(S)	$7,214	5-M	5,938	396
Messiah Coll, Grantham, PA 17027	1909	$23,290		$7,060	2-B	2,854	284
Methodist Univ, Fayetteville, NC 28311-1498	1956	$20,080		$7,550	2-M	2,082	212
Metro Coll of New York, New York, NY 10013-1919 (4)	1964	$16,460		NA	1-M	1,238	224
Metro State Coll of Denver, Denver, CO 80217-3362	1963	$3,431	(S)	NA	5-B	20,761	1,141
Metro State Univ, St. Paul, MN 55106-5000	1971	$5,082	(S)	NA	5-M	6,543	509
Miami Intl Univ of Art & Design, Miami, FL 33132-1418	1965	$18,960		$6,150	3-M	1,406	110
Miami Univ, Oxford, OH 45056	1809	$10,502	(S)	$8,140	12-D	16,329	1,272
Michigan State Univ, East Lansing, MI 48824	1855	$8,843	(S)	$6,044	5-D	45,520	2,910
Michigan Tech Univ, Houghton, MI 49931-1295	1885	$8,910	(S)	$6,840	5-D	6,550	489
MidAmerica Nazarene Univ, Olathe, KS 66062-1899	1966	$15,968		$5,830	2-M	1,779	173
Mid-Continent Univ, Mayfield, KY 42066-9007	1949	$12,050		$6,000	2-B	1,169	71
Middle Tennessee State Univ, Murfreesboro, TN 37132	1911	$4,670	(S)	$5,626	5-D	22,863	NA
Middlebury Coll, Middlebury, VT 05753-6002	1800	$44,330	(C)	NA	1-D	2,406	307
Midway Coll, Midway, KY 40347-1120 (3)	1847	$14,850		$6,000	2-B	1,316	138
Midwestern State Univ, Wichita Falls, TX 76308	1922	$4,716	(S)	$5,220	5-M	6,042	314
Midwestern Univ, Glendale Campus, Glendale, AZ 85308	1996	$15,556		$8,785	1-D	1,117	NA
Miles Coll, Birmingham, AL 35208	1905	$6,410		$5,200	2-B	1,738	147
Millersville Univ of Pennsylvania, Millersville, PA 17551-0302	1855	$6,398	(S)	$6,566	5-M	8,194	433
Millikin Univ, Decatur, IL 62522-2084	1901	$23,845		$7,210	2-M	2,488	267
Mills Coll, Oakland, CA 94613-1000	1852	$33,024		$10,240	1-D	1,410	189
Millsaps Coll, Jackson, MS 39210-0001	1890	$23,352		$8,368	2-M	1,084	99
Milwaukee School of Engineering, Milwaukee, WI 53202-3109	1903	$25,980		$6,501	1-M	2,427	224
Minnesota State Univ Mankato, Mankato, MN 56001	1868	$5,840	(S)	$5,099	5-M	14,148	717
Minnesota State Univ Moorhead, Moorhead, MN 56563-0002	1885	$5,721	(S)	$5,420	5-M	7,652	303
Minot State Univ, Minot, ND 58707-0002	1913	$4,492	(S)	$5,294	5-M	3,712	278
Mississippi Coll, Clinton, MS 39058	1826	$12,494		$5,500	2-F	4,039	344
Mississippi State Univ, Mississippi State, MS 39762	1878	$4,596	(S)	$6,331	5-D	16,206	1,032
Mississippi Univ for Women, Columbus, MS 39701-9998 (4)	1884	NA		NA	5-M	2,328	214
Mississippi Valley State Univ, Itta Bena, MS 38941-1400	1946	$4,297	(S)	$4,242	5-M	3,132	168
Missouri Baptist Univ, St. Louis, MO 63141-8660	1964	$14,810		$5,990	2-M	4,511	191
Missouri Southern State Univ, Joplin, MO 64801-1595	1937	$4,276	(S)	$4,720	5-M	5,675	307
Missouri State Univ, Springfield, MO 65804-0094	1905	$5,738	(S)	$5,358	5-D	19,218	1,027
Missouri Valley Coll, Marshall, MO 65340-3197	1889	$15,450		$5,850	2-B	1,606	119
Missouri Western State Univ, St. Joseph, MO 64507-2294	1915	$5,168	(S)	$4,756	5-B	5,276	308
Molloy Coll, Rockville Centre, NY 11571-5002	1955	$17,310		NA	1-M	3,673	403
Monmouth Univ, West Long Branch, NJ 07764-1898	1853	$20,200		$5,750	2-M	6,399	535
Monmouth Coll, Monmouth, IL 61462-1998	1853	$21,868		$8,472	1-M	1,345	155
Monroe Coll, Bronx, NY 10468-5407	1933	$10,200		$10,120	3-M	4,361	251
Monroe Coll, New Rochelle, NY 10801-6410	1933	$9,760		$6,900	3-M	1,781	72
Montana State Univ, Bozeman, MT 59717	1893	$5,673	(S)	$6,450	5-D	12,338	805
Montana State Univ–Billings, Billings, MT 59101-0298	1927	$5,055	(S)	$4,310	5-M	4,799	286
Montana State Univ–Northern, Havre, MT 59501-7751	1929	NA		NA	5-M	1,589	103
Montana Tech of The Univ of Montana, Butte, MT 59701-8997	1895	$5,605	(S)	$5,594	5-M	2,951	149
Montclair State Univ, Montclair, NJ 07043-1624	1908	$8,404	(S)	$8,988	5-D	16,076	1,197
Montreat Coll, Montreat, NC 28757-1267	1916	$16,182		$5,258	2-M	1,039	86
Moody Bible Inst, Chicago, IL 60610-3284	1886	$2,150		$7,320	2-F	2,687	100
Moravian Coll, Bethlehem, PA 18018-6650	1742	$26,775		$7,760	2-F	1,965	196
Morehead State Univ, Morehead, KY 40351	1922	$4,870	(S)	$5,208	5-M	9,025	528
Morehouse Coll, Atlanta, GA 30314 (1)	1867	$17,982		$9,928	1-B	2,933	229
Morgan State Univ, Baltimore, MD 21251	1867	$6,204	(S)	$7,310	5-D	6,621	458
Morningside Coll, Sioux City, IA 51106	1894	$19,902		$6,227	2-M	1,722	152
Mount Aloysius Coll, Cresson, PA 16630-1999	1939	$15,350		$6,470	2-M	1,587	168
Mount Holyoke Coll, South Hadley, MA 01075 (3)	1837	$34,266		$10,040	1-M	2,153	242

Name, address	Year Founded	Tuition & Fees	Rm. & Board	Control Degree	Enroll-ment	Faculty
Mount Ida Coll, Newton, MA 02459-3310	1899	$21,330	$10,635	1-B	1,367	170
Mount Marty Coll, Yankton, SD 57078-3724	1936	$16,582	$4,958	2-M	1,220	97
Mount Mary Coll, Milwaukee, WI 53222-4597	1913	$19,204	$6,195	2-M	1,732	213
Mount Mercy Coll, Cedar Rapids, IA 52402-4797	1928	$18,930	$5,970	2-B	1,482	153
Mount Olive Coll, Mount Olive, NC 28365	1951	$13,126	$5,300	2-B	3,155	274
Mount Saint Mary Coll, Newburgh, NY 12550-3494	1960	$18,290	$9,040	1-M	2,601	215
Mount St. Mary's Coll, Los Angeles, CA 90049-1599 (4)	1925	$24,150	$8,747	2-M	2,384	327
Mount St. Mary's Univ, Emmitsburg, MD 21727-7799.	1808	$25,890	$9,130	2-F	2,186	190
Mount Union Coll, Alliance, OH 44601-3993	1846	$20,970	$6,350	2-B	2,193	226
Mount Vernon Nazarene Univ, Mount Vernon, OH 43050-9500	1964	$18,064	$5,286	2-M	2,670	244
Mountain State Univ, Beckley, WV 25802-9003	1933	$7,800	$5,636	1-M	4,420	368
Mt. Sierra Coll, Monrovia, CA 91016	1990	$12,768	NA	3-B	1,100	50
Muhlenberg Coll, Allentown, PA 18104-5586	1848	$30,715	$7,525	2-B	2,500	267
Murray State Univ, Murray, KY 42071	1922	$5,418 (S)	$5,670	5-M	10,298	590
Muskingum Coll, New Concord, OH 43762	1837	$17,380	$6,840	2-M	2,396	139
Myers Univ, Cleveland, OH 44114-4624	1848	$9,840	NA	1-M	1,177	165
Naropa Univ, Boulder, CO 80302-6697	1974	$19,426	$6,894	1-F	1,136	206
Natl Univ, La Jolla, CA 92037-1011	1971	$9,132	NA	1-M	25,992	3,195
Natl-Louis Univ, Chicago, IL 60603	1886	$17,760	NA	1-D	7,345	284
Nazareth Coll of Rochester, NY 14618-3790	1924	$21,640	$9,080	1-D	3,179	341
Nebraska Wesleyan Univ, Lincoln, NE 68504-2796	1887	$19,302	$5,165	2-M	2,068	217
Neumann Coll, Aston, PA 19014-1298	1965	$18,632	$8,418	2-M	2,969	263
Nevada State Coll at Henderson, Henderson, NV 89015	2002	$1,992 (S)	NA	5-B	1,959	141
New Coll of California, San Francisco, CA 94102-5206	1971	$13,530	NA	1-M	1,316	192
New England Coll, Henniker, NH 03242-3293	1946	$24,136	$8,456	1-M	1,340	107
New England Inst of Art, Brookline, MA 02445	NA	$18,742	$10,476	3-B	1,293	115
New Jersey City Univ, Jersey City, NJ 07305-1597	1927	$7,537 (S)	$7,880	5-M	8,523	627
New Jersey Inst of Tech, Newark, NJ 07102.	1881	$10,506 (S)	$8,980	5-D	8,209	646
New Mexico Highlands Univ, Las Vegas, NM 87701	1893	$2,444 (S)	$4,476	5-M	3,750	109
New Mexico Inst of Mining & Tech, Socorro, NM 87801	1889	$3,971 (S)	$5,090	5-D	1,846	147
New Mexico State Univ, Las Cruces, NM 88003-8001	1888	$4,230 (S)	$5,576	5-D	16,415	908
New School for General Studies, New York, NY 10011-8603.	1919	$19,810	$11,750	1-D	1,628	492
New York Inst of Tech, Old Westbury, NY 11568-8000	1955	$20,358	$11,452	1-D	11,404	849
New York Univ, New York, NY 10012-1019	1831	$33,420	$11,780	1-D	40,870	4,380
Newbury Coll, Brookline, MA 02445	1962	$17,800	$8,975	1-B	1,311	93
Newman Univ, Wichita, KS 67213-2097	1933	$17,308	$5,372	2-M	2,104	85
Niagara Univ, Niagara University, NY 14109.	1856	$21,240	$8,850	2-M	3,881	335
Nicholls State Univ, Thibodaux, LA 70310	1948	$3,470 (S)	$4,038	5-M	6,805	283
Nichols Coll, Dudley, MA 01571-5000.	1815	$23,900	$8,800	1-M	1,470	65
Norfolk State Univ, Norfolk, VA 23504	1935	NA	NA	5-M	NA	NA
North Carolina Agr & Tech State Univ, Greensboro, NC 27411	1891	$3,872 (S)	$6,686	5-D	11,098	495
North Carolina Central Univ, Durham, NC 27707-3129.	1910	$3,456 (S)	$4,972	5-F	8,675	553
North Carolina State Univ, Raleigh, NC 27695	1887	$5,117 (S)	$7,373	5-D	31,130	1,845
North Carolina Wesleyan Coll, Rocky Mount, NC 27804-8677	1956	$17,600	$6,870	2-B	1,629	165
North Central Coll, Naperville, IL 60566-7063.	1861	$23,115	$7,440	2-M	2,556	225
North Central Univ, Minneapolis, MN 55404-1322	1930	$12,946	$4,612	2-B	1,241	80
North Dakota State Univ, Fargo, ND 58105	1890	$5,722 (S)	$5,477	5-D	12,258	630
North Georgia Coll & State Univ, Dahlonega, GA 30597	1873	$3,452 (S)	$4,780	5-M	4,922	327
North Greenville Univ, Tigerville, SC 29688-1892.	1892	$11,180	NA	2-B	1,948	139
North Park Univ, Chicago, IL 60625-4895.	1891	$15,160	$7,050	2-D	2,181	121
Northcentral Univ, Prescott, AZ 86314	NA	NA	NA	3-D	1,401	301
Northeastern Illinois Univ, Chicago, IL 60625-4699	1961	$6,261 (S)	NA	5-M	12,056	701
Northeastern State Univ, Tahlequah, OK 74464-2399	1846	$3,489 (S)	$3,600	5-F	9,540	459
Northeastern Univ, Boston, MA 02115-5096.	1898	$30,309	$10,970	1-D	20,605	1,273
Northern Arizona Univ, Flagstaff, AZ 86011	1899	$4,546 (S)	$6,260	5-D	20,562	1,492
Northern Illinois Univ, De Kalb, IL 60115-2854	1895	$7,125 (S)	$6,848	5-D	25,313	1,193
Northern Kentucky Univ, Highland Heights, KY 41099	1968	$5,448 (S)	$5,690	5-F	14,617	1,089
Northern Michigan Univ, Marquette, MI 49855-5301.	1899	$6,141 (S)	$6,874	5-M	9,353	471
Northern State Univ, Aberdeen, SD 57401-7198	1901	$4,962 (S)	$4,102	5-M	2,407	93
Northwest Missouri State Univ, Maryville, MO 64468-6001	1905	$4,668 (S)	NA	5-M	6,220	284
Northwest Nazarene Univ, Nampa, ID 83686-5897	1913	$19,970	$5,300	2-M	1,749	93
Northwest Univ, Kirkland, WA 98033	1934	$19,762	$6,578	2-M	1,265	97
Northwestern Coll, Orange City, IA 51041-1996	1882	$18,296	$5,210	2-B	1,342	130
Northwestern Coll, St. Paul, MN 55113-1598	1902	$20,990	$6,750	2-M	1,781	174
Northwestern Oklahoma State Univ, Alva, OK 73717-2799	1897	$3,450 (S)	$3,310	5-M	2,024	144
Northwestern State Univ of Louisiana, Natchitoches, LA 71497	1884	$3,553 (S)	$4,686	5-M	9,431	607
Northwestern Univ, Evanston, IL 60208	1851	$33,559	$10,266	1-D	17,460	1,192
Northwood Univ, Midland, MI 48640-2398	1959	$16,455	$7,194	1-M	4,125	82
Norwich Univ, Northfield, VT 05663	1819	$22,832	$7,964	1-M	2,707	272
Notre Dame Coll, South Euclid, OH 44121-4293	1922	$20,130	$6,850	2-M	1,393	118
Notre Dame de Namur Univ, Belmont, CA 94002-1908	1851	$24,650	$10,580	2-M	1,583	156
Nova Southeastern Univ, Fort Lauderdale, FL 33314-7796	1964	$18,650	$6,012	1-D	25,960	1,553
Nyack Coll, Nyack, NY 10960-3698	1882	$15,400	$7,600	2-F	3,063	NA
Oakland City Univ, Oakland City, IN 47660-1099	1885	$14,220	$5,400	2-D	1,900	183
Oakland Univ, Rochester, MI 48309-4401	1957	$6,638 (S)	$6,354	5-D	17,737	906
Oakwood Coll, Huntsville, AL 35896	1896	$12,668	$7,170	2-B	1,771	178
Oberlin Coll, Oberlin, OH 44074	1833	$34,426	$8,720	1-M	2,841	334
Occidental Coll, Los Angeles, CA 90041-3314	1887	$35,333	$9,500	1-M	1,825	220
Oglala Lakota Coll, Kyle, SD 57752-0490	1970	NA	NA	11	1,000	NA
Oglethorpe Univ, Atlanta, GA 30319-2797	1835	$23,510	$8,000	1-M	1,030	102
Ohio Dominican Univ, Columbus, OH 43219-2099	1911	$20,570	$6,800	2-M	3,054	217
Ohio Northern Univ, Ada, OH 45810-1599	1871	$28,260	$7,080	2-F	3,620	307
Ohio State Univ at Lima, Lima, OH 45804	1960	$6,240 (S)	NA	5-M	1,214	79
Ohio State Univ at Marion, Marion, OH 43302-5695.	1958	$6,240 (S)	NA	5-M	1,538	112
Ohio State Univ, Columbus, OH 43210.	1870	$8,559 (S)	$6,720	5-D	51,818	4,031
Ohio State Univ–Mansfield Campus, Mansfield, OH 44906-1599.	1958	$6,240 (S)	$4,803	5-M	1,464	91
Ohio State Univ–Newark Campus, Newark, OH 43055-1797	1957	$6,240 (S)	$4,989	5-M	2,310	135
Ohio Univ, Athens, OH 45701-2979	1804	$8,847 (S)	$7,839	5-D	20,593	1,188
Ohio Univ–Chillicothe, Chillicothe, OH 45601-0629	1946	$153/hr. (S)	NA	5-M	2,000	106
Ohio Univ–Eastern, St. Clairsville, OH 43950-9724	1957	$131/cr. hr. (A)	NA	5-B	1,118	114
Ohio Univ–Lancaster, Lancaster, OH 43130-1097	1968	$144/cr. hr. (S)	NA	5-M	1,744	104
Ohio Univ–Southern Campus, Ironton, OH 45638-2214	1956	$136/cr. hr. (S)	NA	5-M	1,746	155
Ohio Univ–Zanesville, Zanesville, OH 43701-2695.	1946	$4,596 (S)	NA	5-M	1,679	130
Ohio Wesleyan Univ, Delaware, OH 43015.	1842	$30,290	$7,790	2-B	1,935	182
Oklahoma Baptist Univ, Shawnee, OK 74804	1910	$14,666	$4,330	2-M	1,883	119

Name, address	Year Founded	Tuition & Fees		Rm. & Board	Control, Degree	Enrollment	Faculty
Oklahoma Christian Univ, Oklahoma City, OK 73136-1100	1950	$15,796		$6,060	2-M	2,120	181
Oklahoma City Univ, Oklahoma City, OK 73106-1402	1904	$19,400		$6,560	2-F	3,713	285
Oklahoma Panhandle State Univ, Goodwell, OK 73939-0430	1909	$3,521	(S)	$3,200	5-B	1,136	92
Oklahoma State Univ, Stillwater, OK 74078	1890	$4,997	(S)	$6,015	5-D	23,307	1,245
Oklahoma Wesleyan Univ, Bartlesville, OK 74006-6299	1909	$15,500		$5,800	2-M	1,159	35
Old Dominion Univ, Norfolk, VA 23529	1930	$6,107	(S)	$6,640	5-D	21,625	1,017
Olivet Coll, Olivet, MI 49076-9701	1844	$17,594		$6,060	2-M	1,069	67
Olivet Nazarene Univ, Bourbonnais, IL 60914-2271	1907	$17,590		$6,400	2-M	4,364	123
Oral Roberts Univ, Tulsa, OK 74171-0001	1963	$17,400		$7,350	2-D	3,244	291
Oregon Health & Sci Univ, Portland, OR 97239-3098	1974	$11,540	(S)	NA	12-D	2,418	836
Oregon Inst of Tech, Klamath Falls, OR 97601-8801	1947	$5,919	(S)	$6,480	5-M	3,146	223
Oregon State Univ, Corvallis, OR 97331	1868	$5,643	(S)	$7,344	5-D	19,362	1,166
Otis Coll of Art & Design, Los Angeles, CA 90045-9785	1918	$28,346		NA	1-M	1,125	257
Otterbein Univ, Westerville, OH 43081	1847	$23,871		$6,789	2-M	3,176	275
Ouachita Baptist Univ, Arkadelphia, AR 71998-0001	1886	$17,950		$5,400	2-B	1,452	145
Our Lady of Holy Cross Coll, New Orleans, LA 70131-7399	1916	NA		NA	2-M	1,446	123
Our Lady of the Lake Coll, Baton Rouge, LA 70808 (4)	1990	$7,280		NA	2-M	2,046	159
Our Lady of the Lake Univ of San Antonio, San Antonio, TX 78207-4689	1895	$18,400		$5,767	2-D	2,783	240
Pace Univ, New York, NY 10038	1906	$30,086		$9,570	1-D	13,463	1,190
Pacific Lutheran Univ, Tacoma, WA 98447	1890	$23,450		$7,140	2-M	3,640	266
Pacific Oaks Coll, Pasadena, CA 91103 (4)	1945	$19,140		NA	1-M	1,028	125
Pacific Union Coll, Angwin, CA 94508-9707	1882	$20,265		$5,652	2-M	1,397	95
Pacific Univ, Forest Grove, OR 97116-1797	1849	$26,670		$7,170	1-D	2,790	119
Palm Beach Atlantic Univ, West Palm Beach, FL 33416-4708	1968	$18,740		$6,780	2-F	3,264	274
Palmer Coll of Chiropractic, Davenport, IA 52803-5287	1897	$6,416		NA	1-F	1,505	136
Park Univ, Parkville, MO 64152-3795	1875	$7,340		$5,406	1-M	13,182	376
Parsons The New School for Design, New York, NY 10011-8878	1896	$30,930		$11,750	1-M	3,598	941
Peirce Coll, Philadelphia, PA 19102-4699	1865	$13,240		NA	1-B	2,179	167
Penn State Abington, Abington, PA 19001	1950	$10,520	(S)	NA	12-B	3,141	226
Penn State Altoona, Altoona, PA 16601-3760	1939	$10,958	(S)	$6,850	12-B	3,833	294
Penn State Berks, Reading, PA 19610-6009	1924	$10,958	(S)	$7,490	12-B	2,660	177
Penn State Erie, The Behrend Coll, Erie, PA 16563-0001	1948	$10,958	(S)	$6,850	12-M	3,839	265
Penn State Harrisburg, Middletown, PA 17057-4898	1966	$10,948	(S)	$8,430	12-D	3,799	293
Penn State Univ Park, University Park, PA 16802-1503	1855	$12,164	(S)	$6,850	12-D	42,914	2,582
Pennsylvania Coll of Tech, Williamsport, PA 17701-5778	1965	$10,620	(S)	$7,300	12-B	6,569	483
Pepperdine Univ, Malibu, CA 90263	1937	$32,740		$9,500	2-D	7,593	707
Peru State Coll, Peru, NE 68421	1867	$3,831	(S)	$4,620	5-M	1,677	130
Pfeiffer Univ, Misenheimer, NC 28109-0960	1885	$16,450		$6,650	2-M	2,116	162
Philadelphia Biblical Univ, Langhorne, PA 19047-2990	1913	$15,875		$6,550	2-F	1,389	156
Philadelphia Univ, Philadelphia, PA 19144-5497	1884	$23,818		$8,212	1-D	3,256	412
Piedmont Coll, Demorest, GA 30535-0010	1897	$16,500		$6,000	2-M	2,118	217
Pikeville Coll, Pikeville, KY 41501	1889	$12,750		$5,000	2-F	1,098	69
Pittsburg State Univ, Pittsburg, KS 66762	1903	$3,790	(S)	$4,844	5-M	6,859	391
Plymouth State Univ, Plymouth, NH 03264-1595	1871	$7,766	(S)	$7,893	5-M	5,872	367
Point Loma Nazarene Univ, San Diego, CA 92106-2899	1902	$23,730		$7,470	2-M	3,437	NA
Point Park Univ, Pittsburgh, PA 15222-1984	1960	$17,770		$7,880	1-M	3,546	431
Polytechnic Univ of Puerto Rico, Hato Rey, PR 00919	1966	$6,033		NA	1-M	5,844	300
Polytechnic Univ, Brooklyn Campus, Brooklyn, NY 11201-2990	1854	$29,789		$8,500	1-D	2,919	273
Pomona Coll, Claremont, CA 91711	1887	$31,865		$11,291	1-B	1,545	203
Pontifical Catholic Univ of Puerto Rico, Ponce, PR 00717-0777	1948	$5,098		$3,565	2-D	7,412	366
Portland State Univ, Portland, OR 97207-0751	1946	$5,600	(S)	$8,940	5-D	24,254	1,260
Post Univ, Waterbury, CT 06723-2540	1890	$21,500		$8,400	1-B	1,101	122
Prairie View A&M Univ, Prairie View, TX 77446-0519	1878	$7,726	(A)	$7,226	5-D	8,023	484
Pratt Inst, Brooklyn, NY 11205-3899	1887	$31,080		$8,918	1-F	4,673	960
Presbyterian Coll, Clinton, SC 29325	1880	$26,320		$7,610	2-B	1,224	111
Prescott Coll, Prescott, AZ 86301	1966	$18,711		$1,560	1-M	1,053	77
Princeton Univ, Princeton, NJ 08544-1019	1746	$33,000		$10,980	1-D	7,242	1,025
Providence Coll, Providence, RI 02918	1917	$27,345		$9,765	2-M	4,835	379
Purchase Coll, State Univ of New York, Purchase, NY 10577-1400	1967	$5,709	(S)	$9,078	5-M	3,901	362
Purdue Univ Calumet, Hammond, IN 46323-2094	1951	$5,467	(S)	$4,150	5-M	9,303	499
Purdue Univ North Central, Westville, IN 46391-9542	1967	$4,962	(S)	NA	5-M	3,724	260
Purdue Univ, West Lafayette, IN 47907	1869	$7,096	(S)	$7,546	5-D	39,228	2,347
Queens Coll of the City Univ of New York, Flushing, NY 11367-1597	1937	$4,377	(S)	NA	11-M	18,107	1,337
Queens Univ of Charlotte, Charlotte, NC 28274-0002	1857	$19,450		$6,980	2-M	2,118	116
Quincy Univ, Quincy, IL 62301-2699	1860	$19,600		$7,390	2-M	1,250	130
Quinnipiac Univ, Hamden, CT 06518-1940	1929	$28,720		$11,200	1-D	7,341	778
Radford Univ, Radford, VA 24142	1910	$5,746	(S)	$6,218	5-M	9,220	580
Ramapo Coll of New Jersey, Mahwah, NJ 07430-1680	1969	$9,496	(S)	$9,924	5-M	5,499	430
Randolph-Macon Coll, Ashland, VA 23005-5505	1830	$25,345		$7,695	2-B	1,146	152
Reed Coll, Portland, OR 97202-8199	1908	$34,530		$9,000	1-M	1,436	132
Regent Univ, Virginia Beach, VA 23464-9800	1977	$12,000		NA	1-D	4,266	165
Regis Coll, Weston, MA 02493	1927	$23,680		$10,580	2-M	1,314	109
Regis Univ, Denver, CO 80221-1099	1877	$26,900		$8,830	2-D	16,004	1,342
Reinhardt Coll, Waleska, GA 30183-2981	1883	$14,970		$6,018	2-B	1,060	122
Rensselaer Polytechnic Inst, Troy, NY 12180-3590	1824	$33,496		$9,915	1-D	7,433	471
Rhode Island Coll, Providence, RI 02908-1991	1854	$4,958	(S)	$7,560	5-D	8,939	696
Rhode Island School of Design, Providence, RI 02903-2784	1877	$33,118		$9,860	1-F	2,259	503
Rhodes Coll, Memphis, TN 38112-1690	1848	$29,112		$7,180	2-M	1,696	180
Rice Univ, Houston, TX 77251-1892	1912	$28,900		$10,250	1-D	5,119	701
Richard Stockton Coll of New Jersey, Pomona, NJ 08240-0195	1969	$9,058	(S)	$8,446	5-M	7,212	440
Rider Univ, Lawrenceville, NJ 08648-3001	1865	$24,790		$9,280	1-M	5,790	518
Ringling Coll of Art & Design, Sarasota, FL 34234-5895	1931	$23,125		$9,999	1-B	1,090	124
Rivier Coll, Nashua, NH 03060-5086	1933	$21,695		$7,942	2-M	2,320	178
Roanoke Coll, Salem, VA 24153-3794	1842	$24,653		$8,152	2-B	1,970	187
Robert Morris Coll, Chicago, IL 60605	1913	$16,800		NA	1-M	4,701	343
Robert Morris Univ, Moon Township, PA 15108-1189	1921	$16,290		$8,410	1-D	5,065	364
Roberts Wesleyan Coll, Rochester, NY 14624-1997	1866	$21,656		$7,774	2-M	1,903	246
Rochester Coll, Rochester Hills, MI 48307-2764	1959	$13,088		$6,820	2-M	1,055	135
Rochester Inst of Tech, Rochester, NY 14623-5603	1829	$25,011		$8,748	1-D	15,557	1,203
Rockford Coll, Rockford, IL 61108-2393	1847	$22,950		$6,750	1-M	1,426	152
Rockhurst Univ, Kansas City, MO 64110-2561	1910	$22,990		$6,200	2-D	3,066	226
Roger Williams Univ, Bristol, RI 02809	1956	$25,759		$10,943	1-F	5,172	464
Rogers State Univ, Claremore, OK 74017-3252	1909	$3,540	(S)	$6,300	5-B	3,952	204
Rollins Coll, Winter Park, FL 32789-4499	1885	$30,860		$9,626	1-M	2,454	233
Roosevelt Univ, Chicago, IL 60605-1394	1945	$16,980		$8,750	1-D	7,186	621

Name, address	Year Founded	Tuition & Fees		Rm. & Board	Control/Degree	Enrollment	Faculty
Rose-Hulman Inst of Tech, Terre Haute, IN 47803-3999 (2).	1874	$28,995		$7,869	1-M	1,963	161
Rowan Univ, Glassboro, NJ 08028-1701	1923	$9,330	(S)	$8,742	5-D	9,578	1,063
Rush Univ, Chicago, IL 60612-3832	1969	$21,310		$5,885	1-D	1,362	796
Rutgers, The State Univ of New Jersey, Camden, Camden, NJ 08102-1401	1927	$9,758	(S)	$8,596	5-F	5,165	401
Rutgers, The State Univ of New Jersey, New Brunswick, New Brunswick, NJ 08901-1281	1766	$9,958	(S)	$9,312	5-D	34,392	2,212
Rutgers, The State Univ of New Jersey, Newark, Newark, NJ 07102.	1892	$9,534	(S)	$9,535	5-D	10,203	606
Sacred Heart Univ, Fairfield, CT 06825-1000	1963	$25,400		$10,320	2-D	5,756	497
Sage Coll of Albany, Albany, NY 12208-3425.	1957	$17,670		$8,520	1-B	1,074	87
Saginaw Valley State Univ, University Center, MI 48710	1963	$5,543	(S)	$6,380	5-M	9,543	570
Saint Anselm Coll, Manchester, NH 03102-1310	1889	$24,660		$9,070	2-B	1,986	177
Saint Augustine's Coll, Raleigh, NC 27604-2298	1867	$12,456		$6,372	2-B	1,395	97
Saint Francis Univ, Loretto, PA 15940-0600	1847	$22,224		$7,640	2-M	2,014	187
Saint John's Univ, Collegeville, MN 56321 (2).	1857	$24,924		$6,496	2-F	2,044	164
Saint Joseph Coll, West Hartford, CT 06117-2700	1932	$23,490		$11,500	2-M	1,803	212
Saint Joseph's Coll of Maine, Standish, ME 04084-5263	1912	$21,760		$9,030	2-M	1,050	126
Saint Joseph's Coll, Rensselaer, IN 47978	1889	$20,960		$6,720	2-M	1,031	89
Saint Joseph's Univ, Philadelphia, PA 19131-1395.	1851	$29,095		$10,170	2-D	7,535	602
Saint Leo Univ, Saint Leo, FL 33574-6665	1889	$16,420		$8,102	2-D	2,774	129
Saint Louis Univ, St. Louis, MO 63103-2097.	1818	$26,648		$8,230	2-D	12,034	1,004
Saint Martin's Univ, Lacey, WA 98503-1297	1895	$20,965		$6,400	2-M	1,463	162
Saint Mary-of-the-Woods Coll, Saint Mary-of-the-Woods, IN 47876	1840	$20,180		$7,380	2-M	1,668	67
Saint Mary's Coll of California, Moraga, CA 94575	1863	$29,050		$10,566	2-D	3,962	539
Saint Mary's Coll, Notre Dame, IN 46556 (3)	1844	$26,872		$8,678	2-B	1,527	205
Saint Mary's Univ of Minnesota, Winona, MN 55987-1399	1912	$22,398		$6,130	2-D	5,566	569
Saint Michael's Coll, Colchester, VT 05439.	1904	$28,515		$6,990	2-M	2,437	220
Saint Peter's Coll, Jersey City, NJ 07306-5997.	1872	$22,650		$9,260	2-M	3,117	271
Saint Vincent Coll, Latrobe, PA 15650-2690.	1846	$23,000		$7,242	2-M	1,818	187
Saint Xavier Univ, Chicago, IL 60655-3105.	1847	$19,860		$7,414	2-M	5,657	405
Salem Coll, Winston-Salem, NC 27108-0548	1772	$17,949		$9,551	2-M	1,094	103
Salem State Coll, Salem, MA 01970-5353	1854	$5,970	(S)	$5,380	5-M	10,230	717
Salisbury Univ, Salisbury, MD 21801-6837	1925	$6,412	(S)	$7,058	5-M	7,383	489
Salve Regina Univ, Newport, RI 02840-4192	1934	$25,175		$9,800	2-D	2,589	252
Sam Houston State Univ, Huntsville, TX 77341	1879	$4,896	(S)	$5,880	5-D	15,935	681
Samford Univ, Birmingham, AL 35229-0002.	1841	$16,000		$6,060	2-D	4,478	407
Samuel Merritt Coll, Oakland, CA 94609-3108 (4)	1909	$29,576		$5,903	1-D	1,178	171
San Diego State Univ, San Diego, CA 92182	1897	$3,160	(S)	$10,093	5-D	34,305	1,725
San Francisco State Univ, San Francisco, CA 94132-1722	1899	$3,166	(S)	$9,544	5-M	29,628	1,807
San Jose State Univ, San Jose, CA 95192-0001	1857	$3,296	(S)	$9,096	5-M	29,604	NA
Santa Clara Univ, Santa Clara, CA 95053	1851	$30,900		$10,380	2-D	7,952	766
Sarah Lawrence Coll, Bronxville, NY 10708-5999.	1926	$36,088		$12,152	1-M	1,709	236
Savannah Coll of Art & Design, Savannah, GA 31402-3146	1978	$24,890		$10,015	1-M	8,236	508
Savannah State Univ, Savannah, GA 31404	1890	$3,178	(S)	$5,010	5-M	3,188	167
School of the Art Inst of Chicago, Chicago, IL 60603-3103.	1866	$31,020		$8,900	1-M	2,873	468
School of Visual Arts, New York, NY 10010-3994.	1947	$22,080		$12,300	3-M	3,715	861
Seattle Pacific Univ, Seattle, WA 98119-1997	1891	$23,391		$7,818	2-D	3,830	364
Seattle Univ, Seattle, WA 98122-1090	1891	$24,615		$7,503	2-D	7,226	594
Seton Hall Univ, South Orange, NJ 07079-2697.	1856	$24,720		$10,466	2-D	9,637	926
Seton Hill Univ, Greensburg, PA 15601	1883	$23,380		$7,230	2-M	1,895	192
Sewanee: The Univ of the South, Sewanee, TN 37383-1000.	1857	$30,660		$8,780	2-D	1,611	174
Shaw Univ, Raleigh, NC 27601-2399	1865	$10,020		$6,410	2-F	2,882	284
Shawnee State Univ, Portsmouth, OH 45662-4344	1986	$5,832	(S)	$6,939	5-B	3,889	317
Shenandoah Univ, Winchester, VA 22601-5195	1875	$21,240		$7,650	2-D	3,105	340
Shepherd Univ, Shepherdstown, WV 25443-3210	1871	$4,348	(S)	$6,456	5-M	4,091	288
Shippensburg Univ of Pennsylvania, Shippensburg, PA 17257-2299.	1871	$6,549	(S)	$5,962	5-M	7,516	378
Shorter Coll, Rome, GA 30165	1873	$14,300		$6,600	2-B	1,044	124
Siena Coll, Loudonville, NY 12211-1462.	1937	$21,460		$8,475	2-B	3,220	307
Siena Heights Univ, Adrian, MI 49221-1796	1919	NA		NA	2-M	2,153	164
Simmons Coll, Boston, MA 02115.	1899	$26,705		$10,710	1-D	4,849	374
Simpson Coll, Indianola, IA 50125-1297	1860	$23,596		$6,655	2-B	2,060	181
Simpson Univ, Redding, CA 96003-8606	1921	$18,600		$6,400	2-M	1,015	104
Sinte Gleska Univ, Rosebud, SD 57555	1970	NA		NA	1-M	1,200	NA
Skidmore Coll, Saratoga Springs, NY 12866-1632	1903	$34,694		$9,556	1-M	2,816	338
Slippery Rock Univ of Pennsylvania, Slippery Rock, PA 16057-1383.	1889	$6,363	(S)	$4,998	5-D	8,230	361
Smith Coll, Northampton, MA 01063	1871	$32,558		$10,880	1-D	3,092	313
Sojourner-Douglass Coll, Baltimore, MD 21205-1814 (4)	1980	$6,748		NA	1-M	1,124	136
Sonoma State Univ, Rohnert Park, CA 94928-3609	1960	$3,648	(S)	NA	5-M	7,749	542
South Carolina State Univ, Orangeburg, SC 29117-0001.	1896	$7,278	(S)	$7,658	5-D	4,384	274
South Dakota School of Mines & Tech, Rapid City, SD 57701-3995	1885	$5,330	(S)	$4,410	5-D	2,124	137
South Dakota State Univ, Brookings, SD 57007	1881	$5,052	(S)	$5,029	5-D	11,303	598
South Univ, Savannah, GA 31406-4805	1899	$15,800		NA	3-D	1,077	97
Southeast Missouri State Univ, Cape Girardeau, MO 63701-4799.	1873	$5,505	(S)	$5,647	5-M	10,477	579
Southeastern Baptist Theological Seminary, Wake Forest, NC 27588-1889	1950	NA		NA	2-D	1,979	90
Southeastern Louisiana Univ, Hammond, LA 70402.	1925	$3,423	(S)	$5,750	5-M	15,118	683
Southeastern Oklahoma State Univ, Durant, OK 74701-0609	1909	$3,574	(S)	$5,348	5-M	3,872	229
Southeastern Univ, Lakeland, FL 33801-6099	1935	$13,480		$6,430	2-B	2,901	138
Southern Adventist Univ, Collegedale, TN 37315-0370	1892	$15,596		$4,734	2-M	2,593	221
Southern Arkansas Univ–Magnolia, Magnolia, AR 71753.	1909	$4,650	(S)	$3,970	5-M	3,057	184
Southern Connecticut State Univ, New Haven, CT 06515-1355.	1893	$6,591	(S)	$8,432	5-D	12,326	1,024
Southern Illinois Univ Carbondale, Carbondale, IL 62901-4701	1869	$8,071	(S)	$6,666	5-D	21,003	1,097
Southern Illinois Univ Edwardsville, Edwardsville, IL 62026-0001	1957	$7,118	(S)	$6,500	5-F	13,449	815
Southern Methodist Univ, Dallas, TX 75275	1911	$30,880		$10,825	2-D	10,941	924
Southern Nazarene Univ, Bethany, OK 73008	1899	$15,024		$5,378	2-M	2,218	176
Southern New Hampshire Univ, Manchester, NH 03106-1045.	1932	$23,346		$8,970	1-D	3,490	380
Southern Oregon Univ, Ashland, OR 97520	1926	$4,986	(S)	$6,468	5-M	4,675	289
Southern Polytechnic State Univ, Marietta, GA 30060-2896.	1948	$3,348	(S)	$5,610	5-M	4,206	226
Southern Univ & Agr & Mech Coll, Baton Rouge, LA 70813.	1880	$3,666	(S)	$5,030	5-D	8,619	546
Southern Univ at New Orleans, New Orleans, LA 70126-1009.	1959	$2,990	(S)	NA	5-M	5,000	NA
Southern Utah Univ, Cedar City, UT 84720-2498.	1897	$4,069	(S)	$4,154	5-M	7,029	285
Southern Wesleyan Univ, Central, SC 29630-1020	1906	$16,150		$5,800	2-M	2,557	234
Southwest Baptist Univ, Bolivar, MO 65613-2597.	1878	$14,100		$4,200	2-D	3,503	248
Southwest Minnesota State Univ, Marshall, MN 56258.	1963	$6,240	(S)	$5,360	5-M	6,126	195
Southwestern Adventist Univ, Keene, TX 76059.	1894	$12,484		$5,806	2-M	1,191	92
Southwestern Assemblies of God Univ, Waxahachie, TX 75165-5735.	1927	NA		NA	2-M	1,676	95
Southwestern Coll, Winfield, KS 67156-2499	1885	$16,900		$5,438	2-M	1,557	180
Southwestern Oklahoma State Univ, Weatherford, OK 73096-3098.	1901	$3,450	(S)	$3,330	5-F	5,164	225

Name, address	Year Founded	Tuition & Fees		Rm. & Board	Control, Degree	Enrollment	Faculty
Southwestern Univ, Georgetown, TX 78626	1840	$25,740		$8,710	2-B	1,277	166
Spalding Univ, Louisville, KY 40203-2188	1814	$15,900		$3,672	2-D	1,641	174
Spelman Coll, Atlanta, GA 30314-4399 (3)	1881	$17,005		$8,750	1-B	2,290	249
Spring Arbor Univ, Spring Arbor, MI 49283-9799	1873	$17,386		$6,070	2-M	3,714	133
Spring Hill Coll, Mobile, AL 36608-1791	1830	$22,000		$8,120	2-M	1,446	147
Springfield Coll, Springfield, MA 01109-3797	1885	$22,715		$8,130	1-D	3,155	342
St. Ambrose Univ, Davenport, IA 52803-2898	1882	$640/sem. hr.		NA	2-D	3,780	310
St. Augustine Coll, Chicago, IL 60640-3501	1980	$7,128		NA	1-B	1,279	132
St. Bonaventure Univ, St. Bonaventure, NY 14778-2284	1858	$22,515		$7,760	2-M	2,614	207
St. Cloud State Univ, St. Cloud, MN 56301-4498	1869	$5,718	(S)	$5,194	5-M	15,964	934
St. Edward's Univ, Austin, TX 78704	1885	$20,400		$7,460	2-M	5,224	472
St. Francis Coll, Brooklyn Heights, NY 11201-4398	1884	$14,020		NA	2-M	2,258	213
St. John Fisher Coll, Rochester, NY 14618-3597	1948	$20,710		$8,880	2-M	3,704	345
St. John's Univ, Queens, NY 11439	1870	$24,970		$11,470	2-D	20,069	1,486
St. Joseph's Coll, New York, Brooklyn, NY 11205-3688	1916	$12,946		NA	1-M	1,310	137
St. Joseph's Coll, Suffolk Campus, Patchogue, NY 11772-2399	1916	$13,610		NA	1-M	3,833	380
St. Lawrence Univ, Canton, NY 13617-1455	1856	$33,910		$8,630	1-M	2,303	189
St. Louis Coll of Pharmacy, St. Louis, MO 63110-1088	1864	$19,750		$7,823	1-F	1,126	101
St. Mary's Coll of Maryland, St. Mary's City, MD 20686-3001	1840	$11,989	(S)	$8,855	5-B	1,957	210
St. Mary's Univ of San Antonio, San Antonio, TX 78228-8507	1852	$19,934		$6,780	2-D	3,904	333
St. Norbert Coll, De Pere, WI 54115-2099	1898	$23,497		$6,319	2-M	2,072	179
St. Olaf Coll, Northfield, MN 55057-1098	1874	$30,600		$7,900	2-B	3,041	324
St. Thomas Aquinas Coll, Sparkill, NY 10976	1952	$18,900		$9,400	1-M	2,232	144
St. Thomas Univ, Miami Gardens, FL 33054-6459	1961	$18,750		$5,910	2-F	2,517	231
Stanford Univ, Stanford, CA 94305-9991	1891	$32,994		$10,367	1-D	17,747	1,041
State Univ of New York at Binghamton, Binghamton, NY 13902-6000	1946	$5,910	(S)	$8,588	5-D	14,373	889
State Univ of New York at Fredonia, Fredonia, NY 14063-1136	1826	$5,482	(S)	$8,120	5-M	5,540	444
State Univ of New York at New Paltz, New Paltz, NY 12561	1828	$5,340	(S)	$7,630	5-M	7,699	703
State Univ of New York at Oswego, Oswego, NY 13126	1861	$5,322	(S)	$8,940	5-M	8,183	507
State Univ of New York at Plattsburgh, Plattsburgh, NY 12901-2681	1889	$5,337	(S)	$7,728	5-M	6,217	487
State Univ of New York Coll at Brockport, Brockport, NY 14420-2997	1867	$5,356	(S)	$7,830	5-M	8,312	615
State Univ of New York Coll at Cortland, Cortland, NY 13045	1868	$4,350	(S)	$7,850	5-M	6,995	537
State Univ of New York Coll at Geneseo, Geneseo, NY 14454-1401	1871	$5,560	(S)	$7,788	5-M	5,530	329
State Univ of New York Coll at Old Westbury, Old Westbury, NY 11568-0210	1965	$5,076	(S)	$8,083	5-M	3,450	264
State Univ of New York Coll at Oneonta, Oneonta, NY 13820-4015	1889	$5,412	(S)	$7,696	5-M	5,786	475
State Univ of New York Coll at Potsdam, Potsdam, NY 13676	1816	$5,357	(S)	$8,220	5-M	4,332	366
State Univ of New York Coll of Agriculture & Tech at Cobleskill, Cobleskill, NY 12043	1916	$5,650	(S)	$8,630	5-B	2,506	192
State Univ of New York Coll of Environmental Sci & Forestry, Syracuse, NY 13210-2779	1911	$5,069	(S)	$10,600	5-D	2,069	159
State Univ of New York Downstate Medical Ctr, Brooklyn, NY 11203-2098	1858	$4,745	(S)	$12,260	5-D	1,609	981
State Univ of New York Empire State Coll, Saratoga Springs, NY 12866-4391	1971	$4,575	(S)	NA	5-M	12,038	1,118
State Univ of New York Inst of Tech, Utica, NY 13504-3050	1966	$5,317	(S)	$7,600	5-M	2,587	167
State Univ of New York Maritime Coll, Throggs Neck, NY 10465-4198 (2)	1874	$6,550	(S)	$8,919	5-M	1,316	107
State Univ of New York Upstate Medical Univ, Syracuse, NY 13210-2334	1950	$9,166	(S)	$3,930	5-D	1,236	685
Stephen F. Austin State Univ, Nacogdoches, TX 75962	1923	$5,232	(S)	$6,544	5-D	11,756	627
Stetson Univ, DeLand, FL 32723	1883	$28,780		$7,968	1-F	3,762	259
Stevens Inst of Tech, Hoboken, NJ 07030	1870	$33,115		$10,000	1-D	4,829	329
Stillman Coll, Tuscaloosa, AL 35403-9990	1876	NA		NA	2-B	1,458	86
Stonehill Coll, Easton, MA 02357-5510	1948	$26,345		$11,040	2-M	2,386	255
Stony Brook Univ, State Univ of New York, Stony Brook, NY 11794	1957	$5,631	(S)	$8,394	5-D	22,522	1,440
Strayer Univ, Washington, DC 20005-2603	1892	$10,935		NA	3-M	20,138	881
Suffolk Univ, Boston, MA 02108-2770	1906	$22,690		$12,756	1-D	8,863	980
Sul Ross State Univ, Alpine, TX 79832	1920	$4,336	(S)	$5,650	5-M	1,954	NA
Sullivan Univ, Louisville, KY 40205	1864	$14,265		$4,320	3-M	4,505	269
Susquehanna Univ, Selinsgrove, PA 17870	1858	$27,620		$7,600	2-B	2,009	189
Swarthmore Coll, Swarthmore, PA 19081-1397	1864	$33,232		$10,300	1-B	1,484	202
Syracuse Univ, Syracuse, NY 13244	1870	$29,965		$10,420	1-D	17,492	1,432
Tarleton State Univ, Stephenville, TX 76402	1899	$4,626	(S)	$5,802	5-D	9,464	528
Taylor Univ, Upland, IN 46989-1001	1846	$22,028		$5,867	2-M	1,854	192
Temple Univ, Philadelphia, PA 19122-6096	1884	$10,180	(S)	$8,230	12-D	33,865	2,716
Tennessee State Univ, Nashville, TN 37209-1561	1912	$4,564	(S)	$5,000	5-D	9,038	637
Tennessee Tech Univ, Cookeville, TN 38505	1915	$4,590	(S)	$5,964	5-D	9,733	560
Texas A&M Intl Univ, Laredo, TX 78041-1900	1969	$4,738	(S)	$6,500	5-D	4,917	298
Texas A&M Univ at Galveston, Galveston, TX 77553-1675	1962	$4,743	(S)	$4,870	5-M	1,553	170
Texas A&M Univ, College Station, TX 77843	1876	$6,966	(S)	$7,660	5-D	45,380	2,446
Texas A&M Univ—Commerce, Commerce, TX 75429-3011	1889	$5,242	(S)	$5,740	5-D	8,556	849
Texas A&M Univ—Corpus Christi, Corpus Christi, TX 78412-5503	1947	$5,148	(S)	NA	5-D	8,585	496
Texas A&M Univ—Kingsville, Kingsville, TX 78363	1925	$4,326	(S)	NA	5-D	7,126	438
Texas A&M Univ—Texarkana, Texarkana, TX 75505-5518	1971	$2,644	(S)	NA	5-M	1,670	108
Texas Christian Univ, Fort Worth, TX 76129-0002	1873	$23,020		$7,520	2-D	8,865	803
Texas Lutheran Univ, Seguin, TX 78155-5999	1891	$18,840		$5,600	2-B	1,429	143
Texas Southern Univ, Houston, TX 77004-4584	1947	$4,998	(S)	$6,402	5-D	11,224	576
Texas State Univ-San Marcos, San Marcos, TX 78666	1899	$5,652	(S)	$5,878	5-D	27,485	1,671
Texas Tech Univ, Lubbock, TX 79409	1923	$6,459	(S)	$7,288	5-D	27,996	1,154
Texas Wesleyan Univ, Fort Worth, TX 76105-1536	1890	$15,715		$5,500	2-F	2,930	258
Texas Woman's Univ, Denton, TX 76201 (4)	1901	$5,832	(S)	$5,846	5-D	11,832	654
Thiel Coll, Greenville, PA 16125-2181	1866	$18,720		$7,574	2-B	1,279	113
Thomas Edison State Coll, Trenton, NJ 08608-1176	1972	$4,081/year		NA	5-M	13,175	NA
Thomas Jefferson Univ, Philadelphia, PA 19107	1824	$22,884		$3,021	1-D	2,867	266
Thomas More Coll, Crestview Hills, KY 41017-3495	1921	$21,220		$6,250	2-M	1,400	129
Tiffin Univ, Tiffin, OH 44883-2161	1888	$15,870		$6,775	1-M	1,977	137
Touro Coll, New York, NY 10010	1971	NA		NA	1-D	11,447	999
Touro Univ Intl, Cypress, CA 90630	NA	$8,000		NA	1-D	2,743	213
Towson Univ, Towson, MD 21252-0001	1866	$7,164	(S)	$7,506	5-D	18,921	1,289
Transylvania Univ, Lexington, KY 40508-1797	1780	$22,300		$7,130	2-B	1,117	97
Trevecca Nazarene Univ, Nashville, TN 37210-2877	1901	$14,774		$6,470	2-D	2,217	219
Trinity (Washington) Univ, Washington, DC 20017-1094	1897	$17,360		$7,574	2-M	1,672	158
Trinity Christian Coll, Palos Heights, IL 60463-0929	1959	$18,115		$7,010	2-B	1,310	148
Trinity Coll, Hartford, CT 06106-3100	1823	$35,130		$8,970	1-M	2,528	243
Trinity Intl Univ, Deerfield, IL 60015-1284	1897	$20,106		$6,550	2-D	2,855	381
Trinity Univ, San Antonio, TX 78212-7200	1869	$25,022		$8,270	2-M	2,693	293
Tri-State Univ, Angola, IN 46703-1764	1884	$21,210		$6,240	1-M	1,210	99
Troy Univ, Troy, AL 36082	1887	$4,104	(S)	$5,491	5-M	27,938	1,489
Truman State Univ, Kirksville, MO 63501-4221	1867	$6,342	(S)	$5,570	5-M	5,762	363
Tufts Univ, Medford, MA 02155	1852	$34,730		$9,770	1-D	9,638	1,056
Tulane Univ, New Orleans, LA 70118-5669	1834	$34,896		$8,397	1-D	10,606	1,319

Name, address	Year Founded	Tuition & Fees		Rm. & Board	Control, Degree	Enrollment	Faculty
Tusculum Coll, Greeneville, TN 37743-9997	1794	$16,215		$6,500	2-M	2,923	150
Tuskegee Univ, Tuskegee, AL 36088	1881	$14,615		$6,783	1-D	2,842	256
Union Coll, Barbourville, KY 40906-1499	1879	$15,650		$5,000	2-M	1,389	85
Union Coll, Schenectady, NY 12308-2311	1795	$44,043	(C)	NA	1-B	2,212	223
Union Inst & Univ, Cincinnati, OH 45206-1925	1969	$8,910		NA	1-D	2,379	169
Union Univ, Jackson, TN 38305-3697	1823	$17,900		NA	2-D	2,934	290
United States Air Force Acad, USAF Academy, CO 80840-5025 (2)	1954	$0	(C)	NA	4-B	4,524	563
United States Military Acad, West Point, NY 10996 (2)	1802	$0	(C)	NA	4-B	4,231	604
United States Naval Acad, Annapolis, MD 21402-5000 (2)	1845	$0	(C)	NA	4-B	4,479	581
United Talmudical Seminary, Brooklyn, NY 11211-7900 (1)	1949	NA		NA	2-M	1,670	NA
Univ at Albany, State Univ of New York, Albany, NY 12222-0001	1844	$5,939	(S)	$8,605	5-D	17,434	1,214
Univ at Buffalo, the State Univ of New York, Buffalo, NY 14260	1846	$6,128	(S)	$8,108	5-D	27,220	1,748
Univ of Advancing Tech, Tempe, AZ 85283-1042	1983	$16,400		$8,400	3-M	1,227	64
Univ of Akron, Akron, OH 44325	1870	$8,382	(S)	$7,640	5-D	21,882	1,497
Univ of Alabama at Birmingham, Birmingham, AL 35294	1969	$4,792	(S)	$7,111	5-D	16,561	915
Univ of Alabama in Huntsville, Huntsville, AL 35899	1950	$4,848	(S)	$5,110	5-D	7,091	469
Univ of Alabama, Tuscaloosa, AL 35487	1831	$5,278	(S)	$5,380	5-D	23,838	1,168
Univ of Alaska Anchorage, Anchorage, AK 99508-8060	1954	$3,600	(S)	$8,030	5-M	17,023	1,199
Univ of Alaska Fairbanks, Fairbanks, AK 99775-7520	1917	$4,308	(S)	$6,030	5-D	8,341	658
Univ of Alaska Southeast, Juneau, AK 99801	1972	$4,396	(S)	$5,790	5-M	2,965	239
Univ of Arizona, Tucson, AZ 85721	1885	$4,766	(S)	$7,850	5-D	36,805	1,455
Univ of Arkansas at Fort Smith, Fort Smith, AR 72913-3649	1928	$3,340	(S)	$2,880	11-B	6,767	368
Univ of Arkansas at Little Rock, Little Rock, AR 72204-1099	1927	$5,511	(S)	$3,100	5-D	11,905	749
Univ of Arkansas at Monticello, Monticello, AR 71656	1909	$4,150	(S)	$3,440	5-M	3,179	208
Univ of Arkansas at Pine Bluff, Pine Bluff, AR 71601-2799	1873	$4,454	(S)	$5,940	5-M	3,128	225
Univ of Arkansas for Medical Sci, Little Rock, AR 72205-7199	1879	NA		NA	5-D	2,016	NA
Univ of Arkansas, Fayetteville, AR 72701-1201	1871	$5,808	(S)	$6,522	5-D	17,926	863
Univ of Baltimore, Baltimore, MD 21201-5779	1925	$6,070	(S)	NA	5-D	4,948	363
Univ of Bridgeport, Bridgeport, CT 06604	1927	$21,710		$9,600	1-D	4,018	380
Univ of California, Berkeley, Berkeley, CA 94720-1500	1868	$6,654	(S)	$13,074	5-D	33,933	2,026
Univ of California, Davis, Davis, CA 95616	1905	$7,593	(S)	$11,354	5-D	29,628	1,888
Univ of California, Irvine, Irvine, CA 92697	1965	$6,141	(S)	$9,815	5-D	25,229	1,925
Univ of California, Los Angeles, Los Angeles, CA 90095	1919	$7,143	(S)	$11,141	5-D	38,218	2,505
Univ of California, Riverside, Riverside, CA 92521-0102	1954	$6,591	(S)	$10,200	5-D	16,875	857
Univ of California, San Diego, La Jolla, CA 92093	1959	$6,685	(S)	$9,657	5-D	26,465	1,149
Univ of California, Santa Barbara, Santa Barbara, CA 93106	1909	$7,277	(S)	$11,178	5-D	21,062	1,067
Univ of California, Santa Cruz, Santa Cruz, CA 95064	1965	$7,962	(S)	$11,805	5-D	15,364	759
Univ of Central Arkansas, Conway, AR 72035-0001	1907	$6,012	(S)	$4,320	5-D	12,330	651
Univ of Central Florida, Orlando, FL 32816	1963	$3,492	(S)	$8,000	5-D	46,719	1,664
Univ of Central Missouri, Warrensburg, MO 64093	1871	$5,835	(S)	$5,109	5-M	10,711	596
Univ of Central Oklahoma, Edmond, OK 73034-5209	1890	$3,539	(S)	$4,763	5-M	15,723	803
Univ of Charleston, Charleston, WV 25304-1099	1888	$21,000		$7,600	1-M	1,202	90
Univ of Chicago, Chicago, IL 60637-1513	1891	$34,005		$10,608	1-D	11,730	1,630
Univ of Cincinnati, Cincinnati, OH 45221	1819	$9,399	(S)	$9,246	5-D	27,932	1,241
Univ of Colorado at Boulder, Boulder, CO 80309	1876	$5,643	(S)	$8,300	5-D	31,399	1,845
Univ of Colorado at Colorado Springs, Colorado Springs, CO 80933-7150	1965	$6,537	(S)	$7,662	5-D	8,583	556
Univ of Colorado at Denver & Health Sci Ctr, Denver, CO 80217-3364	1912	$5,177	(S)	NA	5-D	19,766	1,362
Univ of Connecticut, Storrs, CT 06269	1881	$8,842	(S)	$8,850	5-D	23,557	1,308
Univ of Dallas, Irving, TX 75062-4736	1955	$23,267		$7,615	2-D	2,941	233
Univ of Dayton, Dayton, OH 45469-1300	1850	$23,970		$7,190	2-D	10,503	914
Univ of Delaware, Newark, DE 19716	1743	$7,740	(S)	$7,366	12-D	19,742	1,421
Univ of Denver, Denver, CO 80208	1864	$30,372		$9,228	1-D	10,374	1,050
Univ of Detroit Mercy, Detroit, MI 48219-0900	1877	$23,970		$7,622	2-D	5,521	708
Univ of Dubuque, Dubuque, IA 52001-5099	1852	$17,420		$5,950	2-D	1,441	158
Univ of Evansville, Evansville, IN 47722	1854	$22,980		$7,120	2-M	2,879	239
Univ of Findlay, Findlay, OH 45840-3653	1882	$22,794		$7,792	2-M	6,182	299
Univ of Florida, Gainesville, FL 32611	1853	$3,206	(S)	$6,590	5-D	50,822	2,311
Univ of Georgia, Athens, GA 30602	1785	$4,964	(S)	$6,848	5-D	33,959	2,159
Univ of Guam, Mangilao, GU 96923	1952	$4,854	(S)	$7,785	7-M	3,176	249
Univ of Hartford, West Hartford, CT 06117-1599	1877	$26,996		$10,418	1-D	7,308	787
Univ of Hawai`i at Hilo, Hilo, HI 96720-4091	1970	$3,148	(S)	$6,292	5-M	3,507	377
Univ of Hawai`i at Manoa, Honolulu, HI 96822	1907	$5,390	(S)	$7,185	5-D	20,357	1,272
Univ of Houston, Houston, TX 77204	1927	$6,909	(S)	$6,418	5-D	34,334	1,823
Univ of Houston-Clear Lake, Houston, TX 77058-1098	1971	$4,653	(S)	NA	5-M	7,853	524
Univ of Houston-Downtown, Houston, TX 77002-1001	1974	$3,656	(S)	NA	5-M	11,449	565
Univ of Houston-Victoria, Victoria, TX 77901-4450	1973	$4,680	(S)	NA	5-M	2,652	137
Univ of Idaho, Moscow, ID 83844-2282	1889	$4,200	(S)	$5,696	5-D	11,739	590
Univ of Illinois at Chicago, Chicago, IL 60607-7128	1946	$9,742	(S)	$7,446	5-D	24,654	1,519
Univ of Illinois at Springfield, Springfield, IL 62703-5407	1969	$7,244	(S)	$7,495	5-D	4,761	334
Univ of Illinois at Urbana–Champaign, Champaign, IL 61820	1867	$11,130	(S)	$8,196	5-D	42,728	2,051
Univ of Indianapolis, Indianapolis, IN 46227-3697	1902	$18,850		$7,380	2-D	4,389	447
Univ of Iowa, Iowa City, IA 52242-1316	1847	$6,293	(S)	NA	5-D	28,816	1,673
Univ of Kansas, Lawrence, KS 66045	1866	$6,153	(S)	$5,747	5-D	28,924	1,283
Univ of Kentucky, Lexington, KY 40506-0032	1865	$7,096	(S)	$5,970	5-D	26,382	1,724
Univ of La Verne, La Verne, CA 91750-4443	1891	$25,590		$9,750	1-D	3,876	402
Univ of Louisiana at Lafayette, Lafayette, LA 70504	1898	$3,382	(S)	$3,770	5-D	16,302	695
Univ of Louisiana at Monroe, Monroe, LA 71209-0001	1931	$93/cr. hr.	(S)	NA	5-D	8,571	429
Univ of Louisville, Louisville, KY 40292-0001	1798	$6,252	(S)	$5,096	5-D	20,804	1,335
Univ of Maine at Augusta, Augusta, ME 04330-9410	1965	$5,445	(S)	NA	5-B	5,257	324
Univ of Maine at Farmington, Farmington, ME 04938-1990	1863	$6,408	(S)	$6,312	5-B	2,424	171
Univ of Maine at Fort Kent, Fort Kent, ME 04743-1292	1878	NA		NA	5-B	1,076	72
Univ of Maine at Machias, Machias, ME 04654-1321	1909	$5,245	(S)	$5,962	5-B	1,259	77
Univ of Maine at Presque Isle, Presque Isle, ME 04769-2888	1903	$5,380	(S)	$5,658	5-B	1,548	116
Univ of Maine, Orono, ME 04469	1865	$7,464	(S)	$7,125	5-D	11,435	823
Univ of Mary Hardin-Baylor, Belton, TX 76513	1845	$15,660		$5,728	2-M	2,738	227
Univ of Mary Washington, Fredericksburg, VA 22401-5358	1908	$6,084	(S)	$6,244	5-M	4,862	354
Univ of Mary, Bismarck, ND 58504-9652	1959	$11,780		$4,260	2-D	2,765	313
Univ of Maryland Eastern Shore, Princess Anne, MD 21853-1299	1886	$5,908	(S)	$6,330	5-D	3,762	234
Univ of Maryland Univ Coll, Adelphi, MD 20783	1947	$5,520	(S)	NA	5-D	33,096	1,590
Univ of Maryland, Baltimore County, Baltimore, MD 21250	1963	$8,622	(S)	$8,381	5-D	11,798	762
Univ of Maryland, Coll Park, College Park, MD 20742	1856	$7,906	(S)	$8,422	5-D	35,300	2,070
Univ of Massachusetts Amherst, Amherst, MA 01003	1863	$9,595	(S)	$6,989	5-D	25,593	1,346
Univ of Massachusetts Boston, Boston, MA 02125-3393	1964	$8,546	(S)	NA	5-D	12,362	815
Univ of Massachusetts Dartmouth, North Dartmouth, MA 02747-2300	1895	$8,309	(S)	$8,162	5-D	8,756	583
Univ of Massachusetts Lowell, Lowell, MA 01854-2881	1894	$8,444	(S)	$6,365	5-D	11,208	629

Name, address	Year Founded	Tuition & Fees		Rm. & Board	Control, Degree	Enrollment	Faculty
Univ of Memphis, Memphis, TN 38152	1912	$5,256	(S)	$4,720	5-D	20,562	1,279
Univ of Miami, Coral Gables, FL 33124	1925	$33,070		$9,606	1-D	15,670	1,292
Univ of Michigan, Ann Arbor, MI 48109	1817	$9,798	(S)	$7,838	5-D	40,025	2,987
Univ of Michigan–Dearborn, Dearborn, MI 48128-1491	1959	$7,392	(S)	NA	5-M	8,566	481
Univ of Michigan–Flint, Flint, MI 48502-1950	1956	$6,902	(S)	NA	5-F	6,527	445
Univ of Minnesota, Crookston, Crookston, MN 56716-5001	1966	$9,065	(S)	$5,750	5-B	2,414	108
Univ of Minnesota, Duluth, Duluth, MN 55812-2496	1947	$9,439	(S)	$5,722	5-F	11,090	523
Univ of Minnesota, Morris, Morris, MN 56267-2134	1959	$9,112	(S)	$6,260	5-B	1,740	174
Univ of Minnesota, Twin Cities Campus, Minneapolis, MN 55455-0213	1851	$9,173	(S)	$6,996	5-D	50,402	1,974
Univ of Mississippi Medical Ctr, Jackson, MS 39216-4505	1955	$9,206	(S)	$3,400	5-D	2,092	836
Univ of Mississippi, University, MS 38677	1844	$4,602	(S)	$5,892	5-D	15,220	797
Univ of Missouri–Columbia, Columbia, MO 65211	1839	$7,308	(S)	$6,977	5-D	28,253	1,126
Univ of Missouri–Kansas City, Kansas City, MO 64110-2499	1929	$7,592	(S)	$6,823	5-D	14,213	1,100
Univ of Missouri–Rolla, Rolla, MO 65409-0910	1870	$7,889	(S)	$6,185	5-D	5,858	418
Univ of Missouri–St. Louis, St. Louis, MO 63121	1963	$7,968	(S)	$7,178	5-D	15,540	811
Univ of Mobile, Mobile, AL 36613	1961	$13,390		$7,140	2-M	1,639	146
Univ of Montana, Missoula, MT 59812-0002	1893	$4,977	(S)	$5,860	5-D	13,558	NA
Univ of Montana–Western, Dillon, MT 59725-3598	1893	$4,212	(S)	$5,250	5-B	1,176	85
Univ of Montevallo, Montevallo, AL 35115	1896	$5,664	(S)	$4,084	5-M	2,895	216
Univ of Nebraska at Kearney, Kearney, NE 68849-0001	1903	$4,765	(S)	$5,686	5-M	6,468	377
Univ of Nebraska at Omaha, Omaha, NE 68182	1908	$5,118	(S)	$6,630	5-D	13,906	865
Univ of Nebraska Medical Ctr, Omaha, NE 68198	1869	$4,830	(S)	NA	5-D	2,995	1,007
Univ of Nebraska–Lincoln, Lincoln, NE 68588	1869	$5,867	(S)	$6,183	5-D	22,106	1,060
Univ of Nevada, Las Vegas, Las Vegas, NV 89154-9900	1957	$4,167	(S)	$8,857	5-D	27,933	1,677
Univ of Nevada, Reno, Reno, NV 89557	1874	$3,496	(S)	$8,199	5-D	16,663	988
Univ of New England, Biddeford, ME 04005-9526	1831	$23,790		$9,255	1-F	3,379	279
Univ of New Hampshire at Manchester, Manchester, NH 03101-1113	1967	$7,788	(S)	NA	5-M	1,013	91
Univ of New Hampshire, Durham, NH 03824	1866	$10,401	(S)	$7,584	5-D	14,848	948
Univ of New Haven, West Haven, CT 06516-1916	1920	$24,645		$10,130	1-M	4,649	444
Univ of New Mexico, Albuquerque, NM 87131-2039	1889	$4,336	(S)	$6,680	5-D	26,172	1,411
Univ of New Orleans, New Orleans, LA 70148	1958	$3,810	(S)	$4,734	5-D	11,747	654
Univ of North Alabama, Florence, AL 35632-0001	1830	$4,651	(S)	$4,372	5-M	6,810	375
Univ of North Carolina at Asheville, Asheville, NC 28804-3299	1927	$3,882	(S)	$5,880	5-M	3,635	304
Univ of North Carolina at Chapel Hill, Chapel Hill, NC 27599	1789	$5,033	(S)	$6,846	5-D	27,717	1,613
Univ of North Carolina at Charlotte, Charlotte, NC 28223-0001	1946	$3,895	(S)	$5,790	5-D	21,519	1,245
Univ of North Carolina at Greensboro, Greensboro, NC 27412-5001	1891	$4,029	(S)	$6,051	5-D	16,728	1,001
Univ of North Carolina at Pembroke, Pembroke, NC 28372-1510	1887	$5,262	(S)	$5,517	5-M	5,827	416
Univ of North Carolina Wilmington, Wilmington, NC 28403-3297	1947	$4,160	(S)	$6,722	5-D	11,793	784
Univ of North Dakota, Grand Forks, ND 58202	1883	$5,792	(S)	$5,085	5-D	12,834	627
Univ of North Florida, Jacksonville, FL 32224-2645	1965	$3,353	(S)	$6,268	5-D	15,954	696
Univ of North Texas, Denton, TX 76203	1890	$6,112	(S)	$5,625	5-D	33,443	1,546
Univ of Northern Colorado, Greeley, CO 80639	1890	$3,950	(S)	$6,832	5-D	12,981	632
Univ of Northern Iowa, Cedar Falls, IA 50614	1876	$6,112	(S)	$5,740	5-D	12,327	810
Univ of Notre Dame, Notre Dame, IN 46556	1842	$35,187		$9,290	2-D	11,603	1,273
Univ of Oklahoma Health Sci Ctr, Oklahoma City, OK 73190	1890	$4,428	(S)	NA	5-D	3,726	423
Univ of Oklahoma, Norman, OK 73019-0390	1890	$5,110	(S)	$6,863	5-D	26,002	1,296
Univ of Oregon, Eugene, OR 97403	1872	$5,838	(S)	$7,827	5-D	20,348	1,129
Univ of Pennsylvania, Philadelphia, PA 19104	1740	$34,156		$9,804	1-D	18,809	1,701
Univ of Phoenix Online Campus, Phoenix, AZ 85034-7209	1989	$14,180		NA	3-D	160,150	6,237
Univ of Phoenix–Atlanta Campus, Sandy Springs, GA 30350-4153	NA	$11,558		NA	3-M	2,518	890
Univ of Phoenix–Bay Area Campus, Pleasanton, CA 94588-3677	NA	$13,390		NA	3-M	3,139	1,426
Univ of Phoenix–Central Florida Campus, Maitland, FL 32751-7057	1996	$10,058		NA	3-M	2,072	525
Univ of Phoenix–Central Valley Campus, Fresno, CA 93720	2004	$12,350		NA	3-M	2,145	652
Univ of Phoenix–Charlotte Campus, Charlotte, NC 28273-3409	2003	$10,770		NA	3-M	1,604	227
Univ of Phoenix–Chicago Campus, Schaumburg, IL 60173-4399	2002	$11,190		NA	3-M	1,590	437
Univ of Phoenix–Dallas Campus, Dallas, TX 75251-2009	2001	$11,190		NA	3-M	2,539	450
Univ of Phoenix–Denver Campus, Lone Tree, CO 80124-5453	NA	$9,750		NA	3-M	2,948	955
Univ of Phoenix–Fort Lauderdale Campus, Fort Lauderdale, FL 33309	NA	$10,058		NA	3-M	3,121	264
Univ of Phoenix–Hawai`i Campus, Honolulu, HI 96813-4317	NA	$11,700		NA	3-M	1,730	430
Univ of Phoenix–Houston Campus, Houston, TX 77079-2004	2001	$11,190		NA	3-M	4,532	772
Univ of Phoenix–Kansas City Campus, Kansas City, MO 64131-4517	2002	$11,064		NA	3-M	1,201	241
Univ of Phoenix–Las Vegas Campus, Las Vegas, NV 89128	1994	$10,200		NA	3-M	3,484	668
Univ of Phoenix–Louisiana Campus, Metairie, LA 70001-2082	1976	$9,090		NA	3-M	2,747	304
Univ of Phoenix–Maryland Campus, Columbia, MD 21045-5424	NA	$11,820		NA	3-M	1,823	436
Univ of Phoenix–Metro Detroit Campus, Troy, MI 48098-2623	NA	$11,700		NA	3-M	3,918	772
Univ of Phoenix–Nashville Campus, Nashville, TN 37214	2003	$10,470		NA	3-M	1,290	240
Univ of Phoenix–New Mexico Campus, Albuquerque, NM 87109-4645	NA	$9,750		NA	3-M	4,586	658
Univ of Phoenix–North Florida Campus, Jacksonville, FL 32216-0959	1976	$10,058		NA	3-M	2,211	255
Univ of Phoenix–Oklahoma City Campus, Oklahoma City, OK 73116-8244	1976	$9,750		NA	3-M	1,080	265
Univ of Phoenix–Oregon Campus, Tigard, OR 97223	1976	$10,770		NA	3-M	1,836	495
Univ of Phoenix–Philadelphia Campus, Wayne, PA 19087-2121	1999	$13,050		NA	3-M	1,611	286
Univ of Phoenix–Phoenix Campus, Phoenix, AZ 85040-1958	1976	$9,630		NA	3-M	8,497	784
Univ of Phoenix–Puerto Rico Campus, Guaynabo, PR 00968	1995	$5,880		NA	3-M	2,853	65
Univ of Phoenix–Sacramento Valley Campus, Sacramento, CA 95833-3632	1993	$12,900		NA	3-M	4,585	1,303
Univ of Phoenix–San Diego Campus, San Diego, CA 92123	1988	$12,450		NA	3-M	3,781	978
Univ of Phoenix–Southern Arizona Campus, Tucson, AZ 85712-2732	1979	$9,990		NA	3-M	2,839	610
Univ of Phoenix–Southern California Campus, Costa Mesa, CA 92626	1980	$13,710		NA	3-M	14,760	3,228
Univ of Phoenix–Southern Colorado Campus, Colorado Springs, CO 80919-2335	1999	$9,750		NA	3-M	1,090	431
Univ of Phoenix–Tulsa Campus, Tulsa, OK 74146-3801	1998	$9,750		NA	3-M	1,169	309
Univ of Phoenix–Utah Campus, Salt Lake City, UT 84123-4617	1984	$10,200		NA	3-M	3,986	761
Univ of Phoenix–Washington Campus, Seattle, WA 98188-7500	1997	$11,190		NA	3-M	1,758	258
Univ of Phoenix–West Florida Campus, Temple Terrace, FL 33637	NA	$10,058		NA	3-M	2,659	359
Univ of Phoenix–West Michigan Campus, Walker, MI 49544	2000	$11,400		NA	3-M	1,004	370
Univ of Phoenix–Wisconsin Campus, Brookfield, WI 53045-6608	2001	$11,010		NA	3-M	1,132	238
Univ of Pittsburgh at Bradford, Bradford, PA 16701-2812	1963	$10,894	(S)	$6,650	12-B	1,319	124
Univ of Pittsburgh at Greensburg, Greensburg, PA 15601-5860	1963	$11,612	(S)	$6,680	12-B	1,796	138
Univ of Pittsburgh at Johnstown, Johnstown, PA 15904-2990	1927	$10,876	(S)	$6,200	12-B	3,142	NA
Univ of Pittsburgh, Pittsburgh, PA 15260	1787	$12,138	(S)	$7,800	12-D	26,860	2,157
Univ of Portland, Portland, OR 97203-5798	1901	$26,390		$7,850	2-M	3,478	306
Univ of Puerto Rico at Arecibo, Arecibo, PR 00613	1967	$1,707	(S)	NA	6-B	4,146	274
Univ of Puerto Rico at Bayamón, Bayamón, PR 00959	1971	$2,083	(S)	NA	6-B	4,638	319
Univ of Puerto Rico at Humacao, Humacao, PR 00791	1962	$1,707	(S)	NA	6-B	4,306	282
Univ of Puerto Rico at Ponce, Ponce, PR 00732-7186	1970	$2,264	(S)	NA	6-B	3,486	182
Univ of Puerto Rico at Utuado, Utuado, PR 00641-2500	1979	$2,054	(S)	NA	6-B	1,514	NA
Univ of Puerto Rico, Aguadilla Univ Coll, Aguadilla, PR 00604-0160	1972	$2,049	(S)	NA	6-B	3,231	133

Name, address	Year Founded	Tuition & Fees	Rm. & Board	Control, Degree	Enroll-ment	Faculty
Univ of Puerto Rico, Cayey Univ Coll, Cayey, PR 00736	1967	$1,707 (S)	NA	6-B	3,634	219
Univ of Puerto Rico, Mayagüez Campus, Mayagüez, PR 00681-9000	1911	$1,856 (S)	NA	6-D	12,380	766
Univ of Puerto Rico, Medical Sci Campus, San Juan, PR 00936-5067 (4)	1950	NA	NA	6-D	2,289	693
Univ of Puerto Rico, Río Piedras, San Juan, PR 00931-3300	1903	$1,104 (S)	$4,940	6-D	20,528	1,431
Univ of Puget Sound, Tacoma, WA 98416	1888	$30,060	$7,670	1-F	2,819	274
Univ of Redlands, Redlands, CA 92373-0999	1907	$28,776	$9,360	1-M	2,407	316
Univ of Rhode Island, Kingston, RI 02881	1892	$7,724 (S)	$8,466	5-D	15,062	706
Univ of Richmond, University of Richmond, VA 23173	1830	$37,610	$7,200	1-F	3,554	343
Univ of Rio Grande, Rio Grande, OH 45674	1876	$3,280	$6,788	1-M	2,429	308
Univ of Rochester, Rochester, NY 14627-0250	1850	$35,190 (A)	$10,640	1-D	8,846	763
Univ of Saint Francis, Fort Wayne, IN 46808-3994	1890	$18,478	$5,834	2-M	2,039	223
Univ of San Diego, San Diego, CA 92110-2492	1949	$32,564	$10,960	2-D	7,483	723
Univ of San Francisco, San Francisco, CA 94117-1080	1855	$31,180	$10,730	2-D	8,549	871
Univ of Sci & Arts of Oklahoma, Chickasha, OK 73018	1908	$3,720 (S)	$4,360	5-B	1,492	89
Univ of Scranton, Scranton, PA 18510	1888	$25,938	$10,224	2-D	5,353	509
Univ of Sioux Falls, Sioux Falls, SD 57105-1699	1883	$17,940	$5,400	2-D	1,675	140
Univ of South Alabama, Mobile, AL 36688-0002	1963	$4,502 (S)	$4,428	5-D	13,090	992
Univ of South Carolina Aiken, Aiken, SC 29801-6309	1961	$6,700 (S)	$6,370	5-M	3,380	265
Univ of South Carolina Beaufort, Beaufort, SC 29902-4601	1959	$5,794 (S)	$6,900	5-B	1,386	101
Univ of South Carolina Upstate, Spartanburg, SC 29303-4999	1967	$7,314 (S)	$5,240	5-M	4,610	374
Univ of South Carolina, Columbia, SC 29208	1801	$7,808 (S)	$6,520	5-D	27,390	1,673
Univ of South Dakota, Vermillion, SD 57069-2390	1862	$5,379 (S)	$4,964	5-D	8,746	335
Univ of South Florida, Tampa, FL 33620-9951	1956	$3,490 (S)	$7,180	5-D	43,636	1,937
Univ of Southern California, Los Angeles, CA 90089	1880	$33,892	$10,144	1-D	33,389	2,570
Univ of Southern Indiana, Evansville, IN 47712-3590	1965	$4,520 (S)	$6,492	5-M	10,021	629
Univ of Southern Maine, Portland, ME 04104-9300	1878	$6,327 (S)	$7,444	5-D	10,478	704
Univ of Southern Mississippi, Hattiesburg, MS 39406-0001	1910	$4,714 (S)	$5,070	5-D	14,777	860
Univ of St. Francis, Joliet, IL 60435-6169	1920	$19,540	$7,280	2-M	2,060	206
Univ of St. Thomas, Houston, TX 77006-4696	1947	$17,868	$6,700	2-D	3,607	275
Univ of St. Thomas, St. Paul, MN 55105-1096	1885	$24,808	$6,882	2-D	10,712	776
Univ of Tampa, Tampa, FL 33606-1490	1931	$19,628	$7,254	1-M	5,381	435
Univ of Tennessee at Chattanooga, Chattanooga, TN 37403-2598	1886	$5,628 (S)	$6,500	5-D	8,923	733
Univ of Tennessee at Martin, Martin, TN 38238-1000	1900	$4,665 (S)	$4,410	5-M	6,893	446
Univ of Tennessee, Knoxville, TN 37996	1794	$5,864 (S)	$6,358	5-D	28,901	1,625
Univ of Texas at Arlington, Arlington, TX 76019	1895	$6,400 (S)	$5,553	5-D	24,825	1,100
Univ of Texas at Austin, Austin, TX 78712-1011	1883	$7,630 (S)	$8,176	5-D	49,697	2,814
Univ of Texas at Brownsville, Brownsville, TX 78520-4991	1973	$3,657 (S)	$2,300	5-M	15,688	693
Univ of Texas at Dallas, Richardson, TX 75083-0688	1969	$7,570 (S)	$6,540	5-D	14,523	697
Univ of Texas at El Paso, El Paso, TX 79968-0001	1913	$5,262 (S)	$4,185	5-D	19,842	1,083
Univ of Texas at San Antonio, San Antonio, TX 78249-0617	1969	$6,699 (S)	$8,169	5-D	28,380	1,138
Univ of Texas at Tyler, Tyler, TX 75799-0001	1971	$4,476 (S)	NA	5-M	5,926	378
Univ of Texas Health Sci Ctr at Houston, Houston, TX 77225-0036	1972	$5,602 (S)	NA	5-D	3,399	1,247
Univ of Texas Health Sci Ctr at San Antonio, San Antonio, TX 78229-3900	1976	$4,535 (A)	NA	5-D	2,754	1,372
Univ of Texas Medical Branch, Galveston, TX 77555	1891	$4,302 (S)	$3,060	5-D	2,255	NA
Univ of Texas of the Permian Basin, Odessa, TX 79762-0001	1969	NA	NA	5-M	2,695	158
Univ of Texas Southwestern Medical Ctr at Dallas, Dallas, TX 75390	1943	$4,105 (S)	NA	5-D	2,434	103
Univ of Texas–Pan American, Edinburg, TX 78541-2999	1927	$4,165 (S)	$5,095	5-D	17,337	830
Univ of the Arts, Philadelphia, PA 19102-4944	1870	$25,680	$6,300	1-M	2,315	472
Univ of the Cumberlands, Williamsburg, KY 40769-1372	1889	$13,658	$6,626	2-M	1,884	126
Univ of the District of Columbia, Washington, DC 20008-1175	1976	$3,140 (A)	NA	9-M	5,534	435
Univ of the Incarnate Word, San Antonio, TX 78209-6397	1881	$19,060	$6,994	2-D	5,619	445
Univ of the Pacific, Stockton, CA 95211-0197	1851	$27,350	$8,700	1-D	6,251	656
Univ of the Sacred Heart, San Juan, PR 00914-0383	1935	$4,980	$2,100	2-M	5,345	343
Univ of the Sci in Philadelphia, Philadelphia, PA 19104-4495	1821	$25,392	$9,936	1-D	2,857	235
Univ of the Virgin Islands, Saint Thomas, VI 00802-9990	1962	$3,726 (S)	$7,550	7-M	2,487	260
Univ of Toledo, Toledo, OH 43606-3390	1872	$7,927 (S)	$7,894	5-D	19,374	1,145
Univ of Tulsa, Tulsa, OK 74104-3189	1894	$21,770	$7,404	2-D	4,125	376
Univ of Utah, Salt Lake City, UT 84112-1107	1850	$4,663 (S)	$5,828	5-D	28,619	1,758
Univ of Vermont, Burlington, VT 05405	1791	$11,324 (S)	$7,642	5-D	11,870	767
Univ of Virginia, Charlottesville, VA 22903	1819	$7,845 (S)	$6,909	5-D	24,068	1,295
Univ of Virginia's Coll at Wise, Wise, VA 24293	1954	$6,151 (S)	$6,984	5-B	1,911	149
Univ of Washington, Bothell, Bothell, WA 98011-8246	1990	$5,859 (S)	NA	5-M	1,683	103
Univ of Washington, Seattle, WA 98195	1861	$5,988 (S)	$6,561	5-D	39,524	3,617
Univ of Washington, Tacoma, Tacoma, WA 98402-3100	1990	$6,327 (S)	NA	5-F	2,292	142
Univ of West Alabama, Livingston, AL 35470	1835	$4,326 (S)	$3,438	5-M	3,633	100
Univ of West Florida, Pensacola, FL 32514-5750	1963	$3,311 (S)	$6,600	5-D	9,819	575
Univ of West Georgia, Carrollton, GA 30118	1933	$3,460 (S)	$5,162	5-D	10,163	490
Univ of Wisconsin–Eau Claire, Eau Claire, WI 54702-4004	1916	$5,502 (S)	$4,936	5-M	10,505	518
Univ of Wisconsin–Green Bay, Green Bay, WI 54311-7001	1968	$5,716 (S)	$4,700	5-M	5,803	285
Univ of Wisconsin–La Crosse, La Crosse, WI 54601-3742	1909	$5,555 (S)	$4,970	5-M	9,818	443
Univ of Wisconsin–Madison, Madison, WI 53706-1380	1848	$6,726 (S)	$6,920	5-D	41,466	2,975
Univ of Wisconsin–Milwaukee, Milwaukee, WI 53201-0413	1956	$7,392 (S)	$5,314	5-D	28,309	1,444
Univ of Wisconsin–Oshkosh, Oshkosh, WI 54901	1871	$5,364 (S)	$5,164	5-M	11,080	560
Univ of Wisconsin–Parkside, Kenosha, WI 53141-2000	1968	$5,386 (S)	$5,277	5-M	4,914	271
Univ of Wisconsin–Platteville, Platteville, WI 53818-3099	1866	$5,450 (S)	$4,880	5-M	6,732	356
Univ of Wisconsin–River Falls, River Falls, WI 54022-5001	1874	$5,728 (S)	$4,586	5-M	5,862	330
Univ of Wisconsin–Stevens Point, Stevens Point, WI 54481-3897	1894	$5,459 (S)	$4,542	5-M	8,842	439
Univ of Wisconsin–Stout, Menomonie, WI 54751	1891	$6,963 (S)	$4,884	5-M	8,327	390
Univ of Wisconsin–Superior, Superior, WI 54880-4500	1893	$5,567 (S)	$4,576	5-M	2,924	173
Univ of Wisconsin–Whitewater, Whitewater, WI 53190-1790	1868	$6,407 (S)	$4,190	5-M	10,502	502
Univ of Wyoming, Laramie, WY 82070	1886	$3,554 (S)	$7,274	5-D	13,203	720
Universidad del Este, Carolina, PR 00983	1949	$4,022	NA	1-M	10,366	439
Universidad del Turabo, Gurabo, PR 00778-3030	1972	$4,022	NA	1-M	14,769	410
Universidad Metropolitana, San Juan, PR 00928-1150	1980	$4,022	NA	1-M	10,566	358
Urbana Univ, Urbana, OH 43078-2091	1850	$16,254	$6,612	1-M	1,551	120
Ursinus Coll, Collegeville, PA 19426-1000	1869	$33,350	$7,600	1-B	1,589	155
Ursuline Coll, Pepper Pike, OH 44124-4398	1871	$20,090	$6,684	2-M	1,639	213
Utah State Univ, Logan, UT 84322	1888	$3,949 (S)	$4,400	5-D	14,444	739
Utah Valley State Coll, Orem, UT 84058-5999	1941	$3,308 (S)	NA	5-B	23,305	1,256
Utica Coll, Utica, NY 13502-4892	1946	$23,440	$9,510	1-F	2,952	290
Valdosta State Univ, Valdosta, GA 31698	1906	$3,490 (S)	$5,680	5-D	10,888	563
Valley City State Univ, Valley City, ND 58072	1890	$5,307 (S)	$3,716	5-B	1,037	91
Valparaiso Univ, Valparaiso, IN 46383	1859	$24,000	$6,640	2-F	3,868	378
Vanderbilt Univ, Nashville, TN 37240-1001	1873	$33,440	$10,890	1-D	11,607	NA
Vanguard Univ of Southern California, Costa Mesa, CA 92626-9601	1920	$21,564	$3,568	2-M	2,146	204

Name, address	Year Founded	Tuition & Fees		Rm. & Board	Control, Degree	Enrollment	Faculty
Vassar Coll, Poughkeepsie, NY 12604	1861	$36,030		$8,130	1-M	2,424	318
Vaughn Coll of Aeronautics & Tech, Flushing, NY 11369-1037 (2).	1932	$14,280		$10,000	1-B	1,097	96
Vermont Tech Coll, Randolph Center, VT 05061-0500	1866	$8,704	(A)	$6,942	5-1	1,454	139
Villa Julie Coll, Stevenson, MD 21153	1952	$16,770		$9,188	1-M	3,123	373
Villanova Univ, Villanova, PA 19085-1699	1842	$31,135		$9,560	2-D	10,456	904
Virginia Coll at Birmingham, Birmingham, AL 35209	1989	$10,950		NA	3-B	2,407	201
Virginia Commonwealth Univ, Richmond, VA 23284-9005	1838	$4,227	(S)	$7,473	5-D	30,381	2,813
Virginia Military Inst, Lexington, VA 24450 (2)	1839	$7,609	(S)	$5,930	5-B	1,362	151
Virginia Polytechnic Inst & State Univ, Blacksburg, VA 24061	1872	$6,973	(S)	$4,700	5-D	28,470	1,586
Virginia State Univ, Petersburg, VA 23806-0001	1882	$5,440	(S)	$6,884	5-D	4,872	336
Virginia Union Univ, Richmond, VA 23220-1170	1865	$12,770		$5,662	2-D	1,700	140
Virginia Wesleyan Coll, Norfolk, VA 23502-5599	1961	$23,136		$6,850	2-B	1,414	185
Viterbo Univ, La Crosse, WI 54601-4797	1890	$18,590		$6,140	2-M	2,991	205
Wagner Coll, Staten Island, NY 10301-4495.	1883	$27,400		$8,400	1-M	2,280	231
Wake Forest Univ, Winston-Salem, NC 27109	1834	$34,330		$9,500	1-D	6,739	600
Walden Univ, Minneapolis, MN 55401	1970	$8,640		NA	3-D	27,633	1,254
Walla Walla Coll, College Place, WA 99324-1198	1892	$21,014		$4,710	2-M	1,876	181
Walsh Coll of Accountancy & Business Administration, Troy, MI 48007-7006	1922	$9,526		NA	1-M	3,105	128
Walsh Univ, North Canton, OH 44720-3396	1958	$18,900		$7,430	2-M	2,396	217
Wartburg Coll, Waverly, IA 50677-0903	1852	$22,410		$6,715	2-B	1,769	164
Washburn Univ, Topeka, KS 66621	1865	$5,312	(S)	$5,170	10-F	7,153	536
Washington & Jefferson Coll, Washington, PA 15301	1781	$28,080		$7,602	1-B	1,515	145
Washington & Lee Univ, Lexington, VA 24450-0303	1749	$31,875		$8,920	1-F	2,148	214
Washington Coll, Chestertown, MD 21620-1197	1782	$30,200		$6,450	1-M	1,381	146
Washington State Univ, Pullman, WA 99164	1890	$6,447	(S)	$6,890	5-D	23,655	1,501
Washington Univ in St. Louis, St. Louis, MO 63130-4899	1853	$35,524		$11,252	1-D	13,355	1,076
Wayland Baptist Univ, Plainview, TX 79072-6998	1908	$10,800		$3,584	2-M	1,072	93
Wayne State Coll, Wayne, NE 68787	1910	$4,013	(S)	$4,470	5-M	3,407	204
Wayne State Univ, Detroit, MI 48202	1868	$6,812	(S)	$6,575	5-D	33,137	1,917
Waynesburg Coll, Waynesburg, PA 15370-1222	1849	$15,780		$6,370	2-M	2,159	135
Weber State Univ, Ogden, UT 84408-1001	1889	$3,433	(S)	$5,328	5-M	18,303	909
Webster Univ, St. Louis, MO 63119-3194	1915	$18,240		$7,403	1-D	7,840	749
Wellesley Coll, Wellesley, MA 02481 (3)	1870	$33,072		$10,216	1-B	2,318	320
Wentworth Inst of Tech, Boston, MA 02115-5998	1904	$19,300		$9,300	1-B	3,613	269
Wesley Coll, Dover, DE 19901-3875	1873	$17,579		$7,800	2-M	2,306	157
Wesleyan Univ, Middletown, CT 06459-0260	1831	$35,144		$9,540	1-D	3,220	365
West Chester Univ of Pennsylvania, West Chester, PA 19383	1871	$6,293	(S)	$6,342	5-M	12,882	806
West Liberty State Coll, West Liberty, WV 26074	1837	$3,996	(S)	$5,734	5-B	2,246	161
West Texas A&M Univ, Canyon, TX 79016-0001	1909	$4,920	(S)	$5,440	5-D	7,412	312
West Virginia State Univ, Institute, WV 25112-1000	1891	$3,776	(S)	$5,600	5-M	3,502	198
West Virginia Univ Inst of Tech, Montgomery, WV 25136	1895	NA		NA	5-M	2,468	176
West Virginia Univ, Morgantown, WV 26506	1867	$4,476	(S)	$6,630	5-D	27,115	1,135
West Virginia Wesleyan Coll, Buckhannon, WV 26201	1890	$20,980		$6,160	2-M	1,222	137
Western Carolina Univ, Cullowhee, NC 28723	1889	$4,610	(S)	$5,210	5-D	8,861	701
Western Connecticut State Univ, Danbury, CT 06810-6885	1903	$6,731	(S)	$7,784	5-D	6,086	481
Western Governors Univ, Salt Lake City, UT 84107	1998	$5,735		NA	1-M	2,821	51
Western Illinois Univ, Macomb, IL 61455-1390	1899	$7,411	(S)	$6,446	5-D	13,602	731
Western Intl Univ, Phoenix, AZ 85021-2718	1978	$7,992		NA	3-M	2,229	385
Western Kentucky Univ, Bowling Green, KY 42101	1906	$5,952	(S)	$5,348	5-M	18,660	1,109
Western Michigan Univ, Kalamazoo, MI 49008-5202	1903	$6,866	(S)	$6,877	5-D	24,841	1,412
Western New England Coll, Springfield, MA 01119	1919	$37,658		$9,998	1-F	3,653	294
Western New Mexico Univ, Silver City, NM 88062-0680	1893	$3,065	(S)	$4,590	5-M	3,074	145
Western Oregon Univ, Monmouth, OR 97361-1394	1856	$4,683	(S)	$7,030	5-M	4,885	312
Western State Coll of Colorado, Gunnison, CO 81231	1901	$3,349	(S)	$6,976	5-B	2,094	146
Western Washington Univ, Bellingham, WA 98225-5996	1893	$5,003	(S)	$6,785	5-M	14,035	651
Westfield State Coll, Westfield, MA 01086	1838	$5,950	(S)	$6,470	5-M	5,426	363
Westminster Coll, New Wilmington, PA 16172-0001	1852	$24,325		$7,070	2-M	1,593	149
Westminster Coll, Salt Lake City, UT 84105-3697	1875	$21,030		$6,140	1-M	2,479	246
Westmont Coll, Santa Barbara, CA 93108-1099	1937	$29,470		$9,232	2-B	1,337	142
Wheaton Coll, Norton, MA 02766	1834	$34,610		$8,150	1-B	1,561	158
Wheaton Coll, Wheaton, IL 60187-5593	1860	$22,450		$7,040	2-D	2,924	295
Wheeling Jesuit Univ, Wheeling, WV 26003-6295	1954	$23,490		$7,230	2-D	1,402	77
Wheelock Coll, Boston, MA 02215-4176 (4)	1888	$24,890		$9,910	1-M	1,023	179
Whitman Coll, Walla Walla, WA 99362-2083	1859	$30,806		$7,840	1-B	1,455	191
Whittier Coll, Whittier, CA 90608-0634	1887	$28,206		$8,542	1-F	1,307	127
Whitworth Univ, Spokane, WA 99251-0001	1890	$25,692		$7,294	2-M	2,504	291
Wichita State Univ, Wichita, KS 67260	1895	$4,481	(S)	$5,276	5-D	14,298	524
Widener Univ, Chester, PA 19013-5792	1821	$26,750		$9,640	1-D	6,460	587
Wilkes Univ, Wilkes-Barre, PA 18766-0002	1933	$22,990		$9,860	1-F	4,777	345
Willamette Univ, Salem, OR 97301-3931	1842	$30,018		$7,250	2-F	2,747	312
William Carey Univ, Hattiesburg, MS 39401-5499	1906	$8,715		$3,615	2-M	2,493	210
William Jewell Coll, Liberty, MO 64068-1843	1849	$21,400		$5,840	2-B	1,404	154
William Paterson Univ of New Jersey, Wayne, NJ 07470-8420	1855	$9,422	(S)	$9,380	5-M	10,600	NA
William Penn Univ, Oskaloosa, IA 52577-1799	1873	$16,880		$5,042	2-B	1,861	52
William Woods Univ, Fulton, MO 65251-1098	1870	$15,570		$6,100	2-M	2,893	274
Williams Coll, Williamstown, MA 01267	1793	$33,700		$8,950	1-M	2,049	313
Wilmington Coll, New Castle, DE 19720-6491	1967	$8,060		NA	1-D	7,911	946
Wilmington Coll, Wilmington, OH 45177	1870	$20,656		$7,406	2-M	1,704	122
Wingate Univ, Wingate, NC 28174-0159	1896	$17,650		$6,750	2-F	1,809	162
Winona State Univ, Winona, MN 55987-5838	1858	$7,100	(S)	$6,300	5-M	8,220	456
Winston-Salem State Univ, Winston-Salem, NC 27110-0003	1892	$3,109	(S)	$5,476	5-M	5,650	400
Winthrop Univ, Rock Hill, SC 29733	1886	$9,500	(S)	$5,570	5-M	6,292	543
Wittenberg Univ, Springfield, OH 45501-0720	1845	$31,400		$7,870	2-M	2,089	195
Wofford Coll, Spartanburg, SC 29303-3663	1854	$26,110		$7,260	2-B	1,240	129
Woodbury Univ, Burbank, CA 91504-1099	1884	$23,572		$8,104	1-M	1,485	237
Worcester Polytechnic Inst, Worcester, MA 01609-2280	1865	$33,318		$9,950	1-D	3,918	314
Worcester State Coll, Worcester, MA 01602-2597	1874	$5,539	(S)	$5,738	5-M	5,440	385
Wright State Univ, Dayton, OH 45435	1964	$7,278	(S)	$7,180	5-D	16,207	647
Xavier Univ of Louisiana, New Orleans, LA 70125-1098.	1925	$13,900		$7,200	2-F	3,012	181
Xavier Univ, Cincinnati, OH 45207	1831	$23,880		$8,640	2-D	6,666	601
Yale Univ, New Haven, CT 06520	1701	$33,030		$10,020	1-D	11,416	1,559
Yeshiva Univ, New York, NY 10033-3201	1886	NA		NA	1-D	5,998	NA
York Coll of Pennsylvania, York, PA 17405-7199	1787	$11,160		$6,950	1-M	5,664	427
York Coll of the City Univ of New York, Jamaica, NY 11451-0001	1967	$4,180	(S)	NA	11-B	6,185	456
Youngstown State Univ, Youngstown, OH 44555-0001	1908	$6,697	(S)	$6,490	5-D	13,178	969

UNITED STATES GOVERNMENT

EXECUTIVE BRANCH	LEGISLATIVE BRANCH	JUDICIAL BRANCH
PRESIDENT **Vice President** **Executive Office of the President** White House Office* Office of the Vice President Council of Economic Advisers Council on Environmental Quality National Security Council Office of Administration Office of Management and Budget Office of National Drug Control Policy Office of Science and Technology Policy Office of the U.S. Trade Representative	**CONGRESS** **Senate** **House** Architect of the Capitol U.S. Botanic Garden Government Accountability Office Government Printing Office Library of Congress Congressional Budget Office Medicare Payment Advisory Commission Stennis Center for Public Service	**Supreme Court of the United States** Courts of Appeals District Courts Territorial Courts Court of International Trade Bankruptcy Courts Court of Federal Claims Tax Court Court of Appeals for the Armed Forces Court of Appeals for Veterans Claims Administrative Office of the Courts Federal Judicial Center Sentencing Commission Judicial Panel on Multidistrict Litigation

*Includes Domestic Policy Council, Homeland Security Council, National Economic Council, Office of Faith-Based and Community Initiatives, Office of the First Lady, Office of National AIDS Policy, Privacy and Civil Liberties Oversight Board, USA Freedom Corps, White House Fellows Office, White House Military Office.

The Bush Administration

As of Oct. 1, 2007; mailing addresses are for Washington, DC, except for the Pentagon.

Terms of office of the president and vice president: Jan. 20, 2005 to Jan. 20, 2009.

President: By law, Pres. George W. Bush receives an annual salary of $400,000 (taxable) and an annual expense allowance of $50,000 (nontaxable) for costs resulting from official duties. In addition, up to $100,000 a year may be spent on travel expenses and $19,000 on official entertainment (both nontaxable). This does not include amounts available for expenditures within the Executive Office of the President, including $3,850,000 for necessary expenses for the White House and amounts for travel and entertainment.

Website: www.whitehouse.gov/president; **E-mail:** comments@whitehouse.gov

Vice President: By law, Vice Pres. Dick Cheney receives an annual salary of $215,700 (taxable), plus $90,000 for official entertainment expenses (nontaxable).

Website: www.whitehouse.gov/vicepresident; **E-mail:** vice_president@whitehouse.gov

The Cabinet Department Heads

(Salary: $186,600 per year)

Secretary of State: Condoleezza Rice
Secretary of the Treasury: Henry M. Paulson Jr.
Secretary of Defense: Robert M. Gates
Attorney General: Peter D. Kiesler, acting
Secretary of the Interior: Dirk Kempthorne
Secretary of Agriculture: Chuck Conner, acting
Secretary of Commerce: Carlos M. Gutierrez
Secretary of Labor: Elaine L. Chao
Secretary of Health and Human Services: Michael O. Leavitt
Secretary of Housing and Urban Development: Alphonso Jackson
Secretary of Transportation: Mary E. Peters
Secretary of Energy: Samuel W. Bodman
Secretary of Education: Margaret Spellings
Secretary of Veterans Affairs: Gordon H. Mansfield, acting
Secretary of Homeland Security: Michael Chertoff

The White House Staff

1600 Pennsylvania Ave. NW 20500;
www.whitehouse.gov

Counselor to the President: Edward W. Gillespie
Physician to the President: Richard Tubb
Director, National Intelligence: Mike McConnell
Assistants to the President:
Chief of Staff: Joshua B. Bolten
Deputy Chief of Staff for Operations: Joe Hagin
Deputy Chief of Staff for Policy: Joel D. Kaplan
Counsel to the President: Fred F. Fielding
White House Press Secretary: Dana M. Perino
Deputy National Security Advisor: James F. Jeffrey
Staff Secretary: Raul Yanes
Communications: Kevin Sullivan
Domestic Policy: Karl Zinsmeister
Economic Policy and Director of the National Economic Council: Allan Hubbard
Homeland Security and Counterterrorism: Frances Fragos Townsend
Legislative Affairs: Candida Wolff
National Security Advisor: Stephen Hadley
Presidential Personnel: Liza Wright
Speechwriting: William McGurn
Chief of Staff to the Vice President: David Addington

Special Assistant to the President & White House Social Secretary: Amy S. Zantzinger
Assistant to the President and Chief of Staff to the First Lady: Anita McBride
Press Secretary, Office of the First Lady: Sally McDonough Niemac

Executive Agencies

Council of Economic Advisers: Edward P. Lazear, chair; www.whitehouse.gov/cea
Office of Administration: John Straub, dir.; www.whitehouse.gov/oa
Office of Science & Technology Policy: John H. Marburger III, dir.; www.ostp.gov
Office of Natl. Drug Control Policy: John P. Walters, dir.; www.whitehousedrugpolicy.gov
Office of Management and Budget: Jim Nussle, dir.; www.whitehouse.gov/omb
U.S. Trade Representative: Amb. Susan C. Schwab; www.ustr.gov
Council on Environ. Quality: James L. Connaughton, chair; www.whitehouse.gov/ceq

Department of State

2201 C St. NW 20520; www.state.gov

Secretary of State: Condoleezza Rice
Deputy Secretary: John D. Negroponte
U.S. Permanent Rep. to the United Nations: Zalmay Khalilzad
U.S. Agency for Intl. Dev. (USAID) Admin.: Henrietta H. Fore, act.
Under Sec. for Political Affairs: R. Nicholas Burns
Under Sec. for Management: Henrietta H. Fore
Under Sec. for Democracy & Global Affairs: Paula J. Dobriansky
Under Sec. for Economic, Energy, & Agricultural Affairs: Reuben Jeffery III
Under Sec. for Arms Control & International Security: vacant
Under Sec. for Public Diplomacy & Public Affairs: Karen P. Hughes
Policy Planning Director: David F. Gordon
Chief of Protocol: Amb. Nancy G. Brinker
Inspector General: Howard J. Krongard
Legal Adviser: John B. Bellinger III
Coord. for Counterterrorism: Amb. Dell L. Dailey
Director General of the Foreign Service & Director of Human Resources: George M. Staples

Assistant Secretaries of Bureaus for:
Administration: Rajkumar Chellaraj
African Affairs: Jendayi E. Frazer
Consular Affairs: Maura Harty
Democracy, Human Rights, & Labor: Barry F. Lowenkron
Diplomatic Security: Richard J. Griffin
East Asian & Pacific Affairs: Christopher R. Hill
Education & Cultural Affairs: Miller Crouch, act.
European & Eurasian Affairs: Daniel Fried
Intelligence & Research: Randall M. Fort
International Narcotics & Law Enforcement Affairs: Thomas A. Schweich, act.
International Organizations: Kristen Silverberg
International Security and Nonproliferation: John C. Rood
Legislative Affairs: Dr. Jeffrey T. Bergner
Near Eastern Affairs: C. David Welch
Oceans, International Environmental, & Scientific Affairs: Claudia A. McMurray
Political-Military Affairs: Stephen Mull, act.
Population, Refugees, & Migration: Ellen R. Sauerbrey
Public Affairs: Sean McCormack
Resource Management; Chief Financial Officer: Bradford R. Higgins
South & Central Asian Affairs: Richard A. Boucher
Verification, Compliance, & Implementation: Paula A. DeSutter
Western Hemisphere Affairs: Thomas A. Shannon Jr.

Department of the Treasury

1500 Pennsylvania Ave. NW 20220; www.ustreas.gov

Secretary of the Treasury: Henry M. Paulson Jr.
Deputy Sec. of the Treasury: Robert M. Kimmitt
Chief of Staff: Jim Wilkinson
Executive Secretary: Taiya Smith
White House Liaison: Denise Dick
Under Sec. for Domestic Finance: Robert Steel
Under Sec. for International Affairs: David H. McCormick
Under Sec. for Terrorism & Financial Intelligence: Stuart Levey
General Counsel: Robert Hoyt
Inspector General: Dennis Schindel, act.
Inspector General for Tax Admin.: J. Russell George
Treasurer of the U.S.: Anna Escobedo Cabral
Assistant Secretaries for:
Economic Policy: Phillip L. Swagel
Financial Institutions: David Nason
Financial Markets: Anthony Ryan
Fiscal Affairs: Kenneth E. Carfine
Intelligence & Analysis: Janice B. Gardner
International Affairs: Clay Lowery
Legislative Affairs: Kevin I. Fromer
Management/CFO: Peter B. McCarthy
Public Affairs: Michele Davis
Tax Policy: Eric Solomon
Terrorist Financing: Patrick M. O'Brien
Bureaus:
Alcohol and Tobacco Tax and Trade: John Manfreda, adm.
Comptroller of the Currency: John Dugan
Engraving & Printing: Larry R. Felix, dir.
Financial Crimes Enforcement Network: James H. Freis Jr., dir.
Financial Management Service: Kenneth Papaj, comm.
Internal Revenue Service: Kevin Brown, act.
U.S. Mint: Edmund C. Moy, dir.
Office of Thrift Supervision: John Reich, dir.
Public Debt: Van Zeck, comm.

Department of Defense

The Pentagon, Arlington, VA 20301; www.defenselink.mil

Secretary of Defense: Robert M. Gates
Deputy Sec. of Defense: Gordon England
Under Sec. Comptroller/CFO: Tina W. Jonas
Under Sec. for Acquis., Tech., & Logistics: Kenneth J. Krieg
Under Sec. for Intelligence: James R. Clapper Jr.
Under Sec. for Personnel & Readiness: David S. C. Chu
Under Sec. for Policy: Eric S. Edelman
Assistant Secretaries for:
Health Affairs: S. Ward Casscells
Homeland Defense: Paul McHale
International Security Affairs: vacant
International Security Policy: Peter C. W. Flory
Legislative Affairs: Hon. Robert Wilkie
Networks & Info Integration/CIO: Hon. John G. Grimes

Nuclear & Chemical & Biological Defense Programs: Jean D. Reed
Public Affairs: J. Dorrance Smith
Reserve Affairs: Thomas F. Hall
Special Ops. & Low-Intensity Conflict: Michael G. Vickers
Inspector General: Claude M. Kicklighter
General Counsel: William J. Haynes II
Operational Test & Evaluation: Charles E. McQueary, dir.
Chairman, Joint Chiefs of Staff: Adm. Michael G. Mullen
Secretary of the Army: Pete Geren
Secretary of the Navy: Dr. Donald C. Winter
Commandant of the Marine Corps: James T. Conway
Secretary of the Air Force: Michael W. Wynne

Department of Justice

950 Pennsylvania Avenue, NW 20530; www.usdoj.gov

Attorney General: Peter D. Keisler, act.
Deputy Attorney General: Craig S. Morford, act.
Associate Attorney General: Gregory G. Katsas, act.
Office of Dispute Resolution: Joanna M. Jacobs, act. dir.
Solicitor General: Paul D. Clement
Inspector General: Glenn A. Fine
Assistant Attorney Generals for:
Antitrust Division: Thomas O. Barnett
Civil Division: Peter D. Keisler
Civil Rights Division: Wan J. Kim
Criminal Division: Alice S. Fisher
Environ. & Nat. Resources Division: Ronald J. Tenpas
Justice Programs: vacant
Legal Counsel: Steven G. Bradbury, act.
Legal Policy: Brett G. Gerry, act.
Legislative Affairs: Richard A. Hertling, act.
National Security Division: Kenneth L. Wainstein
Tax Division: vacant
Office of Public Affairs: Brian Roehrkasse, dir.
Office of Information & Privacy: Melanie Ann Pustay, dir.
Community Oriented Policing Services: Carl R. Peed
Federal Bureau of Investigation: Robert S. Mueller III, dir.
Bureau of Alcohol, Tobacco, Firearms, & Explosives: Michael J. Sullivan, act. dir.
Exec. Office for Immigration Review: Kevin A. Ohlson, dir.
Bureau of Prisons: Harley G. Lappin, dir.
Community Relations Service: Sharee M. Freeman, dir.
Drug Enforcement Admin.: Karen P. Tandy, administrator
Office of Professional Responsibility: H. Marshall Jarrett, counsel
Professional Responsibility Advisory Office: Barbara Kammerman, act. dir.
Office of Tribal Justice: Tracy Toulou, dir.
Exec. Off. for U.S. Trustees: Clifford J. White III, dir.
Foreign Claims Settlement Comm.: Mauricio J. Tamargo, chair
Exec. Office for U.S. Attorneys: Kenneth E. Melson, dir.
Pardon Attorney: Roger C. Adams
U.S. Parole Commission: Edward F. Reilly Jr.
U.S. Marshals Service: John F. Clark
U.S. Natl. Central Bureau of INTERPOL: Martin Renkiewicz
Office of Intergovt. & Public Liaison: Jennifer Korn, dir.
Off. on Violence Against Women: Mary Beth Buchanan, act. dir.
National Drug Intelligence Center: Michael F. Walther

Department of the Interior

1849 C St. NW 20240; www.doi.gov

Secretary of the Interior: Dirk Kempthorne
Deputy Secretary: P. Lynn Scarlett
Solicitor: David Bernhardt
Assistant Secretaries for:
Fish, Wildlife, & Parks: vacant
Indian Affairs: Carl J. Artman
Land & Minerals Management: C. Stephen Allred
Policy, Management, & Budget: vacant
Water & Science: vacant
Bureau of Land Management: James L. Caswell, dir.
Bureau of Reclamation: Robert W. Johnson
Fish & Wildlife Service: Dale Hall
Geological Survey: Mark Myers, dir.
Inspector General: Earl E. Devaney
Minerals Management Service: Randall Luthi, dir.
National Park Service: Mary A. Bomar, dir.
National Indian Gaming Comm.: Phil Hogen, chair
Office of Surface Mining Reclamation & Enforcement: Brent Wahlquist, dir.
Special Trustee for American Indians: Ross Swimmer
Chief Information Officer: W. Hord Tipton

Department of Agriculture

1400 Independence Ave. SW 20250; www.usda.gov

Secretary of Agriculture: Chuck Conner, act.
Deputy Secretary: Chuck Conner
Chief of Staff: Dale Moore
Under Secretaries for:
 Farm & Foreign Agric. Services: Mark Keenum
 Food, Nutrition, & Consumer Services: Nancy Montanez Johner
 Food Safety: Dr. Richard Raymond
 Marketing & Regulatory Progs.: Bruce I. Knight
 Natural Resources & Environment: Mark E. Rey
 Research, Education, & Economics: Gale A. Buchanan
 Rural Development: Thomas C. Dorr
Assistant Secretaries for:
 Administration: Boyd K. Rutherford
 Civil Rights: Margo M. McKay
 Congressional Relations: Linda Avery Strachan
General Counsel: Marc L. Kesselman
Inspector General: Phyllis K. Fong
CFO/CIO: Charles R. Christopherson Jr.
Chief Economist: Keith Collins
Communications: Terri Teuber, dir.

Department of Commerce

1401 Constitution Ave. NW 20230; www.commerce.gov

Secretary of Commerce: Carlos M. Gutierrez
Deputy Secretary: vacant
Chief of Staff: Claire Buchan
General Counsel: John J. Sullivan
Chief Information Officer: Barry C. West
Inspector General: vacant
Under Secretaries for:
 Industry and Security: Mark Foulon, act.
 Economic Affairs: Cynthia A. Glassman
 Export Administration: Christopher A. Padilla
 International Trade: vacant
 NOAA: Vice Admiral Conrad C. Lautenbacher Jr., admin.
 Intellectual Property and Director USPTO: Jon W. Dudas
 Technology: Robert C. Cresanti
Assistant Secretaries for:
 Administration & Chief Financial Officer: Otto J. Wolff
 Telecommunications and Information: John M.R. Kneuer
 Economic Development Administration: Sandy K. Baruah
 Import Administration: David Spooner
 Legislative and Intergovt. Affairs: Nathaniel Wienecke
 Oceans and Atmosphere: John (Jack) J. Kelley Jr.
 Manufacturing and Services: William G. Sutton Jr.
 Market Access and Compliance: David Bohigian
Business Liaison: Dan McCardell
Policy and Strategic Planning: Joel Harris
Public Affairs: E. Richard Mills
White House Liaison: Jeffrey S. Cavanaugh
Bureau of the Census: Charles Louis Kincannon, dir.
Bureau of Economic Analysis: J. Steven Landefeld, dir.
Minority Business Development Agency: Ronald Langston
Natl. Institute of Standards and Technology: Dr. William A. Jeffrey

Department of Labor

200 Constitution Ave. NW 20210; www.dol.gov

Secretary of Labor: Elaine L. Chao
Deputy Secretary: Howard M. Radzely, act.
Assistant Secretaries for:
 Admin. & Management: Patrick Pizzella
 Congressional & Intergovt. Affairs: Kristine Iverson
 Disability Employment Policy: vacant
 Employee Benefits Security Admin.: Bradford P. Campbell
 Employment & Training: Emily Stover DeRocco
 Employment Standards: Victoria A. Lipnic
 Occupational Safety & Health: Edwin G. Foulke Jr.
 Mine Safety & Health: Richard E. Stickler
 Policy: Leon R. Sequeira
 Public Affairs: David W. James
 Veterans' Employment & Training: Charles S. Ciccollela
Solicitor: Jonathan L. Snare, act.
Intl. Labor Affairs: Charlotte Ponticelli, dpty. under sec.
21st Century Workforce: Karen M. Czarnecki, dir.
Small Business Programs: José (Joe) A. Lira, dir.
Women's Bureau: Shinae Chun, dir.
Inspector General: Gordon S. Heddell
Chief Financial Officer: vacant
Bureau of Labor Statistics: vacant

Department of Health and Human Services

200 Independence Ave. SW 20201; www.hhs.gov

Secretary of Health & Human Services: Michael O. Leavitt
Deputy Secretary: Tevi D. Troy
Chief of Staff: Rich McKeown
Centers for Disease Control and Prevention: Julie Louise Gerberding, dir.
Food & Drug Admin.: Andrew von Eschenbach, M.D., comm.
Health Resources and Services: Elizabeth M. Duke, Ph.D.
Healthcare Research & Quality: Carolyn M. Clancy, dir.
Indian Health Service: Charles W. Grim, D.D.S., M.H.S.A., dir.
National Institutes of Health: Elias A. Zerhouni, dir.
Substance Abuse & Mental Health: Terry Cline, Ph.D., admin.
Assistant Secretaries for:
 Administration & Management: Joe Ellis
 Aging: Josefina G. Carbonell
 Children & Families: Daniel C. Schneider, act.
 Health: Dr. Anand K. Parekh, act.
 Legislation: Vincent J. Ventimiglia Jr.
 Planning & Evaluation: vacant
 Preparedness & Response: W. Craig Vanderwagen
 Public Affairs: Christina Pearson, act.
 Resources and Technology: Charles E. Johnson
General Counsel: Daniel Meron
Inspector General: Daniel R. Levinson
Office for Civil Rights: Winston Wilkinson, dir.
Office on Disability: Dr. Margaret Giannini, M.D., F.A.A.P., dir.
Office of Intergovernmental Affairs: Laura M. Caliguiri, dir.
Office of Medicare Hearings & Appeals: Hon. Perry Rhew, dir.
Surgeon General: Rear Adm. Kenneth Moritsugu, act.
Ctrs. for Medicare & Medicaid Services: Kerry Weems, act. adm.

Department of Housing and Urban Development

451 7th St. SW 20410; www.hud.gov

Secretary of Housing & Urban Development: Alphonso Jackson
Deputy Secretary: Roy A. Bernardi
Chief of Staff: Camille T. Pierce
Assistant Secretaries for:
 Administration: Keith Nelson
 Community Planning & Development: vacant
 Congressional & Intergovt. Relations: vacant
 Fair Housing & Equal Opportunity: Kim Kendrick
 Housing/Federal Housing Comm.: Brian Montgomery
 Policy Development & Research: Darlene Williams
 Public & Indian Housing: Orlando J. Cabrera
General Counsel: Robert M. Couch
Inspector General: Kenneth M. Donohue Sr.
Chief Executive Officer: Marcella E. Belt
Chief Financial Officer: John W. Cox
Chief Information Officer: Lisa Schlosser
Chief Procurement Officer: Joseph A. Neurauter
Govt. Natl. Mortgage Assn. (Ginnie Mae): vacant

Department of Transportation

1200 New Jersey Ave. SE 20590 ; www.dot.gov

Secretary of Transportation: Mary E. Peters
Deputy Secretary: Vice Adm. Thomas J. Barrett
Chief of Staff: Robert Johnson
Under Secretary for Policy: Jeffrey N. Shane
General Counsel: David James Gribbin IV
Assistant Secretaries for:
 Administration: Linda J. Washington
 Aviation & International Affairs: Andrew B. Steinberg
 Budget & Programs/CFO: Phyllis F. Scheinberg
 Governmental Affairs: vacant
 Public Affairs: Brian Turmail
 Transportation Policy: Tyler Duvall
Bureau of Transportation Statistics: Steven D. Dillingham
Federal Aviation Admin.: vacant
Federal Highway Admin.: J. Richard Capka
Federal Motor Carrier Safety Admin.: John Hill
Federal Railroad Admin.: Joseph H. Boardman
Federal Transit Admin.: James S. Simpson
Maritime Admin.: Sean T. Connaughton
Natl. Highway Traffic Safety Admin.: Nicole Nason
Inspector General: Calvin Scovel
Pipeline & Hazardous Materials Safety Admin.: Krista L. Edwards, act.
Research & Innovative Technology: Paul Brubaker, adm.
St. Lawrence Seaway Devel. Corp.: Collister Johnson Jr.

Department of Energy

1000 Independence Ave. SW 20585; www.energy.gov

Secretary of Energy: Samuel W. Bodman
Deputy Secretary: Clay Sell
Chief of Staff: Jeffrey Kupfer
Under Sec. of Energy: Clarence H. Albright Jr.
Under Sec. for Science: Dr. Raymond L. Orbach
Under Sec. for Nuclear Security: Thomas D'Agostino, adm.
General Counsel: David R. Hill
Inspector General: Gregory Friedman
Assistant Secretaries for:
  Congressional & Intergovt. Affairs: Lisa E. Epifani
  Electricity Delivery and Energy Reliability: Kevin Kolevar
  Energy Efficiency & Renewable Energy: Alexander Karsner
  Environmental Management: James A. Rispoli
  Fossil Energy: Tom Shope, act.
  Policy & International Affairs: Karen A. Harbert
  Nuclear Energy: Dennis Spurgeon
Directors of Offices for:
  Civilian Radioactive Waste Management: Edward Sproat
  Economic Impact & Diversity: Theresa Alvillar-Speake
  Hearings & Appeals: Fred L. Brown, act.
  Intelligence & Counterintelligence: Rolf Mowatt-Larssen
  Legacy Management: Michael W. Owen
  Management: Ingrid Kolb
  Public Affairs: Andrew C. Beck
Chief Financial Officer: Steven J. Isakowitz
Chief Information Officer: Tom Pyke
Energy Advisory Board: Hon. M. Peter McPherson, chair
Energy Information Admin.: Guy F. Caruso
Health, Safety and Security: Glenn Podonsky, chief
Human Capital Management: Jeff T.H. Pon, chief

Department of Education

400 Maryland Ave. SW 20202; www.ed.gov

Secretary of Education: Margaret Spellings
Deputy Secretary: Raymond J. Simon
Under Secretary: Sara Martinez Tucker
Chief of Staff: David Dunn
Assistant Secretaries for:
  Civil Rights: Stephanie Monroe
  Communications and Outreach: Lauren Maddox
  Elementary and Secondary Education: Kerri L. Briggs
  Legislation & Congressional Affairs: Terrell Halaska
  Management: Michell Clark
  Planning, Evaluation, & Policy Development: Doug Mesecar, act.
  Postsecondary Education: Diane A. Jones
  Special Education & Rehabilitative Services: vacant
  Vocational & Adult Education: Troy Justesen
Chief Financial Officer: Lawrence A. Warder
Federal Student Aid: Lawrence A. Warder, act., chf. op. off.
General Counsel: Kent D. Talbert
Inspector General: John P. Higgins Jr.
Institute of Education Sciences: Grover J. Whitehurst, dir.
Office of Educational Technology: Timothy J. Magner, dir.

Department of Veterans Affairs

810 Vermont Ave. NW 20420; www.va.gov

Secretary of Veterans Affairs: Gordon H. Mansfield, act.
Deputy Secretary: Gordon H. Mansfield
Chief of Staff: Thomas G. Bowman
Under Sec. for Health: Dr. Michael J. Kussman
Under Sec. for Benefits: Daniel L. Cooper
Under Sec. for Memorial Affairs: William F. Tuerk
Assistant Secretaries for:
  Congressional and Legislative Affairs: Thomas E. Harvey

Human Resources: vacant
Information and Technology/CIO: Robert T. Howard
Management: Robert J. Henke
Operations, Security, & Preparedness: Charles Hopkins III
Policy and Planning: Patrick W. Dunne
Public and Intergovernmental Affairs: Lisette M. Mondello
General Counsel: Paul J. Hutter, act.
Inspector General: George J. Opfer
Board of Veterans' Appeals: James P. Terry, chair.

Department of Homeland Security

20528 (no street address used); www.dhs.gov

Secretary of Homeland Security: Michael Chertoff
Deputy Secretary: Michael P. Jackson
Chief of Staff: Chad Sweet
Executive Secretary: Fred L. Schwien
Under Sec. for Management: Paul A. Schneider
Under Sec. for Preparedness: vacant
Under Sec. for Natl. Protection & Program: Robert D. Jamison, act.
Under Sec. for Science & Tech: Rear Adm. Jay M. Cohen
Assistant Secretaries for:
  Cyber Security and Communications: Gregory Garcia
  Grants and Training: Tracy Henke
  Health Affairs: Dr. Jeffrey W. Runge, act.
  Immigration & Customs Enforcement: Julie L. Myers
  Infrastructure Protection: Robert B. Stephan
  Intergovernmental Programs: Anne P. Petera
  International Affairs: Marisa R. Lino
  Legislative Affairs: Donald H. Kent Jr.
  Intelligence & Analysis: Charles E. Allen
  Policy: Stewart A. Baker
  Policy Development: Richard C. Barth, Ph.D.
  Private Sector Office: Alfonso Martinez-Fonts
  Public Affairs: J. Edward Fox
  Strategic Plans: Eric Fagerholm, act.
  Transportation Security Administration: Kip Hawley
Chief Administrative Services Officer: Donald G. Bathurst
Chief Financial Officer: David Norquist
Chief Human Capital Officer: Marta B. Pérez
Chief Information Officer: Scott Charbo
Chief Medical Officer: Dr. Jeffrey W. Runge
Chief Privacy Officer: Hugo Teufel III
Chief Procurement Officer: Elaine C. Duke
Chief Security Officer: Jerry Williams
Citizenship & Immigration Services: Emilio T. Gonzalez, dir./Prakash I. Khatri, ombudsman.
Counternarcotics Enforcement: Uttam Dhillon, dir.
Customs & Border Protection: W. Ralph Basham, comm.
Domestic Nuclear Detection Office: Vayl Oxford, dir.
Federal Coordinator of Gulf Coast Rebuilding: Donald E. Powell
Federal Law Enforcement Training: Connie L. Patrick, dir.
Federal Emergency Management Agency: R. David Paulison, admin.
General Counsel: Gus P. Coldebella
Homeland Security Advisory Council: William H. Webster, chair
Inspector General: Richard L. Skinner
Officer for Civil Rights & Civil Liberties: Daniel W. Sutherland
Operations Coordination: Roger T. Rufe Jr, dir.
Screening Coordination: Kathleen L. Kraninger, dir.
Sr. Military Advisor: Rear Admiral Daniel B. Lloyd
U.S. Coast Guard Commandant: Adm. Thad W. Allen
U.S. Secret Service: Mark J. Sullivan, dir.

Notable U.S. Government Agencies

Source: The U.S. Government Manual; National Archives and Records Administration; World Almanac research
All addresses are Washington, DC, unless otherwise noted; as of September 2007

* = independent agency

Bureau of Alcohol, Tobacco, Firearms and Explosives: Michael J. Sullivan, act. (Dept. of Justice, 650 Mass. Ave NW, 20226); www.atf.gov
Bureau of the Census: Charles Louis Kincannon, dir. (Dept. of Commerce, 4700 Silver Hill Rd., 20233); www.census.gov
Bureau of Citizenship & Immigration Services: Emilio T. Gonzalez, dir. (Dept. of Homeland Security, 20 Massachusetts Avenue NW, 20529); www.uscis.gov

Bureau of Economic Analysis: J. Steven Landefeld, dir. (Dept. of Commerce, 1441 L St. NW, 20005); www.bea.gov
Bureau of Prisons: Harley G. Lappin, dir. (Dept. of Justice, 320 First St. NW, 20534); www.bop.gov
Centers for Disease Control & Prevention: Julie Louise Gerberding, dir. (Dept. of HHS, 1600 Clifton Rd., Atlanta, GA 30333); www.cdc.gov
***Central Intelligence Agency:** Gen. Michael V. Hayden, dir. (Wash., DC 20505); www.cia.gov

*Commission on Civil Rights: Gerald A. Reynolds, chair (624 9th St. NW, 20425); www.usccr.gov

*Commodity Futures Trading Commission: Walter Lukken, act. chair (3 Lafayette Centre, 1155 21st St. NW, 20581); www.cftc.gov

*Consumer Product Safety Commission: Nancy Nord, act. chair (4330 East-West Hwy., Bethesda, MD 20814); www.cpsc.gov

*Environmental Protection Agency: Stephen L. Johnson, adm. (Ariel Rios Bldg., 1200 Pennsylvania Ave. NW, 20460); www.epa.gov

*Equal Employment Opportunity Commission: Naomi C. Earp, chair (1801 L St. NW, 20507); www.eeoc.gov

*Export-Import Bank of the United States: James H. Lambright, pres. and chair (811 Vermont Avenue NW, 20571); www.exim.gov

*Farm Credit Administration: Nancy C. Pellett, chair (1501 Farm Credit Drive, McLean, VA 22102); www.fca.gov

Federal Bureau of Investigation: Robert S. Mueller III, dir. (Dept. of Justice, J. Edgar Hoover Building, 935 Pennsylvania Ave. NW, 20535); www.fbi.gov

*Federal Communications Commission: Kevin J. Martin, chair (445 12th St. SW, 20554); www.fcc.gov

*Federal Deposit Insurance Corporation: Sheila C. Bair, chair (550 17th St. NW, 20429); www.fdic.gov

*Federal Election Commission: Robert D. Lenhard, chair (999 E St. NW, 20463); www.fec.gov

Federal Emergency Management Agency: R. David Paulison, admin. (Dept. of Homeland Security, 500 C St. SW, 20472); www.fema.gov

*Federal Energy Regulatory Commission: Joseph T. Kelliher, chair (888 1st St. NE, 20426); www.ferc.gov

Federal Highway Administration: J. Richard Capka, admin. (Dept. of Trans., 1200 New Jersey Ave. SE 20590); www.fhwa.dot.gov

*Federal Maritime Commission: vacant chair (800 N. Capitol St. NW, 20573); www.fmc.gov

*Federal Mine Safety & Health Review Commission: Michael F. Duffy, chair (601 New Jersey Ave. NW, Ste. 9500, 20001); www.fmshrc.gov

*Federal Reserve System: Ben S. Bernanke, chair, Board of Governors (20th St. & Constitution Ave. NW, 20551); www.federalreserve.gov

*Federal Trade Commission: Deborah Platt Majoras, chair (600 Pennsylvania Ave. NW, 20580); www.ftc.gov

Fish & Wildlife Service: H. Dale Hall, dir. (Dept. of the Interior, 1849 C St. NW, 20240); www.fws.gov

Food and Drug Administration: Andrew C. von Eschenbach, comm. (Dept. of HHS, 5600 Fishers Lane, Rockville, MD 20857); www.fda.gov

Forest Service: Gail Kimbell, chief (Dept. of Agriculture, 1400 Independence Ave. SW, 20250); www.fs.fed.us

Government Accountability Office: (cong. agency) David M. Walker, comptroller gen. (441 G St. NW, 20548); www.gao.gov

*General Services Administration: Lurita A. Doan, admin. (1800 F St. NW, 20405); www.gsa.gov

Government Printing Office: (cong. agency) Richard G. Davis, act. Superintendent of Documents (732 N. Capitol St. NW, 20401); www.gpoaccess.gov

*Inter-American Foundation: Larry Palmer, pres. (901 N Stuart St., 10th floor, Arlington, VA 22203); www.iaf.gov

Internal Revenue Service: Linda E. Stiff, comm. (Dept. of Treas., 1111 Constitution Ave. NW, 20224); www.irs.gov

Library of Congress: (cong. agency) James H. Billington, Librarian of Congress (101 Indep. Ave. SE, 20540); www.loc.gov

*National Aeronautics and Space Administration: Michael Griffin, adm. (300 E St. SW, 20546). www.nasa.gov

*National Archives & Records Administration: Allen Weinstein, archivist (8601 Adelphi Road, College Park, MD 20740-6001); www.archives.gov

*National Endowment for the Arts: Dana Gioia, chair (1100 Pennsylvania Ave. NW, 20506); www.arts.gov

*National Endowment for the Humanities: Bruce Cole, chair (1100 Pennsylvania Ave. NW, 20506); www.neh.gov

National Institutes of Health: Elias A. Zerhouni, dir. (Dept. of HHS, 9000 Rockville Pike, Bethesda, MD 20892); www.nih.gov

*National Labor Relations Board: Robert J. Battista, chair (1099 14th St. NW, 20570); www.nlrb.gov

National Oceanic and Atmospheric Administration: Vice Adm. Conrad C. Lautenbacher Jr., admin. (Dept. of Commerce, 14th & Constitution Ave. NW, 20230); www.noaa.gov

National Park Service: Mary A. Bomar, dir. (Dept. of the Interior, 1849 C St. NW, 20240); www.nps.gov

*National Railroad Passenger Corp. (Amtrak): Alexander Kummant, pres. and CEO (60 Mass. Ave. NE, 20002); www.amtrak.com

*National Science Foundation: Dr. Arden L. Bement Jr., dir., National Science Foundation; Steven C. Beering, chair, National Science Board (4201 Wilson Blvd., Arlington, VA 22230); www.nsf.gov

*National Transportation Safety Board: Mark V. Rosenker, chair (490 L'Enfant Plaza SW, 20594); www.ntsb.gov

*Nuclear Regulatory Commission: Dale E. Klein, chair (U.S. Nuclear Regulatory Commission 20555); www.nrc.gov

Occupational Safety & Health Administration: Edwin G. Foulke Jr. (Dept. of Labor, 200 Constitution Ave. NW, 20210); www.osha.gov

*Occupational Safety & Health Review Commission: Horace A. Thompson, chair (1120 20th St. NW, 9th Floor, 20036); www.oshrc.gov

*Office of Government Ethics: Robert I. Cusick, dir. (1201 New York Ave. NW, Suite 500, 20005); www.usoge.gov

*Office of Personnel Management: Linda M. Springer, dir. (1900 E St. NW, 20415-0001); www.opm.gov

*Office of Special Counsel: Scott J. Bloch, spec. counsel (1730 M St. NW, Suite 218, 20036); www.osc.gov

*Peace Corps: Ronald A. Tschetter, dir. (1111 20th St., NW, 20526); www.peacecorps.gov

*Postal Rate Commission: Dan G. Blair, chair (901 New York Avenue, NW, Ste. 200, 20268); www.prc.gov

*Securities and Exchange Commission: Christopher Cox, chair (100 F Street NE, 20549); www.sec.gov

*Selective Service System: William A. Chatfield, dir. (National Headquarters, 1515 Wilson Blvd., Arlington, VA 22209-2425); www.sss.gov

*Small Business Administration: Steven C. Preston, adm. (409 Third St. SW, Ste. 7800, 20416); www.sba.gov

Smithsonian Institution: (quasi-official agency) Cristián Samper, act. sec. (PO Box 37012, SI Building, Rm. 153, MRC 010, 20013); www.si.edu

*Social Security Administration: Michael J. Astrue, comm. (6401 Security Blvd., Baltimore, MD 21235); www.ssa.gov

Surgeon General: Rear Adm. Kenneth Moritsugu, act. (Dept. of HHS, 200 Independence Ave SW, 20201); www.surgeongeneral.gov

*Tennessee Valley Authority: Tom Kilgore, Chief Executive Officer and President (400 W. Summit Hill Dr., Knoxville, TN 37902); www.tva.gov

*Trade and Development Agency: Leocadia I. Zak, act. dir. (1000 Wilson Blvd. Ste. 1600, Arlington, VA 22209); www.tda.gov

*U.S. Agency for International Development: Henrietta H. Fore, act. adm. (1300 Pennsylvania Ave. NW, 20523-1000); www.usaid.gov

United States Coast Guard: Adm. Thad W. Allen, commandant (Dept. of Homeland Security, 2100 2nd St. SW, 20593); www.uscg.mil

U.S. Customs and Border Protection: W. Ralph Basham, comm. (Dept. of Homeland Security, 1300 Pennsylvania Ave. NW, 20229); www.cbp.gov

United States Fire Administration: Gregory B. Cade, asst. adm. (Dept. of Homeland Security, 16825 S. Seton Ave., Emmitsburg, MD 21727) www.usfa.dhs.gov

United States Geological Survey: Mark Myers, dir. (Dept. of the Interior, 12201 Sunrise Valley Dr., Reston, VA 20192); www.usgs.gov

*United States International Trade Commission: Daniel R. Pearson, chair (Dept. of Commerce, 500 E St. SW, 20436); www.usitc.gov

United States Mint: Edmund C. Moy, dir. (Dept. of Treas., U.S. Mint Headquarters, 801 9th St., NW, 20220); www.usmint.gov

*United States Postal Service: John E. Potter, Postmaster General (475 L'Enfant Plaza SW, 20260); www.usps.com

United States Secret Service: Mark J. Sullivan, dir. (Dept. of Homeland Security, 245 Murray Dr., Bldg. 410, 20223); www.secretservice.gov

CABINETS OF THE U.S.

The U.S. Cabinet and Its Role

The heads of major executive departments of government constitute the Cabinet. This institution, not provided for in the U.S. Constitution, developed as an advisory body out of the desire of presidents to consult on policy matters. Aside from its advisory role, the Cabinet as a body has no formal function and wields no executive authority. Individual members exercise authority as heads of their departments, reporting to the president.

In addition to the heads of federal departments as listed below, the Cabinet commonly includes other officials designated by the president as of Cabinet rank.

The officials so designated by Pres. George W. Bush include: Vice Pres. Richard B. Cheney, Chief of Staff to the President Joshua B. Bolten, Environmental Protection Agency Administrator Steve Johnson, Office of Management and Budget Director Jim Nussle, Office of National Drug Control Policy Director John P. Walters, and United States Trade Representative Susan Schwab.

The Cabinet meets at times set by the president. Members of Pres. Bush's Cabinet listed in this chapter are as of Oct. 1, 2007.

Secretaries of State

The Department of Foreign Affairs was created by act of Congress on July 27, 1789, and the name changed to Department of State on Sept. 15, 1789.

President	Secretary	Home	Sworn In
Washington	Thomas Jefferson	VA	1789
	Edmund Randolph	VA	1794
	Timothy Pickering	PA	1795
Adams, J.	Timothy Pickering	PA	1797
	John Marshall	VA	1800
Jefferson	James Madison	VA	1801
Madison	Robert Smith	MD	1809
	James Monroe	VA	1811
Monroe	John Quincy Adams	MA	1817
Adams, J.Q.	Henry Clay	KY	1825
Jackson	Martin Van Buren	NY	1829
	Edward Livingston	LA	1831
	Louis McLane	DE	1833
	John Forsyth	GA	1834
Van Buren	John Forsyth	GA	1837
Harrison, W.H.	Daniel Webster	MA	1841
Tyler	Daniel Webster	MA	1841
	Abel P. Upshur	VA	1843
	John C. Calhoun	SC	1844
Polk	John C. Calhoun	SC	1845
	James Buchanan	PA	1845
Taylor	James Buchanan	PA	1849
	John M. Clayton	DE	1849
Fillmore	John M. Clayton	DE	1850
	Daniel Webster	MA	1850
	Edward Everett	MA	1852
Pierce	William L. Marcy	NY	1853
Buchanan	William L. Marcy	NY	1857
	Lewis Cass	MI	1857
	Jeremiah S. Black	PA	1860
Lincoln	Jeremiah S. Black	PA	1861
	William H. Seward	NY	1861
Johnson, A.	William H. Seward	NY	1865
Grant	Elihu B. Washburne	IL	1869
	Hamilton Fish	NY	1869
Hayes	Hamilton Fish	NY	1877
	William M. Evarts	NY	1877
Garfield	William M. Evarts	NY	1881
	James G. Blaine	ME	1881
Arthur	James G. Blaine	ME	1881
	F.T. Frelinghuysen	NJ	1881
Cleveland	F.T. Frelinghuysen	NJ	1885
	Thomas F. Bayard	DE	1885
Harrison, B.	Thomas F. Bayard	DE	1889
Harrison, B.	James G. Blaine	ME	1889
	John W. Foster	IN	1892
Cleveland	Walter Q. Gresham	IN	1893
	Richard Olney	MA	1895
McKinley	Richard Olney	MA	1897
	John Sherman	OH	1897
	William R. Day	OH	1898
	John Hay	DC	1898
Roosevelt, T.	John Hay	DC	1901
	Elihu Root	NY	1905
	Robert Bacon	NY	1909
Taft	Robert Bacon	NY	1909
	Philander C. Knox	PA	1909
Wilson	Philander C. Knox	PA	1913
	William J. Bryan	NE	1913
	Robert Lansing	NY	1915
	Bainbridge Colby	NY	1920
Harding	Charles E. Hughes	NY	1921

President	Secretary	Home	Sworn In
Coolidge	Charles E. Hughes	NY	1923
	Frank B. Kellogg	MN	1925
Hoover	Frank B. Kellogg	MN	1929
	Henry L. Stimson	NY	1929
Roosevelt, F.D.	Cordell Hull	TN	1933
	E.R. Stettinius Jr.	VA	1944
Truman	E.R. Stettinius Jr.	VA	1945
	James F. Byrnes	SC	1945
	George C. Marshall	PA	1947
	Dean G. Acheson	CT	1949
Eisenhower	John Foster Dulles	NY	1953
	Christian A. Herter	MA	1959
Kennedy	Dean Rusk	NY	1961
Johnson, L.B.	Dean Rusk	NY	1963
Nixon	William P. Rogers	NY	1969
	Henry A. Kissinger	DC	1973
Ford	Henry A. Kissinger	DC	1974
Carter	Cyrus R. Vance	NY	1977
	Edmund S. Muskie	ME	1980
Reagan	Alexander M. Haig Jr.	CT	1981
	George P. Shultz	CA	1982
Bush, G.H.W.	James A. Baker III	TX	1989
	Lawrence S. Eagleburger	MI	1992
Clinton	Warren M. Christopher	CA	1993
	Madeleine K. Albright	DC	1997
Bush, G.W.	Colin L. Powell	NY	2001
	Condoleezza Rice	AL	2005

Secretaries of the Treasury

The Treasury Department was organized by act of Congress on Sept. 2, 1789.

President	Secretary	Home	Sworn In
Washington	Alexander Hamilton	NY	1789
	Oliver Wolcott	CT	1795
Adams, J.	Oliver Wolcott	CT	1797
	Samuel Dexter	MA	1801
Jefferson	Samuel Dexter	MA	1801
	Albert Gallatin	PA	1801
Madison	Albert Gallatin	PA	1809
	George W. Campbell	TN	1814
	Alexander J. Dallas	PA	1814
	William H. Crawford	GA	1816
Monroe	William H. Crawford	GA	1817
Adams, J.Q.	Richard Rush	PA	1825
Jackson	Samuel D. Ingham	PA	1829
	Louis McLane	DE	1831
	William J. Duane	PA	1833
	Roger B. Taney	MD	1833
	Levi Woodbury	NH	1834
Van Buren	Levi Woodbury	NH	1837
Harrison, W.H.	Thomas Ewing	OH	1841
Tyler	Thomas Ewing	OH	1841
	Walter Forward	PA	1841
	John C. Spencer	NY	1843
	George M. Bibb	KY	1844
Polk	Robert J. Walker	MS	1845
Taylor	William M. Meredith	PA	1849
Fillmore	Thomas Corwin	OH	1850
Pierce	James Guthrie	KY	1853
Buchanan	Howell Cobb	GA	1857
	Phillip F. Thomas	MD	1860
	John A. Dix	NY	1861
Lincoln	Salmon P. Chase	OH	1861
	William P. Fessenden	ME	1864
	Hugh McCulloch	IN	1865
Johnson, A.	Hugh McCulloch	IN	1865

President	Secretary	Home	Sworn In
Grant	George S. Boutwell	MA	1869
	William A. Richardson	MA	1873
	Benjamin H. Bristow	KY	1874
	Lot M. Morrill	ME	1876
Hayes	John Sherman	OH	1877
Garfield	William Windom	MN	1881
Arthur	Charles J. Folger	NY	1881
	Walter Q. Gresham	IN	1884
	Hugh McCulloch	IN	1884
Cleveland	Daniel Manning	NY	1885
	Charles S. Fairchild	NY	1887
Harrison, B.	William Windom	MN	1889
	Charles Foster	OH	1891
Cleveland	John G. Carlisle	KY	1893
McKinley	Lyman J. Gage	IL	1897
Roosevelt, T.	Lyman J. Gage	IL	1901
	Leslie M. Shaw	IA	1902
	George B. Cortelyou	NY	1907
Taft	Franklin MacVeagh	IL	1909
Wilson	William G. McAdoo	NY	1913
	Carter Glass	VA	1918
	David F. Houston	MO	1920
Harding	Andrew W. Mellon	PA	1921
Coolidge	Andrew W. Mellon	PA	1923
Hoover	Andrew W. Mellon	PA	1929
	Ogden L. Mills	NY	1932
Roosevelt, F.D.	William H. Woodin	NY	1933
	Henry Morgenthau, Jr.	NY	1934
Truman	Fred M. Vinson	KY	1945
	John W. Snyder	MO	1946
Eisenhower	George M. Humphrey	OH	1953
	Robert B. Anderson	CT	1957
Kennedy	C. Douglas Dillon	NJ	1961
Johnson, L.B.	C. Douglas Dillon	NJ	1963
	Henry H. Fowler	VA	1965
	Joseph W. Barr	IN	1968
Nixon	David M. Kennedy	IL	1969
	John B. Connally	TX	1971
	George P. Shultz	IL	1972
	William E. Simon	NJ	1974
Ford	William E. Simon	NJ	1974
Carter	W. Michael Blumenthal	MI	1977
	G. William Miller	RI	1979
Reagan	Donald T. Regan	NY	1981
	James A. Baker III	TX	1985
	Nicholas F. Brady	NJ	1988
Bush, G.H.W.	Nicholas F. Brady	NJ	1989
Clinton	Lloyd Bentsen	TX	1993
	Robert E. Rubin	NY	1995
	Lawrence H. Summers	CT	1999
Bush, G.W.	Paul H. O'Neill	MO	2001
	John W. Snow	OH	2003
	Henry M. Paulson	FL	2006

Secretaries of Defense

The Department of Defense, originally designated the National Military Establishment, was created on Sept. 18, 1947. It is headed by the secretary of defense, who is a member of the president's Cabinet. The departments of the army, of the navy, and of the air force function within the Defense Department, and since 1947 the secretaries of these departments have not been members of the president's Cabinet.

President	Secretary	Home	Sworn In
Truman	James V. Forrestal	NY	1947
	Louis A. Johnson	WV	1949
	George C. Marshall	PA	1950
	Robert A. Lovett	NY	1951
Eisenhower	Charles E. Wilson	MI	1953
	Neil H. McElroy	OH	1957
	Thomas S. Gates Jr.	PA	1959
Kennedy	Robert S. McNamara	MI	1961
Johnson, L.B.	Robert S. McNamara	MI	1963
	Clark M. Clifford	MD	1968
Nixon	Melvin R. Laird	WI	1969
	Elliot L. Richardson	MA	1973
	James R. Schlesinger	VA	1973
Ford	James R. Schlesinger	VA	1974
	Donald H. Rumsfeld	IL	1975
Carter	Harold Brown	CA	1977

President	Secretary	Home	Sworn In
Reagan	Caspar W. Weinberger	CA	1981
	Frank C. Carlucci	PA	1987
Bush, G.H.W.	Richard B. Cheney	WY	1989
Clinton	Les Aspin	WI	1993
	William J. Perry	CA	1994
	William S. Cohen	ME	1997
Bush, G.W.	Donald H. Rumsfeld	IL	2001
	Robert M. Gates	TX	2006

Secretaries of War

The War Department (which included jurisdiction over the navy until 1798) was created by act of Congress on Aug. 7, 1789, and Gen. Henry Knox was commissioned secretary of war under that act on Sept. 12, 1789.

President	Secretary	Home	Sworn In
Washington	Henry Knox	MA	1789
	Timothy Pickering	PA	1795
	James McHenry	MD	1796
Adams, J.	James McHenry	MD	1797
	Samuel Dexter	MA	1800
Jefferson	Henry Dearborn	MA	1801
Madison	William Eustis	MA	1809
	John Armstrong	NY	1813
	James Monroe	VA	1814
	William H. Crawford	GA	1815
Monroe	John C. Calhoun	SC	1817
Adams, J.Q.	James Barbour	VA	1825
	Peter B. Porter	NY	1828
Jackson	John H. Eaton	TN	1829
	Lewis Cass	MI	1831
	Benjamin F. Butler	NY	1837
Van Buren	Joel R. Poinsett	SC	1837
Harrison, W.H.	John Bell	TN	1841
Tyler	John Bell	TN	1841
	John C. Spencer	NY	1841
	James M. Porter	PA	1843
	William Wilkins	PA	1844
Polk	William L. Marcy	NY	1845
Taylor	George W. Crawford	GA	1849
Fillmore	Charles M. Conrad	LA	1850
Pierce	Jefferson Davis	MS	1853
Buchanan	John B. Floyd	VA	1857
	Joseph Holt	KY	1861
Lincoln	Simon Cameron	PA	1861
	Edwin M. Stanton	PA	1862
Johnson, A.	Edwin M. Stanton	PA	1865
	John M. Schofield	IL	1868
Grant	John A. Rawlins	IL	1869
	William T. Sherman	OH	1869
	William W. Belknap	IA	1869
	Alphonso Taft	OH	1876
	James D. Cameron	PA	1876
Hayes	George W. McCrary	IA	1877
	Alexander Ramsey	MN	1879
Garfield	Robert T. Lincoln	IL	1881
Arthur	Robert T. Lincoln	IL	1881
Cleveland	William C. Endicott	MA	1885
Harrison, B.	Redfield Proctor	VT	1889
	Stephen B. Elkins	WV	1891
Cleveland	Daniel S. Lamont	NY	1893
McKinley	Russel A. Alger	MI	1897
	Elihu Root	NY	1899
Roosevelt, T.	Elihu Root	NY	1901
	William H. Taft	OH	1904
	Luke E. Wright	TN	1908
Taft	Jacob M. Dickinson	TN	1909
	Henry L. Stimson	NY	1911
Wilson	Lindley M. Garrison	NJ	1913
	Newton D. Baker	OH	1916
Harding	John W. Weeks	MA	1921
Coolidge	John W. Weeks	MA	1923
	Dwight F. Davis	MO	1925
Hoover	James W. Good	IL	1929
	Patrick J. Hurley	OK	1929
Roosevelt, F.D.	George H. Dern	UT	1933
	Harry H. Woodring	KS	1937
	Henry L. Stimson	NY	1940
Truman	Robert P. Patterson	NY	1945
	Kenneth C. Royall[1]	NC	1947

(1) Last member of the Cabinet with this title. The War Department became the Department of the Army and became a branch of the Department of Defense in 1947.

Secretaries of the Navy

The Navy Department was created by act of Congress on Apr. 30, 1798.

President	Secretary	Home	Sworn In
Adams, J.	Benjamin Stoddert	MD	1798
Jefferson	Benjamin Stoddert	MD	1801
	Robert Smith	MD	1801
Madison	Paul Hamilton	SC	1809
	William Jones	PA	1813
	Benjamin W. Crowninshield	MA	1814
Monroe	Benjamin W. Crowninshield	MA	1817
	Smith Thompson	NY	1818
	Samuel L. Southard	NJ	1823
Adams, J.Q.	Samuel L. Southard	NJ	1825
Jackson	John Branch	NC	1829
	Levi Woodbury	NH	1831
	Mahlon Dickerson	NJ	1834
Van Buren	Mahlon Dickerson	NJ	1837
	James K. Paulding	NY	1838
Harrison, W.H.	George E. Badger	NC	1841
Tyler	George E. Badger	NC	1841
	Abel P. Upshur	VA	1841
	David Henshaw	MA	1843
	Thomas W. Gilmer	VA	1844
	John Y. Mason	VA	1844
Polk	George Bancroft	MA	1845
	John Y. Mason	VA	1846
Taylor	William B. Preston	VA	1849
Fillmore	William A. Graham	NC	1850
	John P. Kennedy	MD	1852
Pierce	James C. Dobbin	NC	1853
Buchanan	Isaac Toucey	CT	1857
Lincoln	Gideon Welles	CT	1861
Johnson, A.	Gideon Welles	CT	1865
Grant	Adolph E. Borie	PA	1869
	George M. Robeson	NJ	1869
Hayes	Richard W. Thompson	IN	1877
	Nathan Goff Jr.	WV	1881
Garfield	William H. Hunt	LA	1881
Arthur	William E. Chandler	NH	1882
Cleveland	William C. Whitney	NY	1885
Harrison, B.	Benjamin F. Tracy	NY	1889
Cleveland	Hilary A. Herbert	AL	1893
McKinley	John D. Long	MA	1897
Roosevelt, T.	John D. Long	MA	1901
	William H. Moody	MA	1902
	Paul Morton	IL	1904
	Charles J. Bonaparte	MD	1905
	Victor H. Metcalf	CA	1906
	Truman H. Newberry	MI	1908
Taft	George von L. Meyer	MA	1909
Wilson	Josephus Daniels	NC	1913
Harding	Edwin Denby	MI	1921
Coolidge	Edwin Denby	MI	1923
	Curtis D. Wilbur	CA	1924
Hoover	Charles Francis Adams	MA	1929
Roosevelt, F.D.	Claude A. Swanson	VA	1933
	Charles Edison	NJ	1940
	Frank Knox	IL	1940
	James V. Forrestal	NY	1944
Truman	James V. Forrestal[1]	NY	1945

(1) Last member of Cabinet with this title. The Navy Department became a branch of the Department of Defense when the latter was created on Sept. 18, 1947.

Attorneys General

The Office of Attorney General was established by act of Congress on Sept. 24, 1789. It officially reached Cabinet rank in Mar. 1792, when the first attorney general, Edmund Randolph, attended his initial Cabinet meeting. The Department of Justice, headed by the attorney general, was created June 22, 1870.

President	Secretary	Home	Sworn In
Washington	Edmund Randolph	VA	1789
	William Bradford	PA	1794
	Charles Lee	VA	1795
Adams, J.	Charles Lee	VA	1797
Jefferson	Levi Lincoln	MA	1801
	John Breckenridge	KY	1805
	Caesar A. Rodney	DE	1807
Madison	Caesar A. Rodney	DE	1807
	William Pinkney	MD	1811
	Richard Rush	PA	1814
Monroe	Richard Rush	PA	1817
	William Wirt	VA	1817
Adams, J.Q.	William Wirt	VA	1825
Jackson	John M. Berrien	GA	1829
	Roger B. Taney	MD	1831
	Benjamin F. Butler	NY	1833
Van Buren	Benjamin F. Butler	NY	1837
	Felix Grundy	TN	1838
	Henry D. Gilpin	PA	1840
Harrison, W.H.	John J. Crittenden	KY	1841
Tyler	John J. Crittenden	KY	1841
	Hugh S. Legare	SC	1841
	John Nelson	MD	1843
Polk	John Y. Mason	VA	1845
	Nathan Clifford	ME	1846
	Isaac Toucey	CT	1848
Taylor	Reverdy Johnson	MD	1849
Fillmore	John J. Crittenden	KY	1850
Pierce	Caleb Cushing	MA	1853
Buchanan	Jeremiah S. Black	PA	1857
	Edwin M. Stanton	PA	1860
Lincoln	Edward Bates	MO	1861
	James Speed	KY	1864
Johnson, A.	James Speed	KY	1865
	Henry Stanbery	OH	1866
	William M. Evarts	NY	1868
Grant	Ebenezer R. Hoar	MA	1869
	Amos T. Akerman	GA	1870
	George H. Williams	OR	1871
	Edwards Pierrepont	NY	1875
	Alphonso Taft	OH	1876
Hayes	Charles Devens	MA	1877
Garfield	Wayne MacVeagh	PA	1881
Arthur	Benjamin H. Brewster	PA	1882
Cleveland	Augustus Garland	AR	1885
Harrison, B.	William H. H. Miller	IN	1889
Cleveland	Richard Olney	MA	1893
	Judson Harmon	OH	1895
McKinley	Joseph McKenna	CA	1897
	John W. Griggs	NJ	1898
	Philander C. Knox	PA	1901
Roosevelt, T.	Philander C. Knox	PA	1901
	William H. Moody	MA	1904
	Charles J. Bonaparte	MD	1906
Taft	George W. Wickersham	NY	1909
Wilson	J.C. McReynolds	TN	1913
	Thomas W. Gregory	TX	1914
	A. Mitchell Palmer	PA	1919
Harding	Harry M. Daugherty	OH	1921
Coolidge	Harry M. Daugherty	OH	1923
	Harlan F. Stone	NY	1924
	John G. Sargent	VT	1925
Hoover	William D. Mitchell	MN	1929
Roosevelt, F.D.	Homer S. Cummings	CT	1933
	Frank Murphy	MI	1939
	Robert H. Jackson	NY	1940
	Francis Biddle	PA	1941
Truman	Thomas C. Clark	TX	1945
	J. Howard McGrath	RI	1949
	J.P. McGranery	PA	1952
Eisenhower	Herbert Brownell Jr	NY	1953
	William P. Rogers	MD	1957
Kennedy	Robert F. Kennedy	MA	1961
Johnson, L.B.	Robert F. Kennedy	MA	1963
	N. deB. Katzenbach	IL	1964
	Ramsey Clark	TX	1967
Nixon	John N. Mitchell	NY	1969
	Richard G. Kleindienst	AZ	1972
	Elliot L. Richardson	MA	1973
	William B. Saxbe	OH	1974

President	Secretary	Home	Sworn In
Ford	William B. Saxbe	OH	1974
	Edward H. Levi	IL	1975
Carter	Griffin B. Bell	GA	1977
	Benjamin R. Civiletti	MD	1979
Reagan	William French Smith	CA	1981
	Edwin Meese III	CA	1985
	Richard Thornburgh	PA	1988
Bush, G.H.W.	Richard Thornburgh	PA	1989
	William P. Barr	NY	1991
Clinton	Janet Reno	FL	1993
Bush, G.W.	John Ashcroft	MO	2001
	Alberto Gonzales[1]	TX	2005

(1) Alberto Gonzales resigned Sept. 17, 2007.

Secretaries of the Interior

The Department of the Interior was created by act of Congress on Mar. 3, 1849.

President	Secretary	Home	Sworn In
Taylor	Thomas Ewing	OH	1849
Fillmore	Thomas M. T. McKennan	PA	1850
	Alex H. H. Stuart	VA	1850
Pierce	Robert McClelland	MI	1853
Buchanan	Jacob Thompson	MS	1857
Lincoln	Caleb B. Smith	IN	1861
	John P. Usher	IN	1863
Johnson, A.	John P. Usher	IN	1865
	James Harlan	IA	1865
	Orville H. Browning	IL	1866
Grant	Jacob D. Cox	OH	1869
	Columbus Delano	OH	1870
	Zachariah Chandler	MI	1875
Hayes	Carl Schurz	MO	1877
Garfield	Samuel J. Kirkwood	IA	1881
Arthur	Henry M. Teller	CO	1882
Cleveland	Lucius Q.C. Lamar	MS	1885
	William F. Vilas	WI	1888
Harrison, B.	John W. Noble	MO	1889
Cleveland	Hoke Smith	GA	1893
	David R. Francis	MO	1896
McKinley	Cornelius N. Bliss	NY	1897
	Ethan A. Hitchcock	MO	1898
Roosevelt, T.	Ethan A. Hitchcock	MO	1901
	James R. Garfield	OH	1907
Taft	Richard A. Ballinger	WA	1909
	Walter L. Fisher	IL	1911
Wilson	Franklin K. Lane	CA	1913
	John B. Payne	IL	1920
Harding	Albert B. Fall	NM	1921
	Hubert Work	CO	1923
Coolidge	Hubert Work	CO	1923
	Roy O. West	IL	1929
Hoover	Ray Lyman Wilbur	CA	1929
Roosevelt, F.D.	Harold L. Ickes	IL	1933
Truman	Harold L. Ickes	IL	1945
	Julius A. Krug	WI	1946
	Oscar L. Chapman	CO	1949
Eisenhower	Douglas McKay	OR	1953
	Fred A. Seaton	NE	1956
Kennedy	Stewart L. Udall	AZ	1961
Johnson, L.B.	Stewart L. Udall	AZ	1963
Nixon	Walter J. Hickel	AK	1969
	Rogers C.B. Morton	MD	1971
Ford	Rogers C.B. Morton	MD	1971
	Stanley K. Hathaway	WY	1975
	Thomas S. Kleppe	ND	1975
Carter	Cecil D. Andrus	ID	1977
Reagan	James G. Watt	CO	1981
	William P. Clark	CA	1983
	Donald P. Hodel	OR	1985
Bush, G.H.W.	Manuel Lujan	NM	1989
Clinton	Bruce Babbitt	AZ	1993
Bush, G.W.	Gale Norton	CO	2001
	Dirk Kempthorne	ID	2006

Secretaries of Agriculture

The Department of Agriculture was created by act of Congress on May 15, 1862. On Feb. 8, 1889, its commissioner was renamed secretary of agriculture and became a member of the Cabinet.

President	Secretary	Home	Sworn In
Cleveland	Norman J. Colman	MO	1889
Harrison, B.	Jeremiah M. Rusk	WI	1889
Cleveland	J. Sterling Morton	NE	1893
McKinley	James Wilson	IA	1897
Roosevelt, T.	James Wilson	IA	1901
Taft	James Wilson	IA	1909
Wilson	David F. Houston	MO	1913
	Edwin T. Meredith	IA	1920
Harding	Henry C. Wallace	IA	1921
Coolidge	Henry C. Wallace	IA	1923
	Howard M. Gore	WV	1924
	William M. Jardine	KS	1925
Hoover	Arthur M. Hyde	MO	1929
Roosevelt, F.D.	Henry A. Wallace	IA	1933
	Claude R. Wickard	IN	1940
Truman	Clinton P. Anderson	NM	1945
Truman	Charles F. Brannan	CO	1948
Eisenhower	Ezra Taft Benson	UT	1953
Kennedy	Orville L. Freeman	MN	1961
Johnson, L.B.	Orville L. Freeman	MN	1963
Nixon	Clifford M. Hardin	IN	1969
	Earl L. Butz	IN	1971
Ford	Earl L. Butz	IN	1974
	John A. Knebel	VA	1976
Carter	Bob Bergland	MN	1977
Reagan	John R. Block	IL	1981
	Richard E. Lyng	CA	1986
Bush, G.H.W.	Clayton K. Yeutter	NE	1989
	Edward Madigan	IL	1991
Clinton	Mike Espy	MS	1993
	Dan Glickman	KS	1995
Bush, G.W.	Ann M. Veneman	CA	2001
	Mike Johanns[1]	NE	2005

(1) Mike Johanns announced his resignation Sept. 20, 2007.

Secretaries of Commerce and Labor

The Department of Commerce and Labor, created by Congress on Feb. 14, 1903, was divided by Congress Mar. 4, 1913, into separate departments of Commerce and Labor. The secretary of each was made a Cabinet member.

Secretaries of Commerce and Labor

President	Secretary	Home	Sworn In
Roosevelt, T.	George B. Cortelyou	NY	1903
	Victor H. Metcalf	CA	1904
	Oscar S. Straus	NY	1906
Taft	Charles Nagel	MO	1909

Secretaries of Labor

President	Secretary	Home	Sworn In
Wilson	William B. Wilson	PA	1913
Harding	James J. Davis	PA	1921
Coolidge	James J. Davis	PA	1923
Hoover	James J. Davis	PA	1929
	William N. Doak	VA	1930
Roosevelt, F.D.	Frances Perkins	NY	1933
Truman	L.B. Schwellenbach	WA	1945
	Maurice J. Tobin	MA	1949
Eisenhower	Martin P. Durkin	IL	1953
	James P. Mitchell	NJ	1953
Kennedy	Arthur J. Goldberg	IL	1961
	W. Willard Wirtz	IL	1962
Johnson, L.B.	W. Willard Wirtz	IL	1963
Nixon	George P. Shultz	IL	1969
	James D. Hodgson	CA	1970
	Peter J. Brennan	NY	1973
Ford	Peter J. Brennan	NY	1974
	John T. Dunlop	CA	1975
	W.J. Usery Jr.	GA	1976
Carter	F. Ray Marshall	TX	1977
Reagan	Raymond J. Donovan	NJ	1981
	William E. Brock	TN	1985
	Ann D. McLaughlin	DC	1987
Bush, G.H.W.	Elizabeth Hanford Dole	NC	1989
	Lynn Martin	IL	1991
Clinton	Robert B. Reich	MA	1993
	Alexis M. Herman	AL	1997
Bush, G.W.	Elaine L. Chao	KY	2001

Secretaries of Commerce

President	Secretary	Home	Sworn In
Wilson	William C. Redfield	NY	1913
	Joshua W. Alexander	MO	1919
Harding	Herbert C. Hoover	CA	1921
Coolidge	Herbert C. Hoover	CA	1923
	William F. Whiting	MA	1928
Hoover	Robert P. Lamont	IL	1929
	Roy D. Chapin	MI	1932
Roosevelt, F.D.	Daniel C. Roper	SC	1933
	Harry L. Hopkins	NY	1939
	Jesse Jones	TX	1940
	Henry A. Wallace	IA	1945
Truman	Henry A. Wallace	IA	1945
	W. Averell Harriman	NY	1947
	Charles Sawyer	OH	1948
Eisenhower	Sinclair Weeks	MA	1953
	Lewis L. Strauss	NY	1958
	Frederick H. Mueller	MI	1959
Kennedy	Luther H. Hodges	NC	1961
Johnson, L.B.	Luther H. Hodges	NC	1963
	John T. Connor	NJ	1965
	Alex B. Trowbridge	NJ	1967
	Cyrus R. Smith	NY	1968
Nixon	Maurice H. Stans	MN	1969
	Peter G. Peterson	IL	1972
	Frederick B. Dent	SC	1973
Ford	Frederick B. Dent	SC	1974
	Rogers C.B. Morton	MD	1975
	Elliot L. Richardson	MA	1975
Carter	Juanita M. Kreps	NC	1977
	Philip M. Klutznick	IL	1979
Reagan	Malcolm Baldrige	CT	1981
	C. William Verity Jr.	OH	1987
Bush, G.H.W.	Robert A. Mosbacher	TX	1989
	Barbara H. Franklin	PA	1992
Clinton	Ronald H. Brown	DC	1993
	Mickey Kantor	CA	1996
	William M. Daley	IL	1997
	Norman Y. Mineta	CA	2000
Bush, G.W.	Donald L. Evans	TX	2001
	Carlos Gutierrez	MI	2005

Secretaries of Housing and Urban Development

The Department of Housing and Urban Development was created by act of Congress on Sept. 9, 1965.

President	Secretary	Home	Sworn In
Johnson, L.B.	Robert C. Weaver	WA	1966
	Robert C. Wood	MA	1969
Nixon	George W. Romney	MI	1969
	James T. Lynn	OH	1973
Ford	James T. Lynn	OH	1974
	Carla Anderson Hills	CA	1975
Carter	Patricia Roberts Harris	DC	1977
	Moon Landrieu	LA	1979
Reagan	Samuel R. Pierce Jr.	NY	1981
Bush, G.H.W.	Jack F. Kemp	NY	1989
Clinton	Henry G. Cisneros	TX	1993
	Andrew M. Cuomo	NY	1997
Bush, G.W.	Mel Martinez	FL	2001
	Alphonso Jackson	TX	2004

Secretaries of Transportation

The Department of Transportation was created by act of Congress on Oct. 15, 1966.

President	Secretary	Home	Sworn In
Johnson, L.B.	Alan S. Boyd	FL	1966
	John A. Volpe	MA	1969
Nixon	Claude S. Brinegar	CA	1973
	Claude S. Brinegar	CA	1974
Ford	William T. Coleman Jr.	PA	1975
	Brock Adams	WA	1977
Carter	Neil E. Goldschmidt	OR	1979
	Andrew L. Lewis Jr.	PA	1981
	Elizabeth Hanford Dole	NC	1983
Reagan	James H. Burnley	NC	1987
	Samuel K. Skinner	IL	1989
Bush, G.H.W.	Andrew H. Card Jr.	MA	1992
	Federico F. Peña	CO	1993
Clinton	Rodney E. Slater	AR	1997
Bush, G.W.	Norman Y. Mineta	CA	2001
	Mary E. Peters	AZ	2006

Secretaries of Energy

The Department of Energy was created by federal law on Aug. 4, 1977.

President	Secretary	Home	Sworn In
Carter	James R. Schlesinger	VA	1977
	Charles Duncan Jr.	WY	1979
Reagan	James B. Edwards	SC	1981
	Donald P. Hodel	OR	1982
	John S. Herrington	CA	1985
Bush, G.H.W.	James D. Watkins	CA	1989
Clinton	Hazel R. O'Leary	MN	1993
	Federico F. Peña	CO	1997
	Bill Richardson	NM	1998
Bush, G.W.	Spencer Abraham	MI	2001
	Samuel W. Bodman	MA	2005

Secretaries of Health, Education, and Welfare

The Department of Health, Education, and Welfare was created by Congress on Apr. 11, 1953. On Sept. 27, 1979, it was divided by Congress into the departments of Education and of Health and Human Services, with the secretary of each being a Cabinet member.

President	Secretary	Home	Sworn In
Eisenhower	Oveta Culp Hobby	TX	1953
	Marion B. Folsom	NY	1955
	Arthur S. Flemming	OH	1958
Kennedy	Abraham A. Ribicoff	CT	1961
	Anthony J. Celebrezze	OH	1962
Johnson, L.B.	Anthony J. Celebrezze	OH	1963
	John W. Gardner	NY	1965
	Wilbur J. Cohen	MI	1968
Nixon	Robert H. Finch	CA	1969
	Elliot L. Richardson	MA	1970
	Caspar W. Weinberger	CA	1973
Ford	Caspar W. Weinberger	CA	1974
	Forrest D. Mathews	AL	1975
Carter	Joseph A. Califano Jr.	DC	1977
	Patricia Roberts Harris	DC	1979

Secretaries of Health and Human Services

President	Secretary	Home	Sworn In
Carter	Patricia Roberts Harris	DC	1979
Reagan	Richard S. Schweiker	PA	1981
	Margaret M. Heckler	MA	1983
Reagan	Otis R. Bowen	IN	1985
Bush, G.H.W.	Louis W. Sullivan	GA	1989
Clinton	Donna E. Shalala	WI	1993
Bush, G.W.	Tommy Thompson	WI	2001
	Michael O. Leavitt	UT	2005

Secretaries of Education

President	Secretary	Home	Sworn In
Carter	Shirley Hufstedler	CA	1979
Reagan	Terrel Bell	UT	1981
	William J. Bennett	NY	1985
	Lauro F. Cavazos	TX	1988
Bush, G.H.W.	Lauro F. Cavazos	TX	1989
	Lamar Alexander	TN	1991
Clinton	Richard W. Riley	SC	1993
Bush, G.W.	Roderick R. Paige	TX	2001
	Margaret Spellings	TX	2005

Secretaries of Veterans Affairs

The Department of Veterans Affairs was created on Oct. 25, 1988, when Pres. Ronald Reagan signed a bill that made the Veterans Administration into a Cabinet department, effective Mar. 15, 1989.

President	Secretary	Home	Sworn In
Bush, G.H.W.	Edward J. Derwinski	IL	1989
Clinton	Jesse Brown	IL	1993
	Togo D. West Jr.	NC	1998
Clinton	Hershel W. Gober (acting)	AR	2000
Bush, G.W.	Anthony Principi	CA	2001
	R. James Nicholson[1]	CO	2005

(1) R. James Nicholson resigned Oct. 1, 2007.

Secretaries of Homeland Security

The Department of Homeland Security was created by act of Congress on Nov. 25, 2002.

President	Secretary	Home	Sworn In
Bush, G.W.	Thomas Ridge	PA	2003
	Michael Chertoff	DC	2005

U.S. SUPREME COURT

(data as of Sept. 2007)

Justices of the U.S. Supreme Court

The Supreme Court comprises the chief justice of the U.S. and 8 associate justices, all appointed for life by the president with advice and consent of the Senate. Names of chief justices are in **boldface**. Terms of service begin with the year each justice took the Judicial oath. Service years are the number of complete years served by a justice. Current salaries: chief justice, $212,100; associate justice, $203,000. The U.S. Supreme Court Bldg. is at 1 First St. NE, Washington, DC 20543. The Court website is www.supremecourtus.gov

Members at start of 2007-2008 term (Oct. 1, 2007): Chief justice: John G. Roberts Jr; assoc. justices in seniority order: John Paul Stevens, Antonin Scalia, Anthony M. Kennedy, David H. Souter, Clarence Thomas, Ruth Bader Ginsburg, Stephen G. Breyer, Samuel A. Alito Jr.

Name, apptd. from	Term	Yrs	Born	Died
John Jay, NY	1789-1795	5	1745	1829
John Rutledge, SC[1]	1790-1791	1	1739	1800
William Cushing, MA	1790-1810*	20	1732	1810
James Wilson, PA	1789-1798	8	1742	1798
John Blair, VA	1790-1795*	5	1732	1800
James Iredell, NC	1790-1799	9	1751	1799
Thomas Johnson, MD	1792-1793	<1	1732	1819
William Paterson, NJ	1793-1806	13	1745	1806
John Rutledge, SC[2,3]	1795	<1	1739	1800
Samuel Chase, MD	1796-1811	15	1741	1811
Oliver Ellsworth, CT	1796-1800	4	1745	1807
Bushrod Washington, VA	1799-1829*	30	1762	1829
Alfred Moore, NC	1800-1804	3	1755	1810
John Marshall, VA	1801-1835	34	1755	1835
William Johnson, SC	1804-1834	30	1771	1834
Henry B. Livingston, NY	1807-1823	16	1757	1823
Thomas Todd, KY	1807-1826	18	1765	1826
Gabriel Duvall, MD	1811-1835	23	1752	1844
Joseph Story, MA	1812-1845*	33	1779	1845
Smith Thompson, NY	1823-1843	20	1768	1843
Robert Trimble, KY	1826-1828	2	1777	1828
John McLean, OH	1830-1861*	31	1785	1861
Henry Baldwin, PA	1830-1844	14	1780	1844
James M. Wayne, GA	1835-1867	32	1790	1867
Roger B. Taney, MD	1836-1864	28	1777	1864
Philip P. Barbour, VA	1836-1841	4	1783	1841
John Catron, TN	1837-1865	28	1786	1865
John McKinley, AL	1838-1852*	14	1780	1852
Peter V. Daniel, VA	1842-1860*	18	1784	1860
Samuel Nelson, NY	1845-1872	27	1792	1873
Levi Woodbury, NH	1845-1851	5	1789	1851
Robert C. Grier, PA	1846-1870	23	1794	1870
Benjamin R. Curtis, MA	1851-1857	5	1809	1874
John A. Campbell, AL	1853-1861*	8	1811	1889
Nathan Clifford, ME	1858-1881	23	1803	1881
Noah H. Swayne, OH	1862-1881	18	1804	1884
Samuel F. Miller, IA	1862-1890	28	1816	1890
David Davis, IL	1862-1877	14	1815	1886
Stephen J. Field, CA	1863-1897	33	1816	1899
Salmon P. Chase, OH	1864-1873	8	1808	1873
William Strong, PA	1870-1880	10	1808	1895
Joseph P. Bradley, NJ	1870-1892	21	1813	1892
Ward Hunt, NY	1873-1882	9	1810	1886
Morrison R. Waite, OH	1874-1888	14	1816	1888
John M. Harlan, KY	1877-1911	33	1833	1911
William B. Woods, GA	1881-1887	6	1824	1887
Stanley Matthews, OH	1881-1889	7	1824	1889
Horace Gray, MA	1882-1902	20	1828	1902
Samuel Blatchford, NY	1882-1893	11	1820	1893
Lucius Q.C. Lamar, MS	1888-1893	5	1825	1893
Melville W. Fuller, IL	1888-1910	21	1833	1910
David J. Brewer, KS	1890-1910	20	1837	1910
Henry B. Brown, MI	1891-1906	15	1836	1913
George Shiras Jr, PA	1892-1903	10	1832	1924
Howell E. Jackson, TN	1893-1895	2	1832	1895
Edward D. White, LA[1]	1894-1910	16	1845	1921
Rufus W. Peckham, NY	1896-1909	13	1838	1909
Joseph McKenna, CA	1898-1925	26	1843	1926
Oliver W. Holmes, MA	1902-1932	29	1841	1935
William R. Day, OH	1903-1922	19	1849	1923
William H. Moody, MA	1906-1910	3	1853	1917
Horace H. Lurton, TN	1910-1914	4	1844	1914
Charles E. Hughes, NY[1]	1910-1916	5	1862	1948
Willis Van Devanter, WY	1911-1937	26	1859	1941
Joseph R. Lamar, GA	1911-1916	5	1857	1916
Edward D. White, LA[2]	1910-1921	10	1845	1921
Mahlon Pitney, NJ	1912-1922	10	1858	1924
James C. McReynolds, TN	1914-1941	26	1862	1946
Louis D. Brandeis, MA	1916-1939	22	1856	1941
John H. Clarke, OH	1916-1922	5	1857	1945
William H. Taft, CT	1921-1930	8	1857	1930
George Sutherland, UT	1922-1938	15	1862	1942
Pierce Butler, MN	1923-1939	16	1866	1939
Edward T. Sanford, TN	1923-1930	7	1865	1930
Harlan F. Stone, NY[1]	1925-1941	16	1872	1946
Charles E. Hughes, NY[2]	1930-1941	11	1862	1948
Owen J. Roberts, PA	1930-1945	15	1875	1955
Benjamin N. Cardozo, NY	1932-1938	6	1870	1938
Hugo L. Black, AL	1937-1971	34	1886	1971
Stanley F. Reed, KY	1938-1957	19	1884	1980
Felix Frankfurter, MA	1939-1962	23	1882	1965
William O. Douglas, CT	1939-1975	36[4]	1898	1980
Frank Murphy, MI	1940-1949	9	1890	1949
Harlan F. Stone, NY[2]	1941-1946	4	1872	1946
James F. Byrnes, SC	1941-1942	1	1879	1972
Robert H. Jackson, NY	1941-1954	13	1892	1954
Wiley B. Rutledge, IA	1943-1949	6	1894	1949
Harold H. Burton, OH	1945-1958	13	1888	1964
Fred M. Vinson, KY	1946-1953	7	1890	1953
Tom C. Clark, TX	1949-1967	17	1899	1977
Sherman Minton, IN	1949-1956	7	1890	1965
Earl Warren, CA	1953-1969	15	1891	1974
John Marshall Harlan, NY	1955-1971	16	1899	1971
William J. Brennan Jr, NJ	1956-1990	33	1906	1997
Charles E. Whittaker, MO	1957-1962	5	1901	1973
Potter Stewart, OH	1958-1981	22	1915	1985
Byron R. White, CO	1962-1993	31	1917	2002
Arthur J. Goldberg, IL	1962-1965	2	1908	1990
Abe Fortas, TN	1965-1969	3	1910	1982
Thurgood Marshall, NY	1967-1991	24	1908	1993
Warren E. Burger, VA	1969-1986	17	1907	1995
Harry A. Blackmun, MN	1970-1994	24	1908	1999
Lewis F. Powell Jr, VA	1972-1987	15	1907	1998
William H. Rehnquist, AZ[1]	1972-1986	14	1924	2005
John Paul Stevens, IL	1975-		1920	
Sandra Day O'Connor, AZ	1981-2006	24	1930	
William H. Rehnquist, VA[2]	1986-2005	18	1924	2005
Antonin Scalia, VA	1986-		1936	
Anthony M. Kennedy, CA	1988-		1936	
David H. Souter, NH	1990-		1939	
Clarence Thomas, GA	1991-		1948	
Ruth Bader Ginsburg, NY	1993-		1933	
Stephen G. Breyer, MA	1994-		1938	
John G. Roberts Jr, MD	2005-		1955	
Samuel A. Alito Jr, NJ	2006-		1950	

*Date oath taken from questionable source. (1) Later, chief justice, as listed. (2) Formerly assoc. justice. (3) Named as acting chief justice; confirmation rejected by the Senate. (4) Longest term of service.

CONGRESS

The One Hundred and Tenth Congress, With Official 2006 Election Results

The 110th Congress convened Jan. 4, 2007.

Source: Federal Election Commission general election results

The Senate

Rep., 49; Dem., 49; Ind., 2; Total, 100. Boldface denotes the 2006 election winner. *Incumbent.

Terms are for 6 years and end Jan. 3 of the year preceding the senator's name in the following table. Annual salary, $165,200; President Pro Tempore, Majority Leader, and Minority Leader, $183,500. To be eligible for the Senate, one must be at least 30 years old, a U.S. citizen for at least 9 years, and a resident of the state from which chosen. The address is U.S. Senate, Washington DC 20510; telephone, 202-224-3121; website, www.senate.gov

Senate officials as of September 2007 were: Pres. Pro Tempore, Robert C. Byrd (WV); Majority Leader, Harry Reid (NV); Majority Whip, Richard Durbin (IL); Minority Leader, Mitch McConnell (KY); Minority Whip, Trent Lott (MS). The Senate had 16 women (11 D, 5 R), two more than in the previous Senate; 2 Asian Americans (Daniel Inouye & Daniel K. Akaka, both D, HI), same number as in previous Senate; 3 Hispanics (Mel Martinez, R, FL, Ken Salazar, D, CO, & Robert Menendez, D, NJ), same number as in previous Senate; 1 African American (Barack Obama, D, IL), same number as in previous Senate; no Native Americans.

As of Sept. 2007, 4 Senators (4 R) did not plan to seek reelection at the end of their term. Marked in list with #.

D-Democrat; R-Republican; CFL-Connecticut for Lieberman; DFL-Dem.-Farmer-Labor; DNL-Dem.-Nonpartisan League; I-Independent; L-Libertarian

Term ends	Senator (Party); Service from[1]	2006 election
Alabama		
2009	Jeff Sessions (R); 1/7/97	
2011	Richard Shelby (R); 1/6/87	
Alaska		
2009	Ted Stevens (R); 12/24/68	
2011	Lisa Murkowski (R); 12/20/02	
Arizona		
2011	John McCain (R); 1/6/87	
2013	**Jon Kyl* (R); 1/4/95**	814,398
	Jim Pederson (D).	664,141
Arkansas		
2009	Mark Pryor (D); 1/7/03	
2011	Blanche L. Lincoln (D); 1/6/99	
California		
2011	Barbara Boxer (D); 1993	
2013	**Dianne Feinstein* (D); 11/10/92**	5,076,289
	Richard "Dick" Mountjoy (R)	2,990,822
Colorado		
2009	Wayne Allard# (R); 1/7/97	
2011	Ken Salazar (D); 2005	
Connecticut		
2011	Christopher J. Dodd (D); 1981	
2013	**Joseph Lieberman* (CFL); 1989**	564,095
	Ned Lamont (D)	450,844
Delaware		
2009	Joseph Biden Jr. (D); 1973	
2013	**Thomas R. Carper* (D); 2001**	170,567
	Jan Ting (R).	69,734
Florida		
2011	Mel Martinez (R); 2005	
2013	**Bill Nelson* (D); 2001**	2,890,548
	Katherine Harris (R).	1,826,127
Georgia		
2009	Saxby Chambliss (R); 1/7/03	
2011	Johnny Isakson (R); 2005	
Hawaii		
2011	Daniel K. Inouye (D); 1963	
2013	**Daniel K. Akaka* (D); 4/28/90**	210,330
	Cynthia Thielen (R)	126,097
Idaho		
2009	Larry Craig# (R); 1991	
2011	Mike Crapo (R); 1/6/99	
Illinois		
2009	Richard J. Durbin (D); 1/7/97	
2011	Barack Obama (D); 2005	
Indiana		
2011	Evan Bayh (D); 1/6/99	
2013	**Richard G. Lugar (R)*; 1977**	1,171,553
	Steve Osborn (L)	168,820
Iowa		
2009	Tom Harkin (D); 1985	
2011	Chuck Grassley (R); 1981	
Kansas		
2009	Pat Roberts (R); 1/7/97	
2011	Sam Brownback (R); 11/27/96	
Kentucky		
2009	Mitch McConnell (R); 1985	
2011	Jim Bunning (R); 1/6/99	
Louisiana		
2009	Mary L. Landrieu (D); 1/7/97	
2011	David Vitter (R); 2005	
Maine		
2011	Susan M. Collins (R); 1/7/97	
2013	**Olympia J. Snowe* (R); 1/4/95**	402,598
	Jean M. Hay Bright (D)	111,984
Maryland		
2011	Barbara Ann Mikulski (D); 1/6/87	
2013	**Benjamin L. Cardin (D); 2007**	965,477
	Michael S. Steele (R)	787,182
Massachusetts		
2009	John F. Kerry (D); 1/2/85	
2013	**Edward M. Kennedy* (D); 11/7/62**	1,500,738
	Kenneth G. Chase (R)	661,532
Michigan		
2009	Carl Levin (D); 1979	
2013	**Debbie Stabenow* (D); 2001**	2,151,278
	Michael Bouchard (R)	1,559,597
Minnesota		
2009	Norm Coleman (R); 1/7/03	
2013	**Amy Klobuchar (DFL); 2007**	1,278,849
	Mark Kennedy (R)	835,653
Mississippi		
2009	Thad Cochran (R); 12/27/78	
2013	**Trent Lott* (R); 1989**	388,399
	Erik R. Fleming (D)	213,000
Missouri		
2011	Christopher (Kit) Bond (R); 1/6/87	
2013	**Claire McCaskill (D); 2007**	1,055,255
	Jim Talent* (R); 11/23/02	1,006,941
Montana		
2009	Max Baucus (D); 12/15/78	
2013	**Jon Tester (D); 2007**	199,845
	Conrad Burns* (R); 1989	196,283
Nebraska		
2009	Chuck Hagel# (R); 1/7/97	
2013	**Ben Nelson* (D); 2001**	378,388
	Pete Ricketts (R).	213,928
Nevada		
2011	Harry Reid (D); 1/6/87	
2013	**John Ensign* (R); 2001**	322,501
	Jack Carter (D)	238,796
New Hampshire		
2009	John Sununu (R); 1/7/03	
2011	Judd Gregg (R); 1993	
New Jersey		
2009	Frank Lautenberg (D); 1/7/03	
2013	**Robert Menendez (D); 1/18/06**	1,200,843
	Thomas H. Kean Jr. (R)	997,775

Term ends	Senator (Party); Service from[1]	2006 election
	New Mexico	
2009	Pete V. Domenici (R); 1973	
2013	**Jeff Bingaman* (D); 1983**	**394,365**
	Allen W. McCulloch, MD (R)	163,826
	New York	
2011	Charles E. Schumer (D); 1/6/99	
2013	**Hillary Rodham Clinton* (D); 2001**	**3,008,428**
	John Spencer (R)	1,392,189
	North Carolina	
2009	Elizabeth H. Dole (R); 1/7/03	
2011	Richard Burr (R); 2005	
	North Dakota	
2011	Byron L. Dorgan (D); 12/14/92	
2013	**Kent Conrad* (DNL); 1/6/87**	**150,146**
	Dwight Grotberg (R)	64,417
	Ohio	
2011	George V. Voinovich (R); 1/6/99	
2013	**Sherrod Brown (D); 2007**	**2,257,369**
	Mike DeWine* (R); 1/4/95	1,761,037
	Oklahoma	
2009	James M. Inhofe (R); 11/21/94	
2011	Tom Coburn (R); 2005	
	Oregon	
2009	Gordon Smith (R); 1/7/97	
2011	Ron Wyden (D); 2/6/96	
	Pennsylvania	
2011	Arlen Specter (R); 1981	
2013	**Bob Casey, Jr. (D); 2007**	**2,392,984**
	Rick Santorum* (R); 1/4/95	1,684,778
	Rhode Island	
2009	John F. Reed (D); 1/7/97	
2013	**Sheldon Whitehouse (D); 2007**	**206,110**
	Lincoln D. Chafee* (R); 11/2/99	179,001
	South Carolina	
2009	Lindsey Graham (R); 1/7/03	
2011	Jim DeMint (R); 2005	
	South Dakota	
2009	Tim Johnson (D); 1/7/97	
2011	John Thune (R); 2005	

Term ends	Senator (Party); Service from[1]	2006 election
	Tennessee	
2009	Lamar Alexander (R); 1/7/03	
2013	**Bob Corker (R); 2007**	**929,911**
	Harold Ford, Jr. (D)	879,976
	Texas	
2009	John Cornyn (R); 12/2/02	
2013	**Kay Bailey Hutchison* (R); 6/5/93**	**2,661,789**
	Barbara Ann Radnofsky (D)	1,555,202
	Utah	
2011	Robert F. Bennett (R); 1993	
2013	**Orrin G. Hatch* (R); 1977**	**356,238**
	Pete Ashdown (D)	177,459
	Vermont	
2011	Patrick Leahy (D); 1975	
2013	**Bernard Sanders (I); 2007**	**171,638**
	Rich Tarrant (R)	84,924
	Virginia	
2009	John W. Warner# (R); 1/2/79	
2013	**James H. "Jim" Webb, Jr. (D); 2007**	**1,175,606**
	George F. Allen* (R); 2001	1,166,277
	Washington	
2011	Patty Murray (D); 1993	
2013	**Maria Cantwell* (D); 2001**	**1,184,659**
	Mike McGavick (R)	832,106
	West Virginia	
2009	John D. Rockefeller IV (D); 1/15/85	
2013	**Robert C. Byrd* (D); 1959**	**296,276**
	John R. Raese (R)	155,043
	Wisconsin	
2011	Russ Feingold (D); 1993	
2013	**Herb Kohl* (D); 1989**	**1,439,214**
	Robert Gerald Lorge (R)	630,299
	Wyoming	
2009	Michael B. Enzi (R); 1/7/97	
2013	**Craig Thomas* (R)[2]; 1/4/95**	**135,174**
	Dale Groutage (D)	57,671

(1) Jan. 3, unless otherwise noted. (2) John Barrasso (R) was appointed June 22, 2007, to fill the vacancy due to the death of Craig Thomas, June 4, 2007.

The House of Representatives

Rep., 201; Dem., 232; Vac., 2; Total, 435. Boldface denotes the 2006 election winner. *Incumbent. Listed are winner, runner-up, and any candidate who received at least 5% of votes cast.

Terms are for 2 years ending Jan. 3, 2009. Annual salary, $165,200; Speaker of the House, $212,100; Majority Leader and Minority Leader, $183,500. To be eligible for membership, a person must be at least 25 years of age, a U.S. citizen for at least 7 years, and a resident of the state from which he or she is chosen. The address is U.S. House of Representatives, Washington, DC 20515; telephone, 202-224-3121; website, www.house.gov

House officials as of September 2007 were: Speaker of the House, Nancy Pelosi (CA); Majority Leader, Steny Hoyer (MD); Majority Whip, James Clyburn (SC); Minority Leader, John Boehner (OH); Minority Whip, Roy Blunt (MO). Including delegates, there were 74 women in the House (53 D, 21 R), 3 more than in the previous House. There were 42 African Americans (all D), same number as in previous House, 24 Hispanics (20 D, 4 R), an increase of 1; 6 Asian Americans, an increase of 1; and 1 Native American.

As of Sept. 2007, 11 representatives (2 D, 9 R) did not plan to seek reelection at the end of their term. Marked in list with #.

D-Democrat; **R**-Republican; **AIP**-American Independent; **CRP**-CO Reform Party; **C**-Constitution; **CRV**-Conservative; **DFL**-Dem.-Farmer-Labor; **DNL**-Dem.-Nonpartisan League; **G**-Green; **IDP**-Independence; **IG**-Ind. Green; **I**-Independent; **L**-Libertarian; **SWP**-Socialist Workers Party; **U**-Unenrolled; **WF**-Working Families

Dist.	Representative (Party)	2006 Election
	Alabama	
1	**Jo Bonner* (R)**	**112,944**
	Vivian Sheffield Beckerle (D)	52,770
2	**Terry Everett*# (R)**	**124,302**
	Charles (Chuck) Dean James (D)	54,450
3	**Mike Rogers* (R)**	**98,257**
	Greg A. Pierce (D)	63,559
4	**Robert B. Aderholt* (R)**	**128,484**
	Barbara Bobo (D)	54,382
5	**Bud Cramer* (D)**	**Unopposed**
6	**Spencer Bachus* (R)**	**Unopposed**
7	**Artur Davis* (D)**	**Unopposed**
	Alaska	
	Don E. Young* (R)	**132,743**
	Diane E. Benson (D)	93,879

Dist.	Representative (Party)	2006 Election
	Arizona	
1	**Rick Renzi*# (R)**	**105,646**
	Ellen Simon (D)	88,691
2	**Trent Franks* (R)**	**135,150**
	John Thrasher (D)	89,671
3	**John Shadegg* (R)**	**112,519**
	Herb Paine (D)	72,586
4	**Ed Pastor* (D)**	**56,464**
	Don Karg (R)	18,627
5	**Harry Mitchell (D)**	**101,838**
	J.D. Hayworth* (R)	93,815
6	**Jeff Flake* (R)**	**152,201**
	Jason M. Blair (L)	51,285
7	**Raul Grijalva* (D)**	**80,354**
	Ron Drake (R)	46,498

Dist.	Representative (Party)	2006 Election
8	Gabrielle Giffords (D)	137,655
	Randy Graf (R)	106,790

Arkansas

Dist.	Representative (Party)	2006 Election
1	Marion Berry* (D)	127,577
	Mickey "Stubby" Stumbaugh (R)	56,611
2	Vic Snyder* (D)	124,871
	Andy Mayberry (R)	81,432
3	John Boozman* (R)	125,039
	Woodrow Anderson (D)	75,885
4	Mike Ross* (D)	128,236
	Joe Ross (R)	43,360

California

Dist.	Representative (Party)	2006 Election
1	Mike Thompson* (D)	144,409
	John W. Jones (R)	63,194
2	Wally Herger* (R)	134,911
	A. J. Sekhon (D)	68,234
3	Dan Lungren* (R)	135,709
	Bill Durston (D)	86,318
4	John T. Doolittle* (R)	135,818
	Charlie Brown (D)	126,999
5	Doris O. Matsui* (D)	105,676
	Claire Yan (R)	35,106
6	Lynn Woolsey* (D)	173,190
	Todd Hooper (R)	64,405
7	George Miller* (D)	118,000
	Camden McConnell (L)	22,486
8	Nancy Pelosi* (D)	148,435
	Mike DeNunzio (R)	19,800
9	Barbara Lee* (D)	167,245
	John "J.D." den Dulk (R)	20,786
10	Ellen O. Tauscher* (D)	130,859
	Darcy Linn (R)	66,069
11	Jerry McNerney (D)	109,868
	Richard W. Pombo* (R)	96,396
12	Tom Lantos* (D)	138,650
	Mike Moloney (R)	43,674
13	Fortney Pete Stark* (D)	110,756
	George I. Bruno (R)	37,141
14	Anna G. Eshoo* (D)	141,153
	Rob Smith (R)	48,097
15	Mike Honda* (D)	115,532
	Raymond L. Chukwu (R)	44,186
16	Zoe Lofgren* (D)	98,929
	Charel Winston (R)	37,130
17	Sam Farr* (D)	120,750
	Anthony R. De Maio (R)	35,932
18	Dennis A. Cardoza* (D)	71,182
	John A. Kanno (R)	37,531
19	George P. Radanovich* (R)	110,246
	T. J. Cox (D)	71,748
20	Jim Costa* (D)	Unopposed
21	Devin G. Nunes* (R)	95,214
	Steven Haze (D)	42,718
22	Kevin McCarthy (R)	133,278
	Sharon Beery (D)	55,226
23	Lois Capps* (D)	114,661
	Victor D. Tognazzini (R)	61,272
24	Elton Gallegly* (R)	129,812
	Jill M. Martinez (D)	79,461
25	Howard P. "Buck" McKeon* (R)	93,987
	Robert Rodriguez (D)	55,913
26	David Dreier* (R)	102,028
	Cynthia Rodriguez Matthews (D)	67,878
27	Brad Sherman* (D)	92,650
	Peter Hankwitz (R)	42,074
28	Howard L. Berman* (D)	79,866
	Stanley Kimmel Kesselman (R)	20,629
29	Adam Schiff* (D)	91,014
	William J. Bodell (R)	39,321
30	Henry A. Waxman* (D)	151,284
	David Nelson Jones (R)	55,904
31	Xavier Becerra* (D)	Unopposed
32	Hilda L. Solis* (D)	76,059
	Leland Faegre (L)	15,627
33	Diane E. Watson* (D)	Unopposed
34	Lucille Roybal-Allard* (D)	57,459
	Wayne Miller (R)	17,359

Dist.	Representative (Party)	2006 Election
35	Maxine Waters* (D)	82,498
	Gordon Michael Mego (AIP)	8,343
	Paul T. Ireland (L)	7,665
36	Jane Harman* (D)	105,323
	Brian Gibson (R)	53,068
37	Juanita Millender-McDonald* (D)[1]	80,716
	Herb Peters (L)	17,246
38	Grace F. Napolitano* (D)	75,181
	Sidney W. Street (R)	24,620
39	Linda T. Sanchez* (D)	72,149
	James L. Andion (R)	37,384
40	Ed Royce* (R)	100,995
	Florice Orea Hoffman (D)	46,418
41	Jerry Lewis* (R)	109,761
	Louie A. Contreras (D)	54,235
42	Gary G. Miller* (R)	Unopposed
43	Joe Baca* (D)	52,791
	Scott Folkens (R)	29,069
44	Ken Calvert* (R)	89,555
	Louis Vandenberg (D)	55,275
45	Mary Bono* (R)	99,638
	David Roth (D)	64,613
46	Dana Rohrabacher* (R)	116,176
	Jim Brandt (D)	71,573
47	Loretta Sanchez* (D)	47,134
	Tan Nguyen (R)	28,485
48	John Campbell* (R)	120,130
	Steve Young (D)	74,647
49	Darrell Issa* (R)	98,831
	Jeeni Criscenzo (D)	52,227
50	Brian P. Bilbray (R)	118,018
	Francine Busby (D)	96,612
51	Bob Filner* (D)	78,114
	Blake L. Miles (R)	34,931
52	Duncan Hunter*# (R)	123,696
	John Rinaldi (D)	61,208
53	Susan A. Davis* (D)	97,541
	John "Woody" Woodrum (R)	43,312

(1) Juanita Millender-McDonald died on April 22, 2007. Laura Richardson (D) was elected Aug. 21, 2007 in special election and took office on Sept. 4.

Colorado

Dist.	Representative (Party)	2006 Election
1	Diana L. DeGette* (D)	129,446
	Thomas D. Kelly (G)	32,825
2	Mark Udall* (D)	157,850
	Rich Mancuso (R)	65,481
3	John Salazar* (D)	146,488
	Scott Tipton (R)	86,930
4	Marilyn N. Musgrave* (R)	109,732
	Angie Paccione (D)	103,748
	Eric Eidsness (CRP)	27,133
5	Doug Lamborn (R)	123,264
	Jay Fawcett (D)	83,431
6	Tom Tancredo* (R)	158,806
	Bill Winter (D)	108,007
7	Ed Perlmutter (D)	103,918
	Rick O'Donnell (R)	79,571

Connecticut

Dist.	Representative (Party)	2006 Election
1	John B. Larson* (D)	154,539
	Scott MacLean (R)	53,010
2	Joe Courtney (D)	121,248
	Rob Simmons* (R)	121,165
3	Rosa L. DeLauro* (D)	150,436
	Joseph Vollano (R)	44,386
4	Christopher Shays* (R)	106,510
	Diane Farrell (D)	99,450
5	Chris Murphy (D)	117,186
	Nancy L. Johnson* (R)	94,824

Delaware

	Representative (Party)	2006 Election
	Michael N. Castle* (R)	143,897
	Dennis Spivack (D)	97,565

Florida

Dist.	Representative (Party)	2006 Election
1	Jeff Miller* (R)	135,786
	Joe Roberts (D)	62,340
2	Allen Boyd* (D)	Unopposed
3	Corrine Brown* (D)	Unopposed
4	Ander Crenshaw* (R)	141,759
	Robert J. Harms (D)	61,704

Dist.	Representative (Party)	2006 Election
5	Virginia "Ginny" Brown-Waite* (R)	162,421
	John T. Russell (D)	108,959
6	Clifford "Cliff" B. Stearns* (R)	136,601
	David E. Bruderly (D)	91,528
7	John L. Mica* (R)	149,656
	John F. Chagnon (D)	87,584
8	Ric Keller* (R)	95,258
	Charlie Stuart (D)	82,526
9	Gus Michael Bilirakis (R)	123,016
	Phyllis Busansky (D)	96,978
10	C.W. Bill Young* (R)	131,488
	Samm Simpson (D)	67,950
11	Kathy Castor* (D)	97,470
	Eddie Adams, Jr. (R)	42,454
12	Adam H. Putnam* (R)	124,452
	Joe Viscusi (I)	34,976
	Ed Bowlin (I)	20,636
13	Vern Buchanan (R)	119,309
	Christine Jennings (D)	118,940
14	Connie Mack* (R)	151,615
	Robert M. Neeld (D)	83,920
15	Dave Weldon* (R)	125,965
	Bob Bowman (D)	97,834
16	Tim Mahoney (D)	115,832
	Joe Negron (R)	111,415
17	Kendrick B. Meek* (D)	Unopposed
18	Ileana Ros-Lehtinen* (R)	79,631
	David "Big Dave" Patlak (D)	48,499
19	Robert Wexler* (D)	Unopposed
20	Debbie Wasserman Schultz* (D)	Unopposed
21	Lincoln Diaz-Balart* (R)	66,784
	Frank J. Gonzalez (D)	45,522
22	Ron Klein (D)	108,688
	E. Clay Shaw* (R)	100,663
23	Alcee L. Hastings* (D)	Unopposed
24	Tom Feeney* (R)	123,795
	Clint Curtis (D)	89,863
25	Mario Diaz-Balart* (R)	60,765
	Michael Calderin (D)	43,168

Georgia

Dist.	Representative (Party)	2006 Election
1	Jack Kingston* (R)	94,961
	Jim Nelson (D)	43,668
2	Sanford Bishop* (D)	88,662
	Bradley C. Hughes (R)	41,967
3	Lynn Westmoreland* (R)	130,428
	Mike McGraw (D)	62,371
4	Henry C. "Hank" Johnson, Jr. (D)	106,352
	Catherine Davis (R)	34,778
5	John Lewis* (D)	Unopposed
6	Tom Price* (R)	144,958
	Steve Sinton (D)	55,294
7	John Linder* (R)	130,561
	Allan Burns (D)	53,553
8	Jim Marshall* (D)	80,660
	Mac Collins (R)	78,908
9	Nathan Deal* (R)	128,685
	John D. Bradbury (D)	39,240
10	Charlie Norwood* (R)[2]	117,721
	Terry Holley (D)	57,032
11	Phil Gingrey* (R)	118,524
	Patrick Samuel Pillion (D)	48,261
12	John Barrow* (D)	71,651
	Max Burns (R)	70,787
13	David Scott* (D)	103,019
	Deborah Travis Honeycutt (R)	45,770

(2) Charlie Norwood died on Feb. 13, 2007. Paul C. Broun (R) was elected July 17, 2007 in special election and took office on July 25.

Hawaii

Dist.	Representative (Party)	2006 Election
1	Neil Abercrombie* (D)	112,904
	Richard (Noah) Hough (R)	49,890
2	Mazie K. Hirono (D)	106,906
	Bob Hogue (R)	68,244

Idaho

Dist.	Representative (Party)	2006 Election
1	Bill Sali (R)	115,843
	Larry Grant (D)	103,935
2	Mike Simpson* (R)	132,262
	Jim Hansen (D)	73,441

Illinois

Dist.	Representative (Party)	2006 Election
1	Bobby L. Rush* (D)	146,623
	Jason E. Tabour (R)	27,804
2	Jesse L. Jackson, Jr.* (D)	146,347
	Robert Belin (R)	20,395
3	Daniel William Lipinski* (D)	127,768
	Raymond G. Wardingley (R)	37,954
4	Luis V. Gutierrez*# (D)	69,910
	Ann Melichar (R)	11,532
5	Rahm Emanuel* (D)	114,319
	Kevin Edward White (R)	32,250
6	Peter J. Roskam (R)	91,382
	L. Tammy Duckworth (D)	86,572
7	Danny K. Davis* (D)	143,071
	Charles Hutchinson (R)	21,939
8	Melissa Bean* (D)	93,355
	David McSweeney (R)	80,720
9	Janice D. Schakowsky* (D)	122,852
	Michael P. Shannon (R)	41,858
10	Mark Steven Kirk* (R)	107,929
	Daniel J. Seals (D)	94,278
11	Gerald C. "Jerry" Weller*# (R)	109,009
	John Pavich (D)	88,846
12	Jerry F. Costello* (D)	Unopposed
13	Judy Biggert* (R)	119,720
	Joseph Shannon (D)	85,507
14	J. Dennis Hastert*# (R)	117,870
	Jonathan "John" Laesch (D)	79,274
15	Timothy V. Johnson* (R)	116,810
	David Gill (D)	86,025
16	Donald A. Manzullo* (R)	125,951
	Richard D. Auman (D)	63,627
17	Phil Hare (D)	115,025
	Andrea Zinga (R)	86,161
18	Ray LaHood*# (R)	150,194
	Steve Waterworth (D)	73,052
19	John M. Shimkus* (R)	143,491
	Danny L. Stover (D)	92,861

Indiana

Dist.	Representative (Party)	2006 Election
1	Peter J. Visclosky* (D)	104,195
	Mark J. Leyva (R)	40,146
2	Joe Donnelly (D)	103,561
	J. Christopher Chocola* (R)	88,300
3	Mark E. Souder* (R)	95,421
	Thomas E. Hayhurst (D)	80,357
4	Steve Buyer* (R)	111,057
	David Avram Sanders (D)	66,986
5	Dan Burton* (R)	133,118
	Katherine Fox Carr (D)	64,362
6	Mike Pence* (R)	115,266
	Barry A. Welsh (D)	76,812
7	Julia M. Carson* (D)	74,750
	Eric Dickerson (R)	64,304
8	Brad Ellsworth (D)	131,019
	John N. Hostettler* (R)	83,704
9	Baron P. Hill (D)	110,454
	Michael E. Sodrel* (R)	100,469

Iowa

Dist.	Representative (Party)	2006 Election
1	Bruce Braley (D)	114,322
	Mike Whalen (R)	89,729
2	David Loebsack* (D)	107,683
	James A. Leach* (R)	101,707
3	Leonard L. Boswell* (D)	115,769
	Jeff Lamberti (R)	103,722
4	Tom Latham* (R)	121,650
	Selden E. Spencer (D)	90,982
5	Steve King* (R)	105,580
	Joyce Schulte (D)	64,181

Kansas

Dist.	Representative (Party)	2006 Election
1	Jerry Moran* (R)	156,728
	John Doll (D)	39,781
2	Nancy Boyda (D)	114,139
	Jim Ryun* (R)	106,329
3	Dennis Moore* (D)	153,105
	Chuck Ahner (R)	79,824
4	Todd Tiahrt* (R)	116,386
	Garth J. McGinn (D)	62,166

Dist.	Representative (Party)	2006 Election
	Kentucky	
1	Ed Whitfield* (R)	123,618
	Tom Barlow (D)	83,865
2	Ron Lewis* (R)	118,548
	Mike Weaver (D)	95,415
3	John Yarmuth* (D)	122,489
	Anne M. Northup* (R)	116,568
4	Geoff Davis* (R)	105,845
	Ken Lucas (D)	88,822
5	Harold "Hal" Rogers* (R)	147,201
	Kenneth Stepp (D)	52,367
6	Ben Chandler* (D)	158,765
	Paul Ard (L)	27,015
	Louisiana	
1	"Bobby" Jindal* (R)	130,508
	David Gereighty (D)	10,919
2	William J. Jefferson* (D)[3]	28,283
	Karen Carter (D)[3]	20,364
	Derrick Shepherd (D)	16,799
	Joseph "Joe" Lavigne (R)	12,511
	Troy "C" Carter (D)	11,304
3	"Charlie" Melancon* (D)	75,023
	Craig Romero (R)	54,950
4	"Jim" McCrery* (R)	77,078
	Artis R. Cash, Sr. (D)	22,757
	Patti Cox (D)	17,788
	Chester T. Kelley (R)	16,649
5	Rodney Alexander* (R)	78,211
	Gloria Williams Hearn (D)	33,233
6	Richard H. Baker* (R)	94,658
	Richard M. Fontanesi (L)	19,648
7	Charles W. Boustany, Jr.* (R)	113,720
	Mike Stagg (D)	47,133

(3) In a runoff election Dec. 9, 2006, William Jefferson received 35,153 votes, Karen Carter 27,011.

Dist.	Representative (Party)	2006 Election
	Maine	
1	Thomas H. Allen*# (D)	170,949
	Darlene J. Curley (R)	88,009
2	Michael H. Michaud* (D)	179,732
	Laurence S. D'Amboise (R)	75,146
	Maryland	
1	Wayne T. Gilchrest* (R)	185,177
	Jim Corwin (D)	83,738
2	C. A. Dutch Ruppersberger* (D)	135,818
	Jimmy Mathis (R)	60,195
3	John P. Sarbanes (D)	150,142
	John White (R)	79,174
4	Albert R. Wynn* (D)	141,897
	Michael Moshe Starkman (R)	32,792
5	Steny H. Hoyer* (D)	168,114
	Steve Warner	33,464
6	Roscoe G. Bartlett* (R)	141,200
	Andrew Duck (D)	92,030
7	Elijah Cummings* (D)	Unopposed
8	Chris Van Hollen* (D)	168,872
	Jeffrey M. Stein (R)	48,324
	Massachusetts	
1	John W. Olver* (D)	158,057
	William H. Szych (U)	48,574
2	Richard E. Neal* (D)	Unopposed
3	James P. McGovern* (D)	Unopposed
4	Barney Frank* (D)	Unopposed
5	Martin T. Meehan* (D)[4]	Unopposed
6	John F. Tierney* (D)	168,056
	Richard W. Barton (R)	72,997
7	Edward J. Markey* (D)	Unopposed
8	Michael E. Capuano* (D)	125,515
	Laura Garza (SWP)	12,449
9	Stephen F. Lynch* (D)	169,420
	Jack E. Robinson (R)	47,114
10	William D. Delahunt* (D)	171,812
	Jeffrey K. Beatty (R)	78,439

(4) Martin Meehan resigned July 1, 2007 to become Chancellor of the Univ. of Massachusetts-Lowell. A special election for his replacement between Jim Ogonowski (R) and Niki Tsongas (D) was scheduled for Oct. 16, 2007.

Dist.	Representative (Party)	2006 Election
	Michigan	
1	Bart Stupak* (D)	180,448
	Don Hooper (R)	72,753
2	Peter Hoekstra* (R)	183,006
	Kimon Kotos (D)	86,950
3	Vernon J. Ehlers* (R)	171,212
	James R. Rinck (D)	93,846
4	Dave Camp* (R)	160,041
	Mike Huckleberry (D)	100,260
5	Dale E. Kildee* (D)	176,171
	Eric J. Klammer (R)	60,967
6	Fred Upton* (R)	142,125
	Kim Clark (D)	88,978
7	Tim Walberg (R)	122,348
	Sharon Marie Renier (D)	112,665
8	Mike Rogers* (R)	157,237
	Jim Marcinkowski (D)	122,107
9	Joe Knollenberg* (R)	142,390
	Nancy Skinner (D)	127,620
10	Candice S. Miller* (R)	179,072
	Robert Denison (D)	84,689
11	Thaddeus G. McCotter* (R)	143,658
	Tony Trupiano (D)	114,248
12	Sander Levin* (D)	168,494
	Randell J. Shafer (R)	62,689
13	Carolyn Cheeks Kilpatrick* (D)	Unopposed
14	John Conyers, Jr.* (D)	158,755
	Chad Miles (R)	27,367
15	John D. Dingell* (D)	181,946
	Smith Aimee (G)	9,447
	Minnesota	
1	Tim Walz (DFL)	141,556
	Gil Gutknecht* (R)	126,486
2	John Kline* (R)	163,269
	Coleen Rowley (DFL)	116,343
3	Jim Ramstad*# (R)	184,333
	Wendy Wilde (DFL)	99,588
4	Betty McCollum* (DFL)	172,096
	Obi Sium (R)	74,797
5	Keith Ellison (DFL)	136,060
	Alan Fine (R)	52,263
	Tommy Lee (IDP)	51,546
6	Michele Bachmann (R)	151,248
	Patty Wetterling (DFL)	127,144
7	Collin C. Peterson* (DFL)	179,164
	Michael J. Barrett (R)	74,557
8	James L. Oberstar* (DFL)	180,670
	Rod Grams (R)	97,683
	Mississippi	
1	Roger F. Wicker* (R)	95,098
	James K. "Ken" Hurt (D)	49,174
2	Bennie G. Thompson* (D)	100,160
	Yvonne R. Brown (R)	55,672
3	Chip Pickering*# (R)	125,421
	Jim Giles (I)	25,999
4	Gene Taylor* (D)	110,996
	Randy McDonnell (R)	28,117
	Missouri	
1	Lacy Clay* (D)	141,574
	Mark J. Byrne (R)	47,893
2	Todd Akin* (R)	176,452
	George D. Weber (D)	105,242
3	Russ Carnahan* (D)	145,219
	David Bertelsen (D)	70,189
4	Ike Skelton* (D)	159,303
	James A. "Jim" Noland (R)	69,254
5	Emanuel Cleaver II* (D)	136,149
	Jacob Turk (R)	68,456
6	Sam Graves* (R)	150,882
	Sara Jo Shettles (D)	87,477
7	Roy Blunt* (R)	160,942
	Jack Truman (D)	72,592
8	Jo Ann Emerson* (R)	156,164
	Veronica J. Hambacker (D)	57,557
9	Kenny C. Hulshof* (R)	149,114
	Duane N. Burghard (D)	87,145

Dist.	Representative (Party)	2006 Election
Montana		
	Denny Rehberg* (R)	**239,124**
	Monica J. Lindeen (D)	158,916
Nebraska		
1	**Jeff Fortenberry* (R)**	**121,015**
	Maxine B. Moul (D)	86,360
2	**Lee Terry* (R)**	**99,475**
	Jim Esch (D)	82,504
3	**Adrian Smith (R)**	**113,687**
	Scott Kleeb (D)	93,046
Nevada		
1	**Shelley Berkley* (D)**	**85,025**
	Kenneth Wegner (R)	40,917
2	**Dean Heller (R)**	**117,168**
	Jill Derby (D)	104,593
3	**Jon Porter* (R)**	**102,232**
	Tessa M. Hafen (D)	98,261
New Hampshire		
1	**Carol Shea-Porter (D)**	**100,691**
	Jeb Bradley* (R)	95,527
2	**Paul W. Hodes (D)**	**108,743**
	Charles Bass* (R)	94,088
New Jersey		
1	**Robert E. Andrews* (D)**	**Unopposed**
2	**Frank A. LoBiondo* (R)**	**111,245**
	Viola Thomas-Hughes (D)	64,279
3	**Jim Saxton* (R)**	**122,559**
	Rich Sexton (D)	86,113
4	**Christopher H. Smith* (R)**	**124,482**
	Carol E. Gay (D)	62,905
5	**Scott Garrett* (R)**	**112,142**
	Paul Aronsohn (D)	89,503
6	**Frank Pallone, Jr.* (D)**	**98,615**
	Leigh-Ann Bellew (R)	43,539
7	**Mike Ferguson* (R)**	**98,399**
	Linda Stender (D)	95,454
8	**Bill Pascrell, Jr.* (D)**	**97,568**
	Jose M. Sandoval (R)	39,053
9	**Steven R. Rothman* (D)**	**105,853**
	Vincent Micco (R)	40,879
10	**Donald M. Payne* (D)**	**Unopposed**
11	**Rodney Frelinghuysen* (R)**	**126,085**
	Tom Wyka (D)	74,414
12	**Rush Holt* (D)**	**125,468**
	Joseph S. Sinagra (R)	65,509
13	**Albio Sires (D)**	**77,238**
	John J. Guarini (R)	19,284
New Mexico		
1	**Heather A. Wilson* (R)**	**105,986**
	Patricia A. Madrid (D)	105,125
2	**Steve Pearce* (R)**	**92,620**
	Albert D. Kissling (D)	63,119
3	**Tom Udall* (D)**	**144,880**
	Ronald M. Dolin (R)	49,219
New York		
1	**Timothy H. Bishop* (D/IDP/WF)**	**104,360**
	Italo A. Zanzi (R/CRV)	63,328
2	**Steve J. Israel* (D/IDP/WF)**	**105,276**
	John W. Bugler (R/CRV)	44,212
3	**Peter T. King* (R/CRV/IDP)**	**101,787**
	David L. Mejias (D/WF)	79,843
4	**Carolyn McCarthy* (D/IDP/WF)**	**101,861**
	Martin W. Blessinger (R/CRV)	55,050
5	**Gary L. Ackerman* (D/IDP/WF)**	**Unopposed**
6	**Gregory W. Meeks* (D)**	**Unopposed**
7	**Joseph Crowley* (D/WF)**	**63,997**
	Kevin Brawley (R/CRV)	12,220
8	**Jerrold L. Nadler* (D/WF)**	**108,536**
	Eleanor Friedman (R)	17,413
9	**Anthony D. Weiner* (D/WF)**	**Unopposed**
10	**Edolphus Towns* (D)**	**72,171**
	Jonathan H. Anderson (R)	4,666
11	**Yvette D. Clarke (D/WF)**	**88,334**
	Stephen Finger (R/L)	7,447
12	**Nydia M. Velazquez* (D/WF)**	**62,847**
	Allan E. Romaguera (R/CRV)	7,182
13	**Vito Fossella* (R/CRV/IDP)**	**59,334**
	Stephen A. Harrison (D/WF)	45,131
14	**Carolyn B. Maloney* (D/IDP/WF)**	**119,582**
	Danniel Maio (R)	21,969
15	**Charles B. Rangel* (D/WF)**	**103,916**
	Edward Daniels (R)	6,592
16	**Jose E. Serrano* (D/WF)**	**56,124**
	Ali Mohamed (R/CRV)	2,759
17	**Eliot L. Engel* (D/WF)**	**93,614**
	Jim Faulkner (R/CRV/IDP)	28,842
18	**Nita M. Lowey* (D/WF)**	**124,256**
	Richard A. Hoffman (R/CRV)	51,450
19	**John Hall (D)**	**100,119**
	Sue W. Kelly* (R/CRV/IDP)	95,359
20	**Kirsten E. Gillibrand (D)**	**125,168**
	John E. Sweeney* (R/CRV/IDP)	110,554
21	**Michael R. McNulty* (D/CRV/IDP/WF)**	**167,604**
	Warren Redlich (R)	46,752
22	**Maurice D. Hinchey* (D/IDP/WF)**	**Unopposed**
23	**John M. McHugh* (R/CRV/IDP)**	**106,781**
	Robert J. Johnson (D/WF)	62,318
24	**Michael A. Arcuri (D/IDP/WF)**	**109,686**
	Raymond A. Meier (R/CRV)	91,504
25	**James T. Walsh* (R/CRV/IDP)**	**110,525**
	Dan Maffei (D/WF)	107,108
26	**Thomas M. Reynolds* (R/CRV)**	**109,257**
	Jack Davis (D/IDP/WF)	100,914
27	**Brian M. Higgins* (D/IDP/WF)**	**140,027**
	Michael J. McHale (R)	36,614
28	**Louise M. Slaughter* (D/IDP/WF)**	**111,386**
	John E. Donnelly (R/CRV)	40,844
29	**John Randy Kuhl, Jr.* (R/CRV/IDP)**	**106,077**
	Eric J. Massa (D/WF)	100,044
North Carolina		
1	**G.K. Butterfield* (D)**	**Unopposed**
2	**Bob Etheridge* (D)**	**85,993**
	Dan Mansell (R)	43,271
3	**Walter B. Jones* (R)**	**99,519**
	Craig Weber (D)	45,458
4	**David Price* (D)**	**127,340**
	Steve Acuff (R)	68,599
5	**Virginia Foxx* (R)**	**96,138**
	Roger Sharpe (D)	72,061
6	**Howard Coble* (R)**	**108,433**
	Rory Blake (D)	44,661
7	**Mike McIntyre* (D)**	**101,787**
	Shirley Davis (R)	38,033
8	**Robert C. "Robin" Hayes* (R)**	**60,926**
	Larry Kissell (D)	60,597
9	**Sue Myrick* (R)**	**106,206**
	Bill Glass (D)	53,437
10	**Patrick McHenry* (R)**	**94,179**
	Richard Carsner (D)	58,214
11	**Heath Shuler (D)**	**124,972**
	Charles H. Taylor* (R)	107,342
12	**Mel Watt* (D)**	**71,345**
	Ada M. Fisher (R)	35,127
13	**Brad Miller* (D)**	**98,540**
	Vernon Robinson (R)	56,120
North Dakota		
	Earl Pomeroy* (DNL)	**142,934**
	Matt Mechtel (R)	74,687
Ohio		
1	**Steve Chabot* (R)**	**105,680**
	John Cranley (D)	96,584
2	**Jean Schmidt* (R)**	**120,112**
	Victoria Wulsin (D)	117,595
3	**Michael R. Turner* (R)**	**127,978**
	Richard Chema (D)	90,650
4	**Jim Jordan (R)**	**129,958**
	Richard E. Siferd (D)	86,678
5	**Paul E. Gillmor* (R)[5]**	**129,813**
	Robin Weirauch (D)	98,544
6	**Charles A. Wilson, Jr. (D)**	**135,628**
	Chuck Blasdel (R)	82,848
7	**Dave Hobson* (R)**	**137,899**
	William R. Conner (D)	89,579

Dist.	Representative (Party)	2006 Election
8	**John A. Boehner* (R)**	**136,863**
	Mort Meier (D)	77,640
9	**Marcy Kaptur* (D)**	**153,880**
	Bradley S. Leavitt (R)	55,119
10	**Dennis J. Kucinich* (D)**	**138,393**
	Michael D. Dovilla (R)	69,996
11	**Stephanie Tubbs Jones* (D)**	**146,799**
	Lindsey N. String (R)	29,125
12	**Pat Tiberi* (R)**	**145,943**
	Bob Shamansky (D)	108,746
13	**Betty Sutton (D)**	**135,639**
	Craig Foltin (R)	85,922
14	**Steven C. LaTourette* (R)**	**144,069**
	Lewis R. Katz (D)	97,753
15	**Deborah Pryce*# (R)**	**110,714**
	Mary Jo Kilroy (D)	109,659
16	**Ralph Regula* (R)**	**137,167**
	Thomas Shaw (D)	97,955
17	**Tim Ryan* (D)**	**170,369**
	Don Manning, II (R)	41,925
18	**Zack Space (D)**	**129,646**
	Joy Padgett (R)	79,259

(5) Paul Gillmor died on Sept. 5, 2007. A special election for his replacement was scheduled for Dec. 11, 2007.

Oklahoma

Dist.	Representative (Party)	2006 Election
1	**John Sullivan* (R)**	**116,920**
	Alan Gentges (D)	56,724
2	**Dan Boren* (D)**	**122,347**
	Patrick K. Miller (R)	45,861
3	**Frank D. Lucas* (R)**	**128,042**
	Sue Barton (D)	61,749
4	**Tom Cole* (R)**	**118,266**
	Hal Spake (D)	64,775
5	**Mary Fallin (R)**	**108,936**
	David Hunter (D)	67,293

Oregon

Dist.	Representative (Party)	2006 Election
1	**David Wu* (D)**	**169,409**
	Derrick Kitts (R)	90,904
2	**Greg Walden* (R)**	**181,529**
	Carol Voisin (D)	82,484
3	**Earl Blumenauer* (D)**	**186,380**
	Bruce Broussard (R)	59,529
4	**Peter A. DeFazio* (D)**	**180,607**
	Jim Feldkamp (R)	109,105
5	**Darlene Hooley* (D)**	**146,973**
	Mike Erickson (R)	116,424

Pennsylvania

Dist.	Representative (Party)	2006 Election
1	**Robert A. Brady* (D)**	**Unopposed**
2	**Chaka Fattah* (D)**	**165,867**
	Michael Gessner (R)	17,291
3	**Phil English* (R)**	**108,525**
	Steven Porter (D)	85,110
4	**Jason Altmire (D)**	**131,847**
	Melissa A. Hart* (R)	122,049
5	**John E. Peterson* (R)**	**115,126**
	Donald L. Hilliard (D)	76,456
6	**Jim Gerlach* (R)**	**121,047**
	Lois Murphy (D)	117,892
7	**Joe Sestak (D)**	**147,898**
	Curt Weldon* (R)	114,426
8	**Patrick J. Murphy (D)**	**125,656**
	Michael G. Fitzpatrick* (R)	124,138
9	**Bill Shuster* (R)**	**121,069**
	Tony Barr (D)	79,610
10	**Christopher Carney (D)**	**110,115**
	Don Sherwood* (R)	97,862
11	**Paul E. Kanjorski* (D)**	**134,340**
	Joseph F. Leonardi (R)	51,033
12	**John P. Murtha* (D)**	**123,472**
	Diana Irey (R)	79,612
13	**Allyson Schwartz* (D)**	**147,368**
	Raj Peter Bhakta (R)	75,492
14	**Mike Doyle* (D)**	**161,075**
	Titus North (G)	17,720
15	**Charles W. Dent* (R)**	**106,153**
	Charles Dertinger (D)	86,186

Dist.	Representative (Party)	2006 Election
16	**Joseph R. Pitts* (R)**	**115,741**
	Lois K. Herr (D)	80,915
17	**Tim Holden* (D)**	**137,253**
	Matthew A. Wertz (R)	75,455
18	**Tim Murphy* (R)**	**144,632**
	Chad Kluko (D)	105,419
19	**Todd Platts* (R)**	**142,512**
	Philip J. Avillo, Jr. (D)	74,625

Rhode Island

Dist.	Representative (Party)	2006 Election
1	**Patrick J. Kennedy* (D)**	**124,676**
	Jonathan P. Scott (R)	41,856
2	**James R. Langevin* (D)**	**140,352**
	Rod Driver (I)	52,743

South Carolina

Dist.	Representative (Party)	2006 Election
1	**Henry Brown* (R)**	**115,766**
	Randy Maatta (D)	73,218
2	**Joe Wilson* (R)**	**127,811**
	Michael Ray Ellisor (D)	76,090
3	**J. Gresham Barrett* (R)**	**111,882**
	Lee Ballenger (D)	66,039
4	**Bob Inglis* (R)**	**115,553**
	William Griff Griffith (D)	57,490
5	**John Spratt* (D)**	**99,669**
	Ralph Norman (R)	75,422
6	**James E. "Jim" Clyburn* (D)**	**100,213**
	Gary McLeod (R)	53,181

South Dakota

	Representative (Party)	2006 Election
	Stephanie Herseth* (D)	**230,468**
	Bruce W. Whalen (R)	97,864

Tennessee

Dist.	Representative (Party)	2006 Election
1	**David Davis (R)**	**108,336**
	Rick Trent (D)	65,538
2	**John J. Duncan, Jr.* (R)**	**157,095**
	John Greene (D)	45,025
3	**Zach Wamp* (R)**	**130,791**
	Brett Benedict (D)	68,324
4	**Lincoln Davis* (D)**	**123,666**
	Kenneth Martin (R)	62,449
5	**Jim Cooper* (D)**	**122,919**
	Thomas F. Kovach (R)	49,702
6	**Bart Gordon* (D)**	**129,069**
	David R. Davis (R)	60,392
7	**Marsha Blackburn* (R)**	**152,288**
	Bill Morrison (D)	73,369
8	**John Tanner* (D)**	**129,610**
	John Farmer (R)	47,492
9	**Steve Cohen (D)**	**103,341**
	Jake Ford (I)	38,243
	Mark White (R)	31,002

Texas

Dist.	Representative (Party)	2006 Election
1	**Louie Gohmert* (R)**	**104,099**
	Roger L. Owen (D)	46,303
2	**Ted Poe* (R)**	**90,490**
	Gary E. Binderim (D)	45,080
3	**Sam Johnson* (R)**	**88,690**
	Dan Dodd (D)	49,529
4	**Ralph M. Hall* (R)**	**106,495**
	Glenn Melancon (D)	55,278
5	**Jeb Hensarling* (R)**	**88,478**
	Charlie Thompson (D)	50,983
6	**Joe L. Barton* (R)**	**91,927**
	David T. Harris (D)	56,369
7	**John Culberson* (R)**	**99,318**
	Jim Henley (D)	64,514
8	**Kevin Brady* (R)**	**105,665**
	James "Jim" Wright (D)	51,393
9	**Al Green* (D)**	**Unopposed**
10	**Michael T. McCaul* (R)**	**97,726**
	Ted Ankrum (D)	71,415
11	**Mike Conaway* (R)**	**Unopposed**
12	**Kay Granger* (R)**	**98,371**
	John R. Morris (D)	45,676
13	**Mac Thornberry* (R)**	**108,107**
	Roger J. Waun (D)	33,460
14	**Ron Paul* (R)**	**94,380**
	Shane Sklar (D)	62,429

Dist.	Representative (Party)	2006 Election
15[6]	**Rubén Hinojosa* (D)**	**43,236**
	Paul B. Haring (R)	16,601
	Eddie Zamora (R)	10,150
16	**Sylvestre Reyes* (D)**	**61,116**
	Gordon R. Strickland (L)	16,572
17	**Chet Edwards* (D)**	**92,478**
	Van Taylor (R)	64,142
18	**Sheila Jackson Lee* (D)**	**65,936**
	Ahmad R. Hassan (R)	16,448
19	**Randy Neugebauer* (R)**	**94,785**
	Robert Ricketts (D)	41,676
20	**Charles A. Gonzalez* (D)**	**68,348**
	Michael Idrogo (L)	9,897
21[6]	**Lamar Smith* (R)**	**122,486**
	John Courage (D)	49,957
	Gene Kelley (D)	18,355
22	**Nick Lampson (D)**	**76,775**
	Shelley Sekula-Gibbs (write-in R)[7]	61,938
	Bob Smither (L)	9,009
23[6]	**Ciro D. Rodriguez (D)[8]**	**24,594**
	Henry Bonilla* (R)[8]	60,175
	Albert Uresti (D)	14,552
	Lukin Gilliland (D)	13,728
24	**Kenny E. Marchant* (R)**	**83,835**
	Gary R. Page (D)	52,075
25[6]	**Lloyd Doggett* (D)**	**109,911**
	Grant Rostig (L)	42,975
26	**Michael C. Burgess* (R)**	**94,219**
	Tim Barnwell (D)	58,271
27	**Solomon P. Ortiz* (D)**	**62,058**
	William "Willie" Vaden (R)	42,538
28[6]	**Henry Cuellar* (D)**	**52,574**
	Frank Enriquez (D)	15,798
	Ron Avery (C)	9,383
29	**Gene Green* (D)**	**37,174**
	Eric Story (R)	12,347
30	**Eddie Bernice Johnson* (D)**	**81,348**
	Wilson Aurbach (R)	17,850
31	**John R. Carter* (R)**	**90,869**
	Mary Beth Harrell (D)	60,293
32	**Pete Sessions* (R)**	**71,461**
	Will Pryor (D)	52,269

(6) The boundaries for districts 15, 21, 23, 25, and 28 were redrawn on Aug. 4, 2006. Court-ordered special general elections were held on Nov. 7. (7) Rep. Tom Delay (R) won a primary election March 7, 2006 but resigned June 9 and withdrew from the election. No Republican was listed on the general election ballot. (8) No candidate received a majority of the votes cast. In a special runoff election held Dec. 12, 2006, Ciro Rodriguez received 38,256 votes, Henry Bonilla 32,217.

Utah

Dist.	Representative (Party)	2006 Election
1	**Rob Bishop* (R)**	**112,546**
	Steven Olsen (D)	57,922
2	**Jim Matheson* (D)**	**133,231**
	LaVar Christensen (R)	84,234
3	**Chris Cannon* (R)**	**95,455**
	Christian Burridge (D)	53,330

Vermont

	Representative (Party)	2006 Election
	Peter Welch (D)	**139,815**
	Martha Rainville (R)	117,023

Virginia

Dist.	Representative (Party)	2006 Election
1	**Jo Ann S. Davis* (R)**	**143,889**
	Shawn O'Donnell (D)	81,083
2	**Thelma D. Drake* (R)**	**88,777**
	Philip J. Kellam (D)	83,901
3	**Bobby Scott* (D)**	**Unopposed**
4	**J. Randy Forbes* (R)**	**150,967**
	Albert P. Burckard, Jr. (IG)	46,487
5	**Virgil H. Goode, Jr.* (R)**	**125,370**
	Al Weed (D)	84,682
6	**R. W. "Bob" Goodlatte* (R)**	**153,187**
	Barbara Jean Pryor (I)	25,129
	Andre D. Peery (I)	24,731
7	**Eric I. Cantor* (R)**	**163,706**
	Jim Nachman (D)	88,206
8	**James P. Moran, Jr.* (D)**	**144,700**
	Tom M. O'Donoghue (R)	66,639
9	**Rick Boucher* (D)**	**129,705**
	Bill Carrico (R)	61,574
10	**Frank R. Wolf* (R)**	**138,213**
	Judy M. Feder (D)	98,769
11	**Thomas M. Davis* III (R)**	**130,468**
	Andrew L. Hurst (D)	102,511

Washington

Dist.	Representative (Party)	2006 Election
1	**Jay Inslee* (D)**	**163,832**
	Larry W. Ishmael (R)	78,105
2	**Rick Larsen* (D)**	**157,064**
	Doug Roulstone (R)	87,730
3	**Brian Baird* (D)**	**147,065**
	Michael Messmore (R)	85,915
4	**Doc Hastings* (R)**	**115,246**
	Richard Wright (D)	77,054
5	**Cathy McMorris* (R)**	**134,967**
	Peter J. Goldmark (D)	104,357
6	**Norm Dicks* (D)**	**158,202**
	Doug Cloud (R)	65,883
7	**Jim McDermott* (D)**	**195,462**
	Steve Beren (R)	38,715
8	**Dave Reichert* (R)**	**129,362**
	Darcy Burner (D)	122,021
9	**Adam Smith* (D)**	**119,038**
	Steven C. Cofchin (R)	62,082

West Virginia

Dist.	Representative (Party)	2006 Election
1	**Alan B. Mollohan* (D)**	**100,939**
	Chris Wakim (R)	55,963
2	**Shelley Moore Capito* (R)**	**94,110**
	Mike Callaghan (D)	70,470
3	**Nick Joe Rahall* II (D)**	**92,413**
	Kim Wolfe (R)	40,820

Wisconsin

Dist.	Representative (Party)	2006 Election
1	**Paul Ryan* (R)**	**161,320**
	Jeffrey C. Thomas (D)	95,761
2	**Tammy Baldwin* (D)**	**191,414**
	Dave Magnum (R)	113,015
3	**Ron Kind* (D)**	**163,322**
	Paul R. Nelson (R)	88,523
4	**Gwen Moore* (D)**	**136,735**
	Perfecto Rivera (R)	54,486
5	**F. James Sensenbrenner, Jr.* (R)**	**194,669**
	Bryan Kennedy (D)	112,451
6	**Tom Petri* (R)**	**Unopposed**
7	**David R. Obey* (D)**	**161,903**
	Nick Reid (R)	91,069
8	**Steven L. Kagen* (D)**	**141,570**
	John Gard (R)	135,622

Wyoming

	Representative (Party)	2006 Election
	Barbara Cubin* (R)	**93,336**
	Gary Trauner (D)	92,324

Nonvoting Members of Congress

Representative (Party)	2006 Election
American Samoa	
Eni F.H. Faleomavaega Hunkin* (D)	5,195
Amata Aumua Coleman (R)	4,493
Muavaefaatasi Ae Ae, Jr. (I)	1,345
District of Columbia	
Eleanor Holmes Norton* (D)	Unopposed

Representative (Party)	2006 Election
Guam	
Madeleine Z. Bordallo* (D)	Unopposed
Puerto Rico (Resident Commissioner)	
2009 Luis G. Fortuno (R); 2005	
Virgin Islands	
Donna M. Christensen* (D)	19,593
Warren B. Mosler (I)	11,201

Floor Leaders in the U.S. Senate Since the 1920s
(as of Sept. 2007)

Majority Leaders				Minority Leaders			
Name	**Party**	**State**	**Tenure**	**Name**	**Party**	**State**	**Tenure**
Charles Curtis[1]	Rep.	KS	1925-1929	Oscar W. Underwood[2]	Dem.	AL	1920-1923
James E. Watson	Rep.	IN	1929-1933	Joseph T. Robinson	Dem.	AR	1923-1933
Joseph T. Robinson	Dem.	AR	1933-1937	Charles L. McNary	Rep.	OR	1933-1944
Alben W. Barkley	Dem.	KY	1937-1947	Wallace H. White	Rep.	ME	1944-1947
Wallace H. White	Rep.	ME	1947-1949	Alben W. Barkley	Dem.	KY	1947-1949
Scott W. Lucas	Dem.	IL	1949-1951	Kenneth S. Wherry	Rep.	NE	1949-1951
Ernest W. McFarland	Dem.	AZ	1951-1953	Henry Styles Bridges	Rep.	NH	1952-1953
Robert A. Taft	Rep.	OH	1953	Lyndon B. Johnson	Dem.	TX	1953-1955
William F. Knowland	Rep.	CA	1953-1955	William F. Knowland	Rep.	CA	1955-1959
Lyndon B. Johnson	Dem.	TX	1955-1961	Everett M. Dirksen	Rep.	IL	1959-1969
Mike Mansfield	Dem.	MT	1961-1977	Hugh D. Scott	Rep.	PA	1969-1977
Robert C. Byrd	Dem.	WV	1977-1981	Howard H. Baker Jr.	Rep.	TN	1977-1981
Howard H. Baker Jr.	Rep.	TN	1981-1985	Robert C. Byrd	Dem.	WV	1981-1987
Robert J. Dole	Rep.	KS	1985-1987	Robert J. Dole	Rep.	KS	1987-1995
Robert C. Byrd	Dem.	WV	1987-1989	Thomas A. Daschle	Dem.	SD	1995-2001[3]
George J. Mitchell	Dem.	ME	1989-1995	Trent Lott	Rep.	MS	2001-2002[3,4]
Robert J. Dole	Rep.	KS	1995-1996	Thomas A. Daschle	Dem.	SD	2003-2005[5]
Trent Lott	Rep.	MS	1996-2001[3]	Harry M. Reid	Dem.	NV	2005-2007
Thomas A. Daschle	Dem.	SD	2001-2003[3]	Mitch McConnell	Rep.	KY	2007-
William Frist	Rep.	TN	2003-2007[4]				
Harry M. Reid	Dem.	NV	2007-				

Note: The offices of party (majority and minority) leaders in the Senate did not evolve until the 20th century. (1) First Republican to be designated floor leader. (2) First Democrat to be designated floor leader. (3) Democrats held the majority Jan. 3, 2001, until Dick Cheney (R) was installed as vice pres., Jan. 20. Republicans regained the majority Jan. 20 until Jim Jeffords (VT) switched from Republican to Independent, June 6, and gave Democrats the majority. (4) Trent Lott resigned from Republican leadership Dec. 20, 2002. William Frist was elected Republican leader Dec. 23, 2002, and began service Jan. 7, 2003, as majority leader. (5) Thomas Daschle was defeated in the 2004 election, and retired from the Senate Jan. 3, 2005; Democratic Whip Harry M. Reid was elected to the post for the 109th Congress.

Speakers of the House of Representatives
(as of Sept. 2007)

Name	**Party**	**State**	**Tenure**	**Name**	**Party**	**State**	**Tenure**
Frederick Muhlenberg	Federalist	PA	1789-1791	James G. Blaine	Rep.	ME	1869-1875
Jonathan Trumbull	Federalist	CT	1791-1793	Michael C. Kerr	Dem.	IN	1875-1876
Frederick Muhlenberg	Federalist	PA	1793-1795	Samuel J. Randall	Dem.	PA	1876-1881
Jonathan Dayton	Federalist	NJ	1795-1799	J. Warren Keifer	Rep.	OH	1881-1883
Theodore Sedgwick	Federalist	MA	1799-1801	John G. Carlisle	Dem.	KY	1883-1889
Nathaniel Macon	Dem.-Rep.	NC	1801-1807	Thomas B. Reed	Rep.	ME	1889-1891
Joseph B. Varnum	Dem.-Rep.	MA	1807-1811	Charles F. Crisp	Dem.	GA	1891-1895
Henry Clay	Dem.-Rep.	KY	1811-1814	Thomas B. Reed	Rep.	ME	1895-1899
Langdon Cheves	Dem.-Rep.	SC	1814-1815	David B. Henderson	Rep.	IA	1899-1903
Henry Clay	Dem.-Rep.	KY	1815-1820	Joseph G. Cannon	Rep.	IL	1903-1911
John W. Taylor	Dem.-Rep.	NY	1820-1821	Champ Clark	Dem.	MO	1911-1919
Philip P. Barbour	Dem.-Rep.	VA	1821-1823	Frederick H. Gillett	Rep.	MA	1919-1925
Henry Clay	Dem.-Rep.	KY	1823-1825	Nicholas Longworth	Rep.	OH	1925-1931
John W. Taylor	Dem.	NY	1825-1827	John N. Garner	Dem.	TX	1931-1933
Andrew Stevenson	Dem.	VA	1827-1834	Henry T. Rainey	Dem.	IL	1933-1934
John Bell	Dem.	TN	1834-1835	Joseph W. Byrns	Dem.	TN	1935-1936
James K. Polk	Dem.	TN	1835-1839	William B. Bankhead	Dem.	AL	1936-1940
Robert M. T. Hunter	Dem.	VA	1839-1841	Sam Rayburn	Dem.	TX	1940-1947
John White	Whig.	KY	1841-1843	Joseph W. Martin Jr.	Rep.	MA	1947-1949
John W. Jones	Dem.	VA	1843-1845	Sam Rayburn	Dem.	TX	1949-1953
John W. Davis	Dem.	IN	1845-1847	Joseph W. Martin Jr.	Rep.	MA	1953-1955
Robert C. Winthrop	Whig.	MA	1847-1849	Sam Rayburn	Dem.	TX	1955-1961
Howell Cobb	Dem.	GA	1849-1851	John W. McCormack	Dem.	MA	1962-1971
Linn Boyd	Dem.	KY	1851-1855	Carl Albert	Dem.	OK	1971-1977
Nathaniel P. Banks	American	MA	1856-1857	Thomas P. O'Neill Jr.	Dem.	MA	1977-1987
James L. Orr	Dem.	SC	1857-1859	James Wright	Dem.	TX	1987-1989
William Pennington	Rep.	NJ	1860-1861	Thomas S. Foley	Dem.	WA	1989-1995
Galusha A. Grow	Rep.	PA	1861-1863	Newt Gingrich	Rep.	GA	1995-1999
Schuyler Colfax	Rep.	IN	1863-1869	J. Dennis Hastert	Rep.	IL	1999-2007
Theodore M. Pomeroy	Rep.	NY	1869	Nancy Pelosi	Dem.	CA	2007-

Political Divisions of the U.S. Senate and House of Representatives, 1901-2007
Source: Office of the Clerk; Congressional Research Service

Note: all figures reflect immediate post-election party breakdown; **boldface** denotes party in majority immediately after election.

		SENATE					HOUSE OF REPRESENTATIVES				
Congress	**Years**	**Total Sens.**	**Dem.**	**Rep.**	**Other parties**	**Vacant**	**Total Members**	**Dem.**	**Rep.**	**Other parties**	**Vacant**
57th	1901-03	90	32	**56**	2		357	151	**200**	6	
58th	1903-05	90	33	**57**			386	176	**207**	3	
59th	1905-07	90	32	**58**			386	135	**251**		
60th	1907-09	92	31	**61**			391	167	**223**	1	
61st	1909-11	92	32	**60**			391	172	**219**		
62nd	1911-13	96	44	**52**			394	**230**	162	2	
63rd	1913-15	96	**51**	44	1		435	**291**	134	10	
64th	1915-17	96	**56**	40			435	**230**	196	9	
65th	1917-19	96	**54**	42			435	214[1]	**215**	6	
66th	1919-21	96	47	**49**			435	192	**240**	2	1
67th	1921-23	96	37	**59**			435	131	**302**	2	
68th	1923-25	96	42	**53**	1		435	207	**225**	3	
69th	1925-27	96	41	**54**	1		435	183	**247**	5	
70th	1927-29	96	46	**48**	1	1	435	194	**238**	3	
71st	1929-31	96	39	**56**	1		435	164	**270**	1	
72nd	1931-33	96	47	**48**	1		435	216[2]	**218**	1	

Congress	Years	SENATE Total Sens.	Dem.	Rep.	Other parties	Vacant	HOUSE OF REPRESENTATIVES Total Members	Dem.	Rep.	Other parties	Vacant
73rd	1933-35	96	59	36	1		435	313	117	5	
74th	1935-37	96	69	25	2		435	322	103	10	
75th	1937-39	96	76	16	4		435	334	88	13	
76th	1939-41	96	69	23	4		435	262	169	4	
77th	1941-43	96	66	28	2		435	267	162	6	
78th	1943-45	96	57	38	1		435	222	209	4	
79th	1945-47	96	57	38	1		435	242	191	2	
80th	1947-49	96	45	51			435	188	246	1	
81st	1949-51	96	54	42			435	263	171	1	
82nd	1951-53	96	49	47			435	235	199	1	
83rd	1953-55	96	47	48	1		435	213	221	1	
84th	1955-57	96	48	47	1		435	232	203		
85th	1957-59	96	49	47			437[3]	234	201		
86th	1959-61	100	65	35			437[4]	283	153	1	
87th	1961-63	100	64	36			435	263	174		
88th	1963-65	100	66	34			435	259	176		
89th	1965-67	100	68	32			435	295	140		
90th	1967-69	100	64	36			435	247	187		1
91st	1969-71	100	57	43			435	243	192		
92nd	1971-73	100	54	44	2		435	255	180		
93rd	1973-75	100	56	42	2		435	242	192	1	
94th	1975-77	100	60	38	2		435	291	144		
95th	1977-79	100	61	38	1		435	292	143		
96th	1979-81	100	58	41	1		435	277	158		
97th	1981-83	100	46	53	1		435	242	192	1	
98th	1983-85	100	46	54			435	269	166		
99th	1985-87	100	47	53			435	253	182		
100th	1987-89	100	55	45			435	258	177		
101st	1989-91	100	55	45			435	260	175		
102nd	1991-93	100	56	44			435	267	167	1	
103rd	1993-95	100	57	43			435	258	176	1	
104th	1995-97	100	48	52			435	204	230	1	
105th	1997-99	100	45	55			435	206	228	1	
106th	1999-2001	100	45	55			435	211	223	1	
107th	2001-03	100	50	50[5]			435	212	221	2	
108th	2003-05	100	48	51	1		435	204	229	1	1
109th	2005-07	100	44	55	1		435	202	232	1	
110th	2007-09	100	49[6]	49	2		435	233	202		

(1) Democrats organized the House with help of other parties. (2) Democrats organized House because of Republican deaths. (3) Proclamation declaring Alaska a state issued Jan. 3, 1959. (4) Proclamation declaring Hawaii a state issued Aug. 21, 1959. (5) While the Senate was split 50-50, control was held by whichever party had an incumbent vice president. Republican Sen. James M. Jeffords (VT) changed his party designation to Independent on June 6, 2001, switching control of the Senate to Democrats from Republicans. (6) Both Independent senators chose to caucus with the Democrats.

Congressional Bills Vetoed, 1789-2007

Source: Senate Library

President	Regular vetoes	Pocket vetoes	Total vetoes	Vetoes overridden	President	Regular vetoes	Pocket vetoes	Total vetoes	Vetoes overridden
Washington	2	—	2	—	Benjamin Harrison	19	25	44	1
John Adams	—	—	—	—	Cleveland[2]	42	128	170	5
Jefferson	—	—	—	—	McKinley	6	36	42	—
Madison	5	2	7	—	Theodore Roosevelt	42	40	82	1
Monroe	1	—	1	—	Taft	30	9	39	1
John Q. Adams	—	—	—	—	Wilson	33	11	44	6
Jackson	5	7	12	—	Harding	5	1	6	—
Van Buren	—	1	1	—	Coolidge	20	30	50	4
William Harrison	—	—	—	—	Hoover	21	16	37	3
Tyler	6	4	10	1	Franklin Roosevelt	372	263	635	9
Polk	2	1	3	—	Truman	180	70	250	12
Taylor	—	—	—	—	Eisenhower	73	108	181	2
Fillmore	—	—	—	—	Kennedy	12	9	21	—
Pierce	9	—	9	5	Lyndon Johnson	16	14	30	—
Buchanan	4	3	7	—	Nixon	26	17	43	7
Lincoln	2	5	7	—	Ford	48	18	66	12
Andrew Johnson	21	8	29	15	Carter	13	18	31	2
Grant	45	48	93	4	Reagan	39	39	78	9
Hayes	12	1	13	1	George H. W. Bush[3]	29	15	44	1
Garfield	—	—	—	—	Clinton[4]	36	1	37	2
Arthur	4	8	12	1	George W. Bush[5]	3	—	3	—
Cleveland[1]	304	110	414	2	**Total**[3,4,5]	**1,487**	**1,066**	**2,553**	**106**

— = 0. (1) First term only. (2) Second term only. (3) Excluded from the figures are 2 additional bills, which Pres. George H. W. Bush claimed to be vetoed but Congress considered enacted into law because the president failed to return them to Congress during a recess period. (4) Does not include line-item vetoes, which were ruled unconstitutional by the Supreme Court on June 25, 1998. (5) As of Sept. 2007.

Librarians of Congress

Librarian	Served	Appointed by President	Librarian	Served	Appointed by President
John J. Beckley	1802-1807	Jefferson	Herbert Putnam	1899-1939	McKinley
Patrick Magruder	1807-1815	Jefferson	Archibald MacLeish	1939-1944	F. D. Roosevelt
George Watterston	1815-1829	Madison	Luther H. Evans	1945-1953	Truman
John Silva Meehan	1829-1861	Jackson	L. Quincy Mumford	1954-1974	Eisenhower
John G. Stephenson	1861-1864	Lincoln	Daniel J. Boorstin	1975-1987	Ford
Ainsworth Rand Spofford	1864-1897	Lincoln	James H. Billington	1987-	Reagan
John Russell Young	1897-1899	McKinley			

Governors of States and Puerto Rico

As of Sept. 2007. Of the 50 state governors, 22 are Republicans, 28 are Democrats.

State	Capital, ZIP Code	Governor	Party	Term years	Term expires	Annual salary
Alabama	Montgomery 36104	Bob Riley	Rep.	4	Jan. 2007	$112,895
Alaska	Juneau 99801	Sarah Palin[1]	Rep.	4	Dec. 2010	125,000
Arizona	Phoenix 85007	Janet Napolitano	Dem.	4	Jan. 2011	95,000
Arkansas	Little Rock 72201	Mike Beebe[1]	Dem.	4	Jan. 2011	82,465
California	Sacramento 95814	Arnold Schwarzenegger[2]	Rep.	4	Jan. 2011	212,179
Colorado	Denver 80203	Bill Ritter	Dem.	4	Jan. 2011	90,000
Connecticut	Hartford 06106	M. Jodi Rell	Rep.	4	Jan. 2011	150,000
Delaware	Dover 19901	Ruth Ann Minner	Dem.	4	Jan. 2011	132,500
Florida	Tallahassee 32301	Charlie Crist[1]	Rep.	4	Jan. 2011	136,176
Georgia	Atlanta 30334	Sonny Perdue	Rep.	4	Jan. 2011	130,192
Hawaii	Honolulu 96813	Linda Lingle	Rep.	4	Dec. 2010	117,600
Idaho	Boise 83702	C. L. "Butch" Otter[1]	Rep.	4	Jan. 2011	105,560
Illinois	Springfield 62706	Rod R. Blagojevich	Dem.	4	Jan. 2011	150,691
Indiana	Indianapolis 46204	Mitch E. Daniels Jr.	Rep.	4	Jan. 2009	95,000
Iowa	Des Moines 50319	Chester J. Culver[1]	Dem.	4	Jan. 2011	130,000
Kansas	Topeka 66612	Kathleen Sebelius	Dem.	4	Jan. 2011	108,007
Kentucky	Frankfort 40601	Ernie Fletcher	Rep.	4	Dec. 2007	138,000
Louisiana	Baton Rouge 70802	Kathleen Babineaux Blanco	Dem.	4	Jan. 2008	95,000
Maine	Augusta 04330	John E. Baldacci	Dem.	4	Jan. 2011	70,000
Maryland	Annapolis 21401	Martin O'Malley[1]	Dem.	4	Jan. 2011	150,000
Massachusetts	Boston 02133	Deval Patrick[1]	Dem.	4	Jan. 2011	140,535
Michigan	Lansing 48933	Jennifer M. Granholm	Dem.	4	Jan. 2011	177,000
Minnesota	St. Paul 55101	Tim Pawlenty	Rep.	4	Jan. 2011	120,303
Mississippi	Jackson 39201	Haley Barbour	Rep.	4	Jan. 2008	122,160
Missouri	Jefferson City 65101	Matt Blunt	Rep.	4	Jan. 2009	129,922
Montana	Helena 59620	Brian Schweitzer	Dem.	4	Jan. 2009	100,120
Nebraska	Lincoln 68509	David Heineman	Rep.	4	Jan. 2011	105,000
Nevada	Carson City 89701	Jim Gibbons[1]	Rep.	4	Jan. 2011	141,000
New Hampshire	Concord 03301	John H. Lynch	Dem.	2	Jan. 2009	108,990
New Jersey	Trenton 08625	Jon Corzine[2]	Dem.	4	Jan. 2010	175,000
New Mexico	Santa Fe 87501	Bill Richardson	Dem.	4	Jan. 2011	110,000
New York	Albany 12224	Eliot Spitzer[1]	Dem.	4	Jan. 2011	179,000
North Carolina	Raleigh 27601	Mike Easley	Dem.	4	Jan. 2009	135,854
North Dakota	Bismarck 58501	John Hoeven	Rep.	4	Jan. 2011	96,183
Ohio	Columbus 43215	Ted Strickland[1]	Dem.	4	Jan. 2011	144,831
Oklahoma	Oklahoma City 73105	Brad Henry	Dem.	4	Jan. 2011	140,000
Oregon	Salem 97301	Ted Kulongoski	Dem.	4	Jan. 2011	93,600
Pennsylvania	Harrisburg 17120	Edward G. Rendell	Dem.	4	Jan. 2011	164,396
Rhode Island	Providence 02903	Donald L. Carcieri	Rep.	4	Jan. 2011	105,194
South Carolina	Columbia 29201	Mark Sanford	Rep.	4	Jan. 2011	106,078
South Dakota	Pierre 57501	Mike Rounds	Rep.	4	Jan. 2011	108,711
Tennessee	Nashville 37243	Phil Bredesen	Dem.	4	Jan. 2011	159,960
Texas	Austin 78701	Rick Perry	Rep.	4	Jan. 2011	150,000
Utah	Salt Lake City 84103	John M. Huntsman Jr.	Rep.	4	Jan. 2009	107,700
Vermont	Montpelier 05602	Jim Douglas	Rep.	2	Jan. 2009	150,067
Virginia	Richmond 23218	Timothy M. Kaine	Dem.	4	Jan. 2010	175,000
Washington	Olympia 98501	Christine Gregoire	Dem.	4	Jan. 2009	163,618
West Virginia	Charleston 25301	Joe Manchin III	Dem.	4	Jan. 2009	95,000
Wisconsin	Madison 53702	Jim Doyle	Dem.	4	Jan. 2011	137,092
Wyoming	Cheyenne 82001	Dave Freudenthal	Dem.	4	Jan. 2011	105,000
Puerto Rico	San Juan 00901	Aníbal Acevedo Vilá	PDP[3]	4	Jan. 2009	70,000

(1) New governor; began first term after 2006 elections. (2) Does not accept salary. (3) Popular Democratic Party.

State Elected Officials, Salaries, Party Membership

As of Sept. 2007, 22 state legislatures were controlled by Democrats; 14 by Republicans; 13 were split; Nebraska's legislature is non-partisan. Some salaries may be rounded to the nearest dollar.

Alabama

Governor: Bob Riley, R, $112,895
Lt. Gov.: Jim Folsom Jr., D, $12 per day, plus $50 per day, plus $5,350 per mo expenses
Atty. Gen.: Troy King, R, $155,828
Sec. of State: Beth Chapman, R, $79,580
Treasurer: Kay Ivey, R, $79,580
Auditor: Samantha Shaw, R, $79,580
Legislature: meets annually at Montgomery 1st Tues. in Mar., 1st year of term of office; 1st Tues. in Feb., 2nd and 3rd yrs.; 2nd Tues. in Jan., 4th yr. Members receive $10 per day salary, plus $50 per day and $3,850 per month for expenses.
Senate: Dem., 23; Rep., 11; 1 vacancy. Total, 35.
House: Dem., 62; Rep., 43. Total, 105.

Alaska

Governor: Sarah Palin, R, $125,000
Lt. Gov.: Sean Parnell, R, $100,000
Atty. Gen.: Talis Colberg, R, $122,640
Legislature: meets annually on 3rd Tues. in Jan. at Juneau for 90 days with a 10-day extension possible upon 2/3 vote. Members receive $24,012 annually, plus $163 or $218 session per diem, depending on season.
Senate: Dem., 9; Rep., 11. Total, 20.
House: Dem., 17; Rep., 23. Total, 40.

Arizona

Governor: Janet Napolitano, D, $95,000
Sec. of State: Jan Brewer, R, $70,000
Atty. Gen.: Terry Goddard, D, $90,000
Treasurer: Dean Martin, R, $70,000
Legislature: meets annually in Jan. at Phoenix. Each member receives an annual salary of $24,000 plus a per diem.
Senate: Dem., 13; Rep., 17. Total, 30.
House: Dem., 27; Rep., 33. Total, 60.

Arkansas

Governor: Mike Beebe, D, $82,465
Lt. Gov.: Bill Halter, D, $39,857
Sec. of State: Charlie Daniels, D, $51,540
Atty. Gen.: Dustin McDaniel, D, $68,720
Treasurer: Martha Shoffner, D, $51,540
Auditor: Jim Wood, D, $51,540
General Assembly: meets odd years in Jan. at Little Rock. Members receive $15,060 annually.
Senate: Dem., 27; Rep., 8. Total, 35.
House: Dem., 75; Rep., 25. Total, 100.

California

Governor: Arnold Schwarzenegger, R, $212,179[1]
Lt. Gov.: John Garamendi, D, $159,134
Sec. of State: Debra Bowen, R, $159,134
Atty. Gen.: Edmund G. Brown Jr., D, $184,301
Controller: John Chiang, D, $169,743

Treasurer: Bill Lockyer, D, $169,743
Legislature: meets at Sacramento on the 1st Mon. in Dec. of even-numbered years; each session lasts 2 years. Members receive $116,208 annually, plus $162 per diem. High-ranking legislators earn an extra $16,964 or more, depending on post.
Senate: Dem., 25; Rep., 15. Total, 40
House: Dem., 48; Rep., 32. Total, 80
(1) Does not accept salary.

Colorado
Governor: Bill Ritter, D, $90,000
Lt. Gov.: Barbara O'Brien, D, $68,500
Sec. of State: Mike Coffman, R, $68,500
Atty. Gen.: John Suthers, R, $80,000
Treasurer: Cary Kennedy, R, $68,500
General Assembly: meets annually in Jan. at Denver. Members receive $30,000 annually plus $99 per diem for attendance at interim committee meetings.
Senate: Dem., 20; Rep., 15. Total, 35
House: Dem., 39; Rep., 26. Total, 65

Connecticut
Governor: M. Jodi Rell, R, $150,000
Lt. Gov.: Michael Fedele, R, $110,000
Sec. of State: Susan Bysiewicz, D, $110,000
Treasurer: Denise Nappier, D, $110,000
Comptroller: Nancy S. Wyman, D, $110,000
Atty. Gen.: Richard Blumenthal, D, $110,000
General Assembly: meets annually odd years in Jan. and even years in Feb., at Hartford. Members receive $28,000 annually, plus $5,500 (senator), $4,500 (representative) per year for expenses.
Senate: Dem., 24; Rep., 12. Total, 36
House: Dem., 107; Rep., 44. Total, 151

Delaware
Governor: Ruth Ann Minner, D, $132,500
Lt. Gov.: John C. Carney Jr., D, $76,250
Sec. of State: Harriet Smith Windsor, D, $123,850
Atty. Gen.: Joseph H. Biden III, D, $140,950
Treasurer: Jack A. Markell, D, $110,050
General Assembly: meets annually the 2nd Tues. in Jan. and continues each Tues., Wed., and Thurs. until June 30, at Dover. Members receive $42,750 annually.
Senate: Dem., 13; Rep., 8. Total, 21
House: Dem., 19; Rep., 22. Total, 41

Florida
Governor: Charlie Crist, R, $136,176
Lt. Gov.: Jeff Kottkamp, R, $130,508
Chief Financial Officer: Alex Sink, D, $134,815
Atty. Gen.: Bill McCollum, R, $134,815
Comm. of Agriculture: Charles H. Bronson, R, $134,815
Legislature: meets at Tallahassee. Members receive $31,982 annually, plus expense allowance.
Senate: Dem., 14; Rep., 26. Total, 40
House: Dem., 42; Rep., 78. Total, 120

Georgia
Governor: Sonny Perdue, R, $130,192
Lt. Gov.: Casey Cagle, R, $85,595
Sec. of State: Karen Handel, R, $121,120
Atty. Gen.: Thurbert Baker, D, $128,745
General Assembly: meets annually at Atlanta on 2nd Mon. in Jan. Members receive $16,524 annually.
Senate: Dem., 22; Rep., 34. Total, 56
House: Dem., 74; Rep., 106. Total, 180

Hawaii
Governor: Linda Lingle, R, $117,600
Lt. Gov.: James R. Aiona Jr., R, $105,000
Atty. Gen.: Mark J. Bennett, R, $114,708
Comptroller: Russ K. Saito, $109,248
Dir. of Budget & Finance: Georgina K. Kawamura, R, $109,248
Legislature: meets annually on 3rd Wed. in Jan. at Honolulu. Members receive $35,900 annually; presiding officers, $43,400.
Senate: Dem., 20; Rep., 5. Total, 25
House: Dem., 43; Rep., 8. Total, 51

Idaho
Governor: C. L. "Butch" Otter, R, $105,560
Lt. Gov.: Jim Risch, R, $27,820
Sec. of State: Ben Ysursa, R, $85,800
Treasurer: Ron Crane, R, $85,800
Atty. Gen.: Lawrence Wasden, R, $95,160
Legislature: meets annually the Mon. on or nearest Jan. 9 at Boise. Members receive $15,646 annually, plus $99 per day during session if required to maintain a 2nd residence, $38 if no 2nd residence; plus $1,700 unvouchered constituent service allowance.
Senate: Dem., 7; Rep., 28. Total, 35
House: Dem., 19; Rep., 51. Total, 70

Illinois
Governor: Rod R. Blagojevich, D, $150,691
Lt. Gov.: Patrick Quinn, D, $115,235
Sec. of State: Jesse White, D, $132,963
Comptroller: Daniel Hynes, D, $115,235
Atty. Gen.: Lisa Madigan, D, $132,963

Treasurer: Judy Baar Topinka, R, $115,235
General Assembly: meets annually in Nov. and Jan. at Springfield. Members receive $57,619 annually.
Senate: Dem., 37; Rep., 22. Total, 59
House: Dem., 67; Rep., 51. Total, 118

Indiana
Governor: Mitch E. Daniels Jr., R, $95,000
Lt. Gov.: Becky Skillman, R, $76,000
Sec. of State: Todd Rokita, R, $66,000
Atty. Gen.: Steve Carter, R, $79,400
Treasurer: Richard Mourdock, R, $66,000
Auditor: Tim Berry, R, $66,000
Superintendent of Public Instruction: Dr. Suellen Reed, R, $79,400
General Assembly: meets annually on the Tues. after 2nd Mon. in Jan. at Indianapolis. Members receive $11,600 annually, plus $137 per day in session, $55 per day while not in session.
Senate: Dem., 17; Rep., 33. Total, 50
House: Dem., 51; Rep., 49. Total, 100

Iowa
Governor: Chester J. Culver, D, $130,000
Lt. Gov.: Patty Judge, D, $103,212
Sec. of State: Michael A. Mauro, D, $103,212
Atty. Gen.: Tom Miller, D, $123,669
Treasurer: Michael L. Fitzgerald, D, $103,212
Auditor: David A. Vaudt, R, $103,212
Sec. of Agriculture: Bill Northey, R, $103,212
General Assembly: meets annually in Jan. at Des Moines. Members receive $25,000 annually, plus expense allowance.
Senate: Dem., 30; Rep., 20. Total, 50
House: Dem., 53; Rep., 47. Total, 100

Kansas
Governor: Kathleen Sebelius, D, $108,007
Lt. Gov.: Mark Parkinson, D, $30,549
Sec. of State: Ron Thornburgh, R, $83,905
Atty. Gen.: Paul J. Morrison, D, $96,489
Treasurer: Lynn Jenkins, R, $83,905
Insurance Commissioner: Sandy Praeger, R, $83,905
Legislature: meets annually on the 2nd Mon. of Jan. at Topeka, for a maximum of 90 days. Members receive $87 per day salary, plus $99 per diem in session.
Senate: Dem., 10; Rep., 30. Total, 40
House: Dem., 47; Rep., 78. Total, 125

Kentucky
Governor: Ernie Fletcher, R, $138,000
Lt. Gov.: Stephen Pence, R, $99,059
Sec. of State: Trey Grayson, R, $99,059
Atty. Gen.: Gregory Stumbo, D, $99,059
Treasurer: Jonathan Miller, D, $99,059
Auditor: Crit (Eugenia) Luallen, D, $99,059
General Assembly: meets annually on the 1st Tues. after the 1st Mon. in Jan. at Frankfort. Members receive $166 per day, plus $100 per day expenses during session and $1,581 per month for expenses for interim.
Senate: Dem., 16; Rep., 21; 1 ind. Total, 38
House: Dem., 61; Rep., 39. Total, 100
Note: Elections for all government offices listed here (excluding members of the General Assembly) were expected to be held Nov. 6, 2007.

Louisiana
Governor: Kathleen Babineaux Blanco, D, $95,000
Lt. Gov.: Mitch Landrieux, D, $85,000
Sec. of State: Jay Dardenne, R, $85,000
Atty. Gen.: Charles C. Foti Jr., D, $85,000
Treasurer: John Kennedy, R, $85,000
Legislature: meets in even-numbered years at Baton Rouge starting last Mon. in Mar., for 60 legislative days of 85 calendar days; meets in odd-numbered years on last Mon. in Apr. for 45 days of 60 calendar days. Members receive $16,800 annually, plus $121 per day expenses while in session and $500 per month as an unvouchered expense allowance.
Senate: Dem., 25; Rep., 14. Total, 39
House: Dem., 60; Rep., 43; 1 ind.; 1 vacancy. Total, 105
Note: Elections for all government offices listed here (including members of the legislature) were expected to be held Nov. 17, 2007. Gov. Blanco planned to retire.

Maine
Governor: John E. Baldacci, D, $70,000
Sec. of State: Matthew Dunlap, D, $74,859
Atty. Gen.: G. Steven Rowe, D, $94,952
Treasurer: David G. Lemoine, D, $74,859
State Auditor: Neria R. Douglass, D, $88,046
Legislature: meets in odd-numbered years on Wed. in Dec.; meets in even-numbered years on Wed. after first Tues. in Jan. Members receive $12,713 for first regular session, $9,353 (est.) for 2nd, plus a daily expense allowance.
Senate: Dem., 18; Rep., 17. Total, 35
House: Dem., 89; Rep., 60; unenrolled, 2. Total, 151

Maryland

Governor: Martin O'Malley, D, $150,000
Lt. Gov.: Anthony Brown, D, $125,000
Comptroller: Peter Franchot, D, $125,000
Atty. Gen.: Douglas F. Gansler, D, $125,000
Sec. of State: Vacant, $87,500
Treasurer: Nancy Kopp, D, $125,000
General Assembly: meets 90 consecutive days annually beginning on 2nd Wed. in Jan. at Annapolis. Members receive $43,500 annually, plus expenses.
Senate: Dem., 32; Rep., 14. Total, 46
House: Dem., 104; Rep., 37. Total, 141

Massachusetts

Governor: Deval Patrick, D, $140,535
Lt. Gov.: Timothy Murray, D, $127,523
Sec. of the Commonwealth: William F. Galvin, D, $124,920
Atty. Gen.: Martha Coakley, D, $127,523
Treasurer: Timothy P. Cahill, D, $124,920
State Auditor: A. Joseph DeNucci, D, $124,920
General Court (legislature): meets Jan. annually in Boston. Members receive $53,380 annually.
Senate: Dem., 34; Rep., 5; 1 vacancy. Total, 40
House: Dem., 140; Rep., 19; 1 vacancy. Total, 160

Michigan

Governor: Jennifer M. Granholm, D, $177,000
Lt. Gov.: John Cherry, D, $123,900
Sec. of State: Terri Lynn Land, R, $124,900
Atty. Gen.: Michael Cox, R, $124,900
Treasurer: Robert J. Kleine, D, $174,204
Legislature: meets annually in Jan. at Lansing. Members receive $79,650 annually.
Senate: Dem., 17; Rep., 21. Total, 38
House: Dem., 58; Rep., 52. Total, 110

Minnesota

Governor: Tim Pawlenty, R, $120,303
Lt. Gov.: Carol Molnau, R, $78,197
Sec. of State: Mark Ritchie, DFL, $90,227
Atty. Gen.: Lori Swanson, DFL, $114,288
Auditor: Rebecca Otto, DFL, $102,258
Legislature: meets for up to 120 days total within every 2 years, at St. Paul. Members receive $31,141 annually, plus expense allowance during session.
Senate: DFL, 44; Rep., 23. Total, 67
House: DFL, 85; Rep., 49. Total, 134
Note: DFL=Democratic-Farmer-Labor Party

Mississippi

Governor: Haley Barbour, R, $122,160
Lt. Gov.: Amy Tuck, R, $60,000
Sec. of State: Eric Clark, D, $90,000
Atty. Gen.: Jim Hood, D, $108,960
Treasurer: Tate Reeves, R, $90,000
Auditor: Phil Bryant, R, $90,000
Legislature: meets annually in Jan. at Jackson. Members receive $10,000 per regular session, plus travel allowance, and $1,500 per month when not in session.
Senate: Dem., 26; Rep., 26. Total, 52
House: Dem., 75; Rep., 47. Total, 122
Note: Elections for all government offices listed here (including members of the legislature) were expected to be held Nov. 6, 2007.

Missouri

Governor: Matt Blunt, R, $129,922
Lt. Gov.: Peter Kinder, R, $83,965
Sec. of State: Robin Carnahan, D, $104,608
Atty. Gen.: Jeremiah W. Nixon, D, $113,046
Treasurer: Sarah Steelman, R, $104,608
State Auditor: Susan Montec, D, $104,608
General Assembly: meets annually at Jefferson City beginning 1st Wed. after 1st Mon. in Jan. Members receive $31,351 annually.
Senate: Dem., 14; Rep., 20. Total, 34
House: Dem., 71; Rep., 92. Total, 163

Montana

Governor: Brian Schweitzer, D, $100,120
Lt. Gov.: John Bohlinger, R, $79,007
Sec. of State: Brad Johnson, R, $79,129
Atty. Gen.: Mike McGrath, D, $89,602
Legislature: meets odd years in Jan. at Helena. Members receive $76.80 per legislative day, plus $94.05 per diem while in session.
Senate: Dem., 26; Rep., 24. Total, 50
House: Dem., 49; Rep., 50; Constitution Party, 1. Total, 100

Nebraska

Governor: David Heineman, R, $105,000
Lt. Gov.: Rick Sheehy, R, $75,000
Sec. of State: John A. Gale, R, $85,000
Atty. Gen.: Jon Bruning, R, $95,000
Treasurer: Shane Osborn, R, $85,000
Auditor of Public Accounts: Mike Foley, R, $85,000
Legislature: Unicameral body composed of 49 members who are elected on a nonpartisan ballot and are called senators; meets annually in Jan. at Lincoln. Members receive $12,000 annually, plus expenses.

Nevada

Governor: Jim Gibbons, R, $141,000
Lt. Gov.: Brian Krolicki, R, $60,000
Sec. of State: Ross Miller, D, $97,000
Controller: Kim Wallin, D, $97,000
Atty. Gen.: Catherine Cortez Masto, D, $133,000
Treasurer: Kate Marshall, D, $97,000
Legislature: meets at Carson City odd years starting on 1st Mon. in Feb. for 120 days. Members receive $138 per day salary, plus a per diem during session of $147 per day (subject to an overall limit of $6,800 during regular sessions and $1,000 during special sessions).
Senate: Dem., 10; Rep., 11. Total, 21
Assembly: Dem., 27; Rep., 15. Total, 42

New Hampshire

Governor: John H. Lynch, D, $108,990
Sec. of State: William M. Gardner, D, $94,584
Atty. Gen.: Kelly A. Ayotte, R, $105,396
Treasurer: Catherine A. Provencher, $94,584
General Court (legis.): meets every year in Jan. at Concord. Members receive $200, presiding officers $250, biannually.
Senate: Dem., 14; Rep., 10. Total, 24
House: Dem., 239; Rep., 161. Total, 400

New Jersey

Governor: Jon Corzine, D, $175,000[1]
Sec. of State: Nina Mitchell Wells, D, $141,000
Atty. Gen.: Anne Milgram, D, $141,000
Acting Treasurer: Michelline Davis, D, $127,500
Legislature: meets throughout the year at Trenton. Members receive $49,000 annually, except president of Senate: and speaker of Assembly:, who receive 1/3 more.
Senate: Dem., 22; Rep., 18. Total, 40
Assembly: Dem., 50; Rep., 30. Total, 80
(1) Does not accept salary.

New Mexico

Governor: Bill Richardson, D, $110,000
Lt. Gov.: Diane D. Denish, D, $85,000
Sec. of State: Mary Herrera, D, $85,000
Atty. Gen.: Gary King, D, $95,000
Treasurer: James B. Lewis, D, $85,000
Auditor: Hector H. Balderas, D, $85,000
Commissioner of Public Lands: Patrick Lyons, R, $90,000
Legislature: meets starting on the 3rd Tues. in Jan. at Santa Fe; odd years for 60 days, even years for 30 days. Members receive $145 per day while in session.
Senate: Dem., 24; Rep., 18. Total, 42
House: Dem., 42; Rep., 28. Total, 70

New York

Governor: Eliot Spitzer, D, $179,000
Lt. Gov.: David Paterson, D, $151,500
Sec. of State: Lorraine A. Cortés-Vásquez, D, $120,800
Comptroller: Thomas Dinapoli, D, $151,500
Atty. Gen.: Andrew Cuomo, D, $151,500
Legislature: meets annually on the 1st Wed. after the 1st Mon. in Jan. at Albany. Members receive $79,500 annually, plus $143 per diem.
Senate: Dem., 29; Rep., 33. Total, 62
Assembly: Dem., 108; Rep., 42. Total, 150

North Carolina

Governor: Mike Easley, D, $135,854
Lt. Gov.: Beverly Perdue, D, $119,901
Sec. of State: Elaine F. Marshall, D, $119,901
Atty. Gen.: Roy Cooper, D, $119,901
Treasurer: Richard H. Moore, D, $119,901
General Assembly: meets odd years starting on the 3rd Wed. following the 2nd Mon. in Jan. at Raleigh. Members receive $13,951 annually and a $559 monthly expense allowance, plus travel and other allowances in session. Also meets in even years for a short session (about 6-8 weeks), usually in May.
Senate: Dem., 31; Rep., 19. Total, 50
House: Dem., 68; Rep., 52. Total, 120

North Dakota

Governor: John Hoeven, R, $96,183
Lt. Gov.: John S. Dalrymple III, R, $74,668
Sec. of State: Alvin A. Jaeger, R, $76,511
Atty. Gen.: Wayne Stenehjem, R, $83,991
Treasurer: Kelly Schmidt, R, $72,253
Legislative Assembly: meets odd years in Jan. at Bismarck. Members receive $364 per month salary, plus $130 per calendar day salary during session and $50 per day expenses, plus any additional state or local taxes on lodging, with a limit of $900 per month.
Senate: Dem., 21; Rep., 26. Total, 47
House: Dem., 33; Rep., 61. Total, 94

Ohio

Governor: Ted Strickland, D, $144,831
Lt. Gov.: Lee Fisher, D, $75,916
Sec. of State: Jennifer Brunner, D, $106,990
Atty. Gen.: Marc Dann, D, $106,990
Treasurer: Richard Cordray, D, $106,990
Auditor: Mary Taylor, R, $106,990

General Assembly: meets odd years at Columbus starting on 1st Mon. in Jan. Members receive $58,934 annually.
Senate: Dem., 12; Rep., 21. Total, 33
House: Dem., 46; Rep., 43. Total, 99

Oklahoma

Governor: Brad Henry, D, $140,000
Lt. Gov.: Jari Askins, D, $109,250
Sec. of State: M. Susan Savage, D, $90,000
Atty. Gen.: Drew Edmondson, D, $126,500
Treasurer: Scott Meacham, D, $109,250
Auditor: Jeff A. McMahan, D, $109,250
Legislature: meets annually the first Mon. in Feb. at Oklahoma City. In odd-numbered years, the session includes one day (1st Tues. after 1st Mon.) in Jan. Members receive $38,400 annually.
Senate: Dem., 24; Rep., 24. Total, 48
House: Dem., 44; Rep., 57. Total, 101

Oregon

Governor: Ted Kulongoski, D, $93,600
Sec. of State: Bill Bradbury, D, $72,000
Atty. Gen.: Hardy Myers, D, $77,200
Treasurer: Randall Edwards, D, $72,000
Legislative Assembly: meets odd years in Jan. at Salem. Members receive $1,534 monthly, $99 expenses per diem during session and when attending meetings during the interim, plus between $450 and $750 expense account during interim.
Senate: Dem., 18; Rep., 11; Ind., 1. Total, 30
House: Dem., 31; Rep., 29. Total, 60

Pennsylvania

Governor: Edward G. Rendell, D, $164,396
Lt. Gov.: Catherine Baker Knoll, D, $138,091
Sec. of the Commonwealth: Pedro A. Cortés, D, $118,366
Atty. Gen.: Tom Corbett, D, $136,778
Auditor: Jack Wagner, D, $136,778
Treasurer: Robin L. Wiessman, D, $136,778
General Assembly: convenes annually on the 1st Tues. in Jan. at Harrisburg. Members receive $73,614 annually, plus expenses.
Senate: Dem., 21; Rep., 29. Total, 50
House: Dem., 102; Rep., 101. Total, 203

Rhode Island

Governor: Donald L. Carcieri, R, $105,194
Lt. Gov.: Elizabeth Roberts, D, $88,584
Sec. of State: A. Ralph Mollis, D, $88,584
Atty. Gen.: Patrick C. Lynch, D, $94,121
Treasurer: Frank D. Caprio, D, $88,584
General Assembly: meets annually in Jan. at Providence. Members receive $10,000 annually (plus mileage and cost-of-living increase).
Senate: Dem., 33; Rep., 5. Total, 38
House: Dem., 62; Rep., 13. Total, 75

South Carolina

Governor: Mark Sanford, R, $106,078
Lt. Gov.: R. André Bauer, R, $46,545
Sec. of State: Mark Hammond, R, $92,007
Comptroller: Richard A. Eckstrom, R, $92,007
Atty. Gen.: Henry McMaster, R, $92,007
Treasurer: Converse A. Chellis III, R, $92,007
General Assembly: meets annually on the 2nd Tues. in Jan. at Columbia. Members receive $10,400 annually, plus $130 per diem.
Senate: Dem., 19; Rep., 25; 2 vacancies. Total, 46
House: Dem., 51; Rep., 72; 1 vacancy. Total, 124

South Dakota

Governor: Mike Rounds, R, $108,711
Lt. Gov.: Dennis M. Daugaard, R, $15,832
Sec. of State: Chris Nelson, R, $73,865
Atty. Gen.: Larry Long, R, $92,307
Treasurer: Vernon L. Larson, R, $73,865
Auditor: Rich Sattgast, R, $73,865
Legislature: meets annually beginning the 2nd Tues. in Jan. at Pierre, for 40-day session in odd-numbered years, and 35-day session in even-numbered years. Members receive $12,000 per 2-year term plus $110 per diem for days in session.
Senate: Dem., 15; Rep., 20. Total, 35
House: Dem., 20; Rep., 50. Total, 70

Tennessee

Governor: Phil Bredesen, D, $159,960
Lt. Gov./Speaker of the Senate: Ron Ramsey, R, $54,363
Sec. of State: Riley C. Darnell, D, $180,000
Treasurer: Dale Sims, D, $180,000
Comptroller: John Morgan, D, $180,000
Atty. Gen.: Robert E. Cooper Jr., D, $154,800
General Assembly: meets annually on the 2nd Tues. in Jan. at Nashville. Members receive $18,121 annual salary, plus $153 per diem while in session and $1,000 monthly office allowance.
Senate: Dem., 16; Rep., 16; Ind., 1. Total, 33
House: Dem., 53; Rep., 46. Total, 99

Texas

Governor: Rick Perry, R, $150,000
Lt. Gov.: David Dewhurst, R, $7,200 (plus $139 per day during legislative sessions)
Sec. of State: Phil Wilson, R, $117,516

Comptroller: Susan Combs, R, $150,000
Atty. Gen.: Greg W. Abbott, R, $150,000
Railroad Commissioners: Michael L. Williams, R, Chair; Elizabeth Jones, R; Victor G. Carrillo, R; $137,500
Legislature: meets odd years in Jan. at Austin. Members receive $7,200 annually, plus $139 per diem while in session.
Senate: Dem., 11; Rep., 20. Total, 31
House: Dem., 69; Rep., 81. Total, 150

Utah

Governor: Jon M. Huntsman Jr., R, $107,700
Lt. Gov.: Gary R. Herbert, R, $102,315
Atty. Gen.: Mark Shurtleff, R, $102,315
Auditor: Auston G. Johnson, R, $86,400
Treasurer: Edward T. Alter, R, $83,800
Legislature: convenes for 45 days, starting on 3rd Mon. in Jan. each year at Salt Lake City. Members receive $130 per day, plus $39 a day expenses.
Senate: Dem., 8; Rep., 21. Total, 29
House: Dem., 20; Rep., 54. Total, 74

Vermont

Governor: Jim Douglas, R, $150,067
Lt. Gov.: Brian E. Dubie, R, $63,701
Sec. of State: Deborah L. Markowitz, D, $95,156
Atty. Gen.: William H. Sorrell, D, $113,915
Treasurer: Jeb (George B.) Spaulding, D, $95,156
Auditor: Thomas M. Salmon, D, $95,156
General Assembly: meets in Jan. at Montpelier (annual and biennial session). Members receive $601 per 4-day week while in session plus $105 per day for special session, plus expenses.
Senate: Dem., 23; Rep., 7. Total, 30
House: Dem., 93; Rep., 49; VT Progressive, 6; 2 Ind. Total, 150

Virginia

Governor: Timothy M. Kaine, D, $175,000
Lt. Gov.: Bill Bolling, R, $36,321
Atty. Gen.: Bob McDonnell, R, $150,000
Sec. of the Commonwealth: Kate Hanley, D, $146,940
Treasurer: J. Braxton Powell, D, $128,371
General Assembly: meets annually in Jan. at Richmond. Members receive $18,000 (senate) or $17,640 (house) annually, plus expense and mileage allowances.
Senate: Dem., 17; Rep., 23. Total, 40
House: Dem., 40; Rep., 57; Ind., 3. Total, 100

Washington

Governor: Christine Gregoire, D, $163,618
Lt. Gov.: Brad Owen, D, $92,106
Sec. of State: Sam Reed, R, $114,657
Atty. Gen.: Rob McKenna, R, $148,744
Treasurer: Mike Murphy, D, $114,657
Auditor: Brian Sonntag, D, $114,657
Legislature: meets annually in Jan. at Olympia. Members receive $41,280 annually, plus $101 per diem while in session, and $101 per diem for attending meetings during interim.
Senate: Dem., 32; Rep., 17. Total, 49
House: Dem., 62; Rep., 57. Total, 98

West Virginia

Governor: Joe Manchin III, D, $95,000
Sec. of State: Betty Ireland, R, $75,000
Atty. Gen.: Darrell V. McGraw Jr., D, $80,000
Treasurer: John D. Perdue, D, $75,000
Comm. of Agric.: Gus R. Douglass, D, $75,000
Auditor: Glen B. Gainer III, D, $75,000
Legislature: meets annually in Jan. at Charleston, except after gubernatorial elections, when the legislature meets in Feb. Members receive $15,000 annually.
Senate: Dem., 23; Rep., 11. Total, 34
House: Dem., 72; Rep., 28. Total, 100

Wisconsin

Governor: Jim Doyle, D, $137,092
Lt. Gov.: Barbara Lawton, D, $72,394
Sec. of State: Douglas La Follette, D, $65,079
Treasurer: Jack Voight, D, $65,079
Atty. Gen.: Peggy A. Lautenschlager, D, $133,033
Legislature: meets in Jan. of odd-numbered years for a 2-year session at Madison. Members receive $47,413 annually, plus $88 per day expenses.
Senate: Dem., 18; Rep., 15. Total, 33
Assembly: Dem., 47; Rep., 52. Total, 99

Wyoming

Governor: Dave Freudenthal, D, $105,000
Sec. of State: Max Maxfield, R, $92,000
Atty. Gen.: Bruce Salzburg, D, $95,000
Treasurer: Joseph B. Meyer, R, $92,000
State Auditor: Rita C. Meyer, R, $92,000
Legislature: meets odd years in Jan., even years in Feb., at Cheyenne. Members receive $150 per day while in session, plus $85 per diem.
Senate: Dem., 7; Rep., 23. Total, 30
House: Dem., 16; Rep., 44. Total, 60

THE **WORLD**
AT A GLANCE

THE AMERICAN PEOPLE

U.S. Population (pp. 588-604)

Male: 49% Female: 51%

Race and Hispanic Origin

White only 80.1%
Black only 12.8%
Asian-American only 4.4%
Am. Indian & Alaska Native 1.0%
Hawaiian/Pacific Islander only 0.2%
Two or more races 1.6%
Hispanic or Latino 14.8%

Age (2005)

Under 5 . . . . .7.0%
Under 21 . . . . .29.1%
65 and over 12.1%
85 and over 1.3%

Projected population over 65 by 2050 . . . . 22.1%
Projected population over 85 by 2050 . . . . 5.0%

The Foreign-Born Population (pp. 597-601)

U.S. population that is foreign-born. 12.1%
Most common ancestry claimed by Americans (2005). . . . . German, 49.2 mil people
#1 country of origin for foreign-born residents (2005). . . . . .Mexico, 11.0 mil people
#1 country of origin for unauthorized immigrants . . . . Mexico, 6.6 mil people
#1 state of intended residence for new immigrants . . . . California, 264,677 people
#1 metropolitan area of intended residence for new immigrants . . . . . . New York-N. New Jersey-Long Island, 224,444 people
#1 country for foreign adoptions . . . . .China, 6,520 adoptions (p. 159)
#1 language spoken at home, after English (2005) . . . . Spanish or Spanish Creole, 32.2 mil speakers
#2 language spoken at home, after English (2005) . . . . Chinese, 2.3 mil speakers

---

Health and Vital Statistics (pp. 132-164)

Top U.S. Baby Names: Jacob and Emily

Births in U.S. . . . . 4.3 mil
Deaths in U.S. . . . . 2.4 mil

Marriages per 1,000 people 7.3
Divorces per 1,000 people 3.6

Marriage

Households headed by married couples. . . . . in 1960: 74% . . . . in 2006: 51%
Men's median age at first marriage . . . . in 1960: 22.8 . . . . in 2006: 27.5
Women's median age at first marriage . . . . in 1960: 20.3 . . . . in 2006: 25.9
Population (age 15 and older) that has never been married. . . . . 29% (p. 600)

Sex

Median lifetime opposite-sex sexual partners, for people age 15-44 . . . . Men: 5.6 . . . . Women: 3.3
High schoolers who had intercourse in the past three months (2005) . . . . Boys: 33.3% . . . . Girls: 34.6%
People age 75-85 who were sexually active with a partner in the past 12 months . . . . . . Men: 38.5% . . . . . . Women: 16.7%

Death, Drugs, Illness

#1 cause of death (2004). . . . . Heart disease, 652,486 deaths
#1 emergency room complaint (2005) . . . . Stomach pain, 7.8 mil emergency visits
#1 drug type prescribed in physicians' offices (2005). Antidepressants, 107 mil prescriptions
Average projected lifespan for a U.S. citizen born . . . . in 1900: 47.3 years . . . . in 2004: 77.8 years
Percent of population in 2001-04 that was . . . . overweight: 65.2% . . . . obese: 31.1%
Americans who have used an illicit drug . . . . . . in their lifetime: 45.4% . . . in past year: 14.5% . . . . . . in past month: 8.3%

Accidental deaths				Drug use among high school seniors			
	1970	2005	% Change		1975	2006	% Change
Motor vehicle	54,633	45,800	−16.2%	Marijuana	47.3%	42.3%	-10.6%
Firearms	2,406	730	−69.7%	Cigarettes	73.6%	47.1%	-36.0%
Poisoning	5,299	20,900	+294.4%	LSD	11.3%	3.3%	-70.8%

Crime and Punishment (pp. 110-119)

Property crimes committed . . . . 10.0 mil
Violent crimes committed . . . . 1.4 mil
People arrested . . . . 14.4 mil
State with highest violent crime rate . . . . .South Carolina, 765.5 per 1,000 pop.
State with lowest violent crime rate . . . . Maine, 115.5 per 1,000 pop.

People in prison . . . . 2.2 mil
People on death row (end of 2005) 3,254
Number of executions (2005) 60

The American Presidents (pp. 515-544)

Shortest president . . . . James Madison, 5 ft 4 in
First to be impeached . . . . Andrew Johnson (1868)
Only bachelor president . . . . James Buchanan

Tallest president . . . . Abraham Lincoln, 6 ft 4 in
First to hold an Internet chat . . . . Bill Clinton (1999)
Only divorced president . . . . Ronald Reagan

---

American Societies and Associations (pp. 387-394)

American Political Items Collectors . . . . .www.apic.us
Bald-Headed Men of America . . . . members.aol.com/baldusa
Brewery Collectibles Club of America. . . . . www.bcca.com
International Wizard of Oz Club. . . . . www.ozclub.org
National Button Society. . . . . www.nationalbuttonsociety.org
Ships in Bottles Association of America . . . . www.shipsinbottles.org

---

Note: All figures are for 2006 unless otherwise noted.

UNITED STATES FACTS

Superlative U.S. Statistics[1]

Source: U.S. Geological Survey, Dept. of the Interior; U.S. Bureau of the Census, Dept. of Commerce; World Almanac research

Total Area for 50 states and Washington, DC (Land, 3,537,440 sq mi; Water, 256,648 sq mi)		3,794,085 sq mi[2]
Largest state	Alaska	663,267 sq mi
Smallest state	Rhode Island	1,545 sq mi
Largest county (excluding Alaska)	San Bernardino County, CA	20,105 sq mi
Smallest county	Arlington County, VA[3]	26 sq mi
Largest incorporated city	Sitka, AK	4,812 sq mi
Northernmost city	Barrow, AK.	71°17′ N
Northernmost point	Point Barrow, AK	71°23′ N
Southernmost city	Hilo, HI	19°44′ N
Southernmost settlement	Naalehu, HI	19°03′ N
Southernmost point	Ka Lae (South Cape), Island of Hawaii	18° 55′ N (155°41′ W)
Easternmost city	Eastport, ME	66° 59′05′′ W
Easternmost settlement[4]	Amchitka Isl., AK	179°15′ E
Easternmost point[4]	Pochnoi Point, on Semisopochnoi Isl., AK	179°46′ E
Westernmost city	Atka, AK.	174° 12′ W
Westernmost settlement	Adak Station, AK	176° 39′ W
Westernmost point	Amatignak Isl., AK	179° 06′ W
Lowest settlement	Bombay Beach, CA	−223 ft
Highest point on Atlantic coast	Cadillac Mountain, Mount Desert Isl., ME	1,530 ft
Oldest national park	Yellowstone National Park (1872), WY-MT-ID	2,219,791 acres
Largest national park	Wrangell-St. Elias, AK	8,323,148 acres
Highest waterfall	Yosemite Falls—Total in 3 sections.	2,425 ft
	(Upper Yosemite Fall, 1,430 ft; Cascades, 675 ft; Lower Yosemite Fall, 320 ft)	
Longest river system	Mississippi-Missouri-Red Rock	3,710 mi
Highest mountain	Mount McKinley (Denali), AK.	20,320 ft
Lowest point	Death Valley, CA	−282 ft
Deepest lake	Crater Lake, OR.	1,932 ft
Rainiest spot	Mount Waialeale, HI	Annual avg rainfall 433 in
Largest gorge	Grand Canyon, Colorado River, AZ	277 mi long, 600 ft to 18 mi wide, 1 mi deep
Deepest gorge	Hells Canyon, Snake River, OR-ID	7,900 ft
Largest dam	New Cornelia Tailings, Ten Mile Wash, AZ[5]	274,026,000 cu yds material used
Tallest building	Sears Tower, Chicago, IL	1,450 ft
Largest building	Boeing Manufacturing Plant, Everett, WA	472,000,000 cu ft; covers 98 acres
Largest office building	Pentagon, Arlington, VA	77,025,000 cu ft; covers 29 acres
Tallest structure	TV tower, Blanchard, ND.	2,063 ft
Longest bridge span	Verrazano-Narrows, NY.	4,260 ft
Highest bridge	Royal Gorge, CO	1,053 ft above water
Deepest well	Bertha Rogers gas well, Washita County, OK.	31,441 ft

The 48 Contiguous States

Total Area for 48 states and Washington, DC (Land, 2,959,066 sq mi; Water, 160,824 sq mi)		3,119,887 sq mi[2]
Largest state	Texas	268,581 sq mi
Northernmost city	Bellingham, WA	48°46′ N
Northernmost settlement	Angle Inlet, MN	49°21′ N
Northernmost point	Northwest Angle, MN.	49°23′ N
Southernmost city	Key West, FL	24°33′ N
Southernmost mainland city	Florida City, FL.	25°27′ N
Southernmost point	Key West, FL.	24°33′ N
Easternmost settlement	Lubec, ME	66°58′49′′ W
Easternmost point	West Quoddy Head, ME	66°57′ W
Westernmost town	La Push, WA	124°38′ W
Westernmost point	Cape Alava, WA.	124°44′ W
Highest mountain	Mount Whitney, CA	14,494 ft

(1) All areas are total area, including water, unless otherwise noted. (2) Does not add, because of rounding. (3) Smallest county by land area is New York County (Manhattan) at 23 sq mi; its total area including water is 34 square miles. Superlative shown is for smallest total area. (4) Alaska's Aleutian Islands extend into the eastern hemisphere (across 180° longitude) and thus technically contain the easternmost point and settlement in the U.S. (5) The New Cornelia Tailings Dam is a privately owned industrial dam composed of tailings, remnants of a mining process.

Geodetic Datum of North America

In July 1986, the National Oceanic and Atmospheric Administration's National Geodetic Survey (NGS), in cooperation with Canada and Mexico, completed readjustment and redefinition of the system of latitudes and longitudes. The resulting North American Datum of 1983 (NAD 83) replaces the North American Datum of 1927, as well as local reference systems for Hawaii, Puerto Rico, and the Virgin Islands. The change was prompted by Hawaii's increased need for accurate coordinate information. To facilitate use of satellite surveying and navigation systems, such as the Global Positioning System (GPS), the new datum was redefined using the Geodetic Reference System 1980 as the reference ellipsoid because this model more closely approximates the true size and shape of the earth. In addition, the origin of the coordinate system is referenced to the mass center of the Earth to coincide with the orbital orientation of the GPS satellites. Positional changes resulting from the datum redefinition can reach 330 ft in the continental U.S., Canada, and Mexico. Changes that exceed 660 ft can be expected in Alaska, Puerto Rico, and the Virgin Islands. Hawaii's coordinates changed about 1,300 ft.

Additional Statistical Information About the U.S.

The annual *Statistical Abstract of the United States,* published by the U.S. Commerce Dept., Bureau of Census, contains additional data. For information, write Supt. of Documents, P.O. Box 371954, Pittsburgh, PA 15250-7954, call 1-866-512-1800, or e-mail ContactCenter@gpo.gov. For electronic products, write Supt. of Documents, Government Printing Office, Attn: Electronic Products, P.O. Box 37082, Washington, DC 20013-7082. The *Statistical Abstract* can be viewed on the Internet at: www.census.gov/compendia/statab

Highest and Lowest Altitudes in U.S. States and Territories

Source: U.S. Geological Survey, Dept. of the Interior

(Minus sign means below sea level)

State	HIGHEST POINT Name	County	Elev. (ft)	LOWEST POINT Name	County	Elev. (ft)
Alabama	Cheaha Mountain	Cleburne	2,407	Gulf of Mexico		Sea level
Alaska	Mount McKinley	Denali	20,320	Pacific Ocean		Sea level
American Samoa	Lata Mountain	Tau Island	3,160	Pacific Ocean		Sea level
Arizona	Humphreys Peak	Coconino	12,633	Colorado R.	Yuma	70
Arkansas	Magazine Mountain	Logan	2,753	Ouachita R.	Ashley-Union	55
California	Mount Whitney	Inyo-Tulare	14,494	Death Valley	Inyo	−282
Colorado	Mount Elbert	Lake	14,433	Arikaree R.	Yuma	3,315
Connecticut	S. slope of Mt. Frissell	Litchfield	2,380	Long Island Sound		Sea level
Delaware	Ebright Azimuth	New Castle	448	Atlantic Ocean		Sea level
Dist. of Columbia	Tenleytown	NW part	410	Potomac R.		1
Florida	Britton Hill	Walton	345	Atlantic Ocean		Sea level
Georgia	Brasstown Bald	Towns-Union	4,784	Atlantic Ocean		Sea level
Guam	Mount Lamlam	Agat District	1,332	Pacific Ocean		Sea level
Hawaii	Mauna Kea	Hawaii	13,796	Pacific Ocean		Sea level
Idaho	Borah Peak	Custer	12,662	Snake R.	Nez Perce	710
Illinois	Charles Mound	Jo Daviess	1,235	Mississippi R.	Alexander	279
Indiana	Hoosier Hill	Wayne	1,257	Ohio R.	Posey	320
Iowa	Hawkeye Point	Osceola	1,670	Mississippi R.	Lee	480
Kansas	Mount Sunflower	Wallace	4,039	Verdigris R.	Montgomery	679
Kentucky	Black Mountain	Harlan	4,145	Mississippi R.	Fulton	257
Louisiana	Driskill Mountain	Bienville	535	New Orleans	Orleans	−8
Maine	Mount Katahdin	Piscataquis	5,268	Atlantic Ocean		Sea level
Maryland	Hoye Crest	Garrett	3,360	Atlantic Ocean		Sea level
Massachusetts	Mount Greylock	Berkshire	3,491	Atlantic Ocean		Sea level
Michigan	Mount Arvon	Baraga	1,979	Lake Erie		571
Minnesota	Eagle Mountain	Cook	2,301	Lake Superior		601
Mississippi	Woodall Mountain	Tishomingo	806	Gulf of Mexico		Sea level
Missouri	Taum Sauk Mountain	Iron	1,772	St. Francis R.	Dunklin	230
Montana	Granite Peak	Park	12,799	Kootenai R.	Lincoln	1,800
Nebraska	Panorama Point	Kimball	5,424	Missouri R.	Richardson	840
Nevada	Boundary Peak	Esmeralda	13,147	Colorado R.	Clark	479
New Hampshire	Mount Washington	Coos	6,288	Atlantic Ocean		Sea level
New Jersey	High Point	Sussex	1,803	Atlantic Ocean		Sea level
New Mexico	Wheeler Peak	Taos	13,161	Red Bluff Res.	Eddy	2,842
New York	Mount Marcy	Essex	5,344	Atlantic Ocean		Sea level
North Carolina	Mount Mitchell	Yancey	6,684	Atlantic Ocean		Sea level
North Dakota	White Butte	Slope	3,506	Red R. of the North	Pembina	750
Ohio	Campbell Hill	Logan	1,550	Ohio R.	Hamilton	455
Oklahoma	Black Mesa	Cimarron	4,973	Little R.	McCurtain	289
Oregon	Mount Hood	Clackamas-Hood R.	11,239	Pacific Ocean		Sea level
Pennsylvania	Mount Davis	Somerset	3,213	Delaware R.	Delaware	Sea level
Puerto Rico	Cerro de Punta	Ponce District	4,390	Atlantic Ocean		Sea level
Rhode Island	Jerimoth Hill	Providence	812	Atlantic Ocean		Sea level
South Carolina	Sassafras Mountain	Pickens	3,560	Atlantic Ocean		Sea level
South Dakota	Harney Peak	Pennington	7,242	Big Stone Lake	Roberts	966
Tennessee	Clingmans Dome	Sevier	6,643	Mississippi R.	Shelby	178
Texas	Guadalupe Peak	Culberson	8,749	Gulf of Mexico		Sea level
Utah	Kings Peak	Duchesne	13,528	Beaver Dam Wash	Washington	2,000
Vermont	Mount Mansfield	Chittenden	4,393	Lake Champlain		95
Virginia	Mount Rogers	Grayson-Smyth	5,729	Atlantic Ocean		Sea level
Virgin Islands	Crown Mountain	St. Thomas Island	1,556	Atlantic Ocean		Sea level
Washington	Mount Rainier	Pierce	14,411	Pacific Ocean		Sea level
West Virginia	Spruce Knob	Pendleton	4,863	Potomac R.	Jefferson	240
Wisconsin	Timms Hill	Price	1,951	Lake Michigan		579
Wyoming	Gannett Peak	Fremont	13,804	Belle Fourche R.	Crook	3,099

U.S. Coastline by States

Source: National Oceanic and Atmospheric Administration, U.S. Dept. of Commerce

(in statute miles)

	Coastline[1]	Shoreline[2]		Coastline[1]	Shoreline[2]
ATLANTIC COAST	**2,069**	**28,673**	**GULF COAST**	**1,631**	**17,141**
Connecticut	0	618	Alabama	53	607
Delaware	28	381	Florida	770	5,095
Florida	580	3,331	Louisiana	397	7,721
Georgia	100	2,344	Mississippi	44	359
Maine	228	3,478	Texas	367	3,359
Maryland	31	3,190			
Massachusetts	192	1,519	**PACIFIC COAST**	**7,623**	**40,298**
New Hampshire	13	131	Alaska	5,580	31,383
New Jersey	130	1,792	California	840	3,427
New York	127	1,850	Hawaii	750	1,052
North Carolina	301	3,375	Oregon	296	1,410
Pennsylvania	0	89	Washington	157	3,026
Rhode Island	40	384			
South Carolina	187	2,876	**ARCTIC COAST**	**1,060**	**2,521**
Virginia	112	3,315	**UNITED STATES**	**12,383**	**88,633**

(1) Figures are lengths of general outline of seacoast. Measurements were made with a unit measure of 30 minutes of latitude on charts as near the scale of 1:1,200,000 as possible. Coastline of sounds and bays is included to a point where they narrow to width of unit measure, and includes the distance across at such point. (2) Figures obtained in 1939-40 with a recording instrument on the largest-scale charts and maps then available. Shoreline of outer coast, offshore islands, sounds, bays, rivers, and creeks is included to the head of tidewater or to a point where tidal waters narrow to a width of 100 ft.

States: Capitals, Key Dates, Geographic Data

The 13 colonies that declared independence from Great Britain and fought the War of Independence (American Revolution) became the 13 original states. They were (in the order in which they ratified the Constitution): Delaware, Pennsylvania, New Jersey, Georgia, Connecticut, Massachusetts, Maryland, South Carolina, New Hampshire, Virginia, New York, North Carolina, and Rhode Island.

State	Settled[1]	Capital	Date	Order	Long (approx. mean)	Wide (approx. mean)	Land	Water	Total	Rank in area[2]
AL	1702	Montgomery	Dec. 14, 1819	22	330	190	50,744	1,675	52,419	30
AK	1784	Juneau	Jan. 3, 1959	49	1,480[3]	810	571,951	91,316	663,267	1
AZ	1776	Phoenix	Feb. 14, 1912	48	400	310	113,635	364	113,998	6
AR	1686	Little Rock	June 15, 1836	25	260	240	52,068	1,110	53,179	29
CA	1769	Sacramento	Sept. 9, 1850	31	770	250	155,959	7,736	163,696	3
CO	1858	Denver	Aug. 1, 1876	38	380	280	103,718	376	104,094	8
CT	1634	Hartford	Jan. 9, 1788	5	110	70	4,845	699	5,543	48
DE	1638	Dover	Dec. 7, 1787	1	100	30	1,954	536	2,489	49
DC	NA	NA	NA	NA	NA	NA	61	7	68	51
FL	1565	Tallahassee	Mar. 3, 1845	27	500	160	53,927	11,828	65,755	22
GA	1733	Atlanta	Jan. 2, 1788	4	300	230	57,906	1,519	59,425	24
HI	1820	Honolulu	Aug. 21, 1959	50	NA	NA	6,423	4,508	10,931	43
ID	1842	Boise	July 3, 1890	43	570	300	82,747	823	83,570	14
IL	1720	Springfield	Dec. 3, 1818	21	390	210	55,584	2,331	57,914	25
IN	1733	Indianapolis	Dec. 11, 1816	19	270	140	35,867	551	36,418	38
IA	1788	Des Moines	Dec. 28, 1846	29	310	200	55,869	402	56,272	26
KS	1727	Topeka	Jan. 29, 1861	34	400	210	81,815	462	82,277	15
KY	1774	Frankfort	June 1, 1792	15	380	140	39,728	681	40,409	37
LA	1699	Baton Rouge	Apr. 30, 1812	18	380	130	43,562	8,278	51,840	31
ME	1624	Augusta	Mar. 15, 1820	23	320	190	30,862	4,523	35,385	39
MD	1634	Annapolis	Apr. 28, 1788	7	250	90	9,774	2,633	12,407	42
MA	1620	Boston	Feb. 6, 1788	6	190	50	7,840	2,715	10,555	44
MI	1668	Lansing	Jan. 26, 1837	26	490	240	56,804	39,912	96,716	11
MN	1805	St. Paul	May 11, 1858	32	400	250	79,610	7,329	86,939	12
MS	1699	Jackson	Dec. 10, 1817	20	340	170	46,907	1,523	48,430	32
MO	1735	Jefferson City	Aug. 10, 1821	24	300	240	68,886	818	69,704	21
MT	1809	Helena	Nov. 8, 1889	41	630	280	145,552	1,490	147,042	4
NE	1823	Lincoln	Mar. 1, 1867	37	430	210	76,872	481	77,354	16
NV	1849	Carson City	Oct. 31, 1864	36	490	320	109,826	735	110,561	7
NH	1623	Concord	June 21, 1788	9	190	70	8,968	382	9,350	46
NJ	1660	Trenton	Dec. 18, 1787	3	150	70	7,417	1,304	8,721	47
NM	1610	Santa Fe	Jan. 6, 1912	47	370	343	121,356	234	121,589	5
NY	1614	Albany	July 26, 1788	11	330	283	47,214	7,342	54,556	27
NC	1660	Raleigh	Nov. 21, 1789	12	500	150	48,711	5,108	53,819	28
ND	1812	Bismarck	Nov. 2, 1889	39	340	211	68,976	1,724	70,700	19
OH	1788	Columbus	Mar. 1, 1803	17	220	220	40,948	3,877	44,825	34
OK	1889	Oklahoma City	Nov. 16, 1907	46	400	220	68,667	1,231	69,898	20
OR	1811	Salem	Feb. 14, 1859	33	360	261	95,997	2,384	98,381	9
PA	1682	Harrisburg	Dec. 12, 1787	2	283	160	44,817	1,239	46,055	33
RI	1636	Providence	May 29, 1790	13	40	30	1,045	500	1,545	50
SC	1670	Columbia	May 23, 1788	8	260	200	30,109	911	32,020	40
SD	1859	Pierre	Nov. 2, 1889	40	380	210	75,885	1,232	77,116	17
TN	1769	Nashville	June 1, 1796	16	440	120	41,217	926	42,143	36
TX	1682	Austin	Dec. 29, 1845	28	790	660	261,797	6,784	268,581	2
UT	1847	Salt Lake City	Jan. 4, 1896	45	350	270	82,144	2,755	84,899	13
VT	1724	Montpelier	Mar. 4, 1791	14	160	80	9,250	365	9,614	45
VA	1607	Richmond	June 25, 1788	10	430	200	39,594	3,180	42,774	35
WA	1811	Olympia	Nov. 11, 1889	42	360	240	66,544	4,756	71,300	18
WV	1727	Charleston	June 20, 1863	35	240	130	24,078	152	24,230	41
WI	1766	Madison	May 29, 1848	30	310	260	54,310	11,188	65,498	23
WY	1834	Cheyenne	July 10, 1890	44	360	280	97,100	713	97,814	10

Note: Land and water areas may not add to totals because of rounding. NA = Not applicable. (1) First permanent settlement by Europeans. (2) Rank is based on total area as shown. (3) Aleutian Islands and Alexander Archipelago not included.

The Continental Divide of the U.S.

The Continental Divide of the U.S., also known as the Great Divide, is located at the watershed created by the mountain ranges, or tablelands, of the Rocky Mountains. This watershed separates the waters that drain easterly into the Atlantic Ocean and its marginal seas, such as the Gulf of Mexico, from those waters that drain westerly into the Pacific Ocean. The majority of easterly flowing water in the U.S. drains into the Gulf of Mexico before reaching the Atlantic Ocean. The majority of westerly flowing water, before reaching the Pacific Ocean, drains either through the Columbia River or through the Colorado River, which flows into the Gulf of California before reaching the Pacific Ocean.

The location and route of the Continental Divide across the U.S. can briefly be described as follows:

Beginning at the U.S.-Mexican boundary, near long. 108° 45′ W, the Divide, in a northerly direction, crosses New Mexico along the W edge of the Rio Grande drainage basin, entering Colorado near long. 106° 41′ W.

From there by a very irregular route north across Colorado along the W summits of the Rio Grande and of the Arkansas, the South Platte, and the North Platte river basins, and across Rocky Mountain National Park, entering Wyoming near long. 106° 52′ W.

From there in a northwesterly direction, forming the W rims of the North Platte, the Big Horn, and the Yellowstone river basins, crossing the SW portion of Yellowstone National Park.

From there in a westerly and then a northerly direction forming the common boundary of Idaho and Montana, to a point on said boundary near long. 114° 00′ W.

From there northeasterly and northwesterly through Montana and the Glacier National Park, entering Canada near long. 114° 04′ W.

Chronological List of Territories, With State Admissions to Union

Source: National Archives and Records Service

Name of territory	Date of act creating territory	When act took effect	Admission as state	Years as terr.
Northwest Territory[1]	July 13, 1787	No fixed date	Mar. 1, 1803[2]	16
Territory southwest of Ohio River	May 26, 1790	No fixed date	June 1, 1796[3]	6
Mississippi	Apr. 7, 1798	When president acted	Dec. 10, 1817	19
Indiana	May 7, 1800	July 4, 1800	Dec. 11, 1816	16
Orleans	Mar. 26, 1804	Oct. 1, 1804	Apr. 30, 1812[4]	7
Michigan	Jan. 11, 1805	June 30, 1805	Jan. 26, 1837	31
Louisiana-Missouri[5]	Mar. 3, 1805	July 4, 1805	Aug. 10, 1821	16
Illinois	Feb. 3, 1809	Mar. 1, 1809	Dec. 3, 1818	9
Alabama	Mar. 3, 1817	When MS became a state	Dec. 14, 1819	2
Arkansas	Mar. 2, 1819	July 4, 1819	June 15, 1836	17
Florida	Mar. 30, 1822	No fixed date	Mar. 3, 1845	23
Wisconsin	Apr. 20, 1836	July 3, 1836	May 29, 1848	12
Iowa	June 12, 1838	July 3, 1838	Dec. 28, 1846	8
Oregon	Aug. 14, 1848	Date of act	Feb. 14, 1859	10
Minnesota	Mar. 3, 1849	Date of act	May 11, 1858	9
New Mexico	Sept. 9, 1850	On president's proclamation	Jan. 6, 1912	61
Utah	Sept. 9, 1850	Date of act	Jan. 4, 1896	46
Washington	Mar. 2, 1853	Date of act	Nov. 11, 1889	36
Nebraska	May 30, 1854	Date of act	Mar. 1, 1867	12
Kansas	May 30, 1854	Date of act	Jan. 29, 1861	6
Colorado	Feb. 28, 1861	Date of act	Aug. 1, 1876	15
Nevada	Mar. 2, 1861	Date of act	Oct. 31, 1864	3
Dakota	Mar. 2, 1861	Date of act	Nov. 2, 1889	28
Arizona	Feb. 24, 1863	Date of act	Feb. 14, 1912	49
Idaho	Mar. 3, 1863	Date of act	July 3, 1890	27
Montana	May 26, 1864	Date of act	Nov. 8, 1889	25
Wyoming	July 25, 1868	When officers were qualified	July 10, 1890	22
Alaska[6]	May 17, 1884	No fixed date	Jan. 3, 1959	75
Oklahoma	May 2, 1890	Date of act	Nov. 16, 1907	17
Hawaii	Apr. 30, 1900	June 14, 1900	Aug. 21, 1959	59

(1) Included what is now Ohio, Indiana, Illinois, Michigan, Wisconsin, E Minnesota, admitted. (2) Ohio was the first state of NW territory admitted. (3) Admitted as the state of Tennessee. (4) Admitted as the state of Louisiana. (5) The act creating Missouri (June 4, 1812) became effective Dec. 7, 1812. (6) Although the May 17, 1884, act actually constituted Alaska as a district, it was often referred to as a territory, and administered as such. The Territory of Alaska was formally organized by an act of Aug. 24, 1912.

Geographic Centers, U.S. and Each State

Source: U.S. Geological Survey, Dept. of the Interior

There is no generally accepted definition of geographic center and no uniform method for determining it. Following the U.S. Geological Survey, the geographic center of an area is defined here as the center of gravity of the surface, or that point on which the surface would balance if it were a plane of uniform thickness. All locations in the following list are approximate.

No marked or monumented point has been officially established by any government agency as the geographic center of the 50 states, the conterminous U.S. (48 states), or the North American continent. A group of private citizens erected a monument in Lebanon, KS, marking it as geographic center of the conterminous U.S., and a cairn erected in Rugby, ND, asserts that location as the center of the North American continent.

Geographic centers as reported by the U.S. Geological Survey are indicated below:

United States, including Alaska and Hawaii—W of Castle Rock, Butte County, SD; lat. 44° 58′ N, long. 103° 46′ W
Conterminous U.S. (48 states)—Near Lebanon, Smith Co., Kansas, lat. 39° 50′ N, long. 98° 35′ W
North American continent—6 mi W of Balta, Pierce County, North Dakota; lat. 48° 10′ N, long. 100° 10′ W
Alabama—Chilton, 12 mi SW of Clanton
Alaska—lat. 63° 50′ N, long. 152° W; approx. 60 mi NW of Mt. McKinley
Arizona—Yavapai, 55 mi E-SE of Prescott
Arkansas—Pulaski, 12 mi NW of Little Rock
California—Madera, 38 mi E of Madera
Colorado—Park, 30 mi NW of Pikes Peak
Connecticut—Hartford, at East Berlin
Delaware—Kent, 11 mi S of Dover
District of Columbia—Near 4th and L Sts. NW
Florida—Hernando, 12 mi N-NW of Brooksville
Georgia—Twiggs, 18 mi SE of Macon
Hawaii—lat. 20° 15′ N, long. 156° 20′ W, off Maui
Idaho—Custer, SW of Challis
Illinois—Logan, 28 mi NE of Springfield
Indiana—Boone, 14 mi N-NW of Indianapolis
Iowa—Story, 5 mi NE of Ames
Kansas—Barton, 15 mi NE of Great Bend
Kentucky—Marion, 3 mi N-NW of Lebanon
Louisiana—Avoyelles, 3 mi SE of Marksville
Maine—Piscataquis, 18 mi N of Dover
Maryland—Prince George's, 4.5 mi NW of Davidsonville
Massachusetts—Worcester, N part of city
Michigan—Wexford, 5 mi N-NW of Cadillac
Minnesota—Crow Wing, 10 mi SW of Brainerd
Mississippi—Leake, 9 mi W-NW of Carthage
Missouri—Miller, 20 mi SW of Jefferson City
Montana—Fergus, 11 mi W of Lewistown
Nebraska—Custer, 10 mi NW of Broken Bow
Nevada—Lander, 26 mi SE of Austin
New Hampshire—Belknap, 3 mi E of Ashland
New Jersey—Mercer, 5 mi SE of Trenton
New Mexico—Torrance, 12 mi S-SW of Willard
New York—Madison, 12 mi S of Oneida and 26 mi SW of Utica
North Carolina—Chatham, 10 mi NW of Sanford
North Dakota—Sheridan, 5 mi SW of McClusky
Ohio—Delaware, 25 mi N-NE of Columbus
Oklahoma—Oklahoma, 8 mi N of Oklahoma City
Oregon—Crook, 25 mi S-SE of Prineville
Pennsylvania—Centre, 2.5 mi W of Bellefonte
Rhode Island—Kent, 1 mi S-SW of Crompton
South Carolina—Richland, 13 mi SE of Columbia
South Dakota—Hughes, 8 mi NE of Pierre
Tennessee—Rutherford, 5 mi NE of Murfreesboro
Texas—McCulloch, 15 mi NE of Brady
Utah—Sanpete, 3 mi N of Manti
Vermont—Washington, 3 mi E of Roxbury
Virginia—Buckingham, 5 mi W of Buckingham
Washington—Chelan, 10 mi W-SW of Wenatchee
West Virginia—Braxton, 4 mi E of Sutton
Wisconsin—Wood, 9 mi SE of Marshfield
Wyoming—Fremont, 58 mi E-NE of Lander

International Boundary Lines of the U.S.

The length of the N boundary of the conterminous U.S.—the U.S.-Canadian border, excluding Alaska—is 3,987 mi according to the U.S. Geological Survey, Dept. of the Interior. The length of the Alaskan-Canadian border is 1,538 mi. The U.S.-Mexican border, from the Gulf of Mexico to the Pacific Ocean, is about 1,933 mi (1963 boundary agreement).

Origins of the Names of U.S. States

Source: State officials, Smithsonian Institution, and Topographic Division, U.S. Geological Survey, Dept. of the Interior

Alabama—Indian for tribal town, later a tribe (Alabamas or Alibamons) of the Creek confederacy.

Alaska—Russian version of Aleutian (Eskimo) word, *alakshak*, for "peninsula," "great lands," or "land that is not an island."

Arizona—Spanish version of Pima Indian word for "little spring place," or Aztec *arizuma*, meaning "silver-bearing."

Arkansas—Algonquin name for the Quapaw Indians, meaning "south wind."

California—Bestowed by the Spanish conquistadors (possibly by Cortez). It was the name of an imaginary island, an earthly paradise, in *Las Serges de Esplandian*, a Spanish romance written by Montalvo in 1510. *Baja California* (Lower California, in Mexico) was first visited by Spanish in 1533. The present U.S. state was called *Alta* (Upper) *California*.

Colorado—From Spanish for "red," first applied to Colorado River.

Connecticut—From Mohican and other Algonquin words meaning "long river place."

Delaware—Named for Lord De La Warr, early governor of Virginia; first applied to river, then to Indian tribe (Lenni-Lenape), and the state.

District of Columbia—For Christopher Columbus, 1791.

Florida—Named by Ponce de León *Pascua Florida*, "Flowery Easter," on Easter Sunday, 1513.

Georgia—For King George II of England, by James Oglethorpe, colonial administrator, 1732.

Hawaii—Possibly derived from native word for homeland, *Hawaiki* or *Owhyhee*.

Idaho—Said to be a coined name with an invented meaning: "gem of the mountains"; originally suggested for the Pikes Peak mining territory (Colorado), then applied to the new mining territory of the Pacific Northwest. Another theory suggests *Idaho* may be a Kiowa Apache term for the Comanche.

Illinois—French for *Illini* or "land of *Illini*," Algonquin word meaning "men" or "warriors."

Indiana—Means "land of the Indians."

Iowa—Indian word variously translated as "here I rest" or "beautiful land." Named for the Iowa R., which was named for the Iowa Indians.

Kansas—Sioux word for "south wind people."

Kentucky—Indian word that is variously translated as "dark and bloody ground," "meadowland," and "land of tomorrow."

Louisiana—Part of territory called Louisiana by Sieur de La Salle for French King Louis XIV.

Maine—From Maine, ancient French province. Also: descriptive, referring to the mainland as distinct from the many coastal islands.

Maryland—For Queen Henrietta Maria, wife of Charles I of England.

Massachusetts—From Indian tribe named after "large hill place" identified by Capt. John Smith as being near Milton, MA.

Michigan—From Chippewa words, *mici gama*, meaning "great water," after the lake of the same name.

Minnesota—From Dakota Sioux word meaning "cloudy water" or "sky-tinted water" of the Minnesota River.

Mississippi—Probably Chippewa; *mici zibi*, "great river" or "gathering-in of all the waters." Also: Algonquin word, *messipi*.

Missouri—An Algonquin Indian term meaning "river of the big canoes."

Montana—Latin or Spanish for "mountainous."

Nebraska—From Omaha or Otos Indian word meaning "broad water" or "flat river," describing the Platte River.

Nevada—Spanish, meaning "snow-clad."

New Hampshire—Named, 1629, by Capt. John Mason of Plymouth Council for his home county in England.

New Jersey—The Duke of York, 1664, gave a patent to John Berkeley and Sir George Carteret to be called Nova Caesaria, or New Jersey, after England's Isle of Jersey.

New Mexico—Spaniards in Mexico applied term to land north and west of Rio Grande in the 16th century.

New York—For Duke of York and Albany, who received patent to New Netherland from his brother Charles II and sent an expedition to capture it, 1664.

North Carolina—In 1619 Charles I gave a large patent to Sir Robert Heath to be called Province of Carolana, from *Carolus*, Latin name for Charles. A new patent was granted by Charles II to Earl of Clarendon and others. Divided into North and South Carolina, 1710.

North Dakota—*Dakota* is Sioux for "friend" or "ally."

Ohio—Iroquois word for "fine or good river."

Oklahoma—Choctaw word meaning "red man," proposed by Rev. Allen Wright, Choctaw-speaking Indian.

Oregon—Origin unknown. One theory holds that the name may have been derived from that of the Wisconsin River, shown on a 1715 French map as "Ouaricon-sint."

Pennsylvania—William Penn, the Quaker who was made full proprietor of this area by King Charles II in 1681, suggested "Sylvania," or "woodland," for his tract. The king's government owed Penn's father, Admiral William Penn, 16,000 pounds, and the land was granted as partial settlement. Charles II added the "Penn" to Sylvania, against the desires of the modest proprietor, in honor of the admiral.

Puerto Rico—Spanish for "rich port."

Rhode Island—Exact origin is unknown. One theory notes that Giovanni de Verrazano recorded an island about the size of Rhodes in the Mediterranean in 1524, but others believe the state was named *Roode Eylandt* by Adriaen Block, Dutch explorer, because of its red clay.

South Carolina—See North Carolina.

South Dakota—See North Dakota.

Tennessee—*Tanasi* was the name of Cherokee villages on the Little Tennessee River. From 1784 to 1788 this was the State of Franklin, or Frankland.

Texas—Variant of word used by Caddo and other Indians meaning "friends" or "allies," and applied to them by the Spanish in eastern Texas. Also written *Texias, Tejas, Teysas*.

Utah—From a Navajo word meaning "upper," or "higher up," as applied to a Shoshone tribe called Ute. Spanish form is *Yutta*. The English is *Uta* or *Utah*. Proposed name *Deseret*, "land of honeybees," from Book of Mormon, was rejected by Congress.

Vermont—From French words *vert* (green) and *mont* (mountain). The Green Mountains were said to have been named by Samuel de Champlain. When the state was formed, 1777, Dr. Thomas Young suggested combining *vert* and *mont* into Vermont.

Virginia—Named by Sir Walter Raleigh, who fitted out the expedition of 1584, in honor of Queen Elizabeth, the Virgin Queen of England.

Washington—Named after George Washington. When the bill creating the Territory of Columbia was introduced in the 32nd Congress, the name was changed to Washington because of the existence of the District of Columbia.

West Virginia—So named when western counties of Virginia refused to secede from the U.S. in 1863.

Wisconsin—An Indian name, spelled *Ouisconsin* and *Mesconsing* by early chroniclers. Believed to mean "grassy place" in Chippewa. Congress made it *Wisconsin*.

Wyoming—From the Algonquin words for "large prairie place," "at the big plains," or "on the great plain."

Territorial Sea of the U.S.

According to a Dec. 27, 1988, proclamation by Pres. Ronald Reagan: "The territorial sea of the United States henceforth extends to 12 nautical miles from the baselines of the United States determined in accordance with international law. In accordance with international law, as reflected in the applicable provisions of the 1982 United Nations Convention on the Law of the Sea, within the territorial sea of the United States, the ships of all countries enjoy the right of innocent passage and the ships and aircraft of all countries enjoy the right of transit passage through international straits."

Major Accessions of Territory by the U.S.

Source: U.S. Dept. of the Interior; Bureau of the Census, U.S. Dept. of Commerce

Not including territories such as Panama Canal Zone and the Philippines which are no longer under U.S. jurisdiction; area figures are for total area and may differ from figures for current areas given elsewhere.

	Acquisition date	Area (sq mi)		Acquisition date	Area (sq mi)		Acquisition date	Area (sq mi)
Territory in 1790[1]	NA	888,685	Mexican Cession	1848	529,017	Guam[3]	1899	212
Louisiana Purchase	1803	827,192	Gadsden Purchase	1853	29,640	American Samoa[4]	1900	76
Treaty of Florida	1819	72,003	Alaska	1867	586,412	U.S. Virgin Islands	1917	133
Texas	1845	390,143	Hawaii	1898	6,450	Northern Marianas[5]	1986	179
Oregon Territory	1846	285,680	Puerto Rico[2]	1899	3,435			

NA = Not applicable. (1) Includes that part of a drainage basin of Red River of the North, S of 49th parallel, sometimes considered part of Louisiana Purchase. (2) Ceded by Spain in 1898, ratified in 1899, and became the Commonwealth of Puerto Rico by Act of Congress on July 25, 1952. (3) Acquired in 1898; ratified 1899. (4) Acquired in 1899; ratified 1900. (5) Formerly a part of the U.S. administered Trust Territory of the Pacific Islands; became a U.S. commonwealth, Nov. 3, 1986.

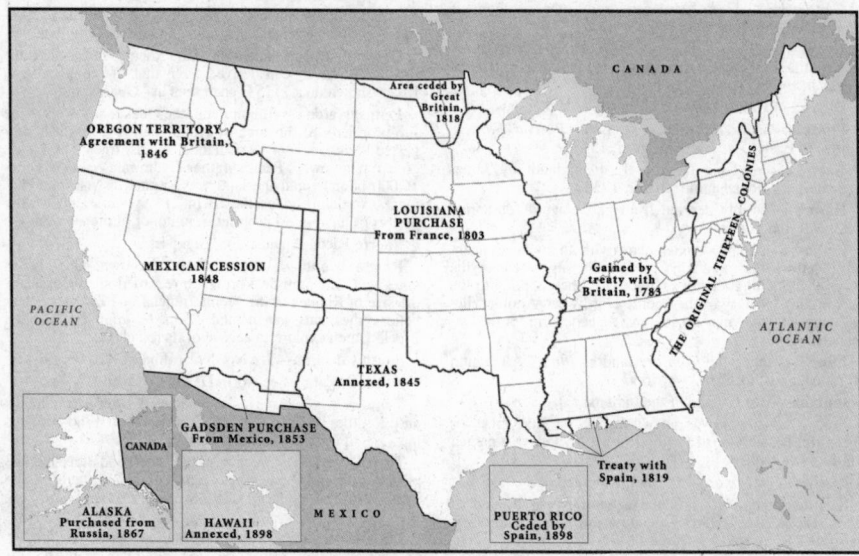

Special Areas Administered by the U.S. Forest Service, 2006

Source: U.S. Forest Service, Dept. of Agriculture

NHL=National Historic Landmark; NS(A)=Nat. Scenic (Area); NM=National Monument; NP=National Preserve; NRA=National Recreation Area; NVM=Nat. Volcanic Monument; SRA=Scenic Recreation Area

Area name	Location	Estab.	Acres[1]	Area name	Location	Estab.	Acres[1]
Admiralty Island NM	AK	1980	974,278	Mount Pleasant NSA	VA	1994	7,580
Allegheny NRA	PA	1984	24,350	Mount Rogers NRA	VA	1966	118,509
Arapaho NRA	CO	1978	32,414	Mount St. Helens NVM	WA	1989	112,605
Beech Creek NS & Botanic Area	OK	1988	6,200	Newberry NVM	OR	1990	54,822
Cascade Head NS Research Area	OR	1974	6,637	North Cascades NSA	WA	1984	87,600
Columbia River Gorge NSA	OR-WA	1986	70,848	Opal Creek SRA	OR	1996	12,645
Coosa Bald NSA	GA	1991	7,100	Oregon Dunes NRA	OR	1972	27,232
Ed Jenkins NRA	GA	1991	23,166	Pine Ridge NRA	NE	1986	6,600
Flaming Gorge NRA	UT-WY	1968	189,825	Rattlesnake NRA	MT	1980	59,119
Giant Sequoia NM	CA	2000	327,769	Santa Rosa and San Jacinto Mts. NM	CA	2000	64,400
Grand Island NRA	MI	1990	12,961	Sawtooth NRA	ID	1972	729,428
Grey Towers NHL	PA	1963	102	Smith River NRA	CA	1990	305,169
Hells Canyon NRA	OR-ID	1975	537,759	Spring Mt. NRA	NV	1993	314,367
Indian Nations NS & Wildlife Area	OK	1988	39,171	Spruce Knob-Seneca Rocks NRA	WV	1965	57,237
Jemez NRA	NM	1993	57,000	Valles Caldera NP	NM	2000	89,716
Land Between the Lakes NRA	KY-TN	1998	170,310	Whiskeytown-Shasta-Trinity NRA	CA	1965	176,367
Misty Fiords NM	AK	1980	2,293,627	White Rocks NRA	VT	1984	36,400
Mono Basin NSA	CA	1984	115,600	Winding Stair Mt. NRA	OK	1988	25,890
Mount Baker NRA	WA	1984	8,473				

(1) Area administered by the Forest Service or federally owned.

20 Most-Visited Sites in the National Park System, 2006
Source: National Park Service, Dept. of the Interior
Attendance at all areas administered by the National Park Service in 2006 totaled 272,623,980 recreation visits.

Site (location)	Recreation visits	Site (location)	Recreation visits
Blue Ridge Parkway (NC-VA)	18,953,478	San Francisco Maritime Natl. Historical Park (CA)	3,984,645
Golden Gate National Recreation Area (CA)	13,486,824	National World War II Memorial (DC)	3,865,430
Great Smoky Mountains National Park (NC-TN)	9,289,215	Lincoln Memorial (DC)	3,810,347
Gateway National Recreation Area (NJ-NY)	8,456,456	National Capital Parks Central (DC)	3,803,244
Lake Mead National Recreation Area (AZ-NV)	7,777,753	Vietnam Veterans Memorial (DC)	3,629,739
George Washington Memorial Pkwy (VA-MD-DC)	6,872,213	Independence National Historical Park (PA)	3,532,245
Natchez Trace Parkway (MS-AL-TN)	5,713,583	Castle Clinton National Monument (NY)	3,415,397
Delaware Water Gap Natl. Recreation Area (NJ-PA)	5,254,216	Colonial National Historical Park (VA)	3,344,018
Cape Cod National Seashore (MA)	4,487,716	Statue of Liberty National Monument (NJ-NY)	3,263,585
Grand Canyon National Park (AZ)	4,279,439	Korean War Veterans Memorial (DC)	3,248,757

National Parks, Other Areas Administered by National Park Service

As of April 30, 2007, the National Park Service administered 84,337,466 acres of federal land across 391 sites. Dates when sites were authorized for initial protection by Congress or by presidential proclamation are given in parentheses. If different, the date the area got its current designation, or was transferred to the National Park Service, follows. Gross area in acres, as of Sept. 30, 2006, follows date(s). Not listed are 28 NPS-affiliated areas, 37 Natl. Heritage Areas, 16 Natl. Hist. Trails, and some units administered by the National Capital Region.

NATIONAL PARKS

Acadia, ME (1916/1929): 47,388. Includes Mount Desert Isl., half of Isle au Haut, Schoodic Peninsula on mainland. Highest elevation on Eastern seaboard.

American Samoa, AS (1988): 9,000. Features a paleotropical rain forest and a coral reef.

Arches, UT (1929/1971): 76,679. Contains giant red sandstone arches and other products of erosion.

Badlands, SD (1929/1978): 242,756. Reformations and native prairie. Animal fossils 23-37 mil years old.

Big Bend, TX (1935): 801,163. Rio Grande, Chisos Mts.

Biscayne, FL (1968/1980): 172,971. Aquatic park encompassing chain of islands south of Miami.

Black Canyon of the Gunnison, CO (1933/1999): 30,750. Has a canyon 2,900 ft deep and 40 ft wide at its narrowest part.

Bryce Canyon, UT (1923/1928): 35,835. Spectacularly colorful and unusual display of erosion effects.

Canyonlands, UT (1964): 337,598. At junction of Colorado and Green rivers; extensive evidence of prehistoric Indians.

Capitol Reef, UT (1937/1971): 241,904. A 70-mi uplift of sandstone cliffs dissected by high-walled gorges.

Carlsbad Caverns, NM (1923/1930): 46,766. Largest known caverns; not yet fully explored.

Channel Islands, CA (1938/1980): 249,561. Sea lion breeding place, nesting sea birds, unique plants.

Congaree, SC (1976/1988): 26,546. Last significant tract of southern bottomland hardwood forest in the U.S.

Crater Lake, OR (1902): 183,224. Extraordinary blue lake in the crater of Mt. Mazama, a volcano that erupted about 7,700 years ago; deepest U.S. lake.

Cuyahoga Valley, OH (1974/2000): 32,864. Rural landscape along Ohio and Erie Canal system between Akron and Cleveland.

Death Valley, CA-NV (1933/1994): 3,372,402. Large desert area. Includes the lowest point in the Western Hemisphere; also includes Scotty's Castle.

Denali, AK (1917/1980): 4,740,912. Name changed from Mt. McKinley National Park. Contains highest mountain in U.S.; wildlife.

Dry Tortugas, FL (1935/1992): 64,701. Ft. Jefferson and seven coral reef and sand islands near Key West.

Everglades, FL (1934): 1,508,540. Largest remaining subtropical wilderness in continental U.S.

Gates of the Arctic, AK (1978/1984): 7,523,898. Vast wilderness in north central region. Limited federal facilities.

Glacier, MT (1910): 1,013,322. Superb Rocky Mt. scenery, numerous glaciers and glacial lakes. Part of Waterton-Glacier Intl. Peace Park established by U.S. and Canada in 1932.

Glacier Bay, AK (1925/1986): 3,224,840. Great tidewater glaciers that move down mountainsides and break up into the sea; much wildlife.

Grand Canyon, AZ (1893/1919): 1,217,403. Most spectacular part of Colorado River's greatest canyon.

Grand Teton, WY (1929): 309,995. Most impressive part of the Teton Mts., winter feeding ground of largest American elk herd.

Great Basin, NV (1922/1986): 77,180. Includes Wheeler Pk., Lexington Arch, and Lehman Caves.

Great Sand Dunes, CO (1932/2000): 44,246. North America's tallest dunes.

Great Smoky Mountains, NC-TN (1926/1934): 522,052. Largest Eastern U.S. mountain range, magnificent forests.

Guadalupe Mountains, TX (1966): 86,416. Extensive Permian limestone fossil reef; tremendous earth fault.

Haleakala, HI (1916/1960): 29,111. Dormant volcano on Maui with large colorful craters.

Hawaii Volcanoes, HI (1916/1961): 323,431. Contains Kilauea and Mauna Loa, active volcanoes.

Hot Springs, AR (1832/1921): 5,550. Bathhouses are furnished with thermal waters from the park's 47 hot springs; these waters are used for bathing and drinking.

Isle Royale, MI (1931): 571,790. Largest island in Lake Superior, noted for its wilderness area and wildlife.

Joshua Tree, CA (1936/1994): 789,866. Desert region includes Joshua trees, other plant and animal life.

Katmai, AK (1918/1980): 3,674,540. "Valley of Ten Thousand Smokes," scene of 1912 volcanic eruption.

Kenai Fjords, AK (1978/1980): 669,983. Abundant marine mammals, birdlife; the Harding Icefield, one of the 4 major icecaps in U.S.

Kings Canyon, CA (1890/1940): 461,901. Mountain wilderness, dominated by Kings River Canyons and High Sierra; contains giant sequoias.

Kobuk Valley, AK (1978/1980): 1,750,717. Contains geological and recreational sites. Limited federal facilities.

Lake Clark, AK (1978/1980): 2,619,733. Across Cook Inlet from Anchorage. A scenic wilderness rich in fish and wildlife. Limited federal facilities.

Lassen Volcanic, CA (1907/1916): 106,372. Contains Lassen Peak, recently active volcano, and other volcanic phenomena.

Mammoth Cave, KY (1926/1941): 52,830. 365 mi of explored underground passages, beautiful natural formations, river 300 ft below surface.

Mesa Verde, CO (1906): 52,122. Most notable and best preserved prehistoric cliff dwellings in the U.S.

Mount Rainier, WA (1899): 236,381. Greatest single-peak glacial system in the U.S.

North Cascades, WA (1968): 504,781. Spectacular mountainous region with many glaciers, lakes.

Olympic, WA (1909/1938): 922,651. Mountain wilderness containing finest remnant of Pacific Northwest rainforest, active glaciers, Pacific shoreline, rare elk.

Petrified Forest, AZ (1906/1962): 221,621. Extensive petrified wood and Indian artifacts. Contains part of Painted Desert.

Redwood, CA (1968): 112,512. 40 mi of Pacific coastline, groves of ancient redwoods and world's tallest trees.

Rocky Mountain, CO (1915): 265,828. On the Continental Divide; includes peaks over 14,000 ft.

Saguaro, AZ (1933/1994): 91,440. Part of the Sonoran Desert; includes the giant saguaro cacti, unique to the region.

Sequoia, CA (1890): 404,051. Groves of giant sequoias, highest mountain in conterminous U.S.: Mt. Whitney (14,494 ft). World's largest tree.

Shenandoah, VA (1926): 199,073. Portion of the Blue Ridge Mts.; overlooks Shenandoah Valley; Skyline Drive.

Theodore Roosevelt, ND (1947/1978): 70,447. Contains part of T.R.'s ranch and scenic badlands.

Virgin Islands, VI (1956): 14,686. Authorized to cover 75% of St. John Isl. and Hassel Isl.; lush growth, lovely beaches, Carib Indian petroglyphs, evidence of colonial Danes.

Voyageurs, MN (1971): 218,200. Abundant lakes, forests, wildlife, canoeing, boating.

Wind Cave, SD (1903): 28,295. Limestone caverns in Black Hills. Extensive wildlife includes a herd of bison.

Wrangell-St. Elias, AK (1978/1980): 8,323,148. Largest area in park system, most peaks over 16,000 ft, abundant wildlife; day's drive east of Anchorage. No federal facilities.

Yellowstone, ID-MT-WY (1872): 2,219,791. World's first national park. World's greatest geyser area has about 10,000 geysers and hot springs; spectacular falls and impressive canyons of the Yellowstone River; grizzly bear, moose, and bison.

Yosemite, CA (1890): 761,266. Yosemite Valley, the nation's highest waterfall, grove of sequoias, and mountains.

Zion, UT (1909/1919): 146,598. Unusual shapes and landscapes resulting from erosion and faulting; evidence of past volcanic activity; contains "The Great White Throne," 2,394-ft. monolith.

NATIONAL HISTORICAL PARKS

Adams, MA (1946/1998): 24. Home of Pres. John Adams, John Quincy Adams, and celebrated descendants.

Appomattox Court House, VA (1930/1954): 1,774. Where Lee surrendered to Grant.

Boston, MA (1974): 43. Includes Faneuil Hall, Old North Church, Bunker Hill, Paul Revere House.

Cane River Creole (and heritage area), LA (1994): 207. Preserves the Creole culture as it developed along the Cane R.

Cedar Creek & Belle Grove, VA (2002): 3,590. Civil War battle site and an antebellum plantation in the Shenandoah Valley.

Chaco Culture, NM (1907/1980): 33,960. Ruins of pueblos built by prehistoric Indians including the Pueblo, Hopi and Navajo.

Chesapeake and Ohio Canal, MD-DC-WV (1938/1971): 19,611. 184-mi historic canal; DC to Cumberland, MD.

Colonial, VA (1930/1936): 8,677. Includes most of Jamestown Isl., site of first successful English colony; Yorktown, site of Cornwallis's surrender to George Washington; and Colonial Parkway.

Cumberland Gap, KY-TN-VA (1940): 20,516. Mountain pass of the Wilderness Road, which carried the first great migration of pioneers into America's interior.

Dayton Aviation Heritage, OH (1992): 86. Commemorates the area's aviation heritage.

George Rogers Clark, IN (1966): 26. Commemorates American defeat of British in West during Revolution.

Harpers Ferry, MD-VA-WV (1944/1963): 3,646. At the confluence of the Shenandoah and Potomac rivers, the site of John Brown's 1859 raid on the Army arsenal.

Hopewell Culture, OH (1923/1992): 1,170. Remains of ceremonial mounds built in the Ohio River Valley, 200 BC–500 AD.

Independence, PA (1948): 44. Contains several properties associated with the American Revolution and the founding of the U.S. Includes Independence Hall and the Liberty Bell Center.

Jean Lafitte (and preserve), LA (1907/1978): 20,005. Includes Chalmette, site of 1815 Battle of New Orleans; French Quarter.

Kalaupapa, HI (1980): 10,779. Molokai's former leper colony.

Kaloko-Honokohau, HI (1978): 1,161. Preserves the native culture of Hawaii.

Keweenaw, MI (1992): 1,869. Site of first significant copper mine in U.S.

Klondike Gold Rush, AK-WA (1976): 13,192. Preserves Chilkoot Trail used in 1898 Gold Rush. Museum in Seattle.

Lewis & Clark, OR-WA (1958/2004): 1,574. Lewis and Clark encampment, 1805-06. Incorporates former Fort Clatsop Natl. Mem. Park and OR-WA state parks.

Lowell, MA (1978): 141. Textile mills, canal, 19th-cent. structures; park shows planned city of Industrial Revolution.

Lyndon B. Johnson, TX (1969/1980): 1,570. President's birthplace, boyhood home, ranch.

Marsh-Billings-Rockefeller, VT (1992): 643. Boyhood home of conservationist George Perkins Marsh.

Minute Man, MA (1959): 961. Where the Minute Men battled the British, Apr. 19, 1775. Also contains Hawthorne's home.

Morristown, NJ (1933): 1,711. Sites of important military encampments during the American Revolution; Washington's headquarters, 1779-80.

Natchez, MS (1988): 105. Mansions, townhouses, and villas related to history of Natchez.

New Bedford Whaling, MA (1996): 34. Preserves structures and relics associated with the city's 19th-cent. whaling industry.

New Orleans Jazz, LA (1994): 5. Preserves, educates, and interprets jazz as it has evolved in New Orleans.

Nez Perce, ID-MT-OR-WA (1965): 3,208. Illustrates the history and culture of the Nez Perce Indian country (38 separate sites).

Pecos, NM (1965/1990): 6,669. Ruins of ancient Pueblo of Pecos, archaeological sites, and 2 associated Spanish colonial missions from the 17th and 18th centuries.

Pu'uhonua o Honaunau, HI (1955/1978): 420. Until 1819, a sanctuary for Hawaiians vanquished in battle and for those guilty of crimes or breaking taboos.

Rosie the Riveter/WWII Home Front, CA (2000): 145. Site of a shipyard that employed thousands of women in WWII; commemorates women who worked in war-time industries.

Salt River Bay (and ecological preserve), St. Croix, VI (1992): 978. The only known site where, in 1493, members of a Columbus party landed on what is now territory of the U.S.

San Antonio Missions, TX (1978): 826. Four of finest Spanish missions in U.S., 18th-cent. irrigation system.

San Francisco Maritime, CA (1988): 50. Artifacts, photographs, and historic vessels related to the development of the Pacific Coast.

San Juan Island, WA (1966): 1,752. Commemorates peaceful relations between the U.S., Canada, and Great Britain since the 1872 boundary disputes.

Saratoga, NY (1938): 3,394. Scene of a major 1777 battle that became a turning point in the American Revolution.

Sitka, AK (1910/1972): 112. Scene of last major resistance of the Tlingit Indians to the Russians, 1804.

Tumacacori, AZ (1908/1990): 360. Historic Spanish mission building stands near site first visited by Father Kino in 1691.

Valley Forge, PA (1976): 3,466. Continental Army campsite in 1777-78 winter.

War in the Pacific, GU (1978): 2,037. Seven distinct units illustrating the Pacific theater of WWII. Limited federal facilities.

Women's Rights, NY (1980): 7. Seneca Falls site where Lucretia Mott, Elizabeth Cady Stanton organized movement in 1848.

NATIONAL BATTLEFIELDS/PARKS/SITES

Antietam, MD (1890/1978): 3,228. Battle here ended first Confederate invasion of North, Sept. 17, 1862.

Big Hole, MT (1910/1963): 1,011. Site of major battle with Nez Perce Indians, Aug. 9-10, 1877.

Brices Cross Roads Site, MS (1929): 1. Civil War battlefield.

Cowpens, SC (1929/1972): 842. American Revolution battlefield, Jan. 17, 1781.

Fort Donelson, TN-KY (1928/1985): 1,006. Site of first major Union victory, Feb. 14-16, 1862.

Fort Necessity, PA (1931/1961): 903. Site of first battle of French and Indian War, July 3, 1754.

Kennesaw Mountain Park, GA (1917/1935): 2,888. Site of major battle of Atlanta campaign in Civil War.

Manassas Park, VA (1940): 5,073. Scene of two battles in Civil War, 1861 and 1862.

Monocacy, MD (1934/1976): 1,647. Civil War battle in defense of Washington, DC, fought here, July 9, 1864.

Moores Creek, NC (1926/1980): 88. Feb. 27, 1776 battle between Patriots and Loyalists commemorated here.

Petersburg, VA (1926/1962): 2,740. Scene of 10-month Union campaigns, 1864-65.

Richmond Park, VA (1936): 7,127. Site of battles defending Confederate capital.

Stones River, TN (1927/1960): 709. Scene of battle that began federal offensive to trisect the Confederacy, Dec. 31, 1862-Jan. 2, 1863.

Tupelo, MS (1929/1961): 1. Site of crucial battle over Sherman's supply line, July 14-15, 1865.

Wilson's Creek, MO (1960/1970): 2,369. Scene of Civil War battle for control of Missouri, Aug. 10, 1861.

NATIONAL MILITARY PARKS

Chickamauga and Chattanooga, GA-TN (1890): 9,036. Site where Gen. Sherman and Union armies gained control of TN, 1863.

Fredericksburg and Spotsylvania County, VA (1927/1933): 8,382. Sites of several major Civil War battles and campaigns.

Gettysburg, PA (1895/1933): 5,990. Site of decisive Confederate defeat in North, July 1863, and of Gettysburg Address.

Guilford Courthouse, NC (1917/1933): 230. American Revolution battle site.

Horseshoe Bend, AL (1956): 2,040. On Tallapoosa River, where Gen. Andrew Jackson's forces broke the power of the Upper Creek Indian Confederacy on March 27, 1814.

Kings Mountain, SC (1931/1933): 3,945. Site of American Revolution battle, fought on Oct. 7, 1780.

Pea Ridge, AR (1956): 4,300. Scene of Civil War battle, fought Mar. 7-8, 1862.

Shiloh, TN (1894/1933): 5,065. Major Civil War battlesite; includes some well-preserved Indian burial mounds.

Vicksburg, MS (1899/1933): 1,795. Union victory gave North control of the Mississippi and split the Confederate forces.

NATIONAL MEMORIALS

Arkansas Post, AR (1960): 758. First permanent French settlement in the lower Mississippi River valley.

Arlington House, The Robert E. Lee Memorial, VA (1925/1972): 28. Lee's home overlooking the Potomac.

Chamizal, El Paso, TX (1966/1974): 55. Commemorates 1963 settlement of 99-year dispute with Mexico.

Coronado, AZ (1941/1952): 4,750. Commemorates first European exploration of the Southwest.

De Soto, FL (1948): 27. Commemorates 16th-cent. Spanish explorations.

Federal Hall, NY (1939/1955): 0.45. First seat of U.S. government under the Constitution.

Flight 93, Shanksville, PA (2002): 2,262. Commemorates the passengers and crew of Flight 93, who died thwarting an attack on Sept. 11, 2001. In planning stages; no federal facilities.

Fort Caroline, FL (1950): 138. On St. Johns River, overlooks site of a French Huguenot colony.

Franklin Delano Roosevelt, DC (1982): 8. Statues of Pres. Roosevelt and Eleanor Roosevelt; waterfalls and gardens.

General Grant, NY (1958): 0.76. Tomb of Ulysses Grant and wife.

Hamilton Grange, NY (1962): 1. Home of Alexander Hamilton.

Jefferson National Expansion, MO (1935): 91. Commemorates westward expansion.

Johnstown Flood, PA (1964): 178. Commemorates tragic flood of 1889.

Korean War Veterans, DC (1986): 2. Dedicated in 1995; honors those who served in the Korean War.

Lincoln Boyhood, IN (1962): 200. Site of Lincoln cabin, Lincoln's boyhood home, and gravesite of Lincoln's mother.

Lincoln Memorial, DC (1911/1933): 107. Marble statue of the 16th U.S. president.

Lyndon Baines Johnson Memorial Grove on the Potomac, DC (1973): 17. Overlooks the Potomac R.; vista of the Capitol.

Mount Rushmore, SD (1925): 1,278. World-famous sculpture of 4 presidents: Washington, Jefferson, Lincoln, T. Roosevelt.

Perry's Victory and International Peace Memorial, Put-in-Bay, OH (1936/1972): 25. The world's most massive Doric column, constructed 1912-15, promotes pursuit of peace through arbitration and disarmament.

Roger Williams, Providence, RI (1965): 5. Memorial to founder of Rhode Island.

Thaddeus Kosciuszko, PA (1972): 0.02. Memorial to Polish hero of American Revolution.

Theodore Roosevelt Island, DC (1932/1933): 89. Statue of Roosevelt in wooded island sanctuary.

Thomas Jefferson, DC (1934): 18. Statue of Jefferson in an inscribed circular, colonnaded structure.

USS Arizona, HI (1980): 11. Memorializes American losses at Pearl Harbor.

Vietnam Veterans, DC (1980): 2. Black granite wall inscribed with names of those missing or killed in action in Vietnam War.

Washington Monument, DC (1848/1933): 106. Obelisk honoring the first U.S. president.

World War II, DC (1994/2004): 7. Oval plaza with central pool commemorating those who fought and died.

Wright Brothers, NC (1927/1953): 428. Site of first powered flight.

NATIONAL HISTORIC SITES

Abraham Lincoln Birthplace, Hodgenville, KY (1916/1959): 345. Memorial building, sinking spring.

Allegheny Portage Railroad, PA (1964): 1,284. Linked the Pennsylvania Canal system and the West.

Andersonville, GA (1970): 515. Noted Civil War prisoner-of-war camp.

Andrew Johnson, Greeneville, TN (1935/1963): 17. Two homes and the tailor shop of the 17th U.S. president.

Bent's Old Fort, CO (1960): 799. Replica of S. Plains outpost.

Boston African-American, MA (1980): 0.35. Pre-Civil War black-owned structures.

Brown v. Board of Education, KS (1992): 2. Commemorates the landmark 1954 U.S. Supreme Court decision, which ended legal segregation in schools.

Carl Sandburg Home, Flat Rock, NC (1968): 264.

Charles Pinckney, SC (1988): 28. Statesman's farm. Pinckney was a principal author and signer of the Constitution.

Christiansted, St. Croix, VI (1952/1961): 27. Commemorates Danish colony.

Clara Barton, MD (1974): 9. Home of founder of American Red Cross.

Edgar Allan Poe, Philadelphia, PA (1978/1980): 0.52. Writer's home, where he wrote short stories.

Edison, West Orange, NJ (1955/1962): 21. Inventor's home and laboratory.

Eisenhower, Gettysburg, PA (1967): 690. Home of 34th president.

Eleanor Roosevelt, Hyde Park, NY (1977): 181. The former first lady's personal retreat.

Eugene O'Neill, Danville, CA (1976): 13. Playwright's home where he wrote his final plays, including *The Iceman Cometh.*

First Ladies, Canton, OH (2000): 0.33. Home of first lady Ida Sexton McKinley. Library now devoted to America's first ladies.

Ford's Theatre, DC (1866/1970): 0.29. Includes theater, now restored, where Lincoln was assassinated, house where he died, and Lincoln Museum.

Fort Bowie, AZ (1964): 1,000. Focal point of operations against Geronimo and the Apaches.

Fort Davis, TX (1961): 474. Frontier outpost in West Texas. Established to guard the San Antonio-El Paso Road.

Fort Laramie, WY (1938/1960): 833. Military post on Oregon Trail.

Fort Larned, KS (1964/1966): 718. Military post on Santa Fe Trail.

Fort Point, San Francisco, CA (1970): 29. West Coast fortification. Protected San Francisco during and after Civil War.

Fort Raleigh, NC (1941): 513. First attempted English settlement in North America.

Fort Scott, KS (1965/1978): 17. Commemorates U.S. frontier of 1840s and '50s. Was a major focal point of black troop activity and training during Civil War.

Fort Smith, AR-OK (1961): 75. One of the earliest U.S. posts in Missouri Territory, active 1817-90.

Fort Union Trading Post, MT-ND (1966): 444. Principal fur-trading post on upper Missouri, 1829-67.

Fort Vancouver, WA-OR (1948/1961): 194. Headquarters for Hudson's Bay Company in 1825. Early political seat.

Frederick Douglass, DC (1962/1988): 9. Home of famous black abolitionist, writer, and orator.

Frederick Law Olmsted, MA (1979): 7. Home of city planner., famous for designing Central Park in NYC.

Friendship Hill, PA (1978): 675. Home of Albert Gallatin, Jefferson's and Madison's secretary of treasury.

Golden Spike, UT (1957): 2,735. Commemorates completion of first transcontinental railroad in 1869.

Grant-Kohrs Ranch, MT (1972): 1,618. Ranch house owned by John Grant, a 19th-cent. range-cattle industry pioneer.

Hampton, MD (1948): 62. 18th-cent. Georgian mansion, which in 1790 was the largest house in the U.S.

Harry S. Truman, MO (1983): 7. Home of pres. after 1919.

Herbert Hoover, West Branch, IA (1965): 187. Birthplace and boyhood home of 31st president.

Home of Franklin D. Roosevelt, Hyde Park, NY (1944): 456. FDR's birthplace, home, and "summer White House."

Hopewell Furnace, PA (1938/1985): 848. 19th-cent. iron-making village.

Hubbell Trading Post, AZ (1965): 160. Trading post that allowed interaction between the Navajo and white traders in the late 19th and 20th century. Still active today.

James A. Garfield, Mentor, OH (1980): 8. Home of 20th president. Site of his front-porch campaign.

Jimmy Carter, GA (1987): 72. Birthplace and home of 39th president.

John Fitzgerald Kennedy, Brookline, MA (1967): 0.09. Birthplace and childhood home of 35th president.

John Muir, Martinez, CA (1964): 345. Home of Sierra Club founder and "Father of the National Park Service."

Knife River Indian Villages, ND (1974): 1,758. Remnants of villages last occupied by Hidatsa and Mandan Indians.

Lincoln Home, Springfield, IL (1971): 12. Lincoln's residence at the time he was elected 16th president, 1860.

Little Rock Central High School, AR (1998): 27. Commemorates 1957 desegregation during which federal troops had to be called in to protect 9 black students.

Longfellow, Cambridge, MA (1972): 2. Poet's home, 1837-82; Washington's headquarters during Boston siege, 1775-76.

Maggie L. Walker, VA (1978): 1. Richmond home of black leader and first female bank president, daughter of an ex-slave.

Manzanar, Lone Pine, CA (1992): 814. Commemorates Manzanar War Relocation Ctr., a Japanese-American internment camp during WWII.

Martin Luther King, Jr., Atlanta, GA (1980): 39. Birthplace, grave, church of the civil rights leader.

Martin Van Buren, NY (1974): 40. Lindenwald, home of 8th president, near Kinderhook.

Mary McLeod Bethune Council House, DC (1982/1991): 0.07. Commemorates Bethune's leadership in the black women's movement.

Minuteman Missile, SD (1999): 15. Missile launch facilities dating back to the Cold War era.

Nicodemus, KS (1996): 161. Only remaining western town established by African Americans during Reconstruction.

Ninety Six, SC (1976): 1,022. Colonial trading village and the site of Gen. Nathaniel Greene's siege in 1781.

Palo Alto Battlefield, TX (1978): 3,407. Scene of first battle of the Mexican War.

Pennsylvania Avenue, DC (1965): 0.26 Includes area between Capitol and White House, encompassing the U.S. Navy Memorial, Freedom Plaza, the Old Post Office Pavilion, and other sites.

Puukohola Heiau, HI (1972): 86. Ruins of temple built by King Kamehameha, first king of united Hawaiian islands.

Sagamore Hill, Oyster Bay, NY (1962): 83. Home of Pres. Theodore Roosevelt from 1885 until his death in 1919.

Saint-Gaudens, Cornish, NH (1964): 148. Home, studio, and gardens of American sculptor Augustus Saint-Gaudens.

Saint Paul's Church, New York, NY (1943): 6. Site associated with John Peter Zenger's "freedom of press" trial.

Salem Maritime, MA (1938): Major fishing and whaling port famous for 1692 witchcraft trials.

San Juan, PR (1949): 75. 16th-cent. Span. fortifications.

Sand Creek Massacre, Sand Creek, CO (2000): 12,583. Site where more than 160 Cheyenne and Arapaho Indians were killed by U.S. soldiers in 1864.

Saugus Iron Works, MA (1974): 9. Reconstructed 17th-cent. colonial ironworks.

Springfield Armory, MA (1974): 55. Small-arms manufacturing center for nearly 200 years.

Steamtown, PA (1986): 62. Railyard, roadhouse, repair shops of former Delaware, Lackawanna & Western Railroad.

Theodore Roosevelt Birthplace, New York, NY (1962): 0.11. Reconstructed brownstone where the president was born.

Theodore Roosevelt Inaugural, Buffalo, NY (1966): 1. Wilcox House where he took oath of office, 1901.

Thomas Stone, MD (1978): 328. Home of signer of Declaration of Independence.

Tuskegee Airmen, AL (1998): 90. Airfield where pilots of all-black air corps unit of WWII received flight training.

Tuskegee Institute, AL (1974): 58. College founded by Booker T. Washington in 1881 for blacks.

Ulysses S. Grant, St. Louis Co., MO (1989): 10. Home of Grant during pre-Civil War years.

Vanderbilt Mansion, Hyde Park, NY (1940): 212. Mansion of 19th-cent. financier.

Washita Battlefield, OK (1996): 315. Scene of Nov. 27, 1868, battle between Plains tribes and the U.S. army.

Weir Farm, Wilton, CT (1990): 74. Home and studio of American impressionist painter J. Alden Weir.

Whitman Mission, WA (1936/1963): 139. Site of Protestant Missionaries to the Cayuse Indians during the Mid 19th-cent.

William Howard Taft, Cincinnati, OH (1969): 3. Birthplace and early home of the 27th president.

NATIONAL MONUMENTS

Name	State	Year[1]	Acreage
African Burial Ground[4]	NY	2006	0.35
Agate Fossil Beds	NE	1965	3,058
Alibates Flint Quarries	TX	1965	1,371
Aniakchak[2]	AK	1978	137,176
Aztec Ruins	NM	1923	318
Bandelier	NM	1916	33,677
Booker T. Washington	VA	1956	239
Buck Island Reef	VI	1961	19,016
Cabrillo	CA	1913	160
Canyon de Chelly	AZ	1931	83,840
Cape Krusenstern[3]	AK	1978	649,085
Capulin Volcano	NM	1916	793
Casa Grande Ruins	AZ	1889	473
Castillo de San Marcos	FL	1924	18
Castle Clinton	NY	1946	1
Cedar Breaks	UT	1933	6,155
Chiricahua	AZ	1924	11,985
Colorado	CO	1911	20,534
Craters of the Moon	ID	1924	53,571
Devils Postpile	CA	1911	798
Devils Tower	WY	1906	1,347
Dinosaur	CO-UT	1915	210,278
Effigy Mounds	IA	1949	2,526
El Malpais	NM	1987	114,277
El Morro	NM	1906	1,279
Florissant Fossil Beds	CO	1969	5,998
Fort Frederica	GA	1936	241
Fort Matanzas	FL	1924	300
Fort McHenry (and Historic Shrine)	MD	1925	43
Fort Pulaski	GA	1924	5,623
Fort Stanwix	NY	1935	16
Fort Sumter	SC	1948	200
Fort Union	NM	1954	721
Fossil Butte	WY	1972	8,198
George Washington Birthplace	VA	1930	662
George Washington Carver	MO	1943	210
Gila Cliff Dwellings	NM	1907	533
Governors Island	NY	2001	23
Grand Portage	MN	1951	710
Hagerman Fossil Beds	ID	1988	4,351
Hohokam Pima[4]	AZ	1972	1,690
Homestead NM of America	NE	1936	211
Hovenweep	CO-UT	1923	785
Jewel Cave	SD	1908	1,274
John Day Fossil Beds	OR	1974	13,944
Lava Beds	CA	1925	46,560
Little Bighorn Battlefield	MT	1879	765
Minidoka Internment[2]	ID	2001	73
Montezuma Castle	AZ	1906	858
Muir Woods	CA	1908	554
Natural Bridges	UT	1908	7,636
Navajo	AZ	1909	360
Ocmulgee	GA	1934	702
Oregon Caves	OR	1909	488
Organ Pipe Cactus	AZ	1937	330,689
Papahanaumokuakea Marine	HI	2006	88,190,080
Petroglyph	NM	1990	7,232
Pinnacles	CA	1908	26,481
Pipe Spring	AZ	1923	40
Pipestone	MN	1937	282
Poverty Point[2]	LA	1988	911
Rainbow Bridge[3]	UT	1910	160
Russell Cave	AL	1961	310
Salinas Pueblo Missions	NM	1909	1,071
Scotts Bluff	NE	1919	3,005
Statue of Liberty	NJ-NY	1924	61
Sunset Crater Volcano	AZ	1930	3,040
Timpanogos Cave	UT	1922	250
Tonto	AZ	1907	1,120
Tuzigoot	AZ	1939	812
Virgin Islands Coral Reef	VI	2001	13,893
Walnut Canyon	AZ	1915	3,580
White Sands	NM	1933	143,733
Wupatki	AZ	1924	35,422
Yucca House[2]	CO	1919	34
Little River Canyon[3]	AL	1992	13,633
Mojave	CA	1994	1,531,480
Noatak	AK	1978	6,569,904
Tallgrass Prairie	KS	1996	10,894
Timucuan Ecological & Historic	FL	1988	46,295
Wrangell-St. Elias	AK	1978	4,852,753
Yukon-Charley Rivers[3]	AK	1978	2,526,512

NATIONAL PRESERVES

Name	State	Year[1]	Acreage
Aniakchak	AK	1978	464,118
Bering Land Bridge	AK	1978	2,697,393
Big Cypress	FL	1974	720,561
Big Thicket	TX	1974	97,805
Craters of the Moon	ID	2002	410,733
Denali	AK	1917	1,334,118
Gates of the Arctic	AK	1978	948,608
Glacier Bay	AK	1925	58,406
Great Sand Dunes	CO	2000	41,686
Katmai	AK	1918	418,699
Lake Clark	AK	1978	1,410,292

NATIONAL SEASHORES

Name	State	Year[1]	Acreage
Assateague Island	MD-VA	1965	39,727
Canaveral	FL	1975	57,662
Cape Cod	MA	1961	43,609
Cape Hatteras	NC	1937	30,351
Cape Lookout	NC	1966	28,243
Cumberland Island	GA	1972	36,347
Fire Island	NY	1964	19,579
Gulf Islands	FL-MS	1971	137,991
Padre Island	TX	1962	130,434
Point Reyes	CA	1962	71,070

NATIONAL PARKWAYS

Name	State	Year[1]	Acreage
Blue Ridge	NC-VA	1933	93,792
George Washington Memorial	VA-MD-DC	1930	7,007
John D. Rockefeller Jr. Mem.	WY	1972	23,777
Natchez Trace	MS-AL-TN	1938	52,299

NATIONAL LAKESHORES

Name	State	Year[1]	Acreage
Apostle Islands	WI	1970	69,372
Indiana Dunes	IN	1966	15,091
Pictured Rocks	MI	1966	73,236
Sleeping Bear Dunes	MI	1970	71,291

NATIONAL RESERVES

Name	State	Year[1]	Acreage
City of Rocks	ID	1988	14,107
Ebey's Landing Historical	WA	1978	19,324

NATIONAL RIVERS

Name	State	Year[1]	Acreage
Big South Fork (& Recreation Area)	KY-TN	1976	125,310
Buffalo	AR	1972	94,293
Mississippi (& Recreation Area)	MN	1988	53,775
New River Gorge	WV	1978	72,189
Ozark Riverways	MO	1964	80,785

NATIONAL WILD AND SCENIC RIVERS

Name	State	Year[1]	Acreage
Alagnak Wild	AK	1980	30,666
Bluestone Scenic[2]	WV	1978	4,310
Delaware Scenic	NY-NJ-PA	1978	1,973
Great Egg Harbor Wild & Scenic	NJ	1992	43,311
Missouri Recreational	NE-SD	1991	34,159
Niobrara Scenic	NE	1991	23,074
Obed Wild & Scenic	TN	1976	5,073
Rio Grande Wild & Scenic[3]	TX	1978	9,600
Saint Croix Scenic	MN-WI	1968	67,469
Upper Delaware Scenic & Recreational	NY-PA	1978	75,000

NATIONAL RECREATION AREAS

Name	State	Year[1]	Acreage
Amistad	TX	1965	58,500
Bighorn Canyon	MT-WY	1966	120,296
Boston Harbor Islands	MA	1996	1,482
Chattahoochee R.	GA	1978	9,357
Chickasaw	OK	1902	9,899
Curecanti	CO	1965	41,972
Delaware Water Gap	NJ-PA	1965	68,712
Gateway	NJ-NY	1972	26,607
Gauley R.[3]	WV	1988	11,507
Glen Canyon	AZ-UT	1958	1,254,117
Golden Gate	CA	1972	79,285
Lake Chelan	WA	1968	61,947
Lake Mead	AZ-NV	1936	1,495,664
Lake Meredith	TX	1965	44,978
Lake Roosevelt[5]	WA	1946	100,390
Ross Lake	WA	1968	117,575
Santa Monica Mts.[3]	CA	1978	154,109
Whiskeytown-Shasta-Trinity	CA	1965	42,503

OTHER DESIGNATIONS

Name	State	Year[1]	Acreage
Catoctin Mountain	MD	1954	5,810
Constitution Gardens	DC	1974	52
Fort Washington	MD	1930	341
Greenbelt	MD	1950	1,175
National Capital	DC	1933	6,695
National Mall	DC	1933	146
Piscataway	MD	1961	4,695
Prince William Forest	VA	1948	15,985
Rock Creek	DC	1890	1,755
White House	DC	1933	18
Wolf Trap Farm Park for the Performing Arts	VA	1966	130

INTERNATIONAL HISTORIC SITE

Name	State	Year[1]	Acreage
Saint Croix Island[3]	ME	1949	45

NATIONAL SCENIC TRAILS

Name	State	Year[1]	Length (mi)
Appalachian	ME to GA	1968	2,175
Ice Age	WI	1980	1,000
Natchez Trace	MS-TN	1983	64
North Country	NY to ND	1980	3,200
Potomac Heritage	VA to PA	1983	520

(1) Year first designated. (2) No federal facilities. (3) Limited federal facilities. (4) Not open to the public. (5) Formerly Coulee Dam National Recreation Area.

457

AFGHANISTAN ALBANIA ALGERIA ANDORRA ANGOLA

ANTIGUA AND BARBUDA | ARGENTINA | ARMENIA | AUSTRALIA | AUSTRIA

AZERBAIJAN | THE BAHAMAS | BAHRAIN | BANGLADESH | BARBADOS

BELARUS | BELGIUM | BELIZE | BENIN | BHUTAN

BOLIVIA | BOSNIA AND HERZEGOVINA | BOTSWANA | BRAZIL | BRUNEI

BULGARIA | BURKINA FASO | BURUNDI | CAMBODIA | CAMEROON

CANADA | CAPE VERDE | CENTRAL AFRICAN REPUBLIC | CHAD | CHILE

CHINA | COLOMBIA | COMOROS | CONGO, DEM. REP. OF THE | CONGO REPUBLIC

COSTA RICA | CÔTE D'IVOIRE | CROATIA | CUBA | CYPRUS

CZECH REPUBLIC | DENMARK | DJIBOUTI | DOMINICA | DOMINICAN REPUBLIC

ECUADOR | EGYPT | EL SALVADOR | EQUATORIAL GUINEA | ERITREA

Note: Flag proportions have been standardized to fit page.

458

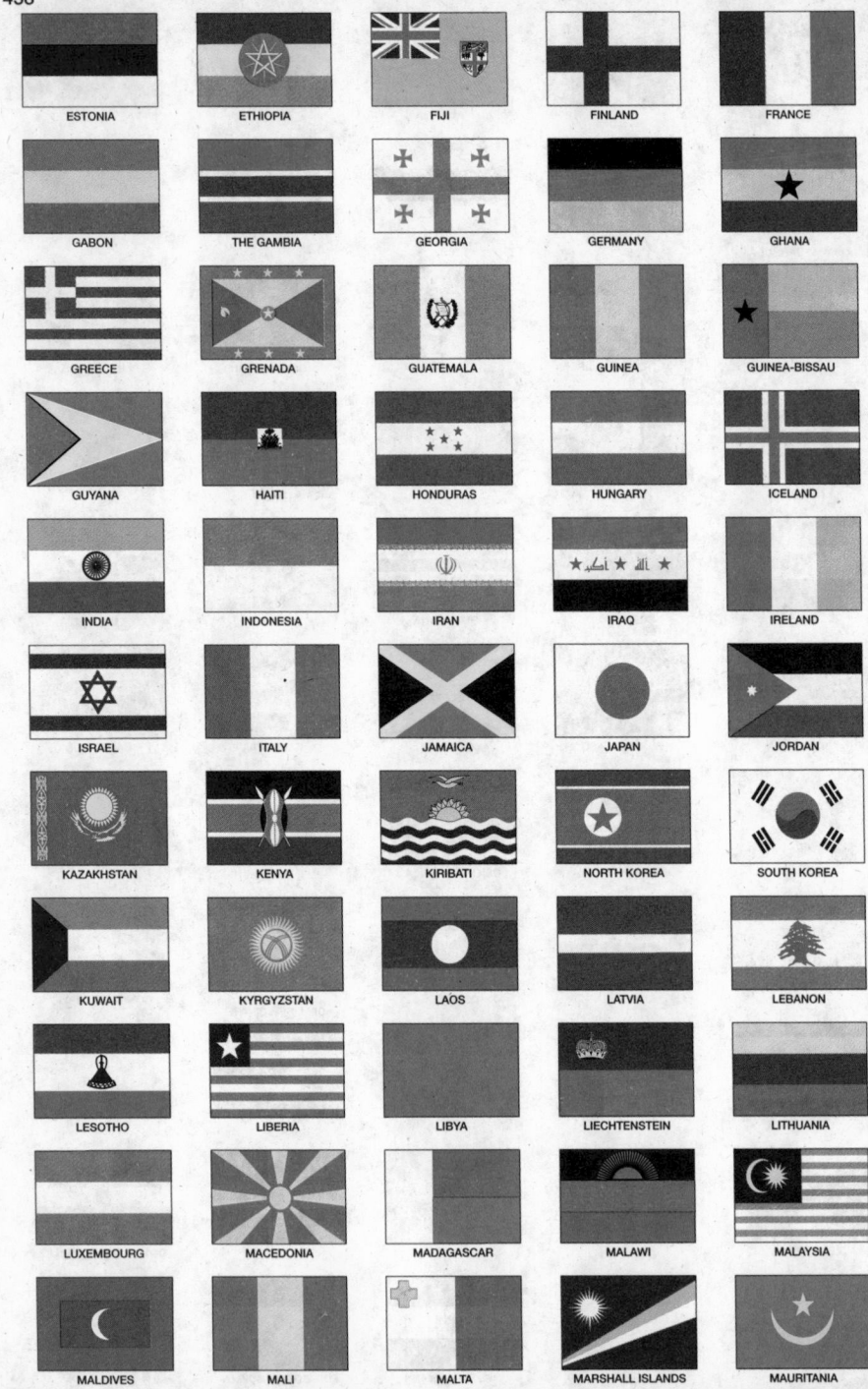

ESTONIA

ETHIOPIA

FIJI

FINLAND

FRANCE

GABON

THE GAMBIA

GEORGIA

GERMANY

GHANA

GREECE

GRENADA

GUATEMALA

GUINEA

GUINEA-BISSAU

GUYANA

HAITI

HONDURAS

HUNGARY

ICELAND

INDIA

INDONESIA

IRAN

IRAQ

IRELAND

ISRAEL

ITALY

JAMAICA

JAPAN

JORDAN

KAZAKHSTAN

KENYA

KIRIBATI

NORTH KOREA

SOUTH KOREA

KUWAIT

KYRGYZSTAN

LAOS

LATVIA

LEBANON

LESOTHO

LIBERIA

LIBYA

LIECHTENSTEIN

LITHUANIA

LUXEMBOURG

MACEDONIA

MADAGASCAR

MALAWI

MALAYSIA

MALDIVES

MALI

MALTA

MARSHALL ISLANDS

MAURITANIA

Note: Flag proportions have been standardized to fit page.

MAURITIUS

MEXICO

MICRONESIA

MOLDOVA

MONACO

MONGOLIA

MONTENEGRO

MOROCCO

MOZAMBIQUE

MYANMAR (BURMA)

NAMIBIA

NAURU

NEPAL

NETHERLANDS

NEW ZEALAND

NICARAGUA

NIGER

NIGERIA

NORWAY

OMAN

PAKISTAN

PALAU

PANAMA

PAPUA NEW GUINEA

PARAGUAY

PERU

PHILIPPINES

POLAND

PORTUGAL

QATAR

ROMANIA

RUSSIA

RWANDA

ST. KITTS AND NEVIS

ST. LUCIA

ST. VINCENT AND
THE GRENADINES

SAMOA

SAN MARINO

SÃO TOMÉ AND PRÍNCIPE

SAUDI ARABIA

SENEGAL

SERBIA

SEYCHELLES

SIERRA LEONE

SINGAPORE

SLOVAKIA

SLOVENIA

SOLOMON ISLANDS

SOMALIA

SOUTH AFRICA

SPAIN

SRI LANKA

SUDAN

SURINAME

SWAZILAND

Note: Flag proportions have been standardized to fit page.

SWEDEN

SWITZERLAND

SYRIA

TAIWAN

TAJIKISTAN

TANZANIA

THAILAND

TIMOR-LESTE
(EAST TIMOR)

TOGO

TONGA

TRINIDAD AND TOBAGO

TUNISIA

TURKEY

TURKMENISTAN

TUVALU

UGANDA

UKRAINE

UNITED ARAB EMIRATES

UNITED KINGDOM

UNITED STATES

URUGUAY

UZBEKISTAN

VANUATU

VATICAN CITY

VENEZUELA

VIETNAM

YEMEN

ZAMBIA

ZIMBABWE

INTERNATIONAL TIME ZONES

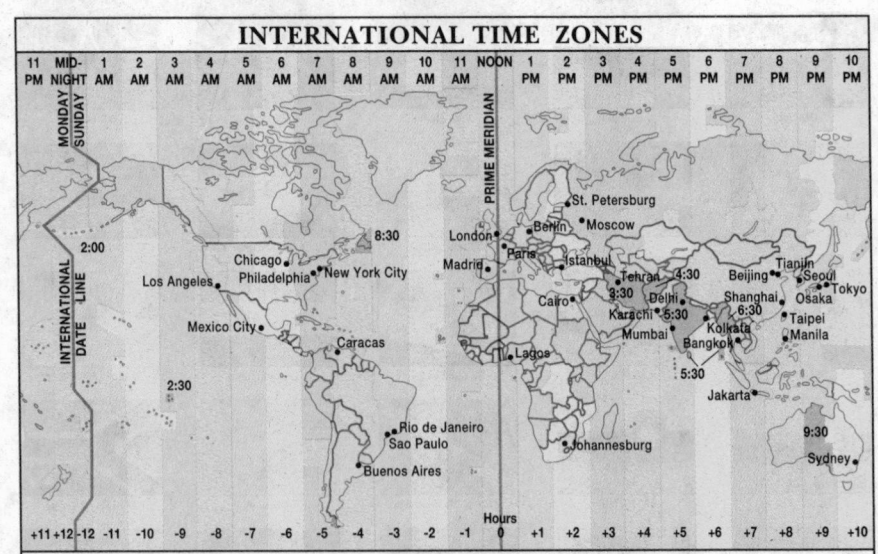

The world is divided into 24 time zones, each 15° longitude wide. The longitudinal meridian passing through Greenwich, England, is the starting point, and is called the *prime meridian*. The 12th zone is divided by the 180th meridian (International Date Line). When the line is crossed going west, the date is advanced one day; when crossed going east, the date becomes a day earlier. © GeoNova

Note: Flag proportions have been standardized to fit page.

UNITED STATES

463

NORTH AMERICA AND THE CARIBBEAN

© GeoNova

Map labels

ATLANTIC OCEAN

PACIFIC OCEAN

Caribbean Sea

Gulf of Mexico

Bay of Campeche

Gulf of California

Straits of Florida

THE BAHAMAS

UNITED STATES

MEXICO

Greater Antilles

Lesser Antilles

CUBA

HAITI

DOMINICAN REPUBLIC

JAMAICA

GUATEMALA

HONDURAS

NICARAGUA

COSTA RICA

PANAMA

BELIZE

EL SALVADOR

YUCATAN PENINSULA

VENEZUELA

COLOMBIA

BRAZIL

SOUTH AMERICA

Nova Scotia

Cape Sable

Cities and places

Montreal, Ottawa, Sherbrooke, Bangor, Portland, N.H., Boston, Mass., R.I., Conn., N.Y., Rochester, Buffalo, Hamilton, Toronto, Cleveland, Detroit, Chicago, Milwaukee, Green Bay, Duluth, Sudbury

New York, Philadelphia, Pa., N.J., Baltimore, Del., Md., Washington, D.C., W. Va., Richmond, Virginia, Norfolk, Raleigh, N. Carolina, Cape Hatteras, Charlotte, S. Carolina, Charleston, Savannah, Jacksonville

Pittsburgh, Columbus, Ohio, Cincinnati, Indianapolis, Ind., Louisville, Kentucky, Nashville, Tennessee, Atlanta, Georgia, Birmingham, Alabama, Miss., Jackson, Mobile, New Orleans, Baton Rouge, La., Memphis

St. Louis, Mo., Des Moines, Iowa, Wisconsin, Minneapolis, St. Paul, Minnesota, Fargo, Bismarck, N. Dakota, S. Dakota, Rapid City, Sioux Falls, Omaha, Nebraska, Kansas City, Kansas, Wichita, Oklahoma City, Oklahoma, Little Rock, Arkansas

Montana, Billings, Butte, Idaho, Boise, Pocatello, Wyoming, Casper, Cheyenne, Colorado, Denver, Colorado Springs, Pueblo, Amarillo, Lubbock, Dallas, Fort Worth, Texas, Austin, San Antonio, Houston, Shreveport

New Mexico, Albuquerque, El Paso, Santa Fe, Utah, Salt Lake City, Great Salt Lake, Nevada, Reno, Arizona, Phoenix, Tucson, Nogales

California, Sacramento, San Francisco, San Jose, Fresno, Santa Barbara, Point Conception, Los Angeles, San Diego, Tijuana, Mexicali, Eureka, Oregon, Eugene, Portland

Death Valley, Lowest point in North America, Mt. Whitney 4418 m (14,494 ft)

GREAT BASIN, COLORADO PLATEAU, MOUNTAIN, PLAINS, ROCKY MOUNTAINS, SIERRA NEVADA, COAST RANGES, CASCADES, APPALACHIAN MTS., COASTAL PLAIN

Mt. Mitchell 2037 m (6684 ft)

Mississippi, Missouri, Platte, Snake, Rio Grande, Colorado, Arkansas, Ohio, L. Superior, L. Michigan, L. Huron, L. Ontario, L. Erie

BAJA CALIFORNIA, False Cape, La Paz, Mazatlan, Culiacan, Durango, Obregon, Ciudad Obregon, Hermosillo, Chihuahua, Ciudad Juarez, Torreon, Monterrey, Matamoros, Nuevo Laredo, Ciudad Victoria, Tampico, Potosi, San Luis Potosi, Leon, Guadalajara, Colima, Tepic, Puebla, Mexico City, Veracruz, Villahermosa, Tuxtla Gutierrez, Oaxaca, Acapulco, Merida, Cancun, Campeche

SIERRA MADRE OCCIDENTAL, SIERRA MADRE ORIENTAL

Cerro Mohinora 3250 m (10,663 ft)

Tajumulco 4220 m (13,846 m), Pico de Orizaba 5747 m (18,855 ft)

Guatemala City, San Salvador, Tegucigalpa, Managua, Lake Nicaragua, San Jose, Panama City, Belmopan

Bogotá, Caracas

Freeport, Nassau, Havana, Isla de la Juventud, Santa Clara, Camaguey, Holguin, Santiago de Cuba, Guantanamo, Cayman Is. (U.K.), Montego Bay, Kingston, Santiago, Port-au-Prince, Santo Domingo, Ponce, San Juan, Puerto Rico (U.S.), Virgin Is. (U.K.&U.S.)

Turks & Caicos Is. (U.K.)

ANTIGUA & BARBUDA, Anguilla (U.K.), St. KITTS & NEVIS, Guadeloupe (Fr.), DOMINICA, Martinique (Fr.), ST. LUCIA, ST. VINCENT & THE GRENADINES, BARBADOS, GRENADA, TRINIDAD & TOBAGO, Port of Spain

Bermuda (U.K.)

Miami, Cape Sable, Tampa, St. Petersburg, Sarasota, Florida

Tropic of Cancer

Miles: 0, 250, 500, 750 Miles
Kilometers: 0, 250, 500, 750, 1,000 Kilometers

ATLANTIC

OCEAN

Natal
João
Pessoa
Recife
Maceió
Aracaju
Mossoró
Juazeiro
do Norte
Campina Grande
Fortaleza
Salvador
Alagoinhas
Parnaíba
Patrolina
Feira de
Santana
Jequié
Itabuna
Ilhéus
São Luís
Caxias
Teresina
Vitória da
Conquista
Governador
Valadares
Vitória
Floriano
Montes Claros
Teófilo
Otoni
Belém
Imperatriz
Araguaína
Pico da Bandeira
2890 m (9,482 ft)
Juiz de Fora
Volta Redonda
Niterói
Marajó
Island
Marabá
Carajas
Belo Horizonte
Ribeirão
Preto
Campinas
Jundiaí
Macapá
Anápolis
Brasília
Goiânia
Uberlândia
São José do
Rio Preto
Bauru
Sorocaba
Londrina
TRINIDAD AND TOBAGO
Margarita I.
Bonaire (Neth.)
Curaçao (Neth.)
Aruba (Neth.)
Kourou
Cayenne
Paramaribo
New Amsterdam
Georgetown
Port of Spain
Santarém
Altamira
Cuiabá
Rondonópolis
Jataí
Presidente
Prudente
BRAZILIAN
HIGHLANDS
BRAZIL
MATO GROSSO
PLATEAU
Campo
Grande
Dourados
Concepción
Coari
Manaus
Porto Velho
Ji-Paraná
Itaituba
AMAZON
SELVAS
BASIN
LLANOS
French
Guiana
(Fr.)
SURINAME
GUYANA
GUIANA HIGHLANDS
Boa Vista
El Tigre
Ciudad Guayana
Ciudad
Bolívar
Cumaná
Barcelona
Caracas
Coro
Maracay
Valencia
Barquisimeto
Maracaibo
Cabimas
Valera
Mérida
San Cristóbal
Cúcuta
Bucaramanga
Medellín
Pico do Neblina
3014 m (9,889 ft)
San Fernando
de Apure
Puerto
Ayacucho
VENEZUELA
Santa Marta
Barranquilla
Cartagena
Sincelejo
Montería
Manizales
Pereira
Armenia
Cali
Popayán
Buenaventura
Pasto
Ibagué
Palmira
COLOMBIA
Tunja
Bogotá
Villavicencio
Neiva
Nevado del Huila 5750 m (18,865 ft)
Florencia
Valledupar
Caribbean Sea
Pico Cristóbal Colón
5775 m (18,947 ft)
Letícia
Benjamin
Constant
Crocerio do Sul
Iquitos
Yurimaguas
Pucallpa
Riberalta
Cobija
Puerto
Maldonado
Cuzco
Guajará-Mirim
Trinidad
Cochabamba
Santa Cruz
Gamir
BOLIVIA
La Paz
Sucre
Potosí
Oruro
ALTIPLANO
ANDES
CHACO
Paraguay
San Salvador
Concepción
PERU
LA MONTAÑA
Nev. Ausangate
6384 m (20,945 ft)
Cerro de Pasco
Huánuco
Huancayo
Ayacucho
Abancay
Lima
Callao
Ica
Puno
Arequipa
Tacna
Arica
Iquique
Antofagasta
ATACAMA DESERT
Calama
Juliaca
Nev. Yerupajá
6635 m (21,769 ft)
Chiclayo
Trujillo
Chimbote
Cajamarca
Piura
Sullana
Talara
Aguja
Point
Tumbes
Machala
Guayaquil
Portoviejo
Manta
Ambato
Riobamba
Cuenca
Loja
Esmeraldas
Quito
Chimborazo 6310 m (20,702 ft)
Cotopaxi 5897 m (19,347 ft)
Tumaco
ECUADOR
Equator
Galapagos
Islands
(Ecuador)
PACIFIC

OCEAN

PANAMA
Panama
City
Tegucigalpa
HONDURAS
San
Salvador
SALVADOR
Managua
San José
COSTA
RICA
NICARAGUA
CENTRAL

AMERICA

10°
0°
20°
40°
50°
60°
70°
80°
90°
10°

Orinoco
Negro
Amazon
Purus
Japurá
Juruá
Madeira
Xingu
Tapajós
Tocantins
Araguaia
São Francisco
Paraná
Ucayali
Marañón
Branco
Putumayo
Magdalena
Río
Branco

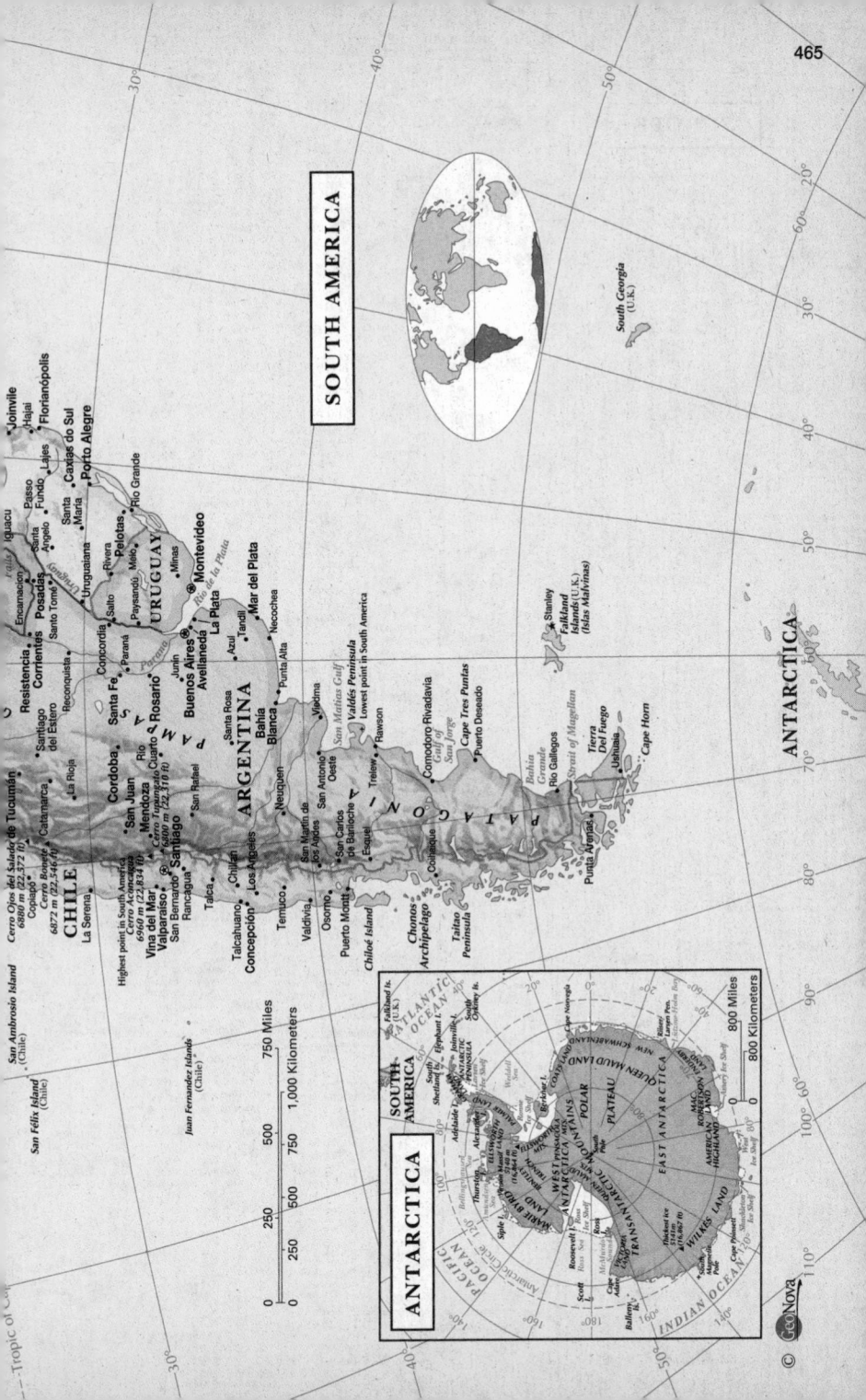

SOUTH AMERICA

ANTARCTICA

EUROPE

GREENLAND
(KALAALLIT NUNAAT)
(Denmark)

Isafjordhur

Akureyri
Keflavik
ICELAND
Reykjavik

Seydhisfjordhur

Norwegian Sea

Namsos

Torshavn *Faroe Islands (Den.)*

Trondheim
Molde
Alesund

NORWAY   SWEDE

Shetland Islands (U.K.)

Bergen

Orkney Islands
Thurso

Haugesund
Stavanger

Drammen   Oslo
Skien

Karlstad   Orebro

Uppsa

Stockho
Link

Kristiansand

Inverness

Scotland   Aberdeen

Dundee

Vänern
Vättern

Goteborg
Norrkoping
Jonkoping

ATLANTIC
OCEAN

Londonderry
Northern Ireland
Belfast

Glasgow
Ayr   Edinburgh

Aalborg
Halmstad   Vaxjo

Jutland

North Sea

Esbjerg   Arhus

Copenhagen   Helsingborg
Malmo

Galway
IRELAND
Limerick

Dublin

UNITED
KINGDOM   Newcastle

DENMARK   Odense

Bornho
(Den.)

Cork   Waterford

Liverpool
Manchester

Leeds
Kingston upon Hull
Sheffield

Kiel   Lübeck   Rostock

Groningen

Hamburg   Szczecin

NORTHE

Birmingham
Wales   Swansea
Cardiff   England
Bristol

Coventry

Norwich

Bremen   Bydgos:

Hannover
Bielefeld   Magdeburg

Berlin

POLA

Plymouth

Land's End

Portsmouth

London   Amsterdam
The Hague   Rotterdam
Dover   Antwerp   Essen
Brussels   Cologne
Lille   Liege   Bonn

NETHERLANDS

Thames

GERMANY   Po

Kassel

Leipzig

Dresden   Wro

Erfurt   Chemnitz   Liberec

Channel Is.
(U.K.)

Brest

English Channel

Le Havre
Caen

Wiesbaden
LUXEMBOURG   Frankfurt
Mannheim   Prague

Saarbrucken

Ostr
Plzen   Bri

CZECH REP.

Wal

Rouen

BELGIUM

Luxembourg

Rennes

Paris
Le Mans
Orleans

Nancy
Strasbourg

Nurnberg
Stuttgart   Regensburg

Nantes

Seine

Tours

Loire

Dijon

Augsburg   Munich   Linz
Basel

Limoges

FRANCE

Clermont-Ferrand
Saint-Etienne

Lyon

SWITZERLAND   Zürich
Geneva   Bern

Mt. Blanc
4807 m (15,771 ft)

Salzburg

Innsbruck

Danub

Bra

Vienna

AUSTRIA

Klagenfurt

Graz   Gy

LIECHTENSTEIN

Bordeaux

Grenoble

A L P S

Matterhorn
4505 m (14,690 ft)

SLOVENIA

Toulouse

PYRENEES

Montpellier

Torino

Milan
Bergamo

Udine
Trieste   Ljubljana   Zagre

Rijeka

Venice

CROATI

A Coruña
Vigo

Gijon
Santander
Bilbao

Donostia-
San Sebastian

Pamplona

Avignon

Marseille   Nice

Bologna

Genoa
Parma

Verona

Po

DINARI

Porto   Braga

Leon

Vitoria-Gasteiz
Valladolid

Zaragoza

Duero

IBERIAN

Salamanca

Pico de Aneto
3404 m
(11,169 ft)

ANDORRA

Toulon

MONACO

Pisa

Florence

SAN
MARINO

Ancona

Perugia

BO

Adriati

Split   Sara

Coimbra

Lisbon

PORTUGAL

Setubal

Madrid

Badajoz

Tagus

Toledo

Barcelona

Tarragona

Corsica
(Fr.)

Ajaccio

Elba

VATICAN CITY

Rome

ITALY

Dubrov

SPAIN

Castellon de la Plana

Valencia

Sardinia
(It.)

Naples   Foggia

Vesuvius
1277 m (4,190 ft)

Salerno

Tara

Cape
St. Vincent

Cadiz

PENINSULA

Cordoba

Seville

Malaga   Granada

Alicante
Murcia

Palma de
Mallorca

Majorca   Minorca

Balearic
Is.
(Sp.)

Sassari

Cagliari

Tyrrhenian

Sea

Io

Strait of
Gibraltar

GIBRALTER
(U.K.)

Almeria

Cartagena

Mediterranean

Palermo   Messina
Etna
3369 m (11,053 ft)

Sicily
(It.)

Reggio di
Calabria

Catania

Rabat

AFRICA

Algiers

Tunis

Sea

MALTA   Valletta

Se

MOROCCO   ALGERIA   TUNISIA

0   250   500 Miles
0   250   500   750 Kilometers

Barents Sea

ASIA

North Cape
nerfest
Vardo

RUSSIA

Novaya Zemlya

Naryan-Mar
Pechora

Murmansk
Apatity **KOLA PENINSULA**
Ukhta

Ivalo
runa **LAPLAND**
so

Rovaniemi
White Sea
Arkhangelsk

Belomorsk

Syktyvkar

URAL MOUNTAINS

lea
Oulu
Skelleftea

Berezniki
Perm

FINLAND
Dvina
Kotlas

Vaasa
Kuopio
Lake Onega
Kirov
Izhevsk
Ufa
Sterlitamak

Jyvaskyla
Lake Ladoga
Petrozavodsk

ori
Tampere
Lahti

Turku
Kotka
Cherepovets
Vologda
Yoshkar Ola
Naberezhnye Chelny
Kama

Aland Is.
(in.)
Helsinki
St. Petersburg
Rybinsk
Yaroslavl
Kostroma
Nizhniy Novgorod
Kazan
Cheboksary
Orsk
Orenburg

Tallinn
Velikiy Novgorod
Ivanovo
Ulyanovsk

ESTONIA
Tartu
Pskov
Tver
Vladimir
Saransk
Tolyatti
Samara

LATVIA
Riga
Liepaja
Moscow
Kaluga
Ryazan
Penza
Volga
Ural

Daugavpils
Smolensk
Tula
KAZAKHSTAN

LITHUANIA
Klaipeda
Vitsyebsk
Tambov
Saratov

Kaunas
Vilnius
Orsha
Lipetsk

(RUSSIA)
Kaliningrad
PLAIN
Mahilyow
Bryansk
Voronezh

Hrodna
Minsk
Babruysk

Bialystok
Homyel
Kursk
Volgograd

Warsaw
Brest
Pinsk
Chernihiv
Belgorod
Astrakhan

Lublin
BELARUS
Sumy
Kharkiv
Poltava

Kielce
Kyiv (Kiev)
Cherkasy
Luhansk
Horlivka
Don

wice
Zhytomyr
UKRAINE
Donetsk
Rostov-na-Donu

rakow
Lviv
Vinnytsia
Dnipropetrovsk
Zaporizhzhia
Mariupol
Caspian

AKIA
Kosice
Chernivtsi
MOLDOVA
Kryvyi Rih
Mykolaiv
Sea of Azov
Sea

pest
Debrecen
Iasi
Chisinau
Odesa
Krasnodar
Stavropol
Grozny
Makhachkala

 RY
Oradea
Cluj-Napoca
CRIMEA PENINSULA
Simferopol
Mt. Elbrus 5642 m (18,510 ft) Highest point in Europe
Nalchik
Vladikavkaz

Szeged
ROMANIA
Brasov
Galati
Sevastopol
CAUCASUS MTS.
Baku

Novi Sad
Timisoara
Ploiesti
GEORGIA
Tbilisi

SERBIA
Belgrade
Bucharest
Craiova
Constanta
Black Sea
ARMENIA
AZERBAIJAN

Nis
Ruse
Yerevan
AZER.

TENEGRO
Danube
Pleven
Varna

gorica
BULGARIA
Stara Zagora
Burgas
Tehran

koder
Sofia
Plovdiv

MACEDONIA
Istanbul
IRAN

PENINSULA
Kavala
Thessaloniki

BANIA
Olympus 2917 m (9,570 ft)
TURKEY
Ankara
ASIA

Larisa
Ioannina
Aegean Sea
Dardanelles

GREECE
Volos
Athens

Patras
Corinth
Baghdad

Peloponnese
Sparta
SYRIA
IRAQ

Kalamata
Cyclades

Nicosia
LEBANON
© GeoNova

Rhodes (Gr.)
CYPRUS
Beirut
Damascus

Crete
Hania
Iraklion
Sea of Crete

ASIA

Chukchi Sea

Bering Strait

Provideniya

Wrangel I.

East Siberian Sea

New Siberian Islands

Laptev Sea

Tiksi

Bering Sea

Anadyr

Cherskiy

KOLYMA MOUNTAINS

Zyryanka

Verkhoyansk

Susuman

Magadan

Shiveluch
3168 m (10,771 ft)
Klyuchevskaya
4750 m (15,584 ft)
Karymsky
1536 m (5,039 ft)
Petropavlovsk-Kamchatskiy

KAMCHATKA PEN.

VERKHOYANSK RA.

Vilyuysk

Yakutsk

Okhotsk

Sea of Okhotsk

Alaid
2339 m
(7,674 ft)

Lensk

Aldan

Berkakit

STANOVOY RANGE

Tynda

Komsomolsk-na-Amure

Svobodnyy

Blagoveshchensk

Sarycheva
1496 m
(4,908 ft)

Okha

Sakhalin

Kuril Is.
(Russia)

Ust-Kut

Bodaybo

Chita

YABLONOVY RANGE

Khabarovsk

Yuzhno-Sakhalinsk

Tiatia
1819 m
(5,968 ft)

Lake Baykal

Ulan-Ude

GREATER KHINGAN RANGE

Amur

Hokkaido

Sapporo

Hailar

Yichun

Jixi

Ussuriysk

Vladivostok

Hakodate

Darhan

Choybalsan

Ulaanbaatar

Qiqihar

Harbin

Jilin

*Sea of Japan
(East Sea)*

Akita

Sendai

Niigata

Honshu

MONGOLIA

MONGOLIAN PLATEAU

GOBI DESERT

Changchun

Fushun

Shenyang

N. KOREA

Hamhung

JAPAN

Tokyo

Yokohama

Kyoto

Nagoya

Mt. Fuji 3776 m (12,388 ft)

Hohhot

Beijing

Anshan

Dalian

Pyongyang

Seoul

Kobe

Osaka

Shikoku

Baotou

Tianjin

Incheon

Busan

Hiroshima

Kitakyushu

Yinchuan

Shijiazhuang

S. KOREA

Daegu

Fukuoka

Xining

Taiyuan

Jinan

Qingdao

Nagasaki

Kyushu

Kagoshima

Lanzhou

Handan

Yellow Sea

Xian

Luoyang

Xuzhou

Zhengzhou

Nanjing

Ryukyu Is.
(Japan)

Huainan

Hefei

Shanghai

Hangzhou

Okinawa

Naha

CHINA

Chengdu

Wuhan

Jingdezhen

Nanchang

Wenzhou

East China Sea

Chongqing

Zigong

Shaoyang

Changsha

Ganzhou

Fuzhou

Gulyang

Guilin

Xiamen

Kunming

Liuzhou

Guangzhou

Taipei

TAIWAN

Kaohsiung

Nanning

Macao

Hong Kong

Tropic of Cancer

*PACIFIC
OCEAN*

Haiphong

Zhanjiang

Laoag

Luzon

*Philippine
Sea*

LAOS

Hanoi

Haikou

Baguio

PHILIPPINES

Northern
Mariana
Islands
(U.S.)

Vientiane

Vinh

*Hainan
(China)*

Quezon City

Naga

PALAU

THAILAND

Hue

Da Nang

Manila

Samar

Ratchasima

Mindoro

Tacloban

Leyte

VIETNAM

*South
China
Sea*

Iloilo

Panay

Cebu

Butuan

Bangkok

CAMBODIA

Nha Trang

Puerto
Princesa

Negros

Mindanao

Davao

Phnom Penh

Ho Chi Minh City

Palawan

*Sulu
Sea*

Zamboanga

Can Tho

Jayapura

PAPUA
NEW GUINEA

*Gulf of
Thailand*

Kota Kinabalu

Sandakan

*Celebes
Sea*

Ternate

Halmahera

Port Moresby

Hat Yai

Bandar Seri Begawan

BRUNEI

Tarakan

*New
Guinea*

George
Town

MALAYSIA

Natuna Is.

Manado

Gorontalo

Kuala
Lumpur

Kuching

Samainda

Celebes

Ambon

*Arafura
Sea*

Singapore

SINGAPORE

Pontianak

Borneo

Balikpapan

Palopo

*Banda
Sea*

Pekanbaru

Sampit

Banjarmasin

Parepare

Baubau

Jambi

Makassar

Moluccas

Ceram

Padang

Sumatra

Palembang

Java Sea

INDONESIA

AUSTRALIA

Bandar Lampung

Jakarta

Semarang

Surabaya

Dili

TIMOR LESTE

Bandung

Yogyakarta

Java

Malang

Bali

Mataram

Sumba

Ende

Timor

Kupang

*Timor
Sea*

| 0 | 500 | 1,000 Miles |

| 0 | 500 | 1,000 | 1,500 Kilometers |

470

AFRICA

SEYCHELLES

INDIAN OCEAN

ATLANTIC OCEAN

COMOROS
Moroni
Mayotte (Fr.)

MADAGASCAR
Antsiranana
Antalaha
Mahajanga
Toamasina
Antananarivo
Antsirabe
Fianarantsoa
Tolanaro
Toliara

Mozambique Channel

Mozambique

KENYA
Eldoret
Nakuru
Nairobi
Machakos
Mt. Kenya 5199 m (17,058 ft)
Margherita Pk. 5119 m (16,795 ft)

Mogadishu
Marka
Kismaayo

HIGHLANDS
Kilimanjaro 5895 m (19,340 ft) Highest point in Africa
Mombasa
Tanga
Pemba I.
Zanzibar I.
Zanzibar
Dar es Salaam
Mtwara

SERENGETI PLAIN
Mt. Meru 4565 m (14,979 ft)
Kampala
Jinja
Kisumu
Kigali
RWANDA
Bukavu
BURUNDI
Bujumbura
Goma
Kindu
Kigoma
Tabora
Dodoma
Morogoro
Iringa
Mbeya
Songea
Mwanza
Mbala
Lake Victoria
Lake Tanganyika

TANZANIA
BENIN

Nacala
Nampula
Quelimane
Blantyre
MALAWI
Lilongwe
Chipata
Tete
MOZAMBIQUE
Chimoio
Beira
Mutare
HARARE
Chinhoyi

Lake Nyasa

CONGO BASIN
REPUBLIC OF THE CONGO
Brazzaville
Franceville
GABON
Libreville
Lambaréné
Port-Gentil

DEMOCRATIC REPUBLIC OF THE CONGO
Kisangani
Mbandaka
Mbuji-Mayi
Kananga
Tshikapa
Kikwit
Bandundu
Kinshasa
Mbanza-Ngungu
Matadi
Boma
Kabinda
Mwene-Ditu
Kamina
Kalemie
Kabalo
Boende
Ilebo
Luena
Kolwezi
Likasi
Lubumbashi
KATANGA

Congo
Kasai
Kwango
Ubangi

SAO TOME AND PRINCIPE
Sao Tome
Principe
Annobon (Eq. Guinea)

ANGOLA
Luanda
Malanje
Huambo
Lobito
Benguela
Namibe
Menongue
Lubango
Cabinda (Angola)
Pointe-Noire
Loubomo

ZAMBIA
Lusaka
Kitwe
Ndola
Kabwe
Livingstone
PLATEAU
Lake Kariba
Zambezi

Victoria Falls

ZIMBABWE
Bulawayo
Gweru
Masvingo
Francistown

BOTSWANA
KALAHARI DESERT
Gaborone
Serowe
Mbabane
SWAZILAND

NAMIBIA
Windhoek
Grootfontein
Tsumeb
Keetmanshoop
Lüderitz
Walvis Bay
NAMIB DESERT

Orange
Okavango

SOUTH AFRICA
Johannesburg
Pretoria
Vereeniging
Welkom
Klerksdorp
Kimberley
Upington
Springbok
Bloemfontein
LESOTHO
Maseru
Newcastle
Pietermaritzburg
Durban
Umtata
Bisho
East London
Port Elizabeth
Worcester
Cape Town
Cape of Good Hope
Cape Agulhas
Middelburg
Mmabatho

Maputo
Xai-Xai
Inhambane
Thohoyandou
Messina
Polokwane
Limpopo

Tropic of Capricorn

Equator

Ascension (U.K.)

0 250 500 750 Miles
0 250 500 750 1,000 Kilometers

© GeoNova

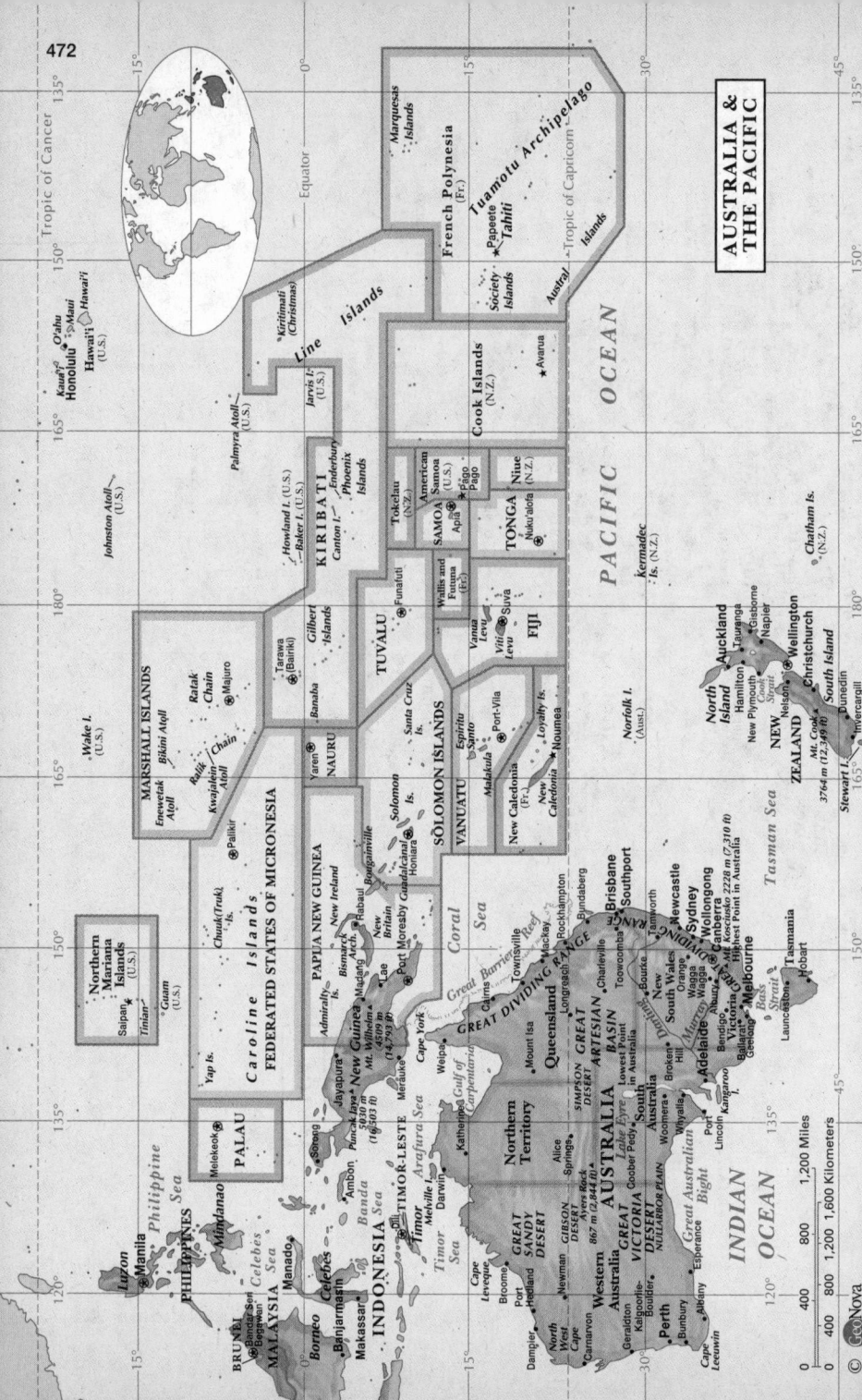

472

AUSTRALIA &
THE PACIFIC

UNITED STATES HISTORY

Chronology of Events

1492
Christopher Columbus and crew sighted land Oct. 12 in present-day Bahamas.

1513
Juan Ponce de León explored Florida coast.

1524
Giovanni da Verrazano led French expedition along coast from Carolina north to Nova Scotia; entered New York Harbor.

1526
San Miguel de Guadalupe, **first European settlement** in what became U.S. territory, was established in the summer off South Carolina coast; abandoned in October.

Ponce de León

1539
Hernando de Soto landed in Florida May 28; crossed Mississippi River, **1541**.

1540
Francisco Vásquez de Coronado explored Southwest north of Rio Grande. **Hernando de Alarcón** reached Colorado River; **García López de Cárdenas** reached Grand Canyon. Others explored California coast.

1562
First French colony in what became U.S. territory founded on Parris Island off South Carolina coast; abandoned, **1564**.

1565
St. Augustine, FL, oldest continuously occupied European settlement in U.S., founded Sept. 8 by Pedro Menéndez de Avilés. Spain ceded settlement to U.S. in **1821**.

1579
Sir Francis Drake entered San Francisco Bay and claimed region for Britain.

1585
First English colony in America, sponsored by Sir Walter Raleigh, founded on **Roanoke Island**, off North Carolina coast; colony failed.

1587
Second colony attempted on Roanoke Island. Virginia Dare of colony became **first English infant born** in the New World. Settlers of second colony found to have vanished, **1590**.

1607
Capt. **John Smith** and 105 cavaliers in 3 ships landed on Virginia coast, started Jamestown, **first permanent English settlement** in New World.

1609
Henry Hudson, English explorer of Northwest Passage, employed by Dutch, sailed into New York Harbor in September and up Hudson to Albany. **Samuel de Champlain** explored Lake Champlain, to the north.
Spaniards settled **Santa Fe, NM**.

1619
House of Burgesses, **first representative assembly** in New World, elected July 30 at Jamestown, VA.
First black laborers—indentured servants—in English North American colonies, brought by Dutch to Jamestown in August. Chattel slavery legally recognized, **1650**.

1620
Pilgrims, Puritan separatists, left Plymouth, England, Sept. 16 on *Mayflower*; reached Cape Cod Nov. 19; 103 passengers landed at Plymouth, Dec. 26. **Mayflower Compact**, signed Nov. 11, was agreement to form a self-government. Half of colony died during harsh winter.

1624
Dutch colonies started in Albany and in New York area, where **New Netherland** was established in May.

1626
Peter Minuit bought **Manhattan** for Dutch West India Co. from Manahatta Indians during summer for goods valued at $24; named island **New Amsterdam**.

1630
Settlement of **Boston** established by Massachusetts colonists led by John Winthrop; Winthrop began *The History of New England*.
William Bradford, a governor of Plymouth Colony, began his chronicle *History of Plymouth Plantation (1620-1647)*, first published in entirety in **1856**.

1634
Maryland founded as Catholic colony under charter to Lord Baltimore. Act of Toleration passed **1649** provided for religious tolerance.

1635
Boston Latin School, **oldest public school** in continuous existence in U.S., founded Apr. 23.

1636
Roger Williams founded **Providence, RI**, in June, as a democratically ruled colony with separation of church and state. Charter granted, **1644**.
Harvard College founded; **oldest institution of higher learning** in U.S.

1640
First book printed in America, the so-called *Bay Psalm Book*.

1647
Liberal constitution drafted in Rhode Island.
First law in America providing for **free compulsory basic education** enacted in Massachusetts.

1660
British Parliament passed first **Navigation Act** Dec. 1, regulating colonial commerce to suit English needs.

1661
A version of the New Testament translated into Algonquian became the **first Bible printed** in the colonies.

1664
British troops Sept. 8 seized New Netherland from Dutch. Charles II granted New Netherland and city of New Amsterdam to brother, Duke of York; both renamed **New York**. Dutch recaptured colony **1673**, but ceded it to Britain Nov. 10, **1674**.

1670
Charles Town, SC, founded by English colonists in April.

1673
Regular mail service on horseback instituted Jan. 1 between New York and Boston.
Jacques Marquette and **Louis Jolliet** reached the upper Mississippi and traveled down it.

1674
Future **Salem witch trial** judge Samuel Sewall began renowned diary covering events through **1729**.

1676
Bloody **Indian war** in New England ended Aug. 12. King Philip, Wampanoag chief, and Narragansett Indians killed.
Nathaniel Bacon led planters against autocratic British Gov. Sir William Berkeley, burned Jamestown, VA, Sept. 19. Rebellion collapsed when Bacon died; 23 followers executed.

1678
A book of poetry by **Anne Bradstreet** (first published in Britain) revised and expanded for posthumous publication in Massachusetts. Considered first female poet in American colonies.

1679
Fire destroyed 150 houses in Boston. City imported **first fire engines** from England.

1681
John Bunyan's *The Pilgrim's Progress* published in America; became best seller.

1682

Robert Cavelier, Sieur de La Salle, claimed lower Mississippi River country for France and called it **Louisiana** Apr. 9. Had French outposts built in Illinois and Texas, **1684.** Killed during mutiny, **1687.**

Spanish colonists became the **first Europeans to settle Texas**, at site of present-day El Paso.

1683

William Penn signed treaty with Delaware Indians Apr. 23 and made payment for **Pennsylvania** lands. The **first German colonists** in America settled near Philadelphia.

1689

New York's English colonial governor, **Sir Edmund Andros**, resigned after armed uprising in Boston on Apr. 18.

1690

First colonial newspaper, *Publick Occurrences*, published by Benjamin Harris but promptly shut down for lack of official permission. Harris also published *New England Primer* for use as elementary school textbook.

Large-scale **whaling** operations began in Nantucket, MA.

1692

Witchcraft delusion at Salem, MA; 20 alleged witches executed by special court.

1697

The Essays of **Sir Francis Bacon**, first published in England in **1597**, was published in America; it became a best seller.

1699

Former privateer Capt. **William Kidd** arrested and sent to England; hanged for piracy, **1701.**

French settlements made in **Mississippi, Louisiana**.

1702

Legislation enacted making **Church of England** the established church in Maryland.

1704

Indians attacked Deerfield, MA, Feb. 28-29; killed 40, carried off 100.

Boston News Letter, **first regular newspaper**, started by postmaster John Campbell.

1710

British-colonial troops captured French fort, Port Royal, Nova Scotia, in **Queen Anne's War, 1702-13**. France yielded Nova Scotia by treaty, **1713**.

1712

Slaves revolted in New York Apr. 6; 21 were executed. Second uprising, **1741**; 13 slaves hanged, 13 burned, 71 deported.

1716

First theater in colonies opened in Williamsburg, VA.

1726

Great Awakening, general revival of evangelical religion, began in colonies.

Benjamin Franklin

1731

America's **first circulating library** founded in Philadelphia by Benjamin Franklin.

1732

Benjamin Franklin published the **first** *Poor Richard's Almanack*; published annually until **1757.**

Last of 13 colonies, **Georgia**, chartered.

1733

Influenza epidemic swept through New York City and Philadelphia.

1735

Editor **John Peter Zenger** was acquitted of libel Aug. 5 in New York after criticizing the British governor's conduct in office.

1739

A series of **slave uprisings** put down in South Carolina.

1741

Famous sermon "Sinners in the Hands of an Angry God," delivered at Enfield, MA, July 8, by Jonathan Edwards, a major figure in revivalist **Great Awakening**.

Danish navigator **Vitus Bering**, commanding Russian expedition, reached Alaska.

1744

King George's War pitted British and colonials versus French. Colonials captured Louisbourg, Cape Breton Isl., Nova Scotia, June 17, **1745**. Returned to France **1748** by Treaty of Aix-la-Chapelle.

1752

Benjamin Franklin, flying kite in thunderstorm, proved lightning is electricity, June 15; invented lightning rod.

Liberty Bell, cast in England, was delivered to Pennsylvania.

1754

French and Indian War began with Ft. Necessity campaign in Pennsylvania. Skirmish May 28, battle at fort July 3-4. British moved Acadian French from Nova Scotia to Louisiana Oct. 8, **1755.** British captured Québec Sept. 18, **1759**, in battles in which French Gen. Joseph de Montcalm and British Gen. James Wolfe were killed. Peace pact signed Feb. 10, **1763.** French lost Canada and Midwest.

Delegates from 7 colonies to New York for **Albany Congress**, July 19, approved plan of union by Benjamin Franklin; plan rejected by the colonies.

1757

First streetlights appeared in Philadelphia.

1764

Sugar Act, Apr. 5, placed duties on lumber, foodstuffs, molasses, and rum in colonies, to pay French and Indian War debts.

1765

Stamp Act, enacted by Parliament Mar. 22, required revenue stamps to help fund royal troops. Nine colonies, at Stamp Act Congress in New York Oct. 7-25, adopted Declaration of Rights. Stamp Act repealed Mar. 17, **1766.**

Quartering Act, requiring colonists to house British troops, went into effect Mar. 24.

1767

Townshend Acts levied taxes on glass, painter's lead, paper, and tea. In **1770** all duties except on tea were repealed.

1770

British troops fired Mar. 5 into Boston mob, killed 5 including **Crispus Attucks**, a black man, reportedly leader of group; later called **Boston Massacre**.

1773

East India Co. tea ships turned back at Boston, New York, and Philadelphia in May. Cargo ship burned at Annapolis, Oct. 14; cargo thrown overboard at **Boston Tea Party**, Dec. 16, to protest the tea tax.

First museum in the colonies was officially established in Charleston, SC; later named the Charleston Museum.

1774

"Intolerable Acts" of Parliament curtailed Massachusetts self-rule; barred use of Boston Harbor until tea was paid for.

First Continental Congress held in Philadelphia Sept. 5-Oct. 26; called for civil disobedience against British.

Rhode Island **abolished slavery.**

1775

Patrick Henry addressed Virginia convention, Mar. 23, said, "Give me liberty or give me death!"

Paul Revere, William Dawes, and Dr. **Samuel Prescott**, Apr. 18, rode to alert patriots that British were on their way to Concord to destroy arms. At **Lexington**, MA, Apr. 19, Minutemen lost 8. On return from **Concord**, British suffered 273 casualties.

Col. Ethan Allen (joined by Col. Benedict Arnold) captured **Ft. Ticonderoga** in New York, May 10, also Crown Point. Colonials headed for **Bunker Hill**, fortified Breed's Hill, Charlestown, MA. Repulsed British under Gen. William Howe twice before retreating, June 17.

Continental Congress June 15 named George Washington commander in chief. Established a postal system, July 26; Benjamin Franklin became the **first postmaster general**.

1776

Thomas Paine

Thomas Paine's *Common Sense*, famous pro-independence pamphlet, published Jan. 10; quickly sold some 100,000 copies.

France and Spain agreed May 2 to provide arms to U.S.

In Continental Congress June 7, Richard Henry Lee (VA) moved "that these united colonies are, and of right ought to be, free and independent states." Resolution adopted July 2. **Declaration of Independence** approved July 4, signed Aug. 2.

Col. William Moultrie's batteries at **Charleston, SC**, repulsed British sea attack June 28. Washington lost **Battle of Long Island** Aug. 27; evacuated New York.

Nathan Hale executed as spy by British Sept. 22.

Brig. Gen. Arnold's **Lake Champlain** fleet was defeated at Valcour Oct. 11, but British returned to Canada. Howe failed to destroy Washington's army at White Plains, Oct. 28. Hessians captured Ft. Washington, Manhattan, and 3,000 men, Nov. 16; captured Ft. Lee, NJ, Nov. 20.

Washington, in Pennsylvania, recrossed **Delaware River** Dec. 25-26, defeated Hessians at Trenton, NJ, Dec. 26.

1777

Washington defeated Lord Cornwallis at **Princeton** Jan. 3.

Continental Congress, June 14, authorized an **American flag**, the Stars and Stripes.

Maj. Gen. John Burgoyne's force of 8,000 from Canada, captured **Ft. Ticonderoga**, July 6. Americans beat back Burgoyne at Bemis Heights, Oct. 7, cut off British escape route. Burgoyne surrendered 5,000 men at Saratoga, NY, Oct. 17.

Articles of Confederation adopted by Continental Congress, Nov. 15; took effect Mar. 1, **1781**.

1778

France signed treaty of aid with U.S. Feb. 6. Sent fleet; British evacuated Philadelphia in consequence, June 18.

1779

George Rogers Clark took Ft. Vincennes in what is now Indiana in February.

John Paul Jones on the *Bonhomme Richard* defeated *Serapis* in British North Sea waters, Sept. 23.

1780

Charleston, SC, fell to the British May 12, but a British force was defeated near **Kings Mountain, NC**, Oct. 7 by militia.

Benedict Arnold found to be a traitor Sept. 23. Arnold escaped, made brigadier general in British army.

1781

Bank of North America, **first commercial bank**, incorporated May 26.

Cornwallis retired to **Yorktown, VA**. Adm. Francois Joseph de Grasse landed 3,000 French and stopped British fleet in **Hampton Roads**. Washington and Jean Baptiste de Rochambeau joined forces, arrived near Williamsburg, Sept. 26. Siege of Cornwallis began, Oct. 6; **Cornwallis surrendered** Oct. 19.

1782

New British cabinet agreed in March to **recognize U.S. independence**. Preliminary agreement signed in Paris, Nov. 30.

Use of **scarlet letter A**, sewn on clothing or branded on skin of adulterers, discontinued in New England.

1783

Massachusetts Supreme Court decision in final Quock Walker trial **legally ended slavery**.

Newspapers typically published weekly. **First regular daily newspaper**, *Pennsylvania Evening Post*, went on sale in Philadelphia, May 30.

Britain, U.S. signed **Paris peace treaty**, Sept. 3, recognizing American independence. Congress ratified it Jan. 14, **1784**.

Washington ordered army disbanded Nov. 3, bade farewell to his officers at Fraunces Tavern, New York City, Dec. 4.

1784

Thomas Jefferson's proposal to **ban slavery in new territories** after 1802 was narrowly defeated, Mar. 1.

1785

Regular stagecoach routes established between Albany, New York City, and Philadelphia.

1786

Delegates from 5 states at Annapolis, MD, Sept. 11-14 asked Congress to call a **constitutional convention**.

1787

Shays's Rebellion of debt-ridden farmers in Massachusetts failed, Jan. 25.

Constitutional convention opened in Philadelphia, May 25, with Washington presiding. Constitution accepted by delegates, Sept. 17; Delaware became first state to ratify it, Dec. 7; Pennsylvania and New Jersey followed.

Northwest Ordinance adopted July 13 by Continental Congress for Northwest Territory, north of Ohio River, west of New York; made rules for statehood. Guaranteed freedom of religion, support for schools, no slavery.

Federalist Papers first appeared in *NY Independent Journal*.

1788

A **large fire in New Orleans**, then a Spanish territory, destroyed much of the city, Mar. 21.

Constitution adopted June 21 after being ratified by the requisite ninth state (New Hampshire); also ratified by **Georgia, Connecticut, Massachusetts, Maryland, South Carolina, Virginia, and New York** throughout the year.

First U.S. senators elected Sept. 30, from Pennsylvania.

1789

George Washington chosen president by all electors voting (73 eligible, 69 voting, 4 absent); **John Adams**, vice president, got 34 votes. **First Congress** met at Federal Hall, New York City, and declared Constitution in effect, Mar. 4; Washington inaugurated there Apr. 30; **first inaugural ball** held May 7.

U.S. **State Dept.** established by Congress July 27. (Thomas Jefferson installed as first secretary of state Feb. **1790**.) **War Dept.** created Aug. 7, with Henry Knox as secretary; **Treasury Dept.** created Sept. 2, with Alexander Hamilton to be secretary.

Supreme Court created by Federal Judiciary Act, Sept. 24; **John Jay** confirmed by Congress as **first Supreme Court chief justice**, Sept. 26.

1790

First Supreme Court session held Feb. 2 in New York City.

Congress, Mar. 1, authorized decennial **U.S. census**. Collection of data took 18 months.

Naturalization Act (2-year residency) passed Mar. 26.

John Carroll consecrated as **first American Catholic bishop**, Aug. 15.

Congress met in **Philadelphia**, new temporary capital, Dec. 6.

1791

Bill of Rights, submitted to states, Sept. 25, **1789**, went into effect Dec. 15.

First Bank of the United States, **first bank to be chartered by federal government**, established in Philadelphia.

1792

Coinage Act established **U.S. Mint** in Philadelphia, Apr. 2.

Gen. **"Mad" Anthony Wayne** made commander in Ohio-Indiana area, trained American Legion, established string of forts. Routed Indians at Fallen Timbers on Maumee River, Aug. 20, **1794**, checked British at Fort Miami, OH, same year.

White House cornerstone laid Oct. 13.

1793

Washington inaugurated for second term, Mar. 4, having received 132 electoral votes; **John Adams** again became vice president, having received second highest total, 77.

Washington declared **U.S. neutrality**, Apr. 22, in war between Britain and France.

Eli Whitney invented **cotton gin**, reviving Southern slavery.

1794

Whiskey Rebellion, western Pennsylvania farmers protesting liquor tax of **1791**, suppressed by federal militia in September.

Jay's Treaty, controversial treaty with Britain negotiated by John Jay, signed Nov. 19, ratified June 24, **1795**. This treaty intended to settle long-standing differences between U.S. and Britain.

1795

U.S. bought peace from **Algerian pirates** by paying $1 mil ransom for 115 seamen Sept. 5, followed by annual tributes.

Gen. Wayne signed **Treaty of Greenville** with Indians, opening Northwest Territory to settlers.

Univ. of North Carolina became **first operating state university**.

1796

Washington's farewell address as president delivered Sept. 17. Warned against permanent alliances with foreign powers, big public debt, large military establishment, and devices of "small, artful, enterprising minority."

1797

John Adams inaugurated as second president Mar. 4, having received 71 electoral votes; **Thomas Jefferson** became vice president, having received 68.

U.S. frigate *United States* launched at Philadelphia, July 10; *Constellation* at Baltimore, Sept. 7; *Constitution* (Old Ironsides) at Boston, Sept. 20.

1798

Alien and Sedition Acts passed by Federalists June-July; intended to silence political opposition.

War with France threatened over French raids on U.S. shipping and rejection of U.S. diplomats. Navy (45 ships) and 365 privateers captured 84 French ships. USS *Constellation* took French warship *Insurgente*, **1799**. Napoleon stopped French raids after becoming first consul.

1800
Federal government moved to **Washington, DC**.

1801
John Marshall named Supreme Court chief justice, Jan. 20.

Thomas Jefferson, who had received same number of electoral votes as Aaron Burr in **1800** election, won out over Burr in House vote reached Feb. 17; Burr named vice president.

Tripoli declared war June 10 against U.S., which refused added tribute to commerce-raiding Arab corsairs. Land and naval campaigns forced Tripoli to negotiate peace, June 4, **1805**.

Oldest U.S. art institution, Pennsylvania Academy of Fine Arts, founded in Philadelphia.

1802
Congress established U.S. Military Academy at **West Point**, NY.

1803
Supreme Court, in *Marbury v. Madison*, overturned U.S. law for first time, Feb. 24.

Napoleon sold all of Louisiana, stretching to Canadian border, to U.S. for $11,250,000 in bonds, plus $3,750,000 indemnities to American citizens with claims against France. U.S. took title Dec. 20. **Louisiana Purchase** doubled U.S. area.

Meriwether Lewis   William Clark

1804
Meriwether Lewis and **William Clark** expedition ordered by Pres. Thomas Jefferson to explore what is now Northwest U.S. Started from St. Louis May 14; ended Sept. 23, **1806**, back in St. Louis.

Vice Pres. **Aaron Burr** shot Alexander Hamilton in duel July 11 in Weehawken, NJ; Hamilton died next day.

1805
U.S. Marines aided by Arab mercenaries, Apr. 27, captured Tripolitan port of Derna. Major victory in war against **Barbary pirates**; inspiration for "to the shores of Tripoli" in Marines Corps song.

1807

Robert Fulton made **first practical steamboat trip**; left New York City Aug. 17, reached Albany, 150 mi away, in 32 hrs.

Embargo Act banned all trade with foreign countries, forbidding ships to set sail for foreign ports Dec. 22.

1808
Slave importation outlawed. Some 250,000 slaves were illegally imported **1808-60**.

Robert Fulton

1810
Third U.S. Census found population of 7,239,814. The slave population was put at 1,191,364, and the population of all other non-white free persons at 186,446.

1811
Indiana Territory governor William Henry Harrison defeated Indians led by Tenskwatawa, called the Prophet, in **Battle of Tippecanoe**, Nov. 7.

Construction began on **Cumberland Road** in Cumberland, MD; road became important route to West.

About 400 **slaves revolted** in Louisiana, killing the son of a plantation owner and marching on New Orleans. The insurrection was suppressed; some 75 slaves killed.

1812
War of 1812 had 3 main causes: Britain seized U.S. ships trading with France; Britain had seized 4,000 naturalized U.S. sailors by **1810**; Britain armed Indians, who raided Western border. U.S. stopped trade with Europe **1807** and **1809**. Trade with Britain only was stopped **1810**.

Unaware that Britain had raised blockade against France two days before, **Congress declared war** June 18.

British took **Detroit** Aug. 16.

1813
Oliver H. Perry defeated British fleet at **Battle of Lake Erie**, Sept. 10. U.S. won **Battle of the Thames**, Ontario, Oct. 5, but failed in Canadian invasion attempts. York (Toronto) and Buffalo were burned.

1814
Troops under Andrew Jackson defeated Creek Indians led by Chief Weatherford at **Battle of Horseshoe Bend** in Alabama, Mar. 29, ending **Creek Indian War**, begun a year earlier.

British landed in Maryland in August, defeated U.S. force Aug. 24, **burned Capitol and White House**. Maryland militia stopped British advance, Sept. 12. British bombardment of Ft. McHenry, Baltimore, for 25 hours, Sept. 13-14, failed, inspiring **Francis Scott Key** to write the words to **"The Star-Spangled Banner."**

U.S. won naval **Battle of Lake Champlain** Sept. 11. Peace treaty with Great Britain signed at Ghent, Dec. 24.

1815
Some 5,300 British, unaware of peace treaty, attacked U.S. entrenchments near **New Orleans**, Jan. 8. British had more than 2,000 casualties; Americans lost 71.

U.S. flotilla finally ended attacks by **pirates from Ottoman states** from Ottoman states of Algiers, Tunis, Tripoli.

1816
Second Bank of the U.S. chartered Apr. 10.

The **American Colonization Society**, which sought to address slavery issue by transporting freed blacks to Africa, formed in Washington, DC, Dec. **1816**-Jan. **1817**.

1817
Thomas Hopkins Gallaudet established the **first free public school for the deaf** in Hartford, CT.

1818
Connecticut **expanded suffrage** among white male voters. Massachusetts followed suit in **1820**, and New York in **1821**, reducing or eliminating property qualifications.

1819
Spain ceded **Florida** to U.S. Feb. 22.

American steamship *Savannah* made **first part-steam-powered, part-sail-powered crossing of Atlantic**, traveling from Savannah,,GA, to Liverpool, England, in 29 days.

Washington Irving's *Sketch Book* became best seller.

1820
First organized immigration of blacks to Africa from U.S. began with 86 free blacks sailing to Sierra Leone in February.

Henry Clay's **Missouri Compromise** bill passed by Congress, Mar. 3. Slavery was allowed in Missouri but not west of the Mississippi River, north of 36°30´ (the southern line of Missouri). Repealed **1854**.

1821
Emma Willard founded Troy Female Seminary, **first U.S. women's college**.

Stephen Austin established **first American community in Texas**, San Felipe de Austin.

James Fenimore Cooper's *The Spy*, novel set during the American Revolution, published and became a best seller.

1822

Tension between sports and academics surfaced when Yale College Pres. Timothy Dwight **banned a primitive form of football**, setting fines for violators.

Emma Willard

1823
Monroe Doctrine, opposing European intervention in the Americas, enunciated by Pres. James Monroe Dec. 2.

The **Hudson River School**, painters who focused on the beauties of nature, began to come to public attention.

1824
Pawtucket, RI, **weavers strike**, first such action by women workers.

Slavery abolished in state of Illinois Aug. 2.

1825
After a deadlocked election, **John Quincy Adams** was elected president by the House, Feb. 9.

Erie Canal opened; first boat left Buffalo Oct. 26, reached New York City Nov. 4.

John Stevens, of Hoboken, NJ, built and operated **first experimental steam locomotive** in U.S.

1826
Thomas Jefferson and **John Adams** both died July 4.
James Fenimore Cooper's *The Last of the Mohicans* published.

1827
Massachusetts became first state to pass a law providing for **tax-supported public high schools**.

1828
Baltimore & Ohio, the **first U.S. passenger railroad**, began operations July 4.
South Carolina Dec. 19 declared right of **state nullification of federal laws**, opposing the "Tariff of Abominations."
Noah Webster published his *American Dictionary of the English Language*.

Noah Webster

1829
Andrew Jackson inaugurated as president, Mar. 4.

1830
Famous **debate** Jan. 27 between Sen. **Daniel Webster** (MA) and Robert Hayne (SC), on state right to nullify federal law.
Mormon church organized by Joseph Smith in Fayette, NY, Apr. 6.
Pres. Jackson, May 28, signed **Indian Removal Act**, providing land and some pay to Indians who agree to resettle in West.

1831
William Lloyd Garrison began **abolitionist newspaper** *The Liberator* Jan. 1.
Nat Turner, black slave in Virginia, led local slave rebellion, starting Aug. 21; 57 whites killed. Troops called in, 100 slaves killed. Turner captured, tried, hanged Nov. 11.

1832
Black Hawk War in Illinois and Wisconsin Apr.-Sept. pushed Sauk and Fox Indians west across Mississippi.

1833
American Anti-Slavery Society founded in Philadelphia, Dec. 4.
Oberlin College became **first to adopt coeducation** in U.S.

1835
Liberty Bell cracked July 8 while tolling death of Chief Justice John Marshall.
Seminole Indians in Florida under Osceola began attacks Nov. 1, protesting forced removal. The unpopular war ended Aug. 14, **1842**; most of the Indians sent to Oklahoma.
Texas proclaimed right to secede from Mexico; **Sam Houston** put in command of Texas army, Nov. 2-4.
Gold discovered on Cherokee land in Georgia. Indians forced to cede lands, Dec. 20, and to cross Mississippi.

1836
Texans besieged at **Alamo** in San Antonio by Mexicans under Santa Anna, Feb. 23-Mar. 6; entire garrison killed. Texas independence declared, Mar. 2. At San Jacinto Apr. 21, Sam Houston and Texans defeated Mexicans.
Ralph Waldo Emerson published his first work, *Nature*, espousing his philosophy of **transcendentalism**.
Marcus Whitman, H. H. Spaulding, and wives reached Fort Walla Walla on Columbia River, OR. **First white women to cross plains**.

1838
Cherokee Indians forced to walk **"Trail of Tears"** from Georgia to Oklahoma starting in October.

1841
First emigrant wagon train bound for California, 47 persons, left Independence, MO, May 1, reached California Nov. 4.
Edgar Allan Poe published one of the **first American detective stories**, *The Murders in the Rue Morgue*.

1842
Webster-Ashburton Treaty signed Aug. 9, fixing U.S.-Canada border in Maine and Minnesota.
First use of anesthetic (sulfuric ether gas).

1843
More than 1,000 settlers left Independence, MO, for Oregon May 22, arriving in October via **Oregon Trail**.

1844
First message over first telegraph line sent May 24 by inventor Samuel F. B. Morse from Washington to Baltimore: "What hath God wrought!"

1845
Congress **overrode a presidential veto for the first time,** Mar. 3, after Pres. John Tyler vetoed a tariff bill.
Congress of **Texas voted for annexation** by U.S., July 4. Texas admitted to Union, Dec. 29.
Edgar Allan Poe's poem "The Raven" published.

1846
Mexican War began after Pres. James K. Polk ordered Gen. Zachary Taylor to seize disputed Texan land settled by Mexicans. After border clash, U.S. declared war May 13; Mexico declared war May 23. About 12,000 U.S. troops took Vera Cruz Mar. 27, **1847**, and Mexico City Sept. 14, **1847**. Treaty signed Feb. 2, **1848**, ended war, and Mexico ceded claims to Texas, California, and other territory.
Bear flag of **Republic of California** raised by American settlers at Sonoma, June 14.
Treaty with Britain June 15 set **Oregon territory boundary** at 49th parallel (extension of existing line). Expansionists had used slogan "54° 40´ or fight." The term **"manifest destiny,"** coined by journalist in **1845**, also came into play.
Mormons, after violent clashes with settlers over polygamy, left Nauvoo, IL, for West under Brigham Young. They settled July **1847** at Salt Lake City, UT.
Elias Howe invented **sewing machine**.

1847
First adhesive U.S. postage stamps—Benjamin Franklin 5¢, Washington 10¢—sold July 1.
Henry Wadsworth Longfellow's *Evangeline* published.

1848
Gold discovered Jan. 24 in California; 80,000 prospectors emigrated in **1849**.
Lucretia Mott and **Elizabeth Cady Stanton** led **Seneca Falls, NY, Women's Rights Convention** July 19-20.

1850
Sen. Henry Clay's **Compromise of 1850** admitted California as 31st state Sept. 9, with slavery

Lucretia Mott

forbidden; made Utah and New Mexico territories; made **Fugitive Slave Law** more harsh; and ended District of Columbia slave trade.
Nathaniel Hawthorne's *The Scarlet Letter* published.

1851
Herman Melville's *Moby-Dick* published.

1852
Harriet Beecher Stowe's *Uncle Tom's Cabin* published.

1853
Japan receives Comm. Matthew C. Perry, July 14. He negotiated **treaty to open Japan** to U.S. ships.
New York City hosted **first World's Fair** in the U.S., beginning July 14.
Stephen Foster published "My Old Kentucky Home."

1854
Republican Party formed at Ripon, WI, Feb. 28. Opposed Kansas-Nebraska Act, which left issue of slavery to vote of settlers. Act became law May 30.
Treaty ratified with Mexico Apr. 25, providing for **Gadsden Purchase** of a strip of land.
Henry David Thoreau's *Walden* published.

1855
First railroad train crossed Mississippi River on river's first bridge, between Rock Island, IL, and Davenport, IA, Apr. 21.
Walt Whitman's *Leaves of Grass* published.

1856
Republican Party's **first presidential nominee, John C. Fremont**, defeated. Abraham Lincoln made 50 speeches for him.
Proslavery group sacked Lawrence, KS, May 21; abolitionist John Brown led antislavery contingent against Missourians at Osawatomie, KS, Aug. 30.
First U.S. kindergarten opened in Watertown, WI.

Walt Whitman

Dred Scott

1857

In **Dred Scott** case, which involved determination of constitutionality of already-repealed Missouri Compromise, Supreme Court decided Mar. 6 that slaves did not become free in a free state, and blacks were not and could not be citizens.

Currier & Ives, firm of American lithographers, issued their first print.

1858

First Atlantic cable completed, by Cyrus W. Field Aug. 5.
Lincoln-Douglas debates in Illinois, Aug. 21-Oct. 15.

1859

Edwin L. Drake drilled the **first commercially productive oil well** near Titusville, PA, Aug. 27.
Abolitionist **John Brown**, with 21 men, seized U.S. Armory at **Harpers Ferry**, WV, Oct. 16. U.S. Marines captured raiders, killing several. Brown was hanged for treason Dec. 2.

1860

Shoeworkers in Lynn, MA, went on strike Feb. 22. Within a week, strike spread to about 20,000 shoeworkers throughout New England in country's **largest strike to date**.
First Pony Express between Sacramento, CA, and St. Joseph, MO, started Apr. 3.
Republican **Abraham Lincoln** elected president Nov. 6 in 4-way race.

1861

Seven southern states set up **Confederate States of America** Feb. 8, with **Jefferson Davis** as president. **Civil War** began as Confederates fired on **Ft. Sumter** in Charleston, SC, Apr. 12. They captured it Apr. 14.
Pres. Lincoln called for 75,000 volunteers Apr. 15. By May, 11 states had **seceded**. Lincoln blockaded Southern ports Apr. 19, cutting off vital exports and aid.
Confederates repelled Union forces at first **Battle of Bull Run**, July 21.
First transcontinental telegraph line put in operation.

1862

Union forces were victorious in Western campaigns, took New Orleans May 1. Battles in East were largely inconclusive despite heavy casualties. The **Battle of Antietam**, in western Maryland Sept. 17, was bloodiest one-day battle of war; each side lost over 2,000 men.
Homestead Act, which granted free farms to settlers, approved May 20.
Land Grant Act, which provided for public land sale to benefit agricultural education, approved July 7. It eventually led to establishment of state university systems.

1863

Pres. Lincoln issued **Emancipation Proclamation** Jan. 1, freeing "all slaves in areas still in rebellion."
Entire Mississippi River was in Union hands by July 4. Union forces won major victory at Gettysburg, PA, July 1-3. Pres. Lincoln gave his **Gettysburg Address** Nov. 19.
Confederate forces under siege surrendered **Vicksburg, MS**, to Union forces under Gen. Ulysses S. Grant, July 4.
About 1,000 were killed or wounded in **draft riots** in New York City; some blacks were hanged by mobs July 13-16.
Pres. Lincoln declared **Thanksgiving** to be a national holiday.

1864

Gen. **William Tecumseh Sherman** marched through Georgia, taking Atlanta Sept. 1 and Savannah Dec. 22.
Sand Creek massacre of Cheyenne and Arapaho Indians Nov. 29. Soldiers drove Indians out of village; about 150 killed.

1865

Gen. **Robert E. Lee surrendered** 27,800 Confederate troops to Gen. Grant at Appomattox Court House in VA, Apr. 9. J. E. Johnston surrendered 31,200 to Sherman at Durham Station, NC, Apr. 18. Last rebel troops surrendered May 26.
Pres. **Lincoln** shot Apr. 14 by **John Wilkes Booth** in Ford's Theater, Washington, DC. Died the following morning. Vice Pres. **Andrew Johnson** was sworn in as president. Booth was hunted down and fatally wounded, perhaps by his own hand, Apr. 26. Four co-conspirators were hanged July 7.
13th Amendment, abolishing slavery, ratified Dec. 6.

1866

Congress took control of Southern **Reconstruction**, backed freedmen's rights in legislation vetoed by Johnson; veto overridden by Congress, Apr. 9.
Ku Klux Klan formed secretly in South to terrorize blacks who voted. Disbanded 1869-71.

1867

Alaska sold to U.S. by Russia for $7.2 mil Mar. 30, through efforts of Sec. of State William H. Seward.
Fraternal society the **Grange** was organized Dec. 4 to protect farmer interests.
Horatio Alger's *Ragged Dick* published.

1868

Pres. Johnson again dismissed Sec. of War Edwin M. Stanton after first dismissing him in **1867**. **Johnson impeached** by the House Feb. 24 for violation of Tenure of Office Act but actually in response to his opposition to congressional Reconstruction. He was acquitted by the Senate March-May.
14th Amendment, providing for citizenship of all persons born or naturalized in U.S. and subject to the jurisdiction thereof, ratified July 9.
Louisa May Alcott's *Little Women* published.
The World Almanac, a publication of the *New York World*, appeared for first time.

1869

Transcontinental railroad completed; golden spike driven at Promontory, UT, May 10, marking junction of Central Pacific and Union Pacific lines.
Attempt to "corner" gold led to financial **"Black Friday"** in New York Sept. 24.
Woman suffrage law passed in Wyoming Territory Dec. 10.
Knights of Labor labor union formed in Philadelphia. By **1886**, it had 700,000 members nationally.

1870

15th Amendment, making race no bar to voting rights, ratified Feb. 8.
First U.S. boardwalk completed, in Atlantic City, NJ.
U.S. Weather Bureau founded.

1871

Great Chicago fire destroyed city Oct. 8-11.
National Rifle Association founded.

1872

Amnesty Act May 22 restored civil rights to citizens of the South, except for 500 Confederate leaders.
Congress established Yellowstone, **first national park**.
James McNeill Whistler painted famous portrait known informally as **"Whistler's Mother."**

1873

First U.S. postal card issued May 1.
Jesse James and his gang robbed their first passenger train July 21.
Banks failed, panic began in September. **Depression** lasted 5 years.
"Boss" William Tweed of New York City was convicted Nov. 19 of stealing public funds. He died in jail in **1878**.
New York's Bellevue Hospital started **first nursing school**.

1874

Women's Christian Temperance Union established in Cleveland.
First public zoo in U.S. established in Philadelphia.

1875

Congress passed **Civil Rights Act** Mar. 1, giving equal rights to blacks in public accommodations and jury duty. Act invalidated in **1883** by Supreme Court.
First Kentucky Derby held May 17.
First **Jim Crow segregation law** enacted, in Tennessee.

1876

Democrat **Samuel J. Tilden** received majority of popular votes for president over Republican **Rutherford B. Hayes**, but 22 electoral votes were in dispute. Congress agreed to certify Hayes as winner in Feb. **1877** after Republicans agreed to end federal Reconstruction of South.
Alexander Graham Bell patented the telephone Mar. 7.

Col. **George A. Custer** and 264 soldiers of the 7th Cavalry were killed June 25 in "last stand," **Battle of the Little Bighorn**, MT, in Sioux Indian War.

1877

Molly Maguires—Irish terrorist society in mining areas of Scranton, PA—was broken up by hanging, June 21, of 11 leaders for murders of mine officials and police.

Pres. Rutherford B. Hayes sent federal troops to control violent national **railroad strike**.

1878

First commercial telephone exchange opened, New Haven, CT, Jan. 28.

Thomas A. Edison founded Edison Electric Light Co. on Oct. 15.

1879

F. W. Woolworth opened his first five-and-ten store, in Utica, NY, Feb. 22.

French actress **Sarah Bernhardt** made her U.S. debut Nov. 8 at New York City's Booth Theater.

Economist and social philosopher **Henry George** published *Progress & Poverty*, advocating single tax on land.

1880

Chinese Exclusion Treaty signed with China, Nov. 17, providing for restitution of Chinese nationals entering U.S.

1881

Clara Barton founded **American Red Cross** May 21.

Pres. **James A. Garfield** shot in Washington, DC, July 2; died Sept. 19.

Famous gun battle between the Earp brothers and outlaw rustlers Oct. 26 near the **OK Corral**, Tombstone, AZ.

Clara Barton

Booker T. Washington founded Tuskegee Institute for blacks.

Helen Hunt Jackson's *A Century of Dishonor*, about mistreatment of Indians, published.

1882

Chinese Exclusion Act, barring Chinese immigration, passed by Congress May 6.

1883

Civil Service Act, or **Pendleton Act**, passed Jan. 16, created foundations of American civil service system.

The **Brooklyn Bridge** opened May 24 as world's longest suspension bridge.

The **Northern Pacific Railroad** was completed Sept. 8.

Buffalo Bill Cody's Wild West Show began its 30-year touring run.

1884

First long-distance telephone call completed, Mar. 27, between Boston and New York.

First roller coaster in U.S. opened at Coney Island in New York City.

Mark Twain's *The Adventures of Huckleberry Finn* published.

1885

Washington Monument dedicated Feb. 21.

1886

Haymarket riot and bombing, May 4, followed labor battles for 8-hour day in Chicago; 7 police and 4 workers died. Eight anarchists found guilty Aug. 20; 4 hanged Nov. 11.

Coca-Cola first sold, May 8, at Jacob's Pharmacy in Atlanta.

Apache Indian **Geronimo** surrendered Sept. 4, ending last major Indian war.

Statue of Liberty dedicated Oct. 28.

American Federation of Labor (AFL) formed Dec. 8 by 25 craft unions.

Geronimo

1887

Interstate Commerce Act enacted Feb. 4, created Interstate Commerce Commission.

1888

Great blizzard struck Eastern U.S. Mar. 11-14, causing about 400 deaths.

Ernest Thayer's poem **"Casey at the Bat"** recited for first time in public at New York City theater in May.

1889

U.S. opened **Oklahoma** to white settlement Apr. 22; within 24 hours claims for 2 mil acres were staked by 50,000 "sooner" settlers.

More than 2,200 lives lost in **Johnstown, PA, flood** May 31.

Electric lights installed at White House.

1890

Sherman Antitrust Act passed July 2, began federal effort to curb monopolies.

Massacre at **Wounded Knee**, SD, Dec. 29, the last major conflict between Indians and U.S. troops. About 200 Indian men, women, and children and 29 soldiers were killed.

Jacob Riis's *How the Other Half Lives*, about city slums, published, instigating reform legislation in New York City.

Emily Dickinson's poems published, 4 years after her death.

1891

Forest Reserve Act, Mar. 3, let president close public forest land to settlement for establishment of national parks.

Carnegie Hall, in New York City, opened May 5.

1892

Ellis Island, in New York Bay, opened Jan. 1 to receive immigrants; closed **1954**.

Homestead, PA, strike at Carnegie steel mills; 7 guards and 11 strikers and spectators shot to death July 6.

James J. Corbett defeated John L. Sullivan Sept. 7 to become **first world heavyweight champion** under Marquess of Queensbury rules.

1893

Columbian Exposition world's fair held May-Oct. in Chicago.

Financial panic led to 4-year **depression**.

Mormon Temple dedicated in Salt Lake City, UT.

1894

Thomas A. Edison's **kinetoscope**, for motion pictures (invented **1887**), given first public showing Apr. 14.

Jacob S. Coxey led army of unemployed from the Midwest, reaching Washington, DC, Apr. 30. Coxey arrested May 1 for trespassing on Capitol grounds; his army disbanded.

Pullman strike began May 11 at railroad car plant in Chicago.

Milton Hershey started **Hershey Chocolate Company**.

1895

"America, the Beautiful" appeared for first time, in church publication, July 4.

Stephen Crane's *The Red Badge of Courage* published.

1896

Supreme Court, in *Plessy v. Ferguson*, May 18, approved racial segregation under the **"separate but equal"** doctrine.

William Jennings Bryan delivered "Cross of Gold" speech July 9; won Democratic Party nomination.

John Philip Sousa composed "Stars and Stripes Forever" on Dec. 25.

1897

Olney-Pauncefote Treaty with Britain, Jan. 11, gave wide scope to arbitration in settling disputes; never ratified by U.S.

John J. McDermott won **first Boston Marathon** Apr. 19.

First Klondike gold arrived in San Francisco July 14, helping set off **Klondike gold rush**.

First subway service in country opens to public in Boston, Sept. 1.

1898

U.S. battleship *Maine* blown up Feb. 15 in Havana, Cuba; 260 killed.

U.S. blockaded Cuba Apr. 22 in aid of independence forces. U.S. declared **war on Spain** Apr. 24; destroyed Spanish fleet in Philippines May 1; took Guam June 20. U.S. took **Puerto Rico** July 25-Aug. 12. Spain agreed Dec. 10 to cede Philippines, Puerto Rico, and Guam, and approved independence for Cuba.

Annexation of **Hawaii** signed by Pres. William McKinley, July 7.

1899

Filipino insurgents, unable to get recognition of independence from U.S., started guerrilla war Feb. 4. Their leader, Emilio Aguinaldo, captured May 23, **1901**. **Philippine insurrection** ended **1902**. Killed were 20,000 Filipino troops and some 200,000 civilians, mostly from disease and starvation.

Pres. McKinley signed treaty officially ending **Spanish-American War**, Feb. 10.

U.S. declared **Open Door Policy** Sept. 6, to make China an open international market.

Philosopher **John Dewey**'s *School and Society*, advocating progressive education ("learn by doing"), published.

Pianist Scott Joplin's "Maple Leaf Rag" published, popularizing **ragtime music**.

1900
International Ladies' Garment Workers Union founded in New York City June 3. Fought sweatshop working conditions.

Carry Nation, Kansas temperance leader, began raiding saloons with a hatchet.

U.S. helped suppress **Boxer Rebellion** in Beijing.

Eastman Kodak Co. introduced the **Brownie camera**, popularizing picture-taking.

1901
Texas had first significant oil strike at **Spindletop** well near Beaumont, Jan. 10.

Pres. **McKinley** shot Sept. 6 in Buffalo, NY, by anarchist Leon Czolgosz; died Sept. 14. Vice Pres. **Theodore Roosevelt** sworn in as **youngest-ever president**, at age 42 years, 11 months.

Booker T. Washington's *Up from Slavery* published.

1902
Permanent **Bureau of the Census** established Mar. 6.

U.S. withdrew troops from **Cuba** May 20, and Cuba became independent.

Helen Keller autobiography appeared in serial form.

1903
Treaty between U.S. and Colombia to have U.S. dig **Panama Canal** signed Jan. 22, rejected by Colombia. Panama declared independence from Colombia with U.S. support Nov. 3; recognized by Pres. Theodore Roosevelt Nov. 6. U.S., Panama signed canal treaty Nov. 18.

Wisconsin set first **direct primary voting system**, May 23.

Henry Ford founded Ford Motor Co., June 16.

Boston defeated Pittsburgh, 5 games to 3, Oct. 13 in **first modern World Series**.

Kitty Hawk, Dec. 17, 1903

First successful flight in heavier-than-air mechanically propelled airplane by **Orville Wright** Dec. 17 near Kitty Hawk, NC, 120 ft. in 12 secs. Later flight same day by **Wilbur Wright**, 852 ft. in 59 secs. Improved plane patented, 1906.

Iroquois Theater fire in Chicago killed about 600 out of 1,900 in audience, Dec. 30.

Pioneering film *Great Train Robbery* produced.

1904
St. Louis hosted **first Olympics in U.S.**, July 1-Nov. 23.

First section of New York subway system opened, Oct. 27.

Ida Tarbell published muckraking *The History of the Standard Oil Company*.

Henry James's last great novel, *The Golden Bowl*, published.

1905
Industrial Workers of the World, which advocated Marxian theory of class struggle between workers and capitalists, founded in Chicago, June 27.

Rotary, oldest service club organization in U.S., founded in Chicago.

1906
San Francisco earthquake and fire, Apr. 18-19, caused more than 3,000 deaths and $400 mil in damages.

Pure Food and Drug Act and **Meat Inspection Act** both passed June 30.

Upton Sinclair's *The Jungle* published.

1907
Financial panic and **depression** started Mar. 13.

Pres. Roosevelt sent **"Great White Fleet"** of 16 U.S. battleships around the world in show of power.

1908
Springfield, IL, torn by **anti-black rioting**, Aug. 14-15.

Henry Ford introduced **Model T** car, priced at $850, Oct. 1.

1909
Adm. Robert E. Peary claimed to have reached **North Pole** Apr. 6 on sixth attempt, accompanied by black explorer Matthew Henson and 4 Inuit; may have fallen short.

Matthew Henson

National Conference on the Negro convened May 30, leading to founding of **National Association for the Advancement of Colored People** (NAACP).

1910
Boy Scouts of America founded Feb. 8.

Former Pres. Roosevelt called for **"new nationalism"** in famous speech in Kansas, Aug. 10.

1911
Building with New York City's **Triangle Shirtwaist Co.** factory caught fire Mar. 25; 146 died.

Supreme Court ruled May 15 that **Standard Oil Co.** must be dissolved because it unreasonably restrained trade.

First transcontinental airplane flight (with numerous stops) by C. P. Rodgers, from New York to Pasadena, CA, Sept. 17-Nov. 5; time in air 82 hrs., 4 mins.

1912
American Girl Guides founded Mar. 12; name changed in **1913** to **Girl Scouts**.

U.S. Marines, Aug. 14, sent to **Nicaragua**, which was in default of loans to U.S. and Europe.

1913
16th Amendment, authorizing federal income tax, ratified Feb. 3.

The **Armory Show** in New York City brought modern art to U.S. for first time, Feb. 17.

17th Amendment, providing for direct popular election of U.S. senators, ratified Apr. 8.

Federal Reserve System authorized Dec. 23, in major reform of U.S. banking and finance.

1914
Ford Motor Co. raised basic wage rates from $2.40 for 9-hr. day to $5 for 8-hr. day, Jan. 5, increasing stability in labor force.

When U.S. sailors were arrested at Tampico, Mexico, Apr. 9, Atlantic fleet was sent to **Veracruz**, occupied city.

Pres. Woodrow Wilson proclaimed **U.S. neutrality** in the European war, Aug. 4.

The **Panama Canal** officially opened Aug. 15.

The **Clayton Antitrust Act** passed Oct. 15, strengthening federal antimonopoly powers.

1915
First transcontinental telephone call, New York to San Francisco, completed Jan. 25 by Alexander Graham Bell and Thomas A. Watson.

Lusitania

British ship *Lusitania* sunk May 7 by German submarine; 1,198 passengers died, including 128 Americans. (In notice in morning newspapers the day *Lusitania* set sail, Germany had warned Americans against taking passage on British vessels.) As result of U.S. campaign, Germany issued apology and promise of payments, Oct. 5. Pres. Wilson asked for a military fund increase, Dec. 7.

U.S. troops landed in **Haiti**, July 28. Haiti became virtual U.S. protectorate under Sept. 16 treaty.

D. W. Griffith's film *The Birth of a Nation* released. William J. Simmons partly inspired by film to revive **Ku Klux Klan**, which peaks in 1920s.

1916
Gen. **John J. Pershing** entered Mexico to pursue **Francisco (Pancho) Villa**, who had raided U.S. border areas. Forces withdrew Feb. 5, **1917**.

Rural Credits Acts passed July 17, followed by **Warehouse Act** Aug. 11; both provided financial aid to farmers.

Bomb exploded during **San Francisco Preparedness Day parade** July 22, killed 10. Thomas J. Mooney, labor organizer, and Warren K. Billings, shoeworker, convicted **1917**; both later pardoned.

U.S. bought **Virgin Islands** from Denmark Aug. 4.

U.S. established military government in the **Dominican Republic** Nov. 29.

Jeannette Rankin (R-MT) elected **first female House Representative**.

1917

Germany, suffering from British blockade, declared almost unrestricted **submarine warfare** Jan. 31. U.S. cut diplomatic ties with Germany Feb. 3 and formally **declared war** Apr. 6.

Jones Act, passed Mar. 2, made **Puerto Rico** a U.S. territory, its inhabitants U.S. citizens.

Conscription law passed May 18. First U.S. troops arrived in Europe June 26.

1918

Pres. Wilson set out his **14 Points** as basis for peace, Jan. 8.

More than 1 mil American troops were in Europe by July. Allied counteroffensive launched at Château-Thierry July 18. War ended with signing of **armistice** Nov. 11.

Influenza epidemic killed an estimated 20 mil worldwide, 548,000 in U.S.

1919

18th Amendment, providing for prohibition of manufacture, sale, or transportation of alcoholic beverages, ratified Jan. 16, to take effect on Jan. 16, **1920**.

First transatlantic flight, by U.S. Navy seaplane, left Rockaway, NY, May 8, stopped at Newfoundland, Azores, Lisbon May 27.

Boston police strike Sept. 9, earliest strike conducted by government employees.

About 250 **foreign-born radicals** deported Dec. 21 to Soviet Union.

Sherwood Anderson's *Winesburg, Ohio* published.

1920

In national **Red Scare**, some 2,700 Communists, anarchists, and other radicals were arrested Jan.-May.

League of Women Voters founded Feb. 14.

Senate refused Mar. 19 to ratify **League of Nations Covenant**.

Nicola Sacco and **Bartolomeo Vanzetti** accused of killing 2 men in Massachusetts payroll holdup Apr. 15. Found guilty **1921**. A 7-year campaign for their release failed; both executed Aug. 23, **1927**. Verdict repudiated **1977** by proclamation of Massachusetts Gov. Michael Dukakis.

19th Amendment ratified Aug. 18, giving women the vote.

First regular licensed radio broadcasting began Aug. 20.

Wall St. bombing in New York City killed 30, injured 100, did $2 mil damage, Sept. 16.

Sinclair Lewis's *Main Street*, **F. Scott Fitzgerald**'s *This Side of Paradise*, and **Edith Wharton**'s *The Age of Innocence* published.

1921

Congress sharply curbed immigration, set **national quota system** May 19.

Joint congressional resolution declaring **peace with Germany, Austria, and Hungary** signed July 2 by Pres. Warren G. Harding; treaties were signed in Aug.

In so-called **Black Sox scandal**, 8 Chicago White Sox players were banned from baseball Aug. 4 for conspiring with gamblers to throw the 1919 World Series.

Limitation of Armaments Conference met in Washington, DC, Nov. 12-Feb. 6, **1922**. Major powers agreed to curtail naval construction, outlaw poison gas, restrict submarine attacks on merchant vessels, and respect China's integrity.

1922

During nationwide coal strike, union miners killed some 21 strike-breakers at Herrin, IL, June 21-22, in incident referred to as the **Herrin Massacre**.

Reader's Digest founded.

T. S. Eliot's *The Waste Land* published in London.

1923

First sound-on-film motion picture, *Phonofilm*, shown at Rivoli Theater, New York City, beginning in April.

Pres. Calvin Coolidge addressed Congress, Dec. 6; **first official broadcast of presidential speech**.

1924

Law approved by Congress June 15 made all **Native Americans U.S. citizens**.

Nellie Tayloe Ross elected governor of Wyoming and **Miriam (Ma) Ferguson** elected governor of Texas Nov. 9. Ross inaugurated as nation's **first female governor** Jan. 5, **1925**. Ferguson installed Jan. 20, **1925**.

George Gershwin wrote "Rhapsody in Blue."

1925

John T. Scopes found guilty of having taught **evolution** in Dayton, TN, high school, fined $100 and costs, July 24.

F. Scott Fitzgerald's *The Great Gatsby* published.

1926

Dr. Robert H. Goddard demonstrated practicality of rockets Mar. 16 in Auburn, MA, with **first liquid-fuel rocket**; rocket traveled 184 ft. in 2.5 secs.

Congress established **Army Air Corps** July 2.

Air Commerce Act passed Nov. 2, established government agencies for development of airports, radio navigation, and other services.

Ernest Hemingway's *The Sun Also Rises* published.

1927

Capt. **Charles A. Lindbergh** left Roosevelt Field, NY, May 20 alone in *Spirit of St. Louis* on first New York-Paris nonstop flight. Reached Le Bourget airfield May 21, 3,610 mi. in 33½ hrs.

The Jazz Singer, **first feature-length film** in which **spoken dialogue was part of narrative action**, released Oct. 6. Noted for line, "You ain't heard nothin' yet!"

Charles A. Lindbergh

Show Boat, Jerome Kern and Oscar Hammerstein II's adaptation of Edna Ferber's novel, opened in New York Dec. 27. Considered musical with first serious libretto.

1928

Amelia Earhart became first woman to fly across the Atlantic, June 17.

Herbert Hoover elected president Nov. 6, defeating New York Gov. Alfred E. Smith, a Catholic.

Amelia Earhart

1929

Gangsters killed 7 rivals in Chicago **St. Valentine's Day massacre** Feb. 14, which won Al Capone control of Chicago's underworld.

Stock market crash Oct. 29 marked end of past prosperity as stock prices plummeted. Stock losses for 1929-31 estimated at $50 bil; beginning of **Great Depression**.

Albert B. Fall, former secretary of the interior, was convicted of accepting $10,000 bribe in leasing of the **Elk Hills (Teapot Dome)** naval oil reserve; sentenced Nov. 1 to a year in prison and fined.

Thomas Wolfe's *Look Homeward, Angel* and **William Faulkner**'s *The Sound and the Fury* published.

1930

London **Naval Reduction Treaty** signed by U.S., Britain, Italy, France, and Japan Apr. 22; in effect Jan. 1, **1931**; expired Dec. 31, **1936**.

Hawley-Smoot Tariff signed; rate hikes slash world trade.

Sinclair Lewis became first American to win a **Nobel Prize in literature**.

1931

Empire State Building opened in New York City May 1, displacing Chrysler Building as world's tallest.

Al Capone convicted of tax evasion Oct. 17.

Pearl Buck's *The Good Earth* published.

1932

Reconstruction Finance Corp. established Jan. 22 to stimulate banking and business. Unemployment at 12 mil.

Nineteen-month-old **Charles Lindbergh Jr.** kidnapped Mar. 1; found dead May 12. Bruno Hauptmann found guilty, Feb. **1935**; executed Apr. 3, **1936**.

Unemployed World War I veterans demanding Congress pay promised bonus early launched **Bonus March** on Washington, DC, May 29.

Franklin D. Roosevelt elected president for first time in Democratic landslide, Nov. 8.

Chicago Bears won **first NFL title game** Dec. 18, defeating the Portsmouth (OH) Spartans, 9-0.

Frances Perkins

1933

Pres. Roosevelt named **Frances Perkins** U.S. secretary of labor; **first woman in U.S. cabinet.**

Pres. Roosevelt ordered **all U.S. banks closed** Mar. 6.

In a "100 days" special session, Mar. 9-June 16, Congress passed **New Deal**, including measures to regulate banks, distribute funds to the jobless, create jobs, raise agricultural prices, and set wage and production standards for industry.

Gold standard dropped by U.S. in favor of "modified gold bullion standard"; announced by Pres. Roosevelt Apr. 19, ratified by Congress June 5.

Tennessee Valley Authority created by act of Congress, May 18.

Prohibition ended in the U.S. as 36th state ratified **21st Amendment** Dec. 5.

Pres. Roosevelt foreswore armed intervention in **Western Hemisphere** nations, Dec. 26.

1934

Pres. Roosevelt signed law creating **Securities and Exchange Commission**, June 6.

U.S. troops pulled out of **Haiti**, Aug. 6.

1935

Works Progress Administration **(WPA)** instituted May 6. Rural Electrification Administration created May 11. National Industrial Recovery Act struck down by Supreme Court May 27.

Boulder Dam (later renamed **Hoover Dam**) completed, May 29.

Social Security Act passed by Congress Aug. 14.

Comedian **Will Rogers** and aviator Wiley Post killed Aug. 15 in Alaska plane crash.

Huey Long, Louisiana senator and national political leader, shot Sept. 8; died Sept. 10.

George Gershwin's jazz opera *Porgy and Bess* opened Oct. 10 in New York.

Committee for Industrial Organization (later Congress of Industrial Organizations) formed to expand industrial unionism Nov. 9.

1936

Jesse Owens won 4 gold medals at the **Berlin Olympics** in August, first American to do so in track-and-field events at single Olympics.

Baseball Hall of Fame founded in Cooperstown, NY.

Margaret Mitchell's *Gone with the Wind* published.

1937

Airship *Hindenburg* caught fire, was destroyed May 6 as it was landing in Lakehurst, NJ.

Golden Gate Bridge opened May 27, becoming suspension bridge with world's longest span.

Joe Louis knocked out James J. Braddock to become world heavyweight champ June 22.

Aviator **Amelia Earhart** and copilot Fred Noonan disappeared July 2 near Howland Island, in the Pacific.

Pres. Roosevelt asked for 6 additional Supreme Court justices; **"packing" plan** defeated.

Auto, steel labor unions won first big contracts.

Zora Neale Hurston's *Their Eyes Were Watching God* published.

1938

National minimum wage enacted June 25.

Orson Welles's radio dramatization of H. G. Wells's *War of the Worlds*, Oct. 30, caused Martian invasion scare.

Seabiscuit beat War Admiral in match race of the century, at Pimlico track, MD, Nov. 1.

Artist Anna Mary Robertson, **"Grandma Moses,"** discovered.

Thornton Wilder's *Our Town* produced on Broadway.

1939

Opera singer **Marian Anderson** performed for integrated crowd of 75,000 at Lincoln Memorial Apr. 9. First Lady Eleanor Roosevelt had quit Daughters of the American Revolution after organization refused to let Anderson sing in DC's Constitution Hall.

New York World's Fair—theme: "The World of Tomorrow"—opened Apr. 30, closed Oct. 31. Reopened for second season May 11, **1940**, ended Oct. 27.

Lou Gehrig, seriously ill, said farewell to fans at Yankee Stadium, July 4.

Albert Einstein alerted Pres. Roosevelt to **A-bomb possibilities** in Aug. 2 letter.

U.S. declared its neutrality in European war Sept. 5.

Pres. Roosevelt proclaimed limited **national emergency** Sept. 8, unlimited emergency May 27, **1941**. Both ended by Pres. Harry Truman, Apr. 28, **1952**.

John Steinbeck's *The Grapes of Wrath* published.

Pocket Books, **first paperback publisher** in U.S., established.

Film versions of *Gone with the Wind* and *The Wizard of Oz* released.

1940

U.S. OK'd sale of **surplus war material** to Britain June 3; announced transfer of 50 overaged destroyers Sept. 3.

First peacetime military draft in U.S. history approved, Sept. 14.

Forty-hour work week went into effect, Oct. 24.

Pres. **Roosevelt** elected Nov. 5 to third presidential term.

Richard Wright's *Native Son* published.

1941

Four Freedoms—freedom of speech and religion, freedom from want and fear—termed essential by Pres. Roosevelt in speech to Congress Jan. 6.

Lend-Lease Act signed Mar. 11 provided $7 bil in military credits for Britain. Lend-lease for USSR approved in Nov.

Pres. Roosevelt signed executive order June 25 barring federal government and war contractors from **racial discrimination**. Order also established Fair Employment Practice Committee.

The **Atlantic Charter**, 8-point declaration of principles, issued by Pres. Roosevelt and British Prime Min. Winston Churchill, Aug. 14.

Pearl Harbor

Japan attacked **Pearl Harbor**, Hawaii, 7:55 AM Hawaiian time, Dec. 7; 19 ships sunk or damaged, 2,300 dead. Pres. Roosevelt called it "a date that will live in infamy." U.S. declared war on Japan Dec. 8. Germany and Italy declared war on U.S. Dec. 11. U.S. responded with declaration of war later on same day. Japanese invaded **Philippines**, Dec. 22; Wake Island fell, Dec. 23.

1942

Japanese troops took **Bataan** peninsula Apr. 8, took **Corregidor** May 6.

Federal government began forcibly moving 110,000 Japanese-Americans from West Coast to **detention camps**. Exclusion lasted 3 years.

Battle of Midway June 4-7 was Japan's first major defeat.

Marines landed on **Guadalcanal** Aug. 7; last Japanese not expelled until Feb. 9, **1943**.

U.S., Britain invaded **North Africa** Nov. 8.

First nuclear chain reaction (fission of uranium isotope U-235) produced at Univ. of Chicago under physicists Arthur Compton, Enrico Fermi, others, Dec. 2.

1943

Oklahoma! opened Mar. 31 on Broadway.

Pres. Roosevelt signed June 10 pay-as-you-go income tax bill. Starting July 1, wage and salary earners were subject to **paycheck withholding tax**.

Detroit race riot June 21 left 34 dead, 700 injured. Six killed in riot in New York City's **Harlem** section Aug. 2.

U.S., Britain invaded **Sicily** July 9, Italian **mainland** Sept. 3.

Marines in Nov. recaptured the **Gilbert Islands**, captured by Japan in **1941** and **1942**.

1944

U.S., Allied forces invaded Europe at Normandy, France, on **"D Day,"** June 6, in greatest amphibious landing in history.

Battle of the Bulge, failed Nazi counteroffensive, waged Dec. 16 to Jan. 28, **1945**.

GI Bill of Rights, providing benefits to veterans, signed by Pres. Roosevelt June 22.

Representatives of the U.S. and other major powers met at **Dumbarton Oaks**, Washington, DC, Aug. 21-Oct. 7, to work out formation of postwar world organization that became the **United Nations.**

U.S. forces landed on **Leyte**, Philippines, Oct. 20.

Pres. **Roosevelt** elected to fourth term as president Nov. 7.

1945

Yalta Conference met in the Crimea, USSR, Feb. 4-11. Pres. Roosevelt, Prime Min. Churchill, and Soviet leader Joseph Stalin agreed that their 3 countries, plus France, would occupy Germany and that the Soviet Union would enter war against Japan.

Marines landed on **Iwo Jima** Feb. 19, won control Mar. 16 after heavy casualties. U.S. forces invaded **Okinawa** Apr. 1, captured it June 21.

Pres. **Roosevelt** died in Warm Springs, GA, Apr. 12; Vice Pres. **Harry S. Truman** became president.

Germany surrendered May 7; May 8 proclaimed **V-E Day**.

First atomic bomb, produced at Los Alamos, NM, exploded at Alamogordo, NM, July 16. Bomb dropped on **Hiroshima** Aug. 6, killing about 75,000; bomb dropped on **Nagasaki** Aug. 9, killing about 40,000. Japan agreed to surrender Aug. 14; formally surrendered Sept. 2.

At **Potsdam Conference**, July 17-Aug. 2, leaders of U.S., USSR, and Britain agreed on disarmament of Germany, occupation zones, war crimes trials.

Empire State Building struck accidentally by Army B-25 bomber, July 28, killing 14.

U.S. forces entered **Korea** south of 38th parallel to displace Japanese Sept. 8.

Gen. **Douglas MacArthur** took over supervision of Japan Sept. 9.

1946

Steel strike by 750,000 started Jan. 21, settled in 4 weeks. Strike by 400,000 **mine workers** began Apr. 1 (settled May 29); other industries (including rail, maritime) followed.

Winston Churchill employed the phrase **"iron curtain"** in Mar. 5 speech at Westminster College in Fulton, MO.

Atomic bomb tested off **Bikini Atoll** in Pacific, July 1. In all, U.S. conducted 23 nuclear tests between 1946 and **1958**.

Philippines given independence by U.S. July 4.

Mother Frances Xavier Cabrini **first American to be canonized**, July 7.

Dr. **Benjamin Spock**'s *Baby and Child Care* published as **baby boom** began.

John Hersey's *Hiroshima* published.

1947

Pres. Truman asked Congress for financial and military aid for Greece and Turkey to help combat Communist subversion **(Truman Doctrine)**, Mar. 12. Approved May 15.

UN Security Council voted Apr. 2 to place under U.S. trusteeship the **Pacific islands** formerly mandated to Japan.

Jackie Robinson joined Brooklyn Dodgers Apr. 11, breaking color barrier in major league baseball.

Jackie Robinson

The **Marshall Plan** for U.S. aid to European countries proposed by Sec. of State George C. Marshall June 5. Congress authorized some $12 bil in next 4 years.

Taft-Hartley Labor Act restricting labor union power vetoed by Pres. Truman June 20; Congress overrode veto.

Air Force Capt. **Chuck Yeager** broke sound barrier, Oct. 14, in X-1 rocket plane.

1948

Organization of American States founded Apr. 30 by 21 countries.

USSR halted all surface traffic into **West Berlin** June 24; in response, U.S. and British troops launched an **airlift**. Soviet blockade halted May 12, **1949**; airlift ended Sept. 30.

Pres. **Truman** elected Nov. 2, defeating Gov. Thomas E. Dewey in historic upset.

Alger Hiss indicted Dec. 15 for perjury, after denying he had passed secret documents to Whittaker Chambers to go to a Communist spy ring. Convicted Jan. 21, **1950**.

Kinsey Report on sexuality in the human male published.

1949

North Atlantic Treaty Organization **(NATO)** established Aug. 24 by U.S., Canada, and 10 Western European nations, agreeing that an armed attack against one would be considered an attack against all.

Eleven leaders of U.S. **Communist Party** convicted Oct. 14 of advocating violent overthrow of U.S. government; sentenced to prison. Supreme Court upheld convictions, **1951**.

Pres. Truman, Oct. 26, signed legislation raising **federal minimum wage** from 40¢ an hour to 75¢.

Arthur Miller's *Death of a Salesman* opened on Broadway.

1950

Masked bandits robbed **Brink's, Inc.**, Boston express office, Jan. 17 of $2.8 mil. Case solved **1956**; 8 sentenced to life.

Pres. Truman authorized production of **H-bomb** Jan. 31.

Sen. **Estes Kefauver** (D-TN) chaired Special Committee to Investigate Organized Crime in Interstate Commerce, organized May 3. Also known as Kefauver Committee.

North Korean forces **invaded South Korea** June 25. UN asked for troops to restore peace. Pres. Truman ordered Air Force and Navy to Korea June 27. Truman approved ground forces, air strikes against North Korea June 30.

U.S. sent 35 military advisers to **South Vietnam** June 27 and agreed to aid anti-Communist government.

Army **seized all railroads** Aug. 27 on Truman's order to prevent general strike; returned to owners in **1952**.

U.S. forces landed at **Inchon**, South Korea, Sept. 15. UN forces took Pyongyang Oct. 20, reached China border Nov. 20; China sent troops across border Nov. 26.

Charles Schulz's *Peanuts* comic strip first appeared in newspapers, Oct. 2.

Two members of **Puerto Rican nationalist movement** tried to kill Pres. Truman Nov. 1.

U.S. banned shipments Dec. 8 to **Communist China** and to Asiatic ports trading with it.

Variety show *Your Show of Shows* debuted on TV.

David Riesman's *The Lonely Crowd* published.

1951

22nd Amendment, limiting presidential term of office, ratified Feb. 27.

Ethel and Julius Rosenberg

Julius Rosenberg, his wife, **Ethel Rosenberg**, and **Morton Sobell** found guilty Mar. 29 of conspiracy to commit wartime espionage. Rosenbergs received death penalty. Sobell sentenced to 30 years; released **1969**.

Pres. Truman removed Gen. **Douglas MacArthur** from Korea command Apr. 11 for unauthorized policy statements.

Korea cease-fire talks began in July; lasted 2 years. Fighting ended July 27, **1953**.

Transcontinental TV began Sept. 4 with Pres. Truman's address at Japanese Peace Treaty Conference in San Francisco.

Japanese peace treaty signed in San Francisco Sept. 8 by U.S., Japan, and 47 other nations.

J. D. Salinger's *Catcher in the Rye* published.

1952

Pres. Truman ordered **seizure of nation's steel mills** Apr. 8 to avert strike. Ruled illegal by Supreme Court June 2.

Peace contract between West Germany, U.S., Great Britain, and France signed May 26.

Last racial and ethnic barriers to naturalization removed, June 26-27, with passage of **Immigration and Naturalization Act of 1952**.

Puerto Rico proclaimed commonwealth July 25, after referendum Mar. 3.

Richard Nixon, as vice-pres. candidate, gave **"Checkers" speech**, so called because of sentimental reference to his dog Checkers, Sept. 23.

First hydrogen device explosion Nov. 1 in Pacific.

Ralph Ellison's *Invisible Man* published.

1953

Federal jury in New York convicted 13 **Communist** leaders on conspiracy charges, Jan. 20.

Julius and Ethel Rosenberg executed in Sing Sing Prison electric chair, Ossining, NY, June 19, for relaying nuclear secrets to Soviet Union.

Korean War armistice signed July 27.

California Gov. **Earl Warren** sworn in Oct. 5 as 14th chief justice of U.S. Supreme Court.

1954

Nautilus, **first atomic-powered submarine**, launched at Groton, CT, Jan. 21.

Five members of Congress were wounded in the House Mar. 1 by 4 **Puerto Rican independence supporters** who fired at random from a spectators' gallery.

At televised Army-McCarthy hearings, Apr. 22-June 17, before a Senate subcommittee, Army officials accused Sen. **Joseph McCarthy** (R-WI) of seeking preferential treatment for a draftee, and McCarthy accused Army of hindering probe of Communist infiltration into Army. McCarthy was cleared in the hearings, but the Senate later voted to condemn him, 67-22, for his abuse of the Senate during hearings and debates.

Supreme Court ruled unanimously May 17 that **racial segregation** was unconstitutional, in *Brown v. Board of Education of Topeka*.

Ernest Hemingway won Nobel Prize in literature for *The Old Man and the Sea*.

1955

U.S. agreed Feb. 12 to help train **South Vietnamese army**.

Rosa Parks

Supreme Court ordered "all deliberate speed" in **integration** of public schools, May 31.

A **summit meeting** of leaders of **Big 4**—U.S., Britain, France, and USSR—took place July 18-23 in Geneva, Switzerland.

Rosa Parks refused Dec. 1 to give her seat to white man on bus in Montgomery, AL. Her arrest, detention, and conviction sparked boycott of bus system, organized by Rev. **Martin Luther King Jr.**, by Montgomery's black community, Dec. 5. Bus segregation ordinance declared unconstitutional by federal court in **1956**. Boycott ended Dec. 23 of that year.

America's 2 largest labor organizations merged Dec. 5, creating **AFL-CIO**.

Russian-born U.S. citizen **Vladimir Nabokov**'s *Lolita* published.

1956

Massive resistance to **Supreme Court desegregation rulings** was called for Mar. 12 by 101 Southern congressmen.

U.S. Supreme Court, Apr. 23, unanimously ruled against **racial segregation** on intrastate buses.

Federal-Aid Highway Act signed June 29, creating **interstate highway system**.

First transatlantic telephone cable activated Sept. 25.

On Oct. 8, in Game 5, Yankee right-hander Don Larsen pitched **only perfect World Series game**.

Eugene O'Neill's *Long Day's Journey into Night*, autobiographical play about dissolution of his family, opened in November on Broadway.

1957

Congress approved **Civil Rights Act of 1957**, Apr. 29, first such bill since Reconstruction to protect voting rights.

The U.S. surgeon general July 12 said studies showed "direct link" between cigarette **smoking and lung cancer**.

Arkansas Gov. Orval Faubus called National Guardsmen Sept. 4 to bar 9 black students from entering all-white high school in **Little Rock**. Faubus complied Sept. 21 with federal court order to remove Guardsmen, but local authorities ordered black students to withdraw. Pres. Eisenhower sent troops Sept. 24 to enforce court order.

Pres. Eisenhower signed **Civil Rights Act** into law Sept. 9. Provided for creation of Civil Rights Commission.

Jack Kerouac's *On the Road* published.

1958

Army launched **first U.S. Earth-orbiting satellite**, *Explorer I*, Jan. 31 from Cape Canaveral, FL; discovered Van Allen radiation belt.

U.S. Marines sent to **Lebanon** to protect elected government from threatened overthrow July-Oct.

Nuclear sub *Nautilus* made **first undersea crossing of North Pole** Aug. 5.

Presidential aide **Sherman Adams** resigned Sept. 22 over scandal involving alleged improper gifts.

First domestic jet airline passenger service in U.S. opened by National Airlines Dec. 10 between New York and Miami.

1959

Alaska admitted as 49th state, Jan. 3; **Hawaii** admitted as 50th, Aug. 21.

Completion of **St. Lawrence Seaway** Apr. 25 allowed passage of oceangoing vessels between Atlantic Ocean and Great Lakes.

Vice Pres. Richard Nixon, on tour of USSR, held **"kitchen debate,"** July 24, with Soviet Prem. Nikita Khrushchev at U.S. exhibit in Moscow.

Prem. **Khrushchev** paid unprecedented visit to U.S. Sept. 15-27; made transcontinental tour.

Pres. Eisenhower issued injunction Oct. 12, upheld and made effective by Supreme Court Nov. 7, ending **record 116-day steel strike**.

In **quiz show scandal**, Columbia Univ. Prof. Charles Van Doren admitted to U.S. House subcommittee Nov. 2 that he had been coached before appearances on NBC-TV's *21* in 1956; he had won $129,000.

1960

Sit-ins began Feb. 1 when 4 black college students in Greensboro, NC, refused to move from a Woolworth lunch counter after being denied service. By Sept. 1961, over 70,000 students, whites and blacks, had participated in sit-ins.

A U.S. **U-2 reconnaissance plane** was shot down in the Soviet Union May 1; pilot Gary Powers captured. The incident led to cancellation of a Paris summit conference.

Pres. Eisenhower signed **Civil Rights Act** May 6.

A **birth control pill** approved as safe for first time by Food and Drug Administration May 9.

Vice Pres. **Richard Nixon** and Sen. **John F. Kennedy** faced each other Sept. 26 in first in series of televised debates. Kennedy defeated Nixon to win presidency, Nov. 8.

U.S. announced Dec. 15 its backing of rightist group in **Laos**, which took power the next day.

1961

U.S. severed diplomatic and consular relations with Cuba Jan. 3, after disputes over nationalizations of U.S. firms, U.S. military presence at Guantanamo base. U.S.-directed invasion of Cuba's **Bay of Pigs** Apr. 17 by Cuban exiles unsuccessfully attempted to overthrow the regime of Prem. Fidel Castro.

Peace Corps created by executive order, Mar. 1.

23rd Amendment, giving DC citizens the right to vote in presidential elections, ratified Mar. 29.

Comdr. Alan B. Shepard Jr. rocketed from Cape Canaveral, FL, in a Mercury capsule May 5, in **first U.S.-crewed suborbital space flight**.

"Freedom Rides" from Washington, DC, across Deep South were launched May 20 to protest segregation in interstate transportation.

John Updike's *Rabbit, Run* and **Joseph Heller**'s *Catch-22* published.

1962

John H. Glenn Jr.

Pres. Kennedy said Feb. 14 that U.S. military advisers in **Vietnam** would fire if fired upon.

Lt. Col. John H. Glenn Jr. became **first American in orbit** Feb. 20 when he circled the Earth 3 times in the Mercury capsule *Friendship 7*.

In *Baker v. Carr*, Mar. 26, Supreme Court ruled that constitutional challenges to unequal distribution of voters among legislative districts could be resolved by federal courts.

James Meredith became first black student at Univ. of Mississippi Oct. 1 after 3,000 troops put down riots.

A Soviet **offensive missile buildup** in Cuba was revealed Oct. 22 by Pres. Kennedy, who ordered naval and air quarantine on shipment of offensive military equipment to the island. He and Soviet Prem. Khrushchev agreed Oct. 28 on formula to end crisis. Kennedy announced Nov. 2 that missile bases in Cuba were being dismantled.

Rachel Carson's *Silent Spring* launched environmentalist movement.

1963

In *Gideon v. Wainwright*, Mar. 18, Supreme Court ruled that all criminal defendants must have counsel.

March for civil rights began May 2 in Birmingham, AL, led to desegregation accord, which in turn sparked rioting and violence.

University of Alabama **desegregated** after Gov. George Wallace stepped aside when confronted by federally deployed National Guard troops June 11.

Civil rights leader **Medgar Evers** assassinated June 12.

Supreme Court ruled June 17 that laws requiring **recitation of Lord's Prayer or Bible verses** in public schools were unconstitutional.

Pres. Kennedy, on Europe trip, addressed huge crowd in **West Berlin**, June 23.

Limited **nuclear test-ban treaty** agreed upon July 25 by the U.S., the Soviet Union, and Britain.

On Aug. 28, 200,000 joined in **March on Washington** in support of black demands for equal rights led by Rev. Martin Luther King Jr.; highlight was King's **"I have a dream" speech.**

Four black girls killed in bombing of **16th St. Baptist Church** in Birmingham, AL, Sept. 15.

South Vietnam Pres. **Ngo Dinh Diem** assassinated Nov. 2; U.S. had earlier withdrawn support.

Pres. **Kennedy** shot and fatally wounded Nov. 22 as he rode in motorcade through downtown Dallas, TX. Vice Pres. **Lyndon B. Johnson** sworn in as president. **Lee Harvey Oswald** arrested and charged with murder; Oswald was shot and fatally wounded Nov. 24. Nightclub owner **Jack Ruby** convicted of Oswald's murder; he died in **1967** while awaiting retrial following reversal of his conviction.

Betty Friedan's feminist work *The Feminine Mystique* published.

1964

Panama suspended relations with U.S. Jan. 9 after riots. U.S. offered Dec. 18 to negotiate new canal treaty.

The Beatles

The Beatles arrived in U.S. for first time; appeared Feb. 9 on *The Ed Sullivan Show*.

Supreme Court ruled Feb. 17 in *Wesberry v. Sanders* that **congressional districts** as near as practicable be equal in population so that "one man's vote in a Congressional election is to be worth as much as another's."

U.S. reported May 27 it was sending military planes to **Laos.**

Three **civil rights workers** reported missing in Mississippi June 22; bodies found Aug. 4. Eighteen white men tried. On Oct. 20, **1967**, an all-white federal jury convicted 7 of conspiracy in the slayings.

Omnibus **civil rights bill** signed by Pres. Johnson July 2, banning discrimination in voting, jobs, public accommodations.

Congress Aug. 7 passed **Tonkin Gulf Resolution**, authorizing presidential action in Vietnam, after North Vietnamese boats reportedly attacked 2 U.S. destroyers Aug. 2.

Congress approved **War on Poverty** bill Aug. 11, providing for a domestic Peace Corps **(VISTA)**, **Job Corps**, and antipoverty funding.

The **Warren Commission** released a report Sept. 27 concluding that Lee Harvey Oswald was solely responsible for the Kennedy assassination.

Pres. **Johnson** elected to full term, Nov. 3, defeating Sen. **Barry Goldwater** (R-AZ) in landslide.

Verrazano-Narrows Bridge opened in New York City Nov. 21, with world's longest suspension span.

1965

In State of the Union address Jan. 4, Pres. Johnson outlined plans for **"Great Society"**, program of civil rights, antipoverty, and health-care legislation.

Pres. Johnson in Feb. ordered continuous bombing of **North Vietnam** below 20th parallel.

Malcolm X assassinated Feb. 21 at New York City rally.

March from Selma to Montgomery, AL, Mar. 21-25, by Rev. Martin Luther King Jr. to demand federal protection of blacks' voting rights. New **Voting Rights Act**, which banned literacy tests and other voter qualification tests, signed Aug. 6.

Some 14,000 U.S. troops sent to **Dominican Republic** during civil war Apr. 28. All troops withdrawn by next year.

Bill establishing **Medicare**, government health insurance program for elderly, signed by Pres. Johnson July 30.

Watts riot by blacks living in that section of Los Angeles resulted in 34 deaths and $200 mil in property damage Aug. 11-16.

National **immigration quota system** abolished Oct. 3.

Electric power failure blacked out most of northeastern U.S., parts of 2 Canadian provinces the night of Nov. 9-10.

1966

U.S. forces began firing into **Cambodia** May 1.

Bombing of **Hanoi** area of North Vietnam by U.S. planes began June 29. By Dec. 31, 385,300 U.S. troops were stationed in South Vietnam, plus 60,000 offshore and 33,000 in Thailand.

Supreme Court ruled June 13, in *Miranda v. Arizona*, that suspects must be read their rights before police questioning.

Medicare began July 1.

In 96-minute shooting rampage, 25-year-old student **Charles Whitman** killed 15 and wounded 31 from atop a tower at the **Univ. of Texas**, Austin, Aug. 1; shot dead by police. Whitman had earlier killed his mother and wife.

Dept. of Transportation created, Oct. 15.

Edward Brooke (R-MA) elected Nov. 8 as **first black U.S. senator** in 85 years.

Robert C. Weaver named secretary of newly created Dept. of Housing and Urban Development, becoming **first black cabinet member.**

1967

Green Bay Packers beat Kansas City Chiefs, 35-10, in **first Super Bowl**, Jan. 15, in Los Angeles.

Three astronauts died Jan. 27 in *Apollo 1* fire on ground at Cape Canaveral, FL.

25th Amendment, providing for presidential succession, ratified Feb. 10.

Rep. **Adam Clayton Powell** (D-NY) was denied seat Mar. 1 because of charges he misused government funds. Seated following reelection in **1968** but was fined and stripped of seniority.

Pres. **Johnson** and Soviet Prem. **Aleksei Kosygin** met June 23 and 25 at **Glassboro State College** in New Jersey; agreed not to let any crisis push them into war.

Riots by blacks in **Newark**, NJ, July 12-17 killed 26, injured 1,500; more than 1,000 arrested. In **Detroit**, MI, July 23-30, 43 died, 2,000 injured; 5,000 left homeless by rioting, looting, and burning in city's black neighborhoods.

Thurgood Marshall sworn in Oct. 2 as **first black Supreme Court justice.**

Antiwar march on Washington, DC, Oct. 21-22, drew 50,000 participants.

Carl B. Stokes (D, Cleveland) and Richard G. Hatcher (D, Gary, IN) elected **first black mayors** of major U.S. cities Nov. 7.

Thurgood Marshall

1968

In **"Tet offensive,"** Communist troops attacked several provincial capitals and other major cities, including Saigon, Jan. 30, but suffered heavy casualties.

Pres. Johnson **curbed bombing** of North Vietnam Mar. 31. Peace talks began in Paris May 10. All bombing of North halted Oct. 31.

Rev. **Martin Luther King Jr.** assassinated Apr. 4 in Memphis, TN. **James Earl Ray**, an escaped convict, pleaded guilty to slaying, was sentenced to 99 years.

Students at **Columbia Univ.**, Apr. 23-24, seized school buildings in protest demonstrations.

Martin Luther King Jr.

Sen. **Robert F. Kennedy** (D-NY) shot June 5 in Los Angeles after celebrating presidential primary victories. Died June 6. **Sirhan Bishara Sirhan** convicted of murder, **1969**; death sentence commuted to life in prison, **1972**.

Vice Pres. **Hubert Humphrey** nominated for president at **Democratic National Convention** in Chicago, marked by clash between police and antiwar protestors, Aug. 26-29. Republican nominee **Richard Nixon** won presidency, defeating Humphrey in close race Nov. 5.

Apollo 8 orbited moon in 5-day mission, Dec. 21-27.

USS *Pueblo* and 83-man crew seized in Sea of Japan Jan. 23 by North Koreans; 82 men released Dec. 22.

1969

Expanded 4-party **Vietnam peace talks** began Jan. 18. U.S. force peaked at 543,400 in April. Withdrawal started July 8. Pres. Nixon set Vietnamization policy Nov. 3.

Earl Warren retired upon swearing in **Warren Burger**, June 23, as Supreme Court chief justice.

In incident that marked birth of gay rights movement, police clashed with patrons of gay bar, the **Stonewall** Inn, in New York City June 27.

U.S. astronaut **Neil Armstrong**, commander of the *Apollo 11* mission, became the **first person to set foot on the moon**, July 20, followed by astronaut **Edwin "Buzz" Aldrin**. Astronaut **Michael Collins** remained aboard command module.

Woodstock rock music festival near Bethel, NY, drew 300,000-500,000 people, Aug. 15-18.

Anti—Vietnam War demonstrations held in cities across the U.S., marking Vietnam Moratorium day, Oct. 15; on Nov. 15, some 250,000 marched in Washington, DC.

Massacre of hundreds of civilians by U.S. troops at **My Lai**, South Vietnam, in **1968** reported Nov. 16.

Sesame Street launched on public TV.

Kurt Vonnegut Jr.'s *Slaughterhouse Five* published.

1970

A federal jury Feb. 18 found the **"Chicago 7"** antiwar activists innocent of conspiring to incite riots during **1968** Democratic National Convention. However, 5 were convicted of crossing state lines with intent to incite riots.

Three astronauts safely returned to Earth Apr. 17 after oxygen tank on *Apollo 13* ruptured. Lunar landing cancelled.

Millions of Americans participated in antipollution demonstrations Apr. 22 to mark **first Earth Day**.

U.S. and South Vietnamese forces crossed **Cambodian** borders Apr. 30 to get at enemy bases.

Four students killed May 4 at **Kent State Univ.** in Ohio by National Guardsmen during war protest. In protest at **Jackson State Univ.** in Mississippi, 2 killed when police fired on protesters.

Anna Mae Hayes of Army Nurse Corps and Elizabeth P. Hoisington, director of Women's Army Corps, became **first female generals** June 11.

Postal reform measure signed Aug. 12 created an independent U.S. Postal Service.

Pres. Nixon, Dec. 31, signed **clean air bill** calling for development of cleaner auto engine and national air quality standards for 10 major pollutants.

Garry Trudeau's *Doonesbury* comic strip launched in 30 papers.

1971

Charles Manson and 3 of his cult followers found guilty Jan. 25 of first-degree murder in **1969** slaying of actress Sharon Tate and 6 others.

A court-martial jury Mar. 29 convicted Lt. William L. Calley Jr. in murder of 22 South Vietnamese at **My Lai** on Mar. 16, **1968**. He was sentenced to life in prison Mar. 31, later reduced to 20 years.

Pres. Nixon, Apr. 14, relaxed 20-year **trade embargo with China**.

26th Amendment, lowering the voting age to 18 in all elections, ratified June 30.

New York Times began publishing June 13 classified **Pentagon Papers**, secret Pentagon study on U.S. involvement in Vietnam. Supreme Court June 30 upheld, 6-3, right of the *Times* and *Washington Post* to publish the documents.

Pres. Nixon, Aug. 15, instituted 90-day **wage and price freeze**.

U.S. bombers initiated massive 5-day strike Dec. 26 in North Vietnam in retaliation for alleged violations of agreements reached prior to **1968** bombing halt.

1972

Pres. Nixon arrived in **Beijing** Feb. 21 for 8-day visit to China, in "journey for peace." Joint communiqué released Feb. 27 called for increased Sino-U.S. contacts.

Senate, Mar. 22, approved **Equal Rights Amendment** banning discrimination on basis of sex; sent measure to states for ratification.

North Vietnamese forces launched biggest attacks in 4 years across the demilitarized zone Mar. 30. The U.S. responded Apr. 15 with **resumption of bombing** of Hanoi and Haiphong after 4-year lull. Pres. Nixon announced May 8 the mining of North Vietnam ports. Last U.S. combat troops left Aug. 11.

Gov. **George C. Wallace** (D-AL), campaigning for president at Laurel, MD, shopping center May 15, shot and seriously wounded. **Arthur Bremer** convicted Aug. 4, sentenced to 63 years for shooting Wallace and 3 others.

In **first visit of U.S. president to Moscow**, Pres. Nixon arrived May 22 for summit talks with Kremlin leaders that culminated in landmark strategic arms pact (**SALT I**).

Five men arrested June 17 for breaking into Democratic National Committee offices in **Watergate** office complex in Washington, DC.

Supreme Court in *Furman v. Georgia* June 29 ruled **capital punishment** as currently practiced was unconstitutional.

Mark Spitz won 7 gold medals in world record times at the Munich Olympics in Aug.-Sept.

Billie Jean King defeated Bobby Riggs in 3 straight sets in tennis's nationally televised "Battle of the Sexes," Sept. 20.

Pres. **Nixon** reelected Nov. 7 in landslide, carrying 49 states to defeat Sen. George McGovern (D-SD).

Three astronauts, part of *Apollo 17*, made sixth and last lunar landing on Dec. 11.

Full-scale **bombing of North Vietnam** resumed after Paris peace negotiations reached impasse Dec. 18.

1973

Five of 7 defendants in **Watergate** break-in trial pleaded guilty Jan. 11 and 15; the other 2 were convicted Jan. 30.

In *Roe v. Wade*, Supreme Court ruled, 7-2, Jan. 22, fetus not a person with constitutional rights and that right to privacy protected woman's decision to have abortion; states may not ban abortions during first 3 months of pregnancy and may regulate, but not ban, abortions during second trimester.

Four-party **Vietnam peace pact** signed in Paris Jan. 27, and North Vietnam released some 590 U.S. prisoners by Apr. 1. Last U.S. troops left Mar. 29.

End of military draft announced Jan. 27.

Pres. Nixon announced, Apr. 30, resignation of top Nixon aides **H. R. Haldeman** and **John D. Ehrlichman** and Attorney Gen. **Richard G. Kleindienst**, firing of White House Counsel **John W. Dean III**, as a consequence of the widening Watergate scandal.

Skylab, **first U.S. space station**, launched May 14.

Secretariat became first Triple Crown winner since Citation in 1948 by winning Belmont Stakes June 9 in record time.

John Dean told Senate hearings June 25 that Pres. Nixon, his staff and campaign aides, and the Justice Dept. had conspired to cover up **Watergate** facts.

The U.S. officially ceased bombing in **Cambodia** at midnight Aug. 14 in accord with June congressional action.

Vice Pres. **Spiro Agnew**, Oct. 10, resigned and pleaded no contest to charge of tax evasion on payments made to him by contractors when he was Maryland governor. **Gerald R. Ford**, Oct. 12, became **first appointed vice president** under 25th Amendment; sworn in Dec. 6.

A total **ban on oil exports** to U.S. was imposed by Arab oil-producing nations Oct. 19-21 after outbreak of an Arab-Israeli war. Ban was lifted Mar. 18, **1974**.

The **"Saturday Night Massacre"** occurred Oct. 20, when Pres. Nixon ordered Attorney Gen. **Elliot Richardson** to fire Watergate special prosecutor **Archibald Cox**, who had sought handover of Nixon's subpoenaed White House tapes. Richardson refused to comply and resigned; Dep. Attorney Gen. **William Ruckelshaus** refused and was fired. Solicitor Gen. **Robert Bork**, as acting attorney gen., then fired Cox. Nixon administration named **Leon Jaworski**, Nov. 1, to succeed Cox.

Congress overrode Nov. 7 Pres. Nixon's veto of **war powers bill**, which curbed president's power to commit forces to hostilities abroad without congressional approval.

1974

On Apr. 8, **Hank Aaron** of the Atlanta Braves hit his 715th career home run to break Babe Ruth's record.

House Judiciary Committee opened **impeachment** hearings May 9 against Pres. Nixon.

John D. Ehrlichman and 3 **White House "plumbers"** found guilty July 12 of conspiring to violate the civil rights of the psychiatrist of Pentagon Papers leaker Daniel Ellsberg by breaking into psychiatrist's office.

Supreme Court ruled, 8-0, July 24 that Pres. Nixon had to turn over 64 **tapes of White House conversations**.

House Judiciary Committee, in televised hearings July 24-30, recommended 3 **articles of impeachment** against Pres. Nixon, involving conspiracy to obstruct justice in Watergate cover-up, abuses of power, and defiance of committee subpoenas. The House voted Aug. 20, 412-3, to accept the committee report, which included the impeachment articles.

Pres. **Nixon** announced his **resignation**, Aug. 8, and stepped down the next day. His support in Congress had begun to collapse Aug. 5, after release of tapes appearing to implicate him in Watergate cover-up. Vice Pres. **Ford** sworn in Aug. 9 as 38th U.S. president.

Pres. Ford, Aug. 20, nominated **Nelson Rockefeller** to be vice president; Rockefeller sworn in Dec. 10.

Pres. Ford, Sept. 8, issued **pardon** to ex-Pres. Nixon for any federal crimes he committed while president.

1975
Former Atty. Gen. John Mitchell and ex-presidential advisers H. R. Haldeman and John Ehrlichman found guilty Jan. 1 of **Watergate cover-up** charges. Mitchell released **1979**, last of 25 jailed over scandal to leave prison.

U.S. launched **evacuation from Saigon** of Americans and some South Vietnamese Apr. 29 as Communist forces completed takeover of South Vietnam; Government of **South Vietnamese** government officially surrendered Apr. 30.

U.S. merchant ship *Mayaguez* and its crew of 39 seized by Cambodian forces in Gulf of Siam May 12. In rescue operation, U.S. Marines attacked Tang Island, planes bombed air base; Cambodia surrendered ship and crew.

Congress voted $405 mil for **South Vietnam refugees** May 16; 140,000 flown to U.S.

Illegal CIA operations described by panel headed by Vice Pres. Rockefeller June 10.

Publishing heiress **Patricia (Patty) Hearst**, kidnapped Feb. 5, **1974**, by Symbionese Liberation Army, captured in San Francisco Sept. 18 with other militants. She was convicted Mar. 20, **1976**, of bank robbery.

1976
In **"right to die"** case, New Jersey Supreme Court, Mar. 31, allowed comatose Karen Ann Quinlan to be removed from respirator. She survived, dying in nursing home in **1985**.

Supreme Court reinstated **death penalty**, July 2, subject to conditions.

U.S. celebrated **200th anniversary of independence** July 4 with festivals, parades, and New York City's Operation Sail, gathering of tall ships from around the world.

"Legionnaire's disease" killed 29 people who attended American Legion convention July 21-24 in Philadelphia.

Viking II set down on Utopia Plains of **Mars** Sept. 3, following successful landing by *Viking I* on Chryse Plains, July 20.

Two U.S. officers on routine mission near DMZ slain by **North Korean soldiers** Aug. 18; North Korea stated "regret," Aug. 21.

1977
Convicted murderer Gary Gilmore executed by Utah firing squad Jan. 17; **first use of capital punishment** in U.S. since **1967**.

Pres. Jimmy Carter Jan. 21 pardoned most Vietnam War **draft evaders**.

Natural gas shortage caused by severe winter weather led Congress Feb. 2 to approve emergency gas bill temporarily authorizing reallocation of interstate gas from surplus areas to shortage areas.

Pres. Carter signed act Aug. 4 creating new cabinet-level **energy department**.

FBI Dec. 7 released 40,000 pages of previously secret files relating to **Kennedy assassination**.

George Lucas's **first** *Star Wars* **film** produced.

1978
Senate voted, Apr. 18 to turn over **Panama Canal** to Panama on Dec. 31, **1999**; Mar. 16 vote had given approval to treaty guaranteeing area's neutrality after the year **2000**.

Californians, June 6, approved **Proposition 13**, state constitutional amendment slashing property taxes.

Supreme Court, June 28, ruled that special admissions program—under which set number of places reserved for minorities—violated civil rights act, which forbids anyone from being excluded from federally funded program because of race, in *Regents of the Univ. of California v. Bakke.*

Egyptian Pres. **Anwar al-Sadat** and Israeli Prem. **Menachem Begin** reached accord on "framework for peace," Sept. 17, after Pres. Carter-mediated talks at **Camp David**.

New York's Chemical Bank Dec. 20 initiated industry-wide move to raise **lending rate** to near-record 11.75%.

1979
Partial meltdown released radioactive material Mar. 28 at nuclear reactor on **Three Mile Island** near Middletown, PA.

American Airlines DC-10 **jetliner crashed** May 25 after takeoff from Chicago, killing 275 people.

In speech July 15, Pres. Carter spoke of national "crisis of confidence" and outlined proposed 10-year $140 bil program to **reduce dependence on foreign oil.**

Three Mile Island

Militant followers of **Ayatollah Khomeini** took hostage some 90 people, including 66 Americans, Nov. 4 at **American embassy in Tehran**, Iran. Khomeini demanded return of former Shah Muhammad Reza Pahlavi, who was undergoing medical treatment in New York City.

1980
Pres. Carter announced, Jan. 4, economic sanctions against USSR in retaliation for Soviet invasion of Afghanistan. At Carter's request, U.S. Olympic Committee voted, Apr. 12, against U.S. participation in **Moscow Summer Olympics.**

Lake Placid, NY, hosted the **Winter Olympics** for the second time. The U.S. hockey team defeated heavily favored Russian team Feb. 22 en route to winning gold medal.

Eight Americans killed and 5 wounded, Apr. 24, in **ill-fated hostage rescue attempt** held by Iranian militants.

Mt. St. Helens, in Washington state, erupted May 18. The blast, with others May 25 and June 12, left 57 dead.

In sweeping victory, Nov. 4, **Ronald Reagan** (R) was elected 40th president, defeating incumbent Pres. Carter. Republicans gained control of Senate.

Former Beatle **John Lennon** was shot and killed by **Mark David Chapman**, Dec. 8, in New York City.

1981
Minutes after Reagan's inauguration Jan. 20, 52 **American hostages in Iran** were freed after being held for 444 days.

Pres. **Reagan** was shot and seriously wounded, Mar. 30, in Washington, DC; also seriously wounded were a Secret Service agent, a policeman, and Press Sec. **James Brady. John W. Hinckley Jr.** arrested, found not guilty by reason of insanity in **1982**, committed to mental institution.

World's **first reusable spacecraft**, space shuttle *Columbia*, sent into space, Apr. 12. It performed its first operational mission in **1982**.

Members of the **Professional Air Traffic Controllers Organization**, Aug. 3, went on strike. Most defied a back-to-work order and were dismissed by Pres. Reagan Aug. 5 for violating federal law.

Pres. Reagan signed into law Aug. 13 **tax-cut legislation**, expected to save taxpayers $750 bil over 5 years, largest tax cut to date.

The Senate confirmed, Sept. 21, appointment of **Sandra Day O'Connor** as **first female Supreme Court justice.**

Sandra Day O'Connor

1982
The 13-year-old Justice Dept. lawsuit against **AT&T** was settled Jan. 8. AT&T agreed to give up 22 Bell System companies and was allowed to expand.

Equal Rights Amendment, sent to states in **1972**, defeated when deadline for ratification passed June 30 with only 35 of 38 necessary number of states supporting amendment.

Centers for Disease Control, July 16, reported evidence of growing **AIDS epidemic**, responsible for 184 deaths in country since first reported in U.S. in June **1981**.

The economy showed signs of recovery from **recession** that began in mid-**1981**, as Dow Jones Industrial Average hit 1016.93 Oct. 13, its highest level in 18 months.

NFL strike ended Nov. 16 after 57 days when players and team owners settled with $1.6 bil pact.

Retired dentist Dr. Barney B. Clark became **first permanent artificial heart recipient**, Dec. 2; he died Mar. 23, **1983**.

The House, Dec. 16, cited EPA administrator Anne Gorsuch for contempt after refusing to produce certain documents concerning the **Superfund**, law that established fund for cleanup and authorized prosecution of hazardous waste dumpers.

1983

Pres. Reagan, Jan. 3, declared Times Beach, MO, a federal disaster area because of toxic **dioxin** in soil.

Harold Washington elected Apr. 12 as **first black mayor of Chicago.**

On Apr. 20, Pres. Reagan signed compromise bipartisan bill designed to save **Social Security** from bankruptcy.

Sally Ride became **first American woman to travel in space**, June 18, when space shuttle *Challenger* launched from Cape Canaveral, FL.

On Sept. 1, **South Korean passenger jet** infringing on Soviet air space and apparently misidentified was shot down; 269 people, including 61 Americans, killed.

On Oct. 23, 241 U.S. Marines and sailors were killed when TNT-laden **suicide truck bomb** blew up Marine barracks at **Beirut** International Airport in Lebanon.

U.S. troops, with small force from 6 Caribbean nations, invaded **Grenada** Oct. 25. After a few days, Grenadian militia and Cuban "construction workers" were overcome, U.S. citizens were evacuated, and the Marxist regime was deposed.

1984

Seven regional companies took over **local telephone service** from AT&T, Jan. 1.

On space shuttle *Challenger*'s fourth trip, launched Feb. 3, two astronauts became **first humans to fly free of a spacecraft.**

On May 7, Vietnam War veterans reached out-of-court settlement with 7 chemical companies in class-action suit over the herbicide **Agent Orange.**

Former Vice Pres. **Walter Mondale** won Democratic presidential nomination, June 6. He chose Rep. **Geraldine Ferraro** (D-NY) as vice presidential candidate, first woman to be nominated for position by major political party.

Pres. Reagan signed bill July 17 cutting federal transportation aid to states that keep their **drinking age** under 21.

Pres. **Reagan** reelected Nov. 6 in Republican landslide, carrying 49 states for record 525 electoral votes.

Bernhard Goetz shot and wounded 4 allegedly menacing teenage boys on NYC subway train, Dec. 22; later acquitted of major charges but was successfully sued.

1985

Visiting Germany, Pres. Reagan, May 5, laid wreath at Bergen-Belsen Nazi concentration camp site and also at military cemetery at **Bitburg**, where some Nazis were buried.

Philadelphia police bombed a rowhouse occupied by **MOVE** radical group, May 13; 11 killed, and fire damaged 2 blocks of houses.

On June 14, **terrorists seized TWA jet** after takeoff from Athens, Greece, with 153 passengers and crew. Thirty-nine Americans held hostage for 17 days; 1 U.S. service member killed.

Reversing an earlier decision to market "new" Coke, the **Coca-Cola Co.** said, July 10, it would resume marketing soda made under its original "Classic" formula.

Live Aid, a rock concert broadcast around the world July 13, raised $70 mil for starving peoples of Africa.

On Oct. 7, 4 **Palestinian hijackers** seized Italian cruise ship *Achille Lauro* in the Mediterranean for 2 days. One American, **Leon Klinghoffer**, was killed.

For first time in 6 years U.S. and Soviet leaders met at **summit in Geneva**, Nov. 19-20.

General Electric agreed Dec. 11 to buy RCA Corp. for $6.28 bil, largest merger to date outside oil industry.

1986

The U.S. officially observed **Martin Luther King Jr. Day** for the first time Jan. 20.

Space shuttle *Challenger* exploded 73 seconds after liftoff, Jan. 28, killing 6 astronauts and Teacher in Space Project participant Christa McAuliffe.

In 4-day extravaganza in July, the U.S. celebrated 100th birthday of the **Statue of Liberty.**

The Senate confirmed, Sept. 17, Reagan's nomination of William **Rehnquist** as chief justice and **Antonin Scalia** as associate justice of Supreme Court.

Congress completed action Oct. 2 overriding a veto to place economic sanctions on **South Africa**.

Space Shuttle Challenger

Lebanese newspaper first broke news of **Iran-Contra scandal** Nov. 3, involving secret U.S. sale of arms to Iran and use of some proceeds to support right-wing Nicaraguan guerrilla movement.

Ivan Boesky, accused of insider trading, agreed Nov. 14 to pay $100 million in fines and illicit profits and to plead guilty to an unspecified criminal count. Largest penalty to date imposed for insider trading.

Robert Penn Warren named America's **first poet laureate** by the Library of Congress.

1987

Pres. Reagan produced nation's **first trillion-dollar budget**, Jan. 5.

Dow Jones closed above 2,000 for first time, Jan. 8.

The FDA approved, Mar. 20, AZT—first drug shown to be effective in **fight against AIDS**.

Nearly 1.4 mil **illegal aliens** met May 4 deadline for applying for **amnesty** under new federal policy.

Joint public hearings by Senate and House committees investigating **Iran-Contra affair** opened May 5. Lt. Col. **Oliver North**, former National Security Council staff member, said he had believed all his activities were authorized by his superiors. Hearings end Aug. 3. Pres. Reagan, Aug. 12, denied knowing of diversion of funds to contras.

An **Iraqi missile** killed 37 sailors on the USS *Stark* in the Persian Gulf, May 17. Iraq called it an accident.

The 200th anniversary of **U.S. Constitution** signing was observed, Sept. 17, in Philadelphia and around the U.S.

Stock market crashed, Oct. 19, with the Dow Jones plummeting a record 508 points to 1,738, ending bull market that began mid-**1982**.

Pres. Reagan and Soviet leader Mikhail Gorbachev Dec. 8, signed **pact to dismantle** all 1,752 U.S. and 859 Soviet **missiles** with 300- to 3,400-mi. range.

1988

In report issued May 16, Surgeon Gen. C. Everett Koop declared **cigarettes addictive**.

Congress approved, in June, greatest expansion yet of **Medicare** benefits, to protect the elderly and disabled against "catastrophic" medical costs. The act was repealed in November **1989**.

Much of U.S. suffered **worst drought** in over 50 years; by late June half the nation's agricultural counties had been declared disaster areas.

A missile, fired from U.S. Navy warship *Vincennes* in the Persian Gulf, mistakenly struck a commercial **Iranian airliner**, July 3, killing all 290 aboard.

George H. W. Bush (R) elected 41st U.S. president, Nov. 8, decisively defeating Massachusetts Gov. **Michael Dukakis** (D).

Pan Am Flight 103 exploded and crashed, due to terrorist bomb, into town of **Lockerbie, Scotland**, Dec. 21, killing all 259 people aboard and 11 on the ground.

Drexel Burnham Lambert agreed, Dec. 21, to plead guilty to insider trading and other violations, and pay penalties of $650 mil, largest such settlement ever.

1989

Major oil spill occurred when *Exxon Valdez* struck Bligh Reef in Alaska's Prince William Sound, Mar. 24.

Oliver North convicted, May 4, on charges related to **Iran-Contra scandal**. Conviction thrown out on appeal in **1991** because of his immunized testimony.

A measure to rescue **savings and loan industry** signed into law, Aug. 9, by Pres. Bush, launching largest federal rescue to date.

Army Gen. **Colin Powell** became **first black chairman of Joint Chiefs of Staff** after being nominated Aug. 10 by Pres. Bush.

Baseball legend **Pete Rose** banned from game for life Aug. 24 for involvement with gamblers.

Hurricane Hugo swept through the Caribbean and the Carolinas Sept. 10-22, causing at least 86 deaths and $7 bil in damage in the Carolinas alone.

Just before a World Series game, Oct. 17, an **earthquake** struck the San Francisco Bay area, causing 63 deaths.

L. Douglas Wilder (D) declared governor of Virginia Nov. 27, **first elected black governor** of state in U.S. history.

U.S. troops **invaded Panama**, Dec. 20, overthrowing the government of **Manuel Noriega**. Noriega, wanted by U.S. authorities on drug charges, surrendered Jan. 3, **1990**.

1990

Junk bond financier **Michael Milken** pleaded guilty to fraud-related charges, Apr. 14; agreed to pay $500 mil in restitution; sentenced Nov. 21 to 10 years in prison.

Justice **William Brennan** announced, July 20, resignation from U.S. Supreme Court. His replacement, Judge **David Souter**, confirmed Sept. 27.

Pres. Bush signed **Americans with Disabilities Act**, barring discrimination against the disabled, July 26.

Operation Desert Shield forces left for Saudi Arabia Aug. 7, to defend that country following invasion of **Kuwait** by Iraq, Aug. 2.

Pres. Bush Nov. 15 signed into law **Clean Air Act**, strengthened version of Clean Air Act of **1970**; focus on urban pollution, cancer-causing emissions from industrial sources.

1991

The U.S. and its allies defeated Iraq in **Persian Gulf War** and liberated Kuwait, which Iraq had invaded the previous year. On Jan. 17, the allies launched a devastating air attack. In rapid ground war starting Feb. 24, which lasted just 100 hours, U.S.-led forces killed or captured thousands of Iraqi soldiers and sent the rest into retreat before Pres. Bush ordered ceasefire Feb. 27.

An 8-month **recession** showed signs of having ended in Mar. The **Dow Jones** Industrial Average closed above 3,000 for first time, Apr. 17.

House Speaker announced Oct. 3 closure of **House Bank** by end of year after revelations that House members had written 8,331 bad checks worth hundreds of thousands of dollars.

Justice **Thurgood Marshall**, first black to sit on U.S. Supreme Court, announced, June 17, plans to retire. Senate approved, Oct. 15, nomination of **Clarence Thomas** to replace Marshall, despite allegations of sexual harassment against him by former aide Anita Hill. Thomas became second black person to serve on Court.

Hurricane Andrew

1992

Retail giant **R.H. Macy & Co.** filed for bankruptcy, Jan. 27. Major U.S. carrier Trans World Airlines (**TWA**), filed for bankruptcy, Jan. 31.

Riots swept South Central **Los Angeles** Apr. 29 after jury acquitted 4 white police officers on all but one count in **1991** videotaped beating of black motorist **Rodney King**. Death toll in L.A. violence was put at 52.

27th Amendment, regarding congressional pay raises, ratified May 7.

Hurricane Andrew ravaged South Florida and Louisiana Aug. 24-26, causing 65 deaths.

White supremacist and fugitive Randall Weaver surrendered Aug. 31 after 11-day FBI **siege** at his **Ruby Ridge**, ID, cabin, during which his wife, son, and a deputy sheriff were killed in exchanges of gunfire.

Bill Clinton (D) elected 42nd president, Nov. 3, defeating Pres. **Bush** (R) and independent **Ross Perot**.

A UN-sanctioned military force, led by U.S. troops, arrived in **Somalia** Dec. 9.

Presidents of U.S., Canada, and Mexico Dec. 17 signed **North American Free Trade Agreement** (NAFTA), which took effect Jan. 1, **1994**.

More than 1.1 mil votes were cast to choose portrait of the late **Elvis Presley** for **postage stamp**, first in the U.S. to honor a rock performer.

1993

A bomb exploded in a parking garage beneath the **World Trade Center** in New York City, Feb. 26, killing 6 people. Four men found guilty, Mar. 4, **1994**. Two Islamic militants convicted in bombing, Nov. 12, **1997**.

Four federal agents killed, Feb. 28, during an unsuccessful raid on **Branch Davidian** compound near **Waco**, TX. A 51-day siege by agents ended Apr. 19, when the compound burned down, leaving more than 70 cult members dead. Eleven cult members acquitted Feb. 26, **1994**, of charges in deaths of the federal agents. U.S. agents cleared of wrongdoing in **2000**.

Janet Reno became **first female attorney general** Mar. 12.

Federal jury, Apr. 17, found 2 Los Angeles police officers guilty and 2 not guilty of violating civil rights of motorist **Rodney King** in **1991** videotaped beating. Mostly white state jury had acquitted 4 of the officers on all charges in **1992**, sparking riots in L.A. and other cities. State charge against fourth officer had been dropped when federal charges leveled against all 4 that same year.

Defense Sec. Les Aspin, Apr. 28, removed restrictions on **aerial combat roles for women** in the armed forces.

In a May 14 plebiscite, voters in **Puerto Rico** supported continuing commonwealth status with U.S.

"Motor-voter" bill was signed by Pres. Clinton, May 20, allowing citizens to register to vote by mail when applying for a driver's license or certain benefits.

The **"Great Flood of 1993"** inundated at least 15 mil acres in 9 Midwestern states in summer, leaving 50 dead and $15 bil in damages.

Pres. Clinton, July 2, approved recommendations that 33 major U.S. military bases be closed. On July 19 he announced **"don't ask, don't tell, don't pursue"** policy for homosexuals in the military.

Judge **Ruth Bader Ginsburg** sworn in, Aug. 10, as 107th justice and second woman on Supreme Court.

Pres. Clinton, Aug. 10, signed measure designed to **cut federal budget deficits** by $496 bil over 5 years, through spending cuts and new taxes.

Brady Bill, a major gun-control measure named after Sarah Brady and former Reagan press sec. James Brady, was signed into law by Pres. Clinton Nov. 30.

1994

A predawn **earthquake** in the Los Angeles area, Jan. 17, claimed 61 lives and caused widespread devastation.

Pres. Clinton Feb. 3 lifted 19-year ban on U.S. trade with **Vietnam**.

Byron De La Beckwith convicted Feb. 5 of **1963** murder of civil rights leader **Medgar Evers**.

Longtime CIA officer **Aldrich Ames** and his wife charged, Feb. 21, with spying. Under plea bargain, he received life in prison, while she drew 63 months.

U.S. troops, Mar. 25, officially ended peacekeeping and humanitarian aid mission in **Somalia**, begun in **1992**.

Congressional committees, late July, began **Whitewater** hearings. **Kenneth Starr** named Aug. 5 as independent counsel to probe Whitewater affair.

Major league **baseball players** went on **strike** following Aug. 11 games. World Series canceled; strike ended Apr. 25, **1995**.

Senate Majority Leader George Mitchell (D-ME), Sept. 26, dropped efforts to pass Pres. Clinton's **health-care reform** package.

1995

104th Congress opened, Jan. 4. A bill to end Congress's exemption from federal labor laws, first in series of measures in Republicans' **"Contract with America,"** cleared Congress Jan. 17; signed into law Jan. 23.

Pres. Clinton invoked emergency authority, Jan. 31, to extend **$20 bil loan to Mexico** to help it avert financial collapse.

Last UN peacekeeping troops withdrew from **Somalia** Feb. 28-Mar. 3, with aid of U.S. Marines. In **Haiti**, peacekeeping responsibilities were transferred from U.S. to UN forces Mar. 31, with the U.S. providing 2,400 soldiers.

A truck bomb exploded outside an **Oklahoma City federal office building** Apr. 19, killing 168 people in deadliest terrorist attack yet on U.S. soil. **Timothy McVeigh** was first and key suspect arrested, Apr. 21.

The U.S. space shuttle *Atlantis* made first in series of dockings with Russian space station *Mir*, June 29-July 4.

The U.S. announced July 11 it was reestablishing diplomatic **relations with Vietnam**.

Shannon Faulkner won legal fight to gain admission to previously all-male cadet corps of **The Citadel** in South Carolina, Aug. 11, though she dropped out after a few days of training.

Ten Muslim militants convicted, Oct. 1, in failed plot to blow up **UN Headquarters** and other buildings and assassinate political leaders.

Former football star **O. J. Simpson** found not guilty Oct. 3 of June **1994** murders of his former wife, Nicole Brown Simpson, and her friend Ron Goldman.

Hundreds of thousands of black men participated in **Million Man March** and rally in Washington, DC, Oct. 16, organized by Rev. **Louis Farrakhan**.

Five Americans among 7 killed, Nov. 13, in **bombing** of U.S. military post in **Riyadh**, Saudi Arabia.

A budget impasse between Congress and Pres. Clinton led to a **partial government shutdown** beginning Nov. 14. Operations resumed Nov. 20 under continuing resolutions.

After talks outside Dayton, OH, warring parties in **Bosnia and Herzegovina** reached agreement Nov. 21 to end their conflict; treaty signed Dec. 14, after which first of some 20,000 U.S. peacekeeping troops arrived in Bosnia.

A **1973** federal law imposing **55-mph speed limit** was repealed by measure signed Nov. 28, returning authority to states.

1996

Senate, Jan. 26, approved, 87-4, Second Strategic Arms Reduction Treaty (**START II**).

Congress, in March, approved **line item veto** bill, giving president power to delete from spending bills any items containing expenditures he or she disapproves of, but it was struck down by Supreme Court, June 25, **1998**.

James and Susan McDougal convicted May 28 of fraud and conspiracy in **Whitewater** case. Arkansas Gov. Jim Guy Tucker convicted of similar charges by same jury.

The antitax **Freemen** surrendered to federal authorities June 13 after 81-day standoff near Jordan, MT; 4 were convicted, July 8, **1998**, of conspiring to defraud banks.

A bomb exploded at **Khobar Towers** military complex near Dhahran, **Saudi Arabia**, June 25, killing 19 American service personnel.

Homemade pipe bomb exploded July 27 in Atlanta, GA, during **Summer Olympics**. One person killed by blast. **Eric Robert Rudolph** pleaded guilty to bombing in 2005.

Major **welfare reform bill** signed into law, Aug. 22.

U.S. signed **Comprehensive Test Ban Treaty**, Sept. 24, which banned all nuclear weapons tests and other nuclear explosions. Senate failed to ratify treaty in **1999**.

Shannon Lucid, Sept. 26, completed **record space voyage** of 188 days, longest by women and by U.S. astronaut.

Pres. **Clinton** reelected to second term, Nov. 5.

1997

Bombs detonated at Atlanta, GA, **women's clinic** that performed abortions, Jan. 16, and at gay nightclub, Feb. 21. **Eric Robert Rudolph** pled guilty in 2005 to both bombings as well as Jan. **1998** bombing of women's clinic in Birmingham, AL, which killed 1.

Madeleine Albright sworn in as secretary of state Jan. 23, becoming **first female State Dept. head.**

Former CIA official **Harold Nicholson** pleaded guilty, Mar. 3, to spying for Russia.

Thirty-nine members of **Heaven's Gate religious cult** found dead in Rancho Santa Fe, CA, house Mar. 26, in apparent mass suicide.

Madeleine Albright

Timothy McVeigh convicted of conspiracy and murder, June 2, in **1995** Oklahoma City bombing.

Islamic militants **Ramzi Ahmed Yousef** and **Eyad Ismoil Yousef** convicted, Nov. 12, in **1993** bombing of **World Trade Center**.

On Nov. 19, Bobbi McCaughey delivered **first set of live septuplets** to survive more than a month.

Terry Nichols convicted Dec. 23 on charges related to the **1995** Oklahoma City bombing.

1998

It was reported Jan. 21 that Whitewater independent counsel Kenneth Starr had evidence of **sexual relationship** between Pres. Clinton and former White House intern **Monica Lewinsky**. Clinton denied it.

"Unabomber" Theodore Kaczynski, arrested in Montana in **1993**, pleaded guilty Jan. 22 in California and New Jersey bombings that killed 3 people and injured 2.

The state of Texas, Feb. 3, **executed its first female convict** in 135 years—Karla Faye Tucker.

Two youths, aged 11 and 13, were arrested, Mar. 24, in killing of 4 students and a teacher outside **Jonesboro, AR, school**; later committed to juvenile detention center.

Monica Lewinsky, Aug. 6, testified to having had a sexual relationship with Pres. Clinton, but said she was never asked to lie. In grand jury testimony and address to the nation, Aug. 17, Clinton acknowledged an inappropriate relationship with Lewinsky. On Sept. 9, independent counsel Starr sent the House what he called "credible information that may constitute grounds" for **impeachment**.

Mark McGwire, Sept. 8, hit his 62nd **home run** of the season, breaking Roger Maris's **1961** season record.

On Sept. 30, Pres. Clinton announced federal **budget surplus** of $70 bil for fiscal year 1998, the first since **1969**.

Terrorist **bombs** in **U.S. embassies** in Nairobi, Kenya, and Dar-es-Salaam, Tanzania, killed at least 257, Aug. 7. The U.S. launched retaliatory strikes, Aug. 20, against alleged terrorist-related targets in Afghanistan and Sudan.

House Judiciary Committee, Oct. 5, voted 21-16 along party lines to recommend that Clinton **impeachment** investigation proceed. The House concurred Oct. 8, voting 258-176; 31 Democrats voted yes.

John Glenn, first U.S. astronaut to orbit Earth, returned to space at age 77 aboard shuttle *Discovery*, Oct. 29-Nov. 7.

Pres. **Clinton**, Nov. 13, settled suit by agreeing to pay $850,000 to **Paula Corbin Jones**, who had alleged that he had made an unwanted sexual advance on her in **1991**.

Country's 4 largest **tobacco companies**, in settlement, Nov. 23, with 46 states, DC, and 4 territories, agreed to pay $206 bil over 25 years to cover public health costs related to smoking.

The House, Dec. 19, approved 2 articles of **impeachment** charging Pres. Clinton with grand jury **perjury** (228-206) and **obstruction of justice** (221-212) in cover-up of his sexual relationship with Lewinsky; 2 other impeachment articles failed.

1999

Pres. **Clinton's impeachment trial**—second such trial in U.S. history—began in GOP-controlled Senate Jan. 7. He was acquitted, Feb. 12. Perjury article failed with 45 votes; obstruction of justice article drew 50-50 vote, with two-thirds vote needed for conviction.

Dr. **Jack Kevorkian**, who claimed to have helped 130 people kill themselves, convicted of 2nd-degree murder Mar. 26 in one death; sentenced to 10-25 years in prison.

One man pled guilty in April, another convicted in November in **1998** kidnapping and beating death of **Matthew Shepard**, an openly gay student at the Univ. of Wyoming.

Eric Harris, 18, and **Dylan Klebold**, 17, killed 12 fellow students and a teacher Apr. 20 at **Columbine High School** in Littleton, CO, then fatally shot themselves.

One NYC police officer pleaded guilty to 6 charges, May 25, and another was convicted on an assault charge, June 8, in connection with **1997** torture and sodomizing of Haitian immigrant **Abner Louima** in police station.

John F. Kennedy Jr., son of former president, died in a plane crash, July 16, along with his wife and sister-in-law.

2000

Across U.S., midnight celebrations marked changeover to the year 2000 on Jan. 1; feared **Y2K** computer glitch caused only minor problems.

Vermont governor Howard Dean signed legislation Apr. 2 allowing same-sex couples in **civil unions** to gain same legal rights as heterosexual married couples. Closest law to date granting gays right to marry.

Teams of scientists from U.S. and Britain announced jointly, June 26, that they had determined structure of the **human genome**.

Following bitter international custody dispute, 6-year-old **Elián González** was returned to father in Cuba June 28, 7 months after he was rescued from a boat wreck in which his mother and other refugees had drowned off the Florida coast.

Tiger Woods became youngest player, at age 24, to win all 4 of golf's majors, with record score in the British Open, July 23.

The Food and Drug Administration announced, Sept. 28, approval of **RU-486**, a pill that induces abortions.

Seventeen U.S. sailors killed Oct. 12 in terrorist bombing of **USS Cole**, which was refueling in Aden, Yemen.

On **election night**, Nov. 7, winner of Florida's 25 deciding electoral votes remained uncertain. The Florida Supreme Court, Dec. 8, ordered manual recount of all ballots that did not have a vote for president recorded by machine. On Dec. 12, Supreme Court reversed that decision. Vice Pres. **Gore** conceded the presidential election to Texas Gov. **George W. Bush** (R) in televised address, Dec. 13.

2001

Congress, Jan. 6, certified **George W. Bush** as president by electoral vote of 271-266 (1 Gore elector abstained). He was sworn in as 43rd president Jan. 20.

AOL-Time Warner merger completed Jan. 11 after Federal Trade Commission approved it Dec. **2000**. Largest merger to date.

Outgoing Pres. Clinton issued 176 pardons and commutations, Jan. 20, including that of **Marc Rich**, fugitive commodities trader whose ex-wife was Clinton financial backer.

FBI agent **Robert Hanssen** arrested Feb. 20 and charged 2 days later with spying for the Soviet Union and Russia.

U.S. **Navy spy plane** collided with Chinese fighter plane over South China Sea Apr. 1, killing the fighter pilot. The 24 U.S. crew members were detained in Hainan until U.S. officials expressed apology, Apr. 12.

Sen. **James Jeffords** (R-VT) announced May 24 he was leaving his party and becoming an independent, giving Democrats control of Senate.

Pres. Bush signed, June 7, **$1.35 tril tax-cut package**, touted as largest tax cut in a generation.

Oklahoma City bomber **Timothy McVeigh** executed June 11 by lethal injection in Terre Haute, IN.

Bush announced Aug. 9 he would allow federal funding of limited **stem-cell research** using human embryos.

On morning of **Sept. 11**, 2 hijacked commercial airliners struck the **World Trade Center twin towers** in New York City in **worst-ever terrorist attack** on American soil. A third hijacked plane destroyed a portion of the **Pentagon**; a fourth crashed in a field in Somerset County, **Pennsylvania**. Some 3,000 people were killed, including about 2,800 at the World Trade Center. U.S. observed a national day of mourning, Sept. 14. Congress, Sept. 21, approved $15 bil **bailout package for airline industry.**

Ground Zero, Sept 17

Five people died, and 14 became ill, from exposure to **anthrax** traveling through the U.S. postal system, Oct. 4-Nov. 21.

The U.S. and Britain, Oct. 7, launched sustained **air-strike campaign** against Afghan-based terrorist organization al-Qaeda and the country's ruling Taliban militia.

On Oct. 7, San Francisco Giants outfielder **Barry Bonds** hit his 73rd **home run** for a single-season record.

Pres. Bush created **Office of Homeland Security**, Oct. 8 and signed a federal **antiterrorism bill**, Oct. 26.

The **Taliban** surrendered Kabul, the Afghan capital, Nov. 13, and fled from Kandahar, their stronghold, Dec. 7.

Taliban member and U.S. citizen **John Walker Lindh** captured Dec. 2 by U.S. forces in Afghanistan.

Leading energy-trading company **Enron** became largest firm thus far to file for bankruptcy, Dec. 2.

The U.S. government, Dec. 11, indicted **Zacarias Moussaoui** as alleged Sept. 11 co-conspirator.

Pres. Bush announced Dec. 13 that U.S. would withdraw from **1972 Antiballistic Missile Treaty**.

2002

Taliban and al-Qaeda fighters captured in Afghanistan were flown to U.S. naval base at **Guantanamo Bay** in Cuba, with first 20 arriving Jan. 11.

A House committee, Jan. 14, released parts of a letter from Sherron Watkins, an Enron employee, to CEO **Kenneth Lay**, warning him company could "implode" in scandal. Lay resigned Jan. 23. Congress, Jan. 24, began public hearings into **Enron bankruptcy**.

In his first State of the Union address, Jan. 29, Pres. Bush called Iran, Iraq, and North Korea part of an **"axis of evil."**

Eight U.S. troops killed Mar. 2-4 in assault against Taliban and al-Qaeda forces in eastern Afghanistan. By Mar. 6, 1,200 U.S. troops were involved in **Operation Anaconda**, which ended Mar. 12.

Final independent prosecutor's report, Mar. 20, found insufficient evidence that Pres. Clinton or his wife had committed any crime in connection with **Whitewater**.

Pres. Bush, Mar. 27, signed into law major **campaign-finance reform bill** that banned unregulated, unrestricted "soft money" donations.

Ceremonial last girder removed May 30 from site of **World Trade Center** towers in New York, signaling end of massive clean-up and recovery operation.

Coleen Rowley testified before congressional committee June 6 that Washington FBI agents had stymied investigative efforts in Minneapolis prior to Sept. 11.

U.S. **Roman Catholic bishops**, meeting in Dallas, TX, June 13-15, approved stringent policies dealing with priests who sexually abuse minors; revised rules formulated with Vatican approval were adopted by bishops, Nov. 13.

Federal jury convicted **Arthur Andersen** accounting firm of obstruction of justice, June 15. Supreme Court overturned conviction in **2005**, ruling that flawed jury instructions invalidated it.

WorldCom announced June 25 that it had overstated its cash flow by billions; on July 21, it displaced Enron as **largest U.S. company to declare bankruptcy**.

Pres. Bush told UN General Assembly Sept. 12 that he would work with Security Council to deal with threat posed by Iraq's **weapons of mass destruction**.

Richard Reid pleaded guilty Oct. 4 to all charges stemming from incident aboard a Paris-to-Miami flight in Dec. **2001**, when he tried to ignite explosives in his shoes.

Former Pres. **Jimmy Carter** named Oct. 10 as winner of a Nobel Peace Prize.

On Oct. 10-11 the House, 296-133, and Senate, 77-23, gave Bush backing to use military force against **Iraq**.

The Bush administration revealed Oct. 16 that **North Korea** had acknowledged it was developing **nuclear arms**.

John Muhammad and **Lee Malvo** arrested Oct. 24 in connection with series of random **sniper shootings** in Washington, DC, area that left 10 dead.

An **antitrust settlement** between **Microsoft Corp.** and Justice Dept. approved Nov. 1 by a federal judge.

Republicans emerged from elections, Nov. 5, with majority in Senate and increased margin in House.

House Democrats elected Rep. **Nancy Pelosi** (CA) Nov. 14 to head their caucus in new Congress, **first woman to lead either party in House**.

Pres. Bush, Nov. 25, signed legislation creating cabinet-level **Dept. of Homeland Security**.

Cardinal **Bernard Law**, Dec. 13, resigned as archbishop of Boston after being criticized for allegedly covering up instances of children being sexually abused by Catholic priests.

Trent Lott (R-MS) bowed out as new Senate majority leader Dec. 20 shortly after being chosen amid furor over comment made apparently supporting segregation; Sen. **Bill Frist** (R-TN) elected as leader Dec. 23.

2003

On Jan. 10-11, shortly before leaving office, Gov. **George Ryan** (R-IL) **pardoned or commuted death sentences** of 171 Illinois death row convicts.

The Senate, Jan. 22, approved Pres. Bush's nomination of **Tom Ridge** to be **first secretary of homeland security**.

Space shuttle **Columbia** broke apart Feb. 1 over southwestern U.S. during its descent toward planned landing; all 7 crew members killed. Official report issued Aug. 26 found immediate cause to be damage sustained during liftoff when chunk of foam came loose and hit the left wing; it also cited a "broken safety culture" at NASA.

The Senate, Mar. 6, approved the **Strategic Offensive Reductions Treaty**, or **Moscow Treaty**, signed in 2002 by U.S. and Russian leaders. It required the 2 countries to reduce their deployed nuclear warheads to 1,700-2,200 by **2012**.

A U.S.-led military offensive aimed at ousting **Saddam Hussein** got underway Mar. 19, when 40 Tomahawk cruise missiles hit targets in Baghdad; strikes continued in succeeding nights. U.S. forces Mar. 21 seized major oil fields near Basra. On Apr. 1, U.S. forces announced the rescue from an Iraqi hospital of injured Army Pfc. **Jessica Lynch**, one of group of soldiers ambushed near Nasiriya.

On Apr. 3, U.S. Marines crossed the Tigris River and moved close to **Baghdad**. By Apr. 8, major government buildings had been occupied and organized resistance had dropped. U.S. forces report control over much of Baghdad, Apr. 9. Statue of Hussein in downtown Baghdad toppled. With collapse of regime, services in major cities were disrupted, and looting became widespread. Pres. Bush, speaking from the aircraft carrier *Abraham Lincoln*, declared on May 1 the **end of major combat operations**. However, insurgents continued to mount attacks against both military and civilian targets.

Pres. Bush signed a measure May 28 providing $330 bil in **tax cuts**, third largest in history.

Under settlement in private antitrust suit brought by Netscape (unit of AOL), **Microsoft** agreed May 29 to pay **AOL Time Warner** $750 mil.

On June 23, the Supreme Court in *Grutter v. Bollinger*, upheld **affirmative action program** providing preference to minorities for admission to Univ. of Michigan law school. But the Court, in *Gratz v. Bollinger*, rejected an undergraduate affirmative action program at the university that employed numerical formulas.

U.S. soldiers killed **Uday and Qusay Hussein**, 2 sons of Saddam Hussein, in gun battle in Mosul, northern Iraq, July 22.

A **power failure** spread rapidly through Ohio, Michigan, and the Northeast, as well as eastern Canada, on Aug. 14. Some 50 mil people in 8 states and province of Ontario were left without electricity for as long as 2 days.

On Sept. 9, Roman Catholic archdiocese of Boston and lawyers representing about 550 victims of **sexual abuse by priests** announced settlement worth up to $85 mil.

California voters, Oct. 7, voted to recall Democratic Gov. Gray Davis from office and replace him with Republican actor-turned-politician **Arnold Schwarzenegger**.

Rev. V. Gene Robinson consecrated Nov. 2 as Episcopal bishop of New Hampshire, becoming **first openly gay prelate** in the Episcopal Church U.S.A.

The Senate, Nov. 3, approved by voice vote the $87.5 bil that Pres. Bush sought for **U.S. military forces in Iraq** and for help rebuilding the country. The House had given its approval Oct. 31.

A Virginia jury, Nov. 17, found **John Muhammad** guilty in **2002** Washington, DC, area **sniper attacks**; he was sentenced to death. Another Virginia jury found **Lee Malvo** guilty of 2 counts of murder in the attacks, Dec. 18; he was sentenced to life in prison without parole.

Massachusetts Supreme Judicial Court decided 4-3, Nov. 18, that **gay couples had right to marry** under state constitution.

Pres. Bush signed a bill Dec. 8 overhauling **Medicare**. The program would offer in **2006** its first-ever prescription drug benefit, and private insurance companies would have larger role in covering Medicare beneficiaries.

Saddam Hussein captured by U.S. military forces Dec. 13, in underground hideout southeast of Tikrit.

The Bush administration announced Dec. 23 that a Holstein in Washington State had tested positive for **mad-cow disease**; the animal, first in U.S. to be so identified, had already been slaughtered.

2004

Sen. **John Kerry** (MA) became Democratic frontrunner in candidacy for presidency by winning Jan. 19 Iowa caucus and Jan. 27 New Hampshire primary.

On Feb. 12, San Francisco began issuing **marriage licenses to same-sex couples**. On Mar. 11, state supreme court issued stay blocking the practice.

The **National World War II Memorial** in Washington, DC, opened to the public Apr. 29, was dedicated May 29.

Photos showing abuse of **Abu Ghraib prison inmates** in Iraq by American soldiers emerged Apr. 30, provoking outrage.

Ronald Reagan, 40th U.S. president, died at home in Los Angeles, June 5. He had been diagnosed with Alzheimer's disease in **1994**.

The U.S.-led coalition formally transferred power to an **interim Iraqi government** on June 28.

The U.S. Supreme Court, June 28, issued three separate decisions regarding **rights of terrorism detainees** that generally curtailed sweeping powers claimed by Pres. Bush as military commander in chief.

The **9/11 Commission Report**, released to the public July 22, summarized what was known about events of that day and called for restructuring of U.S. intelligence operations.

In Boston, July 26-29, Democrats nominated Sen. **John Kerry** (MA) for president and Sen. **John Edwards** (NC) for vice president.

Four hurricanes—Charley, Frances, Ivan, and Jeanne—hit Florida and surrounding states Aug. 13-Sept. 25. Storms blamed for over 50 deaths and more than $20 bil in damage in U.S. Flooding severe in Alabama, Georgia, Louisiana, and South Carolina.

Pres. **Bush** and Vice Pres. **Cheney** renominated Sept. 1 on **Republican ticket** at party convention in New York.

Number of **U.S. soldiers killed** in the Iraqi conflict reached 1,000 on Sept. 7, including 755 in combat.

CBS, Sept. 8, aired *60 Minutes* story claiming it had obtained documents showing that Pres. Bush had failed to meet his responsibilities while in the **National Guard** in the 1970s. CBS Evening News managing editor and anchorman, Dan Rather, admitted on air Sept. 20, however, that documents could not be authenticated.

The Supreme Court announced Oct. 25 that Chief Justice **William H. Rehnquist** was being treated for thyroid cancer. Rehnquist did not attend oral arguments at the Court for remainder of year.

The **Boston Red Sox** swept their last 8 games to win the World Series Oct. 27, for first time since **1918**.

Pres. **Bush** reelected Nov. 2, capturing 31 states with 286 electoral votes, just 16 more than the 270 needed. Republicans gained 4 Senate seats for new 55-44 majority. Republicans won a majority in House for sixth consecutive election. The newly elected House had 232 Republicans, 202 Democrats, and 1 independent.

After a weeklong campaign, U.S. forces took control of the Iraqi city of **Fallujah** from insurgents, Nov. 14.

In episode broadcast Nov. 30, **Ken Jennings** ended his record-setting 74-game *Jeopardy!* winning streak, having won over $2.5 mil.

Pres. Bush signed intelligence reform bill Dec. 17, based on 9/11 Commission's findings. The bill created a **director of national intelligence** to oversee nation's intelligence agencies.

2005

Army Reserve Spec. **Charles Graner Jr.** found guilty, Jan. 14, of assault and other charges in connection with **Abu Ghraib** prisoner abuses in Iraq and sentenced to 10 years in prison. Army Reserve Pfc. **Lynndie England**, who had been photographed posing with prisoners, convicted Sept. 26 and sentenced to 3 years in prison.

Pres. **Bush** inaugurated for second term, Jan. 20.

Condoleezza Rice became **first black woman secretary of state**, Jan. 26.

Alberto Gonzales became **first Hispanic U.S. attorney general**, Feb. 3.

The Supreme Court, Mar. 1, ruled in *Roper v. Simmons* that **executing** convicts who committed their crimes **before age 18** violated constitutional ban on cruel and unusual punishment.

Terri Schiavo, in a persistent vegetative state since **1990**, died Mar. 31, 13 days after feeding tube removed. She had been at the center of legal dispute between her husband, who was her legal guardian, and her parents.

Zacarias Moussaoui, a French citizen with Moroccan roots, pleaded guilty to 6 counts of conspiracy, Apr. 22. He said Osama bin Laden had instructed him to fly a plane into the White House but denied he was to be one of the Sept. 11 hijackers.

A report in *Newsweek*, contending that Guantanamo Bay interrogators had **flushed copy of the Koran** down a toilet, sparked riots in Afghanistan, May 10, and anti-American protests in several Muslim countries, May 27. *Newsweek* issued retraction May 16, saying its source could no longer confirm the incident.

Bipartisan group of 14 Senators reached compromise, May 23, averting deadlock over judicial nominees. Democrats had threatened **filibuster** to prevent an up or down vote on nominees they thought extreme. Majority Leader Bill Frist (R-TN) had said he was prepared to invoke **"nuclear option"**—changing Senate rules to reduce from 60 to 51 number of votes needed to cut off debate on judicial nominees.

Vanity Fair article revealed May 31 that former FBI official **W. Mark Felt** was **"Deep Throat"**—a source for *Washington Post* reporters Bob Woodward and Carl Bernstein when they investigated **1972** Watergate break-in.

Supreme Court Justice **Sandra Day O'Connor** announced, July 1, that she would retire, effective when her replacement was confirmed.

Lance Armstrong won record-setting 7th straight **Tour de France,** July 24.

The **Teamsters** and **Service Employees International Union** declared July 25 that they were pulling out of the **AFL-CIO** to form their own coalition. The **United Food and Commercial Workers** announced its secession July 29.

Discovery blasted off from Cape Canaveral, FL, July 26, in first shuttle launch since fleet grounded following the **2003** *Columbia* disaster. NASA announced, July 27, however, that it was suspending future shuttle missions until continuing problems with foam insulation and heat shield were resolved.

New Orleans after Hurricane Katrina

Pres. Bush, Aug. 23, rejected calls from war protesters—including **Cindy Sheehan,** whose son was killed in Iraq—for the U.S. to withdraw its troops from Iraq.

After striking Florida's Atlantic coast, Aug. 26, **Hurricane Katrina** struck the Gulf Coast, Aug. 29, causing devastation in Louisiana, Mississippi, and Alabama. Breech in a levee on Lake Pontchartrain, Aug. 30, flooded **New Orleans,** forcing more than 10,000 refugees to crowd into the Superdome sports arena.

Chief Justice **William H. Rehnquist** died Sept. 3. Bush Sept. 5 nominated as successor Judge **John G. Roberts Jr.,** who Bush had earlier nominated to replace Justice O'Connor. Roberts sworn in as 17th chief justice Sept. 29. Roberts, at 50 years of age, became **youngest chief justice since 1801.**

House Majority Leader Rep. **Tom DeLay** (R-TX) indicted in Texas Sept. 28 for allegedly conspiring to launder illegal contributions. He temporarily stepped down from his leadership post after indictment. Majority Whip Rep. **Roy Blunt** (MO) chosen interim leader.

White House counsel **Harriet Miers,** nominated Oct. 3 to Supreme Court, withdrew her name in letter to the president Oct. 27. In her place, Pres. Bush, Oct. 31, named Judge **Samuel A. Alito Jr.**

Civil rights icon **Rosa Parks** died Oct. 24. On Oct. 30, she became the **first woman to lie in honor** in **Capitol rotunda** and the 31st person overall.

The **Chicago White Sox,** Oct. 26, defeated the Houston Astros to win their first **World Series** title since **1917.**

A federal grand jury indicted **I. Lewis (Scooter) Libby,** chief of staff for Vice Pres. Cheney and an assistant to Pres. Bush, on 5 counts of obstruction of justice, false statements, and perjury, Oct. 28, in connection with leaking of identity of CIA agent **Valerie Plame Wilson.** Libby resigned same day.

New York Times, Dec. 16, reported that Pres. Bush in **2002** had secretly authorized National Security Agency to **eavesdrop on people in the U.S.** who were suspected of terrorist activities, without the need to first obtain **court-approved warrants.**

Judge John Jones III struck down, Dec. 20, requirement by Pennsylvania school district that 9th grade biology students be read a statement promoting **intelligent design** as an alternative to evolution.

The Senate, Dec. 21, passed $453 bil **defense appropriations bill** after inclusion of **anti-torture amendment.** Provision that would have allowed oil drilling in Alaska's **Arctic National Wildlife Refuge** removed after Republican leaders realized they would not have enough votes to end debate.

Tropical Storm Zeta, Dec. 29, was season's 28th tropical storm, ending **most active hurricane season** on record.

2006

Former top Republican lobbyist **Jack Abramoff** pleaded guilty Jan. 3 to 3 felony counts of conspiracy to bribe public officials, fraud, and tax evasion. In plea agreement with federal prosecutors, Abramoff promised to cooperate with investigation into his dealings with Congressional members.

Senate voted, Jan. 31, to confirm Supreme Court nomination of **Samuel A. Alito Jr.** Alito replaced retiring Justice Sandra Day O'Connor.

Vice Pres. Cheney, Feb. 11, accidentally shot and wounded 78-year-old hunting partner, **Harry Whittington,** during quail-shooting outing at South Texas ranch. Incident became White House public-relations problem; Cheney drew increasing criticism for failing to appear in public to explain what had happened.

Dubai Ports World, Mar. 9, announced it would "transfer" to unnamed U.S. company the management of operations in 6 major U.S. ports, which it had been in the process of acquiring through purchase of British company. Democrats and Republicans had objected to operation of port facilities by DP World, owned by government of Dubai in United Arab Emirates, claiming it would undermine U.S. antiterrorism efforts.

Federal jury recommended, May 3, that **Zacarias Moussaoui** be sentenced to life in prison for role in Sept. 11 terrorist attacks; prosecutors had sought death sentence.

Former Enron CEO **Jeffrey Skilling** convicted May 25 on 19 charges of fraud, conspiracy, and insider trading related to Enron's **2001** bankruptcy. **Kenneth Lay,** Enron's founder and Skilling's successor as CEO, found guilty of 6 counts of fraud and conspiracy.

Pres. Bush, June 13, made unannounced **visit to Baghdad** to demonstrate support for new Iraqi government led by Prem. Nouri Kamel al-Maliki. During trip, Bush reaffirmed that U.S. military forces would not be withdrawn until Iraqi government fully self-sufficient and capable of ensuring national security.

Supreme Court ruled June 29, 5-3 in *Hamdan v. Rumsfeld,* that Pres. Bush's system for **trying terrorism detainees at Guantanamo Bay,** Cuba, military base was unauthorized under federal law and international law, as defined by Geneva Conventions.

Pres. Bush, July 19, issued **first veto** of his administration to reject bill that would have ended federal funding constraints on **human embryonic stem cell research.** House fell 51 votes short of two-thirds majority needed to override veto. Bush in Aug. **2001** had authorized federal funding for embryonic stem cell research but had effectively limited it to roughly 20 cell lines already in existence. Under vetoed legislation, stem cells could be harvested from surplus embryos at fertility clinics that would otherwise be destroyed.

British authorities announced Aug. 10 that they had foiled "major terrorist plot" to use **liquid explosives** on transatlantic passenger flights between Britain and U.S. New security restrictions prohibited passengers in U.S. from transporting liquids, except baby formula and medication, in carry-on luggage.

Pres. Bush in speech Sept. 6 announced transfer of 14 top-ranking terrorist suspects from CIA custody to Guantanamo Bay, Cuba, prison camp; called for Congress to immediately pass legislation allowing government to try them using military tribunals. Speech marked first time Bush had confirmed existence of **secret overseas prisons** for terrorism suspects run by CIA. Defense Dept. released same day new Army Field Manual delineating permissible **methods of interrogation** and banning several techniques that had been criticized as **torture.**

Rep. **Mark Foley** (R-FL) resigned his House seat and abandoned bid for 7th term Sept. 29 after he was questioned by ABC News about sexually suggestive computer messages that he had exchanged with teenage House page. Revelations of Foley's contacts with other teenage boys who had served as House pages also emerged.

Pres. Bush signed bill Oct. 26 that authorized construction of 700-mile, double-layered fence along U.S.-Mexico border, calling bill "an important step toward **immigration reform.**" Bush had endorsed more comprehensive approach to combating illegal immigration—approved by Senate but not the House—that included giving at least some of the estimated 12 mil illegal immigrants in U.S. chance to gain citizenship.

Democratic Party won control of House and Senate in midterm congressional elections Nov. 7. Republican majority had ruled House since **1994** elections, and the Senate as well except for a period in **2001-02.** Representative **Nancy Pelosi** (D-CA) poised to make history as **first woman speaker of the House.** Pres. Bush announced Nov. 8 that Defense Sec. **Donald Rumsfeld,** a focus of criticism over Iraq war, had resigned.

Gerald R. Ford, 38th U.S. president, died Dec. 26 at home in Rancho Mirage, California, at age of 93. He lived longer than any other former president, enjoying three decades in retirement.

For events of 2007, see Year in Review—Chronology (pp. 12-28).

Patrick Henry's Speech to the Virginia Convention

The following is an excerpt from Patrick Henry's speech to the Virginia Convention, which met at St. John's Church in Richmond, on Mar. 23, 1775, to react to British oppression.

Gentlemen may cry, peace, peace—but there is no peace. The war is actually begun! The next gale that sweeps from the north will bring to our ears the clash of resounding arms! Our brethren are already in the field! Why stand we here idle? What is it that gentlemen wish? What would they have? Is life so dear, or peace so sweet, as to be purchased at the price of chains and slavery? Forbid it, Almighty God! I know not what course others may take; but as for me, give me liberty, or give me death!

How the Declaration of Independence Was Adopted

On June 7, 1776, Richard Henry Lee, who had issued the first call for a congress of the colonies, introduced in the Continental Congress at Philadelphia a resolution declaring "that these United Colonies are, and of right ought to be, free and independent states, that they are absolved from all allegiance to the British Crown, and that all political connection between them and the state of Great Britain, is, and ought to be, totally dissolved."

The resolution, seconded by John Adams on behalf of the Massachusetts delegation, came up again on June 11 when a committee of five, headed by Thomas Jefferson, was appointed to express the purpose of the resolution in a declaration of independence. The other four were John Adams, Benjamin Franklin, Robert R. Livingston, and Roger Sherman.

Drafting the Declaration was assigned to Jefferson, who worked on a portable desk of his own construction in a room at Market and 7th St. The committee reported the result on June 28, 1776. The members of the Congress suggested a number of changes, which Jefferson called "deplorable." They did not approve Jefferson's arraignment of the British people and King George III for encouraging and fostering the slave trade, which Jefferson called "an execrable commerce." They eliminated 630 words and added 146, leaving 1,322 words in the final draft. In its final form, capitalization was erratic. Jefferson had written that men were endowed with "inalienable" rights; in the final copy it came out as "unalienable" and has been thus ever since.

The Lee-Adams resolution of independence was adopted by 12 "yeas" on July 2—the actual date of the act of independence. The Declaration, which explains the act, was adopted July 4.

After the Declaration was adopted, July 4, 1776, it was turned over to John Dunlap, printer, to be printed on broadsides. The original copy was lost and one of his broadsides was attached to a page in the journal of the Congress. It was read aloud July 8 in Philadelphia, PA, Easton, PA, and Trenton, NJ. On July 9, it was read by order of Gen. George Washington to the troops assembled on the Common in New York City (City Hall Park).

The Continental Congress of July 19, 1776, adopted the following resolution:

"Resolved, That the Declaration passed on the 4th, be fairly engrossed on parchment with the title and stile of 'The Unanimous Declaration of the thirteen United States of America' and that the same, when engrossed, be signed by every member of Congress."

Not all delegates who signed the engrossed Declaration were present on July 4. Robert Morris (PA), William Williams (CT), and Samuel Chase (MD) signed on Aug. 2; Oliver Wolcott (CT), George Wythe (VA), Richard Henry Lee (VA), and Elbridge Gerry (MA) signed in August and September; Matthew Thornton (NH) joined the Congress Nov. 4 and signed later. Thomas McKean (DE) rejoined Washington's army before signing and said later that he signed in 1781.

Charles Carroll of Carrollton was appointed a delegate by Maryland on July 4, 1776, presented his credentials July 18, and signed the engrossed Declaration on Aug. 2. Born Sept. 19, 1737, he was 95 years old and the last surviving signer when he died on Nov. 14, 1832.

Two Pennsylvania delegates who did not support the Declaration on July 4 were replaced. The four New York delegates did not have authority from their state to vote on July 4. On July 9, the New York state convention authorized its delegates to approve the Declaration, and the Congress was so notified on July 15, 1776. The four signed the Declaration on Aug. 2.

The original engrossed Declaration is preserved at the National Archives in Washington, DC.

Declaration of Independence

The Declaration of Independence was adopted by the Continental Congress in Philadelphia on July 4, 1776. John Hancock was president of the Congress, and Charles Thomson was secretary. A copy of the Declaration, engrossed on parchment, was signed by members of Congress on and after Aug. 2, 1776. On Jan. 18, 1777, Congress ordered that "an authenticated copy, with the names of the members of Congress subscribing the same, be sent to each of the United States, and that they be desired to have the same put on record." Authenticated copies were printed in broadside form in Baltimore, where the Continental Congress was then in session. The following text is that of the original printed by John Dunlap at Philadelphia for the Continental Congress. The original is on display at the National Archives.

IN CONGRESS, July 4, 1776.

A DECLARATION

By the REPRESENTATIVES of the

UNITED STATES OF AMERICA,

In GENERAL CONGRESS assembled

When in the Course of human Events, it becomes necessary for one People to dissolve the Political Bands which have connected them with another, and to assume among the Powers of the Earth, the separate and equal Station to which the Laws of Nature and of Nature's God entitle them, a decent Respect to the Opinions of Mankind requires that they should declare the causes which impel them to the Separation.

We hold these Truths to be self-evident, that all Men are created equal, that they are endowed by their Creator with certain unalienable Rights, that among these are Life, Liberty, and the Pursuit of Happiness—That to secure these Rights, Governments are instituted among Men, deriving their just Powers from the Consent of the Governed, that whenever any Form of Government becomes destructive of these Ends, it is the Right of the People to alter or to abolish it, and to institute new Government, laying its Foundation on such Principles, and organizing its Powers in such Form, as to them shall seem most likely to effect their Safety and Happiness. Prudence, indeed, will dictate that Governments long established should not be changed for light and transient Causes; and accordingly all Experience hath shewn, that Mankind are more disposed to suffer, while Evils are sufferable, than to right themselves by abolishing the Forms to which they are accustomed. But when a long Train of Abuses and Usurpations, pursuing invariably the same Object, evinces a Design to reduce them under absolute Despotism, it is their Right, it is their Duty, to throw off such Government, and to provide new Guards for their future Security. Such has been the patient Sufferance of these Colonies; and such is now the Necessity which constrains them to alter their former Systems of Government. The History of the present King of Great-Britain is a History of repeated Injuries and Usurpations, all having in direct Object the Establishment of an absolute Tyranny over these States. To prove this, let Facts be submitted to a candid World.

He has refused his Assent to Laws, the most wholesome and necessary for the public Good.

He has forbidden his Governors to pass Laws of immediate and pressing Importance, unless suspended in their Operation till his Assent should be obtained; and when so suspended, he has utterly neglected to attend to them.

He has refused to pass other Laws for the Accommodation of large Districts of People, unless those People would relinquish the Right of Representation in the Legislature, a Right inestimable to them, and formidable to Tyrants only.

He has called together Legislative Bodies at Places unusual, uncomfortable, and distant from the Depository of their Public Records, for the sole Purpose of fatiguing them into Compliance with his Measures.

He has dissolved Representative Houses repeatedly, for opposing with manly Firmness his Invasions on the Rights of the People.

He has refused for a long Time, after such Dissolutions, to cause others to be elected; whereby the Legislative Powers, incapable of Annihilation, have returned to the People at large for their exercise; the State remaining in the mean time exposed to all the Dangers of Invasion from without, and Convulsions within.

He has endeavoured to prevent the Population of these States; for that Purpose obstructing the Laws for Naturalization of Foreigners; refusing to pass others to encourage their Migrations hither, and raising the Conditions of new Appropriations of Lands.

He has obstructed the Administration of Justice, by refusing his Assent to Laws for establishing Judiciary Powers.

He has made Judges dependent on his Will alone, for the Tenure of their Offices, and the Amount and payment of their Salaries.

He has erected a Multitude of new Offices, and sent hither Swarms of Officers to harrass our People, and eat out their Substance.

He has kept among us, in Times of Peace, Standing Armies, without the consent of our Legislatures.

He has affected to render the Military independent of, and superior to the Civil Power.

He has combined with others to subject us to a Jurisdiction foreign to our Constitution, and unacknowledged by our Laws; giving his Assent to their Acts of pretended Legislation:

For quartering large Bodies of Armed Troops among us:

For protecting them, by a mock Trial, from Punishment for any Murders which they should commit on the Inhabitants of these States:

For cutting off our Trade with all Parts of the World:

For imposing Taxes on us without our Consent:

For depriving us, in many Cases, of the Benefits of Trial by Jury:

For transporting us beyond Seas to be tried for pretended Offences:

For abolishing the free System of English Laws in a neighbouring Province, establishing therein an arbitrary Government, and enlarging its Boundaries, so as to render it at once an Example and fit Instrument for introducing the same absolute Rule into these Colonies:

For taking away our Charters, abolishing our most valuable Laws, and altering fundamentally the Forms of our Governments:

For suspending our own Legislatures, and declaring themselves invested with Power to legislate for us in all Cases whatsoever.

He has abdicated Government here, by declaring us out of his Protection and waging War against us.

He has plundered our Seas, ravaged our Coasts, burnt our towns, and destroyed the Lives of our People.

He is, at this Time, transporting large Armies of foreign Mercenaries to complete the works of Death, Desolation, and Tyranny, already begun with circumstances of Cruelty and Perfidy, scarcely paralleled in the most barbarous Ages, and totally unworthy the Head of a civilized Nation.

He has constrained our fellow Citizens taken Captive on the high Seas to bear Arms against their Country, to become the Executioners of their Friends and Brethren, or to fall themselves by their Hands.

He has excited domestic Insurrections amongst us, and has endeavoured to bring on the Inhabitants of our Frontiers, the merciless Indian Savages, whose known Rule of Warfare, is an undistinguished Destruction, of all Ages, Sexes and Conditions.

In every stage of these Oppressions we have Petitioned for Redress in the most humble Terms: Our repeated Petitions have been answered only by repeated Injury. A Prince, whose Character is thus marked by every act which may define a Tyrant, is unfit to be the Ruler of a free People.

Nor have we been wanting in Attentions to our British Brethren. We have warned them from Time to Time of Attempts by their Legislature to extend an unwarrantable Jurisdiction over us. We have reminded them of the Circumstances of our Emigration and Settlement here. We have appealed to their native Justice and Magnanimity, and we have conjured them by the Ties of our common Kindred to disavow these Usurpations, which, would inevitably interrupt our Connections and Correspondence. They too have been deaf to the Voice of Justice and of Consanguinity. We must, therefore, acquiesce in the Necessity, which denounces our Separation, and hold them, as we hold the rest of Mankind, Enemies in War, in Peace, Friends.

We, therefore, the Representatives of the UNITED STATES OF AMERICA, in General Congress, Assembled, appealing to the Supreme Judge of the World for the Rectitude of our Intentions, do, in the Name, and by Authority of the good People of these Colonies, solemnly Publish and Declare, That these United Colonies are, and of Right ought to be, Free and Independent States; that they are absolved from all Allegiance to the British Crown, and that all political Connection between them and the State of Great-Britain, is and ought to be totally dissolved; and that as Free and Independent States, they have full Power to levy War, conclude Peace, contract Alliances, establish Commerce, and to do all other Acts and Things which Independent States may of right do. And for the support of this declaration, with a firm Reliance on the Protection of Divine Providence, we mutually pledge to each other our lives, our Fortunes, and our sacred Honor.

JOHN HANCOCK, President

Attest.

CHARLES THOMSON, Secretary.

Signers of the Declaration of Independence

Delegate (state)	Occupation	Birthplace	Born	Died
Adams, John (MA)	Lawyer	Braintree (Quincy), MA	Oct. 30, 1735	July 4, 1826
Adams, Samuel (MA)	Political leader	Boston, MA	Sept. 27, 1722	Oct. 2, 1803
Bartlett, Josiah (NH)	Physician, judge	Amesbury, MA	Nov. 21, 1729	May 19, 1795
Braxton, Carter (VA)	Farmer	Newington Plantation, VA	Sept. 10, 1736	Oct. 10, 1797
Carroll, Charles of Carrollton (MD)	Merchant	Annapolis, MD	Sept. 19, 1737	Nov. 14, 1832
Chase, Samuel (MD)	Judge	Princess Anne, MD	Apr. 17, 1741	June 19, 1811
Clark, Abraham (NJ)	Surveyor	Elizabethtown, NJ	Feb. 15, 1726	Sept. 15, 1794
Clymer, George (PA)	Merchant	Philadelphia, PA	Mar. 16, 1739	Jan. 23, 1813
Ellery, William (RI)	Lawyer	Newport, RI	Dec. 22, 1727	Feb. 15, 1820
Floyd, William (NY)	Soldier	Brookhaven, NY	Dec. 17, 1734	Aug. 4, 1821
Franklin, Benjamin (PA)	Printer, publisher	Boston, MA	Jan. 17, 1706	Apr. 17, 1790
Gerry, Elbridge (MA)	Merchant	Marblehead, MA	July 17, 1744	Nov. 23, 1814
Gwinnett, Button (GA)	Merchant	Gloucester, England	c. 1735	May 19, 1777
Hall, Lyman (GA)	Physician	Wallingford, CT	Apr. 12, 1724	Oct. 19, 1790
Hancock, John (MA)	Merchant	Braintree (Quincy), MA	Jan. 12, 1737	Oct. 8, 1793
Harrison, Benjamin (VA)	Farmer	Charles City County, VA	Apr. 5, 1726	Apr. 24, 1791
Hart, John (NJ)	Farmer	Stonington, CT	c. 1711	May 11, 1779
Hewes, Joseph (NC)	Merchant	Kingston, NJ	Jan. 23, 1730	Nov. 10, 1779
Heyward, Thos. Jr. (SC)	Lawyer, farmer	St. Luke's Parish, SC	July 28, 1746	Mar. 6, 1809
Hooper, William (NC)	Lawyer	Boston, MA	June 17, 1742	Oct. 14, 1790
Hopkins, Stephen (RI)	Judge, educator	Providence, RI	Mar. 7, 1707	July 13, 1785
Hopkinson, Francis (NJ)	Judge, author	Philadelphia, PA	Oct. 2, 1737	May 9, 1791
Huntington, Samuel (CT)	Judge	Windham, CT	July 3, 1731	Jan. 5, 1796
Jefferson, Thomas (VA)	Lawyer	Shadwell, VA	Apr. 13, 1743	July 4, 1826
Lee, Francis Lightfoot (VA)	Farmer	Westmoreland County, VA	Oct. 14, 1734	Jan. 11, 1797
Lee, Richard Henry (VA)	Farmer	Westmoreland County, VA	Jan. 20, 1732	June 19, 1794
Lewis, Francis (NY)	Merchant	Llandaff, Wales	Mar. 21, 1713	Dec. 31, 1802
Livingston, Philip (NY)	Merchant	Albany, NY	Jan. 15, 1716	June 12, 1778
Lynch, Thomas Jr. (SC)	Farmer	Winyah, SC	Aug. 5, 1749	(at sea) 1779
McKean, Thomas (DE)	Lawyer	New London, PA	Mar. 19, 1734	June 24, 1817
Middleton, Arthur (SC)	Farmer	Charleston, SC	June 26, 1742	Jan. 1, 1787
Morris, Lewis (NY)	Farmer	Morrisania (Bronx County), NY	Apr. 8, 1726	Jan. 22, 1798
Morris, Robert (PA)	Merchant	Liverpool, England	Jan. 31, 1734	May 8, 1806
Morton, John (PA)	Judge	Ridley, PA	c. 1724	Apr. 1777
Nelson, Thos. Jr. (VA)	Farmer	Yorktown, VA	Dec. 26, 1738	Jan. 4, 1789
Paca, William (MD)	Judge	Abingdon, MD	Oct. 31, 1740	Oct. 23, 1799
Paine, Robert Treat (MA)	Judge	Boston, MA	Mar. 11, 1731	May 12, 1814
Penn, John (NC)	Lawyer	Caroline County, VA	May 17, 1741	Sept. 14, 1788
Read, George (DE)	Judge	Cecil County, MD	Sept. 18, 1733	Sept. 21, 1798
Rodney, Caesar (DE)	Judge	Dover, DE	Oct. 7, 1728	June 29, 1784
Ross, George (PA)	Judge	New Castle, DE	May 10, 1730	July 14, 1779
Rush, Benjamin (PA)	Physician	Byberry, PA (Philadelphia)	Jan. 4, 1746	Apr. 19, 1813
Rutledge, Edward (SC)	Lawyer	Charleston, SC	Nov. 23, 1749	Jan. 23, 1800
Sherman, Roger (CT)	Lawyer	Newton, MA	Apr. 19, 1721	July 23, 1793
Smith, James (PA)	Lawyer	Northern Ireland	c. 1719	July 11, 1806
Stockton, Richard (NJ)	Lawyer	Princeton, NJ	Oct. 1, 1730	Feb. 28, 1781
Stone, Thomas (MD)	Lawyer	Charles County, MD	c. 1743	Oct. 5, 1787
Taylor, George (PA)	Ironmaster	Ireland	c. 1716	Feb. 23, 1781
Thornton, Matthew (NH)	Physician	Ireland	c. 1714	June 24, 1803
Walton, George (GA)	Judge	Cumberland County, VA	c. 1741	Feb. 2, 1804
Whipple, William (NH)	Merchant, judge	Kittery, ME	Jan. 14, 1730	Nov. 28, 1785
Williams, William (CT)	Merchant	Lebanon, CT	Apr. 8, 1731	Aug. 2, 1811
Wilson, James (PA)	Judge	Carskerdo, Scotland	Sept. 14, 1742	Aug. 21, 1798
Witherspoon, John (NJ)	Clergyman, educator	Gifford, Scotland	Feb. 5, 1723	Nov. 15, 1794
Wolcott, Oliver (CT)	Judge	Windsor, CT	Nov. 20, 1726	Dec. 1, 1797
Wythe, George (VA)	Lawyer	Elizabeth City Co., VA	c. 1726	June 8, 1806

Origin of the Constitution

The War of Independence was conducted by delegates from the original 13 states, who comprised the Congress of the United States of America, known as the Continental Congress. In 1777 the Congress submitted to the legislatures of the states the Articles of Confederation and Perpetual Union, which were ratified by New Hampshire, Massachusetts, Rhode Island, Connecticut, New York, New Jersey, Pennsylvania, Delaware, Virginia, North Carolina, South Carolina, Georgia, and finally, in 1781, Maryland.

The first article read: "The stile of this confederacy shall be the United States of America." This did not signify a sovereign nation, because the states delegated only those powers they could not handle individually, such as to wage war, make treaties, and contract debts for general expenses (e.g., paying the army). Taxes for payment of such debts were lev-ied by the individual states. The president signed himself "President of the United States in Congress assembled," but here the United States were considered in the plural, a cooperating group.

When the war was won, it became evident that a stronger federal union was needed. The Congress left the initiative to the legislatures. Virginia in Jan. 1786 appointed commissioners to meet with representatives of other states; delegates from Virginia, Delaware, New York, New Jersey, and Pennsylvania met at Annapolis. Alexander Hamilton prepared their call asking delegates from all states to meet in Philadelphia in May 1787 "to render the Constitution of the federal government adequate to the exigencies of the union." Congress endorsed the plan on Feb. 21, 1787. Delegates were appointed by all states except Rhode Island.

The convention was called for May 14, 1787, but a quorum was not present until May 25. George Washington was chosen president (presiding officer). The states certified 65 delegates, but 10 did not attend. The work was done by 55, not all of whom were present at all sessions. Of the 55 attending delegates, 16 failed to sign, and 39 actually signed Sept. 17, 1787, some with reservations. Some historians have said 74 delegates (9 more than the 65 actually certified) were named, and 19 failed to attend. These 9 additional persons refused the appointment, were never delegates, and were never counted as absentees. Washington sent the Constitution to Congress, and that body, Sept. 28, 1787, ordered it sent to the legislatures, "in order to be submitted to a convention of delegates chosen in each state by the people thereof."

The Constitution was ratified by votes of state conventions as follows: Delaware, Dec. 7, 1787, unanimous; Penn-sylvania, Dec. 12, 1787, 46 to 23; New Jersey, Dec. 18, 1787, unanimous; Georgia, Jan. 2, 1788, unanimous; Connecticut, Jan. 9, 1788, 128 to 40; Massachusetts, Feb. 6, 1788, 187 to 168; Maryland, Apr. 28, 1788, 63 to 11; South Carolina, May 23, 1788, 149 to 73; New Hampshire, June 21, 1788, 57 to 46; Virginia, June 25, 1788, 89 to 79; New York, July 26, 1788, 30 to 27. Nine states were needed to establish the operation of the Constitution "between the states so ratifying the same," and New Hampshire was the 9th state. The government did not declare the Constitution in effect until the first Wednesday in Mar. 1789, which was Mar. 4. After that, North Carolina ratified it on Nov. 21, 1789, 194 to 77; and Rhode Island, May 29, 1790, 34 to 32. Vermont in convention ratified it on Jan. 10, 1791, and by act of Congress approved on Feb. 18, 1791, was admitted into the Union as the 14th state, Mar. 4, 1791.

Constitution of the United States
The Original 7 Articles

The text of the Constitution given here (except for Amendment XXVII) is from the pocket-size edition of the Constitution published by the U.S. Government Printing Office as a result of a congressional resolution to print the Constitution in its original form as amended through July 5, 1971. *Text in brackets* indicates that an item has been superseded or amended, or provides background information. **Boldface text preceding** an article, section, or amendment is a brief summary, added by *The World Almanac.*

PREAMBLE

We, the People of the United States, in Order to form a more perfect Union, establish Justice, insure domestic Tranquility, provide for the common defence, promote the general Welfare, and secure the Blessings of Liberty to ourselves and our Posterity, do ordain and establish this Constitution for the United States of America.

ARTICLE I.

Section 1—Legislative powers; in whom vested.

All legislative Powers herein granted shall be vested in a Congress of the United States, which shall consist of a Senate and House of Representatives.

Section 2—House of Representatives, how and by whom chosen. Qualifications of a Representative. Representatives and direct taxes, how apportioned. Enumeration. Vacancies to be filled. Power of choosing officers, and of impeachment.

The House of Representatives shall be composed of Members chosen every second Year by the People of the several States, and the Electors in each State shall have the Qualifications requisite for Electors of the most numerous Branch of the State Legislature.

No person shall be a Representative who shall not have attained to the Age of twenty-five Years, and been seven Years a Citizen of the United States, and who shall not, when elected, be an Inhabitant of that State in which he shall be chosen.

[Representatives and direct taxes shall be apportioned among the several States which may be included within this Union, according to their respective Numbers, which shall be determined by adding to the whole Number of free Persons, including those bound to Service for a Term of Years, and excluding Indians not taxed, three-fifths of all other persons.] [The previous sentence was superseded by Amendment XIV, section 2.] The actual Enumeration shall be made within three Years after the first Meeting of the Congress of the United States, and within every subsequent Term of ten Years, in such Manner as they shall by Law direct. The Number of Representatives shall not exceed one for every thirty Thousand, but each State shall have at Least one Representative; and until such enumeration shall be made, the State of New Hampshire shall be entitled to chuse three, Massachusetts eight, Rhode-Island and Providence Plantations one, Connecticut five, New-York six, New Jersey four,

Pennsylvania eight, Delaware one, Maryland six, Virginia ten, North Carolina five, South Carolina five, and Georgia three.

When vacancies happen in the Representation from any State, the Executive Authority thereof shall issue Writs of Election to fill such Vacancies.

The House of Representatives shall chuse their Speaker and other Officers; and shall have the sole Power of Impeachment.

Section 3—Senators, how and by whom chosen. How classified. Qualifications of a Senator. President of the Senate, his right to vote. President pro tem., and other officers of the Senate, how chosen. Power to try impeachments. When President is tried, Chief Justice to preside. Sentence.

The Senate of the United States shall be composed of two Senators from each State, *[chosen by the Legislature thereof] [The preceding five words were superseded by Amendment XVII.]* for six Years; and each Senator shall have one Vote.

Immediately after they shall be assembled in Consequence of the first Election, they shall be divided as equally as may be into three Classes. The Seats of the Senators of the first Class shall be vacated at the Expiration of the second Year, of the second Class at the Expiration of the fourth Year, and of the third Class at the Expiration of the Sixth year, so that one-third may be chosen every second Year; *[and if Vacancies happen by Resignation, or otherwise, during the Recess of the Legislature of any State, the Executive thereof may make temporary Appointments until the next Meeting of the Legislature, which shall then fill such Vacancies.] [The words in brackets were superseded by Amendment XVII.]*

No person shall be a Senator who shall not have attained to the Age of thirty Years, and been nine Years a Citizen of the United States, and who shall not, when elected, be an Inhabitant of that State for which he shall be chosen.

The Vice President of the United States shall be President of the Senate, but shall have no Vote, unless they be equally divided.

The Senate shall chuse their other Officers, and also a President pro tempore, in the absence of the Vice President, or when he shall exercise the Office of President of the United States.

The Senate shall have the sole Power to try all Impeachments. When sitting for that Purpose, they shall be on Oath or Affirmation. When the President of the United States is tried, the Chief Justice shall preside: And no Person shall be convicted without the Concurrence of two thirds of the Members present.

Judgment in Cases of Impeachment shall not extend further than to removal from Office, and disqualification to hold and enjoy any Office of honor, Trust or Profit under the United States: but the Party convicted shall nevertheless be liable and subject to Indictment, Trial, Judgment and Punishment, according to Law.

Section 4—Times, etc., of holding elections, how prescribed. One session each year.

The Times, Places and Manner of holding Elections for Senators and Representatives, shall be prescribed in each State by the Legislature thereof; but the Congress may at any time by Law make or alter such Regulations, except as to the Place of Chusing Senators.

The Congress shall assemble at least once in every Year, and such Meeting shall be *[on the first Monday in December,] [The words in brackets were superseded by Amendment XX, section 2.]* unless they shall by Law appoint a different Day.

Section 5—Membership, quorum, adjournments, rules. Power to punish or expel. Journal. Time of adjournments, how limited, etc.

Each House shall be the Judge of the Elections, Returns and Qualifications of its own Members, and a Majority of each shall constitute a Quorum to do Business; but a smaller number may adjourn from day to day, and may be authorized to compel the Attendance of absent Members, in such manner, and under such Penalties as each House may provide.

Each House may determine the Rules of its Proceedings, punish its members for disorderly Behavior, and, with the Concurrence of two thirds, expel a Member.

Each House shall keep a Journal of its Proceedings, and from time to time publish the same, excepting such Parts as may in their Judgment require Secrecy; and the Yeas and Nays of the Members of either House on any question shall, at the Desire of one fifth of those Present, be entered on the Journal.

Neither House, during the Session of Congress, shall, without the Consent of the other, adjourn for more than three days, nor to any other Place than that in which the two Houses shall be sitting.

Section 6—Compensation, privileges, disqualifications in certain cases.

The Senators and Representatives shall receive a Compensation for their Services, to be ascertained by Law, and paid out of the Treasury of the United States. They shall in all Cases, except Treason, Felony and Breach of the Peace, be privileged from Arrest during their Attendance at the Session of their respective Houses, and in going to and returning from the same; and for any Speech or Debate in either House, they shall not be questioned in any other Place.

No Senator or Representative shall, during the Time for which he was elected, be appointed to any civil Office under the Authority of the United States, which shall have been created, or the Emoluments whereof shall have been encreased during such time; and no Person holding any Office under the United States, shall be a Member of either House during his Continuance in Office.

Section 7—House to originate all revenue bills. Veto. Bill may be passed by two-thirds of each House, notwithstanding, etc. Bill, not returned in ten days, to become a law. Provisions as to orders, concurrent resolutions, etc.

All bills for raising Revenue shall originate in the House of Representatives; but the Senate may propose or concur with Amendments as on other Bills.

Every Bill which shall have passed the House of Representatives and the Senate, shall, before it become a Law, be presented to the President of the United States; If he approve he shall sign it, but if not he shall return it, with his Objections to that House in which it shall have originated, who shall enter the Objections at large on their Journal, and proceed to reconsider it. If after such Reconsideration two thirds of that House shall agree to pass the Bill, it shall be sent, together with the Objections, to the other House, by which it shall likewise be reconsidered, and if approved by two thirds of that House, it shall become a Law. But in all such Cases the Votes of both Houses shall be determined by Yeas and Nays, and the Names of the Persons voting for and against the Bill shall be entered on the Journal of each House respectively. If any Bill shall not be returned by the President within ten Days (Sundays excepted) after it shall have been presented to him, the Same shall be a Law, in like Manner as if he had signed it, unless the Congress by their Adjournment prevent its Return, in which Case it shall not be a Law.

Every order, Resolution, or Vote to which the Concurrence of the Senate and House of Representatives may be necessary (except on a question of Adjournment) shall be presented to the President of the United States; and before the Same shall take Effect, shall be approved by him, or being disapproved by him, shall be repassed by two thirds of the Senate and House of Representatives, according to the Rules and Limitations prescribed in the Case of a Bill.

Section 8—Powers of Congress.

The Congress shall have Power To lay and collect Taxes, Duties, Imposts and Excises, to pay the Debts and provide for the common Defence and general Welfare of the United States; but all Duties, Imposts and Excises shall be uniform throughout the United States;

To borrow money on the credit of the United States;

To regulate Commerce with foreign Nations, and among the several States, and with the Indian Tribes;

To establish an uniform Rule of Naturalization, and uniform Laws on the subject of Bankruptcies throughout the United States;

To coin Money, regulate the Value thereof, and of foreign Coin, and fix the Standard of Weights and Measures;

To provide for the Punishment of counterfeiting the Securities and current Coin of the United States;

To establish Post Offices and post Roads;

To promote the Progress of Science and useful Arts, by securing for limited Times to Authors and Inventors the exclusive Right to their respective Writings and Discoveries;

To constitute Tribunals inferior to the supreme Court;

To define and punish Piracies and Felonies committed on the high Seas, and Offenses against the Law of Nations;

To declare War, grant Letters of Marque and Reprisal, and make Rules concerning Captures on Land and Water;

To raise and support Armies, but no Appropriation of Money to that Use shall be for a longer Term than two Years;

To provide and maintain a Navy;

To make Rules for the Government and Regulation of the land and naval Forces;

To provide for calling forth the Militia to execute the Laws of the Union, suppress Insurrections and repel Invasions;

To provide for organizing, arming, and disciplining the Militia, and for governing such Part of them as may be employed in the Service of the United States, reserving to the States respectively, the Appointment of the Officers, and the Authority of training the Militia according to the discipline prescribed by Congress;

To exercise exclusive Legislation in all Cases whatsoever, over such District (not exceeding ten Miles square) as may, by Cession of particular States, and the acceptance of Congress, become the Seat of the Government of the United States, and to exercise like Authority over all Places purchased by the Consent of the Legislature of the State in which the Same shall be, for the Erection of Forts, Magazines, Arsenals, dock-Yards, and other needful Buildings;—And

To make all Laws which shall be necessary and proper for carrying into Execution the foregoing Powers, and all other Powers vested by this Constitution in the Government of the United States, or in any Department or Officer thereof.

Section 9—Provision as to migration or importation of certain persons. Habeas corpus, bills of attainder, etc. Taxes, how apportioned. No export duty. No commercial preference. Money, how drawn from Treasury, etc. No titular nobility. Officers not to receive presents, etc.

The Migration or Importation of such Persons as any of the States now existing shall think proper to admit, shall not be prohibited by the Congress prior to the Year one thousand eight hundred and eight, but a tax or duty may be imposed on such Importation, not exceeding ten dollars for each Person.

The privilege of the Writ of Habeas Corpus shall not be suspended, unless when in Cases of Rebellion or Invasion the public Safety may require it.

No Bill of Attainder or ex post facto Law shall be passed.

No capitation, or other direct, Tax shall be laid, unless in Proportion to the Census or Enumeration herein before directed to be taken. *[Modified by Amendment XVI.]*

No Tax or Duty shall be laid on Articles exported from any State.

No Preference shall be given by any Regulation of Commerce or Revenue to the Ports of one State over those of another: nor shall Vessels bound to, or from, one State, be obliged to enter, clear, or pay Duties in another.

No Money shall be drawn from the Treasury, but in Consequence of Appropriations made by Law; and a regular Statement and Account of the Receipts and Expenditures of all public Money shall be published from time to time.

No Title of Nobility shall be granted by the United States: and no Person holding any Office of Profit or Trust under them, shall, without the Consent of the Congress, accept of any present, Emolument, Office, or Title, of any kind whatever, from any King, Prince, or foreign State.

Section 10—States prohibited from the exercise of certain powers.

No State shall enter into any Treaty, Alliance, or Confederation; grant Letters of Marque and Reprisal; coin Money; emit Bills of Credit; make any Thing but gold and silver Coin a Tender in Payment of Debts; pass any Bill of Attainder, ex post facto Law, or Law impairing the Obligation of Contracts, or grant any Title of Nobility.

No State shall, without the Consent of the Congress, lay any Imposts or Duties on Imports or Exports, except what may be absolutely necessary for executing its inspection Laws: and the net Produce of all Duties and Imposts, laid by any State on Imports or Exports, shall be for the Use of the Treasury of the United States; and all such Laws shall be subject to the Revision and Control of the Congress.

No State shall, without the Consent of Congress, lay any duty of Tonnage, keep Troops, or Ships of War in time of Peace, enter into any Agreement or Compact with another State, or with a foreign Power, or engage in War, unless actually invaded, or in such imminent Danger as will not admit of delay.

ARTICLE II.

Section 1—President: his term of office. Electors of President; number and how appointed. Electors to vote on same day. Qualification of President. On whom his duties devolve in case of his removal, death, etc. President's compensation. His oath of office.

The executive Power shall be vested in a President of the United States of America. He shall hold his Office during the Term of four Years, and, together with the Vice President, chosen for the same Term, be elected, as follows.

Each State shall appoint, in such Manner as the Legislature thereof may direct, a Number of Electors, equal to the whole Number of Senators and Representatives to which the State may be entitled in the Congress: but no Senator or Representative, or Person holding an Office of Trust or Profit under the United States, shall be appointed an Elector.

[The Electors shall meet in their respective States, and vote by Ballot for two persons, of whom one at least shall not be an Inhabitant of the same State with themselves. And they shall make a List of all the Persons voted for, and of the Number of Votes for each; which List they shall sign and certify, and transmit sealed to the Seat of the Government of the United States, directed to the President of the Senate. The President of the Senate shall, in the Presence of the Senate and House of Representatives, open all the Certificates, and the Votes shall then be counted. The Person having the greatest Number of Votes shall be the President, if such

Number be a Majority of the whole Number of Electors appointed; and if there be more than one who have such Majority, and have an equal Number of Votes, then the House of Representatives shall immediately chuse by Ballot one of them for President; and if no Person have a Majority, then from the five highest on the List the said House shall in like Manner chuse the President. But in chusing the President, the Votes shall be taken by States, the Representation from each State having one Vote; a quorum for this Purpose shall consist of a Member or Members from two thirds of the States, and a Majority of all the States shall be necessary to a Choice. In every Case, after the Choice of the President, the Person having the greatest Number of Votes of the Electors shall be the Vice President. But if there should remain two or more who have equal Votes, the Senate shall chuse from them by Ballot the Vice-President.] [This clause was superseded by Amendment XII.]

The Congress may detemine the Time of chusing the Electors, and the Day on which they shall give their Votes; which Day shall be the same throughout the United States.

No person except a natural born Citizen, or a Citizen of the United States, at the time of the Adoption of this Constitution, shall be eligible to the Office of President; neither shall any Person be eligible to that Office who shall not have attained to the Age of thirty-five Years, and been fourteen Years a Resident within the United States. *[For qualification of the Vice President, see Amendment XII.]*

[In Case of the Removal of the President from Office, or of his Death, Resignation, or Inability to discharge the Powers and Duties of the said Office, the same shall devolve on the Vice President, and the Congress may by Law, provide for the Case of Removal, Death, Resignation or Inability, both of the President and Vice President, declaring what Officer shall then act as President, and such Officer shall act accordingly, until the Disability be removed, or a President shall be elected. [This clause was superseded by Amendments XXV.]

The President shall, at stated Times, receive for his Services, a Compensation, which shall neither be encreased nor diminished during the Period for which he shall have been elected, and he shall not receive within that Period any other Emolument from the United States, or any of them.

Before he enter on the Execution of his Office, he shall take the following Oath or Affirmation:–"I do solemnly swear (or affirm) that I will faithfully execute the Office of President of the United States, and will to the best of my Ability, preserve, protect and defend the Constitution of the United States."

Section 2—President to be Commander-in-Chief. He may require opinions of cabinet officers, etc., may pardon. Treaty-making power. Nomination of certain officers. When President may fill vacancies.

The President shall be Commander in Chief of the Army and Navy of the United States, and of the Militia of the several States, when called into the actual Service of the United States; he may require the Opinion in writing, of the principal Officer in each of the executive Departments, upon any subject relating to the Duties of their respective Offices, and he shall have Power to Grant Reprieves and Pardons for Offenses against the United States, except in Cases of Impeachment.

He shall have Power, by and with the Advice and Consent of the Senate, to make Treaties, provided two-thirds of the Senators present concur; and he shall nominate, and by and with the Advice and Consent of the Senate, shall appoint Ambassadors, other public Ministers and Consuls, Judges of the supreme Court, and all other Officers of the United States, whose Appointments are not herein otherwise provided for, and which shall be established by Law: but the Congress may by Law vest the Appointment of such inferior Officers, as they think proper, in the President alone, in the Courts of Law, or in the Heads of Departments.

The President shall have Power to fill up all Vacancies that may happen during the Recess of the Senate, by granting Commissions which shall expire at the End of their next Session.

Section 3—President shall communicate to Congress. He may convene and adjourn Congress, in case of disagreement, etc. Shall receive ambassadors, execute laws, and commission officers.

He shall from time to time give to the Congress Information of the State of the Union, and recommend to their Consideration such Measures as he shall judge necessary and expedient; he may, on extraordinary Occasions, convene both Houses, or either of them, and in Case of Disagreement between them, with Respect to the Time of Adjournment, he may adjourn them to such Time as he shall think proper; he shall receive Ambassadors and other public Ministers; he shall take Care that the Laws be faithfully executed, and shall Commission all the Officers of the United States.

Section 4—All civil offices forfeited for certain crimes.

The President, Vice President and all civil Officers of the United States, shall be removed from Office on Impeachment for, and Conviction of, Treason, Bribery, or other high Crimes and Misdemeanors.

ARTICLE III.

Section 1—Judicial powers, tenure. Compensation.

The judicial Power of the United States, shall be vested in one supreme Court, and in such inferior Courts as the Congress may from time to time ordain and establish. The Judges, both of the supreme and inferior Courts, shall hold their Offices during good Behaviour, and shall, at stated Times, receive for their Services, a Compensation, which shall not be diminished during their Continuance in Office.

Section 2—Judicial power; to what cases it extends. Original jurisdiction of Supreme Court; appellate jurisdiction. Trial by jury, etc. Trial, where.

The judicial Power shall extend to all Cases, in Law and Equity, arising under this Constitution, the Laws of the United States, and Treaties made, or which shall be made, under their Authority;–to all Cases affecting Ambassadors, other public Ministers and Consuls;–to all Cases of admiralty and maritime Jurisdiction;–to Controversies to which the United States shall be a Party;–to Controversies between two or more States; *[–between a State and Citizens of another State;–]* between Citizens of different States; –between Citizens of the same State claiming Lands under Grants of different States, *[and between a State, or the Citizens thereof, and foreign States, Citizens or Subjects.] [This section is modified by Amendment XI.]*

In all Cases affecting Ambassadors, other public Ministers and Consuls, and those in which a State shall be Party, the supreme Court shall have original Jurisdiction. In all the other Cases before mentioned, the supreme Court shall have appellate Jurisdiction, both as to Law and Fact, with such Exceptions, and under such Regulations as the Congress shall make.

The trial of all Crimes, except in Cases of Impeachment, shall be by Jury; and such Trial shall be held in the State where the said Crimes shall have been committed; but when not committed within any State, the Trial shall be at such Place or Places as the Congress may by Law have directed.

Section 3—Treason Defined. Proof of. Punishment of.

Treason against the United States, shall consist only in levying War against them, or in adhering to their Enemies, giving them Aid and Comfort. No Person shall be convicted of Treason unless on the Testimony of two Witnesses to the same overt Act, or on Confession in open Court.

The Congress shall have Power to declare the Punishment of Treason, but no Attainder of Treason shall work Corruption of Blood, or Forfeiture except during the Life of the Person attainted.

ARTICLE IV.

Section 1—Each State to give credit to the public acts, etc., of every other State.

Full Faith and Credit shall be given in each State to the public Acts, Records, and judicial Proceedings of every other State. And the Congress may by general Laws prescribe the Manner in which such Acts, Records and Proceedings shall be proved, and the Effect thereof.

The judicial Power of the United States, shall be vested in one supreme Court, and in such inferior Courts as the Congress may from time to time ordain and establish. The Judges, both of the supreme and inferior Courts, shall hold their Offices during good Behaviour, and shall, at stated Times, receive for their Services, a Compensation, which shall not be diminished during their Continuance in Office.

Section 2—Privileges of citizens of each State. Fugitives from justice to be delivered up. Persons held to service having escaped, to be delivered up.

The Citizens of each State shall be entitled to all Privileges and Immunities of Citizens in the several States.

A Person charged in any State with Treason, Felony, or other Crime, who shall flee from Justice, and be found in another State, shall on demand of the executive Authority of the State from which he fled, be delivered up, to be removed to the State having Jurisdiction of the Crime.

[No Person held to Service or Labour in one State, under the Laws thereof, escaping into another, shall, in Consequence of any Law or Regulation therein, be discharged from such Service or Labour, but shall be delivered up on Claim of the Party to whom such Service or Labour may be due.] [This clause was superseded by Amendment XIII.]

Section 3—Admission of new States. Power of Congress over territory and other property.

New States may be admitted by the Congress into this Union; but no new State shall be formed or erected within the Jurisdiction of any other State; nor any State be formed by the Junction of two or more States, or parts of States, without the Consent of the Legislatures of the States concerned as well as of the Congress.

The Congress shall have Power to dispose of and make all needful Rules and Regulations respecting the Territory or other Property belonging to the United States; and nothing in this Constitution shall be so construed as to Prejudice any Claims of the United States, or of any particular State.

Section 4—Republican form of government guaranteed. Each State to be protected.

The United States shall guarantee to every State in this Union a Republican Form of Government, and shall protect each of them against Invasion; and on Application of the Legislature, or of the Executive (when the Legislature cannot be convened) against domestic Violence.

ARTICLE V.

Constitution: how amended; proviso.

The Congress, whenever two-thirds of both Houses shall deem it necessary, shall propose Amendments to this Constitution, or, on the Application of the Legislatures of two-thirds of the several States, shall call a Convention for proposing Amendments, which, in either Case, shall be valid to all Intents and Purposes, as part of this Constitution, when ratified by the Legislatures of three-fourths of the several States, or by Conventions in three-fourths thereof, as the one or the other Mode of Ratification may be proposed by the Congress: Provided that no Amendment which may be made prior to the Year One thousand eight hundred and eight shall in any Manner affect the first and fourth Clauses in the Ninth Section of the first Article; and that no State, without its Consent, shall be deprived of its equal Suffrage in the Senate.

ARTICLE VI.

Certain debts, etc., declared valid. Supremacy of Constitution, treaties, and laws of the United States. Oath to support Constitution, by whom taken. No religious test.

All Debts contracted and Engagements entered into, before the Adoption of this Constitution, shall be as valid against the United States under this Constitution, as under the Confederation.

This Constitution, and the Laws of the United States which shall be made in Pursuance thereof; and all Treaties made, or which shall be made, under the Authority of the United States, shall be the supreme Law of the Land; and the Judges in every State shall be bound thereby, any Thing in the Constitution or Laws of any State to the Contrary notwithstanding.

The Senators and Representatives before mentioned, and the Members of the several State Legislatures, and all executive and judicial Officers, both of the United States and of the several States, shall be bound by Oath or Affirmation, to support this Constitution; but no religious Test shall ever be required as a Qualification to any Office or public Trust under the United States.

ARTICLE VII.

What ratification shall establish Constitution.

The Ratification of the Conventions of nine States shall be sufficient for the Establishment of this Constitution between the States so ratifying the Same.

Done in Convention by the Unanimous Consent of the States present the Seventeenth Day of September in the Year of our Lord one thousand seven hundred and Eighty seven and of the Independence of the United States of America the Twelfth.

In Witness whereof We have hereunto subscribed our Names.

Go WASHINGTON, Presidt and deputy from Virginia

New Hampshire—John Langdon, Nicholas Gilman

Massachusetts—Nathaniel Gorham, Rufus King

Connecticut—Wm. Saml. Johnson, Roger Sherman

New York—Alexander Hamilton

New Jersey—Wil: Livingston, David Brearley, Wm. Paterson, Jona: Dayton

Pennsylvania—B Franklin, Thomas Mifflin, Robt Morris, Geo. Clymer, Thos. FitzSimons, Jared Ingersoll, James Wilson, Gouv Morris

Delaware—Geo: Read, Gunning Bedford jun, John Dickinson, Richard Bassett, Jaco: Broom

Maryland—James McHenry, Dan of St Thos. Jenifer, Danl Carroll

Virginia—John Blair, James Madison Jr.

North Carolina—Wm. Blount, Rich'd Dobbs Spaight, Hu Williamson

South Carolina—J. Rutledge, Charles Cotesworth Pinckney, Charles Pinckney, Pierce Butler

Georgia—William Few, Abr Baldwin

Attest: William Jackson, Secretary.

Ten Original Amendments: The Bill of Rights
In force Dec. 15, 1791

[The First Congress, at its first session in the City of New York, Sept. 25, 1789, submitted to the states 12 amendments to clarify certain individual and state rights not named in the Constitution. They are generally called the Bill of Rights.

Influential in framing these amendments was the Declaration of Rights of Virginia, written by George Mason (1725-92) in 1776. Mason, a Virginia delegate to the Constitutional Convention, did not sign the Constitution and opposed its ratification on the ground that it did not sufficiently oppose slavery or safeguard individual rights.

In the preamble to the resolution offering the proposed amendments, Congress said: "The conventions of a number of the States having at the time of their adopting the Constitution, expressed a desire, in order to prevent misconstruction or abuse of its powers, that further declaratory and restrictive clauses should be added, and as extending the ground of public confidence in the government will best insure the beneficent ends of its institution, be it resolved," etc.

Ten of these amendments, now commonly known as one to 10 inclusive, but originally 3 to 12 inclusive, were ratified by the states as follows: New Jersey, Nov. 20, 1789; Maryland, Dec. 19, 1789; North Carolina, Dec. 22, 1789; South Carolina, Jan. 19, 1790; New Hampshire, Jan. 25, 1790; Delaware, Jan. 28, 1790; New York, Feb. 27, 1790; Pennsylvania, Mar. 10, 1790; Rhode Island, June 7, 1790; Vermont, Nov. 3, 1791; Virginia, Dec. 15, 1791; Massachusetts, Mar. 2, 1939; Georgia, Mar. 18, 1939; Connecticut, Apr. 19, 1939. These original 10 ratified amendments follow as Amendments I to X inclusive.

Of the two original proposed amendments that were not ratified promptly by the necessary number of states, the first related to apportionment of Representatives; the second, relating to compensation of members of Congress, was ratified in 1992 and became Amendment 27.]

AMENDMENT I.
Religious establishment prohibited. Freedom of speech, of press, right to assemble and to petition.
Congress shall make no law respecting an establishment of religion, or prohibiting the free exercise thereof; or abridging the freedom of speech, or of the press; or the right of the people peaceably to assemble, and to petition the Government for a redress of grievances.

AMENDMENT II.
Right to keep and bear arms.
A well regulated Militia, being necessary to the security of a free State, the right of the people to keep and bear Arms, shall not be infringed.

AMENDMENT III.
Conditions for quarters for soldiers.
No Soldier shall, in time of peace be quartered in any house, without the consent of the Owner, nor in time of war, but in a manner to be prescribed by law.

AMENDMENT IV.
Protection from unreasonable search and seizure.
The right of the people to be secure in their persons, houses, papers, and effects, against unreasonable searches and seizures, shall not be violated, and no Warrants shall issue, but upon probable cause, supported by Oath or affirmation, and particularly describing the place to be searched, and the persons or things to be seized.

AMENDMENT V.
Provisions concerning prosecution and due process of law. Double jeopardy restriction. Private property not to be taken without compensation.
No person shall be held to answer for a capital, or otherwise infamous crime, unless on a presentment or indictment of a Grand Jury, except in cases arising in the land or naval forces, or in the Militia, when in actual service in time of War or public danger; nor shall any person be subject for the same offence to be twice put in jeopardy of life or limb; nor shall be compelled in any criminal case to be a witness against himself, nor be deprived of life, liberty, or property, without due process of law; nor shall private property be taken for public use, without just compensation.

AMENDMENT VI.
Right to speedy trial, witnesses, etc.
In all criminal prosecutions, the accused shall enjoy the right to a speedy and public trial, by an impartial jury of the State and district wherein the crime shall have been committed, which district shall have been previously ascertained by law, and to be informed of the nature and cause of the accusation; to be confronted with the witnesses against him; to have compulsory process for obtaining witnesses in his favor, and to have the Assistance of Counsel for his defence.

AMENDMENT VII.
Right of trial by jury.
In suits at common law, where the value in controversy shall exceed twenty dollars, the right of trial by jury shall be preserved, and no fact tried by a jury, shall be otherwise reexamined in any Court of the United States, than according to the rules of the common law.

AMENDMENT VIII.
Excessive bail or fines; cruel and unusual punishment.
Excessive bail shall not be required, nor excessive fines imposed, nor cruel and unusual punishments inflicted.

AMENDMENT IX.
Rule of construction of Constitution.
The enumeration in the Constitution, of certain rights, shall not be construed to deny or disparage others retained by the people.

AMENDMENT X.
Rights of States under Constitution.
The powers not delegated to the United States by the Constitution, nor prohibited by it to the States, are reserved to the States respectively, or to the people.

Amendments Since the Bill of Rights

AMENDMENT XI.
Judicial powers construed.
The Judicial power of the United States shall not be construed to extend to any suit in law or equity, commenced or prosecuted against one of the United States by Citizens of another State, or by Citizens or Subjects of any Foreign State.

[This amendment was proposed to the Legislatures of the several States by the Third Congress on March 4, 1794, and was declared to have been ratified in a message from the President to Congress, dated Jan. 8, 1798.

[It was on Jan. 5, 1798, that Secretary of State Pickering received from 12 of the States authenticated ratifications, and informed President John Adams of that fact.

[As a result of later research in the Department of State, it is now established that Amendment XI became part of the Constitution on Feb. 7, 1795, for on that date it had been ratified by 12 States as follows:

[1. New York, Mar. 27, 1794. 2. Rhode Island, Mar. 31, 1794. 3. Connecticut, May 8, 1794. 4. New Hampshire, June 16, 1794. 5. Massachusetts, June 26, 1794. 6. Vermont, between Oct. 9, 1794, and Nov. 9, 1794. 7. Virginia, Nov. 18, 1794. 8. Georgia, Nov. 29, 1794. 9. Kentucky, Dec. 7, 1794. 10. Maryland, Dec. 26, 1794. 11. Delaware, Jan. 23, 1795. 12. North Carolina, Feb. 7, 1795]

[On June 1, 1796, more than a year after Amendment XI had become a part of the Constitution—but before anyone was officially aware of this—Tennessee had been admitted as a State; but not until Oct. 16, 1797, was a certified copy of the resolution of Tennessee proposing the amendment sent to the Governor of Tennessee, John Sevier, by Secretary of State Pickering, whose office was then at Trenton, New Jersey, because of the epidemic of yellow fever at Philadelphia; it seems, however, that the Legislature of Tennessee took no action on Amendment XI, owing doubtless to the fact that public announcement of its adoption was made soon thereafter.]

[Besides the necessary 12 States, one other, South Carolina, ratified Amendment XI, but this action was not taken until Dec. 4, 1797; the two remaining States, New Jersey and Pennsylvania, failed to ratify.]

AMENDMENT XII.

Manner of choosing President and Vice-President.

[Proposed by Congress Dec. 9, 1803; ratified June 15, 1804.]

The Electors shall meet in their respective states and vote by ballot for President and Vice-President, one of whom, at least, shall not be an inhabitant of the same state with themselves; they shall name in their ballots the person voted for as President, and in distinct ballots the person voted for as Vice-President, and they shall make distinct lists of all persons voted for as President, and of all persons voted for as Vice-President, and of the number of votes for each, which lists they shall sign and certify, and transmit sealed to the seat of the government of the United States, directed to the President of the Senate;–The President of the Senate shall, in presence of the Senate and House of Representatives, open all the certificates and the votes shall then be counted;—The person having the greatest number of votes for President, shall be the President, if such number be a majority of the whole number of Electors appointed; and if no person have such majority, then from the persons having the highest numbers not exceeding three on the list of those voted for as President, the House of Representatives shall choose immediately, by ballot, the President. But in choosing the President, the votes shall be taken by states, the representation from each state having one vote; a quorum for this purpose shall consist of a member or members from two-thirds of the states, and a majority of all the states shall be necessary to a choice. *[And if the House of Representatives shall not choose a President whenever the right of choice shall devolve upon them, before the fourth day of March next following, then the Vice-President shall act as President, as in the case of the death or other constitutional disability of the President.] [The words in brackets were superseded by Amendment XX, section 3.]* The person having the greatest number of votes as Vice-President, shall be the Vice-President, if such number be a majority of the whole number of Electors appointed, and if no person have a majority, then from the two highest numbers on the list, the Senate shall choose the Vice-President; a quorum for the purpose shall consist of two-thirds of the whole number of Senators, and a majority of the whole number shall be necessary to a choice. But no person constitutionally ineligible to the office of President shall be eligible to that of Vice-President of the United States.

THE RECONSTRUCTION AMENDMENTS

[Amendments XIII, XIV, and XV are commonly known as the Reconstruction Amendments, inasmuch as they followed the Civil War, and were drafted by Republicans who were bent on imposing their own policy of reconstruction on the South. Postbellum legislatures there— Mississippi, South Carolina, Georgia, for example—had set up laws which, it was charged, were contrived to perpetuate Negro slavery under other names.]

AMENDMENT XIII.

Slavery abolished.

[Proposed by Congress Jan. 31, 1865; ratified Dec. 6, 1865. The amendment, when first proposed by a resolution in Congress, was passed by the Senate, 38 to 6, on Apr. 8, 1864, but was defeated in the House, 95 to 66 on June 15, 1864. On reconsideration by the House, on Jan. 31, 1865, the resolution passed, 119 to 56. It was approved by President Lincoln on Feb. 1, 1865, although the Supreme Court had decided in 1798 that the President has nothing to do with the proposing of amendments to the Constitution, or their adoption.]

1. Neither slavery nor involuntary servitude, except as a punishment for crime whereof the party shall have been duly convicted, shall exist within the United States, or any place subject to their jurisdiction.

2. Congress shall have power to enforce this article by appropriate legislation.

AMENDMENT XIV.

Citizenship rights not to be abridged.

[The following amendment was proposed to the Legislatures of the several states by the 39th Congress, June 13, 1866, ratified July 9, 1868, and declared to have been ratified in a proclamation by the Secretary of State, July 28, 1868.]

[The 14th amendment was adopted only by virtue of ratification subsequent to earlier rejections. Newly constituted legislatures in both North Carolina and South Carolina (respectively July 4 and 9, 1868), ratified the proposed amendment, although earlier legislatures had rejected the proposal. The Secretary of State issued a proclamation, which, though doubtful as to the effect of attempted withdrawals by Ohio and New Jersey, entertained no doubt as to the validity of the ratification by North and South Carolina. The following day (July 21, 1868), Congress passed a resolution which declared the 14th Amendment to be a part of the Constitution and directed the Secretary of State so to promulgate it. The Secretary waited, however, until the newly constituted Legislature of Georgia had ratified the amendment, subsequent to an earlier rejection, before the promulgation of the ratification of the new amendment.]

1. All persons born or naturalized in the United States, and subject to the jurisdiction thereof, are citizens of the United States and of the State wherein they reside. No State shall make or enforce any law which shall abridge the privileges or immunities of citizens of the United States; nor shall any State deprive any person of life, liberty, or property, without due process of law; nor deny to any person within its jurisdiction the equal protection of the laws.

2. Representatives shall be apportioned among the several States according to their respective numbers, counting the whole number of persons in each State, excluding Indians not taxed. But when the right to vote at any election for the choice of electors for President and Vice-President of the United States, Representatives in Congress, the Executive and Judicial officers of a State, or the members of the Legislature thereof, is denied to any of the male inhabitants of such State, being twenty-one years of age, and citizens of the United States, or in any way abridged, except for

participation in rebellion, or other crime, the basis of representation therein shall be reduced in the proportion which the number of such male citizens shall bear to the whole number of male citizens twenty-one years of age in such State.

3. No person shall be a Senator or Representative in Congress, or elector of President and Vice-President, or hold any office, civil or military, under the United States, or under any State, who, having previously taken an oath, as a member of Congress, or as an officer of the United States, or as a member of any State legislature, or as an executive or judicial officer of any State, to support the Constitution of the United States, shall have engaged in insurrection or rebellion against the same, or given aid or comfort to the enemies thereof. But Congress may by a vote of two-thirds of each House, remove such disability.

4. The validity of the public debt of the United States, authorized by law, including debts incurred for payment of pensions and bounties for services in suppressing insurrection or rebellion, shall not be questioned. But neither the United States nor any State shall assume or pay any debt or obligation incurred in aid of insurrection or rebellion against the United States, or any claim for the loss or emancipation of any slave; but all such debts, obligations and claims shall be held illegal and void.

The Congress shall have power to enforce, by appropriate legislation, the provisions of this article.

AMENDMENT XV.

Race no bar to voting rights.

[The following amendment was proposed to the legislatures of the several States by the 40th Congress, Feb. 26, 1869, and ratified Feb. 3, 1870.]

1. The right of citizens of the United States to vote shall not be denied or abridged by the United States or by any State on account of race, color, or previous condition of servitude–

2. The Congress shall have power to enforce this article by appropriate legislation.

AMENDMENT XVI.

Income taxes authorized.

[Proposed by Congress July 12, 1909; ratified Feb. 3, 1913.]

The Congress shall have power to lay and collect taxes on incomes, from whatever source derived, without apportionment among the several States, and without regard to any census or enumeration.

AMENDMENT XVII.

United States Senators to be elected by direct popular vote.

[Proposed by Congress May 13, 1912; ratified Apr. 8, 1913.]

The Senate of the United States shall be composed of two Senators from each State, elected by the people thereof, for six years; and each Senator shall have one vote. The electors in each State shall have the qualifications requisite for electors of the most numerous branch of the State legislatures.

When vacancies happen in the representation of any State in the Senate, the executive authority of such State shall issue writs of election to fill such vacancies: *Provided,* That the legislature of any State may empower the executive thereof to make temporary appointments until the people fill the vacancies by election as the legislature may direct.

This amendment shall not be so construed as to affect the election or term of any Senator chosen before it becomes valid as part of the Constitution.

AMENDMENT XVIII.

Liquor prohibition amendment.

[Proposed by Congress Dec. 18, 1917; ratified Jan. 16, 1919. Repealed by Amendment XXI, effective Dec. 5, 1933.]

1. After one year from the ratification of this article the manufacture, sale, or transportation of intoxicating liquors within, the importation thereof into, or the exportation thereof from the United States and all territory subject to the jurisdiction thereof for beverage purposes is hereby prohibited.

2. The Congress and the several States shall have concurrent power to enforce this article by appropriate legislation.

3. This article shall be inoperative unless it shall have been ratified as an amendment to the Constitution by the legislatures of the several States as provided in the Constitution, within seven years from the date of the submission hereof to the States by the Congress.

[The total vote in the Senates of the various States was 1,310 for, 237 against—84.6% dry. In the lower houses of the States the vote was 3,782 for, 1,035 against—78.5% dry.

[The amendment ultimately was adopted by all the States except Rhode Island.]

AMENDMENT XIX.

Giving nationwide suffrage to women.

[Proposed by Congress June 4, 1919; ratified Aug. 18, 1920.]

The right of citizens of the United States to vote shall not be denied or abridged by the United States or by any State on account of sex.

Congress shall have power to enforce this Article by appropriate legislation.

AMENDMENT XX.

Terms of President and Vice President to begin on Jan. 20; those of Senators, Representatives, Jan. 3.

[Proposed by Congress Mar. 2, 1932; ratified Jan. 23, 1933.]

1. The terms of the President and Vice President shall end at noon on the 20th day of January, and the terms of Senators and Representatives at noon on the 3d day of January, of the years in which such terms would have ended if this article had not been ratified; and the terms of their successors shall then begin.

2. The Congress shall assemble at least once in every year, and such meeting shall begin at noon on the 3d day of January, unless they shall by law appoint a different day.

3. If, at the time fixed for the beginning of the term of the President, the President elect shall have died, the Vice President elect shall become President. If a President shall not have been chosen before the time fixed for the beginning of his term, or if the President elect shall have failed to qualify, then the Vice President elect shall act as President until a President shall have qualified; and the Congress may by law provide for the case wherein neither a President elect nor a Vice President elect shall have qualified, declaring who shall then act as President, or the manner in which one who is to act shall be selected, and such person shall act accordingly until a President or Vice President shall have qualified.

4. The Congress may by law provide for the case of the death of any of the persons from whom the House of Representatives may choose a President whenever the right of choice shall have devolved upon them, and for the case of the death of any of the persons from whom the Senate may choose a Vice President whenever the right of choice shall have devolved upon them.

5. Sections 1 and 2 shall take effect on the 15th day of October following the ratification of this article (Oct. 1933).

6. This article shall be inoperative unless it shall have been ratified as an amendment to the Constitution by the

legislatures of three-fourths of the several States within seven years from the date of its submission.

AMENDMENT XXI.

Repeal of Amendment XVIII.

[Proposed by Congress Feb. 20, 1933; ratified Dec. 5, 1933.]

1. The eighteenth article of amendment to the Constitution of the United States is hereby repealed.

2. The transportation or importation into any State, Territory, or possession of the United States for delivery or use therein of intoxicating liquors, in violation of the laws thereof, is hereby prohibited.

3. This article shall be inoperative unless it shall have been ratified as an amendment to the Constitution by conventions in the several States, as provided in the Constitution, within seven years from the date of the submission hereof to the States by the Congress.

AMENDMENT XXII.

Limiting Presidential terms of office.

[Proposed by Congress Mar. 24, 1947; ratified Feb. 27, 1951.]

1. No person shall be elected to the office of the President more than twice, and no person who has held the office of President, or acted as President, for more than two years of a term to which some other person was elected President shall be elected to the office of the President more than once. But this Article shall not apply to any person holding the office of President when this Article was proposed by the Congress, and shall not prevent any person who may be holding the office of President, or acting as President, during the term within which this Article becomes operative from holding the office of President or acting as President during the remainder of such term.

2. This article shall be inoperative unless it shall have been ratified as an amendment to the Constitution by the legislatures of three-fourths of the several States within seven years from the date of its submission to the States by the Congress.

AMENDMENT XXIII.

Presidential vote for District of Columbia.

[Proposed by Congress June 16, 1960; ratified Mar. 29, 1961.]

1. The District constituting the seat of Government of the United States shall appoint in such manner as the Congress may direct:

A number of electors of President and Vice President equal to the whole number of Senators and Representatives in Congress to which the District would be entitled if it were a State, but in no event more than the least populous State; they shall be in addition to those appointed by the States, but they shall be considered, for the purposes of the election of President and Vice President, to be electors appointed by a State; and they shall meet in the District and perform such duties as provided by the twelfth article of amendment.

2. The Congress shall have power to enforce this article by appropriate legislation.

AMENDMENT XXIV.

Barring poll tax in federal elections.

[Proposed by Congress Sept. 14, 1962; ratified Jan. 23, 1964.]

1. The right of citizens of the United States to vote in any primary or other election for President or Vice President, for electors for President or Vice President, or for Senator or Representative in Congress, shall not be denied or abridged by the United States or any State by reason of failure to pay any poll tax or other tax.

2. The Congress shall have power to enforce this article by appropriate legislation.

AMENDMENT XXV.

Presidential disability and succession.

[Proposed by Congress July 6, 1965; ratified Feb. 10, 1967.]

1. In case of the removal of the President from office or of his death or resignation, the Vice President shall become President.

2. Whenever there is a vacancy in the office of the Vice President, the President shall nominate a Vice President who shall take office upon confirmation by a majority vote of both houses of Congress.

3. Whenever the President transmits to the President pro tempore of the Senate and the Speaker of the House of Representatives his written declaration that he is unable to discharge the powers and duties of his office, and until he transmits to them a written declaration to the contrary, such powers and duties shall be discharged by the Vice President as Acting President.

4. Whenever the Vice President and a majority of either the principal officers of the executive departments or of such other body as Congress may by law provide, transmit to the President pro tempore of the Senate and the Speaker of the House of Representatives their written declaration that the President is unable to discharge the powers and duties of his office, the Vice President shall immediately assume the powers and duties of the office as Acting President.

Thereafter, when the President transmits to the President pro tempore of the Senate and the Speaker of the House of Representatives his written declaration that no inability exists, he shall resume the powers and duties of his office unless the Vice President and a majority of either the principal officers of the executive department or of such other body as Congress may by law provide, transmit within four days to the President pro tempore of the Senate and the Speaker of the House of Representatives their written declaration that the President is unable to discharge the powers and duties of his office. Thereupon Congress shall decide the issue, assembling within forty-eight hours for that purpose if not in session. If the Congress, within twenty-one days after receipt of the latter written declaration, or, if Congress is not in session, within twenty-one days after Congress is required to assemble, determines by two-thirds vote of both Houses that the President is unable to discharge the powers and duties of his office, the Vice President shall continue to discharge the same as Acting President; otherwise, the President shall resume the powers and duties of his office.

AMENDMENT XXVI.

Lowering voting age to 18 years.

[Proposed by Congress Mar. 23, 1971; ratified July 1, 1971.]

1. The right of citizens of the United States, who are eighteen years of age or older, to vote shall not be denied or abridged by the United States or by any State on account of age.

2. The Congress shall have the power to enforce this article by appropriate legislation.

AMENDMENT XXVII.

Congressional pay.

[Proposed by Congress Sept. 25, 1789; ratified May 7, 1992.]

No law, varying the compensation for the services of the Senators and Representatives, shall take effect, until an election of Representatives shall have intervened.

How a Bill Becomes a Law

A senator or representative introduces a bill in Congress by sending it to the clerk of the House or the Senate, who assigns it a number and title. This procedure is termed the first reading. The clerk then refers the bill to the appropriate committee of the Senate or House.

If the committee opposes the bill, it will table, or kill, it. Otherwise, the committee holds hearings to listen to opinions and facts offered by members and other interested people. The committee then debates the bill and possibly offers amendments. A vote is taken, and if favorable, the bill is sent back to the clerk of the House or Senate.

The clerk reads the bill to the house—the second reading. Members may then debate the bill and suggest amendments.

After debate and possibly amendment, the bill is given a third reading, simply of the title, and put to a voice or roll-call vote.

If passed, the bill goes to the other house, where it may be defeated or passed, with or without amendments. If defeated, the bill dies. If passed with amendments, a conference committee made up of members of both houses works out the differences and arrives at a compromise.

After passage of the final version by both houses, the bill is sent to the president. If the president signs it, the bill becomes a law. The president may, however, veto the bill by refusing to sign it and sending it back to the house where it originated, with reasons for the veto.

The president's objections are then read and debated, and a roll-call vote is taken. If the bill receives less than a two-thirds majority, it is defeated. If it receives at least two-thirds, it is sent to the other house. If that house also passes it by at least a two-thirds majority, the one veto is overridden, and the bill becomes a law.

If the president neither signs nor vetoes the bill within 10 days—not including Sundays—it automatically becomes a law even without the president's signature. However, if Congress has adjourned within those 10 days, the bill is automatically killed; this indirect rejection is termed a pocket veto.

Note: Under the Line Item Veto Act, effective Jan. 1, 1997, the president was authorized, under certain circumstances, to veto a bill in part, but the legislation was found unconstitutional by the Supreme Court, June 25, 1998.

Confederate States and Secession

The American Civil War (1861-65) grew out of sectional disputes over the continued existence of slavery in the South and the contention of Southern legislators that the states retained many rights, including the right to secede.

The war was not fought by state against state but by one federal regime against another, the Confederate government in Richmond assuming control over the economic, political, and military life of the South, under protest from Georgia and South Carolina.

South Carolina voted an ordinance of secession from the Union, repealing its 1788 ratification of the U.S. Constitution on Dec. 20, 1860, to take effect on Dec. 24. Other states seceded in 1861. Their votes in conventions were: Mississippi, Jan. 9, 84-15; Florida, Jan. 10, 62-7; Alabama, Jan. 11, 61-39; Georgia, Jan. 19, 208-89; Louisiana, Jan. 26, 113-17; Texas, Feb. 1, 166-7, ratified by popular vote on Feb. 23 (for 34,794, against 11,325); Virginia, Apr. 17, 88-55, ratified by popular vote on May 23 (for 128,884; against 32,134); Arkansas, May 6, 69-1; Tennessee, May 7, ratified by popular

vote on June 8 (for 104,019, against 47,238); North Carolina, May 20.

Missouri Unionists stopped secession in conventions Feb. 28 and Mar. 9. The legislature condemned secession Mar. 7. Under the protection of Confederate troops, secessionist members of the legislature adopted a resolution of secession at Neosho, Oct. 31. The Confederate Congress seated the secessionists' representatives.

Kentucky did not secede, and its government remained Unionist. In a part of the state occupied by Confederate troops, Kentuckians approved secession, and the Confederate Congress admitted their representatives.

The Maryland legislature voted against secession Apr. 27, 53-13. Delaware did not secede. Western Virginia held conventions at Wheeling, named a pro-Union governor on June 11, 1861, and was admitted to the Union as West Virginia on June 20, 1863. Its constitution provided for gradual abolition of slavery.

Confederate Government

Forty-two delegates from South Carolina, Georgia, Alabama, Mississippi, Louisiana, and Florida met in convention at Montgomery, AL, on Feb. 4, 1861. They adopted a provisional constitution of the Confederate States of America and elected Jefferson Davis (MS) as provisional president and Alexander H. Stephens (GA) as provisional vice president.

A permanent constitution was adopted Mar. 11. It abolished the African slave trade, but it did not bar interstate

commerce in slaves. On July 20 the Congress moved to Richmond, VA. Davis was elected president in November and was inaugurated on Feb. 22, 1862.

The Congress adopted a flag, consisting of a red field with a white stripe, and a blue jack with a circle of white stars. Later the more popular flag was the red field with blue diagonal crossbars that held 13 white stars, for the 11 states in the Confederacy plus Kentucky and Missouri.

Lincoln's Address at Gettysburg, 1863

Fourscore and seven years ago our fathers brought forth on this continent a new nation, conceived in liberty and dedicated to the proposition that all men are created equal.

Now we are engaged in a great civil war, testing whether that nation or any nation so conceived and so dedicated can long endure. We are met on a great battle field of that war. We have come to dedicate a portion of that field, as a final resting-place for those who here gave their lives that that nation might live. It is altogether fitting and proper that we should do this.

But, in a larger sense, we can not dedicate—we can not consecrate—we can not hallow—this ground. The brave men, living and dead, who struggled here, have consecrated

it, far above our poor power to add or detract. The world will little note, nor long remember, what we say here, but it can never forget what they did here. It is for us the living, rather, to be dedicated here to the unfinished work which they who fought here have thus far so nobly advanced. It is rather for us to be here dedicated to the great task remaining before us—that from these honored dead we take increased devotion to that cause for which they gave the last full measure of devotion—that we here highly resolve that these dead shall not have died in vain—that this nation, under God, shall have a new birth of freedom—and that government of the people, by the people, for the people, shall not perish from the earth.

Selected Landmark Decisions of the U.S. Supreme Court, 1803-2007

See also Year in Review: Notable Supreme Court Decisions, 2006-07.

1803: *Marbury v. Madison.* The Court ruled that Congress exceeded its power in the Judiciary Act of 1789; the Court thus established its power to review acts of Congress and declare invalid those it found in conflict with the Constitution.

1819: *McCulloch v. Maryland.* The Court ruled that Congress had the authority to charter a national bank, under the Constitution's granting of the power to enact all laws "necessary and proper" to responsibilities of government.

1819: *Trustees of Dartmouth College v. Woodward.* The Court ruled that a state could not arbitrarily alter the terms of a college's contract. (The Court later used a similar principle to limit the states' ability to interfere with business contracts.)

1857: *Dred Scott v. Sanford.* The Court declared unconstitutional the already-repealed Missouri Compromise of 1820 because it deprived a person of his or her property—a slave—without due process of law. The Court also ruled that slaves were not citizens of any state nor of the U.S. (The latter part of the decision was overturned by ratification of the 14th Amendment in 1868.)

1896: *Plessy v. Ferguson.* The Court ruled that a state law requiring federal railroad trains to provide separate but equal facilities for black and white passengers neither infringed upon federal authority to regulate interstate commerce nor violated the 13th and 14th Amendments. (The "separate but equal" doctrine remained effective until the 1954 *Brown v. Board of Education* decision.)

1904: *Northern Securities Co. v. U.S.* The Court ruled that a holding company formed solely to eliminate competition between two railroad lines was a combination in restraint of trade, violating the federal antitrust act.

1908: *Muller v. Oregon.* The Court upheld a state law limiting the working hours of women. (Louis D. Brandeis, counsel for the state, cited evidence from social workers, physicians, and factory inspectors that the number of hours women worked affected their health and morals.)

1911: *Standard Oil Co. of New Jersey et al. v. U.S.* The Court ruled that the Standard Oil Trust must be dissolved because of its unreasonable restraint of trade.

1919: *Schenck v. U.S.* The Court sustained the Espionage Act of 1917, maintaining that freedom of speech and press could be constrained if "the words used . . . create a clear and present danger."

1925: *Gitlow v. New York.* The Court ruled that the 1st Amendment prohibition against government abridgment of the freedom of speech applied to the states as well as to the federal government. The decision was the first of a number of rulings holding that the 14th Amendment extended the guarantees of the Bill of Rights to state action.

1935: *Schechter Poultry Corp. v. U.S.* The Court ruled that Congress exceeded its authority to delegate legislative powers and to regulate interstate commerce when it enacted the National Industrial Recovery Act, which afforded the U.S. president too much discretionary power.

1951: *Dennis et al. v. U.S.* The Court upheld convictions under the Smith Act of 1940 for invoking Communist theory advocating the forcible overthrow of the government. In *Yates v. U.S.* [1957], the Court moderated this ruling by allowing such advocacy in the abstract, if not connected to action to achieve the goal.)

1954: *Brown v. Board of Education of Topeka.* The Court ruled that separate public schools for black and white students were inherently unequal, so that state-sanctioned segregation in public schools violated the equal protection guarantee of the 14th Amendment. And in *Bolling v. Sharpe* the same year, the Court ruled that the congressionally mandated segregated public school system in the District of Columbia violated the 5th Amendment's due process guarantee of personal liberty. (The Brown ruling also led to abolition of state-sponsored segregation in other public facilities.)

1957: *Roth v. U.S.; Alberts v. California.* The Court ruled obscene material was not protected by 1st Amendment guarantees of freedom of speech and press, defining obscene as "utterly without redeeming social value" and appealing to "prurient interests" in the average person's view. This definition was modified in later decisions, and the "average person" standard was replaced by the "local community" standard in *Miller v. California* (1973).

1961: *Mapp v. Ohio.* The Court ruled that evidence obtained in violation of the 4th Amendment guarantee against unreasonable search and seizure must be excluded from use at state as well as federal trials.

1962: *Engel v. Vitale.* The Court held that government bodies could not encourage the recitation of a state-composed prayer in public schools, even if nondenominational, because this would be an unconstitutional attempt to establish religion.

1962: *Baker v. Carr.* The Court held that the constitutional challenges to the unequal distribution of voters among legislative districts could be resolved by federal courts.

1963: *Gideon v. Wainwright.* The Court ruled that state and federal defendants charged with serious crimes must have access to an attorney, at state expense if necessary.

1964: *New York Times Co. v. Sullivan.* The Court ruled that the 1st Amendment protected the press from libel suits for defamatory reports about public officials unless an injured party could prove that a defamatory report was made out of malice or "reckless disregard" for the truth.

1965: *Griswold v. Connecticut.* The Court ruled that a state unconstitutionally interfered with personal privacy in the marriage relationship when it prohibited anyone, including married couples, from using contraceptives.

1966: *Miranda v. Arizona.* The Court ruled that, under the guarantee of due process, suspects in custody, before being questioned, must be informed that they have the right to remain silent, that anything they say may be used against them, and that they have the right to counsel.

1973: *Roe v. Wade; Doe v. Bolton.* The Court ruled that the fetus was not a "person" with constitutional rights and that a right to privacy inherent in the 14th Amendment's due process guarantee of personal liberty protected a woman's decision to have an abortion. During the 1st trimester of pregnancy, the Court maintained, the decision should be left entirely to a woman and her physician. Some regulation of abortion procedures was allowed in the 2nd trimester, and some restriction of abortion in the 3rd.

1974: *U.S. v. Nixon.* The Court ruled that neither the separation of powers nor the need to preserve the confidentiality of presidential communications could alone justify an absolute executive privilege of immunity from judicial demands for evidence to be used in a criminal trial.

1976: *Gregg v. Georgia; Proffit v. Florida; Jurek v. Texas.* The Court held that death, as a punishment for persons convicted of 1st degree murder, was not in and of itself cruel and unusual punishment in violation of the 8th Amendment. But the Court ruled that the sentencing judge and jury must consider the individual character of the offender and the circumstances of the particular crime.

1978: *Regents of the Univ. of Calif. v. Bakke.* The Court ruled that a special admissions program for a state medical school, under which a set number of places were reserved for minorities, violated the 1964 Civil Rights Act, which forbids excluding anyone, because of race, from a federally funded program. However, the Court ruled that race could be considered as one of a complex of factors.

1986: *Bowers v. Hardwick.* The Court refused to extend any constitutional right of privacy to homosexual activity, upholding a Georgia antisodomy law that in effect made such activity a crime. However, the law was struck down by the state supreme court in 1998, and in *Lawrence v. Texas* (2003), the U.S. Supreme Court struck down all state antisodomy laws, as violations of liberty prohibited in the 14th Amendment's due process clause. Also, in *Romer v. Evans* (1996), the Court struck down a Colorado constitutional provision that it ruled violated the 14th Amendment's Equal Protection Clause because it barred legislation whereby "homosexual orientation, conduct, practices, or relationships" granted a person "minority status, quota preferences, protected status, or claim of discrimination."

1990: *Cruzan v. Missouri.* The Court ruled that a person had the right to refuse life-sustaining medical treatment. However, the Court also ruled that, before treatment could be withheld from a comatose patient, a state could require "clear and convincing evidence" that the patient would not have wanted to live. In two **1997** rulings, *Washington v. Glucksberg* and *Vacco v. Quill,* the Court ruled that states could ban doctor-assisted suicide.

1995: *Adarand Constructors, Inc., v. Peña.* The Court held that federal programs that classify people by race, unless "narrowly tailored" to accomplish a "compelling governmental interest," may violate the right to equal protection.

1995: *U.S. Term Limits Inc. v. Thornton.* The Court ruled that neither states nor Congress could limit terms of members of Congress, since the Constitution reserves to the people the right to choose federal lawmakers.

1997: *Clinton v. Jones.* Rejecting an appeal by Pres. Clinton in a sexual harassment suit, the Court ruled that a sitting president did not have temporary immunity from a lawsuit for actions outside the realm of official duties.

1997: *City of Boerne v. Flores.* The Court overturned a 1993 law banning enforcement of laws that "substantially burden" religious practice unless there is a "compelling need" to do so. The Court held that the act was an unwarranted intrusion by Congress on states' prerogatives and an infringement of the judiciary's role.

1997: *Reno v. ACLU.* Citing the right to free expression, the Court overturned a provision making it a crime to display or distribute "indecent" or "patently offensive" material on the Internet. The Court ruled, however, in *NEA v. Finley* **(1998)** that "general standards of decency" may be used as a criterion in federal arts funding.

1998: *Clinton v. City of New York.* The Court struck down the Line-Item Veto Act (1996), holding that it unconstitutionally gave the president "the unilateral power to change the text of duly enacted statutes."

1998: *Faragher v. City of Boca Raton*; *Burlington Industries, Inc. v. Ellerth.* The Court issued new guidelines for workplace sexual harassment suits, holding employers responsible for misconduct by supervisory employees. And in *Oncale v. Sundowner Offshore Services,* the Court ruled that the law against sexual harassment applies regardless of whether harasser and victim are the same sex.

1999: *Dept. of Commerce v. U.S. House.* Upholding a challenge to plans for the 2000 census, the Court prohibited statistical sampling, favored by Democrats, in the apportioning of seats in the U.S. House of Representatives. The Court maintained that an actual head count was required.

1999: *Alden v. Maine*; *Florida Prepaid v. College Savings Bank*; *College Savings Bank v. Florida.* In a series of rulings, the Court applied the principle of "sovereign immunity" to shield states in large part from being sued under federal law.

2000: *Boy Scouts of America v. Dale.* The Court ruled that the Boy Scouts could dismiss a troop leader after learning he was gay, holding that the right to freedom of association outweighed a New Jersey antidiscrimination statute.

2000: *Stenberg v. Carhart.* The Court struck down a Nebraska law that banned so-called partial-birth abortion. It argued that the law could be interpreted as banning other abortion procedures and that it should have made exception for reasons of health. (*See* **1973:** *Roe v. Wade.*)

2000: *Bush v. Gore.* The Court ruled that manual recounts of presidential ballots in the Nov. 2000 election could

not proceed because inconsistent evaluation standards in different counties violated the equal protection clause. In effect, the ruling meant existing official results leaving George W. Bush as narrow winner of the election would prevail.

2001: *Easley v. Cromartie.* The Court ruled that North Carolina's 12th Congressional District, whose irregular shape had been challenged as an unconstitutional racial gerrymander, was the permissible result of attempts to create a majority-Democrat district.

2001: *Good News Club v. Milford Central School.* The justices found that religious and secular organizations were entitled to equal access to public elementary school grounds for after-school meetings.

2002: *Atkins v. Virginia.* The Court ruled that the execution of mentally retarded felons violated the 8th Amendment ban on "cruel and unusual punishment."

2002: *Ring v. Arizona.* The Court found that only a jury, not a judge, could decide to impose the death penalty.

2002: *Zelman v. Simmons-Harris.* The Court ruled that publicly funded tuition vouchers could be used at religious schools without violating the separation of church and state.

2002: *Federal Maritime Commission v. South Carolina State Ports Authority.* The Court ruled that the 11th Amendment gave states immunity from private lawsuits involving federal agencies.

2003: *Grutter v. Bollinger*; *Gratz v. Bollinger.* The Court upheld affirmative action in admission policies at the Univ. of Michigan Law School. However, in a second decision, the Court ruled against a strict point system based on racial and ethnic backgrounds, as used in the university's undergraduate admissions process.

2004: *Rasul v. Bush*; *Al Odah v. U.S.* The Court ruled that terrorism detainees held at the U.S. naval base at Guantanamo Bay, Cuba, could challenge their detentions in U.S. courts.

2004: *Tennessee v. Lane.* The Court ruled that disabled individuals could sue states under the Americans with Disabilities Act for failing to provide adequate access to state courthouses, despite states' usual immunity from private lawsuits in federal court.

2004: *Locke v. Davey.* The justices decided that a scholarship program provided by the state of Washington did not violate the right to free exercise of religion in denying aid to students preparing for the clergy.

2004: *Ashcroft v. ACLU et al.* The Court struck down the Child Online Protection Act, which Congress passed in 1998 to restrict access to online pornography by minors, on the basis that the law, as written, violated the 1st Amendment right of free speech.

2005: *Kelo v. City of New London.* The Court ruled that local governments could force property owners to sell their land in order to facilitate private development projects deemed to be economically beneficial to the community.

2005: *Roper v. Simmons.* The Court ruled that executions of convicts who committed their crimes before age 18 were prohibited under the 8th Amendment ban on cruel and unusual punishment.

2006: *Garcetti v. Ceballos.* The Court ruled that the 1st Amendment guarantee of free speech did not protect statements made by public employees in the course of their official duties.

2006: *Hamdan v. Rumsfeld.* The Court ruled that Pres. George W. Bush's system for trying terrorism detainees at the U.S. military base in Guantanamo Bay, Cuba, was unauthorized under both federal law and the international Geneva Conventions.

2007: *Gonzales v. Carhart et al*; *Gonzales v. Planned Parenthood Federation of America.* The Court upheld a 2003 federal law prohibiting the abortion procedure known as intact dilation and extraction, or "partial-birth" abortion.

2007: *Parents Involved in Community Schools v. Seattle School District No. 1*; *Madison v. Jefferson County Board of Education.* The Court ruled that two school districts could not, to encourage diversity, use "racial classifications in making school assignments."

Presidential Oath of Office

The Constitution (Article II) directs that the president-elect shall take the following oath or affirmation to be inaugurated as president: "I do solemnly swear [affirm] that I will faithfully execute the office of President of the United States, and will, to the best of my ability, preserve, protect, and defend the Constitution of the United States." (Custom decrees the addition of the words "So help me God" at the end of the oath when taken by the president-elect, with the left hand on the Bible for the duration of the oath, and the right hand slightly raised.)

Law on Succession to the Presidency

If by reason of death, resignation, removal from office, inability, or failure to qualify there is neither a president nor vice president to discharge the powers and duties of the office of president, then the speaker of the House of Representatives shall upon his resignation as speaker and as representative, act as president. The same rule shall apply in the case of the death, resignation, removal from office, or inability of an individual acting as president.

If at the time when a speaker is to begin the discharge of the powers and duties of the office of president there is no speaker, or the speaker fails to qualify as acting president, then the president pro tempore of the Senate, upon his resignation as president pro tempore and as senator, shall act as president.

An individual acting as president shall continue to act until the expiration of the then current presidential term, except that (1) if his discharge of the powers and duties of the office is founded in whole or in part in the failure of both the president-elect and the vice president-elect to qualify, then he shall act only until a president or vice president qualifies, and (2) if his discharge of the powers and duties of the office is founded in whole or in part on the inability of the president or vice president, then he shall act only until the removal of the disability of one of such individuals.

If, by reason of death, resignation, removal from office, or failure to qualify, there is no president pro tempore to act as president, then the officer of the United States who is highest on the following list, and who is not under any disability to discharge the powers and duties of president shall act as president; the secretaries of state, treasury, defense, attorney general; secretaries of interior, agriculture, commerce, labor, health and human services, housing and urban development, transportation, energy, education, veterans affairs.

[Legislation approved July 18, 1947; amended Sept. 9, 1965, Oct. 15, 1966, Aug. 4, 1977, and Sept. 27, 1979. See also Constitutional Amendment XXV.]

Origin of the United States National Motto

In God We Trust, designated as the U.S. National Motto by Congress in 1956, originated during the Civil War as an inscription for U.S. coins, although it was used by Francis Scott Key in a slightly different form when he wrote "The Star-Spangled Banner" in 1814. On Nov. 13, 1861, when Union morale had been shaken by battlefield defeats, the Rev. M. R. Watkinson, of Ridleyville, PA, wrote to Sec. of the Treasury Salmon P. Chase. "From my heart I have felt our national shame in disowning God as not the least of our present national disasters," the minister wrote, suggesting "recognition of the Almighty God in some form on our coins." Sec. Chase ordered designs prepared with the inscription *In God We Trust* and backed coinage legislation that authorized use of this slogan. The motto first appeared on some U.S. coins in 1864, and disappeared and reappeared on various coins until 1955, when Congress ordered it placed on all paper money and all coins.

The Great Seal of the U.S.

On July 4, 1776, the Continental Congress appointed a committee consisting of Benjamin Franklin, John Adams, and Thomas Jefferson "to bring in a device for a seal of the United States of America." The designs submitted by this and a subsequent committee were considered unacceptable. After many delays, a third committee, appointed early in 1782, presented a design prepared by lawyer William Barton. Charles Thomson, the secretary of Congress, suggested certain changes, and Congress finally approved the design on June 20, 1782. The obverse side of the seal shows an American bald eagle. In its mouth is a ribbon bearing the motto *E Pluribus Unum* (out of many, one). In the eagle's talons are 13 arrows of war and an olive branch of peace. The reverse side shows an unfinished pyramid with an eye (the Eye of Providence) above it.

The Flag of the U.S.—The Stars and Stripes

The 50-star flag of the United States was raised for the first time officially at 12:01 AM on July 4, 1960, at Fort McHenry National Monument in Baltimore, MD. The 50th star had been added for Hawaii; a year earlier the 49th, for Alaska. Before that, no star had been added since 1912, when New Mexico and Arizona were admitted to the Union.

The true history of the Stars and Stripes has become so cluttered by myth and tradition that the facts are difficult, and in some cases impossible, to establish. For example, it is not certain who designed the Stars and Stripes, who made the first such flag, or even whether it ever flew in any sea fight or land battle of the American Revolution.

All agree, however, that the Stars and Stripes originated as the result of a resolution offered by the Marine Committee of the Second Continental Congress at Philadelphia and adopted on June 14, 1777. It read:

Resolved: that the flag of the United States be thirteen stripes, alternate red and white; that the union be thirteen stars, white in a blue field, representing a new constellation.

Congress gave no hint as to the designer of the flag, no instructions as to the arrangement of the stars, and no information on its appropriate uses. Historians have been unable to find the original flag law.

The resolution establishing the flag was not even published until Sept. 2, 1777. Despite repeated requests, Washington did not get the flags until 1783, after the American Revolution was over. And there is no certainty that they were the Stars and Stripes.

Early Flags

Many historians consider the first flag of the U.S. to have been the Grand Union (sometimes called Great Union) flag, although the Continental Congress never officially adopted it. This flag was a modification of the British Meteor flag, which had the red cross of St. George and the white cross of St. Andrew combined in the blue canton. For the Grand Union flag, 6 horizontal stripes were imposed on the red field, dividing it into 13 alternating red and white stripes. On

Jan. 1, 1776, when the Continental Army came into formal existence, this flag was unfurled on Prospect Hill, Somerville, MA. Washington wrote that "we hoisted the Union Flag in compliment to the United Colonies."

One of several flags about which controversy has raged for years is at Easton, PA. Containing the devices of the national flag in reversed order, this flag has been in the public library at Easton for more than 150 years. Some contend that this flag was actually the first Stars and Stripes, first displayed on July 8, 1776. This flag has 13 red and white stripes in the canton, 13 white stars centered in a blue field.

A flag was hastily improvised from garments by the defenders of Ft. Schuyler at Rome, NY, Aug. 3-22, 1777. Historians believe it was the Grand Union Flag.

The Sons of Liberty had a flag of 9 red and white stripes, to signify 9 colonies, when they met in New York in 1765 to oppose the Stamp Tax. By 1775, the flag had grown to 13 red and white stripes, with a rattlesnake on it.

At Concord, Apr. 19, 1775, the minutemen from Bedford, MA, are said to have carried a flag having a silver arm with sword on a red field. At Cambridge, MA, the Sons of Liberty used a plain red flag with a green pine tree on it.

In June 1775, Washington went from Philadelphia to Boston to take command of the army, escorted to New York by the Philadelphia Light Horse Troop. It carried a yellow flag that had an elaborate coat of arms—the shield charged with 13 knots, the motto "For These We Strive"—and a canton of 13 blue and silver stripes.

In Feb. 1776, Col. Christopher Gadsden, a member of the Continental Congress, gave the South Carolina Provincial Congress a flag "such as is to be used by the commander-in-chief of the American Navy." It had a yellow field, with a rattlesnake about to strike and the words "Don't Tread on Me."

At the Battle of Bennington, Aug. 16, 1777, patriots used a flag of 7 white and 6 red stripes with a blue canton extending down 9 stripes and showing an arch of 11 white stars over the figure 76 and a star in each of the upper corners. The stars are 7-pointed. This flag is preserved in the historical museum in Bennington, VT.

At the Battle of Cowpens, Jan. 17, 1781, the 3d Maryland Regiment is said to have carried a flag of 13 red and white stripes, with a blue canton containing 12 stars in a circle around one star.

Who Designed the Flag? No one knows for certain. Francis Hopkinson, designer of a naval flag, declared he also had designed the flag and in 1781 asked Congress to reimburse him for his services. Congress did not do so. Dumas Malone

of Columbia University wrote: "This talented man . . . designed the American flag."

Who Called the Flag "Old Glory"? The flag is said to have been named Old Glory by William Driver, a sea captain of Salem, MA. One legend has it that when he raised the flag on his brig, the *Charles Doggett*, in 1824, he said: "I name thee Old Glory." But his daughter, who presented the flag to the Smithsonian Institution, said he named it at his 21st birthday celebration on Mar. 17, 1824, when his mother presented the homemade flag to him.

The Betsy Ross Legend. The widely publicized legend that Betsy Ross made the first Stars and Stripes in June 1776, at the request of a committee composed of George Washington, Robert Morris, and George Ross, an uncle, was first made public in 1870, by a grandson of Ms. Ross. Historians have been unable to find a historical record of such a meeting or committee.

Adding New Stars

The flag of 1777 was used until 1795. Then, on the admission of Vermont and Kentucky to the Union, Congress passed and Pres. Washington signed an act that after May 1, 1795, the flag should have 15 stripes, alternating red and white, and 15 white stars on a blue field.

When new states were admitted, it became evident that the flag would become burdened with stripes. Congress thereupon ordered that after July 4, 1818, the flag should have 13 stripes, symbolizing the 13 original states; that the union have 20 stars, and that whenever a new state was admitted a new star should be added on the July 4 following admission.

No law designates the permanent arrangement of the stars. However, since 1912, when a new state has been admitted, the new design has been announced by executive order. No star is specifically identified with any state.

Code of Etiquette for Display and Use of the U.S. Flag

Reviewed by National Flag Foundation

Although the Stars and Stripes originated in 1777, it was not until 146 years later that there was a serious attempt to establish a uniform code of etiquette for the U.S. flag. On Feb. 15, 1923, the War Department issued a circular on the rules of flag usage. These rules were adopted almost in their entirety June 14, 1923, by a conference of 68 patriotic organizations in Washington, DC. Finally, on June 22, 1942, a joint resolution of Congress, amended by Public Law 94-344, July 7, 1976, codified "existing rules and customs pertaining to the display and use of the flag."

When to Display the Flag—The flag should be displayed on all days, especially on legal holidays and other special occasions, on official buildings when in use, in or near polling places on election days, and in or near schools when in session. Citizens may fly the flag at any time. It is customary to display it only from sunrise to sunset on buildings and on stationary flagstaffs in the open. It may be displayed at night, however, on special occasions, preferably lighted. The flag now flies over the White House both day and night.

It flies over the Senate wing of the Capitol when the Senate is in session and over the House wing when that body is in session. It flies day and night over the east and west fronts of the Capitol, without floodlights at night but receiving illumination from the Capitol Dome. It flies 24 hours a day at several other places, including the Ft. McHenry National Monument in Baltimore, where it inspired Francis Scott Key to write "The Star Spangled Banner." The flag also flies 24 hours a day, properly illuminated, at U.S. Customs ports of entry.

Flying the Flag at Half-Staff—Flying the flag at half-staff, that is, halfway up the staff, is a signal of mourning. The flag should be hoisted to the top of the staff for an instant before being lowered to half-staff. It should be hoisted to the peak again before being lowered for the day or night.

As provided by presidential proclamation, the flag should fly at half-staff for 30 days from the day of death of a president or former president; for 10 days from the day of death of a vice president, chief justice or retired chief justice of the U.S., or speaker of the House of Representatives; from day of death until burial of an associate justice of the Supreme Court, cabinet member, former vice president, Senate president pro tempore, or majority or minority Senate or House leader; for a U.S. senator, representative, territorial delegate, or the resident commissioner of Puerto Rico, on day of death and the following day within the metropolitan area of the District of Columbia and from day of death until burial within the decedent's state, congressional district, territory or commonwealth; and for the death of the governor of a state, territory, or possession of the U.S., from day of death until burial.

On Memorial Day, the flag should fly at half-staff until noon and then be raised to the peak. The flag should also fly at half-staff on Korean War Veterans Armistice Day (July 27), National Pearl Harbor Remembrance Day (Dec. 7), and Peace Officers Memorial Day (May 15).

How to Fly the Flag—The flag should be hoisted briskly and lowered ceremoniously and should never be allowed to touch the ground or the floor. When the flag is hung over a sidewalk from a rope extending from a building to a pole, the union should be away from the building. When the flag is hung over the center of a street the union should be to the north in an east-west street and to the east in a north-south street. No other flag may be flown above or, if on the same level, to the right of the U.S. flag, except that at the United Nations Headquarters the UN flag may be placed above flags of all member nations and other national flags may be flown with equal prominence or honor with the flag of the U.S. At services by Navy chaplains at sea, the church pennant may be flown above the flag.

When two flags are placed against a wall with crossed staffs, the U.S. flag should be at right—its own right, and its staff should be in front of the staff of the other flag; when a number of flags are grouped and displayed from staffs, it should be at the center and highest point of the group.

Church and Platform Use—In an auditorium, the flag may be displayed flat, above and behind the speaker. When displayed from a staff in a church or in a public auditorium, the flag should hold the position of superior prominence, in advance of the audience, and in the position of honor at the speaker's right as she or he faces the audience. Any other flag so displayed should be placed on the left of the speaker or to the right of the audience.

When the flag is displayed horizontally or vertically against a wall, the stars should be uppermost and at the observer's left.

When used to cover a casket, the flag should be placed so that the union is at the head and over the left shoulder. It should not be lowered into the grave nor touch the ground.

How to Dispose of Worn Flags—When the flag is in such condition that it is no longer a fitting emblem for display, it should be destroyed in a dignified way, preferably by burning.

When to Salute the Flag—All persons present should face the flag, stand at attention, and salute on the following occasions: (1) when the flag is passing in a parade or in a review, (2) during the ceremony of hoisting or lowering, (3) when the national anthem is played, and (4) during the Pledge of Allegiance. Those present in uniform should render the military salute. Those not in uniform should place the right hand over the heart. A man wearing a hat should remove it with his right hand and hold it to his left shoulder during the salute.

Prohibited Uses of the Flag—The flag should not be dipped to any person or thing. (An exception—customarily, ships salute by dipping their colors.) It should never be displayed with the union down save as a distress signal. It should never be carried flat or horizontally, but always aloft and free.

It should not be displayed on a float, an automobile, or a boat except from a staff. It should never be used as a covering for a ceiling, nor have placed on it any word, design, or drawing. It should never be used as a receptacle for carrying anything. It should not be used to cover a statue or a monument.

The flag should never be used for advertising purposes, nor be embroidered on such articles as cushions or handkerchiefs, printed or otherwise impressed on boxes or anything that is designed for temporary use and discard; or used as a costume or athletic uniform. Advertising signs should not be fastened to its staff or halyard.

The flag should never be used as drapery of any sort, never festooned, drawn back, nor up, in folds, but always allowed to fall free. Bunting of blue, white, and red, always arranged with the blue above and the white in the middle, should be used for covering a speaker's desk, draping the front of a platform, and for decoration in general.

An act of Congress approved on Feb. 8, 1917, provided certain penalties for the desecration, mutilation, or improper use of the flag within the District of Columbia. A 1968 federal law provided penalties of as much as a year's imprisonment or a $1,000 fine or both for publicly burning or otherwise desecrating any U.S. flag. In addition, many states have laws against flag desecration. In 1989, the Supreme Court ruled that no laws could prohibit political protesters from burning the flag. The decision had the effect of declaring unconstitutional the flag desecration laws of 48 states, as well as a similar federal statute, in cases of peaceful political expression.

The Supreme Court, in June 1990, declared that a new federal law making it a crime to burn or deface the American flag violated the free-speech guarantee of the First Amendment. The 5-4 Court decision led to renewed calls in Congress for a constitutional amendment to make it possible to prosecute flag burners.

Pledge of Allegiance to the Flag

I pledge allegiance to the flag of the United States of America and to the republic for which it stands, one nation under God, indivisible, with liberty and justice for all.

This, the current official version of the Pledge of Allegiance, has developed from the original pledge, which was first published in the Sept. 8, 1892, issue of *Youth's Companion*, a weekly magazine then published in Boston. The original pledge contained the phrase "my flag," which was changed more than 30 years later to "flag of the United States of America." A 1954 act of Congress added the words "under God." (In 2002, the 9th Circuit U.S. Court of Appeals ruled that recitation of the pledge in public schools could not include that phrase. In 2004, however, the U.S. Supreme Court voted to decline to decide the case on a technicality. The lower court's decision was thus overturned.)

The authorship of the pledge was in dispute for many years. The *Youth's Companion* stated in 1917 that the original draft was written by James B. Upham, an executive of the magazine who died in 1910. A leaflet circulated by the magazine later named Upham as the originator of the draft "afterwards condensed and perfected by him and his associates of the Companion force."

Francis Bellamy, a former member of *Youth's Companion* editorial staff, publicly claimed authorship of the pledge in 1923. In 1939, the United States Flag Association, acting on the advice of a committee named to study the controversy, upheld the claim of Bellamy, who had died 8 years earlier. In 1957 the Library of Congress issued a report attributing the authorship to Bellamy.

The History of the National Anthem

"The Star-Spangled Banner" was ordered played by the military and naval services by Pres. Woodrow Wilson in 1916. It was designated the national anthem by Act of Congress, Mar. 3, 1931. The words were written by Francis Scott Key, of Georgetown, MD, during the bombardment of Fort McHenry, Baltimore, Sept. 13-14, 1814. Key was a lawyer, a graduate of St. John's College, Annapolis, and a volunteer in a light artillery company. When a friend, Dr. Beanes, a Maryland physician, was taken aboard Admiral Cockburn's British squadron for interfering with ground troops, Key and J. S. Skinner, carrying a note from Pres. Madison, went to the fleet under a flag of truce on a cartel ship to ask Beanes's release. Cockburn consented, but as the fleet was about to sail up the Patapsco to bombard Fort McHenry, he detained them, first on HMS *Surprise* and then on a supply ship.

Key witnessed the bombardment from his own vessel. It began at 7 AM, Sept. 13, 1814, and lasted, with intermissions, for 25 hrs. The British fired more than 1,500 shells, each weighing as much as 220 lbs. They were unable to approach closely because the U.S. had sunk 22 vessels. Only 4 Americans were killed and 24 wounded. A British bomb-ship was disabled.

During the event, Key wrote a stanza on the back of an envelope. Next day at Indian Queen Inn, Baltimore, he wrote out the poem and gave it to his brother-in-law, Judge J. H. Nicholson. Nicholson suggested use of the tune, "Anacreon in Heaven" (attributed to a British composer named John Stafford Smith), and had the poem printed on broadsides, of which 2 survive. On Sept. 20 it appeared in the *Baltimore American.* Later Key made 3 copies; one is in the Library of Congress, and one in the Pennsylvania Historical Society. The copy Key wrote on Sept. 14 remained in the Nicholson family for 93 years. In 1907 it was sold to Henry Walters of Baltimore. In 1934 it was bought at auction by the Walters Art Gallery, Baltimore, for $26,400. In 1953 it was sold to the Maryland Historical Society for the same price.

The flag that Key saw during the bombardment is preserved in the Smithsonian Institution, Washington, DC. It measures 30 by 42 ft and has 15 alternating red and white stripes and 15 stars, for the original 13 states plus Kentucky and Vermont. It was made by Mary Young Pickersgill. The Baltimore Flag House, a museum, occupies her premises, which were restored in 1953.

The Star-Spangled Banner

Note: The 2nd and 3rd stanzas are commonly omitted as a courtesy to the British.

I

Oh, say can you see by the dawn's early light
What so proudly we hailed at the twilight's last gleaming?
Whose broad stripes and bright stars thru the perilous fight,
O'er the ramparts we watched were so gallantly streaming?
And the rocket's red glare, the bombs bursting in air,
Gave proof through the night that our flag was still there.
Oh, say does that star-spangled banner yet wave
O'er the land of the free and the home of the brave?

II

On the shore, dimly seen through the mists of the deep,
Where the foe's haughty host in dread silence reposes,
What is that which the breeze, o'er the towering steep,
As it fitfully blows, half conceals, half discloses?
Now it catches the gleam of the morning's first beam,
In full glory reflected now shines in the stream:
'Tis the star-spangled banner! Oh long may it wave
O'er the land of the free and the home of the brave!

III

And where is that band who so vauntingly swore
That the havoc of war and the battle's confusion,
A home and a country should leave us no more!
Their blood has washed out their foul footsteps' pollution.
No refuge could save the hireling and slave
From the terror of flight, or the gloom of the grave:
And the star-spangled banner in triumph doth wave
O'er the land of the free and the home of the brave!

IV

Oh! thus be it ever, when freemen shall stand
Between their loved home and the war's desolation!
Blest with victory and peace, may the heav'n rescued land
Praise the Power that hath made and preserved us a nation.
Then conquer we must, when our cause it is just,
And this be our motto: "In God is our trust."
And the star-spangled banner in triumph shall wave
O'er the land of the free and the home of the brave!

America (My Country 'Tis of Thee)

First sung in public on July 4, 1831, at a service in the Park Street Church, Boston, the words were written by Rev. Samuel Francis Smith, a Baptist clergyman, who set them to a melody he found in a German songbook, unaware that it was the tune for the British anthem, "God Save the King/Queen."

My country, 'tis of thee,
Sweet land of liberty,
Of thee I sing.
Land where my fathers died!
Land of the Pilgrims' pride!
From ev'ry mountainside,
Let freedom ring!

My native country, thee,
Land of the noble free,
Thy name I love.
I love thy rocks and rills,
Thy woods and templed hills;
My heart with rapture thrills
Like that above.

Let music swell the breeze,
And ring from all the trees
Sweet freedom's song.
Let mortal tongues awake;
Let all that breathe partake;
Let rocks their silence break,
The sound prolong.

Our fathers' God, to Thee,
Author of liberty,
To Thee we sing.
Long may our land be bright
With freedom's holy light;
Protect us by Thy might,
Great God, our King!

America, the Beautiful

Words composed by Katharine Lee Bates, a Massachusetts educator and author, in 1893, inspired by the view she experienced atop Pikes Peak in Colorado. The final form was established in 1911, and it is set to the music of Samuel A. Ward's "Materna."

O beautiful for spacious skies.
For amber waves of grain,
For purple mountain majesties
Above the fruited plain.
America! America!
God shed His grace on thee,
And crown thy good with brotherhood
From sea to shining sea.

O beautiful for pilgrim feet
Whose stern impassion'd stress
A thorough-fare for freedom beat
Across the wilderness.
America! America!
God mend thine ev'ry flaw,
Confirm thy soul in self control,
Thy liberty in law.

O beautiful for heroes prov'd
In liberating strife,
Who more than self their country lov'd
And mercy more than life.
America! America!
May God thy gold refine
Till all success be nobleness,
And ev'ry gain divine.

O beautiful for patriot dream
That sees beyond the years,
Thine alabaster cities gleam,
Undimmed by human tears.
America! America!
God shed His grace on thee,
And crown thy good with brotherhood
From sea to shining sea.

The Liberty Bell: Its History and Significance

The Liberty Bell is housed in the Liberty Bell Center, located in Philadelphia's National Historical Park.

The original bell was ordered by Assembly Speaker and Chairman of the State House Superintendents Isaac Norris and was ordered from Thomas Lester, Whitechapel Foundry, London. It reached Philadelphia at the end of August 1752. It bore an inscription from Leviticus 25:10: "PROCLAIM LIBERTY THROUGHOUT ALL THE LAND UNTO ALL THE INHABITANTS THEREOF."

The bell was cracked by a stroke of its clapper in Sept. 1752 while it hung on a truss in the State House yard for testing. Pass & Stow, Philadelphia founders, recast the bell, adding 1½ ounces of copper to a pound of the original "Whitechapel" metal to reduce its high tone and brittleness. It was found that the bell contained too much copper, injuring its tone, so Pass & Stow recast it again, this time successfully.

In June 1753 the bell was hung in the old wooden steeple of the State House. In use while the Continental Congress was in session in the State House, it rang out in defiance of British tax and trade restrictions, and it proclaimed the Boston Tea Party and, on July 8, 1776, the first public reading of the Declaration of Independence.

On Sept. 18, 1777, when the British Army was about to occupy Philadelphia, the Liberty Bell was moved in a baggage train of the American Army to Allentown, PA, where it was hidden until June 27, 1778. The bell was moved back to Philadelphia after the British left the city.

In July 1781 the wooden steeple became insecure and had to be taken down. The bell was lowered into the brick section of the tower, where it remained until 1828. Between 1828 and 1844 the old State House bell continued to ring during special occasions. According to tradition, it cracked in 1835 as it tolled the death of Chief Justice John Marshall. It rang for the last time on Feb. 23, 1846. In 1852 it was placed on exhibition in the Declaration Chamber of Independence Hall.

In 1876, when thousands of Americans visited Philadelphia for the Centennial Exposition, the bell was placed in its old wooden support in the tower hallway. In 1877 it was hung from the ceiling of the tower by a chain of 13 links. It was returned again to the Declaration Chamber and in 1896 taken back to the tower hall, where it occupied a glass case. In 1915 the case was removed so that the public might touch it. On Jan. 1, 1976, just after midnight to mark the opening of the Bicentennial Year, the bell was moved to a new glass and steel pavilion behind Independence Hall for easier viewing.

On Oct. 9, 2003, the bell was transferred from Liberty Bell Pavilion to its present location, where exhibits and displays explain the history of the bell.

The measurements of the bell are as follows: circumference around the lip, 12 ft ½ in; circumference around the crown, 6 ft 11¼ in; lip to the crown, 3 ft; height over the crown, 2 ft 3 in; thickness at lip, 3 in; thickness at crown, 1¼ in; weight, 2,080 lbs; length of clapper, 3 ft 2 in.

Statue of Liberty National Monument

Since 1886, the Statue of Liberty, formally known as "Liberty Enlightening the World," has stood as a symbol of freedom in New York harbor. It also commemorates French-American friendship, for it was given by the people of France and designed by French sculptor Frederic Auguste Bartholdi (1834-1904).

On Washington's Birthday, Feb. 22, 1877, Congress approved the use of a site on Bedloe's Island suggested by Bartholdi. This island of 12 acres had been owned in the 17th century by a Walloon named Isaac Bedloe. It was called Bedloe's until Aug. 3, 1956, when Pres. Dwight Eisenhower approved a measure changing the name to Liberty Island.

The statue was finished on May 21, 1884, and presented to the U.S. minister to France, Levi Parsons Morton, July 4, 1884, by Ferdinand de Lesseps, head of the Franco-American Union, promoter of the Panama Canal, and builder of the Suez Canal.

On Aug. 5, 1884, the Americans laid the cornerstone for the pedestal, to be built on the foundations of Fort Wood, erected by the government in 1811. The American committee had raised $125,000, but this was inadequate. Joseph Pulitzer, owner of the New York World, appealed on Mar. 16, 1885, for general donations. By Aug. 11, 1885, he had raised $100,000. The statue itself arrived dismantled, in 214 packing cases, from Rouen, France, in June 1885. The last rivet of the statue was driven on Oct. 28, 1886, when Pres. Grover Cleveland dedicated the monument.

The Statue of Liberty National Monument was designated as such in 1924. It is administered by the National Park Service. A $2.5 million building housing the American Museum of Immigration was opened by Pres. Richard Nixon on

Sept. 26, 1972, at the base of the statue. It houses a permanent exhibition tracing the history of American immigration.

Four years of restoration work funded and led by the Statue of Liberty-Ellis Island Foundation were completed before the statue's 1986 centennial. Among other repairs, the $87-million project included replacing the 1,600 wrought iron bands that hold the statue's copper skin to its frame, replacing its torch, and installing an elevator. A 4-day "Liberty Weekend" extravaganza of concerts, tall ships, ethnic festivals, and fireworks, July 3-6, 1986, celebrated the 100th anniversary. Chief Justice Warren E. Burger swore in 5,000 new citizens on Ellis Island, while 20,000 others across the country were sworn in through a satellite telecast. Other ceremonies followed on Oct. 28, 1986, the statue's exact 100th birthday.

Following the Sept. 11 terrorist attacks, Liberty Island was closed to visitors. On Dec. 20, 2001, the secretary of the interior reopened the island after installing airport-type screening facilities at passenger embarkation areas at Battery Park in Manhattan and Liberty State Park in New Jersey.

To open the statue, the federal government needed to increase security throughout the park. In addition to federally funded security upgrades, significant safety improvements were made to meet building codes. The National Park Service turned to the Statue of Liberty-Ellis Island Foundation, which began a fund-raising campaign to help finance safety renovations inside the statue, additional exits, improved handicapped access, and upgraded fire suppression and emergency warning systems. The federal investment in upgrades amounted to about $30 million, with the private sector contributing an additional $7 million. Access to the statue was finally restored on Aug. 3, 2004.

Two tours are now available (they must be reserved in advance). Reservations are available by visiting www.statuereservations.com or by calling 1-866-STATUE4. A limited number of "walk up" reservations are also available at ferry embarkation areas. The Promenade Tour goes along the promenade above the fort on which the statue and pedestal were built. The Observatory Tour incorporates the Promenade Tour and also goes up the pedestal by elevator to a panoramic observation deck; on that level is a view of the statue's interior. Both tours are ranger-guided and include a visit to the original torch, taken down during renovation in the 1980s, and the museum. The entire statue above the pedestal, including the crown, remains closed. (For more information, visit www.nps.gov/stli and www.statueofliberty.org)

Statue Statistics

The statue weighs 450,000 lbs., or 225 tons. The copper sheeting weighs 200,000 lbs. There are 167 steps from the land level to the top of the pedestal, 168 steps inside the statue to the head, and 54 rungs on the ladder leading to the arm that holds the torch.

	Ft	In		Ft	In
Height from base to torch tip	151	1	Nose, length	4	6
Foundation of pedestal to torch tip	305	1	Right arm, length	42	0
Heel to top of head	111	1	Right arm, max. thickness	12	0
Hand, length	16	5	Thickness of waist	35	0
Index finger, length	8	0	Mouth, width	3	0
Size of fingernail		13x10	Tablet, length	23	7
Head from chin to cranium	17	3	Tablet, width	13	7
Head thickness, ear to ear	10	0			

Emma Lazarus's Famous Poem

Engraved on pedestal below the statue.

The New Colossus

Not like the brazen giant of Greek fame,
With conquering limbs astride from land to land;
Here at our sea-washed, sunset gates shall stand
A mighty woman with a torch, whose flame
Is the imprisoned lightning, and her name
Mother of Exiles. From her beacon-hand
Glows world-wide welcome; her mild eyes command

The air-bridged harbor that twin cities frame.
"Keep ancient lands, your storied pomp!" cries she
With silent lips. "Give me your tired, your poor,
Your huddled masses yearning to breathe free,
The wretched refuse of your teeming shore.
Send these, the homeless, tempest-tost to me,
I lift my lamp beside the golden door!"

Ellis Island

Ellis Island was the gateway to America for over 12 mil immigrants between 1892 and 1924. In the late 18th century, Samuel Ellis, a New York City merchant, purchased the island and gave it his name. From Ellis, it passed to New York State, and the U.S. government bought it in 1808. On Jan. 1, 1892, the government opened the first federal immigration center in the U.S. there. The 27½-acre site eventually supported more than 35 buildings, including the Main Building with its Great Hall, in which as many as 5,000 people a day were processed.

Closed as an immigration station in 1954, Ellis Island was proclaimed part of the Statue of Liberty National Monument in 1965 by Pres. Lyndon B. Johnson. After a 6-year, $170 million restoration project funded by the Statue of Liberty-Ellis Island Foundation, Ellis Island was reopened as a museum in 1990. Artifacts, historic photographs and documents, oral histories, and ethnic music depicting 400 years of American immigration are housed in the museum. The museum also includes The American Immigrant Wall of Honor (www.wallofhonor.com), which is inscribed with more than 600,000 names that have been placed in tribute. Registrations are still being accepted for inclusion in the memorial.

The American Family Immigration History Center® opened in April 2001. It contains an electronic database of ship passenger arrival information through the Port of New York and Ellis Island from 1892 to 1924. Data on over 25 million individuals are available, as well as an interactive database which features a Living Family Archive, multimedia presentations on various immigration groups and patterns, reproductions of original ships' passenger manifests, and pictures of over 800 immigrant ships (www.ellisisland.org).

In 1998, the Supreme Court ruled that nearly 90% of the island (the 24.2 acres which are landfill) lies in New Jersey, while the original 3.3 acres, on which the museum is located, are in New York.

U.S. Presidents

	Name	Politics	Born	Birthplace	Inaug.	Age at inaug.	Died	Death age
1.	George Washington	Fed.	1732, Feb. 22	VA	1789	57	1799, Dec. 14	67
2.	John Adams	Fed.	1735, Oct. 30	MA	1797	61	1826, July 4	90
3.	Thomas Jefferson	Dem.-Rep.	1743, Apr. 13	VA	1801	57	1826, July 4	83
4.	James Madison	Dem.-Rep.	1751, Mar. 16	VA	1809	57	1836, June 28	85
5.	James Monroe	Dem.-Rep.	1758, Apr. 28	VA	1817	58	1831, July 4	73
6.	John Quincy Adams	Dem.-Rep.	1767, July 11	MA	1825	57	1848, Feb. 23	80
7.	Andrew Jackson	Dem.	1767, Mar. 15	SC	1829	61	1845, June 8	78
8.	Martin Van Buren	Dem.	1782, Dec. 5	NY	1837	54	1862, July 24	79
9.	William Henry Harrison	Whig	1773, Feb. 9	VA	1841	68	1841, Apr. 4	68
10.	John Tyler	Whig	1790, Mar. 29	VA	1841	51	1862, Jan. 18	71
11.	James Knox Polk	Dem.	1795, Nov. 2	NC	1845	49	1849, June 15	53
12.	Zachary Taylor	Whig	1784, Nov. 24	VA	1849	64	1850, July 9	65
13.	Millard Fillmore	Whig	1800, Jan. 7	NY	1850	50	1874, Mar. 8	74
14.	Franklin Pierce	Dem.	1804, Nov. 23	NH	1853	48	1869, Oct. 8	64
15.	James Buchanan	Dem.	1791, Apr. 23	PA	1857	65	1868, June 1	77
16.	Abraham Lincoln	Rep.	1809, Feb. 12	KY	1861	52	1865, Apr. 15	56
17.	Andrew Johnson	(1)	1808, Dec. 29	NC	1865	56	1875, July 31	66
18.	Ulysses S. Grant	Rep.	1822, Apr. 27	OH	1869	46	1885, July 23	63
19.	Rutherford Birchard Hayes	Rep.	1822, Oct. 4	OH	1877	54	1893, Jan. 17	70
20.	James Abram Garfield	Rep.	1831, Nov. 19	OH	1881	49	1881, Sept. 19	49
21.	Chester Alan Arthur	Rep.	1829, Oct. 5	VT	1881	51	1886, Nov. 18	57
22.	Grover Cleveland	Dem.	1837, Mar. 18	NJ	1885	47	1908, June 24	71
23.	Benjamin Harrison	Rep.	1833, Aug. 20	OH	1889	55	1901, Mar. 13	67
24.	Grover Cleveland	Dem.	1837, Mar. 18	NJ	1893	55	1908, June 24	71
25.	William McKinley	Rep.	1843, Jan. 29	OH	1897	54	1901, Sept. 14	58
26.	Theodore Roosevelt	Rep.	1858, Oct. 27	NY	1901	42	1919, Jan. 6	60
27.	William Howard Taft	Rep.	1857, Sept. 15	OH	1909	51	1930, Mar. 8	72
28.	(Thomas) Woodrow Wilson	Dem.	1856, Dec. 28	VA	1913	56	1924, Feb. 3	67
29.	Warren Gamaliel Harding	Rep.	1865, Nov. 2	OH	1921	55	1923, Aug. 2	57
30.	(John) Calvin Coolidge	Rep.	1872, July 4	VT	1923	51	1933, Jan. 5	60
31.	Herbert Clark Hoover	Rep.	1874, Aug. 10	IA	1929	54	1964, Oct. 20	90
32.	Franklin Delano Roosevelt	Dem.	1882, Jan. 30	NY	1933	51	1945, Apr. 12	63
33.	Harry S. Truman	Dem.	1884, May 8	MO	1945	60	1972, Dec. 26	88
34.	Dwight David Eisenhower	Rep.	1890, Oct. 14	TX	1953	62	1969, Mar. 28	78
35.	John Fitzgerald Kennedy	Dem.	1917, May 29	MA	1961	43	1963, Nov. 22	46
36.	Lyndon Baines Johnson	Dem.	1908, Aug. 27	TX	1963	55	1973, Jan. 22	64
37.	Richard Milhous Nixon (2)	Rep.	1913, Jan. 9	CA	1969	56	1994, Apr. 22	81
38.	Gerald Rudolph Ford	Rep.	1913, July 14	NE	1974	61	2006, Dec. 26	93
39.	James Earl (Jimmy) Carter	Dem.	1924, Oct. 1	GA	1977	52		
40.	Ronald Wilson Reagan	Rep.	1911, Feb. 6	IL	1981	69	2004, June 5	93
41.	George Herbert Walker Bush	Rep.	1924, June 12	MA	1989	64		
42.	Wm. Jefferson (Bill) Clinton	Dem.	1946, Aug. 19	AR	1993	46		
43.	George Walker Bush	Rep.	1946, July 6	CT	2001	54		

(1) Andrew Johnson, a Democrat, was nominated vice president by Republicans and elected with Lincoln on National Union ticket. (2) Resigned Aug. 9, 1974.

U.S. Presidents, Vice Presidents, Congresses

President	Service	Vice President	Congresses
1. George Washington	Apr. 30, 1789-Mar. 3, 1797	1. John Adams	1, 2, 3, 4
2. John Adams	Mar. 4, 1797-Mar. 3, 1801	2. Thomas Jefferson	5, 6
3. Thomas Jefferson	Mar. 4, 1801-Mar. 3, 1805	3. Aaron Burr	7, 8
	Mar. 4, 1805-Mar. 3, 1809	George Clinton	9, 10
4. James Madison	Mar. 4, 1809-Mar. 3, 1813	4. George Clinton (1)	11, 12
	Mar. 4, 1813-Mar. 3, 1817	5. Elbridge Gerry (2)	13, 14
5. James Monroe	Mar. 4, 1817-Mar. 3, 1825	6. Daniel D. Tompkins	15, 16, 17, 18
6. John Quincy Adams	Mar. 4, 1825-Mar. 3, 1829	John C. Calhoun	19, 20
7. Andrew Jackson	Mar. 4, 1829-Mar. 3, 1833	7. John C. Calhoun (3)	21, 22
	Mar. 4, 1833-Mar. 3, 1837	8. Martin Van Buren	23, 24
8. Martin Van Buren	Mar. 4, 1837-Mar. 3, 1841	9. Richard M. Johnson	25, 26
9. William Henry Harrison (4)	Mar. 4, 1841-Apr. 4, 1841	10. John Tyler	27
10. John Tyler	Apr. 6, 1841-Mar. 3, 1845	(None)	27, 28
11. James K. Polk	Mar. 4, 1845-Mar. 3, 1849	11. George M. Dallas	29, 30
12. Zachary Taylor (4)	Mar. 5, 1849-July 9, 1850	12. Millard Fillmore	31
13. Millard Fillmore	July 10, 1850-Mar. 3, 1853	(none)	31, 32
14. Franklin Pierce	Mar. 4, 1853-Mar. 3, 1857	13. William R. King (5)	33, 34
15. James Buchanan	Mar. 4, 1857-Mar. 3, 1861	14. John C. Breckinridge	35, 36
16. Abraham Lincoln (4)	Mar. 4, 1861-Mar. 3, 1865	15. Hannibal Hamlin	37, 38
	Mar. 4, 1865-Apr. 15, 1865	16. Andrew Johnson	39
17. Andrew Johnson	Apr. 15, 1865-Mar. 3, 1869	(None)	39, 40
18. Ulysses S. Grant	Mar. 4, 1869-Mar. 3, 1873	17. Schuyler Colfax	41, 42
	Mar. 4, 1873-Mar. 3, 1877	18. Henry Wilson (6)	43, 44
19. Rutherford B. Hayes	Mar. 4, 1877-Mar. 3, 1881	19. William A. Wheeler	45, 46
20. James A. Garfield (4)	Mar. 4, 1881-Sept. 19, 1881	20. Chester A. Arthur	47
21. Chester A. Arthur	Sept. 20, 1881-Mar. 3, 1885	(None)	47, 48
22. Grover Cleveland (7)	Mar. 4, 1885-Mar. 3, 1889	21. Thomas A. Hendricks (8)	49, 50
23. Benjamin Harrison	Mar. 4, 1889-Mar. 3, 1893	22. Levi P. Morton	51, 52
24. Grover Cleveland (7)	Mar. 4, 1893-Mar. 3, 1897	23. Adlai E. Stevenson	53, 54
25. William McKinley	Mar. 4, 1897-Mar. 3, 1901	24. Garret A. Hobart (9)	55, 56
(4)	Mar. 4, 1901-Sept. 14, 1901	25. Theodore Roosevelt	57
26. Theodore Roosevelt	Sept. 14, 1901-Mar. 3, 1905	(None)	57, 58
	Mar. 4, 1905-Mar. 3, 1909	26. Charles W. Fairbanks	59, 60

President	Service	Vice President	Congresses
27. William H. Taft	Mar. 4, 1909-Mar. 3, 1913	27. James S. Sherman (10)	61, 62
28. Woodrow Wilson	Mar. 4, 1913-Mar. 3, 1921	28. Thomas R. Marshall	63, 64, 65, 66
29. Warren G. Harding (4)	Mar. 4, 1921-Aug. 2, 1923	29. Calvin Coolidge	67
30. Calvin Coolidge	Aug. 3, 1923-Mar. 3, 1925	(None)	68
	Mar. 4, 1925-Mar. 3, 1929	30. Charles G. Dawes	69, 70
31. Herbert C. Hoover	Mar. 4, 1929-Mar. 3, 1933	31. Charles Curtis	71, 72
32. Franklin D. Roosevelt (11)	Mar. 4, 1933-Jan. 20, 1941	32. John N. Garner	73, 74, 75, 76, 77
	Jan. 20, 1941-Jan. 20, 1945	33. Henry A. Wallace	77, 78, 79
(4)	Jan. 20, 1945-Apr. 12, 1945	34. Harry S. Truman	79
33. Harry S. Truman	Apr. 12, 1945-Jan. 20, 1949	(None)	79, 80, 81
	Jan. 20, 1949-Jan. 20, 1953	35. Alben W. Barkley	81, 82, 83
34. Dwight D. Eisenhower	Jan. 20, 1953-Jan. 20, 1961	36. Richard M. Nixon	83, 84, 85, 86, 87
35. John F. Kennedy (4)	Jan. 20, 1961-Nov. 22, 1963	37. Lyndon B. Johnson	87, 88
36. Lyndon B. Johnson	Nov. 22, 1963-Jan. 20, 1965	(None)	88, 89
	Jan. 20, 1965-Jan. 20, 1969	38. Hubert H. Humphrey	89, 90, 91
37. Richard M. Nixon	Jan. 20, 1969-Jan. 20, 1973	39. Spiro T. Agnew (12)	91, 92, 93
(13)	Jan. 20, 1973-Aug. 9, 1974	40. Gerald R. Ford (14)	93
38. Gerald R. Ford (15)	Aug. 9, 1974-Jan. 20, 1977	41. Nelson A. Rockefeller (16)	93, 94, 95
39. Jimmy Carter	Jan. 20, 1977-Jan. 20, 1981	42. Walter F. Mondale	95, 96, 97
40. Ronald W. Reagan	Jan. 20, 1981-Jan. 20, 1989	43. George H. W. Bush	97, 98, 99, 100, 101
41. George H. W. Bush	Jan. 20, 1989-Jan. 20, 1993	44. Dan Quayle	101, 102, 103
42. Bill Clinton	Jan. 20, 1993-Jan. 20, 2001	45. Al Gore	103, 104, 105, 106, 107
43. George W. Bush	Jan. 20, 2001-	46. Dick Cheney	107, 108, 109, 110

(1) Died Apr. 20, 1812. (2) Died Nov. 23, 1814. (3) Resigned Dec. 28, 1832, to become U.S. senator. (4) Died in office. (5) Died Apr. 18, 1853. (6) Died Nov. 22, 1875. (7) Terms not consecutive. (8) Died Nov. 25, 1885. (9) Died Nov. 21, 1899. (10) Died Oct. 30, 1912. (11) First president to be inaugurated under 20th Amendment, Jan. 20, 1937. (12) Resigned Oct. 10, 1973. (13) Resigned Aug. 9, 1974. (14) First nonelected vice president, chosen under 25th Amendment procedure. (15) First president never elected president or vice president. (16) Second nonelected vice president, chosen under 25th Amendment. Confirmed Dec. 19, 1974.

Vice Presidents of the U.S.

The numerals given vice presidents do not coincide with those given presidents, because some presidents (Tyler, Fillmore, A. Johnson, Arthur) had none, and some had more than one.

Name	Birthplace	Year	Home	Inaug.	Politics	Place of death	Year	Death age
1. John Adams	Quincy, MA	1735	MA	1789	Fed.	Quincy, MA	1826	90
2. Thomas Jefferson	Shadwell, VA	1743	VA	1797	Dem.-Rep.	Monticello, VA	1826	83
3. Aaron Burr	Newark, NJ	1756	NY	1801	Dem.-Rep.	Staten Island, NY	1836	80
4. George Clinton	Little Britain, NY	1739	NY	1805	Dem.-Rep.	Washington, DC	1812	73
5. Elbridge Gerry	Marblehead, MA	1744	MA	1813	Dem.-Rep.	Washington, DC	1814	70
6. Daniel D. Tompkins	Scarsdale, NY	1774	NY	1817	Dem.-Rep.	Staten Island, NY	1825	51
7. John C. Calhoun (1)	Abbeville, SC	1782	SC	1825	Dem.-Rep.	Washington, DC	1850	68
8. Martin Van Buren	Kinderhook, NY	1782	NY	1833	Dem.	Kinderhook, NY	1862	79
9. Richard M. Johnson (2)	Louisville, KY	1780	KY	1837	Dem.	Frankfort, KY	1850	70
10. John Tyler	Greenway, VA	1790	VA	1841	Whig	Richmond, VA	1862	71
11. George M. Dallas	Philadelphia, PA	1792	PA	1845	Dem.	Philadelphia, PA	1864	72
12. Millard Fillmore	Cayuga Co., NY	1800	NY	1849	Whig	Buffalo, NY	1874	74
13. William R. King	Sampson Co., NC	1786	AL	1853	Dem.	Cahaba, AL	1853	67
14. John C. Breckinridge	Lexington, KY	1821	KY	1857	Dem.	Lexington, KY	1875	54
15. Hannibal Hamlin	Paris, ME	1809	ME	1861	Rep.	Bangor, ME	1891	81
16. Andrew Johnson	Raleigh, NC	1808	TN	1865	(3)	Carter Co., TN	1875	66
17. Schuyler Colfax	New York, NY	1823	IN	1869	Rep.	Mankato, MN	1885	62
18. Henry Wilson	Farmington, NH	1812	MA	1873	Rep.	Washington, DC	1875	63
19. William A. Wheeler	Malone, NY	1819	NY	1877	Rep.	Malone, NY	1887	68
20. Chester A. Arthur	Fairfield, VT	1829	NY	1881	Rep.	New York, NY	1886	57
21. Thomas A. Hendricks	Zanesville, OH	1819	IN	1885	Dem.	Indianapolis, IN	1885	66
22. Levi P. Morton	Shoreham, VT	1824	NY	1889	Rep.	Rhinebeck, NY	1920	96
23. Adlai E. Stevenson (4)	Christian Co., KY	1835	IL	1893	Dem.	Chicago, IL	1914	78
24. Garret A. Hobart	Long Branch, NJ	1844	NJ	1897	Rep.	Paterson, NJ	1899	55
25. Theodore Roosevelt	New York, NY	1858	NY	1901	Rep.	Oyster Bay, NY	1919	60
26. Charles W. Fairbanks	Unionville Centre, OH	1852	IN	1905	Rep.	Indianapolis, IN	1918	66
27. James S. Sherman	Utica, NY	1855	NY	1909	Rep.	Utica, NY	1912	57
28. Thomas R. Marshall	N. Manchester, IN	1854	IN	1913	Dem.	Washington, DC	1925	71
29. Calvin Coolidge	Plymouth Notch, VT	1872	MA	1921	Rep.	Northampton, MA	1933	60
30. Charles G. Dawes	Marietta, OH	1865	IL	1925	Rep.	Evanston, IL	1951	85
31. Charles Curtis	Topeka, KS	1860	KS	1929	Rep.	Washington, DC	1936	76
32. John Nance Garner	Red River Co., TX	1868	TX	1933	Dem.	Uvalde, TX	1967	98
33. Henry A. Wallace	Adair County, IA	1888	IA	1941	Dem.	Danbury, CT	1965	77
34. Harry S. Truman	Lamar, MO	1884	MO	1945	Dem.	Kansas City, MO	1972	88
35. Alben W. Barkley	Graves County, KY	1877	KY	1949	Dem.	Lexington, VA	1956	78
36. Richard M. Nixon	Yorba Linda, CA	1913	CA	1953	Rep.	New York, NY	1994	81
37. Lyndon B. Johnson	Stonewall, TX	1908	TX	1961	Dem.	San Antonio, TX	1973	64
38. Hubert H. Humphrey	Wallace, SD	1911	MN	1965	Dem.	Waverly, MN	1978	66
39. Spiro T. Agnew (5)	Baltimore, MD	1918	MD	1969	Rep.	Berlin, MD	1996	77
40. Gerald R. Ford (6)	Omaha, NE	1913	MI	1973	Rep.	Rancho Mirage, CA	2006	93
41. Nelson A. Rockefeller (7)	Bar Harbor, ME	1908	NY	1974	Rep.	New York, NY	1979	70
42. Walter F. Mondale	Ceylon, MN	1928	MN	1977	Dem.			
43. George H. W. Bush	Milton, MA	1924	TX	1981	Rep.			
44. J. Dan Quayle	Indianapolis, IN	1947	IN	1989	Rep.			
45. Al Gore	Washington, DC	1948	TN	1993	Dem.			
46. Dick Cheney	Lincoln, NE	1941	WY	2001	Rep.			

(1) Resigned Dec. 28, 1832, having been elected to the Senate to fill a vacancy. (2) Richard M. Johnson was the only vice president to be chosen by the Senate because of a tied vote in the Electoral College. (3) Andrew Johnson was a Democrat, nominated vice president by Republicans, and elected with Lincoln on the National Union Ticket. (4) Grandfather of Democratic candidate for president in 1952 and 1956. (5) Resigned Oct. 10, 1973. (6) First nonelected vice president, chosen under 25th Amendment procedure. (7) Second nonelected vice president, chosen under 25th Amendment.

Biographies of the Presidents

George Washington (1789-97), 1st president, Federalist, was born on Feb. 22, 1732, in Wakefield on Pope's Creek, Westmoreland Co., VA, the son of Augustine and Mary Ball Washington. He spent his early childhood on a farm near Fredericksburg. His father died when Washington was 11. He studied mathematics and surveying, and at 16, he went to live with his elder half brother, Lawrence, who built and named Mount Vernon in Virginia. Washington surveyed the lands of Thomas Fairfax in the Shenandoah Valley. He accompanied Lawrence to Barbados, West Indies, where he contracted smallpox and was deeply scarred. Lawrence died in 1752, and Washington inherited his property. He valued land, and when he died, he owned 70,000 acres in Virginia and 40,000 acres in what is now West Virginia.

Washington's military service began in 1753, when Lt. Gov. Robert Dinwiddie of Virginia sent him on missions deep into Ohio country. He clashed with the French and had to surrender Fort Necessity on July 3, 1754. He was an aide to the British general Edward Braddock and was at his side when the army was ambushed and defeated (July 9, 1755) on a march to Fort Duquesne. He helped take Fort Duquesne from the French in 1758.

After Washington's marriage to Martha Dandridge Custis, a widow, in 1759, he managed his family estate at Mount Vernon. Although not at first for independence, he opposed the repressive measures of the British crown and took charge of the Virginia troops before war broke out. He was made commander of the newly created Continental Army by the Continental Congress on June 15, 1775.

The American victory was due largely to Washington's leadership. He was resourceful, a disciplinarian, and the one dependable force for unity. Washington favored a federal government. He became chairman of the Constitutional Convention of 1787 and helped get the Constitution ratified. Unanimously elected president by the electoral college, he was inaugurated Apr. 30, 1789, on the balcony of New York's Federal Hall. He was reelected in 1792. Washington made an effort to avoid partisan politics as president.

Refusing to consider a 3rd term, Washington retired to Mount Vernon in March 1797. He suffered acute laryngitis after a ride in snow and rain around his estate, was bled profusely, and died Dec. 14, 1799.

John Adams (1797-1801), 2nd president, Federalist, was born on Oct. 30, 1735, in Braintree (now Quincy), MA, the son of John and Susanna Boylston Adams. He was a great-grandson of Henry Adams, who came from England in 1636. He graduated from Harvard in 1755, then taught school and studied law. He married Abigail Smith in 1764. In 1765 he argued against taxation without representation before the royal governor. In 1770, he successfully defended in court the British soldiers who fired on civilians in the Boston Massacre. He was a delegate to the Continental Congress and a signer of the Declaration of Independence. In 1778, Congress sent Adams and John Jay to join Benjamin Franklin as diplomatic representatives in Europe. Because he ran second to Washington in electoral college balloting in Feb. 1789, Adams became the nation's first vice president, a post he characterized as highly insignificant; he was reelected in 1792.

In 1796 Adams was chosen president by the electors. His administration was marked by growing conflict with fellow Federalist Alexander Hamilton and with others in his own cabinet who supported Hamilton's strongly anti-French position. Adams avoided full-scale war with France but became unpopular, especially after securing passage of the Alien and Sedition Acts in 1798. His foreign policy contributed significantly to the election of Thomas Jefferson in 1800.

Adams lived for a quarter century after he left office, during which time he wrote extensively. He died July 4, 1826, on the same day as his rival Thomas Jefferson (the 50th anniversary of the Declaration of Independence).

Thomas Jefferson (1801-09), 3rd president, Democratic-Republican, was born on Apr. 13, 1743, in Shadwell in Goochland (now Albemarle) Co., VA, the son of Peter and Jane Randolph Jefferson. His father died when Jefferson was 14, leaving him 2,750 acres and his slaves. Jefferson attended (1760-62) the College of William and Mary, read Greek and Latin classics, and played the violin. In 1769 he was elected to the Virginia House of Burgesses. In 1770 he began building his home, Monticello, and in 1772 he married Martha Wayles Skelton, a wealthy widow. Jefferson helped establish the Virginia Committee of Correspondence. As a member of the 2nd Continental Congress he drafted the Declaration of Independence. He also was a member of the Virginia House of Delegates (1776-79) and was elected governor of Virginia in 1779, succeeding Patrick Henry. He was reelected in 1780 but resigned in 1781 after British troops invaded Virginia. During his term he wrote the statute on religious freedom. After his wife's death in 1782, Jefferson again became a delegate to the Congress, and in 1784 he drafted the report that was the basis for the Ordinances of 1784, 1785, and 1787. He was minister to France from 1785 to 1789, when George Washington appointed him secretary of state.

Jefferson's strong faith in the consent of the governed conflicted with the emphasis on executive control, favored by Sec. of the Treasury Alexander Hamilton, and Jefferson resigned on Dec. 31, 1793. In the 1796 election Jefferson was the Democratic-Republican candidate for president; John Adams won the election, and Jefferson became vice president. In 1800, Jefferson and Aaron Burr received equal electoral college votes; the House of Representatives elected Jefferson president. Jefferson was a strong advocate of westward expansion; major events of his first term were the Louisiana Purchase (1803) and the Lewis and Clark expedition. An important development during his second term was passage of the Embargo Act, barring U.S. ships from setting sail to foreign ports. Jefferson established the Univ. of Virginia and designed its buildings. He died July 4, 1826, on the same day as John Adams (the 50th anniversary of the Declaration of Independence).

Analysis of DNA taken from descendants of Jefferson and Sally Hemings, one of his slaves, revealed a very high probability of Jefferson fathering at least one, perhaps all, of her six known children.

James Madison (1809-17), 4th president, Democratic-Republican, was born on Mar. 16, 1751, in Port Conway, King George Co., VA, the son of James and Eleanor Rose Conway Madison. Madison graduated from the College of New Jersey in 1771. He served in the Virginia Constitutional Convention (1776), and, in 1780, became a delegate to the 2nd Continental Congress. He was chief recorder at the Constitutional Convention in 1787 and supported ratification in the *Federalist Papers*, written with Alexander Hamilton and John Jay. In 1789, Madison was elected to the House of Representatives, where he helped frame the Bill of Rights and fought against passage of the Alien and Sedition Acts. In the 1790s, he helped found the Democratic-Republican Party, which ultimately became the Democratic Party. He became Jefferson's secretary of state in 1801.

Madison was elected president in 1808. His first term was marked by tensions with Great Britain, and his conduct of foreign policy was criticized by the Federalists and by his own party. Nevertheless, he was reelected in 1812, the year war was declared on Great Britain. The war that many considered a second American revolution ended with a treaty that did not settle any of the issues. Madison's most important action after the war was demilitarizing the U.S.-Canadian border.

In 1817, Madison retired to his estate, Montpelier, where he served as an elder statesman. He edited his famous papers on the Constitutional Convention and helped found the Univ. of Virginia, of which he became rector in 1826. He died June 28, 1836.

James Monroe (1817-25), 5th president, Democratic-Republican, was born on Apr. 28, 1758, in Westmoreland Co., VA, the son of Spence and Elizabeth Jones Monroe. He entered the College of William and Mary in 1774 but left to serve in the 3rd Virginia Regiment during the American Revolution. After the war, he studied law with Thomas Jefferson. In 1782 he was elected to the Virginia House of Delegates, and he served (1783-86) as a delegate to the Continental Congress. He opposed ratification of the Constitution because it lacked a bill of rights. Monroe was elected to the U.S. Senate in 1790. In 1794, Pres. Washington appointed Monroe minister to France. He served twice as governor of Virginia (1799-1802, 1811). Pres. Jefferson also sent him to France as minister (1803), and from 1803 to 1807, he served as minister to Great Britain.

In 1816 Monroe was elected president; he was reelected in 1820 with all but one electoral college vote. His administration became known as the Era of Good Feeling. He obtained Florida from Spain, settled boundary disputes with Britain over Canada, and eliminated border forts. He supported the antislavery position that led to the Missouri Compromise. His most significant contribution was the Monroe Doctrine, which opposed European intervention in the Western Hemisphere and became a cornerstone of U.S. foreign policy.

Although Monroe retired to Oak Hill, VA, financial problems forced him to sell his property and move to New York City. He died there on July 4, 1831.

John Quincy Adams (1825-29), 6th president, independent Federalist, later Democratic-Republican, was born on July 11, 1767, in Braintree (now Quincy), MA, the son of John and Abigail Adams. His father was the 2nd president. He studied abroad and at Harvard College, from which he graduated in 1787. In 1803, he was elected to the U.S. Senate. President Monroe chose him as his secretary of state in 1817. In this capacity he negotiated the cession of Florida from Spain, supported exclusion of slavery in the Missouri Compromise, and helped formulate the Monroe Doctrine. In 1824, Adams was elected president by the House of Representatives after he failed to win an electoral college majority. His expansion of executive powers was strongly opposed, and in the 1828 election he lost to Andrew Jackson. In 1831 he entered the House of Representatives and served 17 years with distinction. He opposed slavery, the annexation of Texas, and the Mexican War. He helped establish the Smithsonian Institution.

Adams suffered a stroke in the House and died in the Speaker's Room on Feb. 23, 1848.

Andrew Jackson (1829-37), 7th president, Democratic-Republican, later a Democrat, was born on Mar. 15, 1767, in the Waxhaw district, on the border of North Carolina and South Carolina, the son of Andrew and Elizabeth Hutchinson Jackson. At the age of 13, he joined the militia to fight in the American Revolution and was captured. Orphaned at the age of 14, Jackson was brought up by a well-to-do uncle. By age 20, he was practicing law, and he later served as prosecuting attorney in Nashville, TN. In 1796 he helped draft the constitution of Tennessee, and for a year he occupied its one seat in the House of Representatives. The next year Jackson served in the U.S. Senate.

In the War of 1812, Jackson crushed the Creek Indians at Horseshoe Bend, AL (1814), and, with a greatly outnumbered army consisting chiefly of backwoods militia members and volunteers, defeated Gen. Edward Pakenham's British troops at the Battle of New Orleans (1815). Nicknamed "Old Hickory" for his toughness, he emerged as a national hero.

In 1818 Jackson briefly invaded Spanish Florida to quell Seminoles and outlaws who harassed frontier settlements. He ran for president against John Quincy Adams in 1824, but, although he won the most popular and electoral votes, he did not have a majority. The House of Representatives decided the election and chose Adams. In the 1828 election, however, Jackson defeated Adams, carrying the West and the South.

As president, Jackson introduced what became known as the spoils system—rewarding party members with government posts. Perhaps his most controversial act, however, was depositing federal funds in so-called pet banks, those directed by Democratic bankers, rather than in the Bank of the United States. "Let the people rule" was his slogan. In 1832, Jackson killed the congressional caucus for nominating presidential candidates and substituted the national convention. When South Carolina refused to collect imports under his protective tariff, he ordered army and naval forces to Charleston. After leaving office in 1837, he retired to the Hermitage, outside Nashville, where he died on June 8, 1845.

Martin Van Buren (1837-41), 8th president, Democrat, was born on Dec. 5, 1782, in Kinderhook, NY, the son of Abraham and Maria Hoes Van Buren. After attending local schools, he studied law and became a lawyer at the age of 20. A consummate politician, Van Buren began his career in the New York state senate and then served as state attorney general from 1816 to 1819. He was elected to the U.S. Senate in 1821. He helped swing Eastern support to Andrew Jackson in the 1828 election and then served as Jackson's secretary of state from 1829 to 1831. In 1832 he was elected vice president. Known as the "Little Magician," Van Buren was extremely influential in Jackson's administration.

In 1836, Van Buren defeated William Henry Harrison for president and took office as the financial panic of 1837 initiated a nationwide depression. Although he instituted the independent treasury system, his refusal to spend land revenues led to his defeat by William Henry Harrison in 1840. In 1844 he lost the Democratic nomination to James K. Polk. In 1848 he again ran for president on the Free Soil ticket but lost. He died in Kinderhook on July 24, 1862.

William Henry Harrison (1841), 9th president, Whig, who served only 31 days, was born on Feb. 9, 1773, in Berkeley, Charles City Co., VA, the son of Benjamin Harrison, a signer of the Declaration of Independence, and of Elizabeth Bassett Harrison. He attended Hampden-Sydney College. Harrison served as secretary of the Northwest Territory in 1798 and was its delegate to the House of Representatives in 1799. He was the first governor of Indiana Territory and served as superintendent of Indian affairs. With 900 men he put down a Shawnee uprising at Tippecanoe, IN, on Nov. 7, 1811. A generation later, in 1840, he waged a rousing presidential campaign, using the slogan "Tippecanoe and Tyler Too." The Tyler of the slogan was his running mate, John Tyler.

Although born to one of the wealthiest, most prestigious, and most influential families in Virginia, Harrison was elected president with the slogan, "Log Cabin and Hard Cider." He caught pneumonia during his inauguration and died Apr. 4, 1841, after only one month in office.

John Tyler (1841-45), 10th president, independent Whig, was born on Mar. 29, 1790, in Greenway, Charles City Co., VA, the son of John and Mary Armistead Tyler. His father was governor of Virginia (1808-11). Tyler graduated from the College of William and Mary in 1807 and in 1811 was elected to the Virginia legislature. In 1816 he was chosen for the U.S. House of Representatives. He served in the Virginia legislature again from 1823 to 1825, when he was elected governor of Virginia. After a stint in the U.S. Senate (1827-36), he was elected vice president (1840).

When William Henry Harrison died only a month after taking office, Tyler succeeded him. Because he was the first person to occupy the presidency without having been elected to that office, he was referred to as "His Accidency." He gained passage of the Preemption Act of 1841, which gave squatters on government land the right to buy 160 acres at the minimum auction price. His last act as president was to sign a resolution annexing Texas. Tyler accepted renomination in 1844 from some Democrats but withdrew in favor of the official party candidate, James K. Polk. A strong advocate of states' rights, he served briefly in the Confederate House of Representatives before he died in Richmond, VA, on Jan. 18, 1862.

James Knox Polk (1845-49), 11th president, Democrat, was born on Nov. 2, 1795, in Mecklenburg Co., NC, the son of Samuel and Jane Knox Polk. He graduated from the Univ. of North Carolina in 1818 and served in the Tennessee state legislature from 1823 to 1825. He served in the U.S. House of Representatives from 1825 to 1839, the last 4 years as Speaker. He was governor of Tennessee from 1839 to 1841. In 1844, after the Democratic National Convention became deadlocked, it nominated Polk, who became the first "dark horse" candidate for president. He was nominated primarily because he favored annexation of Texas.

As president, Polk reestablished the independent treasury system originated by Van Buren. He was so intent on acquiring California from Mexico that he sent troops to the Mexican border and, when Mexicans attacked, declared that a state of war existed. The Mexican War ended with the annexation of California and much of the Southwest as part of America's "manifest destiny." Polk compromised on the Oregon boundary ("54-40 or fight!") by accepting the 49th parallel and yielding Vancouver Island to the British. Polk died in Nashville, TN, on June 15, 1849, a few months after leaving office.

Zachary Taylor (1849-50), 12th president, Whig, who served only 16 months, was born on Nov. 24, 1784, in Orange Co., VA, the son of Richard and Sarah Strother Taylor. He grew up on his father's plantation near Louisville, KY, where he was educated by private tutors. In 1808 Taylor joined the regular army and was commissioned first lieutenant. He fought in the War of 1812, the Black Hawk War (1832), and the second Seminole War (beginning in 1837). He was called "Old Rough and Ready." In 1846 Pres. Polk sent him with an army to the Rio Grande. When the Mexicans attacked him, Polk declared war. Outnumbered 4-1, Taylor defeated Santa Anna at Buena Vista (1847).

A national hero, Taylor received the Whig nomination in 1848 and was elected president, even though he had never bothered to vote. He resumed the spoils system and, though a slaveholder, worked to admit California as a free state. He fell ill and died in office on July 9, 1850.

Millard Fillmore (1850-53), 13th president, Whig, was born on Jan. 7, 1800, in Cayuga Co., NY, the son of Nathaniel and Phoebe Millard Fillmore. Although he had little schooling, he became a law clerk at the age of 22 and a year later was admitted to the bar. He was elected to the New York state assembly in 1828 and served until 1831. From 1833 until 1835 and again from 1837 to 1843, he represented his district in the U.S. House of Representatives. He opposed the entrance of Texas as a slave state and voted for a protective tariff. In 1844 he was defeated for governor of New York.

In 1848 he was elected vice president, and he succeeded as president after Taylor's death. Fillmore favored the Compromise of 1850 and signed the Fugitive Slave Law. His policies pleased neither expansionists nor slaveholders, and he was not renominated in 1852. In 1856 he was nominated by the American (Know-Nothing) Party, but despite the support of the Whigs, he was defeated by James Buchanan. He died in Buffalo, NY, on Mar. 8, 1874.

Franklin Pierce (1853-57), 14th president, Democrat, was born on Nov. 23, 1804, in Hillsboro, NH, the son of Benjamin Pierce, Revolutionary War general and governor of New Hampshire, and Anna Kendrick. He graduated from Bowdoin College in 1824 and was admitted to the bar in 1827. He was elected to the New Hampshire state legislature in 1829 and was chosen Speaker in 1831. He went to the U.S. House in 1833 and was elected a U.S. senator in 1837. He enlisted in the Mexican War and became brigadier general under Gen. Winfield Scott.

In 1852 Pierce was nominated as the Democratic presidential candidate on the 49th ballot. He decisively defeated Gen. Scott, his Whig opponent, in the election. Although he was against slavery, Pierce was influenced by proslavery Southerners. He supported the controversial Kansas-Nebraska Act, which left the question of slavery in the new territories of Kansas and Nebraska to popular vote. Pierce signed a reciprocity treaty with Canada and approved the Gadsden Purchase of a border area on a proposed railroad route, from Mexico. Denied renomination, he spent most of his remaining years in Concord, NH, where he died on Oct. 8, 1869.

James Buchanan (1857-61), 15th president, Federalist, later Democrat, was born on Apr. 23, 1791, near Mercersburg, PA, the son of James and Elizabeth Speer Buchanan. He graduated from Dickinson College in 1809 and was admitted to the bar in 1812. He fought in the War of 1812 as a volunteer. He was twice elected to the Pennsylvania general assembly, and in 1821 he entered the U.S. House of Representatives. After briefly serving (1832-33) as minister to Russia, he was elected U.S. senator from Pennsylvania. As Polk's secretary of state (1845-49), he ended the Oregon dispute with Britain and supported the Mexican War and annexation of Texas. As minister to Great Britain, he signed the Ostend Manifesto (1854), declaring a U.S. right to take Cuba by force should efforts to purchase it fail.

Nominated by Democrats, Buchanan was elected president in 1856. On slavery he favored popular sovereignty and choice by state constitutions but did not consistently uphold this position. He denied the right of states to secede but opposed coercion and attempted to keep peace by not provoking secessionists. Buchanan left office having failed to deal decisively with the situation. He died at Wheatland, his estate, near Lancaster, PA, on June 1, 1868.

Abraham Lincoln (1861-65), 16th president, Whig, then Republican, was born on Feb. 12, 1809, in a log cabin on a farm in Hardin (now Larue) Co., KY, the son of Thomas and Nancy Hanks Lincoln. The Lincolns moved to Spencer Co., IN, near Gentryville, when Lincoln was 7. After Lincoln's mother died, his father married Mrs. Sarah Bush Johnston in 1819. In 1830 the family moved to Macon Co., IL.

Defeated in 1832 in a race for the state legislature, Lincoln was elected on the Whig ticket two years later and served in the lower house from 1834 to 1842. In 1837 Lincoln was admitted to the bar and became partner in a Springfield, IL, law office. He soon won recognition as an effective and resourceful attorney. In 1846, he was elected to the U.S. House of Representatives, where he attracted attention during a single term for his opposition to the Mexican War and his position on slavery. In 1856 he campaigned for the newly founded Republican Party, and in 1858 he became its senatorial candidate against Stephen A. Douglas. Although he lost the election, Lincoln gained national recognition from his debates with Douglas.

In 1860, Lincoln was nominated for president by the Republican Party on a platform of restricting slavery. He ran against Douglas, a northern Democrat; John C. Breckinridge, a Southern proslavery Democrat; and John Bell, of the Constitutional Union Party. As a result of Lincoln's winning the election, South Carolina seceded from the Union on Dec. 20, 1860, followed in 1861 by 10 other Southern states.

The Civil War erupted when Fort Sumter, which Lincoln decided to resupply, was attacked by Confederate forces on Apr. 12, 1861. Lincoln called successfully for recruits from the North. On Sept. 22, 1862, five days after the Battle of Antietam, Lincoln announced that slaves in territory then in rebellion would be free Jan. 1, 1863, the date of the Emancipation Proclamation. His speeches, including his Gettysburg and inaugural addresses, are remembered for their eloquence.

Lincoln was reelected, in 1864, over Gen. George B. McClellan, Democrat. Gen. Robert E. Lee surrendered on Apr. 9, 1865. On Apr. 14, Lincoln was shot by actor John Wilkes Booth in Ford's Theater, in Washington, DC. He died the next day.

Andrew Johnson (1865-69), 17th president, Democrat, was born on Dec. 29, 1808, in Raleigh, NC, the son of Jacob and Mary McDonough Johnson. He was apprenticed to a tailor as a youth, but ran away after two years and eventually settled in Greeneville, TN. He became popular with the townspeople and in 1829 was elected councilman and later mayor. In 1835 he was sent to the state general assembly. In 1843 he was elected to the U.S. House of Representatives, where he served for 10 years. Johnson was also governor of Tennessee from 1853 to 1857, when he was elected to the U.S. Senate. He supported John C. Breckinridge against Lincoln in the 1860 election. Although Johnson had held slaves, he opposed secession and tried to prevent Tennessee from seceding. In Mar. 1862, Lincoln appointed him military governor of occupied Tennessee.

In 1864, in order to balance Lincoln's ticket with a Southern Democrat, the Republicans nominated Johnson for vice president. He was elected vice president with Lincoln and then succeeded to the presidency upon Lincoln's death. Soon afterward, in a controversy with Congress over the president's power over the South, he proclaimed an amnesty to all Confederates, except certain leaders, if they would ratify the 13th Amendment abolishing slavery. States doing so added anti-Negro provisions that enraged Congress, which restored military control over the South. When Johnson removed Sec. of War Edwin M. Stanton, without notifying the Senate, the House impeached him in Feb. 1868. Charging him with thereby having violated the Tenure of Office Act, the House was actually responding to his opposition to harsh congressional Reconstruction, expressed in repeated vetoes. He was tried by the Senate, and in May, in two separate votes on different counts, Johnson was acquitted, both times by only one vote.

Johnson was denied renomination but remained politically active. He was reelected to the Senate in 1874. Johnson died July 31, 1875, at Carter Station, TN.

Ulysses S. Grant (1869-77), 18th president, Republican, was born on Apr. 27, 1822, in Point Pleasant, OH, the son of Jesse R. and Hannah Simpson Grant. The next year the family moved to Georgetown, OH. Grant was named Hiram Ulysses. Upon entering West Point in 1839, he found his name had been put down as Ulysses S. Grant, with his middle name first and his mother's maiden name as his middle name. He eventually adopted it as his true name but maintained the "S" did not stand for anything. Grant graduated in 1843. During the Mexican War, Grant served under both Gen. Zachary Taylor and Gen. Winfield Scott. In 1854, he resigned his commission because of loneliness and drinking problems, and in the following years he engaged in generally unsuccessful farming and business ventures. With the start of the Civil War, he was named colonel and then brigadier general of the Illinois Volunteers. He took Forts Henry and Donelson and fought at Shiloh. His brilliant campaign against Vicksburg and his victory at Chattanooga made him so prominent that Lincoln placed him in command of all

Union armies. Grant accepted Lee's surrender at Appomattox Court House on Apr. 9, 1865. Pres. Johnson appointed Grant secretary of war when he suspended Stanton, but Grant was not confirmed.

Grant was nominated for president by the Republicans in 1868 and elected over Democrat Horatio Seymour. The 15th Amendment, the amnesty bill, and peaceful settlement of disputes with Great Britain were events of his administration. The Liberal Republicans and Democrats opposed him with Horace Greeley in the 1872 election, but Grant was reelected. His second administration was marked by scandals, including the Crédit Mobelier affair, the Whiskey Ring, in which high-ranked officials conspired to defraud the government of taxes, and the impeachment of his Secretary of War. An attempt by the Stalwarts (Old Guard Republicans) to nominate him in 1880 failed. In 1884 the collapse of an investment firm in which he was a partner left Grant penniless. He wrote his personal memoirs while ill with cancer and completed them shortly before his death at Mt. McGregor, NY, on July 23, 1885.

Rutherford Birchard Hayes (1877-81), 19th president, Republican, was born on Oct. 4, 1822, in Delaware, OH, the son of Rutherford and Sophia Birchard Hayes. He was reared by his uncle, Sardis Birchard. Hayes graduated from Kenyon College in 1842 and from Harvard Law School in 1845. He practiced law in Lower Sandusky (now Fremont), OH, and was city solicitor of Cincinnati from 1858 to 1861. During the Civil War, he was major of the 23rd Ohio Volunteers. He was wounded several times, and by the end of the war he had risen to the rank of brevet major general. While serving (1865-67) in the U.S. House of Representatives, Hayes supported Reconstruction and Johnson's impeachment. He was twice elected governor of Ohio (1867, 1869). After losing a race for the U.S. House in 1872, he was reelected governor of Ohio in 1875.

In 1876, Hayes was nominated for president and believed he had lost the election to Democrat Samuel J. Tilden. But a few Southern states submitted two sets of electoral votes, and the result was in dispute. An electoral commission, consisting of 8 Republicans and 7 Democrats, awarded all disputed votes to Hayes, allowing him to become president by one electoral vote. Hayes, keeping a promise to Southerners, withdrew troops from areas still occupied in the South, ending the era of Reconstruction. He proposed civil service reforms, alienating those favoring the spoils system, and advocated repeal of the Tenure of Office Act restricting presidential power to dismiss officials. He supported sound money and specie payments.

Hayes died in Fremont, OH, on Jan. 17, 1893.

James Abram Garfield (1881), 20th president, Republican, was born on Nov. 19, 1831, in Orange, Cuyahoga Co., OH, the son of Abram and Eliza Ballou Garfield. His father died in 1833, and he was reared in poverty by his mother. He worked as a canal bargeman, a farmer, and a carpenter. He attended Western Reserve Eclectic Institute and graduated from Williams College in 1856. He returned to Western Reserve to teach and in 1857, at age 25, he became the school's president. In 1859 he was elected to the Ohio legislature. Antislavery and antisecession, he volunteered for military service in the Civil War, becoming colonel of the 42nd Ohio Infantry and brigadier in 1862. He fought at Shiloh, TN, was chief of staff for Gen. William Starke Rosecrans, and was made major general for gallantry at Chickamauga, GA. He entered Congress as a radical Republican in 1863, calling for execution or exile of Confederate leaders, but he moderated his views after the Civil War. On the electoral commission in 1877 he voted for Hayes against Tilden on strict party lines.

Garfield was a senator-elect in 1880 when he became the Republican nominee for president. He was chosen as a compromise over Gen. Grant, James G. Blaine, and John Sherman, and won election despite some bitterness among

Grant's supporters. For much of his brief tenure as president, Garfield was concerned with a fight with New York Sen. Roscoe Conkling, who opposed two major appointments made by Garfield. On July 2, 1881, Garfield was shot and seriously wounded by a mentally disturbed office seeker, Charles J. Guiteau, while entering a railroad station in Washington, DC. He lingered on in the White House before finally succumbing on Sept. 19, 1881, in Elberon, NJ.

Chester Alan Arthur (1881-85), 21st president, Republican, was born on Oct. 5, 1829, in Fairfield, VT, to William and Malvina Stone Arthur. He graduated from Union College in 1848, taught school in Vermont, then studied law and practiced in New York City. In 1853, he argued in a fugitive slave case that slaves transported through New York State were thereby freed. In 1871, he was appointed collector of the Port of New York. Pres. Hayes, an opponent of the spoils system, forced him to resign in 1878. This made the New York machine enemies of Hayes. Arthur and the Stalwarts (Old Guard Republicans) tried to nominate Grant for a 3rd term as president in 1880. When Garfield was nominated, Arthur was nominated for vice president in the interests of harmony.

Upon Garfield's assassination, Arthur became president. Despite his past connections, he signed major civil service reform legislation. Arthur tried to dissuade Congress from enacting the high protective tariff of 1883. He was defeated for renomination in 1884 by James G. Blaine. He died in New York City on Nov. 18, 1886.

Grover Cleveland (1885-89; 1893-97) *(According to a State Dept. ruling, Grover Cleveland should be counted as both the 22nd and the 24th president, because his two terms were not consecutive.)* Democrat, was born Stephen Grover Cleveland on Mar. 18, 1837, in Caldwell, NJ, the son of Richard F. and Ann Neal Cleveland. When he was a small boy, his family moved to New York. Prevented by his father's death from attending college, he studied by himself and was admitted to the bar in Buffalo, NY, in 1859. In succession he became assistant district attorney (1863), sheriff (1871), mayor (1881), and governor of New York (1882). He was an independent, honest administrator who hated corruption. Cleveland was nominated for president over Tammany Hall opposition in 1884 and defeated Republican James G. Blaine.

As president, he enlarged the civil service and vetoed many pension raids on the Treasury. In the 1888 election he was defeated by Benjamin Harrison, although his popular vote was larger. Reelected over Harrison in 1892, he faced a money crisis brought about by a lowered gold reserve, circulation of paper, and exorbitant silver purchases under the Sherman Silver Purchase Act. He obtained a repeal of the Sherman Act but was unable to secure effective tariff reform. A severe economic depression and labor troubles racked his administration, but he refused to interfere in business matters and rejected Jacob Coxey's demand for unemployment relief. In 1894, he broke the Pullman strike. Cleveland was not renominated in 1896.

He died in Princeton, NJ, on June 24, 1908.

Benjamin Harrison (1889-93), 23rd president, Republican, was born on Aug. 20, 1833, in North Bend, OH, the son of John Scott and Elizabeth Irwin Harrison. His great-grandfather, Benjamin Harrison, was a signer of the Declaration of Independence; his grandfather, William Henry Harrison, was 9th president; his father was a member of Congress. He attended school on his father's farm and graduated from Miami University in Oxford, OH, in 1852. He was admitted to the bar in 1854 and practiced in Indianapolis, IN. During the Civil War, he rose to the rank of brevet brigadier general and fought at Kennesaw Mountain, Peachtree Creek, Nashville, and in the Atlanta campaign. He

lost the 1876 gubernatorial election in Indiana but succeeded in becoming a U.S. senator in 1881.

In 1888 he defeated Cleveland for president despite receiving fewer popular votes. As president, he expanded the pension list and signed the McKinley high tariff bill, the Sherman Antitrust Act, and the Sherman Silver Purchase Act. During his administration, six states were admitted to the Union. He was defeated for reelection in 1892. He died in Indianapolis, IN, on Mar. 13, 1901.

William McKinley (1897-1901), 25th president, Republican, was born on Jan. 29, 1843, in Niles, OH, the son of William and Nancy Allison McKinley. McKinley briefly attended Allegheny College. When the Civil War broke out in 1861, he enlisted and served for the duration. He rose to captain and in 1865 was made brevet major. After studying law in Albany, NY, he opened a law office in Canton, OH (1867). He served twice in the U.S. House (1877-83; 1885-91) and led the fight there for the McKinley Tariff, passed in 1890; he was not reelected to the House as a result. He served two terms (1892-96) as governor of Ohio.

In 1896 he was elected president as a proponent of a protective tariff and sound money (gold standard) over William Jennings Bryan, the Democrat and a proponent of free silver. McKinley was reluctant to intervene in Cuba, but the loss of the battleship *Maine* at Havana crystallized opinion. He demanded Spain's withdrawal from Cuba; Spain made some concessions, but Congress announced a state of war as of Apr. 21, 1898. He was reelected in the 1900 campaign, defeating Bryan's anti-imperialist arguments with the promise of a "full dinner pail." McKinley was respected for his conciliatory nature and for his conservative stance on business issues. On Sept. 6, 1901, while welcoming citizens at the Pan-American Exposition, in Buffalo, NY, he was shot by Leon Czolgosz, an anarchist. He died Sept. 14.

Theodore Roosevelt (1901-09), 26th president, Republican, was born on Oct. 27, 1858, in New York City, the son of Theodore and Martha Bulloch Roosevelt. He was a 5th cousin of Franklin D. Roosevelt and an uncle of Eleanor Roosevelt. Roosevelt graduated from Harvard University in 1880. He attended Columbia Law School briefly but abandoned law to enter politics. He was elected to the New York State Assembly in 1881 and served until 1884. He spent the next two years ranching and hunting in the Dakota Territory. In 1886, he ran unsuccessfully for mayor of New York City. He was civil service commissioner in Washington, DC, from 1889 to 1895. From 1895 to 1897, he served as New York City's police commissioner. He was assistant secretary of the Navy under McKinley. The Spanish-American War made him nationally known. He organized the 1st U.S. Volunteer Cavalry (Rough Riders) and, as lieutenant colonel, led the charge up Kettle Hill in San Juan. Elected New York governor in 1898, he fought the spoils system and achieved taxation of corporation franchises.

Nominated for vice president in 1900, Roosevelt became the nation's youngest president when McKinley was assassinated. He was reelected in 1904. As president he fought corruption of politics by big business, dissolved the Northern Securities Co. and others for violating antitrust laws, intervened in the 1902 coal strike on behalf of the public, obtained the Elkins Law (1903) forbidding rebates to favored corporations, and helped pass the Hepburn Railway Rate Act of 1906 (extending jurisdiction of the Interstate Commerce Commission). He helped obtain passage of the Pure Food and Drug Act (1906) and of employers' liability laws. Roosevelt vigorously organized conservation efforts. He mediated the peace between Japan and Russia in 1905, for which he won the Nobel Peace Prize. He abetted the 1903 revolution in Panama that led to U.S. acquisition of territory for the Panama Canal.

In 1908 Roosevelt obtained the nomination of William H. Taft, who was elected. Feeling that Taft had abandoned his policies, he unsuccessfully sought the nomination in 1912.

He then ran on the Progressive "Bull Moose" ticket against Taft and Woodrow Wilson, splitting the Republicans and ensuring Wilson's election. During the campaign he was shot by a mentally deranged man but was not seriously wounded. In 1916, after unsuccessfully seeking the presidential nomination, he supported the Republican candidate, Charles E. Hughes. A strong friend of Britain, he fought for U.S. intervention in World War I.

Roosevelt was a voracious reader and wrote some 40 books, including *The Winning of the West.* He died Jan. 6, 1919, at Sagamore Hill, Oyster Bay, NY.

William Howard Taft (1909-13), 27th president, Republican, and 10th chief justice of the U.S., was born on Sept. 15, 1857, in Cincinnati, OH, the son of Alphonso and Louisa Maria Torrey Taft. His father was secretary of war and attorney general in Grant's cabinet and minister to Austria and Russia under Arthur. Taft graduated from Yale in 1878 and from Cincinnati Law School in 1880. After working as a law reporter for Cincinnati newspapers, he served as assistant prosecuting attorney (1881-82), assistant county solicitor (1885), superior court judge (1887), U.S. solicitor-general (1890), and federal circuit judge (1892). In 1900 he became head of the U.S. Philippines Commission and was the first civil governor of the Philippines (1901-04). In 1904 he served as secretary of war, and in 1906 he was sent to Cuba to help avert a threatened revolution.

Taft was groomed for the presidency by Theodore Roosevelt and elected over William Jennings Bryan in 1908. Taft vigorously continued Roosevelt's trust-busting, instituted the Dept. of Labor, and drafted the amendments calling for direct election of senators and the income tax. However, his tariff and conservation policies angered progressives. Although renominated in 1912, he was opposed by Roosevelt, who ran on the Progressive Party ticket; the result was Democrat Woodrow Wilson's election.

Taft, with some reservations, supported the League of Nations. After leaving office, he was professor of constitutional law at Yale (1913-21) and chief justice of the U.S. (1921-30). Taft was the only person in U.S. history to have been both president and chief justice. He died in Washington, DC, on Mar. 8, 1930.

(Thomas) Woodrow Wilson (1913-21), 28th president, Democrat, was born on Dec. 28, 1856, in Staunton, VA, the son of Joseph Ruggles and Janet (Jessie) Woodrow Wilson. He grew up in Georgia and South Carolina. He attended Davidson College in North Carolina before graduating from Princeton University in 1879. He studied law at the Univ. of Virginia and political science at Johns Hopkins Univ., where he received his PhD in 1886. He taught at Bryn Mawr (1885-88) and at Wesleyan (1888-90) before joining the faculty at Princeton. He was president of Princeton from 1902 until 1910, when he was elected governor of New Jersey. In 1912 he was nominated for president with the aid of William Jennings Bryan, who sought to block James "Champ" Clark and Tammany Hall. Wilson won because the Republican vote for Taft was split by the Progressives.

As president, Wilson protected American interests in revolutionary Mexico and fought for American rights on the high seas. He oversaw the creation of the Federal Reserve system, cut the tariff, and developed a reputation as a reformer. His sharp warnings to Germany led to the resignation of his secretary of state, Bryan, a pacifist. In 1916 he was reelected by a slim margin with the slogan, "He kept us out of war," although his attempts to mediate in the war failed. After several American ships were sunk by the Germans, he secured a declaration of war against Germany on Apr. 6, 1917.

Wilson outlined his peace program on Jan. 8, 1918, in the Fourteen Points, a state paper that had worldwide influence. He enunciated a doctrine of self-determination for the settlement of territorial disputes. The Germans accepted his terms and an armistice on Nov. 11, 1918.

Wilson went to Paris to help negotiate the peace treaty, the crux of which he considered the League of Nations. The Senate demanded reservations that would not make the U.S. subordinate to the votes of other nations in case of war. Wilson refused and toured the country to get support. He suffered a stroke in Oct. 1919. An invalid, he clung to his office while his wife and doctors effectively functioned as president.

Wilson was awarded the 1919 Nobel Peace Prize, but the treaty embodying the League of Nations was ultimately rejected by the Senate in 1920. He left the White House in Mar. 1921. He died in Washington, DC, on Feb. 3, 1924.

Warren Gamaliel Harding (1921-23), 29th president, Republican, was born on Nov. 2, 1865, near Corsica (now Blooming Grove), OH, the son of George Tyron and Phoebe Elizabeth Dickerson Harding. He attended Ohio Central College, studied law, and became editor and publisher of a county newspaper. He entered the political arena as state senator (1901-04) and then served as lieutenant governor (1904-06). In 1910 he ran unsuccessfully for governor of Ohio; in 1914 he was elected to the U.S. Senate. In the Senate he voted for antistrike legislation, women's suffrage, and the Volstead Prohibition Enforcement Act over Pres. Wilson's veto. He opposed the League of Nations.

In 1920 he was nominated for president and defeated James M. Cox in the election. The Republicans capitalized on war weariness and fear that Wilson's League of Nations would curtail U.S. sovereignty. Harding stressed a return to "normalcy" and worked for tariff revision and the repeal of excess profits law and high income taxes. His secretary of the interior, Albert B. Fall, became involved in the Teapot Dome scandal, over the leasing of U.S. government-owned oil reserves.

As rumors began to circulate about the corruption in his administration, Harding fell ill after a trip to Alaska, and he died suddenly in San Francisco on Aug. 2, 1923.

(John) Calvin Coolidge (1923-29), 30th president, Republican, was born on July 4, 1872, in Plymouth Notch, VT, the son of John Calvin and Victoria J. Moor Coolidge. Coolidge graduated from Amherst College in 1895. He entered Republican state politics and served as mayor of Northampton, MA, as state senator, as lieutenant governor, and, in 1919, as governor. In Sept. 1919, Coolidge attained national prominence by calling out the state guard in the Boston police strike. He declared, "There is no right to strike against the public safety by anybody, anywhere, anytime." This brought his name before the Republican convention of 1920, where he was nominated for vice president.

Coolidge succeeded to the presidency on Harding's death. As president, he opposed the League of Nations and the soldiers' bonus bill, which was passed over his veto. In 1924 he was elected to the presidency by a huge majority. He substantially reduced the national debt. He twice vetoed the McNary-Haugen farm bill, which would have provided relief to financially hard-pressed farmers.

With Republicans eager to renominate him, Coolidge simply announced on Aug. 2, 1927, "I do not choose to run for president in 1928." He died in Northampton, MA, on Jan. 5, 1933.

Herbert Clark Hoover (1929-33), 31st president, Republican, was born on Aug. 10, 1874, in West Branch, IA, the son of Jesse Clark and Hulda Randall Minthorn Hoover. Hoover grew up in Indian Territory (now Oklahoma) and Oregon and graduated from Stanford University with a degree in geology in 1895. He worked briefly with the U.S. Geological Survey and then managed mines in Australia, Asia, Europe, and Africa. While chief engineer of imperial mines in China, he directed food relief for victims of the Boxer Rebellion. He gained a reputation not only as an engineer but as a humanitarian as he directed the American Relief Committee, London (1914-15) and the U.S. Commission for Relief in Belgium (1915-19). He was U.S. Food Administrator (1917-19), American Relief Administrator (1918-23), and in charge of Russian Relief (1918-23). He served as secretary of commerce under both Harding and Coolidge. Some historians believe that he was the most effective secretary of commerce ever to hold that office.

In 1928 Hoover was elected president over Alfred E. Smith. In 1929 the stock market crashed, and the economy collapsed. During the Great Depression, Hoover inaugurated some government assistance programs, but he was opposed to administration of aid through a federal bureaucracy. As the effects of the depression continued, he was defeated in the 1932 election by Franklin D. Roosevelt. Hoover remained active after leaving office. President Truman named him coordinator of the European Food Program (1946) and chairman of the Commission on Organization of the Executive Branch (1947-49; 1953-55).

Hoover died in New York City on Oct. 20, 1964.

Franklin Delano Roosevelt (1933-45), 32nd president, Democrat, was born on Jan. 30, 1882, in Hyde Park, NY, the son of James and Sara Delano Roosevelt. He graduated from Harvard University in 1903. He attended Columbia University Law School without taking a degree and was admitted to the New York State bar in 1907. His political career began when he was elected to the New York State senate in 1910. In 1913 Pres. Wilson appointed him assistant secretary of the navy, a post he held during World War I.

In 1920 Roosevelt ran for vice president with James Cox and was defeated. From 1921 to 1928 he worked in his New York law office and was also vice president of a bank. In Aug. 1921, he was stricken with poliomyelitis, which left his legs paralyzed. As a result of therapy he was able to stand, or walk a few steps, with the aid of leg braces.

Roosevelt served two terms as governor of New York (1929-33). In 1932, Democratic convention delegate W. G. McAdoo, pledged to nominee John N. Garner, threw his votes to Roosevelt, who was nominated for president. The Depression and the promise to repeal Prohibition ensured his election. He asked for emergency powers, proclaimed the New Deal, and put into effect a vast number of administrative changes. Foremost was the use of public funds for relief and public works, resulting in deficit financing. He greatly expanded the federal government's regulation of business and by an excess profits tax and progressive income taxes produced a redistribution of earnings on an unprecedented scale. He also promoted legislation establishing the Social Security system. He was the last president inaugurated on Mar. 4 (1933) and the first inaugurated on Jan. 20 (1937).

Roosevelt was the first president to use radio for "fireside chats." When the Supreme Court nullified some New Deal laws, he sought power to "pack" the Court with additional justices, but Congress refused to give him the authority. He was the first president to break the "no 3rd term" tradition (1940) and was elected to a 4th term in 1944, despite failing health.

Roosevelt was openly hostile to fascist governments before World War II and launched a lend-lease program on behalf of the Allies. With British Prime Min. Winston Churchill he wrote a declaration of principles to be followed after Nazi defeat (the Atlantic Charter of Aug. 14, 1941) and urged the Four Freedoms (freedom of speech, of worship, from want, from fear) Jan. 6, 1941. When Japan attacked Pearl Harbor on Dec. 7, 1941, the U.S. entered the war. Roosevelt guided the nation through the war and conferred with allied heads of state at Casablanca, Morocco (Jan. 1943), Quebec, Canada (Aug. 1943), Tehran, Iran (Nov.- Dec. 1943), Cairo, Egypt (Nov. and Dec. 1943), and Yalta, Ukraine (Feb. 1945).

Roosevelt did not, however, live to see the end of the war. He died of a cerebral hemorrhage in Warm Springs, GA, on Apr. 12, 1945.

Harry S. Truman (1945-53), 33rd president, Democrat, was born on May 8, 1884, in Lamar, MO, the son of John Anderson and Martha Ellen Young Truman. A family disagreement on whether his middle name should be Shipp or Solomon, after his two grandfathers, resulted in his using only the middle initial S. After graduating from high school in Independence, MO, he worked for the *Kansas City Star* (1901) as a railroad timekeeper and as a clerk in Kansas City banks until about 1905. He ran his family's farm from 1906 to 1917, then served in France during World War I. After the war he opened a haberdashery, was a judge on the Jackson Co. Court (1922-24), and attended Kansas City School of Law (1923-25).

Truman was elected to the U.S. Senate in 1934 and re-elected in 1940. In 1944, with Roosevelt's backing, he was nominated for vice president and elected. On Roosevelt's death in 1945, Truman became president. In 1948, in a famous upset victory, he defeated Republican Thomas E. Dewey to win election to a new term.

Truman authorized the first uses of the atomic bomb (Hiroshima and Nagasaki, Aug. 6 and 9, 1945), bringing World War II to a rapid end. He was responsible for what came to be called the Truman Doctrine to aid nations such as Greece and Turkey, threatened by Communist takeover, and his strong commitment to NATO and to the Marshall Plan helped bring the two about. In 1948-49, he broke a Soviet blockade of West Berlin with a massive airlift. When Communist North Korea invaded South Korea (June 1950), he won UN approval for a "police action" and, without prior congressional consent, sent in forces under Gen. Douglas MacArthur. When MacArthur opposed his policy of limited objectives, Truman removed him.

He died in Kansas City, MO, on Dec. 26, 1972.

Dwight David Eisenhower (1953-61), 34th president, Republican, was born on Oct. 14, 1890, in Denison, TX, the son of David Jacob and Ida Elizabeth Stover Eisenhower. He grew up on a small farm in Abilene, KS, and graduated from West Point in 1915. He was on the staff of Gen. Douglas MacArthur in the Philippines from 1935 to 1939. In 1942, he was made commander of Allied forces landing in North Africa; the next year he was made full general. He became supreme Allied commander in Europe that same year and as such led the Normandy invasion (June 6, 1944). On Dec. 20, 1944, he was given the rank of general of the Army, which was made permanent in 1946.

On May 7, 1945, Eisenhower received the surrender of Germany at Rheims, France. He returned to the U.S. to serve as chief of staff (1945-48). His war memoir, *Crusade in Europe* (1948), was a best-seller. In 1948 he became president of Columbia University; in 1950 he became commander of NATO forces.

Eisenhower resigned from the army and was nominated for president by the Republicans in 1952. He defeated Adlai E. Stevenson in the 1952 election and again in 1956. Eisenhower called himself a moderate, favored the "free market system" versus government price and wage controls, kept government out of labor disputes, reorganized the defense establishment, and promoted missile programs. He continued foreign aid, helped negotiate a cease fire truce in the Korean War, endorsed Taiwan and SE Asia defense treaties, backed the UN in condemning the Anglo-French raid on Egypt, and advocated the "open skies" policy of mutual inspection with the USSR. He sent U.S. troops into Little Rock, AR, in Sept. 1957, to enforce school integration.

Eisenhower died on Mar. 28, 1969, in Washington, DC.

John Fitzgerald Kennedy (1961-63), 35th president, Democrat, was born on May 29, 1917, in Brookline, MA, the son of Joseph P. and Rose Fitzgerald Kennedy. He graduated from Harvard University in 1940. While serving in the Navy (1941-45), he commanded a patrol torpedo (PT) boat in the Solomons and won the Navy and Marine Corps Medal. In 1956, while recovering from spinal surgery, he wrote *Profiles in Courage*, biographical sketches of political heroes, which won a Pulitzer Prize in 1957. He served in the House of Representatives from 1947 to 1953 and was elected to the Senate in 1952 and 1958. In 1960, he won the Democratic nomination for president and narrowly defeated Republican Vice Pres. Richard M. Nixon. Kennedy was the youngest president ever elected to the office and the first Catholic.

Despite the image of youth and vigor he conveyed to the public, Kennedy suffered from serious medical problems, including Addison's disease and severe chronic back pain that required him to wear a back brace. The public was not aware of the extent of these problems, or of his many marital infidelities, including an affair with a young White House press aide that only became known in 2003.

In Apr. 1961, the new Kennedy administration suffered a severe setback when an invasion force of anti-Castro Cubans, trained and directed by the CIA, failed to establish a beachhead at the Bay of Pigs in Cuba. One of Kennedy's most important acts as president was his successful demand on Oct. 22, 1962, that the Soviet Union dismantle its missile bases in Cuba. Kennedy also defied Soviet attempts to force the Allies out of Berlin. He started the Peace Corps, backed civil rights, and expanded medical care for the aged. Space exploration was greatly developed during his administration.

On Nov. 22, 1963, President Kennedy was assassinated while riding in a motorcade in Dallas, TX. A commission chaired by Chief Justice Earl Warren concluded in Sept. 1964 that the sole assassin had been Lee Harvey Oswald, a former U.S. Marine and, at the time of the shooting, an ardent Marxist. Oswald was captured a short time after the assassination and charged with the crime. Two days afte the assassination, before he could go on trial, he was shot dead by nightclub owner Jack Ruby while being moved to a county jail.

Lyndon Baines Johnson (1963-69), 36th president, Democrat, was born on Aug. 27, 1908, near Stonewall, TX, the son of Sam Ealy and Rebekah Baines Johnson. He graduated from Southwest Texas State Teachers College in 1930 and attended Georgetown University Law School. He taught public speaking in Houston (1930-31) and then served as secretary to Rep. R. M. Kleberg (1931-35). In 1937 Johnson won an election to fill the vacancy caused by the death of a U.S. representative and in 1938 was elected to the full term, after which he returned for four terms. During 1941 and 1942 he also served in the Navy in the Pacific, earning a Silver Star for bravery. He was elected U.S. senator in 1948 and reelected in 1954. He became Democratic leader of the Senate in 1953. Johnson had strong support for the Democratic presidential nomination at the 1960 convention, where the nominee, John F. Kennedy, asked him to run for vice president. His campaigning helped overcome religious bias against Kennedy in the South.

Johnson became president when Kennedy was assassinated. He was elected to a full term in 1964. Johnson's domestic program was of considerable importance. He won passage of major civil rights, anti-poverty, aid to education, and health-care (Medicare, Medicaid) legislation—the "Great Society" program. However, his escalation of the war in Vietnam came to overshadow the achievements of his administration. In the face of increasing division in the nation and in his own party over his handling of the war, Johnson declined to seek another term.

Johnson died on Jan. 22, 1973, in San Antonio, TX.

Richard Milhous Nixon (1969-74), 37th president, Republican, was born on Jan. 9, 1913, in Yorba Linda, CA, the son of Francis Anthony and Hannah Milhous Nixon. He graduated from Whittier College in 1934 and from Duke University Law School in 1937. After practicing law in Whittier, CA, and serving briefly in the Office of Price Administration in 1942, he entered the Navy and served in the South Pacific. Nixon was elected to the House of Representatives in 1946 and 1948. He achieved prominence as the House Un-American Activities Committee member who forced the showdown leading to the Alger Hiss perjury conviction. In 1950 he was elected to the Senate.

Nixon was elected vice president in the Eisenhower landslides of 1952 and 1956. He won the Republican nomination for president in 1960 but was narrowly defeated by John F. Kennedy. He ran unsuccessfully for governor of California in 1962. In 1968 he again won the GOP presidential nomination, then defeated Hubert Humphrey for the presidency.

As president, Nixon appointed four Supreme Court justices, including the chief justice, moving the court to the right. As a "new federalist," he sought to shift responsibility to state and local governments. He dramatically altered relations with China, which he visited in 1972—the first U.S. president to do so. With foreign affairs adviser Henry Kissinger, he pursued détente with the Soviet Union, signing major arms limitation and other treaties and increasing trade. He began a gradual withdrawal from Vietnam, but U.S. troops remained there through his first term. He ordered an incursion into Cambodia (1970) and the bombing of Hanoi and mining of Haiphong Harbor (1972). Reelected by a large majority in Nov. 1972, he secured a Vietnam cease-fire in Jan. 1973.

Nixon's 2nd term was cut short by scandal, after disclosures relating to a June 1972 burglary of Democratic Party headquarters in the Watergate office complex in DC. The courts and Congress sought tapes of Nixon's office conversations and called for criminal proceedings against former White House aides and for a House inquiry into possible impeachment. Nixon claimed executive privilege, but the Supreme Court ruled against him. In July 1974, the House Judiciary Committee recommended adoption of three impeachment articles charging him with obstruction of justice, abuse of power, and contempt of Congress. On Aug. 5, he released transcripts of conversations that linked him to cover-up activities. He resigned on Aug. 9, becoming the first president ever to do so.

In later years, Nixon emerged as an elder statesman. He died Apr. 22, 1994, in New York City.

Gerald Rudolph Ford (1974-77), 38th president, Republican, was born on July 14, 1913, in Omaha, NE, the son of Leslie and Dorothy Gardner King, and was named Leslie Lynch King Jr. When he was 2, his parents divorced, and he and his mother moved to Grand Rapids, MI. There she met and married Gerald R. Ford, who formally adopted him and gave him his name. Ford graduated from the Univ. of Michigan in 1935 and from Yale Law School in 1941. He began practicing law in Grand Rapids, but in 1942, he joined the Navy and served in the Pacific, leaving the service in 1946 as a lieutenant commander. He entered the House of Representatives in 1949 and spent 25 years in the House, eight of them as Republican leader.

On Oct. 12, 1973, after Vice Pres. Spiro T. Agnew resigned, Pres. Nixon nominated Ford to replace him. It was the first use of the procedures set out in the 25th Amendment. When Nixon resigned, Aug. 9, 1974, because of the Watergate scandal, Ford became president; he was the only president who was never elected either to the presidency or to the vice presidency.

Ford was widely credited with having contributed to rebuilding morale after the Nixon presidency. But he was also criticized by many when, in a controversial move, he pardoned Nixon for any federal crimes he might have committed as president. Ford vetoed 48 bills in his first 21 months in office, mostly in the interest of fighting high inflation; he was less successful in curbing high unemployment. In foreign policy, Ford continued to pursue détente.

Ford was narrowly defeated in the 1976 election. In 1999, he received the Medal of Freedom, the country's highest civilian award, and the Congressional Gold Medal, in recognition of his public service.

Ford died Dec. 26, 2006, at home in Rancho Mirage, CA.

James Earl (Jimmy) Carter (1977-81), 39th president, Democrat, was the first president from the Deep South since before the Civil War. He was born on Oct. 1, 1924, in Plains, GA, the son of James and Lillian Gordy Carter. Carter graduated from the U.S. Naval Academy in 1946 and in 1952 entered the Navy's nuclear submarine program as an aide to Capt. (later Adm.) Hyman Rickover. He studied nuclear physics at Union College.

Carter's father died in 1953, and he left the Navy to take over the family peanut farming businesses. He served in the Georgia state senate (1963-67) and as governor of Georgia (1971-75). In 1976, Carter won the Democratic nomination and defeated Pres. Gerald R. Ford.

On his first full day in office, Carter pardoned all Vietnam draft evaders. He played a major role in the negotiations leading to the 1979 peace treaty between Israel and Egypt, and he won passage of new treaties with Panama providing for U.S. control of the Panama Canal to end in 2000. Carter was widely criticized, however, for the poor state of the economy and was viewed by some as weak in his handling of foreign policy. In Nov. 1979, Iranian student militants attacked the U.S. embassy in Tehran and held members of the embassy staff hostage. Efforts to obtain release of the hostages were a major preoccupation during the rest of his term. He reacted to the Soviet invasion of Afghanistan by imposing a grain embargo and boycotting the Moscow Olympic Games.

Carter was defeated by Ronald Reagan in the 1980 election. The 52 American hostages in Iran were finally released on Inauguration Day, 1981, just after Reagan officially became president. In 2007, the Carter Center celebrated its 25th anniversary. Since its founding by Carter and his wife, Rosalynn Carter, in 1982, the Center has observed more than 67 elections in 26 countries with struggling democracies and reduced incidents of Guinea worm disease. In large part for his diplomatic efforts in office and subsequently, he was awarded the Nobel Peace Prize in 2002.

Ronald Wilson Reagan (1981-89), 40th president, Republican, was born on Feb. 6, 1911, in Tampico, IL, the son of John Edward and Nellie Wilson Reagan. Reagan graduated from Eureka College in 1932, after which he worked as a sports announcer in Des Moines, IA. He began a successful career as an actor in 1937, starring in numerous movies, and later in television, until the 1960s. During World War II Reagan served in the Army Air Force, making training films. He was president of the Screen Actors Guild in 1947-52 and in 1959-60. Reagan was elected governor of California in 1966 and reelected in 1970.

In 1980, Reagan gained the Republican presidential nomination and won a landslide victory over Jimmy Carter. He was easily reelected in 1984. Reagan forged a bipartisan coalition in Congress, which led to enactment of his program of large-scale tax cuts, cutbacks in many government programs, and a major defense buildup. He signed a Social Security reform bill designed to provide for the long-term solvency of the system. In 1986, he signed into law a major tax-reform bill. He was shot and seriously wounded in 1981 by a would-be assassin who was later declared insane.

In 1982, the U.S. joined France and Italy in maintaining a peacekeeping force in Beirut, Lebanon, and the next year Reagan sent a task force to invade Grenada after two Marxist coups on the island. Reagan's opposition to international terrorism led to the U.S. bombing of Libyan military installations in 1986. He strongly supported El Salvador, the Nicaraguan contras, and other anticommunist governments and

forces throughout the world. He also held four summit meetings with Soviet leader Mikhail Gorbachev. At the 1987 meeting in Washington, DC, a historic treaty eliminating short- and medium-range missiles from Europe was signed.

Reagan faced a crisis in 1986-87. It was revealed that the U.S. had sold weapons through Israeli brokers to Iran in exchange for the release of U.S. hostages being held in Lebanon and that subsequently some of the money had been diverted to the Nicaraguan contras (Congress had barred U.S. aid to the contras). The scandal led to the resignation of leading White House aides. As Reagan left office in Jan. 1989, the nation was experiencing its 6th consecutive year of economic prosperity. Over the same period, however, the federal government recorded large budget deficits.

In 1994, in a letter to the American people, Reagan revealed that he was suffering from Alzheimer's disease. He died on June 5, 2004, in Los Angeles, CA, from complications of the disease.

George Herbert Walker Bush (1989-93), 41st president, Republican, was born on June 12, 1924, in Milton, MA, the son of Prescott and Dorothy Walker Bush. He served as a U.S. Navy pilot in World War II. After graduating from Yale University in 1948, he settled in Texas, where, in 1953, he helped found an oil company. After losing a bid for a U.S. Senate seat in 1964, he was elected to the House of Representatives in 1966 and 1968. He lost a second U.S. Senate race in 1970. Subsequently he served as U.S. ambassador to the United Nations (1971-73), headed the U.S. Liaison Office in Beijing (1974-75), and was director of central intelligence (1976-77).

Following an unsuccessful bid for the 1980 Republican presidential nomination, Bush became Ronald Reagan's running mate, and served as vice president from 1981 to 1989.

In 1988, Bush gained the GOP presidential nomination and defeated Michael Dukakis. Bush took office faced with U.S. budget and trade deficits, and insolvent U.S. savings and loan institutions. He faced a severe budget deficit annually, struggled with military cutbacks, and vetoed abortion-rights legislation. In 1990 he agreed to a budget deficit-reduction plan that included tax hikes.

Bush supported Soviet reforms, Eastern Europe democratization, and good relations with Beijing. In Dec. 1989, Bush sent troops to Panama; they overthrew the government and captured military dictator Gen. Manuel Noriega.

Bush reacted to Iraq's Aug. 1990 invasion of Kuwait by sending U.S. forces to the Persian Gulf area and assembling a UN-backed coalition, including NATO and Arab League members. After a month-long air war, in Feb. 1991, Allied forces retook Kuwait in a 4-day ground assault. The quick victory, with extremely light casualties on the U.S. side, gave Bush at that time one of the highest presidential approval ratings in history. His popularity plummeted by the end of 1991, however, as the economy slipped into recession. He was defeated by Bill Clinton in the 1992 election. In 2005, he led campaigns with former Pres. Clinton to raise money for the victims of the Indian Ocean tsunami and Hurricane Katrina.

William Jefferson (Bill) Clinton (1993-2001), 42nd president, Democrat, was born on Aug. 19, 1946, in Hope, AR, son of William Blythe and Virginia Cassidy Blythe, and was named William Jefferson Blythe IV. Blythe died in an automobile accident before his son was born. His widow married Roger Clinton, and at the age of 16, William Jefferson Blythe IV changed his last name to Clinton.

Clinton became interested in politics in high school and went on to Georgetown University, where he graduated with high honors in 1968. He then attended Oxford University for 2 years as a Rhodes scholar. During that time he legally avoided the draft and possible service in Vietnam, according to some critics by misleading his draft board. He earned a degree from Yale Law School in 1973.

Clinton worked on George McGovern's 1972 presidential campaign. He taught at the University of Arkansas from 1973 to 1976, when he was elected state attorney general. In 1978, he was elected governor, becoming the nation's youngest at the time. Defeated for reelection in 1980, he was returned to office several times thereafter. He married Hillary Rodham in 1975.

Clinton won most of the 1992 presidential primaries, moving his party toward the center as he tried to broaden his appeal; as the Democratic party's presidential nominee he defeated Pres. George H. W. Bush and Reform Party candidate Ross Perot in the November election. In 1993, Clinton won passage of a measure to reduce the federal budget deficit and won congressional approval of the North American Free Trade Agreement. His administration's plan for major health-care reform legislation died in Congress. After 1994 midterm elections, Clinton faced Republican majorities in both houses of Congress. He followed a centrist course at home, sent troops to Bosnia to help implement a peace settlement, and cultivated relations with Russia and China.

Though accused of improprieties in his involvement in the Whitewater Development Corp., an Arkansas land-development venture, Clinton won reelection with 49% of the popular vote in 1996. Independent prosecutor Kenneth Starr did not find substantial and credible evidence of impeachable wrongdoing by the Clintons. He submitted a report to Congress, however, providing evidence of an affair between Clinton and former White House intern Monica Lewinsky. In 1998, Clinton became only the second U.S. president to be impeached by the House of Representatives. He was charged with perjury and obstruction of justice in connection with his attempted cover-up of the affair but was acquitted by the Senate the following year. He retained wide popularity, aided by a strong economy.

In 1999, the United States, under Clinton, joined other NATO nations in an aerial bombing campaign that induced Serbia to withdraw troops from the Kosovo region, where they had been terrorizing ethnic Albanians. In 2000 he became the first president since the Vietnam War to visit Vietnam. On Clinton's last full day in office, Robert Ray, Starr's successor as independent counsel, agreed to conclude the Whitewater investigation. As part of the deal, Clinton acknowledged giving false testimony about his affair with Lewinsky, gave up his law license for 5 years, and paid a $25,000 fine.

After leaving office, Clinton remained active in political affairs. His wife was elected in 2000 to the U.S. Senate from New York, and in 2007 she campaigned for the 2008 Democratic presidential nomination.

George Walker Bush (2001-), 43rd president, Republican, was born on July 6, 1946, in New Haven, CT. He was the first of six children born to George Herbert Walker Bush and his wife, the former Barbara Pierce, a close collateral descendant of Pres. Franklin Pierce. Bush was the first son of a former president to win the White House since John Quincy Adams took office in 1825.

The young George Bush grew up in Midland and Houston, TX. In 1961 he was sent to the Phillips Academy in Andover, MA, the same prep school his father had attended. In 1964 he entered Yale University, his father's alma mater, where he majored in history. Eligible for the draft upon graduation during the Vietnam War, he signed on with the Texas Air National Guard. Bush received an honorable discharge. After earning a master's degree from Harvard Business School, he returned to Midland in 1975 and went into the oil business. Two years later he married Laura Welch; in 1981 she gave birth to twin daughters.

Bush, who had lost a race for Congress in 1978, returned to the oil business, but success proved elusive. After aiding in his father's successful 1988 presidential campaign, he joined a group of investors to buy the Texas Rangers baseball club. Bush ran for governor in 1994, defeating popular incumbent Ann Richards. He won reelection by a landslide in 1998. As governor, he built personal bonds with Democratic leaders and backed education reforms.

The Nov. 2000 presidential election was one of the closest in history. While Bush came out behind in the popular vote—by about 540,000 out of more than 100 million cast—the electoral vote total hinged on the outcome in Florida, where official totals, challenged by Democrats, gave him a razor-thin lead. In December the Supreme Court in effect ended a Democratic-backed effort to recount the vote there, and Florida's 25 electoral votes decided the election in Bush's favor. Among the issues Bush had campaigned on was that of lowering federal taxes, and in May 2001, he won approval from Congress for a tax cut package projected to cost $1.35 tril over the next decade.

After the Sept. 11, 2001 terrorist attacks, Bush vowed to punish those responsible. In a "war against terrorism," the U.S. military attacked and deposed Afghanistan's Taliban regime, which was sheltering elements of the al-Qaeda terrorist network, held responsible for the attacks. The Taliban and al-Qaeda, however, continued to function in parts of Afghanistan, and al-Qaeda was blamed for staging terrorist acts in a number of other countries. In 2002 Bush won congressional approval to create a cabinet-level department for homeland security.

Bush met in May 2002 with Russian Pres. Vladimir Putin in Moscow, where they signed a pact cutting nuclear armaments in each country. In July, with corporate scandals and a slumping stock market fueling demands for tighter regulation of business, Bush signed legislation aimed at curbing financial abuses.

In March 2003, the United States, aided mainly by forces from Great Britain, launched an air and ground war against Iraq and deposed the dictatorial regime of Pres. Saddam Hussein. The regime was accused of harboring weapons of mass destruction and of violating other UN resolutions. A Senate Intelligence Committee report issued in July 2004 concluded that pre-war intelligence on illicit weapons in Iraq had been seriously flawed. Despite Hussein's capture in Iraq, Dec. 13, 2003, and the formation of a new Iraqi government in June 2004, insurgent violence continued into 2007.

Bush was elected to a second term in Nov. 2004. The administration's Iraq policy, its conduct of the war and reconstruction efforts, and domestic security were major issues.

In 2005, Bush continued to press for Social Security reform, but his plans met with public and congressional resistance. Hurricane Katrina devastated the Gulf Coast in Aug. and left hundreds of thousands of people homeless as the flooded city of New Orleans was evacuated and shut down. Pres. Bush and the Federal Emergency Management Agency (FEMA) were criticized for what was widely perceived as a slow and ineffective response to the disaster. In Sept., Justice Sandra Day O'Connor resigned, creating the first Supreme Court vacancy in more than 11 years; Chief Justice William H. Rehnquist died later that month. Appeals court judge John G. Roberts, initially nominated to succeed O'Connor, was quickly confirmed as new chief justice, and judge Samuel A. Alito was appointed to fill O'Connor's seat.

In his Nov. 2005 outline for winning the war in Iraq, Bush warned against any "artificial deadline" for withdrawing U.S. troops. He held a steady position on Iraq and the global war on terror through 2007, despite a sinking public approval rating. On Sept. 6, 2006, Bush revealed that prisoners had been held at secret facilities in other countries, and that men linked to the 9-11 attacks were being transferred from CIA custody to the U.S. prison in Guantanamo Bay. Democrats used public dissatisfaction with the war to win majorities in both the House and Senate in Nov. 7, 2006 midterm elections. Defense Sec. Donald Rumsfeld, one of the chief architects of the war, resigned Nov. 8.

In 2006 and 2007, Bush failed in attempts to create a temporary worker or guest-worker program that would grant legal status to some of the estimated 12 mil illegal immigrants in the U.S. He exercised his veto for the first time in July 2006, rejecting legislation that would have eased restrictions on federal funding for stem cell research.

In Jan. 2007, Bush announced a "surge" of more than 20,000 additional troops to Iraq. Bush sparred verbally with Iranian Pres. Mahmoud Ahmadinejad through 2007, pressing for greater transparency in Iran's nuclear program. Bush embarked on a 5-nation Latin American tour in March 2007, and on May 29 rebuked the government of Sudan for not co-operating with international efforts to end the crisis in Dar-fur, saying he would enforce sanctions and push the UN for an arms embargo on Sudan. In Sept., North Korea an-nounced that it would end its nuclear weapons programs by the end of the year, in exchange for a variety of incentives still under consideration by the Bush administration and its partners (China, Japan, South Korea, and Russia) in six-party talks, aimed at securing North Korea's nuclear disar-mament.

Wives and Children of the Presidents

Name (born-died; married)	State	Sons/ daughters	Name (born-died; married)	State	Sons/ daughters
Martha Dandridge Custis Washington (1731-1802; 1759)	VA	None	Caroline Lavinia Scott Harrison (1832-92; 1853)	OH	1/1
Abigail Smith Adams (1744-1818; 1764)	MA	3/2	Mary Scott Lord Dimmick Harrison (1858-1948; 1896)	PA	0/1
Martha Wayles Skelton Jefferson (1748-82; 1772)	VA	1/5	Ida Saxton McKinley (1847-1907; 1871)	OH	0/2
Dolley Payne Todd Madison (1768-1849; 1794)	NC	None	Alice Hathaway Lee Roosevelt (1861-84; 1880)	MA	0/1
Elizabeth Kortright Monroe (1768-1830; 1786)	NY	1/2	Edith Kermit Carow Roosevelt (1861-1948; 1886)	CT	4/1
Louisa Catherine Johnson Adams (1775-1852; 1797)	MD[1]	3/1	Helen Herron Taft (1861-1943; 1886)	OH	2/1
Rachel Donelson Robards Jackson (1767-1828; 1791)	VA	1[2]	Ellen Louise Axson Wilson (1860-1914; 1885)	GA	0/3
Hannah Hoes Van Buren (1783-1819; 1807)	NY	4/0	Edith Bolling Galt Wilson (1872-1961; 1915)	VA	None
Anna Tuthill Symmes Harrison (1775-1864; 1795)	NJ	6/4	Florence Kling De Wolfe Harding (1860-1924; 1891)	OH	None
Letitia Christian Tyler (1790-1842; 1813)	VA	3/5	Grace Anna Goodhue Coolidge (1879-1957; 1905)	VT	2/0
Julia Gardiner Tyler (1820-89; 1844)	NY	5/2	Lou Henry Hoover (1875-1944; 1899)	IA	2/0
Sarah Childress Polk (1803-91; 1824)	TN	None	Anna Eleanor Roosevelt (1884-1962; 1905)	NY	5/1
Margaret (Peggy) Mackall Smith Taylor (1788-1852; 1810)	MD	1/5	Elizabeth Virginia (Bess) Wallace Truman (1885-1982; 1919)	MO	0/1
Abigail Powers Fillmore (1798-1853; 1826)	NY	1/1	Mamie Geneva Doud Eisenhower (1896-1979; 1916)	IA	2/0
Caroline Carmichael McIntosh Fillmore (1813-81; 1858)	NJ	None	Jacqueline Lee Bouvier Kennedy (1929-94; 1953)	NY	2/1
Jane Means Appleton Pierce (1806-63; 1834)	NH	3/0	Claudia (Lady Bird) Alta Taylor Johnson (1912-2007; 1934)	TX	0/2
Mary Todd Lincoln (1818-82; 1842)	KY	4/0	Thelma Catherine Patricia Ryan Nixon (1912-93; 1940)	NV	0/2
Eliza McCardle Johnson (1810-76; 1827)	TN	3/2	Elizabeth (Betty) Bloomer Warren Ford (1918; 1948)	IL	3/1
Julia Boggs Dent Grant (1826-1902; 1848)	MO	3/1	Rosalynn Smith Carter (1927; 1946)	GA	3/1
Lucy Ware Webb Hayes (1831-89; 1852)	OH	7/1	Anne Frances (Nancy) Robbins Davis Reagan (1921; 1952)	NY	1/1[3]
Lucretia Rudolph Garfield (1832-1918; 1858)	OH	5/2	Barbara Pierce Bush (1925; 1945)	NY	4/2
Ellen Lewis Herndon Arthur (1837-80; 1859)	VA	2/1	Hillary Rodham Clinton (1947; 1975)	IL	0/1
Frances Folsom Cleveland (1864-1947; 1886)	NY	2/3	Laura Welch Bush (1946; 1977)	TX	0/2

Note: Pres. Buchanan was unmarried. (1) Born in London, father a MD citizen. (2) Adopted. (3) Pres. Reagan's first wife, whom he later divorced, was Jane Wyman. They had a daughter who died in infancy, a daughter who lived past infancy, and an adopted son.

First Lady Laura Welch Bush

Laura Welch Bush was born in Midland, TX, Nov. 4, 1946. She graduated from Southern Methodist University, earned a master's in library science at the Univ. of Texas at Austin, and became a librarian and teacher in Dallas and Houston public schools. She and George W. Bush were married in 1977; in 1981, their twin daughters, Jenna and Barbara, were born.

As First Lady of Texas (1995-2001), Laura Bush worked for educational reform and stressed literacy programs. She launched an early childhood development initiative and also worked to promote breast cancer awareness.

Laura Bush's first solo appearance as First Lady came at the launch of DC Teaching Fellows, a program encouraging pro-fessionals to become teachers. In Nov. 2001 she became the first First Lady to give a speech of her own in place of the presi-dent's weekly radio address. In 2005, she toured Afghanistan and the Middle East, seeking to promote women's rights and democracy in the region. She continues her involvement in such issues as early childhood education and the preservation of the cultural and natural heritage of the U.S. She is also a strong promoter of literacy and reading and, along with the Library of Congress, created the National Book Festival in 2001.

Burial Places of the Presidents

President	Burial place	President	Burial place	President	Burial place
Washington	Mt. Vernon, VA	Pierce	Concord, NH	Wilson	Wash. Natl. Cathedral, DC
J. Adams	Quincy, MA	Buchanan	Lancaster, PA	Harding	Marion, OH
Jefferson	Charlottesville, VA	Lincoln	Springfield, IL	Coolidge	Plymouth Notch, VT
Madison	Montpelier Station, VA	A. Johnson	Greeneville, TN	Hoover	West Branch, IA
Monroe	Richmond, VA	Grant	New York, NY	F. Roosevelt	Hyde Park, NY
J. Q. Adams	Quincy, MA	Hayes	Fremont, OH	Truman	Independence, MO
Jackson	Nashville, TN	Garfield	Cleveland, OH	Eisenhower	Abilene, KS
Van Buren	Kinderhook, NY	Arthur	Albany, NY	Kennedy	Arlington Natl. Cemetery
W. H. Harrison	North Bend, OH	Cleveland	Princeton, NJ	L. B. Johnson	Stonewall, TX
Tyler	Richmond, VA	B. Harrison	Indianapolis, IN	Nixon	Yorba Linda, CA
Polk	Nashville, TN	McKinley	Canton, OH	Ford	Grand Rapids, MI
Taylor	Louisville, KY	T. Roosevelt	Oyster Bay, NY	Reagan	Simi Valley, CA
Fillmore	Buffalo, NY	Taft	Arlington Natl. Cemetery		

Presidential Facts

Oldest president: Ronald Reagan, who was 77 when he left office

Youngest president: Theodore Roosevelt, who was 42 when sworn in after McKinley's death

Youngest person elected president: John F. Kennedy, who was 43 when elected in 1960

Tallest president: Abraham Lincoln, who was 6 feet, 4 inches

Shortest president: James Madison, who was 5 feet, 4 inches

Heaviest president: William Howard Taft, who was 332 pounds in 1911

First president to live in the White House: John Adams, who moved there in 1800

First president inaugurated in Washington, DC: Thomas Jefferson, in 1801

First president whose parents were immigrants: Andrew Jackson; his parents immigrated from Ireland in 1765

First president born a U.S. citizen: Martin Van Buren, in Kinderhook, NY, 1782

First president born outside the original colonies: Abraham Lincoln, in Kentucky, 1809

Most common presidential home state: Virginia, with 8 presidents

First president of all 50 states: Dwight D. Eisenhower, first inaugurated in 1953

First president born in the 20th century: John F. Kennedy, in 1917

First president to be photographed while in office: James K. Polk, in 1849

First president to have a telephone in the White House: Rutherford B. Hayes, in 1879

First president to address the nation on radio: Warren G. Harding, in 1922

First president to appear on TV: Franklin D. Roosevelt, at opening ceremonies for the 1939 World's Fair

First president to give a live, televised news conference: John F. Kennedy, in 1961

First president to hold an Internet chat: Bill Clinton, in 1999

Only presidents who lost the popular vote while winning election: John Quincy Adams, in 1824 (elected by the House after general election failed to produce a majority); Rutherford B. Hayes, in 1876; Benjamin Harrison, in 1888; George W. Bush, in 2000. Popular vote totals are unknown.

Only presidents chosen by the House of Representatives: Thomas Jefferson (1st term) and John Quincy Adams

Most common Alma Mater (undergraduate): Harvard, with 5 presidents

Only left-handed presidents: James Garfield, Herbert Hoover, Harry Truman, Gerald Ford, Ronald Reagan, George H. W. Bush, and Bill Clinton

Only Catholic elected president: John F. Kennedy; the most common religious affiliations have been Episcopalian (11) and Presbyterian (7)

Only bachelor presidents: James Buchanan, who never married, and Grover Cleveland, who married Frances Folsom in the White House in 1886

Only divorced president: Ronald Reagan; divorced from actress Jane Wyman in 1948, married Nancy Davis in 1952

Presidents who died on July 4: John Adams and Thomas Jefferson (both 1826) and James Monroe (1831)

Only president buried in Washington, DC: Woodrow Wilson, who was interred at the Washington National Cathedral

Presidential Libraries

Presidential libraries are coordinated by the National Archives and Records Administration (www.archives.gov/presidential-libraries). Materials for presidents before Herbert Hoover are held by private institutions.

Herbert Hoover Library and Museum
210 Parkside Dr.
West Branch, IA 52358
PHONE: 319-643-5301
E-MAIL: hoover.library@nara.gov
WEBSITE: hoover.archives.gov

Dwight D. Eisenhower Library
200 SE 4th St.
Abilene, KS 67410-2900
PHONE: 877-RING-IKE
E-MAIL: eisenhower.library@nara.gov
WEBSITE: eisenhower.archives.gov

Richard Nixon Library and Museum
CA OFFICE: 18001 Yorba Linda Blvd.
Yorba Linda, CA 92886-3903
CA PHONE: 714-983-9120
E-MAIL: nixon@nara.gov
WEBSITE: www.nixonlibrary.org
MD OFFICE: 8601 Adelphi Rd.
College Park, MD 20740-6001
PHONE: 301-837-3290

Ronald Reagan Library and Museum
40 Presidential Dr.
Simi Valley, CA 93065-0600
PHONE: 800-410-8354
E-MAIL: reagan.library@nara.gov
WEBSITE: www.reagan.utexas.edu

Franklin D. Roosevelt Library and Museum
4079 Albany Post Rd.
Hyde Park, NY 12538-1990
PHONE: 800-FDR-VISIT
E-MAIL: roosevelt.library@nara.gov
WEBSITE: www.fdrlibrary.marist.edu

John F. Kennedy Library and Museum
Columbia Pt.
Boston, MA 02125-3312
PHONE: 866-JFK-1960
E-MAIL: kennedy.library@nara.gov
WEBSITE: www.jfklibrary.org

Gerald R. Ford Library and Museum
LIBRARY: 1000 Beal Ave.
Ann Arbor, MI 48109-2109
PHONE: 734-205-0555
MUSEUM: 303 Pearl St. NW
Grand Rapids, MI 49504-5353
PHONE: 616-254-0400
E-MAIL: ford.library@nara.gov
WEBSITE: www.fordlibrarymuseum.gov

George Bush Library and Museum
1000 George Bush Dr. West
College Station, TX 77845
PHONE: 979-691-4000
E-MAIL: library.bush@nara.gov
WEBSITE: bushlibrary.tamu.edu

Harry S. Truman Library and Museum
500 West U.S. Hwy. 24
Independence, MO 64050-2481
PHONE: 800-833-1225
E-MAIL: truman.library@nara.gov
WEBSITE: www.trumanlibrary.org

Lyndon Baines Johnson Library and Museum
2313 Red River St.
Austin, TX 78705-5737
PHONE: 512-721-0200
E-MAIL: johnson.library@nara.gov
WEBSITE: www.lbjlib.utexas.edu

Jimmy Carter Library and Museum
441 Freedom Pkwy.
Atlanta, GA 30307-1496
PHONE: 404-865-7100
E-MAIL: carter.library@nara.gov
WEBSITE: www.jimmycarterlibrary.gov

William J. Clinton Library and Museum
1200 President Clinton Ave.
Little Rock, AR 72201
PHONE: 501-374-4242
E-MAIL: clinton.library@nara.gov
WEBSITE: www.clintonlibrary.gov

Presidential Impeachment in U.S. History

The U.S. Constitution provides for impeachment and removal from office of federal officials on grounds of "Treason, Bribery, or other high Crimes and Misdemeanors" (Article II, Sect. 4). Impeachment is the bringing of charges by the House of Representatives. It is followed by a Senate trial; a two-thirds majority vote of Senators present is needed for conviction and removal from office.

In 1868, **Andrew Johnson** became the first president impeached by the House. He was tried but not convicted.

In 1974, impeachment articles against Pres. **Richard Nixon**, in connection with the Watergate scandal, were voted by the House Judiciary Committee. He resigned Aug. 9, and the House accepted the committee report without taking further action. In 1998, Pres. **Bill Clinton** was impeached by the House in connection with covering up a sexual relationship with former White House intern Monica Lewinsky. He was tried in the Senate in 1999 and acquitted.

PRESIDENTIAL ELECTIONS

Electoral and Popular Vote, 2004 and 2000

Source: Federal Election Commission (2004); Voter News Service (2000).

State	2004 Electoral Vote Kerry	Bush	Nader	Democrat Kerry	Republican Bush	Indep.[1] Nader	2000 Electoral Vote Gore	Bush	Nader	Buchanan	Democrat Gore	Republican Bush	Green[1] Nader	Reform[1] Buchanan
AL	0	9	0	693,933	1,176,394	6,701	0	9	0	0	692,611	941,173	18,323	6,303
AK	0	3	0	111,025	190,889	5,069	0	3	0	0	79,004	167,398	28,747	4,194
AZ	0	10	—	893,524	1,104,294	—	0	8	0	0	685,341	781,652	45,645	10,903
AR	0	6	0	469,953	572,898	6,171	0	6	0	0	422,768	472,940	13,421	10,936
CA	55	0	0	6,745,485	5,509,826	—	54	0	0	0	5,861,203	4,567,429	418,707	39,897
CO	0	9	0	1,001,732	1,101,255	12,718	0	8	0	0	738,227	883,748	91,434	10,282
CT	7	0	0	857,488	693,826	12,969	8	0	0	0	816,015	561,094	64,452	4,382
DE	3	0	0	200,152	171,660	2,153	3	0	0	0	180,068	137,288	8,307	775
DC	3	0	0	202,970	21,256	1,485	2[2]	0	0	0	171,923	18,073	10,576	—
FL	0	27	0	3,583,544	3,964,522	32,971	0	25	0	—	2,912,253	2,912,790	97,488	17,356
GA	0	15	—	1,366,149	1,914,254	—	0	13	—	0	1,116,230	1,419,720	—	10,868
HI	4	0	—	231,708	194,191	—	4	0	0	0	205,286	137,845	21,623	1,071
ID	0	4	—	181,098	409,235	—	0	4	0	—	138,637	336,937	—	7,687
IL	21	0	—	2,891,550	2,345,946	—	22	0	0	0	2,589,026	2,019,421	103,759	16,060
IN	0	11	—	969,011	1,479,438	—	0	12	0	—	901,980	1,245,836	—	17,173
IA	0	7	0	741,898	751,957	5,973	7	0	0	0	638,517	634,373	29,374	6,942
KS	0	6	0	434,993	736,456	9,348	0	6	0	0	399,276	622,332	36,086	7,239
KY	0	8	0	712,733	1,069,439	8,856	0	8	0	0	638,923	872,520	23,118	4,181
LA	0	9	0	820,299	1,102,169	7,032	0	9	0	0	792,344	927,871	20,473	14,478
ME	4	0	0	396,842	330,201	8,069	4	0	0	0	319,951	286,616	37,127	4,315
MD	10	0	0	1,334,493	1,024,703	11,854	10	0	0	0	1,144,008	813,827	53,768	4,067
MA	12	0	0	1,803,800	1,071,109	—	12	0	0	0	1,616,487	878,502	173,564	11,086
MI	17	0	0	2,479,183	2,313,746	24,035	18	0	0	—	2,170,418	1,953,139	84,165	—
MN	9[3]	0	0	1,445,014	1,346,695	18,683	10	0	0	0	1,168,266	1,109,659	126,696	22,256
MS	0	6	0	458,094	684,981	3,177	0	7	0	0	404,614	572,844	8,122	2,233
MO	0	11	—	1,259,171	1,455,713	—	0	11	0	0	1,111,138	1,189,924	38,515	9,806
MT	0	3	0	173,710	266,063	6,168	0	3	0	0	137,126	240,178	24,437	5,735
NE	0	5	0	254,328	512,814	5,698	0	5	0	0	231,780	433,862	24,540	3,431
NV	0	5	0	397,190	418,690	4,838	0	4	0	0	279,978	301,575	15,008	4,747
NH	4	0	0	340,511	331,237	4,479	0	4	0	0	266,348	273,559	22,198	2,603
NJ	15	0	0	1,911,430	1,670,003	19,418	15	0	0	0	1,788,850	1,284,173	94,554	6,868
NM	0	5	0	370,942	376,930	4,053	5	0	0	0	286,783	286,417	21,251	1,279
NY	31	0	0	4,314,280	2,962,567	99,873	33	0	0	0	4,112,965	2,405,570	244,360	33,202
NC	0	15	—	1,525,849	1,961,166	—	0	14	—	0	1,257,692	1,631,163	—	8,971
ND	0	3	0	111,052	196,651	3,756	0	3	0	0	95,284	174,852	9,486	7,330
OH	0	20	—	2,741,167	2,859,768	—	0	21	0	0	2,186,190	2,351,209	117,857	25,980
OK	0	7	—	503,966	959,792	—	0	8	—	0	474,276	744,337	—	9,014
OR	7	0	—	943,163	866,831	—	7	0	0	0	720,342	713,577	77,357	5,706
PA	21	0	—	2,938,095	2,793,847	—	23	0	0	0	2,485,967	2,281,127	103,392	16,879
RI	4	0	0	259,765	169,046	4,651	4	0	0	0	249,508	130,555	25,052	2,250
SC	0	8	0	661,699	937,974	5,520	0	8	0	0	566,039	786,892	20,279	3,540
SD	0	3	0	149,244	232,584	4,320	0	3	—	0	118,804	190,700	—	3,314
TN	0	11	0	1,036,477	1,384,375	8,992	0	11	0	0	981,720	1,061,949	19,781	4,218
TX	0	34	—	2,832,704	4,526,917	—	0	32	0	0	2,433,746	3,799,639	137,994	12,423
UT	0	5	0	241,199	663,742	11,305	0	5	0	0	203,053	515,096	35,850	9,277
VT	3	0	0	184,067	121,180	4,494	3	0	0	0	149,022	119,775	20,374	2,182
VA	0	13	—	1,454,742	1,716,959	—	0	13	0	0	1,217,290	1,437,490	59,398	5,578
WA	11	0	0	1,510,201	1,304,894	23,283	11	0	0	0	1,247,652	1,108,864	103,002	4,953
WV	0	5	0	326,541	423,778	4,063	0	5	0	0	295,497	336,475	10,680	3,101
WI	10	0	0	1,489,504	1,478,120	16,390	11	0	0	0	1,242,987	1,237,279	94,070	11,206
WY	0	3	0	70,776	167,629	2,741	0	3	0	0	60,481	147,947	—	2,724
Total	**251**	**286**	**0**	**59,028,444**	**62,040,610**	**411,306**	**266**	**271**	**0**	**0**	**51,003,894**	**50,459,211**	**2,834,410**	**441,001**

(—) = Not listed on state's ballot. (1) Listed on the ballot in some states as particular party. (2) One Washington, DC, elector abstained. (3) One Minnesota elector voted for Democratic vice-presidential candidate Sen. John Edwards (NC) for both president and vice president.

2004 Official Presidential General Election Results

Source: Federal Election Commission

Candidate (Party)	Popular Vote	Percent of Pop. Vote	Candidate (Party)	Popular Vote	Percent of Pop. Vote
George W. Bush (Republican)	62,040,610	50.73	Thomas J. Harens (Christian Freedom)	2,387	0.00
John Kerry (Democrat)	59,028,444	48.27	Gene Amondson (Concerns of People)	1,944	0.00
Ralph Nader (Independent)	465,650	0.38*	Bill Van Auken (Socialist Equality)	1,857	0.00
Michael Badnarik (Libertarian)	397,265	0.32	John Parker (Workers World)	1,646	0.00
Michael Anthony Peroutka (Independent)	143,630	0.12	Charles Jay (Personal Choice)	946	0.00
David Cobb (Green)	119,859	0.10	Stanford E. Andress (Unaffiliated)	804	0.00
Leonard Peltier (Peace and Freedom)	27,607	0.02	Earl F. Dodge (Prohibition Party)	140	0.00
Walter F. Brown (Socialist)	10,837	0.01	Write-in (other)	37,240	0.03
James Harris (Socialist Workers)	7,102	0.01	None of These Candidates	3,688	0.00
Róger Calero (Socialist Workers)	3,689	0.00	**Total**	**122,295,645**	**100.00**

Note: Party designations may vary from one state to another. Percents do not add because of rounding. *Includes write-in votes in states where Nader was not on the ballot.

PRESIDENTIAL ELECTION RESULTS BY STATE SINCE 1948

Results for New England states are for selected cities or towns.

Source: Federal Election Commission. Not all write-ins are included.

Alabama

2004: Bush, R., 1,176,394; Kerry, D., 693,933; Nader, Ind., 6,701; Badnarik, Ind., 3,529; Peroutka, Ind., 1,994.

2000: Bush, R., 941,173; Gore, D., 692,611; Nader, Ind., 18,323; Buchanan, Ind., 6,351; Browne, Libertarian, 5,893; Phillips, Ind., 775 Hagelin, Ind., 447.

1996: Dole, R., 769,044; Clinton, D., 662,165; Perot, Ind. (Ref.), 92,149; Browne, Libertarian, 5,290; Phillips, Ind., 2,365; Hagelin, Natural Law, 1,697; Harris, Ind., 516.

1992: Bush, R., 804,283; Clinton, D., 690,080; Perot, Ind., 183,109; Marrou, Libertarian, 5,737; Fulani, New Alliance, 2,161.

1988: Bush, R., 815,576; Dukakis, D., 549,506; Paul, Lib., 8,460; Fulani, Ind., 3,311.

1984: Reagan, R., 872,849; Mondale, D., 551,899; Bergland, Libertarian, 9,504.

1980: Reagan, R., 654,192; Carter, D., 636,730; Anderson, Independent, 16,481; Rarick, Amer. Ind., 15,010; Clark, Libertarian, 13,318; Bubar, Statesman, 1,743; Hall, Com., 1,629; DeBerry, Soc. Workers, 1,303; McReynolds, Socialist, 1,006; Commoner, Citizens, 517.

1976: Carter, D., 659,170; Ford, R., 504,070; Maddox, Amer. Ind., 9,198; Bubar, Proh., 6,669; Hall, Com., 1,954; MacBride, Libertarian, 1,481.

1972: Nixon, R., 728,701; McGovern, D., 219,108 plus 37,815 Natl. Dem. Party of Alabama; Schmitz, Conservative, 11,918; Munn., Proh., 8,551.

1968: Wallace, 3rd Party, 691,425; Humphrey, D., 196,579; Nixon, R., 146,923; Munn, Proh., 4,022.

1964: Goldwater, R., 479,085; Dem. (electors unpledged), 209,848; scattered, 105.

1960: Kennedy, D., 324,050; Nixon, R., 237,981; Faubus, States' Rights, 4,367; Decker, Proh., 2,106; King, Afro-Americans, 1,485; scattered, 236.

1956: Stevenson, D., 290,844; Eisenhower, R., 195,694; Ind. electors, 20,323.

1952: Stevenson, D., 275,075; Eisenhower, R., 149,231; Hamblen, Proh., 1,814.

1948: Thurmond, States' Rights, 171,443; Dewey, R., 40,930; Wallace, Prog., 1,522; Watson, Proh., 1,085.

Alaska

2004: Bush, R., 190,889; Kerry, D., 111,025; Nader, Populist, 5,069; Peroutka, AK Ind., 2,092; Badnarik, Libertarian, 1,675; Cobb, Green, 1,058.

2000: Bush, R., 167,398; Gore, D., 79,004; Nader, Green, 28,747; Buchanan, Reform, 5,192; Browne, Libertarian, 2,636; Hagelin, Natural Law, 919; Phillips, Constitution, 596.

1996: Dole, R., 122,746; Clinton, D., 80,380; Perot, Ref., 26,333; Nader, Green, 7,597; Browne, Libertarian, 2,276; Phillips, Taxpayers, 925; Hagelin, Natural Law, 729.

1992: Bush, R., 102,000; Clinton, D., 78,294; Perot, Ind., 73,481; Gritz, Populist/America First, 1,379; Marrou, Libertarian, 1,378.

1988: Bush, R., 119,251; Dukakis, D., 72,584; Paul, Lib., 5,484; Fulani, New Alliance, 1,024.

1984: Reagan, R., 138,377; Mondale, D., 62,007; Bergland, Libertarian, 6,378.

1980: Reagan, R., 86,112; Carter, D., 41,842; Clark, Libertarian, 18,479; Anderson, Ind., 11,155; write-in, 857.

1976: Ford, R., 71,555; Carter, D., 44,058; MacBride, Libertarian, 6,785.

1972: Nixon, R., 55,349; McGovern, D., 32,967; Schmitz, Amer., 6,903.

1968: Nixon, R., 37,600; Humphrey, D., 35,411; Wallace, 3rd Party, 10,024.

1964: Johnson, D., 44,329; Goldwater, R., 22,930.

1960: Nixon, R., 30,953; Kennedy, D., 29,809.

Arizona

2004: Bush, R., 1,104,294; Kerry, D., 893,524; Badnarik, Libertarian, 11,856.

2000: Bush, R., 781,652; Gore, D., 685,341; Nader, Green, 45,645; Buchanan, R., 12,373; Smith, Libertarian, 5,775; Hagelin, Natural Law, 1,120.

1996: Clinton, D., 653,288; Dole, R., 622,073; Perot, Ref., 112,072; Browne, Libertarian, 14,358.

1992: Bush, R., 572,086; Clinton, D., 543,050; Perot, Ind., 353,741; Gritz, Populist/America First, 8,141; Marrou, Libertarian, 6,759; Hagelin, Natural Law, 2,267.

Arkansas

2004: Bush, R., 572,898; Kerry, D., 469,953; Nader, Populist, 6,171; Badnarik, Libertarian, 2,352; Peroutka, Constitution, 2,083; Cobb, Green, 1,488.

2000: Bush, R., 472,940; Gore, D., 422,768; Nader, Green, 13,421; Buchanan, Reform, 7,358; Browne, Libertarian, 2,781; Phillips, Constitution, 1,415; Hagelin, Natural Law, 1,098.

1996: Clinton, D., 475,171; Dole, R., 325,416; Perot, Ref., 69,884; Nader, Ind., 3,649; Browne, Ind., 3,076; Phillips, Ind., 2,065; Forbes, Ind., 932; Collins, Ind., 823; Masters, Ind., 749; Moorehead, Ind., 747; Hagelin, Ind., 729; Hollis, Ind., 538; Dodge, Ind., 483.

1992: Clinton, D., 505,823; Bush, R., 337,324; Perot, Ind., 99,132; Phillips, U.S. Taxpayers, 1,437; Marrou, Libertarian, 1,261; Fulani, New Alliance, 1,022.

1988: Bush, R., 466,578; Dukakis, D., 349,237; Duke, Chr. Pop., 5,146; Paul, Lib., 3,297.

1984: Reagan, R., 534,774; Mondale, D., 338,646; Bergland, Libertarian, 2,220.

1980: Reagan, R., 403,164; Carter, D., 398,041; Anderson, Ind., 22,468; Clark, Libertarian, 8,970; Commoner, Citizens, 2,345; Bubar, Statesman, 1,350; Hall, Com., 1,244.

1976: Carter, D., 498,604; Ford, R., 267,903; McCarthy, Ind., 639; Anderson, Amer., 389.

1972: Nixon, R., 445,751; McGovern, D., 198,899; Schmitz, Amer., 3,016.

1968: Wallace, 3rd Party, 235,627; Nixon, R., 189,062; Humphrey, D., 184,901.

1964: Johnson, D., 314,197; Goldwater, R., 243,264; Kasper, Natl. States' Rights, 2,965.

1960: Kennedy, D., 215,049; Nixon, R., 184,508; Natl. States' Rights, 28,952.

1956: Stevenson, D., 213,277; Eisenhower, R., 186,287; Andrews, Ind., 7,008.

1952: Stevenson, D., 226,300; Eisenhower, R., 177,155; Hamblen, Proh., 886; MacArthur, Christian Nat., 458; Hass, Soc. Labor, 1.

1948: Truman, D., 149,659; Dewey, R., 50,959; Thurmond, States' Rights, 40,068; Thomas, Soc., 1,037; Wallace, Prog., 751; Watson, Proh., 1.

California

2004: Kerry, D., 6,745,485; Bush, R., 5,509,826; Badnarik, Libertarian, 50,165; Cobb, Green, 40,771; Peltier, Peace & Freedom, 27,607; Peroutka, Amer. Ind., 26,645.

2000: Gore, D., 5,861,203; Bush, R., 4,567,429; Nader, Green, 418,707; Browne, Libertarian, 45,520; Buchanan, Reform, 44,987; Phillips, Amer. Ind., 17,042; Hagelin, Natural Law, 10,934.

1996: Clinton, D., 5,119,835; Dole, R., 3,828,380; Perot, Ref., 697,847; Nader, Green, 237,016; Browne, Libertarian, 73,600; Feinland, Peace & Freedom, 25,332; Phillips, Amer. Ind., 21,202; Hagelin, Natural Law, 15,403.

1992: Clinton, D., 5,121,325; Bush, R., 3,630,575; Perot, Ind., 2,296,006; Marrou, Libertarian, 48,139; Daniels, Ind., 18,597; Phillips, U.S. Taxpayers, 12,711.

1988: Bush, R., 5,054,917; Dukakis, D., 4,702,233; Paul, Lib., 70,105; Fulani, Ind., 31,181.

1984: Reagan, Rep. 5,305,410; Mondale, D., 3,815,947; Bergland, Libertarian, 48,400.

1980: Reagan, Rep. 4,524,858; Carter, Dem., 3,083,661; Anderson, Ind., 739,833; Clark, Libertarian, 148,434; Commoner, Ind., 61,063; Smith, Peace and Freedom, 18,116; Rarick, Amer. Ind., 9,856.

1976: Ford, R., 3,882,244; Carter, D., 3,742,284; write-in, McCarthy, 58,412; MacBride, Libertarian, 56,388; Maddox, Amer. Ind., 51,098; Wright, People's, 41,731; Camejo, Soc. Workers, 17,259; Hall, Com., 12,766; write-in, 4,935.

1972: Nixon, R., 4,602,096; McGovern, D., 3,475,847; Schmitz, Amer., 232,554; Spock, Peace and Freedom, 55,167; Hospers, Libertarian, 980; Jenness, Soc. Workers, 574; Hall, Com., 373; Fisher, Soc. Labor, 197; Munn, Proh., 53; Green, Universal, 21.

1968: Nixon, R., 3,467,664; Humphrey, D., 3,244,318; Wallace, 3rd Party, 487,270; Peace and Freedom, 27,707; McCarthy, Alternative, 20,721; Gregory, write-in, 3,230; Blomen, Soc. Labor, 341; Mitchell, Com., 260; Munn, Proh., 59; Soeters, Defense, 17.

1964: Johnson, D., 4,171,877; Goldwater, R., 2,879,108; Hass, Soc. Labor, 489; DeBerry, Soc. Workers, 378; Munn, Proh., 305; Hensley, Universal, 19.

1960: Nixon, R., 3,259,722; Kennedy, D., 3,224,099; Decker, Proh., 21,706; Hass, Soc. Labor, 1,051.

1956: Eisenhower, R., 3,027,668; Stevenson, D., 2,420,136; Holtwick, Proh., 11,119; Andrews, Constitution, 6,087; Hass, Soc. Labor, 300; Hoopes, Soc., 123; Dobbs, Soc. Workers, 96; Smith, Christian Natl., 8.

1952: Eisenhower, R., 2,897,310; Stevenson, D., 2,197,548; Hallinan, Prog., 24,106; Hamblen, Proh., 15,653; MacArthur, (Tenny Ticket), 3,326; Hass, Soc. Labor, 273; Hoopes, Soc., 206; (Kellems Ticket) 178; scattered, 3,249.

1948: Truman, D., 1,913,134; Dewey, R., 1,895,269; Wallace, Prog., 190,381; Watson, Proh., 16,926; Thomas, Soc., 3,459; Thurmond, States' Rights, 1,228; Teichert, Soc. Labor, 195; Dobbs, Soc. Workers, 133.

Colorado

2004: Bush, R., 1,101,255; Kerry, D., 1,001,732; Nader, Ref., 12,718; Badnarik, Libertarian, 7,664; Peroutka, Amer. Const., 2,562; Cobb, Green, 1,591; Andress, Ind., 804; Amondson, Concerns of People, 378; Van Auken, Soc. Equal., 329; Harris, Soc. Wkrs., 241; Brown, Soc., 216; Dodge, Prohib., 140.

2000: Bush, R., 883,748; Gore, Dem 738,227; Nader, Green, 91,434; Browne, Libertarian, 12,799; Buchanan, Reform, 10,465; Hagelin, Reform, 2,240; Phillips, Amer. Constitution, 1,319; McReynolds, Soc., 712; Harris, Soc. Workers, 216; Dodge, Proh., 208.

1996: Dole, R., 691,848; Clinton, D., 671,152; Perot, Ref., 99,629; Nader, Green, 25,070; Browne, Libertarian, 12,392; Phillips, Amer. Constitution, 2,813; Collins, Ind., 2,809; Hagelin, Natural Law, 2,547; Hollis, Soc., 669; Moorehead, Workers World, 599; Templin, Amer., 557; Dodge, Proh., 375; Harris, Soc. Workers, 244.

1992: Clinton, D., 629,681; Bush, R., 562,850; Perot, Ind., 366,010; Marrou, Libertarian, 8,669; Fulani, New Alliance, 1,608.

1988: Bush, R., 728,177; Dukakis, D., 621,453; Paul, Lib., 15,482; Dodge, Proh., 4,604.

1984: Reagan, R., 821,817; Mondale, D., 454,975; Bergland, Libertarian, 11,257.

1980: Reagan, R., 652,264; Carter, D., 367,973; Anderson, Ind., 130,633; Clark, Libertarian, 25,744; Commoner, Citizens, 5,614; Bubar, Statesman, 1,180; Pulley, Socialist, 520; Hall, Com., 487.

1976: Ford, R., 584,367; Carter, D., 460,353; McCarthy, Ind., 26,107; MacBride, Libertarian, 5,330; Bubar, Proh., 2,882.

1972: Nixon, R., 597,189; McGovern, D., 329,980; Schmitz, Amer., 17,269; Fisher, Soc. Labor, 4,361; Spock, Peoples, 2,403; Hospers, Libertarian, 1,111; Jenness, Soc. Workers, 555; Munn, Proh., 467; Hall, Com., 432.

1968: Nixon, R., 409,345; Humphrey, D., 335,174; Wallace, 3rd Party, 60,813; Blomen, Soc. Labor, 3,016; Gregory, New-party, 1,393; Munn, Proh., 275; Halstead, Soc. Workers, 235.

1964: Johnson, D., 476,024; Goldwater, R., 296,767; DeBerry, Soc. Workers, 2,537; Munn, Proh., 1,356; Hass, Soc. Labor, 302.

1960: Nixon, R., 402,242; Kennedy, D., 330,629; Hass, Soc. Labor, 2,803; Dobbs, Soc. Workers, 572.

1956: Eisenhower, R., 394,479; Stevenson, D., 263,997; Hass, Soc. Lab., 3,308; Andrews, Ind., 759; Hoopes, Soc., 531.

1952: Eisenhower, R., 379,782; Stevenson, D., 245,504; MacArthur, Constitution, 2,181; Hallinan, Prog., 1,919; Hoopes, Soc., 365; Hass, Soc. Labor, 352.

1948: Truman, D., 267,288; Dewey, R., 239,714; Wallace, Prog., 6,115; Thomas, Soc., 1,678; Dobbs, Soc. Workers, 228; Teichert, Soc. Labor, 214.

Connecticut

2004: Kerry, D., 857,488; Bush, R., 693,826; Nader, Petitioning Cand., 12,969; Cobb, Green, 9,564; Badnarik, Libertarian, 3,367; Peroutka, Concerned Citizens, 1,543.

2000: Gore, D., 816,015; Bush, R., 561,094; Nader, Green, 64,452; Phillips, Concerned Citizens, 9,695; Buchanan, Reform, 4,731; Browne, Libertarian, 3,484.

1996: Clinton, D., 735,740; Dole, R., 483,109; Perot, Ref., 139,523; Nader, Green, 24,321; Browne, Libertarian, 5,788; Phillips, Concerned Citizens, 2,425; Hagelin, Natural Law, 1,703.

1992: Clinton, D., 682,318; Bush, R., 578,313; Perot, Ind., 348,771; Marrou, Libertarian, 5,391; Fulani, New Alliance, 1,363.

1988: Bush, R., 750,241; Dukakis, D., 676,584; Paul, Lib., 14,071; Fulani, New Alliance, 2,491.

1984: Reagan, R., 890,877; Mondale, D., 569,597.

1980: Reagan, R., 677,210; Carter, D., 541,732; Anderson, Ind., 171,807; Clark, Libertarian, 8,570; Commoner, Citizens, 6,130; scattered, 836.

1976: Ford, R., 719,261; Carter, D., 647,895; Maddox, George Wallace Party, 7,101; LaRouche, U.S. Labor, 1,789.

1972: Nixon, R., 810,763; McGovern, D., 555,498; Schmitz, Amer., 17,239; scattered, 777.

1968: Humphrey, D., 621,561; Nixon, R., 556,721; Wallace, 3rd Party, 76,650; scattered, 1,300.

1964: Johnson, D., 826,269; Goldwater, R., 390,996; scattered, 1,313.

1960: Kennedy, D., 657,055; Nixon, R., 565,813.

1956: Eisenhower, R., 711,837; Stevenson, D., 405,079; scattered, 205.

1952: Eisenhower, R., 611,012; Stevenson, D., 481,649; Hoopes, Soc., 2,244; Hallinan, Peoples, 1,466; Hass, Soc. Labor, 535; write-in, 5.

1948: Dewey, R., 437,754; Truman, D., 423,297; Wallace, Prog., 13,713; Thomas, Soc., 6,964; Teichert, Soc. Labor, 1,184; Dobbs, Soc. Workers, 606.

Delaware

2004: Kerry, D., 200,152; Bush, R., 171,660; Nader, Ind., 2,153; Badnarik, Libertarian, 586; Peroutka, Constitution, 289; Cobb, Green, 250; Brown, Nat. Law, 100.

2000: Gore, D., 180,068; Bush, R., 137,288; Nader, Green, 8,307; Buchanan, Reform, 777; Browne, Libertarian, 774; Phillips, Constitution, 208; Hagelin, Natural Law, 107.

1996: Clinton, D., 140,355; Dole, R., 99,062; Perot, Ind. (Ref.), 28,719; Browne, Libertarian, 2,052; Phillips, Taxpayers, 348; Hagelin, Natural Law, 274.

1992: Clinton, D., 126,054; Bush, R., 102,313; Perot, Ind., 59,213; Fulani, New Alliance, 1,105.

1988: Bush, R., 139,639; Dukakis, D., 108,647; Paul, Lib., 1,162; Fulani, New Alliance, 443.

1984: Reagan, R., 152,190; Mondale, D., 101,656; Bergland, Libertarian, 268.

1980: Reagan, R., 111,252; Carter, D., 105,754; Anderson, Ind., 16,288; Clark, Libertarian, 1,974; Greaves, Amer., 400.

1976: Carter, D., 122,596; Ford, R., 109,831; McCarthy, non-partisan, 2,437; Anderson, Amer., 645; LaRouche, U.S. Labor, 136; Bubar, Proh., 103; Levin, Soc. Labor, 86.

1972: Nixon, R., 140,357; McGovern, D., 92,283; Schmitz, Amer., 2,638; Munn, Proh., 238.

1968: Nixon, R., 96,714; Humphrey, D., 89,194; Wallace, 3rd Party, 28,459.

1964: Johnson, D., 122,704; Goldwater, R., 78,078; Munn, Proh., 425; Hass, Soc. Labor, 113.

1960: Kennedy, D., 99,590; Nixon, R., 96,373; Faubus, States' Rights, 354; Decker, Proh., 284; Hass, Soc. Labor, 82.

1956: Eisenhower, R., 98,057; Stevenson, D., 79,421; Oltwick, Proh., 400; Hass, Soc. Labor, 110.

1952: Eisenhower, R., 90,059; Stevenson, D., 83,315; Hass, Soc. Lab., 242; Hamblen, Proh., 234; Hallinan, Prog., 155; Hoopes, Soc., 20.

1948: Dewey, R., 69,688; Truman, D., 67,813; Wallace, Prog., 1,050; Watson, Proh., 343; Thomas, Soc., 250; Teichert, Soc. Labor, 29.

District of Columbia

2004: Kerry, D., 202,970; Bush, R., 21,256; Nader, Ind., 1,485; Cobb, DC Statehd Green Pty., 737; Badnarik, Libertarian, 502; Harris, Soc. Wkrs., 130.

2000: Gore, D., 171,923; Bush, R., 18,073; Nader, Green, 10,576; Browne, Libertarian, 669; Harris, Soc. Workers, 114.

1996: Clinton, D., 158,220; Dole, R., 17,339; Nader, Green, 4,780; Perot, Ref., 3,611; Browne, Libertarian, 588; Hagelin, Natural Law, 283; Harris, Soc. Workers, 257.

1992: Clinton, D., 192,619; Bush, R., 20,698; Perot, Ind., 9,681; Fulani, New Alliance, 1,459; Daniels, Ind., 1,186.

1988: Dukakis, D., 159,407; Bush, R., 27,590; Fulani, New Alliance, 2,901; Paul, Lib., 554.

1984: Mondale, D., 180,408; Reagan, R., 29,009; Bergland, Libertarian, 279.

1980: Carter, D., 130,231; Reagan, R., 23,313; Anderson, Ind., 16,131; Commoner, Citizens, 1,826; Clark, Libertarian, 1,104; Hall, Com., 369; DeBerry, Soc. Workers, 173; Griswold, Workers World, 52; write-in, 690.

1976: Carter, D., 137,818; Ford, R., 27,873; Camejo, Soc. Workers, 545; MacBride, Libertarian, 274; Hall, Com., 219; LaRouche, U.S. Labor, 157.

1972: McGovern, D., 127,627; Nixon, R., 35,226; Reed, Soc. Workers, 316; Hall, Com., 252.

1968: Humphrey, D., 139, 566; Nixon, R., 31,012.

1964: Johnson, D., 169,796; Goldwater, R., 28,801.

Florida

2004: Bush, R., 3,964,522; Kerry, D., 3,583,544; Nader, Ref., 32,971; Badnarik, Libertarian, 11,996; Peroutka, Constitution, 6,626; Cobb, Green, 3,917; Brown, Soc., 3,502; Harris, Soc. Wkrs., 2,732.

2000: Bush, R., 2,912,790; Gore, D., 2,912,253; Nader, Green, 97,488; Buchanan, Reform, 17,484; Browne, Libertarian, 16,415; Hagelin, Nat. Law, 2,281; Moorehead, Wkrs. World, 1,804; Phillips, Constit., 1,371; McReynolds, Soc., 622; Harris, Soc. Wkrs., 562.

1996: Clinton, D., 2,545,968; Dole, R., 2,243,324; Perot, Ref., 483,776; Browne, Libertarian, 23,312.

1992: Bush, R., 2,171,781; Clinton, D., 2,071,651; Perot, Ind., 1,052,481; Marrou, Libertarian, 15,068.

1988: Bush, R., 2,616,597; Dukakis, D., 1,655,851; Paul, Lib., 19,796, Fulani, New Alliance, 6,655.

1984: Reagan, R., 2,728,775; Mondale, D., 1,448,344.

1980: Reagan, R., 2,046,951; Carter, D., 1,419,475; Anderson, Ind., 189,692; Clark, Libertarian, 30,524; write-in, 285.

1976: Carter, D., 1,636,000; Ford, R., 1,469,531; McCarthy, Ind., 23,643; Anderson, Amer., 21,325.

1972: Nixon, R., 1,857,759; McGovern, D., 718,117; scattered, 7,407.

1968: Nixon, R., 886,804; Humphrey, D., 676,794; Wallace, 3rd Party, 624,207.

1964: Johnson, D., 948,540; Goldwater, R., 905,941.

1960: Nixon, R., 795,476; Kennedy, D., 748,700.

1956: Eisenhower, R., 643,849; Stevenson, D., 480,371.

1952: Eisenhower, R., 544,036; Stevenson, D., 444,950; scattered, 351.

1948: Truman, D., 281,988; Dewey, R., 194,280; Thurmond, States' Rights, 89,755; Wallace, Prog., 11,620.

Georgia

2004: Bush, R., 1,914,254; Kerry, D., 1,366,149; Badnarik, Libertarian, 18,387.

2000: Bush, R., 1,419,720; Gore, D., 1,116,230; Browne, Libertarian, 36,332; Buchanan, Independent, 10,926.

1996: Dole, R., 1,080,843; Clinton, D., 1,053,849; Perot, Ref., 146,337; Browne, Libertarian, 17,870.

1992: Clinton, D., 1,008,966; Bush, R., 995,252; Perot, Ind., 309,657; Marrou, Libertarian, 7,110.

1988: Bush, R., 1,081,331; Dukakis, D., 714,792; Paul, Lib., 8,435; Fulani, New Alliance, 5,099.

1984: Reagan, R., 1,068,722; Mondale, D., 706,628.

1980: Carter, D., 890,955; Reagan, R., 654,168; Anderson, Ind., 36,055; Clark, Libertarian, 15,627.

1976: Carter, D., 979,409; Ford, R., 483,743; write-in, 4,306.

1972: Nixon, R., 881,496; McGovern, D., 289,529; Schmitz, Amer., 812; scattered, 2,993.

1968: Wallace, 3rd Party, 535,550; Nixon, R., 380,111; Humphrey, D., 334,440; write-in, 162.

1964: Goldwater, R., 616,600; Johnson, D., 522,557.

1960: Kennedy, D., 458,638; Nixon, R., 274,472; write-in, 239.

1956: Stevenson, D., 444,388; Eisenhower, R., 222,778; Andrews, Ind., write-in, 1,754.

1952: Stevenson, D., 456,823; Eisenhower, R., 198,979; Liberty Party, 1.

1948: Truman, D., 254,646; Thurmond, States' Rights, 85,055; Dewey, R., 76,691; Wallace, Prog., 1,636; Watson, Proh., 732.

Hawaii

2004: Kerry, D., 231,708; Bush, R., 194,191; Cobb, Green, 1,737; Badnarik, Libertarian, 1,377.

2000: Gore, D., 205,286; Bush, R., 137,845; Nader, Green, 21,623; Browne, Libertarian, 1,477; Buchanan, Reform, 1,071; Phillips, Constitution, 343; Hagelin, Natural Law, 306.

1996: Clinton, D., 205,012; Dole, R., 113,943; Perot, Ref., 27,358; Nader, Green, 10,386; Browne, Libertarian, 2,493; Hagelin, Natural Law, 570; Phillips, Taxpayers, 358.

1992: Clinton, D., 179,310; Bush, R., 136,822; Perot, Ind., 53,003; Gritz, Populist/America First, 1,452; Marrou, Libertarian, 1,119.

1988: Dukakis, D., 192,364; Bush, R., 158,625; Paul, Lib., 1,999; Fulani, New Alliance, 1,003.

1984: Reagan, R., 184,934; Mondale, D., 147,098; Bergland, Libertarian, 2,167.

1980: Carter, D., 135,879; Reagan, R., 130,112; Anderson, Ind., 32,021; Clark, Libertarian, 3,269; Commoner, Citizens, 1,548; Hall, Com., 458.

1976: Carter, D., 147,375; Ford, R., 140,003; MacBride, Libertarian, 3,923.

1972: Nixon, R., 168,865; McGovern, D., 101,409.

1968: Humphrey, D., 141,324; Nixon, R., 91,425; Wallace, 3rd Party, 3,469.

1964: Johnson, D., 163,249; Goldwater, R., 44,022.

1960: Kennedy, D., 92,410; Nixon, R., 92,295.

Idaho

2004: Bush, R., 409,235; Kerry, D., 181,098; Badnarik, Libertarian, 3,844; Peroutka, Constitution, 3,084.

2000: Bush, R., 336,937; Gore, D., 138,637; Buchanan, Reform, 7,615; Browne, Libertarian, 3,488; Phillips, Constitution, 1,469; Hagelin, Natural Law, 1,177.

1996: Dole, R., 256,595; Clinton, D., 165,443; Perot, Ref., 62,518; Browne, Libertarian, 3,325; Phillips, Taxpayers, 2,230; Hagelin, Natural Law, 1,600.

1992: Bush, R., 202,645; Clinton, D., 137,013; Perot, Ind., 130,395; Gritz, Populist/America First, 10,281; Marrou, Libertarian, 1,167.

1988: Bush, R., 253,881; Dukakis, D., 147,272; Paul, Lib., 5,313; Fulani, Ind., 2,502.

1984: Reagan, R., 297,523; Mondale, D., 108,510; Bergland, Libertarian, 2,823.

1980: Reagan, R., 290,699; Carter, D., 110,192; Anderson, Ind., 27,058; Clark, Libertarian, 8,425; Rarick, Amer., 1,057.

1976: Ford, R., 204,151; Carter, D., 126,549; Maddox, Amer., 5,935; MacBride, Libertarian, 3,558; LaRouche, U.S. Labor, 739.

1972: Nixon, R., 199,384; McGovern, D., 80,826; Schmitz, Amer., 28,869; Spock, Peoples, 903.

1968: Nixon, R., 165,369; Humphrey, D., 89,273; Wallace, 3rd Party, 36,541.

1964: Johnson, D., 148,920; Goldwater, Rep., 143,557.

1960: Nixon, R., 161,597; Kennedy, D., 138,853.

1956: Eisenhower, R., 166,979; Stevenson, D., 105,868; Andrews, Ind., 126; write-in, 16.

1952: Eisenhower, R., 180,707; Stevenson, D., 95,081; Hallinan, Prog., 443; write-in, 23.

1948: Truman, D., 107,370; Dewey, R., 101,514; Wallace, Prog., 4,972; Watson, Proh., 628; Thomas, Soc., 332.

Illinois

2004: Kerry, D., 2,891,550; Bush, R., 2,345,946; Badnarik, Libertarian, 32,442.

2000: Gore, D., 2,589,026; Bush, R., 2,019,421; Nader, Green, 103,759; Buchanan, Ind., 16,106; Browne, Libertarian, 11,623; Hagelin, Reform, 2,127.

1996: Clinton, D., 2,341,744; Dole, R., 1,587,021; Perot, Ref., 346,408; Browne, Libertarian, 22,548; Phillips, Taxpayers, 7,606; Hagelin, Natural Law, 4,606.

1992: Clinton, D., 2,453,350; Bush, R., 1,734,096; Perot, Ind., 840,515; Marrou, Libertarian, 9,218; Fulani, New Alliance, 5,267; Gritz, Populist/America First, 3,577; Hagelin, Natural Law, 2,751; Warren, Soc. Workers, 1,361.

1988: Bush, R., 2,310,939; Dukakis, D., 2,215,940; Paul, Lib., 14,944; Fulani, Solid., 10,276.

1984: Reagan, R., 2,707,103; Mondale, D., 2,086,499; Bergland, Libertarian, 10,086.

1980: Reagan, R., 2,358,049; Carter, D., 1,981,413; Anderson, Ind., 346,754; Clark, Libertarian, 38,939; Commoner, Citizens, 10,692; Hall, Com., 9,711; Griswold, Workers World, 2,257; DeBerry, Soc. Workers, 1,302; write-in, 604.

1976: Ford, R., 2,364,269; Carter, D., 2,271,295; McCarthy, Ind., 55,939; Hall, Com., 9,250; MacBride, Libertarian, 8,057; Camejo, Soc. Workers, 3,615; Levin, Soc. Labor, 2,422; LaRouche, U.S. Labor, 2,018; write-in, 1,968.

1972: Nixon, Rep. 2,788,179; McGovern, D., 1,913,472; Fisher, Soc. Labor, 12,344; Hall, Com., 4,541; Schmitz, Amer., 2,471; others, 2,229.

1968: Nixon, R., 2,174,774; Humphrey, D., 2,039,814; Wallace, 3rd Party, 390,958; Blomen, Soc. Labor, 13,878; write-in, 325.

1964: Johnson, D., 2,796,833; Goldwater, R., 1,905,946; write-in, 62.

1960: Kennedy, D., 2,377,846; Nixon, R., 2,368,988; Hass, Soc. Labor, 10,560; write-in, 15.

1956: Eisenhower, R., 2,623,327; Stevenson, D., 1,775,682; Hass, Soc. Labor, 8,342; write-in, 56.

1952: Eisenhower, R., 2,457,327; Stevenson, D., 2,013,920; Hass, Soc. Labor, 9,363; write-in, 448.

1948: Truman, D., 1,994,715; Dewey, R., 1,961,103; Watson, Proh., 11,959; Thomas, Soc., 11,522; Teichert, Soc. Labor, 3,118.

Indiana

2004: Bush, R., 1,479,438; Kerry, D., 969,011; Badnarik, Libertarian, 18,058.

2000: Bush, R., 1,245,836; Gore, D., 901,980; Buchanan, Ind., 16,959; Browne, Libertarian, 15,530.

1996: Dole, R., 1,006,693; Clinton, D., 887,424; Perot, Ref., 224,299; Browne, Libertarian, 15,632.

1992: Bush, R., 989,375; Clinton, D., 848,420; Perot, Ind., 455,934; Marrou, Libertarian, 7,936; Fulani, New Alliance, 2,583.

1988: Bush, R., 1,297,763; Dukakis, D., 860,643; Fulani, New Alliance, 10,215.

1984: Reagan, R., 1,377,230; Mondale, D., 841,481; Bergland, Libertarian, 6,741.

1980: Reagan, R., 1,255,656; Carter, D., 844,197; Anderson, Ind., 111,639; Clark, Libertarian, 19,627; Commoner, Citizens, 4,852; Greaves, Amer., 4,750; Hall, Com., 702; DeBerry, Soc., 610.

1976: Ford, R., 1,185,958; Carter, D., 1,014,714; Anderson, Amer., 14,048; Camejo, Soc. Workers, 5,695; LaRouche, U.S. Labor, 1,947.

1972: Nixon, R., 1,405,154; McGovern, D., 708,568; Reed, Soc. Workers, 5,575; Spock, Peace and Freedom, 4,544; Fisher, Soc. Labor, 1,688.

1968: Nixon, R., 1,067,885; Humphrey, D., 806,659; Wallace, 3rd Party, 243,108; Munn, Proh., 4,616; Halstead, Soc. Workers, 1,293; Gregory, write-in, 36.

1964: Johnson, D., 1,170,848; Goldwater, R., 911,118; Munn, Proh., 8,266; Hass, Soc. Labor, 1,374.

1960: Nixon, R., 1,175,120; Kennedy, D., 952,358; Decker, Proh., 6,746; Hass, Soc. Labor, 1,136.

1956: Eisenhower, R., 1,182,811; Stevenson, D., 783,908; Holtwick, Proh., 6,554; Hass, Soc. Labor, 1,334.

1952: Eisenhower, R., 1,136,259; Stevenson, D., 801,530; Hamblen, Proh., 15,335; Hallinan, Prog., 1,222; Hass, Soc. Labor, 979.

1948: Dewey, R., 821,079; Truman, D., 807,833; Watson, Proh., 14,711; Wallace, Prog., 9,649; Thomas, Soc., 2,179; Teichert, Soc. Labor, 763.

Iowa

2004: Bush, R., 751,957; Kerry, D., 741,898; Nader, Petitioning Cand., 5,973; Badnarik, Libertarian, 2,992; Peroutka, Constitution, 1,304; Cobb, Green, 1,141; Harris, Soc. Wkrs., 373; Van Auken, Petitioning Cand., 176.

2000: Gore, D., 638,517; Bush, R., 634,373; Nader, Green, 29,374; Buchanan, Reform, 5,731; Browne, Libertarian, 3,209; Hagelin, Ind., 2,281; Phillips, Constitution, 613; Harris, Soc. Workers, 190; McReynolds, Soc., 107.

1996: Clinton, D., 620,258; Dole, R., 492,644; Perot, Ref., 105,159; Nader, Green, 6,550; Hagelin, Natural Law, 3,349; Browne, Libertarian, 2,315; Phillips, Taxpayers, 2,229; Harris, Soc. Workers, 331.

1992: Clinton, D., 586,353; Bush, R., 504,891; Perot, Ind., 253,468; Hagelin, Natural Law, 3,079; Gritz, Populist/America First, 1,177; Marrou, Libertarian, 1,076.

1988: Dukakis, D., 670,557; Bush, R., 545,355; LaRouche, Ind., 3,526; Paul, Lib., 2,494.

1984: Reagan, R., 703,088; Mondale, D., 605,620; Bergland, Libertarian, 1,844.

1980: Reagan, R., 676,026; Carter, D., 508,672; Anderson, Ind., 115,633; Clark, Libertarian, 13,123; Commoner, Citizens, 2,273; McReynolds, Socialist, 534; Hall, Com., 298; DeBerry, Soc. Wrkrs., 244; Greaves, Amer., 189; Bubar, Statesman, 150; scattered, 519.

1976: Ford, R., 632,863; Carter, D., 619,931; McCarthy, Ind., 20,051; Anderson, Amer., 3,040; MacBride, Libertarian, 1,452.

1972: Nixon, R., 706,207; McGovern, D., 496,206; Schmitz, Amer., 22,056; Jenness, Soc. Workers, 488; Hall, Com., 272; Green, Universal, 199; Fisher, Soc. Labor, 195; scattered, 321.

1968: Nixon, R., 619,106; Humphrey, D., 476,699; Wallace, 3rd Party, 66,422; Halstead, Soc. Workers, 3,377; Cleaver, Peace and Freedom, 1,332; Munn, Proh., 362; Blomen, Soc. Labor, 241.

1964: Johnson, D., 733,030; Goldwater, R., 449,148; Munn, Proh., 1,902; Hass, Soc. Labor, 182; DeBerry, Soc. Workers, 159.

1960: Nixon, R., 722,381; Kennedy, D., 550,565; Hass, Soc. Labor, 230; write-in, 634.

1956: Eisenhower, R., 729,187; Stevenson, D., 501,858; Andrews (A.C.P. of Iowa), 3,202; Hoopes, Soc., 192; Hass, Soc. Labor, 125.

1952: Eisenhower, R., 808,906; Stevenson, D., 451,513; Hallinan, Prog., 5,085; Hamblen, Proh., 2,882; Hoopes, Soc., 219; Hass, Soc. Labor, 139; scattered, 29.

1948: Truman, D., 522,380; Dewey, R., 494,018; Wallace, Prog., 12,125; Teichert, Soc. Labor, 4,274; Watson, Proh., 3,382; Thomas, Soc., 1,829; Dobbs, Soc. Workers, 26.

Kansas

2004: Bush, R., 736,456; Kerry, D., 434,993; Nader, Ref., 9,348; Badnarik, Libertarian, 4,013; Peroutka, Ind., 2,899.

2000: Bush, R., 622,332; Gore, D., 399,276; Nader, Ind., 36,086; Buchanan, Reform, 7,370; Browne, Libertarian, 4,525; Hagelin, Ind., 1,373; Phillips, Constitution, 1,254.

1996: Dole, R., 583,245; Clinton, D., 387,659; Perot, Ref., 92,639; Browne, Libertarian, 4,557; Phillips, Ind., 3,519; Hagelin, Ind., 1,655.

1992: Bush, R., 449,951; Clinton, D., 390,434; Perot, Ind., 312,358; Marrou, Libertarian, 4,314.

1988: Bush, R., 554,049; Dukakis, D., 422,636; Paul, Ind., 12,553; Fulani, Ind., 3,806.

1984: Reagan, R., 674,646; Mondale, D., 332,471; Bergland, Libertarian, 3,585.

1980: Reagan, R., 566,812; Carter, D., 326,150; Anderson, Ind., 68,231; Clark, Libertarian, 14,470; Shelton, Amer., 1,555; Hall, Com., 967; Bubar, Statesman, 821; Rarick, Conservative, 789.

1976: Ford, R., 502,752; Carter, D., 430,421; McCarthy, Ind., 13,185; Anderson, Amer., 4,724; MacBride, Libertarian, 3,242; Maddox, Conservative, 2,118; Bubar, Proh., 1,403.

1972: Nixon, R., 619,812; McGovern, D., 270,287; Schmitz, Conservative, 21,808; Munn, Proh., 4,188.

1968: Nixon, R., 478,674; Humphrey, D., 302,996; Wallace, 3rd Party, 88,921; Munn, Proh., 2,192.

1964: Johnson, D., 464,028; Goldwater, R., 386,579; Munn, Proh., 5,393; Hass, Soc. Labor, 1,901.

1960: Nixon, R., 561,474; Kennedy, D., 363,213; Decker, Proh., 4,138.

1956: Eisenhower, R., 566,878; Stevenson, D., 296,317; Holtwick, Proh., 3,048.

1952: Eisenhower, R., 616,302; Stevenson, D., 273,296; Hamblen, Proh., 6,038; Hoopes, Soc., 530.

1948: Dewey, R., 423,039; Truman, D., 351,902; Watson, Proh., 6,468; Wallace, Prog., 4,603; Thomas, Soc., 2,807.

Kentucky

2004: Bush, R., 1,069,439; Kerry, D., 712,733; Nader, Ind., 8,856; Badnarik, Libertarian, 2,619; Peroutka, Constitution, 2,213.

2000: Bush, R., 872,520; Gore, D., 638,923; Nader, Green, 23,118; Buchanan, Reform, 4,152; Browne, Libertarian, 2,885; Hagelin, Natural Law, 1,513; Phillips, Constitution, 915.

1996: Clinton, D., 636,614; Dole, R., 623,283; Perot, Ref., 120,396; Browne, Libertarian, 4,009; Phillips, Taxpayers, 2,204; Hagelin, Natural Law, 1,493.

1992: Clinton, D., 665,104; Bush, R., 617,178; Perot, Ind., 203,944; Marrou, Libertarian, 4,513.

1988: Bush, R., 734,281; Dukakis, D., 580,368; Duke, Pop., 4,494; Paul, Lib., 2,118.

1984: Reagan, R., 815,345; Mondale, D., 536,756.

1980: Reagan, R., 635,274; Carter, D., 616,417; Anderson, Ind., 31,127; Clark, Libertarian, 5,531; McCormack, Respect For Life, 4,233; Commoner, Citizens, 1,304; Pulley, Socialist, 393; Hall, Com., 348.

1976: Carter, D., 615,717; Ford, R., 531,852; Anderson, Amer., 8,308; McCarthy, Ind., 6,837; Maddox, Amer. Ind., 2,328; MacBride, Libertarian, 814.

1972: Nixon, R., 676,446; McGovern, D., 371,159; Schmitz, Amer., 17,627; Spock, Peoples, 1,118; Jenness, Soc. Workers, 685; Hall, Com., 464.

1968: Nixon, R., 462,411; Humphrey, D., 397,547; Wallace, 3rd Party, 193,098; Halstead, Soc. Workers, 2,843.

1964: Johnson, D., 669,659; Goldwater, R., 372,977; Kasper, Natl. States Rights, 3,469.

1960: Nixon, R., 602,607; Kennedy, D., 521,855.

1956: Eisenhower, R., 572,192; Stevenson, D., 476,453; Byrd, States' Rights, 2,657; Holtwick, Proh., 2,145; Hass, Soc. Labor, 358.

1952: Stevenson, D., 495,729; Eisenhower, R., 495,029; Hamblen, Proh., 1,161; Hass, Soc. Labor, 893; Hallinan, Proh., 336.

1948: Truman, D., 466,756; Dewey, R., 341,210; Thurmond, States' Rights, 10,411; Wallace, Prog., 1,567; Thomas, Soc., 1,284; Watson, Proh., 1,245; Teichert, Soc. Labor, 185.

Louisiana

2004: Bush, R., 1,102,169; Kerry, D., 820,299; Nader, Better Life, 7,032; Peroutka, Constitution, 5,203; Badnarik, Libertarian, 2,781; Brown, Protect Wking Fam., 1,795; Amondson, Prohib., 1,566; Cobb, Green, 1,276; Harris, Soc. Wkrs., 985.

2000: Bush, R., 927,871; Gore, D., 792,344; Nader, Green, 20,473; Buchanan, Reform, 14,356; Phillips, Constitution, 5,483; Browne, Libertarian, 2,951; Harris, Soc. Workers, 1,103; Hagelin, Natural Law, 1,075.

1996: Clinton, D., 927,837; Dole, R., 712,586; Perot, Ref., 123,293; Browne, Libertarian, 7,499; Nader, Liberty, Ecology, Community, 4,719; Phillips, Taxpayers, 3,366; Hagelin, Natural Law, 2,981; Moorehead, Workers World, 1,678.

1992: Clinton, D., 815,971; Bush, R., 733,386; Perot, Ind., 211,478; Gritz, Populist/America First, 18,545; Marrou, Libertarian, 3,155; Daniels, Ind., 1,663; Phillips, U.S. Taxpayers, 1,552; Fulani, New Alliance, 1,434; LaRouche, Ind., 1,136.

1988: Bush, R., 883,702; Dukakis, D., 717,460; Duke, Pop., 18,612; Paul, Lib., 4,115.

1984: Reagan, R., 1,037,299; Mondale, D., 651,586; Bergland, Libertarian, 1,876.

1980: Reagan, R., 792,853; Carter, D., 708,453; Anderson, Ind., 26,345; Rarick, Amer. Ind., 10,333; Clark, Libertarian, 8,240; Commoner, Citizens, 1,584; DeBerry, Soc. Work., 783.

1976: Carter, D., 661,365; Ford, R., 587,446; Maddox, Amer., 10,058; Hall, Com., 7,417; McCarthy, Ind., 6,588; MacBride, Libertarian, 3,325.

1972: Nixon, R., 686,852; McGovern, D., 298,142; Schmitz, Amer., 52,099; Jenness, Soc. Workers, 14,398.

1968: Wallace, 3rd Party, 530,300; Humphrey, D., 309,615; Nixon, R., 257,535.

1964: Goldwater, R., 509,225; Johnson, D., 387,068.

1960: Kennedy, D., 407,339; Nixon, R., 230,890; States' Rights (unpledged), 169,572.

1956: Eisenhower, R., 329,047; Stevenson, D., 243,977; Andrews, States' Rights, 44,520.

1952: Stevenson, D., 345,027; Eisenhower, R., 306,925.

1948: Thurmond, States' Rights, 204,290; Truman, D., 136,344; Dewey, R., 72,657; Wallace, Prog., 3,035.

Maine

2004: Kerry, D., 396,842; Bush, R., 330,201; Nader, Better Life, 8,069; Cobb, Green, 2,936; Badnarik, Libertarian, 1,965; Peroutka, Constitution, 735.

2000: Gore, D., 319,951; Bush, R., 286,616; Nader, Green, 37,127; Buchanan, Reform, 4,443; Browne, Libertarian, 3,074; Phillips, Constitution, 579.

1996: Clinton, D., 312,788; Dole, R., 186,378; Perot, Ref., 85,970; Nader, Green, 15,279; Browne, Libertarian, 2,996; Phillips, Taxpayers, 1,517; Hagelin, Natural Law, 825.

1992: Clinton, D., 263,420; Perot, Ind., 206,820; Bush, R., 206,504; Marrou, Libertarian, 1,681.

1988: Bush, R., 307,131; Dukakis, D., 243,569; Paul, Lib., 2,700; Fulani, New Alliance, 1,405.

1984: Reagan, R., 336,500; Mondale, D., 214,515.

1980: Reagan, R., 238,522; Carter, D., 220,974; Anderson, Ind., 53,327; Clark, Libertarian, 5,119; Commoner, Citizens, 4,394; Hall, Com., 591; write-in, 84.

1976: Ford, R., 236,320; Carter, D., 232,279; McCarthy, Ind., 10,874; Bubar, Proh., 3,495.

1972: Nixon, R., 256,458; McGovern, D., 160,584; scattered, 229.

1968: Humphrey, D., 217,312; Nixon, R., 169,254; Wallace, 3rd Party, 6,370.

1964: Johnson, D., 262,264; Goldwater, R., 118,701.

1960: Nixon, R., 240,608; Kennedy, D., 181,159.

1956: Eisenhower, R., 249,238; Stevenson, D., 102,468.

1952: Eisenhower, R., 232,353; Stevenson, D., 118,806; Hallinan, Prog., 332; Hass, Soc. Labor, 156; Hoopes, Soc., 138; scattered, 1.

1948: Dewey, R., 150,234; Truman, D., 111,916; Wallace, Prog., 1,884; Thomas, Soc., 547; Teichert, Soc. Labor, 206.

Maryland

2004: Kerry, D., 1,334,493; Bush, R., 1,024,703; Nader, Populist, 11,854; Badnarik, Libertarian, 6,094; Cobb, Green, 3,632; Peroutka, Constitution, 3,421.

2000: Gore, D., 1,144,008; Bush, R., 813,827; Nader, Green, 53,768; Browne, Libertarian, 5,310; Buchanan, Reform., 4,248; Phillips, Constitution, 918.

1996: Clinton, D., 966,207; Dole, R., 681,530; Perot, Ref., 115,812; Browne, Libertarian, 8,765; Phillips, Taxpayers, 3,402; Hagelin, Natural Law, 2,517.

1992: Clinton, D., 988,571; Bush, R., 707,094; Perot, Ind., 281,414; Marrou, Libertarian, 4,715; Fulani, New Alliance, 2,786.

1988: Bush, R., 876,167; Dukakis, D., 826,304; Paul, Lib., 6,748; Fulani, New Alliance, 5,115.

1984: Reagan, R., 879,918; Mondale, D., 787,935; Bergland, Libertarian, 5,721.

1980: Carter, D., 726,161; Reagan, R., 680,606; Anderson, Ind., 119,537; Clark, Libertarian, 14,192.

1976: Carter, D., 759,612; Ford, R., 672,661.

1972: Nixon, R., 829,305; McGovern, D., 505,781; Schmitz, Amer., 18,726.

1968: Humphrey, D., 538,310; Nixon, R., 517,995; Wallace, 3rd Party, 178,734.

1964: Johnson, D., 730,912; Goldwater, R., 385,495; write-in, 50.

1960: Kennedy, D., 565,800; Nixon, R., 489,538.

1956: Eisenhower, R., 559,738; Stevenson, D., 372,613.

1952: Eisenhower, R., 499,424; Stevenson, D., 395,337; Hallinan, Prog., 7,313.

1948: Dewey, R., 294,814; Truman, D., 286,521; Wallace, Prog., 9,983; Thomas, Soc., 2,941; Thurmond, States' Rights, 2,476; Wright, write-in, 2,294.

Massachusetts

2004: Kerry, D., 1,803,800; Bush, R., 1,071,109; Badnarik, Libertarian, 15,022; Cobb, Green, 10,623.

2000: Gore, D., 1,616,487; Bush, R., 878,502; Nader, Green, 173,564; Browne, Libertarian, 16,366; Buchanan, Reform, 11,149; Hagelin, Natural Law, 2,884.

1996: Clinton, D., 1,571,509; Dole, R., 718,058; Perot, Ref., 227,206; Browne, Libertarian, 20,424; Hagelin, Natural Law, 5,183; Moorehead, Workers World, 3,276.

1992: Clinton, D., 1,318,639; Bush, R., 805,039; Perot, Ind., 630,731; Marrou, Libertarian, 9,021; Fulani, New Alliance, 3,172; Phillips, U.S. Taxpayers, 2,218; Hagelin, Natural Law, 1,812; LaRouche, Ind., 1,027.

1988: Dukakis, D., 1,401,415; Bush, R., 1,194,635; Paul, Lib., 24,251; Fulani, New Alliance, 9,561.

1984: Reagan, R., 1,310,936; Mondale, D., 1,239,606.

1980: Reagan, R., 1,057,631; Carter, D., 1,053,802; Anderson, Ind., 382,539; Clark, Libertarian, 22,038; DeBerry, Soc. Workers, 3,735; Commoner, Citizens, 2,056; McReynolds, Soc., 62; Bubar, Statesman, 34; Griswold, Workers World, 19; scattered, 2,382.

1976: Carter, D., 1,429,475; Ford, R., 1,030,276; McCarthy, Ind., 65,637; Camejo, Soc. Workers, 8,138; Anderson, Amer., 7,555; La Rouche, U.S. Labor, 4,922; MacBride, Libertarian, 135.

1972: McGovern, D., 1,332,540; Nixon, R., 1,112,078; Jenness, Soc. Workers, 10,600; Schmitz, Amer., 2,877; Fisher, Soc. Labor, 129; Spock, Peoples, 101; Hall, Com., 46; Hospers, Libertarian, 43; scattered, 342.

1968: Humphrey, D., 1,469,218; Nixon, R., 766,844; Wallace, 3rd Party, 87,088; Blomen, Soc. Labor, 6,180; Munn, Proh., 2,369; scattered, 53; blanks, 25,394.

1964: Johnson, D., 1,786,422; Goldwater, R., 549,727; Hass, Soc. Labor, 4,755; Munn, Proh., 3,735; scattered, 159; blank, 48,104.

1960: Kennedy, D., 1,487,174; Nixon, R., 976,750; Hass, Soc. Labor, 3,892; Decker, Proh., 1,633; others, 31; blank and void, 26,024.

1956: Eisenhower, R., 1,393,197; Stevenson, D., 948,190; Hass, Soc. Labor, 5,573; Holtwick, Proh., 1,205; others, 341.

1952: Eisenhower, R., 1,292,325; Stevenson, D., 1,083,525; Hallinan, Prog., 4,636; Hass, Soc. Labor, 1,957; Hamblen, Proh., 886; scattered, 69; blanks, 41,150.

1948: Truman, D., 1,151,788; Dewey, R., 909,370; Wallace, Prog., 38,157; Teichert, Soc. Labor, 5,535; Watson, Proh., 1,663.

Michigan

2004: Kerry, D., 2,479,183; Bush, R., 2,313,746; Nader, Ind., 24,035; Badnarik, Libertarian, 10,552; Cobb, Green, 5,325; Peroutka, U.S. Taxpayers, 4,980; Brown, Nat. Law, 1,431.

2000: Gore, D., 2,170,418; Bush, R., 1,953,139; Nader, Green, 84,165; Browne, Libertarian, 16,711; Phillips, U.S. Taxpayers, 3,791; Hagelin, Natural Law, 2,426.

1996: Clinton, D., 1,989,653; Dole, R., 1,481,212; Perot, Ref., 336,670; Browne, Libertarian, 27,670; Hagelin, Natural Law, 4,254; Moorehead, Workers World, 3,153; White, Soc. Equality, 1,554.

1992: Clinton, D., 1,871,182; Bush, R., 1,554,940; Perot, Ind., 824,813; Marrou, Libertarian, 10,175; Phillips, U.S. Taxpayers, 8,263; Hagelin, Natural Law, 2,954.

1988: Bush, R., 1,965,486; Dukakis, D., 1,675,783; Paul, Lib., 18,336; Fulani, Ind., 2,513.

1984: Reagan, R., 2,251,571; Mondale, D., 1,529,638; Bergland, Libertarian, 10,055.

1980: Reagan, R., 1,915,225; Carter, D., 1,661,532; Anderson, Ind., 275,223; Clark, Libertarian, 41,597; Commoner, Citizens, 11,930; Hall, Com., 3,262; Griswold, Workers World, 30; Greaves, Amer., 21; Bubar, Statesman, 9.

1976: Ford, R., 1,893,742; Carter, D., 1,696,714; McCarthy, Ind., 47,905; MacBride, Libertarian, 5,406; Wright, People's, 3,504; Camejo, Soc. Workers, 1,804; LaRouche, U.S. Labor, 1,366; Levin, Soc. Labor, 1,148; scattered, 2,160.

1972: Nixon, R., 1,961,721; McGovern, D., 1,459,435; Schmitz, Amer., 63,321; Fisher, Soc. Labor, 2,437; Jenness, Soc. Workers, 1,603; Hall, Com., 1,210.

1968: Humphrey, D., 1,593,082; Nixon, R., 1,370,665; Wallace, 3rd Party, 331,968; Halstead, Soc. Workers, 4,099; Blomen, Soc. Labor, 1,762; Cleaver, New Politics, 4,585; Munn, Proh., 60; scattered, 29.

1964: Johnson, D., 2,136,615; Goldwater, R., 1,060,152; DeBerry, Soc. Workers, 3,817; Hass, Soc. Labor, 1,704; Proh. (no candidate listed), 699; scattered, 145.

1960: Kennedy, D., 1,687,269; Nixon, R., 1,620,428; Dobbs, Soc. Workers, 4,347; Decker, Proh., 2,029; Daly, Tax Cut, 1,767; Hass, Soc. Labor, 1,718; Ind. Amer., 539.

1956: Eisenhower, R., 1,713,647; Stevenson, D., 1,359,898; Holtwick, Proh., 6,923.

1952: Eisenhower, R., 1,551,529; Stevenson, D., 1,230,657; Hamblen, Proh., 10,331; Hallinan, Prog., 3,922; Hass, Soc. Labor, 1,495; Dobbs, Soc. Workers, 655; scattered, 3.

1948: Dewey, R., 1,038,595; Truman, D., 1,003,448; Wallace, Prog., 46,515; Watson, Proh., 13,052; Thomas, Soc., 6,063; Teichert, Soc. Labor, 1,263; Dobbs, Soc. Workers, 672.

Minnesota

2004: Kerry, D., 1,445,014; Bush, R., 1,346,695; Nader, Better Life, 18,683; Badnarik, Libertarian, 4,639; Cobb, Green, 4,408; Peroutka, Constitution, 3,074; Harens, other, 2,387; Van Auken, Soc. Equal., 539; Calero, Soc. Wkrs., 416.

2000: Gore, D., 1,168,266; Bush, R., 1,109,659; Nader, Green, 126,696; Buchanan, Reform Minnesota, 22,166; Browne, Libertarian, 5,282; Phillips, Constitution, 3,272; Hagelin, Reform, 2,294; Harris, Soc. Workers, 1,022.

1996: Clinton, D., 1,120,438; Dole, R., 766,476; Perot, Ref., 257,704; Nader, Green, 24,908; Browne, Libertarian, 8,271; Peron, Grass Roots, 4,898; Phillips, Taxpayers, 3,416; Hagelin, Natural Law, 1,808; Birrenbach, Ind. Grass Roots, 787; Harris, Soc. Workers, 684; White, Soc. Equality, 347.

1992: Clinton, D., 1,020,997; Bush, R., 747,841; Perot, Ind., 562,506; Marrou, Libertarian, 3,373; Gritz, Populist/America First, 3,363; Hagelin, Natural Law, 1,406.

1988: Dukakis, D., 1,109,471; Bush, R., 962,337; McCarthy, Minn. Prog., 5,403; Paul, Lib., 5,109.

1984: Mondale, D., 1,036,364; Reagan, R., 1,032,603; Bergland, Libertarian, 2,996.

1980: Carter, D., 954,173; Reagan, R., 873,268; Anderson, Ind., 174,997; Clark, Libertarian, 31,593; Commoner, Citizens, 8,406; Hall, Com., 1,117; DeBerry, Soc. Workers, 711; Griswold, Workers World, 698; McReynolds, Soc., 536; write-in, 281.

1976: Carter, D., 1,070,440; Ford, R., 819,395; McCarthy, Ind., 35,490; Anderson, Amer., 13,592; Camejo, Soc. Workers, 4,149; MacBride, Libertarian, 3,529; Hall, Com., 1,092.

1972: Nixon, R., 898,269; McGovern, D., 802,346; Schmitz, Amer., 31,407; Fisher, Soc. Labor, 4,261; Spock, Peoples, 2,805; Jenness, Soc. Workers, 940; Hall, Com., 662; scattered, 962.

1968: Humphrey, D., 857,738; Nixon, R., 658,643; Wallace, 3rd Party, 68,931; Cleaver, Peace, 935; Halstead, Soc. Workers, 808; McCarthy, write-in, 585; Mitchell, Com., 415; Blomen, Ind. Gov't., 285; scattered, 2,613.

1964: Johnson, D., 991,117; Goldwater, R., 559,624; Hass, Industrial Gov., 2,544; DeBerry, Soc. Workers, 1,177.

1960: Kennedy, D., 779,933; Nixon, R., 757,915; Dobbs, Soc. Workers, 3,077; Industrial Gov., 962.

1956: Eisenhower, R., 719,302; Stevenson, D., 617,525; Hass, Soc. Labor (Ind. Gov.), 2,080; Dobbs, Soc. Workers, 1,098.

1952: Eisenhower, R., 763,211; Stevenson, D., 608,458; Hallinan, Prog., 2,666; Hass, Soc. Labor, 2,383; Hamblen, Proh., 2,147; Dobbs, Soc. Workers, 618.

1948: Truman, D., 692,966; Dewey, R., 483,617; Wallace, Prog., 27,866; Thomas, Soc., 4,646; Teichert, Soc. Labor, 2,525; Dobbs, Soc. Workers, 606.

Mississippi

2004: Bush, R., 684,981; Kerry, D., 458,094; Nader, Ref., 3,177; Badnarik, Libertarian, 1,793; Peroutka, Constitution, 1,759; Harris, Ind., 1,268; Cobb, Green, 1,073.

2000: Bush, R., 572,844; Gore, D., 404,614; Nader, Ind., 8,122; Phillips, Constitution, 3,267; Buchanan, Reform, 2,265; Browne, Libertarian, 2,009; Harris, Ind., 613; Hagelin, Natural Law, 450.

1996: Dole, R., 439,838; Clinton, D., 394,022; Perot, Ind. (Ref.), 52,222; Browne, Libertarian, 2,809; Phillips, Taxpayers, 2,314; Hagelin, Natural Law, 1,447; Collins, Ind., 1,205.

1992: Bush, R., 487,793; Clinton, D., 400,258; Perot, Ind., 85,626; Fulani, New Alliance, 2,625; Marrou, Libertarian, 2,154; Phillips, U.S. Taxpayers, 1,652; Hagelin, Natural Law, 1,140.

1988: Bush, R., 557,890; Dukakis, D., 363,921; Duke, Ind., 4,232; Paul, Lib., 3,329.

1984: Reagan, R., 582,377; Mondale, D., 352,192; Bergland, Libertarian, 2,336.

1980: Reagan, R., 441,089; Carter, D., 429,281; Anderson, Ind., 12,036; Clark, Libertarian, 5,465; Griswold, Workers World, 2,402; Pulley, Soc. Workers, 2,347.

1976: Carter, D., 381,309; Ford, R., 366,846; Anderson, Amer., 6,678; McCarthy, Ind., 4,074; Maddox, Ind., 4,049; Camejo, Soc. Workers, 2,805; MacBride, Libertarian, 2,609.

1972: Nixon, R., 505,125; McGovern, D., 126,782; Schmitz, Amer., 11,598; Jenness, Soc. Workers, 2,458.

1968: Wallace, 3rd Party, 415,349; Humphrey, D., 150,644; Nixon, R., 88,516.

1964: Goldwater, R., 356,528; Johnson, D., 52,618.

1960: Democratic unpledged electors, 116,248; Kennedy, D., 108,362; Nixon, R., 73,561. Mississippi's victorious slate of 8 unpledged Democratic electors cast their votes for Sen. Harry F. Byrd (D, VA).

1956: Stevenson, D., 144,498; Eisenhower, R., 56,372; Black and Tan Grand Old Party, 4,313; total, 60,685; Byrd, Ind., 42,966.

1952: Stevenson, D., 172,566; Eisenhower, Ind. vote pledged to Rep. candidate, 112,966.

1948: Thurmond, States' Rights, 167,538; Truman, D., 19,384; Dewey, R., 5,043; Wallace, Prog., 225.

Missouri

2004: Bush, R., 1,455,713; Kerry, D., 1,259,171; Badnarik, Libertarian, 9,831; Peroutka, Constitution, 5,355.

2000: Bush, R., 1,189,924; Gore, D., 1,111,138; Nader, Green, 38,515; Buchanan, Reform, 9,818; Browne, Libertarian, 7,436; Phillips, Constitution, 1,957; Hagelin, Natural Law, 1,104.

1996: Clinton, D., 1,025,935; Dole, R., 890,016; Perot, Ref., 217,188; Phillips, Taxpayers, 11,521; Browne, Libertarian, 10,522; Hagelin, Natural Law, 2,287.

1992: Clinton, D., 1,053,873; Bush, R., 811,159; Perot, Ind., 518,741; Marrou, Libertarian, 7,497.

1988: Bush, R., 1,084,953; Dukakis, D., 1,001,619; Fulani, New Alliance, 6,656; Paul, write-in, 434.

1984: Reagan, R., 1,274,188; Mondale, D., 848,583.

1980: Reagan, R., 1,074,181; Carter, D., 931,182; Anderson, Ind., 77,920; Clark, Libertarian, 14,422; DeBerry, Soc. Workers, 1,515; Commoner, Citizens, 573; write-in, 31.

1976: Carter, D., 999,163; Ford, R., 928,808; McCarthy, Ind., 24,329.

1972: Nixon, R., 1,154,058; McGovern, D., 698,531.

1968: Nixon, R., 811,932; Humphrey, D., 791,444; Wallace, 3rd Party, 206,126.

1964: Johnson, D., 1,164,344; Goldwater, R., 653,535.

1960: Kennedy, D., 972,201; Nixon, R., 962,221.

1956: Stevenson, D., 918,273; Eisenhower, R., 914,299.

1952: Eisenhower, R., 959,429; Stevenson, D., 929,830; Hallinan, Prog., 987; Hamblen, Proh., 885; MacArthur, Christian Nationalist, 302; America First, 233; Hoopes, Soc., 227; Hass, Soc. Labor, 169.

1948: Truman, D., 917,315; Dewey, R., 655,039; Wallace, Prog., 3,998; Thomas, Soc., 2,222.

Montana

2004: Bush, R., 266,063; Kerry, D., 173,710; Nader, Ind., 6,168; Peroutka, Constitution, 1,764; Badnarik, Libertarian, 1,733; Cobb, Green, 996.

2000: Bush, Rep, 240,178; Gore, D., 137,126; Nader, Green, 24,437; Buchanan, Reform, 5,697; Browne, Libertarian, 1,718; Phillips, Constitution, 1,155; Hagelin, Natural Law, 675.

1996: Dole, R., 179,652; Clinton, D., 167,922; Perot, Ref., 55,229; Browne, Libertarian, 2,526; Hagelin, Natural Law, 1,754.

1992: Clinton, D., 154,507; Bush, R., 144,207; Perot, Ind., 107,225; Gritz, Populist/America First, 3,658.

1988: Bush, R., 190,412; Dukakis, D., 168,936; Paul, Lib., 5,047; Fulani, New Alliance, 1,279.

1984: Reagan, R., 232,450; Mondale, D., 146,742; Bergland, Libertarian, 5,185.

1980: Reagan, R., 206,814; Carter, D., 118,032; Anderson, Ind., 29,281; Clark, Libertarian, 9,825.

1976: Ford, R., 173,703; Carter, D., 149,259; Anderson, Amer., 5,772.

1972: Nixon, R., 183,976; McGovern, D., 120,197; Schmitz, Amer., 13,430.

1968: Nixon, R., 138,835; Humphrey, D., 114,117; Wallace, 3rd Party, 20,015; Munn, Proh., 510; Caton, New Reform, 470; Halstead, Soc. Workers, 457.

1964: Johnson, D., 164,246; Goldwater, R., 113,032; Kasper, Natl. States' Rights, 519; Munn, Proh., 499; DeBerry, Soc. Workers, 332.

1960: Nixon, R., 141,841; Kennedy, D., 134,891; Decker, Proh., 456; Dobbs, Soc. Workers, 391.

1956: Eisenhower, R., 154,933; Stevenson, D., 116,238.

1952: Eisenhower, R., 157,394; Stevenson, D., 106,213; Hallinan, Prog., 723; Hamblen, Proh., 548; Hoopes, Soc., 159.

1948: Truman, D., 119,071; Dewey, R., 96,770; Wallace, Prog., 7,313; Thomas, Soc., 695; Watson, Proh., 429.

Nebraska

2004: Bush, R., 512,814; Kerry, D., 254,328; Nader, Petitioning Cand., 5,698; Badnarik, Libertarian, 2,041; Peroutka, Nebraska, 1,314; Cobb, Green, 978; Calero, Petitioning Cand., 82.

2000: Bush, R., 433,862; Gore, D., 231,780; Nader, Green, 24,540; Buchanan, Ind., 3,646; Browne, Libertarian, 2,245; Hagelin, Natural Law, 478; Phillips, Ind., 468.

1996: Dole, R., 363,467; Clinton, D., 236,761; Perot, Ref., 71,278; Browne, Libertarian, 2,792; Phillips, Ind., 1,928; Hagelin, Natural Law, 1,189.

1992: Bush, R., 343,678; Clinton, D., 216,864; Perot, Ind., 174,104; Marrou, Libertarian, 1,340.

1988: Bush, R., 397,956; Dukakis, D., 259,235; Paul, Lib., 2,534; Fulani, New Alliance, 1,740.

1984: Reagan, R., 459,135; Mondale, D., 187,475; Bergland, Libertarian, 2,075.

1980: Reagan, R., 419,214; Carter, D., 166,424; Anderson, Ind., 44,854; Clark, Libertarian, 9,041.

1976: Ford, R., 359,219; Carter, D., 233,287; McCarthy, Ind., 9,383; Maddox, Amer. Ind., 3,378; MacBride, Libertarian, 1,476.

1972: Nixon, R., 406,298; McGovern, D., 169,991; scattered, 817.

1968: Nixon, R., 321,163; Humphrey, D., 170,784; Wallace, 3rd Party, 44,904.

1964: Johnson, D., 307,307; Goldwater, R., 276,847.

1960: Nixon, R., 380,553; Kennedy, D., 232,542.

1956: Eisenhower, R., 378,108; Stevenson, D., 199,029.

1952: Eisenhower, R., 421,603; Stevenson, D., 188,057.

1948: Dewey, R., 264,774; Truman, D., 224,165.

Nevada

2004: Bush, R., 418,690; Kerry, D., 397,190; Nader, Ind., 4,838; "None of These Candidates," Ind., 3,688; Badnarik, Libertarian, 3,176; Peroutka, Indep. Amer., 1,152; Cobb, Green, 853.

2000: Bush, R., 301,575; Gore, D., 279,978; Nader, Green, 15,008; Buchanan, Citizens First, 4,747; "None of These Candidates," 3,315; Browne, Libertarian, 3,311; Phillips, Ind. Amer., 621; Hagelin, Natural Law, 415.

1996: Clinton, D., 203,974; Dole, R., 199,244; Perot, Ref., 43,986; "None of These Candidates," 5,608; Nader, Green, 4,730; Browne, Libertarian, 4,460; Phillips, Ind. Amer., 1,732; Hagelin, Natural Law, 545.

1992: Clinton, D., 189,148; Bush, R., 175,828; Perot, Ind., 132,580; Gritz, Populist/America First, 2,892; Marrou, Libertarian, 1,835.

1988: Bush, R., 206,040; Dukakis, D., 132,738; Paul, Lib., 3,520; Fulani, New Alliance, 835.

1984: Reagan, R., 188,770; Mondale, D., 91,655; Bergland, Libertarian, 2,292.

1980: Reagan, R., 155,017; Carter, D., 66,666; Anderson, Ind., 17,651; Clark, Libertarian, 4,358.

1976: Ford, R., 101,273; Carter, D., 92,479; MacBride, Libertarian, 1,519; Maddox, Amer. Ind., 1,497; scattered, 5,108.

1972: Nixon, R., 115,750; McGovern, D., 66,016.

1968: Nixon, R., 73,188; Humphrey, D., 60,598; Wallace, 3rd Party, 20,432.

1964: Johnson, D., 79,339; Goldwater, R., 56,094.

1960: Kennedy, D., 54,880; Nixon, R., 52,387.

1956: Eisenhower, R., 56,049; Stevenson, D., 40,640.

1952: Eisenhower, R., 50,502; Stevenson, D., 31,688.

1948: Truman, D., 31,291; Dewey, R., 29,357; Wallace, Prog., 1,469.

New Hampshire

2004: Kerry, D., 340,511; Bush, R., 331,237; Nader, Ind., 4,479.

2000: Bush, R., 273,559; Gore, D., 266,348; Nader, Green, 22,198; Browne, Libertarian, 2,757; Buchanan, Independence, 2,615; Phillips, Constitution, 328.

1996: Clinton, D., 246,166; Dole, R., 196,486; Perot, Ref., 48,387; Browne, Libertarian, 4,214; Phillips, Taxpayers, 1,344.

1992: Clinton, D., 209,040; Bush, R., 202,484; Perot, Ind., 121,337; Marrou, Libertarian, 3,548.

1988: Bush, R., 281,537; Dukakis, D., 163,696; Paul, Lib., 4,502; Fulani, New Alliance, 790.

1984: Reagan, R., 267,051; Mondale, D., 120,377; Bergland, Libertarian, 735.

1980: Reagan, R., 221,705; Carter, D., 108,864; Anderson, Ind., 49,693; Clark, Libertarian, 2,067; Commoner, Citizens, 1,325; Hall, Com., 129; Griswold, Workers World, 76; DeBerry, Soc. Workers, 72; scattered, 68.

1976: Ford, R., 185,935; Carter, D., 147,645; McCarthy, Ind., 4,095; MacBride, Libertarian, 936; Reagan, write-in, 388; La Rouche, U.S. Labor, 186; Camejo, Soc. Workers, 161; Levin, Soc. Labor, 66; scattered, 215.

1972: Nixon, R., 213,724; McGovern, D., 116,435; Schmitz, Amer., 3,386; Jenness, Soc. Workers, 368; scattered, 142.

1968: Nixon, R., 154,903; Humphrey, D., 130,589; Wallace, 3rd Party, 11,173; New Party, 421; Halstead, Soc. Workers, 104.

1964: Johnson, D., 182,065; Goldwater, R., 104,029.

1960: Nixon, R., 157,989; Kennedy, D., 137,772.

1956: Eisenhower, R., 176,519; Stevenson, D., 90,364; Andrews, Const., 111.

1952: Eisenhower, R., 166,287; Stevenson, D., 106,663.

1948: Dewey, R., 121,299; Truman, D., 107,995; Wallace, Prog., 1,970; Thomas, Soc., 86; Teichert, Soc. Labor, 83; Thurmond, States' Rights, 7.

New Jersey

2004: Kerry, D., 1,911,430; Bush, R., 1,670,003; Nader, Ind., 19,418; Badnarik, Ind., 4,514; Peroutka, Ind., 2,750; Cobb, Ind., 1,807; Brown, Ind., 664; Van Auken, Ind., 575; Calero, Ind., 530.

2000: Gore, D., 1,788,850; Bush, R., 1,284,173; Nader, Ind., 94,554; Buchanan, Ind., 6,989; Browne, Ind., 6,312; Hagelin, Ind., 2,215; McReynolds, Ind., 1,880; Phillips, Ind., 1,409; Harris, Ind., 844.

1996: Clinton, D., 1,652,361; Dole, R., 1,103,099; Perot, Ref., 262,134; Nader, Green, 32,465; Browne, Libertarian, 14,763; Hagelin, Natural Law, 3,887; Phillips, Taxpayers, 3,440; Harris, Soc. Workers, 1,837; Moorehead, Workers World, 1,337; White, Soc. Equality, 537.

1992: Clinton, D., 1,436,206; Bush, R., 1,356,865; Perot, Ind., 521,829; Marrou, Libertarian, 6,822; Fulani, New Alliance, 3,513; Phillips, U.S. Taxpayers, 2,670; LaRouche, Ind., 2,095; Warren, Soc. Workers, 2,011; Daniels, Ind., 1,996; Gritz, Populist/America First, 1,867; Hagelin, Natural Law, 1,353.

1988: Bush, R., 1,740,604; Dukakis, D., 1,317,541; Lewin, Peace and Freedom, 9,953; Paul, Lib., 8,421.

1984: Reagan, R., 1,933,630; Mondale, D., 1,261,323; Bergland, Libertarian, 6,416.

1980: Reagan, R., 1,546,557; Carter, D., 1,147,364; Anderson, Ind., 234,632; Clark, Libertarian, 20,652; Commoner, Citizens, 8,203; McCormack, Right to Life, 3,927; Lynen, Middle Class, 3,694; Hall, Com., 2,555; Pulley, Soc. Workers, 2,198; McReynolds, Soc., 1,973; Gahres, Down With Lawyers, 1,718; Griswold, Workers World, 1,288; Wendelken, Ind., 923.

1976: Ford, R., 1,509,688; Carter, D., 1,444,653; McCarthy, Ind., 32,717; MacBride, Libertarian, 9,449; Maddox, Amer., 7,716; Levin, Soc. Labor, 3,686; Hall, Com., 1,662; LaRouche, U.S. Labor, 1,650; Camejo, Soc. Workers, 1,184; Wright, People's, 1,044; Bubar, Proh., 554; Zeidler, Soc., 469.

1972: Nixon, R., 1,845,502; McGovern, D., 1,102,211; Schmitz, Amer., 34,378; Spock, Peoples, 5,355; Fisher, Soc. Labor, 4,544; Jenness, Soc. Workers, 2,233; Mahalchik, Amer. First, 1,743; Hall, Com., 1,263.

1968: Nixon, R., 1,325,467; Humphrey, D., 1,264,206; Wallace, 3rd Party, 262,187; Halstead, Soc. Workers, 8,667; Gregory, Peace and Freedom, 8,084; Blomen, Soc. Labor, 6,784.

1964: Johnson, D., 1,867,671; Goldwater, R., 963,843; DeBerry, Soc. Workers, 8,181; Hass, Soc. Labor, 7,075.

1960: Kennedy, D., 1,385,415; Nixon, R., 1,363,324; Dobbs, Soc. Workers, 11,402; Lee, Cons., 8,708; Hass, Soc. Labor, 4,262.

1956: Eisenhower, R., 1,606,942; Stevenson D., 850,337; Holtwick, Proh., 9,147; Hass, Soc. Labor, 6,736; Andrews, Cons., 5,317; Dobbs, Soc. Workers, 4,004; Krajewski, Amer. Third Party, 1,829.

1952: Eisenhower, R., 1,373,613; Stevenson, D., 1,015,902; Hoopes, Soc., 8,593; Hass, Soc. Labor, 5,815; Hallinan, Prog., 5,589; Krajewski, Poor Man's, 4,203; Dobbs, Soc. Workers, 3,850; Hamblen, Proh., 989.

1948: Dewey, R., 981,124; Truman, D., 895,455; Wallace, Prog., 42,683; Watson, Proh., 10,593; Thomas, Soc., 10,521; Dobbs, Soc. Workers, 5,825; Teichert, Soc. Labor, 3,354.

New Mexico

2004: Bush, R., 376,930; Kerry, D., 370,942; Nader, Ind., 4,053; Badnarik, Libert., 2,382; Cobb, Green, 1,226; Peroutka, Constitution, 771.

2000: Gore, D., 286,783; Bush, R., 286,417; Nader, Green, 21,251; Browne, Libertarian, 2,058; Buchanan, Reform, 1,392; Hagelin, Natural Law, 361; Phillips, Constitution, 343.

1996: Clinton, D., 273,495; Dole, R., 232,751; Perot, Ref., 32,257; Nader, Green, 13,218; Browne, Libertarian, 2,996; Phillips, Taxpayers, 713; Hagelin, Natural Law, 644.

1992: Clinton, D., 261,617; Bush, R., 212,824; Perot, Ind., 91,895; Marrou, Libertarian, 1,615.

1988: Bush, R., 270,341; Dukakis, D., 244,497; Paul, Lib., 3,268; Fulani, New Alliance, 2,237.

1984: Reagan, R., 307,101; Mondale, D., 201,769; Bergland, Libertarian, 4,459.

1980: Reagan, R., 250,779; Carter, D., 167,826; Anderson, Ind., 29,459; Clark, Libertarian, 4,365; Commoner, Citizens, 2,202; Bubar, Statesman, 1,281; Pulley, Soc. Workers, 325.

1976: Ford, R., 211,419; Carter, D., 201,148; Camejo, Soc. Wkrs., 2,462; MacBride, Libert., 1,110; Zeidler, Soc., 240; Bubar, Proh., 211.

1972: Nixon, R., 235,606; McGovern, D., 141,084; Schmitz, Amer., 8,767; Jenness, Soc. Workers, 474.

1968: Nixon, R., 169,692; Humphrey, D., 130,081; Wallace, 3rd Party, 25,737; Chavez, 1,519; Halstead, Soc. Workers, 252.

1964: Johnson, D., 194,017; Goldwater, R., 131,838; Hass, Soc. Labor, 1,217; Munn, Proh., 543.

1960: Kennedy, D., 156,027; Nixon, R., 153,733; Decker, Proh., 777; Hass, Soc. Labor, 570.

1956: Eisenhower, R., 146,788; Stevenson, D., 106,098; Holtwick, Proh., 607; Andrews, Ind., 364; Hass, Soc. Labor, 69.

1952: Eisenhower, R., 132,170; Stevenson, D., 105,661; Hamblen, Proh., 297; Hallinan, Ind. Prog., 225; MacArthur, Christian National, 220; Hass, Soc. Labor, 35.

1948: Truman, D., 105,464; Dewey, R., 80,303; Wallace, Prog., 1,037; Watson, Proh., 127; Thomas, Soc., 83; Teichert, Soc. Lab., 49.

New York

2004: Kerry, D., 4,314,280; Bush, R., 2,962,567; Nader, Ind., 99,873; Badnarik, Libertarian, 11,607; Calero, Soc. Wkrs., 2,405.

2000: Gore, D., 4,112,965; Bush, R., 2,405,570; Nader, Green, 244,360; Buchanan, Reform, 31,554; Hagelin, Independence, 24,369; Browne, Libertarian, 7,664; Harris, Soc. Workers, 1,790; Phillips, Constitution, 1,503.

1996: Clinton, D., 3,756,177; Dole, R., 1,933,492; Perot, Ind. (Ref.), 503,458; Nader, Green, 75,956; Phillips, Right to Life, 23,580; Browne, Libertarian, 12,220; Hagelin, Natural Law, 5,011; Moorehead, Workers World, 3,473; Harris, Soc. Workers, 2,762.

1992: Clinton, D., 3,444,450; Bush, R., 2,346,649; Perot, Ind., 1,090,721; Warren, Soc. Workers, 15,472; Marrou, Libertarian, 13,451; Fulani, New Alliance, 11,318; Hagelin, Natural Law, 4,420.

1988: Dukakis, D., 3,347,882; Bush, R., 3,081,871; Marra, Right to Life, 20,497; Fulani, New Alliance, 15,845.

1984: Reagan, R., 3,664,763; Mondale, D., 3,119,609; Bergland, Libertarian, 11,949.

1980: Reagan, R., 2,893,831; Carter, D., 2,728,372; Anderson, Ind., 467,801; Clark, Libertarian, 52,648; McCormack, Right To Life, 24,159; Commoner, Citizens, 23,186; Hall, Com., 7,414; DeBerry, Soc. Wkrs., 2,068; Griswold, Wkrs. World, 1,416; scattered, 1,064.

1976: Carter, D., 3,389,558; Ford, R., 3,100,791; MacBride, Libertarian, 12,197; Hall, Com., 10,270; Camejo, Soc. Workers, 6,996; LaRouche, U.S. Labor, 5,413; blank, void, or scattered, 143,037.

1972: Nixon, R., 3,824,642; McGovern, D., 2,767,956; Lib., 183,128; total, 2,951,084; Reed, Cons., 368,136; Soc. Wkrs., 7,797; Fisher, Soc. Labor, 4,530; Hall, Com., 5,641; blank, void, or scattered, 161,641.

1968: Humphrey, D., 3,378,470; Nixon, R., 3,007,932; Wallace, 3rd Party, 358,864; Gregory, Freedom and Peace, 24,517; Halstead, Soc. Workers, 11,851; Blomen, Soc. Labor, 8,432; blank, void, and scattered, 171,624.

1964: Johnson, D., 4,913,156; Goldwater, R., 2,243,559; Hass, Soc. Labor, 6,085; DeBerry, Soc. Workers, 3,215; scattered, 188; blank and void, 151,383.

1960: Kennedy, D., 3,423,909; Liberal, 406,176; total, 3,830,085; Nixon, R., 3,446,419; Dobbs, Soc. Workers, 14,319; scattered, 256; blank and void, 88,896.

1956: Eisenhower, R., 4,340,340; Stevenson, D., 2,458,212, Liberal, 292,557, total, 2,750,769; write-in votes for Andrews, 1,027; Werdel, 492; Hass, 150; Hoopes, 82; others, 476.

1952: Eisenhower, R., 3,952,815; Stevenson, D., 2,687,890; Liberal, 416,711; total, 3,104,601; Hallinan, Amer. Lab., 64,211; Hoopes, Soc., 2,664; Dobbs, Soc. Workers, 2,212; Hass, Ind. Gov't., 1,560; scattered, 178; blank and void, 87,813.

1948: Dewey, R., 2,841,163; Truman, D., 2,557,642; Liberal, 222,562; total, 2,780,204; Wallace, Amer. Lab., 509,559; Thomas, Soc., 40,879; Teichert, Ind. Gov't., 2,729; Dobbs, Soc. Wkrs., 2,675.

North Carolina

2004: Bush, R., 1,961,166; Kerry, D., 1,525,849; Badnarik, Libertarian, 11,731.

2000: Bush, R., 1,631,163; Gore, D., 1,257,692; Browne, Libertarian, 13,891; Buchanan, Reform, 8,874.

1996: Dole, R., 1,225,938; Clinton, D., 1,107,849; Perot, Ref., 168,059; Browne, Libertarian, 8,740; Hagelin, Natural Law, 2,771.

1992: Bush, R., 1,134,661; Clinton, D., 1,114,042; Perot, Ind., 357,864; Marrou, Libertarian, 5,171.

1988: Bush, R., 1,237,258; Dukakis, D., 890,167; Fulani, New Alliance, 5,682; Paul, write-in, 1,263.

1984: Reagan, R., 1,346,481; Mondale, D., 824,287; Bergland, Libertarian, 3,794.

1980: Reagan, R., 915,018; Carter, D., 875,635; Anderson, Ind., 52,800; Clark, Libertarian, 9,677; Commoner, Citizens, 2,287; DeBerry, Soc. Workers, 416.

1976: Carter, D., 927,365; Ford, R., 741,960; Anderson, Amer., 5,607; MacBride, Libertarian, 2,219; LaRouche, U.S. Labor, 755.

1972: Nixon, R., 1,054,889; McGovern, D., 438,705; Schmitz, Amer., 25,018.

1968: Nixon, R., 627,192; Wallace, 3rd Party, 496,188; Humphrey, D., 464,113.

1964: Johnson, D., 800,139; Goldwater, R., 624,844.

1960: Kennedy, D., 713,136; Nixon, R., 655,420.
1956: Stevenson, D., 590,530; Eisenhower, R., 575,062.
1952: Stevenson, D., 652,803; Eisenhower, R., 558,107.
1948: Truman, D., 459,070; Dewey, R., 258,572; Thurmond, States' Rights, 69,652; Wallace, Prog., 3,915.

North Dakota

2004: Bush, R., 196,651; Kerry, D., 111,052; Nader, Ind., 3,756; Badnarik, Libertarian, 851; Peroutka, Constitution, 514.
2000: Bush, R., 174,852; Gore, D., 95,284; Nader, Ind., 9,486; Buchanan, Reform, 7,288; Browne, Ind., 660; Phillips, Constitution, 373; Hagelin, Ind., 313.
1996: Dole, R., 125,050; Clinton, D., 106,905; Perot, Ref., 32,515; Browne, Libertarian, 847; Phillips, Ind., 745; Hagelin, Natural Law, 349.
1992: Bush, R., 136,244; Clinton, D., 99,168; Perot, Ind., 71,084.
1988: Bush, R., 166,559; Dukakis, D., 127,739; Paul, Lib., 1,315; LaRouche, Natl. Econ. Recovery, 905.
1984: Reagan, R., 200,336; Mondale, D., 104,429; Bergland, Libertarian, 703.
1980: Reagan, R., 193,695; Carter, D., 79,189; Anderson, Ind., 23,640; Clark, Libertarian, 3,743; Commoner, Libertarian, 429; McLain, Natl. People's League, 296; Greaves, Amer., 235; Hall, Com., 93; DeBerry, Soc. Workers, 89; McReynolds, Soc., 82; Bubar, Statesman, 54.
1976: Ford, R., 153,470; Carter, D., 136,078; Anderson, Amer., 3,698; McCarthy, Ind., 2,952; Maddox, Amer. Ind., 269; MacBride, Libertarian, 256; scattered, 371.
1972: Nixon, R., 174,109; McGovern, D., 100,384; Schmitz, Amer., 5,646; Jenness, Soc. Workers, 288; Hall, Com., 87.
1968: Nixon, R., 138,669; Humphrey, D., 94,769; Wallace, 3rd Party, 14,244; Halstead, Soc. Workers, 128; Munn, Prohibition, 38; Troxell, Ind., 34.
1964: Johnson, D., 149,784; Goldwater, R., 108,207; DeBerry, Soc. Workers, 224; Munn, Proh., 174.
1960: Nixon, R., 154,310; Kennedy, D., 123,963; Dobbs, Soc. Workers, 158.
1956: Eisenhower, R., 156,766; Stevenson, D., 96,742; Andrews, Amer., 483.
1952: Eisenhower, R., 191,712; Stevenson, D., 76,694; MacArthur, Christian Nationalist, 1,075; Hallinan, Prog., 344; Hamblen, Proh., 302.
1948: Dewey, R., 115,139; Truman, D., 95,812; Wallace, Prog., 8,391; Thomas, Soc., 1,000; Thurmond, States' Rights, 374.

Ohio

2004: Bush, R., 2,859,768; Kerry, D., 2,741,167; Badnarik, nonpartisan, 14,676; Peroutka, nonpartisan, 939.
2000: Bush, R., 2,351,209; Gore, D., 2,186,190; Nader, Ind., 117,857; Buchanan, Ind., 26,724; Browne, Libertarian, 13,475; Hagelin, Natural Law, 6,169; Phillips, Ind., 3,823.
1996: Clinton, D., 2,148,222; Dole, R., 1,859,883; Perot, Ref., 483,207; Browne, Ind., 12,851; Moorehead, Ind., 10,813; Hagelin, Natural Law, 9,120; Phillips, Ind., 7,361.
1992: Clinton, D., 1,984,942; Bush, R., 1,894,310; Perot, Ind., 1,036,426; Marrou, Libertarian, 7,252; Fulani, New Alliance, 6,413; Gritz, Populist/America First, 4,699; Hagelin, Natural Law, 3,437; LaRouche, Ind., 2,446.
1988: Bush, R., 2,416,549; Dukakis, D., 1,939,629; Fulani, Ind., 12,017; Paul, Ind., 11,926.
1984: Reagan, R., 2,678,559; Mondale, D., 1,825,440; Bergland, Libertarian, 5,886.
1980: Reagan, R., 2,206,545; Carter, D., 1,752,414; Anderson, Ind., 254,472; Clark, Libertarian, 49,033; Commoner, Citizens, 8,564; Hall, Com., 4,729; Congress, Ind., 4,029; Griswold, Workers World, 3,790; Bubar, Statesman, 27.
1976: Carter, D., 2,011,621; Ford, R., 2,000,505; McCarthy, Ind., 58,258; Maddox, Amer. Ind., 15,529; MacBride, Libertarian, 8,961; Hall, Com., 7,817; Camejo, Soc. Workers, 4,717; LaRouche, U.S. Labor, 4,335; scattered, 130.
1972: Nixon, R., 2,441,827; McGovern, D., 1,558,889; Schmitz, Amer., 80,067; Fisher, Soc. Labor, 7,107; Hall, Com., 6,437; Wallace, Ind., 460.
1968: Nixon, R., 1,791,014; Humphrey, D., 1,700,586; Wallace, 3rd Party, 467,495; Gregory, 372; Blomen, Soc. Labor, 120; Halstead, Soc. Workers, 69; Mitchell, Com., 23; Munn, Proh., 19.
1964: Johnson, D., 2,498,331; Goldwater, R., 1,470,865.
1960: Nixon, R., 2,217,611; Kennedy, D., 1,944,248.
1956: Eisenhower, R., 2,262,610; Stevenson, D., 1,439,655.
1952: Eisenhower, R., 2,100,391; Stevenson, D., 1,600,367.
1948: Truman, D., 1,452,791; Dewey, R., 1,445,684; Wallace, Prog., 37,596.

Oklahoma

2004: Bush, R., 959,792; Kerry, D., 503,966.
2000: Bush, R., 744,337; Gore, D., 474,276; Buchanan, Reform, 9,014; Browne, Libertarian, 6,602.
1996: Dole, R., 582,315; Clinton, D., 488,105; Perot, Ref., 130,788; Browne, Libertarian, 5,505.
1992: Bush, R., 592,929; Clinton, D., 473,066; Perot, Ind., 319,878; Marrou, Libertarian, 4,486.
1988: Bush, R., 678,367; Dukakis, D., 483,423; Paul, Lib., 6,261; Fulani, New Alliance, 2,985.
1984: Reagan, R., 861,530; Mondale, D., 385,080; Bergland, Libertarian, 9,066.
1980: Reagan, R., 695,570; Carter, D., 402,026; Anderson, Ind., 38,284; Clark, Libertarian, 13,828.
1976: Ford, R., 545,708; Carter, D., 532,442; McCarthy, Ind., 14,101.
1972: Nixon, R., 759,025; McGovern, D., 247,147; Schmitz, Amer., 23,728.
1968: Nixon, R., 449,697; Humphrey, D., 301,658; Wallace, 3rd Party, 191,731.
1964: Johnson, D., 519,834; Goldwater, R., 412,665.
1960: Nixon, R., 533,039; Kennedy, D., 370,111.
1956: Eisenhower, R., 473,769; Stevenson, D., 385,581.
1952: Eisenhower, R., 518,045; Stevenson, D., 430,939.
1948: Truman, D., 452,782; Dewey, R., 268,817.

Oregon

2004: Kerry, D., 943,163; Bush, R., 866,831; Badnarik, Libertarian, 7,260; Cobb, Pac. Green, 5,315; Peroutka, Constitution, 5,257.
2000: Gore, D., 720,342; Bush, R., 713,577; Nader, Green, 77,357; Browne, Libertarian, 7,447; Buchanan, Ind., 7,063; Hagelin, Reform, 2,574; Phillips, Constitution, 2,189.
1996: Clinton, D., 649,641; Dole, R., 538,152; Perot, Ref., 121,221; Nader, Pacific, 49,415; Browne, Libertarian, 8,903; Phillips, Taxpayers, 3,379; Hagelin, Natural Law, 2,798; Hollis, Soc., 1,922.
1992: Clinton, D., 621,314; Bush, R., 475,757; Perot, Ind., 354,091; Marrou, Libertarian, 4,277; Fulani, New Alliance, 3,030.
1988: Dukakis, D., 616,206; Bush, R., 560,126; Paul, Lib., 14,811; Fulani, Ind., 6,487.
1984: Reagan, R., 658,700; Mondale, D., 536,479.
1980: Reagan, R., 571,044; Carter, D., 456,890; Anderson, Ind., 112,389; Clark, Libertarian, 25,838; Commoner, Citizens, 13,642; scattered, 1,713.
1976: Ford, R., 492,120; Carter, D., 490,407; McCarthy, Ind., 40,207; write-in, 7,142.
1972: Nixon, R., 486,686; McGovern, D., 392,760; Schmitz, Amer., 46,211; write-in, 2,289.
1968: Nixon, R., 408,433; Humphrey, D., 358,866; Wallace, 3rd Party, 49,683; write-in, McCarthy, 1,496; N. Rockefeller, 69; others, 1,075.
1964: Johnson, D., 501,017; Goldwater, R., 282,779; write-in, 2,509.
1960: Nixon, R., 408,060; Kennedy, D., 367,402.
1956: Eisenhower, R., 406,393; Stevenson, D., 329,204.
1952: Eisenhower, R., 420,815; Stevenson, D., 270,579; Hallinan, Ind., 3,665.
1948: Dewey, R., 260,904; Truman, D., 243,147; Wallace, Prog., 14,978; Thomas, Soc., 5,051.

Pennsylvania

2004: Kerry, D., 2,938,095; Bush, R., 2,793,847; Badnarik, Libertarian, 21,185; Cobb, Green, 6,319; Peroutka, Constitution, 6,318.
2000: Gore, D., 2,485,967; Bush, R., 2,281,127; Nader, Green, 103,392; Buchanan, Reform, 16,023; Phillips, Constitution, 14,428; Browne, Libertarian, 11,248.
1996: Clinton, D., 2,215,819; Dole, R., 1,801,169; Perot, Ref., 430,984; Browne, Libertarian, 28,000; Phillips, Constitutional, 19,552; Hagelin, Natural Law, 5,783.
1992: Clinton, D., 2,239,164; Bush, R., 1,791,841; Perot, Ind., 902,667; Marrou, Libertarian, 21,477; Fulani, New Alliance, 4,661.
1988: Bush, R., 2,300,087; Dukakis, D., 2,194,944; McCarthy, Consumer, 19,158; Paul, Lib., 12,051.
1984: Reagan, R., 2,584,323; Mondale, D., 2,228,131; Bergland, Libertarian, 6,982.
1980: Reagan, R., 2,261,872; Carter, D., 1,937,540; Anderson, Ind., 292,921; Clark, Libertarian, 33,263; DeBerry, Soc. Workers, 20,291; Commoner, Consumer, 10,430; Hall, Com., 5,184.

1976: Carter, D., 2,328,677; Ford, R., 2,205,604; McCarthy, Ind., 50,584; Maddox, Const., 25,344; Camejo, Soc. Workers, 3,009; LaRouche, U.S. Labor, 2,744; Hall, Com., 1,891; others, 2,934.

1972: Nixon, R., 2,714,521; McGovern, D., 1,796,951; Schmitz, Amer., 70,593; Jenness, Soc. Workers, 4,639; Hall, Com., 2,686; others, 2,715.

1968: Humphrey, D., 2,259,405; Nixon, R., 2,090,017; Wallace, 3rd Party, 378,582; Gregory, Peace and Freedom, 7,821; Blomen, Soc. Labor, 4,977; Halstead, Soc. Workers, 4,862; others, 2,264.

1964: Johnson, D., 3,130,954; Goldwater, R., 1,673,657; DeBerry, Soc. Workers, 10,456; Hass, Soc. Labor, 5,092; scattered, 2,531.

1960: Kennedy, D., 2,556,282; Nixon, R., 2,439,956; Hass, Soc. Labor, 7,185; Dobbs, Soc. Workers, 2,678; scattered, 440.

1956: Eisenhower, R., 2,585,252; Stevenson, D., 1,981,769; Hass, Soc. Labor, 7,447; Dobbs, Militant Workers, 2,035.

1952: Eisenhower, R., 2,415,789; Stevenson, D., 2,146,269; Hamblen, Proh., 8,771; Hallinan, Prog., 4,200; Hoopes, Soc., 2,684; Dobbs, Militant Workers, 1,502; Hass, Ind. Gov., 1,347; scattered, 155.

1948: Dewey, R., 1,902,197; Truman, D., 1,752,426; Wallace, Prog., 55,161; Thomas, Soc., 11,325; Watson, Proh., 10,338; Dobbs, Militant Workers, 2,133; Teichert, Soc. Labor, 1,461.

Rhode Island

2004: Kerry, D., 259,765; Bush, R., 169,046; Nader, Ref., 4,651; Cobb, Green, 1,333; Badnarik, Libertarian, 907; Peroutka, Constitution, 339; Parker, Workers World, 253.

2000: Gore, D., 249,508; Bush, R., 130,555; Nader, Ind., 25,052; Buchanan, Reform, 2,273; Browne, Ind., 742; Hagelin, Ind., 271; Moorehead, Ind., 199; Phillips, Ind., 97; McReynolds, Ind., 52; Harris, Ind., 34.

1996: Clinton, D., 233,050; Dole, R., 104,683; Perot, Ref., 43,723; Nader, Green, 6,040; Browne, Libertarian, 1,109; Phillips, Taxpayers, 1,021; Hagelin, Natural Law, 435; Moorehead, Workers World, 186.

1992: Clinton, D., 213,299; Bush, R., 131,601; Perot, Ind., 105,045; Fulani, New Alliance, 1,878.

1988: Dukakis, D., 225,123; Bush, R., 177,761; Paul, Lib., 825; Fulani, New Alliance, 730.

1984: Reagan, R., 212,080; Mondale, D., 197,106; Bergland, Libertarian, 277.

1980: Carter, D., 198,342; Reagan, R., 154,793; Anderson, Ind., 59,819; Clark, Libertarian, 2,458; Hall, Com., 218; McReynolds, Soc., 170; DeBerry, Soc. Workers, 90; Griswold, Workers World, 77.

1976: Carter, D., 227,636; Ford, R., 181,249; MacBride, Libertarian, 715; Camejo, Soc. Workers, 462; Hall, Com., 334; Levin, Soc. Labor, 188.

1972: Nixon, R., 220,383; McGovern, D., 194,645; Jenness, Soc. Workers, 729.

1968: Humphrey, D., 246,518; Nixon, R., 122,359; Wallace, 3rd Party, 15,678; Halstead, Soc. Workers, 383.

1964: Johnson, D., 315,463; Goldwater, R., 74,615.

1960: Kennedy, D., 258,032; Nixon, R., 147,502.

1956: Eisenhower, R., 225,819; Stevenson, D., 161,790.

1952: Eisenhower, R., 210,935; Stevenson, D., 203,293; Hallinan, Prog., 187; Hass, Soc. Labor, 83.

1948: Truman, D., 188,736; Dewey, R., 135,787; Wallace, Prog., 2,619; Thomas, Soc., 429; Teichert, Soc. Labor, 131.

South Carolina

2004: Bush, R., 937,974; Kerry, D., 661,699; Nader, Ind., 5,520; Peroutka, Constitution, 5,317; Badnarik, Libertarian, 3,608; Brown, United Citizen, 2,124; Cobb, Green, 1,488.

2000: Bush, R., 786,892; Gore, D., 566,039; Nader, United Citizens, 20,279; Browne, Libertarian, 4,898; Buchanan, Reform, 3,309; Phillips, Constitution, 1,682; Hagelin, Natural Law, 943.

1996: Dole, R., 573,458; Clinton, D., 506,283; Perot, Ref./ Patriot, 64,386; Browne, Libertarian, 4,271; Phillips, Taxpayers, 2,043; Hagelin, Natural Law, 1,248.

1992: Bush, R., 577,507; Clinton, D., 479,514; Perot, Ind., 138,872; Marrou, Libertarian, 2,719; Phillips, U.S. Taxpayers, 2,680; Fulani, New Alliance, 1,235.

1988: Bush, R., 606,443; Dukakis, D., 370,554; Paul, Lib., 4,935; Fulani, United Citizens, 4,077.

1984: Reagan, R., 615,539; Mondale, D., 344,459; Bergland, Libertarian, 4,359.

1980: Reagan, R., 439,277; Carter, D., 428,220; Anderson, Ind., 13,868; Clark, Libertarian, 4,807; Rarick, Amer. Ind., 2,086.

1976: Carter, D., 450,807; Ford, R., 346,149; Anderson, Amer., 2,996; Maddox, Amer. Ind., 1,950; write-in, 681.

1972: Nixon, R., 477,044; McGovern, D., 184,559; Schmitz, Amer., 10,075; United Citizens, 2,265; write-in, 17.

1968: Nixon, R., 254,062; Wallace, 3rd Party, 215,430; Humphrey, D., 197,486.

1964: Goldwater, R., 309,048; Johnson, D., 215,700; write-in: Wallace, 5; Nixon, 1; Powell, 1; Thurmond, 1.

1960: Kennedy, D., 198,129; Nixon, R., 188,558; write-in, 1.

1956: Stevenson, D., 136,372; Byrd, Ind., 88,509; Eisenhower, R., 75,700; Andrews, Ind., 2.

1952: Stevenson, D., 173,004. Under state law votes cast for 2 Eisenhower slates of electors could not be combined. Eisenhower, Ind., 158,289; R., 9,793; total, 168,082. Hamblen, Proh., 1.

1948: Thurmond, States' Rights, 102,607; Truman, D., 34,423; Dewey, R., 5,386; Wallace, Prog., 154; Thomas, Soc., 1.

South Dakota

2004: Bush, R., 232,584; Kerry, D., 149,244; Nader, Ind., 4,320; Peroutka, Constitution, 1,103; Badnarik, Libertarian, 964.

2000: Bush, R., 190,700; Gore, D., 118,804; Buchanan, Reform, 3,322; Phillips, Ind., 1,781; Browne, Libertarian, 1,662.

1996: Dole, R., 150,543; Clinton, D., 139,333; Perot, Ref., 31,250; Browne, Libertarian, 1,472; Phillips, Taxpayers, 912; Hagelin, Natural Law, 316.

1992: Bush, R., 136,718; Clinton, D., 124,888; Perot, Ind., 73,295.

1988: Bush, R., 165,415; Dukakis, D., 145,560; Paul, Lib., 1,060; Fulani, New Alliance, 730.

1984: Reagan, R., 200,267; Mondale, D., 116,113.

1980: Reagan, R., 198,343; Carter, D., 103,855; Anderson, Ind., 21,431; Clark, Libertarian, 3,824; Pulley, Soc. Workers, 250.

1976: Ford, R., 151,505; Carter, D., 147,068; MacBride, Libertarian, 1,619; Hall, Com., 318; Camejo, Soc. Workers, 168.

1972: Nixon, R., 166,476; McGovern, D., 139,945; Jenness, Soc. Workers, 994.

1968: Nixon, R., 149,841; Humphrey, D., 118,023; Wallace, 3rd Party, 13,400.

1964: Johnson, D., 163,010; Goldwater, R., 130,108.

1960: Nixon, R., 178,417; Kennedy, D., 128,070.

1956: Eisenhower, R., 171,569; Stevenson, D., 122,288.

1952: Eisenhower, R., 203,857; Stevenson, D., 90,426.

1948: Dewey, R., 129,651; Truman, D., 117,653; Wallace, Prog., 2,801.

Tennessee

2004: Bush, R., 1,384,375; Kerry, D., 1,036,477; Nader, Ind., 8,992; Badnarik, Ind., 4,866; Peroutka, Ind., 2,570.

2000: Bush, R., 1,061,949; Gore, D., 981,720; Nader, Green, 19,781; Browne, Libertarian, 4,284; Buchanan, Reform, 4,250; Brown, Ind., 1,606; Phillips, Ind., 1,015; Hagelin, Reform, 613; Venson, Ind., 535.

1996: Clinton, D., 909,146; Dole, R., 863,530; Perot, Ind. (Ref.), 105,918; Nader, Ind., 6,427; Browne, Ind., 5,020; Phillips, Ind., 1,818; Collins, Ind., 688; Hagelin, Ind., 636; Michael, Ind., 408; Dodge, Ind., 324.

1992: Clinton, D., 933,521; Bush, R., 841,300; Perot, Ind., 199,968; Marrou, Libertarian, 1,847.

1988: Bush, R., 947,233; Dukakis, D., 679,794; Paul, Ind., 2,041; Duke, Ind., 1,807.

1984: Reagan, R., 990,212; Mondale, D., 711,714; Bergland, Libertarian, 3,072.

1980: Reagan, R., 787,761; Carter, D., 783,051; Anderson, Ind., 35,991; Clark, Libertarian, 7,116; Commoner, Citizens, 1,112; Bubar, Statesman, 521; McReynolds, Soc., 519; Hall, Com., 503; DeBerry, Soc. Workers, 490; Griswold, Workers World, 400; write-in, 152.

1976: Carter, D., 825,879; Ford, R., 633,969; Anderson, Amer., 5,769; McCarthy, Ind., 5,004; Maddox, Amer. Ind., 2,303; MacBride, Libertarian, 1,375; Hall, Com., 547; LaRouche, U.S. Labor, 512; Bubar, Proh., 442; Miller, Ind., 316; write-in, 230.

1972: Nixon, R., 813,147; McGovern, D., 357,293; Schmitz, Amer., 30,373; write-in, 369.

1968: Nixon, R., 472,592; Wallace, 3rd Party, 424,792; Humphrey, D., 351,233.

1964: Johnson, D., 635,047; Goldwater, R., 508,965; write-in, 34.

1960: Nixon, R., 556,577; Kennedy, D., 481,453; Faubus, States' Rights, 11,304; Decker, Proh., 2,458.

1956: Eisenhower, R., 462,288; Stevenson, D., 456,507; Andrews, Ind., 19,820; Holtwick, Proh., 789.

1952: Eisenhower, R., 446,147; Stevenson, D., 443,710; Hamblen, Proh., 1,432; Hallinan, Prog., 885; MacArthur, Christian Nationalist, 379.

1948: Truman, D., 270,402; Dewey, R., 202,914; Thurmond, States' Rights, 73,815; Wallace, Prog., 1,864; Thomas, Soc., 1,288.

Texas

2004: Bush, R., 4,526,917; Kerry, D., 2,832,704; Badnarik, Libertarian, 38,787.

2000: Bush, R., 3,799,639; Gore, D., 2,433,746; Nader, Green, 137,994; Browne, Libertarian, 23,160; Buchanan, Ind., 12,394.

1996: Dole, R., 2,736,167; Clinton, D., 2,459,683; Perot, Ind. (Ref.), 378,537; Browne, Libertarian, 20,256; Phillips, Taxpayers, 7,472; Hagelin, Natural Law, 4,422.

1992: Bush, R., 2,496,071; Clinton, D., 2,281,815; Perot, Ind., 1,354,781; Marrou, Libertarian, 19,699.

1988: Bush, R., 3,036,829; Dukakis, D., 2,352,748; Paul, Lib., 30,355; Fulani, New Alliance, 7,208.

1984: Reagan, R., 3,433,428; Mondale, D., 1,949,276.

1980: Reagan, R., 2,510,705; Carter, D., 1,881,147; Anderson, Ind., 111,613; Clark, Libertarian, 37,643; write-in, 528.

1976: Carter, D., 2,082,319; Ford, R., 1,953,300; McCarthy, Ind., 20,118; Anderson, Amer., 11,442; Camejo, Soc. Workers, 1,723; write-in, 2,982.

1972: Nixon, R., 2,298,896; McGovern D., 1,154,289; Jenness, Soc. Workers, 8,664; Schmitz, Amer., 6,039; others, 3,393.

1968: Humphrey, D., 1,266,804; Nixon, R., 1,227,844; Wallace, 3rd Party, 584,269; write-in, 489.

1964: Johnson, D., 1,663,185; Goldwater, R., 958,566; Lightburn, Constitution, 5,060.

1960: Kennedy, D., 1,167,932; Nixon, R., 1,121,699; Sullivan, Constitution, 18,169; Decker, Proh., 3,870; write-in, 15.

1956: Eisenhower, R., 1,080,619; Stevenson, D., 859,958; Andrews, Ind., 14,591.

1952: Eisenhower, R., 1,102,878; Stevenson, D., 969,228; Hamblen, Proh., 1,983; MacArthur, Christian Nationalist, 833; MacArthur, Constitution, 730; Hallinan, Prog., 294.

1948: Truman, D., 750,700; Dewey, R., 282,240; Thurmond, States' Rights, 106,909; Wallace, Prog., 3,764; Watson, Proh., 2,758; Thomas, Soc., 874.

Utah

2004: Bush, R., 663,742; Kerry, D., 241,199; Nader, Ind., 11,305; Peroutka, Constitution, 6,841; Badnarik, Libertarian, 3,375; Jay, Pers. Choice, 946; Harris, Soc. Wkrs., 393.

2000: Bush, R., 515,096; Gore, D., 203,053; Nader, Green, 35,850; Buchanan, Reform, 9,319; Browne, Libertarian, 3,616; Phillips, Ind. Amer., 2,709; Hagelin, Natural Law, 763; Harris, Soc. Workers, 186; Youngkin, Ind., 161.

1996: Dole, R., 361,911; Clinton, D., 221,633; Perot, Ref., 66,461; Nader, Green, 4,615; Browne, Libertarian, 4,129; Phillips, Taxpayers, 2,601; Templin, Ind. Amer., 1,290; Crane, Ind., 1,101; Hagelin, Natural Law, 1,085; Moorehead, Workers World, 298; Harris, Soc. Workers, 235; Dodge, Proh., 111.

1992: Bush, R., 322,632; Perot, Ind., 203,400; Clinton, D., 183,429; Gritz, Populist/America First, 28,602; Marrou, Libertarian, 1,900; Hagelin, Natural Law, 1,319; LaRouche, Ind., 1,089.

1988: Bush, R., 428,442; Dukakis, D., 207,352; Paul, Lib., 7,473; Dennis, Amer., 2,158.

1984: Reagan, R., 469,105; Mondale, D., 155,369; Bergland, Libertarian, 2,447.

1980: Reagan, R., 439,687; Carter, D., 124,266; Anderson, Ind., 30,284; Clark, Libertarian, 7,226; Commoner, Citizens, 1,009; Greaves, Amer., 965; Rarick, Amer. Ind., 522; Hall, Com., 139; DeBerry, Soc. Workers, 124.

1976: Ford, R., 337,908; Carter, D., 182,110; Anderson, Amer., 13,304; McCarthy, Ind., 3,907; MacBride, Libertarian, 2,438; Maddox, Amer. Ind., 1,162; Camejo, Soc. Workers, 268; Hall, Com., 121.

1972: Nixon, R., 323,643; McGovern, D., 126,284; Schmitz, Amer., 28,549.

1968: Nixon, R., 238,728; Humphrey, D., 156,665; Wallace, 3rd Party, 26,906; Peace and Freedom, 180; Halstead, Soc. Workers, 89.

1964: Johnson, D., 219,628; Goldwater, R., 181,785.

1960: Nixon, R., 205,361; Kennedy, D., 169,248; Dobbs, Soc. Workers, 100.

1956: Eisenhower, R., 215,631; Stevenson, D., 118,364.

1952: Eisenhower, R., 194,190; Stevenson, D., 135,364.

1948: Truman, D., 149,151; Dewey, R., 124,402; Wallace, Prog., 2,679; Dobbs, Soc. Workers, 73.

Vermont

2004: Kerry, D., 184,067; Bush, R., 121,180; Nader, Ind., 4,494; Badnarik, Libertarian, 1,102; Parker, Liberty Union, 265; Calero, Soc. Wkrs., 244.

2000: Gore, D., 149,022; Bush, R., 119,775; Nader, Green, 20,374; Buchanan, Reform, 2,192; Lane, Grass Roots, 1,044; Browne, Libertarian, 784; Hagelin, Natural Law, 219; McReynolds, Liberty Union, 161; Phillips, Constitution, 153; Harris, Soc. Workers, 70.

1996: Clinton, D., 137,894; Dole, R., 80,352; Perot, Ref., 31,024; Nader, Green, 5,585; Browne, Libertarian, 1,183; Hagelin, Natural Law, 498; Peron, Grass Roots, 480; Phillips, Taxpayers, 382; Hollis, Liberty Union, 292; Harris, Soc. Workers, 199.

1992: Clinton, D., 133,590; Bush, R., 88,122; Perot, Ind., 65,985.

1988: Bush, R., 124,331; Dukakis, D., 115,775; Paul, Lib., 1,000; LaRouche, Ind., 275.

1984: Reagan, R., 135,865; Mondale, D., 95,730; Bergland, Libertarian, 1,002.

1980: Reagan, R., 94,598; Carter, D., 81,891; Anderson, Ind., 31,760; Commoner, Citizens, 2,316; Clark, Libertarian, 1,900; McReynolds, Liberty Union, 136; Hall, Com., 118; DeBerry, Soc. Workers, 75; scattered, 413.

1976: Ford, R., 100,387; Carter, D., 77,798; Carter, Ind. Vermonter, 991; total, 79,789; McCarthy, Ind., 4,001; Camejo, Soc. Workers, 430; LaRouche, U.S. Labor, 196; scattered, 99.

1972: Nixon, R., 117,149; McGovern, D., 68,174; Spock, Liberty Union, 1,010; Jenness, Soc. Workers, 296; scattered, 318.

1968: Nixon, R., 85,142; Humphrey, D., 70,255; Wallace, 3rd Party, 5,104; Gregory, New Party, 579; Halstead, Soc. Workers, 295.

1964: Johnson, D., 107,674; Goldwater, R., 54,868.

1960: Nixon, R., 98,131; Kennedy, D., 69,186.

1956: Eisenhower, R., 110,390; Stevenson, D., 42,549; scattered, 39.

1952: Eisenhower, R., 109,717; Stevenson, D., 43,355; Hallinan, Prog., 282; Hoopes, Soc., 185.

1948: Dewey, R., 75,926; Truman, D., 45,557; Wallace, Prog., 1,279; Thomas, Soc., 585.

Virginia

2004: Bush, R., 1,716,959; Kerry, D., 1,454,742; Badnarik, Libertarian, 11,032; Peroutka, Constitution, 10,161.

2000: Bush, R., 1,437,490; Gore, D., 1,217,290; Nader, Green, 59,398; Browne, Libertarian, 15,198; Buchanan, Reform, 5,455; Phillips, Constitution, 1,809.

1996: Dole, R., 1,138,350; Clinton, D., 1,091,060; Perot, Ref., 159,861; Phillips, Taxpayers, 13,687; Browne, Libertarian, 9,174; Hagelin, Natural Law, 4,510.

1992: Bush, R., 1,150,517; Clinton, D., 1,038,650; Perot, Ind., 348,639; LaRouche, Ind., 11,937; Marrou, Libertarian, 5,730; Fulani, New Alliance, 3,192.

1988: Bush, R., 1,309,162; Dukakis, D., 859,799; Fulani, Ind., 14,312; Paul, Lib., 8,336.

1984: Reagan, R., 1,337,078; Mondale, D., 796,250.

1980: Reagan, R., 989,609; Carter, D., 752,174; Anderson, Ind., 95,418; Commoner, Citizens, 14,024; Clark, Libertarian, 12,821; DeBerry, Soc. Workers, 1,986.

1976: Ford, R., 836,554; Carter, D., 813,896; Camejo, Soc. Workers, 17,802; Anderson, Amer., 16,686; LaRouche, U.S. Labor, 7,508; MacBride, Libertarian, 4,648.

1972: Nixon, R., 988,493; McGovern, D., 438,887; Schmitz, Amer., 19,721; Fisher, Soc. Labor, 9,918.

1968: Nixon, R., 590,319; Humphrey, D., 442,387; Wallace, 3rd Party, *320,272; Blomen, Soc. Labor, 4,671; Gregory, Peace and Freedom, 1,680; Munn, Proh., 601. *10,561 votes for Wallace were omitted in the count.

1964: Johnson, D., 558,038; Goldwater, R., 481,334; Hass, Soc. Labor, 2,895.

1960: Nixon, R., 404,521; Kennedy, D., 362,327; Coiner, Cons., 4,204; Hass, Soc. Labor, 397.

1956: Eisenhower, R., 386,459; Stevenson, D., 267,760; Andrews, States' Rights, 42,964; Hoopes, Soc. D., 444; Hass, Soc. Labor, 351.

1952: Eisenhower, R., 349,037; Stevenson, D., 268,677; Hass, Soc. Labor, 1,160; Hoopes, Soc. D., 504; Hallinan, Prog., 311.

1948: Truman, D., 200,786; Dewey, R., 172,070; Thurmond, States' Rights, 43,393; Wallace, Prog., 2,047; Thomas, Soc., 726; Teichert, Soc. Labor, 234.

Washington

2004: Kerry, D., 1,510,201; Bush, R., 1,304,894; Nader, Ind., 23,283; Badnarik, Libertarian, 11,955; Peroutka, Constitution, 3,922; Cobb, Green, 2,974; Parker, Workers World, 1,077; Harris, Soc. Wkrs., 547; Van Auken, Soc. Equal., 231.

2000: Gore, D., 1,247,652; Bush, R., 1,108,864; Nader, Green, 103,002; Browne, Libertarian, 13,135; Buchanan, Freedom, 7,171; Hagelin, Natural Law, 2,927; ; Phillips, Constitution, 1,989; Moorehead, Wkrs. World, 1,729; McReynolds, Soc., 660; Harris, Soc. Wkrs., 304.

1996: Clinton, D., 1,123,323; Dole, R., 840,712; Perot, Ref., 201,003; Nader, Ind., 60,322; Browne, Libertarian, 12,522; Hagelin, Natural Law, 6,076; Phillips, Taxpayers, 4,578; Collins, Ind., 2,374; Moorehead, Workers World, 2,189; Harris, Soc. Workers, 738.

1992: Clinton, D., 993,037; Bush, R., 731,234; Perot, Ind., 541,780; Marrou, Libertarian, 7,533; Gritz, Populist/America First, 4,854; Hagelin, Natural Law, 2,456; Phillips, U.S. Taxpayers, 2,354; Fulani, New Alliance, 1,776; Daniels, Ind., 1,171.

1988: Dukakis, D., 933,516; Bush, R., 903,835; Paul, Lib., 17,240; LaRouche, Ind., 4,412.

1984: Reagan, R., 1,051,670; Mondale, D., 798,352; Bergland, Libertarian, 8,844.

1980: Reagan, R., 865,244; Carter, D., 650,193; Anderson, Ind., 185,073; Clark, Libertarian, 29,213; Commoner, Citizens, 9,403; DeBerry, Soc. Workers, 1,137; McReynolds, Soc., 956; Hall, Com., 834; Griswold, Workers World, 341.

1976: Ford, R., 777,732; Carter, D., 717,323; McCarthy, Ind., 36,986; Maddox, Amer. Ind., 8,585; Anderson, Amer., 5,046; MacBride, Libertarian, 5,042; Wright, People's, 1,124; Camejo, Soc. Workers, 905; LaRouche, U.S. Labor, 903; Hall, Com., 817; Levin, Soc. Labor, 713; Zeidler, Soc., 358.

1972: Nixon, R., 837,135; McGovern, D., 568,334; Schmitz, Amer., 58,906; Spock, Ind., 2,644; Hospers, Libertarian, 1,537; Fisher, Soc. Labor, 1,102; Jenness, Soc. Workers, 623; Hall, Com., 566.

1968: Humphrey, D., 616,037; Nixon, R., 588,510; Wallace, 3rd Party, 96,990; Cleaver, Peace and Freedom, 1,609; Blomen, Soc. Labor, 488; Mitchell, Free Ballot, 377; Halstead, Soc. Workers, 270.

1964: Johnson, D., 779,699; Goldwater, R., 470,366; Hass, Soc. Labor, 7,772; DeBerry, Freedom Soc., 537.

1960: Nixon, R., 629,273; Kennedy, D., 599,298; Hass, Soc. Labor, 10,895; Curtis, Constitution, 1,401; Dobbs, Soc. Workers, 705.

1956: Eisenhower, R., 620,430; Stevenson, D., 523,002; Hass, Soc. Labor, 7,457.

1952: Eisenhower, R., 599,107; Stevenson, D., 492,845; MacArthur, Christian Nationalist, 7,290; Hallinan, Prog., 2,460; Hass, Soc. Labor, 633; Hoopes, Soc., 254; Dobbs, Soc. Workers, 119.

1948: Truman, D., 476,165; Dewey, R., 386,315; Wallace, Prog., 31,692; Watson, Proh., 6,117; Thomas, Soc., 3,534; Teichert, Soc. Labor, 1,133; Dobbs, Soc. Workers, 103.

West Virginia

2004: Bush, R., 423,778; Kerry, D., 326,541; Nader, Ind., 4,063; Badnarik, Libertarian, 1,405.

2000: Bush, R., 336,475; Gore, D., 295,497; Nader, Green, 10,680; Buchanan, Reform, 3,169; Browne, Libertarian, 1,912; Hagelin, Natural Law, 367.

1996: Clinton, D., 327,812; Dole, R., 233,946; Perot, Ref., 71,639; Browne, Libertarian, 3,062.

1992: Clinton, D., 331,001; Bush, R., 241,974; Perot, Ind., 108,829; Marrou, Libertarian, 1,873.

1988: Dukakis, D., 341,016; Bush, R., 310,065; Fulani, New Alliance, 2,230.

1984: Reagan, R., 405,483; Mondale, D., 328,125.

1980: Carter, D., 367,462; Reagan, R., 334,206; Anderson, Ind., 31,691; Clark, Libertarian, 4,356.

1976: Carter, D., 435,864; Ford, R., 314,726.

1972: Nixon, R., 484,964; McGovern, D., 277,435.

1968: Humphrey, D., 374,091; Nixon, R., 307,555; Wallace, 3rd Party, 72,560.

1964: Johnson, D., 538,087; Goldwater, R., 253,953.

1960: Kennedy, D., 441,786; Nixon, R., 395,995.

1956: Eisenhower, R., 449,297; Stevenson, D., 381,534.

1952: Stevenson, D., 453,578; Eisenhower, R., 419,970.

1948: Truman, D., 429,188; Dewey, R., 316,251; Wallace, Prog., 3,311.

Wisconsin

2004: Kerry, D., 1,489,504; Bush, R., 1,478,120; Nader, Ind., 16,390; Badnarik, Libertarian, 6,464; Cobb, Green, 2,661; Brown, Ind., 471; Harris, Ind., 411.

2000: Gore, D., 1,242,987; Bush, R., 1,237,279; Nader, Green, 94,070; Buchanan, Reform, 11,446; Browne, Libertarian, 6,640; Phillips, Constitution, 2,042; Moorehead, Workers World, 1,063; Hagelin, Reform, 878; Harris, Soc. Workers, 306.

1996: Clinton, D., 1,071,971; Dole, R., 845,029; Perot, Ref., 227,339; Nader, Green, 28,723; Phillips, Taxpayers, 8,811; Browne, Libertarian, 7,929; Hagelin, Natural Law, 1,379; Moorehead, Workers World, 1,333; Hollis, Soc., 848; Harris, Soc. Workers, 483.

1992: Clinton, D., 1,041,066; Bush, R., 930,855; Perot, Ind., 544,479; Marrou, Libertarian, 2,877; Gritz, Populist/America First, 2,311; Daniels, Ind., 1,883; Phillips, U.S. Taxpayers, 1,772; Hagelin, Natural Law, 1,070.

1988: Dukakis, D., 1,126,794; Bush, R., 1,047,499; Paul, Lib., 5,157; Duke, Pop., 3,056.

1984: Reagan, R., 1,198,584; Mondale, D., 995,740; Bergland, Libertarian, 4,883.

1980: Reagan, R., 1,088,845; Carter, D., 981,584; Anderson, Ind., 160,657; Clark, Libertarian, 29,135; Commoner, Citizens, 7,767; Rarick, Constitution, 1,519; McReynolds, Soc., 808; Hall, Com., 772; Griswold, Workers World, 414; DeBerry, Soc. Workers, 383; scattered, 1,337.

1976: Carter, D., 1,040,232; Ford, R., 1,004,987; McCarthy, Ind., 34,943; Maddox, Amer. Ind., 8,552; Zeidler, Soc., 4,298; MacBride, Libertarian, 3,814; Camejo, Soc. Workers, 1,691; Wright, People's, 943; Hall, Com., 749; LaRouche, U.S. Lab., 738; Levin, Soc. Labor, 389; scattered, 2,839.

1972: Nixon, R., 989,430; McGovern, D., 810,174; Schmitz, Amer., 47,525; Spock, Ind., 2,701; Fisher, Soc. Labor, 998; Hall, Com., 663; Reed, Ind., 506; scattered, 893.

1968: Nixon, R., 809,997; Humphrey, D., 748,804; Wallace, 3rd Party, 127,835; Blomen, Soc. Labor, 1,338; Halstead, Soc. Workers, 1,222; scattered, 2,342.

1964: Johnson, D., 1,050,424; Goldwater, R., 638,495; DeBerry, Soc. Workers, 1,692; Hass, Soc. Labor, 1,204.

1960: Nixon, R., 895,175; Kennedy, D., 830,805; Dobbs, Soc. Workers, 1,792; Hass, Soc. Labor, 1,310.

1956: Eisenhower, R., 954,844; Stevenson, D., 586,768; Andrews, Ind., 6,918; Hoopes, Soc., 754; Hass, Soc. Labor, 710; Dobbs, Soc. Workers, 564.

1952: Eisenhower, R., 979,744; Stevenson, D., 622,175; Hallinan, Ind., 2,174; Dobbs, Ind., 1,350; Hoopes, Ind., 1,157; Hass, Ind., 770.

1948: Truman, D., 647,310; Dewey, R., 590,959; Wallace, Prog., 25,282; Thomas, Soc., 12,547; Teichert, Soc. Labor, 399; Dobbs, Soc. Workers, 303.

Wyoming

2004: Bush, R., 167,629; Kerry, D., 70,776; Nader, Ind., 2,741; Badnarik, Libertarian, 1,171; Peroutka, Ind., 631.

2000: Bush, R., 147,947; Gore, D., 60,481; Buchanan, Reform, 2,724; Browne, Libertarian, 1,443; Phillips, Ind., 720; Hagelin, Natural Law, 411.

1996: Dole, R., 105,388; Clinton, D., 77,934; Perot, Ind. (Ref.), 25,928; Browne, Libertarian, 1,739; Hagelin, Natural Law, 582.

1992: Bush, R., 79,347; Clinton, D., 68,160; Perot, Ind., 51,263.

1988: Bush, R., 106,867; Dukakis, D., 67,113; Paul, Lib., 2,026; Fulani, New Alliance, 545.

1984: Reagan, R., 133,241; Mondale, D., 53,370; Bergland, Libertarian, 2,357.

1980: Reagan, R., 110,700; Carter, D., 49,427; Anderson, Ind., 12,072; Clark, Libertarian, 4,514.

1976: Ford, R., 92,717; Carter, D., 62,239; McCarthy, Ind., 624; Reagan, Ind., 307; Anderson, Amer., 290; MacBride, Libertarian, 89; Brown, Ind., 47; Maddox, Amer. Ind., 30.

1972: Nixon, R., 100,464; McGovern, D., 44,358; Schmitz, Amer., 748.

1968: Nixon, R., 70,927; Humphrey, D., 45,173; Wallace, 3rd Party, 11,105.

1964: Johnson, D., 80,718; Goldwater, R., 61,998.

1960: Nixon, R., 77,451; Kennedy, D., 63,331.

1956: Eisenhower, R., 74,573; Stevenson, D., 49,554.

1952: Eisenhower, R., 81,047; Stevenson, D., 47,934; Hamblen, Proh., 194; Hoopes, Soc., 40; Haas, Soc. Labor, 36.

1948: Truman, D., 52,354; Dewey, R., 47,947; Wallace, Prog., 931; Thomas, Soc., 137; Teichert, Soc. Labor, 56.

The Electoral College

The president and the vice president are the only elective federal officials not chosen by direct vote of the people. They are elected by the members of the Electoral College, an institution provided for in the U.S. Constitution.

On presidential election day, the first Tuesday after the first Monday in November of every 4th year, each state chooses as many electors as it has senators and representatives in Congress. In 1964, for the first time, as provided by the 23rd Amendment to the Constitution, the District of Columbia voted for 3 electors. Thus, with 100 senators and 435 representatives, there are 538 members of the Electoral College, with a majority of 270 electoral votes needed to elect the president and vice president.

Although political parties were not part of the original plan created by the Founding Fathers, today political parties customarily nominate their slates of electors at their respective state conventions. Some states print names of the candidates for president and vice president at the top of the Nov. ballot; others list only the electors' names. In either case, the electors of the party receiving the highest vote are elected. Two states, Maine and Nebraska, allow for proportional allocation.

The electors meet on the first Monday after the 2nd Wednesday in December in their respective state capitals or in some other place prescribed by state legislatures. By long-established custom, they vote for their party nominees, although this is not required by federal law; some states do require it.

The Constitution requires electors to cast a ballot for at least one person who is not an inhabitant of that elector's home state. This ensures that presidential and vice presidential candidates from the same party will not be from the same state. (In 2000, Republican vice presidential nominee Dick Cheney changed his voter registration to Wyoming from Gov. George W. Bush's home state of Texas.) Also, an elector cannot be a member of Congress or hold federal office.

Certified and sealed lists of the votes of the electors in each state are sent to the president of the U.S. Senate, who then opens them in the presence of the members of the Senate and House of Representatives in a joint session held in early Jan., and the electoral votes of all the states are then officially counted.

If no candidate for president has a majority, the House of Representatives chooses a president from the top 3 candidates, with all representatives from each state combining to cast one vote for that state. The House decided the outcome of the 1800 and 1824 presidential elections. If no candidate for vice president has a majority, the Senate chooses from the top 2, with the senators voting as individuals. The Senate chose the vice president following the 1836 election.

Under the electoral college system, a candidate who fails to be the top vote getter in the popular vote still may win a majority of electoral votes. This happened in the elections of 1876, 1888, and 2000.

Electoral Votes for President

Electoral votes based on the 2000 Census were in force beginning with the 2004 elections.

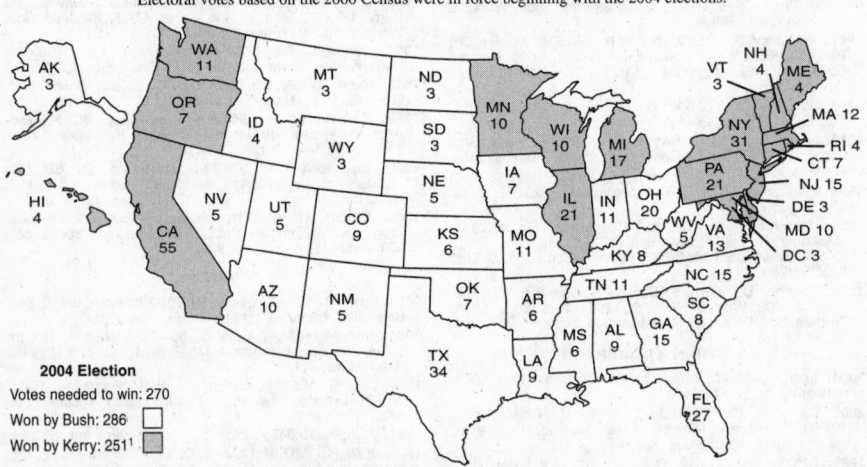

2004 Election

Votes needed to win: 270

Won by Bush: 286 ☐

Won by Kerry: 251[1] ▨

(1) A Minnesota elector pledged to Kerry voted for his running mate, Sen. John Edwards.

Voter Turnout in Presidential Elections, 1932-2004

Source: Federal Election Commission; Commission for Study of American Electorate; *Congressional Quarterly*

	Candidates	Voter Participation (% of voting-age population)		Candidates	Voter Participation (% of voting-age population)
1932	Roosevelt-Hoover	52.4	1972	Nixon-McGovern	55.2[1]
1936	Roosevelt-Landon	56.0	1976	Carter-Ford	53.5
1940	Roosevelt-Willkie	58.9	1980	Reagan-Carter	54.0
1944	Roosevelt-Dewey	56.0	1984	Reagan-Mondale	53.1
1948	Truman-Dewey	51.1	1988	Bush-Dukakis	50.2
1952	Eisenhower-Stevenson	61.6	1992	Clinton-Bush-Perot	55.9
1956	Eisenhower-Stevenson	59.3	1996	Clinton-Dole-Perot	49.0
1960	Kennedy-Nixon	62.8	2000	Bush-Gore	51.3
1964	Johnson-Goldwater	61.9	2004	Bush-Kerry	60.7
1968	Nixon-Humphrey	60.9			

(1) The sharp drop in 1972 followed the expansion of eligibility with the enfranchisement of 18- to 20-year-olds.

Major-Party Nominees for President and Vice President, 1856-2004

Asterisk (*) denotes winning ticket

	Democratic			Republican	
Year	**President**	**Vice President**	**Year**	**President**	**Vice President**
1856	James Buchanan*	John Breckinridge	1856	John Frémont	William Dayton
1860	Stephen A. Douglas (1)	Herschel V. Johnson	1860	Abraham Lincoln*	Hannibal Hamlin
1864	George McClellan	G.H. Pendleton	1864	Abraham Lincoln*	Andrew Johnson
1868	Horatio Seymour	Francis Blair	1868	Ulysses S. Grant*	Schuyler Colfax
1872	Horace Greeley	B. Gratz Brown	1872	Ulysses S. Grant*	Henry Wilson
1876	Samuel J. Tilden	Thomas Hendricks	1876	Rutherford B. Hayes*	William Wheeler
1880	Winfield Hancock	William English	1880	James A. Garfield*	Chester A. Arthur
1884	Grover Cleveland*	Thomas Hendricks	1884	James G. Blaine	John Logan
1888	Grover Cleveland	A.G. Thurman	1888	Benjamin Harrison*	Levi Morton
1892	Grover Cleveland*	Adlai Stevenson	1892	Benjamin Harrison	Whitelaw Reid
1896	William J. Bryan	Arthur Sewall	1896	William McKinley*	Garret Hobart
1900	William J. Bryan	Adlai Stevenson	1900	William McKinley*	Theodore Roosevelt
1904	Alton Parker	Henry Davis	1904	Theodore Roosevelt*	Charles Fairbanks
1908	William J. Bryan	John Kern	1908	William H. Taft*	James Sherman
1912	Woodrow Wilson*	Thomas Marshall	1912	William H. Taft	James Sherman (2)
1916	Woodrow Wilson*	Thomas Marshall	1916	Charles E. Hughes	Charles Fairbanks
1920	James M. Cox	Franklin D. Roosevelt	1920	Warren G. Harding*	Calvin Coolidge
1924	John W. Davis	Charles W. Bryan	1924	Calvin Coolidge*	Charles G. Dawes
1928	Alfred E. Smith	Joseph T. Robinson	1928	Herbert Hoover*	Charles Curtis
1932	Franklin D. Roosevelt*	John N. Garner	1932	Herbert Hoover	Charles Curtis
1936	Franklin D. Roosevelt*	John N. Garner	1936	Alfred M. Landon	Frank Knox
1940	Franklin D. Roosevelt*	Henry A. Wallace	1940	Wendell L. Willkie	Charles McNary
1944	Franklin D. Roosevelt*	Harry S. Truman	1944	Thomas E. Dewey	John W. Bricker
1948	Harry S. Truman*	Alben W. Barkley	1948	Thomas E. Dewey	Earl Warren
1952	Adlai E. Stevenson	John J. Sparkman	1952	Dwight D. Eisenhower*	Richard M. Nixon
1956	Adlai E. Stevenson	Estes Kefauver	1956	Dwight D. Eisenhower*	Richard M. Nixon
1960	John F. Kennedy*	Lyndon B. Johnson	1960	Richard M. Nixon	Henry Cabot Lodge
1964	Lyndon B. Johnson*	Hubert H. Humphrey	1964	Barry M. Goldwater	William E. Miller
1968	Hubert H. Humphrey	Edmund S. Muskie	1968	Richard M. Nixon*	Spiro T. Agnew
1972	George S. McGovern	R. Sargent Shriver Jr. (3)	1972	Richard M. Nixon*	Spiro T. Agnew
1976	Jimmy Carter*	Walter F. Mondale	1976	Gerald R. Ford	Bob Dole
1980	Jimmy Carter	Walter F. Mondale	1980	Ronald Reagan*	George H. W. Bush
1984	Walter F. Mondale	Geraldine Ferraro	1984	Ronald Reagan*	George H. W. Bush
1988	Michael S. Dukakis	Lloyd Bentsen	1988	George H.W. Bush*	Dan Quayle
1992	Bill Clinton*	Al Gore	1992	George H.W. Bush	Dan Quayle
1996	Bill Clinton*	Al Gore	1996	Bob Dole	Jack Kemp
2000	Al Gore	Joseph Lieberman	2000	George W. Bush*	Richard Cheney
2004	John Kerry	John Edwards	2004	George W. Bush*	Richard Cheney

(1) Douglas and Johnson were nominated at the Baltimore convention. An earlier convention in Charleston, SC, failed to reach a consensus and resulted in a split in the party. The Southern faction of the Democrats nominated John Breckinridge for president and Joseph Lane for vice president. (2) Died Oct. 30; replaced on ballot by Nicholas Butler. (3) Chosen by Democratic National Committee after Thomas Eagleton withdrew because of controversy over past treatments for depression.

Third-Party and Independent Presidential Candidates

Although many "third party" candidates or independents have pursued the presidency, only 10 of these from 1832 to 2000 have polled more than a million votes. In most elections since 1860, fewer than one vote in 20 has been cast for a third-party candidate. Major vote getters among third-party and independent candidates include James B. Weaver (People's Party), 1892; former Pres. Theodore Roosevelt (Progressive Party), 1912; Robert M. La Follette (Progressive Party), 1924; George C. Wallace (American Independent Party), 1968; and H. Ross Perot, as an independent in 1992 and with the Reform Party in 1996. In these 6 elections non-major-party candidates combined polled at least 10% of the vote.

Roosevelt outpolled the Republican candidate, William Howard Taft, in 1912, capturing 28% of the popular vote and 88 electoral votes. In 1948, Strom Thurmond was able to capture 39 electoral votes (from 5 Southern states); however, all third parties received only 5.75% of the popular vote in the election. Twenty years later, George Wallace's popularity in the same region allowed him to get 46 electoral votes and 13.5% of the popular vote.

In 1992 Perot captured 19% of the popular vote; however, he did not win a single state. In 1996, Perot won 8% of the popular vote; all third-party candidates combined won just over 10%. In 2000, Ralph Nader won about 3% of the vote.

Despite the difficulty in winning the presidency, independent and third-party candidates often bring attention to their most prominent issues. They can also affect the outcome between major-party candidates.

Notable Third Party and Independent Campaigns by Year

Party	Presidential nominee	Year	Issues	Strength in . . .
Anti-Masonic	William Wirt	1832	Against secret societies and oaths	PA, VT
Liberty	James G. Birney	1844	Anti-slavery	North
Free Soil	Martin Van Buren	1848	Anti-slavery	NY, OH
American (Know-Nothing)	Millard Fillmore	1856	Anti-immigrant	Northeast, South
Greenback	Peter Cooper	1876	For "cheap money," labor rights	National
Greenback	James B. Weaver	1880	For "cheap money," labor rights	National
Prohibition	John P. St. John	1884	Anti-liquor	National
People's (Populists)	James B. Weaver	1892	For "cheap money," end of national banks	South, West
Socialist	Eugene V. Debs	1900-12; 1920	For public ownership	National
Progressive (Bull Moose)	Theodore Roosevelt	1912	Against high tariffs	Midwest, West
Progressive	Robert M. La Follette	1924	Farmer and labor rights	Midwest, West
Socialist	Norman Thomas	1928-48	Liberal reforms	National
Union	William Lemke	1936	Anti-New Deal	National
States' Rights (Dixiecrats)	Strom Thurmond	1948	For states' rights	South
Progressive	Henry A. Wallace	1948	Anti-Cold War	NY, CA
American Independent	George C. Wallace	1968	For states' rights	South
American	John G. Schmitz	1972	For "law and order"	Far West, OH, LA
Liberal	John B. Anderson	1980	A 3rd choice	National
None (Independent)	H. Ross Perot	1992	Federal budget deficit	National
Reform	H. Ross Perot	1996	Deficit; campaign finance	National
Green, Independent	Ralph Nader	2000, 2004	Corporate power; domestic priorities	National

Popular and Electoral Vote for President, 1789-2004

(D) Democrat; (DR) Democratic Republican; (F) Federalist; (LR) Liberal Republican; (NR) National Republican;
(P) People's; (PR) Progressive; (R) Republican; (RF) Reform; (SR) States' Rights; (W) Whig; Asterisk (*)—See notes at bottom.

Year	President elected	Popular	Elec.	Major losing candidate(s)	Popular	Elec.
1789	George Washington (F)	Unknown	69	No opposition	—	—
1792	George Washington (F)	Unknown	132	No opposition	—	—
1796	John Adams (F)	Unknown	71	Thomas Jefferson (DR)	Unknown	68
1800*	Thomas Jefferson (DR)	Unknown	73	Aaron Burr (DR)	Unknown	73
1804	Thomas Jefferson (DR)	Unknown	162	Charles Pinckney (F)	Unknown	14
1808	James Madison (DR)	Unknown	122	Charles Pinckney (F)	Unknown	47
1812	James Madison (DR)	Unknown	128	DeWitt Clinton (F)	Unknown	89
1816	James Monroe (DR)	Unknown	183	Rufus King (F)	Unknown	34
1820	James Monroe (DR)	Unknown	231	John Quincy Adams (DR)	Unknown	1
1824*	John Quincy Adams (DR)	113,122	84	Andrew Jackson (DR)	151,271	99
				Henry Clay (DR)	46,587	37
				William H. Crawford (DR)	44,282	41
1828	Andrew Jackson (D)	642,553	178	John Quincy Adams (NR)	500,897	83
1832	Andrew Jackson (D)	701,780	219	Henry Clay (NR)	484,205	49
1836	Martin Van Buren (D)	764,176	170	William H. Harrison (W)	550,816	73
1840	William H. Harrison (W)	1,275,390	234	Martin Van Buren (D)	1,128,854	60
1844	James K. Polk (D)	1,339,494	170	Henry Clay (W)	1,300,004	105
1848	Zachary Taylor (W)	1,361,393	163	Lewis Cass (D)	1,223,460	127
				Martin Van Buren (Free Soil)	291,501	—
1852	Franklin Pierce (D)	1,607,510	254	Winfield Scott (W)	1,386,942	42
1856	James Buchanan (D)	1,836,072	174	John C. Fremont (R)	1,342,345	114
				Millard Fillmore (American)	873,053	8
1860	Abraham Lincoln (R)	1,865,908	180	Stephen A. Douglas (D)	848,019	12
				John C. Breckinridge (D)	845,763	72
				John Bell (Const. Union)	589,581	39
1864	Abraham Lincoln (R)	2,218,388	212	George McClellan (D)	1,812,807	21
1868	Ulysses S. Grant (R)	3,013,650	214	Horatio Seymour (D)	2,708,744	80
1872*	Ulysses S. Grant (R)	3,598,235	286	Horace Greeley (D-LR)	2,834,671	—
1876*	Rutherford B. Hayes (R)	4,034,311	185	Samuel J. Tilden (D)	4,288,546	184
1880	James A. Garfield (R)	4,446,158	214	Winfield S. Hancock (D)	4,444,260	155
1884	Grover Cleveland (D)	4,874,621	219	James G. Blaine (R)	4,848,936	182
1888	Benjamin Harrison (R)	5,443,892	233	Grover Cleveland (D)	5,534,488	168
1892	Grover Cleveland (D)	5,551,883	277	Benjamin Harrison (R)	5,179,244	145
				James Weaver (P)	1,027,329	22
1896	William McKinley (R)	7,108,480	271	William J. Bryan (D-P)	6,511,495	176
1900	William McKinley (R)	7,218,039	292	William J. Bryan (D)	6,358,345	155
1904	Theodore Roosevelt (R)	7,626,593	336	Alton B. Parker (D)	5,082,898	140
1908	William H. Taft (R)	7,676,258	321	William J. Bryan (D)	6,406,801	162
1912	Woodrow Wilson (D)	6,293,152	435	Theodore Roosevelt (PR)	4,119,207	88
				William H. Taft (R)	3,483,922	8
1916	Woodrow Wilson (D)	9,126,300	277	Charles E. Hughes (R)	8,546,789	254
1920	Warren G. Harding (R)	16,153,115	404	James M. Cox (D)	9,133,092	127
1924	Calvin Coolidge (R)	15,719,921	382	John W. Davis (D)	8,386,704	136
				Robert M. La Follette (PR)	4,822,856	13
1928	Herbert Hoover (R)	21,437,277	444	Alfred E. Smith (D)	15,007,698	87
1932	Franklin D. Roosevelt (D)	22,829,501	472	Herbert Hoover (R)	15,760,684	59
1936	Franklin D. Roosevelt (D)	27,757,333	523	Alfred Landon (R)	16,684,231	8
1940	Franklin D. Roosevelt (D)	27,313,041	449	Wendell Willkie (R)	22,348,480	82
1944	Franklin D. Roosevelt (D)	25,612,610	432	Thomas E. Dewey (R)	22,117,617	99
1948	Harry S. Truman (D)	24,179,345	303	Thomas E. Dewey (R)	21,991,291	189
				Strom Thurmond (SR)	1,169,021	39
				Henry A. Wallace (PR)	1,157,172	—
1952	Dwight D. Eisenhower (R)	33,936,234	442	Adlai E. Stevenson (D)	27,314,992	89
1956*	Dwight D. Eisenhower (R)	35,590,472	457	Adlai E. Stevenson (D)	26,022,752	73
1960*	John F. Kennedy (D)	34,226,731	303	Richard M. Nixon (R)	34,108,157	219
1964	Lyndon B. Johnson (D)	43,129,566	486	Barry M. Goldwater (R)	27,178,188	52
1968	Richard M. Nixon (R)	31,785,480	301	Hubert H. Humphrey (D)	31,275,166	191
				George C. Wallace (3rd party)	9,906,473	46
1972*	Richard M. Nixon (R)	47,169,911	520	George S. McGovern (D)	29,170,383	17
1976*	Jimmy Carter (D)	40,830,763	297	Gerald R. Ford (R)	39,147,793	240
1980	Ronald Reagan (R)	43,904,153	489	Jimmy Carter (D)	35,483,883	49
				John B. Anderson (independent)	5,719,437	—
1984	Ronald Reagan (R)	54,455,075	525	Walter F. Mondale (D)	37,577,185	13
1988*	George H. W. Bush (R)	48,886,097	426	Michael S. Dukakis (D)	41,809,074	111
1992	Bill Clinton (D)	44,908,254	370	George H. W. Bush (R)	39,102,343	168
				H. Ross Perot (independent)	19,741,065	—
1996	Bill Clinton (D)	45,590,703	379	Bob Dole (R)	37,816,307	159
				H. Ross Perot (RF)	7,866,284	—
2000*	George W. Bush (R)	50,459,211	271	Al Gore (D)	51,003,894	266
				Ralph Nader (Green)	2,834,410	—
2004*	George W. Bush (R)	62,040,610	286	John Kerry (D)	59,028,444	251
				Ralph Nader (Independent)	411,306	—

*1800—Elected by House of Representatives because of tied electoral vote. 1824—Elected by House of Representatives because no candidate had polled a majority. By 1824, the Democratic Republicans had become a loose coalition of competing political groups. By 1828, the supporters of Jackson were known as Democrats, and the John Q. Adams and Henry Clay supporters as National Republicans. 1872—Greeley died Nov. 29, 1872. His electoral votes were split among 4 individuals. 1876—FL, LA, OR, and SC election returns were disputed. Congress in joint session (Mar. 2, 1877) declared Hayes and Wheeler elected president and vice president. 1956—Democrats elected 74 electors, but one from Alabama refused to vote for Stevenson. 1960—Sen. Harry F. Byrd (D, VA) received 15 electoral votes. 1972—John Hospers of California received one vote from an elector of Virginia. 1976—Ronald Reagan of CA received one vote from an elector of Washington. 1988—Sen. Lloyd Bentsen (D, TX) received 1 vote from an elector of West Virginia. 2000—One Gore elector from Washington, DC, abstained. Nader was listed as "Independent" on the ballot in some states, and was not on the ballot in all states. 2004—One Minnesota elector voted for VP candidate John Edwards for both president and vice president.

100 MOST POPULOUS U.S. CITIES

Source: Bureau of Labor Statistics: employment; Bureau of Econ. Analysis: per cap. income; other data U.S. Census Bureau.

Included here are the 100 most populous U.S. cities, using 2006 Census Bureau estimates. Population rank indicated by figure in parentheses. Most data are for the city proper. Some statistics, where noted, apply to the whole Metropolitan Statistical Area (MSA). Employment figures are for 2006 (except for New Orleans, LA); per capita income figures for 2005. Mayors are as of Sept. 2007. Inc.=incorporated; est.=established. **Note:** Websites are as of Sept. 2007 and subject to change. For a listing of the 100 largest U.S. cities, ranked by population, *see* p. 479.

Akron, Ohio

Population (2006): 209,704 (92); **Pop. density:** 3,377; **Pop. change (2000-2006):** –3.4%. **Area:** 62.1 sq mi. **Employment (2006):** 101,258 employed; 5.9% unemployed. **Per capita income (MSA):** $33,396; increase (2004-2005): 3.8%.

Mayor: Donald L. Plusquellic, Democrat

History: settled 1825; inc. as city 1865; located on Ohio-Erie Canal and is a port of entry; polymer center of the Americas.

Transportation: 1 intl., 1 regional airport; major trucking industry; Conrail, Amtrak; metro transit system. **Communications:** 6 TV, 8 radio stations; 1 daily newspaper. **Medical facilities:** 6 hosp. **Educational facilities:** 1 univ. and colleges, 57 pub. schools. **Further information:** Greater Akron Chamber, One Cascade Plaza, 17th Floor, Akron, OH 44308; www.ci.akron.oh.us; www.greaterakronchamber.com

Albuquerque, New Mexico

Population (2006): 504,949 (33); **Pop. density:** 2,796; **Pop. change (2000-2006):** 12.6%. **Area:** 180.6 sq mi. **Employment (2006):** 252,382 employed; 3.6% unemployed. **Per capita income (MSA):** $30,884; increase (2004-2005): 3.5%.

Mayor: Martin J. Chavez, Democrat

History: founded 1706 by the Spanish; inc. 1890.

Transportation: 1 intl. airport; 1 railroad; bus system. **Communications:** 15 TV, 24 radio stations, 1 daily newspaper. **Medical facilities:** 19 major hosp. **Educational facilities:** 132 pub. schools, 1 univ., 25 colleges. **Further information:** Albuquerque Convention & Visitors Bureau, PO Box 26866, Albuquerque, NM 87125-6866; www.itsatrip.org; www.cabq.gov

Anaheim, California

Population (2006): 334,425 (54); **Pop. density:** 6,839; **Pop. change (2000-2006):** 1.7%. **Area:** 48.9 sq mi. **Employment (2006):** 167,659 employed; 4.4% unemployed. **Per capita income (MSA):** $36,746; increase (2004-2005): 4.6%.

Mayor: Curt Pringle, Republican

History: founded 1857; inc. 1870; home of Disneyland Resort, the Mighty Ducks of Anaheim, and the Los Angeles Angels of Anaheim.

Transportation: Amtrak, Metrolink (2 sta.), OCTA bus service. **Communications:** 1 daily newspaper, 2 TV, 2 radio stations (MSA). **Medical facilities:** 5 hosp.; 5 medical centers. **Educational facilities:** 22 colleges and trade schools, 60 pub. schools. **Further information:** City Hall, 200 South Anaheim Blvd., Ste. 733, Anaheim, CA 92805; www.anaheim.net; www.anaheimoc.org

Anchorage, Alaska

Population (2006): 278,700 (65); **Pop. density:** 164; **Pop. change (2000-2006):** 7.1%. **Area:** 1,697.20 sq mi. **Employment (2006):** 142,853 employed; 5.3% unemployed. **Per capita income (MSA):** $38,421; increase (2004-2005): 4.4%.

Mayor: Mark Begich, Democrat

History: founded 1914 as a construction camp for railroad; HQ of Alaska Defense Command, WWII; severely damaged in earthquake 1964, now rebuilt; current population center of Alaska.

Transportation: 1 intl., 1 regional airport; 2 seaplane bases; 2 airfields; 1 railroad; transit system, 1 port. **Communications:** 1 daily newspaper, 13 TV, 25 radio stations. **Medical facilities:** 5 hosp. **Educational facilities:** 2 univ., 8 trade schools/colleges, 96 pub. schools. **Further information:** Anchorage Chamber of Commerce, 1016 W 6th Ave., Ste. 303, Anchorage, AK, 99501; www.muni.org; www.anchoragechamber.org

Arlington, Texas

Population (2006): 367,197 (49); **Pop. density:** 3,833; **Pop. change (2000-2006):** 10.2%. **Area:** 95.8 sq mi. **Employment (2006):** 197,725 employed; 4.5% unemployed. **Per capita income (MSA):** $37,209; increase (2004-2005): 4.8%.

Mayor: Robert N. Cluck, Republican

History: settled in 1840s; inc. 1884.

Transportation: 1 mun. airport; freight railways. **Communications:** 2 TV, 1 radio station. **Medical facilities:** 7 hosp. **Educational facilities:** 1 univ., 8 colleges and trade schools, 74 pub. schools. **Further information:** Arlington Chamber of Commerce, 505 E. Border St., Arlington, TX 76010; City of Arlington, 101 W. Abram, Arlington, TX 76010; www.ci.arlington.tx.us; www.arlingtontx.com

Atlanta, Georgia

Population (2006): 486,411 (34); **Pop. density:** 3,693; **Pop. change (2000-2006):** 16.8%. **Area:** 131.7 sq mi. **Employment (2006):** 210,992 employed; 5.2% unemployed. **Per capita income (MSA):** $34,825; increase (2004-2005): 3.8%.

Mayor: Shirley Franklin, Democrat

History: founded as "Terminus" 1837; renamed Atlanta 1845; inc. 1847; played major role in Civil War; became permanent state capital 1877; birthplace of civil rights movement; host to 1996 Centennial Olympic Games.

Transportation: 1 intl., 1 regional airport; 3 railroad lines; MARTA bus and rapid rail service. **Communications:** 3 daily newspapers, 21 TV, 24 radio stations. **Medical facilities:** 19 hosp.; VA hosp.; U.S. Centers for Disease Control and Prevention; American Cancer Society. **Educational facilities:** 6 univ., 10 colleges; 89 pub. schools. **Further information:** Metro Atlanta Chamber of Commerce, 235 Andrew Young Intl. Blvd. NW, Atlanta, GA 30303; www.metroatlantachamber.com; www.atlantaga.gov

Aurora, Colorado

Population (2006): 303,582 (59); **Pop. density:** 2,130; **Pop. change (2000-2006):** 10.0%. **Area:** 142.5 sq mi. **Employment (2006):** 161,921 employed; 5.3% unemployed. **Per capita income (MSA):** $42,369; increase (2004-2005): 4.4%.

Mayor: Ed Tauer, Republican

History: founded in 1891 and originally called Fletcher; renamed Aurora in 1907; inc. 1929. Early growth stimulated by presence of military bases; fast-growing trade, technology, and medical science center.

Transportation: adjacent to Denver Intl. Airport; bus system. **Communications:** 1 daily newspaper, 2 TV, 3 radio stations. **Medical facilities:** 3 hosp. **Educational facilities:** 2 univ., 6 colleges and technical schools, 49 pub. schools, 4 private schools. **Further information:** Aurora Planning Dept., 15151 E. Alameda Pkwy., Aurora, CO 80012; www.auroragov.org; www.aurorachamber.org

Austin, Texas

Population (2006): 709,893 (16); **Pop. density:** 2,823; **Pop. change (2000-2006):** 7.6%. **Area:** 251.5 sq mi. **Employment (2006):** 393,661 employed; 3.9% unemployed. **Per capita income (MSA):** $34,441; increase (2004-2005): 5.2%.

Mayor: Will Wynn, Non-Partisan

History: first permanent settlement 1835; capital of Rep. of Texas 1839; named after Stephen Austin; inc. 1840.

Transportation: 1 intl. airport; 2 railroads; bus system. **Communications:** 2 daily newspapers, 15 TV, 12 radio stations. **Medical facilities:** 20 hosp. **Educational facilities:** 4 univ., 17 colleges and trade schools. **Further information:** Greater Austin Chamber, 210 Barton Springs Rd., Ste. 400, Austin, TX 78704; www.austinchamber.com; www.austintexas.org

Bakersfield, California

Population (2006): 308,392 (58); **Pop. density:** 2,727; **Pop. change (2000-2006):** 26.7%. **Area:** 113.1 sq mi. **Employment (2006):** 137,165 employed; 5.2% unemployed. **Per capita income (MSA):** $24,999; increase (2004-2005): 3.9%.

Mayor: Harvey L. Hall, Non-Partisan

History: named after Col. Thomas Baker, an early settler; inc. 1898.

Transportation: 2 airports; 3 railroads; local bus system. **Communications:** 1 daily newspaper, 20 TV, 20 radio stations. **Medical facilities:** 7 hosp. **Educational facilities:** 4 univ., 5 colleges/technical schools, 43 public schools. **Further information:** Greater Bakersfield Chamber of Commerce, 1725 Eye St., Bakersfield, CA 93301; www.bakersfieldchamber.org; www.bakersfieldcity.us

Baltimore, Maryland

Population (2006): 631,366 (19); **Pop. density:** 7,814; **Pop. change (2000-2006):** –3.0%. **Area:** 80.8 sq mi. **Employment (2006):** 262,024 employed; 6.4% unemployed. **Per capita income (MSA):** $41,320; increase (2004-2005): 5.9%.

Mayor: Sheila Dixon, Democrat

History: founded by Maryland legislature 1729; inc. 1797; War of 1812 British artillery barrage of Ft. McHenry (1814) inspired Francis Scott Key to write "Star-Spangled Banner"; birthplace of America's railroads 1828; rebuilt after fire 1904; site of National Aquarium 1981.

Transportation: 1 intl. airport; 3 railroads; bus system; subway system; light rail system; Inner Harbor water taxi system; 2

underwater tunnels. **Communications:** 3 daily newspapers, 8 TV, 21 radio stations. **Medical facilities:** 23 hosp. **Educational facilities:** 12 univ., 18 colleges and trade schools; 203 pub. schools. **Further information:** Greater Baltimore Committee, 111 S. Calvert St., Ste. 1700, Baltimore, MD 21202-6180; www.gbc.org; www.baltimore.org

Baton Rouge, Louisiana

Population (2006): 229,553 (79); **Pop. density:** 2,989; **Pop. change (2000-2006):** 0.7%. **Area:** 76.8 sq mi. **Employment (2006):** 106,017 employed; 4.1% unemployed. **Per capita income (MSA):** $29,654; increase (2004-2005): 6.7%.

Mayor: Melvin "Kip" Holden, Democrat

History: claimed by Spain at time of Louisiana Purchase 1803; est. independence by rebellion 1810; inc. as town 1817; became state capital 1849; Union-held most of Civil War.

Transportation: 1 airport; 1 bus line; 3 railroad trunk lines. **Communications:** 1 daily newspaper, 13 TV, 18 radio stations. **Medical facilities:** 17 hosp. **Educational facilities:** 2 univ., 24 colleges and trade schools; 94 pub., 52 priv. schools. **Further information:** The Chamber of Greater Baton Rouge, 564 Laurel St., Baton Rouge, LA, 70801; www.brgov.com; www.brac.org

Birmingham, Alabama

Population (2006): 229,424 (80); **Pop. density:** 1,531; **Pop. change (2000-2006):** –5.4%. **Area:** 149.9 sq mi. **Employment (2006):** 99,515 employed; 4.4% unemployed. **Per capita income (MSA):** $35,663; increase (2004-2005): 5.5%.

Mayor: Bernard Kincaid, Democrat

History: settled 1871 at the intersection of 2 major railroads, within proximity of elements needed for iron and steel production.

Transportation: 1 intl. airport; 4 major rail freight lines, Amtrak; 1 bus line; 75 truck line terminals; 5 air cargo cos.; 7 barge lines. **Communications:** 1 daily newspaper, 9 TV, 21 radio stations; 1 educational TV, 1 educational radio station. **Medical facilities:** 16 hosp., VA hosp. **Educational facilities:** 66 pub. schools, 7 univ., 16 colleges. **Further information:** Birmingham Area Chamber of Commerce, 505 N. 20th St., Birmingham, AL, 35203; www.birminghamchamber.com; www.informationbirmingham.com

Boston, Massachusetts

Population (2006): 590,763 (22); **Pop. density:** 12,206; **Pop. change (2000-2006):** 0.3%. **Area:** 48.4 sq mi. **Employment (2006):** 274,451 employed; 5.3% unemployed. **Per capita income (MSA):** $47,168; increase (2004-2005): 4.4%.

Mayor: Thomas M. Menino, Democrat

History: settled 1630 by John Winthrop; capital of Mass. Bay Colony; figured strongly in Am. Revolution, earning distinction as the "Cradle of Liberty"; inc. 1822.

Transportation: 1 intl. airport; 2 railroads; city rail and subway system; 3 underwater tunnels; port. **Communications:** 3 daily newspapers, 11 TV, 21 radio stations. **Medical facilities:** 39 hosp. **Educational facilities:** 31 univ. and colleges. **Further information:** Greater Boston Convention and Visitors Bureau, 2 Copley Pl., Suite 105, Boston, MA 02116; www.bostonusa.com; www.cityofboston.gov

Buffalo, New York

Population (2006): 276,059 (66); **Pop. density:** 6,799; **Pop. change (2000-2006):** –5.7%. **Area:** 40.6 sq mi. **Employment (2006):** 115,769 employed; 6.1% unemployed. **Per capita income (MSA):** $32,071; increase (2004-2005): 3.7%.

Mayor: Byron W. Brown, Democrat

History: settled 1780 by Seneca Indians; raided twice by British, War of 1812; served as western terminus for Erie Canal, became a center for trade and manufacturing; inc. 1832; last stop on the Underground Railroad; key point for Canada-U.S. political, trade, and social relations.

Transportation: 1 intl. airport; 4 Class I railroads; Amtrak metro rail system; water service to Great Lakes-St. Lawrence Seaway system and Atlantic seaboard. **Communications:** 12 TV, 18 radio stations. **Medical facilities:** 16 hosp., 40 research centers. **Educational facilities:** 15 colleges and univ.; 71 pub. schools. **Further information:** Buffalo Niagara Visitor Center, Market Arcade/Walden Galleria, 617 Main Street, Ste. 200, Buffalo, NY 14203; www.ci.buffalo.ny.us; buffaloniagara.org

Chandler, Arizona

Population (2006): 240,595 (76); **Pop. density:** 4,155; **Pop. change (2000-2006):** 35.9%. **Area:** 57.9 sq mi. **Employment (2006):** 121,035 employed; 2.7% unemployed. **Per capita income (MSA):** $32,414; increase (2004-2005): 4.9%.

Mayor: Boyd W. Dunn, Non-Partisan

History: town formed 1912; population doubled in 1990s as "the high-tech oasis of the Silicon Desert."

Transportation: 1 muni. airport; mass transit system. **Communications:** 2 TV, 1 radio station. **Medical facilities:** 2 hosp. **Educational facilities:** 2 univ., 1 community coll.; 25 elem., 6 junior high, 3 high schools; 13 charter schools **Further information:** Chandler Chamber, 25 South Arizona Pl., Suite 201, Chandler, AZ 85225; www.chandlerchamber.com; www.chandleraz.gov

Charlotte, North Carolina

Population (2006): 630,478 (20); **Pop. density:** 2,602; **Pop. change (2000-2006):** 11.2%. **Area:** 242.3 sq mi. **Employment (2006):** 325,793 employed; 4.2% unemployed. **Per capita income (MSA):** $36,761; increase (2004-2005): 4.8%.

Mayor: Patrick McCrory, Republican

History: settled by Scotch-Irish immigrants 1740s; inc. 1768 and named after Queen Charlotte, George III's wife; scene of first major U.S. gold discovery 1799.

Transportation: 1 intl. airport; 2 major railway lines; 1 bus line; 605 trucking firms. **Communications:** 2 daily newspapers, 8 TV, 13 radio stations. **Medical facilities:** 8 hosp. **Educational facilities:** 9 univ., 9 colleges, 94 elem. schools, 32 middle schools, 25 high schools. **Further information:** Chamber of Commerce, PO Box 32785, Charlotte, NC 28232; www.charlottechamber.com

Chesapeake, Virginia

Population (2006): 220,560 (84); **Pop. density:** 647; **Pop. change (2000-2006):** 10.7%. **Area:** 340.7 sq mi. **Employment (2006):** 110,321 employed; 3.2% unemployed. **Per capita income (MSA):** $33,163; increase (2004-2005): 5.0%.

Mayor: Dalton S. Edge, Republican

History: region settled in 1620s with first English colonies on banks of Elizabeth River; home to Great Dismal Swamp Canal, first envisioned by George Washington in 1763; Battle of Great Bridge fought here Dec. 1775; inc. as a city 1963.

Transportation: Freight rail service; bus service; 2 regional airports. **Communications:** 3 TV, 5 radio stations. **Medical facilities:** 1 hosp. **Educational facilities:** 6 colleges and univ.; 56 pub. schools and educational centers. **Further information:** City of Chesapeake, Public Communications Dept., 306 Cedar Rd., Chesapeake, VA 23322; www.cityofchesapeake.net

Chicago, Illinois

Population (2006): 2,833,321 (3); **Pop. density:** 12,476; **Pop. change (2000-2006):** –2.2%. **Area:** 227.1 sq mi. **Employment (2006):** 1,255,442 employed; 5.2% unemployed. **Per capita income (MSA):** $38,951; increase (2004-2005): 4.5%.

Mayor: Richard M. Daley, Democrat

History: site acquired from Indians 1795; significant white settlement began with Erie Canal 1825; chartered as city 1837; boomed with arrival of railroads and canal to Mississippi R.; one-third of city destroyed by fire 1871; major grain and livestock market.

Transportation: 2 intl. airports; major railroad system, trucking industry. **Communications:** 16 TV, 38 radio stations. **Medical facilities:** 44 hosp. **Educational facilities:** 63 insts. of higher learning, 623 pub. schools. **Further information:** Chicagoland Chamber of Commerce, Aon Center, 200 E. Randolph St., Ste. 2200, Chicago, IL 60601-6436; www.cityofchicago.org; www.chicagolandchamber.com

Chula Vista, California

Population (2006): 212,756 (89); **Pop. density:** 4,351; **Pop. change (2000-2006):** 22.6%. **Area:** 48.9 sq mi. **Employment (2006):** 84,188 employed; 4.7% unemployed. **Per capita income (MSA):** $40,569; increase (2004-2005): 5.3%.

Mayor: Cheryl Cox, Republican

History: visited by Spanish in 1542; became part of Spanish land grant in 1795; came into the U.S. during the Mexican War in 1847; inc. 1911. WWII brought aircraft industry and growth.

Transportation: bus system; DART. **Communications:** See San Diego, CA. **Medical facilities:** 2 hosp. **Educational facilities:** 65 pub. schools, 5 colleges. **Further information:** Chula Vista Chamber of Commerce, 233 Fourth Ave., Chula Vista, CA 91910. www.chulavistachamber.org

Cincinnati, Ohio

Population (2006): 332,252 (56); **Pop. density:** 4,260; **Pop. change (2000-2006):** 0.3%. **Area:** 78 sq mi. **Employment (2006):** 145,838 employed; 5.7% unemployed. **Per capita income (MSA):** $34,961; increase (2004-2005): 3.6%.

Mayor: Mark Mallory, Democrat

History: founded 1788 and named after the Society of Cincinnati, an organization of Revolutionary War officers; chartered as village 1802; inc. as city 1819.

Transportation: 1 intl., 2 muni. airports; 3 railroads; 2 bus systems. **Communications:** 3 daily newspapers, 9 TV, 17 radio stations. **Medical facilities:** 28 hosp.; Cincinnati Children's

Hosp. Medical Center; VA hosp. **Educational facilities:** 65 pub. schools; 4 univ., 12 colleges, 8 technical & 2-year colleges. **Further information:** Chamber of Commerce, 441 Vine St., Ste. 300, Cincinnati, OH 45202; www.cincinnatichamber.com; www.cincinnatiusa.com

Cleveland, Ohio

Population (2006): 444,313 (40); **Pop. density:** 5,726; **Pop. change (2000-2006):** –6.9%. **Area:** 77.6 sq mi. **Employment (2006):** 175,639 employed; 7.1% unemployed. **Per capita income (MSA):** $35,423; increase (2004-2005): 3.9%.

Mayor: Frank G. Jackson, Democrat

History: surveyed in 1796; given recognition as village 1815, inc. as city 1836; annexed Ohio City 1854.

Transportation: 1 intl., 2 muni. airports; rail service; major port; rapid transit system. **Communications:** 10 TV, 23 radio stations. **Medical facilities:** 14 hosp. **Educational facilities:** 8 univ. and colleges; 127 pub. schools. **Further information:** Greater Cleveland Partnership, The Highbee Building, 100 Public Sq., Ste. 210, Cleveland, OH 44113-2291; www.city.cleveland.oh.us; www.gcpartnership.com

Colorado Springs, Colorado

Population (2006): 372,437 (48); **Pop. density:** 2,006; **Pop. change (2000-2006):** 3.1%. **Area:** 185.7 sq mi. **Employment (2006):** 205,182 employed; 4.5% unemployed. **Per capita income (MSA):** $33,569; increase (2004-2005): 5.8%.

Mayor: Lionel Rivera, Republican

History: founded 1871 at the foot of Pike's Peak; inc. 1872.

Transportation: 2 muni. airports; 1 bus line. **Communications:** 7 TV, 17radio stations. **Medical facilities:** 6 hosp. **Educational facilities:** 11 univ., 5 colleges; 185 public schools. **Further information:** Chamber of Commerce, 2 N. Cascade Ave., Ste. 110, Colorado Springs, CO 80903; www.springs gov.com; www.coloradospringschamber.org

Columbus, Ohio

Population (2006): 733,203 (15); **Pop. density:** 3,486; **Pop. change (2000-2006):** 3.0%. **Area:** 210.3 sq mi. **Employment (2006):** 392,316 employed; 4.7% unemployed. **Per capita income (MSA):** $34,960; increase (2004-2005): 3.7%.

Mayor: Michael B. Coleman, Democrat

History: first settlement 1797; laid out as new capital 1812 with current name; became city 1834.

Transportation: 2 intl., 2 muni. airports, 2 airfields; 2 railroads; 2 intercity bus lines. **Communications:** 13 TV, 20 radio stations. **Medical facilities:** 13 hosp. **Educational facilities:** 11 univ. and colleges; 8 technical/2-year schools; 128 pub. schools. **Further information:** Greater Columbus Chamber of Commerce, 37 N. High St., Columbus, OH 43215. Experience Columbus, 90 N. High St., Columbus, OH 43215; www.columbus-chamber.org; www.experiencecolumbus.org; www.cityofcolumbus.org

Corpus Christi, Texas

Population (2006): 285,267 (63); **Pop. density:** 1,845; **Pop. change (2000-2006):** 2.8%. **Area:** 154.6 sq mi. **Employment (2006):** 136,822 employed; 4.8% unemployed. **Per capita income (MSA):** $28,603; increase (2004-2005): 5.7%.

Mayor: Henry Garrett, Non-Partisan

History: settled 1839 and inc. 1852.

Transportation: 1 intl. airport; 2 bus lines, metro bus system; 3 freight railroads. **Communications:** 23 TV, 15 radio stations. **Medical facilities:** 8 hosp. **Educational facilities:** 2 univ., 1 college, 60 pub. schools. **Further information:** Corpus Christi Regional Economic Development Corp., One Shoreline Plz., 800 N. Shoreline Bl., Ste. 1300 South, Corpus Christi, TX 78401; www.ccredc.com; www.cctexas.com

Dallas, Texas

Population (2006): 1,232,940 (9); **Pop. density:** 3,600; **Pop. change (2000-2006):** 3.7%. **Area:** 342.5 sq mi. **Employment (2006):** 573,002 employed; 5.2% unemployed. **Per capita income (MSA):** $37,209; increase (2004-2005): 4.8%.

Mayor: Tom Leppert, Republican

History: first settled 1841; platted 1846; inc. 1871; developed as the financial and commercial center of Southwest; headquarters of regional Federal Reserve Bank; major center for distribution and high-tech manufacturing.

Transportation: 1 intl., 1 natl., 1 muni. airport, 1 charter/corp. airport, 2 airfields; Amtrak; transit system. **Communications:** 11 TV, 19 radio stations. **Medical facilities:** 33 hosp. **Educational facilities:** 225 pub. schools, 12 univ. and colleges, 3 community college campuses. **Further information:** Greater Dallas Chamber, Resource Center, 700 N. Pearl St., Ste. 1200, Dallas, TX 75201; www.dallaschamber.org; www.dallascityhall.com

Denver, Colorado

Population (2006): 566,974 (26); **Pop. density:** 3,696; **Pop. change (2000-2006):** 2.4%. **Area:** 153.4 sq mi. **Employment (2006):** 295,796 employed; 4.9% unemployed. **Per capita income (MSA):** $42,369; increase (2004-2005): 4.4%.

Mayor: John W. Hickenlooper, Democrat

History: settled 1858 by gold prospectors and miners; inc. 1861; became territorial capital 1867; growth spurred by gold and silver boom; became financial, industrial, cultural center of Rocky Mt. region.

Transportation: 1 intl., 1 regional, 2 muni. airports; 5 rail freight lines, Amtrak; 1 bus line. **Communications:** 22 TV, 23 radio stations. **Medical facilities:** 15 hosp. **Educational facilities:** 15 four-yr. colleges and univ.; 8 two-yr. and community colleges; 151 pub. schools. **Further information:** Denver Metro Chamber of Commerce, 1445 Market St., Denver, CO 80202-1729; www.denverchamber.org; www.denvergov.org

Detroit, Michigan

Population (2006): 871,121 (11); **Pop. density:** 6,276; **Pop. change (2000-2006):** –8.4%. **Area:** 138.8 sq mi. **Employment (2006):** 317,997 employed; 13.7% unemployed. **Per capita income (MSA):** $37,515; increase (2004-2005): 3.9%.

Mayor: Kwame M. Kilpatrick, Democrat

History: founded by French 1701; controlled by British 1760; acquired by U.S. 1796; destroyed by fire 1805; fought over during War of 1812; inc. as city 1815; capital of state 1837-47; auto manufacturing began 1890.

Transportation: 1 intl., 1 muni. airport; 10 railroads (4 Class I); major intl. port; pub. transit system. **Communications:** 11 TV, 23 radio stations. **Medical facilities:** 14 hosp. **Educational facilities:** 2 univ., 3 colleges, 1 community college, 227 pub. schools. **Further information:** Detroit Regional Chamber, One Woodward Ave., Ste. 1900, PO Box 33840, Detroit, MI 48232-0840; www.detroitchamber.com, www.detroitmi.gov

Durham, North Carolina

Population (2006): 209,009 (93); **Pop. density:** 2,209; **Pop. change (2000-2006):** 11.3%. **Area:** 94.6 sq mi. **Employment (2006):** 108,912 employed; 3.8% unemployed. **Per capita income (MSA):** $35,097; increase (2004-2005): 3.4%.

Mayor: William V. Bell, Democrat

History: Inc. 1869; Trinity College moved to Durham in 1892, renamed Duke Univ. in 1924.

Transportation: 2 area bus systems; 1 intl. airport; 1 train station. **Communications:** 5 TV, 8 radio stations. **Medical facilities:** 5 hosp. **Educational facilities:** 46 pub. schools; 1 comm. coll.; school of nursing; 2 univ. **Further information:** Durham Convention and Visitors Bureau, 101 E. Morgan St., Durham, NC 2770-3333; www.durham-nc.com; www.ci.durham.nc.us

El Paso, Texas

Population (2006): 609,415 (21); **Pop. density:** 2,446; **Pop. change (2000-2006):** 8.1%. **Area:** 249.1 sq mi. **Employment (2006):** 237,149 employed; 6.3% unemployed. **Per capita income (MSA):** $23,256; increase (2004-2005): 5.4%.

Mayor: John Cook, Non-Partisan

History: first settled 1598; inc. 1873; arrival of railroad 1881 boosted city's population and industries.

Transportation: 1 intl. airport, 1 airfield; 2 rail providers; 4 intl. ports of entry. **Communications:** 9 TV, 22 radio stations. **Medical facilities:** 16 hosp. **Educational facilities:** 5 univ., 2 colleges; 2 grad. and doctoral programs; 92 pub. schools. **Further information:** Greater El Paso Chamber of Commerce, 10 Civic Center Plaza, El Paso, TX 79901; www.elpaso.org; www.elpaso texas.gov

Fort Wayne, Indiana

Population (2006): 248,637 (70); **Pop. density:** 3,147; **Pop. change (2000-2006):** –0.6%. **Area:** 79 sq mi. **Employment (2006):** 110,771 employed; 5.3% unemployed. **Per capita income (MSA):** $31,223; increase (2004-2005): 3.4%.

Mayor: Graham A. Richard, Democrat

History: French fort 1680; U.S. fort 1794; settled by 1832; inc. 1840 prior to Wabash-Erie canal completion 1843.

Transportation: 1 intl. airport, 1 airfield; 3 railroads; 6 bus lines. **Communications:** 6 TV, 16 radio stations, 11 newspapers. **Medical facilities:** 7 hosp. **Educational facilities:** 5 univ., 4 colleges, 3 bus. schools; 53 pub. schools. **Further information:** Chamber of Commerce, 826 Ewing Street, Fort Wayne, IN 46802-2182; www.fwchamber.org; www.ci.ft-wayne.in.us

Fort Worth, Texas

Population (2006): 653,320 (18); **Pop. density:** 2,234; **Pop. change (2000-2006):** 20.7%. **Area:** 292.5 sq mi. **Employment (2006):** 289,465 employed; 5% unemployed. **Per capita income (MSA):** $37,209; increase (2004-2005): 4.8%.

Mayor: Mike J. Moncrief, Democrat

History: established as military post 1849; inc. 1873; oil discovered 1917.

Transportation: 2 intl. airport, 2 muni. airports, 4 airfields, 1 industrial airport; 4 major railroads, Amtrak; local bus service; 1 transcontinental, 1 intrastate bus lines. **Communications:** 7 TV, 11 radio stations. **Medical facilities:** 15 hosp. **Educational facilities:** 5 univ. and colleges, 144 pub. schools. **Further information:** Chamber of Commerce, 777 Taylor St. #900, Fort Worth, TX 76102; www.fortworthgov.org; www.fortworthchamber.com

Fremont, California

Population (2006): 201,691 (97); **Pop. density:** 2,630; **Pop. change (2000-2006):** −0.8%. **Area:** 76.7 sq mi. **Employment (2006):** 105,629 employed; 3.1% unemployed. **Per capita income (MSA):** $52,543; increase (2004-2005): 5.1%.

Mayor: Bob Wasserman, Non-Partisan

History: area first settled by Spanish 1769; inc. 1956 with consolidation of 5 communities.

Transportation: intracity bus line; Bay Area Rapid Transit System (southern terminal). **Communications:** 2 radio stations. **Medical facilities:** 2 hosp.; 2 major medical centers; 18 clinics. **Educational facilities:** 1 community college; 51 pub. schools. **Further information:** Chamber of Commerce, 39488 Stevenson Place, Ste. 100, Fremont, CA 94539; www.fremont business.com

Fresno, California

Population (2006): 466,714 (36); **Pop. density:** 4,470; **Pop. change (2000-2006):** 8.8%. **Area:** 104.4 sq mi. **Employment (2006):** 202,401 employed; 7.5% unemployed. **Per capita income (MSA):** $25,961; increase (2004-2005): 2.8%.

Mayor: Alan Autry, Non-Partisan

History: founded 1872; inc. as city 1885.

Transportation: 1 intl. airport, 1 corp/charter airport, 1 muni. airport; Amtrak; 1 bus line; intra-city bus system. **Communications:** 16 TV, 26 radio stations. **Medical facilities:** 9 hosp. **Educational facilities:** 9 colleges; 88 pub. schools. **Further information:** Greater Fresno Area Chamber of Commerce, 2331 Fresno St., Fresno, CA 93721; www.fresnochamber.com; www.fresno.gov

Garland, Texas

Population (2006): 217,963 (86); **Pop. density:** 3,817; **Pop. change (2000-2006):** 1.0%. **Area:** 57.1 sq mi. **Employment (2006):** 108,810 employed; 4.9% unemployed. **Per capita income (MSA):** $37,209; increase (2004-2005): 4.8%.

Mayor: Ronald Jones, Non-Partisan

History: settled 1850s; inc. 1891.

Transportation: 30 min. from Dallas/Ft. Worth Intl. Airport; 2 railroads. **Communications:** 2 TV, 2 radio stations. **Medical facilities:** 2 hosp. **Educational facilities:** 3 univ., 2 community colleges; 67 pub. schools. **Further information:** Chamber of Commerce, 914 S. Garland Ave., Garland, TX 75040; www.garlandchamber.com; www.ci.garland.tx.us

Glendale, Arizona

Population (2006): 246,531 (72); **Pop. density:** 4,426; **Pop. change (2000-2006):** 12.7%. **Area:** 55.7 sq mi. **Employment (2006):** 135,105 employed; 3.6% unemployed. **Per capita income (MSA):** $32,414; increase (2004-2005): 4.9%.

Mayor: Elaine M. Scruggs, Non-Partisan

History: est. 1892; inc. 1910.

Transportation: 1 muni. airport. **Communications:** 1 TV, 4 radio stations. **Medical facilities:** 4 hosp. **Educational facilities:** 12 institutes of higher education, 82 pub. schools. **Further information:** City of Glendale Marketing/Communications Department, 5850 W. Glendale Ave, Glendale, AZ 85301; www.glendaleazchamber.org

Glendale, California

Population (2006): 199,463 (99); **Pop. density:** 6,518; **Pop. change (2000-2006):** 2.3%. **Area:** 30.6 sq mi. **Employment (2006):** 100,208 employed; 4.1% unemployed. **Per capita income (MSA):** $36,746; increase (2004-2005): 4.6%.

Mayor: Ara Najarian, Non-Partisan

History: became a town in 1887; inc. 1906.

Transportation: 1 natl. airport; commuter trains, Amtrak; bus system. **Communications:** 2 radio stations. **Medical facilities:** 3 hosp. **Educational facilities:** 1 community college; 31 pub. schools. **Further information:** City of Glendale Public Information Officer, 613 E. Broadway, Glendale, CA 91206; www.ci.glendale.ca.us; www.glendalechamber.com

Greensboro, North Carolina

Population (2006): 236,865 (77); **Pop. density:** 2,262; **Pop. change (2000-2006):** 4.6%. **Area:** 104.7 sq mi. **Employment (2006):** 122,136 employed; 4.6% unemployed. **Per capita income (MSA):** $31,464; increase (2004-2005): 3.8%.

Mayor: Keith Holliday, Democrat

History: settled 1749; site of Revolutionary War conflict 1781 between Generals Nathanael Greene and Cornwallis; inc. 1807, origin of civil rights sit-in movement.

Transportation: 1 intl. airport, 2 airfields; 2 railroads; Trailways/Greyhound bus service. **Communications:** 3 TV, 10 radio stations. **Medical facilities:** 2 hosp. **Educational facilities:** 3 univ., 4 colleges; 94 pub. schools. **Further information:** Chamber of Commerce, 342 N. Elm St., Greensboro, NC 27401; www.greensboro-nc.gov; www.greensboro.org

Henderson, Nevada

Population (2006): 240,614 (75); **Pop. density:** 3,019; **Pop. change (2000-2006):** 37.2%. **Area:** 79.7 sq mi. **Employment (2006):** 132,245 employed; 3.2% unemployed. **Per capita income (MSA):** $34,980; increase (2004-2005): 5.8%.

Mayor: James B. Gibson, Democrat

History: early growth spurred by World War II magnesium mining; inc. 1953.

Transportation: Henderson Executive Airport; Citizens Area Transit (CAT) public transportation. **Communications:** 2 TV, 8 radio stations. **Medical facilities:** 3 hosp. **Educational facilities:** 5 coll.; 2 vocational schools; 29 elem., 4 middle, 9 high schools. **Further information:** City of Henderson Public Information Office, 240 Water St., Henderson, NV 89015; www.ci.henderson.nv.us; www.hendersonchamber.com

Hialeah, Florida

Population (2006): 217,141 (87); **Pop. density:** 11,309; **Pop. change (2000-2006):** −4.1%. **Area:** 19.2 sq mi. **Employment (2006):** 91,885 employed; 4.6% unemployed. **Per capita income (MSA):** $37,507; increase (2004-2005): 5.4%.

Mayor: Julio Robaina, Republican

History: founded 1917, inc. 1925; industrial and residential city NW of Miami; Hialeah Park Horse Racing Track.

Transportation: 5 mi from Miami Intl. Airport; access to Port of Miami; Amtrak; 2 rail freight lines; Metrorail, Metrobus systems. **Communications:** 2 radio stations. **Medical facilities:** 3 hosp. **Educational facilities:** 8 univ. and colleges, 25 pub., 39 private schools. **Further information:** Hialeah-Dade Development, Inc., 501 Palm Ave., Hialeah, FL 33010; www.ci.hialeah.fl.us

Honolulu, Hawaii

Population (2006): 377,357 (46); **Pop. density:** 4,403; **Pop. change (2000-2006):** 1.5%. **Area:** 85.7 sq mi. **Employment (2006):** 439,852 employed; 2.3% unemployed. **Per capita income (MSA):** $36,828; increase (2004-2005): 5.7%.

Mayor: Mufi Hannemann, Non-Partisan

History: harbor entered by Europeans 1778; declared capital of kingdom by King Kamehameha III 1850; Pearl Harbor naval base attacked by Japanese Dec. 7, 1941.

Transportation: 1 intl. airport; 3 commercial harbors. **Communications:** 14 TV, 32 radio stations. **Medical facilities:** 10 hospitals. **Educational facilities:** 7 univ., 7 community colleges; 81 pub. schools. **Further information:** Hawaii Visitors and Convention Bureau, 2270 Kalakaua Ave., 8th Fl., Honolulu, HI 96815; www.honolulu.gov; www.gohawaii.com

Houston, Texas

Population (2006): 2,144,491 (4); **Pop. density:** 3,701; **Pop. change (2000-2006):** 8.8%. **Area:** 579.4 sq mi. **Employment (2006):** 949,129 employed; 5.2% unemployed. **Per capita income (MSA):** $39,199; increase (2004-2005): 6.9%.

Mayor: Bill White, Democrat

History: founded 1836; inc. 1837; capital of Repub. of Texas 1837-39; developed rapidly after construction of channel to Gulf of Mexico 1914; world center of oil and natural gas technology.

Transportation: 1 intl., 1 natl., 1 regional, 4 muni. , 2 corp/charter airports; 6 airfields; 2 mainline railroads; major bus and rail transit system; major intl. port. **Communications:** 16 TV, 27 radio stations. **Medical facilities:** 52 hospitals. **Educational facilities:** 35 univ. and colleges (Harris Co.); 306 pub. schools. **Further information:** Greater Houston Partnership, 1200 Smith St., Ste. 700, Houston, TX 77002-4400; www.houston.org; www.houstontx.gov

Indianapolis, Indiana

Population (2006): 785,597 (13); **Pop. density:** 2,173; **Pop. change (2000-2006):** 0.5%. **Area:** 361.5 sq mi. **Employment (2006):** 412,098 employed; 4.9% unemployed. **Per capita income (MSA):** $36,391; increase (2004-2005): 3.4%.

Mayor: Bart Peterson, Democrat

History: settled 1820; became capital 1825.

Transportation: 1 intl., 4 muni. , 1 corp/charter airport; 2 airfields; 5 railroads; 3 interstate bus lines. **Communications:** 14 TV, 21 radio stations. **Medical facilities:** 17 hosp. **Educational facilities:** 8 univ. and colleges; 80 pub. schools. **Further information:** Greater Indianapolis Chamber of Commerce, 111 Monument Circle, Ste. 1950, Indianapolis, IN 46204; www.indy gov.org; www.indychamber.com

Jacksonville, Florida

Population (2006): 794,555 (12); **Pop. density:** 1,049; **Pop. change (2000-2006):** 8.0%. **Area:** 757.7 sq mi. **Employment (2006):** 389,719 employed; 3.4% unemployed. **Per capita income (MSA):** $34,288; increase (2004-2005): 3.9%.

Mayor: John Peyton, Republican

History: settled 1816 as Cowford; renamed after Andrew Jackson 1822; inc. 1832; rechartered 1851; scene of conflicts in Seminole and Civil wars.

Transportation: 1 intl., 3 muni. airports; 3 railroads; 2 interstate bus lines; 2 seaports. **Communications:** 15 TV, 22 radio stations. **Medical facilities:** 9 hosp. **Educational facilities:** 7 univ., 5 colleges, 1 community college; 278 pub. schools, 114 private schools. **Further information:** Chamber of Commerce, 3 Independent Drive, Jacksonville, FL 32202; www.coj.net; www.myjaxchamber.com; www.expandinjax.com

Jersey City, New Jersey

Population (2006): 241,789 (73); **Pop. density:** 16,227; **Pop. change (2000-2006):** 0.7%. **Area:** 14.9 sq mi. **Employment (2006):** 106,427 employed; 6% unemployed. **Per capita income (MSA):** $45,268; increase (2004-2005): 4.1%.

Mayor: Jerramiah Healy, Democrat

History: site bought from Indians 1630; chartered as town by British 1668; scene of Revolutionary War conflict 1779; chartered under present name 1838; important station on Underground Railroad.

Transportation: Intercity bus and subway system; ferry service to Manhattan. **Communications:** 3 radio stations. **Medical facilities:** 3 hosp. **Educational facilities:** 2 colleges, 1 univ., 38 pub. schools. **Further information:** Hudson County Chamber of Commerce, 660 Newark Ave., Ste. 220, Jersey City, NJ 07306; www.cityofjerseycity.com

Kansas City, Missouri

Population (2006): 447,306 (39); **Pop. density:** 1,427; **Pop. change (2000-2006):** 1.3%. **Area:** 313.5 sq mi. **Employment (2006):** 221,965 employed; 6.3% unemployed. **Per capita income (MSA):** $35,769; increase (2004-2005): 3.7%.

Mayor: Mark Funkhouser, Democrat

History: settled by 1838 at confluence of the Missouri and Kansas rivers; inc. 1850.

Transportation: 1 intl., 1 muni. airport; a major rail center; more than 300 motor freight carriers; 7 barge lines. **Communications:** 11 TV, 17 radio stations. **Medical facilities:** 17 hosp. **Educational facilities:** 22 univ. and colleges. **Further information:** Greater Kansas City Chamber of Commerce, 911 Main St., Ste. 2600, Kansas City, MO 64105; www.kcchamber.com; www.kc mo.org

Laredo, Texas

Population (2006): 215,484 (88); **Pop. density:** 2,745; **Pop. change (2000-2006):** 21.3%. **Area:** 78.5 sq mi. **Employment (2006):** 79,881 employed; 5.2% unemployed. **Per capita income (MSA):** $18,809; increase (2004-2005): 6.5%.

Mayor: Raul G. Salinas, Non-Partisan

History: founded by Spanish colonists in 1755; part of U.S. from 1848; fast growth fueled by immigration; became principal port of entry into Mexico.

Transportation: 1 intl. airport; 2 railroads; 3 interstate bus lines, 2 local bus lines. **Communications:** 8 TV, 9 radio stations. **Medical facilities:** 4 hosp. **Educational facilities:** 1 univ., 1 community college; 62 public schools, 29 private schools; 7 vocational training centers. **Further information:** Laredo Chamber of Commerce, P.O. Box 790, Laredo, TX 78042; www.laredo chamber.com; www.cityoflaredo.com

Las Vegas, Nevada

Population (2006): 552,539 (28); **Pop. density:** 4,877; **Pop. change (2000-2006):** 15.1%. **Area:** 113.3 sq mi. **Employment (2006):** 273,503 employed; 4.2% unemployed. **Per capita income (MSA):** $34,980; increase (2004-2005): 5.8%.

Mayor: Oscar B. Goodman, Democrat

History: occupied by Mormons 1855-57; bought by railroad 1903; city of Las Vegas inc. 1911; gambling legalized 1931.

Transportation: 1 intl., 1 muni. airport; 1 railroad; monorail; bus system. **Communications:** 19 TV, 27 radio stations. **Medical facilities:** 21 hosp. **Educational facilities:** 1 univ., 2 state colleges; 277 pub. schools in area. **Further information:** Las Vegas Chamber of Commerce, 3720 Howard Hughes Parkway, Las Vegas, NV 89169-0916; www.lvchamber.com; www.lasvegasnevada.gov

Lexington, Kentucky

Population (2006): 270,789 (68); **Pop. density:** 952; **Pop. change (2000-2006):** 3.9%. **Area:** 284.5 sq mi. **Employment (2006):** 142,864 employed; 4.3% unemployed. **Per capita income (MSA):** $33,737; increase (2004-2005): 3.7%.

Mayor: Jim Newberry, Democrat

History: site was founded and named in 1775 by hunters after the site of the opening battle of the Revolutionary War at Lexington, Mass.; settled 1779; chartered 1782; inc. as a city 1832.

Transportation: 1 regional airport; 2 railroads; city buses. **Communications:** 5 TV, 9 radio stations. **Medical facilities:** 13 hosp. **Educational facilities:** 2 univ., 4 colleges, 53 public schools: 6 high schools, 10 middle schools, 35 elementary schools, 2 technology schools. **Further information:** Commerce Lexington, 330 E. Main St., Lexington, KY 40507; www.lfucg.com

Lincoln, Nebraska

Population (2006): 241,167 (74); **Pop. density:** 3,233; **Pop. change (2000-2006):** 6.5%. **Area:** 74.6 sq mi. **Employment (2006):** 137,793 employed; 2.5% unemployed. **Per capita income (MSA):** $33,316; increase (2004-2005): 2.8%.

Mayor: Chris Beutler, Democrat

History: originally called Lancaster; chosen state capital 1867, renamed after Abraham Lincoln; inc. 1869.

Transportation: 1 regional airport; Greyhound; Amtrak, 2 railroads. **Communications:** 6 TV, 14 radio stations. **Medical facilities:** 8 hosp. **Educational facilities:** 3 univ., 3 voc.-tech./ business colleges; 55 pub., 30 private schools, 3 focus programs. **Further information:** Chamber of Commerce, PO Box 83006, Lincoln, NE 68501-3006; www.lincoln.org; www.lincoln. ne.gov, www.lcoc.com

Long Beach, California

Population (2006): 472,494 (35); **Pop. density:** 9,375; **Pop. change (2000-2006):** 2.4%. **Area:** 50.4 sq mi. **Employment (2006):** 221,854 employed; 5.2% unemployed. **Per capita income (MSA):** $36,746; increase (2004-2005): 4.6%.

Mayor: Bob Foster, Democrat

History: settled as early as 1784 by Spanish; by 1884 present site developed on harbor; inc. 1888; oil discovered 1921.

Transportation: 1 natl. airport; 3 railroads; major intl. port; 4 bus co. with 40 bus lines, light rail service. **Communications:** 3 radio, 1 TV stations. **Medical facilities:** 7 hosp. **Educational facilities:** 1 univ., 1 community college (2 campuses); 87 pub. schools in district. **Further information:** Long Beach City Hall, 333 W. Ocean Blvd., Long Beach, CA 90802; www.long beach.gov; www.lbchamber.com

Los Angeles, California

Population (2006): 3,849,378 (2); **Pop. density:** 8,206; **Pop. change (2000-2006):** 4.2%. **Area:** 469.1 sq mi. **Employment (2006):** 1,790,669 employed; 5.2% unemployed. **Per capita income (MSA):** $36,746; increase (2004-2005): 4.6%.

Mayor: Antonio Villaraigosa, Democrat

History: founded by Spanish 1781; captured by U.S. 1846; inc. 1850; grew rapidly after coming of railroads, 1876 & 1885; Hollywood a district of L.A.

Transportation: 1 intl., 1 muni. airport; 3 railroads; major freeway system; intracity bus and rail system. **Communications:** 20 TV, 32 radio stations. **Medical facilities:** 30 hosp. **Educational facilities:** 158 univ. and colleges (incl. junior, community, and other); 1,858 pub. schools; 1,120 private schools. **Further information:** Los Angeles Area Chamber of Commerce, 350 S. Bixel St., Los Angeles, CA 90017; www.ci.la.ca.us; www.lachamber.org; www.lacvb.com

Louisville, Kentucky

Population (2006): 554,496 (27); **Pop. density:**; **Pop. change (2000-2006):** 0.6%. **Area:** TKTK sq mi. **Employment (2006):** 339,832 employed; 5.6% unemployed. **Per capita income (MSA):** $33,749; increase (2004-2005): 3.8%.

Mayor: Jerry E. Abramson, Democrat

History: settled 1778; named for Louis XVI of France; inc. 1828; base for Union forces in Civil War.

Transportation: 1 intl., 1 regional airport; 1 terminal, 4 trunkline railroads; metro bus line, Greyhound station; 5 barge lines. **Communications:** 9 TV, 19 radio stations. **Medical facilities:** 16 hosp. **Educational facilities:** 10 univ. and colleges, 32 business and vocational schools. **Further information:** Greater Louisville, Inc. Metro Chamber of Commerce, 614 W. Main St., Ste. 6000, Louisville, KY 40202; www.greaterlouisville.com; www.louisvilleky.com www.gotolouisville.com

Lubbock, Texas

Population (2006): 212,169 (90); **Pop. density:** 1,848; **Pop. change (2000-2006):** 6.2%. **Area:** 114.8 sq mi. **Employment (2006):** 112,799 employed; 3.9% unemployed. **Per capita income (MSA):** $28,098; increase (2004-2005): 6.0%.

Mayor: David Miller, Republican

History: settled 1879; laid out 1891; inc. 1909 through merger of two towns.

Transportation: 1 intl. airport, 1 airfield; 2 railroads, bus line. **Communications:** 16 TV, 18 radio stations. **Medical facilities:** 7 hosp. **Educational facilities:** 3 univ., 1 junior college; 51 pub. schools. **Further information:** Chamber of Commerce, 1301 Broadway, Ste. 101, Lubbock, TX 79401; www.ci.lubbock.tx.us; www.lubbockchamber.com

Madison, Wisconsin

Population (2006): 223,389 (82); **Pop. density:** 3,252; **Pop. change (2000-2006):** 6.8%. **Area:** 68.7 sq mi. **Employment (2006):** 137,316 employed; 3.2% unemployed. **Per capita income (MSA):** $38,993; increase (2004-2005): 4.0%.

Mayor: Dave Cieslewicz, Democrat

History: first white settlement 1832; selected as site for state capital, named after James Madison, 1836; chartered 1856.

Transportation: 1 natl. airport, 1 airfield; 1 intracity, 3 intercity bus systems; 3 freight rail lines. **Communications:** 6 TV, 15 radio stations. **Medical facilities:** 5 hosp. **Educational facilities:** 7 colleges and univ., including main branch of Univ. of Wisconsin; 30 elem. schools, 11 middle schools, 5 high schools. **Further information:** Greater Madison Chamber of Commerce, PO Box 71, Madison, WI 53701-0071; www.cityofmadison.com; www.madisonchamber.com

Memphis, Tennessee

Population (2006): 670,902 (17); **Pop. density:** 2,402; **Pop. change (2000-2006):** −1.8%. **Area:** 279.3 sq mi. **Employment (2006):** 292,170 employed; 6.4% unemployed. **Per capita income (MSA):** $33,529; increase (2004-2005): 3.7%.

Mayor: Willie W. Herenton, Democrat

History: French, Spanish, and U.S. forts by 1797; settled by 1819; inc. as town 1826, as city 1840; surrendered charter to state 1879 after yellow fever epidemics; rechartered as city 1893.

Transportation: 1 intl. airport; 5 railroads; 1 bus system. **Communications:** 9 TV, 20 radio stations. **Medical facilities:** 15 hosp. **Educational facilities:** 17 univ. and colleges; 191 public schools. **Further information:** Memphis Regional Chamber, 22 N. Front St., 2nd Floor, Memphis, TN 38101; www.ci.memphis.tn.us; www.memphischamber.com

Mesa, Arizona

Population (2006): 447,541 (38); **Pop. density:** 3,580; **Pop. change (2000-2006):** 12.5%. **Area:** 125 sq mi. **Employment (2006):** 242,044 employed; 3.2% unemployed. **Per capita income (MSA):** $32,414; increase (2004-2005): 4.9%.

Mayor: Keno Hawker, Republican

History: founded by Mormons 1878; inc. 1883; population boomed fivefold 1960-80.

Transportation: 1 muni. airport, 1 airfield; metro bus service. **Communications:** 3 TV, 4 radio stations. **Medical facilities:** 7 hosp. **Educational facilities:** 5 univ., 7 colleges; 82 pub. schools. **Further information:** Convention and Visitor's Bureau and Mesa Chamber of Commerce, 120 N. Center, Mesa, AZ 85201; www.mesacvb.com; www.mesachamber.org; www.cityofmesa.org

Miami, Florida

Population (2006): 404,048 (43); **Pop. density:** 11,318; **Pop. change (2000-2006):** 11.5%. **Area:** 35.7 sq mi. **Employment (2006):** 158,965 employed; 4% unemployed. **Per capita income (MSA):** $37,507; increase (2004-2005): 5.4%.

Mayor: Manuel A. Diaz, Independent

History: site of fort 1836; settlement began 1870; inc. 1896; modern city developed into financial and recreation center; land speculation in 1920s added to city's growth, as did Cuban, Central and South American, and Haitian immigration since 1960.

Transportation: 1 intl., 1 regional, 1 corp. airport; 2 airfields, 1 seaplane base; seaport; Amtrak, transit rail system; 2 bus lines; 65 truck lines. **Communications:** 23 TV, 21 radio stations. **Medical facilities:** 19 hosp. **Educational facilities:** 6 univ. and colleges. **Further information:** Greater Miami Chamber of Commerce, Omni Mall Complex, 1601 Biscayne Blvd., Miami, FL 33132; www.greatermiami.com; www.miamigov.com

Milwaukee, Wisconsin

Population (2006): 573,358 (25); **Pop. density:** 5,966; **Pop. change (2000-2006):** −4.0%. **Area:** 96.1 sq mi. **Employment (2006):** 249,281 employed; 7% unemployed. **Per capita income (MSA):** $38,164; increase (2004-2005): 4.1%.

Mayor: Tom Barrett, Democrat

History: Indian trading post by 1674; settlement began 1835; inc. as city 1848; famous beer industry.

Transportation: 1 intl. airport, 1 airfield; 3 railroads; major port; 4 bus lines. **Communications:** 14 TV, 19 radio stations. **Medical facilities:** 17 hosp. **Educational facilities:** 7 univ. and colleges, 182 pub. schools. **Further information:** Visit Milwaukee, 648 N. Plankinton Ave. Ste. 425, Milwaukee, WI 53203-2917; www.visitmilwaukee.org; www.milwaukee.gov

Minneapolis, Minnesota

Population (2006): 372,833 (47); **Pop. density:** 6,791; **Pop. change (2000-2006):** −2.6%. **Area:** 54.9 sq mi. **Employment (2006):** 209,711 employed; 3.8% unemployed. **Per capita income (MSA):** $42,091; increase (2004-2005): 2.9%.

Mayor: R.T. Rybak, Democrat

History: site visited by Hennepin 1680; included in area of military reservations 1819; inc. 1867.

Transportation: 1 intl., 2 regional, 1 muni. airports, 1 airfield; 5 railroads. **Communications:** 10 TV, 17 radio stations. **Medical facilities:** 7 hosp. **Educational facilities:** 10 univ. and colleges; 121 pub., 28 private schools. **Further information:** City of Minneapolis Office of Pub. Affairs, 301M City Hall, 350 S. Fifth Street, Minneapolis, MN 55415; www.ci.minneapolis.mn.us; www.minneapolis.org

Modesto, California

Population (2006): 205,721 (95); **Pop. density:** 5,746; **Pop. change (2000-2006):** 9.0%. **Area:** 35.8 sq mi. **Employment (2006):** 91,974 employed; 6.8% unemployed. **Per capita income (MSA):** $26,810; increase (2004-2005): 3.5%.

Mayor: Jim Ridenour, Republican

History: founded 1870 after the Gold Rush of 1849 brought an influx of settlers to the region; recent growth boosted by agriculture and immigration.

Transportation: 1 muni. airport. **Communications:** 4 TV, 12 radio stations. **Medical facilities:** 4 hosp. **Educational facilities:** 1 junior college, 5 public high schools. **Further information:** Modesto Convention & Visitor Bureau, 1150 Ninth St., Ste. C, Modesto, CA 95354; www.visitmodesto.com; www.ci.modesto.ca.us

Montgomery, Alabama

Population (2006): 201,998 (96); **Pop. density:** 1,300; **Pop. change (2000-2006):** 0.1%. **Area:** 155.4 sq mi. **Employment (2006):** 93,995 employed; 3.6% unemployed. **Per capita income (MSA):** $31,958; increase (2004-2005): 5.7%.

Mayor: Bobby N. Bright, Democrat

History: inc. as town 1819, as city 1837; became state capital 1846; first capital of Confederacy 1861.

Transportation: 1 regional airport; 2 railroads; 2 bus lines; Alabama R. navigable to Gulf of Mexico. **Communications:** 6 TV, 14 radio stations. **Medical facilities:** 7 hosp. **Educational facilities:** 9 colleges and univ.; 35 pub., 35 private schools. **Further information:** Montgomery Area Chamber of Commerce, 41 Commerce St., PO Box 79, Montgomery, AL 36101; www.montgomerychamber.com; www.montgomeryal.gov

Nashville, Tennessee

Population (2006): 552,120 (29); **Pop. density:** 1,167; **Pop. change (2000-2006):** 1.2%. **Area:** 473.3 sq mi. **Employment (2006):** 299,345 employed; 4.2% unemployed. **Per capita income (MSA):** $36,655; increase (2004-2005): 5.1%.

Mayor: Bill Purcell, Democrat

History: settled 1779; first chartered 1806; became permanent state capital 1843; home of Grand Ole Opry.

Transportation: 1 intl. airport, 2 airfields; 1 railroad; bus line; transit system of buses and trolleys. **Communications:** 15 TV, 18 radio stations. **Medical facilities:** 14 hosp. **Educational facilities:** 17 universities and colleges, 129 pub. schools. **Further information:** Chamber of Commerce, 211 Commerce St., Ste 100, Nashville, TN 37201; www.nashvillechamber.com; www.nashville.gov

Newark, New Jersey

Population (2006): 281,402 (64); **Pop. density:** 11,824; **Pop. change (2000-2006):** 3.3%. **Area:** 23.8 sq mi. **Employment (2006):** 97,352 employed; 8.5% unemployed. **Per capita income (MSA):** $45,268; increase (2004-2005): 4.1%.

Mayor: Cory Booker, Democrat

History: settled by Puritans 1666; used as supply base by Washington 1776; inc. as town 1833, as city 1836.

Transportation: 1 intl. airport; 1 intl. seaport, 4 railroads; bus system; subways. **Communications:** 3 TV, 5 radio stations, 1 daily newspaper, 8 weekly newspapers. **Medical facilities:** 6 hosp. **Educational facilities:** 5 univ. and colleges; 58 pub. elementary schools, 13 junior and senior high schools, 10 special schools, 2 vocational schools, and 40 private schools. **Further information:** Newark Public Information Office, City of Newark, 920 Broad St. #214, Newark, NJ 07102; www.ci.newark.nj.us; www.rbp.org

New Orleans, Louisiana

Hurricane Katrina struck New Orleans Aug. 29, 2005, causing widespread damage to the city's levee system, resulting in massive flooding. Many residents have since returned to the city. As a result of these events, updated 2006 employment and unemployment statistics are not available.

Population (2006): 223,388 (83); **Pop. density:** 1,237; **Pop. change (2000-2006):** −53.9%. **Area:** 180.6 sq mi. **Employment (2006):** NA. **Per capita income (MSA):** $20,210; decrease (2004-2005): −34%.

Mayor: C. Ray Nagin, Democrat

History: founded by French 1718; became major seaport on Mississippi R.; acquired by U.S. as part of Louisiana Purchase 1803; inc. as city 1805; Americans defeated British forces at the Battle of New Orleans in 1815.

Transportation: 1 intl., 1 regional airport; major railroad center; street car and bus lines. **Communications:** 15 TV, 23 radio stations. **Medical facilities:** 13 hosp. **Educational facilities:** 10 univ. and 9 colleges. **Further information:** New Orleans Metropolitan Convention & Visitors Bureau, Inc., 2020 St. Charles Ave., New Orleans, LA 70130; www.neworleanscvb.com; www.cityofno.com

New York, New York

Population (2006): 8,214,426 (1); **Pop. density:** 27,084; **Pop. change (2000-2006):** 2.6%. **Area:** 303.3 sq mi. **Employment (2006):** 3,616,432 employed; 4.9% unemployed. **Per capita income (MSA):** $45,268; increase (2004-2005): 4.1%.

Mayor: Michael R. Bloomberg, Independent

History: trading post established 1624; British took control from Dutch 1664 and named city New York; briefly U.S. capital; Washington inaugurated as president 1789; under new charter, 1898, city expanded to include 5 boroughs: The Bronx, Brooklyn, Queens, and Staten Island, as well as Manhattan; Sept. 11, 2001, terrorist attack destroyed World Trade Center, killed about 2,800.

Transportation: 3 intl. airports serve area; 2 seaplane bases; 2 rail terminals; major subway network that includes 26 routes; 244 bus routes; ferry system; 4 underwater tunnels. **Communications:** 13 TV, 38 radio stations. **Medical facilities:** 70 hosp.; 6 academic medical centers. **Educational facilities:** 54 univ. and colleges; 1,198 pub. schools. **Further information:** Convention and Visitors Bureau, 810 Seventh Ave., New York, NY 10019; www.nyc.gov; www.nycvisit.com

Norfolk, Virginia

Population (2006): 229,112 (81); **Pop. density:** 4,267; **Pop. change (2000-2006):** −2.3%. **Area:** 53.7 sq mi. **Employment (2006):** 93,488 employed; 4.1% unemployed. **Per capita income (MSA):** $33,163; increase (2004-2005): 5.0%.

Mayor: Paul D. Fraim, Non-Partisan.

History: founded 1682; burned by patriots to prevent capture by British during Revolutionary War; rebuilt and inc. as town 1805, as city 1845; site of world's largest naval base; major east coast commercial port and cruise terminal.

Transportation: 1 intl., 1 charter/corp. airport, 1 airfield; 2 railroads; Amtrak; bus system; free downtown shuttle. **Communications:** 5 TV, 15 radio stations. **Medical facilities:** 8 hosp. **Educational facilities:** 2 univ., 2 colleges, 1 medical school; 59 pub. schools. **Further information:** Norfolk Convention and Visitors Bureau, 232 E. Main St., Norfolk, VA 23510; www.norfolk.gov; www.norfolkcvb.com

Oakland, California

Population (2006): 397,067 (44); **Pop. density:** 7,078; **Pop. change (2000-2006):** −0.6%. **Area:** 56.1 sq mi. **Employment (2006):** 179,575 employed; 6.9% unemployed. **Per capita income (MSA):** $52,543; increase (2004-2005): 5.1%.

Mayor: Ron Dellums, Democrat

History: area settled by Spanish 1820; inc. as city under present name 1854.

Transportation: 1 intl. airport; western terminus for 2 railroads; underground, 75-mi underwater subway. **Communications:** 1 TV, 3 radio stations. **Medical facilities:** 4 hosp. **Educational facilities:** 12 East Bay colleges and univ.; 81 pub. schools. **Further information:** Oakland Metropolitan Chamber of Commerce, 475 14th St., Oakland, CA 94612-1903; www.oaklandchamber.com; www.oaklandnet.com

Oklahoma City, Oklahoma

Population (2006): 537,734 (30); **Pop. density:** 886; **Pop. change (2000-2006):** 6.2%. **Area:** 607 sq mi. **Employment (2006):** 250,295 employed; 4.3% unemployed. **Per capita income (MSA):** $32,875; increase (2004-2005): 4.9%.

Mayor: Mick Cornett, Republican

History: settled during land rush in Midwest 1889; inc. 1890; became capital 1910; oil discovered 1928. Bomb in 1995 destroyed federal office bldg., killed 168 people.

Transportation: 1 intl., 1 regional airport, 2 airfields; 2 railroad; pub. transit system; 1 major bus line. **Communications:** 18 TV, 17 radio stations. **Medical facilities:** 23 hosp. **Educational facilities:** 20 univ. and colleges; 83 pub., 37 private schools. **Further information:** Chamber of Commerce, Economic Development Division, 123 Park Ave., Oklahoma City, OK 73102; www.okc.gov; www.okccvb.org; www.greateroklahomacity.com.

Omaha, Nebraska

Population (2006): 419,545 (42); **Pop. density:** 3,626; **Pop. change (2000-2006):** 7.2%. **Area:** 115.7 sq mi. **Employment (2006):** 217,468 employed; 3% unemployed. **Per capita income (MSA):** $37,444; increase (2004-2005): 3.5%.

Mayor: Mike Fahey, Democrat

History: founded 1854; inc. 1857; large food-processing, telecommunications, information-processing center.

Transportation: 1 natl. airport, 1 airfield; 3 major railroads; intercity bus line. **Communications:** 10 TV, 17 radio stations. **Medical facilities:** 12 hosp. **Educational facilities:** 5 univ., 6 colleges; 243 pub., 78 private schools. **Further information:** Greater Omaha Chamber of Commerce, 1301 Harney St., Omaha, NE 68102; www.ci.omaha.ne.us; www.accessomaha.com

Orlando, Florida

Population (2006): 220,186 (85); **Pop. density:** 2,355; **Pop. change (2000-2006):** 14.5%. **Area:** 93.5 sq mi. **Employment (2006):** 121,233 employed; 3% unemployed. **Per capita income (MSA):** $31,557; increase (2004-2005): 5.0%.

Mayor: Buddy Dyer, Democrat

History: Fort Gatlin built just south of present-day Orlando in 1838; name changed from Jernigan to Orlando, 1856; inc. 1875; Walt Disney World opened in 1971.

Transportation: 2 intl., 1 regional, 1 corp./charter airport; 2 bus lines. **Communications:** 18 TV, 11 radio stations. **Medical facilities:** 3 hosp. **Educational facilities:** 153 public schools; 4 tech schools; 5 colleges and univ. **Further Information:** Orlando/Orange County Convention and Visitors Bureau, 6700 Forum Dr., Ste. 100, Orlando, FL 32821-8087; www.orlandoinfo.com; www.ci.orlando.fl.us

Philadelphia, Pennsylvania

Population (2006): 1,448,394 (6); **Pop. density:** 10,721; **Pop. change (2000-2006):** −4.6%. **Area:** 135.1 sq mi. **Employment (2006):** 584,038 employed; 6.3% unemployed. **Per capita income (MSA):** $40,727; increase (2004-2005): 4.8%.

Mayor: John F. Street, Democrat

History: first settled by Swedes 1638; Swedes surrendered to Dutch 1654; settled by English and Scottish Quakers 1678; named Philadelphia 1682; chartered 1701; Continental Congresses convened 1774, 1775; Declaration of Independence signed here 1776; national capital 1790-1800; state capital 1683-1799.

Transportation: 1 intl., 2 muni. airports; 3 railroads; major freshwater port; subway, el, rail commuter, bus, and streetcar system. **Communications:** 2 major daily newspapers, 13 TV, 29 radio stations. **Medical facilities:** 29 hosp. **Educational facilities:** 27 univ. and colleges. **Further information:** Greater Philadelphia Chamber of Commerce, Business Information Center, 200 S. Broad St., Suite 700, Philadelphia PA 19102; www.phila.gov; www.philachamber.com

Phoenix, Arizona

Population (2006): 1,512,986 (5); **Pop. density:** 3,186; **Pop. change (2000-2006):** 14.5%. **Area:** 474.9 sq mi. **Employment (2006):** 796,587 employed; 4.1% unemployed. **Per capita income (MSA):** $32,414; increase (2004-2005): 4.9%.

Mayor: Phil Gordon, Democrat

History: founded 1867; inc. as city 1881; became territorial capital 1889.

Transportation: 1 intl., 2 muni. airports; 2 transcontinental and 10 intrastate railroads; transcontinental bus line; pub. transit system. **Communications:** 22 TV, 22 radio stations. **Medical facilities:** 24 hosp. **Educational facilities:** 36 institutions of higher learning; 380 pub. schools (247 elem. and junior high schools, 35 senior high schools, 98 charter schools). **Further information:** Greater Phoenix Chamber of Commerce, 201 N. Central Ave., 27th fl., Phoenix, AZ 85004; www.phoenix.gov; www.phoenixchamber.com

Pittsburgh, Pennsylvania

Population (2006): 312,819 (57); **Pop. density:** 5,626; **Pop. change (2000-2006):** −6.5%. **Area:** 55.6 sq mi. **Employment (2006):** 144,708 employed; 4.9% unemployed. **Per capita income (MSA):** $36,530; increase (2004-2005): 4.9%.

Mayor: Luke Ravenstahl, Democrat

History: settled around Ft. Pitt 1758; inc. as city 1816; became an inland port; by Civil War, already a center for iron production.

Transportation: 1 intl., 1 regional airport; 1 airfield; 20 railroads; 2 bus lines; trolley/subway system. **Communications:** 12 TV, 22 radio stations. **Medical facilities:** 18 hosp. **Educational facilities:** 3 univ., 6 colleges; 93 pub. schools. **Further information:** Greater Pittsburgh Convention & Visitors Bureau, Regional Enterprise Tower, 30th Floor, 425 Sixth Ave., Pittsburgh, PA 15219; Pittsburgh Regional Alliance, Regional Enterprise Tower, Ste. 1100, 425 Sixth Ave., Pittsburgh, PA 15219; www.visitpittsburgh.com; www.pghgov.com

Plano, Texas

Population (2006): 255,009 (69); **Pop. density:** 3,562; **Pop. change (2000-2006):** 14.9%. **Area:** 71.6 sq mi. **Employment (2006):** 139,473 employed; 4.2% unemployed. **Per capita income (MSA):** $37,209; increase (2004-2005): 4.8%.
Mayor: Pat Evans, Republican
History: settled 1846; inc. as city 1873.
Transportation: DART bus line. **Communications:** 1 TV, 2 radio stations. **Medical facilities:** 7 hosp. **Educational facilities:** 5 institutions of higher learning, 64 pub. schools. **Further information:** City of Plano Public Information Dept. 1520 K Ave., Suite 320, Plano, TX 75074; Plano Chamber of Commerce, 1200 E. 15th St., Plano, TX 75074; www.plano.gov; www.planochamber.org

Portland, Oregon

Population (2006): 537,081 (31); **Pop. density:** 3,999; **Pop. change (2000-2006):** 1.5%. **Area:** 134.3 sq mi. **Employment (2006):** 282,202 employed; 5.2% unemployed. **Per capita income (MSA):** $35,430; increase (2004-2005): 4.2%.
Mayor: Tom Potter, Democrat
History: settled by pioneers 1845; developed as trading center, aided by California Gold Rush 1849; city chartered 1851.
Transportation: 1 intl. airport; 2 major rail freight lines, Amtrak; mass transit bus, light rail, and street car system; marine port. **Communications:** 11 TV, 25 radio stations. **Medical facilities:** 8 hosp. **Educational facilities:** 25 univ. and colleges, 1 community college. **Further information:** Portland Business Alliance, 200 SW Market St., Ste. 1770, Portland, OR 97201; www.portlandalliance.com; www.portlandonline.com

Raleigh, North Carolina

Population (2006): 356,321 (51); **Pop. density:** 3,109; **Pop. change (2000-2006):** 25.0%. **Area:** 114.6 sq mi. **Employment (2006):** 190,677 employed; 3.5% unemployed. **Per capita income (MSA):** $35,624; increase (2004-2005): 2.9%.
Mayor: Charles Meeker, Democrat
History: named after Sir Walter Raleigh; site chosen for capital 1788; laid out 1792; inc. 1795; occupied by Gen. Sherman 1865.
Transportation: 1 intl. airport, 1 airfield; 3 railroads; 2 bus lines. **Communications:** 8 TV, 13 radio stations. **Medical facilities:** 7 hosp. **Educational facilities:** 6 univ. and colleges; 1 community college; 140 pub. schools (county). **Further information:** Chamber of Commerce, 800 S. Salisbury St., Raleigh, NC 27602; www.raleigh-wake.org; www.raleighchamber.org, www.raleigh-nc.org

Reno, Nevada

Population (2006): 210,255 (91); **Pop. density:** 3,043; **Pop. change (2000-2006):** 14.8%. **Area:** 69.1 sq mi. **Employment (2006):** 108,277 employed; 4% unemployed. **Per capita income (MSA):** $41,284; increase (2004-2005): 3.0%.
Mayor: Robert Cashell, Republican
History: Founded in 1857. Originally named Lakes Crossing. Name changed to Reno, after a Union Civil War general, in 1868 with the arrival of the transcontinental railroad.
Transportation: 1 intl. airport, 1 airfield; local and national bus lines; Amtrak, Union Pacific Railroad. **Communications:** 11 TV, 14 radio stations. **Medical Facilities:** 8 hosp. **Educational Facilities:** 58 public schools; 1 univ. **Further information:** City of Reno, NV PO Box 1900, Reno, NV 89505; www.cityofreno.com; www.reno-sparkschamber.org

Riverside, California

Population (2006): 293,761 (61); **Pop. density:** 3,761; **Pop. change (2000-2006):** 14.9%. **Area:** 78.1 sq mi. **Employment (2006):** 147,917 employed; 5.1% unemployed. **Per capita income (MSA):** $26,618; increase (2004-2005): 3.6%.
Mayor: Ronald O. Loveridge, Non-Partisan
History: founded 1870; inc. 1886; known for its citrus industry; home of the parent navel orange tree and the historic Mission Inn.
Transportation: 1 muni. airport, intl. airport nearby; rail freight lines, commuter line; trolley/bus system; interstate freeways. **Communications:** 3 TV, 7 radio stations. **Medical facilities:** 3 hosp. **Educational facilities:** 3 univ., 1 community college. **Further information:** Chamber of Commerce, 3985 University Avenue, Riverside, CA 92501; www.riversideca.com; www.riverside-chamber.com

Rochester, New York

Population (2006): 208,123 (94); **Pop. density:** 5,813; **Pop. change (2000-2006):** −5.3%. **Area:** 35.8 sq mi. **Employment (2006):** 90,407 employed; 5.7% unemployed. **Per capita income (MSA):** $33,857; increase (2004-2005): 4.1%.
Mayor: Robert Duffy, Democrat
History: first permanent settlement 1812; inc. as village 1817, as city 1834; developed as Erie Canal town.
Transportation: 1 intl. airport; Amtrak; 2 bus lines; intracity transit service; Port of Rochester. **Communications:** 10 TV, 17 radio stations. **Medical facilities:** 5 hosp. **Educational facilities:** 11 colleges, 3 community colleges. **Further information:** Rochester Business Alliance, 150 State St., Ste. 400, Rochester, NY 14614; www.rochesterbusinessalliance.com; www.cityofrochester.gov

Sacramento, California

Population (2006): 453,781 (37); **Pop. density:** 4,669; **Pop. change (2000-2006):** 11.5%. **Area:** 97.2 sq mi. **Employment (2006):** 202,036 employed; 5.6% unemployed. **Per capita income (MSA):** $35,463; increase (2004-2005): 4.6%.
Mayor: Heather Fargo, Democrat
History: settled 1839; important trading center during California Gold Rush 1840s; became state capital 1854.
Transportation: 1 intl., 1 corp./charter, 2 muni. airports; 2 mainline transcontinental rail carriers; bus and light rail system; Port of Sacramento. **Communications:** 15 TV, 21 radio stations. **Medical facilities:** 10 hosp. **Educational facilities:** 7 colleges and univ., 5 community colleges, 81 pub. schools. **Further information:** Sacramento Metropolitan Chamber of Commerce, One Capitol Mall, Ste. 300, Sacramento, CA 95814; www.metrochamber.org; www.cityofsacramento.org

St. Louis, Missouri

Population (2006): 347,181 (52); **Pop. density:** 5,609; **Pop. change (2000-2006):** −0.3%. **Area:** 61.9 sq mi. **Employment (2006):** 147,427 employed; 6.8% unemployed. **Per capita income (MSA):** $35,573; increase (2004-2005): 4.6%.
Mayor: Francis Slay, Democrat
History: founded 1764 as a fur trading post by French; acquired by U.S. 1803; chartered as city 1822; became independent city 1876; lies on Mississippi R., near confluence with Missouri R.
Transportation: 1 intl., 1 muni. airport; 1 airfield; 2nd largest rail center, 7 trunk-line railroads; 3rd largest inland port; bus & light rail; 32 barge lines, 550 motor freight carriers. **Communications:** 2 TV, 2 radio stations. **Medical facilities:** 23 hosp. **Educational facilities:** 8 univ., 13 colleges and seminaries; 63 public schools; 29 parochial schools; 5 magnet/charter high schools. **Further information:** St. Louis Planning & Urban Design Agency, 1015 Locust St., Ste. 1200, St. Louis, MO 63101; www.stlouis.missouri.org; www.explorestlouis.com

St. Paul, Minnesota

Population (2006): 273,535 (67); **Pop. density:** 5,181; **Pop. change (2000-2006):** −4.6%. **Area:** 52.8 sq mi. **Employment (2006):** 140,585 employed; 4.1% unemployed. **Per capita income (MSA):** $42,091; increase (2004-2005): 2.9%.
Mayor: Chris Coleman, Democrat
History: founded in early 1840s as "Pig's Eye Landing"; became capital of the Minnesota territory 1849 and chartered as St. Paul 1854.
Transportation: 1 intl., 2 muni. airports; 6 major rail lines; 2 interstate bus lines; pub. transit system. **Communications:** 7 TV, 2 radio stations. **Medical facilities:** 7 hosp. **Educational facilities:** 5 univ., 5 colleges; 1 technical, 3 law schools, 1 art and design college; 65 public, 39 private schools. **Further information:** St. Paul Area Chamber of Commerce, 401 N. Robert St., Ste. 150, St. Paul, MN 55101; www.visitsaintpaul.com; www.ci.stpaul.mn.us

St. Petersburg, Florida

Population (2006): 248,098 (71); **Pop. density:** 4,163; **Pop. change (2000-2006):** −0.1%. **Area:** 59.6 sq mi. **Employment (2006):** 127,812 employed; 3.1% unemployed. **Per capita income (MSA):** $33,250; increase (2004-2005): 3.9%.
Mayor: Rick Baker, Democrat
History: founded 1888; inc. 1903.
Transportation: 1 intl., 1 regional airport; Amtrak bus connection; county-wide public bus system; downtown 'Looper' bus service; has largest muni. marina in Florida; 1 cruise port. **Communications:** 1 radio station, 2 daily newspapers. **Medical facilities:** 8 hosp. **Educational facilities:** 1 univ., 1 college, 1 law school; 27 elem., 9 middle, 5 high schools; 3 alternative/vocational schools; 100 private schools. **Further information:** City of St. Petersburg, 175 5th St. N., St. Petersburg, FL 33701; www.stpete.org, www.stpete.com

San Antonio, Texas

Population (2006): 1,296,682 (7); **Pop. density:** 3,181; **Pop. change (2000-2006):** 11.8%. **Area:** 407.6 sq mi. **Employment (2006):** 583,344 employed; 4.5% unemployed. **Per capita income (MSA):** $30,383; increase (2004-2005): 4.9%.

Mayor: Phil Hardberger, Democrat

History: first Spanish garrison 1718; Battle at the Alamo in 1836; city briefly captured by Texans; inc. 1837; 1st town meeting in Texas took place here in 1845.

Transportation: 1 intl., 1 muni. airport; 6 airfields; 2 railroads; 3 bus lines; pub. transit system. **Communications:** 27 TV, 26 radio stations. **Medical facilities:** 31 hosp. **Educational facilities:** 18 univ. and colleges; 16 pub. school districts. **Further information:** Chamber of Commerce, 602 E. Commerce St., San Antonio, TX 78205; www.sachamber.org; www.sanantonio.gov

San Bernardino, California

Population (2006): 198,985 (100); **Pop. density:** 3,384; **Pop. change (2000-2006):** 7.0%. **Area:** 58.8 sq mi. **Employment (2006):** 79,069 employed; 6.5% unemployed. **Per capita income (MSA):** $26,618; increase (2004-2005): 3.6%.

Mayor: Patrick J. Morris, Democrat

History: Named by Spanish Franciscan missionaries in 1810. Major Mormon settlement in the 1850s, later recalled to Utah. Population grew in 1860s when gold was discovered nearby. Later became a transportation hub. Inc. 1854.

Transportation: 1 intl. airport; commuter rail; local bus lines. **Communications:** 5 TV, 9 radio stations. **Medical facilities:** 3 hosp. **Educational facilities:** 3 univ.; 66 public schools. **Further information:** San Bernardino Convention & Visitors Bureau, 1955 Hunts Ln., Ste. 102, San Bernardino, CA 92408; www.sanbernardino.com

San Diego, California

Population (2006): 1,256,951 (8); **Pop. density:** 3,876; **Pop. change (2000-2006):** 2.7%. **Area:** 324.3 sq mi. **Employment (2006):** 650,665 employed; 4% unemployed. **Per capita income (MSA):** $40,569; increase (2004-2005): 5.3%.

Mayor: Jerry Sanders, Republican

History: claimed by the Spanish 1542; first mission est. 1769; scene of conflict during Mexican-American War 1846; inc. 1850.

Transportation: 1 intl., 2 muni. airports; 1 railroad; major freeway system; bus system; trolley system. **Communications:** 13 TV, 23 radio stations. **Medical facilities:** 15 hosp. **Educational facilities:** 25 colleges and univ.; 177 pub. schools. **Further information:** San Diego Regional Chamber of Commerce, 402 W. Broadway, Ste. 1000, San Diego, CA 92101; www.sandiego.gov; www.sdchamber.com

San Francisco, California

Population (2006): 744,041 (14); **Pop. density:** 15,932; **Pop. change (2000-2006):** –4.2%. **Area:** 46.7 sq mi. **Employment (2006):** 403,666 employed; 4.2% unemployed. **Per capita income (MSA):** $52,543; increase (2004-2005): 5.1%.

Mayor: Gavin Newsom, Democrat

History: nearby Farallon Islands sighted by Spanish 1542; city settled by 1776; claimed by U.S. 1846; became a major city during California Gold Rush 1849; inc. as city 1850; earthquake devastated city 1906.

Transportation: 1 intl. airport; intracity railway system; 2 railway transit systems; bus and railroad service; ferry system; 1 underwater tunnel. **Communications:** 13 TV; 30 radio stations. **Medical facilities:** 10 hosp. **Educational facilities:** 18 univ. and colleges, 113 pub. schools, 5 charter schools. **Further information:** San Francisco Visitors Information Center, 900 Market St., San Francisco, CA 94102; www.ci.sf.ca.us; www.sfchamber.com; www.onlyinsanfrancisco.com

San Jose, California

Population (2006): 929,936 (10); **Pop. density:** 5,317; **Pop. change (2000-2006):** 3.9%. **Area:** 174.9 sq mi. **Employment (2006):** 413,711 employed; 5% unemployed. **Per capita income (MSA):** $50,468; increase (2004-2005): 4.6%.

Mayor: Chuck Reed, Democrat

History: founded by the Spanish 1777 between San Francisco and Monterey; state cap. 1849-51; inc. 1850.

Transportation: 1 intl., 1 muni. airport; 2 railroads; light rail system; bus system. **Communications:** 5 TV, 10 radio stations. **Medical facilities:** 5 hosp. **Educational facilities:** 6 univ. and colleges. **Further information:** San Jose Convention and Visitors Bureau, 408 Almaden Blvd., San Jose, CA 95110; www.sanjoseca.gov; www.sanjose.gov

Santa Ana, California

Population (2006): 340,024 (53); **Pop. density:** 12,547; **Pop. change (2000-2006):** 0.6%. **Area:** 27.1 sq mi. **Employment (2006):** 149,761 employed; 5.6% unemployed. **Per capita income (MSA):** $36,746; increase (2004-2005): 4.6%.

Mayor: Miguel Pulido, Democrat

History: founded 1769; inc. as city 1869.

Transportation: 1 natl. airport; 5 major freeways including main Los Angeles-San Diego artery; Amtrak. **Communications:** 2 TV, 3 radio stations. **Medical facilities:** 3 hosp. **Educational facilities:** 1 community college. **Further information:** Santa Ana Chamber of Commerce, 2020 N. Broadway, 2nd floor, Santa Ana, CA 92706; www.santaanachamber.com; www.ci.santa-ana.ca.us

Scottsdale, Arizona

Population (2006): 231,127 (78); **Pop. density:** 1,255; **Pop. change (2000-2006):** 14.1%. **Area:** 184.2 sq mi. **Employment (2006):** 136,517 employed; 2.6% unemployed. **Per capita income (MSA):** $32,414; increase (2004-2005): 4.9%.

Mayor: Mary Manross, Democrat

History: founded 1888 by Army Chaplain Winfield Scott; inc. June 25, 1951; slogan "West's Most Western Town," by Mayor Malcolm White, adopted 1951.

Transportation: 1 muni. airport; regional bus system; local bus system; taxi system. **Communications:** 3 radio stations. **Medical facilities:** 6 hosp. **Educational facilities:** 1 univ. nearby, 1 community college; 3 unified school districts. **Further information:** Scottsdale Convention and Visitors Bureau, Galleria Corporate Center, 4343 N. Scottsdale Rd., Ste. 170, Scottsdale, AZ 85251; www.scottsdaleaz.gov; www.scottsdalecvb.com

Seattle, Washington

Population (2006): 582,454 (23); **Pop. density:** 6,942; **Pop. change (2000-2006):** 3.4%. **Area:** 83.9 sq mi. **Employment (2006):** 341,707 employed; 4% unemployed. **Per capita income (MSA):** $41,608; increase (2004-2005): 0%.

Mayor: Greg Nickels, Democrat

History: settled 1851; inc. 1869; suffered severe fire 1889; played prominent role during Alaska Gold Rush 1897; growth followed opening of Panama Canal 1914; center of aircraft industry WWII.

Transportation: 2 intl. airports, 2 seaplane bases; 2 railroads; ferries serve Puget Sound, Alaska, Canada. **Communications:** 8 TV, 26 radio stations. **Medical facilities:** 13 hosp. **Educational facilities:** 7 univ., 6 colleges, 11 community colleges. **Further information:** Greater Seattle Chamber of Commerce, 1301 5th Ave., Ste. 2500, Seattle, WA 98101-2611; www.seattle.gov; www.seattlechamber.com

Shreveport, Louisiana

Population (2006): 200,199 (98); **Pop. density:** 1,942; **Pop. change (2000-2006):** –0.3%. **Area:** 103.1 sq mi. **Employment (2006):** 89,244 employed; 4% unemployed. **Per capita income (MSA):** $30,004; increase (2004-2005): 3.7%.

Mayor: Cedric B. Glover, Democrat

History: founded 1836 near site of a 180-mi logjam cleared by Capt. Henry Shreve; inc. 1839; oil discovered 1905.

Transportation: 1 regional, 1 muni. airport; 3 bus lines. **Communications:** 7 TV, 16 radio stations. **Medical facilities:** 12 hosp. **Educational facilities:** 2 univ., 4 colleges; approx. 100 pub. schools. **Further information:** Chamber of Commerce, 400 Edwards St., Shreveport, LA 71101; www.shreveportchamber.org; www.ci.shreveport.la.us

Stockton, California

Population (2006): 290,141 (62); **Pop. density:** 5,304; **Pop. change (2000-2006):** 19.0%. **Area:** 54.7 sq mi. **Employment (2006):** 108,276 employed; 9.1% unemployed. **Per capita income (MSA):** $26,071; increase (2004-2005): 2.0%.

Mayor: Ed Chavez, Non-Partisan

History: site purchased 1842; settled 1849; inc. 1850; chief distributing point for agric. products of San Joaquin Valley.

Transportation: 1 muni. airport, 1 seaplane base; deepwater inland seaport; 4 railroads; 2 bus lines, county bus system. **Communications:** 5 TV, 8 radio stations. **Medical facilities:** 3 hosp.; regional burn, cancer, heart centers. **Educational facilities:** 9 univ. and colleges; 58 pub. schools. **Further information:** Chamber of Commerce, 445 W. Weber Ave., Ste. 220, Stockton, CA 95203; www.stocktongov.com; www.stocktonchamber.org

Tampa, Florida

Population (2006): 332,888 (55); **Pop. density:** 2,970; **Pop. change (2000-2006):** 9.7%. **Area:** 112.1 sq mi. **Employment (2006):** 158,137 employed; 3.2% unemployed. **Per capita income (MSA):** $33,250; increase (2004-2005): 3.9%.

Mayor: Pam Iorio, Democrat

History: U.S. army fort on site 1824; inc. 1851; Ybor City National Historical Landmark district.

Transportation: 1 intl., 2 muni. airports; Port of Tampa; CSX rail, Amtrak Rail; bus system; downtown streetcar. **Communications:** 16 TV, 11 radio stations. **Medical facilities:** 11 hosp. **Educational facilities:** 5 univ. and colleges; 193 pub. schools. **Further information:** Greater Tampa Chamber of Commerce, 615 Channelside Drive, Ste. 108, PO Box 420, Tampa, FL 33602; www.tampachamber.com; www.tampagov.net

Toledo, Ohio

Population (2006): 298,446 (60); **Pop. density:** 3,703; **Pop. change (2000-2006):** -4.9%. **Area:** 80.6 sq mi. **Employment (2006):** 136,418 employed; 6.8% unemployed. **Per capita income (MSA):** $30,915; increase (2004-2005): 3.2%.

Mayor: Carleton S. Finkbeiner, Democrat

History: site of Ft. Industry 1794; Battles of Ft. Meigs and Ft. Timbers 1812; figured in "Toledo War" 1835-36 between Ohio and Michigan over borders; inc. 1837.

Transportation: 2 muni. airports; 4 railroads; 53 motor freight lines; 16 interstate bus lines. **Communications:** 10 TV, 11 radio stations. **Medical facilities:** 4 hosp. **Educational facilities:** 6 univ. and colleges. **Further information:** Toledo Area Chamber of Commerce, 300 Madison Ave., Ste. 200, Toledo, OH 43604; www.toledochamber.com; www.ci.toledo.oh.us

Tucson, Arizona

Population (2006): 518,956 (32); **Pop. density:** 9,267; **Pop. change (2000-2006):** 6.5%. **Area:** 56 sq mi. **Employment (2006):** 249,667 employed; 4.4% unemployed. **Per capita income (MSA):** $28,869; increase (2004-2005): 5.1%.

Mayor: Robert E. Walkup, Republican

History: settled 1775 by Spanish as a presidio; acquired by U.S. in Gadsden Purchase 1853; inc. 1877.

Transportation: 1 intl., 1 muni. airport; 1 airfield; 2 railroads; 1 bus system, 1 trolley. **Communications:** 16 TV, 27 radio stations. **Medical facilities:** 13 hosp. **Educational facilities:** 1 univ., 1 community college; 216 pub. schools. **Further information:** Tucson Metropolitan Chamber of Commerce, 465 St. Mary's Rd., PO Box 991, Tucson, AZ 85701; www.tucsonaz.gov; www.tucsonchamber.org

Tulsa, Oklahoma

Population (2006): 382,872 (45); **Pop. density:** 2,097; **Pop. change (2000-2006):** -2.6%. **Area:** 182.6 sq mi. **Employment (2006):** 198,497 employed; 4.1% unemployed. **Per capita income (MSA):** $34,685; increase (2004-2005): 6.1%.

Mayor: Kathryn L. Taylor, Democrat

History: settled in 1836 by Creek Indians; modern town founded 1882 and inc. 1898; oil discovered early 20th century; emerging as telecommunications hub.

Transportation: 1 intl., 1 regional airport; 1 airfield; 5 rail lines; 5 bus lines; transit bus system. **Communications:** 25 TV, 15 radio stations. **Medical facilities:** 18 hosp. **Educational facilities:** 8 univ. and colleges; 85 pub., 39 private schools. **Further information:** Tulsa Metro Chamber, 2 West 2nd St., Williams Tower II, Ste. 150, Tulsa, OK 74103; www.tulsachamber.com; www.cityoftulsa.org

Virginia Beach, Virginia

Population (2006): 435,619 (41); **Pop. density:** 1,754; **Pop. change (2000-2006):** 2.4%. **Area:** 248.3 sq mi. **Employment (2006):** 217,901 employed; 2.9% unemployed. **Per capita income (MSA):** $33,163; increase (2004-2005): 5.0%.

Mayor: Meyera E. Oberndorf, Independent

History: area founded by Capt. John Smith 1607; formed by merger with Princess Anne Co. 1963.

Transportation: 1 private airfield; 2 railroads; 1 bus line; pub. transit system. **Communications:** 4 TV, 4 radio stations. **Medical facilities:** 3 hosp. **Educational facilities:** 1 univ., 2 colleges; 87 pub. schools. **Further information:** Virginia Beach Dept. of Economic Development, 222 Central Park Ave., Suite 1000, Virginia Beach, VA 23462; Virginia Beach Convention and Visitors Bureau, 2100 Parks Ave., Virginia Beach, VA 23451; www.yesvirginiabeach.com; www.vbgov.com; www.vbfun.com

Washington, District of Columbia

Population (2006): 581,530 (24); **Pop. density:** 9,471; **Pop. change (2000-2006):** 1.7%. **Area:** 61.4 sq mi. **Employment (2006):** 296,957 employed; 6% unemployed. **Per capita income (MSA):** $48,697; increase (2004-2005): 5.2%.

Mayor: Adrian M. Fenty, Democrat

History: U.S. capital; site at Potomac R. chosen by George Washington 1790 on land ceded from VA and MD (portion S of Potomac returned to VA 1846); Congress first met 1800; inc. 1802; sacked by British, War of 1812; 125 killed during Sept. 11, 2001 terrorist attack on the Pentagon.

Transportation: 3 intl. airports in area; Amtrak, 6 other passenger & cargo rail lines; Metrobus/Metrorail transit system; bus line. **Communications:** 18 TV, 20 radio stations. **Medical facilities:** 17 hosp. **Educational facilities:** 10 univ. and colleges. **Further information:** DC Chamber of Commerce, 1213 K Street NW, Washington, DC 20005; www.dc.gov; www.dcchamber.org

Wichita, Kansas

Population (2006): 357,698 (50); **Pop. density:** 2,634; **Pop. change (2000-2006):** 1.8%. **Area:** 135.8 sq mi. **Employment (2006):** 177,198 employed; 5.1% unemployed. **Per capita income (MSA):** $33,671; increase (2004-2005): 6.1%.

Mayor: Carl Brewer, Democrat

History: founded 1864; inc. 1871.

Transportation: 1 natl., 1 muni. airport; 4 airfields; 3 major rail freight lines; 2 bus lines. **Communications:** 8 TV, 15 radio stations. **Medical facilities:** 12 hosp. **Educational facilities:** 3 univ., 1 medical school; 96 pub. schools. **Further information:** Chamber of Commerce, 350 W. Douglas Ave., Wichita, KS 67202; www.wichitakansas.org; www.wichita.gov; www.gwedc.org

Fastest-Growing Big Cities*

	City	2006 population	2000 population	% change
1.	Henderson, NV	240,614	175,416	37.2
2.	Chandler, AZ	240,595	177,000	35.9
3.	Bakersfield, CA	308,392	243,451	26.7
4.	Raleigh, NC	356,321	285,143	25.0
5.	Chula Vista, CA	212,756	173,555	22.6
6.	Laredo, TX	215,484	177,622	21.3
7.	Fort Worth, TX	653,320	541,272	20.7
8.	Stockton, CA	290,141	243,854	19.0
9.	Atlanta, GA	486,411	416,423	16.8
10.	Las Vegas, NV	552,539	480,189	15.1

Fastest-Shrinking Big Cities*

	City	2006 population	2000 population	% change
1.	New Orleans, LA	223,388	484,674	-53.9
2.	Detroit, MI	871,121	951,291	-8.4
3.	Cleveland, OH	444,313	477,472	-6.9
4.	Pittsburgh, PA	312,819	334,563	-6.5
5.	Buffalo, NY	276,059	292,648	-5.7
6.	Birmingham, AL	229,424	242,434	-5.4
7.	Rochester, NY	208,123	219,774	-5.3
8.	Toledo, OH	298,446	313,782	-4.9
9.	St. Paul, MN	273,535	286,788	-4.6
10.	Philadelphia, PA	1,448,394	1,517,550	-4.6

*Among those with populations of 200,000 or more, based on 2006 U.S. Census Bureau estimates.

Percent of Population by Race and Hispanic Origin, 10 Largest Cities,[1] 2000

	City	White	Black or African-Amer.	Amer. Indian, Alaska Native	Asian	Hawaiian & Other Pacific Isl.	Some other race[2]	Two or more races	Hispanic or Latino (of any race)
1.	New York, NY	44.7	26.6	0.5	9.8	0.1	13.4	4.9	27.0
2.	Los Angeles, CA	46.9	11.2	0.8	10.0	0.2	25.7	5.2	46.5
3.	Chicago, IL	42.0	36.8	0.4	4.3	0.1	13.6	2.9	26.0
4.	Houston, TX	49.3	25.3	0.4	5.3	0.1	16.5	3.1	37.4
5.	Philadelphia, PA	45.0	43.2	0.3	4.5	0.0	4.8	2.2	8.5
6.	Phoenix, AZ	71.1	5.1	2.0	2.0	0.1	16.4	3.3	34.1
7.	San Antonio, TX	67.7	6.8	0.8	1.6	0.1	19.3	3.7	58.7
8.	San Diego, CA	60.2	7.9	0.6	13.6	0.5	12.4	4.8	25.4
9.	Dallas, TX	50.8	25.9	0.5	2.7	0.0	17.2	2.7	35.6
10.	San Jose, CA	47.5	3.5	0.8	26.9	0.4	15.9	5.0	30.2

(1) Top 10 cities as determined by 2004 Census Bureau estimates. (2) Persons who, instead of checking off a race shown, filled in a designation under "some other race."

——— STATES AND OTHER AREAS OF THE U.S. ———

Sources: Population: U.S. Commerce Dept., Bureau of the Census—Census 2000: April 1, 2000, and July 2006 est. (including armed forces stationed in the state). Area: Bureau of the Census, Geography Division. Acres forested: Agriculture Dept., Forest Service. Chief airports: Transportation Dept., Federal Aviation Admin. Chief manuf. goods: Bureau of the Census, Manufacturing and Construction Division. Chief crops & Livestock: Agriculture Dept., Natl. Agricultural Stat. Serv. Lumber production: Bureau of the Census, Industry Division. Nonfuel minerals: Dept. of Interior, Office of Mineral Information. Commercial fishing: Commerce Dept., Natl. Marine Fisheries Service. Gross state product & Personal per capita income: Commerce Dept., Bureau of Economic Analysis. Sales tax: Fed. of Tax Admin. Employment distribution & Unemployment: Labor Dept., Bureau of Labor Statistics. New private housing: Bureau of the Census, Residential Construction Branch. Finance: Federal Deposit Insurance Corp. Lottery figures (not all states have a lottery): North American Assn. of State and Provincial Lotteries, for local fiscal year. Federal employees: Labor Dept., Office of Personnel Management. Energy: Energy Dept., Energy Information Administration. Other information from sources in individual states. Some data on Outlying U.S. Areas & Other Islands provided by the CIA World Factbook. For information about tourism earnings, see Transportation and Tourism.

NOTE: Pop. density is for land area only. Categories under racial distribution may not add to 100% due to rounding. "Nat. AK" (Native Alaskans) includes Eskimos and Aleuts. **Hispanic population may be any race** and is dispersed among racial categories, besides being listed separately. Chief airports had 500,000+ boardings in 2005. Nonfuel mineral values for some states exclude small amounts to avoid disclosing proprietary data. Categories under employment distribution are not all-inclusive. Commercial bank and savings institution figures are for FDIC-insured institutions only. Postal Service, TN Valley Auth., and some other agencies are not included in federal govt. numbers. Notable federal facilities marked with an asterisk (*) have been recommended for realignment or closure by the U.S. Dept. of Defense, which had until Sept. 15, 2007 to begin the process, to be completed by Sept. 15, 2011. Electricity prod. excludes independent power producers. **Famous Persons lists may include nonnatives** associated with the state as well as persons born there. Websites are subject to change and are not endorsed by *The World Almanac*.

Alabama (AL)
Heart of Dixie, Camellia State

People. Population (2006 est.): 4,599,030; rank: 23; **net change** (2005-2006): 1.1%. **Pop. density:** 90.8 per sq mi. **Racial distribution** (2005): 71.4% white; 26.4% black; 0.8% Asian; 0.5% Native/Nat. AK; 0.04% Hawaiian/Pacific Islander; 2 or more races, 0.9%. **Hispanic pop.** (any race): 2.3%.

Geography. Total area: 52,419 sq mi; rank: 30. **Land area:** 50,744 sq mi; rank: 28. **Acres forested:** 23.0 mil. **Location:** East South Central state extending N-S from Tenn. to the Gulf of Mexico; E of the Mississippi River. **Climate:** long, hot summers; mild winters; generally abundant rainfall. **Topography:** coastal plains, including Prairie Black Belt, give way to hills, broken terrain; highest elevation, 2,407 ft. **Capital:** Montgomery. **Chief airports at:** Birmingham, Huntsville.

Economy. Chief industries: pulp & paper, chemicals, electronics, apparel, textiles, primary metals, lumber and wood products, food processing, fabricated metals, automotive tires, oil and gas exploration. **Chief manuf. goods:** animal slaughtering & processing, chemicals & synthetics, paper & paperboard, iron & steel, petroleum, tires, aerospace, aluminum, auto body & electronics. **Chief crops:** cotton, greenhouse & nursery, hay, peanuts, corn, soy beans. **Livestock** (Jan. 2007): 1.3 mil cattle/calves; (Dec. 2006): 165,000 hogs/pigs, 14.3 mil chickens (excl. broilers), 1.1 bil broilers. **Timber/lumber** (est. 2006): 2.7 mil bd. ft.; pine, hardwoods. **Nonfuel minerals** (preliminary 2006): $1.2 bil; cement (portland), stone (crushed), lime, sand and gravel (construction), cement (masonry). **Commercial fishing** (2005): $39.9 mil. **Chief port:** Mobile. **Gross state product** (est. 2006): $160.6 bil. **Sales tax** (2007): 4.0%. **Employment distrib.** (May 2007): 18.8% govt.; 19.5% trade/trans./util.; 14.9% mfg.; 10.3% ed./health; 11.0% prof./bus. serv.; 8.8% leisure/hosp.; 4.9% finance; 5.6% constr.; 4.0% other serv.; 1.5% info. **Unemployment** (2006): 3.6%. **Per cap. pers. income** (2006): $31,295. **New private housing** (2006): 32,034 units/$4.4 bil. **Commercial banks** (2006): 168; **deposits:** $68.3 bil. **Savings institutions** (2006): 14; **deposits:** $3.0 bil.

Federal govt. Fed. civ. employees (Mar. 2006): 33,997; **avg. salary:** $64,078. **Notable fed. facilities:** Redstone Arsenal; Ft. Rucker; Marshall Space Flight Ctr.; Anniston Army Depot; *Maxwell/Gunter AFB; U.S. Corps of Engineers.

Energy. Electricity production (est. 2006 kWh by source): Coal: 77.7 bil; Gas: 7.4 bil; Hydroelectric: 7.5 bil; Nuclear: 31.9 bil; Petroleum: 88 mil.

State data. Motto: We dare defend our rights. **Flower:** Camellia. **Bird:** Yellowhammer. **Tree:** Southern Longleaf pine. **Song:** Alabama. **Entered union** Dec. 14, 1819; rank, 22nd. **State fair:** Regional and county fairs held in Sept. and Oct.; no state fair.

History. Alabama was inhabited by the Creek, Cherokee, Chickasaw, Alabama, and Choctaw peoples when Spanish explorers arrived in the early 1500s. The French made the first permanent settlement at Fort Louis, 1702, and founded Mobile, 1711. France later gave up the entire region to England under the Treaty of Paris, 1763. Spanish forces took control of the Mobile Bay area, 1780, and it remained under Spanish control until seized by U.S. troops, 1813. Most of present-day Alabama was held by the Creeks until Gen. Andrew Jackson broke their power, 1814. When Alabama became a state, 1819, black slaves made up about 1/3 of the population. The Indian Removal Act of 1830 forced most remaining Creeks west. The state seceded, 1861, and the Confederate states were organized Feb. 4, at Montgomery, the first capital; the state was readmitted, 1868. Birmingham, founded 1871, became a center for iron- and steel-making. The Montgomery bus boycott, 1955, sparked by Rosa Parks, helped launch the civil rights movement; other confrontations came at Birmingham, 1963, and Selma, 1965. The leading political figure from the 1960s through the '80s, 4-term Gov. George Wallace, started as a segregationist but later won with black support. Growth in the auto industry boosted the state economy as the 21st cent. began.

Tourist attractions. First White House of the Confederacy, Civil Rights Memorial, Alabama Shakespeare Festival, in Montgomery; Ivy Green (Helen Keller's birthplace), Tuscumbia; Civil Rights Museum, statue of Vulcan, in Birmingham; Carver Museum, Tuskegee; W. C. Handy Home, Museum, & Library, Florence; Alabama Space and Rocket Center, Huntsville; Moundville State Monument; Pike Pioneer Museum, Troy; USS *Alabama* Memorial Park, Mobile; Russell Cave Natl. Monument, near Bridgeport: a detailed record of occupancy by humans from about 10,000 BCE to 1650 CE.

Famous Alabamians. Hank Aaron, Tallulah Bankhead, Hugo L. Black, Paul "Bear" Bryant, George Washington Carver, Nat King Cole, William C. Handy, Bo Jackson, Helen Keller, Coretta Scott King, Harper Lee, Joe Louis, Willie Mays, John Hunt Morgan, Jim Nabors, Jesse Owens, Condoleezza Rice, George Wallace, Booker T. Washington, Hank Williams.

Tourist information. Bureau of Tourism and Travel, 401 Adams Avenue, Suite 126, PO Box 4927, Montgomery, AL 36103; 1-800-ALABAMA, (334) 242-4169; www.touralabama.org

Website. www.alabama.gov

Alaska (AK)
The Last Frontier (unofficial)

People. Population (2006 est.): 670,053; rank: 47; **net change** (2005-2006): 1.0%. **Pop. density:** 1.2 per sq mi. **Racial distribution** (2005): 70.5% white; 3.7% black; 4.6% Asian; 16.0% Native/Nat. AK; 0.6% Hawaiian/Pacific Islander; 2 or more races, 4.7%. **Hispanic pop.** (any race): 5.1%.

Geography. Total area: 663,267 sq mi; rank: 1. **Land area:** 571,951 sq mi; rank: 1. **Acres forested:** 126.9 mil. **Location:** NW corner of North America, bordered on E by Canada. **Climate:** SE, SW, and central regions, moist and mild; far north extremely dry. Extended summer days, winter nights, throughout. **Topography:** includes Pacific and Arctic mountain systems, central plateau, and Arctic slope. Mt. McKinley, 20,320 ft, is the highest point in North America. **Capital:** Juneau. **Chief airport at:** Anchorage.

Economy. Chief industries: petroleum, tourism, fishing, mining, forestry, transportation, aerospace. **Chief manuf. goods:** petroleum, seafood. **Chief crops:** greenhouse products, barley, oats, hay, potatoes, carrots. **Livestock** (Jan. 2007): 16,000 cattle/calves; (Dec. 2006): 900 hogs/pigs. **Timber/lumber** (est. 2006): figs. undisclosed; spruce, yellow cedar, hemlock. **Nonfuel minerals** (preliminary 2006): $2.9 bil; zinc, gold, lead, silver, sand and gravel (construction). **Commercial fishing** (2005): $1.3 bil. **Chief ports:** Anchorage, Dutch Harbor, Kodiak, Seward, Skagway, Juneau, Sitka, Valdez, Wrangell. **Gross state product** (est. 2006): $41.1 bil. **Sales tax** (2007): none. **Employment distrib.** (May 2007): 25.9% govt.; 20.5% trade/trans./util.; 3.1% mfg.; 11.8% ed./health; 7.9% prof./bus. serv.; 10.4% leisure/hosp.; 4.7% finance; 5.7% constr.; 3.6% other serv.; 2.2% info. **Unemployment** (2006): 6.7%. **Per cap. pers. income** (2006): $37,271. **New private housing** (2006): 2,739 units/$511.5 mil. **Commercial banks** (2006): 7; **deposits:** $6.4 bil. **Savings institutions** (2006): 2; **deposits:** $348 mil.

Federal govt. Fed. civ. employees (Mar. 2006): 11,922; **avg. salary:** $56,525. **Notable fed. facilities:** *Elmendorf AFB; *Ft. Richardson; Ft. Wainwright; *Eilson AFB; Ft. Greely.

Energy. Electricity production (est. 2006, kWh by source): Coal: 210 mil.; Gas: 3.9 bil; Hydroelectric: 1.4 bil; Petroleum: 546 mil.

State data. Motto: North to the future. **Flower:** Forget-Me-Not. **Bird:** Willow ptarmigan. **Tree:** Sitka spruce. **Song:** Alaska's Flag. **Entered union** Jan. 3, 1959; rank, 49th. **State fair** at Palmer; late Aug.–early Sept.

History. Early inhabitants included the Tlingit-Haida and Athabascan peoples. Ancestors of the Aleut and Inuit (Eskimo) probably arrived from Siberia between 10,000 and 6,000 years ago. Vitus Bering, a Dane sailing for Russia, was the first European to land in Alaska, 1741. Russians, pursuing the fur trade, established a permanent settlement on Kodiak Island, 1784. Sec. of State William H. Seward bought Alaska from Russia for $7.2 mil in 1867, a bargain some called "Seward's Folly." Discovery of gold in the Klondike region of Canada's Yukon Territory, 1896, triggered an Alaskan gold rush. Alaska became a territory, 1912, and a state, 1959. A huge oil find at Prudhoe Bay, 1968, led to construction of the Trans-Alaska Pipeline, 1974-77. The *Exxon Valdez* supertanker ran aground, 1989, spilling about 11 mil gallons of crude oil; the cleanup cost more than $2.2 bil. Repeated attempts by Congress members to allow oil and gas drilling in the Arctic National Wildlife Refuge have failed.

Tourist attractions. Inside Passage; Portage Glacier; Mendenhall Glacier; Ketchikan Totems; Glacier Bay Natl. Park and Preserve; Denali Natl. Park, one of N. America's great wildlife sanctuaries, surrounding Mt. McKinley, N. America's highest peak; Mt. Roberts Tramway, Juneau; Pribilof Islands fur seal rookeries; restored St. Michael's Russian Orthodox Cathedral, Sitka; White Pass & Yukon Route railroad; Skagway; Katmai Natl. Park & Preserve.

Famous Alaskans. Tom Bodett, Susan Butcher, Ernest Gruening, Jewel (Kilcher), Gov. Tony Knowles, Sydney Laurence, Libby Riddles, Jefferson "Soapy" Smith.

Tourist information. Alaska Travel Industry Association, 2600 Cordova St., Ste. 201, Anchorage, AK 99503; 1-800-327-9372; www.travelalaska.com

Website. www.state.ak.us

Arizona (AZ)
Grand Canyon State

People. Population (2006 est.): 6,166,318; rank: 16; **net change** (2005-2006): 3.6%. **Pop. density:** 54.3 per sq mi. **Racial distribution** (2005): 87.4% white; 3.6% black; 2.2% Asian; 5.1% Native/Nat. AK; 0.2% Hawaiian/Pacific Islander; 2 or more races, 1.5%. **Hispanic pop.** (any race): 28.5%.

Geography. Total area: 113,998 sq mi; rank: 6. **Land area:** 113,635 sq mi; rank: 6. **Acres forested:** 19.4 mil. **Location:** in the southwestern U.S. **Climate:** clear and dry in the southern regions and northern plateau; high central areas have heavy winter snows. **Topography:** Colorado plateau in the N, containing the Grand Canyon; Mexican Highlands running diagonally NW to SE; Sonoran Desert in the SW. **Capital:** Phoenix. **Chief airports at:** Tucson, Phoenix.

Economy. Chief industries: manufacturing, construction, tourism, mining, agriculture. **Chief manuf. goods:** aerospace, semiconductors, navigational instruments, cement, plastics, structural metals, dairy, printing, furniture. **Chief crops:** cotton, grapes, apples, lettuce, hay, potatoes, sorghum, barley, corn, wheat. **Livestock** (Jan. 2007): 940,000 cattle/calves, 110,000 sheep/lambs; (Dec. 2006): 148,000 hogs/pigs. **Timber/lumber** (est. 2006): 93 mil bd. ft.; pine, fir, spruce. **Nonfuel minerals** (preliminary 2006): $6.7 bil; copper, molybdenum concentrates, sand and gravel (construction), cement (portland), lime. **Gross state product** (est.

2006): $232.5 bil. **Sales tax** (2007): 5.6%. **Employment distrib.** (May 2007): 15.6% govt.; 19.2% trade/trans./util.; 6.8% mfg.; 11.0% ed./health; 15.2% prof./bus. serv.; 10.3% leisure/hosp.; 6.9% finance; 9.0% constr.; 3.9% other serv.; 1.6% info. **Unemployment** (2006): 4.1%. **Per cap. pers. income** (2006): $31,458. **New private housing** (2006): 65,363 units/ $11.2 bil. **Commercial banks** (2006): 69; **deposits:** $72.0 bil. **Savings institutions** (2006): 14; **deposits:** $6.8 bil. **Lottery** (2006): total sales: $468.7 mil; profit: $141.1 mil.

Federal govt. Fed. civ. employees (Mar. 2006): 33,871; **avg. salary:** $55,393. **Notable fed. facilities:** *Luke AFB, Davis-Monthan AFB; *Ft. Huachuca; Yuma Proving Grounds.

Energy. Electricity production (est. 2006, kWh by source): Coal: 40.1 bil; Gas: 13.2 bil; Hydroelectric: 6.8 bil; Nuclear: 24.0 bil; Petroleum: 72 mil; Other: 35 mil.

State data. Motto: Ditat Deus (God enriches). **Flower:** Blossom of the Saguaro cactus. **Bird:** Cactus wren. **Tree:** Paloverde. **Song:** Arizona. **Entered union** Feb. 14, 1912; rank, 48th. **State fair** at Phoenix; Oct.–early Ncv.

History. Paleoindians hunted large game in the area at least 12,000 years ago. Anasazi, Mogollon, and Hohokam civilizations lived there c. 300 BCE-1300 CE; Navajo and Apache came c. 15th cent. Marcos de Niza, a Franciscan, and Estevanico, a black former slave, explored, 1539; Spanish explorer Francisco Vásquez de Coronado visited, 1540. Eusebio Francisco Kino, a Jesuit missionary, taught Indians 1692-1711, and left missions. Tubac, a Spanish fort, became the first European settlement, 1752. Spain ceded Arizona to Mexico, 1821. The U.S. took over, 1848, after the Mexican War. The area below the Gila River came from Mexico in the Gadsden Purchase, 1853. Arizona became a territory, 1863. Apache wars ended with Geronimo's surrender, 1886. Arizona became a state, 1912, and grew rapidly after 1960 with a fourfold rise in population over the next 4 decades. Barry Goldwater was a leading conservative voice in the U.S. Senate (1953-65, 1969-87). The border with Mexico is a major gateway for illegal immigration to the U.S.

Tourist attractions. The Grand Canyon; Painted Desert; Petrified Forest Natl. Park; Canyon de Chelly; Meteor Crater; London Bridge, Lake Havasu City; Biosphere 2, Oracle; Navajo Natl. Monument.

Famous Arizonans. Bruce Babbitt, Cochise, Alice Cooper, Geronimo, Barry Goldwater, Zane Grey, Carl Hayden, George W. P. Hunt, Helen Jacobs, Bil Keane, Percival Lowell, John McCain, William H. Pickering, John J. Rhodes, Morris Udall, Stewart Udall, Frank Lloyd Wright.

Tourist information. Arizona Office of Tourism, 1110 W. Washington St., Ste. 155, Phoenix, AZ 85007; 1-866-275-5816; www.arizonaguide.com

Website. www.az.gov

Arkansas (AR)
The Natural State, The Razorback State

People. Population (2006 est.): 2,810,872; rank: 32; **net change** (2005-2006): 1.3%. **Pop. density:** 54.0 per sq mi. **Racial distribution** (2005): 81.3% white; 15.7% black; 1.0% Asian; 0.7% Native/Nat. AK; 0.09% Hawaiian/Pacific Islander; 2 or more races, 1.2%. **Hispanic pop.** (any race): 4.7%.

Geography. Total area: 53,179 sq mi; rank: 29. **Land area:** 52,068 sq mi; rank: 27. **Acres forested:** 18.8 mil. **Location:** in the west south-central U.S. **Climate:** long, hot summers, mild winters; generally abundant rainfall. **Topography:** eastern delta and prairie, southern lowland forests, and the northwestern highlands, which include the Ozark Plateaus. **Capital:** Little Rock. **Chief airports at:** Cave Springs, Little Rock.

Economy. Chief industries: manufacturing, agriculture, tourism, forestry. **Chief manuf. goods:** poultry processing, motor vehicles & parts, iron & steel, paper & paperboard, plastics, preserved fruits & vegetables, aerospace, rubber. **Chief crops:** rice, soybeans, cotton, hay, wheat, corn, sorghum, tomatoes, peaches, watermelons, pecans, blueberries, grapes. **Livestock** (Jan. 2007): 1.8 mil cattle/calves; (Dec. 2006): 260,000 hogs/pigs, 23.4 mil chickens (excl. broilers), 1.2 bil broilers. **Timber/lumber** (est. 2006): 3.1 bil bd. ft.; oak, hickory, gum, cypress, pine. **Nonfuel minerals** (preliminary 2006): $617 mil; stone (crushed), bromine, cement (portland), sand and gravel (construction), lime. **Chief ports:** Little Rock, Pine Bluff, Osceola, Helena, Fort Smith, Van Buren, Camden, Dardanelle, North Little Rock, West Memphis, Crossett, McGehee, Morrilton. **Gross state product** (est. 2006): $91.8 bil. **Sales tax** (2007): 6%. **Employ-

ment distrib. (May 2007): 17.6% govt.; 20.7% trade/trans./util.; 15.8% mfg.; 12.7% ed./health; 9.6% prof./bus. serv.; 8.4% leisure/hosp.; 4.4% finance; 4.8% constr.; 3.7% other serv.; 1.7% info. **Unemployment** (2006): 5.3%. **Per cap. pers. income** (2006): $27,935. **New private housing** (2006): 13,885 units/$1.8 bil. **Commercial banks** (2006): 162; **deposits:** $42.7 bil. **Savings institutions** (2006): 8; **deposits:** $1.5 bil.

Federal govt. Fed. civ. employees (Mar. 2006): 12,090; **avg. salary:** $54,176. **Notable fed. facilities:** Little Rock AFB; Pine Bluff Arsenal; Natl. Ctr. for Toxicological Research, Jefferson.

Energy. Electricity production (est. 2006, kWh by source): Coal: 24.1 bil; Gas: 847 mil; Hydroelectric: 1.5 bil; Nuclear: 15.2 bil; Petroleum: 95 mil.

State data. Motto: Regnat Populus (The people rule). **Flower:** Apple blossom. **Bird:** Mockingbird. **Tree:** Pine. **Song:** Arkansas. **Entered union** June 15, 1836; rank, 25th. **State fair** at Little Rock; mid-Oct.

History. Quapaw, Caddo, Osage, Cherokee, and Choctaw peoples lived in the area at the time of European contact. The first European explorers were de Soto, 1541; Marquette and Jolliet, 1673; and La Salle, 1682. French fur trader Henri de Tonty founded the first settlement, 1686, at Arkansas Post. In 1762, the area was ceded by France to Spain, then given back again, 1800, and was part of the Louisiana Purchase, 1803. It was made a territory, 1819, and entered the Union as a slave state, 1836. Arkansas seceded in 1861, after the Civil War began, and was readmitted, 1868. Pres. Eisenhower sent federal troops, 1957, to keep Gov. Orval Faubus from blocking racial integration at Central High School in Little Rock. Wal-Mart, now the world's leading retailer, opened its first store at Rogers, 1962. Elected 5 times as governor, Bill Clinton later served 2 terms in the White House (1993-2001); his presidential library opened, 2004, in Little Rock.

Tourist attractions. Hot Springs Natl. Park (water ranging from 95°F-147°F); Eureka Springs; Ozark Folk Center, Blanchard Caverns, near Mountain View; Crater of Diamonds (only U.S. diamond mine) near Murfreesboro; Toltec Mounds Archeological State Park, Little Rock; Buffalo Natl. River; Mid-America Museum, Hot Springs; Pea Ridge Natl. Military Park; Tanyard Springs, Morrilton; Wiederkehr Wine Village.

Famous Arkansans. Daisy Bates, Dee Brown, Paul "Bear" Bryant, Glen Campbell, Johnny Cash, Hattie Caraway, Wesley Clark, Bill Clinton, "Dizzy" Dean, Orval Faubus, James W. Fulbright, John Grisham, John H. Johnson, Douglas MacArthur, John L. McClellan, James S. McDonnell, Scottie Pippen, Dick Powell, Brooks Robinson, Billy Bob Thornton, Winthrop Rockefeller, Mary Steenburgen, Edward Durell Stone, Sam Walton, Archibald Yell.

Tourist information. Arkansas Dept. of Parks & Tourism, 1 Capitol Mall, Little Rock, AR 72201; 1-800-NATURAL; www.arkansas.com

Website. www.state.ar.us

California (CA)
Golden State

People. Population (2006 est.): 36,457,549; rank: 1; **net change** (2005-2006): 0.8%. **Pop. density:** 234.0 per sq mi. **Racial distribution** (2005): 77.0% white; 6.7% black; 12.2% Asian; 1.2% Native/Nat. AK; 0.4% Hawaiian/Pacific Islander; 2 or more races, 2.4%. **Hispanic pop.** (any race): 35.2%.

Geography. Total area: 163,696 sq mi; rank: 3. **Land area:** 155,959 sq mi; rank: 3. **Acres forested:** 40.2 mil. **Location:** on western coast of the U.S. **Climate:** moderate temperatures and rainfall along the coast; extremes in the interior. **Topography:** long mountainous coastline; central valley; Sierra Nevada on the east; desert basins of the southern interior; rugged mountains of the north. **Capital:** Sacramento. **Chief airports at:** Burbank, Fresno, Long Beach, Los Angeles, Oakland, Ontario, Palm Springs, Sacramento, San Diego, San Francisco, San Jose, Santa Ana.

Economy. Chief industries: agriculture, tourism, apparel, electronics, telecommunications, entertainment. **Chief manuf. goods:** petroleum, aerospace, precision instruments, semiconductors, telecom. & broadcasting equip., pharmaceutical, wineries, plastics, medical equip., preserved fruits & vegetables, printing, dairy, cut & sew apparel, motor vehicles. **Chief crops:** grapes, nursery products, almonds, lettuce, hay, strawberries, floriculture, tomatoes, cotton, oranges, pistachios, walnuts, broccoli, carrots, rice, peaches, lemons. **Livestock** (Jan. 2007): 5.5 mil cattle/calves, 610,000

sheep/lambs; (Dec. 2006): 145,000 hogs/pigs, 23.3 mil chickens (excl. broilers). **Timber/lumber** (est. 2006): 2.8 bil bd. ft.; fir, pine, redwood, oak. **Nonfuel minerals** (preliminary 2006): $4.5 bil; sand and gravel (construction), cement (portland), boron minerals, stone (crushed), soda ash. **Commercial fishing** (2005): $115.0 mil. **Chief ports:** Long Beach, Los Angeles, San Diego, Oakland, San Francisco, Sacramento, Stockton. **Gross state product** (est. 2006): $1.7 trillion. **Sales tax** (2007): 7.25%. **Employment distrib.** (May 2007): 16.6% govt.; 18.8% trade/trans./util.; 9.8% mfg.; 10.9% ed./health; 14.8% prof./bus. serv.; 10.2% leisure/hosp.; 6.1% finance; 6.1% constr.; 3.4% other serv.; 3.1% info. **Unemployment** (2006): 4.9%. **Per cap. pers. income** (2006): $38,956. **New private housing** (2006): 160,502 units/$29.6 bil. **Commercial banks** (2006): 297; **deposits:** $530.1 bil. **Savings institutions** (2006): 36; **deposits:** $195.7 bil. **Lottery** (2006): total sales: $3.6 bil; profit: $1.2 bil.

Federal govt. Fed. civ. employees (Mar. 2006): 139,804; **avg. salary:** $66,212. **Notable fed. facilities:** San Diego; *USMC Camp Pendleton; Naval Base Coronado; Twentynine Palms; Miramar; Travis AFB; Naval Research Lab., Monterey; Lawrence Livermore Natl. Lab; Berkeley Natl. Lab; NASA Jet Propulsion Lab; Edwards AFB (NASA Dryden Flight Research Ctr., AF Flight Test Ctr.); San Francisco Mint.

Energy. Electricity production (est. 2006, kWh by source): Gas: 16.3 bil; Hydroelectric: 47.4 bil; Nuclear: 32.0 bil; Petroleum: 61 mil; Other: 1.3 bil.

State data. Motto: Eureka (I have found it). **Flower:** Golden poppy. **Bird:** California valley quail. **Tree:** California redwood. **Song:** I Love You, California. **Entered union** Sept. 9, 1850; rank, 31st. **State fair** at Sacramento; late Aug.–early Sept.

History. Early inhabitants included more than 100 different Native American tribes with multiple dialects. The first European explorers were Cabrillo, 1542, and Drake, 1579. The first settlement was the Spanish Alta California mission at San Diego, 1769, first in a string founded by Franciscan Father Junípero Serra. California became a province of independent Mexico, 1821. U.S. traders and settlers arrived in the 19th cent. and staged the Bear Flag revolt, 1846, in protest against Mexican rule; later that year U.S. forces occupied California. At the end of the Mexican War, Mexico ceded the territory to the U.S., 1848; that same year gold was discovered, and the famed gold rush began. California became a state, 1850. An economic downturn in the 1870s spurred riots against Chinese immigrants, who had come as laborers in the boom years. An earthquake and related fires devastated San Francisco, 1906. During World War II, Japanese Americans, many of them U.S. citizens, were held in detention camps, 1942-45. Ronald Reagan, a former movie actor, became state governor (1967-75) and U.S. president (1981-89). A budget crisis, 2003, resulted in the recall of Gov. Gray Davis and the election of another former actor, Arnold Schwarzenegger. Led by Hollywood in entertainment and Silicon Valley in high-tech, the state's economy dwarfs that of most nations.

Tourist attractions. The *Queen Mary*, Aquarium of the Pacific, in Long Beach; Palomar Mountain; Disneyland, Anaheim; Getty Center, Universal Studios, in Los Angeles; Tournament of Roses & Rose Bowl, Pasadena; Golden State Museum, Sacramento; San Diego Zoo; Yosemite Valley; Lassen and Sequoia-Kings Canyon natl. parks; Lake Tahoe; Mojave and Colorado deserts; San Francisco Bay; Napa Valley; Monterey Peninsula; oldest living things on earth believed to be a stand of Bristlecone pines in the Inyo Natl. Forest, est. 4,700 years old; Redwood Natl. & State Parks.

Famous Californians. Edmund G. (Pat) Brown, Jerry Brown, Luther Burbank, Julia Child, Ted Danson, Cameron Diaz, Leonardo DiCaprio, Joe DiMaggio, Dianne Feinstein, John C. Fremont, Tom Hanks, Bret Harte, William Randolph Hearst, Helen Hunt, Jack Kemp, Monica Lewinsky, Jack London, George Lucas, Mark McGwire, Marilyn Monroe, John Muir, Richard M. Nixon, George S. Patton Jr., Gregory Peck, Nancy Pelosi, Ronald Reagan, Sally K. Ride, William Saroyan, Father Junípero Serra, O.J. Simpson, Kevin Spacey, Leland Stanford, John Steinbeck, Arnold Schwarzenegger, Shirley Temple, Earl Warren, Ted Williams, Serena Williams, Venus Williams, Tiger Woods.

Tourist information. California Division of Tourism, PO Box 1499, Sacramento, CA 95812-1499; 1-800-862-2543; www.gocalif.com

Website. www.state.ca.us

Colorado (CO)
Centennial State

People. Population (2006 est.): 4,753,377; rank: 22; **net change** (2005-2006): 1.9%. **Pop. density:** 45.9 per sq mi. **Racial distribution** (2005): 90.3% white; 4.1% black; 2.6% Asian; 1.1% Native/Nat. AK; 0.1% Hawaiian/Pacific Islander; 2 or more races, 1.8%. **Hispanic pop.** (any race): 19.5%.

Geography. Total area: 104,094 sq mi; rank: 8. **Land area:** 103,718 sq mi; rank: 8. **Acres forested:** 21.6 mil. **Location:** in W central U.S. **Climate:** low relative humidity, abundant sunshine, wide daily, seasonal temp. ranges; alpine conditions in the high mountains. **Topography:** eastern dry high plains; hilly to mountainous central plateau; western Rocky Mountains of high ranges, with broad valleys, deep, narrow canyons. **Capital:** Denver. **Chief airports at:** Denver, Colorado Springs.

Economy. Chief industries: manufacturing, construction, government, tourism, agriculture, aerospace, electronics equipment. **Chief manuf. goods:** animal slaughtering, beer, petroleum, pharmaceuticals, aerospace, medical equip., precision instruments, printing, semiconductors. **Chief crops:** hay, corn, potatoes, wheat, onions, dry edible beans, sunflowers, sugarbeets, barley, proso millet, cabbage, peaches, lettuce, apples, cantaloupes. **Livestock** (Jan. 2007): 2.7 mil cattle/calves, 400,000 sheep/lambs; (Dec. 2006): 830,000 hogs/pigs, 4.6 mil chickens (excl. broilers). **Timber/lumber** (est. 2006): 106 mil bd. ft.; oak, ponderosa pine, Douglas fir. **Nonfuel minerals** (preliminary 2006): $1.7 bil; molybdenum concentrates, sand and gravel (construction), cement (portland), gold, stone (crushed). **Gross state product** (est. 2006): $230.5 bil. **Sales tax** (2007): 2.9%. **Employment distrib.** (May 2007): 16.5% govt.; 18.0% trade/trans./util.; 6.4% mfg.; 10.3% ed./health; 15.0% prof./bus. serv.; 11.4% leisure/hosp.; 6.9% finance; 7.1% constr.; 4.0% other serv.; 3.3% info. **Unemployment** (2006): 4.3%. **Per cap. pers. income** (2006): $39,186. **New private housing** (2006): 38,343 units/$7.8 bil. **Commercial banks** (2006): 185; **deposits:** $68.2 bil. **Savings institutions** (2006): 17; **deposits:** $8.2 bil. **Lottery** (2006): total sales: $468.8 mil; profit $125.6 mil.

Federal govt. Fed. civ. employees (Mar. 2006): 33,196; **avg. salary:** $67,679. **Notable fed. facilities:** *U.S. Air Force Academy; Peterson AFB; Denver Mint; Ft. Carson; Natl. Renewable Energy Labs; U.S. Rail Transportation Test Ctr.; Cheyenne Mtn. Operations Ctr. (NORAD, U.S. Space Comm.); Denver Federal Ctr.; Natl. Ctr. for Atmospheric Research; Natl. Inst. for Standards & Technology, Boulder; Natl. Wildlife Res. Ctr.; NOAA Env. Technology Lab.

Energy. Electricity production (est. 2006, kWh by source): Coal: 35.8 bil; Gas: 4.5 bil; Hydroelectric: 1.5 bil; Petroleum: 13 mil; Other: 71 mil.

State data. Motto: Nil Sine Numine (Nothing Without Providence). **Flower:** Rocky Mountain columbine. **Bird:** Lark bunting. **Tree:** Colorado blue spruce. **Song:** Where the Columbines Grow. **Entered union:** Aug. 1, 1876; rank 38th. **State fair** at Pueblo; mid-Aug.–early Sept.

History. Paleoindians hunted big game in the area at least 11,000 years ago. Anasazi cliff dwellers flourished around Mesa Verde until about 1300 CE; other Native Americans were the Ute, Pueblo, Cheyenne, and Arapaho. The region was claimed by Spain, but passed to France, 1800. The U.S. acquired eastern Colorado in the Louisiana Purchase, 1803. Lt. Zebulon M. Pike explored the area, 1806, sighting the peak that bears his name. After the Mexican War, 1846-48, U.S. immigrants settled in the east, former Mexicans in the south. Gold was discovered in 1858, causing a population boom. Congress created Colorado Territory, 1861. Conflict between newcomers and displaced Native Americans led to the Sand Creek Massacre, 1864, in which U.S. soldiers and settlers killed some 150 Cheyenne and Arapaho. Most Native Americans were later removed to Oklahoma Territory. The 1870s brought statehood, 1876, and rich silver finds that turned Leadville into a boomtown. Federal military and civilian employment in Colorado surged in the 1940s and '50s; since then, tourism and high-tech industries have fueled the economy. The state's Hispanic population grew from 5.8% in 1980 to 19.5% in 2006.

Tourist attractions. Rocky Mountain and Black Canyon of the Gunnison natl. parks; Aspen Ski Resort; Garden of the Gods, Colorado Springs; Great Sand Dunes, Dinosaur, and Colorado natl. monuments; Pikes Peak and Mt. Evans highways; Mesa Verde Natl. Park (ancient Anasazi Indian cliff dwellings); Grand Mesa Natl. Forest; mining towns of Central City, Silverton, Cripple Creek; Burlington's Old Town; Bent's Fort, near La Junta; Georgetown Loop Historic Mining Railroad Park, Cumbres & Toltec Scenic Railroad; limited stakes gaming in Central City, Blackhawk, Cripple Creek, Ignacio, and Towaoe.

Famous Coloradans. Tim Allen, Frederick Bonfils, Henry Brown, Molly Brown, William N. Byers, M. Scott Carpenter, Lon Chaney, Jack Dempsey, Mamie Eisenhower, Douglas Fairbanks, Barney Ford, Scott Hamilton, John Kerry, Chief Ourey, "Baby Doe" Tabor, Lowell Thomas, Byron R. White, Paul Whiteman.

Tourist information. Colorado Tourism Office, 1625 Broadway, Ste. 1700, Denver, CO 80202; 1-800-COLORADO; www.colorado.com
Website. www.colorado.gov

Connecticut (CT)
Constitution State, Nutmeg State

People. Population (2006 est.): 3,504,809; rank: 29; **net change** (2005-2006): 0.1%. **Pop. density:** 723.4 per sq mi. **Racial distribution** (2005): 84.9% white; 10.1% black; 3.2% Asian; 0.3% Native/Nat. AK; 0.08% Hawaiian/Pacific Islander; 2 or more races, 1.4%. **Hispanic pop.** (any race): 10.9%.

Geography. Total area: 5,543 sq mi; rank: 48. **Land area:** 4,845 sq mi; rank: 48. **Acres forested:** 1.9 mil. **Location:** New England state in NE corner of the U.S. **Climate:** moderate; winters avg. slightly below freezing; warm, humid summers. **Topography:** western upland, the Berkshires, in NW, highest elevations; narrow central lowland N-S; hilly eastern upland drained by rivers. **Capital:** Hartford. **Chief airport at:** Windsor Locks.

Economy. Chief industries: manufacturing, retail trade, government, services, finances, insurance, real estate. **Chief manuf. goods:** aerospace, chemicals, fabricated metals, precision instruments, toiletries, medical equip., printing, plastics. **Chief crops:** nursery stock, Christmas trees, mushrooms, sweet corn, apples, tobacco, hay. **Livestock** (Jan. 2007): 53,000 cattle/calves; (Dec. 2006): 3,600 hogs/pigs, 4.0 mil chickens (excl. broilers) **Timber/lumber** (est. 2006): 37 mil bd. ft.; oak, birch, beech, maple. **Nonfuel minerals** (preliminary 2006): $169 mil; stone (crushed), sand and gravel (construction), stone (dimension), clays (common), gemstones (natural). **Commercial fishing** (2005): $37.6 mil. **Chief ports:** New Haven, Bridgeport, New London. **Gross state product** (est. 2006): $204.1 bil. **Sales tax** (2007): 6.0%. **Employment distrib.** (May 2007): 14.6% govt.; 18.3% trade/trans./util.; 11.3% mfg.; 16.7% ed./health; 12.3% prof./bus. serv.; 8.1% leisure/hosp.; 8.5% finance; 4.1% constr.; 3.8% other serv.; 2.2% info. **Unemployment** (2006): 4.3%. **Per cap. pers. income** (2006): $49,852. **New private housing** (2006): 9,236 units/$1.9 bil. **Commercial banks** (2006): 35; **deposits:** $44.6 bil. **Savings institutions** (2006): 38; **deposits:** $34.6 bil. **Lottery** (2006): total sales: $970.3 mil; profit: $284.9 mil.

Federal govt. Fed. civ. employees (Mar. 2006): 6,854; **avg. salary:** $66,343. **Notable fed. facilities:** U.S. Coast Guard Academy; *Navy Sub Base New London.

Energy. Electricity production (est. 2006, kWh by source): Hydroelectric: 322 mil.

State data. Motto: Qui Transtulit Sustinet (He who transplanted still sustains). **Flower:** Mountain laurel. **Bird:** American robin. **Tree:** White oak. **Song:** Yankee Doodle. **Fifth of** the 13 original states to ratify the Constitution, Jan. 9, 1788. **State Fair:** district and local fairs, largest at Durham, late Sept.; no state fair.

History. At the time of European contact, inhabitants of the area were Algonquian peoples, including the Mohegan and Pequot. Dutch explorer Adriaen Block was the first European visitor, 1614. By 1634, settlers from Plymouth Bay had started colonies along the Connecticut River; in 1637 they defeated the Pequots. The Colony of Connecticut was chartered by England, 1662, adding New Haven, 1665. A Patriot stronghold in the American Revolution, the state actively supported the antislavery movement and the Union cause in the Civil War. The state economy prospered in the 20th cent. from insurance- and defense-related industries. *Nautilus*, the first nuclear-powered submarine, was launched at Groton, 1954.

Tourist attractions. Mark Twain House, Hartford; Yale University's Art Gallery, Peabody Museum, in New Haven; Mystic Seaport, Marine Life Aquarium; P. T. Barnum Museum, Bridgeport; Gillette Castle, Hadlyme; U.S.S. *Nautilus* Memorial, Groton (1st nuclear-powered submarine); Mashantucket Pequot Museum & Research Ctr., Foxwoods Resort & Casino, in Ledyard; Mohegan Sun, Uncasville; Lake Compounce, Bristol.

Famous "Nutmeggers." Ethan Allen, Phineas T. Barnum, G.W. Bush, Samuel Colt, Jonathan Edwards, Nathan Hale, Katharine Hepburn, Isaac Hull, Robert Mitchum, J. Pierpont Morgan, Ralph Nader, Israel Putnam, Wallace Stevens, Harriet Beecher Stowe, Mark Twain, Noah Webster, Eli Whitney.

Tourist information. Connecticut Commission on Culture and Tourism, One Financial Plaza, 755 Main St., Hartford, CT 06103; 1-888-CTVISIT, (860) 256-2800; www.ctvisit.com

Website. www.ct.gov

Delaware (DE)
First State, Diamond State

People. Population (2006 est.): 853,476; rank: 45; **net change** (2005-2006): 1.4%. **Pop. density:** 437.3 per sq mi. **Racial distribution** (2005): 74.9% white; 20.7% black; 2.7% Asian; 0.4% Native/Nat. AK; 0.06% Hawaiian/Pacific Islander; 2 or more races, 1.4%. **Hispanic pop.** (any race): 6.0%.

Geography. Total area: 2,489 sq mi; rank: 49. **Land area:** 1,954 sq mi; rank: 49. **Acres forested:** 0.4 mil. **Location:** occupies the Delmarva Peninsula on the Atlantic coastal plain. **Climate:** moderate. **Topography:** Piedmont plateau to the N, sloping to a near sea-level plain. **Capital:** Dover.

Economy. Chief industries: chemicals, agriculture, finance, poultry, shellfish, tourism, auto assembly, food processing, transportation equipment. **Chief manuf. goods:** pharmaceuticals, poultry processing, soap & cleaning compounds, precision instruments, basic chemicals, plastics. **Chief crops:** soybeans, corn, greenhouse & nursery, wheat, potatoes, barley, hay, watermelons, lima beans, green peas, pumpkins, mushrooms, cabbage. **Livestock** (Jan. 2007): 23,000 cattle/calves; (Dec. 2006): 10,500 hogs/pigs, 269.1 mil broilers. **Timber/lumber:** figs. undisclosed; hardwoods and softwoods. **Nonfuel minerals** (preliminary 2006): $22.2 mil; Sand and gravel (construction), magnesium compounds, stone(crushed), gemstones (natural). **Commercial fishing** (2005): $6.1 mil. **Chief port:** Wilmington. **Gross state product** (est. 2006): $60.4 bil. **Sales tax** (2007): none. **Employment distrib.** (May 2007): 14.2% govt.; 18.7% trade/trans./util.; 7.4% mfg.; 13.2% ed./health; 14.4% prof./bus. serv.; 9.7% leisure/hosp.; 9.7% finance; 6.6% constr.; 4.6% other serv.; 1.6% info. **Unemployment** (2006): 3.6%. **Per cap. pers. income** (2006): $39,022. **New private housing** (2006): 6,504 units/$785.5 mil. **Commercial banks** (2006): 35; **deposits:** $86.2 bil. **Savings institutions** (2006): 8; **deposits:** $67.7 bil. **Lottery** (2006): total sales: $728.0 mil; profit: $248.8 mil.

Federal govt. Fed. civ. employees (Mar. 2006): 2,864; **avg. salary:** $57,176. **Notable fed. facilities:** Dover AFB, Federal Wildlife Refuge, Bombay Hook.

Energy. Electricity production (est. 2006, kWh by source): Petroleum: 4 mil.

State data. Motto: Liberty and independence. **Flower:** Peach blossom. **Bird:** Blue hen chicken. **Tree:** American holly. **Song:** Our Delaware. **First** of original 13 states to ratify the Constitution, Dec. 7, 1787. **State fair** at Harrington; mid–late July.

History. The Lenni Lenape (Delaware) people lived in the region at the time of European contact. Henry Hudson located the Delaware R., 1609, and in 1610, English explorer Samuel Argall entered Delaware Bay, naming the area after Virginia's governor, Lord De La Warr. Dutch, Swedish, and Finnish settlers were followed by the British, who took control in 1664. After 1682, Delaware became part of Pennsylvania, and in 1704 it was granted its own assembly. It adopted a constitution as the state of Delaware, 1776, and was first to ratify the federal Constitution, 1787. Although it remained in the Union during the Civil War, Delaware retained slavery until the 13th Amendment abolished it in 1865. The Du Pont company, founded as a gunpowder mill in 1802, became an industrial giant in the 20th century, making nylon, Teflon, and other synthetics. Pro-business laws drew many out-of-state firms to incorporate in Delaware. In 2000, Ruth Ann Minner was elected Delaware's first woman governor.

Tourist attractions. Ft. Christina Monument, site of founding of New Sweden, Holy Trinity (Old Swedes) Church, erected 1698, the oldest Protestant church in the U.S. still in use, in Wilmington; Hagley Museum, Winterthur Museum and Gardens, near Wilmington; New Castle historic district; John

Dickinson "Penman of the Revolution" home, Dover; Rehoboth Beach; Dover Downs Intl. Speedway.

Famous Delawareans. Thomas F. Bayard, Joseph Biden, Henry Seidel Canby, E. I. du Pont, John P. Marquand, Howard Pyle, Caesar Rodney.

Tourist information. Delaware Tourism Office, 99 Kings Highway, Dover, DE 19901; 1-866-2VISITDE; www.visitdelaware.net

Website. www.delaware.gov

Florida (FL)
Sunshine State

People. Population (2006 est.): 18,089,888; rank: 4; **net change** (2005-2006): 1.8%. **Pop. density:** 337.1 per sq mi. **Racial distribution** (2005): 80.4% white; 15.7% black; 2.1% Asian; 0.4% Native/Nat. AK; 0.08% Hawaiian/Pacific Islander; 2 or more races, 1.2%. **Hispanic pop.** (any race): 19.5%.

Geography. Total area: 65,755 sq mi; rank: 22. **Land area:** 53,927 sq mi; rank: 26. **Acres forested:** 16.3 mil. **Location:** peninsula jutting southward 500 mi between the Atlantic and the Gulf of Mexico. **Climate:** subtropical N of Bradenton-Lake Okeechobee-Vero Beach line; tropical S of line. **Topography:** land is flat or rolling; highest point is 345 ft in the NW. **Capital:** Tallahassee. **Chief airports at:** Fort Lauderdale, Fort Myers, Jacksonville, Miami, Orlando, Pensacola, Sanford, Sarasota/Bradenton, Tallahassee, Tampa, West Palm Beach.

Economy. Chief industries: tourism, agriculture, manufacturing, construction, services, international trade. **Chief manuf. goods:** navigational instruments, medical equip., cement, broadcasting equip., beverages, phosphatic fertilizer, preserved fruits & vegetables, structural metal, printing. **Chief crops:** greenhouse & nursery, oranges, sugarcane, tomatoes, green peppers, grapefruit, strawberries, snap beans, sweet corn, potatoes, cucumbers, tangerines. **Livestock** (Jan. 2007): 1.7 mil cattle/calves; (Dec. 2006): 20,000 hogs/pigs, 13.7 mil chickens (excl. broilers), 75.0 mil broilers. **Timber/lumber** (est. 2006): 1.1 bil bd. ft.; pine, cypress, cedar. **Nonfuel minerals** (preliminary 2006): $2.8 bil; stone (crushed), phosphate rock, cement (portland), sand and gravel (construction), cement (masonry). **Commercial fishing** (2005): $168.4 mil. **Chief ports:** Pensacola, Tampa, Manatee, Miami, Port Everglades, Jacksonville, St. Petersburg, Canaveral. **Gross state product** (est. 2006): $713.5 bil. **Sales tax** (2007): 6.0%. **Employment distrib.** (May 2007): 13.8% govt.; 19.7% trade/trans./util.; 4.9% mfg.; 12.3% ed./health; 16.8% prof./bus. serv.; 11.6% leisure/hosp.; 6.8% finance; 7.7% constr.; 4.3% other serv.; 2.0% info. **Unemployment** (2006): 3.3%. **Per cap. pers. income** (2006): $35,798. **New private housing** (2006): 203,238 units/$35.7 bil. **Commercial banks** (2006): 312; **deposits:** $296.9 bil. **Savings institutions** (2006): 53; **deposits:** $66.5 bil. **Lottery** (2006): total sales: $4.0 bil; profit: $1.2 bil.

Federal govt. Fed. civ. employees (Mar. 2006): 71,858; **avg. salary:** $60,807. **Notable fed. facilities:** John F. Kennedy Space Ctr.; Eglin AFB; MacDill AFB; *Pensacola NAS; Jacksonville NAS; Mayport Naval Sta.

Energy. Electricity production (est. 2006, kWh by source): Coal: 60.4 bil; Gas: 85.4 bil; Hydroelectric: 216 mil; Nuclear: 31.4 bil; Petroleum: 15.5 bil; Other: 82 mil.

State data. Motto: In God we trust. **Flower:** Orange blossom. **Bird:** Mockingbird. **Tree:** Sabal palmetto palm. **Song:** Old Folks at Home. **Entered union** Mar. 3, 1845; rank, 27th. **State fair** at Tampa; early–mid Feb.

History. Florida has been inhabited for at least 12,000 years. Timucua, Apalachee, and Calusa peoples were living in the region when the earliest Europeans came; later the Seminole migrated from Georgia to Florida, becoming dominant there in the early 18th cent. The first European to see Florida was Ponce de León, 1513. France established a colony, Fort Caroline, on the St. Johns River, 1564. Spain settled St. Augustine, 1565, and Spanish troops massacred most of the French. Britain's Sir Francis Drake burned St. Augustine, 1586. In 1763, Spain ceded Florida to Great Britain, which held the area 20 years before returning it to Spain. Florida was ceded to the U.S. in the Adams-Onís Treaty, 1819. The Seminole War, 1835-42, resulted in removal of most Native Americans to Indian Territory. Florida joined the Union in 1845, seceded in 1861, and was readmitted in 1868. In the late 19th cent., hotel and railroad builder Henry M. Flagler laid the foundations of the tourism industry. The state experienced phenomenal population growth in the 20th cent., especially after 1950. The first U.S. astronaut was launched into space from Cape Canaveral, 1961. Walt Disney World opened near Orlando, 1971. Hurricane Andrew slammed S. Florida, 1992, causing at least $25 bil in property damage. A dispute over Florida's presidential vote in 2000 led to the U.S. Supreme Court decision awarding the White House to George W. Bush; his brother Jeb was state governor 1999-2007. Cuban expatriates wield major political influence in the Miami area.

Tourist attractions. Miami Beach; Castillo de San Marcos, St. Augustine (oldest permanent European settlement in U.S.); Walt Disney World Resort, Sea World, Universal Studios, near Orlando; Kennedy Space Center & U.S. Astronaut Hall of Fame; Everglades Natl. Park; Ringling Museums of Art & the Circus, in Sarasota; Cypress Gardens, Winter Haven; Busch Gardens, Tampa; Florida Caverns State Park, near Mariana; Church St. Station, Orlando; Silver Springs, Ocala.

Famous Floridians. Edna Buchanan, Jeb Bush, Marjory Stoneman Douglas, Henry M. Flagler, Carl Hiaasen, Zora Neale Hurston, James Weldon Johnson, MacKinlay Kantor, John D. MacDonald, Chief Osceola, Claude Pepper, Henry B. Plant, A. Philip Randolph, Marjorie Kinnan Rawlings, Janet Reno, Joseph W. Stilwell, Charles P. Summerall, Ben Vereen.

Tourist information. Visit Florida, 661 E. Jefferson St., Ste. 300, Tallahassee, FL 32301; 1-888-7FLA-USA; www.visitflorida.com

Website. www.myflorida.com

Georgia (GA)

Empire State of the South, Peach State

People. Population (2006 est.): 9,363,941; rank: 9; **net change** (2005-2006): 2.5%. **Pop. density:** 162.8 per sq mi. **Racial distribution** (2005): 66.1% white; 29.8% black; 2.7% Asian; 0.3% Native/Nat. AK; 0.08% Hawaiian/Pacific Islander; 2 or more races, 1.0%. **Hispanic pop.** (any race): 7.1%.

Geography. Total area: 59,425 sq mi; rank: 24. **Land area:** 57,906 sq mi; rank: 21. **Acres forested:** 24.4 mil. **Location:** South Atlantic state. **Climate:** maritime tropical air masses dominate in summer; polar air masses in winter; E central area drier. **Topography:** most southerly of the Blue Ridge Mts. cover NE and N central; central Piedmont extends to the fall line of rivers; coastal plain levels to the coast flatlands. **Capital:** Atlanta. **Chief airports at:** Atlanta, Savannah.

Economy. Chief industries: services, manufacturing, retail trade. **Chief manuf. goods:** carpet & rugs, animal slaughtering & processing, motor vehicles & parts, plastics, aircrafts, paper, chemicals, food. **Chief crops:** cotton, greenhouse & nursery, peanuts, pecans, corn, tomatoes, cucumbers, onions, watermelons, tobacco, squash, blueberries, hay, cabbage, soybeans, peaches, snap beans, wheat. **Livestock** (Jan. 2007): 1.2 mil cattle/calves; (Dec. 2006): 245,000 hogs/pigs, 28.0 mil chickens (excl. broilers), 1.4 bil broilers. **Timber/lumber** (est. 2006): 3.0 bil bd. ft.; pine, hardwood. **Nonfuel minerals** (preliminary 2006): $2.0 bil; clays (kaolin), stone (crushed), clays (fuller's earth), sand and gravel (construction), cement (portland). **Commercial fishing** (2005): $13.5 mil. **Chief ports:** Savannah, Brunswick. **Gross state product** (est. 2006): $379.6 bil. **Sales tax** (2007): 4.0%. **Employment distrib.** (May 2007): 16.3% govt.; 21.2% trade/trans./util.; 10.7% mfg.; 10.8% ed./health; 13.4% prof./bus. serv.; 9.6% leisure/hosp.; 5.6% finance; 5.4% constr.; 3.9% other serv.; 2.8% info. **Unemployment** (2006): 4.6%. **Per cap. pers. income** (2006): $31,891. **New private housing** (2006): 104,200 units/$14.5 bil. **Commercial banks** (2006): 350; **deposits:** $162.8 bil. **Savings institutions** (2006): 25; **deposits:** $6.7 bil. **Lottery** (2006): total sales: $3.2 bil; profit: $822.4 mil.

Federal govt. Fed. civ. employees (Mar. 2006): 66,314; **avg. salary:** $61,376. **Notable fed. facilities:** Ft. Benning; Ft. Stewart; Fed. Law Enforcement Training Ctr., Glynco; Robins AFB; Ft. Gordon; King's Bay Naval Base; Moody AFB; *Navy Supply Corps School; *Ft. McPherson; Centers for Disease Control; Marine Corps Logistics.

Energy. Electricity production (est. 2006, kWh by source): Coal: 85.7 bil; Gas: 7.4 bil; Hydroelectric: 3.0 bil; Nuclear: 32.0 bil; Petroleum: 87 mil.

State data. Motto: Wisdom, justice and moderation. **Flower:** Cherokee rose. **Bird:** Brown thrasher. **Tree:** Live oak. **Song:** Georgia On My Mind. **Fourth** of the 13 original states

to ratify the Constitution, Jan. 2, 1788. **State fair** at Macon, late Sept.–Oct.

History. Creek and Cherokee peoples were living in the region when Spaniards founded Santa Catalina mission, 1566, on Saint Catherines Island. Gen. James Oglethorpe established a colony at Savannah, 1733, for the poor and religiously persecuted. Oglethorpe defeated a Spanish army from Florida at Bloody Marsh, 1742. Georgia was a battleground in the American Revolution, with the British finally evacuating Savannah in 1782. When Georgia entered the Union, 1788, its plantation economy relied on slaves for rice and cotton growing. The Cherokee were removed to Indian Territory, 1838-39, and thousands died on the long march, known as the Trail of Tears. By 1860 the number of slaves exceeded 462,000 (44% of the total population). Georgia seceded from the Union, 1861, and was invaded by Union forces, 1864, under Gen. William T. Sherman, who took Atlanta, Sept. 2, and proceeded on his famous "march to the sea," ending in Dec., in Savannah. Georgia was readmitted, 1870. Born 1929 in Atlanta, Martin Luther King Jr., made the city his home base during the civil rights struggles of the 1960s. Atlanta became the leading city of the "New South," world headquarters of Coca-Cola and CNN, and host of the 1996 Summer Olympic Games. Hispanics are a rapidly growing economic and political force in the state.

Tourist attractions. State Capitol, Stone Mt. Park, Six Flags Over Georgia, Kennesaw Mt. Natl. Battlefield Park, Martin Luther King Jr. Natl. Historic Site, Underground Atlanta, Jimmy Carter Library & Museum, all Atlanta; Chickamauga and Chattanooga Natl. Military Park, near Dalton; Chattahoochee Natl. Forest; Helen alpine village; Dahlonega, site of America's first gold rush; Brasstown Bald Mt.; Lake Lanier; Franklin D. Roosevelt's Little White House, Warm Springs; Callaway Gardens, Pine Mt.; Andersonville Natl. Historic Site; Okefenokee Swamp, near Waycross; Jekyll, St. Simons, Cumberland islands; Savannah historic riverfront district.

Famous Georgians. Kim Basinger, Griffin Bell, James Bowie, James Brown, Erskine Caldwell, Jimmy Carter, Ray Charles, Lucius D. Clay, Ty Cobb, James Dickey, John C. Fremont, Newt Gingrich, Joel Chandler Harris, "Doc" Holliday, Holly Hunter, Alan Jackson, Jasper Johns, Martin Luther King Jr., Gladys Knight, Sidney Lanier, Little Richard, Juliette Gordon Low, Margaret Mitchell, Sam Nunn, Flannery O'Connor, Otis Redding, Burt Reynolds, Julia Roberts, Jackie Robinson, Clarence Thomas, Travis Tritt, Ted Turner, Carl Vinson, Alice Walker, Herschel Walker, Joseph Wheeler, Joanne Woodward, Trisha Yearwood, Andrew Young.

Tourist information. Dept. of Economic Development, 75 Fifth St., NW, Ste. 1200, Atlanta, GA 30308; 1-800-VISITGA; www.georgia.org

Website. www.georgia.gov

Hawai'i (HI)

Aloha State

People. Population (2006 est.): 1,285,498; rank: 42; **net change** (2005-2006): 1.0%. **Pop. density:** 200.2 per sq mi. **Racial distribution** (2005): 26.8% white; 2.3% black; 41.5% Asian; 0.3% Native/Nat. AK; 9.0% Hawaiian/Pacific Islander; 2 or more races, 20.1%. **Hispanic pop.** (any race): 8.0%.

Geography. Total area: 10,931 sq mi; rank: 43. **Land area:** 6,423 sq mi; rank: 47. **Acres forested:** 1.7 mil. **Location:** Hawaiian Islands lie in the North Pacific, 2,397 mi SW from San Francisco. **Climate:** subtropical, with wide variations in rainfall; Waialeale, on Kaua'i, wettest spot in U.S. (annual rainfall 460 in.) **Topography:** islands are tops of a chain of submerged volcanic mountains; active volcanoes: Mauna Loa, Kilauea. **Capital:** Honolulu. **Chief airports at:** Hilo, Honolulu, Kahului, Kailua Kona, Lihue.

Economy. Chief industries: tourism, defense, sugar, pineapples. **Chief manuf. goods:** concrete, printing, baked goods, sugar, preserved fruits & vegetables, apparel. **Chief crops:** flowers & nursery, pineapples, seed crops, sugarcane, macadamia nuts, coffee, algae, papayas, tomatoes, bananas, basil, ginger. **Livestock** (Jan. 2007): 158,000 cattle/calves; (Dec. 2006): 16,000 hogs/pigs, 470,000 chickens (excl. broilers). **Timber/lumber:** figs. undisclosed. **Nonfuel minerals** (preliminary 2006): $107 mil; stone (crushed), sand and gravel (construction), gemstones (natural). **Commercial fishing** (2005): $70.8 mil. **Chief ports:** Honolulu, Hilo, Kailua. **Gross state product** (est. 2006): $58.3 bil. **Sales tax** (2007): 4.0%. **Employment distrib.** (May 2007): 19.9%

govt.; 19.0% trade/trans./util.; 2.4% mfg.; 11.6% ed./health; 13.0% prof./bus. serv.; 17.4% leisure/hosp.; 4.8% finance; 6.0% constr.; 4.2% other serv.; 1.7% info. **Unemployment** (2006): 2.4%. **Per cap. pers. income** (2006): $36,299. **New private housing** (2006): 7,530 units/$1.8 bil. **Commercial banks** (2006): 9; **deposits:** $19.9 bil. **Savings institutions** (2006): 3; **deposits:** $5.8 bil.

Federal govt. Fed. civ. employees (Mar. 2006): 20,759; **avg. salary:** $55,470. **Notable fed. facilities:** Pearl Harbor Naval Shipyard; Schofield Barracks; Marine Corps Base-Kaneohe Bay; *Hickam AFB; Tripler Army Med. Ctr.; Ft. Shafter; Wheeler AFB; Prince Kuhio Federal Bldg.

Energy. Electricity production (est. 2006, kWh by source): Petroleum: 6.6 bil; Other: 1 mil.

State data. Motto: The life of the land is perpetuated in righteousness. **Flower:** Yellow hibiscus. **Bird:** Hawaiian goose. **Tree:** Kukui (Candlenut). **Song:** Hawai'i Pono'i. **Entered union** Aug. 21, 1959; rank, 50th. **State fair** at Honolulu, late May–June.

History. Polynesians from islands 2,000 mi to the S settled the Hawaiian Islands, probably 300-600 CE. The first European visitor was British captain James Cook, 1778. King Kamehameha I united the islands by 1810. Christian missionaries arrived, 1819, bringing Western culture. Under the reign, 1825-54, of King Kamehameha III, a constitution, legislature, and public school system were instituted. Sugar production began, 1835, and it became the dominant industry. Queen Liliuokalani was deposed, 1893, and a republic was established, 1894, headed by Sanford B. Dole. Annexation by the U.S. came in 1898. The Japanese attack on Pearl Harbor, Dec. 7, 1941, brought the U.S. into World War II. Hawai'i attained statehood, 1959. Hurricane Iniki pounded Kauai, 1992, causing about $1 bil in damage. In 2006, Pres. George W. Bush designated the Northwestern Hawaiian Islands National Monument, a marine area of 140,000 sq mi.

Tourist attractions. Hawaii Volcanoes, Haleakala natl. parks; Natl. Memorial Cemetery of the Pacific, Waikiki Beach, Diamond Head, in Honolulu; U.S.S. *Arizona* Memorial, Pearl Harbor; Hanauma Bay; Polynesian Cultural Center, Laie; Nu'uanu Pali; Waimea Canyon; Wailoa and Wailuku River state parks.

Famous Islanders. Bernice Pauahi Bishop, Tia Carrere, Father Damien de Veuster, Don Ho, Duke Kahanamoku, King Kamehameha, Brook Mahealani Lee, Daniel K. Inouye, Jason Scott Lee, Queen Liliuokalani, Bette Midler, Ellison Onizuka.

Tourist information. Hawaii Visitors and Conventions Bureau, 2270 Kalakaua Ave., Ste. 801, Honolulu, HI 96815; 1-800-GOHAWAII; **Website.** www.gohawaii.com

Idaho (ID)
Gem State

People. Population (2006 est.): 1,466,465; rank: 39; **net change** (2005-2006): 2.6%. **Pop. density:** 17.7 per sq mi. **Racial distribution** (2005): 95.5% white; 0.6% black; 1.0% Asian; 1.4% Native/Nat. AK; 0.1% Hawaiian/Pacific Islander; 2 or more races, 1.3%. **Hispanic pop.** (any race): 9.1%.

Geography. Total area: 83,570 sq mi; rank: 14. **Land area:** 82,747 sq mi; rank: 11. **Acres forested:** 21.6 mil. **Location:** northwestern Mountain state bordering on British Columbia. **Climate:** tempered by Pacific westerly winds; drier, colder, continental climate in SE; altitude an important factor. **Topography:** Snake R. plains in the S; central region of mountains, canyons, gorges (Hells Canyon, 7,900 ft, deepest in N. America); subalpine northern region. **Capital:** Boise. **Chief airport at:** Boise.

Economy. Chief industries: manufacturing, agriculture, tourism, lumber, mining, electronics. **Chief manuf. goods:** computers & electronics, preserved fruits & vegetables, cheese, lumber. **Chief crops:** potatoes, wheat, hay, sugar beets, barley, greenhouse & nursery, onions, dry beans, corn, mint, apples, hops, peaches, lentils, peas, cherries, plums & prunes, oats. **Livestock** (Jan. 2007): 2.2 mil cattle/calves, 260,000 sheep/lambs; (Dec. 2006): 25,000 hogs/pigs, 844,000 chickens (excl. broilers). **Timber/lumber:** (est. 2006): 1.5 bil bd. ft.; pine, fir, spruce. **Nonfuel minerals** (preliminary 2006): $810 mil; molybdenum (concentrates), sand and gravel (construction), phosphate rock, silver, stone (crushed). **Chief port:** Lewiston. **Gross state product** (est. 2006): $49.9 bil. **Sales tax** (2007): 6.0%. **Employment distrib.** (May 2007): 18.4% govt.; 20.1% trade/trans./util.; 9.9%

mfg.; 11.0% ed./health; 13.0% prof./bus. serv.; 9.5% leisure/hosp.; 5.0% finance; 8.0% constr.; 2.9% other serv.; 1.7% info. **Unemployment** (2006): 3.4%. **Per cap. pers. income** (2006): $29,952. **New private housing** (2006): 17,075 units/$3.0 bil. **Commercial banks** (2006): 27; **deposits:** $14.4 bil. **Savings institutions** (2006): 7; **deposits:** $2.5 bil. **Lottery** (2006): total sales: $131.1 mil; profit: $33.0 mil.

Federal govt. Fed. civ. employees (Mar. 2006): 7,788; **avg. salary:** $58,057. **Notable fed. facilities:** Idaho Natl. Lab; *Mountain Home AFB.

Energy. Electricity production (est. 2006, kWh by source): 70 mil; Hydroelectric: 10.1 bil.

State data. Motto: Esto Perpetua (It is perpetual). **Flower:** Syringa. **Bird:** Mountain bluebird. **Tree:** White pine. **Song:** Here We Have Idaho. **Entered union** July 3, 1890; rank, 43rd. **State fair** at Boise, late Aug.; at Blackfoot, early Sept.

History. Paleoindian hunters roamed the land over 13,000 years ago; later inhabitants included Shoshone, Northern Paiute, Bannock, and Nez Percé peoples. Lewis and Clark expedition explored, 1805-6. Next came fur traders, 1809-34, and missionaries, 1830s-50s. Mormons made their first permanent settlement at Franklin, 1860. Idaho's gold rush began the same year and brought thousands of permanent settlers. A series of Indian wars followed, including a remarkable campaign by Chief Joseph and the Nez Percé that ended with his surrender in Montana, 1877. Idaho became a territory, 1863, and a state, 1890. In the 20th cent., it emerged as a leader in potato, lumber, and silver output. The Sun Valley ski resort opened in 1936, boosting tourism. Startup of Lewiston's river port, 1975, opened Idaho to oceangoing trade. Fueled by high-tech job growth, the state's population jumped 13.3% in 2000-06.

Tourist attractions. Hells Canyon, deepest gorge in N. America; World Center for Birds of Prey, Boise; Craters of the Moon Natl. Monument; Sun Valley, in Sawtooth Mts.; Shoshone Falls; Lava Hot Springs; Lake Pend Oreille; Lake Coeur d'Alene; Sawtooth Natl. Recreation Area, Redfish Lake; River of No Return Wilderness Area.

Famous Idahoans. William E. Borah, Frank Church, Lou Dobbs, Fred T. Dubois, Chief Joseph, Harmon Killebrew, Ezra Pound, Sacagawea, Picabo Street, Lana Turner.

Tourist information. Division of Tourism Development, 700 W. State St., PO Box 83720, Boise, ID 83720; (208) 334-2470; www.visitid.org

Website. www.state.id.us

Illinois (IL)
Prairie State

People. Population (2006 est.): 12,831,970; rank: 5; **net change** (2005-2006): 0.5%. **Pop. density:** 231.0 per sq mi. **Racial distribution** (2005): 79.4% white; 15.1% black; 4.1% Asian; 0.3% Native/Nat. AK; 0.06% Hawaiian/Pacific Islander; 2 or more races, 1.1%. **Hispanic pop.** (any race): 14.3%.

Geography. Total area: 57,914 sq mi; rank: 25. **Land area:** 55,584 sq mi; rank: 24. **Acres forested:** 4.3 mil. **Location:** East North Central state; western, southern, and eastern boundaries formed by Mississippi, Ohio, and Wabash rivers, respectively. **Climate:** temperate; typically cold, snowy winters, hot summers. **Topography:** prairie and fertile plains throughout; open hills in the southern region. **Capital:** Springfield. **Chief airports at:** Chicago (2).

Economy. Chief industries: services, manufacturing, travel, wholesale and retail trade, finance, insurance, real estate, construction, health care, agriculture. **Chief manuf. goods:** food, petroleum, plastics, chemicals, agricultural machinery, pharmaceuticals, motor vehicles, printing. **Chief crops:** corn, soybeans, hay, wheat, greenhouse & nursery, apples, peaches, sorghum. **Livestock** (Jan. 2007): 1.3 mil cattle/calves, 70,000 sheep/lambs; (Dec. 2006): 4.2 mil hogs/pigs, 5.6 mil chickens (excl. broilers). **Timber/lumber:** (est. 2006): 173 mil bd. ft.; oak, hickory, maple, cottonwood. **Nonfuel minerals** (preliminary 2006): $1.3 bil; stone (crushed), cement (portland), sand and gravel (construction), sand and gravel (industrial), clays (fuller's earth). **Chief port:** Chicago. **Gross state product** (est. 2006): $589.6 bil. **Sales tax** (2007): 6.25%. **Employment distrib.** (May 2007): 14.2% govt.; 19.9% trade/trans./util.; 11.3% mfg.; 12.9% ed./health; 14.5% prof./bus. serv.; 9.1% leisure/hosp.; 6.8% finance; 4.7% constr.; 4.3% other serv.; 1.9% info. **Unemployment** (2006): 4.5%. **Per cap. pers. income** (2006): $38,215. **New private housing** (2006): 58,802 units/$9.5 bil. **Commercial banks** (2006): 646; **deposits:** $292.9 bil. **Savings institu-**

tions (2006): 100; **deposits:** $36.7 bil. **Lottery** (2006): total sales: $2.0 bil; profit: $637.7 mil.

Federal govt. Fed. civ. employees (Mar. 2006): 42,382; **avg. salary:** $67,385. **Notable fed. facilities:** *Great Lakes Naval Station; Fermi Natl. Accelerator Lab; Argonne Natl. Lab; Scott AFB; *Rock Island Arsenal.

Energy. Electricity production (est. 2006, kWh by source): Coal: 10.6 bil; Gas: 372 mil; Hydroelectric: 50 mil; Petroleum: 36 mil; Other: 12 mil.

State data. Motto: State sovereignty—national union. **Flower:** Native violet. **Bird:** Cardinal. **Tree:** White oak. **Song:** Illinois. **Entered union** Dec. 3, 1818; rank, 21st. **State fair** at Springfield, mid-Aug.; DuQuoin, late Aug.–Sept.

History. The region has been inhabited for at least 10,000 years; seminomadic Algonquian peoples, including the Peoria, Illinois, Kaskaskia, and Tamaroa, lived there at the time of European contact. Fur traders were the first Europeans in Illinois, followed shortly by Jolliet and Marquette, 1673, and La Salle, 1680, who built a fort near present-day Peoria. French priests established the first permanent settlements, at Cahokia, near present-day St. Louis, 1699, and Kaskaskia, 1703. France ceded the area to Britain, 1763, and in 1778, American Gen. George Rogers Clark took Kaskaskia from the British without a shot. Illinois became a separate territory, 1809, and a state, 1818. Defeat of Native American tribes in the Black Hawk War, 1832, and canal, rail, and road construction brought rapid change. Mormon settlers at Nauvoo, 1839, met with hostility, and a Carthage mob killed Mormon leader Joseph Smith and his brother, 1844. The great Chicago Fire, 1871, destroyed the city's downtown. Illinois became a center for the labor movement, leading to bitter conflicts such as the Haymarket riot, 1886, and Pullman strike, 1894. Social reformer Jane Addams founded Hull House, 1889, to aid immigrants and the poor. During 1900-70, as manufacturing expanded, many African Americans arrived from the southern U.S. Chicago police violently suppressed antiwar protests at the 1968 Democratic National Convention. Dennis Hastert was the longest serving Republican Speaker of the House, 1999-2007. Barack Obama, elected in 2004, is the first male African American Democrat to serve in the U.S. Senate.

Tourist attractions. Chicago museums and parks; Illinois State Museum, Abraham Lincoln Presidential Library and Museum, in Springfield; Cahokia Mounds, Collinsville; Starved Rock State Park; Crab Orchard Wildlife Refuge; Mormon settlement at Nauvoo; Fts. Kaskaskia, Chartres, Massac (parks); Shawnee Natl. Forest; Dickson Mounds Museum, Lewistown.

Famous Illinoisans. Jane Addams, John Ashcroft, Saul Bellow, Jack Benny, Ray Bradbury, Gwendolyn Brooks, William Jennings Bryan, St. Frances Xavier Cabrini, Hillary Rodham Clinton, Clarence Darrow, John Deere, Stephen A. Douglas, James T. Farrell, George W. Ferris, Marshall Field, Betty Friedan, Benny Goodman, Ulysses S. Grant, Dennis Hastert, Ernest Hemingway, Charlton Heston, Wild Bill Hickok, Henry J. Hyde, Abraham Lincoln, Vachel Lindsay, Edgar Lee Masters, Oscar Mayer, Cyrus McCormick, Ronald Reagan, Donald Rumsfeld, Carl Sandburg, Adlai Stevenson, James Watson, Frank Lloyd Wright, Philip Wrigley.

Tourist information. Illinois Bureau of Tourism, 620 E. Adams St., 4th fl., Springfield, IL 62701; 1-800-2-CONNECT; www.enjoyillinois.com

Website. www.illinois.gov

Indiana (IN)

Hoosier State

People. Population (2006 est.): 6,313,520; rank: 15; **net change** (2005-2006): 0.8%. **Pop. density:** 176.2 per sq mi. **Racial distribution** (2005): 88.6% white; 8.8% black; 1.2% Asian; 0.3% Native/Nat. AK; 0.05% Hawaiian/Pacific Islander; 2 or more races, 1.1%. **Hispanic pop.** (any race): 4.5%.

Geography. Total area: 36,418 sq mi; rank: 38. **Land area:** 35,867 sq mi; rank: 38. **Acres forested:** 4.5 mil. **Location:** East North Central state; Lake Michigan on N border. **Climate:** 4 distinct seasons with a temperate climate. **Topography:** hilly southern region; fertile rolling plains of central region; flat, heavily glaciated north; dunes along Lake Michigan shore. **Capital:** Indianapolis. **Chief airport at:** Indianapolis.

Economy: Chief industries: manufacturing, services, agriculture, government, wholesale and retail trade, transportation and public utilities. **Chief manuf. goods:** motor vehicles & parts, iron & steel mills, pharmaceuticals, petroleum, plas-

tics, medical equipment, printing. **Chief crops:** corn, soybeans, greenhouse & nursery, wheat, hay, tomatoes, watermelons, apples. **Livestock** (Jan. 2007): 900,000 cattle/calves, 53,000 sheep/lambs; (Dec. 2006): 3.3 mil hogs/pigs, 31.7 mil chickens (excl. broilers). **Timber/lumber** (est. 2006): 343 mil bd. ft.; oak, tulip, beech, sycamore. **Nonfuel minerals** (preliminary 2006): $963 mil; stone (crushed), cement (portland), sand and gravel (construction), lime, cement (masonry). **Chief ports:** Burns Harbor, Portage; Southwind Maritime, Mt. Vernon; Clark Maritime, Jeffersonville. **Gross state product** (est. 2006): $248.9 bil. **Sales tax** (2007): 6.0%. **Employment distrib.** (May 2007): 14.7% govt.; 19.7% trade/trans./util.; 18.6% mfg.; 12.9% ed./health; 9.4% prof./bus. serv.; 9.6% leisure/hosp.; 4.7% finance; 5.3% constr.; 3.8% other serv.; 1.3% info. **Unemployment** (2006): 5.0%. **Per cap. pers. income** (2006): $32,526. **New private housing** (2006): 29,069 units/$4.7 bil. **Commercial banks** (2006): 163; **deposits:** $76.1 bil. **Savings institutions** (2006): 57; **deposits:** $11.1 bil. **Lottery** (2006): total sales: $816.4 mil; profit: $218.0 mil.

Federal govt. Fed. civ. employees (Mar. 2006): 18,577; **avg. salary:** $60,658. **Notable fed. facilities:** Nav. Surface Warfare Ctr., Crane Div.

Energy. Electricity production (est. 2006, kWh by source): Coal: 116.5 bil; Gas: 552 mil; Hydroelectric: 450 mil; Petroleum: 135 mil.

State data. Motto: Crossroads of America. **Flower:** Peony. **Bird:** Cardinal. **Tree:** Tulip poplar. **Song:** On the Banks of the Wabash, Far Away. **Entered union** Dec. 11, 1816; rank, 19th. **State fair** at Indianapolis, mid-Aug.

History. When the Europeans arrived, Miami, Potawatomi, Kickapoo, Piankashaw, Wea, and Shawnee peoples inhabited the region. La Salle visited the present South Bend area, 1679 and 1681. The first French fort was built near present-day Lafayette, 1717. A French trading post was established, 1731-32, at Vincennes. France ceded the area to Britain, 1763. During the American Revolution, American Gen. George Rogers Clark captured Vincennes, 1778, and defeated British forces, 1779. Indiana became a territory, 1800, and a state, 1816. The Miami were beaten, 1794, at Fallen Timbers, and Gen. William H. Harrison defeated Tecumseh's Indian confederation, 1811, at Tippecanoe. Manufacturing grew rapidly after the Civil War. U.S. Steel founded Gary, 1906. An automotive test track was the site of the first Indianapolis 500 race, 1911. The auto industry remains key to the state economy; in 2006, Honda announced it would build a $550-mil plant near Greensburg.

Tourist attractions. Lincoln Log Cabin Historic Site, near Charleston; George Rogers Clark Park, Vincennes; Wyandotte Caves; Tippecanoe Battlefield Park, near Lafayette; Benjamin Harrison home, Indianapolis 500 raceway and museum, in Indianapolis; Indiana Dunes, Chesterton; National College Football Hall of Fame, South Bend; Hoosier Natl. Forest.

Famous "Hoosiers." Larry Bird, Ambrose Burnside, Hoagy Carmichael, Jim Davis, James Dean, Eugene V. Debs, Theodore Dreiser, Paul Dresser, Jeff Gordon, Benjamin Harrison, Gil Hodges, Michael Jackson, David Letterman, Carole Lombard, John Mellencamp, Jane Pauley, Cole Porter, Gene Stratton Porter, Ernie Pyle, Dan Quayle, James Whitcomb Riley, Oscar Robertson, Red Skelton, Booth Tarkington, Kurt Vonnegut, Lew Wallace, Wendell L. Willkie, Wilbur Wright.

Tourist information. Indiana Office of Tourism Development, 1 North Capital, Suite 100, Indianapolis, IN 46204; 1-800-677-9800; www.enjoyindiana.com

Website. www.in.gov

Iowa (IA)

Hawkeye State

People. Population (2006 est.): 2,982,085; rank: 30; **net change** (2005-2006): 0.6%. **Pop. density:** 53.4 per sq mi. **Racial distribution** (2005): 94.9% white; 2.3% black; 1.4% Asian; 0.3% Native/Nat. AK; 0.04% Hawaiian/Pacific Islander; 2 or more races, 0.9%. **Hispanic pop.** (any race): 3.7%.

Geography. Total area: 56,272 sq mi; rank: 26. **Land area:** 55,869 sq mi; rank: 23. **Acres forested:** 2.1 mil. **Location:** West North Central state bordered by Mississippi R. on the E and Missouri R. on the W. **Climate:** humid, continental. **Topography:** Watershed from NW to SE; soil especially rich and land level in the N central counties. **Capital:** Des Moines. **Chief airports at:** Cedar Rapids, Des Moines.

Economy. Chief industries: agriculture, communications, construction, finance, insurance, trade, services, manufacturing. **Chief manuf. goods:** machinery, vegetable oils, animal slaughtering & processing, laundry equipment, plastics, motor vehicles & parts. **Chief crops:** corn, soybeans, hay, greenhouse & nursery, oats. **Livestock** (Jan. 2007): 4.0 mil cattle/calves, 235,000 sheep/lambs; (Dec. 2006): 17.2 mil hogs/pigs, 61.6 mil chickens (excl. broilers). **Timber/lumber** (est. 2006): 80 mil bd. ft.; red cedar. **Nonfuel minerals** (preliminary 2006): $704 mil; cement (portland), stone (crushed), sand and gravel (construction), gypsum (crude), lime. **Gross state product** (est. 2006): $124.0 bil. **Sales tax** (2007): 5.0%. **Employment distrib.** (May 2007): 16.7% govt.; 20.3% trade/trans./util.; 15.1% mfg.; 13.3% ed./health; 7.8% prof./bus. serv.; 9.0% leisure/hosp.; 6.6% finance; 5.1% constr.; 3.7% other serv.; 2.2% info. **Unemployment** (2006): 3.7%. **Per cap. pers. income** (2006): $33,236. **New private housing** (2006): 13,357 units/$2.0 bil. **Commercial banks** (2006): 399; **deposits:** $49.6 bil. **Savings institutions** (2006): 23; **deposits:** $4.5 bil. **Lottery** (2006): total sales: $339.5 mil; profit: $80.9 mil.

Federal govt. Fed. civ. employees (Mar. 2006): 7,468; **avg. salary:** $55,799. **Notable fed. facilities:** Ames Lab; Natl. Animal Disease Ctr.

Energy. Electricity production (est. 2006, kWh by source): Coal: 33.2 bil; Gas: 2.4 bil; Hydroelectric: 894 mil; Nuclear: 378 mil; Petroleum: 96 mil; Other: 1.2 bil.

State data. Motto: Our liberties we prize, and our rights we will maintain. **Flower:** Wild rose. **Bird:** Eastern goldfinch. **Tree:** Oak. **Rock:** Geode. **Entered union** Dec. 28, 1846; rank, 29th. **State fair** at Des Moines; mid-Aug.

History. Early inhabitants were Mound Builders who dwelt on Iowa's fertile plains. Later, Iowa and Yankton Sioux lived in the area. The first Europeans, Marquette and Jolliet, gave France its claim to the area, 1673. In 1762, France ceded the region to Spain, but Napoleon took it back, 1800. It became part of the U.S. through the Louisiana Purchase, 1803. Native American Sauk and Fox tribes moved into the area but relinquished their land in defeat, after the 1832 uprising led by the Sauk chieftain Black Hawk. Iowa became a territory in 1838, and entered as a free state, 1846, strongly supporting the Union. Fertile land lured farmers from eastern states, 1850-1900 and the population rose rapidly. Growth slowed in the 20th cent., as farming became mechanized. Surging demand for ethanol fuel from Iowa corn contributed more than $2.6 bil to the state economy in 2005. Every 4 years, the Iowa caucuses have traditionally posed an early test for politicians hoping to win their party's presidential nomination.

Tourist attractions. Herbert Hoover birthplace and library, West Branch; Effigy Mounds Natl. Monument, prehistoric Indian burial site, Marquette; Amana Colonies; Grant Wood's paintings and memorabilia, Davenport Municipal Art Gallery; Living History Farms, Des Moines; Adventureland, Prairie Meadows horse racing, in Altoona; Boone & Scenic Valley Railroad; Greyhound Parks, in Dubuque and Council Bluffs; riverboat cruises and casino gambling, Mississippi and Missouri Rivers; Iowa Great Lakes, Okoboji.

Famous Iowans. Tom Arnold, Johnny Carson, Marquis Childs, Buffalo Bill Cody, Mamie Dowd Eisenhower, Bob Feller, George Gallup, Susan Glaspell, James Norman Hall, Harry Hansen, Herbert Hoover, Ann Landers, Glenn Miller, Lillian Russell, Billy Sunday, James A. Van Allen, Abigail Van Buren, Carl Van Vechten, Henry Wallace, John Wayne, Meredith Willson, Grant Wood.

Tourist information. Iowa Tourism Office, Iowa Dept. of Economic Development, 200 E. Grand Ave., Des Moines, IA 50309; (515) 242-4700; www.traveliowa.com

Website. www.iowa.gov

Kansas (KS)
Sunflower State

People. Population (2006 est.): 2,764,075; rank: 33; **net change** (2005-2006): 0.6%. **Pop. density:** 33.8 per sq mi. **Racial distribution** (2005): 89.4% white; 5.9% black; 2.1% Asian; 0.9% Native/Nat. AK; 0.07% Hawaiian/Pacific Islander; 2 or more races, 1.6%. **Hispanic pop.** (any race): 8.3%.

Geography. Total area: 82,277 sq mi; rank: 15. **Land area:** 81,815 sq mi; rank: 13. **Acres forested:** 1.5 mil. **Location:** West North Central state, with Missouri R. on E. **Climate:** temperate but continental, with great extremes between summer and winter. **Topography:** hilly Osage Plains

in the E; central region level prairie and hills; high plains in the W. **Capital:** Topeka. **Chief airport at:** Wichita.

Economy. Chief industries: manufacturing, finance, insurance, real estate, services. **Chief manuf. goods:** animal slaughtering, aerospace, petroleum, plastics, machinery, navigational instruments, printing. **Chief crops:** wheat, corn, soybeans, hay, sorghum, sunflowers, cotton, potatoes. **Livestock** (Jan. 2007): 6.4 mil cattle/calves, 107,000 sheep/lambs; (Dec. 2006): 1.8 mil hogs/pigs. **Timber/lumber:** figs. undisclosed; oak, walnut. **Nonfuel minerals** (preliminary 2006): $913 mil; cement (portland), helium (grade-A), stone (crushed), salt, helium (crude). **Chief port:** Kansas City. **Gross state product** (est. 2006): $111.7 bil. **Sales tax** (2007): 5.3%. **Employment distrib.** (May 2007): 19.1% govt.; 19.0% trade/trans./util.; 13.4% mfg.; 12.3% ed./health; 10.3% prof./bus. serv.; 8.6% leisure/hosp.; 5.2% finance; 4.8% constr.; 3.9% other serv.; 2.8% info. **Unemployment** (2006): 4.5%. **Per cap. pers. income** (2006): $34,743. **New private housing** (2006): 14,619 units/$2.0 bil. **Commercial banks** (2006): 367; **deposits:** $42.8 bil. **Savings institutions** (2006): 18; **deposits:** $7.9 bil. **Lottery** (2006): total sales: $236.1 mil; profit: $67.1 mil.

Federal govt. Fed. civ. employees (Mar. 2006): 15,796; **avg. salary:** $57,528. **Notable fed. facilities:** Fts. Riley, Leavenworth; Leavenworth Fed. Pen.; McConnell AFB; Colmery-O'Neal Veterans Hospital.

Energy. Electricity production (est. 2006, kWh by source): Coal: 33.2 bil; Gas: 1.8 bil; Nuclear: 9.4 bil; Petroleum: 55 mil; Other: 106 mil.

State data. Motto: Ad Astra per Aspera (To the stars through difficulties). **Flower:** Native sunflower. **Bird:** Western meadowlark. **Tree:** Cottonwood. **Song:** Home on the Range. **Entered union** Jan. 29, 1861; rank, 34th. **State fair** at Hutchinson; begins Friday after Labor Day.

History. Wichita, Pawnee, Kansa, and Osage peoples lived in the area when Coronado explored it in 1541. These Native Americans—hunters who also farmed—were joined on the Plains by the nomadic Cheyenne, Arapaho, Comanche, and Kiowa about 1800. France claimed the region, 1682, ceded its claim to Spain, 1762, then regained control, 1800, before selling it to the U.S. in the Louisiana Purchase, 1803. After 1830, thousands of Native Americans were removed from more eastern states to Kansas. Organized as a territory, 1854, the area witnessed violent clashes between pro- and antislavery settlers and became known as "Bleeding Kansas." It entered the Union as a free state, 1861. After the Civil War, rail construction and huge cattle drives from Texas turned Abilene and Dodge City into cowboy capitals. Russian Mennonite immigrants brought a new strain of winter wheat, 1874, transforming Kansas agriculture. Carry Nation launched her anti-saloon crusade in the 1890s. Part of the "Dust Bowl," the state experienced drought and depression in the 1930s. Topeka was the focus of the famous *Brown v. Board of Education* decision, 1954, that led to desegregation of U.S. public schools. Bob Dole represented Kansas in the U.S. Senate (1969-96) but failed in several efforts to win higher office.

Tourist attractions. Eisenhower Center, Abilene; Natl. Agricultural Ctr. & Hall of Fame, Bonner Springs; Dodge City-Boot Hill; Old Cowtown Museum, Wichita; Ft. Scott and Ft. Larned, restored 1800s cavalry forts; Kansas Cosmosphere and Space Center, Hutchinson; Woodlands Racetrack, Kansas City; U.S. Cavalry Museum, Ft. Riley; Heartland Park Raceway, Topeka.

Famous Kansans. Kirstie Alley, Roscoe "Fatty" Arbuckle, Ed Asner, Gwendolyn Brooks, John Brown, George Washington Carver, Wilt Chamberlain, Walter P. Chrysler, Glenn Cunningham, John Stuart Curry, Robert Dole, Amelia Earhart, Wyatt Earp, Dwight D. Eisenhower, Ron Evans, Maurice Greene, Wild Bill Hickok, Cyrus Holliday, Dennis Hopper, William Inge, Don Johnson, Walter Johnson, Nancy Landon Kassebaum, Buster Keaton, Emmett Kelly, Alf Landon, Edgar Lee Masters, Hattie McDaniel, Oscar Micheaux, Carry Nation, Georgia Neese-Gray, Charlie Parker, Gordon Parks, Jim Ryun, Barry Sanders, Vivian Vance, William Allen White, Jess Willard.

Tourist information. Kansas Dept. of Commerce, Travel and Tourism Div., 1000 SW Jackson St., Ste. 100, Topeka, KS 66612; (785) 296-2009; www.travelks.com

Website. www.kansas.gov

Kentucky (KY)
Bluegrass State

People. Population (2006 est.): 4,206,074; rank: 26; **net change** (2005-2006): 0.8%. **Pop. density:** 106.5 per sq mi. **Racial distribution** (2005): 90.4% white; 7.5% black; 0.9% Asian; 0.2% Native/Nat. AK; 0.05% Hawaiian/Pacific Islander; 2 or more races, 1.0%. **Hispanic pop.** (any race): 2.0%.

Geography. Total area: 40,409 sq mi; rank: 37. **Land area:** 39,728 sq mi; rank: 36. **Acres forested:** 12.7 mil. **Location:** East South Central state, bordered on N by Illinois, Indiana, Ohio; on E by West Virginia and Virginia; on S by Tennessee; on W by Missouri. **Climate:** moderate, with plentiful rainfall. **Topography:** mountainous in E; rounded hills of the Knobs in the N; Bluegrass, heart of state; wooded rocky hillsides of the Pennyroyal; Western Coal Field; the fertile Purchase in the SW. **Capital:** Frankfort. **Chief airports at:** Covington, Lexington, Louisville.

Economy. Chief industries: manufacturing, services, finance, insurance and real estate, retail trade, public utilities. **Chief manuf. goods:** motor vehicles & parts, aluminum, basic chemicals, plastics, iron & steel, rubber, printing. **Chief crops:** hay, corn, soybeans, tobacco, wheat. **Livestock** (Jan. 2007): 2.5 mil cattle/calves, 37,000 sheep/lambs; (Dec. 2006): 310,000 hogs/pigs, 6.6 mil chickens (excl. broilers), 289.0 mil broilers. **Timber/lumber** (est. 2006): 619 mil bd. ft.; hardwoods, pines. **Nonfuel minerals** (preliminary 2006): $918 mil; stone (crushed), lime, cement (portland), sand and gravel (construction), clays (ball). **Chief ports:** Paducah, Louisville, Covington, Owensboro, Ashland, Henderson County, Lyon County, Hickman-Fulton County. **Gross state product** (est. 2006): $146.0 bil. **Sales tax** (2007): 6.0%. **Employment distrib.** (May 2007): 17.3% govt.; 20.5% trade/trans./util.; 13.8% mfg.; 12.9% ed./health; 9.6% prof./bus. serv.; 9.4% leisure/hosp.; 5.0% finance; 4.6% constr.; 4.1% other serv.; 1.6% info. **Unemployment** (2006): 5.7%. **Per cap. pers. income** (2006): $29,352. **New private housing** (2006): 16,628 units/$2.3 bil. **Commercial banks** (2006): 224; **deposits:** $58.4 bil. **Savings institutions** (2006): 27; **deposits:** $2.2 bil. **Lottery:** total sales: $742.3 mil; profit: $204.3 mil.

Federal govt. Fed. civ. employees (Mar. 2006): 20,737; **avg. salary:** $52,242. **Notable fed. facilities:** U.S. Gold Bullion Depository, Ft. Knox; Ft. Campbell; Fed. Correctional Institution, Lexington; Army Corps of Engineers, Louisville.

Energy. Electricity production (est. 2006, kWh by source): Coal: 83.3 bil; Gas: 964 mil; Hydroelectric: 2.6 bil; Petroleum: 79 mil; Other: 60 mil.

State data. Motto: United we stand, divided we fall. **Flower:** Goldenrod. **Bird:** Cardinal. **Tree:** Tulip Poplar. **Song:** My Old Kentucky Home. **Entered union** June 1, 1792; rank, 15th. **State fair** at Louisville; mid-Aug.

History. Paleoindians first arrived about 14,000 years ago. Much later, Shawnee, Wyandot, Delaware, and Cherokee peoples also used the area mostly for hunting. Explored by Thomas Walker and Christopher Gist, 1750-51, Kentucky was the first area W of the Alleghenies settled by American pioneers. The first permanent settlement was Harrodsburg, 1774. Daniel Boone blazed the Wilderness Trail through the Cumberland Gap and founded Ft. Boonesborough, 1775. Clashes with Native Americans were frequent, 1774-94. Virginia dropped its claims to the region, and Kentucky became a state, 1792. Tobacco growing, horse breeding, coal mining, and bourbon whiskey making were major industries in the 19th cent. A slave state, Kentucky tried to stay neutral in the Civil War, but then opted for the Union; many Kentuckians sided with the Confederacy. The U.S. gold depository at Fort Knox opened, 1937. Led by Toyota, Ford, and GM, auto manufacturing has grown in recent decades; about 10% of cars and trucks built in the U.S. each year are made in Kentucky.

Tourist attractions. Churchill Downs (Kentucky Derby), Louisville; Land Between the Lakes Natl. Recreation Area, lakes Kentucky & Barkley; Mammoth Cave Natl. Park; Lake Cumberland; Lincoln's birthplace, Hodgenville; My Old Kentucky Home State Park, Bardstown; Cumberland Gap Natl. Historical Park, Middlesboro; Kentucky Horse Park, Lexington; Shaker Village, Pleasant Hill.

Famous Kentuckians. Muhammad Ali, John James Audubon, Alben W. Barkley, Daniel Boone, Louis D. Brandeis, John C. Breckinridge, Kit Carson, Albert B. "Happy" Chandler, Henry Clay, Jefferson Davis, D. W. Griffith, "Casey" Jones, Abraham Lincoln, Mary Todd Lincoln, Thomas Hunt Morgan, Carry Nation, Col. Harland Sanders, Diane Sawyer, Adlai Stevenson, Jesse Stuart, Zachary Taylor, Hunter S. Thompson, Robert Penn Warren, Whitney Young Jr.

Tourist information. Kentucky Dept. of Tourism, Capital Plaza Tower, 22nd fl., 500 Mero St., Frankfort, KY 40601; 1-800-225-8747; www.kentuckytourism.com
Website. www.kentucky.gov

Louisiana (LA)
Pelican State

People. Population (2006 est.): 4,287,768; rank: 25; **net change** (2005-2006): -4.9%. **Pop. density:** 99.2 per sq mi. **Racial distribution** (2005): 64.1% white; 33.1% black; 1.4% Asian; 0.6% Native/Nat. AK; 0.03% Hawaiian/Pacific Islander; 2 or more races, 0.8%. **Hispanic pop.** (any race): 2.8%.

Geography. Total area: 51,840 sq mi; rank: 31. **Land area:** 43,562 sq mi; rank: 33. **Acres forested:** 13.8 mil. **Location:** West South Central state on the Gulf Coast. **Climate:** subtropical, affected by continental weather patterns. **Topography:** lowlands of marshes and Mississippi R. flood plain; Red R. Valley lowlands; upland hills in the Florida Parishes; average elevation, 100 ft. **Capital:** Baton Rouge. **Chief airports at:** Baton Rouge, Metairie.

Economy. Chief industries: wholesale and retail trade, tourism, manufacturing, construction, transportation, communication, public utilities, finance, insurance, mining. **Chief manuf. goods:** petroleum, chemicals, plastics material & resin, pesticides & fertilizers, cleaning products, paper & paperboard, ships, structural metals. **Chief crops:** sugarcane, cotton, rice, soybeans, corn, sweet potatoes. **Livestock** (Jan. 2007): 860,000 cattle/calves; (Dec. 2006): 14,000 hogs/pigs, 2.5 mil chickens (excl. broilers). **Timber/lumber** (est. 2006): 1.7 bil bd. ft.; pines, hardwoods, oak. **Nonfuel minerals** (preliminary 2006): $362 mil; salt, sand and gravel (construction), stone (crushed), clays (common), sand and gravel (industrial). **Commercial fishing** (2005): $251.8 mil. **Chief ports:** New Orleans, Baton Rouge, Lake Charles, Port of S. Louisiana (La Place), Shreveport, Plaquemine, St. Bernard, Alexandria. **Gross state product** (est. 2006): $193.1 bil. **Sales tax** (2007): 4.0%. **Employment distrib.** (May 2007): 18.6% govt.; 20.0% trade/trans./util.; 8.1% mfg.; 12.8% ed./health; 10.5% prof./bus. serv.; 10.2% leisure/hosp.; 5.1% finance; 7.1% constr.; 3.6% other serv.; 1.3% info. **Unemployment** (2006): 4.0%. **Per cap. pers. income** (2006): $30,952. **New private housing** (2006): 28,671 units/$3.8 bil. **Commercial banks** (2006): 147; **deposits:** $67.9 bil. **Savings institutions** (2006): 27; **deposits:** $4.0 bil. **Lottery** (2006): total sales: $332.1 mil; profit: $118.8 mil.

Federal govt. Fed. civ. employees (Mar. 2006): 19,011; **avg. salary:** $57,446. **Notable federal facilities:** Ft. Polk (Joint Readiness Training Ctr.); Barksdale AFB; Strategic Petroleum Reserve, Michoud Assembly Plant, Southern Regional Research Ctr., Army Corps of Engineers, all New Orleans; New Orleans NAS.

Energy. Electricity production (est. 2006, kWh by source): Coal: 11.5 bil; Gas: 10.7 bil; Nuclear: 16.7 bil; Petroleum: 195 mil.

State data. Motto: Union, justice, and confidence. **Flower:** Magnolia. **Bird:** Eastern brown pelican. **Tree:** Cypress. **Song:** Give Me Louisiana. **Entered union** Apr. 30, 1812; rank, 18th. **State fair** at Shreveport; late Oct.–early Nov.

History. Caddo, Tunica, Choctaw, Chitimacha, and Chawash peoples lived in the region at the time of European contact. Spanish explorers in the early 16th cent. reached the mouth of the Mississippi. La Salle, 1682, claimed the region for France. Early French and Spanish settlers were the ancestors of Louisiana Creoles. Cajuns descended from the Acadians, French settlers expelled by the British from Nova Scotia, Canada, in 1755. France ceded the Louisiana region to Spain, 1762, took it back, 1800, and sold it to the U.S., 1803, in the Louisiana Purchase. Admitted as a state in 1812, Louisiana witnessed the Battle of New Orleans, 1815. Cotton and sugar plantations relied on black slaves, who made up 47% of the population in 1860, on the eve of the Civil War. Louisiana seceded, 1861, and was readmitted, 1868. Jazz was born in New Orleans in the early 20th cent. As governor (1928-32), Huey Long pushed populist programs. The offshore oil and gas industry developed after World War II. Many tropical storms and floods have battered Louisiana, including Hurricane Katrina, 2005, which devastated New Orleans.

Tourist attractions. French Quarter and other New Orleans attractions; Jean Lafitte Natl. Hist. Park, Chalmette; Longfellow-Evangeline State Hist. Site, St. Martinville; Kent Plantation House, Alexandria; Hodges Gardens, Natchitoches; USS *Kidd* Memorial, Baton Rouge.

Famous Louisianans. Louis Armstrong, Pierre Beauregard, Judah P. Benjamin, Braxton Bragg, Kate Chopin, Johnnie Cochraw, Harry Connick Jr., Ellen DeGeneres, Fats Domino, Lillian Hellman, Grace King, Elmore Leonard, Bob Livingston, Huey Long, Eli & Peyton Manning, Wynton Marsalis, Leonidas K. Polk, Anne Rice, Henry Miller Shreve, Britney Spears, Edward D. White Jr.

Tourist information. Louisiana Office of Tourism, 1051 N. 3rd St., PO Box 94291, Baton Rouge, LA 70804-9291; (225) 342-8100; www.louisianatravel.com

Website. www.louisiana.gov

Maine (ME)
Pine Tree State

People. Population (2006 est.): 1,321,574; rank: 40; **net change** (2005-2006): 0.3%. **Pop. density:** 42.8 per sq mi. **Racial distribution** (2005): 96.9% white; 0.8% black; 0.8% Asian; 0.6% Native/Nat. AK; 0.03% Hawaiian/Pacific Islander; 2 or more races, 0.9%. **Hispanic pop.** (any race): 1.0%.

Geography. Total area: 35,385 sq mi; rank: 39. **Land area:** 30,862 sq mi; rank: 39. **Acres forested:** 17.7 mil. **Location:** New England state at northeastern tip of U.S. **Climate:** Southern interior and coastal, influenced by air masses from the S and W; northern clime harsher, avg. over 100 in. snow in winter. **Topography:** Appalachian Mts. extend through state; western borders have rugged terrain; long sand beaches on southern coast; northern coast mainly rocky promontories, peninsulas, fjords. **Capital:** Augusta. **Chief airport at:** Portland.

Economy. Chief industries: manufacturing, agriculture, fishing, services, trade, government, finance, insurance, real estate, construction. **Chief manuf. goods:** paper, ships & boats, cardboard, frozen/canned fruits & vegetables, plastics, baked goods. **Chief crops:** potatoes, greenhouse & nursery, wild blueberries, apples, hay, maple syrup. **Livestock** (Jan. 2007): 86,000 cattle/calves; (Dec. 2006): 4,800 hogs/pigs, 5.7 mil chickens (excl. broilers). **Timber/lumber** (est. 2006): 985 mil bd. ft.; pine, spruce, fir. **Nonfuel minerals** (preliminary 2006): $155 mil; sand and gravel (construction), cement (portland), stone (crushed), stone (dimension), peat. **Commercial fishing** (2005): $393.2 mil. **Chief ports:** Searsport, Portland, Eastport. **Gross state product** (est. 2006): $47.0 bil. **Sales tax** (2007): 5.0%. **Employment distrib.** (May 2007): 17.4% govt.; 20.0% trade/trans./util.; 9.6% mfg.; 18.7% ed./health; 8.6% prof./bus. serv.; 9.7% leisure/hosp.; 5.3% finance; 5.3% constr.; 3.1% other serv.; 1.8% info. **Unemployment** (2006): 4.6%. **Per cap. pers. income** (2006): $32,348. **New private housing** (2006): 7,293 units/$1.1 bil. **Commercial banks** (2006): 19; **deposits:** $12.2 bil. **Savings institutions** (2006): 22; **deposits:** $7.3 bil. **Lottery** (2006): total sales: $229.7 mil; profit: $51.7 mil.

Federal govt. Fed. civ. employees (Mar. 2006): 9,128; **avg. salary:** $57,336. **Notable fed. facilities:** Portsmouth Naval Shipyard, *Brunswick NAS.

Energy. Electricity production (est. 2006, kWh, by source): Hydroelectric: 6 mil.

State data. Motto: Dirigo (I direct). **Flower:** White pine cone and tassel. **Bird:** Chickadee. **Tree:** Eastern white pine. **Song:** State of Maine Song. **Entered union** Mar. 15, 1820; rank, 23rd. **State fair** at Bangor, late July–early Aug.; at Skowhegan, mid-Aug.

History. Paleoindians arrived about 11,500 years ago. Maine was inhabited by Algonquian peoples including the Abnaki, Penobscot, and Passamaquoddy at the time of European contact. French settled, 1604, at the St. Croix River, English, c. 1607, on the Kennebec; both settlements failed. A royal charter, 1691, made Maine part of Massachusetts. Maine broke off, 1819, and became a separate state, 1820. Drawing on vast forest resources, the pulp and paper industry developed after the Civil War. Bath Iron Works began building U.S. Navy vessels and other ships in the 1890s. Mail-order and retail giant L.L. Bean was founded, 1912. Women have fared well in state politics: Margaret Chase Smith became the first woman to serve in both houses of Congress (House, 1940-49; Senate, 1949-73), and Olympia Snowe and Susan

Collins have represented Maine in the Senate since the mid-1990s.

Tourist attractions. Acadia Natl. Park, Bar Harbor, on Mt. Desert Island; Old Orchard Beach; Portland's Old Port; Kennebunkport; Common Ground Country Fair, Unity; Portland Head Light; Baxter State Pk.; Freeport/L. L. Bean.

Famous "Down Easters." Leon Leonwood (L.L.) Bean, James G. Blaine, Cyrus H. K. Curtis, Hannibal Hamlin, Sarah Jewett, Stephen King, Henry Wadsworth Longfellow, Sir Hiram and Hudson Maxim, Edna St. Vincent Millay, George Mitchell, Edmund Muskie, Judd Nelson, Edwin Arlington Robinson, Joan Benoit Samuelson, Liv Tyler, Kate Douglas Wiggin, Ben Ames Williams.

Tourist information. Maine Office of Tourism, 59 State House Station, Augusta, ME 04333; 1-888-624-6345 (from within the United States and Canada); www.visitmaine.com.

Website. www.state.me.us

Maryland (MD)
Old Line State, Free State

People. Population (2006 est.): 5,615,727; rank: 19; **net change** (2005-2006): 0.5%. **Pop. density:** 578.6 per sq mi. **Racial distribution** (2005): 64.0% white; 29.3% black; 4.8% Asian; 0.3% Native/Nat. AK; 0.06% Hawaiian/Pacific Islander; 2 or more races, 1.5%. **Hispanic pop.** (any race): 5.7%.

Geography. Total area: 12,407 sq mi; rank: 42. **Land area:** 9,774 sq mi; rank: 42. **Acres forested:** 2.6 mil. **Location:** South Atlantic state stretching from the Ocean to the Allegheny Mts. **Climate:** continental in the west; humid subtropical in the east. **Topography:** Eastern Shore of coastal plain and Maryland Main of coastal plain, piedmont plateau, and the Blue Ridge, separated by the Chesapeake Bay. **Capital:** Annapolis. **Chief airport at:** Glen Burnie.

Economy. Chief industries: manufacturing, biotechnology and information technology, services, tourism. **Chief manuf. goods:** navigational instruments, pharmaceutical & medicine, broadcasting equip., plastics, printing, milk & ice cream. **Chief crops:** greenhouse & nursery, corn, soybeans, wheat, hay, tomatoes, watermelons, barley, potatoes, apples. **Livestock** (Jan. 2007): 220,000 cattle/calves, 23,000 sheep/lambs; (Dec. 2006): 34,000 hogs/pigs, 3.5 mil chickens (excl. broilers), 271.8 mil broilers. **Timber/lumber** (est. 2006): 231 mil bd. ft.; hardwoods. **Nonfuel minerals** (preliminary 2006): $596 mil; stone (crushed), cement (portland), sand and gravel (construction), cement (masonry), stone (dimension). **Commercial fishing** (2005): $63.7 mil. **Chief port:** Baltimore. **Gross state product** (est. 2006): $257.8 bil. **Sales tax** (2007): 5.0%. **Employment distrib.** (May 2007): 18.4% govt.; 18.0% trade/trans./util.; 5.1% mfg.; 14.1% ed./health; 15.4% prof./bus. serv.; 9.1% leisure/hosp.; 6.1% finance; 7.4% constr.; 4.5% other serv.; 1.9% info. **Unemployment** (2006): 3.9%. **Per cap. pers. income** (2006): $44,077. **New private housing** (2006): 23,262 units/$3.9 bil. **Commercial banks** (2006): 91; **deposits:** $75.6 bil. **Savings institutions** (2006): 55; **deposits:** $17.2 bil. **Lottery** (2006): total sales: $1.6 bil; profit: $501.0 mil.

Federal govt. Fed. civ. employees (Mar. 2006): 103,438; **avg. salary:** $79,319. **Notable fed. facilities:** U.S. Naval Academy; Natl. Agriculture Res. Ctr.; Ft. Meade, Aberdeen Proving Ground; Naval Air Sys. Command; Goddard Space Flight Ctr.; Natl. Inst. of Health; Natl. Inst. of Standards & Technology; Food & Drug Admin.; Bureau of the Census; Natl. Naval Med. Ctr., Bethesda; Natl. Marine Fisheries Serv.; Natl. Oceanic and Atmospheric Admin.

Energy. Electricity production (est. 2006, kWh by source): Petroleum: 25 mil.

State data. Motto: Fatti Maschii, Parole Femine (Manly deeds, womanly words). **Flower:** Black-eyed Susan. **Bird:** Baltimore oriole. **Tree:** White oak. **Song:** Maryland, My Maryland. **Seventh** of the original 13 states to ratify the U.S. Constitution, Apr. 28, 1788. **State fair** at Timonium; late Aug.–early Sept.

History. Europeans encountered Algonquian-speaking Nanticoke and Piscataway and Iroquois-speaking Susquehannock when they first visited the area. Italian navigator Verrazano reached the Chesapeake region in the early 16th cent. English Capt. John Smith explored and mapped the area, 1608. William Claiborne set up a trading post on Kent Island in Chesapeake Bay, 1631. King Charles I granted land to Cecilius Calvert, Lord Baltimore, 1632; Calvert's brother Leonard, with about 200 settlers, founded St. Marys, 1634.

During the Revolutionary War, Baltimore (1776-77) and Annapolis (1783-84) served as temporary capitals of the U.S. In the War of 1812, when a British fleet tried to take Ft. McHenry, Marylander Francis Scott Key wrote "The Star-Spangled Banner," 1814. Born into slavery at Tuckahoe in 1818, Frederick Douglass became a leading abolitionist. Although a slaveholding state, Maryland stayed in the Union during the Civil War and was the site of the battle of Antietam, 1862. Gov. Spiro Agnew elected U.S. Vice Pres. 1968, 1972; pleaded no contest to tax evasion and resigned 1973. Israeli and Egyptian leaders reached a historic peace accord at the Camp David presidential retreat, 1978. A major effort is under way to clean up pollution in the Chesapeake Bay watershed.

Tourist attractions. Laurel Park (Maryland Million); Ocean City; restored Ft. McHenry—near which Francis Scott Key wrote "The Star-Spangled Banner," Pimlico track (The Preakness), Edgar Allan Poe house, Camden Yards, Natl. Aquarium, Harborplace, all Baltimore; Antietam Battlefield, near Hagerstown; South Mountain Battlefield; U.S. Naval Academy, Maryland State House (oldest still in legislative use in the U.S.), in Annapolis; Natl. Cryptologic Museum, Ft. Meade.

Famous Marylanders. John Astin, Benjamin Banneker, Tom Clancy, Jonathan Demme, Francis Scott Key, H. L. Mencken, Kweisi Mfume, Ogden Nash, Charles Willson Peale, William Pinkney, Edgar Allan Poe, Cal Ripken Jr., Babe Ruth, Upton Sinclair, Roger B. Taney, John Waters, Montel Williams.

Tourist information. Maryland Office of Tourism Development, 217 E. Redwood St., Baltimore, MD 21202; 1-866-MD-WELCOME; www.mdwelcome.org
Website. www.maryland.gov

Massachusetts (MA)
Bay State, Old Colony

People. Population (2006 est.): 6,437,193; rank: 13; **net change** (2005-2006): 0.1%. **Pop. density:** 822.4 per sq mi. **Racial distribution** (2005): 86.7% white; 6.9% black; 4.7% Asian; 0.3% Native/Nat. AK; 0.08% Hawaiian/Pacific Islander; 2 or more races, 1.3%. **Hispanic pop.** (any race): 7.9%.

Geography. Total area: 10,555 sq mi; rank: 44. **Land area:** 7,840 sq mi; rank: 45. **Acres forested:** 3.1 mil. **Location:** New England state along Atlantic seaboard. **Climate:** temperate, with colder and drier clime in western region. **Topography:** jagged indented coast from Rhode Island around Cape Cod; flat land yields to stony upland pastures near central region and gentle hilly country in west; except in west, land is rocky, sandy, and not fertile. **Capital:** Boston. **Chief airport at:** Boston.

Economy. Chief industries: services, trade, manufacturing. **Chief manuf. goods:** electronics & instruments, pharmaceuticals, telecom. & broadcasting equip., plastics, medical equip., printing. **Chief crops:** greenhouse & nursery, cranberries, tomatoes, sweet corn, apples, hay, tobacco. **Livestock** (Jan. 2007): 44,000 cattle/calves; (Dec. 2006): 13,000 hogs/pigs, 246,000 chickens (excl. broilers). **Timber/lumber** (est. 2006): 51 mil bd. ft.; white pine, oak, other hard woods. **Nonfuel minerals** (preliminary 2006): $262 mil; stone (crushed), sand and gravel (construction), lime, stone (dimension), clays (common). **Commercial fishing** (2005): $426.9 mil. **Chief ports:** Boston, Fall River, New Bedford, Salem, Gloucester, Plymouth. **Gross state product** (est. 2006): $337.6 bil. **Sales tax** (2007): 5.0%. **Employment distrib.** (May 2007): 13.5% govt.; 17.4% trade/trans./util.; 9.0% mfg.; 18.8% ed./health; 14.7% prof./bus. serv.; 9.2% leisure/hosp.; 6.8% finance; 4.3% constr.; 3.6% other serv.; 2.7% info. **Unemployment** (2006): 5.0%. **Per cap. pers. income** (2006): $45,877. **New private housing** (2006): 19,580 units/$3.2 bil. **Commercial banks** (2006): 50; **deposits:** $109.3 bil. **Savings institutions** (2006): 161; **deposits:** $66.4 bil. **Lottery** (2006): total sales: $4.5 bil; profit: $951.2 mil.

Federal govt. Fed. civ. employees (Mar. 2006): 24,532; **avg. salary:** $67,035. **Notable fed. facilities:** Thomas P. O'Neill Jr. Fed. Bldg.; J.W. McCormack Bldg.; JFK Fed. Bldg.; Hanscom AFB; *Natick Army Soldier Systems Ctr.

Energy. Electricity production (est. 2006, kWh by source): Coal: 1.1 bil; Gas: 337 mil; Hydroelectric: 237 mil; Petroleum: 33 mil.

State data. Motto: Ense Petit Placidam Sub Libertate Quietem (By the sword we seek peace, but peace only under liberty). **Flower:** Mayflower. **Bird:** Chickadee. **Tree:** American elm. **Song:** All Hail to Massachusetts. **Sixth** of the original 13 states to ratify Constitution, Feb. 6, 1788. **State fair** at West Springfield, mid-Sept.–early Oct.

History. Early inhabitants were Algonquian peoples: Nauset, Wampanoag, Massachuset, Pennacook, Nipmuc, and Pocumtuc. Pilgrims settled in Plymouth, 1620, giving thanks for their survival with the first Thanksgiving Day, 1621. About 20,000 new settlers arrived, 1630-40. Colonist-Native American relations deteriorated, leading to King Philip's War, 1675-76, which the colonists won. Witch trials at Salem, 1692, led to the execution of about 20 people. Demonstrations against British restrictions set off the Boston Massacre, 1770, and the Boston Tea Party, 1773. The first bloodshed of American Revolution was at Lexington, 1775. After statehood, Massachusetts prospered from shipbuilding, seafaring, and the making of textiles, shoes, and metal goods, while artists, writers, and social reformers flourished. The controversial Sacco-Vanzetti case, 1920-27, ended with the execution of 2 Italian immigrants on murder and robbery charges. After World War II, old industries declined, knowledge-intensive enterprises thrived, and the Kennedys became a dominant political family. The state's highest court ruled, 2003, that same-sex couples could legally marry.

Tourist attractions. Provincetown arts colony; Cape Cod; Plymouth Rock, Plimoth Plantation, Mayflower II, all Plymouth; Freedom Trail, Museum of Fine Arts, New England Aquarium, and other Boston attractions; Tanglewood, Hancock Shaker Village, Berkshire Scenic Railway Museum, Norman Rockwell Museum, and other Berkshires attractions; Salem; Old Sturbridge Village; Old Deerfield Historic District; Walden Pond, Concord; Naismith Memorial Basketball Hall of Fame, Springfield.

Famous "Bay Staters." John Adams, John Quincy Adams, Samuel Adams, Louisa May Alcott, Horatio Alger, Susan B. Anthony, Crispus Attucks, Clara Barton, Alexander Graham Bell, Stephen Breyer, George H. W. Bush, John Cheever, E. E. Cummings, Emily Dickinson, Charles Eliot, Ralph Waldo Emerson, William Lloyd Garrison, Edward Everett Hale, John Hancock, Nathaniel Hawthorne, Oliver Wendell Holmes, Winslow Homer, Elias Howe, John F. Kennedy, John Kerry, Jack Kerouac, Jack Lemmon, James Russell Lowell, Cotton Mather, Samuel F. B. Morse, Edgar Allan Poe, Paul Revere, Norman Rockwell, Dr. Seuss (Theodor Seuss Geisel), Henry David Thoreau, Barbara Walters, James McNeil Whistler, John Greenleaf Whittier.

Tourist information. Massachusetts Office of Travel & Tourism, 10 Park Plaza, Ste. 4510, Boston, MA 02116; 1-800-227-MASS; www.massvacation.com
Website. www.mass.gov

Michigan (MI)
Great Lakes State, Wolverine State

People. Population (2006 est.): 10,095,642; rank: 8; **net change** (2005-2006): -0.1%. **Pop. density:** 178.6 per sq mi. **Racial distribution** (2005): 81.3% white; 14.3% black; 2.2% Asian; 0.6% Native/Nat. AK; 0.04% Hawaiian/Pacific Islander; 2 or more races, 1.5%. **Hispanic pop.** (any race): 3.8%.

Geography. Total area: 96,716 sq mi; rank: 11. **Land area:** 56,804 sq mi; rank: 22. **Acres forested:** 19.3 mil. **Location:** East North Central state bordering on 4 of the 5 Great Lakes, divided into an Upper and Lower Peninsula by the Straits of Mackinac, which link lakes Michigan and Huron. **Climate:** well-defined seasons tempered by the Great Lakes. **Topography:** low rolling hills give way to northern tableland of hilly belts in Lower Peninsula; Upper Peninsula is level in the east, with swampy areas; western region is higher and more rugged. **Capital:** Lansing. **Chief airports at:** Detroit, Flint, Grand Rapids.

Economy. Chief industries: manufacturing, services, tourism, agriculture, forestry/lumber. **Chief manuf. goods:** motor vehicles & parts, plastics, metalworking machinery, non-wood office furniture, fabricated metals. **Chief crops:** greenhouse & nursery, soybeans, corn, wheat, sugar beets, apples, blueberries, potatoes, dry beans, cherries, hay, cucumbers, tomatoes, grapes. **Livestock** (Jan. 2007): 1.1 mil. cattle/calves, 81,000 sheep/lambs; (Dec. 2006): 1.0 mil hogs/pigs, 11.4 mil chickens (excl. broilers). **Timber/lumber** (est. 2006): 927 mil bd. ft.; maple, oak, aspen. **Nonfuel min-**

erals (preliminary 2006): $2.0 bil; iron ore (usable shipped); cement (portland), sand and gravel (construction), stone (crushed), salt. Commercial fishing (2005): $6.1 mil. Chief ports: Detroit, Saginaw River, Escanaba, Muskegon, Sault Ste. Marie, Port Huron, Marine City. Gross state product (est. 2006): $381.0 bil. Sales tax (2007): 6.0%. Employment distrib. (May 2007): 15.7% govt.; 18.1% trade/trans./util.; 14.5% whle.; 13.7% ed./health; 13.5% prof./bus. serv.; 9.8% leisure/hosp.; 4.9% finance; 3.9% constr.; 4.1% other serv.; 1.5% info. Unemployment (2006): 6.9%. Per cap. pers. income (2006): $33,847. New private housing (2006): 29,191 units/$4.5 bil. Commercial banks (2006): 176; deposits: $140.5 bil. Savings institutions (2006): 20; deposits: $12.1 bil. Lottery (2006): total sales: $2.2 bil; profit: $688.0 mil.

Federal govt. Fed. civ. employees (Mar. 2006): 23,345; avg. salary: $65,576. Notable fed. facilities: Isle Royal, Sleeping Bear Dunes national parks; Army TACOM Life Cycle Mgmt. Command; Hart-Dole-Inouye Fed. Ctr.

Energy. Electricity production (est. 2006, kWh by source): Coal: 67.1 bil; Gas: 1.3 bil; Hydroelectric: 1.1 bil; Nuclear: 29.1 bil; Petroleum: 277 mil.

State data. Motto: Si Quaeris Peninsulam Amoenam, Circumspice (If you seek a pleasant peninsula, look about you). Flower: Apple blossom. Bird: Robin. Tree: White pine. Song: Michigan, My Michigan. Entered union Jan. 26, 1837; rank, 26th. State fair at Detroit, late Aug.–early Sept.; at Escanaba, mid-Aug.

History. Hunting and fishing peoples lived in the region as early as 11,000 years ago. Ojibwa, Ottawa, Miami, Potawatomi, and Huron inhabited the area at the time of European contact. French fur traders and missionaries arrived in the 17th cent. and established a settlement at Sault Ste. Marie, 1668. British took over, 1763, and crushed a Native American uprising led by Ottawa chieftain Pontiac. Treaty of Paris ceded the area to U.S., 1783, but British remained until 1796. Michigan was organized as a territory, 1805. The British seized Ft. Mackinac and Detroit, 1812, but the U.S. regained control, 1814. The opening of the Erie Canal, 1825, and new land laws and Native American cessions led the way for a flood of settlers. Strongly antislavery, Michigan became a state, 1837, and supplied 90,000 soldiers to the Union army in the Civil War. In the 20th cent., automobile manufacturing was the backbone of the economy. Henry Ford launched the Model T car, 1908; the United Auto Workers union was founded, 1935. Motown music flourished in Detroit in the 1960s, but riots in 1967 dealt the city a heavy blow. As the auto industry faltered, Michigan lost nearly 300,000 jobs in 2000-06.

Tourist attractions. Henry Ford Museum/Greenfield Village, Dearborn; Frederick Meijer Gardens and Sculpture Park, Grand Rapids; Tahquamenon (Hiawatha) Falls; De Zwaan windmill and Tulip Festival, Holland; "Soo Locks," St. Mary's Falls Ship Canal, Sault Ste. Marie; Air Zoo, Kalamazoo; Mackinac Island; Museum of African-American History, Motown Historical Museum, in Detroit.

Famous Michiganders. Ralph Bunche, Francis Ford Coppola, Paul de Kruif, Thomas Edison, Edna Ferber, Gerald R. Ford, Henry Ford, Aretha Franklin, Edgar Guest, Lee Iacocca, Robert Ingersoll, Magic Johnson, Casey Kasem, Will Kellogg, Ring Lardner, Elmore Leonard, Charles Lindbergh, Joe Louis, Madonna, Malcolm X, Terry McMillan, Michael Moore, Pontiac, Gilda Radner, Diana Ross, Glenn Seaborg, Tom Selleck, Sinbad (David Adkins), John Smoltz, Lily Tomlin, Stewart Edward White, Serena Williams.

Tourist information. Michigan Economic Development Corp., 300 N. Washington Square, Lansing, MI 48913; 1-800-644-2489; travel.michigan.org

Website. www.michigan.gov

Minnesota (MN)
North Star State, Gopher State

People. Population (2006 est.): 5,167,101; rank: 21; net change (2005-2006): 0.8%. Pop. density: 64.9 per sq mi. Racial distribution (2005): 89.6% white; 4.3% black; 3.4% Asian; 1.2% Native/Nat. AK; 0.05% Hawaiian/Pacific Islander; 2 or more races, 1.4%. Hispanic pop. (any race): 3.6%.

Geography. Total area: 86,939 sq mi; rank: 12. Land area: 79,610 sq mi; rank: 14. Acres forested: 16.7 mil. Location: West North Central state bounded on the E by Wisconsin and Lake Superior, on the N by Canada, on the W

by the Dakotas, and on the S by Iowa. Climate: northern part of state lies in the moist Great Lakes storm belt; the western border lies at the edge of the semi-arid Great Plains. Topography: central hill and lake region covering approx. half the state; to the NE, rocky ridges and deep lakes; to the NW, flat plain; to the S, rolling plains and deep river valleys. Capital: St. Paul. Chief airport at: Minneapolis.

Economy. Chief industries: agribusiness, forest products, mining, manufacturing, tourism. Chief manuf. goods: petroleum & asphalt, computers & electronics, milk & cheese, printing, animal slaughtering, paper & product, medical equip. Chief crops: corn, soybeans, hay, sugar beets, wheat, potatoes, greenhouse & nursery, dry edible beans, green peas, sunflowers. Livestock (Jan. 2007): 2.4 mil cattle/calves, 150,000 sheep/lambs; (Dec. 2006): 6.8 mil hogs/pigs, 14.2 mil chickens (excl. broilers), 45.9 mil broilers. Timber/lumber (est. 2006): 167 mil bd. ft.; needle-leaves and hardwoods. Nonfuel minerals (preliminary 2006): $2.7 bil; iron ore (usable shipped), sand and gravel (construction), stone (crushed), sand and gravel (industrial), stone (dimension). Commercial fishing (2005): $184,387. Chief ports: Duluth, St. Paul, Minneapolis. Gross state product (est. 2006): $244.5 bil. Sales tax (2007): 6.5%. Employment distrib. (May 2007): 15.2% govt.; 19.1% trade/trans./util.; 12.2% mfg.; 15.0% ed./health; 11.7% prof./bus. serv.; 9.0% leisure/hosp.; 6.6% finance; 4.7% constr.; 4.2% other serv.; 2.0% info. Unemployment (2006): 4.0%. Per cap. pers. income (2006): $38,712. New private housing (2006): 26,352 units/$4.8 bil. Commercial banks (2006): 454; deposits: $93.6 bil. Savings institutions (2006): 31; deposits: $3.5 bil. Lottery (2006): total sales: $450.0 mil; profit: $121.3 mil.

Federal govt. Fed. civ. employees (Mar. 2006): 14,298; avg. salary: $62,953.

Energy. Electricity production (est. 2006, kWh by source): Coal: 29.2 bil; Gas: 1.6 bil; Hydroelectric: 468 mil; Nuclear: 13.2 bil; Petroleum: 88 mil; Other: 232 mil.

State data. Motto: L'Etoile du Nord (The star of the north). Flower: Pink and white lady's-slipper. Bird: Common loon. Tree: Red pine. Song: Hail! Minnesota. Entered union May 11, 1858; rank, 32nd. State fair at St. Paul; late Aug.–early Sept.

History. Inhabited for at least 10,000 years, the region was home to Dakota Sioux when Europeans arrived. French fur traders Pierre Esprit Radisson and Médard Chouart, sieur des Groseilliers, explored in the mid-17th cent. In 1679, Daniel Greysolon, sieur Duluth, claimed the entire region for France. Ojibwa arrived in the 18th cent. and warred with the Sioux for over 100 years. Britain took the area east of the Mississippi, 1763. The U.S. took over that portion after the American Revolution and gained the western area, 1803, in the Louisiana Purchase. The U.S. built Ft. St. Anthony (now Ft. Snelling), 1819, and bought Native American lands, 1837, spurring an influx of settlers from the east. Minnesota became a territory, 1849, and a state, 1858. Sioux staged a bloody uprising, the Battle of Wood Lake, 1862, and were driven from the state. Railroad construction after the Civil War spurred the growth of the grain, timber, and iron mining industries. Opening of the St. Lawrence Seaway, 1959, aided the port of Duluth. Elected as a reformer, colorful former wrestler Jesse Ventura served as governor, 1999-2003. Two-term Sen. Paul Wellstone, one of a long line of liberal Minnesota Democrats, died when his campaign plane crashed, 2002. The I-35W Mississippi River Bridge in Minneapolis collapsed Aug. 1, 2007, killing 13.

Tourist attractions. Minneapolis Institute of Arts, Walker Art Center, Minneapolis Sculpture Garden, Minnehaha Falls (Hiawatha), Guthrie Theater, all Minneapolis; Ordway Theater, Winter Carnival, in St. Paul; Voyageurs Natl. Park; Mayo Clinic, Rochester; North Shore (of Lake Superior).

Famous Minnesotans. Warren Burger, Ethan and Joel Coen, William O. Douglas, Bob Dylan, F. Scott Fitzgerald, Al Franken, Judy Garland, Cass Gilbert, Hubert Humphrey, Garrison Keillor, Sister Elizabeth Kenny, Jessica Lange, Sinclair Lewis, Paul Manship, Roger Maris, E. G. Marshall, William and Charles Mayo, Eugene McCarthy, Walter F. Mondale, Prince (Rodgers Nelson), Charles Schulz, Harold Stassen, Thorstein Veblen, Jesse Ventura, Paul Wellstone.

Tourist information. Explore Minnesota Tourism, Metro Square, 121 7th Pl. E., Ste. 100, St. Paul, MN 55101. 1-888-TOURISM; www.exploreminnesota.com

Website. www.state.mn.us

Mississippi (MS)
Magnolia State

People. Population (2006 est.): 2,910,540; rank: 31; **net change** (2005-2006): 0.1%. **Pop. density:** 62.1 per sq mi. **Racial distribution** (2005): 61.2% white; 36.9% black; 0.7% Asian; 0.4% Native/Nat. AK; 0.03% Hawaiian/Pacific Islander; 2 or more races, 0.6%. **Hispanic pop.** (any race): 1.7%.

Geography. Total area: 48,430 sq mi; rank: 32. **Land area:** 46,907 sq mi; rank: 31. **Acres forested.** 18.6 mil. **Location:** East South Central state bordered on the W by the Mississippi R. and on the S by the Gulf of Mexico. **Climate:** semi-tropical, with abundant rainfall, long growing season, and extreme temperatures unusual. **Topography:** low, fertile delta between the Yazoo and Mississippi rivers; loess bluffs stretching around delta border; sandy gulf coastal terraces followed by piney woods and prairie; rugged, high sandy hills in extreme NE followed by Black Prairie Belt, Pontotoc Ridge, and flatwoods into the north central highlands. **Capital:** Jackson. **Chief airport at:** Jackson.

Economy. Chief industries: warehousing & distribution, services, manufacturing, government, wholesale and retail trade. **Chief manuf. goods:** petroleum, upholstered furniture, poultry processing, motor vehicle parts, plastics, ships & boats, misc. chemicals. **Chief crops:** cotton, soybeans, rice, hay, corn, sweet potatoes. **Livestock** (Jan. 2007): 980,000 cattle/calves; (Dec. 2006): 335,000 hogs/pigs, 10.7 mil chickens (excl. broilers), 803.8 mil broilers. **Timber/lumber** (est. 2006): 2.7 bil bd. ft.; pine, oak, hardwoods. **Nonfuel minerals** (preliminary 2006): $212 mil; sand and gravel (construction), stone (crushed), cement (portland), clays (fuller's earth), clays (ball). **Commercial fishing** (2005): $23.4 mil. **Chief ports:** Pascagoula, Vicksburg, Gulfport, Natchez, Greenville. **Gross state product** (est. 2006): $84.2 bil. **Sales tax** (2007): 7.0%. **Employment distrib.** (May 2007): 21.0% govt.; 19.8% trade/trans./util.; 14.9% mfg.; 10.9% ed./health; 8.3% prof./bus. serv.; 10.7% leisure/hosp.; 4.0% finance; 5.2% constr.; 3.2% other serv.; 1.2% info. **Unemployment** (2006): 6.8%. **Per cap. pers. income** (2006): $26,535. **New private housing** (2006): 16,618 units/$2.0 bil. **Commercial banks** (2006): 104; **deposits:** $$39.8 bil. **Savings institutions** (2006): 6; **deposits:** $417 mil.

Federal govt. Fed. civ. employees (Mar. 2006) 16,576; **avg. salary:** $56,978. **Notable fed. facilities:** *Keesler AFB; Meridian NAS; Columbus AFB; NASA Stennis Space Ctr.; Army Corps of Engineers Waterways Experiment Sta.; Naval Constr. Battalion Ctr., Gulfport.

Energy. Electricity production (est. 2006, kWh by source): Coal: 14.9 bil; Gas: 8.4 bil; Nuclear: 10.4 bil; Petroleum: 397 mil.

State data. Motto: Virtute et Armis (By valor and arms). **Flower:** Magnolia. **Bird:** Mockingbird. **Tree:** Magnolia. **Song:** Go, Mississippi! **Entered union** Dec. 10, 1817; rank, 20th. **State fair** at Jackson; begins first Wed. in Oct.

History. Choctaw, Chickasaw, and Natchez peoples were living in the region at the time of European contact. The Spaniard Hernando de Soto explored the area, 1540-41. La Salle traced the Mississippi River from Illinois to its mouth and claimed the entire Mississippi Valley for France, 1682. The first settlement, was the French Ft. Maurepas, 1699, on Biloxi Bay. The region was ceded to Britain, 1763, and claimed by Spain, 1779-98, then became a U.S. territory, 1798, and a state, 1817. Slavery spread along with cotton plantations, and slaves made up 55% of the population, 1860. Mississippi seceded, 1861. In the Civil War, Union forces captured Vicksburg, 1863, and caused extensive damage elsewhere. Mississippi reentered the Union, 1870. For the next 100 years, resistance to desegregation and violence against blacks made the state a battleground for the African American civil rights movement. Hurricanes Camille, 1969, and Katrina, 2005, caused substantial damage to the Gulf Coast. Since the early 1990s, casino gambling has boosted the economy.

Tourist attractions. Vicksburg Natl. Military Park and Cemetery, other Civil War sites; Hattiesburg; Natchez Trace; Indian mounds; Antebellum homes; pilgrimages in Natchez and some 25 other cities; The Elvis Presley Birthplace & Museum, Tupelo; Smith Robertson Museum, Mynelle Gardens, in Jackson; Mardi Gras, Shrimp Festival, in Biloxi; Gulf Islands Natl. Seashore.

Famous Mississippians. Margaret Walker Alexander, Dana Andrews, Jimmy Buffett, Hodding Carter III, Bo Diddley, William Faulkner, Brett Favre, Shelby Foote, Morgan Freeman, John Grisham, Fannie Lou Hamer, Jim Henson, Faith Hill, John Lee Hooker, Robert Johnson, James Earl Jones, B. B. King, L. Q. C. Lamar, Trent Lott, Gerald McRaney, Willie Morris, Walter Payton, Elvis Presley, Leontyne Price, Charley Pride, LeAnn Rimes, Muddy Waters, Eudora Welty, Tennessee Williams, Oprah Winfrey, Johnny Winter, Richard Wright, Tammy Wynette.

Tourist information. Mississippi Division of Tourism. PO Box 849, Jackson, MS 39205-0849; 1-888-SEE-MISS; www.visitmississippi.org

Website. www.ms.gov

Missouri (MO)
Show Me State

People. Population (2006 est.): 5,842,713; rank: 18; **net change** (2005-2006): 0.8%. **Pop. density:** 85.0 per sq mi. **Racial distribution** (2005): 85.4% white; 11.5% black; 1.3% Asian; 0.4% Native/Nat. AK; 0.07% Hawaiian/Pacific Islander; 2 or more races, 1.3%. **Hispanic pop.** (any race): 2.7%.

Geography. Total area: 69,704 sq mi; rank: 21. **Land area:** 68,886 sq mi; rank: 18. **Acres forested:** 14.0 mil. **Location:** West North Central state near the geographic center of the conterminous U.S.; bordered on the E by the Mississippi R., on the NW by the Missouri R. **Climate:** continental, susceptible to cold Canadian air, moist, warm gulf air, and drier SW air. **Topography:** rolling hills, open, fertile plains, and well-watered prairie N of the Missouri R.; south of the river land is rough and hilly with deep, narrow valleys; alluvial plain in the SE; low elevation in the west. **Capital:** Jefferson City. **Chief airports at:** Kansas City, St. Louis.

Economy. Chief industries: agriculture, manufacturing, aerospace, tourism. **Chief manuf. goods:** motor vehicles & parts, aerospace, pharmaceuticals, plastics, soap, animal slaughtering & processing, printing. **Chief crops:** soybeans, corn, hay, cotton & cottonseed, wheat, rice, sorghum. **Livestock** (Jan. 2007): 4.5 mil cattle/calves, 78,000 sheep/lambs; (Dec. 2006): 2.8 mil hogs/pigs, 9.4 mil chickens (excl. broilers). **Timber/lumber** (est. 2006): 507 mil bd. ft.; oak, hickory. **Nonfuel minerals** (preliminary 2006): $2.1 bil; stone (crushed), cement (portland), lead, lime, zinc. **Gross state product** (est. 2006): $225.9 bil. **Sales tax** (2007): 4.225%. **Employment distrib.** (May 2007): 15.9% govt.; 19.5% trade/trans./util.; 10.6% mfg.; 13.6% ed./health; 11.9% prof./bus. serv.; 10.5% leisure/hosp.; 5.9% finance; 5.4% constr.; 4.3% other serv.; 2.2% info. **Unemployment** (2006): 4.8%. **Per cap. pers. income** (2006): $32,705. **New private housing** (2006): 29,172 units/$4.1 bil. **Commercial banks** (2006): 369; **deposits:** $93.2 bil. **Savings institutions** (2006): 33; **deposits:** $4.9 bil. **Lottery** (2006): total sales: $913.5 mil; profit: $260.7 mil.

Federal govt. Fed. civ. employees (Mar. 2006): 32,947; **avg. salary:** $56,159. **Notable fed. facilities:** Federal Reserve banks; *Ft. Leonard Wood; Jefferson Barracks Natl. Cem.; Whiteman AFB.

Energy. Electricity production (est. 2006, kWh by source): Coal: 77.1 bil; Gas: 3.5 bil; Hydroelectric: 299 mil; Nuclear: 10.1 bil; Petroleum: 62 mil.

State data. Motto: Salus Populi Suprema Lex Esto (The welfare of the people shall be the supreme law). **Flower:** Hawthorn. **Bird:** Bluebird. **Tree:** Dogwood. **Song:** Missouri Waltz. **Entered union** Aug. 10, 1821; rank, 24th. **State fair** at Sedalia, mid-Aug.; at Bethany, late Aug.–early Sept.

History. In the 17th cent., when French explorers arrived, Algonquian Sauk, Fox, and Illinois and Siouan Osage, Missouri, Iowa, and Kansa peoples were living in the region; few remained by the 1830s. French hunters and lead miners made the first settlement c. 1735, at Ste. Genevieve. The territory was ceded to Spain by the French, 1762, then returned to France, 1800, and acquired by the U.S. in the Louisiana Purchase, 1803. Powerful earthquakes rocked New Madrid, 1811-12. Missouri became a territory, 1812, and entered the Union as a slave state, 1821. St. Louis became the gateway for pioneers heading West. Though Missouri stayed with the Union, pro- and antislavery forces battled there during the Civil War. In the late 19th cent. railroad building and the cattle trade made Kansas City a boomtown. The most notable Missourian of the 20th cent., Harry S. Truman, was U.S. president, 1945-53. The state, a political bellwether, voted for the winner in every presidential election from 1960 to 2004.

Tourist attractions. Silver Dollar City, Branson; Mark Twain Area, Hannibal; Pony Express Museum, St. Joseph; Harry S. Truman Library, Independence; Gateway Arch, St.

Louis; Worlds of Fun, Kansas City; Lake of the Ozarks; Churchill Mem., Fulton; State Capitol, Jefferson City.

Famous Missourians. Maya Angelou, Robert Altman, Burt Bacharach, Josephine Baker, Scott Bakula, Thomas Hart Benton, Tom Berenger, Yogi Berra, Chuck Berry, George Caleb Bingham, Daniel Boone, Omar Bradley, William Burroughs, Kate Capshaw, Dale Carnegie, George Washington Carver, Bob Costas, Walter Cronkite, Walt Disney, T. S. Eliot, Richard Gephardt, John Goodman, Betty Grable, Edwin Hubble, Jesse James, Rush Limbaugh, Marianne Moore, Reinhold Niebuhr, J. C. Penney, John J. Pershing, Brad Pitt, Joseph Pulitzer, Ginger Rogers, Bess Truman, Harry S. Truman, Kathleen Turner, Tina Turner, Mark Twain, Dick Van Dyke, Tennessee Williams, Lanford Wilson, Shelley Winters, Jane Wyman.

Tourist information. Missouri Division of Tourism. PO Box 1055, Jefferson City, MO 65102; 1-800-519-2100; www.visitmo.com

Website. www.state.mo.us

Montana (MT)
Treasure State

People. Population (2006 est.): 944,632; rank: 44; **net change** (2005-2006): 1.1%. **Pop. density:** 6.5 per sq mi. **Racial distribution** (2005): 91.1% white; 0.4% black; 0.5% Asian; 6.5% Native/Nat. AK; 0.05% Hawaiian/Pacific Islander; 2 or more races, 1.5%. **Hispanic pop.** (any race): 2.4%.

Geography. Total area: 147,042 sq mi; rank: 4. **Land area:** 145,552 sq mi; rank: 4. **Acres forested:** 23.3 mil. **Location:** Mountain state bounded on the E by the Dakotas, on the S by Wyoming, on the SSW by Idaho, and on the N by Canada. **Climate:** colder, continental climate with low humidity. **Topography:** Rocky Mts. in western third of the state; eastern two-thirds gently rolling northern Great Plains. **Capital:** Helena.

Economy. Chief industries: agriculture, timber, mining, tourism, oil and gas. **Chief manuf. goods:** sawmills, softwood veneer & plywood, petroleum. **Chief crops:** wheat, barley, hay, sugar beets, potatoes, dry beans, flaxseed, cherries, corn, oats. **Livestock** (Jan. 2007): 2.4 mil cattle/calves, 290,000 sheep/lambs; (Dec. 2006): 180,000 hogs/pigs, 490,000 chickens (excl. broilers). **Timber/lumber** (est. 2006): 976 mil bd. ft.; Douglas fir, pines, larch. **Nonfuel minerals** (preliminary 2006): $1.0 bil; copper, molybdenum (concentrates), platinum metal, metal, sand and gravel (construction). **Gross state product** (est. 2006): $32.3 bil. **Sales tax** (2007): none. **Employment distrib.** (May 2007): 20.1% govt.; 20.5% trade/trans./util.; 4.6% mfg.; 13.1% ed./health; 9.0% prof./bus. serv.; 12.9% leisure/hosp.; 5.0% finance; 7.4% constr.; 3.8% other serv.; 1.7% info. **Unemployment** (2006): 3.2%. **Per cap. pers. income** (2006): $30,688. **New private housing** (2006): 4,542 units/$723.1 mil. **Commercial banks** (2006): 83; **deposits:** $13.5 bil. **Savings institutions** (2006): 2; **deposits:** $235 mil. **Lottery** (2006): total sales: $39.9 mil; profit: $9.1 mil.

Federal govt. Fed. civ. employees (Mar. 2006): 8,858; **avg. salary:** $55,997. **Notable fed. facilities:** Malmstrom AFB & missile silos; Ft. Peck, Hungry Horse, Libby, Yellowtail, and other dams.

Energy. Electricity production (est. 2006, kWh by source): Coal: 291 mil.; Hydroelectric: 6.6 bil.

State data. Motto: Oro y Plata (Gold and silver). **Flower:** Bitterroot. **Bird:** Western meadowlark. **Tree:** Ponderosa pine. **Song:** Montana. **Entered union** Nov. 8, 1889; rank, 41st. **State fair** at Great Falls; late July–early Aug.

History. Paleoindian hunters reached the area over 12,000 years ago. Cheyenne, Blackfoot, Crow, Assiniboin, Salish (Flatheads), Kootenai, and Kalispel peoples lived in the region before Europeans arrived. French explorers visited the region, 1742. The U.S. acquired the area partly through the Louisiana Purchase, 1803, partly through explorations of Lewis and Clark, 1805-6. Fur traders and missionaries established posts in the early 19th cent. Gold was discovered at Grasshopper Creek, 1862, and Montana Territory was established, 1864. Indian uprisings reached their peak with the defeat of Gen. George Custer at the Battle of Little Bighorn, 1876. Chief Joseph and the Nez Percé tribe surrendered here, 1877, after a long trek across the state. Mining activity and the coming of the Northern Pacific Railway, 1883, brought population growth. Montana became a state, 1889. Copper wealth from the Butte pits resulted in the turn of the century "War of Copper Kings" as feuding factions contended

for "the richest hill on earth." During the first half of the 20th cent., the Anaconda Copper firm wielded enormous political influence. Jeannette Rankin, a suffragist and pacifist, was the first woman elected to Congress, 1916. Mike Mansfield served 34 years in Congress and was Senate Democratic leader, 1961-77. An 18-year hunt for notorious "Unabomber" Theodore Kaczynski ended with his arrest, 1996, at his cabin near Lincoln.

Tourist attractions. Glacier Natl. Park; Yellowstone Natl. Park; Museum of the Rockies, Bozeman; Museum of the Plains Indian, Blackfeet Reservation, near Browning; Little Bighorn Battlefield Natl. Monument and Custer Natl. Cemetery; Flathead Lake; Helena; Lewis and Clark Caverns State Park, near Whitehall; Lewis and Clark Interpretive Center, Great Falls.

Famous Montanans. Dana Carvey, Gary Cooper, Marcus Daly, Chet Huntley, Will James, Myrna Loy, David Lynch, Mike Mansfield, Brent Musburger, Jeannette Rankin, Charles M. Russell, Lester Thurow.

Tourist information. Travel Montana, Dept. of Commerce, PO Box 200533, 301 S. Park, Helena, MT 59601; 1-800-VISITM; www.visitmt.org

Website. www.state.mt.gov

Nebraska (NE)
Cornhusker State

People. Population (2006 est.): 1,768,331; rank: 38; **net change** (2005-2006): 0.6%. **Pop. density:** 23.0 per sq mi. **Racial distribution** (2005): 92.0% white; 4.3% black; 1.6% Asian; 0.9% Native/Nat. AK; 0.07% Hawaiian/Pacific Islander; 2 or more races, 1.1%. **Hispanic pop.** (any race): 7.1%.

Geography. Total area: 77,354 sq mi; rank: 16. **Land area:** 76,872 sq mi; rank: 15. **Acres forested:** 0.9 mil. **Location:** West North Central state with the Missouri R. for a NE and E border. **Climate:** continental semi-arid. **Topography:** till plains of the central lowland in the eastern third rising to the Great Plains and hill country of the north central and NW. **Capital:** Lincoln. **Chief airport at:** Omaha.

Economy. Chief industries: agriculture, manufacturing. **Chief manuf. goods:** animal slaughtering, grain & oilseed, farm machinery, medical equip., motor vehicle parts, printing, structural metals. **Chief crops:** corn, sorghum, soybeans, hay, wheat, dry beans, oats, potatoes, sugar beets. **Livestock** (Jan. 2007): 6.7 mil cattle/calves, 95,000 sheep/lambs; (Dec. 2006): 3.0 mil hogs/pigs, 13.2 mil chickens (excl. broilers), 5.1 mil broilers. **Timber/lumber:** figs. undisclosed; oak, hickory, and elm. **Nonfuel minerals** (preliminary 2006): $112 mil; cement (portland), sand and gravel (construction), stone (crushed), lime, clays (common). **Chief ports:** Omaha, Sioux City, Brownville, Blair, Plattsmouth, Nebraska City. **Gross state product** (est. 2006): $75.7 bil. **Sales tax** (2007): 5.5%. **Employment distrib.** (May 2007): 17.2% govt.; 21.2% trade/trans./util.; 10.4% mfg.; 13.9% ed./health; 11.0% prof./bus. serv.; 8.6% leisure/hosp.; 6.9% finance; 5.2% constr.; 3.7% other serv.; 2.0% info. **Unemployment** (2006): 3.0%. **Per cap. pers. income** (2006): $34,397. **New private housing** (2006): 8,230 units/$1.1 bil. **Commercial banks** (2006): 255; **deposits:** $31.1 bil. **Savings institutions** (2006): 14; **deposits:** $2.8 bil. **Lottery** (2006): total sales: $113.1 mil; profit: $30.3 mil.

Federal govt. Fed. civ. employees (Mar. 2006): 8,826; **avg. salary:** $47,406. **Notable fed. facilities:** *Offutt AFB.

Energy. Electricity production (est. 2006, kWh by source): Coal: 20.7 bil; Gas: 795 mil; Hydroelectric: 840 mil; Nuclear: 9.0 bil; Petroleum: 19 mil; Other: 316 mil.

State data. Motto: Equality before the law. **Flower:** Goldenrod. **Bird:** Western meadowlark. **Tree:** Cottonwood. **Song:** Beautiful Nebraska. **Entered union** Mar. 1, 1867; rank, 37th. **State fair** at Lincoln; late Aug.–early Sept.

History. When Europeans arrived, Pawnee, Ponca, Omaha, and Oto peoples lived in the region. Spanish and French explorers and fur traders visited the area prior to its acquisition in the Louisiana Purchase, 1803. Lewis and Clark passed through, 1804-6. The first permanent settlement was Bellevue, near Omaha, 1823. The 1834 Indian Intercourse Act declared Nebraska Indian country and excluded white settlement, but conflicts with settlers eventually forced Native Americans to move to reservations. Nebraska became a territory, 1854, and a state, 1867. Many Civil War veterans settled under free land terms of the 1862 Homestead Act; as agriculture grew, struggles followed between homesteaders and ranchers. Since the mid-1930s, Nebraska has been the only state with a unicameral legislature. A leader in agribusiness, Nebraska has also become a major telemarketing center. The "Oracle of Omaha," investor Warren Buffett, one of the world's wealthiest men, announced in 2006 he would give most of his $44 bil fortune to charity.

Tourist attractions. State Museum (Elephant Hall), State Capitol, in Lincoln; Stuhr Museum of the Prairie Pioneer, Grand Island; Museum of the Fur Trade, Chadron; Henry Doorly Zoo, Joslyn Art Museum, in Omaha; Ashfall Fossil Beds, Strategic Air and Space Museum, Ashland; Boys Town, Omaha; Arbor Lodge State Park, Nebraska City; Buffalo Bill Ranch State Hist. Park, North Platte; Pioneer Village, Minden; Oregon Trail landmarks; Scotts Bluff Natl. Monument; Chimney Rock Natl. Historic Site; Ft. Robinson; Hastings Museum of Natural & Cultural Hist.

Famous Nebraskans. Grover Cleveland Alexander, Fred Astaire, Marlon Brando, Charles W. Bryan, William Jennings Bryan, Warren Buffett, Johnny Carson, Willa Cather, Dick Cavett, Dick Cheney, William F. "Buffalo Bill" Cody, Loren Eiseley, Rev. Edward J. Flanagan, Henry Fonda, Gerald R. Ford, Bob Gibson, Rollin Kirby, Harold Lloyd, Malcolm X, J. Sterling Morton, John Neihardt, Nick Nolte, George Norris, Tom Osborne, John J. Pershing, Roscoe Pound, Chief Red Cloud, Mari Sandoz, Robert Taylor, Darryl F. Zanuck.

Tourist Infomation. Nebraska Division of Travel and Tourism, PO Box 98907, Lincoln, NE 68509-8907; 1-877-NE-BRASKA; www.visitnebraska.org

Website. www.nebraska.gov

Nevada (NV)

Sagebrush State, Battle Born State, Silver State

People. Population (2006 est.): 2,495,529; rank: 35; **net change** (2005-2006): 3.5%. **Pop. density:** 22.7 per sq mi. **Racial distribution** (2005): 82.0% white; 7.7% black; 5.7% Asian; 1.4% Native/Nat. AK; 0.5% Hawaiian/Pacific Islander; 2 or more races, 2.6%. **Hispanic pop.** (any race): 23.5%.

Geography. Total area: 110,561 sq mi; rank: 7. **Land area:** 109,826 sq mi; rank: 7. **Acres forested:** 10.2 mil. **Location:** Mountain state bordered on N by Oregon and Idaho, on E by Utah and Arizona, on SE by Arizona, and on SW and W by California. **Climate:** semi-arid and arid. **Topography:** rugged N-S mountain ranges; highest elevation, Boundary Peak, 13,140 ft; southern area is within the Mojave Desert; lowest elevation, Colorado River at southern tip of state, 479 ft. **Capital:** Carson City. **Chief airports at:** Las Vegas, Reno.

Economy. Chief industries: gaming, tourism, mining, manufacturing, government, retailing, warehousing, trucking. **Chief manuf. goods:** gaming machines, cement & concrete, plastics, printing, architectural & structural metals, electricity instruments. **Chief crops:** hay, onions, potatoes, alfalfa, wheat, garlic, mint, barley. **Livestock** (Jan. 2007): 500,000 cattle/calves, 75,000 sheep/lambs; (Dec. 2006): 3,500 hogs/pigs. **Timber/lumber** (est. 2006): <0.5 mil bd. ft.; piñon, juniper, other pines. **Nonfuel minerals** (preliminary 2006): $5.2 bil; gold, copper, sand and gravel (construction), lime, silver. **Gross state product** (est. 2006): $118.4 bil. **Sales tax** (2007): 6.5%. **Employment distrib.** (May 2007): 12.2% govt.; 17.7% trade/trans./util.; 3.9% mfg.; 7.0% ed./health; 12.4% prof./bus. serv.; 26.0% leisure/hosp.; 5.0% finance; 10.8% constr.; 2.9% other serv.; 1.2% info. **Unemployment** (2006): 4.2%. **Per cap. pers. income** (2006): $37,089. **New private housing** (2006): 39,445 units/$5.4 bil. **Commercial banks** (2006): 44; **deposits:** $49.6 bil. **Savings institutions** (2006): 9; **deposits** $76.6 bil.

Federal govt. Fed. civ. employees (Mar. 2006): 9,146; **avg. salary:** $59,831. **Notable fed. facilities:** Nevada Test Site; Hawthorne Army Depot; Nellis AFB & Range Complex; Fallon NAS; Natl. Wild Horse & Burro Ctr. at Palomino Valley.

Energy. Electricity production (est. 2006, kWh by source): Coal: 6.4 bil; Gas: 5.3 bil; Hydroelectric: 2.1 bil; Petroleum: 17 mil.

State data. Motto: All for our country. **Flower:** Sagebrush. **Bird:** Mountain bluebird. **Trees:** Single-leaf piñon and bristlecone pine. **Song:** Home Means Nevada. **Entered union** Oct. 31, 1864; rank, 36th. **State fair** at Reno; late Aug.

History. Shoshone, Paiute, Bannock, and Washoe peoples lived in the area at the time of European contact. Nevada was first explored by Spaniards, 1776. In the 1820s, fur traders Peter Skene Ogden and Jedediah Smith separately explored the area. It was acquired by the U.S., 1848, at the end of the Mexican War. A trading post at Mormon Station, now Genoa, was established, 1850. Discovery of the Comstock Lode, rich in gold and silver, 1859, spurred a population boom. Nevada became a territory, 1861, and a state, 1864. Hoover Dam was built, 1931-36. With gambling legal since 1931, a surge in resort casino construction after World War II turned Las Vegas into one of the nation's most popular tourist destinations. An influx of Hispanics and Asians, attracted by service-industry and construction jobs, helped make Nevada the fastest-growing state in the U.S. during 1990-2005.

Tourist attractions. Legalized gambling at: Lake Tahoe, Reno, Las Vegas, Laughlin, Elko County, and elsewhere; Hoover Dam; Lake Mead; Great Basin Natl. Park; Valley of Fire State Park; Virginia City; Red Rock Canyon Natl. Conservation Area; Liberace Museum, The Strip, Fremont St., Atomic Testing Museum, Pinball Hall of Fame, all Las Vegas; Lamoille Canyon; Pyramid Lake; Lost City Museum, Overton; Skiing near Lake Tahoe.

Famous Nevadans. Andre Agassi, Walter Van Tilburg Clark, George Ferris, Sarah Winnemucca Hopkins, Paul Laxalt, Dat So La Lee, John William Mackay, Anne Martin, Pat McCarran, Key Pittman, William Morris Stewart.

Tourist information. Commission on Tourism, 401 N. Carson St., Carson City, NV 89701; 1-800-NEVADA8; www.travelnevada.com

Website. www.nv.gov

New Hampshire (NH)

Granite State

People. Population (2006 est.): 1,314,895; rank: 41; **net change** (2005-2006): 0.6%. **Pop. density:** 146.9 per sq mi. **Racial distribution** (2005): 96.1% white; 1.0% black; 1.7% Asian; 0% Native/Nat. AK; 0.04% Hawaiian/Pacific Islander; 2 or more races, 1.0%. **Hispanic pop.** (any race): 2.2%.

Geography. Total area: 9,350 sq mi; rank: 46. **Land area:** 8,968 sq mi; rank: 44. **Acres forested:** 4.8 mil. **Location:** New England state bounded on S by Massachusetts, on W by Vermont, on N and NW by Canada, on E by Maine and the Atlantic Ocean. **Climate:** highly varied, due to its nearness to high mountains and ocean. **Topography:** low, rolling coast followed by countless hills and mountains rising out of a central plateau. **Capital:** Concord. **Chief airport at:** Manchester.

Economy. Chief industries: tourism, manufacturing, agriculture, trade, mining. **Chief manuf. goods:** navigational instr., circuit boards, electrical equip., fabricated metal, machinery, medical equip., plastics. **Chief crops:** greenhouse & nursery, apples, sweet corn, hay, Christmas trees, berries, maple syrup. **Livestock** (Jan. 2007): 35,000 cattle/calves; (Dec. 2006): 2,800 hogs/pigs, 223,000 chickens (excl. broilers). **Timber/lumber** (est. 2006): 246 mil bd. ft.; white pine, hemlock, oak, birch. **Nonfuel minerals** (preliminary 2006): $100 mil; stone (crushed), sand and gravel (construction), stone (dimension), gemstones (natural). **Commercial fishing** (2005): $22.2 mil. **Chief ports:** Portsmouth, Hampton, Rye. **Gross state product** (est. 2006): $56.3 bil. **Sales tax** (2007): none. **Employment distrib.** (May 2007): 14.6% govt.; 22.1% trade/trans./util.; 11.6% mfg.; 15.9% ed./health; 9.8% prof./bus. serv.; 9.8% leisure/hosp.; 6.1% finance; 4.5% constr.; 3.4% other serv.; 2.0% info. **Unemployment** (2006): 3.4%. **Per cap. pers. income** (2006): $39,311. **New private housing** (2006): 5,677 units/$1.0 bil. **Commercial banks** (2006): 17; **deposits:** $9.4 bil. **Savings institutions** (2006): 22; **deposits:** $11.1 bil. **Lottery** (2006): total sales: $262.7 mil; profit: $80.3 mil.

Federal govt. Fed. civ. employees (Mar. 2006): 3,433; **avg. salary:** $75,990. **Notable fed. facilities:** Army Cold Regions Res. & Engineering Lab.

Energy. Electricity production (est. 2006, kWh by source): Coal: 3.9 bil; Gas: 61 mil; Hydroelectric: 342 mil; Nuclear: 230 mil; Other: 55 mil.

State data. Motto: Live free or die. **Flower:** Purple lilac. **Bird:** Purple finch. **Tree:** White birch. **Song:** Old New Hampshire. **Ninth** of the original 13 states to ratify the Constitution, June 21, 1788. **State fair:** many agricultural fairs statewide, July through Sept.; no official State fair.

History. The area has been inhabited for about 10,000 years. Algonquian-speaking peoples, including the Pennacook, lived in the region when the Europeans arrived. The first explorers to visit the area were England's Martin Pring, 1603, and France's Champlain, 1605. The first settlement was Odiorne's Point (now part of Rye), 1623. Before the American Revolution, New Hampshire residents raided a British fort at Portsmouth, 1774, and drove the royal governor out, 1775. New Hampshire became the first colony to adopt its own constitution, 1776. After statehood, 1788, New Hampshire became a textile manufacturing center. The mill towns declined in the first half of the 20th cent., but tourism and high-technology industries, lured by low taxes, have revived the economy since the 1960s. A state law requires it to hold the first primary of the presidential campaign season.

Tourist attractions. Mt. Washington, highest peak in Northeast; Lake Winnipesaukee; Crawford, Franconia, Pinkham notches, Flume Gorge, Canon Mt. aerial tramway, all White Mt. region; Strawbery Banke, Portsmouth; Canterbury Shaker Village; Saint-Gaudens, Natl. Historic Site, Cornish; Mt. Monadnock.

Famous New Hampshirites. Salmon P. Chase, Ralph Adams Cram, Mary Baker Eddy, Daniel Chester French, Robert Frost, Horace Greeley, Sarah Buell Hale, Franklin Pierce, Augustus Saint-Gaudens, Adam Sandler, Alan Shepard, David H. Souter, Daniel Webster.

Tourist information. Division of Travel & Tourism Development, 172 Pembroke Rd., PO Box 1856; Concord, NH 03302-1856; 1-800-FUNINNH; www.visitnh.gov

Website. www.state.nh.us

New Jersey (NJ)
Garden State

People. Population (2006 est.): 8,724,560; rank: 11; **net change** (2005-2006): 0.2%. **Pop. density:** 1,183.9 per sq mi. **Racial distribution** (2005): 76.6% white; 14.5% black; 7.2% Asian; 0.3% Native/Nat. AK; 0.08% Hawaiian/Pacific Islander; 2 or more races, 1.3%. **Hispanic pop.** (any race): 15.2%.

Geography. Total area: 8,721 sq mi; rank: 47. **Land area:** 7,417 sq mi; rank: 46. **Acres forested:** 2.1 mil. **Location:** Middle Atlantic state bounded on N and E by New York and Atlantic Ocean, on S and W by Delaware and Pennsylvania. **Climate:** moderate, with marked difference bet. NW and SE extremities. **Topography:** Appalachian Valley in the NW also has highest elevation, High Pt., 1,801 ft; Appalachian Highlands, flat-topped NE-SW mountain ranges; Piedmont Plateau, low plains broken by high ridges (Palisades) rising 400-500 ft; Coastal Plain, covering three-fifths of state in SE, rises from sea level to gentle slopes. **Capital:** Trenton. **Chief airport at:** Newark.

Economy. Chief industries: pharmaceuticals, telecommunications, biotechnology, printing & publishing. **Chief manuf. goods:** petroleum, pharmaceuticals, toiletries, chemicals, plastics, printing, navigational instr., medical equip., paper prod. **Chief crops:** greenhouse & nursery, blueberries, peaches, corn, hay, tomatoes, bell peppers, cranberries, soybeans, apples. **Livestock** (Jan. 2007): 38,000 cattle/calves; (Dec. 2006): 7,000 hogs/pigs, 1.4 mil chickens (excl. broilers). **Timber/lumber** (est. 2006): 29 mil bd. ft.; pine, cedar, mixed hardwoods. **Nonfuel minerals** (preliminary 2006): $369 mil; stone (crushed), sand and gravel (construction), sand and gravel (industrial), greensand marl, peat. **Commercial fishing** (2005): $159.0 mil. **Chief ports:** Newark, Elizabeth, Hoboken, Camden. **Gross state product** (est. 2006): $453.2 bil. **Sales tax** (2007): 7.0%. **Employment distrib.** (May 2007): 16.1% govt.; 21.2% trade/trans./util.; 7.7% mfg.; 14.1% ed./health; 14.9% prof./bus. serv.; 8.4% leisure/hosp.; 6.9% finance; 4.3% constr.; 4.0% other serv.; 2.4% info. **Unemployment** (2006): 4.6%. **Per cap. pers. income** (2006): $46,344. **New private housing** (2006): 34,233 units/$4.4 bil. **Commercial banks** (2006): 94; **deposits:** $153.1 bil. **Savings institutions** (2006): 80; **deposits:** $60.2 bil. **Lottery** (2006): total sales: $2.5 bil; profit: $849.3 mil.

Federal govt. Fed. civ. employees (Mar. 2006): 26,682; **avg. salary:** $72,313. **Notable fed. facilities:** McGuire AFB; *Ft. Monmouth; Picatinny Arsenal; *Lakehurst Naval Air Engineering Ctr.; Ft. Dix; FAA William J. Hughes Technical Ctr.

Energy. Electricity production (est. 2006, kWh by source): Coal: 1.3 bil; Petroleum: 92 mil.

State data. Motto: Liberty and prosperity. **Flower:** Purple violet. **Bird:** Eastern goldfinch. **Tree:** Red oak. **Third** of the original 13 states to ratify the Constitution, Dec. 18, 1787. **State fair** at Augusta; late July–early Aug.

History. The Lenni Lenape (Delaware) peoples lived in the region and had mostly peaceful relations with European colonists, who arrived after the explorers Verrazano, 1524, and Hudson, 1609. The first permanent European settlement was Dutch, at Bergen (now Jersey City), 1660. When the British took New Netherland, 1664, the area between the Delaware and Hudson Rivers was given to Lord John Berkeley and Sir George Carteret. During the American Revolution, New Jersey was the scene of many major battles, including Trenton,

1776; Princeton, 1777; and Monmouth, 1778. New Jersey was the third state to ratify the Constitution, 1787, and the first to approve the Bill of Rights, 1789. In a duel at Weehawken, 1804, Vice Pres. Aaron Burr fatally shot Alexander Hamilton. Canal and railroad building stimulated the growth of cities and industries in the 19th cent. The 20th cent. arrival of large numbers of African Americans, Italians, Irish, European Jews, Puerto Ricans, Asian Indians, and other groups made New Jersey one of the most diverse states in the U.S. Construction of resort casinos in Atlantic City from the late 1970s revitalized tourism. Gov. James McGreevey resigned, 2004, after acknowledging an extramarital affair with a man later identified as his former homeland security adviser.

Tourist attractions. 127 mi of beaches, boardwalks at Atlantic City (with gambling), Seaside Heights, Ocean City, Wildwood; Grover Cleveland birthplace, Caldwell; Cape May Historic District; Edison Natl. Historic Site, W. Orange; Six Flags Great Adventure, Jackson; Liberty State Park, Liberty Science Center, in Jersey City; Pine Barrens wilderness area; Princeton University; Revolutionary War sites; Adventure Aquarium, Battleship NJ, Walt Whitman house, in Camden.

Famous New Jerseyans. Jason Alexander, Samuel Alito, Count Basie, Judy Blume, Jon Bon Jovi, Bill Bradley, Aaron Burr, Grover Cleveland, James Fenimore Cooper, Stephen Crane, Danny DeVito, Thomas Edison, Albert Einstein, James Gandolfini, Allen Ginsberg, Alexander Hamilton, Ed Harris, Whitney Houston, Buster Keaton, Joyce Kilmer, Norman Mailer, Jack Nicholson, Thomas Paine, Dorothy Parker, Joe Pesci, Molly Pitcher, Paul Robeson, Philip Roth, Antonin Scalia, Wally Schirra, H. Norman Schwarzkopf, Frank Sinatra, Bruce Springsteen, Martha Stewart, Meryl Streep, Dave Thomas, John Travolta, Walt Whitman, William Carlos Williams, Woodrow Wilson.

Tourist information. Dept. of State, Division of Travel and Toursim, PO Box 460, Trenton, NJ 08625; 1-800-VISITNJ; www.visitnj.org

Website. www.state.nj.us

New Mexico (NM)
Land of Enchantment

People. Population (2006 est.): 1,954,599; rank: 36; **net change** (2005-2006): 1.5%. **Pop. density:** 16.1 per sq mi. **Racial distribution** (2005): 84.5% white; 2.4% black; 1.3% Asian; 10.2% Native/Nat. AK; 0.1% Hawaiian/Pacific Islander; 2 or more races, 1.5%. **Hispanic pop.** (any race): 43.4%.

Geography. Total area: 121,589 sq mi; rank: 5. **Land area:** 121,356 sq mi; rank: 5. **Acres forested:** 16.7 mil. **Location:** southwestern state bounded by Colorado on the N, Oklahoma, Texas, and Mexico on the E and S, and Arizona on the W. **Climate:** dry, with temperatures rising or falling 5°F with every 1,000 ft elevation. **Topography:** eastern third, Great Plains; central third, Rocky Mts. (85% of the state is over 4,000-ft elevation); western third, high plateau. **Capital:** Santa Fe. **Chief airport at:** Albuquerque.

Economy. Chief industries: government, services, trade. **Chief manuf. goods:** semiconductors, medical equip., navigational/measuring/medical/control instruments, aircrafts, chemicals, jewelry. **Chief crops:** hay, pecans, corn, greenhouse & nursery, chiles, onions, cotton, wheat, peanuts. **Livestock** (Jan. 2007): 1.6 mil cattle/calves, 130,000 sheep/ lambs; (Dec. 2006): 2,000 hogs/pigs. **Timber/lumber:** figs. undisclosed; ponderosa pine, Douglas fir. **Nonfuel minerals** (preliminary 2006): $1.5 bil; copper, potash, sand and gravel (construction), molybdenum (concentrates), cement (portland). **Gross state product** (est. 2006): $75.9 bil. **Sales tax** (2007): 5.0%. **Employment distrib.** (May 2007): 23.3% govt.; 16.9% trade/trans./util.; 4.4% mfg.; 13.1% ed./health; 12.8% prof./bus. serv.; 10.5% leisure/hosp.; 4.2% finance; 7.0% constr.; 3.4% other serv.; 2.0% info. **Unemployment** (2006): 4.2%. **Per cap. pers. income** (2006): $29,673. **New private housing** (2006): 13,573 units/$2.3 bil. **Commercial banks** (2006): 55; **deposits:** $18.9 bil. **Savings institutions** (2006): 9; **deposits:** $2.0 bil. **Lottery** (2006): total sales: $154.7 mil; profit: $36.9 mil.

Federal govt. Fed. civ. employees (Mar. 2006): 22,298; **avg. salary:** $58,693. **Notable fed. facilities:** Kirtland, *Cannon, *Holloman AF bases; Los Alamos Natl. Lab; *White Sands Missile Range; Natl. Solar Observatory; Natl. Radio Astronomy Observatory; Sandia Natl. Labs.

Energy. Electricity production (est. 2006, kWh by source): Coal: 29.9 bil; Gas: 4.0 bil; Hydroelectric: 189 mil; Petroleum: 37 mil.

State data. Motto: Crescit Eundo (It grows as it goes). **Flower:** Yucca. **Bird:** Roadrunner. **Tree:** Piñon. **Song:** O, Fair New Mexico; Asi Es Nuevo Mexico. **Entered union** Jan. 6, 1912; rank, 47th. **State fair** at Albuquerque, mid-Sept.; at Las Cruces, early Oct.; at Roswell, early Oct.; at Deming, early Oct.

History. Inhabited for more than 10,000 years, the region was home to Sandia, Clovis, Folsom, Mogollon, and Anasazi cultures, followed by the Pueblo people, Anasazi descendants; later, nomadic Navajo and Apache came. Franciscan Marcos de Niza and a former black slave, Estevanico, explored the area, 1539, seeking gold; Coronado followed, 1540. First settlements were near San Juan Pueblo, 1598, and at Santa Fe, 1610. Settlers alternately traded and fought with the Apache, Comanche, and Navajo. Trade on the Santa Fe Trail to Missouri started, 1821. After the Mexican War began, 1846, Gen. Stephen Kearny took Santa Fe without firing a shot, and declared New Mexico part of the U.S. All Hispanic New Mexicans and Pueblo became U.S. citizens by terms of the 1848 treaty ending the war. New Mexico became a territory, 1850, but did not attain statehood until 1912. Pancho Villa raided Columbus, 1916, and U.S. troops were sent to the area. The world's first atomic bomb was exploded at a test site near Alamogordo, 1945. An underground nuclear waste depository opened near Carlsbad, 1999. Construction on a "spaceport" for space tourism, partially financed by the state, was to begin in 2008.

Tourist attractions. Carlsbad Caverns Natl. Park, with world's largest natural underground chamber; Santa Fe, oldest capital in U.S.; White Sands Natl. Monument, world's largest gypsum deposit; Chaco Culture Natl. Hist. Park; Acoma Pueblo, "sky city" built atop a 357-ft mesa; Taos Art Colony & Ski Valley; Ute Lake State Park; Shiprock; Roswell.

Famous New Mexicans. Ben Abruzzo, Maxie Anderson, Jeff Bezos, Billy (the Kid) Bonney, Kit Carson, Bob Foster, Peter Hurd, Tony Hillerman, Archbishop Jean Baptiste Lamy, Nancy Lopez, Bill Mauldin, Georgia O'Keeffe, Bill Richardson, Kim Stanley, Al Unser, Bobby Unser, Lew Wallace.

Tourist information. New Mexico Dept. of Tourism, 491 Old Santa Fe Tr., Santa Fe, NM 87501; 1-800-733-6396; www.newmexico.org

Website. www.newmexico.gov

New York (NY)
Empire State

People. Population (2006 est.): 19,306,183; rank: 3; **net change** (2005-2006): 0.0%. **Pop. density:** 409.0 per sq mi. **Racial distribution** (2005): 73.8% white; 17.4% black; 6.7% Asian; 0.5% Native/Nat. AK; 0.09% Hawaiian/Pacific Islander; 2 or more races, 1.5%. **Hispanic pop.** (any race): 16.1%.

Geography. Total area: 54,556 sq mi; rank: 27. **Land area:** 47,214 sq mi; rank: 30. **Acres forested:** 18.4 mil. **Location:** Middle Atlantic state, bordered by the New England states, Atlantic Ocean, New Jersey and Pennsylvania, Lakes Ontario and Erie, and Canada. **Climate:** variable; the SE region moderated by the ocean. **Topography:** highest and most rugged mountains in the NE Adirondack upland; St. Lawrence-Champlain lowlands extend from Lake Ontario NE along the Canadian border; Hudson-Mohawk lowland follows the flows of the rivers N and W, 10-30 mi wide; Atlantic coastal plain in the SE; Appalachian Highlands, covering half the state westward from the Hudson Valley, include the Catskill Mts., Finger Lakes; plateau of Erie-Ontario lowlands. **Capital:** Albany. **Chief airports at:** Albany, Buffalo, Islip, New York (2), Rochester, Syracuse.

Economy. Chief industries: manufacturing, finance, communications, tourism, transportation, services. **Chief manuf. goods:** pharmaceuticals, photographic chemicals, electronics, automotive parts, toiletries, printing, plastics, apparel. **Chief crops:** greenhouse & nursery, apples, corn, hay, cabbage, onions, soybeans, potatoes, snap beans, grapes, squash, pumpkins, tomatoes, wheat, cucumbers, green peas. **Livestock** (Jan. 2007): 1.4 mil cattle/calves, 74,000 sheep/lambs; (Dec. 2006): 98,000 hogs/pigs, 5.6 mil chickens (excl. broilers). **Timber/lumber** (est. 2006): 591 mil bd. ft.; birch, sugar and red maple, basswood, hemlock, pine, oak, ash. **Nonfuel minerals** (preliminary 2006): $1.3 bil; stone (crushed), cement (portland), salt, sand and gravel (construction), wollastonite. **Commercial fishing** (2005): $56.5 mil. **Chief ports:** New York, Buffalo, Albany. **Gross state product** (est. 2006): $1.0 trillion. **Sales tax** (2007): 4.0%. **Employment distrib.** (May 2007): 17.3% govt.; 17.3%

trade/trans./util.; 6.3% mfg.; 18.5% ed./health; 12.9% prof./bus. serv.; 8.0% leisure/hosp.; 8.4% finance; 4.1% constr.; 4.1% other serv.; 3.1% info. **Unemployment** (2006): 4.5%. **Per cap. pers. income** (2006): $42,392. **New private housing** (2006): 54,382 units/$7.1 bil. **Commercial banks** (2006): 158; **deposits:** $691.7 bil. **Savings institutions** (2006): 76; **deposits:** $98.6 bil. **Lottery** (2006): total sales: $6.8 bil; profit: $2.2 bil.

Federal govt. Fed. civ. employees (Mar. 2006): 57,472; **avg. salary:** $65,010. **Notable fed. facilities:** Ft. Drum; West Point Military Academy; Merchant Marine Academy; AF Research Labs., Rome; Watervliet Arsenal; Brookhaven Natl. Lab.

Energy. Electricity production (est. 2006, kWh by source): Coal: 1.2 bil; Gas: 15.3 bil; Hydroelectric: 21.1 bil; Petroleum: 3.9 bil.

State data. Motto: Excelsior (Ever upward). **Flower:** Rose. **Bird:** Bluebird. **Tree:** Sugar maple. **Song:** I Love New York. **Eleventh** of the original 13 states to ratify the Constitution, July 26, 1788. **State fair** at Syracuse; late Aug.–early Sept.

History. When Europeans arrived, Algonquians including the Mahican, Wappinger, and Lenni Lenape inhabited the region, as did the Iroquoian Mohawk, Oneida, Onondaga, Cayuga, and Seneca tribes, who established the League of the Five Nations. Verrazano entered New York harbor, 1524. In 1609, Henry Hudson visited the river later named for him, and Champlain explored the lake that now bears his name. The first permanent settlement was Dutch, near present-day Albany, 1624. New Amsterdam was settled, 1626, at the S tip of Manhattan island. A British fleet seized New Netherland, 1664. Key battles of the American Revolution included Saratoga, 1777. In the 19th cent., New York City emerged as one of the world's great metropolitan areas, a center for trade, finance, and arts, and a haven for millions of immigrants. Completion of Erie Canal, 1825, established the state as a gateway to the West. The first women's rights convention was held in Seneca Falls, 1848. Although the state backed the Union in the Civil War, the military draft, 1863, triggered 3 days of riots in New York City. Industry declined in the 20th cent., and California and Texas passed New York in population. Attica was the scene of a bloody prison revolt, 1971. New Yorkers, 2000, elected former First Lady Hillary Rodham Clinton to the U.S. Senate. Two jet aircraft hijacked by terrorists on Sept. 11, 2001, destroyed the World Trade Center in lower Manhattan.

Tourist attractions. New York City; Adirondack and Catskill Mts.; Finger Lakes; Great Lakes; Thousand Islands; Niagara Falls; Saratoga Springs; Philipsburg Manor, Sunnyside (Washington Irving's home), Dutch Church of Sleepy Hollow, near Tarrytown; Corning Museum of Glass; Fenimore House, Natl. Baseball Hall of Fame and Museum, in Cooperstown; Ft. Ticonderoga; Empire State Plaza, Albany; Lake Placid; Franklin D. Roosevelt Natl. Historic Site, Hyde Park; Long Island beaches; Theodore Roosevelt estate, Sagamore Hill, Oyster Bay; Turning Stone Casino.

Famous New Yorkers. Woody Allen, Susan B. Anthony, James Baldwin, Lucille Ball, Ann Bancroft, L. Frank Baum, Milton Berle, Humphrey Bogart, Barbara Boxer, Mel Brooks, Benjamin Cardozo, De Witt Clinton, Peter Cooper, Aaron Copland, Tom Cruise, Robert De Niro, George Eastman, Millard Fillmore, Lou Gehrig, George and Ira Gershwin, Ruth Bader Ginsburg, Rudolph Giuliani, Jackie Gleason, Stephen Jay Gould, Julia Ward Howe, Charles Evans Hughes, Washington Irving, Henry and William James, John Jay, Michael Jordan, Edward Koch, Fiorello LaGuardia, Herman Melville, Arthur Miller, J. Pierpont Morgan Jr., Eddie Murphy, Joyce Carol Oates, Carroll O'Connor, Rosie O'Donnell, Eugene O'Neill, Jerry Orbach, George Pataki, Colin Powell, Nancy Reagan, John D. Rockefeller, Nelson Rockefeller, John Roberts, Richard Rodgers, Ray Romano, Eleanor Roosevelt, Franklin D. Roosevelt, Theodore Roosevelt, Tim Russert, J. D. Salinger, Caroline Kennedy Schlossberg, Jerry Seinfeld, Al Sharpton, Paul Simon, Alfred E. Smith, Elizabeth Cady Stanton, Barbra Streisand, Donald Trump, William (Boss) Tweed, Martin Van Buren, Luther Vandross, Gore Vidal, Denzel Washington, Edith Wharton, Walt Whitman.

Tourist information. Empire State Development, Travel Information Center, 30 South Pearl St., Albany, NY 12245; 1-800-CALLNYS from U.S. states and territories and Canada; (518) 474-4116 from other areas; www.iloveny.com

Website. www.state.ny.us

North Carolina (NC)

Tar Heel State, Old North State

People. Population (2006 est.): 8,856,505; rank: 10; **net change** (2005-2006): 2.1%. **Pop. density:** 182.2 per sq mi. **Racial distribution** (2005): 74.1% white; 21.8% black; 1.8% Asian; 1.3% Native/Nat. AK; 0.07% Hawaiian/Pacific Islander; 2 or more races, 1.0%. **Hispanic pop.** (any race): 6.4%.

Geography. Total area: 53,819 sq mi; rank: 28. **Land area:** 48,711 sq mi; rank: 29. **Acres forested:** 19.3 mil. **Location:** South Atlantic state bounded by Virginia, South Carolina, Georgia, Tennessee, and the Atlantic Ocean. **Climate:** sub-tropical in SE, medium-continental in mountain region; tempered by the Gulf Stream and the mountains in W. **Topography:** coastal plain and tidewater, two-fifths of state, extending to the fall line of the rivers; piedmont plateau, another two-fifths, of gentle to rugged hills; southern Appalachian Mts. contains the Blue Ridge and Great Smoky Mts. **Capital:** Raleigh. **Chief airports at:** Charlotte, Greensboro, Raleigh.

Economy. Chief industries: manufacturing, agriculture, tourism. **Chief manuf. goods:** transportation, tobacco, pharmaceuticals, toiletries, plastics, animal slaughtering & processing, household furniture, fabric & apparel. **Chief crops:** greenhouse & nursery, tobacco, cotton, soybeans, corn, Christmas trees, sweet potatoes, wheat, peanuts, blueberries, cucumbers, tomatoes, hay, potatoes. **Livestock** (Jan. 2007): 850,000 cattle/calves, 21,000 sheep/lambs; (Dec. 2006): 9.5 mil hogs/pigs, 19.2 mil chickens (excl. broilers), 749.0 mil broilers. **Timber/lumber** (est. 2006): 2.7 bil bd. ft.; yellow pine, oak, hickory, poplar, maple. **Nonfuel minerals** (preliminary 2006): \$872 mil; stone (crushed), phosphate rock, sand and gravel (construction), sand and gravel (industrial), feldspar. **Commercial fishing** (2005): \$64.9 mil. **Chief ports:** Morehead City, Wilmington. **Gross state product** (est. 2006): \$374.5 bil. **Sales tax** (2007): 4%. **Employment distrib.** (May 2007): 17.0% govt.; 18.5% trade/trans./util.; 13.3% mfg.; 12.3% ed./health; 11.9% prof./bus. serv.; 9.5% leisure/hosp.; 5.1% finance; 6.2% constr.; 4.4% other serv.; 1.8% info. **Unemployment** (2006): 4.8%. **Per cap. pers. income** (2006): \$32,234. **New private housing** (2006): 99,979 units/\$16.1 bil. **Commercial banks** (2006): 97; **deposits:** \$189.2 bil. **Savings institutions** (2006): 39; **deposits:** \$6.0 bil. **Lottery** (2006): total sales: \$229.5 mil; profit: \$64.6 mil.

Federal govt. Fed. civ. employees (Mar. 2006): 33,163; **avg. salary:** \$57,319. **Notable fed. facilities:** Ft. Bragg; *Camp LeJeune Marine Base. *Cherry Point Marine Air Station; Natl. Inst. of Environmental Health Sciences, EPA Research & Dev. Labs, all in Research Triangle Park.

Energy. Electricity production (est. 2006, kWh by source): Coal: 72.3 bil; Gas: 2.1 bil; Hydroelectric: 2.9 bil; Nuclear: 40.0 bil; Petroleum: 220 mil.

State data. Motto: Esse Quam Videri (To be rather than to seem). **Flower:** Dogwood. **Bird:** Cardinal. **Tree:** Pine. **Song:** The Old North State. **Twelfth** of the original 13 states to ratify the Constitution, Nov. 21, 1789. **State fair** at Raleigh, mid-Oct.; at Fletcher, mid-Sept.

History. Algonquian, Siouan, and Iroquoian peoples lived in the region at the time of European contact. Sir Walter Raleigh tried to found a colony, 1584-87; the "Lost Colony" on Roanoke Island, 1587, disappeared without a trace. Permanent settlers came from Virginia in the mid-17th cent. The province's congress was the first to vote for independence, 1776. In the Revolutionary War, Cornwallis's forces were defeated at Kings Mountain, 1780, and forced out after Guilford Courthouse, 1781. The state ratified the Constitution, 1789, only after Congress passed the Bill of Rights. North Carolina, with a slave population of 1/3, seceded from the Union,1861, and provided more troops to the Confederacy than any other state; it was readmitted, 1868. The Wright brothers made the first powered airplane flight at Kitty Hawk, 1903. Sit-ins at segregated Greensboro lunch counters, 1960, drew national attention to the civil rights movement. Long reliant on tobacco, textiles, and wood products, North Carolina has prospered since the 1960s from advanced technologies in the Raleigh-Durham-Chapel Hill area and banking in Charlotte. The hurricane-prone state was hit hard by Hazel, 1954, Fran, 1996, and Floyd, 1999.

Tourist attractions. Cape Hatteras and Cape Lookout natl. seashores; Great Smoky Mts.; Guilford Courthouse and Moore's Creek parks; 66 American Revolution battle sites; Bennett Place (where last Confederate army surrendered), near Durham; Ft. Raleigh, Roanoke Island; Wright Brothers Natl. Memorial, Kitty Hawk; Battleship *North Carolina*, Wilmington; NC Zoo, Asheboro; NC Symphony, Exploris, NC museums of Art, Nat. Sciences, History, in Raleigh; Carl Sandburg Home, Hendersonville; Biltmore House & Gardens, Asheville.

Famous North Carolinians. David Brinkley, Shirley Caesar, John Coltrane, Rick Dees, Elizabeth Hanford Dole, John Edwards, Ava Gardner, Richard J. Gatling, Billy Graham, Andy Griffith, O. Henry, Andrew Jackson, Andrew Johnson, Michael Jordan, Wm. Rufus King, Charles Kuralt, Meadowlark Lemon, Dolley Madison, Thelonious Monk, Edward R. Murrow, Arnold Palmer, Richard Petty, James K. Polk, Charlie Rose, Carl Sandburg, Enos Slaughter, Dean Smith, James Taylor, Thomas Wolfe.

Tourist information. North Carolina Dept. of Commerce, Tourism Services, 4301 Mail Service Center, Raleigh, NC 27699; 1-800-VISIT-NC; (919) 733-4151 (local calls); www.visitnc.com

Website. www.nc.gov

North Dakota (ND)

Peace Garden State

People. Population (2006 est.): 635,867; rank: 48; **net change** (2005-2006): 0.2%. **Pop. density:** 9.2 per sq mi. **Racial distribution** (2005): 92.3% white; 0.8% black; 0.7% Asian; 5.3% Native/Nat. AK; 0.04% Hawaiian/Pacific Islander; 2 or more races, 1.0%. **Hispanic pop.** (any race): 1.6%.

Geography. Total area: 70,700 sq mi; rank: 19. **Land area:** 68,976 sq mi; rank: 17. **Acres forested:** 0.7 mil. **Location:** West North Central state, situated exactly in the middle of North America, bounded on the N by Canada, on the E by Minnesota, on the S by South Dakota, on the W by Montana. **Climate:** continental, with a wide range of temperature and moderate rainfall. **Topography:** Central Lowland in the E comprises the flat Red River Valley and the Rolling Drift Prairie; Missouri Plateau of the Great Plains on the W. **Capital:** Bismarck.

Economy. Chief industries: agriculture, mining, tourism, manufacturing, telecommunications, energy, food processing. **Chief manuf. goods:** machinery, wood product, motor vehicles & parts, furniture, processed foods. **Chief crops:** wheat, soybeans, corn, sugar beets, barley, dry beans, sunflowers, canola, potatoes, flaxseed, hay, dry peas, lentils, oats. **Livestock** (Jan. 2007): 1.9 mil cattle/calves, 100,000 sheep/lambs; (Dec. 2006): 169,000 hogs/pigs. **Timber/lumber** (est. 2006): 1 mil bd. ft.; oak, ash, cottonwood, aspen. **Nonfuel minerals** (preliminary 2006): \$56 mil; sand and gravel (construction), lime, sand and gravel (industrial), stone (crushed), clays (common). **Gross state product** (est. 2006): \$26.4 bil. **Sales tax** (2007): 5.0%. **Employment distrib.** (May 2007): 21.5% govt.; 21.2% trade/trans./util.; 7.2% mfg.; 14.0% ed./health; 8.4% prof./bus. serv.; 9.1% leisure/hosp.; 5.4% finance; 5.5% constr.; 4.2% other serv.; 2.1% info. **Unemployment** (2006): 3.2%. **Per cap. pers. income** (2006): \$32,552. **New private housing** (2006): 3,529 units/\$462.3 mil. **Commercial banks** (2006): 103; **deposits:** \$12.2 bil. **Savings institutions** (2006): 2; **deposits:** \$752 mil. **Lottery** (2006): total sales: \$22.3 mil; profit: \$6.9 mil.

Federal govt. Fed. civ. employees (Mar. 2006): 5,581; **avg. salary:** \$54,141. **Notable fed. facilities:** Minot AFB; *Grand Forks AFB; Northern Prairie Wildlife Res. Ctr.; Garrison Dam Nat. Fish Hatchery; Theodore Roosevelt Natl. Park; Grand Forks Human Nutrition Res. Ctr.; Ft. Union Natl. Hist. Site.

Energy. Electricity production (est. 2006, kWh by source): Coal: 29.2 bil; Hydroelectric: 1.5 bil; Petroleum: 39 mil; Other: 6 mil.

State data. Motto: Liberty and union, now and forever, one and inseparable. **Flower:** Wild prairie rose. **Bird:** Western meadowlark. **Tree:** American elm. **Song:** North Dakota Hymn. **Entered union** Nov. 2, 1889; rank, 39th. **State fair** at Minot; late July.

History. Paleoindian peoples hunted in the area at least 11,000 years ago. At the time of European contact, the Ojibwa, Yanktonai and Teton Sioux, Mandan, Arikara, and Hidatsa peoples lived in the region. Pierre de Varennes, sieur de La Vérendrye, was the first French fur trader in the area, 1738, followed by the English at the end of the 18th cent. Lewis and Clark built Ft. Mandan, near present-day Washburn, 1804-5, and wintered there. The first permanent settlement was at Pembina, 1812. Missouri River steamboats reached the area, 1832. Dakota Territory was organized,

1861. The first railroad arrived, 1872. The "bonanza farm" craze of the 1870s-80s led to statehood, 1889. The Nonpartisan League, a farmers' group favoring state ownership of industries, helped elect Lynn Frazier as governor, 1916, but he and others were ousted in a recall vote, 1921. The predominantly agricultural state had a 6.5% drop in population, 1930-2005.

Tourist attractions. North Dakota Heritage Center, Bismarck; Bonanzaville, Fargo; Ft. Union Trading Post Natl. Historic Site; Lake Sakakawea; Intl. Peace Garden; Theodore Roosevelt Natl. Park, including Elkhorn Ranch, Badlands; Ft. Abraham Lincoln State Park and Museum, near Mandan; Dakota Dinosaur Museum, Dickinson; Knife River Indian Villages-Natl. Hist. Site.

Famous North Dakotans. Maxwell Anderson, Angie Dickinson, John Bernard Flannagan, Phil Jackson, Louis L'Amour, Peggy Lee, Eric Sevareid, Ann Sothern, Vilhjalmur Stefansson, Lawrence Welk.

Tourist information. North Dakota Tourism Division, Century Center, 1600 E. Century Ave., Ste. 2, PO Box 2057, Bismarck, ND 58502; 1-800-435-5663; www.ndtourism.com

Website. www.nd.gov

Ohio (OH)
Buckeye State

People. Population (2006 est.): 11,478,006; rank: 7; **net change** (2005-2006): 0.1%. **Pop. density:** 280.8 per sq mi. **Racial distribution** (2005): 85.1% white; 11.9% black; 1.4% Asian; 0.2% Native/Nat. AK; 0.03% Hawaiian/Pacific Islander; 2 or more races, 1.3%. **Hispanic pop.** (any race): 2.3%.

Geography. Total area: 44,825 sq mi; rank: 34. **Land area:** 40,948 sq mi; rank: 35. **Acres forested:** 7.9 mil. **Location:** East North Central state bounded on the N by Michigan and Lake Erie; on the E and S by Pennsylvania, West Virginia, and Kentucky; on the W by Indiana. **Climate:** temperate but variable; weather subject to much precipitation. **Topography:** generally rolling plain; Allegheny plateau in E; Lake Erie plains extend southward; central plains in the W. **Capital:** Columbus.

Economy. Chief industries: manufacturing, trade, services. **Chief manuf. goods:** motor vehicles & parts, petroleum, plastics & rubber, iron & steel, aircraft, machinery, fabricated metal, printing. **Chief crops:** corn, soybeans, hay, wheat, grapes, potatoes, tomatoes, apples, strawberries, tobacco. **Livestock** (Jan. 2007): 1.3 mil cattle/calves, 141,000 sheep/lambs; (Dec. 2006): 1.7 mil hogs/pigs, 33.5 mil chickens (excl. broilers), 45.6 mil broilers. **Timber/lumber** (est. 2006): 371 mil bd. ft.; oak, ash, maple, walnut, beech. **Nonfuel minerals** (preliminary 2006): $1.3 bil; stone (crushed), sand and gravel (construction), salt, lime, cement (portland). **Commercial fishing** (2005): $3.3 mil. **Chief ports:** Toledo, Conneaut, Cleveland, Ashtabula. **Gross state product** (est. 2006): $461.3 bil. **Sales tax** (2007): 5.5%. **Employment distrib.** (May 2007): 14.9% govt.; 19.1% trade/trans./util.; 14.3% mfg.; 14.4% ed./health; 12.1% prof./bus. serv.; 9.4% leisure/hosp.; 5.6% finance; 4.3% constr.; 4.1% other serv.; 1.6% info. **Unemployment** (2006): 5.5%. **Per cap. pers. income** (2006): $33,338. **New private housing** (2006): 34,422 units/$5.9 bil. **Commercial banks** (2006): 190; **deposits:** $181.0 bil. **Savings institutions** (2006): 106; **deposits:** $27.6 bil. **Lottery** (2006): total sales: $2.2 bil; profit: $646.3 mil.

Federal govt. Fed. civ. employees (Mar. 2006): 41,445; **avg. salary:** $67,638. **Notable fed. facilities:** Wright-Patterson AFB; Defense Supply Ctr., Columbus; *NASA John H. Glenn Res. Ctr.; *Lima Army Tank Plant.

Energy. Electricity production (est. 2006, kWh by source): Coal: 127.6 bil; Gas: 669 mil; Hydroelectric: 515 mil; Nuclear: 16.8 bil; Petroleum: 281 mil; Other: 20 mil.

State data. Motto: With God, all things are possible. **Flower:** Scarlet carnation. **Bird:** Cardinal. **Tree:** Buckeye. **Song:** Beautiful Ohio. **Entered union** Mar. 1, 1803; rank, 17th. **State fair** at Columbus; early Aug.

History. Paleoindians hunted in the area about 11,000 years ago; the Adena and Hopewell cultures followed. Wyandot, Delaware, Miami, and Shawnee peoples sparsely occupied the area when the first Europeans arrived. La Salle visited the region, 1669. France claimed it, 1682, but ceded it to Britain, 1763. After the American Revolution, Ohio became part of the Northwest Territory, 1787. The first permanent settlement was at Marietta, 1788. Cincinnati was also founded, 1788; Cleveland, 1796. Indian warfare abated with the Treaty of Greenville, 1795. Ohio became a state, 1803. In the War of 1812, Oliver Hazard Perry's victory on Lake Erie and William Henry Harrison's invasion of Canada, 1813, ended British incursions. Columbus, founded 1812, became the state capital, 1816. Before the Civil War, Ohioans aided the Underground Railroad, helping runaway slaves. Agricultural for much of the 19th cent., the state became an industrial powerhouse in the 20th. Manufacturing jobs dropped by 24%, 1998-2007. No Republican has ever won the presidency without carrying Ohio, and the state's 20 electoral votes proved crucial to Pres. George W. Bush in 2004.

Tourist attractions. Mound City Group, Hopewell Culture Natl. Hist. Park; Neil Armstrong Air and Space Museum, Wapakoneta; Air Force Museum, Dayton; Pro Football Hall of Fame, Canton; King's Island amusement park, Mason; Lake Erie Islands, Cedar Point amusement park, in Sandusky; birthplaces, homes of, and memorials to U.S. Pres. W. H. Harrison, Grant, Garfield, Hayes, B. Harrison, McKinley, Harding, Taft; Amish Region, Tuscarawas/Holmes counties; German Village, Columbus; Jack Nicklaus' Golf Center, Mason; Bob Evans Farm, Rio Grande; Rock and Roll Hall of Fame and Museum, Cleveland.

Famous Ohioans. Sherwood Anderson, Neil Armstrong, George Bellows, Halle Berry, Ambrose Bierce, Erma Bombeck, Drew Carey, Hart Crane, George Custer, Clarence Darrow, Paul Laurence Dunbar, Thomas Edison, Clark Gable, John Glenn, Zane Grey, Bob Hope, William Dean Howells, Toni Morrison, Jack Nicklaus, Jesse Owens, Jack Paar, Pontiac, Eddie Rickenbacker, John D. Rockefeller Sr. and Jr., Roy Rogers, Pete Rose, Arthur Schlesinger Jr., Gen. William Sherman, Steven Spielberg, Gloria Steinem, Harriet Beecher Stowe, Charles Taft, Robert A. Taft, William H. Taft, Tecumseh, James Thurber, Ted Turner, Orville and Wilbur Wright.

Tourist information. Division of Travel and Tourism, 77 S. High St., PO Box 1001, Columbus, OH 43216; 1-800-BUCK-EYE; www.discoverohio.com

Website. www.ohio.gov

Oklahoma (OK)
Sooner State

People. Population (2006 est.): 3,579,212; rank: 28; **net change** (2005-2006): 1.0%. **Pop. density:** 52.1 per sq mi. **Racial distribution** (2005): 78.5% white; 7.7% black; 1.5% Asian; 8.1% Native/Nat. AK; 0.09% Hawaiian/Pacific Islander; 2 or more races, 4.0%. **Hispanic pop.** (any race): 6.6%.

Geography. Total area: 69,898 sq mi; rank: 20. **Land area:** 68,667 sq mi; rank: 19. **Acres forested:** 7.7 mil. **Location:** West South Central state bounded on the N by Colorado and Kansas; on the E by Missouri and Arkansas; on the S and W by Texas and New Mexico. **Climate:** temperate; southern humid belt merging with colder northern continental; humid eastern and dry western zones. **Topography:** high plains predominate in the W, hills and small mountains in the E; the east central region is dominated by the Arkansas R. Basin, and the Red R. Plains, in the S. **Capital:** Oklahoma City. **Chief airports at:** Oklahoma City, Tulsa.

Economy. Chief industries: manufacturing, mineral and energy exploration and production, agriculture, services. **Chief manuf. goods:** animal slaughtering & processing, petroleum, plastics & rubber, fabricated metals, machinery, motor vehicles & parts. **Chief crops:** wheat, greenhouse & nursery, hay, cotton, corn, soybeans, pecans, sorghum, peanuts. **Livestock** (Jan. 2007): 5.3 mil cattle/calves, 80,000 sheep/lambs; (Dec. 2006): 2.3 mil hogs/pigs, 4.5 mil chickens (excl. broilers), 249.4 mil broilers. **Timber/lumber** (est. 2006): 391 mil bd. ft.; pine, oak, hickory. **Nonfuel minerals** (preliminary 2006): $622 mil; stone (crushed), cement (portland), sand and gravel (construction), sand and gravel (industrial), iodine (crude). **Chief ports:** Catoosa, Muskogee. **Gross state product** (est. 2006): $134.7 bil. **Sales tax** (2007): 4.5%. **Employment distrib.** (May 2007): 20.7% govt.; 18.0% trade/trans./util.; 9.5% mfg.; 12.1% ed./health; 11.3% prof./bus. serv.; 8.9% leisure/hosp.; 5.3% finance; 4.6% constr.; 4.9% other serv.; 1.9% info. **Unemployment** (2006): 4.0%. **Per cap. pers. income** (2006): $32,210. **New private housing** (2006): 15,840 units/$2.3 bil. **Commercial banks** (2006): 276; **deposits:** $49.0 bil. **Savings institutions** (2006): 8; **deposits:** $4.3 bil. **Lottery** (2006): total sales: $204.8 mil; profit: $69.0 mil.

Federal govt. Fed. civ. employees (Mar. 2006): 33,652; **avg. salary:** $56,603. **Notable fed. facilities:** Tinker AFB; FAA Mike Monroney Aeronautical Ctr.; *Ft. Sill; *Altus AFB;

McAlester Army Ammunition Plant; Vance AFB; Natl. Inst. for Petroleum & Energy Res.; Natl. Severe Storms Lab.

Energy. Electricity production (est. 2006, kWh by source): Coal: 32.3 bil; Gas: 19.1 bil; Hydroelectric: 1.2 bil; Petroleum: 23 mil; Other: 3 mil.

State data. Motto: Labor Omnia Vincit.(Labor conquers all things). **Flower:** Mistletoe. **Bird:** Scissor-tailed flycatcher. **Tree:** Redbud. **Song:** Oklahoma! **Entered union** Nov. 16, 1907; rank, 46th. **State fair** at Oklahoma City, mid-Sept.; at Tulsa, 4th Thursday after Labor Day–2nd Sunday of Oct.

History. Few Native Americans inhabited the region when the Spanish explorer Coronado arrived, 1541; in the 16th and 17th cent., French traders visited. Part of the Louisiana Purchase, 1803, Oklahoma was known as Indian Country and, from 1834, Indian Territory. It became home to the "Five Civilized Tribes"—Cherokee, Choctaw, Chickasaw, Creek, and Seminole—after the forced removal of Indians from the eastern U.S., 1828-46. The land was also used by Comanche, Osage, and other Plains Indians. As white settlers pressed west, land was opened for homesteading by "runs" and lottery. The first run was in 1889; the most famous run, 1893, was to the Cherokee Outlet. Oklahoma became a state, 1907. In the early 20th cent., oil finds brought wealth to the Tulsa area; the Greenwood section of the city, then known as the "Negro Wall Street," was devastated by a white mob, 1921. Depression and drought drove many "Okies" from the Dust Bowl to California in the 1930s. A truck bomb in Oklahoma City, 1995, destroyed a federal office building, killing 168 people; Timothy McVeigh was executed for the crime, 2001.

Tourist attractions. Cherokee Heritage Center, Tahlequah; Oklahoma City Natl. Memorial; Natl. Cowboy Hall of Fame, Remington Park Race Track, White Water Bay and Frontier City theme pks., in Oklahoma City; Will Rogers Memorial, Claremore; Ft. Gibson; Ouachita Natl. Forest; Philbrook Museum of Art, Gilcrease Museum, in Tulsa; Tulsa's art deco district; Wichita Mts. Wildlife Refuge; Woolaroc Museum & Wildlife Preserve, Bartlesville; Sequoyah's Home Site, Sallisaw.

Famous Oklahomans. Troy Aikman, Carl Albert, Gene Autry, Johnny Bench, William "Hopalong Cassidy" Boyd, Garth Brooks, Lon Chaney, L. Gordon Cooper, Walter Cronkite, Jerome "Dizzy" Dean, Ralph Ellison, John Hope Franklin, James Garner, Geronimo, Woody Guthrie, Paul Harvey, Ron Howard, Gen. Patrick J. Hurley, Ben Johnson, Jeane Kirkpatrick, Louis L'Amour, Shannon Lucid, Mickey Mantle, Reba McEntire, Wiley Post, Tony Randall, Oral Roberts, Will Rogers, Sam Snead, Barry Switzer, Maria Tallchief, Jim Thorpe, J.C. Watts Jr.

Tourist information. Travel and Tourism Division, 120 N. Robinson, 6th Fl., PO Box 52002, Oklahoma City, OK 73152-2002; 1-800-652-6552; www.travelok.com

Website. www.ok.gov

Oregon (OR)
Beaver State

People. Population (2006 est.): 3,700,758; rank: 27; **net change** (2005-2006): 1.7%. **Pop. density:** 38.6 per sq mi. **Racial distribution** (2005): 90.8% white; 1.8% black; 3.4% Asian; 1.4% Native/Nat. AK; 0.3% Hawaiian/Pacific Islander; 2 or more races, 2.3%. **Hispanic pop.** (any race): 9.9%.

Geography. Total area: 98,381 sq mi; rank: 9. **Land area:** 95,997 sq mi; rank: 10. **Acres forested:** 29.7 mil. **Location:** Pacific state, bounded on N by Washington; on E by Idaho; on S by Nevada and California; on W by the Pacific. **Climate:** coastal mild and humid climate; continental dryness and extreme temperatures in the interior. **Topography:** Coast Range of rugged mountains; fertile Willamette R. Valley to E and S; Cascade Mt. Range of volcanic peaks E of the valley; plateau E of Cascades, remaining two-thirds of state. **Capital:** Salem. **Chief airport at:** Portland.

Economy. Chief industries: manufacturing, services, trade, finance, insurance, real estate, government, construction. **Chief manuf. goods:** wood products, frozen produce, printing, computers & electronics, transportation equipment, industrial machinery. **Chief crops:** greenhouse & nursery, grass seed, hay, wheat, potatoes, Christmas trees, onions, pears, hazelnuts, corn, grapes, cherries, blackberries, blueberries, peppermint, snap beans, apples, hops. **Livestock** (Jan. 2007): 1.3 mil cattle/calves, 215,000 sheep/lambs; (Dec. 2006): 25,000 hogs/pigs, 3.4 mil chickens (excl. broilers). **Timber/lumber** (est. 2006): 6.8 bil bd. ft.; Douglas fir, hemlock, ponderosa pine. **Nonfuel minerals** (preliminary

2006): \$428 mil; sand and gravel (construction), stone (crushed), cement (portland), diatomite, lime. **Commercial fishing** (2005): \$87.8 mil. **Chief ports:** Portland, Astoria, Coos Bay. **Gross state product** (est. 2006): \$151.3 bil. **Sales tax** (2007): none. **Employment distrib.** (May 2007): 17.2% govt.; 19.6% trade/trans./util.; 11.6% mfg.; 12.1% ed./health; 11.4% prof./bus. serv.; 9.9% leisure/hosp.; 6.1% finance; 5.9% constr.; 3.5% other serv.; 2.1% info. **Unemployment** (2006): 5.4%. **Per cap. pers. income** (2006): \$33,666. **New private housing** (2006): 26,623 units/\$4.9 bil. **Commercial banks** (2006): 50; **deposits:** \$37.8 bil. **Savings institutions** (2006): 8; **deposits:** \$7.5 bil. **Lottery** (2006): total sales: \$1.1 bil; profit: \$483.0 mil.

Federal govt. Fed. civ. employees (Mar. 2006): 17,649; **avg. salary:** \$60,818. **Notable fed. facilities:** Bonneville Power Administration.

Energy. Electricity production (est. 2006, kWh by source): Coal: 2.4 bil; Gas: 3.0 bil; Hydroelectric: 37.2 bil; Petroleum: 4 mil; Other: 69 mil.

State data. Motto: She flies with her own wings. **Flower:** Oregon grape. **Bird:** Western meadowlark. **Tree:** Douglas fir. **Song:** Oregon, My Oregon. **Entered union** Feb. 14, 1859; rank, 33rd. **State fair** at Salem; 11 days ending with Labor Day.

History. More than 100 Native American tribes inhabited the area at the time of European contact, including the Chinook, Yakima, Cayuse, Modoc, and Nez Percé. Capt. Robert Gray sighted and sailed into the Columbia River, 1792. Lewis and Clark, traveling overland, wintered at its mouth, 1805-6. Fur traders sent by John Jacob Astor established the Astoria trading post in the Columbia River region, 1811. Settlers arrived in the Willamette Valley, 1834. In 1843, the first large wave of settlers arrived via the Oregon Trail. Oregon became a territory, 1848, and a state, 1859. Early in the 20th cent., the "Oregon System"—political reforms that included initiative, referendum, recall, direct primary, and woman suffrage—was adopted. Originally dominated by forest products, the economy diversified after World War II, with high-tech firms clustering in the "Silicon Forest" area around Portland. Oregonians were the first in the U.S. to pass measures allowing physician-assisted suicide for terminally ill patients, 1994, and establishing an all-mail voting system, 1998.

Tourist attractions. John Day Fossil Beds Natl. Monument; Columbia River Gorge; Timberline Lodge, Mt. Hood Natl. Forest; Crater Lake Natl. Park; Oregon Dunes Natl. Recreation Area; Ft. Clatsop Natl. Memorial; Oregon Caves Natl. Monument; Oregon Museum of Science and Industry, Portland; Shakespeare Festival, Ashland; High Desert Museum, Bend; Multnomah Falls; Diamond Lake; "Spruce Goose," Evergreen Aviation Museum, McMinnville.

Famous Oregonians. Ernest Bloch, Bill Bowerman, Ernest Haycox, Chief Joseph, Ken Kesey, Phil Knight, Ursula K. Le Guin, Edwin Markham, Tom McCall, Dr. John McLoughlin, Joaquin Miller, Bob Packwood, Linus Pauling, Steve Prefontaine, John Reed, Alberto Salazar, Mary Decker Slaney, William Simon U'Ren.

Tourist information. Oregon Tourism Commission, 670 Hawthorne SE, Ste. 240, Salem, OR 97301; 1-800-547-7842; www.traveloregon.com

Website. www.oregon.gov

Pennsylvania (PA)
Keystone State

People. Population (2006 est.): 12,440,621; rank: 6; **net change** (2005-2006): 0.3%. **Pop. density:** 278.0 per sq mi. **Racial distribution** (2005): 86.0% white; 10.6% black; 2.2% Asian; 0.2% Native/Nat. AK; 0.05% Hawaiian/Pacific Islander; 2 or more races, 1.0%. **Hispanic pop.** (any race): 4.1%.

Geography. Total area: 46,055 sq mi; rank: 33. **Land area:** 44,817 sq mi; rank: 32. **Acres forested:** 16.9 mil. **Location:** Middle Atlantic state, bordered on the E by the Delaware R.; on the S by the Mason-Dixon Line; on the W by West Virginia and Ohio; on the N/NE by Lake Erie and New York. **Climate:** continental with wide fluctuations in seasonal temperatures. **Topography:** Allegheny Mts. run SW to NE, with Piedmont and Coast Plain in the SE triangle; Allegheny Front a diagonal spine across the state's center; N and W rugged plateau falls to Lake Erie Lowland. **Capital:** Harrisburg. **Chief airports at:** Harrisburg, Philadelphia, Pittsburgh.

Economy. Chief industries: agribusiness, advanced manufacturing, health care, travel & tourism, depository institutions, biotechnology, printing & publishing, research & consulting, trucking & warehousing, transportation by air, engineering & management, legal services. **Chief manuf. goods:** petroleum, pharmaceuticals, plastics, iron & steel, printing, paper & paperboard, confectionery & snacks, animal slaughtering & processing. **Chief crops:** greenhouse & nursery, mushrooms, corn, hay, soybeans, apples, tomatoes, wheat, grapes, peaches, potatoes, strawberries, tobacco. **Livestock** (Jan. 2007): 1.6 mil cattle/calves, 108,000 sheep/lambs; (Dec. 2006): 1.1 mil hogs/pigs, 28.3 mil chickens (excl. broilers), 144.9 mil broilers. **Timber/lumber** (est. 2006): 1.1 bil bd. ft.; pine, oak, maple. **Nonfuel minerals** (preliminary 2006): $1.7 bil; stone (crushed), cement (portland), sand and gravel (construction), lime, cement (masonry). **Commercial fishing** (2005): $39,063. **Chief ports:** Philadelphia, Pittsburgh, Erie. **Gross state product** (est. 2006): $510.3 bil. **Sales tax** (2007): 6.0%. **Employment distrib.** (May 2007): 13.1% govt.; 19.4% trade/trans./util.; 11.3% mfg.; 18.6% ed./health; 11.9% prof./bus. serv.; 8.7% leisure/hosp.; 5.7% finance; 4.6% constr.; 4.5% other serv.; 1.9% info. **Unemployment** (2006): 4.7%. **Per cap. pers. income** (2006): $36,680. **New private housing** (2006): 39,128 units/$6.4 bil. **Commercial banks** (2006): 186; **deposits:** $172.9 bil. **Savings institutions** (2006): 99; **deposits:** $77.3 bil. **Lottery** (2006): total sales: $3.1 bil; profit: $975.9 mil.

Federal govt. Fed. civ. employees (Mar. 2006): 62,486; **avg. salary:** $59,092. **Notable fed. facilities:** Army War College, Carlisle Barracks; *Naval Inventory Control Point, Mechanicsburg; Philadelphia Mint, Defense Supply Ctr., Naval Surface Warfare Ctr., in Phila.; Defense Distribution Ctr., New Cumberland; *Tobyhanna Army Depot; *Letterkenny Army Depot; *NAS Willow Grove; *Charles E. Kelly Support Facility.

Energy. Electricity production (est. 2006, kWh by source): Coal: 18.6 bil; Hydroelectric: 1.4 bil; Nuclear: 12.1 bil; Petroleum: 33 mil.

State data. Motto: Virtue, liberty and independence. **Flower:** Mountain laurel. **Bird:** Ruffed grouse. **Tree:** Hemlock. **Song:** Pennsylvania. **Second** of the original 13 states to ratify the Constitution, Dec. 12, 1787. **State fair** at Harrisburg, early Jan.; at Bensalem, late May–early June; county and community fairs, Mar.–Oct.; no official "State Fair."

History. When Europeans came, Algonquian-speaking Lenni Lenape (Delaware) and Shawnee and the Iroquoian Susquehannocks, Erie, and Seneca occupied the region. Swedish explorers made the first permanent settlement, 1643, on Tinicum Island. The Dutch seized the settlement, 1655, but lost it to the British, 1664. The region was given by Charles II to William Penn, 1681. Philadelphia ("brotherly love") was the capital of the colonies during most of the American Revolution, and of the U.S., 1790-1800; the Declaration of Independence, 1776, and Constitution, 1787, were signed here. Philadelphia was taken by the British, 1777; Washington's troops encamped at Valley Forge in the bitter winter of 1777-78. Slavery was abolished, 1780. Union victory at the Battle of Gettysburg, July 1-3, 1863, marked a turning point in the Civil War. A dam collapse at Johnstown, 1889, killed at least 2,200 people. From the late 19th cent. to the mid-20th, Pittsburgh prospered from coal and steel; later, heavy industry declined, but the city revived as a hub of finance, health care, and research. The Three Mile Island nuclear plant near Harrisburg had a near-meltdown, 1979. One of 4 hijacked planes on Sept. 11, 2001, crashed near Shanksville; a national memorial was designated on the site in 2002.

Tourist attractions. Independence Natl. Historic Park, Franklin Institute Science Museum, Philadelphia Museum of Art, in Philadelphia; Valley Forge Natl. Historic Park; Gettysburg Natl. Military Park; Pennsylvania Dutch Country; Hershey; Duquesne Incline, Carnegie Institute, Heinz Hall, in Pittsburgh; Pocono Mts.; Pennsylvania's Grand Canyon, Tioga County; Allegheny Natl. Forest; Laurel Highlands; Presque Isle State Park; Fallingwater, Mill Run; Johnstown; Steamtown, Scranton; U.S. Brig Niagara, Erie; Oil Heritage Region, Northwest PA.

Famous Pennsylvanians. Marian Anderson, Maxwell Anderson, George Blanda, James Buchanan, Andrew Carnegie, Rachel Carson, Perry Como, Bill Cosby, Thomas Eakins, Stephen Foster, Benjamin Franklin, Robert Fulton, Martha Graham, Milton Hershey, Gene Kelly, Grace Kelly (Princess Grace of Monaco), Dan Marino, George C. Marshall, Chris Matthews, John J. McCloy, Margaret Mead, Andrew W. Mellon, Joe Montana, Stan Musial, Joe Namath, John O'Hara, Arnold Palmer, Robert E. Peary, Mike Piazza, Tom Ridge, Mary Roberts Rinehart, Fred Rogers, Betsy Ross, Will Smith, Jimmy Stewart, Jim Thorpe, Johnny Unitas, John Updike, Honus Wagner, and Andy Warhol, Benjamin West.

Tourist information. Department of Community and Economic Development, Office of Tourism, 400 North St., 4th Fl., Harrisburg, PA 17120-0225; 1-800-VISITPA; www.visit pa.com

Website. www.state.pa.us

Rhode Island (RI)
Little Rhody, Ocean State

People. Population (2006 est.): 1,067,610; rank: 43; **net change** (2005-2006): -0.6%. **Pop. density:** 1,032.8 per sq mi. **Racial distribution** (2005): 88.9% white; 6.2% black; 2.7% Asian; 0.6% Native/Nat. AK; 0.1% Hawaiian/Pacific Islander; 2 or more races, 1.5%. **Hispanic pop.** (any race): 10.7%.

Geography. Total area: 1,545 sq mi; rank: 50. **Land area:** 1,045 sq mi; rank: 50. **Acres forested:** 0.4 mil. **Location:** New England state. **Climate:** invigorating and changeable. **Topography:** eastern lowlands of Narragansett Basin; western uplands of flat and rolling hills. **Capital:** Providence. **Chief airport at:** Warwick.

Economy. Chief industries: services, manufacturing. **Chief manuf. goods:** plastics, fabricated metals, electrical equip., jewelry. **Chief crops:** greenhouse & nursery, sweet corn, berries, potatoes, apples, hay. **Livestock** (Jan. 2007): 4,900 cattle/calves; (Dec. 2006): 1,900 hogs/pigs. **Timber/lumber** (est. 2006): 6 mil bd. ft.; **Nonfuel minerals** (preliminary 2006): $38.4 mil; sand and gravel (construction), stone (crushed), sand and gravel (industrial), gemstones (natural). **Commercial fishing** (2005): $91.8 mil. **Chief ports:** Providence, Quonset Point, Newport. **Gross state product** (est. 2006): $45.7 bil. **Sales tax** (2007): 7.0%. **Employment distrib.** (May 2007): 13.1% govt.; 15.9% trade/trans./util.; 10.2% mfg.; 19.9% ed./health; 11.7% prof./bus. serv.; 10.4% leisure/hosp.; 7.2% finance; 4.9% constr.; 4.6% other serv.; 2.2% info. **Unemployment** (2006): 5.1%. **Per cap. pers. income** (2006): $37,388. **New private housing** (2006): 2,370 units/$383.8 mil. **Commercial banks** (2006): 12; **deposits:** $19.7 bil. **Savings institutions** (2006): 13; **deposits:** $4.0 bil. **Lottery** (2006): total sales: $1.7 bil; profit: $323.9 mil.

Federal govt. Fed. civ. employees (Mar. 2006): 5,882; **avg. salary:** $73,502. **Notable fed. facilities:** Naval War College; Naval Underwater Warfare Ctr.; NE Fisheries Science Ctr.; EPA Atlantic Ecology Div. Lab.

Energy. Electricity production (est. 2006, kWh by source): Petroleum: 7 mil.

State data. Motto: Hope. **Flower:** Violet. **Bird:** Rhode Island red. **Tree:** Red maple. **Song:** Rhode Island. **Thirteenth** of original 13 states to ratify the Constitution, May 29, 1790. **State fair:** largest fair at Richmond, mid-Aug.; no state fair.

History. When Europeans arrived, Narragansett, Niantic, Nipmuc, and Wampanoag peoples lived in the region. Verrazano visited the area, 1524. The first permanent settlement was founded at Providence, 1636, by Roger Williams, who was exiled from the Massachusetts Bay Colony; Anne Hutchinson, also exiled, settled Portsmouth, 1638. Quaker and Jewish immigrants seeking freedom of worship began arriving, 1650s-60s. The colonists broke the power of the Narragansett in the Great Swamp Fight, 1675, the decisive battle in King Philip's War. The colony was the first to formally renounce all allegiance to King George III, May 4, 1776. Initially opposed to joining the Union, Rhode Island was the last of the 13 colonies to ratify the Constitution, 1790. Trade, textiles, and metal goods dominated the economy in the 19th cent., and Newport became a fashionable resort after the Civil War. Immigration from Ireland, Italy, Portugal, French Canada, and most recently Latin America have given Rhode Island the highest proportion of Roman Catholics of any state, 64% in 2006.

Tourist attractions. Newport mansions; yachting races including Newport to Bermuda; Block Island; Touro Synagogue (oldest in U.S.) Newport; First Baptist Church in America, Providence; Slater Mill Historic Site, Pawtucket; Gilbert Stuart birthplace, Saunderstown.

Famous Rhode Islanders. Ambrose Burnside, George M. Cohan, Nelson Eddy, Jabez Gorham, Nathanael Greene, Christopher and Oliver La Farge, John McLaughlin, Matthew C. and Oliver Hazard Perry, Gilbert Stuart.

Tourist information. Rhode Island Tourism Division, 351 Iron Horse Way, Ste. 101, Providence, RI 02908; 1-800-556-2484; www.visitrhodeisland.com

Website. www.state.ri.us

South Carolina (SC)

Palmetto State

People. Population (2006 est.): 4,321,249; rank: 24; **net change** (2005-2006): 1.7%. **Pop. density:** 143.6 per sq mi. **Racial distribution** (2005): 68.4% white; 29.2% black; 1.1% Asian; 0.4% Native/Nat. AK; 0.05% Hawaiian/Pacific Islander; 2 or more races, 0.8%. **Hispanic pop.** (any race): 3.3%.

Geography. Total area: 32,020 sq mi; rank: 40. **Land area:** 30,109 sq mi; rank: 40. **Acres forested:** 12.5 mil. **Location:** South Atlantic state, bordered by North Carolina on the N; Georgia on the SW and W; the Atlantic Ocean on the E, SE, and S. **Climate:** humid subtropical. **Topography:** Blue Ridge province in NW has highest peaks; piedmont lies between the mountains and the fall line; coastal plain covers two-thirds of the state. **Capital:** Columbia. **Chief airports at:** Charleston, Columbia, Greer, Myrtle Beach.

Economy. Chief industries: tourism, agriculture, manufacturing. **Chief manuf. goods:** chemicals & synthetics, motor vehicles & parts, plastics, paper & paper product, turbines, rubber, textiles. **Chief crops:** greenhouse & nursery, tobacco, soybeans, cotton, corn, peaches, wheat, tomatoes, peanuts. **Livestock** (Jan. 2007): 400,000 cattle/calves; (Dec. 2006): 295,000 hogs/pigs, 6.8 mil chickens (excl. broilers), 227.1 mil broilers. **Timber/lumber** (est. 2006): 1.4 bil bd. ft.; pine, oak. **Nonfuel minerals** (preliminary 2006): $730 mil; stone (crushed), cement (portland), cement (masonry), sand and gravel (construction), sand and gravel (industrial). **Commercial fishing** (2005): $15.2 mil. **Chief ports:** Charleston, Georgetown, Royal. **Gross state product** (est. 2006): $149.2 bil. **Sales tax** (2007): 6.0%. **Employment distrib.** (May 2007): 17.4% govt.; 19.3% trade/trans./util.; 12.6% mfg.; 10.6% ed./health; 11.3% prof./bus. serv.; 11.2% leisure/hosp.; 5.4% finance; 6.5% constr.; 4.1% other serv.; 1.4% info. **Unemployment** (2006): 6.5%. **Per cap. pers. income** (2006): $29,515. **New private housing** (2006): 50,776 units/$7.6 bil. **Commercial banks** (2006): 85; **deposits:** $53.5 bil. **Savings institutions** (2006): 24; **deposits:** $5.6 bil. **Lottery** (2006): total sales: $1.1 bil; profit: $319.4 mil.

Federal govt. Fed. civ. employees (Mar. 2006): 17,158; **avg. salary:** $57,057. **Notable fed. facilities:** *Ft. Jackson; *Charleston AFB; *Naval Weapons Station Charleston; Parris Island; Shaw AFB; USMC Air Station Beaufort; Savannah River Site.

Energy. Electricity production (est. 2006, kWh by source): Coal: 39.2 bil; Gas: 4.7 bil; Hydroelectric: 1.9 bil; Nuclear: 50.8 bil; Petroleum: 118 mil; Other: 389 mil.

State data. Motto: Dum Spiro Spero (While I breathe, I hope). **Flower:** Yellow jessamine. **Bird:** Carolina wren. **Tree:** Palmetto. **Song:** Carolina. **Eighth** of the original 13 states to ratify the Constitution, May 23, 1788. **State fair** at Columbia, mid-Oct.; at Aiken, late Oct.

History. When Europeans arrived, Cherokee, Catawba, and Muskogean peoples lived in the area. Spanish and French came in the 16th cent. The first English colonists settled near the Ashley River, 1670, and moved to the site of present-day Charleston, 1680. The colonists seized the government, 1775, and the royal governor fled. The British took Charleston, 1780, but were defeated at Kings Mountain that same year, and at Cowpens, 1781. In the 1830s, South Carolinians, angered by federal protective tariffs, adopted the Nullification Doctrine, holding that a state can void an act of Congress. Plantation agriculture relied on slave labor to cultivate rice and cotton; slaves made up 57% of the population in 1860, when South Carolina was the first state to secede from the Union. Confederate troops fired on and forced the surrender of U.S. troops at Ft. Sumter, in Charleston Harbor, 1861, launching the Civil War. The state was readmitted to the Union, 1868. Strom Thurmond, who ran for president as a segregationist in 1948, later served 48 years in the U.S. Senate (1955-2003). Formerly dependent on textiles, the state has attracted new industries by courting foreign investment.

Tourist attractions. Historic Charleston, Charleston Museum (est. 1773, oldest in U.S.); Ft. Sumter Natl. Monument, in Charleston Harbor; Middleton Place, Magnolia Plantation, Cypress Gardens, Drayton Hall, all near Charleston; other gardens at Brookgreen, Edisto, Glencairn; Myrtle Beach; Hilton Head Island; Revolutionary War battle sites; Andrew Jackson State Park; SC State Museum, Riverbanks Zoo, in Columbia.

Famous South Carolinians. Charles Bolden, James F. Byrnes, John C. Calhoun, Joe Frazier, DuBose Heyward, Ernest F. Hollings, Andrew Jackson, Jesse Jackson, "Shoeless" Joe Jackson, James Longstreet, Francis Marion, Andie McDowell, Ronald McNair, Charles Pinckney, John Rutledge, Thomas Sumter, Strom Thurmond, John B. Watson.

Tourist information. SC Dept. of Parks, Recreation, & Tourism, 1205 Pendleton St., Columbia, SC 29201; 1-866-224-9339; (803) 734-1700; www.discoversouthcarolina.com **Website.** www.sc.gov

South Dakota (SD)

Coyote State, Mount Rushmore State

People. Population (2006 est.): 781,919; rank: 46; **net change** (2005-2006): 0.9%. **Pop. density:** 10.3 per sq mi. **Racial distribution** (2005): 88.5% white; 0.8% black; 0.7% Asian; 8.8% Native/Nat. AK; 0.04% Hawaiian/Pacific Islander; 2 or more races, 1.2%. **Hispanic pop.** (any race): 2.1%.

Geography. Total area: 77,116 sq mi; rank: 17. **Land area:** 75,885 sq mi; rank: 16. **Acres forested:** 1.6 mil. **Location:** West North Central state bounded on the N by North Dakota; on the E by Minnesota and Iowa; on the S by Nebraska; on the W by Wyoming and Montana. **Climate:** characterized by extremes of temperature, persistent winds, low precipitation and humidity. **Topography:** Prairie Plains in the E; rolling hills of the Great Plains in the W; the Black Hills, rising 3,500 ft, in the SW corner. **Capital:** Pierre.

Economy. Chief industries: agriculture, services, manufacturing. **Chief manuf. goods:** animal slaughtering, machinery, semiconductors, surgical appliances. **Chief crops:** corn, soybeans, wheat, hay, sunflowers, sorghum, oats, barley. **Livestock** (Jan. 2007): 3.7 mil cattle/calves, 380,000 sheep/lambs; (Dec. 2006): 1.3 mil hogs/pigs, 3.6 mil chickens (excl. broilers). **Timber/lumber:** figs. undisclosed; ponderosa pine. **Nonfuel minerals** (preliminary 2006): $204 mil; cement (portland), sand and gravel (construction), stone (crushed), stone (dimension), gold. **Gross state product** (est. 2006): $32.3 bil. **Sales tax** (2007): 4.0%. **Employment distrib.** (May 2007): 18.8% govt.; 20.0% trade/trans./util.; 10.3% mfg.; 14.5% ed./health; 6.5% prof./bus. serv.; 10.9% leisure/hosp.; 7.5% finance; 5.6% constr.; 3.9% other serv.; 1.7% info. **Unemployment** (2006): 3.2%. **Per cap. pers. income** (2006): $33,929. **New private housing** (2006): 5,304 units/$658.8 mil. **Commercial banks** (2006): 91; **deposits:** $74.0 bil. **Savings institutions** (2006): 6; **deposits:** $1.2 bil. **Lottery** (2006): total sales: $686.2 mil; profit: $119.0 mil.

Federal govt. Fed. civ. employees (Mar. 2006): 7,166; **avg. salary:** $53,000. **Notable fed. facilities:** *Ellsworth AFB.

Energy. Electricity production (est. 2006, kWh by source): Coal: 3.3 bil; Gas: 254 mil; Hydroelectric: 3.4 bil; Petroleum: 7 mil; Other: 6 mil.

State data. Motto: Under God, the people rule. **Flower:** Pasqueflower. **Bird:** Chinese ring-necked pheasant. **Tree:** Black Hills spruce. **Song:** Hail, South Dakota. **Entered union** Nov. 2, 1889; rank, 40th. **State fair** at Huron; late Aug.–early Sept.

History. Paleoindians hunted in the region at least 11,500 years ago. At the time of first European contact, Mandan, Hidatsa, Arikara, and Sioux lived in the area. The French Vérendrye brothers explored the region, 1742-43. The U.S. acquired the territory in the Louisiana Purchase, 1803, and Lewis and Clark passed through, 1804-6. In 1817 a trading post opened at what would become Fort Pierre. Dakota Territory was established, 1861. Gold was discovered, 1874, in the Black Hills on Sioux land; the "Great Dakota Boom" began in 1879. South Dakota became a state, 1889. The massacre of Native American families at Wounded Knee, 1890, ended Sioux resistance; 83 years later, armed supporters of the American Indian Movement, a Native American rights group, occupied the area, leading to a 70-day standoff. Major economic activities include agribusiness and, since the 1980s, credit card services. Republicans scored a key election victory, 2004, with the defeat of 3-term U.S. Sen. Tom Daschle, a national Democratic leader.

Tourist attractions. Black Hills; Mt. Rushmore; Needles Highway; Harney Peak, tallest E. of Rockies; Deadwood, 1876 Gold Rush town; Custer State Park; Jewel Cave Natl. Monument; Badlands Natl. Park "moonscape"; "Great Lakes of S. Dakota"; Ft. Sisseton; Great Plains Zoo & Museum,

Sioux Falls; Corn Palace, Mitchell; Wind Cave Natl. Park; Crazy Horse Memorial, mountain carving in progress.

Famous South Dakotans. Sparky Anderson, Black Elk, Bob Barker, Tom Brokaw, Crazy Horse, Thomas Daschle, Myron Floren, Mary Hart, Cheryl Ladd, Dr. Ernest O. Lawrence, George McGovern, Billy Mills, Allen Neuharth, Pat O'Brien, Sitting Bull.

Tourist information. Department of Tourism and State Development, Capitol Lake Plaza, 711 E. Wells Ave., c/o 500 E. Capitol Ave., Pierre, SD 57501-5070; 1-800-SDAKOTA; www.travelsd.com

Website. www.state.sd.us

Tennessee (TN)
Volunteer State

People. Population (2006 est.): 6,038,803; rank: 17; **net change** (2005-2006): 1.4%. **Pop. density:** 146.5 per sq mi. **Racial distribution** (2005): 80.7% white; 16.8% black; 1.2% Asian; 0.3% Native/Nat. AK; 0.05% Hawaiian/Pacific Islander; 2 or more races, 1.0%. **Hispanic pop.** (any race): 3.0%.

Geography. Total area: 42,143 sq mi; rank: 36. **Land area:** 41,217 sq mi; rank: 34. **Acres forested:** 14.4 mil. **Location:** East South Central state bounded on the N by Kentucky and Virginia; on the E by North Carolina; on the S by Georgia, Alabama, and Mississippi; on the W by Arkansas and Missouri. **Climate:** humid continental to the N; humid subtropical to the S. **Topography:** rugged country in the E; the Great Smoky Mts. of the Unakas; low ridges of the Appalachian Valley; the flat Cumberland Plateau; slightly rolling terrain and knobs of the Interior Low Plateau, the largest region; Eastern Gulf Coastal Plain to the W, laced with streams; Mississippi Alluvial Plain, a narrow strip of swamp and flood plain in the extreme W. **Capital:** Nashville. **Chief airports at:** Maryville, Memphis, Nashville.

Economy. Chief industries: manufacturing, trade, services, tourism, finance, insurance, real estate. **Chief manuf. goods:** motor vehicles & parts, computers & electronics, food, chemicals, plastics, printing, appliances, aluminum. **Chief crops:** greenhouse & nursery, soybeans, cotton, corn, tobacco, hay, tomatoes, wheat. **Livestock** (Jan. 2007): 2.3 mil cattle/calves, 25,000 sheep/lambs; (Dec. 2006): 220,000 hogs/pigs, 1.9 mil chickens (excl. broilers), 213.5 mil broilers. **Timber/lumber:** (est. 2006): 1.0 bil bd. ft.; red oak, white oak, yellow poplar, hickory. **Nonfuel minerals** (preliminary 2006): $807 mil; stone (crushed), cement (portland), sand and gravel (construction), clays (ball), sand and gravel (industrial). **Chief ports:** Memphis, Nashville, Chattanooga, Knoxville. **Gross state product** (est. 2006): $238.0 mil. **Sales tax** (2007): 7.0%. **Employment distrib.** (May 2007): 14.9% govt.; 21.7% trade/trans./util.; 13.9% mfg.; 12.3% ed./health; 11.3% prof./bus. serv.; 10.1% leisure/hosp.; 5.1% finance; 5.0% constr.; 3.6% other serv.; 1.8% info. **Unemployment** (2006): 5.2%. **Per cap. pers. income** (2006): $32,304. **New private housing** (2006): 46,003 units/$6.8 bil. **Commercial banks** (2006): 215; **deposits:** $97.9 bil. **Savings institutions** (2006): 20; **deposits:** $4.0 bil. **Lottery** (2006): total sales: $996.3 mil; profit: $277.7 mil.

Federal govt. Fed. civ. employees (Mar. 2006): 23,514; **avg. salary:** $57,349. **Notable fed. facilities:** Tennessee Valley Authority; Oak Ridge Natl. Lab; Arnold Engineering Development Ctr.; Ft. Campbell; NSA Mid-South, Millington.

Energy. Electricity production (est. 2006, kWh by source): Coal: 59.1 bil; Gas: 493 mil; Hydroelectric: 7.2 bil; Nuclear: 24.7 bil; Petroleum: 137 mil; Other: 2 mil.

State data. Motto: Agriculture and commerce. **Flower:** Iris. **Bird:** Mockingbird. **Tree:** Tulip poplar. **Songs:** My Homeland, Tennessee; When It's Iris Time in Tennessee; My Tennessee; Tennessee Waltz; Rocky Top. **Entered union** June 1, 1796; rank, 16th. **State fair** at Nashville, early Sept.; at Clarksville, mid-July; at Jackson, mid-Sept.

History. Inhabited for at least 20,000 years, the region was home to Creek and Yuchi peoples when the first Europeans arrived; the Cherokee moved into the region in the early 18th cent. Spanish explorers visited the area, 1540. English traders crossed the Great Smoky Mtns. from the east, while France's Marquette and Jolliet sailed down the Mississippi on the west, 1673. The first permanent settlement was of Virginians on the Watauga River, 1769. After the American Revolution, in which Tennesseans fought in eastern campaigns, the region became a territory, 1790, and a state, 1796. Slavery was widespread in western Tennessee, where cotton was the main crop, but much less common in the east. The state se-

ceded, 1861, and saw many Civil War engagements; some 187,000 Tennesseans fought for the Confederacy and 51,000 for the Union. Tennessee was readmitted in 1866, the only former Confederate state not to have a postwar military government. The famous Scopes trial, 1925, questioned the teaching of evolution in public schools. In the 1930s, the Tennessee Valley Authority, a federal program, brought electric power to rural areas. Nashville became the capital of country music, while Memphis fostered the blues and, with Elvis Presley in the 1950s, rock 'n' roll. Martin Luther King Jr., was assassinated in Memphis, 1968. Since the 1970s, auto plants have become major employers, as has Federal Express. Al Gore Jr., U.S. vice pres. (1993-2001), lost his 2000 presidential bid partly because he failed to carry his home state of Tennessee.

Tourist attractions. Reelfoot Lake; Lookout Mountain, Tennessee Aquarium, in Chattanooga; Fall Creek Falls; Great Smoky Mts. Natl. Park; Lost Sea, Sweetwater; Cherokee Natl. Forest; Cumberland Gap Natl. Park; Andrew Jackson's home, the Hermitage, near Nashville; homes of Pres. Polk and Andrew Johnson; American Museum of Science and Energy, Oak Ridge; Parthenon, Grand Old Opry, Opryland USA, all Nashville; Dollywood theme park, Pigeon Forge; Graceland, home of Elvis Presley, Memphis; Alex Haley Home and Museum, Henning; Casey Jones Village, Jackson.

Famous Tennesseans. Roy Acuff, Davy Crockett, David Farragut, Ernie Ford, Aretha Franklin, Morgan Freeman, Bill Frist, Al Gore Jr., Alex Haley, William C. Handy, Sam Houston, Cordell Hull, Andrew Jackson, Andrew Johnson, Casey Jones, Estes Kefauver, Grace Moore, Dolly Parton, Minnie Pearl, James Polk, Elvis Presley, Dinah Shore, Bessie Smith, Fred Thompson, Hank Williams Jr., Alvin York.

Tourist information. Dept. of Tourist Development, Wm. Snodgrass/Tennessee Tower, 312 8th Ave., 25th Fl., Nashville, TN 37243; (615) 741-2159; www.tnvacation.com

Website. www.tn.gov

Texas (TX)
Lone Star State

People. Population (2006 est.): 23,507,783; rank: 2; **net change** (2005-2006): 2.5%. **Pop. density:** 90.0 per sq mi. **Racial distribution** (2005): 83.2% white; 11.7% black; 3.3% Asian; 0.7% Native/Nat. AK; 0.1% Hawaiian/Pacific Islander; 2 or more races, 1.1%. **Hispanic pop.** (any race): 35.1%.

Geography. Total area: 268,581 sq mi; rank: 2. **Land area:** 261,797 sq mi; rank: 2. **Acres forested:** 17.1 mil. **Location:** Southwestern state, bounded on the SE by the Gulf of Mexico; on the SW by Mexico, separated by the Rio Grande; surrounding states are Louisiana, Arkansas, Oklahoma, New Mexico. **Climate:** extremely varied; driest region is the Trans-Pecos; wettest is the NE. **Topography:** Gulf Coast Plain in the S and SE; North Central Plains slope upward with some hills; the Great Plains extend over the Panhandle, are broken by low mountains; the Trans-Pecos is the southern extension of the Rockies. **Capital:** Austin. **Chief airports at:** Austin, Dallas, El Paso, Fort Worth, Houston (2), Lubbock, San Antonio.

Economy. Chief industries: manufacturing, trade, oil and gas extraction, services. **Chief manuf. goods:** petroleum, chemicals & resins, computers & electronics, animal slaughtering & processing, plastics, aerospace. **Chief crops:** cotton, greenhouse & nursery, corn, wheat, sorghum, hay, peanuts, onions, rice, pecans, grapefruit. **Livestock** (Jan. 2007): 14.0 mil cattle/calves, 1 mil sheep/lambs; (Dec. 2006): 930,000 hogs/pigs, 24.9 mil chickens (excl. broilers), 628.3 mil broilers. **Timber/lumber:** (est. 2006): 1.9 bil bd. ft.; pine, cypress. **Nonfuel minerals** (preliminary 2006): $2.9 bil; cement (portland), stone (crushed), sand and gravel (construction), salt, lime. **Commercial fishing** (2005): $172.3 mil. **Chief ports:** Houston, Galveston, Brownsville, Beaumont, Port Arthur, Corpus Christi. **Gross state product** (est. 2006): $1.1 trillion. **Sales tax** (2007): 6.25%. **Employment distrib.** (May 2007): 17.1% govt.; 20.0% trade/trans./util.; 9.0% mfg.; 12.1% ed./health; 12.4% prof./bus. serv.; 9.6% leisure/hosp.; 6.2% finance; 6.1% constr.; 3.4% other serv.; 2.1% info. **Unemployment** (2006): 4.9%. **Per cap. pers. income** (2006): $34,257. **New private housing** (2006): 216,642 units/$29.2 bil. **Commercial banks** (2006): 651; **deposits:** $351.5 bil. **Savings institutions** (2006): 52; **deposits:** $50.9 bil. **Lottery** (2006): total sales: $3.8 bil; profit: $1.0 bil.

Federal govt. Fed. civ. employees (Mar. 2006): 113,364; **avg. salary:** $59,618. **Notable fed. facilities:** Forts *Hood, *Bliss, *Sam Houston; *Lackland, *Randolph, *Sheppard, *Dyess, Goodfellow AF Bases; NASA Johnson Space Ctr.; Naval Air Training School, Corpus Christi NAS; Kingsville NAS; Ft. Worth Western Currency Facility.

Energy. Electricity production (est. 2006, kWh by source): Coal: 59.5 bil; Gas: 34.2 bil; Hydroelectric: 870 mil; Petroleum: 67 mil.

State data. Motto: Friendship. **Flower:** Bluebonnet. **Bird:** Mockingbird. **Tree:** Pecan. **Song:** Texas, Our Texas. **Entered union** Dec. 29, 1845; rank, 28th. **State fair** at Dallas, late Sept.-mid-Oct.; at Beaumont, mid-Oct.; at Belton, late Aug.–early Sept.; at Denton, mid-Aug.; at Tyler, late Sept.

History. Humans have lived in the region for at least 12,000 years. Coahuiltecan, Karankawa, Caddo, Jumano, and Tonkawa peoples were in the area when the first Europeans came; later, Apache, Comanche, Cherokee, and Wichita arrived. Early Spanish explorers included Pineda, who sailed along the Texas coast, 1519; Cabeza de Vaca, shipwrecked near Galveston along with the former slave Estevanico, 1528; and Coronado, who crossed the Panhandle, 1541. Spaniards made the first settlement at Ysleta, near El Paso, 1682. Americans moved into the land early in the 19th cent. Mexico, of which Texas was a part, won independence from Spain, 1821. Texans rebelled, 1836, losing to Santa Anna at the Alamo, but winning decisively under Sam Houston at San Jacinto. With Houston as president, 1836-38 & 1841-44, the Republic of Texas functioned as a nation until admitted to the Union. With a slave population of 30%, Texas seceded, 1861; mostly unscathed by the Civil War, it was readmitted, 1870. In 1900 a powerful hurricane lashed Galveston, killing at least 8,000. Cotton and cattle were dominant until 1901, when the Spindletop gusher, near Beaumont, launched the petroleum and petrochemical industries. By 2000 the state population ranked 2nd in the U.S. With wealth and population came political power, notably in the presidencies of Lyndon B. Johnson, 1963-69, George H. W, Bush, 1989-93, and George W. Bush, since 2001.

Tourist attractions. Padre Island Natl. Seashore; Big Bend, Guadalupe Mts. natl. parks; Ft. Davis; Six Flags Over Texas, Arlington SeaWorld, Six Flags Fiesta Texas, The Alamo, San Antonio Missions Natl. Hist. Park, all San Antonio; Cowgirl Hall of Fame, Kimball Art Museum, in Fort Worth; Lyndon B. Johnson Natl. Historical Park, Johnson City; Lyndon B. Johnson Library and Museum, Austin; Texas State Aquarium, Corpus Christi; George Bush Library, College Station.

Famous Texans. Lance Armstrong, Stephen F. Austin, Lloyd Bentsen, James Bowie, Carol Burnett, George H. W. Bush, George W. Bush, Joan Crawford, J. Frank Dobie, Dwight D. Eisenhower, Morgan Fairchild, Farrah Fawcett, Sam Houston, Howard Hughes, Kay Bailey Hutchison, Molly Ivins, Lyndon B. Johnson, Tommy Lee Jones, Janis Joplin, Barbara Jordan, Mary Martin, Chester Nimitz, Sandra Day O'Connor, H. Ross Perot, Katherine Anne Porter, Dan Rather, Sam Rayburn, Ann Richards, Sissy Spacek, Kenneth Starr, George Strait.

Tourist information. Texas Tourism, PO Box 12428, Austin, TX 78711; (512) 936-0101; www.traveltex.com

Website. www.state.tx.us

Utah (UT)
Beehive State

People. Population (2006 est.): 2,550,063; rank: 34; **net change** (2005-2006): 2.4%. **Pop. density:** 31.1 per sq mi. **Racial distribution** (2005): 93.8% white; 1.0% black; 1.9% Asian; 1.3% Native/Nat. AK; 0.7% Hawaiian/Pacific Islander; 2 or more races, 1.3%. **Hispanic pop.** (any race): 10.9%.

Geography. Total area: 84,899 sq mi; rank: 13. **Land area:** 82,144 sq mi; rank: 12. **Acres forested:** 15.7 mil. **Location:** Middle Rocky Mountain state; its southeastern corner touches Colorado, New Mexico, and Arizona, and is the only spot in the U.S. where 4 states join. **Climate:** arid; ranging from warm desert in SW to alpine in NE. **Topography:** high Colorado plateau is cut by brilliantly colored canyons of the SE; broad, flat, desert-like Great Basin of the W; the Great Salt Lake and Bonneville Salt Flats to the NW; Middle Rockies in the NE run E-W; valleys and plateaus of the Wasatch Front. **Capital:** Salt Lake City. **Chief airport at:** Salt Lake City.

Economy. Chief industries: services, trade, manufacturing, government, transportation, utilities. **Chief manuf. goods:** food, petroleum, nonferrous metal, motor vehicles & parts, aerospace, sporting goods, fabricated metal, computers & electronics. **Chief crops:** hay, greenhouse & nursery, wheat, cherries, onions, apples, barley, peaches, corn. **Livestock** (Jan. 2007): 830,000 cattle/calves, 295,000 mil sheep/lambs; (Dec. 2006): 680,000 hogs/pigs, 4.4 mil chickens (excl. broilers). **Timber/lumber** (est. 2006): 49 mil bd. ft.; aspen, spruce, pine. **Nonfuel minerals** (preliminary 2006): $4.0 bil; copper, molybdenum (concentrates), gold, cement (portland), sand and gravel (construction). **Gross state product** (est. 2006): $97.7 bil. **Sales tax** (2007): 4.75%. **Employment distrib.** (May 2007): 16.7% govt.; 19.3% trade/trans./util.; 10.2% mfg.; 10.9% ed./health; 13.0% prof./bus. serv.; 8.9% leisure/hosp.; 6.0% finance; 8.7% constr.; 2.9% other serv.; 2.7% info. **Unemployment** (2006): 2.9%. **Per cap. pers. income** (2006): $29,108. **New private housing** (2006): 25,873 units/$4.8 bil. **Commercial banks** (2006): 74; **deposits:** $132.5 bil. **Savings institutions** (2006): 8; **deposits:** $10.8 bil.

Federal govt. Fed. civ. employees (Mar. 2006): 27,438; **avg. salary:** $54,379. **Notable fed. facilities:** *Hill AFB; *Tooele Army Depot; Army Dugway Proving Ground.

Energy. Electricity production (est. 2006, kWh by source): Coal: 35.8 bil; Gas: 2.9 bil; Hydroelectric: 782 mil; Petroleum: 34 mil; Other: 191 mil.

State data. Motto: Industry. **Flower:** Sego lily. **Bird:** Seagull. **Tree:** Blue spruce. **Song:** Utah, This is the Place. **Entered union** Jan. 4, 1896; rank, 45th. **State fair** at Salt Lake City; early Sept.

History. Ute, Gosiute, Southern Paiute, and Navajo peoples lived in the region at the time of European contact. Spanish Franciscans visited the area, 1776; American fur traders followed. Permanent settlement began with the arrival of the Latter-day Saints, or Mormons, 1847; they made the arid land bloom and created a prosperous economy. Organized in 1849, the State of Deseret asked admission to the Union; instead, Congress established Utah Territory, 1850, and Brigham Young was appointed governor. The Union Pacific and Central Pacific railroads met near Promontory Point, May 10, 1869, creating the first transcontinental railroad. Statehood was not achieved until 1896, after a long controversy over the Mormon practices of economic isolationism and polygamy, which the church renounced in 1890. The 20th cent. brought expansion in mining, defense-related industries, and, more recently, information technologies. More than 2/3 of Utahans are Mormons; the church has its world headquarters in Salt Lake City. Utah experienced 43% population growth, 1990-2005, and had the highest birthrate and lowest median age of any state in the U.S.

Tourist attractions. Temple Square, Mormon Church headquarters, in Salt Lake City; Great Salt Lake; Zion, Canyonlands, Bryce Canyon, Arches, and Capitol Reef natl. parks; Dinosaur, Rainbow Bridge, Timpanogos Cave, and Natural Bridges natl. monuments; Lake Powell; Flaming Gorge Natl. Recreation Area.

Famous Utahans. Maude Adams, Ezra Taft Benson, John Moses Browning, Mariner Eccles, Philo Farnsworth, James Fletcher, David M. Kennedy, J. Willard Marriott, Merlin Olsen, Osmond family, Ivy Baker Priest, George Romney, Roseanne, Wallace Stegner, Brigham Young, Loretta Young.

Tourist information. Utah Office of Tourism, Council Hall/ Captiol Hill, 300 N. State St., Salt Lake City, UT 84114; 1-800-200-1160 or 1-800-UTAH-FUN; www.utah.com

Website. www.utah.gov

Vermont (VT)
Green Mountain State

People. Population (2006 est.): 623,908; rank: 49; **net change** (2005-2006): 0.2%. **Pop. density:** 67.6 per sq mi. **Racial distribution** (2005): 96.9% white; 0.6% black; 1.0% Asian; 0.4% Native/Nat. AK; 0.03% Hawaiian/Pacific Islander; 2 or more races, 1.1%. **Hispanic pop.** (any race): 1.1%.

Geography. Total area: 9,614 sq mi; rank: 45. **Land area:** 9,250 sq mi; rank: 43. **Acres forested:** 4.6 mil. **Location:** northern New England state. **Climate:** temperate, with considerable temperature extremes; heavy snowfall in mountains. **Topography:** Green Mts. N-S backbone 20-36 mi wide; avg. altitude 1,000 ft. **Capital:** Montpelier. **Chief airport at:** Burlington.

Economy. Chief industries: manufacturing, tourism, agriculture, trade, finance, insurance, real estate, government. **Chief manuf. goods:** dairy, plastics, printing, wood furniture, sporting goods, metalworking machinery. **Chief crops:** greenhouse & nursery, hay, maple syrup, apples, berries, sweet corn. **Livestock** (Jan. 2007): 265,000 cattle/calves; (Dec. 2006): 2,500 hogs/pigs, 235,000 chickens (excl. broilers). **Timber/lumber** (est. 2006): 173 mil bd. ft.; pine, spruce, fir, hemlock. **Nonfuel minerals** (preliminary 2006): $101 mil; stone (crushed), sand and gravel (construction), stone (dimension), talc (crude), gemstones (natural). **Gross state product** (est. 2006): $24.2 bil. **Sales tax** (2007): 6.0%. **Employment distrib.** (May 2007): 18.0% govt.; 19.3% trade/trans./util.; 11.6% mfg.; 18.1% ed./health; 7.3% prof./bus. serv.; 10.0% leisure/hosp.; 4.3% finance; 5.8% constr.; 3.2% other serv.; 2.0% info. **Unemployment** (2006): 3.6%. **Per cap. pers. income** (2006): $34,264. **New private housing** (2006): 2,626 units/$421.9 mil. **Commercial banks** (2006): 17; **deposits:** $8.6 bil. **Savings institutions** (2006): 7; **deposits:** $1.3 bil. **Lottery** (2006): total sales: $104.9 mil; profit: $22.9 mil.

Federal govt. Fed. civ. employees (Mar. 2006): 3,537; **avg. salary:** $57,279. **Notable fed. facilities:** Law Enforcement Support Ctr.

Energy. Electricity production (est. 2006, kWh by source): Gas: 2 mil; Hydroelectric: 358 mil; Petroleum: 6 mil; Other: 273 mil.

State data. Motto: Freedom and unity. **Flower:** Red clover. **Bird:** Hermit thrush. **Tree:** Sugar maple. **Song:** These Green Mountains. **Entered union** Mar. 4, 1791; rank, 14th. **State fair** at Rutland; early Sept.

History. Inhabited for 10,000 years or more, the region attracted Abenaki and Mahican peoples before Europeans arrived. Champlain explored the lake that now bears his name, 1609. The first European settlement was on Isle la Motte, in Lake Champlain, 1666. During the American Revolution, Ethan Allen and the Green Mountain Boys captured Ft. Ticonderoga (NY), 1775. Under a constitution that provided for public schools and abolished slavery, settlers declared a republic, 1777. Vermont joined the Union, 1791. Agriculture dominated in the 19th cent. Still mainly rural, the state expanded tourism and manufacturing after World War II, and IBM became the largest private employer. In 2000, with Howard Dean as governor (1991-2003), Vermont became the first state in the U.S. to legalize same-sex civil unions.

Tourist attractions. Shelburne Museum; Rock of Ages Quarry, Graniteville; Vermont Marble Museum, Proctor; Bennington Battle Monument; Pres. Calvin Coolidge homestead, Plymouth; Maple Grove Maple Museum, St. Johnsbury; Ben & Jerry's Factory, N. Waterbury.

Famous Vermonters. Ethan Allen, Chester A. Arthur, Calvin Coolidge, Howard Dean, John Deere, George Dewey, John Dewey, Stephen A. Douglas, Dorothy Canfield Fisher, James Fisk, James Jeffords, Rudy Vallee.

Tourist information. Vermont Dept. of Tourism and Marketing, Ntl. Life Building 6th Floor, Drawer 20, Montpelier, VT 05620; (802) 828-3237; 1-800-VERMONT; www.vermontvacation.com

Website. www.vermont.gov

Virginia (VA)

Old Dominion

People. Population (2006 est.): 7,642,884; rank: 12; **net change** (2005-2006): 1.0%. **Pop. density:** 193.5 per sq mi. **Racial distribution** (2005): 73.6% white; 19.9% black; 4.6% Asian; 0.3% Native/Nat. AK; 0.08% Hawaiian/Pacific Islander; 2 or more races, 1.6%. **Hispanic pop.** (any race): 6.0%.

Geography. Total area: 42,774 sq mi; rank: 35. **Land area:** 39,594 sq mi; rank: 37. **Acres forested:** 16.1 mil. **Location:** South Atlantic state bounded by the Atlantic Ocean on the E and surrounded by North Carolina, Tennessee, Kentucky, West Virginia, and Maryland. **Climate:** mild and equable. **Topography:** mountain and valley region in the W, including the Blue Ridge Mts.; rolling piedmont plateau; tidewater, or coastal plain, including the eastern shore. **Capital:** Richmond. **Chief airports at:** Arlington, Dulles, Highland Springs, Newport News, Norfolk.

Economy. Chief industries: services, trade, government, manufacturing, tourism, agriculture. **Chief manuf. goods:** beverages & tobacco, transportation equip., animal slaughtering & processing, plastics, textiles, paper & paper product, printing, pharmaceuticals, furniture, chemicals. **Chief crops:** greenhouse & nursery, soybeans, tomatoes, corn, tobacco, hay, cotton, apples, wheat, peanuts, potatoes. **Livestock** (Jan. 2007): 1.6 mil cattle/calves, 72,000 sheep/lambs; (Dec. 2006): 365,000 hogs/pigs, 4.5 mil chickens (excl. broilers), 256.2 mil broilers. **Timber/lumber** (est. 2006): 1.6 bil bd. ft.; pine and hardwoods. **Nonfuel minerals** (preliminary 2006): $1.2 bil; stone (crushed), cement (portland), sand and gravel (construction), lime, zirconium (concentrates). **Commercial fishing** (2005): $155.3 mil. **Chief ports:** Hampton Roads, Richmond, Alexandria. **Gross state product** (est. 2006): $369.3 bil. **Sales tax** (2007): 5.0%. **Employment distrib.** (May 2007): 18.1% govt.; 17.7% trade/trans./util.; 7.5% mfg.; 11.0% ed./health; 17.0% prof./bus. serv.; 9.3% leisure/hosp.; 5.2% finance; 6.6% constr.; 4.9% other serv.; 2.4% info. **Unemployment** (2006): 3.0%. **Per cap. pers. income** (2006): $39,173. **New private housing** (2006): 47,704 units/$7.7 bil. **Commercial banks** (2006): 151; **deposits:** $127.5 bil. **Savings institutions** (2006): 19; **deposits:** $45.3 bil. **Lottery** (2006): total sales: $1.4 bil; profit: $454.9 mil.

Federal govt. Fed. civ. employees (Mar. 2006): 121,337; **avg. salary:** $73,224. **Notable fed. facilities:** Pentagon; *Norfolk Naval Sta., Shipyard, & other Hampton Roads; *Ft. Belvoir; *Langley AFB; NASA Langley Res. Ctr.; CIA George Bush Ctr. for Intelligence, Langley; Quantico USMC Base, FBI Academy; *Dahlgren Nav. Surface Warfare Ctr. & Lab; USDA Food and Nutrition Serv.; U.S. Geological Survey Natl. Ctr.

Energy. Electricity production (est. 2006, kWh by source): Coal: 28.6 bil; Gas: 3.8 bil; Hydroelectric: 1.3 bil; Nuclear: 27.6 bil; Petroleum: 661 mil; Other: 483 mil.

State data. Motto: Sic Semper Tyrannis (Thus always to tyrants). **Flower:** Dogwood. **Bird:** Cardinal. **Tree:** Dogwood. **Song Emeritus:** Carry Me Back to Old Virginia. **Tenth** of the original 13 states to ratify the Constitution, June 25, 1788. **State fair** at Richmond; late Sept.–early Oct.

History. Cherokee and Susquehanna peoples and the Algonquians of the Powhatan Confederacy were in the region when Europeans arrived. English settlers founded Jamestown, 1607. Virginians were indispensable to the founding of the American republic, and 4 of the first 5 U.S. presidents—Washington, Jefferson, Madison, and Monroe—came from there. The conclusive battle of the American Revolution took place at Yorktown, 1781. The state profited from tobacco, cotton, and the slave trade; in 1860, slaves made up nearly 1/3 of the population. Virginia seceded from the Union, 1861, and Richmond became the capital of the Confederacy, but Western counties, loyal to the Union, split off to become West Virginia, 1863. The war ended with Lee's surrender to Grant at Appomattox, 1865, and Virginia was readmitted to the Union, 1870. In the 20th cent., expansion of federal civilian jobs and military facilities transformed the economy. State officials pledged "massive resistance" to racial integration in the mid-1950s, but eventually accommodated. In 1989, L. Douglas Wilder became the first elected black governor in U.S. history. On Sept. 11, 2001, terrorist hijackers crashed a jet into U.S. defense headquarters at the Pentagon, in Arlington.

Tourist attractions. Colonial Williamsburg; Busch Gardens Williamsburg; Wolf Trap Farm, near Vienna; Arlington Natl. Cemetery; Mt. Vernon, home of George Washington; Jamestown Settlement; Yorktown; Jefferson's Monticello, Charlottesville; Robert E. Lee's birthplace, Stratford Hall, and grave, Lexington; Appomattox; Shenandoah Natl. Park; Blue Ridge Parkway; Virginia Beach; Kings Dominion, near Richmond.

Famous Virginians. Richard E. Byrd, James B. Cabell, Henry Clay, Katie Couric, Jubal Early, Jerry Falwell, William Henry Harrison, Patrick Henry, A.P. Hill, Thomas Jefferson, Joseph E. Johnston, Robert E. Lee, Meriwether Lewis and William Clark, James Madison, John Marshall, George Mason, James Monroe, George Pickett, Pocahontas, Edgar Allan Poe, John Randolph, Walter Reed, Rev. Pat Robertson, John Smith, J.E.B. Stuart, William Styron, Zachary Taylor, John Tyler, Maggie Walker, Booker T. Washington, George Washington, L. Douglas Wilder, Woodrow Wilson.

Tourist Information. Virginia Tourism Corp., 901 E. Byrd St., Richmond, VA 23219; 1-800-VISITVA; www.virginia.org

Website. www.virginia.gov

Washington (WA)
Evergreen State

People. Population (2006 est.): 6,395,798; rank: 14; **net change** (2005-2006): 1.7%. **Pop. density:** 96.1 per sq mi. **Racial distribution** (2005): 85.0% white; 3.5% black; 6.4% Asian; 1.7% Native/Nat. AK; 0.5% Hawaiian/Pacific Islander; 2 or more races, 3.0%. **Hispanic pop.** (any race): 8.8%.

Geography. Total area: 71,300 sq mi; rank: 18. **Land area:** 66,544 sq mi; rank: 20. **Acres forested:** 21.8 mil. **Location:** Pacific state bordered by Canada on the N; Idaho on the E; Oregon on the S; and the Pacific Ocean on the W. **Climate:** mild, dominated by the Pacific Ocean and protected by the Cascades. **Topography:** Olympic Mts. on NW peninsula; open land along coast to Columbia R.; flat terrain of Puget Sound Lowland; Cascade Mts. region's high peaks to the E; Columbia Basin in central portion; highlands to the NE; mountains to the SE. **Capital:** Olympia. **Chief airports at:** Seattle, Spokane.

Economy. Chief industries: advanced technology, aerospace, biotechnology, intl. trade, forestry, tourism, recycling, agriculture & food processing. **Chief manuf. goods:** aerospace, petroleum, food, paper, milled lumber, plastics, structural metals, computers & electronics. **Chief crops:** apples, potatoes, wheat, hay, cherries, greenhouse & nursery, forest products, pears, grapes, onions, hops, sweet corn, Christmas trees, mint, raspberries. **Livestock** (Jan. 2007): 1.1 mil cattle/calves, 51,000 mil sheep/lambs; (Dec. 2006): 36,000 hogs/pigs, 6.1 mil chickens (excl. broilers). **Timber/lumber** (est. 2006): 5.0 bil bd. ft.; Douglas fir, hemlock, cedar, pine. **Nonfuel minerals** (preliminary 2006): $720 mil; sand and gravel (construction), zinc, stone (crushed), cement (portland), diatomite. **Commercial fishing** (2005): $191.4 mil. **Chief ports:** Seattle, Tacoma, Vancouver, Kelso-Longview. **Gross state product** (est. 2006): $293.5 bil. **Sales tax** (2007): 6.5%. **Employment distrib.** (May 2007): 18.4% govt.; 18.8% trade/trans./util.; 10.0% mfg.; 11.9% ed./health; 11.6% prof./bus. serv.; 9.6% leisure/hosp.; 5.4% finance; 6.9% constr.; 3.6% other serv.; 3.5% info. **Unemployment** (2006): 5.0%. **Per cap. pers. income** (2006): $37,423. **New private housing** (2006): 50,033 units/$8.5 bil. **Commercial banks** (2006): 101; **deposits:** $76.6 bil. **Savings institutions** (2006): 21; **deposits:** $22.9 bil. **Lottery** (2006): total sales: $477.9 mil; profit: $117.0 mil.

Federal govt. Fed. civ. employees (Mar. 2006): 45,948; **avg. salary:** $62,571. **Notable fed. facilities:** Bonneville Power Admin.; *Ft. Lewis; *McChord AFB; DOE Hanford Nuclear Site; Naval Base Kitsap (Bremerton & Bangor); Whidbey Island NAS; Naval Sta., Everett; Pacific Northwest Natl. Lab.

Energy. Electricity production (est. 2006, kWh by source): Gas: 1.8 bil; Hydroelectric: 81.8 bil; Nuclear: 9.3 bil; Petroleum: 6 mil; Other: 1.2 bil.

State data. Motto: Alki (By and by). **Flower:** Western rhododendron. **Bird:** Willow goldfinch. **Tree:** Western hemlock. **Song:** Washington, My Home. **Entered union** Nov. 11, 1889; rank, 42nd. **State fairs:** county and area fairs, April-Sept.; no state fair.

History. People of the Clovis culture lived in the region 11,000 years ago. At the time of European contact, Native Americans in the area included Nez Percé, Spokane, Yakima, Cayuse, Okanogan, Walla Walla, and Colville peoples in the interior, and Nooksak, Chinook, Nisqually, Clallam, Makah, Quinault, and Puyallup peoples along the coast. Spain's Bruno Hezeta sailed the coast, 1775. In 1792, British naval officer George Vancouver mapped the Puget Sound area, and American Capt. Robert Gray sailed up the Columbia River. Fur traders and missionaries arrived in the first half of the 19th cent. Final agreement on the border of Washington and Canada was made with Britain, 1846. Completion in 1883 of a transcontinental rail link between Puget Sound and the eastern U.S. aided immigration, and Washington became a state in 1889. In the 20th cent., cheap hydroelectric power spurred growth in the aluminum and aircraft industries; founded in 1975, Microsoft became a computer software giant. Mt. St. Helens erupted, 1980. With grunge music, Starbucks coffee, and Amazon.com, Seattle became a national trendsetter in the 1990s; violent street protests disrupted a World Trade Organization meeting there in 1999. Gary Locke, in office 1997-2005, was the first U.S. governor of Chinese ancestry.

Tourist attractions. Seattle Center, Space Needle, waterfront, Museum of Flight, Underground Tour, all Seattle; Mt. Rainier, Olympic, and North Cascades natl. parks; Mt. St. Helens; Puget Sound; San Juan Islands; Grand Coulee Dam; Columbia R. Gorge Natl. Scenic Area; Spokane's Riverfront Park.

Famous Washingtonians. Raymond Carver, Kurt Cobain, Bing Crosby, William O. Douglas, Bill Gates, Jimi Hendrix, Henry M. Jackson, Gary Larson, Mary McCarthy, Robert Motherwell, Edward R. Murrow, Theodore Roethke, Ann Rule, Hilary Swank, Julia Sweeney, Adam West, Marcus Whitman, Minoru Yamasaki.

Tourist information. WA State Tourism, 128 10th Ave. SW, PO Box 42500, Olympia, WA 98504; 1-800-544-1800; www.experiencewashington.com

Website. www.access.wa.gov

West Virginia (WV)
Mountain State

People. Population (2006 est.): 1,818,470; rank: 37; **net change** (2005-2006): 0.2%. **Pop. density:** 75.5 per sq mi. **Racial distribution** (2005): 95.2% white; 3.2% black; 0.6% Asian; 0.2% Native/Nat. AK; 0.02% Hawaiian/Pacific Islander; 2 or more races, 0.8%. **Hispanic pop.** (any race): 0.9%.

Geography. Total area: 24,230 sq mi; rank: 41. **Land area:** 24,078 sq mi; rank: 41. **Acres forested:** 12.1 mil. **Location:** South Atlantic state bounded on the N by Ohio, Pennsylvania, Maryland; on the S and W by Virginia, Kentucky, Ohio; on the E by Maryland and Virginia. **Climate:** humid continental climate except for marine modification in the lower panhandle. **Topography:** ranging from hilly to mountainous; Allegheny Plateau in the W, covers two-thirds of the state; mountains here are the highest in the state, over 4,000 ft. **Capital:** Charleston.

Economy. Chief industries: manufacturing, services, mining, tourism. **Chief manuf. goods:** chemicals, aluminum, motor vehicle parts, lumber & plywood, primary & fabricated metals. **Chief crops:** hay, apples, corn, peaches, soybeans, tobacco, wheat. **Livestock** (Jan. 2007): 420,000 cattle/calves, 34,000 sheep/lambs; (Dec. 2006): 11,000 hogs/pigs, 2.1 mil chickens (excl. broilers), 89.7 mil broilers. **Timber/lumber** (est. 2006): 670 mil bd. ft.; oak, yellow poplar, hickory, walnut, cherry. **Nonfuel minerals** (preliminary 2006): $211 mil; stone (crushed), cement (portland), lime, sand and gravel (industrial), cement (masonry). **Chief port:** Huntington. **Gross state product** (est. 2006): $55.7 bil. **Sales tax** (2007): 6.0%. **Employment distrib.** (May 2007): 19.3% govt.; 18.8% trade/trans./util.; 7.8% mfg.; 14.8% ed./health; 7.9% prof./bus. serv.; 9.5% leisure/hosp.; 4.0% finance; 5.3% constr.; 7.4% other serv.; 1.5% info. **Unemployment** (2006): 4.9%. **Per cap. pers. income** (2006): $27,897. **New private housing** (2006): 5,645 units/$944.4 mil. **Commercial banks** (2006): 83; **deposits:** $24.0 bil. **Savings institutions** (2006): 7; **deposits:** $805 mil. **Lottery** (2006): total sales: $1.5 bil; profit: $610.0 mil.

Federal govt. Fed. civ. employees (Mar. 2006): 13,292; **avg. salary:** $58,964. **Notable fed. facilities:** Natl. Radio Astronomy Observatory, Green Bank; Bureau of Public Debt Bldg.; Harpers Ferry Natl. Park; Alderson Fed. Prison for Women; FBI Natl. Crime Info. Ctr.

Energy. Electricity production (est. 2006, kWh by source): Coal: 59.4 bil; Gas: 87 mil; Hydroelectric: 383 mil; Petroleum: 124 mil.

State data. Motto: Montani Semper Liberi (Mountaineers are always free). **Flower:** Big rhododendron. **Bird:** Cardinal. **Tree:** Sugar maple. **Songs:** The West Virginia Hills; This Is My West Virginia; West Virginia, My Home, Sweet Home. **Entered union** June 20, 1863; rank, 35th. **State fair** at Lewisburg; mid-Aug.

History. Sparsely inhabited at the time of European contact, the area was primarily Native American hunting grounds. British explorers Thomas Batts and Robert Fallam reached the New River, 1671. Coal, discovered in 1742, was mined extensively by the mid-19th cent. White settlement led to conflicts with Native Americans, including a major battle in which frontiersmen defeated an Indian confederacy at Point Pleasant, 1774. The region joined the Union as part of Virginia, 1788. Longstanding tensions between the E and W parts of the state came to a head in 1861, when Virginia seceded. Delegates of W counties, meeting at Wheeling, repudiated the act and created a new state, Kanawha, later renamed West Virginia, which was admitted to the Union in 1863. Poverty has been a problem for much of the state's subsequent history. West Virginia continues to rank low in per capita personal income, despite billions of dollars in federal contracts brought to the state by 9-term U.S. Sen. Robert Byrd; in 2006 he became the longest-serving member in Senate history.

Tourist attractions. Harpers Ferry Natl. Historic Park; Clay Center & Avampato Discovery Museum, Charleston; White Sulphur Springs (The Greenbrier) and Berkeley Springs mineral water spas; New River Gorge Natl. River; Beckley Exhibition Coal Mine; Monongahela Natl. Forest; Fenton Glass, Williamstown; Blenko Glass, Milton; Sternwheel Regatta, Charleston; Mountain State Forest Festival, Elkins; skiing at Canaan Valley, Snowshoe, Timberline, Winterplace; Mountain State Art & Craft Festival, Ripley; Oglebay Resort, Wheeling; white water rafting on New and Gauley rivers.

Famous West Virginians. Newton D. Baker, Pearl Buck, Robert Byrd, John W. Davis, Thomas "Stonewall" Jackson, Don Knotts, Dwight Whitney Morrow, Michael Owens, Mary Lou Retton, Walter Reuther, Cyrus Vance, Jerry West, Charles "Chuck" Yeager.

Tourist information. West Virginia Division of Tourism, 90 MacCorkle Ave., SW, South Charleston, WV 25303; 1-800-CALLWVA; www.wvtourism.com

Website. www.wv.gov

Wisconsin (WI)
Badger State

People. Population (2006 est.): 5,556,506; rank: 20; **net change** (2005-2006): 0.5%. **Pop. density:** 102.5 per sq mi. **Racial distribution** (2005): 90.1% white; 6.0% black; 2.0% Asian; 0.9% Native/Nat. AK; 0.04% Hawaiian/Pacific Islander; 2 or more races, 1.0%. **Hispanic pop.** (any race): 4.5%.

Geography. Total area: 65,498 sq mi; rank: 23. **Land area:** 54,310 sq mi; rank: 25. **Acres forested:** 16.0 mil. **Location:** East North Central state, bounded on the N by Lake Superior and Upper Michigan; on the E by Lake Michigan; on the S by Illinois; on the W by the St. Croix and Mississippi rivers. **Climate:** long, cold winters and short, warm summers tempered by the Great Lakes. **Topography:** narrow Lake Superior Lowland plain met by Northern Highland, which slopes gently to the sandy crescent Central Plain; Western Upland in the SW; 3 broad parallel limestone ridges running N-S are separated by wide and shallow lowlands in the SE. **Capital:** Madison. **Chief airports at:** Madison, Milwaukee.

Economy. Chief industries: services, manufacturing, trade, government, agriculture, tourism. **Chief manuf. goods:** transportation, dairy, animal slaughtering & processing, paper, printing, plastics, computers & electronics. **Chief crops:** corn, greenhouse & nursery, soybeans, potatoes, cranberries, hay, wheat, snap beans, apples, peas. **Livestock** (Jan. 2007): 3.4 mil cattle/calves, 92,000 mil sheep/lambs; (Dec. 2006): 440,000 hogs/pigs, 6.5 mil chickens (excl. broilers), 38.3 mil broilers. **Timber/lumber** (est. 2006): 540 mil bd. ft.; maple, birch, oak, evergreens. **Nonfuel minerals** (preliminary 2006): $591 mil; stone (crushed), sand and gravel (construction), lime, sand and gravel (industrial), stone (dimension). **Commercial fishing** (2005): $2.6 mil. **Chief ports:** Superior, Ashland, Milwaukee, Green Bay, Kewaunee, Pt. Washington, Manitowoc, Sheboygan, Marinette, Kenosha. **Gross state product** (est. 2006): $227.2 bil. **Sales tax** (2007): 5.0%. **Employment distrib.** (May 2007): 14.8% govt.; 19.1% trade/trans./util.; 17.1% mfg.; 13.7% ed./health; 9.5% prof./bus. serv.; 9.2% leisure/hosp.; 5.6% finance; 4.5% constr.; 4.7% other serv.; 1.7% info. **Unemployment** (2006): 4.7%. **Per cap. pers. income** (2006): $34,701. **New private housing** (2006): 27,329 units/$4.4 bil. **Commercial banks** (2006): 278; **deposits:** $88.0 bil. **Savings institutions** (2006): 42; **deposits:** $5.5 bil. **Lottery** (2006): total sales: $508.9 mil; profit: $150.6 mil.

Federal govt. Fed. civ. employees (Mar. 2006): 11,494; **avg. salary:** $57,404. **Notable fed. facilities:** *Ft. McCoy; USDA Forest Products Lab.

Energy. Electricity production (est. 2006, kWh by source): Coal: 38.7 bil; Gas: 2.4 bil; Hydroelectric: 1.2 bil; Nuclear: 12.2 bil; Petroleum: 89 mil; Other: 255 mil.

State data. Motto: Forward. **Flower:** Wood violet. **Bird:** Robin. **Tree:** Sugar maple. **Song:** On, Wisconsin! **Entered union** May 29, 1848; rank, 30th. **State fair** at West Allis; early Aug.

History. At the time of European contact, Ojibwa, Menominee, Winnebago, Kickapoo, Sauk, Fox, and Potawatomi peoples inhabited the area. French explorer Jean Nicolet reached Green Bay, 1634; French missionaries and fur traders followed. The British took over, 1763. The U.S. won the land after the American Revolution but did not wield control until forts were established at Green Bay and Prairie du Chien, 1816. Native Americans rebelled against the seizure of tribal lands in the Black Hawk War, 1832, but were defeated and relocated to reservations. Wisconsin became a territory, 1836, and a state, 1848. Some 96,000 soldiers served the Union cause during the Civil War. Many immigrants arrived from Germany, Poland, and Scandinavia. Wisconsin agriculture focused on dairy; Milwaukee became a manufacturing center. As gov., 1901-06, Robert La Follette pushed Progressive reforms such as direct primary voting and consumer protection laws. An era of "McCarthyism" ended when anti-Communist crusader Sen. Joseph McCarthy (R, WI) was censured by the U.S. Senate, 1954.

Tourist attractions. Old Wade House & Carriage Museum, Greenbush; Villa Louis, Prairie du Chien; Circus World Museum, Baraboo; Wisconsin Dells; Old World Wisconsin, Eagle; Door County peninsula; Chequamegon and Nicolet natl. forests; Lake Winnebago; House on the Rock, Dodgeville; Monona Terrace, Madison.

Famous Wisconsinites. Don Ameche, Carrie Chapman Catt, Willem Dafoe, Edna Ferber, Hamlin Garland, King Camp Gillette, Harry Houdini, Robert La Follette, Alfred Lunt, Pat O'Brien, Georgia O'Keeffe, William H. Rehnquist, John Ringling, Donald K. "Deke" Slayton, Spencer Tracy, Thorstein Veblen, Orson Welles, Laura Ingalls Wilder, Thornton Wilder, Frank Lloyd Wright.

Tourist information. Wisconsin Dept. of Tourism, 201 W. Washington Ave., PO Box 8690, Madison, WI 53708-8690; 1-800-432-TRIP; www.travelwisconsin.com

Website. www.wisconsin.gov

Wyoming (WY)
Equality State, Cowboy State

People. Population (2006 est.): 515,004; rank: 51; **net change** (2005-2006): 1.2%. **Pop. density:** 5.3 per sq mi. **Racial distribution** (2005): 94.8% white; 0.9% black; 0.6% Asian; 2.4% Native/Nat. AK; 0.07% Hawaiian/Pacific Islander; 2 or more races, 1.2%. **Hispanic pop.** (any race): 6.7%.

Geography. Total area: 97,814 sq mi; rank: 10. **Land area:** 97,100 sq mi; rank: 9. **Acres forested:** 11.0 mil. **Location:** Mountain state lying in the high western plateaus of the Great Plains. **Climate:** semi-desert conditions throughout; true desert in the Big Horn and Great Divide basins. **Topography:** the eastern Great Plains rise to the foothills of the Rocky Mts.; the Continental Divide crosses the state from the NW to the SE. **Capital:** Cheyenne.

Economy. Chief industries: mineral extraction, oil, natural gas, tourism and recreation, agriculture. **Chief manuf. goods:** petroleum, chemicals, fabricated metal, beet sugar, lumber. **Chief crops:** hay, sugar beets, barley, dry beans, wheat, corn, greenhouse & nursery, oats. **Livestock** (Jan. 2007): 1.4 mil cattle/calves; 460,000 mil sheep/lambs; (Dec. 2006): 100,000 hogs/pigs, 16,000 chickens (excl. broilers). **Timber/lumber** (est. 2006): 164 mil bd. ft.; ponderosa & lodgepole pine, Douglas fir, Engelmann spruce. **Nonfuel minerals** (preliminary 2006): $1.3 bil; soda ash, clays (bentonite), helium (grade-A), sand and gravel (construction), cement (portland). **Gross state product** (est. 2006): $29.6 bil. **Sales tax** (2007): 4.0%. **Employment distrib.** (May 2007): 23.7% govt.; 19.1% trade/trans./util.; 3.5% mfg.; 8.1% ed./health; 6.3% prof./bus. serv.; 11.4% leisure/hosp.; 4.0% finance; 8.9% constr.; 3.9% other serv.; 1.4% info. **Unemployment** (2006): 3.2%. **Per cap. pers. income** (2006): $40,676. **New private housing** (2006): 3,537 units/$638.8 mil. **Commercial banks** (2006): 49; **deposits:** $9.1 bil. **Savings institutions** (2006): 4; **deposits:** $383 mil. **Lottery** (2006): total sales: $508.9 mil; profit: $150.6 mil.

Federal govt. Fed. civ. employees (Mar. 2006): 4,759; **avg. salary:** $54,952. **Notable fed. facilities:** Warren AFB.

Energy. Electricity production (est. 2006, kWh by source): Coal: 42.6 bil; Gas: 59 mil; Hydroelectric: 846 mil; Petroleum: 45 mil; Other: 20 mil.

State data. Motto: Equal Rights. **Flower:** Indian Paintbrush. **Bird:** Western Meadowlark. **Tree:** Plains Cottonwood. **Song:** Wyoming. **Entered union** July 10, 1890; rank, 44th. **State fair** at Douglas; mid-Aug.

History. Inhabited for at least 12,000 years, the region supported Shoshone, Crow, Cheyenne, Oglala Sioux, and Arapaho peoples when Europeans arrived. France's Vérendrye brothers were the first Europeans to see the region, 1742-43. John Colter, an American, traversed the Yellowstone area, 1807-8. Trappers and fur traders followed in the 1820s. Forts Laramie and Bridger became important stops on trails to the West Coast. Population grew after the Union Pacific crossed the state, 1867-68. Wyoming became a territory, 1868, and the first to extend full voting rights to women, 1869. Statehood was attained, 1890. Disputes between large landowners and small ranchers culminated in the Johnson County Cattle War, 1892; federal troops were called in to restore order. Nellie Tayloe Ross was the first woman governor to take office in the U.S., 1925. Wyoming, the least populous state, has relied on the energy, tourism, and ranching industries in recent decades. Dick Cheney, Wyoming's representative in the U.S. House, 1979-89, became U.S. vice pres., 2001.

Tourist attractions. Yellowstone Natl. Park, the first U.S. national park, est. 1872; Grand Teton Natl. Park; Natl. Elk Refuge; Devils Tower Natl. Monument; Ft. Laramie Natl. Hist. Site and nearby pioneer trail ruts; Buffalo Bill Historical Center, Cody; Cheyenne Frontier Days.

Famous Wyomingites. James Bridger, William F. "Buffalo Bill" Cody, Curt Gowdy, Esther Hobart Morris, Jackson Pollock, Nellie Tayloe Ross.

Tourist information. Wyoming Travel and Tourism, I-25 at College Dr., Cheyenne, WY 82002; 1-800-225-5996; www.wyomingtourism.org

Website. www.wyoming.gov

District of Columbia (DC)

People. Population (2006 est.): 581,530; rank: 50; **net change** (2005-2006): -0.1%. **Pop. density:** 9,518.7 per sq mi. **Racial distribution** (2005): 38.0% white; 57.0% black; 3.1% Asian; 0.3% Native/Nat. AK; 0.07% Hawaiian/Pacific Islander; 2 or more races, 1.6%. **Hispanic pop.** (any race): 8.6%.

Geography. Total area: 68 sq mi; rank: 51. **Land area:** 61 sq mi; rank: 51. **Location:** at the confluence of the Potomac and Anacostia rivers, flanked by Maryland on the N, E, and SE and by Virginia on the SW. **Climate:** hot humid summers, mild winters. **Topography:** low hills rise toward the N away from the Potomac R. and slope to the S; highest elevation, 410 ft, lowest Potomac R., 1 ft.

Economy. Chief industries: government, legal, publishing, medical, service, tourism. **Gross product** (est. 2006): $87.7 bil. **Sales tax** (2007): 5.75%. **Employment distrib.** (May 2007): 33.3% govt.; 4.0% trade/trans./util.; 0.2% mfg.; 13.4% ed./health; 22.9% prof./bus. serv.; 8.1% leisure/hosp.; 4.3% finance; 1.8% constr.; 8.7% other serv.; 3.2% info. **Unemployment** (2006): 6.0%. **Per cap. pers. income** (2006): $55,755. **New private housing** (2006): 2,105 units/ $299.5 mil. **Commercial banks** (2006): 24; **deposits:** $20.9 bil. **Savings institutions** (2006): 8; **deposits:** $3.3 bil. **Lottery** (2006): total sales: $266.2 mil; profit: $73.4 mil.

Federal govt. Fed. civ. employees (Mar. 2006): 138,622; **avg. salary:** $87,195.

District data. Motto: Justitia omnibus (Justice for all). **Flower:** American beauty rose. **Tree:** Scarlet oak. **Bird:** Wood thrush.

History. The District of Columbia, coextensive with the city of Washington, is the seat of the U.S. federal government. It lies on the west central edge of Maryland on the Potomac River, opposite Virginia. The Piscataway, an Algonquian-speaking people, were living in the region when Europeans arrived in the 17th cent. Proposals for a "federal town" for the deliberations of the Continental Congress were made in 1783. Authorized by Congress, 1790, Pres. George Washington chose the Potomac site and persuaded landowners to sell their holdings to the government. Its area was originally 100 sq mi taken from the sovereignty of Maryland and Virginia. Virginia's portion south of the Potomac was given back to that state in 1846.

Pres. Washington chose Pierre Charles L'Enfant, a Frenchman, to plan the capital. Surveyor Andrew Ellicott finished the official map and design of the city, assisted by Benjamin Banneker, a black architect and astronomer. Pres. Washington laid the cornerstone of the north wing of the Capitol building, 1793, and Pres. John Adams moved to the new national capital, 1800. The City of Washington was incorporated, 1802. British troops invaded, 1814, setting fire to the Capitol, the President's House (as the White House was then called), and other buildings. Pres. Lincoln ended slavery in the district, 1862. Many African Americans arrived after the Civil War, but racial segregation remained legal until the mid-20th cent. After federal government expansion spurred population growth, 1930-50, an exodus to the suburbs shrank the city's population, 1950-2005.

The 23rd Amendment (1961) granted residents the right to vote for president and vice president. Congress, which has legislative authority over the District under the Constitution, approved legislation in 1970 giving the District one delegate to the House of Representatives, who could vote in committee but not on the floor. Voters approved, 1974, a congressionally drafted charter giving them the right to elect their own mayor and city council. The district won the right to levy taxes, but Congress retained power to veto council actions and approve the city budget. Security measures were dramatically increased after terrorists attacked the U.S. on Sept. 11, 2001. After a 34-year absence, major league baseball returned to the city in 2005.

Tourist attractions. *See* Washington, DC, Capital of the U.S., page 586.

Famous Washingtonians. Edward Albee, Frederick Douglass, John Foster Dulles, Duke Ellington, Katherine Graham, Goldie Hawn, J. Edgar Hoover, Pete Sampras, John Philip Sousa.

Tourist information. Washington, DC Convention and Tourism Corp., 901 7th St NW, 4th Fl., Washington, D.C., 20001-3719; (202) 789-7000; www.washington.org

Website. www.dc.gov

OUTLYING U.S. AREAS

American Samoa (AS)

People. Population (July 2007 est.): 57,663. **Population growth rate** (2006-07 est.): −0.3%. **Pop. density:** 749 per sq mi. **Ethnic distrib.** (2000): 92.9% Pacific Islander; 2.9% Asian; 1.2% white; 2.8% 2 or more races. **Languages:** Samoan, English.

Geography. Total area: 77 sq mi. **Land area:** 77 sq mi. **Location:** American Samoa is the most southerly of all lands under U.S. sovereign, about 2,300 mi. SW of Honolulu. It is an unincorporated territory consisting of 7 small islands of the Samoan group: **Tutuila** (52.59 sq mi), **Aunu'u** (0.59 sq mi), **Manu'a Group: Ta'u** (17.57 sq mi), **Olosega** (2.03 sq mi), **Ofu** (2.83 sq mi) and the atolls **Rose** (0.03 sq mi) and **Swains** (1.38 sq mi). **Climate:** Marine tropical, avg. temp 82°F with little seasonal variation; avg. annual rainfall about 36 in. **Topography:** volcanic islands, rugged peaks, and limited coastal plains. About 70% of the land is bush and mountains. **Capital:** Pago Pago on Tutuila. **Chief airport at:** Pago Pago.

Economy. Chief industries: tuna fishing and processing, trade, services, tourism. **Chief crops:** giant taro, taro, yams,

coconuts, breadfruits, bananas, papayas. **Livestock** (2003): 300 cattle; 68,372 chickens; 64,208 hogs/pigs. **Commercial fishing** (2006): $11.7 mil. **Fed. employees** (2005): 70. **Unemployment** (2005): 29.8%. **Gross domestic product** (2003 est.): $510 mil. **Commercial banks** (2006): 2; **deposits:** $177 mil.

Energy. Electricity production (2005): 189 mil. kWh.

Misc. data: Motto: Samoa Muamua le Atua (In Samoa, God Is First). **Song:** Amerika Samoa. **Flower:** Paogo (Ula-fala). **Plant:** Ava.

History. A tripartite agreement between Great Britain, Germany, and the U.S. in 1899 gave the U.S. sovereignty over the eastern islands of the Samoan group; these islands became American Samoa. Local chiefs ceded Tutuila and Aunu'u to the U.S. in 1900, and the Manu'a group and Rose Island in 1904; Swains Island was annexed in 1925. Samoa (Western), comprising the larger islands of the Samoan group, was a New Zealand mandate and UN Trusteeship until it became independent Jan. 1, 1962 (now called Samoa).

From 1900 to 1951, American Samoa was under the jurisdiction of the U.S. Navy. Since 1951, it has been under the Interior Dept. On Jan. 3, 1978, the first popularly elected Samoan governor and lieutenant governor were inaugurated. Previously, the governor was appointed by the Sec. of the Interior. American Samoa has a bicameral legislature and elects a delegate to the U.S. House of Representatives who has a voice but no vote, except in committees.

Hurricane Val, 1991, caused $80 mil in damages. Scientists discovered a rapidly growing volcano, Vailulu'u, between Ta'u and Rose in 1975.

American Samoans are of Polynesian origin. They are nationals of the U.S.; as of 2000, 91,029 lived in the U.S., including 16,166 in Hawaii, 37,498 in California, and 8,049 in Washington.

Tourist attractions. Rose Atoll; Vaitogi coast; Natl. Park of American Samoa; tropical rainforest.

Tourist information. Office of Tourism, Dept. of Commerce, American Samoa Govt., PO Box 1147, Pago Pago, AS 96799; (684) 699-9411; www.amsamoa.com/tourism

Website. www.americansamoa.gov

Guam (GU)

People. Population (July 2007 est.): 173,456. **Population growth rate** (2006-07 est.): 1.4%. **Pop. density:** 818 per sq mi. **Ethnic distrib.** (2000): 37.1% Chamorro, 26.3% Filipino, 11.3% other Pacific Islander, 6.9% white, 6.3% Asian, 2.3% other, 9.8% two or more race/ethnicities. **Languages:** English, Chamorro, Philippine/other Pacific Island languages.

Geography. Total area: 212 sq mi. **Land area:** 212 sq mi. **Location:** largest and southernmost of the Mariana Islands in the West Pacific, 3,700 mi W of Hawaii. **Climate:** tropical, with temperatures from 70° to 90° F; rainy July to Nov., avg. annual rainfall, about 80 to 100 in. **Topography:** coralline limestone plateau in the N; southern chain of low volcanic mountains sloping gently to the W, more steeply to coastal cliffs on the E; general elevation, 500 ft; highest point, Mt. Lamlam, 1,334 ft. **Capital:** Hagåtña. **Chief airport at:** Hagåtña.

Economy. Chief industries: U.S. military, tourism, construction, shipping, concrete products, printing & publishing. **Chief manuf. goods:** textiles, foods. **Chief crops:** watermelons, cucumbers, eggplant, long beans, bananas, bitter melons, taro, squash. **Livestock** (2002): 154 cattle; 2,703 chickens; 675 hogs/pigs. **Commercial fishing** (2006): $722,466. **Nonfuel minerals** (est. 2004): $13 mil; crushed stone. **Chief port:** Apra Harbor. **Gross domestic product** (2005 est.): $2.5 bil. **Employment distrib.** (Dec. 2005): 33.1% trade/trans; 26.2% serv.; 25.5% govt.; 7.7% constr.; 2.9% mfg.; 0.3% agric. **Unemployment** (2005): 7.0%. **Mean earner's income** (2003): $21,778. **Commercial banks** (2006): 6; **deposits:** $1.6 bil. **Savings institutions** (2006): 1; **deposits:** $44 mil.

Energy. Electricity production (2006): 1.8 bil. kWh.

Federal govt. Fed. employees (2005): 3,300. **Notable fed. facilities:** *Anderson AFB.

Misc. data. Motto: Where America's Day Begins. **Flower:** Puti Tai Nobio (Bougainvillea). **Bird:** Ko'ko (Guam Rail). **Tree:** Ifit (Intsia bijuga). **Song:** Stand Ye Guamanians.

History. Guam was probably settled by voyagers from the Indonesian-Philippine archipelago by 3rd cent. BCE. Pottery, rice cultivation, and megalithic technology show strong East Asian cultural influence. Centralized, village clan-based communities engaged in agriculture and offshore fishing. The estimated population by the early 16th cent. was 50,000-75,000. Magellan arrived in the Marianas Mar. 6, 1521. They were colonized in 1668 by Spanish missionaries, who named them the Mariana Islands in honor of Maria Anna, queen of Spain. When Spain ceded Guam to the U.S., it sold the other Marianas to Germany. Japan obtained a League of Nations mandate over the German islands in 1919; in Dec. 1941 it seized Guam, which was retaken by the U.S. in July-August 1944.

Guam is a self-governing organized unincorporated U.S. territory. The Organic Act of 1950 provided for a governor, elected to a 4-year term, and a 21-member unicameral legislature, elected biennially by the residents, who are American citizens. In 1970, the first governor was elected. In 1972, a U.S. law gave Guam one delegate to the U.S. House of Representatives who has a voice but no vote, except in committees.

Guam's quest to change its status to a U.S. Commonwealth began in the late 1970s. The Guam Commission on Self-Determination, created in 1984, developed a draft Com-

monwealth Act. In 1993, legislation proposing a change of status was submitted to the U.S. Congress. In 1994, the U.S. Congress passed legislation transferring 3,200 acres of land on Guam from federal to local control.

Typhoon Omar damaged 75-90% of the island's buildings, 1992. A Korean Air jetliner crashed and burned near Agana, 1997, killing 228 of 254 aboard.

Tourist attractions. Tropical climate, oceanic marine environment; Tarzan Falls; Plaza de España; beaches; water sports; duty-free port shopping.

Tourist information. Guam Visitors Bureau, 401 Pale San Vitores Rd., Tamuning, Guam 96913; (671) 646-5278; www.visitguam.org

Website. www.guam.gov

Commonwealth of the Northern Mariana Islands (MP)

People. Population (July 2007 est.): 84,546. **Population growth rate** (2006-07 est.): 2.5%. **Pop. density:** 459 per sq mi. **Ethnic distrib.** (2000): 56.3% Asian, 36.3% Pacific Islander, 1.8% white, 0.8% other, 4.8% two or more races/ethnicities. **Languages:** Philippine languages, Chinese, Chamorro, English.

Geography. Total area: 184.2 sq mi. **Land area:** 184.2 sq mi. **Location:** Between Guam and the Tropic of Cancer, the 14 islands of the Northern Marianas form a 300-mi. long archipelago. The indigenous population is concentrated on the 3 largest of the 6 inhabited islands: **Saipan,** the seat of government and commerce, **Rota,** and **Tinian. Climate.** Tropical, with avg. temperature around 82°F, moderated by northeast trade winds; avg. annual rainfall, 80-100 in. **Topography:** Limestone S islands with even terraces and coral reefs; volcanic N isles. **Capital:** Saipan. **Chief airport at:** Saipan.

Economy. Chief industries: mining, tourism, apparel mfg., retail. **Chief manuf. goods:** apparel, stone, clay and glass products. **Chief crops:** bananas, cucumbers, sweetpotatoes, chinese cabbage, taro. **Livestock** (2002): 1,319 cattle; 2,242 hogs/pigs; 7,027 chickens. **Commercial fishing** (2006): $815,108. **Chief port:** Saipan. **Gross domestic product** (2005): $900 mil. **Employment distrib.** (1999 est.): 35% manuf.; 18% managerial; 16% serv. **Fed. employees** (2005): 124. **Unemployment** (2002): 3.4%. **Commercial banks** (2006): 3; **deposits:** $471 mil. **Savings institutions** (2006): 1; **deposits:** $10 mil.

Misc. data. Flower: Plumeria. **Bird:** Mariana Fruit-dove. **Tree:** Flame Tree. **Song:** Gi Talo Gi Halom Tasi (In the middle of the sea).

History. The people of the Northern Marianas are predominantly of Chamorro cultural extraction, although Carolinians and immigrants from other areas of E. Asia and Micronesia have also settled in the islands. English is among the several languages commonly spoken.

The German-controlled Northern Marianas were placed under Japanese control by a League of Nations mandate after World War I. The U.S. captured the islands during World War II. From July 18, 1947, the U.S. had administered the Northern Marianas under a trusteeship agreement with the UN Security Council. In 1975, the residents voted to become a U.S. commonwealth.

The Northern Mariana Islands has been self-governing since 1978, when a constitution drafted and adopted by the people became effective and a popularly elected bicameral legislature (2-year term), with offices of governor (4-year term) and lieut. governor, was inaugurated. Pres. Ronald Reagan proclaimed the Northern Marianas a commonwealth, 1986, and the UN formally ended its trusteeship, 1990.

Under the 1976 Commonwealth Covenant with the U.S., the islands are exempt from federal immigration and import laws, and minimum wage is lower than on the mainland. The garment making industry, which has since boomed, has drawn accusations of sweatshop conditions from some critics. Legislation passed in 2007 will raise the minimum wage to the federal rate by 2015.

Tourist attractions. WWII sites; House of Taga; beaches; water sports; resorts; gambling.

Tourist information. Marianas Visitors Authority, PO Box 500861, Saipan, MP 96950; (670) 664-3200; www.mymarianas.com

Website. www.gov.mp

Commonwealth of Puerto Rico (PR)

(Estado Libre Asociado de Puerto Rico)

People. Population (2006 est.): 3,927,776 (about 3.8 mil. more Puerto Ricans reside in the mainland U.S.) **Population growth rate:** (2005-2006): 0.4%. **Pop. density:** 1,147 per sq mi. **Racial distribution** (2000): 80.5% white; 8.0% black; 0.2% Asian; 0.4% Native American/Nat. AK; 6.8% other; 2 or more races, 4.2%. **Hispanic pop.** (any race): 98.8%. **Languages:** Spanish and English are joint official languages.

Geography. Total area: 3,515 sq mi. **Land area:** 3,459 sq mi. **Location:** island lying between the Atlantic to the N and the Caribbean to the S; it is easternmost of the West Indies group called the Greater Antilles, of which Cuba, Hispaniola, and Jamaica are the larger islands. **Climate:** mild, with a mean temperature of 77°F. **Topography:** mountainous throughout three-fourths of its rectangular area, surrounded by a broken coastal plain; highest peak, Cerro de Punto, 4,390 ft. **Capital:** San Juan. **Chief airport at:** San Juan.

Economy. Chief industries: manufacturing, service, tourism. **Chief manuf. goods:** pharmaceuticals, medical equip., electronics, apparel, food products. **Chief crops:** pineapples, pumpkins, coffee, watermelons, plantains, bananas. **Livestock** (2005): 420,000 cattle; (Dec. 2006) 1.4 mil. chickens; 100,000 hogs/pigs; 16,000 sheep. **Commercial fishing** (2006): $3.8 mil. **Nonfuel minerals** (est. 2004): $187 mil; mostly crushed stone, portland cement. **Chief port:** San Juan. **Gross domestic product:** (est. 2006) $86.5 bil. **Employment distrib.** (May 2007): 28.7% govt.; 17.7% trade/trans./util.; 10.0% mfg.; 10.7% ed./health; 10.2% prof./bus. serv.; 7.0% leisure/hosp.; 4.9% finance; 6.5% constr.; 2.3% other serv.; 2.1% info. **Unemployment** (2006): 10.4%. **Per capita pers. income** (est. 2006): $12,997. **Commercial banks** (2006): 12; **deposits:** $59.1 bil. **Lottery** (2006): total sales: $334.5 mil; profit: $115.9 mil.

Federal govt. Fed. civ. employees (2005): 11,308. **Notable fed. facilities:** P.R. Natl. Guard Training Area at Camp Santiago, and at Ft. Allen, Juana Diaz; *U.S. Army Station at Ft. Buchanan; Int. Inst. of Tropical Forestry; Vieques Natl. Wildlife Ref.; USGS Caribbean Water Science Ctr.

Energy. Electricity production (2005): 24.5 bil kWh.

Misc. data. Motto: Joannes Est Nomen Eius (John is his name). **Flower:** Maga. **Bird:** Reinita. **Tree:** Ceiba. **National anthem:** La Borinqueña.

History. Puerto Rico (or Borinquen, after the original Arawak Indian name, Boriquen) was visited by Columbus on his second voyage, Nov. 19, 1493. In 1508, the Spanish arrived.

Sugarcane was introduced, 1515, and slaves were imported 3 years later. Gold mining petered out, 1570. Spaniards fought off a series of British and Dutch attacks; slavery was abolished, 1873. Under the treaty of Paris, Puerto Rico was ceded to the U.S. after the Spanish-American War, 1898. In 1952 the people voted in favor of Commonwealth status.

The Commonwealth of Puerto Rico is a self-governing part of the U.S. with a primarily Hispanic culture. The island's citizens have virtually the same control over their internal affairs as do the 50 states of the U.S. However, they do not vote in national general elections, only in national primaries.

Puerto Rico is represented in the U.S. House of Representatives by a Resident Commissioner who has a voice but no vote, except in committees.

No federal income tax is collected from residents on income earned from local sources in Puerto Rico. Nevertheless, as part of the U.S. legal system, Puerto Rico is subject to the provisions of the U.S. Constitution; most federal laws apply as they do in the 50 states.

Puerto Rico's famous "Operation Bootstrap," begun in the late 1940s, succeeded in changing the island from "The Poorhouse of the Caribbean" to an area with the highest per capita income in Latin America. This program encouraged manufacturing and development of the tourist trade by selective tax exemption, low-interest loans, and other incentives. Despite the marked success of Puerto Rico's development efforts over an extended period of time, per capita income in Puerto Rico is low in comparison to that of the 50 states.

In plebiscites held in 1967, 1993, and 1998, voters chose to retain Commonwealth status. Protests mounted in the late-1990s over the U.S. Navy's use of Vieques Island for live ammunition training; official military exercises there were terminated, 2003.

Tourist attractions. Ponce Museum of Art; Forts El Morro and San Cristobal; Old Walled City of San Juan; Arecibo Observatory; Cordillera Central and state parks; El Yunque Rain Forest; San Juan Cathedral; Porta Coeli Chapel and Museum of Religious Art, Interamerican Univ., San Germán; Condado Convention Center; Casa Blanca, Ponce de León family home, Puerto Rican Family Museum of 16th and 17th centuries, and Fine Arts Center, all in San Juan.

Cultural facilities and events. Festival Casals classical music concerts, mid-June; Puerto Rico Symphony Orchestra at Music Conservatory; Botanical Garden and Museum of Anthropology, Art, and History at the University of Puerto Rico; Institute of Puerto Rican Culture, at the Dominican Convent.

Famous Puerto Ricans. Julia de Burgos, Marta Casals Istomin, Pablo Casals, José Celso Barbosa, Orlando Cepeda, Roberto Clemente, José de Diego, José Feliciano, Doña Felisa Rincón de Gautier, Luis A. Ferré, José Ferrer, Commodore Diégo E. Hernández, Miguel Hernández Agosto, Rafael Hernández (El Jibarito), Rafael Hernández Colón, Raúl Julía, René Marqués, Ricky Martin, Concha Meléndez, Rita Moreno, Luis Muñoz Marín, Luis Palés Matos, Adm. Horacio Rivero.

Tourist information. The Puerto Rico Tourism Company, La Princesa Bldg., #2 Paseo La Princesa, Old San Juan, PR 00902; 1-800-866-7827; www.gotopuertorico.com

Website. www.gobierno.pr (site is in Spanish)

Virgin Islands (VI)

St. John, St. Croix, St. Thomas

People. Population (July 2007 est.): 108,448. **Population growth rate** (2006-07 est.): −0.2%. **Pop. density:** 803 per sq mi. **Ethnic distrib.** (2000): 76.2% black; 13.1% white; 1.1% Asian; 6.1% other races; 3.5% two or more races. **Languages:** English (official), Spanish, Creole.

Geography. Total area: 136 sq mi. **Land area:** 135 sq mi. **Location:** 3 larger and 50 smaller islands and cays in the S and W of the V.I. group (British V.I. colony to the N and E), which is situated 70 mi E of Puerto Rico, located W of the Anegada Passage, a major channel connecting the Atlantic Ocean and the Caribbean Sea. **Climate:** subtropical; the sun tempered by gentle trade winds; humidity is low; average temperature, 78° F. **Topography:** St. Thomas is mainly a ridge of hills running E and W, and has little tillable land; St. Croix rises abruptly in the N but slopes to the S to flatlands and lagoons; St. John has steep, lofty hills and valleys with little level tillable land. **Capital:** Charlotte Amalie on St. Thomas. **Chief airport at:** Charlotte Amalie.

Economy. Chief industries: retail, petroleum, tourism, prof. consulting. **Chief manuf. goods:** rum, stone, glass & clay products, electronics, textiles. **Chief crops:** cucumbers, mangoes, tomatoes, bananas, lettuce. **Livestock** (2002): 2,223 cattle; 1,830 chickens; 1,085 hogs/pigs; 2,389 sheep; 2,223 goats. **Commercial fishing** (2006): $10.7 mil. **Minerals:** stone, crushed limestone, traprock. **Chief port:** Charlotte Amalie. **Gross domestic product** (2004 est.): $1.6 bil. **Fed. employees** (2005): 690. **Unemployment** (2006 est.): 6.2%. **Per capita income** (2001 est.): $19,000. **Commercial banks** (2006): 4; **deposits:** $1.9 bil.

Energy. Electricity production (2004): 980 mil. kWh.

Misc. data. Motto: United in Pride and Hope. **Flower:** Yellow cedar. **Bird:** Yellow breast. **Song:** Virgin Islands March.

History. The islands were visited by Columbus in 1493. Spanish forces, 1555, defeated the Caribes and claimed the territory; by 1596 the native population was annihilated. First permanent settlement in the U.S. territory, 1672, by the Danes; U.S. purchased the islands, 1917, for defense purposes.

The Virgin Islands has a republican form of government, headed by a governor and lieut. governor elected, since 1970, by popular vote for 4-year terms. There is a 15-member unicameral legislature, elected by popular vote for a 2-year term. Residents of the V.I. have been U.S. citizens since 1927. Since 1973 they have elected a delegate to the U.S. House of Representatives, who has a voice but no vote, except in committees.

Hurricane Hugo, 1989, caused $500 mil in damages; U.S. troops were deployed to suppress looting and unrest.

Tourist attractions. Magens Bay, St. Thomas; duty-free shopping; Virgin Islands Natl. Park; beaches, Indian relics, and evidence of colonial Danes.

Tourist information. USVI Division of Tourism, 78-123 Estate Contant, Charlotte Amalie, St. Thomas 00804; 1-800-372-USVI; www.usvitourism.vi
Website. www.vi.gov

Other Islands

Navassa lies between Haiti and Jamaica, 100 mi S of Guantanamo Bay, Cuba, in the Caribbean; it covers 1,147 acres, and is uninhabited. Claimed 1857, USCG lighthouse built 1917, now inoperative. Natl. Wildlife Refuge since 1999. Administered by the Dept. of Interior.

The three coral islands of **Wake Atoll**—**Wake, Wilkes,** and **Peale**—lie in the Pacific Ocean on the direct route from Hawaii to Hong Kong, about 2,300 mi W of Honolulu and 1,500 mi NE of Guam. The group is 4.5 mi long, 1.5 mi wide. Land area totals 2.5 sq mi. The U.S. annexed Wake Atoll Jan. 17, 1899. Japan occupied Wake 1941-45. Designated a Natl. Hist. Landmark in 1985. Wake is owned by the U.S. Air Force, administered by the Dept. of Interior, but used by the Army as a missile launch facility. The population consists of military

personnel and contractors. Most infrastructure damaged by super typhoon Ioke in 2006.

The following mostly uninhabited islands are part of **The Pacific/Remote Islands Natl. Wildlife Refuge Complex** administered by the Dept. of Interior: **Midway Atoll,** acquired in 1867, has 3 main islands—Sand, Spit, and Eastern—1,250 mi WNW of Honolulu, with an area of about 1,500 acres. Naval activity ended in 1997. Has the world's largest colony of Laysan albatross. **Johnston Atoll,** 800 mi WSW of Honolulu, is 2 natural & 2 man-made islands across 107 sq mi administered by the Navy. Johnston was a nuclear test site in 1958, 1962; the Army disposed of chemical weapons 1990-2000. Cleanup ended in 2005. **Kingman Reef** is a barren, coral atoll 932 mi S of Hawaii, annexed 1922. **Palmyra Atoll** is 54 islets over 753 sq mi, 1,052 mi S of Hawaii; annexed with Hawaii in 1898. Part privately owned by the Nature Conservancy. **Jarvis Island** covers 1,086 acres, 1,300 mi S of Honolulu near the equator. West of Jarvis are **Howland & Baker Islands,** 36 mi apart and about 1,600 mi SW of Honolulu.

WASHINGTON, DC, CAPITAL OF THE U.S.

Most attractions are free. All times are subject to change. For more details call the Washington, DC, Convention and Visitors Association at 1-800-422-8644, or visit www.washington.org

Bureau of Engraving and Printing

The **Bureau of Engraving and Printing** of the U.S. Treasury Dept. is the headquarters for the making of U.S. paper money. Public tours are offered Mon.-Fri., 9-10:45 AM, 12:30-2 PM (later in summer), except on federal holidays. 14th and C Sts. SW; 866-874-2330. **Website:** www.moneyfactory.gov

Capitol

The **United States Capitol** was originally designed by Dr. William Thornton, an amateur architect, who submitted a plan in 1793 that won him $500 and a city lot. Three other architects designed or supervised the construction of the Capitol before its completion.

The present cast iron dome at its greatest exterior height measures 135 ft, 5 in. and is topped by the bronze Statue of Freedom, which stands 19½ ft and weighs 14,985 lb. On its base are the words E Pluribus Unum ("Out of Many, One").

The Capitol is open to the public, for guided tours only, Mon.-Sat., 9 AM-4:30 PM. It is closed Jan. 1, Thanksgiving Day, and Dec. 25.

To observe debate while Congress is in session, those living in the U.S. may obtain tickets from their U.S. representative or senator. Visitors from other countries may obtain passes at the Capitol. Between Constitution & Independence Aves., at Pennsylvania Ave.; (202) 225-6827.
Website: www.aoc.gov

Federal Bureau of Investigation

The **Federal Bureau of Investigation** offers guided one-hour tours of its headquarters. Visitors learn about the history of the FBI and see weapons confiscated from famous gangsters, photos of most-wanted fugitives, the DNA laboratory, goods forfeited/seized in narcotics operations, and a sharp-shooting demonstration.

Tours have been suspended for building renovation. J. Edgar Hoover Bldg., Pennsylvania Ave., between 9th and 10th Sts. NW; (202) 324-3447. **Website:** www.fbi.gov

Folger Shakespeare Library

The **Folger Shakespeare Library,** on Capitol Hill, is a research institution holding rare books and manuscripts of the Renaissance period and the largest collection of Shakespearean materials in the world. Exhibit may be visited Mon.-Sat., 10 AM-4 PM, 201 E. Capitol St., SE; (202) 544-4600. **Website:** www.folger.edu

Holocaust Memorial Museum

The **U.S. Holocaust Memorial Museum** opened on Apr. 21, 1993. The museum documents the events of the Holocaust through permanent and temporary displays, interactive videos, and special lectures. The permanent exhibition is not recommended for children under age 11.

The museum is open daily, 10 AM-5:30 PM, except Yom Kippur and Dec. 25; extended hours Tues. and Thurs. (10 AM-7:50 PM) from Apr.-June. A limited number of free tickets are available at the door; advance tickets may be ordered for a

small fee at 1-800-400-9373. 100 Raoul Wallenberg Pl. SW; (202) 488-0400. **Website:** www.ushmm.org

Jefferson Memorial

Dedicated Apr. 13, 1943, the **Thomas Jefferson Memorial** stands on the south shore of the Tidal Basin in West Potomac Park. It is a circular stone structure that combines architectural elements of the dome of the Pantheon in Rome and the rotunda designed by Jefferson for the Univ. of Virginia.

The memorial is open daily, 24 hrs., staffed 9:30 AM-11:30 PM; closed Dec. 25. Has elevator and curb ramps for handicapped; (202) 426-6841. **Website:** www.nps.gov/thje

John F. Kennedy Center

The **John F. Kennedy Center for the Performing Arts** opened Sept. 8, 1971. Designed by Edward Durell Stone, it includes an opera house, a concert hall, several theaters, 2 restaurants, and a library. Free tours are available Mon.-Fri., 10 AM-5 PM and Sat. & Sun., 10 AM-1 PM. 2700 F St. NW; (202) 467-4600; 1-800-444-1324.
Website: www.kennedy-center.org

Korean War Veterans Memorial

Dedicated on July 27, 1995, the **Korean War Veterans Memorial** honors Americans who served in the war. Situated at the west end of the Mall, the triangular-shaped stone and steel memorial features a multiservice formation of 19 combat-ready troops clad in ponchos with the wind at their back. A granite wall, with images of men and women who served, juts into a pool of water, the Pool of Remembrance.

The memorial is open 8 AM-11:45 pm; closed Dec. 25. French Dr., SW across from Lincoln Memorial; (202) 426-6841. **Website:** www.nps.gov/kwvm

Library of Congress

Established by and for Congress in 1800, the **Library of Congress** extends its services to other government agencies and libraries, scholars, and the general public. It contains more than 134 mil. items in some 460 languages.

Exhibit halls are open to the public Mon.-Fri., 8:30 AM-9:30 PM; Sat., 8:30 AM-6:30 PM. The Library is closed all federal holidays. 101 Independence Ave., SE; (202) 707-8000. **Website:** www.loc.gov

Lincoln Memorial

Designed by Henry Bacon, the **Lincoln Memorial** in West Potomac Park is a large marble hall enclosing a statue of Abraham Lincoln seated on an armchair. The memorial was dedicated May 30, 1922. The statue was designed by Daniel Chester French and sculpted by French and the Piccirilli brothers. The text of the Gettysburg Address is in the south chamber; that of Lincoln's Second Inaugural speech is in the north chamber. Each is engraved on a stone tablet.

The memorial is open daily, 24 hrs., staffed 9:30 AM-11:30 PM, and is wheelchair-accessible. W. Potomac Park at 23rd St. NW; (202) 426-6841. **Website:** www.nps.gov/linc

National Archives and Records

Original copies of the Declaration of Independence, the Constitution, and the Bill of Rights are on display in the **National Archives** Exhibition Hall. The National Archives also holds other valuable U.S. government records and historic maps, photographs, and manuscripts. Central Research and Microfilm Research Rooms are also available to the public for genealogical research.

Exhibition Hall is open daily 10 AM-5:30PM (later in spring and summer). 7th & Pennsylvania Ave. NW; (202) 357-5450. **Website:** www.archives.gov

National Gallery of Art

The **National Gallery of Art** was established by Congress, Mar. 24, 1937, and opened Mar. 17, 1941. The original West building was designed by John Russell Pope. The East building, opened in 1978, was designed by I. M. Pei. Open daily, Mon.-Sat. 10 AM-5 PM, Sunday 11 AM-6 PM. Closed Jan. 1 and Dec. 25. 4th & Constitution Ave NW; (202) 737-4215. **Website:** www.nga.gov

Franklin Delano Roosevelt Memorial

Opened May 2, 1997, the **FDR Memorial** features 9 bronze sculptural ensembles depicting FDR, Eleanor Roosevelt, and events from the Great Depression and World War II. This 7.5-acre memorial is located near the Tidal Basin in a park-like setting and is wheelchair accessible.

Grounds, staffed daily, 8 AM-midnight, except Dec. 25. 1850 W. Basin Dr. SW; (202) 426-6841. **Website:** www.nps.gov/fdrm

Smithsonian Institution

The **Smithsonian Institution**, established in 1846, is the world's largest museum complex. It holds some 144 mil. artifacts and specimens in its trust. There are 15 museums and the National Zoo in the D.C. area. The **Smithsonian Information Center** is located in "the Castle" on the Mall. Also on the Mall are the **National Museum of American History** (closed until Summer '08), the **National Museum of Natural History**, the **National Air and Space Museum**, the **National Museum of the American Indian**, the **Hirshhorn Museum and Sculpture Garden**, the **Arthur M. Sackler & Freer Galleries of Art**, the **National Museum of African Art**, and the **Arts and Industries Building** (closed for renovation). Located nearby are the **National Postal Museum**, the **National Museum of American Art**, the **National Portrait Gallery**, and the **Renwick Gallery.** Farther away, at 1901 Fort Place SE, is the **Anacostia Museum.** The **Air and Space Museum's Udvar-Hazy Center** is near Dulles Airport in Virginia.

Most museums are open daily, except Dec. 25, 10 AM-5:30 PM (later in summer); (202) 633-1000. **Website:** www.si.edu

Vietnam Veterans Memorial

Originally dedicated Nov. 13, 1982, the **Vietnam Veterans Memorial** recognizes the men and women who served in the armed forces in the Vietnam War. The names of more than 58,000 Americans who lost their lives or remain missing are inscribed on a V-shaped black-granite wall, designed by Maya Ying Lin.

Since 1982, 2 additions have been made to the Memorial. The 1st, dedicated on Nov. 11, 1984, is the Frederick Hart sculpture *Three Servicemen*. On Nov. 11, 1993, the Vietnam Women's Memorial, designed by Glenna Goodacre, was dedicated, honoring the more than 11,500 women who served in Vietnam.

The memorial is open daily, 24 hrs., staffed 9:30 AM-11:30 PM. Constitution Ave. & Bacon Dr. NW; (202) 426-6841. **Website:** www.nps.gov/vive

Washington Monument

The **Washington Monument**, dedicated in 1885, is a tapering shaft, or obelisk, of white marble, 555 ft, 5 $1/8$ inches in height and 55 ft, 1½ in. square at base. Eight small windows, 2 on each side, are located at the 500-ft level.

Open daily, 9 AM-4:45 PM, except July 1, Dec. 25. Free timed passes are available; advance passes are available for a small fee. 15th & Constitution Ave. NW; (202) 426-6841. **Website:** www.nps.gov/wash

White House

The **White House,** the President's residence, stands on 18 acres on the south side of Pennsylvania Ave., between the Treasury and the old Executive Office Building. The walls are of sandstone, quarried at Aquia Creek, VA. The building was first made white with lime-based whitewash in 1798, but the name did not become official until 1901.

The White House is normally open for free self-guided tours of 10 or more Tues.-Sat., 7:30 AM-12:30 pm. (Tour requests must be made at least one month in advance through your member of Congress.) Only the public rooms on the ground floor and state floor may be visited. 1600 Pennsylvania Ave. The White House Visitor Center at 1450 Pennsylvania Ave. is open daily 7:30 AM-4 PM; (202) 456-7041. **Website:** www.whitehouse.gov

National World War II Memorial

The **National WWII Memorial** is dedicated to the approx. 16 mil. veterans who served and the more than 400,000 who died in the war. It rests on 7.4 acres of land at the east end of the reflecting pool on the Mall. The memorial opened on April 29, 2004, and was dedicated on May 29.

At the north and south entrances are 43-ft. archways, representing the Atlantic and Pacific theaters. Inside the grounds is a large, oval plaza with a wall of 4,000 gold stars; each represents 100 American deaths. Fifty-six pillars ringing the center represent the states, territories, and District of Columbia. There is also a garden enclosed by a stone wall, the Circle of Remembrance.

The memorial is wheelchair-accessible and open daily, 24 hrs., staffed 9:30 AM-11:30 PM, except Dec. 25. Located on 17th St. between Constitution and Independence Aves.; (202) 426-6841. **Website:** www.nps.gov/nwwm

Attractions Near Washington, DC

Arlington National Cemetery

Arlington National Cemetery, on the former Custis-Lee estate in Arlington, VA, is the site of the **Tomb of the Unknowns** and is the final resting place of Pres. W.H. Taft, John F. Kennedy and his wife, Jacqueline Bouvier Kennedy Onassis. An eternal flame burns over the grave site. Many other famous Americans are buried at Arlington, as well as more than 300,000 U.S. military personnel, from every major war.

North of the National Cemetery stands the **U.S. Marine Corps War Memorial**, also known as Iwo Jima. The memorial is a bronze statue of the raising of the U.S. flag on Mt. Suribachi, Feb. 23, 1945, during World War II, executed by Felix de Weldon from the photograph by Joe Rosenthal.

On the southern side of the Memorial Bridge, near the cemetery entrance, a memorial honoring the women in the military was dedicated Oct. 18, 1997. The **Women in Military Service for America Memorial** is a semicircular retaining wall 226 ft. long with a central niche 30 ft. high.

Open daily, 8 AM-5 PM (8 AM-7 PM, Apr.-Sept.), Arlington, VA; (703) 607-8000. **Website:** www.arlingtoncemetery.org

Mount Vernon

Mount Vernon, George Washington's estate, is on the south bank of the Potomac R., 16 mi from Washington, DC, in northern Virginia. The present house is believed to be an enlargement of one built by Augustine Washington in 1735. His son Lawrence renamed the estate after British Navy Adm. Edward Vernon. George Washington, Lawrence's half brother, inherited it in 1761. The estate has been restored to its 18th-century appearance and includes many original furnishings. Washington and his wife, Martha, are buried on the grounds.

Open 365 days, Apr.-Aug. 8 AM-5 PM; Mar., Sept.-Oct. 9 AM-5 PM; Nov.-Feb. 9 AM-4 PM; (703) 780-2000; 1-800-429-1520. Admission: adults $13, seniors (62+) $12, children (6-11) $6, age 5 and under free. **Website:** www.mountvernon. org

The Pentagon

The **Pentagon,** headquarters of the Dept. of Defense, is the largest office building in the U.S. It houses more than 23,000 employees in offices occupying 3,705,793 sq ft. The building was severely damaged when struck by a plane Sept. 11, 2001.

Group tours available to government agencies, educational institutions, or military units by reservation only. General public must contact their member of Congress to request a tour. Non U.S. citizens must contact their national embassy. Arlington, VA (I-395 South to Boundary Channel Drive exit); (703) 697-1776. **Website:** pentagon.afis.osd.mil

UNITED STATES POPULATION

Population Profile: New Milestones for Minorities, Rapid Growth in South and West

Source: U.S. Census Bureau, U.S. Dept. of Commerce

The U.S. reached a well-publicized population milestone in October 2006: an estimated population of 300 million. More recent population estimates show that the nation's minorities surpassed several other major milestones that year, including an overall minority population of 100 million—more than the 92.2 mil total population of the U.S. in 1910—as well as a black population of 40 million, and a Native Hawaiian and Pacific Islander population of 1 million. Hispanics remained the fastest-growing minority group, however, increasing by 3.4% between 2005 and 2006, and accounting for almost half of total U.S. population growth over that period. Asians ranked second with a growth rate of 3.2%; in comparison, the non-Hispanic, white-only population grew by a mere 0.3% over the same period.

Swelling Ranks of Majority-Minority States

Nearly 10% of U.S. counties, four states (Hawaii, New Mexico, California, and Texas), and the District of Columbia also achieved or maintained "majority-minority" status in 2006, with populations that were more than 50% minority. Denver County, CO, and East Baton Rouge, LA, were the two largest counties to achieve this milestone, while Los Angeles County retained its rank as the county with the largest minority population in the U.S.: 7 million, or 71% of the county's total population. Notably, Los Angeles County also had the largest population of non-Hispanic white-only residents (2.9 million). The county with the largest numerical increase in its minority population was Harris County, TX (home to the city of Houston), which gained 121,400 minority residents over this period.

Biggest, Fastest Growth Concentrated in West and South

Maricopa County, AZ, led all U.S. counties in sheer numerical population growth, gaining 696,000 residents between 2000 and 2006—bringing its total population to 3.8 million, the fourth-largest in the nation and a major contributor to Arizona's place as the fastest-growing U.S. state (up 3.6%) in 2005-06. Harris County, TX came in second, adding 486,000 residents to reach a total of 3.9 million. Three of the 10 counties that added the largest number of residents were in Texas and three in California.

Between 2005 and 2006, Texas gained more people (579,275) than any other state, followed by Florida (321,697) and California (303,402). Ranked by percentage growth, the West was the fastest-growing region, up 1.5%, followed closely by the South (1.4%) and more distantly by the Midwest (0.4%). Measured in numerical growth, the South led with an increase of 1.5 million residents between 2005 and 2006, followed by the West with 1 million, and only 281,000 in the Midwest. As of July 2006, 36% of all U.S. residents lived in the South, 23% in the West, 22% in the Midwest, and 18% in the Northeast.

Metropolitan areas with large numerical gains were also concentrated in the West and South, led by Atlanta with an 890,211-resident gain between 2000 and 2006—one of only six metropolitan areas that gained more than 500,000 people

in that period. Dallas-Forth Worth came in second, with an increase of 842,449, followed by Houston (824,547), Phoenix (787,306), and Riverside-San Bernardino-Ontario, CA (771,314). Twenty-five of the top 50 fastest-growing metro areas were located in the South, and 23 in the West; the fastest-growing metropolitan area in the Northeast, York-Hanover, PA, was ranked 95th in the nation.

New York City remained the most populous U.S. city, with 8.2 million residents—more than twice the population of Los Angeles, with 3.8 million. Yet after clocking the single largest population increase (43,000) of any U.S. city between 2005 and 2006, Phoenix displaced Philadelphia as the fifth most populous U.S. city in 2006, dramatically illustrating a century-long shift in U.S. population. The Census Bureau noted that in 1910, the 10 most populous cities were within approximately 500 miles of the Canadian border; nearly 100 years later, seven of the top 10 and three of the top five were in states bordering Mexico.

Predictably, New Orleans showed the largest population loss among cities with 100,000 or more people, losing more than half of its population from mid-2005 (452,170) to mid-2006 (223,388). The city with the second highest rate of loss, Hialeah, FL, dropped just 1.6% of its population over the same period. Among cities with a population of 100,000 or more, many of the fastest-growing were suburbs, first among them North Las Vegas, NV, with an increase of 11.9% in 2006. It was followed by three cities near Dallas: McKinney (in second place), Grand Prairie (sixth place) and Denton (tenth). Texas also boasted five of the top 10 cities with the highest numerical population gains from 2005 to 2006.

Households Shrink, but Little Change in Single-Parent Households

Despite these major population gains, the percentage of households headed by single parents has changed very little since 1994, remaining at approximately 9%. In 2006 there were 12.9 million single-parent households in the U.S., most of them headed by single women (10.4 million). Among children 17 and younger, 67% lived with two married parents in 2006; there were also an estimated 5.8 million stay-at-home parents, 5.6 million of them women.

Significant Earnings Gap Tied to Educational Attainment

In 2005, the latest year for which this data is available, adults 18 and older with an advanced degree earned an average of $79,946, more than four times the average of $19,915 earned by adults with less than a high school diploma. Adults with only a bachelor's degree earned an average of $54,689, and those with only a high school diploma earned $19,915. Fortunately, 86% of all adults 25 and older had completed high school, and 28% had earned a bachelor's degree or higher. Minnesota and Alaska were the states with the highest proportions of adults with at least a high school diploma, while the District of Columbia had the highest proportion with at least a bachelor's degree.

Census Origins and Methods

The U.S. census is conducted every 10 years as mandated by the Constitution, Article 1, Section 2. The primary purpose is to apportion seats in the House of Representatives and determine state legislative district boundaries. The data are also critical for a vast array of government programs and for providing demographic information to individuals and businesses.

The first U.S. census was conducted in 1790, a little more than a year after George Washington became president. It counted the number of free white males age 16 and over (to measure how many men might be available for military service), the number under 16, the number of free white females, all other free persons (including any American Indians who paid taxes), and slaves. It took 18 months to collect the data, at a cost of about $1 million in today's dollars. Census results from each enumeration district were re-

quired to be publicly displayed within that district, a practice that lasted through the 1840 census. The 1790 census, which counted a total of 3.9 million people, resulted in an increase of 41 seats (65 to 106) in the House of Representatives.

As the nation expanded, so did the scope of the census data. The first inquiry on manufacturing industries was made in 1810. Questions on agriculture, mining, and fisheries were added in 1840. In 1850, the census included questions on social issues—taxation, churches, poverty, and crime.

The 1880 census had so many questions that it took the full 10 years between censuses to publish all the results. Because of this delay, Congress limited the 1900 census to questions on population, manufactures, agriculture, and mortality. Many of the dropped topics reappeared in later censuses.

Today, the secretary of commerce and the Census Bureau are directed by law to take censuses of population, housing, agriculture, irrigation, manufactures, mineral industries, other businesses (wholesale trade, retail trade, services), construction, transportation, and governments at stated intervals, and may take surveys related to any of these subjects.

U.S. marshals supervised the first 9 censuses and reported to the president (1790), the secretary of state (1800-40), or the secretary of the interior (1850-70). There was no continuity of personnel from one census to the next. In 1902, Congress authorized a permanent Census Office in the Interior Dept. In 1903, the agency was transferred to the new Dept. of Commerce and Labor, and when the department split in 1913, the Bureau of the Census was placed in the Commerce Dept.

The Census Bureau began using statistical sampling techniques in the 1940s, computers in the 1950s, and mail enumeration in the 1960s, all in an effort to publish more data sooner and at a lower cost, and with less burden on the public. For the 2010 Census, the Census Bureau plans to continue mailing questionnaires to most housing units in the country, but to use handheld computers, rather than paper and pencil, in doing follow-up interviews at nonresponding households.

Also, the 2010 Census will consist only of a short-form questionnaire. In previous censuses, about 5 in 6 households received the short form while 1 in 6 households received the long-form questionnaire, which asked questions about details such as ancestry, marital status, and occupation. The American Community Survey (ACS) replaces the need in 2010 for the long form. First implemented nationwide in 2005 and conducted yearly, the ACS gathers detailed demographic, economic, and housing information about America's communities.

25 Largest Counties, by Population, 2000, 2006

Source: Annual Population Estimates, 2000 Census, U.S. Census Bureau, U.S. Dept of Commerce
(ranked by 2006 population counts)

County	2006 population[1]	2000 population	Percent change	County	2006 population[1]	2000 population	Percent change
Los Angeles County, CA ...	9,948,081	9,519,338	4.5	King County, WA.........	1,826,732	1,737,034	5.2
Cook County, IL..........	5,288,655	5,376,741	-1.6	Broward County, FL	1,787,636	1,623,018	10.1
Harris County, TX.......	3,886,207	3,400,578	14.3	Clark County, NV........	1,777,539	1,375,765	29.2
Maricopa County, AZ......	3,768,123	3,072,149	22.7	Santa Clara County, CA ...	1,731,281	1,682,585	2.9
Orange County, CA	3,002,048	2,846,289	5.5	Tarrant County, TX	1,671,295	1,446,219	15.6
San Diego County, CA....	2,941,454	2,813,833	4.5	New York County, NY	1,611,581	1,537,195	4.8
Kings County, NY........	2,508,820	2,465,326	1.8	Bexar County, TX	1,555,592	1,392,931	11.7
Miami-Dade County, FL....	2,402,208	2,253,362	6.6	Suffolk County, NY	1,469,715	1,419,369	3.5
Dallas County, TX	2,345,815	2,218,899	5.7	Middlesex County, MA	1,467,016	1,465,396	0.1
Queens County, NY......	2,255,175	2,229,379	1.2	Alameda County, CA.....	1,457,426	1,443,741	0.9
Riverside County, CA.....	2,026,803	1,545,387	31.2	Philadelphia County, PA ...	1,448,394	1,517,550	-4.6
San Bernardino County, CA.	1,999,332	1,709,434	17.0	Sacramento County, CA...	1,374,724	1,223,499	12.4
Wayne County, MI	1,971,853	2,061,162	-4.3				

Note on least populated counties: The following are the 10 smallest counties by mid-year 2006 population: Loving County, TX (60); Kalawao County, HI (120); King County, TX (287); Arthur County, NE (372); Kenedy County, TX (402); Petroleum County, MT (474); Blaine County, NE (492); McPherson County, NE (497); San Juan County, CO (578); and Thomas County, NE (629).
(1) Population estimates are for July 1.

Population by State, 2000, 2006

Source: Annual Population Estimates, 2000 Census, U.S. Census Bureau, U.S. Dept. of Commerce
(ranked by 2006 population counts)

Rank	State	2006 population[1]	2000 population	Percent change 2000-06	Rank	State	2006 population[1]	2000 population	Percent change 2000-06
1.	California........	36,457,549	33,871,648	7.6	27.	Oregon	3,700,758	3,421,399	8.2
2.	Texas...........	23,507,783	20,851,820	12.7	28.	Oklahoma	3,579,212	3,450,654	3.7
3.	New York.......	19,306,183	18,976,457	1.7	29.	Connecticut.....	3,504,809	3,405,565	2.9
4.	Florida..........	18,089,888	15,982,378	13.2	30.	Iowa	2,982,085	2,926,324	1.9
5.	Illinois	12,831,970	12,419,293	3.3	31.	Mississippi	2,910,540	2,844,658	2.3
6.	Pennsylvania.....	12,440,621	12,281,054	1.3	32.	Arkansas.......	2,810,872	2,673,400	5.1
7.	Ohio............	11,478,006	11,353,140	1.1	33.	Kansas........	2,764,075	2,688,418	2.8
8.	Michigan	10,095,643	9,938,444	1.6	34.	Utah	2,550,063	2,233,169	14.2
9.	Georgia	9,363,941	8,186,453	14.4	35.	Nevada........	2,495,529	1,998,257	24.9
10.	North Carolina....	8,856,505	8,049,313	10.0	36.	New Mexico.....	1,954,599	1,819,046	7.5
11.	New Jersey.....	8,724,560	8,414,350	3.7	37.	West Virginia.....	1,818,470	1,808,344	0.6
12.	Virginia	7,642,884	7,078,515	8.0	38.	Nebraska.......	1,768,331	1,711,263	3.3
13.	Massachusetts ...	6,437,193	6,349,097	1.4	39.	Idaho..........	1,466,465	1,293,953	13.3
14.	Washington	6,395,798	5,894,121	8.5	40.	Maine	1,321,574	1,274,923	3.7
15.	Indiana	6,313,520	6,080,485	3.8	41.	New Hampshire ..	1,314,895	1,235,786	6.4
16.	Arizona	6,166,318	5,130,632	20.2	42.	Hawaii.........	1,285,498	1,211,537	6.1
17.	Tennessee.......	6,038,803	5,689,283	6.1	43.	Rhode Island	1,067,610	1,048,319	1.8
18.	Missouri........	5,842,713	5,595,211	4.4	44.	Montana	944,632	902,195	4.7
19.	Maryland	5,615,727	5,296,486	6.0	45.	Delaware	853,476	783,600	8.9
20.	Wisconsin	5,556,506	5,363,675	3.6	46.	South Dakota	781,919	754,844	3.6
21.	Minnesota	5,167,101	4,919,479	5.0	47.	Alaska.........	670,053	626,932	6.9
22.	Colorado	4,753,377	4,301,261	10.5	48.	North Dakota	635,867	642,200	-1.0
23.	Alabama	4,599,030	4,447,100	3.4	49.	Vermont	623,908	608,827	2.5
24.	South Carolina...	4,321,249	4,012,012	7.7	50.	District of Columbia	581,530	572,059	1.7
25.	Louisiana	4,287,768	4,468,976	-4.1	51.	Wyoming	515,004	493,782	4.3
26.	Kentucky........	4,206,074	4,041,769	4.1		**Total resident pop.[2]....**	**299,398,484**	**281,421,906**	**6.4**

(1) Population estimates are for July 1. (2) Resident population excludes military personnel and others living abroad and allocated to the state in total population count.

Density of Population by State, 1930-2000

Source: Decennial Censuses, U.S. Census Bureau, U.S. Dept. of Commerce

(per square mile, land area only)

State	1930	1960	1980	1990	2000	State	1930	1960	1980	1990	2000
AL......	51.8	64.2	76.6	79.6	87.6	MT......	3.7	4.6	5.4	5.5	6.2
AK	0.1	0.4	0.7	1.0	1.1	NE......	18.0	18.4	20.5	20.5	22.3
AZ......	3.8	11.5	23.9	32.3	45.2	NV......	0.8	2.6	7.3	10.9	18.2
AR......	35.2	34.2	43.9	45.1	51.3	NH......	51.6	67.2	102.4	123.7	137.8
CA	36.2	100.4	151.4	190.8	217.2	NJ	537.3	805.5	986.2	1,042.0	1,134.5
CO	10.0	16.9	27.9	31.8	41.5	NM......	3.5	7.8	10.7	12.5	15.0
CT	328.0	520.6	637.8	678.4	702.9	NY......	262.6	350.6	370.6	381.0	401.9
DE	120.5	225.2	307.6	340.8	401.0	NC......	64.5	93.2	120.4	136.1	165.2
DC	7,981.5	12,523.9	10,132.3	9,882.8	9,378.0	ND......	9.7	9.1	9.4	9.3	9.3
FL......	27.1	91.5	180.0	239.6	296.4	OH......	161.6	236.6	263.3	264.9	277.3
GA	49.7	67.8	94.1	111.9	141.4	OK......	34.6	33.8	44.1	45.8	50.3
HI	57.5	98.5	150.1	172.5	188.6	OR......	9.9	18.4	27.4	29.6	35.6
ID	5.4	8.1	11.5	12.2	15.6	PA......	213.8	251.4	264.3	265.1	274.0
IL	136.4	180.4	205.3	205.6	223.4	RI......	649.8	819.3	897.8	960.3	1,003.2
IN	89.4	128.8	152.8	154.6	169.5	SC......	56.8	78.7	103.4	115.8	133.2
IA	44.1	49.2	52.1	49.7	52.4	SD......	9.1	9.0	9.1	9.2	9.9
KS	22.9	26.6	28.9	30.3	32.9	TN......	62.4	86.2	111.6	118.3	138.0
KY	65.2	76.2	92.3	92.8	101.7	TX......	22.1	36.4	54.3	64.9	79.6
LA	46.5	72.2	94.5	96.9	102.6	UT......	6.2	10.8	17.8	21.0	27.2
ME	25.7	31.3	36.3	39.8	41.3	VT......	38.8	42.0	55.2	60.8	65.8
MD	165.0	313.5	428.7	489.2	541.9	VA......	60.7	99.6	134.7	156.3	178.8
MA	537.4	657.3	733.3	767.6	809.8	WA......	23.3	42.8	62.1	73.1	88.6
MI.......	84.9	137.7	162.6	163.6	175.0	WV......	71.8	77.2	80.8	74.5	75.1
MN	32.0	43.1	51.2	55.0	61.8	WI......	53.7	72.6	86.5	90.1	98.8
MS	42.4	46.0	53.4	54.9	60.6	WY......	2.3	3.4	4.9	4.7	5.1
MO	52.4	62.6	71.3	74.3	81.2	**U.S......**	**41.2**	**50.6**	**64.0**	**70.3**	**79.6**

Note: For purposes of comparison, Alaska and Hawaii are included in above tabulation for 1930, even though not states then.

U.S. Area and Population, 1790-2000

Source: Decennial Censuses, U.S. Census Bureau, U.S. Dept. of Commerce

Census date	AREA (square miles)			POPULATION		Increase over preceding census	
	Gross area[1]	Land area	Water area[1]	Number	Per sq mi of land	Number	%
1790 (Aug. 2)	891,364	864,746	24,065	3,929,214	4.5	—	—
1800 (Aug. 4)	891,364	864,746	24,065	5,308,483	6.1	1,379,269	35.1
1810 (Aug. 6)	1,722,685	1,681,828	34,175	7,239,881	4.3	1,931,398	36.4
1820 (Aug. 7)	1,792,552	1,749,462	38,544	9,638,453	5.5	2,398,572	33.1
1830 (June 1)[2]	1,792,552	1,749,462	38,544	12,866,020	7.4	3,227,567	33.5
1840 (June 1)[2]	1,792,552	1,749,462	38,544	17,069,453	9.8	4,203,433	32.7
1850 (June 1)	2,991,655	2,940,042	52,705	23,191,876	7.9	6,122,423	35.9
1860 (June 1)	3,021,295	2,969,640	52,747	31,443,321	10.6	8,251,445	35.6
1870 (June 1)	3,612,299	3,540,705	52,747	39,818,449[3]	11.2	8,375,128	26.6
1880 (June 1)	3,612,299	3,540,705	52,747	50,189,209	14.2	10,370,760	26.0
1890 (June 1)	3,612,299	3,540,705	52,747	62,979,766	17.8	12,790,557	25.5
1900 (June 1)	3,618,770	3,547,314	52,553	76,212,168	21.5	13,232,402	21.0
1910 (Apr. 15)	3,618,770	3,547,045	52,822	92,228,496	26.0	16,016,328	21.0
1920 (Jan. 1)	3,618,770	3,546,931	52,936	106,021,537	29.9	13,793,041	15.0
1930 (Apr. 1)	3,618,770	3,551,608	45,259	123,202,624	34.7	17,181,087	16.2
1940 (Apr. 1)	3,618,770	3,551,608	45,259	132,164,569	37.2	8,961,945	7.3
1950 (Apr. 1)	3,618,770	3,552,206	63,005	151,325,798	42.6	19,161,229	14.5
1960 (Apr. 1)	3,618,770	3,540,911	74,212	179,323,175	50.6	27,997,377	18.5
1970 (Apr. 1)	3,618,770	3,536,855	78,444	203,302,031	57.5	23,978,856	13.4
1980 (Apr. 1)[4]	3,618,770	3,539,289	79,481	226,542,199	64.0	23,240,168	11.4
1990 (Apr. 1)[5]	3,717,796	3,536,278	181,518	248,718,302	70.3	22,176,103	9.8
2000 (Apr. 1)[6]	3,794,083	3,537,438	256,645	281,424,602	79.6	32,706,300	13.1

Note: Percent changes are computed on the basis of change in population since the preceding census date, so the period covered is not always exactly 10 years. Population density figures given for various years represent the area within the boundaries of the U.S. that was under its jurisdiction on the date in question—including, in some cases, considerable areas not organized or settled and not actually covered by the census. In 1870, for example, Alaska was not covered by the census, but its area is included in density calculations. Population figures shown here may reflect corrections made to the initial tabulated census counts. (1) Figure for 1990 includes inland, coastal, and Great Lakes water. Figure for 2000 includes additional territorial water as determined by presidential decree in Dec. 1998. Figures for 1790 to 1980 cover inland water only. (2) The U.S. total includes persons (5,318 in 1830; 6,100 in 1840) on public ships in the service of the U.S. not credited to any region, division, or state. (3) Revised to include adjustments for underenumeration in southern states; unrevised number is 38,558,371. (4) Total pop. count has been revised since the 1980 census publications. Numbers by age, race, Hispanic origin, and sex have not been corrected. (5) Census count includes count question resolution corrections processed through Dec. 1997 and does not include adjustments for census coverage errors. (6) Total pop. count reflects modifications to the 2000 census population as documented in the Count Question Resolution program.

Congressional Apportionment
Source: Decennial Censuses, U.S. Census Bureau, U.S. Dept. of Commerce

The Constitution, in Article 1, Section 2, provided for a census of the population every 10 years to serve as a basis for apportionment of representatives among the states. This apportionment largely determines the number of electoral votes allotted to each state.

The number of representatives of each state in Congress is determined by the state's population, though each state is entitled to one representative regardless of population size. A congressional apportionment has been made after each decennial census except that of 1920. (The year above each column is the year of the census on which apportionment for the next election year is based.) Prior to 1870, $3/5$ the number of slaves were added to the total free population. Indians "not taxed" were excluded until 1940.

Under provisions of a law that became effective Nov. 15, 1941, representatives are apportioned by the method of equal proportions. In the application of this method, the apportionment is made so that the average population per representative has the least possible variation between one state and any other.

The first House of Representatives, in 1789, had 65 members, as provided by the Constitution. Of these, the largest numbers were from Virginia (10), Massachusetts (8), and Pennsylvania (8).

As the nation's population grew, the number of representatives was increased, but the total membership of the House has been fixed at 435 since the apportionment based on the 1910 census.

State	2000	1990	1980	1970	1950	1900	1850	State	2000	1990	1980	1970	1950	1900	1850
AL	7	7	7	7	9	9	7	NE	3	3	3	3	4	6	NA
AK	1	1	1	1	1	NA	NA	NV	3	2	2	1	1	1	NA
AZ	8	6	5	4	2	NA	NA	NH	2	2	2	2	2	2	3
AR	4	4	4	4	6	7	2	NJ	13	13	14	15	14	10	5
CA	53	52	45	43	30	8	2	NM	3	3	3	2	2	NA	NA
CO	7	6	6	5	4	3	NA	NY	29	31	34	39	43	37	33
CT	5	6	6	6	6	5	4	NC	13	12	11	11	12	10	8
DE	1	1	1	1	1	1	1	ND	1	1	1	1	2	2	NA
FL	25	23	19	15	8	3	1	OH	18	19	21	23	23	21	21
GA	13	11	10	10	10	11	8	OK	5	6	6	6	6	5	NA
HI	2	2	2	2	1	NA	NA	OR	5	5	5	4	4	2	1
ID	2	2	2	2	2	1	NA	PA	19	21	23	25	30	32	25
IL	19	20	22	24	25	25	9	RI	2	2	2	2	2	2	2
IN	9	10	10	11	11	13	11	SC	6	6	6	6	6	7	6
IA	5	5	6	6	8	11	2	SD	1	1	1	2	2	2	NA
KS	4	4	5	5	6	8	NA	TN	9	9	9	8	9	10	10
KY	6	6	7	7	8	11	10	TX	32	30	27	24	22	16	2
LA	7	7	8	8	8	7	4	UT	3	3	3	2	2	1	NA
ME	2	2	2	2	3	4	6	VT	1	1	1	1	1	2	3
MD	8	8	8	8	7	6	6	VA	11	11	10	10	10	10	13
MA	10	10	11	12	14	14	11	WA	9	9	8	7	7	3	NA
MI	15	16	18	19	18	12	4	WV	3	3	4	4	6	5	NA
MN	8	8	8	8	9	9	2	WI	8	9	9	9	10	11	3
MS	4	5	5	5	6	8	5	WY	1	1	1	1	1	1	NA
MO	9	9	9	10	11	16	7	**TOTAL**	435	435	435	435	435	391	237
MT	1	1	2	2	2	1	NA								

NA = Not applicable.

U.S. Slave and "Free Colored" Population, 1790, 1820, 1860[1]
Source: Decennial Censuses, U.S. Census Bureau, U.S. Dept. of Commerce

	1790 CENSUS			1820 CENSUS			1860 CENSUS		
	Slaves	% slaves	Free colored	Slaves	% slaves	Free colored	Slaves	% slaves	Free colored
Northern states[2]	40,370	2.1	33,016	18,001	0.3	92,351	18	0.0	225,224
Connecticut	2,759	1.2	2,801	97	0.0	7,844	0	0.0	8,627
New Jersey	11,423	6.2	2,762	7,557	2.7	12,460	18	0.0	25,318
New York	21,324	6.3	4,654	10,088	0.7	29,279	0	0.0	49,005
Pennsylvania	3,737	0.9	6,537	211	0.0	30,202	0	0.0	56,949
Border/disputed states	123,753	27.4	12,056	248,860	22.4	55,794	429,403	20.6	118,652
Delaware	8,887	15.0	3,899	4,509	6.2	12,958	1,798	1.6	19,829
Kansas	....			....			2	0.0	625
Kentucky	11,830	16.2	114	126,732	22.5	2,759	225,483	19.5	10,684
Maryland	103,036	32.2	8,043	107,397	26.4	39,730	87,189	12.7	83,942
Missouri	....			10,222	15.4	347	114,931	9.7	3,572
Southern states	533,774	35.4	20,301	1,263,780	37.8	74,381	3,521,110	34.3	132,760
Alabama	....			41,879	32.7	571	435,080	45.1	2,690
Arkansas	....			1,617	11.3	59	111,115	25.5	144
Florida	....			....			61,745	44.0	932
Georgia	29,264	35.5	398	149,654	43.9	1,763	462,198	43.7	3,500
Louisiana	....			69,064	45.2	10,476	331,726	46.9	18,647
Mississippi	....			32,814	43.5	458	436,631	55.2	773
North Carolina	100,572	25.5	4,975	205,017	32.1	14,612	331,059	33.4	30,463
South Carolina	107,094	43.0	1,801	258,475	51.4	6,826	402,406	57.2	9,914
Tennessee	3,417	9.5	361	80,107	18.9	2,727	275,719	24.8	7,300
Texas	....			....			182,566	30.2	355
Virginia	293,427	39.2	12,766	425,153	39.9	36,889	490,865	30.7	58,042
Total territories[3]	....			6,377	19.3	4,048	3,229	1.1	11,434
Total states and territories	697,897	17.8	59,466	1,538,125	16.0	233,504	3,953,760	12.6	488,070

(1) "Free colored" was an official Census Bureau designation in these decades. All pop. figures for slaves and free colored include both blacks and those of mixed-race background. (2) Some states had negligible slave populations that are not listed separately but are included in regional totals (relevant census years in parentheses): California (1860), Illinois (1820, 1860), Indiana (1820, 1860), Iowa (1860), Maine (1820, 1860), Massachusetts (1790, 1820, 1860), Michigan (1860), Minnesota (1860), New Hampshire (1790, 1820, 1860), Ohio (1820, 1860), Oregon (1860), Rhode Island (1790, 1820, 1860), Vermont (1820, 1860), and Wisconsin (1860). (3) Incl. Colorado (1860), Dakota (1860), the District of Columbia (1820, 1860), Nebraska (1860), Nevada (1860), New Mexico (1860), Utah (1860), and Washington (1860).

U.S. Population by Official
Source: Decennial Censuses, U.S. Census Bureau

State	1790[1]	1800[1]	1810[1]	1820[1]	1830[1]	1840[1]	1850[1]	1860	1870	1880	1890	1900	1910
AL[2]	....	1	9	128	310	591	772	964,201	996,992	1,262,505	1,513,401	1,828,697	2,138,093
AK	....	....	....	....	....	....	....	....	....	33,426	32,052	63,592	64,356
AZ	....	....	....	....	....	....	....	....	9,658	40,440	88,243	122,931	204,354
AR	....	....	1	14	30	98	210	435,450	484,471	802,525	1,128,211	1,311,564	1,574,449
CA	....	....	....	....	....	....	93	379,994	560,247	864,694	1,213,398	1,485,053	2,377,549
CO	....	....	....	....	....	....	....	34,277	39,864	194,327	413,249	539,700	799,024
CT	238	251	262	275	298	310	371	460,147	537,454	622,700	746,258	908,420	1,114,756
DE	59	64	73	73	77	78	92	112,216	125,015	146,608	168,493	184,735	202,322
DC	....	8	16	23	30	34	52	75,080	131,700	177,624	230,392	278,718	331,069
FL	....	....	....	....	35	54	87	140,424	187,748	269,493	391,422	528,542	752,619
GA	83	163	252	341	517	69	906	1,057,286	1,184,109	1,542,180	1,837,353	2,216,331	2,609,121
HI	....	....	....	....	....	....	....	....	....	....	....	154,001	191,909
ID	....	....	....	....	....	....	....	....	14,999	32,610	88,548	161,772	325,594
IL	....	....	12	55	157	476	851	1,711,951	2,539,891	3,077,871	3,826,352	4,821,550	5,638,591
IN	....	6	25	147	343	686	988	1,350,428	1,680,637	1,978,301	2,192,404	2,516,462	2,700,876
IA	....	....	....	....	....	43	192	674,913	1,194,020	1,624,615	1,912,297	2,231,853	2,224,771
KS	....	....	....	....	....	....	....	107,206	364,399	996,096	1,428,108	1,470,495	1,690,949
KY	74	221	407	564	688	780	982	1,155,684	1,321,011	1,648,690	1,858,635	2,147,174	2,289,905
LA	....	....	77	153	216	352	518	708,002	726,915	939,946	1,118,588	1,381,625	1,656,388
ME[3]	97	152	229	298	399	502	583	628,279	626,915	648,936	661,086	694,466	742,371
MD	320	342	381	407	447	470	583	687,049	780,894	934,943	1,042,390	1,188,044	1,295,346
MA[3]	379	423	472	523	610	738	995	1,231,066	1,457,351	1,783,085	2,238,947	2,805,346	3,366,416
MI	....	....	5	9	32	212	398	749,113	1,184,059	1,636,937	2,093,890	2,420,982	2,810,173
MN	....	....	....	....	....	....	6	172,023	439,706	780,773	1,310,283	1,751,394	2,075,708
MS[2]	....	8	31	75	137	376	607	791,305	827,922	1,131,597	1,289,600	1,551,270	1,797,114
MO	....	....	20	67	140	384	682	1,182,012	1,721,295	2,168,380	2,679,185	3,106,665	3,293,335
MT	....	....	....	....	....	....	....	....	20,595	39,159	142,924	243,329	376,053
NE	....	....	....	....	....	....	....	28,841	122,993	452,402	1,062,656	1,066,300	1,192,214
NV	....	....	....	....	....	....	....	6,857	42,491	62,266	47,355	42,335	81,875
NH	142	184	214	244	269	285	318	326,073	318,300	346,991	376,530	411,588	430,572
NJ	184	211	246	278	321	373	490	672,035	906,096	1,131,116	1,444,933	1,883,669	2,537,167
NM[4]	....	....	....	....	....	....	62	93,516	91,874	119,565	160,282	195,310	327,301
NY	340	589	959	1,373	1,919	2,429	3,097	3,880,735	4,382,759	5,082,871	6,003,174	7,268,894	9,113,614
NC	394	478	556	639	736	753	869	992,622	1,071,361	1,399,750	1,617,949	1,893,810	2,206,287
ND[5]	....	....	....	....	....	....	....	....	2,405	36,909	190,983	319,146	577,056
OH	....	45	231	581	938	1,519	1,980	2,339,511	2,665,260	3,198,062	3,672,329	4,157,545	4,767,121
OK	....	....	....	....	....	....	....	....	....	....	258,657	790,391	1,657,155
OR[6]	....	....	....	....	....	....	12	52,465	90,923	174,768	317,704	413,536	672,765
PA	434	602	810	1,049	1,348	1,724	2,312	2,906,215	3,521,951	4,282,891	5,258,113	6,302,115	7,665,111
RI	69	69	77	83	97	109	148	174,620	217,353	276,531	345,506	428,556	542,610
SC	249	346	415	503	581	594	669	703,708	705,606	995,577	1,151,149	1,340,316	1,515,400
SD[5]	....	....	....	....	....	....	....	4,837	11,776	98,268	348,600	401,570	583,888
TN	36	106	262	423	682	829	1,003	1,109,801	1,258,520	1,542,359	1,767,518	2,020,616	2,184,789
TX	....	....	....	....	....	....	213	604,215	818,579	1,591,749	2,235,527	3,048,710	3,896,542
UT	....	....	....	....	....	....	11	40,273	86,786	143,963	210,779	276,749	373,351
VT	85	154	218	236	281	292	314	315,098	330,551	332,286	332,422	343,641	355,956
VA[7]	692	808	878	938	1,044	1,025	1,120	1,219,630	1,225,163	1,512,565	1,655,980	1,854,184	2,061,612
WA[6,8]	....	....	....	....	....	....	1	11,594	23,955	75,116	357,232	518,103	1,141,990
WV[7]	56	79	105	137	177	225	302	376,688	442,014	618,457	762,794	958,800	1,221,119
WI	....	....	....	....	....	31	305	775,881	1,054,670	1,315,497	1,693,330	2,069,042	2,333,860
WY	....	....	....	....	....	....	....	....	9,118	20,789	62,555	92,531	145,965
U.S.[9]	3,929	5,308	7,240	9,638	12,866	17,063	23,192	31,443,321	38,553,371	50,189,209	62,979,766	76,212,168	92,228,531

Note: Where possible, population shown is that of the 2000 area of the state. Members of the Armed Forces overseas or other U.S. nationals abroad are not included. Totals revised to include corrections of initial tabulated counts. (1) Totals for 1790 through 1850 are in thousands. (2) 1800 and 1810 figures are for those parts of Mississippi Territory now part of present states of AL and MS. (3) 1790-1810 figures for MA do not include the pop. of the district taken from MA to form the state of ME in 1820. (4) 1850 figure incl. pop. for parts of Territory of New Mexico now part of present states of AZ, NM, CO, and NV. 1860 figure incl. pop. in parts taken to form part of Arizona Territory in 1863. (5) 1860 figure is for Dakota Territory, which comprised the present states of ND and SD. 1870 and 1880 figures are for parts of Dakota Territory that became the two states in 1889. (6) 1850 pop. figure for parts of Oregon Territory taken to form part of Washington Territory in 1853 and 1859 are listed under WA. (7) 1790-1860 figures for VA do not include the pop. of areas taken from VA to form the state of WV in 1863. (8) 1860 figure incl. pop. in present-day ID and parts of MT and WY. (9) 1830 and 1840 pop. totals incl. persons (5,318 in 1830; 6,100 in 1840) on public ships in the service of the U.S. not credited to any region, division, or state.

Estimated Population of American Colonies, 1630-1780
Source: U.S. Census Bureau, U.S. Dept. of Commerce
(numbers in thousands)

Colony	1630	1650	1670	1690	1700	1720	1740	1750	1770	1780
TOTAL	4.6	50.4	111.9	210.4	250.9	466.2	905.6	1,170.8	2,148.1	2,780.4
Maine (counties)[1]	0.4	1.0	...	...	...	...	...	...	31.3	49.1
New Hampshire[2]	0.5	1.3	1.8	4.2	5.0	9.4	23.3	27.5	62.4	87.8
Vermont[3]	...	...	...	...	...	...	...	...	10.0	47.6
Plymouth and Massachusetts[1,2,4]	0.9	15.6	35.3	56.9	55.9	91.0	151.6	188.0	235.3	268.6
Rhode Island[2]	...	0.8	2.2	4.2	5.9	11.7	25.3	33.2	58.2	52.9
Connecticut[2]	...	4.1	12.6	21.6	26.0	58.8	89.6	111.3	183.9	206.7
New York[2]	0.4	4.1	5.8	13.9	19.1	36.9	63.7	76.7	162.9	210.5
New Jersey[2]	...	...	1.0	8.0	14.0	29.8	51.4	71.4	117.4	139.6
Pennsylvania[2]	...	...	...	11.4	18.0	31.0	85.6	119.7	240.1	327.3
Delaware[2]	...	0.2	0.7	1.5	2.5	5.4	19.9	28.7	35.5	45.4
Maryland[2]	...	4.5	13.2	24.0	29.6	66.1	116.1	141.1	202.6	245.5
Virginia[2]	2.5	18.7	35.3	53.0	58.6	87.8	180.4	231.0	447.0	538.0
North Carolina[2]	...	...	3.9	7.6	10.7	21.3	51.8	73.0	197.2	270.1
South Carolina[2]	...	...	0.2	3.9	5.7	17.0	45.0	64.0	124.2	180.0
Georgia[2]	...	...	...	...	...	...	2.0	5.2	23.4	56.1
Kentucky[5]	...	...	...	...	...	...	...	...	15.7	45.0
Tennessee[6]	...	...	...	...	...	...	...	...	1.0	10.0

(1) For 1660-1750, Maine counties are included with Massachusetts. Maine was part of Massachusetts until it became a separate state in 1820. (2) One of the original 13 states. (3) Admitted to statehood in 1791. (4) Plymouth became a part of the Province of Massachusetts in 1691. (5) Admitted to statehood in 1792. (6) Admitted to statehood in 1796.

Census, 1790-2000
U.S. Dept. of Commerce

1920	1930	1940	1950	1960	1970	1980	1990	2000	State
2,348,174	2,646,248	2,832,961	3,061,743	3,266,740	3,444,165	3,893,888	4,040,587	4,447,100	AL
55,036	59,278	72,524	128,643	226,167	300,382	401,851	550,043	626,932	AK
334,162	435,573	499,261	749,587	1,302,161	1,770,900	2,718,215	3,665,228	5,130,632	AZ
1,752,204	1,854,482	1,949,387	1,909,511	1,786,272	1,923,295	2,286,435	2,350,725	2,673,400	AR
3,426,861	5,677,251	6,907,387	10,586,223	15,717,204	19,953,134	23,667,902	29,760,021	33,871,648	CA
939,629	1,035,791	1,123,296	1,325,089	1,753,947	2,207,259	2,889,964	3,294,394	4,301,261	CO
1,380,631	1,606,903	1,709,242	2,007,280	2,535,234	3,031,709	3,107,576	3,287,116	3,405,565	CT
223,003	238,380	266,505	318,085	446,292	548,104	594,338	666,168	783,600	DE
437,571	486,869	663,091	802,178	763,956	756,510	638,333	606,900	572,059	DC
968,470	1,468,211	1,897,414	2,771,305	4,951,560	6,789,443	9,746,324	12,937,926	15,982,378	FL
2,895,832	2,908,506	3,123,723	3,444,578	3,943,116	4,589,575	5,463,105	6,478,216	8,186,453	GA
255,912	368,336	422,330	499,794	632,772	768,561	964,691	1,108,229	1,211,537	HI
431,866	445,032	524,873	588,637	667,191	712,567	943,935	1,006,749	1,293,953	ID
6,485,280	7,630,654	7,897,241	8,712,176	10,081,158	11,113,976	11,426,518	11,430,602	12,419,293	IL
2,930,390	3,238,503	3,427,796	3,934,224	4,662,498	5,193,669	5,490,224	5,544,159	6,080,485	IN
2,404,021	2,470,939	2,538,268	2,621,073	2,757,537	2,824,376	2,913,808	2,776,755	2,926,324	IA
1,769,257	1,880,999	1,801,028	1,905,299	2,178,611	2,246,578	2,363,679	2,477,574	2,688,418	KS
2,416,630	2,614,589	2,845,627	2,944,806	3,038,156	3,218,706	3,660,777	3,685,296	4,041,769	KY
1,798,509	2,101,593	2,363,880	2,683,516	3,257,022	3,641,306	4,205,900	4,219,973	4,468,976	LA
768,014	797,423	847,226	913,774	969,265	992,048	1,124,660	1,227,928	1,274,923	ME
1,449,661	1,631,526	1,821,244	2,343,001	3,100,689	3,922,399	4,216,975	4,781,468	5,296,486	MD
3,852,356	4,249,614	4,316,721	4,690,514	5,148,578	5,689,170	5,737,037	6,016,425	6,349,097	MA
3,668,412	4,842,325	5,256,106	6,371,766	7,823,194	8,875,083	9,262,078	9,295,297	9,938,444	MI
2,387,125	2,563,953	2,792,300	2,982,483	3,413,864	3,804,971	4,075,970	4,375,099	4,919,479	MN
1,790,618	2,009,821	2,183,796	2,178,914	2,178,141	2,216,912	2,520,638	2,573,216	2,844,658	MS
3,404,055	3,629,367	3,784,664	3,954,653	4,319,813	4,676,501	4,916,686	5,117,073	5,595,211	MO
548,889	537,606	559,456	591,024	674,767	694,409	786,690	799,065	902,195	MT
1,296,372	1,377,963	1,315,834	1,325,510	1,411,330	1,483,493	1,569,825	1,578,385	1,711,263	NE
77,407	91,058	110,247	160,083	285,278	488,738	800,493	1,201,833	1,998,257	NV
443,083	465,293	491,524	533,242	606,921	737,681	920,610	1,109,252	1,235,786	NH
3,155,900	4,041,334	4,160,165	4,835,329	6,066,782	7,168,164	7,364,823	7,730,188	8,414,350	NJ
360,350	423,317	531,818	681,187	951,023	1,016,000	1,302,894	1,515,069	1,819,046	NM
10,385,227	12,588,066	13,479,142	14,830,192	16,782,304	18,236,967	17,558,072	17,990,455	18,976,457	NY
2,559,123	3,170,276	3,571,623	4,061,929	4,556,155	5,082,059	5,881,766	6,628,637	8,049,313	NC
646,872	680,845	641,935	619,636	632,446	617,761	652,717	638,800	642,200	ND
5,759,394	6,646,697	6,907,612	7,946,627	9,706,397	10,652,017	10,797,630	10,847,115	11,353,140	OH
2,028,283	2,396,040	2,336,434	2,233,351	2,328,284	2,559,229	3,025,290	3,145,585	3,450,654	OK
783,389	953,786	1,089,684	1,521,341	1,768,687	2,091,385	2,633,105	2,842,321	3,421,399	OR
8,720,017	9,631,350	9,900,180	10,498,012	11,319,366	11,793,909	11,863,895	11,881,643	12,281,054	PA
604,397	687,497	713,346	791,896	859,488	949,723	947,154	1,003,464	1,048,319	RI
1,683,724	1,738,765	1,899,804	2,117,027	2,382,594	2,590,516	3,121,820	3,486,703	4,012,012	SC
636,547	692,849	642,961	652,740	680,514	665,507	690,768	696,004	754,844	SD
2,337,885	2,616,556	2,915,841	3,291,718	3,567,089	3,923,687	4,591,120	4,877,185	5,689,283	TN
4,663,228	5,824,715	6,414,824	7,711,194	9,579,677	11,196,730	14,229,191	16,986,510	20,851,820	TX
449,396	507,847	550,310	688,862	890,627	1,059,273	1,461,037	1,722,850	2,233,169	UT
352,428	359,611	359,231	377,747	389,881	444,330	511,456	562,758	608,827	VT
2,309,187	2,421,851	2,677,773	3,318,680	3,966,949	4,648,494	5,346,818	6,187,358	7,078,515	VA
1,356,621	1,563,396	1,736,191	2,378,963	2,853,214	3,409,169	4,132,156	4,866,692	5,894,121	WA
1,463,701	1,729,205	1,901,974	2,005,552	1,860,421	1,744,237	1,949,644	1,793,477	1,808,344	WV
2,632,067	2,939,006	3,137,587	3,434,575	3,951,777	4,417,731	4,705,767	4,891,769	5,363,675	WI
194,402	225,565	250,742	290,529	330,066	332,416	469,557	453,588	493,782	WY
106,021,568	123,202,660	132,164,569	151,325,798	179,323,175	203,211,926	226,545,805	248,709,873	281,421,906	U.S.

U.S. Center of Population, 1790-2000

Source: Decennial Censuses, U.S. Census Bureau, U.S. Dept. of Commerce.

The **U.S. center of population (mean)** is considered here to be the center of population gravity, or that point upon which the U.S. would balance if it were a rigid plane without weight and the population distributed thereon, with each individual assumed to have equal weight and to exert an influence on a central point proportional to his or her distance from that point.

Census year	N Lat °	'	"	W Long °	'	"	Approximate location
1790	39	16	30	76	11	12	Kent Co., MD, 23 miles east of Baltimore
1800	39	16	6	76	56	30	Howard Co., MD, 18 miles west of Baltimore
1810	39	11	30	77	37	12	Loudoun Co., VA, 40 miles northwest by west of Washington, D.C.
1820	39	5	42	78	33	0	Hardy Co., WV, 16 miles east of Moorefield[1]
1830	38	57	54	79	16	54	Grant Co., WV, 19 miles west-southwest of Moorefield[1]
1840	39	2	0	80	18	0	Upshur Co., WV, 16 miles south of Clarksburg[1]
1850	38	59	0	81	19	0	Wirt Co., WV, 23 miles southeast of Parkersburg[1]
1860	39	0	24	82	48	48	Pike Co., OH, 20 miles south by east of Chillicothe
1870	39	12	0	83	35	42	Highland Co., OH, 48 miles east by north of Cincinnati
1880	39	4	8	84	39	40	Boone Co., KY, 8 miles west by south of Cincinnati, OH
1890	39	11	56	85	32	53	Decatur Co., IN, 20 miles east of Columbus
1900	39	9	36	85	48	54	Bartholomew Co., IN, 6 miles southeast of Columbus
1910	39	10	12	86	32	20	Monroe Co., IN, in the city of Bloomington
1920	39	10	21	86	43	15	Owen Co., IN, 8 miles south-southeast of Spencer
1930	39	3	45	87	8	6	Greene Co., IN, 3 miles northeast of Linton
1940	38	56	54	87	22	35	Sullivan Co., IN, 2 miles southeast by east of Carlisle
1950 (incl. Alaska & Hawaii)	38	48	15	88	22	8	Clay Co., IL, 3 miles northeast of Louisville
1960	38	35	58	89	12	35	Clinton Co., IL, 6½ miles northwest of Centralia
1970	38	27	47	89	42	22	St. Clair Co., IL, 5 miles east-southeast of Mascoutah
1980	38	8	13	90	34	26	Jefferson Co., MO, ¼ mile west of DeSoto
1990	37	52	20	91	12	55	Crawford Co., MO, 9.7 miles southwest of Steelville
2000	37	41	49	91	48	34	Phelps Co., MO, 2.8 miles east of Edgar Springs

(1) West Virginia was set off from Virginia on Dec. 31, 1862, and was admitted as a state on June 20, 1863.

Metropolitan Area Populations, 1990-2006

Source: Annual Population Estimates, Decennial Censuses, U.S. Census Bureau, U.S. Dept. of Commerce

(ranked by 2006 population counts)

Metropolitan Statistical Areas (MSAs) are defined for federal statistical use by the Office of Management and Budget (OMB), with technical assistance from the U.S. Census Bureau. MSAs must have at least one urbanized area of 50,000 or more inhabitants, plus an adjacent area closely integrated socially and economically with the core as measured by commuting ties. Micropolitan Statistical Areas (not listed here) must in general have at least one urban cluster with a population of at least 10,000 but no more than 50,000. The standards used to define metropolitan areas are reviewed and revised before each decennial census. The areas currently in use were defined in 2003, using 2000 standards and 2000 census data. Updates to these areas are made annually to reflect changes in population estimates.

The OMB has designated 371 MSAs in the U.S. and Puerto Rico as of Dec. 2006.

About 83.9% of the total U.S. population resided in MSAs in 2000. This number represented an increase of 28.9 mil (13.9%) since 1990.

			Population		Percent change
Rank	Metropolitan Statistical Area (MSA)	2006[1]	2000	1990	2000-06
1.	New York-Northern New Jersey-Long Island, NY-NJ-PA	18,818,536	18,323,002	16,846,046	2.7
2.	Los Angeles-Long Beach-Santa Ana, CA	12,950,129	12,365,627	11,273,720	4.7
3.	Chicago-Naperville-Joliet, IL-IN-WI	9,505,748	9,098,316	8,182,076	4.5
4.	Dallas-Fort Worth-Arlington, TX	6,003,967	5,161,544	3,989,294	16.3
5.	Philadelphia-Camden-Wilmington, PA-NJ-DE-MD	5,826,742	5,687,147	5,435,550	2.5
6.	Houston-Sugar Land-Baytown, TX	5,539,949	4,715,407	3,767,233	17.5
7.	Miami-Fort Lauderdale-Miami Beach, FL	5,463,857	5,007,564	4,056,228	9.1
8.	Washington-Arlington-Alexandria, DC-VA-MD-WV	5,290,400	4,796,183	4,122,259	10.3
9.	Atlanta-Sandy Springs-Marietta, GA	5,138,223	4,247,981	3,068,975	21.0
10.	Detroit-Warren-Livonia, MI	4,468,966	4,452,557	4,248,699	0.4
11.	Boston-Cambridge-Quincy, MA-NH	4,455,217	4,391,344	4,133,895	1.5
12.	San Francisco-Oakland-Fremont, CA	4,180,027	4,123,740	3,684,112	1.4
13.	Phoenix-Mesa-Scottsdale, AZ	4,039,182	3,251,876	2,238,498	24.2
14.	Riverside-San Bernardino-Ontario, CA	4,026,135	3,254,821	2,588,793	23.7
15.	Seattle-Tacoma-Bellevue, WA	3,263,497	3,043,878	2,559,136	7.2
16.	Minneapolis-St. Paul-Bloomington, MN-WI	3,175,041	2,968,806	2,538,776	6.9
17.	San Diego-Carlsbad-San Marcos, CA	2,941,454	2,813,833	2,498,016	4.5
18.	St. Louis, MO-IL	2,796,368	2,698,687	2,580,720	3.6
19.	Tampa-St. Petersburg-Clearwater, FL	2,697,731	2,395,997	2,067,959	12.6
20.	Baltimore-Towson, MD	2,658,405	2,552,994	2,382,172	4.1
21.	Denver-Aurora, CO	2,408,750	2,179,240	1,650,489	10.5
22.	Pittsburgh, PA	2,370,776	2,431,087	2,468,289	-2.5
23.	Portland-Vancouver-Beaverton, OR-WA	2,137,565	1,927,881	1,523,741	10.9
24.	Cleveland-Elyria-Mentor, OH	2,114,155	2,148,143	2,102,248	-1.6
25.	Cincinnati-Middletown, OH-KY-IN	2,104,218	2,009,632	1,844,915	4.7
26.	Sacramento-Arden-Arcade-Roseville, CA	2,067,117	1,796,857	1,481,220	15.0
27.	Orlando-Kissimmee, FL	1,984,855	1,644,561	1,224,844	20.7
28.	Kansas City, MO-KS	1,967,405	1,836,038	1,636,527	7.2
29.	San Antonio, TX	1,942,217	1,711,703	1,407,745	13.5
30.	San Jose-Sunnyvale-Santa Clara, CA	1,787,123	1,735,819	1,534,274	3.0
31.	Las Vegas-Paradise, NV	1,777,539	1,375,765	741,368	29.2
32.	Columbus, OH	1,725,570	1,612,694	1,405,168	7.0
33.	Indianapolis-Carmel, IN	1,666,032	1,525,104	1,294,217	9.2
34.	Virginia Beach-Norfolk-Newport News, VA-NC	1,649,457	1,576,370	1,450,855	4.6
35.	Providence-New Bedford-Fall River, RI-MA	1,612,989	1,582,997	1,509,789	1.9
36.	Charlotte-Gastonia-Concord, NC-SC	1,583,016	1,330,448	1,024,690	19.0
37.	Austin-Round Rock, TX	1,513,565	1,249,763	846,227	21.1
38.	Milwaukee-Waukesha-West Allis, WI	1,509,981	1,500,741	1,432,149	0.6
39.	Nashville-Davidson-Murfreesboro, TN	1,455,097	1,311,789	1,048,216	10.9
40.	Jacksonville, FL	1,277,997	1,122,750	925,213	13.8
41.	Memphis, TN-MS-AR	1,274,704	1,205,204	1,067,263	5.8
42.	Louisville-Jefferson County, KY-IN	1,222,216	1,161,975	1,056,156	5.2
43.	Richmond, VA	1,194,008	1,096,957	949,244	8.8
44.	Hartford-West Hartford-East Hartford, CT	1,188,841	1,148,618	1,123,678	3.5
45.	Oklahoma City, OK	1,172,339	1,095,421	971,042	7.0
46.	Buffalo-Niagara Falls, NY	1,137,520	1,170,111	1,189,340	-2.8
47.	Birmingham-Hoover, AL	1,100,019	1,052,238	956,646	4.5
48.	Salt Lake City, UT	1,067,722	968,858	768,075	10.2
49.	Rochester, NY	1,035,435	1,037,831	1,002,410	-0.2
50.	New Orleans-Metairie-Kenner, LA	1,024,678	1,316,510	1,264,383	-22.2
51.	Raleigh-Cary, NC	994,551	797,071	544,020	24.8
52.	Tucson, AZ	946,362	843,746	666,957	12.2
53.	Honolulu, HI	909,863	876,156	836,231	3.8
54.	Bridgeport-Stamford-Norwalk, CT	900,440	882,567	827,645	2.0
55.	Tulsa, OK	897,752	859,532	761,019	4.4
56.	Fresno, CA	891,756	799,407	667,490	11.6
57.	Albany-Schenectady-Troy, NY	850,957	825,875	809,642	3.0
58.	New Haven-Milford, CT	845,244	824,008	804,219	2.6
59.	Dayton, OH	838,940	848,153	843,835	-1.1
60.	Omaha-Council Bluffs, NE-IA	822,549	767,041	685,797	7.2
61.	Albuquerque, NM	816,811	729,649	599,416	11.9
62.	Allentown-Bethlehem-Easton, PA-NJ	800,336	740,395	686,688	8.1
63.	Oxnard-Thousand Oaks-Ventura, CA	799,720	753,197	669,016	6.2
64.	Worcester, MA	784,992	750,963	709,705	4.5
65.	Bakersfield, CA	780,117	661,645	544,981	17.9
66.	Grand Rapids-Wyoming, MI	774,084	740,482	645,918	4.5
67.	Baton Rouge, LA	766,514	705,973	623,850	8.6
68.	El Paso, TX	736,310	679,622	591,610	8.3
69.	Columbia, SC	703,771	647,158	548,936	8.7
70.	Akron, OH	700,943	694,960	657,575	0.9

(1) Population estimates are for July 1.

Population of 100 Largest U.S. Cities, 1850-2006

Source: Annual Population Estimates, Decennial Censuses, U.S. Census Bureau, U.S. Dept. of Commerce

(ranked by 2006 population counts)

Rank City	2006[1]	2000	1990	1980	1970	1950	1900	1850
1. New York, NY	8,214,426	8,008,278	7,322,564	7,071,639	7,895,563	7,891,957	3,437,202	696,115
2. Los Angeles, CA	3,849,378	3,694,820	3,485,398	2,968,528	2,811,801	1,970,358	102,479	1,610
3. Chicago, IL	2,833,321	2,896,016	2,783,726	3,005,072	3,369,357	3,620,962	1,698,575	29,963
4. Houston, TX	2,144,491	1,953,631	1,630,553	1,595,138	1,233,535	596,163	44,633	2,396
5. Phoenix, AZ	1,512,986	1,321,045	983,403	789,704	584,303	106,818	5,544	...
6. Philadelphia, PA	1,448,394	1,517,550	1,585,577	1,688,210	1,949,996	2,071,605	1,293,697	121,376
7. San Antonio, TX	1,296,682	1,144,646	935,933	785,940	654,153	408,442	53,321	3,488
8. San Diego, CA	1,256,951	1,223,400	1,110,549	875,538	697,471	334,387	17,700	...
9. Dallas, TX	1,232,940	1,188,580	1,006,877	904,599	844,401	434,462	42,638	...
10. San Jose, CA	929,936	894,943	782,248	629,400	459,913	95,280	21,500	...
11. Detroit, MI	871,121	951,270	1,027,974	1,203,368	1,514,063	1,849,568	285,704	21,019
12. Jacksonville, FL	794,555	735,617	635,230	540,920	504,265	204,517	28,429	1,045
13. Indianapolis, IN[2]	785,597	781,870	741,952	700,807	736,856	427,173	169,164	8,091
14. San Francisco, CA	744,041	776,733	723,959	678,974	715,674	775,357	342,782	34,776
15. Columbus, OH	733,203	711,470	632,910	565,021	540,025	375,901	125,560	17,882
16. Austin, TX	709,893	656,562	465,622	345,890	253,539	132,459	22,258	629
17. Memphis, TN	670,902	650,100	610,337	646,174	623,988	396,000	102,320	8,841
18. Fort Worth, TX	653,320	534,694	447,619	385,164	393,455	278,778	26,688	...
19. Baltimore, MD	631,366	651,154	736,014	786,741	905,787	949,708	508,957	169,054
20. Charlotte, NC	630,478	540,828	395,934	315,474	241,420	134,042	18,091	1,065
21. El Paso, TX	609,415	563,662	515,342	425,259	322,261	130,485	15,906	...
22. Boston, MA	590,763	589,141	574,283	562,994	641,071	801,444	560,892	136,881
23. Seattle, WA	582,454	563,374	516,259	493,846	530,831	467,591	80,671	...
24. Washington, DC	581,530	572,059	606,900	638,432	756,668	802,178	278,718	40,001
25. Milwaukee, WI	573,358	596,974	628,088	636,297	717,372	637,392	285,315	20,061
26. Denver, CO	566,974	554,636	467,610	492,686	514,678	415,786	133,859	...
27. Louisville-Jefferson, KY[2]	554,496	256,207	269,063	298,694	361,706	369,129	204,731	43,194
28. Las Vegas, NV	552,539	478,434	258,295	164,674	125,787	24,624	...	...
29. Nashville-Davidson, TN[2]	552,120	545,524	510,784	455,651	426,029	174,307	80,865	10,165
30. Oklahoma City, OK	537,734	506,132	444,719	404,014	368,164	243,504	10,037	...
31. Portland, OR	537,081	529,121	437,319	368,148	379,967	373,628	90,426	...
32. Tucson, AZ	518,956	486,699	405,390	330,537	262,933	45,454	7,531	...
33. Albuquerque, NM	504,949	448,607	384,736	332,920	244,501	96,815	6,238	...
34. Atlanta, GA	486,411	416,474	394,017	425,022	495,039	331,314	89,872	2,572
35. Long Beach, CA	472,494	461,522	429,433	361,498	358,879	250,767	2,252	...
36. Fresno, CA	466,714	427,652	354,202	217,491	165,655	91,669	12,470	...
37. Sacramento, CA	453,781	407,018	369,365	275,741	257,105	137,572	29,282	6,820
38. Mesa, AZ	447,541	396,375	288,091	152,404	63,049	16,790	722	...
39. Kansas City, MO	447,306	441,545	435,146	448,028	507,330	456,622	163,752	...
40. Cleveland, OH	444,313	478,403	505,616	573,822	750,879	914,808	381,768	17,034
41. Virginia Beach, VA	435,619	425,257	393,069	262,199	172,106	5,390	...	...
42. Omaha, NE	419,545	390,007	335,795	313,939	346,929	251,117	102,555	...
43. Miami, FL	404,048	362,470	358,548	346,681	334,859	249,276	1,681	...
44. Oakland, CA	397,067	399,484	372,242	339,337	361,561	384,575	66,960	...
45. Tulsa, OK	382,872	393,049	367,302	360,919	330,350	182,740	1,390	...
46. Honolulu, HI[3]	377,357	371,657	365,272	365,048	324,871	248,034	39,306	...
47. Minneapolis, MN	372,833	382,618	368,383	370,951	434,400	521,718	202,718	...
48. Colorado Springs, CO	372,437	360,890	281,140	215,105	135,517	45,472	21,085	...
49. Arlington, TX	367,197	332,969	261,721	160,113	90,229	7,692	1,079	...
50. Wichita, KS	357,698	344,284	304,011	279,838	276,554	168,279	24,671	...
51. Raleigh, NC	356,321	276,093	207,951	150,255	122,830	65,679	13,643	4,518
52. St. Louis, MO	347,181	348,189	396,685	452,801	622,236	856,796	575,238	77,860
53. Santa Ana, CA	340,024	337,977	293,742	204,023	155,710	45,533	4,933	...
54. Anaheim, CA	334,425	328,014	266,406	219,494	166,408	14,556	1,456	...
55. Tampa, FL	332,888	303,447	280,015	271,577	277,714	124,681	15,839	...
56. Cincinnati, OH	332,252	331,285	364,040	385,409	453,514	503,998	325,902	115,435
57. Pittsburgh, PA	312,819	334,563	369,879	423,959	520,089	676,806	321,616	46,601
58. Bakersfield, CA	308,392	247,057	174,820	105,611	69,515	34,784	4,836	...
59. Aurora, CO	303,582	276,393	222,103	158,588	74,974	11,421	202	...
60. Toledo, OH	298,446	313,619	332,943	354,635	383,062	303,616	131,822	3,829
61. Riverside, CA	293,761	255,166	226,505	170,591	140,089	46,764	7,973	...
62. Stockton, CA	290,141	243,771	210,943	148,283	109,963	70,853	17,506	...
63. Corpus Christi, TX	285,267	277,454	257,453	232,134	204,525	108,287	4,703	...
64. Newark, NJ	281,402	273,546	275,221	329,248	381,930	438,776	246,070	38,894
65. Anchorage, AK	278,700	260,283	226,338	174,431	48,081	11,254	...	...
66. Buffalo, NY	276,059	292,648	328,123	357,870	462,768	580,132	352,387	42,261
67. St. Paul, MN	273,535	287,151	272,235	270,230	309,866	311,349	163,065	1,112
68. Lexington, KY	270,789	260,512	225,366	204,165	108,137	55,534	26,369	8,159
69. Plano, TX	255,009	222,030	128,713	72,331	17,872	2,126	1,304	...
70. Fort Wayne, IN	248,637	205,727	173,072	172,391	178,269	133,607	45,115	4,282
71. St. Petersburg, FL	248,098	248,232	238,629	238,647	216,159	96,738	1,575	...
72. Glendale, AZ	246,531	218,812	148,134	96,988	36,228	8,179	...	...
73. Jersey City, NJ	241,789	240,055	228,537	223,532	260,350	299,017	206,433	6,856
74. Lincoln, NE	241,167	225,581	191,972	171,932	149,518	98,884	40,169	...
75. Henderson, NV	240,614	175,381	64,942	23,376	16,400	5,717	...	...
76. Chandler, AZ	240,595	176,581	89,862	29,673	13,763	3,799	...	...
77. Greensboro, NC	236,865	223,891	183,521	155,642	144,076	74,389	10,035	...
78. Scottsdale, AZ	231,127	202,705	130,069	88,364	67,823	2,032	...	...
79. Baton Rouge, LA	229,553	227,818	219,531	220,394	165,921	125,629	11,269	3,905

Rank City	2006[1]	2000	1990	1980	1970	1950	1900	1850
80. Birmingham, AL	229,424	242,820	265,968	284,413	300,910	326,037	38,415	...
81. Norfolk, VA	229,112	234,403	261,229	266,979	307,951	213,513	46,624	14,326
82. Madison, WI	223,389	208,054	191,262	170,616	171,809	96,056	19,164	1,525
83. New Orleans, LA	223,388	484,674	496,938	557,927	593,471	570,445	287,104	116,375
84. Chesapeake, VA	220,560	199,184	151,976	114,486	89,580	...	...	...
85. Orlando, FL	220,186	185,951	164,693	128,394	99,006	52,367	2,481	...
86. Garland, TX	217,963	215,768	180,650	138,857	81,437	10,571	819	...
87. Hialeah, FL	217,141	226,419	188,004	145,254	102,452	19,676	...	...
88. Laredo, TX	215,484	176,576	122,899	91,449	69,024	51,910	13,429	...
89. Chula Vista, CA	212,756	173,556	135,163	83,927	67,901	31,339	...	...
90. Lubbock, TX	212,169	199,564	186,206	174,361	149,101	71,747	...	...
91. Reno, NV	210,255	180,480	134,230	100,756	72,863	32,497	4,500	...
92. Akron, OH	209,704	217,074	223,019	237,177	275,425	274,605	42,728	3,266
93. Durham, NC	209,009	187,035	136,611	100,831	95,438	71,311	6,679	...
94. Rochester, NY	208,123	219,773	231,636	241,741	295,011	332,488	162,608	36,403
95. Modesto, CA	205,721	188,856	164,730	106,963	61,712	17,389	2,024[4]	...
96. Montgomery, AL	201,998	201,568	187,106	177,857	133,386	106,525	30,346	8,728
97. Fremont, CA	201,691	203,413	173,339	131,945	100,869	...	...	...
98. Shreveport, LA	200,199	200,145	198,525	206,989	182,064	127,206	16,013	1,728
99. Arlington, VA[3]	199,776	189,453	170,936	152,599	174,284	135,449	6,430	...
100. Glendale, CA	199,463	194,973	180,038	139,060	132,664	95,702	...	...

(1) Population estimates are for July 1. (2) Part of a consolidated city-county government. The populations of other incorporated places within the county have been excluded from population totals above. For years that predate the establishment of a consolidated city-county government, city population is shown. (3) A census designated place, or CDP. Although not incorporated, CDPs are recognized as statistical equivalents for census purposes. Honolulu CDP is coextensive with Honolulu Judicial District within the city and county of Honolulu. Arlington CDP is coextensive with Arlington County. (4) Estimated.

Mobility, by Selected Characteristics, 2004-05

Source: Annual Social and Economic Supplement, Current Population Survey, U.S. Census Bureau, U.S. Dept. of Commerce

(numbers in thousands)

	Total movers[1]	MOVED TO					Total movers[1]	MOVED TO			
		Same county	Diff. county, same state	Diff. state	Abroad			Same county	Diff. county, same state	Diff. state	Abroad
Marital status[2]						**Income[2]**					
Married, spouse present	11,656	6,370	2,374	2,392	520	Without income	3,925	1,993	682	706	544
Married, spouse absent	732	317	91	152	172	Under $5,000	3,066	1,571	637	679	179
Widowed	808	425	183	181	19	$5,000-$9,999	3,204	1,859	645	566	134
Divorced	3,462	1,975	768	668	51	$10,000-$19,999	6,090	3,663	1,170	1,019	238
Separated	1,106	647	234	192	33	$20,000-$29,999	4,964	2,909	984	882	189
Never married	12,877	7,340	2,584	2,222	731	$30,000-$39,999	3,379	1,942	757	596	84
						$40,000-$49,999	2,081	1,114	499	428	40
Educational attainment[3]						$50,000-$59,999	1,189	647	255	252	35
Less than 9th grade	1,376	766	203	172	235	$60,000-$74,999	1,043	540	226	247	30
Grades 9-12, no diploma	2,120	1,249	424	353	94	$75,000-$99,999	822	412	186	205	19
High school graduate	6,568	3,744	1,295	1,314	215	$100,000 and over	878	424	193	227	34
Some college or AA degree	5,602	3,110	1,275	1,053	164	**Ownership status[4]**					
Bachelor's degree	4,209	2,209	847	960	193	Owner-occupied unit	15,446	8,494	3,477	3,048	427
Prof. or graduate degree	1,899	901	372	498	128	Renter-occupied unit	24,443	14,242	4,370	4,394	1,437
						All movers[4]	39,889	22,736	7,847	7,441	1,865

(1) People who moved to a new residence in the 12 months preceding the March 2005 survey. (2) Ages 15 and older. (3) Ages 25 and older. (4) Ages 1 and older.

U.S. Population, by Age, Sex, and Household, 2005[1]

Source: American Community Survey, 2000 Census, U.S. Census Bureau, U.S. Dept. of Commerce

	Number	%
Total population	288,378,137	100.0
AGE		
Under 5 years	20,267,176	7.0
5 to 9 years	19,512,288	6.8
10 to 14 years	20,800,182	7.2
15 to 19 years	19,544,895	6.8
20 to 24 years	19,302,837	6.7
25 to 34 years	38,785,474	13.4
35 to 44 years	43,237,594	15.0
45 to 54 years	42,045,357	14.6
55 to 59 years	17,122,367	5.9
60 to 64 years	12,999,440	4.5
65 to 74 years	18,359,809	6.4
75 to 84 years	12,589,992	4.4
85 years and over	3,810,726	1.3
18 years and over	215,246,449	74.6
Male	103,883,099	36.0
Female	111,363,350	38.6
21 years and over	204,456,378	70.9
62 years and over	42,320,186	14.7
65 years and over	34,760,527	12.1

	Number	%
SEX		
Male	141,274,964	49.0
Female	147,103,173	51.0
HOUSEHOLDS BY TYPES		
Total population in households	288,378,137	100.0
Total households	111,090,617	100.0
Family households (families)	74,341,149	66.9
Married-couple family	55,224,773	49.7
Female householder, no husband present	14,018,712	12.6
2-person household	31,523,480	28.4
3-person household	17,022,702	15.3
4-person household	15,010,949	13.5
5-or-more-person household	10,784,018	9.7
Nonfamily households	36,749,468	33.1
Householder living alone	30,073,238	27.1
2-person household	5,472,669	4.9
3-or-more-person household	1,203,561	1.1
Householder 65 years and over	6,676,230	6.0
Persons per household	2.60	NA

NA = Not applicable. (1) 2005 data are limited to the household population and exclude the population living in institutions, college dormitories, and other group quarters. Data based on a sample and are subject to sampling variability.

U.S. Foreign-Born Population

Source: Annual Social and Economic Supplements, Current Population Surveys, U.S. Census Bureau, U.S. Dept. of Commerce

Percentage of Population That Is Foreign-Born, 1900-2006

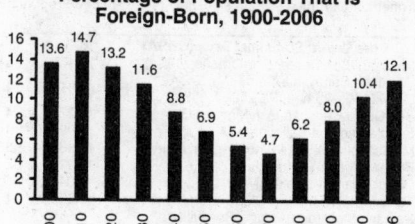

U.S. Foreign-Born Population by Regional Origin, 1995-2006

(numbers in thousands)

Region	2006	%	2000	1995
Europe	4,340	12.2	4,355	3,937
Under 18	263	18.7	250	232
Asia	9,239	25.9	7,246	6,121
Under 18	665	22.0	657	767
Latin America	16,111	45.2	14,477	11,777
Under 18	1,583	52.4	1,684	1,481
Other	5,969	16.7	2,301	2,658
Under 18	510	16.9	245	275
ALL REGIONS	**35,659**	**100.0**	**28,379**	**24,493**
Under 18	**3,021**	**100.0**	**2,837**	**2,726**

Foreign-Born Population: Top Countries of Origin, 1880-2005

Source: American Community Survey, Decennial Censuses, U.S. Census Bureau, U.S. Dept. of Commerce

(numbers in thousands; % is percent of all foreign-born)

1880 Country	No.	%	1920 Country	No.	%	1960 Country	No.	%	2000 Country	No.	%	2005[4] Country	No.	%
Germany	1,967	29.4	Germany	1,686	12.1	Italy	1,257	12.9	Mexico	9,177	29.5	Mexico	10,967	30.7
Ireland	1,855	27.8	Italy	1,610	11.6	Germany	990	10.2	China[2]	1,519	4.9	China[2]	1,761	4.9
Gr. Britain	918	13.7	U.S.S.R.	1,400	10.1	Canada	953	9.8	Philippines	1,369	4.4	Philippines	1,593	4.5
Canada	717	10.7	Poland	1,140	8.2	Gr. Britain	765	7.9	India	1,023	3.3	India	1,422	4.0
Sweden	194	2.9	Canada	1,138	8.2	Poland	748	7.7	Vietnam	988	3.2	Vietnam	1,066	3.0
Norway	182	2.7	Gr. Britain	1,135	8.2	U.S.S.R.	691	7.1	Cuba	873	2.8	El Salvador	987	2.8
France	107	1.6	Ireland	1,037	7.5	Mexico	576	5.9	Korea[3]	864	2.8	Korea[3]	983	2.8
China[1]	104	1.6	Sweden	626	4.5	Ireland	339	3.5	Canada	821	2.6	Cuba	896	2.5
Switzerland	89	1.3	Austria	576	4.1	Austria	305	3.1	El Salvador	817	2.6	Canada	819	2.3
Czech.	85	1.3	Mexico	486	3.5	Hungary	245	2.5	Germany	707	2.3	Dominican Republic	701	2.0
Total	**6,680**	**100.0**	**Total**	**13,921**	**100.0**	**Total**	**9,738**	**100.0**	**Total**	**31,108**	**100.0**	**Total**	**35,689**	**100.0**

(1) Includes Taiwan. (2) Includes Hong Kong and Taiwan. (3) Includes N. and S. Korea. (4) Data based on a sample and are subject to sampling variability.

Languages Spoken at Home by the U.S. Population[1], 2005

Source: American Community Survey, U.S. Census Bureau, U.S. Dept. of Commerce

(numbers in thousands)

Language	Speakers	Language	Speakers	Language	Speakers
Total	**268,111**	German	1,120	Other Indic languages	586
Speak only English	216,176	Korean	984	African languages	582
Speak other language	**51,935**	Russian	812	French Creole	549
Spanish or Spanish Creole	32,184	Italian	802	Other Asian languages	544
Chinese	2,300	Arabic	687	Hindi	462
French (including Patois, Cajun)	1,383	Portuguese or Portuguese Creole	662	Japanese	458
Tagalog	1,377			Other Indo-European languages	385
Vietnamese	1,142	Polish	608	Persian	326

Note: Does not include population living in institutions, college dormitories, and other group quarters. Data based on a sample and are subject to sampling variability. (1) 5 years and older.

Immigrants Admitted, by State of Intended Residence, 2006

Source: *Yearbook of Immigration Statistics*, Office of Immigration Statistics, U.S. Dept. of Homeland Security

(fiscal year 2006, ranked by numbers of immigrants admitted)

State	Immigrants	State	Immigrants	State	Immigrants	State	Immigrants
Total	**1,266,264**	Michigan	20,911	Utah	5,749	Louisiana	2,693
California	264,677	North Carolina	18,989	Kentucky	5,506	Idaho	2,377
New York	180,165	Connecticut	18,700	South Carolina	5,292	Delaware	2,265
Florida	155,996	Minnesota	18,254	Rhode Island	4,778	Maine	1,719
Texas	89,037	Ohio	16,592	Oklahoma	4,591	Alaska	1,554
New Jersey	65,934	Nevada	14,714	Kansas	4,280	Mississippi	1,480
Illinois	52,459	Colorado	12,714	Alabama	4,278	South Dakota	1,013
Virginia	38,488	Tennessee	10,042	Iowa	4,086	Vermont	895
Massachusetts	35,560	Oregon	9,192	New Mexico	3,805	West Virginia	764
Georgia	32,202	Wisconsin	8,341	Nebraska	3,795	North Dakota	649
Maryland	30,204	Indiana	8,125	District of Columbia	3,775	Montana	505
Pennsylvania	25,958	Hawaii	7,501	New Hampshire	2,990	Wyoming	376
Washington	23,805	Other[1]	7,175	Arkansas	2,926	Unknown	1
Arizona	21,530	Missouri	6,857				

(1) Includes U.S. dependencies and Armed Services posts.

Immigrants Admitted, by Top 25 Metropolitan Areas of Intended Residence, 2006

Source: Office of Immigration Statistics, U.S. Dept. of Homeland Security
(fiscal year 2006)

Core Based Statistical Areas (CBSAs) refer collectively to metropolitan and micropolitan statistical areas. (See Metropolitan Area Populations on page 594 for more information.)

Core Based Statistical Area (CBSA)	2006	%	Core Based Statistical Area (CBSA)	2006	%
Total immigrants admitted to U.S.	1,266,264	100.0	Riverside-San Bernardino-Ontario, CA	19,467	1.5
New York-Northern New Jersey-Long Island, NY-NJ-PA.	224,444	17.7	San Jose-Sunnyvale-Santa Clara, CA	18,261	1.4
Los Angeles-Long Beach-Santa Ana, CA . . .	120,880	9.5	Orlando-Kissimmee, FL.	17,409	1.4
Miami-Fort Lauderdale-Miami Beach, FL. . . .	98,922	7.8	San Diego-Carlsbad-San Marcos, CA.	17,273	1.4
Washington-Arlington-Alexandria-Rockville, DC-VA-MD-WV	54,556	4.3	Seattle-Tacoma-Bellevue, WA	17,095	1.4
Chicago-Naperville-Joliet, IL-IN-WI	49,755	3.9	Minneapolis-St. Paul-Bloomington, MN-WI . . .	15,831	1.3
San Francisco-Oakland-Fremont, CA	38,350	3.0	Phoenix-Mesa-Scottsdale, AZ.	15,220	1.2
Houston-Sugar Land-Baytown, TX	31,557	2.5	Detroit-Warren-Livonia, MI	14,041	1.1
Boston-Cambridge-Quincy, MA-NH	28,473	2.2	Tampa-St. Petersburg-Clearwater, FL	13,544	1.1
Dallas-Fort Worth-Arlington, TX	26,654	2.1	Sacramento-Arden-Arcade-Roseville-Woodland, CA.	12,767	1.0
Atlanta-Sandy Springs-Marietta, GA	25,270	2.0	Las Vegas-Paradise, NV.	12,696	1.0
Philadelphia-Camden-Wilmington, PA-NJ-DE-MD	20,757	1.6	Baltimore-Towson, MD	8,623	0.7
			Denver-Aurora, CO	8,401	0.7
			Portland-Vancouver-Beaverton, OR-WA.	8,204	0.6

U.S. Population by Reported Ancestry, 2005

Source: American Community Survey, U.S. Census Bureau, U.S. Dept. of Commerce
(numbers in thousands)

Ancestry[1]	Pop.	%	Ancestry[1]	Pop.	%	Ancestry[1]	Pop.	%
German	49,179	17.1	Scottish	5,859	2.0	West Indian[2] (except Hispanic groups)	2,233	0.8
Irish	34,669	12.0	Scotch-Irish	5,289	1.8	Czech.	1,556	0.5
English	27,762	9.6	Dutch	5,079	1.8	Hungarian.	1,522	0.5
Unclassified or not reported	25,581	8.9	Norwegian	4,601	1.6	Danish	1,434	0.5
American	20,536	7.1	Swedish	4,260	1.5	Arab	1,400	0.5
Italian	17,235	6.0	Russian	3,010	1.0	Portuguese.	1,379	0.5
Polish	9,771	3.4	European	2,527	0.9	Total.	288,378	100.0
French (except Basque).	9,530	3.3	French Canadian	2,266	0.8			

Note: Data based on a sample and are subject to sampling variability. (1) Ancestry listed in this table refers to the total number of people who claimed a particular ancestry on the American Community Survey. Race and Hispanic origin groups are not included because official data for those groups are tracked elsewhere by the Census Bureau. Data exclude population living in institutions, college dormitories, and other group quarters. (2) Incl. Bahamian, Barbadian, Belizean, Bermudan, British West Indian, Dutch West Indian, Haitian, Jamaican, Trinidadian and Tobagonian, U.S. Virgin Islander, West Indian, and Other West Indian.

The Elderly U.S. Population, 1900-2050

Source: Decennial Censuses, Annual Population Estimates, U.S. Interim Projections, U.S. Census Bureau, U.S. Dept. of Commerce
(numbers in thousands)

Year	65 AND OVER Number	65 AND OVER Percent	85 AND OVER Number[1]	85 AND OVER Percent	Year	65 AND OVER Number	65 AND OVER Percent	85 AND OVER Number[1]	85 AND OVER Percent
1900[1]	3,080	4.1	122	0.2	2001[2]	35,330	12.4	4,418	1.5
1910[1]	3,950	4.3	167	0.2	2002[2]	35,589	12.4	4,547	1.6
1920[1]	4,933	4.7	210	0.2	2003[2]	35,952	12.4	4,716	1.6
1930[1]	6,634	5.4	272	0.2	2004[2]	36,333	12.4	4,867	1.7
1940[1]	9,019	6.8	365	0.3	2005[2]	36,790	12.4	5,096	1.7
1950[1]	12,270	8.1	577	0.4	2006[2]	37,260	12.4	5,297	1.8
1960	16,560	9.2	929	0.5	2010[3]	40,244	13.0	6,123	2.0
1970	20,066	9.9	1,511	0.7	2020[3]	54,632	16.3	7,269	2.2
1980	25,549	11.3	2,240	1.0	2030[3]	71,453	19.7	9,603	2.6
1990	31,242	12.6	3,080	1.2	2040[3]	80,049	19.1	15,409	3.9
1995[2]	33,619	12.8	3,685	1.4	2050[3]	86,705	22.1	20,861	5.0
2000	34,992	12.4	4,240	1.5					

(1) Figures for 1900 to 1950 exclude Alaska and Hawaii. (2) Population estimate is for July 1. (3) Projected.

Projections of Total U.S. Population, by Age, 2010-50

Source: U.S. Interim Projections, U.S. Census Bureau, U.S. Dept. of Commerce
(numbers in thousands; % distribution may not add to totals due to overlapping categories and rounding)

Age	2010 Pop.	2010 % Distrib.	2020 Pop.	2020 % Distrib.	2030 Pop.	2030 % Distrib.	2040 Pop.	2040 % Distrib.	2050 Pop.	2050 % Distrib.
TOTAL	308,936	100	335,805	100	363,584	100	391,946	100	419,854	100
Under 5 years.	21,426	6.9	22,932	6.8	24,272	6.7	26,299	6.7	28,080	6.7
5-14 years	40,473	13.1	44,478	13.2	47,329	13.0	50,503	12.9	54,495	13.0
15-24 years	43,012	13.9	42,229	12.6	46,639	12.8	49,721	12.7	52,869	12.6
25-34 years	41,646	13.5	45,065	13.4	44,935	12.4	49,755	12.7	52,804	12.6
35-44 years	41,121	13.3	42,816	12.8	46,676	12.8	47,008	12.0	51,796	12.3
45-54 years	44,827	14.5	40,921	12.2	42,902	11.8	46,981	12.0	47,383	11.3
55-64 years	36,186	11.7	42,732	12.7	39,378	10.8	41,629	10.6	45,721	10.9
65 years and over . . .	40,244	13.0	54,632	16.3	71,453	19.7	80,050	20.4	86,706	20.7
85 years and over . .	6,123	2.0	7,269	2.2	9,603	2.6	15,409	3.9	20,861	5.0

Note: Interim projections of U.S. population consistent with Census 2000, as enumerated. Projections are for July 1 of the given year, exclude Armed Forces and U.S. citizens residing outside of the U.S., and are based on middle series projections for births, deaths, and net migration.

Disability Status of the Elderly (65 and Over)[1], 2005

Source: American Community Survey, U.S. Census Bureau, U.S. Dept. of Commerce
(numbers in thousands)

	Number	%		Number	%
Population 65 years and over	34,761	100.0	Mental disability[4]	3,988	11.5
With one or more disabilities	14,037	40.5	Self-care disability[5]	3,358	9.7
Sensory disability[2]	5,707	16.4	Go-outside-home disability[6]	5,778	16.6
Physical disability[3]	10,712	30.8	With no disability	20,697	59.5

Note: Data based on a sample and are subject to sampling variability. (1) Civilian noninstitutionalized population. (2) Blindness, deafness, severe vision, or hearing impairment. (3) Walking, climbing stairs, reaching, lifting, or carrying. (4) Learning, remembering, or concentrating. (5) Dressing, bathing, or getting around inside the home. (6) Going outside the home alone to shop or visit a doctor's office.

Young Adults Living at Home or Dormitory in the U.S., 1960-2006

Source: Decennial Censuses, Annual Social and Economic Supplements,
Current Population Surveys, U.S. Census Bureau, U.S. Dept. of Commerce
(numbers in thousands)

	18-24 years old						25-34 years old					
	Male			Female				Male			Female	
Year	Total	At home[1]	%	Total	At home[1]	%	Year	Total	At home[1]	%	Total	At home[1]	%
1960	6,842	3,583	52	7,876	2,750	35	1960	10,896	1,185	11	11,587	853	7
1970	10,398	5,641	54	11,959	4,941	41	1970	11,929	1,129	10	12,637	829	7
1980	14,278	7,755	54	14,844	6,336	43	1980	18,107	1,894	11	18,689	1,300	7
1985	13,695	8,172	60	14,149	6,758	48	1985	20,184	2,685	13	20,673	1,661	8
1990	12,450	7,232	58	12,860	6,135	48	1990	21,462	3,213	15	21,779	1,774	8
1995	12,545	7,328	58	12,613	5,896	47	1995	20,589	3,166	15	20,800	1,759	9
1996	12,402	7,327	59	12,441	5,955	48	1996	20,390	3,213	16	20,528	1,810	9
1997	12,534	7,501	60	12,452	6,006	48	1997	20,039	2,909	15	20,217	1,745	9
1998	12,633	7,399	59	12,568	5,974	48	1998	19,526	2,845	15	19,828	1,680	9
1999	12,936	7,440	58	13,031	6,389	49	1999	18,924	2,636	14	19,551	1,699	9
2000	13,291	7,593	57	13,242	6,232	47	2000	18,563	2,387	13	19,222	1,602	8
2001[2]	13,412	7,385	55	13,361	6,068	45	2001[2]	19,308	2,520	13	19,527	1,583	8
2002[2]	13,696	7,575	55	13,602	6,252	46	2002[2]	19,220	2,610	14	19,428	1,618	8
2003[2]	13,811	7,569	55	13,592	6,215	46	2003[2]	19,543	2,631	14	19,659	1,375	7
2004[2]	14,165	8,010	57	13,611	6,327	47	2004[2]	19,553	2,720	14	19,587	1,559	8
2005[2]	14,060	7,448	53	13,933	6,413	46	2005[2]	19,656	2,660	14	19,632	1,597	8
2006[2]	14,100	7,573	54	13,841	6,466	47	2006[2]	19,824	2,840	14	19,653	1,731	9

(1) Includes young adults living in their parent(s)' home and unmarried college students living in dormitories. (2) Data uses population controls based on Census 2000 and an expanded sample of households.

Living Arrangements of Children, 1970-2005

Source: Annual Social and Economic Supplements, Current Population Surveys, U.S. Census Bureau, U.S. Dept. of Commerce

			Percentage of children who live with—							
				MOTHER ONLY						
Race, Hispanic origin, and year	Number (1,000)	BOTH PARENTS	Total	Divorced	Married spouse absent	Single[1]	Widowed	FATHER ONLY	NEITHER PARENT
White									
1970	58,790	90	8	3	3	Z	2	1	2
1980	52,242	83	14	7	4	1	2	2	2
1990	51,390	79	16	8	4	3	1	3	2
1999	56,265	74	18	NA	NA	NA	NA	4	3
2000	56,455	75	17	NA	NA	NA	NA	4	3
2001	56,135	75	18	8	1	5	1	4	3
2002	58,276	75	18	8	1	5	1	5	3
2003	55,920	74	18	8	1	5	1	5	3
2004	55,902	74	18	8	1	6	1	4	3
2005	56,259	74	18	8	1	6	1	5	3
2006	42,744	76	16	8	1	4	1	5	3
Black									
1970	9,422	59	30	5	16	4	4	2	10
1980	9,375	42	44	11	16	13	4	2	12
1990	10,018	38	51	10	12	27	2	4	8
1999	11,425	35	51	NA	NA	NA	NA	4	10
2000	11,412	38	49	NA	NA	NA	NA	4	9
2001	11,578	38	48	8	2	30	2	5	10
2002	11,646	39	48	9	2	31	1	5	8
2003	11,340	36	51	11	2	30	1	5	9
2004	11,424	35	50	9	2	31	2	6	9
2005	11,295	35	50	9	2	32	1	5	10
2006	11,225	35	51	9	2	32	1	5	9
Hispanic[2]									
1970[3]	4,006	78	NA	NA	NA	NA	NA	NA	NA
1980	5,459	75	20	6	8	4	2	2	4
1990	7,174	67	27	7	10	8	2	3	3
1999	11,236	63	27	NA	NA	NA	NA	5	5
2000	11,613	65	25	NA	NA	NA	NA	4	5
2001	12,446	65	25	6	2	11	1	5	6
2002	12,817	65	25	6	2	11	1	5	5
2003	13,284	65	25	5	2	11	1	6	5
2004	13,752	65	25	6	1	11	1	5	5
2005	14,248	65	25	6	2	11	1	5	5
2006	14,697	66	25	6	2	11	1	4	5

NA = Not available. Z = Less than 0.5%. Note: Excludes persons under 18 years of age who maintained households or resided in group quarters. (1) Never married. (2) Hispanic persons may be of any race. (3) Incl. all persons under 18 years old.

Children by Relationship to Householder, 2000

Source: 2000 Census, U.S. Census Bureau, U.S. Dept. of Commerce
(numbers in thousands; figures may not add to totals due to rounding)

	All ages Total	All ages %	Under 6 Total	Under 6 %	6-17 yrs Total	6-17 yrs %	18 yrs+ Total	18 yrs+ %
Children of householder	83,714	100	20,120	100	44,532	100	19,062	100
Adopted children	2,059	2.5	389	1.9	1,197	2.7	473	2.5
Stepchildren	4,385	5.2	328	1.6	2,964	6.7	1,092	5.7
Biological children	77,271	92.3	19,402	96.4	40,371	90.7	17,497	91.8

Marital Status of the U.S. Population, 1990-2006

Source: Annual Social and Economic Supplements, Current Population Surveys, U.S. Census Bureau, U.S. Dept. of Commerce

(numbers in millions; figures may not add to totals due to rounding)

Marital status	Total 1990	Total 1995	Total 2000	Total 2006	Male 1990	Male 1995	Male 2000	Male 2006	Female 1990	Female 1995	Female 2000	Female 2006
Total pop.[1]	191.8	202.7	213.8	233.0	92.0	97.7	103.1	113.1	99.8	105.0	110.7	120.0
Never married	50.2	55.0	60.0	68.5	27.5	30.3	32.3	37.1	22.7	24.7	27.8	31.4
Married	112.6	116.6	120.2	122.8	55.8	57.6	59.7	61.6	56.8	59.0	60.5	61.2
Widowed	13.8	13.4	13.7	13.9	2.3	2.3	2.6	2.6	11.5	11.1	11.1	11.3
Divorced	15.1	17.7	19.9	22.8	6.3	7.4	8.6	9.7	8.8	10.3	11.3	13.1
Percent of total pop.[1]												
Never married	26.2	27.1	28.1	29.4	29.9	31.0	31.3	32.8	22.8	23.5	25.1	26.2
Married	58.7	57.5	56.2	52.7	60.7	58.9	57.9	54.5	56.9	56.2	54.7	51.0
Widowed	7.2	6.6	6.4	6.0	2.5	2.3	2.5	2.3	11.5	10.6	10.0	9.4
Divorced	7.9	8.7	9.3	9.8	6.8	7.6	8.3	8.6	8.9	9.8	10.2	10.9

(1) Ages 15 and older.

U.S. Households Headed by Couples, 1960-2006

Source: Annual Social and Economic Supplements, Current Population Surveys, U.S. Census Bureau, U.S. Dept. of Commerce

(numbers in thousands)

Year	Total households	Married-couple households	% of total	Unmarried-couple households[1]	% of total	Year	Total households	Married-couple households	% of total	Unmarried-couple households[1]	% of total
1960	52,799	39,254	74	439	0.8	1993	96,426	53,090	55	3,510	3.6
1970	63,401	44,728	71	523	0.8	1994	97,107	53,171	55	3,661	3.8
1980	80,776	49,112	61	1,589	2.0	1995	98,990	53,858	54	3,668	3.7
1981	82,368	49,294	60	1,808	2.2	1996	99,627	53,567	54	3,958	4.0
1982	83,527	49,630	59	1,863	2.2	1997	101,018	53,604	53	4,130	4.1
1983	83,918	49,908	59	1,891	2.3	1998	102,528	54,317	53	4,236	4.1
1984	85,407	50,090	59	1,988	2.3	1999	103,874	54,770	53	4,486	4.3
1985	86,789	50,350	58	1,983	2.3	2000	104,705	55,311	53	4,736	4.5
1986	88,458	50,933	58	2,220	2.5	2001	108,209	56,592	52	4,893	4.5
1987	89,479	51,537	58	2,334	2.6	2002	109,297	56,747	52	4,898	4.5
1988	91,124	51,675	57	2,588	2.8	2003	111,278	57,320	52	5,054	4.5
1989	92,830	52,100	56	2,764	3.0	2004	112,000	57,719	52	5,080	4.5
1990	93,347	52,317	56	2,856	3.1	2005	113,146	58,109	51	4,855	4.3
1991	94,312	52,147	55	3,039	3.2	2006	114,384	58,179	51	5,012	4.4
1992	95,669	52,457	55	3,308	3.5						

(1) Does not include same-sex couples or families living in U.S. military barracks or emergency/homeless shelters.

Unmarried-Partner Households by Sex of Partners, 2005

Source: American Community Survey, U.S. Census Bureau, U.S. Dept. of Commerce

Household	Number	Household	Number
Total U.S. households	111,090,617	Female householder and female partner	363,848
Unmarried-partner households	5,966,106	Female householder and male partner	2,528,729
Male householder and male partner	413,095	All other households	105,124,511
Male householder and female partner	2,660,434		

Note: Does not include families living in institutions, college dormitories, and other group quarters. Data based on a sample and are subject to sampling variability.

Population, by Sex, Race, Residence, and Median Age, 1790-2006

Source: Decennial Censuses, Annual Population Estimates, U.S. Census Bureau, U.S. Dept. of Commerce

(numbers in thousands, except as indicated)

	SEX Male	SEX Female	RACE White	RACE Black Number	RACE Black Percent	RACE Other[5]	RESIDENCE Urban	RESIDENCE Rural	MEDIAN AGE (years) All races	MEDIAN AGE (years) White	MEDIAN AGE (years) Black
Conterminous U.S.[1]											
1790 (Aug. 2)	NA	NA	3,172	757	19.3	NA	202	3,728	NA	NA	NA
1810 (Aug. 6)	NA	NA	5,862	1,378	19.0	NA	525	6,714	NA	16.0	NA
1820 (Aug. 7)	4,897	4,742	7,867	1,772	18.4	NA	693	8,945	16.7	16.6	17.2
1840 (June 1)	8,689	8,381	14,196	2,874	16.8	NA	1,845	15,218	17.8	17.9	17.6
1860 (June 1)	16,085	15,358	26,923	4,442	14.1	79	6,217	25,227	19.4	19.7	17.5
1870 (June 1)	19,494	19,065	33,589	4,880	12.7	89	9,902	28,656	20.2	20.4	18.5
1880 (June 1)	25,519	24,637	43,403	6,581	13.1	172	14,130	36,059	20.9	21.4	18.0
1890 (June 1)	32,237	30,711	55,101	7,489	11.9	358	22,106	40,841	22.0	22.5	17.8
1900 (June 1)	38,816	37,178	66,809	8,834	11.6	351	30,215	45,997	22.9	23.4	19.4
1920 (Jan. 1)	53,900	51,810	94,821	10,463	9.9	427	54,158	51,553	25.3	25.5	22.3
1930 (Apr. 1)	62,137	60,638	110,287	11,891	9.7	597	69,161	53,820	26.5	26.9	23.5
1940 (Apr. 1)	66,062	65,608	118,215	12,866	9.8	589	74,705	57,246	29.0	29.5	25.3

	SEX		RACE				RESIDENCE		MEDIAN AGE (years)		
				Black							
	Male	Female	White	Number	Percent	Other[5]	Urban	Rural	All races	White	Black
United States											
1950 (Apr. 1)	74,833	75,864	135,150	15,045	9.9	1,131	90,128	54,230	30.2	30.8	26.1
1960 (Apr. 1)	88,331	90,992	158,832	18,872	10.5	1,620	125,269	54,054	29.5	30.3	23.5
1970 (Apr. 1)[2]......	98,912	104,300	177,749	22,580	11.1	2,883	149,647	53,565	28.1	28.9	22.4
1980 (Apr. 1)[3]......	110,053	116,493	194,713	26,683	11.8	5,150	167,051	59,495	30.0	30.9	24.9
1985 (July 1, est.)....	115,730	122,194	202,031	28,569	12.0	7,324	NA	NA	31.4	32.3	26.6
1990 (Apr. 1)	121,239	127,470	199,686	29,986	12.1	9,233	187,053	61,656	32.9	34.4	28.1
1991 (July 1, est.)....	122,984	129,122	210,979	31,107	12.3	10,020	NA	NA	33.1	34.1	28.1
1992 (July 1, est.)....	124,506	130,496	212,885	31,670	12.4	10,446	NA	NA	33.4	34.4	28.4
1993 (July 1, est.)....	125,938	131,858	214,760	32,168	12.5	10,867	NA	NA	33.7	34.7	28.7
1994 (July 1, est.)....	127,216	133,076	216,413	32,653	12.5	11,227	NA	NA	34.0	35.0	29.0
1995 (July 1, est.)....	128,569	134,321	218,149	33,095	12.6	11,646	NA	NA	34.3	35.3	29.2
1996 (July 1, est.)....	129,746	135,434	219,686	33,514	12.6	11,979	NA	NA	34.6	35.7	29.5
1997 (July 1, est.)....	131,016	136,618	221,334	33,947	12.7	12,355	NA	NA	34.9	36.0	29.7
1998 (July 1, est.)....	132,263	137,766	222,932	34,370	12.7	12,727	NA	NA	35.3	36.3	29.9
1999 (July 1, est.)....	133,352	139,526	224,692	34,903	12.8	13,283	NA	NA	35.5	36.6	30.1
2000 (Apr. 1)[4]	138,054	143,368	228,104	35,704	12.7	13,716	222,361	59,061	35.3	36.6	30.0
2001 (July 1, est.)[4]...	138,054	143,368	228,104	35,704	12.7	13,716	NA	NA	35.3	36.6	30.0
2002 (July 1, est.)[4]...	140,079	145,147	230,589	36,260	12.7	14,322	NA	NA	35.5	36.9	30.2
2003 (July 1, est.)[4]...	141,592	146,534	232,465	36,676	12.7	14,803	NA	NA	35.7	37.1	30.4
2004 (July 1, est.)[4]...	142,938	147,858	234,191	37,045	12.7	15,252	NA	NA	35.9	37.3	30.6
2005 (July 1, est.)[4]...	144,467	149,171	236,036	37,473	12.8	15,686	NA	NA	36.0	37.5	30.8
2006 (July 1, est.)[4]...	145,974	150,534	237,885	37,905	12.8	16,138	NA	NA	36.2	37.6	30.9

NA = Not available. **Note:** For 2000 "urban" includes residents of Urban Areas (densely settled areas with 50,000 or more inhabitants); or Urban Clusters (densely settled areas with at least 2,500 but fewer than 50,000). These definitions differ from previous Census years. (1) Excludes Alaska and Hawaii. (2) The revised 1970 resident population count is 203,302,031, which incorporates changes due to errors found after tabulations were completed. The race and sex data shown here reflect the official 1970 census count; the residence data come from the tabulated count. (3) The race data shown for Apr. 1, 1980, have been modified. (4) Race data are for one race alone. (5) "Other" consists of American Indians, Alaska Natives, Asians, Native Hawaiians and other Pacific Islanders.

U.S. Population by Race and Hispanic Origin, 1990-2000
Source: Decennial Censuses, U.S. Census Bureau, U.S. Dept. of Commerce

	2000 Census		1990 Census		% change, 1990-2000[4]	
	One race only	One race or more[3]	Number	% of total pop.	Using one race only for 2000 Census	Using one race only or in combination for 2000 Census
RACE[1]						
Total population[2]	281,421,906	281,421,906	248,709,873	100.0	13.2	13.2
White.............	211,460,626	216,930,975	199,686,070	80.3	5.9	8.6
Black or African American ..	34,658,190	36,419,434	29,986,060	12.1	15.6	21.5
American Indian and Alaska Native ..	2,475,956	4,119,301	1,959,234	0.8	26.4	110.3
Asian.............	10,242,998	11,898,828	6,908,638	2.8	48.3	72.2
Native Hawaiian and Other Pac. Isl. ..	398,835	874,414	365,024	0.1	9.3	139.5
Some other race	15,359,073	18,521,486	9,804,847	3.9	56.6	88.9
HISPANIC ORIGIN AND RACE						
Total population[2]	281,421,906	281,421,906	248,709,873	100.0	13.2	13.2
Hispanic or Latino (of any race)[2].....	35,305,818	35,305,818	22,354,059	9.0	57.9	57.9
Not Hispanic or Latino[2]...........	246,116,088	246,116,088	226,355,814	91.0	8.7	8.7
White	194,552,774	198,177,900	188,128,296	75.6	3.4	5.3
Black or African American	33,947,837	35,383,751	29,216,293	11.7	16.2	21.1
American Indian and Alaska Native .	2,068,883	3,444,700	1,793,773	0.7	15.3	92.0
Asian.........	10,123,169	11,579,494	6,642,481	2.7	52.4	74.3
Native Hawaiian and Other Pac. Isl..	353,509	748,149	325,878	0.1	8.5	129.6
Some other race	467,770	1,770,645	249,093	0.1	87.8	610.8

(1) Because individuals could report only one race in 1990 and could report more than one race in 2000, and because of other changes in the census questionnaire, the race data for 1990 and 2000 are not directly comparable. (2) The differences in data for the total population, Hispanic or Latino population, and total Not Hispanic or Latino population are not affected by the changes cited in (1). Hispanic or Latino persons may be of any race. (3) One race in or in combination with one or more of the other five races listed. (4) Columns 5 and 6 provide, respectively, a "minimum-maximum" range for the percent change in population of each race between 1990 and 2000.

Unauthorized Immigrant Population, 2006, 2000
Source: Office of Immigration Statistics, U.S. Dept. of Homeland Security

Country of Birth			State of Residence		
	Est. population[1]			Est. population[1]	
Country of birth	2006	2000	State of residence	2006	2000
All countries	11,550,000	8,460,000	All states	11,550,000	8,460,000
Mexico.................	6,570,000	4,680,000	California...............	2,830,000	2,510,000
El Salvador.............	510,000	430,000	Texas.................	1,640,000	1,090,000
Guatemala.............	430,000	290,000	Florida	980,000	800,000
Philippines	280,000	200,000	Illinois	550,000	440,000
Honduras	280,000	160,000	New York.............	540,000	540,000
India..................	270,000	120,000	Arizona	500,000	330,000
Korea[2].................	250,000	180,000	Georgia...............	490,000	220,000
Brazil	210,000	100,000	New Jersey	430,000	350,000
China	190,000	190,000	North Carolina	370,000	260,000
Vietnam	160,000	160,000	Washington	280,000	170,000
Other countries.........	2,410,000	1,950,000	Other states............	2,950,000	1,750,000

Note: Unauthorized immigrant pop. estimates are made using the "residual" method. The estimated size of the legally resident foreign-born pop. (i.e., legal permanent residents; asylees; refugees; nonimmigrant students, temporary workers, and exchange visitors) is subtracted from the estimated size of the total foreign-born pop. Figures may not add to totals because of rounding. (1) Population estimates are for January of year listed. (2) Includes N. and S. Korea.

Hispanic Voting Power

Source: Tomás Rivera Policy Institute; Pew Hispanic Center, Pew Research Center; National Association of Latino Elected and Appointed Officials (NALEO); Current Population Survey, U.S. Census Bureau, U.S. Dept. of Commerce

Data compiled by the Tomás Rivera Policy Institute show that Hispanic voter turnout in presidential elections increased from 2,453,000 in 1980 to 5,934,000 by 2000. In the Nov. 2004 U.S. election, the Hispanic turnout rose to 7,587,000. Though that number represented only 28% of all Hispanics 18 years of age and over, the turnout was 81.5% of all registered Hispanic voters.

Two states—California and Texas—account for more than half of all Hispanic registered voters. In Florida, a hotly contested state in both the 2000 and 2004 presidential elections, the proportion of registered Hispanics to all registered voters is approaching 1 in 8. Except for Hispanics of Cuban origin, who are more likely to be Republican, most Hispanics vote Democrat or independent. According to NALEO, the number of elected Hispanic officeholders at all levels of government rose from 3,743 in 1996 to 5,129 in 2007, an increase of about 37%. There were no Hispanics in the U.S. Senate in 1996. In 2007, the Senate claims three Hispanic members—Mel Martinez of Florida, Ken Salazar of Colorado, and Robert Menendez of New Jersey. New Mexico Gov. Bill Richardson, who is Hispanic, campaigned for the 2008 Democratic presidential nomination in 2007.

Top 10 States in Hispanic Percent of All Registered Voters, 2004

Source: Univision

(ranked by Hispanic % of all registered voters)

Rank	State (electoral votes)	Hispanics registered	% of elig. Hispanic reg.	Hispanic % of all reg. voters
1.	New Mexico (5)	259,000	56.1	32.5
2.	Texas (34)	2,035,000	60.0	21.7
3.	Arizona (10)	331,000	49.3	16.4
4.	California (55)	2,032,000	55.0	14.6
5.	Florida (27)	857,000	63.4	12.0
6.	Colorado (9)	213,000	57.0	10.7
7.	New York (31)	606,000	56.0	7.3
8.	Nevada (5)	59,000	47.2	7.1
9.	New Jersey (15)	218,000	61.4	5.4
10.	Illinois (21)	267,000	65.5	4.6

Party Affiliation of Latino Voters by Origin, 2004

Source: Pew Hispanic Center/Kaiser Family Foundation

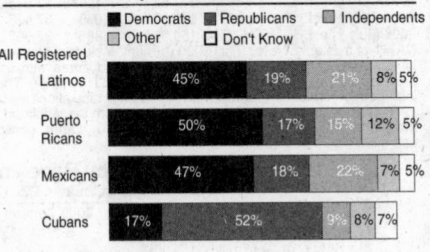

Race and Minority Group Populations by Age, 2005

Source: American Community Survey, U.S. Census Bureau, U.S. Dept. of Commerce

(resident population)

Hispanic Americans were the youngest of the population groups below, with a median age of 27.2 in 2005. The median age for blacks was 31.3; for Asians, 35.1; and for whites, 40.4.

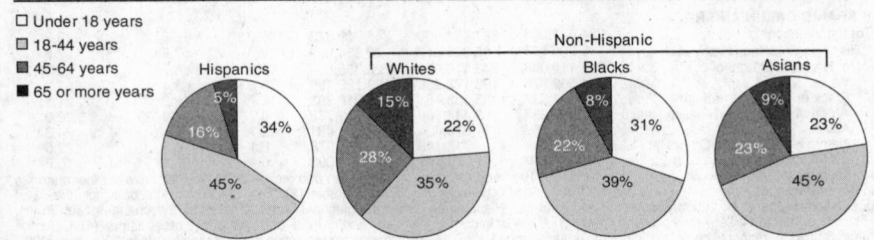

Note: Data based on a sample and are subject to sampling variability.

Educational Attainment of the U.S. Population 25 Years of Age and Over, 2005

Source: American Community Survey; U.S. Census Bureau, U.S. Dept. of Commerce

Group	Pop. (in thousands)	High school grad.[1] or more	Some college no degree, or more	Bachelor's degree or more
Hispanics (of any race)	22,663	59.3%	32.3%	12.2%
Non-Hispanic whites	134,106	89.0%	58.7%	30.0%
Blacks	20,518	79.9%	47.0%	17.3%
Asians	8,520	85.6%	68.8%	49.1%
American Indian and Alaska Native	1,406	76.3%	45.1%	13.6%
Two or more races	2,230	84.1%	57.3%	23.7%
U.S. total	**188,951**	**84.2%**	**54.7%**	**27.2%**

Note: Data are limited to the household population and exclude the population living in institutions, college dormitories, and other group quarters. Data based on a sample and are subject to sampling variability. (1) Incl. equivalency.

U.S. Population Growth by Race and Hispanic Origin, 1970-2020[1]

Source: Decennial Censuses, American Community Survey, U.S. Interim Projecitons, U.S. Census Bureau, U.S. Dept. of Commerce

(figures in millions)

350
300
250
200
150
100
50
0
Others2
Asian3
Blacks
Whites
Hispanics4
203.2
9.6
226.5
14.6
248.7
22.4
281.4
35.3
296.4
41.9
308.9
47.8
335.8
59.8
1970
1980
1990
2000
2005
2010*
2020*

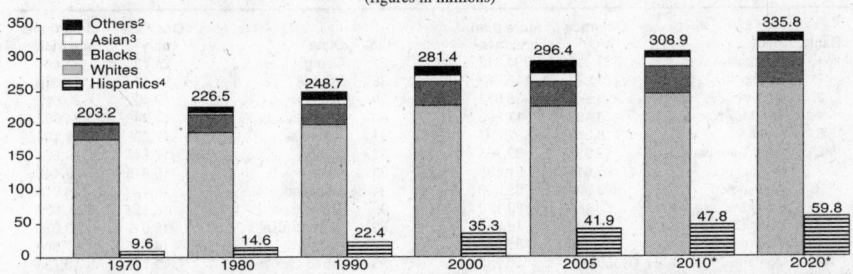

*Projected. (1) Because of changes in census questions and methods, data on race and Hispanic origin may not be wholly comparable over time. (2) Includes American Indians, Alaska Natives, and other races. From 2000 on, this category also includes Native Hawaiians, other Pacific Islanders, and persons reporting 2 or more races. (3) Figures for 1970-90 include Pacific Islanders. (4) May be of any race.

Race and Minority Groups, Percentage by State

Source: American Community Survey, except where noted; U.S. Census Bureau, U.S. Dept. of Commerce

Non-Hispanic White Population Percentage by State, 2005

% by state
1.1 - 29.7
42.8 - 63.0
65.6 - 75.3
76.9 - 87.0
88.8 - 96.0

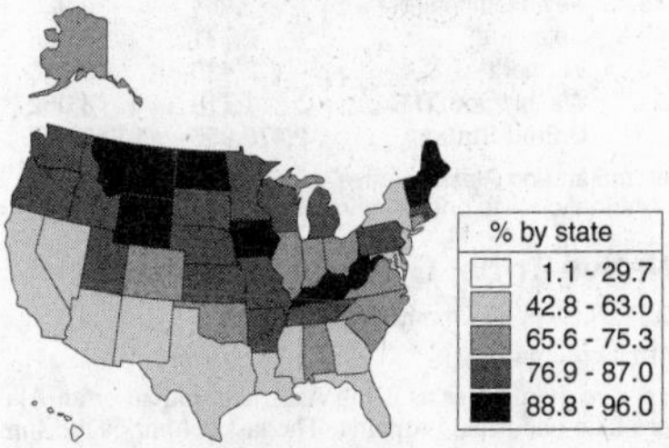

Black Population Percentage by State, 2005

% by state
0.4 - 2.2
3.1 - 6.11
7.1 - 11.5
13.5 - 21.0
25.8 - 56.8*
*Washington, DC

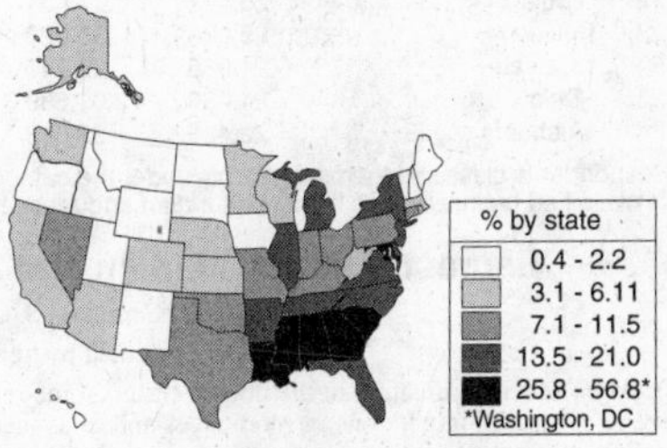

Hispanic Population Percentage by State, 2000

Source: 2000 Census

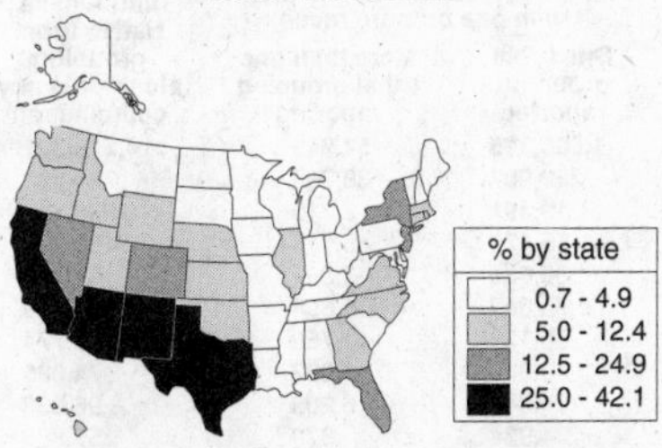

% by state
0.7 - 4.9
5.0 - 12.4
12.5 - 24.9
25.0 - 42.1

Asian Population Percentage by State, 2005

% by state
0.2 - 1.7
1.8 - 3.3
3.5 - 5.8
6.6 - 12.4
42.0*
*Hawaii

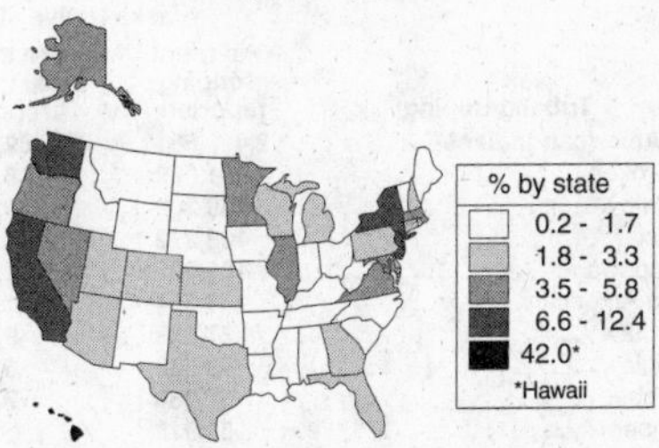

American Indian and Alaska Native Population Percentage by State, 2005

% by state
0.1 - 0.4
0.5 - 0.9
1.1 - 1.9
4.7 - 9.6
14.2*
*Alaska

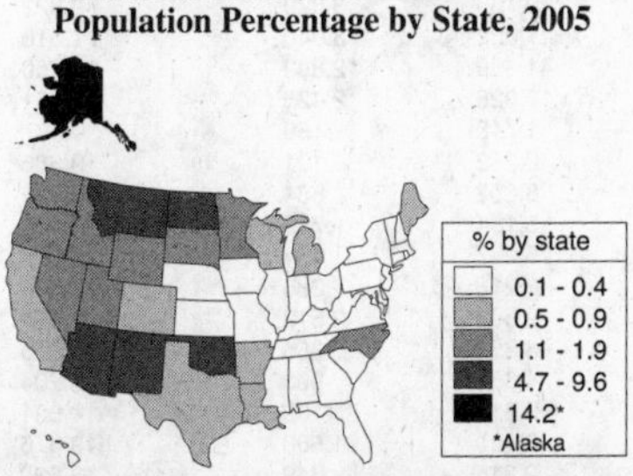

Two or More Races Population Percentage by State, 2005

% by state
0.9 - 1.2
1.4 - 2.2
2.4 - 3.3
4.9 - 6.9
21.0*
*Hawaii

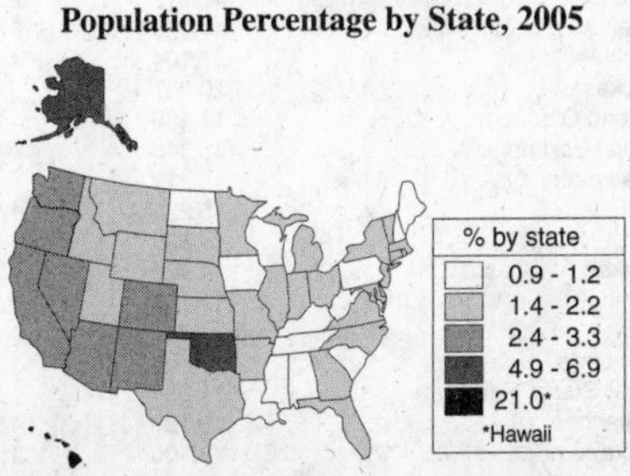

Note: 2005 data are based on a sample and are subject to sampling variability.

U.S. States Ranked by American Indian and Alaska Native Population, 2000

Source: 2000 Census, U.S. Census Bureau, U.S. Dept. of Commerce

(ranked by totals shown in first column)

Rank	State	One race only[1]	More than one race[2]	Rank	State	One race only[1]	More than one race[2]
1.	California	333,346	294,216	27.	Georgia	21,737	31,460
2.	Oklahoma	273,230	118,719	28.	Virginia	21,172	31,692
3.	Arizona	255,879	36,673	29.	New Jersey	19,492	29,612
4.	New Mexico	173,483	17,992	30.	Pennsylvania	18,348	34,302
5.	Texas	118,362	97,237	31.	Arkansas	17,808	19,194
6.	North Carolina	99,551	32,185	32.	Idaho	17,645	9,592
7.	Alaska	98,043	21,198	33.	Indiana	15,815	23,448
8.	Washington	93,301	65,639	34.	Maryland	15,423	24,014
9.	New York	82,461	89,120	35.	Tennessee	15,152	24,036
10.	South Dakota	62,283	5,998	36.	Massachusetts	15,015	23,035
11.	Michigan	58,479	65,933	37.	Nebraska	14,896	7,308
12.	Montana	56,068	10,252	38.	South Carolina	13,718	13,738
13.	Minnesota	54,967	26,107	39.	Mississippi	11,652	7,903
14.	Florida	53,541	64,339	40.	Wyoming	11,133	3,879
15.	Wisconsin	47,228	22,158	41.	Connecticut	9,639	14,849
16.	Oregon	45,211	40,456	42.	Iowa	8,989	9,257
17.	Colorado	44,241	35,448	43.	Kentucky	8,616	15,936
18.	North Dakota	31,329	3,899	44.	Maine	7,098	6,058
19.	Illinois	31,006	42,155	45.	Rhode Island	5,121	5,604
20.	Utah	29,684	10,761	46.	West Virginia	3,606	7,038
21.	Nevada	26,420	15,802	47.	Hawaii	3,535	21,347
22.	Louisiana	25,477	17,401	48.	New Hampshire	2,964	4,921
23.	Missouri	25,076	35,023	49.	Delaware	2,731	3,338
24.	Kansas	24,936	22,247	50.	Vermont	2,420	3,976
25.	Ohio	24,486	51,589	51.	Washington, D.C.	1,713	3,062
26.	Alabama	22,430	22,019		United States	2,475,956	1,643,345

(1) Respondents classified themselves only under the category "American Indian and Alaska Native" on Census 2000. (2) Respondents classified themselves as "American Indian and Alaska Native" in combination with one or more other races.

Largest American Indian and Alaska Native Tribal Groupings, 2000

Source: 2000 Census, U.S. Census Bureau, U.S. Dept. of Commerce

(ranked by totals shown in first column)

Based on self-identification in the 2000 Census. Some respondents reported themselves as being American Indian or an Alaska Native in combination with one or more races and/or as members of more than one tribal grouping. The last column is the sum of preceding columns.

Tribal grouping	American Indian and Alaska Native alone		American Indian and Alaska Native in combination with one or more races		American Indian and Alaska Native tribal grouping alone or in any combination
	One tribal grouping reported	More than one tribal grouping reported	One tribal grouping reported	More than one tribal grouping reported	
All American Indians[1]	2,423,531	52,425	1,585,396	57,949	4,119,301
Cherokee	281,069	18,793	390,902	38,769	729,533
Navajo	269,202	6,789	19,491	2,715	298,197
Sioux	108,272	4,794	35,179	5,115	153,360
Chippewa	105,907	2,730	38,635	2,397	149,669
Latin American	104,354	1,850	73,042	1,694	180,940
Choctaw	87,349	9,552	50,123	11,750	158,774
Pueblo	59,533	3,527	9,943	1,082	74,085
Apache	57,060	7,917	24,947	6,909	96,833
Lumbee	51,913	642	4,934	379	57,868
Eskimo	45,919	1,418	6,919	505	54,761
Iroquois	45,212	2,318	29,763	3,529	80,822
Creek	40,223	5,495	21,652	3,940	71,310
Blackfeet	27,104	4,358	41,389	12,899	85,750
Chickasaw	20,887	3,014	12,025	2,425	38,351
Tohono O'odham	17,466	714	1,748	159	20,087
Inupiat Eskimo	16,047	845	2,282	191	19,365
Potawatomi	15,817	592	8,602	584	25,595
Yaqui	15,224	1,245	5,184	759	22,412
Tlingit-Haida	14,825	1,059	6,047	434	22,365
Alaskan Athabascan	14,520	815	3,218	285	18,838
Seminole	12,431	2,982	9,505	2,513	27,431
Aleut	11,941	832	3,850	355	16,978
Cheyenne	11,191	1,365	4,655	993	18,204
Puget Sound Salish	11,034	226	3,212	159	14,631
Comanche	10,120	1,568	6,120	1,568	19,376
Paiute	9,705	1,163	2,315	349	13,532

(1) Totals include tribal groupings not listed separately.

U.S. Places of 5,000 or More Population—With ZIP and Area Codes

Source: U.S. Bureau of the Census, Dept. of Commerce; NeuStar Inc.

The following is a list of places of 5,000 or more inhabitants recognized by the Bureau of the Census, U.S. Dept. of Commerce, based on July 1, 2006 Census Bureau estimates. Also given are 1990 census populations. This list includes **places that are incorporated** under the laws of their respective states as cities, boroughs, towns, and villages, as well as boroughs in Alaska and towns in the 6 New England states, New York, and Wisconsin. Townships are not included.

Places that the Census Bureau designates as **"census designated places" (CDPs)** are also included; these are marked (c). The Census Bureau does not calculate estimates for CDPs; for these places, the 2000 Census figure is given, in *italics*, in place of the 2006 estimate. CDP boundaries can change from one census to another.

This list also includes, in *italics*, **minor civil divisions (MCDs)**, for Connecticut, Maine, Massachusetts, New Hampshire, Rhode Island, and Vermont. MCDs are not incorporated and not recognized as CDPs, but are often the primary political or administrative divisions of a county.

An asterisk (*) denotes that the ZIP code given is for general delivery; named streets and/or P.O. boxes within the community may differ; consult www.usps.com. Telephone **area codes** are given in parentheses. Some regions have 2 or more area codes intermixed (where new customers receive the newer area code); these are known as **overlays.** States where this occurs are noted. When 2 or more area codes are listed for one place, consult local operators for assistance. Area codes based on latest information as of Aug. 2007. For a listing in numerical order of specific area codes in the U.S., Canada, and the Caribbean, see Computers and Telecommunications chapter, page 350.

For some places listed, no area code and/or ZIP code is available. — = Not available.

Alabama

ZIP	Place	Area Code	2006	1990
*35007	Alabaster.................	(205)	28,240	14,619
*35950	Albertville...............	(256)	19,205	14,507
*35010	Alexander City...........	(256)	15,085	14,917
36420	Andalusia................	(334)	8,740	9,269
36201	Anniston.................	(256)	23,799	26,638
35016	Arab.....................	(256)	7,632	6,321
*35611	Athens...................	(256)	21,851	16,901
*36502	Atmore..................	(251)	7,485	8,046
35954	Attalla..................	(256)	6,455	6,859
*36830	Auburn..................	(334)	51,906	33,830
36507	Bay Minette..............	(251)	7,697	7,168
*35020	Bessemer................	(205)	28,416	33,581
35201	Birmingham..............	(205)	229,424	265,347
*35956	Boaz....................	(256)	8,117	6,928
36426	Brewton..................	(251)	5,326	5,885
35040	Calera...................	(205)	8,329	2,136
35243	Cahaba Heights (c)........	(205)	*5,203*	4,778
*35215	Center Point.............	(205)	*15,438*	22,658
36611	Chickasaw................	(251)	6,042	6,651
*35045	Clanton..................	(205)	8,512	7,669
35055	Cullman.................	(256)	14,828	13,367
36526	Daphne..................	(251)	18,996	11,291
*35601	Decatur.................	(256)	55,778	49,917
36732	Demopolis................	(334)	7,565	7,512
*36301	Dothan..................	(334)	64,053	54,131
*36330	Enterprise...............	(334)	23,653	20,119
*36027	Eufaula.................	(334)	13,350	13,220
35064	Fairfield................	(205)	11,477	12,200
36532	Fairhope................	(251)	16,164	9,189
*35630	Florence................	(256)	36,721	36,426
36535	Foley...................	(251)	12,712	4,937
35214	Forestdale (c)............	(205)	*10,509*	10,395
*35967	Fort Payne..............	(256)	13,771	11,838
36362	Fort Rucker (c)..........	(334)	*6,052*	7,593
35068	Fultondale...............	(205)	6,905	6,400
*35901	Gadsden.................	(256)	37,291	42,523
35071	Gardendale...............	(205)	13,042	9,251
35905	Glencoe.................	(256)	5,291	4,687
35235	Grayson Valley (c)........	(205)	*5,447*	—
36037	Greenville...............	(334)	7,087	7,847
*36542	Gulf Shores..............	(251)	8,814	3,261
35976	Guntersville.............	(256)	8,009	7,038
35570	Hamilton................	(205)	6,517	6,171
35640	Hartselle................	(256)	13,479	11,114
35080	Helena..................	(205)	13,863	4,303
*35209	Homewood................	(205)	23,780	23,644
*35244	Hoover..................	(205)	68,707	39,988
*35023	Hueytown................	(205)	15,876	15,280
*35801	Huntsville...............	(256)	168,132	159,880
35210	Irondale................	(205)	9,510	9,458
36545	Jackson.................	(251)	5,273	5,819
36265	Jacksonville.............	(256)	9,114	10,283
*35501	Jasper..................	(205)	14,117	13,553
35242	Lake Purdy (c)...........	(205)	*5,799*	1,840
36863	Lanett..................	(334)	7,541	8,985
35094	Leeds...................	(205)	11,092	10,009
35096	Lincoln..................	(256)	5,047	—
*35758	Madison.................	(256)	36,824	14,792
35228	Midfield.................	(205)	5,246	5,559
36054	Millbrook................	(334)	15,580	6,046
*36601	Mobile..................	(251)	192,830	199,973
36460	Monroeville..............	(251)	6,577	6,993
35115	Montevallo...............	(205)	5,201	4,239
*36104	Montgomery..............	(334)	201,998	190,350
35004	Moody...................	(205)	11,758	4,921
35811	Moores Mill (c)..........	(256)	*5,178*	3,362
*35223	Mountain Brook...........	(205)	20,927	19,810
35661	Muscle Shoals............	(256)	12,703	9,611
*35476	Northport................	(205)	21,890	17,297
35121	Oneonta.................	(205)	6,690	4,844
*36801	Opelika..................	(334)	24,563	22,122
36467	Opp.....................	(334)	6,718	7,011
36561	Orange Beach.............	(251)	5,319	2,253
*36203	Oxford..................	(256)	20,198	9,537
*36360	Ozark...................	(334)	14,710	13,030
35124	Pelham..................	(205)	20,120	9,356
*35125	Pell City................	(205)	11,894	7,945
*36867	Phenix City..............	(334)	30,067	25,311
36272	Piedmont................	(256)	5,009	—
35126	Pinson (c)................	(205)	*5,033*	10,987
35127	Pleasant Grove...........	(205)	10,283	8,458
36067	Prattville...............	(334)	31,119	19,816
35610	Prichard................	(251)	28,151	34,320
*35906	Rainbow City.............	(256)	9,000	7,667
36274	Roanoke.................	(334)	6,661	6,362
*35653	Russellville..............	(256)	8,857	7,812
36206	Saks (c).................	(256)	*10,698*	11,138
36571	Saraland................	(251)	12,771	11,784
36572	Satsuma................	(251)	5,991	5,194
*35768	Scottsboro...............	(256)	14,951	13,786
*36701	Selma...................	(334)	19,265	23,755
35660	Sheffield................	(256)	9,232	10,380
35907	Southside...............	(256)	8,118	5,580
*36527	Spanish Fort.............	(251)	5,601	3,732
35150	Sylacauga...............	(256)	12,932	12,520
35160	Talladega................	(256)	17,131	18,175
36078	Tallassee................	(334)	5,072	5,112
35217	Tarrant.................	(205)	6,608	8,046
36081	Troy....................	(334)	14,049	13,051
35173	Trussville...............	(205)	17,796	8,283
*35401	Tuscaloosa..............	(205)	83,052	77,866
35674	Tuscumbia...............	(256)	8,202	8,413
36083	Tuskegee................	(334)	11,499	12,257
*36854	Valley..................	(334)	8,931	9,556
*35216	Vestavia Hills............	(205)	31,051	19,550
*36092	Wetumpka................	(334)	7,313	4,670

Alaska (907)

ZIP	Place	2006	1990
*99501	Anchorage..............	278,700	226,338
*99559	Bethel.................	6,356	4,674
*99708	College (c).............	*11,402*	11,249
99702	Eielson AFB (c).........	*5,400*	5,251
*99701	Fairbanks..............	31,142	30,843
99603	Homer.................	5,524	3,660
*99801	Juneau................	30,737	26,751
*99611	Kenai.................	7,533	6,327
*99901	Ketchikan..............	7,446	8,263
99654	Knik-Fairview (c)........	*7,049*	272
*99615	Kodiak................	6,259	6,365
99654	Lakes (c)...............	*6,706*	—
99645	Palmer................	7,443	2,901
*99835	Sitka..................	8,920	8,588
*99654	Wasilla................	9,236	4,028

Arizona

ZIP	Place	Area Code	2006	1990
*85220	Apache Junction..........	(480)	31,046	18,092
85323	Avondale................	(623)	75,403	17,595
85653	Avra Valley (c)..........	(520)	*5,038*	3,403
86351	Big Park (c).............	(928)	*5,245*	3,024
85603	Bisbee..................	(520)	6,095	6,288
85326	Buckeye................	(623)	29,615	4,436
*86442	Bullhead City............	(928)	40,225	21,951
86322	Camp Verde..............	(928)	10,610	6,243
85704	Casas Adobes (c).........	(520)	*54,011*	—
85738	Catalina (c).............	(520)	*7,025*	4,864
85718	Catalina Foothills (c)......	(520)	*53,794*	—
85222	Casa Grande.............	(520)	34,554	19,076
*85225	Chandler................	(480)	240,595	89,862
86323	Chino Valley.............	(928)	10,503	4,837
85228	Coolidge................	(520)	7,892	6,934
86326	Cottonwood..............	(928)	11,171	5,918
86326	Cottonwood-Verde Village (c)	(928)	*10,610*	7,037
86327	Dewey-Humboldt (c).......	(928)	*6,295*	3,640
85607	Douglas.................	(520)	17,016	13,908
85746	Drexel Heights (c)........	(520)	*23,849*	—
85335	El Mirage...............	(623)	25,531	5,001
85231	Eloy...................	(520)	10,746	7,211
*86004	Flagstaff................	(928)	58,213	45,857
85232	Florence................	(520)	17,009	7,321
85705	Flowing Wells (c)........	(520)	*15,050*	14,013
85367	Fortuna Foothills (c)......	(928)	*20,478*	7,737
85268	Fountain Hills (c)........	(480)	24,669	10,030
85234	Gilbert.................	(480)	191,517	29,149
*85301	Glendale................	(623)	246,531	147,070
*85501	Globe..................	(928)	7,141	6,062

ZIP	Place	Area Code	2006	1990
85219	Gold Camp (c)	(480)	6,029	—
85338	Goodyear	(623)	47,359	6,258
*85614	Green Valley (c)	(520)	17,283	13,231
85283	Guadalupe	(480)	5,467	5,458
86025	Holbrook	(928)	5,154	4,770
*86401	Kingman	(928)	27,271	13,208
*86403	Lake Havasu City	(928)	56,355	24,363
85340	Litchfield Park	(623)	5,514	—
85653	Marana	(520)	29,989	2,565
85238	Maricopa	(520)	30,518	—
*85201	Mesa	(480)	447,541	289,199
*86440	Mohave Valley (c)	(928)	13,694	6,962
86401	New Kingman-Butler (c)	(928)	14,810	11,627
*85087	New River (c)	(623)	10,740	—
*85621	Nogales	(520)	20,768	19,489
*85737	Oro Valley	(520)	39,308	9,024
*86040	Page	(928)	6,827	6,598
85253	Paradise Valley	(480)	14,479	11,903
*85541	Payson	(928)	15,257	8,377
*85345	Peoria	(623)	142,024	51,080
*85034	Phoenix	(602)	1,512,986	988,015
85743	Picture Rocks (c)	(520)	8,139	4,026
*86301	Prescott	(928)	41,528	26,592
*86314	Prescott Valley	(928)	36,122	8,904
85242	Queen Creek	(480)	20,818	2,639
*85546	Safford	(928)	8,981	7,359
85629	Sahuarita	(928)	13,027	—
85349	San Luis	(928)	22,634	4,212
*85251	Scottsdale	(480)	231,127	130,099
*86336	Sedona	(928)	11,323	7,720
*85901	Show Low	(928)	11,027	5,020
*85635	Sierra Vista	(520)	42,706	32,983
85650	Sierra Vista Southeast (c)	(520)	9,042	9,237
*85937	Snowflake	(928)	5,157	—
85350	Somerton	(928)	10,806	5,293
85713	South Tucson	(520)	5,571	5,171
*85351	Sun City (c)	(623)	38,309	38,126
*85375	Sun City West (c)	(623)	26,344	15,997
85248	Sun Lakes (c)	(480)	11,936	6,578
*85374	Surprise	(623)	85,914	7,122
85749	Tanque Verde (c)	(520)	16,195	—
*85282	Tempe	(480)	169,712	141,993
85736	Three Points (c)	(520)	5,273	2,175
85353	Tolleson	(623)	6,812	4,483
86045	Tuba City (c)	(928)	8,225	7,323
*85726	Tucson	(520)	518,956	415,444
85735	Tucson Estates (c)	(520)	9,755	2,662
*85941	Whiteriver (c)	(928)	5,220	3,775
*85390	Wickenburg	(928)	6,423	4,515
86047	Winslow	(928)	9,958	9,279
*85364	Yuma	(928)	87,423	56,966

Arkansas

ZIP	Place	Area Code	2006	1990
*71923	Arkadelphia	(870)	10,475	10,014
*72501	Batesville	(870)	9,577	9,187
72012	Beebe	(501)	5,926	4,809
*72714	Bella Vista (c)	(479)	16,582	9,083
*72015	Benton	(501)	27,077	18,177
72712	Bentonville	(479)	32,049	11,257
72616	Berryville	(870)	5,099	—
*72315	Blytheville	(870)	16,403	22,523
*72022	Bryant	(501)	13,613	5,940
72023	Cabot	(501)	22,186	8,319
*71701	Camden	(870)	11,965	14,701
72719	Centerton	(479)	6,743	491
72830	Clarksville	(479)	8,446	5,833
*72032	Conway	(501)	55,334	26,481
71635	Crossett	(870)	5,679	6,282
71832	De Queen	(870)	5,873	4,633
72065	East End (c)	(501)	5,623	—
*71730	El Dorado	(870)	20,351	23,146
*72701	Fayetteville	(479)	68,726	42,247
*72335	Forrest City	(870)	13,831	13,364
*72901	Fort Smith	(479)	83,461	72,798
*72936	Greenwood	(479)	8,240	3,984
*72601	Harrison	(870)	12,986	9,936
*72543	Heber Springs	(501)	7,064	5,628
72342	Helena–West Helena	(870)	13,046	7,491
*71801	Hope	(870)	10,484	9,768
*71901	Hot Springs	(501)	38,468	33,095
*71909	Hot Springs Village (c)	(501)	8,397	6,361
*72076	Jacksonville	(501)	30,506	29,101
*72401	Jonesboro	(870)	60,489	46,535
*72201	Little Rock	(501)	184,422	175,727
72745	Lowell	(479)	7,050	1,224
*71753	Magnolia	(870)	10,321	11,151
*72104	Malvern	(501)	9,046	9,236
72364	Marion	(870)	10,151	4,405
*72113	Maumelle	(501)	14,901	6,714
71953	Mena	(479)	5,634	5,475
*71655	Monticello	(870)	9,128	8,119
72110	Morrilton	(501)	6,558	6,551
*72653	Mountain Home	(870)	12,215	9,027
72112	Newport	(870)	7,208	7,459
*72114	North Little Rock	(501)	58,896	61,829
72370	Osceola	(870)	8,031	9,165
*72450	Paragould	(870)	24,248	18,540
*71601	Pine Bluff	(870)	51,758	57,140

ZIP	Place	Area Code	2006	1990
72455	Pocahontas	(870)	6,845	6,151
*72756	Rogers	(479)	52,181	24,692
*72801	Russellville	(479)	26,014	21,260
*72143	Searcy	(501)	20,993	15,180
*72120	Sherwood	(501)	23,422	18,890
*72761	Siloam Springs	(479)	14,141	8,151
*72764	Springdale	(479)	63,082	29,945
72160	Stuttgart	(870)	9,260	10,420
71854	Texarkana	(870)	29,856	22,631
72472	Trumann	(870)	6,831	6,346
*72956	Van Buren	(479)	21,818	14,899
71671	Warren	(870)	6,263	6,455
*72301	West Memphis	(870)	28,092	28,259
*71602	White Hall	(870)	5,140	3,849
72396	Wynne	(870)	8,497	8,187

California

ZIP	Place	Area Code	2006	1990
92301	Adelanto	(760)	27,105	6,815
*91376	Agoura Hills	(818)	22,666	20,396
*94501	Alameda	(510)	70,699	73,979
94507	Alamo (c)	(925)	15,626	12,277
94706	Albany	(510)	15,965	16,327
*91802	Alhambra	(626)	87,506	82,087
92656	Aliso Viejo	(949)	41,489	7,612
90249	Alondra Park (c)	(310)	8,622	12,215
*91901	Alpine (San Diego Co.) (c)	(619)	13,143	9,695
*91003	Altadena (c)	(626)	42,610	42,658
95945	Alta Sierra (c)	(530)	6,522	5,709
95127	Alum Rock (c)	(408)	13,479	—
94589	American Canyon	(707)	15,919	7,734
*92803	Anaheim	(714)	334,425	266,406
96007	Anderson	(530)	10,418	8,299
*94509	Antioch	(925)	100,586	62,195
*92307	Apple Valley	(760)	68,886	46,079
95003	Aptos (c)	(831)	9,396	9,061
*91006	Arcadia	(626)	56,486	48,284
95521	Arcata	(707)	16,888	15,211
95825	Arden-Arcade (c)	(916)	96,025	92,040
93420	Arroyo Grande	(805)	16,415	14,432
*90701	Artesia	(562)	16,583	15,464
93203	Arvin	(661)	14,930	9,286
94577	Ashland (c)	(510)	20,793	16,590
93422	Atascadero	(805)	27,343	23,138
94027	Atherton	(650)	7,293	7,163
95301	Atwater	(209)	27,152	22,282
*95603	Auburn	(530)	12,995	10,653
95202	August (c)	(209)	7,808	6,376
93204	Avenal	(559)	16,837	9,770
91702	Azusa	(626)	47,074	41,203
*93302	Bakersfield	(661)	308,392	176,264
91706	Baldwin Park	(626)	78,568	69,330
92220	Banning	(951)	29,266	20,572
*92312	Barstow	(760)	23,628	21,472
94565	Bay Point (c)	(925)	21,534	17,453
—	Bayview-Montalvin (c)	(510)	5,004	3,988
93402	Baywood-Los Osos (c)	(805)	14,351	14,377
95903	Beale AFB (c)	(530)	5,115	6,912
92223	Beaumont	(951)	26,625	9,685
*90201	Bell	(323)	37,332	34,365
90202	Bell Gardens	(213)/(323)/(562)	45,285	42,315
*90706	Bellflower	(562)	74,351	61,815
94002	Belmont	(650)	24,665	24,165
94510	Benicia	(707)	26,597	24,437
*94704	Berkeley	(510)	101,555	102,724
92203	Bermuda Dunes (c)	(760)	6,229	4,571
*90210	Beverly Hills	(213)/(310)/(323)	34,979	31,971
92314	Big Bear City (c)	(909)	5,779	4,920
92315	Big Bear Lake	(909)	6,169	5,351
94526	Blackhawk-Camino Tassajara (c)	(925)	10,048	6,199
92316	Bloomington (c)	(951)	19,318	15,116
92225	Blythe	(760)	22,427	10,835
93637	Bonadelle Ranchos-Madera Ranchos (c)	(559)	7,300	5,705
*91902	Bonita (c)	(619)	12,401	12,542
92021	Bostonia (c)	(619)	15,169	13,670
95416	Boyes Hot Springs (c)	(707)	6,665	5,973
92227	Brawley	(760)	22,582	18,923
*92822	Brea	(562)/(714)	38,585	32,873
94513	Brentwood	(925)	47,547	7,563
—	Bret Harte (c)	(209)	5,161	—
*90622	Buena Park	(714)	79,664	68,784
*91510	Burbank (Los Angeles Co.)	(818)	104,317	93,649
—	Burbank (Santa Clara Co.) (c)	(408)	5,239	4,902
*94010	Burlingame	(650)	27,573	26,666
91372	Calabasas	(818)	22,432	16,577
*92231	Calexico	(760)	37,243	18,633
93504	California City	(760)	12,659	5,955
92320	Calimesa	(909)	7,470	6,654
92233	Calipatria	(760)	7,692	2,701
94515	Calistoga	(707)	5,214	4,468
*93010	Camarillo	(805)	62,489	52,297
93428	Cambria (c)	(805)	6,232	5,382
95682	Cameron Park (c)	(530)	14,549	11,897
*95008	Campbell	(408)	37,520	36,088
92054	Camp Pendleton North (c)	(760)	8,197	10,373
92055	Camp Pendleton South (c)	(760)	8,854	11,299
92587	Canyon Lake	(951)	11,347	9,991

ZIP	Place	Area Code	2006	1990
95010	Capitola	(831)	9,507	10,171
*92008	Carlsbad	(760)	92,928	63,292
*95608	Carmichael (c)	(916)	49,742	48,702
*93013	Carpinteria	(805)	13,490	13,747
*90745	Carson	(310)	93,805	83,995
92077	Casa de Oro-Mt. Helix (c)	(619)	18,874	30,727
*94546	Castro Valley (c)	(510)	57,292	48,619
*95012	Castroville (c)	(831)	6,724	9,5012
*92235	Cathedral City	(760)	52,461	30,085
95307	Ceres	(209)	42,245	26,413
90703	Cerritos	(562)	52,353	53,244
91724	Charter Oak (c)	(626)	9,027	8,858
94541	Cherryland (c)	(510)	13,837	11,088
*95926	Chico	(530)	73,316	39,970
*91708	Chino	(909)	79,289	59,682
91709	Chino Hills	(909)	75,282	37,868
93610	Chowchilla	(559)	18,560	5,930
*91910	Chula Vista	(619)	212,756	135,160
91702	Citrus (c)	(626)	10,581	9,481
*95621	Citrus Heights	(916)	84,547	107,439
91711	Claremont	(909)	35,103	32,610
94517	Clayton	(925)	11,191	7,317
95422	Clearlake	(707)	14,877	11,804
95425	Cloverdale	(707)	8,129	4,924
93612	Clovis	(559)	89,316	50,323
92236	Coachella	(760)	36,145	16,896
93210	Coalinga	(559)	17,597	8,212
*92324	Colton	(909)	51,427	40,213
95932	Colusa	(530)	5,841	4,934
90040	Commerce	(323)	13,557	12,135
90221	Compton	(310)	95,701	90,454
*94520	Concord	(925)	122,204	111,308
93212	Corcoran	(559)	23,403	13,360
*96021	Corning	(530)	7,279	5,870
92877	Corona	(951)	150,253	75,943
*92118	Coronado	(619)	26,518	26,540
*94925	Corte Madera (c)	(415)	9,313	8,272
*92628	Costa Mesa	(714)/(949)	109,809	96,357
94931	Cotati	(707)	7,170	5,714
92679	Coto de Caza (c)	(949)	13,057	2,853
94556	Country Club (c)	(209)	9,462	9,325
*91722	Covina	(626)	47,833	43,332
95531	Crescent City	(707)	7,860	—
92325	Crestline (c)	(909)	7,825	8,594
90201	Cudahy	(323)	24,873	22,817
*90230	Culver City	(310)	39,403	38,793
*95014	Cupertino	(408)	52,948	39,967
90630	Cypress	(714)	47,606	42,655
*94015	Daly City	(415)/(650)	101,005	92,088
*92629	Dana Point	(949)	35,945	31,896
*94526	Danville	(925)	41,540	31,306
*95616	Davis	(530)	60,964	46,322
90250	Del Aire (c)	(310)	9,012	8,040
*93215	Delano	(661)	50,310	22,762
95315	Delhi (c)	(209)	8,022	3,280
*92240	Desert Hot Springs	(760)	22,824	11,668
91765	Diamond Bar	(909)	57,759	53,672
93618	Dinuba	(559)	19,603	12,743
95620	Dixon	(707)	17,652	10,417
90239	Downey	(562)	109,376	91,444
94514	Discovery Bay (c)	(925)	8,981	5,351
*91009	Duarte	(626)	22,165	20,716
94568	Dublin	(925)	41,840	23,229
*95938	Durham (c)	(530)	5,220	4,784
93219	Earlimart (c)	(661)	6,583	5,881
90220	East Compton (c)	(310)	9,286	7,967
—	East Foothills (c)	(408)	8,133	14,898
92343	East Hemet (c)	(951)	14,823	17,611
90638	East La Mirada (c)	(562)	9,538	9,367
90022	East Los Angeles (c)	(323)	124,283	126,379
94303	East Palo Alto	(650)	32,784	23,451
91107	East Pasadena (c)	(626)	6,045	5,910
93257	East Porterville (c)	(559)	6,730	5,790
91775	East San Gabriel (c)	(626)	14,512	12,736
*93524	Edwards AFB (c)	(661)	5,909	7,423
*92020	El Cajon	(619)	91,756	88,118
*92244	El Centro	(760)	40,563	31,405
94530	El Cerrito	(510)	22,600	22,869
95762	El Dorado Hills (c)	(916)	18,016	6,395
94018	El Granada (c)	(650)	5,724	4,426
*91734	El Monte	(626)	123,162	106,162
*93446	El Paso de Robles (Paso Robles)	(805)	27,973	18,583
93030	El Rio (c)	(805)	6,193	6,419
90245	El Segundo	(310)	16,473	15,223
*94803	El Sobrante (c)	(510)	12,260	9,852
*95624	Elk Grove	(916)	129,184	17,483
*94608	Emeryville	(510)	8,751	5,740
*92024	Encinitas	(760)	59,260	55,406
95320	Escalon	(209)	7,257	4,437
*92025	Escondido	(760)	133,510	108,648
*95501	Eureka	(707)	25,435	27,025
93221	Exeter	(559)	10,160	7,276
*94930	Fairfax	(415)	7,120	6,931
94533	Fairfield	(707)	104,897	78,650
95628	Fair Oaks (c)	(916)	28,008	26,867
94541	Fairview (c)	(510)	9,470	9,045
*92028	Fallbrook (c)	(760)	29,100	22,095
93223	Farmersville	(559)	10,019	6,235
*93015	Fillmore	(805)	15,027	11,992
93622	Firebaugh	(559)	6,961	4,429
90001	Florence-Graham (c)	(323)	60,197	57,147
95828	Florin (c)	(916)	27,653	24,330
*95630	Folsom	(916)	66,123	29,802
92334	Fontana	(909)	170,099	87,535
95841	Foothill Farms (c)	(916)	17,426	17,135
92610	Foothill Ranch (c)	(949)	10,899	—
94537	Fort Bragg	(707)	6,785	6,078
*95540	Fortuna	(707)	11,208	8,788
94404	Foster City	(650)	28,937	28,176
*92728	Fountain Valley	(714)	55,857	53,691
93625	Fowler	(559)	5,063	—
95019	Freedom (c)	(831)	6,000	8,361
*94537	Fremont	(510)	201,691	173,339
*93706	Fresno	(559)	466,714	354,091
*92834	Fullerton	(714)	132,418	114,144
95632	Galt	(209)	23,396	8,889
95205	Garden Acres (c)	(209)	9,747	8,547
*92842	Garden Grove	(714)	166,296	142,965
*90247	Gardena	(310)	59,733	51,481
*95020	Gilroy	(408)	48,313	31,487
92509	Glen Avon (c)	(951)	14,853	12,663
*91209	Glendale	(818)	199,463	180,038
*91741	Glendora	(626)	50,370	47,832
93561	Golden Hills (c)	(661)	7,434	5,423
95670	Gold River (c)	(916)	8,023	—
93116	Goleta	(805)	29,182	—
93926	Gonzales	(831)	8,647	4,660
92324	Grand Terrace	(951)	12,250	10,946
95746	Granite Bay (c)	(916)	19,388	—
95945	Grass Valley	(530)	12,426	9,048
93927	Greenfield	(831)	14,264	7,464
95948	Gridley	(530)	5,912	4,631
*93433	Grover Beach	(805)	12,802	11,602
93434	Guadalupe	(805)	6,490	5,479
95322	Gustine	(209)	5,180	4,137
91745	Hacienda Heights (c)	(626)	53,122	52,354
94019	Half Moon Bay	(650)	12,308	8,886
*93230	Hanford	(559)	48,655	30,463
90716	Hawaiian Gardens	(562)	15,422	13,639
*90250	Hawthorne	(310)/(323)	85,438	71,349
*94544	Hayward	(510)	140,606	114,705
95448	Healdsburg	(707)	10,961	9,469
92546	Hemet	(951)	70,136	43,366
94547	Hercules	(510)	24,776	16,829
90254	Hermosa Beach	(310)	19,544	18,219
*92340	Hesperia	(760)	83,351	50,418
92346	Highland	(909)	51,550	34,439
94010	Hillsborough	(650)	10,714	10,667
*95023	Hollister	(831)	35,690	19,318
92250	Holtville	(760)	5,400	4,820
91720	Home Gardens (c)	(951)	9,461	7,780
95326	Hughson	(209)	6,351	2,918
*92647	Huntington Beach	(714)	194,436	181,519
90255	Huntington Park	(323)	62,165	56,129
93234	Huron	(559)	7,172	4,766
*92251	Imperial	(760)	11,754	4,113
*91932	Imperial Beach	(619)	26,137	26,512
92210	Indian Wells	(760)	5,015	—
*92201	Indio	(760)	76,896	36,850
*90301	Inglewood	(310)/(323)	114,914	109,602
—	Interlaken (c)	(831)	7,328	6,404
95640	Ione	(209)	7,649	6,516
*92619	Irvine	(714)/(949)	193,956	110,330
93117	Isla Vista (c)	(805)	18,344	20,395
91935	Jamul (c)	(619)	5,920	2,258
94914	Kentfield (c)	(415)	6,351	6,030
93630	Kerman	(559)	12,191	5,448
93930	King City	(831)	11,225	7,634
93631	Kingsburg	(559)	11,188	7,245
91011	La Cañada Flintridge	(818)	20,989	19,378
90045	Ladera Heights (c)	(310)	6,568	6,316
94549	Lafayette	(925)	24,877	23,366
—	Laguna (c)	(916)	34,309	9,828
*92652	Laguna Beach	(949)	24,161	23,170
*92654	Laguna Hills	(949)	32,156	22,719
92607	Laguna Niguel	(949)	64,771	44,723
—	Laguna West-Lakeside (c)		8,414	—
*92654	Laguna Woods	(949)	18,210	—
*90631	La Habra	(562)/(714)	59,264	51,263
90631	La Habra Heights	(562)	5,970	6,226
92352	Lake Arrowhead (c)	(909)	8,934	6,539
*92531	Lake Elsinore	(951)	45,033	19,733
92630	Lake Forest	(949)	76,323	56,036
92530	Lakeland Village (c)	(909)	5,626	5,159
93535	Lake Los Angeles (c)	(661)	11,523	7,977
95453	Lakeport	(707)	5,234	4,567
92040	Lakeside(c)	(619)	19,560	39,412
*90714	Lakewood	(562)	80,055	73,553
*91941	La Mesa	(619)	53,043	52,911
*90638	La Mirada	(562)/(714)	49,733	40,452
93241	Lamont (c)	(661)	13,296	11,517
*93539	Lancaster	(661)	140,804	97,300
90623	La Palma	(562)/(714)	15,776	15,392
—	La Presa (c)	(619)	32,721	—
*91747	La Puente	(626)	41,526	36,955
*92253	La Quinta	(760)	41,328	11,215
95401	La Riviera (c)	(916)	10,273	10,986
95403	Larkfield-Wikiup (c)	(707)	7,479	6,779
*94939	Larkspur	(415)	11,746	11,068
92688	Las Flores (c)	(949)	5,625	—

ZIP	Place	Area Code	2006	1990
95330	Lathrop	(209)	14,924	6,841
91750	La Verne	(909)	33,316	30,843
*90260	Lawndale	(310)	32,016	27,331
*91945	Lemon Grove	(619)	23,869	23,984
93245	Lemoore	(559)	22,916	13,622
90304	Lennox (c)	(310)	22,950	22,757
95648	Lincoln	(916)	39,566	7,248
95901	Linda (c)	(530)	13,474	13,033
93247	Lindsay	(559)	10,860	8,338
95062	Live Oak (Santa Cruz Co.) (c)	(831)	16,628	15,212
95953	Live Oak (Sutter Co.)	(530)	8,042	4,320
*94550	Livermore	(925)	79,438	56,741
95334	Livingston	(209)	12,906	7,317
*95240	Lodi	(209)	62,451	51,874
92354	Loma Linda	(951)	21,263	18,470
90717	Lomita	(310)	20,482	19,442
*93436	Lompoc	(805)	39,883	37,649
*90801	Long Beach	(310)/(562)	472,494	429,321
95560	Loomis	(916)	6,699	5,705
*90720	Los Alamitos	(562)/(949)	11,696	11,788
*94022	Los Altos	(650)	27,483	26,599
94022	Los Altos Hills	(650)	8,308	7,514
*90086	Los Angeles	(213)/(310)/(323)/(818)	3,849,378	3,485,557
93635	Los Banos	(209)	34,171	14,519
*95030	Los Gatos	(408)	28,366	27,357
94903	Lucas Valley-Marinwood (c)	(415)	6,357	5,982
90262	Lynwood	(213)/(310)/(323)	71,061	61,945
93250	McFarland	(661)	12,093	7,005
95521	McKinleyville (c)	(707)	13,599	10,749
*93638	Madera	(559)	54,959	29,283
93637	Madera Acres (c)	(559)	7,741	5,245
95954	Magalia (c)	(530)	10,569	8,987
*90265	Malibu	(310)	13,176	11,730
93546	Mammoth Lakes	(760)	7,406	4,785
*90266	Manhattan Beach	(310)	36,665	32,063
*95336	Manteca	(209)	63,709	40,773
93933	Marina	(831)	18,156	26,512
*90291	Marina del Rey (c)	(310)	8,176	7,431
94553	Martinez	(925)	35,593	31,800
95901	Marysville	(530)	11,949	12,324
—	Mayflower Village (c)	—	5,081	4,978
90270	Maywood	(323)	28,714	27,893
93640	Mendota	(559)	9,752	6,821
*94025	Menlo Park	(650)	29,981	28,403
92359	Mentone (c)	(909)	7,803	5,675
*95340	Merced	(209)	76,313	56,155
94030	Millbrae	(650)	20,461	20,414
94941	Mill Valley	(415)	13,323	13,029
*95035	Milpitas	(408)	64,292	50,690
91752	Mira Loma (c)	(951)	17,617	15,786
*93641	Miramonte (c)	(805)	7,177	7,744
92690	Mission Viejo	(949)	94,848	79,464
*95350	Modesto	(209)	205,721	164,746
91017	Monrovia	(626)	38,006	35,733
91763	Montclair	(909)	35,544	28,434
90640	Montebello	(323)	62,968	59,564
*93940	Monterey	(831)	28,803	31,954
*91754	Monterey Park	(323)/(626)/(818)	62,183	60,738
*93021	Moorpark	(805)	35,668	25,494
94556	Moraga	(925)	16,946	15,987
*92552	Moreno Valley	(951)	183,571	118,779
*95037	Morgan Hill	(408)	35,982	23,928
*93442	Morro Bay	(805)	10,135	9,664
94041	Mountain View	(650)	70,090	67,365
*92564	Murrieta	(951)	90,457	18,557
92407	Muscoy (c)	(714)	8,919	7,541
*94558	Napa	(707)	74,966	61,865
*91950	National City	(619)	60,960	54,249
92363	Needles	(760)	5,330	5,475
94560	Newark	(510)	41,891	37,861
95360	Newman	(209)	9,951	4,158
*92658	Newport Beach	(949)	80,006	66,643
93444	Nipomo (c)	(805)	12,626	7,109
91760	Norco	(951)	27,051	23,302
*90650	Norwalk	(562)	105,240	94,279
95603	North Auburn (c)	(530)	11,847	10,301
94025	North Fair Oaks (c)	(650)	15,440	13,912
95660	North Highlands (c)	(916)	44,187	42,105
*94947	Novato	(415)	51,518	47,585
95361	Oakdale	(209)	19,296	11,978
*94617	Oakland	(510)	397,067	372,242
94561	Oakley	(925)	26,822	18,374
93445	Oceano (c)	(805)	7,260	6,169
*92056	Oceanside	(760)	165,803	128,090
93308	Oildale (c)	(661)	27,885	26,553
*93023	Ojai	(805)	7,861	7,613
95961	Olivehurst (c)	(530)	11,061	9,708
*91761	Ontario	(909)	173,351	133,179
95060	Opal Cliffs (c)	(831)	6,458	5,468
*92863	Orange	(714)	135,070	110,658
93646	Orange Cove	(559)	9,946	5,604
95662	Orangevale (c)	(916)	26,705	26,266
*93457	Orcutt (c)	(805)	28,830	—
94563	Orinda	(925)	18,348	16,642
95963	Orland	(530)	7,050	5,052
93647	Orosi (c)	(559)	7,318	5,486
*95965	Oroville	(530)	13,505	11,530
*93030	Oxnard	(805)	184,463	142,560
94044	Pacifica	(650)	37,327	37,670
93950	Pacific Grove	(831)	14,865	16,117
95968	Palermo (c)	(530)	5,720	5,260
93590	Palmdale	(661)	138,790	73,314
*92260	Palm Desert	(760)	47,047	23,252
92262	Palm Springs	(760)	47,806	40,144
*94303	Palo Alto	(650)	57,809	55,900
90274	Palos Verdes Estates	(310)	13,770	13,512
*95969	Paradise	(530)	26,389	25,401
90723	Paramount	(562)	56,369	47,669
95823	Parkway-So. Sacramento (c)	(916)	36,468	31,903
93648	Parlier	(559)	13,124	7,938
*91109	Pasadena	(323)/(626)/(818)	144,133	131,586
—	Paso Robles. See El Paso de Robles			
95363	Patterson	(209)	18,404	8,626
92509	Pedley (c)	(951)	11,207	8,869
*92572	Perris	(951)	51,397	21,500
*94952	Petaluma	(707)	54,660	43,166
—	Phoenix Lake-Cedar Ridge (c)	—	5,123	3,569
*90660	Pico Rivera	(562)	64,336	59,177
*94611	Piedmont	(510)	10,540	10,602
*94564	Pinole	(510)	18,875	17,460
*93449	Pismo Beach	(805)	8,384	7,669
94565	Pittsburg	(925)	63,017	47,607
*92871	Placentia	(714)	49,943	41,259
95667	Placerville	(530)	10,086	8,286
94523	Pleasant Hill	(925)	33,191	31,583
94566	Pleasanton	(925)	66,397	50,570
*91769	Pomona	(909)	154,271	131,700
*93257	Porterville	(559)	45,716	29,521
*93041	Port Hueneme	(805)	21,814	20,322
92679	Portola Hills (c)	(949)	6,391	2,677
*92064	Poway	(858)	48,117	43,396
93907	Prunedale (c)	(831)	16,432	7,393
93551	Quartz Hill (c)	(661)	9,890	9,626
92065	Ramona (c)	(760)	15,691	13,040
*95670	Rancho Cordova	(916)	59,921	48,731
91729	Rancho Cucamonga	(909)	170,714	101,409
92270	Rancho Mirage	(760)	16,710	9,778
90275	Rancho Palos Verdes	(310)	41,754	41,667
91941	Rancho San Diego (c)	(619)	20,155	6,977
92688	Rancho Santa Margarita	(949)	50,618	11,390
96080	Red Bluff	(530)	14,005	12,363
*96049	Redding	(530)	90,033	66,176
*92373	Redlands	(909)	70,382	62,667
*90277	Redondo Beach	(310)	67,346	60,167
*94063	Redwood City	(650)	73,691	66,072
93654	Reedley	(559)	22,805	15,791
*92377	Rialto	(909)	99,467	72,395
*94802	Richmond	(510)	102,120	86,019
*93556	Ridgecrest	(760)	26,170	28,295
95003	Rio del Mar (c)	(831)	9,198	8,919
95673	Rio Linda (c)	(916)	10,466	9,481
94571	Rio Vista	(707)	7,305	3,488
95366	Ripon	(209)	14,047	7,455
95367	Riverbank	(209)	20,346	8,591
*92502	Riverside	(951)	293,761	226,546
95677	Rocklin	(916)	50,131	18,806
*94572	Rodeo (c)	(510)	8,717	7,589
94928	Rohnert Park	(707)	41,083	36,326
*90274	Rolling Hills Estates	(310)	8,096	7,789
95360	Rosamond (c)	(661)	14,349	7,430
—	Rosedale (c)	(805)	8,445	4,673
95407	Roseland (c)	(707)	6,369	8,779
*91770	Rosemead	(626)	54,991	51,638
95826	Rosemont (c)	(916)	22,904	22,851
*95678	Roseville	(916)	107,158	44,685
90720	Rossmoor (c)	(714)	10,298	9,893
91748	Rowland Heights (c)	(626)	48,553	42,647
*92519	Rubidoux (c)	(951)	29,100	24,367
92382	Running Springs (c)	(909)	5,125	4,195
*95814	Sacramento	(916)	453,781	369,365
94574	Saint Helena	(707)	5,904	4,990
95368	Salida (c)	(831)	12,560	4,499
*93907	Salinas	(831)	145,032	108,777
*94960	San Anselmo	(415)	12,043	11,735
*92401	San Bernardino	(909)	198,985	170,036
94066	San Bruno	(650)	39,986	38,961
93001	San Buenaventura (Ventura)	(805)	104,092	92,557
94070	San Carlos	(650)	27,002	26,382
*92674	San Clemente	(949)	61,050	41,100
*92138	San Diego	(619)/(858)	1,256,951	1,110,623
*92065	San Diego Country Estates (c)	(760)	9,262	6,874
91773	San Dimas	(909)	35,714	32,398
*91341	San Fernando	(818)	24,119	22,580
*94142	San Francisco	(415)	744,041	723,959
*91778	San Gabriel	(626)	41,024	37,120
93657	Sanger	(559)	23,963	16,839
*92581	San Jacinto	(951)	35,060	17,614
*95113	San Jose	(408)	929,936	782,224
*92690	San Juan Capistrano	(949)	34,839	26,183
*94577	San Leandro	(510)	78,030	68,223
*93401	San Luis Obispo	(805)	42,963	41,958
*92069	San Marcos	(760)	76,501	38,974
*91108	San Marino	(626)	13,094	12,959
*94402	San Mateo	(650)	91,601	85,619
94806	San Pablo	(510)	31,044	25,158
*94915	San Rafael	(415)	56,008	48,410
*94583	San Ramon	(925)	49,589	35,303
*92711	Santa Ana	(714)/(949)	340,024	293,827
*93102	Santa Barbara	(805)	85,681	85,571
*95050	Santa Clara	(408)	108,518	93,613

ZIP	Place	Area Code	2006	1990
*91380	Santa Clarita	(661)	168,008	120,050
*95060	Santa Cruz	(831)	54,778	49,711
90670	Santa Fe Springs	(562)	17,112	15,520
*93454	Santa Maria	(805)	84,712	61,552
*90401	Santa Monica	(310)	88,050	86,905
*93060	Santa Paula	(805)	28,531	25,062
*95402	Santa Rosa	(707)	154,212	113,261
*92071	Santee	(619)	52,530	52,902
*95070	Saratoga	(408)	30,045	28,061
*94965	Sausalito	(415)	7,207	7,152
*95066	Scotts Valley	(831)	11,150	8,667
90740	Seal Beach	(562)	24,358	25,098
93955	Seaside	(831)	34,066	38,826
*95472	Sebastopol	(707)	7,557	7,008
93662	Selma	(559)	22,710	14,757
—	Shackelford (c)	—	5,170	
*93263	Shafter	(661)	14,887	9,404
*96019	Shasta Lake	(916)	10,228	8,821
*91025	Sierra Madre	(626)	10,977	10,762
*90806	Signal Hill	(562)	11,017	8,371
*93065	Simi Valley	(805)	121,288	100,218
92075	Solana Beach	(858)	12,649	12,956
93960	Soledad	(831)	27,701	13,426
*93463	Solvang	(805)	5,121	4,741
95476	Sonoma	(707)	9,897	8,168
95073	Soquel	(831)	5,081	9,188
91733	South El Monte	(626)	21,631	20,850
90280	South Gate	(323)/(562)	98,434	86,284
*96151	South Lake Tahoe	(530)	23,844	21,586
95965	South Oroville (c)	(530)	7,695	7,463
*91030	So. Pasadena	(213)/(323)/626)/(818)	24,884	23,936
*94080	South San Francisco	(650)	61,354	54,312
91770	South San Gabriel (c)	(626)	7,595	7,700
91744	South San Jose Hills (c)	(626)	20,218	17,814
90605	South Whittier (c)	(562)	55,193	49,514
95991	South Yuba City (c)	(530)	12,651	8,816
*91977	Spring Valley (c)	(619)	26,663	55,331
*94309	Stanford (c)	(650)	13,315	18,097
90680	Stanton	(714)	37,640	30,491
*95208	Stockton	(209)	290,141	210,943
95375	Strawberry (c)	(209)	5,302	4,377
*94585	Suisun City	(707)	26,917	22,704
*92586	Sun City (c)	(951)	17,773	14,930
*94086	Sunnyvale	(408)	130,519	117,324
*96130	Susanville	(530)	18,108	12,130
93268	Taft	(661)	9,150	5,902
94941	Tamalpais-Homestead Val. (c)	(415)	10,691	9,601
94806	Tara Hills (c)	(510)	5,332	4,998
93581	Tehachapi	(661)	11,979	6,182
92589	Temecula	(951)	89,392	27,177
91780	Temple City	(626)	37,890	31,153
95965	Thermalito (c)	(530)	6,045	5,646
*91359	Thousand Oaks	(805)	124,207	104,381
92276	Thousand Palms (c)	(760)	5,120	4,122
94920	Tiburon	(415)	8,717	7,554
*90503	Torrance	(310)	142,350	133,107
95376	Tracy	(209)	80,308	33,558
*96161	Truckee	(916)	16,084	8,848
*93274	Tulare	(559)	52,109	33,249
*95380	Turlock	(209)	68,492	42,224
*92781	Tustin	(714)/(949)	69,665	50,689
92705	Tustin Foothills (c)	(714)	24,044	24,358
92277	Twentynine Palms	(760)	30,531	11,821
92278	Twentynine Palms Base (c)	(760)	8,413	10,606
95060	Twin Lakes (c)	(831)	5,533	5,379
*95482	Ukiah	(707)	15,385	14,632
94587	Union City	(510)	69,477	53,762
*91785	Upland	(909)	73,379	63,374
*95687	Vacaville	(707)	92,691	71,476
91744	Valinda (c)	(626)	21,776	18,735
*94590	Vallejo	(707)	116,844	109,199
92343	Valle Vista (c)	(951)	10,488	8,751
92082	Valley Center (c)	(760)	7,323	1,711
93437	Vandenberg AFB (c)	(805)	6,151	9,846
93436	Vandenberg Village (c)	(805)	5,802	5,971
*92393	Victorville	(760)	98,662	50,103
90043	View Park-Windsor Hills (c)	(310)	10,958	11,769
92861	Villa Park (c)	(714)	6,020	6,299
—	Vincent (c)	—	15,097	13,713
—	Vineyard (c)	—	10,109	
*93291	Visalia	(559)	113,487	75,659
*92083	Vista	(760)	89,891	71,861
—	Waldon (c)	—	5,133	
*91788	Walnut	(626)	31,294	29,105
*94596	Walnut Creek	(925)	63,701	60,569
90255	Walnut Park (c)	(213)	16,180	14,722
93280	Wasco	(661)	24,279	12,412
95386	Waterford	(209)	8,812	4,771
*95076	Watsonville	(831)	48,709	31,099
90044	West Athens (c)	(310)	9,101	8,859
90502	West Carson (c)	(310)	21,138	20,143
90247	West Compton (c)	(310)	5,435	5,451
*91790	West Covina	(626)	107,745	96,226
90069	West Hollywood	(310)/(323)	36,514	36,118
*91359	Westlake Village	(805)	8,584	7,455
*92685	Westminster	(714)	89,520	78,293
—	West Modesto (c)	—	6,096	
90047	Westmont (c)	(323)	31,623	31,044
91746	West Puente Valley (c)	(626)	22,589	20,254
*95691	West Sacramento	(916)	44,162	28,898
*90606	West Whittier-Los Nietos (c)	(562)	25,129	24,164
*90605	Whittier	(562)	84,015	77,671
92595	Wildomar (c)	(951)	14,064	10,411
*95490	Willits	(707)	5,055	5,027
90222	Willowbrook (c)	(323)	34,138	32,772
95988	Willows	(530)	6,293	5,988
95492	Windsor	(707)	25,294	12,002
—	Winter Gardens (c)	—	19,771	
95694	Winters	(530)	6,731	4,639
95388	Winton (c)	(209)	8,832	7,559
92504	Woodcrest (c)	(951)	8,342	7,796
93286	Woodlake	(559)	7,336	5,678
*95695	Woodland	(530)	51,144	40,230
94061	Woodside	(650)	5,509	5,034
*92885	Yorba Linda	(714)	65,314	52,422
96097	Yreka	(530)	7,502	6,948
*95991	Yuba City	(530)	60,360	27,385
92399	Yucaipa	(909)	50,223	32,819
*92286	Yucca Valley	(760)	20,331	16,539

Colorado

Area code (720) overlays area code (303). See introductory note.

ZIP	Place	Area Code	2006	1990
*80840	Air Force Academy (c)	(719)	7,526	9,062
*81101	Alamosa	(719)	8,679	7,579
80401	Applewood (c)	(303)	7,123	11,069
*80004	Arvada	(303)	104,830	89,261
*81611	Aspen	(970)	5,728	5,049
*80017	Aurora	(303)	303,582	222,103
81620	Avon	(970)	6,399	1,798
80221	Berkley (c)	(303)	10,743	
80513	Berthoud	(970)	5,120	3,087
*80908	Black Forest (c)	(719)	13,247	8,143
*80302	Boulder	(303)	91,481	85,127
*80601	Brighton	(303)	29,750	14,203
*80020	Broomfield	(303)	45,116	24,638
80723	Brush	(970)	5,205	4,165
*81212	Canon City	(719)	16,124	12,687
81623	Carbondale	(970)	6,013	3,004
80104	Castle Pines (c)	(303)	5,958	
*80104	Castle Rock	(303)	39,682	8,710
80120	Castlewood (c)	(303)	25,567	24,392
80015	Centennial	(303)	98,270	
*80110	Cherry Hills Village	(303)	6,185	5,245
81222	Cimarron Hills (c)	(719)	15,194	11,160
81520	Clifton (c)	(970)	17,345	12,671
*80903	Colorado Springs	(719)	372,437	280,430
80120	Columbine (c)	(303)	24,095	23,969
*80022	Commerce City	(303)	38,887	16,466
81321	Cortez	(970)	8,448	7,284
*81625	Craig	(970)	9,251	8,091
81416	Delta	(970)	8,306	3,789
*80202	Denver	(303)	566,974	467,610
80022	Derby (c)	(303)	6,423	6,043
*81301	Durango	(970)	15,614	12,439
80214	Edgewater	(303)	5,159	4,613
81632	Edwards (c)	(970)	8,257	
*80110	Englewood	(303)	32,286	29,396
80516	Erie	(303)	14,125	1,258
80517	Estes Park	(970)	6,006	3,184
80620	Evans	(970)	17,977	5,876
*80439	Evergreen (c)	(303)	9,216	7,582
80221	Federal Heights	(303)	11,744	9,342
*80504	Firestone	(303)	7,124	1,358
80913	Fort Carson (c)	(719)	10,566	11,309
*80525	Fort Collins	(970)	129,467	87,491
80621	Fort Lupton	(303)	7,424	5,159
*80701	Fort Morgan	(970)	10,807	9,068
80817	Fountain	(719)	19,374	10,754
*80530	Frederick	(303)	7,395	988
81521	Fruita	(970)	7,055	4,045
*81504	Fruitvale (c)	(970)	6,936	5,222
*81601	Glenwood Springs	(970)	8,765	6,561
*80401	Golden	(303)	17,239	13,127
*81501	Grand Junction	(970)	46,898	32,893
*80631	Greeley	(970)	89,046	60,454
*80111	Greenwood Village	(303)	13,440	7,589
80501	Gunbarrel (c)	(303)	9,435	9,388
*81230	Gunnison	(970)	5,309	4,636
81637	Gypsum	(970)	5,307	
80163	Highlands Ranch (c)	(303)	70,931	10,181
80534	Johnstown	(303)	8,237	1,579
80127	Ken Caryl (c)	(303)	30,887	24,391
80026	Lafayette	(303)	24,211	14,708
81050	La Junta	(719)	7,242	7,678
*80226	Lakewood	(303)	140,024	126,475
81052	Lamar	(719)	8,356	8,343
*80126	Littleton	(303)	40,324	33,711
80124	Lone Tree	(303)	9,003	1,261
*80501	Longmont	(303)	82,646	51,976
80027	Louisville	(303)	18,417	12,363
80538	Loveland	(970)	61,122	37,357
80829	Manitou Springs	(719)	5,072	4,540
80543	Milliken	(970)	5,881	1,605
81401	Montrose	(970)	16,449	8,854
80233	Northglenn	(303)	33,045	27,195
80649	Orchard Mesa (c)	(970)	6,456	5,977
*80134	Parker	(303)	41,406	5,450
*81003	Pueblo	(719)	103,730	98,640

ZIP	Place	Area Code	2006	1990
81007	Pueblo West (c)	(719)	16,899	4,386
81503	Redlands (c)	(970)	8,043	9,355
81650	Rifle	(970)	8,446	4,858
*81201	Salida	(719)	5,410	4,737
80911	Security-Widefield (c)	(719)	29,845	23,822
80110	Sheridan	(303)	5,460	4,976
80221	Sherrelwood (c)	(303)	17,657	16,636
80122	Southglenn (c)	(303)	43,520	43,087
*80477	Steamboat Springs	(970)	9,315	6,695
80751	Sterling	(970)	12,581	10,362
80134	Stonegate (c)	(719)	6,284	—
80906	Stratmoor (c)	(719)	6,650	5,854
80027	Superior	(303)	10,262	255
80134	The Pinery (c)	(303)	7,253	4,885
*80229	Thornton	(303)	109,155	55,031
81082	Trinidad	(719)	9,134	8,580
81251	Twin Lakes (c)	(719)	6,301	—
80229	Welby (c)	(303)	12,973	10,218
*80030	Westminster	(303)	105,753	74,619
*80033	Wheat Ridge	(303)	30,979	29,419
80550	Windsor	(970)	15,976	5,062
*80863	Woodland Park	(719)	6,729	4,610
80132	Woodmoor (c)	(719)	7,177	3,858

Connecticut
See introductory note.

ZIP	Place	Area Code	2006	1990
06401	Ansonia	(203)	18,614	18,403
06001	Avon	(860)	17,315	13,937
06403	Beacon Falls	(203)	5,700	5,083
06037	Berlin	(860)	20,105	16,787
06524	Bethany	(203)	5,514	—
06801	Bethel	(203)	18,599	17,541
06002	Bloomfield	(860)	20,611	19,483
06043	Bolton	(860)	5,133	—
06405	Branford	(203)	29,027	27,603
06405	Branford Center (c)	(203)	5,735	5,688
*06602	Bridgeport	(203)	137,912	141,686
*06010	Bristol	(860)	61,161	60,640
06804	Brookfield	(203)	16,398	14,113
06234	Brooklyn	(860)	7,801	6,681
*06013	Burlington	(860)	9,134	7,026
06331	Canterbury	(860)	5,092	—
06019	Canton	(860)	10,065	8,268
06040	Central Manchester (c)	(860)	30,595	30,934
*06410	Cheshire	(203)	28,833	25,684
06410	Cheshire Village (c)	(203)	5,789	5,759
06413	Clinton	(860)	13,623	12,767
*06415	Colchester	(860)	15,385	10,980
06237	Columbia	(860)	5,361	4,510
06340	Conning Towers-Nautilus Pk. (c)	(860)	10,241	10,013
06238	Coventry	(860)	12,194	10,063
06416	Cromwell	(860)	13,526	12,286
*06810	Danbury	(203)	79,285	65,585
06820	Darien	(203)	20,393	18,196
06418	Derby	(203)	12,457	12,199
06422	Durham	(860)	7,350	5,732
06026	East Granby	(860)	5,074	4,302
06423	East Haddam	(860)	8,847	6,676
*06424	East Hampton	(860)	12,446	10,428
*06108	East Hartford	(860)	48,857	50,452
*06512	East Haven	(203)	28,686	26,144
06333	East Lyme	(860)	18,283	15,340
06612	Easton	(203)	7,437	6,303
06088	East Windsor	(860)	10,546	10,081
06029	Ellington	(860)	14,346	11,197
06082	Enfield	(860)	45,231	45,532
06426	Essex	(860)	6,769	5,904
*06825	Fairfield	(203)	57,829	53,418
*06032	Farmington	(860)	25,000	20,608
06033	Glastonbury	(860)	33,025	27,901
06033	Glastonbury Center (c)	(860)	7,157	7,082
06035	Granby	(860)	11,169	9,369
*06830	Greenwich	(203)	62,077	58,441
06351	Griswold	(860)	11,238	10,384
06340	Groton	(860)	9,311	45,144
06437	Guilford	(203)	22,333	19,848
06438	Haddam	(860)	7,734	6,769
*06514	Hamden	(203)	57,841	52,434
*06101	Hartford	(860)	124,512	139,739
06791	Harwinton	(860)	5,595	5,228
06248	Hebron	(860)	9,222	7,079
06037	Kensington (c)	(860)	8,541	8,306
*06239	Killingly	(860)	17,646	15,889
06419	Killingworth	(860)	6,431	4,814
06249	Lebanon	(860)	7,302	6,041
06339	Ledyard	(860)	15,064	14,913
*06759	Litchfield	(860)	8,743	8,365
06443	Madison	(203)	18,755	15,485
*06040	Manchester	(860)	55,650	51,618
*06250	Mansfield	(860)	24,756	21,103
06447	Marlborough	(860)	6,311	5,535
06450	Meriden	(203)	59,439	59,479
*06762	Middlebury	(203)	7,132	6,145
06457	Middletown	(860)	47,481	42,762
*06460	Milford	(203)	55,020	48,168
06468	Monroe	(203)	19,562	16,896
06353	Montville	(860)	19,619	16,673
06770	Naugatuck	(203)	31,872	30,625

ZIP	Place	Area Code	2006	1990
*06050	New Britain	(860)	70,746	75,491
*06840	New Canaan	(203)	19,939	17,864
06812	New Fairfield	(203)	14,221	12,911
06057	New Hartford	(860)	6,788	5,769
*06511	New Haven	(203)	124,001	130,474
06320	New London	(860)	25,926	28,540
06776	New Milford	(860)	28,671	23,629
06470	Newtown	(203)	26,985	20,779
06471	North Branford	(203)	14,450	12,996
06473	North Haven	(203)	24,031	22,247
06359	North Stonington	(860)	5,197	4,907
*06856	Norwalk	(203)	84,187	78,331
06360	Norwich	(860)	36,324	37,391
06779	Oakville (c)	(860)	8,618	8,741
06371	Old Lyme	(860)	7,410	6,535
06475	Old Saybrook	(860)	10,570	9,552
06477	Orange	(203)	13,852	12,830
06478	Oxford	(203)	12,309	8,685
06379	Pawcatuck (c)	(860)	5,474	5,289
06374	Plainfield	(860)	15,417	14,363
06062	Plainville	(860)	17,285	17,392
06782	Plymouth	(860)	12,154	11,822
06480	Portland	(860)	9,585	8,418
06712	Prospect	(203)	9,264	7,775
*06260	Putnam	(860)	9,307	9,031
06260	Putnam District (c)	(860)	6,746	6,835
06896	Redding	(203)	8,902	7,927
*06877	Ridgefield (c)	(203)	7,212	6,363
06877	Ridgefield	(203)	23,999	20,919
06066	Rockville (c)	(860)	7,708	—
06067	Rocky Hill	(860)	18,806	16,554
*06483	Seymour	(203)	16,218	14,288
06484	Shelton	(203)	40,142	35,418
06082	Sherwood Manor (c)	(860)	5,689	6,357
*06070	Simsbury	(860)	23,623	22,023
06070	Simsbury Center (c)	(860)	5,603	5,577
06071	Somers	(860)	10,873	9,108
06488	Southbury	(203)	19,686	15,818
06489	Southington	(860)	42,182	38,518
06074	South Windsor	(860)	25,989	22,090
06082	Southwood Acres (c)	(860)	8,067	8,963
*06075	Stafford	(860)	11,806	11,091
*06904	Stamford	(203)	119,261	108,056
06378	Stonington	(860)	18,220	16,919
*06268	Storrs (c)	(860)	10,996	12,198
06602	Stratford	(203)	49,514	49,389
*06078	Suffield	(860)	15,106	11,427
06786	Terryville (c)	(860)	5,360	5,426
06787	Thomaston	(860)	7,916	6,947
06277	Thompson	(860)	9,306	8,668
06082	Thompsonville (c)	(860)	8,125	8,458
06084	Tolland	(860)	14,674	11,001
*06790	Torrington	(860)	35,903	33,687
06611	Trumbull	(860)	34,963	32,016
06066	Vernon	(860)	29,622	29,841
*06492	Wallingford	(203)	44,740	40,822
06492	Wallingford Center (c)	(203)	17,509	17,827
*06702	Waterbury	(203)	107,251	108,961
*06385	Waterford	(860)	18,766	17,930
06795	Watertown	(860)	22,339	20,456
06498	Westbrook	(860)	6,610	5,414
*06101	West Hartford	(860)	60,700	60,110
06516	West Haven	(203)	52,721	54,021
06883	Weston	(203)	10,251	8,648
*06880	Westport	(203)	26,592	24,410
*06101	Wethersfield	(860)	26,016	25,651
06226	Willimantic (c)	(860)	15,823	14,746
06279	Willington	(860)	6,195	5,979
06897	Wilton	(203)	17,854	15,989
*06094	Winchester	(860)	10,861	11,524
06280	Windham	(860)	23,770	22,039
06095	Windsor	(860)	28,658	27,817
06096	Windsor Locks	(860)	12,424	12,358
*06098	Winsted (c)	(860)	7,321	8,254
*06716	Wolcott	(203)	16,269	13,700
06525	Woodbridge	(203)	9,228	7,924
06798	Woodbury	(203)	9,757	8,131
06281	Woodstock	(860)	8,187	6,008

Delaware (302)

ZIP	Place	2006	1990
19701	Bear (c)	17,593	—
19713	Brookside (c)	14,806	15,307
19703	Claymont (c)	9,220	9,800
*19901	Dover	34,735	27,630
*19809	Edgemoor (c)	5,992	5,853
19805	Elsmere (c)	5,731	5,935
19702	Glasgow (c)	12,840	—
19707	Hockessin (c)	12,902	—
19709	Middletown (c)	10,272	3,834
19963	Milford	7,852	6,032
*19711	Newark	30,014	26,463
19702	Pike Creek (c)	19,751	10,163
19973	Seaford	7,080	5,689
19977	Smyrna	7,837	5,231
*19899	Wilmington	72,826	71,529
19720	Wilmington Manor (c)	8,262	8,568

District of Columbia (202)

ZIP	Place		2006	1990
*20090	Washington		581,530	606,900

Florida

Area code (321) overlays area code (407). Area code (754) overlays (954). Area code (786) overlays (305). See introductory note.

ZIP	Place	Area Code	2006	1990
*32615	Alachua	(386)	8,493	4,667
*32714	Altamonte Springs	(407)	40,613	35,167
33169	Andover (c)	(305)	8,489	6,251
33572	Apollo Beach (c)	(813)	7,444	6,025
*32712	Apopka	(407)	35,563	13,611
*34266	Arcadia	(863)	7,084	6,488
*32233	Atlantic Beach	(904)	13,268	11,636
33823	Auburndale	(863)	13,038	8,846
33160	Aventura	(305)	30,027	14,914
*33825	Avon Park	(863)	9,056	8,078
32807	Azalea Park (c)	(407)	11,073	8,926
*33830	Bartow	(863)	16,455	14,716
33154	Bay Harbor Islands	(305)	5,014	4,703
32819	Bay Hill (c)	(407)	5,177	5,346
34667	Bayonet Point (c)	(727)	23,577	21,860
33507	Bayshore Gardens (c)	(941)	17,350	17,062
33589	Beacon Square (c)	(727)	7,263	6,265
34233	Bee Ridge (c)	(941)	8,744	6,406
33756	Bellair-Meadowbrook Terrace (c)	(904)	16,539	15,606
33430	Belle Glade	(561)	15,233	16,177
*32802	Belle Isle	(407)	6,457	5,272
*34420	Belleview	(352)	21,201	19,386
33465	Beverly Hills (c)	(352)	8,317	6,163
33043	Big Pine Key (c)	(305)	5,032	4,206
*33509	Bloomingdale (c)	(813)	19,839	13,912
33433	Boca Del Mar (c)	(561)	21,832	17,754
33431	Boca Raton	(561)	86,396	61,486
*34135	Bonita Springs	(239)	40,877	13,600
33547	Boyette (c)	(813)	64,775	5,895
33436	Boynton Beach	(561)	68,284	46,284
*34206	Bradenton	(941)	53,662	43,769
*33509	Brandon (c)	(813)	77,895	57,985
32503	Brent (c)	(850)	22,257	21,624
33317	Broadview Park (c)	(954)	6,798	6,109
33313	Broadview-Pompano Park (c)	(954)	5,314	5,230
*34601	Brooksville	(352)	7,609	7,589
33142	Brownsville (c)	(305)	14,393	15,607
32404	Callaway	(850)	14,145	12,253
*32920	Cape Canaveral	(321)	10,363	8,014
*33920	Cape Coral	(239)	151,389	74,991
*33055	Carol City (c)	(305)	59,443	53,331
32707	Casselberry	(407)	24,647	20,736
32404	Cedar Grove	(850)	5,183	1,479
33401	Century Village (c)	(305)	7,616	8,363
33549	Cheval (c)	(813)	7,602	—
33624	Citrus Park (c)	(813)	20,226	—
*32966	Citrus Ridge (c)	(772)	12,015	—
*33758	Clearwater	(727)	107,742	98,669
*34711	Clermont	(352)	11,982	6,910
33440	Clewiston	(863)	7,281	6,085
*32922	Cocoa	(321)	16,743	17,710
*32931	Cocoa Beach	(321)	12,171	12,123
*32922	Cocoa West (c)	(321)	5,921	6,160
*33097	Coconut Creek	(954)	50,120	27,269
33064	Collier Manor-Cresthaven (c)	(954)	7,741	7,322
33801	Combee Settlement (c)	(863)	5,436	5,463
32809	Conway (c)	(407)	14,394	13,159
*33328	Cooper City	(954)	29,945	21,335
*33114	Coral Gables	(305)	42,794	40,091
*33073	Coral Springs	(954)	129,805	78,864
33157	Coral Terrace (c)	(305)	24,380	23,255
33015	Country Club (c)	(305)	36,310	3,408
33196	Country Walk (c)	(305)	10,653	—
*32536	Crestview	(850)	18,215	9,886
33803	Crystal Lake (c)	(863)	5,341	5,300
*33157	Cutler (c)	(305)	17,920	16,201
*33157	Cutler Ridge (c)	(305)	24,781	21,268
33884	Cypress Gardens (c)	(863)	8,844	9,188
33919	Cypress Lake (c)	(239)	12,072	10,491
*33525	Dade City	(352)	6,987	5,633
*33004	Dania Beach	(954)	28,802	—
*33329	Davie	(954)	85,583	47,143
*32114	Daytona Beach	(386)	64,183	61,991
*32713	DeBary	(386)	16,427	9,327
*33441	Deerfield Beach	(954)	76,215	46,997
*32720	De Land	(386)	25,873	16,622
*32444	Delray Beach	(561)	64,630	47,184
*32783	Deltona	(407)	84,273	49,429
*32541	Destin	(850)	12,745	8,090
32819	Doctor Phillips (c)	(407)	9,548	7,963
*33178	Doral	(305)	21,313	3,516
*34698	Dunedin	(727)	36,640	34,427
33610	East Lake (c)	(813)	29,394	—
33610	East Lake-Orient Park (c)	(813)	5,703	6,171
33157	East Perrine (c)	(305)	7,079	—
*32132	Edgewater	(386)	21,486	15,351
32542	Eglin AFB (c)	(850)	8,082	8,347
33614	Egypt Lake-Leto (c)	(813)	32,782	—
34680	Elfers (c)	(727)	13,161	12,356
*34295	Englewood (c)	(941)	16,196	15,025
32534	Ensley (c)	(850)	18,752	16,362
33928	Estero (c)	(239)	9,503	3,177

ZIP	Place	Area Code	2006	1990
*32726	Eustis	(352)	18,305	12,856
32804	Fairview Shores (c)	(305)	13,898	13,192
*32034	Fernandina Beach	(904)	11,324	8,765
32730	Fern Park (c)	(407)	8,318	8,294
32514	Ferry Pass (c)	(850)	27,176	26,301
*33034	Florida City	(305)	9,445	5,978
32960	Florida Ridge (c)	(772)	15,217	12,218
32714	Forest City (c)	(407)	12,612	10,638
*33310	Fort Lauderdale	(954)	185,804	149,238
33841	Fort Meade	(863)	5,734	5,151
*33902	Fort Myers	(239)	60,531	44,947
*33931	Fort Myers Beach	(239)	6,559	9,284
*33922	Fort Myers Shores (c)	(239)	5,793	5,460
*34981	Fort Pierce	(772)	39,365	36,830
*33452	Fort Pierce North (c)	(772)	7,386	5,833
*34982	Fort Pierce South (c)	(772)	5,672	5,320
32548	Fort Walton Beach	(850)	19,339	21,407
33172	Fountainbleau (c)	(305)	59,549	—
*32259	Fruit Cove (c)	(904)	16,077	5,904
34232	Fruitville (c)	(941)	12,741	9,808
33823	Fussels Corner (c)	(863)	5,313	3,840
*32602	Gainesville	(352)	108,655	91,482
33534	Gibsonton (c)	(813)	8,752	7,706
32960	Gifford (c)	(772)	7,599	6,278
33138	Gladeview (c)	(954)	14,468	15,637
33143	Glenvar Heights (c)	(305)	16,243	14,823
34116	Golden Gate (c)	(239)	20,951	14,148
33055	Golden Glades (c)	(305)	32,623	25,474
33411	Golden Lakes (c)	(561)	6,694	3,867
32733	Goldenrod (c)	(407)	12,871	12,362
32560	Gonzalez (c)	(850)	11,365	7,669
33170	Goulds (c)	(305)	7,453	7,284
33624	Greater Carrollwood (c)	(813)	33,519	—
33624	Greater Northdale (c)	(813)	20,461	16,318
33573	Greater Sun Center (c)	(813)	16,321	—
*33454	Greenacres	(561)	32,395	18,683
32043	Green Cove Springs	(904)	6,387	4,497
34736	Groveland	(352)	5,812	—
*32561	Gulf Breeze	(850)	6,446	5,530
33581	Gulf Gate Estates (c)	(941)	11,647	11,622
*33737	Gulfport	(727)	12,533	11,709
*33844	Haines City	(863)	17,595	11,683
*33009	Hallandale Beach	(305)/(954)	39,372	30,997
33434	Hamptons at Boca Raton (c)	(561)	11,306	11,686
34442	Hernando (c)	(352)	8,253	2,103
*33010	Hialeah	(305)	217,141	188,000
*33016	Hialeah Gardens	(305)	19,658	7,727
33455	Hobe Sound (c)	(772)	11,376	11,507
*34690	Holiday (c)	(727)	21,904	19,360
32125	Holly Hill	(386)	13,325	11,141
*33022	Hollywood	(954)	145,794	121,720
*34218	Holmes Beach	(941)	5,071	4,826
*33030	Homestead	(305)	53,767	26,694
34447	Homosassa Springs (c)	(352)	12,458	6,271
*34667	Hudson (c)	(727)	12,765	7,344
32837	Hunters Creek (c)	(407)	9,369	—
*34142	Immokalee (c)	(239)	19,763	14,120
32937	Indian Harbour Beach	(321)	8,472	6,933
32963	Indian River Estates (c)	(772)	5,793	4,858
33785	Indian Rocks Beach	(727)	5,216	3,963
34956	Indiantown (c)	(772)	5,588	4,794
*34450	Inverness	(352)	7,215	5,797
34452	Inverness Highlands South (c)	(352)	5,781	—
33880	Inwood (c)	(863)	6,925	6,824
33908	Iona (c)	(239)	11,756	9,565
*33036	Islamorada, Village of Islands	(305)	6,451	—
33162	Ives Estates (c)	(305)	17,586	13,531
*32203	Jacksonville	(904)	794,555	635,230
*32250	Jacksonville Beach	(904)	21,698	17,839
33880	Jan Phyl Village (c)	(863)	5,633	5,308
33568	Jasmine Estates (c)	(727)	18,213	17,136
*34957	Jensen Beach (c)	(772)	11,100	9,884
*33458	Jupiter	(561)	48,647	26,753
33183	Kendale Lakes (c)	(305)	56,901	48,524
33256	Kendall (c)	(305)	75,226	87,271
33193	Kendall West (c)	(305)	38,034	—
33149	Key Biscayne (c)	(305)	10,033	8,854
33037	Key Largo (c)	(305)	11,886	11,336
33556	Keystone (c)	(813)	14,627	—
*33040	Key West	(305)	23,262	24,832
*33573	Kings Point (c)	(305)	12,207	12,422
*34744	Kissimmee	(407)	60,894	30,337
*32159	Lady Lake	(352)	13,584	8,071
34786	Lake Butler (c)	—	7,062	—
32055	Lake City	(386)	11,953	9,626
33804	Lakeland	(863)	90,207	70,576
33801	Lakeland Highlands (c)	(863)	12,557	9,972
32569	Lake Lorraine (c)	(850)	7,106	6,779
33054	Lake Lucerne (c)	(305)	9,132	9,478
33612	Lake Magdalene (c)	(813)	28,755	15,973
32746	Lake Mary	(407)	14,718	5,929
33403	Lake Park	(561)	8,893	6,704
33189	Lakes by the Bay (c)	(305)	9,055	5,615
32073	Lakeside (c)	(904)	30,927	29,137
33853	Lake Wales	(863)	13,687	9,670
34951	Lakewood Park (c)	(772)	10,458	7,211
*33461	Lake Worth	(561)	35,980	28,564
33461	Lake Worth Corridor (c)	—	18,663	—
*34639	Land O'Lakes (c)	(813)	20,971	7,892
*33465	Lantana	(561)	10,334	8,392

ZIP	Place	Area Code	2006	1990
*33770	Largo	(727)	73,796	65,910
*33062	Lauderdale-by-the-Sea	(954)	5,991	4,014
*33313	Lauderdale Lakes	(954)	31,911	27,341
*33313	Lauderhill	(954)	59,482	49,015
34272	Laurel (c)	(941)	8,393	8,245
*34461	Lecanto (c)	(352)	5,161	1,243
*34748	Leesburg	(352)	19,835	14,783
*33936	Lehigh Acres (c)	(239)	33,430	13,611
*33033	Leisure City (c)	(305)	22,152	19,379
*33074	Lighthouse Point	(954)	11,292	10,378
*32060	Live Oak	(386)	7,024	6,332
32810	Lockhart (c)	(407)	12,944	11,636
34228	Longboat Key	(941)	7,414	5,937
*32750	Longwood	(407)	13,529	13,316
*33549	Lutz (c)	(813)	17,081	10,552
32444	Lynn Haven	(850)	15,654	9,270
33919	McGregor (c)	(904)	7,136	6,504
32063	Macclenny	(904)	5,484	3,966
*32751	Maitland	(407)	14,172	8,932
33550	Mango (c)	(813)	8,842	8,700
33050	Marathon	(305)	9,789	8,857
*34145	Marco Island	(239)	16,069	—
*33093	Margate	(954)	55,974	42,985
32446	Marianna	(850)	6,286	6,292
34753	Mascotte	(352)	5,028	—
32824	Meadow Woods (c)	(407)	11,286	4,876
33811	Medulla (c)	(863)	6,637	3,977
*32901	Melbourne	(321)	76,963	60,034
32666	Melrose Park (c)	(954)	7,114	6,477
33561	Memphis (c)	(941)	7,264	6,760
*32953	Merritt Island (c)	(321)	36,090	32,886
*33101	Miami	(305)	404,048	358,648
*33152	Miami Beach	(305)	86,916	92,639
33023	Miami Gardens	(305)	98,989	—
*33014	Miami Lakes	(305)	22,206	12,750
*33153	Miami Shores	(305)	9,882	10,084
*33266	Miami Springs	(305)	12,962	13,268
32976	Micco (c)	(772)	9,498	8,757
*32068	Middleburg (c)	(904)	10,338	6,223
*32570	Milton	(850)	8,118	7,216
32754	Mims (c)	(321)	9,147	9,412
*34755	Minneola	(352)	8,999	1,515
*33023	Miramar	(954)	108,072	40,663
*32757	Mount Dora	(352)	11,564	7,294
32526	Myrtle Grove (c)	(850)	17,211	17,402
*34102	Naples	(239)	21,975	19,505
34113	Naples Manor (c)	(239)	5,186	4,574
34102	Naples Park (c)	(239)	6,741	8,002
32266	Neptune Beach	(904)	6,884	6,816
*34653	New Port Richey	(727)	17,200	14,044
33552	New Port Richey East (c)	(727)	9,916	9,683
*32168	New Smyrna Beach	(386)	22,732	16,549
*32578	Niceville	(850)	12,277	10,509
33269	Norland (c)	(305)	22,995	22,109
33308	North Andrews Gardens (c)	(305)	9,656	9,002
33141	North Bay Village	(305)	8,061	5,383
*33918	North Fort Myers (c)	(239)	40,214	30,027
*33068	North Lauderdale	(954)	42,220	26,473
*33261	North Miami	(305)	57,670	50,001
*33160	North Miami Beach	(305)	39,030	35,361
*33408	North Palm Beach	(561)	12,457	11,538
*34287	North Port	(941)	50,523	11,973
34234	North Sarasota (c)	(941)	6,738	6,702
*33307	Oakland Park	(305)	42,384	26,326
*33860	Oak Ridge (c)	(407)	22,349	15,388
*34478	Ocala	(352)	52,488	42,045
32548	Ocean City (c)	(850)	5,594	5,422
34761	Ocoee	(407)	30,644	12,778
*33163	Ojus (c)	(305)	16,642	15,519
*34972	Okeechobee	(863)	5,926	4,943
34677	Oldsmar	(813)	13,443	8,361
*33265	Olympia Heights (c)	(305)	13,452	37,792
*33054	Opa-Locka	(305)	15,596	15,283
*33054	Opa-Locka North (c)	(305)	6,224	6,568
*32763	Orange City	(386)	9,267	5,372
*32073	Orange Park	(904)	9,496	9,488
*32802	Orlando	(407)	220,186	164,674
32811	Orlo Vista (c)	(407)	6,047	5,990
*32174	Ormond Beach	(386)	38,504	29,721
32074	Ormond By-The-Sea (c)	(386)	8,430	8,157
*32765	Oviedo	(407)	30,618	11,114
32571	Pace (c)	(850)	7,393	6,277
33476	Pahokee	(561)	6,581	6,822
*32177	Palatka	(386)	11,005	10,447
*32905	Palm Bay	(321)	97,748	62,543
33480	Palm Beach	(561)	9,731	9,814
33408	Palm Beach Gardens	(561)	48,914	24,139
*34990	Palm City (c)	(772)	20,097	3,925
*32135	Palm Coast	(386)	68,013	14,287
*34221	Palmetto	(813)	14,002	9,268
33157	Palmetto Bay	(305)/(786)	23,354	—
33157	Palmetto Estates (c)	(305)	13,675	12,293
*34683	Palm Harbor (c)	(727)	59,248	50,256
*33601	Palm River-Clair Mel (c)	(813)	17,589	13,691
*33406	Palm Springs	(561)	15,587	9,763
33012	Palm Springs North (c)	(305)	5,460	5,300
32082	Palm Valley (c)	(904)	19,860	9,960
*32401	Panama City	(850)	36,807	34,396
*32417	Panama City Beach	(850)	13,565	4,051
*33067	Parkland	(954)	23,329	3,773
34108	Pelican Bay (c)	(239)	5,686	—
*34029	Pembroke Pines	(954)	150,064	65,566
*32502	Pensacola	(850)	53,248	59,198
*32347	Perry	(850)	6,804	7,151
32839	Pine Castle (c)	(407)	8,803	8,276
33156	Pinecrest	(305)	19,033	—
32858	Pine Hills (c)	(407)	41,764	35,322
33324	Pine Island Ridge (c)	(954)	5,199	5,244
*33781	Pinellas Park	(727)	47,354	43,571
*34465	Pine Ridge (c)	(352)	5,490	—
33168	Pinewood (c)	(305)	16,523	15,518
*33318	Plantation	(954)	85,938	66,814
*33566	Plant City	(813)	31,727	22,754
*34758	Poinciana (c)	(407)	13,647	—
*33060	Pompano Beach	(954)	104,402	72,411
33064	Pompano Beach Highlands (c)	(941)	6,505	17,915
33952	Port Charlotte (c)	(941)	46,451	41,535
*32129	Port Orange	(904)	54,851	35,399
*32927	Port St. John (c)	(321)	12,112	8,933
*34981	Port St. Lucie	(772)	143,868	55,761
34983	Port St. Lucie-River Park (c)	(772)	5,175	4,874
*34992	Port Salerno (c)	(772)	10,141	7,786
*33032	Princeton (c)	(305)	10,090	7,073
*33950	Punta Gorda	(941)	17,126	10,637
*32351	Quincy	(850)	6,913	7,452
*33156	Richmond Heights (c)	(305)	8,479	8,583
33177	Richmond West (c)	(305)	28,082	—
34231	Ridge Wood Heights (c)	(941)	5,028	4,851
*33569	Riverview (c)	(813)	12,035	6,478
*33419	Riviera Beach	(561)	35,846	27,646
32955	Rockledge	(321)	24,290	16,023
33947	Rotonda (c)	(941)	6,574	3,576
*33411	Royal Palm Beach	(561)	30,851	15,532
*33570	Ruskin (c)	(813)	8,321	6,046
*34695	Safety Harbor	(727)	17,363	15,120
*33706	Saint Pete Beach	(727)	10,085	9,200
*33733	Saint Petersburg	(727)	248,098	240,318
33912	San Carlos Park (c)	(239)	16,317	11,785
33432	Sandalfoot Cove (c)	(305)	16,582	14,214
*32771	Sanford	(407)	49,124	32,387
33957	Sanibel	(239)	5,812	5,468
*34230	Sarasota	(941)	52,942	50,897
33577	Sarasota Springs (c)	(941)	15,875	16,088
32937	Satellite Beach	(321)	9,937	9,889
33055	Scott Lake (c)	(305)	14,401	14,541
*32958	Sebastian	(772)	20,255	10,248
*33870	Sebring	(863)	10,648	8,841
*33584	Seffner (c)	(813)	5,467	5,371
*33770	Seminole	(727)	19,219	9,251
34610	Shady Hills (c)	(727)	7,798	—
34242	Siesta Key (c)	(941)	7,150	7,772
*34472	Silver Springs Shores (c)	(352)	6,690	6,421
32809	Sky Lake (c)	(407)	5,651	6,202
32703	South Apopka (c)	(407)	5,800	6,360
33505	South Bradenton (c)	(941)	21,587	20,398
32121	South Daytona	(386)	13,541	12,488
34266	Southeast Arcadia (c)	(863)	6,064	4,145
34277	Southgate (c)	(941)	7,455	7,324
34233	South Gate Ridge (c)	(941)	5,655	5,924
33760	South Highpoint (c)	(727)	8,839	—
33243	South Miami	(305)	11,025	10,404
33157	South Miami Heights (c)	(305)	33,522	30,030
33707	South Pasadena	(727)	5,652	5,644
32937	South Patrick Shores (c)	(321)	8,913	10,249
34230	South Sarasota (c)	(941)	5,314	5,298
33595	South Venice (c)	(941)	13,539	11,951
33331	Southwest Ranches	(954)	7,411	—
32206	Springfield	(850)	8,956	8,719
*34604	Spring Hill (c)	(352)	69,078	31,117
32091	Starke	(904)	5,863	5,226
*34994	Stuart	(772)	16,155	11,936
34446	Sugarmill Woods (c)	(352)	6,409	4,073
33160	Sunny Isles Beach (c)	(305)	15,207	—
*33325	Sunrise	(954)	90,793	65,683
*33283	Sunset (c)	(305)	17,150	15,810
33144	Sweetwater	(305)	13,532	13,909
*32301	Tallahassee	(850)	159,012	124,773
*33320	Tamarac	(954)	60,644	44,822
33144	Tamiami (c)	(305)	54,788	33,845
*33601	Tampa	(813)	332,888	280,015
*34689	Tarpon Springs	(727)	23,214	17,874
32778	Tavares	(352)	12,802	7,488
*33687	Temple Terrace	(813)	22,415	16,444
33469	Tequesta	(561)	5,942	4,499
33186	The Crossings (c)	(305)	23,557	—
33196	The Hammocks (c)	(305)	47,379	—
32159	The Villages (c)	(352)	8,333	—
33592	Thonotosassa (c)	(813)	6,091	—
33186	Three Lakes (c)	(305)	6,955	—
33025	Timber Pines (c)	(352)	5,840	3,182
*32780	Titusville	(321)	44,027	39,394
32615	Town 'n' Country (c)	(813)	72,523	60,946
*33706	Treasure Island	(727)	7,561	7,266
32817	Union Park (c)	(407)	10,191	6,890
33024	University (c)	(813)	30,736	—
*33165	University Park (c)	(305)	26,538	—

ZIP	Place	Area Code	2006	1990
32401	Upper Grand Lagoon (c)	(850)	10,889	7,855
32580	Valparaiso	(850)	6,089	6,316
*33594	Valrico (c)	(813)	6,582	—
34231	Vamo (c)	(941)	5,285	3,325
*34285	Venice	(941)	20,952	17,052
33595	Venice Gardens (c)	(941)	7,466	7,701
*32960	Vero Beach	(772)	16,939	17,350
32960	Vero Beach South (c)	(772)	20,362	16,973
33901	Villas (c)	(239)	11,346	9,898
32507	Warrington (c)	(850)	15,207	16,040
32791	Wekiva Springs (c)	(407)	23,169	23,026
*33414	Wellington	(561)	54,993	20,670
33543	Wesley Chapel (c)	(813)	5,691	—
33714	West and East Lealman (c)	(727)	21,753	—
33626	Westchase (c)	(813)	11,116	—
33165	Westchester (c)	(305)	30,271	29,883
33409	Westgate-Belvedere Homes (c)	(561)	8,134	6,880
33138	West Little River (c)	(305)	32,498	33,575
*32912	West Melbourne	(321)	15,137	8,398
*33144	West Miami	(305)	5,743	5,727
33326	Weston	(954)	65,720	—
*33416	West Palm Beach	(561)	98,774	67,764
33023	West Park	(954)	14,835	—
32505	West Pensacola (c)	(850)	21,939	22,107
33157	West Perrine (c)	(305)	8,600	—
34208	West Samoset (c)	(941)	5,507	3,819
32966	West Vero Corridor (c)	(772)	7,695	—
33168	Westview (c)	(305)	9,692	9,668
33165	Westwood Lakes (c)	(305)	12,005	11,522
33496	Whisper Walk (c)	(561)	5,135	3,037
32821	Williamsburg (c)	(407)	6,736	3,093
*33305	Wilton Manors (c)	(954)	12,909	11,804
33803	Winston (c)	(813)	9,024	9,118
34787	Winter Garden (c)	(407)	27,045	9,863
33880	Winter Haven	(863)	30,978	24,725
*32789	Winter Park	(407)	28,083	24,260
*32707	Winter Springs	(407)	32,598	22,151
32547	Wright (c)	(850)	21,697	18,945
34972	Yeehaw Junction (c)	(407)	21,778	—
*32097	Yulee (c)	(904)	8,392	6,915
*33540	Zephyrhills	(813)	12,763	8,220
33541	Zephyrhills West (c)	(813)	5,242	4,249

Georgia

Area code (678) overlays (770). Area code (762) overlays (706). See introductory note.

ZIP	Place	Area Code	2006	1990
*30101	Acworth	(770)	18,790	4,519
31620	Adel	(229)	5,389	5,093
31706	Albany	(229)	75,335	78,804
*30004	Alpharetta	(770)	43,424	13,002
31709	Americus	(229)	16,514	16,516
*30603	Athens-Clarke County[1]	(706)	112,787	86,522
*30301	Atlanta	(404)	486,411	393,929
30011	Auburn	(770)	7,261	3,139
*30903	Augusta-Richmond County[2]	(706)	194,398	186,616
*30168	Austell	(770)	6,766	4,173
39818	Bainbridge	(229)	12,087	10,803
30204	Barnesville	(770)	5,982	4,747
30032	Belvedere Park (c)	(404)	18,945	18,089
31723	Blakely	(229)	5,419	5,595
30110	Bremen	(770)	5,487	4,353
*31520	Brunswick	(912)	16,074	16,433
*30518	Buford	(404)	11,160	8,771
39827	Cairo	(229)	9,605	9,035
*30701	Calhoun	(706)	14,015	7,135
31730	Camilla	(229)	5,609	5,124
30032	Candler-McAfee (c)	(404)	28,294	29,491
*30114	Canton	(770)	19,553	4,817
30117	Carrollton	(770)	21,878	16,029
*30120	Cartersville	(770)	17,407	12,037
30125	Cedartown	(770)	9,870	7,976
31028	Centerville	(478)	6,857	3,509
30366	Chamblee	(404)	10,532	7,668
30021	Clarkston	(404)	7,508	5,385
30337	College Park	(404)	20,533	20,645
31908	Columbus	(706)	188,660	178,683
*30529	Commerce	(770)	6,088	4,108
30288	Conley (c)	(404)	6,188	5,528
*30013	Conyers	(404)	12,529	7,380
31015	Cordele	(229)	11,511	10,833
31525	Country Club Estates (c)	(912)	7,594	7,500
*30014	Covington	(770)	14,272	9,860
*30040	Cumming	(770)	5,877	2,798
31805	Cusseta-Chattahoochee County	(706)	14,041	1,107
*30132	Dallas	(770)	9,437	2,810
*30720	Dalton	(706)	33,045	22,218
*30030	Decatur	(404)	19,053	17,304
31520	Dock Junction (c)	(912)	6,951	7,094
*30362	Doraville	(404)	10,306	7,626
31533	Douglas	(912)	11,246	10,464
*30134	Douglasville	(404)	28,870	11,635
30333	Druid Hills (c)	(404)	12,741	12,174
31021	Dublin	(478)	17,263	16,312
*30096	Duluth	(404)	25,838	9,821
*30362	Dunwoody (c)	(404)	32,808	26,302
31023	Eastman	(478)	5,518	5,153
30364	East Point	(404)	42,204	34,595
31024	Eatonton	(706)	6,732	6,479

ZIP	Place	Area Code	2006	1990
30809	Evans (c)	(706)	17,727	13,713
30213	Fairburn	(770)	9,580	4,013
30060	Fair Oaks (c)	(404)	8,443	6,996
30535	Fairview (c)	(706)	6,601	6,444
*30214	Fayetteville	(404)	14,998	5,827
31750	Fitzgerald	(229)	9,139	8,901
*30297	Forest Park	(404)	22,080	16,958
31905	Fort Benning South (c)	(706)	11,737	14,617
30742	Fort Oglethorpe	(706)	9,400	5,880
31313	Fort Stewart (c)	(912)	11,205	13,774
31030	Fort Valley	(478)	8,142	8,198
30501	Gainesville	(770)	33,340	17,885
*31418	Garden City	(912)	9,477	7,410
31754	Georgetown (c)	(912)	10,599	5,554
30427	Glennville	(912)	5,131	3,676
30316	Gresham Park (c)	(404)	9,215	9,000
*30223	Griffin	(770)	23,424	21,325
30813	Grovetown	(706)	8,139	3,596
30354	Hapeville	(404)	6,148	5,483
31313	Hinesville	(912)	29,554	21,596
30142	Holly Springs	(770)	6,334	2,406
30238	Irondale (c)	—	7,727	3,352
30549	Jefferson	(706)	6,456	2,763
*31546	Jesup	(912)	10,138	8,958
*30144	Kennesaw	(404)	30,936	8,936
31548	Kingsland	(912)	12,438	6,089
30728	LaFayette	(706)	6,859	6,655
*30240	LaGrange	(706)	27,652	25,574
30045	Lawrenceville	(404)	28,851	17,250
*30047	Lilburn	(404)	11,542	9,295
30052	Loganville	(770)	9,547	3,180
30126	Mableton (c)	(404)	29,733	25,725
30253	McDonough	(770)	16,853	2,929
*31201	Macon	(478)	94,693	107,365
30060	Marietta	(404)	63,152	44,129
30907	Martinez (c)	(706)	27,749	33,731
31061	Midway-Hardwick (c)	—	5,135	4,910
31061	Milledgeville	(478)	19,761	17,727
30655	Monroe	(770)	12,631	9,759
30260	Morrow	(770)	5,395	5,074
31768	Moultrie	(229)	15,260	14,865
30087	Mountain Park (c)	(404)	11,753	11,025
30263	Newnan	(770)	27,097	12,497
*30071	Norcross	(404)	10,111	5,947
30319	North Atlanta (c)	(404)	38,579	27,812
30033	North Decatur (c)	(404)	15,270	13,936
30033	North Druid Hills (c)	(404)	18,852	14,170
30032	Panthersville (c)	(404)	11,791	9,874
*30269	Peachtree City	(404)	34,947	19,027
31069	Perry	(478)	11,340	9,452
31322	Pooler	(912)	11,782	4,649
30127	Powder Springs	(404)	14,964	6,862
30074	Redan (c)	(404)	33,841	24,376
31324	Richmond Hill	(912)	9,806	2,934
31326	Rincon	(912)	6,922	2,992
30274	Riverdale	(404)	15,502	9,495
*30161	Rome	(706)	36,142	30,425
30077	Roswell	(404)	87,802	47,986
31558	Saint Marys	(912)	15,967	8,204
31522	Saint Simons (c)	(912)	13,381	12,026
31082	Sandersville	(478)	6,138	6,290
30358	Sandy Springs[3]	(404)	85,771	67,842
*31402	Savannah	(912)	127,889	137,812
30079	Scottdale (c)	(404)	9,803	8,636
31411	Skidaway Island (c)	(912)	6,494	4,495
*30080	Smyrna	(404)	48,632	32,453
*30078	Snellville	(770)	19,983	12,084
30458	Statesboro	(912)	25,583	20,770
30281	Stockbridge	(404)	13,668	3,359
*30086	Stone Mountain	(404)	7,522	6,544
30518	Sugar Hill	(404)	16,170	4,519
30024	Suwanee	(770)	14,034	2,412
30401	Swainsboro	(478)	7,532	7,361
31791	Sylvester	(229)	5,888	6,023
30286	Thomaston	(706)	9,140	9,127
*31792	Thomasville	(229)	18,988	17,554
30824	Thomson	(706)	6,911	6,862
*31794	Tifton	(229)	16,650	14,215
30577	Toccoa	(706)	9,069	8,720
*30084	Tucker (c)	(404)	26,532	25,781
30290	Tyrone	(770)	6,273	2,724
30291	Union City	(404)	16,407	9,347
31603	Valdosta	(229)	45,529	40,038
*30474	Vidalia	(912)	11,163	11,118
30180	Villa Rica	(770)	11,045	3,916
30339	Vinings (c)	(404)	9,677	7,417
*31088	Warner Robins	(478)	58,672	43,861
31501	Waycross	(912)	14,813	16,410
30830	Waynesboro	(706)	5,863	5,669
31410	Whitemarsh Island (c)	(912)	5,824	2,824
31410	Wilmington Island (c)	(912)	14,213	11,230
30680	Winder	(770)	13,161	7,373
*30188	Woodstock	(770)	21,482	4,361

(1) Athens merged with Clarke County in 1991. The 2006 and 1990 populations are for all of Clarke County except Winterville and Bogart, which are part of the county but are also separate incorporated places. (2) Augusta merged with Richmond County in 1996. The 2006 and 1990 populations are for all of Richmond County except Blythe and Hephzibah, which are part of the county but are also separate incorporated places. (3) 1990 population of Sandy Springs is for Sandy Springs CDP. The city was incorporated in 2005.

Hawaii (808)

ZIP	Place	2006	1990
96744	Ahuimanu (c)	8,506	8,387
96701	Aiea (c)	9,019	8,906
96706	Ewa Beach(c)	14,650	14,315
96708	Haiku-Pauwela (c)	6,578	4,509
96701	Halawa (c)	13,891	13,408
96778	Hawaiian Paradise Park (c)	7,051	3,389
96853	Hickam Housing (c)	5,471	6,553
*96720	Hilo (c)	40,759	37,808
96725	Holualoa (c)	6,107	3,834
*96820	Honolulu (c)[1]	377,357	377,059
*96732	Kahului (c)	20,146	16,889
96734	Kailua (Hawaii Co.) (c)	9,870	9,126
96863	Kailua (Honolulu Co.) (c)	36,513	36,818
96740	Kalaoa (c)	6,794	4,490
*96744	Kaneohe (c)	34,970	35,448
96863	Kaneohe Station (c)	11,827	11,662
96746	Kapaa (c)	9,472	8,149
96753	Kihei (c)	16,749	11,107
*96761	Lahaina (c)	9,118	9,073
96766	Lihue (c)	5,674	5,536
96792	Maili (c)	5,943	6,059
96792	Makaha (c)	7,753	7,990
96706	Makakilo (c)	13,156	9,828
96768	Makawao (c)	6,527	5,405
96789	Mililani Town (c)	28,608	29,359
96792	Nanakuli (c)	10,814	9,575
96761	Napili-Honokowai (c)	6,788	4,332
96782	Pearl City (c)	30,976	30,993
96788	Pukalani (c)	7,380	5,879
96857	Schofield Barracks (c)	14,428	19,597
96797	Village Park (c)	9,625	7,407
*96786	Wahiawa (c)	16,151	17,386
96792	Waianae (c)	10,506	8,758
96793	Waihee-Waiehu (c)	7,310	4,004
96753	Wailea-Makena (c)	5,671	3,799
96793	Wailuku (c)	12,296	10,688
96701	Waimalu (c)	29,371	29,967
96796	Waimea (c)	7,028	5,972
96797	Waipahu (c)	33,108	31,435
96797	Waipio (c)	11,672	11,812
96786	Waipio Acres (c)	5,298	5,304

(1) Population estimate for Honolulu CDP has been updated for 2006.

Idaho (208)

ZIP	Place	2006	1990
*83401	Ammon	12,065	5,002
83221	Blackfoot	11,007	9,646
*83707	Boise	198,638	126,685
83318	Burley	9,174	8,702
*83605	Caldwell	37,056	18,586
83202	Chubbuck	10,861	7,794
*83814	Coeur d'Alene	41,328	24,561
83616	Eagle	18,419	3,327
83617	Emmett	6,284	4,601
*83714	Garden City	11,353	6,369
83333	Hailey	7,751	3,575
83835	Hayden	12,349	4,888
*83402	Idaho Falls	52,786	43,973
83338	Jerome	8,687	6,529
*83634	Kuna	11,510	1,955
83501	Lewiston	31,293	28,082
*83642	Meridian	59,832	9,596
*83843	Moscow	22,352	18,398
83647	Mountain Home	11,656	7,913
83648	Mountain Home AFB (c)	8,894	5,936
*83653	Nampa	76,587	28,365
83661	Payette	7,624	5,672
*83201	Pocatello	53,932	46,117
*83854	Post Falls	24,515	7,349
83263	Preston	5,089	3,710
83858	Rathdrum	6,308	2,014
*83440	Rexburg	26,657	14,298
*83350	Rupert	5,214	5,455
*83864	Sandpoint	8,206	5,561
*83301	Twin Falls	40,380	27,634
83672	Weiser	5,425	4,571

Illinois

Area code (224) overlays area code (847). Area code (331) overlays area code (630). Area code (779) overlays area code (815). See introductory note.

ZIP	Place	Area Code	2006	1990
60101	Addison	(630)	37,035	32,053
*60102	Algonquin	(847)	29,886	11,764
60803	Alsip	(708)	18,940	18,227
62002	Alton	(618)	29,269	33,060
62906	Anna	(618)	5,068	4,805
60002	Antioch	(847)	13,491	6,105
*60005	Arlington Heights	(847)	74,138	75,463
*60505	Aurora	(630)	170,617	99,672
*60010	Barrington	(847)	10,270	9,538
*60103	Bartlett	(630)	40,344	19,395
61607	Bartonville	(309)	6,146	6,555
*60510	Batavia	(630)	27,401	17,076
*60083	Beach Park	(847)	12,942	9,492
62618	Beardstown	(217)	5,914	5,270
*62220	Belleville	(618)	41,095	42,806
60104	Bellwood	(708)	19,326	20,241
61008	Belvidere	(815)	25,682	16,059
*60106	Bensenville	(630)	20,477	17,767
62812	Benton	(618)	6,952	7,216
60402	Berwyn	(708)	50,820	45,426
62010	Bethalto	(618)	9,749	9,507
*60108	Bloomingdale	(630)	21,967	16,614
*61701	Bloomington	(309)	70,970	51,889
*60406	Blue Island	(708)	22,547	21,203
*60440	Bolingbrook	(630)	69,881	40,843
60538	Boulder Hill (c)	(630)	8,169	8,169
60914	Bourbonnais	(815)	17,454	13,929
60915	Bradley	(815)	14,201	10,954
60408	Braidwood	(815)	6,601	3,584
*60455	Bridgeview	(708)	14,966	14,402
*60153	Broadview	(708)	7,763	8,538
60513	Brookfield	(708)	18,257	18,876
*60089	Buffalo Grove	(847)	43,231	36,417
60459	Burbank	(708)	27,669	27,600
60527	Burr Ridge	(630)	11,082	8,247
62206	Cahokia	(618)	15,430	17,550
60409	Calumet City	(708)	37,399	37,840
*60643	Calumet Park	(708)	8,031	8,418
61520	Canton	(309)	14,797	13,959
*62901	Carbondale	(618)	24,881	27,033
62626	Carlinville	(217)	5,714	5,416
62821	Carmi	(618)	5,343	5,735
*60188	Carol Stream	(630)	40,067	31,759
60110	Carpentersville	(847)	37,397	23,049
62918	Carterville	(618)	5,190	3,630
60013	Cary	(847)	19,633	10,025
62801	Centralia	(618)	13,732	14,476
62207	Centreville	(618)	5,773	7,489
*61821	Champaign	(217)	73,685	63,502
60410	Channahon	(815)	13,410	4,266
61920	Charleston	(217)	20,182	20,398
62629	Chatham	(217)	10,039	6,074
62233	Chester	(618)	7,840	8,204
*60607	Chicago	(312)(773)	2,833,321	2,783,726
*60411	Chicago Heights	(708)	31,055	32,966
60415	Chicago Ridge	(708)	13,539	13,643
61523	Chillicothe	(309)	5,812	5,959
60804	Cicero	(708)	81,823	67,436
60514	Clarendon Hills	(630)	8,572	6,994
61727	Clinton	(217)	7,331	7,437
60616	Coal City	(815)	5,341	3,907
62234	Collinsville	(618)	25,610	22,424
61241	Colona	(309)	5,276	2,237
62236	Columbia	(618)	9,109	5,524
60478	Country Club Hills	(708)	16,740	15,431
60525	Countryside	(708)	5,836	5,961
60435	Crest Hill	(815)	20,516	10,999
60445	Crestwood	(708)	11,168	10,823
60417	Crete	(708)	8,982	6,773
61610	Creve Coeur	(309)	5,233	5,938
*60014	Crystal Lake	(815)	41,533	24,692
*61832	Danville	(217)	32,760	33,828
60561	Darien	(630)	22,600	20,556
*62525	Decatur	(217)	77,047	83,900
60015	Deerfield	(847)	19,664	17,327
60115	DeKalb	(815)	42,559	35,076
*60018	Des Plaines	(847)	57,033	53,414
61021	Dixon	(815)	15,347	15,134
60419	Dolton	(708)	24,241	23,956
*60515	Downers Grove	(630)	49,136	47,464
62832	Du Quoin	(618)	6,427	6,697
62024	East Alton	(618)	6,571	7,063
61244	East Moline	(309)	21,134	20,147
*61611	East Peoria	(309)	22,549	21,378
*62201	East St. Louis	(618)	29,448	40,944
62025	Edwardsville	(618)	24,270	14,582
62401	Effingham	(217)	12,447	11,927
*60120	Elgin	(847)	101,903	77,014
*60009	Elk Grove Village	(847)	33,666	33,429
60126	Elmhurst	(630)	45,203	42,029
60707	Elmwood Park	(708)	24,295	23,206
61530	Eureka	(309)	5,161	—
*60201	Evanston	(847)	75,543	73,233
60805	Evergreen Park	(708)	19,669	20,874
62837	Fairfield	(618)	5,170	5,439
*62208	Fairview Heights	(618)	16,587	14,768
60422	Flossmoor	(708)	9,397	8,651
*60130	Forest Park	(708)	15,329	14,918
60020	Fox Lake	(847)	11,015	7,539
60021	Fox River Grove	(847)	5,114	3,629
60423	Frankfort	(815)	16,928	7,180
60423	Frankfort Square (c)	(815)	7,766	6,227
*60131	Franklin Park	(847)	18,273	18,485
61032	Freeport	(815)	25,254	25,840
60030	Gages Lake (c)	(847)	10,415	8,349
*61401	Galesburg	(309)	31,738	33,530
61254	Geneseo	(309)	6,523	5,990
60134	Geneva	(630)	23,975	12,625
60136	Gilberts	(847)	5,245	—
62034	Glen Carbon	(618)	12,349	7,774
60022	Glencoe	(847)	9,011	8,954
*60139	Glendale Heights	(630)	32,349	27,915
60137	Glen Ellyn	(630)	27,295	24,919
*60025	Glenview	(847)	46,321	38,436
60425	Glenwood	(708)	8,600	9,289
62035	Godfrey	(618)	17,051	15,675
60441	Goodings Grove (c)	(815)	17,084	14,054

ZIP	Place	Area Code	2006	1990
62040	Granite City	(618)	30,593	32,766
60030	Grayslake	(847)	21,387	7,388
62246	Greenville	(618)	7,134	5,108
60031	Gurnee	(847)	30,942	13,715
60133	Hanover Park	(630)	37,161	32,918
62946	Harrisburg	(618)	9,573	9,318
60033	Harvard	(815)	9,694	5,975
*60426	Harvey	(708)	28,501	29,771
*60656	Harwood Heights	(708)	8,125	7,680
60047	Hawthorn Woods	(847)	7,752	4,423
60429	Hazel Crest	(708)	14,274	13,334
62948	Herrin	(618)	11,835	10,857
60457	Hickory Hills	(708)	13,443	13,021
62249	Highland	(618)	9,373	7,546
60035	Highland Park	(847)	31,614	30,575
60040	Highwood	(847)	5,471	5,358
62049	Hillsboro	(217)	6,267	—
*60162	Hillside	(708)	7,683	7,672
60521	Hinsdale	(630)	18,178	16,029
*60195	Hoffman Estates	(847)	52,479	46,363
60491	Homer Glen	(708)	25,415	—
*60430	Homewood	(708)	18,734	19,278
60942	Hoopeston	(217)	5,722	5,871
60142	Huntley	(847)	20,047	2453
*60067	Inverness	(847)	7,434	6,516
60042	Island Lake	(847)	8,533	4,449
60143	Itasca	(630)	8,453	6,947
*62650	Jacksonville	(217)	19,448	19,327
62052	Jerseyville	(618)	8,291	7,382
*60050	Johnsburg	(815)	6,494	—
*60436	Joliet	(815)	142,702	77,217
60458	Justice	(708)	12,612	11,137
60901	Kankakee	(815)	26,480	27,541
61443	Kewanee	(309)	12,563	12,969
60525	La Grange	(708)	15,401	15,362
60526	La Grange Park	(708)	12,598	12,861
*60010	Lake Barrington	(847)	5,035	3,855
60044	Lake Bluff	(847)	6,282	5,486
60045	Lake Forest	(847)	21,320	17,836
*60102	Lake in the Hills	(847)	29,359	5,882
60050	Lakemoor	(815)	5,154	1,332
60046	Lake Villa	(847)	8,614	2,857
*60047	Lake Zurich	(847)	20,386	14,927
60438	Lansing	(708)	27,093	28,131
61301	La Salle	(815)	9,511	9,717
*60439	Lemont	(630)	15,475	7,359
*60048	Libertyville	(847)	21,955	19,174
62656	Lincoln	(217)	14,822	15,418
60069	Lincolnshire	(847)	7,333	4,928
*60645	Lincolnwood	(847)	11,945	11,365
60532	Lisle	(630)	23,364	19,584
62056	Litchfield	(217)	6,793	6,883
60441	Lockport	(815)	23,840	9,401
60148	Lombard	(630)	42,792	39,408
*60047	Long Grove	(847)	8,058	4,747
*61130	Loves Park	(815)	23,744	15,457
60411	Lynwood	(708)	7,864	6,535
60534	Lyons	(708)	10,381	9,828
*60050	McHenry	(815)	25,884	16,343
*61115	Machesney Park	(815)	22,423	19,042
61455	Macomb	(309)	18,422	19,952
61853	Mahomet	(217)	5,802	3,499
60442	Manhattan	(815)	6,118	2,059
60950	Manteno	(815)	8,305	3,709
60152	Marengo	(815)	7,499	4,768
62959	Marion	(618)	17,282	14,597
*60426	Markham	(708)	12,248	13,136
62062	Maryville	(618)	6,906	2,576
*62258	Mascoutah	(618)	6,209	5,511
*60443	Matteson	(708)	16,446	11,378
61938	Mattoon	(217)	17,340	18,441
*60153	Maywood	(708)	25,506	27,139
*60160	Melrose Park	(708)	22,250	20,859
61342	Mendota	(815)	7,072	7,017
62960	Metropolis	(618)	6,415	6,734
60445	Midlothian	(708)	13,821	14,372
61264	Milan	(309)	5,213	5,753
60447	Minooka	(815)	9,718	2,561
60448	Mokena	(708)	18,279	6,128
*61265	Moline	(309)	42,916	43,080
61462	Monmouth	(309)	9,151	9,489
60538	Montgomery	(630)	13,667	4,487
61856	Monticello	(217)	5,345	4,775
60450	Morris	(815)	13,282	10,274
61550	Morton	(309)	15,757	13,799
60053	Morton Grove	(847)	22,462	22,373
62863	Mount Carmel	(618)	7,635	8,287
60056	Mount Prospect	(847)	54,140	53,168
62864	Mount Vernon	(618)	16,407	17,082
62549	Mount Zion	(217)	5,061	4,522
60060	Mundelein	(847)	33,063	21,224
62966	Murphysboro	(618)	8,241	9,176
*60540	Naperville	(630)	142,901	85,806
60451	New Lenox	(815)	24,039	9,698
60714	Niles	(847)	29,065	28,375
*61761	Normal	(309)	50,681	40,023
*60634	Norridge	(708)	14,046	14,459
60542	North Aurora	(630)	14,930	6,010
*60062	Northbrook	(708)	34,142	32,565
*60064	North Chicago	(847)	34,068	34,978
60093	Northfield	(847)	5,488	4,924
60164	Northlake	(708)	11,251	12,505
60546	North Riverside	(708)	6,320	6,180
*60521	Oak Brook	(630)	8,863	9,087
60452	Oak Forest	(708)	27,970	26,202
*60303	Oak Lawn	(708)	53,777	56,182
60303	Oak Park	(708)	50,272	53,648
62269	O'Fallon	(618)	25,822	16,064
62450	Olney	(618)	8,426	8,873
60477	Orland Hills	(708)	7,303	5,510
60462	Orland Park	(708)	55,520	35,720
60543	Oswego	(630)	26,252	3,949
61350	Ottawa	(815)	19,058	17,574
*60067	Palatine	(847)	67,396	41,554
60463	Palos Heights	(708)	12,558	11,478
60465	Palos Hills	(708)	17,146	17,803
62557	Pana	(217)	5,501	5,796
61944	Paris	(217)	8,857	9,105
60085	Park City	(847)	6,761	4,677
60466	Park Forest	(708)	22,855	24,656
60068	Park Ridge	(847)	36,887	37,075
*61554	Pekin	(309)	33,368	32,254
*61601	Peoria	(309)	113,107	113,508
61616	Peoria Heights	(309)	6,257	6,930
61354	Peru	(815)	9,833	9,302
62274	Pinckneyville	(618)	5,460	3,372
*60544	Plainfield	(815)	31,968	4,557
60545	Plano	(630)	9,415	5,104
61764	Pontiac	(815)	11,353	11,428
62040	Pontoon Beach	(618)	6,051	4,013
61356	Princeton	(815)	7,555	7,197
60070	Prospect Heights	(847)	16,244	15,236
*62301	Quincy	(217)	40,034	39,682
61866	Rantoul	(217)	12,309	17,212
60471	Richton Park	(708)	12,937	10,523
60827	Riverdale	(708)	14,418	13,671
60305	River Forest	(708)	11,192	11,669
60171	River Grove	(708)	10,157	9,961
60546	Riverside	(708)	8,396	8,774
60472	Robbins	(708)	6,306	7,498
62454	Robinson	(618)	6,446	6,740
61068	Rochelle	(815)	9,771	8,769
61071	Rock Falls	(815)	9,448	9,669
*61125	Rockford	(815)	155,138	142,815
*61201	Rock Island	(309)	38,442	40,630
61072	Rockton	(815)	5,424	2,928
60008	Rolling Meadows	(847)	23,682	22,598
*60446	Romeoville	(815)	36,837	14,101
61073	Roscoe	(815)	8,742	2,079
60172	Roselle	(630)	23,174	20,803
60073	Round Lake	(847)	16,220	3,550
60073	Round Lake Beach	(847)	28,283	16,406
60073	Round Lake Park	(847)	6,236	4,045
*60174	Saint Charles	(630)	32,609	22,636
62881	Salem	(618)	7,551	7,470
60548	Sandwich	(815)	7,083	5,607
60411	Sauk Village	(708)	10,410	10,734
*60194	Schaumburg	(847)	72,690	68,586
*60176	Schiller Park	(847)	11,482	11,189
*62269	Shiloh	(618)	10,575	2,655
61282	Silvis	(309)	7,801	6,926
*60077	Skokie	(847)	66,659	59,432
61080	South Beloit	(815)	5,507	4,072
60177	South Elgin	(847)	21,005	7,474
60473	South Holland	(708)	21,365	22,105
*62703	Springfield	(217)	116,482	105,412
60081	Spring Grove	(815)	5,541	1,066
61362	Spring Valley	(815)	5,375	5,246
62088	Staunton	(618)	5,182	4,806
60475	Steger	(708)	10,586	9,251
61081	Sterling	(815)	15,347	15,142
*60402	Stickney	(708)	5,853	5,678
60107	Streamwood	(630)	37,535	31,197
61364	Streator	(815)	13,899	14,121
60554	Sugar Grove	(630)	9,025	2,123
60501	Summit	(708)	10,318	9,971
*62221	Swansea	(618)	12,582	8,201
60178	Sycamore	(815)	16,270	9,896
62568	Taylorville	(217)	11,194	11,133
60477	Tinley Park	(708)	58,595	37,115
62294	Troy	(618)	9,578	6,194
60466	University Park	(708)	8,253	6,204
*61801	Urbana	(217)	38,658	36,383
62471	Vandalia	(618)	6,823	6,114
*60061	Vernon Hills	(847)	24,200	15,319
60181	Villa Park	(630)	22,528	22,279
60555	Warrenville	(630)	13,193	11,389
61571	Washington	(309)	13,365	10,136
*62204	Washington Park	(618)	5,675	7,431
62298	Waterloo	(618)	9,435	5,030
60970	Watseka	(815)	5,543	5,424
60084	Wauconda	(847)	11,823	6,294
*60085	Waukegan	(847)	92,066	69,481
60154	Westchester	(708)	15,991	17,301
*60185	West Chicago	(630)	26,738	14,808
60118	West Dundee	(847)	7,964	3,728
60558	Western Springs	(708)	12,574	11,956
62896	West Frankfort	(618)	8,316	8,526

ZIP	Place	Area Code	2006	1990
60559	Westmont	(630)	25,059	21,402
*60187	Wheaton	(630)	54,611	51,441
*60090	Wheeling	(847)	36,432	29,911
60527	Willowbrook	(630)	8,863	8,651
60480	Willow Springs	(708)	5,963	4,509
60091	Wilmette	(847)	26,737	26,694
60481	Wilmington	(815)	6,127	4,743
60190	Winfield	(630)	10,027	7,096
60093	Winnetka	(847)	12,433	12,210
60096	Winthrop Harbor	(847)	7,220	6,240
60097	Wonder Lake (c)	(815)	7,463	6,664
*60191	Wood Dale	(630)	13,518	12,394
60517	Woodridge	(630)	34,386	26,359
62095	Wood River	(618)	10,933	11,490
60098	Woodstock	(815)	22,777	14,368
60482	Worth	(708)	10,561	11,208
60560	Yorkville	(630)	12,596	3,974
60099	Zion	(847)	24,895	19,783

Indiana

ZIP	Place	Area Code	2006	1990
46001	Alexandria	(765)	5,888	5,709
*46011	Anderson	(765)	57,496	59,518
46703	Angola	(260)	7,922	5,851
46706	Auburn	(260)	12,802	9,386
46123	Avon	(317)	9,847	—
47006	Batesville	(812)	6,444	4,720
47421	Bedford	(812)	13,581	13,817
46107	Beech Grove	(317)	14,082	13,383
*47408	Bloomington	(812)	69,247	62,735
46714	Bluffton	(260)	9,463	9,104
47601	Boonville	(812)	6,761	6,686
47834	Brazil	(812)	8,212	7,640
47025	Bright (c)	(812)	5,405	3,945
46112	Brownsburg	(317)	18,850	7,751
*46032	Carmel	(317)	60,570	25,380
46303	Cedar Lake	(219)	10,211	8,885
47111	Charlestown	(812)	7,200	5,889
46304	Chesterton	(219)	12,456	9,118
*47129	Clarksville	(812)	21,308	19,838
46725	Columbia City	(260)	8,121	5,883
*47201	Columbus	(812)	39,690	33,948
47331	Connersville	(765)	14,213	15,550
*47933	Crawfordsville	(219)	15,150	13,584
*46307	Crown Point	(219)	23,493	17,728
46229	Cumberland	(317)	5,398	4,557
46122	Danville	(317)	7,827	4,345
46733	Decatur	(574)	9,513	8,642
46517	Dunlap (c)	(574)	5,887	5,705
46311	Dyer	(219)	15,481	10,923
46312	East Chicago	(219)	30,594	33,892
46515	Elkhart	(574)	52,748	44,661
47429	Ellettsville	(812)	5,589	3,275
46036	Elwood	(765)	9,096	9,494
*47708	Evansville	(812)	115,738	126,272
46038	Fishers	(317)	61,840	7,189
*46802	Fort Wayne	(260)	248,637	195,680
*46041	Frankfort	(765)	16,475	14,754
46131	Franklin	(317)	22,356	12,932
46738	Garrett	(260)	5,752	5,349
*46401	Gary	(219)	97,715	116,646
46933	Gas City	(765)	5,791	6,311
*46526	Goshen	(574)	31,882	23,794
46530	Granger (c)	(574)	28,284	20,241
46135	Greencastle	(765)	10,085	8,984
46140	Greenfield	(317)	17,453	11,657
47240	Greensburg	(812)	10,538	9,286
*46142	Greenwood	(317)	44,767	26,507
46319	Griffith	(219)	16,484	17,914
*46320	Hammond	(219)	78,292	84,236
47348	Hartford City	(765)	6,543	6,960
*46322	Highland	(219)	22,961	23,696
46342	Hobart	(219)	28,043	24,440
47542	Huntingburg	(812)	6,069	5,236
46750	Huntington	(260)	16,846	16,389
*46206	Indianapolis	(317)	795,484	731,278
*47546	Jasper	(812)	13,976	10,030
*47130	Jeffersonville	(812)	29,220	24,016
46755	Kendallville	(260)	10,199	7,984
*46902	Kokomo	(765)	45,923	44,996
*47901	Lafayette	(765)	61,244	45,933
46307	Lakes of the Four Seasons (c)	(219)	7,291	6,556
46405	Lake Station	(219)	13,467	13,899
*46350	La Porte	(219)	21,231	21,507
46226	Lawrence	(317)	41,791	26,849
46052	Lebanon	(765)	15,186	12,059
47441	Linton	(812)	5,786	5,814
46947	Logansport	(574)	19,083	16,865
47250	Madison	(812)	12,575	12,006
*46952	Marion	(765)	30,528	32,607
46151	Martinsville	(765)	11,791	11,677
46410	Merrillville	(219)	31,896	27,257
*46360	Michigan City	(219)	32,116	33,822
46544	Mishawaka	(574)	48,912	42,635
47960	Monticello	(574)	5,438	5,237
46158	Mooresville	(317)	11,347	5,779
47620	Mount Vernon	(812)	7,186	7,217
*47302	Muncie	(765)	65,287	71,170

ZIP	Place	Area Code	2006	1990
46321	Munster	(219)	22,346	19,949
46550	Nappanee	(574)	7,070	5,474
*47150	New Albany	(812)	36,963	36,322
47362	New Castle	(765)	18,663	17,753
46774	New Haven	(260)	13,678	11,234
46184	New Whiteland	(317)	5,515	—
*46600	Noblesville	(317)	40,115	17,655
46962	North Manchester	(260)	5,932	6,383
47265	North Vernon	(812)	6,424	5,129
47130	Oak Park (c)	(812)	5,379	5,630
*46970	Peru	(765)	12,719	12,843
46168	Plainfield	(317)	24,734	14,953
46563	Plymouth	(574)	11,025	8,291
46368	Portage	(219)	36,300	29,062
46304	Porter	(219)	5,313	3,242
47371	Portland	(260)	6,180	6,483
47670	Princeton	(812)	8,641	8,127
47978	Rensselaer	(219)	6,259	5,045
*47374	Richmond	(765)	37,371	38,705
46975	Rochester	(574)	6,460	5,969
46173	Rushville	(765)	5,619	5,533
46373	Saint John	(219)	11,710	4,921
47167	Salem	(812)	6,515	5,619
46375	Schererville	(219)	28,881	20,155
47170	Scottsburg	(812)	5,992	5,334
47172	Sellersburg	(812)	6,152	5,936
47274	Seymour	(812)	19,111	15,605
46176	Shelbyville	(765)	18,372	15,841
*46624	South Bend	(574)	104,905	105,511
46383	South Haven (c)	(219)	5,609	6,112
46224	Speedway	(317)	12,416	13,092
47586	Tell City	(812)	7,595	8,088
*47808	Terre Haute	(765)	57,259	57,475
46072	Tipton	(765)	5,203	4,751
*46383	Valparaiso	(219)	29,516	24,414
47591	Vincennes	(812)	17,997	19,867
46992	Wabash	(260)	11,108	12,127
*46580	Warsaw	(574)	13,082	10,968
47501	Washington	(812)	11,279	10,864
46074	Westfield	(317)	13,444	3,304
46580	West Lafayette	(765)	28,997	26,144
46391	Westville	(219)	5,198	5,234
46077	Zionsville	(317)	12,352	6,207

Iowa

ZIP	Place	Area Code	2006	1990
50511	Algona	(515)	5,478	6,015
50009	Altoona	(515)	13,394	7,242
*50010	Ames	(515)	51,557	47,198
52205	Anamosa	(319)	5,653	5,100
*50021	Ankeny	(515)	38,726	18,482
50022	Atlantic	(712)	6,896	7,432
52722	Bettendorf	(563)	32,394	28,139
*50036	Boone	(515)	12,773	12,392
52601	Burlington	(319)	25,464	27,208
51401	Carroll	(712)	9,985	9,579
*50613	Cedar Falls	(319)	36,940	34,298
*52401	Cedar Rapids	(319)	124,417	108,772
52544	Centerville	(641)	5,686	5,936
*50616	Charles City	(641)	7,604	7,878
51632	Clarinda	(712)	5,573	5,104
50428	Clear Lake	(641)	7,889	8,183
*52732	Clinton	(563)	27,042	29,201
50325	Clive	(515)	14,062	7,446
52241	Coralville	(319)	18,017	10,347
*51501	Council Bluffs	(712)	60,271	54,315
50801	Creston	(641)	7,435	7,911
*52802	Davenport	(563)	99,514	95,333
52101	Decorah	(563)	8,080	8,063
51442	Denison	(712)	7,422	6,604
*50318	Des Moines	(515)	193,886	193,966
50742	De Witt	(563)	5,319	4,514
*52001	Dubuque	(563)	57,696	57,538
51334	Estherville	(712)	6,319	6,720
52556	Fairfield	(641)	9,379	9,955
50501	Fort Dodge	(515)	25,466	26,057
52627	Fort Madison	(319)	10,916	11,614
51534	Glenwood	(712)	5,769	4,960
50111	Grimes	(515)	7,005	2,653
*50112	Grinnell	(641)	9,369	8,902
51537	Harlan	(712)	5,134	5,148
52233	Hiawatha	(319)	6,625	5,354
50644	Independence	(319)	6,114	5,972
50125	Indianola	(515)	14,227	11,340
*52240	Iowa City	(319)	62,649	59,735
50126	Iowa Falls	(641)	5,059	5,435
50131	Johnston	(515)	14,513	4,702
52632	Keokuk	(319)	10,687	12,451
*50138	Knoxville	(641)	7,476	8,232
51031	Le Mars	(712)	9,363	8,454
52060	Maquoketa	(563)	6,021	6,130
52302	Marion	(319)	31,084	20,422
50158	Marshalltown	(641)	25,957	25,178
*50401	Mason City	(641)	27,740	29,040
52641	Mount Pleasant	(319)	8,893	7,959
52761	Muscatine	(563)	22,719	22,881
50201	Nevada	(515)	6,328	6,009
50208	Newton	(641)	15,469	14,799
52317	North Liberty	(319)	9,994	2,926

ZIP	Place	Area Code	2006	1990
50211	Norwalk	(515)	8,246	5,726
50662	Oelwein	(319)	6,322	6,691
51041	Orange City	(712)	5,860	4,940
52577	Oskaloosa	(641)	11,028	10,600
52501	Ottumwa	(641)	24,845	24,488
50219	Pella	(641)	10,245	9,270
50220	Perry	(515)	8,752	6,652
*50317	Pleasant Hill	(515)	7,225	3,671
*51566	Red Oak	(712)	5,949	6,264
*51601	Shenandoah	(712)	5,221	5,572
51250	Sioux Center	(712)	6,611	5,074
*51101	Sioux City	(712)	83,262	80,505
51301	Spencer	(712)	11,059	11,066
50588	Storm Lake	(712)	9,882	8,769
*50322	Urbandale	(515)	37,173	23,775
52349	Vinton	(319)	5,214	5,103
52353	Washington	(319)	7,244	7,074
*50701	Waterloo	(319)	65,998	66,467
50263	Waukee	(515)	10,950	2,512
50677	Waverly	(319)	9,347	8,539
50595	Webster City	(515)	8,018	7,894
*50265	West Des Moines	(515)	53,945	31,702

Kansas

ZIP	Place	Area Code	2006	1990
67410	Abilene	(785)	6,444	6,242
67002	Andover	(316)	9,546	4,204
67005	Arkansas City	(620)	11,416	12,762
66002	Atchison	(913)	10,154	10,656
67010	Augusta	(316)	8,696	7,848
*66952	Bel Aire	(316)	6,653	3,695
66012	Bonner Springs	(913)	7,093	6,413
66720	Chanute	(620)	8,887	9,488
67337	Coffeyville	(620)	10,387	12,917
66901	Concordia	(785)	5,281	6,152
67037	Derby	(316)	21,101	14,691
66018	De Soto	(913)	5,244	2,291
*67801	Dodge City	(620)	26,101	21,129
67042	El Dorado	(316)	12,718	11,495
66801	Emporia	(620)	26,188	25,512
66025	Eudora	(785)	6,027	3,006
66442	Fort Riley North (c)	(785)	8,114	12,848
66701	Fort Scott	(620)	7,976	8,362
*67846	Garden City	(620)	27,175	24,097
*66030	Gardner	(913)	15,597	4,277
67530	Great Bend	(620)	15,537	15,427
*67601	Hays	(785)	19,726	18,632
67060	Haysville	(316)	10,029	8,364
*67501	Hutchinson	(620)	41,085	39,308
67301	Independence	(620)	9,317	10,000
66749	Iola	(620)	5,966	6,351
*66441	Junction City	(785)	16,106	20,642
*66102	Kansas City	(913)	143,801	151,521
66043	Lansing	(913)	10,705	7,120
*66044	Lawrence	(785)	88,605	65,608
*66048	Leavenworth	(913)	34,993	38,495
*66209	Leawood	(913)	30,702	19,693
*66214	Lenexa	(913)	44,520	34,110
*67901	Liberal	(620)	20,384	16,573
67460	McPherson	(620)	13,594	12,422
*66502	Manhattan	(785)	50,737	43,081
*66202	Merriam	(913)	10,773	11,819
*66201	Mission	(913)	9,736	9,504
67110	Mulvane	(316)	5,755	4,683
*67114	Newton	(316)	18,093	16,700
*66061	Olathe	(913)	114,662	63,402
66067	Ottawa	(785)	12,792	10,667
*66204	Overland Park	(913)	166,722	111,790
66071	Paola	(913)	5,339	4,698
*67219	Park City	(316)	7,412	5,081
67357	Parsons	(620)	11,237	11,919
*66762	Pittsburg	(620)	19,120	17,789
*66208	Prairie Village	(913)	21,414	23,186
67124	Pratt	(620)	6,408	6,687
66205	Roeland Park	(913)	6,954	7,706
*67401	Salina	(785)	46,140	42,299
*66203	Shawnee	(913)	59,252	37,962
*66601	Topeka	(785)	122,113	119,883
67880	Ulysses	(620)	5,669	5,474
67147	Valley Center	(316)	5,958	4,272
67152	Wellington	(620)	7,991	8,517
*67202	Wichita	(316)	357,698	304,017
*67156	Winfield	(620)	11,741	11,931

Kentucky

ZIP	Place	Area Code	2006	1990
41001	Alexandria	(859)	8,002	5,592
*41101	Ashland	(606)	21,570	23,622
40004	Bardstown	(502)	11,128	6,712
*41073	Bellevue	(859)	5,943	6,997
*40403	Berea	(859)	13,606	9,129
42101	Bowling Green	(270)	53,176	41,688
40218	Buechel (c)	(502)	7,272	7,081
41005	Burlington (c)	(859)	10,779	6,070
42718	Campbellsville	(270)	10,890	9,592
*42330	Central City	(270)	5,779	4,979
40701	Corbin	(606)	8,299	7,644
41011	Covington	(859)	42,797	43,646

ZIP	Place	Area Code	2006	1990
41031	Cynthiana	(859)	6,300	6,497
40422	Danville	(859)	15,385	14,454
*41024	Dayton	(859)	5,508	6,576
40243	Douglass Hills	(502)	5,737	5,431
*41017	Edgewood	(859)	8,869	8,143
*42701	Elizabethtown	(270)	23,406	18,167
41018	Elsmere	(859)	7,884	6,847
41018	Erlanger	(859)	16,965	15,979
40118	Fairdale (c)	(502)	7,658	6,563
40291	Fern Creek (c)	(502)	17,870	16,406
40118	Flatwoods	(606)	7,641	7,799
*41042	Florence	(859)	26,929	18,586
42223	Fort Campbell North (c)	(270)	14,338	13,861
40121	Fort Knox (c)	(270)	12,377	21,495
41017	Fort Mitchell	(859)	7,554	7,438
41075	Fort Thomas	(859)	15,413	16,032
41011	Fort Wright	(859)	5,420	6,404
*40601	Frankfort	(502)	27,077	26,535
*42134	Franklin	(270)	8,110	7,607
40324	Georgetown	(502)	20,685	11,414
*42141	Glasgow	(270)	14,107	12,777
40330	Harrodsburg	(859)	8,156	7,335
*42420	Henderson	(270)	27,915	25,945
*41076	Highland Heights	(859)	5,754	4,223
40228	Highview (c)	(502)	15,161	14,814
40129	Hillview	(502)	7,452	6,119
*42240	Hopkinsville	(270)	27,415	29,809
41051	Independence	(859)	20,254	10,444
*40269	Jeffersontown	(502)	25,907	23,223
*40031	La Grange	(502)	6,180	3,901
40342	Lawrenceburg	(502)	9,656	5,911
40033	Lebanon	(270)	5,957	5,695
*42754	Leitchfield	(270)	6,520	4,965
*40507	Lexington	(859)	270,789	225,366
40741	London	(606)	7,864	5,757
*40232	Louisville/Jefferson County[1]	(502)	554,496	269,555
40252	Lyndon	(502)	10,528	8,037
42431	Madisonville	(270)	19,303	18,693
42066	Mayfield	(270)	10,336	9,935
41056	Maysville	(606)	9,179	8,113
40965	Middlesborough	(606)	10,116	11,328
*40253	Middletown	(502)	6,404	5,016
42633	Monticello	(606)	6,106	5,357
40351	Morehead	(606)	7,578	8,357
40353	Mount Sterling	(859)	6,499	5,362
40047	Mount Washington	(502)	11,761	5,256
42071	Murray	(270)	15,725	14,442
40219	Newburg (c)	(502)	20,636	21,647
*41071	Newport	(859)	15,721	18,871
*40356	Nicholasville	(859)	24,791	13,603
41042	Oakbrook (c)	(859)	7,726	4,113
42262	Oak Grove	(270)	7,223	2,863
*40259	Okolona (c)	(502)	17,807	18,902
*42301	Owensboro	(270)	55,525	53,577
*42003	Paducah	(270)	25,661	27,256
*40361	Paris	(859)	9,304	8,730
*41501	Pikeville	(606)	6,343	6,324
*40268	Pleasure Ridge Park (c)	(502)	25,776	25,131
42445	Princeton	(270)	6,421	6,940
40059	Prospect	(502)	5,129	
*40160	Radcliff	(502)	21,652	19,778
*40475	Richmond	(859)	31,431	21,183
42276	Russellville	(270)	7,331	7,454
40216	Saint Dennis (c)	(502)	9,177	10,326
*40207	Saint Matthews	(502)	17,681	15,691
*40066	Shelbyville	(502)	10,994	6,155
40165	Shepherdsville	(502)	9,035	4,805
40256	Shively	(502)	15,616	15,535
*42501	Somerset	(606)	12,219	10,735
41015	Taylor Mill	(859)	6,715	5,530
*40272	Valley Station (c)	(502)	22,946	22,840
*40383	Versailles	(859)	7,733	7,269
41017	Villa Hills	(859)	7,707	7,370
40769	Williamsburg	(606)	5,163	5,493
40390	Wilmore	(859)	5,876	4,215
*40391	Winchester	(859)	16,556	15,799

(1) Louisville merged with Jefferson County in 2003. The 2006 and 1990 populations are for all of Jefferson County except the separate incorporated places of Anchorage, Middletown, and Jeffersontown.

Louisiana

ZIP	Place	Area Code	2006	1990
*70510	Abbeville	(337)	11,836	11,769
*71301	Alexandria	(318)	45,836	49,049
70032	Arabi (c)	(504)	8,093	8,787
*70094	Avondale (c)	(504)	5,441	5,813
70714	Baker	(225)	13,699	13,087
71220	Bastrop	(318)	12,345	13,916
*70821	Baton Rouge	(225)	229,553	219,531
70364	Bayou Cane (c)	(985)	17,046	15,876
*70037	Belle Chasse (c)	(504)	9,848	8,512
*70427	Bogalusa	(985)	13,002	14,280
*71111	Bossier City	(318)	61,306	52,721
70517	Breaux Bridge	(337)	8,001	6,694
*70094	Bridge City (c)	(504)	8,323	8,327
70518	Broussard	(337)	7,344	3,213
70811	Brownfields (c)	(225)	5,222	5,229
71292	Brownsville-Bawcomville (c)	(318)	7,616	7,397
70520	Carencro	(337)	6,434	5,518

ZIP	Place	Area Code	2006	1990
*70043	Chalmette (c)	(504)	32,069	31,860
70443	Claiborne (c)	(318)	9,830	8,300
*70433	Covington	(985)	9,692	7,691
*70526	Crowley	(337)	14,070	13,983
70345	Cut Off (c)	(985)	5,635	5,325
*70726	Denham Springs	(225)	10,439	8,381
70634	DeRidder	(337)	10,115	10,475
70047	Destrehan (c)	(985)	11,260	8,031
70346	Donaldsonville	(225)	7,733	7,949
70458	Eden Isle (c)	(504)	6,261	3,768
70072	Estelle (c)	(504)	15,880	14,091
70535	Eunice	(337)	11,622	11,162
71459	Fort Polk South (c)	(337)	11,000	11,911
70538	Franklin	(337)	7,879	9,004
70354	Galliano (c)	(985)	7,356	4,294
70810	Gardere (c)	(225)	8,992	7,209
*70737	Gonzales	(225)	9,019	7,208
*70053	Gretna	(504)	16,285	17,208
*70401	Hammond	(985)	19,134	15,871
70123	Harahan	(504)	9,242	9,927
*70058	Harvey (c)	(504)	22,226	21,222
*70360	Houma	(985)	32,657	30,495
70544	Jeanerette	(337)	6,036	6,205
70121	Jefferson (c)	(504)	11,843	14,521
70546	Jennings	(337)	10,631	11,305
70548	Kaplan	(337)	5,205	4,535
*70062	Kenner	(504)	66,592	72,033
*70501	Lafayette	(337)	114,214	101,865
*70601	Lake Charles	(337)	70,224	70,580
71254	Lake Providence (c)	(318)	5,104	5,380
*70068	Laplace (c)	(985)	27,684	24,194
*70373	Larose (c)	(985)	7,306	5,772
*71446	Leesville	(337)	5,853	7,638
70070	Luling (c)	(985)	11,512	2,803
*70471	Mandeville	(985)	12,158	7,474
71052	Mansfield	(318)	5,478	5,389
71351	Marksville	(318)	5,774	5,526
*70072	Marrero (c)	(504)	36,165	36,671
70075	Meraux (c)	(504)	10,192	8,849
70812	Merrydale (c)	(225)	10,427	10,395
*70009	Metairie (c)	(504)	146,136	149,428
*71055	Minden	(318)	13,251	13,661
*71207	Monroe	(318)	51,555	54,909
*70380	Morgan City	(985)	11,930	14,531
70611	Moss Bluff (c)	(337)	10,535	8,039
*71457	Natchitoches	(318)	17,730	16,609
*70560	New Iberia	(337)	32,981	31,828
*70140	New Orleans	(504)	223,388	496,938
71463	Oakdale	(318)	8,022	6,837
70810	Oak Hills Place (c)	(225)	7,996	5,479
70817	Old Jefferson (c)	(225)	5,631	4,531
*70570	Opelousas	(337)	23,222	19,091
70392	Patterson	(985)	5,222	5,166
*71360	Pineville	(318)	14,500	15,308
*70764	Plaquemine	(225)	6,691	7,101
*70454	Ponchatoula	(985)	6,156	5,499
70767	Port Allen	(225)	5,168	6,277
70605	Prien (c)	(337)	7,215	6,448
70394	Raceland (c)	(985)	10,224	5,564
70578	Rayne	(337)	8,645	8,502
71037	Red Chute (c)	(318)	5,984	5,431
*70084	Reserve (c)	(985)	9,111	8,847
70123	River Ridge (c)	(504)	14,588	14,800
*71270	Ruston	(318)	20,522	20,071
70776	Saint Gabriel	(225)	5,605	3,854
70582	Saint Martinville	(337)	7,023	7,226
70087	Saint Rose (c)	(504)	6,540	6,259
70395	Schriever (c)	(985)	5,880	4,958
70583	Scott	(337)	8,104	4,912
70817	Shenandoah (c)	(318)	17,070	13,429
*71102	Shreveport	(318)	200,199	198,518
*70458	Slidell	(985)	28,089	24,124
71075	Springhill	(318)	5,186	5,668
*70663	Sulphur	(337)	19,512	20,125
*71282	Tallulah	(318)	8,042	8,526
70056	Terrytown (c)	(504)	25,430	23,787
*70301	Thibodaux	(985)	14,510	14,125
70056	Timberlane (c)	(504)	11,405	12,614
70810	Village Saint George (c)	(225)	6,993	6,242
70586	Ville Platte	(337)	8,316	9,037
70092	Violet (c)	(504)	8,555	8,574
70094	Waggaman (c)	(504)	9,435	9,405
70785	Walker	(225)	6,104	3,846
*71291	West Monroe	(318)	13,028	14,096
*70094	Westwego	(504)	10,003	11,218
71483	Winnfield	(318)	5,250	6,138
70592	Youngsville	(337)	5,922	1,195
70791	Zachary	(225)	13,259	9,036

Maine (207)

See introductory note.

ZIP	Place	2006	1990
*04210	Auburn	23,156	24,309
*04330	Augusta	18,560	21,325
*04401	Bangor	31,008	33,181
04609	Bar Harbor	5,150	4,443
04530	Bath	9,184	9,799
04915	Belfast	6,803	6,355
03901	Berwick	7,433	5,995

ZIP	Place	2006	1990
*04005	Biddeford	21,898	20,710
04412	Brewer	9,079	9,021
04011	Brunswick (c)	14,816	14,683
04011	Brunswick	21,915	20,906
04093	Buxton	8,171	6,494
*04843	Camden	5,316	5,060
04107	Cape Elizabeth	8,826	8,854
04736	Caribou	8,283	9,415
04021	Cumberland	7,653	5,836
03903	Eliot	6,383	5,329
04605	Ellsworth	7,075	5,975
04937	Fairfield	6,787	6,718
04105	Falmouth	10,557	7,610
04938	Farmington	7,580	7,436
*04032	Freeport	8,151	6,905
04345	Gardiner	6,175	6,746
04038	Gorham	15,402	11,856
04039	Gray	7,420	5,904
04444	Hampden	6,771	5,974
04079	Harpswell	5,204	5,012
04401	Hermon	5,168	—
*04730	Houlton (c)	5,278	5,627
04730	Houlton	6,283	6,613
04043	Kennebunk	11,505	8,004
03904	Kittery	10,495	9,372
04027	Lebanon	5,589	—
*04240	Lewiston	35,734	39,757
04457	Lincoln	5,231	5,587
04250	Lisbon	9,419	9,457
04462	Millinocket (c)	5,190	6,922
04260	New Gloucester	5,367	3,878
04963	Oakland	5,202	5,595
04064	Old Orchard Beach	9,349	7,789
04064	Old Orchard Beach (c)	8,856	7,789
04468	Old Town	7,723	8,317
04473	Orono	9,712	10,573
04473	Orono (c)	8,253	9,789
04271	Paris	5,015	—
04274	Poland	5,353	—
*04101	Portland	63,011	64,157
04769	Presque Isle	9,253	10,550
04841	Rockland	7,578	7,972
04276	Rumford	6,409	7,078
04072	Saco	18,289	15,181
04073	Sanford (c)	10,133	10,296
04073	Sanford	21,534	20,463
*04074	Scarborough	18,880	12,518
04976	Skowhegan (c)	6,696	6,990
04976	Skowhegan	8,876	8,725
03908	South Berwick	7,252	5,877
*04106	South Portland	23,784	23,163
04084	Standish	9,832	7,678
04086	Topsham (c)	6,271	6,147
04086	Topsham	9,940	8,746
04282	Turner	5,540	4,293
04572	Waldoboro	5,090	4,601
04087	Waterboro	7,300	4,510
*04901	Waterville	15,639	17,173
04090	Wells	10,038	7,778
04092	Westbrook	16,201	16,121
*04092	Windham	16,546	13,020
04901	Winslow	7,743	5,436
04901	Winslow (c)	7,944	7,997
04364	Winthrop	6,475	5,968
04096	Yarmouth	8,132	7,862
03909	York	13,306	9,818

Maryland

Area code (240) overlays area code (301). Area code (443) overlays (410). See introductory note.

ZIP	Place	Area Code	2006	1990
21001	Aberdeen	(410)	14,130	13,087
20607	Accokeek (c)	(301)	7,349	4,477
*20783	Adelphi (c)	(301)	14,998	13,524
20762	Andrews AFB (c)	(301)	7,925	10,228
*21401	Annapolis	(410)	36,408	33,195
21227	Arbutus (c)	(410)	20,116	19,750
21012	Arnold (c)	(410)	23,422	20,261
*20916	Aspen Hill (c)	(301)	50,228	45,494
21220	Ballenger Creek (c)		13,518	5,546
*21203	Baltimore	(410)	631,366	736,014
*21014	Bel Air	(410)	10,039	8,942
21050	Bel Air North (c)	(410)	25,798	14,880
21014	Bel Air South (c)	(410)	39,711	26,421
*20705	Beltsville (c)	(301)	15,690	14,476
20603	Bennsville (c)	(301)	7,325	—
*20814	Bethesda (c)	(301)	55,277	62,936
20710	Bladensburg (c)	(301)	7,813	8,064
*20715	Bowie	(301)	53,325	37,642
21220	Bowleys Quarters (c)	(410)	6,314	5,595
*21225	Brooklyn Park (c)	(410)	10,938	10,987
*21716	Brunswick	(301)	5,230	5,091
*20866	Burtonsville (c)	(301)	7,305	5,853
20619	California (c)	(410)	9,307	7,626
20705	Calverton (c)	(301)	12,610	12,046
21613	Cambridge	(410)	11,468	11,514
*20748	Camp Springs (c)	(301)	17,968	16,392
21401	Cape St. Clair (c)	(410)	8,022	7,878

ZIP	Place	Area Code	2006	1990
21234	Carney (c)	(410)	28,264	25,578
*21228	Catonsville (c)	(410)	39,820	35,233
20657	Chesapeake Ranch Estates-Drum Point (c)	(301)	11,503	5,423
*20784	Cheverly (c)	(301)	6,582	6,023
*20815	Chevy Chase (c)	(301)	9,381	8,559
20782	Chillum (c)	(301)	34,252	31,309
20735	Clinton (c)	(301)	26,064	19,987
20904	Cloverly (c)	(301)	7,835	7,904
21030	Cockeysville (c)	(410)	19,388	18,668
*20914	Colesville (c)	(301)	19,810	18,819
20740	College Park	(301)	27,410	23,714
*21045	Columbia (c)	(410)/(301)	88,254	75,883
20743	Coral Hills (c)	(410)	10,720	11,032
21502	Cresaptown-Bel Air (c)	(301)	5,884	4,586
21114	Crofton (c)	(410)	20,091	12,781
*21502	Cumberland	(301)	20,758	23,712
20872	Damascus (c)	(301)	11,430	9,817
*20874	Darnestown (c)	(301)	6,378	—
*20747	District Heights	(301)	6,224	6,711
21222	Dundalk (c)	(410)	62,306	65,800
*21601	Easton	(410)	13,954	9,372
20737	East Riverdale (c)	(301)	14,961	14,187
21219	Edgemere (c)	(410)	9,248	9,226
21040	Edgewood (c)	(410)	23,378	23,903
21784	Eldersburg (c)	(410)	27,741	9,720
21075	Elkridge (c)	(410)	22,042	12,953
*21921	Elkton	(410)	14,753	9,073
*21043	Ellicott City (c)	(410)	56,397	41,396
21221	Essex (c)	(410)	39,078	40,872
20904	Fairland (c)	(301)	21,738	19,828
21047	Fallston (c)	(410)	8,427	5,730
21061	Ferndale (c)	(410)	16,056	16,355
20902	Forest Glen (c)	(301)	7,344	—
*20747	Forestville (c)	(301)	12,707	16,731
20755	Fort Meade (c)	(301)	9,882	12,509
*20744	Fort Washington (c)	(301)	23,845	24,032
*21701	Frederick	(301)	58,882	40,186
20744	Friendly (c)	(301)	10,938	9,028
21532	Frostburg	(301)	7,865	8,069
*20877	Gaithersburg	(301)	57,934	39,676
21117	Garrison (c)	(410)	7,969	5,045
*20874	Germantown (c)	(301)	55,419	41,145
20706	Glenarden	(301)	6,304	5,025
*21061	Glen Burnie (c)	(410)	38,922	37,305
20769	Glenn Dale (c)	(301)	12,609	9,689
20706	Goddard (c)	(301)	5,554	4,576
20785	Greater Landover (c)	(301)	22,900	—
20772	Greater Upper Marlboro (c)	(301)	18,720	11,528
*20770	Greenbelt	(301)	21,972	20,561
21122	Green Haven (c)	(410)	17,415	14,416
21771	Green Valley (c)	(301)	12,262	9,424
*21740	Hagerstown	(301)	39,008	35,306
21740	Halfway (c)	(301)	10,065	8,873
21074	Hampstead	(410)	5,480	2,608
21211	Hampton (c)	(410)	5,004	4,926
21078	Havre de Grace	(410)	12,498	8,952
20748	Hillcrest Heights (c)	(301)	16,359	17,136
*20780	Hyattsville (c)	(301)	15,091	13,864
20794	Jessup (c)	(301)	7,865	6,537
21085	Joppatowne (c)	(410)	11,391	11,084
20901	Kemp Mill (c)	(301)	9,956	—
*20772	Kettering (c)	(301)	11,008	9,901
20721	Lake Arbor (c)	(301)	8,533	—
*21122	Lake Shore (c)	(410)	13,065	13,269
*20787	Langley Park (c)	(301)	16,214	17,474
20706	Lanham-Seabrook (c)	(301)	18,190	16,792
21227	Lansdowne-Baltimore Highlands (c)	(410)	15,724	15,509
20646	La Plata	(301)	8,739	5,841
20772	Largo (c)	(301)	8,408	9,475
*20707	Laurel	(301)	21,945	19,086
20653	Lexington Park (c)	(410)	11,021	9,943
21701	Linganore-Bartonsville (c)	(301)	12,529	4,079
21090	Linthicum (c)	(410)	7,539	7,547
21207	Lochearn (c)	(410)	25,269	25,240
21037	Londontowne (c)	(410)	7,595	6,992
*21093	Lutherville-Timonium (c)	(410)	15,814	16,442
*20748	Marlow Heights (c)	(301)	6,059	5,885
20772	Marlton (c)	(301)	7,798	5,523
20724	Maryland City (c)	(301)	6,814	6,813
21093	Mays Chapel (c)	(410)	11,427	10,132
21220	Middle River (c)	(410)	23,958	24,616
21207	Milford Mill (c)	(410)	26,527	22,547
*20717	Mitchellville (c)	(301)	9,611	12,593
*20886	Montgomery Village (c)	(301)	38,051	32,315
21771	Mount Airy	(301)/(410)	8,703	3,730
20712	Mount Rainier	(301)	8,627	7,954
20784	New Carrollton	(301)	12,651	12,002
*20815	North Bethesda (c)	(301)	38,610	29,656
20895	North Kensington (c)	(301)	8,940	8,607
20707	North Laurel (c)	(301)	20,468	15,008
20878	North Potomac (c)	(301)	23,044	18,456
*21842	Ocean City	(410)	7,031	5,146
21811	Ocean Pines (c)	(410)	10,496	4,251
21113	Odenton (c)	(410)	20,534	12,833
20832	Olney (c)	(301)	31,438	23,019
21206	Overlea (c)	(410)	12,148	12,137
21117	Owings Mills (c)	(410)	20,193	9,474
*20750	Oxon Hill-Glassmanor (c)	(301)	35,355	35,794
21234	Parkville (c)	(410)	31,118	31,617
21401	Parole (c)	(410)	14,031	10,054
*21122	Pasadena (c)	(410)	12,093	10,012
21128	Perry Hall (c)	(410)	28,705	22,723
*21282	Pikesville (c)	(410)	29,123	24,815
20837	Poolesville (c)	(301)	5,529	3,796
*20850	Potomac (c)	(301)	44,822	45,634
21227	Pumphrey (c)	(410)	5,317	5,483
21133	Randallstown (c)	(410)	30,870	26,277
20855	Redland (c)	(301)	16,998	16,145
*21136	Reisterstown (c)	(410)	22,438	19,314
*20737	Riverdale Park	(301)	6,550	4,843
21017	Riverside (c)	(301)	6,128	—
*21122	Riviera Beach (c)	(410)	12,695	11,376
*20850	Rockville	(301)	59,114	44,830
20772	Rosaryville (c)	(301)	12,322	8,976
21237	Rosedale (c)	(410)	19,199	18,703
20906	Rossmoor (c)	(301)	7,569	6,182
21221	Rossville (c)	(410)	11,515	9,492
20602	Saint Charles (c)	(301)	33,379	28,717
*21801	Salisbury	(410)	27,172	20,592
20763	Savage-Guilford (c)	(301)	12,918	9,669
21144	Severn (c)	(410)	35,076	24,499
21146	Severna Park (c)	(410)	28,507	25,879
20764	Shady Side (c)	(410)	5,559	4,107
*20907	Silver Spring (c)	(301)	76,540	76,046
21061	South Gate (c)	(410)	28,672	27,564
20895	South Kensington (c)	(301)	7,887	8,777
20707	South Laurel (c)	(301)	20,479	18,591
21666	Stevensville (c)	(410)	5,686	1,862
*20752	Suitland-Silver Hills (c)	(301)	33,515	35,111
*20913	Takoma Park	(301)	18,497	16,724
21787	Taneytown	(410)	5,479	3,695
*20748	Temple Hills (c)	(301)	7,792	6,865
21788	Thurmont	(301)	6,027	3,398
*21204	Towson (c)	(410)	51,793	49,445
20854	Travilah (c)	(301)	7,442	—
*20602	Waldorf (c)	(301)	22,312	15,058
20743	Walker Mill (c)	(301)	11,104	10,920
21793	Walkersville (c)	(301)	5,590	4,145
*21157	Westminster	(410)	17,870	13,060
*20902	Wheaton-Glenmont (c)	(301)	57,694	53,720
21162	White Marsh (c)	(410)	8,485	8,183
20903	White Oak (c)	(301)	20,973	18,671
21207	Woodlawn (c) (Baltimore Co.)	(410)	36,079	32,907
21284	Woodlawn (c) (Pr. George's Co.)	(301)	6,251	5,329
20721	Woodmore (c)	(240)/(301)	6,077	2,874

Massachusetts

Area code (339) overlays area code (781). Area code (351) overlays (978). Area code (774) overlays (508). Area code (857) overlays (617). See introductory note.

ZIP	Place	Area Code	2006	1990
02351	Abington	(781)	16,378	13,817
*01720	Acton	(978)	20,586	17,872
*02743	Acushnet (c)	(508)	10,518	9,554
01220	Adams (c)	(413)	8,371	9,445
01220	Adams (c)	(413)	5,784	6,356
01001	Agawam (c)	(413)	28,510	27,323
01913	Amesbury	(978)	16,542	14,997
01913	Amesbury (c)	(978)	12,327	12,109
*01002	Amherst (c)	(413)	34,049	35,228
*01002	Amherst Center (c)	(413)	17,050	17,824
*01810	Andover (c)	(978)	8,740	8,242
*01810	Andover	(978)	33,475	29,151
02205	Arlington	(781)	41,075	44,630
01430	Ashburnham (c)	(978)	5,998	5,433
01721	Ashland (c)	(508)	15,678	12,066
*01331	Athol (c)	(978)	11,661	11,451
01331	Athol (c)	(978)	8,370	8,732
02703	Attleboro	(508)	43,283	38,383
01501	Auburn (c)	(508)	16,375	15,005
*01432	Ayer (c)	(978)	7,315	6,871
*02630	Barnstable (c)	(508)	47,380	40,949
01005	Barre (c)	(978)	5,427	1,094
*01730	Bedford (c)	(781)	12,884	12,996
01007	Belchertown (c)	(413)	14,103	10,579
02019	Bellingham (c)	(508)	15,896	14,877
*02478	Belmont (c)	(781)	23,308	24,720
02779	Berkley (c)	(508)	6,391	4,237
01915	Beverly	(978)	39,538	38,195
*01821	Billerica (c)	(978)	41,391	37,609
01504	Blackstone (c)	(508)	9,032	8,023
02748	Bliss Corner (c)	(508)	5,466	4,908
*02205	Boston	(617)	590,763	574,283
02532	Bourne (c)	(508)	19,224	16,064
01719	Boxborough (c)	(978)	5,073	—
01921	Boxford (c)	(978)	8,127	6,266
*02185	Braintree (c)	(781)	34,185	33,836
02631	Brewster (c)	(508)	10,143	8,440
*02324	Bridgewater (c)	(508)	6,664	7,242
02324	Bridgewater (c)	(508)	25,695	21,249
02303	Brockton	(508)	94,191	92,788
*02446	Brookline (c)	(617)	55,241	54,718
*01803	Burlington (c)	(781)	24,895	23,302
*02139	Cambridge	(617)	101,365	95,802
02021	Canton (c)	(781)	21,772	18,530
*02330	Carver (c)	(508)	11,578	10,590

ZIP	Place	Area Code	2006	1990
01507	Charlton	(508)	12,567	9,576
02633	Chatham	(508)	6,783	6,579
01824	Chelmsford	(978)	33,707	32,383
02150	Chelsea	(617)	32,792	28,710
*01020	Chicopee	(413)	54,428	56,632
01510	Clinton	(978)	14,163	13,222
01510	Clinton (c)	(978)	7,884	7,943
01778	Cochituate (c)	(508)	6,768	6,046
02025	Cohasset	(781)	7,223	7,075
01742	Concord	(978)	16,789	17,076
*01226	Dalton	(413)	6,657	7,155
01923	Danvers	(978)	25,833	24,174
*02714	Dartmouth	(508)	31,366	27,244
*02026	Dedham	(781)	23,615	23,782
02638	Dennis	(508)	15,691	13,864
02715	Dighton	(508)	6,715	5,631
01516	Douglas	(508)	7,957	5,438
02030	Dover	(508)	5,641	4,915
01826	Dracut	(978)	29,385	25,594
01571	Dudley	(508)	10,830	9,540
*02332	Duxbury	(781)	14,599	13,895
02333	East Bridgewater	(508)	13,937	11,104
02536	East Falmouth (c)	(508)	6,615	5,577
02642	Eastham	(508)	5,509	4,462
01027	Easthampton	(413)	16,082	15,537
*01028	East Longmeadow	(413)	14,937	13,367
*02334	Easton	(508)	23,031	19,807
02149	Everett	(617)	37,008	35,701
02719	Fairhaven	(508)	16,266	16,132
*02722	Fall River	(508)	91,474	92,703
02540	Falmouth	(508)	33,590	27,960
01420	Fitchburg	(978)	40,050	41,194
02035	Foxborough	(508)	16,274	14,637
02035	Foxborough (c)	(508)	5,509	5,706
*01701	Framingham	(508)	64,762	64,989
02038	Franklin	(508)	31,267	22,095
02702	Freetown	(508)	8,963	8,522
*01440	Gardner	(978)	20,805	20,125
01833	Georgetown	(978)	8,110	6,384
*01930	Gloucester	(978)	30,564	28,716
01519	Grafton	(508)	17,405	13,035
01033	Granby	(413)	6,347	5,565
01230	Great Barrington	(413)	7,437	7,725
*01301	Greenfield	(413)	17,699	18,666
01301	Greenfield (c)	(413)	13,716	14,016
*01450	Groton	(978)	10,585	7,511
01834	Groveland	(978)	6,769	5,214
02338	Halifax	(781)	7,787	6,526
*01936	Hamilton	(978)	8,267	7,280
01036	Hampden	(413)	5,328	—
02339	Hanover	(781)	14,115	11,912
*02341	Hanson	(781)	9,989	9,028
01451	Harvard	(978)	6,051	12,329
02645	Harwich	(508)	12,537	10,275
*01830	Haverhill	(978)	60,176	51,418
*02018	Hingham (c)	(781)	5,352	5,454
*02043	Hingham	(781)	21,784	19,821
02343	Holbrook	(781)	10,730	11,041
01520	Holden	(508)	16,667	14,628
01746	Holliston	(508)	13,896	12,926
*01040	Holyoke	(413)	39,765	43,704
01747	Hopedale	(508)	6,226	5,666
01748	Hopkinton	(508)	14,172	9,191
01749	Hudson	(978)	19,447	17,233
01749	Hudson (c)	(978)	14,388	14,267
02045	Hull	(781)	11,231	10,466
02601	Hyannis (c)	(508)	11,050	14,120
01938	Ipswich	(978)	13,293	11,873
02364	Kingston (c)	(781)	5,380	4,774
02364	Kingston	(781)	12,475	9,045
02347	Lakeville	(508)	10,641	7,785
01523	Lancaster	(978)	6,970	6,661
*01842	Lawrence	(978)	70,662	70,207
*01238	Lee	(413)	5,858	5,849
01524	Leicester	(508)	11,003	10,191
01240	Lenox	(413)	5,159	5,069
01453	Leominster	(978)	41,549	38,145
*02420	Lexington	(781)	30,231	28,974
01773	Lincoln	(781)	7,948	7,666
01460	Littleton	(978)	8,648	7,051
*01028	Longmeadow	(413)	15,481	15,467
*01853	Lowell	(978)	103,229	103,439
01056	Ludlow	(413)	21,951	18,820
01462	Lunenburg	(978)	10,010	9,117
01901	Lynn	(781)	87,991	81,245
01940	Lynnfield	(781)	11,443	11,049
02148	Malden	(781)	55,595	53,884
01944	Manchester-by-the-Sea	(978)	5,290	5,286
*02048	Mansfield	(508)	23,096	16,568
02048	Mansfield Center (c)	(508)	7,320	7,170
01945	Marblehead	(781)	20,231	19,971
02738	Marion	(508)	5,285	4,496
01752	Marlborough	(508)	38,062	31,813
*02050	Marshfield	(781)	24,836	21,531
02649	Mashpee	(508)	14,343	7,884
02739	Mattapoisett	(508)	6,471	5,850
01754	Maynard	(978)	10,180	10,325
02052	Medfield (c)	(508)	6,670	5,985
02052	Medfield	(508)	12,297	10,531
*02155	Medford	(781)	55,681	57,407

ZIP	Place	Area Code	2006	1990
02053	Medway	(508)	12,817	9,931
02176	Melrose	(781)	26,666	28,150
01756	Mendon	(508)	5,767	—
01860	Merrimac	(978)	6,392	5,166
01844	Methuen	(978)	44,259	39,990
*02346	Middleborough	(508)	21,305	17,867
02346	Middleborough Center (c)	(508)	6,913	6,837
01949	Middleton	(978)	9,319	4,921
01757	Milford	(508)	27,523	25,355
01757	Milford (c)	(508)	24,230	23,339
*01527	Millbury	(508)	13,609	12,228
02054	Millis	(508)	7,972	7,613
02186	Milton	(617)	25,902	25,725
01057	Monson	(413)	8,792	7,776
01351	Montague	(413)	8,368	8,316
*02584	Nantucket	(508)	10,240	6,012
01760	Natick	(508)	31,886	30,510
*02494	Needham	(781)	28,368	27,557
*02740	New Bedford	(508)	92,538	99,922
01951	Newbury	(978)	6,954	5,623
01950	Newburyport	(978)	17,303	16,317
*02456	Newton	(617)	82,819	82,585
02056	Norfolk	(508)	10,598	9,259
01247	North Adams	(413)	13,842	16,797
01059	North Amherst (c)	(413)	6,019	6,239
*01060	Northampton	(413)	28,592	11,929
01845	North Andover	(978)	27,196	29,289
*02760	North Attleborough	(508)	27,946	22,792
02760	North Attleborough Center (c)	(508)	16,796	16,178
01532	Northborough (c)	(508)	6,257	5,761
01532	Northborough	(508)	14,681	13,371
01534	Northbridge	(508)	14,425	12,002
01864	North Reading	(978)	13,950	25,038
02060	North Scituate (c)	(781)	5,065	4,891
02766	Norton	(508)	19,242	14,265
02061	Norwell	(781)	10,369	9,279
02062	Norwood	(781)	28,365	28,700
02065	Ocean Bluff-Brant Rock (c)	(781)	5,100	4,541
*01364	Orange	(978)	7,736	7,312
02653	Orleans	(508)	6,398	5,838
01540	Oxford (c)	(508)	5,899	5,969
01540	Oxford	(508)	13,712	12,588
01069	Palmer	(413)	12,926	12,054
*01960	Peabody	(978)	51,734	47,264
02359	Pembroke	(781)	18,739	14,544
01463	Pepperell	(978)	11,412	10,098
01866	Pinehurst (c)	(978)	6,941	6,614
*01201	Pittsfield	(413)	43,497	48,622
02762	Plainville	(508)	8,110	6,871
02360	Plymouth (c)	(508)	7,658	7,258
02360	Plymouth	(508)	55,516	45,608
*02169	Quincy	(617)	91,058	84,985
02368	Randolph	(781)	30,326	30,093
*02767	Raynham	(508)	13,665	9,867
01867	Reading	(781)	23,086	22,539
02769	Rehoboth	(508)	11,374	8,656
02151	Revere	(781)	46,833	42,786
02770	Rochester	(508)	5,406	—
02370	Rockland	(781)	17,896	16,123
01966	Rockport (c)	(978)	5,606	5,448
01966	Rockport	(978)	7,687	7,482
01969	Rowley	(978)	5,875	4,452
01543	Rutland	(508)	7,608	4,936
*01970	Salem	(978)	41,343	38,091
01952	Salisbury	(978)	8,438	6,882
*02563	Sandwich	(508)	20,508	15,489
01906	Saugus	(781)	27,107	25,549
02066	Scituate (c)	(781)	5,069	5,180
02066	Scituate	(508)	18,083	16,786
02771	Seekonk	(508)	13,648	13,046
02067	Sharon	(781)	17,142	15,517
02067	Sharon (c)	(781)	5,941	5,893
01464	Shirley	(978)	7,661	6,118
*01545	Shrewsbury	(508)	33,262	24,146
*02725	Somerset	(508)	18,430	17,655
*02143	Somerville	(617)	74,554	76,210
01002	South Amherst (c)	(413)	5,039	5,053
01073	Southampton	(413)	5,933	4,478
*01772	Southborough	(508)	9,551	6,628
01550	Southbridge	(508)	17,117	17,816
01550	Southbridge (c)	(508)	12,878	13,631
01075	South Hadley	(413)	17,034	16,685
01077	Southwick	(413)	9,603	7,667
01562	Spencer (c)	(508)	6,032	6,306
01562	Spencer	(508)	12,095	11,645
*01101	Springfield	(413)	151,176	156,983
01564	Sterling	(978)	7,847	6,481
02180	Stoneham	(781)	21,471	22,203
02072	Stoughton	(781)	26,901	26,777
01775	Stow	(978)	6,218	5,328
*01566	Sturbridge	(508)	8,969	7,775
01776	Sudbury	(978)	17,027	14,358
01590	Sutton	(508)	9,038	6,824
01907	Swampscott	(781)	14,134	13,650
02777	Swansea	(508)	16,222	15,411
*02780	Taunton	(508)	56,074	49,832
01468	Templeton	(978)	7,696	6,438
01876	Tewksbury	(978)	29,418	27,266

ZIP	Place	Area Code	2006	1990
01883	Topsfield	(978)	6,130	5,754
01469	Townsend	(978)	9,327	8,496
01879	Tyngsborough	(978)	11,542	8,642
01568	Upton	(508)	6,484	4,677
01569	Uxbridge	(508)	12,613	10,415
01880	Wakefield	(781)	24,588	24,825
*02081	Walpole (c)	(508)	5,867	5,495
02081	Walpole	(508)	23,165	20,223
*02451	Waltham	(781)	59,352	57,878
01082	Ware (c)	(413)	6,174	6,533
01082	Ware	(413)	9,982	9,808
02571	Wareham	(508)	21,324	19,232
01083	Warren	(413)	5,097	—
*02471	Watertown	(781)	32,165	33,284
01778	Wayland	(508)	12,970	11,874
01570	Webster (c)	(508)	16,826	16,196
01570	Webster	(508)	11,600	11,849
*02457	Wellesley	(781)	26,987	26,615
01581	Westborough	(508)	18,634	14,133
01583	West Boylston	(508)	7,779	6,611
02379	West Bridgewater	(508)	6,769	6,389
01742	West Concord (c)	(508)	5,632	5,761
01085	Westfield	(413)	40,460	38,372
01886	Westford	(978)	21,507	16,392
*01473	Westminster	(978)	7,422	6,191
02493	Weston	(781)	11,646	10,200
02790	Westport	(508)	15,137	13,852
*01089	West Springfield	(413)	27,849	27,537
02090	Westwood	(781)	13,832	12,557
02673	West Yarmouth (c)	(508)	6,460	5,409
*02188	Weymouth	(781)	53,606	54,063
01588	Whitinsville (c)	(508)	6,340	5,639
02382	Whitman	(781)	14,460	13,240
01095	Wilbraham	(413)	14,044	12,635
01267	Williamstown	(413)	8,189	8,220
01887	Wilmington	(978)	21,525	17,651
01475	Winchendon	(978)	10,146	8,805
01890	Winchester	(781)	21,092	20,267
02152	Winthrop	(617)	17,222	18,127
*01801	Woburn	(781)	37,010	35,943
*01613	Worcester	(508)	175,454	169,759
*02093	Wrentham	(508)	11,135	9,006
*02675	Yarmouth	(508)	24,354	21,174
02675	Yarmouth Port (c)	(508)	5,395	4,271

Michigan

Area code (947) overlays area code (248). See introductory note.

ZIP	Place	Area Code	2006	1990
49221	Adrian	(517)	21,703	22,097
49224	Albion	(517)	9,237	10,066
49401	Allendale (c)	(616)	11,555	6,950
48101	Allen Park	(313)	27,616	31,092
*48801	Alma	(989)	9,240	9,034
49707	Alpena	(989)	10,637	11,354
*48106	Ann Arbor	(734)	113,206	109,608
*48321	Auburn Hills	(248)	20,986	17,076
*49016	Battle Creek	(269)	52,777	53,516
*48707	Bay City	(989)	34,449	38,936
48505	Beecher (c)	(810)	12,793	14,465
*48809	Belding	(616)	5,870	5,969
*49022	Benton Harbor	(269)	10,641	12,818
49022	Benton Heights (c)	(269)	5,458	5,449
48072	Berkley	(248)	14,980	16,960
48025	Beverly Hills	(248)	10,012	10,610
49307	Big Rapids	(231)	10,565	12,603
*48012	Birmingham	(248)	19,185	19,997
*48301	Bloomfield (c)	(248)	43,021	42,137
48722	Bridgeport (c)	(989)	7,849	8,569
*48116	Brighton	(810)	7,263	5,686
48601	Buena Vista (c)	(989)	7,845	8,196
48509	Burton	(810)	30,875	27,437
49601	Cadillac	(231)	10,308	10,104
*48184	Canton (c)	(734)	76,366	57,047
48724	Carrollton (c)	(989)	6,602	6,521
48015	Center Line	(586)	8,247	9,026
48813	Charlotte	(517)	9,017	8,083
49721	Cheboygan	(231)	5,135	4,997
*48017	Clawson	(248)	12,239	13,874
*48046	Clinton (c)	(517)	95,648	85,866
49036	Coldwater	(517)	10,653	9,607
49321	Comstock Park (c)	(616)	10,674	5,916
49508	Cutlerville (c)	(616)	15,114	11,228
48423	Davison	(810)	5,323	5,693
48120	Dearborn	(313)	92,382	89,286
48127	Dearborn Heights	(313)	55,278	60,838
48231	Detroit	(313)	871,121	1,027,974
*49047	Dowagiac	(269)	5,931	6,418
*49506	East Grand Rapids	(616)	10,373	10,807
48826	East Lansing	(517)	46,009	50,677
48021	Eastpointe	(586)	32,949	35,283
49001	Eastwood (c)	(269)	6,265	6,340
48827	Eaton Rapids	(517)	5,318	4,695
48229	Ecorse	(313)	10,530	12,180
49829	Escanaba	(906)	12,575	13,659
49022	Fair Plain (c)	(269)	7,828	8,051
*48333	Farmington	(248)	9,993	10,170
*48333	Farmington Hills	(248)	79,793	74,614
48430	Fenton	(810)	11,931	8,434
48220	Ferndale	(248)	21,312	25,084
48134	Flat Rock	(734)	9,560	7,290
*48501	Flint	(810)	117,068	140,925
48433	Flushing	(810)	8,056	8,542
49506	Forest Hills (c)	(616)	20,942	16,690
48026	Fraser	(586)	15,104	13,899
48623	Freeland (c)	(989)	5,147	1,421
*48135	Garden City	(734)	28,473	31,846
48173	Gibraltar	(734)	5,133	4,297
49837	Gladstone	(906)	5,223	4,565
48439	Grand Blanc	(810)	7,806	7,760
49417	Grand Haven	(616)	10,573	11,951
48837	Grand Ledge	(517)	7,718	7,562
*49501	Grand Rapids	(616)	193,083	189,126
*49418	Grandville	(616)	16,774	15,624
48838	Greenville	(616)	8,333	8,101
48138	Grosse Ile (c)	(734)	10,894	9,781
*48230	Grosse Pointe	(313)	5,331	5,681
48230	Grosse Pointe Farms	(313)	9,174	10,092
48230	Grosse Pointe Park	(313)	11,698	12,857
48230	Grosse Pointe Woods	(313)	16,128	17,715
*48212	Hamtramck	(313)	21,615	18,372
48225	Harper Woods	(313)	13,392	14,903
48625	Harrison (c)	(989)	24,461	24,685
48840	Haslett (c)	(517)	11,283	10,230
49058	Hastings	(269)	7,081	6,549
48030	Hazel Park	(248)	18,302	20,051
48203	Highland Park	(313)	15,300	20,121
49242	Hillsdale	(517)	7,894	8,175
*49423	Holland	(616)	34,245	30,745
48442	Holly	(248)	6,378	5,595
48842	Holt (c)	(517)	11,315	11,744
*49931	Houghton	(906)	7,014	7,498
*48844	Howell	(517)	9,854	8,147
49426	Hudsonville	(616)	7,039	6,170
48070	Huntington Woods	(248)	5,902	6,419
48141	Inkster	(313)/(734)	28,443	30,772
48846	Ionia	(616)	12,449	10,349
*49801	Iron Mountain	(906)	7,980	8,525
49938	Ironwood	(906)	5,590	6,849
*49849	Ishpeming	(906)	6,469	7,200
49204	Jackson	(517)	34,554	37,425
*49428	Jenison (c)	(616)	17,211	17,882
49001	Kalamazoo	(269)	72,161	80,277
*49518	Kentwood	(616)	46,574	37,826
49802	Kingsford	(906)	5,437	5,480
48144	Lambertville (c)	(734)	9,299	7,860
*48901	Lansing	(517)	114,276	127,321
48446	Lapeer	(810)	9,330	7,759
48146	Lincoln Park	(313)	37,595	41,832
*48150	Livonia	(734)	96,736	100,850
49431	Ludington	(231)	8,450	8,507
48071	Madison Heights	(248)	30,042	32,196
49660	Manistee	(231)	6,597	6,734
49855	Marquette	(906)	20,488	21,977
*49068	Marshall	(269)	7,265	6,941
48040	Marysville	(810)	10,078	8,515
48854	Mason	(517)	8,056	6,768
48122	Melvindale	(313)	10,494	11,216
49858	Menominee	(906)	8,604	9,398
48640	Midland	(989)	41,551	38,053
48160	Milan	(734)	5,579	4,040
*48381	Milford	(248)	6,578	5,500
48161	Monroe	(734)	21,840	22,902
*48046	Mount Clemens	(586)	16,989	18,405
*48804	Mount Pleasant	(989)	26,203	23,299
49440	Muskegon	(231)	39,608	39,809
49444	Muskegon Heights	(231)	11,741	13,176
*48047	New Baltimore	(586)	11,308	5,798
49120	Niles	(269)	11,571	12,458
49505	Northview (c)	(616)	14,730	13,712
48167	Northville	(248)	6,228	6,226
49441	Norton Shores	(231)	23,429	21,755
*48375	Novi	(248)	54,105	32,998
48237	Oak Park	(248)	30,960	30,468
48805	Okemos (c)	(517)	22,805	20,216
48867	Owosso	(989)	15,388	16,322
49770	Petoskey	(231)	6,112	6,056
48170	Plymouth	(734)	9,037	9,560
48170	Plymouth Township (c)	(734)	27,798	23,646
48343	Pontiac	(248)	67,124	71,136
49081	Portage	(269)	45,236	41,042
48061	Port Huron	(810)	31,302	33,694
48239	Redford (c)	(313)	51,622	54,387
48062	Richmond	(586)	5,685	4,028
48218	River Rouge	(313)	9,031	11,314
48192	Riverview	(734)	12,537	13,894
48308	Rochester	(248)	11,239	7,130
48306	Rochester Hills	(248)	69,833	61,766
49341	Rockford	(616)	5,176	3,750
48174	Romulus	(313)/(734)	24,137	22,897
48066	Roseville	(586)	47,406	51,412
48068	Royal Oak	(248)	57,984	65,410
48605	Saginaw	(989)	57,523	69,512
48604	Saginaw Township North (c)	(989)	24,994	23,018
48603	Saginaw Township South (c)	(989)	13,801	13,987
48079	Saint Clair	(810)	5,437	5,116
48080	Saint Clair Shores	(313)	61,162	68,107
48879	Saint Johns	(989)	7,381	7,392
49085	Saint Joseph	(269)	8,623	9,214

ZIP	Place	Area Code	2006	1990
48880	Saint Louis	(989)	6,474	3,828
48176	Saline	(734)	8,817	6,663
*49783	Sault Sainte Marie	(906)	14,272	14,689
49455	Shelby (c)	(231)	65,159	48,655
48609	Shields (c)	(989)	6,590	6,634
*48037	Southfield	(248)	76,090	75,727
48195	Southgate	(734)	29,215	30,771
49090	South Haven	(269)	5,160	5,563
48178	South Lyon	(248)	11,072	6,479
48161	South Monroe (c)	(734)	6,370	5,266
49015	Springfield	(269)	5,140	5,582
*48311	Sterling Heights	(586)	127,991	117,810
49091	Sturgis	(269)	11,065	10,130
48473	Swartz Creek	(810)	5,358	4,851
48180	Taylor	(313)/(734)	64,240	70,811
49286	Tecumseh	(517)	8,848	7,462
48182	Temperance (c)	(734)	7,757	6,542
49093	Three Rivers	(269)	7,286	7,464
*49684	Traverse City	(231)	14,407	15,155
48183	Trenton	(734)	19,068	20,586
*48099	Troy	(248)	81,118	72,884
49534	Walker	(616)	23,556	17,279
*48390	Walled Lake	(248)	6,954	6,278
*48090	Warren	(586)	134,589	144,864
*48329	Waterford (c)	(248)	73,150	66,692
48917	Waverly (c)	(517)	16,194	15,614
48184	Wayne	(734)	18,289	19,899
*48323	West Bloomfield Township (c)	(248)	64,862	54,843
*48185	Westland	(313)/(734)	84,504	84,724
49009	Westwood (c)	(269)	9,122	8,957
48189	Whitmore Lake (c)	(734)	6,574	3,251
48393	Wixom	(248)	13,568	8,550
48183	Woodhaven	(734)	13,381	11,631
*48192	Wyandotte	(734)	26,473	30,938
*49509	Wyoming	(616)	70,155	63,891
*48197	Ypsilanti	(734)	21,746	24,846
49464	Zeeland	(616)	5,478	5,417

Minnesota

ZIP	Place	Area Code	2006	1990
56007	Albert Lea	(507)	17,758	18,310
55301	Albertville	(763)	6,001	1,252
56308	Alexandria	(320)	10,852	8,029
*55304	Andover	(763)	30,222	15,216
*55303	Anoka	(612)/(763)	17,501	17,192
55124	Apple Valley	(952)	50,109	34,598
*55112	Arden Hills	(651)	9,815	9,199
55912	Austin	(507)	23,331	21,926
*56425	Baxter	(218)	7,885	3,695
*56601	Bemidji	(218)	13,291	11,165
55309	Big Lake	(763)	9,323	3,113
*55014	Blaine	(651)/(763)	55,144	38,975
*55420	Bloomington	(952)	80,869	86,335
*56401	Brainerd	(218)	13,722	12,353
*55429	Brooklyn Center	(763)	27,371	28,887
*55443	Brooklyn Park	(763)	69,942	56,381
55313	Buffalo	(763)	13,853	7,302
*55337	Burnsville	(651)/(952)	59,321	51,288
55008	Cambridge	(763)	7,377	5,094
55316	Champlin	(763)	23,294	16,849
55317	Chanhassen	(952)	23,520	11,736
55318	Chaska	(952)	23,736	11,339
55014	Circle Pines	(763)/(651)	5,418	4,704
55720	Cloquet	(218)	11,479	10,885
55421	Columbia Heights	(612)/(763)	17,969	18,910
*55433	Coon Rapids	(763)	62,207	52,978
*55340	Corcoran	(763)	5,692	5,199
55016	Cottage Grove	(651)	32,969	22,935
56716	Crookston	(218)	7,809	8,119
*55428	Crystal	(763)	21,494	23,788
*56501	Detroit Lakes	(218)	8,039	7,141
*55806	Duluth	(218)	84,167	85,493
*55121	Eagan	(651)/(952)	63,736	47,409
*55005	East Bethel	(763)	12,096	8,050
56721	East Grand Forks	(218)	7,857	8,658
*55344	Eden Prairie	(612)/(952)	60,952	39,311
*55424	Edina	(952)	45,305	46,075
55330	Elk River	(763)	22,285	11,143
*56031	Fairmont	(507)	10,403	11,265
*55113	Falcon Heights	(651)	5,438	5,380
55021	Faribault	(507)	22,206	17,085
*55024	Farmington	(651)/(952)	18,207	5,940
56537	Fergus Falls	(218)	13,839	12,362
55025	Forest Lake	(651)	17,458	5,833
*55432	Fridley	(763)	26,289	28,335
55336	Glencoe	(320)	5,627	4,648
*55427	Golden Valley	(763)	19,921	20,971
*55744	Grand Rapids	(218)	8,337	7,976
*55304	Ham Lake	(763)	14,889	8,924
55033	Hastings	(651)	21,360	15,478
*55810	Hermantown	(218)	9,106	6,761
*55746	Hibbing	(218)	16,295	18,046
*55343	Hopkins	(952)	16,704	16,529
55038	Hugo	(651)	11,658	4,417
55350	Hutchinson	(320)	13,963	11,459
56649	International Falls	(218)	6,418	8,325
*55076	Inver Grove Heights	(651)	33,470	22,477
55040	Isanti	(763)	5,774	1,128
55352	Jordan	(952)	5,312	3,514

ZIP	Place	Area Code	2006	1990
55944	Kasson	(507)	5,573	3,514
55947	La Crescent	(507)	5,083	4,311
55041	Lake City	(651)	5,374	4,490
55042	Lake Elmo	(651)	7,590	5,900
*55044	Lakeville	(952)	53,074	24,854
*55014	Lino Lakes	(651)	19,879	8,807
55355	Litchfield	(320)	6,645	6,041
*55117	Little Canada	(651)	9,537	8,971
56345	Little Falls	(320)	8,180	7,581
55115	Mahtomedi	(651)	8,016	5,633
*56001	Mankato	(507)	34,970	31,459
*55311	Maple Grove	(763)	60,584	38,736
55109	Maplewood	(651)	35,484	30,954
56258	Marshall	(507)	12,464	12,023
*55118	Mendota Heights	(651)	11,339	9,388
*55440	Minneapolis	(612)/(763)/(952)	372,833	368,383
*55345	Minnetonka	(952)	49,928	48,370
55359	Minnetrista	(952)	5,726	3,439
56265	Montevideo	(763)	5,324	5,499
*55362	Monticello	(763)	11,414	5,045
*56560	Moorhead	(218)	34,749	32,295
56267	Morris	(320)	5,072	5,613
55364	Mound	(952)	9,408	9,634
55112	Mounds View	(763)	12,023	12,541
55112	New Brighton	(651)	20,875	22,207
*55427	New Hope	(763)	20,393	21,853
56071	New Prague	(952)	6,759	3,575
56073	New Ulm	(507)	13,406	13,132
55056	North Branch	(651)/(763)	10,485	4,267
*55057	Northfield	(507)	19,177	14,684
*56001	North Mankato	(507)	12,259	10,662
55109	North Saint Paul	(651)	11,293	12,376
*55128	Oakdale	(651)	27,206	18,377
*55011	Oak Grove	(763)	8,266	5,488
*55323	Orono	(952)	7,928	7,285
*55330	Otsego	(763)	12,067	5,219
*55060	Owatonna	(507)	24,533	19,386
*55446	Plymouth	(763)	70,102	50,889
55372	Prior Lake	(952)	22,674	11,482
55303	Ramsey	(763)	22,955	12,408
55066	Red Wing	(651)	15,754	15,134
56283	Redwood Falls	(507)	5,194	4,859
*55423	Richfield	(612)	33,262	35,710
*55422	Robbinsdale	(763)	13,340	14,396
*55901	Rochester	(507)	96,975	70,729
55374	Rogers	(763)	6,277	722
55068	Rosemount	(651)/(952)	20,468	8,622
55113	Roseville	(651)	31,909	33,485
*55418	Saint Anthony	(612)	7,754	7,727
*56301	Saint Cloud	(320)	66,228	48,812
55070	Saint Francis	(763)	7,312	2,479
55374	Saint Joseph	(320)	5,822	3,294
*55426	Saint Louis Park	(952)	43,145	43,787
55376	Saint Michael	(763)	14,858	2,506
*55101	Saint Paul	(651)	273,535	272,235
55071	Saint Paul Park	(651)	5,271	4,965
*55107	Saint Peter	(507)	10,693	9,481
56082	Sartell	(320)	13,241	5,409
56377	Sauk Rapids	(320)	11,560	7,823
56379	Savage	(952)	27,292	9,906
*55378	Shakopee	(612)	32,865	11,739
*55379	Shoreview	(651)	26,726	24,587
55126	Shorewood	(952)	7,461	5,913
*55331	South Saint Paul	(651)	19,321	20,197
*55075	Spring Lake Park	(651)	6,633	6,532
*55432	Stewartville	(507)	5,518	4,520
55976	Stillwater	(651)	17,781	13,882
*55082	Thief River Falls	(218)	8,444	8,010
*56701	Vadnais Heights	(651)	12,525	11,041
*55127	Victoria	(952)	6,203	2,354
*55386	Virginia	(218)	8,550	9,432
*55792	Waconia	(952)	9,031	3,498
*55387	Waite Park	(320)	6,770	5,020
56387	Waseca	(507)	9,491	8,385
56093	West Saint Paul	(651)	18,842	19,248
*55118	White Bear Lake	(651)	23,586	24,622
55110	Willmar	(320)	18,067	17,531
56201	Winona	(507)	26,533	25,435
*55987	Woodbury	(651)	54,365	20,075
55125	Worthington	(507)	11,056	9,977
56187	Zimmerman	(763)	5,073	—
55398				

Mississippi

Area code (769) overlays area code (601). See introductory note.

ZIP	Place	Area Code	2006	1990
39730	Aberdeen	(662)	6,172	6,837
38821	Amory	(662)	7,368	7,093
38606	Batesville	(662)	7,729	6,403
*39520	Bay Saint Louis	(228)	(1)	8,063
*39530	Biloxi	(228)	44,342	46,319
38829	Booneville	(662)	8,664	7,955
*39042	Brandon	(601)	20,096	11,089
*39601	Brookhaven	(601)	9,983	10,243
39272	Byram (c)	(601)	7,386	—
39046	Canton	(601)	12,578	11,723
*38614	Clarksdale	(662)	18,883	21,180
38732	Cleveland	(662)	12,671	15,384
*39056	Clinton	(601)	26,212	21,847
39429	Columbia	(601)	6,523	6,815

ZIP	Place	Area Code	2006	1990
*39701	Columbus	(662)	24,213	23,799
*38834	Corinth	(662)	14,290	11,820
39059	Crystal Springs	(601)	5,939	5,643
39525	Diamondhead (c)	(228)	5,912	2,661
39540	D'Iberville	(228)	7,064	6,566
39232	Flowood	(601)	6,914	2,770
39074	Forest	(601)	6,008	5,062
39553	Gautier	(228)	16,251	10,088
38701	Greenville	(662)	37,801	45,226
*38930	Greenwood	(662)	16,742	18,906
38901	Grenada	(662)	14,546	10,864
39564	Gulf Hills (c)	(228)	5,900	5,004
39501	Gulfport	(228)	64,316	64,045
*39401	Hattiesburg	(601)	48,012	45,325
38632	Hernando	(662)	10,580	3,125
*38635	Holly Springs	(662)	7,964	7,261
38637	Horn Lake	(662)	22,763	9,069
*38751	Indianola	(662)	11,264	11,809
39205	Jackson	(601)	176,614	202,062
39090	Kosciusko	(662)	7,335	6,986
*39440	Laurel	(601)	18,450	18,827
38756	Leland	(662)	5,065	6,366
39560	Long Beach	(228)	(1)	15,804
39339	Louisville	(662)	6,708	7,165
*39648	McComb	(601)	17,191	11,797
*39110	Madison	(601)	13,607	7,471
*39302	Meridian	(601)	38,200	41,036
39563	Moss Point	(228)	14,583	17,837
*39120	Natchez	(601)	17,162	19,460
38652	New Albany	(662)	8,065	6,775
*39564	Ocean Springs	(228)	17,140	15,221
38654	Olive Branch	(662)	29,861	3,567
38655	Oxford	(662)	14,051	10,026
*39567	Pascagoula	(228)	23,719	25,899
39571	Pass Christian	(228)	(1)	5,557
*39288	Pearl	(601)	23,986	19,588
39465	Petal	(601)	10,266	7,883
39350	Philadelphia	(601)	7,705	6,758
39466	Picayune	(601)	11,759	10,633
38863	Pontotoc	(662)	5,917	4,570
39218	Richland	(601)	7,118	4,014
*39157	Ridgeland	(601)	21,535	11,714
38663	Ripley	(662)	5,656	5,371
39532	Saint Martin (c)	(228)	6,676	6,349
38668	Senatobia	(601)	6,878	4,772
*38671	Southaven	(662)	41,295	18,705
*39759	Starkville	(662)	22,638	18,458
*38801	Tupelo	(662)	35,930	30,685
*39180	Vicksburg	(601)	25,740	26,886
39576	Waveland	(228)	(1)	5,369
39367	Waynesboro	(601)	5,669	5,143
39402	West Hattiesburg (c)	(601)	6,305	5,450
39773	West Point	(662)	11,529	8,489
39194	Yazoo City	(662)	11,822	12,427

(1) In Bay Saint Louis, Long Beach, Pass Christian, and Waveland, the Census Bureau was unable to obtain reliable data to estimate population change caused by hurricane Katrina and is therefore not releasing 2006 estimates for these cities.

Missouri

ZIP	Place	Area Code	2006	1990
63123	Affton (c)	(314)	20,535	21,106
63010	Arnold	(636)	20,766	18,828
65605	Aurora	(417)	7,377	6,459
*63011	Ballwin	(636)	30,264	27,054
63012	Barnhart (c)	(314)	6,108	4,911
63137	Bellefontaine Neighbors	(314)	10,508	10,918
64012	Belton	(816)	24,124	18,145
*63134	Berkeley	(314)	9,531	12,250
63033	Black Jack	(314)	6,904	6,131
*64015	Blue Springs	(816)	53,885	40,103
*65613	Bolivar	(417)	10,563	6,845
63628	Bonne Terre	(573)	6,563	3,871
65233	Boonville	(660)	8,755	7,095
63334	Bowling Green	(573)	5,165	3,046
*65615	Branson	(417)	7,435	3,706
63144	Brentwood	(314)	7,292	8,150
*63044	Bridgeton	(314)	15,173	17,732
64429	Cameron	(816)	9,119	4,782
*63701	Cape Girardeau	(573)	36,621	34,475
64834	Carl Junction	(417)	6,847	4,123
64836	Carthage	(417)	13,343	10,747
*63830	Caruthersville	(573)	6,363	7,389
63834	Charleston	(573)	5,187	5,131
63017	Chesterfield	(636)	46,635	42,325
64601	Chillicothe	(660)	8,740	8,799
*63105	Clayton	(314)	16,019	13,926
64735	Clinton	(660)	9,511	8,703
*65201	Columbia	(573)	94,428	69,133
*63128	Concord (c)	(314)	16,689	19,859
63126	Crestwood	(314)	11,579	11,229
63141	Creve Coeur	(314)	16,997	12,289
*63366	Dardenne Prairie	(636)	7,423	1,769
63020	De Soto	(636)	6,565	5,993
*63131	Des Peres	(636)	8,626	8,395
63601	Desloge	(573)	5,172	4,150
63841	Dexter	(573)	7,652	7,506

ZIP	Place	Area Code	2006	1990
*63011	Ellisville	(636)	9,286	7,183
63025	Eureka	(636)	9,072	4,683
64024	Excelsior Springs	(816)	11,650	10,373
63640	Farmington	(573)	15,498	11,596
*63135	Ferguson	(314)	21,296	22,290
63028	Festus	(636)	11,202	8,105
*63033	Florissant	(314)	51,387	51,038
65473	Fort Leonard Wood (c)	(573)	13,666	15,863
65251	Fulton	(573)	12,324	10,033
*64118	Gladstone	(816)	27,542	26,243
63137	Glasgow Village (c)	(573)	5,234	5,199
63122	Glendale	(314)	5,555	5,945
64029	Grain Valley	(816)	9,430	1,898
64030	Grandview	(816)	24,373	24,973
63401	Hannibal	(573)	17,637	18,004
64701	Harrisonville	(816)	9,804	7,696
*63042	Hazelwood	(314)	25,523	15,512
*64050	Independence	(816)	109,400	112,301
63755	Jackson	(573)	13,255	9,256
*65101	Jefferson City	(573)	39,274	35,517
63136	Jennings	(314)	14,829	15,841
*64801	Joplin	(417)	47,994	41,175
64108	Kansas City	(816)	447,306	434,829
64060	Kearney	(816)	7,891	1,790
63857	Kennett	(573)	10,950	10,941
63501	Kirksville	(660)	16,988	17,152
63122	Kirkwood	(314)	26,936	28,318
63124	Ladue (St. Louis Co.)	(314)	8,226	8,795
63367	Lake Saint Louis	(636)	13,708	7,536
65536	Lebanon	(417)	13,774	9,983
*64063	Lee's Summit	(816)	81,913	46,418
63125	Lemay (c)	(314)	17,215	18,005
*64068	Liberty	(816)	29,581	20,459
63552	Macon	(660)	5,466	5,571
*63011	Manchester	(636)	18,808	6,506
63143	Maplewood	(314)	8,770	9,962
65340	Marshall	(660)	12,334	12,711
65706	Marshfield	(417)	6,987	4,374
63043	Maryland Heights	(314)	26,339	25,440
64468	Maryville	(816)	10,556	10,663
63129	Mehlville (c)	(314)	28,822	27,557
65265	Mexico	(573)	11,016	11,290
65270	Moberly	(660)	13,992	12,839
65708	Monett	(417)	8,726	6,529
63026	Murphy (c)	(636)	9,048	9,342
*64850	Neosho	(417)	11,243	9,254
64772	Nevada	(417)	8,479	8,597
65714	Nixa	(417)	17,391	4,893
64116	North Kansas	(816)	5,494	4,130
64075	Oak Grove	(816)	6,849	4,565
63129	Oakville (c)	(314)	35,309	31,750
63366	O'Fallon	(636)	72,477	17,427
63132	Olivette	(314)	7,442	7,573
63114	Overland	(314)	15,906	17,987
65721	Ozark	(417)	16,354	4,401
*63069	Pacific	(636)	7,159	4,350
*63601	Park Hills	(573)	8,640	7,866
64152	Parkville	(816)	5,107	2,402
*63775	Perryville	(573)	8,034	6,933
64080	Pleasant Hill	(816)	6,903	3,827
*63901	Poplar Bluff	(573)	17,059	16,841
64083	Raymore	(816)	16,544	5,592
*64133	Raytown	(816)	28,577	30,601
65738	Republic	(417)	11,354	6,290
64085	Richmond	(816)	6,052	5,738
63117	Richmond Heights	(314)	9,228	10,448
*65401	Rolla	(573)	17,985	14,090
63074	Saint Ann	(314)	12,972	14,449
*63301	Saint Charles	(636)	63,009	50,634
63114	Saint John	(314)	6,495	7,502
*64501	Saint Joseph	(816)	72,651	71,852
*63166	Saint Louis	(314)	347,181	396,685
*63376	Saint Peters	(636)	54,839	40,660
63126	Sappington (c)	(314)	7,287	10,917
64485	Savannah	(816)	5,100	
*65301	Sedalia	(660)	20,669	19,800
63119	Shrewsbury	(314)	6,332	6,416
*63801	Sikeston	(573)	17,164	17,641
64089	Smithville	(816)	7,471	2,525
63138	Spanish Lake (c)	(314)	21,337	20,322
*65801	Springfield	(417)	150,797	140,494
63080	Sullivan	(573)	6,657	5,661
63127	Sunset Hills	(314)	8,301	4,915
63011	Town and Country	(314)	10,773	10,944
64683	Trenton	(660)	6,086	6,129
63379	Troy	(314)	10,985	3,811
63084	Union	(636)	9,447	6,196
63130	University City	(314)	36,847	40,087
63088	Valley Park	(636)	6,351	4,165
64093	Warrensburg	(660)	17,965	15,244
63383	Warrenton	(636)	6,903	3,564
63090	Washington	(636)	14,228	11,367
64870	Webb City	(417)	10,982	7,538
63119	Webster Groves	(314)	22,686	22,992
63385	Wentzville	(636)	20,749	4,640
65775	West Plains	(417)	11,592	9,214
*63011	Wildwood	(314)	34,549	16,742

Montana (406)

ZIP	Place	2006	1990
59711	Anaconda-Deer Lodge County	8,888	10,356
59714	Belgrade	7,323	3,422
*59101	Billings	100,148	81,125
*59718	Bozeman	35,061	22,660
*59701	Butte–Silver Bow	32,110	33,336
59901	Evergreen (c)	6,215	4,109
*59401	Great Falls	56,215	55,125
59501	Havre	9,451	10,201
59601	Helena	27,885	24,609
59635	Helena Valley Southeast (c)	7,141	4,601
59602	Helena Valley West Central (c)	6,983	6,327
*59901	Kalispell	19,432	11,917
59044	Laurel	6,421	5,686
59457	Lewistown	6,083	6,097
59047	Livingston	7,279	6,701
59301	Miles City	8,083	8,461
*59801	Missoula	64,081	42,918
59801	Orchard Homes (c)	5,199	10,317
59937	Whitefish	7,723	4,368

Nebraska

ZIP	Place	Area Code	2006	1990
69301	Alliance	(308)	8,155	9,765
68310	Beatrice	(402)	12,921	12,352
*68108	Bellevue	(402)	47,594	39,240
*68008	Blair	(402)	7,916	6,860
69337	Chadron	(308)	5,208	5,588
68108	Chalco (c)	(402)	10,736	7,337
*68601	Columbus	(402)	21,414	19,480
68333	Crete	(402)	6,305	4,841
68022	Elkhorn	(402)	8,327	1,398
*68025	Fremont	(402)	25,417	23,680
69341	Gering	(308)	7,681	7,946
*68802	Grand Island	(308)	44,632	39,487
69341	Gering	(308)	5,970	
68901	Hastings	(402)	25,144	22,837
*68949	Holdrege	(308)	5,325	5,671
*68847	Kearney	(308)	29,385	24,396
68128	La Vista	(402)	16,041	9,992
68850	Lexington	(308)	10,251	6,600
*68501	Lincoln	(402)	241,167	191,972
69001	McCook	(308)	7,542	8,112
68410	Nebraska City	(402)	7,137	6,547
*68701	Norfolk	(402)	23,896	21,476
69101	North Platte	(308)	24,386	22,605
68113	Offutt AFB (c)	(402)	8,901	
68005	Omaha	(402)	419,545	344,463
*68046	Papillion	(402)	21,271	13,892
68048	Plattsmouth	(402)	7,047	6,415
68127	Ralston	(402)	6,163	6,236
68661	Schuyler	(402)	5,212	4,052
*69361	Scottsbluff	(308)	14,738	13,711
68434	Seward	(402)	6,869	5,641
*69162	Sidney	(308)	6,372	5,959
68776	South Sioux City	(402)	12,137	9,677
68787	Wayne	(402)	5,176	5,142
68467	York	(402)	7,955	7,940

Nevada

ZIP	Place	Area Code	2006	1990
*89005	Boulder City	(702)	15,005	12,567
*89701	Carson City	(775)	55,289	40,443
89403	Dayton (c)	(775)	5,907	2,217
*89801	Elko	(775)	16,980	14,836
89139	Enterprise (c)	(702)	14,676	6,412
*89406	Fallon	(775)	8,403	6,430
89408	Fernley	(775)	12,093	5,164
89410	Gardnerville Ranchos (c)	(775)	11,054	7,455
89015	Henderson	(702)	240,614	64,948
*89450	Incline Village-Crystal Bay (c)	(775)	9,952	7,119
*89125	Las Vegas	(702)	552,539	258,877
*89028	Laughlin (c)	(702)	7,076	4,791
89506	Lemmon Valley-Golden Valley(c)	(702)	6,855	—
*89024	Mesquite	(702)	14,799	1,871
89040	Moapa Valley (c)	(702)	5,784	3,444
89191	Nellis AFB (c)	(702)	8,896	8,377
89030	North Las Vegas	(702)	197,567	47,849
*89041	Pahrump (c)	(775)	24,631	7,424
89109	Paradise (c)	(702)	186,070	124,682
*89501	Reno	(775)	210,255	134,230
89436	Spanish Springs (c)	(775)	9,018	
*89431	Sparks	(775)	83,959	53,367
89815	Spring Creek (c)	(775)	10,548	5,866
89147	Spring Valley (c)	(702)	117,390	51,726
89110	Sunrise Manor (c)	(702)	156,120	95,362
89433	Sun Valley (c)	(775)	19,461	11,391
89883	West Wendover (c)	(775)	5,091	
89101	Winchester (c)	(702)	26,958	23,365
89445	Winnemucca City	(775)	7,934	6,134

New Hampshire (603)
See introductory note.

ZIP	Place	2006	1990
03809	Alton	5,109	—
03031	Amherst	11,703	9,068
03811	Atkinson	6,601	5,188
03032	Auburn	5,163	
03825	Barrington	8,275	6,164
03110	Bedford	20,986	12,563
03220	Belmont	7,268	5,796
03570	Berlin	9,954	11,824
03304	Bow	8,098	5,500
03743	Claremont	13,264	13,902
*03301	Concord	42,378	36,006
03818	Conway	9,214	7,940
03038	Derry (c)	22,661	20,446
03038	Derry	34,103	29,603
*03820	Dover	28,422	25,042
03824	Durham (c)	12,904	9,236
03824	Durham	13,313	11,818
03042	Epping	6,169	5,162
03833	Exeter (c)	9,759	9,556
03833	Exeter	14,754	12,481
03835	Farmington	6,575	5,739
03235	Franklin	8,785	8,304
03246	Gilford	7,453	5,867
03045	Goffstown	17,696	14,621
03841	Hampstead	8,832	6,732
*03842	Hampton (c)	9,126	7,989
*03842	Hampton	15,442	12,278
03755	Hanover Compact (c)	8,162	6,538
03755	Hanover	11,151	9,212
03242	Henniker	5,081	
03244	Hillsborough	5,462	4,698
03049	Hollis	7,748	5,705
03106	Hooksett	13,439	9,002
03229	Hopkinton	5,617	4,806
03051	Hudson (c)	7,814	7,626
03051	Hudson	24,729	19,530
03452	Jaffrey	5,694	5,361
*03431	Keene	22,672	22,430
03848	Kingston	6,229	5,591
*03246	Laconia	17,060	15,743
*03766	Lebanon	12,586	12,183
03052	Litchfield	8,582	5,516
03561	Littleton	6,162	5,827
03053	Londonderry (c)	11,417	10,114
03053	Londonderry	24,879	19,781
03307	Loudon	5,117	—
*03103	Manchester	109,497	99,332
03253	Meredith	6,667	4,837
03054	Merrimack	26,613	22,156
03055	Milford (c)	8,293	8,015
03055	Milford	15,054	11,795
*03060	Nashua	87,157	79,662
03071	New Ipswich	5,134	
03857	Newmarket (c)	5,124	4,917
03857	Newmarket	9,521	7,157
03773	Newport	6,528	6,110
03276	Northfield	5,185	—
03076	Pelham	12,514	9,408
03275	Pembroke	7,390	6,561
03458	Peterborough	6,100	5,239
03102	Pinardville (c)	5,779	4,654
03865	Plaistow	7,705	7,316
03264	Plymouth	6,336	5,811
*03801	Portsmouth	20,618	25,925
03077	Raymond	10,188	8,713
03461	Rindge	6,391	4,941
*03867	Rochester	30,117	26,630
03870	Rye	5,214	—
03079	Salem	29,580	25,746
03873	Sandown	5,776	—
03874	Seabrook	8,513	6,503
03878	Somersworth	11,783	11,249
03106	South Hooksett (c)	5,282	3,638
03885	Stratham	7,170	4,955
03275	Suncook (c)	5,362	5,214
03446	Swanzey	7,320	6,236
03281	Weare	8,925	6,193
03087	Windham	12,939	9,000
03894	Wolfeboro	6,625	4,807

New Jersey

Area code (551) overlays area code (201). Area code (848) overlays (732). Area code (862) overlays (973). See introductory note.

ZIP	Place	Area Code	2006	1990
*08201	Absecon	(609)	8,065	7,298
07401	Allendale	(201)	6,713	5,900
07712	Asbury Park	(732)	16,546	16,799
08034	Ashland (c)	(856)	8,375	
*08401	Atlantic City	(609)	39,958	37,986
08106	Audubon	(856)	8,981	9,205
07001	Avenel (c)	(732)	17,552	15,504
08034	Barclay-Kingston (c)	(856)	10,728	—
08007	Barrington	(856)	7,004	6,792
07002	Bayonne	(201)	58,844	61,464
08722	Beachwood	(732)	10,744	9,324
07109	Belleville (c)	(973)	35,928	34,213
*08031	Bellmawr	(856)	11,193	12,603
*07719	Belmar	(732)	5,875	5,877
07621	Bergenfield	(201)	26,194	24,458
07922	Berkeley Heights (c)	(908)	13,407	11,980
08009	Berlin	(856)	7,910	5,672
07924	Bernardsville	(908)	7,688	6,597

ZIP	Place	Area Code	2006	1990
07403	Bloomingdale	(973)	7,604	7,530
07603	Bogota	(201)	8,108	7,824
07005	Boonton	(973)	8,600	8,343
08805	Bound Brook	(732)	10,225	9,487
08302	Bridgeton	(856)	24,389	18,942
08203	Brigantine	(609)	12,886	11,354
08015	Browns Mills (c)	(609)	11,257	11,429
07828	Budd Lake (c)	(973)	8,100	7,272
08016	Burlington	(609)	9,715	9,835
07405	Butler	(973)	8,074	7,392
*07006	Caldwell	(973)	7,373	7,542
*08101	Camden	(856)	79,318	87,492
07072	Carlstadt	(201)	6,037	5,510
08069	Carney's Point (c)	(856)	6,914	8,443
07008	Carteret	(732)	22,264	19,025
07009	Cedar Grove (c)	(973)	12,300	12,053
07928	Chatham	(973)	8,390	8,007
08002	Cherry Hill Mall (c)	(856)	13,238	—
07066	Clark (c)	(732)/(908)	14,597	14,629
08312	Clayton	(856)	7,469	6,155
07010	Cliffside Park	(201)	22,970	20,393
*07015	Clifton	(973)	79,606	71,984
07624	Closter	(201)	8,730	8,094
08108	Collingswood	(856)	13,961	15,289
07067	Colonia (c)	(732)	17,811	18,238
07016	Cranford (c)	(908)	22,578	22,633
07626	Cresskill	(201)	8,437	7,558
08759	Crestwood Village (c)	(732)	8,392	8,030
08810	Dayton (c)	(732)	6,235	—
*07627	Demarest	(201)	5,106	4,800
*07801	Dover	(973)	18,387	15,115
07628	Dumont	(201)	17,365	17,187
08812	Dunellen	(732)	6,940	6,528
08816	East Brunswick (c)	(732)	46,756	43,548
*07019	East Orange	(973)	67,247	73,552
07073	East Rutherford	(201)/(973)	8,931	7,902
*07724	Eatontown	(732)	14,022	13,800
08043	Echelon (c)	(856)	10,440	—
07020	Edgewater	(201)	9,628	5,001
*08818	Edison (c)	(732)/(908)	97,687	88,680
*07207	Elizabeth	(908)	126,179	110,002
*07407	Elmwood Park	(201)	18,805	17,623
07630	Emerson	(201)	7,318	6,930
07631	Englewood	(201)	27,824	24,850
07632	Englewood Cliffs	(201)	5,793	5,634
08002	Erlton-Ellisburg (c)	(856)	8,168	—
08618	Ewing (c)	(609)	35,707	34,185
07004	Fairfield (Essex Co.) (c)	(973)	7,063	7,615
07704	Fair Haven	(732)	5,885	5,270
07410	Fair Lawn	(201)/(973)	31,246	30,548
07022	Fairview (Bergen Co.)	(201)	13,628	10,733
07023	Fanwood	(908)	7,211	7,115
08518	Florence-Roebling (c)	(609)	8,200	8,564
07932	Florham Park	(973)	12,605	8,521
08863	Fords (c)	(732)	15,032	14,392
08640	Fort Dix (c)	(609)	7,464	10,205
07024	Fort Lee	(201)	37,008	31,997
07416	Franklin (Sussex Co.) (c)	(973)	5,210	4,977
07417	Franklin Lakes	(201)	11,340	9,873
07728	Freehold	(732)	11,394	10,742
07026	Garfield	(862)/(973)	29,644	26,727
08028	Glassboro	(856)	19,360	15,614
07028	Glen Ridge	(973)	6,908	7,076
07452	Glen Rock	(201)	11,396	10,883
*08030	Gloucester City	(856)	11,482	12,649
08053	Greentree (c)	(856)	11,536	—
07093	Guttenberg	(201)	10,717	8,268
*07602	Hackensack	(201)	43,671	37,049
07840	Hackettstown	(908)	9,478	8,120
08033	Haddonfield	(856)	11,515	11,633
08035	Haddon Heights	(856)	7,365	7,860
*07508	Haledon	(973)	8,358	6,951
08037	Hammonton	(609)	13,572	12,208
07029	Harrison	(973)	13,942	13,425
07604	Hasbrouck Heights	(201)	11,621	11,488
*07506	Hawthorne	(973)	18,166	17,084
07422	Highland Lake (c)	(973)	5,051	4,550
08904	Highland Park	(732)	14,175	13,279
08520	Hightstown	(609)	5,300	5,126
07642	Hillsdale	(201)	10,053	9,750
07205	Hillside (c)	(908)/(973)	21,747	21,044
07030	Hoboken	(201)	39,853	33,397
08753	Holiday City-Berkeley (c)	(732)	13,884	14,293
07843	Hopatcong	(973)	15,884	15,586
07111	Irvington (c)	(973)	60,695	59,774
08830	Iselin (c)	(732)	16,698	16,141
08831	Jamesburg	(732)	6,429	5,294
*07303	Jersey City	(201)	241,789	228,517
07734	Keansburg	(732)	10,573	11,069
*07032	Kearny	(201)/(973)	38,008	34,874
08824	Kendall Park (c)	(908)	9,006	7,127
07033	Kenilworth	(908)	7,741	7,574
07735	Keyport	(732)	7,471	7,586
07405	Kinnelon	(973)	9,681	8,470
07871	Lake Mohawk (c)	(973)	9,755	8,930
08701	Lakewood	(732)	36,065	26,095
08879	Laurence Harbor (c)	(732)	6,227	6,361
*08733	Leisure Village West-Pine Lake Park (c)	(732)	11,085	10,139
07605	Leonia	(201)	8,799	8,365
07035	Lincoln Park	(973)	10,856	10,978
07738	Lincroft (c)	(732)	6,255	6,193
07036	Linden	(732)/(908)	39,874	36,701
08021	Lindenwold	(856)	17,160	18,734
08221	Linwood	(609)	7,354	6,866
07424	Little Falls (c)	(973)	10,855	11,294
07643	Little Ferry	(201)	10,715	9,989
07739	Little Silver	(732)	6,089	5,721
07039	Livingston (c)	(973)	27,391	26,609
07644	Lodi	(201)/(973)	24,310	22,355
07740	Long Branch	(732)	32,314	28,658
07071	Lyndhurst (c)	(201)	19,383	18,262
08641	McGuire AFB (c)	(609)	6,478	7,580
07940	Madison	(973)	16,016	15,850
08859	Madison Park (c)	(732)	6,929	7,490
08736	Manasquan	(732)	6,199	5,369
08835	Manville	(908)	10,481	10,567
07040	Maplewood (c)	(973)	23,868	21,756
08402	Margate City	(609)	8,601	8,431
08053	Marlton (c)	(856)	10,260	10,228
07747	Matawan	(732)	8,781	9,239
07607	Maywood	(201)	9,374	9,536
07945	Mendham	(973)	5,176	4,890
08619	Mercerville-Hamilton Sq. (c)	(609)	26,419	26,873
08840	Metuchen	(732)	13,216	12,804
08846	Middlesex	(732)	13,746	13,055
07432	Midland Park	(201)	6,906	7,047
07041	Millburn (c)	(973)	19,765	18,630
08850	Milltown	(732)	7,038	6,968
08332	Millville	(856)	28,194	25,992
*07042	Montclair (c)	(973)	38,977	37,729
07645	Montvale	(201)	7,308	6,946
08057	Moorestown-Lenola (c)	(856)	13,860	13,242
07751	Morganville (c)	(732)	11,255	—
07950	Morris Plains	(973)	5,601	5,219
*07960	Morristown	(973)	18,922	16,189
08085	Mountainside	(908)	6,644	6,657
07856	Mount Arlington	(973)	5,708	3,630
08087	Mystic Islands (c)	(609)	8,694	7,400
07753	Neptune City (c)	(732)	5,150	4,997
*07102	Newark	(973)	281,402	275,221
*08901	New Brunswick	(732)	50,172	41,711
07646	New Milford	(201)	16,243	15,990
07974	New Providence	(908)	11,915	11,439
07860	Newton	(973)	8,337	7,521
07031	North Arlington	(201)	15,077	13,790
08902	North Brunswick Twp. (c)	(732)	36,287	31,287
07006	North Caldwell	(973)	7,207	6,706
08225	Northfield	(609)	8,003	7,305
*07508	North Haledon	(973)	9,039	7,987
*07060	North Plainfield	(908)	21,738	18,820
07648	Norwood	(201)	6,267	4,858
07110	Nutley (c)	(973)	27,362	27,099
07436	Oakland	(201)	13,558	11,997
*08050	Ocean Acres (c)	(609)	13,155	5,587
08226	Ocean City	(609)	15,124	15,512
07757	Oceanport	(732)	5,751	6,146
08857	Old Bridge (c)	(732)	22,833	22,151
07675	Old Tappan	(201)	6,013	4,254
07649	Oradell	(201)	7,957	8,024
*07051	Orange (c)	(973)	32,868	29,925
07650	Palisades Park	(201)	19,306	14,536
08065	Palmyra	(856)	7,598	7,056
07652	Paramus	(201)	26,548	25,004
07656	Park Ridge	(201)	8,945	8,102
07055	Passaic	(973)	67,974	58,041
*07510	Paterson	(973)	148,708	140,891
08066	Paulsboro	(856)	6,062	6,577
*08110	Pennsauken (c)	(856)	35,737	34,738
08070	Pennsville (c)	(856)	11,657	12,218
*08861	Perth Amboy	(732)	48,607	41,967
08865	Phillipsburg	(908)	14,831	15,757
08021	Pine Hill	(856)	11,275	9,854
08071	Pitman	(856)	9,199	9,365
*07061	Plainfield	(908)	47,353	46,577
08232	Pleasantville	(609)	18,982	16,027
08742	Point Pleasant	(732)	5,398	18,177
08742	Point Pleasant Beach	(732)	19,882	5,112
07442	Pompton Lakes	(973)	11,243	10,539
*08540	Princeton	(609)	13,684	12,016
08536	Princeton Meadows (c)	(609)	13,430	—
*07508	Prospect Park	(973)	5,720	5,053
07065	Rahway	(732)	27,843	25,325
08057	Ramblewood (c)	(856)	6,003	6,181
07446	Ramsey	(201)	14,775	13,228
07731	Ramtown (c)	(732)	5,932	—
*08869	Raritan	(908)	6,427	5,798
*07701	Red Bank	(732)	11,850	10,636
07657	Ridgefield	(201)	10,996	9,996
07660	Ridgefield Park	(201)	12,665	12,454
*07451	Ridgewood	(201)/(973)	24,639	24,152
07456	Ringwood	(973)	12,814	12,623
07661	River Edge	(201)	10,862	10,603
07866	Rockaway	(973)	6,410	6,243
07068	Roseland	(973)	5,400	4,847
07203	Roselle	(908)	21,158	20,314
07204	Roselle Park	(908)	13,124	12,805
07760	Rumson	(732)	7,194	6,701
08078	Runnemede	(856)	8,461	9,042
07070	Rutherford	(201)	17,871	17,790

ZIP	Place	Area Code	2006	1990
08079	Salem	(856)	5,784	6,883
*08872	Sayreville	(732)	42,560	34,998
*07094	Secaucus	(201)	15,562	14,061
08083	Somerdale	(856)	5,123	5,440
08244	Somers Point	(609)	11,573	11,216
08876	Somerville	(908)	12,550	11,632
08879	South Amboy	(732)	7,865	7,851
07080	South Plainfield	(732)/(908)	22,795	20,489
*08882	South River	(732)	15,822	13,692
08884	Spotswood	(732)	8,179	7,983
07762	Spring Lake Heights	(732)	5,106	5,341
08084	Stratford	(856)	7,122	7,614
*07901	Summit	(908)	21,103	19,757
07670	Tenafly	(201)	14,390	13,326
*07724	Tinton Falls	(732)	17,082	12,361
*07512	Totowa	(973)	10,634	10,177
08650	Trenton	(609)	83,923	88,675
07083	Union (Union Co.) (c)	(908)	66,167	50,024
07735	Union Beach	(732)	6,631	6,156
*07087	Union City	(201)	63,930	58,012
07458	Upper Saddle River	(201)	8,531	7,198
08406	Ventnor City	(609)	12,564	11,005
*08360	Vineland	(856)	58,271	54,780
07463	Waldwick	(201)	9,621	9,757
07057	Wallington	(201)/(973)	11,430	10,828
07465	Wanaque	(201)/(973)	11,171	9,711
07882	Washington	(908)	6,841	6,474
07069	Watchung	(908)	6,284	5,110
*07091	Westfield	(732)/(908)	29,944	28,870
07764	West Long Branch	(732)	8,312	7,690
07093	West New York	(201)	46,398	38,125
07424	West Paterson	(973)	11,234	10,982
*07675	Westwood	(201)	10,934	10,446
07885	Wharton	(973)	6,211	5,405
08260	Wildwood	(609)	5,309	4,484
*08096	Woodbury	(856)	10,410	10,904
07677	Woodcliff Lake	(201)	5,953	5,303
07075	Wood-Ridge	(201)/(973)	7,594	7,506

New Mexico (505)

ZIP	Place		2006	1990
*88310	Alamogordo		36,069	27,596
*87101	Albuquerque		504,949	384,915
88021	Anthony (c)		7,904	5,160
*88210	Artesia		10,597	10,610
87410	Aztec		7,056	5,480
87002	Belen		7,142	6,547
87004	Bernalillo		7,158	5,864
87413	Bloomfield		7,409	5,214
*88220	Carlsbad		25,410	24,952
88021	Chaparral (c)		6,117	2,962
*88101	Clovis		33,258	30,954
87048	Corrales		7,893	5,453
*88030	Deming		15,296	11,422
87031	El Cerro-Monterey Park (c)		5,483	
87505	Eldorado at Santa Fe (c)		5,799	2,260
*87532	Espanola		9,629	8,389
*87401	Farmington		43,573	33,997
*87301	Gallup		19,301	19,157
87020	Grants		8,965	8,626
*88240	Hobbs		29,292	29,121
87417	Kirtland (c)		6,190	3,552
*88001	Las Cruces		86,268	62,360
*87701	Las Vegas		13,889	14,753
87544	Los Alamos (c)		11,909	11,455
87002	Los Chaves (c)		5,033	3,872
87031	Los Lunas		11,803	6,013
*87107	Los Ranchos de Albuquerque		5,416	6,075
88260	Lovington		9,693	9,322
87107	North Valley (c)		11,923	12,507
*88130	Portales		11,308	10,690
87740	Raton		6,781	7,372
*87124	Rio Rancho		71,607	32,512
*88201	Roswell		45,582	44,260
*88345	Ruidoso		9,359	4,600
*87501	Santa Fe		72,056	56,537
87420	Shiprock (c)		8,156	7,687
*88061	Silver City		9,992	10,683
87801	Socorro		8,604	8,159
87105	South Valley (c)		39,060	35,701
*88063	Sunland Park		14,234	8,179
87571	Taos		5,193	4,065
87901	Truth or Consequences		6,915	6,221
*88401	Tucumcari		5,249	6,827
87544	White Rock (c)		6,045	6,192
87327	Zuni Pueblo (c)		6,367	5,857

New York

Area code (347) overlays area code (718). Area codes (646) and (917) overlay (212). See introductory note.

ZIP	Place	Area Code	2006	1990
*10901	Airmont	(845)	8,647	7,674
*12201	Albany	(518)	93,963	100,031
11507	Albertson (c)	(516)	5,200	5,166
14411	Albion	(585)	5,729	5,863
*11701	Amityville	(516)/(631)	9,417	9,286
12010	Amsterdam	(518)	17,758	20,714
12603	Arlington (c)	(845)	12,481	11,948

ZIP	Place	Area Code	2006	1990
*13021	Auburn	(315)	27,766	31,258
11702	Babylon	(631)	12,506	12,249
11510	Baldwin (c)	(516)	23,455	22,719
11510	Baldwin Harbor (c)	(516)	8,147	7,899
13027	Baldwinsville	(315)	7,103	6,591
12020	Ballston Spa	(518)	5,518	5,194
*14020	Batavia	(585)	15,473	16,310
14810	Bath	(607)	5,545	5,801
11705	Bayport (c)	(631)	8,662	7,702
11706	Bay Shore (c)	(631)	23,852	21,279
11709	Bayville	(516)	7,082	7,193
12508	Beacon	(845)	14,908	13,243
11710	Bellmore (c)	(516)	16,441	16,438
11714	Bethpage (c)	(516)	16,543	15,761
*13902	Binghamton	(607)	45,217	53,008
10913	Blauvelt (c)	(845)	5,207	4,838
11716	Bohemia (c)	(631)	9,871	9,556
11717	Brentwood (c)	(631)	53,917	45,218
10510	Briarcliff Manor	(914)	7,993	7,070
14610	Brighton (c)	(585)	35,584	34,455
14420	Brockport	(585)	8,129	8,749
10708	Bronxville	(914)	6,486	6,028
14240	Buffalo	(716)	276,059	328,175
11933	Calverton (c)	(631)	5,704	4,759
*14424	Canandaigua	(585)	11,317	10,725
13617	Canton	(315)	6,076	6,379
11514	Carle Place (c)	(516)	5,247	5,107
10512	Carmel Hamlet (c)	(845)	5,650	4,800
11516	Cedarhurst	(516)	6,031	5,716
11720	Centereach (c)	(631)	27,285	26,720
11934	Center Moriches (c)	(631)	6,655	5,987
11721	Centerport (c)	(631)	5,446	5,333
11722	Central Islip (c)	(516)	31,950	26,028
10514	Chappaqua (c)	(914)	9,468	
14225	Cheektowaga (c)	(716)	79,988	84,387
*10977	Chestnut Ridge	(845)	7,904	7,517
12047	Cohoes	(518)	15,011	16,825
12205	Colonie (c)	(518)	8,346	8,019
11725	Commack (c)	(631)	36,367	36,124
10920	Congers (c)	(845)	8,303	8,003
11726	Copiague (c)	(631)	21,922	20,769
11727	Coram (c)	(631)	34,923	30,111
*14830	Corning	(607)	10,478	11,938
13045	Cortland	(607)	18,423	19,801
*10520	Croton-on-Hudson	(914)	7,899	7,018
11729	Deer Park (c)	(631)	28,316	28,840
12054	Delmar (c)	(518)	8,292	8,360
14043	Depew	(716)	15,607	17,673
11746	Dix Hills (c)	(631)	26,024	25,849
10522	Dobbs Ferry	(914)	11,138	9,940
*14048	Dunkirk	(716)	12,299	13,989
14052	East Aurora	(585)/(716)	6,340	6,647
10709	Eastchester (c)	(914)	18,564	18,537
12302	East Glenville (c)	(518)	6,064	6,518
*11576	East Hills (c)	(516)	6,690	6,746
11730	East Islip (c)	(631)	14,078	14,325
11758	East Massapequa (c)	(516)	19,565	19,550
11554	East Meadow (c)	(516)	37,461	36,909
11731	East Northport (c)	(631)	20,845	20,411
11772	East Patchogue (c)	(631)	20,824	20,195
14445	East Rochester (c)	(585)	6,977	6,932
11518	East Rockaway	(516)	10,177	10,152
11786	East Shoreham (c)	(631)	5,809	5,461
*14901	Elmira	(607)	29,567	33,724
11003	Elmont (c)	(516)	32,657	28,612
11731	Elwood (c)	(631)	10,916	10,916
*13760	Endicott	(607)	12,562	13,531
13762	Endwell (c)	(607)	11,706	12,602
13219	Fairmount (c)	(315)	10,795	12,266
14450	Fairport	(585)	5,496	5,943
12601	Fairview (c)	(845)	5,421	4,811
*11735	Farmingdale	(516)	8,639	8,022
*11001	Floral Park	(516)	15,602	15,947
13603	Fort Drum (c)	(315)	12,123	11,578
11768	Fort Salonga (c)	(631)	9,634	9,176
11010	Franklin Square (c)	(516)	29,342	28,205
14063	Fredonia	(716)	11,127	10,436
11520	Freeport	(516)	43,144	39,894
13069	Fulton	(315)	11,459	12,929
*11530	Garden City	(516)	21,811	21,675
11040	Garden City Park (c)	(516)	7,554	7,437
14624	Gates-North Gates (c)	(585)	15,138	14,995
14454	Geneseo	(585)	7,809	7,187
14456	Geneva	(315)	13,367	14,143
11542	Glen Cove	(516)	26,438	24,149
12801	Glens Falls	(518)	14,078	15,023
12801	Glens Falls North (c)	(518)	8,061	7,978
12078	Gloversville	(518)	15,175	16,656
10924	Goshen	(845)	5,547	5,255
*11021	Great Neck	(516)	9,719	8,745
11020	Great Neck Plaza	(516)	6,867	5,897
14616	Greece (c)	(585)	14,614	15,632
11740	Greenlawn (c)	(631)	13,286	13,208
*10583	Greenville (Westchester Co.) (c)	(914)	8,648	9,528
14075	Hamburg (c)	(716)	9,495	10,442
11946	Hampton Bays (c)	(631)	12,236	7,893
10528	Harrison (c)	(914)	26,337	23,308
10530	Hartsdale (c)	(914)	9,830	9,587
10706	Hastings-on-Hudson	(914)	7,843	8,000

ZIP	Place	Area Code	2006	1990
*11788	Hauppauge (c)	(631)	20,100	19,750
10927	Haverstraw	(845)	10,672	9,438
10532	Hawthorne (c)	(845)	5,083	4,764
*11551	Hempstead	(516)	52,526	45,982
13350	Herkimer	(315)	7,162	7,945
11557	Hewlett	(516)	7,060	6,620
*11802	Hicksville (c)	(516)	41,260	40,174
12528	Highland	(845)	5,060	4,492
10977	Hillcrest (c)	(845)	7,106	6,447
14468	Hilton	(585)	6,091	5,216
14843	Hornell	(607)	8,705	9,877
*14845	Horseheads	(607)	6,293	6,802
12534	Hudson	(518)	6,985	8,034
12839	Hudson Falls	(518)	6,772	7,651
11743	Huntington (c)	(631)	18,403	18,243
11746	Huntington Station (c)	(631)	29,910	28,247
13357	Ilion	(315)	8,237	8,888
11096	Inwood (c)	(516)	9,325	7,767
14617	Irondequoit (c)	(585)	52,354	52,322
10533	Irvington	(914)	6,656	6,348
11751	Islip (c)	(631)	20,575	18,924
11752	Islip Terrace (c)	(631)	5,641	5,530
*14850	Ithaca	(607)	29,829	29,541
*14702	Jamestown	(716)	29,918	34,681
10535	Jefferson Valley-Yorktown (c)	(914)	14,891	14,118
11753	Jericho (c)	(516)	13,045	13,141
13790	Johnson City	(607)	14,889	16,578
12095	Johnstown	(518)	8,502	9,058
*14217	Kenmore	(716)	15,318	17,180
11754	Kings Park (c)	(631)	16,146	17,773
11024	Kings Point	(516)	5,178	4,843
*12401	Kingston	(845)	22,828	23,095
10950	Kiryas Joel	(845)	20,071	7,437
14218	Lackawanna	(716)	17,926	20,585
10512	Lake Carmel (c)	(845)	8,663	8,489
11755	Lake Grove	(631)	10,621	9,612
10547	Lake Mohegan (c)	(914)	5,979	—
11779	Lake Ronkonkoma (c)	(631)	19,701	18,997
11552	Lakeview	(516)	5,607	5,476
*14086	Lancaster	(716)	11,328	11,940
10538	Larchmont	(914)	6,530	6,181
11559	Lawrence	(516)	6,442	6,513
11756	Levittown	(516)	53,067	53,286
11757	Lindenhurst	(631)	27,937	26,879
*14094	Lockport	(716)	21,035	24,426
11561	Long Beach	(516)	35,111	33,510
11563	Lynbrook	(516)	19,457	19,208
12953	Malone	(518)	5,903	6,777
11565	Malverne	(516)	8,751	9,054
10543	Mamaroneck	(914)	18,472	17,325
11030	Manhasset (c)	(516)	8,362	7,718
11050	Manorhaven	(516)	6,307	5,672
11949	Manorville (c)	(631)	11,131	6,198
11758	Massapequa (c)	(516)	22,652	22,018
11762	Massapequa Park	(516)	17,115	18,044
13662	Massena	(315)	10,800	11,716
11950	Mastic (c)	(631)	15,436	13,778
11951	Mastic Beach (c)	(631)	11,543	10,293
13211	Mattydale (c)	(315)	6,367	6,418
10940	Mechanicstown (c)	(845)	6,061	—
11763	Medford (c)	(631)	21,985	21,274
14103	Medina	(585)/(716)	6,191	6,686
11747	Melville (c)	(631)	14,533	12,586
11566	Merrick (c)	(516)	22,764	23,042
11953	Middle Island (c)	(631)	9,702	7,848
*10940	Middletown	(845)	26,005	24,160
11764	Miller Place (c)	(631)	10,580	9,315
11501	Mineola	(516)	18,808	19,005
*10950	Monroe	(845)	8,141	6,672
10952	Monsey (c)	(845)	14,504	13,986
*12701	Monticello	(845)	6,635	6,597
10970	Mount Ivy (c)	(845)	6,536	6,013
10549	Mount Kisco	(914)	10,441	9,108
11766	Mount Sinai (c)	(631)	8,734	8,023
*10551	Mount Vernon	(914)	68,395	67,153
12590	Myers Corner (c)	(845)	5,546	5,599
10954	Nanuet (c)	(845)	16,707	14,065
11767	Nesconset (c)	(631)	11,992	10,712
14513	Newark	(315)	9,284	9,849
*12550	Newburgh	(845)	28,345	26,454
11590	New Cassel (c)	(516)	13,298	10,257
10956	New City (c)	(845)	34,038	33,673
*11040	New Hyde Park	(516)	9,393	9,728
12561	New Paltz	(845)	6,714	5,470
*10802	New Rochelle	(914)	73,464	67,265
10977	New Square	(845)	6,715	2,623
*12550	New Windsor (c)	(845)	8,898	
*10001	New York	(212)/(718)	8,214,426	7,322,564
*14302	Niagara Falls	(716)	52,326	61,840
11701	North Amityville (c)	(631)	16,572	13,849
11703	North Babylon (c)	(631)	17,877	18,081
11706	North Bay Shore (c)	(631)	14,992	12,799
11710	North Bellmore (c)	(516)	20,079	19,707
11713	North Bellport (c)	(631)	9,007	8,182
11757	North Lindenhurst (c)	(631)	11,767	10,563
11758	North Massapequa (c)	(516)	19,152	19,365
11566	North Merrick (c)	(516)	11,844	12,113
11040	North New Hyde Park (c)	(516)	14,542	14,359
11772	North Patchogue (c)	(631)	7,825	7,374
11768	Northport	(631)	7,494	7,572
13212	North Syracuse	(315)	6,694	7,363
14120	North Tonawanda	(716)	31,770	34,989
11580	North Valley Stream (c)	(516)	15,789	14,574
11793	North Wantagh (c)	(516)	12,156	12,276
13815	Norwich	(607)	7,203	7,613
10960	Nyack	(845)	6,706	6,558
11769	Oakdale (c)	(631)	8,075	7,875
11572	Oceanside (c)	(516)	32,733	32,423
13669	Ogdensburg	(315)	11,346	13,521
11804	Old Bethpage (c)	(516)	5,400	5,610
11568	Old Westbury	(516)	5,387	3,897
14760	Olean	(585)/(716)	14,584	16,946
13421	Oneida	(315)	10,935	10,850
13820	Oneonta	(607)	13,238	13,954
12550	Orange Lake (c)	(845)	6,085	5,196
10562	Ossining	(914)	23,578	22,582
13126	Oswego	(315)	17,638	19,195
11771	Oyster Bay (c)	(516)	6,826	6,687
11772	Patchogue	(631)	11,812	11,060
10965	Pearl River (c)	(845)	15,553	15,314
10566	Peekskill	(914)	24,601	19,536
10803	Pelham	(914)	6,404	5,443
10803	Pelham Manor	(914)	5,427	6,413
14527	Penn Yan	(315)	5,213	5,248
11714	Plainedge (c)	(516)	9,195	8,739
11803	Plainview (c)	(516)	25,637	26,207
12901	Plattsburgh	(518)	19,298	21,255
10570	Pleasantville	(914)	7,169	6,592
10573	Port Chester	(914)	28,006	24,728
11777	Port Jefferson	(631)	7,844	7,455
11776	Port Jefferson Station (c)	(631)	7,527	7,232
*12771	Port Jervis	(845)	9,160	9,060
11050	Port Washington (c)	(516)	15,215	15,387
*13676	Potsdam	(315)	9,829	10,251
*12601	Poughkeepsie	(845)	30,050	28,844
12144	Rensselaer	(518)	7,812	8,255
11961	Ridge (c)	(631)	13,380	11,734
11901	Riverhead (c)	(631)	10,513	8,814
*14692	Rochester	(585)	208,123	230,356
*11571	Rockville Centre	(516)	24,029	24,727
11778	Rocky Point (c)	(631)	10,185	8,596
*13440	Rome	(315)	34,220	44,350
11779	Ronkonkoma (c)	(631)	20,029	20,391
11575	Roosevelt (c)	(516)	15,854	15,030
11577	Roslyn Heights (c)	(516)	6,295	6,405
12303	Rotterdam (c)	(518)	20,536	21,228
10580	Rye	(914)	15,109	14,936
10573	Rye Brook	(914)	9,671	7,765
11780	Saint James (c)	(631)	13,268	12,703
14779	Salamanca	(716)	5,762	6,566
13454	Salisbury (c)	(315)	12,341	12,226
12866	Saratoga Springs	(518)	28,499	25,001
11782	Sayville (c)	(631)	16,735	16,550
10583	Scarsdale	(914)	17,886	16,987
*12301	Schenectady	(518)	61,560	65,566
10940	Scotchtown (c)	(845)	8,954	8,765
12302	Scotia	(518)	8,086	7,359
11783	Seaford (c)	(631)	15,791	15,597
11507	Searingtown (c)	(516)	5,034	5,020
11784	Selden (c)	(631)	21,861	20,608
13148	Seneca Falls	(315)	6,800	7,370
10591	Sleepy Hollow[1]	(914)	10,124	8,152
11787	Smithtown (c)	(631)	26,901	25,638
13209	Solvay	(315)	6,554	6,717
11789	Sound Beach (c)	(631)	9,807	9,102
11735	South Farmingdale (c)	(516)	15,061	15,377
14850	South Hill (c)	(607)	6,003	5,423
11746	South Huntington (c)	(631)	9,465	9,624
14094	South Lockport (c)	(716)	8,552	7,112
11971	Southold (c)	(631)	5,465	5,192
14904	Southport (c)	(607)	7,396	7,753
11581	South Valley Stream (c)	(516)	5,638	5,243
10977	Spring Valley	(845)	25,424	21,802
*11790	Stony Brook (c)	(631)	13,727	13,726
10980	Stony Point (c)	(845)	11,744	10,587
*11901	Suffern	(845)	10,954	11,055
11791	Syosset (c)	(516)	18,544	18,967
*13220	Syracuse	(315)	140,658	163,860
10983	Tappan (c)	(845)	6,757	6,867
10591	Tarrytown	(914)	11,477	10,739
11776	Terryville (c)	(631)	10,589	10,275
10594	Thornwood (c)	(914)	5,980	7,025
*14150	Tonawanda	(716)	15,107	17,284
*12180	Troy	(518)	47,952	54,269
10707	Tuckahoe	(914)	6,300	6,302
11553	Uniondale (c)	(516)	23,011	20,328
*13504	Utica	(315)	59,082	68,637
10595	Valhalla (c)	(914)	5,379	—
10989	Valley Cottage (c)	(845)	9,269	9,007
11582	Valley Stream	(516)	35,477	33,946
10952	Viola (c)	(845)	5,931	4,504
11792	Wading River (c)	(631)	6,668	5,317
12586	Walden	(845)	6,832	5,836
12590	Wappingers Falls	(845)	5,149	4,605
11793	Wantagh (c)	(516)	18,971	18,567
10990	Warwick	(845)	6,630	5,984
10992	Washingtonville	(845)	6,194	4,906
13165	Waterloo	(315)	5,108	5,116
*13601	Watertown	(315)	26,712	29,429

ZIP	Place	Area Code	2006	1990
12189	Watervliet	(518)	9,802	11,061
14580	Webster	(585)	5,025	5,464
10952	Wesley Hills	(845)	5,087	4,308
*11704	West Babylon (c)	(631)	43,452	42,410
*11590	Westbury	(516)	14,582	13,060
14905	West Elmira (c)	(607)	5,136	5,218
12801	West Glens Falls (c)	(518)	6,721	5,964
10993	West Haverstraw	(845)	9,919	9,183
11743	West Hills (c)	(631)	5,607	5,849
11795	West Islip (c)	(631)	28,907	28,419
12203	Westmere (c)	(518)	7,188	6,750
*10996	West Point (c)	(845)	7,138	8,024
11796	West Sayville (c)	(631)	5,003	4,680
14224	West Seneca (c)	(716)	45,943	47,866
13219	Westvale (c)	(315)	5,166	5,952
11798	Wheatley Heights (c)	(631)	5,013	5,027
*10602	White Plains	(914)	57,081	48,718
*14231	Williamsville	(716)	5,254	5,583
11596	Williston Park	(516)	7,051	7,516
11797	Woodbury (c)	(516)	9,010	8,008
11598	Woodmere (c)	(516)	16,447	15,578
11798	Wyandach (c)	(631)	10,546	8,950
11980	Yaphank (c)	(631)	5,025	4,637
*10702	Yonkers	(914)	197,852	188,082
10598	Yorktown Heights (c)	(914)	7,972	7,690

(1) North Tarrytown changed its name to Sleepy Hollow on Dec. 12, 1996.

North Carolina

Area code (980) overlays area code (704). See introductory note.

ZIP	Place	Area Code	2006	1990
28315	Aberdeen	(910)	15,414	—
*28001	Albemarle	(704)	5,052	14,940
*27502	Apex	(919)	30,208	4,789
27263	Archdale	(336)	9,451	6,975
*27203	Asheboro	(336)	24,130	16,362
*28802	Asheville	(828)	72,789	63,379
28012	Belmont	(704)	8,990	8,434
28016	Bessemer City	(704)	5,386	4,698
28711	Black Mountain	(828)	7,667	7,156
*28607	Boone	(828)	13,328	12,949
28712	Brevard	(828)	6,654	5,452
*27215	Burlington	(336)	48,399	39,498
27509	Butner (c)	(919)	5,192	4,679
28428	Carolina Beach	(910)	5,625	4,002
27510	Carrboro	(919)	16,577	12,134
*27511	Cary	(919)	112,414	44,394
*27514	Chapel Hill	(919)	49,919	38,719
*28204	Charlotte	(704)	630,478	419,558
28021	Cherryville	(704)	5,533	4,756
*27520	Clayton	(919)	13,842	4,756
27012	Clemmons (c)	(336)	16,730	5,982
*28328	Clinton	(910)	8,797	8,385
*28025	Concord	(704)	62,587	29,591
28613	Conover	(828)	7,128	5,311
28031	Cornelius	(704)	20,449	2,581
*28036	Davidson	(704)	8,760	4,046
*28334	Dunn	(910)	9,972	9,258
*27701	Durham	(919)	209,009	138,894
*27288	Eden	(336)	15,643	15,238
*27909	Elizabeth City	(252)	19,056	16,087
27244	Elon	(336)	7,121	4,394
*28302	Fayetteville	(910)	168,003	75,850
28043	Forest City	(828)	7,324	7,475
*28307	Fort Bragg (c)	(910)	29,183	34,744
27526	Fuquay-Varina	(919)	13,669	4,447
27529	Garner	(919)	23,741	14,716
*28052	Gastonia	(704)	69,904	54,725
*27530	Goldsboro	(919)	38,203	40,736
27253	Graham	(336)	14,144	10,368
*27420	Greensboro	(336)	236,865	185,125
*27834	Greenville	(252)	72,052	46,274
28540	Half Moon (c)	(910)	6,645	6,306
28345	Hamlet	(910)	5,749	6,722
28075	Harrisburg	(704)	5,347	1,625
*28532	Havelock	(252)	21,906	20,300
*27536	Henderson	(252)	16,204	15,655
28739	Hendersonville	(828)	11,808	7,284
*28603	Hickory	(828)	40,583	28,474
*27260	High Point	(336)	97,796	69,428
27278	Hillsborough	(919)	5,403	4,263
27540	Holly Springs	(919)	17,425	1,203
28348	Hope Mills	(910)	12,630	8,272
*28070	Huntersville	(704)	38,796	3,014
28079	Indian Trail	(704)	17,491	1,942
*28540	Jacksonville	(910)	69,688	78,031
28560	James City (c)	(252)	5,420	4,279
*28081	Kannapolis	(704)	40,223	31,592
*27284	Kernersville	(336)	21,862	11,860
27948	Kill Devil Hills	(252)	6,614	4,238
27021	King	(336)	6,578	4,059
28405	Kings Grant (c)	(910)	7,738	—
28086	Kings Mountain	(704)	10,919	8,768
*28502	Kinston	(252)	22,729	25,295
27545	Knightdale	(919)	6,479	1,884
*28352	Laurinburg	(910)	15,766	16,111
*28645	Lenoir	(828)	18,018	16,337
27023	Lewisville	(336)	12,444	6,433
*27292	Lexington	(336)	20,382	16,583
*28092	Lincolnton	(704)	10,599	6,955
*28358	Lumberton	(910)	21,894	18,656
28752	Marion	(828)	5,057	4,765
28403	Masonboro (c)	(910)	11,812	7,010
*28105	Matthews	(704)	26,296	13,756
27302	Mebane	(919)	9,285	4,754
28759	Mills River	(828)	6,088	—
28227	Mint Hill	(704)	18,663	13,637
*28110	Monroe	(704)	30,871	18,623
*28115	Mooresville	(704)	20,944	9,563
28557	Morehead City	(252)	9,293	6,473
*28655	Morganton	(828)	17,224	15,085
*27560	Morrisville	(919)	12,513	1,022
27030	Mount Airy	(336)	8,457	7,156
28120	Mount Holly	(704)	9,804	7,710
28411	Murraysville (c)	(910)	7,279	—
28409	Myrtle Grove (c)	(910)	7,125	4,275
28562	New Bern	(252)	27,650	20,728
28658	Newton	(828)	13,160	11,134
28465	Oak Island	(910)	8,152	—
28411	Ogden (c)	(910)	5,481	3,228
27565	Oxford	(919)	8,550	7,965
*28374	Pinehurst	(910)	11,830	5,825
28399	Piney Green (c)	(910)	11,658	8,919
*27611	Raleigh	(919)	356,321	218,859
*27320	Reidsville	(336)	14,859	14,086
27870	Roanoke Rapids	(252)	16,505	15,722
28379	Rockingham	(910)	9,171	9,399
*27801	Rocky Mount	(252)	57,057	53,078
*27573	Roxboro	(336)	8,732	7,332
28704	Royal Pines (c)	(828)	5,334	4,418
28601	Saint Stephens (c)	(828)	9,439	8,734
*28144	Salisbury	(704)	28,480	23,626
*27330	Sanford	(919)	27,771	18,881
27576	Selma	(919)	6,779	4,600
*28150	Shelby	(704)	21,378	15,460
27344	Siler City	(919)	8,449	4,808
28412	Silver Lake (c)	(910)	5,788	4,071
27577	Smithfield	(919)	12,271	10,180
*28387	Southern Pines	(910)	12,212	9,213
28052	South Gastonia (c)	(704)	5,433	5,487
28390	Spring Lake	(910)	8,079	7,552
*28677	Statesville	(704)	25,511	20,647
27358	Summerfield	(336)	7,423	2,051
27886	Tarboro	(252)	10,564	11,037
*27360	Thomasville	(336)	26,200	15,915
27370	Trinity	(336)	6,988	5,469
28110	Unionville	(704)	6,996	—
28170	Wadesboro	(704)	5,171	—
*27587	Wake Forest	(919)	22,651	5,832
27889	Washington	(252)	10,060	9,160
*28786	Waynesville	(828)	9,432	7,282
28104	Weddington	(704)	9,029	3,803
28472	Whiteville	(910)	5,235	5,340
27892	Williamston	(252)	5,583	5,870
*28402	Wilmington	(910)	95,944	55,530
*27893	Wilson	(252)	47,380	38,400
*27102	Winston-Salem	(336)	196,990	162,292

North Dakota (701)

ZIP	Place	2006	1990
*58501	Bismarck	58,333	49,272
58301	Devils Lake	6,718	7,782
*58601	Dickinson	15,636	16,097
*58102	Fargo	90,056	74,084
*58201	Grand Forks	50,372	49,417
*58401	Jamestown	14,813	15,571
58554	Mandan	17,449	15,177
*58701	Minot	34,745	34,544
*58701	Minot AFB (c)	7,599	9,095
58072	Valley City	6,388	7,163
*58075	Wahpeton	7,907	8,751
58078	West Fargo	21,508	12,287
*58801	Williston	12,303	13,136

Ohio

Area code (234) overlays area code (330). Area code (567) overlays (419). See introductory note.

ZIP	Place	Area Code	2006	1990
45810	Ada	(419)	5,841	5,428
*44309	Akron	(330)	209,704	223,019
44601	Alliance	(330)	22,770	23,376
44001	Amherst	(440)	11,841	10,332
44805	Ashland	(419)	21,852	20,079
*44004	Ashtabula	(440)	20,177	21,633
45701	Athens	(740)	20,896	21,265
44202	Aurora	(330)	14,402	9,192
44515	Austintown (c)	(330)	31,627	32,371
44011	Avon	(440)	16,455	7,337
44012	Avon Lake	(440)	22,117	15,066
44203	Barberton	(330)	27,063	27,623
44140	Bay Village	(440)	14,976	17,000
44122	Beachwood	(216)	11,350	10,664
45434	Beavercreek	(937)	39,366	33,626
45069	Beckett Ridge (c)	(513)	8,663	4,505
44146	Bedford	(216)/(440)	13,320	14,822
*44146	Bedford Heights	(216)/(440)	10,663	12,131
45305	Bellbrook	(937)	6,906	6,511
43311	Bellefontaine	(937)	12,808	12,126

ZIP	Place	Area Code	2006	1990
44811	Bellevue	(419)	7,995	8,157
45714	Belpre	(740)	6,534	6,796
44017	Berea	(440)	18,139	19,051
43209	Bexley	(614)	12,283	13,088
43004	Blacklick Estates (c)	(614)	9,518	10,080
*45242	Blue Ash	(513)	11,537	11,923
44513	Boardman (c)	(330)	37,215	38,596
*43402	Bowling Green	(419)	29,725	28,303
44141	Brecksville	(440)	13,106	11,818
45211	Bridgetown North (c)	(513)	12,569	11,748
44147	Broadview Heights	(440)	17,563	12,219
44144	Brooklyn	(216)	10,692	11,706
44142	Brook Park	(216)/(440)	19,699	22,865
45309	Brookville	(937)	5,313	4,621
44212	Brunswick	(330)	35,107	28,218
43506	Bryan	(419)	8,357	8,348
44820	Bucyrus	(419)	12,581	13,496
*43725	Cambridge	(740)	11,454	11,748
44405	Campbell	(330)	8,726	10,038
44614	Canal Fulton	(330)	5,111	4,157
43110	Canal Winchester	(614)	5,819	2,652
44406	Canfield	(330)	7,061	5,409
*44711	Canton	(330)	78,924	84,161
45005	Carlisle	(937)	5,882	4,872
*45822	Celina	(419)	10,396	9,945
*45458	Centerville (Montgomery Co.)	(937)	23,046	21,082
44024	Chardon	(440)	5,284	4,446
45211	Cheviot	(513)	8,049	9,616
45601	Chillicothe	(740)	22,216	21,923
*45202	Cincinnati	(513)	332,252	364,114
43113	Circleville	(740)	13,630	11,666
45315	Clayton	(937)	13,069	713
*44101	Cleveland	(216)	444,313	505,616
*44118	Cleveland Heights	(216)	47,097	54,052
43410	Clyde	(419)	6,164	6,087
44408	Columbiana	(330)	5,935	4,961
*43216	Columbus	(614)	733,203	632,945
44030	Conneaut	(440)	12,561	13,241
44410	Cortland	(330)	6,542	5,652
43812	Coshocton	(740)	11,643	12,193
45238	Covedale (c)	(513)	6,360	6,669
44827	Crestline	(419)	5,086	—
*44222	Cuyahoga Falls	(330)	50,398	48,950
*45401	Dayton	(937)	156,771	182,011
45236	Deer Park	(513)	5,496	6,181
43512	Defiance	(419)	16,212	16,787
43015	Delaware	(740)	32,100	19,966
45833	Delphos	(419)	6,816	7,093
*45247	Dent (c)	(513)	7,612	6,416
44622	Dover	(330)	12,504	11,329
45663	Dry Run (c)	(614)	6,553	5,389
*43016	Dublin	(614)/(740)	36,565	16,366
*44112	East Cleveland	(216)	25,213	33,096
44095	Eastlake	(440)	19,669	21,161
43920	East Liverpool	(330)	12,305	13,654
45320	Eaton	(937)	8,213	7,396
*44035	Elyria	(440)	55,745	56,746
*45322	Englewood	(937)	12,771	11,402
*44117	Euclid	(216)	48,717	54,875
45324	Fairborn	(937)	31,696	31,300
*45011	Fairfield	(513)	42,248	39,709
44334	Fairlawn	(330)	7,159	5,779
44126	Fairview Park	(440)	16,212	18,028
*45839	Findlay	(419)	38,173	35,703
45224	Finneytown (c)	(513)	13,492	13,096
45240	Forest Park	(513)	17,700	18,621
45230	Forestville (c)	(513)	10,978	9,185
44830	Fostoria	(419)	13,337	14,971
45005	Franklin	(513)	12,695	11,026
43420	Fremont	(419)	16,970	17,619
43230	Gahanna	(614)	33,080	23,898
44833	Galion	(419)	11,158	11,859
*44125	Garfield Heights	(216)	28,518	31,739
44041	Geneva	(440)	6,435	6,597
*45325	Germantown	(937)	5,098	4,916
44420	Girard	(330)	10,377	11,304
44044	Grafton	(440)	5,869	3,423
43212	Grandview Heights	(614)	6,209	7,010
43023	Granville	(740)	5,281	4,315
44232	Green	(330)	23,532	19,179
*45123	Greenfield	(937)	5,142	5,172
45331	Greenville	(937)	13,037	12,863
45253	Groesbeck (c)	(513)	7,202	6,684
43123	Grove City	(614)	31,820	19,661
*45011	Hamilton	(513)	62,130	61,438
45030	Harrison	(513)	8,313	7,520
43056	Heath	(740)	8,892	7,231
44134	Highland Heights	(440)	8,620	6,249
43026	Hilliard	(614)/(740)	26,812	11,794
45133	Hillsboro	(937)	6,694	6,235
44484	Howland Center (c)	(330)	6,481	6,732
44425	Hubbard	(330)	7,921	8,248
45424	Huber Heights	(937)	37,667	38,696
*44236	Hudson	(330)	23,154	5,159
44839	Huron	(419)	7,459	7,067
44131	Independence	(216)/(440)	6,789	6,500
45638	Ironton	(740)	11,416	12,751
45640	Jackson	(740)	6,232	6,167
*44240	Kent	(330)	27,946	28,835
43326	Kenton	(419)	8,149	8,356
43606	Kenwood (c)	(513)	7,423	7,469
*45429	Kettering	(937)	54,666	60,569
*44094	Kirtland	(440)	7,309	5,881
44107	Lakewood	(216)	52,194	59,718
43130	Lancaster	(740)	36,507	34,507
45039	Landen (c)	(513)	12,766	9,263
45036	Lebanon	(513)	20,346	10,461
*45802	Lima	(419)	38,219	45,553
43228	Lincoln Village (c)	(614)	9,482	9,958
43138	Logan	(740)	7,368	6,725
	London	(614)/(740)	9,496	7,807
*44052	Lorain	(440)	70,592	71,245
44641	Louisville	(330)	9,442	8,087
45140	Loveland	(513)	11,154	10,122
44124	Lyndhurst	(216)/(440)	14,195	15,982
*44056	Macedonia	(330)	10,418	7,509
45233	Mack South (c)	(513)	5,837	5,767
45243	Madeira	(513)	8,153	9,141
*44901	Mansfield	(419)	50,212	50,627
44137	Maple Heights	(216)	24,293	27,089
45750	Marietta	(740)	14,189	15,026
43302	Marion	(740)	36,138	34,075
43935	Martins Ferry	(740)	6,804	8,003
43040	Marysville	(937)	17,621	10,362
45040	Mason	(513)	29,491	11,450
44646	Massillon	(330)	32,315	30,969
43537	Maumee	(419)	14,149	15,561
44124	Mayfield Heights	(440)	18,110	19,847
44256	Medina	(330)	26,350	19,231
44060	Mentor	(440)	51,593	47,491
44060	Mentor-on-the-Lake	(216)	8,293	8,271
*45343	Miamisburg	(937)	19,878	17,834
44130	Middleburg Heights	(216)/(440)	15,237	14,702
45042	Middletown	(513)	51,290	46,758
45150	Milford	(513)	6,317	5,660
45050	Monroe	(513)	11,226	5,380
45242	Montgomery	(513)	9,856	9,733
44333	Montrose-Ghent (c)	(330)	5,261	4,906
45439	Moraine	(937)	6,595	5,989
45231	Mount Healthy	(513)	6,461	7,580
43050	Mount Vernon	(740)	15,908	14,550
44262	Munroe Falls	(330)	5,260	5,359
43545	Napoleon	(419)	9,419	8,884
45764	Nelsonville	(740)	5,423	4,563
43054	New Albany	(614)	6,345	1,621
*43055	Newark	(740)	47,242	44,396
45344	New Carlisle	(937)	5,616	6,049
44657	New Franklin	(330)	15,013	—
44663	New Philadelphia	(330)	17,433	15,698
44446	Niles	(330)	19,824	21,128
45239	Northbrook (c)	(513)	11,076	11,471
*44720	North Canton	(330)	16,755	14,904
45239	North College Hill	(513)	9,157	11,002
45251	Northgate (c)	(513)	8,016	7,864
44057	North Madison (c)	(440)	8,451	8,699
44070	North Olmsted	(440)	32,126	34,204
45502	Northridge (c) (Clark Co.)	(937)	6,853	5,939
45414	Northridge (c) (Montgomery Co.)	(937)	8,487	9,448
*44039	North Ridgeville	(440)	27,197	21,564
44133	North Royalton	(440)	29,465	23,197
*43619	Northwood	(419)	5,482	5,506
44203	Norton	(330)	11,549	11,477
44857	Norwalk	(419)	16,576	14,731
45212	Norwood	(513)	19,532	23,674
*45873	Oakwood	(937)	8,611	8,957
44074	Oberlin	(440)	8,239	8,191
44138	Olmsted Falls	(440)	8,333	6,741
44862	Ontario	(419)	5,302	4,026
*43616	Oregon	(419)	19,110	18,334
44667	Orrville	(330)	8,466	7,955
45056	Oxford	(513)	22,394	19,013
44077	Painesville	(440)	17,933	15,769
*44129	Parma	(216)/(440)	80,009	87,876
44130	Parma Heights	(216)/(440)	20,293	21,448
43062	Pataskala	(740)	12,643	3,046
44124	Pepper Pike	(216)/(440)	5,738	6,185
44646	Perry Heights (c)	(330)	8,900	9,055
*43551	Perrysburg	(419)	16,902	12,551
43147	Pickerington	(614)/(740)	16,575	5,668
45356	Piqua	(937)	20,865	20,612
45231	Pleasant Run (c)	(513)	5,267	4,964
44319	Portage Lakes (c)	(330)	9,870	13,373
*43452	Port Clinton	(419)	6,263	7,106
*45662	Portsmouth	(740)	20,132	22,676
43065	Powell	(614)	11,494	2,154
44266	Ravenna	(330)	11,422	12,069
*45215	Reading	(513)	10,090	12,038
43068	Reynoldsburg	(614)/(740)	33,078	25,748
44143	Richmond Heights	(216)/(440)	10,372	9,611
44270	Rittman	(330)	6,301	6,147
45431	Riverside	(937)	22,462	1,471
44116	Rocky River	(440)	19,377	20,410
43460	Rossford	(419)	6,359	5,861
43950	Saint Clairsville	(740)	5,081	5,136
45885	Saint Marys	(419)	8,203	8,441
44460	Salem	(330)	11,974	12,233
*44870	Sandusky	(419)	26,216	29,764
44870	Sandusky South (c)	(419)	6,599	6,336
*44131	Seven Hills	(216)/(440)	11,915	12,339
*44122	Shaker Heights	(216)	27,245	30,955

ZIP	Place	Area Code	2006	1990
*45241	Sharonville	(513)	12,884	13,121
44054	Sheffield Lake	(440)	9,085	9,825
44875	Shelby	(419)	9,489	9,610
44878	Shiloh (c)	(419)	*11,272*	11,607
*45365	Sidney	(937)	20,139	18,710
44139	Solon	(440)	22,257	18,548
*44121	South Euclid	(216)	21,791	23,866
45066	Springboro	(513)	16,963	6,574
45246	Springdale	(513)	9,640	10,621
*45501	Springfield	(937)	62,844	70,487
*43952	Steubenville	(740)	19,199	22,125
44224	Stow	(330)	34,335	27,998
44241	Streetsboro	(330)	14,185	9,932
*44136	Strongsville	(440)	43,347	35,308
44471	Struthers	(330)	11,077	12,284
45244	Summerside (c)	(513)	*5,523*	4,573
43560	Sylvania	(419)	19,109	17,489
44278	Tallmadge	(330)	17,370	14,870
45243	The Village of Indian Hill	(513)	5,644	5,383
44883	Tiffin	(419)	17,347	18,604
45371	Tipp City	(937)	9,360	6,483
*43601	Toledo	(419)	298,446	332,943
43964	Toronto	(740)	5,361	6,127
45067	Trenton	(513)	10,664	6,189
*45426	Trotwood	(937)	26,403	29,358
*45373	Troy	(937)	22,331	19,478
44087	Twinsburg	(330)	17,484	9,606
44683	Uhrichsville	(740)	5,611	5,604
45322	Union	(937)	6,261	5,531
*44122	University Heights	(216)	13,015	14,787
*43221	Upper Arlington	(614)	31,326	34,128
43351	Upper Sandusky	(419)	6,398	5,906
43078	Urbana	(937)	11,586	11,353
45377	Vandalia	(937)	14,226	13,872
45891	Van Wert	(419)	10,442	10,922
*44089	Vermilion	(440)	10,896	11,127
*44281	Wadsworth	(330)	20,155	15,718
*45895	Wapakoneta	(419)	9,579	9,214
*44481	Warren	(330)	45,256	50,793
*44122	Warrensville Heights	(216)	13,967	15,884
*43160	Washington	(740)	13,612	13,080
43566	Waterville	(419)	5,223	4,594
43567	Wauseon	(419)	7,355	6,322
45692	Wellston	(740)	6,005	6,049
*45449	West Carrollton City	(937)	13,005	14,403
*43081	Westerville	(614)	34,971	30,269
44145	Westlake	(440)	31,025	27,018
45694	Wheelersburg (c)	(740)	*6,471*	5,113
43213	Whitehall	(614)	17,894	20,572
45239	White Oak (c)	(513)	*13,277*	12,430
44092	Wickliffe	(440)	13,097	14,558
*44890	Willard	(419)	6,766	6,210
*44094	Willoughby	(440)	22,356	20,510
*44094	Willoughby Hills	(440)	8,449	8,427
*44095	Willowick	(440)	13,870	15,269
45177	Wilmington	(937)	12,694	11,199
45459	Woodbourne-Hyde Park (c)	(937)	*7,910*	7,837
44691	Wooster	(330)	25,791	22,427
43085	Worthington	(614)	13,079	14,869
45433	Wright-Patterson AFB (c)	(937)	*6,656*	8,579
*45215	Wyoming	(513)	7,575	8,128
45385	Xenia	(937)	23,438	24,836
*44501	Youngstown	(330)	81,520	95,732
*43701	Zanesville	(740)	25,361	26,778

Oklahoma

ZIP	Place	Area Code	2006	1990
*74820	Ada	(580)	15,919	15,765
*73521	Altus	(580)	19,525	21,910
73005	Anadarko	(405)	6,534	6,586
*73401	Ardmore	(580)	24,535	23,079
*74003	Bartlesville	(918)	34,885	34,256
73008	Bethany	(405)	19,559	20,075
74008	Bixby	(918)	19,294	9,502
74631	Blackwell	(580)	7,193	7,538
73010	Blanchard	(405)	6,145	—
*74012	Broken Arrow	(918)	88,314	58,082
74015	Catoosa	(918)	6,608	2,954
*73018	Chickasha	(405)	17,163	14,988
73020	Choctaw	(405)	10,803	8,545
*74017	Claremore	(918)	17,314	13,280
73601	Clinton	(580)	8,448	9,298
74429	Coweta	(918)	8,675	6,159
74023	Cushing	(918)	8,456	7,218
*73115	Del City	(405)	21,904	23,928
*73533	Duncan	(580)	22,487	21,732
*74701	Durant	(580)	15,050	12,929
*73034	Edmond	(405)	76,644	52,310
*73644	Elk City	(580)	11,002	10,428
73036	El Reno	(405)	16,222	15,414
*73701	Enid	(580)	46,514	45,309
74033	Glenpool	(918)	9,142	6,688
*74344	Grove	(918)	6,011	4,020
73044	Guthrie	(405)	10,924	10,440
73942	Guymon	(580)	10,696	7,803
74437	Henryetta	(918)	6,100	5,872
74848	Holdenville	(405)	5,564	4,893
74743	Hugo	(580)	5,573	5,978
74745	Idabel	(580)	6,918	6,957
74037	Jenks	(918)	14,123	7,484
*73501	Lawton	(580)	87,540	80,561
73443	Lone Grove	(580)	5,156	4,114
*74501	McAlester	(918)	18,333	16,739
*74354	Miami	(918)	13,635	13,142
*73140	Midwest City	(405)	55,161	52,267
*73153	Moore	(405)	49,277	40,318
*74401	Muskogee	(918)	40,004	37,708
73064	Mustang	(405)	16,443	10,434
73065	Newcastle	(405)	6,688	4,214
73068	Noble	(405)	5,591	4,710
*73069	Norman	(405)	102,827	80,071
*73125	Oklahoma City	(405)	537,734	444,724
74447	Okmulgee	(918)	12,829	13,441
*74055	Owasso	(918)	24,938	11,151
73075	Pauls Valley	(405)	6,186	6,150
73077	Perry	(580)	5,068	4,978
73078	Piedmont	(405)	5,008	—
*74601	Ponca City	(580)	24,710	26,359
74953	Poteau	(918)	8,304	7,210
*74361	Pryor Creek	(918)	9,294	8,327
73080	Purcell	(405)	5,968	4,784
74955	Sallisaw	(918)	8,736	7,122
74063	Sand Springs	(918)	18,246	15,339
*74066	Sapulpa	(918)	20,871	18,074
*74868	Seminole	(405)	6,950	7,071
*74801	Shawnee	(405)	29,989	26,017
74070	Skiatook	(918)	6,363	4,910
*74074	Stillwater	(405)	44,818	36,676
*74464	Tahlequah	(918)	16,237	10,586
74873	Tecumseh	(405)	6,643	5,750
73120	The Village	(405)	9,772	10,353
*74103	Tulsa	(918)	382,872	367,302
73089	Tuttle	(405)	5,704	2,807
74301	Vinita	(918)	5,992	5,804
*74467	Wagoner	(918)	8,001	6,894
*73123	Warr Acres	(405)	9,426	9,288
73772	Watonga	(580)	5,609	3,408
73096	Weatherford	(580)	9,938	10,124
*73801	Woodward	(580)	12,033	12,340
*73099	Yukon	(405)	22,279	20,935

Oregon

Area code (971) overlays area code (503). See introductory note.

ZIP	Place	Area Code	2006	1990
*97321	Albany	(541)	46,213	33,523
*97006	Aloha (c)	(503)	*41,741*	34,284
97601	Altamont (c)	(541)	*19,603*	18,591
97520	Ashland	(541)	20,881	16,252
97103	Astoria	(503)	9,917	10,069
97814	Baker City	(541)	9,648	9,140
*97005	Beaverton	(503)	89,643	53,307
*97701	Bend	(541)	71,892	23,740
97415	Brookings	(541)	6,344	4,400
97013	Canby	(503)	15,334	8,990
97225	Cedar Hills (c)	(503)	*8,949*	9,294
97291	Cedar Mill (c)	(503)	*12,597*	9,697
97502	Central Point	(541)	16,150	7,512
97058	City of the Dalles	(541)	11,926	11,021
97015	Clackamas (c)	(503)	*5,177*	2,578
97420	Coos Bay	(541)	15,999	15,076
97113	Cornelius	(503)	11,260	6,148
*97333	Corvallis	(541)	49,807	44,757
*97424	Cottage Grove	(541)	8,859	7,403
97338	Dallas	(503)	14,748	9,422
97009	Damascus	(503)	9,658	—
97524	Eagle Point	(541)	7,982	3,026
*97440	Eugene	(541)	146,356	112,733
97024	Fairview	(503)	9,462	2,588
97439	Florence	(541)	8,122	5,171
97116	Forest Grove	(503)	20,111	13,559
97301	Four Corners (c)	(503)	*13,922*	12,156
97223	Garden Home-Whitford (c)	(503)	*6,931*	6,652
97027	Gladstone	(503)	12,152	10,152
*97526	Grants Pass	(541)	29,693	17,503
97470	Green (c)	(541)	*6,174*	5,076
*97030	Gresham	(503)	97,105	68,285
*97015	Happy Valley	(503)	9,945	1,552
97303	Hayesville (c)	(503)	*18,222*	14,318
97838	Hermiston	(541)	14,891	10,047
*97123	Hillsboro	(503)	87,732	37,598
97031	Hood River	(541)	6,673	4,632
97351	Independence	(503)	8,764	4,425
97222	Jennings Lodge (c)	(503)	*7,036*	6,530
97448	Junction City	(541)	5,362	3,961
97307	Keizer	(503)	35,027	21,884
*97601	Klamath Falls	(541)	19,785	17,737
97850	La Grande	(541)	12,318	11,766
*97034	Lake Oswego	(503)	36,713	30,576
97739	La Pine (c)	(541)	*5,799*	—
97355	Lebanon	(541)	14,416	10,950
97367	Lincoln City	(541)	7,944	5,903
97128	McMinnville	(503)	5,296	17,894
97741	Madras	(541)	30,410	3,443
*97501	Medford	(541)	71,168	47,021
97862	Milton-Freewater	(541)	6,402	5,533
*97269	Milwaukie	(503)	20,988	18,670
97038	Molalla	(503)	7,012	3,651
97361	Monmouth	(503)	9,476	6,288

ZIP	Place	Area Code	2006	1990
97132	Newberg	(503)	21,576	13,086
*97365	Newport	(541)	9,896	8,437
97459	North Bend	(541)	9,846	9,614
97268	Oak Grove (c)	(503)	12,808	12,576
97006	Oak Hills (c)	(503)	9,050	6,450
97267	Oatfield (c)	(503)	15,750	15,348
97914	Ontario	(541)	11,093	9,394
97045	Oregon City	(503)	30,667	14,698
97801	Pendleton	(541)	16,589	15,142
*97208	Portland	(503)	537,081	485,975
97754	Prineville	(541)	9,313	5,355
97225	Raleigh Hills (c)	(503)	5,865	6,066
97756	Redmond	(541)	22,786	7,165
97527	Redwood (c)	(541)	5,844	3,702
97229	Rockcreek (c)	(503)	9,404	8,282
97470	Roseburg	(541)	20,991	18,389
97470	Roseburg North (c)	(541)	5,473	6,831
97051	Saint Helens	(503)	12,351	7,535
*97309	Salem	(503)	152,239	107,793
97055	Sandy	(503)	8,286	4,154
97056	Scappoose	(503)	6,056	3,550
97138	Seaside	(503)	6,187	5,359
97378	Sheridan	(503)	5,666	3,950
97140	Sherwood	(503)	17,068	3,093
97381	Silverton	(503)	8,993	5,635
*97477	Springfield	(541)	55,848	44,664
97383	Stayton	(503)	7,314	5,011
97015	Sunnyside (c)	(503)	6,791	4,423
97479	Sutherlin	(541)	7,306	5,020
97386	Sweet Home	(541)	8,576	6,850
97540	Talent	(541)	6,076	3,274
*97281	Tigard	(503)	49,100	29,435
97060	Troutdale	(503)	15,030	7,852
97062	Tualatin	(503)	26,208	14,664
97882	Umatilla	(541)	5,350	3,058
97225	West Haven-Sylvan (c)	(503)	7,147	6,009
97068	West Linn	(503)	25,209	16,389
*97225	West Slope (c)	(503)	6,442	7,959
97503	White City (c)	(541)	5,466	5,891
97070	Wilsonville	(503)	16,533	7,510
97071	Woodburn	(503)	22,035	13,404

Pennsylvania

Area code (267) overlays area code (215). Area code (484) overlays (610).
Area code (878) overlays (412). See introductory note.

ZIP	Place	Area Code	2006	1990
15001	Aliquippa	(724)	10,956	13,374
*18105	Allentown	(610)	107,294	105,301
*16603	Altoona	(814)	46,954	51,881
19002	Ambler	(215)	6,270	6,609
15003	Ambridge	(724)	7,219	8,133
18403	Archbald	(570)	6,396	6,291
19003	Ardmore (c)	(610)	12,616	12,646
15210	Arlington Heights (c)	(412)	5,132	4,768
15068	Arnold	(724)	5,344	6,113
19407	Audubon (c)	(610)	6,549	6,328
18612	Back Mountain (c)	(570)	26,699	—
15234	Baldwin	(12)	18,622	21,923
*18013	Bangor	(610)	5,286	5,383
15010	Beaver Falls	(724)	9,274	10,687
16823	Bellefonte	(814)	6,131	6,358
15202	Bellevue	(412)	8,110	9,126
18603	Berwick	(570)	10,306	10,976
15102	Bethel Park	(412)	31,891	33,823
*18016	Bethlehem	(610)	72,704	71,427
19508	Birdsboro	(610)	5,206	4,222
18447	Blakely	(570)	6,810	7,222
*17815	Bloomsburg	(570)	12,883	12,439
19422	Blue Bell (c)	(215)/(610)	6,395	6,091
19061	Boothwyn (c)	(610)	5,206	5,069
16701	Bradford	(814)	8,578	9,625
15227	Brentwood	(412)	9,678	10,823
15017	Bridgeville	(412)	9,771	5,445
19007	Bristol	(215)	7,827	10,405
19015	Brookhaven	(610)	8,578	8,570
19008	Broomall (c)	(610)	11,046	10,930
*16001	Butler	(724)	14,361	15,714
15419	California	(724)	5,947	5,748
*17011	Camp Hill	(717)	7,414	7,831
15317	Canonsburg	(724)	8,825	9,200
18407	Carbondale	(570)	9,319	10,664
*17013	Carlisle	(717)	18,272	18,419
15106	Carnegie	(412)	8,046	9,278
15108	Carnot-Moon (c)	(412)	10,637	10,187
15234	Castle Shannon	(412)	8,152	9,135
18032	Catasauqua	(610)	6,565	6,662
17201	Chambersburg	(717)	17,946	16,647
*19013	Chester	(610)	36,801	41,856
15025	Clairton	(412)	7,963	9,656
16214	Clarion	(814)	5,257	6,457
18411	Clarks Summit	(570)	5,008	5,433
16830	Clearfield	(814)	6,288	6,633
19018	Clifton Heights	(610)	6,609	7,111
19320	Coatesville	(610)	11,631	11,038
19426	Collegeville	(610)	5,008	—
19023	Collingdale	(610)	8,467	9,175
17109	Colonial Park (c)	(717)	13,259	13,777
17512	Columbia	(717)	10,070	10,701
15425	Connellsville	(724)	8,592	9,229

ZIP	Place	Area Code	2006	1990
*19428	Conshohocken	(610)	8,488	8,064
15108	Coraopolis	(412)	5,671	6,747
16407	Corry	(814)	6,496	7,216
15205	Crafton	(412)	6,204	7,188
19021	Croydon (c)	(215)	9,993	9,967
19023	Darby	(610)	10,007	11,140
19036	Darby Twp. (c)	(610)	9,622	10,955
19333	Devon-Berwyn (c)	(610)	5,067	5,019
18519	Dickson City	(570)	5,949	6,276
15033	Donora	(724)	5,356	5,928
15216	Dormont	(412)	8,564	9,772
*19335	Downingtown	(610)	7,885	7,749
18901	Doylestown	(215)	8,211	8,575
19026	Drexel Hill (c)	(610)	29,364	29,744
15801	DuBois	(814)	7,801	8,286
*18512	Dunmore	(570)	13,937	15,403
15110	Duquesne	(412)	6,778	8,525
19401	East Norriton (c)	(610)	13,211	13,324
*18042	Easton	(610)	26,209	26,276
18301	East Stroudsburg	(570)	10,476	8,781
17402	East York (c)	(717)	8,782	8,487
15027	Economy	(724)	9,212	9,305
*16412	Edinboro	(814)	6,682	7,736
17022	Elizabethtown	(717)	11,897	9,952
16117	Ellwood City	(724)	8,140	8,894
18049	Emmaus	(610)	11,401	11,157
17025	Enola (c)	(717)	5,627	5,961
17522	Ephrata	(717)	13,085	12,133
*16501	Erie	(814)	102,036	108,718
18643	Exeter	(570)	5,991	5,691
19030	Fairless Hills (c)	(215)	8,365	9,026
16121	Farrell	(724)	5,914	6,835
19053	Feasterville-Trevose (c)	(215)	6,425	6,696
16063	Fernway (c)	(724)	12,188	9,072
19032	Folcroft	(610)	6,890	7,506
19033	Folsom (c)	(610)	8,072	8,173
15221	Forest Hills	(412)	6,336	7,335
15238	Fox Chapel	(412)	5,179	5,319
16323	Franklin	(814)	6,811	7,329
15237	Franklin Park	(412)	11,840	10,109
18052	Fullerton (c)	(610)	14,268	13,127
*17325	Gettysburg	(717)	8,103	7,025
19036	Glenolden	(610)	7,287	7,260
19038	Glenside (c)	(215)	7,914	8,704
*15601	Greensburg	(724)	15,604	16,318
16125	Greenville	(724)	6,277	6,734
16127	Grove City	(412)	7,688	8,240
15101	Hampton Twp. (c) (Allegheny Co.)	(412)	17,526	15,568
*17331	Hanover	(717)	15,015	14,399
19438	Harleysville (c)	(215)	8,795	7,400
*17105	Harrisburg	(717)	47,164	52,376
15065	Harrison Twp. (c) (Allegheny Co.)	(412)	10,934	11,763
19040	Hatboro	(215)	7,204	7,382
*18201	Hazleton	(570)	22,037	24,730
18055	Hellertown	(610)	5,617	5,662
16148	Hermitage	(724)	16,530	15,260
17033	Hershey (c)	(717)	12,771	11,860
16648	Hollidaysburg	(814)	5,538	5,624
16001	Homeacre-Lyndora (c)	(724)	6,685	7,511
19044	Horsham (c)	(215)	14,779	15,051
16652	Huntingdon	(814)	6,827	6,843
15701	Indiana	(724)	14,817	15,174
15644	Jeannette	(724)	10,096	11,221
15025	Jefferson Hills	(412)	9,620	—
*15907	Johnstown	(814)	22,269	28,124
15108	Kennedy Twp. (c)	(412)	7,504	7,152
19348	Kennett Square	(610)	5,292	5,218
19406	King of Prussia (c)	(610)	18,511	18,406
18704	Kingston	(570)	13,131	14,507
19443	Kulpsville (c)	(215)	8,005	5,183
19530	Kutztown	(610)	5,038	—
*17604	Lancaster	(717)	54,779	55,551
19446	Lansdale	(215)	15,720	16,362
19050	Lansdowne	(610)	10,759	11,712
15650	Latrobe	(724)	8,561	9,265
17540	Leacock-Leola-Bareville (c)	(717)	6,625	5,685
17042	Lebanon	(717)	24,180	24,800
18235	Lehighton	(610)	5,494	5,914
19055	Levittown (c)	(215)	53,966	55,362
*17837	Lewisburg	(570)	5,578	5,785
17044	Lewistown	(717)	8,582	9,341
17112	Linglestown (c)	(717)	6,414	5,862
19353	Lionville-Marchwood (c)	(610)	6,298	6,468
17543	Lititz	(717)	9,029	8,280
17745	Lock Haven	(570)	8,652	9,230
17011	Lower Allen (c)	(717)	6,619	6,329
15068	Lower Burrell	(724)	12,350	12,251
15237	McCandless Twp. (c)	(412)	29,022	28,781
15134	McKeesport	(412)	22,408	26,016
15136	McKees Rocks	(412)	6,109	7,691
19002	Maple Glen (c)	(215)	7,042	5,881
*16335	Meadville	(814)	13,421	14,318
17055	Mechanicsburg	(717)	8,802	9,452
19063	Media	(610)	5,456	5,957
17057	Middletown (Dauphin Co.)	(717)	8,858	9,254
18017	Middletown (c) (Northampton Co.)	(610)	7,378	6,866
17551	Millersville	(717)	7,271	8,099
17847	Milton	(570)	6,406	6,746
15061	Monaca	(724)	5,886	6,739
15062	Monessen	(724)	8,219	9,901

ZIP	Place	Area Code	2006	1990
18936	Montgomeryville (c)	(215)	12,031	9,114
18507	Moosic	(570)	5,765	5,397
19067	Morrisville (Bucks Co.)	(215)	9,746	9,765
18707	Mountain Top (c)	(570)	15,269	—
17851	Mount Carmel	(570)	5,970	7,196
17552	Mount Joy	(717)	7,056	6,398
15228	Mount Lebanon (c)	(412)	33,017	34,414
15120	Munhall	(412)	11,358	13,158
*15146	Municipality of Monroeville	(412)	27,857	29,169
15668	Municipality of Murrysville	(724)	19,472	17,240
18634	Nanticoke	(570)	10,341	12,267
18064	Nazareth	(610)	6,055	5,713
19086	Nether Providence Twp. (c)	(610)	13,456	12,730
15066	New Brighton	(724)	6,231	6,854
*16108	New Castle	(724)	24,732	28,334
17070	New Cumberland	(717)	7,115	7,665
17557	New Holland	(717)	5,146	4,484
*15068	New Kensington	(724)	13,935	15,894
*19403	Norristown	(610)	30,337	30,754
18067	Northampton	(610)	9,765	8,717
15104	North Braddock	(412)	5,915	7,036
15137	North Versailles (c)	(412)	11,125	13,294
16421	Northwest Harborcreek (c)	(814)	8,658	7,485
19074	Norwood	(610)	5,834	6,162
15139	Oakmont	(412)	6,505	6,961
15238	O'Hara Twp. (c)	(412)	8,856	9,096
16301	Oil City	(814)	10,849	11,949
18518	Old Forge	(570)	8,569	8,834
19075	Oreland (c)	(215)	5,509	5,695
18071	Palmerton	(610)	5,259	5,394
17078	Palmyra	(717)	6,962	6,910
19301	Paoli (c)	(610)	5,425	5,277
16801	Park Forest Village (c)	(814)	8,830	6,703
17331	Parkville (c)	(717)	6,593	5,009
17112	Paxtonia (c)	(570)	5,254	4,862
15235	Penn Hills (c)	(412)	46,809	57,632
19096	Penn Wynne (c)	(610)	5,382	5,807
18944	Perkasie	(215)	8,726	7,878
*19104	Philadelphia	(215)	1,448,394	1,585,577
*19460	Phoenixville (c)	(610)	15,811	15,066
15233	Pittsburgh	(412)	312,819	369,879
*18640	Pittston	(570)	7,658	9,389
15236	Pleasant Hills (c)	(412)	7,841	8,884
15239	Plum	(412)	26,298	25,609
18651	Plymouth	(570)	6,128	7,134
19462	Plymouth Meeting (c)	(610)	5,593	6,241
19464	Pottstown	(610)	21,409	21,831
17901	Pottsville	(570)	14,643	16,603
17109	Progress (c)	(717)	9,647	9,654
19076	Prospect Park	(610)	6,425	6,764
15767	Punxsutawney	(814)	6,073	6,782
18951	Quakertown	(215)	8,768	8,982
19087	Radnor Twp. (c)	(610)	30,878	27,676
*19612	Reading	(610)	81,183	78,380
17356	Red Lion	(717)	6,091	6,130
18954	Richboro (c)	(215)	6,678	5,141
19078	Ridley Park	(610)	7,049	7,592
15237	Ross Twp. (c)	(412)	32,551	35,102
15857	Saint Marys	(814)	13,719	14,020
19464	Sanatoga (c)	(610)	7,734	3,723
18840	Sayre	(570)	5,585	5,791
17972	Schuylkill Haven	(570)	5,239	5,610
15106	Scott Twp. (c)	(412)	17,288	20,413
*18505	Scranton	(570)	72,861	81,805
17870	Selinsgrove	(570)	5,343	5,384
15116	Shaler Twp. (c)	(412)	29,757	33,694
17872	Shamokin	(570)	7,468	9,184
*16146	Sharon	(724)	15,286	17,533
19079	Sharon Hill	(610)	5,343	5,771
17976	Shenandoah	(570)	5,248	6,221
19607	Shillington	(610)	5,049	5,062
17404	Shiloh (c)	(717)	10,192	5,315
17257	Shippensburg	(717)	5,602	5,331
*15501	Somerset	(814)	6,468	6,454
18964	Souderton	(215)	6,637	5,957
15129	South Park Twp. (c)	(412)	14,340	14,292
17702	South Williamsport	(570)	6,102	6,496
19064	Springfield (c) (Delaware Co.)	(610)	23,677	25,326
*16804	State College	(814)	38,436	38,981
17113	Steelton	(717)	5,609	5,152
15136	Stowe Twp. (c)	(412)	6,706	9,202
18360	Stroudsburg	(570)	6,350	5,312
—	Sugarcreek	(814)	5,068	5,532
*17801	Sunbury	(570)	9,944	11,591
19081	Swarthmore	(610)	6,150	6,157
15218	Swissvale	(412)	8,909	10,637
18252	Tamaqua	(570)	6,696	7,943
18517	Taylor	(570)	6,211	6,944
16354	Titusville	(814)	5,806	6,434
19401	Trooper (c)	(610)	6,061	7,370
15145	Turtle Creek	(412)	5,628	6,556
16686	Tyrone (c)	(814)	5,295	5,743
15401	Uniontown	(724)	11,853	12,034
19063	Upper Providence Twp. (c)	(610)	10,509	9,477
15241	Upper Saint Clair (c)	(412)	20,053	19,023
15690	Vandergrift	(724)	5,131	5,904
19013	Village Green-Green Ridge (c)	(610)	8,279	9,026
*16365	Warren	(814)	9,605	11,122
15301	Washington (Wash. Co.)	(724)	14,767	15,864
17268	Waynesboro	(717)	9,755	9,578

ZIP	Place	Area Code	2006	1990
17315	Weigelstown (c)	(717)	10,117	8,665
*19380	West Chester	(610)	18,224	18,041
19380	West Goshen (c)	(610)	8,472	8,948
*15122	West Mifflin	(412)	20,957	23,644
—	Westmont	(814)	5,173	5,789
19401	West Norriton (c)	(610)	14,901	15,209
15229	West View	(412)	6,771	7,734
18052	Whitehall (Allegheny Co.)	(412)	13,556	14,451
15131	White Oak	(412)	8,108	8,761
*18703	Wilkes-Barre	(570)	41,288	47,523
15221	Wilkinsburg	(412)	17,771	21,080
15145	Wilkins Twp. (c)	(412)	6,917	7,487
*17701	Williamsport	(570)	29,814	31,933
19090	Willow Grove (c)	(215)	16,234	16,325
17584	Willow Street (c)	(717)	7,258	5,817
15025	Wilson	(412)	7,718	7,830
19094	Woodlyn (c)	(610)	10,036	10,151
19038	Wyndmoor (c)	(215)	5,601	5,682
19610	Wyomissing	(610)	10,456	7,332
19050	Yeadon (c)	(610)	11,479	11,980
*17405	York	(717)	40,454	42,192

Rhode Island (401)
See introductory note.

ZIP	Place		2006	1990
02806	Barrington		16,566	15,849
02809	Bristol		24,498	21,625
02830	Burrillville		16,545	16,230
02863	Central Falls		18,994	17,637
02813	Charlestown		8,208	6,478
02816	Coventry		34,672	31,083
*02905	Cranston		81,479	76,060
02864	Cumberland		34,345	29,038
02864	Cumberland Hill (c)		7,738	6,379
02818	East Greenwich		13,462	11,865
02914	East Providence		49,123	50,380
02822	Exeter		6,206	5,461
02814	Glocester		10,597	9,227
02828	Greenville (c)		8,626	8,303
02833	Hopkinton		8,051	6,873
02835	Jamestown		5,535	4,999
02919	Johnston		28,855	26,542
02881	Kingston (c)		5,446	6,504
02865	Lincoln		22,061	18,045
02842	Middletown		16,431	19,460
02882	Narragansett		16,708	15,004
02840	Newport		24,409	28,227
02843	Newport East (c)		11,463	11,080
02852	North Kingstown		26,734	23,786
02908	North Providence		32,993	32,090
02896	North Smithfield		11,288	10,497
*02860	Pawtucket		72,998	72,644
02871	Portsmouth		17,011	16,857
*02904	Providence		175,255	160,728
02812	Richmond		7,740	5,351
02857	Scituate		10,916	9,796
02917	Smithfield		21,698	19,163
02879	South Kingstown		29,457	24,612
02878	Tiverton (c)		7,282	7,259
02878	Tiverton		15,215	14,312
02864	Valley Falls (c)		11,599	11,175
*02879	Wakefield-Peacedale (c)		8,468	7,134
02885	Warren		11,192	11,385
02886	Warwick		85,925	85,427
02891	Westerly (c)		17,682	16,477
02891	Westerly		23,424	21,605
02817	West Greenwich		6,430	—
02893	West Warwick		29,564	29,268
02895	Woonsocket		43,940	43,877

South Carolina

ZIP	Place	Area Code	2006	1990
29620	Abbeville	(864)	5,683	5,778
*29801	Aiken	(803)	28,829	20,386
*29621	Anderson	(864)	26,242	26,385
*29070	Batesburg-Leesville	(803)	5,610	6,107
29920/29906	Beaufort	(843)	12,029	9,576
29841	Belvedere (c)	(803)	5,631	6,133
29512	Bennettsville	(843)	10,692	10,095
29611	Berea (c)	(864)	14,158	13,535
29902	Burton (c)	(843)	7,180	6,917
29020	Camden	(803)	7,022	6,696
29033	Cayce	(803)	12,597	10,824
29625	Centerville (c)	(864)	5,181	4,866
*29402	Charleston	(843)	107,845	88,256
29520	Cheraw	(843)	5,431	5,553
29706	Chester	(803)	6,123	7,158
29631	Clemson	(864)	12,444	11,145
29325	Clinton	(864)	9,034	9,603
*29201	Columbia	(803)	119,961	110,734
29526	Conway	(843)	14,056	9,819
*29532	Darlington	(843)	6,548	7,310
29204	Dentsville (c)	(803)	13,009	11,839
29536	Dillon	(843)	6,382	6,829
29640	Easley (c)	(864)	19,194	15,179
29681	Five Forks (c)	(864)	8,064	—
*29501	Florence	(843)	31,284	29,913
29206	Forest Acres	(803)	9,906	7,181
*29715	Fort Mill	(803)	8,560	4,930

ZIP	Place	Area Code	2006	1990
29644	Fountain Inn	(864)	7,097	4,388
*29341	Gaffney	(864)	12,949	13,149
29605	Gantt (c)	(864)	13,962	13,891
29576	Garden City (c)	(843)	9,357	6,305
*29442	Georgetown	(843)	8,706	9,517
29445	Goose Creek	(843)	31,914	24,692
*29602	Greenville	(864)	57,428	58,256
29646	Greenwood	(864)	22,407	20,807
29650	Greer	(864)	22,473	10,322
29406	Hanahan	(843)	13,846	13,176
29550	Hartsville	(843)	7,473	8,372
*29928	Hilton Head Island	(843)	33,838	23,694
29621	Homeland Park (c)	(864)	6,337	6,569
29063	Irmo	(803)	11,338	11,284
29456	Ladson (c)	(843)	13,264	13,540
29560	Lake City	(843)	6,666	7,153
*29720	Lancaster	(803)	8,374	8,914
29902	Laurel Bay (c)	(843)	6,625	4,972
29360	Laurens	(864)	9,849	9,694
*29072	Lexington	(803)	14,110	4,046
29566	Little River (c)	(843)	7,027	3,470
29078	Lugoff (c)	(803)	6,278	3,211
29571	Marion	(843)	6,959	7,658
29662	Mauldin	(864)	19,806	11,662
*29461	Moncks Corner	(843)	6,572	5,599
*29465	Mount Pleasant	(843)	59,113	30,108
29576	Murrells Inlet (c)	(843)	5,519	3,334
*29575	Myrtle Beach	(803)	28,597	24,848
29108	Newberry	(803)	10,874	10,543
*29841	North Augusta	(803)	19,926	15,684
*29410	North Charleston	(843)	87,482	70,304
*29582	North Myrtle Beach	(843)	14,972	8,731
29565	Oak Grove (c)	(843)	8,183	7,173
*29115	Orangeburg	(803)	13,563	13,772
29935	Port Royal	(843)	9,848	2,985
29611	Parker (c)	(864)	10,760	11,072
29642	Powderville (c)	(864)	5,362	—
29072	Red Bank (c)	(803)	8,811	5,950
29020	Red Hill (c)	(843)	10,509	6,112
*29730	Rock Hill	(803)	61,620	42,112
29417	Saint Andrews (c)	(843)	21,814	25,692
29609	Sans Souci (c)	(864)	7,836	7,612
*29678	Seneca	(864)	8,030	7,726
29210	Seven Oaks (c)	(803)	15,755	15,722
*29681	Simpsonville	(864)	16,017	11,744
29577	Socastee (c)	(843)	14,295	10,426
*29306	Spartanburg	(864)	38,561	43,479
*29483	Summerville	(843)	41,575	22,519
29150	Sumter	(803)	39,159	40,977
29687	Taylors (c)	(864)	20,125	19,619
29379	Union	(864)	8,241	9,840
29607	Wade Hampton (c)	(864)	20,458	20,014
29488	Walterboro	(843)	5,545	5,595
29611	Welcome (c)	(864)	6,590	6,560
*29169	West Columbia	(803)	13,670	10,974
29206	Woodfield (c)	(803)	9,238	8,862
29745	York	(803)	7,465	6,709

South Dakota (605)

ZIP	Place	2006	1990
*57401	Aberdeen	24,071	24,995
57005	Brandon	7,643	3,545
*57006	Brookings	18,802	16,270
*57350	Huron	10,909	12,448
57042	Madison	6,258	6,257
57301	Mitchell	14,857	13,798
57501	Pierre	14,095	12,906
*57701	Rapid City	62,715	54,523
*57701	Rapid Valley (c)	61,459	5,968
*57101	Sioux Falls	142,396	100,836
*57783	Spearfish	9,647	6,966
57785	Sturgis	6,132	5,537
57069	Vermillion	9,862	10,034
57201	Watertown	20,526	17,623
*57078	Yankton	13,767	12,703

Tennessee

ZIP	Place	Area Code	2006	1990
37701	Alcoa	(865)	8,463	6,400
*37303	Athens	(423)	14,068	12,054
38004	Atoka	(901)	6,298	659
*38184	Bartlett	(901)	46,932	27,038
37660	Bloomingdale (c)	(423)	10,350	10,953
38008	Bolivar	(731)	5,639	5,969
*37027	Brentwood	(615)	33,789	16,392
*37621	Bristol	(423)	25,351	23,421
38012	Brownsville	(731)	10,567	10,017
*37401	Chattanooga	(423)	155,190	152,393
37642	Church Hill	(423)	6,552	5,208
*37040	Clarksville	(931)	113,175	75,542
*37311	Cleveland	(423)	38,627	32,236
*37716	Clinton	(865)	9,504	8,972
37315	Collegedale	(423)	7,323	5,048
*38017	Collierville	(901)	38,678	14,501
37663	Colonial Heights (c)	(423)	7,067	6,716
38401	Columbia	(931)	33,811	28,583
*38501	Cookeville	(931)	28,340	21,744
38019	Covington	(901)	9,100	7,487
*38555	Crossville	(931)	10,840	6,930

ZIP	Place	Area Code	2006	1990
37321	Dayton	(423)	6,661	5,671
*37055	Dickson	(615)	13,062	10,487
*38024	Dyersburg	(731)	17,401	16,321
37411	East Brainerd (c)	(423)	14,132	11,594
37412	East Ridge	(423)	19,756	21,101
*37643	Elizabethton	(423)	13,933	13,007
37650	Erwin	(423)	5,806	5,318
37062	Fairview	(615)	7,483	4,210
*37922	Farragut	(865)	19,348	12,802
37334	Fayetteville	(931)	7,092	7,158
37215	Forest Hills (c)	(615)	5,319	—
*37064	Franklin	(615)	55,870	20,098
37066	Gallatin	(615)	27,723	18,794
*38138	Germantown	(901)	37,476	33,159
37072	Goodlettsville	(615)	15,584	11,219
37073	Greenbrier	(615)	6,236	3,062
*37743	Greeneville	(423)	15,537	13,532
37215	Green Hill (c)	(615)	7,068	6,763
37748	Harriman	(865)	6,717	7,119
*37341	Harrison (c)	(423)	7,630	7,191
37074	Hartsville-Trousdale	(615)	7,811	2,222
38340	Henderson	(731)	6,433	4,760
37075	Hendersonville	(615)	46,218	32,188
38343	Humboldt	(731)	9,264	9,651
38301	Jackson	(731)	62,711	49,145
37760	Jefferson City	(865)	8,028	5,875
*37601	Johnson City	(423)	59,866	50,354
*37662	Kingsport	(423)	44,191	40,457
37763	Kingston	(423)	5,553	4,552
*37950	Knoxville	(865)	182,337	169,761
*37766	La Follette	(423)	8,183	7,201
*37086	La Vergne	(615)	7,946	7,496
38002	Lakeland	(901)	27,255	1,204
38464	Lawrenceburg	(931)	10,819	10,397
37087	Lebanon	(615)	23,702	15,208
*37771	Lenoir City	(865)	7,703	6,147
37091	Lewisburg	(931)	10,834	9,879
38351	Lexington	(731)	7,780	5,810
37352	Lynchburg	(931)	6,070	4,721
38201	McKenzie	(731)	5,420	5,168
37110	McMinnville	(931)	13,311	11,194
37355	Manchester	(931)	9,671	7,709
38237	Martin	(731)	10,104	8,600
37801	Maryville	(865)	26,433	19,208
*38101	Memphis	(901)	670,902	618,652
37343	Middle Valley (c)	(423)	11,884	12,255
38358	Milan	(731)	7,885	7,512
37072	Millersville	(615)	6,233	2,575
38053	Millington	(901)	10,336	17,866
37813	Morristown	(423)	27,020	22,513
37645	Mount Carmel	(423)	5,356	4,268
37122	Mount Juliet	(615)	19,369	5,389
38058	Munford	(901)	6,062	2,944
37130	Murfreesboro	(615)	92,559	44,922
*37202	Nashville-Davidson	(615)	552,120	488,366
37821	Newport	(423)	7,391	7,123
*37830	Oak Ridge	(865)	27,638	27,310
37363	Ooltewah (c)	(423)	5,681	4,903
38242	Paris	(731)	9,981	9,332
*37862	Pigeon Forge	(865)	5,913	3,027
37148	Portland	(615)	10,721	5,539
38478	Pulaski	(931)	7,875	7,916
37415	Red Bank	(423)	11,632	12,320
38063	Ripley	(731)	7,719	6,634
37854	Rockwood	(865)	5,451	5,348
38372	Savannah	(731)	7,248	6,547
*37862	Sevierville	(865)	15,489	7,178
*37865	Seymour (c)	(865)	8,850	7,026
*37160	Shelbyville	(931)	19,149	14,042
37377	Signal Mountain	(423)	7,107	7,034
37167	Smyrna	(615)	34,491	14,720
37379	Soddy-Daisy	(423)	12,030	8,240
37311	South Cleveland (c)	(423)	6,216	5,372
37172	Springfield	(615)	16,523	11,227
37174	Spring Hill	(931)	20,768	1,464
37874	Sweetwater	(423)	6,314	5,066
*37388	Tullahoma	(931)	18,913	16,761
38261	Union City	(731)	10,786	10,513
*38188	White House	(615)	9,184	2,987
37398	Winchester	(931)	7,841	6,305

Texas

Area codes (281) and (832) overlay area code (713). Area code (430) overlays (903). Area code (682) overlays (817). Area codes (972) and (469) overlay (214). See introductory note.

ZIP	Place	Area Code	2006	1990
*79604	Abilene	(325)	114,797	106,707
—	Abram-Perezville (c)	(956)	5,444	3,999
75001	Addison	(214)	13,813	8,783
78516	Alamo	(956)	16,287	8,352
78209	Alamo Heights	(210)	7,093	6,502
77039	Aldine (c)	(713)	13,979	11,133
*78332	Alice	(361)	19,744	19,788
*75002	Allen	(214)	73,298	19,315
*79830	Alpine	(432)	6,035	5,622
78574	Alton	(956)	7,428	3,048
78572	Alton North (c)	(956)	5,051	—
*77511	Alvin	(713)	22,405	19,220
*79105	Amarillo	(806)	185,525	157,571

ZIP	Place	Area Code	2006	1990
78750	Anderson Mill (c)	(512)	*8,953*	9,468
79714	Andrews	(432)	9,548	10,678
*77515	Angleton	(979)	18,727	17,140
78336	Aransas Pass	(361)	8,960	7,180
*76004	Arlington	(817)	367,197	261,717
77346	Atascocita (c)	(281)	*35,757*	—
*75751	Athens	(903)	12,604	10,982
75551	Atlanta	(214)	5,625	6,118
*78712	Austin	(512)	709,893	472,020
*76020	Azle	(817)	10,796	8,868
77518	Bacliff (c)	(409)	*19,343*	5,549
75180	Balch Springs	(214)	19,818	17,406
78602	Bastrop	(512)	7,591	4,044
*77414	Bay City	(979)	18,263	18,170
*77520	Baytown	(713)	68,714	63,843
77707	Beaumont	(409)	109,856	114,323
76021	Bedford	(817)	48,752	43,762
78102	Beeville	(361)	13,634	13,547
77401	Bellaire	(713)	17,596	13,844
*76115	Bellmead	(254)	9,532	8,336
76513	Belton	(254)	16,091	12,463
76126	Benbrook	(817)	22,307	19,564
79720	Big Spring	(432)	24,222	23,093
78006	Boerne	(830)	8,707	4,361
75418	Bonham	(903)	10,661	6,688
*79007	Borger	(806)	13,262	15,675
76230	Bowie	(940)	5,566	4,990
76825	Brady	(325)	5,396	5,946
76424	Breckenridge	(254)	5,671	5,665
76020	Briar (c)	(817)	*5,350*	3,899
*77833	Brenham	(979)	14,752	11,952
77611	Bridge City	(409)	8,725	8,010
76426	Bridgeport	(940)	5,818	3,581
79316	Brownfield	(806)	9,152	9,560
*78520	Brownsville	(956)	172,437	107,027
*76801	Brownwood	(325)	19,763	18,387
78717	Brushy Creek (c)	(512)	*15,371*	5,833
*77801	Bryan	(979)	67,266	55,002
76354	Burkburnett	(940)	10,291	10,145
*76028	Burleson	(817)	31,660	16,113
78611	Burnet	(512)	5,643	3,423
76520	Cameron	(254)	5,855	5,635
78526	Cameron Park (c)	(956)	*5,961*	3,802
79835	Canutillo (c)	(915)	*5,129*	4,442
*79015	Canyon	(806)	13,572	11,365
78130	Canyon Lake (c)	(830)	*16,870*	9,975
78834	Carrizo Springs	(830)	5,682	5,745
*75006	Carrollton	(214)	121,604	82,169
75633	Carthage	(903)	6,604	6,496
*75104	Cedar Hill	(214)	42,932	19,988
*78613	Cedar Park	(512)	52,058	5,161
75935	Center	(936)	5,805	4,950
77530	Channelview (c)	(713)	*29,685*	25,564
79201	Childress	(940)	6,649	5,055
78108	Cibolo	(210)	10,085	1,757
77450	Cinco Ranch (c)	(281)	*11,196*	—
*76031	Cleburne	(817)	29,689	22,205
*77327	Cleveland	(713)	8,046	7,124
77015	Cloverleaf (c)	(713)	*23,508*	18,230
77531	Clute	(979)	10,737	9,467
*77840	College Station	(979)	74,125	52,443
76034	Colleyville	(817)	23,210	12,724
*75428	Commerce	(903)	9,419	6,825
*77301	Conroe	(936)	49,760	27,675
78109	Converse	(210)	13,937	8,887
*75019	Coppell	(214)	39,175	16,881
76522	Copperas Cove	(254)	29,722	24,079
*76205	Corinth	(940)	19,556	3,944
*78469	Corpus Christi	(361)	285,267	257,428
*75110	Corsicana	(903)	26,422	22,911
75835	Crockett	(936)	6,981	7,024
76036	Crowley	(817)	10,998	6,974
78839	Crystal City	(830)	7,362	8,263
77954	Cuero	(361)	6,632	6,700
79022	Dalhart	(806)	7,023	6,246
*75221	Dallas	(214)	1,232,940	1,007,618
77535	Dayton	(936)	7,286	5,042
76234	Decatur	(214)	6,249	4,245
77536	Deer Park	(713)	29,784	27,424
*78840	Del Rio	(830)	36,491	30,705
*75020	Denison	(903)	23,957	21,505
*76201	Denton	(940)	109,561	66,270
*75115	DeSoto	(214)	45,954	30,544
75941	Diboll	(936)	5,501	4,341
77539	Dickinson	(281)	18,018	11,692
78537	Donna	(956)	16,449	12,652
79029	Dumas	(806)	14,046	12,871
*75138	Duncanville	(214)	35,583	35,008
76135	Eagle Mountain (c)	(817)	*6,599*	5,847
*78852	Eagle Pass	(830)	26,401	20,651
*78539	Edinburg	(956)	66,672	31,091
77957	Edna	(361)	5,867	5,436
78852	Eidson Road (c)	(830)	*9,348*	—
77437	El Campo	(979)	10,816	10,511
78621	Elgin	(512)	9,287	4,846
*79910	El Paso	(915)	609,415	515,342
78543	Elsa	(956)	6,608	5,242
*75119	Ennis	(214)	19,086	13,869
*76039	Euless	(817)	52,016	38,149
76140	Everman	(817)	5,748	5,672
79838	Fabens (c)	(915)	*8,043*	5,599
*78015	Fair Oaks Ranch	(210)	5,900	1,886
75069	Fairview	(214)	6,709	—
78355	Falfurrias	(361)	5,071	5,788
*75381	Farmers Branch	(214)	26,583	24,250
78114	Floresville	(830)	7,250	5,247
*75022	Flower Mound	(214)	65,851	15,527
76119	Forest Hill	(817)	13,668	11,482
75126	Forney	(214)	12,526	4,070
79906	Fort Bliss (c)	(915)	*8,264*	11,737
76544	Fort Hood (c)	(254)	*33,711*	35,580
79735	Fort Stockton	(432)	7,404	8,524
*76161	Fort Worth	(817)	653,320	447,619
78624	Fredericksburg	(830)	10,752	6,934
*77541	Freeport	(979)	12,603	11,389
*77546	Friendswood	(281)	33,478	22,814
*75034	Frisco	(214)	80,499	6,138
*76240	Gainesville	(940)	16,571	14,256
77547	Galena Park	(713)	10,226	10,033
*77550	Galveston	(409)	57,523	59,067
*75040	Garland	(214)	217,963	180,635
76528	Gatesville	(254)	15,489	11,492
*78626	Georgetown	(512)	42,467	14,840
78942	Giddings	(979)	5,469	4,093
*75644	Gilmer	(903)	5,143	4,822
75647	Gladewater	(903)	6,319	6,027
75154	Glenn Heights	(214)	10,244	4,564
78629	Gonzales	(830)	7,496	6,527
77479	Greatwood (c)	(713)	*6,640*	—
76450	Graham	(940)	8,691	8,986
*76048	Granbury	(817)	7,753	4,045
75051	Grand Prairie	(214)	153,812	99,606
*76051	Grapevine	(817)	48,583	29,407
*75401	Greenville	(903)	25,883	23,071
77619	Groves	(409)	14,742	16,744
*75147	Gun Barrel City	(903)	6,051	3,526
*76117	Haltom City	(817)	39,987	32,856
*76548	Harker Heights	(254)	22,842	12,932
*78550	Harlingen	(956)	64,202	48,746
75032	Heath	(214)	6,853	2,128
78023	Helotes	(210)	6,460	1,556
77445	Hempstead	(979)	6,837	3,598
*75652	Henderson	(903)	11,584	11,139
79045	Hereford	(806)	14,531	14,745
76643	Hewitt	(254)	13,207	8,983
78557	Hidalgo	(956)	11,357	3,292
*75205	Highland Park	(214)	9,035	8,739
77562	Highlands (c)	(713)	*7,089*	6,632
75067	Highland Village	(214)	15,738	7,027
76645	Hillsboro	(254)	9,064	7,072
77563	Hitchcock	(409)	7,265	5,868
79938	Homestead Meadows South (c)	(915)	*6,807*	—
78861	Hondo	(830)	8,933	6,018
*79927	Horizon City	(915)	10,709	2,308
*77052	Houston	(281)/(713)/(832)	2,144,491	1,654,348
*77338	Humble	(713)	14,927	12,060
*77340	Huntsville	(936)	37,537	30,628
*76053	Hurst	(817)	38,182	33,574
78634	Hutto	(512)	9,572	—
78362	Ingleside	(361)	9,357	5,696
76367	Iowa Park	(940)	6,142	6,072
*75015	Irving	(214)	196,084	155,037
77029	Jacinto City	(713)	9,939	9,343
*75766	Jacksonville	(903)	14,402	12,765
75951	Jasper	(409)	7,465	7,160
*77040	Jersey Village	(713)	7,138	4,826
78729	Jollyville (c)	(512)	*15,813*	15,206
76058	Joshua	(817)	5,574	3,634
*77449	Katy	(713)	13,561	8,004
75142	Kaufman	(214)	8,058	5,251
76059	Keene	(817)	6,196	3,944
*76248	Keller	(817)	36,925	13,683
76060	Kennedale	(817)	6,736	4,096
79745	Kermit	(432)	5,204	6,875
*78028	Kerrville	(830)	22,361	17,384
*75662	Kilgore	(903)	12,040	11,066
*76540	Killeen	(254)	102,003	63,535
*78363	Kingsville	(361)	24,394	25,276
78219	Kirby	(210)	8,574	8,326
78640	Kyle	(512)	20,655	2,225
78236	Lackland AFB (c)	(210)	*7,123*	9,352
76705	Lacy-Lakeview	(254)	5,762	3,617
78559	La Feria	(956)	6,856	4,360
78645	Lago Vista	(512)	5,794	2,199
78572	La Homa (c)	(956)	*10,433*	1,403
75065	Lake Dallas	(940)	7,261	3,656
77566	Lake Jackson	(979)	27,614	22,771
*78734	Lakeway	(512)	9,545	4,044
77568	La Marque	(409)	14,033	14,120
79331	Lamesa	(806)	9,259	10,809
76550	Lampasas	(512)	7,828	6,382
*75146	Lancaster	(214)	33,790	22,117
*77571	La Porte	(713)	33,886	27,923
*78041	Laredo	(956)	215,484	122,893
*77573	League City	(281)	65,351	30,159
78641	Leander	(512)	20,451	3,354
78268	Leon Valley	(210)	9,795	9,581
79336	Levelland	(806)	12,674	13,986
*75067	Lewisville	(214)	94,589	46,521
77575	Liberty	(936)	8,443	7,690

ZIP	Place	Area Code	2006	1990
75068	Little Elm	(214)	21,287	1,242
79339	Littlefield	(806)	6,246	6,489
*78233	Live Oak	(210)	11,704	10,023
*77351	Livingston	(936)	6,430	5,019
78644	Lockhart	(512)	13,642	9,205
*75606	Longview	(903)	76,524	70,311
78566	Los Fresnos	(956)	5,345	2,473
79408	Lubbock	(806)	212,169	186,206
*75901	Lufkin	(936)	33,863	30,210
78648	Luling	(830)	5,398	4,661
77657	Lumberton	(409)	9,728	6,640
78501	McAllen	(956)	126,411	84,021
*75070	McKinney	(214)	107,530	21,283
76063	Mansfield	(817)	41,564	15,615
*78654	Marble Falls	(830)	7,186	4,017
76661	Marlin	(254)	6,158	6,386
*75670	Marshall	(903)	23,965	23,682
78368	Mathis	(361)	5,473	5,423
77477	Meadows Place	(281)/(713)	6,626	4,663
78570	Mercedes	(956)	14,734	12,694
*75149	Mesquite	(214)	131,447	101,484
76667	Mexia	(254)	6,708	6,933
*79701	Midland	(432)	102,073	89,343
76065	Midlothian	(214)	14,452	5,040
75773	Mineola	(903)	5,091	—
76067	Mineral Wells	(940)	17,065	14,935
*78572	Mission	(956)	63,272	28,653
77083	Mission Bend (c)	(713)	30,831	24,945
*77489	Missouri City	(713)	73,679	36,143
79756	Monahans	(432)	6,392	8,101
*75455	Mount Pleasant	(903)	15,202	12,291
*75094	Murphy	(214)	12,789	1,603
*75961	Nacogdoches	(936)	31,135	30,872
*77868	Navasota	(936)	7,378	6,296
77627	Nederland	(409)	16,454	16,192
*78130	New Braunfels	(830)	49,969	27,334
77479	New Territory (c)	(281)	13,861	—
*76161	North Richland Hills	(817)	62,306	45,895
78539	Nurillo (c)	(956)	5,056	—
*79761	Odessa	(432)	95,163	89,699
*77630	Orange	(409)	17,891	19,370
77465	Palacios	(361)	5,160	4,418
*75801	Palestine	(903)	18,166	18,042
78572	Palmhurst	(956)	5,032	—
78572	Palmview South (c)	(956)	6,219	—
*79065	Pampa	(806)	17,089	19,959
*75460	Paris	(903)	26,490	24,799
*77501	Pasadena	(713)	144,793	119,604
*77581	Pearland	(713)	68,305	18,927
78061	Pearsall	(830)	7,768	6,924
78721	Pecan Grove (c)	(254)	13,551	9,502
79772	Pecos	(432)	8,118	12,069
79070	Perryton	(806)	8,236	7,619
*78660	Pflugerville	(512)	29,747	4,444
78577	Pharr	(956)	61,360	32,921
*79072	Plainview	(806)	22,088	21,698
*75074	Plano	(214)	255,009	127,885
78064	Pleasanton	(830)	9,543	7,678
*77640	Port Arthur	(409)	55,745	58,551
78578	Port Isabel	(956)	5,379	4,740
78374	Portland	(361)	16,420	12,224
77979	Port Lavaca	(361)	11,696	10,886
77651	Port Neches	(409)	12,897	12,908
78579	Progreso	(956)	5,309	2,808
75078	Prosper	(972)	5,158	—
*75580	Raymondville	(956)	9,574	8,880
75154	Red Oak	(214)	8,031	3,660
76028	Rendon (c)	(817)	9,022	7,658
*75080	Richardson	(214)	99,822	74,840
*76118	Richland Hills	(817)	8,076	7,978
*77469	Richmond	(713)	13,660	10,042
78043	Rio Bravo	(956)	5,745	—
78582	Rio Grande City	(956)	13,836	10,725
76114	River Oaks	(817)	6,925	6,580
76701	Robinson	(254)	9,716	7,111
78380	Robstown	(361)	12,422	12,849
76567	Rockdale	(512)	6,035	5,235
*78382	Rockport	(361)	9,264	5,619
*75087	Rockwall	(214)	32,224	10,486
78584	Roma	(956)	11,173	8,059
77471	Rosenberg	(713)	31,846	20,183
*78681	Round Rock	(512)	92,392	30,923
*75088	Rowlett	(214)	54,869	23,260
75159	Royse	(649)/(214)/(972)	7,129	2,206
75785	Rusk	(903)	5,170	4,366
75048	Sachse	(214)	17,597	5,346
*76179	Saginaw	(817)	18,739	8,551
*76902	San Angelo	(325)	88,300	84,462
*78265	San Antonio	(210)	1,296,682	976,514
78586	San Benito	(956)	25,005	20,125
79849	San Elizario (c)	(915)	11,046	4,385
76266	Sanger	(940)	6,984	3,602
78589	San Juan	(956)	32,319	12,561
*78666	SanMarcos	(512)	47,181	28,738
*77510	Santa Fe	(409)	10,590	8,429
78154	Schertz	(210)	28,289	10,597
77586	Seabrook	(281)	11,182	6,685
75159	Seagoville	(214)	11,377	8,969
77474	Sealy	(979)	6,150	4,541
*78155	Seguin	(830)	24,909	18,692

ZIP	Place	Area Code	2006	1990
79360	Seminole	(432)	6,078	6,342
78739	Shady Hollow (c)	(512)	5,140	—
*75090	Sherman	(903)	37,623	31,584
77656	Silsbee	(409)	6,788	6,368
78387	Sinton	(361)	5,512	5,549
79364	Slaton	(806)	5,697	6,078
*79549	Snyder	(325)	10,567	12,195
79927	Socorro	(915)	31,080	22,995
77587	South Houston	(713)	16,282	14,207
76092	Southlake	(817)	25,748	7,082
77373	Spring	(713)	36,385	33,111
77477	Stafford	(713)	19,825	8,395
76401	Stephenville	(254)	16,058	13,502
77478	Sugar Land	(713)	79,943	33,712
75482	Sulphur Springs	(903)	15,290	14,062
79556	Sweetwater	(325)	10,623	11,967
76574	Taylor	(512)	15,322	11,472
76501	Temple	(254)	54,984	46,150
78209	Terrell Hills	(210)	5,121	4,592
*75160	Terrell	(214)	18,506	12,490
75501	Texarkana	(903)	36,054	32,294
77590	Texas City	(409)	45,070	40,822
*75056	The Colony	(214)	40,206	22,113
77387	The Woodlands	(713)	55,649	29,205
78258	Timberwood Park (c)	(210)	5,889	2,578
77375	Tomball	(713)	10,053	6,370
76262	Trophy Club	(817)	7,644	3,922
*75702	Tyler	(903)	94,146	75,450
78148	Universal City	(830)	17,773	13,057
75205	University Park	(214)	24,182	22,259
*78801	Uvalde	(830)	16,507	14,729
76384	Vernon	(940)	11,217	12,001
*77901	Victoria	(361)	62,169	55,076
77662	Vidor	(409)	11,193	10,935
*76702	Waco	(254)	121,496	103,590
75501	Wake Village	(903)	5,505	4,761
76148	Watauga	(817)	23,685	20,009
75165	Waxahachie	(214)	26,709	17,984
*76086	Weatherford	(817)	24,630	14,804
77598	Webster	(281)	9,930	4,678
78728	Wells Branch (c)	(512)	11,271	7,094
78596	Weslaco	(956)	32,092	22,739
77351	West Livingston (c)	(936)	6,612	—
79764	West Odessa (c)	(432)	17,799	16,568
77005	West University Place	(713)	15,122	12,920
77488	Wharton	(979)	9,345	9,011
75791	Whitehouse	(903)	7,327	4,018
75693	White Oak	(903)	6,255	5,136
76108	White Settlement	(817)	15,943	15,472
76307	Wichita Falls	(940)	99,354	96,259
78239	Windcrest	(210)	5,149	5,331
78660	Windemere (c)	(512)	6,868	3,207
76712	Woodway	(254)	8,698	8,695
75098	Wylie	(214)	32,696	8,716
77995	Yoakum	(361)	5,677	5,611

Utah

ZIP	Place	Area Code	2006	1990
84004	Alpine	(801)	9,204	3,492
84003	American Fork	(801)	25,596	15,722
84065	Bluffdale	(801)	7,088	2,142
*84010	Bountiful	(801)	41,161	37,544
84302	Brigham City	(435)	18,463	15,644
84109	Canyon Rim (c)	(801)	10,428	10,527
*84720	Cedar City	(435)	25,665	13,443
84062	Cedar Hills	(801)	8,410	708
84014	Centerville	(801)	15,075	11,500
*84015	Clearfield	(801)	27,241	21,435
84015	Clinton	(801)	18,811	7,945
84121	Cottonwood Heights[1]	(801)	34,954	28,766
84121	Cottonwood West (c)	(801)	18,727	17,476
84020	Draper	(801)	36,873	7,143
84043	Eagle Mountain	(801)	12,232	30
84109	East Millcreek (c)	(801)	21,385	21,184
84627	Ephraim	(435)	5,085	—
84025	Farmington	(801)	15,540	9,049
84029	Grantsville	(435)	8,016	4,500
84404	Harrisville	(801)	5,247	3,004
84032	Heber	(435)	9,775	4,782
84065	Herriman	(801)	14,643	—
84003	Highland	(801)	13,889	5,007
*84117	Holladay	(801)	25,308	14,095
84737	Hurricane	(435)	12,084	3,915
84319	Hyrum	(435)	5,971	4,829
84738	Ivins	(435)	7,205	1,639
84037	Kaysville	(801)	23,563	13,961
84118	Kearns (c)	(801)	33,659	28,374
84041	Layton	(801)	62,716	41,784
84043	Lehi	(801)	36,021	8,475
84042	Lindon	(801)	9,758	3,818
84093	Little Cottonwood Creek Valley (c)	(801)	7,221	5,042
84321	Logan	(435)	47,660	32,771
84044	Magna (c)	(801)	22,770	17,829
84664	Mapleton	(801)	7,157	3,572
84047	Midvale	(801)	27,249	11,886
84109	Millcreek (c)	(801)	30,377	32,230
*84117	Mount Olympus (c)	(801)	7,103	7,413
*84157	Murray	(801)	44,844	31,274

ZIP	Place	Area Code	2006	1990
84648	Nephi	(435)	5,207	3,515
84341	North Logan	(435)	7,558	3,775
*84404	North Ogden	(801)	16,798	11,593
84054	North Salt Lake	(801)	11,598	6,464
*84401	Ogden	(801)	78,086	63,943
84084	Oquirrh (c)	(801)	10,390	7,593
*84057	Orem	(801)	90,857	67,561
*84060	Park City	(435)	8,044	4,468
*84651	Payson	(801)	16,748	9,510
84062	Pleasant Grove	(801)	30,729	13,476
*84404	Pleasant View	(801)	6,486	3,597
84501	Price	(435)	8,010	8,712
84332	Providence	(435)	5,540	3,344
*84601	Provo	(801)	113,984	86,835
84701	Richfield	(435)	7,104	5,593
84405	Riverdale	(801)	7,979	6,419
*84065	Riverton	(801)	35,543	11,261
*84067	Roy	(801)	35,100	24,560
*84770	Saint George	(435)	67,614	28,572
84653	Salem	(801)	5,632	—
*84101	Salt Lake City	(801)	178,858	159,928
*84070	Sandy	(801)	94,203	75,240
84765	Santa Clara	(435)	6,280	2,323
84655	Santaquin	(801)	7,035	2,522
84043	Saratoga Springs	(801)	7,283	—
84335	Smithfield	(435)	7,455	5,566
84095	South Jordan	(801)	44,009	12,215
84403	South Ogden	(801)	15,328	12,105
84165	South Salt Lake	(801)	21,354	10,129
*84403	South Weber	(801)	5,807	2,853
84660	Spanish Fork	(801)	27,717	11,272
84663	Springville	(801)	25,998	13,950
84098	Summit Park (c)	(435)	6,597	—
84075	Syracuse	(801)	19,534	4,658
84118	Taylorsville	(801)	58,048	51,550
84074	Tooele	(435)	29,062	13,887
84337	Tremonton	(435)	6,289	4,262
*84078	Vernal	(435)	8,163	6,640
84780	Washington	(435)	15,217	4,198
84405	Washington Terrace	(801)	8,292	8,189
84087	West Bountiful	(801)	5,185	—
84401	West Haven	(801)	6,122	—
*84084	West Jordan	(801)	94,300	42,915
84015	West Point	(801)	8,186	4,258
*84170	West Valley City	(801)	119,841	86,969
84070	White City (c)	(801)	5,988	6,506
*84087	Woods Cross	(801)	8,168	5,384

(1) 1990 population of Cottonwood Heights is for Cottonwood Heights CDP. The city was incorporated in 2005.

Vermont (802)
See introductory note.

ZIP	Place	2006	1990
05641	Barre	9,078	9,482
05641	Barre	8,077	7,411
05201	Bennington (c)	9,168	9,532
05201	Bennington	15,349	16,451
*05301	Brattleboro	11,741	12,241
*05301	Brattleboro (c)	8,289	8,612
*05401	Burlington	38,358	39,127
*05446	Colchester	17,180	14,731
*05451	Essex	19,264	—
*05451	Essex Junction	8,902	16,498
05047	Hartford	10,829	9,404
05465	Jericho	5,089	1,405
05849	Lyndon	5,709	5,371
05753	Middlebury (c)	6,252	6,007
*05753	Middlebury Town	8,193	8,034
05468	Milton	10,347	8,404
*05602	Montpelier	7,954	8,247
05661	Morristown	5,550	4,733
05855	Newport	5,289	4,434
05663	Northfield	5,810	5,610
05060	Randolph	5,091	—
05101	Rockingham	5,076	—
*05701	Rutland	16,964	18,230
*05478	Saint Albans	7,409	7,339
05478	Saint Albans City	6,030	4,606
05819	Saint Johnsbury (c)	6,319	6,424
05819	Saint Johnsbury	7,556	7,608
05482	Shelburne	7,063	5,871
*05403	South Burlington	17,014	12,809
05156	Springfield	8,792	9,579
05488	Swanton	6,472	5,636
05676	Waterbury	5,243	4,614
05495	Williston	8,278	4,887
05404	Winooski	6,318	6,649

Virginia
Area code (571) overlays area code (703). See introductory note.

ZIP	Place	Area Code	2006	1990
*24210	Abingdon	(276)	7,933	7,003
*22313	Alexandria	(703)	136,974	111,182
22003	Annandale (c)	(703)	54,994	50,975
22554	Aquia Harbour (c)	(703)	7,856	6,308
*22210	Arlington[1] (c)	(703)	199,776	170,897
23005	Ashland	(804)	7,052	5,864
*22041	Bailey's Crossroads (c)	(703)	23,166	19,507
24523	Bedford	(540)	6,249	6,177

ZIP	Place	Area Code	2006	1990
22306	Belle Haven (c)	(757)	6,269	6,427
24219	Big Stone Gap	(276)	5,498	4,847
*24060	Blacksburg	(540)	39,284	34,590
24605	Bluefield	(276)	5,226	—
23235	Bon Air (c)	(804)	16,213	16,413
22812	Bridgewater	(540)	5,399	3,918
*24203	Bristol	(276)	17,496	18,426
24416	Buena Vista	(540)	6,457	6,406
20109	Bull Run (c)	(703)	11,337	5,525
*22150	Burke (c)	(703)	57,737	57,734
24018	Cave Spring (c)	(540)	24,941	24,053
20120	Centreville (c)	(703)	48,661	29,585
20151	Chantilly (c)	(703)	41,041	29,337
*22906	Charlottesville	(434)	40,315	40,475
*23320	Chesapeake	(757)	220,560	151,982
23831	Chester (c)	(804)	17,890	14,986
24073	Christiansburg	(540)	17,853	15,004
24078	Collinsville (c)	(276)	7,777	7,280
23834	Colonial Heights	(804)	17,676	16,064
24426	Covington	(540)	6,073	7,198
*22701	Culpeper	(540)	13,011	8,581
22193	Dale City (c)	(703)	55,971	47,170
*24541	Danville	(434)	45,586	53,056
23228	Dumbarton (c)	(804)	6,674	8,526
22027	Dunn Loring (c)	(703)	7,861	6,509
23222	East Highland Park (c)	(804)	12,488	11,850
23847	Emporia	(434)	5,625	5,479
23803	Ettrick (c)	(804)	5,627	5,290
22030	Fairfax	(703)	22,422	19,894
*22046	Falls Church	(703)	10,799	9,522
*23901	Farmville	(434)	6,898	6,505
24551	Forest (c)	(434)	8,006	5,624
22060	Fort Belvoir (c)	(703)	7,176	8,590
22308	Fort Hunt (c)	(703)	12,923	12,989
23801	Fort Lee (c)	(804)	7,269	6,895
22310	Franconia (c)	(703)	31,907	19,882
23851	Franklin	(757)	8,800	7,864
*22404	Fredericksburg	(540)	21,273	19,027
22630	Front Royal	(540)	14,561	11,880
24333	Galax	(276)	6,682	6,699
*23060	Glen Allen (c)	(804)	12,562	9,010
23062	Gloucester Point (c)	(804)	9,429	8,509
22066	Great Falls (c)	(703)	8,549	6,945
22306	Groveton (c)	(703)	21,296	19,997
*23670	Hampton	(757)	145,017	133,811
*22801	Harrisonburg	(540)	40,885	30,707
20170	Herndon	(703)	21,877	16,139
23075	Highland Springs (c)	(804)	15,137	13,823
24019	Hollins (c)	(540)	14,309	13,305
23860	Hopewell	(804)	22,731	23,101
22303	Huntington (c)	(703)	8,325	7,489
22306	Hybla Valley (c)	(703)	16,721	15,491
22043	Idylwood (c)	(703)	16,005	14,710
22042	Jefferson (c)	(703)	27,422	25,782
22041	Lake Barcroft (c)	(703)	8,906	8,686
22963	Lake Monticello (c)	(434)	6,852	2,331
22191	Lake Ridge (c)	(540)	30,404	23,862
23228	Lakeside (c)	(804)	11,157	12,081
23060	Laurel (c)	(804)	14,875	13,011
20175	Leesburg	(703)	37,476	16,202
24450	Lexington	(540)	6,739	6,959
22312	Lincolnia (c)	(703)	15,788	13,041
20136	Linton Hall (c)	(703)	8,620	—
22079	Lorton (c)	(703)	17,786	15,385
*24506	Lynchburg	(434)	67,720	66,049
*22101	McLean (c)	(703)	38,929	38,168
24572	Madison Heights (c)	(434)	11,584	11,700
20110	Manassas (c)	(703)	36,638	27,957
20113	Manassas Park (c)	(703)	11,642	6,734
22030	Mantua (c)	(703)	7,485	6,804
24354	Marion	(276)	6,130	6,630
*24112	Martinsville	(276)	14,945	16,162
*23111	Mechanicsville (c)	(804)	30,464	22,027
22116	Merrifield (c)	(703)	11,170	8,399
22026	Montclair (c)	(703)	15,728	11,399
23231	Montrose (c)	(804)	7,018	6,405
22121	Mount Vernon (c)	(703)	28,582	27,485
22122	Newington (c)	(703)	19,784	17,965
*23607	Newport News	(757)	178,281	171,439
*23501	Norfolk	(757)	229,112	261,250
22151	North Springfield (c)	(703)	9,173	8,996
22124	Oakton (c)	(703)	29,348	24,610
*23804	Petersburg	(804)	32,445	37,027
22043	Pimmit Hills (c)	(703)	6,152	6,019
23662	Poquoson	(757)	11,918	11,005
*23707	Portsmouth	(757)	101,377	103,910
24301	Pulaski	(540)	9,062	9,985
22134	Quantico Station (c)	(703)	6,571	7,425
*24141	Radford	(540)	14,525	15,940
20190	Reston (c)	(703)	56,407	48,556
*23232	Richmond	(804)	192,913	202,798
24022	Roanoke	(540)	91,552	96,509
24281	Rose Hill (c)	(276)	15,058	12,675
24153	Salem	(540)	24,825	23,797
22044	Seven Corners (c)	(703)	8,701	7,280
23430	Smithfield	(757)	7,000	4,686
24592	South Boston	(434)	8,064	6,997
*22150	Springfield (c)	(703)	30,417	23,706
*24402	Staunton	(540)	23,334	24,461
*24477	Stuarts Draft (c)	(540)	8,367	5,087

ZIP	Place	Area Code	2006	1990
23162	Sudley (c)	(540)	7,719	7,321
*23434	Suffolk	(757)	81,071	52,143
24502	Timberlake (c)	(434)	10,683	10,314
22172	Triangle (c)	(703)	5,500	4,740
23229	Tuckahoe (c)	(804)	43,242	42,629
22101	Tysons Corner (c)	(703)	18,540	13,124
*22180	Vienna	(703)	14,873	14,852
24179	Vinton	(540)	7,905	7,643
*23450	Virginia Beach	(757)	435,619	393,089
*20186	Warrenton	(540)	8,733	4,882
22980	Waynesboro	(540)	21,454	18,549
22110	West Gate (c)	(703)	7,493	6,565
22152	West Springfield (c)	(703)	28,378	28,126
*23185	Williamsburg	(757)	11,793	11,409
*22601	Winchester	(540)	25,265	21,947
24592	Wolf Trap (c)	(703)	14,001	13,133
*22191	Woodbridge (c)	(703)	31,941	26,401
23059	Wyndham (c)	(804)	6,176	—
24382	Wytheville	(276)	8,136	8,036
22110	Yorkshire (c)	(703)	6,732	5,699

(1) Population estimate for Arlington CDP has been updated for 2006.

Washington

ZIP	Place	Area Code	2006	1990
98520	Aberdeen	(360)	16,389	16,565
98036	Alderwood Manor (c)	(425)	15,329	22,945
*98221	Anacortes	(360)	16,633	11,451
98223	Arlington	(360)	16,090	4,037
98335	Artondale (c)	(360)	8,630	7,141
*98002	Auburn	(253)	48,886	33,650
98110	Bainbridge Island	(206)	22,178	—
98315	Bangor Trident Base (c)	(360)	7,253	3,702
98604	Battle Ground	(360)	13,399	3,758
*98009	Bellevue	(425)	118,186	95,213
*98225	Bellingham	(360)	75,150	52,179
*98390	Bonney Lake	(360)	15,099	7,494
*98011	Bothell	(425)	31,353	12,575
*98337	Bremerton	(360)	35,295	38,142
98036	Brier	(425)	6,382	5,633
98178	Bryn Mawr-Skyway (c)	(206)	13,977	12,514
*98166	Burien	(206)	31,131	27,507
98233	Burlington	(360)	8,642	4,349
98292	Camano (c)	(360)	13,347	—
98607	Camas	(360)	17,480	6,762
98055	Cascade-Fairwood (c)	(425)	34,580	30,107
98531	Centralia	(360)	15,597	12,101
98532	Chehalis	(360)	7,224	6,527
99004	Cheney	(509)	10,360	7,723
99403	Clarkston	(509)	7,244	6,753
99403	Clarkston Heights-Vineland (c)	(509)	6,117	2,832
99324	College Place	(509)	8,980	6,308
99114	Colville	(509)	5,049	4,360
98072	Cottage Lake (c)	(206)	24,330	—
99218	Country Homes (c)	(509)	5,203	5,126
98042	Covington	(253)	17,509	—
98198	Des Moines	(206)	28,992	20,830
99213	Dishman (c)	(509)	10,031	9,671
98327	DuPont	(253)	6,008	592
98019	Duvall	(360)	5,868	2,640
98031	East Hill-Meridian (c)	(253)/(425)	29,308	42,696
98366	East Port Orchard (c)	(360)	5,116	5,409
98056	East Renton Highlands (c)	(425)	13,264	13,218
98802	East Wenatchee	(360)	8,927	3,886
98801	East Wenatchee Bench (c)	(509)	13,658	12,539
*98371	Edgewood (c)	(253)	9,765	8,702
*98020	Edmonds	(425)	40,126	30,743
98387	Elk Plain (c)	(360)	15,697	12,197
*98926	Ellensburg	(509)	16,831	12,360
98022	Enumclaw	(360)	10,983	7,243
98823	Ephrata	(509)	7,298	5,349
*98201	Everett	(425)	98,514	70,937
99218	Fairwood (c)	(509)	6,764	5,807
*98002	Federal Way	(253)	84,166	67,535
98685	Felida (c)	(360)	5,683	3,109
98248	Ferndale	(360)	10,333	5,398
98424	Fife	(253)	6,456	3,864
99336	Finley (c)	(509)	5,770	4,897
98466	Fircrest	(253)	6,262	5,270
98597	Five Corners (c)	(360)	12,207	6,776
98433	Fort Lewis (c)	(253)	19,089	22,224
98373	Frederickson (c)	(206)	5,758	3,502
*98329	Gig Harbor	(253)	6,672	3,236
98338	Graham (c)	(253)	8,739	—
98930	Grandview	(509)	9,124	7,169
99016	Green Acres (c)	(509)	5,158	4,626
98660	Hazel Dell North (c)	(360)	9,261	6,924
98665	Hazel Dell South (c)	(360)	6,605	5,796
98025	Hobart (c)	(425)	6,251	—
98606	Hockinson (c)	(360)	5,136	—
98550	Hoquiam	(360)	9,061	8,972
98011	Inglewood-Finn Hill (c)	(425)	22,661	29,132
*98027	Issaquah	(425)	18,373	7,786
98626	Kelso	(360)	12,120	11,767
98028	Kenmore	(425)	19,980	8,917
99336	Kennewick	(509)	62,276	42,148
*98031	Kent	(253)/(425)	83,501	37,960
98033	Kingsgate (c)	(425)	12,222	14,259
*98033	Kirkland	(425)	46,476	40,059
*98509	Lacey	(360)	35,412	19,279
98155	Lake Forest Park	(206)	12,548	4,031
98002	Lakeland North (c)	(253)	15,085	14,402
98002	Lakeland South (c)	(253)	11,436	9,027
98842	Lake Morton-Berrydale (c)	(425)	9,659	—
98665	Lake Shore (c)	(360)	6,670	6,268
98258	Lake Stevens	(425)	8,007	3,435
*98498	Lakewood	(253)	57,575	55,937
98092	Lea Hill (c)	(253)	10,871	6,876
99019	Liberty Lake	(509)	5,848	2,015
98632	Longview	(360)	36,767	31,499
98264	Lynden	(360)	10,912	5,709
*98046	Lynnwood	(425)	33,685	28,637
98290	Maltby (c)	(360)	8,267	—
98038	Maple Valley	(425)	16,440	1,211
98012	Martha Lake (c)	(425)	12,633	10,155
*98270	Marysville	(360)	31,938	12,248
98040	Mercer Island	(206)	23,463	20,816
98444	Midland (c)	(253)	7,414	5,587
*98082	Mill Creek	(425)	15,586	7,180
98682	Mill Plain (c)	(360)	7,400	—
98354	Milton	(253)	6,702	4,995
98661	Minnehaha (c)	(360)	7,689	9,661
98272	Monroe	(360)	16,152	4,275
98837	Moses Lake	(509)	17,272	11,235
98043	Mountlake Terrace	(425)	20,225	19,320
*98273	Mount Vernon	(360)	29,984	17,647
98686	Mount Vista (c)	(360)	5,770	—
98275	Mukilteo	(425)	20,308	11,575
*98059	Newcastle	(425)	9,592	4,649
*98166	Normandy Park	(206)	6,228	6,794
98012	North Creek (c)	(425)	25,742	23,236
98270	North Marysville (c)	(425)	21,161	18,711
98277	Oak Harbor	(360)	22,713	17,176
*98501	Olympia	(360)	44,645	33,729
99214	Opportunity (c)	(509)	25,065	22,326
98662	Orchards (c)	(360)	17,852	—
98360	Orting	(360)	5,462	—
*99327	Othello	(509)	6,293	4,638
99027	Otis Orchards-East Farms (c)	(360)	6,318	5,811
98047	Pacific	(253)	5,859	4,622
98204	Paine Field-Lake Stickney (c)	(425)	24,383	18,670
98444	Parkland (c)	(253)	24,053	20,882
98366	Parkwood (c)	(360)	7,213	6,853
*99301	Pasco	(509)	49,927	20,337
98037	Picnic Point-North Lynnwood (c)	(425)	22,953	—
98362	Port Angeles	(360)	18,984	17,710
98366	Port Orchard	(360)	7,992	4,984
98368	Port Townsend	(360)	9,134	7,001
98370	Poulsbo	(360)	7,808	4,848
98390	Prairie Ridge (c)	(360)	11,688	8,278
99350	Prosser	(509)	5,121	4,492
*99163	Pullman	(509)	25,357	23,478
98371	Puyallup	(253)	36,605	23,878
98848	Quincy	(509)	5,585	3,738
*98052	Redmond	(425)	48,739	35,800
*98058	Renton	(425)	58,534	41,688
*99352	Richland	(509)	44,668	32,315
98188	Riverton-Boulevard Park (c)	(206)	11,188	15,337
98686	Salmon Creek (c)	(360)	16,767	11,989
98074	Sammamish	(425)	35,164	—
*98148	SeaTac	(253)	25,336	22,760
*98101	Seattle	(206)/(425)	582,454	516,259
98208	Seattle Hill-Silver Firs (c)	(425)	35,311	—
98284	Sedro-Woolley	(360)	10,402	6,333
98942	Selah	(509)	6,947	5,113
98382	Sequim	(360)	5,688	—
98584	Shelton	(360)	9,236	7,241
*98133	Shoreline	(206)	52,315	46,979
*98315	Silverdale (c)	(360)	15,816	7,660
98290	Snohomish	(360)	8,841	6,499
*98065	Snoqualmie	(425)	6,862	1,546
98373	South Hill (c)	(253)	31,623	12,963
98387	Spanaway (c)	(253)	21,588	15,001
*99210	Spokane	(509)	198,081	177,165
*99211	Spokane Valley	(509)	83,533	—
98292	Stanwood	(360)	5,448	1,961
98388	Steilacoom	(253)	6,147	5,728
98371	Summit (c)	(253)	8,041	6,312
*98390	Sumner	(253)	9,474	7,535
98944	Sunnyside	(509)	14,828	11,238
*98402	Tacoma	(253)	196,532	176,664
98501	Tanglewilde-Thompson Place (c)	(360)	5,670	6,061
98901	Terrace Heights (c)	(509)	6,447	4,223
98948	Toppenish	(509)	9,186	7,419
*98138	Tukwila	(206)	17,111	14,506
*98501	Tumwater	(360)	13,593	9,976
*98901	Union Gap	(509)	5,693	3,120
98053	Union Hill-Novelty Hill (c)	(425)	11,265	—
98467	University Place	(253)	30,610	26,724
*98661	Vancouver	(360)	158,855	62,065
*98013	Vashon (c)	(206)	10,123	—
99037	Veradale (c)	(509)	9,387	7,836
99362	Walla Walla	(509)	30,945	26,482
98443	Waller (c)	(253)	9,200	6,415
98661	Walnut Grove (c)	(360)	7,164	3,906
98671	Washougal	(360)	11,326	4,764
*98801	Wenatchee	(509)	29,968	21,746
98027	West Lake Sammamish (c)	(425)	5,937	6,087
98258	West Lake Stevens (c)	(425)	18,071	12,453
*99353	West Richland	(509)	10,199	3,962

ZIP	Place	Area Code	2006	1990
99181	West Valley (c)	(509)	10,433	6,594
98166	White Center (c)	(206)	20,975	20,531
*98072	Woodinville	(425)	10,101	7,628
*98903	Yakima	(509)	82,805	58,427
98597	Yelm	(360)	5,038	—

West Virginia (304)

ZIP	Place	2006	1990
*25801	Beckley	16,828	18,274
24701	Bluefield	11,053	12,756
26330	Bridgeport	7,756	6,837
26201	Buckhannon	5,579	5,909
*25301	Charleston	50,846	57,287
*26507	Cheat Lake (c)	6,396	3,992
*26301	Clarksburg	16,459	17,970
25301	Cross Lanes (c)	10,353	10,878
25064	Dunbar	7,675	8,697
26241	Elkins	7,046	7,494
*26554	Fairmont	19,145	20,210
26354	Grafton	5,386	5,524
*25704	Huntington	49,007	54,844
25526	Hurricane	6,071	4,461
26726	Keyser	5,334	5,870
*25401	Martinsburg	16,392	14,073
*26505	Morgantown	28,654	25,879
26041	Moundsville	9,455	10,753
26155	New Martinsville	5,649	6,705
25143	Nitro	6,739	6,851
*25901	Oak Hill	7,272	6,812
*26101	Parkersburg	31,755	33,862
25705	Pea Ridge (c)	6,363	6,535
24740	Princeton	6,200	7,043
25177	Saint Albans	11,063	12,241
*25303	South Charleston	12,578	13,645
25569	Teays Valley (c)	12,704	8,436
*26105	Vienna	10,691	10,862
26062	Weirton	19,250	22,124
26003	Wheeling	29,330	34,882

Wisconsin

ZIP	Place	Area Code	2006	1990
54301	Allouez	(920)	14,837	14,431
54720	Altoona	(715)	6,416	5,889
54409	Antigo	(715)	8,266	8,284
*54911	Appleton	(920)	70,191	65,695
54806	Ashland	(715)	8,202	8,695
*54304	Ashwaubenon	(920)	17,106	16,376
53913	Baraboo	(608)	10,980	9,203
53916	Beaver Dam	(920)	15,522	14,196
54311	Bellevue Town	(920)	14,571	7,541
*53511	Beloit	(608)	36,348	35,571
54923	Berlin	(920)	5,210	5,371
*53045	Brookfield	(262)	39,613	35,184
*53209	Brown Deer	(414)	11,586	12,236
53105	Burlington	(262)	10,524	8,851
53108	Caledonia	(262)	25,427	—
53012	Cedarburg	(262)	11,210	10,086
*54729	Chippewa Falls	(715)	13,131	12,749
53527	Cottage Grove	(608)	5,325	1,131
53110	Cudahy	(414)	18,051	18,659
53532	De Forest	(608)	8,654	4,882
53018	Delafield	(262)	6,918	5,347
53115	Delavan	(262)	8,441	6,073
54115	De Pere	(920)	22,499	16,594
*54703	Eau Claire	(715)	63,297	56,806
53534	Edgerton	(608)	5,194	4,254
53121	Elkhorn	(262)	9,080	5,337
53122	Elm Grove	(262)	6,088	6,261
*53711	Fitchburg	(608)	22,506	15,648
*54935	Fond du Lac	(920)	42,341	37,755
53538	Fort Atkinson	(920)	11,979	10,213
53217	Fox Point	(414)	6,705	7,238
53132	Franklin	(414)	33,812	21,855
53022	Germantown	(262)	19,345	13,658
*53209	Glendale	(414)	12,811	14,088
53024	Grafton	(262)	11,568	9,340
*54303	Green Bay	(920)	100,353	96,466
53129	Greendale	(414)	13,791	15,128
*53220	Greenfield	(414)	35,444	33,403
*53130	Hales Corners	(414)	7,566	7,623
53027	Hartford	(262)	13,265	8,188
53029	Hartland	(262)	8,689	6,906
54313	Hobart	(920)	5,834	4,284
54636	Holmen	(608)	7,342	3,220
*54303	Howard	(920)	16,219	9,874
*54016	Hudson	(715)	11,913	6,378
53037	Jackson	(262)	6,085	2,603
*53545	Janesville	(608)	62,998	52,210
53549	Jefferson	(920)	7,721	6,078
54130	Kaukauna	(920)	15,095	11,982
*53140	Kenosha	(262)	96,240	80,426
54136	Kimberly	(920)	6,398	5,406
54455	Kronenwetter	(715)	6,351	4,850
*54601	La Crosse	(608)	50,266	51,140
53147	Lake Geneva	(262)	8,155	5,979
54729	Lake Hallie	(715)	5,775	—
53551	Lake Mills	(920)	5,401	4,143
54140	Little Chute	(920)	11,035	9,207
53558	McFarland	(608)	7,504	5,232
*53714	Madison	(608)	223,389	190,766
*54220	Manitowoc	(920)	33,635	32,521
54143	Marinette	(715)	11,009	11,843
*54449	Marshfield	(715)	19,136	19,293
53050	Mayville	(920)	5,367	4,374
54952	Menasha	(920)	16,709	14,711
*53051	Menomonee Falls	(262)	34,370	26,840
54751	Menomonie	(715)	15,318	13,547
*53097	Mequon	(262)	23,600	18,885
54452	Merrill	(715)	9,897	9,860
53562	Middleton	(608)	16,595	13,785
53563	Milton	(608)	5,720	4,574
*53201	Milwaukee	(414)	573,358	628,088
53716	Monona	(608)	7,938	8,637
53566	Monroe	(608)	10,599	10,241
53572	Mount Horeb	(608)	6,573	4,182
53406	Mount Pleasant	(262)	25,828	20,884
53149	Mukwonago	(262)	6,815	4,495
53150	Muskego	(414)	22,760	16,813
54956	Neenah	(920)	24,831	23,219
53186	New Berlin	(262)	39,234	33,592
54961	New London	(920)	7,019	6,658
54017	New Richmond	(715)	7,963	5,106
53154	Oak Creek	(414)	32,341	19,513
53066	Oconomowoc	(262)	14,167	10,993
54650	Onalaska	(608)	16,186	12,201
53575	Oregon	(608)	8,810	4,519
*54901	Oshkosh	(920)	64,084	55,006
53072	Pewaukee (city)	(262)	12,789	—
53072	Pewaukee (village)	(262)	9,000	5,287
53818	Platteville	(608)	9,748	9,862
*53158	Pleasant Prairie	(262)	18,942	12,037
54467	Plover	(715)	11,378	8,176
53073	Plymouth	(920)	8,280	6,769
53901	Portage	(608)	9,782	8,640
53074	Port Washington	(262)	11,039	9,338
53821	Prairie du Chien	(608)	5,745	5,657
*53401	Racine	(262)	79,592	84,298
*53959	Reedsburg	(608)	8,533	5,834
54501	Rhinelander	(715)	7,821	7,382
54401	Rib Mountain (c)	(715)	6,059	4,634
54868	Rice Lake	(715)	8,413	7,998
53581	Richland Center	(608)	5,147	5,018
54971	Ripon	(920)	7,303	7,241
54022	River Falls	(715)	13,657	10,610
54474	Rothschild	(715)	5,197	3,310
*53235	Saint Francis	(414)	8,871	9,245
54166	Shawano	(715)	8,730	7,598
*53081	Sheboygan	(920)	48,598	49,587
53085	Sheboygan Falls	(920)	7,663	5,823
53211	Shorewood	(414)	13,254	14,116
53172	South Milwaukee	(414)	20,716	20,958
54656	Sparta	(608)	9,022	7,788
*54481	Stevens Point	(715)	24,368	23,002
53589	Stoughton	(608)	12,564	8,786
54235	Sturgeon Bay	(920)	9,171	9,176
53177	Sturtevant	(262)	6,446	3,803
*54173	Suamico	(920)	10,775	5,214
*53590	Sun Prairie	(608)	26,429	15,352
54880	Superior	(715)	26,960	27,134
53089	Sussex	(262)	10,134	5,039
54660	Tomah	(608)	8,723	7,572
53181	Twin Lakes	(262)	5,522	3,989
*54241	Two Rivers	(920)	12,010	13,030
53593	Verona	(608)	10,048	5,374
*53094	Watertown	(920)	23,127	19,142
53186	Waukesha	(262)	67,814	56,894
53597	Waunakee	(608)	10,646	5,897
54981	Waupaca	(715)	5,820	4,946
53963	Waupun	(920)	10,676	8,844
*54403	Wausau	(715)	38,435	37,060
*53213	Wauwatosa	(414)	44,798	49,366
*53214	West Allis	(414)	58,710	63,221
*53095	West Bend	(262)	29,853	24,470
*54476	Weston	(715)	13,177	9,714
*53217	Whitefish Bay	(414)	13,535	14,272
53190	Whitewater	(262)	14,065	12,636
53185	Wind Lake (c)	(262)	5,202	3,748
*54494	Wisconsin Rapids	(715)	17,739	18,245

Wyoming (307)

ZIP	Place	2006	1990
*82609	Casper	52,089	46,765
*82009	Cheyenne	55,314	50,008
82414	Cody	9,217	7,897
82633	Douglas	5,643	5,076
*82930	Evanston	11,567	10,904
*82716	Gillette	23,899	17,545
*82935	Green River	11,933	12,711
*83002	Jackson	9,215	4,708
82520	Lander	7,047	7,023
*82072	Laramie	25,688	26,687
82435	Powell	5,381	5,292
*82301	Rawlins	8,861	9,380
82501	Riverton	9,728	9,202
*82901	Rock Springs	19,324	19,050
82801	Sheridan	16,429	13,904
82240	Torrington	5,487	5,651

Populations and Areas of Counties and States

Source: U.S. Bureau of the Census, Dept. of Commerce; World Almanac research

Counties are the primary legal divisions of most states and generally are functioning governmental units. In **Alaska**, however, the chief units of local government are boroughs; outside the boroughs there are "census areas," delineated for statistical purposes. In **Louisiana**, the primary legal divisions are known as parishes.

State population figures are estimates for July 1, 2006. **For counties**, July 1, 2006, population estimates and Apr. 1, 1990, decennial census figures are given. **Land areas** are from 2000 census. County areas may not add to state areas because of rounding.

Alabama
(67 counties, 50,744 sq. mi. land; pop. 4,599,030)

County	County seat or courthouse	2006 Pop.	1990 Pop.	Land area sq. mi.
Autauga	Prattville	49,730	34,222	596
Baldwin	Bay Minette	169,162	98,280	1,596
Barbour	Clayton	28,171	25,417	885
Bibb	Centreville	21,482	16,598	623
Blount	Oneonta	56,436	39,248	646
Bullock	Union Springs	10,906	11,042	625
Butler	Greenville	20,520	21,892	777
Calhoun	Anniston	112,903	116,032	608
Chambers	Lafayette	35,176	36,876	597
Cherokee	Centre	24,863	19,543	553
Chilton	Clanton	41,953	32,458	694
Choctaw	Butler	14,656	16,018	914
Clarke	Grove Hill	27,248	27,240	1,238
Clay	Ashland	13,829	13,252	605
Cleburne	Heflin	14,700	12,730	553
Coffee	Elba	46,027	40,240	679
Colbert	Tuscumbia	54,766	51,666	595
Conecuh	Evergreen	13,403	14,054	851
Coosa	Rockford	11,044	11,063	652
Covington	Andalusia	37,234	36,478	1,034
Crenshaw	Luverne	13,719	13,635	610
Cullman	Cullman	80,187	67,613	738
Dale	Ozark	48,392	49,633	561
Dallas	Selma	43,945	48,130	981
De Kalb	Fort Payne	68,014	54,651	778
Elmore	Wetumpka	75,688	49,210	621
Escambia	Brewton	37,849	35,518	947
Etowah	Gadsden	103,362	99,840	535
Fayette	Fayette	18,005	17,962	628
Franklin	Russellville	30,847	27,814	636
Geneva	Geneva	25,868	23,647	576
Greene	Eutaw	9,374	10,153	646
Hale	Greensboro	18,236	15,498	644
Henry	Abbeville	16,706	15,374	562
Houston	Dothan	95,660	81,331	580
Jackson	Scottsboro	53,745	47,796	1,079
Jefferson	Birmingham	656,700	651,520	1,113
Lamar	Vernon	14,548	15,715	605
Lauderdale	Florence	87,891	79,661	669
Lawrence	Moulton	34,312	31,513	693
Lee	Opelika	125,781	87,146	609
Limestone	Athens	72,446	54,135	568
Lowndes	Hayneville	12,759	12,658	718
Macon	Tuskegee	22,594	24,928	611
Madison	Huntsville	304,307	238,912	805
Marengo	Linden	21,842	23,084	977
Marion	Hamilton	30,165	29,830	741
Marshall	Guntersville	87,185	70,832	567
Mobile	Mobile	404,157	378,643	1,233
Monroe	Monroeville	23,342	23,968	1,026
Montgomery	Montgomery	223,571	209,085	790
Morgan	Decatur	115,237	100,043	582
Perry	Marion	11,186	12,759	719
Pickens	Carrollton	20,133	20,699	881
Pike	Troy	29,620	27,595	671
Randolph	Wedowee	22,673	19,881	581
Russell	Phenix City	50,085	46,860	641
Saint Clair	Ashville & Pell City	75,232	49,811	634
Shelby	Columbiana	178,182	99,363	795
Sumter	Livingston	13,606	16,174	905
Talladega	Talladega	80,271	74,109	740
Tallapoosa	Dadeville	41,010	38,826	718
Tuscaloosa	Tuscaloosa	171,159	150,500	1,324
Walker	Jasper	70,034	67,670	794
Washington	Chatom	17,651	16,694	1,081
Wilcox	Camden	12,911	13,568	889
Winston	Double Springs	24,634	22,053	614

Alaska
(27 divisions, 571,951 sq. mi. land; pop. 670,053)

Borough or Census Division	2006 Pop.	1990 Pop.	Land area sq. mi.
Aleutians East Borough	2,647	2,464	6,988
Aleutians West Census Area	5,239	9,478	4,397
Anchorage Municipality	278,700	226,338	1,697
Bethel Census Area	17,147	13,660	40,633
Bristol Bay Borough	1,042	1,410	505
Denali Borough	1,846	1,682	12,750
Dillingham Census Area	4,970	4,010	18,675
Fairbanks North Star Borough	86,754	77,720	7,366
Haines Borough	2,257	2,117	2,344
Juneau Borough	30,737	26,752	2,717
Kenai Peninsula Borough	52,304	40,802	16,013
Ketchikan Gateway Borough	13,384	13,828	1,233
Kodiak Island Borough	13,072	13,309	6,560
Lake and Peninsula Borough	1,548	1,666	23,782
Matanuska-Susitna Borough	80,480	39,683	24,682
Nome Census Area	9,245	8,288	23,001
North Slope Borough	6,608	5,986	88,817
Northwest Arctic Borough	7,511	6,106	35,898
Prince of Wales-Outer Ketchikan Census Area	5,688	6,278	7,411
Sitka Borough	8,920	8,588	2,874
Skagway-Hoonah-Angoon Census Area	3,100	3,679	7,896
Southeast Fairbanks Census Area	6,773	5,925	24,815
Valdez-Cordova Census Area	9,872	9,920	34,319
Wade Hampton Census Area	7,580	5,789	17,194
Wrangell-Petersburg Census Area	6,096	7,042	5,835
Yakutat Borough	689	725	7,650
Yukon-Koyukuk Census Area	5,844	6,798	145,900

Arizona
(15 counties, 113,635 sq. mi. land; pop. 6,166,318)

County	County seat or courthouse	2006 Pop.	1990 Pop.	Land area sq. mi.
Apache	Saint Johns	71,118	61,591	11,205
Cochise	Bisbee	127,757	97,624	6,169
Coconino	Flagstaff	124,953	96,591	18,617
Gila	Globe	52,209	40,216	4,768
Graham	Safford	33,660	26,554	4,629
Greenlee	Clifton	7,738	8,008	1,847
La Paz	Parker	20,256	13,844	4,500
Maricopa	Phoenix	3,768,123	2,122,101	9,203
Mohave	Kingman	193,035	93,497	13,312
Navajo	Holbrook	111,399	77,674	9,953
Pima	Tucson	946,362	666,957	9,186
Pinal	Florence	271,059	116,397	5,370
Santa Cruz	Nogales	43,080	29,676	1,238
Yavapai	Prescott	208,014	107,714	8,123
Yuma	Yuma	187,555	106,895	5,514

Arkansas
(75 counties, 52,068 sq. mi. land; pop. 2,810,872)

County	County seat or courthouse	2006 Pop.	1990 Pop.	Land area sq. mi.
Arkansas	DeWitt & Stuttgart	19,884	21,653	988
Ashley	Hamburg	22,843	24,319	921
Baxter	Mountain Home	41,307	31,186	554
Benton	Bentonville	196,045	97,530	846
Boone	Harrison	36,405	28,297	591
Bradley	Warren	12,111	11,793	651
Calhoun	Hampton	5,558	5,826	628
Carroll	Berryville & Eureka Springs	27,339	18,623	630
Chicot	Lake Village	12,915	15,713	644
Clark	Arkadelphia	22,913	21,437	865
Clay	Corning & Piggott	16,497	18,107	639
Cleburne	Heber Springs	25,485	19,411	553
Cleveland	Rison	8,858	7,781	595
Columbia	Magnolia	24,440	25,691	766
Conway	Morrilton	20,694	19,151	556
Craighead	Jonesboro & Lake City	88,244	68,956	711
Crawford	Van Buren	58,785	42,493	595
Crittenden	Marion	52,083	49,939	610
Cross	Wynne	19,056	19,225	616
Dallas	Fordyce	8,350	9,614	667
Desha	Arkansas City	14,181	16,798	765
Drew	Monticello	18,387	17,369	828
Faulkner	Conway	100,685	60,006	647
Franklin	Charleston & Ozark	18,276	14,897	610
Fulton	Salem	11,756	10,037	618
Garland	Hot Springs	95,164	73,397	677
Grant	Sheridan	17,493	13,948	632
Greene	Paragould	40,091	31,804	578
Hempstead	Hope	23,347	21,621	729
Hot Spring	Malvern	31,730	26,115	615
Howard	Nashville	14,415	13,569	587
Independence	Batesville	34,909	31,192	764
Izard	Melbourne	13,356	11,364	581
Jackson	Newport	17,426	18,944	634
Jefferson	Pine Bluff	80,655	85,487	885
Johnson	Clarksville	24,453	18,221	662
Lafayette	Lewisville	7,896	9,643	527
Lawrence	Walnut Ridge	16,899	17,455	587

County	County seat or courthouse	2006 Pop.	1990 Pop.	Land area sq. mi.
Lee.	Marianna	11,379	13,053	602
Lincoln	Star City	14,125	13,690	561
Little River	Ashdown	13,074	13,966	532
Logan.	Booneville & Paris	22,903	20,557	710
Lonoke	Lonoke	62,902	39,268	766
Madison	Huntsville	15,361	11,618	837
Marion	Yellville	16,931	12,001	598
Miller	Texarkana	43,055	38,467	624
Mississippi	Blytheville & Osceola	47,517	57,525	898
Monroe	Clarendon	9,095	11,333	607
Montgomery	Mount Ida	9,272	7,841	781
Nevada	Prescott	9,471	10,101	620
Newton	Jasper	8,411	7,666	823
Ouachita	Camden	26,710	30,574	732
Perry	Perryville	10,411	7,969	551
Phillips	Helena	23,331	28,830	693
Pike	Murfreesboro	10,859	10,086	603
Poinsett	Harrisburg	25,086	24,664	758
Polk	Mena	20,363	17,347	859
Pope	Russellville	57,671	45,883	812
Prairie	Des Arc & De Valls Bluff	8,927	9,518	646
Pulaski	Little Rock	367,319	349,773	771
Randolph	Pocahontas	18,448	16,558	652
Saint Francis	Forrest City	27,535	28,497	634
Saline	Benton	94,024	64,183	723
Scott	Waldron	11,415	10,205	894
Searcy	Marshall	8,075	7,841	667
Sebastian	Fort Smith & Greenwood	120,322	99,590	536
Sevier	De Queen	16,297	13,637	564
Sharp	Ash Flat	17,963	14,109	604
Stone	Mountain View	11,981	9,775	607
Union	El Dorado	44,170	46,719	1,039
Van Buren	Clinton	16,718	14,008	712
Washington	Fayetteville	186,521	113,409	950
White	Searcy	72,560	54,676	1,034
Woodruff	Augusta	7,905	9,520	587
Yell	Danville & Dardanelle	21,834	17,759	928

California
(58 counties, 155,959 sq. mi. land; pop. 36,457,549)

County	County seat or courthouse	2006 Pop.	1990 Pop.	Land area sq. mi.
Alameda	Oakland	1,457,426	1,304,347	738
Alpine	Markleeville	1,180	1,113	739
Amador	Jackson	38,941	30,039	593
Butte	Oroville	215,881	182,120	1,639
Calaveras	San Andreas	47,722	31,998	1,020
Colusa	Colusa	21,272	16,275	1,151
Contra Costa	Martinez	1,024,319	803,731	720
Del Norte	Crescent City	28,893	23,460	1,008
El Dorado	Placerville	178,066	125,995	1,711
Fresno	Fresno	891,756	667,479	5,963
Glenn	Willows	28,061	24,798	1,315
Humboldt	Eureka	128,330	119,118	3,572
Imperial	El Centro	160,301	109,303	4,175
Inyo	Independence	17,980	18,281	10,203
Kern	Bakersfield	780,117	544,981	8,141
Kings	Hanford	146,153	101,469	1,391
Lake	Lakeport	65,933	50,631	1,258
Lassen	Susanville	34,715	27,598	4,557
Los Angeles	Los Angeles	9,948,081	8,863,052	4,061
Madera	Madera	146,345	88,090	2,136
Marin	San Rafael	248,742	230,096	520
Mariposa	Mariposa	18,401	14,302	1,451
Mendocino	Ukiah	88,109	80,345	3,509
Merced	Merced	245,658	178,403	1,929
Modoc	Alturas	9,597	9,678	3,944
Mono	Bridgeport	12,754	9,956	3,044
Monterey	Salinas	410,206	355,660	3,322
Napa	Napa	133,522	110,765	754
Nevada	Nevada City	98,764	78,510	958
Orange	Santa Ana	3,002,048	2,410,668	789
Placer	Auburn	326,242	172,796	1,404
Plumas	Quincy	21,263	19,739	2,554
Riverside	Riverside	2,026,803	1,170,413	7,207
Sacramento	Sacramento	1,374,724	1,066,789	966
San Benito	Hollister	55,842	36,697	1,389
San Bernardino	San Bernardino	1,999,332	1,418,380	20,053
San Diego	San Diego	2,941,454	2,498,016	4,200
San Francisco	San Francisco	744,041	723,959	47
San Joaquin	Stockton	673,170	480,628	1,399
San Luis Obispo	San Luis Obispo	257,005	217,162	3,304
San Mateo	Redwood City	705,499	649,623	449
Santa Barbara	Santa Barbara	400,335	369,608	2,737
Santa Clara	San Jose	1,731,281	1,497,577	1,291
Santa Cruz	Santa Cruz	249,705	229,734	445
Shasta	Redding	179,951	147,036	3,785
Sierra	Downieville	3,455	3,318	953
Siskiyou	Yreka	45,091	43,531	6,287
Solano	Fairfield	411,680	339,469	829
Sonoma	Santa Rosa	466,891	388,222	1,576
Stanislaus	Modesto	512,138	370,522	1,494

County	County seat or courthouse	2006 Pop.	1990 Pop.	Land area sq. mi.
Sutter	Yuba City	91,410	64,409	603
Tehama	Red Bluff	61,686	49,625	2,951
Trinity	Weaverville	14,313	13,063	3,179
Tulare	Visalia	419,909	311,932	4,824
Tuolumne	Sonora	56,855	48,456	2,235
Ventura	Ventura	799,720	669,016	1,845
Yolo	Woodland	188,085	141,212	1,013
Yuba	Marysville	70,396	58,234	631

Colorado
(64 counties, 103,718 sq. mi. land; pop. 4,753,377)

County	County seat or courthouse	2006 Pop.	1990 Pop.	Land area sq. mi.
Adams[1]	Brighton	414,338	265,038	1,192
Alamosa	Alamosa	15,225	13,617	723
Arapahoe	Littleton	537,197	391,572	803
Archuleta	Pagosa Springs	12,386	5,345	1,350
Baca	Springfield	4,017	4,556	2,556
Bent	Las Animas	5,551	5,048	1,514
Boulder[1]	Boulder	282,304	225,339	742
Broomfield[2]	Broomfield	45,116	NA	27
Chaffee	Salida	16,918	12,684	1,013
Cheyenne	Cheyenne Wells	1,906	2,397	1,781
Clear Creek	Georgetown	9,130	7,619	395
Conejos	Conejos	8,406	7,453	1,287
Costilla	San Luis	3,378	3,190	1,227
Crowley	Ordway	5,386	3,946	789
Custer	Westcliffe	3,926	1,926	739
Delta	Delta	30,401	20,980	1,142
Denver	Denver	566,974	467,549	153
Dolores	Dove Creek	1,911	1,504	1,067
Douglas	Castle Rock	263,621	60,391	840
Eagle	Eagle	49,085	21,928	1,688
Elbert	Kiowa	23,181	9,646	1,851
El Paso	Colorado Springs	576,884	397,014	2,126
Fremont	Canon City	48,010	32,273	1,533
Garfield	Glenwood Springs	51,908	29,974	2,947
Gilpin	Central City	5,042	3,070	150
Grand	Hot Sulphur Springs	13,406	7,966	1,847
Gunnison	Gunnison	14,331	10,273	3,239
Hinsdale	Lake City	819	467	1,118
Huerfano	Walsenburg	7,808	6,009	1,591
Jackson	Walden	1,406	1,605	1,613
Jefferson[1]	Golden	526,994	438,430	772
Kiowa	Eads	1,413	1,688	1,771
Kit Carson	Burlington	7,590	7,140	2,161
Lake	Leadville	7,814	6,007	377
La Plata	Durango	47,936	32,284	1,692
Larimer	Fort Collins	276,253	186,136	2,601
Las Animas	Trinidad	15,564	13,765	4,772
Lincoln	Hugo	5,458	4,529	2,586
Logan	Sterling	20,780	17,567	1,839
Mesa	Grand Junction	134,189	93,145	3,328
Mineral	Creede	929	558	876
Moffat	Craig	13,680	11,357	4,742
Montezuma	Cortez	25,217	18,672	2,037
Montrose	Montrose	38,559	24,423	2,241
Morgan	Fort Morgan	28,109	21,939	1,285
Otero	La Junta	19,452	20,185	1,263
Ouray	Ouray	4,307	2,295	540
Park	Fairplay	17,157	7,174	2,201
Phillips	Holyoke	4,601	4,189	688
Pitkin	Aspen	14,798	12,661	970
Prowers	Lamar	13,776	13,347	1,640
Pueblo	Pueblo	152,912	123,051	2,389
Rio Blanco	Meeker	6,180	6,051	3,221
Rio Grande	Del Norte	12,006	10,770	912
Routt	Steamboat Springs	21,580	14,088	2,362
Saguache	Saguache	7,006	4,619	3,168
San Juan	Silverton	578	745	387
San Miguel	Telluride	7,143	3,653	1,287
Sedgwick	Julesburg	2,467	2,690	548
Summit	Breckenridge	25,399	12,881	608
Teller	Cripple Creek	22,243	12,468	557
Washington	Akron	4,630	4,812	2,521
Weld[1]	Greeley	236,857	131,821	3,992
Yuma	Wray	9,829	8,954	2,366

NA = Not available. (1) Parts of these counties were taken to create Broomfield County in 2001. (2) Created in 2001.

Connecticut
(8 counties, 4,845 sq. mi. land; pop. 3,504,809)

County	County seat or courthouse	2006 Pop.	1990 Pop.	Land area sq. mi.
Fairfield	Bridgeport	900,440	827,645	626
Hartford	Hartford	876,927	851,783	735
Litchfield	Litchfield	190,119	174,092	920
Middlesex	Middletown	163,774	143,196	369
New Haven	New Haven	845,244	804,219	606
New London	New London	263,293	254,957	666
Tolland	Rockville	148,140	128,699	410
Windham	Willimantic	116,872	102,525	513

Delaware
(3 counties, 1,954 sq. mi. land; pop. 853,476)

County	County seat or courthouse	2006 Pop.	1990 Pop.	Land area sq. mi.
Kent	Dover	147,601	110,993	590
New Castle	Wilmington	525,587	441,946	426
Sussex	Georgetown	180,288	113,229	938

District of Columbia
(61 sq. mi. land; pop. 581,530)
Has no counties; coextensive with city of Washington.

Florida
(67 counties, 53,927 sq. mi. land; pop. 18,089,888)

County	County seat or courthouse	2006 Pop.	1990 Pop.	Land area sq. mi.
Alachua	Gainesville	227,120	181,596	874
Baker	Macclenny	25,203	18,486	585
Bay	Panama City	163,505	126,994	764
Bradford	Starke	28,384	22,515	293
Brevard	Titusville	534,359	398,978	1,018
Broward	Fort Lauderdale	1,787,636	1,255,531	1,205
Calhoun	Blountstown	13,410	11,011	567
Charlotte	Punta Gorda	154,438	110,975	694
Citrus	Inverness	138,143	93,513	584
Clay	Green Cove Springs	178,899	105,986	601
Collier	Naples	314,649	152,099	2,025
Columbia	Lake City	67,007	42,613	797
De Soto	Arcadia	35,315	23,865	637
Dixie	Cross City	14,964	10,585	704
Duval	Jacksonville	837,964	672,971	774
Escambia	Pensacola	295,426	262,445	662
Flagler	Bunnell	83,084	28,701	485
Franklin	Apalachicola	10,264	8,967	544
Gadsden	Quincy	46,658	41,116	516
Gilchrist	Trenton	16,865	9,667	349
Glades	Moore Haven	11,230	7,591	774
Gulf	Port Saint Joe	14,043	11,504	555
Hamilton	Jasper	14,215	10,930	515
Hardee	Wauchula	28,621	19,499	637
Hendry	La Belle	40,459	25,773	1,153
Hernando	Brooksville	165,409	101,115	478
Highlands	Sebring	97,987	68,432	1,028
Hillsborough	Tampa	1,157,738	834,054	1,051
Holmes	Bonifay	19,285	15,778	482
Indian River	Vero Beach	130,100	90,208	503
Jackson	Marianna	49,288	41,375	916
Jefferson	Monticello	14,677	11,296	598
Lafayette	Mayo	8,045	5,578	543
Lake	Tavares	290,435	152,104	953
Lee	Fort Myers	571,344	335,113	804
Leon	Tallahassee	245,625	192,493	667
Levy	Bronson	39,076	25,912	1,118
Liberty	Bristol	7,782	5,569	836
Madison	Madison	19,210	16,569	692
Manatee	Bradenton	313,298	211,707	741
Marion	Ocala	316,183	194,835	1,579
Martin	Stuart	139,393	100,900	556
Miami-Dade	Miami	2,402,208	1,937,194	1,946
Monroe	Key West	74,737	78,024	997
Nassau	Fernandina Beach	66,707	43,941	652
Okaloosa	Crestview	180,291	143,777	936
Okeechobee	Okeechobee	40,406	29,627	774
Orange	Orlando	1,043,500	677,491	907
Osceola	Kissimmee	244,045	107,728	1,322
Palm Beach	West Palm Beach	1,274,013	863,503	1,974
Pasco	Dade City	450,171	281,131	745
Pinellas	Clearwater	924,413	851,659	280
Polk	Bartow	561,606	405,382	1,874
Putnam	Palatka	74,083	65,070	722
Saint Johns	Saint Augustine	169,224	83,829	609
Saint Lucie	Fort Pierce	252,724	150,171	572
Santa Rosa	Milton	144,561	81,961	1,017
Sarasota	Sarasota	369,535	277,776	572
Seminole	Sanford	406,875	287,521	308
Sumter	Bushnell	68,768	31,577	546
Suwannee	Live Oak	39,494	26,780	688
Taylor	Perry	19,842	17,111	1,042
Union	Lake Butler	14,842	10,252	240
Volusia	De Land	496,575	370,737	1,103
Wakulla	Crawfordville	29,542	14,202	607
Walton	De Funiak Springs	52,270	27,759	1,058
Washington	Chipley	22,720	16,919	580

Georgia
(159 counties, 57,906 sq. mi. land; pop. 9,363,941)

County	County seat or courthouse	2006 Pop.	1990 Pop.	Land area sq. mi.
Appling	Baxley	17,860	15,744	509
Atkinson	Pearson	8,047	6,213	338
Bacon	Alma	10,482	9,566	285
Baker	Newton	4,098	3,615	343
Baldwin	Milledgeville	45,275	39,530	258
Banks	Homer	16,445	10,308	234
Barrow	Winder	63,702	29,721	162
Bartow	Cartersville	91,266	55,915	459
Ben Hill	Fitzgerald	17,635	16,245	252
Berrien	Nashville	16,756	14,153	452
Bibb	Macon	154,903	150,137	250
Bleckley	Cochran	12,353	10,430	217
Brantley	Nahunta	15,735	11,077	444
Brooks	Quitman	16,464	15,398	494
Bryan	Pembroke	29,648	15,438	442
Bulloch	Statesboro	63,207	43,125	682
Burke	Waynesboro	22,986	20,579	830
Butts	Jackson	23,561	15,326	187
Calhoun	Morgan	6,094	5,013	280
Camden	Woodbine	45,118	30,167	630
Candler	Metter	10,674	7,744	247
Carroll	Carrollton	107,325	71,422	499
Catoosa	Ringgold	62,016	42,464	162
Charlton	Folkston	10,882	8,496	781
Chatham	Savannah	241,411	216,774	438
Chattahoochee	Cusseta	14,041	16,934	249
Chattooga	Summerville	26,442	22,236	313
Cherokee	Canton	195,327	90,204	424
Clarke	Athens	112,787	87,594	121
Clay	Fort Gaines	3,180	3,364	195
Clayton	Jonesboro	271,240	181,436	143
Clinch	Homerville	6,897	6,160	809
Cobb	Marietta	679,325	447,745	340
Coffee	Douglas	40,242	29,592	599
Colquitt	Moultrie	44,821	36,645	552
Columbia	Appling	106,887	66,031	290
Cook	Adel	16,333	13,456	229
Coweta	Newnan	115,291	53,853	443
Crawford	Knoxville	12,823	8,991	325
Crisp	Cordele	22,051	20,011	274
Dade	Trenton	16,233	13,183	174
Dawson	Dawsonville	20,643	9,429	211
Decatur	Bainbridge	28,665	25,517	597
DeKalb	Decatur	723,602	546,174	268
Dodge	Eastman	19,700	17,607	500
Dooly	Vienna	11,748	9,901	393
Dougherty	Albany	94,773	96,321	330
Douglas	Douglasville	119,557	71,120	199
Early	Blakely	12,065	11,854	511
Echols	Statenville	4,274	2,334	404
Effingham	Springfield	48,954	25,687	479
Elbert	Elberton	20,768	18,949	369
Emanuel	Swainsboro	22,600	20,546	686
Evans	Claxton	11,425	8,724	185
Fannin	Blue Ridge	22,319	15,992	386
Fayette	Fayetteville	106,671	62,415	197
Floyd	Rome	95,322	81,251	513
Forsyth	Cumming	150,968	44,083	226
Franklin	Carnesville	21,691	16,650	263
Fulton	Atlanta	960,009	648,776	529
Gilmer	Ellijay	28,175	13,368	427
Glascock	Gibson	2,720	2,357	144
Glynn	Brunswick	73,630	62,496	422
Gordon	Calhoun	51,419	35,067	356
Grady	Cairo	25,082	20,279	458
Greene	Greensboro	15,534	11,793	388
Gwinnett	Lawrenceville	757,104	352,910	433
Habersham	Clarkesville	41,112	27,622	278
Hall	Gainesville	173,256	95,434	394
Hancock	Sparta	9,677	8,908	473
Haralson	Buchanan	28,616	21,966	282
Harris	Hamilton	28,785	17,788	464
Hart	Hartwell	24,276	19,712	232
Heard	Franklin	11,472	8,628	296
Henry	McDonough	178,033	58,741	323
Houston	Perry	127,530	89,208	377
Irwin	Ocilla	10,403	8,649	357
Jackson	Jefferson	55,778	30,005	342
Jasper	Monticello	13,624	8,453	370
Jeff Davis	Hazlehurst	13,278	12,032	333
Jefferson	Louisville	16,768	17,408	528
Jenkins	Millen	8,725	8,247	350
Johnson	Wrightsville	9,626	8,329	304
Jones	Gray	26,973	20,739	394
Lamar	Barnesville	16,679	13,038	185
Lanier	Lakeland	7,723	5,531	187
Laurens	Dublin	47,316	39,988	812
Lee	Leesburg	32,495	16,250	356
Liberty	Hinesville	62,571	52,745	519
Lincoln	Lincolnton	8,257	7,442	211
Long	Ludowici	11,452	6,202	401
Lowndes	Valdosta	97,844	75,981	504
Lumpkin	Dahlonega	25,462	14,573	284
McDuffie	Thomson	21,917	20,119	260
McIntosh	Darien	11,248	8,634	433
Macon	Oglethorpe	13,817	13,114	403
Madison	Danielsville	27,837	21,050	284
Marion	Buena Vista	7,276	5,590	367
Meriwether	Greenville	22,881	22,411	503
Miller	Colquitt	6,239	6,280	283
Mitchell	Camilla	23,852	20,275	512
Monroe	Forsyth	24,443	17,113	396

County	County seat or courthouse	2006 Pop.	1990 Pop.	Land area sq. mi.
Montgomery	Mount Vernon	9,067	7,379	245
Morgan	Madison	17,908	12,883	350
Murray	Chatsworth	41,398	26,147	344
Muscogee	Columbus	188,660	179,280	216
Newton	Covington	91,451	41,808	276
Oconee	Watkinsville	30,858	17,618	186
Oglethorpe	Lexington	13,997	9,763	441
Paulding	Dallas	121,530	41,611	313
Peach	Fort Valley	24,785	21,189	151
Pickens	Jasper	29,640	14,432	232
Pierce	Blackshear	17,452	13,328	343
Pike	Zebulon	16,801	10,224	218
Polk	Cedartown	41,091	33,815	311
Pulaski	Hawkinsville	9,887	8,108	247
Putnam	Eatonton	19,930	14,137	345
Quitman	Georgetown	2,486	2,210	152
Rabun	Clayton	16,354	11,648	371
Randolph	Cuthbert	7,357	8,023	429
Richmond	Augusta	194,398	189,719	324
Rockdale	Conyers	80,332	54,091	131
Schley	Ellaville	4,198	3,590	168
Screven	Sylvania	15,190	13,842	648
Seminole	Donalsonville	9,168	9,010	238
Spalding	Griffin	62,185	54,457	198
Stephens	Toccoa	25,143	23,436	179
Stewart	Lumpkin	4,754	5,654	459
Sumter	Americus	32,490	30,232	485
Talbot	Talbotton	6,605	6,524	393
Taliaferro	Crawfordville	1,877	1,915	195
Tattnall	Reidsville	23,492	17,722	484
Taylor	Butler	8,792	7,642	377
Telfair	McRae	13,268	11,000	441
Terrell	Dawson	10,657	10,653	335
Thomas	Thomasville	45,135	38,943	548
Tift	Tifton	41,685	34,998	265
Toombs	Lyons	27,623	24,072	367
Towns	Hiawassee	10,525	6,754	167
Treutlen	Soperton	6,852	5,994	201
Troup	La Grange	63,245	55,532	414
Turner	Ashburn	9,322	8,703	286
Twiggs	Jeffersonville	10,184	9,806	360
Union	Blairsville	20,652	11,993	323
Upson	Thomaston	27,676	26,300	325
Walker	La Fayette	64,606	58,310	447
Walton	Monroe	79,388	38,586	329
Ware	Waycross	35,748	35,471	902
Warren	Warrenton	5,949	6,078	286
Washington	Sandersville	20,723	19,112	680
Wayne	Jesup	28,895	22,356	645
Webster	Preston	2,252	2,263	210
Wheeler	Alamo	6,908	4,903	298
White	Cleveland	24,738	13,006	242
Whitfield	Dalton	92,999	72,462	290
Wilcox	Abbeville	8,712	7,008	380
Wilkes	Washington	10,468	10,597	471
Wilkinson	Irwinton	9,995	10,228	447
Worth	Sylvester	21,938	19,744	570

Hawaii
(5 counties, 6,423 sq. mi. land; pop. 1,285,498)

County	County seat or courthouse	2006 Pop.	1990 Pop.	Land area sq. mi.
Hawaii	Hilo	171,191	120,317	4,028
Honolulu	Honolulu	909,863	836,231	600
Kalawao[1]		120	130	13
Kauai	Lihue	63,004	51,177	622
Maui	Wailuku	141,320	100,374	1,159

(1) Administered by state government.

Idaho
(44 counties, 82,747 sq. mi. land; pop. 1,466,465)

County	County seat or courthouse	2006 Pop.	1990 Pop.	Land area sq. mi.
Ada	Boise	359,035	205,775	1,055
Adams	Council	3,485	3,254	1,365
Bannock	Pocatello	78,443	66,026	1,113
Bear Lake	Paris	6,167	6,084	971
Benewah	Saint Maries	9,347	7,937	776
Bingham	Blackfoot	44,051	37,583	2,095
Blaine	Hailey	21,501	13,552	2,645
Boise	Idaho City	7,641	3,509	1,902
Bonner	Sandpoint	41,275	26,622	1,738
Bonneville	Idaho Falls	94,630	72,207	1,868
Boundary	Bonners Ferry	10,831	8,332	1,269
Butte	Arco	2,781	2,918	2,233
Camas	Fairfield	1,088	727	1,075
Canyon	Caldwell	173,302	90,076	590
Caribou	Soda Springs	6,996	6,963	1,766
Cassia	Burley	21,365	19,532	2,566
Clark	Dubois	920	762	1,765
Clearwater	Orofino	8,324	8,505	2,461
Custer	Challis	4,180	4,133	4,925
Elmore	Mountain Home	28,114	21,205	3,078
Franklin	Preston	12,494	9,232	665

County	County seat or courthouse	2006 Pop.	1990 Pop.	Land area sq. mi.
Fremont	Saint Anthony	12,369	10,937	1,867
Gem	Emmett	16,558	11,844	563
Gooding	Gooding	14,404	11,633	731
Idaho	Grangeville	15,762	13,768	8,485
Jefferson	Rigby	22,350	16,543	1,095
Jerome	Jerome	20,130	15,138	600
Kootenai	Coeur d'Alene	131,507	69,795	1,245
Latah	Moscow	35,029	30,617	1,077
Lemhi	Salmon	7,930	6,899	4,564
Lewis	Nez Perce	3,756	3,516	479
Lincoln	Shoshone	4,522	3,308	1,206
Madison	Rexburg	31,393	23,674	472
Minidoka	Rupert	19,041	19,361	760
Nez Perce	Lewiston	38,324	33,754	849
Oneida	Malad City	4,176	3,492	1,200
Owyhee	Murphy	11,104	8,392	7,678
Payette	Payette	22,595	16,434	408
Power	American Falls	7,914	7,086	1,406
Shoshone	Wallace	13,180	13,931	2,634
Teton	Driggs	7,838	3,439	450
Twin Falls	Twin Falls	71,575	53,580	1,925
Valley	Cascade	8,836	6,109	3,678
Washington	Weiser	10,202	8,550	1,456

Illinois
(102 counties, 55,584 sq. mi. land; pop. 12,831,970)

County	County seat or courthouse	2006 Pop.	1990 Pop.	Land area sq. mi.
Adams	Quincy	67,221	66,090	857
Alexander	Cairo	8,635	10,626	236
Bond	Greenville	18,055	14,991	380
Boone	Belvidere	52,617	30,806	281
Brown	Mount Sterling	6,701	5,836	306
Bureau	Princeton	35,257	35,688	869
Calhoun	Hardin	5,177	5,322	254
Carroll	Mount Carroll	16,035	16,805	444
Cass	Virginia	13,766	13,437	376
Champaign	Urbana	185,682	173,025	997
Christian	Taylorville	35,063	34,418	709
Clark	Marshall	16,987	15,921	502
Clay	Louisville	14,028	14,460	469
Clinton	Carlyle	36,633	33,944	474
Coles	Charleston	50,949	51,644	508
Cook	Chicago	5,288,655	5,105,044	946
Crawford	Robinson	19,825	19,464	444
Cumberland	Toledo	11,000	10,670	346
DeKalb	Sycamore	100,139	77,932	634
De Witt	Clinton	16,768	16,516	398
Douglas	Tuscola	19,791	19,464	417
DuPage	Wheaton	932,670	781,689	334
Edgar	Paris	19,183	19,595	624
Edwards	Albion	6,617	7,440	222
Effingham	Effingham	34,429	31,704	479
Fayette	Vandalia	21,774	20,893	716
Ford	Paxton	14,211	14,275	486
Franklin	Benton	39,862	40,319	412
Fulton	Lewistown	37,378	38,080	866
Gallatin	Shawneetown	6,159	6,909	324
Greene	Carrollton	14,255	15,317	543
Grundy	Morris	45,828	32,337	420
Hamilton	McLeansboro	8,335	8,499	435
Hancock	Carthage	19,031	21,373	795
Hardin	Elizabethtown	4,585	5,189	178
Henderson	Oquawka	7,819	8,096	379
Henry	Cambridge	50,339	51,159	823
Iroquois	Watseka	30,598	30,787	1,116
Jackson	Murphysboro	57,778	61,067	588
Jasper	Newton	9,880	10,609	494
Jefferson	Mount Vernon	40,523	37,020	571
Jersey	Jerseyville	22,628	20,539	369
Jo Daviess	Galena	22,594	21,821	601
Johnson	Vienna	13,360	11,347	345
Kane	Geneva	493,735	317,471	520
Kankakee	Kankakee	109,090	96,255	677
Kendall	Yorkville	88,158	39,413	321
Knox	Galesburg	52,906	56,393	716
Lake	Waukegan	713,076	516,418	448
La Salle	Ottawa	113,065	106,913	1,135
Lawrence	Lawrenceville	15,887	15,972	372
Lee	Dixon	35,701	34,392	725
Livingston	Pontiac	38,658	39,301	1,044
Logan	Lincoln	30,302	30,798	618
McDonough	Macomb	31,823	35,244	589
McHenry	Woodstock	312,373	183,241	604
McLean	Bloomington	161,202	129,180	1,184
Macon	Decatur	109,309	117,206	581
Macoupin	Carlinville	48,841	47,679	864
Madison	Edwardsville	265,303	249,238	725
Marion	Salem	40,088	41,561	572
Marshall	Lacon	13,003	12,846	386
Mason	Havana	15,503	16,269	539
Massac	Metropolis	15,135	14,752	239
Menard	Petersburg	12,588	11,164	314
Mercer	Aledo	16,786	17,290	561
Monroe	Waterloo	31,876	22,422	388
Montgomery	Hillsboro	30,367	30,728	704

County	County seat or courthouse	2006 Pop.	1990 Pop.	Land area sq. mi.
Morgan	Jacksonville	35,666	36,397	569
Moultrie	Sullivan	14,383	13,930	336
Ogle	Oregon	54,826	45,957	759
Peoria	Peoria	182,495	182,827	620
Perry	Pinckneyville	22,865	21,412	441
Piatt	Monticello	16,688	15,548	440
Pike	Pittsfield	16,840	17,577	830
Pope	Golconda	4,184	4,373	371
Pulaski	Mound City	6,726	7,523	201
Putnam	Hennepin	6,005	5,730	160
Randolph	Chester	33,028	34,583	578
Richland	Olney	15,724	16,545	360
Rock Island	Rock Island	147,545	148,723	427
Saint Clair	Belleville	260,919	262,852	664
Saline	Harrisburg	26,062	26,551	383
Sangamon	Springfield	193,524	178,386	868
Schuyler	Rushville	6,984	7,498	437
Scott	Winchester	5,377	5,644	251
Shelby	Shelbyville	22,112	22,261	759
Stark	Toulon	6,233	6,534	288
Stephenson	Freeport	47,388	48,052	564
Tazewell	Pekin	130,559	123,692	649
Union	Jonesboro	18,261	17,619	414
Vermilion	Danville	81,941	88,257	899
Wabash	Mount Carmel	12,457	13,111	223
Warren	Monmouth	17,480	19,181	543
Washington	Nashville	14,927	14,965	563
Wayne	Fairfield	16,602	17,241	714
White	Carmi	15,078	16,522	495
Whiteside	Morrison	59,880	60,186	685
Will	Joliet	668,217	357,313	837
Williamson	Marion	63,740	57,733	423
Winnebago	Rockford	295,635	252,913	514
Woodford	Eureka	37,904	32,653	528

Indiana
(92 counties, 35,867 sq. mi. land; pop. 6,313,520)

County	County seat or courthouse	2006 Pop.	1990 Pop.	Land area sq. mi.
Adams	Decatur	33,719	31,095	339
Allen	Fort Wayne	347,316	300,836	657
Bartholomew	Columbus	74,444	63,657	407
Benton	Fowler	9,050	9,441	406
Blackford	Hartford City	13,603	14,067	165
Boone	Lebanon	53,526	38,147	423
Brown	Nashville	15,071	14,080	312
Carroll	Delphi	20,526	18,809	372
Cass	Logansport	39,902	38,413	413
Clark	Jeffersonville	103,569	87,774	375
Clay	Brazil	27,021	24,705	358
Clinton	Frankfort	34,217	30,974	405
Crawford	English	11,137	9,914	306
Daviess	Washington	30,220	27,533	431
Dearborn	Lawrenceburg	49,663	38,835	305
Decatur	Greensburg	24,948	23,645	373
De Kalb	Auburn	41,902	35,324	363
Delaware	Muncie	114,879	119,659	393
Dubois	Jasper	41,212	36,616	430
Elkhart	Goshen	198,105	156,198	464
Fayette	Connersville	24,648	26,015	215
Floyd	New Albany	72,570	64,404	148
Fountain	Covington	17,486	17,808	396
Franklin	Brookville	23,373	19,580	386
Fulton	Rochester	20,622	18,840	369
Gibson	Princeton	33,396	31,913	489
Grant	Marion	69,825	74,169	414
Greene	Bloomfield	33,360	30,410	542
Hamilton	Noblesville	250,979	108,936	398
Hancock	Greenfield	65,050	45,527	306
Harrison	Corydon	36,992	29,890	485
Hendricks	Danville	131,204	75,717	408
Henry	New Castle	46,947	48,139	393
Howard	Kokomo	84,500	80,827	293
Huntington	Huntington	38,026	35,427	383
Jackson	Brownstown	42,404	37,730	509
Jasper	Rensselaer	32,296	24,823	560
Jay	Portland	21,605	21,512	384
Jefferson	Madison	32,668	29,797	361
Jennings	Vernon	28,473	23,661	377
Johnson	Franklin	133,316	88,109	320
Knox	Vincennes	38,241	39,884	516
Kosciusko	Warsaw	76,541	65,294	538
Lagrange	Lagrange	37,291	29,477	380
Lake	Crown Point	494,202	475,594	497
La Porte	La Porte	110,479	107,066	598
Lawrence	Bedford	46,413	42,836	449
Madison	Anderson	130,575	130,669	452
Marion	Indianapolis	865,504	797,159	396
Marshall	Plymouth	47,295	42,182	444
Martin	Shoals	10,340	10,369	336
Miami	Peru	35,552	36,897	376
Monroe	Bloomington	122,613	108,978	394
Montgomery	Crawfordsville	38,173	34,436	505
Morgan	Martinsville	70,290	55,920	406
Newton	Kentland	14,293	13,551	402
Noble	Albion	47,918	37,877	411

County	County seat or courthouse	2006 Pop.	1990 Pop.	Land area sq. mi.
Ohio	Rising Sun	5,826	5,315	87
Orange	Paoli	19,659	18,409	400
Owen	Spencer	22,741	17,281	385
Parke	Rockville	17,021	15,410	445
Perry	Tell City	18,843	19,107	381
Pike	Petersburg	12,855	12,509	336
Porter	Valparaiso	160,105	128,932	418
Posey	Mount Vernon	26,765	25,968	409
Pulaski	Winamac	13,861	12,780	434
Putnam	Greencastle	36,978	30,315	480
Randolph	Winchester	26,581	27,148	453
Ripley	Versailles	27,748	24,616	446
Rush	Rushville	17,684	18,129	408
Saint Joseph	South Bend	266,678	247,052	457
Scott	Scottsburg	23,704	20,991	190
Shelby	Shelbyville	44,114	40,307	413
Spencer	Rockport	20,596	19,490	399
Starke	Knox	23,069	22,747	309
Steuben	Angola	33,683	27,446	309
Sullivan	Sullivan	21,542	18,993	447
Switzerland	Vevay	9,721	7,738	221
Tippecanoe	Lafayette	156,169	130,598	500
Tipton	Tipton	16,377	16,119	260
Union	Liberty	7,291	6,976	162
Vanderburgh	Evansville	173,354	165,058	235
Vermillion	Newport	16,645	16,773	257
Vigo	Terre Haute	103,009	106,107	403
Wabash	Wabash	33,559	35,069	413
Warren	Williamsport	8,701	8,176	365
Warrick	Boonville	57,090	44,920	384
Washington	Salem	28,062	23,717	514
Wayne	Richmond	68,846	71,951	404
Wells	Bluffton	28,199	25,948	370
White	Monticello	24,396	23,265	505
Whitley	Columbia City	32,556	27,651	336

Iowa
(99 counties, 55,869 sq. mi. land; pop. 2,982,085)

County	County seat or courthouse	2006 Pop.	1990 Pop.	Land area sq. mi.
Adair	Greenfield	7,714	8,409	569
Adams	Corning	4,192	4,866	424
Allamakee	Waukon	14,796	13,855	640
Appanoose	Centerville	13,442	13,743	496
Audubon	Audubon	6,278	7,334	443
Benton	Vinton	26,962	22,429	716
Black Hawk	Waterloo	126,106	123,798	567
Boone	Boone	26,584	25,186	571
Bremer	Waverly	23,837	22,813	438
Buchanan	Independence	21,045	20,844	571
Buena Vista	Storm Lake	20,091	19,965	575
Butler	Allison	15,073	15,731	580
Calhoun	Rockwell City	10,437	11,508	570
Carroll	Carroll	20,963	21,423	569
Cass	Atlantic	14,124	15,128	564
Cedar	Tipton	18,326	17,444	580
Cerro Gordo	Mason City	44,384	46,733	568
Cherokee	Cherokee	12,094	14,098	577
Chickasaw	New Hampton	12,412	13,295	505
Clarke	Osceola	9,156	8,287	431
Clay	Spencer	16,801	17,585	569
Clayton	Elkader	18,251	19,054	779
Clinton	Clinton	49,782	51,040	695
Crawford	Denison	16,948	16,775	714
Dallas	Adel	54,525	29,755	586
Davis	Bloomfield	8,602	8,312	503
Decatur	Leon	8,656	8,338	532
Delaware	Manchester	17,848	18,035	578
Des Moines	Burlington	40,885	42,614	416
Dickinson	Spirit Lake	16,924	14,909	381
Dubuque	Dubuque	92,384	86,403	608
Emmet	Estherville	10,479	11,569	396
Fayette	West Union	20,996	21,843	731
Floyd	Charles City	16,441	17,058	501
Franklin	Hampton	10,708	11,364	582
Fremont	Sidney	7,737	8,226	511
Greene	Jefferson	9,809	10,045	568
Grundy	Grundy Center	12,320	12,029	503
Guthrie	Guthrie Center	11,344	10,935	591
Hamilton	Webster City	16,087	16,071	577
Hancock	Garner	11,680	12,638	571
Hardin	Eldora	17,791	19,094	569
Harrison	Logan	15,745	14,730	697
Henry	Mount Pleasant	20,405	19,226	434
Howard	Cresco	9,677	9,809	473
Humboldt	Dakota City	9,975	10,756	434
Ida	Ida Grove	7,180	8,365	432
Iowa	Marengo	16,140	14,630	586
Jackson	Maquoketa	20,290	19,950	636
Jasper	Newton	37,409	34,795	730
Jefferson	Fairfield	15,945	16,310	435
Johnson	Iowa City	118,038	96,119	614
Jones	Anamosa	20,505	19,444	575
Keokuk	Sigourney	11,081	11,624	579
Kossuth	Algona	16,011	18,591	973

County	County seat or courthouse	2006 Pop.	1990 Pop.	Land area sq. mi.
Lee	Fort Madison & Keokuk	36,338	38,687	517
Linn	Cedar Rapids	201,853	168,767	717
Louisa	Wapello	11,858	11,592	402
Lucas	Chariton	9,543	9,070	431
Lyon	Rock Rapids	11,636	11,952	588
Madison	Winterset	15,547	12,483	561
Mahaska	Oskaloosa	22,298	21,532	571
Marion	Knoxville	32,987	30,001	554
Marshall	Marshalltown	39,555	38,276	572
Mills	Glenwood	15,595	13,202	437
Mitchell	Osage	10,856	10,928	469
Monona	Onawa	9,343	10,034	693
Monroe	Albia	7,725	8,114	433
Montgomery	Red Oak	11,365	12,076	424
Muscatine	Muscatine	42,883	39,907	439
O'Brien	Primghar	14,409	15,444	573
Osceola	Sibley	6,629	7,267	399
Page	Clarinda	16,263	16,870	535
Palo Alto	Emmetsburg	9,549	10,669	564
Plymouth	Le Mars	24,906	23,388	864
Pocahontas	Pocahontas	7,794	9,525	578
Polk	Des Moines	408,888	327,140	569
Pottawattamie	Council Bluffs	90,218	82,628	954
Poweshiek	Montezuma	19,007	19,033	585
Ringgold	Mount Ayr	5,289	5,420	538
Sac	Sac City	10,682	12,324	576
Scott	Davenport	162,621	150,973	458
Shelby	Harlan	12,489	13,230	591
Sioux	Orange City	32,525	29,903	768
Story	Nevada	80,145	74,252	573
Tama	Toledo	17,890	17,419	721
Taylor	Bedford	6,540	7,114	534
Union	Creston	12,093	12,750	424
Van Buren	Keosauqua	7,836	7,676	485
Wapello	Ottumwa	36,010	35,696	432
Warren	Indianola	43,926	36,033	572
Washington	Washington	21,529	19,612	569
Wayne	Corydon	6,542	7,067	526
Webster	Fort Dodge	38,960	40,342	715
Winnebago	Forest City	11,216	12,122	400
Winneshiek	Decorah	21,263	20,847	690
Woodbury	Sioux City	102,972	98,276	873
Worth	Northwood	7,698	7,991	400
Wright	Clarion	13,419	14,269	581

Kansas
(105 counties, 81,815 sq. mi. land; pop. 2,764,075)

County	County seat or courthouse	2006 Pop.	1990 Pop.	Land area sq. mi.
Allen	Iola	13,677	14,638	503
Anderson	Garnett	8,051	7,803	583
Atchison	Atchison	16,745	16,932	432
Barber	Medicine Lodge	4,974	5,874	1,134
Barton	Great Bend	27,511	29,382	894
Bourbon	Fort Scott	14,950	14,966	637
Brown	Hiawatha	10,236	11,128	571
Butler	El Dorado	63,147	50,580	1,428
Chase	Cottonwood Falls	3,070	3,021	776
Chautauqua	Sedan	3,953	4,407	642
Cherokee	Columbus	21,451	21,374	587
Cheyenne	Saint Francis	2,911	3,243	1,020
Clark	Ashland	2,206	2,418	975
Clay	Clay Center	8,625	9,158	644
Cloud	Concordia	9,594	11,023	716
Coffey	Burlington	8,701	8,404	630
Comanche	Coldwater	1,884	2,313	788
Cowley	Winfield	34,931	36,915	1,126
Crawford	Girard	38,059	35,582	593
Decatur	Oberlin	3,120	4,021	894
Dickinson	Abilene	19,322	18,958	848
Doniphan	Troy	7,865	8,134	392
Douglas	Lawrence	112,123	81,798	457
Edwards	Kinsley	3,138	3,787	622
Elk	Howard	3,077	3,327	647
Ellis	Hays	26,926	26,004	900
Ellsworth	Ellsworth	6,332	6,586	716
Finney	Garden City	39,097	33,070	1,302
Ford	Dodge City	33,783	27,463	1,099
Franklin	Ottawa	26,513	21,994	574
Geary	Junction City	24,174	30,453	385
Gove	Gove	2,721	3,231	1,071
Graham	Hill City	2,677	3,543	898
Grant	Ulysses	7,552	7,159	575
Gray	Cimarron	5,852	5,396	869
Greeley	Tribune	1,331	1,774	778
Greenwood	Eureka	7,067	7,847	1,140
Hamilton	Syracuse	2,594	2,388	996
Harper	Anthony	5,952	7,124	801
Harvey	Newton	33,643	31,028	539
Haskell	Sublette	4,171	3,886	577
Hodgeman	Jetmore	2,071	2,177	860
Jackson	Holton	13,500	11,525	656
Jefferson	Oskaloosa	18,848	15,905	536
Jewell	Mankato	3,324	4,251	909
Johnson	Olathe	516,731	355,021	477
Kearny	Lakin	4,469	4,027	871
Kingman	Kingman	7,975	8,292	863
Kiowa	Greensburg	2,969	3,660	722
Labette	Oswego	22,203	23,693	649
Lane	Dighton	1,797	2,375	717
Leavenworth	Leavenworth	73,628	64,371	463
Lincoln	Lincoln	3,396	3,653	719
Linn	Mound City	9,962	8,254	599
Logan	Oakley	2,675	3,081	1,073
Lyon	Emporia	35,369	34,732	851
McPherson	McPherson	29,380	27,268	900
Marion	Marion	12,760	12,888	943
Marshall	Marysville	10,349	11,705	903
Meade	Meade	4,561	4,247	978
Miami	Paola	30,900	23,466	577
Mitchell	Beloit	6,299	7,203	700
Montgomery	Independence	34,692	38,816	645
Morris	Council Grove	6,046	6,198	697
Morton	Elkhart	3,138	3,480	730
Nemaha	Seneca	10,374	10,446	718
Neosho	Erie	16,298	17,035	572
Ness	Ness City	2,946	4,033	1,075
Norton	Norton	5,584	5,947	878
Osage	Lyndon	16,958	15,248	704
Osborne	Osborne	3,978	4,867	892
Ottawa	Minneapolis	6,168	5,634	721
Pawnee	Larned	6,515	7,555	754
Phillips	Phillipsburg	5,444	6,590	886
Pottawatomie	Westmoreland	19,220	16,128	844
Pratt	Pratt	9,436	9,702	735
Rawlins	Atwood	2,643	3,404	1,070
Reno	Hutchinson	63,706	62,389	1,254
Republic	Belleville	5,033	6,482	716
Rice	Lyons	10,295	10,610	727
Riley	Manhattan	62,527	67,139	610
Rooks	Stockton	5,290	6,039	888
Rush	LaCrosse	3,317	3,842	718
Russell	Russell	6,740	7,835	885
Saline	Salina	54,110	49,301	720
Scott	Scott City	4,643	5,289	718
Sedgwick	Wichita	470,895	403,662	999
Seward	Liberal	23,404	18,743	640
Shawnee	Topeka	172,693	160,976	550
Sheridan	Hoxie	2,600	3,043	895
Sherman	Goodland	5,981	6,926	1,056
Smith	Smith Center	4,024	5,078	895
Stafford	Saint John	4,435	5,365	792
Stanton	Johnson	2,232	2,333	680
Stevens	Hugoton	5,287	5,048	728
Sumner	Wellington	24,441	25,841	1,182
Thomas	Colby	7,468	8,258	1,075
Trego	WaKeeney	2,993	3,694	888
Wabaunsee	Alma	6,895	6,603	797
Wallace	Sharon Springs	1,557	1,821	914
Washington	Washington	5,944	7,073	898
Wichita	Leoti	2,288	2,758	719
Wilson	Fredonia	9,889	10,289	574
Woodson	Yates Center	3,507	4,116	501
Wyandotte	Kansas City	155,509	162,026	151

Kentucky
(120 counties, 39,728 sq. mi. land; pop. 4,206,074)

County	County seat or courthouse	2006 Pop.	1990 Pop.	Land area sq. mi.
Adair	Columbia	17,650	15,360	407
Allen	Scottsville	18,788	14,628	346
Anderson	Lawrenceburg	20,885	14,571	203
Ballard	Wickliffe	8,245	7,902	251
Barren	Glasgow	40,737	34,001	491
Bath	Owingsville	11,707	9,692	279
Bell	Pineville	29,544	31,506	361
Boone	Burlington	110,080	57,589	246
Bourbon	Paris	19,839	19,236	291
Boyd	Catlettsburg	49,371	51,096	160
Boyle	Danville	28,444	25,590	182
Bracken	Brooksville	8,655	7,766	203
Breathitt	Jackson	15,924	15,703	495
Breckinridge	Hardinsburg	19,225	16,312	572
Bullitt	Shepherdsville	72,851	47,567	299
Butler	Morgantown	13,397	11,245	428
Caldwell	Princeton	12,916	13,232	347
Calloway	Murray	35,421	30,735	386
Campbell	Newport	86,866	83,866	152
Carlisle	Bardwell	5,317	5,238	192
Carroll	Carrollton	10,521	9,292	130
Carter	Grayson	27,365	24,340	411
Casey	Liberty	16,326	14,211	446
Christian	Hopkinsville	66,989	68,941	721
Clark	Winchester	35,275	29,496	254
Clay	Manchester	24,052	21,746	471

County	County seat or courthouse	2006 Pop.	1990 Pop.	Land area sq. mi.
Clinton	Albany	9,566	9,135	197
Crittenden	Marion	9,070	9,196	362
Cumberland	Burkesville	7,046	6,784	306
Daviess	Owensboro	93,613	87,189	462
Edmonson	Brownsville	12,054	10,357	303
Elliott	Sandy Hook	7,187	6,455	234
Estill	Irvine	15,163	14,614	254
Fayette	Lexington	270,789	225,366	285
Fleming	Flemingsburg	14,576	12,292	351
Floyd	Prestonsburg	42,282	43,586	394
Franklin	Frankfort	48,183	44,143	210
Fulton	Hickman	6,949	8,271	209
Gallatin	Warsaw	8,153	5,393	99
Garrard	Lancaster	16,933	11,579	231
Grant	Williamstown	24,769	15,737	260
Graves	Mayfield	37,872	33,550	556
Grayson	Leitchfield	25,425	21,050	504
Green	Greensburg	11,641	10,371	289
Greenup	Greenup	37,374	36,796	346
Hancock	Hawesville	8,636	7,864	189
Hardin	Elizabethtown	97,087	89,240	628
Harlan	Harlan	31,692	36,574	467
Harrison	Cynthiana	18,592	16,248	310
Hart	Munfordville	18,547	14,890	416
Henderson	Henderson	45,666	43,044	440
Henry	New Castle	16,025	12,823	289
Hickman	Clinton	4,974	5,566	244
Hopkins	Madisonville	46,830	46,126	551
Jackson	McKee	13,810	11,955	346
Jefferson	Louisville	701,500	665,123	385
Jessamine	Nicholasville	44,790	30,508	173
Johnson	Paintsville	24,188	23,248	262
Kenton	Covington & Independence	154,911	142,005	162
Knott	Hindman	17,536	17,906	352
Knox	Barbourville	32,527	29,676	388
Larue	Hodgenville	13,791	11,679	263
Laurel	London	56,979	43,438	436
Lawrence	Louisa	16,321	13,998	419
Lee	Beattyville	7,648	7,422	210
Leslie	Hyden	11,973	13,642	404
Letcher	Whitesburg	24,520	27,000	339
Lewis	Vanceburg	14,012	13,029	484
Lincoln	Stanford	25,361	20,096	336
Livingston	Smithland	9,797	9,062	316
Logan	Russellville	27,363	24,416	556
Lyon	Eddyville	8,273	6,624	216
McCracken	Paducah	64,950	62,879	251
McCreary	Whitley City	17,354	15,603	428
McLean	Calhoun	9,844	9,628	254
Madison	Richmond	79,015	57,508	441
Magoffin	Salyersville	13,449	13,077	309
Marion	Lebanon	18,979	16,499	346
Marshall	Benton	31,278	27,205	305
Martin	Inez	12,093	12,526	231
Mason	Maysville	17,271	16,666	241
Meade	Brandenburg	27,994	24,170	309
Menifee	Frenchburg	6,788	5,092	204
Mercer	Harrodsburg	21,818	19,148	251
Metcalfe	Edmonton	10,334	8,963	291
Monroe	Tompkinsville	11,771	11,401	331
Montgomery	Mount Sterling	24,887	19,561	199
Morgan	West Liberty	14,306	11,648	381
Muhlenberg	Greenville	31,561	31,318	475
Nelson	Bardstown	42,102	29,710	423
Nicholas	Carlisle	6,958	6,725	197
Ohio	Hartford	23,844	21,105	594
Oldham	La Grange	55,285	33,263	189
Owen	Owenton	11,428	9,035	352
Owsley	Booneville	4,690	5,036	198
Pendleton	Falmouth	15,334	12,062	281
Perry	Hazard	29,753	30,283	342
Pike	Pikeville	66,860	72,584	788
Powell	Stanton	13,825	11,686	180
Pulaski	Somerset	59,749	49,489	662
Robertson	Mount Olivet	2,332	2,124	100
Rockcastle	Mount Vernon	16,857	14,803	318
Rowan	Morehead	22,234	20,353	281
Russell	Jamestown	17,174	14,716	254
Scott	Georgetown	41,605	23,867	285
Shelby	Shelbyville	39,717	24,824	384
Simpson	Franklin	17,180	15,145	236
Spencer	Taylorsville	16,475	6,801	186
Taylor	Campbellsville	23,771	21,146	270
Todd	Elkton	12,101	10,940	376
Trigg	Cadiz	13,399	10,361	443
Trimble	Bedford	9,074	6,090	149
Union	Morganfield	15,371	16,557	345
Warren	Bowling Green	101,266	77,720	545
Washington	Springfield	11,444	10,441	301
Wayne	Monticello	20,504	17,468	459
Webster	Dixon	14,083	13,955	335
Whitley	Williamsburg	38,142	33,326	440
Wolfe	Campton	7,095	6,503	223
Woodford	Versailles	24,386	19,955	191

Louisiana
(64 parishes, 43,562 sq. mi. land; pop. 4,287,768)

Parish	Parish seat or courthouse	2006 Pop.	1990 Pop.	Land area sq. mi.
Acadia	Crowley	60,457	55,882	655
Allen	Oberlin	25,447	21,226	765
Ascension	Donaldsonville	97,335	58,214	292
Assumption	Napoleonville	23,472	22,753	339
Avoyelles	Marksville	42,663	39,159	832
Beauregard	De Ridder	35,130	30,083	1,160
Bienville	Arcadia	15,168	16,232	811
Bossier	Benton	107,270	86,088	839
Caddo	Shreveport	253,118	248,253	882
Calcasieu	Lake Charles	184,524	168,134	1,071
Caldwell	Columbia	10,615	9,806	529
Cameron	Cameron	7,792	9,260	1,313
Catahoula	Harrisonburg	10,567	11,065	704
Claiborne	Homer	16,210	17,405	755
Concordia	Vidalia	19,460	20,828	696
De Soto	Mansfield	26,390	25,668	877
East Baton Rouge	Baton Rouge	429,073	380,105	455
East Carroll	Lake Providence	8,699	9,709	421
East Feliciana	Clinton	20,922	19,211	453
Evangeline	Ville Platte	35,911	33,274	664
Franklin	Winnsboro	20,455	22,387	624
Grant	Colfax	19,879	17,526	645
Iberia	New Iberia	75,509	68,297	575
Iberville	Plaquemine	32,974	31,049	619
Jackson	Jonesboro	15,202	15,859	570
Jefferson	Gretna	431,361	448,306	307
Jefferson Davis	Jennings	31,418	30,722	652
Lafayette	Lafayette	203,091	164,762	270
Lafourche	Thibodaux	93,554	85,860	1,085
La Salle	Jena	14,093	13,662	624
Lincoln	Ruston	41,857	41,745	471
Livingston	Livingston	114,805	70,523	648
Madison	Tallulah	12,328	12,463	624
Morehouse	Bastrop	29,761	31,938	794
Natchitoches	Natchitoches	38,719	37,254	1,255
Orleans	New Orleans	223,388	496,938	181
Ouachita	Monroe	149,259	142,191	611
Plaquemines	Pointe a la Hache	22,512	25,575	845
Pointe Coupee	New Roads	22,648	22,540	557
Rapides	Alexandria	130,201	131,556	1,323
Red River	Coushatta	9,438	9,526	389
Richland	Rayville	20,554	20,629	558
Sabine	Many	23,934	22,646	865
Saint Bernard	Chalmette	15,514	66,631	465
Saint Charles	Hahnville	52,761	42,437	284
Saint Helena	Greensburg	10,759	9,874	408
Saint James	Convent	21,721	20,879	246
Saint John the Baptist	Edgard	48,537	39,996	219
Saint Landry	Opelousas	91,528	80,312	929
Saint Martin	Saint Martinville	51,341	44,097	740
Saint Mary	Franklin	51,867	58,086	613
Saint Tammany	Covington	230,605	144,500	854
Tangipahoa	Amite	113,137	85,709	790
Tensas	Saint Joseph	6,138	7,103	602
Terrebonne	Houma	109,348	96,982	1,255
Union	Farmerville	22,964	20,796	878
Vermilion	Abbeville	56,021	50,055	1,174
Vernon	Leesville	46,748	61,961	1,328
Washington	Franklinton	44,750	43,185	670
Webster	Minden	41,301	41,989	595
West Baton Rouge	Port Allen	22,463	19,419	191
West Carroll	Oak Grove	11,732	12,093	359
West Feliciana	Saint Francisville	15,535	12,915	406
Winn	Winnfield	15,835	16,498	950

Maine
(16 counties, 30,862 sq. mi. land; pop. 1,321,574)

County	County seat or courthouse	2006 Pop.	1990 Pop.	Land area sq. mi.
Androscoggin	Auburn	107,552	105,259	470
Aroostook	Houlton	73,008	86,936	6,672
Cumberland	Portland	274,598	243,135	836
Franklin	Farmington	30,017	29,008	1,698
Hancock	Ellsworth	53,597	46,948	1,588
Kennebec	Augusta	121,068	115,904	868
Knox	Rockland	41,096	36,310	366
Lincoln	Wiscasset	35,234	30,357	456
Oxford	South Paris	57,118	52,602	2,078
Penobscot	Bangor	147,180	146,601	3,396
Piscataquis	Dover-Foxcroft	17,585	18,653	3,966
Sagadahoc	Bath	36,837	33,535	254
Somerset	Skowhegan	52,249	49,767	3,927
Waldo	Belfast	38,715	33,018	730
Washington	Machias	33,288	35,308	2,568
York	Alfred	202,232	164,587	991

Maryland
(23 counties, 1 ind. city, 9,774 sq. mi. land; pop. 5,615,727)

County	County seat or courthouse	2006 Pop.	1990 Pop.	Land area sq. mi.
Allegany	Cumberland	72,831	74,946	425
Anne Arundel	Annapolis	509,300	427,239	416
Baltimore	Towson	787,384	692,134	599
Calvert	Prince Frederick	88,804	51,372	215
Caroline	Denton	32,617	27,035	320
Carroll	Westminster	170,260	123,372	449
Cecil	Elkton	99,506	71,347	348
Charles	La Plata	140,416	101,154	461
Dorchester	Cambridge	31,631	30,236	558
Frederick	Frederick	222,938	150,208	663
Garrett	Oakland	29,859	28,138	648
Harford	Bel Air	241,402	182,132	440
Howard	Ellicott City	272,452	187,328	252
Kent	Chestertown	19,983	17,842	279
Montgomery	Rockville	932,131	762,875	496
Prince George's	Upper Marlboro	841,315	722,705	485
Queen Anne's	Centreville	46,241	33,953	372
Saint Mary's	Leonardtown	98,854	75,974	361
Somerset	Princess Anne	25,774	23,440	327
Talbot	Easton	36,062	30,549	269
Washington	Hagerstown	143,748	121,393	458
Wicomico	Salisbury	91,987	74,339	377
Worcester	Snow Hill	48,866	35,028	473
Independent City				
Baltimore		631,366	736,014	81

Massachusetts
(14 counties, 7,840 sq. mi. land; pop. 6,437,193)

County	County seat or courthouse	2006 Pop.	1990 Pop.	Land area sq. mi.
Barnstable	Barnstable	224,816	186,605	396
Berkshire	Pittsfield	131,117	139,352	931
Bristol	Taunton	545,379	506,325	556
Dukes	Edgartown	15,515	11,639	104
Essex	Salem	735,958	670,080	501
Franklin	Greenfield	72,183	70,086	702
Hampden	Springfield	460,520	456,310	618
Hampshire	Northampton	153,471	146,568	529
Middlesex	East Cambridge	1,467,016	1,398,468	823
Nantucket	Nantucket	10,240	6,012	48
Norfolk	Dedham	654,753	616,087	400
Plymouth	Plymouth	493,623	435,276	661
Suffolk	Boston	687,610	663,906	59
Worcester	Worcester	784,992	709,711	1,513

Michigan
(83 counties, 56,804 sq. mi. land; pop. 10,095,643)

County	County seat or courthouse	2006 Pop.	1990 Pop.	Land area sq. mi.
Alcona	Harrisville	11,759	10,145	674
Alger	Munising	9,665	8,972	918
Allegan	Allegan	113,501	90,509	827
Alpena	Alpena	30,067	30,605	574
Antrim	Bellaire	24,463	18,185	477
Arenac	Standish	17,024	14,906	367
Baraga	L'Anse	8,742	7,954	904
Barry	Hastings	59,899	50,057	556
Bay	Bay City	108,390	111,723	444
Benzie	Beulah	17,652	12,200	321
Berrien	Saint Joseph	161,705	161,378	571
Branch	Coldwater	45,875	41,502	507
Calhoun	Marshall	137,991	135,982	709
Cass	Cassopolis	51,329	49,477	492
Charlevoix	Charlevoix	26,422	21,468	417
Cheboygan	Cheboygan	27,282	21,398	716
Chippewa	Sault Sainte Marie	38,674	34,604	1,561
Clare	Harrison	31,307	24,952	567
Clinton	Saint Johns	69,909	57,893	571
Crawford	Grayling	14,928	12,260	558
Delta	Escanaba	38,156	37,780	1,170
Dickinson	Iron Mountain	27,447	26,831	766
Eaton	Charlotte	107,237	92,879	576
Emmet	Petoskey	33,607	25,040	468
Genesee	Flint	441,966	430,459	640
Gladwin	Gladwin	27,008	21,896	507
Gogebic	Bessemer	16,524	18,052	1,102
Grand Traverse	Traverse City	84,952	64,273	465
Gratiot	Ithaca	42,107	38,982	570
Hillsdale	Hillsdale	47,206	43,431	599
Houghton	Houghton	35,334	35,446	1,012
Huron	Bad Axe	34,143	34,951	837
Ingham	Mason	276,898	281,912	559
Ionia	Ionia	64,821	57,024	573
Iosco	Tawas City	26,831	30,209	549
Iron	Crystal Falls	12,377	13,175	1,166
Isabella	Mount Pleasant	65,818	54,624	574
Jackson	Jackson	163,851	149,756	707
Kalamazoo	Kalamazoo	240,720	223,411	562
Kalkaska	Kalkaska	17,330	13,497	561
Kent	Grand Rapids	599,524	500,631	856
Keweenaw	Eagle River	2,183	1,701	541
Lake	Baldwin	11,793	8,583	567

County	County seat or courthouse	2006 Pop.	1990 Pop.	Land area sq. mi.
Lapeer	Lapeer	93,761	74,768	654
Leelanau	Leland	22,112	16,527	348
Lenawee	Adrian	102,195	91,476	751
Livingston	Howell	184,511	115,645	568
Luce	Newberry	6,684	5,763	903
Mackinac	Saint Ignace	11,050	10,674	1,022
Macomb	Mount Clemens	832,861	717,400	480
Manistee	Manistee	25,067	21,265	544
Marquette	Marquette	64,675	70,887	1,821
Mason	Ludington	29,045	25,537	495
Mecosta	Big Rapids	42,252	37,308	556
Menominee	Menominee	24,698	24,920	1,044
Midland	Midland	83,792	75,651	521
Missaukee	Lake City	15,197	12,147	567
Monroe	Monroe	155,035	133,600	551
Montcalm	Stanton	63,977	53,059	708
Montmorency	Atlanta	10,478	8,936	548
Muskegon	Muskegon	175,231	158,983	509
Newaygo	White Cloud	49,840	38,206	842
Oakland	Pontiac	1,214,255	1,083,592	873
Oceana	Hart	28,639	22,455	540
Ogemaw	West Branch	21,665	18,681	564
Ontonagon	Ontonagon	7,202	8,854	1,312
Osceola	Reed City	23,584	20,146	566
Oscoda	Mio	9,140	7,842	565
Otsego	Gaylord	24,711	17,957	515
Ottawa	Grand Haven	257,671	187,768	566
Presque Isle	Rogers City	14,144	13,743	660
Roscommon	Roscommon	26,064	19,776	521
Saginaw	Saginaw	206,300	211,946	809
Saint Clair	Port Huron	171,725	145,607	724
Saint Joseph	Centreville	62,777	58,913	504
Sanilac	Sandusky	44,448	39,928	964
Schoolcraft	Manistique	8,744	8,302	1,178
Shiawassee	Corunna	72,912	69,770	539
Tuscola	Caro	57,878	55,498	812
Van Buren	Paw Paw	79,018	70,060	611
Washtenaw	Ann Arbor	344,047	282,937	710
Wayne	Detroit	1,971,853	2,111,687	614
Wexford	Cadillac	31,994	26,360	565

Minnesota
(87 counties, 79,610 sq. mi. land; pop. 5,167,101)

County	County seat or courthouse	2006 Pop.	1990 Pop.	Land area sq. mi.
Aitkin	Aitkin	16,149	12,425	1,819
Anoka	Anoka	327,005	243,641	424
Becker	Detroit Lakes	32,230	27,881	1,310
Beltrami	Bemidji	43,169	34,384	2,505
Benton	Foley	38,688	30,185	408
Big Stone	Ortonville	5,510	6,285	497
Blue Earth	Mankato	58,254	54,044	752
Brown	New Ulm	26,361	26,984	611
Carlton	Carlton	34,116	29,259	860
Carver	Chaska	87,545	47,915	357
Cass	Walker	29,036	21,791	2,018
Chippewa	Montevideo	12,721	13,228	583
Chisago	Center City	50,344	30,521	418
Clay	Moorhead	54,476	50,422	1,045
Clearwater	Bagley	8,440	8,309	995
Cook	Grand Marais	5,329	3,868	1,451
Cottonwood	Windom	11,659	12,694	640
Crow Wing	Brainerd	61,009	44,249	997
Dakota	Hastings	388,001	275,210	570
Dodge	Mantorville	19,770	15,731	440
Douglas	Alexandria	35,467	28,674	634
Faribault	Blue Earth	15,283	16,937	714
Fillmore	Preston	21,151	20,777	861
Freeborn	Albert Lea	31,636	33,060	708
Goodhue	Red Wing	45,807	40,690	758
Grant	Elbow Lake	6,078	6,246	546
Hennepin	Minneapolis	1,122,093	1,032,431	557
Houston	Caledonia	19,832	18,497	558
Hubbard	Park Rapids	18,890	14,939	922
Isanti	Cambridge	38,576	25,921	439
Itasca	Grand Rapids	44,729	40,863	2,665
Jackson	Jackson	11,150	11,677	702
Kanabec	Mora	16,276	12,802	525
Kandiyohi	Willmar	41,088	38,761	796
Kittson	Hallock	4,691	5,767	1,097
Koochiching	International Falls	13,658	16,299	3,102
Lac qui Parle	Madison	7,464	8,924	765
Lake	Two Harbors	10,966	10,415	2,099
Lake of the Woods	Baudette	4,327	4,076	1,297
Le Sueur	Le Center	27,895	23,239	449
Lincoln	Ivanhoe	5,963	6,890	537
Lyon	Marshall	24,640	24,789	714
McLeod	Glencoe	37,279	32,030	492
Mahnomen	Mahnomen	5,072	5,044	556
Marshall	Warren	9,951	10,993	1,772
Martin	Fairmont	20,768	22,914	709
Meeker	Litchfield	23,405	20,846	609
Mille Lacs	Milaca	26,169	18,670	574
Morrison	Little Falls	32,919	29,604	1,125
Mower	Austin	38,666	37,385	712

County	County seat or courthouse	2006 Pop.	1990 Pop.	Land area sq. mi.
Murray	Slayton	8,778	9,660	704
Nicollet	Saint Peter	31,313	28,076	452
Nobles	Worthington	20,445	20,098	715
Norman	Ada	6,850	7,975	876
Olmsted	Rochester	137,521	106,470	653
Otter Tail	Fergus Falls	57,817	50,714	1,980
Pennington	Thief River Falls	13,709	13,306	617
Pine	Pine City	28,419	21,264	1,411
Pipestone	Pipestone	9,423	10,491	466
Polk	Crookston	31,088	32,589	1,970
Pope	Glenwood	11,212	10,745	670
Ramsey	Saint Paul	493,215	485,760	156
Red Lake	Red Lake Falls	4,168	4,525	432
Redwood	Redwood Falls	15,791	17,254	880
Renville	Olivia	16,531	17,673	983
Rice	Faribault	61,980	49,183	498
Rock	Luverne	9,535	9,806	483
Roseau	Roseau	16,201	15,026	1,663
Saint Louis	Duluth	196,067	198,232	6,225
Scott	Shakopee	124,092	57,846	357
Sherburne	Elk River	84,995	41,945	436
Sibley	Gaylord	15,126	14,366	589
Stearns	Saint Cloud	144,096	119,324	1,345
Steele	Owatonna	36,221	30,729	430
Stevens	Morris	9,827	10,634	562
Swift	Benson	10,307	10,724	744
Todd	Long Prairie	24,375	23,363	942
Traverse	Wheaton	3,799	4,463	574
Wabasha	Wabasha	22,282	19,744	525
Wadena	Wadena	13,445	13,154	535
Waseca	Waseca	19,469	18,079	423
Washington	Stillwater	225,000	145,860	392
Watonwan	Saint James	11,164	11,682	435
Wilkin	Breckenridge	6,634	7,516	751
Winona	Winona	49,288	47,828	626
Wright	Buffalo	114,787	68,710	661
Yellow Medicine	Granite Falls	10,430	11,684	758

Mississippi
(82 counties, 46,907 sq. mi. land; pop. 2,910,540)

County	County seat or courthouse	2006 Pop.	1990 Pop.	Land area sq. mi.
Adams	Natchez	32,626	35,356	460
Alcorn	Corinth	35,589	31,722	400
Amite	Liberty	13,466	13,328	730
Attala	Kosciusko	19,644	18,481	735
Benton	Ashland	7,873	8,046	407
Bolivar	Cleveland & Rosedale	38,352	41,875	876
Calhoun	Pittsboro	14,647	14,908	587
Carroll	Carrollton & Vaiden	10,326	9,237	628
Chickasaw	Houston & Okolona	18,998	18,085	502
Choctaw	Ackerman	9,401	9,071	419
Claiborne	Port Gibson	11,487	11,370	487
Clarke	Quitman	17,631	17,313	691
Clay	West Point	21,210	21,120	409
Coahoma	Clarksdale	28,420	31,665	554
Copiah	Hazlehurst	29,223	27,592	777
Covington	Collins	20,447	16,527	414
De Soto	Hernando	144,706	67,910	478
Forrest	Hattiesburg	76,372	68,314	467
Franklin	Meadville	8,269	8,377	565
George	Lucedale	21,828	16,673	478
Greene	Leakesville	13,103	10,220	713
Grenada	Grenada	22,861	21,555	422
Hancock	Bay Saint Louis	40,421	31,760	477
Harrison	Gulfport	171,875	165,365	581
Hinds	Jackson & Raymond	249,012	254,441	869
Holmes	Lexington	20,866	21,604	756
Humphreys	Belzoni	10,393	12,134	418
Issaquena	Mayersville	1,805	1,909	413
Itawamba	Fulton	23,352	20,017	532
Jackson	Pascagoula	130,577	115,243	727
Jasper	Bay Springs & Paulding	18,197	17,114	676
Jefferson	Fayette	9,194	8,653	519
Jefferson Davis	Prentiss	13,184	14,051	408
Jones	Ellisville & Laurel	66,715	62,031	694
Kemper	De Kalb	10,108	10,356	766
Lafayette	Oxford	40,865	31,826	631
Lamar	Purvis	46,240	30,424	497
Lauderdale	Meridian	76,724	75,555	704
Lawrence	Monticello	13,457	12,458	431
Leake	Carthage	22,769	18,436	583
Lee	Tupelo	79,714	65,579	450
Leflore	Greenwood	35,752	37,341	592
Lincoln	Brookhaven	34,404	30,278	586
Lowndes	Columbus	59,773	59,308	502
Madison	Canton	87,419	53,794	717
Marion	Columbia	25,730	25,544	542
Marshall	Holly Springs	35,853	30,361	706
Monroe	Aberdeen	37,572	36,582	764
Montgomery	Winona	11,754	12,387	407
Neshoba	Philadelphia	30,125	24,800	570
Newton	Decatur	22,413	20,291	578
Noxubee	Macon	12,051	12,604	695
Oktibbeha	Starkville	41,633	38,375	458
Panola	Batesville & Sardis	35,427	29,996	684
Pearl River	Poplarville	57,099	38,714	811
Perry	New Augusta	12,132	10,865	647
Pike	Magnolia	40,240	36,882	409
Pontotoc	Pontotoc	28,887	22,237	497
Prentiss	Booneville	25,615	23,278	415
Quitman	Marks	9,289	10,490	405
Rankin	Brandon	135,830	87,161	775
Scott	Forest	28,790	24,137	609
Sharkey	Rolling Fork	5,851	7,066	428
Simpson	Mendenhall	27,972	23,953	589
Smith	Raleigh	15,970	14,798	636
Stone	Wiggins	15,608	10,750	445
Sunflower	Indianola	31,833	35,129	694
Tallahatchie	Charleston & Sumner	13,798	15,210	644
Tate	Senatobia	26,723	21,432	404
Tippah	Ripley	21,248	19,523	458
Tishomingo	Iuka	19,112	17,683	424
Tunica	Tunica	10,419	8,164	455
Union	New Albany	27,008	22,085	415
Walthall	Tylertown	15,543	14,352	404
Warren	Vicksburg	49,308	47,880	587
Washington	Greenville	58,007	67,935	724
Wayne	Waynesboro	21,087	19,517	810
Webster	Walthall	10,041	10,222	422
Wilkinson	Woodville	10,239	9,678	677
Winston	Louisville	19,708	19,433	607
Yalobusha	Coffeeville & Water Valley	13,401	12,033	467
Yazoo	Yazoo City	27,929	25,506	919

Missouri
(114 counties, 1 ind. city, 68,886 sq. mi. land; pop. 5,842,713)

County	County seat or courthouse	2006 Pop.	1990 Pop.	Land area sq. mi.
Adair	Kirksville	24,461	24,577	567
Andrew	Savannah	17,117	14,632	435
Atchison	Rockport	6,132	7,457	545
Audrain	Mexico	25,739	23,599	693
Barry	Cassville	36,404	27,547	779
Barton	Lamar	13,015	11,312	594
Bates	Butler	17,116	15,025	848
Benton	Warsaw	18,728	13,859	706
Bollinger	Marble Hill	12,323	10,619	621
Boone	Columbia	146,048	112,379	685
Buchanan	Saint Joseph	84,955	83,083	410
Butler	Poplar Buff	41,582	38,765	698
Caldwell	Kingston	9,313	8,380	429
Callaway	Fulton	43,072	32,809	839
Camden	Camdenton	40,283	27,495	655
Cape Girardeau	Jackson	71,892	61,633	579
Carroll	Carrollton	10,058	10,748	695
Carter	Van Buren	5,956	5,515	508
Cass	Harrisonville	95,781	63,808	699
Cedar	Stockton	13,998	12,093	476
Chariton	Keytesville	8,046	9,202	752
Christian	Ozark	70,514	32,644	563
Clark	Kahoka	7,305	7,547	507
Clay	Liberty	206,957	153,411	396
Clinton	Plattsburg	20,671	16,595	419
Cole	Jefferson City	73,296	63,579	391
Cooper	Boonville	17,441	14,835	565
Crawford	Steelville	24,009	19,173	743
Dade	Greenfield	7,804	7,449	490
Dallas	Buffalo	16,696	12,646	542
Daviess	Gallatin	8,072	7,865	567
De Kalb	Maysville	12,309	9,967	424
Dent	Salem	15,276	13,702	754
Douglas	Ava	13,658	11,876	815
Dunklin	Kennett	32,277	33,112	546
Franklin	Union	100,067	80,603	923
Gasconade	Hermann	15,634	14,006	521
Gentry	Albany	6,389	6,854	492
Greene	Springfield	254,779	207,949	675
Grundy	Trenton	10,239	10,536	436
Harrison	Bethany	8,898	8,469	725
Henry	Clinton	22,719	20,044	702
Hickory	Hermitage	9,243	7,335	399
Holt	Oregon	4,997	6,034	462
Howard	Fayette	9,949	9,631	466
Howell	West Plains	38,734	31,447	928
Iron	Ironton	10,279	10,726	551
Jackson	Independence	664,078	633,234	605
Jasper	Carthage	112,505	90,465	640
Jefferson	Hillsboro	216,469	171,380	657
Johnson	Warrensburg	50,646	42,514	830
Knox	Edina	4,093	4,482	506
Laclede	Lebanon	35,091	27,158	766
Lafayette	Lexington	33,186	31,107	629
Lawrence	Mount Vernon	37,400	30,236	613
Lewis	Monticello	10,152	10,233	505
Lincoln	Troy	50,123	28,892	630
Linn	Linneus	12,865	13,885	620

County	County seat or courthouse	2006 Pop.	1990 Pop.	Land area sq. mi.
Livingston	Chillicothe	14,291	14,592	535
McDonald	Pineville	22,949	16,938	540
Macon	Macon	15,651	15,345	804
Madison	Fredericktown	12,109	11,127	497
Maries	Vienna	9,099	7,976	528
Marion	Palmyra	28,425	27,682	438
Mercer	Princeton	3,584	3,723	454
Miller	Tuscumbia	24,989	20,700	592
Mississippi	Charleston	13,770	14,442	413
Moniteau	California	15,092	12,298	417
Monroe	Paris	9,396	9,104	646
Montgomery	Montgomery City	12,170	11,355	537
Morgan	Versailles	20,716	15,574	597
New Madrid	New Madrid	18,314	20,928	678
Newton	Neosho	56,047	44,445	626
Nodaway	Maryville	21,660	21,709	877
Oregon	Alton	10,407	9,470	791
Osage	Linn	13,498	12,018	606
Ozark	Gainesville	9,393	8,598	742
Pemiscot	Caruthersville	19,163	21,921	493
Perry	Perryville	18,639	16,648	475
Pettis	Sedalia	40,520	35,437	685
Phelps	Rolla	42,289	35,248	673
Pike	Bowling Green	18,566	15,969	673
Platte	Platte City	83,061	57,867	420
Polk	Bolivar	29,596	21,826	637
Pulaski	Waynesville	44,022	41,307	547
Putnam	Unionville	5,153	5,079	518
Ralls	New London	9,925	8,476	471
Randolph	Huntsville	25,438	24,370	482
Ray	Richmond	23,999	21,968	569
Reynolds	Centerville	6,547	6,661	811
Ripley	Doniphan	13,937	12,303	629
Saint Charles	Saint Charles	338,719	212,751	560
Saint Clair	Osceola	9,589	8,457	677
Sainte Genevieve	Sainte Genevieve	18,248	16,037	502
Saint Francois	Farmington	62,181	48,904	449
Saint Louis	Clayton	1,000,510	993,508	508
Saline	Marshall	22,896	23,523	756
Schuyler	Lancaster	4,271	4,236	308
Scotland	Memphis	4,922	4,822	438
Scott	Benton	41,068	39,376	421
Shannon	Eminence	8,503	7,613	1,004
Shelby	Shelbyville	6,645	6,942	501
Stoddard	Bloomfield	29,754	28,895	827
Stone	Galena	31,382	19,078	463
Sullivan	Milan	6,785	6,326	651
Taney	Forsyth	43,770	25,561	632
Texas	Houston	23,566	21,476	1,179
Vernon	Nevada	20,455	19,041	834
Warren	Warrenton	29,685	19,534	431
Washington	Potosi	24,182	20,380	760
Wayne	Greenville	12,997	11,543	761
Webster	Marshfield	35,507	23,753	593
Worth	Grant City	2,186	2,440	267
Wright	Hartville	18,397	16,758	682

Independent City

County	County seat or courthouse	2006 Pop.	1990 Pop.	Land area sq. mi.
Saint Louis		347,181	396,685	62

Montana
(56 counties, 145,552 sq. mi. land; pop. 944,632)

County	County seat or courthouse	2006 Pop.	1990 Pop.	Land area sq. mi.
Beaverhead	Dillon	8,743	8,424	5,542
Big Horn	Hardin	13,035	11,337	4,995
Blaine	Chinook	6,615	6,728	4,226
Broadwater	Townsend	4,572	3,318	1,191
Carbon	Red Lodge	9,903	8,080	2,048
Carter	Ekalaka	1,321	1,503	3,340
Cascade	Great Falls	79,385	77,691	2,698
Chouteau	Fort Benton	5,417	5,452	3,973
Custer	Miles City	11,151	11,697	3,783
Daniels	Scobey	1,774	2,266	1,426
Dawson	Glendive	8,624	9,505	2,373
Deer Lodge	Anaconda	8,888	10,356	737
Fallon	Baker	2,777	3,103	1,620
Fergus	Lewistown	11,496	12,083	4,339
Flathead	Kalispell	85,314	59,218	5,098
Gallatin	Bozeman	80,921	50,484	2,606
Garfield	Jordan	1,244	1,589	4,668
Glacier	Cut Bank	13,578	12,121	2,995
Golden Valley	Ryegate	1,150	912	1,175
Granite	Philipsburg	2,909	2,548	1,727
Hill	Havre	16,403	17,654	2,896
Jefferson	Boulder	11,256	7,939	1,657
Judith Basin	Stanford	2,142	2,282	1,870
Lake	Polson	28,606	21,041	1,494
Lewis & Clark	Helena	59,302	47,495	3,461
Liberty	Chester	1,863	2,295	1,430
Lincoln	Libby	19,226	17,481	3,613
McCone	Circle	1,760	2,276	2,643
Madison	Virginia City	7,404	5,989	3,587
Meagher	White Sulphur Springs	1,968	1,819	2,392
Mineral	Superior	4,057	3,315	1,220
Missoula	Missoula	101,417	78,687	2,598
Musselshell	Roundup	4,586	4,106	1,867
Park	Livingston	16,084	14,515	2,802
Petroleum	Winnett	474	519	1,654
Phillips	Malta	4,098	5,163	5,140
Pondera	Conrad	6,032	6,433	1,625
Powder River	Broadus	1,756	2,090	3,297
Powell	Deer Lodge	6,997	6,620	2,326
Prairie	Terry	1,074	1,383	1,737
Ravalli	Hamilton	40,582	25,010	2,394
Richland	Sidney	9,295	10,716	2,084
Roosevelt	Wolf Point	10,496	10,999	2,356
Rosebud	Forsyth	9,261	10,505	5,012
Sanders	Thompson Falls	11,138	8,669	2,762
Sheridan	Plentywood	3,447	4,732	1,677
Silver Bow	Butte	32,801	33,941	718
Stillwater	Columbus	8,646	6,536	1,795
Sweet Grass	Big Timber	3,760	3,154	1,855
Teton	Choteau	6,115	6,271	2,273
Toole	Shelby	5,073	5,046	1,911
Treasure	Hysham	680	874	979
Valley	Glasgow	6,995	8,239	4,921
Wheatland	Harlowton	1,959	2,246	1,423
Wibaux	Wibaux	909	1,191	889
Yellowstone	Billings	138,213	113,419	2,635

Nebraska
(93 counties, 76,872 sq. mi. land; pop. 1,768,331)

County	County seat or courthouse	2006 Pop.	1990 Pop.	Land area sq. mi.
Adams	Hastings	33,185	29,625	563
Antelope	Neligh	6,931	7,965	857
Arthur	Arthur	372	462	715
Banner	Harrisburg	783	852	746
Blaine	Brewster	492	675	711
Boone	Albion	5,668	6,667	687
Box Butte	Alliance	11,132	13,130	1,075
Boyd	Butte	2,185	2,835	540
Brown	Ainsworth	3,354	3,657	1,221
Buffalo	Kearney	43,954	37,447	968
Burt	Tekamah	7,341	7,868	493
Butler	David City	8,595	8,601	584
Cass	Plattsmouth	25,963	21,318	559
Cedar	Hartington	8,819	10,131	740
Chase	Imperial	3,811	4,381	895
Cherry	Valentine	5,934	6,307	5,961
Cheyenne	Sidney	9,865	9,494	1,196
Clay	Clay Center	6,564	7,123	573
Colfax	Schuyler	10,113	9,139	413
Cuming	West Point	9,660	10,117	572
Custer	Broken Bow	11,242	12,270	2,576
Dakota	Dakota City	20,587	16,742	264
Dawes	Chadron	8,466	9,021	1,396
Dawson	Lexington	25,018	19,940	1,013
Deuel	Chappell	1,958	2,237	440
Dixon	Ponca	6,170	6,143	476
Dodge	Fremont	36,171	34,500	534
Douglas	Omaha	492,003	416,444	331
Dundy	Benkelman	2,109	2,582	920
Fillmore	Geneva	6,259	7,103	576
Franklin	Franklin	3,348	3,938	575
Frontier	Stockville	2,729	3,101	975
Furnas	Beaver City	5,003	5,553	718
Gage	Beatrice	23,365	22,794	855
Garden	Oshkosh	1,995	2,460	1,704
Garfield	Burwell	1,790	2,141	570
Gosper	Elwood	1,978	1,928	458
Grant	Hyannis	660	769	776
Greeley	Greeley	2,454	3,006	569
Hall	Grand Island	55,555	48,925	546
Hamilton	Aurora	9,490	8,862	544
Harlan	Alma	3,446	3,810	553
Hayes	Hayes Center	1,029	1,222	713
Hitchcock	Trenton	2,926	3,750	710
Holt	O'Neill	10,610	12,599	2,413
Hooker	Mullen	756	793	721
Howard	Saint Paul	6,736	6,057	569
Jefferson	Fairbury	7,874	8,759	573
Johnson	Tecumseh	4,683	4,673	376
Kearney	Minden	6,701	6,629	516
Keith	Ogallala	8,250	8,584	1,061
Keya Paha	Springview	892	1,029	773
Kimball	Kimball	3,710	4,108	952
Knox	Center	8,812	9,564	1,108
Lancaster	Lincoln	267,135	213,641	839
Lincoln	North Platte	35,865	32,508	2,564
Logan	Stapleton	749	878	571
Loup	Taylor	656	683	570
McPherson	Tryon	497	546	859
Madison	Madison	35,279	32,655	573
Merrick	Central City	7,954	8,062	485
Morrill	Bridgeport	5,171	5,423	1,424
Nance	Fullerton	3,705	4,275	441
Nemaha	Auburn	7,247	7,980	409
Nuckolls	Nelson	4,650	5,786	575
Otoe	Nebraska City	15,747	14,252	616

County	County seat or courthouse	2006 Pop.	1990 Pop.	Land area sq. mi.
Pawnee	Pawnee City	2,804	3,317	432
Perkins	Grant	2,992	3,367	883
Phelps	Holdrege	9,442	9,715	540
Pierce	Pierce	7,564	7,827	574
Platte	Columbus	31,962	29,820	678
Polk	Osceola	5,349	5,655	439
Red Willow	McCook	10,865	11,705	717
Richardson	Falls City	8,656	9,937	553
Rock	Bassett	1,544	2,019	1,008
Saline	Wilber	14,155	12,715	575
Sarpy	Papillion	142,637	102,583	241
Saunders	Wahoo	20,344	18,285	754
Scotts Bluff	Gering	36,546	36,025	739
Seward	Seward	16,835	15,450	575
Sheridan	Rushville	5,571	6,750	2,441
Sherman	Loup City	3,083	3,718	566
Sioux	Harrison	1,403	1,549	2,067
Stanton	Stanton	6,570	6,244	430
Thayer	Hebron	5,317	6,635	575
Thomas	Thedford	629	851	713
Thurston	Pender	7,273	6,936	394
Valley	Ord	4,373	5,169	568
Washington	Blair	20,044	16,607	390
Wayne	Wayne	9,196	9,364	443
Webster	Red Cloud	3,701	4,279	575
Wheeler	Bartlett	823	948	575
York	York	14,502	14,428	576

Nevada

(16 counties, 1 ind. city, 109,826 sq. mi. land; pop. 2,495,529)

County	County seat or courthouse	2006 Pop.	1990 Pop.	Land area sq. mi.
Churchill	Fallon	25,036	17,938	4,929
Clark	Las Vegas	1,777,539	741,368	7,910
Douglas	Minden	45,909	27,637	710
Elko	Elko	47,114	33,463	17,179
Esmeralda	Goldfield	790	1,344	3,589
Eureka	Eureka	1,480	1,547	4,176
Humboldt	Winnemucca	17,446	12,844	9,648
Lander	Battle Mountain	5,272	6,266	5,494
Lincoln	Pioche	4,738	3,775	10,634
Lyon	Yerington	51,231	20,001	1,994
Mineral	Hawthorne	4,868	6,475	3,756
Nye	Tonopah	42,693	17,781	18,147
Pershing	Lovelock	6,414	4,336	6,037
Storey	Virginia City	4,132	2,526	263
Washoe	Reno	396,428	254,667	6,342
White Pine	Ely	9,150	9,264	8,876
Independent City				
Carson City		55,289	40,443	143

New Hampshire

(10 counties, 8,968 sq. mi. land; pop. 1,314,895)

County	County seat or courthouse	2006 Pop.	1990 Pop.	Land area sq. mi.
Belknap	Laconia	61,562	49,216	401
Carroll	Ossipee	47,475	35,410	934
Cheshire	Keene	77,393	70,121	707
Coos	Lancaster	33,019	34,828	1,800
Grafton	North Haverhill	85,336	74,929	1,713
Hillsborough	Nashua	402,789	335,838	876
Merrimack	Concord	148,085	120,240	934
Rockingham	Brentwood	296,267	245,845	695
Strafford	Dover	119,990	104,233	369
Sullivan	Newport	42,979	38,592	537

New Jersey

(21 counties, 7,417 sq. mi. land; pop. 8,724,560)

County	County seat or courthouse	2006 Pop.	1990 Pop.	Land area sq. mi.
Atlantic	Mays Landing	271,620	224,327	561
Bergen	Hackensack	904,037	825,380	234
Burlington	Mount Holly	450,627	395,066	805
Camden	Camden	517,001	502,824	222
Cape May	Cape May Court House	97,724	95,089	255
Cumberland	Bridgeton	154,823	138,053	489
Essex	Newark	786,147	777,964	126
Gloucester	Woodbury	282,031	230,082	325
Hudson	Jersey City	601,146	553,099	47
Hunterdon	Flemington	130,783	107,852	430
Mercer	Trenton	367,605	325,759	226
Middlesex	New Brunswick	786,971	671,712	310
Monmouth	Freehold	635,285	553,192	472
Morris	Morristown	493,160	421,330	469
Ocean	Toms River	562,335	433,203	636
Passaic	Paterson	497,093	470,872	185
Salem	Salem	66,595	65,294	338
Somerset	Somerville	324,186	240,222	305
Sussex	Newton	153,384	130,936	521
Union	Elizabeth	531,088	493,819	103
Warren	Belvidere	110,919	91,675	358

New Mexico

(33 counties, 121,356 sq. mi. land; pop. 1,954,599)

County	County seat or courthouse	2006 Pop.	1990 Pop.	Land area sq. mi.
Bernalillo	Albuquerque	615,099	480,577	1,166
Catron	Reserve	3,476	2,563	6,928
Chaves	Roswell	62,474	57,849	6,071
Cibola	Grants	27,481	23,794	4,539
Colfax	Raton	13,514	12,925	3,757
Curry	Clovis	45,513	42,207	1,406
DeBaca	Fort Sumner	1,991	2,252	2,325
Dona Ana	Las Cruces	193,888	135,510	3,807
Eddy	Carlsbad	51,815	48,605	4,182
Grant	Silver City	29,792	27,676	3,966
Guadalupe	Santa Rosa	4,365	4,156	3,030
Harding	Mosquero	718	987	2,125
Hidalgo	Lordsburg	5,087	5,958	3,446
Lea	Lovington	57,312	55,765	4,393
Lincoln	Carrizozo	21,223	12,219	4,831
Los Alamos	Los Alamos	19,022	18,115	109
Luna	Deming	27,205	18,110	2,965
McKinley	Gallup	71,875	60,686	5,449
Mora	Mora	5,151	4,264	1,931
Otero	Alamogordo	62,744	51,928	6,627
Quay	Tucumcari	9,155	10,823	2,875
Rio Arriba	Tierra Amarilla	40,949	34,365	5,858
Roosevelt	Portales	18,291	16,702	2,449
Sandoval	Bernalillo	113,772	63,319	3,709
San Juan	Aztec	126,473	91,605	5,514
San Miguel	Las Vegas	29,325	25,743	4,717
Santa Fe	Santa Fe	142,407	98,928	1,909
Sierra	Truth or Consequences	12,669	9,912	4,180
Socorro	Socorro	18,240	14,764	6,646
Taos	Taos	31,832	23,118	2,203
Torrance	Estancia	17,551	10,285	3,345
Union	Clayton	3,801	4,124	3,830
Valencia	Los Lunas	70,389	45,235	1,068

New York

(62 counties, 47,214 sq. mi. land; pop. 19,306,183)

County	County seat or courthouse	2006 Pop.	1990 Pop.	Land area sq. mi.
Albany	Albany	297,556	292,812	523
Allegany	Belmont	50,267	50,470	1,030
Bronx[1]	Bronx	1,361,473	1,203,789	42
Broome	Binghamton	196,269	212,160	707
Cattaraugus	Little Valley	81,534	84,234	1,310
Cayuga	Auburn	81,243	82,313	693
Chautauqua	Mayville	135,357	141,895	1,062
Chemung	Elmira	88,641	95,195	408
Chenango	Norwich	51,787	51,768	894
Clinton	Plattsburgh	82,166	85,969	1,039
Columbia	Hudson	62,955	62,982	636
Cortland	Cortland	48,483	48,963	500
Delaware	Delhi	46,977	47,352	1,446
Dutchess	Poughkeepsie	295,146	259,462	802
Erie	Buffalo	921,390	968,584	1,044
Essex	Elizabethtown	38,649	37,152	1,797
Franklin	Malone	50,968	46,540	1,631
Fulton	Johnstown	55,435	54,191	496
Genesee	Batavia	58,830	60,060	494
Greene	Catskill	49,822	44,739	648
Hamilton	Lake Pleasant	5,162	5,279	1,720
Herkimer	Herkimer	63,332	65,809	1,411
Jefferson	Watertown	114,264	110,943	1,272
Kings[1]	Brooklyn	2,508,820	2,300,664	71
Lewis	Lowville	26,685	26,796	1,275
Livingston	Geneseo	64,173	62,372	632
Madison	Wampsville	70,197	69,166	656
Monroe	Rochester	730,807	713,968	659
Montgomery	Fonda	49,112	51,981	405
Nassau	Mineola	1,325,662	1,287,873	287
New York[1]	New York	1,611,581	1,487,536	23
Niagara	Lockport	216,130	220,756	523
Oneida	Utica	233,954	250,836	1,213
Onondaga	Syracuse	456,777	468,973	780
Ontario	Canandaigua	104,353	95,101	644
Orange	Goshen	376,392	307,571	816
Orleans	Albion	43,213	41,846	391
Oswego	Oswego	123,077	121,785	953
Otsego	Cooperstown	62,583	60,390	1,003
Putnam	Carmel	100,603	83,941	231
Queens[1]	Jamaica	2,255,175	1,951,598	109
Rensselaer	Troy	155,292	154,429	654
Richmond[1]	Saint George	477,377	378,977	58
Rockland	New City	294,965	265,475	174
Saint Lawrence	Canton	111,284	111,974	2,686
Saratoga	Ballston Spa	215,473	181,276	812
Schenectady	Schenectady	150,440	149,285	206
Schoharie	Schoharie	32,196	31,840	622
Schuyler	Watkins Glen	19,415	18,662	329
Seneca	Waterloo	34,724	33,683	325
Steuben	Bath	98,236	99,088	1,393
Suffolk	Riverhead	1,469,715	1,321,339	912
Sullivan	Monticello	76,588	69,277	970
Tioga	Owego	51,285	52,337	519

County	County seat or courthouse	2006 Pop.	1990 Pop.	Land area sq. mi.
Tompkins	Ithaca	100,407	94,097	476
Ulster	Kingston	182,742	165,380	1,126
Warren	Lake George	66,087	59,209	869
Washington	Hudson Falls	63,368	59,330	835
Wayne	Lyons	92,889	89,123	604
Westchester	White Plains	949,355	874,866	433
Wyoming	Warsaw	42,613	42,507	593
Yates	Penn Yan	24,732	22,810	338

(1) New York City comprises 5 counties: Bronx, Kings (Brooklyn), New York (Manhattan), Queens, and Richmond (Staten Island).

North Carolina
(100 counties, 48,711 sq. mi. land; pop. 8,856,505)

County	County seat or courthouse	2006 Pop.	1990 Pop.	Land area sq. mi.
Alamance	Graham	142,661	108,213	430
Alexander	Taylorsville	36,177	27,544	260
Alleghany	Sparta	10,912	9,590	235
Anson	Wadesboro	25,472	23,474	532
Ashe	Jefferson	25,499	22,209	426
Avery	Newland	17,674	14,867	247
Beaufort	Washington	46,355	42,283	828
Bertie	Windsor	19,094	20,388	699
Bladen	Elizabethtown	32,921	28,663	875
Brunswick	Bolivia	94,945	50,985	855
Buncombe	Asheville	222,174	174,357	656
Burke	Morganton	90,054	75,740	507
Cabarrus	Concord	156,395	98,935	364
Caldwell	Lenoir	79,841	70,709	472
Camden	Camden	9,271	5,904	241
Carteret	Beaufort	63,584	52,407	520
Caswell	Yanceyville	23,546	20,662	425
Catawba	Newton	153,784	118,412	400
Chatham	Pittsboro	60,052	38,979	683
Cherokee	Murphy	26,309	20,170	455
Chowan	Edenton	14,695	13,506	173
Clay	Hayesville	10,008	7,155	215
Cleveland	Shelby	98,373	84,958	465
Columbus	Whiteville	54,637	49,587	935
Craven	New Bern	94,875	81,812	708
Cumberland	Fayetteville	299,060	274,713	653
Currituck	Currituck	23,770	13,736	262
Dare	Manteo	33,935	22,746	384
Davidson	Lexington	156,236	126,688	552
Davie	Mocksville	40,035	27,859	265
Duplin	Kenansville	52,790	39,995	818
Durham	Durham	246,896	181,844	290
Edgecombe	Tarboro	53,964	56,692	505
Forsyth	Winston-Salem	332,355	265,855	410
Franklin	Louisburg	55,886	36,414	492
Gaston	Gastonia	199,397	174,769	356
Gates	Gatesville	11,527	9,305	341
Graham	Robbinsville	7,995	7,196	292
Granville	Oxford	54,473	38,341	531
Greene	Snow Hill	20,157	15,384	265
Guilford	Greensboro	451,905	347,431	649
Halifax	Halifax	55,521	55,516	725
Harnett	Lillington	106,283	67,833	595
Haywood	Waynesville	56,447	46,948	554
Henderson	Hendersonville	99,033	69,747	374
Hertford	Winton	23,581	22,317	353
Hoke	Raeford	42,303	22,856	391
Hyde	Swan Quarter	5,341	5,411	613
Iredell	Statesville	146,206	93,205	576
Jackson	Sylva	35,562	26,835	491
Johnston	Smithfield	152,143	81,306	792
Jones	Trenton	10,204	9,361	472
Lee	Sanford	56,908	41,370	257
Lenoir	Kinston	57,662	57,274	400
Lincoln	Lincolnton	71,894	50,319	299
McDowell	Marion	43,414	35,681	442
Macon	Franklin	32,395	23,504	516
Madison	Marshall	20,355	16,953	449
Martin	Williamston	24,342	25,078	461
Mecklenburg	Charlotte	827,445	511,211	526
Mitchell	Bakersville	15,681	14,433	221
Montgomery	Troy	27,638	23,359	492
Moore	Carthage	83,162	59,000	698
Nash	Nashville	92,312	76,677	540
New Hanover	Wilmington	182,591	120,284	199
Northampton	Jackson	21,247	21,004	536
Onslow	Jacksonville	150,673	149,838	767
Orange	Hillsborough	120,100	93,662	400
Pamlico	Bayboro	12,785	11,368	337
Pasquotank	Elizabeth City	39,591	31,298	227
Pender	Burgaw	48,630	28,855	871
Perquimans	Hertford	12,337	10,447	247
Person	Roxboro	37,341	30,180	392
Pitt	Greenville	145,619	108,480	652
Polk	Columbus	19,226	14,458	238
Randolph	Asheboro	140,410	106,546	787
Richmond	Rockingham	46,555	44,511	474
Robeson	Lumberton	129,021	105,170	949
Rockingham	Wentworth	93,063	86,064	566
Rowan	Salisbury	136,254	110,605	511
Rutherford	Rutherfordton	63,867	56,956	564

County	County seat or courthouse	2006 Pop.	1990 Pop.	Land area sq. mi.
Sampson	Clinton	63,561	47,297	945
Scotland	Laurinburg	37,094	33,763	319
Stanly	Albemarle	59,358	51,765	395
Stokes	Danbury	46,168	37,224	452
Surry	Dobson	72,687	61,704	537
Swain	Bryson City	13,445	11,268	528
Transylvania	Brevard	29,780	25,520	378
Tyrrell	Columbia	4,187	3,856	390
Union	Monroe	175,272	84,210	637
Vance	Henderson	43,810	38,892	254
Wake	Raleigh	786,522	426,311	832
Warren	Warrenton	19,605	17,265	429
Washington	Plymouth	13,227	13,997	348
Watauga	Boone	42,700	36,952	313
Wayne	Goldsboro	113,847	104,666	553
Wilkes	Wilkesboro	67,310	59,393	757
Wilson	Wilson	76,624	66,061	371
Yadkin	Yadkinville	38,056	30,488	336
Yancey	Burnsville	18,421	15,419	312

North Dakota
(53 counties, 68,976 sq. mi. land; pop. 635,867)

County	County seat or courthouse	2006 Pop.	1990 Pop.	Land area sq. mi.
Adams	Hettinger	2,332	3,174	988
Barnes	Valley City	10,955	12,545	1,492
Benson	Minnewaukan	6,997	7,198	1,381
Billings	Medora	829	1,108	1,151
Bottineau	Bottineau	6,650	8,011	1,669
Bowman	Bowman	2,991	3,596	1,162
Burke	Bowbells	1,947	3,002	1,104
Burleigh	Bismarck	75,384	60,131	1,633
Cass	Fargo	132,525	102,874	1,765
Cavalier	Langdon	4,099	6,064	1,488
Dickey	Ellendale	5,398	6,107	1,131
Divide	Crosby	2,092	2,899	1,260
Dunn	Manning	3,443	4,005	2,010
Eddy	New Rockford	2,502	2,951	630
Emmons	Linton	3,645	4,830	1,510
Foster	Carrington	3,583	3,983	635
Golden Valley	Beach	1,691	2,108	1,002
Grand Forks	Grand Forks	65,435	70,683	1,438
Grant	Carson	2,588	3,549	1,659
Griggs	Cooperstown	2,456	3,303	709
Hettinger	Mott	2,564	3,445	1,132
Kidder	Steele	2,453	3,332	1,351
La Moure	La Moure	4,262	5,383	1,147
Logan	Napoleon	1,999	2,847	993
McHenry	Towner	5,429	6,528	1,874
McIntosh	Ashley	2,956	4,021	975
McKenzie	Watford City	5,700	6,383	2,742
McLean	Washburn	8,543	10,457	2,110
Mercer	Stanton	8,234	9,808	1,045
Morton	Mandan	25,754	23,700	1,926
Mountrail	Stanley	6,442	7,021	1,824
Nelson	Lakota	3,289	4,410	982
Oliver	Center	1,808	2,381	724
Pembina	Cavalier	7,906	9,238	1,119
Pierce	Rugby	4,221	5,052	1,018
Ramsey	Devils Lake	11,267	12,681	1,185
Ransom	Lisbon	5,695	5,921	863
Renville	Mohall	2,425	3,160	875
Richland	Wahpeton	16,888	18,148	1,437
Rolette	Rolla	13,903	12,772	902
Sargent	Forman	4,198	4,549	859
Sheridan	McClusky	1,408	2,148	972
Sioux	Fort Yates	4,282	3,761	1,094
Slope	Amidon	713	907	1,218
Stark	Dickinson	22,167	22,832	1,338
Steele	Finley	1,943	2,420	712
Stutsman	Jamestown	20,761	22,241	2,221
Towner	Cando	2,417	3,627	1,025
Traill	Hillsboro	8,178	8,752	862
Walsh	Grafton	11,362	13,840	1,282
Ward	Minot	55,270	57,921	2,013
Wells	Fessenden	4,432	5,864	1,271
Williams	Williston	19,456	21,129	2,070

Ohio
(88 counties, 40,048 sq. mi. land; pop. 11,478,006)

County	County seat or courthouse	2006 Pop.	1990 Pop.	Land area sq. mi.
Adams	West Union	28,516	25,371	584
Allen	Lima	105,788	109,755	404
Ashland	Ashland	54,727	47,507	424
Ashtabula	Jefferson	102,703	99,880	702
Athens	Athens	61,860	59,549	507
Auglaize	Wapakoneta	47,060	44,585	401
Belmont	Saint Clairsville	68,771	71,074	537
Brown	Georgetown	44,423	34,966	492
Butler	Hamilton	354,992	291,479	467
Carroll	Carrollton	29,189	26,521	395
Champaign	Urbana	39,921	36,019	429
Clark	Springfield	141,872	147,538	400
Clermont	Batavia	192,706	150,094	452

County	County seat or courthouse	2006 Pop.	1990 Pop.	Land area sq. mi.
Clinton	Wilmington	43,399	35,444	411
Columbiana	Lisbon	110,542	108,276	532
Coshocton	Coshocton	36,976	35,427	564
Crawford	Bucyrus	45,047	47,870	402
Cuyahoga	Cleveland	1,314,241	1,412,140	458
Darke	Greenville	52,780	53,617	600
Defiance	Defiance	39,091	39,350	411
Delaware	Delaware	156,697	66,929	442
Erie	Sandusky	78,116	76,781	255
Fairfield	Lancaster	140,591	103,468	505
Fayette	Washington Court House	28,305	27,466	407
Franklin	Columbus	1,095,662	961,437	540
Fulton	Wauseon	42,900	38,498	407
Gallia	Gallipolis	31,313	30,954	469
Geauga	Chardon	95,676	81,087	404
Greene	Xenia	152,298	136,731	415
Guernsey	Cambridge	40,876	39,024	522
Hamilton	Cincinnati	822,596	866,228	407
Hancock	Findlay	73,824	65,536	531
Hardin	Kenton	31,966	31,111	470
Harrison	Cadiz	15,799	16,085	404
Henry	Napoleon	29,520	29,108	417
Highland	Hillsboro	42,833	35,728	553
Hocking	Logan	28,973	25,533	423
Holmes	Millersburg	41,574	32,849	423
Huron	Norwalk	60,313	56,238	493
Jackson	Jackson	33,543	30,230	420
Jefferson	Steubenville	70,125	80,298	410
Knox	Mount Vernon	58,561	47,473	527
Lake	Painesville	232,892	215,500	228
Lawrence	Ironton	63,179	61,834	455
Licking	Newark	156,287	128,300	687
Logan	Bellefontaine	46,189	42,310	458
Lorain	Elyria	301,993	271,126	493
Lucas	Toledo	445,281	462,361	340
Madison	London	41,496	37,078	465
Mahoning	Youngstown	251,026	264,806	415
Marion	Marion	65,583	64,274	404
Medina	Medina	169,353	122,354	422
Meigs	Pomeroy	23,092	22,987	429
Mercer	Celina	41,303	39,443	463
Miami	Troy	101,914	93,184	407
Monroe	Woodsfield	14,606	15,497	456
Montgomery	Dayton	542,237	573,809	462
Morgan	McConnelsville	14,821	14,194	418
Morrow	Mount Gilead	34,529	27,749	406
Muskingum	Zanesville	86,125	82,068	665
Noble	Caldwell	14,165	11,336	399
Ottawa	Port Clinton	41,331	40,029	255
Paulding	Paulding	19,432	20,488	416
Perry	New Lexington	35,313	31,557	410
Pickaway	Circleville	53,606	48,248	502
Pike	Waverly	28,269	24,249	441
Portage	Ravenna	155,012	142,585	492
Preble	Eaton	42,491	40,113	425
Putnam	Ottawa	34,744	33,819	484
Richland	Mansfield	127,010	126,137	497
Ross	Chillicothe	75,556	69,330	688
Sandusky	Fremont	61,625	61,963	409
Scioto	Portsmouth	76,441	80,327	612
Seneca	Tiffin	57,255	59,733	551
Shelby	Sidney	48,884	44,915	409
Stark	Canton	380,575	367,585	576
Summit	Akron	545,931	514,990	413
Trumbull	Warren	217,362	227,795	616
Tuscarawas	New Philadelphia	91,766	84,090	568
Union	Marysville	46,702	31,969	437
Van Wert	Van Wert	29,303	30,464	410
Vinton	McArthur	13,519	11,098	414
Warren	Lebanon	201,871	113,973	400
Washington	Marietta	61,867	62,254	635
Wayne	Wooster	113,950	101,461	555
Williams	Bryan	38,719	36,956	422
Wood	Bowling Green	124,183	113,269	617
Wyandot	Upper Sandusky	22,553	22,254	406

Oklahoma

(77 counties, 68,667 sq. mi. land; pop. 3,579,212)

County	County seat or courthouse	2006 Pop.	1990 Pop.	Land area sq. mi.
Adair	Stilwell	22,317	18,421	576
Alfalfa	Cherokee	5,673	6,416	867
Atoka	Atoka	14,340	12,778	978
Beaver	Beaver	5,336	6,023	1,814
Beckham	Sayre	19,271	18,812	902
Blaine	Watonga	12,734	11,470	928
Bryan	Durant	38,395	32,089	909
Caddo	Anadarko	30,063	29,550	1,278
Canadian	El Reno	101,335	74,409	900
Carter	Ardmore	47,503	42,919	824
Cherokee	Tahlequah	44,910	34,049	751
Choctaw	Hugo	15,334	15,302	774
Cimarron	Boise City	2,807	3,301	1,835

County	County seat or courthouse	2006 Pop.	1990 Pop.	Land area sq. mi.
Cleveland	Norman	228,594	174,253	536
Coal	Coalgate	5,634	5,780	518
Comanche	Lawton	109,181	111,486	1,069
Cotton	Walters	6,491	6,651	637
Craig	Vinita	15,046	14,104	761
Creek	Sapulpa	69,146	60,915	956
Custer	Arapaho	25,566	26,897	987
Delaware	Jay	40,061	28,070	741
Dewey	Taloga	4,475	5,551	1,000
Ellis	Arnett	3,912	4,497	1,229
Garfield	Enid	57,068	56,735	1,058
Garvin	Pauls Valley	27,375	26,605	807
Grady	Chickasha	50,490	41,747	1,101
Grant	Medford	4,653	5,689	1,001
Greer	Mangum	5,864	6,559	639
Harmon	Hollis	3,042	3,793	538
Harper	Buffalo	3,348	4,063	1,039
Haskell	Stigler	12,155	10,940	577
Hughes	Holdenville	13,893	13,014	807
Jackson	Altus	26,042	28,764	803
Jefferson	Waurika	6,385	7,010	759
Johnston	Tishomingo	10,436	10,032	645
Kay	Newkirk	45,889	48,056	919
Kingfisher	Kingfisher	14,316	13,212	903
Kiowa	Hobart	9,778	11,347	1,015
Latimer	Wilburton	10,562	10,333	722
Le Flore	Poteau	50,079	43,270	1,586
Lincoln	Chandler	32,645	29,216	958
Logan	Guthrie	36,971	29,011	744
Love	Marietta	9,162	7,788	515
McClain	Purcell	31,038	22,795	570
McCurtain	Idabel	34,018	33,433	1,852
McIntosh	Eufaula	19,899	16,779	620
Major	Fairview	7,329	8,055	957
Marshall	Madill	14,558	10,829	371
Mayes	Pryor	39,774	33,366	656
Murray	Sulphur	12,945	12,042	418
Muskogee	Muskogee	71,018	68,078	814
Noble	Perry	11,152	11,045	732
Nowata	Nowata	10,785	9,992	565
Okfuskee	Okemah	11,370	11,551	625
Oklahoma	Oklahoma City	691,266	599,611	709
Okmulgee	Okmulgee	39,670	36,490	697
Osage	Pawhuska	45,549	41,645	2,251
Ottawa	Miami	33,026	30,561	471
Pawnee	Pawnee	16,844	15,575	569
Payne	Stillwater	73,818	61,507	686
Pittsburg	McAlester	45,002	40,950	1,306
Pontotoc	Ada	35,350	34,119	720
Pottawatomie	Shawnee	68,638	58,760	788
Pushmataha	Antlers	11,641	10,997	1,397
Roger Mills	Cheyenne	3,293	4,147	1,142
Rogers	Claremore	82,435	55,170	675
Seminole	Wewoka	24,650	25,412	633
Sequoyah	Sallisaw	41,356	33,828	674
Stephens	Duncan	43,243	42,299	874
Texas	Guymon	20,238	16,419	2,037
Tillman	Frederick	8,482	10,384	872
Tulsa	Tulsa	577,795	503,341	570
Wagoner	Wagoner	66,313	47,883	563
Washington	Bartlesville	49,241	48,066	417
Washita	Cordell	11,583	11,441	1,003
Woods	Alva	8,385	9,103	1,287
Woodward	Woodward	19,231	18,976	1,242

Oregon

(36 counties, 95,997 sq. mi. land; pop. 3,700,758)

County	County seat or courthouse	2006 Pop.	1990 Pop.	Land area sq. mi.
Baker	Baker City	16,243	15,317	3,068
Benton	Corvallis	79,061	70,811	676
Clackamas	Oregon City	374,230	278,850	1,868
Clatsop	Astoria	37,315	33,301	827
Columbia	Saint Helens	49,163	37,557	657
Coos	Coquille	64,820	60,273	1,600
Crook	Prineville	22,941	14,111	2,979
Curry	Gold Beach	22,358	19,327	1,627
Deschutes	Bend	149,140	74,976	3,018
Douglas	Roseburg	105,117	94,649	5,037
Gilliam	Condon	1,775	1,717	1,204
Grant	Canyon City	7,250	7,853	4,529
Harney	Burns	6,888	7,060	10,134
Hood River	Hood River	21,533	16,903	522
Jackson	Medford	197,071	146,387	2,785
Jefferson	Madras	20,352	13,676	1,781
Josephine	Grants Pass	81,688	62,649	1,640
Klamath	Klamath Falls	66,438	57,702	5,944
Lake	Lakeview	7,473	7,186	8,136
Lane	Eugene	337,870	282,912	4,554
Lincoln	Newport	46,199	38,889	980
Linn	Albany	111,489	91,227	2,292
Malheur	Vale	31,247	26,038	9,887
Marion	Salem	311,304	228,483	1,184
Morrow	Heppner	11,753	7,625	2,032

County	County seat or courthouse	2006 Pop.	1990 Pop.	Land area sq. mi.
Multnomah	Portland	681,454	583,887	435
Polk	Dallas	73,296	49,541	741
Sherman	Moro	1,699	1,918	823
Tillamook	Tillamook	25,380	21,570	1,102
Umatilla	Pendleton	72,928	59,249	3,215
Union	La Grande	24,345	23,598	2,037
Wallowa	Enterprise	6,875	6,911	3,145
Wasco	The Dalles	23,712	21,683	2,381
Washington	Hillsboro	514,269	311,554	724
Wheeler	Fossil	1,404	1,396	1,715
Yamhill	McMinnville	94,678	65,551	716

Pennsylvania
(67 counties, 44,817 sq. mi. land; pop. 12,440,621)

County	County seat or courthouse	2006 Pop.	1990 Pop.	Land area sq. mi.
Adams	Gettysburg	101,105	78,274	520
Allegheny	Pittsburgh	1,223,411	1,336,449	730
Armstrong	Kittanning	70,096	73,478	654
Beaver	Beaver	175,736	186,093	434
Bedford	Bedford	49,927	47,919	1,015
Berks	Reading	401,149	336,523	859
Blair	Hollidaysburg	126,494	130,542	526
Bradford	Towanda	62,471	60,967	1,151
Bucks	Doylestown	623,205	541,174	607
Butler	Butler	182,901	152,013	789
Cambria	Ebensburg	146,967	163,062	688
Cameron	Emporium	5,489	5,913	397
Carbon	Jim Thorpe	62,567	56,803	381
Centre	Bellefonte	140,953	124,812	1,108
Chester	West Chester	482,112	376,389	756
Clarion	Clarion	40,385	41,699	602
Clearfield	Clearfield	82,442	78,097	1,147
Clinton	Lock Haven	37,232	37,182	891
Columbia	Bloomsburg	65,014	63,202	486
Crawford	Meadville	89,389	86,166	1,013
Cumberland	Carlisle	226,117	195,257	550
Dauphin	Harrisburg	254,176	237,813	525
Delaware	Media	555,996	547,658	184
Elk	Ridgway	33,179	34,878	829
Erie	Erie	279,811	275,575	802
Fayette	Uniontown	145,760	145,351	790
Forest	Tionesta	6,506	4,802	428
Franklin	Chambersburg	139,991	121,082	772
Fulton	McConnellsburg	14,783	13,837	438
Greene	Waynesburg	40,432	39,550	576
Huntingdon	Huntingdon	45,771	44,164	874
Indiana	Indiana	88,234	89,994	829
Jefferson	Brookville	45,725	46,083	655
Juniata	Mifflintown	23,512	20,625	392
Lackawanna	Scranton	209,728	219,097	459
Lancaster	Lancaster	494,486	422,822	949
Lawrence	New Castle	91,795	96,246	360
Lebanon	Lebanon	126,883	113,744	362
Lehigh	Allentown	335,544	291,130	347
Luzerne	Wilkes-Barre	313,020	328,149	891
Lycoming	Williamsport	117,668	118,710	1,235
McKean	Smethport	44,065	47,131	982
Mercer	Mercer	118,551	121,003	672
Mifflin	Lewistown	46,057	46,197	412
Monroe	Stroudsburg	165,685	95,681	609
Montgomery	Norristown	775,688	678,193	483
Montour	Danville	17,934	17,735	131
Northampton	Easton	291,306	247,110	374
Northumberland	Sunbury	91,654	96,771	460
Perry	New Bloomfield	45,087	41,172	554
Philadelphia	Philadelphia	1,448,394	1,585,577	135
Pike	Milford	58,195	28,032	547
Potter	Coudersport	17,568	16,717	1,081
Schuylkill	Pottsville	147,405	152,585	778
Snyder	Middleburg	38,226	36,680	331
Somerset	Somerset	78,508	78,218	1,075
Sullivan	Laporte	6,277	6,104	450
Susquehanna	Montrose	41,889	40,380	823
Tioga	Wellsboro	41,137	41,126	1,134
Union	Lewisburg	43,387	36,176	317
Venango	Franklin	55,488	59,381	675
Warren	Warren	41,742	45,050	883
Washington	Washington	206,432	204,584	857
Wayne	Honesdale	50,929	39,944	729
Westmoreland	Greensburg	366,440	370,321	1,025
Wyoming	Tunkhannock	28,093	28,076	397
York	York	416,322	339,574	904

Rhode Island
(5 counties, 1,045 sq. mi. land; pop. 1,067,610)

County	County seat or courthouse	2006 Pop.	1990 Pop.	Land area sq. mi.
Bristol	Bristol	52,256	48,859	25
Kent	East Greenwich	170,053	161,143	170
Newport	Newport	82,144	87,194	104
Providence	Providence	635,596	596,270	413
Washington	West Kingston	127,561	109,998	333

South Carolina
(46 counties, 30,110 sq. mi. land; pop. 4,321,249)

County	County seat or courthouse	2006 Pop.	1990 Pop.	Land area sq. mi.
Abbeville	Abbeville	25,935	23,862	508
Aiken	Aiken	151,800	120,991	1,073
Allendale	Allendale	10,748	11,727	408
Anderson	Anderson	177,963	145,177	718
Bamberg	Bamberg	15,678	16,902	393
Barnwell	Barnwell	23,265	20,293	548
Beaufort	Beaufort	142,045	86,425	587
Berkeley	Moncks Corner	152,282	128,658	1,098
Calhoun	Saint Matthews	15,026	12,753	380
Charleston	Charleston	331,917	295,159	919
Cherokee	Gaffney	53,886	44,506	393
Chester	Chester	32,875	32,170	581
Chesterfield	Chesterfield	43,191	38,575	799
Clarendon	Manning	33,339	28,450	607
Colleton	Walterboro	39,467	34,377	1,056
Darlington	Darlington	67,551	61,851	561
Dillon	Dillon	30,984	29,114	405
Dorchester	Saint George	118,979	83,060	575
Edgefield	Edgefield	25,261	18,360	502
Fairfield	Winnsboro	23,810	22,295	687
Florence	Florence	131,297	114,344	800
Georgetown	Georgetown	60,860	46,302	815
Greenville	Greenville	417,166	320,127	790
Greenwood	Greenwood	68,213	59,567	456
Hampton	Hampton	21,268	18,186	560
Horry	Conway	238,493	144,053	1,134
Jasper	Ridgeland	21,809	15,487	656
Kershaw	Camden	57,490	43,599	726
Lancaster	Lancaster	63,628	54,516	549
Laurens	Laurens	70,374	58,132	715
Lee	Bishopville	20,559	18,437	410
Lexington	Lexington	240,160	167,526	699
McCormick	McCormick	10,226	8,868	360
Marion	Marion	34,684	33,899	489
Marlboro	Bennettsville	29,152	29,716	480
Newberry	Newberry	37,762	33,172	631
Oconee	Walhalla	70,567	57,494	625
Orangeburg	Orangeburg	90,845	84,804	1,106
Pickens	Pickens	114,446	93,896	497
Richland	Columbia	348,226	286,321	756
Saluda	Saluda	19,059	16,441	452
Spartanburg	Spartanburg	271,087	226,793	811
Sumter	Sumter	104,430	101,276	665
Union	Union	28,306	30,337	514
Williamsburg	Kingstree	36,105	36,815	934
York	York	199,035	131,497	682

South Dakota
(66 counties, 75,885 sq. mi. land; pop. 781,919)

County	County seat or courthouse	2006 Pop.	1990 Pop.	Land area sq. mi.
Aurora	Plankinton	2,905	3,135	708
Beadle	Huron	15,643	18,253	1,259
Bennett	Martin	3,543	3,206	1,185
Bon Homme	Tyndall	7,281	7,089	563
Brookings	Brookings	28,195	25,207	794
Brown	Aberdeen	34,645	35,580	1,713
Brule	Chamberlain	5,167	5,485	819
Buffalo	Gannvalley	2,109	1,759	471
Butte	Belle Fourche	9,374	7,914	2,249
Campbell	Mound City	1,494	1,965	736
Charles Mix	Lake Andes	9,224	9,131	1,098
Clark	Clark	3,683	4,403	958
Clay	Vermillion	12,867	13,186	412
Codington	Watertown	26,347	22,698	688
Corson	McIntosh	4,288	4,195	2,473
Custer	Custer	7,944	6,179	1,558
Davison	Mitchell	19,035	17,503	435
Day	Webster	5,778	6,978	1,029
Deuel	Clear Lake	4,301	4,522	624
Dewey	Timber Lake	6,112	5,523	2,303
Douglas	Armour	3,168	3,746	434
Edmunds	Ipswich	4,062	4,356	1,146
Fall River	Hot Springs	7,304	7,353	1,740
Faulk	Faulkton	2,339	2,744	1,000
Grant	Milbank	7,278	8,372	683
Gregory	Burke	4,268	5,359	1,016
Haakon	Philip	1,864	2,624	1,813
Hamlin	Hayti	5,616	4,974	507
Hand	Miller	3,323	4,272	1,437
Hanson	Alexandria	3,690	2,994	435
Harding	Buffalo	1,205	1,669	2,671
Hughes	Pierre	16,946	14,817	741
Hutchinson	Olivet	7,426	8,262	813
Hyde	Highmore	1,551	1,696	861
Jackson	Kadoka	2,900	2,811	1,869
Jerauld	Wessington Springs	2,071	2,425	530
Jones	Murdo	1,067	1,324	971
Kingsbury	De Smet	5,464	5,925	838
Lake	Madison	11,170	10,550	563
Lawrence	Deadwood	22,685	20,655	800
Lincoln	Canton	35,239	15,427	578
Lyman	Kennebec	3,929	3,638	1,640

County	County seat or courthouse	2006 Pop.	1990 Pop.	Land area sq. mi.
McCook	Salem	5,851	5,688	575
McPherson	Leola	2,565	3,228	1,137
Marshall	Britton	4,430	4,844	838
Meade	Sturgis	24,425	21,878	3,471
Mellette	White River	2,099	2,137	1,306
Miner	Howard	2,553	3,272	570
Minnehaha	Sioux Falls	163,281	123,809	810
Moody	Flandreau	6,644	6,507	520
Pennington	Rapid City	94,338	81,343	2,776
Perkins	Bison	3,025	3,932	2,872
Potter	Gettysburg	2,321	3,190	866
Roberts	Sisseton	10,024	9,914	1,101
Sanborn	Woonsocket	2,517	2,833	569
Shannon	(Attached to Fall River)	13,824	9,902	2,094
Spink	Redfield	6,923	7,981	1,504
Stanley	Fort Pierre	2,815	2,453	1,443
Sully	Onida	1,435	1,589	1,007
Todd	(Attached to Tripp)	10,088	8,352	1,388
Tripp	Winner	6,066	6,924	1,614
Turner	Parker	8,540	8,576	617
Union	Elk Point	13,745	10,189	460
Walworth	Selby	5,425	6,087	708
Yankton	Yankton	21,779	19,252	522
Ziebach	Dupree	2,706	2,220	1,962

Tennessee
(95 counties, 41,217 sq. mi. land; pop. 6,038,803)

County	County seat or courthouse	2006 Pop.	1990 Pop.	Land area sq. mi.
Anderson	Clinton	73,579	68,250	338
Bedford	Shelbyville	43,413	30,411	474
Benton	Camden	16,378	14,524	395
Bledsoe	Pikeville	13,030	9,669	406
Blount	Maryville	118,186	85,962	559
Bradley	Cleveland	93,538	73,712	329
Campbell	Jacksboro	40,848	35,079	480
Cannon	Woodbury	13,448	10,467	266
Carroll	Huntingdon	29,096	27,514	599
Carter	Elizabethton	59,157	51,505	341
Cheatham	Ashland City	39,018	27,140	303
Chester	Henderson	16,043	12,819	289
Claiborne	Tazewell	31,347	26,137	434
Clay	Celina	8,055	7,238	236
Cocke	Newport	35,220	29,141	434
Coffee	Manchester	51,625	40,343	429
Crockett	Alamo	14,392	13,378	265
Cumberland	Crossville	52,344	34,736	682
Davidson	Nashville	578,698	510,786	502
Decatur	Decaturville	11,426	10,472	334
De Kalb	Smithville	18,360	14,360	305
Dickson	Charlotte	46,583	35,061	490
Dyer	Dyersburg	37,886	34,854	511
Fayette	Somerville	36,102	25,559	705
Fentress	Jamestown	17,480	14,669	499
Franklin	Winchester	41,319	34,923	555
Gibson	Trenton	48,461	46,315	603
Giles	Pulaski	29,269	25,741	611
Grainger	Rutledge	22,453	17,095	280
Greene	Greeneville	65,945	55,832	622
Grundy	Altamont	14,499	13,362	361
Hamblen	Morristown	61,026	50,480	161
Hamilton	Chattanooga	312,905	285,536	542
Hancock	Sneedville	6,713	6,739	222
Hardeman	Bolivar	28,176	23,377	668
Hardin	Savannah	26,089	22,633	578
Hawkins	Rogersville	56,850	44,565	487
Haywood	Brownsville	19,405	19,437	533
Henderson	Lexington	26,750	21,844	520
Henry	Paris	31,837	27,888	562
Hickman	Centerville	23,812	16,754	613
Houston	Erin	8,076	7,018	200
Humphreys	Waverly	18,394	15,813	532
Jackson	Gainesboro	10,918	9,297	309
Jefferson	Dandridge	49,372	33,016	274
Johnson	Mountain City	18,043	13,766	298
Knox	Knoxville	411,967	335,749	508
Lake	Tiptonville	7,406	7,129	163
Lauderdale	Ripley	26,732	23,491	470
Lawrence	Lawrenceburg	40,934	35,303	617
Lewis	Hohenwald	11,588	9,247	282
Lincoln	Fayetteville	32,728	28,157	570
Loudon	Loudon	44,566	31,255	229
McMinn	Athens	52,020	42,383	430
McNairy	Selmer	25,722	22,422	560
Macon	Lafayette	21,726	15,906	307
Madison	Jackson	95,894	77,982	557
Marion	Jasper	27,942	24,683	498
Marshall	Lewisburg	28,884	21,539	375
Maury	Columbia	78,309	54,812	613
Meigs	Decatur	11,698	8,033	195
Monroe	Madisonville	44,163	30,541	635
Montgomery	Clarksville	147,114	100,498	539
Moore	Lynchburg	6,070	4,696	129
Morgan	Wartburg	20,108	17,300	522
Obion	Union City	32,184	31,717	545
Overton	Livingston	20,740	17,636	433

County	County seat or courthouse	2006 Pop.	1990 Pop.	Land area sq. mi.
Perry	Linden	7,653	6,612	415
Pickett	Byrdstown	4,855	4,548	163
Polk	Benton	15,939	13,643	435
Putnam	Cookeville	68,284	51,373	401
Rhea	Dayton	30,347	24,344	316
Roane	Kingston	53,293	47,227	361
Robertson	Springfield	62,187	41,492	476
Rutherford	Murfreesboro	228,829	118,570	619
Scott	Huntsville	21,926	18,358	532
Sequatchie	Dunlap	13,002	8,863	266
Sevier	Sevierville	81,382	51,050	592
Shelby	Memphis	911,438	826,330	755
Smith	Carthage	18,753	14,143	314
Stewart	Dover	12,998	9,479	458
Sullivan	Blountville	153,239	143,596	413
Sumner	Gallatin	149,416	103,281	529
Tipton	Covington	57,380	37,568	459
Trousdale	Hartsville	7,811	5,920	114
Unicoi	Erwin	17,663	16,549	186
Union	Maynardville	19,086	13,694	224
Van Buren	Spencer	5,448	4,846	273
Warren	McMinnville	40,016	32,992	433
Washington	Jonesborough	114,316	92,336	326
Wayne	Waynesboro	16,828	13,935	734
Weakley	Dresden	33,357	31,972	580
White	Sparta	24,482	20,090	377
Williamson	Franklin	160,781	81,021	583
Wilson	Lebanon	104,035	67,675	571

Texas
(254 counties, 261,797 sq. mi. land; pop. 23,507,783)

County	County seat or courthouse	2006 Pop.	1990 Pop.	Land area sq. mi.
Anderson	Palestine	57,064	48,024	1,071
Andrews	Andrews	12,952	14,338	1,501
Angelina	Lufkin	82,524	69,884	802
Aransas	Rockport	24,831	17,892	252
Archer	Archer City	9,266	7,973	910
Armstrong	Claude	2,120	2,021	914
Atascosa	Jourdanton	43,876	30,533	1,232
Austin	Bellville	26,407	19,832	653
Bailey	Muleshoe	6,597	7,064	827
Bandera	Bandera	20,203	10,562	792
Bastrop	Bastrop	71,684	38,263	888
Baylor	Seymour	3,805	4,385	871
Bee	Beeville	33,176	25,135	880
Bell	Belton	257,897	191,073	1,060
Bexar	San Antonio	1,555,592	1,185,394	1,247
Blanco	Johnson City	9,250	5,972	711
Borden	Gail	648	799	899
Bosque	Meridian	18,058	15,125	989
Bowie	Boston	91,455	81,665	888
Brazoria	Angleton	287,898	191,707	1,386
Brazos	Bryan	159,006	121,862	586
Brewster	Alpine	9,048	8,653	6,193
Briscoe	Silverton	1,598	1,971	900
Brooks	Falfurrias	7,731	8,204	943
Brown	Brownwood	38,970	34,371	944
Burleson	Caldwell	16,932	13,625	666
Burnet	Burnet	42,896	22,677	996
Caldwell	Lockhart	36,720	26,392	546
Calhoun	Port Lavaca	20,705	19,053	512
Callahan	Baird	13,491	11,859	899
Cameron	Brownsville	387,717	260,120	906
Camp	Pittsburg	12,410	9,904	198
Carson	Panhandle	6,595	6,576	923
Cass	Linden	29,955	29,982	937
Castro	Dimmitt	7,449	9,070	898
Chambers	Anahuac	28,779	20,088	599
Cherokee	Rusk	48,513	41,049	1,052
Childress	Childress	7,717	5,953	710
Clay	Henrietta	11,104	10,024	1,098
Cochran	Morton	3,214	4,377	775
Coke	Robert Lee	3,623	3,424	899
Coleman	Coleman	8,761	9,710	1,260
Collin	McKinney	698,851	264,036	848
Collingsworth	Wellington	2,930	3,573	919
Colorado	Columbus	20,824	18,383	963
Comal	New Braunfels	101,181	51,832	561
Comanche	Comanche	13,887	13,381	938
Concho	Paint Rock	3,654	3,044	991
Cooke	Gainesville	38,946	30,777	874
Coryell	Gatesville	72,667	64,226	1,052
Cottle	Paducah	1,679	2,247	901
Crane	Crane	3,845	4,652	786
Crockett	Ozona	3,879	4,078	2,807
Crosby	Crosbyton	6,549	7,304	900
Culberson	Van Horn	2,525	3,407	3,812
Dallam	Dalhart	6,143	5,461	1,505
Dallas	Dallas	2,345,815	1,852,691	880
Dawson	Lamesa	14,174	14,349	902
Deaf Smith	Hereford	18,623	19,153	1,497
Delta	Cooper	5,561	4,857	277
Denton	Denton	584,238	273,644	889
DeWitt	Cuero	20,167	18,840	909

County	County seat or courthouse	2006 Pop.	1990 Pop.	Land area sq. mi.	County	County seat or courthouse	2006 Pop.	1990 Pop.	Land area sq. mi.
Dickens	Dickens	2,596	2,571	904	Martin	Stanton	4,441	4,956	915
Dimmit	Carrizo Springs	10,385	10,433	1,331	Mason	Mason	3,902	3,423	932
Donley	Clarendon	3,848	3,696	930	Matagorda	Bay City	37,824	36,928	1,114
Duval	San Diego	12,437	12,918	1,793	Maverick	Eagle Pass	52,298	36,378	1,280
Eastland	Eastland	18,293	18,488	926	Medina	Hondo	43,913	27,312	1,328
Ector	Odessa	127,462	118,934	901	Menard	Menard	2,210	2,252	902
Edwards	Rocksprings	1,935	2,266	2,120	Midland	Midland	124,380	106,611	900
Ellis	Waxahachie	139,300	85,167	940	Milam	Cameron	25,286	22,946	1,017
El Paso	El Paso	736,310	591,610	1,013	Mills	Goldthwaite	5,184	4,531	748
Erath	Stephenville	34,289	27,991	1,086	Mitchell	Colorado City	9,327	8,016	910
Falls	Marlin	17,547	17,712	769	Montague	Montague	19,810	17,274	931
Fannin	Bonham	33,337	24,804	891	Montgomery	Conroe	398,290	182,201	1,044
Fayette	La Grange	22,521	20,095	950	Moore	Dumas	20,591	17,865	900
Fisher	Roby	4,027	4,842	901	Morris	Daingerfield	13,002	13,200	255
Floyd	Floydada	7,053	8,497	992	Motley	Matador	1,276	1,532	989
Foard	Crowell	1,519	1,794	707	Nacogdoches	Nacogdoches	61,079	54,753	947
Fort Bend	Richmond	493,187	225,421	875	Navarro	Corsicana	49,440	39,926	1,008
Franklin	Mount Vernon	10,367	7,802	286	Newton	Newton	14,090	13,569	933
Freestone	Fairfield	18,803	15,818	877	Nolan	Sweetwater	14,812	16,594	912
Frio	Pearsall	16,336	13,472	1,133	Nueces	Corpus Christi	321,457	291,145	836
Gaines	Seminole	15,008	14,123	1,502	Ochiltree	Perryton	9,550	9,128	918
Galveston	Galveston	283,551	217,396	398	Oldham	Vega	2,133	2,278	1,501
Garza	Post	4,877	5,143	896	Orange	Orange	84,243	80,509	356
Gillespie	Fredericksburg	23,527	17,204	1,061	Palo Pinto	Palo Pinto	27,797	25,055	953
Glasscock	Garden City	1,248	1,447	901	Panola	Carthage	22,989	22,035	801
Goliad	Goliad	7,192	5,980	854	Parker	Weatherford	106,266	64,785	904
Gonzales	Gonzales	19,566	17,205	1,068	Parmer	Farwell	9,714	9,863	882
Gray	Pampa	21,919	23,967	928	Pecos	Fort Stockton	16,139	14,675	4,764
Grayson	Sherman	118,478	95,019	934	Polk	Livingston	46,995	30,687	1,057
Gregg	Longview	117,090	104,948	274	Potter	Amarillo	121,328	97,841	909
Grimes	Anderson	25,552	18,843	794	Presidio	Marfa	7,713	6,637	3,856
Guadalupe	Seguin	108,410	64,873	711	Rains	Emory	11,514	6,715	232
Hale	Plainview	36,317	34,671	1,005	Randall	Canyon	111,472	89,673	914
Hall	Memphis	3,668	3,905	903	Reagan	Big Lake	3,022	4,514	1,175
Hamilton	Hamilton	8,186	7,733	836	Real	Leakey	3,061	2,412	700
Hansford	Spearman	5,237	5,848	920	Red River	Clarksville	13,440	14,317	1,050
Hardeman	Quanah	4,250	5,283	695	Reeves	Pecos	11,466	15,852	2,636
Hardin	Kountze	51,483	41,320	894	Refugio	Refugio	7,596	7,976	770
Harris	Houston	3,886,207	2,818,101	1,729	Roberts	Miami	835	1,025	924
Harrison	Marshall	63,819	57,483	899	Robertson	Franklin	16,214	15,511	855
Hartley	Channing	5,335	3,634	1,462	Rockwall	Rockwall	69,155	25,604	129
Haskell	Haskell	5,438	6,820	903	Runnels	Ballinger	10,724	11,294	1,051
Hays	San Marcos	130,325	65,614	678	Rusk	Henderson	48,354	43,735	924
Hemphill	Canadian	3,412	3,720	910	Sabine	Hemphill	10,457	9,586	490
Henderson	Athens	80,222	58,543	874	San Augustine	San Augustine	8,888	7,999	528
Hidalgo	Edinburg	700,634	383,545	1,570	San Jacinto	Coldspring	24,760	16,372	571
Hill	Hillsboro	35,806	27,146	962	San Patricio	Sinton	69,522	58,749	692
Hockley	Levelland	22,609	24,199	908	San Saba	San Saba	5,993	5,401	1,134
Hood	Granbury	49,238	28,981	422	Schleicher	Eldorado	2,776	2,990	1,311
Hopkins	Sulphur Springs	33,496	28,833	782	Scurry	Snyder	16,202	18,634	903
Houston	Crockett	23,044	21,375	1,231	Shackelford	Albany	3,194	3,316	914
Howard	Big Spring	32,463	32,343	903	Shelby	Center	26,575	22,034	794
Hudspeth	Sierra Blanca	3,320	2,915	4,571	Sherman	Stratford	2,936	2,858	923
Hunt	Greenville	83,338	64,343	841	Smith	Tyler	194,635	151,309	928
Hutchinson	Stinnett	22,460	25,689	887	Somervell	Glen Rose	7,773	5,360	187
Irion	Mertzon	1,814	1,629	1,051	Starr	Rio Grande City	61,780	40,518	1,223
Jack	Jacksboro	9,110	6,981	917	Stephens	Breckenridge	9,610	9,010	895
Jackson	Edna	14,249	13,039	829	Sterling	Sterling City	1,246	1,438	923
Jasper	Jasper	35,293	31,102	937	Stonewall	Aspermont	1,402	2,013	919
Jeff Davis	Fort Davis	2,315	1,946	2,264	Sutton	Sonora	4,281	4,135	1,454
Jefferson	Beaumont	243,914	239,389	904	Swisher	Tulia	7,830	8,133	900
Jim Hogg	Hebbronville	5,027	5,109	1,136	Tarrant	Fort Worth	1,671,295	1,170,103	863
Jim Wells	Alice	41,131	37,679	865	Taylor	Abilene	124,927	119,655	916
Johnson	Cleburne	149,016	97,165	729	Terrell	Sanderson	983	1,410	2,358
Jones	Anson	19,645	16,490	931	Terry	Brownfield	12,387	13,218	890
Karnes	Karnes City	15,270	12,455	750	Throckmorton	Throckmorton	1,678	1,880	912
Kaufman	Kaufman	93,241	52,220	786	Titus	Mount Pleasant	30,306	24,009	411
Kendall	Boerne	30,213	14,589	662	Tom Green	San Angelo	103,938	98,458	1,522
Kenedy	Sarita	402	460	1,457	Travis	Austin	921,006	576,407	989
Kent	Jayton	734	1,010	902	Trinity	Groveton	14,296	11,445	693
Kerr	Kerrville	47,254	36,304	1,106	Tyler	Woodville	20,557	16,646	923
Kimble	Junction	4,570	4,122	1,251	Upshur	Gilmer	37,923	31,370	588
King	Guthrie	287	354	912	Upton	Rankin	3,134	4,447	1,242
Kinney	Brackettville	3,342	3,119	1,363	Uvalde	Uvalde	27,050	23,340	1,557
Kleberg	Kingsville	30,353	30,274	871	Val Verde	Del Rio	48,145	38,721	3,170
Knox	Benjamin	3,702	4,837	849	Van Zandt	Canton	52,916	37,944	849
Lamar	Paris	49,863	43,949	917	Victoria	Victoria	86,191	74,361	883
Lamb	Littlefield	14,244	15,072	1,016	Walker	Huntsville	63,304	50,917	787
Lampasas	Lampasas	20,758	13,521	712	Waller	Hempstead	35,185	23,374	514
La Salle	Cotulla	5,969	5,254	1,489	Ward	Monahans	10,352	13,115	835
Lavaca	Hallettsville	18,970	18,690	970	Washington	Brenham	31,912	26,154	609
Lee	Giddings	16,573	12,854	629	Webb	Laredo	231,470	133,239	3,357
Leon	Centerville	16,538	12,665	1,072	Wharton	Wharton	41,475	39,955	1,090
Liberty	Liberty	75,685	52,726	1,160	Wheeler	Wheeler	4,854	5,879	914
Limestone	Groesbeck	22,720	20,946	909	Wichita	Wichita Falls	125,158	122,378	628
Lipscomb	Lipscomb	3,114	3,143	932	Wilbarger	Vernon	14,218	15,121	971
Live Oak	George West	11,522	9,556	1,036	Willacy	Raymondville	20,645	17,705	597
Llano	Llano	18,269	11,631	935	Williamson	Georgetown	353,830	139,551	1,123
Loving	Mentone	60	107	673	Wilson	Floresville	38,829	22,650	807
Lubbock	Lubbock	254,862	222,636	899	Winkler	Kermit	6,609	8,626	841
Lynn	Tahoka	6,212	6,758	892	Wise	Decatur	57,891	34,679	905
McCulloch	Brady	8,016	8,778	1,069	Wood	Quitman	41,776	29,380	650
McLennan	Waco	226,189	189,123	1,042	Yoakum	Plains	7,438	8,786	800
McMullen	Tilden	913	817	1,113	Young	Graham	18,021	18,126	922
Madison	Madisonville	13,310	10,931	470	Zapata	Zapata	13,615	9,279	997
Marion	Jefferson	10,970	9,984	381	Zavala	Crystal City	12,036	12,162	1,298

Utah
(29 counties, 82,144 sq. mi. land; pop. 2,550,063)

County	County seat or courthouse	2006 Pop.	1990 Pop.	Land area sq. mi.
Beaver	Beaver	6,294	4,765	2,590
Box Elder	Brigham City	47,197	36,485	5,723
Cache	Logan	98,662	70,183	1,165
Carbon	Price	19,469	20,228	1,478
Daggett	Manila	947	690	698
Davis	Farmington	276,259	187,941	304
Duchesne	Duchesne	15,701	12,645	3,238
Emery	Castle Dale	10,698	10,332	4,452
Garfield	Panguitch	4,534	3,980	5,174
Grand	Moab	8,999	6,620	3,682
Iron	Parowan	40,544	20,789	3,298
Juab	Nephi	9,420	5,817	3,392
Kane	Kanab	6,532	5,169	3,992
Millard	Fillmore	12,390	11,333	6,589
Morgan	Morgan	8,134	5,528	609
Piute	Junction	1,347	1,277	758
Rich	Randolph	2,040	1,725	1,029
Salt Lake	Salt Lake City	978,701	725,956	737
San Juan	Monticello	14,265	12,621	7,820
Sanpete	Manti	24,196	16,259	1,588
Sevier	Richfield	19,640	15,431	1,910
Summit	Coalville	35,469	15,518	1,871
Tooele	Tooele	53,552	26,601	6,930
Uintah	Vernal	27,955	22,211	4,477
Utah	Provo	464,760	263,590	1,998
Wasatch	Heber City	20,255	10,089	1,177
Washington	Saint George	126,312	48,560	2,427
Wayne	Loa	2,544	2,177	2,460
Weber	Ogden	213,247	158,330	576

Vermont
(14 counties, 9,250 sq. mi. land; pop. 623,908)

County	County seat or courthouse	2006 Pop.	1990 Pop.	Land area sq. mi.
Addison	Middlebury	37,057	32,953	770
Bennington	Bennington	36,929	35,845	676
Caledonia	Saint Johnsbury	30,842	27,846	651
Chittenden	Burlington	150,069	131,761	539
Essex	Guildhall	6,567	6,405	665
Franklin	Saint Albans	48,187	39,980	637
Grand Isle	North Hero	7,751	5,318	83
Lamoille	Hyde Park	24,592	19,735	461
Orange	Chelsea	29,440	26,149	689
Orleans	Newport	27,718	24,053	698
Rutland	Rutland	63,641	62,142	933
Washington	Montpelier	59,564	54,928	689
Windham	Newfane	43,898	41,588	789
Windsor	Woodstock	57,653	54,055	971

Virginia
(95 counties, 39 ind. cities, 39,594 sq. mi. land; pop. 7,642,884)

County	County seat or courthouse	2006 Pop.	1990 Pop.	Land area sq. mi.
Accomack	Accomac	39,345	31,703	455
Albemarle	Charlottesville	92,035	68,177	723
Alleghany[1]	Covington	16,600	12,815	445
Amelia	Amelia Court House	12,502	8,787	357
Amherst	Amherst	32,239	28,578	475
Appomattox	Appomattox	14,128	12,300	334
Arlington	Arlington	199,776	170,895	26
Augusta	Staunton	70,910	54,557	970
Bath	Warm Springs	4,814	4,799	532
Bedford	Bedford	66,507	45,553	755
Bland	Bland	6,903	6,514	359
Botetourt	Fincastle	32,228	24,992	543
Brunswick	Lawrenceville	17,938	15,987	566
Buchanan	Grundy	24,409	31,333	504
Buckingham	Buckingham	16,099	12,873	581
Campbell	Rustburg	52,667	47,499	504
Caroline	Bowling Green	26,731	19,217	533
Carroll	Hillsville	29,450	26,519	476
Charles City	Charles City	7,221	6,282	183
Charlotte	Charlotte Court	12,491	11,688	475
Chesterfield	Chesterfield	296,718	209,599	426
Clarke	Berryville	14,565	12,101	177
Craig	New Castle	5,179	4,372	331
Culpeper	Culpeper	44,622	27,791	381
Cumberland	Cumberland	9,465	7,825	298
Dickenson	Clintwood	16,182	17,620	332
Dinwiddie	Dinwiddie	25,695	22,279	504
Essex	Tappahannock	10,633	8,689	258
Fairfax	Fairfax	1,010,443	818,310	395
Fauquier	Warrenton	66,170	48,700	650
Floyd	Floyd	14,789	11,965	381
Fluvanna	Palmyra	25,058	12,429	287
Franklin	Rocky Mount	50,784	39,549	692
Frederick	Winchester	71,187	45,723	415
Giles	Pearisburg	17,403	16,366	357
Gloucester	Gloucester	38,293	30,131	217
Goochland	Goochland	20,085	14,163	284
Grayson	Independence	16,159	16,278	443
Greene	Stanardsville	17,709	10,297	157
Greensville	Emporia	11,006	8,553	295

County	County seat or courthouse	2006 Pop.	1990 Pop.	Land area sq. mi.
Halifax	Halifax	36,149	36,030	819
Hanover	Hanover	98,983	63,306	473
Henrico	Richmond	284,399	217,878	238
Henry	Collinsville	56,208	56,942	382
Highland	Monterey	2,510	2,635	416
Isle of Wight	Isle of Wight	34,723	25,053	316
James City	Williamsburg	59,741	34,779	143
King and Queen	King and Queen Court House	6,903	6,289	316
King George	King George	21,780	13,527	180
King William	King William	15,381	10,913	275
Lancaster	Lancaster	11,519	10,896	133
Lee	Jonesville	23,787	24,496	437
Loudoun	Leesburg	268,817	86,185	520
Louisa	Louisa	31,226	20,325	497
Lunenburg	Lunenburg	13,219	11,419	432
Madison	Madison	13,613	11,949	321
Mathews	Mathews	9,184	8,348	86
Mecklenburg	Boydton	32,381	29,241	624
Middlesex	Saluda	10,615	8,653	130
Montgomery	Christiansburg	84,541	73,913	388
Nelson	Lovingston	15,161	12,778	472
New Kent	New Kent	16,852	10,466	210
Northampton	Eastville	13,609	13,061	207
Northumberland	Heathsville	12,820	10,524	192
Nottoway	Nottoway	15,572	14,993	315
Orange	Orange	31,740	21,421	342
Page	Luray	24,104	21,690	311
Patrick	Stuart	19,212	17,473	483
Pittsylvania	Chatham	61,501	55,672	971
Powhatan	Powhatan	27,649	15,328	261
Prince Edward	Farmville	20,530	17,320	353
Prince George	Prince George	36,184	27,390	266
Prince William	Manassas	357,503	214,954	338
Pulaski	Pulaski	35,055	34,496	321
Rappahannock	Washington	7,203	6,622	267
Richmond	Warsaw	9,142	7,273	191
Roanoke	Salem	90,482	79,278	251
Rockbridge	Lexington	21,337	18,350	600
Rockingham	Harrisonburg	72,564	57,482	851
Russell	Lebanon	28,790	28,667	475
Scott	Gate City	22,882	23,204	537
Shenandoah	Woodstock	40,051	31,636	512
Smyth	Marion	32,506	32,370	452
Southampton	Courtland	17,814	17,022	600
Spotsylvania	Spotsylvania	119,529	57,397	401
Stafford	Stafford	120,170	62,255	270
Surry	Surry	7,119	6,145	279
Sussex	Sussex	12,249	10,248	491
Tazewell	Tazewell	44,608	45,960	520
Warren	Front Royal	36,102	26,142	214
Washington	Abingdon	51,984	45,887	563
Westmoreland	Montross	17,188	15,480	229
Wise	Wise	41,905	39,573	404
Wythe	Wytheville	28,640	25,471	463
York	Yorktown	61,879	42,434	106

Independent Cities

Alexandria		136,974	111,183	15
Bedford		6,249	6,176	7
Bristol		17,496	18,426	13
Buena Vista		6,457	6,406	7
Charlottesville		40,315	40,470	10
Chesapeake		220,560	151,982	341
Colonial Heights		17,676	16,064	7
Covington		6,073	7,352	6
Danville		45,586	53,056	43
Emporia		5,625	5,556	7
Fairfax		22,422	19,945	6
Falls Church		10,799	9,464	2
Franklin		8,800	8,392	8
Fredericksburg		21,273	19,033	11
Galax		6,682	6,745	8
Hampton		145,017	133,773	52
Harrisonburg		40,885	30,707	18
Hopewell		22,731	23,101	10
Lexington		6,739	6,959	2
Lynchburg		67,720	66,120	49
Manassas		36,638	27,757	10
Manassas Park		11,642	6,798	2
Martinsville		14,945	16,162	11
Newport News		178,281	171,477	68
Norfolk		229,112	261,250	54
Norton		3,643	4,247	8
Petersburg		32,445	37,071	23
Poquoson		11,918	11,005	16
Portsmouth		101,377	103,910	33
Radford		14,525	15,940	10
Richmond		192,913	202,713	60
Roanoke		91,552	96,487	43
Salem		24,825	23,835	15
Staunton		23,334	24,581	20
Suffolk		81,071	52,143	400
Virginia Beach		435,619	393,089	248
Waynesboro		21,454	18,549	15
Williamsburg		11,793	11,600	9
Winchester		25,265	21,947	9

(1) The independent city of Clifton Forge became part of Alleghany County in 2001.

Washington
(39 counties, 66,544 sq. mi. land; pop. 6,395,798)

County	County seat or courthouse	2006 Pop.	1990 Pop.	Land area sq. mi.
Adams	Ritzville	16,887	13,603	1,925
Asotin	Asotin	21,247	17,605	635
Benton	Prosser	159,463	112,560	1,703
Chelan	Wenatchee	71,034	52,250	2,921
Clallam	Port Angeles	70,400	56,210	1,739
Clark	Vancouver	412,938	238,053	628
Columbia	Dayton	4,087	4,024	869
Cowlitz	Kelso	99,905	82,119	1,139
Douglas	Waterville	35,772	26,205	1,821
Ferry	Republic	7,560	6,295	2,204
Franklin	Pasco	66,570	37,473	1,242
Garfield	Pomeroy	2,223	2,248	711
Grant	Ephrata	82,612	54,798	2,681
Grays Harbor	Montesano	71,587	64,175	1,917
Island	Coupeville	81,489	60,195	208
Jefferson	Port Townsend	29,279	20,406	1,814
King	Seattle	1,826,732	1,507,305	2,126
Kitsap	Port Orchard	240,604	189,731	396
Kittitas	Ellensburg	37,189	26,725	2,297
Klickitat	Goldendale	20,335	16,616	1,872
Lewis	Chehalis	73,585	59,358	2,408
Lincoln	Davenport	10,376	8,864	2,311
Mason	Shelton	55,951	38,341	961
Okanogan	Okanogan	40,040	33,350	5,268
Pacific	South Bend	21,735	18,882	933
Pend Oreille	Newport	12,951	8,915	1,400
Pierce	Tacoma	766,878	586,203	1,679
San Juan	Friday Harbor	15,298	10,035	175
Skagit	Mount Vernon	115,700	79,545	1,735
Skamania	Stevenson	10,833	8,289	1,656
Snohomish	Everett	669,887	465,628	2,089
Spokane	Spokane	446,706	361,333	1,764
Stevens	Colville	42,632	30,948	2,478
Thurston	Olympia	234,670	161,238	727
Wahkiakum	Cathlamet	4,026	3,327	264
Walla Walla	Walla Walla	57,721	48,439	1,271
Whatcom	Bellingham	185,953	127,780	2,120
Whitman	Colfax	39,838	38,775	2,159
Yakima	Yakima	233,105	188,823	4,296

West Virginia
(55 counties, 24,078 sq. mi. land; pop. 1,818,470)

County	County seat or courthouse	2006 Pop.	1990 Pop.	Land area sq. mi.
Barbour	Philippi	15,788	15,699	341
Berkeley	Martinsburg	97,534	59,253	321
Boone	Madison	25,512	25,870	503
Braxton	Sutton	14,810	12,998	513
Brooke	Wellsburg	24,132	26,992	89
Cabell	Huntington	93,904	96,827	282
Calhoun	Grantsville	7,381	7,885	281
Clay	Clay	10,256	9,983	342
Doddridge	West Union	7,459	6,994	320
Fayette	Fayetteville	46,610	47,952	664
Gilmer	Glenville	6,965	7,669	340
Grant	Petersburg	11,915	10,428	477
Greenbrier	Lewisburg	34,850	34,693	1,021
Hampshire	Romney	22,480	16,498	642
Hancock	New Cumberland	30,911	35,233	83
Hardy	Moorefield	13,420	10,977	583
Harrison	Clarksburg	68,745	69,371	416
Jackson	Ripley	28,451	25,938	466
Jefferson	Charles Town	50,443	35,926	210
Kanawha	Charleston	192,419	207,619	903
Lewis	Weston	17,129	17,223	382
Lincoln	Hamlin	22,357	21,382	437
Logan	Logan	36,218	43,032	454
McDowell	Welch	23,882	35,233	535
Marion	Fairmont	56,706	57,249	310
Marshall	Moundsville	33,896	37,356	307
Mason	Point Pleasant	25,756	25,178	432
Mercer	Princeton	61,278	64,980	420
Mineral	Keyser	26,928	26,697	328
Mingo	Williamson	27,100	33,739	423
Monongalia	Morgantown	84,752	75,509	361
Monroe	Union	13,510	12,406	473
Morgan	Berkeley Springs	16,337	12,128	229
Nicholas	Summersville	26,446	26,775	649
Ohio	Wheeling	44,662	50,871	106
Pendleton	Franklin	7,679	8,054	698
Pleasants	St. Marys	7,280	7,546	131
Pocahontas	Marlinton	8,755	9,008	940
Preston	Kingwood	30,384	29,037	648
Putnam	Winfield	54,982	42,835	346

County	County seat or courthouse	2006 Pop.	1990 Pop.	Land area sq. mi.
Raleigh	Beckley	79,302	76,819	607
Randolph	Elkins	28,465	27,803	1,040
Ritchie	Harrisville	10,628	10,233	454
Roane	Spencer	15,583	15,120	484
Summers	Hinton	13,531	14,204	361
Taylor	Grafton	16,304	15,144	173
Tucker	Parsons	6,856	7,728	419
Tyler	Middlebourne	9,264	9,796	258
Upshur	Buckhannon	23,685	22,867	355
Wayne	Wayne	41,647	41,636	506
Webster	Webster Springs	9,696	10,729	556
Wetzel	New Martinsville	16,685	19,258	359
Wirt	Elizabeth	5,980	5,192	233
Wood	Parkersburg	86,597	86,915	367
Wyoming	Pineville	24,225	28,990	501

Wisconsin
(72 counties, 54,310 sq. mi. land; pop. 5,556,506)

County	County seat or courthouse	2006 Pop.	1990 Pop.	Land area sq. mi.
Adams	Friendship	20,843	15,682	648
Ashland	Ashland	16,511	16,307	1,044
Barron	Barron	45,889	40,750	863
Bayfield	Washburn	15,147	14,008	1,476
Brown	Green Bay	240,213	194,594	529
Buffalo	Alma	13,897	13,584	684
Burnett	Siren	16,490	13,084	822
Calumet	Chilton	44,579	34,291	320
Chippewa	Chippewa Falls	60,300	52,360	1,010
Clark	Neillsville	34,094	31,647	1,216
Columbia	Portage	55,440	45,088	774
Crawford	Prairie du Chien	17,060	15,940	573
Dane	Madison	463,826	367,085	1,202
Dodge	Juneau	88,983	76,559	882
Door	Sturgeon Bay	28,200	25,690	483
Douglas	Superior	44,061	41,758	1,309
Dunn	Menomonie	41,975	35,909	852
Eau Claire	Eau Claire	94,741	85,183	638
Florence	Florence	4,941	4,590	488
Fond du Lac	Fond du Lac	99,243	90,083	723
Forest	Crandon	9,899	8,776	1,014
Grant	Lancaster	49,362	49,266	1,148
Green	Monroe	35,688	30,339	584
Green Lake	Green Lake	19,147	18,651	354
Iowa	Dodgeville	23,756	20,150	763
Iron	Hurley	6,502	6,153	757
Jackson	Black River Falls	19,853	16,588	987
Jefferson	Jefferson	80,025	67,783	557
Juneau	Mauston	26,855	21,650	768
Kenosha	Kenosha	162,001	128,181	273
Kewaunee	Kewaunee	20,832	18,878	343
La Crosse	La Crosse	109,404	97,904	453
Lafayette	Darlington	16,298	16,074	634
Langlade	Antigo	20,631	19,505	873
Lincoln	Merrill	30,151	26,993	883
Manitowoc	Manitowoc	81,911	80,421	592
Marathon	Wausau	130,223	115,400	1,545
Marinette	Marinette	43,208	40,548	1,402
Marquette	Montello	15,227	12,321	455
Menominee	Keshena	4,597	4,075	358
Milwaukee	Milwaukee	915,097	959,212	242
Monroe	Sparta	43,028	36,633	901
Oconto	Oconto	37,958	30,226	998
Oneida	Rhinelander	36,779	31,679	1,125
Outagamie	Appleton	172,734	140,510	640
Ozaukee	Port Washington	86,321	72,894	232
Pepin	Durand	7,325	7,107	232
Pierce	Ellsworth	39,373	32,765	576
Polk	Balsam Lake	44,784	34,773	917
Portage	Stevens Point	67,484	61,405	806
Price	Phillips	15,000	15,600	1,253
Racine	Racine	196,096	175,034	333
Richland	Richland Center	18,341	17,521	586
Rock	Janesville	159,153	139,510	720
Rusk	Ladysmith	15,054	15,079	913
Saint Croix	Hudson	80,015	50,251	722
Sauk	Baraboo	58,261	46,975	838
Sawyer	Hayward	17,080	14,181	1,256
Shawano	Shawano	41,401	37,157	893
Sheboygan	Sheboygan	114,756	103,877	514
Taylor	Medford	19,605	18,901	975
Trempealeau	Whitehall	28,078	25,263	734
Vernon	Viroqua	29,188	25,617	795
Vilas	Eagle River	22,379	17,707	874
Walworth	Elkhorn	101,007	75,000	555

County	County seat or courthouse	2006 Pop.	1990 Pop.	Land area sq. mi.	County	County seat or courthouse	2006 Pop.	1990 Pop.	Land area sq. mi.
Washburn	Shell Lake	16,674	13,772	810	Crook	Sundance	6,255	5,294	2,859
Washington	West Bend	127,578	95,328	431	Fremont	Lander	37,163	33,662	9,182
Waukesha	Waukesha	380,985	304,715	556	Goshen	Torrington	12,129	12,373	2,225
Waupaca	Waupaca	52,687	46,104	751	Hot Springs	Thermopolis	4,588	4,809	2,004
Waushara	Wautoma	24,915	19,385	626	Johnson	Buffalo	8,014	6,145	4,166
Winnebago	Oshkosh	160,593	140,320	439	Laramie	Cheyenne	85,384	73,142	2,686
Wood	Wisconsin Rapids. .	74,774	73,605	793	Lincoln	Kemmerer	16,383	12,625	4,069

Wyoming
(23 counties, 97,100 sq. mi. land; pop. 515,004)

County	County seat or courthouse	2006 Pop.	1990 Pop.	Land area sq. mi.		County seat or courthouse	2006 Pop.	1990 Pop.	Land area sq. mi.
					Natrona	Casper	70,401	61,226	5,340
					Niobrara	Lusk	2,253	2,499	2,626
					Park	Cody	27,094	23,178	6,942
					Platte	Wheatland	8,588	8,145	2,085
					Sheridan	Sheeridan	27,673	23,562	2,523
Albany	Laramie	30,360	30,797	4,273	Sublette	Pinedale	7,359	4,843	4,883
Big Horn	Basin	11,390	10,525	3,137	Sweetwater	Green River	38,763	38,823	10,425
Campbell	Gillette	38,934	29,370	4,797	Teton	Jackson	19,288	11,173	4,008
Carbon	Rawlins	15,325	16,659	7,896	Uinta	Evanston	20,213	18,705	2,082
Converse	Douglas	12,866	11,128	4,255	Washakie	Worland	7,819	8,388	2,240
					Weston	Newcastle	6,762	6,518	2,398

Population of Outlying Areas
Source: Bureau of the Census, U.S. Dept. of Commerce; World Almanac research

Population estimates for July 1, 2006, are given for Puerto Rican municipios (a municipio is the governmental unit that is the primary legal subdivision of Puerto Rico; the Census Bureau treats the municipio as the statistical equivalent of a county). All other population counts and all land area figures are from the 2000 census. Because only selected areas are shown, the population and land area figures may not equal the total reported.

ZIP codes with an asterisk (*) are general delivery ZIP codes. Consult the local postmaster or www.usps.com for more specific delivery information. Wake Atoll, Johnston Atoll, and Midway Atoll receive mail through APO and FPO addresses.

Commonwealth of Puerto Rico
(78 municipios, 3,425 sq. mi. land; pop. 3,927,776)

ZIP code	Municipio	2006 Pop.	Land area sq. mi.	ZIP code	Municipio	2006 Pop.	Land area sq. mi.	ZIP code	Municipio	2006 Pop.	Land area sq. mi.
00601*	Adjuntas	18,583	67	00738	Fajardo	41,986	30	00718	Naguabo	24,209	52
00602	Aguada	45,165	31	00650	Florida	15,203	15	00719	Naranjito	29,918	27
00605*	Aguadilla	66,926	37	00653	Guánica	22,735	37	00720	Orocovis	24,654	63
00703	Aguas Buenas	31,053	31	00785*	Guayama	45,205	65	00723	Patillas	20,026	47
00705	Aibonito	27,146	31	00656	Guayanilla	23,653	42	00624	Peñuelas	29,045	44
00610	Añasco	29,888	39	00970*	Guaynabo	102,525	27	00732*	Ponce	181,267	115
00613*	Arecibo	102,216	126	00778	Gurabo	42,142	28	00678	Quebradillas	27,612	23
00714	Arroyo	19,038	15	00659	Hatillo	42,483	42	00677	Rincón	16,155	14
00617	Barceloneta	23,028	19	00660	Hormigüeros	17,414	11	00745	Río Grande	55,894	61
00794	Barranquitas	30,254	34	00791*	Humacao	60,569	45	00637	Sabana Grande	27,404	36
00958*	Bayamón	221,546	44	00662	Isabela	47,301	55	00751	Salinas	31,985	69
00623	Cabo Rojo	52,123	70	00664	Jayuya	18,194	45	00683	San Germán	37,485	55
00726*	Caguas	142,769	59	00795	Juana Díaz	52,770	60	00936*	San Juan	426,618	48
00627	Camuy	38,803	46	00777	Juncos	40,129	27	00754	San Lorenzo	43,921	53
00729	Canóvanas	46,781	33	00667	Lajas	27,583	60	00685	San Sebastián	47,145	70
00984*	Carolina	187,578	45	00669	Lares	37,164	61	00757	Santa Isabel	22,763	34
00963*	Cataño	27,036	5	00670	Las Marías	11,948	46	00954*	Toa Alta	77,599	27
00737*	Cayey	47,378	52	00771	Las Piedras	38,631	34	00950*	Toa Baja	95,000	23
00735	Ceiba	17,991	29	00772	Loíza	33,634	19	00976*	Trujillo Alto	84,396	21
00638	Ciales	20,581	67	00773	Luquillo	20,452	26	00641	Utuado	34,799	113
00739	Cidra	47,294	36	00674	Manatí	48,996	45	00692	Vega Alta	39,372	28
00769	Coamo	39,265	78	00606	Maricao	6,300	37	00694*	Vega Baja	64,379	46
00782	Comerío	19,460	28	00707	Maunabo	12,679	21	00765	Vieques	9,205	51
00783	Corozal	38,625	43	00681*	Mayagüez	94,478	78	00766	Villalba	29,762	35
00775	Culebra	2,077	12	00676	Moca	43,664	50	00767	Yabucoa	40,332	55
00646	Dorado	36,002	23	00687	Morovis	32,379	39	00698	Yauco	48,008	68

Other U.S. External Territories

American Samoa
(77 sq. mi. land; 2000 pop. 57,291; Zip code 96799)

Guam
(210 sq. mi. land; pop. 154,805)

ZIP code	Location	2000 Pop.	Land area sq. mi.
96910*	Agaña Hts.	3,940	1
96928	Agat	5,656	10
96910*	Asan	2,090	6
96913*	Barrigada	8,652	8
96924	Chalan Pago-Ordot	5,923	6
96929	Dededo	42,980	31
96910*	Hagatña	1,100	1
96915	Inarajan	3,052	19
96913	Mangilao	13,313	10
96915	Merizo	2,163	6
96910*	Mongmong-Toto-Maite	5,845	2

ZIP code	Location	2000 Pop.	Land area sq. mi.
96915	Piti	1,666	7
96915	Santa Rita	7,500	16
96910	Sinajana	2,853	1
96915	Talofofo	3,215	18
96913*	Tamuning	18,012	6
96915	Umatac	887	6
96929	Yigo	19,474	35
96915	Yona	6,484	20

Commonwealth of the Northern Mariana Islands
(4 municipalities, 179 sq. mi. land; pop. 69,221)

ZIP code	Municipality	2000 Pop.	Land area sq. mi.
96950	Northern Islands...	6	60
96951	Rota	3,283	33
96950	Saipan	62,392	45
96952	Tinian	3,540	42

Virgin Islands
(134 sq. mi. land; pop. 108,612)

ZIP code	Location	2000 Pop.	Land area sq. mi.
00820	Saint Croix	53,234	83
00820*	Christiansted	2,637	<1
00841*	Frederiksted	732	<1
00830*	Saint John	4,197	20
00804*	Saint Thomas	51,181	31
00802*	Charlotte Amalie	11,004	<1

WORLD HISTORY

Chronology of World History
Reviewed by Helen A. Gaudette, Ph.D.

Note: In this section, the notation BCE (before the common era) is applied to years dating to the traditional BC (before Christ) era, and CE (common era) is applied to AD (anno domini) dates. This notation is now preferred in scientific and academic publications. The traditional Gregorian Calendar system and its dates and years are unaltered except by these labels.

Other abbreviations used in this chapter include: MYA = million years ago, BP = years before the present, c. = circa, fl. = flourished, r. = ruled, b. = born, d. = died.

Prehistory: Our Ancestors Emerge
Reviewed by G. A. Clark, Ph.D.

Evidence of the origins of *Homo sapiens sapiens*, the genus, species, and subspecies to which all living humans belong, comes from fossils, genetic and anatomical studies, and interpretation of the geological and archaeological records. The current body of evidence suggests that humans evolved from apelike primate ancestors that lived in E and central Africa 5-7 million years ago (MYA). Although humans living today are members of a single subspecies, the fossil record confirms that our ancestors coexisted with other similar species. Current theories trace the first hominid (upright, bipedal, humanlike primate) to Africa 4-6 MYA. Different genera lived in a variety of environments throughout the continent. In addition to *Australopithecus afarensis*—better known as "Lucy," an Ethiopian specimen found in 1974 that dates to 3.5 MYA—these early hominids include such recent discoveries as *Sahelanthropus* (c. 6.5 MYA, from Chad), *Ardipithecus* (c. 5 MYA, Kenya), *Kenyanthropus* (c. 3.5 MYA, Kenya), and *Orrorin* (c. 5 MYA, Kenya).

Our genus, *Homo*, arose 2-3 MYA, when hominids began to produce primitive stone tools. The oldest tools are dated to c. 2.5 MYA from the Kada Gona site, in Ethiopia, and were made by systematically removing sharp flakes from a stone core. This produced tools used for scraping and cutting meat, sinew, and wood, as well as implements used to break bones open to obtain fat and marrow. Although we cannot determine whether they had the ability to speak, early hominids were social animals, who lived in groups of c. 12-20 individuals, aggregated and dispersed seasonally, used campsites repeatedly, and subsisted by gathering plants and small animals or scavenging larger predators' kills. A closer ancestor, *Homo erectus*, appeared in E Africa around 1.9 MYA and was the first to leave the continent, spreading throughout Eurasia by c. 1.8 MYA. *Homo erectus* hunted, learned to control fire (by c. 500,000 years ago), and may have had primitive language skills.

Europe has provided a particularly rich set of fossil evidence dating to about 250,000 years ago and after. Neanderthals, who appeared c. 200,000 BP (years before the present), were proficient hunters of game, had sophisticated tools, developed social organizations, and were well-adapted to harsh Ice Age European climates. Recent advances in molecular biology support the theory that Neanderthals were a distinct population or species that coexisted with—but evidently did not interbreed with—early modern humans (also called Crô-Magnons). A similar situation may have occurred in Asia, where more primitive *Homo* species coexisted with early modern humans after c. 40,000 BP, and possibly as recently as 18,000 years ago, on Flores. Further study of *Homo antecessor*, a species identified at the Trinchera Dolina site in Spain, might help clarify the relationship between the earliest representatives of *Homo* in W Europe, and the Neanderthals.

Genetic evidence indicates that the first *Homo sapiens* originated in E Africa. The oldest existing modern human fossils are dated to c. 160,000 BP, and were found in Ethiopia's Middle Awash valley. Our species quickly spread. Modern humans were living in Israel by c. 100,000 BP, and in Romania by c. 35,000 BP. Migration from Asia to Australia took place as early as 60,000 BP. First confirmation for the crossing from Asia to the Americas by the Bering land bridge dates to the end of the last Ice Age, at 14,000 BP; however, genetic data and the Monte Verde site in Chile suggest that small, isolated groups of people arrived in the Americas 18,000 to 14,000 years ago, settling in both continents.

As human cognitive capacities slowly expanded over the Pleistocene (1.7–0.01 MYA), a variety of behavioral modes—in toolmaking, diet, shelter, social arrangements, and spiritual expression—arose as humans adapted to different geographic and climatic zones. By about 20,000 years ago, sites from all over the world show seasonal migration patterns and efficient exploitation of a wide range of plant and animal foods.

The ability to make fire enormously expanded the human diet. Fire-making began as early as 1 MYA in Africa and is documented in Asia and Europe after c. 500,000 years ago. Hearths were found to be in N Israel by c. 750,000 BP, and by 465,000 BP in SW France. Fire-hardened wooden throwing spears c. 3 m long were fashioned by big-game hunters c. 400,000 years ago in Germany. Scraping tools, dated to after 750,000 BP in Europe, N Africa, the Middle East, and Central Asia, suggest the preparation of hides for clothing. The oldest relatively unambiguous evidence of personal adornment, perforated snail shell beads, dates to c. 120,000 BP at Skhul Cave on Mount Carmel in Israel. By the time Australia was settled, human ancestors had learned to navigate in boats over open water. The earliest bone tools found so far were fashioned some 90,000 years ago at Semliki, in the Congo basin, by fishermen who crafted bone harpoons.

About 60,000 BP the earliest immigrants to Australia carved and painted designs on rocks. Although the painted caves of Cosquer and Chauvet in southern France date to c. 35,000 years ago, it was after c. 15,000 BP that painting and decoration flourished in Europe, along with stone and ivory sculpture. A few musical instruments—bone flutes with precisely bored holes—have been found in sites dated after 40,000 BP.

Over the course of the Upper Pleistocene (c. 130,000-12,000 years ago), the number of people surviving long enough to become grandparents slowly increased. With more adults available to provide child care, humans began to develop more complex, multigenerational social systems. The 'reach' of social memory increased accordingly. Shortly after 10,000 BCE, among widely separated foraging communities in both hemispheres, a series of dramatic technological and social changes occurred, marking the Neolithic Age, or New Stone Age. As the world climate became drier and warmer, the population-to-resource ratio became imbalanced, eventually creating increased human interference in the life cycles of certain plants and animals. Domesticated plants and animals facilitated population growth and the appearance of permanent settlements, which in turn reduced birth spacing and spurred more population growth. Manufacture of pottery and cloth began shortly thereafter. Genetic research suggests that mutations related to traits currently found in human populations, such as unusually light skin pigmentation and the ability to process lactose amongst Europeans, arose after c. 12,000 years ago.

Sites in the Americas, SE Europe, and the Middle East show roughly contemporaneous (10,000-8000 BCE) evidence of Neolithic domestication economies. Adaptation to the Neolithic domestication economy in E and S Asia, W Europe, and sub-Saharan Africa dates to between c. 8000-5000 BCE. Farming and sheep- and goat-herding spread rapidly throughout the Mediterranean basin, perhaps in as few as 100-200 years. The variety of crops—wheat, barley, rice, maize, squash, beans, and tubers—and other characteristics suggest that this adaptation occurred independently in as many as 12 or 13 places in both hemispheres. Evidence for fermented beverages likewise coincides with the early Neolithic farming lifestyle. Northern Chinese farmers concocted a wine-like drink from rice, honey, and fruit between 7000 and 6000 BCE. Vintners in what today is Iran were fermenting grapes and making wine by c. 5400 BCE. The domestication economies of the Neolithic Revolution provided the basis for subsequent social and cultural evolution worldwide.

Major Gods & Goddesses of Ancient Egypt

Name	Relations	Sphere or Position	Emblem/Attribute
Ra (Re)/Atum/Amon	Self-created	The sun, creation	Hawk
Thoth (Djeheuty)	Son of Ra	The moon, wisdom, writing	Ibis/baboon
Ptah	Creator of Atum	Creation, craftsmen	—
Osiris	Brother of Set(h) & Isis	The underworld (dead), fertility, resurrection, vegetation	Bull
Isis	Sister/consort of Osiris	The underworld (dead)	—
Set(h)	Brother of Osiris	Evil, trickery, chaos	Boar, pig
Horus (several)	Sons of Osiris & Isis and Ra & Hathor	The earth	Falcon
Hathor	Consort of Ra	Motherhood, love	Cow
Anubis	Son of Osiris	Embalmer & judge of the dead	Jackal/dog

Earliest Civilizations: 4000-1000 BCE

Mesopotamia. If history began with writing, the first chapter opened in Mesopotamia, the Tigris-Euphrates river valley. The Sumerians used clay tablets with pictographs to keep records after 4000 BCE. A **cuneiform** (wedge-shaped) script evolved by 3000 BCE as a full syllabic alphabet. Neighboring peoples adapted the script for their own use.

Sumerian life centered, from 4000 BCE, on large cities (Eridu, Ur, Uruk, Nippur, Kish, and Lagash) organized around temples and priestly bureaucracies, with surrounding plains watered by vast irrigation works and worked with traction plows. Sailboats, wheeled vehicles, potter's wheels, and kilns were used. Copper was smelted and tempered from c. 4000 BCE; bronze was produced not long after. Ores, as well as precious stones and metals, were obtained through long-distance ship and caravan trade. Iron was used from c. 2000 BCE. Improved ironworking, developed partly by the Hittites, became widespread by 1200 BCE.

Sumerian political primacy passed among cities and their kingly dynasties. Semitic-speaking peoples, with cultures derived from the Sumerian, founded a succession of dynasties that ruled in Mesopotamia and neighboring areas for most of 1,800 years; among them were the **Akkadians** (first under Sargon I, c. 2350 BCE), the Amorites (whose laws, codified by **Hammurabi**, c. 1792-1750 BCE, have biblical parallels), and the Assyrians, with interludes of rule by the Hittites, Kassites, and Mitanni.

Mesopotamian learning, maintained by scribes and preserved in vast libraries, was practically oriented. Lists of astronomical phenomena, plants, animals, and stones were maintained; medical texts listed ailments and herbal cures. The Sumerians worshiped anthropomorphic gods representing natural forces. Sacrifices were made at **ziggurats**—huge stepped temples.

The Syria-Palestine area, site of some of the earliest urban remains (Jericho, 7000 BCE), and of the recently uncovered **Ebla** civilization (fl. 2500 BCE), experienced Egyptian cultural and political influence along with Mesopotamian. The **Phoenician** coast was an active commercial center. A phonetic alphabet was invented here before 1600 BCE. It became the ancestor of many other alphabets.

Egypt. Agricultural villages along the Nile River were united by around 3300 BCE into 2 kingdoms, Upper and Lower Egypt, unified (c. 3100 BCE) under the pharaoh Menes. A bureaucracy supervised construction of canals and monuments (**pyramids** starting 2700 BCE. Control over Nubia to the S was asserted from 2600 BCE. Brilliant **Old Kingdom** Period achievements in architecture, sculpture, and painting reached their height during the 3rd and 4th Dynasties. **Hieroglyphic writing** appeared by 3200 BCE, recording a sophisticated literature that included religious writings, philosophy, history, and science. An ordered hierarchy of gods, including totemistic animal elements, was served by

Egyptian hieroglyphics

a powerful priesthood in Memphis. The pharaoh was identified with the falcon god Horus. Other trends included belief in an afterlife and short-lived quasi-monotheistic reforms introduced by the pharaoh **Akhenaton** (c. 1379-1362 BCE), also the husband of Nefertiti.

After a period of dominance by Semitic Hyksos from Asia (c. 1700-1550 BCE), the **New Kingdom** established an empire in Syria. Egypt became increasingly embroiled in Asiatic wars and diplomacy. Conquered by Persia in 525 BCE, it eventually faded away as an independent culture.

India. An urban civilization with an as-yet undeciphered writing system stretched across the Indus Valley and along the Arabian Sea c. 3000-1500 BCE. Major sites are Harappa and **Mohenjo-Daro** in Pakistan, well-planned geometric cities with underground sewers and vast granaries. The entire region may have been ruled as a single state. Bronze was used, and arts and crafts were well developed. Religious life apparently took the form of fertility cults. Indus civilization was probably in decline when it was destroyed by **Aryans** who arrived from the NW, speaking an Indo-European language. Led by a warrior aristocracy whose legendary deeds are in the **Rig Veda**, the Aryans spread E and S, bringing their sky gods, priestly (Brahman) ritual, and the beginnings of the caste system; local customs and beliefs were assimilated by the conquerors.

Europe. On Crete, the Bronze Age **Minoan civilization** emerged c. 2500 BCE. A prosperous economy and richly decorative art was supported by seaborne commerce. Mycenae and other cities in mainland Greece and Asia Minor (e.g., **Troy**) preserved elements of the culture until c. 1200 BCE. Cretan Linear A script (c. 2000-1700 BCE) remains undeciphered; Linear B script (c. 1300-1200 BCE) records an early Greek dialect. The possible connection between Mycenaean monumental stonework and the megalithic monuments of W Europe, Iberia, and Malta (c. 4000-1500 BCE) is unclear.

China. Proto-Chinese neolithic cultures had long covered N and SE China when the first large political state was organized in the N by the **Shang dynasty** (c. 1523 BCE). Shang kings called themselves Sons of Heaven, and they presided over a cult of human and animal sacrifice to ancestors and nature gods. The Chou dynasty, starting c. 1027 BCE, expanded the area of the Son of Heaven's dominion, but feudal states exercised most temporal power. A writing system with 2,000 characters was already in use under the Shang, with **pictographs** later supplemented by phonetic characters. Many of its principles and symbols, despite changes in spoken Chinese, were preserved in later writing systems. Technical advances allowed urban specialists to create fine ceramic and jade products, and bronze casting after 1500 BCE was the most advanced in the world. Bronze artifacts discovered in N Thailand date from 3600 BCE, hundreds of years before initial Middle Eastern finds.

Americas. Olmecs settled (1500 BCE) on the Gulf coast of Mexico and developed the first known civilization in the western hemisphere. Temple cities and huge stone sculpture date from 1200 BCE. A rudimentary calendar and writing system existed. Olmec religion, centering on a jaguar god, and Olmec art forms influenced later Meso-American cultures.

Formation of Classical Societies: 1000 BCE-400 BCE

Homer

Greece. After a period of decline during the Dorian Greek invasions (1200-1000 BCE), the Aegean area developed a unique civilization. Drawing on Mycenaean traditions, Mesopotamian learning (weights and measures, lunisolar calendar, astronomy, musical scales), the Phoenician alphabet (modified for Greek), and Egyptian art, **Greek city-states** saw a rich elaboration of intellectual life. The two great epic poems attributed to **Homer**, the *Iliad* and the *Odyssey,* were probably composed around the 8th cent. BCE. Long-range commerce was aided by metal coinage (introduced by the Lydians in Asia Minor before 700 BCE); colonies were founded around the Mediterranean (Cumae in Italy in 760 BCE; Massalia in France c. 600 BCE) and Black Sea shores.

Philosophy, starting with Ionian speculation on the nature of matter (Thales, c. 634-546 BCE), continued by other "Pre-Socratics" (e.g., Heraclitus, c. 535-415 BCE; Parmenides, b. c. 515 BCE), reached a high point in Athens in the rationalist idealism of **Plato** (c. 428-347 BCE), a disciple of **Socrates** (c. 469-399 BCE; executed for alleged impiety), and in **Aristotle** (384-322 BCE), a pioneer in many fields, from natural sciences to logic, ethics, and metaphysics. The **arts** were highly valued. Architecture culminated in the **Parthenon** (438 BCE) by Phidias (fl. 490-430 BCE). Poetry (Sappho, c. 610-580 BCE; Pindar, c. 518-438 BCE) and **drama** (Aeschylus, 525-456 BCE; Sophocles, c. 496-406 BCE; Euripides, c. 484-406 BCE) thrived. Male beauty and strength, a chief artistic theme, were celebrated at the national games at Olympia.

Ruled by local tyrants or **oligarchies**, the Greeks were not politically united, but managed to resist inclusion in the Persian Empire—Persian king Darius was defeated at Marathon (490 BCE), his son Xerxes at Salamis (480 BCE), and the Persian army at Plataea (479 BCE). Democracy sprouted in Athens as statesman Pericles (495-429 BCE) sought participation in government from all citizens. Local warfare was common; the Peloponnesian Wars (431-404 BCE) ended in Sparta's victory over Athens. Greek political power subsequently waned, but Greek cultural forms spread far and wide.

Hebrews. Nomadic Hebrew tribes entered Canaan before 1200 BCE, settling among other Semitic peoples speaking the same language. They brought from the desert a **monotheistic** faith said to have been revealed to Abraham in Canaan c. 1800 BCE and Moses at Mt. Sinai c. 1250 BCE, after the Hebrews' escape from bondage in Egypt. David (r. 1000-961 BCE) and Solomon (r. 961-922 BCE) united them in a kingdom that briefly dominated the area. **Phoenicians** to the N founded Mediterranean colonies (Carthage, c. 814 BCE) and sailed into the Atlantic.

A temple in Jerusalem became the national religious center, with sacrifices performed by a hereditary priesthood. Polytheistic influences, especially of the fertility cult of Baal, were opposed by **prophets** (Elijah, Amos, Isaiah).

Divided into **two kingdoms** after Solomon, the Hebrews were unable to resist the revived Assyrian empire, which conquered Israel, the N kingdom, in 722 BCE. Judah, the S kingdom, was conquered in 586 BCE by the Babylonians under Nebuchadnezzar II. With the fixing of most of the biblical canon by the mid-4th cent. BCE and the emergence of rabbis, Judaism successfully survived the loss of Hebrew autonomy. A Jewish kingdom was revived under the Hasmoneans (168-42 BCE).

China. During the **Eastern Chou** dynasty (770-256 BCE), Chinese culture spread E to the sea and S to the Yangtze R. Large feudal states on the periphery of the empire contended for preeminence, but continued to recognize the Son of Heaven (king), who retained a purely ritual role enriched with courtly music and dance. In the Age of Warring States (403-221 BCE), when the first sections of the **Great Wall** were built, the Ch'in state in the W gained supremacy and finally united all of China.

Iron tools entered China c. 500 BCE, and casting techniques were advanced, aiding agriculture. Peasants owned their land and owed civil and military service to nobles. China's cities grew in number and size; barter remained the chief trade medium.

Intellectual ferment among noble scribes and officials produced the Classical Age of Chinese literature and philosophy. **Confucius** (551-479 BCE) urged a restoration of a supposedly harmonious social order of the past through proper conduct in accordance with one's station and through filial and ceremonial piety. The *Analects* attributed to him are revered throughout E Asia.

The Seven Wonders of the Ancient World

These ancient works of art and architecture were considered awe-inspiring by the Greek and Roman world of the first few centuries BCE. Later classical writers disagreed as to which works belonged, but the following were usually included:

The Pyramids of Egypt: The only surviving ancient Wonder, these monumental structures of masonry, located at Giza on the W bank of the Nile R above Cairo, were built from c. 2700 to 2500 BCE as royal tombs. Three—Khufu (Cheops), Khafra (Chephren), and Menkaurus (Mycerimus)—were often grouped as the first Wonder of the World. The largest, the Great Pyramid of Khufu covers 13 acres. It is estimated to contain 2.3 million blocks of stone, the stones themselves averaging 2½ tons and some weighing 30 tons. Its construction reputedly took 100,000 laborers 20 years.

The Hanging Gardens of Babylon: These gardens were laid out on a brick terrace 400 ft square and 75 ft above the ground. To irrigate the plants, screws were turned to lift water from the Euphrates R. The gardens were probably built by King Nebuchadnezzar II about 600 BCE. The Walls of Babylon, long, thick, and made of colorfully glazed brick, were also considered by some among the Seven Wonders.

The Pharos (Lighthouse) of Alexandria: This structure was designed about 270 BCE, during the reign of Ptolemy II, by the Greek architect Sostratos. Estimates of its height range from 200 to 600 ft.

The Colossus of Rhodes: A bronze statue of the sun god Helios, the Colossus was worked on for 12 years in the third cent. BCE by the sculptor Chares. It was probably 120 ft high. A symbol of the city of Rhodes at its height, the statue stood on a promontory overlooking the harbor.

The Temple of Artemis (Diana) at Ephesus: This largest and most complex temple of ancient times was built about 550 BCE and was made of marble except for its tile-covered wooden roof. It was begun in honor of a non-Hellenic goddess who later became identified with the Greek goddess of the same name. Ephesus was one of the greatest of the Ionian cities.

The Mausoleum at Halicarnassus: The source of our word *mausoleum*, this marble tomb was built in what is now SE Turkey by Artemisia for her husband Mausolus, king of Caria in Asia Minor, who died in 353 BCE. About 135 ft high, the tomb was adorned with the works of 4 sculptors.

The Statue of Zeus (Jupiter) at Olympia: This statue showed Zeus seated on a throne. His flesh was made of ivory, his robe and ornaments of gold. Reputedly 40 ft high, the statue was made by Phidias and was placed in the great temple of Zeus in the sacred grove of Olympia about 457 BCE.

Among other thinkers, **Mencius** (d. 289 BCE) added the view that the Mandate of Heaven can be removed from an unjust dynasty. The Legalists sought to curb the supposed natural wickedness of people through new institutions and harsh laws. The Naturalists emphasized the balance of opposites—yin, yang—in the world. **Taoists** sought mystical knowledge through meditation and disengagement.

India. The political and cultural center of India shifted from the Indus to the Ganges River Valley. Buddhism, Jainism, and mystical revisions of orthodox Vedism all developed c. 500-300 BCE. The *Upanishads*, last part of the *Veda*, urged escape from the cycle of rebirth into the physical world. Vedism remained the preserve of the Brahman caste.

In contrast, **Buddhism**, founded by Siddhartha Gautama (c. 563-c. 483 BCE)—Buddha ("Enlightened One")—appealed to merchants in the urban centers and took hold at first (and most lastingly) on the geographic fringes of Indian civilization. The classic Indian epics were composed in this era: the **Ramayana** perhaps c. 300 BCE, the **Mahabharata** over a period starting around 400 BCE.

N India was divided into a large number of monarchies and aristocratic republics, probably derived from tribal groupings, when the Magadha kingdom was formed in Bihar c. 542 BCE. It soon became the dominant power. The **Maurya dynasty**, founded by Chandragupta c. 321 BCE, expanded the kingdom, uniting most of N India in a centralized bureaucratic empire. The third Mauryan king, **Asoka** (reigned c. 274-236 BCE), conquered most of the subcontinent. He converted to Buddhism and inscribed its tenets on pillars throughout India. He downplayed the caste system.

Before its final decline in India, Buddhism developed into a popular worship of heavenly Bodhisattvas ("enlightened beings"), and it produced a refined architecture (the Great Stupa [shrine] at Sanchi, 100 CE) and sculpture (Gandhara reliefs, 1-400) CE.

Persia. Aryan peoples (Persians, Medes) dominated the area of present Iran by the beginning of the 1st millennium BCE. The prophet **Zoroaster** (born c. 628 BCE) introduced a dualistic religion in which the forces of good (Ahura Mazda, "Lord of Wisdom") and evil (Ahriman) battle for dominance; individuals are judged by their actions and earn damnation or salvation. Zoroaster's hymns (*Gathas*) are included in the *Avesta*, the Zoroastrian scriptures. A version of this faith became the established religion of the Persian Empire.

Africa. Nubia, periodically occupied by Egypt since about 2600 BCE, ruled Egypt c. 750-661 BCE and survived as an independent Egyptianized kingdom (**Kush;** capital Meroe) for 1,000 years. The Iron Age Nok culture flourished c. 500 BCE- 200 CE on the Benue Plateau of **Nigeria.**

Americas. The Chavin culture controlled N Peru c. 900 BCE to 200 BCE. Its ceremonial centers, featuring the jaguar god, survived long after. Its architecture, ceramics, and textiles had influenced other Peruvian cultures. **Mayan civilization** began to develop in Central America as early as 1500 BCE.

Great Empires Unite the Classical World: 400 BCE-400 CE

Persia and Alexander the Great. Cyrus, ruler of a small kingdom in Persia from 559 BCE, united the Persians and Medes within 10 years and conquered Asia Minor and Babylonia in another 10. His son Cambyses, followed by **Darius** (r. 522-486 BCE), added vast lands to the E and N as far as the Indus Valley and Central Asia, as well as Egypt and Thrace. The whole empire was ruled by an international bureaucracy and army, with Persians holding the chief positions. The resources and styles of all the subject civilizations were exploited to create a rich syncretic art.

The kingdom of Macedon, which under Philip II dominated the Greek world and Egypt, was passed on to his son **Alexander** in 336 BCE. Within 13 years, Alexander had conquered all the Persian dominions. Imbued by his tutor Aristotle with Greek ideals, Alexander encouraged colonization, and Greek-style cities were founded. After his death in 323 BCE, wars of succession divided the empire into 3 significant dynasties—the Antigonids in Asia Minor and **Macedon,** the Ptolemies in Egypt, and the **Seleucids** in Mesopotamia. In the ensuing 300 years (the **Hellenistic Era**), a cosmopolitan Greek-oriented culture permeated the ancient world from W Europe to the borders of India, absorbing native elites everywhere.

Hellenistic philosophy stressed the private individual's search for happiness. The Cynics followed Diogenes (c. 372-287 BCE), who stressed self-sufficiency and restriction of desires and expressed contempt for luxury and social convention. Zeno (c. 335-c.263 BCE) and the **Stoics** exalted reason, identified it with virtue, and counseled an ascetic disregard for misfortune. The **Epicureans** tried to build lives of moderate pleasure without political or emotional involvement. Hellenistic arts imitated life realistically, especially in sculpture and literature (comedies of Menander, 342-292 BCE).

The sciences thrived, especially at Alexandria, where the Ptolemies financed a great library and museum. Fields of study included mathematics (**Euclid's** geometry, c. 300 BCE); astronomy (heliocentric theory of Aristarchus, 310-230 BCE; Julian calendar, 45 BCE; **Ptolemy**'s *Almagest,* c. 150 CE); geography (world map of Eratosthenes, 276-194 BCE); hydraulics (**Archimedes,** 287-212 BCE); medicine (Galen, 130-200 CE); and chemistry. Inventors refined uses for siphons, valves, gears, springs, screws, levers, cams, and pulleys.

A restored Persian empire under the **Parthians** (northern Iranian tribesmen) controlled the eastern Hellenistic world from 250 BCE to 229 CE. The Parthians and the succeeding Sassanian dynasty (c. 224-651 CE) fought with Rome periodically. The **Sassanians** revived Zoroastrianism as a state religion and patronized a nationalistic artistic and scholarly renaissance.

Rome. The city of Rome was founded, according to legend, by Romulus in 753 BCE. Through military expansion and colonization, and by granting citizenship to conquered tribes, the city annexed all of Italy S of the Po in the 100-year period before 268 BCE. The Latin and other Italic tribes were annexed first, followed by the **Etruscans** (founders of a great civilization, N of Rome) and the Greek colonies in the S. With a large standing army and reserve forces of several hundred thousand, Rome was able to defeat Carthage in the 3 **Punic Wars** (264-241, 218-201, 149-146 BCE), despite the invasion of Italy by **Hannibal** (218 BCE), thus gaining Sicily and territory in Spain and N Africa.

Rome exploited local disputes to conquer Greece and Asia Minor in the 2nd cent. BCE, and Egypt in the 1st (after the defeat and suicide of **Antony and Cleopatra,** 30 BCE). The Mediterranean civilized world, up to the disputed Parthian border, was now Roman and remained so for 500 years. Less civilized regions were added to the Empire: Gaul (conquered by **Julius Caesar,** 58-51 BCE), Britain (43 CE), and Dacia NE of the Danube (107 CE).

Julius Caesar

The original aristocratic republican government, with democratic features added in the 5th and 4th cent. BCE, deteriorated under the pressures of empire and class conflict (**Gracchus** brothers, social reformers, murdered in 133 BCE and 121 BCE; slave revolts in 135 BCE and 73 BCE). After a series of civil wars (Marius vs. Sulla, 88-82 BCE; Caesar vs. **Pompey,** 49-45 BCE; triumvirate vs. Caesar's assassins, 44-43 BCE; Antony vs. Octavian, 32-30 BCE), the empire came under the rule of a deified monarch (first emperor, **Augustus,** 27 BCE-14 CE).

Major Gods & Goddesses of the Classical World

Greek	Roman	Relations	Sphere or Position
Aphrodite	Venus	Daughter of Zeus & Dione	Love
Apollo	——	Son of Zeus & Leto	Healing, poetry, light
Ares	Mars	Son of Zeus & Hera	War
Artemis	Diana	Daughter of Zeus & Leto	Hunting, chastity
Athena	Minerva	Daughter of Zeus & Metis	Wisdom, crafts, war
Cronus	Saturn	Father of Zeus	Titans' ruler
Demeter	Ceres	Sister of Zeus	Agriculture, fertility
Dionysus	Bacchus	Son of Zeus & Semele	Wine, fertility, ecstasy
Eros	Cupid	Son of Ares & Aphrodite	Love
Hades	Pluto	Brother of Zeus	The underworld, death
Hephaestus	Vulcan	Son of Zeus & Hera	Fire
Hera	Juno	Wife & sister of Zeus	Earth
Hermes	Mercury	Son of Zeus & Maia	Travel, commerce, gods' messenger
Hestia	Vesta	Sister of Zeus	The hearth
Pan	——	Son of Hermes & a wood nymph	Forests, flocks, shepherds
Persephone	Proserpina	Daughter of Zeus & Demeter	Grain
Poseidon	Neptune	Brother of Zeus	The sea
Rhea	Ops	Mother of Zeus	The earth
Uranus	Uranus	Father of Titans (elder gods)	The heavens
Zeus	Jupiter	Son of Cronus & Rhea	Ruler of the gods

Provincials (nearly all granted citizenship by Caracalla, 212 CE) came to dominate the army and civil service. Traditional **Roman law**, systematized and interpreted by independent jurists, and local self-rule in provincial cities were supplanted by a vast tax-collecting bureaucracy in the 3rd and 4th cent. The legal rights of women, children, and slaves were strengthened.

Roman innovations in **civil engineering** included water mills, windmills, and rotary mills and use of cement that hardened under water. Monumental architecture (baths, theaters, temples) relied on the arch and the dome. The network of roads (some still standing) stretched 53,000 mi, passing through mountain tunnels as long as 3.5 mi. Aqueducts brought water to cities; underground sewers removed waste.

Roman art and literature were to a large extent derivative of Greek models. Innovations were made in sculpture (naturalistic busts, equestrian statues), decorative wall painting (as at Pompeii), satire (**Juvenal**, 60-127 CE), history (**Tacitus**, 56-120 CE), prose romance (Petronius, d. 66 CE). Gladiatorial contests dominated public amusements, which were supported by the state.

India. The **Gupta** monarchs reunited N India c. 320 CE. Their peaceful and prosperous reign saw a revival of Hindu religious thought and Brahman power. The old Vedic traditions were combined with devotion to many indigenous deities (who were seen as manifestations of Vedic gods). Caste lines were reinforced, and Buddhist practices gradually disappeared or were integrated with **Hindu** traditions. The art (often erotic), architecture, and literature of the period, patronized by the Gupta court, are considered among India's finest achievements (Kalidasa, poet and dramatist, fl. c. 400

CE). Mathematical innovations included use of the zero and decimal numbers. Invasions by White Huns from the NW destroyed the empire c. 550 CE.

Rich cultures also developed in S India during this period. Emotional Tamil religious poetry contributed to the Hindu revival. The Pallava kingdom controlled much of S India c. 350-880 CE and helped to spread Indian civilization to SE Asia.

China. The Ch'in ruler Shih Huang Ti (r. 221-210 BCE), known as the First Emperor, centralized political authority, standardized the written language, laws, weights, measures, and coinage, and conducted a census, but tried to destroy most philosophical texts. The **Han dynasty** (202 BCE-220 CE) instituted the Mandarin bureaucracy, which lasted 2,000 years. Local officials were selected by examination in Confucian classics and trained at the imperial university and provincial schools.

The invention of **paper** facilitated this bureaucratic system. Agriculture was promoted, but peasants bore most of the tax burden. Irrigation was improved, water clocks and sundials were used, astronomy and mathematics thrived, and landscape painting was perfected.

With the expansion S and W (to nearly the present borders of today's China), trade was opened with India, SE Asia, and the Middle East, over sea and caravan routes. Indian missionaries brought Mahayana Buddhism to China by the 1st cent. CE and spawned a variety of sects. Taoism was revived and merged with popular superstitions. **Taoist and Buddhist monasteries** and convents multiplied in the turbulent centuries after the collapse of the Han dynasty.

Monotheism Spreads: 1-750 CE

Roman Empire. Polytheism was practiced in the Roman Empire, and religions indigenous to particular Middle Eastern nations became international. Roman citizens worshiped **Isis** of Egypt, **Mithras** of Persia, **Demeter** of Greece, and the great mother **Cybele** of Phrygia. Their cults centered on mysteries (secret ceremonies) and the promise of an afterlife, symbolized by the death and rebirth of the god. The Jews of the empire preserved their monotheistic religion, Judaism, the world's oldest (c. 1300 BCE) continuous religion. Its teachings are contained in the Bible (the Old Testament). 1st-cent. Judaism embraced several sects, including the **Sadducees**, mostly drawn from the Temple priesthood, who were culturally Hellenized; the **Pharisees**, who upheld the full range of traditional customs and practices as of equal weight to literal scriptural law and elaborated synagogue

worship; and the **Essenes**, an ascetic, millennarian sect. Messianic fervor led to repeated, unsuccessful rebellions against Rome (66-70, 135). As a result, the Temple in Jerusalem was destroyed and the population decimated; this event marked the beginning of the Diaspora (living in exile). To preserve the faith, a program of codification of law was begun at the academy of Yavneh. The work continued for some 500 years in Palestine and in Babylonia, ending in the final redaction (c. 600) of the **Talmud**, a huge collection of legal and moral debates, rulings, liturgy, biblical exegesis, and legendary materials.

Christianity, which emerged as a distinct sect by the 2nd half of the 1st cent., is based on the teachings of **Jesus**, whom believers considered the Savior (Messiah or Christ) and son of God. Missionary activities of the Apostles and such early leaders as **Paul of Tarsus** spread the faith. Intermittent persecution, as in Rome under Nero in 64 CE, on grounds of suspected disloyalty, failed to disrupt the Christian communities. Each congregation, generally urban and of plebeian character, was tightly organized under a leader (bishop), elders (presbyters or priests), and assistants (deacons). The four **Gospels** (accounts of the life and teachings of Jesus) and the Acts of the Apostles were written down in the late 1st and early 2nd cent. and circulated along with letters of Paul and other Christian leaders. An authoritative canon of these writings was not fixed until the 4th cent.

A school for priests was established at Alexandria in the 2nd cent. Its teachers (**Origen** c. 182-251) helped define doctrine and promote the faith in Greek-style philosophical works. Neoplatonism underwent Christian coloration in the writings of Church Fathers such as **Augustine** (354-430). Christian hermits began to associate in monasteries, first in Egypt (St. Pachomius c. 290-345), then in other eastern lands, then in the W (**St. Benedict's rule,** 529). Devotion to saints, especially Mary, mother of Jesus, spread. Under **Constantine** (r. 306-37), Christianity became in effect the established religion of the Empire. Pagan temples were expropriated, state funds were used to build churches and support the hierarchy, and laws were adjusted in accordance with Christian ideas. Pagan worship was banned by the end of the 4th cent., and severe restrictions were placed on Judaism.

The newly established church was rocked by doctrinal disputes, often exacerbated by regional rivalries. Chief heresies (as defined by church councils, backed by imperial authority) were **Arianism,** which denied the divinity of Jesus; **Monophysitism,** denying the human nature of Christ; **Donatism,** which regarded as invalid any sacraments administered by sinful clergy; and **Pelagianism,** which denied the necessity of unmerited divine aid (grace) for salvation.

Islam. The earliest Arab civilization emerged by the end of the 2nd millennium BCE in the watered highlands of Yemen. Seaborne and caravan trade in frankincense and myrrh connected the area with the Nile and Fertile Crescent. The Minaean, Sabean (Sheba), and Himyarite states successively held sway. By Muhammad's time (7th cent. CE), the region was a province of Sassanian Persia. In the N, the Nabataean kingdom at Petra and the kingdom of Palmyra were Aramaicized, Romanized, and finally absorbed, as neighboring Judea had been, into the Roman Empire. Nomads shared the central region with a few trading towns and oases. Wars between tribes and raids on communities were common and were celebrated in a poetic tradition that by the 6th cent. helped establish a classic literary Arabic.

About 610, **Muhammad,** a 40-year-old Arab man of Mecca, emerged as a prophet. He proclaimed a revelation from the one true God, calling on contemporaries to abandon idolatry and restore the faith of Abraham. He introduced his religion as "**Islam,**" meaning "submission" to the one God,

Allah, as a continuation of the biblical faith of Abraham, Moses, and Jesus, all respected as prophets in this system. His teachings, recorded in the **Koran** (al-Qur'an in Arabic), in many ways were inclusive of Abrahamic monotheistic ideas known to the Jews and Christians in Arabia. A key aspect of the Abrahamic connection was insistence on justice in society, which led to severe opposition among the aristocrats in Mecca. As conditions worsened for Muhammad and his followers, he decided in 622 to make a **hegira** ("flight") to Medina, 200 mi to the N. This event marks the beginning of the Muslim lunar calendar. Hostilities between Mecca and Medina increased, and in 629 Muhammad conquered Mecca. By the time he died in 632, nearly all the Arabian peninsula accepted his political and religious leadership.

After his death the majority of Muslims (later known as **Sunni** Muslims) recognized the leadership of the **caliph** ("successor") Abu Bakr (632-34), followed by Umar (634-44), Uthman (644-56), and Ali (656-60). A minority, the **Shiites,** insisted instead on the leadership of Ali, Muhammad's cousin and son-in-law. By 644, **Muslim rule** over Arabia was confirmed. Muslim armies had threatened the Byzantine and Persian empires, which were weakened by wars and disaffection among subject peoples (including Coptic and Syriac Christians opposed to the Byzantine Orthodox establishment). Syria, Palestine, Egypt, Iraq, and Persia fell to Muslim armies. The new administration assimilated existing systems in the region; hence the conquered peoples participated in running the empire. The Koran recognized the so-called Peoples of the Book, i.e., Christians, Jews, and Zoroastrians, as tolerated monotheists, and Muslim policy was relatively tolerant to minorities living as "protected" peoples. An expanded tax system, based on conquests of the Persian and Byzantine empires, provided revenue to organize campaigns against neighboring non-Muslim regions.

Under the **Umayyads** (661-750) and **Abbasids** (750-1256), territorial expansion led Muslim armies across N Africa and into Spain (711). Muslim armies in the W were stopped at Tours (France) in 732 by the Frankish ruler **Charles Martel.** Asia Minor, the Indus Valley, and Transoxiana were conquered in the E. The conversion of conquered peoples to Islam was gradual. In many places the official Arabic language supplanted the local tongues. But in the eastern regions the Arab rulers and their armies adopted Persian cultures and language as part of their Muslim identity.

Disputes over succession, and pious opposition to injustices in society, led to a number of oppositional movements, which also led to the factionalization of Muslim community. The **Shiites** supported leadership candidates descended from Muhammad, believing them to be carriers of some kind of divine authority. The **Kharijites** supported an egalitarian system derived from the Koran, opposing and even engaging in battle against those who did not agree with them.

New Peoples Enter World History: 400-900 CE

Barbarian invasions. Germanic tribes infiltrated S and E from their Baltic homeland during the 1st millennium BCE, reaching S Germany by 100 BCE and the Black Sea by 214 CE. Organized into large federated tribes under elected kings, most resisted Roman domination and raided the empire in time of civil war (Goths took Dacia in 214, raided Thrace in 251-69). Germanic troops and commanders dominated the Roman armies by the end of the 4th cent. **Huns,** invaders from Asia, entered Europe in 372, driving more Germans into the W empire. Emperor Valens allowed Visigoths to cross the Danube in 376. Huns under Attila (d. 453) raided Gaul, Italy, and the Balkans.

The W empire, weakened by overtaxation and social stagnation, was overrun in the 5th cent. Gaul was effectively lost in 406-7, Spain in 409, Britain in 410, Africa in 429-39. Rome was sacked in 410 by Visigoths under Alaric and in 455 by Vandals. **The last western emperor,** Romulus Augustulus, was deposed in 476 by the Germanic chief Odovacar.

Celts. Celtic cultures, which in pre-Roman times covered

most of W Europe, were confined almost entirely to the British Isles after the Germanic invasions. **St. Patrick** completed (c. 457-92) the conversion of Ireland and a strong monastic tradition took hold. Irish monastic missionaries in Scotland, England, and the continent (Columba c. 521-97; Columbanus c. 543-615) helped restore Christianity after the Germanic invasions. **Monasteries** became centers of classic and Christian learning and presided over the recording of a Christianized Celtic mythology, elaborated by secular writers and bards. An intricate decorative art style developed, especially in book illumination (Lindisfarne Gospels, c. 700; Book of Kells, 8th cent.).

Successor states. The Visigothic kingdom in Spain (from 419) and much of France (to 507) saw continuation of Roman administration, language, and law (Breviary of Alaric, 506) until its destruction by the Muslims (711). The Vandal kingdom in Africa (from 429) was conquered by the Byzantines in 533. Italy was ruled successively by an Ostrogothic kingdom under Byzantine suzerainty (489-554), direct Byzantine government, and German Lombards (568-774). The

Major Norse Gods & Goddesses

Name	Relations	Sphere or Position	Emblem/Attribute
Odin	Father of the Aesir (gods)	War and death, poetry, wisdom, magic	Spear, mead, ring/One-eyed
Thor	Son of Odin	Thunder, lightning, rain; champion of the gods	Hammer, belt
Njord	Father of Freyja & Freyr	Wind and sea, wealth and prosperity	——
Frigg	Wife of Odin	Marriage and motherhood, home	——
Freyja (Freya)	Daughter of Njord	Fertility, birth, crops	Necklace
Freyr	Son of Njord	Agriculture, sun, rain	Magic ship, golden boar
Tyr	Son of Odin[1]	Justice, war	Spear/One-handed
Heimdall	Son of nine giantesses	Watchman of the gods; keen sight & hearing	Horn
Balder (Baldur)	Son of Odin	Light, purity	——
Loki	Son of giants; father of Hel (goddess of death), Jormungand (serpent encompassing the world), Fenrir (the wolf).	Malicious trickster	——

(1) Referred to as the son of Hymir in some mythologies.

Lombards divided the peninsula with the Byzantines and papacy under the dynamic reformer **Pope Gregory the Great** (590-604) and successors.

King Clovis (r. 481-511) united the Franks on both sides of the Rhine and, after his conversion to Christianity, defeated the Arian heretics, Burgundians (after 500), and Visigoths (507) with the support of native clergy and the papacy. Under the **Merovingian** kings, a feudal system emerged: Power was fragmented among hierarchies of military landowners. Social stratification, which in late Roman times had acquired legal, hereditary sanction, was reinforced.

Charlemagne

The Carolingians (747-987) expanded the kingdom and restored central power. **Charlemagne** (r. 768-814) conquered nearly all the Germanic lands, including Lombard Italy, and was crowned Emperor by Pope Leo III in Rome in 800. A centuries-long decline in commerce and arts was reversed under Charlemagne's patronage. He welcomed Jews to his kingdom, which became a center of Jewish learning (Rashi, 1040-1105). He sponsored the Carolingian Renaissance of learning under the Anglo-Latin scholar Alcuin (c. 732-804), who reformed church liturgy.

Byzantine Empire. Under **Diocletian** (r. 284-305) the Roman empire had been divided into 2 parts to facilitate administration and defense. **Constantine** founded (330) **Constantinople** (at old Byzantium) as a fully Christian city. Commerce and taxation financed a sumptuous, orientalized court, a class of hereditary bureaucratic families, and magnificent urban construction (Hagia Sophia, 532-37). The city's fortifications and naval innovations repelled assaults by Goths, Huns, Slavs, Bulgars, Avars, Arabs, and Scandinavians. Greek replaced Latin as the official language by c. 700. **Byzantine art**, a solemn, sacral, and stylized variation of late classical styles (mosaics at the Church of San Vitale, Ravenna, Italy 526-48), was a starting point for medieval art in E and W Europe.

Justinian (r. 527-65) reconquered parts of Spain, N Africa, and Italy, codified **Roman law** (Codex Justinianus [529] was medieval Europe's chief legal text), closed the Platonic Academy at Athens, and ordered all pagans to convert. Lombards in Italy and Arabs in Africa retook most of his conquests. The Isaurian dynasty from Anatolia (from

717) and the Macedonian dynasty (867-1054) restored military and commercial power. The Iconoclast controversy (726-843) over the permissibility of images helped alienate the Eastern Church from the papacy.

Abbasid Empire. Baghdad (est. 762), became seat of the **Abbasid dynasty** (est. 750), while Ummayads continued to rule in Spain. A brilliant cosmopolitan civilization emerged, inaugurating a Muslim-Arab golden age. Arabic was the lingua franca of the empire; intellectual sources from Persian, Sanskrit, Greek, and Syriac were rendered into Arabic. Christians and Jews equally participated in this translation movement, which also involved interaction between Jewish legal thought and Islamic law, as much as between Christian theology and Muslim scholasticism. Persian-style court life, with art and music, flourished at the court of **Harun al-Rashid** (786-809), celebrated in the masterpiece known to English readers as *The Arabian Nights*. The sciences, medicine, and mathematics were pursued at Baghdad, Cordova, and Cairo (est. 969). The culmination of this intellectual synthesis in Islamic civilization came with the scientific and philosophical works of **Avicenna** (Ibn Sina, 980-1037), **Averroes** (Ibn Rushd, 1126-98), and **Maimonides** (1135-1204), a Jew who wrote in Arabic. This intellectual tradition was translated into Latin and opened a new period in Christian thought.

The decentralization of the **Abbasid** empire, from 874, led to establishment of various Muslim dynasties under different ethnic groups. Persians, Berbers, and Turks ruled different regions, retaining connection with the Abbasid caliph at the religious level. The Abbasid period also saw various religious movements against the orthodox position held by governing authorities. This situation in Muslim religion led to the establishment of different legal, theological, and mystical schools of thought. The most influential mass movement was **Sufism**, which aimed at the reaching out of the average individual in quest of a spiritual path. Al-Ghazali (1058-1111) is credited with reconciling personal Sufism with the orthodox Sunni tradition.

Africa. Immigrants from Saba in S Arabia helped set up the **Axum** kingdom in Ethiopia in the 1st cent. (their language, Ge'ez, is preserved by the Ethiopian Church). In the 3rd cent., when the kingdom became Christianized, it defeated Kushite Meroe and expanded its influence into Yemen. Axum was the center of a vast ivory trade and controlled the Red Sea coast until c. 1100. Arab conquest in Egypt cut Axum's political and economic ties with Byzantium.

The Iron Age entered W Africa by the end of the 1st millennium BCE. **Ghana**, the first known sub-Saharan state, ruled in the upper Senegal-Niger region c. 400-1240, controlling the trade of gold from mines in the S to trans-Sahara caravan routes to the N. The **Bantu** peoples, probably of W African origin, began to spread E and S perhaps 2,000 years ago, displacing the Pygmies and Bushmen of central and S Africa during a 1,500-year period.

Japan. The advanced Neolithic Yayoi period, when irrigation, rice farming, and iron and bronze casting techniques were introduced from China or Korea, persisted to c. 400 CE. The myriad Japanese states were then united by the **Yamato** clan, under an emperor who acted as chief priest of the animistic Shinto cult. Japanese political and military intervention by the 6th cent. in Korea, then under strong Chinese influence, quickened a Chinese cultural invasion of Japan, bringing Buddhism, the Chinese language (which long remained a literary and governmental medium), Chinese ideographs, and Buddhist styles in painting, sculpture, literature, and architecture (7th cent., Horyu-ji temple at Nara). The Taika Reforms (646) tried unsuccessfully to centralize Japan according to Chinese bureaucratic and Buddhist philosophical values.

A nativist reaction against the Buddhist **Nara period** (710-94) ushered in the **Heian period** (794-1185) centered at the new capital, Kyoto. Japanese elegance and simplicity modified Chinese styles in architecture, scroll painting, and literature; the writing system was also simplified. The courtly novel *Tale of Genji* (1010-20) testifies to the enhanced role of women in medieval Japanese literature and culture.

Southeast Asia. The historic peoples of SE Asia began arriving some 2,500 years ago from China and Tibet, displacing scattered aborigines. Their agriculture relied on rice and yams. Indian cultural influences were strongest; literacy and Hindu and Buddhist ideas followed the S India-China trade route. From the S tip of Indochina, the kingdom of **Funan** (1st-7th cent.) traded as far W as Persia. It was absorbed by Chenla, itself conquered by the **Khmer Empire** (600-1300). The Khmers, under Hindu god-kings (Suryavarman II, 1113-c. 1150), built the monumental Angkor Wat temple center for the royal phallic cult. The Nam-Viet king-dom in Annam, dominated by China and Chinese culture for 1,000 years, emerged in the 10th cent., growing at the expense of the Khmers, who also lost ground in the NW to the new, highly organized **Thai** kingdom. On Sumatra, the **Srivijaya** Empire controlled vital sea lanes (7th to 10th cent.). A Buddhist dynasty, the Sailendras, ruled central **Java** (8th-9th cent.), building at Borobudur one of the largest stupas in the world.

China. The Sui dynasty (581-618) ushered in a period of commercial, artistic, and scientific achievement in China, continuing under the **Tang** dynasty (618-906). Inventions like the magnetic compass, gunpowder, the abacus, and printing were introduced or perfected. Medical innovations included cataract surgery. The state, from its cosmopolitan capital, Chang-an, supervised foreign trade, which exchanged Chinese silks, porcelains, and art for spices, ivory, etc., over Central Asian caravan routes and sea routes reaching Africa. A golden age of poetry bequeathed valuable works to later generations (Tu Fu, 712-70; Li Po, 701-62). Landscape painting flourished.

Commercial and industrial expansion continued under the **Northern Sung** dynasty (960-1126), facilitated by paper money and credit notes. But commerce never achieved respectability; government monopolies expropriated successful merchants. The population, long stable at 50 million, doubled in 200 years with the introduction of early-ripening rice and the double harvest. In art, native Chinese styles were revived.

Americas. From 300 to 600 a Native American empire stretched from the Valley of Mexico to Guatemala, centering on the huge city **Teotihuacán** (founded 100 BCE). To the S, in Guatemala, a high **Mayan** civilization developed (150-900) around hundreds of rural ceremonial centers. The Mayans improved on Olmec writing and the calendar and pursued astronomy and mathematics. In South America, a widespread pre-Inca culture grew from **Tiahuanacu**, Bolivia, near Lake Titicaca (Gateway of the Sun, c. 700).

Christian Europe Regroups and Expands: 900-1300

Scandinavians. Pagan Danish and Norse (Viking) adventurers, traders, and pirates raided the coasts of the British Isles (Dublin, est. c. 831), France, and even the Mediterranean for over 200 years beginning in the late 8th cent. Inland settlement in the W was limited to Great Britain (King Canute, 994-1035) and Normandy, settled (911) under Rollo, as a fief of France. Vikings also reached Iceland (874), Greenland (c. 986), and North America (**Leif Ericson** and others, c. 1000). Norse traders (**Varangians**) developed Russian river commerce from the 8th to the 11th cent. and helped set up a state at Kiev in the late 9th cent. Conversion to Christianity occurred in the 10th cent., reaching Sweden 100 years later. In the 11th cent. Norman bands conquered S Italy and Sicily, and Duke **William of Normandy** conquered (1066) England, bringing feudal government and the French language, essential elements in later English civilization.

Central and East Europe. Slavs began to expand from about 150 CE in all directions in Europe, and by the 7th cent. they reached as far S as the Adriatic and Aegean seas. In the Balkan Peninsula they dislocated Romanized local populations or assimilated newcomers (Bulgarians, a Turkic people). The first **Slavic states** were Moravia (628) in Central Europe and the Bulgarian state (680) in the Balkans. Missions of St. Methodius and Cyril (whose Greek-based cyrillic alphabet is still used by some S and E Slavs) converted (863) Moravia.

The Eastern Slavs, part-civilized under the overlordship of the Turkish-Jewish **Khazar** trading empire (7th-10th cent.), gravitated toward Constantinople by the 9th cent. The **Kievan state** adopted (989) Eastern Christianity under Prince Vladimir. King Boleslav I (992-1025) began **Poland's** long history of conquest. The Magyars (Hungari-ans), in present-day Hungary since 896, accepted (1001) Latin Christianity.

Germany. The German kingdom that emerged after the breakup of Charlemagne's W Empire remained a confederation of largely autonomous states. Otto I, a Saxon who was king from 936, established the **Holy Roman Empire**—a union of Germany and N Italy—in alliance with Pope John XII, who crowned (962) him emperor; he defeated (955) the Magyars. Imperial power was greatest under the **Hohenstaufens** (1138-1254), despite the growing opposition of the papacy, which ruled central Italy, and the Lombard League cities. Frederick II (1194-1250) improved administration and patronized the arts; after his death, German influence was removed from Italy.

Christian Spain. From its N mountain redoubts, Christian rule slowly migrated S through the 11th cent., when Muslim unity collapsed. After the capture (1085) of **Toledo**, the kingdoms of Portugal, Castile, and Aragon undertook repeated crusades of reconquest, finally completed in 1492. Elements of Islamic civilization persisted in recaptured areas, influencing all Western Europe.

Crusades. Pope Urban II called for a crusade (1095) to restore Asia Minor to Byzantium and the Holy Land to Christendom, respectively. This first crusade captured Jerusalem and led to the foundation of 4 Frankish states in the Levant. The defeat inflicted upon crusaders at the Battle of Hattin (1187) by **Saladin** (c. 1137-93), the Kurdish ruler of Egypt and Syria, effectively negated territorial gains. Many crusades followed until 1291. The 4th crusade sacked Constantinople (1204). Other crusades were launched against Christian heretics (Albigensian Crusade, 1229), pagans, and enemies of the papacy.

Economy. The agricultural base of European life benefited from improvements in **plow design** (c. 1000) and by draining of lowlands and clearing of forests, leading to a rural population increase. Towns grew in N Italy, Flanders, and N Germany (Hanseatic League). Improvements in **loom design** permitted factory textile production. **Guilds** dominated urban trades from the 12th cent. Banking (centered in Italy, 12th-15th cent.) facilitated long-distance trade.

The Church. The split between the Eastern and Western churches was formalized in 1054. Western and Central Europe was divided into 500 bishoprics under one united hierarchy, but conflicts between secular and church authorities were frequent (German **Investiture Controversy**, 1075-1122). Clerical power was first strengthened through the international monastic reform begun at Cluny in 910. Popular religious enthusiasm often expressed itself in heretical movements (Waldensians from 1173), but was channeled by the **Dominican** (1215) and **Franciscan** (1223) friars into the religious mainstream.

Arts. Romanesque architecture (9th-mid-12th cent.) expanded on late Roman models, using the rounded arch and massed stone to support enlarged basilicas. Painting and sculpture followed Byzantine models. The literature of **chivalry** was exemplified by the epic (*Chanson de Roland*, c. 1100) and by courtly love poems of the troubadours of Provence and minnesingers of Germany. **Gothic** architecture emerged in France (church of St. Denis, c. 1140) and spread along with French cultural influence. Rib vaulting and pointed arches were used to combine soaring heights with delicacy, and they freed walls for display of stained glass. Exteriors were covered with painted relief sculpture and embellished with elaborate architectural detail.

Learning. Law, medicine, and philosophy were advanced at independent **universities** (Bologna, Paris, 12th cent.), originally corporations of students and masters. Twelfth-cent. translations of Greek classics, especially Aristotle, encouraged an analytic approach. Scholastic philosophy, from Anselm (1033-1109) to **Aquinas** (1225-74), attempted to understand revelation through reason.

Apogee of Central Asian Power and the Spread of Islam: 1250-1500

Turks. Turkic peoples, of Central Asian ancestry, were a military threat to the Byzantine and Persian Empires from the 6th cent. After several waves of invasions, during which most of the Turks adopted Islam, the **Seljuk Turks** took (1055) Baghdad. They ruled Persia, Iraq and, after 1071, Asia Minor, where massive numbers of Turks settled. The empire was divided in the 12th cent. into smaller states ruled by Seljuks, Kurds, and Mamluks (a military caste of former Turk, Kurd, and Circassian slaves), which governed Egypt and the Middle East until the Ottoman era (c. 1290-1922).

Osman I (r. c. 1290-1326) and succeeding sultans united Anatolian Turkish warriors in a militaristic state that waged holy war against Byzantium and Balkan Christians. Most of the Balkans had been subdued, and Anatolia united, when Constantinople fell (1453). By the mid-16th cent., Hungary, the Middle East, and N Africa had been conquered. The Turkish advance was stopped at Vienna (1529) and at the naval battle of Lepanto (1571) by Spain, Venice, and the papacy.

The Ottoman state was governed in accordance with orthodox Muslim law. Greek, Armenian, and Jewish communities were segregated and were ruled by religious leaders responsible for taxation; they dominated trade. State offices and most army ranks were filled by slaves through a system of child conscription among Christians.

India. Mahmud of Ghazni (971-1030) led repeated Turkish raids into N India. Turkish power was consolidated in 1206 with the start of the **Sultanate at Delhi.** Centralization of state power under the early Delhi sultans went far beyond traditional Indian practice. Muslim rule of most of the subcontinent lasted until the British conquest 600 years later.

Kublai Khan

Mongols. Genghis Khan (c. 1167-1227) first united the feuding Mongol tribes, and built their armies into an effective offensive force around a core of highly mobile cavalry. He and his immediate successors created the largest land empire in history; by 1279 it stretched from the E coast of Asia to the Danube, from the Siberian steppes to the Arabian Sea. East-West trade and contacts were facilitated (Marco Polo, c. 1254-1324).

The western Mongols were Islamized by 1295; successor states soon lost their Mongol character by assimilation. They were briefly reunited under the Turk Tamerlane (1336-1405).

Kublai Khan ruled China from his new capital Beijing (est. c. 1264). Naval campaigns against Japan (1274, 1281) and Java (1293) were defeated, the latter by the Hindu-Bud-

dhist maritime kingdom of Majapahit. The Yuan dynasty used Mongols and other foreigners (including Europeans) in official posts and tolerated the return of Nestorian Christianity (suppressed 841-45) and the spread of Islam in the S and W. A native reaction expelled the Mongols in 1367-68.

Russia. The Kievan state in Russia, weakened by the decline of Byzantium and the rise of the Catholic Polish-Lithuanian state, was overrun (1238-40) by the Mongols. Only the northern trading republic of Novgorod remained independent. The grand dukes of Moscow emerged as leaders of a coalition of princes that eventually (by 1481) defeated the Mongols. After the fall of Constantinople in 1453, the **Tsars** (Caesars) at Moscow (from Ivan III, r. 1462-1505) set up an independent Russian Orthodox Church. Commerce failed to revive. The isolated Russian state remained agrarian, with the peasant class falling into serfdom.

Persia. A revival of Persian literature, making use of the Arab alphabet and literary forms, began in the 10th cent. (epic of Firdausi, 935-1020). An art revival, influenced by Chinese styles introduced after the Mongols came to power in Iran, began in the 13th cent. Persian cultural and political forms, and often the Persian language, were used for centuries by Turkish and Mongol elites from the Balkans to India. Persian mystics from Rumi (1207-73) to Jami (1414-92) promoted Sufism in their poetry.

Africa. Two militant Islamic Berber dynasties emerged from the Sahara to carve out empires from the Sahel to central Spain—the **Almoravids** (c. 1050-1140) and the fanatical **Almohads** (c. 1125-1269). The Ghanaian empire was replaced in the upper Niger by Mali (c. 1230-1340), whose Muslim rulers imported Egyptians to help make **Timbuktu** a center of commerce (in gold, leather, and slaves) and learning. The Songhay empire (to 1590) replaced Mali. To the S, forest kingdoms produced refined artworks (Ife terra cotta, **Benin** bronzes).

Other **Muslim states** in Nigeria (Hausas) and Chad originated in the 11th cent. and continued in some form until the 19th-cent. European conquest. Less-developed Bantu kingdoms existed across central Africa.

Some 40 Muslim Arab-Persian trading colonies and city-states were established all along the E African coast from the 10th cent. (Kilwa, Mogadishu). The interchange with Bantu peoples produced the **Swahili** language and culture. Gold, palm oil, and slaves were brought from the interior, stimulating the growth of the Monamatapa kingdom of the Zambezi (15th cent.). The Christian Ethiopian empire (from 13th cent.) continued the traditions of Axum.

Southeast Asia. Islam was introduced into Malaya and the Indonesian islands by Arab, Persian, and Indian traders. Coastal Muslim cities and states (starting before 1300) soon dominated the interior. Chief among these was the **Malacca** state (c. 1400-1511), on the Malay peninsula.

Arts and Statecraft Thrive in Europe: 1350-1600

Dante

Italy. Distinctive Italian achievements in literature and fine arts during the late Middle Ages (**Dante,** 1265-1321; Giotto, 1276-1337) led to the vigorous new styles of the Renaissance (14th-16th cent.). Patronized by the rulers of the quarreling petty states of Italy (**Medicis** in Florence and the papacy, c. 1400-1737), the plastic arts perfected realistic techniques, including **perspective** (Masaccio, 1401-28, **Leonardo da Vinci,** 1452-1519). Classical motifs were used in architecture, and increased talent and expense were put into secular buildings. The Florentine dialect was refined as a national literary language (**Petrarch,** 1304-74). Greek refugees from the E strengthened the respect of humanist scholars for the classic sources. Soon an international movement aided by the spread of **printing** (Gutenberg, c. 1397(?)-1468), **humanism** was optimistic about the power of human reason (Erasmus of Rotterdam, 1466-1536, More's *Utopia,* 1516) and valued individual effort in the arts and in politics (**Machiavelli,** 1469-1527).

France. The French monarchy, strengthened in its repeated struggles with powerful nobles (Burgundy, Flanders, Aquitaine) by alliances with the growing commercial towns, consolidated bureaucratic control under Philip IV (r. 1285-1314) and extended French influence into Germany and Italy (popes at Avignon, France, 1309-1417). The **Hundred Years War** (1337-1453) ended English dynastic claims in France (battles of Crécy, 1346, and Poitiers, 1356; Joan of Arc executed, 1431). A French Renaissance, dating from royal invasions (1494, 1499) of Italy, was encouraged at the court of Francis I (r. 1515-47), who centralized taxation and law. French vernacular literature consciously asserted its independence (La Pléiade, 1549).

England. The evolution of England's unique political institutions began with the **Magna Carta** (1215), by which King John guaranteed the privileges of nobles and church against the monarchy and assured jury trial. After the **Wars of the Roses** (1455-85), the **Tudor dynasty** reasserted royal prerogatives (Henry VIII, r. 1509-47), but the trend toward independent departments and ministerial government also continued. English trade (wool exports from c. 1340) was protected by the nation's growing maritime power (**Spanish Armada** destroyed, 1588).

English replaced French and Latin in the late 14th cent. in law and literature (**Chaucer,** c. 1340-1400) and English translation of the Bible began (Wycliffe, 1380s). **Elizabeth I** (r. 1558-1603) presided over a confident flowering of poetry (Spenser, 1552-99), drama (**Shakespeare,** 1564-1616), and music.

German Empire. From among a welter of minor feudal states, church lands, and independent cities, the **Habsburgs** assembled a far-flung territorial domain, based in Austria from 1276. Family members held the title of Holy Roman Emperor from 1438 to the Empire's dissolution in 1806, but failed to centralize its domains, leaving Germany disunited for centuries. Resistance to Turkish expansion brought Hungary under Austrian control from the 16th cent. The Netherlands, Luxembourg, and Burgundy were added in 1477, curbing French expansion.

The Flemish painting tradition of naturalism, technical proficiency, and bourgeois subject matter began in the 15th cent. (**Jan Van Eyck,** c. 1390-1441), the earliest northern manifestation of the Renaissance. Albrecht **Dürer** (1471-1528) typified the merging of late Gothic and Italian trends in 16th-cent. German art. Imposing civic architecture flourished in the prosperous commercial cities.

Spain. Despite the unification of Castile and Aragon in 1479, the 2 countries retained separate governments, and the nobility, especially in Aragon and Catalonia, retained many privileges. Spanish lands in Italy (Naples, Sicily) and the Netherlands entangled the country in European wars through the mid-17th cent., while explorers, traders, and conquerors built up a Spanish empire in the Americas and the Philippines.

From the late 15th cent., a **golden age** of literature and art produced works of social satire (plays of Lope de Vega, 1562-1635; **Cervantes,** 1547-1616), as well as spiritual intensity (**El Greco,** 1541-1614; **Velazquez,** 1599-1660).

Black Death. The bubonic plague reached Europe from the E in 1348, killing up to half the population by 1350 (and recurring periodically in most areas until the early 18th cent. Labor scarcity forced wages to rise and brought greater freedom to the peasantry, making possible **peasant uprisings** (Jacquerie in France, 1358; Wat Tyler's rebellion in England, 1381).

Explorations. Organized European maritime exploration began, seeking to evade the Venice-Ottoman monopoly of E trade and to promote Christianity. Beginning in 1418, expeditions from Portugal explored the W coast of Africa, until Vasco da Gama rounded the Cape of Good Hope in 1497 and reached India. A Portuguese trading empire was consolidated by the seizure of Goa (1510) and Malacca (1551). Japan was reached in 1542. The voyages of Christopher **Columbus** (1492-1504) uncovered a world new to Europeans, which Spain hastened to subdue. Navigation schools in Spain and Portugal, the development of large sailing ships (carracks) mounted with cannons, and the invention (c. 1475) of the rifle aided European penetration.

Mughals and Safavids. E of the Ottoman Empire, 2 Muslim dynasties ruled unchallenged in the 16th and 17th cent. The Mughal dynasty of India, founded by Persianized Turkish invaders from the NW under Babur, dates from their 1526 conquest of the Delhi Sultanate. The dynasty ruled most of India for more than

Taj Mahal

200 years, surviving nominally until 1857. **Akbar** (r. 1556-1605) consolidated administration at his glorious court, where the Urdu language (Persian-influenced Hindi) developed. Trade relations with Europe increased. Under Shah Jahan (1629-58), a secularized art fusing Hindu and Muslim elements flourished in miniature painting and in architecture (**Taj Mahal**). Sikhism (founded c. 1519) combined elements of both faiths. Suppression of Hindus and Shi'ite Muslims in S India in the late 17th cent. weakened the empire.

Fanatical devotion to the Shi'ite sect characterized the Safavids (1502-1736) of Persia and led to hostilities with the Sunni Ottomans for more than a century. The prosperity and the strength of the empire are evidenced by the mosques at its capital city, **Isfahan**. The Safavids enhanced Iranian national consciousness.

China. The **Ming** emperors (1368-1644), the last native dynasty in China, wielded unprecedented personal power, while the Confucian bureaucracy began to suffer from inertia. European trade (Portuguese monopoly through **Macao** from 1557) was strictly controlled. Jesuit scholars and scientists (Matteo Ricci, 1552-1610) introduced some Western science; their writings familiarized the West with China. Chinese technological inventiveness declined from this era, but the arts thrived, especially in the areas of painting and ceramics.

Japan. After the decline of the first hereditary shogunate (chief generalship) at **Kamakura** (1185-1333), fragmentation of power accelerated, as did the consequent social mobility. Under Kamakura and the Ashikaga shogunate (1338-1573), the daimyos (lords) and samurai (warriors) grew more powerful and promoted a martial ideology. Japanese pirates and traders plied the China coast. Popular Buddhist movements included the nationalist Nichiren sect (from c. 1250) and **Zen** (brought from China, 1191), which stressed meditation and a disciplined esthetic (tea ceremony, gardening, martial arts, *No* drama).

Reformed Europe Expands Overseas: 1500-1700

Reformation. Theological debate and protests against real and perceived clerical corruption existed in the medieval Christian world, expressed by such dissenters as John **Wycliffe** (c. 1320-84) and his followers (the Lollards) in England, and **Huss** (burned as a heretic, 1415) in Bohemia.

Martin **Luther** (1483-1546) preached that faith alone leads to salvation, without the mediation of clergy or good works. He attacked the authority of the pope, rejected priestly celibacy, and recommended individual study of the Bible (which he translated into German c. 1525). His 95 Theses (1517) led to his excommunication (1521). John **Calvin** (1509-64) said that God's elect were predestined for salvation and all others for damnation; good conduct and success were signs of election. Calvin in Geneva and John **Knox** (1505-72) in Scotland established theocratic states.

Henry VIII asserted English national authority and secular power by breaking away (1534) from the Catholic Church, creating what would become the Anglican Church. Monastic property was confiscated, and some Protestant doctrines given official sanction.

Religious wars. A century and a half of religious wars began with a S German peasant uprising (1524), repressed with Luther's support. Radical sects—democratic, pacifist, millennarian—arose (Anabaptists ruled Münster in 1534-35) and were suppressed violently. Civil war in France from 1562 between **Huguenots** (Protestant nobles and merchants) and Catholics ended with the 1598 **Edict of Nantes**, tolerating Protestants (revoked 1685). Habsburg attempts to restore Catholicism in Germany were resisted in 25 years of fighting; the 1555 Peace of Augsburg guarantee of religious independence to local princes and cities was confirmed only after the **Thirty Years War** (1618-48), when much of Germany was devastated by local and foreign armies (Sweden, France).

A Catholic Reformation, or **Counter Reformation**, met the Protestant challenge, defining an official theology at the Council of Trent (1545-63). The **Jesuit** order (Society of Jesus), founded in 1534 by Ignatius Loyola (1491-1556), helped reconvert large areas of Poland, Hungary, and S Germany and sent missionaries to the New World, India, and China, while the **Inquisition** suppressed heresy in Catholic countries. A revival of religious fervor appeared in devotional literature (Teresa of Avila, 1515-82) and in grandiose **Baroque** art (Bernini, 1598-1680).

Galileo Galilei

Scientific Revolution. The late nominalist thinkers (Ockham, c. 1300-49) of Paris and Oxford challenged Aristotelian orthodoxy, allowing for a freer scientific approach. At the same time, metaphysical values, such as the Neoplatonic faith in an orderly, mathematical cosmos, still motivated and directed inquiry. Nicolaus **Copernicus** (1473-1543) promoted the heliocentric theory, which was confirmed when Johannes **Kepler** (1571-1630) discovered the mathematical laws describing the elliptical orbits of the planets. The traditional Christian-Aristotelian belief that the heavens and the earth were fundamentally different collapsed when **Galileo Galilei** (1564-1642) discovered moving sunspots, irregular moon topography, and moons around Jupiter, though he did face religious opposition (Galileo's retraction, 1633). He and Sir Isaac **Newton** (1642-1727) developed a mechanics that unified cosmic and earthly phenomena. Newton and Gottfried von **Leibniz** (1646-1716) invented calculus. René **Descartes** (1596-1650), best known for his influential philosophy, also invented analytic geometry.

An explosion of **observational science** included the discovery of blood circulation (Harvey, 1578-1657) and microscopic life (Leeuwenhoek, 1632-1723), and advances in anatomy (Vesalius, 1514-64, dissected corpses) and chemistry (Boyle, 1627-91). Scientific research institutes were founded: Florence (1657), London (**Royal Society**, 1660), Paris (1666). Inventions proliferated (Savery's steam engine, 1696).

Arts. Mannerist trends of the High Renaissance (**Michelangelo**, 1475-1564) exploited virtuosity, grace, novelty, and exotic subjects and poses. The notion of artistic genius was promoted. Private connoisseurs entered the art market. These trends were elaborated in the 17th cent. **Baroque** era on a grander scale. Dynamic movement in painting and sculpture was emphasized by sharp lighting effects, rich materials (colored marble, gilt), and realistic details. Curved facades, broken lines, rich detail, and ceiling decoration characterized Baroque architecture. Monarchs, princes, and prelates, usually Catholic, used Baroque art to enhance and embellish their authority, as in royal portraits (Velazquez, 1599-1660; Van Dyck, 1599-1641).

National styles emerged. In France, a taste for rectilinear order and serenity (Poussin, 1594-1665), linked to the new rational philosophy, was expressed in classical forms. The influence of **classical values** in French literature (tragedies of **Racine**, 1639-99) gave rise to the "battle of the Ancients and Moderns." New forms included the essay (**Montaigne**, 1533-92) and novel (*Princesse de Cleves*, La Fayette, 1678).

Dutch painting of the 17th cent. was unique in its wide social distribution. The Flemish tradition of undemonstrative realism reached its peak in **Rembrandt** (1606-69) and Jan Vermeer (1632-75).

Economy. European economic expansion, known as the **commercial revolution**, was stimulated by new trade with the East, by New World gold and silver, and by a doubling of population (50 million in 1450, 100 million in 1600). **New business and financial techniques** were developed and refined, such as joint-stock companies, insurance, and letters of credit and exchange. The Bank of Amsterdam (1609) and the Bank of England (1694) broke the old monopoly of private banking families. The rise of a business mentality was typified by the spread of clock towers in cities in the 14th cent. By the mid-15th cent., portable clocks were available; the first watch was invented in 1502.

By 1650, most governments had adopted the **mercantile system**, in which they sought to amass metallic wealth by protecting merchants' foreign and colonial trade monopolies. The rise in prices and the new coin-based economy undermined craft guild and feudal manorial systems. Expanding industries (clothweaving, mining) benefited from technical advances. Coal replaced wood as the chief fuel; it was used to fuel new 16th-cent. blast furnaces making cast iron.

New World. The **Aztecs** united much of the Meso-American area in a militarist empire by 1519, from their capital, Tenochtitlán (pop. 300,000), which was the center of a cult requiring ritual human sacrifice. Most of the civilized areas of South America were ruled by the centralized Inca Empire (1476-1534), stretching 2,000 mi from Ecuador to NW Argentina. Lavish and sophisticated traditions in pottery, weaving, sculpture, and architecture were maintained in both regions.

Hernán Cortés

These empires, beset by revolts, fell in 2 short campaigns to gold-seeking Spanish forces based in the Antilles and Panama. Hernán **Cortés** took Mexico (1519-21); Francisco **Pizarro**, Peru (1532-35). From these centers, land and sea expeditions claimed most of North and South America for Spain. The indigenous high cultures did not survive the impact of **Christian missionaries** and the new upper class of whites and mestizos. Although the Spanish administration intermittently concerned itself with their welfare, the population was reduced by European diseases and remained impoverished at most levels. New World silver and such native products as potatoes, tobacco, corn, peanuts, chocolate, and rubber exercised a major economic influence on Europe.

Brazil, which the Portuguese reached in 1500 and settled after 1530, and the Caribbean colonies of several European nations developed a plantation economy where sugarcane, tobacco, cotton, coffee, rice, indigo, and lumber were grown by slaves. From the early 16th to late 19th cent., 10 million Africans were transported to **slavery** in the Americas and Caribbean islands.

Netherlands. The urban, Calvinist N provinces of the Netherlands rebelled (1568) against Habsburg Spain and founded an oligarchic mercantile republic. Their control of the Baltic grain market enabled them to exploit Mediterranean food shortages. Religious refugees—French and Belgian Protestants, Iberian Jews—added to the commercial talent pool. After Spain absorbed Portugal (1580), the Dutch seized Portuguese possessions and created a vast but short-lived commercial empire in Brazil, the Antilles, Africa, India, Ceylon, Malacca, Indonesia, and Taiwan. The Dutch also challenged or supplanted Portuguese traders in China and Japan. Revolution in 1640 restored Portuguese independence.

England. Anglicanism became firmly established under **Elizabeth I** after a brief Catholic interlude under "Bloody Mary" (1553-58). But religious and political conflicts led to a rebellion (1642) by Parliament. Forces of the Roundheads (Puritans) defeated the Cavaliers (Royalists); Charles I was beheaded (1649). The new Commonwealth was

Queen Elizabeth I

ruled as a military dictatorship by Oliver **Cromwell**, who also brutally crushed (1649-51) an Irish rebellion. Conflicts within the Puritan camp (democratic Levelers defeated, 1649) aided the Stuart restoration (1660), but Parliament was strengthened and the peaceful **"Glorious Revolution"** (1688) advanced political and religious liberties (writings of **Locke**, 1632-1704). British privateers (Drake, 1540-96)

challenged Spanish control of the New World and penetrated Asian trade routes (Madras taken, 1639). North American colonies (Jamestown, 1607; Plymouth, 1620) provided an outlet for private enterprise and religious dissenters from Europe.

France. Emerging from the religious civil wars in 1628, France regained military and commercial great power status (under the ministries of **Richelieu**, Mazarin, and Colbert). Under **Louis XIV** (reigned 1643-1715), royal absolutism triumphed over nobles and local *parlements* (defeat of Fronde, 1648-53). Permanent colonies were founded in Canada (1608), the Caribbean (1626), and India (1674).

Sweden. Sweden seceded from the Scandinavian Union in 1523. The thinly populated agrarian state (with copper, iron, and timber exports) was united by the Vasa kings, whose conquests by the mid-17th cent. made Sweden the dominant Baltic power. The empire collapsed in the Great Northern War (1700-21).

Poland. After the union with Lithuania in 1447, Poland ruled vast territories from the Baltic to the Black Sea, resisting German and Turkish incursions. Catholic nobles failed to gain the loyalty of their Orthodox Christian subjects in the E; commerce and trades were practiced by German and Jewish immigrants. The bloody 1648-49 Cossack uprising began the kingdom's dismemberment.

China. A new dynasty, the **Manchus**, invaded from the NE, seized power in 1644, and expanded Chinese control to its greatest extent in Central and SE Asia. Trade and diplomatic contact with Europe grew, carefully controlled by China. New crops (sweet potato, maize, peanut) allowed economic and population growth (pop. 300 million, in 1800). Traditional arts and literature were pursued with increased sophistication (*Dream of the Red Chamber*, novel, mid-18th cent.).

Japan. Tokugawa Ieyasu, shogun from 1603, finally unified and pacified feudal Japan. Hereditary nobles (daimyos and samurai) monopolized government office and the professions. An urban merchant class grew, literacy spread, and a cultural renaissance occurred (**haiku**, a verse innovation of the poet Basho, 1644-94). Fear of European domination led to persecution of Christian converts from 1597 and to stringent isolation from outside contact from 1640.

Philosophy, Industry, and Revolution: 1700-1800

Science and Reason. Greater faith in reason and empirical observation, instead of tradition and religious beliefs, espoused since the Renaissance (Francis Bacon, 1561-1626), was bolstered by scientific discoveries. René **Descartes** (1596-1650) used a rationalistic approach modeled on geometry and introspection to discover "self-evident" truths as a foundation of knowledge. Sir

Isaac Newton

Isaac **Newton** emphasized induction from experimental observation. Baruch de **Spinoza** (1632-77), who called for political and intellectual freedom, developed a systematic rationalistic philosophy in his classic work *Ethics*.

French philosophers assumed leadership of the **Enlightenment** in the 18th cent. Montesquieu (1689-1755) used British history to support his notions of limited government. **Voltaire's** (1694-1778) diaries and novels of exotic travel illustrated the intellectual trends toward secular ethics and relativism. Jean-Jacques **Rousseau's** (1712-1778) radical concepts of the **social contract** and of the inherent goodness of the common man gave impetus to antimonarchical republicanism. The *Encyclopedia* (1751-72, edited by Diderot and d'Alembert), designed as a monument to reason, was largely devoted to practical technology.

In England, ideals of liberty were connected with empiricist philosophy and science in the followers of John **Locke**.

But British empiricism, especially as developed by the skeptical David **Hume** (1711-76), radically reduced the role of reason in philosophy, as did the evolutionary approach to law and politics of Edmund Burke (1729-97) and the utilitarian ethics of Jeremy Bentham (1748-1832). Adam Smith (1723-90) and other **physiocrats** called for a rationalization of economic activity by removing artificial barriers to a supposedly natural free exchange of goods known as **laissez-faire**.

German writers participated in the new philosophical trends popularized by Christian von Wolff (1679-1754). Immanuel **Kant's** (1724-1804) transcendental idealism, unifying an empirical epistemology with a priori moral and logical concepts, directed German thought away from skepticism. Italian contributions included work on electricity (Galvani, 1737-98; Volta, 1745-1827), the pioneer historiography of Vico (1668-1744), and writings on penal reform (Beccaria, 1738-94). Benjamin Franklin (1706-90) was celebrated in Europe for his varied achievements.

The growth of the **press** (*Spectator*, 1711-12) and the wide distribution of realistic but sentimental **novels** attested to the increase of a large bourgeois public.

Arts. Rococo art, characterized by extravagant decorative effects, asymmetries copied from organic models, and artificial pastoral subjects, was favored by the continental aristocracy for most of the cent. (Watteau, 1684-1721) and had musical analogies in the ornamentalized polyphony of late Baroque. The **Neoclassical** art after 1750, associated with the new scientific archaeology, was more streamlined and was infused with the supposed moral and geometric rectitude of the Roman Republic (David, 1748-1825). In England, **town planning** on a grand scale began.

Industrial Revolution in England. Agricultural improvements, such as the sowing drill (1701) and livestock breeding, were implemented on the large fields provided by enclosure of common lands by private owners. Profits from agriculture and from colonial and foreign trade (1800 volume, £54 million) were channeled through hundreds of banks and the **Stock Exchange** (est. 1773) into new industrial processes.

The Newcomen steam pump (1712) aided coal mining. Coal fueled the new efficient steam engines patented by James Watt in 1769, and coke-smelting produced cheap, sturdy iron for machinery by the 1730s. The **flying shuttle** (1733) and **spinning jenny** (c. 1764) were used in the large new cotton textile factories, where women and children were much of the work force. Goods were transported cheaply over **canals** (2,000 mi; built 1760-1800).

American Revolution. The British colonies in North America attracted a mass immigration of religious dissenters and poor people throughout the 17th and 18th cent., coming from the British Isles, Germany, the Netherlands, and other countries. The population reached 3 million non-natives by the 1770s. The small native population was greatly reduced by European diseases and by wars with the various colonies. British attempts to control colonial trade and to tax the colonists to pay for the costs of colonial administration and defense clashed with local self-government and eventually provoked the colonies to a successful rebellion.

Central and East Europe. The monarchs of the three states that dominated E Europe—Austria, Prussia, and Russia—accepted the advice and legitimation of philosophes in creating modern, centralized institutions in their kingdoms, which were enlarged by the division (1772-95) of Poland.

Under **Frederick II** (called the Great) (r. 1740-86) Prussia, with its efficient modern army, doubled in size. State monopolies and tariff protection fostered industry, and some legal reforms were introduced. Austria's heterogeneous realms were unified under **Maria Theresa** (r. 1740-80) and **Joseph II** (r. 1780-90). Reforms in education, law, and religion were enacted, and the Austrian serfs were freed (1781). With its defeat in the Seven Years' War in 1763, Austria failed to regain Silesia, which had been seized by Prussia, but it was compensated by expansion to the E and S (Hungary, Slavonia, 1699; Galicia, 1772).

Russia, whose borders continued to expand, adopted some Western bureaucratic and economic policies under **Peter I** (r. 1682-1725) and **Catherine II** (r. 1762-96). Trade and cultural contacts with the West multiplied from the new Baltic Sea capital, **St. Petersburg** (est. 1703).

French Revolution. The growing French middle class lacked political power and resented aristocratic tax privileges, especially in light of the successful American Revolution. Peasants lacked adequate land and were burdened with feudal obligations to nobles. War with Britain led to the loss of French Canada and drained the treasury, finally forcing the king to call the **Estates-General** in 1789 (first time since 1614), in an atmosphere of food riots (poor crop in 1788).

Aristocratic resistance to absolutism was soon overshadowed by the reformist Third Estate (middle class), which proclaimed itself the **National Constituent Assembly** June 17 and took the "Tennis Court oath" on June 20 to secure a constitution. The storming of the **Bastille** on July 14, 1789, by Parisian artisans was followed by looting and seizure of aristocratic property throughout France. Assembly reforms included abolition of class and regional privileges, a Declaration of Rights, suffrage by taxpayers (75% of males), and the **Civil Constitution of the Clergy** providing for election and loyalty oaths for priests. A republic was declared Sept. 22, 1792, in spite of royalist pressure from Austria and Prussia, which had declared war in April (joined by Britain the next year). Louis XVI was beheaded Jan. 21, 1793, and Queen Marie Antoinette was beheaded Oct. 16, 1793.

Royalist uprisings in La Vendée and military reverses led to institution of a **reign of terror** in which tens of thousands of opponents of the Revolution and criminals were executed. Radical reforms in the **Convention** period (Sept. 1793-Oct. 1795) included the abolition of colonial slavery, economic measures to aid the poor, support of public education, and a short-lived de-Christianization.

Division among radicals (execution of Hebert, Danton, and Robespierre, 1794) aided the ascendancy of a moderate **Directory**, which consolidated military victories. **Napoleon Bonaparte** (1769-1821), a popular young general, exploited political divisions and participated in a coup Nov. 9, 1799, making himself first consul (dictator).

India. Sikh and Hindu rebels (Rajputs, Marathas) and Afghans destroyed the power of the Mughals during the 18th cent. After France's defeat (1763) in the Seven Years' War, Britain was the primary European trade power in India. Its control of inland **Bengal and Bihar** was recognized (1765) by the Mughal shah, who granted the **British East India Co.** (under Clive, 1725-74) the right to collect land revenue there. Despite objections from Parliament (1784 India Act), the company's involvement in local wars and politics led to repeated acquisitions of new territory. The company exported Indian textiles, sugar, and indigo.

Nationalism Gathers Momentum: 1800-40

French ideals and empire spread. Inspired by the ideals of the French Revolution, and supported by the expanding French armies, new republican regimes arose near France: the **Batavian** Republic in the Netherlands (1795-1806), the **Helvetic** Republic in Switzerland (1798-1803), the **Cisalpine** Republic in N Italy (1797-1805), the **Ligurian** Republic in Genoa (1797-1805), and the **Parthenopian** Republic in S Italy (1799). A Roman Republic existed briefly in 1798 after Pope Pius VI was arrested by French troops. In Italy and Germany, new nationalist sentiments were stimulated both in imitation of and in reaction to developments in France (anti-French and anti-Jacobin peasant uprisings in Italy, 1796-99).

From 1804, when Napoleon declared himself emperor, to 1812, a succession of military victories (Austerlitz, 1805; Jena, 1806) extended his control over most of Europe, through puppet states (**Confederation of the Rhine** united W German states for the first time and **Grand Duchy of Warsaw** revived Polish national hopes), expansion of the empire, and alliances.

Among the lasting reforms initiated under Napoleon's absolutist reign were: establishment of the Bank of France, centralization of tax collection, codification of law along Roman models (Code Napoléon), and reform and extension of secondary and university education. In an 1801 concordat, the papacy recognized the effective autonomy of the French Catholic Church.

Napoleon's continental successes were offset by British victory under Adm. Horatio Nelson in the **Battle of Trafalgar** (1805).

In all, some 400,000 French soldiers were killed in the Napoleonic Wars, along with about 600,000 foreign troops.

Last gasp of old regime. The disastrous 1812 invasion of Russia exposed Napoleon's overextension. After Napoleon's 1814 exile at Elba, his armies were defeated (1815) at **Waterloo**, by British and Prussian troops.

At the **Congress of Vienna**, the monarchs and princes of Europe redrew their boundaries, to the advantage of Prussia (in Saxony and the Ruhr), Austria (in Illyria and Venetia), and Russia (in Poland and Finland). British conquest of Dutch and French colonies (S Africa, Ceylon, Mauritius) was recognized, and France, under the restored Bourbons, retained its expanded 1792 borders. The settlement brought 50 years of international peace to Europe.

But the Congress was unable to check the advance of liberal ideals and of nationalism among the smaller European nations. The 1825 **Decembrist uprising** by liberal officers in Russia was easily suppressed. But an independence movement in **Greece**, stirred by commercial prosperity and a cultural revival, succeeded in expelling Ottoman rule by 1831, with the aid of Britain, France, and Russia.

A constitutional monarchy was secured in France by the **1830 Revolution**; Louis Philippe became king. The revolutionary contagion spread to **Belgium**, which gained its independence (1830) from the Dutch monarchy, to **Poland**, whose rebellion was defeated (1830-31) by Russia, and to Germany.

Romanticism. A new style in intellectual and artistic life replaced Neoclassicism and Rococo after the mid-18th cent. By the early 19th cent., Romanticism prevailed in Europe.

Rousseau had begun the reaction against rationalism; in education (*Émile*, 1762) he stressed subjective spontaneity over regularized instruction. German writers (Lessing, 1729-81; Herder, 1744-1803) favorably compared the German folk song to classical forms and began a cult of Shakespeare, whose passion and "natural" wisdom was a model for the romantic *Sturm und Drang* (Storm and Stress) movement. **Goethe's** *Sorrows of Young Werther* (1774) set the model for the tragic, passionate genius.

A new interest in **Gothic architecture** in England after 1760 (Walpole, 1717-97) spread through Europe, associated with an aesthetic Christian and mystic revival (**Blake**, 1757-1827). Celtic, Norse, and German mythology and folk tales were revived or imitated (Macpherson's Ossian translation, 1762; Grimm's Fairy Tales, 1812-22). The medieval revival (Scott's *Ivanhoe*, 1819) led to a new interest in history, stressing national differences and organic growth (**Carlyle**, 1795-1881; Michelet, 1798-1874), corresponding to theories of natural evolution (Lamarck's *Philosophie Zoologique*, 1809; Lyell's *Geology*, 1830-33). A reaction against classicism characterized the English **romantic poets** (beginning with **Wordsworth,** 1770-1850). Revolution and war fed an emphasis on freedom and conflict, expressed by both poets (**Byron,** 1788-1824; **Hugo,** 1802-85) and philosophers (**Hegel,** 1770-1831).

Wild gardens replaced the formal French variety, and painters favored rural, stormy, and mountainous landscapes (**Turner,** 1775-1851; **Constable,** 1776-1837). Clothing became freer, with wigs, hoops, and ruffles discarded. Originality and genius were expected in the life as well as the work of inspired artists (Murger's *Scenes from Bohemian Life*, 1847-49). Exotic locales and themes (as in Gothic horror stories) were used in art and literature (Delacroix, 1798-1863; **Poe**, 1809-49).

Music exhibited the new dramatic style and a breakdown of classical forms (**Beethoven,** 1770-1827). The use of folk melodies and modes aided the growth of distinct national traditions (Glinka in Russia, 1804-57).

Latin America. Francois **Toussaint L'Ouverture** led a successful slave revolt in Haiti, which subsequently became the first Latin American state to achieve independence (1804). The mainland Spanish colonies won their independence (1810-24), under such leaders as Simón **Bolívar** (1783-1830). Brazil became an independent empire (1822) under the Portuguese prince regent. A new class of military officers divided power with large landholders and the church.

United States. Territory under U.S. control nearly doubled in size with the **Louisiana Purchase** (1803). Heavy immigration and exploitation of ample natural resources fueled rapid economic growth. The spread of the franchise, public education, and antislavery sentiment were signs of a widespread democratic ethic.

China. Failure to keep pace with Western arms technology exposed China to greater European influence and hampered efforts to bar imports of opium, which had damaged Chinese society and drained wealth overseas. In the **Opium War** (1839-42), Britain forced China to expand trade opportunities and to cede Hong Kong.

Triumph of Progress: 1840-80

Idea of Progress. As a result of the cumulative scientific, economic, and political changes of the preceding eras, the idea took hold among literate people in the West that continuing growth and improvement was the usual state of human and natural life.

Charles Darwin's statement of the theory of evolution and survival of the fittest (*On the Origin of Species*, 1859), defended by intellectuals and scientists against theological objections, was taken as confirmation that progress was the natural direction of life. The controversy helped define popular ideas of the dedicated scientist and of science's increasing control over the world (Foucault's demonstration of earth's rotation, 1851; Pasteur's germ theory, 1861).

Liberals following Ricardo (1772-1823) in their faith that unrestrained competition would bring continuous economic expansion sought to adjust political life to new social realities and believed that unregulated competition of ideas would yield truth

Charles Darwin

(**Mill**, 1806-73). In England, successive reform bills (1832, 1867, 1884) gave representation to the new industrial towns and extended the franchise to the middle and lower classes and to Catholics, Dissenters, and Jews. On both sides of the Atlantic, reformists tried to improve conditions for the mentally ill (**Dix**, 1802-87), women (Anthony, 1820-1906), and prisoners. Slavery was barred in the British Empire (1833), the U.S. (1865), and Brazil (1888).

Socialist theories based on ideas of human perfectibility or progress were widely disseminated. Utopian socialists such as Saint-Simon (1760-1825) envisaged an orderly, just society directed by a technocratic elite. A model factory town, New Lanark, Scotland, was set up by utopian Robert Owen (1771-1858), and communal experiments were tried in the U.S. (Brook Farm, Mass., 1841-47). Bakunin's (1814-76) anarchism represented the opposite extreme of total freedom. Karl Marx (1818-83) posited the inevitable triumph of socialism in industrial countries through a dialectical process of class conflict.

Spread of industry. The technical processes and managerial innovations of the English industrial revolution spread to Europe (especially Germany) and the U.S., causing an explosion of industrial production, demand for raw materials, and competition for markets. Inventors, both trained and self-taught, provided means for larger-scale production (Bessemer steel, 1856; sewing machine, 1846). Many inventions were shown at the universal prosperity-themed 1851 London Great Exhibition at the **Crystal Palace**.

Local specialization and long-distance trade were aided by a revolution in transportation and communication. Railroads were first introduced in the 1820s in England and the U.S. Over 150,000 mi of track had been laid worldwide by 1880, with another 100,000 mi laid in the next decade. Steamships were improved (*Savannah* crossed Atlantic, 1819). The **telegraph**, perfected by 1844 (Morse), connected the Old and New Worlds by cable in 1866 and quickened the pace of international commerce and politics. The first commercial **telephone** exchange went into operation in the U.S. in 1878.

The new class of industrial workers, uprooted from their rural homes, lacked job security and suffered from dangerous overcrowding at work and at home. Many responded by organizing **trade unions** (legalized in England, 1824; France, 1884). The U.S. Knights of Labor had 700,000 members by 1886. The First International (1864-76) tried to unite workers worldwide around a Marxist program. The quasi-Socialist Paris Commune uprising (1871) was violently suppressed. Acts to reduce child labor and regulate conditions were passed (1833-50 in England). Social security measures were introduced by the Bismarck regime (1883-89) in Germany.

Revolutions of 1848. Among the causes of the continent-wide revolutions were an international collapse of credit and resulting unemployment, bad harvests in 1845-47, and a cholera epidemic. The new urban proletariat and expanding bourgeoisie demanded greater political roles. Republics were proclaimed in France, Rome, and Venice. Nationalist feelings reached fever pitch in the Habsburg empire, as Hungary declared independence under Kossuth, as a Slav Congress demanded equality, and as Piedmont tried to drive Austria from Lombardy. A national liberal assembly at Frankfurt called for German unification.

Karl Marx

But riots fueled bourgeois fear of socialism (**Marx and Engels**, *Communist Manifesto*, 1848), and peasants remained conservative. The old establishment—the Papacy, the Habsburgs with the help of the Czarist Russian army—was able to rout the revolutionaries by 1849. The French Republic succumbed to a renewed monarchy by 1852 (Emperor Napoleon III).

Great nations unified. Using the "blood and iron" tactics of Bismarck from 1862, Prussia controlled N Germany by 1867 (war with Denmark, 1864; Austria, 1866). After defeating France in 1870 (annexation of Alsace-Lorraine), it won the allegiance of S German states. A new **German Empire** was proclaimed (1871). **Italy**, inspired by Giuseppe Mazzini (1805-72) and Giuseppe Garibaldi (1807-82), was unified by the reformed Piedmont kingdom through uprisings, plebiscites, and war.

The **U.S.**, its area expanded after the 1846-48 Mexican War, defeated (1861-65) a secession attempt by southern states in the **Civil War**. Canadian provinces were united in an autonomous **Dominion of Canada** (1867). Control in **India** was removed from the East India Co. and centralized under British administration after the 1857-58 Sepoy rebellion, laying the groundwork for the modern Indian State. Queen Victoria was named Empress of India (1876).

Europe dominates Asia. The Ottoman Empire began to collapse in the face of Balkan nationalisms and European imperial incursions in N Africa (**Suez Canal**, 1869). The Turks had lost control of most of both regions by 1882. Russia completed its expansion S by 1884 (despite the temporary setback of the **Crimean War** with Turkey, Britain, and France, 1853-56), taking Turkestan, all the Caucasus, and Chinese areas in the E and sponsoring Balkan Slavs against the Turks. A succession of reformist and reactionary regimes presided over a slow modernization (serfs freed, 1861). Persian independence suffered as Russia and British India competed for influence.

China was forced to sign a series of unequal treaties with European powers and Japan. Overpopulation and an inefficient dynasty brought misery and caused rebellions (Taiping, Muslims) leaving tens of millions dead. **Japan** was forced by the U.S. (Commodore Perry's visits, 1853-54) and Europe to end its isolation. The Meiji restoration (1868) gave power to a Westernizing oligarchy. Intensified empire-building gave Burma to Britain (1824-85) and Indochina to France (1862-95). Christian missionary activity followed imperial and trade expansion in Asia.

Respectability. Fine arts were expected to reflect and encourage the good morals and manners among the Victorians. Prudery, exaggerated delicacy, and familial piety were heralded by **Bowdler's** expurgated Shakespeare edition (1818). Government-supported mass education sought to inculcate a work ethic as a means to escape poverty (**Horatio Alger,** 1832-99).

The official **Beaux Arts** school in Paris set an international style of imposing public buildings (Paris Opera, 1861-74; Vienna Opera, 1861-69) and uplifting statues (Bartholdi's Statue of Liberty, 1884). Realist painting, influenced by photography (Daguerre, 1837), appealed to a new mass audience with social or historical narrative (Wilkie, 1785-1841; Poynter, 1836-1919) or with serious religious, moral, or social messages (pre-Raphaelites, Millet's *Angelus*, 1858), often drawn from ordinary life. The **Impressionists** (Monet, 1840-1926; Pissarro, 1830-1903; Renoir, 1841-1919) rejected the formalism, sentimentality, and precise techniques of academic art in favor of a spontaneous, undetailed rendering of the world through careful representation of the effect of natural light on objects.

Realistic **novelists** presented the full panorama of social classes and personalities, but retained sentimentality and moral judgment (**Dickens**, 1812-70; **Eliot**, 1819-80; **Tolstoy**, 1828-1910; **Balzac**, 1799-1850).

Veneer of Stability: 1880-1900

Imperialism triumphant. The vast **African** interior, visited by European explorers (Barth, 1821-65; Livingstone, 1813-73), was conquered by the European powers in rapid, competitive thrusts from their coastal bases after 1880, mostly for domestic political and international strategic reasons. W African Muslim kingdoms (Fulani), Arab slave traders (Zanzibar), and Bantu military confederations (Zulu) were alike subdued. Only Christian Ethiopia (defeat of Italy, 1896) and Liberia resisted successfully. France (W Africa) and Britain ("Cape to Cairo", **Boer War**, 1899-1902) were the major beneficiaries. The ideology of "the white man's burden" (Kipling, *Barrack Room Ballads*, 1892) or of a "civilizing mission" (France) justified the conquests.

W European foreign capital investment soared to nearly $40 billion by 1914, but most was in E Europe (France, Germany), the Americas (Britain), and Europe's colonies. The foundation of the modern interdependent world economy was laid, with cartels dominating raw material trade.

An industrious world. Industrial and technological proficiency characterized the 2 new great powers—Germany and the U.S. Coal and iron deposits enabled Germany to reach 2nd or 3rd place status in iron, steel, and shipbuilding by the 1900s. German electrical and chemical industries were world leaders. The U.S. post-Civil War boom (interrupted by "panics"—1884, 1893, 1896) was shaped by massive immigration from S and E Europe from 1880, government subsidy of railroads, and huge private monopolies (Standard Oil, 1870; U.S. Steel, 1901). The **Spanish-American War**, 1898 (Philippine Insurrection, 1899-1902), and the **Open Door policy** in China (1899) made the U.S. a world power.

England led in **urbanization**, with **London** the world capital of finance, insurance, and shipping. Sewer systems (Paris, 1850s), electric subways (London, 1890), parks, and bargain department stores helped improve living standards for most of the urban population of the industrial world.

Westernization of Asia. Asian reaction to European economic, military, and religious incursions took the form of imitation of Western techniques and adoption of Western ideas of progress and freedom. The Chinese "self-strengthening" movement of the 1860s and 1870s included rail, port, and arsenal improvements and metal and textile mills. Reformers such as **K'ang Yu-wei** (1858-1927) won liberalizing reforms in 1898, right after the European and Japanese "scramble for concessions."

A universal education system in Japan and importation of foreign industrial, scientific, and military experts aided Japan's rapid modernization after 1868, under the authoritarian Meiji regime. Japan's victory in the **Sino-Japanese War** (1894-95) put Formosa and Korea in its power.

In India, the British alliance with the remaining princely states masked reform sentiment among the Westernized urban elite; higher education had been conducted largely in English for 50 years. The **Indian National Congress**, founded in 1885, demanded a larger government role for Indians.

Fin-de-siècle sophistication. Naturalist writers pushed realism to its extreme limits, adopting a quasi-scientific attitude and writing about formerly taboo subjects such as sex, crime, extreme poverty, and corruption (Flaubert, 1821-80; Zola, 1840-1902; Hardy, 1840-1928). Unseen or repressed psychological motivations were explored in the clinical and theoretical works of Sigmund **Freud** (1856-1939) and in works of fiction (**Dostoyevsky**, 1821-81; James, 1843-1916; Schnitzler, 1862-1931).

A contempt for bourgeois life or a desire to shock a complacent audience was shared by the French **symbolist** poets (Verlaine, 1844-96; Rimbaud, 1854-91), by neopagan English writers (Swinburne, 1837-1909), by continental dramatists (**Ibsen**, 1828-1906), and by satirists (**Wilde**, 1854-1900). The German philosopher Friedrich **Nietzsche** (1844-1900) was influential in his elitism and pessimism.

Postimpressionist art neglected long-cherished conventions of representation (Cézanne, 1839-1906) and showed a willingness to learn from primitive and non-European art (Gauguin, 1848-1903; Japanese prints).

Racism. Gobineau (1816-82) gave a pseudobiological foundation to modern racist theories, which spread in Europe in the latter 19th cent., along with **Social Darwinism**, the belief that societies are and should be organized as a struggle for survival of the fittest. The medieval period was interpreted as an era of natural Germanic rule (Chamberlain, 1855-1927), and notions of racial superiority were associated with German national aspirations (Treitschke, 1834-96). **Anti-Semitism**, with a new racist rationale, became a significant political force in Germany (Anti-Semitic Petition, 1880), Austria (Lueger, 1844-1910), and France (**Dreyfus affair**, 1894-1906).

Last Respite: 1900-9

Alliances. While the peace of Europe (and its dependencies) continued to hold (1907 **Hague Conference** extended the rules of war and international arbitration procedures), imperial rivalries, protectionist trade practices (in Germany and France), and the escalating arms race (British *Dreadnought* battleship launched; Germany widens Kiel canal, 1906) exacerbated minor disputes (German-French Moroccan "crises," 1905, 1911).

Security was sought through balance-of-power alliances: **Triple Alliance** (Germany, Austria-Hungary, Italy; renewed in 1902 and 1907); Anglo-Japanese Alliance (1902), Franco-Russian Alliance (1899), **Entente Cordiale** (Britain, France, 1904), Anglo-Russian Treaty (1907), German-Ottoman friendship.

Ottomans decline. The inefficient, corrupt Ottoman government was unable to resist further loss of territory. Nearly all European lands were lost in 1912 to Serbia, Greece, Montenegro, and Bulgaria. Italy took Libya and the Dodecanese islands the same year, and Britain took Kuwait (1899) and the Sinai (1906). The **Young Turk** revolution in 1908 forced the sultan to restore a constitution, and it introduced some social reform, industrialization, and secularization.

British Empire. British trade and cultural influence remained dominant in the empire, but constitutional reforms presaged its eventual dissolution: The colonies of **Australia** were united in 1901 under a self-governing commonwealth. **New Zealand** acquired dominion status in 1907. The old Boer republics joined Cape Colony and Natal in the self-governing Union of **South Africa** in 1910.

The 1909 Indian Councils Act enhanced the role of elected province legislatures in **India**. The Muslim League (founded 1906) sought separate communal representation.

East Asia. Japan exploited its growing industrial power to expand its empire. Victory in the 1904-5 war against Russia (naval battle of Tsushima, 1905) assured Japan's domination of **Korea** (annexed 1910) and Manchuria (Port Arthur taken, 1905).

In China, central authority began to crumble (empress died, 1908). Reforms (Confucian exam system ended 1905, modernization of the army, building of railroads) were inadequate, and secret societies of reformers and nationalists, inspired by the Westernized **Sun Yat-sen** (1866-1925) fomented periodic uprisings in the S.

Sun Yat-sen

Siam, whose independence had been guaranteed by Britain and France in 1896, was split into spheres of influence by those countries in 1907.

Russia. The population of the Russian Empire approached 150 million in 1900. Reforms in education, in law, and in local institutions (*zemstvos*) and an industrial boom starting in the 1880s (oil, railroads) created the beginnings of a modern state, despite the autocratic tsarist regime. Liberals (1903 Union of Liberation), Socialists (Social Democrats founded 1898, Bolsheviks split off 1903), and populists (Social Revolutionaries founded 1901) were periodically repressed, and national minorities were persecuted (anti-Jewish pogroms, 1903, 1905-6).

An industrial crisis after 1900 and harvest failures aggravated poverty among urban workers, and the 1904-5 defeat by Japan (which checked Russia's Asian expansion) sparked the **Revolution of 1905-6**. A Duma (parliament) was created, and an agricultural reform (under Stolypin, prime minister 1906-11) created a large class of land-owning peasants (*kulaks*).

The world shrinks. Developments in transportation and communication and mass population movements helped create an awareness of an interdependent world. Early **automobiles** (Daimler, Benz, 1885) were experimental or were designed as luxuries. Assembly-line mass production (Ford Motor Co., 1903) made the invention practical, and by 1910 nearly 500,000 motor vehicles were registered in the U.S. alone. **Heavier-than-air flights** began in 1903 in the U.S. (Wright brothers' *Flyer*), preceded by glider, balloon, and model plane advances in several countries. Trade was advanced by improvements in ship design (gyrocompass, 1910), speed (*Lusitania* crossed Atlantic in 5 days, 1907), and reach (Panama Canal begun, 1904).

The first transatlantic **radio** telegraphic transmission occurred in 1901, 6 years after Marconi discovered radio. Radio transmission of human speech had been made in 1900. Telegraphic transmission of photos was achieved in 1904, lending immediacy to news reports. **Phonographs**, popularized by Caruso's recordings (starting 1902), made for quick international spread of musical styles (ragtime). **Motion pictures**, perfected in the 1890s (Dickson, Lumière brothers), became a popular and artistic medium after 1900; newsreels appeared in 1909.

Emigration from crowded European centers soared in the decade: 9 million migrated to the U.S., and millions more went to Siberia, Canada, Argentina, Australia, South Africa, and Algeria. Some 70 million Europeans emigrated in the cent. before 1914. Several million Chinese, Indians, and Japanese migrated to SE Asia, where their urban skills often enabled them to take a predominant economic role.

Social reform. The social and economic problems of the poor were kept in the public eye by realist fiction writers (Dreiser's *Sister Carrie*, 1900; Gorky's *Lower Depths*, 1902; Sinclair's *The Jungle*, 1906), journalists (U.S. **muckrakers**—Steffens, Tarbell), and artists (Ashcan school). Frequent labor strikes and occasional assassinations by anarchists or radicals (Empress Elizabeth of Austria, 1898; King Umberto I of Italy, 1900; U.S. Pres. McKinley, 1901; Russian Interior Minister Plehve, 1904; Portugal's King Carlos, 1908) added to social tension and fear of revolution.

But democratic reformism prevailed. In Germany, Bernstein's (1850-1932) **revisionist Marxism**, downgrading revolution, was accepted by the powerful Social Democrats and trade unions. The British Fabian Society (the Webbs, Shaw) and the Labour Party (founded 1906) worked for reforms such as social security and union rights (1906), while woman suffragists grew more militant. U.S. **progressives** fought big business (Pure Food and Drug Act, 1906). In France, the 10-hour work day (1904) and separation of church and state (1905) were reform victories, as was universal suffrage in Austria (1907).

Arts. An unprecedented period of experimentation, centered in France, produced several **new painting styles**: Fauvism exploited bold color areas (Matisse, *Woman With Hat*, 1905); expressionism reflected powerful inner emotions (the Brücke group, 1905); cubism combined several views of an object on one flat surface (Picasso's *Demoiselles*, 1906-7); futurism tried to depict speed and motion (Italian Futurist Manifesto, 1910). **Architects** explored new uses of steel structures, with facades either neoclassical (Adler and Sullivan in U.S.); curvilinear Art Nouveau (Gaudi's Casa Mila, 1905-10); or functionally streamlined (Wright's Robie House, 1909).

Music and dance shared the experimental spirit. Ruth St. Denis (1877-1968) and Isadora Duncan (1878-1927) pioneered modern dance, while Sergei Diaghilev in Paris revitalized classic ballet from 1909. Composers explored atonal music (Debussy, 1862-1918) and dissonance (Schoenberg, 1874-1951) or revolutionized classical forms (Stravinsky, 1882-1971), often showing jazz or folk music influences.

War and Revolution: 1910-19

War threatens. Germany under Wilhelm II sought a political and imperial role consonant with its industrial strength, challenging Britain's world supremacy and threatening France, which was still resenting the loss (1871) of Alsace-Lorraine. Austria wanted to curb an expanded Serbia (after 1912) and the threat it posed to its own Slav lands. Russia feared Austrian and German political and economic aims in the Balkans and Turkey.

An accelerated arms race resulted from these circumstances. The German standing army rose to more than 2 million men by 1914. Russia and France had more than a million each, and Austria and the British Empire nearly a million each. Dozens of enormous battleships were built by the powers after 1906.

The **assassination of Austrian Archduke Franz Ferdinand** by a Serbian, June 28, 1914, was the pretext for war. The system of alliances made the conflict Europe-wide; Germany's invasion of Belgium to outflank France forced Britain to enter the war. Patriotic fervor was nearly unanimous among all classes in most countries.

World War I. German forces were stopped in France in one month. The rival armies dug **trench networks**. Artillery and improved machine guns prevented either side from any lasting advance despite repeated assaults (600,000 dead at **Verdun**, Feb.-July 1916). Poison gas, used by Germany in 1915, proved ineffective. The entrance of more than 1 million U.S. troops tipped the balance after mid-1917, forcing Germany to sue for peace the next year. The formal armistice was signed on Nov. 11, 1918.

In the E, the Russian armies were thrown back (battle of **Tannenberg**, Aug. 20, 1914), and the war grew unpopular in Russia. An allied attempt to relieve Russia through Turkey failed (**Gallipoli**, 1915). The **Russian Revolution** (1917) abolished the monarchy. The new Bolshevik regime signed the capitulatory Brest-Litovsk peace in March 1918. Italy entered the war on the allied side in May 1915 but was pushed back by Oct. 1917. A renewed offensive with Allied aid in Oct.-Nov. 1918 forced Austria to surrender.

The British Navy successfully blockaded Germany, which responded with submarine U-boat attacks; **unrestricted submarine warfare** against neutrals after Jan. 1917 helped bring the U.S. into the war. Other battlefields included Palestine and Mesopotamia, both of which Britain wrested from the Turks in 1917, and the African and Pacific colonies of Germany, most of which fell to Britain, France, Australia, Japan, and South Africa.

Settlement. At the **Paris Peace Conference** (Jan.-June 1919), concluded by the **Treaty of Versailles**, and in subsequent negotiations and local wars (Russian-Polish War, 1920), the **map of Europe** was **redrawn** with a nod to U.S. Pres. Woodrow Wilson's principle of self-determination. Austria and Hungary were separated, and much of their land was given to Yugoslavia (formerly Serbia), Romania, Italy, and the newly independent Poland and Czechoslovakia.

Germany lost territory in the W, N, and E, while Finland and the Baltic states were detached from Russia. Turkey lost nearly all its Arab lands to British-sponsored Arab states or to direct French and British rule. Belgium's sovereignty was recognized.

From 1916, the civilian populations and economies of both sides were mobilized to an unprecedented degree. Hardships intensified among fighting nations in 1917 (French mutiny crushed in May). More than 10 million soldiers died in the war.

A huge **reparations** burden and partial demilitarization were imposed on Germany. Pres. Wilson obtained approval for a League of Nations, but the U.S. Senate refused to allow the U.S. to join.

Vladimir Lenin

Russian revolution. Military defeats and high casualties caused a contagious lack of confidence in Tsar Nicholas, who was forced to abdicate Mar. 1917. A liberal provisional government failed to end the war, and massive desertions, riots, and fighting between factions followed. A moderate socialist government under Aleksandr Kerensky was overthrown (Nov. 1917) in a violent coup by the **Bolsheviks** in Petrograd under **Lenin,** who later disbanded the elected Constituent Assembly.

The Bolsheviks brutally suppressed all opposition and ended the war with Germany in Mar. 1918. **Civil war** broke out in the summer between the Red Army (the Bolsheviks and their supporters), and monarchists, anarchists, minority nationalities (Ukrainians, Georgians, Poles), and others. Small U.S., British, French, and Japanese units also opposed the Bolsheviks (1918-19; Japan in Vladivostok to 1922). The civil war, anarchy, and pogroms devastated the country until the 1920 Red Army victory. The **Communist Party** leadership retained absolute power.

Other European revolutions. An unpopular monarchy in **Portugal** was overthrown in 1910. The new republic took severe anticlerical measures in 1911.

After a century of Home Rule agitation, during which **Ireland** was devastated by famine (1 million dead, 1846-47) and emigration, republican militants staged an unsuccessful uprising in Dublin during **Easter 1916**. The execution of the leaders and mass arrests by the British won popular support for the rebels. The **Irish Free State,** comprising all but the 6 N counties, achieved dominion status in 1922.

In the aftermath of the world war, radical revolutions were attempted in Germany (**Spartacist** uprising, Jan. 1919), **Hungary** (Kun regime, 1919), and elsewhere. All were suppressed or failed for lack of support.

Chinese revolution. The Manchu Dynasty was overthrown and a republic proclaimed in Oct. 1911. First Pres.

Sun Yat-sen resigned in favor of strongman Yuan Shih-k'ai. Sun organized the parliamentarian **Kuomintang** party.

Students launched protests on May 4, 1919, against League of Nations concessions in China to Japan. Nationalist, liberal, and socialist ideas and political groups spread. The **Communist Party** was founded in 1921. A Communist regime took power in Mongolia with Soviet support in 1921.

India restive. Indian objections to British rule erupted in nationalist riots as well as in the nonviolent tactics of Mahatma **Gandhi** (1869-1948). Nearly 400 unarmed demonstrators were shot at **Amritsar** in Apr. 1919. Britain approved limited self-rule that year.

Mexican revolution. Under the long Diaz dictatorship (1877-1911) the economy advanced, but Indian and mestizo lands were confiscated, and concessions to foreigners (mostly U.S.) damaged the middle class. A **revolution in**

1910 led to civil wars and U.S. intervention (1914, 1916-17). Land reform and a more democratic constitution (1917) were achieved.

Sciences. Scientific specialization prevailed by the 20th cent. Advances in knowledge and technological aptitude increased with the geometric rise in the number of practitioners. Physicists challenged common-sense views of causality, observation, and a mechanistic universe, putting science further beyond popular grasp (**Einstein's** general theory of relativity, 1916; Bohr's quantum mechanics, 1913; Heisenberg's uncertainty principle, 1927).

Albert Einstein

The Aftermath of War: 1920-29

U.S. Easy credit, technological ingenuity, and war-related industrial decline in Europe caused a long economic boom, in which ownership of new products—**autos, phones, radios**—became more democratized. **Prosperity,** an increase in women workers, women's suffrage (19th Amendment ratified, 1920), and drastic change in fashion (flappers, mannish bob for women, clean-shaven men) created a wide perception of social change, despite prohibition of alcoholic beverages (1919-33). Union membership and strikes increased. Fear of radicals led to Palmer raids (1919-20) and the Sacco/Vanzetti case (1921-27).

Europe sorts itself out. Germany's liberal **Weimar constitution** (1919) could not guarantee a stable government in the face of rightist violence (Rathenau assassinated, 1922) and Communist refusal to cooperate with Socialists. Reparations and Allied occupation of the Rhineland caused staggering inflation that destroyed middle-class savings, but economic expansion resumed after mid-decade, aided by U.S. loans. A sophisticated, **innovative culture** developed in architecture and design (Bauhaus, 1919-28), film (Lang, M, 1931), painting (Grosz), music (Weill, *Threepenny Opera*, 1928), theater (Brecht, *A Man's a Man*, 1926), criticism (Benjamin), philosophy (Jung), and fashion. This culture was considered decadent and socially disruptive by rightists.

England elected its first Labour governments (Jan. 1924, June 1929). A 10-day general strike in support of coal miners failed in May 1926. In **Italy**, strikes, political chaos, and violence by small Fascist bands culminated in the Oct. 1922 Fascist March on Rome, which established **Mussolini's** dictatorship. Strikes were outlawed (1926), and Italian influence was pressed in the Balkans (Albania a protectorate, 1926). A conservative dictatorship was also established in **Portugal** in a 1926 military coup.

Czechoslovakia, the only stable democracy to emerge from the war in Central or E Europe, faced opposition from Germans (in the Sudetenland), Ruthenians, and some Slovaks. As the industrial heartland of the old Habsburg empire, it remained fairly prosperous. With French backing, it formed the Little Entente with Yugoslavia (1920) and **Romania** (1921) to block Austrian or Hungarian irredentism. Croats and Slovenes in **Yugoslavia** demanded a federal state until King Alexander I proclaimed (1929) a royal dictatorship. Poland faced internal nationality problems as well (Germans, Ukrainians, Jews); Pilsudski ruled as dictator from 1926. The Baltic states were threatened by traditionally dominant ethnic Germans and by Soviet-supported Communists.

An economic collapse and famine in **Russia** (1921-22) claimed 5 million lives. The New Economic Policy (1921) allowed land ownership by peasants and some private commerce and industry. **Stalin** was absolute ruler within 4 years of Lenin's death (1924). He inaugurated a brutal collectivization program (1929-32) and used foreign Communist parties for Soviet state advantage.

Internationalism. Revulsion against World War I led to pacifist agitation, to the Kellogg-Briand Pact renouncing aggressive war (1928), and to **naval disarmament** pacts (Washington, 1922; London, 1930). But the League of Nations was able to arbitrate only minor disputes (Greece-Bulgaria, 1925).

Middle East. Mustafa Kemal (**Ataturk**) led **Turkish** nationalists in resisting Italian, French, and Greek military advances (1919-23). The sultanate was abolished (1922), and elaborate reforms were passed, including secularization of law and adoption of the Latin alphabet. Ethnic conflict led to persecution of **Armenians** (more than 1 million dead in 1915, 1 million expelled), Greeks (forced Greek-Turk population exchange, 1923), and Kurds (1925 uprising).

With evacuation of the Turks from **Arab** lands, the puritanical Wahabi dynasty of E Arabia conquered (1919-25) what is now Saudi Arabia. British, French, and Arab dynastic and nationalist maneuvering resulted in the creation of 2 more Arab monarchies in 1921—Iraq and Transjordan (both under British control)—and 2 French mandates—Syria and Lebanon. Jewish immigration into British-mandated **Palestine,** inspired by the Zionist movement, was resisted by Arabs, at times violently (1921, 1929 massacres).

Reza Khan ruled **Persia** after his 1921 coup (shah from 1925), centralized control, and created the trappings of a modern secular state.

In 1922, English archaeologist Howard Carter discovered the **tomb** of the boy pharaoh **Tutankhamen** in the Valley of the Kings in Egypt.

China. The Kuomintang under **Chiang Kai-shek** (1887-1975) subdued the warlords by 1928. The Communists were brutally suppressed after their alliance with the Kuomintang was broken in 1927. Relative peace thereafter allowed for industrial and financial improvements, with some Russian, British, and U.S. cooperation.

Chiang Kai-shek

Arts. Nearly all bounds of subject matter, style, and attitude were broken in the arts of the period. **Abstract** art first took inspiration from natural forms or narrative themes (Kandinsky from 1911 and then worked free of any representational aims (Malevich's suprematism, 1915-19; Mondrian's geometric style from 1917). The **Dada** movement (from 1916) mocked artistic pretension with absurd collages and constructions. Paradox, illusion, and psychological taboos were exploited by **surrealists** by the late 1920s (Dali, Magritte). Architectural schools celebrated industrial values, whether vigorous abstract constructivism (Tatlin, *Monument to 3rd International,* 1919) or the machined, streamlined **Bauhaus** style, which was extended to many design fields (Helvetica typeface).

Prose writers explored revolutionary narrative modes related to dreams (Kafka's *Trial*, 1925), internal monologue (Joyce's *Ulysses*, 1922), and word play (Stein's *Making of Americans*, 1925). Poets and novelists wrote of modern alienation (Eliot's *Waste Land*, 1922) and aimlessness ("The Lost Generation").

Rise of Totalitarians: 1930-39

Depression. A worldwide financial panic and economic depression began with the Oct. 1929 U.S. stock market crash and the May 1931 failure of the Austrian Credit-Anstalt. A credit crunch caused international bankruptcies and **unemployment**: 12 million jobless by 1932 in the U.S., 5.6 million in Germany, 2.7 million in England. Governments responded with **tariff restrictions** (Smoot-Hawley Act, 1930; Ottawa Imperial Conference, 1932), which dried up world trade. Government public works programs were vitiated by deflationary budget balancing.

Mussolini & Hitler

Germany. Years of agitation by violent extremists were brought to a head by the Depression. Nazi leader Adolf Hitler was named chancellor in Jan. 1933 and given dictatorial power by the Reichstag in March. Opposition parties were disbanded, strikes banned, and all aspects of economic, cultural, and religious life were brought under central government and Nazi party control and manipulated by sophisticated propaganda. Severe persecution of Jews began (**Nuremberg Laws**, Sept. 1935). Many Jews, political opponents, and others were sent to concentration camps (Dachau, 1933), where thousands died or were killed. Public works, renewed conscription (1935), arms production, and a 4-year plan (1936) all but ended unemployment.

Hitler's expansionism started with reincorporation of the Saar (1935), occupation of the **Rhineland** (Mar. 1936), and annexation of Austria (Mar. 1938). At **Munich** (Sept. 1938) Britain and France attempted to appease Hitler and avoid war by successfully encouraging Czechoslovakia's surrender of the Sudetenland territory.

Russia. Rapid industrialization was achieved through successive **5-year plans** starting in 1928, using severe labor discipline and mass forced labor. Industry was financed by a decline in living standards and exploitation of agriculture, which was almost totally collectivized by the early 1930s (*kolkhoz*, collective farm; *sovkhoz*, state farm, often in newly worked lands). Successive **purges** increased the role of professionals and management at the expense of workers. Millions perished in a series of manufactured disasters: extermination (1929-34) of kulaks (peasant landowners), severe famine (1932-33), party purges and show trials (Great Purge, 1936-38), suppression of nationalities, and poor conditions in labor camps.

Spain. An industrial revolution during World War I created an urban proletariat, which was attracted to socialism and anarchism; Catalan nationalists challenged central authority. The 5 years after King Alfonso left Spain in Apr. 1931 were dominated by tension between intermittent leftist and anticlerical governments and clericals, monarchists, and other rightists. Anarchist and Communist rebellions were crushed, but a July 1936 extreme right rebellion led by Gen. Francisco **Franco** and aided by Nazi Germany and Fascist Italy succeeded, after a 3-year **civil war** (more than 1 million dead in battles and atrocities). The war polarized international public opinion.

Italy. Despite propaganda for the ideal of the Corporate State, few domestic reforms were attempted. An entente with Hungary and Austria (Mar. 1934), a pact with Germany and Japan (Nov. 1937), and intervention by 50,000-75,000 troops in Spain (1936-39) sealed Italy's identification with the fascist bloc (anti-Semitic laws after Mar. 1938). Ethiopia was conquered (1935-36), and Albania annexed (Jan. 1939) in conscious imitation of ancient Rome.

Eastern Europe. Repressive regimes fought for power against an active opposition (liberals, socialists, Communists, peasants, Nazis). Minority groups and Jews were restricted within national boundaries that did not coincide with ethnic population patterns. In the destruction of **Czechoslovakia**, Hungary occupied S Slovakia (Nov. 1938) and Ruthenia (Mar. 1939), and a pro-Nazi regime took power in the rest of Slovakia. Other boundary disputes (e.g., Poland-Lithuania, Yugoslavia-Bulgaria, and Romania-Hungary) doomed attempts to build joint fronts against Germany or Russia. Economic depression was severe.

East Asia. After a period of liberalism in **Japan**, nativist militarists dominated the government with popular support. Manchuria was seized (Sept. 1931-Feb. 1932), and a puppet state was set up (Manchukuo). Adjacent Jehol (Inner Mongolia) was occupied in 1933. China proper was invaded in July 1937; large areas were conquered by Oct. 1938. Hundreds of thousands of rapes, murders, and other atrocities were attributed to the Japanese.

In **China** Communist forces left Kuomintang-besieged strongholds in the S in a Long March (1934-35) to the N. The Kuomintang-Communist civil war was suspended in Jan. 1937 in the face of threatening Japan.

Democracies. The Roosevelt Administration, in office Mar. 1933, embarked on an extensive program of **New Deal** social reform and economic stimulation, including protection for labor unions (heavy industries organized), Social Security, public works, wage-and-hour laws, and assistance to farmers. Isolationist sentiment (1937 Neutrality Act) prevented U.S. intervention in Europe, but military expenditures were increased in 1939.

French political instability and polarization prevented resolution of economic and international security questions. The **Popular Front** government under Leon Blum (June 1936-Apr. 1938) passed social reforms (40-hr week) and raised arms spending. National coalition governments, which ruled Britain from Aug. 1931, brought economic recovery but failed to define a consistent international policy until Chamberlain's government (from May 1937), which practiced **appeasement** of Germany and Italy.

India. Twenty years of agitation for autonomy and then for independence (Gandhi's **salt march**, 1930) achieved some constitutional reform (extended provincial powers, 1935) despite Muslim-Hindu strife. Social issues assumed prominence with peasant uprisings (1921), strikes (1928), Gandhi's efforts for untouchables (1932 "fast unto death"), and social and agrarian reform by the provinces after 1937.

Mahatma Gandhi

Arts. The streamlined, geometric design motifs of Art Deco (from 1925) prevailed through the 1930s. **Abstract art** flourished (Moore sculptures from 1931) alongside a new **realism** related to social and political concerns (Socialist Realism, the official Soviet style from 1934; Mexican muralist Rivera, 1886-1957; and Orozco, 1883-1949), which were also expressed in fiction and poetry (Steinbeck's *Grapes of Wrath*, 1939; Sandburg's *The People, Yes*, 1936). Modern architecture (International Style, 1932) was unchallenged in its use of artificial materials (concrete, glass), lack of decoration, and monumentality (Rockefeller Center, 1929-40). Larger-than-life U.S.-made films captured a worldwide audience (*Gone With the Wind*, *The Wizard of Oz*, both 1939).

War, Hot and Cold: 1940-49

War in Asia-Pacific. Japan occupied Indochina in Sept. 1940, dominated Thailand in Dec. 1941, and attacked Hawaii (**Pearl Harbor**), the Philippines, Hong Kong, and Malaya on Dec. 7, 1941 (precipitating U.S. entrance into the war). Indonesia was

Pearl Harbor

attacked in Jan. 1942, and Burma was conquered in Mar. 1942. The Battle of **Midway** (June 1942) turned back the Japanese advance. "Island-hopping" battles (**Guadalcanal**, Aug. 1942-Jan. 1943; **Leyte Gulf**, Oct. 1944; Iwo Jima, Feb.-Mar. 1945; **Okinawa**, Apr. 1945) and massive bombing raids on Japan from June 1944 wore out Japanese defenses. U.S. atom bombs, dropped Aug. 6 and 9 on **Hiroshima** and Nagasaki, forced Japan to agree, on Aug. 14, to surrender; formal surrender was on Sept. 2, 1945.

War in Europe. The Nazi-Soviet nonaggression pact (Aug. 1939) freed Germany to attack Poland (Sept. 1939). Britain and France, which had guaranteed Polish independence, declared war on Germany. Russia seized E Poland (Sept. 1939), attacked Finland (Nov. 1939), and took the Baltic states (July 1940). Mobile German forces staged *blitzkrieg* attacks during Apr.-June 1940, conquering neutral Denmark, Norway, and the Low Countries and defeating France; 350,000 British and French troops were evacuated at **Dunkirk** (May). The **Battle of Britain** (June-Dec. 1940) denied Germany air superiority. German-Italian campaigns won the Balkans by Apr. 1941. Three million Axis troops **invaded Russia** in June 1941, marching through Ukraine to the Caucasus, and through White Russia and the Baltic republics to Moscow and Leningrad. Russian winter counterthrusts (1941-42 and 1942-43) stopped the German advance (**Stalingrad**, Sept. 1942-Feb. 1943). Sustain-

Stalin, Roosevelt & Churchill

ing great casualties, the Russians drove the Axis from all E Europe and the Balkans in the next 2 years. Invasions of N Africa (Nov. 1942), Italy (Sept. 1943), and **Normandy** (launched on D-Day, June 6, 1944) brought U.S., British, Free French, and allied troops to Germany by spring 1945. In Feb. 1945, the 3 Allied leaders, Winston **Churchill** (Britain), Joseph **Stalin** (USSR), and Franklin D. Roosevelt (U.S.), met in Yalta to discuss strategy and resolve political issues, including the postwar Allied occupation of Germany. Germany surrendered May 7, 1945.

Atrocities. The war brought 20th-cent. cruelty to its peak. The Nazi regime systematically killed an estimated 5-6 million Jews, including some 3 million who died in death camps (e.g., **Auschwitz**). Gypsies, political opponents, people with mental or physical disabilities, and others deemed undesirable were also murdered by the Nazis, as were vast numbers of Slavs.

Civilian deaths. German bombs killed 70,000 British civilians. More than 100,000 Chinese civilians were killed by Japanese forces in the capture and occupation of Nanking. Severe retaliation by the Soviet army, E European partisans, Free French, and others took a heavy toll. U.S. and British bombing of Germany killed hundreds of thousands, as did U.S. bombing of Japan (80,000-200,000 at Hiroshima alone). Some 45 million people died in the war.

Settlement. The **United Nations** charter was signed in San Francisco on June 26, 1945, by 50 nations. The International Tribunal at **Nuremberg** convicted 22 German leaders for war crimes in Sept. 1946; 23 Japanese leaders were convicted in Nov. 1948. Postwar border changes included large gains in territory for the USSR, losses for Germany, a shift to the W in Polish borders, and minor losses for Italy. Communist regimes, supported by Soviet troops, took power in most of E Europe, including Soviet-occupied Germany (GDR, aka East Germany, proclaimed Oct. 1949). Japan lost all overseas lands.

Recovery. Basic political and social changes were imposed on Japan and W Germany by the western allies (Japan constitution adopted, May 1947; W German basic law, May 1949). U.S. **Marshall Plan** aid ($12 billion, 1947-51) spurred W European economic recovery after a period of severe inflation and strikes in Europe and the U.S. The British Labour Party introduced a national health service and nationalized basic industries in 1946.

Cold War. Western fears of further Soviet advances (Cominform formed in Oct. 1947; Czechoslovakia coup, Feb. 1948; Berlin blockade, Apr. 1948-Sept. 1949) led to the formation of **NATO**. Civil War in Greece and Soviet pressure on Turkey led to U.S. aid under the **Truman Doctrine** (Mar. 1947). Other anti-Communist security pacts were the Organization of American States (Apr. 1948) and the SE Asia Treaty Organization (Sept. 1954). A new wave of **Soviet purges** and repression intensified in the last years of Stalin's rule, extending to E Europe (Slansky trial in Czechoslovakia, 1951). Only Yugoslavia resisted Soviet control (expelled by Cominform, June 1948; U.S. aid, June 1949).

China, Korea. Communist forces emerged from World War II strengthened by the Soviet takeover of industrial Manchuria. In 4 years of fighting, the Kuomintang was driven from the mainland; the People's Republic of China was proclaimed Oct. 1, 1949. Korea was divided by USSR and U.S. occupation forces. Separate republics were proclaimed in the 2 zones in Aug.-Sept. 1948.

India. India and Pakistan became independent dominions on Aug. 15, 1947. Millions of Hindu and Muslim refugees were created by the partition; riots (1946-47) took hundreds of thousands of lives; Mahatma **Gandhi** was assassinated in Jan. 1948. Burma became completely independent in Jan. 1948; Ceylon took dominion status in Feb.

Middle East. The UN approved partition of Palestine into Jewish and Arab states. **Israel** was proclaimed a state, May 14, 1948. Arabs rejected partition, but failed to defeat Israel in war (May 1948-July 1949). Immigration from Europe and the Middle East swelled Israel's Jewish population. British and French forces left Lebanon and Syria in 1946. Transjordan occupied most of Arab Palestine.

Southeast Asia. Communists and others fought against restoration of French rule in **Indochina** from 1946; a non-Communist government was recognized by France in Mar. 1949, but fighting continued. Both Indonesia and the Philippines became independent; the former in 1949 after 4 years of war with Netherlands, the latter in 1946. Philippine economic and military ties with the U.S. remained strong; a Communist-led peasant rising was checked in 1948.

Arts. New York became the center of the world art market; **abstract expressionism** was the chief mode (Pollock from 1943, de Kooning from 1947). Literature and philosophy explored **existentialism** (Camus's *The Stranger*, 1942; Sartre's *Being and Nothingness*, 1943). Non-Western attempts to revive or create regional styles (Senghor's Négritude, Mishima's novels) only confirmed the emergence of a universal culture. Radio and phonograph records spread American popular music (swing, bebop) around the world.

The American Decade: 1950-59

Polite decolonization. The peaceful decline of European political and military power in Asia and Africa accelerated in the 1950s. Nearly all of **N Africa** was freed by 1956, but France fought a bitter war to retain Algeria, with its large European minority, until 1962. **Ghana**, independent in 1957, led a parade of new black African nations (more than 2 dozen by 1962), which altered the political character of the UN. Ethnic disputes often exploded in the new nations after decolonization (UN troops in Cyprus, 1964; **Nigerian civil war**, 1967-70). Leaders of the new states, mostly sharing socialist ideologies, tried to create an Afro-Asian bloc (Bandung Conference, 1955), but Western economic influence and U.S. political ties remained strong (Baghdad Pact, 1955).

Trade. World trade volume soared, in an atmosphere of monetary stability assured by international accords (**Bretton Woods**, 1944). In Europe, economic integration advanced (**European Economic Community, 1957**; European Free Trade Association, 1960). Comecon (1949) coordinated the economies of Soviet-bloc countries.

U.S. Economic growth produced an abundance of consumer goods (9.3 million motor vehicles sold, 1955). Suburban housing changed life patterns for middle and working classes (Levittown, 1947-51). Pres. Dwight **Eisenhower's** landslide election victories (1952, 1956) reflected consensus politics. A system of alliances and military bases bolstered U.S. influence on all continents. Trade and payments surpluses were balanced by overseas investments and foreign aid ($50 billion, 1950-59).

USSR. In the "thaw" after Stalin's death in 1953, relations with the West improved (evacuation of Vienna, Geneva summit conference, both 1955). Repression of scientific and cultural life eased, and many prisoners were freed culminating in **de-Stalinization** (1956). Nikita **Khrushchev's** leadership aimed at consumer sector growth, but farm production lagged, despite the virgin lands program (from 1954). Soviet crushing of the 1956 Hungarian revolution, the 1960 U-2 spy plane episode, and other incidents renewed East-West tension and domestic curbs.

Eastern Europe. Resentment of Russian domination and Stalinist repression combined with nationalist, economic, and religious factors to produce periodic violence. E Berlin workers rioted (1953), Polish workers rioted in Poznan (June 1956), and a broad-based **revolution** broke out in **Hungary** (Oct. 1956). All were suppressed by Soviet force or threats (at least 7,000 dead in Hungary), but Poland was allowed to restore private ownership of farms, and a degree of personal and economic freedom returned to Hungary. Yugoslavia experimented with worker self-management and a market economy.

Korea. The 1945 division of Korea along the 38th parallel left industry in the N, which was organized into a militant regime and armed by the USSR. The S was politically disunited. More than 60,000 N Korean troops invaded the S on June 25, 1950. The U.S., backed by the UN Security Council, sent troops. UN troops reached the Chinese border in Nov. Some 200,000 Chinese troops crossed the Yalu R. and drove back UN forces. By spring 1951 battle lines had become stabilized near the original 38th parallel border, but heavy fighting continued. Finally, an armistice was signed on July 27, 1953. U.S. troops remained in the S, and U.S. economic and military aid continued. The war stimulated rapid economic recovery in Japan.

China. Starting in 1952, industry, agriculture, and social institutions were forcibly collectivized. In a massive purge, as many as several million people were executed as Kuomintang supporters or as class and political enemies. The **Great Leap Forward** (1958-60) unsuccessfully tried to force the pace of development by substituting labor for investment.

Indochina. Ho Chi Minh's forces, aided by the USSR and the new Chinese Communist government, fought French and pro-French Vietnamese forces to a standstill and captured the strategic **Dienbienphu** camp in May 1954. The Geneva Agreements divided Vietnam in half pending elections (never held) and recognized Laos and Cambodia as independent. The U.S. aided the anti-Communist Republic of Vietnam in the S.

Middle East. Arab revolutions placed leftist, militantly nationalist regimes in power in Egypt (1952) and Iraq (1958). But Arab unity attempts failed (United Arab Republic joined Egypt, Syria, Yemen, 1958-61). Arab refusal to recognize Israel (Arab League economic blockade began Sept. 1951) led to a permanent **state of war**, with repeated incidents (Gaza, 1955). Israel occupied Sinai, and Britain and France took (Oct. 1956) the Suez Canal, but were replaced by the UN Emergency Force. The Mossadegh government in Iran nationalized (May 1951) the British-owned oil industry in May, but was overthrown (Aug. 1953) in a U.S.-aided coup.

Latin America. Argentinian dictator Juan **Perón**, in office 1946, crushed opposition and enforced land reform, some nationalization, welfare state measures, and curbs on the Roman Catholic Church. A Sept. 1955 coup deposed Perón. The 1952 revolution in Bolivia brought land reform, nationalization of tin mines, and improvement in the status of Native Americans, who nevertheless remained poor. The Batista regime in Cuba was overthrown (Jan. 1959) by Fidel **Castro**, who imposed a Communist dictatorship, aligned Cuba with the USSR and improved education and health care. A U.S.-backed anti-Castro invasion (**Bay of Pigs**, Apr. 1961) was crushed. Self-government advanced in the British Caribbean.

Technology. Large outlays on research and development in the U.S. and the USSR focused on military applications (H-bomb in U.S., 1952; USSR, 1953; Britain, 1957; intercontinental missiles, late 1950s). Soviet launching of the **Sputnik** satellite (Oct. 4, 1957) spurred increases in U.S. science education funds (National Defense Education Act).

Literature and film. Alienation from social and literary conventions reached an extreme in the theater of the absurd (Beckett's *Waiting for Godot*, 1952), the "new novel" (Robbe-Grillet's *Voyeur*, 1955), and avant-garde film (Antonioni's *L'Avventura*, 1960). U.S. beatniks (Kerouac's *On the Road*, 1957) and others rejected the supposed conformism of Americans (Riesman's *The Lonely Crowd*, 1950).

Rising Expectations: 1960-69

Economic boom. The longest sustained economic boom on record spanned almost the entire decade in the capitalist world; the closely watched GNP figure doubled (1960-70) in the U.S., fueled by Vietnam War-related budget deficits. The **General Agreement on Tariffs and Trade** (1967) stimulated W European prosperity, which spread to peripheral areas (Spain, Italy, E Germany). Japan became a top economic power. Foreign investment aided the industrialization of Brazil. There were limited Soviet economic reform attempts.

Reform and radicalization. Pres. John F. **Kennedy**, inaugurated 1961, emphasized youthful idealism and vigor; his assassination Nov. 22, 1963, was a national trauma. A series of political and social reform movements took root in the U.S. and other countries. Blacks demonstrated nonviolently and with partial success against segregation and poverty (1963 March on Washington; 1964 **Civil Rights Act**), but some urban areas erupted in extensive riots (Watts, 1965; Detroit, 1967; **Martin Luther King** assassination, Apr. 4, 1968). New concern for the poor (Harrington's *Other America*, 1963) helped lead to Pres. Lyndon Johnson's **"Great Society"** programs (Medicare, Water Quality Act, Higher Education Act, all 1965). Concern for the environment surged (Carson's *Silent Spring*, 1962).

Feminism revived as a cultural and political movement (Friedan's *Feminine Mystique*, 1963; National Organization for Women founded 1966), and a movement for homosexual rights emerged (Stonewall riot in NYC, 1969). Pope John XXIII called the **Second Vatican Council** (1962-65), which liberalized Roman Catholic liturgy and some other aspects of Catholicism.

Opposition to U.S. involvement in Vietnam, especially among university students (**Moratorium** protest, Nov. 1969), turned violent (Weatherman Chicago riots, Oct. 1969). **New Left** and Marxist theories became popular, and membership in radical groups (Students for a Democratic Society, Black Panthers) increased. Maoist groups, especially in Europe, called for total transformation of society. In France, students sparked a nationwide strike affecting 10 million workers in May-June 1968, but an electoral reaction barred revolutionary change.

China. China's revolutionary militancy under **Mao Zedong** caused disputes with the USSR under "revisionist" Khrushchev, starting in 1960. The 2 powers exchanged fire in 1969 border disputes. China used force to capture (1962) areas disputed with India. The **"Great Proletarian Cultural Revolution"** tried to impose a utopian egalitarian program in China and

Mao Zedong

spread revolution abroad; political struggle, often violent, convulsed China in 1965-68.

Indochina. Communist-led guerrillas aided by N Vietnam fought from 1960 against the S Vietnam government of Ngo Dinh Diem (killed 1963). The U.S. military role increased after the 1964 **Tonkin Gulf** incident. U.S. forces peaked at 543,400 in Apr. 1969. Massive numbers of N Vietnamese troops also fought. Laotian and Cambodian neutrality were threatened by Communist insurgencies, with N Vietnamese aid, and U.S. intrigues.

Developing World. A bloc of authoritarian leftist regimes among the newly independent nations emerged in political opposition to the U.S.-led Western alliance and came to dominate the conference of nonaligned nations (Belgrade, 1961; Cairo, 1964; Lusaka, 1970). Soviet political ties and military bases were established in Cuba, Egypt, Algeria, Guinea, and other countries whose leaders were regarded as revolutionary heroes by opposition groups in pro-Western or colonial countries. Some leaders were ousted in coups by pro-Western groups—Zaire's Patrice Lumumba (killed 1961), Ghana's Kwame Nkrumah (exiled 1966), and Indo-

nesia's Sukarno (effectively ousted in 1965 after a Communist coup failed).

Middle East. Arab-Israeli tension erupted into a brief war June 1967. Israel emerged from the war as a major regional power. Military shipments before and after the war brought much of the Arab world into the Soviet political sphere. Most Arab states broke U.S. diplomatic ties, while Communist countries cut their ties to Israel. Intra-Arab disputes continued: Egypt and Saudi Arabia supported rival factions in a bloody Yemen civil war 1962-70; Lebanese troops fought Palestinian commandos 1969.

East Europe. To stop the large-scale exodus of citizens, E German authorities built (Aug. 1961) a **fortified wall across Berlin.** Soviet sway in the Balkans was weakened by Albania's support of China (USSR broke ties in Dec. 1961) and Romania's assertion (1964) of industrial and foreign policy autonomy. Liberalization (spring 1968) in Czechoslovakia was crushed with massive force by troops of 5 Warsaw Pact countries. W German treaties (1970) with the USSR and Poland facilitated the transfer of German technology and confirmed postwar boundaries.

Arts and styles. The boundary between fine and popular arts was blurred to some extent by Pop Art (Warhol) and rock musicals (*Hair*, 1968). Informality and exaggeration prevailed in fashion (beards, miniskirts). A nonpolitical "counterculture" developed, rejecting traditional bourgeois life goals and personal habits, and use of marijuana and hallucinogens spread (**Woodstock** festival, Aug. 1969). Indian influence was felt in religion (Ram Dass) and fashion, and **The Beatles,** who brought unprecedented sophistication to rock music, became for many a symbol of the decade.

Science. Achievements in space (**humans on the moon,** July 1969) and electronics (lasers, integrated circuits) encouraged a faith in scientific solutions to problems in agriculture ("green revolution"), medicine (heart transplants, 1967), and other areas.

Buzz Aldrin on Moon, 1969

Harmful technology, it was believed, could be controlled (1963 nuclear weapon test ban treaty, 1968 nonproliferation treaty).

Disillusionment: 1970-79

U.S.: Caution and neoconservatism. A relatively sluggish economy, energy shortages, and environmental problems contributed to a **"limits of growth"** philosophy. Suspicion of science and technology killed or delayed major projects (supersonic transport dropped, 1971; Seabrook nuclear power plant protests, 1977-78) and was fed by the Three Mile Island nuclear reactor accident (Mar. 1979).

There were signs of growing mistrust of big government and less support for new social policies. School busing and racial quotas were opposed (Bakke decision, June 1978); the proposed Equal Rights Amendment for women languished; civil rights legislation aimed at protecting homosexuals was opposed (Dade County referendum, June 1977).

Completion of Communist forces' takeover of **South Vietnam** (evacuation of U.S. civilians, Apr. 1975), revelations of Central Intelligence Agency misdeeds (Rockefeller Commission report, June 1975), and **Watergate** scandals (Nixon resigned in Aug. 1974) reduced faith in U.S. moral and material capacity to influence world affairs. Revelations of Soviet crimes (Solzhenitsyn's *Gulag Archipelago*, 1974) and Soviet intervention in Africa helped foster a revival of anti-Communist sentiment.

Economy sluggish. The 1960s boom faltered in the 1970s; a severe recession in the U.S. and Europe (1974-75) followed a huge oil price hike (Dec. 1973). Monetary instability (U.S. cut ties to gold in Aug. 1971), the decline of the dollar, and protectionist moves by industrial countries (1977-78) threatened trade. Business investment and spending for research declined. Severe inflation plagued many countries (25% in Britain, 1975; 18% in U.S., 1979).

China picks up pieces. After the 1976 deaths of Mao Zedong and Zhou Enlai, struggle for the leadership succession was won by pragmatists. A nationwide purge of orthodox Maoists was carried out, and the **Gang of Four,** led by Mao's widow, Chiang Ching, arrested. The new leaders freed more than 100,000 political prisoners and reduced public adulation of Mao. Political and trade ties were expanded with Japan, Europe, and the U.S. in the late 1970s, as relations worsened with the USSR, Cuba, and Vietnam (4-week invasion by China, 1979). Ideological guidelines in industry, science, education, and the armed forces, which the ruling faction said had caused chaos and decline, were reversed (bonuses to workers, Dec. 1977; exams for college entrance, Oct. 1977). Severe restrictions on cultural expression were eased.

Europe. European unity moves (EEC-EFTA trade accord, 1972) faltered as economic problems appeared (Britain floated pound, 1972; France floated franc, 1974). Germany and Switzerland curbed guest workers from southern Europe. Greece and Turkey quarreled over Cyprus and Aegean oil rights.

All non-Communist Europe was under democratic rule after free elections (June 1976) in **Spain** 7 months after the death of Franco. The conservative, colonialist regime in **Portugal** was overthrown in Apr. 1974. In **Greece** the 7-year-old military dictatorship yielded power in 1974. Northern Europe, though ruled mostly by Socialists (**Swedish** Socialists unseated in 1976 after 44 years in power), turned more conservative. The **British** Labour government imposed (1975) wage curbs and suspended nationalization schemes. Terrorism in **Germany** (1972 Munich Olympics killings) led to laws curbing some civil liberties. French "new philosophers" rejected leftist ideologies, and the Socialist-Communist coalition lost a 1978 election bid.

Religion and politics. The improvement in **Muslim** countries' political fortunes by the 1950s (with the exception of Central Asia under Soviet and Chinese rule) and the growth of Arab oil wealth were followed by a resurgence of traditional religious fervor. Libyan dictator Muammar al-Qaddafi mixed Islamic laws with socialism and called for Muslim return to Spain and Sicily. The illegal Muslim Brotherhood in **Egypt** was accused of violence, while extreme groups bombed (1977) theaters to protest Western and secular values.

In **Turkey**, the National Salvation Party was the first Islamic group to share (1974) power since secularization in the 1920s. In **Iran**, Ayatollah Ruhollah Khomeini led a revolution that deposed the secular shah (Jan. 1979) and created an Islamic republic there. Religiously motivated Muslims took part in an insurrection in Saudi Arabia that briefly seized (1979) the Grand Mosque in Mecca. Muslim puritan opposition to **Pakistan** Pres. Zulfikar Ali-Bhutto helped lead to his overthrow in July 1977. Muslim solidarity, however, could not prevent Pakistan's eastern province (**Bangladesh**) from declaring (Dec. 1971) independence after a bloody civil war.

Muslim and Hindu resentment of coerced sterilization in **India** helped defeat the Indira Gandhi government, which was replaced (Mar. 1977) by a coalition including religious Hindu parties. Muslims in the S **Philippines**, aided by Libya, rebelled against central rule from 1973.

The Buddhist Soka Gakkai movement launched (1964) the Komeito party in **Japan**, which became a major opposition party in 1972 and 1976 elections.

Evangelical Protestant groups grew in the U.S. A revival of interest in Orthodox Christianity occurred among **Russian** intellectuals (Solzhenitsyn). The secularist **Israeli** Labor party, after decades of rule, was ousted in 1977 by conservatives led by Menachem Begin; religious militants founded settlements on the disputed West Bank, part of biblically promised Israel. U.S. Reform Judaism revived many previously discarded traditional practices.

Sadat, Carter, Begin

Religious wars raged intermittently in **Northern Ireland** (Catholic vs. Protestant, 1969-1997) and **Lebanon** (Christian vs. Muslim, 1975-), while religious militancy complicated the Israel-Arab dispute (1973 Israel-Arab war). The Camp David Accords in 1978, negotiated by Egyptian Pres. Anwar al-Sadat, Israeli Prime Min. Menachem Begin, and U.S. Pres. Jimmy Carter, facilitated the landmark 1979 **Egypt-Israel peace treaty**, but increased militancy on the West Bank impeded further progress.

Latin America. Repressive conservative regimes strengthened their hold on most of the continent, with a violent coup against the elected (Sept. 1973) Allende government in **Chile**, a 1976 military coup in **Argentina**, and coups against reformist regimes in **Bolivia** (1971, 1979) and **Peru** (1976). In Central America increasing liberal and leftist militancy led to the ouster (1979) of the Somoza regime of **Nicaragua** and to civil conflict in **El Salvador**.

Indochina. Communist victories in Vietnam, Cambodia, and Laos by May 1975 led to new turmoil. The **Pol Pot regime** ordered millions of city-dwellers to resettle in rural areas, in a program of forced labor and terrorism that cost more than 1 million lives (1975-79) and caused hundreds of thousands of ethnic Chinese and others to flee. The Vietnamese invasion of Cambodia (1979) swelled the refugee population and contributed to widespread starvation.

Russian expansion. Soviet influence, checked in some countries (troops ousted by Egypt, 1972), was projected farther afield, often with the use of Cuban troops (Angola, 1975-89; Ethiopia, 1977-88) and aided by a growing navy, a merchant fleet, and international banking ability. **Détente** with the West—1972 Berlin pact, 1972 strategic arms pact (**SALT**)—gave way to a more antagonistic relationship in the late 1970s, exacerbated by the Soviet invasion (1979) of **Afghanistan**.

Africa. The last remaining European colonies were granted independence (**Spanish Sahara**, 1976; **Djibouti**, 1977) and, after 10 years of civil war and many negotiation sessions, a black government took over (1979) in Zimbabwe (Rhodesia); white domination remained in **South Africa**. Great power involvement in local wars (Russia in **Angola, Ethiopia**; France in **Chad, Zaire, Mauritania**) and the use of tens of thousands of Cuban troops were denounced by some African leaders. Ethnic or tribal clashes made Africa a locus of sustained warfare during the late 1970s.

Arts. Traditional modes of painting, architecture, and music received increased popular and critical attention in the 1970s. These more conservative styles coexisted with modernist works in an atmosphere of increased variety and tolerance.

Revitalization of Capitalism, Demand for Democracy: 1980-89

USSR, Eastern Europe. A troublesome 1980-85 for the USSR was followed by 5 years of astonishing change: the surrender of the Communist monopoly, the remaking of the Soviet state, and the beginning of the disintegration of the Soviet empire. After the deaths of Gen. Sec. Leonid Brezhnev (1982) and 2 successors (Andropov in 1984 and Chernenko in 1985), the harsh treatment of dissent and restriction of emigration, and the Soviet invasion (Dec. 1979) of Afghanistan, Gen. Sec. Mikhail Gorbachev (in office 1985-1991) promoted *glasnost* and *perestroika*—economic, political, and social reform. Supported by the Communist Party (July 1988), he signed (Dec. 1987) the INF disarmament treaty, and he pledged (1988) to cut the military budget. Military withdrawal from Afghanistan was completed in Feb. 1989, the process of democratization went ahead unhindered in Poland and Hungary, and the Soviet people

chose (Mar. 1989) part of the new Congress of People's Deputies from competing candidates. By decade's end the **Cold War** appeared to be fading away.

In **Poland, Solidarity**, the labor union founded (1980) by Lech Walesa, was outlawed in 1982 and then legalized in 1988, after years of unrest. Poland's first free election since the Communist takeover brought Solidarity victory (June 1989); Tadeusz Mazowiecki, a Walesa adviser, became (Aug. 1989) prime minister in a government with the Communists. In the fall of 1989 the failure of Marxist economies in **Hungary, East Germany, Czechoslovakia, Bulgaria**, and **Romania** brought the collapse of the Communist monopoly and a demand for democracy. In a historic step, the **Berlin Wall** was opened in Nov. 1989.

U.S. "The Reagan Years" (1981-88) brought the **longest economic boom** yet in U.S. history via budget and tax cuts, deregulation, "junk bond" financing, leveraged buy-outs, and mergers and takeovers. However, there was a stock market crash (Oct. 1987), and federal budget deficits and the trade deficit increased. Foreign policy showed a **strong anti-Communist stance**, via increased defense spending, aid to anti-Communists in Cen-

Reagan and Gorbachev

tral America, invasion of Cuba-threatened Grenada, and championing of the MX missile system and "Star Wars" missile defense program. Four Reagan-Gorbachev summits (1985-88) climaxed in the INF treaty (1987), as the Cold War began to wind down. The Iran-contra affair (North's TV testimony, July 1987) was a major political scandal. Homelessness and drug abuse (especially "crack" cocaine) were growing social problems. In 1988, Vice Pres. George Bush was elected to succeed Ronald Reagan as president.

Middle East. The Middle East remained militarily unstable, with sharp divisions along economic, political, racial, and religious lines. In **Iran**, the Islamic revolution of 1979 created a strong anti-U.S. stance (hostage crisis, Nov. 1979-Jan. 1981). In Sept. 1980, **Iraq** repudiated its border agreement with Iran and began major hostilities that led to an 8-year war in which millions were killed.

Libya's support for international terrorism induced the U.S. to close (May 1981) its diplomatic mission there and embargo (Mar. 1982) Libyan oil. The U.S. accused Libyan leader Muammar al-Qaddafi of aiding (Dec. 1985) terrorists in Rome and of Vienna airport attacks, and retaliated by bombing Libya (Apr. 1986).

Israel affirmed (July 1980) all Jerusalem as its capital, destroyed (1981) an Iraqi atomic reactor, and invaded (1982) Lebanon, forcing the PLO to agree to withdraw. A **Palestinian uprising**, including women and children hurling rocks and bottles at troops, began (Dec. 1987) in Israeli-occupied Gaza and spread to the West Bank; troops responded with force, killing 300 by the end of 1988, with 6,000 more in detention camps.

Israeli withdrawal from **Lebanon** began in Feb. 1985 and ended in June 1985, as Lebanon continued torn by military and political conflict. Artillery duels (Mar.-Apr. 1989) between Christian East Beirut and Muslim West Beirut left 200 dead and 700 wounded. At decade's end, violence still dominated.

Latin America. In **Nicaragua**, the leftist Sandinista National Liberation Front, in power after the 1979 civil war, faced problems as a result of Nicaragua's military aid to leftist guerrillas in El Salvador and U.S. backing of antigovernment contras. The U.S. CIA admitted (1984) having directed the mining of Nicaraguan ports, and the U.S. sent humanitarian (1985) and military (1986) aid. Profits from secret arms sales to Iran were found (1987) diverted to contras. Cease-fire talks between the Sandinista government and contras came in 1988, and elections were held in Nicaragua in Feb. 1990.

In **El Salvador**, a military coup (Oct. 1979) failed to halt extreme right-wing violence and left-wing terrorism. Archbishop Oscar Romero was assassinated in Mar. 1980; from Jan. to June some 4,000 civilians were killed in the civil unrest. In 1984, newly elected Pres. José Napoleon Duarte worked to stem human rights abuses, but violence continued.

In **Chile**, Gen. Augusto Pinochet yielded the presidency after a democratic election (Dec. 1989), but remained as head of the army. He had ruled the country since 1973, imposing harsh measures against leftists and dissidents; at the same time he introduced economic programs that restored prosperity to Chile.

Africa. 1980-85 marked a rapid decline in the economies of virtually all African countries, a result of accelerating desertification, the world economic recession, heavy indebtedness to overseas creditors, rapid population growth, and political instability. Some 60 million Africans faced prolonged hunger in 1981; much of Africa had one of the worst droughts ever in 1983, and by year's end, one-third of the population, or about 150 million, were near **famine**. "Live Aid," a marathon rock concert, was presented in July 1985, and the U.S. and Western nations sent aid in Sept. 1985. Economic hardship fueled political unrest and coups. Wars in Ethiopia and Sudan and military strife in several other nations continued. AIDS took a heavy toll.

South Africa. Anti-apartheid sentiment gathered force in South Africa as demonstrations and violent police response grew. White voters approved (Nov. 1983) the first constitution to give "Coloureds" and Asians a voice, while still excluding blacks (70% of the population). The U.S. imposed economic sanctions in Aug. 1985, and 11 Western nations followed in September. P. W. **Botha**, 1980s president, was succeeded by F. W. **de Klerk**, in Sept. 1989, who promised "evolutionary" change via negotiation with the black population.

Asia. Benazir Bhutto became the first woman to lead a majority-Muslim nation as prime minister of Pakistan (Dec. 1988). The "people power" revolt in the Philippines ousted Ferdinand Marcos (Feb. 1986) after 2 decades as presidnet

China. During the 1980s the Communist government and paramount leader **Deng Xiaoping** pursued **far-reaching changes**, expanding commercial and technical ties to the industrialized world and increasing the role of market forces in stimulating urban development. Apr. 1989 brought new demands for political reforms; student demonstrators camped out in Tiananmen Square, Beijing, in a massive peaceful protest. Some 100,000 students and workers marched, and at least 20 other cities saw protests. In response, martial law was imposed; army troops crushed the demonstration in and around Tiananmen Square on June 3-4, with death toll estimates at 500-7,000, up to 10,000 dissidents arrested, 31 people tried and executed. The conciliatory Communist Party chief was ousted; the Politburo adopted (July 1989) reforms against official corruption.

Japan. Japan's relations with other nations, especially the U.S., were dominated by **trade imbalances favoring Japan**. In 1985, the U.S. trade deficit with Japan was $49.7 billion, one-third of the total U.S. trade deficit. After Japan was found (Apr. 1986) to sell semiconductors and computer memory chips below cost, the U.S. was assured a "fair share" of the market, but charged (Mar. 1987) Japan with failing to live up to the agreement.

European Community. With the addition of Greece, Portugal, and Spain, the EC became a common market of more than **300 million people**, the West's largest trading entity. Margaret **Thatcher** became the first British prime minister in the 20th century to win a 3rd consecutive term (1987). France elected (1981) its first socialist president, François **Mitterrand**, who was reelected in 1988. Italy elected (1983) its first socialist premier, Bettino **Craxi**.

International terrorism. With the 1979 overthrow of the shah of Iran, terrorism became a prominent tactic. It increased through the 1980s, but with fewer high-profile attacks after 1985. In 1979-81, Iranian militants held 52 **U.S. hostages in Iran** for 444 days; in 1983 a TNT-laden suicide terrorist blew up U.S. Marine headquarters in Beirut, killing 241 Americans, and a truck bomb blew up a French paratroop barracks, killing 58. The *Achille Lauro* cruise ship was hijacked in 1986, and an American passenger killed; the U.S. subsequently intercepted the Egyptian plane flying the terrorists to safety. Incidents rose to 700 in 1985, and to 1,000 in 1988. **Assassinated leaders** included Egypt's Pres. Anwar al-**Sadat** (1981), India's Prime Min. Indira **Gandhi** (1984), and Lebanese Premier Rashid **Karami** (1987).

Post–Cold War World: 1990-99

Soviet Empire breakup. The world community witnessed the extraordinary disintegration of the **Soviet Union** into 15 independent states. The 1980s had already seen internal reforms and a decline of Communist power both within the Soviet Union and in Eastern Europe. The Soviet breakup began in earnest with declarations of independence adopted by the Baltic republics of **Lithuania, Latvia,** and **Estonia** during an abortive coup against reformist leader Mikhail **Gorbachev** (Aug. 1991). Other republics soon took the same step. In Dec. 1991, **Russia, Ukraine,** and **Belarus** declared the Soviet Union dead; Gorbachev resigned, and the Soviet Parliament went out of existence. The Warsaw Pact and the Council for Mutual Economic Assistance (Comecon) were disbanded. Most of the former Soviet republics joined in a loose confederation called the **Commonwealth of Independent States.** Russia remained the predominant country after the breakup, but its people soon suffered severe economic hardship as the nation, under Pres. Boris **Yeltsin,** moved to revamp the economy and adopt a free market system. In Oct. 1993, **anti-Yeltsin forces** occupied the Parliament building and were ousted by the army; about 140 people died in the fighting.

The Muslim republic of **Chechnya** declared independence from the rest of Russia, but this was met with an invasion by Russian troops (Dec. 1994). After almost 21 months of vicious fighting, a cease-fire took hold in 1996, and the Russians withdrew. In 1999 Russia forcibly suppressed Muslim insurgents in Dagestan and entered neighboring Chechnya, again fighting to gain control over separatist rebels there. Yeltsin resigned office Dec. 31, 1999, to be replaced by Vladimir **Putin** (elected in his own right, Mar. 2000).

Europe. Yugoslavia broke apart, and hostilities ensued among the republics along ethnic and religious lines. **Croatia, Slovenia,** and **Macedonia** declared independence (1991), followed by **Bosnia-Herzegovina** (1992). **Serbia** and **Montenegro** remained as the republic of Yugoslavia. Bitter fighting followed, especially in Bosnia, where Serbs reportedly engaged in **"ethnic cleansing"** of the Muslim population; a peace plan (Dayton accord), brokered by the United States, was signed by **Bosnia, Serbia,** and **Croatia** (Dec. 1995), with **NATO** responsible for policing its implementation. In spring 1999, NATO conducted a bombing campaign aimed at stopping Yugoslavia from its campaign to drive out ethnic Albanians from the Kosovo region; a peace accord was reached in June under which NATO peacekeeping troops entered Kosovo.

The two **Germanys** were reunited after 45 years (Oct. 1990). The union was greeted with jubilation, but stresses became apparent when free market principles were applied to the aging East German industries, resulting in many plant closings and rising unemployment. West German chancellor Helmut **Kohl,** a Christian Democrat, lost power after 16 years, in Sept. 1998 elections; Gerhard **Schroeder,** a Social Democrat, took over. Czechoslovakia broke apart peacefully (Jan. 1993), becoming the **Czech Republic** and **Slovakia.** In **Poland,** Lech **Walesa** was elected president (Dec. 1991) but was defeated in his bid for a 2nd term (Nov. 1995).

NATO approved the **Partnership for Peace** Program (Jan. 1994) coordinating the defense of **Eastern** and **Central European** countries; Russia joined the program later that year. NATO signed a pact with **Russia** (1997) providing for NATO expansion into the former Soviet-bloc countries; a similar treaty was set up with **Ukraine.** The **Czech Republic, Hungary,** and **Poland** became members in Jan. 1999; in that year **NATO** celebrated its 50th anniversary. Efforts toward European unity continued with adoption of a single market (Jan. 1993) and conversion of the European Community to the **European Union** as the Maastricht Treaty took effect (Nov. 1993). Agreement was reached for 11 EU members to participate in Economic and Monetary Union, adopting a common currency **(euro)** in Jan. 1999.

Margaret Thatcher

An intraparty revolt forced Margaret **Thatcher** out as prime minister of **Great Britain,** to be succeeded by John **Major** (Nov. 1990); 7 years later, Major suffered an overwhelming defeat at the hands of the new Labour Party leader, Tony **Blair** (May 1997). The divorce of Prince **Charles and Diana,** followed by the death of Diana in a car accident (Aug. 1997), made headlines around the world. Talks on peace in **Northern Ireland** that included participation of Sinn Fein, political arm of the IRA, led to a ground-breaking peace plan, approved in an all-Ireland vote (May 1998). In Dec. 1999, Northern Ireland was granted home rule under a power-sharing cabinet. In **Scotland** voters overwhelmingly approved establishment of a regional legislature (1997), and in **Wales** voters narrowly approved establishment of a local assembly (1997). In a historic innovation, the Church of England **ordained 32 women** as priests (Mar. 1994).

Middle East. In Aug. 1990, **Iraq's Saddam Hussein** ordered his troops to invade **Kuwait.** The UN approved military action in response (Nov. 1990), and an international military force, led by the U.S., bombed Iraq (Jan. 1991) and launched a land attack, crushing the invasion (Feb. 1991). After Iraq accepted the allied terms of the formal cease-fire (Apr. 1991), U.S. troops withdrew, but "no-fly" zones were set up over northern Iraq to protect the Kurds and over southern Iraq to protect Shiite Muslims. The **UN** imposed **sanctions** on Iraq for failure to abide by the cease-fire. Iraq's reported failure to cooperate with UN arms inspectors seeking to eliminate "weapons of mass destruction" led to repeated air strikes by the U.S. and Britain (1998, 2001).

The last Western hostages were freed in **Lebanon,** June 1992. **Israel** and the **Palestine Liberation Organization** signed a peace accord (Sept. 1993) providing for Palestinian self-government in the West Bank and Gaza Strip. Prime Min. Yitzhak **Rabin** and Foreign Min. Shimon **Peres** of Israel and Yasir **Arafat** of the PLO received the Nobel Peace Prize for their efforts (1994). Six Arab nations relaxed their boycott against Israel (1994), and Israel and **Jordan** signed a peace treaty (Oct. 1994). **Rabin was assassinated** (Nov. 1995) by an Israeli opponent of the peace process. After new elections (May 1996), Benjamin Netanyahu as prime minister adopted a harder line in peace negotiations. **Arafat** was elected to the presidency of the Palestinian Authority (Jan. 1996). A Labour government under Ehud **Barak** took power after May 1999 elections.

King **Hussein** of Jordan died (Feb. 1999), to be succeeded by his son Abdullah.

Jiang Zemin

Asia and the Pacific. Hong Kong was returned to **China** (July 1997) after 156 years as a British colony, and **Macao** reverted to Chinese sovereignty (Dec. 1999) after over 400 years of Portuguese rule. Both were to retain their legal and capitalist economic systems for 50 years. **Jiang Zemin,** general secretary of the Chinese Communist Party, assumed the additional post of president of China (Mar. 1993) and emerged as the key leader after the death of leader **Deng Xiaoping** (Feb. 1997). China released from prison—and exiled—some well-known dissidents but continued to be criticized for detentions and other alleged widespread **human rights abuses.** In Nov. 1999 the U.S. and China signed a landmark pact normalizing trade relations.

After years of prosperity, **Thailand, Indonesia**, and **South Korea** in 1997 began to suffer economic reverses that had a worldwide ripple effect. These countries received billion-dollar IMF bailout packages. In **Indonesia**, protests over mismanagement led to the resignation of Pres. **Suharto** (May 1998) after 32 years of nearly autocratic rule. Abdurraham Wahid was elected (Oct. 1999) in the country's first fully democratic elections. In a referendum (Aug. 1999), **East Timor** voted overwhelmingly for independence from Indonesia; pro-Indonesian militias then rampaged through the territory, but a multinational peacekeeping force was allowed in (Sept. 1999) to help restore order. In **South Korea**, former dissident **Kim Dae Jung** was elected president (Dec. 1997). Two previous presidents, Roh Tae Woo and Chun Doo Hwan, were convicted of crimes committed in office but were given amnesty by the new president.

In **Japan** members of a religious cult released the nerve gas sarin on 5 Tokyo subway cars, killing 12 people and injuring more than 5,500 (Mar. 1995). Tamil rebels continued their armed conflict in **Sri Lanka**. In **Afghanistan** the **Taliban**, an extreme Islamic fundamentalist group, gained control of Kabul (Sept. 1996) and, eventually, most of the country. In **North Korea**, longtime dictator **Kim Il Sung** died (July 1994), to be succeeded by his son, **Kim Jong Il**. In the same year the country signed an agreement with the U.S. setting a timetable for North Korea to eliminate its nuclear program. The country also suffered a severe drought, and widespread starvation was feared.

India was beset by riots following destruction of a mosque by Hindu militants (Dec. 1992); Indian army troops repeatedly clashed with pro-independence demonstrators in the disputed Muslim region of **Kashmir**, exacerbating relations with **Pakistan**. Uneasy relations between India and Pakistan reached a new level when both nations conducted nuclear tests in 1998. Conflict in Pakistan between government and the military led to a bloodless coup (Oct. 1999).

Africa. South Africa was transformed as the white-dominated government abandoned **apartheid** and the country made the transition to a nonracial democratic government. Pres. F. W. **de Klerk** released Nelson **Mandela** from prison (Feb. 1990), after he had been held by the government for 27 years, and lifted a ban on the African National Congress. The white government repealed its apartheid laws (1990, 1991). **Mandela** was elected **president** (Apr. 1994), and a new constitution became law (Dec. 1996). Thabo **Mbeki**, the ANC's candidate to succeed Mandela, was overwhelmingly elected president in June 1999. In **Nigeria**, Gen. Olusegun **Obasanjo** was elected president (Feb. 1999), to become the country's first civilian leader in 15 years.

The decades-long rule of **Mobutu** Sese Seko in **Zaire** came to an end (May 1997) at the hands of rebel forces led by Laurent **Kabila**; an ailing Mobutu fled the country and soon after died. Kabila changed the country's name back to **Democratic Republic of the Congo**; conditions remained unstable.

After the presidents of **Burundi** and **Rwanda** were killed in an airplane crash (Apr. 1994), violence erupted in Rwanda between Hutu and Tutsi factions; hundreds of thousands were slain in genocidal fashion. The conflict spread to refugee camps in neighboring Zaire and Burundi. Factional fighting also erupted in **Somalia** after Pres. Muhammad Siad Barre was ousted (Jan. 1991). The UN sent a U.S.-led **peacekeeping force**, but it was unsuccessful in restoring order. Some soldiers of the peacekeeping force were killed, including 23 Pakistanis (June 1993) and 18 U.S. Rangers (Oct. 1993). The UN ended its mission (Mar. 1995) with no durable government in place. **Liberia** endured factional fighting that lasted almost 5 years and claimed over 150,000 lives; a cease-fire was concluded in Aug. 1995. The World Health Organization reported (1995) that Africa accounted for 70% of **AIDS** cases worldwide.

A 16-year civil war appeared to end in **Angola** (May 1991) when the government signed a peace accord with the rebel UNITA faction. But despite the inauguration of a national unity government (Apr. 1997), insurgents continued to fight and gain territory. **Namibia** officially became independent in Mar. 1990. Claimed by South Africa since 1919 and placed under UN authority in 1971, it had long been a focus of colonial rivalries. In **Algeria**, the army cancelled a 2nd round of parliamentary elections (Jan. 1992) after the Islamic party won a first round. Islamic fundamentalists then began a terrorist campaign that, along with killings by progovernment squads, eventually claimed thousands of lives. A peace plan was worked out with the militants in 1999.

North America. The **North American Free Trade Agreement** (NAFTA), liberalizing trade between the United States, Canada, and Mexico, went into effect Jan. 1, 1994. In **Canada**, the Progressive Conservative Party suffered a crushing defeat in general elections (Oct. 1993), and liberal Jean **Chrétien** became prime minister. The map of Canada was altered in Apr. 1999 to create a new territory, **Nunavut**, out of an area that had been part of Northwest Territories.

In the **United States'** 1992 presidential election, Democrat Bill **Clinton** defeated Pres. George Bush, but in 1994 congressional elections Republicans gained control of Congress. Clinton won reelection in 1996; the new administration was plagued by scandals but remained popular amid continued economic prosperity. Clinton proposed (Feb. 1998) the first balanced federal budget in nearly 30 years. In Dec. 1998 Clinton was **impeached** by the U.S. House on charges related to the Monica Lewinsky scandal; he was **acquitted** by the Senate in Feb. 1999.

The U.S. Army and Navy were torn by sexual scandals involving abuse of women personnel. The **United States** suffered embarrassment with the discovery of espionage by CIA agents (Aldrich Ames, Harold Nicholson).

In **Mexico**, Ernesto **Zedillo** of the ruling PRI party was elected president (July 1994) after the party's first candidate was assassinated. The country soon faced a crisis affecting the value of the peso, but recovered with the help of a bailout package from the U.S. A peasant revolt spearheaded by the **Zapatista National Liberation Army** erupted in the state of Chiapas (Jan. 1994) and was suppressed.

Central America and the Caribbean. In **Haiti**, Jean-Bertrand **Aristide** was elected president (Dec. 1990) but was ousted in a military coup after 9 months in office. The UN approved a U.S.-led invasion to restore the elected leader; shortly before troops arrived, a delegation headed by former U.S. Pres. Jimmy Carter arranged (Sept. 1994) for the junta to step aside for Aristide, who served until 1996. In **Nicaragua**, Violetta Chamorro defeated Daniel **Ortega** in the presidential election (Feb. 1990), thus ousting the Sandinistas. In **Panama**, U.S. troops invaded and overthrew the government of Manuel **Noriega** (Dec. 1989), who was wanted on drug charges; Noriega was captured Jan. 1990. On Dec. 31, 1999, Panama assumed full control of the **Panama Canal**, in accord with a treaty with the U.S. In **El Salvador** (1992) and **Guatemala** (1996) the governments signed agreements with rebel factions aimed at ending long-running civil conflicts.

South America. Alberto **Fujimori** was elected president of **Peru** in June 1990 and, despite his suppression of the constitution (1992), was reelected in 1995. Peru succeeded in capturing (Sept. 1992) the leader of the **Shining Path** guerrilla movement. Leftist guerrillas took hostages at an ambassador's residence in Lima (Dec. 1996); one hostage was killed during a government assault rescuing the rest (Apr. 1997). Peronist Pres. Carlos Saúl **Menem** served as **Argentina**'s president for much of the decade (elected 1989, reelected 1995), imposing stringent economic measures; he was succeeded in 1999 by Fernando de la **Rúa**.

Former Chilean Pres. Gen. Augusto **Pinochet** continued to head the army until Mar. 1998; he was arrested in London (Oct. 1998) on human rights charges but was judged medically unfit for trial and returned to Chile (Mar. 2000).

In **Brazil**, Fernando Henrique **Cardoso** was elected president (Oct. 1994) and reelected in 1998 amid a growing economic slump; the IMF announced a $42 billion aid package (Nov. 1998). The first UN Conference on Environment and Development, or **Earth Summit**, was held (June 1992) in **Rio de Janeiro**, with delegates from 178 nations.

Terrorism and Crime. Terrorism, often linked to Mideastern sources continued to target the U.S. and Europe. A terrorist bomb exploded in a garage beneath New York City's **World Trade Center**, killing 6 people (Feb. 1993). Bombings of a U.S. military training center (Nov. 1995) and a barracks holding U.S. airmen (June 1996), both in **Saudi Arabia**, killed 7 and 19, respectively. Bombs exploded outside **U.S. embassies** in Kenya and Tanzania, Aug. 1998, killing over 220 people; the U.S. retaliated with missiles fired at alleged terrorist-linked sites in Afghanistan and Sudan. The Alfred P. Murrah Federal Building in **Oklahoma City**, OK, was destroyed by a bomb that killed 168 people (Apr. 1995).

Science and Technology. The powerful **Hubble Space Telescope** was launched in Apr. 1990; flaws in its mirrors and solar panels were repaired by space-walking astronauts (Dec. 1993). U.S. space shuttle *Atlantis* docked with the orbiting Russian space station *Mir* (June 1995) in first of several joint missions in a spirit of post-Cold-War cooperation.

In Nov. 1998 the first component for a new **International Space Station** was launched into space from Kazakhstan.

Mir *and Shuttle* Atlantis

Scottish scientist Ian Wilmut announced (Feb. 1997) the **cloning** of a sheep, nicknamed Dolly—the first mammal successfully cloned from a cell from an adult animal.

Tim Berners-Lee launched the first **World Wide Web** server (1990) from the European Center for Nuclear Research (CERN) in Switzerland; CERN announced (1993) that the technology could be used for free. User-friendly graphical browsers (Mosaic, 1993; Netscape, 1994) and affordable Internet service providers (America Online for Macs, 1989, and Windows, 1993) rapidly expanded the reach of the **Internet**.

Opening a New Century: 2000-2006

Terrorism. In Oct. 2000, 17 American sailors were killed aboard the USS *Cole* in Aden, **Yemen**, when a small boat exploded alongside it in a terrorist attack. On **Sept. 11, 2001**, hijackers crashed 2 jetliners into the twin towers of the **World Trade Center** in New York City and another into the **Pentagon** outside Washington, DC; a 4th crashed in a field in Pennsylvania. The attacks, which destroyed both towers and damaged the Pentagon, killed about 3,000 people, including all 265 aboard the planes. Saudi exile Osama bin Laden and his **al-Qaeda terrorist network**, based in **Afghanistan** and backed by the Taliban government there, emerged as responsible for the attacks. A U.S.-led military campaign launched in Oct. 2001 **ousted the Taliban**, and a transitional government was installed (Dec. 2001), although al-Qaeda remained active in some areas of Afghanistan and elsewhere, and Bin Laden remained at large. Conspirator Zacarias Moussaoui was tried and sentenced to life (May 2006) for his role in the attacks.

Among incidents elsewhere, a bomb exploded in a truck outside a synagogue in **Tunisia** (Apr. 2002), killing 17 (including the driver). A car bomb on the Indonesian island of **Bali** (Oct. 2002) killed about 200, mostly foreign tourists; Muslim extremists were arrested. Chechen guerrillas seized a Moscow movie theater (Oct. 2002); more than 100 hostages were killed in a subsequent raid by Russian troops. A terrorist explosion in **Moscow subways** killed 39 (Feb. 2004), and 89 died when 2 Russian planes were destroyed apparently by bombs (Aug. 2004). Chechen guerrillas took over a **Beslan, Russia, school**; 330 hostages, many students, and 31 guerrillas were killed in the standoff (Sept. 2004). The bombing of an Israeli-owned **hotel in Kenya** (Nov. 2002) killed 13 (including the 3 bombers). Suicide attacks against Western targets in **Riyadh**, Saudi Arabia (May 2003), killed 34 people (including 9 attackers). Suicide bombings in **Istanbul**, Turkey (Nov. 2003), hit two Jewish synagogues and British targets, killing about 60 people in all.

Four **commuter trains were bombed** in Madrid, Spain, killing 191 (Mar. 2004); elections held a week later ousted Spain's premier. Three subway trains and a bus were **bombed in London** during rush hour (June 2005); 56 people were killed, including 4 bombers. Three suicide bombers killed 20 others on Indonesian resort island **Bali** (Oct. 2005). Al-Qaeda in Iraq claimed responsibility (Nov. 2005) for **hotel bombings** in Jordan that killed 59, excluding the suicide bombers. Eight coordinated explosions killed 207 on commuter trains in Mumbai, India (July 2006); the attacks were tied to an Islamic separatist organization. British authorities thwarted (Aug. 2006) an alleged terrorist plot to detonate **liquid explosives** on transatlantic flights.

The U.S. Supreme Court struck down attempts to use military tribunals to try suspected terrorists (June 2006); Pres. Bush acknowledged (Sept. 2006) the existence of CIA-run overseas prisons for terrorism suspects.

War in Iraq. The U.S., with Great Britain, launched an **invasion of Iraq** (Mar. 2003), aimed at ousting the dictatorial regime of **Saddam Hussein**. Troops took control of Baghdad and other cities, and Pres. Bush declared major combat ended, May 1, but **insurgents** caused continuing casualties among troops and civilians. Searches for **weapons of mass destruction**, cited as major grounds for the invasion, yielded no evidence. **Saddam Hussein** was captured by U.S. troops (Dec. 2003), put on trial by Iraqis, sentenced to death, and **executed** (Dec. 2006).

An interim government was installed (June 2004). Photographic evidence that U.S. soldiers at **Abu Ghraib** prison in Iraq abused detainees arose in Apr. 2004. U.S. military deaths topped 3,000 (Dec. 2006) as attacks by insurgents continued. Despite threats by insurgents, Iraqis turned out in large numbers to vote in national elections (Jan. 2005); the transitional national assembly appointed a Kurdish president and Shiite premier (Apr. 2005). In a referendum, **Iraqis approved a constitution** (Oct. 2005), and voted again in parliamentary elections (Dec. 2005). Sectarian violence in Iraq between the **Sunni and Shiite** factions continued to raise fears of civil war; in late 2006, at least 100 people were dying each day as a result of sectarian attacks. Violent demonstrations followed an attack (Feb. 2006) on Iraq's **"Golden Mosque"** shrine, one of the holiest sites in Shia Islam. The elected government of Premier Nouri Kamel al-Maliki took office (May 2006) representing a Shiite coalition.

Middle East. The peace process languished as **violence between Israelis and Palestinians** escalated, with **suicide bombings** by Palestinians and retaliation by Israeli armed forces. In response to Palestinian suicide attacks that killed 26, Israeli forces stormed the compound of Palestinian leader Yasir Arafat (Mar. 2002), keeping him confined there until early May.

Abbas, Rice & Olmert

Arafat died in a Paris hospital (Nov. 2004) and was succeeded by Mahmoud Abbas following elections. The U.S., Russia, UN, and European Union (EU) formally initiated (Apr. 2003) a "**road map**" plan for Israeli-Palestinian **peace negotiations**, but little progress was made. Israel completed (Aug. 2005) evacuation of 25 Jewish settlements in the **West Bank** and **Gaza Strip**. Israeli Prime Min. Ariel Sharon suffered a severe stroke (Jan. 2006); leadership was passed to Ehud Olmert, who went on to lead a coalition government following elections (Apr. 2006). The militant Palestinian political party **Hamas**, which did not acknowledge the right of Israel to exist, won a majority of parliamentary seats over the long-ruling Fatah party (Jan.

2006), casting the peace process into greater doubt, though talks with other parties, including U.S. Sec. of State Condoleezza Rice, continued.

Israel launched air and ground **attacks on Lebanon** (July 2006) in response to a raid into northern Israel by Lebanon-based **Hezbollah** guerrillas; a ceasefire was declared a month later.

Syrian Pres. Hafez al-**Assad died** (June 2000); succeeded by his son. Iran was censured (Dec. 2003) by the UN Intl. Atomic Energy Agency for covering up aspects of its nuclear weapons program, which it claimed was for peaceful purposes, and defied an Aug. 2006 deadline to suspend uranium enrichment.

Europe. In Oct. 2000, Yugoslav strongman Slobodan **Milosevic yielded power** to Vojislav Kostunica, who had declared himself president in the face of anti-Milosevic protests after a disputed election. Milosevic surrendered to Serbian authorities; he went on trial (Feb. 2002) for **war crimes** allegedly committed during 1990s ethnic conflicts in the Balkans but died (Mar. 2006) before a verdict was reached. The first-ever **Concorde jet crash**, near Paris, killed 113 people (July 2000). The Russian nuclear sub *Kursk* **sank** (Aug. 2000) in the Barents Sea, killing 118 crew members.

By early 2002 the **euro** was the common currency in 12 European Union nations. The EU admitted 10 Eastern European nations (May 2004). The deadline to ratify the EU constitution was extended (June 2005) after voters defeated referenda in France and the Netherlands. Germany elected its first East German chancellor (Nov. 2005), Angela Merkel, also the first woman head of state in Germany.

Angela Merkel

Some 35,000 people across Europe, including over 11,000 in France, reportedly died in 2003 **summer heat waves.**

Pope **John Paul II**, the leader of the world's Roman Catholics, died (Apr. 2005); German cardinal Joseph Ratzinger was elected his successor, taking the name Pope Benedict XVI.

Rioting shook France's immigrant communities in 300 cities and towns (Nov. 2005); over 3,000 arrests were made.

A Danish newspaper's publication of cartoon **caricatures of the Prophet Muhammad** sparked violent worldwide protests by Muslims (Feb. 2006).

Asia. South Korean Pres. **Kim Dae Jung** and North Korean ruler **Kim Jong Il** held a summit meeting and agreed to seek peace and reunification (June 2000), but tensions rose after North Korea admitted conducting a covert nuclear weapons development program (Oct. 2002). North Korea **withdrew** (Jan. 2003) from the Nuclear Nonproliferation Treaty; multi-nation talks were held in Beijing (Aug. 2003) about the status of its **nuclear program**. Multiparty talks broke down in 2005 and apparent nuclear (Oct. 2006) and missile (July 2006) testing in North Korea continued to cause alarm.

Nepal's King **Birendra** and other Nepalese royals were shot to death inside their palace, apparently by Crown Prince Dipendra, who then killed himself (June 2001). **Chinese** Pres. Jiang Zemin and **Russian** Pres. Vladimir Putin signed a **friendship treaty** (July 2001). With Jiang's retirement **Hu Jintao** was named as China's new Communist party chief (Nov. 2002) and president (Mar. 2003).

Pakistan and India **restored diplomatic ties** (May 2003) and declared a **cease-fire** in disputed territory (Nov. 2003). Pakistani Pres. Gen. Pervez Musharraf twice **escaped assassination** by Islamic militants (Dec. 2003). Afghanistan held its first presidential elections and selected Hamid Karzai (Oct.-Nov 2004).

A massive **tsunami** in the Indian Ocean (Dec. 2004) devastated parts of Indonesia, Thailand, India, Sri Lanka, and other Asian and African nations and left some 200,000 dead.

An **earthquake** struck the disputed territory of Kashmir and parts of N. Pakistan and India (Oct. 2005); nearly 80,000 were killed.

The military carried out a bloodless coup in Thailand (Sept. 2006), ousting the premier and dissolving the government.

Africa. The 13th International **AIDS Conference**, held in Durban, South Africa (July 2000), focused on ways of controlling surging AIDS rates in developing countries. **Ethiopia** and **Eritrea** signed a **peace treaty** (Dec. 2000). Laurent **Kabila**, president of the Democratic Republic of the **Congo**, was **shot to death** by a bodyguard (Jan. 2001). Liberian Pres. Charles Taylor went into voluntary exile (Aug. 2003) as part of a deal to end a 14-year-old civil war; other accords were reached aimed at **ending civil wars** in Angola (Apr. 2002) and Côte d'Ivoire (Jan. 2003).

A peace agreement in the Dem. Rep. of **Congo** (Apr. 2003) did not end violence there. Civil war between the Muslim-led government and rebels from Christian areas in **Sudan** continued, with massive casualties. Sudanese government-backed militias (**janjaweed**) in the Darfur region were accused of displacing 2 mil. people in acts bordering on genocide; it was estimated in 2006 that more than 200,000 had been killed there since 2003. Sudan rejected a U.N. peacekeeping force aiming to curb violence in Darfur, which was ongoing despite a peace deal (May 2006), but African Union peacekeeping troops remained. Zimbabwean Pres. Robert Mugabe pulled his country out of the **Commonwealth** (Dec. 2003) after the group reaffirmed suspension of **Zimbabwe** for alleged fraud in the 2002 election. **Libya** agreed (Dec. 2003) to abandon programs pursuing weapons of mass destruction.

Americas and the Caribbean. Vicente **Fox** of the center-right National Action Party (PAN) was elected **president of Mexico** (July 2000), in a historic defeat for the long-supreme Institutional Revolutionary Party (PRI). Peruvian Pres. Alberto **Fujimori stepped down** during his 3rd term (Nov. 2000), amid scandal, and did not seek reelection. In Jan. 2001, George W. **Bush was inaugurated** as U.S. president, after one of the tightest and most controversial elections in U.S. history; he was reelected in Nov. 2004. Power in both houses of the U.S. Congress was transferred to the Democratic Party following Nov. 2006 elections. Defense Sec. Donald Rumsfeld, one of the chief architects of the Iraq War, resigned the day after the Nov. 2006 elections.

Venezuelan Pres. Hugo Chavez regained power after 48-hr. coup (Dec. 2002). Argentina's **record default** on International Monetary Fund loans resulted (Sept. 2003) in a **$12.5 billion debt-refinancing** agreement. **Haiti** was wracked by anti-government protests, leading to the resignation of Jean-Bertrand **Aristide** in Feb. 2004. Tropical storm Jeanne caused mudslides and flooding that killed more than 1,500 in Haiti, Sept. 2004.

Hurricanes and subsequent flooding and landslides in 2005 killed thousands in the U.S. and abroad: **Katrina**, U.S. Gulf Coast (Aug.); Stan, S. Mexico and N. Central America (Oct.).

For the first time in 12 years, the Liberal Party handed control of Canada's government to the Conservative Party, led by Prime Minister Stephen Harper (Jan. 2006). Cuban Pres. Fidel **Castro** temporarily ceded power for the first time in 47 years to undergo surgery (July 2006), although it was unclear when he would be able to return.

Space. The U.S. space shuttle *Columbia* broke up on re-entering Earth's atmosphere Feb. 1, 2003, killing all 7 crew members. The NASA space shuttle program resumed with the July 2005 launch of *Discovery*.

Environment. Negotiators from 178 countries agreed to adopt the **Kyoto Protocol** July 2001, calling for a reduction of greenhouse gases in developed nations; 141 nations had ratified the treaty when it took effect (Feb. 2005). The Intergovernmental Panel on Climate Change called (Feb. 2007) global warming "unequivocal," declaring man-made greenhouse gases a "very likely" cause.

For events of 2007, see Year in Review—Chronology (pp. 12-28).

HISTORICAL FIGURES

Ancient Greeks and Romans

Greeks

Aeschines, orator, 389-314 BCE
Aeschylus, dramatist, 525-456 BCE
Aesop, fableist, c. 620-c. 560 BCE
Alcibiades, politician, 450-404 BCE
Anacreon, poet, c. 582-c. 485 BCE
Anaxagoras, philosopher, c. 500-428 BCE
Anaximander, philosopher, 611-546 BCE
Anaximenes, philosopher, c. 570-500 BCE
Antiphon, speechwriter, c. 480-411 BCE
Apollonius, mathematician, c. 265-170 BCE
Archimedes, mathematician, 287-212 BCE
Aristophanes, dramatist, c. 448-380 BCE
Aristotle, philosopher, 384-322 BCE
Athenaeus, scholar, fl. c. 200
Callicrates, architect, fl. 5th cent. BCE
Callimachus, poet, c. 305-240 BCE
Cratinus, comic dramatist, 520-421 BCE
Democritus, philosopher, c. 460-370 BCE
Demosthenes, orator, 384-322 BCE
Diodorus, historian, fl. 20 BCE
Diogenes, philosopher, 372-c. 287 BCE
Dionysius, historian, d. c. 7 BCE
Empedocles, philosopher, c. 490-430 BCE
Epicharmus, dramatist, c. 530-440 BCE
Epictetus, philosopher, c. 55-c. 135
Epicurus, philosopher, 341-270 BCE
Eratosthenes, scientist, 276-194 BCE
Euclid, mathematician, fl. c. 300 BCE
Euripides, dramatist, c. 484-406 BCE
Galen, physician, 129-216
Heraclitus, philosopher, c. 540-c. 475 BCE
Herodotus, historian, c. 484-420 BCE
Hesiod, poet, 8th cent. BCE
Hippocrates, physician, c. 460-377 BCE
Homer, poet, fl. c. 8th cent. BCE
Isocrates, orator, 436-338 BCE
Menander, dramatist, 342-292 BCE
Parmenides, philosopher, b. c. 515 BCE
Pericles, statesman, c. 495-429 BCE
Phidias, sculptor, c. 500-435 BCE
Pindar, poet, c. 518-c. 438 BCE
Plato, philosopher, c. 428-347 BCE
Plutarch, biographer, c. 46-120
Polybius, historian, c. 200-c. 118 BCE
Praxiteles, sculptor, 400-330 BCE
Pythagoras, phil., math., c. 580-c. 500 BCE
Sappho, poet, c. 610-c. 580 BCE
Simonides, poet, 556-c. 468 BCE
Socrates, philosopher, 469-399 BCE
Solon, statesman, 640-560 BCE
Sophocles, dramatist, c. 496-406 BCE
Strabo, geographer, c. 63 BCE-24 CE
Thales, philosopher, c. 634-546 BCE
Themistocles, politician, c. 524-c. 460 BCE
Theocritus, poet, c. 310-250 BCE
Theophrastus, phil., c. 372-c. 287 BCE
Thucydides, historian, fl. 5th cent. BCE
Timon, philosopher, c. 320-c. 230 BCE
Xenophon, historian, c. 434-c. 355 BCE
Zeno, philosopher, c. 335-c. 263 BCE

Romans

Ammianus, historian, c. 330-395
Apuleius, satirist, c. 124-c. 170
Boethius, scholar, c. 480-524
Caesar, Julius, leader, 100-44 BCE
Catiline, politician, c. 108-62 BCE
Cato (Elder), statesman, 234-149 BCE
Catullus, poet, c. 84-54 BCE
Cicero, orator, 106-43 BCE
Claudian, poet, c. 370-c. 404
Ennius, poet, 239-170 BCE
Gellius, author, c. 130-c. 165
Horace, poet, 65-8 BCE
Juvenal, satirist, 60-127
Livy, historian, 59 BCE-17 CE
Lucan, poet, 39-65
Lucilius, poet, c. 180-c.102 BCE
Lucretius, poet, c. 99-c. 55 BCE
Martial, epigrammatist, c. 38-c. 103
Nepos, historian, c. 100-c. 25 BCE
Ovid, poet, 43 BCE-17 CE
Persius, satirist, 34-62
Plautus, dramatist, c. 254-c. 184 BCE
Pliny the Elder, scholar, 23-79
Pliny the Younger, author, 62-113
Quintilian, rhetorician, c. 35-c. 97
Sallust, historian, 86-34 BCE
Seneca, philosopher, 4 BCE-65 CE
Silius, poet, c. 25-101
Statius, poet, c. 45-c. 96
Suetonius, biographer, c. 69-c. 122
Tacitus, historian, 56-120
Terence, dramatist, 185-c. 159 BCE
Tibullus, poet, c. 55-c. 19 BCE
Vergil, poet, 70-19 BCE
Vitruvius, architect, fl. 1st cent. BCE

Roman Rulers

From Romulus to the end of the Empire in the West. Rulers in the East sat in Constantinople and, for a brief period, in Nicaea, until the capture of Constantinople by the Turks in 1453, when Byzantium was succeeded by the Ottoman Empire.

The Kingdom

BCE
753 Romulus (Quirinus)
716 Numa Pompilius
673 Tullus Hostilius
640 Ancus Marcius
616 L. Tarquinius Priscus
578 Servius Tullius
534 L. Tarquinius Superbus

The Republic

509 Consulate established
509 Quaestorship instituted
498 Dictatorship introduced
494 Plebeian Tribunate created
494 Plebeian Aedileship created
444 Consular Tribunate organized
435 Censorship instituted
366 Praetorship established
366 Curule Aedileship created
362 Military Tribune elected
326 Proconsulate introduced
311 Naval Duumvirate elected
217 Dictatorship of Fabius Maximus
133 Tribunate of Tiberius Gracchus
123 Tribunate of Gaius Gracchus
82 Dictatorship of Sulla
60 First Triumvirate formed (Caesar, Pompeius, Crassus)
46 Dictatorship of Caesar
43 Second Triumvirate formed (Octavianus, Antonius, Lepidus)

The Empire

27 Augustus (Octavian)
CE
14 Tiberius I
37 Caligula
41 Claudius I
54 Nero
68 Galba
69 Galba; Otho, Vitellius
69 Vespasianus
79 Titus
81 Domitianus

96 Nerva
98 Trajanus
117 Hadrianus
138 Antoninus Pius
161 Marcus Aurelius and Lucius Verus
169 Marcus Aurelius (alone)
180 Commodus
193 Pertinax; Julianus I
193 Septimius Severus
211 Caracalla and Geta
212 Caracalla (alone)
217 Macrinus
218 Elagabalus (Heliogabalus)
222 Alexander Severus
235 Maximinus I (the Thracian)
238 Gordianus I and Gordianus II; Pupienus and Balbinus
238 Gordianus III
244 Philippus (the Arabian)
249 Decius
251 Gallus and Volusianus
253 Aemilianus
253 Valerianus and Gallienus
258 Gallienus (alone)
268 Claudius Gothicus
270 Quintillus
270 Aurelianus
275 Tacitus
276 Florianus
276 Probus
282 Carus
283 Carinus and Numerianus
286 Diocletianus and Maximianus
305 Galerius and Constantius I
306 Galerius, Maximinus II, Severus I
307 Galerius, Maximinus II, Constantinus I, Licinius, Maxentius
311 Maximinus II, Constantinus I, Licinius, Maxentius
314 Maximinus II, Constantinus I, Licinius
314 Constantinus I and Licinius
324 Constantinus I (the Great)

337 Constantinus II, Constans I, Constantius II
340 Constantinus II and Constans I
350 Constantius II
361 Julianus II (the Apostate)
363 Jovianus

West (Rome) and East (Constantinople)

364 Valentinianus I (West), Valens (East)
367 Valentinianus I with Gratianus (West), Valens (East)
375 Gratianus with Valentinianus II (West), Valens (East)
378 Gratianus with Valentinianus II (West), Theodosius I (East)
383 Valentinianus II (West), Theodosius I (East)
394 Theodosius I (the Great)
395 Honorius (West), Arcadius (East)
408 Honorius (West), Theodosius II (East)
423 Valentinianus III (West), Theodosius II (East)
450 Valentinianus III (West), Marcianus (East)
455 Maximus (West), Avitus (West); Marcianus (East)
456 Avitus (West), Marcianus (East)
457 Majorianus (West), Leo I (East)
461 Severus II (West), Leo I (East)
467 Anthemius (West), Leo I (East)
472 Olybrius (West), Leo I (East)
473 Glycerius (West), Leo I (East)
474 Julius Nepos (West), Leo II (East)
475 Romulus Augustulus (West), Zeno (East)
476 End of Empire in West with deposing of Romulus Augustulus by Germanic chief Odovacar, who proclaimed self king. Odovacar murdered by King Theodoric of Ostrogoths, 493

Rulers of England and Great Britain

Reign began	Name	Age at death[1]
	ENGLAND	
	Saxons and Danes	
829	Egbert, King of Wessex, won allegiance of all English	NA
839	Ethelwulf, son of Egbert, King of Wessex, Sussex, Kent, Essex	NA
858	Ethelbald, son of Ethelwulf, displaced father in Wessex	NA
860	Ethelbert, 2nd son of Ethelwulf, united Kent and Wessex	NA
866	Ethelred I, 3rd son of Ethelwulf, King of Wessex; fought Danes	NA
871	Alfred (the Great), 4th son of Ethelwulf; defeated Danes; fortified London	52
899	Edward (the Elder), son of Alfred, united English, claimed Scotland	55
924	Athelstan (the Glorious), son of Edward, King of Mercia, Wessex	45
940	Edmund, 3rd son of Edward, King of Wessex, Mercia	25
946	Edred, 4th son of Edward	32
955	Edwy (the Fair), eldest son of Edmund, King of Wessex	18
959	Edgar (the Peaceful), 2nd son of Edmund, ruled all English	32
975	Edward (the Martyr), eldest son of Edgar, murdered by stepmother	17
978; 1014[2]	Ethelred II (the Unready), 2nd son of Edgar, married Emma of Normandy	48
1016	Edmund II (Ironside), son of Ethelred II, King of London	27
1016	Canute (the Dane), gave Wessex to Edmund, married Emma, Ethelred II's widow	40
1035	Harold I (Harefoot), illegitimate son of Canute	NA
1040	Hardecanute, son of Canute by Emma, also King of Denmark	24
1042	Edward (the Confessor), son of Ethelred II, canonized 1161	62
1066	Harold II, Edward's brother-in-law, last Saxon King	44
	House of Normandy	
1066	William I (the Conqueror), defeated Harold II at Hastings	60
1087	William II (Rufus), 3rd son of William I, killed by arrow	43
1100	Henry I (Beauclerc), youngest son of William I	67
	House of Blois	
1135	Stephen, son of Adela, daughter of William I, and Count of Blois	50
	House of Plantagenet	
1154	Henry II, son of Geoffrey Plantagenet (Angevin) by Matilda, daughter of Henry I	56
1189	Richard I (Coeur de Lion), son of Henry II, crusader	42
1199	John (Lackland), son of Henry II, approved Magna Carta, 1215	50
1216	Henry III, son of John, acceded at 9, under regency until 1227	65
1272	Edward I, son of Henry III	68
1307	Edward II, son of Edward I, deposed by Parliament	43
1327	Edward III (of Windsor), son of Edward II	65
1377	Richard II, grandson of Edward III, minor until 1389, deposed	33
	House of Lancaster	
1399	Henry IV, son of John of Gaunt, Duke of Lancaster, son of Edward III	47
1413	Henry V, son of Henry IV, victor of Agincourt	34
1422; 1470	Henry VI, son of Henry V, overthrown by Edward IV in 1461 but was returned to throne in 1470. Deposed, died in Tower of London, 1471	49
	House of York	
1461; 1471	Edward IV, great-great-grandson of Edward III, son of Duke of York. Acclaimed king by Parliament, 1461. Driven into exile in 1470 but defeated enemies to regain throne, 1471	40
1483	Edward V, son of Edward IV, murdered in Tower of London	13
1483	Richard III, brother of Edward IV, fell at Bosworth Field	32
	House of Tudor	
1485	Henry VII, son of Edmund Tudor, Earl of Richmond, whose father had married the widow of Henry V. Descended from Edward III through mother, Margaret Beaufort, via John of Gaunt. By marrying daughter of Edward IV, united Lancaster and York	53
1509	Henry VIII, son of Henry VII, by Elizabeth, daughter of Edward IV	56
1547	Edward VI, son of Henry VIII, by Jane Seymour, his 3rd queen. Ruled under regents, was forced to name Lady Jane Grey his successor. Council of State proclaimed her queen, July 10, 1553. Mary Tudor won Council, was proclaimed queen, July 19. Mary had Lady Jane Grey beheaded for treason, 1554	16
1553	Mary I, daughter of Henry VIII, by Catherine of Aragon	43
1558	Elizabeth I, daughter of Henry VIII, by Anne Boleyn	69
	GREAT BRITAIN	
	House of Stuart	
1603	James I (James VI of Scotland), son of Mary, Queen of Scots. First to call self King of Great Britain; this became official with Act of Union, 1707	59
1625	Charles I, only surviving son of James I, beheaded, 1649	48
	Commonwealth	
	Declared upon execution of Charles I, 1649	
	Protectorate	
1653	Oliver Cromwell, served on Council of State, executive body of Commonwealth, following overthrow of monarchy. Named Lord Protector upon creation of Protectorate by 1653 Instrument of Government	59
1658	Richard Cromwell, 3rd son of Oliver Cromwell. Resigned as Lord Protector amid civil war, 1659. Died 1712	86
	House of Stuart (Restored)	
1660	Charles II, eldest son of Charles I, Restoration put him back on throne, died without issue	55
1685	James II, second son of Charles I, deposed, 1688	68
1689	William III, son of William, Prince of Orange, by Mary, daughter of Charles I. Offered joint rule of throne with wife by Parliament	51
1689	Mary II, eldest daughter of James II, wife of William III, died 1694	33
1702	Anne, second daughter of James II, assumed throne on William III's death	49
	House of Hanover	
1714	George I, son of Elector of Hanover, by Sophia, granddaughter of James I	67
1727	George II, only son of George I, married Caroline of Brandenburg	77
1760	George III, grandson of George II, married Charlotte of Mecklenburg	81
1820	George IV, eldest son of George III, Prince Regent from Feb. 1811	67
1830	William IV, 3rd son of George III, married Adelaide of Saxe-Meiningen	71
1837	Victoria, daughter of Edward, 4th son of George III; married Prince Albert of Saxe-Coburg and Gotha, 1840, who became Prince Consort	81

House of Saxe-Coburg and Gotha

1901	Edward VII, eldest son of Victoria, married Alexandra, Princess of Denmark	68

House of Windsor[3]

1910	George V, 2nd son of Edward VII, married Princess Mary of Teck	70
1936	Edward VIII, eldest son of George V, acceded Jan. 20, abdicated Dec. 11	77
1936	George VI, 2nd son of George V, married Lady Elizabeth Bowes-Lyon	56
1952	Elizabeth II, elder daughter of George VI, acceded Feb. 6	

NA = Age/birth date not certain. (1) Except where noted, year of death is year of accession of succeeding ruler. (2) King Sweyn I of Denmark invaded England in 1013 and declared himself king. Ethelred II reclaimed the throne upon Sweyn's death in 1014. (3) Name adopted by proclamation of George V, July 17, 1917.

Rulers of Scotland

Reign began	Name
846	Kenneth I MacAlpin, first Scot to rule both Scots and Picts
1005	Malcolm II Mackenneth
1034	Duncan I, first general ruler
1040	Macbeth, seized kingdom, slain by Malcolm III MacDuncan
1057	Malcolm III MacDuncan (Canmore), son of Duncan I. Married Margaret, Saxon princess who had fled from Normans
1093	Donald Bane
1094	Duncan II
1095	Donald Bane (restored)
1097	Edgar, son of Queen Margaret, moved court to Edinburgh
1107	Alexander I, brother of Edgar
1124	David I, brother of Edgar
1153	Malcolm IV (the Maiden), grandson of David I
1165	William (the Lion), brother of Malcolm IV
1214	Alexander II, son of William
1249	Alexander III, son of Alexander II, defeated Norse, regained the Hebrides
1286	Margaret (Maid of Norway), granddaughter of Alexander III, child of Eric of Norway, grandniece of Edward I of England Died 1290 at age 8. (Interregnum, 1290-92)
1292	John Balliol, proclaimed king of Scotland by Edward I of England. (Interregnum, 1296-1306[1])
1306	Robert Bruce (the Bruce), victor at Bannockburn, 1314. Treaty with England and secured throne, 1328
1329	David II, only son of Robert Bruce
1371	Robert II (the Steward), grandson of Robert Bruce, son of Walter, the steward of Scotland. First of so-called Stuart line
1390	Robert III, son of Robert II
1406	James I, son of Robert III
1437	James II, son of James I
1460	James III, eldest son of James II
1488	James IV, eldest son of James III
1513	James V, eldest son of James IV
1542	Mary (Queen of Scots), daughter of James V, became queen before she was 1 week old. Married Francis II, son of Henry II of France, 1558. Francis died in 1560. Married her cousin, Henry Stewart, Lord Darnley, 1565; married James Hepburn, Earl of Bothwell, 1567. Imprisoned by Elizabeth I; beheaded, 1587
1567	James VI, son of Mary and Lord Darnley, became James I, king of England on death of Elizabeth, 1603. Although thrones were thus united, legislative union of Scotland and England did not become official until the Act of Union, 1707

(1) Edward I decreed annexation of Scotland to England, 1296. William Wallace led resistance, 1297-1305.

Prime Ministers of Great Britain

Designations in parentheses describe each government.
W=Whig; T=Tory; Cl=Coalition; P=Peelite; Li=Liberal; C=Conservative[1]; La=Labour

Entered office	Name	Entered office	Name	Entered office	Name
1721	Sir Robert Walpole (W)[2]	1830	Earl Grey (W)	1908	Herbert H. Asquith (Li)
1742	Earl of Wilmington (W)	1834	Viscount Melbourne (W)	1915	Herbert H. Asquith (Cl)
1743	Henry Pelham (W)	1834	Sir Robert Peel (C)	1916	David Lloyd George (Cl)
1754	Duke of Newcastle (W)	1835	Viscount Melbourne (W)	1922	Andrew Bonar Law (C)
1756	Duke of Devonshire (W)	1841	Sir Robert Peel (C)	1923	Stanley Baldwin (C)
1757	Duke of Newcastle (W)	1846	Lord (later Earl) John Russell (W)	1924	James Ramsay MacDonald (La)
1762	Earl of Bute (T)	1852	Earl of Derby (C)	1924	Stanley Baldwin (C)
1763	George Grenville (W)	1852	Earl of Aberdeen (P)	1929	James Ramsay MacDonald (La)
1765	Marquess of Rockingham (W)	1855	Viscount Palmerston (Li)	1931	James Ramsay MacDonald (Cl)
1766	William Pitt the Elder (Earl of Chatham) (W)	1858	Earl of Derby (C)	1935	Stanley Baldwin (Cl)
		1859	Viscount Palmerston (Li)	1937	Neville Chamberlain (C)
1768	Duke of Grafton (W)	1865	Earl Russell (Li)	1940	Winston Churchill (Cl)
1770	Frederick North (Lord North) (T)	1866	Earl of Derby (C)	1945	Winston Churchill (C)
1782	Marquess of Rockingham (W)	1868	Benjamin Disraeli (C)	1945	Clement Attlee (La)
1782	Earl of Shelburne (W)	1868	William E. Gladstone (Li)	1951	Sir Winston Churchill (C)
1783	Duke of Portland (Cl)	1874	Benjamin Disraeli (C)	1955	Sir Anthony Eden (C)
1783	William Pitt the Younger (T)	1880	William E. Gladstone (Li)	1957	Harold Macmillan (C)
1801	Henry Addington (T)	1885	Marquess of Salisbury (C)	1963	Sir Alec Douglas-Home (C)
1804	William Pitt the Younger (T)	1886	William E. Gladstone (Li)	1964	Harold Wilson (La)
1806	William Wyndham Grenville, Baron Grenville (W)	1886	Marquess of Salisbury (C)	1970	Edward Heath (C)
		1892	William E. Gladstone (Li)	1974	Harold Wilson (La)
1807	Duke of Portland (T)	1894	Earl of Rosebery (Li)	1976	James Callaghan (La)
1809	Spencer Perceval (T)	1895	Marquess of Salisbury (C)	1979	Margaret Thatcher (C)
1812	Earl of Liverpool (T)	1902	Arthur J. Balfour (C)	1990	John Major (C)
1827	George Canning (T)	1905	Sir Henry Campbell Bannerman (Li)	1997	Tony Blair (La)
1827	Viscount Goderich (T)			2007	Gordon Brown (La)
1828	Duke of Wellington (T)				

(1) The Conservative Party was formed in 1834, an outgrowth of the Tory party. (2) Walpole is commonly regarded as the first prime minister of Britain, though the title was not commonly used then and did not become official until 1905.

Rulers of France: Kings, Queens, Presidents

Caesar to Charlemagne

Julius Caesar subdued the Gauls, native tribes of Gaul (France), 58 to 51 BCE. The Romans ruled 500 years. The Franks, a Teutonic tribe, reached the Somme from the East c. 250 CE. By the 5th century the Merovingian Franks ousted the Romans. In 451, with the help of Visigoths, Burgundians, and others, they defeated Attila and the Huns at Chalons-sur-Marne.

Childeric I became leader of the Merovingians, 458. His son Clovis I (Chlodwig, Ludwig, Louis), crowned 481, founded the dynasty. After defeating the Alemanni (Germans), 496, he was baptized a Christian and made Paris his capital. His line ruled until Childeric III was deposed, 751.

The West Merovingians were called Neustrians, the eastern Austrasians. Pepin of Herstal (687-714), major domus, or head of the palace, of Austrasia, took over Neustria as dux (leader) of the Franks. Pepin's son, Charles, called Martel (the Hammer), defeated the Saracens at Tours-Poitiers, 732; was succeeded by his son, Pepin the Short, 741, who deposed Childeric III and ruled as king until 768.

His son, Charlemagne, or Charles the Great (742-814), became king of the Franks, 768, with his brother Carloman, who died 771. Charlemagne ruled France, Germany, parts of Italy, Spain, and Austria, and enforced Christianity. Crowned Emperor of the Romans by Pope Leo III in St. Peter's, Rome, Dec. 25, 800. Succeeded by son, Louis I the Pious, 814. At death, 840, Louis left empire to sons, Lothair (Roman emperor); Pepin I (king of Aquitaine); Louis II (of Germany); Charles the Bald (France). They quarreled and, by the Treaty of Verdun, 843, divided the empire.

The date preceding each entry is year of accession.

The Carolingians

- **843** Charles I (the Bald), Roman Emperor, 875
- **877** Louis II (the Stammerer), son
- **879** Louis III (d. 882) and Carloman, brothers
- **885** Charles II (the Fat), Roman Emperor, 881
- **888** Eudes (Odo), elected by nobles
- **898** Charles III (the Simple), son of Louis II, defeated by Robert
- **922** Robert, brother of Eudes, killed in war
- **923** Rudolph (Raoul), Duke of Burgundy
- **936** Louis IV, son of Charles III
- **954** Lothair, son, aged 13, defeated by Capet
- **986** Louis V (the Sluggard), left no heirs

The Capets

- **987** Hugh Capet, son of Hugh the Great
- **996** Robert II (the Pious), his son
- **1031** Henry I, son
- **1060** Philip I (the Fair), son
- **1108** Louis VI (the Fat), son
- **1137** Louis VII (the Younger), son
- **1180** Philip II (Augustus), son, crowned at Reims
- **1223** Louis VIII (the Lion), son
- **1226** Louis IX, son, crusader; Louis IX (1214-70) reigned 44 years, arbitrated disputes with English King Henry III, led crusades, 1248 (captured in Egypt, 1250) and 1270, when he died of plague in Tunis. Canonized 1297 as St. Louis
- **1270** Philip III (the Hardy), son
- **1285** Philip IV (the Fair), son, king at 17
- **1314** Louis X (the Headstrong), son. His posthumous son, John I, lived only 7 days.
- **1316** Philip V (the Tall), brother of Louis X
- **1322** Charles IV (the Fair), brother of Louis X

House of Valois

- **1328** Philip VI (of Valois), grandson of Philip III
- **1350** John II (the Good), his son, retired to England
- **1364** Charles V (the Wise), son
- **1380** Charles VI (the Beloved), son
- **1422** Charles VII (the Victorious), son. In 1429 Joan of Arc (Jeanne d'Arc) promised Charles to oust the English, who occupied northern France. Joan won at Orleans and Patay and had Charles crowned at Reims, July 17, 1429. Joan was captured May 24, 1430, and executed May 30, 1431, at Rouen for heresy. Charles ordered her rehabilitation, effected 1455.
- **1461** Louis XI (the Cruel), son, civil reformer
- **1483** Charles VIII (the Affable), son
- **1498** Louis XII, great-grandson of Charles V
- **1515** Francis I, of Angouleme, nephew, son-in-law. Francis I (1494-1547) reigned 32 years, fought 4 big wars, was patron of the arts, aided Cellini, del Sarto, Leonardo da Vinci, Rabelais, embellished Fontainebleau

- **1547** Henry II, son, killed at a joust in tournament. He was the husband of Catherine de Médicis (1519-89) and the lover of Diane de Poitiers (1499-1566). Catherine was born in Florence, daughter of Lorenzo de Medici. By her marriage to Henry II she became the mother of Francis II, Charles IX, Henry III, and Queen Margaret (Reine Margot), wife of Henry IV. She persuaded Charles IX to order the massacre of Huguenots on the Feast of St. Bartholomew, Aug. 24, 1572, six days after her daughter was married to Henry of Navarre.
- **1559** Francis II, son. Betrothed in 1548 at age 4 to Mary, Queen of Scots, aged 6. They were married 1558. Francis died 1560, aged 16; Mary ruled Scotland, abdicated 1567
- **1560** Charles IX, brother
- **1574** Henry III, brother, assassinated

House of Bourbon

- **1589** Henry IV, of Navarre, assassinated. Henry IV made enemies when he gave tolerance to Protestants by Edict of Nantes, 1598. He was grandson of Queen Margaret of Navarre, literary patron. He married Margaret of Valois, daughter of Henry II and Catherine de Médicis; was divorced. In 1600 married Marie de Médicis, who became Regent of France, 1610-17, for her son, Louis XIII, but was exiled by Richelieu, 1631
- **1610** Louis XIII (the Just), son. Louis XIII (1601-43) married Anne of Austria. He came to be dominated by his chief minister (1622-42), Cardinal Richelieu.
- **1643** Louis XIV (the Sun King), son. Louis XIV was king 72 years. Until 1661, Anne of Austria was regent, with Cardinal Mazarin as chief minister; after that, Louis ruled absolutely. Known for his lavish court and patronage of the arts, he exhausted a prosperous country in wars for thrones and territory.
- **1715** Louis XV, great-grandson. Louis XV married a Polish princess, lost Canada to the English. His favorites, Mme. Pompadour and Mme. Du Barry, influenced policies. Mme. Pompadour's saying "Après moi, le déluge" (After me, the deluge) often incorrectly attributed to Louis XV
- **1774** Louis XVI, grandson; married Marie Antoinette, daughter of Empress Maria Therese of Austria. King and queen beheaded by Revolution, 1793. Their son, called Louis XVII, died in prison, never ruled

First Republic

- **1792** National Convention of the French Revolution
- **1795** Directory, under Barras and others
- **1799** Consulate, Napoleon Bonaparte, first consul. Elected consul for life, 1802

First Empire

- **1804** Napoleon I (Napoleon Bonaparte), emperor. Josephine (de Beauharnais), empress, 1804-09; Marie Louise, empress, 1810-14. Her son, Francois (1811-32), titular King of Rome, later Duke de Reichstadt and "Napoleon II," never ruled. Napoleon abdicated 1814, died 1821

Bourbons Restored

- **1814** Louis XVIII, king, brother of Louis XVI
- **1824** Charles X, brother, reactionary, deposed by the July Revolution, 1830

House of Orleans

- **1830** Louis-Philippe, the "Citizen King"

Second Republic

- **1848** Louis Napoleon Bonaparte, president, nephew of Napoleon I

Second Empire

- **1852** Napoleon III (Louis Napoleon Bonaparte), emperor. Eugenie (de Montijo), empress. Lost Franco-Prussian war, deposed 1870. Son, Prince Imperial (1856-79), died in Zulu War. Eugenie died 1920.

Third Republic—Presidents

- **1871** Thiers, Louis Adolphe (1797-1877)
- **1873** MacMahon, Marshal Patrice M. de (1808-93)
- **1879** Grevy, Paul J. (1807-91)
- **1887** Sadi-Carnot, M. (1837-94), assassinated
- **1894** Casimir-Perier, Jean P. P. (1847-1907)
- **1895** Faure, François Felix (1841-99)
- **1899** Loubet, Emile (1838-1929)
- **1906** Fallieres, C. Armand (1841-1931)
- **1913** Poincare, Raymond (1860-1934)
- **1920** Deschanel, Paul (1856-1922)
- **1920** Millerand, Alexandre (1859-1943)
- **1924** Doumergue, Gaston (1863-1937)
- **1931** Doumer, Paul (1857-1932), assassinated
- **1932** Lebrun, Albert (1871-1950), resigned 1940
- **1940** Vichy govt. under German armistice: Henri Philippe Petain (1856-1951), Chief of State, 1940-44

Provisional govt. after liberation: Charles de Gaulle (1890-1970), Oct. 1944-Jan. 21, 1946; Felix Gouin (1884-1977), Jan. 23, 1946; Georges Bidault (1899-1983), June 24, 1946

Fourth Republic—Presidents
1947 Auriol, Vincent (1884-1966)
1954 Coty, Rene (1882-1962)

Fifth Republic—Presidents
1959 De Gaulle, Charles Andre J. M. (1890-1970)
1969 Pompidou, Georges (1911-74)
1974 Giscard d'Estaing, Valery (1926-   )
1981 Mitterrand, François (1916-96)
1995 Chirac, Jacques (1932-   )
2007 Sarkozy, Nicolas (1955-   )

Rulers of Middle Europe; Rise and Fall of Dynasties; Rulers of Germany

Carolingian Dynasty

Charles the Great, or Charlemagne, ruled France, Italy, and Middle Europe; established Ostmark (later Austria); crowned Roman emperor by pope in Rome, 800 CE; died 814.

Louis I (Ludwig) the Pious, son, crowned by Charlemagne 814; died 840.

Louis II, the German, son, succeeded to East Francia (Germany) 843-76.

Charles the Fat, son, inherited East Francia and West Francia (France) 876, reunited empire, crowned emperor by pope, 881; deposed 887.

Arnulf, nephew, 887-99, partition of empire.

Louis the Child, 899-911, last direct descendant of Charlemagne.

Conrad I, duke of Franconia, first elected German king, 911-18, founded House of Franconia.

Saxon Dynasty; First Reich

Henry I, the Fowler, duke of Saxony, 919-36.

Otto I, the Great, 936-73, son; crowned Holy Roman Emperor by pope, 962.

Otto II, 973-83, son; failed to oust Greeks and Arabs from Sicily.

Otto III, 983-1002, son; crowned emperor at 16.

Henry II, the Saint, duke of Bavaria, 1002-24, great-grandson of Otto the Great.

House of Franconia

Conrad II, 1024-39, elected king of Germany.

Henry III, the Black, 1039-56, son; deposed 3 popes, annexed Burgundy.

Henry IV, 1056-1106, son; regency by his mother, Agnes of Poitou. Banned by Pope Gregory VII, he did penance at Canossa.

Henry V, 1106-25, son; last of Salian Dynasty.

Lothair, duke of Saxony, 1125-37. Crowned emperor in Rome, 1134.

House of Hohenstaufen

Conrad III, duke of Swabia, 1138-52, in 2nd Crusade.

Frederick I, Barbarossa, 1152-90; Conrad's nephew.

Henry VI, 1190-96, took lower Italy from Normans. Son became king of Sicily.

Philip of Swabia, 1197-1208, brother.

Otto IV, of House of Welf, 1198-1215, deposed.

Frederick II, 1215-50, son of Henry VI; king of Sicily; crowned king of Jerusalem in 5th Crusade.

Conrad IV, 1250-54, son; lost lower Italy to Charles of Anjou.

Conradin, 1252-68, son, king of Jerusalem and Sicily, beheaded. Last Hohenstaufen.

Interregnum, 1254-73. Rise of the Electors.

Transition

Rudolph I, of Hapsburg, 1273-91, defeated King Ottocar II of Bohemia. Bequeathed duchy of Austria to eldest son, Albert.

Adolph of Nassau, 1292-98, killed in war with Albert of Austria.

Albert I, king of Germany, 1298-1308, son of Rudolph.

Henry VII, of Luxemburg, 1308-13, crowned emperor in Rome; seized Bohemia, 1310.

Louis IV, of Bavaria (Wittelsbach), 1314-47. Also elected was Frederick of Austria, 1314-30 (Hapsburg). Abolition of papal sanction for election of Holy Roman Emperor.

Charles IV, of Luxemburg, 1347-78, grandson of Henry VII, German emperor and king of Bohemia, Lombardy, Burgundy, took Mark of Brandenburg.

Wenceslaus, 1378-1400, deposed.

Rupert, Duke of Palatine, 1400-10.

Sigismund, 1411-37.

Hungary

Stephen I, House of Arpad, 997-1038. Crowned king, 1000; converted Magyars; canonized 1083. After several centuries of feuds Charles Robert of Anjou became Charles I, 1308-42.

Louis I, the Great, son, 1342-82, joint ruler of Poland with Casimir III, 1370. Defeated Turks.

Mary, daughter, 1382-95, ruled with husband, Sigismund of Luxemburg, 1387-1437, also king of Bohemia. As brother of Wenceslaus he succeeded Rupert as Holy Roman Emperor, 1410.

Albert, 1438-39, son-in-law of Sigismund, also Roman emperor as Albert II (see under Hapsburg).

Ulaszlo I of Poland, 1440-44.

Ladislaus V, posthumous son of Albert II, 1444-57. John Hunyadi (Janos Hunyadi), governor (1446-52), fought Turks, Czechs; died 1456.

Matthias I (Corvinus), son of Hunyadi, 1458-90. Shared rule of Bohemia, captured Vienna, 1485, annexed Austria, Styria, Carinthia.

Ulaszlo II (king of Bohemia), 1490-1516.

Louis II, son, aged 10, 1516-26. Wars with Suleiman, Turk. In 1527, Hungary split between Ferdinand I, Archduke of Austria, brother-in-law of Louis II, and John Zapolya of Transylvania. After Turkish invasion, 1547, Hungary split between Ferdinand, Prince John Sigismund (Transylvania), and the Turks.

House of Hapsburg

Albert V, of Austria, Hapsburg, crowned king of Hungary, Jan. 1438; Roman emperor, March 1438, as Albert II; died 1439.

Frederick III, cousin, 1440-93, fought Turks.

Maximilian I, son, 1493-1519, assumed title of Holy Roman Emperor (German), 1493.

Charles V, grandson, 1519-56. King of Spain with mother co-regent, crowned Roman emperor at Aix, 1520. Confronted Luther at Worms; attempted church reform and religious conciliation; abdicated 1556.

Ferdinand I, king of Bohemia, 1526; of Hungary, 1527; disputed. German king, 1531. Crowned Roman emperor on abdication of brother Charles V, 1556.

Maximilian II, son, 1564-76.

Rudolph II, son, 1576-1612.

Matthias, brother, 1612-19, king of Bohemia and Hungary.

Ferdinand II, of Styria, king of Bohemia, 1617; of Hungary, 1618; Roman emperor, 1619. Bohemian Protestants deposed him, elected Frederick V of Palatine, starting Thirty Years War.

Ferdinand III, son, king of Hungary, 1625, Bohemia, 1627; Roman emperor, 1637. Peace of Westphalia, 1648, ended war.

Leopold I, son, 1658-1705.

Joseph I, son, 1705-11.

Charles VI, brother, 1711-40.

Maria Theresa, daughter, 1740-80, archduchess of Austria, queen of Hungary and Bohemia; ousted pretender, Charles VII, crowned 1742; in 1745 obtained election of her husband Francis I as Roman emperor and co-regent (d. 1765). Fought Seven Years' War with Frederick II of Prussia. Mother of Marie Antoinette.

Joseph II, son, 1765-90, Roman emperor, reformer; powers restricted by Empress Maria Theresa until her death, 1780. First partition of Poland.

Leopold II, brother, 1790-92.

Francis II, son, 1792-1835. Fought Napoleon. Proclaimed first hereditary emperor of Austria, 1804. Forced to abdicate as Roman, 1806; last use of title.

Ferdinand I, son, 1835-48, abdicated during revolution.

Austro-Hungarian Monarchy

Francis Joseph I, nephew, 1848-1916, emperor of Austria, king of Hungary. Dual monarchy of Austria-Hungary formed, 1867. After assassination of her husband Archduke Francis Ferdinand, June 28, 1914, Austrian diplomacy precipitated World War I.

Charles I, grand-nephew, 1916-18, last emperor of Austria and king of Hungary. Abdicated Nov. 11-13, 1918, died 1922.

Rulers of Prussia

Nucleus of Prussia was the Mark of Brandenburg. First margrave Albert the Bear (Albrecht), 1134-70. First Hohenzollern margrave was Frederick, burgrave of Nuremberg, 1417-40.

Frederick William, 1640-88, the Great Elector. Son, Frederick III, 1688-1713, crowned King Frederick of Prussia, 1701.

Frederick William I, son, 1713-40.

Frederick II, the Great, son, 1740-86, annexed Silesia, part of Austria.

Frederick William II, nephew, 1786-97.

Frederick William III, son, 1797-1840, Napoleonic wars.

Frederick William IV, son, 1840-61. Uprising of 1848 and first parliament and constitution.

Second and Third Reich

William I, 1861-88, brother. Annexation of Schleswig and Hanover; Franco-Prussian war, 1870-71; proclamation of German Reich, Jan. 18, 1871, at Versailles; William, German emperor (Deutscher Kaiser); Bismarck, chancellor.

Frederick III, son, 1888.

William II, son, 1888-1918, led Germany in World War I,
abdicated as German emperor and king of Prussia, Nov. 9, 1918. Died in exile in Netherlands, June 4, 1941. Minor rulers of Bavaria, Saxony, Wurttemberg also abdicated.

Germany proclaimed republic at Weimar, July 1, 1919. Presidents included Frederick Ebert, 1919-25; Paul von Hindenburg-Beneckendorff, 1925, reelected 1932, died Aug. 2, 1934. Adolf Hitler, chancellor, chosen successor as Leader-Chancellor (Fuehrer-Reichskanzler) of Third Reich. Annexed Austria, Mar. 1938. Precipitated World War II, 1939-45. Suicide Apr. 30, 1945.

Germany After 1945

Following World War II, Germany was split between democratic West and Soviet-dominated East. West German chancellors: Konrad Adenauer, 1949-63; Ludwig Erhard, 1963-66; Kurt Georg Kiesinger, 1966-69; Willy Brandt, 1969-74; Helmut Schmidt, 1974-82; Helmut Kohl, 1982-90. East German Communist party leaders: Walter Ulbricht, 1946-71; Erich Honecker, 1971-89; Egon Krenz, 1989-90.

Germany reunited Oct. 3, 1990. Post-reunification chancellors: Helmut Kohl, 1990-98; Gerhard Schröder, 1998-2005; Angela Merkel, 2005- .

Rulers of Poland

House of Piasts

Miesko I, 962?-92; Poland Christianized 966. Expansion under 3 Boleslavs: I, 992-1025, son, crowned king 1024; II, 1058-79, great-grandson, exiled after killing bishop Stanislav, who became chief patron saint of Poland; III, 1106-38, nephew, divided Poland among 4 sons, eldest suzerain.

Feudal division, 1138-1306. Founding in Prussia of military order Teutonic Knights, 1226. Invasion by Tartars/Mongols, 1226.

Vladislav I, 1306-33, reunited most Polish territories, crowned king 1320. Casimir III the Great, 1333-70, son, developed economy, cultural life, foreign policy.

House of Anjou

Louis I, 1370-82, nephew, was also Louis I of Hungary.

Jadwiga, 1384-99, daughter, married Jagiello, Grand Duke of Lithuania, 1386.

House of Jagiellonians

Vladislav II, 1386-1434, Christianized Lithuania, founded personal union between Poland and Lithuania. Defeated 1410 Teutonic Knights at Grunwald.

Vladislav III, 1434-44, son, simultaneously king of Hungary. Fought Turks, killed 1444 in battle of Varna.

Casimir IV, 1446-92, brother, competed with Hapsburgs, put son Vladislav on throne of Bohemia, later also of Hungary (Ulaszlo II).

Sigismund I, 1506-48, son, patronized science and arts, his and son's reign "Golden Age."

Sigismund II, 1548-72, son, established 1569 real union of Poland and Lithuania (lasted until 1795).

Elective Kings

Polish nobles in 1572 proclaimed Poland a republic headed by king to be elected by whole nobility.

Stephen Batory, 1576-86, duke of Transylvania, married Ann, sister of Sigismund II August. Fought Russians.

Sigismund III Vasa, 1587-1632, nephew of Sigismund II. 1592-98 also king of Sweden. His generals fought Russians, Turks.

Vladislav II Vasa, 1632-48, son. Fought Russians.

John II Casimir Vasa, 1648-68, brother. Fought Cossacks, Swedes, Russians, Turks, Tatars (the "Deluge"). Abdicated 1668.
John III Sobieski, 1674-96. Won Vienna from besieging Turks, 1683.

Stanislav II, 1764-95, last king. Encouraged reforms; first modern constitution in Europe, 1791. Poland partitioned among Russia, Prussia, Austria, 1772, 1793, 1795. Unsuccessful insurrection against foreign invasion, 1794, under Kosciusko, American-Polish general.

1795-1918: Poland Under Foreign Rule

Grand Duchy of Warsaw created by Napoleon I, Frederick August of Saxony grand duke, 1807-15.

Congress of Vienna proclaimed part of Poland "Kingdom" in personal union with Russia, 1815.

Polish uprisings: against Russia, 1830; against Austria, 1846, 1848; against Russia, 1863—all repressed.

1918-39: Second Republic

Head of State Jozef Pilsudski, 1918-22. Presidents: Gabriel Narutowicz, 1922, assassinated; Stanislav Wojciechowski, 1922-26, had to abdicate after Pilsudski's coup d'état; Ignacy Moscicki, 1926-39, ruled (with Pilsudski until his death, 1935) as virtual dictator.

1939-45: Poland Under Foreign Occupation

Nazi and Soviet invasion, Sept. 1939. Polish government-in-exile, first in France, then in England. Vladislav Raczkiewicz, president; Gen. Vladislav Sikorski, then Stanislav Mikolajczyk, prime ministers. Soviet-sponsored Polish Committee of National Liberation proclaimed at Lublin, July 1944, transformed into government Jan. 1, 1945.

Poland After 1945

In the late 1940s, Poland came increasingly under Soviet control. Communist party ruled in Poland until Aug. 1989, when democratic Solidarity party, led by Lech Walesa, gained control of government. Walesa was elected president in 1990, but lost the office to former communist Aleksander Kwasniewski in 1995. The government remained democratic, and Kwasniewski was reelected in Oct. 2000. He was succeeded by Lech Kaczynski, 2005. Jaroslaw Kaczynski, the president's identical twin, became the country's prime minister in 2006.

Rulers of Denmark, Sweden, Norway

Denmark

Earliest rulers invaded Britain. King Canute, who ruled in London 1016-35, was most famous. The Valdemars furnished kings until the 15th century. In 1282 the Danes won the first national assembly, Danehof, from King Erik V.

Most redoubtable medieval character was Margaret, daughter of Valdemar IV, born 1353, married at 10 to King Haakon VI of Norway. In 1376 she had her first infant son, Olaf, made king of Denmark. After his death, 1387, she was regent of Denmark and Norway. In 1388, Sweden accepted her as sovereign. In 1389, she made her grand-nephew, Duke Erik of Pomerania, titular king of Denmark, Sweden, and Norway, with herself as regent. In 1397, she effected the Union of Kalmar of the three kingdoms and had Erik VII
crowned. In 1439, the three kingdoms deposed him and elected, 1440, Christopher of Bavaria king (Christopher III). On his death, 1448, the union broke up.

Succeeding rulers were unable to enforce their claims as rulers of Sweden until 1520, when Christian II conquered Sweden. He was thrown out 1522, and in 1523, Gustavus Vasa united Sweden. Denmark continued to dominate Norway until the Napoleonic wars, when Frederick VI, 1808-39, joined the Napoleonic cause after Britain destroyed the Danish fleet, 1807. In 1814, he was forced to cede Norway to Sweden and Helgoland to Britain, receiving Lauenburg. Successors Christian VIII, 1839; Frederick VII, 1848; Christian IX, 1863; Frederick VIII, 1906; Christian X, 1912; Frederick IX, 1947; Margrethe II, 1972.

Sweden

Early kings ruled at Uppsala, but did not dominate the country. Sverker, c. 1130-c. 1156, united the Swedes and Goths. In 1435 Sweden obtained the Riksdag, or parliament. After the Union of Kalmar, 1397, the Danes either ruled or harried the country until Christian II of Denmark conquered it anew, 1520. This led to a rising under Gustavus Vasa, who ruled Sweden 1523-60, and established an independent kingdom. Charles IX, 1599-1611, crowned 1604, conquered Moscow. Gustavus II Adolphus, 1611-32, was called the Lion of the North. Later rulers: Christina, 1632; Charles X Gustavus, 1654; Charles XI, 1660; Charles XII (invader of Russia and Poland, defeated at Poltava, June 28, 1709), 1697; Ulrika Eleanora, sister, elected queen, 1718; Frederick I (of Hesse), her husband, 1720; Adolphus Frederick, 1751; Gustavus III, 1771; Gustavus IV Adolphus, 1792; Charles XIII, 1809. (Union with Norway began 1814.) Charles XIV John, 1818 (he was Jean Bernadotte, Napoleon's Prince of Pontecorvo, elected 1810 to succeed Charles XIII). Charles XIV John founded the present dynasty, the House of Bernadotte: Oscar I, 1844; Charles XV, 1859; Oscar II, 1872; Gustavus V, 1907; Gustav VI Adolf, 1950; Carl XVI Gustaf, 1973.

Norway

Overcoming many rivals, Harald Haarfager, 872-930, conquered Norway, Orkneys, and Shetlands. Olaf I, great-grandson, 995-1000, brought Christianity into Norway, Iceland, and Greenland. In 1035 Magnus the Good also became king of Denmark. Haakon V, 1299-1319, had married his daughter to Erik of Sweden. Their son, Magnus, became ruler of Norway and Sweden at 6. His son, Haakon VI, married Margaret of Denmark; their son Olaf IV became king of Norway and Denmark, followed by Margaret's regency and the Union of Kalmar, 1397.

In 1450, Norway became subservient to Denmark. Christian IV, 1588-1648, founded Christiania, now Oslo. After Napoleonic wars, when Denmark ceded Norway to Sweden, a strong nationalist movement forced recognition of Norway as an independent kingdom united with Sweden under the Swedish kings, 1814-1905. In 1905, the union was dissolved, and Prince Charles of Denmark became Haakon VII. He died Sept. 21, 1957; succeeded by son, Olav V. Olav V died Jan. 17, 1991; succeeded by son, Harald V.

Rulers of the Netherlands and Belgium

The Netherlands (Holland)

William Frederick, Prince of Orange, led a revolt against French rule, 1813; crowned king, 1815. Belgium seceded Oct. 4, 1830, after a revolt. The secession was ratified by the two kingdoms by treaty, Apr. 19, 1839.

Succession: William II, son, 1840; William III, son, 1849; Wilhelmina, daughter of William III and his 2nd wife, Princess Emma of Waldeck, 1890; Wilhelmina abdicated, Sept. 4, 1948, in favor of daughter, Juliana. Juliana abdicated, Apr. 30, 1980, in favor of daughter, Beatrix.

Belgium

A national congress elected Prince Leopold of Saxe-Coburg as king; he took the throne July 21, 1831, as Leopold I.

Succession: Leopold II, son, 1865; Albert I, nephew of Leopold II, 1909; Leopold III, son of Albert, 1934; Prince Charles, Regent 1944; Leopold returned 1950, yielded powers to son Baudouin, Prince Royal, Aug. 6, 1950, abdicated July 16, 1951. Baudouin I took throne July 17, 1951, died July 31, 1993; succeeded by brother, Albert II.

Rulers of Modern Italy

After the fall of Napoleon in 1814, the Congress of Vienna, 1815, restored Italy as a political patchwork, comprising the Kingdom of Naples and Sicily, the Papal States, and smaller units. Piedmont and Genoa were awarded to Sardinia, ruled by King Victor Emmanuel I of Savoy.

United Italy emerged under the leadership of Camillo, Count di Cavour (1810-61), Sardinian prime minister. Agitation was led by Giuseppe Mazzini (1805-72) and Giuseppe Garibaldi (1807-82), soldier; Victor Emmanuel I abdicated 1821. After a brief regency for a brother, Charles Albert was king, 1831-49, abdicating when defeated by the Austrians at Novara. Succeeded by Victor Emmanuel II, 1849-61.

In 1859 France forced Austria to cede Lombardy to Sardinia, which gave rights to Savoy and Nice to France. In 1860, Garibaldi led 1,000 volunteers in a campaign, took Sicily and expelled the King of Naples. In 1860 the House of Savoy annexed Tuscany, Parma, Modena, Romagna, the Two Sicilys, the Marches, and Umbria. Victor Emmanuel assumed the title of King of Italy at Turin Mar. 17, 1861.

In 1866, Victor Emmanuel allied with Prussia in the Austro-Prussian War, and with Prussia's victory, received Venetia. On Sept. 20, 1870, his troops under Gen. Raffaele Cadorna entered Rome and took over the Papal States, ending the temporal power of the Roman Catholic Church.

Succession: Umberto I, 1878, assassinated 1900; Victor Emmanuel III, 1900, abdicated 1946, died 1947; Humbert II, 1946, ruled a month. In 1921 Benito Mussolini (1883-1945) formed the Fascist party; he became prime minister Oct. 31, 1922. He entered World War II as an ally of Hitler. He was deposed July 25, 1943.

At a plebiscite June 2, 1946, Italy voted for a republic; Premier Alcide de Gasperi became chief of state June 13, 1946. On June 28, 1946, the Constituent Assembly elected Enrico de Nicola, Liberal, provisional president. Successive presidents: Luigi Einaudi, elected May 11, 1948; Giovanni Gronchi, Apr. 29, 1955; Antonio Segni, May 6, 1962; Giuseppe Saragat, Dec. 28, 1964; Giovanni Leone, Dec. 29, 1971; Alessandro Pertini, July 9, 1978; Francesco Cossiga, July 3, 1985; Oscar Luigi Scalfaro, May 28, 1992; Carlo Azeglio Ciampi, May 18, 1999; Giorgio Napolitano, May 15, 2006.

Rulers of Spain

From 8th to 11th centuries Spain was dominated by the Moors (Arabs and Berbers). The Christian reconquest established small kingdoms (Asturias, Aragon, Castile, Catalonia, Leon, Navarre, and Valencia). In 1474 Isabella, b. 1451, became Queen of Castile and Leon. Her husband, Ferdinand, b. 1452, inherited Aragon, 1479, with Catalonia, Valencia, and the Balearic Islands, became Ferdinand V of Castile. By Isabella's request Pope Sixtus IV established the Inquisition, 1478. Last Moorish kingdom, Granada, fell 1492. Columbus opened New World of colonies, 1492. Isabella died 1504, succeeded by her daughter, Juana "the Mad," but Ferdinand ruled until his death in 1516.

Charles I, b. 1500, son of Juana, grandson of Ferdinand and Isabella, and of Maximilian I of Hapsburg, succeeded later as Holy Roman Emperor, Charles V, 1520; abdicated 1556. Philip II, son, 1556-98, inherited only Spanish throne; conquered Portugal, fought Turks, sent Armada vs. England. Married to Mary I of England, 1554-58. Succession: Philip III, 1598-1621; Philip IV, 1621-65; Charles II, 1665-1700, left Spain to Philip of Anjou, grandson of Louis XIV, who as Philip V, 1700-46, founded Bourbon dynasty; Ferdinand VI, 1746-59; Charles III, 1759-88; Charles IV, 1788-1808, abdicated.

Napoleon now dominated politics and made his brother Joseph King of Spain, 1808, but the Spanish ousted him in 1813. Ferdinand VII, 1808, 1814-33, lost American colonies (except Cuba, Puerto Rico); succeeded by daughter Isabella II, aged 3, with wife Maria Christina of Naples regent until 1843. Isabella deposed by revolution, 1868. Elected king by the Cortes (parliament), Amadeo of Savoy, 1870, abdicated 1873. First republic, 1873-74. Alfonso XII, son of Isabella, 1875-85. His posthumous son was Alfonso XIII, with his mother, Queen Maria Christina regent. Spanish-American War, 1898, Spain lost Cuba, gave up Puerto Rico, Philippines, Sulu Isls., Marianas. Alfonso took throne, 1902, aged 16, married British Princess Victoria Eugenia of Battenberg, 1906. Dictatorship of Primo de Rivera, 1923-30, precipitated revolution of 1931. Alfonso agreed to leave without formal abdication. Monarchy abolished; the second republic established, with socialist backing. Niceto Alcala Zamora was president until 1936, when Manuel Azaña was chosen.

In July 1936, the army in Morocco revolted against the government and General Francisco Franco led the troops into Spain. The revolution succeeded by Feb. 1939, when Azaña resigned. Franco became chief of state, with provisions that if he was incapacitated, the Regency Council by two-thirds vote could propose a king to the Cortes, which needed to have a two-thirds majority to elect him.

Alfonso XIII died in Rome Feb. 28, 1941, aged 54. His property and citizenship had been restored.

A law restoring the monarchy was approved in a 1947 referendum. Prince Juan Carlos, b. 1938, grandson of Alfonso XIII, was designated by Franco and the Cortes in 1969 as future king and chief of state. Franco died in office, Nov. 20, 1975; Juan Carlos I proclaimed king, Nov. 22.

Rulers of Russia; Leaders of the USSR and Russian Federation

First ruler to consolidate Slavic tribes was Rurik, leader of the Russians who established himself at Novgorod, 862 CE. He and his immediate successors had Scandinavian affiliations. They moved to Kiev after 972 and ruled as Dukes of Kiev. In 988, Vladimir was converted and adopted the Byzantine Greek Orthodox service, later modified by Slav influences. Important as organizer and lawgiver was Yaroslav, 1019-54, whose daughters married kings of Norway, Hungary, and France. His grandson, Vladimir II (Monomakh), 1113-25, was progenitor of several rulers, but in 1169, Andrew Bogolubski overthrew Kiev and began the line known as Grand Dukes of Vladimir.

Of the Grand Dukes of Vladimir, Alexander Nevsky, 1246-63, had a son, Daniel, first to be called Duke of Muscovy (Moscow), who ruled 1263-1303. His successors became Grand Dukes of Muscovy. After Dmitri III Donskoi defeated the Tatars in 1380, they also became Grand Dukes of all Russia. Tatar independence and considerable territorial expansion were achieved under Ivan III, 1462-1505.

Tsars of Muscovy: Ivan III was referred to in church ritual as Tsar. He married Sofia, niece of the last Byzantine emperor. His successor, Basil III, died in 1533 when Basil's son Ivan was only 3. He became Ivan IV, "the Terrible," crowned 1547 as Tsar of all the Russias, ruled until 1584. Under the weak rule of his son, Feodor I, 1584-98, Boris Godunov had control. The dynasty died, and after years of tribal strife and intervention by Polish and Swedish armies, the Russians united under 17-year-old Michael Romanov, distantly related to Ivan IV's first wife. He ruled 1613-45, established the Romanov line. Fourth ruler after Michael was Peter I.

Tsars, or Emperors, of Russia (Romanovs): Peter I, 1682-1725, known as Peter the Great, took title of Emperor in 1721. His successors and dates of accession were Catherine, his widow, 1725; Peter II, his grandson, 1727; Anne, Duchess of Courland, 1730, daughter of Peter the Great's brother, Tsar Ivan V; Ivan VI, 1740, great-grandson of Ivan V, while still a child, kept in prison and murdered, 1764; Elizabeth, daughter of Peter I, 1741; Peter III, grandson of Peter I, 1761, deposed 1762 for his consort, Catherine II, former princess of Anhalt Zerbst (Germany), who is known as Catherine the Great; Paul I, her son, 1796, killed 1801; Alexander I, son of Paul, 1801, defeated Napoleon; Nicholas I, his brother, 1825; Alexander II, son of Nicholas, 1855, assassinated 1881 by terrorists; Alexander III, son, 1881. Nicholas II, son, 1894-1917, last Tsar of Russia, was forced to abdicate by the March 1917 Revolu-

tion that followed losses to Germany in WWI. The Tsar, Empress, Tsarevich (Crown Prince), and Tsar's 4 daughters were murdered by the Bolsheviks in Yekaterinburg, July 16, 1918.

Provisional Government: premiers, Prince Georgi Lvov, followed by Alexander Kerensky, 1917.

Union of Soviet Socialist Republics

Bolshevik Revolution, Nov. 7, 1917, removed Kerensky from power; council of People's Commissars formed; Lenin (Vladimir Ilyich Ulyanov) became premier. Lenin died Jan. 21, 1924. Aleksei Rykov (executed 1938) and V. M. Molotov held the office, but actual ruler was Joseph Stalin (Joseph Vissarionovich Djugashvili), general secretary of the Central Committee of the Communist Party. Stalin became president of the Council of Ministers (premier) May 7, 1941; died Mar. 5, 1953. Succeeded by Georgi M. Malenkov, as head of the Council and premier. Malenkov also briefly served as first secretary of Central Committee before giving up position to Nikita S. Khrushchev. Malenkov resigned Feb. 8, 1955, became deputy premier, was dropped July 3, 1957. Marshal Nikolai A. Bulganin became premier Feb. 8, 1955, was demoted, and Khrushchev became premier Mar. 27, 1958.

Khrushchev was ousted Oct. 14-15, 1964, replaced by Leonid I. Brezhnev as first secretary of the party and by Aleksei N. Kosygin as premier. On June 16, 1977, Brezhnev also took office as president. He died Nov. 10, 1982; 2 days later the Central Committee elected former KGB head Yuri V. Andropov president. Andropov died Feb. 9, 1984; on Feb. 13, Konstantin U. Chernenko chosen by Central Committee as its general secretary. Chernenko died Mar. 10, 1985; Mar. 11, he was succeeded as general secretary by Mikhail Gorbachev, who replaced Andrei Gromyko as president on Oct. 1, 1988. Gorbachev resigned Dec. 25, 1991, and the Soviet Union officially disbanded the next day. Each of the 15 former Soviet constituent republics became independent.

Post-Soviet Russia

After adopting a degree of sovereignty, the Russian Republic held elections in June 1991. Boris Yeltsin was sworn in July 10, 1991, as Russia's first elected president. With the Dec. 1991 dissolution of the Soviet Union, Russia (officially Russian Federation) became a founding member of the Commonwealth of Independent States. On Dec. 31, 1999, Yeltsin stepped down as president; he named Vladimir Putin his interim successor. Putin won a presidential election Mar. 26, 2000, and was reelected Mar. 14, 2004.

Leaders in the South American Wars of Liberation

Francisco Antonio Gabriel Miranda (1750-1816), Jose Francisco de San Martin (1778-1850), and Simon Bolivar (1783-1830) led early 19th-century struggles of South American nations to free themselves from Spain. All three, and their contemporaries, operated in periods of factional strife, during which soldiers and civilians suffered.

Miranda, a Venezuela who had served with the French in the American Revolution and commanded parts of the French Revolutionary armies in the Netherlands, attempted to start a revolt in Venezuela in 1806 and failed. In 1810, with British and American backing, he returned and was briefly dictator, until the British withdrew their support. In 1812 he was overcome by the royalists in Venezuela and taken prisoner, dying in a Spanish prison in 1816.

San Martin was born in Argentina and during 1789-1811, served in campaigns of the Spanish armies in Europe and Africa. He first joined the independence movement in Argentina in 1812 and in 1817 invaded Chile with 4,000 men over the mountain passes. Here he and Gen. Bernardo O'Higgins (1778-1842) defeated the Spaniards at Chacabuco, 1817; O'Higgins was named Liberator and became first director of Chile, 1817-23. In 1821 San Martin occupied Lima and Callao, Peru, and became protector of Peru.

Bolivar was born in Venezuela, the son of an aristocratic family. He first served under Miranda in 1812 and in 1813

captured Caracas, where he was named Liberator. Forced out next year by civil strife, he led a campaign that captured Bogota in 1814. In 1817 he was again in control of Venezuela and was named dictator. He organized Nueva Granada with the help of General Francisco de Paula Santander (1792-1840). By joining Nueva Granada, Venezuela, and the area that is now Panama and Ecuador, the republic of Colombia was formed, with Bolivar president. After numerous setbacks he decisively defeated the Spaniards in the second battle of Carabobo, Venezuela, June 24, 1821.

In May 1822, Gen. Antonio Jose de Sucre, Bolivar's lieutenant, took Quito. Bolivar went to Guayaquil to confer with San Martin, who resigned as protector of Peru. With a new army of Colombians and Peruvians, Bolivar defeated the Spaniards in a battle at Junin in 1824 and cleared Peru.

De Sucre organized Charcas (Upper Peru) as Republica Bolivar (now Bolivia) and acted as president in place of Bolivar, who wrote its constitution. De Sucre defeated the Spanish faction of Peru at Ayacucho, Dec. 19, 1824.

Continued civil strife finally caused the Colombian federation to break apart. Santander turned against Bolivar, but the latter defeated him and banished him. In 1828 Bolivar gave up the presidency he had held precariously for 14 years. He became ill from tuberculosis and died Dec. 17, 1830. He is buried in the national pantheon in Caracas.

Governments of China

Where dynastic dates overlap, the rulers or events referred to appeared in different areas of China.

c. 1994-c. 1766 BCE	Hsia dynasty, first hereditary Chinese dynasty
c. 1766-c. 1027 BCE	Shang dynasty
c. 1027-770 BCE	Western Chou dynasty, capital near site of present-day Xi'an
770-256 BCE	Eastern Chou dynasty, new capital established at Luoyang
403-221 BCE	Period of the Warring States
221-206 BCE	Ch'in dynasty, quasi-feudal states unified for first time; name of China derived from this dynasty
206 BCE-9 CE	Earlier, or Western Han dynasty, founded by rebel leader Liu Pang, zenith of power under Emperor Wu Ti, 140-87 BCE, Chinese state expanded
9-23	Hsin dynasty, established by courtier Wang Mang, who deposed infant emperor for whom he had been acting as regent
25-220	Later, or Eastern Han dynasty
220-265[1]	Wei dynasty, established by son of Han general Ts'ao Ts'ao
221-263[1]	Shu Han dynasty in southwest China
222-280[1]	Wu dynasty in southeast China
265-317	Western Chin dynasty, established by Ssu-ma Yen, Wei dynasty general
317-420	Eastern Chin dynasty, established by prince of Ssu-ma family
420-589	Southern dynasties, four short-lived dynasties with capital at Chien-k'ang (present-day Nanjing)
589-618	Sui dynasty, reunified China; first emperor was Yang Chien, military servant who usurped throne of non-Chinese Northern Chou, 581
618-906	T'ang dynasty, founded by Li Yuan, who led rebellion against the Sui. Early rulers included former imperial concubine Empress Wu, 683-705; Hsuan Tsung, 712-56
907-960	Five Dynasties, period of disunion with short-lived dynasties in North China, 10 independent states mostly in South China
907-1125	Liao dynasty, of Khitan Mongols, capital at Yen-ching (present-day Beijing)
960-1126	Northern Sung dynasty, established by military leader Chao K'uang-yin, capital at Kaifeng
1122-1234	Chin dynasty, of Juchen people of Manchuria; drove Sung out of northern China
1127-1279	Southern Sung dynasty, capital at Lin-an (present-day Hangzhou)
1279-1368	Yuan dynasty, of Mongols; Kublai Khan, grandson of Genghis Khan, high point of Mongol power
1368-1644	Ming dynasty, founded by rebel leader Chu Yuan-chang, former Buddhist monk. Country again under Chinese rule, capital in present-day Nanjing, then Beijing after defeat of Mongolian tribes
1644-1912	Manchu, or Ch'ing dynasty, under Manchu rule with capital at Chiang-ning (present-day Nanjing). Power of Chinese empire reached highest point in its 2,000-year history. Last imperial dynasty; Hsuan T'ung, or Pu Yi, last emperor. Sun Yat-sen led revolution, 1911. Republic of China formed, 1912
1912-1949	Rep. of China, Gen. Yüan Shih-k'ai elected first president. Power passed to provincial warlords with Yüan's death, 1916. Gen. Chiang Kai-shek sought to reunify China under Kuomintang (Nationalist party) rule, 1926; Kuomintang established new national government at Nanjing, 1928. War with Japan, then civil war, led to Nationalist authority collapse, Communist declaration of People's Rep. of China, 1949

(1) Also known as the period of the Three Kingdoms because of warfare between the Wei, Shu Han, and Wu dynasties.

Leaders of People's Republic of China Since 1949

Mao Zedong	Chairman, 1949-59; Chinese Communist Party (CPC) Chairman, 1949-76
Zhou Enlai	Premier, 1949-76; foreign minister, 1949-76
Deng Xiaoping	Deputy Premier, 1952-66, 1973-76; "paramount leader," 1977-97
Liu Shaoqi	Chairman, 1959-68
Hua Guofeng	Premier, 1976-80; CPC Chairman, 1976-81
Hu Yaobang	CPC General Secretary, 1980-87; CPC Chairman 1981-82
Zhao Ziyang	Premier, 1980-87; CPC General Secretary, 1987-89
Li Xiannian	President, 1983-88
Yang Shangkun	President, 1988-93
Li Peng	Premier, 1988-98
Jiang Zemin	CPC General Secretary, 1989-2002; President, 1993-2003
Zhu Rongji	Premier, 1998-2003
Hu Jintao	CPC General Secretary, 2002- ; President, 2003-
Wen Jiabao	Premier, 2003-

Historical Periods of Japan

c. 300-592	Yamato	Conquest of Yamato plain, c. 300 CE
592-710	Asuka	Accession of Empress Suiko, 592
710-794	Nara	Heijo (Nara) completed, 710; capital moved to Nagaoka, 784
794-1185	Heian	Heian (Kyoto) completed, 794
858-1160	Fujiwara	Fujiwara-no-Yoshifusa became regent, 858
1160-1185	Taira	Taira-no-Kiyomoro assumed control, 1160; Minamoto-no-Yoritomo victor over Taira, 1185
1192-1333	Kamakura	Yoritomo became shogun, 1192
1334-1392	Namboku	Emperor Godaigo restored, 1334; Godaigo established Southern Court at Yoshino, 1336
1392-1573	Muromachi	Unification of Southern and Northern Courts, 1392
1467-1600	Sengoku	Onin war began, 1467
1573-1603	Momoyama	Oda Nobunaga entered Kyoto, 1568, deposes last Ashikaga shogun, 1573. Tokugawa Ieyasu victor at Sekigahara, 1600
1603-1867	Edo	Ieyasu became shogun, 1603
1868-1912	Meiji	Emperor Mutsuhito (Meiji) ascended throne, 1867; Meiji Restoration and Charter Oath, 1868
1912-1926	Taisho	Accession of Emperor Yoshihito, 1912
1926-1989	Showa	Accession of Emperor Hirohito, 1926
1989-	Heisei	Accession of Emperor Akihito, 1989

WORLD EXPLORATION AND GEOGRAPHY
Early Explorers of the Western Hemisphere
Reviewed by G. A. Clark, Ph.D.

In the light of recent discoveries, theories about how and when the first people arrived in the western hemisphere are being reconsidered. Genetic evidence suggests that beginning 14,000 years before the present (BP), the earliest immigrants crossed a 1,000 km-wide "land bridge" between Siberia and Alaska and spread rapidly south through the Americas to S America's southern tip by c. 10,700 BP. Kennewick Man, found in 1996 in Washington's Columbia River gorge (9,600-9,200 BP), and "Luzia" from Brazil (11,500 BP) are examples of these early arrivals. Modern Native Americans appear to be descended from peoples indigenous to N and central Asia who arrived in subsequent waves of migration. A growing body of genetic, skeletal, and linguistic evidence documents their migration throughout the Americas.

Archaeologists have confirmed evidence of habitation dating to at least 12,900 BP at sites located on the shores of ancient lakes in Chile's Atacama Desert. There is also growing support for the contemporary settlement of the lowlands of south-central Chile, and at eight other sites in Brazil, Chile, and Argentina. Because a glacier covered much of N America from c. 20,000 to 13,000 years ago, those who settled in S America might have traveled there in vessels skirting the pack ice along the west coast, spread south through a controversial 'ice-free corridor,' or arrived before glaciations blocked migration from the north. Controversial skeletal evidence from a burial at Santana do Riacho in Brazil (9460 BP) suggests that some of the early immigrants who came via the land bridge from Siberia may have originated in Africa.

Long before Europeans arrived, the Americas were—for the most part—populated by hunter-gatherers and small-scale horticulturalists. In a few areas (SE U.S., Mesoamerica, Peru, and Chile), complex chiefdoms and state-level societies appeared. Irrigation canals dating to 4700 BP provide evidence for the origins of large-scale agriculture in Peru's Andes Mountains. The earliest known state in the Americas occupied a 700-square-mile area spanning four river valleys in coastal Peru between 3500 and 500 BP.

Norsemen (Norwegian Vikings sailing out of Iceland and Greenland), led by Leif Ericson, are credited with having been the first Europeans to reach America, with at least five voyages occurring about 1000 CE (common era) to areas they called Helluland, Markland, and Vinland-possibly what are known today as Baffin Island, Labrador, and Newfoundland or further south in New England. L'Anse aux Meadows, on the N tip of Newfoundland, is the only documented settlement, with evidence of a church dating to c. 1000 CE.

Sustained contact between the hemispheres began with the first voyage of Christopher Columbus (b. Cristoforo Colombo, c. 1451, near Genoa, Italy). Columbus made four voyages to the New World while trying to find a route to India for the Spanish monarchs Ferdinand II and Isabella. He left Palos, Spain, Aug. 3, 1492, with 88 men and landed at San Salvador (Watling Islands, Bahamas), Oct. 12, 1492. His fleet included three vessels, the *Niña*, *Pinta*, and *Santa María*. He also visited Cuba, Hispaniola, and many smaller Caribbean islands populated by the now-extinct Taino Indians. A second expedition left Cadíz, Spain, Sept. 25, 1493, with 17 ships and 1,400 men, reaching the island of Dominica, in the Lesser Antilles, on Nov. 3rd. His third voyage took him from Sanlucar, Spain (May 30, 1498, with 6 ships), to Trinidad and the adjacent coast of S America. A fourth voyage departed Cadíz on May 9, 1502, and reached the E coast of Mexico, Honduras, Panama, and Santiago (the present-day Jamaica). Columbus died on May 20, 1506, convinced he had reached Asia by sailing west.

In N America, John and Sebastian Cabot, Italian explorers sailing for the English crown, reached Newfoundland and possibly Nova Scotia in 1497. John's second voyage (1498), seeking the fabled Northwest Passage, a new trade route to Asia, resulted in the loss of his entire fleet. For most of the 16th century, exploration of the New World was dominated by Spain and Portugal.

In 1497 and 1499 Amerigo Vespucci (for whom the Americas are named), an Italian explorer sailing for Spain, passed along the N and E coasts of South America. He was the first to argue that the newly discovered lands were previously unknown, and not part of Asia.

Other early explorations are listed below.

Year	Explorer	Nationality (sponsor, if different)	Area reached or explored
1497-98	Vasco da Gama	Portuguese	Cape of Good Hope (Africa), India
1499	Alonso de Ojeda	Spanish	N South American coast, Venezuela
1500, Feb.	Vicente Yañez Pinzon	Spanish	S. American coast, Amazon R.
1500, Apr.	Pedro Álvarez Cabral	Portuguese	Brazil
1501	Rodrigo de Bastidas	Spanish	Central America
1513	Vasco Núñez de Balboa	Spanish	Panama, Pacific Ocean
1513	Juan Ponce de León	Spanish	Florida, Yucatán Peninsula
1515	Juan de Solis	Spanish	Río de la Plata
1519	Alonso de Pineda	Spanish	Mouth of Mississippi R.
1519	Hernán Cortés	Spanish	Mexico
1519-20	Ferdinand Magellan	Portuguese (Spanish)	Straits of Magellan, Tierra del Fuego
1524	Giovanni da Verrazano	Italian (French)	Atlantic coast, incl. New York harbor
1528	Cabeza de Vaca	Spanish	Texas coast and interior
1532	Francisco Pizarro	Spanish	Peru
1534	Jacques Cartier	French	Canada, Gulf of St. Lawrence
1536	Pedro de Mendoza	Spanish	Buenos Aires
1539	Francisco de Ulloa	Spanish	California coast
1539-41	Hernando de Soto	Spanish	Mississippi R., near Memphis
1539	Marcos de Niza	Italian (Spanish)	SW United States
1540	Francisco de Coronado	Spanish	SW United States
1540	Hernando Alarcon	Spanish	Colorado R.
1540	Garcia de Lopez Cardenas	Spanish	Colorado, Grand Canyon
1541	Francisco de Orellana	Spanish	Amazon R.
1542	Juan Rodriguez Cabrillo	Portuguese (Spanish)	W Mexico, San Diego harbor
1565	Pedro Menéndez de Aviles	Spanish	St. Augustine, FL
1576	Sir Martin Frobisher	English	Frobisher Bay, Canada
1577-80	Sir Francis Drake	English	California coast
1582	Antonio de Espejo	Spanish	Southwest U.S. (New Mexico)
1584	Amadas & Barlow (for Raleigh)	English	Virginia
1585-87	Sir Walter Raleigh's men	English	Roanoke Isl., NC
1595	Sir Walter Raleigh	English	Orinoco R.
1603-09	Samuel de Champlain	French	Canadian interior, Lake Champlain
1607	Capt. John Smith	English	Atlantic coast
1609-10	Henry Hudson	English (Dutch)	Hudson R., Hudson Bay
1634	Jean Nicolet	French	Lake Michigan, Wisconsin
1673	Jacques Marquette, Louis Jolliet	French	Mississippi R., S to Arkansas
1682	Robert Cavelier, sieur de La Salle	French	Mississippi R., S to Gulf of Mexico
1727-29	Vitus Bering	Danish (Russian)	Bering Strait and Alaska
1789	Sir Alexander Mackenzie	Canadian	NW Canada
1804-06	Meriwether Lewis and William Clark	American	Missouri R., Rocky Mts., Columbia R.

Arctic Exploration

Early Explorers

1587: John Davis (Eng.). Davis Strait to Sanderson's Hope, 72°12′N.

1596: Willem Barents and Jacob van Heemskerck (Holland). Discovered Bear Isl., touched NW tip of Spitsbergen, 79°49′ N, rounded Novaya Zemlya, wintered at Ice Haven.

1607: Henry Hudson (Eng.). North along Greenland's E coast to Cape Hold-with-Hope, 73°30′, then N of Spitsbergen to 80°23′. Explored Hudson's Touches (Jan Mayen).

1616: William Baffin and Robert Bylot (Eng.). Baffin Bay to Smith Sound.

1728: Vitus Bering (Russ.). Sailed through strait (Bering) proving Asia and America are separate.

1733-40: Great Northern Expedition (Russ.). Surveyed Siberian Arctic coast.

1741: Vitus Bering (Russ.). Sighted Alaska, named Mount St. Elias. His lieutenant, Chirikof, explored coast.

1771: Samuel Hearne (Hudson's Bay Co.). Overland from Prince of Wales Fort (Churchill) on Hudson Bay to mouth of Coppermine R.

1778: James Cook (Brit.). Through Bering Strait to Icy Cape, AK, and North Cape, Siberia.

1789: Alexander Mackenzie (North West Co., Brit.). Montreal to mouth of Mackenzie River.

1806: William Scoresby (Brit.). N of Spitsbergen to 81°30′.

1820-23: Ferdinand von Wrangel (Russ.). Surveyed Siberian Arctic coast. His exploration joined James Cook's at North Cape, confirming separation of the continents.

1878-79: (Nils) Adolf Erik Nordenskjöld (Swed.). The 1st to navigate the Northeast Passage—an ocean route connecting Europe's North Sea, along the Arctic coast of Asia and through the Bering Sea, to the Pacific Ocean.

1881: The U.S. steamer *Jeannette*, led by Lt. Cmdr. George W. DeLong, was trapped in ice and crushed, June 1881. DeLong and 11 others died; 12 survived.

1888: Fridtjof Nansen (Nor.) crossed Greenland icecap.

1893-96: Nansen in *Fram* drifted from New Siberian Isls. to Spitsbergen; tried polar dash in 1895, reached Franz Josef Land, 86°14′N.

1897: Salomon A. Andrée (Sweden) and 2 others started in balloon from Spitsbergen, July 11, to drift across pole to U.S., and disappeared. Aug. 6, 1930, their bodies were found on White Isl., 82°57′N, 29°52′E.

1903-6: Roald Amundsen (Nor.) 1st sailed the Northwest Passage—an ocean route linking the Atlantic Ocean to the Pacific via Canada's marine waterways.

North Pole Exploration

Robert E. Peary explored Greenland's coast, 1891-92; tried for North Pole, 1893. In 1900 he reached N limit of Greenland and 83°50′N; in 1902 he reached 84°17′N; in 1906 he went from Ellesmere Isl. to 87°06′N. He sailed in the *Roosevelt*, July 1908, to winter off Cape Sheridan, Grant Land. The dash for the North Pole began Mar. 1 from Cape Columbia, Ellesmere Isl. Peary reportedly reached the pole, 90°N, Apr. 6, **1909**; however, later research suggests he may have fallen short of his goal by c. 30-60 mi. The first surface expedition independently confirmed to have reached the N Pole was that of Ralph Plaisted in 1968 (see below).

Peary had several support groups carrying supplies until the last group turned back at 87°47′ N. Peary, Matthew Henson, and 4 Eskimos proceeded with dog teams and sleds. They were said to have crossed the pole several times, then built an igloo there and remained 36 hours. Started south, Apr. 7 at 4 PM, for Cape Columbia.

1914: Donald MacMillan (U.S.). Northwest, 200 mi, from Axel Heiberg Is to seek Peary's Crocker Land.

1915-17: Vihjalmur Stefansson (Can.). Discovered Borden, Brock, Meighen, and Lougheed Isls.

1918-20: Roald Amundsen (Nor.) sailed the Northeast Passage.

1925: Amundsen and Lincoln Ellsworth (U.S.) reached 87°44′N in attempt to fly to N Pole from Spitsbergen.

1926: Richard E. Byrd and Floyd Bennett (U.S.) reputedly flew over North Pole, May 9. (Claim to have reached the pole is in dispute, however.)

1926: Amundsen, Ellsworth, and Umberto Nobile (It.) flew from Spitsbergen over N Pole May 12, to Teller, AK, in dirigible *Norge*.

1928: Nobile crossed N Pole in airship, May 24; crashed, May 25. Amundsen died attempting a rescue.

North Pole Exploration Records

On Aug. 3, 1958, submarine *Nautilus,* under Comdr. William R. Anderson, crossed the N Pole beneath the ice.

In Aug. 1960, the nuclear-powered U.S. submarine *Seadragon* (Comdr. George P. Steele 2nd) made the 1st E-W underwater transit through the Northwest Passage. Traveling submerged for the most part, it took 6 days to make the 850-mi trek from Baffin Bay to the Beaufort Sea.

On Apr. 19, 1968, Ralph Plaisted (U.S.) and 3 amateur explorers on snowmobiles became the first independently confirmed surface expedition to reach the N Pole.

On Aug. 16, 1977, the Soviet nuclear icebreaker *Arktika* became the 1st surface ship to reach the N Pole.

On Apr. 30, 1978, Naomi Uemura (Jap.) became the 1st person to reach the N Pole alone, traveling by dog sled in a 54-day, 600-mi trek over the frozen Arctic.

In Apr. 1982, Sir Ranulph Fiennes and Charles Burton, Brit. explorers, reached the N Pole and became the 1st to circle the earth from pole to pole. They had reached the S Pole 16 months earlier. The 52,000-mi trek took 3 years, involved 23 people, and cost an estimated $18 mil.

On May 2, 1986, 6 explorers reached the N Pole assisted only by dogs. They became the 1st to reach the pole without aerial logistics support since at least 1909. The explorers, Amer. Will Steger, Paul Schurke, Ann Bancroft, and Geoff Carroll, and Can. Brent Boddy and Richard Weber, completed the 500-mi journey in 56 days.

On June 15, 1995, Weber and Russ. Mikhail Malakhov became the 1st pair to make it to the N Pole and back without any mechanical assistance. The 940-mi trip, made entirely on skis, took 121 days.

On May 20, 2003, Pen Hadow (U.K.) became the 1st to reach the N Pole from Canada, solo and without resupply. The 377-mile journey across the ice took 64 days.

On April 16, 2006, Prince Albert II of Monaco became the first royal to reach the N Pole.

Antarctic Exploration

Antarctica has been approached since 1773-75, when Capt. James Cook (Brit.) reached 71°10′S. Many sea and landmarks bear names of early explorers. Fabian von Bellingshausen (Russ.) discovered Peter I and Alexander I Isls., 1819-21. Nathaniel Palmer (U.S.) traveled throughout Palmer Peninsula, 60°W, 1820, without realizing that this was a continent. Capt. John Davis (U.S.) made the 1st known landing on the continent on Feb. 7, 1821. Later, in 1823, James Weddell (Brit.) found Weddell Sea, 74°15′S, the southernmost point that had been reached.

First to announce existence of the continent of Antarctica was Charles Wilkes (U.S.), who followed the coast for 1,500 mi, 1840. Adelie Coast, 140°E, was found by Dumont d'Urville (Fr.), 1840. Ross Ice Shelf was found by James Clark Ross (Brit.), 1841-42.

1895: Leonard Kristensen (Nor.) landed a party on the coast of Victoria Land. They were the 1st ashore on the main continental mass. C. E. Borchgrevink, a member of that party, returned in 1899 with a Brit. expedition, 1st to winter on Antarctica.

1902-4: Robert Falcon Scott (Brit.) explored Edward VII Peninsula to 82°17′S, 146°33′E from McMurdo Sound.

1908-9: Ernest Shackleton (Brit.) 1st to use Manchurian ponies in Antarctic sledging. He reached 88°23′S, discovering a route on to the plateau by way of the Beardmore Glacier and pioneering the way to the pole.

1911: Roald Amundsen (Nor.) with 4 men and dog teams reached the S Pole, Dec. 14.

1912: Scott reached the pole from Ross Isl., Jan. 18, with 4 companions. None of Scott's party survived. Their bodies and expedition notes were found, Nov. 12.

1928: 1st person to use an airplane over Antarctica was Sir George Hubert Wilkins (Austral.).

1929: Richard E. Byrd (U.S.) established Little America on Bay of Whales. On 1,600-mi airplane flight begun Nov. 28, he crossed S Pole, Nov. 29, with 3 others.

1934-35: Byrd led 2nd expedition to Little America, explored 450,000 sq mi, wintered alone at 80°08´S.

1934-37: John Rymill led British Graham Land expedition; discovered Palmer Penin. is part of mainland.

1935: Lincoln Ellsworth (U.S.) flew S along E Coast of Palmer Penin., then crossed continent to Little America, making 4 landings.

1939-41: U.S. Navy plane flights discovered about 150,000 sq mi of new land.

1940: Byrd charted most of coast between Ross Sea and Palmer Penin.

1946-47: U.S. Navy undertook Operation Highjump, commanded by Byrd, included 13 ships and 4,000 men. Airplanes photomapped coastline and penetrated beyond pole.

1946-48: Ronne Antarctic Research Expedition Comdr., Finn Ronne, USNR, determined the Antarctic to be only one continent with no strait between Weddell Sea and Ross Sea; explored 250,000 sq mi of land by flights to 79°S.

1955-57: U.S. Navy's Operation Deep Freeze led by Adm. Byrd. Supporting U.S. scientific efforts for the International Geophysical Year (IGY), the operation established 5 coastal stations fronting the Indian, Pacific, and Atlantic oceans and also 3 interior stations; explored more than 1,000,000 sq mi in Wilkes Land.

1957-58: During the IGY, July 1957 through Dec. 1958, scientists from 12 countries conducted Antarctic research at a network of some 60 stations on Antarctica.

Dr. Vivian E. Fuchs led a 12-person Trans-Antarctic Expedition on the 1st land crossing of Antarctica. Starting from the Weddell Sea, they reached Scott Station, Mar. 2, 1958, after traveling 2,158 mi in 98 days.

1958: A group of 5 U.S. scientists led by Edward C. Thiel, seismologist, moving by tractor from Ellsworth Station on Weddell Sea, identified a huge mountain range, 5,000 ft

above the ice sheet and 9,000 ft above sea level. The range, originally seen by a Navy plane, was named the Dufek Massif, for Rear Adm. George Dufek.

1959: Argentina, Australia, Belgium, Chile, France, Japan, New Zealand, Norway, South Africa, USSR, U.K., and U.S. signed a treaty suspending territorial claims for 30 yrs. and reserving the continent, S of 60°S, for research.

1961-62: Scientists discovered the Bentley Trench, running from Ross Ice Shelf into Marie Byrd Land, near the end of the Ellsworth Mts., toward the Weddell Sea.

1962: Nuclear power plant online at McMurdo Sound.

1963: On Feb. 22, a U.S. plane made the region's longest nonstop flight from McMurdo Station S past the pole to Shackleton Mts., SE to the "Area of Inaccessibility," and back to McMurdo Station covering 3,600 mi in 10 hrs.

1964: New Zealanders mapped the mountain area from from Cape Adare W some 400 mi to Pennell Glacier.

1985: Igor A. Zotikov, a Russian researcher, discovered sediments in the Ross Ice Shelf that seem to support the continental drift theory. Ocean Drilling Project finds that the ice sheets of E Antarctica are 37 million yrs. old.

1989: Victoria Murden and Shirley Metz became both the 1st women and the 1st Americans to reach the S Pole overland when they arrived with 9 others on Jan. 17, 1989.

1991: 24 nations approved a protocol to the 1959 Antarctica Treaty, Oct. 4. New conservation provisions, including banning oil and other mineral exploration for 50 yrs.

1994: On Dec. 25, after 50-day trek, Liv Arnesen (Nor.) became 1st woman to ski alone and unaided to the S Pole.

1995: On Dec. 22, a Norwegian, Borge Ousland, reached the S Pole in the fastest time on skis: 44 days.

1996-97 Ousland became 1st person to traverse Antarctica alone; reached S Pole Dec. 19, 1996; traveled 1,675 mi in 64 days, ending Jan. 18, 1997.

2000-2001: On Feb. 11, Ann Bancroft and Liv Arnesen (Nor.) became 1st women to ski unaided across Antarctica. The 1,717-mile journey took 94 days.

Volcanoes

Sources: *Volcanoes of the World*, Geoscience Press; Global Volcanism Network, Smithsonian Institution

Roughly 540 volcanoes are known to have erupted during historical times. Nearly 75% of these historically active volcanoes lie along the so-called **Ring of Fire**, running along the W coast of the Americas from the southern tip of Chile to Alaska, down the E coast of Asia from Kamchatka to Indonesia, and continuing from New Guinea to New Zealand. The Ring of Fire marks the boundary between the mobile tectonic plates underlying the Pacific Ocean and those of the surrounding continents. Other active regions occur along rift zones, where plates pull apart, as in Iceland, or where molten material moves up from the mantle over local "hot spots," as in Hawaii. The vast majority of the earth's volcanism occurs at submarine rift zones. For more information on volcanoes, see the Smithsonian Institution's global volcanism website at www.volcano.si.edu

Notable Volcanic Eruptions

Approximately 7,000 years ago, Mazama, a 9,900-ft volcano in southern Oregon, erupted violently, ejecting large amounts of ash and pumice and voluminous pyroclastic flows. The ash spread over the entire northwestern U.S. and as far away as Saskatchewan, Can. During the eruption, the top of the mountain collapsed, leaving a caldera 6 mi across and about a half mile deep, which filled with rainwater to form what is now called Crater Lake.

In AD 79, Vesuvio, or Vesuvius, a 4,190-ft volcano overlooking Naples Bay, became active after several centuries of apparent inactivity. On Aug. 24 of that year, a heated mud and ash flow swept down the mountain, engulfing the cities of Pompeii, Herculaneum, and Stabiae with debris more than 60 ft deep. About 10% of the population of the 3 towns were killed.

In 1883, an eruption similar to the Mazama eruption occurred on the island of Krakatau. At least 2,000 people died in pyroclastic flows on Aug. 26. The next day, the 2,640-ft peak of the volcano collapsed to 1,000 ft below sea level, sinking most of the island and killing over 3,000. A tsunami (tidal wave) generated by the collapse killed more than 31,000 people in Java and Sumatra, and eventually reached England. Ash from the eruption colored sunsets around the world for 2 years. A similar, even more powerful eruption had taken place 68 years earlier at Mt. Tambora on the Indonesian island of Sumbawa.

Date	Volcano	Deaths (est.)	Date	Volcano	Deaths (est.)
Aug. 24, AD 79	Mt. Vesuvius, Italy	16,000	May 8, 1902	Mt. Pelée, Martinique	28,000
1586	Kelut, Java, Indon.	10,000	Jan. 30, 1911	Mt. Taal, Phil.	1,400
Dec. 15, 1631	Mt. Vesuvius, Italy	4,000	May 19, 1919	Mt. Kelut, Java, Indon.	5,000
Aug. 12, 1772	Mt. Papandayan, Java, Indon.	3,000	Jan. 17-21, 1951	Mt. Lamington, New Guinea	3,000
June 8, 1783	Laki, Iceland	9,350	May 18, 1980	Mt. St. Helens, U.S.	57
May 21, 1792	Mt. Unzen, Japan	14,500	Mar. 28, 1982	El Chichon, Mex.	1,880
Apr. 10-12, 1815	Mt. Tambora, Sumbawa, Indon.	92,000[1]	Nov. 13, 1985	Nevado del Ruiz, Colombia	23,000
Aug. 26-28, 1883	Krakatau, Indon.	36,000	Aug. 21, 1986	Lake Nyos, Cameroon	1,700
Apr. 24, 1902	Santa María, Guatemala	1,000[2]	June 15, 1991	Mt. Pinatubo, Luzon, Phil.	800[3]

(1) Of these, 10,000 were directly related to the eruption; an additional 82,000 were the result of starvation and disease brought on by the event. (2) An additional 3,000 deaths due to a malaria outbreak are sometimes attributed to the eruption. (3) Of these, about 500 were associated with post-eruption lahars (volcanic mudflows), in addition to the 300 deaths caused directly by the eruption.

Notable Active Volcanoes

Active volcanoes display a wide range of activity. In this table, years are given for last display of eruptive activity, as of mid-2007; the list does not include submarine volcanoes. An eruption may involve explosive ejection of new or old fragmental material, escape of liquid lava, or both. Volcanoes are listed by height, which does not reflect eruptive magnitude.

Name (latest eruption)		Height (ft)
Africa		
Mt. Cameroon (2000)	Cameroon	13,435
Nyiragongo (2007)	Congo	11,384
Nyamuragira (2007)	Congo	10,033
Mt. Oku [Lake Nyos] (1986)	Cameroon	9,878
Ol Doinyo Lengai (2006)	Tanzania	9,718
Fogo (1995)	Cape Verde Isls.	9,281
Piton de la Fournaise (2007)	Réunion Isl., Indian O.	8,635
Karthala (2006)	Comoros	7,746
Erta Ale (2007)	Ethiopia	2,011
Antarctica		
Erebus (2007)	Ross Isl.	12,447
Deception Island (1970)	S. Shetland Isl.	1,890
Asia and Oceania		
Kliuchevskoi (2005)	Kamchatka, Russia	15,863
Kerinci (2004)	Sumatra, Indon.	12,467
Fuji (1708)	Honshu, Japan.	12,388
Tolbachik (1976)	Kamchatka, Russia	12,080
Semeru (2007)	Java, Indon.	12,060
Slamet (1999)	Java, Indon.	11,247
Raung (2002)	Java, Indon.	10,932
Shiveluch (2007)	Kamchatka, Russia	10,771
On-take (1980)	Honshu, Japan.	10,049
Merapi (2007)	Java, Indon.	9,737
Bezymianny (2006)	Kamchatka, Russia	9,455
Peuet Sague (2000)	Sumatra, Indon.	9,190
Ruapehu (2006)	New Zealand	9,176
Heard (2007)	Indian Ocean	9,006
Baitoushan (1903)	China/Korea.	9,003
Asama (2004)	Honshu, Japan.	8,425
Mayon (2006)	Luzon, Phil.	8,077
Canlaon (2006)	Negros Isls., Phil.	7,989
Niigata-Yake-yama (1998)	Honshu, Japan.	7,874
Alaid (1996)	Kuril Isl., Russia	7,674
Ulawun (2007)	Papua New Guinea	7,657
Chokai (1974)	Honshu, Japan.	7,326
Galunggung (1984)	Java, Indon.	7,113
Azuma (1977)	Honshu, Japan.	6,676
Tongariro (Ngauruhoe) (1977)	New Zealand	6,489
Sangeang Api (1988)	Lesser Sunda Isl., Indon.	6,394
Nasu (1963)	Honshu, Japan.	6,283
Karkar (1979)	Papua New Guinea	6,033
Tiatia (1981)	Kuril Isl., Russia	5,968
Bandai (1888)	Honshu, Japan.	5,968
Manam (2007)	Papua New Guinea	5,928
Kuju (1996)	Kyushu, Japan.	5,876
Karangetang (Api Siau) (2007)	Sangihe Isls., Indon.	5,853
Soputan (2006)	Sulawesi, Indon.	5,853
Bagana (2007)	Papua New Guinea	5,741
Kelut (1990)	Java, Indon.	5,679
Adatara (1996)	Honshu, Japan.	5,636
Gamalama (2003)	Halmahera, Indon.	5,627
Kirishima (1992)	Kyushu, Japan.	5,577
Gamkonora (1987)	Halmahera, Indon.	5,364
Aso (2004)	Kyushu, Japan.	5,223
Lokon-Empung (2003)	Sulawesi, Indon.	5,184
Bulusan (2007)	Luzon, Phil.	5,134
Karymsky (2007)	Kamchatka, Russia	5,039
Unzen (1996)	Kyushu, Japan.	4,921
Akan (2006)	Hokkaido, Japan	4,918
Sarychev Peak (1989)	Kuril Isl., Russia	4,908
Pinatubo (1993)	Luzon, Phil.	4,875
Lopevi (2006)	Vanuatu	4,636
Akita-Yake-yama (1997)	Honshu, Japan.	4,482
Dukono (2007)	Halmahera, Indon.	4,380
Ambrym (2005)	Vanuatu	4,377
Langila (2007)	Papua New Guinea	4,363
Awu (2004)	Sangihe Isl., Indon.	4,331
Akademia Nauk (1996)	Kamchatka, Russia	3,871
Komaga-take (2000)	Hokkaido, Japan	3,711
Sakura-jima (2007)	Kyushu, Japan.	3,665
Miyake-jima (2006)	Izu Isls., Japan.	2,674
Krakatau (2001)	Indonesia	2,667
Suwanose-jima (2007)	Ryukyu Isls., Japan	2,621
Gaua (1982)	Vanuatu	2,615
Oshima (1990)	Izu Isls., Japan.	2,507
Usu (2001)	Hokkaido, Japan	2,418
Rabaul (2007)	Papua New Guinea	2,257
Pagan (2006)	N. Mariana Isl.	1,870
Taal (1977)	Luzon, Phil.	1,312
Yasur (2007)	Tanna Island, Vanuatu	1,184

Name (latest eruption)		Height (ft)
White Island (2001)	Bay of Plenty, New Zealand	1,053
McDonald Islands (2005)	Indian O., Australia	755
Central America and Caribbean		
Tacaná (1986)	Guatemala	13,320
Acatenango (1972)	Guatemala	13,044
Santa María (2007)	Guatemala	12,375
Fuego (2007)	Guatemala	12,346
Irazú (1994)	Costa Rica	11,260
Turrialba (1866)	Costa Rica	10,958
Póas (2006)	Costa Rica	8,884
Pacaya (2007)	Guatemala	8,373
San Miguel (2002)	El Salvador	6,988
Rincón de la Vieja (1998)	Costa Rica	6,286
San Cristóbal (2006)	Nicaragua	5,725
Concepción (2005)	Nicaragua	5,577
Arenal (2007)	Costa Rica	5,479
Soufrière Guadeloupe (1977)	Guadeloupe	4,813
Pelée (1932)	Martinique	4,583
Momotombo (1905)	Nicaragua	4,255
Soufrière St. Vincent (1979)	St. Vincent.	4,003
Soufrière Hills (2007)	Montserrat.	3,002
Masaya (2005)	Nicaragua	2,083
South America		
Llullaillaco (1877)	Argentina-Chile	22,109
Guallatiri (1960)	Chile	19,918
Tupungatito (1987)	Argentina-Chile	19,685
Cotopaxi (1940)	Ecuador.	19,393
El Misti (1784)	Peru	19,101
Láscar (2007)	Chile	18,346
Nevado del Ruiz (1991)	Colombia.	17,457
Sangay (2007)	Ecuador.	17,159
Irruputuncu (1995)	Chile-Bolivia	16,939
Tungurahua (2007)	Ecuador.	16,479
Guagua Pichincha (2004)	Ecuador.	15,695
Puracé (1977)	Colombia.	15,256
Galeras (2006)	Colombia.	14,029
Llaima (2003)	Chile	10,253
Villarrica (2007)	Chile	9,340
Cerro Hudson (1991)	Chile	6,250
Fernandina (2005)	Galápagos Isls., Ecuad.	4,842
Mid-Pacific		
Mauna Loa (1984)	Hawaii, HI	13,681
Kilauea (2007)	Hawaii, HI	4,009
Mid-Atlantic Ridge		
Jan Mayen (1985)	N. Atlantic O., Norway	7,470
Grímsvötn (2004)	Iceland	5,659
Hekla (2000)	Iceland	4,892
Krafla (1984)	Iceland	2,133
Europe		
Etna (2006)	Italy	10,991
Vesuvius (1944)	Italy	4,203
Stromboli (2007)	Italy	3,031
Santorini (1950)	Greece	1,204
North America		
Pico de Orizaba (1846)	Mexico.	18,619
Popocatépetl (2007)	Mexico.	17,802
Rainier (1894)	Washington.	14,409
Wrangell (1999)	Alaska.	14,163
Shasta (1786)	California.	14,163
Colima (2007)	Mexico.	12,631
Lassen Peak (1917)	California.	10,456
Redoubt (1990)	Alaska.	10,197
Iliamna (1876)	Alaska.	10,016
Shishaldin (2004)	Aleutian Isl., AK.	9,373
St. Helens (2007)	Washington.	8,363
Pavlof (1997)	Alaska.	8,264
Veniaminof (2006)	Alaska.	8,225
Katmai (1912)	Alaska.	6,716
Makushin (1995)	Aleutian Isl., AK.	5,905
Great Sitkin (1974)	Aleutian Isl., AK.	5,709
Cleveland (2006)	Aleutian Isl., AK.	5,676
Gareloi (1989)	Aleutian Isl., AK.	5,161
Korovin [Atka complex] (2006)	Aleutian Isl., AK.	5,029
Akutan (1992)	Aleutian Isl., AK.	4,275
Augustine (2006)	Alaska.	4,108
Kiska (1990)	Aleutian Isl., AK.	4,003
El Chichón (1982)	Mexico.	3,773
Okmok (1997)	Aleutian Isl., AK.	3,520
Seguam (1993)	Aleutian Isl., AK.	3,458

Mountains

United States, Canada, Mexico

Peak, state/country	Height (ft)	Peak, state/country	Height (ft)	Peak, state/country	Height (ft)
McKinley (Denali), Alaska	20,320	Alverstone, Alaska-Yukon	14,565	Shavano, Colorado	14,229
Logan, Yukon	19,551	Browne Tower, Alaska	14,530	Belford, Colorado	14,197
Pico de Orizaba, Mexico	18,855	Whitney, California	14,494	Princeton, Colorado	14,197
St. Elias, Alaska-Yukon	18,008	Elbert, Colorado	14,433	Crestone Needle, Colorado	14,197
Popocatépetl, Mexico	17,930	Massive, Colorado	14,421	Yale, Colorado	14,196
Foraker, Alaska	17,400	Harvard, Colorado	14,420	Bross, Colorado	14,172
Iztaccihuatl, Mexico	17,343	Rainier, Washington	14,410	Kit Carson, Colorado	14,165
Lucania, Yukon	17,147	University Peak, Alaska	14,410	Wrangell, Alaska	14,163
King, Yukon	16,971	Williamson, California	14,375	Shasta, California	14,162
Steele, Yukon	16,644	La Plata Peak, Colorado	14,361	El Diente Peak, Colorado	14,159
Bona, Alaska	16,550	Blanca Peak, Colorado	14,345	Point Success, Washington	14,158
Blackburn, Alaska	16,390	Uncompahgre Peak, Colorado	14,309	Maroon Peak, Colorado	14,156
Kennedy, Alaska	16,286	Crestone Peak, Colorado	14,294	Tabeguache, Colorado	14,155
Sanford, Alaska	16,237	Lincoln, Colorado	14,286	Oxford, Colorado	14,153
Vancouver, Alaska-Yukon	15,979	Grays Peak, Colorado	14,270	Sill, California	14,153
South Buttress, Alaska	15,885	Antero, Colorado	14,269	Sneffels, Colorado	14,150
Wood, Yukon	15,885	Torreys Peak, Colorado	14,267	Democrat, Colorado	14,148
Churchill, Alaska	15,638	Castle Peak, Colorado	14,265	Capitol Peak, Colorado	14,130
Fairweather, Alaska-BC	15,300	Quandary Peak, Colorado	14,265	Liberty Cap, Washington	14,112
Zinantecatl (Toluca), Mexico	15,016	Evans, Colorado	14,264	Pikes Peak, Colorado	14,110
Hubbard, Alaska-Yukon	15,015	Longs Peak, Colorado	14,255	Snowmass, Colorado	14,092
Bear, Alaska	14,831	McArthur, Yukon	14,253	Russell, California	14,088
Walsh, Yukon	14,780	Wilson, Colorado	14,246	Eolus, Colorado	14,083
East Buttress, Alaska	14,730	White Mt. Peak, California	14,246	Windom, Colorado	14,082
Matlalcueyetl, Mexico	14,636	North Palisade, California	14,242	Columbia, Colorado	14,073
Hunter, Alaska	14,753	Cameron, Colorado	14,238	Augusta, Alaska	14,070

The highest point in the West Indies is in the Dominican Republic, Pico Duarte (10,417 ft).

South America

Peak, country	Height (ft)	Peak, country	Height (ft)	Peak, country	Height (ft)
Aconcagua, Argentina	22,834	Coropuna, Peru	21,083	Solo, Argentina	20,492
Ojos del Salado, Arg.-Chile	22,572	Laudo, Argentina	20,997	Polleras, Argentina	20,456
Bonete, Argentina	22,546	Ancohuma, Bolivia	20,958	Pular, Chile	20,423
Tupungato, Argentina-Chile	22,310	Ausangate, Peru	20,945	Chani, Argentina	20,341
Pissis, Argentina	22,241	Toro, Argentina-Chile	20,932	Aucanquilcha, Chile	20,295
Mercedario, Argentina	22,211	Illampu, Bolivia	20,873	Juncal, Argentina-Chile	20,276
Huascaran, Peru	22,205	Tres Cruces, Argentina-Chile	20,853	Negro, Argentina	20,184
Llullaillaco, Argentina-Chile	22,109	Huandoy, Peru	20,852	Quela, Argentina	20,128
El Libertador, Argentina	22,047	Parinacota, Bolivia-Chile	20,768	Condoriri, Bolivia	20,095
Cachi, Argentina	22,047	Tortolas, Argentina-Chile	20,745	Palermo, Argentina	20,079
Incahuasi, Argentina-Chile	21,720	Ampato, Peru	20,702	Solimana, Peru	20,068
Yerupaja, Peru	21,709	El Condor, Argentina	20,669	San Juan, Argentina-Chile	20,049
Galan, Argentina	21,654	Salcantay, Peru	20,574	Sierra Nevada, Argentina-Chile	20,023
El Muerto, Argentina-Chile	21,457	Chimborazo, Ecuador	20,561	Antofalla, Argentina	20,013
Sajama, Bolivia	21,391	Huancarhuas, Peru	20,531	Marmolejo, Argentina-Chile	20,013
Nacimiento, Argentina	21,302	Famatina, Argentina	20,505	Chachani, Peru	19,931
Illimani, Bolivia	21,201	Pumasillo, Peru	20,492		

Africa

Peak, country	Height (ft)	Peak, country	Height (ft)	Peak, country	Height (ft)
Kilimanjaro, Tanzania	19,340	Meru, Tanzania	14,979	Guna, Ethiopia	13,881
Kenya, Kenya	17,058	Karisimbi, Congo-Rwanda	14,787	Gughe, Ethiopia	13,780
Margherita Pk., Uganda-Congo.	16,763	Elgon, Kenya-Uganda	14,178	Toubkal, Morocco	13,661
Ras Dashan, Ethiopia	15,158	Batu, Ethiopia	14,131	Cameroon, Cameroon	13,435

Australia, New Zealand, SE Asian Islands

Peak, country	Height (ft)	Peak, country	Height (ft)	Peak, country	Height (ft)
Jaya, New Guinea	16,500	Wilhelm, New Guinea	14,793	Cook, New Zealand	12,349
Trikora, New Guinea	15,585	Kinabalu, Malaysia	13,455	Semeru, Java, Indonesia	12,060
Mandala, New Guinea	15,420	Kerinci, Sumatra, Indon.	12,467	Kosciusko, Australia	7,310

Other Notable U.S. Mountains

Peak, state	Height (ft)	Peak, state	Height (ft)	Peak, state	Height (ft)
Gannett Peak, WY	13,804	Adams, WA	12,277	Clingmans Dome, NC-TN	6,643
Grand Teton, WY	13,766	San Gorgonio, CA	11,502	Washington, NH	6,288
Kings, UT	13,528	Hood, OR	11,239	Rogers, VA	5,729
Cloud, WY	13,175	Lassen, CA	10,457	Marcy, NY	5,344
Wheeler, NM	13,161	Granite, CA	10,321	Katahdin, ME	5,268
Boundary, NV	13,140	Guadalupe, TX	8,749	Spruce Knob, WV	4,861
Granite, MT	12,799	Olympus, WA	7,965	Mansfield, VT	4,393
Borah, ID	12,662	Harney, SD	7,242	Black Mountain, KY	4,145
Humphreys, AZ	12,633	Mitchell, NC	6,684		

Height of Mount Everest

Mt. Everest, the world's highest mountain, was considered 29,002 ft when Edmund Hillary and Tenzing Norgay became the 1st climbers to scale it, in 1953. This triangulation figure had been accepted since 1850. In 1954 the Surveyor General of the Republic of India set the height at 29,028 ft, plus or minus 10 ft because of snow; this figure was also accepted by the National Geographic Society.

In 1999, a team of climbers sponsored by Boston's Museum of Science and the National Geographic Society measured the height at the summit using sophisticated satellite-based technology. This new measurement, of 29,035 ft, was accepted by the National Geographic Society and other authorities, including the U.S. National Imagery and Mapping Agency.

By May 31, 2007, over 50 years after the 1st climbers had reached the summit, some 2,765 more had followed, and about 193 had died in the attempt.

Europe

Peak, country	Height (ft)	Peak, country	Height (ft)	Peak, country	Height (ft)
Alps		Dent D'Herens, Switzerland	13,686	Gletscherhorn, Switzerland	13,068
Mont Blanc, France-Italy	15,771	Breithorn, It., Switzerland	13,665	Schalihorn, Switzerland	13,040
Monte Rosa (highest peak		Bishorn, Switzerland	13,645	Scerscen, Switzerland	13,028
of group), Switzerland	15,203	Jungfrau, Switzerland	13,642	Eiger, Switzerland	13,025
Dom, Switzerland	14,911	Ecrins, France	13,461	Jagerhorn, Switzerland	13,024
Liskamm, It., Switzerland	14,852	Monch, Switzerland	13,448	Rottalhorn, Switzerland	13,022
Weisshorn, Switzerland	14,780	Pollux, Switzerland	13,422	**Pyrenees**	
Taschhorn, Switzerland	14,733	Schreckhorn, Switzerland	13,379	Aneto, Spain	11,168
Matterhorn, It., Switzerland	14,690	Ober Gabelhorn, Switzerland	13,330	Posets, Spain	11,073
Dent Blanche, Switzerland	14,293	Gran Paradiso, Italy	13,323	Perdido, Spain	11,007
Nadelhorn, Switzerland	14,196	Bernina, It., Switzerland	13,284	Vignemale, France-Spain	10,820
Grand Combin, Switzerland	14,154	Fiescherhorn, Switzerland	13,283	Long, Spain	10,479
Lenzpitze, Switzerland	14,088	Grunhorn, Switzerland	13,266	Estats, Spain	10,304
Finsteraarhorn, Switzerland	14,022	Lauteraarhorn, Switzerland	13,261	Montcalm, Spain	10,105
Castor, Switzerland	13,865	Durrenhorn, Switzerland	13,238	**Caucasus (Europe-Asia)**	
Zinalrothorn, Switzerland	13,849	Allalinhorn, Switzerland	13,213	Elbrus, Russia	18,510
Hohberghorn, Switzerland	13,842	Weissmies, Switzerland	13,199	Shkhara, Georgia	17,064
Alphubel, Switzerland	13,799	Lagginhorn, Switzerland	13,156	Dykh Tau, Russia	17,054
Rimpfischhorn, Switzerland	13,776	Zupo, Switzerland	13,120	Kashtan Tau, Russia	16,877
Aletschorn, Switzerland	13,763	Fletschhorn, Switzerland	13,110	Janqi, Georgia	16,565
Strahlhorn, Switzerland	13,747	Adlerhorn, Switzerland	13,081	Kazbek, Georgia	16,558

Asia (Mainland)

Peak, country	Height (ft)	Peak, country	Height (ft)	Peak, country	Height (ft)
Everest, Nepal-Tibet	29,035	Tirich Mir, Pakistan	25,230	Badrinath, India	23,420
K2 (Godwin Austen), Kashmir	28,250	Makalu II, Nepal-Tibet	25,120	Nunkun, Kashmir	23,410
Kanchenjunga, India-Nepal	28,208	Minya Konka, China	24,900	Lenin Peak, Tajikistan	23,405
Lhotse I (Everest), Nepal-Tibet	27,923	Kula Gangri, Bhutan-Tibet	24,784	Pyramid, India-Nepal	23,400
Makalu I, Nepal-Tibet	27,824	Changtzu (Everest), Nepal-Tibet	24,780	Api, Nepal	23,399
Lhotse II (Everest), Nepal-Tibet	27,560	Muz Tagh Ata, Xinjiang	24,757	Pauhunri, India-Tibet	23,385
Dhaulagiri, Nepal	26,810	Skyang Kangri, Kashmir	24,750	Trisul, India	23,360
Manaslu I, Nepal	26,760	Ismail Semani Peak,Tajikistan	24,590	Kangto, India-Tibet	23,260
Cho Oyu, Nepal-Tibet	26,750	Jongsang Peak, India-Nepal	24,472	Nyenchhe Thanglha, Tibet	23,255
Nanga Parbat, Kashmir	26,660	Jengish Chokusu, Xinjiang-		Trisuli, India	23,210
Annapurna I, Nepal	26,504	Kyrgyzstan	24,406	Pumori, Nepal-Tibet	23,190
Gasherbrum, Kashmir	26,470	Sia Kangri, Kashmir	24,350	Dunagiri, India	23,184
Broad, Kashmir	26,400	Haramosh Peak, Pakistan	24,270	Lombo Kangra, Tibet	23,165
Gosainthan Nepal-Tibet	26,287	Istoro Nal, Pakistan	24,240	Saipal, Nepal	23,100
Annapurna II, Nepal	26,041	Tent Peak, India-Nepal	24,165	Macha Pucchare, Nepal	22,958
Gyachung Kang, Nepal-Tibet	25,910	Chomo Lhari, Bhutan-Tibet	24,040	Numbar, Nepal	22,817
Disteghil Sar, Kashmir	25,868	Chamlang, Nepal	24,012	Kanjiroba, Nepal	22,580
Himalchuli, Nepal	25,801	Kabru, India-Nepal	24,002	Ama Dablam, Nepal	22,350
Nuptse (Everest), Nepal-Tibet	25,726	Alung Gangri, Tibet	24,000	Cho Polu, Nepal	22,093
Masherbrum, Kashmir	25,660	Baltoro Kangri, Kashmir	23,990	Lingtren, Nepal-Tibet	21,972
Nanda Devi, India	25,645	Mussu Shan, Xinjiang	23,890	Khumbutse, Nepal-Tibet	21,785
Rakaposhi, Kashmir	25,550	Mana, India	23,860	Hlako Gangri, Tibet	21,266
Kamet, India-Tibet	25,447	Baruntse, Nepal	23,688	Mt. Grosvenor, China	21,190
Namcha Barwa, Tibet	25,445	Nepal Peak, India-Nepal	23,500	Thagchhab Gangri, Tibet	20,970
Gurla Mandhata, Tibet	25,355	Amne Machin, China	23,490	Damavand, Iran	18,606
Ulugh Muz Tagh, Xinjiang-Tibet	25,340	Gauri Sankar, Nepal-Tibet	23,440	Ararat, Turkey	16,804
Kungur, Xinjiang	25,325				

Antarctica

Peak	Height (ft)	Peak	Height (ft)	Peak	Height (ft)
Vinson Massif	16,864	Miller	13,650	Falla	12,549
Tyree	16,290	Long Gables	13,620	Rucker	12,520
Shinn	15,750	Dickerson	13,517	Goldthwait	12,510
Gardner	15,375	Giovinetto	13,412	Morris	12,500
Epperly	15,100	Wade	13,400	Erebus	12,450
Kirkpatrick	14,855	Fisher	13,386	Campbell	12,434
Elizabeth	14,698	Fridtjof Nansen	13,350	Don Pedro Christophersen	12,355
Markham	14,290	Wexler	13,202	Lysaght	12,326
Bell	14,117	Lister	13,200	Huggins	12,247
Mackellar	14,098	Shear	13,100	Sabine	12,200
Anderson	13,957	Odishaw	13,008	Astor	12,175
Bentley	13,934	Donaldson	12,894	Mohl	12,172
Kaplan	13,878	Ray	12,808	Frankes	12,064
Andrew Jackson	13,750	Sellery	12,779	Jones	12,040
Sidley	13,720	Waterman	12,730	Gjelsvik	12,008
Ostenso	13,710	Anne	12,703	Coman	12,000
Minto	13,668	Press	12,566		

Important Islands and Their Areas

Figures are for total areas in square miles. Boldface figure in parentheses shows rank among the world's 10 largest individual islands. Because some islands have not been surveyed accurately, some areas shown are estimates. Some "islands" listed are island groups. Only the largest islands in a group are listed individually. Only islands over 10 sq miles in area are listed.

Antarctica

Adelaide	1,400
Alexander	16,700
Berkner	18,500
Roosevelt	2,900

Arctic Ocean

Akimiski, Nunavut	1,159
Amund Ringnes, Nun.	2,029
Axel Heiberg, Nun.	16,671
Baffin, Nun. **(5)**	195,928
Banks, Northwest Territories	27,038
Bathurst, Nun.	6,194
Bolsheviks, Russia	4,368
Bolshoy Lyakhovsky, Russia	1,776
Borden, NWT., Nun.	1,079
Bylot, Nun.	4,273
Coats, Nun.	2,123
Cornwallis, Nun.	2,701
Devon, Nun.	21,331
Disko, Greenland	3,312
Ellef Ringnes, Nun.	4,361
Ellesmere, Nun. **(10)**	75,767
Faddayevskiy, Russia	1,930
Franz Josef Land, Russia	8,000
Iturup (Etorofu), Russia	2,596
King William, Nun.	5,062
Komsomolets, Russia	3,477
Mackenzie King, NWT	1,949
Mansel, Nun.	1,228
Melville, NWT, Nun.	16,274
Milne Land, Greenland	1,400
New Siberian Islands, Russia	14,500
Kotelnyy, Russia	4,504
Novaya Zemlya, Russia (2 isls.)	31,730
Oktyabrskoy, Russia	5,471
Prince Charles, NWT	3,676
Prince of Wales, Nun.	12,872
Prince Patrick, NWT.	6,119
Somerset, Nun.	9,570
Southampton, Nun.	15,913
Svalbard (tot. group)	23,957
Nordaustlandet.	5,410
Spitsbergen	15,060
Traill, Greenland	1,300
Victoria, NWT., Nun. **(9)**	83,897
Wrangel, Russia	2,800

Atlantic Ocean

Anticosti, Canada	3,068
Ascension, UK	34
Azores, Portugal (tot. group)	868
Faial	67
San Miguel	291
Bahama Isls. (tot. group)	5,382
Andros, Bahamas	2,300
Bermuda Islands, UK (tot. group)	21
Bioko Isl., Equatorial Guinea	785
Block Islands, RI, U.S.	21
Canary Islands, Spain (tot. group)	2,807
Fuerteventura	688
Gran Canaria	592
Tenerife	795
Cape Breton, Canada	3,981
Cape Verde Islands	1,557
Caviana, Para, Brazil	1,918
Channel Islands, UK (tot. group)	75
Guernsey	24
Jersey	45
Faroe Islands, Denmark	540
Falkland Islands, UK (tot. group)	4,700
East Falkland	2,550
West Falkland	1,750
Great Britain, UK **(8)**	84,200
Greenland, Denmark **(1)**	840,000
Gurupa, Para, Brazil	1,878
Hebrides, Scotland	2,744
Iceland	39,699
Ireland (tot. group)	32,589
Irish Republic	27,137
Northern Ireland (UK)	5,452
Isle of Man, UK	227
Isle of Wight, England	147
Long Island, NY, U.S.	1,320

Atlantic Ocean

Madeira Islands, Portugal	306
Marajo, Brazil	15,444
Martha's Vineyard, MA, U.S.	89
Mount Desert, ME, U.S.	104
Nantucket, MA, U.S.	45
Newfoundland, Canada	42,031
Orkney Islands, Scotland	390
Prince Edward, Canada	2,185
St. Helena, UK	47
Shetland Islands, Scotland	587
Skye, Scotland	670
South Georgia, UK	1,450
Tierra del Fuego, Chile, Arg.	18,800
Tristan da Cunha, UK	40

Baltic Sea

Aland Islands, Finland	590
Bornholm, Denmark	227
Gotland, Sweden	1,159

Caribbean Sea

Antigua	108
Aruba, Netherlands	75
Barbados	166
Cuba	42,804
Isle of Youth	926
Cayman Islands	100
Curacao, Netherlands	171
Dominica	290
Guadeloupe, France	687
Hispaniola (Haiti and Dominican Rep.)	29,389
Jamaica	4,244
Martinique, France	436
Puerto Rico, U.S.	3,339
Tobago	116
Trinidad	1,864
Virgin Islands, UK	59
Virgin Islands, U.S.	134

East Indies

Bali, Indonesia	2,171
Bangka, Indonesia	4,375
Borneo, Indonesia-Malaysia-Brunei **(3)**	280,100
Bougainville, Papua New Guinea	3,880
Buru, Indonesia	3,670
Celebes, Indonesia	69,000
Flores, Indonesia	5,500
Halmahera, Indonesia	6,865
Java (Jawa), Indonesia	48,900
Madura, Indonesia	2,113
Moluccas, Indonesia	32,307
New Britain, Papua New Guinea	14,093
New Guinea, Indon.-PNG **(2)**	306,000
New Ireland, PNG	3,707
Seram, Indonesia	6,621
Sumba, Indonesia	4,306
Sumbawa, Indonesia	5,965
Sumatra, Indonesia **(6)**	165,000
Timor, Indonesia	13,094
Yos Sudarsa, Indonesia	4,500

Indian Ocean

Andaman Isls., India	2,500
Kerguelen	2,247
Madagascar **(4)**	226,658
Mauritius	720
Pemba, Tanzania	380
Reunion, France	970
Seychelles	176
Sri Lanka	25,332
Zanzibar, Tanzania	640

Mediterranean Sea

Balearic Isls., Spain	1,927
Corfu, Greece	229
Corsica, France	3,369
Crete, Greece	3,189
Cyprus	3,572
Elba, Italy	86
Euboea, Greece	1,411
Malta	95
Rhodes, Greece	540
Sardinia, Italy	9,301
Sicily, Italy	9,926

Pacific Ocean

Admiralty, AK, U.S.	1,709
Aleutian Isls., AK, U.S. (tot. group)	6,912
Adak	275
Amchitka	116
Attu	350
Kanaga	142
Kiska	106
Tanaga	195
Umnak	686
Unalaska	1,051
Unimak	1,571
Baranof, AK, U.S.	1,636
Chichagof, AK, U.S.	2,062
Chiloe, Chile	3,241
Christmas, Kiribati	94
Diomede, Big, Russia	11
Easter Isl., Chile	69
Fiji (tot. group)	7,056
Vanua Levu	2,242
Viti Levu	4,109
Galapagos Isls., Ecuador	3,043
Graham Isl., British Columbia	2,456
Guadalcanal, Solomon Isls.	2,180
Guam, U.S.	210
Hainan, China	13,000
Hawaiian Isls., HI, U.S. (tot. group)	6,428
Hawaii	4,028
Oahu	600
Hong Kong, China.	31
Hoste, Chile.	1,590
Japan (tot. group)	145,850
Hokkaido	30,144
Honshu **(7)**	87,805
Kyushu	14,114
Okinawa	459
Shikoku	7,049
Kangaroo, South Australia	1,680
Kodiak, AK, U.S.	3,485
Kupreanof, AK, U.S.	1,084
Marquesas Isls., France	492
Marshall Isls.	70
Melville, N Terr., Australia	2,240
Micronesia.	271
New Caledonia, France.	6,530
New Zealand (tot. group)	104,454
Chatham Isls.	372
North	44,204
South.	58,384
Stewart	674
North Mariana Isls., U.S.	179
Nunivak, AK, U.S.	1,600
Palau	188
Philippines (tot. group)	115,860
Leyte	2,787
Luzon	40,680
Mindanao	36,775
Mindoro	3,690
Negros	4,907
Palawan	4,554
Panay	4,446
Samar	5,050
Prince of Wales, AK, U.S.	2,770
Revillagigedo, AK, U.S.	1,134
Riesco, Chile	1,973
St. Lawrence, AK, U.S.	1,780
Sakhalin, Russia	29,500
Samoa Isls. (tot. group)	1,177
American Samoa, U.S.	77
Tutuila, U.S.	55
Savaii, Samoa	659
Upolu, Samoa	432
Santa Catalina, CA, U.S.	75
Santa Ines, Chile.	1,407
Tahiti, France	402
Taiwan, China (tot. group)	13,969
Jinmen Dao (Quemoy)	56
Tasmania, Australia	26,178
Tonga Isls.	290
Vancouver Isl., Brit. Columbia.	12,079
Vanuatu	4,707
Wellington, Chile	2,549

Persian Gulf

Bahrain	217

Notable Deserts of the World

Deserts are defined as regions of the Earth receiving less than 10 in. of precipitation annually, usually in combination with an evaporation rate exceeding precipitation.

In addition to areas listed below, the continent of Antarctica, with an area of about 5.4 mil square miles (roughly doubled by ice in winter), is generally considered a desert. Annual precipitation averages 8 in. along the coast and far less in the deep interior; however, there is little evaporation.

Arabian (Eastern), 70,000 sq mi in Egypt between the Nile R. and Red Sea, extending southward into Sudan
Atacama, 600-mi-long area rich in nitrate and copper deposits in N Chile
Chihuahuan, 140,000 sq mi in TX, NM, AZ, and Mexico
Dasht-e Kauir, approx. 300 mi long by approx. 100 mi wide in N central Iran
Dasht-e Lut, 20,000 sq mi in E Iran
Death Valley, 3,300 sq mi in CA and NV
Gibson, 120,000 sq mi in the interior of W Australia
Gobi, 500,000 sq mi in Mongolia and China
Great Sandy, 150,000 sq mi in W Australia
Great Victoria, 150,000 sq mi in SW Australia
Kalahari, 225,000 sq mi in S Africa
Kara Kum, 120,000 sq mi in Turkmenistan
Kyzyl Kum, 100,000 sq mi in Kazakhstan and Uzbekistan
Libyan, 450,000 sq mi in the Sahara, extending from Libya through SW Egypt into Sudan

Mojave, 15,000 sq mi in southern CA
Namib, long narrow area (varies from 30-100 mi wide) extending 800 mi along SW coast of Africa
Nubian, 100,000 sq mi in the Sahara in NE Sudan
Painted Desert, section of high plateau in northern AZ extending 150 mi
Patagonia, 300,000 sq mi in S Argentina
Rub al-Khali (Empty Quarter), 250,000 sq mi in the S Arabian Peninsula
Sahara, 3,500,000 sq mi in N Africa, extending westward to the Atlantic. Largest desert in the world.
Sonoran, 70,000 sq mi in southwestern AZ and southeastern CA extending into NW Mexico
Syrian, 100,000-sq-mi arid wasteland extending over much of N Saudi Arabia, E Jordan, S Syria, and W Iraq
Taklimakan, 140,000 sq mi in Xinjiang Prov., China
Thar (Great Indian), 100,000-sq-mi arid area extending 400 mi along India-Pakistan border

Areas and Average Depths of Oceans, Seas, and Gulfs

Geographers and mapmakers recognize at least 4 major bodies of water: the Pacific, the Atlantic, the Indian, and the Arctic oceans. The Atlantic and Pacific oceans are considered divided at the equator into the N and S Atlantic and the N and S Pacific. The Arctic Ocean is the name for waters N of the continental landmasses in the region of the Arctic Circle.

	Area (sq mi)	Avg. depth (ft)		Area (sq mi)	Avg. depth (ft)
Pacific Ocean	64,186,300	12,925	Sea of Japan	391,100	5,468
Atlantic Ocean	33,420,000	11,730	Hudson Bay	281,900	305
Indian Ocean	28,350,500	12,598	East China Sea	256,600	620
Southern Ocean[1]	7,846,000	13,100[2]	Andaman Sea	218,100	3,667
Arctic Ocean	5,105,700	3,407	Black Sea	196,100	3,906
South China Sea	1,148,500	4,802	Red Sea	174,900	1,764
Caribbean Sea	971,400	8,448	North Sea	164,900	308
Mediterranean Sea	969,100	4,926	Baltic Sea	147,500	180
Bering Sea	873,000	4,893	Yellow Sea	113,500	121
Gulf of Mexico	582,100	5,297	Persian Gulf	88,800	328
Sea of Okhotsk	537,500	3,192	Gulf of California	59,100	2,375

(1) The International Hydrographic Organization delimited a fifth world ocean in 2000. The Southern Ocean as defined extends from the coast of Antarctica north to 60° south latitude, covering portions of the Atlantic, Indian, and Pacific oceans. (2) Ranges from 13,100 to 16,400 feet deep.

Principal Ocean Depths

Source: National Imagery and Mapping Agency, U.S. Dept. of Defense

Name of area	Location (lat.)	(long.)	Depth (meters)	(fathoms)	(ft)
Pacific Ocean					
Marianas Trench	11°22′ N	142°36′ E	10,924	5,973	35,840
Tonga Trench	23°16′ S	174°44′ W	10,800	5,906	35,433
Philippine Trench	10°38′ N	126°36′ E	10,057	5,499	32,995
Kermadec Trench	31°53′ S	177°21′ W	10,047	5,494	32,963
Bonin Trench	24°30′ N	143°24′ E	9,994	5,464	32,788
Kuril Trench	44°15′ N	150°34′ E	9,750	5,331	31,988
Izu Trench	31°05′ N	142°10′ E	9,695	5,301	31,808
New Britain Trench	06°19′ S	153°45′ E	8,940	4,888	29,331
Yap Trench	08°33′ N	138°02′ E	8,527	4,663	27,976
Japan Trench	36°08′ N	142°43′ E	8,412	4,600	27,599
Peru-Chile Trench	23°18′ S	71°14′ W	8,064	4,409	26,457
Palau Trench	07°52′ N	134°56′ E	8,054	4,404	26,424
Aleutian Trench	50°51′ N	177°11′ E	7,679	4,199	25,194
New Hebrides Trench	20°36′ S	168°37′ E	7,570	4,139	24,836
North Ryukyu Trench	24°00′ N	126°48′ E	7,181	3,927	23,560
Mid. America Trench	14°02′ N	93°39′ W	6,662	3,643	21,857
Atlantic Ocean					
Puerto Rico Trench	19°55′ N	65°27′ W	8,605	4,705	28,232
S Sandwich Trench	55°42′ S	25°56′ W	8,325	4,552	27,313
Romanche Gap	0°13′ S	18°26′ W	7,728	4,226	25,354
Cayman Trench	19°12′ N	80°00′ W	7,535	4,120	24,721
Brazil Basin	09°10′ S	23°02′ W	6,119	3,346	20,076
Indian Ocean					
Java Trench	10°19′ S	109°58′ E	7,125	3,896	23,376
Ob' Trench	09°45′ S	67°18′ E	6,874	3,759	22,553
Diamantina Trench	35°50′ S	105°14′ E	6,602	3,610	21,660
Vema Trench	09°08′ S	67°15′ E	6,402	3,501	21,004
Agulhas Basin	45°20′ S	26°50′ E	6,195	3,387	20,325
Arctic Ocean					
Eurasia Basin	82°23′ N	19°31′ E	5,450	2,980	17,881
Mediterranean Sea					
Ionian Basin	36°32′ N	21°06′ E	5,150	2,816	16,896

Note: Greater depths have been reported in some areas but are not officially confirmed by research vessels.

Principal World Rivers
For N American rivers, see separate table.

River	Source or upper limit of length	Outflow	Length (mi)
Africa			
Chari	Bamingui-Bangoran region, Central African Republic	Lake Chad	650
Congo	Junction of Lualaba and Luava Rivers	Atlantic Ocean	2,720
Cubango (fmr. Okavango)	Central Angola	Okavango Delta	1,000
Gambia	Fouta Djallon massif, Guinea	Atlantic Ocean	700
Kasai	Central Angola	Congo River	1,100
Limpopo	Junction of Marico and Ngotwane Rivers, South Africa	Indian Ocean	1,100
Lualaba	SE Congo	Congo River	1,100
Niger	Fouta Djallon plateau, Guinea	Gulf of Guinea	2,600
Nile	Luvironza River, Burundi	Mediterranean Sea	4,160
Orange	Maluti mountains, N Lesotho	Atlantic Ocean	1,300
Sénégal	Junction of Bafing and Bakoy rivers, Mali	Atlantic Ocean	1,000
Ubangi	Junction of Uele and Bomu rivers, Congo	Congo River	700
Zambezi	NW Zambia	Indian Ocean	1,700
Asia			
Amu Darya	Junction of Wakhsh and Panj Rivers, Tajikistan	Aral Sea	1,660
Amur	Junction of Shilka and Argun Rivers, China-Russia	Tartar Strait	1,780
Angara	Lake Baykal, Russia	Yenisei River	1,150
Ayeyarwady (fmr. Irrawaddy)	Junction of Mali and Nmai Rivers, Myanmar	Andaman Sea	1,000
Brahmaputra	Kailas range, Himalayas, SW Tibet	Bay of Bengal	1,800
Chang-Jiang	Tibetan plateau, SW Qinghai, China	East China Sea	3,450
Euphrates	Junction of Kara (Sarasu) and Murat Rivers, Turkey	Shatt al-Arab	1,700
Ganges	Gangotri glacier, Himalayas, India	Bay of Bengal	1,560
Godavari	W Ghats, Maharashtra, India	Bay of Bengal	900
Hsi (see Xi)			
Huang-He	Kunlun mountains, Qinghai, China	Yellow Sea	3,000
Indus	Kailas range, Himalayas, Tibet	Arabian Sea	1,900
Irtysh	Kazakhstan-Russia	Ob River	2,650
Jordan	Junction of Dan, Banias, and Hazbani streams, Israel	Dead Sea	200
Kolyma	Kolyma and Cherskogo ranges, Russia	Arctic Ocean	1,500
Krishna	W Ghats, Maharashtra, India	Bay of Bengal	800
Kura	NE Turkey	Caspian Sea	950
Lena	W Baikal range, Russia	Laptev Sea	2,648
Mekong	E Tibetan Plateau, China	South China Sea	2,700
Narmada	Madhya Pradesh, India	Arabian Sea	775
Ob	Junction of Biya and Katun Rivers, Russia	Gulf of Ob	2,300
Salween	E. Tibet, China	Gulf of Martaban	1,750
Songhua Jiang	Changbai mountains, Jilin, China	Amur River	1,150
Sungari (see Songhua Jiang)			
Sutlej	Kailas range, Himalayas, Tibet	Indus River	900
Syr	Junction of Naryn and Kara Darya Rivers, Uzbekistan	Aral Sea	1,380
Tarim	Junction of Kashi and Yarkant Rivers, China	Lop Nor	1,300
Tigris	Taurus mountains, Turkey	Shatt al-Arab	1,150
Xi He	E Yunnan, China	South China Sea	1,250
Yamuna	Uttarkashi dist., Uttar Pradesh, India	Ganges River	850
Yangtze (see Chang-Jiang)			
Yellow (see Huang-He)			
Yenisei	Kyzyl, Tuva Republic, Russia	Kara Sea	2,500
Australia			
Darling	Eastern Highlands, NE New South Wales/SE Queensland	Murray River	1,702
Murray	Australian Alps, SE New South Wales	Indian Ocean	1,609
Murrumbidgee	Australian Alps, SE New South Wales	Murray River	1,050
Europe			
Buh, Southern	NW of Khmel'nyts'kyy, Ukraine	Black Sea	532
Buh, Western	ENE of Zolochiv, Ukraine	Wisla River	500
Danube	Brege and Brigach Rivers, Black Forest, SW Germany	Black Sea	1,770
Dnieper	W of Sychevka, Smolensk, Russia	Black Sea	1,420
Dniester	Carpathian mountains, Ukraine	Black Sea	850
Don	SE of Tula, Russia	Sea of Azov	1,200
Drava	Carnic Alps, N Italy	Danube River	450
Dvina, North	Near Veliki Ustyug, Vologda, Russia	White Sea	465
Dvina, West	Valdai Hills, Russia	Gulf of Riga	635
Ebro	Cantabrian mountains, N Spain	Mediterranean Sea	575
Elbe	Giant mountains, NW Czech Republic	North Sea	725
Garonne	Central Pyrenees, Spain	Bay of Biscay	402
Kama	Ural mountains, N of Kuliga, Russia	Volga River	1,260
Loire	Mt. Gerbier-de-Jonc, Vivrais mountains, France	Atlantic Ocean	630
Marne	Langres plateau, NE France	Seine River	325
Meuse	Langres plateau, NE France	North Sea	560
Oder	Sudetes mountains, NE Czech Republic	Baltic Sea	562
Oka	S of Orël, Russia	Volga River	925
Pechora	N Ural mountains, Russia	Barents Sea	1,120
Po	Cottian Alps, Piedmont, NW Italy	Adriatic Sea	405
Rhine	Swiss Alps	North Sea	820

River	Source or upper limit of length	Outflow	Length (mi)
Rhône	Rhône glacier, NE Valais, Switzerland	Mediterranean Sea	505
Seine	Langres Plateau, N Burgundy, France	English Channel	480
Shannon	Near Cuilcagh Mountain, NW Cavan County, Ireland	Atlantic Ocean	240
Tagus	E of Madrid, Spain	Atlantic Ocean	585
Thames	4 headstreams in the Cotswold Hills, Gloucestershire, England	North Sea	210
Tiber	Etruscan Apennines, Italy	Tyrrhenian Sea	251
Tisza	N of Rakhiv, W Ukraine	Danube River	700
Ural	S Ural mountains, NE Bashkortostan, Russia	Caspian Sea	1,580
Volga	Valday Hills, Smolensk, Russia	Caspian Sea	2,290
Weser	Junction of Fulda and Werra Rivers, Germany	North Sea	273
Wisla	W Beskid range, Carpathian mountains, SW Poland	Gulf of Gdansk	665
South America			
Amazon	Junction of Ucayali and Marañón Rivers, Andes mountains, Peru	Atlantic Ocean	3,900
Araguaía	Serra des Araras, Goiás-Mato Grosso, Brazil	Tocantins River	1,100
Beni	Cordillera Real, La Paz, Bolivia	Madeira River	1,000
Caquetá-Japura	Andes mountains, SW Colombia	Amazon River	1,750
Juruá	Cerros de Canchyuaya, E Peru	Amazon Bay	1,500
Madeira	Junction of Beni and Mamoré Rivers, Bolivia	Amazon River	2,100
Magdalena	Cordillera Central, SW Colombia	Caribbean Sea	1,000
Negro	SE Colombia	Amazon River	1,400
Orinoco	Near Mt. Delgado Chalbaud, Guiana Highlands, S Venezuela	Atlantic Ocean	1,600
Paraguay	Central Mato Grosso highlands, Brazil	Paraná River	1,584
Paraná	Junction of Paranaíba and Rio Grande, SE Brazil	Rio de la Plata	2,485
Pilcomayo	E of Lake Poopó, Bolivia	Paraguay River	1,000
Purus	Andes mountains, E Peru	Amazon River	2,100
Putumayo	Andes mountains, S Colombia	Amazon River	1,000
Rio de la Plata	Estuary of Paraná and Uruguay Rivers, Argentina-Uruguay	Atlantic Ocean	170
São Francisco	Serra de Canastra, SW Minas Gerais, Brazil	Atlantic Ocean	1,800
Tocantins	S central Goiás, Brazil	Para River	1,640
Ucayali	Junction of Apurímac and Urubamba Rivers, E Peru	Marañón River	1,000
Uruguay	S Brazil	Rio de la Plata	1,000
Xingu	Central Mato Grosso, Brazil	Amazon River	1,230

Major Rivers in North America

River	Source or upper limit of length	Outflow	Length (mi)
Alabama	Gilmer County, GA	Mobile River	729
Albany	Lake St. Joseph, Ontario	James Bay	610
Allegheny	Potter County, PA	Ohio River	325
Altamaha-Ocmulgee	Junction of Yellow and South Rivers, Newton County, GA	Atlantic Ocean	392
Apalachicola-Chattahoochee	Towns County, GA	Gulf of Mexico	524
Arkansas	Lake County, CO	Mississippi River	1,459
Assiniboine	Eastern Saskatchewan	Red River	450
Attawapiskat	Attawapiskat, Ontario	James Bay	465
Back (NWT)	Contwoyto Lake	Chantrey Inlet, Arctic Ocean	605
Big Black (MS)	Webster County, MS	Mississippi River	330
Brazos	Junction of Salt and Double Mountain Forks, Stonewall County, TX	Gulf of Mexico	950
Canadian	Las Animas County, CO	Arkansas River	906
Cedar (IA)	Dodge County, MN	Iowa River	329
Cheyenne	Junction of Antelope Creek and Dry Fork, Converse County, WY	Missouri River	290
Churchill, Lab.	Lake Ashuanipi, Labrador	Atlantic Ocean	532
Churchill, Man.	Methy Lake, Saskatchewan	Hudson Bay	1,000
Cimarron	Colfax County, NM	Arkansas River	600
Colorado (AZ)	Rocky Mountain Natl. Park, CO (90 mi in Mexico)	Gulf of California	1,450
Colorado (TX)	West Texas	Matagorda Bay	862
Columbia	Columbia Lake, British Columbia	Pacific Ocean, bet. OR and WA	1,243
Columbia, Upper	Columbia Lake, British Columbia	Mouth of Snake River	890
Connecticut	Third Connecticut Lake, NH	Long Island Sound, CT	407
Coppermine (NWT)	Lac de Gras	Coronation Gulf, Arctic Ocean	525
Cumberland	Letcher County, KY	Ohio River	720
Delaware	Schoharie County, NY	Liston Point, Delaware Bay	390
Fraser	Near Mount Robson (on Continental Divide)	Strait of Georgia	850
Gila	Catron County, NM	Colorado River	649
Green (UT-WY)	Junction of Wells and Trail Creeks, Sublette County, WY	Colorado River	730
Hudson	Henderson Lake, Essex County, NY	Upper NY Bay	306
Illinois	St. Joseph County, IN	Mississippi River	420
James (ND-SD)	Wells County, ND	Missouri River	710
James (VA)	Junction of Jackson and Cowpasture Rivers, Botetourt County, VA	Hampton Roads	340
Kanawha-New	Junction of North and South Forks of New River, NC	Ohio River	352
Kentucky	Junction of North and Middle Forks, Lee County, KY	Ohio River	259
Klamath	Lake Ewauna, Klamath Falls, OR	Pacific Ocean	250

River	Source or upper limit of length	Outflow	Length (mi)
Kootenay	Kootenay Lake, British Columbia	Columbia River	485
Koyukuk	Endicott Mountains, AK	Yukon River	470
Kuskokwim	Alaska Range	Kuskokwim Bay	724
Liard	Southern Yukon, AK	Mackenzie River	693
Little Missouri	Crook County, WY	Missouri River	560
Mackenzie	Great Slave Lake, N.W.T.	Arctic Ocean	1,060
Milk	Junction of North and South Forks, Alberta	Missouri River	625
Minnesota	Big Stone Lake, MN	Mississippi River	332
Mississippi	Lake Itasca, MN	Gulf of Mexico	2,340
Mississippi-Missouri-Red Rock	Source of Red Rock, Beaverhead Co., MT	Gulf of Mexico	3,710
Missouri	Junction of Jefferson, Madison, and Gallatin Rivers, Gallatin County, MT	Mississippi River	2,315
Missouri-Red Rock	Source of Red Rock, Beaverhead Co., MT	Mississippi River	2,540
Mobile-Alabama-Coosa	Gilmer County, GA	Mobile Bay	774
Nelson (Man.)	Lake Winnipeg	Hudson Bay	410
Neosho	Morris County, KS	Arkansas River, OK	460
Niobrara	Niobrara County, WY	Missouri River, NE	431
North Canadian	Union County, NM	Canadian River, OK	800
North Platte	Junction of Grizzly and Little Grizzly Creeks, Jackson County, CO	Platte River, NE	618
Ohio	Junction of Allegheny and Monongahela Rivers, Pittsburgh, PA	Mississippi River	981
Ohio-Allegheny	Potter County, PA	Mississippi River	1,310
Osage	East-central Kansas	Missouri River	500
Ottawa	Lake Capimitchigama	St. Lawrence River	790
Ouachita	Polk County, AR	Black River	605
Peace	Stikine Mountains, B.C.	Slave River	1,210
Pearl	Neshoba County, MS	Gulf of Mexico	411
Pecos	Mora County, NM	Rio Grande	926
Pee Dee-Yadkin	Watauga County, NC	Winyah Bay	435
Pend Oreille-Clark Fork	Near Butte, MT	Columbia River	531
Platte	Junction of North and South Platte Rivers, NE	Missouri River	310
Porcupine	Ogilvie Mountains, AK	Yukon River, AK	569
Potomac	Garrett County, MD	Chesapeake Bay	383
Powder	Junction of South and Middle Forks, WY	Yellowstone River	375
Red (OK-TX-LA)	Curry County, NM	Mississippi River	1,290
Red River of the North	Junction of Otter Tail and Bois de Sioux Rivers, Wilkin County, MN	Lake Winnipeg	545
Republican	Junction of North Fork and Arikaree River, NE	Kansas River	445
Rio Grande	San Juan County, CO	Gulf of Mexico	1,900
Roanoke	Junction of N and S Forks, Montgomery Co., VA	Albemarle Sound	380
Rock (IL-WI)	Dodge County, WI	Mississippi River	300
Sabine	Junction of S and Caddo Forks, Hunt County, TX	Sabine Lake	380
Sacramento	Siskiyou County, CA	Suisun Bay	377
St. Francis	Iron County, MO.	Mississippi River	425
St. John	Northwestern Maine	Bay of Fundy	418
St. Lawrence	Lake Ontario	Gulf of St. Lawrence, Atlantic Ocean	800
Saguenay	Lake St. John, Quebec	St. Lawrence River	434
Salmon (ID)	Custer County, ID	Snake River	420
San Joaquin	Junction of S and Middle Forks, Madera Co., CA	Suisun Bay	350
San Juan	Silver Lake, Archuleta County, CO	Colorado River	360
Santee-Wateree-Catawba	McDowell County, NC	Atlantic Ocean	538
Saskatchewan, North	Rocky Mountains	Saskatchewan R.	800
Saskatchewan, South	Rocky Mountains	Saskatchewan R.	865
Savannah	Junction of Seneca and Tugaloo Rivers, Anderson County, SC	Atlantic Ocean, GA-SC	314
Severn (Ont.)	Sandy Lake	Hudson Bay	610
Smoky Hill	Cheyenne County, CO	Kansas River, KS	540
Snake	Teton County, WY	Columbia River, WA.	1,038
South Platte	Junction of S and Middle Forks, Park County, CO	Platte River	424
Susitna	Alaska Range	Cook Inlet	313
Susquehanna	Huyden Creek, Otsego County, NY	Chesapeake Bay	447
Tallahatchie	Tippah County, MS	Yazoo River	301
Tanana	Wrangell Mountains, AK.	Yukon River	659
Tennessee	Junction of French Broad and Holston Rivers	Ohio River	652
Tennessee-French Broad	Courthouse Creek, Transylvania County, NC	Ohio River	886
Tombigbee	Prentiss County, MS	Mobile River	525
Trinity	North of Dallas, TX	Galveston Bay	360
Wabash	Darke County, OH	Ohio River	512
Washita	Hemphill County, TX	Red River, OK	500
White (AR-MO)	Madison County, AR	Mississippi River	722
Willamette	Douglas County, OR	Columbia River	309
Wind-Bighorn	Junction of Wind and Little Wind Rivers, Fremont Co., WY (Source of Wind R. is Togwotee Pass, Teton Co., WY)	Yellowstone River	338
Wisconsin	Lac Vieux Desert, Vilas County, WI	Mississippi River	430
Yellowstone	Park County, WY	Missouri River	682
Yukon	McNeil R., Yukon Territory	Bering Sea	1,979

Major Natural Lakes of the World

Source: Geological Survey, U.S. Dept. of the Interior; GeoAccess Division, Natural Resources Canada

A lake is generally defined as a body of water surrounded by land. By this definition some bodies of water that are called seas, such as the Caspian Sea and the Aral Sea, are really lakes. In the following table, the word *lake* is omitted when it is part of the name.

Name	Continent	Area (sq mi)	Length (mi)	Maximum depth (ft)	Elevation (ft)
Caspian Sea[1]	Asia-Europe	143,244	760	3,363	−92
Superior	North America	31,700	350	1,330	600
Victoria	Africa	26,828	250	270	3,720
Huron	North America	23,000	206	750	579
Michigan	North America	22,300	307	923	579
Aral Sea[1]	Asia	13,000[2]	260	180	125
Tanganyika	Africa	12,700	420	4,823	2,534
Baykal	Asia	12,162	395	5,315	1,493
Great Bear	North America	12,096	192	1,463	512
Nyasa (Malawi)	Africa	11,150	360	2,280	1,550
Great Slave	North America	11,031	298	2,015	513
Erie	North America	9,910	241	210	570
Winnipeg	North America	9,417	266	200	713
Ontario	North America	7,340	193	802	245
Balkhash[1]	Asia	7,115	376	85	1,115
Ladoga	Europe	6,835	124	738	13
Maracaibo	South America	5,217	133	115	sea level
Onega	Europe	3,710	145	328	108
Eyre[1]	Australia	3,600[3]	90	4	−52
Titicaca	South America	3,200	122	922	12,500
Nicaragua	North America	3,100	102	230	102
Athabasca	North America	3,064	208	407	700
Reindeer	North America	2,568	143	720	1,106
Tonle Sap	Asia	2,500[3]	70	45	NA
Turkana (Rudolf)	Africa	2,473	154	240	1,230
Issyk Kul[1]	Asia	2,355	115	2,303	5,279
Torrens[1]	Australia	2,230[3]	130	(3)	92
Vanern	Europe	2,156	91	328	144
Nettilling	North America	2,140	67	(3)	95
Winnipegosis	North America	2,075	141	38	830
Albert	Africa	2,075	100	168	2,030
Nipigon	North America	1,872	72	540	1,050
Gairdner[1]	Australia	1,840[3]	90	(3)	112
Urmia[1]	Asia	1,815	90	49	4,180
Manitoba	North America	1,799	140	21	813
Chad	Africa	500+[4]	175	24	787

NA = Not available (1) Salt lake. (2) The diversion of feeder rivers since the 1960s has devastated the Aral—once the world's 4th-largest lake (26,000 sq miles). By 2000, the Aral had effectively become three lakes, with the total area shown. (3) Subject to great seasonal variation. (4) Once 4th-largest lake in Africa (about 10,000 sq mi in the 1960s), Chad had shrunk to around 5% of its original size as of 2006 as a result of irrigation and long-term drought.

The Great Lakes

Source: National Ocean Service, U.S. Dept. of Commerce

The Great Lakes form the world's **largest body of fresh water** (in surface area), and with their connecting waterways are the largest inland water transportation unit. Draining the great North Central basin of the U.S., they enable shipping to reach the Atlantic via their outlet, the St. Lawrence R., and to reach the Gulf of Mexico via the Illinois Waterway, from Lake Michigan to the Mississippi R. A 3rd outlet connects with the Hudson R. and then the Atlantic via the New York State Barge Canal System. Traffic on the Illinois Waterway and the N.Y. State Barge Canal System is limited to recreational boating and small shipping vessels.

Only one of the lakes, Lake Michigan, is wholly in the U.S.; the others are shared with Canada. Ships move from the shores of Lake Superior to Whitefish Bay at the E end of the lake, then through the Soo (Sault Ste. Marie) locks, through the St. Mary's R. and into Lake Huron. To reach Gary and the Port of Indiana and South Chicago, IL, ships move W from Lake Huron to Lake Michigan through the Straits of Mackinac. Lake Superior is 601 ft above low water datum at Rimouski, Quebec, on the International Great Lakes Datum (1985). From Duluth, MN, to the E end of Lake Ontario is 1,156 mi.

	Superior	Michigan	Huron	Erie	Ontario
Length in mi	350	307	206	241	193
Breadth in mi	160	118	183	57	53
Deepest soundings in ft	1,333	923	750	210	802
Volume of water in cu mi	2,935	1,180	850	116	393
Area (sq mi) water surface—U.S.	20,600	22,300	9,100	4,980	3,460
Canada	11,100	NA	13,900	4,930	3,880
Area (sq mi) entire drainage basin—U.S.	16,900	45,600	16,200	18,000	15,200
Canada	32,400	NA	35,500	4,720	12,100
TOTAL AREA (sq mi) U.S. and Canada	81,000	67,900	74,700	32,630	34,850
Low water datum above mean water level at Rimouski, Quebec, avg. level in ft (1985)	601.10	577.50	577.50	569.20	243.30
Latitude, N	46°25′	41°37′	43°00′	41°23′	43°11′
	49°00′	46°06′	46°17′	42°52′	44°15′
Longitude, W	84°22′	84°45′	79°43′	78°51′	76°03′
	92°06′	88°02′	84°45′	83°29′	79°53′
National boundary line in mi	282.8	None	260.8	251.5	174.6
United States shoreline (mainland only) mi	863	1,400	580	431	300

Famous Waterfalls

Source: National Geographic Society

The earth has thousands of waterfalls, some of considerable magnitude. Their magnitude is determined not only by height but also by volume of flow, steadiness of flow, crest width, whether the water drops sheerly or over a sloping surface, and whether it descends in one leap or in a succession of leaps. A series of low falls flowing over a considerable distance is known as a **cascade**.

Estimated mean annual flow, in cubic feet per second, of major waterfalls is as follows: Niagara, 212,200; Paulo Afonso, 100,000; Urubupunga, 97,000; Iguazu, 61,000; Patos-Maribondo, 53,000; Victoria, 35,400; and Kaieteur, 23,400.

Height = total drop in feet in one or more leaps. # = falls of more than one leap; * = falls that diminish greatly seasonally; ** = falls that reduce to a trickle or are dry for part of each year. If the river names are not shown, they are same as the falls. R. = river; (C) = cascade.

Name and location	Height (ft)
Africa	
Angola	
Ruacana, Cunene R.	406
Ethiopia	
Fincha	508
Lesotho	
Maletsunyane*	630
Zimbabwe-Zambia	
Victoria, Zambezi R.*	343
South Africa	
Augrabies, Orange R.*	480
Tugela#	2,014
Tanzania-Zambia	
Kalambo*	726
Asia	
India	
Cauvery*	330
Jog (Gersoppa), Sharavathi R.*	830
Japan	
Kegon, Daiya R.*	330
Australia	
New South Wales	
Wentworth	614
Wollomombi	1,100
Queensland	
Tully	885
Wallaman, Stony Cr.#	1,137
New Zealand	
Helena	890
Sutherland, Arthur R.#	1,904
Europe	
Austria	
Gastein#	492
Krimml#	1,312
France	
Gavarnie*	1,385
Great Britain	
Scotland	
Glomach	370
Wales	
Rhaiadr	240
Italy	
Frua, Toce R. (C)	470
Norway	
Mardalsfossen (Northern)	1,535

Name and location	Height (ft)
Mardalsfossen (Southern)#	2,149
Skjeggedal, Nybuai R.#**	1,378
Skykje**	984
Vetti, Morka-Koldedola R.	900
Sweden	
Handol#	427
Switzerland	
Giessbach (C)	984
Reichenbach#	656
Simmen#	459
Staubbach	984
Trummelbach#	1,312
North America	
Canada	
Alberta	
Panther, Nigel Cr.	600
British Columbia	
Della#	1,443
Takakkaw, Daly Glacier#	1,200
Quebec	
Montmorency	274
Canada-United States	
Niagara: American	182
Horseshoe	173
United States	
Alabama	
Noccalula Falls	90
California	
Feather, Fall R.*	640
Yosemite National Park	
Bridalveil*	620
Illilouette*	370
Nevada, Merced R.*	594
Ribbon**	1,612
Silver Strand, Meadow Br.**	1,170
Vernal, Merced R.*	317
Yosemite#**	2,425
Colorado	
Seven Falls, S. Cheyenne Cr.#	300
Hawaii	
Akaka, Kolekole Str.	442
Idaho	
Shoshone, Snake R.**	212
Kentucky	
Cumberland	68

Name and location	Height (ft)
Maryland	
Great, Potomac R. (C)*	71
Minnesota	
Minnehaha**	53
New Jersey	
Passaic	70
New York	
Taughannock*	215
Oregon	
Multnomah#	620
Tennessee	
Fall Creek	256
Washington	
Mt. Rainier Natl. Park	
Sluiskin, Paradise R.	300
Snoqualmie**	268
Wisconsin	
Big Manitou, Black R. (C)*	165
Wyoming	
Yellowstone Natl. Pk. Tower	132
Yellowstone (upper)*	109
Yellowstone (lower)*	308
Mexico	
El Salo	218
South America	
Argentina-Brazil	
Iguazu	230
Brazil	
Glass	1,325
Patos-Maribondo, Grande R.	115
Paulo Afonso, São Francisco R.	275
Urubupunga, Paraná R.	39
Colombia	
Catarvata de Candelas, Cusiana R.	984
Tequendama, Bogota R.*	427
Ecuador	
Agoyan, Pastaza R.*	200
Guyana	
Kaieteur, Potaro R.	741
Great, Kamarang R.	1,600
Marina, Ipobe R.#	500
Venezuela	
Angel#*	3,212
Cuquenan	2,000

Latitude, Longitude, and Altitude of U.S. and Canadian Cities

Source: U.S. geographic positions, U.S. altitudes provided by Geological Survey, U.S. Dept. of the Interior. Canadian geographic positions and altitudes provided by Natural Resources Canada.

City	Lat. N °	′	″	Long. W °	′	″	Elev. (ft)
Abilene, TX	32	26	55	99	43	58	1,718
Akron, OH	41	4	53	81	31	9	1,050
Albany, NY	42	39	9	73	45	24	20
Albuquerque, NM	35	5	4	106	39	2	4,955
Alert, N.W.T.	82	30	0	62	22	0	100
Allentown, PA	40	36	30	75	29	26	350
Amarillo, TX	35	13	19	101	49	51	3,685
Anchorage, AK	61	13	5	149	54	1	101
Ann Arbor, MI	42	16	15	83	43	35	880
Asheville, NC	35	36	3	82	33	15	2,134
Ashland, KY	38	28	42	82	38	17	558
Atlanta, GA	33	44	56	84	23	17	1,050
Atlantic City, NJ	39	21	51	74	25	24	8
Augusta, GA	33	28	15	81	58	30	414
Augusta, ME	44	18	38	69	46	48	45
Austin, TX	30	16	1	97	44	34	501
Bakersfield, CA	35	22	24	119	1	4	408
Baltimore, MD	39	17	25	76	36	45	100
Bangor, ME	44	48	4	68	46	42	158
Baton Rouge, LA	30	27	2	91	9	16	53
Battle Creek, MI	42	19	16	85	10	47	820
Bay City, MI	43	35	40	83	53	20	595
Beaumont, TX	30	5	9	94	6	6	20
Belleville, Ont.	44	14	0	77	21	0	320
Bellingham, WA	48	45	35	122	29	13	100
Berkeley, CA	37	52	18	122	16	18	150
Billings, MT	45	47	0	108	30	0	3,124
Biloxi, MS	30	23	45	88	53	7	25
Binghamton, NY	42	5	55	75	55	6	865
Birmingham, AL	33	31	14	86	48	9	600
Bismarck, ND	46	48	30	100	47	0	1,700
Bloomington, IL	40	29	3	88	59	37	829
Boise, ID	43	36	49	116	12	9	2,730
Boston, MA	42	21	30	71	3	37	20
Bowling Green, KY	36	59	25	86	26	37	510
Brandon, Man.	49	54	35	99	57	03	1,343
Brantford, Ont.	43	08	0	80	16	0	815
Brattleboro, VT	42	51	3	72	33	30	240
Bridgeport, CT	41	10	1	73	12	19	10
Brockton, MA	42	5	0	71	1	8	112
Buffalo, NY	42	53	11	78	52	43	585
Burlington, Ont.	43	23	10	79	50	15	640
Burlington, VT	44	28	33	73	12	45	113
Butte, MT	46	0	14	112	32	2	5,549

City	Lat. N °	′	″	Long. W °	′	″	Elev. (ft)
Calgary, Alta.	51	03	0	114	05	0	3,557
Cambridge, MA	42	22	30	71	6	22	30
Canton, OH	40	47	56	81	22	43	1,100
Carson City, NV	39	9	50	119	45	59	4,730
Cedar Rapids, IA	42	0	30	91	38	38	730
Central Islip, NY	40	47	26	73	12	8	88
Champaign, IL	40	6	59	88	14	36	740
Charleston, SC	32	46	35	79	55	52	118
Charleston, WV	38	20	59	81	37	58	606
Charlotte, NC	35	13	37	80	50	36	850
Charlottetown, P.E.I.	46	14	25	63	08	05	160
Chattanooga, TN	35	2	44	85	18	35	685
Cheyenne, WY	41	8	24	104	49	11	6,067
Chicago, IL	41	51	0	87	39	0	596
Churchill, Man.	58	43	30	94	07	0	94
Cincinnati, OH	39	9	43	84	27	25	683
Cleveland, OH	41	29	58	81	41	44	690
Colorado Springs, CO	38	50	2	104	49	15	6,008
Columbia, MO	38	57	6	92	20	2	758
Columbia, SC	34	0	2	81	2	6	314
Columbus, GA	32	27	39	84	59	16	300
Columbus, OH	39	57	40	82	59	56	800
Concord, NH	43	12	29	71	32	17	288
Corpus Christi, TX	27	48	1	97	23	46	35
Dallas, TX	32	47	0	96	48	0	463
Dawson, Yukon	64	03	45	139	25	50	1,214
Dayton, OH	39	45	32	84	11	30	750
Daytona Beach, FL	29	12	38	81	1	23	10
Decatur, IL	39	50	25	88	57	17	670
Denver, CO	39	44	21	104	59	3	5,260
Des Moines, IA	41	36	2	93	36	32	803
Detroit, MI	42	19	53	83	2	45	585
Dodge City, KS	37	45	10	100	1	0	2,550
Dubuque, IA	42	30	2	90	39	52	620
Duluth, MN	46	47	0	92	6	23	610
Durham, NC	35	59	38	78	53	56	394
Eau Claire, WI	44	48	41	91	29	54	850
Edmonton, Alta.	53	33	0	113	28	0	2,200
Elizabeth, NJ	40	39	50	74	12	40	38
El Paso, TX	31	45	31	106	29	11	3,695
Enid, OK	36	23	44	97	52	41	1,246
Erie, PA	42	7	45	80	5	7	650
Eugene, OR	44	3	8	123	5	8	419
Eureka, CA	40	48	8	124	9	45	44
Evansville, IN	37	58	29	87	33	21	388
Fairbanks, AK	64	50	16	147	42	59	440
Fall River, MA	41	42	5	71	9	20	200
Fargo, ND	46	52	38	96	47	22	900
Flagstaff, AZ	35	11	53	111	39	2	6,900
Flint, MI	43	0	45	83	41	15	750
Ft. Smith, AR	35	23	9	94	23	54	446
Ft. Wayne, IN	41	7	50	85	7	44	781
Ft. Worth, TX	32	43	31	97	19	14	670
Fredericton, N.B.	45	56	43	66	40	0	67
Fresno, CA	36	44	52	119	46	17	296
Gadsden, AL	34	0	51	86	0	24	554
Gainesville, FL	29	39	5	82	19	30	183
Gallup, NM	35	31	41	108	44	31	6,508
Galveston, TX	29	18	4	94	47	51	10
Gary, IN	41	35	36	87	20	47	600
Grand Junction, CO	39	3	50	108	33	0	4,597
Grand Rapids, MI	42	57	48	85	40	5	610
Great Falls, MT	47	30	1	111	18	0	3,334
Green Bay, WI	44	31	9	88	1	11	594
Greensboro, NC	36	4	21	79	47	32	770
Greenville, SC	34	51	9	82	23	39	966
Guelph, Ont.	43	33	0	80	15	0	1,100
Gulfport, MS	30	22	2	89	5	34	25
Halifax, N.S.	44	52	0	63	43	0	477
Hamilton, OH	39	23	58	84	33	41	600
Hamilton, Ont.	43	14	0	79	57	0	780
Harrisburg, PA	40	16	25	76	53	5	320
Hartford, CT	41	45	49	72	41	8	40
Helena, MT	46	35	34	112	2	7	4,090
Hilo, HI	19	43	47	155	5	24	38
Honolulu, HI	21	18	25	157	51	30	18
Houston, TX	29	45	47	95	21	47	40
Huntsville, AL	34	43	49	86	35	10	641
Indianapolis, IN	39	46	6	86	9	29	717
Iowa City, IA	41	39	40	91	31	48	685
Jackson, MI	42	14	45	84	24	5	940
Jackson, MS	32	17	55	90	11	5	294
Jacksonville, FL	30	19	55	81	39	21	12
Jersey City, NJ	40	43	41	74	4	41	83
Johnstown, PA	40	19	36	78	55	20	1200
Joplin, MO	37	5	3	94	30	47	990
Juneau, AK	58	18	7	134	25	11	50
Kalamazoo, MI	42	17	30	85	35	14	755
Kansas City, KS	39	6	51	94	37	38	750
Kansas City, MO	39	5	59	94	34	42	740
Kenosha, WI	42	35	5	87	49	16	610
Key West, FL	24	33	19	81	46	58	8
Kingston, Ont.	44	18	0	76	28	0	305
Kitchener, Ont.	43	27	0	80	29	0	1,040
Knoxville, TN	35	57	38	83	55	15	889
Lafayette, IN	40	25	0	86	52	31	567
Lancaster, PA	40	2	16	76	18	21	368
Lansing, MI	42	43	57	84	33	20	830
Laredo, TX	27	30	22	99	30	26	414
Las Vegas, NV	36	10	30	115	8	11	2,000
Lawrence, MA	42	42	25	71	9	49	50
Lethbridge, Alta.	49	42	0	112	49	0	3,047
Lexington, KY	37	59	19	84	28	40	955
Lihue, HI	21	58	52	159	22	16	206
Lima, OH	40	44	33	84	6	19	875
Lincoln, NE	40	48	0	96	40	0	1,150
Little Rock, AR	34	44	47	92	17	22	350
London, Ont.	42	59	0	81	14	0	875
Los Angeles, CA	34	3	8	118	14	34	330
Louisville, KY	38	15	15	85	45	34	462
Lowell, MA	42	38	0	71	19	0	102
Lubbock, TX	33	34	40	101	51	17	3,195
Macon, GA	32	50	26	83	37	57	400
Madison, WI	43	4	23	89	24	4	863
Manchester, NH	42	59	44	71	27	19	175
Marshall, TX	32	32	41	94	22	2	410
Medicine Hat, Alta.	50	03	0	110	40	0	2,352
Memphis, TN	35	8	58	90	2	56	254
Meriden, CT	41	32	17	72	48	27	190
Miami, FL	25	46	26	80	11	38	11
Milwaukee, WI	43	2	0	87	54	23	634
Minneapolis, MN	44	58	48	93	15	49	815
Minot, ND	48	13	57	101	17	45	1,555
Mobile, AL	30	41	39	88	2	35	16
Moncton, N.B.	46	06	58	64	48	11	232
Montgomery, AL	32	22	0	86	18	0	260
Montpelier, VT	44	15	36	72	34	33	525
Montréal, Que.	45	31	0	73	39	0	221
Moose Jaw, Sask.	50	24	0	105	32	0	1,892
Muncie, IN	40	11	36	85	23	11	952
Nashville, TN	36	9	57	86	47	4	440
Natchez, MS	31	33	37	91	24	11	230
Newark, NJ	40	44	8	74	10	22	95
New Britain, CT	41	39	40	72	46	48	200
New Haven, CT	41	18	29	72	55	43	40
New Orleans, LA	29	57	16	90	4	30	11
New York, NY	40	42	51	74	0	23	55
Niagara Falls, Ont.	43	06	0	79	04	0	589
Nome, AK	64	30	4	165	24	23	25
Norfolk, VA	36	50	48	76	17	8	10
North Bay, Ont.	46	19	0	79	28	0	1,200
Oakland, CA	37	48	16	122	16	11	42
Ogden, UT	41	13	23	111	58	23	4,299
Oklahoma City, OK	35	28	3	97	30	58	1,195
Omaha, NE	41	15	31	95	56	15	1,040
Orlando, FL	28	32	17	81	22	46	106
Ottawa, Ont.	45	16	0	75	45	0	382
Paducah, KY	37	5	0	88	36	0	345
Pasadena, CA	34	8	52	118	8	37	865
Paterson, NJ	40	55	0	74	10	20	70
Pensacola, FL	30	25	16	87	13	1	32
Peoria, IL	40	41	37	89	35	20	470
Peterborough, Ont.	44	18	0	78	19	0	628
Philadelphia, PA	39	57	8	75	9	51	40
Phoenix, AZ	33	26	54	112	4	24	1,090
Pierre, SD	44	22	6	100	21	2	1,484
Pittsburgh, PA	40	26	26	79	59	46	770
Pittsfield, MA	42	27	0	73	14	45	1,039
Pocatello, ID	42	52	17	112	26	41	4,464
Pt. Arthur, TX	29	53	55	93	55	43	10
Portland, ME	43	39	41	70	15	21	25
Portland, OR	45	31	25	122	40	30	50
Portsmouth, NH	43	4	18	70	45	47	21
Portsmouth, VA	36	50	7	76	17	55	10
Prince Rupert, B.C.	54	19	0	130	19	0	116
Providence, RI	41	49	26	71	24	48	80
Provo, UT	40	14	2	111	39	28	4,549
Pueblo, CO	38	15	16	104	36	31	4,662
Québec City, Que.	46	49	0	71	13	0	244

City	Lat. N °	′	″	Long. W °	′	″	Elev. (ft)
Racine, WI	42	43	34	87	46	58	630
Raleigh, NC	35	46	19	78	38	20	350
Rapid City, SD	44	4	50	103	13	50	3,247
Reading, PA	40	20	8	75	55	38	266
Regina, Sask.	50	27	0	104	37	0	1,894
Reno, NV	39	31	47	119	48	46	4,498
Richmond, VA	37	33	13	77	27	38	190
Roanoke, VA	37	16	15	79	56	30	940
Rochester, MN	44	1	18	92	28	11	990
Rochester, NY	43	9	17	77	36	57	515
Rockford, IL	42	16	16	89	5	38	715
Sacramento, CA	38	34	54	121	29	36	20
Saginaw, MI	43	25	10	83	57	3	595
St. Catharines, Ont.	43	10	0	79	15	0	321
St. Cloud, MN	45	33	39	94	9	44	1,040
St. John, N.B.	45	15	33	66	02	20	357
St. John's, Nfld.	47	34	0	52	44	0	461
St. Joseph, MO	39	46	7	94	50	47	850
St. Louis, MO	38	37	38	90	11	52	455
St. Paul, MN	44	56	40	93	5	35	780
St. Petersburg, FL	27	46	14	82	40	46	44
Salem, OR	44	56	35	123	2	2	154
Salina, KS	38	50	25	97	36	40	1,225
Salt Lake City, UT	40	45	39	111	53	25	4,266
San Antonio, TX	29	25	26	98	29	36	650
San Bernardino, CA	34	6	30	117	17	20	1,200
San Diego, CA	32	42	55	117	9	23	40
San Francisco, CA	37	46	30	122	25	6	63
San Jose, CA	37	20	22	121	53	38	87
San Juan, P.R.	18	28	6	66	6	22	8
Santa Barbara, CA	34	25	15	119	41	50	50
Santa Cruz, CA	36	58	27	122	1	47	20
Santa Fe, NM	35	41	13	105	56	14	6,989
Sarasota, FL	27	20	10	82	31	51	27
Saskatoon, Sask.	52	07	0	106	38	0	1,653
Sault Ste. Marie, Ont.	46	31	0	84	20	0	630
Savannah, GA	32	5	0	81	6	0	42
Schenectady, NY	42	48	51	73	56	24	245
Seattle, WA	47	36	23	122	19	51	350
Sheboygan, WI	43	45	3	87	42	52	630
Sherbrooke, Que.	45	24	0	71	54	0	792
Sheridan, WY	44	47	50	106	57	20	3,742
Shreveport, LA	32	31	30	93	45	0	209
Sioux City, IA	42	30	0	96	24	0	1,117
Sioux Falls, SD	43	32	48	96	43	48	1,442
South Bend, IN	41	41	0	86	15	0	725
Spartanburg, SC	34	56	58	81	55	56	816
Spokane, WA	47	39	32	117	25	30	2,000
Springfield, IL	39	48	6	89	38	37	610
Springfield, MA	42	6	5	72	35	25	70
Springfield, MO	37	12	55	93	17	53	1,300
Springfield, OH	39	55	27	83	48	32	1,000
Stamford, CT	41	3	12	73	32	21	35
Steubenville, OH	40	22	11	80	38	3	1,060
Stockton, CA	37	57	28	121	17	23	15
Sudbury, Ont.	46	31	0	80	54	0	1,140
Superior, WI	46	43	15	92	6	14	642
Sydney, N.S.	46	09	0	60	11	0	203
Syracuse, NY	43	2	53	76	8	52	400
Tacoma, WA	47	15	11	122	26	35	380
Tallahassee, FL	30	26	17	84	16	51	188
Tampa, FL	27	56	50	82	27	31	48
Terre Haute, IN	39	28	0	87	24	50	501
Texarkana, TX	33	25	30	94	2	51	324
Thunder Bay, Ont.	48	24	0	89	19	0	653
Timmins, Ont.	48	28	0	81	20	0	967
Toledo, OH	41	39	50	83	33	19	615
Topeka, KS	39	2	54	95	40	40	1,000
Toronto, Ont.	43	37	39	79	23	46	251
Trenton, NJ	40	13	1	74	44	36	54
Trois-Rivières, Que.	46	21	0	72	33	0	198
Troy, NY	42	43	42	73	41	32	35
Tucson, AZ	32	13	18	110	55	33	2,390
Tulsa, OK	36	9	14	95	59	33	804
Urbana, IL	40	6	38	88	12	26	725
Utica, NY	43	6	3	75	13	59	415
Vancouver, B.C.	49	15	0	123	7	0	14
Victoria, B.C.	48	26	0	123	22	0	63
Waco, TX	31	32	57	97	8	47	405
Walla Walla, WA	46	3	53	118	20	31	1,000
Washington, DC	38	53	42	77	2	12	25
Waterloo, IA	42	29	34	92	20	34	850
West Palm Beach, FL	26	42	54	80	3	13	21
Wheeling, WV	40	3	50	80	43	16	672
Whitehorse, Yukon	60	43	0	135	03	0	2,305
White Plains, NY	41	2	2	73	45	48	220
Wichita, KS	37	41	32	97	20	14	1,305
Wilkes-Barre, PA	41	14	45	75	52	54	550
Wilmington, DE	39	44	45	75	32	49	100
Wilmington, NC	34	13	32	77	56	42	50
Windsor, Ont.	42	18	0	83	01	0	622
Winnipeg, Man.	49	54	39	97	14	36	783
Winston-Salem, NC	36	5	59	80	14	40	912
Worcester, MA	42	15	45	71	48	10	480
Yakima, WA	46	36	8	120	30	17	1,066
Yellowknife, N.W.T.	62	27	20	114	21	0	675
Youngstown, OH	41	5	59	80	38	59	861
Yuma, AZ	32	43	31	114	37	25	160
Zanesville, OH	39	56	25	82	0	48	710

Latitude and Longitude of World Cities

Source: National Imagery Mapping Agency, U.S. Dept. of Defense

City	Lat. °		Long. °	
Athens, Greece	37	59 N	23	44 E
Bangkok, Thailand	13	45 N	100	31 E
Beijing, China	39	56 N	116	24 E
Berlin, Germany	52	31 N	13	25 E
Bogotá, Colombia	04	36 N	74	05 W
Buenos Aires, Argentina	34	36 S	58	28 W
Cairo, Egypt	30	03 N	31	15 E
Jakarta, Indonesia	06	10 S	106	48 E
Jerusalem, Israel	31	46 N	35	14 E
Johannesburg, South Africa	26	12 S	28	05 E
Kathmandu, Nepal	27	43 N	85	19 E
Kiev, Ukraine	50	26 N	30	31 E
London, UK (Greenwich)	51	30 N	00	00
Manila, Philippines	14	35 N	121	00 E
Mexico City, Mexico	19	24 N	99	09 W
Moscow, Russia	55	45 N	37	35 E
Mumbai (Bombay), India	18	58 N	72	50 E
New Delhi, India	28	36 N	77	12 E
Panama City, Panama	08	58 N	79	32 W
Paris, France	48	52 N	02	20 E
Quito, Ecuador	00	13 S	78	30 W
Rio de Janeiro, Brazil	22	43 S	43	13 W
Rome, Italy	41	53 N	12	30 E
Santiago, Chile	33	27 S	70	40 W
Seoul, South Korea	37	34 N	127	00 E
Sydney, Australia	33	53 S	151	12 E
Tehran, Iran	35	40 N	51	26 E
Tokyo, Japan	35	42 N	139	46 E
Warsaw, Poland	52	15 N	21	00 E
Wellington, New Zealand	41	18 S	174	47 E

Highest and Lowest Continental Altitudes

Source: National Geographic Society

Continent	Highest point	Elev. (ft)
Asia	Mount Everest, Nepal-Tibet	29,035
South America	Mount Aconcagua, Argentina	22,834
North America	Mount McKinley, Alaska	20,320
Africa	Kilimanjaro, Tanzania	19,340
Europe	Mount Elbrus, Russia	18,510
Antarctica	Vinson Massif	16,864
Australia	Mount Kosciusko, New South Wales	7,310

Continent	Lowest point	ft below sea level
Asia	Dead Sea, Israel-Jordan	1,348
South America	Valdes Peninsula, Argentina	131
North America	Death Valley, California	282
Africa	Lake Assal, Djibouti	512
Europe	Caspian Sea, Russia, Azerbaijan	92
Antarctica	Bentley Subglacial Trench	8,327[1]
Australia	Lake Eyre, South Australia	52

(1) Estimated level of the continental floor. Lower points that have yet to be discovered may exist further beneath the ice.

RELIGION

Membership of Religious Groups in the U.S.

Sources: *2007 Yearbook of American & Canadian Churches,* © National Council of the Churches of Christ in the USA; World Christian Database; *World Almanac* research

These membership figures are the latest available and generally are based on reports made by officials of each group, and not on any religious census. Figures from other sources may vary. Many groups keep careful records; others only estimate. Not all groups report annually. Church membership figures vary from one denomination to another, but generally the figures reported in this table are inclusive and do not refer simply to full communicants or confirmed members.

The number of houses of worship appears in parentheses. * Indicates that the group declines to make membership figures public. Groups reporting fewer than 5,000 members are not included; where membership numbers are not available, only those groups with 50 or more houses of worship are listed.

Religious group (Houses of Worship)	Members
Adventist Churches	
Advent Christian Ch. (1,282)	262,729
Ch. of God General Conference (Oregon, IL and Morrow, GA) (91)	5,396
Seventh-day Adventist Ch. (4,594)	900,985
American Catholic Church (100)	**25,000**
Apostolic Catholic Churches of America (91)	**12,890**
Apostolic Episcopal Church (250)	**18,000**
Baha'i Faith	**669,019[1]**
Baptist Churches	
Alliance of Baptists (126)	64,350
American Baptist Assn. (1,760)	275,000
American Baptist Chs. in the U.S.A. (5,786)	1,442,824
Baptist Bible Fellowship Intl. (4,500)	1,200,000
Baptist General Conference (918)	143,200
Baptist Missionary Assn. of America (1,334)	234,732
Conservative Baptist Assn. of America (1,200)	200,000
Free Will Baptists, National Assn. of (2,470)	197,919
General Baptists, General Assn. of (715)	66,296
National Baptist Convention of America, Inc. (NA)	3,500,000
National Baptist Convention, U.S.A., Inc. (9,000)	5,000,000
National Missionary Baptist Convention of America (NA)	2,500,000
North American Baptist Conference (276)	49,017
Progressive National Baptist Convention, Inc. (2,000)	2,500,000
Regular Baptist Chs., General Assn. of (1,447)	150,000
Separate Baptists in Christ (100)	8,000
Seventh Day Baptist General Conference, USA and Canada (80)	NA
Southern Baptist Convention (42,334)	16,052,92
Sovereign Grace Believers (350)	4,000
Brethren in Christ Church (232)	**20,739**
Brethren (German Baptists)	
Brethren Ch. (Ashland, OH) (119)	10,381
Church of the Brethren (1,070)	134,828
Fellowship of Grace Brethren Chs. (260)	30,371
Old German Baptist Brethren Ch. (55)	6,205
Buddhists	**2,795,460[1]**
Christian Brethren (Plymouth Brethren) (1,125)	**95,000**
Christian Church (Disciples of Christ) (3,717)	**804,842**
Christian Congregation, Inc. (1,439)	**119,391**
Christian and Missionary Alliance (1,727)	**381,677**
Christian Union (112)	5,634
Churches of Christ in Christian Union (216)	**10,104**
Church of Christ (Holiness) U.S.A. (163)	**10,475**
Church of Christ, Scientist (2,250)	**862,000**
Church of the United Brethren in Christ, USA (228)	**23,585**
Churches of Christ (15,000)	**1,500,000**
Christian Chs. and Chs. of Christ (5,579)	1,071,616
Churches of God	
Chs. of God, General Conference (339)	32,429
Ch. of God (Anderson, IN) (2,353)	234,311
Ch. of God (Seventh Day), Denver, CO (200)	11,000
Ch. of God by Faith, Inc. (148)	NA
Ch. of God, Mountain Assembly, Inc. (118)	6,140
Church of the Nazarene (5,070)	**636,564**
Intl. Council of Community Churches (192)	**115,812**
National Assn. of Congregational Christian Churches (432)	**65,392**
Eastern Catholic Churches	
Armenian Catholic Church (9)	36,000
Chaldean Catholic Church (14)	120,000
Maronite Catholic Church (59)	75,232
Melkite Catholic Church (35)	27,207
Romanian Greek Catholic Church (15)	5,000
Ruthenian Byzantine Catholic Church (223)	99,288
Syrian Catholic Church (12)	13,270
Syro-Malabar Catholic Church (8)	100,000
Ukrainian Greek Catholic Church (200)	102,632
Eastern Orthodox Churches	
American Carpatho-Russian Orthodox Greek Catholic Ch. (80)	13,210

Religious group (Houses of Worship)	Members
Antiochian Orthodox Christian Archdiocese of North America (225)	360,000
Apostolic Catholic Assyrian Ch. Of the East, N.A. Dioceses (22)	120,000
Armenian Apostolic Ch. of America (34)	360,000
Armenian Apostolic Ch., Diocese of America (72)	414,000
Coptic Orthodox Ch. (100)	300,000
Greek Orthodox Archdiocese of America (510)	1,500,000
Mar Thoma Syrian Ch. of India (68)	32,000
Orthodox Ch. in America (721)	1,000,000
Patriarchal Parishes of the Russian Orthodox Ch. in the U.S.A. (31)	17,000
Russian Orthodox Ch. Outside of Russia (177)	480,000
Serbian Orthodox Ch. in the U.S.A. and Canada (68)	67,000
Syrian (Syriac) Orthodox Ch. of Antioch (22)	32,500
Syro-Russian Orthodox Catholic Ch. (120)	34,000
Ukrainian Orthodox Ch. of the U.S.A. (115)	13,000
Episcopal Church (7,364)	**2,333,327**
Evangelical Church (133)	**12,475**
Evangelical Congregational Church (149)	**21,463**
Evangelical Covenant Church (800)	**101,003**
Evangelical Free Church of America (1,224)	**242,619**
Friends	
Evangelical Friends Intl. – North American Region (278)	27,057
Friends General Conference (650)	34,000
Friends United Meeting (436)	41,297
Philadelphia Yearly Meeting of the Religious Society of Friends (105)	11,845
Religious Society of Friends (Conservative) (1,200)	104,000
Full Gospel Fellowship of Churches and Ministers Intl. (902)	**326,900**
General Church of the New Jerusalem (34)	**6,364**
Grace Gospel Fellowship (128)	**60,000**
Hindus	**1,330,446[1]**
Independent Fundamental Churches of America Int'l, Inc. (IFCA) (616)	**80,600**
Jehovah's Witnesses (11,706)	**989,403**
Jews	**5,729,147[1]**
Jewish Organizations [2]	
Union for Reform Judaism (900+)	1,500,000
Union of Orthodox Jewish Congregations of America (1,000)	*
United Synagogue of Conservative Judaism, The (760)	1,500,000
Jewish Reconstructionist Federation (103)	180,000
Latter-Day Saints	
Ch. of Jesus Christ (Bickertonites) (63)	2,707
Ch. of Jesus Christ of Latter-day Saints (11,731)	5,310,598
Community of Christ (1,346)	137,844
Reorganized Ch. of Jesus Christ of Latter-Day Saints (1,353)	247,000
The Liberal Catholic Church—Province of the United States of America (24)	**6,500**
Lutheran Churches	
American Assn. of Lutheran Chs. (101)	18,252
Apostolic Lutheran Ch. of America (58)	NA
Ch. of the Lutheran Brethren of America (108)	13,702
Ch. of the Lutheran Confession (76)	8,643
Evangelical Lutheran Ch. in America (10,766)	5,099,877
Evangelical Lutheran Synod (141)	21,333
Free Lutheran Congregations, Assn. of (245)	36,400
Latvian Evangelical Lutheran Ch. in America (68)	13,846
Lutheran Ch—Missouri Synod (LCMS) (6,187)	2,540,045
Wisconsin Evangelical Lutheran Synod (1,244)	720,071
Mennonite Churches	
Beachy Amish Mennonite Chs. (153)	9,205
Ch. of God in Christ (Mennonite) (124)	20,500
Fellowship of Evangelical Chs. (36)	11,604
Hutterian Brethren (444)	43,000
Mennonite Brethren Chs., General Conference of (368)	82,130
Mennonite Ch. USA (994)	118,070
Old Order Amish Ch. (898)	80,820

Religious group (Houses of Worship)	Members
Methodist Churches	
African Methodist Episcopal Ch. (NA)	2,311,398
African Methodist Episcopal Zion Ch. (3,226)	1,447,934
Allegheny Wesleyan Methodist Connection	
(Original Allegheny Conference) (111)	1,830
Christian Methodist Episcopal Ch. (3,250)	850,000
Evangelical Methodist Ch. (123)	8,615
Free Methodist Ch. of North America (978)	69,342
Primitive Methodist Ch. in the U.S.A. (78)	4,717
Southern Methodist Ch. (117)	7,686
United Methodist Ch. (35,469)	8,341,375
Wesleyan Ch. (1,614)	123,274
Messianic Jews	c. 75,000
Metropolitan Community Churches, Universal	
Fellowship Of (300)	44,000
Missionary Church (375)	41,328
Moravian Church in America (Unitas Fratrum)	
(93)	25,872
Muslims	4,760,437[1]
National Organization of the New Apostolic	
Church of North America (380)	36,438
Pentecostal Churches	
Apostolic Faith Mission Ch. of God (21)	10,350
Apostolic Faith Mission of Portland, Oregon (54)	4,500
Assemblies of God (12,084)	2,627,029
Bible Ch. of Christ, Inc. (6)	6,850
Bible Fellowship Ch. (55)	7,197
Christian Ch. of North America, General Council (96)	7,200
Ch. of God (Cleveland, Tennessee) (6,605)	932,024
Ch. of God in Christ (15,300)	5,499,875
Ch. of God of Prophecy (1,876)	77,609
Ch. of Our Lord Jesus Christ of the Apostolic Faith,	
Inc. (500)	NA
Congregational Holiness Ch. (190)	9,565
Elim Fellowship (100)	NA

Religious group (Houses of Worship)	Members
Intl. Ch. of the Foursquare Gospel (1,834)	319,349
Intl. Pentecostal Ch. of Christ (67)	5,610
Intl. Pentecostal Holiness Ch. (1,911)	209,922
Open Bible Standard Chs. (317)	37,000
Pentecostal Assemblies of the World, Inc. (1,750)	1,500,000
Pentecostal Ch. of God (1,186)	102,000
Pentecostal Free Will Baptist Ch., Inc. (150)	28,000
United House of Prayer (135)	NA
United Pentecostal Ch. Intl. (3,790)	NA
United Pentecostal Chs. of Christ (62)	7,059
Presbyterian Churches	
Associate Reformed Presbyterian Ch. (General	
Synod) (257)	40,861
Cumberland Presbyterian Ch. (784)	85,427
Cumberland Presbyterian Ch. in America (152)	15,142
Evangelical Presbyterian Ch. (193)	67,808
Korean Presbyterian Ch. in America, General	
Assembly of the (305)	54,000
Orthodox Presbyterian Ch. (224)	26,090
Presbyterian Ch. in America (1,498)	306,784
Presbyterian Ch. (U.S.A.) (11,142)	3,455,952
Reformed Presbyterian Ch. of North America (86)	6,105
Reformed Churches	
Christian Reformed Ch. in North America (242)	82,453
Hungarian Reformed Ch. in America (27)	6,000
Netherlands Reformed Congregations (26)	9,395
Protestant Reformed Chs. in America (27)	6,825
Reformed Ch. in America (901)	285,453
United Ch. of Christ (5,888)	1,359,105
Reformed Episcopal Church (125)	**6,400**
Roman Catholic Church (23,010)	**67,901,815[1]**
Salvation Army (1,369)	**454,982**
Sikhs	**268,392[1]**
Unitarian Universalist Assn. of Congregations	
(1,051)	**220,000**

(1) Source: World Christian Database. (2) From American Jewish Committee.

Adherents of All Religions by Six Continental Areas, Mid-2006

Source: *2007 Encyclopædia Britannica Book of the Year; figures rounded*

Religion (No. of countries)	Africa	Asia	Europe	Latin America	Northern America	Oceania	World
Baha'is (218)	2,103,000	3,709,000	148,000	851,000	857,000	133,000	7,801,000
Buddhists (130)	156,000	376,365,000	1,645,000	728,000	3,142,000	506,000	382,542,000
Chinese Universists (94)	36,900	385,284,000	271,000	206,000	732,000	137,000	386,666,900
Christians (238)	432,553,000	354,444,000	556,284,600	526,632,700	276,490,800	26,778,300	2,173,183,400
Roman Catholics (235)	151,951,000	126,256,000	278,870,000	489,356,000	80,620,000	8,676,000	1,135,729,000
Independents (221)	93,100,000	186,844,000	24,741,000	45,031,000	80,643,000	1,864,000	432,223,000
Protestants (232)	121,917,000	58,788,000	70,995,000	56,613,000	66,035,000	7,841,000	382,179,000
Orthodox (134)	39,901,000	12,832,000	158,220,000	928,000	6,748,000	804,000	219,433,000
Anglicans (163)	45,586,000	752,000	26,108,000	924,000	2,914,000	4,953,000	81,237,000
Marginal (215)	3,451,000	3,287,000	4,678,000	10,934,000	11,742,000	666,000	34,758,000
Unaffiliated (232)	25,388,000	5,617,000	21,902,600	4,997,700	54,891,800	4,232,300	117,029,400
Confucianists (15)	300	6,376,000	18,300	800	0	51,800	6,447,200
Ethnic religionists (144)	112,254,000	145,057,000	1,242,000	3,501,000	1,468,000	318,000	263,840,000
Hindus (116)	2,749,000	865,072,000	1,478,000	769,000	1,490,000	424,000	871,982,000
Jains (11)	80,600	4,571,000	0	0	8,000	700	4,660,300
Jews (134)	238,000	5,350,000	2,017,000	1,237,000	6,169,000	107,000	15,118,000
Muslims (206)	368,116,300	927,077,000	33,260,800	1,758,000	5,334,600	417,400	1,335,964,100
Neoreligionists (107)	124,000	102,702,000	379,000	791,000	1,567,000	87,300	105,650,300
Shintoists (8)	0	2,729,000	0	0	61,200	0	2,797,700
Sikhs (33)	61,700	24,938,000	241,000	0	614,000	25,400	25,880,100
Spiritists (55)	3,200	2,000	136,000	13,033,000	162,000	7,500	13,343,700
Taoists (5)	0	2,765,000	0	0	12,000	0	2,777,000
Zoroastrians (23)	1,000	152,000	5,300	0	20,400	1,600	180,300
Other religionists (78)	80,000	70,000	260,000	110,000	670,000	10,000	1,200,000
Nonreligious (237)	6,301,000	616,922,000	108,784,000	16,517,000	32,805,000	4,036,000	785,365,000
Atheists (219)	619,000	127,021,000	21,914,000	2,788,000	2,119,000	417,000	154,878,000

Note: Continental Areas. Following current UN demographic terminology, which divides the world into the 6 major areas shown above. Note that "Asia" includes the former Soviet Central Asian states and "Europe" includes all of Russia, extending eastward to the Pacific. **Countries.** Numbers in parentheses are sovereign and nonsovereign countries in which each religion has a statistically significant and organized following. **Adherents.** As defined in the 1948 Universal Declaration of Human Rights, a person's religion is what he or she says it is. Totals are enumerated following the methodology of the *World Christian Encyclopedia*, 2nd ed. (2001) and *World Christian Trends* (2001), using recent censuses, polls, literature, and other data. Totals may conflict with some estimates for total populations. **Buddhists.** 56% Mahayana, 38% Theravada (Hinayana), 6% Tantrayana (Lamaism). **Chinese Universists** (folk religionists). Followers of traditional Chinese religion (local deities, ancestor veneration, Confucian ethics, universism, divination, some Buddhist elements). **Christians.** Followers of Jesus Christ. Unaffiliated Christians profess Christian beliefs but are not named on specific church rolls; Independents follow Christian churches and networks that regard themselves as independent from historic, mainstream Christianity; Marginal Christians belong to churches on the margins of mainstream Christianity, including Unitarians, Mormons, Jehovah's Witnesses, Christian Science, and Religious Science. **Confucianists.** Non-Chinese followers of Confucius and Confucianism, mostly Koreans in Korea. **Ethnic religionists.** Followers of local, tribal, animistic, or shamanistic religions, with members restricted to one ethnic group. **Hindus.** 68% Vaishnavites, 27% Shaivites, 2% neo-Hindus and reform Hindus. **Jews.** Adherents of Judaism. **Muslims.** 84% Sunni Muslims, 14% Shia Muslims (Shi'ites), 2% other schools. **New-Religionists.** Followers of Asian 20th-cent. New Religions, New Religious movements, radical new crisis religions, and non-Christian syncretistic mass religions, all founded since 1800 and most since 1945. **Other religionists.** Including a handful of religions, quasi-religions, pseudoreligions, pararreligions, religious or mystic systems, and religious and semireligious brotherhoods of numerous varieties.

Episcopal Church Liturgical Colors and Calendar, 2007-2011

Source: The Rt. Rev. Barry E. Yingling, Editor, the *Churchman's Ordo Kalendar*

The most common liturgical colors in the Episcopal Church are: **White**—Christmas Day through First Sunday after Epiphany; Maundy Thursday (as an alternative to crimson at the Eucharist); from the Vigil of Easter to the Day of Pentecost (Whitsunday); Trinity Sunday; Feasts of the Lord (except Holy Cross Day); the Confession of St. Peter; the Conversion of St. Paul; St. Joseph; St. Mary Magdalene; St. Mary the Virgin; St. Michael and All Angels; All Saints' Day; St. John the Evangelist; memorials of other saints who were not martyred; Independence Day and Thanksgiving Day; weddings and funerals. **Red**—the Day of Pentecost; Holy Cross Day; feasts of apostles and evangelists (except those listed above); feasts and memorials of martyrs (including Holy Innocents' Day). **Violet**—Advent and Lent. **Crimson** or oxblood (dark red)—Holy Week. **Green**—the seasons after Epiphany and after Pentecost. **Black**—optional alternative for funerals and Good Friday.

The days of fasting are Ash Wednesday and Good Friday. Other days of special devotion (penitence) include the 40 days of Lent. Ember Days are days of prayer for the church's ministry. They fall on the Wednesday, Friday, and Saturday after the first Sunday in Lent, the Day of Pentecost, Holy Cross Day, and December 13. Rogation Days, the 3 days before Ascension Day, are days of prayer for God's blessing on the crops, on commerce and industry, and for conservation of the earth's resources.

Days, etc.	2007	2008	2009	2010	2011
Golden Number	13	14	15	16	17
Sunday Letter	G	F	D	C	b
Sundays after Epiphany	7	4	7	6	9
Ash Wednesday	Feb. 21	Feb. 6	Feb. 25	Feb. 17	Mar. 9
First Sunday in Lent	Feb. 25	Feb. 10	Mar. 1	Feb. 21	Mar. 13
Passion/Palm Sunday	Apr. 1	Mar. 16	Apr. 5	Mar. 28	Apr. 17
Good Friday	Apr. 6	Mar. 21	Apr. 10	Apr. 2	Apr. 22
Easter Day	Apr. 8	Mar. 23	Apr. 12	Apr. 4	Apr. 24
Ascension Day	May 17	May 1	May 21	May 13	June 2
The Day of Pentecost	May 27	May 11	May 31	May 23	June 12
Trinity Sunday	June 3	May 18	June 7	May 30	June 19
Numbered Proper of 2 Pentecost	#5	#3	#6	#5	#8
First Sunday of Advent	Dec. 2	Nov. 30	Nov. 29	Nov. 28	Nov. 27

Greek Orthodox Movable Ecclesiastical Dates, 2007-2011

Feast days and fasting days are determined annually on the basis of the date of Holy Pascha (Easter). This ecclesiastical cycle begins with the first day of the Triodion and ends with the Sunday of All Saints, a total of 18 weeks.

	2007	2008	2009	2010	2011
Triodion begins	Jan. 28	Feb. 17	Feb. 8	Jan. 24	Feb. 13
1st Sat. of Souls	Feb. 10	Mar. 1	Feb. 21	Feb. 6	Feb. 26
Meat Fare	Feb. 11	Mar. 2	Feb. 22	Feb. 7	Feb. 27
2nd Sat. of Souls	Feb. 17	Mar. 8	Feb. 28	Feb. 13	Mar. 5
Lent Begins	Feb. 19	Mar. 10	Mar. 2	Feb. 15	Mar. 7
St. Theodore—3rd Sat. of Souls	Feb. 24	Mar. 15	Mar. 7	Feb. 20	Mar. 12
Sunday of Orthodoxy	Feb. 25	Mar. 16	Mar. 8	Feb. 21	Mar. 13
Sat. of Lazarus	Mar. 31	Apr. 19	April 11	Mar. 27	Apr. 16
Palm Sunday	Apr. 1	Apr. 20	April 12	Mar. 28	Apr. 17
Holy (Good) Friday	Apr. 6	Apr. 25	April 17	April 2	Apr. 22
Western Easter	Apr. 8	Mar. 23	April 12	April 4	Apr. 24
Orthodox Easter	Apr. 8	Apr. 27	April 19	April 4	Apr. 24
Ascension	May 17	June 5	May 28	May 13	June 2
Sat. of Souls	May 26	June 14	June 6	May 22	June 11
Pentecost	May 27	June 15	June 7	May 23	June 12
All Saints	June 3	June 22	June 14	May 30	June 19
Fast of Holy Apostles (First day)	June 4	June 23	June 15	May 31	June 20

Important Islamic Dates, 1427-1431 AH (2007-2011)

Source: Imad-ad-Dean, Inc., Bethesda, MD 20814

The Islamic calendar is a strict lunar calendar reckoned from the year of the Hijra (Anno Hegirae, or AH)—Muhammad's flight from Mecca to Medina, in 622 CE. Each year consists of 12 lunar months of 29 or 30 days beginning and ending with each new moon's visible crescent. Common years have 354 days; leap years have 355 days. Some Muslim countries employ a conventionalized calendar with the leap day added to the last month, Dhûl Hijah, but for religious purposes the leap date is taken into account by tracking each new moon sighting. The dates given below are based on the convention that the first new moon must be seen before the following dawn on the East Coast of the Americas. Actual (local) Western Hemisphere sightings may occur a day later, but never a day earlier, than these dates reflect. Holy days begin at sunset on the previous day.

	(1428) 2007	(1429) 2008	(1430) 2008-09	(1431) 2009-2010	(1432) 2010-2011
New Year's Day (Muharram 1)	Jan. 20, 2007	Jan. 9, 2008	Dec. 28, 2008	Dec. 17, 2009	Dec. 7, 2010
Ashura (Muharram 10)	Jan. 29, 2007	Jan. 18, 2008	Jan. 6, 2009	Dec. 26, 2009	Dec. 8, 2010
Mawlid (Rabi'l 12)	Mar. 31, 2007	Mar. 20, 2008	Mar. 9, 2009	Feb. 26, 2010	Feb. 15, 2011
Ramadan 1	Sept. 12, 2007	Sept. 1, 2008	Aug. 21, 2009	Aug. 11, 2010	Aug. 1, 2011
Eid al-Fitr (Shawwal 1)	Oct. 12, 2007	Sept. 30, 2008	Sept. 20, 2009	Sept. 9, 2010	Aug. 30, 2011
Eid al-Adha (Dhûl-Hijjah 10)	Dec. 20, 2007	Dec. 8, 2008	Nov. 27, 2009	Nov. 16, 2010	Nov. 6, 2011

Jewish Holy Days, Festivals, and Fasts, 5767-5771 (2007-2012)

The Jewish calendar consists of 12 lunar months, alternating between 29 and 30 days. It is lunisolar, and adjusts for the solar cycle by adding an extra month (Adar II) in the 3rd, 6th, 8th, 11th, 14th, 17th, and 19th years of a 19-year cycle. The calendar started on the day of Creation, reckoned in the 2nd-3rd cent. BCE as Tishrei 1, 3,761 years before the common era.

The religious calendar begins with the month Nisan, from which all other months are counted, and the civil calendar with Tishrei. The months are 1) Nisan; 2) Iyar; 3) Sivan; 4) Tammuz; 5) Av (also Abh); 6) Elul; 7) Tishrei; 8) Cheshvan (also Marcheshvan); 9) Kislev; 10) Tevet (also Tebeth); 11) Shevat (also Shebhat); 12) Adar; 12a) Adar Sheni (II), added in leap years. The names are Aramaic versions of the Babylonian months, adopted during the Jews' exile in Babylon in the 4th century BCE. Rosh Hashanah, the New Year, begins on Tishrei 1 (Sept.-Oct.). Yom Kippur is the holiest day of the year. All holidays listed below begin at sunset on the previous day, except where noted.

Holiday	Date on Jewish Cal.	(5768) 2007-08	(5769) 2008-09	(5770) 2009-10	(5771) 2010-11	(5772) 2011-12
Rosh Hashanah (New Year)	Tishrei 1	Sept. 13 Thu.	Sept. 30 Tue.	Sept. 19 Sat.	Sept. 9 Thu.	Sept. 29 Thu.
	Tishrei 2	Sept. 14 Fri.	Oct. 1 Wed.	Sept. 20 Sun.	Sept. 10 Fri.	Sept. 30 Fri.
Fast of Gedalya[1]	Tishrei 3	Sept. 16 Sun.*	Oct. 2 Thu.	Sept. 21 Mon.	Sept. 12 Sun.	Oct. 2 Sun.
Yom Kippur (Day of Atonement)	Tishrei 10	Sept. 22 Sat.	Oct. 9 Thu.	Sept. 28 Mon.	Sept. 18 Sat.	Oct. 8 Sat.
Sukkot	Tishrei 15	Sept. 27 Thu.	Oct. 14 Tue.	Oct. 3 Sat.	Sept. 23 Thu.	Oct. 13 Thu.
	Tishrei 21	Oct. 3 Wed.	Oct. 20 Mon.	Oct. 9 Fri.	Sept. 29 Wed.	Oct. 19 Wed.
Shemini Atzeret	Tishrei 22	Oct. 4 Thu.	Oct. 21 Tue.	Oct. 10 Sat.	Sept. 30 Thu.	Oct. 20 Thu.
Simchat Torah	Tishrei 23	Oct. 5 Fri.	Oct. 22 Wed.	Oct. 11 Sun.	Oct. 1 Fri.	Oct. 21 Fri.
Hanukkah	Kislev 25	Dec. 5 Wed.	Dec. 22 Mon.	Dec. 12 Sat.	Dec. 2 Thu.	Dec. 21 Wed.
	Tevet 2	Dec. 12 Wed.	Dec. 29 Mon.	Dec. 19 Sat.	Dec. 9 Thu.	Dec. 28 Wed.
Fast of the 10th of Tevet[1]	Tevet 10	Dec. 19 Wed.	Jan. 6 Tue.	Dec. 27 Sun.	Dec. 16 Thu.	Jan. 5 Thu.
Tu B'Shevat	Shevat 15	Jan. 22 Tue.	Feb. 9 Mon.	Jan. 30 Sat.	Jan. 20 Thu.	Feb. 8 Wed.
Ta'anis Esther (Fast of Esther)[1]	Adar 13	Mar. 20 Thu.	Mar. 9 Mon.	Feb. 25 Thu.	Mar. 17 Thu.	Mar. 7 Wed.
Purim	Adar 14	Mar. 21 Fri.	Mar. 10 Tue.	Feb. 28 Sun.	Mar. 20 Sun.	Mar. 8 Thu.
Pesach (Passover)	Nisan 15	Apr. 20 Sun.	Apr. 9 Thu.	Mar. 30 Tue.	Apr. 19 Tue.	Apr. 7 Sat.
	Nisan 22	Apr. 27 Sun.	Apr. 16 Thu.	Apr. 6 Tue.	Apr. 26 Tue.	Apr. 14 Sat.
Lag B'Omer	Iyar 18	May 23 Fri.	May 12 Tue.	May 2 Sun.	May 22 Sun.	May 10 Thu.
Shavuot (Pentecost)	Sivan 6	June 9 Mon.	May 29 Fri.	May 19 Wed.	June 8 Wed.	May 27 Sun.
	Sivan 7	June 10 Tue.	May 30 Sat.	May 20 Thu.	June 9 Thu.	May 28 Mon.
Fast of the 17th Day of Tammuz[1]	Tammuz 17	July 20 Sun.	July 9 Thu.	June 29 Tue.	July 19 Tue.	July 8 Sun.
Fast of the 9th Day of Av	Av 9	Aug.10 Sun.	July 30 Thu.	July 20 Tue.	Aug. 9 Thu.	July 29 Sun.

*Date changed to avoid Sabbath. (1) "Minor fasts" begin at sunrise.

Ash Wednesday and Easter Sunday (Western churches), 1901-2100

Year	Ash Wed.	Easter Sunday	Year	Ash Wed.	Easter Sunday	Year	Ash Wed.	Easter Sunday	Year	Ash Wed.	Easter Sunday	Year	Ash Wed.	Easter Sunday
1901	Feb. 20	Apr. 7	1941	Feb. 26	Apr. 13	1981	Mar. 4	Apr. 19	2021	Feb. 17	Apr. 4	2061	Feb. 23	Apr. 10
1902	Feb. 12	Mar. 30	1942	Feb. 18	Apr. 5	1982	Feb. 24	Apr. 11	2022	Mar. 2	Apr. 17	2062	Feb. 8	Mar. 26
1903	Feb. 25	Apr. 12	1943	Mar. 10	Apr. 25	1983	Feb. 16	Apr. 3	2023	Feb. 22	Apr. 9	2063	Feb. 28	Apr. 15
1904	Feb. 17	Apr. 3	1944	Feb. 23	Apr. 9	1984	Mar. 7	Apr. 22	2024	Feb. 14	Mar. 31	2064	Feb. 20	Apr. 6
1905	Mar. 8	Apr. 23	1945	Feb. 14	Apr. 1	1985	Feb. 20	Apr. 7	2025	Mar. 5	Apr. 20	2065	Feb. 11	Mar. 29
1906	Feb. 28	Apr. 15	1946	Mar. 6	Apr. 21	1986	Feb. 12	Mar. 30	2026	Feb. 18	Apr. 5	2066	Feb. 24	Apr. 11
1907	Feb. 13	Mar. 31	1947	Feb. 19	Apr. 6	1987	Mar. 4	Apr. 19	2027	Feb. 10	Mar. 28	2067	Feb. 16	Apr. 3
1908	Mar. 4	Apr. 19	1948	Feb. 11	Mar. 28	1988	Feb. 17	Apr. 3	2028	Mar. 1	Apr. 16	2068	Mar. 7	Apr. 22
1909	Feb. 24	Apr. 11	1949	Mar. 2	Apr. 17	1989	Feb. 8	Mar. 26	2029	Feb. 14	Apr. 1	2069	Feb. 27	Apr. 14
1910	Feb. 9	Mar. 27	1950	Feb. 22	Apr. 9	1990	Feb. 28	Apr. 15	2030	Mar. 6	Apr. 21	2070	Feb. 12	Mar. 30
1911	Feb. 1	Apr. 16	1951	Feb. 7	Mar. 25	1991	Feb. 13	Mar. 31	2031	Feb. 26	Apr. 13	2071	Mar. 4	Apr. 19
1912	Feb. 21	Apr. 7	1952	Feb. 27	Apr. 13	1992	Mar. 4	Apr. 19	2032	Feb. 11	Mar. 28	2072	Feb. 24	Apr. 10
1913	Feb. 5	Mar. 23	1953	Feb. 18	Apr. 5	1993	Feb. 24	Apr. 11	2033	Mar. 2	Apr. 17	2073	Feb. 8	Mar. 26
1914	Feb. 25	Apr. 12	1954	Mar. 3	Apr. 18	1994	Feb. 16	Apr. 3	2034	Feb. 22	Apr. 9	2074	Feb. 28	Apr. 15
1915	Feb. 17	Apr. 4	1955	Feb. 23	Apr. 10	1995	Mar. 1	Apr. 16	2035	Feb. 7	Mar. 25	2075	Feb. 20	Apr. 7
1916	Mar. 8	Apr. 23	1956	Feb. 15	Apr. 1	1996	Feb. 21	Apr. 7	2036	Feb. 27	Apr. 13	2076	Mar. 4	Apr. 19
1917	Feb. 21	Apr. 8	1957	Mar. 6	Apr. 21	1997	Feb. 12	Mar. 30	2037	Feb. 18	Apr. 5	2077	Feb. 24	Apr. 11
1918	Feb. 13	Mar. 31	1958	Feb. 19	Apr. 6	1998	Feb. 25	Apr. 12	2038	Mar. 10	Apr. 25	2078	Feb. 16	Apr. 3
1919	Mar. 5	Apr. 20	1959	Feb. 11	Mar. 29	1999	Feb. 17	Apr. 4	2039	Feb. 23	Apr. 10	2079	Mar. 8	Apr. 23
1920	Feb. 18	Apr. 4	1960	Mar. 2	Apr. 17	2000	Mar. 8	Apr. 23	2040	Feb. 15	Apr. 1	2080	Feb. 21	Apr. 7
1921	Feb. 9	Mar. 27	1961	Feb. 15	Apr. 2	2001	Feb. 28	Apr. 15	2041	Mar. 6	Apr. 21	2081	Feb. 12	Mar. 30
1922	Mar. 1	Apr. 16	1962	Mar. 7	Apr. 22	2002	Feb. 13	Mar. 31	2042	Feb. 19	Apr. 6	2082	Mar. 4	Apr. 19
1923	Feb. 14	Apr. 1	1963	Feb. 27	Apr. 14	2003	Mar. 5	Apr. 20	2043	Feb. 11	Mar. 29	2083	Feb. 17	Apr. 4
1924	Mar. 5	Apr. 20	1964	Feb. 12	Mar. 29	2004	Feb. 25	Apr. 11	2044	Mar. 2	Apr. 17	2084	Feb. 9	Mar. 26
1925	Feb. 25	Apr. 12	1965	Mar. 3	Apr. 18	2005	Feb. 9	Mar. 27	2045	Feb. 22	Apr. 9	2085	Feb. 28	Apr. 15
1926	Feb. 17	Apr. 4	1966	Feb. 23	Apr. 10	2006	Mar. 1	Apr. 16	2046	Feb. 7	Mar. 25	2086	Feb. 13	Mar. 31
1927	Mar. 2	Apr. 17	1967	Feb. 8	Mar. 26	2007	Feb. 21	Apr. 8	2047	Feb. 27	Apr. 14	2087	Mar. 5	Apr. 20
1928	Feb. 22	Apr. 8	1968	Feb. 28	Apr. 14	2008	Feb. 6	Mar. 23	2048	Feb. 19	Apr. 5	2088	Feb. 25	Apr. 11
1929	Feb. 13	Mar. 31	1969	Feb. 19	Apr. 6	2009	Feb. 25	Apr. 12	2049	Mar. 3	Apr. 18	2089	Feb. 16	Apr. 3
1930	Mar. 5	Apr. 20	1970	Feb. 11	Mar. 29	2010	Feb. 17	Apr. 4	2050	Feb. 23	Apr. 10	2090	Mar. 1	Apr. 16
1931	Feb. 18	Apr. 5	1971	Feb. 24	Apr. 11	2011	Mar. 9	Apr. 24	2051	Feb. 15	Apr. 2	2091	Feb. 21	Apr. 8
1932	Feb. 10	Mar. 27	1972	Feb. 16	Apr. 2	2012	Feb. 22	Apr. 8	2052	Mar. 6	Apr. 21	2092	Feb. 13	Mar. 30
1933	Mar. 1	Apr. 16	1973	Mar. 7	Apr. 22	2013	Feb. 13	Mar. 31	2053	Feb. 19	Apr. 6	2093	Feb. 25	Apr. 12
1934	Feb. 14	Apr. 1	1974	Feb. 27	Apr. 14	2014	Mar. 5	Apr. 20	2054	Feb. 11	Mar. 29	2094	Feb. 17	Apr. 4
1935	Mar. 6	Apr. 21	1975	Feb. 12	Mar. 30	2015	Feb. 18	Apr. 5	2055	Mar. 3	Apr. 18	2095	Mar. 9	Apr. 24
1936	Feb. 26	Apr. 12	1976	Mar. 3	Apr. 18	2016	Feb. 10	Mar. 27	2056	Feb. 16	Apr. 2	2096	Feb. 29	Apr. 15
1937	Feb. 10	Mar. 28	1977	Feb. 23	Apr. 10	2017	Mar. 1	Apr. 16	2057	Mar. 7	Apr. 22	2097	Feb. 13	Mar. 31
1938	Mar. 2	Apr. 17	1978	Feb. 8	Mar. 26	2018	Feb. 14	Apr. 1	2058	Feb. 27	Apr. 14	2098	Mar. 5	Apr. 20
1939	Feb. 22	Apr. 9	1979	Feb. 28	Apr. 15	2019	Mar. 6	Apr. 21	2059	Feb. 12	Mar. 30	2099	Feb. 25	Apr. 12
1940	Feb. 7	Mar. 24	1980	Feb. 20	Apr. 6	2020	Feb. 26	Apr. 12	2060	Mar. 3	Apr. 18	2100	Feb. 10	Mar. 28

Roman Catholic Hierarchy
Source: U.S. Catholic Conference; Holy See Press

Supreme Pontiff

At the head of the Roman Catholic Church is the supreme pontiff, Pope Benedict XVI, Joseph Ratzinger, born in Marktl am Inn, in Bavaria, Germany, on April 16, 1927; ordained priest on June 29, 1951, named archbishop of Munich and Feising in March 1977 and elevated to Cardinal three months later. In 1981, he was appointed prefect of the Congregation for the Doctrine of the Faith, and confirmed as dean of the College of Cardinals on November 30, 2002. He was elected pope by the College of Cardinals on April 19, 2005.

Chronological List of Popes
Source: Annuario Pontificio. Table lists year of accession of each pope.

The Roman Catholic Church named the Apostle Peter as founder of the church in Rome and the first pope. He arrived there c. 42, was martyred there c. 67, and was ultimately canonized as a saint. **The pope's temporal title is:** Sovereign of the State of Vatican City. **The pope's spiritual titles are:** Bishop of Rome, Vicar of Jesus Christ, Successor of St. Peter, Prince of the Apostles, Supreme Pontiff of the Universal Church, Patriarch of the West, Primate of Italy, Archbishop and Metropolitan of the Roman Province.

The names of antipopes are *in italics* and followed by an *. Antipopes were illegitimate claimants to the papal throne.

Year	Pope	Year	Pope	Year	Pope	Year	Pope	Year	Pope
	St. Peter	526	St. Felix IV (III)	872	John VIII	1100	*Theodoric**	1417	Martin V
67	St. Linus	530	Boniface II	882	Marinus I	1102	*Albert**	1431	Eugene IV
76	St. Anacletus or Cletus	530	*Dioscorus**	884	St. Adrian III	1105	*Sylvester IV**	1439	*Felix V**
88	St. Clement I	533	John II	885	Stephen V (VI)	1118	Gelasius II	1447	Nicholas V
97	St. Evaristus	535	St. Agapitus I	891	Formosus	1118	*Gregory VIII**	1455	Callistus III
105	St. Alexander I	536	St. Silverius, Martyr	896	Boniface VI	1119	Callistus II	1458	Pius II
115	St. Sixtus I	537	Vigilius	896	Stephen VI (VII)	1124	Honorius II	1464	Paul II
125	St. Telesphorus	556	Pelagius I	897	Romanus	1124	*Celestine II**	1471	Sixtus IV
136	St. Hyginus	561	John III	897	Theodore II	1130	Innocent II	1484	Innocent VIII
140	St. Pius I	575	Benedict I	898	John IX	1130	*Anacletus II**	1492	Alexander VI
155	St. Anicetus	579	Pelagius II	900	Benedict IV	1138	*Victor IV**	1503	Pius III
166	St. Soter	590	St. Gregory I	903	Leo V	1143	Celestine II	1503	Julius II
175	St. Eleutherius	604	Sabinian	903	*Christopher**	1144	Lucius II	1513	Leo X
189	St. Victor I	607	Boniface III	904	Sergius III	1145	Bl. Eugene III	1522	Adrian VI
199	St. Zephyrinus	608	St. Boniface IV	911	Anastasius III	1153	Anastasius IV	1523	Clement VII
217	St. Callistus I	615	St. Deusdedit or Adeodatus	913	Landus	1154	Adrian IV	1534	Paul III
217	*St. Hippolytus**			914	John X	1159	Alexander III	1550	Julius III
222	St. Urban I	619	Boniface V	928	Leo VI	1159	*Victor IV**	1555	Marcellus II
230	St. Pontian	625	Honorius I	928	Stephen VII (VIII)	1164	*Paschal III**	1555	Paul IV
235	St. Anterus	640	Severinus	931	John XI	1168	*Callistus III**	1559	Pius IV
236	St. Fabian	640	John IV	936	Leo VII	1179	*Innocent III**	1566	St. Pius V
251	St. Cornelius	642	Theodore I	939	Stephen VIII (IX)	1181	Lucius III	1572	Gregory XIII
251	*Novatian**	649	St. Martin I, Martyr	942	Marinus II	1185	Urban III	1585	Sixtus V
253	St. Lucius I	654	St. Eugene I	946	Agapitus II	1187	Clement III	1590	Urban VII
254	St. Stephen I	657	St. Vitalian	955	John XII	1187	Gregory VIII	1590	Gregory XIV
257	St. Sixtus II	672	Adeodatus II	963	Leo VIII	1191	Celestine III	1591	Innocent IX
259	St. Dionysius	676	Donus	964	Benedict V	1198	Innocent III	1592	Clement VIII
269	St. Felix I	678	St. Agatho	965	John XIII	1216	Honorius III	1605	Leo XI
275	St. Eutychian	682	St. Leo II	973	Benedict VI	1227	Gregory IX	1605	Paul V
283	St. Caius	684	St. Benedict II	974	*Boniface VII**	1241	Celestine IV	1621	Gregory XV
296	St. Marcellinus	685	John V	974	Benedict VII	1243	Innocent IV	1623	Urban VIII
308	St. Marcellus I	686	Conon	983	John XIV	1254	Alexander IV	1644	Innocent X
309	St. Eusebius	687	*Theodore**	985	John XV	1261	Urban IV	1655	Alexander VII
311	St. Melchiades	687	*Paschal**	996	Gregory V	1265	Clement IV	1667	Clement IX
314	St. Sylvester I	687	St. Sergius I	997	*John XVI**	1271	Bl. Gregory X	1670	Clement X
336	St. Marcus	701	John VI	999	Sylvester II	1276	Bl. Innocent V	1676	Bl. Innocent XI
337	St. Julius I	705	John VII	1003	John XVII	1276	Adrian V	1689	Alexander VIII
352	Liberius	708	Sisinnius	1004	John XVIII	1276	John XXI	1691	Innocent XII
355	*Felix II**	708	Constantine	1009	Sergius IV	1277	Nicholas III	1700	Clement XI
366	St. Damasus I	715	St. Gregory II	1012	Benedict VIII	1281	Martin IV	1721	Innocent XIII
366	*Ursinus**	731	St. Gregory III	1012	*Gregory**	1285	Honorius IV	1724	Benedict XIII
384	St. Siricius	741	St. Zachary	1024	John XIX	1288	Nicholas IV	1730	Clement XII
399	St. Anastasius I	752	Stephen II (III)[1]	1032	Benedict IX	1294	St. Celestine V	1740	Benedict XIV
401	St. Innocent I	757	St. Paul I	1045	Sylvester III	1294	Boniface VIII	1758	Clement XIII
417	St. Zosimus	767	*Constantine**	1045	Benedict IX	1303	Bl. Benedict XI	1769	Clement XIV
418	St. Boniface I	768	*Philip**	1045	Gregory VI	1305	Clement V	1775	Pius VI
418	*Eulalius**	768	Stephen III (IV)	1046	Clement II	1316	John XXII	1800	Pius VII
422	St. Celestine I	772	Adrian I	1047	Benedict IX	1328	*Nicholas V**	1823	Leo XII
432	St. Sixtus III	795	St. Leo III	1048	Damasus II	1334	Benedict XII	1829	Pius VIII
440	St. Leo I	816	Stephen IV (V)	1049	St. Leo IX	1342	Clement VI	1831	Gregory XVI
461	St. Hilary	817	St. Paschal I	1055	Victor II	1352	Innocent VI	1846	Pius IX
468	St. Simplicius	824	Eugene II	1057	Stephen IX (X)	1362	Bl. Urban V	1878	Leo XIII
483	St. Felix III (II)	827	Valentine	1058	*Benedict X**	1370	Gregory XI	1903	St. Pius X
492	St. Gelasius I	827	Gregory IV	1059	Nicholas II	1378	Urban VI	1914	Benedict XV
496	Anastasius II	844	*John**	1061	Alexander II	1378	*Clement VII**	1922	Pius XI
498	St. Symmachus	844	Sergius II	1061	*Honorius II**	1389	Boniface IX	1939	Pius XII
498	*Lawrence** (501-505)	847	St. Leo IV	1073	St. Gregory VII	1394	*Benedict XIII**	1958	John XXIII
514	St. Hormisdas	855	Benedict III	1080	*Clement III**	1404	Innocent VII	1963	Paul VI
523	St. John I, Martyr	855	*Anastasius**	1086	Bl. Victor III	1406	Gregory XII	1978	John Paul I
		858	St. Nicholas I	1088	Bl. Urban II	1409	*Alexander V**	1978	John Paul II
		867	Adrian II	1099	Paschal II	1410	*John XXIII**	2005	Benedict XVI

(1) After St. Zachary, a Roman priest named Stephen was elected, but died before assuming the papacy. Another Stephen was then elected to succeed Zachary as Stephen II. He is sometimes listed as Stephen III.

College of Cardinals

Source: U.S. Conference of Catholic Bishops

Members of the Sacred College of Cardinals are chosen by the pope to be his chief assistants and advisers in the administration of the church. Among their duties is the election of the pope.

In its present form, the College of Cardinals dates from the 12th century. The first cardinals, from about the 6th century, were deacons and priests of the leading churches of Rome and were bishops of neighboring dioceses. The title of cardinal was limited to members of the college in 1567. The number of cardinals was set at 70 in 1586 by Pope Sixtus V. From 1959 Pope John XXIII began to increase the number; however, the number eligible to participate in papal elections was limited to 120. Previous limitations were set aside by Pope John Paul II when he created new cardinals. In 1918 the Code of Canon Law specified that all cardinals must be priests. Pope John XXIII in 1962 established that all cardinals must be bishops, but this can be dispensed with, as in the case of Cardinal Avery Dulles. In 1971, Pope Paul VI decreed that at age 80 cardinals must retire from curial departments and offices and from participation in papal elections.

As of Aug. 2007, there were 182 members of the College, of whom 105 remained eligible to vote.

North American Cardinals

Name	Office	Born	Named Cardinal
Aloysius M. Ambrozic	Archbishop emeritus of Toronto	1930	1998
William W. Baum[1]	Archbishop emeritus of Washington, DC	1926	1976
Anthony J. Bevilacqua[1]	Archbishop emeritus of Philadelphia	1923	1991
Ernesto Corripio Ahumada[1]	Archbishop emeritus of Mexico City	1919	1979
Avery Robert Dulles[1]	Professor, Fordham University, NYC	1918	2001
Edward M. Egan	Archbishop of New York	1932	2001
Edouard Gagnon[1]	Pres. emeritus of the Commission of Intl. Eucharistic Congresses	1918	1985
Francis E. George	Archbishop of Chicago	1937	1998
William Henry Keeler	Archbishop emeritus of Baltimore	1931	1994
Bernard F. Law	Archbishop emeritus of Boston	1931	1985
William Levada	Prefect of the Congregation for the Doctrine of the Faith	1936	2006
Roger Mahony	Archbishop of Los Angeles	1936	1991
Javier Lozano Barragan	Pres. Pontifical Council for Health Care Workers, Mexico	1933	2003
Adam Joseph Maida	Archbishop of Detroit	1930	1994
Luis Aponte Martinez[1]	Archbishop emeritus of San Juan	1922	1973
Sean O'Malley	Archbishop of Boston	1944	2006
Marc Ouellet	Archbishop of Quebec	1944	2003
Justin F. Rigali	Archbishop of Philadelphia	1935	2003
Norberto Rivera Carrera	Archbishop of Mexico City	1942	1998
Juan Sandoval Iniguez	Archbishop of Guadalajara	1933	1994
James F. Stafford	Major Penitentiary of the Apostolic Penitentiary	1932	1998
Adolfo Antonio Suarez Rivera	Archbishop emeritus of Monterrey	1927	1994
Jean-Claude Turcotte	Archbishop of Montreal	1936	1994
Louis-Albert Vachon[1]	Archbishop emeritus of Quebec	1912	1985

(1) Ineligible to take part in papal elections (as of Sept. 2007).

The Ten Commandments

In the Hebrew Bible (Old Testament) the Ten Commandments (also called the Decalogue, from the Greek meaning "ten words") were revealed by God to Moses on Mt. Sinai. They form the covenant between God and the Israelites and the moral code that is the basis for the Jewish and Christian religions. The Ten Commandments appear in 2 places in the Old Testament—Exodus 20:1-17 and Deuteronomy 5:6-21.

Most Protestant, Anglican, and Orthodox Christians follow Jewish tradition, as here, which considers the introduction ("I am the Lord . . .") the first commandment and makes the prohibition against idolatry the second. Roman Catholic and Lutheran traditions combine I and II and split the last commandment into 2 that separately prohibit coveting of a neighbor's wife and a neighbor's goods. This arrangement alters the numbering of the other commandments by one.

Following is the text of the Ten Commandments as it appears in Exodus 20:1-17, in the King James version of the Bible [Roman numerals added]:

And God spake all these words, saying,

I. I *am* the LORD thy God, which have brought thee out of the land of Egypt, out of the house of bondage. Thou shalt have no other gods before me.

II. Thou shalt not make unto thee any graven image, or any likeness of *any thing* that *is* in heaven above, or that *is* in the earth beneath, or that *is* in the water under the earth. Thou shalt not bow down thyself to them, nor serve them: for I the LORD thy God *am* a jealous God, visiting the iniquity of the fathers upon the children unto the third and fourth *generation* of them that hate me; and shewing mercy unto thousands of them that love me, and keep my commandments.

III. Thou shalt not take the name of the LORD thy God in vain: for the LORD will not hold him guiltless that taketh his name in vain.

IV. Remember the sabbath day, to keep it holy. Six days shalt thou labour, and do all thy work: but the seventh day *is* the sabbath of the LORD thy God: *in it* thou shalt not do any work, thou, nor thy son, nor thy daughter, thy manservant, nor thy maidservant, nor thy cattle, nor thy stranger that *is* within thy gates: for *in* six days the LORD made heaven and earth, the sea, and all that in them *is*, and rested the seventh day: wherefore the LORD blessed the sabbath day, and hallowed it.

V. Honour thy father and thy mother: that thy days may be long upon the land which the LORD thy God giveth thee.

VI. Thou shalt not kill.

VII. Thou shalt not commit adultery.

VIII. Thou shalt not steal.

IX. Thou shalt not bear false witness against thy neighbour.

X. Thou shalt not covet thy neighbour's house, thou shalt not covet thy neighbour's wife, nor his manservant, nor his maidservant, nor his ox, nor his ass, nor any thing that *is* thy neighbour's.

Major Christian Denominations:

Brackets indicate some features that tend to

Denom-ination	Origins	Organization	Authority	Special rites
Baptists	In radical Reformation, objections to infant baptism, demands for church and state separation; John Smyth, English Separatist, in 1609; Roger Williams, 1638, Providence, RI.	Congregational; each local church is autonomous.	Scripture; some Baptists, particularly in the South, interpret the Bible literally.	*[Baptism, usually early teen years and after, by total immersion;]* Lord's Supper.
Church of Christ (Disciples)	Among evangelical Presbyterians in KY (1804) and PA (1809), in distress over Protestant factionalism and decline of fervor; organized in 1832.	Congregational.	*["Where the Scriptures speak, we speak; where the Scriptures are silent, we are silent."]*	Adult baptism; Lord's Supper (weekly).
Episco-palians	Henry VIII separated English Catholic Church from Rome, 1534, for political reasons; Protestant Episcopal Church in U.S. founded in 1789.	*[Diocesan bishops, in apostolic succession, are elected by parish represen-tatives; the national Church is headed by General Convention and Presiding Bishop; part of the Anglican Communion.]*	Scripture as interpreted by tradition, especially 39 Articles (1563); tri-annual convention of bishops, priests, and lay people.	Infant baptism, Eucharist, and other sacraments; sacrament taken to be symbolic, but as having real spiritual effect.
Jehovah's Witnesses	Founded in 1870 in PA by Charles Taze Russell; incorporated as Watch Tower Bible and Tract Society of PA, 1884; name Jehovah's Witnesses adopted in 1931.	A governing body located in NY coordinates worldwide activities; each congregation cared for by a body of elders; each Witness considered a minister.	The Bible.	Baptism by immersion; annual Lord's Meal ceremony.
Latter-day Saints (Mormons)	In a vision of the Father and the Son reported by Joseph Smith (1820s) in NY. Smith also reported receiving new scripture on golden tablets: The Book of Mormon.	Theocratic; 1st Presidency (church president, 2 counselors), 12 Apostles preside over international church. Local congregations headed by lay priesthood leaders.	Revelation to living prophet (church president). The Bible, Book of Mormon, and other revelations to Smith and his successors.	Baptism, at age 8; laying on of hands (which confers the gift of the Holy Ghost); Lord's Supper; temple rites: baptism for the dead, marriage for eternity, others.
Lutherans	Begun by Martin Luther in Wittenberg, Germany, in 1517; objection to Catholic doctrine of salvation and sale of indulgences; break complete, 1519.	Varies from congregational to episcopal; in U.S., a combination of regional synods and congregational polities is most common.	Scripture alone. *The Book of Concord* (1580), which includes the three Ecumenical Creeds, is subscribed to as a correct exposition of Scripture.	Infant baptism; Lord's Supper; Christ's true body and blood present "in, with, and under the bread and wine."
Methodists	Rev. John Wesley began movement in 1738, within Church of England; first U.S. denomination, Baltimore (1784).	Conference and superintendent system; *[in United Methodist Church, general superinten-dents are bishops—not a priestly order, only an office—who are elected for life.]*	Scripture as interpreted by tradition, reason, and experience.	Baptism of infants or adults; Lord's Supper commanded; other rites: marriage, ordination, solemnization of personal commitments.
Orthodox	Developed in original Christian proselytizing; broke with Rome in 1054, after centuries of doctrinal disputes and diverging traditions.	Synods of bishops in autonomous, usually national, churches elect a patriarch, archbishop, or metropolitan; these men, as a group, are the heads of the church.	Scripture, tradition, and the first 7 church councils up to Nicaea II in 787; bishops in council have authority in doctrine and policy.	Seven sacraments: infant baptism and anointing, Eucharist, ordination, penance, marriage, and anointing of the sick.
Pentecostal	In Topeka, KS (1901) and Los Angeles (1906), in reaction to perceived loss of evangelical fervor among Methodists and others.	Originally a movement, not a formal organization, Pentecostalism now has a variety of organized forms and continues also as a movement.	Scripture; individual charismatic leaders, the teachings of the Holy Spirit.	*[Spirit baptism, especially as shown in "speaking in tongues"; healing and sometimes exorcism;]* adult baptism; Lord's Supper.
Presby-terians	In 16th-cent. Calvinist reformation; differed with Lutherans over sacraments, church government; John Knox founded Scotch Presbyterian church about 1560.	*[Highly structured representational system of ministers and lay persons (presbyters) in local, regional, and national bodies (synods).]*	Scripture.	Infant baptism; Lord's Supper; bread and wine symbolize Christ's spiritual presence.
Roman Catholics	Traditionally, founded by Jesus who named St. Peter the 1st vicar; developed in early Chris-tian proselytizing, especially after the conversion of imperial Rome in the 4th cent.	*[Hierarchy with supreme power vested in pope elected by cardinals;]* councils of bishops advise on matters of doctrine and policy.	*[The pope, when speaking for the whole church in matters of faith and morals; and tradition (which is expressed in church councils and in part contained in Scripture).]*	Mass; 7 sacraments: baptism, reconciliation, Eucharist, confirmation, marriage, ordination, and anointing of the sick (unction).
United Church of Christ	*[By ecumenical union, in 1957, of Congregationalists and Evangelical & Reformed, repre-senting both Calvinist and Lutheran traditions.]*	Congregational; a General Synod, representative of all congregations, sets general policy.	Scripture.	Infant baptism; Lord's Supper.

How Do They Differ?

distinguish a denomination sharply from others.

Practice	Ethics	Doctrine	Other	Denomination
Worship style varies from staid to evangelistic; extensive missionary activity.	Usually opposed to alcohol and tobacco; some tendency toward a perfectionist ethical standard.	[No creed; true church is of believers only, who are all equal.]	Believing no authority can stand between the believer and God, the Baptists are strong supporters of church and state separation.	**Baptists**
Tries to avoid any rite not considered part of the 1st-century church; some congregations may reject instrumental music.	Some tendency toward perfectionism; increasing interest in social action programs.	Simple New Testament faith; avoids any elaboration not firmly based on Scripture.	Highly tolerant in doctrinal and religious matters; strongly supportive of scholarly education.	**Church of Christ (Disciples)**
Formal, based on "Book of Common Prayer," updated 1979; services range from austerely simple to highly liturgical.	Tolerant, sometimes permissive; some social action programs.	Scripture; the "historic creeds," which include the Apostles, Nicene, and Athanasian, and the "Book of Common Prayer"; ranges from Anglo-Catholic to low church, with Calvinist influences.	Strongly ecumenical, holding talks with many branches of Christendom.	**Episcopalians**
Meetings are held in Kingdom Halls and members' homes for study and worship; [extensive door-to-door visitations.]	High moral code; stress on marital fidelity and family values; avoidance of tobacco and blood transfusions.	[God, by his first creation, Christ, will soon destroy all wickedness; 144,000 faithful ones will rule in heaven with Christ over others on a paradise earth.]	Total allegiance proclaimed only to God's kingdom or heavenly government by Christ; main periodical, The Watchtower, is printed in 115 languages.	**Jehovah's Witnesses**
Simple service with prayers, hymns, sermon; private temple ceremonies may be more elaborate.	Temperance; strict moral code; [tithing]; a strong work ethic with communal self-reliance; [strong missionary activity]; family emphasis.	Jesus Christ is the Son of God, the Eternal Father. Jesus' atonement saves all humans; those who are obedient to God's laws may become joint-heirs with Christ in God's kingdom.	Mormons believe theirs is the true church of Jesus Christ, restored by God through Joseph Smith. Official name: The Church of Jesus Christ of Latter-day Saints.	**Latter-day Saints (Mormons)**
Relatively simple, formal liturgy with emphasis on the sermon.	Generally conservative in personal and social ethics; doctrine of "2 kingdoms" (worldly and holy) supports conservatism in secular affairs.	Salvation by grace alone through faith; Lutheranism has made major contributions to Protestant theology.	Though still somewhat divided along ethnic lines (German, Swedish, etc.), main divisions are between fundamentalists and liberals.	**Lutherans**
Worship style varies widely by denomination, local church, geography.	Originally pietist and perfectionist; always strong social activist elements.	No distinctive theological development; 25 Articles abridged from Church of England's 39, not binding.	In 1968, The United Methodist Church was formed by the union of The Methodist Church and The Evangelical United Brethren Church.	**Methodists**
Elaborate liturgy, usually in the vernacular, though extremely traditional; the liturgy is the essence of Orthodoxy; veneration of icons.	Tolerant; little stress on social action; divorce, remarriage permitted in some cases; bishops are celibate; priests need not be.	Emphasis on Christ's resurrection, rather than crucifixion; the Holy Spirit proceeds from God the Father only.	Orthodox Church in America originally under Patriarch of Moscow, was granted autonomy in 1970; Greek Orthodox do not recognize this autonomy.	**Orthodox**
Loosely structured service with rousing hymns and sermons, culminating in spirit baptism.	Usually, emphasis on perfectionism, with varying degrees of tolerance.	Simple traditional beliefs, usually Protestant, with emphasis on the immediate presence of God in the Holy Spirit.	Once confined to lower-class "holy rollers," Pentecostalism now appears in mainline churches and has established middle-class congregations.	**Pentecostal**
A simple, sober service in which the sermon is central.	Traditionally, a tendency toward strictness, with firm church- and self-discipline; otherwise tolerant.	Emphasizes the sovereignty and justice of God; no longer dogmatic.	Although traces of belief in predestination (that God has foreordained salvation for the "elect") remain, this idea is no longer a central element in Presbyterianism.	**Presbyterians**
Relatively elaborate ritual centered on the Mass; also rosary recitation, novenas, etc.	Traditionally strict, but increasingly tolerant in practice; divorce and remarriage not accepted, but annulments sometimes granted; celibate clergy, except in Eastern rite.	Highly elaborated; salvation by merit gained through grace; dogmatic; special veneration of Mary, the mother of Jesus.	Relatively rapid change followed Vatican Council II; Mass now in vernacular; more stress on social action, tolerance, ecumenism.	**Roman Catholics**
Usually simple services with emphasis on the sermon.	Tolerant; some social action emphasis.	Standard Protestant; "Statement of Faith" (1959) is not binding.	The 2 main churches in the 1957 union represented earlier unions with small groups of almost every Protestant denomination.	**United Church of Christ**

Books of the Bible

	Old Testament—Standard Protestant List				New Testament List		
Genesis	I Kings	Ecclesiastes	Obadiah		Matthew	Ephesians	Hebrews
Exodus	II Kings	Song of Solomon	Jonah		Mark	Philippians	James
Leviticus	I Chronicles	Isaiah	Micah		Luke	Colossians	I Peter
Numbers	II Chronicles	Jeremiah	Nahum		John	I Thessalonians	II Peter
Deuteronomy	Ezra	Lamentations	Habakkuk		Acts	II Thessalonians	I John
Joshua	Nehemiah	Ezekiel	Zephaniah		Romans	I Timothy	II John
Judges	Esther	Daniel	Haggai		I Corinthians	II Timothy	III John
Ruth	Job	Hosea	Zechariah		II Corinthians	Titus	Jude
I Samuel	Psalms	Joel	Malachi		Galatians	Philemon	Revelation
II Samuel	Proverbs	Amos					

The standard Protestant Old Testament consists of the same 39 books as in the Bible of Judaism, but the latter is organized differently. The Old Testament used by Roman Catholics has 7 additional "deuterocanonical" books, plus some additional parts of books. The 7 are: **Tobit, Judith, Wisdom, Sirach (Ecclesiasticus), Baruch, I Maccabees,** and **II Maccabees.** Both Catholic and Protestant versions of the New Testament have 27 books, with the same names.

Figures in the Hebrew Bible (Old Testament)

Aaron: First of Hebrew high priests; brother of Moses and Miriam.

Abel: Second son of Adam and Eve; slain by Cain.

Abraham: Founder of monotheism; patriarch; also called Abram.

Adam: First human according to Genesis.

Amos: Herdsman; prophesied against social injustice and oppression of the poor.

Bathsheba: Seduced by King David; mother of King Solomon.

Cain: Tiller of the soil; son of Adam and Eve; killed his brother Abel.

Cyrus: Persian ruler; sent Jews home from exile.

Daniel: Cast into lion's den by Nebuchadnezzer; saved.

David: Israel's greatest king; shepherd, warrior, musician, psalmist.

Deborah: Prophet and judge; ruled over Israel.

Elijah: Great prophet; was victorious over the priests of the Phoenician god, Baal.

Elisha: Prophet; successor to Elijah.

Esther: Jewish wife of the king of Persia; saved Jews from annihilation.

Eve: First woman according to Genesis.

Ezekiel: Visionary; prophesized hope to exiled Jews in Babylon.

Ezra: Great Jewish leader; rededicated worship and Torah law after exile.

Goliath: Giant Philistine warrior; slain by David.

Hannah: Childless; promised child to God; mother to the prophet Samuel.

Hosea: Enacted prophecy; asked God's forgiveness for Israel's unfaithfulness.

Isaac: Son of Abraham and Sarah; saved from sacrificial altar.

Isaiah: Highly educated prophet; avoided war with Assyria. Israel destroyed. Jerusalem survived.

Jacob: Son of Isaac; father of the Twelve Tribes; renamed "Israel" by angel.

Jeremiah: Confronted leaders; urged surrender to Babylon.

Jezebel: Phoenician queen of King Ahab; had Israelite prophets killed.

Job: "Blameless" man; lost family and possessions but not his faith.

Jonah: Swallowed by a great fish; prophesized repentance in Nineveh.

Jonathan: Son of King Saul; friend of David.

Joseph: Favorite of Jacob; interprets Pharaoh's dreams; brings Hebrews to Egypt.

Josiah: Reformist king; repaired Temple; restored worship; reintroduced Passover.

Joshua: Successor of Moses; led Hebrews into Canaan.

Leah: Matriarch; older sister of Rachel; Jacob's wife.

Micah: Prophet; predicted the end of war and beginning of peace.

Miriam: Prophet and great leader of the Hebrews; sister to Moses and Aaron.

Moses: Most important Hebrew prophet; leader of the Israelites; received the Torah.

Nathan: Prophet; confronted King David over his seduction of Bathsheba.

Nebuchadnezzer: Babylonian king; destroyed Jerusalem.

Nehemiah: Led Jews back to Jerusalem from Babylonian exile.

Noah: A man of great faith who, according to Genesis, saved his family and two of every living thing on Earth from a great flood.

Rachel: Matriarch; younger sister of Leah; Jacob's wife; Joseph's mother.

Rebecca: Matriarch; wife of Isaac; mother of Jacob.

Ruth: Moabite convert; ancestor of David.

Samuel: Prophet; anointed Saul king of Israel and later anointed David to succeed him.

Samson: Judge and military leader of Israel, possessed super-human strength.

Sarah: First matriarch of Israel; wife of Abraham; mother of Isaac.

Saul: First king of Israel; father of Jonathan.

Solomon: King of Israel at its zenith; known for great wisdom.

Zachariah: Prophet; encouraged rebuilding of Temple destroyed by Babylonians.

Figures in the New Testament

Andrew: One of the Twelve Apostles; brother of Peter and former fisherman; one of the earlier disciples.

Barabbas: Imprisoned with Jesus; set free by Pilate on Passover.

Barnabas: Disciple of Jesus; closely connected with Paul.

Bartholomew: A lesser known member of the Twelve Apostles; cheerful and prayed often.

Cornelius: A Roman convert defended by Peter, allowing Gentiles to become Christians.

Elizabeth: Mother of John the Baptist; relation of the Virgin Mary.

Gabriel: Archangel; appeared to the Virgin Mary to announce that she was to give birth to the messiah.

Herod: Two Herods appear in the New Testament: Herod the Great ordered the death of children around the time of Jesus's birth; his son, Herod, imprisoned John the Baptist, leading to his beheading.

James: One of the Twelve; brother of John the apostle.

Jesus: Central figure of the Gospels; believed to be the messiah and son of God; crucified by the Romans.

John (Baptist): Known as "John the Baptist"; important prophet and forerunner to Jesus; relation of the Virgin Mary.

John (Apostle): Beloved disciple of Jesus; one of the Twelve; possible author of 4th Gospel; brother of James.

Joseph: Husband of the Virgin Mary; descendant of King David.

Judas Iscariot: Betrayer of Jesus; prominent member of the apostles; committed suicide.

Judas Thaddeus: One of the Twelve; also called "Jude" to distinguish him from Judas Iscariot.

Lazarus: Brother of the disciples Martha and Mary of Bethany; raised from the dead at their request; possibly the same Lazarus who appears in Jesus's parable of the rich man.

Luke: Traditional author of the Gospel of Luke; possibly a follower of Paul.

Mark: Traditional author of the Gospel of Mark; possibly a disciple of Peter.

Matthew: One of the Twelve; possible author of the Gospel of Matthew; a former tax collector.

Mary Magdalene: Important female disciple of Jesus; witness to his death and resurrection.

Mary, the mother of Jesus: traditionally believed to be a virgin and conceived without sin; wife of Joseph.

Matthias: Often included on lists of the Twelve Apostles as the apostle who replaced Judas Iscariot after his betrayal.

Paul (Saul): Writer of nearly a quarter of the New Testament; a former persecutor of Christians, converted after a vision; played a significant role in spreading Christianity.

Peter: Considered to be the foremost of the Twelve Apostles; traditionally the first pope and "rock" of the Christian church; author of epistles; also called Simon and Simon Peter.

Philip: One of the Twelve; considered pragmatic and sensible.

Pilate, Pontius: A Roman prefect; played large role in the trial and crucifixion of Jesus.

Simon: One of the Twelve; known as "the Zealot" to distinguish from Simon Peter.

Stephen: Fervently preached that Jesus was the Messiah; stoned to death by angry mob, including Saul; important figure in Saul's conversion.

Thomas: One of the Twelve; known as "Doubting Thomas" because he did not believe Jesus was risen until he could touch him.

Timothy: A disciple closely connected with Paul; recipient of epistles.

Zacharias: Father of John the Baptist; husband of Elizabeth; struck dumb when he doubted his barren wife could become pregnant.

Major Non-Christian World Religions

Sources: Hinduism and Judaism reviewed by Anthony Padovano, PhD, STD, Prof. of Literature & Relig. Studies, Ramapo College, NJ, Adj. Prof. of Theol., Fordham U., NYC; Bahai reviewed by the Bahai Community Relations Center; Sikhism reviewed by The Sikh Coalition of New York, NY; Islam reviewed by Natana Delong-Bas, Lecturer in Islamic Studies, Boston College.

Islam

Founded: Muhammad received his first revelation in 610 CE.

Founder: Muhammad (c. 570-632), the Prophet.

Sacred texts: Two texts constitute the Muslim sacred canon, the Qur'an and the *Hadith*. The *Qur'an* provides the foundation for Islamic religion and culture. Regarded as the final, perfect, and complete word of God as revealed to Muhammad over the course of his life. Received by Muhammad in the Arabic language, it is memorized in Arabic by adherents regardless of their native language. It is divided into 114 chapters of unequal length, the shortest containing only five verses, and the longest containing 306 verses. The Qur'an is the ultimate source of everything Islamic, from metaphysics to theology to sacred history, to ethics and law, to art. The Hadith, which describes Muhammad's actions, attitudes and teachings, complements the Qur'an. Due to its long history of oral transmission, the Hadith's lessons are seen as somewhat vulnerable to human error; it does not contain God's unadulterated voice as does the Qur'an, but functions as a powerful spiritual and behavioral code nonetheless.

Divisions: There are 2 major groups: the majority Sunni (84% of the worldwide Muslim population) and the minority Shiites (14%). Sects first appeared in Islam at the time of Muhammad's death. The group that came to be known as Sunni accepted Abu Bakr, an early convert, as his successor (caliph), while a smaller number, which became the Shi'a, believed that Ali ibn Abi Talib, the son-in-law and first cousin of the prophet, should have become his successor (Imam). The Sunni successor is called a Caliph, while the Shiite successor is an Imam. Imams are believed to interpret the Qur'an infallibly. **Shiites** fall into 3 major branches: Fivers, Seveners, and Twelvers, reflecting the number of Imams they recognize. Twelvers believe that the 12th Imam has lived an invisible existence since 874, and will return as the Mahdi (a messiah figure) who will usher in a 1,000-year reign of peace and justice. **Sufism** (mystical dimension of Islam) emphasizes personal relation to God and obedience informed by love of God; it is prevalent among both Sunni and Shiites.

Organization: Muhammad was both the last prophet and a statesman. Muslim leaders have often assumed both civil and moral functions in Islamic states. Within the larger community, there are cultural and national groups, held together by a common religious law, the *Shari'a*. Muslims believe that God is the ultimate law giver and that human beings cannot devise laws that oppose divine laws; still the Shari'a is approached differently in different parts of the Islamic world. Over the centuries, Sunnis have developed 4 major schools of law: the Hanafi, the Shafi'i, the Hanbali, and the Maliki schools. The Ja'fari school is the most important and well-known Shiite school. Before the 20th century, religious scholars known as the ulama held much legal power. Judges (qadis) and law-interpreters (muftis) are people learned in religious law who lead congregational prayers in mosques and perform other religious duties.

Practice: Five duties (of both men and women), known as the "Pillars of Islam," are regarded as cardinal in Islam and as central to the life of the Islamic community. In accordance with Islam's absolute commitment to monotheism, the first duty is the profession of faith (the *Shahadah*): "There is no God but Allah and Muhammad is his Prophet." A Muslim must profess this belief publicly at least once in his or her lifetime; it defines the membership of an individual in the Islamic community. The second duty is that of five daily prayers organized in intervals throughout the day: sunrise, early afternoon, late afternoon, immediately after sunset, and before midnight. During prayer, Muslims face the *Kaaba*, a small, cube-shaped structure in the courtyard toward *al-Haram* (the "inviolate place"), at the great mosque of Mecca. All five prayers in Islam are congregational and are to be offered in a mosque, but they may be offered individually if one cannot be present with a congregation. Congregational prayer is required only at the early afternoon prayer on Friday for men. The third cardinal duty of a Muslim is to pay alms, or *zakat*, which should be 2.5% of one's total wealth. This was originally the tax levied by Muhammad on the wealthy members of the community, primarily to help the poor. Only when zakat has been paid is the rest of a Muslim's property considered purified and legitimate. The fourth duty is the fast of the lunar month of Ramadan. During the fasting month, one must abstain from eating, drinking, smoking, impure thoughts, and sexual intercourse from dawn until sunset, and feed at least one poor person, if able. The fifth duty is the pilgrimage to the Kaaba in the Grand Mosque at Mecca, which a Muslim must undertake, with exceptions for poverty and ill health, at least once during his or her lifetime.

Location: W Africa to Philippines, across a band including E Africa, Central Asia and W China, India, Malaysia, Indonesia. Islam has several million adherents in North America and about 30 mil in Europe.

Beliefs: Strictly monotheistic. God is creator of the universe, omnipotent, omniscient, just, forgiving, and merciful. God revealed the Qur'an to Muhammad to guide humanity to truth and justice. Those who sincerely "submit" (literal meaning of "islam") to God attain salvation.

World's Largest Muslim Populations, 2005
Source: Government sources; World Christian Database

Rank	Country	Muslim population	% of total pop.
1.	Pakistan	151,428,138	95.9%
2.	India	150,951,110	13.7%
3.	Bangladesh	125,573,119	88.5%
4.	Indonesia	124,903,322	56.1%*
5.	Turkey	71,285,299	97.4%
6.	Iran	68,339,642	98.3%
7.	Egypt	62,948,005	85.0%
8.	Nigeria	55,351,357	42.1%
9.	Algeria	31,831,159	96.9%
10.	Morocco	30,887,356	98.5%
11.	Afghanistan	29,706,315	99.5%
12.	Iraq	27,957,938	97.1%
13.	Ethiopia	26,089,537	33.7%
14.	Sudan	25,833,276	71.3%
15.	Saudi Arabia	22,819,076	92.9%
16.	Yemen	20,768,752	99.0%
17.	Uzbekistan	20,319,956	76.4%
18.	China	19,771,965	1.5%
19.	Syria	17,439,383	91.6%
20.	Russia	14,871,762	10.4%

*Includes about 50 million persons classified as Muslim by the Indonesian government, but sometimes classified as New Religionists.

Baha'i

Founded: Mid-19th century

Founder: Mirza Husayn-Ali Nuri (1817-1892), later known as Baha'u'llah (Arabic for "Glory of God")

Sacred Texts: The writings of Baha'u'llah and of his herald the Bab (Siyyid Ali-Muhammad, 1819-1850). The primary text is *Kitab-i-Aqdas* (the Most Holy Book).

Organization: The Baha'i administrative system consists of elected nine-member councils at the local, national, and international levels. There are also more than 180 National Spiritual Assemblies and an elected, international governing body known as the Universal House of Justice.

Practice: Prayer, meditation, and fasting are key components of Baha'i faith. Work performed in a spirit of service to humanity is considered an important form of worship. The Baha'i Faith has no clergy and minimal ritual and congregational worship.

Divisions: In a religion in which unity is perhaps the central spiritual value, the Baha'i Faith has avoided separating into sects with differentiated theologies and practices.

Location: Worldwide, with practitioners in 236 countries.

Beliefs: God has progressively revealed His will and purpose through a series of Divine manifestations including Jesus, Buddha, Muhammad, Zoroaster, and Baha'u'llah. Baha'u'llah's teachings include the oneness of humanity, the equality of men and women, the harmony of science and religion, the abandonment of all forms of prejudice, and the elimination of extremes of poverty and wealth.

Buddhism

Founded: About 525 BCE, reportedly near Benares, India.

Founder: Gautama Siddhartha (c. 563-483 BCE), the Buddha, who achieved enlightenment through intense meditation.

Sacred Texts: The *Tripitaka*, a collection of the Buddha's teachings, rules of monastic life, and philosophical commentaries on the teachings; also a vast body of Buddhist teachings and commentaries, many of which are called *sutras*.

Organization: The basic institution is the *sangha*, or monastic order, through which traditions are passed down. Monastic life tends to be democratic and anti-authoritarian.

Practice: Varies widely according to the sect, and ranges from austere meditation to magical chanting and elaborate temple rites. Many practices, such as exorcism of devils, reflect pre-Buddhist beliefs.

Divisions: A variety of sects grouped into 3 primary branches: Theravada, which emphasizes the importance of pure thought and deed; Mahayana (includes Zen and Soka-gakkai), which ranges from philosophical schools to belief in the saving grace of higher beings or ritual practices and to practical meditative disciplines; and Vajrayana, or Tantrism, a combination of belief in ritual magic and sophisticated philosophy.

Location: Mainly in Asia, from Sri Lanka to Japan.

Beliefs: Life is suffering, and there is no ultimate reality behind it. The cycle of birth and rebirth continues because of desire and attachment to the unreal "self." Meditation and deeds will end the cycle and achieve Nirvana (nothingness, enlightenment).

Hinduism

Founded: About 1500 BCE by Aryans who migrated to India, where their Vedic religion intermixed with the practices and beliefs of the natives.

Sacred texts: The *Veda,* including the *Upanishads,* a collection of rituals and commentaries; a vast number of epic stories about gods, heroes, and saints, including the *Bhagavadgita,* a part of the *Mahabharata,* and the *Ramayana.*

Organization: None, strictly speaking. Generally, rituals should be performed or assisted by Brahmins, the priestly caste, but in practice, simpler rituals can be performed by anyone. Brahmins are the final judges of ritual purity, the vital element in Hindu life. Temples and religious organizations are usually presided over by Brahmins.

Practice: Primarily passage rites (e.g., initiation, marriage, death, etc.) and daily devotions. Of the public rites, the *puja,* a ceremonial dinner for a god, is the most common.

Divisions: There is no concept of orthodoxy in Hinduism, which presents a variety of sects. The 3 major living traditions are those devoted to the gods Vishnu and Shiva and to the goddess Shakti. Numerous folk beliefs and practices, often in amalgamation with the above groups, exist side by side with philosophical schools.

Location: Mainly India, Nepal, Malaysia, Guyana, Suriname, and Sri Lanka.

Beliefs: There is only one divine principle; the many gods are only aspects of that unity. Life in all its forms is an aspect of the divine, but it appears as a separation from the divine, a meaningless cycle of birth and rebirth (*samsara*) determined by the purity or impurity of past deeds (*karma*). To improve one's *karma* or escape *samsara* by pure acts, thought, and/or devotion is the aim of every Hindu.

Judaism

Founded: About 2000 BCE.

Founder: Abraham is regarded as the founding patriarch, The Torah of Moses is the basic source of the teachings.

Sacred Texts: The 5 books of Moses (the Torah).

Organization: Originally theocratic, Judaism has evolved into a congregational polity. The basic institution is the local synagogue or temple, operated by the congregation and led by a rabbi of their choice. Chief rabbis in France and Great Britain have authority only over those who accept it; in Israel, the 2 chief rabbis have civil authority in family law.

Practice: Among traditional practicioners, almost all areas of life are governed by strict discipline. Sabbath and holidays are marked by observances, and attendance at public worship is considered especially important. Chief annual observances are Passover, celebrating liberation of the Israelites from Egypt and marked by the Seder meal in homes, and the 10 days from Rosh Hashanah (New Year) to Yom Kippur (Day of Atonement), a period of penitence.

Divisions: Judaism is an unbroken spectrum from ultraconservative to ultraliberal, largely reflecting different points of view regarding the binding character of the prohibitions and duties—particularly the dietary and Sabbath observations—traditionally prescribed for the daily life of the Jew.

Location: Mainly in Israel and the U.S.

Beliefs: Strictly monotheistic. God is the creator and ruler of the universe. God established a particular relationship with the Hebrew people: by obeying a divine law God gave them, they would be a special witness to God's mercy and justice. Judaism stresses ethical behavior (and, among the traditional, careful ritual obedience) as true worship of God.

Sikhism

Founded: Late 15th century in South Asia.

Founder: Guru Nanak Dev ji, Sikhism's first Guru.

Sacred Texts: The *Guru Granth Sahib* was compiled by the Sikh Gurus and contains their experiences of the Divine. It also contains writing by other saintly figures of different faiths.

Organization: Each Sikh must make her or his own spiritual journey and not depend on clergy. Congregational prayer led by both men and women takes place in local *Gurudwaras.* Harmandir Sahib in Amritsar, Punjab (Northern India) is the central place of worship.

Practice: Prayers are required in the morning, evening, and before sleeping. The most important mode of congregational prayer is the singing of hymns from the *Guru Granth Sahib.* The "Five Ks" are five articles of faith required of all Sikhs: *Kes* (uncut hair), *Kangha* (comb), *Kara* (steel bracelet), *Kirpan* (sword), and *Kaccha* (short pants).

Divisions: The last living Guru, Guru Gobind Singh (1666-1708) crystallized the practices and beliefs of the faith and determined that no future living Guru was needed. Today the religion is guided by joint sovereignty of Guru Granth and Guru Panth. Guru Granth is the Sikh scripture, as the spiritual manifestation of the Guru, while the Guru Panth is the collectivity of all initiated Sikhs worldwide, as the physical manifestation of the Guru.

Location: Many Sikhs are from Punjabi backgrounds. Punjab is divided between India and Pakistan.

Beliefs: Sikhism preaches a message of devotion, remembrance of God at all times, truthful living, equality between all human beings, and social justice, while emphatically denouncing superstitions and blind rituals. Sikhism is a monotheistic religion based on revelation.

Headquarters of Selected Religious Groups in the U.S.

Sources: *2006 Yearbook of American & Canadian Churches*, © National Council of the Churches of Christ in the USA; *World Almanac* research

(Year organized in parentheses)

African Methodist Episcopal Church (1787), 500 8th Ave. South, Nashville, TN 37203; www.ame-church.com; Senior Bishop, Bishop Philip Robert Cousin

African Methodist Episcopal Zion Church (1796), 3225 West Sugar Creek Rd., Charlotte, NC 28269; www.beamezion.org; Pres. Nathaniel Jarrett.

American Baptist Churches U.S.A. (1907), PO Box 851, Valley Forge, PA 19482; www.abc-usa.org; Pres., Margaret Johnson

Antiochian Orthodox Christian Archdiocese of North America (1895), 358 Mountain Rd., Englewood, NJ 07631; www.antiochian.org; Primate, Metropolitan Philip Saliba

Armenian Apostolic Church of America (1887), **Eastern Prelacy:** 138 E. 39th St., New York, NY 10016; www. armenianprelacy.org; Prelate, Archbishop Oshagan Choloyan; **Western Prelacy:** 3325 N. Glenoaks Bl., Burbank, CA 91504; Prelate, Archbishop Hounan Derderian

Assemblies of God (1914), 1445 N. Boonville Ave., Springfield, MO 65802; www.ag.org; Gen. Supt., Thomas E. Trask

Bahá'í Faith, National Spiritual Assembly of the Bahá'í's of the U.S. (1907), 1233 Central St., Evanston, IL 60201; www.bahai.us; Secy. Gen., Dr. Robert C. Henderson

Baptist Bible Fellowship Intl. (1950), Baptist Bible Fellowship Missions Bldg., 720 E. Kearney St., Springfield, MO 65803; www.bbfi.org; Pres., Rev. Gary Grey

Baptist Convention, Southern (1845), 901 Commerce St., Nashville, TN 37203; www.sbc.net; Pres. Morris H. Chapman

Baptist Convention, U.S.A., Inc., National (1895), 1700 Baptist World Center Dr., Nashville, TN 37207; www.national baptist.com; Pres., Dr. William J. Shaw

Baptist Convention of America, National (1880), 777 S. R.L. Thornton Freeway, Ste. 210, Dallas, TX 75203; www.nb-camerica.net; Pres., Rev. Stephen John Thurston

Baptist Convention of America, Natl. Missionary (1988), 1404 E. Firestone, Los Angeles, CA 90001; www.nmbca.com; Pres., Dr. C. C. Robertson

Baptist General Conference (1852), 2002 S. Arlington Heights Rd., Arlington Heights, IL 60005; www.bgcworld.org; Pres. and CEO, Dr. Gerald Sheveland

Brethren in Christ Church (1778), 431 Grantham Rd., Grantham, PA 17027; www.bic-church.org; Moderator, Dr. Warren L. Hoffman

Buddhist Churches of America (1899), 1710 Octavia St., San Francisco, CA 94109; www.buddhistchurchesofamerica. com; Presiding Bishop, Hakubun Watanabe

Christian Church (Disciples of Christ) (1832), Disciples Center, 130 E. Washington St., Indianapolis, IN 46204; www.disciples.org; Pres., Rev. Dr. Sharon E. Watkins

Christian Churches and Churches of Christ, 4210 Bridgetown Rd., Box 11326, Cincinnati, OH 45211

Christian Methodist Episcopal Church (1870), 4466 Elvis Presley Blvd., Memphis, TN 38116; Executive Secretary, Attorney Juanita Bryant

Church of the Brethren (1708), General Offices, 1451 Dundee Ave., Elgin, IL 60120; www.brethren.org; Moderator, Belita D. Mitchell

Church of Christ (1830), Temple Lot, 200 S. River St., PO Box 472, Independence, MO 64051; http://church-of-christ.com; Council of Apostles, Secy., Apostle Smith N. Brickhouse

Church of God (Anderson, IN) (1881), Box 2420, Anderson, IN 46018; www.chog.org; Gen. Dir., Pres. Ronald V. Duncan

Church of God (Cleveland, TN) (1886), 2490 Keith St. NW, Cleveland, TN 37320; www.churchofgod.cc; Gen. Overseer, G. Dennis McGuire

Church of God in Christ (1907), Mason Temple, 938 Mason St., Memphis, TN 38126; www.cogic.org; Presiding Bishop, Bishop Charles Edward Blake

Church of Jesus Christ (Bickertonites) (1862), 6th & Lincoln Sts., Monongahela, PA 15063; www.thechurchofjesus-christ.com; Pres., Paul Palmieri

Church of Jesus Christ of Latter-day Saints (Mormon), The (1830), 47 E. South Temple St., Salt Lake City, UT 84150; www.lds.org; Pres., Thomas S. Monson

Church of the Nazarene (1907), 6401 The Paseo, Kansas City, MO 64131; www.nazarene.org; Gen. Secy., David P. Wilson

Community of Christ (Reorganized Church of Jesus Christ of Latter-Day Saints) (1860), Int'l. Headquarters, 1001 W. Walnut, Independence, MO 64050; www.CofChrist.org; Pres. Stephen M. Veazey

Community Churches, International Council of (1950), 21116 Washington Pkwy., Frankfort, IL 60423; www.ic ccusa.com; Exec. Director, Michael Livingston

Conservative Judaism, United Synagogue of (1913), 155 5th Ave., New York, NY 10010; www.uscj.org; Pres., Dr. Raymond B. Goldstein

Cumberland Presbyterian Church (1810), 1978 Union Ave., Memphis, TN 38104; www.cumberland.org; Exec. Dir., David Gray Jr.

Episcopal Church (1789), 815 Second Ave., New York, NY 10017; www.episcopalchurch.org; Presiding Bishop and Primate, Most Rev. Katharine Jefferts Schori

Evangelical Lutheran Church in America (1988), 8765 W. Higgins Rd., Chicago, IL 60631; www.elca.org; Presiding Bishop, Rev. Mark S. Hanson

First Church of Christ, Scientist, The (1879), Christian Science Plaza, 175 Huntington Ave., Boston, MA 02115; www.tfccs.com; Pres., Cynthia Neely

Free Methodist Church of North America (1860), World Ministries Center, 770 N. High School Rd., Indianapolis, IN 46214; www.freemethodistchurch.org; The Board of Bishops

Friends General Conference (1900), 1216 Arch St., 2B, Philadelphia, PA 19107; www.fgcquaker.org; Gen. Secy., Bruce Birchard

Greek Orthodox Archdiocese of America (1922), 8-10 E. 79th St., New York, NY 10075; www.goarch.org; Primate, Archbishop Demetrios

Islamic Society of North America, 6555 S. 750 East, Plainfield, IN 46168; www.isna.net; Pres., Ingrid Mattson

Jehovah's Witnesses (1884), 25 Columbia Heights, Brooklyn, NY 11201; www.watchtower.org; Pres., Don Adams

Jewish Reconstructionist Federation (1935), Beit Devora, 101 Greenwood Ave., Jenkintown, PA 19406; Pres., Robert Barkin

Lutheran Church—Missouri Synod (1847), 1333 S. Kirkwood Rd., St. Louis, MO 63122; www.lcms.org; Pres., Dr. Gerald B. Kieschnick

Mennonite Brethren Churches, General Conference of (1860), 2700 S. Alpine Ave., Sioux Falls, SD 57110; Moderator, Ed Boschman

Mennonite Church USA (2001), 722 Main St., PO Box 347, Newton, KS 67114. www.MennoniteUSA.org; Exec. Dir., Jim Schrag

Moravian Church in North America (1735), **Northern Prov.:** 1021 Center St., PO Box 1245, Bethlehem, PA 18016; www. moravian.org; Pres., David L. Wickmann; **Southern Prov.:** 459 S. Church St., Winston-Salem, NC 27101; Pres., Rev. Dr. Wayne Burkette; **Alaska Prov.:** PO Box 545, 371 3rd Ave., Bethel, AK 99559; Pres., Rev. Peter Green

North American Shi'a Muslim Communities Organization (NASIMCO), (1986) P.O. Box 29691, Minneapolis, MN 55429; www.nasimco.org; Dir., Dr. Shiraz Datoo

Orthodox Jewish Congregations in America, Union of (1898), 11 Broadway, New York, NY 10004; www.ou.org; Pres., Stephen J. Stavitsky

Pentecostal Assemblies of the World, Inc. (1925), 3919 N. Meadows Dr., Indianapolis, IN 46205; www.pawinc.org; Presiding Bishop, Dr. Horace E. Smith

Presbyterian Church (U.S.A.), (1983), 100 Witherspoon St., Louisville, KY 40202; www.pcusa.org; Exec. Dir., Linda Valentine

Progressive National Baptist Convention, Inc. (1961), 601 50th St., NE, Washington, DC 20019; www.pnbc.org; Pres., Dr. T. DeWitt Smith, Jr.

Reform Judaism, Union for (1873), 633 3rd Ave., New York, NY 10017; www.urj.org; Pres., Rabbi Eric Yoffie

Roman Catholic Church (1634), U.S. Conference of Catholic Bishops, 3211 4th St. NE, Washington, DC 20017; www.usc-cb.org; Gen. Sec. Msgr. David J. Malloy

Seventh-day Adventist Church (1863), 12501 Old Columbia Pike, Silver Spring, MD 20904; www.adventist.org; Pres., Jan Paulsen

Unitarian Universalist Association of Congregations (1961), 25 Beacon St., Boston, MA 02108; www.uua.org; Pres., The Rev. William Sinkford

United Church of Christ (1957), 700 Prospect Ave., Cleveland, OH 44115; www.ucc.org; Pres., Rev. John H. Thomas

United Methodist Church (1968), Council of Bishops, 100 Maryland Ave. NE, Suite 320, Washington, DC 20002; www.umc.org; Pres. Janice Ruggle Huie

United Pentecostal Church Intl. (1945), 8855 Dunn Rd., Hazelwood, MO 63042; www.upci.org; Gen. Sec. Jerry Jones

Wesleyan Church (1968), 13300 Olio Rd., Fishers, IN 46037; www.wesleyan.org; Gen. Sec., Dr. Ronald D. Kelly

LANGUAGE

New Words in English

The following words and definitions were provided by Merriam-Webster Inc., publishers of *Merriam-Webster's Collegiate Dictionary, Eleventh Edition*, released in 2003. The words or meanings are among those that the Merriam-Webster editors decided had achieved enough currency in English to be added to the 2007 printing of the dictionary.

abaya: a loose-fitting full-length robe worn by some Muslim women

agnolotti: pasta in the form of semicircular cases containing a filling (as of meat, cheese, or vegetables)

andropause: a gradual and highly variable decline in the production of androgenic hormones and especially testosterone in the human male together with its associated effects that is held to occur during and after middle age

bobo: a member of a social class of well-to-do professionals who espouse bohemian values and lead bourgeois lives

Bollywood: the motion-picture industry in India

chaebol: a family-controlled industrial conglomerate in South Korea

crunk: a style of Southern rap music featuring repetitive chants and rapid dance rhythms

d'oh or **doh:** used to express sudden recognition of a foolish blunder or an ironic turn of events

flex-cuff: a plastic strip that can be fastened as a restraint around a person's wrists or ankles

ginormous: extremely large : humongous

gray literature: written material (as a report) that is not published commercially or is not generally accessible

hardscape: structures (as fountains, benches, or gazebos) that are incorporated into a landscape

hijab: the traditional covering for the hair and neck that is worn by Muslim women

horndog: a lustful or sexually aggressive man

instant messaging: a means or system for transmitting electronic messages instantly

microgreen: a shoot of a standard salad plant (as celery or arugula)

nocebo: a harmless substance that when taken by a patient is associated with harmful effects due to negative expectations or the psychological condition of the patient

panic attack: an episode of intense fear or apprehension that is of sudden onset

panino: a usually grilled sandwich made with Italian bread

perfect storm: a critical or disastrous situation created by a powerful concurrence of factors

polyamory: the state or practice of having more than one open relationship at a time

screenshot: an image that shows the contents of a computer display

smackdown: 1: the act of knocking down or bringing down an opponent **2:** a contest in entertainment wrestling **3:** a decisive defeat **4:** a confrontation between rivals or competitors

snowboardcross: a snowboard race that includes jumps and turns

soft-serve: smooth semisolid ice cream made in and dispensed from a freezer in which it is aerated and continuously churned

speed dating: an event at which each participant converses individually with all the prospective partners for a few minutes in order to select those with whom dates are desired

sudoku: a puzzle in which several numbers are to be filled into a 9x9 grid of squares so that every row, every column, and every 3x3 box contains the numbers 1 through 9

telenovela: a soap opera produced in and televised in or from many Latin-American countries

viewshed: the natural environment that is visible from one or more viewing points

yellowcake: partially refined uranium ore that is often used as an intermediate step in the production of nuclear weapons

Words About Words

allegory: extended use of symbols, in the form of characters, animals, or events, that represent ideas or themes. Ex: John Bunyan, *Pilgrim's Progress*

alliteration: repetition of same, initial consonant sounds of two or more words in sequence or in short intervals. Ex: "I have **st**ood **st**ill and **st**opped the **s**ound of feet." —Robert Frost, "Acquainted with the Night"

anagram: a word or phrase made by rearranging letters from another word or phrase. Ex: Clint Eastwood=Old West Action

antithesis: an expression in which contrasting ideas are intentionally juxtaposed, usually in parallel structure. Ex: "The world will little note, nor long remember, what we say here, but it can never forget what they did here." —Abraham Lincoln, Gettysburg Address

assonance: repetition of same or similar vowel sounds in words located near each other. Ex: "Green as a dream, and deep as death." —Rupert Brooke, "The Old Vicarage, Grantchester"

back-formation: creation of a word from an existing word, whose forms seem to suggest that the previously existing word derived from the newer word. Ex: The verb "edit" is a back-formation of the word "editor."

cliché: a saying or expression that has been used so often it has lost its effect. Ex: work like a dog

euphemism: a mild, indirect expression used instead of a plainer one that might be harsh, unpleasant, or offensive. Ex: restroom instead of toilet; pass away instead of die

hyperbole: exaggeration for emphasis or effect. Ex: "And fired the shot heard round the world." —Ralph Waldo Emerson, "Concord Hymn"

irony: an expression in which the intended meaning is contrary to its literal meaning; the words say one thing but mean

another. Ex: "Yet Brutus says he was ambitious; / And Brutus is an honorable man." —Shakespeare, *Julius Caesar*

litotes: intentional understatement made by negating the opposite of what is meant. Ex: This was no small matter.

metonymy: substitution of one word for another that it suggests. Ex: The pen is mightier than the sword.

onomatopoeia: words that imitate the sounds they describe. Ex: buzz, murmur

oxymoron: juxtaposition of contradictory words. Ex: deafening silence

palindrome: a type of anagram in which a word, phrase, or sentence reads the same backward and forward. Ex: Ma is a nun as I am.

paradox: a statement that is seemingly contradictory, odd, or opposed to common sense or expectation and yet is presented as true. Ex: "What a pity that youth must be wasted on the young." —George Bernard Shaw

personification: treating ideas or objects as though they were persons. Ex: "Because I could not stop for Death— / He kindly stopped for me." —Emily Dickinson, "Because I Could Not Stop for Death"

simile: a comparison between two dissimilar things using the words "like" or "as." Ex: "My love is like a red, red rose" —Robert Burns, "A Red, Red Rose"

spoonerism: play on words in which the initial sounds of two or more words are transposed, creating different phrases whose meanings when compared can be humorous. Ex: a blushing crow, a crushing blow

synecdoche: (a form of metonymy) the use of a part for the whole, or the whole for the part. Ex: All hands on deck!

tautology: unnecessary repetition of an idea in different words, phrases, or sentences. Ex: close proximity

National Spelling Bee

The Scripps National Spelling Bee, conducted by The E.W. Scripps Company and other newspapers since 1941, was instituted by *The Courier-Journal* of Louisville, KY, in 1925. Students under 16 who are not beyond the 8th grade are eligible to compete for cash prizes at the finals, held annually in Washington, DC. (The experiences of 8 contestants in the 1999 Spelling Bee were highlighted in a 2002 documentary, *Spellbound.*) The 2007 winners were Evan M. O'Dorney (1st place), and Nate Gartke (2nd place), of Edmonton, Alberta, Canada. Joseph Henares of New Haven, CT; Prateek Kohli of Hicksville, NY; and Isabel Jacobson of Madison, WI, tied for 3rd place.

Here are the last words given, and spelled correctly, in each of the years from 1981 to 2007 at the National Spelling Bee.

1981	sarcophagus	1987	staphylococci	1993	kamikaze	1998	chiaroscurist	2003	pococurante
1982	psoriasis	1988	elegiacal	1994	antediluvian	1999	logorrhea	2004	autochthonous
1983	Purim	1989	spoliator	1995	xanthosis	2000	démarche	2005	appoggiatura
1984	luge	1990	fibranne	1996	vivisepulture	2001	succedaneum	2006	ursprache
1985	milieu	1991	antipyretic	1997	euonym	2002	prospicience	2007	serrefine
1986	odontalgia	1992	lyceum						

Names of the Days

ENGLISH	RUSSIAN	HEBREW	FRENCH	ITALIAN	SPANISH	GERMAN	JAPANESE
Sunday	voskresenye	yom rishon	dimanche	domenica	domingo	Sonntag	nichiyoubi
Monday	ponedelnik	yom sheni	lundi	lunedì	lunes	Montag	getsuyoubi
Tuesday	vtornik	yom shlishi	mardi	martedì	martes	Dienstag	kayoubi
Wednesday	sreda	yom ravii	mercredi	mercoledì	miércoles	Mittwoch	suiyoubi
Thursday	chetverg	yom hamishi	jeudi	giovedì	jueves	Donnerstag	mokuyoubi
Friday	pyatnitsa	yom shishi	vendredi	venerdì	viernes	Freitag	kinyoubi
Saturday	subbota	shabbat	samedi	sabato	sábado	Samstag	doyoubi

Foreign Words and Phrases

(A=Arabic; F=French; Ger=German; Gr=Greek; I=Italian; J=Japanese; L=Latin; R=Russian; S=Spanish; Y=Yiddish)

à bientôt (F; ah-bee-en-TOH): so long; see you soon

ad hoc (L; ad-HOK): for the end or purpose at hand; impromptu

ad hominem (L; ad-HOH-mee-nem): emotional rather than intellectual; in a dispute, using slander to obscure issues

al fresco (I; ahl-FRAYS-koh): outdoors

anime (J; A-nuh-may): Japanese-style animation

antebellum (L; AHN-teh-BEL-lum): pre-war

apercu(s) (F; ah-per-SOO): first perception or insight; outline

belles lettres (F; bel-LET-truh): writing aspiring to artistic merit

bête noire (F; bet-NWAHR): a thing or person viewed with particular dislike or fear

Bildungsroman (Ger; BIL-doongs-roh-mahn): novel embodying coming-of-age story

bodega (S; boh-DAY-gah): grocery store

bonhomie (F; boh-noh-MEE): friendliness

bon vivant (F; bon-vee-VAHN): a person with refined tastes, espec. for food and drink

boondocks (Tagalog; BUHN-dahks): rural

bourgeois (F; boo-ZHWAH): middle-class; conventional; materialistic

carte blanche (F; kahrt-BLANSH): full discretionary power

casus belli (L; KAH-soos-BEL-lee): reason for going to war

cause célèbre (F; kawz-suh-LEB): a notorious incident

cognoscenti (I; kahn-yuh-SHEN-tee): experts; connoisseurs

contretemps (F; kon-truh-tahm): awkward situation

coup de grâce (F; kooh-duh-GRAHS): the final blow

cum laude/magna cum laude/summa cum laude (L; kuhm-LOU-day; MAG-na ...; SOO-ma ...): with praise or honor/with great praise or honor/with the highest praise or honor

de facto (L; day-FAK-toh): in fact, if not by law

de jure (L; dee-JOOR-ee, day-YOOR-ay): in accordance with right or law; officially

de rigueur (F; duh-ree-GUR): necessary according to convention or etiquette

détente (F; day-TAHNT): an easing of strained relations

deus ex machina (L; DAY-uhs-eks-MAH-keh-nah): person/ event that provides a solution unexpectedly or suddenly, espec. (in literature) a contrived solution to a plot

double entendre (F; DOO-blahn-TAHN-druh): expression with a double meaning, one meaning of which is often risqué

éminence grise (F; ay-meh-nahns-GREEZ): one who wields power behind the scenes

enfant terrible (F; ahn-FAHN-te-REE-bluh): one who is noteworthy for embarrassing or unconventional behavior

ennui (F; ah-NOOEE): boredom; world-weariness; annoyance

e pluribus unum (L; eh-PLOO-ree-boos-OO-noom): out of many, one (U.S. motto)

ersatz (Ger; EHR-zats): artificial; being a (usually inferior) substitute

ex post facto (L; eks-pohst-FAK-toh): retroactive(ly)

fait accompli (F; fayt-uh-kom-PLEE): an accomplished fact

fatwa (A; FAHT-wah): in Islam, a legal or religious decree

faux pas (F; foh-PAH): false step; a social blunder or breach of etiquette

habeas corpus (L; HAY-bee-ahs-KOR-pus): an order for an accused person to be brought to court

hoi polloi (Gr; hoy-puh-LOY): the masses

impresario (I; im-prah-SAH-ri-oh): manager, promoter, or sponsor of a musical or theatrical program or company

imprimatur (L; im-prah-MAH-toor): approval or official permission to print, espec. by the Roman Catholic church

in loco parentis (L; in-LOH-koh-puh-REN-tis): in place of parent

in medias res (L; in-MAY-dee-oos-rays): into the middle of things

in omnibus (L; in-AHM-ni-buhs): in all things; in all ways

intelligentsia (R; in-te-luh-JEN-see-uh): elite class of society made up of intellectuals and educated people

je ne sais quoi (F; zhuh-nuh-say-KWAH): I don't know what; the little something that eludes description

joie de vivre (F; zhwah-duh-VEEV-ruh): zest for life

leitmotif (Ger; lyt-moh-TEEF): the central theme or idea, particularly in art and literature

mano a mano (S; MAH-noh-ah-MAH-noh): hand to hand; in direct combat

mea culpa (L; MAY-uh-CUL-puh): through my fault

mensch (Y; MENTSCH): an upright, noble, admirable person

modus operandi (L; MOH-duhs-op-uh-RAN-dee): method of operation

mujahideen (A; moo-jah-ha-DEEN): Islamic holy fighters; shares root with the word jihad, which means "a struggle"

noblesse oblige (F; noh-BLES-oh-BLEEZH): the obligation of nobility to help the less fortunate

nolo contendere (L; NOL-loh-kohn-TEN-duh-ree): a plea of no contest whereby a person does not admit guilt but is subject to punishment

non compos mentis (L; non-KOM-puhs-MEN-tis): not of sound mind

non sequitur (L; non-SEH-kwi-tour): a conclusion that does not logically follow from what preceded it

nouveau riche (F; noo-voh-REESH): a newly rich person, espec. one who spends money conspicuously

ombudsman (Swedish; AHM-budz-muhn): person who receives, investigates, and settles complaints

par excellence (F; par-ek-seh-LANS): best of all; incomparable

parvenu (F; par-vuh-NOO): upstart

persona non grata (L; per-SOH-nah-non-GRAH-tah): unwelcome person

pièce de résistance (F; pee-es-duh-ray-ZEES-tonz): the outstanding item in a series or group

pro bono (L; proh-BOH-noh): (legal work) donated for the public good

quid pro quo (L; kwid-proh-KWOH): something given or received for something else

raison d'être (F; RAY-zohnn-DET-ruh): reason for being

savoir faire (F; sav-wahr-FAIR): dexterity in social affairs

Schadenfreude (Ger; SHAH-duhn-froy-deh): joy at another's misfortune

schlemiel (Y; shleh-MEEL): an unlucky, bungling person

schlepp (Y; SHLEP): move slowly, tediously, drag oneself along

semper fidelis (L; SEM-puhr-fee-DAY-lis): always faithful

sobriquet (F; SOH-bri-kay): nickname

terra firma (L; TER-uh-FUR-muh): solid ground

troika (R; TROY-kuh): group of three, espec. a ruling group

vis-à-vis (F; vee-zuh-VEE): compared with; with regard to

voir dire (F; vwar-DEER): examination by lawyers or judge to determine the suitability of a witness or a prospective juror

zeitgeist (Ger; ZITE-gyste): the general intellectual, moral, and cultural climate of an era

Names for Animal Young

calf: cattle, elephant, hippo, camel, others

cheeper: grouse, partridge, quail

chick: chicken, penguin, other birds

cockerel: rooster

codling, sprag: codfish

colt: horse, zebra (male)

cria: llama, alpaca

cub: lion, bear, shark, fox, others

cygnet: swan

duckling: duck

elver: eel

ephyra: jellyfish

eyas: hawk, others

fawn: deer, antelope

filly: horse, zebra (female)

fingerling, fry: fish generally

fledgling, nestling: birds generally

foal: horse, zebra, others

gosling: goose

heifer: cow

hoglet: hedgehog

joey: kangaroo, opossum, wombat, other marsupials

kid: goat

kit: beaver, rabbit, ferret, wolverine, others

kitten, kitty: cat, other small mammals

lamb: sheep

larva: frog, sea urchin, insects generally

parr, smolt, grilse: salmon

peachick: peafowl

piglet, shoat, farrow, suckling: pig

polliwog, tadpole: frog

poult: turkey

puggle: echidna

pullet: hen

pup: dog, fox, seal, rat

spat: oyster, other bivalves

spiderling: spider

spike, blinker, tinker: mackerel

squab: pigeon

whelp: dog, tiger, other carnivorous mammals

yearling: cattle, sheep, horse, others

Names for Animal Collectives

alligators: congregation
ants: army, colony, swarm
apes: shrewdness, troop
bats: colony
bears: sleuth, sloth
bees: colony, swarm, hive, grist
birds: flight, volery
boars/swine: singular, sounder
buffalo: gang, obstinacy
butterflies: flutter
buzzards: wake
camels: caravan, flock, train
cats: clowder, cluster, glaring, pounce
cattle: drove
cheetahs: coalition
clams, oysters: bed
cockroaches: intrusion
cranes: sedge, siege
crocodiles: bask, nest, float
crows: murder
dolphins: pod
doves: dule, pitying
ducks: brace, team
eagles: convocation, aerie
ferrets: business
finches: charm

fish: school, shoal
flamingos: stand, flamboyance
foxes: skulk
geese: flock, gaggle, skein
giraffes: corps, herd, tower
goats: tribe, trip
gorillas: band, whoop
grasshoppers: cloud
hares: down, husk, trip
hawks: cast, kettle
hedgehogs: array, prickle
hippopotami: bloat
horses: pair, team
hounds: cry, mute, pack
hyenas: cackle
iguanas: mess
jellyfish: smack
kangaroos: mob, troop
larks: exaltation
leopards: leap
lions: pride
locusts: plague, swarm
moles: labor
monkeys: troop
mules: barren, span
nightingales: watch

otters: romp
owls: parliament
oxen: yoke
peacocks: muster
pheasants: nest, nide, bouquet
ponies: string
raccoons: gaze
ravens: unkindness
rhinoceroses: crash
seals: pod
sheep: flock, drove, hurtle
snakes: nest
squirrels: dray, scurry
starlings: flock, murmuration
swans: bevy
tigers: streak
toads: knot
trout: hover
turkeys: rafter
turtles: bale
vultures: committee
whales: gam, herd, pod
woodchucks: fall
woodpeckers: descent
zebras: herd, zeal

Some Common Abbreviations and Acronyms

Acronyms are pronounceable words formed from first letters (or syllables) of other words. Some **abbreviations** below (e.g., AIDS, NATO) are thus acronyms. Some acronyms are words coined as abbreviations and written in lower case (e.g., sonar, yuppie). Acronyms do not have periods; usage for other abbreviations varies, but periods have become less common. Capitalization usage may vary from what is shown here. Italicized words preceding parenthetical definitions below are Latin unless otherwise noted. See also other chapters, including Computers and Telecommunications; Weights and Measures.

AA=Alcoholics Anonymous; Associate in Arts; administrative assistant
AAA=American Automobile Association
AARP=American Association of Retired Persons
ABA=American Bar Association
abr.=abridged
AC=alternating current; air-conditioning
AD=*anno Domini* (in the year of the Lord)
ADD=Attention Deficit Disorder
AFL-CIO=American Federation of Labor and Congress of Industrial Organizations
AI=artificial intelligence
AIDS=acquired immune deficiency syndrome
a.m. or AM=*ante meridiem* (before noon)
anon=anonymous
APO=army post office
APR=annual percentage rate
ARM=adjustable rate mortgage
ASCAP=American Society of Composers, Authors, and Publishers
ASCII=American Standard Code for Information Interchange
ASPCA=American Society for the Prevention of Cruelty to Animals
ATM=automated teller machine
AWOL=absent without leave
BA=Bachelor of Arts
bbl=barrel(s)
BC=before Christ
BCE=before the Common Era
bpd=barrels per day
BS=Bachelor of Science
Btu=British thermal unit(s)
bu=bushel(s)
byob=bring your own bottle
C=Celsius, centigrade
c=*circa* (about); copyright
CAFTA=Central American Free Trade Agreement
CAT=computerized axial tomography
CBD=Central Business District
CDC=Centers for Disease Control and Prevention; Community Development Corporation
CE=Common Era
CEO=chief executive officer
cf.=*confer* (compare)

CFO=chief financial officer
CIA=Central Intelligence Agency
CIF=cost, insurance, and freight
CIO=chief information officer
CNM=Certified Nurse Midwife
COD=cash (or collect) on delivery
COL or Col.=Colonel
COLA=cost of living adjustment
colloq.=colloquial
COO=chief operating officer
CPA=certified public accountant
CPI=Consumer Price Index
CPL or Cpl.=Corporal
CPR=cardiopulmonary resuscitation
CPU=central processing unit
CST=Central Standard Time
DA=district attorney
DC=direct current
DD=Doctor of Divinity
DDS=Doctor of Dental Surgery
DHS=Dept. of Homeland Security
DMD=Doctor of Dental Medicine
DMZ=demilitarized zone
DNA=deoxyribonucleic acid
DNR=do not resuscitate
DOA=dead on arrival
DOB=date of birth
dpi=dots per inch
DPT=diphtheria, pertussis, tetanus
DUI=driving under the influence
DVD=digital video disc
DVM=Doctor of Veterinary Medicine
DWI=driving while intoxicated
ed.=edited, edition, editor
EEG=electroencephalogram
e.g.=*exempli gratia* (for example)
EKG=electrocardiogram
EOE=equal opportunity employer
EP=extended play
EPA=Environmental Protection Agency
ERA=Equal Rights Amendment; earned run average
ESL=English as a second language
ESP=extrasensory perception
Esq.=esquire
EST=eastern standard time
et al.=*et alii* (and others)
etc.=*et cetera* (and so forth)
EU=European Union

F=Fahrenheit
FBI=Federal Bureau of Investigation
FDA=Food and Drug Administration
FDIC=Federal Deposit Insurance Corporation
FEMA=Federal Emergency Management Agency
ff.=and those following
FICA=Federal Insurance Contributions Act (Social Security)
fl.=*floruit* (flourished), used for hist. figures when life dates uncertain
FY=fiscal year
FYI=for your information
GATT=General Agreement on Tariffs and Trade
GB=gigabyte(s)
GDP=gross domestic product
GED=general equivalency diploma (for high school)
GIS=geographic information system
GMT=Greenwich mean time
GOP=Grand Old Party (Republican Party)
GPS=Global Positioning System
GUI=graphical user interface
hazmat=HAZardous MATerial
HDTV=high-definition television
HIV=human immunodeficiency virus
HMO=health maintenance organization
HMS=His/Her Majesty's Ship (UK)
Hon.=the Honorable
HOV=high-occupancy vehicle
HRH=her (his) royal highness (UK)
HTML=hypertext markup language
HTTP=hypertext transfer protocol
HVAC=heating, ventilating, and air-conditioning
Hz=hertz
ibid=*ibidem* (in the same place)
i.e.=*id est* (that is)
IMF=International Monetary Fund
IPO=initial public offering
IQ=intelligence quotient
IRA=individual retirement account; Irish Republican Army
IRS=Internal Revenue Service
ISBN=International Standard Book Number
JD=*Juris Doctor* (Doctor of Law)

k=karat
K=Kelvin
kWh=kilowatt-hour(s)
laser=Light Amplification by Stimulated Emission of Radiation
LLP=limited licensed partnership
loc. cit.=*loco citato* (in the place cited)
LP=long playing
LSAT=Law School Admission Test
LT or Lt.=Lieutenant
MA=Master of Arts
MB=megabyte(s)
MBA=Master of Business Administration
MCAT=Medical College Admission Test
MD=*Medicinae Doctor* (Doctor of Medicine)
MIA=missing in action
modem=MOdulator-DEModulator
MP=member of Parliament (UK)
mph=miles per hour
MRI=magnetic resonance imaging
ms, mss=manuscript(s)
MS=Master of Science; multiple sclerosis
MSG=monosodium glutamate
MST=mountain standard time
MVP=most valuable player
NA=not applicable; not available
NAACP=National Association for the Advancement of Colored People
NAFTA=North American Free Trade Agreement
NASA=National Aeronautics and Space Administration
NATO=North Atlantic Treaty Organization
NB or n.b.=*nota bene* (note carefully)
NCAA=National Collegiate Athletic Association
NIH=National Institutes of Health

NOW=National Organization for Women
NPR=National Public Radio
NRA=National Rifle Association
obs.=obsolete
OED=Oxford English Dictionary
op=*opus* (work)
OPEC=Organization of Petroleum Exporting Countries
OTC=over the counter
p, pp=page(s)
PA=public address
PAC=political action committee
PC=personal computer; politically correct
pd.=paid; *per diem*
PDA=Personal Digital Assistant
PhD=*Philosophiae Doctor* (doctor of philosophy)
PIN=personal identification number
p.m. or PM=*post meridiem* (afternoon)
PS=*post scriptum* (postscript)
PST=Pacific Standard Time
pt=part(s); pint(s); point(s)
PVT or Pvt.=Private
QC=Queen's Counsel (UK)
QED=*quod erat demonstrandum* (which was to be demonstrated)
q.v.=*quod vide* (which see)
radar=radio detecting and ranging
RCMP=Royal Canadian Mounted Police
REM=rapid eye movement
Rev.=Reverend
rev.=revised; reviewed
RIP=*requiescat in pace* (may he/she rest in peace)
RN=Registered Nurse
RNA=ribonucleic acid
ROTC=Reserve Officers' Training Corps

rpm=revolutions per minute
RSVP=*répondez s'il vous plaît* (Fr.) (please reply)
SARS=severe acute respiratory syndrome
SASE=self-addressed stamped envelope
SETI=Search for Extraterrestrial Intelligence
SGT or Sgt.=Sergeant
SIDS=sudden infant death syndrome
SJ=Society of Jesus (Jesuits)
sonar=SOund NAvigation and Ranging
SOP=standard operating procedure
SSI=Supplementary Security Income
TBA=to be announced
TBD=to be determined
TEFL=teaching English as a foreign language
UFO=unidentified flying object
UPC=Universal Product Code
URL=Univeral Resource Locator
USS=United States ship
UTC=coordinated universal time
var.=variant
VCR=videocassette recorder
viz=*videlicet* (namely)
VP=vice president
W=watt(s)
WHO=World Health Organization
WMD=weapons of mass destruction
WPM=words per minute
YMCA=Young Men's Christian Association
YTD=year to date
yuppie=young urban professional
ZIP=zone improvement plan (U.S. Postal Service)

Eponyms
(words named for people)

boycott: to avoid trade or dealings with, as a protest; after Charles C. Boycott, an English land agent in County Mayo, Ireland, ostracized in 1880 for refusing to reduce rents

derby: a stiff felt hat with a dome-shaped crown and narrow rolled brim; after Edward Stanley, 12th Earl of Derby, who in 1780 founded the Derby horse race, to which these hats are worn

derrick: a type of crane consisting of a boom connected to the base of an upright mast; after Derrick, early 17th-cent. English hangman who used a gallows that operated via cables and pulleys

draconian: harsh or severe; after Draco, statesman who codified the laws in Athens in 621 BCE

galvanize: to shock with an electric current, to energize or spur; from Luigi Galvano, Italian physicist who invented a process to cover metals with electrons for protection against rust

gerrymander: to draw an election district in such a way as to favor a political party; after Elbridge Gerry, who created (1812) just such an election district (shaped like a salamander) during his governorship of Massachusetts

guillotine: a machine for beheading; after Joseph Guillotin, French physician who proposed its use in 1789 as more humane than hanging

Luddite: one who opposes new technology; from Ned Ludd, leader of a group of textile workers in England who destroyed machinery in the early 1800s

maudlin: excessively sentimental; from Scriptural figure Mary Magdalene, who is often shown weeping in depictions

mesmerize: to hypnotize or enthrall; from Franz Mesmer, 18th-cent. German physicist who developed therapy using magnetism that led to hypnosis

milquetoast: a timid, unassertive person; after Caspar Milquetoast, comic strip character created by American Harold Tucker Webster in 1924

Pollyanna: an overly optimistic person; based on the title character of a novel (1913) by American writer Eleanor Porter

ritzy: opulent; after the elegant Ritz Hotel, which Swiss-born César Ritz opened in Paris in 1898

salmonella: group of bacteria that can cause infections when contaminated food or water is consumed; named after discoverer Daniel Elmer Salmon, American veterinarian and public health official

sandwich: two or more slices of bread with a filling in between; after John Montagu, 4th Earl of Sandwich (1718-92), who supposedly ate these at the gaming table

shrapnel: originally, a projectile with lead balls designed to inflict maximum damage in explosions, later pieces of shell casings; from Henry Shrapnel (1761-1842), British artillery officer who designed the projectile

silhouette: an outline image; from Étienne de Silhouette (1709-67), a stingy French finance minister

Sisyphean: of, or relating to, futile exertions; from Sisyphus, a king in Greek mythology who was eternally condemned to roll a stone to the top of a hill, only to have it roll back down

Zamboni: an ice resurfacing machine; after American inventor Frank Zamboni, who owned an ice skating rink

Contranyms

Words that can have opposite meanings depending on their usage are known as **contranyms** or self-antonyms. They are also called Janus words, after the Roman god of doors and gates, who is often depicted with two faces looking in opposite directions. Contranyms are produced in various ways: For example, two words with different origins and contradictory meanings might acquire the same spelling, or a word's archaic meaning might be the opposite of the word's meaning in current usage. Here are a few examples of contranyms:

cleave:	to split apart	*or*	to stick together
clip:	to cut	*or*	to fasten
sanction:	approval	*or*	punishment
screen:	to shield	*or*	to present
trim:	to cut away	*or*	to ornament

Contranyms may also have similar sounds but different spellings (e.g., *raise* and *raze*).

> **IT'S A FACT:** The top 10 U.S. baby names in 2006, according to the Social Security Administration, were as follows: **boys:** Jacob, Michael, Joshua, Ethan, Matthew, Daniel, Christopher, Andrew, Anthony, William; **girls:** Emily, Emma, Madison, Isabella, Ava, Abigail, Olivia, Hannah, Sophia, Samantha. William and Sophia joined the top 10, displacing Joseph and Ashley.

Top 10 First Names of Americans by Decade of Birth

Source: Compiled by Dr. Cleveland Kent Evans, Bellevue Univ., Bellevue, NE, based on U.S. Social Security Admin. records

BOYS

1880-1889	John, William, Charles, George, James, Frank, Joseph, Harry, Henry, Edward
1890-1899	John, William, George, James, Charles, Joseph, Frank, Robert, Harry, Henry
1900-1909	John, William, James, George, Joseph, Charles, Robert, Frank, Edward, Henry
1910-1919	John, William, James, Robert, Joseph, Charles, George, Edward, Frank, Walter
1920-1929	John, Robert, James, William, Charles, George, Joseph, Richard, Edward, Donald
1930-1939	Robert, James, John, William, Richard, Charles, Donald, George, Thomas, Joseph
1940-1949	James, Robert, John, William, Richard, David, Charles, Thomas, Michael, Ronald
1950-1959	Michael, James, Robert, John, David, William, Steven, Richard, Thomas, Mark
1960-1969	Michael, John, David, James, Robert, Mark, Steven, William, Jeffrey, Richard
1970-1979	Michael, Christopher, Jason, David, James, John, Brian, Robert, Steven, William
1980-1989	Michael, Christopher, Matthew, Joshua, David, Daniel, James, John, Robert, Brian
1990-1999	Michael, Christopher, Matthew, Joshua, Nicholas, Jacob, Andrew, Daniel, Brandon, Tyler

GIRLS

1880-1889	Mary, Anna, Elizabeth, Catherine, Margaret, Emma, Bertha, Minnie, Florence, Clara
1890-1899	Mary, Anna, Margaret, Helen, Catherine, Elizabeth, Florence, Ruth, Rose, Ethel
1900-1909	Mary, Helen, Margaret, Anna, Ruth, Catherine, Elizabeth, Dorothy, Marie, Mildred
1910-1919	Mary, Helen, Dorothy, Margaret, Ruth, Catherine, Mildred, Anna, Elizabeth, Frances
1920-1929	Mary, Dorothy, Betty, Helen, Margaret, Ruth, Virginia, Catherine, Doris, Frances
1930-1939	Mary, Betty, Barbara, Shirley, Patricia, Dorothy, Joan, Margaret, Carol, Nancy
1940-1949	Mary, Linda, Barbara, Patricia, Carol, Sandra, Nancy, Sharon, Judith, Susan
1950-1959	Deborah, Mary, Linda, Patricia, Susan, Barbara, Karen, Nancy, Donna, Catherine
1960-1969	Lisa, Deborah, Mary, Karen, Michelle, Susan, Kimberly, Lori, Teresa, Linda
1970-1979	Jennifer, Michelle, Amy, Melissa, Kimberly, Lisa, Angela, Heather, Kelly, Sarah
1980-1989	Jessica, Jennifer, Ashley, Sarah, Amanda, Stephanie, Nicole, Melissa, Katherine, Megan
1990-1999	Ashley, Jessica, Sarah, Brittany, Emily, Kaitlyn, Samantha, Megan, Brianna, Katherine

Origins of Popular American Given Names

Source: Dr. Cleveland Kent Evans, Bellevue University, Bellevue, NE; World Almanac research

Boys

Andrew: Gr. *andreios*, "man, manly"

Anthony: Roman *Antonius*, pos. from Gr. *anthos*, "flower"

Brandon: Eng. place name, "gorse-covered hill"

Brian: Irish, perhaps Celtic *Brigonos*, "high, noble"

Charles: Ger. *ceorl*, "free man"

Christopher: Gr. *Khristophoros*, "bearing Christ [in one's heart]"

Daniel: Heb. "God is my judge"

David: Heb. *Dodavehu*, perhaps "darling"

Donald: Scots Gaelic *Domhnall*, "world rule"

Edward: Old Eng. *Eadweard*, "wealth-guard"

Ethan: Heb. "solid," "firm"

Frank: Ger. "Frenchman"

George: Gr. *georgos*, "soil tiller, farmer"

Harry: Middle Eng. form of Henry

Henry: Ger. *Haimric*, "home-power"

Jacob: Heb. *Yaakov*, "God protects" or "supplanter"

James: Late Lat. *Iacomus*, form of Jacob

Jason: Gr. *Iason*, "healer"

Jeffrey: Norman Fr., from Ger. *Gaufrid*, "land-peace," or *Gisfrid*, "pledge-peace"

John: Heb. *Yohanan*, "God is gracious"

Joseph: Heb. *Yosef*, "[God] shall add"

Joshua: Heb. *Yoshua*, "God saves"

Mark: Lat. *Marcus*, perhaps from Mars, the war god

Matthew: Heb. *Mattathia*, "gift of God"

Michael: Heb. "Who could ever be like God?"

Nicholas: Gr. *Nikolaos*, "victory-people"

Patrick: Lat. *Patricius*, "belonging to the noble class"

Richard: Ger. "power-hardy"

Robert: Ger. *Hrodberht*, "fame-bright"

Sean: Gaelic form of John

Steven: Gr. *stephanos*, "crown, garland"

Theodore: Gr. *Theodoros*, "gift of God"

Thomas: Aramaic "twin"

Tyler: Old Eng. *tigeler*, "tile layer"

Walter: Ger. *Waldheri*, "rule-army"

William: Ger. *Wilhelm*, "will-helmet"

Girls

Abigail: Heb. "My father is joy"

Alexis: Gr. "helper" or "defender"

Amanda: 17th-cent. invention from Lat., "lovable"

Amy: Old Fr. *Amee*, "beloved"

Angela: Gr. *angelos*, "messenger [of God]"

Ann Eng. form, **Anne:** Eng., Fr., Ger. form of Hannah

Anna: Lat. and Gr. form of Hannah

Ashley: Eng. place name, "ash grove"

Ava: prob. modern form of Eva, Lat. form of Heb. Eve, "to breathe"

Barbara: Gr. *barbarus*, "foreign"

Bertha: Ger. *behrt*, "bright"

Betty: 18th-cent. pet form of Elizabeth

Brianna: modern fem. form of Brian

Brittany: place name, Fr. province settled by Britons

Carol: form of Charles

Clara: Lat. *clarus*, "famous"

Deborah: Heb. "bee"

Donna: Ital. "lady"

Doris: Gr. "woman of the Dorian tribe," name of a sea nymph

Dorothy: Gr. *Dorothea*, "gift of God"

Elizabeth: Heb. *Elisheba*, perhaps "God is my oath" or "God is good fortune"

Emily: Roman *Aemilia*, possibly from Lat. *aemulus*, "rival"

Emma: Ger. *ermen*, "whole, entire"

Ethel: Old Eng. *aethel*, "noble"

Florence: Lat. *florens*, "flourishing"

Frances: fem. form of Francis, "a Frenchman"

Haley: Eng. place name, "hay clearing"

Hannah: Heb. "He has favored me"

Heather: Middle Eng. *hathir*, "heather"

Helen: Gr. *Helene*, possibly "sunbeam"

Isabella, Isabel: Lat., Sp. variant of Elizabeth

Jennifer: Cornish form of Welsh *Gwenhwyfar*, "fair-smooth"

Jessica: Shakesp. invention, prob. fem. form of Jesse, Heb. "God exists"

Joan: Middle Eng. fem. form of John

Judith: Heb. "Jewish woman"

Kaitlyn: American spelling of Caitlin, the Irish form of Katherine

Karen: Danish form of Katherine

Katherine: Egyptian *Aikaterine*, later modified to resemble Gr. *katharos*, "pure"

Kelly: Irish Gaelic *Ceallagh*, perhaps "churchgoer" or "bright-headed"

Kimberly: Eng. place name, "Cyneburgh's clearing"

Linda: Sp. "pretty" or Ger. "tender"

Lisa: pet form of Elizabeth

Lori: pet form of either Lorraine (Fr. "land of Lothar's people") or Laura (Lat. "laurel")

Madison: Middle Eng. surname, "son of Madeline or Maud"

Margaret: Gr. *margaron*, "pearl"
Maria: Lat. form of Mary
Marie: Fr. form of Mary
Mary: Eng. form of Heb. *Maryam*, perhaps "seeress" or "wished-for child"
Megan: Welsh form of Margaret
Melissa: Gr. "bee"
Michelle: Fr. fem. form of Michael
Mildred: Old Eng. *Mildthryth*, "mild-strength"
Minnie: pet form of Wilhelmina, fem. form of William

Nancy: medieval Eng. pet form of Agnes, Gr. *hagnos*, "holy"; later also pet form for Ann
Nicole: Fr. fem. form of Nicholas
Olivia: Lat. *oliva*, "olive tree"
Patricia: Lat. fem. form of Patrick
Rose: Ger. *hros*, "horse," or Lat. *rosa*, "rose"
Ruth: Heb., perhaps "companion"
Samantha: colonial American invention, probably combining Sam from Samuel (Heb. "name of God") with -antha from Gr. *anthos*, "flower"

Sandra: short form of Alessandra, Ital. fem. of Alexander, Gr. "defend-man"
Sarah: Heb. "princess"
Sharon: Biblical place name, Heb. "plain"
Shirley: Eng. place name, "bright clearing" or "shire meadow"
Sophia: Gr. "wisdom"
Stephanie: Fr. fem. form of Steven
Susan: Eng. form of Heb. *Shoshana*, "lily"
Teresa: Sp., perhaps "woman from Therasia"
Virginia: Lat. "virgin-like"

30 Most Common Last Names in the U.S. Population

Source: 1990 Census, U.S. Census Bureau, U.S. Dept. of Commerce

Rank	Name	Frequency[1] (%)	Rank	Name	Frequency[1] (%)	Rank	Name	Frequency[1] (%)	Rank	Name	Frequency[1] (%)
1.	Smith	1.006	9.	Moore....	0.312	17.	Thompson	0.269	24.	Lee	0.220
2.	Johnson ..	0.810	10.	Taylor....	0.311	18.	Garcia....	0.254	25.	Walker. ..	0.219
3.	Williams ..	0.699	11.	Anderson .	0.311	19.	Martinez ..	0.234	26.	Hall	0.200
4.	Jones	0.621	12.	Thomas ..	0.311	20.	Robinson .	0.233	27.	Allen	0.199
5.	Brown....	0.621	13.	Jackson ..	0.310	21.	Clark.....	0.231	28.	Young ...	0.193
6.	Davis	0.480	14.	White	0.279	22.	Rodriguez.	0.229	29.	Hernandez	0.192
7.	Miller	0.424	15.	Harris	0.275	23.	Lewis	0.226	30.	King	0.190
8.	Wilson ...	0.339	16.	Martin....	0.273						

(1) Percent of people in the population sample with the name shown.

Pen Names

Woody Allen.....................	Allen Stewart Konigsberg
Maya Angelou	Marguerite Johnson
Currer, Ellis, and Acton Bell...	Charlotte, Emily, and Anne Brontë
Nellie Bly	Elizabeth Jane Cochrane Seaman
John le Carré	David John Moore Cornwell
Lewis Carroll	Charles Lutwidge Dodgson
Colette	Sidonie Gabrielle Colette
George Eliot	Mary Ann or Marian Evans
Maksim Gorky	Aleksey Maksimovich Peshkov
O. Henry.........................	William Sydney Porter
Hergé	Georges Rémi
P. D. James	Phyllis Dorothy James White
Ann Landers.....................	Esther Pauline Lederer
J. T. LeRoy......................	Laura Albert
André Maurois...................	Émile Herzog
Molière........................	Jean Baptiste Poquelin
Toni Morrison	Chloe Anthony Wofford
Pablo Neruda	Neftalí Ricardo Reyes Basoalto
Frank O'Connor	Michael Donovan
George Orwell.......................	Eric Arthur Blair
Ouida	Marie Louise de la Ramée
Ellery Queen..........	Frederic Dannay and Manfred B. Lee
Ayn Rand	Alice Rosenbaum
Anne Rice.......................	Howard Allen O'Brien
Saki..........................	Hector Hugh Munro
George Sand	Amandine Lucie Aurore Dupin
Dr. Seuss	Theodor Seuss Geisel
Lemony Snicket....................	Daniel Handler
Stendhal.........................	Marie-Henri Beyle
Mark Twain......................	Samuel Clemens
Voltaire	François Marie Arouet

American Manual Alphabet

In the American Manual Alphabet, each letter of the alphabet is represented by a position of the fingers. This system was originally developed in France by Charles Michel de l'Epee in the 1700s. Laurent Clerc and Thomas Gallaudet further refined it into the American Manual Alphabet.

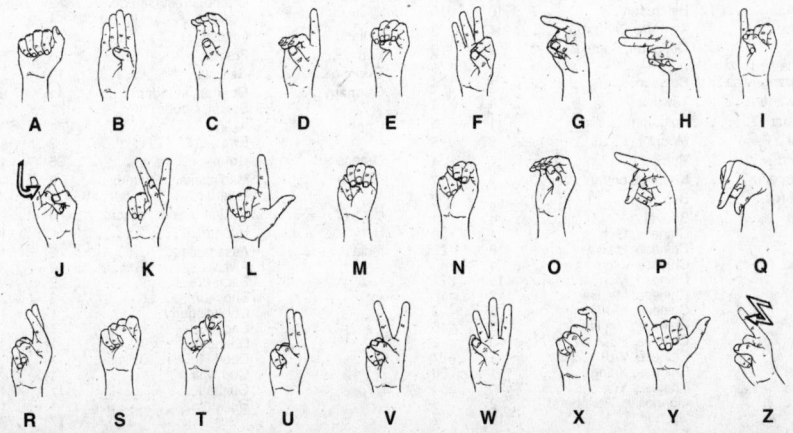

Commonly Misspelled English Words

accidentally	collectible	fascinating	license	opportunity	sacrilegious
accommodate	commitment	February	liaison	optimistic	seize
accumulate	committee	fluorescent	lieutenant	parallel	sergeant
acknowledgment	connoisseur	forty	lightning	patience	separate
acquainted	conscience	gauge	liquefy	performance	sheriff
acquire	conscientious	government	maintenance	permanent	sincerely
a lot	conscious	grammar	marriage	permissible	stubbornness
already	convenience	harass	medieval	perseverance	supersede
amateur	deceive	humorous	millennium	personnel	temperament
appearance	defendant	incidentally	miniature	possess	temperature
appropriate	definitely	independent	miscellaneous	potatoes	transferred
assimilate	desirable	indispensable	Mississippi	prescient	truly
bureau	desperate	innocuous	misspelled	privilege	twelfth
business	deterrent	innovative	mnemonic	propaganda	vaccinate
calendar	eighth	inoculate	mysterious	questionnaire	vacillate
canceled	eligible	irresistible	necessary	receipt	vacuum
Caribbean	eliminate	jewelry	noticeable	receive	vicious
cemetery	embarrass	judgment	occasionally	recommend	Wednesday
changeable	environment	laboratory	occurrence	rhythm	weird
Cincinnati	existence	leisure	omitted	ridiculous	wholly

The Principal Languages of the World

Source: Database of *Ethnologue: Languages of the World*, 15th Edition, www.ethnologue.com. Raymond G. Gordon, Editor. Copyright © 2005, SIL International. Used by permission.

The following tables count only "first language" speakers. All figures are estimates.

Languages Spoken by the Most People

Language	Speakers (millions)	Language	Speakers (millions)	Language	Speakers (millions)
Chinese, Mandarin	873	Bengali	171	Javanese	75
Spanish	322	Russian	145	Telugu	69
English	309	Japanese	122	Marathi	68
Hindi	180	German, standard	95	Vietnamese	67
Portuguese	177	Chinese, Wu	77	Korean	67

Languages Spoken by at Least 2 Million People

A "hub" country is the country of origin, not necessarily the country where the most speakers reside (e.g., Portugal is the "hub" country of Portuguese, although more Portuguese speakers live in Brazil). Number of speakers listed is worldwide total for each language.

Hub	Language	Countries	Speakers (millions)	Hub	Language	Countries	Speakers (millions)
Afghanistan	Farsi, Eastern	3	7		Zhuang, Northern	1	10
	Hazaragi	4	2		Zhuang, Southern	1	4
Albania	Albanian, Tosk	9	2	Congo, Dem. Rep. of	Kituba	1	4
Algeria	Arabic, Algerian spoken	5	21		Lingala	3	2
	Kabyle	3	3		Luba-Kasai	1	6
Angola	Mbundu	1	3	Côte d'Ivoire	Baoulé	1	2
	Umbundu	2	4	Croatia	Croatian	8	6
Armenia	Armenian	30	6	Czech Republic	Czech	10	11
Austria	Bavarian	5	7	Denmark	Danish	8	5
Azerbaijan	Azerbaijani, North	9	7	Egypt	Arabic, Egyptian spoken	9	46
Bangladesh	Bengali	9	171		Arabic, Sa'idi spoken	1	18
	Chittagonian	2	14	Ethiopia	Amharic	4	17
	Sylheti	10	10		Oromo, Borana-Arsi-Guji	3	3
Belarus	Belarusan	16	10		Oromo, Eastern	1	4
Bolivia	Aymara, Central	4	2		Oromo, West Central	2	8
	Quechua, South Bolivian	2	3		Tigrigna	4	5
Bosnia and Herzegovina	Bosnian	1	4	Finland	Finnish	7	5
Botswana	Tswana	4	4	France	French	56	64
Bulgaria	Bulgarian	11	8	Georgia	Georgian	13	4
Burkina Faso	Mòoré	6	5	Germany	German, standard	41	95
Burundi	Rundi	4	4		Saxon, Upper	1	2
Cambodia	Khmer, Central	7	7	Ghana	Akan	1	8
Cameroon	Beti	1	2		Ewé	2	3
China	Bouyei	4	2	Greece	Greek	35	12
	Chinese, Gan	1	20	Guinea	Maninkakan, Eastern	3	2
	Chinese, Hakka	16	29		Pular	6	2
	Chinese, Jinyu	1	45	Haiti	Haitian Creole French	9	7
	Chinese, Mandarin	16	873	Hungary	Hungarian	11	13
	Chinese, Min Bei	2	10	India	Assamese	3	15
	Chinese, Min Dong	6	9		Awadhi	2	20
	Chinese, Min Nan	9	46		Bagri	2	2
	Chinese, Pu-Xian	3	2		Bhojpuri	3	26
	Chinese, Wu	1	77		Chhattisgarhi	1	11
	Chinese, Xiang	1	36		Deccan	1	10
	Chinese, Yue	20	54		Dhundari	1	9
	Mongolian, Peripheral	2	3		Dogri	1	5
	Uyghur	16	7		Garhwali	1	2
					Gujarati	17	46
					Haryanvi	1	13
					Hindi	17	180

Hub	Language	Countries	Speakers (millions)
	Kanauji	1	6
	Kannada	1	35
	Kashmiri	3	4
	Konkani	1	4
	Konkani, Goanese	3	3
	Kumauni	2	2
	Kurux	2	2
	Lambadi	1	2
	Magahi	1	13
	Maithili	2	24
	Malayalam	9	35
	Marathi	3	68
	Marwari	3	13
	Mewati	1	5
	Mundari	3	2
	Oriya	2	31
	Panjabi, Eastern	11	27
	Rajbanshi	3	2
	Sadri	2	2
	Santali	4	6
	Shekhawati	1	3
	Tamil	15	66
	Telugu	7	69
Indonesia	Aceh	1	3
	Bali	1	3
	Banjar	2	3
	Batak Toba	1	2
	Betawi	1	2
	Bugis	2	3
	Indonesian	6	23
	Javanese	4	75
	Madura	2	13
	Malay, Balinese	1	3
	Minangkabau	1	6
	Sasak	1	2
	Sunda	1	27
Iran	Azerbaijani, South	8	24
	Farsi, Western	26	24
	Gilaki	1	3
	Kurdish, Southern	2	5
	Mazanderani	1	3
Iraq	Arabic, Gulf spoken	9	2
	Arabic, Mesopotamian spoken	5	15
	Arabic, North Mesopotamian spoken	4	6
	Kurdish, Central	2	3
Israel	Hebrew	8	5
	Yiddish, Eastern	21	3
Italy	Emiliano-Romagnolo	2	2
	Italian	30	61
	Lombard	3	9
	Napoletano-Calabrese	1	7
	Piemontese	3	3
	Sicilian	1	4
	Venetian	3	2
Jamaica	Jamaican Creole English	7	3
Japan	Japanese	25	122
Jordan	Arabic, South Levantine spoken	8	6
Kazakhstan	Kazakh	13	8
Kenya	Gikuyu	1	5
	Kalenjin	1	2
	Kamba	1	2
	Luo	2	3
	Luyia	2	3
Korea, South	Korean	31	67
Kyrgyzstan	Kirghiz	7	3
Laos	Lao	7	3
Lesotho	Sotho, Southern	3	4
Libya	Arabic, Libyan spoken	3	4
Lithuania	Lithuanian	19	3
Madagascar	Malagasy, Plateau	3	5
Malawi	Nyanja	5	5
Malaysia	Malay	8	17
Mali	Bamanankan	7	2
Mauritania	Hassaniyya	6	2
Mongolia	Mongolian, Halh	4	2
Morocco	Arabic, Moroccan spoken	8	19
	Tachelhit	3	3
	Tamazight, Central Atlas	3	3
Mozambique	Makhuwa	1	2
	Ndau	2	2
Myanmar	Arakanese	3	2
	Burmese	5	32
	Shan	3	2
Nepal	Nepali	4	17
Netherlands	Dutch	8	17
Niger	Zarma	4	2
Nigeria	Hausa	13	24
	Igbo	1	18
	Kanuri, Central	6	3
	Tiv	2	2
	Yoruba	5	19
Pakistan	Balochi, Southern	4	3
	Brahui	4	2
	Panjabi, Western	7	60
	Pashto, Central	1	7
	Pashto, Northern	5	9
	Pashto, Southern	6	2
	Seraiki	3	13
	Sindhi	7	19
	Urdu	21	60
Paraguay	Guaraní, Paraguayan	2	4
Philippines	Bicolano, Central	1	2
	Cebuano	2	20
	Hiligaynon	2	7
	Ilocano	2	8
	Tagalog	7	15
	Waray-Waray	1	2
Poland	Polish	21	42
Portugal	Portuguese	33	177
Romania	Romanian	17	23
Russia	Russian	31	145
Rwanda	Rwanda	4	7
Saudi Arabia	Arabic, Hijazi spoken	2	6
	Arabic, Najdi spoken	7	9
Senegal	Pulaar	6	3
	Wolof	6	3
Serbia and Montenegro*	Albanian, Gheg	7	2
	Serbian	16	11
Slovakia	Slovak	8	5
Somalia	Somali	12	12
South Africa	Afrikaans	10	5
	Sotho, Northern	2	3
	Tsonga	4	3
	Xhosa	3	7
	Zulu	6	9
Spain	Catalan-Valencian-Balear	18	6
	Galician	2	3
	Spanish	43	322
Sri Lanka	Sinhala	6	13
Sudan	Arabic, Sudanese spoken	5	18
Sweden	Swedish	7	8
Switzerland	Schwyzerdütsch	5	6
Syria	Arabic, North Levantine spoken	15	14
Tajikistan	Tajiki	8	4
Tanzania	Sukuma	1	5
Thailand	Malay, Pattani	1	3
	Thai	4	20
	Thai, Northeastern	1	15
	Thai, Northern	2	6
	Thai, Southern	1	5
Tunisia	Arabic, Tunisian spoken	4	9
Turkey	Kurdish, Northern	31	9
	Turkish	35	50
Turkmenistan	Turkmen	13	6
Uganda	Ganda	1	3
Ukraine	Ukrainian	25	39
United Kingdom	English	107	309
Uzbekistan	Uzbek, Northern	12	18
Vietnam	Vietnamese	20	67
Yemen	Arabic, Sanaani spoken	1	7
	Arabic, Ta'izzi-Adeni spoken	5	6
Zambia	Bemba	4	2
Zimbabwe	Shona	4	10

*As of 2006, Montenegro is an independent nation.

BUILDINGS, BRIDGES, AND TUNNELS

Tallest Buildings in the World

Source: Council on Tall Buildings and Urban Habitat, Illinois Inst. of Technology, www.ctbuh.com; Emporis.com, www.emporis.com

Structures under construction as of mid-2007 are denoted by an asterisk (*). Year in parentheses is date of completion or projected completion.

Building	Ht. (ft.)	Stories	Building	Ht. (ft.)	Stories
Taipei 101, Taipei, Taiwan (2004)	1,670	101	Menara Telekom HQ, Kuala Lumpur, Malaysia (1999)	1,017	55
*Shanghai World Financial Center, Shanghai, China (2008)	1,614	101	Emirates Tower Two, Dubai, UAE (2000)	1,014	56
Petronas Tower I, Kuala Lumpur, Malaysia (1998)	1,483	88	*One Island East, Hong Kong, China (2008)	1,011	69
Petronas Tower II, Kuala Lumpur, Malaysia (1998)	1,483	88	AT&T Corporate Center, Chicago, IL, U.S. (1989)	1,007	60
Sears Tower, Chicago, IL, U.S. (1974)	1,451	110	*Burj Dubai Lake Hotel, Dubai, UAE (2008)	1,004	61
Jin Mao Bldg., Shanghai, China (1999)	1,380	88	JP Morgan Chase Tower, Houston, TX, U.S. (1982)	1,002	75
Two International Finance Centre, Hong Kong, China (2003)	1,362	88	Baiyoke Tower II, Bangkok, Thailand (1997)	997	85
CITIC Plaza, Guangzhou, China (1996)	1,283	80	Two Prudential Plaza, Chicago, IL, U.S. (1990)	995	64
Shun Hing Square, Shenzhen, China (1996)	1,260	69	Wells Fargo Plaza, Houston, TX, U.S. (1983)	992	71
Empire State Building, New York, NY, U.S. (1931)	1,250	102	Kingdom Centre, Riyadh, Saudi Arabia (2002)	992	41
Central Plaza, Hong Kong, China (1992)	1,227	78	Aspire Tower, Doha, Qatar (2006)	984	36
Bank of China, Hong Kong, China (1989)	1,205	70	First Canadian Place, Toronto, Canada (1975)	978	72
*Bank of America Tower, New York, NY, U.S. (2008)	1,200	54	Eureka Tower, Melbourne, Australia (2006)	975	91
*Almas Tower, Dubai, UAE (2008)	1,181	68	*Comcast Center, Philadelphia, PA, U.S. (2007)	975	57
Emirates Tower One, Dubai, UAE (1999)	1,165	54	Landmark Tower, Yokohama, Japan (1993)	971	70
Tuntex Sky Tower, Kaohsiung, China (1997)	1,140	85	*Emirates Crown, Dubai, UAE (2008)	971	63
Aon Centre, Chicago, IL, U.S. (1973)	1,136	83	311 South Wacker Drive, Chicago, IL, U.S. (1990)	961	65
The Center, Hong Kong, China (1998)	1,135	73	SEG Plaza, Shenzhen, China (2000)	957	71
John Hancock Center, Chicago, IL, U.S. (1969)	1,127	100	American International Bldg., New York, NY, U.S. (1932)	952	67
*Rose Tower, Dubai, UAE (2007)	1,093	72	Key Tower, Cleveland, OH, U.S. (1991)	947	57
Shimao International Plaza, Shanghai, China (2006)	1,093	60	Plaza 66, Shanghai, China (2001)	945	66
*Minsheng Bank Building, Wuhan, China (2007)	1,087	68	One Liberty Place, Philadelphia, PA, U.S. (1987)	945	61
Ryugyong Hotel, Pyongyang, North Korea (1995)[1]	1,083	105	Millenium Tower, Dubai, UAE (2006)	935	59
*China World Trade Center Tower III, Beijing, China (2008)	1,083	69	Sunjoy Tomorrow Square, Shanghai, China (2003)	934	55
Q1, Gold Coast, Australia (2005)	1,058	78	Columbia Center, Seattle, WA, U.S. (1984)	933	76
Burj al Arab Hotel, Dubai, UAE (1999)	1,053	60	Cheung Kong Centre, Hong Kong, China (1999)	929	63
Nina Tower I, Hong Kong, China (2006)	1,046	80	Chongqing World Trade Center, Chongqing, China (2005)	929	60
Chrysler Building, New York, NY, U.S. (1930)	1,046	77	The Trump Building, New York, NY, U.S. (1930)	927	71
*New York Times Tower, New York, NY, U.S. (2007)	1,046	52	Bank of America Plaza, Dallas, TX, U.S. (1985)	921	72
Bank of America Plaza, Atlanta, GA, U.S. (1993)	1,039	55	United Overseas Bank Plaza, Singapore (1992)	919	66
U.S. Bank Tower, Los Angeles, CA, U.S. (1990)	1,018	73	Republic Plaza, Singapore (1995)	919	66
			Overseas Union Bank Centre, Singapore (1986)	919	63

Note: Burj Dubai, currently under construction in United Arab Emirates, will be the tallest building in the world when it is completed. The actual design figure has not been made public yet, but is likely to top 2,500 ft. and 160 stories. (1) Topped out in 1995, but never completed.

World's 10 Tallest Free-Standing Towers

Structures under construction as of mid-2007 are denoted by an asterisk (*). Year is date of completion or projected completion.

Name	City	Country	Ht. (ft.)	Year	Name	City	Country	Ht. (ft.)	Year
*Guangzhou TV Tower	Guangzhou	China	2,001	2009	*Milad Tower	Tehran	Iran	1,427	2007
CN Tower	Toronto	Canada	1,831	1976	Menara Kuala Lumpur	Kuala Lumpur	Malaysia	1,379	1996
Ostankino Tower	Moscow	Russia	1,772	1967	Tianjin Radio & TV Tower	Tianjin	China	1,362	1991
*Xi'an Broadcasting, Telephone and Television Tower	Xi'an	China	1,542	2008	Central Radio & TV Tower	Beijing	China	1,268	1992
Oriental Pearl TV Tower	Shanghai	China	1,535	1995	Kiev TV Tower	Kiev	Ukraine	1,263	1974

Tall Buildings in Selected North American Cities

Source: Marshall Gerometta and Rick Bronson, Emporis.com, www.emporis.com;
Council on Tall Buildings and Urban Habitat, Illinois Inst. of Technology, www.ctbuh.org

Lists include freestanding towers and other structures that do not have stories and are not technically considered buildings. Structures still under construction as of mid-2007 are denoted by an asterisk (*). Year in parentheses is date of completion or projected completion. Height is generally measured from sidewalk to roof, including penthouse and tower if enclosed as integral part of structure; stories generally counted from street level. NA = Not available or not applicable.

Building	Ht. (ft.)	Stories	Building	Ht. (ft.)	Stories
Atlanta, GA			**Atlantic City, NJ**		
Bank of America Plaza (incl. spire), 600 Peachtree St. NE (1992)	1,039	55	*Harrah's Expansion Tower, 777 Harrah's Blvd. (2008)	557	47
SunTrust Plaza, 303 Peachtree St. NE (1992)[1]	867	60	Borgata Hotel & Casino (2003)	479	40
One Atlantic Center, 1201 W. Peachtree St. (1987)	820	50	*The Water Club at Borgata (2007)	457	39
191 Peachtree Tower (1991)	770	50	*Trump Taj Mahal II, 1000 Boardwalk (2008)	450	40
Westin Peachtree Plaza, 210 Peachtree St. NW (1976)[2]	723	73	Trump Taj Mahal I, 1000 Boardwalk (1990)	429	42
Georgia Pacific Center, 133 Peachtree St. NE (1981)	697	51	**Austin, TX**		
Promenade II (incl. spire), 1230 Peachtree St. NE (1989)	691	40	*360 Condominiums (incl. spire), 360 Nueces St. (2007)	563	44
AT&T Bldg., 675 W. Peachtree St. (1980)	677	47	Frost Bank Tower, 401 N. Congress Ave. (2004)	516	33
*Sovereign, 3344 Peachtree Rd. NE (2008)	665	48	*Altavida, 101 Colorado St. (2008)	416	37
1180 Peachtree (2006)	657	41	**Baltimore, MD**		
GLG Grand/Four Seasons Hotel, 75 14th St. NE (1992)	609	53	Legg Mason Bldg., 100 Light St. (1973)	529	40
*The Mansion on Peachtree (2008)	580	42	Bank of America, 10 Light St. (1924)	509	37
State of Georgia Bldg., 2 Peachtree St. NW (1967)[3]	556	44	William Donald Schaefer Tower, 6 St. Paul Pl. (1992)	493	29
Marriott Marquis, 265 Peachtree Center Ave. NE (1985)	554	52	Commerce Place, 1 South St. (1992)	454	31
*The Atlantic, 270 17th St. NW (2009)	528	46	Marriott Baltimore Inner Harbor East, 700 Aliceanna St. (2001)	430	32
*Twelve Centennial Park Tower I, 400 W. Peachtree St. NW (2007)	520	39	100 E. Pratt St. (1992)	418	28
*Viewpoint, 855 Peachtree St. NE (2008)	501	36	World Trade Center, 401 E. Pratt St. (1977)	405	32
Park Avenue Condominiums, 750 Park Ave. NE (2000)	486	42	**Boston, MA**		
Terminus 100, 3280 Peachtree Rd. NE (2007)	485	27	Hancock Place, 200 Clarendon St. (1976)	790	62
Paramount at Buckhead, 3445 Stratford Rd. NE (2004)	478	40	Prudential Tower, 800 Boylston St. (1964)[1]	750	52
Centennial Tower, 101 Marietta St. (1976)	459	36	Federal Reserve Bldg., 600 Atlantic Ave. (1978)	604	32
Equitable Bldg., 100 Peachtree St. NW (1967)	453	34	Boston Company Bldg., 1 Boston Place (1970)	602	41
Spire, 860 Peachtree St. (2005)	453	28	One International Place, 100 Oliver St. (1987)	600	46
Buckhead Grand, 3338 Peachtree Rd. NE (2004)	451	38	First National Bank of Boston, 100 Federal St. (1971)	591	37
One Park Tower, 34 Peachtree St. (1961)	439	32	One Financial Center, 10 Dewey Sq. (1984)	590	46
1100 Peachtree St. NE (1990)	428	28	111 Huntington Ave. (2002)	554	36
Atlanta Plaza I, 950 E. Paces Ferry Rd. (1986)	425	32	Two International Place (1993)	538	35
Park Place on Peachtree, 2660 Peachtree Rd. NW (1986)	420	38	One Post Office Square (1981)	525	40
2828 Peachtree Luxury Condominiums (2002)	420	33	1 Federal St. (1975)	520	38
1280 West, 1280 W. Peachtree St. NW (1989)	410	38	Exchange Place, 53 State St. (1984)	510	39
*1010 Peachtree (2008)	407	36	Sixty State St. (1977)	509	38
Peachtree Summit No. 1, 401 W. Peachtree NE (1975)	406	31	1 Beacon St. (1972)	507	34
One Coca Cola Plaza, 310 North Ave. NW (1979)	403	29	State Street Financial Center (incl. spire), 1 Lincoln St. (2003)	503	36
Tower Place 100, 3340 Peachtree Rd. NE (1974)	401	29	28 State St. (1970)	500	40
			Marriott's Custom House, 3 McKinley Sq. (1915)	496	32
			John Hancock Bldg., 175 Berkeley St. (1949)	495	26

(1) 902 ft. with antenna. (2) 883 ft. with antenna. (3) 599 ft. with antenna.

Building	Ht. (ft.)	Stories
33 Arch St. (2003)	489	31
225 Franklin St. (1966)	477	33
Millennium Place 1, 10 Avery St. (2001)	475	38
125 High St. (1990)	452	30
100 Summer St. (1975)	450	33
Millennium Place 2, 3 Avery St. (2001)	445	36
McCormack Bldg., 1 Ashburton Pl. (1975)	401	22
Harbor Towers I, 85 E. India Row (1971)	400	40
Keystone Bldg., 99 High St. (1971)	400	32
(1) 836 ft. with antenna.		

Calgary, Alberta

Building	Ht. (ft.)	Stories
*The Bow (2010)	774	58
Petro Canada Centre West Tower, 150 6th Ave. SW (1984)	705	53
Bankers Hall East Tower, 855 2nd St. SW (1989)	645	50
Bankers Hall West Tower, 888 3rd St. SW (2000)	645	50
Calgary Tower, 101 9th Ave. SW (1967)	626	NA
TransCanada Tower, 450 1st St. SW (2001)	581	38
Canterra Tower, 400 3rd Ave. SW (1988)	580	46
*Jamieson Place, 302 4th Ave. SW (2009)	568	38
First Canadian Centre, 350 7th Ave. SW (1982)	547	41
Western Canadian Place—N. Tower, 707 6th St. SW (1983)	538	41
Canada Trust, Calgary Eatons Centre, 421 7th Ave. SW (1991)	530	40
Scotia Square, 700 2nd St. SW (1976)	509	41
Nexen Bldg., 801 7th Ave. SW (1982)	500	37
Two Bow Valley Square, 205 5th Ave. SW (1974)	468	34
Dome Tower, 333 7th Ave. SW (1976)	463	34
5th & 5th Bldg., 605 5th Ave. SW (1980)	460	35
Shell Centre, 400 4th Ave. SW (1977)	460	34
Home Oil Tower, 324 8th Ave. SW (1976)	449	33
Four Bow Valley Square, 250 6th Ave. SW (1982)	441	37
Fifth Avenue Place East Tower, 425 1st St. SW (1981)	435	35
Fifth Avenue Place West Tower, 237 4th Ave. SW (1981)	435	35
Petro-Canada Tower, East Tower, 111 5th Ave. SW (1983)	427	33
*Calgary Courts Centre—North Tower (2007)	423	24
Western Canadian Place—S. Tower, 801 6th St. SW (1983)	420	32
*arriVa Tower, 1,411 11th Ave. SE (2007)	418	34
Altius Centre, 500 4th Ave. SW (1972)	415	32
EnCana Place, 150 9th Ave. SW (1982)	410	28
Hewlett Packard Tower, 715 5th Ave. SW (1975)	408	31
Alberta Stock Exchange, 300 5th Ave. SW (1979)	407	33

Charlotte, NC

Building	Ht. (ft.)	Stories
Bank of America Corporate Center, 100 N. Tryon St. (1992)	871	60
*Wachovia Tower, 534 S. Tryon St. (2009)	764	48
Hearst Tower, 214 N. Tryon St. (2002)	659	50
*210 Trade St. (2008)	601	53
One Wachovia Center, 301 S. College St. (1988)	588	42
Bank of America Plaza, 101 S. Tryon St. (1974)	503	40
Interstate Tower, 121 W. Trade St. (1990)	462	32
201 N. Tryon St. (1997)	447	30
Three Wachovia Center, 401 S. Tryon St. (2000)	440	29
Two Wachovia Plaza, 301 S. Tryon St. (1971)	433	32
*Avenue, 128 W. 5th (2007)	425	36
400 S. Tryon St. (1974)	420	32

Chicago, IL

Building	Ht. (ft.)	Stories
*The Chicago Spire, 400 N. Lake Shore Dr. (2010)	2,000	/150
Sears Tower, 233 S. Wacker Dr. (1974)[1]	1,451	108
*Trump International Hotel & Tower (incl. spire), 401 N. Wabash Ave. (2009)	1,362	96
Aon Center, 200 E. Randolph St. (1973)	1,136	83
John Hancock Center, 875 N. Michigan Ave. (1969)[2]	1,127	100
*Waterview Tower, 111 W. Wacker Dr. (2010)	1,047	89
AT&T Corporate Center (incl. spires), 227 W. Monroe St. (1989)	1,007	60
Two Prudential Plaza (incl. spire), 180 N. Stetson Ave. (1990)	995	64
311 S. Wacker Dr. (1990)	961	65
900 N. Michigan Ave. (1989)	871	66
Water Tower Place, 845 N. Michigan Ave. (1976)	859	74
Chase Tower, 21 S. Clark St. (1969)	850	60
Park Tower, 800 N. Michigan Ave. (2000)	844	67
*The Legacy at Millennium Park, 21-39 S. Wabash Ave. (2009)	822	73
*Aqua, 211 N. Columbus Dr. (2009)	815	82
*300 N. LaSalle St. (2009)	784	60
3 First National Plaza, 70 W. Madison St. (1981)	767	57
Chicago Title & Trust Center, 161 N. Clark St. (1992)	756	50
*One Museum Park, 1215 N. Prairie Ave. (2007)	734	62
Olympia Centre, 737 N. Michigan Ave. (1986)	725	63
*Elysian, 940 N. Rush St. (2008)	700	60
330 N. Wabash Ave. (1973)	695	52
111 S. Wacker Dr. (2005)	681	51
181 W. Madison St. (1990)	680	50
Hyatt Center, 71 S. Wacker Dr. (2005)	679	48
One Magnificent Mile, 980 N. Michigan Ave. (1983)	673	57
340 on the Park, 340 W. Randolph St. (2007)	672	64
R.R. Donnelley Center, 77 W. Wacker Dr. (1992)	668	50
UBS Tower, 1 N. Wacker Dr. (2001)	652	50
Daley Center, 55 W. Washington St. (1965)	648	32
55 E. Erie St. (2004)	647	56
Lake Point Tower, 505 N. Lake Shore Dr. (1968)	645	70
River East Center, 350 E. Illinois St. (2001)	644	58
Grand Plaza I (incl. spire), 540 N. State St. (2003)	641	57

Building	Ht. (ft.)	Stories
*155 N. Wacker (NA)	638	45
Leo Burnett Bldg., 35 W. Wacker Dr. (1989)	635	46
The Heritage at Millennium Park, 125 N. Wabash Ave. (2005)	631	57
NBC Tower (incl. spire), 455 N. Cityfront Plaza Dr. (1989)	627	37
*One Museum Park West, 201 E. Roosevelt Rd. (2009)	620	54
Millennium Centre, 33 W. Ontario St. (2003)	610	58
Chicago Place, 700 N. Michigan Ave. (1991)	608	49
Board of Trade (incl. statue), 141 W. Jackson Blvd. (1930)	605	44
*353 N. Clark St. (2009)	603	40
CNA Plaza, 325 S. Wabash St. (1972)	601	44
Prudential Bldg., 130 E. Randolph St. (1955)[3]	601	41
Heller International Tower, 500 W. Monroe St. (1992)	600	45
One Madison Plaza, 200 W. Madison St. (1982)	599	44
1000 Lake Shore Plaza (1964)	590	55
*The Clare at Water Tower, 55 East Pearson St. (2008)	589	52
Marina City Apts. 1, 300 N. State St. (1964)	588	61
Marina City Apts. 2, 300 N. State St. (1964)	588	61
Citicorp Center, 500 W. Madison St. (1987)	588	42
Park Monroe, 55 E. Monroe St. (1972)	583	40
Smurfit-Stone Bldg., 150 N. Michigan Ave. (1983)	582	41
North Pier Tower, 474 N. Lake Shore Dr. (1990)	581	61
Chase Center, 131 S. Dearborn St. (2003)	580	39
The Fordham, 25 E. Superior St. (2003)	574	52
190 S. LaSalle St. (1987)	573	40
One S. Dearborn St. (2005)	571	39
Onterie Center, 446 E. Ontario St. (1986)	570	58
Chicago Temple, 77 W. Washington St. (1924)	568	23
Palmolive Bldg. (incl. beacon), 919 N. Michigan Ave. (1929)	565	37
Huron Plaza Apts., 30 E. Huron St. (1983)	560	56
Boeing International Headquarters, 100 N. Riverside Plaza (1990)	560	36
The Parkshore, 195 N. Harbor Dr. (1991)	556	56
North Harbor Tower, 175 N. Harbor Dr. (1988)	556	55
Civic Opera Bldg., 20 N. Wacker Dr. (1929)	555	45
Newberry Plaza, 1000 N. State St. (1974)	553	53
Michigan Plaza South, 205 N. Michigan Ave. (1985)	553	46
30 N. LaSalle St. (1975)	553	44
Pittsfield Bldg., 55 E. Washington St. (1927)	551	38
Harbor Point, 155 N. Harbor Dr. (1975)	550	54
One S. Wacker Dr. (1982)	550	40
Kluczynski Federal Bldg., 230 S. Dearborn St. (1975)	545	45
Park Millennium, 222 N. Columbus Dr. (2002)	544	57
USG Bldg., 125 S. Franklin St. (1992)	538	35
The Pinnacle, 21 E. Huron St. (2004)	535	48
LaSalle National Bank, 135 S. LaSalle St. (1934)	535	45
Park Place Tower, 655 W. Irving Park Rd. (1971)	531	56
One N. LaSalle (1930)	530	48
The Elysees, 111 E. Chestnut St. (1973)	529	56
River Plaza, 405 N. Wabash St. (1977)	524	56
35 E. Wacker Drive (1927)	523	40
Unitrin Bldg., 1 E. Wacker Dr. (1962)	522	41
Mather Tower, 75 E. Wacker Dr. (1928)	521	41
Chicago Mercantile Exchange, 10 S. Wacker Dr. (1987)	520	40
Chicago Mercantile Exchange, 30 S. Wacker Dr. (1983)	520	40
The Columbian, 1180 S. Michigan Ave. (2007)	517	47
191 N. Wacker Dr. (2002)	516	37
401 E. Ontario St. (1990)	515	51
One Financial Place, 440 S. LaSalle St. (1985)	515	39
The Streeter, 345 E. Ohio St. (2006)	514	50
5415 N. Sheridan Rd. (1973)	513	54
*600 N. Lake Shore Dr. (2009)	513	47
LaSalle-Wacker Bldg., 221 N. LaSalle St. (1930)[4]	512	41
Harris Bank III, 115 S. LaSalle St. (1974)	510	38
321 N. Clark St. (1987)	510	35
400 E. Ohio St. (1982)	505	50
Carbide & Carbon Bldg., 230 N. Michigan Ave. (1929)	503	37
1 Superior Place, 1 W. Superior St. (1999)	502	52
120 N. LaSalle St. (1992)	501	39
Chase Plaza, 10 S. LaSalle St. (1986)	501	37
*The Tides, 360 E. South Water St. (2007)	500	51
200 S. Wacker Dr. (1981)	500	41
(1) 1,729 ft. with antenna. (2) 1,499 ft. with antenna. (3) 912 ft. with antenna. (4) 543 ft. with antenna.		

Cincinnati, OH

Building	Ht. (ft.)	Stories
Carew Tower, 441 Vine St. (1931)[1]	574	49
PNC Tower, 1 W. 4th St. (1913)	495	31
Scripps Center, 312 Walnut St. (1990)	468	36
Fifth Third Tower, 511 Walnut St. (1969)	423	32
The Center at 600 Vine, 600 Vine St. (1984)	418	29
Chemed Center, 255 5th St. (1990)	410	32
(1) 623 ft. with antenna.		

Cleveland, OH

Building	Ht. (ft.)	Stories
Key Tower (incl. spire), 127 Public Sq. (1991)	947	57
Terminal Tower, 50 Public Sq. (1930)[1]	708	52
200 Public Sq. (1985)	658	45
100 Erieview, 1801 E. 9th St. (1964)	529	40
One Cleveland Center, 1375 E. 9th St. (1983)	450	31
Fifth Third Center, 600 Superior Ave. (1991)	446	28
Carl B. Stokes Federal Courthouse, 801 W. Superior Ave. (2002)	430	24
Justice Center, 1250 Ontario St. (1976)	420	26
Federal Bldg., 1240 E. 9th St. (1967)	419	32
National City Center, 1900 E. 9th St. (1980)	410	35
(1) 771 ft. with flagpole.		

Building	Ht. (ft.)	Stories
Columbus, OH		
James A. Rhodes State Office Tower, 30 E. Broad St. (1973)	624	41
Leveque-Lincoln Tower, 50 W. Broad St. (1927)	555	47
William Green Bldg., 30 W. Spring St. (1990)	530	33
Huntington Center, 41 S. High St. (1983)	512	37
Vern Riffe State Office Tower, 77 S. High St. (1988)	503	33
One Nationwide Plaza (1976)	485	40
Franklin County Courthouse, 373 S. High St. (1991)	464	27
AEP Bldg., One Riverside Plz. (1983)	456	31
Borden Bldg., 180 E. Broad St. (1974)	438	34
Three Nationwide Plaza (1989)	408	27
Dallas, TX		
Bank of America Plaza, 901 Main St. (1985)	921	72
Renaissance Tower (incl. spire), 1201 Elm St. (1974)	886	56
Chase Center, 1717 Main St. (1987)	787	60
JPMorgan Chase Tower, 2200 Ross Ave. (1987)	738	55
Fountain Place, 1445 Ross Ave. (1986)	720	58
Trammel Crow Tower, 2001 Ross Ave. (1984)	686	50
1700 Pacific Ave. (1983)	655	50
*Victory Mandarin Oriental Hotel & Residences (2009)	650	43
Thanksgiving Tower, 1600 Pacific Ave. (1982)	645	50
Energy Plaza, 1601 Bryan St. (1983)	629	49
Elm Place, 1401 Elm St. (1965)	625	52
Republic Center Tower I (incl. spire), 300 N. Ervay St. (1954)	602	36
Republic Center Tower II, 325 N. St. Paul St. (1964)	598	50
One AT&T Plaza, 208 S. Akard St. (1984)	580	37
One Lincoln Plaza, 500 Akard St. (1984)	579	45
Cityplace Center East, 2711 N. Haskell Ave. (1989)	560	42
Reunion Tower, 300 Reunion Blvd. (1976)	560	NA
Adams Mark Hotel Center Tower, 400 Olive St. (1959)	550	42
Mercantile Bldg. (incl. spire), 1700 Main St. (1943)	523	31
2001 Bryan St. (1973)	512	40
Harwood Center, 1999 Bryan St. (1982)	483	36
KMPG Centre, 717 N. Harwood St. (1980)	481	34
San Jacinto Tower, 2121 San Jacinto St. (1982)	456	33
Renaissance Hotel, 2222 Stemmons Fwy. (1983)	451	29
Denver, CO		
Republic Plaza, 330 17th St. (1984)	714	56
1801 California St. (1982)	709	50
Wells Fargo Center, 1700 Lincoln Ave. (1983)	544	43
1999 Broadway (1985)	544	43
707 17th St. (1981)	522	42
555 17th St. (1978)	507	40
*Spire, 1434 Champa St. (2009)	483	41
1670 Broadway (1980)	448	36
Hyatt Regency Denver at the Colorado Convention Center, 650 15th St. (2005)	439	37
17th St. Plaza, 1225 17th St. (1982)	438	32
First Interstate Tower North, 633 17th St. (1974)	434	32
Brooks Towers, 1020 15th St. (1968)	420	42
Denver Place South Tower, 999 18th St. (1981)	416	34
One Tabor Center, 1200 17th St. (1984)	408	32
Johns Manville Plaza, 717 17th St. (1989)	404	29
Detroit, MI		
Marriott Hotel, Renaissance Center I (1977)[1]	727	70
One Detroit Center, 500 Woodward Ave. (1991)[2]	619	45
Penobscot Bldg., 633 Griswold Ave. (1928)	566	46
Renaissance Center 100 Tower (1976)	508	39
Renaissance Center 200 Tower (1976)	508	39
Renaissance Center 300 Tower (1976)	508	39
Renaissance Center 400 Tower (1976)	508	39
Guardian Bldg., 500 Griswold Ave. (1929)	489	36
Book Tower, 1249 Washington Blvd. (1925)	472	35
150 W. Jefferson Ave. (1988)	470	29
Fisher Bldg., 3011 W. Grand Blvd. (1928)	444	28
Cadillac Tower, 65 Cadillac Sq. (1928)	437	40
David Stott Bldg., 1150 Griswold St. (1928)	436	38
One Woodward Ave. (1962)	430	30
(1) 755 ft. with antenna. (2) 665 ft. with antenna.		
Edmonton, Alberta		
Manulife Place, 10170-101 St. NW (1983)	480	36
Telus Plaza South, 10020-100 St. NW (1971)	441	34
Bell Tower, 10104-103 Ave. NW (1982)	426	34
Commerce Place, 10155-102 St. NW (1990)	404	27
Fort Worth, TX		
Burnett Plaza, 801 Cherry St. (1983)	567	40
D.R. Horton Tower, 301 Commerce St. (1984)	547	38
*Omni Convention Center Hotel, 1300 Houston St. (2008)	547	34
Carter Burgess Plaza, 777 Main St. (1982)	525	40
The Tower, 400 Throckmorton St. (1974)	488	36
Wells Fargo Tower, 201 Main St. (1982)	477	33
Hartford, CT		
City Place I, 185 Asylum St. (1980)	535	38
Travelers Tower, 26 Grove St. (1919)	527	34
Goodwin Square, 225 Asylum St. (1990)	522	30
Hartford 21, 221 Trumbull St. (2006)	440	36

Building	Ht. (ft.)	Stories
Honolulu, HI		
First Hawaiian Center, 999 Bishop St. (1996)	429	30
Nauru Tower, 1330 Ala Moana Blvd. (1991)	418	44
Hokua Tower, 1288 Ala Moana Blvd. (2006)	418	40
Moana Pacific East Tower, 1288 Kapiolani Blvd. (2007)	415	46
Moana Pacific West Tower, 1288 Kapiolani Blvd. (2007)	415	46
Ko'olani, 1189 Waimanu St. (2006)	400	47
One Waterfront Tower-Makai, 425 S. King St. (1990)	400	45
One Waterfront Tower-Mauka, 415 S. King St. (1990)	400	45
Hawaiki Tower, 88 Piikoi St. (1999)	400	45
One Archer Lane, 801 S. King St. (1998)	400	41
Imperial Plaza, 725 Kapiolani Blvd. (1992)	400	40
Houston, TX		
JPMorgan Chase Tower, 600 Travis St. (1982)	1,002	75
Wells Fargo Plaza, 1000 Louisiana St. (1983)	992	71
Williams Tower, 2800 Post Oak Blvd. (1983)	901	64
Bank of America Center, 700 Louisiana St. (1983)	780	56
Texaco Heritage Plaza, 1111 Bagby St. (1987)	762	53
Enterprise Plaza, 1100 Louisiana St. (1980)	748	55
Centerpoint Energy Plaza, 1111 Louisiana St. (1974)	741	47
Continental Airlines Center, 1600 Smith St. (1984)	732	55
Fulbright Tower, 1301 McKinney St. (1982)	725	52
One Shell Plaza, 900 Louisiana St. (1970)[1]	714	50
1400 Smith St. (1983)	691	50
3 Allen Center, 333 Clay St. (1980)	685	50
One Houston Center, 1221 McKinney St. (1978)	678	47
First City Tower, 1001 Fannin St. (1984)	662	47
San Felipe Plaza, 5847 San Felipe Blvd. (1984)	625	45
ExxonMobile Bldg., 800 Bell Ave. (1962)	606	44
1500 Louisiana St. (2002)	600	40
America General Center, 2929 Allen Pkwy. (1983)	590	42
Two Houston Center, 909 Fannin St. (1974)	579	40
San Jacinto Column (NA)[2]	570	NA
Marathon Oil Tower, 5555 San Felipe Blvd. (1983)	562	41
Wedge International Tower, 1415 Louisiana St. (1983)	550	44
KBR Tower, 601 Jefferson St. (1973)	550	40
Pennzoil Place I, 700 Milam St. (1976)	523	36
Pennzoil Place II, 700 Louisiana St. (1976)	523	36
Devon Energy Center, 1200 Smith St. (1978)	521	36
Reliant Energy Plaza, 1000 Main St. (2003)	518	36
Total Plaza, 1201 Louisiana St. (1971)	518	35
The Huntington, 2121 Kirby Dr. (1982)	503	34
El Paso Energy Bldg, 1010 Milam St. (1962)	502	33
*One Park Place, 1500 McKinney St. (2009)	501	37
5 Greenway Plaza (1973)	465	31
Calpine Center, 717 Texas Ave. (2003)	453	34
One Allen Center, 500 Dallas St. (1974)	452	34
(1) 999 ft. with antenna. (2) World's tallest memorial column. Located in La Porte, TX, near Houston.		
Indianapolis, IN		
Chase Tower (incl. spires), 111 Monument Cir. (1990)	811	49
One America Tower, 200 N. Illinois St. (1982)	533	38
One Indiana Square, 200 N. Delaware St. (1970)	504	36
Market Tower, 10 W. Market St. (1988)	421	32
300 N. Meridian Bldg. (1988)	408	28
First Indiana Plaza, 135 N. Pennsylvania St. (1988)	401	29
Jacksonville, FL		
Bank of America Tower, 50 N. Laura St. (1990)	617	42
Modis Tower, 1 Independent Dr. (1975)	535	37
The Peninsula, 1357 Riverplace Blvd. (2006)	437	38
BellSouth Tower, 424 N. Pearl St. (1983)	435	27
Riverplace Tower, 1301 Riverplace Blvd. (1967)	433	28
Jersey City, NJ		
30 Hudson St. (2004)	781	42
101 Hudson St. (1992)	548	42
*Trump Plaza I, 88 Morgan St. (2008)	532	55
Newport Tower, 525 Washington Blvd. (1990)	528	37
Exchange Place Center (incl. spire), 10 Exchange Pl. (1990)	516	32
*77 Hudson St. East Tower (2009)	500	48
*77 Hudson St. West Tower (2009)	500	48
Harborside Financial Plaza V, 160 Greene St. (2002)	480	34
Marbella Apts., 425 Washington Blvd. (2003)	427	40
Kansas City, MO		
One Kansas City Place, 1200 Main St. (1988)	632	42
Town Pavilion, 1111 Main St. (1986)	591	38
Hyatt Regency Crown Center, 2345 McGee St. (1980)	504	45
Power & Light Bldg., 1330 Baltimore Ave. (1931)	481	34
909 Walnut St. (1931)	454	35
City Hall, 414 E. 12th St. (1937)	443	29
1201 Walnut St. (1991)	427	30
Commerce Tower, 911 Main St. (1965)	407	32
City Center Square, 1100 Main St. (1977)	404	30
Las Vegas, NV		
Stratosphere Tower, 2000 S. Las Vegas Blvd. (1996)	1,149	NA
*Fontainebleau Resort Hotel, 2755 Las Vegas Blvd. South (2009)	735	63
*The Palazzo (2007)	642	53
*Encore at Wynn Las Vegas, 3145 Las Vegas Blvd. South (2008)	631	48
*Trump International Hotel and Tower 1 (2007)	622	64
Wynn Las Vegas, 3145 Las Vegas Blvd. South (2005)	613	45
*Cosmopolitan Casino Spa Tower, Las Vegas Blvd. and Harmon Ave. (2008)	603	53
*Cosmopolitan Beach Resort Tower, Las Vegas Blvd. and Harmon Ave. (2008)	603	51
*Project CityCenter Hotel and Casino (2009)	600	60

Building	Ht. (ft.)	Stories
*Planet Hollywood Towers (2007)	600	50
*VDARA, 2551 W. Harmon Ave. (2009)	554	50
Eiffel Tower, Paris Hotel and Casino, 3645 Las Vegas Blvd. South (1998)	540	NA
*Mandarin Oriental Hotel Las Vegas, 3750 Las Vegas Blvd. South (2009)	539	56
New York, New York Hotel & Casino, 3790 Las Vegas Blvd. South (1997)	529	48
*Palms Place, 4321 W. Flamingo Rd. (2007)	518	50
Bellagio Hotel & Casino, 3600 Las Vegas Blvd. South (1998)	508	37
Sky Las Vegas, 2780 Las Vegas Blvd. South (2007)	500	45
THEhotel, Mandalay Bay, 3950 Las Vegas Blvd. South (2003)	485	43
*Panorama Tower III, 4631 Industrial Blvd. (2007)	483	43
Mandalay Bay Hotel & Casino, 3950 Las Vegas Blvd. South (1999)	480	43
Turnberry Place I, 2777 Paradise Rd. (2001)	477	38
Turnberry Place II, 2777 Paradise Rd. (2002)	477	38
Turnberry Place III, 2777 Paradise Rd. (2004)	477	38
Turnberry Place IV, 2777 Paradise Rd. (2006)	477	38
The Signature at MGM Grand Tower I, 155 E. Harmon Ave. (2006)	475	38
The Signature at MGM Grand Tower II, 155 E. Harmon Ave. (2006)	475	38
The Signature at MGM Grand Tower III, 155 E. Harmon Ave. (2006)	475	38
Venetian Resort-Hotel-Casino 1, 3355 Las Vegas Blvd. West (1999)	475	35
*Allure Las Vegas I (2007)	466	41
Palms Resort—Fantasy Tower, 4321 W. Flamingo Rd. (2006)	457	40
*Turnberry Towers West Tower, 222 Karen Ave. (2007)	453	45
*Turnberry Towers East Tower, 222 Karen Ave. (2008)	453	45

Los Angeles, CA

Building	Ht. (ft.)	Stories
U.S. Bank Tower, 633 W. 5th St. (1990)	1,018	73
Aon Center, 707 Wilshire Blvd. (1974)	858	62
Two California Plaza, 350 S. Grand Ave. (1992)	750	52
Gas Company Tower, 555 W. 5th St. (1991)	749	52
Bank of America Tower, 333 S. Hope St. (1975)	735	55
777 Tower, 777 S. Figueroa St. (1991)	725	53
Wells Fargo Tower, 333 S. Grand Ave. (1983)	723	54
Figueroa at Wilshire, 601 S. Figueroa St. (1989)	717	52
Paul Hastings Tower, 515 S. Flower St. (1971)	699	52
City National Tower, 555 S. Flower St. (1971)	699	52
Citigroup Center, 444 S. Flower St. (1979)	625	48
611 Place, 611 W. 6th St. (1969)	620	42
One California Plaza, 300 S. Grand Ave. (1985)	578	42
Century Plaza Tower 1, 2029 Century Park East (1973)	571	44
Century Plaza Tower 2, 2049 Century Park East (1973)	571	44
KPMG Tower, 355 S. Grand Ave. (1984)	560	45
Ernst & Young LLP Plaza, 725 S. Figueroa St. (1986)	534	41
SunAmerica Center, 1999 Ave. of the Stars (1989)	533	39
TCW Tower, 865 S. Figueroa St. (1990)	517	37
Union Bank Plaza, 445 S. Figueroa St. (1968)	516	40
10 Universal City Plaza (1984)	506	36
*The Century, 2055 Ave. of the Stars (2009)	497	41
1100 Wilshire, 1100 Wilshire Blvd. (1987)	496	36
Fox Plaza, 2121 Ave. of the Stars (1987)	492	34
Constellation Place, 10250 Constellation Blvd. (2003)	491	35
ARCO Tower, 1055 W. 7th St. (1988)	462	33
Equitable Life, 3435 Wilshire Blvd. (1969)	454	34
City Hall, 200 N. Spring St. (1927)	454	28
SBC Tower, 1150 Olive St. (1965)	452	32

Louisville, KY

Building	Ht. (ft.)	Stories
AEGON Center, 400 W. Market St. (1992)	549	35
National City Tower, 101 S. 5th St. (1972)	512	40
PNC Plaza, 500 W. Jefferson St. (1971)	420	30
Humana Center, 500 W. Main St. (1985)	417	27

Mexico City, Mexico

Building	Ht. (ft.)	Stories
Torre Mayor, Paseo de la Reforma 505 (2003)	738	55
Torre Ejecutiva Pemex, Marina Nacional 329 Col. Huasteca (1984)	702	52
Torre Altus, Paseo de los Laureles 416 (1999)	640	42
Torre Latino Americana (incl. spire), Eje Central Lazaro Cardenas 2 (1956)	597	45
World Trade Center, Montecito 38 Col. Napoles (1972)[1]	565	50
Los Arcos Bosques I, Paeo de los Tamarindos 400 (1997)	529	35
*Los Arcos Bosques II, Paeo de los Tamarindos 400 (NA)	529	35
Santa Fe Flats, Av. Sante Fe 443 (2005)	492	37
Torre Lomas, Paseo de las Palmas 800 (1988)	481	36

(1) 682 ft. with antenna.

Miami, FL

Building	Ht. (ft.)	Stories
*Met 3, 200 SE 2nd St. (2009)	828	76
Four Seasons Hotel & Tower, 1441 Brickell Ave. (2003)	789	64
Wachovia Financial Center, 200 S. Biscayne Blvd. (1983)	764	55
*Infinity II, 1300 S. Miami Ave. (2009)	736	65
*900 Biscayne Bay, 900 Biscayne Blvd. (2008)	712	65
*Marquis, 1100 Biscayne Blvd. (2008)	679	63
*Mint at Riverfront, 90 SW 3rd St. (2009)	631	55
*Infinity at Brickell, 60 W. 13th St. (2008)	630	52
Bank of America Tower, 100 SE 2nd St. (1987)	625	47
*Met 2, 200 SE 3rd St. (2008)	617	46
Marinablue, 888 Biscayne Blvd. (2007)	615	57
*Plaza on Brickell Tower I, 901 Brickell Ave. (2007)	610	56
*Platinum on the Bay, 2955 NE 7th Ave. (2009)	590	56
*Icon Brickell North Tower, 495 Brickell Ave. (2008)	586	58
*Icon Brickell South Tower, 495 Brickell Ave. (2008)	586	58
Ten Museum Park, 1040 Biscayne Blvd. (2007)	585	50
*Paramount at Edgewater Square, 2066 N. Bayshore Dr. (2008)	562	47
50 Biscayne Blvd. (2007)	554	55
*Quantum on the Bay South Tower, 1900 N. Bayshore Dr. (2007)	554	51
*Opera Tower, 1750 N. Bayshore Dr. (2007)	543	56
*Onyx 2 on the Bay, 421 NE 28th St. (2007)	543	49
*Park Place at Brickell (incl. spire), 1450 Brickell Ave. (2009)	540	40
*Everglades on the Bay North Tower, 244 Biscayne Blvd. (2007)	538	49
*Everglades on the Bay South Tower, 244 Biscayne Blvd. (2007)	538	49
*Quantum on the Bay North Tower, 1900 N. Bayshore Dr. (2007)	536	44
Jade at Brickell Bay, 1331 Brickell Bay Dr. (2005)	528	49
*Plaza on Brickell Tower II, 901 Brickell Ave. (2007)	525	48
Santa Maria, 1643 Brickell Ave. (1997)	520	51
*The Ivy, 90-95 SW 3rd St. (2007)	512	45
Stephen P. Clark Center, 111 NW 1st St. (1985)	510	28
*Wind, 330 S. Miami Ave. (2007)	501	41
*Epic Hotel & Residences, 300 Biscayne Blvd. Way (2007)	500	48
*Avenue Brickell Tower, 1060 Brickell Ave. (2007)	495	46
One Biscayne Tower, 2 S. Biscayne Blvd. (1973)	492	39
Espirito Santo Plaza, 1301 Brickell Ave. (2004)	487	36
*Brickell Financial Center Phase I, 680 Brickell Ave. (2009)	484	40
Citicorp Tower at Miami Centre, 201 S. Biscayne Blvd. (1986)	484	35
*Asia, 900 Brickell Key Blvd. (2007)	483	36
Brickell on the River North, 27 SE 5th St. (2005)	482	42
Three Tequesta Point, 848 Brickell Key Dr. (2001)	480	46
Latitude on the River, 615 SW 2nd Ave. (2007)	476	44
*Viceroy, 495 Brickell Ave. (NA)	465	46
One Miami East Tower, 205 S. Brickell Ave. (2005)	460	44
701 Brickell Ave. (1986)	450	33

Miami Beach, FL

Building	Ht. (ft.)	Stories
Blue Diamond Tower, 4779 Collins Ave. (2000)	559	44
Green Diamond Tower, 4775 Collins Ave. (2000)	559	44
Akoya Condominiums, 6365 Collins Ave. (2004)	492	47
Portofino Tower, 300 South Pointe Dr. (1997)	484	44
The Continuum on South Beach, South Tower, 1 South Pointe Dr. (2002)	474	40
ICON South Beach, 450 Alton Rd. (2004)	423	43
*The Continuum on South Beach, North Tower, 200 South Pointe Dr. (2007)	415	37
Murano Grande at Portofino, 400 Alton Rd. (2003)	407	37
Murano at Portofino, 1000 South Pointe Dr. (2001)	402	38

Milwaukee, WI

Building	Ht. (ft.)	Stories
U.S. Bank Center, 777 E. Wisconsin Ave. (1973)	601	42
100 E. Wisconsin Ave. (1989)	549	37
University Club Tower, 825 N. Prospect Ave. (2007)	446	36
Milwaukee Center, 111 E. Kilbourn Ave. (1987)	426	29
411 Bldg., 411 E. Wisconsin Ave. (1983)	408	30

Minneapolis, MN

Building	Ht. (ft.)	Stories
IDS Tower, 80 S. 8th St. (1973)[1]	792	57
225 South Sixth, 225 S. 6th St. (1992)	776	56
Wells Fargo Center, 90 S. 7th St. (1988)	774	57
33 S. 6th St. (1983)	668	52
Campbell Mithun Tower, 222 S. 9th St. (1984)	582	42
U.S. Bank Plaza I, 200 S. 6th St. (1981)	561	41
Dain Rauscher Plaza, 60 S. 6th St. (1992)	539	40
Fifth Street Towers II, 150 S. 5th St. (1988)	503	36
Ameriprise Financial Center, 707 2nd Ave. South (2000)	498	31
Target Plaza South, 1020 Nicollet Mall (2001)	492	33
Plaza VII, 45 S. 7th St. (1987)	475	36
The Carlyle, 220 2nd St. South (2007)	469	41
US Bancorp Center, 800 Nicollet Mall (2000)	468	32
AT&T Tower, 901 Marquette Ave. (1991)	464	34
Accenture Tower, 333 S. 7th St. (1987)	455	33
Foshay Tower, 821 Marquette Ave. (1929)	448	32
Qwest Bldg., 224 5th St. South (1931)	416	26
Fifty South Sixth, 50 S. 6th St. (2001)	404	30
Hennepin Co. Government Center, 300 S. 6th St. (1977)	403	24

(1) 910 ft. with antenna.

Montreal, Quebec

Building	Ht. (ft.)	Stories
1250 Blvd. Rene Levesque (incl. spire) (1992)	743	47
1000 Rue de la Gauchetiere (1992)	673	51
Tour de la Bourse, 800 Place Victoria (1963)	624	47
1 Place Villa Marie (1962)	616	42
La Tour CIBC, 1155 Rene Levesque Blvd. (1962)	604	43
Montreal Tower (1987)	574	NA
Tour McGill College, 1501 McGill College (1992)	519	38
Le Complexe Desjardins Sud (1975)	498	40
Tour KMPG, 600 Maisonneuve (1987)	479	34
Place Montreal Trust, 1800 McGill College (1988)	440	30
500 Place d'Armes (1968)	435	32
Tour TELUS, 630 Rene Levesque Blvd. (1962)	429	32
Le Complexe Desjardins Est (1975)	428	32
Port Royal Apts., 1455 Sherbrooke Ouest (1964)	424	33
Marriott Hotel, 1 Place du Canada (1967)	420	38
Centre Mount Royal, 1000 Sherbrooke Ouest (1974)	420	28
Tour de la Banque Nationale, 600 Rue de la Gauchetiere (1983)	420	28
Tour Bell, 700 Rue de la Gauchetiere (1983)	420	28
Tour Terminal, 800 Rene Levesque Blvd. Ouest (1966)	400	30

Building	Ht. (ft.)	Stories
Nashville, TN		
BellSouth Tower (incl. spires), 333 Commerce St. (1994)	617	33
Financial Center, 424 Church St. (1986)	490	31
William R. Snodgrass Tennessee Tower, 311 7th Ave. North (1970)	452	31
Nashville Life & Casualty Tower, 401 Church St. (1957)	409	30
City Center, 511 Union St. (1987)	402	27
New Orleans, LA		
One Shell Square, 701 Poydras St. (1972)	697	51
CapitalOne Tower, 201 St. Charles Ave. (1985)	645	53
Plaza Tower, 1001 Howard Ave. (1969)	531	45
Energy Centre, 1100 Poydras St. (1984)	530	39
First Bank & Trust Tower, 909 Poydras St. (1987)	481	36
Sheraton Hotel, 500 Canal St. (1985)	478	47
Marriott Hotel, 555 Canal St. (1972)	450	42
Texaco Center, 400 Poydras St. (1983)	442	33
Canal Place One, 365 Canal St. (1979)	439	32
1010 Common St. (1971)	438	31
World Trade Center, 2 Canal St. (1965)	407	33
1450 Poydras St. (1989)	406	26
New York, NY		
*Freedom Tower (incl. spire), One World Trade Center (2011)	1,776	82
Empire State Building, 350 5th Ave. (1931)	1,250	102
*Bank of America (incl. spire), One Bryant Park (2008)	1,200	54
Chrysler Building (incl. spire), 405 Lexington Ave. (1930).	1,046	77
*New York Times Tower (incl. spire), 620 8th Ave. (2007)	1,046	52
American International Bldg. (incl. spire), 70 Pine St. (1932)	952	67
The Trump Bldg., 40 Wall St. (1930)	927	71
Citigroup Center, 153 E. 53rd St. (1977)	915	59
*Beekman Place, 8 Spruce St. (2010)	876	74
Trump World Tower, 845 UN Plaza (2001)	861	72
GE Bldg., 30 Rockefeller Ctr. (1933)	850	70
Cityspire Center, 150 W. 56th St. (1989)	814	75
One Chase Manhattan Plaza (1960)	813	60
Conde Nast Bldg., 4 Times Sq. (1999)[1]	809	48
MetLife Bldg., 200 Park Ave. (1963)	808	59
Bloomberg Tower, 731 Lexington Ave. (2005)[2]	806	54
Woolworth Bldg., 233 Broadway (1913)	792	57
1 Worldwide Plaza, 935 8th Ave. (1989)	778	47
Carnegie Hall Tower, 152 W. 57th St. (1991)	757	60
Bear Stearns World HQ, 383 Madison Ave. (2001).	755	47
7 World Trade Center (2006).	752	52
AXA Center, 787 7th Ave. (1985)	752	51
One Penn Plaza, 250 W. 34th St. (1972)	750	57
Time Warner Center South Tower, 10 Columbus Cir. (2004)	750	55
Time Warner Center North Tower, 10 Columbus Cir. (2004)	750	55
1251 Ave. of the Americas (1971)	750	54
*Goldman Sachs HQ, 200 Murray St. (2009)	749	44
60 Wall St. (1989)	745	55
One Astor Plaza, 1515 Broadway (1970)	745	54
1 Liberty Plaza, 165 Broadway (1973)	743	54
20 Exchange Place (1931)	741	57
Three World Financial Center, 200 Vesey St. (1986)	739	51
Bertelsmann Building (incl. spire), 1540 Broadway (1990)	732	42
Times Square Tower, 1459 Broadway (2004)	726	47
Metropolitan Tower, 142 W. 57th St. (1985)	716	68
JPMorgan Chase World Headquarters, 270 Park Ave. (1960)	707	52
General Motors Bldg., 767 5th Ave. (1968)	705	50
Metropolitan Life Tower, 1 Madison Ave. (1909)	700	50
500 5th Ave. (1931)	697	60
Americas Tower, 1177 Ave. of the Amer. (1992)	692	50
Solow Bldg., 9 W. 57th St. (1974)	689	49
HSBC Bank Bldg., 140 Broadway (1967)	688	52
55 Water St. (1972)	687	53
277 Park Ave. (1963)	687	50
1585 Broadway (1989)	685	42
Random House/Park Imperial, 1739 Broadway (2003)	684	52
Four Seasons Hotel, 57 E. 57th St. (1993)	682	52
McGraw Hill, 1221 Ave. of the Americas (1972)	674	51
Barclay Tower, 10 Barclay St. (2007)	673	56
Lincoln Bldg., 60 E. 42nd St. (1930)	673	53
Paramount Plaza, 1633 Broadway (1970).	670	48
Trump Tower, 725 5th Ave. (1982)	664	58
Citicorp Tower, 1 Court Sq., Queens (1990)	658	50
Bank of New York Bldg., 1 Wall St. (1932)	654	50
599 Lexington Ave. (1986)	653	51
712 5th Ave. (1990).	650	52
Chanin Bldg., 122 E. 42nd St. (1929)	649	56
245 Park Ave. (1967)	648	47
Sony Bldg., 550 Madison Ave. (1983)	647	43
Two World Financial Center, 225 Liberty St. (1986)	645	44
570 Lexington Ave. (1930)	642	50
1 New York Plaza, 1 Water St. (1969).	640	50
1 Dag Hammarskjold Plaza, 885 2nd Ave. (1972)	637	49
345 Park Ave. (1968).	634	44
10 E. 40th St. (1929)	632	48
*123 Washington St. (2008)	631	53
Grace Plaza, 1114 Ave. of the Americas (1972)	630	50
Home Insurance Co., 59 Maiden Ln. (1966)	630	44
Verizon Bldg., 1095 Ave. of the Amer. (1970)	630	40

Building	Ht. (ft.)	Stories
101 Park Ave. (1982)	629	49
Central Park Place, 301 W. 57th St. (1988)	628	56
888 7th Ave. (1971)	628	45
Alliance Capital Bldg., 1345 Ave. of the Amer. (1969)	625	50
Waldorf=Astoria, 301 Park Ave. (1931)	625	47
Trump Palace, 200 E. 69th St. (1991)	623	55
Olympic Tower, 645 5th Ave. (1976)	620	51
425 5th Ave. (2003)	618	55
The Epic, 125 W. 31st St. (2007)	615	58
919 3rd Ave. (1970)	615	47
750 7th Ave. (incl. spire) (1989)	615	35
New York Life, 51 Madison Ave. (1928)	615	33
Tower 49, 12 E. 49th St. (1985)	614	44
Credit Lyonnais Bldg., 1301 Ave. of the Amer. (1964)	609	46
The Orion, 350 W. 42nd St. (2006)	604	58
590 Madison Ave. (1983)	603	41
*Times Square Plaza, 644 8th Ave. (2010)	601	40
Marsh & McLennan Headquarters, 1166 Ave. of the Amer. (1974)	600	44
Hearst Magazine Tower, 959 8th Ave. (2006).	597	46
3 Lincoln Center, 160 W. 66th St. (1993)	595	60
Celanese Bldg., 1211 Ave. of the Amer. (1973)	592	45
Rihga Royal Hotel, 151 W. 54th St. (1990)	590	54
Thurgood Marshall U.S. Court House, 505 Pearl St. (1927)	590	37
The Millennium Hilton Hotel, 55 Church St. (1992)	588	58
*Sky House, 11 E. 29th St. (2007)	588	55
Museum Tower Apts. 21 W. 53rd St. (1985)	588	52
Time & Life, 1271 Ave. of the Americas (1959).	587	48
Jacob K. Javits Federal Bldg., 26 Federal Plz. (1967)	587	41
W Times Square, 1567 Broadway (2000)	584	53
Trump International Hotel & Tower, 15 Columbus Cir. (1970)	583	44
Stevens Tower, 1185 Ave. of the Amer. (1971)	580	42
Municipal Bldg., 1 Centre St. (1914)	580	34
520 Madison Ave. (1981)	577	43
One World Financial Center, 200 Liberty St. (1985)	577	37
Merchandise Mart, 41 Madison Ave. (1973)	576	42
Park Ave. Plaza, 55 E. 52nd St. (1981)	575	44
Lehman Bldg., 745 7th Ave. (2001)	575	38
One Financial Square, 33 Old Slip (1987)	575	37
Marriot Marquis Times Square, 1531 Broadway (1985)	574	50
Westavco Bldg., 299 Park Ave. (1967)	574	42
Ernst & Young Tower, 5 Times Square, 590 7th Ave. (2002)	574	40
Socony Mobil, 150 E. 42nd St. (1956).	572	42
AXA Finance Center, 1290 Ave. of the Amer. (1963)	571	43
Wang Bldg., 780 3rd Ave. (1983)	570	42
600 3rd Ave. (1971).	570	42
450 Lexington Ave. (1991)	568	38
Paramount Tower, 240 E. 39th St. (1998).	567	51
*785 8th Ave. (2008)	566	42
Helmsley Bldg., 230 Park Ave. (1928)	566	35
New York Palace Hotel, 455 Madison Ave. (1980)	563	51
Continental Bank Bldg., 30 Broad St. (1932)	562	48
Park Ave. Tower, 65 E. 55th St. (1986).	561	36
Nelson Tower, 450 7th Ave. (1931).	560	46
Sherry-Netherland, 781 5th Ave. (1927)	560	40
Swiss Bank Tower, 10 E. 50th St. (1990)	560	36
100 UN Plaza, 327 E. 48th St. (1986).	557	52
Continental Can Co., 633 3rd Ave. (1962)	557	39
3 Park Ave. (1975)	556	42
Sperry & Hutchinson, 330 Madison Ave. (1964)	555	41
Continental Corp., 180 Maiden Ln. (1983)	555	41
Reuters Bldg., 3 Times Sq. (2001)[3]	555	30
Madison Belvedere, 14 E. 29th St. (1999)	554	48
Inmont Bldg., 1133 Ave. of the Americas (1970).	552	45
Equitable Trust Co. Bldg., 15 Broad St. (1927)	551	42
Biltmore Tower, 267 W. 47th St. (2003)	550	51
Burroughs Bldg., 605 3rd Ave. (1963).	550	44
2 Grand Central Tower, 140 E. 45th St. (1982).	550	43
The Tower at 15 Central Park West (2007).	550	35
AT&T Long Lines Bldg., 33 Thomas St. (1974).	550	29
Bankers Trust, 33 E. 48th St. (1971).	547	41
The Corinthian, 330 E. 38th St. (1988)	546	55
Transportation Bldg., 225 Broadway (1928)	546	44
MillenniumTower, 101 W. 67th St. (1995)	545	54
Equitable, 120 Broadway (1915).	545	36
Galleria, 117 E. 57th St. (1975).	544	56
2 Gold St. (2005).	543	51
220 Riverside Blvd. at Trump Place (2003).	542	49
17 State St. (1988)	542	41
Grand Central Plaza, 622 3rd Ave. (1973)	542	38
Paine Webber Bldg., 1285 Ave. of the Amer. (1959)	540	42
New York Telephone, 375 Pearl St. (1976).	540	42
Ritz Tower, 109 E. 57th St. (1925)	540	41
Bankers Trust, 16 Wall St. (1912)	540	39
Tribeca Tower, 105 Duane St. (1990)	537	53
Lefcourt Colonial Bldg., 295 Madison Ave. (1929)	537	45
300 Madison Ave. (2003)	535	35
1700 Broadway (1969)	533	41
Westin Hotel New York, 270 W. 43rd St. (2002)	532	45
515 Park Ave. (1999)	532	43
The Metropolis, 150 E. 44th St. (2001)	528	50
North American Plywood, 800 3rd Ave. (1972).	526	41
Hotel Pierre, 2 E. 61st. St. (1928)	525	44
767 3rd Ave. (1980).	525	39
Citibank, 399 Park Ave. (1961)	524	41

Building	Ht. (ft.)	Stories
*William Beaver House, 15 William St. (2008)	523	44
Random House, 825 3rd Ave. (1969)	522	40
Atelier, 625 W. 42nd St. (2007)	521	46
Du Mont Bldg., 515 Madison Ave. (1931)	520	42
26 Broadway (1922)	520	31
Newsweek Bldg., 444 Madison Ave. (1931)	518	42
Downtown Athletic Club, 19 West St. (1930)	518	39
Architects and Designers Bldg., 964 Third Ave. (1969)	518	39
South Park Tower, 124 W. 60th St. (1986)	516	51
High Point Condominium, 250 E. 40th St. (1988)	516	49
House of Seagram, 375 Park Ave. (1958)	516	38
Sterling Drug Bldg., 90 Park Ave. (1964)	515	41
Navarre Bldg., 512 7th Ave. (1930)[4]	513	44
Bank of New York, 48 Wall St. (1927)	513	31
The Belaire, 524 E. 72nd St. (1988)	512	50
Republic National Bank, 1 Hansen Pl., Brooklyn (1929)	512	42
International, Rockefeller Center, 630 5th Ave. (1935)	512	41
1407 Broadway Realty Corp. (1950)	512	41
ITT-American, 437 Madison Ave. (1967)	512	40
Continental Bldg., 1450 Broadway (1931)	511	42
1155 Ave. of the Americas (1984)	511	40
10 Liberty St. (2004)	510	45
810 7th Ave. (1970)	506	41
The Sheffield Apts., 325 W. 56th St. (1978)	505	50
United Nations Secretariat Bldg., 405 E. 42nd St. (1950)	505	39
1 UN Plaza (1975)	505	39
2 UN Plaza (1981)	505	39
2 New York Plaza, 125 Broad St. (1970)	504	40
Johns-Manville Bldg., 22 E. 40th St. (1931)	503	43
60 Broad St. (1962)	503	38
Lefcourt National Bldg., 521 5th Ave. (1928)	503	37
1325 Ave. of the Americas (1989)	502	35
Sheraton Centre, 811 7th Ave. (1962)	501	51
World Apparel Center, 1411 Broadway (1969)	501	39
Bristol Plaza, 200 E. 65th St. (1987)	500	50
Pennmark Towers, 315 W. 33rd St. (2001)	500	35
Four World Financial Center, 250 Vesey St. (1986)	500	34

(1) 1,118 ft. with antenna. (2) 941 ft. with antenna. (3) 659 ft. with antenna. (4) Site of World Almanac offices.

Oklahoma City, OK

Building	Ht. (ft.)	Stories
Chase Tower, 100 N. Broadway Ave. (1971)	500	36
First National Center (incl. spire), 120 N. Robinson St. (1931)	493	33
City Place, 204 N. Robinson St. (1931)	440	32
Oklahoma Tower, 210 Park Ave. (1982)	434	31

Orlando, FL

Building	Ht. (ft.)	Stories
SunTrust Center Tower, 200 S. Orange Ave. (1988)	441	31
Vue at Lake Eola, 136 E. Robinson St. (2006)	426	35
Orange County Courthouse, 425 N. Orange Ave. (1997)	416	24
Bank of America Center, 390 N. Orange Ave. (1988)	409	28

Philadelphia, PA

Building	Ht. (ft.)	Stories
*Comcast Center, 1701 JFK Blvd. (2008)	975	57
One Liberty Place (incl. spire), 1650 Market St. (1987)	945	61
Two Liberty Place (incl. spire), 1601 Chestnut St. (1989)	848	58
Mellon Bank Center, 1735 Market St. (1990)	792	54
Verizon Tower, 1717 Arch St. (1991)	725	53
G. Fred DiBona Jr. Bldg., 1901 Market St. (1990)	625	45
Commerce Square #1, 2005 Market St. (1990)	572	40
Commerce Square #2, 2001 Market St. (1992)	572	40
City Hall (incl. statue) (1901)	548	7
*Residences at Ritz-Carlton, 1416 S. Penn Sq. (2008)	518	48
1818 Market St. (1974)	500	40
The St. James, 700 Walnut St. (2004)	498	45
Loews Philadelphia Hotel, 12 S. 12th St. (1932)	492	39
PNC Bank Bldg., 1600 Market St. (1983)	491	40
Centre Square II, 1542 Market St. (1973)	490	38
5 Penn Center, 1601 Market St. (1970)	488	36
1700 Market St. (1969)	482	32
*The Murano, 2101 Market St. (2008)	475	42
1 South Broad St. (1930)	472	28
Cira Centre, 2929 Arch St. (2005)	437	28
Two Logan Square, 100 N. 18th St. (1988)	435	34
1835 Market St. (1985)	430	29
Aramark Tower, 1101 Market St. (1984)	417	31
Centre Square I, 1500 Market St. (1973)	416	32
Wachovia Bldg., 123 S. Broad St. (1927)	405	30
Ritz-Carlton Hotel, 28 S. Broad St. (1930)	404	30
One Logan Square, 130 N. 18th St. (1982)	400	32

Pittsburgh, PA

Building	Ht. (ft.)	Stories
U.S. Steel Tower, 600 Grant St. (1970)	841	64
One Mellon Bank Center, 500 Grant St. (1983)	725	54
One PPG Place (1984)	635	40
Fifth Ave. Place, 120 5th Ave. (1987)	616	32
One Oxford Centre, 301 Grant St. (1982)	615	46
Gulf Tower, 707 Grant St. (1932)	582	44
University of Pittsburgh Cathedral of Learning, 4200 5th Ave. (1936)	535	42
3 Mellon Bank Center, 525 William Penn Way (1951)	520	41
Freemarkets Center, 210 6th Ave. (1968)	511	39
Grant Bldg., 330 Grant St. (1928)	485	40
Koppers Bldg., 436 7th Ave. (1929)	475	34
Two PNC Plaza, 620 Liberty Ave. (1975)	445	34
Dominion Tower, 625 Liberty Ave. (1987)	430	32
One PNC Plaza, 249 5th Ave. (1972)	424	30
Regional Enterprise Tower, 425 6th Ave. (1953)	410	30

Portland, OR

Building	Ht. (ft.)	Stories
Wells Fargo Center, 1300 SW 5th Ave. (1973)	546	40
U.S. Bancorp Tower, 111 SW 5th Ave. (1983)	536	42
Koin Plaza, 222 SW Columbia St. (1984)	509	31
Pacwest Center, 1211 SW 5th Ave. (1984)	418	30

Raleigh, NC

Building	Ht. (ft.)	Stories
*RBC Centura Headquarters (incl. spire), 300 Fayetteville St. (2008)	538	32
*Soleil Center (2009)	480	47
2 Hanover Square, 434 Fayetteville St. Mall (1991)	431	29
Wachovia Capitol Center, 150 Fayetteville St. Mall (1991)	400	30

St. Louis, MO

Building	Ht. (ft.)	Stories
Gateway Arch, St. Louis Riverfront (1965)	630	NA
Metropolitan Square Tower, 211 N. Broadway (1988)	593	42
AT&T Center, 900 Pine St. (1984)	588	44
Thomas F. Eagleton Federal Courthouse, 111 S. 10th St. (2000)	557	29
One U.S. Bank Plaza, 505 N. 7th St. (1976)	484	35
Laclede Gas Bldg., 720 Olive St. (1969)	400	31

St. Paul, MN

Building	Ht. (ft.)	Stories
Wells Fargo Place, 30 E. 7th St. (1987)	471	36
Jackson Tower, 168 E. 6th St. (1986)	443	46
First National Bank, 332 Minnesota St. (1931)	417	32

San Antonio, TX

Building	Ht. (ft.)	Stories
Tower of the Americas, 600 Hemisphere Way (1968)	622	NA
Marriott Rivercenter (incl. spires), 101 Bowie St. (1988)	546	38
Weston Centre, 112 Pecan St. (1988)	444	32
*Grand Hyatt San Antonio, 600 E. Market St. (2008)	424	34
Tower Life Bldg., 310 S. St. Mary's St. (1929)[1]	404	30

(1) 541 ft. with antenna.

San Diego, CA

Building	Ht. (ft.)	Stories
One American Plaza, 600 W. Broadway (1991)	500	34
Symphony Tower, 759 B St. (1989)	499	34
Manchester Grand Hyatt, 1 Market Pl. (1992)	497	40
Electra, 701 W. Broadway (2007)	475	43
Pinnacle Museum Tower, 500 Front St. (2005)	455	35
Emerald Plaza, 400 W. Broadway (1990)	450	30
Manchester Grand Hyatt Tower 2, 1 Market Pl. (2003)	446	32
One Harbor Drive, 100 Harbor Dr. (1992)	424	41
Two Harbor Drive, 100 Harbor Dr. (1992)	424	41
*Vantage Point (2008)	420	41
The Grande South at Sante Fe Place, 1199 Pacific Hwy. (2004)	420	39
The Grande North at Sante Fe Place, 1205 Pacific Hwy. (2005)	420	39
Advanced Equities Plaza, 655 Broadway (2005)	412	23

San Francisco, CA

Building	Ht. (ft.)	Stories
Transamerica Pyramid, 600 Montgomery St. (1972)	853	48
555 California St. (1969)	779	52
345 California Center (incl. spires) (1986)	695	48
*Millennium Tower, 301 Mission St. (2009)	645	58
*One Ricon Hill South Tower, 425 1st St. (2008)	641	54
101 California St. (1986)	600	48
50 Fremont Ctr. (1983)	600	43
Chevron Tower, 575 Market St. (1975)	573	40
Four Embarcadero Center, 55 Clay St. (1984)	570	45
One Embarcadero Center, 355 Clay St. (1970)	569	45
44 Montgomery St. (1967)	565	43
Spear Tower, 1 Market St. (1976)	565	42
Citicorp Center, 1 Sansome St. (1984)	550	39
Shaklee Terrace Bldg., 444 Market St. (1982)	537	38
McKeeson Plaza, 1 Post St. (1969)	529	38
525 Market St. (1972)	529	38
425 Market St. (1973)	524	38
Telsis Tower, 1 Montgomery St. (1982)	500	38
333 Bush St. (1986)	495	43
Hilton San Francisco & Towers, 201 Mason St. (1971)	493	46
Pacific Gas & Electric, 77 Beale St. (1971)	492	34
50 California St. (1972)	487	37
St. Regis San Francisco, 685 Mission St. (2005)	484	42
*555 Mission St. (2009)	482	33
100 Pine Ctr. (1972)	476	34
45 Fremont Ctr. (1972)	475	34
333 Market Bldg., 333 Market St. (1979)	474	33
650 California St. (1965)	465	33
*The Infinity I, 300 Spear St. (2007)	450	40

Seattle, WA

Building	Ht. (ft.)	Stories
Columbia Center, 701 5th Ave. (1985)[1]	933	76
Washington Mutual Tower, 1201 3rd Ave. (1988)	772	55
Two Union Square, 601 Union St. (1989)	740	56
Seattle Municipal Tower, 700 5th Ave. (1990)	722	57
1001 Fourth Avenue Plaza (1969)	609	50
Space Needle, 203 6th Ave. (1962)	605	NA
WaMu Center, 1301 2nd Ave. (2006)	598	42
U.S. Bank Centre, 1420 5th Ave. (1989)	580	44
Wells Fargo Center, 999 3rd Ave. (1983)	574	47
Bank of America Fifth Avenue Plaza, 800 5th Ave. (1981)	543	42
Union Bank of California Center, 900 4th Ave. (1973)	536	41
Rainier Tower, 1301 5th Ave. (1977)	514	31
IDX Tower at Fourth & Madison, 915 4th Ave. (2003)	512	40
1000 2nd Ave. (1986)	493	40
Henry M. Jackson Bldg., 915 2nd Ave. (1974)	487	37

Building	Ht. (ft.)	Stories
Qwest Plaza, 1600 7th Ave. (1976)	466	33
Smith Tower, 506 2nd Ave. (1914)	462	36
*Olive 8, 737 Olive Way (2008)	460	39
One Union Square, 600 University Ave. (1981)	456	36
1111 3rd Ave. (1980)	454	34
Westin Hotel North Tower, 1900 5th Ave. (1982)	448	44
*Fifteen Twenty-One Second Avenue, 1521 2nd Ave. (2008)	440	38
Westin Bldg., 2001 6th Ave. (1981)	409	34

(1) 963 ft. with antenna

Sunny Isles Beach, FL

Building	Ht. (ft.)	Stories
Trump Palace, 18101 Collins Ave. (2005)	551	43
*Trump Royale, 18201 Collins Ave. (2007)	551	43
Aqualina Ocean Residences, 17875 Collins Ave. (2004)	550	51
*Jade Ocean, 17121 Collins Ave. (2008)	549	51
The Pinnacle, 17555 Collins Ave. (1999)	476	40
La Perla Ocean Residences, 16701 Collins Ave. (2006)	447	42
Ocean Two Condominiums I, 19111 Collins Ave. (2001)	426	40
Ocean Two Condominiums II, 19111 Collins Ave. (2001)	426	40
Ocean Three Condominiums, 18911 Collins Ave. (2003)	405	37

Tampa, FL

Building	Ht. (ft.)	Stories
AmSouth Bldg., 100 N. Tampa St. (1992)	579	42
Bank of America Plaza, 101 E. Kennedy Blvd. (1986)	577	42
One Tampa City Center, 201 N. Franklin St. (1981)	537	39
Suntrust Financial Center, 401 E. Jackson St. (1992)	525	36
*Element, 808 N. Franklin St. (2008)	460	34
Park Tower, 400 N. Tampa St. (1973)	458	36
Rivergate Tower, 400 N. Ashley Dr. (1988)	454	33

Toronto, Ontario

Building	Ht. (ft.)	Stories
CN Tower, 310 Front St. West (1976)	1,815	NA
First Bank Tower, 100 King St. West (1975)[1]	978	72
Scotia Plaza, 40 King St. West (1989)	902	68
BCE Place, Canada Trust Tower (incl. spire), 161 Bay St. (1990)	856	53
Commerce Court West, 199 Bay St. (1973)[2]	784	57
TD Centre—Toronto Dominion Bank Tower, 66 Wellington St. West (1967)	730	56
*Bay-Adelaide Center West Tower, 335 Bay St. (2009)	715	50
*Shangri-La Toronto, 180 University Ave. (2011)	702	65
*Ritz-Carlton Hotel and Residences, 185 Wellington St. West (2009)	699	53
BCE Place, Bay-Wellington Tower, 181 Bay St. (1991)	679	49
*Maple Leaf Square North Tower, 15 York St. (2009)	610	54
TD Centre—Royal Trust Tower, 77 King St. West (1969)	600	46
*RBC Centre, 155 Wellington St. West (2009)	600	40
1 King West, 1 King St. West (2005)	578	51
*Maple Leaf Square South Tower, 15 York St. (2009)	571	50
Royal Bank Plaza—South Tower, 200 Bay St. (1976)	567	41
44 Charles St. West (1974)	545	51
*Quantum 2, 2195 Yonge St. (2008)	525	51
*Uptown Residences, 35 Balmuto St. (2008)	518	48

Building	Ht. (ft.)	Stories
*Festival Tower, 330 King St. West (2010)	514	46
The Residences of College Park North, 763 Bay St. (2006)	505	51
TD Centre—79 Wellington St. West (1985)	504	39
Harbourview Estates Phase 2, 35 Mariner Ter. (2005)	503	49
The 250, 250 Yonge St. (1991)	494	35
Two Bloor West, 2 Bloor St. West (1974)	488	34
*X Condominium, 110 Charles St. East (2009)	487	45
*West One, 11 Brunel Ct. (2007)	486	49
Simcoe Place, 200 Front St. West (1995)	486	33
Exchange Tower, 130 King St. West (1983)	480	30
The Met, 21 Carlton St. (2007)	479	43
CIBC—Commerce Court North, 25 King St. West (1931)	477	34
*Montage, 23 Spadina Ave. (2009)	476	47
Simpson Tower, 401 Bay St. (1968)	473	33
Cadillac-Fairview Tower, 20 Queen St. West (1982)	465	36
*The Residences of College Park South, 761 Bay St. (2007)	463	45
*Success Tower, 33 Bay St. (2008)	459	45
*Murano South Tower, 825 Bay St. (2008)	459	41
Pantages Tower, 210 Victoria St. (2002)	458	45
SPIRE, 33 Lombard St. (2007)	456	45
One Palace Pier Court, Etobicoke (1991)	455	46
Three Palace Pier Court, Etobicoke (1978)	453	46
*Casa Condominium, 33 Charles St. East (2009)	453	45
Continental Bank of Canada, 130 Adelaide St. West (1980)	450	35

(1) 1,116 ft. with antenna. (2) 942 ft. with antenna.

Tulsa, OK

Building	Ht. (ft.)	Stories
One Williams Center, 1 W. 2nd St. (1975)	667	52
Cityplex Central Tower, 2448 E 81st St. (1979)	648	60
First Place Tower, 15 E 5th St. (1973)	516	40
Mid-Continent Tower, 401 S. Boston St. (1984)	513	36
Bank of America Center, 15 W. 6th St. (1967)	412	32
320 S. Boston St. (1928)	400	22

Vancouver, British Columbia

Building	Ht. (ft.)	Stories
*Living Shangri-La, 1120 W. Georgia St. (2008)	646	61
*1133 W. Georgia St. (2011)	600	58
One Wall Centre, 1000 Burrard St. (2001)	491	45
Shaw Tower, 298 Thurlow St. (2004)	489	40
Harbour Centre, 555 W. Hastings St. (1977)[1]	481	30
200 Granville Sq. (1973)	466	32
*The Melville, 1189 Melville St. (2007)	464	43
Royal Centre, 1055 W. Georgia St. (1973)	461	37
Park Place, 666 Burrard St. (1984)	459	35
Bentall V, 550 Burrard St. (2007)	459	34
*Fairmont Pacific Rim Vancouver, 1011 W. Cordova St. (2009)	458	46
Bentall IV, 1055 Dunsmir St. (1981)	454	34
Scotia Tower, 650 W. Georgia St. (1977)	452	36
*Patina, 955 Burrard St. (2009)	418	42
T-D Bank Tower, 700 W. Georgia St. (1970)	417	30
*Capitol Residences, 833 Seymour St. (2008)	414	42
Bentall III, 595 Burrard St. (1974)	400	31

(1) 581 ft. with antenna.

Other Tall Buildings in North American Cities

Lists include freestanding towers and other structures that do not have stories and are not technically considered buildings. Structures still under construction as of mid-2007 are denoted by an asterisk (*). Year in parentheses is date of completion or projected completion. Height is generally measured from sidewalk to roof, including penthouse and tower if enclosed as integral part of structure; stories generally counted from street level. NA = Not available or not applicable.

Building		Ht. (ft.)	Stories
RSA Battle House Tower (incl. spire) (2007)	Mobile, AL	745	35
The Tower at First National Center, (2002)	Omaha, NE	634	45
801 Grand (1991)	Des Moines, IA	630	44
*Torre Aura Altitude (2007)	Guadalajara, Mexico	597	44
Dataflux Tower (2000)	Monterrey, Mexico	597	43
Erastus Corning II Tower (1973)	Albany, NY	589	44
Concourse Corporate Center V (1988)	Sandy Springs, GA	570	34
Concourse Corporate Center VI (1991)	Sandy Springs, GA	553	34
*Absolute World Tower 1 (2010)	Mississauga, Ontario	548	56
Metropolitan Tower (1986)	Little Rock, AK	546	40
One HSBC Ctr. (1970)	Buffalo NY	529	40
Vehicle Assembly Bldg. (1965)	Cape Canaveral, FL	525	40
Skylon (1965)	Niagara Falls, ON	520	NA
*Town Center Westin Hotel and Residences (incl. spire) (2007)	Virginia Beach, VA	508	37
The Beach Club Tower 2 (2006)	Hallandale Beach, FL	505	50
*Absolute World Tower 2 (2010)	Mississauga, Ontario	495	50
*Torre Caney (2007)	Santo Domingo, Domican Republic	492	38
Mohegan Sun Hotel (2002)	Uncasville, CT	487	34
Chase Tower (1972)	Phoenix, AZ	486	40
*Ritz-Carlton Westchester (2008)	White Plains, NY	484	44
*The Residences at Ritz-Carlton Westchester (2008)	White Plains, NY	484	44
Woodmen Tower (1969)	Omaha, NE	478	30
*Ocean Tower (2007)	South Padre Island, TX	470	32
National Newark Bldg. (1931)	Newark, NJ	465	36
*Granby Tower (incl. spire) (2007)	Norfolk, VA	461	31
State Capitol (1932)	Baton Rouge, LA	460	34
Wachovia Center (1995)	Winston-Salem, NC	460	34
*Boise Place (2008)	Boise, ID	460	34
The Tower (1988)	Burbank, CA	460	32
Ruan Center (1974)	Des Moines, IA	457	36
Wachovia Center (1986)	Birmingham, AL	454	34
Regions Center (1975)	Little Rock, AK	454	30
Las Olas River House 1 (2004)	Fort Lauderdale, FL	452	42
*Bellevue Towers Two (2008)	Bellevue, WA	450	43
Lincoln Tower One (2005)	Bellevue, WA	450	42
James Monroe Bldg. (1981)	Richmond, VA	449	29
1180 Raymond Blvd. (1930)	Newark, NJ	448	34
The Westin Diplomat (2002)	Hollywood, FL	444	39
Ravinia #3 (1991)	Dunwoody, GA	444	33
*Trump Hollywood (2008)	Hollywood, FL	443	40
Xerox Tower (1967)	Rochester, NY	443	30
One Summit Square (1981)	Fort Wayne, IN	442	27
The Beach Club Tower 1 (2005)	Hallandale Beach, FL	440	43
*The Beach Club Tower 3 (2007)	Hallandale Beach, FL	440	43
Anadarko Tower (2002)	The Woodlands, TX	439	32
Harbert Plaza (1989)	Birmingham, AL	437	32
The Palisades (2001)	Fort Lee, NJ	434	41
*Bellevue Tower One (2008)	Bellevue, WA	430	42
100 North Main Bldg. (1965)	Memphis, TN	430	38
Bank of America Bldg. (1927)	Providence, RI	428	26
Torre Commercial America (1994)	Monterrey, Mexico	427	35
AmSouth Bank Bldg.(1969)	Mobile, AL	424	33
Wells Fargo Center (1991)	Sacramento, CA	423	30
Wells Fargo Center (1998)	Salt Lake City, UT	422	26
*Trump Plaza (2007)	New Rochelle, NY	420	39
CanWest Global Place (1990)	Winnipeg, Manitoba	420	33
L.D.S. Church Office Bldg. (1972)	Salt Lake City, UT	420	28

Notable Bridges in North America

Source: Office of Bridge Technology, Federal Highway Administration, U.S. Dept. of Transportation; World Almanac research
Asterisk (*) designates railroad bridge. Year is date of completion or projected completion. Span of bridge is the distance between its supports.

Suspension

Year	Bridge	Location	Main span (ft.)
1964	Verrazano-Narrows	New York, NY	4,260
1937	Golden Gate	San Fran. Bay, CA	4,200
1957	Mackinac	Straits of Mackinac, MI	3,800
1931	George Washington	Hudson R., NY–NJ	3,500
1950	Tacoma Narrows	Tacoma, WA	2,800
2007	Tacoma Narrows (new)	Tacoma, WA	2,800
2003	Carquinez (new) (Al Zampa Mem.)	Carquinez Strait, CA	2,388
1936	San Fran.-Oakland Bay (West Span)[1]	San Fran. Bay, CA	2,310
1939	Bronx-Whitestone	East R., NY	2,300
1970	Pierre Laporte	Quebec City, Quebec	2,190
1951	Del. Memorial[2]	Pennsville, NJ–New Castle, DE	2,150
1957	Walt Whitman	Philadelphia, PA	2,000
1929	Ambassador	Detroit, MI–Canada	1,850
1961	Throgs Neck	Long Isl. Sound, NY	1,801
1926	Benjamin Franklin	Philadelphia, PA	1,750
1924	Bear Mtn.	Hudson R., NY	1,632
1903	Williamsburg	East R., NY	1,600
1952	William Preston Lane Jr. Mem.[3]	Sandy Point, MD	1,600
1969	Claiborne Pell/Newport	Narragansett Bay, RI	1,600
1883	Brooklyn	East R., NY	1,596
1938	Lions' Gate	Vancouver, BC	1,550
1963	Vincent Thomas	L.A. Harbor, CA	1,500
1930	Mid-Hudson	Poughkeepsie, NY	1,495
1909	Manhattan	East R., NY	1,470
1955	Angus L. Macdonald	Halifax, Nova Scotia	1,447
1970	A. Murray MacKay	Halifax, Nova Scotia	1,400
1936	Triborough (Harlem R. Lift/Bronx Crossing/East R. Suspension)	East R., NY	1,380
2013	San Fran.-Oakland Bay (Self-Anchored Suspension section, East Span)	San Fran. Bay, CA	1,263
1931	St. Johns	Portland, OR	1,207
1929	Mount Hope	Portsmouth–Bristol, RI	1,200
1960	Ogdensburg-Prescott	Ogdensburg, NY–Canada	1,150
1965	Bidwell Bar	Oroville, CA	1,108
1964	Middle Fork Feather	Butte Co., CA	1,105
1939	Deer Isle	Deer Isle, ME	1,080
1931	Simon Kenton Mem.	Ohio R., Maysville, KY	1,060
1935	Ile d'Orleans	St. Lawrence R., QC	1,059
1867	John A. Roebling/Cincinnati-Covington	Ohio R., KY–Cincinnati, OH	1,057
1971	Dent	Orofino, ID	1,050
1900	Ojuela	Mapimi, Mexico	1,030
1849	Wheeling	Ohio R., WV	1,010
1910	*P&LE RR	Ohio R., PA	750
1930	Ashland-Coal Grove	Ohio R., OH	739
1922	Ironton-Russell[5]	Ohio R., OH–KY	725
1932	Bi-State Vietnam Gold Star	Henderson, KY	720
1979	I-275, Ohio R.	Fort Thomas, KY	720
1962	Champlain	Montreal, Quebec	707
1926	Columbia R.	Cascade Locks, OR	706
1964	John F. Kennedy (I-65)	Ohio R., Louisville, KY	700
1928	Ohio R., B&O RR, HV RR	Pomeroy-Mason, OH	657
1941	*Pit River	Redding, CA	630
1941	Columbia R.	Kettle Falls, WA	600
1954	Columbia R.	Umatilla, OR	600
1965	Bi-State Vietnam Gold Star	Henderson, KY	600
1954	Columbia R.	The Dalles, OR	576
1968	W. 17th St.	Huntington, WV	562

Cantilever

Year	Bridge	Location	Main span (ft.)
1917	Québec	St. Lawrence R., QC	1,801
1974	Commodore Barry	Chester, PA–Bridgeport, NJ	1,644
1958	Greater New Orleans No. 2	Mississippi R., LA	1,594
1958	Greater New Orleans No. 1	Mississippi R., LA	1,575
1995	Gramercy	Mississippi R., Gramercy, LA	1,460
1936	East Bay[4]	San Fran. Bay, CA	1,400
1968	Baton Rouge	Mississippi R., LA	1,235
1955	Tappan Zee	Hudson R., NY	1,212
1930	Lewis and Clark	Longview, WA–OR	1,200
1909	Queensboro	East R., NY	1,182
1958	Carquinez Strait (east)	San Fran. Bay, CA	1,100
1930	Jacques Cartier	Montreal, Quebec	1,097
1921	Isaiah D. Hart	Jacksonville, FL	1,088
1956	Richmond-San Rafael (twin)	San Fran. Bay, CA	1,070
1963	Newburgh-Beacon (north)	Hudson R., NY	1,000
1980	Newburgh-Beacon (south)	Hudson R., NY	1,000
1945	Martin Luther King Jr.	St. Louis, MO	963
1975	Caruthersville	Mississippi R., MO–TN	920
1965	Silver Memorial	Pt. Pleasant, WV–OH	900
1977	Saint Marys	Saint Marys, WV–OH	900
1987	William S. Ritchie	Ohio R., Ravenswood, WV	900
1987	Carl Perkins	Ohio R., OH–KY	900
1941/1988	Natchez-Vidalia, Mississippi R. (twin)	Natchez, MS	875
1938	Blue Water	Pt. Huron, MI–ON	871
1972	I-20, Mississippi R.	Vicksburg, MS	870
1972	N. Fork American R.	Auburn, CA	862
1940	*Baton Rouge	Mississippi R., LA	848
1899	*Cornwall	St. Lawrence R., LA	843
1940	U.S. 82, Mississippi R.	Greenville, MS	840
1961	U.S. 49, Mississippi R.	Helena, AR	840
1963	Brent Spence	KY–Cincinatti, OH	830
1973	*Vicksburg (U.S. 80)	Mississippi R., Vicksburg, MS	825
1963	Mississippi R.	Donaldsonville, LA	825
1929	George Rogers Clark Mem. (U.S. 31)	Ohio R., KY–IN	820
1961	Campbellton-Cross Pt.	New Brunswick, Canada	815
1932	Washington Mem.	Seattle, WA	800
1935	Rip Van Winkle	Catskill, NY	800
1938	Cairo Ohio R.	IL–KY	800
1966	McCullough	Coos Bay, OR	793
1949	Memphis	Mississippi R., TN	790
1935	Huey P. Long[5]	New Orleans, LA	790
1949	Memphis-Arkansas (I-55)	Mississippi R., TN–AR	790

Simple Truss

Year	Bridge	Location	Main span (ft.)
1977	Chester	Chester, WV–OH	745
1929	Irvin S. Cobb (U.S. 45)	Ohio R., IL–KY	716
1923	*Tanana R.	Nenana, AK	700
1967	Williamson-Marietta (I-77)	Ohio R., WV–OH	650
1917	*MacArthur	St. Louis, IL–MO	647
1992	Discovery	Missouri R., MO	625
1958	*Castleton	Hudson R., NY	598
1938	Easton-Phillipsburg	Delaware R., PA	550
1930	Swindell	Pittsburgh, PA	545
1951	Penn. Tpk. Allegheny	Pittsburgh, PA	534
1951	Rankin	Pittsburgh, PA	525
1906	Donora-Webster	Donora-Webster, PA	515
1908	Hulton	Allegheny R., Harmar, PA	505
1967	Alaska Native Veterans' Honor	Nenana R., AK	500

Steel Truss

Year	Bridge	Location	Main span (ft.)
1990	Glade Creek	Raleigh Co., WV	785
1973	U.S. 190, Atchafalaya R.	Krotz Springs, LA	780
1971	Piscataqua R.	Portsmouth, NH–ME	756
1972	Atchafalaya R.	Simmesport, LA	720
1957	Robert O. Norris	Middlesex Co., VA	648
1978	Atchafalaya R.	Morgan City, LA	607
1960	Summit	Summit, DE	600
1968	Reedy Point	Delaware City, DE	600
1955	Interstate (I-5)	Columbia R., OR–WA	531
1910	McKinley[6]	Mississippi R., MO–IL	517
1972	Mississippi R.	Muscatine, IA	512
1896	Newport	Ohio R., KY	511
1931	Lucy Jefferson Lewis	Cumberland R., KY	500
1958	Lake Oahe	Gettysburg, SD	500
1958	Lake Oahe	Mobridge, SD	500
1970	Lake Koocanusa	Lincoln Co., MT	500

Continuous Truss

Year	Bridge	Location	Main span (ft.)
1966	Astoria	Columbia R., OR–WA	1,232
1976	Francis Scott Key	Baltimore, MD	1,200
1981	Ravenswood	Ohio R., Ravenswood, WV	902
1995	Taylor-Southgate	Ohio R., KY–OH	850
1943	Julien Dubuque	Mississippi R., IA–IL	845
1966	Charles Braga	Fall River, MA	840
1956	Earle C. Clements (twin)	Ohio R., IL–KY	825
1953	John E. Mathews	Jacksonville, FL	810
1940	Gov. Nice Memorial	Potomac R., MD–VA	800
1950	Maurice J. Tobin	Boston, MA	800
1957	Kingston-Rhinecliff	Hudson R., NY	800
1992	Cooper River	Charleston, SC	800
1986	Rochester-Monaca	Rochester-Monaca, PA	780
1917	*Sciotoville (twin)	Sciotoville, OH–KY	775
1940	U.S. 231	Ohio R., IN	750
1974	Carroll C. Cropper (I-275)	Ohio R., IN–KY	750
1981	Sewickley	Sewickley, PA	750
1984	13th St.	Ohio R., KY–OH	740
1959	Monaca-E. Rochester	Monaca-E. Rochester, PA	730
1976	Betsy Ross	Philadelphia, PA	729
1929	Milton-Madison	Ohio R., IN–KY	727
1962	Matthew E. Welsh	Ohio R., Mauckport, IN–KY	725
1962	U.S. 41	Ohio R., IN–KY	720
1994	Robert C. Byrd	Huntington, WV	720
1970	Vanport	Vanport, PA	715
1962	Champlain	Montreal, Quebec	707
1962	John F. Kennedy (I-65)	Ohio R., Louisville, KY–IN	700
1973	Girard Point	Philadelphia, PA	700
1956	DE R.-PA Turnpike	Delaware R., NJ–PA	682
1938	Rainbow	Port Arthur-Orange, TX	680
1949	George C. Platt Mem.	Philadelphia, PA	680
1946	Chester	Mississippi R., IL–MO	670
1994	Williamstown-Marietta	Ohio R., WV–OH	650
1955	Jefferson City	Missouri R., MO	640
2000	Mark Twain Mem.	Mississippi R., Hannibal, MO–IL	640
1930	Quincy Memorial	Mississippi R., IL	628
1959	Harbor	Corpus Christi, TX	620
1961	Shippingport	Shippingport, PA	620
1935	Bourne and Sagamore (twin)	Cape Cod Canal, MA	616
1965	I-80, Clarion R.	Clarion, PA	612
1975	Donora-Monessen	Donora-Monessen, PA	608
1961	John A. Blatnik	Superior, WI–Duluth, MN	600
1965	Rio Grande Gorge	Taos, NM	600
1991	Hoffstadt Creek	Mt. St. Helens, WA	600
1991	Jefferson City	Missouri R., MO	596

Year	Bridge	Location	Main span (ft.)
1962	W. Branch Feather R.	Oroville, CA	576
1966	Glenwood	Pittsburgh, PA.	557
1932	Pulaski Skyway (twin)	Newark, NJ.	550
1943	Gold Star Memorial	New London, CT.	540
1968	Emlenton	Emlenton, PA	540
1962	Benicia-Martinez	Benicia-Martinez, CA	528
1914	Brownsville	Brownsville, PA.	518
1971	Grandad	Elk River, ID	504

Continuous Box and Plate Girder

Year	Bridge	Location	Main span (ft.)
1967	San Mateo-Hayward #2	San Fran. Bay, CA	750
1976	Intracoastal Canal	Forked Isl., LA	750
1977	Intracoastal Canal	Gibbstown, LA	750
1969	San Diego-Coronado (twin)	San Diego Bay, CA.	660
1967	Bernard F. Dickman (Poplar St.)	St. Louis, MO	647
1992/1994	Acosta (twin)	Jacksonville, FL	630
1981	Douglas	Juneau, AK.	620
1976	Wax L. Outlet	Calumet, LA	618
1981	Glenn Jackson (I-205)	Columbia R., OR–WA.	600
1976	Archie Stevenot	Stanislaus R., Sonora, CA .	550
1982	Illinois R.	Pekin, IL	550
1982	I-440	Arkansas R., AR	540
1980	Harrison-McGarity, Tenn. R.	Savannah, TN.	525
1965	MacDonald-Cartier	Ottawa, Ontario	520
1988	Mon City	Monongahela, PA	520
1984	I-182, Columbia R.	Richland, WA	450
1986	Veterans	Pittsburgh, PA	440
1987	SR 76, Cumberland R.	Dover, TN	440
1987	SR 20, Tennessee R.	Perryville, TN	440
1970	Abernathy (I-205)	Willamette R., OR.	430
1974	I-430, Arkansas R.	Little Rock, AR	430
1965	I-24, Tennessee R.	Marion Co., TN	420
1974	Dunbar-S. Charleston	S. Charleston, WV	420
1975	36th St.	Charleston, WV	420
1978	Lewiston-Clarkston	Snake R., Clarkston, WA .	420
1984	FAU 3456, Tenn. R.	Chattanooga, TN	420

Continuous Plate

Year	Bridge	Location	Main span (ft.)
1973	Sidney Sherman (I-610)	Houston, TX	630
1971	Atchafalaya Basin (I-10)	Henderson, LA	573
1992	SR 76, Tennessee R.	Paris, TN.	525
1997	SR 114, Tennessee R.	Clifton, TN.	525
1981	Illinois 23	Illinois R., IL	510
1968	IH-45, Trinity R.	Dallas, TX.	480
1978	Antioch	San Joaquin R., CA	460
1977	Thomas Johnson Mem.	Solomons, MD	451
1967	I-90, Mississippi R.	La Crosse, WI	450
1975	I-129	Missouri R., IA–NE	450
1979	Lewis (I. US. 67)	Missouri R., St. Louis, MO .	450
1992	Cuba Landing	Tennessee R., TN	450
1966	I-480	Missouri R., IA–NE	425
1972	Whiskey Bay Pilot	Ramah, LA	425
1972	I-80	Missouri R., IA–NE	425
1972	I-635, Missouri R.	Kansas City, KS–MO	425
1983	US-36	Missouri R., KS–MO	425
1987	I-435	Missouri R., KS–MO	425
1978	I-24	Cumberland R., KY	420
1993	Bob Michel (SR 40)	Peoria, IL	360
1999	SR 53, Clear Fork R.	Fentress/Morgan Co., TN .	350

Cable-Stayed

Year	Bridge	Location	Main span (ft.)
2010	John James Audubon	Pointe Coupee-West Feliciana, LA	1,585
2005	Arthur Ravenel Jr.	Charleston, SC	1,546
1986	Alex Fraser	Vancouver, BC	1,526
2009	U.S. 82, Mississippi R. (new)	Greenville, MS	1,378
1994	Clark	Alton, IL	1,360
1988	Dame Point	Jacksonville, FL	1,300
1995	Fred Hartman	Houston Ship Channel, Baytown, TX	1,250
2003	Sidney Lanier	Brunswick, GA	1,250
1983	Hale Boggs Memorial	Luling, LA	1,222
1987	Sunshine Skyway	Tampa Bay, FL	1,200
2002	William Natcher	Ohio R., KY–IN	1,200
2009	Margaret Hunt Hill	Trinity R., Dallas, TX.	1,198
1988	Tampico	Panuco R., Mexico	1,181
2006	Penobscot Narrows	Bucksport, ME	1,161
2003	Bill Emerson Mem.	Cape Girardeau, MO–IL	1,150
1988	Skybridge (ALRT)[7]	Fraser R., Vancouver, BC .	1,115
1991	Talmadge Mem.	Savannah, GA	1,100
1993	Mezcala	Mex. City-Acapulco Hwy.	1,024
1978	Pasco-Kennewick	Columbia R., WA	981
1984	Coatzacoalcos	Coatzacoalcos R., Mexico .	945
1985	E. Huntington	Huntington, WV–OH	900
1987	Bayview	Quincy, IL	900
2006	U.S. Grant	Portsmouth, OH–KY	876
1990	Weirton-Steubenville	Ohio R., WV–OH	820
1969	Papineau-Leblanc	Montreal, QC	790
1991	Cochrane	Mobile, AL	780
1995	Chesapeake and Delaware Canal	C&D Canal, St. Georges, DE	750
2003	Leonard Zakim Bunker Hill	Boston, MA.	745
1966	Kelly's Creek	New Brunswick, Canada .	713
1967	Hawkshaw	New Brunswick, Canada .	713
1993	Quetzalapa	Quetzalapa, Mexico	699
1996	Burlington	Burlington, IA	660
1991	Veterans Memorial	Neches R., Port Arthur-Bridge City, TX.	640
1990	Varina-Enon	Richmond, VA.	630

I-Beam Girder

Year	Bridge	Location	Main span (ft.)
1980	I-20	Shreveport, LA	438
2001	Moore Haven	Caloosahachee Canal, FL	320
1988	Rte. 18	Weston's Mill Pond, NJ	276

Steel Arch

Year	Bridge	Location	Main span (ft.)
1977	New River Gorge	Fayetteville, WV	1,700
1931	Bayonne (Kill Van Kull)	Bayonne, NJ–NY	1,675
1973	Fremont	Portland, OR.	1,255
1964	Port Mann	Vancouver, BC	1,200
1967	Laviolette	Trois-Rivières, Quebec.	1,100
1990	Roosevelt Lake	Roosevelt Lake, AZ	1,080
1959	Glen Canyon	Page, AZ	1,028
1962	Lewiston-Queenston	Niagara R., NY–Ontario	1,001
1927	Perrine	Twin Falls, ID	993
1917	*Hell Gate	East R., NY.	977
1941	Rainbow	Niagara Falls, NY–Ontario .	950
1997	Blue Water	Port Huron, MI–Ontario	922
1977	Moundsville	Ohio R., WV	912
1972	Hernando DeSoto (I-40) (twin)	Mississippi R., AR–TN	900
1936	Henry Hudson	Harlem R., NY	840
1966	Bob Cummings-Lincoln Trail	Ohio R., IN–KY.	825
1978	I-57, Mississippi R.	Cairo, IL	821
1961	Sherman Minton (I-64)	IN–Louisville, KY	800
1980	I-65, Mobile R.	Mobile, AL	800
1932	West End	Pittsburgh, PA	780
1978	I-470, Ohio R.	Wheeling, WV.	780
1995	Navajo	Marble Canyon, AZ	726
1959	Thaddeus Kosciusko (twin)	Mohawk R., NY	600
1917	Detroit-Superior High Level	Cuyahoga R., Cleveland, OH	591
2004	Gateway Boulevard	Nashville, TN	545
1874	Eads[7]	Mississippi R., St. Louis, MO–IL	520
2000	Paper Mill Road	Baltimore, MD.	500

Concrete Arch

Year	Bridge	Location	Main span (ft.)
2010	Mike O'Callaghan-Pat Tillman Mem. (U.S. 93)	Colorado R., AZ–NV	1,060
1995	Natchez Trace Pkwy.	Franklin, TN	582
1993	Lake Street	Minneapolis, St. Paul, MN .	556
1971	Fred Redmon (twin)	Selah, WA	549
1968	Cowlitz R.	Mossyrock, WA	520
1931	Westinghouse	Pittsburgh, PA	460
1923	Cappelen Memorial	Minneapolis, MN	435
2000	Crooked River	Terrebonne, OR	410
1930	Jack's Run	Pittsburgh, PA	400
1932	Isaac Lee Patterson	Rogue R., Gold Beach, OR .	230

Segmental Concrete

Year	Bridge	Location	Main span (ft.)
1997	Confederation	Prince Edward Isl., NB	820
1978	Shubenacadie R.	S. Maitland, Nova Scotia .	790
1982	Jesse H. Jones Mem.	Houston, TX	750
1992	Jamestown-Verrazano	Narragansett Bay, RI	674
2002	Vietnam Veterans Mem.	James R., Richmond, VA.	672
1986	Umatilla	Columbia R., OR–WA	660
2007	Benicia-Martinez (new)	Carquinez Strait, CA.	659
1978	Stanislaus R.	Parrets Ferry, CA	640
1981	Juneau-Douglas	Gastineau Channel, AK	620
1991	Veterans Mem. Centennial	Coeur d'Alene, ID	520
2001	Smart Road	Blacksburg, VA.	472
1974	Pine Valley Creek	Pine Valley, CA	450
1988	Zilwaukee (twin)	Zilwaukee, MI	392
1985	Red River.	Boyce, LA	370

Twin Concrete Trestle[8]

Year	Bridge	Location	Main span (ft.)
1979	I-55/I-10	Manchac, LA	181,157
1956/1969	L. Pontchartrain Cswy. (twin)	Nr. New Orleans, LA	126,720
1972	Atchafalaya Swamp Frwy.	Baton Rouge, LA	93,984
1983	*I-310	Kenner, LA	25,925

Concrete Slab Dam[8]

Year	Bridge	Location	Main span (ft.)
1927	Conowingo Dam	Susquehanna R., MD	4,611
1952	John H. Kerr	Mecklenburg Co., VA	2,785
1936	Hoover Dam	Lake Mead, NV	1,324

Drawbridges
Vertical Lift

Year	Bridge	Location	Main span (ft.)
1959	*Arthur Kill	NY–NJ	558
1965	Pennsylvania Railroad	Kirkwood-Mt. Pleas., DE ..	548
1935	*Cape Cod Canal	Cape Cod, MA	544
1896	*Delair	Delaware R., NJ	542
1931	Burlington-Bristol	Delaware R., NJ–PA	540
1937	Marine Parkway Gil Hodges Mem.	Jamaica Bay, NY	540
1908	*Willamette R.	Portland, OR.	521
1968	Second Narrows	Vancouver, BC	465
1911	*Armour-Swift-Burlington	Kansas City, MO	428
1945	*Harry S Truman	Kansas City, MO	427
1955	Roosevelt Island	East R., NY.	418
1980	US-17, James R.	Isle of Wight Co., VA	415
1932	*M-K-T RR	Missouri R., MO	416
1969	Cape Fear Mem.	Wilmington, NC	408
1930	Aerial Lift	Duluth, MN	386
1962	Burlington	Ontario, Can.	370
1941	Main Street	Jacksonville, FL	365
1967	SR-156, James R.	Prince George Co., VA.	364
1950	Red R.	Moncla, LA	360
1957	Industrial Canal	New Orleans, LA	360
1936	Triborough	Harlem R., NY	344
1939	U.S. 1&9, Passaic R.	Newark, NJ.	333
1930	*Martinez	Martinez, CA.	328

Year	Bridge	Location	Main span (ft.)
1960	St. Andrews Bay	Panama City, FL	327
1929	*Penn-Lehigh	Newark Bay, PA	322
1987	Industrial Canal	New Orleans, LA	320
1920	*Chattanooga	Tennessee R., TN	310
1960	Broadway	Harlem R., NY	304
1910	Hawthorne	Willamette R., Portland, OR	244

Steel Suspension

Year	Bridge	Location	Main span (ft.)
1931	Maumee R.	Toledo, OH	785

Bascule

Year	Bridge	Location	Main span (ft.)
2008	Woodrow Wilson (I-95)[9]	Potomac R., VA–MD	366
1917	Market Street	Tenn. R., Chattanooga, TN	306
2003	*SW 2nd Avenue	Miami, FL	302
1956	Duwamish R.	Seattle, WA	300
1955	Chehalis R.	Aberdeen, WA	288
1968	Elizabeth R.	Chesapeake, VA	280
1913	Broadway	Portland, OR	278
1936	Siuslaw River	Florence, OR	154

Year	Bridge	Location	Main span (ft.)
		Swing	
1927	Fort Madison[5]	Mississippi R., IA	545
1991	SW Spokane St.	Seattle, WA	480
1930	Rigolets Pass	New Orleans, LA	400
1950	Douglass Memorial	Washington, DC	386
1945	Lord Delaware	Mattaponi R., VA	252
		Swing Span	
1897	*Duluth	St. Louis Bay, MN	486
1899	*C.M.&N. RR	Chicago, IL	474
1913	Rt. 82, Conn. R.	E. Haddam, CT	465
1914	*Coos Bay RR	Coos Bay, OR	458
1936	Umpqua River	Reedsport, OR	430
		Floating Pontoon	
1963	Evergreen Pt.	Seattle, WA	7,578
1993	Lacey V. Murrow[10]	Seattle, WA	6,620
1961	Hood Canal	Hood Canal, WA	6,521
1989	Third Lake Washington	Seattle, WA	5,811

Miscellaneous Bridges

Year	Bridge	Type	Location	Main span (ft.)
2002	Croatan Sound[8]	Continuous postension girder	Manteo, NC	5.2 mi
1987	Powder Point[8]	Tropical hardwood	Duxbury, MA	2,200
1997	Second Blue Water	Continuous tied arch	Pt. Huron, MI–ON	922
1983	Jefferson Barracks (I-255)	Tied arch	Mississippi R., IL–MO	910
1916	C&O RR	Steel girder	Portsmouth, OH	775
1936	Yaquina Bay	Steel braced and concrete tied arches	Newport, OR	600
1958	John Snodgrass	Through truss	Tenn. R., Stevenson, AL	500
1962	International	Arch truss	Sault Ste. Marie, MI–ON	430
1939	O'Neal (U.S. 43)	Through truss	Tenn. R., Florence, AL	420
1958	Tombigbee R.	Steel girder	Choctaw Co., AL	400
1982	SR 193	Seg. box girder	Dauphin Isl., AL	400

(1) Swing span bridge with 2 spans of 2,310 ft. each. (2) A second parallel bridge was completed in 1968. (3) A second parallel bridge was completed in 1978. (4) Currently scheduled for demolition in 2007. (5) Railroad and vehicular bridge. (6) Out of service since 2001. It is currently being renovated and is scheduled to be reopened in fall 2007. (7) ALRT = Automated Light Rail Transit. Transit-only bridge. (8) Length listed is total length of bridge. (9) Consists of twin spans. The bridge's outer span opened in 2006. (10) Replaces the original Lacey V. Murrow bridge, which opened in 1940 and sank in 1990.

Oldest U.S. Bridges in Continuous Use

Built in 1697, the stone-arch Frankford Ave. Bridge crosses Pennypack Creek in Philadelphia, PA. A 3-span bridge with a total length of 75 ft., it was constructed as part of the King's Road, which eventually connected Philadelphia to New York.

The oldest covered bridge, completed in 1829, is the double-span, 278-ft. Bath-Haverhill Bridge, which spans the Ammonoosuc River, between the towns of Bath and Haverhill, NH.

Some Notable International Bridges

Bridges still under construction as of mid-2007 are denoted by asterisk (*). Year is date of completion or projected completion. Span of bridge is the distance between its supports.

Year	Bridge	Location	Main span (ft.)
		Suspension	
1998	Akashi Kaikyo	Japan	6,532
NA	*Izmit Bay[1]	Turkey	5,538
2008	*Xihoumen	China	5,413
1998	Storebælt (East Bridge)	Denmark	5,328
2005	Runyang	China	4,888
1981	Humber	England	4,626
1999	Jiangyin Yangtze	China	4,544
1997	Tsing Ma[2]	China	4,518
2011	*Hardanger	Norway	4,298
1997	Höga Kusten	Sweden	3,970
1988	Minami Bisan-Seto	Japan	3,609
1988	Fatih Sultan Mehmet (Second Bosphorus)	Turkey	3,576
1973	Bosphorus	Turkey	3,524
1999	Kurushima III	Japan	3,379
1999	Kurushima II	Japan	3,346
1966	Tagus River[3]	Portugal	3,323
1964	Forth Road	Scotland	3,300
1988	Kita Bisan-Seto	Japan	3,248
1966	Severn	England	3,241
2001	Yichang	China	3,150

NA = Not available. (1) Project still in planning stages. (2) Double-decked road and rail bridge. (3) Railroad and highway bridge.

Year	Bridge	Location	Main span (ft.)
		Steel Arch	
2008	*Chaotianmen	China	1,811
2003	Lupu	China	1,804
1932	Sydney Harbour	Australia	1,650
2005	Wuhan Yangtze River	China	1,614
2009	*Chenab	India	1,575
2007	*Numata River Gorge	Japan	1,247
2000	Yajisha	China	1,181
1962	Bridge of the Americas	Panama	1,128
1967	Zdakov	China	1,083
1961	Runcorn-Widnes	England	1,082
1935	Birchenough	Zimbabwe	1,080

Year	Bridge	Location	Main span (ft.)
		Concrete Arch	
1997	Wanxian	China	1,378
1980	Krk I	Croatia	1,280
1995	Jiangjiehe	China	1,083
2010	*Mike O'Callaghan-Pat Tillman Mem. (U.S. 93)	U.S.	1,060
1998	Yijiang	China	1,024
1964	Gladesville	Australia	1,000
1965	Amizade	Brazil	951
1984	Bloukrans	South Africa	892
1943	Sandö	Sweden	866
1963	Arrabida	Portugal	886

Year	Bridge	Location	Main span (ft.)
		Cantilever	
1890	Forth (rail)[1]	Scotland	1,709
1974	Minato	Japan	1,673
1943	Howrah	India	1,500

(1) Two spans of 1,709 ft. each.

Year	Bridge	Location	Main span (ft.)
		Steel Plate and Box Girder	
2006	Shibanpo	China	1,083
1974	Rio-Niteroi	Brazil	984
1956	Sava I	Serbia	856
1966	Zoobrücke	Germany	850

Year	Bridge	Location	Main span (ft.)
		Cable-Stayed	
2009	*Sutong	China	3,570
2008	*Stonecutters	China	3,340
1999	Tatara	Japan	2,920
1995	Pont de Normandie	France	2,808
2009	*Second Incheon	South Korea	2,625
2001	Nanjing Second Yangtze River	China	2,060
2000	Wuhan Baishazhou Yangtze River	China	2,028
1996	Quingzhou Minjiang	China	1,985
1993	Yangpu	China	1,975
1997	Xupu	China	1,936
1998	Meiko Chuo	Japan	1,936
2004	Rion-Antirion	Greece	1,837
1999	Skarnsundet	Norway	1,739
1995	Queshi	China	1,699
1995	Tsurumi Tsubasa	Japan	1,673
2002	Jingsha	China	1,640
1991	Oresund	Denmark–Sweden	1,614
1994	Ikuchi	Japan	1,608
1994	Higashi Kobe	Japan	1,591
2010	*John James Audubon	New Roads-St. Francisville, LA	1,585
1998	Zhanjiang	China	1,575
1997	Ting Kau	China	1,558
1992	Arade	Portugal	1,542
1999	Seo Hae Grand	South Korea	1,542
1989	Yokohama Bay	Japan	1,509
1993	Second Hooghly River	Indias	1,499
1995	Second Severn Crossing	England/Wales	1,496
2008	*Hangzhou Bay[1]	China	1,470

(1) Although its main span is not among the world's longest for cable-stayed bridges, Hangzhou Bay will be the longest (22.4 mi) transoceanic bridge in the world when completed.

World's Longest Railway Tunnels

Source: World Almanac research

Asterisk (*) designates planned or under construction as of mid-2007.

Tunnel	Year	Length (mi)	Operating railway	Country
*Gotthard Base	2016	35.4	Swiss Federal Railways	Switzerland-Italy
*Brenner Base	2015	34.2	Austrian Federal Railways	Austria-Italy
Seikan	1988	33.5	Japan Railways	Japan
*Mont d'Ambin Base	2015	33.0	Réseau Ferré de France (RFF) & Rete Ferroviaria Italiana (RFI)	France-Italy
English Channel	1994	31.1	Eurotunnel	UK-France
Lötschberg Base	2007	21.0	BLS Lötschbergbahn AG	Switzerland
Guadarrama	2007	17.6	Renfe	Spain
*Hakkoda	2010	16.4	Japan Railways	Japan
Iwate-Ichinohe	2002	16.0	Japan Railways	Japan
Daishimizu	1982	13.8	Japan Railways	Japan
Wushaoling	2006	12.5	Chinese state	China
Simplon No. 1 and 2	1906/1922	12.3	BLS Lötschbergbahn AG	Switzerland-Italy
Vereina	1999	11.8	Rhätische Bahn (RhB)	Switzerland
London Tunnels (Channel Tunnel Link)	2007	11.8	LCR	UK
Shin-Kanmon	1975	11.6	Japan Railways	Japan
Appennino	1934	11.5	Ferrovie dello Stato (FS)	Italy
Qinling	2002	11.5	Chinese state	China
Vaglia	2006	11.5	Ferrovie dello Stato (FS)	Italy
Rokko	1972	10.1	Japan Railways	Japan
Furka Base	1982	9.6	Matterhorn Gotthard Railway	Switzerland
Haruna	1982	9.6	Japan Railways	Japan
*Ceneri Base	2016	9.6	Swiss Federal Railways	Switzerland
Severomuyskiy	2003	9.5	Russian Railways	Russia
Gorigamine	1997	9.4	Japan Railways	Japan
Firenzuola	2004	9.4	Ferrovie dello Stato (FS)	Italy
Monte Santomarco	1987	9.3	Ferrovie dello Stato (FS)	Italy

Underwater Vehicular Tunnels in North America

Source: World Almanac research

(more than 5,000 ft. in length; year in parentheses is year of completion)

Name	Location	Waterway	Length (ft.)
Brooklyn Battery (twin) (1950)	New York, NY	East River	9,117
Holland (twin) (1927)	New York, NY–Jersey City, NJ	Hudson River	8,558/8,371
Ted Williams (1995)	Boston, MA	Boston Harbor	8,448
Lincoln (center/north/south tubes) (1937/1945/1957)	New York, NY–Weehawken, NJ	Hudson River	8,216/7,482/8,006
Thimble Shoal (1964)	Northampton Co., VA.	Chesapeake Bay	5,734
Chesapeake Channel (1964)	Northampton Co., VA.	Chesapeake Bay	5,423
Fort McHenry (twin) (1985)	Baltimore, MD	Patapsco River	7,920
Hampton Roads (twin) (1957/1976)	Hampton, VA	Hampton Roads	7,479
Baltimore Harbor (twin) (1957)	Baltimore, MD	Baltimore Harbor	7,392
Queens Midtown (twin) (1940)	New York, NY	East River	6,414
Sumner (1934)	Boston, MA	Boston Harbor	5,653
Detroit-Windsor (1930)	Detroit, MI–Windsor, Ont.	Detroit River	5,160
Callahan (1961)	Boston, MA	Boston Harbor	5,070
Louis-Hippolyte Lafontaine (1967)	Montreal, Que.	St. Lawrence River	4,921

Land Vehicular Tunnels in the U.S.

Source: Federal Highway Administration, U.S. Dept. of Transportation; World Almanac research

(more than 3,000 ft. in length)

Name	Location	Length (ft.)	Name	Location	Length (ft.)
Anton Anderson Memorial[1]	Whittier, AK	13,300	Blue Mountain (twin)	PA Turnpike	4,339
Edwin Johnson Memorial	I-70, CO	8,960	Lehigh (twin)	PA Turnpike	4,380
Eisenhower Memorial	I-70, CO	8,939	Wawona	Yosemite Natl. Pk., CA	4,233
Ted Williams[2]	MA Turnpike	8,448	Big Walker Mt. (twin)	Bland Co., VA	4,229
Thomas P. O'Neill Jr.	MA Turnpike	7,920	Squirrel Hill	Pittsburgh, PA	4,225
Allegheny (twin)	PA Turnpike	6,070	Hanging Lake (twin)	Glenwood Canyon, CO	4,000
Liberty (twin)	Pittsburgh, PA	5,920	Caldecott (3 tubes)	Oakland, CA	3,771/3,610
Zion-Mt. Carmel	Zion Natl. Park, UT	5,808	Fort Pitt (twin)	Pittsburgh, PA	3,614
East River Mt. (twin)	VA–WV	5,412	Mount Baker	Seattle, WA	3,456
Tuscarora Mt. (twin)	PA Turnpike	5,326	Dingess	Mingo Co., WV	3,400
Tetsuo Harano (twin)	H-3 Freeway, HI	5,165	Mall	Dist. of Columbia	3,400
Kittatinny Mt. (twin)	PA Turnpike	4,727	Cody	U.S. 14, 16, 20, WY	3,202
Cumberland Gap (twin)	KY–TN	4,600			

(1) Tunnel is used for vehicular and railroad traffic. (2) 3,960 ft. of the tunnel is underwater.

Major U.S. Dams and Reservoirs

Source: 2007 National Inventory of Dams, U.S. Army Corps of Engineers

Highest U.S. Dams

Rank	Dam	River	State	Type	Height Feet	Height Meters	Year completed
1.	Oroville	Feather	California	E	770	235	1968
2.	Hoover	Colorado	Nevada	A	730	221	1935
3.	Dworshak	N. Fork Clearwater	Idaho	G	717	219	1973
4.	Glen Canyon	Colorado	Arizona	A	710	216	1963
5.	New Bullards Bar	North Yuba	California	R	635	194	1970
6.	New Melones	Stanislaus	California	A	625	191	1979
7.	Mossyrock	Cowlitz	Washington	A	606	185	1968
8.	Shasta	Sacramento	California	G	602	183	1945
9.	Don Pedro	Tuolumne	California	G	568	173	1971
10.	Hungry Horse	S. Fork Flathead	Montana	A	564	172	1952

E = Embankment, Earthfill; R = Embankment, Rockfill; G = Gravity; A = Arch.

Largest U.S. Embankment Dams

Rank	Dam	River	State	Volume Cubic yards × 1,000	Cubic meters × 1,000	Year completed
1.	Fort Peck	Missouri	Montana	125,628	96,049	1957
2.	Diamond Valley Lake	Domenigoni Valley Creek	California	110,551	84,522	2000
3.	Oahe	Missouri	South Dakota	92,000	70,339	1966
4.	Oroville	Feather	California	80,000	61,164	1968
5.	B. F. Sisk	San Luis Creek	California	77,664	59,378	1967
6.	Garrison	Missouri	North Dakota	66,500	50,843	1953
7.	Cochiti	Rio Grande	New Mexico	65,693	50,228	1975
8.	Fort Randall	Missouri	South Dakota	50,200	38,381	1954
9.	Castaic	Castaic Creek	California	44,000	33,640	1973
10.	Mansfield	Colorado	Texas	33,890	25,911	1942

Note: All earthfill.

Largest U.S. Reservoirs

Rank	Dam	Reservoir	State	Max. reservoir capacity Acre feet × 1,000	Cubic meters × 1,000	Year completed
1.	Hoover	Lake Mead	Nevada	30,237	37,297	1935
2.	Glen Canyon	Lake Powell	Arizona	29,875	36,850	1963
3.	Garrison	Lake Sakakawea	North Dakota	24,500	30,220	1953
4.	Oahe	Lake Oahe	South Dakota	23,600	29,110	1966
5.	Fort Peck	Fort Peck Lake	Montana	19,100	23,560	1957
6.	Grand Coulee	Lake Roosevelt	Washington	9,562	11,795	1941
7.	Sam Rayburn	Sam Rayburn Lake	Texas	6,520	8,042	1965
8.	Wright Patman	Wright Patman Lake	Texas	6,505	8,024	1954
9.	Fort Randall	Lake Francis Case	South Dakota	6,300	7,771	1954
10.	Wolf Creek	Lake Cumberland	Kentucky	6,089	7,511	1951

Major Dams of the World

Source: Intl. Commission on Large Dams, *World Register of Dams*

Asterisk (*) designates planned or under construction.

World's Highest Dams

Rank	Dam	Country	Height above lowest formation (m)
1.	Rogun*	Tajikistan	335
2.	Nurek	Tajikistan	300
3.	Xiaowan (Yunnan Gorge)	China	292
4.	Grand Dixence	Switzerland	285
5.	Inguri	Georgia	272
6.	Vaiont	Italy	262
7.	Manuel M. Torres	Mexico	261
8.	Tehri*	India	261
9.	Alvaro Obregon	Mexico	260
10.	Mauvoisin	Switzerland	250
11.	Mica	Canada	243
12.	Alberto Lleras C.	Colombia	243
13.	Sayano-Shushenskaya	Russia	242
14.	Ertan	China	240
15.	La Esmeralda	Colombia	237
16.	Kishau*	India	236
17.	Oroville	U.S.	235
18.	El Cajón	Honduras	234
19.	Chirkey	Russia	233
20.	Shuibuya	China	233

World's Largest-Volume Embankment Dams

Rank	Dam	Country	Volume cubic meters × 1,000
1.	Tarbela	Pakistan	127,908
2.	Fort Peck	U.S.	96,049
3.	Tucurui	Brazil	85,200
4.	Ataturk	Turkey	84,500
5.	Diamond Valley Lake	U.S.	84,552
6.	Yacyreta	Argentina/Paraguay	81,000
7.	Rogun*	Tajikistan	75,500
8.	Oahe	U.S.	70,339
9.	Guri	Venezuela	70,000
10.	Parambikulam	India	69,165
11.	High Island West	China	67,000
12.	Gardiner	Canada	65,440
13.	Mangla	Pakistan	64,991
14.	Afsluitdijk	Netherlands	63,400
15.	Oroville	U.S.	61,164
16.	B. F. Sisk	U.S.	59,378
17.	Nurek	Tajikistan	58,000
18.	Tanda	Pakistan	57,250
19.	Garrison	U.S.	50,843
20.	Cochiti	U.S.	50,228

World's Largest-Capacity Hydro Plants

Source: Intl. Commission on Large Dams, *World Register of Dams*

Asterisk (*) designates planned or under construction.

Rank[1]	Dam	Country	Rated capacity planned (MW)
1.	Sanxia (Three Gorges Dam)*	China	18,200
2.	Itaipu	Brazil-Paraguay	14,000
3.	Guri (Raúl Leoni)	Venezuela	10,000
4.	Tucurui	Brazil	8,370
5.	Sayano-Shushenskaya	Russia	6,400
6.	Itaipu	Paraguay	6,300
7.	Krasnoyarsk	Russia	6,000
8.	Bratsk	Russia	4,500
9.	Longtan (Guangxi, Tian'e)	China	4,200
10.	Xiaowan (Yunnan)	China	4,200
11.	Ust-Ilim	Russia	3,840
12.	Ilha Solteira	Brazil	3,444
13.	Ertan	China	3,300
14.	Yacyreta	Argentina/Paraguay	3,100
15.	Xingo	Brazil	3,000
16.	Macagua II	Venezuela	2,940
17.	Gezhouba	China	2,715
18.	Minamiaiki	Japan	2,700
19.	Volgograd	Russia	2,541
20.	Chief Joseph Dam	U.S.	2,512

(1) Ranked by rated capacity planned.

World's Largest-Capacity Reservoirs

Source: Intl. Commission on Large Dams, *World Register of Dams*

Rank	Dam	Country	Capacity cubic meters × 1,000,000
1.	Kariba	Zimbabwe/Zambia	180,600
2.	Bratsk	Russia	169,000
3.	High Aswan	Egypt	162,000
4.	Akosombo (Lake Volta)	Ghana	150,000
5.	Daniel Johnson	Canada	141,851
6.	Guri	Venezuela	135,000
7.	W. A. C. Bennett	Canada	74,300
8.	Krasnoyarsk	Russia	73,300
9.	Zeya	Russia	68,400
10.	Robert-Bourassa	Canada	61,715
11.	La Grande 3	Canada	60,020
12.	Ust-Ilim	Russia	59,300
13.	Boguchany	Russia	58,200
14.	Kuibyshev	Russia	58,000
15.	Serra da Mesa	Brazil	54,400

Timeline of Selected Architectural Styles and Structures

Asterisk (*) denotes part of World Heritage Site.

Style and period	Location; characteristics; significant examples
Mesopotamian c. 3500-539 BCE	City-states of Sumer, Akkad, Babylon, Assyria (modern-day Iraq). Mud brick rectangular temples on oval platforms with simple corbel vaults, later ziggurats. Painted terra-cotta mosaics and murals; carved reliefs on columns and walls. **Ziggurat of Nanna**, Ur (Muqayyar, Iraq), ordered by Ur-Nammu, c. 2100 BCE **Anu Ziggurat and White Temple**, Uruk (Warka, Iraq), c. 3000 BCE
Egyptian c. 3000-30 BCE	Along Nile R. Mud brick and limestone tombs and massive, geometric pyramids, post-and-lintel construction. Highly decorative with colorful hieroglyphics, carvings, columns, obelisks, paintings, and sculpture. ***Stepped Pyramid of Pharaoh Zoser**, Saqqara, by Imhotep, c. 2737-2717 BCE ***Great Pyramid of Khufu** (Giza), c. 2250 BCE ***Great Temple of Amon-Ra** (Karnak), c. 1530-300 BCE ***Mortuary Temple of Queen Hatshepsut**, Deir el Bahari (Thebes), by Senenmut, c. 1479-1458 BCE
Three Dynasties c. 2100-221 BCE	China. Single-level mudbrick or mud-smeared timber structures on earthen platforms with thatched roofs. Later, bracketed wooden-framed structures with brick-tiled floors, roofs with overhanging eaves. **City of Erlitou** (Yanshi, China), c. 1900-1500 BCE
Minoan c. 1800-1450 BCE	Crete. Palaces, tombs in monumental style adapted from Mesopotamia and Egypt. Multi-level stone palaces with large central court, no fortifications. *Polythyron* walls made of doors; stone porticoes and lintels; wooden ceilings and columns; beehive-shaped tombs (*tholi*). **Palace at Knossos** (Heraklion, Crete), c. 1700 BCE
Mycenaean c. 1600-1100 BCE	Greece. Adapted Minoan style, with large stone masonry, huge walls, and fortified citadels with complex palaces (*megaron*). ***Treasury of Atreus** (Mycenae, Greece), c. 1250 BCE
Olmec c. 1200-400 BCE	Mexican Gulf Coast. Many religious structures, including stone temple-pyramids centered in cities; also large stone sculptures and mosaic pavement with natural and animistic themes. **Great Pyramid** (La Venta, Mexico), c. 800-400 BCE
Mayan c. 900 BCE-900 CE	Central America. Religious structures with plaster-surfaced stone temple-pyramids with stairs, containing tombs. Decorative animistic and geometric relief sculptures, lintels, and stone monuments with hieroglyphics. ***Pyramid of the Magician** (Uxmal, Mexico), c. 700-910 CE **North Acropolis** (Tikal, Guatemala), c. 200 CE
Greek c. 750-323 BCE	Greek peninsula, Asia Minor, north Africa, western Mediterranean. Religious, civic buildings in monumental style, inspired by Egypt, based on strict rules of form and human proportion; many ornamental details. Marble and limestone structures (including rectangular temples) with pediment, colonnaded porticos in diverse regional styles, defined by "orders of architecture" like Ionic, Doric, Corinthian. Most early buildings with timber supports; solid stone in later temples. ***Parthenon, Acropolis** (Athens, Greece), by Ictinus and Callicrates, 447-436 BCE ***Temple of Zeus** (Olympia, Greece), by Libon of Elis, (mid-5th cent. BCE) **Mausoleum of Halicarnassus** (Bodrum, Turkey), by Pythis, c. 353 BCE (destroyed) ***Temple of Apollo Epicurius** (Bassae, Greece), by Ictinus, c. 420 BCE
Achaemenid c. 550-334 BCE	Persian empire (Eastern Mediterranean to Indus River). Palatial complexes influenced by cultures absorbed by the empire; limestone and mud brick complexes on raised stone terraces, with ornamental stairways, rectangular pillared audience halls with porticoes and corner towers; pleasure gardens (*bâgh*) as focal point of architecture. ***Pasargadae** (Iran), founded by Cyrus II after 547 BCE ***Persepolis** (Iran), founded by Darius I around 518 BCE
Roman c. 500 BCE-400 CE	Roman Empire. Civic and religious structures with grandiose limestone brick and concrete construction in systematic, practical layout. Adapted Greek orders in many structures, including circular temples and large covered halls (basilica), but emphasized movement with rounded arches and domes, geometric vaults. ***Pantheon** (Rome, Italy), ordered by Emperor Hadrian, 118-28 CE ***Colosseum** (Rome, Italy), ordered by Emperor Vespasian, 70-82 CE ***Roman Forum** (Rome, Italy), 500 BCE-608 CE
Qin & Han c. 221 BCE-220 CE	China. Massive public works, palaces, tombs, and planned cities; systematic layout and design determined by divination techniques (geomancy). Multi-storied timber palace complexes with gardens, courtyards laid along a long hall with a south-north axis for weather; decorative roof with overhanging eaves. ***The Great Wall** (China), ordered by Qin Shi Huang, 220-c. 1600 CE ***Mausoleum of the First Qin Emperor** (Xianyang [Xi'an]), c. 210 BCE
Sassanian 226-651 CE	Iran. Mud brick, mortared rubble, and stone palaces on platforms. Tall, vaulted entry chambers with one open side (iwans). Three-aisled hall chambers covered with rudimentary barrel vaults. Parabolic domes abandoned for square courtyards in later Sassanian period. **Palace of Ardashir I** (Firuzabad, Iran), c. 224 **Taq-i Kisra** [Arch of Khosrau] (Ctesiphon, Iraq), c. 260 or c. 550
Byzantine 330-1453	Byzantine Empire, Italy, Russia. Religious structures with masonry construction based on Roman architecture, many salvaged pieces of old structures. Centralized cross-in-square layout, with large central dome supported by vaults. Highly decorative, with iconographic frescoes, glass mosaics. ***Hagia Sophia** (Istanbul, Turkey), by Anthemius and Isidorous, 532-37 ***St. Mark's Basilica** (Venice, Italy), ordered by Domenico Contarini, 1063-94
Sui-Tang Dynasties 581-906	China. Includes influences from other cultures; geomancy used to enhance "harmony" and social status. Rectangular, multi-story modular timber structures with interlinking corridors; single-eaved roofs with exposed beams. **Daming Palace** (Xi'an, China), 634 (destroyed) **Hall of the Great Buddha** at Foguang Temple (Wutai Mountain), ordered rebuilt by Xuan Zhong, 857
Early Islamic (Umayyad) 692-c. 1000	Syria, Middle East, northern Africa, southern Spain. Mosques in adapted Sassanian style. Austere exteriors; simple columned halls with minarets and mihrab, walled courtyards and gardens, onion domes. Highly decorative interiors with patterned marble, mosaics. **Dome of the Rock** [Qubbat al-Sakhra] (Jerusalem), ordered by Abd al-Malik, 692 **Great Mosque of Córdoba** (Spain), order by Abd al-Rahman I, 784-86
Khmer c. 880-1200s	Indochina. Hindu or Buddhist temple complexes, including brick, later sandstone beehive-shaped shrines with arches atop terraced temple "mountains" symbolizing Mount Meru, Hindu and Buddhist "Mountain of the Gods." Concentric layout of structures mimics the cosmos, relating religious narrative in carved reliefs. ***Angkor Wat** (Cambodia), ordered by Suryavarman II, 12th cent.
Romanesque (Norman) c. 900s-1100s	Western Europe. Churches and monasteries in localized Roman style; many reused material from Roman structures. Austere, heavy, simple, masonry construction with thick walls, concealed buttresses, small windows, barrel arches, and vaults. Churches like Roman basilica with arched central nave, lower side aisles, apse, transept formed Latin cross. Monumental art and ornaments with Christian narrative throughout, especially on façade and portals. ***Durham Cathedral** (England), ordered by Bishop William de Saint-Calais, 1093-1133 ***Cathedral, Baptistery, and "Leaning" Tower** (Pisa, Italy), by various architects, begun in 1063, tower not completed until 1372

Style and period	Location; characteristics; significant examples

Gothic
c. 1100s-1500s*
	France, Europe. Cathedrals meant to inspire spirituality with design like Roman basilica: pointed arches and spires that reach towards heaven, skeletal masonry, revealed structure like flying buttresses, ribbed vaults (to allow better lighting), large stained-glass windows.
	    Abbey Church of Saint-Denis (France), ordered by Abbot Suger, 1136-47
	    *****Cathedral of Notre-Dame** (Paris, France), ordered by Bishop Maurice de Sully, 1163-1351
	    *****Chartres Cathedral** (France), 1194-1260
	    *****Cologne Cathedral** (Cologne, Germany), ordered by Archbishop Konrad von Hochstaden, 1248-1880
	    *****St. Vitus Cathedral** (Prague, Czech Republic), by Matthias of Arras, later Peter Parler, 1344-1929

Yüan & Ming 1279-1644	China. Mongol-influenced timber and some brick structures, influenced by geomancy. Emphasized monumental mass in sprawling yet low-lying structures with simple rectangular pavilions, great halls, elaborate wooden latticework, carved and painted details. *****Forbidden City** (Beijing, China), ordered by Emperor Yung Lo, 1406-20

Renaissance
1420s-1520s
	Italy. The "rebirth" or rediscovery of ancient Roman design, grounded in a scholarly approach to architecture. Followed rules of proportion in perspective and symmetry, classical orders, and simple but perfected geometric forms; emphasis on human scale.
	    *****Pazzi Chapel** (Florence, Italy), by Filippo Brunelleschi, 1429-61
	    *****Palazzo Medici-Riccardi** (Florence, Italy), by Michelozzo di Bartolomeo, 1444-60
	    *****Tempietto San Pietro** (Rome, Italy), by Donato Bramante, 1502-10
	    Villa Almerico Capra "La Rotonda" (near Vicenza, Italy), by Andrea Palladio, later Vincenzo Scamozzi, 1566-1610

Mughal
1526-1858
	India. Monumental palaces and mosques, blending Hindu and Islamic architecture. Sandstone with marble inlay; highly decorative, with semi-precious stones, vegetal and Koranic motifs. Formulaic four-part pleasure gardens (*charbágh*), exemplified by grounds of Taj Mahal.
	    *****Humayun Tomb** (Delhi, India), by Sayyid Muhammad, 1562-72
	    *****Taj Mahal** (Agra, India), ordered by Emperor Shah Jahan, 1631-48

Baroque
1630s-1700s
	Italy, later Western Europe. Elaborate and theatrical religious and civic structures, focused on dramatic overall effect. Complex geometric shapes and elaborate sculptures meant to be viewed from many angles.
	    St. Carlo alle Quattro Fontane, Rome, by Francesco Borromini, 1638-41
	    *****Palace of Versailles** (Versailles, France), royal hunting lodge (built 1631-34) expanded under Louis XIV, 1661-1710
	    Church of San Lorenzo (Turin, Italy), by Guarino Guarini, 1666-79
	    Church of St. John of Nepomuk "Asamkirche" (Munich, Germany), by Cosmas Damian and Egid Quirin Asam, 1733-46

Rococo 1690s-1700s	Europe. Mostly interior, simplified but still fanciful Baroque designs; ornate with natural motifs, gold trim, light and creamy colors, asymmetrical designs and unusual materials. *****Sanssouci Palace** (Potsdam, Germany), by Georg Wenzeslaus von Knobelsdorff, 1745-47

Neoclassicism
1750-1830
	Europe, Americas. Civic, commercial, and religious structures; chaste, non-decorative designs in reaction to Baroque excess. Grounded in enlightenment-era principles and simple, strict adherence to classic (Greek, Roman, Renaissance) forms and details. Palladian style in England, Federal style in U.S.
	    Chiswick House (Chiswick, England), by Richard Boyle, 1725-29
	    *****Monticello** (Charlottesville, VA), by Thomas Jefferson, 1768-1809

Neogothic
1837-1900s
	Britain and U.S. Civic, commercial, and religious structures utilizing Gothic forms in new commercial enterprises like railway stations and hotels. Traditional masonry façade disguised modern structural material like iron and glass.
	    *****Westminster Palace** (London, England), by Charles Barry and A.W.N. Pugin, 1840-47
	    Hotel fronting St. Pancras Railway Station (London, England), by George Gilbert Scott, 1865-71

Arts and Crafts
1850s-1930s
	England and U.S. Residential structures made of brick and other indigenous materials with pastoral and traditional elements like gabled roofs. Conceived as a reaction against homogenization of style following the industrial revolution.
	    Red House (Bexley Heath, England) by Philip Webb, 1859
	    Tigbourne Court (Surrey, England) by Edwin Lutyens, 1898

Beaux-Arts
1870s-1930s
	France, U.S. Grandiose, highly decorative style, using a mix of classical forms taught at the Ecole des Beaux-Arts in Paris: columns, wall projections, elaborate rooftops, high-relief decoration.
	    Boston Public Library (Boston, MA), by McKim, Mead, and White, 1888-95
	    Grand Central Terminal (New York, NY), Reed & Stem and Warren & Wetmore, 1903-13

Art Noveau
1884-1905
	Europe (esp. Brussels, Belgium, France). Civic and residential structures using industrial products like metal and glass to mimic natural forms; airy, fluid, and ornate.
	    Hôtel Tassel (Brussels, Belgium), by Victor Horta, 1892-93
	    Entrances to Metro (Paris, France), by Hector Guimard, 1900

Prairie
1893-1917
	U.S. Mostly residences, some civic buildings in adapted Arts and Crafts style. Inspired by American Midwest and small-town values. Frank Lloyd Wright most notable architect of the style. Buildings centered on chimney, with overhanging eaves and horizontal emphasis, long bands of windows.
	    Robie House (Chicago, IL), by Frank Lloyd Wright, 1908-10
	    National Farmer's Bank (Owatonna, MN), by Louis Sullivan, 1906-08

Futurism 1913-14	Italy. Purely theoretical style that produced no actual structures; emphasized concrete, glass, and steel construction, pure geometric forms and straight lines, and exposed structure and utilities. **La Citta Nuova** (sketches), by Antonio Sant'Elia, 1913
Constructivism 1914-20s	Russia, Europe. Public buildings based on socialist philosophies. Purely utilitarian industrial design, modern materials. **Rusakov Club** (Moscow), by Konstantin Melnikov, 1927-28
De Stijl 1917-31	Netherlands. Building and fixtures designed as a complete, sculpture-like piece of art; emphasis on primary colors, simple but asymmetrical geometry. Name is Dutch for "The Style." **Schröder House** (Utrecht, Netherlands), by Gerrit Thomas Rietveld, 1923-24
Bauhaus 1919-33	Weimar Republic Germany. Art and design school founded by Walter Gropius with philosophy that the machine is the modern medium. Concrete, glass, and steel construction that united industrial crafts and fine arts with simple geometric forms and colors. **Bauhaus** (Dessau, Germany), by Walter Gropius, 1925-26

International Style
1920s-70s
	Asia, Europe, N. America. Reinforced concrete and steel structures, mostly commercial buildings with some residences and civic structures. Post-and-slab construction meant walls no longer support weight so façades could be continuous strip (ribbon) glass "curtain-walls" with modular interiors. Emphasis on simple forms; glass, marble, and stainless steel; minimal decoration.
	    Philadelphia Savings Fund Society Building (Philadelphia, PA), by George Howe and William Lescaze, 1926-32
	    Villa Savoye (Poissy, France), by Le Corbusier, 1928-31
	    Seagram Building (New York, NY), by Ludwig Mies Van Der Rohe with Philip Johnson, 1954-58

Art Deco
1925-30s
	Europe, U.S. Traditional, symmetric, elegant construction (like Beaux-Arts) whimsically mixed with modern styles like geometric forms and steel or chrome features.
	    Chrysler Building (New York, NY), by William van Alen, 1928-30
	    Empire State Building (New York, NY), by Shreve, Lamb, & Harmon, 1930-31

Postmodernism
1970s-present
	Asia, Europe, N. America. Playful reaction against generic, mainstream "orthodox modern architecture" (not all modern architecture). Token references to traditional architectural elements like pediments or gables on houses; aim to present "old clichés in new settings."
	    Vanna Venturi House (Philadelphia, PA), by Robert Venturi, 1962
	    Public Service Building (Portland, OR), by Michael Graves, 1980-83

As of mid-2007, there were **194 nations** in the world. This number includes 2 nations that are not members of the United Nations—Taiwan and Vatican City the Holy See). The 194 nations are profiled below, in alphabetical order. Certain regions and territories that are not independent nations can be found under the entry for the governing nation. Following the nation profiles are comparative statistics, information on international organizations, and other information about nations.

Sources: Intl. Data Base, U.S. Census Bureau; *The World Factbook*, Central Intelligence Agency; U.S. Dept. of Energy; U.S. Dept. of State; United Nations Educational, Scientific, and Cultural Org. (UNESCO); FAO Statistical Database and *Yearbook of Fishery Statistics*, Food and Agriculture Org. of the UN; *Report on the Global AIDS Epidemic*, UNAIDS and World Health Org.; *Intl. Financial Statistics*, Intl. Monetary Fund; Intl. Telecommunication Union; *World Population Prospects* and *World Urbanization Prospects*, Dept. of Economic and Social Affairs, UN Population Division; *Statistical Yearbook*, UN Statistics Division; World Tourism Org.; *The Military Balance*, Intl. Institute for Strategic Studies.

Note: Because of rounding or incomplete enumeration, some percentages may not add to 100%. FY = Fiscal year. **Population** and **health** figures are mid-2007 estimates, unless otherwise noted. Estimated percentage of **urban** population is for 2005. Population figures for **capitals** and **cities** (urban aggr.), i.e., whole metropolitan areas, are 2005 estimates. Where indicated, the latest available population of the city proper is also given. **Defense budget** and **active troops** figures are from mid-2006 unless otherwise noted. **Crude oil reserves** are Jan. 1, 2007, estimates unless otherwise noted. **Livestock** figures are for 2006. **Fish catch** figures, which include the capture and farming of fish, mollusks, and crustaceans, are for 2005. **Electricity prod.** numbers are for 2006. **GDP** figures are 2006 estimates unless otherwise noted; figures are based on purchasing power parity calculations, involving use of intl. dollar price weights applied to quantities of goods and services produced. **Imports** and **exports** estimates and trade partners are from 2006 unless otherwise noted. **Tourism** figures are latest available and represent receipts from international tourism. **Budget** figures are for expenditures and are 2006 estimates unless otherwise noted. Figures for **intl. reserves less gold, gold,** and changes in **consumer prices** are from 2006, unless otherwise noted. **Railroad** and **motor vehicle** statistics are latest available; comm. (commercial) vehicles include trucks and buses. **Civil aviation** statistics are from 2003 unless otherwise noted. Airport figures include total number with paved runways as of mid-2006. **TV sets, radios,** and **daily newspaper circ.** figures are latest available. **Telephone lines** and **Internet** data are for 2006 unless otherwise noted. **Life expect.** is at birth for persons born in 2007. **AIDS rate** is the estimated number of adults, aged 15-49, living with HIV at year-end 2005, divided by the total 2005 population aged 15-49. **Education** figures are from 2006 unless otherwise noted. **Literacy** rates are latest available; they generally measure the percent of population able to read and write on a lower elementary school level, not the (smaller) percent able to read instructions necessary for a job or license. **Embassy** addresses are for Wash., DC, area code (202), unless otherwise noted.

For further details and later information on developments around the world, see the Chronology of the Year's Events. See pages 457-472 for full-color maps and flags of all nations.

Afghanistan

Islamic Republic of Afghanistan

People: Population: 31,889,923. **Age distrib.** (%): <15: 44.6; 65+: 2.4. **Pop. density:** 128 per sq mi, 49 per sq km. **Urban:** 22.9%. **Ethnic groups:** Pashtun 42%, Tajik 27%, Hazara 9%, Uzbek 9%. **Principal languages:** Dari (or Afghan Persian, official), Pashtu (official), Turkic (incl. Uzbek, Turkmen), Balochi, Pashai, many others. **Chief religion:** Muslim (official; Sunni 80%, Shi'a 19%).

Geography: Total area: 250,001 sq mi, 647,500 sq km; **Land area:** 250,001 sq mi, 647,500 sq km. **Location:** In SW Asia, NW of the Indian subcontinent. **Neighbors:** Pakistan on E, S; Iran on W; Turkmenistan, Tajikistan, Uzbekistan on N. The NE tip touches China. **Topography:** The country is landlocked and mountainous, much of it over 4,000 ft. above sea level. The Hindu Kush Mts. tower 16,000 ft. above Kabul and reach a height of 25,000 ft. to the E. Trade with Pakistan flows through the 35-mi-long Khyber Pass. The climate is dry, with extreme temperatures, and there are large desert regions. **Capital:** Kabul, 2,994,000.

Government: Type: Islamic republic. **Head of state and gov.:** Pres. Hamid Karzai; b. Dec. 24, 1957; in office: June 19, 2002. **Local divisions:** 32 provinces. **Defense budget:** NA. **Active troops:** 50,000.

Economy: Industries: textiles, soap, furniture, shoes. **Chief crops:** wheat, fruits, nuts, wool. **Natural resources:** nat. gas, oil, coal, copper, chromite, talc, barite, sulfur, lead, zinc, iron ore, salt, gems. **Arable land:** 12%. **Livestock:** cattle: 3.7 mil; chickens: 8.4 mil; goats: 7.3 mil; sheep: 8.8 mil. **Fish catch:** 1,000 metric tons. **Electricity prod.:** 0.73 bil kWh. **Labor force** (2004 est.): agriculture 80%, industry 10%, services 10%.

Finance: Monetary unit: Afghani (AFN) (Sept. 2007: 49.28 = $1 U.S.). **GDP** (2004 est.): $21.5 bil; **per capita GDP** (2004 est.): $800; **GDP growth:** 8%. **Imports** (2005 est.): $3.9 bil; partners: Pakistan 38.8%, U.S. 12.3%, Germany 7.4%, India 5.2%, Turkmenistan 4%. **Exports** (2005 est.): $471 mil; partners: India 22.1%, Pakistan 21.1%, U.S. 14.7%, UK 6.3%, Denmark 5.5%, Finland 4.3%. **Tourism** (1998): $1 mil. **Budget** (2005 est.): $561 mil.

Transport: Motor vehicles: 8,600 pass. cars; 4,500 comm. vehicles. **Civil aviation** (2000): 88.9 mil pass.-mi; 11 airports. **Chief ports:** Kheyrabad, Shir Khan.

Communications: TV sets: 14 per 1,000 pop. **Radios:** 136 per 1,000 pop. **Telephone lines:** 165,000 main lines. **Daily newspaper circ.:** NA. **Internet:** 535,000 users.

Health: Life expect.: 43.6 male; 44 female. **Births** (per 1,000 pop.): 46.2. **Deaths** (per 1,000 pop.): 20. **Natural inc.:** 2.63%. **Infant mortality** (per 1,000 live births): 157.4. **AIDS rate:** <0.1%.

Education: Compulsory: ages 6-15. **Literacy:** 28%.

Major intl. organizations: UN (FAO, IBRD, ILO, IMF, WHO).

Embassy: 2341 Wyoming Ave. NW 20008; 483-6410.

Website: www.embassyofafghanistan.org

Afghanistan, occupying a favored invasion route since antiquity, has been variously known as Ariana or Bactria (in ancient times) and Khorasan (in the Middle Ages). Foreign empires alternated rule with local emirs and kings until the 18th cent., when a unified kingdom was established. In 1973, a military coup ushered in a republic.

Pro-Soviet leftists took power in a bloody 1978 coup and concluded an economic and military treaty with the USSR. In Dec. 1979 the USSR began a massive airlift into Kabul and backed a new coup, leading to installation of a more pro-Soviet leader. Soviet troops fanned out over Afghanistan and waged a protracted guerrilla war with Muslim rebels, in which some 15,000 Soviet troops reportedly died.

A UN-mediated agreement was signed Apr. 14, 1988, providing for withdrawal of Soviet troops, a neutral Afghan state, and repatriation of refugees. Afghan rebels rejected the pact. The Soviets completed their troop withdrawal Feb. 15, 1989; fighting between Afghan rebels and government forces ensued. Communist Pres. Najibullah resigned Apr. 16, 1992, as competing guerrilla forces advanced on Kabul. The rebels achieved power Apr. 28, ending 14 years of Soviet-backed regimes. More than 2 mil Afghans had been killed and 6 mil had left the country since 1979.

Following the rebel victory there were clashes between moderates and Islamic fundamentalist forces. Burhanuddin Rabbani, a guerrilla leader, became president June 28, 1992, but fierce fighting continued around Kabul and elsewhere. The Taliban, an insurgent Islamic radical faction, gained increasing control and in Sept. 1996 captured Kabul and set up a government. The Taliban executed former Pres. Najibullah and empowered Islamic religious police to enforce codes of dress and behavior that were especially restrictive to women. Rabbani and other ousted leaders fled to the north.

Victories in the northern cities of Mazar-e Sharif, Aug. 8, 1998, and Taloqan, Aug. 8-11, gave the Taliban control over more than 90% of the country. On Aug. 20, U.S. cruise missiles struck southeast of Kabul, hitting facilities the U.S. said were terrorist training camps run by a wealthy Saudi, Osama bin Laden. The UN imposed sanctions Nov. 14, 1999, when Afghanistan refused to turn over bin Laden to the U.S. for prosecution; a UN ban on all military aid to the Taliban took effect Jan. 19, 2001.

After the Sept. 11, 2001, attacks on the World Trade Center and Pentagon, the U.S., blaming bin Laden, demanded that the Taliban surrender him and shut down his al-Qaeda terrorist network. When the Taliban refused, the U.S., with British assistance, began bombing Afghanistan Oct. 7, as part of Operation Enduring Freedom.

Supported by the U.S., the opposition Northern Alliance recaptured Mazar-e Sharif Nov. 9 and took Kabul 4 days later; the Taliban forces abandoned Kandahar, their last stronghold, to southern tribesmen Dec. 7. A power-sharing agreement signed in Bonn, Germany, Dec. 5 by 4 anti-Taliban factions, including the Northern Alliance, provided for an interim government headed by Hamid Karzai, a Pashtun tribal leader. The UN authorized Dec. 20 a multinational security force. Meanwhile, U.S. and allied forces continued to hunt for bin Laden and other top al-Qaeda and Taliban officials.

Meeting June 13, 2002, in Kabul, a traditional council (*loya jirga*) chose Karzai to head a new transitional government. An errant U.S. air strike on the night of June 30-July 1 apparently killed 48 people at Kakarak, north of Kandahar. Gunmen July 6 assassinated Vice Pres. Haji Abdul Qadir, a Pashtun. A car bomb in Kabul killed 30 people Sept. 5; the same day Karzai, guarded by U.S. troops, survived an assassination attempt.

The U.S. announced the end of major combat operations in Afghanistan, May 1, 2003, but resistance continued, with relief and reconstruction workers targeted. NATO officially assumed control of peacekeeping forces (ISAF) Aug. 11.

A new constitution took effect Jan. 26, 2004. Pres. Karzai won reelection Oct. 9 with 55.4% of the vote. During the campaign, insurgents attempted to kill Pres. Karzai, Sept. 16. U.S. troops launched a new offensive, Dec. 11, but were unable to suppress the insurgency.

A prominent anti-Taliban Muslim cleric, Mawlavi Abdullah Fayaz, was assassinated in Kandahar, May 29, 2005; a suicide bomb at his funeral, June 1, killed at least 20 people in a Kandahar mosque, including the police chief of Kabul. Violence continued to rise in the run-up to elections Sept. 18, 2005, for a 249-seat national assembly. Millions defied threats of violence to vote; at least 14 people were killed in more than 20 attacks by insurgents. The new assembly convened Dec. 19, with U.S. Vice Pres. Dick Cheney present. Meeting in London, Jan. 31-Feb.1, 2006, international donors pledged more than $10 bil in aid; prior assistance, 2001-06, had included $10.3 bil in funding from the U.S. and pledges of $9.5 bil from other countries, of which about half had been delivered.

The most intense fighting in more than 4 years erupted Mar. 2006 with a new wave of suicide bombings, rocket and mortar attacks, and other strikes by Taliban insurgents against military and civilian targets. Coalition forces responded in southeastern and eastern regions with Operation Mountain Thrust, beginning mid-May. Erosion of government authority led to an increase in opium growing; a record poppy crop of 8,200 metric tons in 2007 made Afghanistan the source of 93% of the world's illicit opium.

Fighting between Taliban insurgents and U.S. and allied troops in 2007 claimed hundreds of civilian lives. U.S.-led forces killed Mullah Dadullah, a top Taliban field commander, in Helmand Province May 12. The insurgents July 19 kidnapped 23 South Korean Christians riding a bus between Kabul and Kandahar; 2 were killed, but the other 21 were released by Aug. 30.

Between Oct. 2001 and Sept. 2007, some 375 U.S. military personnel died in Afghanistan; casualties from allied countries exceeded 250, with more than 70 each from the U.K. and Canada. Current U.S. troop strength is at least 25,000, of whom 15,000 or more are assigned to NATO's 35,000-member ISAF force. Through the 2007 fiscal year, Congress had appropriated an estimated $126.7 bil for Operation Enduring Freedom.

Albania
Republic of Albania

People: Population: 3,600,523. **Age distrib.** (%): <15: 24.1; 65+: 9.3. **Pop. density:** 340 per sq mi, 131 per sq km. **Urban:** 45.4%. **Ethnic groups:** Albanian 95%, Greek 3%. **Principal languages:** Albanian (Tosk is the official dialect), Greek. **Chief religions:** Muslim 70%, Albanian Orthodox 20%, Roman Catholic 10%.

Geography: Total area: 11,100 sq mi, 28,748 sq km; **Land area:** 10,578 sq mi, 27,398 sq km. **Location:** SE Europe, on SE coast of Adriatic Sea. **Neighbors:** Greece on S; Montenegro, Serbia on N; Macedonia on E. **Topography:** Apart from a narrow coastal plain, Albania consists of hills and mountains covered with scrub forest, cut by small E-W rivers. **Capital:** Tirana, 388,000.

Government: Type: Republic. **Head of state:** Pres. Bamir Topi; b. Apr. 24, 1957; in office: July 24, 2007. **Head of gov.:** Prime Min. Sali Berisha; b. Oct. 15, 1944; in office: Sept. 11, 2005. **Local divisions:** 12 counties divided into 36 districts. **Defense budget:** $147 mil. **Active troops:** 11,020.

Economy: Industries: food proc., textiles, clothing, lumber. **Chief crops:** wheat, corn, potatoes, vegetables, fruits, sugar beets, grapes. **Natural resources:** oil, nat. gas, coal, chromium, copper, timber, nickel, hydropower. **Crude oil reserves:** 198.1 mil bbls. **Arable land:** 20%. **Livestock:** cattle: 634,000; chickens: 4.6 mil; goats: 940,000; pigs: 152,000; sheep: 1.8 mil. **Fish catch:** 5,275 metric tons. **Electricity prod.:** 5.4 bil kWh. **Labor force** (2006 est.): agriculture 58%, industry 15%, services 27%.

Finance: Monetary unit: Lek (ALL) (Sept. 2007: 90.04 = $1 U.S.). **GDP:** $20.5 bil; **per capita GDP:** $5,700; **GDP growth:** 5%. **Imports:** $2.9 bil; Italy 32%, Greece 17.7%, Turkey 8%, Germany 5.6%. **Exports:** $763.2 mil; Italy 67.8%, Serbia and Montenegro 5.8%, Greece 5.4%. **Tourism:** $857 mil. **Budget** (2007 est.): $3.1 bil. **Intl. reserves less gold:** $1.18 bil. **Gold:** 70,000 oz t. **Consumer prices:** 2.37%.

Transport: Railroad: Length: 278 mi. **Motor vehicles:** 174,700 pass. cars; 88,800 comm. vehicles. **Civil aviation:** 75.2 mil pass.-mi; 3 airports. **Chief ports:** Durres, Sarande, Vlore.

Communications: TV sets: 146 per 1,000 pop. **Radios:** 259 per 1,000 pop. **Telephone lines:** 353,600. **Internet:** 471,200 users.

Health: Life expect.: 75 male; 80.5 female. **Births** (per 1,000 pop.): 15.2. **Deaths** (per 1,000 pop.): 5.3. **Natural inc.:** 0.98%. **Infant mortality** (per 1,000 live births): 20. **AIDS rate:** NA.

Major Intl. Organiz.: UN (IBRD, ILO, FAO, IMF, IMO, WHO, WTO), OSCE.

Education: Compulsory: ages 6-13. **Literacy:** 98.7%.

Embassy: 2100 S St. NW 20008; 223-4942.

Website: km.gov.al

Ancient Illyria was conquered by Romans, Slavs, and Turks (15th cent.); the Turks Islamized the population. Independent Albania was proclaimed in 1912; the republic was formed in 1920. King Zog I ruled 1925-39, until Italy invaded.

Communist partisans took over in 1944, allied Albania with USSR, then broke with USSR in 1960 over de-Stalinization. Strong political alliance with China followed, leading to several billion dollars in aid, which was curtailed after 1974. China cut off aid in 1978 when Albania attacked its policies after the death of Chinese ruler Mao Zedong. Large-scale purges of officials occurred during the 1970s.

Enver Hoxha, the nation's ruler for 4 decades, died Apr. 11, 1985. Eventually the new regime introduced some liberalization, including measures in 1990 providing for freedom to travel abroad. Efforts were begun to improve ties with the outside world. Mar. 1991 elections left the former Communists in power, but a general strike and urban opposition led to the formation of a coalition cabinet including non-Communists.

Albania's former Communists were routed in elections Mar. 1992, amid economic collapse and social unrest. Sali Berisha was elected as the first non-Communist president since WWII. Berisha's party claimed a landslide victory in disputed parliamentary elections, May 26 and June 2, 1996. Public protests over the collapse of fraudulent investment schemes in Jan. 1997 led to armed rebellion and anarchy. The UN Security Council, Mar. 28, authorized a 7,000-member force to restore order. Socialists and their allies won parliamentary elections, June 29 and July 6, and international peacekeepers completed their pullout by Aug. 11.

During NATO's air war against Yugoslavia, Mar.-June 1999, Albania hosted some 465,000 Kosovar refugees. Victory by a pro-Berisha coalition in elections July 3, 2005, ended 8 years of Socialist rule. Crowds in Tirana, June 10, 2007, welcomed George W. Bush, the first sitting U.S. president to visit Albania.

Algeria
People's Democratic Republic of Algeria

People: Population: 33,333,216. **Age distrib.** (%): <15: 27.2; 65+: 4.8. **Pop. density:** 36 per sq mi, 14 per sq km. **Urban:** 63.3%. **Ethnic groups:** Arab-Berber 99%. **Principal languages:** Arabic (official), French, Berber dialects. **Chief religion:** Sunni Muslim (official) 99%.

Geography: Total area: 919,595 sq mi, 2,381,740 sq km; **Land area:** 919,595 sq mi, 2,381,740 sq km. **Location:** In NW Africa, from Medit. Sea into Sahara Desert. **Neighbors:** Morocco, Western Sahara on W; Mauritania, Mali, Niger on S; Libya, Tunisia on E. **Topography:** The Tell, located on the coast, comprises fertile plains 50-100 mi wide, with a moderate climate and adequate rain. Two major chains of Atlas Mts., running roughly E-W and reaching 7,000 ft, enclose a dry plateau region. Below lies the Sahara, mostly desert with major mineral resources. **Capital:** Algiers (El Djazair), 3,200,000.

Government: Type: Republic. **Head of state:** Pres. Abdelaziz Bouteflika; b. Mar. 2, 1937; in office: Apr. 27, 1999. **Head of gov.:** Prime Min. Abdelaziz Belkhadem; b. Nov. 8, 1945; in office: May 24, 2006. **Local divisions:** 48 provinces. **Defense budget:** $3.02 bil. **Active troops:** 137,500.

Economy: Industries: oil, nat. gas, light industries, mining, petrochemical, food proc. **Chief crops:** wheat, barley, oats, grapes, olives, citrus. **Natural resources:** oil, nat. gas, iron ore, phosphates, uranium, lead, zinc. **Crude oil reserves:** 12.3 bil bbls. **Arable land:** 3%. **Livestock:** cattle: 1.6 mil; chickens: 125 mil; goats: 3.8 mil; pigs: 5,700; sheep: 19.6 mil. **Fish catch:** 126,627 metric tons. **Electricity prod.:** 31.9 bil kWh. **Labor force** (2003 est.): agriculture 14%, industry 13.4%, construction and public works 10%, trade 14.6%, government 32%, other 16%.

Finance: Monetary unit: Dinar (DZD) (Sept. 2007: 67.93 = $1 U.S.). **GDP:** $250 bil; **per capita GDP:** $7,600; **GDP growth:** 3%. **Imports:** $27.6 bil; France 22.1%, Italy 8.6%, China 8.5%, Germany 5.9%, Spain 5.6%, U.S. 4.8%. **Exports:** $55.6 bil; U.S. 26.7%, Italy 16.6%, Spain 9.1%, France 8.6%, Canada 7.9%, Brazil 6.5%. **Tourism:** $161 mil. **Budget:** $49.1 bil. **Intl. reserves less gold:** $51.79 bil. **Gold:** 5.58 mil oz t. **Consumer prices:** 2.53%.

Transport: Railroad: Length: 2,469 mi. **Motor vehicles:** 1.7 mil pass. cars; 1 mil comm. vehicles. **Civil aviation:** 2.1 bil pass.-mi; 52 airports. **Chief ports:** Algiers, Annaba, Oran.

Communications: TV sets: 107 per 1,000 pop. **Radios:** 242 per 1,000 pop. **Telephone lines:** 2.8 mil. **Daily newspaper circ.:** 27.2 per 1,000 pop. **Internet:** 2.5 mil users.

Health: Life expect.: 71.9 male; 75.2 female. **Births** (per 1,000 pop.): 17.1. **Deaths** (per 1,000 pop.): 4.6. **Natural inc.:** 1.25%. **Infant mortality** (per 1,000 live births): 28.8. **AIDS rate:** 0.1%.

Education: Compulsory: ages 6-14. **Literacy:** 69.9%.

Major intl. organizations: UN (FAO, IBRD, ILO, IMF, IMO, WHO), AL, AU, OPEC.

Embassy: 2118 Kalorama Rd. NW 20008; 265-2800.

Website: www.algeria-us.org

Earliest known inhabitants were ancestors of Berbers, followed by Phoenicians, Romans, Vandals, and, finally, Arabs. Turkey ruled 1518 to 1830, when France took control. Large-scale European immigration followed. Arab nationalists launched a guerrilla war, 1954, that more than 400,000 French troops were unable to suppress. After French Pres. Charles de Gaulle came to power, 1958, colonial rule ended, nearly all Europeans left, and Algeria declared independence July 5, 1962. Ahmed Ben Bella ruled until 1965, when an army coup installed Col. Houari Boumedienne, a former guerrilla leader who held power until his death in 1978.

Hundreds died in antigovernment riots protesting economic hardship in Oct. 1988. In 1989, voters approved a new constitution, which cleared the way for a multiparty system. The government canceled the Jan. 1992 elections that Islamic fundamentalists were expected to win, and banned all nonreligious activities at Algeria's 10,000 mosques. Pres. Mohammed Boudiaf was assassinated June 29, 1992. Over the next 7 years, Muslim fundamentalists carried out attacks on high-ranking officials, security forces, foreigners, and others; pro-government death squads also were active.

Liamine Zeroual won the presidential election of Nov. 16, 1995. A new constitution banning Islamic political parties and increasing the president's powers passed in a referendum on Nov. 28, 1996. Abdelaziz Bouteflika, who became president after a flawed election on Apr. 15, 1999, made peace with rebels and won approval for an amnesty plan in a referendum on Sept. 16. Some 100 people died and thousands were injured in violent protests Apr.-June 2001, chiefly by Algeria's Berber minority. Bouteflika was reelected Apr. 8, 2004, in a landslide; opponents charged fraud.

An earthquake in northern Algeria, May 21, 2003, claimed over 2,200 lives and left 200,000 people homeless. The army launched a campaign against the militant Islamic group GSPC after its members killed 12 soldiers in June. GSPC leader Nabil Sahraoui was killed by Algerian forces, June 20, 2004. Under a reconciliation plan approved by referendum Sept. 29, 2005, the government in Mar. 2006 began freeing Islamists jailed for their role in the 1990s civil war, in which up to 200,000 people were killed, and 8,000 "disappeared."

Radical Islamists bombed 2 police stations Oct. 30, 2006, and 7 more police stations Feb. 13, 2007. Suicide bombings carried out by a local al-Qaeda affiliate Apr. 11 at the Government Palace and a police station in Algiers killed 33 people; more than 50 died in suicide bombings at Batna, Sept. 6, and Dellys, Sept. 8.

Andorra
Principality of Andorra

People: Population: 71,822. **Age distrib.** (%): <15: 14.5; 65+: 14.3. **Pop. density:** 397 per sq mi, 153 per sq km. **Urban:** 90.6%. **Ethnic groups:** Spanish 43%, Andorran 33%, Portuguese 11%, French 7%. **Principal languages:** Catalan (official), Castilian Spanish, French, Portuguese. **Chief religion:** Predominantly Roman Catholic.

Geography: Total area: 181 sq mi, 468 sq km; **Land area:** 181 sq mi, 468 sq km. **Location:** SW Europe, in Pyrenees Mts. **Neighbors:** Spain on S, France on N. **Topography:** High mountains and narrow valleys cover the country. **Capital** (2002): Andorra la Vella, 20,787.

Government: Type: Parliamentary co-principality. **Heads of state:** President of France & Bishop of Urgel (Spain), as co-princes. **Head of gov.:** Albert Pintat Santolària; b. June 23, 1943; in office: May 27, 2005. **Local divisions:** 7 parishes. **Defense budget:** Responsibility of France and Spain.

Economy: Industries: tourism, cattle raising, timber, tobacco, banking. **Chief crops:** rye, wheat, barley, oats. **Natural resources:** hydropower, mineral water, timber, iron ore, lead. **Arable land:** 2%. **Labor force** (2005): agriculture .0.3%, industry 20.3%, services 79.4%.

Finance: Monetary unit: Euro (EUR) (Sept. 2007: 0.72 = $1 U.S.). **GDP** (2005): $2.8 bil; **per capita GDP** (2005): $38,800; **GDP growth** (2005 est.): 3.5%. **Imports** (2005): $1.9 bil; Spain 53.2%, France 21.1%. **Exports** (2005): $148.7 mil; Spain 59.5%, France 17%. **Tourism:** NA. **Budget** (2005): $386.6 mil.

Transport: NA.

Communications: TV sets: 440 per 1,000 pop. **Radios:** 229 per 1,000 pop. **Telephone lines:** 35,400. **Internet:** 23,200 users.

Health: Life expect.: 80.6 male; 86.6 female. **Births** (per 1,000 pop.): 8.5. **Deaths** (per 1,000 pop.): 6.5. **Natural inc.:** 0.2%. **Infant mortality** (per 1,000 live births): 4. **AIDS rate:** NA.

Education: Compulsory: ages 6-16. **Literacy:** 100%.

Major intl. organizations: UN (WHO), OSCE.

Embassy: 2 UN Plaza, 27th Fl., New York, NY 10017; 212-750-8064.

Website: www.andorra.ad

Andorra was a co-principality, with joint sovereignty by France and the bishop of Urgel, from 1278 to 1993. Voters chose to adopt a parliamentary system Mar. 14, 1993.

Tourism, especially skiing, is the economic mainstay. A free port, Andorra attracted more than 11 mil tourists in 2005.

Angola
Republic of Angola

People: Population: 12,263,596. **Age distrib.** (%): <15: 43.7; 65+: 2.8. **Pop. density:** 25 per sq mi, 10 per sq km. **Urban:** 53.3%. **Ethnic groups:** Ovimbundu 37%, Kimbundu 25%, Bakongo 13%. **Principal languages:** Portuguese (official), Bantu, other African languages. **Chief religions:** Indigenous beliefs 47%, Roman Catholic 38%, Protestant 15%.

Geography: Total area: 481,354 sq mi, 1,246,700 sq km; **Land area:** 481,354 sq mi, 1,246,700 sq km. **Location:** In SW Africa on Atlantic coast. **Neighbors:** Namibia on S, Zambia on E, Congo-Kinshasa on N; Cabinda, an enclave separated from rest of country by short Atlantic coast of Congo-Kinshasa, borders Congo-Brazzaville. **Topography:** Mostly plateau elevated 3,000-5,000 ft above sea level, rising from a narrow coastal strip. There is also a temperate highland area in the west-central region, a desert in S, and a tropical rain forest covering Cabinda. **Capital:** Luanda, 2,766,000.

Government: Type: Republic. **Head of state:** Pres. José Eduardo dos Santos; b. Aug. 28, 1942; in office: Sept. 20, 1979. **Head of gov.:** Prime Min. Fernando da Piedade Dias dos Santos; b. Mar.

5, 1952; in office: Dec. 6, 2002. **Local divisions:** 18 provinces. **Defense budget:** $1.56 bil. **Active troops:** 107,000.

Economy: Industries: oil, mining, cement, metals, fish & food proc. **Chief crops:** bananas, sugarcane, coffee, sisal. **Natural resources:** oil, diamonds, iron ore, phosphates, copper, feldspar, gold, bauxite, uranium. **Crude oil reserves:** 8 bil bbls. **Arable land:** 3%. **Livestock:** cattle: 4.2 mil; chickens: 6.8 mil; goats: 2.1 mil; pigs: 780,000; sheep: 340,000. **Fish catch:** 240,000 metric tons. **Electricity prod.:** 2.6 bil kWh. **Labor force** (2003 est.): agriculture 85%, industry and services 15%.

Finance: Monetary unit: Kwanza (AOA) (Sept. 2007: 74.77 = $1 U.S.). **GDP:** $53.1 bil; **per capita GDP:** $4,400; **GDP growth:** 15%. **Imports:** $10.2 bil; South Korea 17.3%, U.S. 14.3%, Portugal 14.1%, China 8.3%, South Africa 6.3%, Brazil 5.9%, France 5.8%. **Exports:** $35.5 bil; U.S. 39.4%, China 35.4%, France 5%, Chile 4.3%. **Tourism:** $66 mil. **Budget:** $9.7 bil. **Intl. reserves less gold:** $5.72 bil. **Consumer prices:** 11.67%.

Transport: Railroad: Length: 1,716 mi. **Motor vehicles:** 117,200 pass. cars; 118,300 comm. vehicles. **Civil aviation:** 297.6 mil pass.-mi; 31 airports. **Chief ports:** Cabinda, Lobito, Luanda.

Communications: TV sets: 15 per 1,000 pop. **Radios:** 67 per 1,000 pop. **Telephone lines:** 98,200. **Daily newspaper circ.:** 11.3 per 1,000 pop. **Internet:** 85,000 users.

Health: Life expect.: 36.7 male; 38.6 female. **Births** (per 1,000 pop.): 44.5. **Deaths** (per 1,000 pop.): 24.8. **Natural inc.:** 1.97%. **Infant mortality** (per 1,000 live births): 184.4. **AIDS rate:** 3.7%.

Education: Compulsory: ages 6-9. **Literacy:** 67.4%.

Major intl. organizations: UN (FAO, IBRD, ILO, IMF, IMO, WHO, WTO), AU, OPEC.

Embassy: 2100-2108 16th St. NW 20009; 785-1156.

Website: www.angola.org

From the early centuries CE to 1500, Bantu tribes penetrated most of the region. Portuguese came in 1583, allied with the Bakongo kingdom in the north, and developed the slave trade. Large-scale colonization did not begin until the 20th cent, when 400,000 Portuguese immigrated.

A guerrilla war begun in 1961 lasted until 1975, when Portugal granted independence. Fighting then erupted between three rival rebel groups—the National Front, based in Zaire (now Congo), the Soviet-backed Popular Movement for the Liberation of Angola (MPLA), and the National Union for the Total Independence of Angola (UNITA), aided by the U.S. and South Africa.

Cuban troops and Soviet aid helped the MPLA win control of most of the country by 1976, although fighting continued through the 1980s. A peace accord between the MPLA government and UNITA was signed May 1, 1991.

Elections were held in Sept. 1992, but fighting again broke out, as UNITA rejected the results. UNITA signed a new peace treaty with the government, Nov. 20, 1994, but the rebels were slow to demobilize. The UN Security Council voted, Aug. 28, 1997, to impose sanctions on UNITA. In Aug. 1998, Angola sent thousands of troops into Congo-Kinshasa (formerly Zaire) to support Laurent Kabila's regime. The UN ended its mission in Angola in Mar. 1999, as the civil war continued.

As of 2001, the UN estimated that the war with UNITA had claimed some 1 mil lives and left another 2.5 mil people homeless. More than 250 died when UNITA rebels ambushed a train Aug. 10. Rebel leader Jonas Savimbi was killed by government troops Feb. 22, 2002. UNITA agreed to a truce Apr. 4 of that year, ending the 27-year-long civil war. Fighting continued, however, between government forces and separatist guerrillas in oil-rich Cabinda; rebels there agreed to a cease-fire July 2006.

With proven petroleum reserves estimated at 9.04 bil barrels, Angola is one of Africa's leading oil producers. Mismanagement and corruption led to the diversion of up to $4.2 bil in oil revenues during 1997-2002, according to a Human Rights Watch report. In Apr. 2004, the govt. arrested nearly 3,000 illegal diamond diggers, many of them foreigners. An outbreak of Marburg hemorrhagic fever, caused by a rare Ebola-like virus, claimed more than 300 lives in 2005. A cholera epidemic beginning Feb. 2006 killed at least 1,600 people.

Antigua and Barbuda

People: Population: 69,481. **Age distrib.** (%): <15: 27.3; 65+: 3.7. **Pop. density:** 406 per sq mi, 157 per sq km. **Urban:** 39.1%. **Ethnic groups:** Black 91%, mixed 4%, white 2%. **Principal languages:** English (official), local dialects. **Chief religions:** Predominantly Protestant; some Roman Catholic.

Geography: Total area: 171 sq mi, 443 sq km; **Land area:** 171 sq mi, 443 sq km. **Location:** E Caribbean. **Neighbors:** St. Kitts & Nevis to W, Guadeloupe (Fr.) to S. **Topography:** These are mostly low-lying and limestone coral islands. Antigua is mostly hilly with an indented coast; Barbuda is a flat island with a large lagoon on W. **Capital** (2004): Saint John's, 23,600.

Government: Type: Constitutional monarchy with British-style parliament. **Head of state:** Queen Elizabeth II; represented by Gov.-Gen. Louise Agnetha Lake-Tack; b. July 26, 1944; in office: July 17, 2007. **Head of gov.:** Prime Min. Baldwin Spencer; b. Oct. 8, 1948; in office: Mar. 24, 2004. **Local divisions:** 6 parishes, 2 dependencies. **Defense budget:** $4.8 mil. **Active troops:** 170.

Economy: Industries: tourism, constr., light mfg. **Chief crops:** cotton, fruits, vegetables. **Arable land:** 18%. **Livestock:** cattle:

14,300; **chickens:** 105,000; **goats:** 36,000; **pigs:** 2,800; **sheep:** 19,000. **Fish catch:** 2,999 metric tons. **Electricity prod.:** 110 mil kWh. **Labor force** (1983): agriculture 7%, industry 11%, services 82%.

Finance: Monetary unit: East Caribbean Dollar (XCD) (Sept. 2007: 2.67 = $1 U.S.). **GDP:** $1.1 bil; **per capita GDP** (2005 est.): $10,900; **GDP growth** (2005 est.): 3.8%. **Imports** (2004 est.): $378 mil; U.S. 21.1%, China 16.4%, Germany 13.3%, Singapore 12.7%, Spain 6.5%. **Exports** (2004 est.): $46.8 mil; Spain 34%, Germany 20.7%, Italy 7.7%, Singapore 5.8%, UK 4.9%. **Tourism:** $337 mil. **Budget** (2000 est.): $145.9 mil. **Intl. reserves less gold:** $95 mil.

Transport: Railroad: Length: NA. **Motor vehicles:** 24,000 pass. cars and comm. vehicles. **Civil aviation:** 201.9 mil pass.-mi; 2 airports. **Chief port:** Saint John's.

Communications: TV sets: 493 per 1,000 pop. **Radios:** 545 per 1,000 pop. **Telephone lines:** 40,000. **Internet:** 32,000 users.

Health: Life expect.: 70 male; 74.9 female. **Births** (per 1,000 pop.): 16.6. **Deaths** (per 1,000 pop.): 5.3. **Natural inc.:** 1.13%. **Infant mortality** (per 1,000 live births): 18.3. **AIDS rate:** NA.

Education: Compulsory: ages 5-16. **Literacy:** 85.8%.

Major intl. organizations: UN (FAO, IBRD, ILO, IMF, IMO, WHO, WTO), Caricom, the Commonwealth, OAS, OECS.

Embassy: 3216 New Mexico Ave. NW 20016; 362-5122.

Website: www.antigua-barbuda.com

Columbus landed on Antigua in 1493. The British colonized it in 1632.

The British associated state of Antigua achieved independence as Antigua and Barbuda on Nov. 1, 1981. The government maintains close relations with the U.S., the UK, and Venezuela. The country was hit hard by Hurricane Luis, Sept. 1995. About 3,000 refugees from the nearby island of Montserrat settled in Antigua following volcanic eruptions there in 1995-97.

Argentina
Argentine Republic

People: Population: 40,301,927. **Age distrib.** (%): <15: 24.9; 65+: 10.7. **Pop. density:** 38 per sq mi, 15 per sq km. **Urban:** 90.1%. **Ethnic groups:** White 97%, Amerindian and other 3%. **Principal languages:** Spanish (official), English, Italian, German, French. **Chief religion:** Roman Catholic (official) 92%.

Geography: Total area: 1,068,302 sq mi, 2,766,890 sq km; **Land area:** 1,056,642 sq mi, 2,736,690 sq km. **Location:** Occupies most of southern S. America. **Neighbors:** Chile on W; Bolivia, Paraguay on N; Brazil, Uruguay on NE. **Topography:** Mountains in W are the Andean, Central, Misiones, and Southern ranges. Aconcagua is the highest peak in the Western Hemisphere, alt. 22,834 ft. E of the Andes are heavily wooded plains, called the Gran Chaco in N, and the fertile, treeless Pampas in the central region. Patagonia, in S, is bleak and arid. Rio de la Plata, an estuary in NE, 170 by 140 mi, is mostly fresh water, from 2,485-mi Parana and 1,000-mi Uruguay rivers. **Capital:** Buenos Aires, 12,550,000 (the Senate has approved moving the capital to the Patagonia Region). **Cities (urban aggr.):** Córdoba, 1,423,000; Rosario, 1,186,000.

Government: Type: Republic. **Head of state and gov.:** Pres. Néstor Kirchner; b. Feb. 25, 1950; in office: May 25, 2003. **Local divisions:** 23 provinces, 1 federal district. **Defense budget:** $1.84 bil. **Active troops:** 71,655.

Economy: Industries: food proc., vehicles, consumer durables, textiles, chemicals. **Chief crops:** sunflower seeds, lemons, soybeans, grapes, corn. **Natural resources:** lead, zinc, tin, copper, iron ore, mang., oil, uranium. **Crude oil reserves:** 2.5 bil bbls. **Arable land:** 10%. **Livestock:** cattle: 50.8 mil; chickens: 95 mil; goats: 4.2 mil; pigs: 1.5 mil; sheep: 12.5 mil. **Fish catch:** 933,902 metric tons. **Electricity prod.:** 101.1 bil kWh. **Labor force:** NA.

Finance: Monetary unit: Peso (ARS) (Sept. 2007: 3.13 = $1 U.S.). **GDP:** $608.8 bil; **per capita GDP:** $15,200; **GDP growth:** 8.5%. **Imports:** $31.7 bil; Brazil 36.1%, U.S. 14.9%, China 6.3%, Germany 5.1%. **Exports:** $46.6 bil; Brazil 16.9%, Chile 8.9%, U.S. 8.4%, China 7.3%. **Tourism:** $2.7 bil. **Budget:** $47.6 bil. **Intl. reserves less gold:** $20.54 bil. **Gold:** 1.76 mil oz t. **Consumer prices:** 10.9%.

Transport: Railroad: Length: 19,823 mi. **Motor vehicles:** 5.4 mil pass. cars; 1 mil comm. vehicles. **Civil aviation:** 7.7 bil pass.-mi; 154 airports. **Chief ports:** Bahia Blanca, Buenos Aires, La Plata, Punta Colorado.

Communications: TV sets: 293 per 1,000 pop. **Radios:** 681 per 1,000 pop. **Telephone lines:** 9.5 mil. **Daily newspaper circ.:** 40.5 per 1,000 pop. **Internet:** 8.2 mil users.

Health: Life expect.: 72.6 male; 80.2 female. **Births** (per 1,000 pop.): 16.5. **Deaths** (per 1,000 pop.): 7.6. **Natural inc.:** 0.9%. **Infant mortality** (per 1,000 live births): 14.3. **AIDS rate:** 0.6%.

Education (2005): Compulsory: ages 5-14. **Literacy:** 97.2%.

Major intl. organizations: UN (FAO, IBRD, ILO, IMF, IMO, WHO, WTO), OAS.

Embassy: 1600 New Hampshire Ave. NW 20009; 238-6401.

Website:

Nomadic Indians roamed the Pampas when Spaniards arrived, 1515-16, led by Juan Diaz de Solis. Nearly all the Indians were killed by the late 19th cent. The colonists won independence,

1816, and a long period of disorder ended in a strong centralized government.

Large-scale Italian, German, and Spanish immigration in the decades after 1880 spurred modernization. Social reforms were enacted in the 1920s, but military coups prevailed 1930-46 until the election of Gen. Juan Perón as president.

Perón, with his wife, Eva Duarte (d. 1952), effected labor reforms but also suppressed speech and press freedoms, closed religious schools, and ran the country into debt. A 1955 coup exiled Perón, who was followed by a series of military and civilian regimes. Perón returned in 1973 and was once more elected president. He died 10 months later, succeeded by his wife Isabel, who had been elected vice president, and who became the first woman head of state in the Western Hemisphere.

A military junta ousted Mrs. Perón in 1976 amid charges of corruption. Under a continuing state of siege, the army conducted a "dirty war" against guerrillas and leftists in which an estimated 30,000 people "disappeared." On Dec. 9, 1985, after a trial of 5 months and nearly 1,000 witnesses, 5 former junta members were found guilty of murder and human rights abuses.

Argentine troops seized control of the British-held Falkland Islands (Islas Malvinas) on Apr. 2, 1982. The British imposed an air and sea blockade around the Falklands. Fighting began May 1. British troops landed on East Falkland May 21. Argentine troops surrendered, June 14; Argentine Pres. Leopoldo Galtieri resigned June 17.

Democratic rule returned in 1983 with a victory by Raul Alfonsín's Radical Civic Union party. By 1989 the nation was plagued by severe financial and political problems, as hyperinflation sparked looting and rioting in several cities. The government of Peronist Pres. Carlos Saúl Menem, installed 1989, introduced harsh economic austerity measures.

About 85 people were killed and nearly 300 injured in the terrorist bombing of a Jewish cultural center in Buenos Aires, July 18, 1994. Following passage of a new constitution in Aug. 1994, Menem was reelected president on May 14, 1995.

Buenos Aires Mayor Fernando de la Rúa won the presidential election Oct. 24, 1999. A prolonged recession and a debt of more than $130 bil left Argentina facing an economic crisis in 2001, which austerity measures and IMF aid failed to remedy. After widespread rioting and looting Dec. 19, de la Rúa resigned.

A 2-week period of protests and political upheavals abated when Congress, Jan. 1, 2002, chose a Peronist, Eduardo Alberto Duhalde, to finish de la Rúa's term. Duhalde devalued the peso by cutting its ties with the U.S. dollar. Further economic decline and renewed protests led Duhalde July 2 to schedule an early presidential election for Mar. 2003; another Peronist, Néstor Kirchner, took office May 25, 2003, after Menem pulled out of a runoff election. Kirchner moved to end corruption and human rights abuses among the military and police. A new IMF aid deal, approved Sept. 10, 2003, rescued Argentina from default.

Fire at a Buenos Aires nightclub, Dec. 30, 2004, killed 194 people. The supreme court, June 14, 2005, overturned amnesty laws that had barred prosecution for "dirty war" crimes committed while the military ruled Argentina. Robust economic growth, 2004-05, allowed Argentina to repay its $9.57 bil debt to the IMF, Jan. 3, 2006. After Pres. Kirchner declined to seek a second term, his wife, Cristina Fernández de Kirchner, ran as the Peronist candidate in elections scheduled for Oct. 28, 2007.

Armenia
Republic of Armenia

People: Population: 2,971,650. **Age distrib.** (%): <15: 19.5; 65+: 11.2. **Pop. density:** 271 per sq mi, 105 per sq km. **Urban:** 64.1%. **Ethnic groups:** Armenian 98%, Kurd 1%, Russian 1%. **Principal languages:** Armenian, Yezidi, Russian. **Chief religions:** Armenian Apostolic 95%, other Christian 4%, Yezidi 2%.

Geography: Total area: 11,506 sq mi, 29,800 sq km; **Land area:** 10,965 sq mi, 28,400 sq km. **Location:** SW Asia. **Neighbors:** Georgia on N, Azerbaijan on E, Iran on S, Turkey on W. **Topography:** Mountainous with many peaks above 10,000 ft. **Capital:** Yerevan, 1,103,000.

Government: Type: Republic. **Head of state:** Pres. Robert Kocharian; b. Aug. 31, 1954; in office: Apr. 9, 1998. **Head of gov.:** Prime Min. Serzh Sargsyan; b. June 30, 1954; in office: Apr. 4, 2007. **Local divisions:** 10 provinces, 1 city. **Defense budget:** $194 mil. **Active troops:** 43,641.

Economy: Industries: machine tools & machines, electric motors, tires, knitted wear. **Chief crops:** grapes, vegetables. **Natural resources:** gold, copper, molybd., zinc, alumina. **Arable land:** 17%. **Livestock:** cattle: 592,067; chickens: 4.7 mil; goats: 42,704; pigs: 137,508; sheep: 548,862. **Fish catch:** 1,033 metric tons. **Electricity prod.:** 6 bil kWh. **Labor force** (2002 est.): agriculture 45%, industry 25%, services 30%.

Finance: Monetary unit: Dram (AMD) (Sept. 2007: 335.75 = $1 U.S.). **GDP:** $16.9 bil; **per capita GDP:** $5,700; **GDP growth:** 13.4%. **Imports:** $1.7 bil; Russia 20.6%, Ukraine 7.4%, Belgium 7.2%, Turkmenistan 6.7%, Italy 5.8%, Germany 5.4%, Iran 5.4%. **Exports:** $1.1 bil; Germany 16.9%, Netherlands 12.6%, Belgium 12.4%, Russia 12.2%, Georgia 7.5%, Israel 6.6%, U.S. 5.7%, Switzerland 5.2%. **Tourism:** $135 mil. **Budget** (2007 est.): $1.6 bil. **Intl. reserves less gold:** $713 mil. **Consumer prices:** 2.89%.

Transport: Railroad: Length: 521 mi. **Civil aviation:** 444.9 mil pass.-mi; 11 airports.

Communications: TV sets: 241 per 1,000 pop. **Radios:** 239 per 1,000 pop. **Telephone lines:** 594,400. **Internet:** 172,800 users.

Health: Life expect.: 68.5 male; 76.3 female. **Births** (per 1,000 pop.): 12.3. **Deaths** (per 1,000 pop.): 8.3. **Natural inc.:** 0.41%. **Infant mortality** (per 1,000 live births): 21.7. **AIDS rate:** 0.1%.

Education: Compulsory: ages 7-14. **Literacy:** 99.4%.

Major intl. organizations: UN (FAO, IBRD, ILO, IMF, WHO, WTO), CIS, OSCE.

Embassy: 2225 R St. NW 20008; 319-1976.

Website: www.armeniaemb.org

Ancient Armenia extended into parts of what are now Turkey and Iran. Present-day Armenia was set up as a Soviet republic Apr. 2, 1921. It joined Georgian and Azerbaijan SSRs Mar. 12, 1922, to form the Transcaucasian SFSR, which became part of the USSR Dec. 30, 1922. Armenia became a constituent republic of the USSR Dec. 5, 1936. An earthquake struck Armenia Dec. 7, 1988; approximately 55,000 were killed and several cities and towns were left in ruins.

Armenia declared independence Sept. 23, 1991, and became an independent state when the USSR disbanded Dec. 26, 1991. Both mostly Christian Armenia and mostly Muslim Azerbaijan claimed Nagorno-Karabakh, an enclave in Azerbaijan that has an ethnic Armenian majority; it seceded from Azerbaijan in 1988. A 1992-94 war that cost 30,000 lives ended in a cease-fire with Armenian forces in control of the enclave. Voters in the breakaway region approved a pro-independence constitution Dec. 10, 2006, but the referendum was rejected by the EU and OSCE.

Voters approved, July 5, 1995, a new constitution increasing presidential powers. Pres. Levon Ter-Petrosian won reelection on Sept. 22, 1996, amid claims of fraud; he resigned Feb. 3, 1998, in a conflict over Nagorno-Karabakh. Robert Kocharian, a nationalist born in the disputed region, won the presidency on Mar. 30, 1998. Gunmen stormed Parliament Oct. 27, 1999, killing Prime Min. Vazgen Sarkissian and 7 others. Kocharian won a second term Mar. 5, 2003, in a runoff vote viewed as flawed by opposition groups and Western observers.

An Armenian airliner crashed into the Black Sea, May 3, 2006, killing all 113 people on board. Prime Min. Andranik Margaryan died of a heart attack Mar. 25, 2007, and was replaced by Def. Min. Serzh Sargsyan.

Australia
Commonwealth of Australia

People: Population: 20,434,176. **Age distrib.** (%): <15: 19.3; 65+: 13.2. **Pop. density:** 7 per sq mi, 3 per sq km. **Urban:** 88.2%.

Ethnic groups: White 92%, Asian 7%, Aborigine and other 1%.

Principal languages: English, Chinese, Italian, Aboriginal languages. **Chief religions:** Roman Catholic 26%, Anglican 21%, other Christian 21%.

Geography: Total area: 2,967,909 sq mi, 7,686,850 sq km; **Land area:** 2,941,299 sq mi, 7,617,930 sq km. **Location:** SE of Asia, Indian O. is W and S, Pacific O. (Coral, Tasman seas) is E; they meet N of Australia in Timor and Arafura seas. Tasmania lies 150 mi S of Victoria state, across Bass Strait. **Neighbors:** Nearest are Indonesia, Papua New Guinea on N; Solomons, Fiji, and New Zealand on E. **Topography:** An island continent. The Great Dividing Range along the E coast has Mt. Kosciusko, 7,310 ft. The W plateau rises to 2,000 ft, with arid areas in the Great Sandy and Great Victoria deserts. The NW part of Western Australia and Northern Terr. are arid and hot. The NE has heavy rainfall and Cape York Peninsula has jungles. **Capital:** Canberra, 381,000. **Cities (urban aggr.):** Sydney, 4,331,000; Melbourne, 3,626,000; Brisbane, 1,758,000; Perth, 1,474,000; Adelaide, 1,134,000.

Government: Type: Democratic, federal state system. **Head of state:** Queen Elizabeth II, represented by Gov.-Gen. Michael Jeffery; b. Dec. 12, 1937; in office: Aug. 11, 2003. **Head of gov.:** Prime Min. John Howard; b. July 26, 1939; in office: Mar. 11, 1996. **Local divisions:** 6 states, 2 territories. **Defense budget:** $14.1 bil. **Active troops:** 51,610.

Economy: Industries: mining, industrial & transp. equip., food proc., chemicals, steel. **Chief crops:** wheat, barley, sugarcane, fruits. **Natural resources:** bauxite, coal, iron ore, copper, tin, silver, uranium, nickel, tungsten, mineral sands, lead, zinc, diamonds, nat. gas, oil. **Crude oil reserves:** 1.6 bil bbls. **Other resources:** Wool (world's leading producer), beef. **Arable land:** 6%. **Livestock:** cattle: 28.6 mil; chickens: 74.5 mil; goats: 461,491; pigs: 2.5 mil; sheep: 100.1 mil. **Fish catch:** 293,022 metric tons. **Electricity prod.:** 236.7 bil kWh. **Labor force** (2004 est.): agriculture 3.6%, industry 21.2%, services 75.2%.

Finance: Monetary unit: Dollar (AUD) (Sept. 2007: 1.19 = $1 U.S.). **GDP:** $674.6 bil; **per capita GDP:** $33,300; **GDP growth:** 2.7%. **Imports:** $127.7 bil; China 14.4%, U.S. 14.1%, Japan 9.6%, Singapore 6%, Germany 5.1%. **Exports:** $117 bil; Japan 19.6%, China 12.3%, South Korea 7.5%, U.S. 6.2%, India 5.5%, New Zealand 5.5%, UK 5%. **Tourism:** $12.7 bil. **Budget:** $258 bil. **Intl.**

reserves less gold: $35.53 bil. **Gold:** 2.57 mil oz t. **Consumer prices:** 3.54%.

Transport: Railroad: Length: 29,663 mi. **Motor vehicles:** 10.6 mil pass. cars; 2.5 mil comm. vehicles. **Civil aviation:** 52.1 bil pass.-mi; 311 airports. **Chief ports:** Brisbane, Fremantle, Gladstone, Melbourne, Sydney.

Communications: TV sets: 716 per 1,000 pop. **Radios:** 1,391 per 1,000 pop. **Telephone lines:** 9.9 mil. **Daily newspaper circ.:** 161 per 1,000 pop. **Internet:** 15.3 mil users.

Health: Life expect.: 77.8 male; 83.6 female. **Births** (per 1,000 pop.): 12. **Deaths** (per 1,000 pop.): 7.6. **Natural inc.:** 0.45%. **Infant mortality** (per 1,000 live births): 4.6. **AIDS rate:** 0.1%.

Education: Compulsory: ages 5-15. **Literacy:** 99%.

Major intl. organizations: UN and all of its specialized agencies, APEC, the Commonwealth, OECD.

Embassy: 1601 Massachusetts Ave. NW 20036; 797-3000.

Website: www.australia.gov.au

Australia harbors many plant and animal species not found elsewhere, including kangaroos, koalas, platypuses, dingos (wild dogs), Tasmanian devils (raccoon-like marsupials), wombats (bear-like marsupials), and barking and frilled lizards.

Capt. James Cook explored the eastern coast in 1770, when the continent was inhabited by a variety of indigenous peoples. The first European settlers, beginning in 1788, were mostly convicts, soldiers, and government officials. By 1830, Britain had claimed the entire continent, and the immigration of free settlers began to accelerate. The Commonwealth was proclaimed Jan. 1, 1901. Northern Terr. was granted limited self-rule July 1, 1978.

State/territory, capital	Area (sq mi)	Population (Dec. 2006 est.)
New South Wales, Sydney	309,500	6,854,800
Victoria, Melbourne	87,900	5,165,400
Queensland, Brisbane	666,990	4,132,000
Western Australia, Perth	975,100	2,081,900
South Australia, Adelaide	379,900	1,575,700
Tasmania, Hobart	26,200	491,700
Australian Capital Terr., Canberra	900	336,400
Northern Terr., Darwin	519,800	212,600

Racially discriminatory immigration policies were abandoned in 1973, after 3 mil Europeans (half British) had entered since 1945. The 50,000 aborigines and 150,000 part-aborigines are mostly detribalized, but there are several preserves in the Northern Territory. They remain economically disadvantaged.

Australia's agricultural success makes the country among the top exporters of beef, lamb, wool, and wheat. Major mineral deposits have been developed, largely for export. Industrialization has been completed. The nation endured a deep recession 1990-93 but has rebounded strongly.

The Labor Party won a majority in Feb. 1983 general elections and was reelected in 1984, 1987, 1990, and 1993. After an election that focused mainly on economic issues, conservatives swept into power in elections Mar. 2, 1996. Incumbent Prime Min. John Howard retained power in the 1998, 2001, and 2004 elections.

Australia led an international peacekeeping force into Timor in Sept. 1999. In a referendum Nov. 6, voters rejected a proposal that would have made Australia a republic. Sydney hosted the Olympics Sept. 15-Oct. 1, 2000.

Australian troops fought in U.S.-led military operations in Afghanistan (2001) and Iraq (2003). Some 2,000 Australian peacekeepers began arriving in the Solomon Is., July 24, 2003; nearly all had been withdrawn by mid-2005. In race riots in Sydney suburbs, Dec. 11-12, 2005, thousands of white youths assaulted people of Middle Eastern ancestry, who then retaliated against whites. Australian troops were dispatched, 2006, to suppress disorders in the Solomon Is. in April and Timor in May. A severe drought spurred water-conservation measures in 2006-07.

Australian External Territories

Norfolk Isl., area 13 sq mi, pop. (2007 est.) 2,114, was taken over, 1914. The soil is very fertile, suitable for citrus, bananas, and coffee. Many of the inhabitants are descendants of the *Bounty* mutineers, moved to Norfolk 1856 from Pitcairn Isl. Australia offered the island limited home rule in 1978.

Coral Sea Isls. Territory, area 1 sq mi, is administered from Norfolk Isl.

Territory of Ashmore and Cartier Isls., area 2 sq mi, in the Indian O., came under Australian authority 1934 and are administered as part of Northern Territory. **Heard Isl. and McDonald Isls.,** area 159 sq mi, are administered by the Dept. of Science.

Cocos (Keeling) Isls., 27 small coral islands in the Indian O. 1,750 mi NW of Australia. Pop. (2007 est.) 596; area 5 sq mi. The residents voted to become part of Australia, Apr. 1984.

Christmas Isl., area 52 sq mi (2007 est.) 1,402; 230 mi S of Java, was transferred by Britain in 1958. It has phosphate deposits.

Australian Antarctic Territory was claimed by Australia in 1933, including 2,362,000 sq mi of territory S of 60th parallel S Lat. and between 160th-45th meridians E Long. It does not include Adelie Coast.

Austria
Republic of Austria

People: Population: 8,199,783. **Age distrib. (%):** <15: 15.1; 65+: 17.5. **Pop. density:** 258 per sq mi, 99 per sq km. **Urban:** 66%. **Ethnic groups:** Austrian 91%, fmr. Yugoslav 4%, Turk 2%, German 1%. **Principal languages:** German, Turkish, Serbian, Croatian. **Chief religions:** Roman Catholic 74%, Protestant 5%.

Geography: Total area: 32,382 sq mi, 83,870 sq km; **Land area:** 31,832 sq mi, 82,444 sq km. **Location:** In S Central Europe. **Neighbors:** Switzerland, Liechtenstein on W; Germany, Czech Rep. on N; Slovakia, Hungary on E; Slovenia, Italy on S. **Topography:** Austria is primarily mountainous, with the Alps and foothills covering the western and southern provinces. The eastern provinces and Vienna are located in the Danube River Basin. **Capital:** Vienna, 2,260,000.

Government: Type: Federal republic. **Head of state:** Pres. Heinz Fischer; b. Oct. 9, 1938; in office: July 8, 2004. **Head of gov.:** Chancellor Alfred Gusenbauer; b. Feb. 8, 1960; in office: Jan. 11, 2007. **Local divisions:** 9 bundeslaender (states). **Defense budget:** $2.32 bil. **Active troops:** 39,600.

Economy: Industries: constr., machinery, vehicles & parts, food, chemicals. **Chief crops:** grains, potatoes, sugar beets, wine. **Natural resources:** iron ore, oil, timber, magnesite, lead, coal, lignite, copper, hydropower. **Crude oil reserves:** 50 mil bbls. **Arable land:** 17%. **Livestock:** cattle: 2 mil; chickens: 14.3 mil; goats: 55,100; pigs: 3.2 mil; sheep: 325,728. **Fish catch:** 2,790 metric tons. **Electricity prod.:** 61 bil kWh. **Labor force (2005 est.):** agriculture 3%, industry 27%, services 70%.

Finance: Monetary unit: Euro (EUR) (Sept. 2007: 0.72 = $1 U.S.). **GDP:** $283.8 bil; **per capita GDP:** $34,600; **GDP growth:** 3.3%. **Imports:** $134.3 bil; Germany 46.5%, Italy 6.8%, Switzerland 4.4%, Netherlands 4%. **Exports:** $133.3 bil; Germany 31.7%, Italy 8.8%, U.S. 5.7%, Switzerland 4.6%, France 4%. **Tourism:** $15.3 bil. **Budget:** $161.6 bil. **Intl. reserves less gold:** $4.66 bil. **Gold:** 9.28 mil oz t. **Consumer prices:** 1.45%.

Transport: Railroad: Length: 3,735 mi. **Motor vehicles:** 4.1 mil pass. cars; 775,000 comm. vehicles. **Civil aviation:** 9 bil pass.-mi; 25 airports. **Chief ports:** Enns, Krems, Linz, Vienna.

Communications: TV sets: 526 per 1,000 pop. **Radios:** 751 per 1,000 pop. **Telephone lines:** 3.6 mil. **Daily newspaper circ.:** 309 per 1,000 pop. **Internet:** 4.2 mil users.

Health: Life expect.: 76.3 male; 82.3 female. **Births** (per 1,000 pop.): 8.7. **Deaths** (per 1,000 pop.): 9.8. **Natural inc.:** –0.12%. **Infant mortality** (per 1,000 live births): 4.5. **AIDS rate:** 0.3%.

Education: Compulsory: ages 6-14. **Literacy:** 98%.

Major intl. organizations: UN and all of its specialized agencies, EU, OECD, OSCE.

Embassy: 3524 International Ct. NW 20008; 895-6700.

Website: www.austria.gv.at

Rome conquered Austrian lands from Celtic tribes around 15 BC. In 788 the territory was incorporated into Charlemagne's empire. By 1300, the House of Hapsburg had gained control; they added vast territories in all parts of Europe to their realm in the next few hundred years.

Austrian dominance of Germany was undermined in the 18th cent. and ended by Prussia by 1866. But the Congress of Vienna, 1815, confirmed Austrian control of a large empire in southeast Europe consisting of Germans, Hungarians, Slavs, Italians, and others. The dual Austro-Hungarian monarchy was established in 1867, giving autonomy to Hungary and almost 50 years of peace.

World War I, started after the June 28, 1914, assassination of Archduke Franz Ferdinand, the Hapsburg heir, by a Serbian nationalist, destroyed the empire. By 1918 Austria was reduced to a small republic, with the borders it has today.

Nazi Germany, ruled by the Austrian-born Adolf Hitler, annexed Austria Mar. 13, 1938. The republic was reestablished in 1945, under Allied occupation. Full independence and neutrality were restored in 1955. Austria joined the EU Jan. 1, 1995.

The rise of the right-wing, anti-immigrant Austrian Freedom Party challenged the dominance of the Austrian Social Democratic Party in the late 1990s. When Freedom Party members joined the cabinet, Feb. 4, 2000, the EU imposed political sanctions on Austria for 7 months. Social Democrats won the parliamentary elections of Oct. 1, 2006.

Azerbaijan
Republic of Azerbaijan

People: Population: 8,120,247. **Age distrib. (%):** <15: 25.4; 65+: 7. **Pop. density:** 244 per sq mi, 94 per sq km. **Urban:** 51.5%. **Ethnic groups:** Azeri 91%, Dagestani 2%, Russian 2%. **Principal languages:** Azeri (official), Lezgi, Russian, Armenian. **Chief religions:** Muslim 93%, Russian Orthodox 3%, Armenian Orthodox 2%.

Geography: Total area: 33,436 sq mi, 86,600 sq km; **Land area:** 33,243 sq mi, 86,100 sq km. **Location:** SW Asia. **Neighbors:** Russia, Georgia on N; Iran on S; Armenia on W; Caspian Sea on E. **Topography:** The Great Caucasus Mts. in N, Karabakh Upland in W border the Kur-Abas lowland; climate is arid except in the subtropical SE. **Capital:** Baku, 1,856,000.

Government: Type: Republic. **Head of state:** Pres. Ilham Aliyev; b. Dec. 24, 1961; in office: Oct. 31, 2003. **Head of gov.:** Prime Min. Artur Rasizade; b. Feb. 26, 1935; in office: Nov. 4, 2003.

Local division: 59 rayons, 11 cities, 1 autonomous republic. **Defense budget:** $306 mil. **Active troops:** 66,740.

Economy: Industries: oil products, oil field equip., steel, iron ore, cement. **Chief crops:** cotton, grain, rice, grapes. **Natural resources:** oil, nat. gas, iron ore, nonferrous metals, alumina. **Crude oil reserves:** 7 bil bbls. **Arable land:** 21%. **Livestock:** cattle: 2.1 mil; chickens: 18.3 mil; goats: 577,917; pigs: 21,317; sheep: 7.3 mil. **Fish catch:** 9,016 metric tons. **Electricity prod.:** 20.1 bil kWh. **Labor force (2001):** agriculture 41%, industry 7%, services 52%.

Finance: Monetary unit: New Manat (AZN) (Sept. 2007: 0.85 = $1 U.S.). **GDP:** $59.7 bil; **per capita GDP:** $7,500; **GDP growth:** 34.5%. **Imports:** $5.2 bil; Russia 19.6%, UK 12.6%, Turkey 9.9%, Germany 8.7%, Singapore 6.2%. **Exports:** $12.5 bil; Italy 30.1%, France 11.7%, Czech Rep. 10.1%, Germany 7.9%, U.S. 7.7%. **Tourism:** $60 mil. **Budget:** $5.8 bil. **Intl. reserves less gold:** $1.66 bil. **Consumer prices:** 8.3%.

Transport: Railroad: Length: 1,837 mi. **Motor vehicles:** 404,000 pass. cars; 108,000 comm. vehicles. **Civil aviation:** 466.6 mil pass.-mi; 27 airports. **Chief port:** Baku.

Communications: TV sets: 257 per 1,000 pop. **Radios:** 23 per 1,000 pop. **Telephone lines:** 1.2 mil. **Daily newspaper circ.:** 9.9 per 1,000 pop. **Internet:** 829,100 users.

Health: Life expect.: 61.9 male; 70.7 female. **Births** (per 1,000 pop.): 17.5. **Deaths** (per 1,000 pop.): 8.4. **Natural inc.:** 0.91%. **Infant mortality** (per 1,000 live births): 58.3. **AIDS rate:** 0.1%.

Education: Compulsory: ages 6-16. **Literacy:** 98.8%.

Major intl. organizations: UN (FAO, IBRD, ILO, IMF, IMO, WHO), CIS, OSCE.

Embassy: 2741 34th St NW 20008; 337-3500.

Website: www.president.az

Azerbaijan was the home of Scythian tribes and part of the Roman Empire. Overrun by Turks in the 11th cent. and conquered by Russia in 1806 and 1813, it joined the USSR Dec. 30, 1922, and became a constituent republic in 1936. Azerbaijan declared independence Aug. 30, 1991, and became an independent state when the Soviet Union disbanded Dec. 26, 1991.

Nagorno-Karabakh, an enclave with a majority population of ethnic Armenians, seceded from Azerbaijan in 1988, triggering a war between mostly Muslim Azerbaijan and most Christian Armenia, 1992-94, in which 30,000 lives were lost (see Armenia).

A National Council in Azerbaijan ousted Communist Pres. Mutaibov and took power May 19, 1992. Abulfez Elchibey became the nation's first democratically elected president June 7 but was ousted from office by Surat Huseynov, commander of a private militia, June 30, 1993. Huseynov became prime minister, and Haydar Aliyev, a pro-Russian former Communist, became president. Huseynov fled the country after his supporters staged an unsuccessful coup attempt Oct. 1994. Voters approved a new constitution expanding presidential powers, Nov. 12, 1995. Pres. Aliyev was reelected Oct. 11, 1998, but international monitors called the vote seriously flawed.

The dying Pres. Aliyev named his son Ilham prime minister Aug. 4, 2003. The younger Aliyev won the presidential election of Oct. 15, in a vote considered fraudulent by international observers; he responded to violent protests Oct. 16 by arresting hundreds of opposition leaders and their supporters. Serious abuses also marred the parliamentary elections of Nov. 6, 2005, won by parties loyal to Aliyev. The opening May 25, 2005, of the Baku-Tbilisi-Ceyhan pipeline, providing an outlet for Azerbaijan's vast Caspian oil reserves, is expected to transform the nation's economy.

The Bahamas
Commonwealth of The Bahamas

People: Population: 305,655. **Age distrib. (%):** <15: 27; 65+: 6.5. **Pop. density:** 79 per sq mi, 30 per sq km. **Urban:** 90.4%. **Ethnic groups:** Black 85%, white 12%. **Principal languages:** English, Creole (among Haitian immigrants). **Chief religions:** Baptist 35%, Anglican 15%, Roman Catholic 14%, other Christian 15%.

Geography: Total area: 5,382 sq mi, 13,940 sq km; **Land area:** 3,888 sq mi, 10,070 sq km. **Location:** In Atlantic O., E of Florida. **Neighbors:** Nearest are U.S. on W, Cuba on S. **Topography:** Nearly 700 islands (29 inhabited) and over 2,000 islets in the W Atlantic O. extend 760 mi NW to SE. **Capital:** Nassau, 233,000.

Government: Type: Independent commonwealth. **Head of state:** Queen Elizabeth II, represented by Gov.-Gen. Arthur Dion Hanna; b. Mar. 7, 1928; in office: Feb. 1, 2006. **Head of gov.:** Prime Min. Hubert Alexander Ingraham; b. Aug. 4, 1947; in office: May 4, 2007. **Local divisions:** 21 districts. **Defense budget:** $42 mil. **Active troops:** 860.

Economy: Industries: tourism, banking, cement, oil refining & shipment, salt, rum. **Chief crops:** citrus, vegetables. **Natural resources:** salt, aragonite, timber. **Arable land:** 1%. **Livestock:** cattle: 750; chickens: 3 mil; goats: 14,500; pigs: 5,000; sheep: 6,500. **Fish catch:** 11,357 metric tons. **Electricity prod.:** 1.9 bil kWh. **Labor force (2005 est.):** agriculture 5%, industry 5%, tourism 50%, other services 40%.

Finance: Monetary unit: Dollar (BSD) (Sept. 2007: 1.00 = $1 U.S.). **GDP:** $6.6 bil; **per capita GDP:** $21,600; **GDP growth:** 4%. **Imports** (2005 est.): $2.2 bil; U.S. 20.9%, South Korea 17.9%, Brazil 16.8%, Japan 11.1%, Spain 6.1%. **Exports** (2005): $451

mil; Spain 23.3%, U.S. 20.7%, Poland 14.1%, Germany 7.2%, UK 6%, Guatemala 5.1%. **Tourism:** $2.1 bil. **Budget** (FY04/05): $1 bil. **Intl. reserves less gold:** $307 mil. **Consumer prices:** 2.39%.
Transport: Motor vehicles: 112,800 pass. cars; 3,500 comm. vehicles. **Civil aviation:** 241.1 mil pass.-mi; 29 airports. **Chief ports:** Freeport, Nassau.
Communications: TV sets: 243 per 1,000 pop. **Radios:** 739 per 1,000 pop. **Telephone lines:** 133,100. **Internet:** 103,000 users.
Health: Life expect.: 62.4 male; 69 female. **Births** (per 1,000 pop.): 17.3. **Deaths** (per 1,000 pop.): 9.1. **Natural inc.:** 0.82%. **Infant mortality** (per 1,000 live births): 24.2. **AIDS rate:** 3.3%.
Education: Compulsory: ages 5-16. **Literacy:** 95.6%.
Major intl. organizations: UN (FAO, IBRD, ILO, IMF, IMO, WHO), Caricom, the Commonwealth, OAS.
Embassy: 2220 Massachusetts Ave. NW 20008; 319-2660.
Website: www.bahamas.com.bs
Christopher Columbus first set foot in the New World on San Salvador (Watling Isl.) in 1492, when Arawak Indians inhabited the islands. British settlement began in 1647; the islands became a British colony in 1783. Internal self-government was granted in 1964; full independence within the Commonwealth was attained July 10, 1973. International banking and investment management have become major industries alongside tourism.

Bahrain
Kingdom of Bahrain

People: Population: 708,573. **Age distrib.** (%): <15: 26.9; 65+: 3.7. **Pop. density:** 2,757 per sq mi, 1,066 per sq km. **Urban:** 96.5%. **Ethnic groups:** Bahraini 62%, non-Bahraini 38%. **Principal languages:** Arabic (official), English, Farsi, Urdu. **Chief religions:** Muslim (Shi'a and Sunni) 81%, Christian 9%.
Geography: Total area: 257 sq mi, 665 sq km; **Land area:** 257 sq mi, 665 sq km. **Location:** SW Asia, in Persian Gulf. **Neighbors:** Nearest are Saudi Arabia on W, Qatar on E. **Topography:** Bahrain Island, and several adjacent, smaller islands, are flat, hot, and humid, with little rain. **Capital:** Manama, 162,000.
Government: Type: Constitutional monarchy. **Head of state:** King Hamad bin Isa al-Khalifa; b. Jan. 28, 1950; in office: as emir Mar. 6, 1999; as king Feb. 14, 2002. **Head of gov.:** Prime Min. Khalifa bin Sulman al-Khalifa; b. 1936; in office: Jan. 19, 1970. **Local divisions:** 12 municipalities. **Defense budget:** $478 mil. **Active troops:** 11,200.
Economy: Industries: oil proc. & refining, aluminum smelting, offshore banking, ship repair. **Chief crops:** fruit, vegetables. **Natural resources:** oil, nat. gas, fish, pearls. **Crude oil reserves:** 124.6 mil bbls. **Arable land:** 3%. **Livestock:** cattle: 9,000; chickens: 470,000; goats: 26,000; sheep: 40,000. **Fish catch:** 11,857 metric tons. **Electricity prod.:** 8.2 bil kWh. **Labor force** (1997 est.): agriculture 1%, industry 79%, services 20%.
Finance: Monetary unit: Dinar (BHD) (Sept. 2007: 0.38 = $1 U.S.). **GDP:** $18 bil; **per capita GDP:** $25,800; **GDP growth:** 7.8%. **Imports:** $9 bil; Saudi Arabia 37.3%, Japan 6.8%, U.S. 6.2%, UK 6.2%, Germany 5%. **Exports:** $12.6 bil; U.S. 3.1%, South Korea 2.3%, Japan 2%. **Tourism:** $864 mil. **Budget:** $4.2 bil. **Intl. reserves less gold** (2004): $1.25 bil. **Gold:** 150,000 oz t. **Consumer prices** (2005): 2.59%.
Transport: Motor vehicles: 187,000 pass. cars; 38,400 comm. vehicles. **Civil aviation:** 2.8 bil pass.-mi; 3 airports. **Chief ports:** Manama, Sitrah.
Communications: TV sets: 446 per 1,000 pop. **Radios:** 64 per 1,000 pop. **Telephone lines:** 193,300. **Internet:** 157,300 users.
Health: Life expect.: 72.2 male; 77.3 female. **Births** (per 1,000 pop.): 17.5. **Deaths** (per 1,000 pop.): 4.2. **Natural inc.:** 1.33%. **Infant mortality** (per 1,000 live births): 16.2. **AIDS rate:** NA.
Education: Compulsory: ages 6-17. **Literacy:** 86.5%.
Major intl. organizations: UN (FAO, IBRD, ILO, IMF, WHO, WTO), AL.
Embassy: 3502 International Dr. NW 20008; 342-1111.
Website: www.bahrainembassy.org
Long ruled by the Khalifa family, Bahrain was a British protectorate from 1861 to Aug. 15, 1971, when it regained independence.
Pearls, shrimp, fruits, and vegetables were the mainstays of the economy until oil was discovered in 1932. By the 1970s, oil reserves were depleted; international banking flourished.
Bahrain took part in the 1973-74 Arab oil embargo against the U.S. and other nations. The government bought controlling interest in the oil industry in 1975. Shiite dissidents have clashed with the Sunni-led government since 1996.
Emir Hamad bin Isa al-Khalifa proclaimed himself king Feb. 14, 2002. Local elections in May marked the first time Bahraini women were allowed to vote and run for office. The first female judge was appointed June 6, 2006.

Bangladesh
People's Republic of Bangladesh

People: Population: 150,448,339. **Age distrib.** (%): <15: 33.1; 65+: 3.5. **Pop. density:** 2,910 per sq mi, 1,124 per sq km. **Urban:** 25.1%. **Ethnic groups:** Bengali 98%. **Principal languages:** Bangla (official, also known as Bengali), English. **Chief religions:** Muslim 83% (official), Hindu 16%.

Geography: Total area: 55,599 sq mi, 144,000 sq km; **Land area:** 51,703 sq mi, 133,910 sq km. **Location:** In S Asia, on N bend of Bay of Bengal. **Neighbors:** India nearly surrounds country on W, N, E; Myanmar on SE. **Topography:** The country is mostly a low plain cut by the Ganges and Brahmaputra rivers and their delta. The land is alluvial and marshy along the coast, with hills only in the extreme SE and NE. A tropical monsoon climate prevails, among the rainiest in the world. **Capital:** Dhaka, 4,030,000. **Cities (urban aggr.):** Chittagong, 4,114,000; Khulna, 1,494,000.
Government: Type: In transition. **Head of state:** Pres. Iajuddin Ahmed; b. Feb. 1,1931; in office: Sept. 6, 2002. **Head of gov.:** Chief Adviser Fakhruddin Ahmed; b. May 1, 1940; in office: Jan. 12, 2007. **Local divisions:** 6 divisions. **Defense budget:** $843 mil. **Active troops:** 126,500.
Economy: Industries: cotton textiles, jute, garments, tea processing, newsprint, cement, chemical fertilizer, light engineering, sugar. **Chief crops:** rice, jute, tea, wheat, sugarcane, potatoes, tobacco. **Natural resources:** nat. gas, timber, coal. **Crude oil reserves:** 28 mil bbls. **Arable land:** 55%. **Livestock:** cattle: 24.5 mil; chickens: 142 mil; goats: 36.9 mil; sheep: 1.3 mil. **Fish catch:** 2,215,957 metric tons. **Electricity prod.:** 21.4 bil kWh. **Labor force** (1995-96): agriculture 63%, industry 11%, services 26%.
Finance: Monetary unit: Taka (BDT) (Sept. 2007: 68.50 = $1 U.S.). **GDP:** $336.7 bil; **per capita GDP:** $2,300; **GDP growth:** 6.6%. **Imports:** $13.8 bil; China 18%, India 12.7%, Kuwait 8%, Singapore 5.6%, Hong Kong 4.2%. **Exports:** $11.2 bil; U.S. 25.2%, Germany 12.7%, UK 9.9%, France 5%. **Tourism:** $70 mil. **Budget:** $8.7 bil. **Intl. reserves less gold:** $2.53 bil. **Gold:** 110,000 oz t. **Consumer prices:** 6.77%.
Transport: Railroad: Length: 1,720 mi. **Motor vehicles:** 65,000 pass. cars; 145,900 comm. vehicles. **Civil aviation:** 2.9 bil pass.-mi; 15 airports. **Chief ports:** Chittagong, Mongla Port.
Communications: TV sets: 7 per 1,000 pop. **Radios:** 50 per 1,000 pop. **Telephone lines:** 1.1 mil. **Internet:** 450,000 users.
Health: Life expect.: 62.8 male; 62.9 female. **Births** (per 1,000 pop.): 29.4. **Deaths** (per 1,000 pop.): 8.1. **Natural inc.:** 2.12%. **Infant mortality** (per 1,000 live births): 59.1. **AIDS rate:** <0.1%.
Education: Compulsory: ages 6-10. **Literacy:** 47.5%.
Major intl. organizations: UN (FAO, IBRD, ILO, IMF, IMO, WHO, WTO), the Commonwealth.
Embassy: 3510 International Dr. NW 20008; 244-0183.
Website: www.bangladesh.gov.bd
Muslim invaders conquered the formerly Hindu area in the 12th cent. British rule lasted from the 18th cent. to 1947, when East Bengal became part of Pakistan.
Opposing domination by West Pakistan, the Awami League, based in the East, won control of the National Assembly in 1971. Assembly sessions were postponed; riots broke out. Pakistani troops attacked Mar. 25; Bangladesh independence was proclaimed the next day. In the ensuing civil war, 1 mil died and 10 mil fled to India.
War between India and Pakistan broke out Dec. 3, 1971. Pakistan surrendered in the East on Dec. 16. Mujibur Rahman, known as Sheikh Mujib, became prime minister; he was killed in a coup Aug. 15, 1975. During the 1970s the country moved into the Indian and Soviet orbits in response to U.S. support of Pakistan, and much of the economy was nationalized.
On May 30, 1981, Pres. Ziaur Rahman was killed in an unsuccessful coup attempt by army rivals. Vice Pres. Abdus Sattar assumed the presidency but was ousted in a coup led by army chief of staff Gen. H. M. Ershad, Mar. 1982. Ershad declared Bangladesh an Islamic Republic in 1988; a parliamentary system of government was adopted in 1991.
Bangladesh is subject to devastating storms and floods that kill thousands. A cyclone struck Apr. 1991, killing over 131,000 people and causing $2.7 bil in damages.
Political turmoil led to the resignation, Mar. 30, 1996, of Prime Min. Khaleda Zia, the widow of Ziaur Rahman. Sheikh Mujib's daughter, Hasina (known as Sheikh Hasina), led the country after the June 12, 1996 election. A cyclone in May 1997 left an estimated 800,000 people homeless. Floods in July-Sept. 1998 inundated most of the country, killed over 1,400 people (many through disease), and stranded at least 30 mil.
Khaleda Zia returned to power following the parliamentary elections of Oct. 1, 2001. Floods July-Aug. 2004 caused at least 950 deaths and $7 bil in property damage. Militant Islamists set off more than 400 small bombs in over 50 cities and towns, Aug. 17, 2005, killing 3 people. Another wave of jihadist bombings, Nov. 29-Dec. 8, killed 22. A Bangladeshi economist, Muhammad Yunus, and his Grameen Bank won the 2006 Nobel Peace Prize for using very small loans (microcredit) to help alleviate poverty, a severe problem in this densely populated country.
Escalating political violence led Pres. Iajuddin Ahmed to declare a state of emergency Jan. 11, 2007, and indefinitely postpone parliamentary elections, which had been scheduled for Jan. 22. A military-backed caretaker government filed criminal charges against Khaleda Zia and Sheikh Hasina, but failed in an attempt to force the two former prime ministers into exile. Monsoon flooding, July-Sept., left at least 840 people dead.

Barbados

People: Population: 280,946. **Age distrib.** (%): <15: 19.7; 65+: 8.9. **Pop. density:** 1,692 per sq mi, 652 per sq km. **Urban:** 52.7%. **Ethnic groups:** Black 90%, white 4%. **Principal language:** English. **Chief religions:** Protestant 67%, Roman Catholic 4%, none 17%, other 12%.

Geography: Total area: 166 sq mi, 431 sq km; **Land area:** 166 sq mi, 431 sq km. **Location:** In Atlantic O., farthest E of West Indies. **Neighbors:** Nearest are St. Lucia and St. Vincent & the Grenadines to the W. **Topography:** The island lies alone in the Atlantic almost completely surrounded by coral reefs. Highest point is Mt. Hillaby, 1,115 ft. **Capital:** Bridgetown, 142,000.

Government: Type: Parliamentary democracy. **Head of state:** Queen Elizabeth II, represented by Gov.-Gen. Sir Clifford Husbands; b. Aug. 5, 1926; in office: June 1, 1996. **Head of gov.:** Prime Min. Owen Arthur; b. Oct. 17, 1949; in office: Sept. 7, 1994. **Local divisions:** 11 parishes and Bridgetown. **Defense budget:** $25 mil. **Active troops:** 610.

Economy: Industries: tourism, sugar, light mfg., component assembly. **Chief crops:** sugarcane, vegetables, cotton. **Natural resources:** oil, fish, nat. gas. **Crude oil reserves:** 2.9 mil bbls. **Other resources:** Fish. **Arable land:** 37%. **Livestock:** cattle: 10,300; chickens: 3.4 mil; cows: 5,100; pigs: 19,000; sheep: 10,800. **Fish catch:** 1,869 metric tons. **Electricity prod.:** 950 mil kWh. **Labor force** (1996 est.): agriculture 10%, industry 15%, services 75%.

Finance: Monetary unit: Dollar (BBD) (Sept. 2007: 2.00 = $1 U.S.). **GDP:** $5.1 bil. **per capita GDP:** $18,400; **GDP growth:** 3.5%. **Imports** (2004 est.): $1.5 bil; US 29.5%, Trinidad and Tobago 26.4%, UK 5.8%, China 5%. **Exports** (2004 est.): $209 mil; Trinidad and Tobago 16.3%, UK 11.1%, U.S. 10.9%, Saint Lucia 9.2%, Jamaica 8.7%, Grenada 5.1%, Saint Vincent and the Grenadines 5%. **Tourism:** $776 mil. **Budget** (2000 est.): $886 mil. **Intl. reserves less gold:** $423 mil. **Consumer prices:** 7.31%.

Transport: Motor vehicles: 62,100 pass. cars; 9,400 comm. vehicles. **Civil aviation:** 1 airport. **Chief port:** Bridgetown.

Communications: TV sets: 290 per 1,000 pop. **Radios:** 651 per 1,000 pop. **Telephone lines:** 134,900. **Daily newspaper circ.:** 155 per 1,000 pop. **Internet:** 160,000 users.

Health: Life expect.: 71 male; 75 female. **Births** (per 1,000 pop.): 12.6. **Deaths** (per 1,000 pop.): 0.4%. **Infant mortality** (per 1,000 live births): 11.6. **AIDS rate:** 1.5%.

Education: Compulsory: ages 5-16. **Literacy:** 99.7%.

Major intl. organizations: UN (FAO, IBRD, ILO, IMF, IMO, WHO, WTO), Caricom, the Commonwealth, OAS.

Embassy: 2144 Wyoming Ave. NW 20008; 939-9200.

Website: www.barbados.gov.bb

Barbados was probably named by Portuguese sailors in reference to bearded fig trees. An English ship visited in 1605, and British settlers arrived on the uninhabited island in 1627. Slaves worked the sugar plantations until slavery was abolished in 1834. Self-rule came gradually, with full independence proclaimed Nov. 30, 1966. British traditions have remained.

Belarus
Republic of Belarus

People: Population: 9,724,723. **Age distrib.** (%): <15: 14.7; 65+: 14.9. **Pop. density:** 121 per sq mi, 47 per sq km. **Urban:** 72.2%. **Ethnic groups:** Belarusian 81%, Russian 11%, Polish 4%. **Principal languages:** Belarusian, Russian. **Chief religions:** Eastern Orthodox 80%, other 20%.

Geography: Total area: 80,155 sq mi, 207,600 sq km; **Land area:** 80,155 sq mi, 207,600 sq km. **Location:** E Europe. **Neighbors:** Poland on W; Latvia, Lithuania on N; Russia on E; Ukraine on S. **Topography:** Belarus is a landlocked country consisting mostly of hilly lowland with significant marsh areas in S. **Capital:** Minsk, 1,778,000.

Government: Type: Republic. **Head of state:** Pres. Aleksandr Lukashenko; b. Aug. 30, 1954; in office: July 20,1994. **Head of gov.:** Prime Min. Syarhey Sidorski; b. Mar. 13, 1954; in office: Dec. 19, 2003 (acting from July 10, 2003). **Local divisions:** 6 oblasts and 1 municipality. **Defense budget:** $279 mil. **Active troops:** 72,940.

Economy: Industries: machine tools, tractors, trucks, earthmovers, motorcycles. **Chief crops:** grain, potatoes, vegetables, sugar beets, flax. **Natural resources:** timber, peat, oil, nat. gas, granite, dolomitic limestone, marl, chalk, sand, gravel, clay. **Crude oil reserves:** 198 mil bbls. **Arable land:** 27%. **Livestock:** cattle: 4 mil; chickens: 28.5 mil; goats: 67,600; pigs: 3.5 mil; sheep: 53,100. **Fish catch:** 5,050 metric tons. **Electricity prod.:** 29.1 bil kWh. **Labor force** (2003 est.): agriculture 14%, industry 34.7%, services 51.3%.

Finance: Monetary unit: Ruble (BYR) (Sept. 2007: 2,150.28 = $1 U.S.). **GDP:** $82.9 bil; **per capita GDP:** $8,100; **GDP growth:** 9.9%. **Imports:** $21.1 bil; Russia 58.6%, Germany 7.5%, Ukraine 5.5%. **Exports:** $19.6 bil; Russia 34.7%, Netherlands 17.7%, UK 7.5%, Ukraine 6.3%, Poland 5.2%. **Tourism:** $251 mil. **Budget:** $7.2 bil. **Intl. reserves less gold:** $730 mil. **Consumer prices:** 7.02%.

Transport: Railroad: Length: 3,425 mi. **Motor vehicles:** 1.7 mil pass. cars. **Civil aviation:** 210 mil pass.-mi; 41 airports. **Chief port:** Mazyr.

Communications: TV sets: 331 per 1,000 pop. **Radios:** 292 per 1,000 pop. **Telephone lines:** 3.4 mil. **Daily newspaper circ.:** 153.9 per 1,000 pop. **Internet:** 5.5 mil users.

Health: Life expect.: 64.3 male; 76.1 female. **Births** (per 1,000 pop.): 9.5. **Deaths** (per 1,000 pop.): 14. **Natural inc.:** −0.45%. **Infant mortality** (per 1,000 live births): 6.6. **AIDS rate:** 0.3%.

Education: Compulsory: ages 6-15. **Literacy:** 99.6%.

Major intl. organizations: UN (FAO, IBRD, ILO, IMF, WHO), CIS, OSCE.

Embassy: 1619 New Hampshire Ave. NW 20009; 986-1604.

Website: www.belarusembassy.org

The region was subject to Lithuanians and Poles in medieval times, and was a prize of war between Russia and Poland beginning in 1503. It became part of the USSR in 1922, although the western part of the region was controlled by Poland. Belarus was overrun by German armies in 1941; recovered by Soviet troops in 1944. Following WWII, Belarus increased in area through Soviet annexation of part of NE Poland. Belarus declared independence Aug. 25, 1991. It became an independent state when the Soviet Union disbanded Dec. 26, 1991.

A new constitution was adopted, Mar. 15, 1994, and a new president was chosen in elections concluding July 1. Russia and Belarus signed a pact Apr. 2, 1996, linking their political and economic systems. An authoritarian constitution enacted in Nov. gave Pres. Aleksandr Lukashenko vast new powers. Opponents charged harassment and fraud in the presidential election of Sept. 9, 2001, won by Lukashenko. In elections on Oct. 17, 2004, considered flawed by foreign observers, nearly all winning candidates were Lukashenko supporters, and a constitutional provision limiting the president to 2 terms was repealed. Lukashenko won a 3rd term, Mar. 19, 2006, in elections criticized by the U.S., EU, and OSCE observers; police in Minsk suppressed postelection protests. The U.S. and EU imposed travel restrictions and financial sanctions on Lukashenko and other top officials.

Belgium
Kingdom of Belgium

People: Population: 10,392,226. **Age distrib.** (%): <15: 16.5; 65+: 17.4. **Pop. density:** 889 per sq mi, 343 per sq km. **Urban:** 97.2%. **Ethnic groups:** Fleming 58%, Walloon 31%. **Principal languages:** Dutch, French, German (all official); Flemish, Luxembourgish. **Chief religions:** Roman Catholic 75%; Protestant, other 25%.

Geography: Total area: 11,787 sq mi, 30,528 sq km; **Land area:** 11,690 sq mi, 30,278 sq km. **Location:** In W Europe, on North Sea. **Neighbors:** France on W and S, Luxembourg on SE, Germany on E, Netherlands on N. **Topography:** Mostly flat, the country is trisected by the Scheldt and Meuse, major commercial rivers. The land becomes hilly and forested in the SE (Ardennes) region. **Capital:** Brussels, 1,012,000.

Government: Type: Parliamentary democracy under a constitutional monarch. **Head of state:** King Albert II; b. June 6, 1934; in office: Aug. 9, 1993. **Head of gov.:** Premier Guy Verhofstadt; b. Apr. 11, 1953; in office: July 12, 1999. **Local divisions:** 10 provinces and Brussels. **Defense budget** (2005): $3.4 bil. **Active troops:** 36,900.

Economy: Industries: engineering & metal products, motor vehicle assembly, proc. food & beverages, chemicals, textiles, glass, oil, coal. **Chief crops:** sugar beets, vegetables, fruits, grain, tobacco. **Natural resources:** coal, nat. gas. **Arable land:** 27%. **Livestock:** cattle: 2.7 mil; chickens: 32.9 mil; goats: 26,209; pigs: 6.3 mil; sheep: 153,976. **Fish catch:** 25,767 metric tons. **Electricity prod.:** 80.8 bil kWh. **Labor force** (2003 est.): agriculture 1.3%, industry 24.5%, services 74.2%.

Finance: Monetary unit: Euro (EUR) (Sept. 2007: 0.72 = $1 U.S.). **GDP:** $342.8 bil; **per capita GDP:** $33,000; **GDP growth:** 3%. **Imports:** $335.5 bil; Netherlands 18.4%, Germany 17.5%, France 11.3%, UK 6.6%, Ireland 5.9%, U.S. 5.3%. **Exports:** $335.3 bil; Germany 19.9%, France 17%, Netherlands 12%, UK 7.9%, U.S. 6.1%, Italy 5.2%. **Tourism:** $9.8 bil. **Budget:** $195.5 bil. **Intl. reserves less gold:** $5.84 bil. **Gold:** 7.32 mil oz t. **Consumer prices:** 1.79%.

Transport: Railroad: Length: 2,188 mi. **Motor vehicles:** 4.9 mil pass. cars; 641,000 comm. vehicles. **Civil aviation:** 2.5 bil pass.-mi; 25 airports. **Chief ports:** Antwerp (one of the world's busiest), Brussels, Ghent, Liege, Oostende, Zeebrugge.

Communications: TV sets: 532 per 1,000 pop. **Radios:** 797 per 1,000 pop. **Telephone lines:** 4.7 mil. **Daily newspaper circ.:** 153 per 1,000 pop. **Internet:** 4.8 mil users.

Health: Life expect.: 75.8 male; 82.2 female. **Births** (per 1,000 pop.): 10.3. **Deaths** (per 1,000 pop.): 10.3. **Natural inc.:** −0.003%. **Infant mortality** (per 1,000 live births): 4.6. **AIDS rate:** 0.3%.

Education: Compulsory: ages 6-18. **Literacy:** 98%.

Major intl. organizations: UN and all of its specialized agencies, EU, NATO, OECD, OSCE.

Embassy: 3330 Garfield St. NW 20008; 333-6900.

Website: belgium.fgov.be

Belgium derives its name from the Belgae, the first recorded inhabitants, probably Celts. The land was conquered by Julius Caesar and was ruled for 1800 years by conquerors, including Rome, the Franks, Burgundy, Spain, Austria, and France. After 1815, Belgium was made a part of the Netherlands, but it became an independent constitutional monarchy in 1830.

Belgian neutrality was violated by Germany in both world wars. King Leopold III surrendered to Germany, May 28, 1940. After the war, he was forced by political pressure to abdicate in favor of his son, King Baudouin. Baudouin was succeeded by his brother, Albert II, Aug. 9, 1993.

The Flemings of northern Belgium speak Dutch, while French is the language of the Walloons in the south. The language difference has been a perennial source of controversy and led to antagonism between the 2 groups. Parliament has passed measures aimed at transferring power from the central government to 3 regions—Wallonia, Flanders, and Brussels. Constitutional changes in 1993 made Belgium a federal state. Sabena, the national airline, went bankrupt Nov. 6, 2001. After elections June 10, 2007, rivalries between Flemings and Walloons led to a political crisis, as Flemish premier-designate Yves Leterme was unable to form new government.

Belize

People: Population: 294,385. **Age distrib. (%):** <15: 38.9; 65+: 3.5. **Pop. density:** 33 per sq mi, 13 per sq km. **Urban:** 48.3%. **Ethnic groups:** Mestizo 49%, Creole 25%, Maya 11%, Garifuna 6%. **Principal languages:** Spanish, Creole, Mayan dialect, English (official), Garifuna, German. **Chief religions:** Roman Catholic 50%, Protestant 27%.

Geography: Total area: 8,867 sq mi, 22,966 sq km; **Land area:** 8,805 sq mi, 22,806 sq km. **Location:** Eastern coast of Central America. **Neighbors:** Mexico on N, Guatemala on W and S. **Topography:** Belize has swampy lowlands in N, Maya Mts. in S, coral reefs and cays near coast. Climate is tropical. **Capital:** Belmopan, 14,000.

Government: Type: Parliamentary democracy. **Head of state:** Queen Elizabeth II, represented by Gov.-Gen. Sir Colville Young; b. Nov. 20, 1932; in office: Nov. 17, 1993. **Head of gov.:** Prime Min. Said Musa; b. Mar. 19, 1944; in office: Aug. 28, 1998. **Local divisions:** 6 districts. **Defense budget:** $16 mil. **Active troops:** 1,050.

Economy: Industries: clothing, food proc., tourism, constr. **Chief crops:** bananas, cacao, citrus, sugar. **Natural resources:** timber, fish, hydropower. **Crude oil reserves: 6.7 mil bbls. Arable land:** 3%. **Livestock:** cattle: 57,800; chickens: 1.6 mil; goats: 165; pigs: 21,224; sheep: 6,265. **Fish catch:** 14,548 metric tons. **Electricity prod.:** 180 mil kWh. **Labor force** (2005 est.): agriculture 22.5%, industry 15.2%, services 62.3%.

Finance: Monetary unit: Dollar (BZD) (Sept. 2007: 1.96 = $1 U.S.). **GDP:** $2.3 bil; **per capita GDP:** $8,400; **GDP growth:** 3.5%. **Imports:** $543 mil; U.S. 34.8%, Mexico 14.6%, Cuba 7.5%, Guatemala 7%, China 4.2%. **Exports:** $359.5 mil; U.S. 32.6%, UK 32.3%, Cote d'Ivoire 3.6%. **Tourism:** $133 mil. **Budget:** $357.5 mil. **Intl. reserves less gold:** $76 mil. **Consumer prices** (2005): 3.64%.

Transport: Motor vehicles: 32,600 pass. cars; 7,800 comm. vehicles. **Civil aviation:** 5 airports. **Chief ports:** Belize City, Big Creek.

Communications: TV sets: 183 per 1,000 pop. **Radios:** 594 per 1,000 pop. **Telephone lines:** 33,900. **Internet:** 34,000 users.

Health: Life expect.: 66.4 male; 70.2 female. **Births** (per 1,000 pop.): 28.3. **Deaths** (per 1,000 pop.): 5.8. **Natural inc.:** 2.26%. **Infant mortality** (per 1,000 live births): 24.4. **AIDS rate:** 2.5%.

Education: Compulsory: ages 5-14. **Literacy:** 76.9%.

Major intl. organizations: UN (FAO, IBRD, ILO, IMF, IMO, WHO, WTO), Caricom, the Commonwealth, OAS.

Embassy: 2535 Massachusetts Ave. NW 20008; 332-9636.

Website: www.belize.gov.bz

Belize (formerly British Honduras) was Britain's last colony on the American mainland; independence was achieved Sept. 21, 1981. Relations with neighboring Guatemala, initially tense, have improved in recent years. Belize has become a center for drug trafficking between Colombia and the U.S.

Benin

Republic of Benin

People: Population: 8,078,314. **Age distrib. (%):** <15: 43.9; 65+: 2.4. **Pop. density:** 189 per sq mi, 73 per sq km. **Urban:** 40.1%. **Ethnic groups:** Fon 39%, Adja 15%, Yoruba 12%, Bariba 9%, Peulh 7%, Ottamari 6%. **Principal languages:** French (official), Fon, Yoruba, various tribal languages. **Chief religions:** Christian 43%, Muslim 24%, Vodun 17%, other 16%.

Geography: Total area: 43,483 sq mi, 112,620 sq km; **Land area:** 42,711 sq mi, 110,620 sq km. **Location:** In W Africa on Gulf of Guinea. **Neighbors:** Togo on W; Burkina Faso, Niger on N; Nigeria on E. **Topography:** Most of Benin is flat and covered with dense vegetation. The coast is hot, humid, and rainy. **Capitals** (2004):Porto-Novo (official), 242,000; Cotonou (administrative), 818,100.

Government: Type: Republic. **Head of state and gov.:** Pres. Thomas Boni Yayi; b. 1952; in office: Apr. 6, 2006. **Local divisions:** 12 departments. **Defense budget** (2005): $71 mil. **Active troops:** 4,750.

Economy: Industries: textiles, food proc., chemical prod., constr. materials. **Chief crops:** cotton, corn, cassava, yams, beans. **Natural resources:** oil, limestone, marble, timber. **Crude oil re-

serves:** 8 mil bbls. **Arable land:** 24%. **Livestock:** cattle: 1.8 mil; chickens: 13 mil; goats: 1.4 mil; pigs: 322,000; sheep: 750,000. **Fish catch:** 38,407 metric tons. **Electricity prod.:** 110 mil kWh. **Labor force:** NA.

Finance: Monetary unit: CFA BCEAO Franc (XOF) (Sept. 2007: 472.78 = $1 U.S.). **GDP:** $9 bil; **per capita GDP:** $1,100; **GDP growth:** 4%. **Imports:** $927.3 mil; China 47.3%, France 7.6%, Thailand 6.1%. **Exports:** $563.1 mil; China 21%, Indonesia 7.8%, India 7.1%, Netherlands 6.3%, Niger 5.7%. **Tourism:** $106 mil. **Budget:** $1.1 bil. **Intl. reserves less gold:** $606 mil. **Consumer prices:** 3.78%.

Transport: Railroad: Length: 359 mi. **Motor vehicles:** 135,700 pass. cars; 19,200 comm. vehicles. **Civil aviation** (2001): 80.8 mil pass.-mi; 1 airport. **Chief port:** Cotonou.

Communications: TV sets: 44 per 1,000 pop. **Radios:** 448 per 1,000 pop. **Telephone lines:** 76,300. **Daily newspaper circ.:** 5.4 per 1,000 pop. **Internet:** 700,000 users.

Health: Life expect.: 52.3 male; 54.6 female. **Births** (per 1,000 pop.): 38.1. **Deaths** (per 1,000 pop.): 11.9. **Natural inc.:** 2.62%. **Infant mortality** (per 1,000 live births): 77.9. **AIDS rate:** 1.8%.

Education: Compulsory: ages 6-11. **Literacy:** 34.7%.

Major intl. organizations: UN (FAO, IBRD, ILO, IMF, IMO, WHO, WTO), AU.

Embassy: 2124 Kalorama Rd. NW 20008; 232-6656.

Website: www.beninembassy.us

The Kingdom of Abomey, rising to power in wars with neighboring kingdoms in the 17th cent., came under French domination in the late 19th cent., and was incorporated into French West Africa by 1904. Under the name Dahomey, the country gained independence Aug. 1, 1960; it became Benin in 1975. In the fifth coup since independence Col. Ahmed Kerekou took power in 1972; two years later he declared a socialist state with a "Marxist-Leninist" philosophy. In Dec. 1989, Kerekou announced Marxism-Leninism would no longer be the state ideology.

In Mar. 1991, Kerekou lost to Nicéphore Soglo in Benin's first free presidential election in 30 years. Kerekou defeated Soglo in Mar. 1996 to reclaim the presidency. He won reelection in a runoff Mar. 22, 2001. Boni Yayi, an economist, won a presidential runoff vote, Mar. 19, 2006. He survived an apparent assassination attempt Mar. 15, 2007.

Bhutan

Kingdom of Bhutan

People: Population: 2,327,849. **Age distrib. (%):** <15: 38.6; 65+: 4. **Pop. density:** 128 per sq mi, 50 per sq km. **Urban:** 11.1%. **Ethnic groups:** Bhote 50%, Nepalese 35%, indigenous tribes 15%. **Principal languages:** Dzongkha (official); Tibetan, Nepalese dialects. **Chief religions:** Lamaistic Buddhist (official) 75%, Hindu 25%.

Geography: Total area: 18,147 sq mi, 47,000 sq km; **Land area:** 18,147 sq mi, 47,000 sq km. **Location:** S Asia, in eastern Himalayan Mts. **Neighbors:** India on W (Sikkim) and S, China on N. **Topography:** Bhutan is comprised of very high mountains in the N, fertile valleys in the center, and thick forests in the Duar Plain in the S. **Capital:** Thimphu, 85,000.

Government: Type: In transition. **Head of state:** King Jigme Khesar Namgyal Wangchuk; b. Feb. 21, 1980; in office: Dec. 14, 2006. **Head of gov.:** Prime Min. Lyonpo Kinzang Dorji; b. 1951; in office July 31, 2007. **Local divisions:** 18 districts. **Defense budget** (2002): $19 mil. **Active troops:** NA.

Economy: Industries: cement, wood products, proc. fruits, alcoholic beverages, calcium carbide. **Chief crops:** rice, corn, root crops, citrus, foodgrains. **Natural resources:** timber, hydropower, gypsum, calcium carbide. **Arable land:** 2%. **Livestock:** cattle: 385,000; chickens: 230,000; goats: 30,000; pigs: 35,000; sheep: 18,000. **Fish catch:** 300 metric tons. **Electricity prod.:** 2 bil kWh. **Labor force** (2004 est.): agriculture 63%, industry 6%, services 31%.

Finance: Monetary unit: Ngultrum (BTN) (Sept. 2007: 40.35 = $1 U.S.). **GDP:** $3.5 bil; **per capita GDP** (2003 est.): $1,400; **GDP growth** (2005 est.): 8.8%. **Imports** (2005): $410 mil; India 75.3%, Hong Kong 16.1%, Mexico 4.9%. **Exports** (2005): $186 mil; India 69.2%, Japan 9.1%, Germany 3.7%. **Tourism:** $12 mil. **Budget** (2005): $350 mil. **Intl. reserves less gold:** $362 mil. **Consumer prices:** 5%.

Transport: Civil aviation: 34.8 mil pass.-mi; 1 airport.

Communications: TV sets: 6 per 1,000 pop. **Radios:** 19 per 1,000 pop. **Telephone lines:** 31,500. **Internet:** 30,000 users.

Health: Life expect.: 55.4 male; 55 female. **Births** (per 1,000 pop.): 33.3. **Deaths** (per 1,000 pop.): 12.5. **Natural inc.:** 2.08%. **Infant mortality** (per 1,000 live births): 96.4. **AIDS rate:** <0.1%.

Education: Compulsory: ages 6-16. **Literacy:** 47%.

Major intl. organizations: UN (FAO, IBRD, IMF, WHO).

Embassy: 2 UN Plaza, 27th Fl., New York, NY 10017; 212-826-1919.

Website: www.bhutan.gov.bt

The region came under Tibetan rule in the 16th cent. British influence grew in the 19th cent. A Buddhist monarchy was set up in 1907. According to a 1910 treaty, Britain guided Bhutan's external affairs, while the country remained internally self-governing. Upon independence, India assumed Britain's role in a 1949 revision of the treaty.

Isolated for much of its history, Bhutan has taken steps toward modernization. King Jigme Singye Wangchuk, in power since 1972, stepped down Dec. 14, 2006, in favor of his son, Jigme Khesar Namgyal Wangchuk. Multiparty parliamentary elections scheduled for Feb. or Mar. 2008 will cap the transition to a constitutional monarchy.

Bolivia
Republic of Bolivia

People: Population: 9,119,152. **Age distrib.** (%): <15: 34.3; 65+: 4.6. **Pop. density:** 22 per sq mi, 8 per sq km. **Urban:** 64.2%. **Ethnic groups:** Quechua 30%, Mestizo 30%, Aymara 25%, white 15%. **Principal languages:** Spanish, Quechua, Aymara (all official). **Chief religion:** Roman Catholic (official) 95%.

Geography: Total area: 424,164 sq mi, 1,098,580 sq km; **Land area:** 418,685 sq mi, 1,084,390 sq km. **Location:** In W central South America, in the Andes Mts. (one of 2 landlocked countries in South America). **Neighbors:** Peru and Chile on W, Argentina and Paraguay on S, Brazil on E and N. **Topography:** The great central plateau, at an altitude of 12,000 ft, over 500 mi long, lies between two great cordilleras having 3 of the highest peaks in South America. Lake Titicaca, on Peruvian border, is highest lake in world on which steamboats ply (12,506 ft). The E central region has semitropical forests; the llanos, or Amazon-Chaco lowlands are in E. **Capitals:** La Paz (administrative), 1,527,000; Sucre (judicial), 227,000. **Cities (urban aggr.):** Santa Cruz, 1,320,000.

Government: Type: Republic. **Head of state and gov.:** Pres. Juan Evo Morales Aima; b. Oct. 26, 1959; in office: Jan. 22, 2006. **Local divisions:** 9 departments. **Defense budget:** $155 mil. **Active troops:** 46,100.

Economy: Industries: mining, smelting, oil, food & beverages, tobacco, handicrafts, clothing. **Chief crops:** soybeans, coffee, coca, cotton, corn, sugarcane, rice, potatoes. **Natural resources:** tin, nat. gas, oil, zinc, tungsten, antimony, silver, iron, lead, gold, timber, hydropower. **Crude oil reserves:** 440 mil bbls. **Other resources:** Timber. **Arable land:** 3%. **Livestock:** cattle: 7.5 mil; chickens: 80.6 mil; goats: 1.9 mil; pigs: 2.5 mil; sheep: 9 mil. **Fish catch:** 7,090 metric tons. **Electricity prod.:** 5 bil kWh. **Labor force:** NA.

Finance: Monetary unit: Boliviano (BOB) (Sept. 2007: 7.76 = $1 U.S.). **GDP:** $27.9 bil; **per capita GDP:** $3,100; **GDP growth:** 4.5%. **Imports:** $2.9 bil; Brazil 24.6%, Argentina 18.8%, Chile 12.2%, U.S. 9.2%, Peru 7.3%. **Exports:** $3.7 bil; Brazil 42.7%, U.S. 12%, Argentina 10.6%, Colombia 7.5%, Japan 6.1%. **Tourism:** $177 mil. **Budget:** $3.6 bil. **Intl. reserves less gold:** $1.74 bil. **Gold:** 910,000 oz t. **Consumer prices:** 4.28%.

Transport: Railroad: Length: 2,187 mi. **Motor vehicles:** 294,000 pass. cars; 174,000 comm. vehicles. **Civil aviation:** 1.1 bil pass.-mi; 16 airports. **Chief port:** Puerto Aguirre.

Communications: TV sets: 118 per 1,000 pop. **Radios:** 675 per 1,000 pop. **Telephone lines:** 666,600. **Daily newspaper circ.:** 98.8 per 1,000 pop. **Internet:** 580,000 users.

Health: Life expect.: 63.5 male; 69 female. **Births** (per 1,000 pop.): 22.8. **Deaths** (per 1,000 pop.): 7.4. **Natural inc.:** 1.54%. **Infant mortality** (per 1,000 live births): 50.4. **AIDS rate:** 0.1%.

Education: Compulsory: ages 6-13. **Literacy:** 86.7%.

Major intl. organizations: UN (FAO, IBRD, ILO, IMF, IMO, WHO, WTO), OAS.

Embassy: 3014 Massachusetts Ave. NW 20008; 483-4410.

Website: www.bolivia.gov.bo

The Incas conquered the region's earlier Indian inhabitants in the 13th cent. Spanish rule began in the 1530s and lasted until Aug. 6, 1825. The country is named after Simon Bolivar, independence fighter.

In a series of wars, Bolivia lost its Pacific coast to Chile, the oil-bearing Chaco to Paraguay, and rubber-growing areas to Brazil, 1879-1935.

Economic unrest, especially among militant mine workers, has contributed to continuing political instability. A reformist government under Victor Paz Estenssoro, 1951-64, nationalized tin mines and attempted to improve conditions for Indian majority but was overthrown by a military junta. A long series of coups and countercoups continued until constitutional government was restored in 1982.

U.S. pressure on the government to reduce the country's coca output, the raw material for cocaine, has led to clashes between police and coca growers and increased anti-U.S. feeling among Bolivians. Gen. Hugo Banzer Suárez, who ruled as a dictator, 1971-78, later governed as president, 1997-2001.

After an inconclusive presidential election June 30, 2002, Congress Aug. 4 chose Gonzalo Sánchez de Lozada, a U.S.-educated mining executive, as head of state. He quit Oct. 17, 2003, after a month of antigovernment protests, led by Bolivian Indians, in which over 70 people died. His successor, Vice Pres. Carlos D. Mesa Gisbert, a former historian and TV reporter, won a referendum July 18, 2004, on his plan to boost exports of Bolivia's huge natural gas reserves. Further protests, mainly over energy issues, forced Mesa to step down.

Juan Evo Morales Aima, a leftist and coca-farmer advocate, won the presidential election, Dec. 18, 2005. In his first year in office, he nationalized the hydrocarbon sector, launched a land-redistribution program to benefit poor farmers, and tightened ties with Venezuela and Cuba. Floods in early 2007 killed at least 54 people and directly affected about 446,500

Bosnia and Herzegovina

People: Population: 4,552,198. **Age distrib.** (%): <15: 15; 65+: 14.6. **Pop. density:** 231 per sq mi, 89 per sq km. **Urban:** 45.7%. **Ethnic groups:** Bosniak 48%, Serbian 37%, Croatian 14%. **Principal languages:** Bosnian (official), Croatian, Serbian. **Chief religions:** Muslim 40%, Orthodox 31%, Roman Catholic 15%, other 14%.

Geography: Total area: 19,741 sq mi, 51,129 sq km; **Land area:** 19,741 sq mi, 51,129 sq km. **Location:** On Balkan Peninsula in SE Europe. **Neighbors:** Serbia, Montenegro on E and SE, Croatia on N and W. **Topography:** Hilly with some mountains. About 36% of the land is forested. **Capital:** Sarajevo, 380,000.

Government: Type: Federal republic. **Heads of state:** Collective presidency with rotating leadership. **Head of gov.:** Prime Min. Nikola Spiric; b. Sept. 4, 1956; in office: Jan. 11, 2007. **Local divisions:** Muslim-Croat Federation, divided into 10 cantons; Serbian-led region (Republika Srpska); internationally supervised Brcko district. **Defense budget:** $144 mil. **Active troops:** 11,865.

Economy: Industries: steel, mining, vehicle assembly, textiles, tobacco products, wooden furniture, tank & aircraft assembly, domestic appliances. **Chief crops:** wheat, corn, fruits, vegetables. **Natural resources:** coal, iron, bauxite, mang., timber, copper, chromium, lead, zinc, hydropower. **Arable land:** 20%. **Livestock:** cattle: 514,869; chickens: 13.3 mil; goats: 73,474; pigs: 712,141; sheep: 994,696. **Fish catch:** 9,070 metric tons. **Electricity prod.:** 12.2 bil kWh. **Labor force:** NA.

Finance: Monetary unit: Convertible Marka (BAM) (Sept. 2007: 1.41 = $1 U.S.). **GDP:** $25.3 bil; **per capita GDP:** $5,600; **GDP growth:** 6%. **Imports:** $8.3 bil; Croatia 25.1%, Germany 14.3%, Slovenia 13%, Italy 9.9%, Austria 5.9%, Hungary 5.1%. **Exports:** $3.5 bil; Croatia 19.1%, Slovenia 17%, Italy 15.6%, Germany 12.5%, Austria 8.8%, Hungary 5.3%. **Tourism:** $488 mil. **Budget:** $5.7 bil. **Intl. reserves less gold:** $2.24 bil.

Transport: Railroad: Length: 378 mi. **Civil aviation:** 29.2 mil pass.-mi; 8 airports.**Chief ports:** Bosanski Brod, Orasje.

Communications: TV sets: 112 per 1,000 pop. **Radios:** 245 per 1,000 pop. **Telephone lines:** 989,000. **Internet:** 950,000 users.

Health: Life expect.: 74.6 male; 82 female. **Births** (per 1,000 pop.): 8.8. **Deaths** (per 1,000 pop.): 8.4. **Natural inc.:** 0.04%. **Infant mortality** (per 1,000 live births): 9.6. **AIDS rate:** <0.1%.

Education: Compulsory: ages 6-15. **Literacy:** 96.7%.

Major intl. organizations: UN (FAO, IBRD, ILO, IMF, IMO, WHO), OSCE.

Embassy: 2109 E St. NW 20037; 337-1500.

Website: www.bhembassy.org

Bosnia was ruled by Croatian kings c. 958 CE, and by Hungary 1000-1200. It became organized c. 1200 and later took control of Herzegovina. The kingdom disintegrated from 1391, with the southern part becoming the independent duchy Herzegovina. It was conquered by Turks in 1463 and made a Turkish province. The area was placed under control of Austria-Hungary in 1878 and made part of the province of **Bosnia and Herzegovina,** which was formally annexed to Austria-Hungary 1908; Bosnia became a province of Yugoslavia in 1918. It was reunited with Herzegovina as a federated republic in the 1946 Yugoslavian constitution.

Bosnia and Herzegovina declared sovereignty Oct. 15, 1991. A referendum for independence was passed Feb. 29, 1992. Ethnic Serbs' opposition to the referendum spurred violent clashes and bombings. The U.S. and EU recognized the republic Apr. 7. Fierce three-way fighting continued between Bosnia's Serbs, Muslims, and Croats. Serb forces massacred thousands of Bosnian Muslims and engaged in "ethnic cleansing" (the expulsion of Muslims and other non-Serbs from areas under Bosnian Serb control). The capital, Sarajevo, was surrounded and besieged by Bosnian Serb forces. Muslims and Croats in Bosnia reached a cease fire Feb. 23, 1994, and signed an accord, Mar. 18, to create a Muslim-Croat confederation in Bosnia. However, by mid-1994, Bosnian Serbs controlled over 70% of the country.

As fighting continued in 1995, the balance of power began to shift toward the Muslim-Croat alliance. Massive NATO air strikes at Bosnian Serb targets beginning Aug. 30 triggered a new round of peace talks, and the siege of Sarajevo was lifted Sept. 15. The new talks produced an agreement in principle to create autonomous regions within Bosnia, with the Serb region (Republika Srpska) constituting 49% of the country. A Croat-Muslim offensive in Sept. recaptured significant territory, leaving Bosnian Serbs in control of approximately half that percentage.

A peace agreement initialed in Dayton, Ohio, Nov. 21, 1995, was signed in Paris, Dec. 14, by leaders of Bosnia, Croatia, and Serbia. Some 60,000 NATO troops (about 20,000 from the U.S.) moved in to police the accord. Meanwhile, a UN tribunal began bringing charges against suspected war criminals. Elections were held Sept. 14, 1996, for a 3-person collective presidency, for seats in a federal parliament, and for regional offices. In Dec. a revamped NATO "stabilization force" (SFOR) of over 30,000 members (more than 8,000 from the U.S.) received an 18-month mandate, which was later extended.

In a landmark verdict Aug. 2, 2001, the UN tribunal found Radislav Krstic, a Bosnian Serb general, guilty in connection with the genocide of thousands of Muslims at Srebrenica in 1995. A European Union peacekeeping force (EUFOR), with 7,000 members, assumed responsibility for SFOR, Dec. 2, 2004. On Sept. 27, 2006, the UN tribunal sentenced former Bosnian Serb leader Momcilo Krajisnik to 27 years for crimes against humanity, but acquitted him of two counts of genocide. As the security situation improved, EUFOR troop strength dropped to 2,500 by mid-2007.

Botswana

Republic of Botswana

People: Population: 1,815,508. **Age distrib.** (%): <15: 35.8; 65+: 3.9. **Pop. density:** 8 per sq mi, 3 per sq km. **Urban:** 57.4%. **Ethnic groups:** Tswana 79%, Kalanga 11%, Basarwa 3%. **Principal languages:** Setswana, Kalanga, Sekgalagadi, English (official). **Chief religions:** Christian 72%.

Geography: Total area: 231,804 sq mi, 600,370 sq km; **Land area:** 226,013 sq mi, 585,370 sq km. **Location:** In southern Africa. **Neighbors:** Namibia on N and W, South Africa on S, Zimbabwe on NE; Botswana claims border with Zambia on N. **Topography:** The Kalahari Desert, supporting nomadic Bushmen and wildlife, spreads over SW; there are swamplands and farming areas in N, and rolling plains in E where livestock are grazed. **Capital:** Gaborone, 210,000.

Government: Type: Parliamentary republic. **Head of state and gov.:** Pres. Festus Mogae; b. Aug. 21, 1939; in office: Apr. 1, 1998. **Local divisions:** 10 districts, 4 town councils. **Defense budget:** $262 mil. **Active troops:** 9,000.

Economy: Industries: diamonds, copper, nickel, salt, soda ash, potash, proc., textiles. **Chief crops:** sorghum, maize, millet, beans, sunflowers. **Natural resources:** diamonds, copper, nickel, salt, soda ash, potash, coal, iron ore, silver. **Arable land:** 1%. **Livestock:** cattle: 3.1 mil; chickens: 4 mil; goats: 2 mil; pigs: 8,000; sheep: 300,000. **Fish catch:** 132 metric tons. **Electricity prod.:** 910 mil kWh. **Labor force:** NA.

Finance: Monetary unit: Pula (BWP) (Sept. 2007: 6.27 = $1 U.S.). **GDP:** $17.9 bil; **per capita GDP:** $10,900; **GDP growth:** 5.4%. **Imports:** $3 bil; Southern African Customs Union 74%, European Free Trade Association 17%, Zimbabwe 4%. **Exports:** $4.8 bil; European Free Trade Association 87%, Southern African Customs Union 7%, Zimbabwe 4%. **Tourism:** $562 mil. **Budget:** $4 bil. **Intl. reserves less gold:** $5.31 bil. **Consumer prices:** 11.56%.

Transport: Railroad: Length: 552 mi. **Motor vehicles:** 74,000 pass. cars; 99,000 comm. vehicles. **Civil aviation:** 51.6 mil pass.-mi; 10 airports.

Communications: TV sets: 21 per 1,000 pop. **Radios:** 154 per 1,000 pop. **Telephone lines:** 136,900. **Daily newspaper circ.:** 24.7 per 1,000 pop. **Internet** (2002): 60,000 users.

Health: Life expect.: 51.6 male; 49.6 female. **Births** (per 1,000 pop.): 23.2. **Deaths** (per 1,000 pop.): 13.6. **Natural inc.:** 0.95%. **Infant mortality** (per 1,000 live births): 44. **AIDS rate:** 24.1%. **Education:** Compulsory: ages 6-15. **Literacy:** 81.2%.

Major intl. organizations: UN (FAO, IBRD, ILO, IMF, WHO, WTO), the Commonwealth, AU.

Embassy: 1531-3 New Hampshire Ave. NW 20036; 244-4990. **Website:** www.gov.bw

First inhabited by bushmen, then Bantus, the region became the British protectorate of Bechuanaland in 1886, halting encroachment by Boers and Germans from the south and southwest. The country became fully independent Sept. 30, 1966, as Botswana. Cattle raising and mining (diamonds, copper, nickel) have contributed to economic growth; its economy is closely tied to South Africa's. According to the UN, about 15% of the total population has HIV/AIDS.

Brazil

Federative Republic of Brazil

People: Population: 190,010,647. **Age distrib.** (%): <15: 25.3; 65+: 6.3. **Pop. density:** 58 per sq mi, 22 per sq km. **Urban:** 84.2%. **Ethnic groups:** White 54%, mulatto 39%, black 6%. **Principal languages:** Portuguese (official), Spanish, English, French. **Chief religions:** Roman Catholic (nominal) 74%, Protestant 15%.

Geography: Total area: 3,286,488 sq mi, 8,511,965 sq km; **Land area:** 3,265,077 sq mi, 8,456,510 sq km. **Location:** Occupies E half of South America. **Neighbors:** French Guiana, Suriname, Guyana, Venezuela on N; Colombia, Peru, Bolivia, Paraguay, on W; Argentina, Uruguay on S. **Topography:** Brazil's Atlantic coastline stretches 4,603 mi. In N is the heavily wooded Amazon basin covering half the country. Its network of rivers is navigable for 15,814 mi. The Amazon itself flows 2,093 mi in Brazil, all navigable. The NE region is semiarid scrubland, heavily settled and poor. The S central region, favored by climate and resources, has almost half of the population, produces 75% of farm goods and 80% of industrial output. The narrow coastal belt includes most of the major cities. Almost the entire country has a tropical or subtropical climate. **Capital:** Brasília, 3,341,000. **Cities (urban aggr.):** São Paulo, 18,333,000; Rio de Janeiro, 11,469,000; Belo Horizonte, 5,304,000.

Government: Type: Federal republic. **Head of state and gov.:** Luiz Inacio Lula da Silva; b. Oct. 27, 1945; in office: Jan. 1, 2003.

Local divisions: 26 states, 1 federal district (Brasília). **Defense budget:** $16.4 bil. **Active troops:** 287,870.

Economy: Industries: textiles, shoes, chemicals, cement, lumber, iron ore, steel, aircraft, motor vehicles & parts. **Chief crops:** coffee, soybeans, wheat, rice, corn, sugarcane, cocoa, citrus. **Natural resources:** bauxite, gold, iron ore, mang., nickel, phosphates, platinum, tin, uranium, oil, hydropower, timber. **Crude oil reserves:** 11.8 bil bbls. **Arable land:** 7%. **Livestock:** cattle: 207.2 mil; chickens: 999 mil; goats: 10.3 mil; pigs: 34.1 mil; sheep: 15.6 mil. **Fish catch:** 1,008,066 metric tons. **Electricity prod.:** 396.4 bil kWh. **Labor force** (2003 est.): agriculture 20%, industry 14%, services 66%.

Finance: Monetary unit: Real (BRL) (Sept. 2007: 1.90 = $1 U.S.). **GDP:** $1.7 tril; **per capita GDP:** $8,800; **GDP growth:** 3.7%. **Imports:** $91.4 bil; U.S. 20.4%, Argentina 8.2%, China 7.8%, Germany 7.5%. **Exports:** $137.5 bil; U.S. 17.9%, Argentina 8.6%, China 8.2%, Germany 4.1%. **Tourism:** $3.9 bil. **Budget** (2007 est.): $219.9 bil. **Intl. reserves less gold:** $56.87 bil. **Gold:** 440,000 oz t. **Consumer prices:** 4.18%.

Transport: Railroad: Length: 18,176 mi. **Motor vehicles:** 16.6 mil pass. cars; 4.5 mil comm. vehicles. **Civil aviation:** 27.5 bil pass.-mi; 714 airports. **Chief ports:** Rio Grande, Rio de Janeiro, Santos, Sepetiba Terminal, Tubarao, Vitoria.

Communications: TV sets: 333 per 1,000 pop. **Radios:** 434 per 1,000 pop. **Telephone lines:** 38.8 mil. **Daily newspaper circ.:** 45.9 per 1,000 pop. **Internet:** 42.6 mil users.

Health: Life expect.: 68.3 male; 76.4 female. **Births** (per 1,000 pop.): 16.3. **Deaths** (per 1,000 pop.): 6.2. **Natural inc.:** 1.01%. **Infant mortality** (per 1,000 live births): 27.6. **AIDS rate:** 0.5%. **Education:** Compulsory: ages 7-14. **Literacy:** 88.6%.

Major intl. organizations: UN and most of its specialized agencies, OAS.

Embassy: 3006 Massachusetts Ave. NW 20008; 238-2700. **Website:** www.brasilemb.org

Pedro Alvares Cabral, a Portuguese navigator, is generally credited as the first European to reach Brazil, in 1500. The country was thinly settled by various Indian tribes. Only a few have survived to the present, mostly in the Amazon basin.

In the next centuries, Portuguese colonists gradually pushed inland, bringing along large numbers of African slaves. (Slavery was not abolished until 1888.) The King of Portugal, fleeing before Napoleon's army, moved the seat of government to Brazil in 1808. Brazil thereupon became a kingdom under Dom Joao VI. After his return to Portugal, his son Pedro proclaimed the independence of Brazil, Sept. 7, 1822, and was crowned emperor. The second emperor, Dom Pedro II, was deposed in 1889, and a republic proclaimed, called the United States of Brazil. In 1967 the country was renamed the Federative Republic of Brazil.

A military junta took control in 1930; dictatorial power was assumed by Getulio Vargas, until finally forced out by the military in 1945. A democratic regime prevailed 1945-64, during which time the capital was moved from Rio de Janeiro to Brasília. In 1964, Pres. Joao Belchoir Marques Goulart instituted economic policies that aggravated Brazil's inflation; he was overthrown by an army revolt. The next 5 presidents were all military leaders. Censorship was imposed, and much of the opposition was suppressed amid charges of torture.

Since 1930, successive governments have pursued industrial and agricultural growth and interior area development. Exploiting vast natural resources and a huge labor force, Brazil became the leading industrial power of Latin America by the 1970s, while agricultural output soared. By the 1990s, Brazil had one of the world's largest economies; income was poorly distributed, however, and more than one out of four Brazilians continued to survive on less than $1 a day. Despite protective environmental legislation, development has destroyed much of the Amazon ecosystem. Brazil hosted delegates from 178 countries at the Earth Summit, June 3-14, 1992.

Democratic presidential elections were held in 1985 as the nation returned to civilian rule. Fernando Collor de Mello was elected president in Dec. 1989. In Sept. 1992, Collor was impeached for corruption. He resigned on Dec. 29 as his trial was beginning, and Itamar Franco, who had been acting president, was sworn in as president. In elections held on Oct. 3, 1994, Fernando Henrique Cardoso was elected president. Reelected Oct. 4, 1998, he guided Brazil through a series of financial crises.

A new civil code guaranteeing legal equality for women was enacted Aug. 15, 2001. The IMF approved a $30 bil loan to Brazil Aug. 7, 2002; by then, Brazil's debt already exceeded $260 bil. Luiz Inacio Lula da Silva, a union leader and reformer, won a presidential runoff Oct. 27 with 61% of the vote. Brazil's space program suffered a setback when a rocket exploded on its launchpad Aug. 22, 2003, killing 21 people; the country successfully launched its first rocket into space Oct. 23, 2004.

A top aide to Pres. Lula resigned June 16, 2005, amid allegations the ruling party bribed legislators in exchange for votes; despite this and other scandals, Lula won a 2nd presidential term Oct. 29, 2006. Brazil's def. min. was replaced after a plane crash July 17, 2007, at São Paulo's Congonhas Airport killed 199 people and exposed chronic problems in the military-controlled aviation system. Gang violence in the slums of Rio de Janeiro and São Paulo has claimed hundreds of lives in recent years.

Brunei
State of Brunei Darussalam

People: Population: 374,577. **Age distrib. (%):** <15: 27.8; 65+: 3.2. **Pop. density:** 184 per sq mi, 71 per sq km. **Urban:** 73.5%. **Ethnic groups:** Malay 67%, Chinese 15%, indigenous 6%. **Principal languages:** Malay (official), English, Chinese. **Chief religions:** Muslim (official) 67%; Buddhist 13%; Christian 10%; indigenous beliefs, other 10%.

Geography: Total area: 2,228 sq mi, 5,770 sq km; **Land area:** 2,035 sq mi, 5,270 sq km. **Location:** In SE Asia, on the N coast of the island of Borneo; it is surrounded on its landward side by the Malaysian state of Sarawak. **Topography:** Brunei has a narrow coastal plain, with mountains in E, hilly lowlands in W. There are swamps in W and NE. Climate is tropical. **Capital:** Bandar Seri Begawan, 64,000.

Government: Type: Independent sultanate. **Head of state and gov.:** Sultan Sir Muda Hassanal Bolkiah Mu'izzadin Waddaulah; b. July 15, 1946; in office: Jan. 1, 1984 (sultan since Oct. 5, 1967). **Local divisions:** 4 districts. **Defense budget:** $343 mil. **Active troops:** 7,000.

Economy: Industries: oil, oil refining, nat. gas liquefaction, constr. **Chief crops:** rice, vegetables, fruits. **Natural resources:** oil, nat. gas, timber. **Crude oil reserves:** 1.1 bil bbls. **Arable land:** 2%. **Livestock:** cattle: 1,300; chickens: 13 mil; goats: 3,000; pigs: 1,800; sheep: 3,000. **Fish catch:** 3,108 metric tons. **Electricity prod.:** 2.7 bil kWh. **Labor force** (2003 est.): agriculture 2.9%, industry 61.1%, services 36%.

Finance: Monetary unit: Dollar (BND) (Sept. 2007: 1.51 = $1 U.S.). **GDP:** $9.6 bil; **per capita GDP:** $25,600; **GDP growth** (2005 est.): 0.4%. **Imports** (2005 est.): $1.5 bil; Singapore 30.7%, Malaysia 18.4%, UK 7.8%, Japan 5.4%, China 5.3%. **Exports** (2005 est.): $6.2 bil; Japan 31.2%, Indonesia 20.3%, South Korea 13.3%, Australia 11.7%, U.S. 7.9%. **Tourism:** $37 mil. **Budget** (2004 est.): $4.8 bil. **Intl. reserves less gold:** $348 mil.

Transport: Railroad: Length: NA. **Motor vehicles:** 226,000 pass. cars; 22,000 comm. vehicles. **Civil aviation:** 2.2 bil pass.-mi; 1 airport. **Chief ports:** Lumut, Muara, Seria.

Communications: TV sets: 637 per 1,000 pop. **Radios:** 302 per 1,000 pop. **Telephone lines:** 80,200. **Internet:** 165,600 users.

Health: Life expect.: 73.1 male; 77.6 female. **Births** (per 1,000 pop.): 18.6. **Deaths** (per 1,000 pop.): 3.3. **Natural inc.:** 1.53%. **Infant mortality** (per 1,000 live births): 13.1. **AIDS rate:** <0.1%.

Education: Compulsory: ages 5-16. **Literacy:** 92.7%.

Major intl. organizations: UN and some of its specialized agencies, APEC, ASEAN, the Commonwealth.

Embassy: 3520 International Ct. NW 20008; 237-1838.

Website: www.brunei.gov.bn

The Sultanate of Brunei was a powerful state in the early 16th cent., with authority over all of the island of Borneo as well as parts of the Sulu Islands and the Philippines. In 1888, a treaty placed the state under the protection of Great Britain.

Brunei became a fully sovereign and independent state on Jan. 1, 1984. Much of the country's oil wealth has been squandered in recent years by members of the royal family.

Bulgaria
Republic of Bulgaria

People: Population: 7,322,858. **Age distrib. (%):** <15: 13.9; 65+: 17.4. **Pop. density:** 172 per sq mi, 66 per sq km. **Urban:** 70%. **Ethnic groups:** Bulgarian 84%, Turk 9%, Roma 5%. **Principal languages:** Bulgarian, Turkish, Roma. **Chief religions:** Bulgarian Orthodox 83%, Muslim 12%.

Geography: Total area: 42,823 sq mi, 110,910 sq km; **Land area:** 42,684 sq mi, 110,550 sq km. **Location:** SE Europe, in E Balkan Peninsula on the Black Sea. **Neighbors:** Romania on N; Serbia, Macedonia on W; Greece, Turkey on S. **Topography:** The Stara Planina (Balkan) Mts. stretch E-W across the center of the country, with the Danubian plain on N, the Rhodope Mts. on SW, and Thracian Plain on SE. **Capital:** Sofia, 1,093,000.

Government: Type: Republic. **Head of state:** Pres. Georgi Parvanov; b. June 28, 1957; in office: Jan. 22, 2002. **Head of gov.:** Prime Min. Sergei Stanishev; b. May 5, 1966; in office: Aug. 16, 2005. **Local divisions:** 28 provinces. **Defense budget:** $739 mil. **Active troops:** 51,000.

Economy: Industries: utilities, food, beverages, tobacco, machinery, metals, chemicals. **Chief crops:** vegetables, fruits, tobacco, wine, wheat, barley, sunflowers, sugar beets. **Natural resources:** bauxite, copper, lead, zinc, coal, timber. **Crude oil reserves:** 15 mil bbls. **Arable land:** 30%. **Livestock:** cattle: 621,797; chickens: 17.2 mil; goats: 608,426; pigs: 942,992; sheep: 1.6 mil. **Fish catch:** 8,579 metric tons. **Electricity prod.:** 41.8 bil kWh. **Labor force** (2006 est.): agriculture 8.5%, industry 33.6%, services 57.9%.

Finance: Monetary unit: Lev (BGN) (Sept. 2007: 1.41 = $1 U.S.). **GDP:** $78.7 bil; **per capita GDP:** $10,700; **GDP growth:** 6.3%. **Imports:** $23.8 bil; Russia 16.8%, Germany 12.4%, Italy 8.7%, Turkey 6.4%, China 5.4%, Greece 5.1%. **Exports:** $15.5 bil; Turkey 10.8%, Italy 10.1%, Germany 9.9%, Greece 8.2%, Belgium 6.4%. **Tourism:** $2.1 bil. **Budget:** $12.2 bil. **Intl. reserves less gold:** $7.27 bil. **Gold:** 1.28 mil oz t. **Consumer prices:** 7.26%.

Transport: Railroad: Length: 2,668 mi. **Motor vehicles:** 2.4 mil pass. cars; 354,000 comm. vehicles. **Civil aviation:** 284 mil pass.-mi; 132 airports. **Chief ports:** Burgas, Varna.

Communications: TV sets: 429 per 1,000 pop. **Radios:** 537 per 1,000 pop. **Telephone lines:** 2.4 mil. **Daily newspaper circ.:** 172.9 per 1,000 pop. **Internet:** 1.9 mil users.

Health: Life expect.: 69 male; 76.4 female. **Births** (per 1,000 pop.): 9.6. **Deaths** (per 1,000 pop.): 14.3. **Natural inc.:** −0.47%. **Infant mortality** (per 1,000 live births): 19.2. **AIDS rate:** <0.1%.

Education: Compulsory: ages 7-14. **Literacy:** 98.2%.

Major intl. organizations: UN (FAO, IBRD, ILO, IMF, IMO, WHO, WTO), EU, NATO, OSCE.

Embassy: 1621 22nd St. NW 20008; 387-0174.

Website: www.government.bg

Bulgaria was settled by Slavs in the 6th cent. Turkic Bulgars arrived in the 7th cent., merged with the Slavs, became Christians by the 9th cent., and set up powerful empires in the 10th and 12th centuries. The Ottomans prevailed in 1396 and remained for 500 years.

An 1876 revolt led to an independent kingdom in 1908. Bulgaria expanded after the first Balkan War but lost its Aegean coastline in WWI, when it sided with Germany. Bulgaria joined the Axis in WWII but withdrew in 1944. Communists took power with Soviet aid; monarchy was abolished Sept. 8, 1946.

On Nov. 10, 1989, Communist Party leader and head of state Todor Zhivkov, who had held power for 35 years, resigned. Zhivkov was imprisoned, Jan. 1990, and convicted, Sept. 1992, of corruption and abuse of power. In Jan. 1990, Parliament voted to revoke the constitutionally guaranteed dominant role of the Communist Party. A new constitution took effect July 13, 1991. An economic austerity program was launched in May 1996. Former Prime Min. Andrei Lukanov, a longtime Communist leader, was assassinated Oct. 2 in Sofia. Petar Stoyanov won a presidential runoff election Nov. 3.

Bulgaria's deteriorating economy provoked nationwide strikes and demonstrations in Jan. 1997. The Union of Democratic Forces, an anti-Communist group, won national elections on Apr. 19, 1997. The UDF lost the elections of June 17, 2001, to a party headed by the former king, Simeon II. Socialist opposition leader Georgi Parvanov won a presidential runoff vote Nov. 18, 2001; he was reelected Oct. 29, 2006.

Bulgaria became a full member of NATO, Apr. 2, 2004, and entered the European Union, Jan. 1, 2007. As part of a broader settlement with the EU, Libya July 24 freed 5 Bulgarian nurses held since 1999 on charges they had infected Libyan children with the AIDS virus; the detentions had drawn protests from human rights groups and the international medical community.

Burkina Faso

People: Population: 14,326,203. **Age distrib. (%):** <15: 46.7; 65+: 2.5. **Pop. density:** 136 per sq mi, 52 per sq km. **Urban:** 18.3%. **Ethnic groups:** Mossi (approx. 40%), Gurunsi, Senufo, Lobi, Bobo, Mande, Fulani. **Principal languages:** French (official), Sudanic languages. **Chief religions:** Muslim 50%, indigenous beliefs 40%, Christian (mainly Roman Catholic) 10%.

Geography: Total area: 105,869 sq mi, 274,200 sq km; **Land area:** 105,715 sq mi, 273,800 km. **Location:** In W Africa, S of the Sahara. **Neighbors:** Mali on NW; Niger on NE; Benin, Togo, Ghana, Côte d'Ivoire on S. **Topography:** Landlocked Burkina Faso is in the savanna region of W Africa. The N is arid, hot, and thinly populated. **Capital:** Ouagadougou, 926,000.

Government: Type: Republic. **Head of state:** Pres. Blaise Compaoré; b. Feb. 3, 1951; in office: Oct. 15, 1987. **Head of gov.:** Prime Min. Tertius Zongo; b. May 18, 1957; in office: June 4, 2007. **Local divisions:** 45 provinces. **Defense budget:** $87 mil. **Active troops:** 10,800.

Economy: Industries: cotton, beverages, agric. proc., soap, cigarettes, textiles, gold. **Chief crops:** cotton, peanuts, shea nuts, sesame, sorghum, millet. **Natural resources:** mang., limestone, marble, gold, antimony, copper, nickel, bauxite, lead, phosphates, zinc, silver. **Arable land:** 18%. **Livestock:** cattle: 8 mil; chickens: 25.7 mil; goats: 10.7 mil; pigs: 2.3 mil; sheep: 7 mil. **Fish catch:** 9,006 metric tons. **Electricity prod.:** 520 mil kWh. **Labor force** (2000 est.): agriculture 90%, industry and services 10%.

Finance: Monetary unit: CFA BCEAO Franc (XOF) (Sept. 2007: 472.78 = $1 U.S.). **GDP:** $18.8 bil; **per capita GDP:** $1,300; **GDP growth:** 6.5%. **Imports:** $1 bil; Cote d'Ivoire 25.4%, France 22.3%, Togo 7%. **Exports:** $543.5 mil; China 40.4%, Singapore 13.9%, Ghana 5.7%, Taiwan 4.9%. **Tourism:** $20 mil. **Budget:** $1.7 bil. **Intl. reserves less gold:** $369 mil. **Consumer prices:** 2.33%.

Transport: Railroad: Length: 386 mi. **Motor vehicles:** 26,500 pass. cars; 22,600 comm. vehicles. **Civil aviation:** 18 mil pass.-mi; 2 airports.

Communications: TV sets: 11 per 1,000 pop. **Radios:** 34 per 1,000 pop. **Telephone lines:** 94,800. **Daily newspaper circ.:** 1.3 per 1,000 pop. **Internet:** 80,000 users.

Health: Life expect.: 47.7 male; 50.8 female. **Births** (per 1,000 pop.): 45.3. **Deaths** (per 1,000 pop.): 15.3. **Natural inc.:** 3%. **Infant mortality** (per 1,000 live births): 89.8. **AIDS rate:** 2%.

Education: Compulsory: ages 6-16. **Literacy:** 23.6%.

Major intl. organizations: UN and many of its specialized agencies, AU.

Embassy: 2340 Massachusetts Ave. NW 20008; 332-5577.
Website: www.burkinaembassy-usa.org

The Mossi people entered the area in the 11th to 13th centuries. Their kingdoms ruled until they were defeated by the Mali and Songhai empires.

French control came by 1896, but Upper Volta (renamed Burkina Faso on Aug. 4, 1984) was not established as a separate territory until 1947. Full independence came Aug. 5, 1960, and a pro-French government was elected. The military seized power in 1980. A 1987 coup established the current regime, which instituted a multiparty system in the early 1990s. Pres. Blaise Compaoré won reelection, Nov. 13, 2005, with 80% of the vote. The country, one of the world's poorest, depends heavily on foreign aid.

Burma
(See Myanmar)

Burundi
Republic of Burundi

Population: 8,390,505. **Age distrib.** (%): <15: 46.3; 65+: 2.6. **Pop. density:** 847 per sq mi, 327 per sq km. **Urban:** 10%. **Ethnic groups:** Hutu 85%, Tutsi 14%, Twa (Pygmy) 1%. **Principal languages:** Kirundi, French (both official); Swahili. **Chief religions:** Roman Catholic 62%, indigenous beliefs 23%, Muslim 10%, Protestant 5%.

Geography: Total area: 10,745 sq mi, 27,830 sq km; **Land area:** 9,904 sq mi, 25,650 sq km. **Location:** In central Africa. **Neighbors:** Rwanda on N, Dem. Rep. of the Congo (formerly Zaire) on W, Tanzania on E and S. **Topography:** Much of the country is grassy highland, with mountains reaching 8,900 ft. The southernmost source of the White Nile is located in Burundi. Lake Tanganyika is the second deepest lake in the world. **Capital:** Bujumbura, 447,000.

Government: Type: Republic. **Head of state and gov.:** Pres. Pierre Nkurunziza; b. Dec. 18, 1963; in office: Aug. 26, 2005. **Local divisions:** 16 provinces. **Defense budget:** $51 mil. **Active troops:** 35,000.

Economy: Industries: light consumer goods, component assembly, constr., food proc. **Chief crops:** coffee, cotton, tea, corn, sorghum, sweet potatoes, bananas. **Natural resources:** nickel, uranium, rare earth oxides, peat, cobalt, copper, platinum, vanadium, hydropower. **Arable land:** 36%. **Livestock:** cattle: 395,741; chickens: 4.3 mil; goats: 750,000; pigs: 70,000; sheep: 242,933. **Fish catch:** 14,200 metric tons. **Electricity prod.:** 140 mil kWh. **Labor force** (2002 est.): agriculture 93.6%, industry 2.3%, services 4.1%.

Finance: Monetary unit: Franc (BIF) (Sept. 2007: 1,104.50 = $1 U.S.). **GDP:** $5.8 bil; **per capita GDP:** $700; **GDP growth:** 3.8%. **Imports:** $207.3 mil; Kenya 19%, Italy 15.1%, Tanzania 11.1%, Belgium 9.7%, Uganda 5.6%. **Exports:** $55.7 mil; Germany 18%, Switzerland 8.6%, Belgium 5.5%, Rwanda 5.4%, Italy 4.6%. **Tourism:** $2 mil. **Budget:** $297 mil. **Intl. reserves less gold:** $87 mil. **Consumer prices:** 2.81%.

Transport: Motor vehicles: 7,000 pass. cars; 9,300 comm. vehicles. **Civil aviation:** 1 airport. **Chief port:** Bujumbura.

Communications: TV sets: 15 per 1,000 pop. **Radios:** 152 per 1,000 pop. **Telephone lines:** 31,100. **Daily newspaper circ.:** 2.5 per 1,000 pop. **Internet:** 60,000 users.

Health: Life expect.: 50.5 male; 52.1 female. **Births** (per 1,000 pop.): 42. **Deaths** (per 1,000 pop.): 13.2. **Natural inc.:** 2.88%. **Infant mortality** (per 1,000 live births): 61.9. **AIDS rate:** 3.3%.

Education: Compulsory: ages 7-12. **Literacy:** 59.3%.

Major intl. organizations: UN (FAO, IBRD, ILO, IMF, WHO, WTO), AU.

Embassy: 2233 Wisconsin Ave. NW, Ste. 212, 20007; 342-2574.

Website: www.burundiembassy-usa.org

The pygmy Twa were the first inhabitants, followed by Bantu Hutus, who were conquered in the 16th cent. by the Tutsi (Watusi), probably from Ethiopia. Under German control in 1899, the area fell to Belgium in 1916, which exercised successively a League of Nations mandate and UN trusteeship over Ruanda-Urundi (now the two countries of Rwanda and Burundi). Burundi became independent July 1, 1962.

An unsuccessful Hutu rebellion in 1972-73 left 10,000 Tutsi and 150,000 Hutu dead. Over 100,000 Hutu fled to Tanzania and Zaire (now Congo). In the 1980s, Burundi's Tutsi-dominated regime pledged itself to ethnic reconciliation and democratic reform. In the nation's first democratic presidential election, in June 1993, a Hutu, Melchior Ndadaye, was elected. He was killed in an attempted coup, Oct. 21, 1993. At least 150,000 Burundians died as a result of ethnic conflict during the next three years. Pres. Cyprien Ntaryamira, elected Jan. 1994, was killed with the president of Rwanda in a mysterious plane crash, Apr. 6. The incident sparked massive carnage in Rwanda; violence in Burundi, initially far more limited, intensified in 1995. Ethnic strife continued after a military coup, July 25, 1996. Former South African Pres. Nelson Mandela mediated peace talks from Dec. 1999; most warring groups signed a draft peace treaty in Arusha, Tanzania, Aug. 28, 2000. Coup attempts were suppressed Apr. 18 and July 23, 2001. A power-sharing government headed by Buyoya was sworn in Nov. 1, but clashes with rebels continued.

Domitien Ndayizeye, a Hutu, became president Apr. 30, 2003. The UN Security Council authorized, May 21, 2004, a 5,650-member peacekeeping force (ONUB) for Burundi. Hutu rebels Aug. 13 attacked a UN camp for Congolese Tutsi refugees in western Burundi, killing more than 160 people, many of them women and children. Approval of a power-sharing constitution by referendum, Feb. 28, 2005, paved the way for local and parliamentary elections. Pierre Nkurunziza, former leader of a Hutu rebel group, became president Aug. 26. ONUB was succeeded, Jan. 1, 2007, by the UN Integrated Office in Burundi (BINUB)

Cambodia
Kingdom of Cambodia

People: Population: 13,995,904. **Age distrib.** (%): <15: 34; 65+: 3.6. **Pop. density:** 205 per sq mi, 79 per sq km. **Urban:** 19.7%. **Ethnic groups:** Khmer 90%, Vietnamese 5%, Chinese 1%. **Principal languages:** Khmer (official), French, English. **Chief religion:** Theravada Buddhist (official) 95%.

Geography: Total area: 69,900 sq mi, 181,040 sq km; **Land area:** 68,155 sq mi, 176,520 sq km. **Location:** SE Asia, on Indochina Peninsula. **Neighbors:** Thailand on W and N, Laos on NE, Vietnam on E. **Topography:** The central area, formed by the Mekong R. basin and Tonle Sap lake, is level. Hills and mountains are in SE, a long escarpment separates the country from Thailand on NW. 76% of the area is forested. **Capital:** Phnom Penh, 1,364,000.

Government: Type: Constitutional monarchy. **Head of state:** King Norodom Sihamoni; b. May 14, 1953; in office: Oct. 14, 2004. **Head of gov.:** Prime Min. Samdech Hun Sen; b. Aug. 5, 1952; in office: Nov. 30, 1998. **Local divisions:** 20 provinces and 4 municipalities. **Defense budget:** $123 mil. **Active troops:** 124,300.

Economy: Industries: tourism, garments, rice milling, fishing, wood & wood products, rubber, cement, gem mining, textiles. **Chief crops:** rice, rubber, corn, vegetables. **Natural resources:** timber, gems, iron ore, mang., phosphates. **Arable land:** 20%. **Livestock:** cattle: 3.3 mil; chickens: 15.1 mil; pigs: 2.7 mil. **Fish catch:** 410,000 metric tons. **Electricity prod.:** 130 mil kWh. **Labor force** (2004 est.): agriculture 75%.

Finance: Monetary unit: Riel (KHR) (Sept. 2007: 4,034.45 = $1 U.S.). **GDP:** $37.7 bil; **per capita GDP:** $2,700; **GDP growth:** 7.2%. **Imports:** $4.4 bil; Thailand 32.3%, China 18%, Hong Kong 14.3%, Singapore 11.8%. **Exports:** $3.4 bil; U.S. 63%, Germany 10%, UK 4.6%. **Tourism:** $604 mil. **Budget:** $931.8 mil. **Intl. reserves less gold:** $769 mil. **Gold:** 400,000 oz t. **Consumer prices:** 4.7%.

Transport: Railroad: Length: 374 mi. **Motor vehicles:** 8,300 pass. cars; 3,100 comm. vehicles. **Civil aviation:** 37.9 mil pass-mi; 6 airports. **Chief ports:** Phnom Penh, Preah Seihanu (Sihanoukville).

Communications: TV sets: 9 per 1,000 pop. **Radios:** 128 per 1,000 pop. **Telephone lines:** 32,800. **Internet:** 44,000 users.

Health: Life expect.: 59.3 male; 63.4 female. **Births** (per 1,000 pop.): 25.5. **Deaths** (per 1,000 pop.): 8.2. **Natural inc.:** 1.73%. **Infant mortality** (per 1,000 live births): 58.5. **AIDS rate:** 1.6%.

Education: Compulsory: ages 6-14. **Literacy:** 73.6%.

Major intl. organizations: UN (FAO, IBRD, ILO, IMF, IMO, WHO, WTO), ASEAN.

Embassy: 4530 16th St. NW 20011; 726-7742.

Website: www.cambodia.gov.kh

Early kingdoms dating from that of Funan in the 1st cent. CE culminated in the great Khmer empire that flourished from the 9th cent. to the 13th, encompassing present-day Thailand, Cambodia, Laos, and southern Vietnam. The peripheral areas were lost to invading Siamese and Vietnamese, and France established a protectorate in 1863. Independence came in 1953.

Prince Norodom Sihanouk, king 1941-55 and head of state from 1960, tried to maintain neutrality. Relations with the U.S. were broken in 1965, after South Vietnam planes attacked Vietcong forces within Cambodia. Relations were restored in 1969, after Sihanouk charged Viet Communists with arming Cambodian insurgents.

In 1970, pro-U.S. Prem. Lon Nol seized power, demanding removal of 40,000 North Viet troops; the monarchy was abolished. Sihanouk formed a government-in-exile in Beijing, and open war began between the government and Communist Khmer Rouge guerrillas. The U.S. provided heavy military and economic aid.

Khmer Rouge forces captured Phnom Penh Apr. 17, 1975. Cities were depopulated and their residents executed or condemned to forced labor. An estimated 1.7 mil people died in "killing fields" or from other hardships under Khmer Rouge rule, 1975-79.

Severe border fighting broke out with Vietnam in 1978 and developed into a full-fledged Vietnamese invasion. Formation of a Vietnamese-backed government was announced, Jan. 8, 1979, one day after the capture of Phnom Penh. Thousands of refugees fled to Thailand, and widespread starvation was reported. Vietnamese troops remained in Cambodia during the 1980s, meeting resistance from Khmer Rouge guerrillas, especially along the Thai border. Vietnam withdrew nearly all its troops by Sept. 1989.

Following UN-sponsored elections in Cambodia that ended May 28, 1993, the 2 leading parties agreed to share power in an interim government until a new constitution was adopted. On Sept. 21, a constitution reestablishing a monarchy was adopted by the National Assembly. It took effect Sept. 24, with Sihanouk as king. The Khmer Rouge, which had boycotted the elections, opposed the new government, and armed violence continued in the mid-1990s. Ieng Sary, a Khmer Rouge leader, broke with the guerrillas, formed a rival group, and announced his support for the monarchy in Aug. 1996, as Khmer Rouge strength rapidly diminished.

Co-Prime Min. Hun Sen staged a coup July 5, 1997, ousting his rival, Prince Norodom Ranariddh. Pol Pot, the Khmer Rouge leader who held power during the late 1970s, was denounced by his former comrades at a show trial, July 25, and sentenced to house arrest; he died Apr. 15, 1998. Hun Sen's party won parliamentary elections on July 26. He retained power in elections July 27, 2003, but without a parliamentary majority. Sihanouk abdicated because of poor health and was succeeded, Oct. 14, 2004, by his son Norodom Sihamoni. Charged with defaming Hun Sen and other members of the ruling coalition, opposition leader Sam Rainsy fled Feb. 3, 2005, after he was stripped of legal immunity; granted a royal pardon, he returned a year later. Arrested in 1999, former Khmer Rouge military chief Ta Mok died July 21, 2006, before he could stand trial for genocide and crimes against humanity.

Cameroon
Republic of Cameroon

People: Population: 18,060,382. **Age distrib.** (%): <15: 41.3; 65+: 3.2. **Pop. density:** 100 per sq mi, 38 per sq km. **Urban:** 54.6%. **Ethnic groups:** Highlanders 31%, Equatorial Bantu 19%, Kirdi 11%, Fulani 10%, NW Bantu 8%, E Nigritic 7%. **Principal languages:** English, French (both official); 24 African lang. groups. **Chief religions:** Indigenous beliefs 40%, Christian 40%, Muslim 20%.

Geography: Total area: 183,568 sq mi, 475,440 sq km; **Land area:** 181,252 sq mi, 469,440 sq km. **Location:** Between W and central Africa. **Neighbors:** Nigeria on NW; Chad, Central African Republic on E; Congo, Gabon, Equatorial Guinea on S. **Topography:** A low coastal plain with rain forests is in S; plateaus in center lead to forested mountains in W, including Mt. Cameroon, 13,435 ft; grasslands in N lead to marshes around Lake Chad. **Capital:** Yaoundé, 1,485,000. **Cities (urban aggr.):** Douala, 1,761,000.

Government: Type: Republic. **Head of state:** Pres. Paul Biya; b. Feb. 13, 1933; in office: Nov. 6, 1982. **Head of gov.:** Prime Min. Ephraïm Inoni; b. Aug. 16, 1947; in office: Dec. 8, 2004. **Local divisions:** 10 provinces. **Defense budget:** $262 mil. **Active troops:** 14,100.

Economy: Industries: oil prod. & refining, food proc., light consumer goods, textiles, lumber. **Chief crops:** coffee, cocoa, cotton, rubber, bananas, oilseed, grains. **Natural resources:** oil, bauxite, iron ore, timber, hydropower. **Crude oil reserves:** 400 mil bbls. **Arable land:** 13%. **Livestock:** cattle: 6 mil; chickens: 31 mil; goats: 4.4 mil; pigs: 1.4 mil; sheep: 3.8 mil. **Fish catch:** 142,682 metric tons. **Electricity prod.:** 4.1 bil kWh. **Labor force:** agriculture 70%, industry 13%, services 17%.

Finance: Monetary unit: CFA BEAC Franc (XAF) (Sept. 2007: 472.78 = $1 U.S.). **GDP:** $42.5 bil; **per capita GDP:** $2,400; **GDP growth:** 3.5%. **Imports:** $3.1 bil; France 23.5%, Nigeria 13.2%, China 7.2%, Belgium 6.2%, U.S. 4.5%. **Exports:** $4.3 bil; Spain 20.9%, Italy 15.2%, France 11.4%, South Korea 7.6%, Netherlands 7.1%, U.S. 5.6%. **Tourism:** $36 mil. **Budget:** $3.2 bil. **Intl. reserves less gold:** $1.14 bil. **Gold:** 30,000 oz t. **Consumer prices:** 5.12%.

Transport: Railroad: Length: 613 mi. **Motor vehicles:** 173,100 pass. cars; 57,400 comm. vehicles. **Civil aviation:** 390.8 mil pass.-mi; 11 airports. **Chief ports:** Douala, Limboth Terminal.

Communications: TV sets: 34 per 1,000 pop. **Radios:** 163 per 1,000 pop. **Telephone lines:** 100,300. **Daily newspaper circ.:** 6.3 per 1,000 pop. **Internet:** 370,000 users.

Health: Life expect.: 52.2 male; 53.6 female. **Births** (per 1,000 pop.): 35.1. **Deaths** (per 1,000 pop.): 12.7. **Natural inc.:** 2.24%. **Infant mortality** (per 1,000 live births): 65.8. **AIDS rate:** 5.4%.

Education: Compulsory: ages 6-11. **Literacy:** 67.9%.

Major intl. organizations: UN (FAO, IBRD, ILO, IMF, IMO, WHO, WTO), the Commonwealth, AU.

Embassy: 2349 Massachusetts Ave. NW 20008; 265-8790.

Website: www.spm.gov.cm

Portuguese sailors were the first Europeans to reach Cameroon, in the 15th cent. The European and American slave trade was very active in the area. German control lasted from 1884 to 1916, when France and Britain divided the territory, later receiving League of Nations mandates and UN trusteeships. French Cameroon became independent Jan. 1, 1960; one part of British Cameroon joined Nigeria in 1961, the other part joined Cameroon. Stability has allowed for development of roads, railways, agriculture, and petroleum production.

Pres. Paul Biya has retained power in a series of elections that were boycotted by opposition parties or disputed as fraudulent. A Kenya Airways jetliner crashed shortly after takeoff from Douala, May 5, 2007, killing all 114 persons on board.

Canada

People: Population: 33,390,141. **Age distrib.** (%): <15: 17.3; 65+: 13.5. **Pop. density:** 10 per sq mi, 4 per sq km. **Urban:** 80.1%. **Ethnic groups:** British 28%, mixed 26%, French 23%, other European 15%, Amerindian 2%. **Principal languages:** English, French (both official). **Chief religions:** Roman Catholic 43%, Protestant 23%.

Geography: Total area: 3,855,103 sq mi, 9,984,670 sq km; **Land area:** 3,511,023 sq mi, 9,093,507 sq km. the largest country in land size in the western hemisphere. **Topography:** Canada stretches 3,426 mi from east to west and extends southward from the North Pole to the U.S. border. Its seacoast includes 36,356 mi of mainland and 115,133 mi of islands, including the Arctic islands almost from Greenland to near the Alaskan border. **Climate:** While generally temperate, varies from freezing winter cold to blistering summer heat. **Capital:** Ottawa, 1,156,000. **Cities (urban aggr.):** Toronto, 5,312,000; Montreal, 3,640,000; Vancouver, 2,188,000; Edmonton, 1,015,000; Calgary, 1,058,000.

Government: Type: Confederation with parliamentary democracy. **Head of state:** Queen Elizabeth II, represented by Gov.-Gen. Michaëlle Jean; b. Sept. 6, 1957; in office: Sept. 27, 2005. **Head of gov.:** Prime Min. Stephen Harper; b. Apr. 30, 1959; in office: Feb. 6, 2006. **Local divisions:** 10 provinces, 3 territories. **Defense budget:** $14.1 bil. **Active troops:** 62,500.

Economy: Industries: transp. equipment, chemicals, minerals, food & fish products, wood & paper products, oil & natural gas. **Chief crops:** wheat, barley, oilseed, tobacco, fruits, vegetables. **Natural resources:** iron ore, nickel, zinc, copper, gold, lead, molybd., potash, silver, fish, timber, wildlife, coal, oil, nat. gas, hydropower. **Crude oil reserves:** 179.2 bil bbls. **Arable land:** 5%. **Livestock:** cattle: 14.8 mil; chickens: 160 mil; goats: 30,000; pigs: 14.7 mil; sheep: 919,000. **Fish catch:** 1,235,065 metric tons. **Electricity prod.:** 609.6 bil kWh. **Labor force** (2004): agriculture 2%, manufacturing 14%, construction 5%, services 75%, other 3%.

Finance: Monetary unit: Dollar (CAD) (Sept. 2007: 1.03 = $1 U.S.). **GDP:** $1.2 tril; **per capita GDP:** $35,600; **GDP growth:** 2.7%. **Imports:** $353.2 bil; U.S. 55.1%, China 8.7%, Mexico 4%. **Exports:** $405 bil; U.S. 82.3%, UK 2.2%, Japan 2.1%. **Tourism:** $12.8 bil. **Budget** (2005 est.): $181.8 bil. **Intl. reserves less gold:** $23.26 bil. **Gold:** 110,000 oz t. **Consumer prices:** 2.01%.

Transport: Railroad: Length: 30,116 mi. **Motor vehicles:** 17.9 mil pass. cars; 675,000 comm. vehicles. **Civil aviation:** 47.4 bil pass.-mi; 509 airports. **Chief ports:** Halifax, Montreal, Port Cartier, Quebec, Saint John's (Newfoundland), Vancouver.

Communications: TV sets: 709 per 1,000 pop. **Radios:** 1,038 per 1,000 pop. **Telephone lines:** 20.8 mil. **Daily newspaper circ.:** 167.9 per 1,000 pop. **Internet:** 22 mil users.

Health: Life expect.: 77 male; 83.9 female. **Births** (per 1,000 pop.): 10.8. **Deaths** (per 1,000 pop.): 7.9. **Natural inc.:** 0.29%. **Infant mortality** (per 1,000 live births): 4.6. **AIDS rate:** 0.3%.

Education: Compulsory: ages 6-16. **Literacy:** 99%.

Major intl. organizations: UN and all of its specialized agencies, APEC, the Commonwealth, NATO, OAS, OECD, OSCE.

Embassy: 501 Pennsylvania Ave. NW 20001; 682-1740.

Website: www.canada.gc.ca

French explorer Jacques Cartier, who reached the Gulf of St. Lawrence in 1534, is generally regarded as Canada's founder. But English seaman John Cabot sighted Newfoundland in 1497, and Vikings are believed to have reached the Atlantic coast centuries before either explorer. Canadian settlement was pioneered by the French who established Quebec City (1608) and Montreal (1642) and declared New France a colony in 1663.

Britain acquired Acadia (later Nova Scotia) in 1717 and, through military victory over French forces in Canada, captured Quebec (1759) and obtained control of the rest of New France in 1763. The French, through the Quebec Act of 1774, retained the rights to their own language, religion, and civil law. The British presence in Canada increased during the American Revolution when many colonials, proudly calling themselves United Empire Loyalists, moved north to Canada. Fur traders and explorers led Canadians westward across the continent. Sir Alexander Mackenzie reached the Pacific in 1793 and scrawled on a rock, "From Canada by land."

In Upper and Lower Canada (later called Ontario and Quebec) and in the Maritimes, legislative assemblies appeared in the 18th cent. and reformers called for responsible government. But the War of 1812 intervened. The war, a conflict between Great Britain and the U.S. fought mainly in Upper Canada, ended in a stalemate in 1814.

In 1837 political agitation for more democratic government culminated in rebellions in Upper and Lower Canada. Britain sent Lord Durham to investigate; in a famous report (1839), he recommended union of the 2 parts into one colony called Canada. The union lasted until Confederation, July 1, 1867, when proclamation of the British North America (BNA) Act (now known as the Constitution Act, 1867) launched the Dominion of Canada, consisting of Ontario, Quebec, and the former colonies of Nova Scotia and New Brunswick.

Since 1840 the Canadian colonies had held the right to internal self-government. The BNA Act, which was the basis for the country's written constitution, established a federal system of government on the model of a British parliament and cabinet structure under the crown. Canada was proclaimed a self-governing Dominion within the British Empire in 1931. With the ratification of the Constitution Act, 1982, Canada severed its last formal legislative link with Britain by obtaining the right to amend its constitution.

The so-called Meech Lake Agreement, 1987, which would have assured constitutional protection for Quebec's efforts to preserve its French language and culture, sparked a separatist revival in Quebec. Subsequently, the Charlottetown agreement, which called for constitutional changes, such as recognition of Quebec as a "distinct society" within the Canadian confederation. It was defeated by a national referendum Oct. 26, 1992.

Canada became the first nation to ratify the North American Free Trade Agreement between Canada, Mexico, and the U.S. June 23, 1993. It went into effect Jan. 1, 1994.

On Feb. 24, 1993, Brian Mulroney resigned as prime minister after more than 8 years in office; he was succeeded by Kim Campbell. In elections Oct. 25, 1993, the ruling Conservatives were defeated in a landslide that left them only 2 of the 295 seats in the House of Commons. Jean Chrétien became prime minister. In a Quebec referendum held Oct. 30, 1995, proponents of secession lost by a razor-thin margin. The elections of June 2, 1997, left the Liberals with a slim majority.

On Jan. 7, 1998, the government apologized to indigenous peoples for 150 years of mistreatment and pledged to set up a "healing fund." Canada's highest court ruled, Aug. 20, that Quebec cannot secede unilaterally, even if a majority of the province approves. Nunavut ("Our Land"), carved from Northwest Territories as a homeland for the Inuit, was established Apr. 1, 1999. Victory by the Liberals in national elections Nov. 27, 2000, made Chrétien the first Canadian prime minister in over 50 years to head a third successive majority government.

Canada sent 5 warships in Oct. 2001 and 850 troops in Feb. 2002, to join U.S. counterterrorism operations in Afghanistan. Relations between Canada and the U.S. cooled after Prime Min. Chrétien refused to contribute troops to the U.S.-led invasion of Iraq in Mar. 2003.

A SARS outbreak killed more than 40 people in the Toronto area in 2003. Chrétien retired Dec. 12, and Paul Martin became prime minister. Weakened by a scandal involving improper payments to Quebec firms for advertising and sponsorship of cultural and sporting events, the Liberals won only 135 of 308 seats in parliamentary elections June 28, 2004. Martin stayed in office as head of a minority government.

Parliament enacted a bill, July 19, 2005, making same-sex marriage (already permitted in 8 of 10 provinces) legal throughout the country. Michaëlle Jean, a Haitian-born TV journalist, was installed Sept. 27 as Canada's first black governor general.

Twelve years of Liberal party rule ended when Conservatives won 124 seats to the Liberals' 103 in parliamentary elections, Jan. 23, 2006. Conservative leader Stephen Harper took office Feb. 6 as head of a minority government. Police and intelligence officials in the Toronto area, June 2-3, arrested and charged 17 people with plotting terrorist attacks in Canada; their targets were said to include the House of Commons and the prime minister. The Supreme Court, Feb. 23, 2007, unanimously struck down a law under which foreign-born terrorism suspects had been indefinitely detained without charge.

Canada's Provinces and Territories

Provinces/Territories	Joined Confed.	Area (sq mi)	Population (2006 census)	Capital	Premier	Party	In office
Alberta	1905	255,287	3,290,350	Edmonton	Ed Stelmach	Prog. Cons.	2006
British Columbia	1871	365,948	4,113,487	Victoria	Gordon Campbell	Liberal	2001
Manitoba	1870	250,947	1,148,401	Winnipeg	Gary Doer	New Democratic	1999
New Brunswick	1867	28,355	729,997	Fredericton	Shawn Graham	Liberal	2006
Newfoundland & Labrador	1949	156,649	505,469	St. John's	Danny Williams	Prog. Cons.	2003
Nova Scotia	1867	21,425	913,462	Halifax	Rodney MacDonald	Prog. Cons.	2006
Ontario	1867	412,581	12,160,282	Toronto	Dalton McGuinty	Liberal	2003
Prince Edward Island	1873	2,185	135,851	Charlottetown	Robert Ghiz	Liberal	2007
Quebec	1867	594,860	7,546,131	Québec	Jean Charest	Liberal	2003
Saskatchewan	1905	251,866	968,157	Regina	Lorne Calvert	New Democratic	2001
Northwest Territories[1]	1871	503,951	41,464	Yellowknife	Joe Handley	non-partisan	2003
Nunavut[1]	(2)	818,959	29,474	Iqaluit	Paul Okalik	non-partisan	1999
Yukon Territory[1]	1898	186,661	30,372	Whitehorse	Dennis Fentie	Yukon	2002

(1) Territories also have federally appointed commissioners to represent federal interests. (2) Territory created in 1999 from eastern portion of Northwest Territories.

Prime Ministers of Canada

Canada is a constitutional monarchy with a parliamentary system of government. It is also a federal state. Canada's official head of state, Queen Elizabeth II, is represented by a resident Governor-General. However, in practice the nation is governed by the Prime Minister, leader of the party that commands the support of a majority of the House of Commons, dominant chamber of Canada's bicameral Parliament.

Name	Party	Term
Sir John A. Macdonald	Conservative	1867-1873
Alexander Mackenzie	Liberal	1873-1878
Sir John A. Macdonald	Conservative	1878-1891
Sir John J. C. Abbott	Conservative	1891-1892
Sir John S. D. Thompson	Conservative	1892-1894
Sir Mackenzie Bowell	Conservative	1894-1896
Sir Charles Tupper	Conservative	1896[1]
Sir Wilfrid Laurier	Liberal	1896-1911
Sir Robert Laird Borden	Cons./Union.[2]	1911-1920
Arthur Meighen	Unionist	1920-1921
W. L. Mackenzie King	Liberal	1921-1926
Arthur Meighen	Conservative	1926[3]
W. L. Mackenzie King	Liberal	1926-1930
Richard Bedford Bennett	Conservative	1930-1935
W. L. Mackenzie King	Liberal	1935-1948
Louis St. Laurent	Liberal	1948-1957
John G. Diefenbaker	Prog. Cons.	1957-1963
Lester Bowles Pearson	Liberal	1963-1968
Pierre Elliott Trudeau	Liberal	1968-1979
Joe Clark	Prog. Cons.	1979-1980
Pierre Elliott Trudeau	Liberal	1980-1984
John Napier Turner	Liberal	1984[4]
Brian Mulroney	Prog. Cons.	1984-1993
Kim Campbell	Prog. Cons.	1993[5]
Jean Chrétien	Liberal	1993-2003
Paul Martin	Liberal	2003-2006
Stephen Harper	Conservative	2006-

(1) May-July. (2) Conservative 1911-17, Unionist 1917-20. (3) June-Sept. (4) June-Sept. (5) June-Oct.

Cape Verde
Republic of Cape Verde

People: Population: 423,613. **Age distrib. (%):** <15: 36.9; 65+: 6.7. **Pop. density:** 272 per sq mi, 105 per sq km. **Urban:** 57.3%. **Ethnic groups:** Creole 71%, African 28%. **Principal languages:** Portuguese (official), Crioulo. **Chief religions:** Roman Catholic (infused with indigenous beliefs), Protestant (mostly Church of the Nazarene).

Geography: Total area: 1,557 sq mi, 4,033 sq km; **Land area:** 1,557 sq mi, 4,033 sq km. **Location:** In Atlantic O., off W tip of Africa. **Neighbors:** Nearest are Mauritania, Senegal to E. **Topography:** Cape Verde Islands are 15 in number, volcanic in origin (active crater on Fogo). The landscape is eroded and stark, with vegetation mostly in interior valleys. **Capital:** Praia, 117,000.

Government: Type: Republic. **Head of state:** Pres. Pedro Pires; b. Apr. 29, 1934; in office: Mar. 22, 2001. **Head of gov.:** Prime Min. José Maria Neves; b. Mar. 28, 1960; in office: Feb. 1, 2001. **Local divisions:** 17 districts. **Defense budget:** $7.4 mil. **Active troops:** 1,200.

Economy: Industries: food & beverages, fish proc., shoes & garments, salt mining, ship repair. **Chief crops:** bananas, corn, beans, sweet potatoes, sugarcane, coffee, peanuts. **Natural resources:** salt, basalt rock, limestone, kaolin, fish. **Arable land:** 11%. **Livestock:** cattle: 23,000; chickens: 460,000; goats: 112,750; pigs: 205,000; sheep: 10,000. **Fish catch:** 7,742 metric tons. **Electricity prod.:** 50 mil kWh. **Labor force:** NA.

Finance: Monetary unit: Escudo (CVE) (Sept. 2007: 79.52 = $1 U.S.). **GDP:** $3.1 bil; **per capita GDP:** $6,000; **GDP growth** (2005 est.): 5.5%. **Imports:** $495.1 mil; Portugal 40.8%, Netherlands 10.5%, Spain 6.2%, Italy 5.5%, Cote d'Ivoire 5.2%, Brazil 5.1%. **Exports:** $96.7 mil; Spain 45.2%, Portugal 22.9%, Netherlands 13.3%, Morocco 4.9%. **Tourism:** $125 mil. **Budget:** $370.4 mil. **Intl. reserves less gold:** $169 mil. **Consumer prices:** 5.37%.

Transport: Motor vehicles: 13,500 pass. cars; 3,100 comm. vehicles. **Civil aviation:** 177.1 mil pass.-mi; 7 airports. **Chief ports:** Mindelo, Praia, Tarrafal.

Communications: TV sets: 5 per 1,000 pop. **Radios:** NA. **Telephone lines:** 71,600. **Internet:** 29,000 users.

Health: Life expect.: 67.7 male; 74.4 female. **Births** (per 1,000 pop.): 24.4. **Deaths** (per 1,000 pop.): 6.5. **Natural inc.:** 1.79%. **Infant mortality** (per 1,000 live births): 45.3. **AIDS rate** (2001): 0.04%.

Education: Compulsory: ages 6-11. **Literacy:** 81.2%.

Major intl. organizations: UN (FAO, IBRD, ILO, IMF, IMO, WHO), AU.

Embassy: 3415 Massachusetts Ave. NW 20007; 965-6820.

Website: virtualcapeverde.net

The first Portuguese colonists landed in 1462; African slaves were brought soon after, and most Cape Verdeans descend from both groups. Cape Verde independence came July 5, 1975. Antonio Mascarenhas Monteiro won the nation's first free presidential election Feb. 17, 1991; he was reelected without opposition five years later. Pedro Pires won a presidential runoff election Feb. 25, 2001, and was reelected Feb. 12, 2006. Remittances from Cape Verdean emigrants are a major source of income.

Central African Republic

People: Population: 4,369,038. **Age distrib.** (%): <15: 41.6; 65+: 4.1. **Pop. density:** 18 per sq mi, 7 per sq km. **Urban:** 38%. **Ethnic groups:** Baya 33%, Banda 27%, Mandjia 13%, Sara 10%, Mboum 7%, M'Baka 4%, Yakoma 4%. **Principal languages:** French (official), Sangho (national), tribal languages. **Chief religions:** Indigenous beliefs 35%, Protestant 25%, Roman Catholic 25%, Muslim 15%.

Geography: Total area: 240,535 sq mi, 622,984 sq km; **Land area:** 240,535 sq mi, 622,984 sq km. **Location:** In central Africa. **Neighbors:** Chad on N, Cameroon on W, Congo-Brazzaville and Congo-Kinshasa (formerly Zaire) on S, Sudan on E. **Topography:** Mostly rolling plateau, average altitude 2,000 ft, with rivers draining S to the Congo and N to Lake Chad. Open, well-watered savanna covers most of the area, with an arid area in NE, and tropical rain forest in SW. **Capital:** Bangui, 541,000.

Government: Type: Republic. **Head of state:** Pres. François Bozizé; b. Oct. 14, 1946; in office: Mar. 15, 2003. **Head of gov.:** Prime Min. Elie Doté; in office: June 13, 2005. **Local divisions:** 14 prefectures, 2 economic prefectures, 1 commune. **Defense budget:** $16 mil. **Active troops:** 3,150.

Economy: Industries: diamond mining, sawmills, breweries, textiles, footwear, bicycle & motorcycle assembly. **Chief crops:** cotton, coffee, tobacco, cassava, yams, millet, corn, bananas. **Natural resources:** diamonds, uranium, timber, gold, oil, hydropower. **Arable land:** 3%. **Livestock:** cattle: 3.4 mil; chickens: 4.8 mil; goats: 3.1 mil; pigs: 805,000; sheep: 259,000. **Fish catch:** 15,000 metric tons. **Electricity prod.:** 110 mil kWh. **Labor force:** NA.

Finance: Monetary unit: CFA BEAC Franc (XAF) (Sept. 2007: 472.78 = $1 U.S.). **GDP:** $5 bil; **per capita GDP:** $1,200; **GDP growth:** 3.5%. **Imports** (2004 est.): $203 mil; France 15.4%, Netherlands 15.1%, U.S. 9.2%, Cameroon 8.9%. **Exports** (2004 est.): $131 mil; Belgium 30.8%, Spain 10.7%, Indonesia 8%, France 7.8%, China 6.9%, Democratic Republic of the Congo 6%, Turkey 5%. **Tourism:** $3 mil. **Budget:** NA. **Intl. reserves less gold:** $83 mil. **Gold:** 10,000 oz t. **Consumer prices** (2005): 2.88%.

Transport: Motor vehicles: 5,300 pass. cars; 6,300 comm. vehicles. **Civil aviation** (2001): 80.8 mil pass.-mi; 3 airports. **Chief ports:** Bangui, Nola.

Communications: TV sets: 6 per 1,000 pop. **Radios:** 83 per 1,000 pop. **Telephone lines:** 10,000. **Daily newspaper circ.:** 1.7 per 1,000 pop. **Internet:** 13,000 users.

Health: Life expect.: 43.7 male; 43.8 female. **Births** (per 1,000 pop.): 33.5. **Deaths** (per 1,000 pop.): 18.5. **Natural inc.:** 1.51%. **Infant mortality** (per 1,000 live births): 84.4. **AIDS rate:** 10.7%.

Education: Compulsory: ages 6-15. **Literacy:** 48.6%.

Major intl. organizations: UN (FAO, IBRD, ILO, IMF, WHO, WTO), AU.

Embassy: 1618 22nd St. NW 20008; 483-7800.

Website: www.state.gov/p/af/ci/ct/

Various Bantu peoples migrated through the region for centuries before French control was asserted in the late 19th cent., when the region was named Ubangi-Shari. Complete independence was attained Aug. 13, 1960.

Pres. Jean-Bedel Bokassa, who seized power in a 1965 military coup, proclaimed himself constitutional emperor of the renamed Central African Empire Dec. 1976. Bokassa's rule was characterized by ruthless authoritarianism and human rights violations. He was ousted in a bloodless coup aided by the French government, Sept. 20, 1979. In 1981, Gen. André Kolingba became head of state in another bloodless coup. Multiparty legislative and presidential elections were held in Oct. 1992 but were canceled by the government when Kolingba was losing. New elections, held in Aug. and Sept. 1993, led to the replacement of Kolingba with civilian rule under Pres. Ange-Félix Patassé.

France sent in troops to suppress army mutinies in 1996 and 1997. After thwarting several coup attempts, Patassé was ousted Mar. 15, 2003, by rebels under former army chief François Bozizé. Bozizé won a presidential runoff election May 8, 2005. As of mid-2007, some 78,000 refugees from fighting in the northern region were living in Chad, Cameroon, or Sudan; another 212,000 were internally displaced.

Chad

Republic of Chad

People: Population: 9,885,661. **Age distrib.** (%): <15: 47.3; 65+: 2.9. **Pop. density:** 20 per sq mi, 8 per sq km. **Urban:** 25.3%. **Ethnic groups:** About 200 groups; largest are Arabs in N, Sara in S. **Principal languages:** French, Arabic (both official); Sara; more than 120 different languages and dialects. **Chief religions:** Muslim 53%, Christian 35%, animist 7%, other 7%.

Geography: Total area: 495,755 sq mi, 1,284,000 sq km; **Land area:** 486,180 sq mi, 1,259,200 sq km. **Location:** In central N Africa. **Neighbors:** Libya on N; Niger, Nigeria, Cameroon on W; Central African Republic on S; Sudan on E. **Topography:** Wooded savanna, steppe, and desert in the S; part of the Sahara in the N. Southern rivers flow N to Lake Chad, surrounded by marshland. **Capital:** N'Djamena, 888,000.

Government: Type: Republic. **Head of state:** Pres. Idriss Déby Itno; b. 1952; in office: Dec. 4, 1990. **Head of gov.:** Prime Min. Delwa Kassiré Koumakoye; b. Dec. 31, 1949; in office: Feb. 26, 2007.

Local divisions: 14 prefectures. **Defense budget:** $60 mil. **Active troops:** 25,350.

Economy: Industries: cotton textiles, meatpacking, beer brewing, sodium carbonate, soap, cigarettes, constr. materials. **Chief crops:** cotton, sorghum, millet, peanuts, rice, potatoes, cassava. **Natural resources:** oil, uranium, natron, kaolin, fish. **Crude oil reserves: 1.5.** **Arable land:** 3%. **Livestock:** cattle: 6.5 mil; chickens: 5.2 mil; goats: 5.8 mil; pigs: 25,000; sheep: 2.6 mil. **Fish catch:** 70,000 metric tons. **Electricity prod.:** 100 mil kWh. **Labor force:** agriculture 80% (subsistence farming, herding, and fishing), industry and services 20%.

Finance: Monetary unit: CFA BEAC Franc (XAF) (Sept. 2007: 472.78 = $1 U.S.). **GDP:** $15 bil; **per capita GDP:** $1,500; **GDP growth:** 1%. **Imports:** $823.1 mil; France 19.1%, Cameroon 18.1%, U.S. 12.9%, Germany 7.5%, Saudi Arabia 5.1%, Belgium 5%. **Exports:** $4.3 bil; U.S. 79.2%, China 10.2%, Taiwan 4%. **Tourism:** $25 mil. **Budget:** $877.6 mil. **Intl. reserves less gold:** $416 mil. **Gold:** 10,000 oz t. **Consumer prices:** 8.04%.

Transport: Motor vehicles: 8,700 pass. cars; 12,400 comm. vehicles. **Civil aviation** (2001): 80.8 mil pass.-mi; 7 airports.

Communications: TV sets: 1 per 1,000 pop. **Radios:** 236 per 1,000 pop. **Telephone lines:** 13,000. **Daily newspaper circ.:** 0.2 per 1,000 pop. **Internet:** 60,000 users.

Health: Life expect.: 46.2 male; 48.3 female. **Births** (per 1,000 pop.): 42.4. **Deaths** (per 1,000 pop.): 16.7. **Natural inc.:** 2.57%. **Infant mortality** (per 1,000 live births): 102.1. **AIDS rate:** 3.5%.

Education: Compulsory: ages 6-11. **Literacy:** 25.7%.

Major intl. organizations: UN (FAO, IBRD, ILO, IMF, WHO, WTO), AU.

Embassy: 2002 R St. NW 20009; 462-4009.

Website: www.state.gov/p/af/ci/cd/

Chad was the site of paleolithic and neolithic cultures before the Sahara Desert formed. A succession of kingdoms and Arab slave traders dominated Chad until France took control around 1900. Independence came Aug. 11, 1960. Northern Muslim rebels have fought animist and Christian southern government and French troops from 1966, despite numerous cease-fires and peace pacts.

Rebel forces, led by Hissène Habré, captured the capital and forced Pres. Goukouni Oueddei to flee the country in June 1982. In Dec. 1990, Habré was overthrown by a Libyan-supported insurgent group, the Patriotic Salvation Movement.

On Feb. 3, 1994, the World Court dismissed a long-standing territorial claim by Libya to the mineral-rich Aozou Strip, on the Libyan border. Following approval of a new constitution in March 1996, Chad's first multiparty presidential election was held in June and July. The U.S. Peace Corps withdrew from Chad in Apr. 1998 because of continuing clashes between rebels and Chad government forces.

Oil began flowing July 15, 2003, through a 665-mi pipeline that allows landlocked Chad to export via Cameroon. Pres. Idriss Déby Itno won a third term, May 3, 2006, in an election boycotted by major opposition groups. Violence along the Sudan border escalated during the year, as Sudanese janjaweed militias and Chadian rebels attacked civilians, and Darfur rebels preyed on refugee camps; by mid-2007, at least 120,000 Chadians had been displaced.

Chile

Republic of Chile

People: Population: 16,284,741. **Age distrib.** (%): <15: 24.1; 65+: 8.5. **Pop. density:** 56 per sq mi, 22 per sq km. **Urban:** 87.6%. **Ethnic groups:** White and white-Amerindian 95%, Amerindian 3%. **Principal languages:** Spanish (official), Araucanian. **Chief religions:** Roman Catholic 70%, Protestant 15%.

Geography: Total area: 292,260 sq mi, 756,950 sq km; **Land area:** 289,113 sq mi, 748,800 sq km. **Location:** Occupies western coast of S South America. **Neighbors:** Peru on N, Bolivia on NE, Argentina on E. **Topography:** Andes Mts. on E border incl. some of the world's highest peaks; on W is 2,650-mile Pacific coast. Width varies 100-250 mi. In N is Atacama Desert, in center are agricultural regions, in S, forests and grazing lands. **Capital:** Santiago, 5,683,000.

Government: Type: Republic. **Head of state and gov.:** Pres. Verónica Michelle Bachelet Jeria; b. Sept. 29, 1951; in office: Mar. 11, 2006. **Local divisions:** 13 regions. **Defense budget:** $1.93 bil. **Active troops:** 75,698.

Economy: Industries: copper, other minerals, foodstuffs, fish proc., iron, steel, wood & wood products, transp. equip., cement, textiles. **Chief crops:** grapes, apples, pears, onions, wheat, corn, oats, peaches, garlic, asparagus, beans. **Natural resources:** copper, timber, iron ore, nitrates, prec. metals, molybd., hydropower. **Crude oil reserves:** 150 mil bbls. **Arable land:** 3%. **Livestock:** cattle: 4.2 mil; chickens: 95 mil; goats: 735,000; pigs: 3.5 mil; sheep: 3.4 mil. **Fish catch:** 5,028,539 metric tons. **Electricity prod.:** 48.2 bil kWh. **Labor force** (2003): agriculture 13.6%, industry 23.4%, services 63%.

Finance: Monetary unit: Peso (CLP) (Sept. 2007: 514.00 = $1 U.S.). **GDP:** $202.7 bil; **per capita GDP:** $12,700; **GDP growth:** 4.2%. **Imports:** $35.4 bil; U.S. 15.6%, Argentina 12.6%, Brazil 11.8%, China 9.7%. **Exports:** $58.2 bil; U.S. 15.6%, Japan 10.5%, China 8.6%, Netherlands 6.7%, South Korea 5.9%. **Tourism:** $1.1 bil. **Budget:** $26.7 bil. **Intl. reserves less gold:** $12.89 bil. **Gold:** 10,000 oz t. **Consumer prices:** 3.39%.

Transport: Railroad: Length: 4,092 mi. **Motor vehicles:** 1.5 mil pass. cars; 756,000 comm. vehicles. **Civil aviation:** 7.6 bil pass.-mi; 73 airports. **Chief ports:** Arica, Antofagasta, Huasco, Iquique, San Antonio, San Vicente, Valparaiso.

Communications: TV sets: 240 per 1,000 pop. **Radios:** 354 per 1,000 pop. **Telephone lines:** 3.3 mil. **Internet:** 4.2 mil users.

Health: Life expect.: 73.7 male; 80.4 female. **Births** (per 1,000 pop.): 15. **Deaths** (per 1,000 pop.): 5.9. **Natural inc.:** 0.92%. **Infant mortality** (per 1,000 live births): 8.4. **AIDS rate:** 0.3%.

Education: Compulsory: ages 6-13. **Literacy:** 95.7%.

Major intl. organizations: UN and all of its specialized agencies, APEC, OAS.

Embassy: 1732 Massachusetts Ave. NW 20036; 785-1746.

Website: www.chileangovernment.cl

Northern Chile was under Inca rule before the Spanish conquest, 1536-40. The southern Araucanian Indians resisted until the late 19th cent. Independence was gained 1810-18, under José de San Martin and Bernardo O'Higgins; the latter, as supreme director 1817-23, sought social and economic reforms until deposed. Chile defeated Peru and Bolivia in 1836-39 and 1879-84, gaining mineral-rich northern land.

In 1970, Salvador Allende Gossens, a Marxist, became president with a narrow plurality of the popular vote. His government improved conditions for the poor, but property seizures by left-wing extremists, poorly planned socialist economic programs, and a destabilization campaign backed by the U.S. led to political and financial chaos.

A military junta seized power Sept. 11, 1973. With the presidential palace under attack, Allende refused to surrender; police said he killed himself. The junta, headed by Gen. Augusto Pinochet Ugarte, named a mostly military cabinet and announced plans to "exterminate Marxism." Repression continued through most of the 1980s.

In Dec. 1989 voters elected a civilian president, although Pinochet continued to head the army until Mar. 10, 1998. In Mar. 1994 a Chilean human rights group estimated that human rights violations had claimed more than 3,100 lives during Pinochet's rule. Initial attempts to prosecute him failed when he was declared mentally unfit to stand trial by courts in Britain and Chile.

Ricardo Lagos Escobar, Chile's first Socialist president since the 1973 coup, took office Mar. 11, 2000. Chile and the U.S. signed a free trade accord June 6, 2003. Verónica Michelle Bachelet Jeria, also a Socialist, won a runoff election Jan. 15, 2006, and took office Mar. 11 as Chile's first woman president. Pinochet died Dec. 10, 2006.

Tierra del Fuego is the largest (18,800 sq mi) island in the archipelago of the same name at the southern tip of S. America, an area of majestic mountains, tortuous channels, and high winds. It was visited 1520 by Magellan and named Land of Fire because of its many Indian bonfires. Part of the island is in Chile, part in Argentina. Punta Arenas, on a mainland peninsula, is a center of sheep raising and the world's southernmost city (pop. [2002 census] 116,005); Puerto Williams is the southernmost settlement.

China

People's Republic of China

(Statistical data do not include Hong Kong or Macao.)

People: Population: 1,321,851,888. **Age distrib.** (%): <15: 20.4; 65+: 7.9. **Pop. density:** 367 per sq mi, 142 per sq km. **Urban:** 40.4%. **Ethnic groups:** 56 groups; Han 92%. Also Zhuang, Manchu, Hui, Miao, Uygur, Yi, Tujia, Tong, Tibetan, Mongol, et al. **Principal languages:** Mandarin (official), Yue (Cantonese), Wu (Shanghaiese), Minbei (Fuzhou), Minnan (Hokkien-Taiwanese), Xiang, Gan, Hakka, minority languages. **Chief religions:** Officially atheist; Buddhism, Taoism, some Muslims, Christians.

Geography: Total area: 3,705,407 sq mi, 9,596,960 sq km; **Land area:** 3,600,947 sq mi, 9,326,410 sq km. **Location:** Occupies most of the habitable mainland of E Asia. **Neighbors:** Mongolia on N; Russia on NE and NW; Afghanistan, Pakistan, Tajikistan, Kyrgystan, Kazakhstan on W; India, Nepal, Bhutan, Myanmar, Laos, Vietnam on S; North Korea on NE. **Topography:** Two-thirds of the vast territory is mountainous or desert; only one-tenth is cultivated. Rolling topography rises to high elevations in the N in the Daxinganlingshanmai separating Manchuria and Mongolia; the Tien Shan in Xinjiang; the Himalayan and Kunlunshanmai in the SW and in Tibet. Length is 1,860 mi from N to S, width E to W is more than 2,000 mi. The eastern half of China is one of the world's best-watered lands. Three great river systems, the Chang (Yangtze), Huang (Yellow), and Xi, provide water for vast farmlands. **Capital:** Beijing, 10,717,000. **Cities (urban aggr.):** Guangzhou, Guangdong 8,425,000; Shanghai 14,503,000; Shenzhen 7,233,000; Tianjin 7,040,000; Wuhan 7,093,000.

Government: Type: Communist Party-led state. **Head of state:** Pres. Hu Jintao; b. Dec. 1942; in office: Mar. 15, 2003 (also gen. secy of Communist Party since Nov. 15, 2002). **Head of gov.:** Premier Wen Jiabao; b. Sept. 1942; in office: Mar. 16, 2003. **Local divisions:** 22 provinces (not including Taiwan), 5 autonomous regions, and 4 municipalities, plus the special administrative regions of Hong Kong (as of July 1, 1997) and Macao (as of Dec. 20, 1999). **Defense budget:** $35.3 bil. **Active troops:** 2,255,000.

Economy: Industries: iron, steel, coal, machine building, armaments, textiles & apparel, oil, cement, chemical fertilizers. **Chief crops:** rice, wheat, potatoes, corn, peanuts, tea, millet, barley, apples, cotton, oilseed. **Natural resources:** coal, iron ore, oil, nat. gas, mercury, tin, tungsten, antimony, mang., molybd., vanadium, magnetite, aluminum, lead, zinc, uranium, hydropower. **Crude oil reserves:** 16 bil bbls. **Arable land:** 15%. **Livestock:** cattle: 117.8 mil; chickens: 4.4 bil; goats: 199 mil; pigs: 510.6 mil; sheep: 173.9 mil. **Fish catch:** 49,467,275 metric tons. **Electricity prod.:** 2,371.8 bil kWh. **Labor force** (2005 est.): agriculture 45%, industry 24%, services 31%.

Finance: Monetary unit: Yuan Renminbi (CNY) (Sept. 2007: 7.52 = $1 U.S.). **GDP:** $10.2 tril; **per capita GDP:** $7,700; **GDP growth:** 10.7%. **Imports:** $777.9 bil; Japan 14.6%, South Korea 11.3%, Taiwan 10.9%, U.S. 7.5%, Germany 4.8%. **Exports:** $974 bil; U.S. 21%, Hong Kong 16%, Japan 9.5%, South Korea 4.6%, Germany 4.2%. **Tourism:** $29.3 bil. **Budget:** $489.6 bil. **Intl. reserves less gold:** $710.25 bil. **Gold:** 19.29 mil oz t. **Consumer prices:** 1.46%.

Transport: Railroad: Length: 46,235 mi. **Motor vehicles:** 17.4 mil pass. cars; 8.9 mil comm. vehicles. **Civil aviation:** 77.4 bil pass.-mi; 403 airports. **Chief ports:** Dalian, Guangzhou, Qinhuangdao, Shanghai.

Communications: TV sets: 291 per 1,000 pop. **Radios:** 342 per 1,000 pop. **Telephone lines:** 367.8 mil. **Daily newspaper circ.:** 59.3 per 1,000 pop. **Internet:** 137 mil users.

Health: Life expect.: 71.1 male; 74.8 female. **Births** (per 1,000 pop.): 13.5. **Deaths** (per 1,000 pop.): 7. **Natural inc.:** 0.65%. **Infant mortality** (per 1,000 live births): 22.1. **AIDS rate:** 0.1%.

Education: Compulsory: ages 6-14. **Literacy:** 90.9%.

Major intl. organizations: UN (FAO, IBRD, ILO, IMF, IMO, WHO, WTO), APEC.

Embassy: 2300 Connecticut Ave. NW 20008; 328-2500.

Website: english.gov.cn

Remains of various humanlike creatures who lived as early as several hundred thousand years ago have been found in many parts of China. Neolithic agricultural settlements dotted the Huang (Yellow) R. basin from about 5000 BCE. Their language, religion, and art were the sources of later Chinese civilization.

Bronze metallurgy reached a peak and Chinese pictographic writing, similar to today's, was in use in the more developed culture of the Shang Dynasty (c. 1500 BCE-c. 1000 BCE), which ruled much of North China.

A succession of dynasties and interdynastic warring kingdoms ruled China for the next 3,000 years. They expanded Chinese political and cultural domination to the south and west, and developed a brilliant technologically and a culturally advanced society. Rule by foreigners (Mongols in the Yuan Dynasty, 1271-1368, and Manchus in the Ch'ing Dynasty, 1644-1911) did not alter the underlying culture.

A period of relative stagnation left China vulnerable to internal and external pressures in the 19th cent. Rebellions left tens of millions dead, and Russia, Japan, Britain, and other powers exercised political and economic control in large parts of the country. China became a republic Jan. 1, 1912, following the Wuchang Uprising inspired by Dr. Sun Yat-sen, founder of the Kuomintang (Nationalist) party. By 1928, the Kuomintang, led by Chiang Kai-shek, succeeded in nominal reunification of China. About the same time, a bloody purge of Communists from the ranks of the Kuomintang fomented hostilities between the two groups that would continue for decades.

For over 50 years, 1894-1945, China was involved in conflicts with Japan. In 1895, China ceded Korea, Taiwan, and other areas. On Sept. 18, 1931, Japan seized the Northeastern Provinces (Manchuria) and set up a puppet state called Manchukuo. The border province of Jehol was cut off as a buffer state in 1933. Taking advantage of Chinese dissension, Japan invaded China proper July 7, 1937. On Nov. 20 the retreating Nationalist government moved its capital to Chongqing (Chungking) from Nanking (Nanjing), which Japanese troops then ravaged Dec. 13.

From 1939 the Sino-Japanese War (1937-45) became part of the broader world conflict. After its defeat in World War II, Japan gave up all seized land, and internal conflicts involving the Kuomintang, Communists, and other factions resumed. China came under the domination of Communist armies, 1949-1950. The Kuomintang government moved to Taiwan, Dec. 8, 1949.

The Chinese People's Political Consultative Conference convened Sept. 21, 1949; The People's Republic of China was proclaimed in Beijing (Peking) Oct. 1, 1949, under Mao Zedong. China and the USSR signed a 30-year treaty of "friendship, alliance, and mutual assistance," Feb. 15, 1950. The U.S. refused recognition of the new regime. On Nov. 26, 1950, the People's Republic sent armies into Korea against U.S. troops and forced a stalemate in the Korean War.

After an initial period of consolidation, 1949-52, industry, agriculture, and social and economic institutions were forcibly molded according to Maoist ideals. However, frequent drastic changes in policy and violent factionalism interfered with economic development. In 1957, Mao admitted an estimated 800,000 people had been executed 1949-54; opponents claimed much higher figures.

The Great Leap Forward, 1958-60, tried to force the pace of economic development through intensive labor on huge new rural communes, and through emphasis on ideological purity. The program caused resistance and was largely abandoned.

By the 1960s, relations with the USSR deteriorated, with disagreements on borders, ideology, and leadership of world Communism. The USSR canceled aid accords, and China, with Albania, launched anti-Soviet propaganda drives.

The Great Proletarian Cultural Revolution, 1965, was an attempt to oppose pragmatism and bureaucratic power and instruct a new generation in revolutionary principles. Massive purges took place. A program of forcibly relocating millions of urban teenagers into the countryside was launched. By 1968 the movement had run its course; many purged officials returned to office in subsequent years, and reforms that had placed ideology above expertise were gradually weakened.

On Oct. 25, 1971, the UN General Assembly ousted the Taiwan government from the UN and seated the People's Republic in its place. The U.S. had supported the mainland's admission but opposed Taiwan's expulsion.

U.S. Pres. Richard Nixon visited China Feb. 21-28, 1972, on invitation from Premier Zhou Enlai, ending years of antipathy between the 2 nations. China and the U.S. opened liaison offices in each other's capitals, May-June 1973. The U.S., Dec. 15, 1978, formally recognized the People's Republic of China as the sole legal government of China; diplomatic relations between the 2 nations were established, Jan. 1, 1979.

Mao died Sept. 9, 1976. By 1978, Vice Premier Deng Xiaoping had consolidated his power, succeeding Mao as "paramount leader" of China. The new ruling group modified Maoist policies in education, culture, and industry, and sought better ties with non-Communist countries. During this "reassessment" of Mao's policies his widow, Jiang Qing, and other "Gang of Four" leftists were convicted of "committing crimes during the 'Cultural Revolution,'" Jan. 25, 1981.

By the mid-1980s, China had enacted far-reaching economic reforms, deemphasizing centralized planning and incorporating market-oriented incentives. Some 100,000 students and workers staged a march in Beijing to demand political reforms, May 4, 1989. As the unrest spread, martial law was imposed, May 20. Troops entered Beijing, June 3-4, and crushed the pro-democracy protests, as tanks and armored personnel carriers rolled through Tiananmen Square. It is estimated that 5,000 died, 10,000 were injured, and hundreds of students and workers were arrested.

Deng Xiaoping died Feb. 19, 1997, leaving Jiang Zemin in control as president. By agreement with the UK, Hong Kong reverted to Chinese sovereignty July 1 (see below). NATO bombs hit the Chinese embassy in Belgrade, Yugoslavia, on May 7, 1999, killing 3 people and wounding 27, for which the U.S. paid compensation. The government banned a popular religious sect, the Falun Gong, July 22, after it staged the largest unauthorized demonstrations in Beijing since 1989. The U.S. and China signed a major trade agreement Nov. 15. Portugal returned Macao to China Dec. 20, 1999.

Beijing was chosen, July 13, 2001, to host the 2008 Summer Olympics. Admission to the WTO Dec. 11 marked an economic milestone, though protested by many human rights and labor organizations. Hu Jintao was named Communist Party general secretary at the 16th party congress, Nov. 15, 2002, and elected president by the 10th National People's Congress, Mar. 15, 2003. A SARS epidemic beginning in late 2002 killed 349 people in mainland China by mid-2003.

In Aug. 2003, China assumed an unprecedented diplomatic role when it hosted multinational talks on N. Korea's nuclear weapons program. With the successful launch and recovery, Oct. 15-16, of the *Shenzhou 5* spacecraft, China became the third nation (after the U.S. and USSR) to send a man into space. Floods in summer 2004 killed more than 1,000 people and caused $8 bil in damage. Pres. Hu Jintao expanded his power when he became China's military chief Sept. 19.

A UN-China survey found that 650,000 Chinese had HIV/AIDS in 2005, less than previously estimated. Floods and mudslides from Tropical Storm Bilis, which hit China July 14, 2006, killed at least 612 people and caused $3.3 bil in damage.

China's industries, exports, and demand for oil have all increased rapidly since the 1980s. Reports in 2007 that China had exported hazardous pet products, toothpaste, tires, and toys focused attention on factories' quality-control problems. Zheng Xiaoyu, the former head of China's food and drug safety agency, was executed July 10 for bribe taking and dereliction of duty.

Manchuria. Home of the Manchus, rulers of China 1644-1911, Manchuria has accommodated millions of Chinese settlers in the 20th cent. Under Japanese rule 1931-45, the area became industrialized. The region is divided into the 3 northeastern provinces of Heilongjiang, Jilin, and Liaoning.

Autonomous Regions

Guangxi Zhuang is in SE China, bounded on the N by Guizhou and Hunan provinces, E and S by Guangdong, on the SW by Vietnam, and on the W by Yunnan. It produces rice in the river valleys and has valuable forest products. **Pop. (2000):** 44.89 mil.

Inner Mongolia was organized by the People's Republic in 1947. Its boundaries have undergone frequent changes, reaching its greatest extent in 1956 (and restored in 1979), with an area of 454,600 sq mi, allegedly in order to dilute the minority Mongol population. Chinese settlers outnumber the Mongols more than 10 to 1. Pop. (2000): 23.76 mil. Capital: Hohhot.

Ningxia Hui, in north central China, is about 60,000 sq mi. Pop. (2000): 5.62 mil. Capital: Yinchuan. Situated mainly at the semiarid Inner Mongolian plateau region with desert areas in the N. The Huang He (Yellow R.) flows across the N furnishes water for irrigation. Coal is mined in the E. Modern industry is relatively undeveloped, and only one railroad crosses the region. The majority of the population is Han, and the Hui (Chinese Muslims) constitute about one-third of the population. The region experienced a significant population boom from 1950-80, which has now stabilized.

Xinjiang Uygur, in Central Asia, is 635,900 sq mi, pop. (2000): 19.25 mil (75% Uygurs, a Turkic Muslim group, with a heavy Chinese increase in recent years). Capital: Urumqi. It is China's richest region in strategic minerals. China has moved to crack down on Uygur separatists, whom Beijing regards as terrorists.

Tibet, 471,700 sq mi, is a thinly populated region of high plateaus and massive mountains, the Himalayas on the S, the Kunluns on the N. High passes connect with India and Nepal; roads lead into China proper. Capital: Lhasa. Average altitude is 15,000 ft. Jiachan, 15,870 ft, is believed to be the highest inhabited town on earth. Agriculture is primitive. Pop. (2000): 2.62 mil (of whom about 500,000 are Chinese). Another 4 mil Tibetans form the majority of the population of vast adjacent areas that have long been incorporated into China.

China ruled all of Tibet from the 18th cent. Independence came in 1911, but China reasserted control in 1951, and a Communist government was installed in 1953, revising the theocratic Lamaist Buddhist rule. Serfdom was abolished, but all land remained collectivized.

A Tibetan uprising within China in 1956 spread to Lhasa in 1959. The rebellion was crushed by Chinese troops, and Buddhism was almost totally suppressed. The Dalai Lama and 100,000 Tibetans fled to India.

Rail service from Beijing to Lhasa began July 1, 2006, with completion of the 710-mi Qinghai-Tibet line, the world's highest railway, an ambitious engineering project that cost more than $4 bil.

Hong Kong

Hong Kong (Xianggang), located at the mouth of the Zhu Jiang (Pearl R.) in SE China, 90 mi S of Canton (Guangzhou), was a British dependency from 1842 until July 1, 1997, when it became a Special Administrative Region of China. Its nucleus is Hong Kong Is., 31 sq mi, occupied by the British in 1841 and formally ceded to them in 1842, on which is located the seat of government. Opposite is Kowloon Peninsula, 3 sq mi, and Stonecutters Is., added to the territory in 1860. An additional 355 sq mi known as the New Territories, a mainland area and islands, were leased from China, 1898, for 99 years. Area 422 sq mi (total); 402 sq mi (land); pop. (2007 est.) 6,980,412, including fewer than 20,000 British.

Hong Kong is a major center for trade and banking. Per capita GDP, $37,300 (2006 est.), is among the highest in the world. Principal industries are textiles and apparel; also tourism ($11.9 bil expenditures in 2004), electronics, shipbuilding, iron and steel, fishing, cement, and small manufactures. Hong Kong's spinning mills are among the best in the world.

Hong Kong harbor was long an important British naval station and one of the world's great transshipment ports. The colony was often a place of refuge for exiles from mainland China. It was occupied by Japan during WWII.

From 1949 to 1962 Hong Kong absorbed more than a million refugees fleeing Communist China. Starting in the 1950s, cheap labor led to a boom in light manufacturing, while liberal tax policies attracted foreign investment; Hong Kong became one of the wealthiest, most productive areas in the Far East. Poor living and working conditions and low wages for many led to political unrest in the 1960s, but legislation and public works programs raised the standard of living by the 1970s.

With the end of the 99-year lease on the New Territories drawing near, Britain and China signed an agreement, Dec. 19, 1984, under which all of Hong Kong was to be returned to China in 1997; under this agreement Hong Kong was to be allowed to keep its capitalist system for 50 years. In Dec. 1996, an electoral college appointed by China chose a shipping magnate, Tung Chee-hwa, to be Hong Kong's chief executive when it reverted to Chinese control.

Following the transfer of government on July 1, Hong Kong retained its street names and its currency, the Hong Kong dollar (HK$7.78 = $1 U.S.), but without the queen's picture. Official languages remained Chinese (Cantonese dialect) and English. Pro-democracy candidates did well in May 24, 1998, elections, despite having been excluded from the provisional government. in 1997. A SARS outbreak in 2003 claimed almost 300 lives and damaged the economy.

Hundreds of thousands of Hong Kong residents turned out July 1, 2003, to protest a proposed anti-subversion law; the bill was withdrawn Sept. 5. Another mass march, July 1, 2004, protested Beijing's refusal to allow greater freedom. Pro-democracy candidates won a majority of the popular vote in elections, Sept. 12, but failed to gain control of the Legislative Council. After Tung Chee-hwa resigned Mar. 10, 2005, Donald Tsang was chosen to serve the remaining 2 years of Tung's term as chief executive; he won a full 5-year term Mar. 25, 2007.

Macao

Macao, area of 11 sq mi, is an enclave, a peninsula and 2 small islands, at the mouth of the Xi (Pearl) R. in China. It was established as a Portuguese trading colony in 1557. In 1849, Portugal claimed sovereignty over the territory; this claim was accepted by China in an 1887 treaty. Portugal granted broad autonomy in 1976. Under a 1987 agreement, Macao reverted to China Dec. 20, 1999. As in the case of Hong Kong, the Chinese government guaranteed Macao it would not interfere in its way of life and capitalist system for a period of 50 years. Tourism is the fastest-growing economic sector; casino gambling revenues reached $7.2 bil in 2006. Pop. (2007 est.): 456,989.

Colombia
Republic of Colombia

People: Population: 44,379,598. **Age distrib.** (%): <15: 29.8; 65+: 5.4. **Pop. density:** 111 per sq mi, 43 per sq km. **Urban:** 72.7%. **Ethnic groups:** Mestizo 58%, white 20%, Creole 14%, black 4%, Amerindian 1%. **Principal language:** Spanish (official). **Chief religion:** Roman Catholic 90%.

Geography: Total area: 439,736 sq mi, 1,138,910 sq km; **Land area:** 401,044 sq mi, 1,038,700 sq km. **Location:** At the NW corner of South America. **Neighbors:** Panama on NW, Ecuador and Peru on S, Brazil and Venezuela on E. **Topography:** Three ranges of Andes—Western, Central, and Eastern Cordilleras—run through the country from N to S. The eastern range consists mostly of high tablelands, densely populated. The Magdalena R. rises in the Andes, flows N to Caribbean, through a rich alluvial plain. Sparsely settled plains in E are drained by Orinoco and Amazon systems. **Capital:** Bogotá (Full name: Santa Fe de Bogotá.), 7,747,000. **Cities (urban aggr.):** Medellin, 3,058,000; Cali, 2,514,000; Barranquilla, 1,857,000.

Government: Type: Republic. **Head of state and gov.:** Pres. Álvaro Uribe Vélez; b. July 4, 1952; in office: Aug. 7, 2002. **Local divisions:** 32 departments, capital district of Bogota. **Defense budget:** $3.77 bil. **Active troops:** 208,600.

Economy: Industries: textiles, food proc., oil, clothing & footwear, beverages, chemicals, cement, mining. **Chief crops:** coffee, cut flowers, bananas, rice, tobacco, corn, sugarcane, cocoa beans. **Natural resources:** oil, nat. gas, coal, iron ore, nickel, gold, copper, emeralds, hydropower. **Crude oil reserves:** 1.5 bil bbls. **Arable land:** 2%. **Livestock:** cattle: 25.7 mil; chickens: 150 mil; goats: 4.1 mil; pigs: 1.7 mil; sheep: 3.3 mil. **Fish catch:** 181,072 metric tons. **Electricity prod.:** 50.5 bil kWh. **Labor force** (2000 est.): agriculture 22.7%, industry 18.7%, services 58.5%.

Finance: Monetary unit: Peso (COP) (Sept. 2007: 2,140.90 = $1 U.S.). **GDP:** $374.4 bil; **per capita GDP:** $8,600; **GDP growth:** 6.8%. **Imports:** $24.3 bil; U.S. 28.2%, Mexico 8.3%, Brazil 6.5%, China 6.3%, Venezuela 5.9%. **Exports:** $24.9 bil; U.S. 35.8%, Venezuela 10.4%, Ecuador 6.6%. **Tourism:** $1 bil. **Budget:** $52.3 bil. **Intl. reserves less gold:** $10.17 bil. **Gold:** 220,000 oz t. **Consumer prices:** 4.3%.

Transport: Railroad: Length: 2,053 mi. **Motor vehicles:** 2.1 mil pass. cars; 343,500 comm. vehicles. **Civil aviation:** 5.2 bil pass.-mi; 101 airports. **Chief ports:** Barranquilla, Buenaventura, Cartagena, Puerto Bolivar, Santa Marta, Turbo.

Communications: TV sets: 279 per 1,000 pop. **Radios:** 539 per 1,000 pop. **Telephone lines:** 7.9 mil. **Daily newspaper circ.:** 26.4 per 1,000 pop. **Internet:** 6.7 mil users.

Health: Life expect.: 68.4 male; 76.2 female. **Births** (per 1,000 pop.): 20.2. **Deaths** (per 1,000 pop.): 5.5. **Natural inc.:** 1.46%. **Infant mortality** (per 1,000 live births): 20.1. **AIDS rate:** 0.6%.

Education: Compulsory: ages 5-14. **Literacy:** 92.8%.

Major intl. organizations: UN (FAO, IBRD, ILO, IMF, IMO, WHO, WTO), OAS.

Embassy: 2118 Leroy Pl. NW 20008; 387-8338.

Website: www.colombiaemb.org

Spain subdued the local Indian kingdoms (Funza, Tunja) by the 1530s and ruled Colombia and neighboring areas as New Granada for 300 years. Independence was won by 1819. Venezuela and Ecuador broke away in 1829-30, and Panama withdrew in 1903.

Colombia is plagued by rural and urban violence. "La Violencia" of 1948-58 claimed 200,000 lives; since 1989, political killings, kidnappings, and "disappearances" have victimized many thousands of civilians, and the internally displaced population has grown to over 3 mil. Attempts at land and social reform and progress in industrialization have not reduced massive social problems.

The government's increased activity against local drug traffickers sparked a series of retaliation killings. On Aug. 18, 1989, Luis Carlos Galán, the ruling party's presidential hopeful for the 1990 election, was assassinated. In 1990, 2 other presidential candidates were assassinated, as drug traffickers carried on a campaign of intimidation.

Right-wing paramilitaries launched a campaign Dec. 22, 2000, against suspected left-wing guerrillas. Legislation expanding the powers of the military was signed Aug. 13, 2001. The collapse of talks with the rebels in Feb. 2002 brought an upsurge of fighting. A hardliner, Álvaro Uribe Vélez, whose father had been killed by leftist rebels in 1983, won a presidential election May 26. A wave of guerrilla violence as he took office led Uribe to declare a "state of unrest" Aug. 12. Police powers were increased Sept. 10 as part of a new government offensive. The constitution was amended, Nov.

30, 2004, to allow the president to seek a second consecutive term; he easily won reelection May 28, 2006. Key political figures, including major allies of Uribe, were arrested in 2007 on charges of colluding with paramilitary death squads.

Colombia produces an estimated 90% of the cocaine reaching the U.S. Since 2000, the U.S. has provided more than $5 bil to Colombia, much of it to combat the drug trade.

Comoros
Union of Comoros

People: Population: 711,417. **Age distrib.** (%): <15: 42.6; 65+: 3. **Pop. density:** 849 per sq mi, 328 per sq km. **Urban:** 37%. **Ethnic groups:** Antalote, Cafre, Makoa, Oimatsaha, Sakalava (all are mostly an African-Arab mix). **Principal languages:** Arabic, French (both official); Shikomoro (a blend of Swahili and Arabic). **Chief religion:** Muslim (official) 98%.

Geography: Total area: 838 sq mi, 2,170 sq km; **Land area:** 838 sq mi, 2,170 sq km. **Location:** 3 islands—Grande Comore (Njazidja), Anjouan (Nzwani), and Moheli (Mwali)—in the Mozambique Channel between NW Madagascar and SE Africa. **Neighbors:** Nearest are Mozambique on W, Madagascar on E. **Topography:** The islands are of volcanic origin, with an active volcano on Grande Comore. **Capital:** Moroni, 44,000.

Government: Type: Republic. **Head of state and gov.:** Pres. Ahmed Abdallah Mohamed Sambi; b. June 5, 1958; in office: May 26, 2006. **Local divisions:** 3 main islands with 4 municipalities.

Economy: Industries: tourism, perfume distillation. **Chief crops:** vanilla, cloves, perfume essences, copra, coconuts, bananas, cassava. **Arable land:** 36%. **Livestock:** cattle: 45,000; chickens: 500,000; goats: 115,000; sheep: 21,000. **Fish catch:** 15,070 metric tons. **Electricity prod.:** 20 mil kWh. **Labor force:** agriculture 80%, industry and services 20%.

Finance: Monetary unit: Franc (TZS) (Sept. 2007: 3.51 = $1 U.S.). **GDP:** $1.3 bil; **per capita GDP** (2005 est.): $600; **GDP growth** (2005 est.): 3%. **Imports** (2004 est.): $115 mil; France 25.1%, UAE 10%, South Africa 6.5%, Pakistan 6.4%, Kenya 5.1%. **Exports** (2004 est.): $34 mil; Netherlands 35.7%, France 18.2%, Italy 12.7%, Singapore 7.8%, Turkey 4.9%, U.S. 4.5%. **Tourism:** $21 mil. **Budget:** NA. **Intl. reserves less gold:** $62 mil.

Transport: Civil aviation: 4 airports. **Chief ports:** Mayotte, Moutsamoudou.

Communications: TV sets: 4 per 1,000 pop. **Radios:** 141 per 1,000 pop. **Telephone lines:** 16,900. **Internet:** 21,000 users.

Health: Life expect.: 60.4 male; 65.2 female. **Births** (per 1,000 pop.): 36.4. **Deaths** (per 1,000 pop.): 8. **Natural inc.:** 2.84%. **Infant mortality** (per 1,000 live births): 70.7. **AIDS rate:** <0.1%.

Education: Compulsory: ages 6-13. **Literacy:** 56.5%.

Major intl. organizations: UN (FAO, IBRD, ILO, IMF, WHO), AL, AU.

Embassy: 420 E. 50th St., New York, NY 10022; 212-972-8010.

Website: www.state.gov/p/af/ci/cn/

The islands were controlled by Muslim sultans until the French acquired them 1841-1909. They became a French overseas territory in 1947. A 1974 referendum favored independence, with only the Christian island of Mayotte preferring association with France. The French National Assembly decided to allow each of the islands to decide its own fate. The Comore Chamber of Deputies declared independence July 6, 1975, with Ahmed Abdallah as president. In a referendum in 1976, Mayotte voted to remain French.

A leftist regime that seized power from Abdallah in 1975 was deposed in a pro-French 1978 coup in which he regained the presidency. In Nov. 1989, Pres. Abdallah was assassinated; soon after, a multiparty system was instituted. A Sept. 1995 military coup, assisted by French mercenaries, ousted Pres. Said Mohamed Djohar. French troops invaded, Oct. 4, and forced coup leaders to surrender.

Attempts to work out a new constitutional relationship between Grande Comore, Anjouan, and Moheli have been ongoing since Anjouan and Moheli seceded from the Comoros in 1997. Unrest on Grande Comore culminated in a military coup, Apr. 30, 1999. Anjouans endorsed secession in a disputed vote Jan. 23, 2000.

Irregularities marred the presidential runoff election of Apr. 14, 2002, won by Azali Assoumani, who led the 1999 coup. Elections for national and island assemblies took place Mar.-Apr. 2004. Ahmed Abdallah Mohamed Sambi won a presidential runoff vote, May 14, 2006. Each of the 3 islands elected its own president in 2002 and 2007.

Congo (formerly Zaire)
Democratic Republic of the Congo

(Congo, officially Democratic Republic of the Congo, is also known as Congo-Kinshasa. It should not be confused with Republic of the Congo, commonly called Congo Republic, and also known as Congo-Brazzaville.)

People: Population: 65,751,512. **Age distrib.** (%): <15: 47.6; 65+: 2.6. **Pop. density:** 75 per sq mi, 29 per sq km. **Urban:** 32.1%. **Ethnic groups:** Over 200 groups. Four largest, the Mongo, Luba, Kongo (all Bantu) and Mangbetu-Azande (Hamitic), make up 45% of pop. **Principal languages:** French (official), Lingala, Kingwana (Swahili dialect), Kikongo, Tshiluba. **Chief religions:** Roman Catholic 50%, Protestant 20%, Kimbanguist 10%, Muslim 10%.

Geography: Total area: 905,568 sq mi, 2,345,410 sq km; **Land area:** 875,525 sq mi, 2,267,600 sq km. **Location:** In central Africa. **Neighbors:** Congo-Brazzaville on W; Central African Republic, Sudan on N; Uganda, Rwanda, Burundi, Tanzania on E; Zambia, Angola on S. **Topography:** Congo includes the bulk of the Congo R. basin. The vast central region is a low-lying plateau covered by rain forest. Mountainous terraces in the W, savannas in the S and SE, grasslands toward the N, and the high Ruwenzori Mts. on the E surround the central region. A short strip of territory borders the Atlantic O. **Capital:** Kinshasa, 6,049,000. **Cities (urban aggr.):** Lubumbashi, 906,000.

Government: Type: In transition. **Head of state and gov.:** Pres. Joseph Kabila; b. June 24, 1971; in office: Jan. 26, 2001. **Local divisions:** 10 provinces, 1 city. **Defense budget:** $163 mil. **Active troops:** 51,000.

Economy: Industries: mining, mineral proc., textiles, footwear, cigarettes, proc. foods & beverages, cement. **Chief crops:** coffee, sugar, rubber, tea, quinine, cassava, palm oil, bananas, root crops, corn, fruits. **Natural resources:** cobalt, copper, cadmium, oil, diamonds, gold, silver, zinc, manganese, uranium, radium, bauxite, iron ore, coal, hydropower, timber. **Crude oil reserves:** 180 mil bbls. **Arable land:** 3%. **Livestock:** cattle: 757,000; chickens: 20 mil; goats: 4 mil; pigs: 960,000; sheep: 900,000. **Fish catch:** 222,965 metric tons. **Electricity prod.:** 7.3 bil kWh. **Labor force:** NA.

Finance: Monetary unit: Franc (CDF) (Sept. 2007: 560.00 = $1 U.S.). **GDP:** $44.4 bil; **per capita GDP:** $700; **GDP growth:** 6.4%. **Imports** (2004 est.): $1.3 bil; South Africa 19.5%, Belgium 11.8%, France 9.4%, Kenya 7.5%, Zambia 6.5%. **Exports** (2004 est.): $1.1 bil; Belgium 33.4%, China 24.1%, Chile 8.9%, Finland 8.2%, U.S. 5.6%. **Tourism:** $20 mil. **Budget:** $2 bil. **Intl. reserves less gold:** NA. **Consumer prices** (2005): 21%.

Transport: Railroad: Length: 3,193 mi. **Motor vehicles:** 172,600 pass. cars; 34,600 comm. vehicles. **Civil aviation:** 25 airports. **Chief ports:** Boma, Kinshasa, Matadi.

Communications: TV sets: 2 per 1,000 pop. **Radios:** 376 per 1,000 pop. **Telephone lines:** 9,700. **Daily newspaper circ.:** 2.8 per 1,000 pop. **Internet:** 180,000.

Health: Life expect.: 55 male; 59.5 female. **Births** (per 1,000 pop.): 43. **Deaths** (per 1,000 pop.): 10.3. **Natural inc.:** 3.26%. **Infant mortality** (per 1,000 live births): 65.5. **AIDS rate:** 3.2%.

Education: Compulsory: ages 6-13. **Literacy:** 67.2%.

Major intl. organizations: UN and most of its specialized agencies, AU.

Embassy: 1726 M St. NW 20036; 234-7690.

Website: www.state.gov/p/af/ci/cg/

The earliest inhabitants of Congo may have been the pygmies, followed by Bantus from the east and Nilotic tribes from the north. The large Bantu Bakongo kingdom ruled much of Congo and Angola when Portuguese explorers visited in the 15th cent.

Leopold II, king of the Belgians, formed an international group to exploit the Congo region in 1876. In 1877 Henry M. Stanley explored the Congo, and in 1878 the king's group sent him back to organize the region and win over the native chiefs. The Conference of Berlin, 1884-85, established the Congo Free State with Leopold as king and chief owner. Exploitation of native laborers on the rubber plantations caused international criticism and led to granting of a colonial charter, 1908; the colony became known as the Belgian Congo. Millions of Congolese are believed to have died between 1880 and 1920 as a result of slave labor and other causes under European rule.

Belgian and Congolese leaders agreed Jan. 27, 1960, that Congo would become independent in June. In the first general elections, May 31, the National Congolese movement of Patrice Lumumba won a plurality in the National Assembly. The Republic of the Congo was proclaimed June 30. Widespread violence caused Europeans and others to flee. The UN Security Council, Aug. 9, called on Belgium to withdraw its troops and sent a UN contingent. Pres. Joseph Kasavubu removed Lumumba as premier in Sept.; Lumumba was murdered Jan. 17, 1961. The last UN troops left the Congo June 30, 1964, and Moise Tshombe became president.

On Sept. 7, 1964, leftist rebels set up a "People's Republic" in Stanleyville (now Kisangani). Tshombe hired foreign mercenaries and sought to rebuild the Congolese Army. In Nov. and Dec. 1964 rebels killed scores of white hostages and thousands of Congolese; Belgian paratroopers, dropped from U.S. transport planes, rescued hundreds. By July 1965 the rebels had lost their effectiveness.

In late 1965 Gen. Joseph D. Mobutu was named president. He later changed his name to Mobutu Sese Seko and ruled as a dictator. The country became the Democratic Republic of the Congo (1966) and the Republic of Zaire (1971). Under Mobutu, economic decline and government corruption plagued Zaire. In 1990, Pres. Mobutu announced an end to a 20-year ban on multiparty politics. He sought to retain power despite mounting international pressure and internal opposition.

During 1994, Zaire was inundated with refugees from the massive ethnic bloodshed in Rwanda. Ethnic violence spread to E Zaire in 1996. In Oct. militant Hutus, who dominated in the refugee camps, fought against rebels (mostly Tutsis) in Zaire, precipitating intervention by government troops. As a result of the fighting, Rwandan refugees abandoned the camps; hundreds of thousands

returned to Rwanda, while hundreds of thousands more were dispersed throughout eastern Zaire. The rebels, led by Gen. Laurent Kabila—a former Marxist and longtime opponent of Mobutu—gained momentum and began to move west across Zaire. On May 17, 1997, Kabila's troops entered Kinshasa and Mobutu went into exile. The country again assumed the name Democratic Republic of the Congo. Mobutu died Sept. 7 in Rabat, Morocco.

Kabila, who ruled by decree, alienated UN officials, international aid donors, and former allies. Rebels assisted by Rwanda and Uganda threatened Kinshasa in Aug. 1998, but the assault was turned back with help from Angola, Namibia, and Zimbabwe. Rebel groups agreed to a cease-fire on Aug. 31, 1999, but the truce was widely violated. Kabila was assassinated Jan. 16, 2001, apparently by one of his bodyguards, and was succeeded by his son Joseph.

The overall death toll from the civil war and related causes was estimated at 3.3 mil through Nov. 2002. By then the war had apparently begun to wind down, with agreements by Rwanda and Uganda to pull out their remaining troops. A power-sharing accord signed Apr. 2, 2003, led to the installation of a new Congolese government in July. A new constitution won legislative approval May 13, 2005. A UN peacekeeping force (MONUC), established in 1999, remained in the country to oversee elections, held July 30-31, 2006, the nation's first multiparty vote since 1960. Kabila defeated former rebel leader Jean-Pierre Bemba in a presidential runoff election, Oct. 29, 2006.

Hundreds reportedly died in Kinshasa, Mar. 22-23, 2007, in clashes between security forces and a militia loyal to Bemba, who departed for Portugal, Apr. 11, for medical treatment. MONUC personnel in Congo at mid-2007 numbered more than 18,000.

Congo Republic
Republic of the Congo

(Congo Republic, officially Republic of the Congo, is also known as Congo-Brazzaville. It should not be confused with Democratic Republic of the Congo [formerly Zaire], now commonly called Congo, and also known as Congo-Kinshasa.)

People: Population: 3,800,610. **Age distrib.** (%): <15: 46.3; 65+: 2.9. **Pop. density:** 29 per sq mi, 11 per sq km. **Urban:** 60.2%. **Ethnic groups:** Kongo 48%, Sangha 20%, M'Bochi 12%, Teke 17%. **Principal languages:** French (official), Lingala, Monokutuba, Kikongo, many local languages and dialects. **Chief religions:** Christian 50%, animist 48%, Muslim 2%.

Geography: Total area: 132,047 sq mi, 342,000 sq km; **Land area:** 131,854 sq mi, 341,500 sq km. **Location:** In W central Africa. **Neighbors:** Gabon and Cameroon on W, Central African Republic on N, Congo-Kinshasa (formerly Zaire) on E, Angola on SW. **Topography:** Much of the Congo is covered by thick forests. A coastal plain leads to the fertile Niari Valley. The center is a plateau; the Congo R. basin consists of flood plains in the lower and savanna in the upper portion. **Capital:** Brazzaville, 1,173,000.

Government: Type: Republic. **Head of state and gov.:** Pres. Denis Sassou-Nguesso; b. 1943; in office: Oct. 25, 1997. **Local divisions:** 10 regions, 6 communes. **Defense budget:** $66 mil. **Active troops:** 10,000.

Economy: Industries: oil, cement, lumber, brewing, sugar, palm oil. **Chief crops:** cassava, sugar, rice, corn, peanuts, vegetables, coffee, cocoa. **Natural resources:** oil, timber, potash, lead, zinc, uranium, copper, phosphates, nat. gas, hydropower. **Crude oil reserves:** 1.6 bil bbls. **Arable land:** 1%. **Livestock:** cattle: 115,000; chickens: 2.4 mil; goats: 295,000; pigs: 46,000; sheep: 99,000. **Fish catch:** 58,448 metric tons. **Electricity prod.:** 350 mil kWh. **Labor force:** NA.

Finance: Monetary unit: CFA BEAC Franc (XAF) (Sept. 2007: 472.78 = $1 U.S.). **GDP:** $5.1 bil; **per capita GDP:** $1,400; **GDP growth:** 7.5%. **Imports:** $2 bil; France 23.5%, China 13.1%, U.S. 7.5%, India 6.9%, Italy 5.6%, Belgium 5.1%. **Exports:** $6 bil; U.S. 38.1%, China 33.3%, Taiwan 10.2%, South Korea 6.2%. **Tourism:** $20 mil. **Budget:** $1.7 bil. **Intl. reserves less gold:** $1.22 bil. **Gold:** 10,000 oz t.

Transport: Railroad: Length: 556 mi. **Motor vehicles:** 29,700 pass. cars; 23,100 comm. vehicles. **Civil aviation:** 19.3 mil pass.-mi; 4 airports. **Chief ports:** Brazzaville, Pointe-Noire.

Communications: TV sets: 13 per 1,000 pop. **Radios:** 126 per 1,000 pop. **Telephone lines:** 15,900. **Daily newspaper circ.:** 6.3 per 1,000 pop. **Internet:** 70,000 users.

Health: Life expect.: 52.1 male; 54.5 female. **Births** (per 1,000 pop.): 42.2. **Deaths** (per 1,000 pop.): 12.6. **Natural inc.:** 2.96%. **Infant mortality** (per 1,000 live births): 83.3. **AIDS rate:** 5.3%.

Education: Compulsory: ages 6-16. **Literacy:** 84.7%.

Major intl. organizations: UN (FAO, IBRD, ILO, IMF, IMO, WHO, WTO), AU.

Embassy: 4891 Colorado Ave. NW 20011; 726-5500.

Website: www.state.gov/p/af/ci/cf/

The Loango Kingdom flourished in the 15th cent., as did the Anzico Kingdom of the Batekes; by the late 17th cent. they had become weakened. By 1885, France established control of the region, then called the Middle Congo. Republic of the Congo gained independence Aug. 15, 1960.

After a 1963 coup sparked by trade unions, the country adopted a Marxist-Leninist stance, with the USSR and China vying for influence. France remained a dominant trade partner and source of technical assistance, however, and French-owned private enterprise retained a major economic role. In 1970, the country was renamed People's Republic of the Congo.

In 1990, Marxism was renounced and opposition parties were legalized. In 1991 the country's name was changed back to Republic of the Congo, and a new constitution was approved. A democratically elected government came into office in 1992. Factional fighting broke out in Brazzaville, June 5, 1997, and intensified during the summer, devastating the capital. Troops loyal to former Marxist dictator Denis Sassou-Nguesso took control of the city Oct. 15. He claimed a lopsided victory in the presidential election of Mar. 10, 2002. The government and "Ninja" rebels in the Pool Region agreed to a cease-fire Mar. 17, 2003.

Oil now accounts for about 65% of the country's GDP and 90% of export revenues.

Costa Rica
Republic of Costa Rica

People: Population: 4,133,884. **Age distrib. (%):** <15: 27.8; 65+: 5.8. **Pop. density:** 211 per sq mi, 82 per sq km. **Urban:** 61.7%. **Ethnic groups:** White and mestizo 94%, black 3%, Amerindian 1%. **Principal languages:** Spanish (official), English spoken around Puerto Limon. **Chief religions:** Roman Catholic (official) 76%, Protestant 14%.

Geography: Total area: 19,730 sq mi, 51,100 sq km; **Land area:** 19,560 sq mi, 50,660 sq km. **Location:** In Central America. **Neighbors:** Nicaragua on N, Panama on S. **Topography:** Lowlands by the Caribbean are tropical. The interior plateau, with an altitude of about 4,000 ft, is temperate. **Capital:** San José, 1,217,000.

Government: Type: Republic. **Head of state and gov.:** Pres. Óscar Arias Sánchez; b. Sept. 13, 1940; in office: May 8, 2006. **Local divisions:** 7 provinces. **Defense budget:** $98 mil (paramilitary budget). **Active troops:** None.

Economy: Industries: microprocessors, food proc., textiles and clothing, constr. materials, fertilizer, plastics. **Chief crops:** bananas, pineapples, coffee, melons, ornamental plants, sugar, corn, rice, beans, potatoes. **Natural resources:** hydropower. **Arable land:** 4%. **Livestock:** cattle: 1 mil; chickens: 19.5 mil; goats: 4,700; pigs: 550,000; sheep: 2,700. **Fish catch:** 46,378 metric tons. **Electricity prod.:** 8.4 bil kWh. **Labor force** (1999 est.): agriculture 20%, industry 22%, services 58%.

Finance: Monetary unit: Colon (CRC) (Sept. 2007: 519.63 = $1 U.S.). **GDP:** $50.9 bil; **per capita GDP:** $12,500; **GDP growth:** 7.9%. **Imports:** $10.9 bil; U.S. 40.9%, Venezuela 5.4%, Mexico 5.3%, Ireland 4.9%, Japan 4.9%, Brazil 4.6%, China 4%. **Exports:** $7.9 bil; U.S. 29.1%, Netherlands 13%, China 12.5%, UK 6.6%. **Tourism:** $1.6 bil. **Budget:** $3.5 bil. **Intl. reserves less gold:** $2.07 bil. **Consumer prices:** 11.47%.

Transport: Railroad: Length: 173 mi. **Motor vehicles:** 621,000 pass. cars; 199,000 comm. vehicles. **Civil aviation:** 1 bil pass.-mi; 32 airports. **Chief ports:** Caldera, Puerto Limon.

Communications: TV sets: 229 per 1,000 pop. **Radios:** 774 per 1,000 pop. **Telephone lines:** 1.4 mil. **Daily newspaper circ.:** 70 per 1,000 pop. **Internet:** 1.2 mil users.

Health: Life expect.: 74.6 male; 79.9 female. **Births** (per 1,000 pop.): 18. **Deaths** (per 1,000 pop.): 4.4. **Natural inc.:** 1.36%. **Infant mortality** (per 1,000 live births): 9.5. **AIDS rate:** 0.3%.

Education: Compulsory: ages 6-15. **Literacy:** 94.9%.

Major intl. organizations: UN (FAO, IBRD, ILO, IMF, IMO, WHO, WTO), OAS.

Embassy: 2114 S St. NW 20008; 234-2945.

Website: www.costarica-embassy.org

Guaymi Indians inhabited the area when Spaniards arrived, 1502. Independence came in 1821. Costa Rica seceded from the Central American Federation in 1838. Since the civil war of 1948-49, there has been little violent social conflict, and free political institutions have been preserved.

Costa Rica, though still a largely agricultural country, has achieved a relatively high standard of living, and land ownership is widespread. Tourism is growing rapidly. Nobel Peace Prize-winner Óscar Arias Sánchez, president 1986-90, won a 2nd term in a close election, Feb. 5, 2006. Corruption charges were filed Aug. 1, 2007, against Miguel Angel Rodríguez, former president of Costa Rica (1998-2002) and OAS secretary-general (2004).

Côte d'Ivoire
Republic of Côte d'Ivoire

People: Population: 18,013,409. **Age distrib. (%):** <15: 40.6; 65+: 2.8. **Pop. density:** 147 per sq mi, 57 per sq km. **Urban:** 45%. **Ethnic groups:** Akan 42%, Voltaiques (Gur) 18%, N Mandes 17%, Krous 11%, S Mandes 10%. **Principal languages:** French (official), Dioula, many native dialects. **Chief religions:** Muslim 35-40%, indigenous beliefs 25-40%, Christian 20-30%.

Geography: Total area: 124,503 sq mi, 322,460 sq km; **Land area:** 122,780 sq mi, 318,000 sq km. **Location:** On S coast of W Africa. **Neighbors:** Liberia, Guinea on W; Mali, Burkina Faso on N; Ghana on E. **Topography:** Forests cover the W half of the country, and range from a coastal strip to halfway to the N on the E. A sparse inland plain leads to low mountains in NW. **Capital** (2003): Yamoussoukro (official), 185,600; Abidjan (de facto), 3,577,000.

Government: Type: In transition. **Head of state:** Pres. Laurent Gbagbo; b. May 31, 1945; in office: Oct. 26, 2000. **Head of gov.:**

Prime Min. Guillaume Soro; b. May 8, 1972; in office: Apr. 4, 2007. **Local divisions:** 58 departments. **Defense budget** (2005): $191 mil. **Active troops:** 17,050.

Economy: Industries: foodstuffs, beverages, wood products, oil refining, truck & bus assembly, textiles, fertilizer, building materials, electricity. **Chief crops:** coffee, cocoa beans, bananas, palm kernels. **Natural resources:** oil, nat. gas, diamonds, mang., iron ore, cobalt, bauxite, copper, hydropower. **Crude oil reserves:** 100 mil bbls. **Arable land:** 10%. **Livestock:** cattle: 1.5 mil; chickens: 33 mil; goats: 1.2 mil; pigs: 345,000; sheep: 1.5 mil. **Fish catch:** 55,866 metric tons. **Electricity prod.:** 5.3 bil kWh. **Labor force:** agriculture 68%.

Finance: Monetary unit: CFA BCEAO Franc (XOF) (Sept. 2007: 472.78 = $1 U.S.). **GDP:** $29.1 bil; **per capita GDP:** $1,600; **GDP growth:** 1.2%. **Imports:** $5.5 bil; Nigeria 27.6%, France 25.4%, China 4.3%. **Exports:** $7.8 bil; France 18.3%, Netherlands 9.7%, U.S. 9.1%, Nigeria 7.2%, Germany 4.2%. **Tourism:** $76 mil. **Budget:** $3.2 bil. **Intl. reserves less gold:** $1.20 bil. **Consumer prices:** 2.47%.

Transport: Railroad: Length: 410 mi. **Motor vehicles:** 113,900 pass. cars; 54,900 comm. vehicles. **Civil aviation** (2001): 80.8 mil pass.-mi; 7 airports. **Chief ports:** Abidjan, Dabou, San-Pédro.

Communications: TV sets: 65 per 1,000 pop. **Radios:** 161 per 1,000 pop. **Telephone lines:** 260,900. **Daily newspaper circ.:** 15.6 per 1,000 pop. **Internet:** 300,000 users.

Health: Life expect.: 46.4 male; 51.7 female. **Births** (per 1,000 pop.): 34.7. **Deaths** (per 1,000 pop.): 14.7. **Natural inc.:** 2%. **Infant mortality** (per 1,000 live births): 87.4. **AIDS rate:** 7.1%.

Education: Compulsory: ages 6-15. **Literacy:** 48.7%.

Major intl. organizations: UN and all of its specialized agencies, AU.

Embassy: 2424 Massachusetts Ave. NW 20008; 797-0300.

Website: cotedivoire.usembassy.gov

A French protectorate from 1842, Côte d'Ivoire became independent in 1960. The name was officially changed from Ivory Coast, Oct. 1985. The country is a leading producer of coffee and cocoa beans.

Students and workers protested, Feb. 1990, demanding the ouster of longtime Pres. Félix Houphouët-Boigny. Côte d'Ivoire held its first multiparty presidential election Oct. 1990, and Houphouët-Boigny retained his office. He died Dec. 7, 1993. The National Assembly named a successor, Henri Konan Bédié, who was reelected Oct. 22, 1995; he was ousted in a military coup Dec. 24, 1999. The coup leader, Robert Guéi, apparently lost a presidential vote Oct. 22, 2000, but claimed victory anyway. After mass protests, he fled, and Laurent Gbagbo became president. Guéi was killed in Abidjan Sept. 19, 2002, after a mutiny broke out there and in Bouaké and Korhogo.

Agreement on power sharing was reached in Mar. 2003, and Gbagbo and former rebel leaders held a ceremony July 5, declaring that the war was over. The country remained divided, however, with rebels holding the north and government forces controlling the south. Under a new accord reached Mar. 4, 2007, rebel leader Guillaume Soro was sworn in as prime min. Apr. 4. A UN peacekeeping force for Côte d'Ivoire (UNOCI), authorized in Feb. 2004, included more than 9,100 uniformed personnel in mid-2007; in Mar., France announced a cut in its own peacekeeping force here from 3,500 to fewer than 3,000.

Croatia
Republic of Croatia

People: Population: 4,493,312. **Age distrib. (%):** <15: 16; 65+: 16.9. **Pop. density:** 206 per sq mi, 80 per sq km. **Urban:** 56.5%. **Ethnic groups:** Croat 90%, Serb 5%. **Principal languages:** Croatian (official), Serbian. **Chief religions:** Roman Catholic 88%, Orthodox 5%.

Geography: Total area: 21,831 sq mi, 56,542 sq km; **Land area:** 21,782 sq mi, 56,414 sq km. **Location:** SE Europe, on the Balkan Peninsula. **Neighbors:** Slovenia, Hungary on N; Bosnia and Herzegovina, Serbia, Montenegro on E. **Topography:** Flat plains in NE; highlands, low mtns. along Adriatic coast. **Capital:** Zagreb, 689,000.

Government: Type: Parliamentary democracy. **Head of state:** Pres. Stipe Mesic; b. Dec. 24, 1934; in office: Feb. 18, 2000. **Head of gov.:** Prime Min. Ivo Sanader; b. June 8, 1953; in office: Dec. 23, 2003. **Local divisions:** 20 counties and Zagreb. **Defense budget:** $712 mil. **Active troops:** 20,800.

Economy: Industries: chemicals, plastics, machine tools, fabricated metal, electronics. **Chief crops:** wheat, corn, sugar beets, sunflower seed, barley. **Natural resources:** oil, coal, bauxite, iron ore, calcium, natural asphalt, silica, mica, clays, salt, hydropower. **Crude oil reserves:** 74.3 mil bbls. **Arable land:** 26%. **Livestock:** cattle: 482,906; chickens: 7 mil; goats: 102,877; pigs: 1.5 mil; sheep: 679,839. **Fish catch:** 48,451 metric tons. **Electricity prod.:** 12 bil kWh. **Labor force** (2004): agriculture 2.7%, industry 32.8%, services 64.5%.

Finance: Monetary unit: Kuna (HRK) (Sept. 2007: 5.28 = $1 U.S.). **GDP:** $60.3 bil; **per capita GDP:** $13,400; **GDP growth:** 4.6%. **Imports:** $21.8 bil; Italy 16.7%, Germany 15.1%, Russia 8.9%, Austria 6.2%, Slovenia 5%. **Exports:** $11.2 bil; Italy 22%, Bosnia and Herzegovina 13.8%, Germany 9.7%, Slovenia 9%,

Austria 7.4%. **Tourism:** $7.4 bil. **Budget:** $19.1 bil. **Intl. reserves less gold:** $7.64 bil. **Consumer prices:** 3.21%.

Transport: Railroad: Length: 1,694 mi. **Motor vehicles:** 1.3 mil pass. cars; 160,000 comm. vehicles. **Civil aviation:** 540 mil pass.-mi; 23 airports. **Chief ports:** Omisalj, Ploce, Rijeka.

Communications: TV sets: 286 per 1,000 pop. **Radios:** 337 per 1,000 pop. **Telephone lines:** 1.8 mil. **Daily newspaper circ.:** 133.8 per 1,000 pop. **Internet:** 1.6 mil users.

Health: Life expect.: 71.2 male; 78.8 female. **Births** (per 1,000 pop.): 9.6. **Deaths** (per 1,000 pop.): 11.5. **Natural inc.:** −0.19%. **Infant mortality** (per 1,000 live births): 6.6. **AIDS rate:** <0.1%.

Education: Compulsory: ages 7-14. **Literacy:** 98.1%.

Major intl. organizations: UN (FAO, IBRD, ILO, IMF, IMO, WHO, WTO), OSCE.

Embassy: 2343 Massachusetts Ave. NW 20008; 588-5899.

Website: www.vlada.hr

From the 7th cent. the area was inhabited by Croats, a south Slavic people. It was formed into a kingdom under Tomislav in 924, and joined with Hungary in 1102. The Croats became westernized and separated from Slavs under Austro-Hungarian influence. The Croats retained autonomy under the Hungarian crown. Slavonia was taken by Turks in the 16th cent.; the northern part was restored by the Treaty of Karlowitz in 1699. Croatia helped Austria put down the Hungarian revolution 1848-49 and as a result was set up with Slavonia as the separate Austrian crownland of Croatia and Slavonia, which was reunited to Hungary as part of Ausgleich in 1867. It united with other Yugoslav areas to proclaim the Kingdom of Serbs, Croats, and Slovenes in 1918. At the reorganization of Yugoslavia in 1929, Croatia and Slavonia became Savska county, which in 1939 was united with Primorje county to form the county of Croatia. A nominally independent state between 1941 and 1945, it became a constituent republic in the 1946 constitution.

On June 25, 1991, Croatia declared independence from Yugoslavia. Fighting began between ethnic Serbs and Croats, with the former gaining control of about 30% of Croatian territory. A ceasefire was declared in Jan. 1992, but new hostilities broke out in 1993. A cease-fire with Serb rebels forming a self-declared republic of Krajina was agreed to Mar. 30, 1994. Croatian government troops recaptured most of the Serb-held territory Aug. 1995. Pres. Franjo Tudjman signed a peace accord with leaders of Bosnia and Serbia in Paris, Dec. 14. Tudjman won reelection June 15, 1997; international monitors called the vote "free but not fair." The last Serb-held enclave, E Slavonia, returned to Croatian control Jan. 15, 1998.

Tudjman died Dec. 10, 1999. Stipe Mesic, a moderate, won a presidential runoff election Feb. 7, 2000, and was reelected Jan. 16, 2005. EU membership talks, scheduled to start Mar. 17, 2005, were postponed because of Croatia's failure to hand over a suspected war criminal, Gen. Ante Gotovina; he was arrested Dec. 7, 2005, in Spain's Canary Islands.

Cuba
Republic of Cuba

People: Population: 11,394,043. **Age distrib.** (%): <15: 18.8; 65+: 10.7. **Pop. density:** 266 per sq mi, 103 per sq km. **Urban:** 75.5%. **Ethnic groups:** Creole 51%, white 37%, black 11%, Chinese 1%. **Principal language:** Spanish (official). **Chief religions:** Roman Catholic, Santeria.

Geography: Total area: 42,803 sq mi, 110,860 sq km; **Land area:** 42,803 sq mi, 110,860 sq km. **Location:** In Caribbean, westernmost of West Indies. **Neighbors:** Bahamas, U.S. to N; Mexico to W; Jamaica to S; Haiti to E. **Topography:** Coastline is about 2,500 mi. The N coast is steep and rocky, the S coast low and marshy. Low hills and fertile valleys cover more than half the country. Sierra Maestra, in E, is the highest of 3 mountain ranges. **Capital:** Havana 2,189,000.

Government: Type: Communist state. **Head of state and gov.:** Acting Pres. Raúl Castro Ruz; b. June 3, 1931; in office: July 31, 2006. **Local divisions:** 14 provinces, 1 special municipality. **Defense budget:** NA. **Active troops:** 49,000.

Economy: Industries: sugar, oil, tobacco, chemicals, constr., services. **Chief crops:** sugar, tobacco, citrus, coffee, rice. **Natural resources:** cobalt, nickel, iron ore, copper, mang., salt, timber, silica, oil. **Crude oil reserves:** 124 mil bbls. **Arable land:** 28%. **Livestock:** cattle: 3.7 mil; chickens: 29.8 mil; goats: 1.2 mil; pigs: 1.8 mil; sheep: 2.8 mil. **Fish catch:** 52,345 metric tons. **Electricity prod.:** 14.7 bil kWh. **Labor force** (2005): agriculture 20%, industry 19.4%, services 60.6%.

Finance: Monetary unit: Peso (CUP) (Sept. 2007: 26.50 = $1 U.S.). **GDP:** $45.5 bil; **per capita GDP:** $4,000; **GDP growth:** 9.5%. **Imports:** $9.5 bil; China 21.6%, Spain 13.3%, Germany 8.8%, Canada 7.6%, Italy 6.1%, U.S. 5.9%, Brazil 5.2%. **Exports:** $3 bil; Canada 20.9%, Netherlands 20.9%, China 18.1%, Spain 5.7%. **Tourism:** $1.9 bil. **Budget:** $36.4 bil.

Transport: Railroad: Length: 2,626 mi. **Motor vehicles:** 24,000 comm. vehicles. **Civil aviation:** 1.3 bil pass.-mi; 78 airports. **Chief ports:** Cienfuegos, Havana, Matanzas.

Communications: TV sets: 248 per 1,000 pop. **Radios:** 352 per 1,000 pop. **Telephone lines:** 972,900. **Daily newspaper circ.:** 53.6 per 1,000 pop. **Internet:** 240,000 users.

Education: Compulsory: ages 6-14. **Literacy:** 99.8%.

Health: Life expect.: 74.9 male; 79.4 female. **Births** (per 1,000 pop.): 11.4. **Deaths** (per 1,000 pop.): 7.1. **Natural inc.:** 0.43%. **Infant mortality** (per 1,000 live births): 6.0. **AIDS rate:** 0.1%.

Major intl. organizations: UN (FAO, ILO, IMO, WHO, WTO). Cuba is an OAS member state, but its current govt. has been excluded from OAS participation since 1962.

Cuban consulate: 2630 16th St. NW 20009; 797-8609.

Website: www.cubagob.cu

Some 50,000 Indians lived in Cuba when it was reached by Columbus in 1492. Its name derives from the Indian Cubanacan. Except for British occupation of Havana, 1762-63, Cuba remained Spanish until 1898. A slave-based sugar plantation economy developed from the 18th cent. Sugar remains the chief product and main export.

A 10-year uprising ended in 1878 with guarantees of rights by Spain, which Spain failed to carry out. A full-scale liberation movement under Jose Martí began Feb. 24, 1895.

The Spanish-American War began Apr. 1898, after the sinking of the USS *Maine* in Havana harbor. Spain, which lost the war, gave up all claims to Cuba. U.S. troops withdrew in 1902, but under 1903 and 1934 agreements, the U.S. continued to lease a site at Guantánamo Bay in the southeast as a naval base (see below). U.S. and other foreign investments acquired a dominant role in the economy. In 1952, former Pres. Fulgencio Batista seized control and established a dictatorship, which grew increasingly harsh and corrupt. Fidel Castro assembled a rebel band in 1956; guerrilla fighting intensified in 1958. Batista fled Jan. 1, 1959, and in the resulting political vacuum Castro took power, becoming premier Feb. 16.

The government began a program of sweeping economic and social changes, without restoring promised liberties. Opponents were imprisoned, and some were executed. Some 700,000 Cubans emigrated in the first years after the Castro takeover, mostly to the U.S. By 1960 all banks and industrial companies had been nationalized, including over $1 bil worth of U.S.-owned properties, mostly without compensation.

In 1961, some 1,400 Cubans, trained and backed by the U.S. Central Intelligence Agency, unsuccessfully tried to invade and overthrow the regime. In the fall of 1962, the U.S. learned the USSR had brought nuclear missiles to Cuba. On Oct. 22, Pres. John F. Kennedy ordered a naval blockade and demanded that the missiles be withdrawn. The crisis ended Oct. 28 when Soviet Prem. Nikita S. Khrushchev agreed to pull out the missiles immediately; in return, the U.S. ended the blockade, pledged not to invade Cuba, and quietly removed its own missiles from Turkey.

In 1977, Cuba and the U.S. signed agreements to exchange diplomats, without restoring full ties, and to regulate offshore fishing. In 1978 and 1980, the U.S. agreed to accept political prisoners released by Cuba, some of whom were criminals and mental patients. A 1987 agreement provided for 20,000 Cubans to emigrate to the U.S. each year; Cuba agreed to take back some 2,500 jailed in the U.S. since 1980. Cuba's support for left-wing regimes and liberation movements in Central America, Africa, and the Caribbean contributed to poor relations with the U.S.

Cuba's economy, hobbled by U.S. sanctions and dependent on aid from other Communist countries, was severely shaken by the collapse of the Communist bloc in the late 1980s. Stiffer trade sanctions enacted by the U.S. in 1992 made things worse. Antigovernment demonstrations in Aug. 1994 prompted Castro to loosen emigration restrictions. A new U.S.-Cuba accord in Sept. ended the exodus of "boat people" after more than 30,000 had left Cuba. In another policy shift, the U.S. announced May 2, 1995, it would admit 20,000 Cuban refugees held at Guantánamo but would send further boat people back to Cuba.

The U.S. imposed additional sanctions after Cuba, Feb. 24, 1996, shot down 2 aircraft operated by anti-Castro exiles. Cuba blamed exile groups for bombings at Havana tourist hotels, July-Sept. 1997. Pope John Paul II visited Cuba, Jan. 21-25, 1998. U.S. restrictions on contact were eased in 1999.

In one of its largest crackdowns in recent years, Cuba arrested about 78 dissidents in Mar. 2003. New U.S. sanctions in May 2004 limited Cuban exiles' visits and remittances to the island, provided funds for U.S. govt. TV and radio broadcasts via airplane, and set aside $36 mil to support Cuban dissidents. On July 31, 2006, the ailing Fidel Castro yielded power to his 75-year-old brother Raúl, who then served as acting president.

The U.S., Jan. 11, 2002, began using its naval base at **Guantánamo Bay** to detain prisoners captured in Afghanistan; in mid-2007, about 360 detainees were still being held at the base. The indefinite detention and aggressive interrogation of Afghan prisoners and others at Guantánamo were criticized by human rights groups. The U.S. Supreme Court ruled, June 29, 2006, that the Bush administration's treatment of detainees and its plan to try them before military commissions violated U.S. law and the Geneva Conventions governing prisoners of war.

Cyprus
Republic of Cyprus

People: Population: 788,457. **Age distrib.** (%): <15: 19.9; 65+: 11.8. **Pop. density:** 221 per sq mi, 85 per sq km. **Urban:** 69.3%. **Ethnic groups:** Greek 77%, Turkish 18%. **Principal languages:**

Greek, Turkish (both official); English. **Chief religions:** Greek Orthodox 78%, Muslim 18%.

Geography: Total area: 3,571 sq mi, 9,250 sq km; **Land area:** 3,568 sq mi, 9,240 sq km. **Location:** In eastern Mediterranean Sea, off Turkish coast. **Neighbors:** Nearest are Turkey on N, Syria and Lebanon on E. **Topography:** Two mountain ranges run E-W, separated by a wide, fertile plain. **Capital:** Nicosia, 211,000.

Government: Type: Republic. **Head of state and gov.:** Pres. Tassos Papadopoulos; b. Jan. 7, 1934; in office: Feb. 28, 2003. **Local divisions:** 6 districts.

Economy: Industries: food, beverages, textiles, chemicals, metal products, tourism. **Chief crops:** citrus, vegetables, barley, grapes, olives. **Natural resources:** copper, pyrites, asbestos, gypsum, timber, salt, marble, clay earth pigment. **Arable land:** 11%. **Livestock:** cattle: 56,109; chickens: 3.1 mil; goats: 344,929; pigs: 452,644; sheep: 272,192. **Fish catch:** 4,249 metric tons. **Electricity prod.:** 4.1 bil kWh. **Labor force** (2004 est.): Greek area: agriculture 7.4%, industry 38.2%, services 54.4%; Turkish area: agriculture 14.5%, industry 29%, services 56.5%.

Finance: Monetary unit: Pound (CYP) (Sept. 2007: 0.42 = $1 U.S.) (will switch to the Euro Jan. 1, 2008). **GDP:** Greek area: $18 bil, Turkish area: $4.5 bil; **per capita GDP:** Greek area: $23,000, Turkish area: $7,135; **GDP growth:** Greek area: 3.8%, Turkish area: 10.6%. **Imports:** Greek: $5.8 bil; Turkish area: $1.2 bil; Greece 17.6%, Italy 11.4%, Germany 9%, UK 8.9%, Israel 6.3%. **Exports:** Greek: $1.34 bil; Turkish area: $68.1 mil; UK 15.1%, Greece 14.2%, France 7.7%, Germany 4.9%, UAE 4.2%. **Tourism:** $2.3 bil. **Budget:** Greek area (2005 est.): $7.7 bil.; Turkish area (2003 est.): $432.8 mil. **Intl. reserves less gold:** $3.75 bil. **Gold:** 470,000 oz t. **Consumer prices:** −2.5%.

Transport: Motor vehicles: 336,000 pass. cars; 126,000 comm. vehicles. **Civil aviation:** 2.4 bil pass.-mi; 13 airports. **Chief ports:** Famagusta, Limassol.

Communications: Television sets: 154 per 1000 pop. **Radios:** 406 per 1,000 pop. **Telephone lines:** 408,300. **Daily newspaper circ.:** 69.5 per 1,000 pop. **Internet:** 356,600 users.

Health: Life expect.: 74.9 male; 79.4 female. **Births** (per 1,000 pop.): 11.4. **Deaths** (per 1,000 pop.): 7.1. **Natural inc.:** 0.43%. **Infant mortality** (per 1,000 live births): 6.9. **AIDS rate:** NA.

Education: Compulsory: ages 6-14. **Literacy:** 96.8%.

Major intl. organizations: UN (FAO, IBRD, ILO, IMF, IMO, WHO, WTO), the Commonwealth, EU, OSCE.

Embassy: 2211 R St. NW 20008; 462-5772.

Website: www.moi.gov.cy

The Ottoman Empire held Cyprus, 1571-1878, until it yielded control over the island to Britain. Agitation for enosis (union) with Greece increased after WWII, with the Turkish minority opposed, and broke into violence in 1955-56. In 1959, Britain, Greece, Turkey, and Cypriot leaders approved a plan for an independent republic, with constitutional guarantees for the Turkish minority and permanent division of offices on an ethnic basis. Greek and Turkish Communal Chambers dealt with religion, education, and other matters.

Archbishop Makarios III, formerly the leader of the enosis movement, was elected president, and full independence became final Aug. 16, 1960. Further communal strife led the United Nations to send a peacekeeping force in 1964; its mandate has been repeatedly renewed.

The Cypriot National Guard, led by officers from the army of Greece, seized the government July 15, 1974. On July 20, Turkey invaded the island; Greece mobilized its forces but did not intervene. A cease-fire was arranged but collapsed. By Aug. 16, Turkish forces had occupied the northeastern 40% of the island, despite the presence of UN peacekeeping forces.

Face-to-face talks between the Greek and Turkish Cypriot leaders resumed Dec. 4, 2001, for the first time in 4 years. Turkish Cyprus opened its border with Greek Cyprus Apr. 23, 2003, for the first time since partition. In separate referendums Apr. 24, 2004, 65% of Turkish Cypriot voters accepted a UN-sponsored reunification plan, but 76% of Greek Cypriots rejected it. Still divided, Cyprus became a full member of the EU on May 1. Beginning July 2006, thousands of refugees from war-torn Lebanon found a temporary haven in Cyprus.

Turkish Republic of Northern Cyprus

A declaration of independence was announced by Turkish-Cypriot leader Rauf Denktash, Nov. 15, 1983. The state is not internationally recognized, but has trade relations with some countries. Mehmet Ali Talat succeeded Denktash as president Apr. 24, 2005. Area of TRNC: 1,295 sq mi; pop. (2006 census, prelim.): 264,172, nearly all Turkish. **Capital:** Lefkosa (Nicosia).

Czech Republic

People: Population: 10,228,744. **Age distrib.** (%): <15: 14.1; 65+: 14.7. **Pop. density:** 343 per sq mi, 132 per sq km. **Urban:** 73.5%. **Ethnic groups:** Czech 90%, Moravian 4%. **Principal languages:** Czech (official), Slovak. **Chief religions:** Roman Catholic 27%, unaffiliated 59%, Protestant 2%.

Geography: Total area: 30,450 sq mi, 78,866 sq km; **Land area:** 29,836 sq mi, 77,276 sq km. **Location:** In E central Europe. **Neighbors:** Poland on N, Germany on N and W, Austria on S, Slovakia on E and SE. **Topography:** Bohemia, in W, is a plateau surrounded by mountains; Moravia is hilly. **Capital:** Prague, 1,171,000.

Government: Type: Republic. **Head of state:** Vaclav Klaus; b. June 19, 1941; in office: Mar. 7, 2003. **Head of gov.:** Prime Min. Mirek Topolanek; b. May 15, 1956; in office: Sept. 4, 2006. **Local divisions:** 13 regions and Prague. **Defense budget:** $2.53 bil. **Active troops:** 24,752.

Economy: Industries: metallurgy, machinery, motor vehicles, glass, armaments. **Chief crops:** wheat, potatoes, sugar beets, hops, fruit. **Natural resources:** coal, kaolin, clay, graphite, timber. **Arable land:** 39%. **Crude oil reserves:** 15 mil bbls. **Livestock:** cattle: 1.4 mil; chickens: 14.7 mil; goats: 14,402; pigs: 2.8 mil; sheep: 148,412. **Fish catch:** 24,697 metric tons. **Electricity prod.:** 77.4 bil kWh. **Labor force** (2003): agriculture 4.1%, industry 37.6%, services 58.3%.

Finance: Monetary unit: Koruna (CZK) (Sept. 2007: 19.83 = $1 U.S.). **GDP:** $224 bil; **per capita GDP:** $21,900; **GDP growth:** 6.1%. **Imports:** $87.7 bil; Germany 32%, Netherlands 6.5%, Slovakia 6.1%, Poland 6.1%, Russia 5.7%. **Exports:** $89.3 bil; Germany 31.9%, Slovakia 8.5%, Poland 5.7%, France 5.6%, Austria 5.1%. **Tourism:** $4.6 bil. **Budget:** $62.5 bil. **Intl. reserves less gold:** $20.73 bil. **Gold:** 430,000 oz t. **Consumer prices:** 2.54%.

Transport: Railroad: Length: 5,948 mi. **Motor vehicles:** 3.8 mil pass. cars; 445,000 comm. vehicles. **Civil aviation:** 3.1 bil pass.-mi; 46 airports. **Chief ports:** Decin, Prague, Ustinad Labem.

Communications: TV sets: 487 per 1,000 pop. **Radios:** 803 per 1,000 pop. **Telephone lines:** 3.2 mil. **Internet:** 3.5 mil users.

Health: Life expect.: 73.1 male; 79.9 female. **Births** (per 1,000 pop.): 9. **Deaths** (per 1,000 pop.): 10.6. **Natural inc.:** −0.17%. **Infant mortality** (per 1,000 live births): 3.9. **AIDS rate:** 0.1%.

Education: Compulsory: ages 6-15. **Literacy:** 99%.

Major intl. organizations: UN (FAO, IBRD, ILO, IMF, IMO, WHO, WTO), Eu, NATO, OECD, OSCE.

Embassy: 3900 Spring of Freedom St. NW 20008; 274-9100.

Website: www.czech.cz

Bohemia and Moravia were part of the Great Moravian Empire in the 9th cent. and later became part of the Holy Roman Empire. Under the kings of Bohemia, Prague in the 14th cent. was the cultural center of Central Europe. Bohemia and Hungary became part of Austria-Hungary.

In 1914-18 Thomas G. Masaryk and Eduard Benes formed a provisional government with the support of Slovak leaders including Milan Stefanik. They proclaimed the Republic of Czechoslovakia Oct. 28, 1918.

Czechoslovakia

By 1938 Nazi Germany had worked up disaffection among German-speaking citizens in Sudetenland and demanded its cession. British Prime Min. Neville Chamberlain, with the acquiescence of France, signed with Hitler at Munich, Sept. 30, 1938, an agreement to the cession, with a guarantee of peace by Hitler and Mussolini. Germany occupied Sudetenland Oct. 1-2.

Hitler on Mar. 15, 1939, dissolved Czechoslovakia, made protectorates of Bohemia and Moravia, and supported the autonomy of Slovakia, proclaimed independent Mar. 14, 1939.

Soviet troops with some Czechoslovak contingents entered eastern Czechoslovakia in 1944 and reached Prague in May 1945; Benes returned as president. In May 1946 elections, the Communist Party won 38% of the votes, and Benes accepted Klement Gottwald, a Communist, as prime minister.

In Feb. 1948, the Communists seized power in advance of scheduled elections. In May 1948 a new constitution was approved. Benes refused to sign it. On May 30 the voters were offered a one-slate ballot and the Communists won full control. Benes resigned June 7 and Gottwald became president. The country was renamed the Czechoslovak Socialist Republic. A harsh Stalinist period followed, with complete and violent suppression of all opposition.

In Jan. 1968 a liberalization movement spread through Czechoslovakia. Antonin Novotny, long the Stalinist ruler, was deposed as party leader and succeeded by Alexander Dubcek, a Slovak, who supported democratic reforms. On Mar. 22 Novotny resigned as president and was succeeded by Gen. Ludvik Svoboda. On Apr. 6, Prem. Joseph Lenart resigned and was succeeded by Oldrich Cernik, a reformer.

In July 1968, the USSR and 4 Warsaw Pact nations demanded an end to liberalization. On Aug. 20, the Soviet, Polish, East German, Hungarian, and Bulgarian armies invaded Czechoslovakia. Despite demonstrations and riots by students and workers, press censorship was imposed, liberal leaders were ousted from office and promises of loyalty to Soviet policies were made by some old-line Communist Party leaders.

On Apr. 17, 1969, Dubcek resigned as leader of the Communist Party and was succeeded by Gustav Husak. In Jan. 1970, Cernik was ousted. Censorship was tightened, and the Communist Party expelled a third of its members. In 1973, amnesty was offered to some of the 40,000 who fled the country after the 1968 invasion, but repressive policies continued.

More than 700 leading Czechoslovak intellectuals and former party leaders signed a human rights manifesto in 1977, called Charter 77, prompting a renewed crackdown by the regime.

The police crushed the largest antigovernment protests since 1968, when tens of thousands of demonstrators took to the streets of Prague, Nov. 17, 1989. As protesters demanded free elections, the Communist Party leadership resigned Nov. 24; millions went on strike Nov. 27.

On Dec. 10, 1989, the first cabinet in 41 years without a Communist majority took power; Vaclav Havel, playwright and human rights campaigner, was chosen president, Dec. 29. In Mar. 1990 the country was officially renamed the Czech and Slovak Federal Republic. Havel failed to win reelection July 3, 1992; his bid was blocked by a Slovak-led coalition.

Slovakia declared sovereignty, July 17. Czech and Slovak leaders agreed, July 23, on a basic plan for a peaceful division of Czechoslovakia into 2 independent states.

Czech Republic

Czechoslovakia split in 2 separate states—the Czech Republic and Slovakia—on Jan. 1, 1993. Havel was elected president of the Czech Republic on Jan. 26. Record floods in July 1997 caused more than $1.7 bil in damage. The country became a full member of NATO on Mar. 12, 1999. Floods Aug. 2002 damaged cultural treasures in Prague.

Vaclav Klaus was chosen Feb. 28, 2003, to replace the retiring Havel. After Czech voters June 13-14, 2003, endorsed joining the EU, the nation became a full EU member May 1, 2004. When his Social Democratic Party fared poorly in EU elections June 11-12, Prime Min. Vladimir Spidla resigned; his successor, Stanislav Gross, 34, was Europe's youngest head of government. A scandal surrounding his 1999 purchase of a luxury apartment in Prague forced Gross to resign Apr. 25, 2005. Inconclusive parliamentary elections, June 2-3, 2006, led to a prolonged political deadlock, after which a minority center-right government took office Sept. 4.

Denmark
Kingdom of Denmark

People: Population: 5,468,120. **Age distrib.** (%): <15: 18.6; 65+: 15.4. **Pop. density:** 334 per sq mi, 129 per sq km. **Urban:** 85.6%. **Ethnic groups:** Scandinavian, Inuit, Faroese, German, Turkish, Iranian, Somali. **Principal languages:** Danish (official), Faroese, Greenlandic (Inuit dialect), German. **Chief religions:** Evangelical Lutheran (official) 95%, other Christian 3%, Muslim 2%.

Geography: Total area: 16,639 sq mi, 43,094 sq km; **Land area:** 16,368 sq mi, 42,394 sq km. **Location:** In N Europe, separating North and Baltic seas. **Neighbors:** Germany on S, Norway on NW, Sweden on NE. **Topography:** Consists of the Jutland Peninsula and about 500 islands, 100 inhabited. Land is flat or gently rolling and is almost all in productive use. **Capital:** Copenhagen, 1,088,000.

Government: Type: Constitutional monarchy. **Head of state:** Queen Margrethe II; b. Apr. 16, 1940; in office: Jan. 14, 1972. **Head of gov.:** Prime Min. Anders Fogh Rasmussen; b. Jan. 26, 1953; in office: Nov. 27, 2001. **Local divisions:** 5 regions. **Defense budget:** $3.41 bil. **Active troops:** 21,620.

Economy: Industries: food proc., machinery, textiles & clothing, chemicals, electronics, constr., furniture. **Chief crops:** barley, wheat, potatoes, sugar beets. **Natural resources:** oil, nat. gas, fish, salt, limestone, stone, gravel, sand. **Crude oil reserves:** 1.3 bil bbls. **Arable land:** 53%. **Livestock:** cattle: 1.6 mil; chickens: 16.8 mil; pigs: 12.6 mil; sheep: 206,000. **Fish catch** 949,625 metric tons. **Electricity prod.:** 34.2 bil kWh. **Labor force** (2004 est.): agriculture 3%, industry 21%, services 76%.

Finance: Monetary unit: Krone (DKK) (Sept. 2007: 5.37 = $1 U.S.). **GDP:** $201.5 bil; **per capita GDP:** $37,000; **GDP growth:** 3.2%. **Imports:** $89.3 bil; Germany 21.3%, Sweden 14.2%, Norway 6.5%, Netherlands 6.2%, UK 5.6%, China 5%. **Exports:** $93.9 bil; Germany 17.4%, Sweden 14.2%, UK 8.9%, U.S. 6.2%, Norway 5.4%, Netherlands 5.1%. **Tourism:** $5.3 bil. **Budget:** $138.9 bil. **Intl. reserves less gold:** $19.76 bil. **Gold:** 2.14 mil oz t. **Consumer prices:** 1.89%.

Transport: Railroad: Length: 1,661 mi. **Motor vehicles:** 1.9 mil pass. cars; 450,000 comm. vehicles. **Civil aviation:** 4.5 bil pass.-mi; 28 airports. **Chief ports:** Alborg, Arhus, Copenhagen, Fredericia, Odense, Roenne.

Communications: TV sets: 776 per 1,000 pop. **Radios:** 1,325 per 1,000 pop. **Telephone lines:** 3.1 mil. **Daily newspaper circ.:** 283.2 per 1,000 pop. **Internet:** 3.8 mil users.

Health: Life expect.: 75.7 male; 80.4 female. **Births** (per 1,000 pop.): 10.9. **Deaths** (per 1,000 pop.): 10.3. **Natural inc.:** 0.06%. **Infant mortality** (per 1,000 live births): 4.5. **AIDS rate:** 0.2%.

Education: Compulsory: ages 7-16. **Literacy:** 99%.

Major intl. organizations: UN and all of its specialized agencies, EU, NATO, OECD, OSCE.

Embassy: 3200 Whitehaven St. NW 20008; 234-4300.

Website: www.denmark.dk

The origin of Copenhagen dates back to ancient times, when the fishing and trading place named Havn (port) grew up on a cluster of islets, but Bishop Absalon (1128-1201) is regarded as the actual founder of the city.

Danes formed a large component of the Viking raiders in the early Middle Ages. The Danish kingdom was a major power until the 17th cent., when it lost its land in southern Sweden. Norway was separated in 1815, and Schleswig-Holstein in 1864. Northern Schleswig was returned in 1920. Denmark was occupied by Nazi

Germany, Apr. 1940-May 1945, but Danes helped more than 7,200 Jews escape to safety in Sweden, Sept. 1943.

Voters ratified the Maastricht Treaty, the basic document of the European Union, in May 1993, after rejecting it in 1992. On Sept. 28, 2000, Danes voted not to join the euro currency zone. The Danish newspaper *Jyllands-Posten* published, Sept. 30, 2005, cartoon images of the prophet Muhammad, offensive to Muslims; the caricatures, republished elsewhere, triggered violent protests and a boycott of Danish products in Islamic countries in early 2006. Police raids Sept. 4, 2007, broke up an alleged terrorist bomb plot with links to al-Qaeda.

The **Faroe Islands** in the North Atlantic, about 300 mi NW of the Shetlands, and 850 mi from Denmark proper, 18 inhabited, have an area of 540 sq mi and pop. (2007 est.) of 47,511. They are an administrative division of Denmark, self-governing in most matters. Torshavn is the capital. Fish is a primary export (641,265 metric tons in 2004).

Greenland (Kalaallit Nunaat)

Greenland, a huge island between the North Atlantic and the Polar Sea, is separated from the North American continent by Davis Strait and Baffin Bay. Its total area is 836,331 sq mi, 81% of which is ice-capped. Most of the island is a lofty plateau 9,000 to 10,000 ft in altitude. The average thickness of the cap is 1,000 ft. Scientists point to accelerated melting of Greenland's ice sheet in recent years as evidence of global warming. The population (2007 est.) is 56,344. Under the 1953 Danish constitution the colony became an integral part of the realm with representatives in the Folketing (Danish legislature). The Danish parliament, 1978, approved home rule for Greenland, effective May 1, 1979. With home rule, Greenlandic place names came into official use. The technically correct name for Greenland is now Kalaallit Nunaat; the official name for its capital is Nuuk, rather than Godthab. Fish is the principal export (261,302 metric tons in 2004).

Djibouti
Republic of Djibouti

People: Population: 496,374. **Age distrib.** (%): <15: 43.4; 65+: 3.4. **Pop. density:** 56 per sq mi, 22 per sq km. **Urban:** 86.1%. **Ethnic groups:** Somali 60%, Afar 35%. **Principal languages:** French, Arabic (both official); Somali; Afar. **Chief religions:** Muslim 94%, Christian 6%.

Geography: Total area: 8,880 sq mi, 23,000 sq km; **Land area:** 8,873 sq mi, 22,980 sq km. **Location:** On E coast of Africa, separated from Arabian Peninsula by strategically vital strait of Bab el-Mandeb. **Neighbors:** Ethiopia on W and SW, Eritrea on NW, Somalia on SE. **Topography:** The territory, divided into a low coastal plain, mountains behind, and an interior plateau, is arid, sandy, and desolate. Climate is generally hot and dry. **Capital:** Djibouti, 555,000.

Government: Type: Republic. **Head of state:** Pres. Ismail Omar Guelleh; b. Nov. 27, 1947; in office: May 8, 1999. **Head of gov.:** Prime Min. Dileita Mohamed Dileita; b. Mar. 12, 1958; in office: Mar. 7, 2001. **Local divisions:** 5 districts. **Defense budget:** $26 mil. **Active troops:** 10,950.

Economy: Industries: constr., agricult. proc. **Chief crops:** fruits, vegetables. **Natural resources:** geothermal areas. **Arable land:** 0.4%. **Livestock:** cattle: 297,000; goats: 512,000; sheep: 466,000. **Fish catch:** 260 metric tons. **Electricity prod.:** 200 mil kWh. **Labor force:** NA.

Finance: Monetary unit: Franc (DJF) (Sept. 2007: 175.82 = $1 U.S.). **GDP:** $1.9 bil; **per capita GDP** (2005 est.): $1,000; **GDP growth** (2005 est.): 3.2%. **Imports** (2004 est.): $987 mil; Saudi Arabia 21.4%, India 17.9%, China 11%, Ethiopia 4.6%. **Exports** (2004 est.): $250 mil; Somalia 66.3%, Ethiopia 21.5%, Yemen 3.4%. **Tourism:** $4 mil. **Budget** (1999 est.): $182 mil. **Intl. reserves less gold:** $80 mil.

Transport: Railroad: Length: 62 mi. **Motor vehicles:** NA. **Civil aviation:** 3 airports. **Chief port:** Djibouti.

Communications: TV sets: 48 per 1,000 pop. **Radios:** 86 per 1,000 pop. **Telephone lines:** 10,800. **Internet:** 11,000 users.

Health: Life expect.: 41.9 male; 44.7 female. **Births** (per 1,000 pop.): 39.1. **Deaths** (per 1,000 pop.): 19.2. **Natural inc.:** 1.98%. **Infant mortality** (per 1,000 live births): 100.8. **AIDS rate:** 3.1%.

Education: Compulsory: ages 6-15. **Literacy:** 67.9%.

Major intl. organizations: UN (FAO, IBRD, ILO, IMF, IMO, WHO, WTO), AL, AU.

Embassy: 1156 15th St. NW, Ste. 515, 20005; 331-0270.

Website: www.state.gov/p/af/ci/dj/

France gained control of the territory in stages between 1862 and 1900. As French Somaliland it became an overseas territory of France in 1945; in 1967 it was renamed the French Territory of the Afars and the Issas.

Ethiopia and Somalia have renounced their claims to the area, but each has accused the other of trying to gain control. There were clashes between Afars (ethnically related to Ethiopians) and Issas (related to Somalis) in 1976. Immigrants from both countries continued to enter the country up to independence, which came June 27, 1977.

French aid is the mainstay of the economy, as well as assistance from Arab countries. A peace accord Dec. 1994 ended a 3-year-long uprising by Afar rebels. An estimated 3,000 French and 1,800 U.S. troops are based in Djibouti.

Dominica
Commonwealth of Dominica

People: Population: 72,377. **Age distrib.** (%): <15: 25.6; 65+: 10.2. **Pop. density:** 249 per sq mi, 96 per sq km. **Urban:** 72.9%. **Ethnic groups:** Black 87%, Creole 9%, Carib Amerindian 3%. **Principal languages:** English (official), French patois. **Chief religions:** Roman Catholic 61%, Protestant 21%.

Geography: Total area: 291 sq mi, 754 sq km; **Land area:** 291 sq mi, 754 sq km. **Location:** In E Caribbean, most northerly Windward Isl. **Neighbors:** Guadeloupe to N, Martinique to S. **Topography:** Mountainous, a central ridge running from N to S, terminating in cliffs; volcanic in origin, with numerous thermal springs; rich deep topsoil on leeward side, red tropical clay on windward coast. **Capital (2004):** Roseau, 20,200.

Government: Type: Parliamentary democracy. **Head of state:** Pres. Nicholas Liverpool; b. 1934; in office: Oct. 2, 2003. **Head of gov.:** Prime Min. Roosevelt Skerrit; b. June 8, 1972; in office: Jan. 8, 2004. **Local divisions:** 10 parishes.

Economy: Industries: soap, coconut oil, tourism, copra, furniture, cement blocks, shoes. **Chief crops:** bananas, citrus, mangoes, root crops, coconuts, cocoa. **Natural resources:** timber, hydropower. **Arable land:** 7%. **Livestock:** cattle: 13,400; chickens: 190,000; goats: 9,700; pigs: 5,000; sheep: 7,600. **Fish catch:** 579 metric tons. **Electricity prod.:** 80 mil kWh. **Labor force:** agriculture 40%, industry and commerce 32%, services 28%.

Finance: Monetary unit: East Caribbean Dollar (XCD) (Sept. 2007: 2.67 = $1 U.S.). **GDP:** $485 mil; **per capita GDP** (2005 est.): $3,800; **GDP growth** (2005 est.): 3.1% **Imports** (2004 est.): $234 mil; U.S. 24.3%, China 21.8%, Trinidad and Tobago 13.2%, South Korea 7.6%. **Exports** (2004 est.): $74 mil; UK 22.7%, Jamaica 10.3%, South Korea 9.1%, Antigua and Barbuda 9%, Guyana 7.6%, China 7.2%. **Tourism:** $51 mil. **Budget** (2001): $84.4 mil. **Intl. reserves less gold:** $42 mil. **Consumer prices:** 2.35%.

Transport: Motor vehicles: 8,700 pass. cars; 3,400 comm. vehicles. **Civil aviation:** 2 airports. **Chief ports:** Portsmouth, Roseau.

Communications: TV sets: 232 per 1,000 pop. **Radios:** 648 per 1,000 pop. **Telephone lines:** 21,000. **Internet:** 26,000 users.

Health: Life expect.: 72.2 male; 78.2 female. **Births** (per 1,000 pop.): 15.7. **Deaths** (per 1,000 pop.): 8.4. **Natural inc.:** 0.73%. **Infant mortality** (per 1,000 live births): 14.6. **AIDS rate:** NA.

Education: Compulsory: ages 5-16. **Literacy:** 94%.

Major intl. organizations: UN (FAO, IBRD, ILO, IMF, IMO, WHO, WTO), Caricom, the Commonwealth, OAS, OECS.

Embassy: 3216 New Mexico Ave. NW 20016; 364-6781.

Website: www.dominica.dm

A British colony since 1805, Dominica was granted self-government in 1967. Independence was achieved Nov. 3, 1978.

Hurricane David struck, Aug. 30, 1979, devastating the island and destroying the banana plantations, Dominica's economic mainstay. Coups were attempted in 1980 and 1981.

Dominica participated in the 1983 U.S.-led invasion of nearby Grenada. Prime Min. Pierre Charles, 49, died of a heart attack Jan. 6, 2004, and was succeeded by Roosevelt Skerrit.

Dominican Republic

People: Population: 9,365,818. **Age distrib.** (%): <15: 32.1; 65+: 5.7. **Pop. density:** 501 per sq mi, 194 per sq km. **Urban:** 66.8%. **Ethnic groups:** Creole 73%, white 16%, black 11%. **Principal language:** Spanish (official). **Chief religion:** Roman Catholic 95%.

Geography: Total area: 18,815 sq mi, 48,730 sq km; **Land area:** 18,680 sq mi, 48,380 sq km. **Location:** In W Indies, sharing isl. of Hispaniola with Haiti. **Neighbors:** Haiti on W, Puerto Rico (U.S.) to E. **Topography:** The Cordillera Central range crosses center of the country, rising to over 10,000 ft, highest in the Caribbean. The Cibao Valley to N is major agricultural area. **Capital:** Santo Domingo, 2,022,000.

Government: Type: Republic. **Head of state and gov.:** Pres. Leonel Fernández Reyna; b. Dec. 26, 1953; in office: Aug. 16, 2004. **Local divisions:** 29 provinces and national district. **Defense budget** (2005): $191 mil. **Active troops:** 24,500.

Economy: Industries: tourism, sugar proc., mining, textiles, cement, tobacco. **Chief crops:** sugarcane, coffee, cotton, cocoa, tobacco, rice, beans. **Natural resources:** nickel, bauxite, gold, silver. **Arable land:** 22%. **Livestock:** cattle: 2.2 mil; chickens: 47.5 mil; goats: 190,000; pigs: 580,000; sheep: 123,000. **Fish catch:** 12,086 metric tons. **Electricity prod.:** 12.2 bil kWh. **Labor force** (1998 est.): agriculture 17%, industry 24.3%, services 58.7%.

Finance: Monetary unit: Peso (DOP) (Sept. 2007: 33.56 = $1 U.S.). **GDP:** $77.1 bil; **per capita GDP:** $8,400; **GDP growth:** 10.7%. **Imports:** $11.4 bil; U.S. 48.6%, Colombia 6.5%, Mexico 6.1%. **Exports:** $6.5 bil; U.S. 72.8%, UK 3.2%, Belgium 2.4%. **Tourism:** $3.5 bil. **Budget:** $5.9 bil. **Intl. reserves less gold:** $1.41 bil. **Gold:** 20,000 oz t. **Consumer prices:** 7.57%.

Transport: Railroad: Length: 321 mi. **Motor vehicles:** 630,000 pass. cars; 341,000 comm. vehicles. **Civil aviation** (1999): 3.1 mil pass.-mi; 14 airports. **Chief ports:** Boca Chica, Puerto Plata, Rio Haina, Santo Domingo.

Communications: TV sets: 96 per 1,000 pop. **Radios:** 178 per 1,000 pop. **Telephone lines:** 897,000. **Daily newspaper circ.:** 27.5 per 1,000 pop. **Internet:** 2 mil users.

Health: Life expect.: 71.3 male; 74.9 female. **Births** (per 1,000 pop.): 22.9. **Deaths** (per 1,000 pop.): 5.3. **Natural inc.:** 1.76%. **Infant mortality** (per 1,000 live births): 27.9. **AIDS rate:** 1.1%.

Education: Compulsory: ages 5-13. **Literacy:** 87%.

Major intl. organizations: UN (FAO, IBRD, ILO, IMF, IMO, WHO, WTO), OAS.

Embassy: 1715 22nd St. NW 20008; 332-6280.

Website: www.domrep.org

Carib and Arawak Indians inhabited the island of Hispaniola when Columbus landed in 1492. The city of Santo Domingo, founded 1496, is the oldest settlement by Europeans in the hemisphere and has the supposed ashes of Columbus in an elaborate tomb in its ancient cathedral.

The western third of the island was ceded to France in 1697. Santo Domingo itself was ceded to France in 1795. Haitian leader Toussaint L'Ouverture seized it, 1801. Spain returned intermittently 1803-21, as several native republics came and went. Haiti ruled again, 1822-44; Spanish occupation occurred 1861-63.

The country was occupied by U.S. Marines from 1916 to 1924, when a constitutionally elected government was installed.

In 1930, Gen. Rafael Leonidas Trujillo Molina was elected president. Trujillo ruled brutally until his assassination in 1961. Pres. Joaquín Balaguer, appointed by Trujillo in 1960, resigned under pressure in 1962.

Juan Bosch, elected president in the first free elections in 38 years, was overthrown in 1963. On Apr. 24, 1965, a revolt was launched by followers of Bosch and others, including a few Communists. Four days later U.S. Marines intervened against pro-Bosch forces. Token units were later sent by 5 South American countries as a peacekeeping force. A provisional government supervised a June 1966 election, in which Balaguer defeated Bosch. Balaguer remained in office for most of the next 28 years, but his May 1994 reelection was widely denounced as fraudulent. He cut short his term and on June 30, 1996, Leonel Fernández Reyna was elected.

Hurricane Georges struck Sept. 22, 1998, causing extensive property damage and claiming more than 200 lives. The leftist candidate, Hipólito Mejía, won a presidential vote May 16, 2000. With the nation reeling from a banking scandal and soaring inflation, Fernández defeated Mejía in the election of May 16, 2004. Floods and mudslides in late May killed about 395 people. A fight between rival prison gangs led to a fire, Mar. 7, 2005, in which 136 inmates died.

East Timor
(*See* Timor-Leste)

Ecuador
Republic of Ecuador

People: Population: 13,755,680. **Age distrib.** (%): <15: 32.6; 65+: 5.1. **Pop. density:** 129 per sq mi, 50 per sq km. **Urban:** 62.8%. **Ethnic groups:** Mestizo 65%, Amerindian 25%, white 7%, black 3%. **Principal languages:** Spanish (official), Amerindian languages (espec. Quechua). **Chief religion:** Roman Catholic 95%.

Geography: Total area: 109,483 sq mi, 283,560 sq km; **Land area:** 106,889 sq mi, 276,840 sq km. **Location:** In NW S. America, on Pacific coast, astride the Equator. **Neighbors:** Colombia on N, Peru on E and S. **Topography:** Two ranges of Andes run N and S, splitting country into 3 zones: hot, humid lowlands on coast; temperate highlands between ranges; and rainy, tropical lowlands to E. **Capital:** Quito, 1,514,000. **Cities (urban aggr.):** Guayaquil, 2,387,000.

Government: Type: Republic. **Head of state and gov.:** Pres. Rafael Correa; b. Apr. 6, 1963; in office: Jan. 15, 2007. **Local divisions:** 22 provinces. **Defense budget:** $653 mil. **Active troops:** 56,500.

Economy: Industries: oil, food proc., textiles, metal work, paper & wood products. **Chief crops:** bananas, coffee, cocoa, rice, potatoes, cassava, plantains, sugarcane. **Natural resources:** oil, fish, timber, hydropower. **Crude oil reserves:** 4.5 bil bbls. **Arable land:** 6%. **Livestock:** cattle: 5 mil; chickens: 104.2 mil; goats: 144,163; pigs: 1.3 mil; sheep: 1.1 mil. **Fish catch:** 486,023 metric tons. **Electricity prod.:** 12.9 bil kWh. **Labor force** (2001): agriculture 8%, industry 24%, services 68%.

Finance: Monetary unit: U.S. Dollar (USD). **GDP:** $61.5 bil; **per capita GDP:** $4,500; **GDP growth:** 4.1%. **Imports:** $10.8 bil; U.S. 24%, Colombia 14.4%, Venezuela 7.7%, Brazil 7%, China 6.3%. **Exports:** $12.6 bil; U.S. 51.4%, Peru 8.2%, Colombia 4.4%, Chile 4.1%. **Tourism:** $486 mil. **Budget:** $10.5 bil. **Intl. reserves less gold:** $990 mil. **Gold:** 850,000 oz t. **Consumer prices:** 3.03%.

Transport: Railroad: Length: 600 mi. **Motor vehicles:** 411,000 pass. cars; 306,000 comm. vehicles. **Civil aviation:** 418.8 mil pass.-mi; 98 airports. **Chief ports:** Esmeraldas, Guayaquil, Manta, Puerto Bolívar.

Communications: TV sets: 213 per 1,000 pop. **Radios:** 406 per 1,000 pop. **Telephone lines:** 1.8 mil. **Daily newspaper circ.:** 98.2 per 1,000 pop. **Internet:** 1.5 mil users.

Health: Life expect.: 73.7 male; 79.6 female. **Births** (per 1,000 pop.): 21.9. **Deaths** (per 1,000 pop.): 4.2. **Natural inc.:** 1.77%. **Infant mortality** (per 1,000 live births): 22.1. **AIDS rate:** 0.3%.

Education: Compulsory: ages 5-14. **Literacy:** 91%.

Major intl. organizations: UN (FAO, IBRD, ILO, IMF, IMO, WHO, WTO), OAS.

Embassy: 2535 15th St. NW 20009; 234-7200.

Website: www.ecuador.org

The region, which was the northern Inca empire, was conquered by Spain in 1533. Liberation forces defeated the Spanish May 24, 1822, near Quito. Ecuador became part of the Great Colombia Republic but seceded, May 13, 1830.

Ecuadoran Indians staged protests in the 1990s to demand greater rights. A border war with Peru flared from Jan. 26, 1995, until a truce took effect Mar. 1. Vice Pres. Alberto Dahik resigned and fled Ecuador, Oct. 11, 1995, to avoid arrest on corruption charges. Elected president in a runoff, July 7, 1996, Abdalá Bucaram—a populist known as El Loco, or "The Crazy One"—imposed stiff price increases and other austerity measures. His rising unpopularity and erratic behavior led the National Congress, Feb. 6, 1997, to dismiss him for "mental incapacity."

Jamil Mahuad Witt, mayor of Quito, won a presidential runoff election July 12, 1998. In Sept. 1998 and Mar. 1999 he imposed emergency measures to cope with a continuing economic crisis. Opposed by Indian groups and military leaders, he was ousted Jan. 21, 2000, and succeeded by Vice Pres. Gustavo Noboa Bejarano. Noboa went ahead with a plan introduced by Mahuad to replace the sucre with the U.S. dollar as Ecuador's currency. Lucio Gutiérrez Borbúa, a leader in the 2000 coup, won a presidential runoff Nov. 24, 2002. Noboa, under investigation for financial mismanagement, went into exile Aug. 23, 2003.

Gutiérrez imposed economic austerity measures, purged opponents from the supreme court, Dec. 2004, and then dissolved the court, Apr. 15, 2005. With street protests rising, the military withdrew support of Gutiérrez. Congress ousted him Apr. 20, and Vice Pres. Alfredo Palacio González became president. The U.S. suspended free-trade talks after Ecuador, May 15, 2006, took over oil assets belonging to U.S.-based Occidental Petroleum. Rafael Correa, a left-wing economist, won a presidential runoff vote Nov. 26, 2006, and took office Jan. 15, 2007. After a power struggle with the National Congress, Correa scored a major triumph when voters Apr. 15 approved his plan to convene an assembly to rewrite the constitution.

The **Galápagos Islands**, pop. (2001 est.) 16,000, about 600 mi to the W, are the home of huge tortoises and other unusual animals. The oil tanker *Jessica* ran aground Jan. 16, 2001, off San Cristóbal Is., spilling some 185,000 gallons of fuel.

Egypt
Arab Republic of Egypt

People: Population: 80,335,036. **Age distrib. (%):** <15: 32.2; 65+: 4.6. **Pop. density:** 209 per sq mi, 81 per sq km. **Urban:** 42.8%. **Ethnic groups:** Egyptian 98%. **Principal languages:** Arabic (official), English, French. **Chief religions:** Muslim (official; mostly Sunni) 90%, Coptic Christian 9%.

Geography: Total area: 386,662 sq mi, 1,001,450 sq km; **Land area:** 384,345 sq mi, 995,450 sq km. **Location:** NE corner of Africa. **Neighbors:** Libya on W; Sudan on S; Israel, Gaza Strip on E. **Topography:** Almost entirely desolate and barren, with hills and mountains in E and along Nile. The Nile Valley, where most of the people live, stretches 550 mi. **Capital:** Cairo, 11,128,000. **Cities (urban aggr.):** Alexandria, 3,770,000.

Government: Type: Republic. **Head of state:** Pres. Hosni Mubarak; b. May 4, 1928; in office: Oct. 14, 1981. **Head of gov.:** Prime Min. Ahmed Nazif; b. July 8, 1952; in office: July 14, 2004. **Local divisions:** 26 governorates. **Defense budget:** $2.9 bil. **Active troops:** 468,500.

Economy: Industries: textiles, food proc., tourism, chemicals, hydrocarbons, constr., cement, metals. **Chief crops:** cotton, rice, corn, wheat, beans, fruits, vegetables. **Natural resources:** oil, nat. gas, iron ore, phosphates, mang., limestone, gypsum, talc, asbestos, lead, zinc. **Crude oil reserves:** 3.7 bil bbls. **Arable land:** 3%. **Livestock:** cattle: 4.5 mil; chickens: 95 mil; goats: 4 mil; pigs: 30,000; sheep: 5.2 mil. **Fish catch:** 889,301 metric tons. **Electricity prod.:** 102.5 bil kWh. **Labor force** (2001 est.): agriculture 32%, industry 17%, services 51%.

Finance: Monetary unit: Pound (EGP) (Sept. 2007: 5.64 = $1 U.S.). **GDP:** $334.4 bil; **per capita GDP:** $4,200; **GDP growth:** 6.8%. **Imports:** $35.9 bil; U.S. 11.4%, China 8.2%, Germany 6.4%, Italy 5.4%, Saudi Arabia 5%. **Exports:** $24.2 bil; Italy 12.2%, U.S. 11.4%, Spain 8.6%, UK 5.6%, France 5.4%, Syria 5.2%. **Tourism:** $6.1 bil. **Budget:** $31.8 bil. **Intl. reserves less gold:** $16.26 bil. **Gold:** 2.43 mil oz t. **Consumer prices:** 7.64%.

Transport: Railroad: Length: 3,146 mi. **Motor vehicles:** 2 mil pass. cars; 715,000 comm. vehicles. **Civil aviation:** 5 bil pass.-mi; 72 airports. **Chief ports:** Alexandria, Damietta, Port Said, Suez.

Communications: TV sets: 170 per 1,000 pop. **Radios:** 317 per 1,000 pop. **Telephone lines:** 10.8 mil. **Daily newspaper circ.:** 31.3 per 1,000 pop. **Internet:** 6 mil users.

Health: Life expect.: 69 male; 74.2 female. **Births** (per 1,000 pop.): 22.5. **Deaths** (per 1,000 pop.): 5.1. **Natural inc.:** 1.74%. **Infant mortality** (per 1,000 live births): 29.5. **AIDS rate:** <0.1%.

Education: Compulsory: ages 6-14. **Literacy:** 71.4%.

Major intl. organizations: UN (FAO, IBRD, ILO, IMF, IMO, WHO, WTO), AL, AU.

Embassy: 3521 International Ct. NW 20008; 895-5400.

Website: www.misr.gov.eg

Archaeological records of ancient Egyptian civilization date back to 4000 BCE. A unified kingdom arose around 3200 BCE and extended its way south into Nubia and as far north as Syria. A high culture of rulers and priests was built on an economic base of serfdom, fertile soil, and annual flooding of the Nile.

Imperial decline facilitated conquest by Asian invaders (Hyksos, Assyrians). The last native dynasty fell in 341 BCE to the Persians, who were in turn replaced by Greeks (Alexander and the Ptolemies), Romans, Byzantines, and Arabs, who introduced Islam and the Arabic language. The ancient Egyptian language is preserved only in Coptic Christian liturgy.

Egypt was ruled as part of larger Islamic empires for many centuries. Britain intervened in Egypt in 1882 and ruled the country as a protectorate, 1914-22. A 1936 treaty strengthened Egyptian autonomy, but Britain retained bases in Egypt and a condominium over the Sudan. When the state of Israel was proclaimed in 1948, Egypt joined other Arab nations invading Israel and was defeated. In 1951 Egypt abrogated the 1936 treaty; the Sudan became independent in 1956.

An uprising on July 23, 1952, overthrew King Farouk and established a republic. Lt. Col. Gamal Abdel Nasser rose to power, becoming premier in 1954 and president in 1956. Nasser emerged as the most influential leader in the Arab world at the time; within Egypt, he pushed construction of the Aswan High Dam, completed in 1970.

After guerrilla raids across its border, Israel invaded Egypt's Sinai Peninsula, Oct. 29, 1956. Egypt rejected a cease-fire demand by Britain and France; on Oct. 31 the 2 nations dropped bombs and on Nov. 5-6 landed forces. Egypt and Israel accepted a UN cease-fire; fighting ended Nov. 7. Subsequently, a UN Emergency Force guarded the border. Full-scale war with Israel broke out again, June 5, 1967; before it ended under a UN cease-fire June 10, Israel had captured Gaza and the Sinai Peninsula and taken control of the E bank of the Suez Canal.

Nasser died Sept. 28, 1970, and was replaced by Vice Pres. Anwar Sadat. In a surprise attack Oct. 6, 1973, Egyptian forces crossed the Suez Canal into the Sinai. (At the same time, Syrian forces attacked Israelis on the Golan Heights.) Egypt was supplied by a USSR military airlift; the U.S. responded with an airlift to Israel. Israel counterattacked, crossed the canal, and surrounded Suez City. A UN cease-fire took effect Oct. 24. Under an agreement signed Jan. 18, 1974, Israeli forces withdrew from the canal's W bank; limited numbers of Egyptian forces occupied a strip along the E bank. A second accord was signed in 1975, with Israel yielding Sinai oil fields.

Pres. Sadat's surprise visit to Jerusalem, Nov. 1977, opened the prospect of peace with Israel. On Mar. 26, 1979, Egypt and Israel signed a formal peace treaty, ending 30 years of war, and establishing diplomatic relations. On Oct. 6, 1981, Pres. Sadat was assassinated by Muslim extremists within the army; he was succeeded by Hosni Mubarak. Israel returned control of the Sinai to Egypt in Apr. 1982.

Egypt saw a rising tide of Islamic fundamentalist violence in the 1990s. U.S. aid to Egypt, totaling more than $50 bil since 1975, helped to keep Mubarak in power. Egypt supported the U.S.-led coalition against Iraq in the Persian Gulf War, 1991. Egyptian security forces conducted raids against Islamic militants, some of whom were executed for terrorism. Naguib Mahfouz, winner of the 1988 Nobel Prize for literature, was stabbed by Islamic militants Oct. 14, 1994. Pres. Mubarak escaped assassination in Ethiopia, June 26, 1995; Egypt blamed Sudan for the attack. On Nov. 17, 1997, near Luxor, Muslim extremists killed 58 foreign tourists and 4 Egyptians.

Mubarak, who was grazed by a knife-wielding assailant Sept. 6, 1999, was confirmed by popular vote Sept. 26 for a 4th presidential term. An EgyptAir jetliner bound from New York to Cairo plunged into the Atlantic near Nantucket Is., Oct. 31, 1999, killing all 217 people on board. Fire on a train bound from Cairo to Luxor, Feb. 20, 2002, left more than 360 people dead. An Egyptian charter plane plunged into the Red Sea shortly after takeoff Jan. 3, 2004, killing 148 people, including 133 French tourists.

Terrorists stepped up their campaign against the economically important tourism industry. Bombs Oct. 7, 2004, in and near Taba (a Sinai tourist site popular with Israelis) killed at least 35 people. Another 88 people were killed in bombings July 23, 2005, at Sharm el Sheikh, a Red Sea resort city. Pressured by the U.S., Mubarak agreed to allow opposition candidates in the Sept. 7 presidential election, which he won with an 88.5% majority; turnout was only 23%. Suicide bombings at the Sinai resort town of Dhab, Apr. 24, 2006, killed at least 18 people and injured 85; security forces May 9 killed Nasser Khamis al-Mallahi, leader of the group blamed for the Taba, Sharm el Sheikh, and Dahab attacks. Constitutional amendments expanding presidential powers and barring religiously-based political parties were approved Mar. 26, 2007, in a referendum criticized as fraudulent by opposition groups and human rights observers.

The **Suez Canal**, 103 mi long, links the Mediterranean and Red seas. It was built by a French corporation 1859-69, but Britain obtained controlling interest in 1875. The last British troops were removed June 13, 1956. On July 26, Egypt nationalized the canal.

El Salvador
Republic of El Salvador

People: Population: 6,948,073. **Age distrib.** (%): <15: 36.1; 65+: 5.2. **Pop. density:** 867 per sq mi, 335 per sq km. **Urban:** 59.8%. **Ethnic groups:** Mestizo 90%, white 9%, Amerindian 1%. **Principal languages:** Spanish (official), Nahua. **Chief religions:** Roman Catholic 83%, many Protestant groups.

Geography: Total area: 8,124 sq mi, 21,040 sq km; **Land area:** 8,000 sq mi, 20,720 sq km. **Location:** In Central America. **Neighbors:** Guatemala on W, Honduras on N. **Topography:** A hot Pacific coastal plain in S rises to a cooler plateau and valley region, densely populated. The N is mountainous, including many volcanoes. **Capital:** San Salvador, 1,517,000.

Government: Type: Republic. **Head of state and gov.:** Pres. Antonio Elías Saca González; b. Mar. 9, 1965; in office: June 1, 2004. **Local divisions:** 14 departments. **Defense budget:** $106 mil. **Active troops:** 15,500.

Economy: Industries: food proc., beverages, oil, chemicals, fertilizer, textiles, furniture, light metals. **Chief crops:** coffee, sugar, corn, rice, beans, oilseed, cotton, sorghum. **Natural resources:** hydropower, geothermal power, oil. **Arable land:** 31%. **Livestock:** cattle: 1.3 mil; chickens: 13.7 mil; goats: 10,750; pigs: 436,360; sheep: 5,100. **Fish catch:** 43,317 metric tons. **Electricity prod.:** 4.7 bil kWh. **Labor force** (2003 est.): agriculture 17.1%, industry 17.1%, services 65.8%.

Finance: Monetary unit: Colon (SVC) (Sept. 2007: 8.75 = $1 U.S.). **GDP:** $33.7 bil; **per capita GDP:** $4,900; **GDP growth:** 4.2%. **Imports:** $7.3 bil; U.S. 30.6%, Guatemala 8.8%, Mexico 8.5%, Germany 6%, China 4.5%, Brazil 4.2%. **Exports:** $3.7 bil; U.S. 49.8%, Guatemala 14.4%, Honduras 8.9%, Nicaragua 5.1%. **Tourism:** $337 mil. **Budget** (2007 est.): $2.9 bil. **Intl. reserves less gold:** $1.21 bil. **Gold:** 230,000 oz t. **Consumer prices:** 4.04%.

Transport: Railroad: Length: 349 mi. **Motor vehicles:** 148,000 pass. cars; 250,800 comm. vehicles. **Civil aviation:** 2.3 bil pass.-mi; 4 airports. **Chief ports:** Acajutla, Puerto Cutuco.

Communications: TV sets: 191 per 1,000 pop. **Radios:** 478 per 1,000 pop. **Telephone lines:** 1 mil. **Daily newspaper circ.:** 28.5 per 1,000 pop. **Internet:** 637,000 users.

Health: Life expect.: 68.2 male; 75.6 female. **Births** (per 1,000 pop.): 26.1. **Deaths** (per 1,000 pop.): 5.6. **Natural inc.:** 2.05%. **Infant mortality** (per 1,000 live births): 22.9. **AIDS rate:** 0.9%.

Education: Compulsory: ages 7-15. **Literacy:** 80.6%.

Major intl. organizations: UN (FAO, IBRD, ILO, IMF, IMO, WHO, WTO), OAS.

Embassy: 1400 16th St. NW, Ste. 100, 20036; 265-9671.

Website: www.elsalvador.org

El Salvador became independent of Spain in 1821, and of the Central American Federation in 1839.

A fight with Honduras in 1969 over the presence of 300,000 Salvadoran workers left 2,000 dead.

A military coup overthrew the government of Pres. Carlos Humberto Romero in 1979, but the ruling military-civilian junta failed to quell a rebellion by leftist insurgents, armed by Cuba and Nicaragua. Extreme right-wing death squads organized to eliminate suspected leftists were blamed for thousands of deaths in the 1980s. The Reagan administration staunchly supported the government with military aid. The 12-year civil war ended Jan. 16, 1992, as the government and leftist rebels signed a formal peace treaty. The civil war had taken the lives of some 75,000 people. The treaty provided for military and political reforms.

Nine soldiers, including 3 officers, were indicted Jan. 1990 in the Nov. 1989 slaying of 6 Jesuit priests in San Salvador. Two of the officers received maximum 30-year jail sentences. They were released Mar. 20, 1993, when the National Assembly passed a sweeping amnesty.

Francisco Flores, candidate of the right-wing ARENA party, won the presidential election of Mar. 7, 1999. Another ARENA nominee, Antonio Saca, a businessman and former sportscaster, won the presidential election of Mar. 21, 2004. Remittances from Salvadorans working in the U.S. are a major source of income.

Equatorial Guinea
Republic of Equatorial Guinea

People: Population: 551,201. **Age distrib.** (%): <15: 41.5; 65+: 3.8. **Pop. density:** 51 per sq mi, 20 per sq km. **Urban:** 38.9%. **Ethnic groups:** Fang 86%, Bubi 7%, Mdowe 4%. **Principal languages:** Spanish, French (both official); Fang; Bubi. **Chief religions:** Nominally Christian and predominantly Roman Catholic, pagan practices.

Geography: Total area: 10,831 sq mi, 28,051 sq km; **Land area:** 10,831 sq mi, 28,051 sq km. **Location:** Bioko Isl. off W Africa coast in Gulf of Guinea, and Rio Muni, mainland enclave. **Neighbors:** Gabon on S, Cameroon on E and N. **Topography:** Bioko Isl. consists of 2 volcanic mountains and connecting valley. Rio Muni, with over 90% of the area, has coastal plain and low hills beyond. **Capital:** Malabo, 96,000.

Government: Type: Republic. **Head of state:** Pres. Teodoro Obiang Nguema Mbasogo; b. June 5, 1942; in office: Aug. 3, 1979. **Head of gov.:** Prime Min. Ricardo Mangue Obama Nfubea; in office: Aug. 14, 2006. **Local divisions:** 7 provinces. **Defense budget** (2005): $7 mil. **Active troops:** 1,320.

Economy: Industries: oil, fishing, sawmilling, nat. gas. **Chief crops:** coffee, cocoa, rice, yams, cassava, bananas. **Natural resources:** oil, timber, gold, mang., uranium. **Crude oil reserves:** 1.1 bil. bbls. **Arable land:** 5%. **Livestock:** cattle: 5,050; chickens: 320,000; goats: 9,000; pigs: 6,100; sheep: 37,600. **Fish catch:** 3,500 metric tons. **Electricity prod.:** 30 mil kWh.

Finance: Monetary unit: CFA BEAC Franc (XAF) (Sept. 2007: 472.78 = $1 U.S.). **GDP** (2005 est.): $25.7 bil; **per capita GDP** (2005 est.): $50,200; **GDP growth** (2005 est.): 18.6%. **Imports:** $2.5 bil; U.S. 40.1%, Spain 10%, Cote d'Ivoire 8.4%, France 6.5%, UK 6.1%, Italy 5.3%. **Exports:** $9 bil; China 31.1%, U.S. 22.4%, Spain 12.7%, Taiwan 7.4%, Portugal 6.1%. **Tourism:** $14 mil. **Budget:** $1.4 bil. **Intl. reserves less gold:** $2.04 bil.

Transport: Motor vehicles: NA. **Civil aviation:** 3 airports. **Civil aviation:** 3 airports. **Chief port:** Malabo.

Communications: TV sets: 116 per 1,000 pop. **Radios:** 429 per 1,000 pop. **Telephone lines:** 10,000. **Daily newspaper circ.:** 4.6 per 1,000 pop. **Internet:** 8,000 users.

Health: Life expect.: 48.1 male; 51 female. **Births** (per 1,000 pop.): 35.2. **Deaths** (per 1,000 pop.): 15. **Natural inc.:** 2.02%. **Infant mortality** (per 1,000 live births): 87.2. **AIDS rate:** 3.2%.

Education: Compulsory: ages 7-11. **Literacy:** 87%.

Major intl. organizations: UN (FAO, IBRD, ILO, IMF, IMO, WHO), AU.

Embassy: 2020 16th St. NW 20009; 518-5700.

Website: www.state.gov/p/af/ci/ek/

Fernando Po (now Bioko) Island was reached by Portugal in the late 15th cent. and ceded to Spain in 1778. Independence came Oct. 12, 1968. Riots occurred in 1969 over disputes between the island and the more backward Rio Muni province on the mainland. Masie Nguema Biyogo, a mainlander, became pres. for life in 1972.

Masie's reign was one of the most brutal in Africa, resulting in a bankrupted nation; most of the nation's 7,000 Europeans emigrated. He was ousted in a military coup, Aug. 1979. Teodoro Obiang Nguema Mbasogo, leader of the coup, became president and installed his family members in key government posts. His regime eventually agreed to elections, held Nov. 21, 1993. These were nominally won by the ruling party, but boycotted by opposition parties that maintained the rules were rigged. Elections for president, Feb. 25, 1996, and Dec. 15, 2002, were similarly condemned.

Oil sales, especially to the U.S., have boomed in recent years. Authorities in Zimbabwe and Equatorial Guinea arrested 85 people in Mar. 2004 on charges of plotting to overthrow the Obiang regime. Mark Thatcher, son of the former British prime min., was arrested in South Africa Aug. 25 for alleged involvement; in a plea bargain Jan. 13, 2005, he agreed to pay a $500,000 fine. Pres. Obiang revamped his entire cabinet in Aug. 2006.

Eritrea
State of Eritrea

People: Population: 4,906,585. **Age distrib.** (%): <15: 43.5; 65+: 3.6. **Pop. density:** 105 per sq mi, 40 per sq km. **Urban:** 19.4%. **Ethnic groups:** Tigrinya 50%, Tigre and Kunama 40%, Afar 4%, Saho 3%. **Principal languages:** Arabic, Tigrinya, Afar, Tigre, Kunama, other Cushitic languages. **Chief religions:** Muslim, Coptic Christian, Roman Catholic, Protestant.

Geography: Total area: 46,842 sq mi, 121,320 sq km; **Land area:** 46,842 sq mi, 121,320 sq km. **Location:** In E Africa on SW coast of Red Sea. **Neighbors:** Ethiopia on S, Djibouti on SE, Sudan on W. **Topography:** Includes many islands of the Dahlak Archipelago, low coastal plains in S, mountain range with peaks to 9,000 ft in N. **Capital:** Asmara, 551,000.

Government: Type: In transition. **Head of state and gov.:** Isaias Afwerki; b. Feb. 2, 1946; in office: May 24, 1993. **Local divisions:** 8 provinces. **Defense budget:** $65 mil. **Active troops:** 201,750.

Economy: Industries: food proc., beverages, clothing, textiles. **Chief crops:** sorghum, lentils, vegetables, corn, cotton, tobacco, sisal. **Natural resources:** gold, potash, zinc, copper, salt, fish. **Arable land:** 5%. **Livestock:** cattle: 2 mil; chickens: 1.4 mil; goats: 1.7 mil; sheep: 2.1 mil. **Fish catch:** 4,027 metric tons. **Electricity prod.:** 270 mil kWh. **Labor force:** agriculture 80%, industry and services 20%.

Finance: Monetary unit: Nakfa (ERN) (Sept. 2007: 15.00 = $1 U.S.). **GDP:** $4.8 bil; **per capita GDP** (2005 est.): $1,000; **GDP growth** (2005 est.): 2%. **Imports:** $701.8 mil; Italy 15.1%, France 11.8%, U.S. 9.5%, Germany 8.6%, Taiwan 7.3%, India 7%, Ireland 6.1%. **Exports:** $17.7 mil; Italy 31.4%, U.S. 11.9%, Belarus 5.9%, France 5.1%, Germany 4.6%, Turkey 4.4%, UK 4%. **Tourism:** $73 mil. **Budget:** $424 mil. **Intl. reserves less gold:** $17 mil.

Transport: Railroad: Length: 190 mi. **Civil aviation:** 4 airports. **Chief ports:** Assab, Massawa.

Communications: TV sets: 16 per 1,000 pop. **Radios:** 484 per 1,000 pop. **Telephone lines:** 37,500. **Internet:** 100,000 users.

Health: Life expect.: 57.9 male; 61.3 female. **Births** (per 1,000 pop.): 34. **Deaths** (per 1,000 pop.): 9.4. **Natural inc.:** 2.46%. **Infant mortality** (per 1,000 live births): 45.2. **AIDS rate:** 2.4%.

Education: Compulsory: ages 7-14. **Literacy:** 58.6%.

Major intl. organizations: UN (FAO, IBRD, ILO, IMF, IMO, WHO), AU.

Embassy: 1708 New Hampshire Ave. NW 20009; 319-1991.

Website: www.shabait.com

Eritrea was part of the Ethiopian kingdom of Aksum. It was an Italian colony from 1890 to 1941, when it was captured by the British. Following a period of British and UN supervision, Eritrea was awarded to Ethiopia as part of a federation in 1952. Ethiopia annexed Eritrea as a province in 1962. This led to a 31-year struggle for independence, which ended when Eritrea formally declared itself an independent nation May 24, 1993. A constitution was ratified in 1997 but not implemented.

A border war with Ethiopia that erupted in June 1998 intensified in May 2000, as Ethiopian troops plunged into western Eritrea; a cease-fire signed June 18 provided for a UN peacekeeping force (UNMEE) to patrol a buffer zone on Eritrean territory. A peace treaty was signed Dec. 12, 2000. UNMEE forces numbered about 1,700 in mid-2007. A UN report in July accused Eritrea of aiding an Islamic insurgency in Somalia.

Estonia
Republic of Estonia

People: Population: 1,315,912. **Age distrib. (%):** <15: 15; 65+: 17.5. **Pop. density:** 79 per sq mi, 30 per sq km. **Urban:** 69.1%. **Ethnic groups:** Estonian 68%, Russian 26%. **Principal languages:** Estonian (official), Russian. **Chief religions:** Unaffiliated 34%, Evangelical Lutheran 14%, Russian Orthodox 13%

Geography: Total area: 17,462 sq mi, 45,226 sq km; **Land area:** 16,684 sq mi, 43,211 sq km. **Location:** E Europe, bordering Baltic Sea and Gulf of Finland. **Neighbors:** Russia on E, Latvia on S. **Topography:** Marshy lowland with numerous lakes and swamps; about 40% forested. Elongated hills show evidence of former glaciation. More than 800 islands on Baltic coast. **Capital:** Tallinn, 392,000.

Government: Type: Republic. **Head of state:** Pres. Toomas Hendrik Ilves; b. Dec. 26, 1953; in office: Oct. 9, 2006. **Head of gov.:** Prime Min. Andrus Ansip; b. Oct. 1, 1956; in office: Apr. 13, 2005. **Local divisions:** 15 counties. **Defense budget:** $240 mil. **Active troops:** 4,100.

Economy: Industries: engineering, electronics, timber, wood products, textiles, telecom. **Chief crops:** potatoes, vegetables. **Natural resources:** oil shale, peat, phosphorite, clay, limestone, sand, dolomite, sea mud. **Arable land:** 25%. **Livestock:** cattle: 249,500; chickens: 1.9 mil; goats: 2,800; pigs: 346,500; sheep: 49,600. **Fish catch:** 99,327 metric tons. **Electricity prod.:** 9.6 bil kWh. **Labor force** (1999 est.): agriculture 11%, industry 20%, services 69%.

Finance: Monetary unit: Kroon (EEK) (Sept. 2007: 11.28 = $1 U.S.). **GDP:** $26.9 bil; **per capita GDP:** $20,300; **GDP growth:** 11.4%. **Imports:** $12 bil; Finland 18.2%, Russia 13.1%, Germany 12.4%, Sweden 9%, Lithuania 6.4%, Latvia 5.7%. **Exports:** $9.7 bil; Finland 18.4%, Sweden 12.4%, Latvia 8.9%, Russia 8.1%, U.S. 5.5%, Germany 5.1%. **Tourism:** $948 mil. **Budget:** $5.7 bil. **Intl. reserves less gold:** $1.85 bil. **Gold:** 10,000 oz t. **Consumer prices:** 4.43%.

Transport: Railroad: Length: 595 mi. **Motor vehicles:** 471,200 pass. cars; 91,000 comm. vehicles. **Civil aviation:** 257.9 mil pass.-mi; 12 airports. **Chief ports:** Muuga, Tallinn.

Communications: TV sets: 567 per 1,000 pop. **Radios:** 191.6 per 1,000 pop. **Telephone lines:** 541,900. **Daily newspaper circ.:** 191.6 per 1,000 pop. **Internet:** 760,000 users.

Health: Life expect.: 66.9 male; 78.1 female. **Births** (per 1,000 pop.): 10.2. **Deaths** (per 1,000 pop.): 13.3. **Natural inc.:** –0.31%. **Infant mortality** (per 1,000 live births): 7.6. **AIDS rate:** 1.3%.

Education: Compulsory: ages 7-15. **Literacy:** 99.8%.

Major intl. organizations: UN (FAO, IBRD, ILO, IMF, IMO, WHO, WTO), EU, NATO, OSCE.

Embassy: 2131 Massachusetts Ave. NW 20008; 588-0101.

Website: www.riik.ee

Estonia was a province of imperial Russia before World War I, and was independent between World Wars I and II. It was conquered by the USSR in 1940 and incorporated as the Estonian SSR. Estonia declared itself an "occupied territory," and proclaimed itself a free nation Mar. 1990. During an abortive Soviet coup, Estonia declared immediate full independence, Aug. 20, 1991; the Soviet Union recognized its independence in Sept. 1991. The first free elections in over 50 years were held Sept. 20, 1992. The last occupying Russian troops were withdrawn by Aug. 31, 1994. Estonia became a full member of the EU and NATO in 2004.

Ethiopia
Federal Democratic Republic of Ethiopia

People: Population: 76,511,887. **Age distrib. (%):** <15: 43.4; 65+: 2.7. **Pop. density:** 177 per sq mi, 68 per sq km. **Urban:** 16%. **Ethnic groups:** Oromo 32%, Amhara 30%, Tigraway 6%, Somali 6%, Gurage 4%, Sidama 4%. **Principal languages:** Amarigna, Ordmigna, Tigrinya, Somaligna, Guaragigna, Sidamigna, Hadiyigna, English. **Chief religions:** Ethiopian Orthodox 51%, Muslim 33%, Protestant 10%, traditional 5%.

Geography: Total area: 435,186 sq mi, 1,127,127 sq km; **Land area:** 432,312 sq mi, 1,119,683 sq km. **Location:** In E Africa. **Neighbors:** Sudan on W; Kenya on S; Somalia, Djibouti on E; Eritrea on N. **Topography:** A high central plateau, 6,000-10,000 ft high, rises to higher mountains near the Great Rift Valley, cutting in from SW. Blue Nile and other rivers cross the plateau, which de-

scends to plains on both W and SE. **Capital:** Addis Ababa, 2,893,000.

Government: Type: Federal republic. **Head of state:** Pres. Girma Wolde Giorgis; b. Dec. 1924; in office: Oct. 8, 2001. **Head of gov.:** Prime Min. Meles Zenawi; b. May 8, 1955; in office: Aug. 23, 1995. **Local divisions:** 9 states, 2 charted cities. **Defense budget:** $345 mil. **Active troops:** 152,500.

Economy: Industries: food proc., beverages, textiles, chemicals, metals proc., cement. **Chief crops:** cereals, pulses, coffee, oilseed, sugarcane, potatoes. **Natural resources:** gold, platinum, copper, potash, nat. gas, hydropower. **Crude oil reserves:** 400,000 bbls. **Arable land:** 12%. **Livestock:** cattle: 43.1 mil; chickens: 34.2 mil; goats: 18.6 mil; pigs: 29,000; sheep: 23.6 mil. **Fish catch:** 9,450 metric tons. **Electricity prod.:** 2.9 bil kWh. **Labor force** (1985): agriculture 80%, industry 8%, government 12%.

Finance: Monetary unit: Birr (ETB) (Sept. 2007: 9.09 = $1 U.S.). **GDP:** $74.9 bil; **per capita GDP:** $1,000; **GDP growth:** 10.6%. **Imports:** $4.1 bil; Saudi Arabia 11%, China 11.4%, India 8.1%, Italy 5.1%. **Exports:** $1.1 bil; China 10.5%, Germany 8.7%, Japan 7.4%, U.S. 6.8%, Saudi Arabia 5.8%, Djibouti 5.8%, Switzerland 5.1%, Italy 5%. **Tourism:** $173 mil. **Budget:** $3.4 bil. **Intl. reserves less gold:** $553 mil. **Consumer prices** (2005): 11.61%.

Transport: Railroad: Length: 423 mi. **Motor vehicles:** 81,200 pass. cars; 44,500 comm. vehicles. **Civil aviation:** 2.2 bil pass.-mi; 14 airports.

Communications: TV sets: 5 per 1,000 pop. **Radios:** 185 per 1,000 pop. **Telephone lines:** 725,000. **Daily newspaper circ.:** 0.4 per 1,000 pop. **Internet:** 164,000 users.

Health: Life expect.: 48.1 male; 50.4 female. **Births** (per 1,000 pop.): 37.4. **Deaths** (per 1,000 pop.): 14.7. **Natural inc.:** 2.27%. **Infant mortality** (per 1,000 live births): 91.9. **AIDS rate:** 1.6%.

Education: Compulsory: ages 7-12. **Literacy:** 35.9%.

Major intl. organizations: UN (FAO, IBRD, ILO, IMF, IMO, WHO), AU.

Embassy: 3506 International Dr. NW 20008; 364-1200.

Website: www.moinfo.gov.et

Ethiopian culture was influenced by Egypt and Greece. The ancient monarchy was invaded by Italy in 1880 but maintained its independence until another Italian invasion in 1936. British forces freed the country in 1941.

A series of droughts in the 1970s killed hundreds of thousands. An army mutiny, strikes, and student demonstrations led to the dethronement, Sept. 12, 1974, of Ethiopia's last emperor, Haile Selassie I, ending his 58-year reign; he died Aug. 1975, while being held by the ruling junta, known as the Dergue. The junta dissolved parliament, abolished the monarchy, established a socialist state, redistributed land, curbed the influence of the Coptic Church, and violently suppressed opposition.

The regime, torn by bloody coups, faced uprisings by tribal and political groups aided in part by Sudan and Somalia. Ties with the U.S., once a major ally, deteriorated, while cooperation accords were signed with the USSR in 1977. In 1978, Soviet advisers and Cuban troops helped defeat Somali forces. Ethiopia and Somalia signed a peace agreement in 1988.

A worldwide relief effort began in 1984, as an extended drought threatened the country with famine; up to 1 mil people may have died as a result of starvation and disease.

The Ethiopian People's Revolutionary Democratic Front (EPRDF), an umbrella group of 6 rebel armies, launched a major push against government forces, Feb. 1991. In May, Pres. Mengistu Haile Mariam resigned, finding refuge in Zimbabwe. The EPRDF took over and set up a transitional government. Ethiopia's first multiparty general elections were held in 1995.

Eritrea, a province on the Red Sea, declared its independence May 24, 1993. Fighting along the border with Eritrea, which erupted in June 1998, intensified in May 2000, as Ethiopian forces plunged into Eritrean territory; a cease-fire was signed June 18 and a peace treaty Dec. 12. The war displaced 350,000 Ethiopians and is estimated to have cost the country nearly $3 bil. A collapse of crop prices in 2001, followed by drought in 2002-03, led to severe food shortages. Ethnic clashes Dec. 2003-Jan. 2004 in western Ethiopia left more than 250 people dead; thousands fled to Sudan.

The ruling EPRDF won parliamentary elections May 15, 2005, but opposition parties made big gains. Police opened fire on anti-government protesters in Addis Ababa, June 8, killing at least 36; the government arrested some 3,000 dissidents. Police suppression of further protests in the capital, Nov. 1-4, left at least 46 dead. As part of a crackdown on Oromo Liberation Front rebels, the government rounded up thousands of Oromo, Nov. 2005-Jan. 2006. In July 2006, Ethiopia sent troops into Somalia in response to advances by Islamist militias there. Tried in absentia, former Pres. Mengistu was convicted of genocide Dec. 12, 2006.

Fiji
Republic of the Fiji Islands

People: Population: 918,675. **Age distrib. (%):** <15: 30.9; 65+: 4.4. **Pop. density:** 130 per sq mi, 50 per sq km. **Urban:** 50.8%. **Ethnic groups:** Fijian 55%, Indian 37%. **Principal languages:** English (official), Fijian, Hindustani. **Chief religions:** Christian 53%, Hindu 34%, Muslim 7%.

Geography: Total area: 7,054 sq mi, 18,270 sq km; **Land area:** 7,054 sq mi, 18,270 sq km. **Location:** In western S Pacific O.

Neighbors: Nearest are Vanuatu to W, Tonga to E. **Topography:** 322 isls. (106 inhabited), many mountainous, with tropical forests and large fertile areas. Viti Levu, the largest isl., has over half the total land area. **Capital:** Suva, 219,000.

Government: Type: In transition. **Head of state:** Pres. Ratu Josefa Iloilo; b. Dec. 29, 1920; in office: July 18, 2000. **Head of gov.:** Interim Prime Min. Vorege (Frank) Bainimarama; b. Apr. 27, 1954; in office: Jan. 5, 2007. **Local divisions:** 4 divisions comprising 14 provinces and 1 dependency. **Defense budget:** $44 mil. **Active troops:** 3,500.

Economy: Industries: tourism, sugar, clothing, copra, gold & silver prod. **Chief crops:** sugarcane, coconuts, cassava, rice, sweet potatoes, bananas. **Natural resources:** timber, fish, gold, copper, oil, hydropower. **Arable land:** 11%. **Livestock:** cattle: 310,000; chickens: 4.3 mil; goats: 260,000; pigs: 140,000; sheep: 5,000. **Fish catch:** 40,099 metric tons. **Electricity prod.:** 1.1 bil kWh. **Labor force** (2001 est.): agriculture 70%, industry and services 30%.

Finance: Monetary unit: Dollar (FJD) (Sept. 2007: 1.61 = $1 U.S.). **GDP:** $5.6 bil; **per capita GDP:** $6,200; **GDP growth:** 3.1%. **Imports** (2005): $1.5 bil; Singapore 28.9%, Australia 23.4%, New Zealand 16.9%, China 4.7%. **Exports** (2005): $719.6 mil; U.S. 16.8%, Australia 13.9%, UK 13.5%, Japan 5.3%, Samoa 4.7%, Tonga 4.1%. **Tourism:** $431 mil. **Budget** (2005): $728.3 mil. **Intl. reserves less gold** (2005): $220 mil. **Gold:** 10,000 oz t. **Consumer prices:** 2.49%.

Transport: Railroad: Length: 371 mi. **Motor vehicles:** 81,000 pass. cars; 57,000 comm. vehicles. **Civil aviation:** 1.4 bil pass.-mi; 3 airports. **Chief ports:** Lambasa, Lautoka, Suva.

Communications: TV sets: 110 per 1,000 pop. **Radios:** 677 per 1,000 pop. **Telephone lines:** 112,500. **Internet:** 80,000 users.

Health: Life expect.: 67.6 male; 72.8 female. **Births** (per 1,000 pop.): 22.4. **Deaths** (per 1,000 pop.): 5.7. **Natural inc.:** 1.67%. **Infant mortality** (per 1,000 live births): 12. **AIDS rate:** 0.1%.

Education: Compulsory: ages 6-17. **Literacy:** 93.7%.

Major intl. organizations: UN (FAO, IBRD, ILO, IMF, IMO, WHO, WTO), the Commonwealth.

Embassy: 2233 Wisconsin Ave. NW, Ste. 240, 20007; 337-8320.

Website: www.fiji.gov.fj

A British colony since 1874, Fiji became independent Oct. 10, 1970. Cultural differences between the Indian community (descendants of contract laborers brought to the islands in the 19th cent.) and indigenous Fijians have led to political polarization. More than 100,000 Indians have left Fiji since the mid-1980s. A new constitution favoring indigenous Fijians was issued July 25, 1990; amendments enacted in July 1997 made the constitution more equitable.

Military coups have been frequent in recent decades. Fiji's first Indian prime minister, Mahendra Chaudhry, took office May 19, 1999. He and other government officials were taken captive May 19, 2000, by indigenous Fijian gunmen led by George Speight. The hostage crisis led to a military takeover, May 29. Release of the last remaining hostages in July 2000 coincided with the installation of an interim military-backed government. Speight was later tried for treason; he was sentenced to life in prison, Feb. 18, 2002. Prime Min. Laisenia Qarase headed an elected civilian government, 2001-06. He retained his office in parliamentary voting, May 6-13, 2006, but was ousted in a military coup Dec. 5.

Finland
Republic of Finland

People: Population: 5,238,460. **Age distrib.** (%): <15: 16.9; 65+: 16.4. **Pop. density:** 45 per sq mi, 17 per sq km. **Urban:** 61.1%. **Ethnic groups:** Finnish 93%, Swedish 6%. **Principal languages:** Finnish, Swedish (both official); Russian; Sami. **Chief religion:** Lutheran National Church 84%.

Geography: Total area: 130,559 sq mi, 338,145 sq km; **Land area:** 117,558 sq mi, 304,473 sq km. **Location:** In N Europe. **Neighbors:** Norway on N, Sweden on W, Russia on E. **Topography:** South and central areas are generally flat areas with low hills and many lakes. The N has mountainous areas, 3,000-4,000 ft above sea level. **Capital:** Helsinki, 1,091,000.

Government: Type: Constitutional republic. **Head of state:** Pres. Tarja Halonen; b. Dec. 24, 1943; in office: Mar. 1, 2000. **Head of gov.:** Prim Min. Matti Vanhanen, b. Nov. 4, 1955; in office: June 24, 2003. **Local divisions:** 6 laanit (provinces). **Defense budget:** $2.9 bil. **Active troops:** 29,300.

Economy: Industries: metal products, electronics, shipbuilding, paper, copper refining, foodstuffs, chemicals, textiles, clothing. **Chief crops:** barley, wheat, sugar beets, potatoes. **Natural resources:** timber, copper, zinc, iron ore, silver. **Arable land:** 7%. **Livestock:** cattle: 949,291; chickens: 5.4 mil; goats: 6,670; pigs: 1.4 mil; sheep: 116,653. **Fish catch:** 146,096 metric tons. **Electricity prod.:** 67.1 bil kWh. **Labor force:** agriculture and forestry 4.4%, industry 17.5%, construction 6%, commerce 22%, finance, insurance, and business services 12%, transport and communications 8%, public services 30.2%.

Finance: Monetary unit: Euro (EUR) (Sept. 2007: 0.72 = $1 U.S.). **GDP:** $176.4 bil; **per capita GDP:** $33,700; **GDP growth:** 5.5%. **Imports:** $71.7 bil; Germany 15.6%, Russia 14%, Sweden 13.7%, Netherlands 6.6%, China 5.4%. **Exports:** $84.7 bil; Germany 11.3%, Sweden 10.5%, Russia 10.1%, UK 6.5%, U.S. 6.5%,

Netherlands 5.1%. **Tourism:** $2.2 bil. **Budget:** $101 bil. **Intl. reserves less gold:** $4.32 bil. **Gold:** 1.58 mil oz t. **Consumer prices:** 1.57%.

Transport: Railroad: Length: 3,567 mi. **Motor vehicles:** 2.3 mil pass. cars; 365,900 comm. vehicles. **Civil aviation:** 5.6 bil pass.-mi; 76 airports. **Chief ports:** Hamina, Helsinki, Kotka, Pori, Rauma, Turku.

Communications: TV sets: 643 per 1,000 pop. **Radios:** 1,564 per 1,000 pop. **Telephone lines:** 1.9 mil. **Daily newspaper circ.:** 445 per 1,000 pop. **Internet:** 2.9 mil users.

Health: Life expect.: 75.2 male; 82.3 female. **Births** (per 1,000 pop.): 10.4. **Deaths** (per 1,000 pop.): 9.9. **Natural inc.:** 0.05%. **Infant mortality** (per 1,000 live births): 3.5. **AIDS rate:** 0.1%.

Education: Compulsory: ages 7-16. **Literacy:** 100%.

Major intl. organizations: UN (FAO, IBRD, ILO, IMF, IMO, WHO, WTO), EU, OECD, OSCE.

Embassy: 3301 Massachusetts Ave. NW 20008; 298-5800.

Website: www.finland.fi

The early Finns probably migrated from the Ural area at about the beginning of the Christian era. Swedish settlers brought the country into Sweden, 1154 to 1809, when Finland became an autonomous grand duchy of the Russian Empire. Russian exactions created a strong national spirit; on Dec. 6, 1917, Finland declared its independence and in 1919 became a republic.

On Nov. 30, 1939, the Soviet Union invaded, and the Finns were forced to cede 16,173 sq mi of territory. After World War II, further cessions were exacted. In 1948, Finland signed a treaty of mutual assistance with the USSR; Finland and Russia nullified this treaty with a new pact in Jan. 1992.

Following approval by Finnish voters in an advisory referendum Oct. 16, 1994, Finland joined the EU effective Jan. 1, 1995. Pres. Tarja Halonen won a 2nd 6-year term, Jan. 29, 2006.

Aland or **Ahvenanmaa**, constituting an autonomous province, is a group of small islands, 590 sq mi, in the Gulf of Bothnia, 25 mi from Sweden, 15 mi from Finland. Mariehamn is the chief port.

France
French Republic

People: Population: 63,718,187. **Age distrib.** (%): <15: 18.6; 65+: 16.2. **Pop. density:** 258 per sq mi, 100 per sq km. **Urban:** 76.7%. **Ethnic groups:** French, with Slavic, N African, Indochinese, Basque minorities. **Principal languages:** French (official), Breton, Alsatian (German), Corsican, Gascon, Provençal, Flemish, Catalan, Basque, Romani. **Chief religions:** Roman Catholic 83%-88%, Muslim 5%-10%.

Geography: Total area: 211,209 sq mi, 547,030 sq km; **Land area:** 210,669 sq mi, 545,630 sq km. **Location:** In W Europe, between Atlantic O. and Medit. Sea. **Neighbors:** Spain, Andorra, Monaco on S; Italy, Switzerland, Germany on E; Luxembourg, Belgium on N. **Topography:** A wide plain covers more than half of the country, in N and W, drained to W by Seine, Loire, Garonne rivers. The Massif Central is a mountainous plateau in center. In E are Alps (Mt. Blanc is tallest in W Europe, 15,771 ft), the lower Jura range, and forested Vosges. The Rhone flows from Lake Geneva to Mediterranean. Pyrenees are in SW, on border with Spain. **Capital:** Paris, 9,820,000. **Cities (urban aggr.):** Lyon, 1,403,000; Marseilles, 1,382,000; Lille, 1,029,000.

Government: Type: Republic. **Head of state:** Pres. Nicolas Sarkozy; b. Jan. 28, 1955; in office: May 16, 2007. **Head of gov.:** Prime Min. François Fillon; b. Mar. 4, 1954; in office: May 17, 2007. **Local divisions:** 22 administrative regions containing 96 departments. **Defense budget:** $45.3 bil. **Active troops:** 254,895.

Economy: Industries: machinery, chemicals, automobiles, metallurgy, aircraft, electronics, textiles, food proc. tourism. **Chief crops:** wheat, cereals, sugar beets, potatoes, wine grapes. **Natural resources:** coal, iron ore, bauxite, zinc, potash, timber, fish. **Crude oil reserves:** 121.5 mil bbls. **Other resources:** Timber, dairy. **Arable land:** 33%. **Livestock:** cattle: 19.4 mil; chickens: 173.7 mil; goats: 1.2 mil; pigs: 14.8 mil; sheep: 8.9 mil. **Fish catch:** 832,793 metric tons. **Electricity prod.:** 543.6 bil kWh. **Labor force** (1999): agriculture 4.1%, industry 24.4%, services 71.5%.

Finance: Monetary unit: Euro (EUR) (Sept. 2007: 0.72 = $1 U.S.). **GDP:** $1.9 tril; **per capita GDP:** $31,100; **GDP growth:** 2.1%. **Imports:** $529.1 bil; Germany 19%, Belgium 11%, Italy 8.3%, Spain 7%, Netherlands 6.7%, UK 6.5%. **Exports:** $490 bil; Germany 15.6%, Spain 9.6%, Italy 8.9%, UK 8.2%, Belgium 7.2%, U.S. 6.7%. **Tourism:** $42.3 bil. **Budget:** $1.2 tril. **Intl. reserves less gold:** $28.35 bil. **Gold:** 87.44 mil oz t. **Consumer prices:** 1.62%.

Transport: Railroad: Length: 18,073 mi. **Motor vehicles:** 29.7 mil pass. cars; 6.4 mil comm. vehicles. **Civil aviation:** 69.8 bil pass.-mi; 292 airports. **Chief ports:** Bordeaux, Dunkerque, Le Havre, Marseille, Nantes, Paris, Rouen, Strasbourg.

Communications: TV sets: 620 per 1,000 pop. **Radios:** 946 per 1,000 pop. **Telephone lines:** 33.9 mil. **Daily newspaper circ.:** 142.1 per 1,000 pop. **Internet:** 30.1 mil users.

Health: Life expect.: 77.6 male; 84.1 female. **Births** (per 1,000 pop.): 12.9. **Deaths** (per 1,000 pop.): 8.4. **Natural inc.:** 0.45%. **Infant mortality** (per 1,000 live births): 3.4. **AIDS rate:** 0.4%.

Education: Compulsory: ages 6-16. **Literacy:** 99%.

Major intl. organizations: UN and most of its specialized agencies, EU, NATO, OECD, OSCE.

Embassy: 4101 Reservoir Rd. NW 20007; 944-6195.
Website: www.diplomatie.gouv.fr

Celtic Gaul was conquered by Julius Caesar 58-51 BCE; Romans ruled for 500 years. Under Charlemagne, Frankish rule extended over much of Europe. After his death France emerged as one of the successor kingdoms.

The monarchy was overthrown by the French Revolution (1789-93) and succeeded by the First Republic, followed by the First Empire under Napoleon (1804-15), a monarchy (1814-48), the Second Republic (1848-52), the Second Empire (1852-70), the Third Republic (1871-1946), the Fourth Republic (1946-58), and the Fifth Republic (1958 to present).

France suffered severe losses in manpower and wealth in WWI, when it was invaded by Germany. By the Treaty of Versailles, France exacted return of Alsace and Lorraine, provinces seized by Germany in 1871. Germany invaded France again in May 1940, and signed an armistice with a government based in Vichy. After France was liberated by the Allies in Sept. 1944, Gen. Charles de Gaulle became head of the provisional government, serving until 1946. De Gaulle again became premier in 1958, during a crisis over Algeria, and obtained voter approval for a new constitution, ushering in the Fifth Republic. He then became president.

France had withdrawn from Indochina in 1954, and from Morocco and Tunisia in 1956. Most of its remaining African territories, including Algeria, were freed 1958-62. In 1966, France withdrew all its troops from the integrated military command of NATO, though 60,000 remained stationed in Germany.

In May 1968 rebellious students in Paris and other centers rioted, battled police, and were joined by workers who launched nationwide strikes. The government awarded pay increases to the strikers May 26. De Gaulle resigned from office in Apr. 1969, after losing a nationwide referendum on constitutional reform. Georges Pompidou, who was elected to succeed him, continued De Gaulle's emphasis on French independence from the U.S. and Soviet Union. After Pompidou's death, in 1974, Valery Giscard d'Estaing was elected president; he continued the basically conservative policies of his predecessors.

On May 10, 1981, France elected François Mitterrand, a Socialist, president. Under Mitterrand the government nationalized 5 major industries and most private banks. After 1986, however, when rightists won a narrow victory in the National Assembly, Mitterrand chose conservative Jacques Chirac as premier. A 2-year period of "cohabitation" ensued, and France began to pursue a privatization program in which many state-owned companies were sold. After Mitterrand was elected to a 2nd 7-year term in 1988, he appointed a Socialist as premier. The center-right won a large majority in 1993 legislative elections, ushering in another period of "cohabitation" with a conservative premier.

Chirac won the presidency in a run-off May 7, 1995. He cut government spending to help the French economy meet the budgetary goals set for the introduction of a common European currency. With unemployment at nearly 13%, legislative elections completed June 1, 1997, produced a decisive victory for the leftist parties. The result was a new period of "cohabitation," this time between a conservative president and a Socialist prime minister, Lionel Jospin. France contributed 7,000 troops to the NATO-led force (KFOR) that entered Kosovo in June 1999.

French voters, disaffected by government scandals, shocked the political establishment in the first round of presidential voting Apr. 21, 2002, by giving Jean-Marie Le Pen, leader of the far-right National Front, a second place finish with 16.9% of the vote; Chirac won only 19.9%, and Jospin was 3rd, with 16.2%. Chirac easily won the May 5 runoff, with 82%, and his center-right allies won parliamentary elections June 9 and 16.

In Mar. 2003, Parliament approved constitutional amendments strengthening regional governments. Parliament gave final approval Mar. 3, 2004, to a law barring the wearing of Islamic head scarves and other religious symbols in public schools.

Displeased with sluggish economic growth, high unemployment, and budget cuts in entitlement programs, voters showed their discontent by rejecting, May 29, 2005, a proposed EU constitution strongly supported by the Chirac government. Prime Min. Jean-Pierre Raffarin resigned May 31 and was replaced by Dominique de Villepin. A state of emergency was declared Nov. 8 after 12 days of riots that began in Paris and spread to some 300 French cities and towns; rioters were mainly young North and West African immigrants. After a wave of mass protests and strikes, Chirac agreed, Apr. 10, 2006, to rescind a law that made it easier for employers to fire inexperienced young workers.

Campaigning as an economic reformer, the conservative, pro-American Nicolas Sarkozy won a presidential runoff election May 6, 2007, defeating Ségolène Royal, a Socialist, by a margin of 53-47%. In parliamentary voting June 10-17, Sarkozy's party held onto a majority, although Socialists made gains.

The island of **Corsica**, in the Mediterranean W of Italy and N of Sardinia, is a territorial collectivity and region of France comprising 2 departments. It elects a total of 2 senators and 3 deputies to the French Parliament. Area: 3,369 sq mi; pop. (2001 census) 260,149. The capital is Ajaccio, birthplace of Napoleon I. Violence by Corsican separatist groups has hurt tourism, a leading industry on the island. Corsicans rejected, 51-49%, a limited autonomy plan in a referendum July 6, 2003.

Overseas Departments

French Guiana is on the NE coast of South America with Suriname on the W and Brazil on the E and S. Its area is 35,135 sq mi (total); 34,421 sq mi (land); pop. (2007 est.) 203,321. Guiana sends one senator and 2 deputies to the French Parliament. Guiana is administered by a prefect and has a Council General of 16 elected members; capital is Cayenne.

The famous penal colony, Devil's Island, was phased out between 1938 and 1951. The European Space Agency maintains a satellite-launching center (established by France in 1964) in the city of Kourou.

Immense forests of rich timber cover 88% of the land. Fishing (especially shrimp), forestry, and gold mining are the most important industries.

Guadeloupe, in the West Indies' Leeward Islands, consists of 2 large islands, Basse-Terre and Grande-Terre, separated by the Salt River, plus Marie Galante and the Saintes group to the S and, to the N, Desirade. (St. Barthelemy and over half of St. Martin [the Netherlands' portion is called St. Maarten], both formerly part of Guadeloupe, voted for secession in 2003 and became separate overseas territorial collectivities in 2007.) A French possession since 1635, the department is represented in the French Parliament; administration consists of a prefect (governor) as well as an elected general and regional councils.

Area of the islands is 525 sq mi; pop. (2007 est., incl. St. Barthelemy and St. Martin) 456,698, mainly descendants of slaves; capital is Basse-Terre on Basse-Terre Island. The land is fertile; sugar, rum, and bananas are exported. Tourism is an important industry.

Martinique, the northernmost of the Windward Islands, in the West Indies, has been a possession since 1635, and a department since Mar. 1946. It is represented in the French Parliament by 2 senators and 4 deputies. The island was the birthplace of Napoleon's Empress Josephine.

It has an area of 425 sq mi (total); 409 sq mi (land); pop. (2007 est.) 439,202, mostly descendants of slaves. The capital is Fort-de-France, pop. (1991) is 101,000. It is a popular tourist stop. The chief exports are rum, bananas, and petroleum products.

Réunion is a volcanic island in the Indian O. about 420 mi E of Madagascar, and has belonged to France since 1665. Area, 972 sq mi (total); 968 sq mi (land); pop. (2007 est.) 798,094, 30% of French extraction. Capital: Saint-Denis. The chief export is sugar. It elects 5 deputies, 3 senators to the French Parliament. St. Barthelemy and St. Martin became overseas territorial collectivities in 2007.

Overseas Territorial Collectivities

Mayotte, claimed by Comoros and administered by France, voted in 1976 to become a territorial collectivity of France. An island NW of Madagascar, area is 144 sq mi, pop. (2007 est.) 208,783. The capital is Mamoudzou.

St. Pierre and Miquelon became a territorial collectivity in 1985. It consists of 2 groups of rocky islands near the SW coast of Newfoundland, inhabited by fishermen. The exports are chiefly fish products. The St. Pierre group has an area of 10 sq mi; Miquelon, 83 sq mi. Total pop. (2007 est.) 7,036. Capital: Saint-Pierre.

Both Mayotte and St. Pierre and Miquelon elect a deputy and a senator to the French Parliament. **St. Barthelemy** and **St. Martin** became overseas territorial collectivities in 2007.

Overseas Territories

Territory of **French Polynesia** comprises 130 islands widely scattered among 5 archipelagos in the South Pacific; administered by a Council of Ministers (headed by a president). Territorial Assembly and the Council have headquarters at Papeete, on Tahiti, one of the **Society Islands** (which include the **Windward** and **Leeward** islands). Two deputies and a senator are elected to the French Parliament.

Other groups are the **Marquesas Islands**, the **Tuamotu Archipelago**, including the **Gambier Islands**, and the **Austral Islands**.

Total area of the islands administered from Tahiti is 1,609 sq mi (total); 1,413 sq mi (land); pop. (2007 est.) 278,963, more than half on Tahiti. Tahiti is picturesque and mountainous with a productive coastline bearing coconuts, citrus, pineapples, and vanilla. Cultured pearls are also produced.

Tahiti was visited by Capt. James Cook in 1769 and by Capt. Bligh in the *Bounty*, 1788-89. Its beauty impressed Herman Melville, Paul Gauguin, and Charles Darwin. A coalition favoring independence for French Polynesia within 20 years gained control of the territorial assembly after elections May 23, 2004.

Territory of the **French Southern and Antarctic Lands** comprises **Adelie Land**, on Antarctica, and 4 island groups in the Indian O. Area: 3,023 sq mi (total); 3,023 sq mi (land).

Adelie, reached 1,840, has a research station, a coastline of 185 mi, and tapers 1,240 mi inland to the South Pole. The U.S. does not recognize national claims in Antarctica. There are 2 huge glaciers, Ninnis, 22 mi wide, 99 mi long, and Mentz, 11 mi wide, 140 mi long. The Indian O. groups are:

Kerguelen Archipelago, visited 1772, consists of one large and 300 small islands. The chief is 87 mi long, 74 mi wide, and has Mt. Ross, 6,429 ft tall. Principal research station is Port-aux-Français. Seals often weigh 2 tons; there are blue whales, coal, peat, semiprecious stones. **Crozet Archipelago**, reached 1772, covers 136 sq mi. Eastern Island rises to 6,560 ft. **Saint Paul**, in southern Indian O., has warm springs with earth at places heating to 120° to 390°F. **Amsterdam** is nearby; both produce cod and rock lobster.

Territory of **New Caledonia** and Dependencies is a group of islands in the Pacific O. about 1,115 mi E of Australia and approx. the same distance NW of New Zealand. Dependencies are the **Loyalty Islands, Isle of Pines, Belep Archipelago,** and **Huon Islands.**

The largest island, New Caledonia, is 6,530 sq mi. Total area of the territory is 7,359 sq mi (total); 7,171 sq mi (land); pop. (2007 est.) 221,943. The group was acquired by France in 1853.

The territory is administered by a High Commissioner. There is a popularly elected Territorial Congress. Two deputies and a senator are elected to the French Parliament. Capital: Noumea.

Mining is the chief industry. New Caledonia is one of the world's largest nickel producers. Other minerals found are chrome, iron, cobalt, manganese, silver, gold, lead, and copper. Agricultural products include yams, sweet potatoes, potatoes, manioc (cassava), corn, and coconuts.

In 1987, New Caledonian voters chose by referendum to remain within the French Republic. There were clashes between French and Melanesians (Kanaks) in 1988. An agreement Apr. 21, 1998, between France and rival New Caledonian factions specified a 15- to 20-year period of "shared sovereignty." The French constitution was amended, July 6, to allow the territory a gradual increase in autonomy, and New Caledonian voters approved the plan Nov. 8, 1998, by a 72% majority.

Territory of the **Wallis and Futuna Islands** comprises 2 island groups in the SW Pacific S of Tuvalu, N of Fiji, and W of Western Samoa; became an overseas territory July 29, 1961. The islands have a total area of 106 sq mi and population (2007 est.) of 16,309. **Alofi,** attached to Futuna, is uninhabited. Capital: Mata-Utu. Chief products are copra, yams, taro roots, bananas, and coconuts. A senator and a deputy are elected to the French Parliament.

Gabon
Gabonese Republic

People: Population: 1,454,867. **Age distrib.** (%): <15: 42.1; 65+: 4. **Pop. density:** 15 per sq mi, 6 per sq km. **Urban:** 83.6%. **Ethnic groups:** Fang, Bapounou, Nzebi, Obamba, European. **Principal languages:** French (official), Fang, Myene, Nzebi, Bapounou/Eschira, Bandjabi. **Chief religions:** Christian 55%-75%, animist.

Geography: Total area: 103,347 sq mi, 267,667 sq km; **Land area:** 99,486 sq mi, 257,667 sq km. **Location:** On Atlantic coast of W central Africa. **Neighbors:** Equatorial Guinea, Cameroon on N; Congo on E and S. **Topography:** Heavily forested, consisting of coastal lowlands; plateaus in N, E, and S; mountains in N, SE, and center. The Ogooue R. system covers most of Gabon. **Capital:** Libreville, 556,000.

Government: Type: Republic. **Head of state:** Pres. Omar Bongo Ondimba; b. Dec. 30, 1935; in office: Dec. 2, 1967. **Head of gov.:** Prime Min. Jean Eyeghe Ndong; b. Feb. 12, 1946; in office: Jan. 20, 2006. **Local divisions:** 9 provinces. **Defense budget** (2005): $19 mil. **Active troops:** 4,700.

Economy: Industries: food & beverages, textiles, lumber, cement, oil, mining, chemicals, ship repair. **Chief crops:** cocoa, coffee, sugar, palm oil, rubber. **Natural resources:** oil, mang., uranium, gold, timber, iron, hydropower. **Crude oil reserves:** 2 bil bbls. **Arable land:** 1%. **Livestock:** cattle: 35,000; chickens: 3.1 mil; goats: 90,000; pigs: 212,000; sheep: 195,000. **Fish catch:** 43,941 metric tons. **Electricity prod.:** 1.5 bil kWh. **Labor force:** agriculture 60%, industry 15%, services 25%.

Finance: Monetary unit: CFA BEAC Franc (XAF) (Sept. 2007: 472.78 = $1 U.S.). **GDP:** $10.2 bil; **per capita GDP:** $7,100; **GDP growth:** 1%. **Imports:** $1.6 bil; France 35.2%, U.S. 7.6%, Netherlands 5.5%, Cameroon 4.5%, Belgium 4.3%. **Exports:** $6.7 bil; U.S. 27.2%, China 15.7%, France 7.7%, Trinidad and Tobago 5.3%, Thailand 4.2%. **Tourism:** $15 mil. **Budget:** $2.2 bil. **Intl. reserves less gold:** $740 mil. **Gold:** 10,000 oz t. **Consumer prices:** 4.09%.

Transport: Railroad: Length: 506 mi. **Motor vehicles:** 23,000 pass. cars; 10,000 comm. vehicles. **Civil aviation:** 407 mil pass.-mi; 11 airports. **Chief ports:** Gamba, Libreville, Owendo, Port-Gentil.

Communications: TV sets: 251 per 1,000 pop. **Radios:** 501 per 1,000 pop. **Telephone lines:** 36,500. **Daily newspaper circ.:** 29 per 1,000 pop. **Internet:** 81,000 users.

Health: Life expect.: 52.9 male; 55.2 female. **Births** (per 1,000 pop.): 36. **Deaths** (per 1,000 pop.): 12.5. **Natural inc.:** 2.35%. **Infant mortality** (per 1,000 live births): 53.7. **AIDS rate:** 7.9%.

Education: Compulsory: ages 6-16. **Literacy:** 84%.

Major intl. organizations: UN (FAO, IBRD, ILO, IMF, IMO, WHO, WTO), AU.

Embassy: 2034 20th St. NW, Ste. 200, 20009; 797-1000.

Website: www.legabon.org

France established control over the region in the second half of the 19th cent. Gabon became independent Aug. 17, 1960. A multi-party political system was introduced in 1990, and a new constitution was enacted Mar. 14, 1991. However, the reelection of longtime Pres. Omar Bongo, on Dec. 5, 1993, prompted rioting and charges of vote fraud. International observers also found fault with the presidential elections of Dec. 6, 1998, and Nov. 27, 2005, which Bongo won by lopsided margins.

Gabon is one of the most prosperous black African countries, thanks to abundant natural resources, foreign private investment, and government development programs.

The Gambia
Republic of The Gambia

People: Population: 1,688,359. **Age distrib.** (%): <15: 44.1; 65+: 2.8. **Pop. density:** 437 per sq mi, 169 per sq km. **Urban:** 53.9%. **Ethnic groups:** Mandinka 42%, Fula 18%, Wolof 16%, Jola 10%, Serahuli 9%. **Principal languages:** English (official), Mandinka, Wolof, Fula, other native dialects. **Chief religions:** Muslim 90%, Christian 9%.

Geography: Total area: 4,363 sq mi, 11,300 sq km; **Land area:** 3,861 sq mi, 10,000 sq km. **Location:** On Atlantic coast near W tip of Africa. **Neighbors:** Surrounded on 3 sides by Senegal. **Topography:** A narrow strip of land on each side of lower Gambia R. **Capital:** Banjul 381,000.

Government: Type: Republic. **Head of state and gov.:** Pres Yahya Jammeh; b. May 25, 1965; in office: July 22, 1994. **Local divisions:** 5 divisions, 1 city. **Defense budget:** $1.6 mil. **Active troops:** 800.

Economy: Industries: peanuts, fish, hides, tourism, beverages, agric. machinery, woodworking, metalworking, clothing. **Chief crops:** rice, millet, sorghum, peanuts, corn, sesame, cassava, palm kernels. **Natural resources:** fish. **Arable land:** 28%. **Livestock:** cattle: 330,000; chickens: 650,000; goats: 270,000; pigs: 19,000; sheep: 148,000. **Fish catch:** 32,000 metric tons. **Electricity prod.:** 150 mil kWh. **Labor force:** agriculture 75%, industry 19%, services 6%.

Finance: Monetary unit: Dalasi (GMD) (Sept. 2007: 21.91 = $1 U.S.). **GDP:** $3.3 bil; **per capita GDP:** $2,000; **GDP growth:** 5.3%. **Imports:** $212.2 mil; China 25%, Senegal 12.6%, Cote d'Ivoire 8%, Brazil 6.2%, Netherlands 4.4%. **Exports:** $130.5 mil; India 36.8%, UK 15.1%, Indonesia 7.5%, France 6.8%, Italy 4.3%, Senegal 4.2%. **Tourism:** $28 mil. **Budget:** $155.1 mil. **Intl. reserves less gold:** $80 mil. **Consumer prices** (2005): 3.17%.

Transport: Motor vehicles: 6,400 pass. cars, 3,500 comm. vehicles. **Civil aviation:** 1 airport. **Chief port:** Banjul.

Communications: TV Sets: 3 per 1,000 pop. **Radios:** 394 per 1,000 pop. **Telephone lines:** 52,900. **Daily newspaper circ.:** 1.7 per 1,000 pop. **Internet:** 58,000 users.

Health: Life expect.: 52.7 male; 56.5 female. **Births** (per 1,000 pop.): 38.9. **Deaths** (per 1,000 pop.): 12. **Natural inc.:** 2.69%. **Infant mortality** (per 1,000 live births): 70.1. **AIDS rate:** 2.4%.

Education: Compulsory: ages 7-12. **Literacy:** 40.1%.

Major intl. organizations: UN (FAO, IBRD, ILO, IMF, IMO, WHO, WTO), the Commonwealth, AU.

Embassy: 1155 15th St. NW, Ste. 1000, 20005; 785-1399.

Website: www.statehouse.gm

The peoples of Gambia were at one time associated with the West African empires of Ghana, Mali, and Songhay. The area became Britain's first African possession in 1588.

Independence came Feb. 18, 1965; republic status within the Commonwealth was achieved in 1970. The country suffered from severe famine in the 1970s. Senegambia, a confederation with Sengal, lasted from 1982 to 1989.

On July 22, 1994, after 24 years in power, Pres. Dawda K. Jawara was deposed in a bloodless coup by a military officer, Yahya Jammeh. Jammeh barred political activity, detained potential opponents, and governed by decree. A new constitution was approved by referendum, Aug. 8, 1996. On Sept. 27 Jammeh won the presidential election. Parliamentary balloting on Jan. 2, 1997, completed the nominal return to civilian rule, but Jammeh retained a firm grip on power. He followed his reelection win on Oct. 18, 2001, with a new crackdown on dissidents. Security forces suppressed an alleged coup plot by army officers Mar. 2006. Pres. Jammeh won a 3rd term Sept. 22, 2006.

Georgia

People: Population: 4,646,003. **Age distrib.** (%): <15: 16.7; 65+: 16.7. **Pop. density:** 173 per sq mi, 67 per sq km. **Urban:** 52.2%. **Ethnic groups:** Georgian 84%, Azeri 7%, Armenian 6%. **Principal languages:** Georgian (official), Russian, Armenian, Azeri, Abkhaz (official in Abkhazia). **Chief religions:** Georgian Orthodox 84%, Muslim 10%.

Geography: Total area: 26,911 sq mi, 69,700 sq km; **Land area:** 26,911 sq mi, 69,700 sq km. **Location:** SW Asia, on E coast of Black Sea. **Neighbors:** Russia on N and NE, Turkey and Armenia on S, Azerbaijan on SE. **Topography:** Separated from Russia on NE by main range of Caucasus Mts. **Capital:** Tbilisi, 1,047,000.

Government: Type: Republic. **Head of state:** Pres. Mikhail Saakashvili; b. Dec. 21, 1967; in office: Jan. 25, 2004. **Head of gov.:** Prime Min. Zurab Noghaideli; b. Oct. 22, 1964; in office: Feb. 17, 2005. **Local divisions:** 53 rayons, 9 cities, and 2 autonomous republics. **Defense budget:** $349 mil. **Active troops:** 11,320.

Economy: Industries: steel, aircraft, machine tools, appliances, mining, chemicals. **Chief crops:** citrus, grapes, tea, hazelnuts, vegetables. **Natural resources:** timber, hydropower, mang., iron ore, copper, coal, oil. **Crude oil reserves:** 35 mil bbls. **Arable land:** 12%. **Livestock:** cattle: 1.3 mil; chickens: 6.9 mil; goats: 95,500; pigs: 455,300; sheep: 719,800. **Fish catch:** 3,072 metric tons. **Electricity prod.:** 7.1 bil kWh. **Labor force** (1999 est.): agriculture 40%, industry 20%, services 40%.

Finance: Monetary unit: Lari (GEL) (Sept. 2007: 1.65 = $1 U.S.). **GDP:** $17.9 bil; **per capita GDP:** $3,800; **GDP growth:** 8%. **Imports:** $3.3 bil; Russia 17%, Turkey 12.3%, U.S. 7.9%, Azerbaijan 7.8%, Ukraine 7.4%, Germany 7.1%. **Exports:** $1.8 bil; UK 21.5%, Turkey 16.9%, U.S. 5.8%, Spain 5.8%, Azerbaijan 5.6%, Turkmenistan 5.1%. **Tourism:** $177 mil. **Budget:** $1.9 bil. **Intl. reserves less gold:** $619 mil. **Consumer prices:** 8.23%.

Transport: Railroad: Length: 1,002 mi. **Motor vehicles:** 377,000 pass. cars; 84,000 comm. vehicles. **Civil aviation:** 238.6 mil pass.-mi; 19 airports. **Chief ports:** Batumi, Póti.

Communications: TV sets: 516 per 1,000 pop. **Radios:** 590 per 1,000 pop. **Telephone lines:** 553,100. **Daily newspaper circ.:** 4.9 per 1,000 pop. **Internet:** 332,000 users.

Health: Life expect.: 73 male; 80.1 female. **Births** (per 1,000 pop.): 10.5. **Deaths** (per 1,000 pop.): 9.4. **Natural inc.:** 0.12%. **Infant mortality** (per 1,000 live births): 17.4. **AIDS rate:** 0.2%.

Education: Compulsory: ages 6-14. **Literacy:** 100%.

Major intl. organizations: UN (FAO, IBRD, ILO, IMF, IMO, WHO, WTO), CIS, OSCE.

Embassy: 2209 Massachusetts Ave. NW 20008; 387-2390.

Website: www.parliament.ge

The region, which contained the ancient kingdoms of Colchis and Iberia, was Christianized in the 4th cent. and conquered by Arabs in the 8th cent. Annexed by Russia in 1801, Georgia was forcibly incorporated into the USSR in 1922.

Georgia declared independence Apr. 9, 1991. It became an independent state when the Soviet Union disbanded Dec. 26, 1991. There was fighting during 1991 between rebel forces and loyalists of Pres. Zviad Gamsakhurdia, who fled the capital Jan. 6, 1992. The ruling Military Council picked former Soviet Foreign Min. Eduard A. Shevardnadze to chair a newly created State Council. An attempted coup by forces loyal to Gamsakhurdia was crushed June 24, 1992. Shevardnadze was later elected president. Gamsakhurdia died Jan. 1994, reportedly by suicide.

Since the country gained independence, rebel movements have challenged the Tbilisi government. In Abkhazia, an autonomous republic within Georgia, ethnic Abkhazis, reportedly aided by Russia, launched a bloody military campaign and, by late 1993, had gained control of much of the region. A cease-fire providing for Russian peacekeepers was signed in Moscow May 14, 1994, but intermittent clashes continued. Georgian government troops also fought South Ossetia secessionists. Chechen rebels based in Pankisi Gorge, northeast of Tbilisi, launched attacks against Russian troops in Chechnya, heightening tensions with Russia.

Shevardnadze was wounded by a car bomb Aug. 29, 1995, while on his way to Parliament to sign a new constitution. He was reelected president Nov. 5. Shevardnadze escaped another assassination attempt, Feb. 9, 1998, when gunmen ambushed his motorcade. A mutiny by more than 200 soldiers was crushed Oct. 19.

Shevardnadze won another 5-year presidential term Apr. 9, 2000. But parliamentary elections Nov. 2, 2003, denounced as fraudulent by opposition groups and international observers, sparked massive antigovernment protests, causing him to resign Nov. 23. Opposition leader Mikhail Saakashvili won the presidential election of Jan. 4, 2004. Prime Min. Zurab Zhvania died Feb. 3, 2005, apparently by carbon-monoxide poisoning from a faulty gas heater; he was succeeded by Zurab Noghaideli. While U.S. Pres. George W. Bush addressed a large crowd in Tbilisi May 10, a live grenade was thrown toward the stage but failed to detonate. The grenade thrower, Vladimir Arutyunian, was convicted Jan. 11, 2006, of trying to assassinate Bush and Saakashvili. Another alleged coup plot was suppressed Sept. 6.

Germany
Federal Republic of Germany

People: Population: 82,400,996. **Age distrib.** (%): <15: 13.9; 65+: 19.8. **Pop. density:** 611 per sq mi, 236 per sq km. **Urban:** 75.2%. **Ethnic groups:** German 92%, Turkish 2%. **Principal language:** German (official). **Chief religions:** Protestant 34%, Roman Catholic 34%, Muslim 4%.

Geography: Total area: 137,847 sq mi, 357,021 sq km; **Land area:** 134,836 sq mi, 349,223 sq km. **Location:** In central Europe. **Neighbors:** Denmark on N; Netherlands, Belgium, Luxembourg, France on W; Switzerland, Austria on S; Czech Rep., Poland on E. **Topography:** Germany is flat in N, hilly in center and W, and mountainous in Bavaria in the S. Chief rivers are Elbe, Weser, Ems, Rhine, and Main, all flowing toward North Sea, and Danube, flowing toward Black Sea. **Capital:** Berlin, 3,389,000. **Cities (urban aggr., 2003):** Rhein-Ruhr North (including Essen), 6.54 mil; Rhein Main (Frankfurt am Mein), 3.68 mil; Rhein-Ruhr Middle (Dusseldorf), 3.24 mil; Rhein-Ruhr South (Cologne), 3.06 mil; Stuttgart, 2.68 mil; **Cities (proper):** Hamburg, 1.73 mil; Munich, 1.23 mil; Cologne, 967,940; Frankfurt-am-Mein, 641,076.

Government: Federal republic. **Head of state:** Pres. Horst Köhler; b. Feb. 22, 1943; in office: July 1, 2004. **Head of gov.:** Chan. Angela Merkel; b. July 17, 1954; in office: Nov. 22, 2005. **Local divisions:** 16 laender (states). **Defense budget:** $35.7 bil. **Active troops:** 245,702.

Economy: Industries: iron, steel, coal, cement, chemicals, machinery, vehicles, machine tools, electronics, food & beverages,

shipbuilding. **Chief crops:** potatoes, wheat, barley, sugar beets, fruit, cabbages. **Natural resources:** iron ore, coal, potash, timber, lignite, uranium, copper, nat. gas, salt, nickel. **Crude oil reserves:** 367 mil bbls. **Arable land:** 33%. **Livestock:** cattle: 12.7 mil; chickens: 107.3 mil; goats: 170,000; pigs: 26.5 mil; sheep: 2.6 mil. **Fish catch:** 330,353 metric tons. **Electricity prod.:** 579.4 bil kWh. **Labor force** (1999): agriculture 2.8%, industry 33.4%, services 63.8%.

Finance: Monetary unit: Euro (EUR) (Sept. 2007: 0.72 = $1 U.S.). **GDP:** $2.6 tril; **per capita GDP:** $31,900; **GDP growth:** 2.7%. **Imports:** $916.4 bil; Netherlands 11.7%, France 8.7%, Belgium 7.6%, UK 5.9%, China 5.9%, Italy 5.5%, U.S. 5.1%. **Exports:** $1.1 tril; France 9.7%, U.S. 8.6%, UK 7.3%, Italy 6.7%, Netherlands 6.2%, Belgium 5.5%, Austria 5.5%. **Tourism:** $29.2 bil. **Budget:** $1.3 tril. **Intl. reserves less gold:** $27.71 bil. **Gold:** 110.04 mil oz t. **Consumer prices:** 1.71%.

Transport: Railroad: Length: 29,329 mi. **Motor vehicles:** 45 mil pass. cars; 3.5 mil comm. vehicles. **Civil aviation:** 93 bil pass.-mi; 332 airports. **Chief ports:** Bremen, Bremerhaven, Frankfurt, Hamburg, Rostock.

Communications: TV sets: 581 per 1,000 pop. **Radios:** 948 per 1,000 pop. **Telephone lines:** 54.2 mil. **Daily newspaper circ.:** 291 per 1,000 pop. **Internet:** 38.6 mil users.

Health: Life expect.: 76 male; 82.1 female. **Births** (per 1,000 pop.): 8.2. **Deaths** (per 1,000 pop.): 10.7. **Natural inc.:** −0.25%. **Infant mortality** (per 1,000 live births): 4.1. **AIDS rate:** 0.1%.

Education: Compulsory: ages 6-18. **Literacy:** 99%.

Major intl. organizations: UN and all of its specialized agencies, EU, NATO, OECD, OSCE.

Embassy: 4645 Reservoir Rd. NW 20007; 298-4000.

Website: www.germany.info

Germany is a central European nation originally composed of numerous states, with a common language and traditions, that were united in one country in 1871; Germany was split into 2 countries from the end of WWII until 1990, when it was reunified.

History and government. Germanic tribes were defeated by Julius Caesar, 55 and 53 BCE, but Roman expansion north of the Rhine was stopped in 9 CE. Charlemagne, ruler of the Franks, consolidated Saxon, Bavarian, Rhenish, Frankish, and other lands; after him the eastern part became the German Empire. The Thirty Years' War, 1618-48, split Germany into small principalities and kingdoms. After Napoleon, Austria contended with Prussia for dominance, but lost the Seven Weeks' War to Prussia, 1866. Otto von Bismarck, Prussian chancellor, formed the North German Confederation, 1867.

In 1870 Bismarck maneuvered Napoleon III into declaring war. After the quick defeat of France, Bismarck formed the **German Empire** and on Jan. 18, 1871, in Versailles, proclaimed King Wilhelm I of Prussia German emperor (Deutscher kaiser).

The German Empire reached its peak before WWI in 1914, with 208,780 sq mi, plus a colonial empire. After that war Germany ceded Alsace-Lorraine to France; West Prussia and Posen (Poznan) province to Poland; part of Schleswig to Denmark; lost all colonies and ports of Memel and Danzig.

Republic of Germany, 1919-33, adopted the Weimar constitution; met reparation payments and elected Friedrich Ebert and Gen. Paul von Hindenburg presidents.

Third Reich, 1933-45, Adolf Hitler led the National Socialist German Workers' (Nazi) party after WWI. In 1923 he attempted to unseat the Bavarian government and was imprisoned. Pres. von Hindenburg named Hitler chancellor Jan. 30, 1933; on Aug. 3, 1934, the day after Hindenburg's death, the cabinet joined the offices of president and chancellor and made Hitler fuehrer (leader). Hitler abolished freedom of speech and assembly, and began a long series of persecutions climaxed by the murder of millions of Jews and others.

He repudiated the Versailles treaty and reparations agreements, remilitarized the Rhineland (1936), and annexed Austria (Anschluss, 1938). At Munich he made an agreement with Neville Chamberlain, British prime minister, which permitted Germany to annex part of Czechoslovakia. He signed a nonaggression treaty with the USSR, 1939 and declared war on Poland Sept. 1, 1939, precipitating WWII. With total defeat near, Hitler committed suicide in Berlin Apr. 1945. The victorious Allies voided all acts and annexations of Hitler's Reich.

Division of Germany. Germany was sectioned into 4 zones of occupation, administered by the Allied Powers (U.S., USSR, UK, and France). The USSR took control of many E German states. The territory E of the so-called Oder-Neisse line was assigned to, and later annexed by, Poland. Northern East Prussia (now Kaliningrad) was annexed by the USSR. Greater Berlin, within but not part of the Soviet zone, was administered by the 4 occupying powers under the Allied Command. In 1948 the USSR withdrew, established its single command in East Berlin, and cut off supplies. The Western Allies utilized a gigantic airlift to bring food to West Berlin, 1948-49.

In 1949, 2 separate German states were established; in May the zones administered by the Western Allies became West Germany; in Oct. the Soviet sector became East Germany. West Berlin was considered an enclave of West Germany, although its status was disputed by the Soviet bloc.

East Germany. The German Democratic Republic (East Germany) was proclaimed in the Soviet sector of Berlin Oct. 7, 1949. It was declared fully sovereign in 1954, but Soviet troops remained on grounds of security and the 4-power Potsdam agreement.

Coincident with the entrance of West Germany into the European defense community in 1952, the East German government decreed a prohibited zone 3 mi deep along its 600-mi border with West Germany and cut Berlin's telephone system in two. Berlin was further divided by erection of a fortified wall in 1961, after over 3 mil East Germans had fled to the West.

East Germany suffered severe economic problems at least until the mid-1960s. Then a "new economic system" was introduced, easing central planning controls and allowing factories to make profits provided they were reinvested in operations or redistributed to workers as bonuses. By the early 1970s, the economy of East Germany was highly industrialized, and the nation was credited with the highest standard of living among Warsaw Pact countries. But growth slowed in the late 1970s, because of shortages of natural resources and labor, and a huge debt to lenders in the West. Comparison with the lifestyle in the West caused many young people to emigrate.

The government firmly resisted following the USSR's policy of glasnost, but by Oct. 1989, was faced with nationwide demonstrations demanding reform. Pres. Erich Honecker, in office since 1976, was forced to resign Oct. 18. On Nov. 4, the border with Czechoslovakia was opened and permission granted for refugees to travel to the West. On Nov. 9, the East German government announced its decision to open the border with the West, signaling the end of the "Berlin Wall," which was the supreme emblem of the cold war. On Aug. 23, 1990, the East German parliament agreed to formal unification with West Germany; this occurred Oct. 3.

West Germany. The Federal Republic of Germany (West Germany) was proclaimed May 23, 1949, in Bonn. The occupying powers, the U.S., Britain, and France, restored civil status, Sept. 21. The Western Allies ended the state of war with Germany in 1951 (the U.S. resumed diplomatic relations July 2), while the USSR did so in 1955. The powers lifted controls, and the republic became fully independent May 5, 1955.

Dr. Konrad Adenauer, Christian Democrat, was made chancellor Sept. 15, 1949, and reelected 1953, 1957, 1961. Willy Brandt, heading a coalition of Social Democrats and Free Democrats, became chancellor Oct. 21, 1969, and pursued a policy of Ostpolitik, or rapprochement with East Germany and the USSR. Brandt resigned May 1974 because of a spy scandal. Terrorist acts on German soil in the 1970s included activities of the Baader-Meinhof gang and the murder of Israeli athletes by Palestinian commandos at the Olympic Games in Munich, Sept. 5, 1972.

Helmut Kohl became chancellor in 1982 and led Christian Democrats to victory in 1983 and 1987. In 1989, changes in the East German government and the opening of the Berlin Wall sparked talk of reunification of the 2 Germanys. In 1990, under Kohl's leadership, West Germany moved rapidly to reunite with East Germany.

A New Era. In May 1990, NATO ministers adopted a package of proposals on reunification, including the inclusion of the united Germany as a full member of NATO and the barring of the new Germany from having its own nuclear, chemical, or biological weapons. In July, the USSR agreed to conditions that would allow Germany to become a member of NATO.

The 2 Germanys agreed to monetary unification under the West German mark beginning in July. The merger of the 2 Germanys took place Oct. 3, and the first all-German elections since 1932 were held Dec. 2. Eastern Germany received over $1 trillion in public and private funds from western Germany between 1990 and 1995. In 1991, Berlin again became the capital of Germany; the legislature, most administrative offices, and most foreign embassies had shifted from Bonn to Berlin by late 1999.

Germany's highest court ruled, July 12, 1994, that German troops could participate in international military missions abroad, when approved by Parliament. General elections Oct. 16 left Chancellor Helmut Kohl's governing coalition with a slim parliamentary majority. On Oct. 31, 1996, after more than 14 years in office, Kohl surpassed Adenauer as Germany's longest-serving chancellor in the 20th cent.

Unemployment hit a postwar high of 12.6% in Jan. 1998. The Kohl era ended with the defeat of the Christian Democrats in parliamentary elections Sept. 27; Gerhard Schröder, of the Social Democratic Party, became chancellor. Germany contributed 8,500 troops to the NATO-led security force (KFOR) that entered Kosovo in June 1999. Kohl resigned as honorary party chairman Jan. 18, 2000, amid allegations of illegal fund-raising. Kohl reached an agreement with prosecutors Feb. 8, 2001, in which he acknowledged committing a "breach of trust" and agreed to pay a fine, but did not plead guilty to any criminal charges.

Despite a stagnant economy, Schröder's coalition of Social Democrats and Greens retained a slim majority in the elections of Sept. 22, 2002; the chancellor was apparently aided by his government's response to devastating summer floods and by his criticism of U.S. policy toward Iraq. In early 2003, Germany worked with France and Russia to block the UN Security Council from endorsing the U.S.-led invasion of Iraq. However, polls showed Schröder's support sharply falling. Schröder's coalition did poorly in elections for the European Parliament, June 13. When his party lost its stronghold of North Rhine-Westphalia in regional voting, May 22, 2005, Schröder called for early elections for Sept. 18. The

Christian Democrats, led by Angela Merkel, won a razor-thin plurality, and after prolonged negotiations she became chancellor Nov. 22, heading a "grand coalition" that included the Socialists.

Germany hosted the G-8 summit in June 2007 but was unable to persuade the U.S. to accept Merkel's plan for a mandatory 50% cut in global emissions of greenhouse gases by 2050. Authorities revealed Sept. 5 that they had foiled a terrorist bomb plot possibly targeting the U.S. Ramstein Air Base and Frankfurt Intl. Airport. As of mid-2007, about 3,000 German troops were serving in Afghanistan as part of a NATO peacekeeping force.

Helgoland, an island of 130 acres in the North Sea, was taken from Denmark by a British Naval Force in 1807 and later ceded to Germany to become part of Schleswig-Holstein province in return for rights in East Africa. The heavily fortified island was surrendered to UK, May 23, 1945, demilitarized in 1947, and returned to West Germany, Mar. 1, 1952. It is a free port.

Ghana
Republic of Ghana

People: Population: 22,931,299. **Age distrib.** (%): <15: 38.2; 65+: 3.6. **Pop. density:** 257 per sq mi, 99 per sq km. **Urban:** 47.8%. **Ethnic groups:** Akan 44%, Moshi-Dagomba 16%, Ewe 13%, Ga 8%, Gurma 3%, Yoruba 1%. **Principal languages:** English (official); about 75 African languages incl. Akan, Mole-Dagbon, Ewe, Ga-Dangme. **Chief religions:** Christian 69%, Muslim 16%, traditional 9%.

Geography: Total area: 92,456 sq mi, 239,460 sq km; **Land area:** 89,166 sq mi, 230,940 sq km. **Location:** On S coast of W Africa. **Neighbors:** Côte d'Ivoire on W, Burkina Faso on N, Togo on E. **Topography:** Mostly low fertile plains and scrubland, cut by rivers and by the artificial Lake Volta. **Capital:** Accra, 1,981,000. **City (urban aggr.):** Kumasi, 1,517,000.

Government: Type: Republic. **Head of state and gov.:** Pres. John Agyekum Kufuor; b. Dec. 8, 1938; in office: Jan. 7, 2001. **Local divisions:** 10 regions. **Defense budget:** $72 mil. **Active troops,** 13,500.

Economy: Industries: mining, lumbering, light mfg., aluminum smelting, food proc. **Chief crops:** cocoa, rice, coffee, cassava, peanuts, corn, shea nuts, bananas. **Natural resources:** gold, timber, diamonds, bauxite, mang., fish, rubber, hydropower. **Crude oil reserves:** 15 mil bbls. **Arable land:** 18%. **Livestock:** cattle: 1.4 mil; chickens: 30 mil; goats: 3.6 mil; pigs: 305,000; sheep: 3.2 mil. **Fish catch:** 393,428 metric tons. **Electricity prod.:** 6.7 bil kWh. **Labor force** (1999 est.): agriculture 60%, industry 15%, services 25%.

Finance: Monetary unit: Cedi (GHC) (Sept. 2007: 9,480.10 = $1 U.S.) (Current denomination will expire Dec. 31, 2007. Re-denomination would make 0.948 Cedi [GHS] = $1 U.S.). **GDP:** $60 bil; **per capita GDP:** $2,700; **GDP growth:** 6%. **Imports:** $5.7 bil; Nigeria 16.4%, China 12.8%, UK 5.6%, Belgium 4.7%, U.S. 4.6%, Brazil 4.3%, South Africa 4.1%, France 4%. **Exports:** $3.286 bil; Netherlands 11.2%, UK 8.6%, U.S. 6.7%, Spain 5.7%, Belgium 5.2%. **Tourism:** $466 mil. **Budget:** $3.9 bil. **Intl. reserves less gold:** $1.39 bil. **Gold:** 280,000 oz t. **Consumer prices:** 10.92%.

Transport: Railroad: Length: 592 mi. **Motor vehicles:** 92,000 pass. cars; 124,000 comm. vehicles. **Civil aviation:** 563 mil pass.-mi; 7 airports. **Chief ports:** Takoradi, Tema.

Communications: TV sets: 115 per 1,000 pop. **Radios:** 680 per 1,000 pop. **Telephone lines:** 356,400. **Daily newspaper circ.:** 13.9 per 1,000 pop. **Internet:** 609,800 users.

Health: Life expect.: 58.3 male; 60 female. **Births** (per 1,000 pop.): 29.9. **Deaths** (per 1,000 pop.): 9.6. **Natural inc.:** 2.03%. **Infant mortality** (per 1,000 live births): 53.6. **AIDS rate:** 2.3%.

Education: Compulsory: ages 6-14. **Literacy:** 57.9%.

Major intl. organizations: UN and all of its specialized agencies, the Commonwealth, AU.

Embassy: 3512 International Dr. NW 20008; 686-4520.

Website: www.ghana.gov.gh

Named for an African empire along the Niger River, 400-1240 CE, Ghana was ruled by Britain for 113 years as the Gold Coast. The UN in 1956 approved merger with the British Togoland trust territory. Independence came Mar. 6, 1957, and republic status within the Commonwealth in 1960.

Pres. Kwame Nkrumah built hospitals and schools, promoted development projects like the Volta R. hydroelectric and aluminum plants but ran the country into debt, jailed opponents, and was accused of corruption. A 1964 referendum gave Nkrumah dictatorial powers and set up a one-party socialist state. Nkrumah was overthrown in 1966 by a police-army coup, which expelled Chinese and East German teachers and technicians. Elections were held in 1969, but 4 further coups occurred in 1972, 1978, 1979, and 1981. The 1979 and 1981 coups were led by Flight Lieut. Jerry Rawlings, were followed by suspension of the constitution and banning of political parties. A new constitution, allowing multiparty politics, was approved in April 1992.

In Feb. 1993 more than 1,000 people were killed in ethnic clashes in northern Ghana. Rawlings won the presidential election of Dec. 7, 1996. Kofi Annan, a career UN diplomat from Ghana, became UN secretary general on Jan. 1, 1997. Opposition leader John Agyekum Kufuor won a runoff vote Dec. 28, 2000, and was sworn in Jan. 7, 2001, marking Ghana's first peaceful transfer of power from one elected president to another. He was reelected Dec. 7, 2004. A major offshore oil find of up to 600 mil barrels was announced in June 2007.

Greece
Hellenic Republic

People: Population: 10,706,290. **Age distrib.** (%): <15: 14.3; 65+: 19. **Pop. density:** 212 per sq mi, 82 per sq km. **Urban:** 59%. **Ethnic groups:** Greek 93%. **Principal language:** Greek (official). **Chief religions:** Greek Orthodox (official) 98%, Muslim 1%.

Geography: Total area: 50,942 sq mi, 131,940 sq km; **Land area:** 50,502 sq mi, 130,800 sq km. **Location:** Occupies S end of Balkan Peninsula in SE Europe. **Neighbors:** Albania, Macedonia, Bulgaria on N; Turkey on E. **Topography:** About three-quarters is nonarable, with mountains in all areas. Pindus Mts. run through the country N to S. The heavily indented coastline is 9,385 mi long. Of over 2,000 islands, only 169 are inhabited, among them Crete, Rhodes, Milos, Kerkira (Corfu), Chios, Lesbos, Samos, Euboea, Delos, Mykonos. **Capital:** Athens, 3,230,000 (1999 city proper: 748,110).

Government: Type: Parliamentary republic. **Head of state:** Pres. Karolos Papoulias; b. June 4, 1929; in office: Mar. 12, 2005. **Head of gov.:** Prime Min. Konstantinos (Costas) Karamanlis; b. Sept. 14, 1956; in office: Mar. 10, 2004. **Local divisions:** 13 regions comprising 51 prefectures. **Defense budget:** $4.76 bil. **Active troops:** 147,100.

Economy: Industries: tourism, food & tobacco proc., textiles, chemicals, metal products, mining, oil. **Chief crops:** wheat, corn, barley, sugar beets, olives, tomatoes, wine. **Natural resources:** bauxite, lignite, magnesite, oil, marble, hydropower potential. **Crude oil reserves:** 5 mil bbls. **Arable land:** 20%. **Livestock:** cattle: 617,128; chickens: 31.4 mil; goats: 5.4 mil; pigs: 948,715; sheep: 8.8 mil. **Fish catch:** 198,946 metric tons. **Electricity prod.:** 56.1 bil kWh. **Labor force** (2004 est.): agriculture 12%, industry 20%, services 68%.

Finance: Monetary unit: Euro (EUR) (Sept. 2007: 0.72 = $1 U.S.). **GDP:** $256.3 bil; **per capita GDP:** $24,000; **GDP growth:** 4.2%. **Imports:** $59.1 bil; Germany 12.6%, Italy 11.6%, Russia 7.1%, France 5.8%, Netherlands 5.2%. **Exports:** $24.4 bil; Germany 11.4%, Italy 11.2%, Bulgaria 6.4%, UK 6%, Cyprus 5.4%, Turkey 5.2%. **Tourism:** $12.7 bil. **Budget:** $106.7 bil. **Intl. reserves less gold:** $376 mil. **Gold:** 3.59 mil oz t. **Consumer prices:** 3.2%.

Transport: Railroad: Length: 1,598 mi. **Motor vehicles:** 4.1 mil pass. cars; 1.2 mil comm. vehicles. **Civil aviation:** 4.8 bil pass.-mi; 66 airports. **Chief ports:** Irakleion, Piraeus, Thessaloníki.

Communications: TV sets: 480 per 1,000 pop. **Radios:** 475 per 1,000 pop. **Telephone lines:** 6.2 mil. **Internet:** 2 mil users.

Health: Life expect.: 76.9 male; 82.1 female. **Births** (per 1,000 pop.): 9.6. **Deaths** (per 1,000 pop.): 10.3. **Natural inc.:** –0.07%. **Infant mortality** (per 1,000 live births): 5.3. **AIDS rate:** 0.2%.

Education: Compulsory: ages 6-14. **Literacy:** 96%.

Major intl. organizations: UN (FAO, IBRD, ILO, IMF, IMO, WHO, WTO), EU, NATO, OECD, OSCE.

Embassy: 2217 Massachusetts Ave. NW 20008; 939-1300.

Website: www.primeminister.gr

The achievements of ancient Greece in art, architecture, science, mathematics, philosophy, drama, literature, and democracy became legacies for succeeding ages. Greece reached the height of its glory and power, particularly in the Athenian city-state, in the 5th cent. BCE. Greece fell under Roman rule in the 2nd and 1st centuries BCE. In the 4th cent. CE it became part of the Byzantine Empire and, after the fall of Constantinople to the Turks in 1453, part of the Ottoman Empire.

Greece won its war of independence from Turkey 1821-29, and became a kingdom. A republic was established 1924; the monarchy was restored, 1935, and George II, King of the Hellenes, resumed the throne. In Oct. 1940, Greece rejected an ultimatum from Italy. Nazi support resulted in its defeat and occupation by Germans, Italians, and Bulgarians. By the end of 1944 the invaders withdrew. Communist resistance forces were defeated by Royalist and British troops. A plebiscite again restored the monarchy.

Communists waged guerrilla war 1947-49 against the government but were defeated with the aid of the U.S. A period of reconstruction and rapid development followed, mainly with conservative governments under Premier Constantine Karamanlis. The Center Union, led by George Papandreou, won elections in 1963 and 1964, but King Constantine, who acceded in 1964, forced Papandreou to resign. A period of political maneuvers ended in the military takeover of April 21, 1967, by Col. George Papadopoulos. King Constantine tried to reverse the consolidation of the harsh dictatorship Dec. 13, 1967, but failed and fled to Italy. Papadopoulos was ousted Nov. 25, 1973.

Greek army officers serving in the National Guard of Cyprus staged a coup on the island July 15, 1974. Turkey invaded Cyprus a week later, precipitating the collapse of the Greek junta, which was implicated in the Cyprus coup. Democratic government returned (and in 1975 the monarchy was abolished).

The 1981 electoral victory of the Panhellenic Socialist Movement (Pasok) of Andreas Papandreou brought substantial changes in Greece's internal and external policies. A scandal centered on George Kostokas, a banker and publisher, led to the arrest or investigation of leading Socialists, implicated Papandreou, and contributed to the defeat of the Socialists at the polls in 1989. However,

Papandreou, who was narrowly acquitted Jan. 1992 of corruption charges, led the Socialists to a comeback victory in general elections Oct. 10, 1993.

Tensions between Greece and the Former Yugoslav Republic of Macedonia eased when the 2 countries agreed to normalize relations Sept. 13, 1995. The ailing Papandreou was replaced as prime minister by Costas Simitis, Jan. 18, 1996. Simitis led the Socialists to victory in the election of Sept. 22.

An earthquake that shook Athens Sept. 7, 1999, killed at least 143 people and left more than 60,000 homeless. The Socialists retained power by a narrow margin in the elections of Apr. 9, 2000. Police in 2002 cracked down on the November 17 terrorist movement, blamed for 23 killings since the mid-1970s.

The conservative New Democracy Party won parliamentary elections, Mar. 7, 2004, and Konstantinos (Costas) Karamanlis became prime minister. Athens hosted the Olympic Summer Games, Aug. 13-29. A Cypriot jetliner crashed near Athens, Aug. 14, 2005, killing all 121 people on board. Rampant wildfires, Aug. 2007, left at least 65 people dead and caused over $1.6 bil in damage. Karamanlis kept his office after early elections Sept. 16.

Grenada

People: Population: 89,971. **Age distrib.** (%): <15: 32.8; 65+: 3.1. **Pop. density:** 676 per sq mi, 262 per sq km. **Urban:** 30.6%. **Ethnic groups:** Black 82%, Creole 13%. **Principal languages:** English (official), French patois. **Chief religions:** Roman Catholic 53%, Anglican 14%, other Protestant 33%.

Geography: Total area: 133 sq mi, 344 sq km; **Land area:** 133 sq mi, 344 sq km. **Location:** In Caribbean, 90 mi N of Venezuela. **Neighbors:** Venezuela, Trinidd & Tobago to S; St. Vincent & the Grenadines to N. **Topography:** Main island is mountainous; country includes Carriacou and Petit Martinique isls. **Capital:** Saint George's, 33,000.

Government: Type: Parliamentary democracy. **Head of state:** Queen Elizabeth II, represented by Gov.-Gen. Sir Daniel Williams; b. Nov. 4, 1935; in office: Aug. 9, 1996. **Head of gov.:** Prime Min. Keith Mitchell; b. Nov. 12, 1946; in office: June 22, 1995. **Local divisions:** 6 parishes, 1 dependency.

Economy: Industries: food, beverages, textiles, light assembly operations, tourism, constr. **Chief crops:** bananas, cocoa, nutmeg, mace, citrus, avocados. **Natural resources:** timber. **Arable land:** 6%. **Livestock:** cattle: 4,450; chickens: 268,000; goats: 7,200; pigs: 2,650; sheep: 13,200. **Fish catch:** 2,050 metric tons. **Electricity prod.:** 150 mil kWh. **Labor force** (1999 est.): agriculture 24%, industry 14%, services 62%.

Finance: Monetary unit: East Caribbean Dollar (XCD) (Sept. 2007: 2.67 = $1 U.S.). **GDP:** $982 mil; **per capita GDP** (2005 est.): $3,900; **GDP growth** (2005 est.): 0.9%. **Imports** (2004 est.): $276 mil; Trinidad and Tobago 32.3%, U.S. 23.2%, Barbados 4.6%, UK 4.1%. **Exports** (2004 est.): $40 mil; Saint Lucia 17.2%, Antigua and Barbuda 11.7%, Saint Kitts and Nevis 10.5%, Dominica 10.5%, U.S. 10.4%. **Tourism:** $92 mil. **Budget** (1997): $102.1 mil. **Intl. reserves less gold:** $66 mil. **Consumer prices:** 3.81%.

Transport: Motor vehicles: 15,800 pass. cars; 4,200 comm. vehicles. **Civil aviation:** 3 airports. **Chief port:** Saint George's.

Communications: TV sets: 376 per 1,000 pop. **Radios:** 613 per 1,000 pop. **Telephone lines:** 27,700. **Internet** (2005): 19,000 users.

Health: Life expect.: 63.4 male; 67.1 female. **Births** (per 1,000 pop.): 21.9. **Deaths** (per 1,000 pop.): 6.6. **Natural inc.:** 1.53%. **Infant mortality** (per 1,000 live births): 13.9. **AIDS rate:** NA.

Education: Compulsory: ages 5-16. **Literacy:** 96%.

Major intl. organizations: UN (FAO, IBRD, ILO, IMF, IMO, WHO, WTO), Caricom, the Commonwealth, OAS, OECS.

Embassy: 1701 New Hampshire Ave. NW 20009; 265-2561.

Website: www.gov.gd

Columbus sighted Grenada in 1498. First European settlers were French, 1650. The island was held alternately by France and England until final British occupation, 1784. Grenada became fully independent Feb. 7, 1974, during a general strike.

On Oct. 14, 1983, a military coup ousted Prime Min. Maurice Bishop, who was put under house arrest, later freed by supporters, rearrested, and, finally, on Oct. 19, executed. U.S. forces, with a token force from 6 area nations, invaded Grenada, Oct. 25. Resistance from the Grenadian army and Cuban advisors was quickly overcome as most people welcomed the invading forces. U.S. troops left Grenada in June 1985. Hurricane Ivan slammed into Grenada, Sept. 7, 2004, killing 39 people and damaging an estimated 90% of the buildings on the island.

Guatemala
Republic of Guatemala

People: Population: 12,728,111. **Age distrib.** (%): <15: 40.8; 65+: 3.6. **Pop. density:** 304 per sq mi, 117 per sq km. **Urban:** 47.2%. **Ethnic groups:** Mestizo 59%, K'iche 9%, Kaqchikel 8%, Mam 8%, Q'eqchi 6%. **Principal languages:** Spanish (official); more than 20 Amerindian languages, incl. Quiche, Cakchiquel, Kekchi, Mam, Garifuna, and Xinca. **Chief religions:** Mostly Roman Catholic; some Protestant, indigenous Mayan beliefs.

Geography: Total area: 42,043 sq mi, 108,890 sq km; **Land area:** 41,865 sq mi, 108,430 sq km. **Location:** In Central America. **Neighbors:** Mexico on N and W, El Salvador on S, Honduras and

Belize on E. **Topography:** The central highland and mountain areas are bordered by the narrow Pacific coast and lowlands and fertile river valleys on the Caribbean. Numerous volcanoes in S, more than half a dozen over 11,000 ft. **Capital:** Guatemala City, 984,000.

Government: Type: Republic. **Head of state and gov.:** Pres. Oscar Berger Perdomo; b. Aug. 11, 1946; in office: Jan. 14, 2004. **Local divisions:** 22 departments. **Defense budget:** $146 mil. **Active troops:** 15,500.

Economy: Industries: sugar, textiles, clothing, furniture, chemicals, oil, metals, rubber, tourism. **Chief crops:** sugarcane, corn, bananas, coffee, beans, cardamom. **Natural resources:** oil, nickel, rare woods, fish, chicle, hydropower. **Crude oil reserves:** 83.1 mil bbls. **Arable land:** 12%. **Livestock:** cattle: 2.8 mil; chickens: 27 mil; goats: 112,000; pigs: 212,000; sheep: 260,000. **Fish catch:** 16,756 metric tons. **Electricity prod.:** 7.3 bil kWh. **Labor force** (1999 est.): agriculture 50%, industry 15%, services 35%.

Finance: Monetary unit: Quetzal (GTQ) (Sept. 2007: 7.70 = $1 U.S.). **GDP:** $61.4 bil; **per capita GDP:** $5,000; **GDP growth:** 4.6%. **Imports:** $9.9 bil; U.S. 31.3%, Mexico 7.9%, China 6.1%, El Salvador 5%, South Korea 5%. **Exports:** $3.7 bil; U.S. 45.2%, El Salvador 12.1%, Honduras 7.3%. **Tourism:** $869 mil. **Budget:** $4.4 bil. **Intl. reserves less gold:** $2.60 bil. **Gold:** 220,000 oz t. **Consumer prices:** 6.45%.

Transport: Railroad: Length: 61 per 1,000 pop. **Motor vehicles:** 1.3 mil pass. cars. **Civil aviation** (1999): 212.5 mil pass.-mi; 11 airports. **Chief ports:** Puerto Quetzal, Santo Tomas de Castilla.

Communications: TV sets: 61 per 1,000 pop. **Radios:** 79 per 1,000 pop. **Telephone lines:** 1.4 mil. **Internet:** 1.3 mil users.

Health: Life expect.: 67.9 male; 71.5 female. **Births** (per 1,000 pop.): 29.1. **Deaths** (per 1,000 pop.): 5.3. **Natural inc.:** 2.38%. **Infant mortality** (per 1,000 live births): 29.8. **AIDS rate:** 0.9%.

Education: Compulsory: ages 7-15. **Literacy:** 69.1%.

Major intl. organizations: UN (FAO, IBRD, ILO, IMF, IMO, WHO, WTO), OAS.

Embassy: 2220 R St. NW 20008; 745-4952.

Website: www.guatemala-embassy.org

A Mayan Indian empire flourished in what is today Guatemala for over 1,000 years before Spaniards came. Guatemala was a Spanish colony 1524-1821. A republic was established in 1839.

The U.S. intervened in Guatemala in 1954 when the Central Intelligence Agency engineered the overthrow of elected Pres. Jacobo Arbenz Guzmán, a left-wing reformer. Since then, the country has experienced a variety of military and civilian governments and periods of insurgency, repression, and civil war.

Dissident army officers seized power Mar. 23, 1982, denouncing a presidential election as fraudulent and pledging to restore "authentic democracy" to the nation. Political violence caused large numbers of Guatemalans to seek refuge in Mexico. Another military coup occurred Oct. 8, 1983. The nation returned to civilian rule in 1986.

The crisis-ridden government of Pres. Jorge Serrano Elías was ousted by the military June 1, 1993. Ramiro de León Carpio was elected president by Congress June 6. A conservative businessman, Alvaro Arzú Irigoyen, won the presidency, Jan. 7, 1996. On Sept. 19 the Guatemalan government and leftist rebels approved a peace accord; the final agreement was signed Dec. 29. During more than 35 years of armed conflict, some 200,000 people were killed or "disappeared" (and are presumed dead); most of these casualties were attributed to the government and its paramilitary allies.

Violent episodes in 1998 included the daylight ambush of a busload of U.S. college students, Jan. 16, resulting in the rape of five young women, and the murder of Bishop Juan José Gerardi, a human rights activist, Apr. 26. U.S. Pres. Bill Clinton, on a visit to Guatemala Mar. 10, 1999, apologized for aid the U.S. had given to forces which he said "engaged in violence and widespread repression." Candidates of the right-wing populist Guatemalan Republican Front won control of Congress, Nov. 7, 1999, and the presidency, Dec. 26.

Drought and weak export prices during 2001-02 worsened the plight of Guatemala's poor, who make up 80% of the population. Oscar Berger Perdomo, the conservative former mayor of Guatemala City, won a presidential runoff election Dec. 28, 2003. Floods and mudslides from Tropical Storm Stan, Oct. 2005, killed at least 669 people; another 844 were missing and presumed dead.

Three Salvadoran lawmakers and their driver were murdered Feb. 19, 2007, while on an official visit to Guatemala; 4 Guatemalan police officers charged with the crime were killed Feb. 25 in the maximum-security prison where they were being held. No candidate won a majority in the 1st round of presidential elections, Sept. 9; a runoff vote was scheduled for Nov. 4.

Guinea

Republic of Guinea

People: Population: 9,947,814. **Age distrib.** (%): <15: 44.3; 65+: 3.2. **Pop. density:** 105 per sq mi, 40 per sq km. **Urban:** 33%. **Ethnic groups:** Peuhl 40%, Malinke 30%, Soussou 20%. **Principal languages:** French (official); many African languages. **Chief religions:** Muslim 85%, Christian 8%, indigenous beliefs 7%.

Geography: Total area: 94,926 sq mi, 245,857 sq km; **Land area:** 94,926 sq mi, 245,857 sq km. **Location:** On Atlantic coast of W Africa. **Neighbors:** Guinea-Bissau, Senegal, Mali on N; Côte d'Ivoire on E; Liberia, Sierra Leone on S. **Topography:** A narrow coastal belt leads to mountainous middle region, source of the Gambia, Senegal, and Niger rivers. Upper Guinea, farther inland, is cooler upland. The SE is forested. **Capital:** Conakry, 1,425,000.

Government: Type: Republic. **Head of state:** Pres. Gen. Lansana Conté; b. 1934; in office: Apr. 5, 1984. **Head of gov.:** Prime Min. Lansana Kouyaté; b. 1950; in office: Mar. 1, 2007. **Local divisions:** 33 prefectures, 1 special zone. **Defense budget:** $36 mil. **Active troops:** 12,300.

Economy: Industries: bauxite, gold, diamonds, aluminum refining, light mfg., agric. proc. **Chief crops:** rice, coffee, pineapples, palm kernels, cassava, bananas, sweet potatoes. **Natural resources:** bauxite, iron ore, diamonds, gold, uranium, hydropower, fish. **Arable land:** 4%. **Livestock:** cattle: 3.8 mil; chickens: 15.9 mil; goats: 1.4 mil; pigs: 74,784; sheep: 1.2 mil. **Fish catch:** 96,571 metric tons. **Electricity prod.:** 770 mil kWh. **Labor force** (2006 est.): agriculture 76%, industry and services 24%.

Finance: Monetary unit: Franc (GNF) (Sept. 2007: 4,073.50 = $1 U.S.). **GDP:** $20.2 bil; **per capita GDP:** $2,100; **GDP growth:** 3.7%. **Imports:** $730 mil; China 8.5%, France 7.9%, Netherlands 4.7%, Belgium 4.3%. **Exports:** $615.1 mil; South Korea 13.1%, Russia 11.1%, Ukraine 9.2%, Spain 7.7%, France 7.4%, U.S. 7.4%, Germany 5.2%. **Tourism:** $30 mil. **Budget:** $556.7 mil. **Intl. reserves less gold** (2005): $67 mil. **Gold** (2004): 10,000 oz t.

Transport: Railroad: Length: 520 mi. **Motor vehicles:** 23,200 pass. cars; 13,000 comm. vehicles. **Civil aviation** (1999): 58.4 mil pass.-mi; 5 airports. **Chief port:** Kamsar.

Communications: TV sets: 47 per 1,000 pop. **Radios:** 52 per 1,000 pop. **Telephone lines:** 26,300. **Internet:** 50,000 users.

Health: Life expect.: 48.5 male; 50.8 female. **Births** (per 1,000 pop.): 41.5. **Deaths** (per 1,000 pop.): 15.3. **Natural inc.:** 2.62%. **Infant mortality** (per 1,000 live births): 88.6. **AIDS rate:** 1.5%.

Education: Compulsory: ages 7-12. **Literacy:** 29.5%.

Major intl. organizations: UN and most of its specialized agencies, AU.

Embassy: 2112 Leroy Pl. NW 20008; 986-4300.

Website: www.state.gov/p/af/ci/gv/

Sékou Touré, Guinea's first president (1958-84), turned to Communist nations for support and set up a one-party state. Thousands of opponents were jailed in the 1970s, after an unsuccessful Portuguese invasion. Many were tortured and killed.

The military took control in a bloodless coup after the March 1984 death of Touré. A new constitution was approved in 1991, but movement toward democracy was slow. When presidential elections were finally held, in Dec. 1993, the incumbent, Gen. Lansana Conté, was the official winner; outside monitors called the elections flawed. Parliamentary elections June 11, 1995, raised similar complaints. Conté suppressed an army mutiny in Conakry, Feb. 2-3, 1996, and won reelection in Dec. 1998.

Fighting in early 2001 along the border with Liberia and Sierra Leone created a refugee crisis in Guinea; efforts to repatriate the Liberians were ongoing in 2007. Major opposition parties boycotted the presidential election Dec. 21, 2003, in which the ailing Conté won 95.6% of the vote. After 2 months in office, Prime Min. François Fall resigned, Apr. 30, 2004, charging Conté with thwarting reform efforts. His successor, Cellou Dalein Diallo, was fired in a power struggle, Apr. 5, 2006. More than 120 died in strikes and protests Jan.-Feb. 2007, until Conté agreed to name a new prime min. from a list approved by union leaders.

Guinea-Bissau

Republic of Guinea-Bissau

People: Population: 1,472,780. **Age distrib.** (%): <15: 41.2; 65+: 3. **Pop. density:** 136 per sq mi, 53 per sq km. **Urban:** 29.6%. **Ethnic groups:** Balanta 30%, Fula 20%, Manjaca 14%, Mandinga 13%, Papel 7%. **Principal languages:** Portuguese (official), Criuolo, African languages. **Chief religions:** Indigenous beliefs 50%, Muslim 45%, Christian 5%.

Geography: Total area: 13,946 sq mi, 36,120 sq km; **Land area:** 10,811 sq mi, 28,000 sq km. **Location:** On Atlantic coast of W Africa. **Neighbors:** Senegal on N, Guinea on E and S. **Topography:** A swampy coastal plain covers most of country; to E is a low savanna region. **Capital:** Bissau, 367,000.

Government: Type: Republic. **Head of state:** Pres. João Bernardo Vieira; b. Apr. 27, 1939; in office: Oct. 1, 2005. **Head of gov.:** Prime Min. Martinho Ndafa Cabi; b. Sept. 17, 1957; in office: Apr. 13, 2007. **Local divisions:** 9 regions. **Defense budget:** $14 mil. **Active troops:** 9,250.

Economy: Industries: agric. proc., beer, soft drinks. **Chief crops:** rice, corn, beans, cassava, cashew nuts, peanuts, palm kernels, cotton. **Natural resources:** fish, timber, phosphates, bauxite, oil. **Arable land:** 8%. **Livestock:** cattle: 530,000; chickens: 1.6 mil; goats: 335,000; pigs: 370,000; sheep: 300,000. **Fish catch:** 6,200 metric tons. **Electricity prod.:** 60 mil kWh. **Labor force** (2000 est.): agriculture 82%, industry and services 18%.

Finance: Monetary unit: CFA BCEAO Franc (XOF) (Sept. 2007: 472.78 = $1 U.S.). **GDP:** $1.2 bil; **per capita GDP:** $900; **GDP growth:** 2.1% **Imports** (2004 est.): $176 mil; Senegal 22.6%, Portugal 17.7%, Italy 12.2%, Pakistan 4.3%. **Exports** (2004 est.): $116 mil; India 72.4%, Nigeria 17.2%, Ecuador 4.1%.

Tourism: $2 mil. **Budget:** NA. **Intl. reserves less gold:** $55 mil. **Consumer prices:** 1.95%.

Transport: Motor vehicles: NA. **Civil aviation:** 3 airports. **Chief ports:** Buba, Cacheu, Farim.

Communications: Radios: 43 per 1,000 pop. **Telephone lines:** 10,200. **Daily newspaper circ.:** 4.8 per 1,000 pop. **Internet:** 37,000 users.

Health: Life expect.: 45.4 male; 49 female. **Births** (per 1,000 pop.): 36.8. **Deaths** (per 1,000 pop.): 16.3. **Natural inc.:** 2.05%. **Infant mortality** (per 1,000 live births): 103.5. **AIDS rate:** 3.8%.

Education: Compulsory: ages 7-12. **Literacy:** 42.4%.

Major intl. organizations: UN (FAO, IBRD, ILO, IMF, IMO, WHO, WTO), AU.

Embassy: 15929 Yukon Ln., Rockville, MD 20855; 301-947-3958.

Website: www.state.gov/p/af/ci/pu/

Portuguese mariners explored the area in the mid-15th cent.; the slave trade flourished in the 17th and 18th centuries, and colonization began in the 19th.

Beginning in the 1960s, an independence movement waged a guerrilla war and formed a government in the interior that had international support. Independence came Sept. 10, 1974, after the Portuguese regime was overthrown.

A November 1980 coup gave army chief João Bernardo Vieira absolute power. Vieira eventually initiated political liberalization; multiparty elections were held July 3, 1994. An army uprising June 7, 1998, triggered a civil war with Senegal and Guinea aiding the Vieira regime. After a peace accord signed on Nov. 2 broke down, rebel troops ousted Vieira on May 7, 1999. Elections Nov. 28-29, 1999, and Jan. 16, 2000, brought a return of civilian rule. Top military officers staged an apparently bloodless coup Sept. 14, 2003. A caretaker government was installed Sept. 28, and legislative elections were held Mar. 2004. Vieira won a presidential runoff election, July 24, 2005, and returned to power Oct. 1.

Guyana
Co-operative Republic of Guyana

People: Population: 769,095. **Age distrib.** (%): <15: 26.1; 65+: 5.3. **Pop. density:** 10 per sq mi, 4 per sq km. **Urban:** 28.2%. **Ethnic groups:** East Indian 50%, black 36%, Amerindian 7%. **Principal languages:** English (official), Amerindian dialects, Creole, Caribbean Hindustani, Urdu. **Chief religions:** Christian 50%, Hindu 35%, Muslim 10%.

Geography: Total area: 83,000 sq mi, 214,970 sq km; **Land area:** 76,004 sq mi, 196,850 sq km. **Location:** On N coast of S. America. **Neighbors:** Venezuela on W, Brazil on S, Suriname on E. **Topography:** Dense tropical forests cover much of land, although flat coastal area up to 40 mi wide, where 90% of the population lives, provides rich alluvial soil for agriculture. A grassy savanna divides the 2 zones. **Capital:** Georgetown, 134,000.

Government: Type: Republic. **Head of state:** Pres. Bharrat Jagdeo; b. Jan. 23, 1964; in office: Aug. 11, 1999. **Head of gov.:** Prime Min. Samuel Hinds; b. Dec. 27, 1943; in office: Dec. 22, 1997. **Local divisions:** 10 regions. **Defense budget:** NA. **Active troops:** 1,100.

Economy: Industries: bauxite, sugar, rice milling, timber, textiles, gold mining. **Chief crops:** sugarcane, rice, wheat, vegetable oils. **Natural resources:** bauxite, gold, diamonds, hardwood timber, shrimp, fish. **Arable land:** 2%. **Livestock:** cattle: 110,000; chickens: 20 mil; goats: 79,000; pigs: 13,000; sheep: 130,000. **Fish catch:** 53,980 metric tons. **Electricity prod.:** 810 mil kWh. **Labor force:** NA.

Finance: Monetary unit: Dollar (GYD) (Sept. 2007: 203.45 = $1 U.S.). **GDP:** $3.7 bil; **per capita GDP:** $4,800; **GDP growth:** 4.5%. **Imports:** $706.9 mil; Trinidad and Tobago 23%, U.S. 21.3%, China 9.7%, Cuba 6.3%, UK 4.5%. **Exports:** $621.6 mil; U.S. 18.7%, Canada 16.3%, UK 8.6%, Portugal 6.5%, Jamaica 6.1%. **Tourism:** $28 mil. **Budget:** $430.3 mil. **Intl. reserves less gold:** $186 mil. **Consumer prices:** 7.24%.

Transport: Railroad: Length: 116 mi. **Motor vehicles:** 61,300 pass. cars; 15,500 comm. vehicles. **Civil aviation** (2001): 108.7 mil pass.-mi; 9 airports. **Chief port:** Georgetown.

Communications: TV sets: 70 per 1,000 pop. **Radios:** 468 per 1,000 pop. **Telephone lines:** 110,100. **Daily newspaper circ.:** 74.8 per 1,000 pop. **Internet:** 160,000 users.

Health: Life expect.: 63.5 male; 69 female. **Births** (per 1,000 pop.): 18.1. **Deaths** (per 1,000 pop.): 8.3. **Natural inc.:** 0.98%. **Infant mortality** (per 1,000 live births): 31.4. **AIDS rate:** 2.4%.

Education: Compulsory: ages 6-15. **Literacy:** 98.8%.

Major intl. organizations: UN (FAO, IBRD, ILO, IMF, IMO, WHO, WTO), Caricom, the Commonwealth, OAS.

Embassy: 2490 Tracy Pl. NW 20008; 265-6900.

Website: www.op.gov.gy

Guyana became a Dutch possession in the 17th cent., but sovereignty passed to Britain in 1815. Indentured servants from India soon outnumbered African slaves. Ethnic tension has affected political life.

Guyana became independent May 26, 1966. A Venezuelan claim to the western half of Guyana was suspended in 1970 but renewed in 1982; an agreement was reached in 1989. The Suriname border is disputed. The government has nationalized most of the economy, which has remained severely depressed.

The Port Kaituma ambush of U.S. Rep. Leo J. Ryan and others investigating mistreatment of American followers of the Rev. Jim Jones's People's Temple cult triggered a mass suicide-execution of 911 cultists at Jonestown in the jungle, Nov. 18, 1978.

The People's National Congress, the party in power since Guyana became independent, was voted out of office with the election of Cheddi Jagan in Oct. 1992. When Pres. Jagan died Mar. 6, 1997, Prime Min. Samuel Hinds succeeded him. Jagan's widow, Janet, became prime min. Mar. 17. She won the presidency in a disputed election Dec. 15. She resigned because of ill health Aug. 11, 1999, and was succeeded by Bharrat Jagdeo, then 35, who became the youngest head of state in the Americas. He won reelection Mar. 19, 2001, and Aug. 28, 2006.

Floods from torrential rains, Jan. 2005, affected about 40% of the population. Gunmen in Georgetown killed Agric. Min. Satyadeow Sawh and 2 members of his family, Apr. 22, 2006.

Haiti
Republic of Haiti

People: Population: 8,706,497. **Age distrib.** (%): <15: 42.1; 65+: 3.5. **Pop. density:** 818 per sq mi, 316 per sq km. **Urban:** 38.8%. **Ethnic groups:** Black 95%, Creole and white 5%. **Principal languages:** French, Creole (both official). **Chief religions:** Roman Catholic 80%, Protestant 16%; Voodoo widely practiced.

Geography: Total area: 10,714 sq mi, 27,750 sq km; **Land area:** 10,641 sq mi, 27,560 sq km. **Location:** In Caribbean, occupies W third of Isl. of Hispaniola. **Neighbors:** Dominican Republic on E, Cuba to W. **Topography:** About two-thirds is mountainous. Much of rest is semiarid. Coastal areas are warm and moist. **Capital:** Port-au-Prince, 2,129,000.

Government: Type: Republic. **Head of state:** Pres. René Préval; b. Jan. 17, 1943; in office May 14, 2006. **Head of gov.:** Prime Min. Jacques Édouard Alexis; b. Sept. 21, 1947; in office: June 9, 2006. **Local divisions:** 9 departments. **Defense budget:** NA. **Active troops:** None.

Economy: Industries: sugar refining, flour milling, textiles, cement, light assembly. **Chief crops:** coffee, mangoes, sugarcane, rice, corn, sorghum. **Natural resources:** bauxite, copper, calcium carbonate, gold, marble, hydropower. **Arable land:** 28%. **Livestock:** cattle: 1.5 mil; chickens: 5.5 mil; goats: 1.9 mil; pigs: 1 mil; sheep: 153,500. **Fish catch:** 8,300 metric tons. **Electricity prod.:** 540 mil kWh. **Labor force:** agriculture 66%, industry 9%, services 25%.

Finance: Monetary unit: Gourde (HTG) (Sept. 2007: 35.47 = $1 U.S.). **GDP:** $14.8 bil; **per capita GDP:** $1,800; **GDP growth:** 2.5% **Imports:** $1.7 bil; U.S. 46%, Netherlands Antilles 11.8%, China 3.4%. **Exports:** $443.7 mil; U.S. 80.4%, Dominican Republic 7.7%, Canada 3%. **Tourism:** $93 mil. **Budget:** $807.7 mil. **Intl. reserves less gold:** $168 mil. **Consumer prices:** 13.07%.

Transport: Railroad: Length: NA. **Motor vehicles:** 93,000 pass. cars; 61,600 comm. vehicles. **Civil aviation:** 4 airports. **Chief port:** Cap-Haitien.

Communications: TV sets: 5 per 1,000 pop. **Radios:** 53 per 1,000 pop. **Telephone lines:** 145,300. **Internet:** 650,000 users.

Health: Life expect.: 55.4 male; 58.8 female. **Births** (per 1,000 pop.): 35.9. **Deaths** (per 1,000 pop.): 10.4. **Natural inc.:** 2.55%. **Infant mortality** (per 1,000 live births): 63.8. **AIDS rate:** 3.8%.

Education: Compulsory: ages 6-11. **Literacy:** 52.9%.

Major intl. organizations: UN and most of its specialized agencies, OAS, Caricom.

Embassy: 2311 Massachusetts Ave. NW 20008; 332-4090.

Website: www.haiti.org

Haiti, visited by Columbus, 1492, and a French colony from 1697, attained its independence, 1804, following the rebellion led by former slave Toussaint L'Ouverture. After a period of political violence, the U.S. occupied the country 1915-34.

François Duvalier, known as Papa Doc, was elected president in Sept. 1957; in 1964 he was named president for life. Upon his death in 1971, he was succeeded by his son, Jean Claude Duvalier, known as Baby Doc. Following weeks of unrest, Jean Claude fled Haiti aboard a U.S. Air Force jet Feb. 7, 1986. His departure ended the Duvalier family's brutal 28-year dictatorship, but political violence, government corruption, poverty, AIDS and other health problems, and deteriorating environmental quality have continued to plague Haiti.

Father Jean-Bertrand Aristide was elected president Dec. 1990, but in Sept. 1991, he was arrested by the military and expelled from the country. Some 35,000 Haitian refugees were intercepted by the U.S. Coast Guard as they tried to enter the U.S., 1991-92. Most were returned to Haiti. There was a new upsurge of refugees starting in late 1993.

The UN authorized, July 31, 1994, an invasion of Haiti by a multinational force. With U.S. troops already en route, a full-scale invasion was averted, Sept. 18, when military leaders agreed to step down. Aristide returned to Haiti and was restored to office Oct. 15. A UN peacekeeping force exercised responsibility in Haiti from Mar. 31, 1995 to Nov. 30, 1997. Aristide transferred power to his elected successor, René Préval, on Feb. 7, 1996.

At least 140 people died and over 160,000 were left homeless when Hurricane Georges struck Haiti Sept. 22, 1998. Aristide won the presidency Nov. 26, 2000, in an election boycotted by opposition groups. An armed uprising in early 2004 and pressure from France and the U.S. toppled Aristide, who went into exile Feb. 29. A U.S.-led contingent, sent in after the upheaval, yielded authority June 1 to a UN stabilization force (MINUSTAH).

Flooding in late May 2004 killed more than 1,000 people, and more than 2,400 were killed in Tropical Storm Jeanne in Sept. Presidential elections Feb. 7, 2006, restored Préval to power. Meeting July 25 in Port-au-Prince, international donors pledged $750 mil in aid. MINUSTAH uniformed personnel in Haiti numbered 8,825 in mid-2007.

Honduras
Republic of Honduras

People: Population: 7,483,763. **Age distrib. (%):** <15: 39.3; 65+: 3.5. **Pop. density:** 173 per sq mi, 67 per sq km. **Urban:** 46.5%. **Ethnic groups:** Mestizo 90%, Amerindian 7%, black 2%, white 1%. **Principal languages:** Spanish (official), Garífuna, Amerindian dialects. **Chief religion:** Roman Catholic 97%.

Geography: Total area: 43,278 sq mi, 112,090 sq km; **Land area:** 43,201 sq mi, 111,890 sq km. **Location:** In Central America. **Neighbors:** Guatemala on W; El Salvador, Nicaragua on S. **Topography:** Caribbean coast is 500 mi long. Pacific coast, on Gulf of Fonseca, is 40 mi long. Country is mountainous, with wide fertile valleys and rich forests. **Capital:** Tegucigalpa, 927,000.

Government: Type: Republic. **Head of state and gov.:** Pres. José Manuel Zelaya Rosales; b. Sept. 20, 1952; in office: Jan. 27, 2006. **Local divisions:** 18 departments. **Defense budget:** $55.6 mil. **Active troops:** 12,000.

Economy: Industries: sugar, coffee, textiles, clothing, wood products. **Chief crops:** bananas, coffee, citrus. **Natural resources:** timber, gold, silver, copper, lead, zinc, iron ore, antimony, coal, fish, hydropower. **Arable land:** 10%. **Livestock:** cattle: 2.5 mil; chickens: 18.7 mil; goats: 24,207; pigs: 490,000; sheep: 14,877. **Fish catch:** 48,580 metric tons. **Electricity prod.:** 5.3 bil kWh. **Labor force** (2003 est.): agriculture 34%, industry 23%, services 43%.

Finance: Monetary unit: Lempira (HNL) (Sept. 2007: 18.90 = $1 U.S.). **GDP:** $22.5 bil; **per capita GDP:** $3,100; **GDP growth:** 6%. **Imports:** $4.9 bil; U.S. 51.7%, Guatemala 6.8%, El Salvador 4.4%, Mexico 4.1%, Costa Rica 4%. **Exports:** $1.9 bil; U.S. 70.3%, Guatemala 3.5%, El Salvador 3.4%. **Tourism:** $396 mil. **Budget:** $2 bil. **Intl. reserves less gold:** $1.75 bil. **Gold:** 20,000 oz t. **Consumer prices:** 5.58%.

Transport: Railroad: Length: 434 mi. **Motor vehicles:** 46,000 pass. cars; 39,300 comm. vehicles. **Civil aviation:** 11 airports. **Chief ports:** Puerto Castilla, Puerto Cortes, San Lorenzo, Tela.

Communications: TV sets: 95 per 1,000 pop. **Radios:** 410 per 1,000 pop. **Telephone lines:** 708,400. **Internet:** 337,300 users.

Health: Life expect.: 67.8 male; 71 female. **Births** (per 1,000 pop.): 27.6. **Deaths** (per 1,000 pop.): 5.3. **Natural inc.:** 2.23%. **Infant mortality** (per 1,000 live births): 25.2. **AIDS rate:** 1.5%.

Education: Compulsory: ages 6-11. **Literacy:** 80%.

Major intl. organizations: UN (FAO, IBRD, ILO, IMF, IMO, WHO, WTO), OAS.

Embassy: 3007 Tilden St. NW, Ste. 4M, 20008; 966-7702.

Website: www.hondurasemb.org

Mayan civilization flourished in Honduras in the 1st millennium CE. Columbus arrived in 1502. Honduras became independent after freeing itself from Spain, 1821, and from the Fed. of Central America, 1838.

Gen. Oswaldo Lopez Arellano, president for most of the period 1963-75 by virtue of one election and 2 coups, was ousted by the army in 1975 over charges of pervasive bribery by United Brands Co. of the U.S. An elected civilian government took power in 1982. Some 3,200 U.S. troops were sent to Honduras after the Honduran border was violated by Nicaraguan forces, Mar. 1988.

Already one of the poorest countries in the Western Hemisphere, Honduras was devastated in late Oct. 1998 by Hurricane Mitch, which killed at least 5,600 people and caused more than $850 mil in damage to crops and livestock.

Ricardo Maduro, a businessman who pledged to crack down on crime, won the presidency Nov. 25, 2001. A fire May 17, 2004, killed 104 inmates at an overcrowded prison in San Pedro Sula. Gunmen in that city Dec. 23 killed 28 passengers on a bus. In mid-Nov. 2005, floods and mudslides from Tropical Storm Gamma left 32 dead. José Manuel Zelaya Rosales of the opposition Liberal Party won the presidential election held Nov. 27.

Hungary
Republic of Hungary

People: Population: 9,956,108. **Age distrib. (%):** <15: 15.3; 65+: 15.4. **Pop. density:** 279 per sq mi, 108 per sq km. **Urban:** 66.3%. **Ethnic groups:** Hungarian 92%, Roma 2%. **Principal languages:** Hungarian (official), Romani, German, Slavic languages, Romanian. **Chief religions:** Roman Catholic 52%, Calvinist 16%; unaffiliated 15%.

Geography: Total area: 35,919 sq mi, 93,030 sq km; **Land area:** 35,653 sq mi, 92,340 sq km. **Location:** In E central Europe. **Neighbors:** Slovakia, Ukraine on N; Austria on W; Slovenia, Serbia, Croatia on S; Romania on E. **Topography:** The Danube R. forms Slovak border in NW, then swings S to bisect the country. Eastern half of Hungary is mainly a great fertile plain, the Alfold; the W and N are hilly. **Capital:** Budapest, 1,693,000.

Government: Type: Parliamentary democracy. **Head of state:** Pres. László Sólyom; b. Jan. 3, 1942; in office: Aug. 5, 2005. **Head of gov.:** Prime Min. Ferenc Gyurcsány; b. June 4, 1961; in office: Sept. 29, 2004. **Local divisions:** 19 counties, 20 urban counties, 1 capital. **Defense budget:** $1.30 bil. **Active troops:** 32,300.

Economy: Industries: mining, metallurgy, constr. materials, proc. foods, textiles, pharm., auto. **Chief crops:** wheat, corn, sunflower seed, potatoes, sugar beets. **Natural resources:** bauxite, coal, nat. gas, fertile soils. **Crude oil reserves:** 20.2 mil bbls. **Arable land:** 50%. **Livestock:** cattle: 708,000; chickens: 31.9 mil; goats: 80,000; pigs: 3.9 mil; sheep: 1.4 mil. **Fish catch:** 21,270 metric tons. **Electricity prod.:** 33.7 bil kWh. **Labor force** (2003): agriculture 5.5%, industry 33.3%, services 61.2%.

Finance: Monetary unit: Forint (HUF) (Sept. 2007: 183.46 = $1 U.S.). **GDP:** $175.2 bil; **per capita GDP:** $17,600; **GDP growth:** 3.9%. **Imports:** $69.8 bil; Germany 27.2%, Russia 8.4%, China 7.1%, Austria 6.2%, France 4.7%, Italy 4.5%, Netherlands 4.3%, Poland 4.2%. **Exports:** $68 bil; Germany 29.5%, Italy 5.6%, Austria 5%, France 5%, UK 4.5%, Romania 4.2%, Poland 4%. **Tourism:** $4.3 bil. **Budget:** $59.6 bil. **Intl. reserves less gold:** $14.31 bil. **Gold:** 100,000 oz t. **Consumer prices:** 3.88%.

Transport: Railroad: Length: 4,932 mi. **Motor vehicles:** 2.8 mil pass. cars; 414,000 comm. vehicles. **Civil aviation:** 1.9 bil pass.-mi; 20 airports. **Chief ports:** Budapest, Dunaujvaros, Gyor-Gonyu.

Communications: TV sets: 447 per 1,000 pop. **Radios:** 690 per 1,000 pop. **Telephone lines:** 3.4 mil. **Daily newspaper circ.:** 162.3 per 1,000 pop. **Internet:** 3.5 mil users.

Health: Life expect.: 68.7 male; 77.4 female. **Births** (per 1,000 pop.): 9.7. **Deaths** (per 1,000 pop.): 13.1. **Natural inc.:** −0.34%. **Infant mortality** (per 1,000 live births): 8.2. **AIDS rate:** 0.1%.

Education: Compulsory: ages 7-16. **Literacy:** 99.4%.

Major intl. organizations: UN (FAO, IBRD, ILO, IMF, IMO, WHO, WTO), EU, NATO, OECD, OSCE.

Embassy: 3910 Shoemaker St. NW 20008; 362-6730.

Website: www.hungary.hu

Earliest settlers, chiefly Slav and Germanic, were overrun by Magyars from the E. Stephen I (997-1038) was made king by Pope Sylvester II in 1000 CE. The country suffered repeated Turkish invasions in the 15th-17th centuries. After the defeats of the Turks, 1686-97, Austria dominated, but Hungary obtained concessions until it regained internal independence in 1867, under a dual monarchy with the emperor of Austria. Defeated with the Central Powers in 1918, Hungary lost Transylvania to Romania, Croatia and Bacska to Yugoslavia, and Slovakia and Carpatho-Ruthenia to Czechoslovakia, all of which had large Hungarian minorities. A republic under Michael Karolyi and a Bolshevist revolt under Bela Kun were followed by a vote for a monarchy in 1920 with Admiral Nicholas Horthy as regent.

Hungary joined Germany in WWII, and was allowed to annex most of its lost territories. Russian troops captured the country, 1944-45. By terms of an armistice with the Allied powers Hungary agreed to give up territory acquired by the 1938 dismemberment of Czechoslovakia and to return to its borders of 1937.

A republic was declared Feb. 1, 1946; Zoltan Tildy was elected president. In 1947 the Communists forced Tildy out, and a hardline, pro-Soviet government was installed. Imre Nagy, who became premier in mid-1953, favored less rigid policies, but he was ousted Apr. 18, 1955. In 1956, popular demands to restore Nagy were heeded Oct. 23. Demonstrations against Communist rule then developed into open revolt. On Nov. 4 Soviet forces launched a massive attack against Budapest with 200,000 troops, 2,500 tanks and armored cars. About 200,000 persons fled the country. Thousands were arrested and executed, including Nagy in June 1958. In spring 1963 the regime freed many captives from the 1956 revolt.

Hungarian troops participated in the 1968 Warsaw Pact invasion of Czechoslovakia. Major economic reforms were launched early in 1968, switching from a central planning system to one based on market forces and profit.

In 1989 Parliament legalized freedom of assembly and association as Hungary shifted away from Communism. In Oct. the Communist Party was formally dissolved. The last Soviet troops left Hungary June 19, 1991. Hungary became a full member of NATO Mar. 12, 1999, and of the EU May 1, 2004.

A leaked recording in which Prime Min. Ferenc Gyurcsány admitted lying "morning, evening, and night" about the economy before Apr. 2006 elections sparked mass protests calling for his resignation in Sept. Tens of thousands of protesters took part in another anti-Gyurcsány rally in Budapest, Mar. 15, 2007.

Iceland
Republic of Iceland

People: Population: 301,931. **Age distrib. (%):** <15: 21.4; 65+: 11.8. **Pop. density:** 8 per sq mi, 3 per sq km. **Urban:** 92.8%. **Ethnic groups:** Icelandic 94%. **Principal languages:** Icelandic (official), English, Nordic languages, German widely spoken. **Chief religion:** Evangelical Lutheran (official) 86%.

Geography: Total area: 39,769 sq mi, 103,000 sq km; **Land area:** 38,707 sq mi, 100,250 sq km. **Location:** Isl. at N end of Atlantic O. **Neighbors:** Nearest is Greenland (Den.) to W. **Topography:** Recent volcanic origin. Three-quarters of surface is wasteland: glaciers, lakes, a lava desert. There are geysers and hot springs, and the climate is moderated by the Gulf Stream. **Capital:** Reykjavík, 185,000.

Government: Type: Constitutional republic. **Head of state:** Pres. Olafur Ragnar Grímsson; b. May 14, 1943; in office: Aug. 1, 1996. **Head of gov.:** Prime Min. Geir H. Haarde; b. Apr. 8, 1951; in office: June 15, 2006. **Local divisions:** 23 counties, 14 independent towns. **Defense budget:** NA. **Active troops:** None (budget mainly for coast guard).

Economy: Industries: fish proc., aluminum smelting, ferrosilicon prod., tourism. **Chief crops:** potatoes, green vegetables. **Natural resources:** fish, hydropower, geothermal power, diatomite. **Arable land:** 1%. **Livestock:** cattle: 63,375; chickens: 213,000; goats: 433; pigs: 41,152; sheep: 451,559. **Fish catch:** 1,669,287 metric tons. **Electricity prod.:** 8.5 bil kWh. **Labor force** (2005): agriculture 5.1%, industry 23%, services 71.4%.

Finance: Monetary unit: Krona (ISK) (Sept. 2007: 64.64 = $1 U.S.). **GDP:** $11.4 bil; **per capita GDP:** $38,000; **GDP growth:** 2.6%. **Imports:** $5.2 bil; Germany 13%, U.S. 9%, Norway 7.6%, Sweden 7.6%, Denmark 6.6%, UK 5.6%, Netherlands 5.2%. **Exports:** $3.6 bil; Netherlands 17.6%, UK 16.4%, Germany 15.9%, Spain 6.8%, U.S. 6.6%. **Tourism:** $368 mil. **Budget:** $6.7 bil. **Intl. reserves less gold:** $1.53 bil. **Gold:** 60,000 oz t. **Consumer prices:** 6.69%.

Transport: Motor vehicles: 175,400 pass. cars; 24,800 comm. vehicles. **Civil aviation:** 1.9 bil pass.-mi; 5 airports. **Chief port:** Reykjavík.

Communications: TV sets: 505 per 1,000 pop. **Radios:** 1,075 per 1,000 pop. **Telephone lines:** 193,700. **Daily newspaper circ.:** 322.3 per 1,000 pop. **Internet:** 194,000 users.

Health: Life expect.: 78.3 male; 82.6 female. **Births** (per 1,000 pop.): 13.6. **Deaths** (per 1,000 pop.): 6.8. **Natural inc.:** 0.68%. **Infant mortality** (per 1,000 live births): 3.3. **AIDS rate:** 0.2%.

Education: Compulsory: ages 6-16. **Literacy:** 99%.

Major intl. organizations: UN (FAO, IBRD, ILO, IMF, IMO, WHO, WTO), EFTA, NATO, OECD, OSCE.

Embassy: 1156 15th St. NW, Ste. 1200, 20005; 265-6653.

Website: www.iceland.is

Iceland was an independent republic from 930 to 1262, when it joined with Norway. Its language has maintained its purity for 1,000 years. The Althing, or assembly, established in 930, is the world's oldest surviving parliament.

Danish rule lasted from 1380-1918; the last ties with the Danish crown were severed in 1941. A continuous 55-year U.S. military presence in Iceland ended with the closure of the Keflavík naval air station in Sept. 2006.

India
Republic of India

People: Population: 1,129,866,154. **Age distrib.** (%): <15: 31.8; 65+: 5.1. **Pop. density:** 984 per sq mi, 380 per sq km. **Urban:** 28.7%. **Ethnic groups:** Indo-Aryan 72%, Dravidian 25%. **Principal languages:** Hindi, English, Bengali, Telugu, Marathi, Tamil, Urdu, Gujarati, Malayalam, Kannada, Oriya, Punjabi, Assamese, Kashmiri, Sindhi, and Sanskrit (all official); Hindustani, a mix of Hindi and Urdu spoken in the north, is popular but not official. **Chief religions:** Hindu 81%, Muslim 13%, Christian 2%, Sikh 2%.

Geography: Total area: 1,269,346 sq mi, 3,287,590 sq km; **Land area:** 1,147,955 sq mi, 2,973,190 sq km. **Location:** Occupies most of Indian subcontinent in S Asia. **Neighbors:** Pakistan on W; China, Nepal, Bhutan on N; Myanmar, Bangladesh on E. **Topography:** The Himalaya Mts., highest in world, stretch across India's northern borders. Below, the Ganges Plain is wide, fertile, and among the most densely populated regions of the world. Area below includes Deccan Peninsula. Close to one quarter of area is forested. The climate varies from tropical heat in S to near-Arctic cold in N. Rajasthan Desert is NW; NE Assam Hills get 400 in. of rain a year. **Capital:** New Delhi, 15,048,000. **Cities** (urban aggr.): Ahmadabad 5,120,000; Bangalore 6,462,000; Chennai (Madras) 6,916,000; Hyderabad 6,115,000; Kolkata (Calcutta) 14,277,000; Mumbai (Bombay) 18,196,000.

Government: Type: Federal republic. **Head of state:** Pres. Pratibha Patil; b. Dec. 19, 1934; in office: July 25, 2007. **Head of gov.:** Prime Min. Manmohan Singh; b. Sept. 26, 1932; in office: May 22, 2004. **Local divisions:** 28 states, 6 union territories, 1 national capital territory. **Defense budget:** $22.3 bil. **Active troops:** 1,316,000.

Economy: Industries: textiles, chemicals, food proc., steel, transp. equip., cement, mining, oil, machinery, software. **Chief crops:** rice, wheat, oilseed, cotton, jute, tea, sugarcane, potatoes. **Natural resources:** coal, iron ore, mang., mica, bauxite, titanium ore, chromite, nat. gas, diamonds, oil, limestone. **Crude oil reserves:** 5.6 bil bbls. **Arable land:** 49%. **Livestock:** cattle: 180.8 mil; chickens: 475 mil; goats: 124.9 mil; pigs: 14 mil; sheep: 62.9 mil. **Fish catch:** 6,318,887 metric tons. **Electricity prod.:** 661.6 bil kWh. **Labor force** (2003): agriculture 60%, industry 12%, services 28%.

Finance: Monetary unit: Rupee (INR) (Sept. 2007: 40.45 = $1 U.S.). **GDP:** $4.2 tril; **per capita GDP:** $3,800; **GDP growth:** 9.2%. **Imports:** $187.9 bil; China 8.5%, U.S. 5.9%, Germany 4.5%, Singapore 4.5%. **Exports:** $112 bil; U.S. 17.4%, UAE 8.5%, China 7.9%, UK 4.4%. **Tourism:** $3.9 bil. **Budget:** $143.8 bil. **Intl. reserves less gold:** $113.49 bil. **Gold:** 11.5 mil oz t. **Consumer prices:** 5.8%.

Transport: Railroad: Length: 39,289 mi. **Motor vehicles:** 8.6 mil pass. cars; 10.9 mil comm. vehicles. **Civil aviation:** 19.4 bil pass.-mi; 243 airports. **Chief ports:** Chennai (Madras), Kandla, Kolkata (Calcutta), Mumbai (Bombay), Vishakhapatnam.

Communications: TV sets: 75 per 1,000 pop. **Radios:** 120 per 1,000 pop. **Telephone lines:** 40.8 mil. **Daily newspaper circ.:** 60 per 1,000 pop. **Internet:** 858.22 mil users.

Health: Life expect.: 66.3 male; 71.2 female. **Births** (per 1,000 pop.): 22.7. **Deaths** (per 1,000 pop.): 6.6. **Natural inc.:** 1.61%. **Infant mortality** (per 1,000 live births): 34.6. **AIDS rate:** 0.9%.

Education: Compulsory: ages 6-14. **Literacy:** 61%.

Major intl. organizations: UN (FAO, IBRD, ILO, IMF, IMO, WHO, WTO), the Commonwealth.

Embassy: 2107 Massachusetts Ave. NW 20008; 939-7000.

Website: www.india.gov.in

India has one of the oldest civilizations in the world. Excavations trace the Indus Valley civilization back for at least 5,000 years. Paintings in the mountain caves of Ajanta, richly carved temples, the Taj Mahal in Agra, and the Kutab Minar in Delhi are among relics of the past.

Aryan tribes, speaking Sanskrit, invaded from the northwest around 1500 BCE. Asoka ruled most of the Indian subcontinent in the 3rd cent. BCE, and established Buddhism. But Hinduism revived and eventually predominated. Under the Guptas, 4th-6th cent. CE, science, literature, and the arts enjoyed a "golden age."

Arab invaders established a Muslim foothold in the west in the 8th cent., and Turkish Muslims gained control of North India by 1200. The Mogul emperors ruled 1526-1857.

Vasco da Gama established Portuguese trading posts 1498-1503. The Dutch followed. The British East India Co. sent Capt. William Hawkins, 1609, to get concessions from the Mogul emperor for spices and textiles. Operating as the East India Co. the British gained control of most of India. The British parliament assumed political direction; under Lord Bentinck, 1828-35, rule by rajahs was curbed. After the Sepoy troops mutinied, 1857-58, the British supported the native rulers.

Nationalism grew rapidly after WWI. The Indian National Congress and the Muslim League demanded constitutional reform. A leader emerged in Mohandas K. Gandhi (called Mahatma, or Great Soul), b. Oct. 2, 1869, assassinated Jan. 30, 1948. He advocated self-rule, nonviolence, and removal of the caste system of untouchability. In 1930 he launched a program of civil disobedience, including a boycott of British goods and rejection of taxes without representation.

In 1935 Britain gave India a constitution providing a bicameral federal congress. Muhammad Ali Jinnah, head of the Muslim League, sought creation of a Muslim nation, Pakistan.

The British government partitioned British India into the dominions of India and Pakistan. India became a member of the UN in 1945, a self-governing member of the Commonwealth in 1947, and a democratic republic, Jan. 26, 1950. More than 12 mil Hindu and Muslim refugees crossed the India-Pakistan borders in a mass transferal of some of the 2 peoples during 1947; about 200,000 were killed in communal fighting.

After Pakistan troops began attacks on Bengali separatists in East Pakistan, Mar. 25, 1971, some 10 mil refugees fled into India. India and Pakistan went to war Dec. 3, 1971, on both the east and west fronts. Pakistan troops in the east surrendered Dec. 16; Pakistan agreed to a cease-fire in the west Dec. 17.

Indira Gandhi, India's prime minister since Jan. 1966, invoked emergency powers in June 1975. Thousands of opponents were arrested and press censorship imposed. These and other actions, including enforcement of coercive birth control measures in some areas, were widely resented. Opposition parties, united in the Janata coalition, turned Gandhi's New Congress Party from power in federal and state parliamentary elections in 1977.

Gandhi became prime minister for the second time, Jan. 14, 1980. She was assassinated by 2 of her Sikh bodyguards Oct. 31, 1984, in response to the government suppression of a Sikh uprising in Punjab in June 1984, which included an assault on the Golden Temple at Amritsar, the holiest Sikh shrine. Widespread rioting followed the assassination; thousands of Sikhs were killed and some 50,000 left homeless. Rajiv, Indira Gandhi's son, replaced her as prime minister. He was swept from office in 1989 amid charges of incompetence and corruption, and assassinated May 21, 1991, while campaigning to regain power.

A gas leak at a Union Carbide chemical plant in Bhopal, in Dec. 1984, eventually killed an estimated 14,000 people. A lawsuit settled in 1989 provided $470 mil in compensation to victims; in 2002 an Indian High Court upheld a culpable homicide conviction against former UC chairman Warren Anderson.

Many died in religious, ethnic, and political conflicts during the 1980s and '90s. To suppress the Sikh insurgency in Punjab, Indian government troops attacked the Golden Temple again in 1988. Nationwide riots followed the destruction of a 16th-cent. mosque by Hindu militants in Dec. 1992. Ethnic clashes in Assam, in northwest

India, killed thousands in Feb. 1993. Bombs jolted Mumbai and Kolkata, Mar. 12-19, killing over 300.

Mother Teresa, renowned for her work among the poor, died Sept. 5, 1997. India's first lowest-caste president, K. R. Narayanan, took office July 25. The Hindu nationalist Bharatiya Janata Party (BJP) won enough seats in parliamentary elections, Feb. 1998, to form a government. Atal Bihari Vajpayee was sworn in as prime minister Mar. 19. India conducted a series of nuclear tests in mid-May, drawing wide condemnation and raising tensions with Pakistan.

An alliance led by Vajpayee won a majority in legislative elections, Sept. 5-Oct. 3, 1999. A cyclone that hit the state of Orissa, East India, on Oct. 29, 1999, left some 10,000 people dead. A powerful earthquake in Gujarat struck on Jan. 26, 2001, claimed more than 20,000 lives. India blamed Pakistani-sponsored terrorist groups for an Oct. 1 suicide attack on the state legislature in Jammu and Kashmir (see below), in which at least 40 people died, and a Dec. 13 assault on the state parliament in New Delhi Dec. 13, which left 13 people dead. Hindu-Muslim clashes in Gujarat Feb. 27-Mar. 11, 2002, claimed more than 700 lives. A. P. J. Abdul Kalam, a Muslim scientist who spearheaded India's nuclear weapons program, became president July 25.

Two bombs in Mumbai, Aug. 25, 2003, killed more than 50 people; Indian authorities blamed Muslim militants. Led by Rajiv Gandhi's Italian-born widow, Sonia, the Congress Party won the most seats in parliamentary elections Apr.-May 2004. When Hindu nationalists objected to her candidacy, she chose not to become prime minister, and Manmohan Singh, a Sikh economist, took office instead.

The Indian Ocean tsunami of Dec. 26, 2004, left more than 10,700 people dead, some 5,600 missing, and over 647,000 displaced. An agreement reached during U.S. Pres. Bush's visit to New Delhi, Mar. 2, 2006, called for the U.S. to allow India to buy nuclear fuel and reactor components, and for India to permit inspections at 14 civilian nuclear plants (but not 8 military nuclear reactors). Islamic extremists were suspected in 3 bombings in New Delhi, Oct. 29, 2005, that killed more than 60 people, and 7 blasts in Mumbai, July 11, 2006, that killed more than 200 on commuter trains. Pratibha Patil took office July 25, 2007 as India's first female president. Monsoon floods, July-Sept., killed more than 2,600 people and severely damaged 575,000 homes.

Despite robust economic growth since the 1990s, especially in high-technology industries, nearly 80% of India's population still earns less than $2 per day. According to the UN, 2.5 mil people in India have HIV/AIDS, fewer than previously estimated.

Sikkim, bordered by Tibet, Bhutan, and Nepal, formerly British protected, became a protectorate of India in 1950. Area, 2,740 sq mi; pop. (2001 census): 540,493; capital: Gangtok. In Sept. 1974, India's parliament voted to make Sikkim an associate state, absorbing it into India.

Kashmir is a predominantly Muslim region in the NW that borders India, Pakistan, Afghanistan, and China. Originally a Hindu kingdom, Muslim rule began in 1341; after almost 200 years under the Moguls, the area was incorporated into British India in 1846. Fighting broke out in the region between India and Pakistan in 1947 following independence from Britain. A cease-fire was negotiated by the UN Jan. 1, 1949; it gave Pakistan control of one-third of the area as Azad Kashmir, in the west and northwest, and India the remaining two-thirds, as the Indian state of Jammu and Kashmir. It is India's only Muslim-majority state. Area: 39,146 sq mi; pop. (2001 census): 10,000,000; capitals: Srinagar (summer) and Jammu (winter). Fighting returned to the area during the 1965 and 1971 wars with Pakistan. China occupied about 14,000 sq mi in the Ladakh district after a war with India in 1962.

In the 1990s there were repeated clashes between Indian army troops and separatist fighters triggered by India's decision to impose central government rule. The clashes strained relations between India and Pakistan, which India charged was aiding the separatists; fighting was especially heavy in May-June 1999. As 2002 began, some 1 mil Indian and Pakistani troops faced each other across the "line of control" that divides Kashmir. Tensions escalated when Muslim gunmen May 14 killed 34 people, many of them women and children, at an army base near Jammu, and Pakistan conducted missile tests May 25-28. U.S. mediation in June helped ease the crisis. Legislative elections were held Sept.-Oct. 2002.

A cease-fire between Indian and Pakistani troops along the line of control took effect Nov. 25, 2003, but clashes between Indian forces and Islamic militants continued. Estimates of conflict-related deaths since 1989 range from 40,000 to over 80,000. A powerful earthquake Oct. 8, 2005, killed about 80,000 and left up to 3 mil homeless in Pakistani-held Kashmir and northern Pakistan.

France, 1952-54, peacefully yielded to India its 5 colonies, former French India, comprising Pondicherry, Karikal, Mahe, Yanaon (which became **Pondicherry Union Territory,** area 190 sq mi; pop. (2001 census): 973,829 and Chandernagor (which was incorporated into the state of **West Bengal.**

Indonesia
Republic of Indonesia

People: Population: 234,693,997. **Age distrib. (%):** <15: 28.7; 65+: 5.7. **Pop. density:** 333 per sq mi, 128 per sq km. **Urban:**
48.1%. **Ethnic groups:** Javanese 41%, Sundanese 15%, Madurese 3%. **Principal languages:** Bahasa Indonesia (official, modified form of Malay), English, Dutch, Javanese, other dialects. **Chief religions:** Muslim 87%, Protestant 6%, Roman Catholic 3%, Hindu 2%, Buddhist 1%.

Geography: Total area: 741,100 sq mi, 1,919,440 sq km; **Land area:** 705,192 sq mi, 1,826,440 sq km. **Location:** Archipelago SE of Asian mainland along the Equator. **Neighbors:** Malaysia on N, Papua New Guinea on E, Timor-Leste on S. **Topography:** Indonesia comprises over 13,500 islands (6,000 inhabited), including Java (one of the most densely populated areas in the world with over 2,000 persons per sq mi), Sumatra, Kalimantan (most of Borneo), Sulawesi (Celebes), and West Irian (Irian Jaya, the W half of New Guinea). Also: Bangka, Billiton, Madura, Bali, Timor. The mountains and plateaus on the major islands have a cooler climate than the tropical lowlands. **Capital:** Jakarta, 13,215,000. **Cities (urban aggr.):** Bandung, 4,126,000; Surabaja, 2,992,000.

Government: Type: Republic. **Head of state and gov.:** Susilo Bambang Yudhoyono; b. Sept. 9, 1949; in office: Oct. 20, 2004. **Local divisions:** 30 provinces, 2 special regions, 1 capital district. **Defense budget:** $2.59 bil. **Active troops:** 302,000.

Economy: Industries: oil & nat. gas, textiles, apparel & footwear, mining, cement, fertilizers, plywood, rubber. **Chief crops:** rice, cassava, peanuts, rubber, cocoa, coffee, palm oil, copra. **Natural resources:** oil, tin, nat. gas, nickel, timber, bauxite, copper, coal, gold, silver. **Crude oil reserves:** 4.3 bil bbls. **Arable land:** 11%. **Livestock:** cattle: 11.2 mil; chickens: 1.4 bil; goats: 14.1 mil; pigs: 7.1 mil; sheep: 8.5 mil. **Fish catch:** 5,578,369 metric tons. **Electricity prod.:** 120.3 bil kWh. **Labor force** (2004 est.): agriculture 43.3%, industry 18%, services 38.7%.

Finance: Monetary unit: Rupiah (IDR) (Sept. 2007: 9,366.10 = $1 U.S.). **GDP:** $948.3 bil; **per capita GDP:** $3,900; **GDP growth:** 5.5%. **Imports:** $77.7 bil; Singapore 30.3%, China 11.5%, Japan 9%, Malaysia 5%, Thailand 4.1%, Australia 4%. **Exports:** $102.3 bil; Japan 19.3%, Singapore 11.8%, U.S. 11.5%, South Korea 7.8%, China 7.7%. **Tourism:** $4.5 bil. **Budget:** $79.5 bil. **Intl. reserves less gold:** $27.21 bil. **Gold:** 2.35 mil oz t. **Consumer prices:** 13.11%.

Transport: Railroad: Length: 4,013 mi. **Motor vehicles:** 3.9 mil pass. cars; 2.8 mil comm. vehicles. **Civil aviation:** 13.2 bil pass.-mi; 159 airports. **Chief ports:** Banjarmasin, Ciwandan, Palembang, Panjang, Sungai Pakning.

Communications: TV sets: 143 per 1,000 pop. **Radios:** 155 per 1,000 pop. **Telephone lines:** 14.8 mil. **Daily newspaper circ.:** 22.9 per 1,000 pop. **Internet:** 16 mil users.

Health: Life expect.: 67.7 male; 72.8 female. **Births** (per 1,000 pop.): 19.7. **Deaths** (per 1,000 pop.): 6.3. **Natural inc.:** 1.34%. **Infant mortality** (per 1,000 live births): 32.1. **AIDS rate:** 0.1%.

Education: Compulsory: ages 7-15. **Literacy:** 90.4%.

Major intl. organizations: UN and all of its specialized agencies, APEC, ASEAN, OPEC.

Embassy: 2020 Massachusetts Ave. NW 20036; 775-5200. **Website:** www.presidenri.go.id

Hindu and Buddhist civilization from India reached Indonesia nearly 2,000 years ago, taking root especially in Java. Islam spread along the maritime trade routes in the 15th cent., and became predominant by the 16th cent. The Dutch replaced the Portuguese as the area's most important European trade power in the 17th cent., securing territorial control over Java by 1750. The outer islands were not finally subdued until the early 20th cent., when the full area of present-day Indonesia was united under one rule for the first time.

Following Japanese occupation, 1942-45, nationalists led by Sukarno and Hatta declared independence. The Netherlands ceded sovereignty Dec. 27, 1949, after 4 years of fighting. A republic was declared, Aug. 17, 1950, with Sukarno as president. West Irian, on New Guinea, remained under Dutch control. After the Dutch in 1957 rejected proposals for new negotiations over West Irian, Indonesia stepped up the seizure of Dutch property. In 1963 the UN turned the area (later renamed Irian Jaya and now known as Papua) over to Indonesia, which promised a plebiscite. In 1969, voting by tribal chiefs favored staying with Indonesia, despite an uprising and widespread opposition.

Sukarno suspended Parliament in 1960 and was named president for life in 1963. He made close alliances with Communist governments. In Sept. 1965 an attempted coup in which several military officers were murdered was successfully put down, but Sukarno was forced to cede power to the army, led by Gen. Suharto, who became acting president in 1967 and ruled Indonesia for the next 31 years. The regime blamed the coup on the Communist Party; more than 300,000 alleged Communists were killed in army-initiated massacres.

Parliament reelected Suharto to a 7th consecutive 5-year term Mar. 10, 1998, as a severe economic downturn focused public anger on nepotism, cronyism, and corruption in the Suharto regime. Price increases in May sparked mass protests and then mob violence in Jakarta and other cities, claiming some 500 lives. Suharto resigned May 21 and was succeeded by his vice-president, Bacharuddin Jusuf Habibie. Abdurrahman Wahid, leader of Indonesia's largest Muslim organization, was elected president Oct. 20, 1999. In Aug. 2000, under pressure from the legislature, he agreed to share power with Vice Pres. Megawati Sukarnoputri, the daughter of the late Pres. Sukarno. Charging Wahid with incompetence and corruption, the legislature ousted him July 23, 2001, and Megawati became Indonesia's first woman president.

Clashes between Muslims and Christians in the Maluku (Molucca) Is., 1999-2002, claimed about 5,000 lives. Ethnic violence in Kalimantan, Borneo, killed more than 400 in Feb. 2001. East Timor, a former Portuguese colony that Indonesia invaded in Dec. 1975 and controlled until Oct. 1999, became a fully independent country May 20, 2002, as Timor-Leste. Separatists in Aceh, NW Sumatra, fought repeatedly against government troops during the 1980s and 90s; peace accords were announced in Dec. 2002 and, after that deal unraveled, in July 2005. The last of 24,000 Indonesian government troops pulled out of Aceh, Dec. 29, 2005.

Investigators blamed the Islamic terrorist group Jemaah Islamiyah, an al-Qaeda affiliate, for bombings that killed 202 people, mostly foreign tourists, at nightclubs in Bali, Oct. 12, 2002, and 12 people at a Marriott hotel in Jakarta, Aug. 5, 2003. A car bomb attack outside the Australian embassy in Jakarta, Sept. 9, 2004, killed 9 people and injured more than 180. Susilo Bambang Yudhoyono, a retired general, defeated Megawati Sept. 20 in a direct presidential runoff vote.

A massive earthquake off northwest Sumatra, Dec. 26, 2004, triggered tsunamis that wreaked havoc in the Indian Ocean region. The death toll in Indonesia alone exceeded 125,000, not counting almost 40,000 missing. Another large quake off northwest Sumatra, Mar. 28, 2005, left at least 1,300 dead. On Java in 2006, an earthquake May 27 killed 5,800, left 1.5 mil homeless, and caused damage estimated at $3.1 bil; a tsunami July 17 claimed at least 650 lives. Floods in Jakarta, Feb. 2007, left 54 people dead and 400,000 displaced. Two top leaders of the Jemaah Islamiyah terror network were arrested in June.

Iran
Islamic Republic of Iran

People: Population: 65,397,521. **Age distrib.** (%): <15: 23.2; 65+: 5.4. **Pop. density:** 104 per sq mi, 40 per sq km. **Urban:** 66.9%. **Ethnic groups:** Persian 51%, Azeri 24%, Gilaki/Mazandarani 8%, Kurd 7%, Arab 3%, Lur 2%, Balochi 2%, Turkmen 2%. **Principal languages:** Farsi/Persian (official), Kurdish, Luri, Balochi, Turkic languages, Arabic, Turkish. **Chief religion:** Muslim (official; Shi'a 89%, Sunni 10%).

Geography: Total area: 636,296 sq mi, 1,648,000 sq km; **Land area:** 631,663 sq mi, 1,636,000 sq km. **Location:** Between the Middle East and S Asia. **Neighbors:** Turkey, Iraq on W; Armenia, Azerbaijan, Turkmenistan on N; Afghanistan, Pakistan on E. **Topography:** Interior highlands and plains surrounded by high mountains, up to 18,000 ft. Large salt deserts cover much of area, but there are many oases and forest areas. Most of population inhabits N and NW. **Capital:** Tehran, 7,314,000. **Cities (urban aggr.):** Esfahan, 1,535,000; Mashhad, 2,134,000.

Government: Type: Islamic republic. **Religious head:** Ayatollah Sayyed Ali Khamenei; b. July 17, 1939; in office: June 4, 1989. **Head of state and gov.:** Pres. Mahmoud Ahmadinejad; b. Oct. 28, 1956; in office: Aug. 3, 2005. **Local divisions:** 28 provinces. **Defense budget:** $6.6 bil. **Active troops:** 545,000.

Economy: Industries: oil, petrochems., textiles, constr. materials, food proc., metal fabricating, armaments. **Chief crops:** wheat, rice, other grains, sugar beets, fruits, nuts, cotton. **Natural resources:** oil, nat. gas, coal, chromium, copper, iron ore, lead, mang., zinc, sulfur. **Crude oil reserves:** 136.3 bil bbls. **Arable land:** 10%. **Livestock:** cattle: 9.4 mil; chickens: 380 mil; goats: 25.8 mil; sheep: 52.2 mil. **Fish catch:** 527,912 metric tons. **Electricity prod.:** 170.4 bil kWh. **Labor force** (2001 est.): agriculture 30%, industry 25%, services 45%.

Finance: Monetary unit: Rial (IRR) (Sept. 2007: 9,314.00 = $1 U.S.). **GDP:** $599.2 bil; **per capita GDP:** $8,700; **GDP growth:** 4.3%. **Imports:** $45.5 bil; Germany 12.1%, China 10.6%, UAE 9.4%, South Korea 6.2%, France 5.6%, Italy 5.4%. **Exports:** $63.2 bil; Japan 14.1%, China 12.9%, Turkey 7.3%, Italy 6.3%, South Korea 5.7%. **Tourism:** $1.1 bil. **Budget:** $100.6 bil. **Consumer prices:** 13.43%.

Transport: Railroad: Length: 4,509 mi. **Motor vehicles:** 1.5 mil pass. cars; 431,200 comm. vehicles. **Civil aviation:** 6.4 bil pass.-mi; 129 airports. **Chief ports:** Assaluyeh, Bushehr.

Communications: TV sets: 154 per 1,000 pop. **Radios:** 265 per 1,000 pop. **Telephone lines:** 22 mil. **Internet:** 18 mil users.

Health: Life expect.: 69.1 male; 72.1 female. **Births** (per 1,000 pop.): 16.6. **Deaths** (per 1,000 pop.): 5.7. **Natural inc.:** 1.09%. **Infant mortality** (per 1,000 live births): 38.1. **AIDS rate:** 0.2%.

Education: Compulsory: ages 6-10. **Literacy:** 82.4%.

Major intl. organizations: UN (FAO, IBRD, ILO, IMF, IMO, WHO), OPEC.

Iranian Interests Section: 2209 Wisconsin Ave. NW 20007; 965-4990.

Website: www.spk-gov.ir

Iran was once called Persia. The Iranians, who supplanted an earlier agricultural civilization, came from the east during the 2nd millennium BCE; they were an Indo-European group related to the Aryans of India. In 549 BCE Cyrus the Great united the Medes and Persians in the Persian Empire; he conquered Babylonia in 538 BCE, and restored Jerusalem to the Jews. Alexander the Great conquered Persia in 333 BCE, but Persians regained independence in the next century under the Parthians, themselves succeeded by

Sassanian Persians in 226 CE. Arabs brought Islam to Persia in the 7th cent., replacing the indigenous Zoroastrian faith. After Persian political and cultural autonomy was reasserted in the 9th cent., arts and sciences flourished.

Turks and Mongols ruled Persia in turn from the 11th cent. to 1502, when Ismael I established the Iranian Safavid dynasty and made Shiite Islam the official religion. The dynasty lasted until 1722. The British and Russian empires vied for influence in the 19th cent.; Afghanistan was severed from Iran by Britain in 1857.

Reza Khan, a military officer, became prime min., 1923, and shah in 1925. He began modernization, curbed foreign influence, and officially changed the country's name from Persia to Iran in 1935. Fearing the shah's Axis sympathies, British and Soviet troops forced him to abdicate, 1941; he was succeeded by his son, Mohammad Reza Pahlavi. With U.S. backing, he brought economic and social change to Iran (the "White Revolution"), but repression, often severe, of opposition groups intensified. Violent protests in 1978 eventually forced the shah to depart, Jan. 16, 1979. Shiite leader Ayatollah Ruhollah Khomeini, exiled by the shah in 1963, returned to Tehran, Feb. 1, and by Feb. 11 pro-Khomeini forces had defeated government troops. Khomeini established an Islamic theocracy.

Iranian militants seized the U.S. embassy Nov. 4, 1979 and took hostages including 62 Americans. Despite international condemnations and U.S. efforts, including an abortive Apr. 1980 rescue attempt, the crisis continued. The U.S. broke diplomatic relations with Iran, Apr. 7. The shah died in Egypt, July 27. The hostage drama ended Jan. 20, 1981, when an accord, involving the release of frozen Iranian assets, was reached.

A dispute over the Shatt al-Arab waterway situated between Iran and Iraq led to a long and costly war between the 2 countries, 1980-88, killing hundreds of thousands of people. In Nov. 1986 it became known that the U.S., which had generally sided with Iraq during the war, had secretly shipped arms to Iran to gain that country's help in obtaining the release of U.S. hostages held in Lebanon. The revelation sparked a major scandal in the U.S. A U.S. Navy warship shot down an Iranian airliner, July 3, 1988, after mistaking it for an F-14 fighter jet; all 290 aboard the plane died.

An earthquake struck northern Iran June 21, 1990, killing more than 45,000, injuring 100,000, and leaving 400,000 homeless. Some 1 mil Kurdish refugees fled from Iraq to Iran following the Persian Gulf War of 1991. To curb Iran's alleged support for international terrorism, the U.S. in 1996 authorized sanctions on foreign companies that invest there.

Mohammad Khatami, a moderate Shiite Muslim cleric, was elected president May 23, 1997, winning nearly 70% of the vote. During the next 3 years, hardline Islamists clashed repeatedly and sometimes violently with reformers, who won a majority in parliamentary elections Feb. 18 and May 5, 2000. Inviting rapprochement with Iran, the U.S. eased some sanctions Mar. 18. Khatami was reelected June 8, 2001, with a 77% majority but continued to face resistance from religious conservatives.

The U.S.-led war in Iraq, beginning Mar. 2003, contributed to a new period of instability in Iran. In June, armed Islamist vigilantes harassed students who were holding pro-democracy protests in Tehran and other cities. An earthquake Dec. 26 in Bam, southeast Iran, killed about 26,000 people. After the Guardian Council, dominated by religious conservatives, disqualified some 2,400 reformist candidates, hardliners won legislative elections Feb. 20, 2004.

The Guardian Council, May 22, 2005, selected 6 candidates out of 1,014 presidential aspirants. The mayor of Tehran, Mahmoud Ahmadinejad, a religious conservative who campaigned as an economic reformer, defeated former Pres. Hashemi Rafsanjani in a runoff election June 24 and took office Aug. 3. The Bush administration, which in 2002 had called Iran part of an "axis of evil," accused the Iranian regime of seeking to build nuclear weapons, aiding Shiite militias in Iraq, and supplying rockets to Hezbollah fighters in Lebanon for use against Israel.

Seeking to halt Iran's uranium-enrichment program, the UN Security Council imposed sanctions, Dec. 23, 2006, and toughened them, Mar. 24, 2007. Easing a diplomatic standoff with the UK, Iran on Apr. 5 freed 15 British sailors and marines who had been seized in the Persian Gulf 2 weeks earlier. Negotiators for Iran and the U.S. met in Baghdad, May 28, for the first direct talks between the 2 countries in 27 years. In a speech to the UN General Assembly, Sept. 25, Ahmadinejad denounced the UN sanctions but said Iran would work with the IAEA on nuclear issues.

Iraq
Republic of Iraq

People: Population: 27,499,638. **Age distrib.** (%): <15: 39.4; 65+: 3. **Pop. density:** 165 per sq mi, 64 per sq km. **Urban:** 66.9%. **Ethnic groups:** Arab 75%-80%, Kurdish 15%-20%. **Principal languages:** Arabic (official), Kurdish (official in Kurdish regions), Assyrian, Armenian. **Chief religion:** Muslim (official; Shi'a 60%-65%, Sunni 32%-37%).

Geography: Total area: 168,754 sq mi, 437,072 sq km; **Land area:** 166,859 sq mi, 432,162 sq km. **Location:** In Middle East, occupying most of historic Mesopotamia. **Neighbors:** Jordan, Syria on W; Turkey on N; Iran on E; Kuwait, Saudi Arabia on S. **Topography:** Mostly an alluvial plain, including the Tigris and Euphrates rivers, descending from mountains in N to desert in SW. Persian

Gulf region is marshland. **Capital:** Baghdad, 5,904,000. **Cities (urban aggr.):** Basra 837,000; Mosul 1,234,000; Erbil 925,000

Government: Type: In transition. **Head of state:** Pres. Jalal Talabani; b. 1933; in office: Apr. 7, 2005. **Head of gov.:** Prime Min. Nouri Kamel al-Maliki; b. 1950; in office: May 20, 2006. **Local divisions:** 18 governorates (1 in Kurdish Autonomous Region). **Defense budget:** NA. **Active troops:** 227,000.

Economy: Industries: oil, chemicals, textiles, constr. materials, food proc. **Chief crops:** wheat, barley, rice, vegetables, dates, cotton. **Natural resources:** oil, nat. gas, phosphates, sulfur. **Arable land:** 13%. **Crude oil reserves:** 115 bil bbls. **Livestock:** cattle: 1.5 mil; chickens: 33 mil; goats: 1.7 mil; sheep: 6.2 mil. **Fish catch:** 32,970 metric tons. **Electricity prod.:** 32 bil kWh. **Labor force:** NA.

Finance: Monetary unit: Dinar (IQD) (Sept. 2007: 1,232.50 = $1 U.S.). **GDP:** $50.7 bil; **per capita GDP:** $2,900; **GDP growth:** 2.4%. **Imports:** $20.8 bil; Syria 26.9%, Turkey 20.6%, U.S. 12%, Jordan 7.3%. **Exports:** $32.2 bil; U.S. 46.6%, Italy 10.7%, Canada 6.2%, Spain 6.1%. **Tourism:** $45 mil. **Budget:** $41 bil. **Intl. reserves less gold:** $12.99 bil. **Gold:** 190,000 oz t.

Transport: Railroad: Length: 1,367 mi. **Motor vehicles:** 753,000 pass. cars; 345,000 comm. vehicles. **Civil aviation:** 77 airports. **Chief ports:** Al Basrah, Umm Qasr.

Communications: TV sets: 82 per 1,000 pop. **Radios:** 229 per 1,000 pop. **Telephone lines:** 1 mil. **Internet:** 36,000 users.

Health: Life expect.: 68 male; 70.7 female. **Births** (per 1,000 pop.): 31.4. **Deaths** (per 1,000 pop.): 5.3. **Natural inc.:** 2.62%. **Infant mortality** (per 1,000 live births): 47. **AIDS rate:** NA.

Education: Compulsory: ages 6-11. **Literacy:** 74.1%.

Major intl. organizations: UN (FAO, IBRD, ILO, IMF, IMO, WHO), AL, OPEC.

Iraqi Interests Section: 1801 P St. NW 20036; 483-7500.

Website: www.iraqigovernment.org

The Tigris-Euphrates valley, formerly called Mesopotamia, was the site of one of the earliest civilizations in the world. Mesopotamia ceased to be a separate entity after the Persian, Greek, and Arab conquests. The Arabs founded Baghdad, from where the caliph ruled a vast Islamic empire in the 8th and 9th centuries. Mongol and Turkish conquests led to a decline in the region's population, economy, cultural life, and irrigation system.

Britain secured a League of Nations mandate over Iraq after WWI. Independence under a king came in 1932. Rebellious army officers killed King Faisal II, July 14, 1958, and established a leftist, pan-Arab republic, which pursued close ties with the USSR. Successive regimes were increasingly dominated by the Baath Arab Socialist Party. A Baath leader, Saddam Hussein, became president of Iraq, July 16, 1979. After purging his enemies, he ruled as a dictator for more than 2 decades, repressing Iraq's Kurds and Shiites and launching disastrous wars against 2 neighboring nations, Iran and Kuwait. Hussein sought weapons of mass destruction; Israeli planes destroyed a nuclear reactor near Baghdad June 7, 1981, claiming it could be used to produce nuclear weapons.

After skirmishing intermittently for 10 months over the sovereignty of the disputed Shatt al-Arab waterway that divides the two countries, Iraq and Iran entered into open warfare on Sept. 22, 1980. Iran repulsed early Iraqi advances, producing a long and costly stalemate; hundreds of thousands of Iraqis lost their lives during the 8-year conflict. Hussein used poison gas against Iraqi Kurds in 1988, killing up to 5,000 people in Halabja, the first mass use of poison gas against civilians since the Holocaust.

Iraq attacked and overran Kuwait Aug. 2, 1990. Backed by the UN, a U.S.-led coalition launched air and missile attacks on Iraq, Jan. 16, 1991. The coalition began a ground attack to retake Kuwait Feb. 23. Iraqi forces showed little resistance and were soundly defeated in 4 days. Over 175,000 Iraqis were taken prisoner, and Iraqi casualties were estimated at over 85,000. As part of the cease-fire agreement, Iraq agreed to scrap all poison gas and germ weapons and allow UN observers to inspect the sites. UN trade sanctions would remain in effect until Iraq complied with all terms.

In Feb. 1991, Iraqi troops drove Kurdish insurgents and civilians to the borders of Iran and Turkey, causing a refugee crisis. The U.S. and allies established havens inside Iraq for the Kurds. The U.S. launched a missile attack aimed at Iraq's intelligence headquarters in Baghdad June 26, 1993, citing evidence that Iraq had sponsored a plot to kill former Pres. George Bush.

Iraqi cooperation with UN weapons inspection teams was intermittent throughout the 1990s. On Dec. 9, 1996, the UN began a program intended to allow Baghdad to sell limited amounts of oil for food and medicine. An independent panel later concluded that there was massive corruption in UN administration of the program, allowing the Iraqi regime to reap huge profits (aside from the large profits through oil smuggling).

Iraqi resistance to UN access to suspected weapons sites touched off diplomatic crises during 1997-98, culminating in intensive U.S. and British aerial bombardment of Iraqi military targets, Dec. 16-19, 1998. After 2 years of sporadic activity, U.S. and British warplanes struck harder at sites near Baghdad on Feb. 16, 2001.

In a speech before the UN, Sept. 12, 2002, Pres. George W. Bush demanded that Iraq eliminate weapons of mass destruction, refrain from supporting terrorism, and end repression. Under Security Council Resolution 1441, approved Nov. 8, Iraq allowed UN inspectors to search for banned weapons, while the U.S. and Britain built up troops in the Persian Gulf. Despite opposition from some

countries, including France, Germany, and Russia, a U.S.-led coalition launched an invasion of Iraq on the evening of Mar. 19, 2003. By Apr. 6 the British controlled Basra and other areas in the south, and the U.S. entered Baghdad Apr. 7. Hussein had disappeared, the Iraqi government had collapsed, and most of Iraq's armed forces had dissolved into the civilian population. On May 1, Pres. Bush declared that major combat there was over. Continuing searches failed to find evidence of usable chemical, biological, or nuclear weapons the U.S. and other countries claimed Iraq had stockpiled.

The U.S. initially governed Iraq through a Coalition Provisional Authority, headed by L. Paul Bremer. A 25-member Iraqi Governing Council was appointed and named a cabinet Sept. 1, 2003. Reconstruction efforts continued but were hampered by guerrilla attacks from Baath remnants, Islamic extremists, and others. Iraqi resistance activities widened with the bombings of the Jordanian embassy, Aug. 7; the UN headquarters in Baghdad, Aug. 19, killing UN special envoy Sergio Vieira de Mello and 21 others; and a blast in Najaf Aug. 29 that killed at least 83 people, including Ayatollah Mohammad Bakir al-Hakim, a Shiite leader. After a second bombing at its Baghdad headquarters Sept. 22, the UN scaled back its presence in Iraq.

Photographs released in Apr. 2004 graphically showed instances of physical abuse and sexual humiliation of Iraqi inmates by U.S. military personnel at Baghdad's Abu Ghraib prison in fall 2003. The images sparked widespread condemnation and U.S. criminal proceedings against some individuals.

Coalition forces succeeded in neutralizing many leaders of the former regime. Two of Hussein's sons, Uday and Qusay, were killed July 22, 2003, by U.S. troops in Mosul. Saddam Hussein was captured in an underground hideout Dec. 13; he appeared before an Iraqi tribunal July 1, 2004, and was charged with crimes against humanity committed in 1982 at the Shiite village of Dujail. His trial, which began Oct. 19, 2005, was marred by murders of several lawyers representing him and his co-defendants. In a 2nd trial, which began Aug. 21, 2006, he faced charges of genocide for crimes against the Kurds in the late 1980s. Before the 2nd trial could be concluded, he was sentenced to death Nov. 5 for the Dujail killings and hanged Dec. 30.

On June 28, 2004, U.S. authorities officially transferred sovereignty to a transitional Iraqi government led by Prime Min. Iyad Allawi. Despite threats by insurgents, an estimated 8 mil people in Iraq, mostly Shiites and Kurds, cast ballots Jan. 30, 2005, for a 275-member transitional national assembly. On Apr. 6, the assembly elected Jalal al-Talabani, a Kurd, as president; Ibrahim al-Jaafari, a Shiite, became prime minister. The insurgents launched new waves of attacks, killing hundreds of police and army recruits. Rumors of a suicide bomber set off a stampede by Shiite pilgrims in northern Baghdad Aug. 31, killing close to 1,000 people. The U.S. blamed Jordanian militant Abu Musab al-Zarqawi, leader of the terrorist group Al Qaeda in Iraq, for directing a series of kidnappings, beheadings, and suicide bombings. He was killed by a U.S. air strike, June 7, 2006.

Legislative elections were held Dec. 15, 2005, and official results announced Jan. 20, 2006, but political wrangling delayed installation of a new government, headed by Shiite leader Nouri Kamel al-Maliki, until May 20. Meanwhile, a bomb Feb. 22 that destroyed the dome of Samarra's Golden Mosque, a Shiite shrine, triggered an intensification of sectarian violence between Sunnis and Shiites, much of it in Baghdad. The Iraqi civilian death toll averaged more than 2,800 per month, Jan.-Dec. 2006, and about 1,900 per month, Jan.-Aug. 2007. At mid-2007, some 1.5 mil Iraqi refugees were in Syria and 750,000 in Jordan; up to 2 mil Iraqis were internally displaced.

In early 2007, Lt. Gen. David H. Petraeus became the top U.S. military commander in Iraq; a "surge" elevated U.S. troop strength from 132,000 in Jan. to 168,000 in Sept., the highest since the war began. Many of the reinforcements were sent to the Baghdad area. U.S. officials claimed the security situation was improving, especially in Anbar Province, where Sunni clan leaders took action against Al Qaeda in Iraq. But insurgents struck elsewhere; one of the worst attacks of the war came Aug. 14 in 2 Kurdish villages near the Syrian border, as truck bombs killed at least 500 and injured 1,500 more. Iraqi religious and factional rivalries continued to impede settlement of key political and economic problems.

Also present in Iraq in Sept. 2007 were about 12,000 allied troops and tens of thousands of U.S. and other civilian advisers and contractors; the role of U.S. private security firms drew heightened scrutiny after a Baghdad shootout involving Blackwater security guards Sept. 16 left at least 8 Iraqi civilians dead. By Sept. 2007, nearly 3,800 U.S. service members had been killed and about 28,000 wounded, many from insurgents' roadside bombs, also known as improvised explosive devices (IEDs). British troop losses totaled about 170; other allies, about 130. Through the 2007 fiscal year, the U.S. Congress had appropriated an estimated $450 bil for war-related operations in Iraq.

Ireland

People: Population: 4,109,086. **Age distrib.** (%): <15: 20.8; 65+: 11.7. **Pop. density:** 154 per sq mi, 60 per sq km. **Urban:** 60.5%. **Ethnic groups:** Celtic, English minority. **Principal languages:** English, Irish Gaelic (both official); Irish Gaelic spoken by small number in western areas. **Chief religions:** Roman Catholic 88%, Church of Ireland 3%.

Geography: Total area: 27,135 sq mi, 70,280 sq km; **Land area:** 26,599 sq mi, 68,890 sq km. **Location:** In Atlantic O. just W of Great Britain. **Neighbors:** United Kingdom (Northern Ireland) on E. **Topography:** Consists of a central plateau surrounded by isolated groups of hills and mountains. Coastline is heavily indented by the Atlantic O. **Capital:** Dublin, 1,037,000.

Government: Type: Parliamentary republic. **Head of state:** Pres. Mary McAleese; b. June 27, 1951; in office: Nov. 11, 1997. **Head of gov.:** Prime Min. Bertie Ahern; b. Sept. 12, 1951; in office: June 26, 1997. **Local divisions:** 26 counties. **Defense budget:** $970 mil. **Active troops:** 10,470.

Economy: Industries: food products, brewing, textiles, clothing, pharm., chemicals. **Chief crops:** turnips, barley, potatoes, sugar beets, wheat. **Natural resources:** zinc, lead, nat. gas, barite, copper, gypsum, limestone, dolomite, peat, silver. **Arable land:** 17%. **Livestock:** cattle: 6.9 mil; chickens: 12.7 mil; goats: 7,300; pigs: 1.6 mil; sheep: 6 mil. **Fish catch:** 322,582 metric tons. **Electricity prod.:** 24.1 bil kWh. **Labor force** (2002 est.): agriculture 8%, industry 29%, services 64%.

Finance: Monetary unit: Euro (EUR) (Sept. 2007: 0.72 = $1 U.S.). **GDP:** $180.7 bil; **per capita GDP:** $44,500; **GDP growth:** 6%. **Imports:** $87.4 bil; UK 37.3%, U.S. 11.6%, Germany 9.5%, Netherlands 4.6%. **Exports:** $119.8 bil; U.S. 18.8%, UK 17.4%, Belgium 15.9%, Germany 7.5%, France 5.6%. **Tourism:** $4.6 bil. **Budget:** $73.1 bil. **Intl. reserves less gold:** $479 mil. **Gold:** 180,000 oz t. **Consumer prices:** 3.94%.

Transport: Railroad: Length: 2,058 mi. **Motor vehicles:** 1.5 mil pass. cars; 264,000 comm. vehicles. **Civil aviation:** 17.1 bil pass.-mi; 15 airports. **Chief ports:** Cork, Dublin.

Communications: TV sets: 406 per 1,000 pop. **Radios:** 697 per 1,000 pop. **Telephone lines:** 2.1 mil. **Daily newspaper circ.:** 147.7 per 1,000 pop. **Internet:** 1.4 mil users.

Health: Life expect.: 75.3 male; 80.7 female. **Births** (per 1,000 pop.): 14.4. **Deaths** (per 1,000 pop.): 7.8. **Natural inc.:** 0.66%. **Infant mortality** (per 1,000 live births): 5.2. **AIDS rate:** 0.2%.

Education: Compulsory: ages 6-15. **Literacy:** 99%.

Major intl. organizations: UN (FAO, IBRD, ILO, IMF, IMO, WHO, WTO), EU, OECD, OSCE.

Embassy: 2234 Massachusetts Ave. NW 20008; 462-3939.

Website: www.irlgov.ie

Celtic tribes invaded the islands about the 4th cent. BCE; their Gaelic culture and literature flourished and spread to Scotland and elsewhere in the 5th cent. CE, the same century in which St. Patrick converted the Irish to Christianity. Invasions by Norsemen began in the 8th cent., ended with defeat of the Danes by the Irish King Brian Boru in 1014. English invasions started in the 12th cent.; for over 700 years the Anglo-Irish struggle continued with bitter rebellions and savage repressions.

The Easter Monday Rebellion in 1916 failed but was followed by guerrilla warfare and harsh reprisals by British troops called the "Black and Tans." The Dail Eireann (Irish parliament) reaffirmed independence in Jan. 1919. The British offered dominion status to Ulster (6 counties) and southern Ireland (26 counties) Dec. 1921. The constitution of the Irish Free State, a British dominion, was adopted Dec. 11, 1922. Northern Ireland remained part of the United Kingdom.

A new constitution adopted by plebiscite came into operation Dec. 29, 1937. It declared the name of the state Eire in the Irish language (Ireland in the English) and declared it a sovereign democratic state. On Dec. 21, 1948, an Irish law declared the country a republic rather than a dominion and withdrew it from the Commonwealth. The British Parliament recognized both actions, 1949, but reasserted its claim to incorporate the 6 northeastern counties in the UK.

Irish governments have favored peaceful unification of all Ireland and cooperated with Britain against terrorist groups. After negotiators in Northern Ireland approved a peace settlement on Good Friday, April 10, 1998, voters in the Irish Republic endorsed the accord, on May 22; the agreement required the removal of the Irish constitution of territorial claims on the north. Irish voters rejected, June 7, 2001, then reversed themselves and approved, Oct. 19, 2002, a plan calling for EU expansion.

Ireland's first woman president, Mary Robinson, resigned Sept. 12, 1997, to become UN high commissioner for human rights, 1997-2002. She was succeeded as president by Mary McAleese, a law professor from Northern Ireland and the first northerner to hold the office. Expansion of educational opportunities and foreign investment in high-tech industries have boosted Ireland's prosperity in recent years.

Israel
State of Israel

People: Population: 6,426,679. **Age distrib.** (%): <15: 26.1; 65+: 9.8. **Pop. density:** 819 per sq mi, 316 per sq km. **Urban:** 91.6%. **Ethnic groups:** Jewish 76%, Arab and other 24%. **Principal languages:** Hebrew, Arabic (both official); English. **Chief religions:** Jewish 76%, Muslim (mostly Sunni) 16%, Christian 2%.

Geography: Total area: 8,019 sq mi, 20,770 sq km; **Land area:** 7,849 sq mi, 20,330 sq km. **Location:** Middle East, on E end of Mediterranean Sea. **Neighbors:** Lebanon on N; Syria, West Bank,

Jordan on E; Gaza Strip, Egypt on W. **Topography:** The Mediterranean coastal plain is fertile and well-watered. In the center is the Judean Plateau. A triangular-shaped semi-desert region, the Negev, extends from S of Beersheba to an apex at head of the Gulf of Aqaba. The E border drops sharply into the Jordan Rift Valley, including Lake Tiberias (Sea of Galilee) and the Dead Sea, which is c. 1,300 ft below sea level, lowest point on earth's surface. **Capital:** Jerusalem (most countries maintain their embassies in Tel Aviv), 711,000. **Cities** (urban aggr.): Tel Aviv-Yafo, 3,012,000; Haifa, 992,000.

Government: Type: Republic. **Head of state:** Pres. Shimon Peres; b. Aug. 1923; in office: July 15, 2007. **Head of gov.:** Prime Min. Ehud Olmert; b. Sept. 30, 1945; in office: Apr. 14, 2006 (acting from Jan. 4). **Local divisions:** 6 districts. **Defense budget:** $7.69 bil. **Active troops:** 168,000.

Economy: Industries: high-tech products, wood & paper products, potash & phosphates, food, beverages, tobacco. **Chief crops:** citrus, vegetables, cotton. **Natural resources:** timber, potash, copper ore, nat. gas, phosphate rock, magnesium bromide, clays, sand. **Crude oil reserves:** 2 mil bbls. **Arable land:** 15%. **Livestock:** cattle: 398,000; chickens: 37.1 mil; goats: 87,000; pigs: 205,000; sheep: 445,000. **Fish catch:** 26,555 metric tons. **Electricity prod.:** 46.9 bil kWh. **Labor force** (1996): agriculture, forestry, and fishing 1.8%; manufacturing 15.7%, construction 5.3%, wholesale and retail trade 12.9%, transport, storage, and communications 6.3%, finance and business 16.9%, personal and other services 11.5%, public services 28.6%.

Finance: Monetary unit: New Shekel (ILS) (Sept. 2007: 4.09 = $1 U.S.). **GDP:** $170.3 bil; **per capita GDP:** $26,800; **GDP growth:** 4.8%. **Imports:** $47.8 bil; U.S. 12.4%, Belgium 8.2%, Germany 6.7%, Switzerland 5.9%, UK 5.1%, China 5.1%. **Exports:** $42.9 bil; U.S. 38.4%, Belgium 6.5%, Hong Kong 5.9%. **Tourism:** $2.8 bil. **Budget:** $49.6 bil. **Intl. reserves less gold:** $19.38 bil. **Consumer prices:** 2.11%.

Transport: Railroad: Length: 530 mi. **Motor vehicles:** 1.6 mil pass. cars; 364,000 comm. vehicles. **Civil aviation:** 7.7 bil pass.-mi; 30 airports. **Chief ports:** Ashdod, Elat, Haifa.

Communications: TV sets: 328 per 1,000 pop. **Radios:** 524 per 1,000 pop. **Telephone lines:** 3 mil. **Internet:** 1.9 mil users.

Health: Life expect.: 77.4 male; 81.9 female. **Births** (per 1,000 pop.): 17.7. **Deaths** (per 1,000 pop.): 6.2. **Natural inc.:** 1.15%. **Infant mortality** (per 1,000 live births): 6.8. **AIDS rate:** NA.

Education: Compulsory: ages 5-15. **Literacy:** 97.1%.

Major intl. organizations: UN (FAO, IBRD, ILO, IMF, IMO, WHO, WTO).

Embassy: 3514 International Dr. NW 20008; 364-5500.

Website: www.mfa.gov.il

Occupying the southwest corner of the ancient Fertile Crescent, Israel contains some of the oldest known evidence of agriculture and of primitive town life. The Hebrews probably arrived early in the 2nd millennium BCE. Under King David and his successors (c. 1000 BCE-597 BCE), Judaism was developed and secured. After conquest by Babylonians, Persians, and Greeks, an independent Jewish kingdom was revived, 168 BCE, but Rome took effective control in the next century, suppressed Jewish revolts in 70 CE and 135 CE, and renamed Judea Palestine, after the earlier coastal inhabitants, the Philistines.

Arab invaders conquered Palestine in 636. The Arabic language and Islam prevailed within a few centuries, but a Jewish minority remained. The land was ruled from the 11th cent. as a part of non-Arab empires by Seljuks, Mamluks, and Ottomans (with a Crusader interval, 1098-1291).

After 4 centuries of Ottoman rule, the land was taken in 1917 by Britain, which pledged in the Balfour Declaration to support a Jewish homeland there. In 1920 a British Palestine Mandate was recognized; in 1922 the land east of the Jordan was detached.

Jewish immigration, begun in the late 19th cent., swelled in the 1930s with refugees from the Nazis; heavy Arab immigration from Syria and Lebanon also occurred. Arab opposition to Jewish immigration turned violent in 1920, 1921, 1929, and 1936. The UN General Assembly voted in 1947 to partition Palestine into an Arab and a Jewish state. Britain withdrew in May 1948.

Israel was declared an independent state May 14, 1948; the Arabs rejected partition. Egypt, Jordan, Syria, Lebanon, Iraq, and Saudi Arabia invaded but failed to destroy the Jewish state, which gained territory. Separate armistices with the Arab nations were signed in 1949; Jordan occupied the West Bank, Egypt occupied Gaza. Neither granted Palestinian autonomy.

After persistent terrorist raids, Israel invaded Egypt's Sinai, Oct. 29, 1956, aided briefly by British and French forces. A UN cease-fire was arranged Nov. 6.

An uneasy truce between Israel and the Arab countries lasted until 1967, when Egypt reoccupied the Gaza Strip and closed the Gulf of Aqaba to Israeli shipping. In a 6-day war that started June 5, the Israelis took the Gaza Strip, occupied the Sinai Peninsula to the Suez Canal, and captured East Jerusalem, Syria's Golan Heights, and Jordan's West Bank. Together, the West Bank and Gaza comprise the Palestinian territories, now represented by the Palestinian Authority (see below).

Egypt and Syria attacked Israel, Oct. 6, 1973 (on Yom Kippur, the most solemn day on the Jewish calendar). Israel counter-attacked, driving the Syrians back, and crossed the Suez Canal. A cease-fire took effect Oct. 24 and a UN peacekeeping force went to the area. Under a disengagement agreement signed Jan. 18, 1974, Israel withdrew from the canal's west bank.Israeli forces raided Entebbe, Uganda, July 3, 1976, and rescued 103 hostages who had been seized by Arab and German terrorists.

Israel's prime ministers, including David Ben-Gurion, Golda Meir, and Yitzhak Rabin, pursued a moderate socialist program, 1948-77. In 1977, the conservative opposition, led by Menachem Begin, was voted into office for the first time. Egypt's Pres. Anwar al-Sadat visited Jerusalem Nov. 1977, and on Mar. 26, 1979, Egypt and Israel signed a formal peace treaty, ending 30 years of war. Israel returned the Sinai to Egypt in 1982.

On June 7, 1981, Israeli jets destroyed an Iraqi atomic reactor near Baghdad that, Israel claimed, would have enabled Iraq to manufacture nuclear weapons. Israeli forces invaded Lebanon, June 6, 1982, to destroy Palestine Liberation Organization (PLO) strongholds there. After massive Israeli bombing of West Beirut, the PLO agreed to evacuate the city. Israeli troops entered West Beirut after newly elected Lebanese Pres. Bashir Gemayel was assassinated on Sept. 14. Israel drew widespread condemnation when Lebanese Christian forces, Sept. 16, entered two West Beirut refugee camps and slaughtered hundreds of Palestinians.

In 1989, violence escalated over the Israeli military occupation of the West Bank and Gaza Strip. In a series of uprisings known as the first intifada, Palestinian protesters defied Israeli troops, who forcibly retaliated. During the Persian Gulf War, 1991, Iraq fired Scud missiles at Israel. The Labor Party of Yitzhak Rabin won parliamentary elections, June 23, 1992.

Ongoing peace talks led to historic agreements between Israel and the PLO, Sept. 1993. The PLO recognized Israel's right to exist; Israel recognized the PLO as the Palestinians' representative. The two sides then signed, Sept. 13, an agreement for limited Palestinian self-rule in the West Bank and Gaza. Israel and Jordan signed, July 25, 1994, in Washington, DC, a declaration ending their 46-year state of war.

Arab and American extremists repeatedly challenged the peace process. A Jewish gunman opened fire on Arab worshippers at a mosque in Hebron, Feb. 25, 1994, killing at least 29 before he himself was killed. On Nov. 4, 1995, an Orthodox Jewish Israeli assassinated Rabin as he left a peace rally in Tel Aviv. Support for Rabin's successor, Shimon Peres, was shaken by a series of suicide bombings and rocket attacks against Israel by Islamic militants. Emphasizing security issues, the candidate of the conservative Likud bloc, Benjamin Netanyahu, was elected prime minister on May 29, 1996.

Under an interim accord brokered by Pres. Bill Clinton and signed by Netanyahu and PLO leader Yasir Arafat at the White House, Oct. 23, 1998, Israel yielded more West Bank territory to the Palestinians, in exchange for new security guarantees. Negotiations bogged down, however, and full implementation did not begin until Sept. 1999. In the interim, Netanyahu lost by a landslide to the Labor candidate, Ehud Barak, in the election of May 17, 1999.

Israel pulled virtually all its troops out of southern Lebanon by May 24, 2000. Marathon summit talks in the U.S. between Barak and Arafat, July 11-25, failed. A second intifada began in late Sept. in Israel and the Palestinian territories. Barak called new elections for prime minister but lost Feb. 6, 2001, to Ariel Sharon, a hardliner. The bloodshed intensified during the summer, as Palestinian suicide bombers launched attacks on Israeli civilians and Israel struck at Palestinian-controlled territory and carried out an assassination campaign against suspected terrorists.

Israel launched a major West Bank offensive Mar. 29, 2002, 2 days after a suicide bomber killed 26 Israeli Jews at a Passover celebration in Netanya. Fighting was particularly fierce at the Jenin refugee camp, where 23 Israeli troops and at least 50 Palestinians were killed. Israel withdrew in early May but, after another wave of suicide bombings, reoccupied much of the West Bank June 21-27.

A U.S.-sponsored "road map" to Middle East peace, unveiled Apr. 30, 2003, made little headway. Israel Sept. 1 vowed "all-out war" against Hamas terrorists. Israeli missile strikes in Gaza City killed Hamas founder and leader Sheikh Ahmed Yassin Mar. 22, 2004, and his successor, Abdel Aziz al-Rantisi, Apr. 17. Hamas suicide bombers Aug. 31 blew up 2 buses in Beersheba, killing 16.

Sharon's decision to pull all Israeli settlers and troops out of Gaza (see below), approved by the cabinet Feb. 20, 2005, led to a realignment in Israeli politics. When right-wing Likud members opposed the plan, Sharon and Deputy Prime Min. Ehud Olmert broke with them and formed the centrist Kadima Party. Sharon suffered a massive stroke Jan. 4, 2006. With Sharon incapacitated, Olmert became prime minister, led Kadima to victory in Mar. 28 elections, and formed a broad coalition government.

Border clashes in which Hamas militants from Gaza (June 25) and Hezbollah fighters from Lebanon (July 12) killed and captured Israeli soldiers rapidly escalated into full-scale war. Israeli air and ground forces hit hard in Gaza, but the fiercest fighting raged on the northern front. Hezbollah (aided by Syria and Iran) bombarded northern Israel with nearly 4,000 rockets, while Israeli forces (backed by the U.S.) blockaded Lebanon, knocked out bridges, roads, and other infrastructure, and pounded southern Lebanon and southern Beirut, damaging Hezbollah but also killing many civilians. By Aug. 14, when a UN-monitored cease-fire took hold, the estimated death toll from the war included nearly 1,150 Lebanese, almost 200 Gaza Palestinians, and 150 Israelis. To police the truce, 15,000 Lebanese govt. troops began moving into southern

Lebanon, and expansion of the UN force in Lebanon (UNIFIL) to 15,000 was authorized.

Israel's inability to gain a decisive victory over Hezbollah led to the resignation of army commander Lt. Gen. Dan Halutz, Jan. 16, 2007; an official report issued Apr. 30 criticized Olmert for a "severe failure" of wartime leadership. Peres became president July 15 after his predecessor, Moshe Katsav, accused of rape, pleaded guilty to lesser charges, received a suspended sentence, and resigned. Crossing into Syria, Sept. 6, Israeli aircraft struck a secret site where Israelis reportedly believed the Syrians were developing a nuclear facility, with North Korean help.

Palestinian Territories

The Palestinian territories comprise the Gaza Strip, often called Gaza, and the West Bank, both occupied by Israel in 1967. Since 1996 the Palestinian Authority has been responsible for civil government in the territories. Elected president Jan. 20, 1996, PLO leader Yasir Arafat headed the Palestinian Authority until his death Nov. 11, 2004. Mahmoud Abbas (also called Abu Mazen), who had succeeded Arafat as PLO chairman and leader of the Fatah faction, was elected president Jan. 9, 2005. A victory by Hamas militants in legislative elections Jan. 25, 2006, led to a power struggle with Abbas, who favored a negotiated settlement with Israel. In bitter fighting, Hamas ousted Fatah from Gaza, June 2007, but Abbas retained power in the West Bank. Since Sept. 2000, when the second intifada began, the Israeli-Palestinian conflict has claimed the lives of more than 1,000 Israelis and at least 4,750 Palestinians.

The Gaza Strip extends northeast from the Sinai Peninsula for 40 km (25 mi), with the Mediterranean Sea to the west and Israel to the east. The Palestinian Authority is responsible for civil government. Nearly all the inhabitants are Palestinian Arabs, more than 35% of whom live in refugee camps. **Population** (2007 est.) 1,482,405. **Area:** 139 sq mi.

Israel captured Gaza from Egypt in the 1967 war. It remained under Israeli occupation until May 1994, when the Israeli Defense Forces withdrew. Agreements between Israel and the PLO in 1993 and 1994 provided for interim self-rule in Gaza, but Israel retained control over security. Israel forcibly evacuated all 9,000 Jewish settlers from Gaza by Aug. 22, 2005, and the last remaining Israeli soldiers pulled out Sept. 12. Israel established a fortified barrier on its Gaza border to block Palestinian infiltrators. After the Hamas takeover, Israel declared Gaza a "hostile entity," Sept. 19, 2007, and intensified military and economic pressures.

The West Bank is located west of the Jordan R. and Dead Sea, bounded by Jordan on the east and by Israel on the north, west, and south. The Palestinian Authority administers several major cities, but Israel retains control over much land, including Jewish settlements. **Population** (2007 est.) 2,535,927. **Area:** 2,263 sq mi.

Israel captured the West Bank from Jordan in the 1967 war. A 1974 Arab summit conference designated the PLO as sole representative of West Bank Arabs. In 1988 Jordan cut legal and administrative ties with the territory. Jericho was returned to Palestinian control in May 1994. An accord between Israel and the PLO expanding Palestinian self-rule in the West Bank was signed Sept. 28, 1995. Later agreements gave Palestinians full or shared control of 40% of West Bank territory.

In June 2002 the Israeli government began building a controversial security barrier in the West Bank to restrict Palestinian access to Israel; in a nonbinding ruling, July 9, 2004, the World Court said the barrier violated international law.

Italy

Italian Republic

People: Population: 58,147,733. **Age distrib.** (%): <15: 13.8; 65+: 19.9. **Pop. density:** 512 per sq mi, 198 per sq km. **Urban:** 67.6%. **Ethnic groups:** Mostly Italian; small minorities of German, Slovene. **Principal languages:** Italian (official), German, French, Slovenian. **Chief religion:** Roman Catholic 90%.

Geography: Total area: 116,306 sq mi, 301,230 sq km; **Land area:** 113,522 sq mi, 294,020 sq km. **Location:** In S Europe, jutting into Mediterranean Sea. **Neighbors:** France on W; Switzerland, Austria on N; Slovenia on E; San Marino, Vatican City. **Topography:** Occupies long boot-shaped peninsula, extending SE from the Alps into Mediterranean, with islands of Sicily and Sardinia offshore. The alluvial Po Valley drains most of N. Rest of the country is rugged and mountainous, except for intermittent coastal plains, like the Campania, S of Rome. Apennine Mts. run down through center of peninsula. **Capital:** Rome, 3,348,000. **Cities (urban aggr.):** Milan, 2,953,000; Naples, 2,245,000; Turin, 1,660,000.

Government: Type: Republic. **Head of state:** Pres. Giorgio Napolitano; b. June 29, 1925; in office: May 15, 2006. **Head of gov.:** Prime Min. Romano Prodi; b. Aug. 9, 1939; in office: May 17, 2006. **Local divisions:** 20 regions divided into 103 provinces. **Defense budget:** $15.5 bil. **Active troops:** 191,152.

Economy: Industries: tourism, machinery, iron & steel, chemicals, food proc., textiles, autos. **Chief crops:** fruits, vegetables, grapes, potatoes, sugar beets, soybeans, grain, olives. **Natural resources:** mercury, potash, marble, sulfur, nat. gas, oil, fish, coal. **Crude oil reserves:** 600 mil bbls. **Arable land:** 26%. **Livestock:** cattle: 6.3 mil; chickens: 100 mil; goats: 945,000; pigs: 9.2 mil; sheep: 8 mil. **Fish catch:** 479,316 metric tons. **Electricity prod.:** 278.6 bil kWh. **Labor force** (2001): agriculture 5%, industry 32%, services 63%.

Finance: Monetary unit: Euro (EUR) (Sept. 2007: 0.72 = $1 U.S.). **GDP:** $1.8 tril; **per capita GDP:** $30,200; **GDP growth:** 1.9%. **Imports:** $445.6 bil; Germany 16.7%, France 9.2%, Netherlands 5.6%, China 5.2%, Belgium 4.2%, Spain 4.1%. **Exports:** $450.1 bil; Germany 13.2%, France 11.7%, U.S. 7.6%, Spain 7.3%, UK 6.1%. **Tourism:** $35.3 bil. **Budget:** $925 bil. **Intl. reserves less gold:** $17.06 bil. **Gold:** 78.83 mil oz t. **Consumer prices:** 2.09%.

Transport: Railroad: Length: 12,091 mi. **Motor vehicles:** 34 mil pass. cars; 4 mil comm. vehicle. **Civil aviation:** 25.4 bil pass.-mi; 98 airports. **Chief ports:** Augusta, Genoa, Livorno, Melilli Oil Terminal, Ravenna, Taranto, Trieste, Venice.

Communications: TV sets: 492 per 1,000 pop. **Radios:** 880 per 1,000 pop. **Telephone lines:** 25 mil. **Daily newspaper circ.:** 109 per 1,000 pop. **Internet:** 28.9 mil users.

Health: Life expect.: 77 male; 83.1 female. **Births** (per 1,000 pop.): 8.5. **Deaths** (per 1,000 pop.): 10.5. **Natural inc.:** −0.2%. **Infant mortality** (per 1,000 live births): 5.7. **AIDS rate:** 0.5%.

Education: Compulsory: ages 6-14. **Literacy:** 98.4%.

Major intl. organizations: UN and all of its specialized agencies, EU, NATO, OECD, OSCE.

Embassy: 3000 Whitehaven St. NW 20008; 612-4400.

Website: english.camera.it

Rome emerged as the major power in Italy after 500 BCE, dominating the Etruscans to the north and Greeks to the south. Under the Empire, which lasted until the 5th cent. CE, Rome ruled most of Western Europe, the Balkans, the Middle East, and North Africa.

After Fascism was overthrown in 1943, Italy declared war on Germany and Japan and contributed to the Allied victory. It surrendered conquered lands and lost its colonies. Mussolini was killed by partisans Apr. 28, 1945. Victor Emmanuel III abdicated May 9, 1946; his son Humbert II was king until June 10, when Italy became a republic after a referendum, June 2-3. In the postwar decades, Italy had a succession of short-lived governments.

Christian Democratic leader and former Prime Min. Aldo Moro was abducted and murdered in 1978 by Red Brigade terrorists. The wave of left-wing political violence, including other kidnappings and assassinations, continued into the 1980s.

In the early 1990s, scandals implicated some of Italy's most prominent politicians. In Mar. 1994 voting, under reformed election rules, right-wing parties won a majority, dislodging Italy's long-powerful Christian Democratic Party. A coalition of center-left parties won the election of Apr. 21, 1996. Italy led a 7,000-member peacekeeping force in Albania, Apr.-Aug. 1997, and contributed 2,000 troops to the NATO-led security force (KFOR) that entered Kosovo in June 1999.

Supporters of Silvio Berlusconi, a multibillionaire media magnate, won the parliamentary elections of May 13, 2001. In 2003, Berlusconi backed the U.S.-led war in Iraq, and a force of up to 3,200 Italian troops served in the coalition. Public opposition to Berlusconi's Iraq policy intensified after U.S. troops at a Baghdad checkpoint fired on a car carrying a freed hostage, Mar. 4, 2005, wounding her and killing the Italian agent who was protecting her. Turin hosted the Winter Olympics, Feb. 10-26, 2006. A coalition of center-left parties led by Romano Prodi scored a narrow win over Berlusconi in parliamentary elections, Apr. 9-10. The national soccer team took the World Cup, July 9. Italy pulled all its troops out of Iraq by Nov. 2006. As of 2007, some 2,500 Italian troops were serving in the UN peacekeeping force in Lebanon.

Sicily, 9,926 sq mi, pop. (2001 est.) 4,866,200 is an island 180 by 120 mi, seat of a region that embraces the island of **Pantelleria,** 32 sq mi, and the **Lipari** group, 44 sq mi, including 2 active volcanoes: **Vulcano,** 1,637ft, and **Stromboli,** 3,038 ft. From prehistoric times Sicily has been settled by various peoples; a Greek state had its capital at Syracuse. Rome took Sicily from Carthage 215 BCE. **Mt. Etna,** an 11,053-ft active volcano, is its tallest peak.

Sardinia, 9,301 sq mi, pop. (2001 est.) 1,599,500, lies in the Mediterranean, 115 mi W of Italy and 7½ mi S of Corsica. It is 160 mi long, 68 mi wide, and mountainous, with mining of coal, zinc, lead, copper. In 1720 Sardinia was added to the possessions of the Dukes of Savoy in Piedmont and Savoy to form the Kingdom of Sardinia. Giuseppe Garibaldi is buried on the nearby isle of Caprera. **Elba,** 86 sq mi, lies 6 mi W of Tuscany. Napoleon I lived in exile on Elba 1814-15.

Jamaica

People: Population: 2,780,132. **Age distrib. (%):** <15: 32.5; 65+: 7.4. **Pop. density:** 665 per sq mi, 257 per sq km. **Urban:** 53.1%. **Ethnic groups:** Black 91%, mixed 6%. **Principal languages:** English, English patois. **Chief religions:** Protestant 63%, other or unspecified 14%.

Geography: Total area: 4,244 sq mi, 10,991 sq km; **Land area:** 4,182 sq mi, 10,831 sq km. **Location:** W Indies. **Neighbors:** Nearest are Cuba to N, Haiti to E. **Topography:** Four-fifths of country covered by mountains. **Capital:** Kingston, 576,000

Government: Type: Constitutional monarchy with parliamentary system based on UK-model. **Head of state:** Queen Elizabeth II, represented by Gov.-Gen. Kenneth Hall; b. Apr. 24, 1941; in office: Feb. 15, 2006. **Head of gov.:** Prime Min. Bruce Golding; b. Dec. 5, 1947; in office: Sept. 11, 2007. **Local divisions:** 14 parishes. **Defense budget** (2005): $58 mil. **Active troops:** 2,830.

Economy: Industries: tourism, bauxite, textiles, food proc., light manufactures, rum, cement, metal, paper, chemical products. **Chief crops:** sugarcane, bananas, coffee, citrus, yams. **Natural resources:** bauxite, gypsum, limestone. **Arable land:** 16%. **Livestock:** cattle: 430,000; chickens: 12.5 mil; goats: 440,000; pigs: 85,000; sheep: 1,280. **Fish catch:** 18,766 metric tons. **Electricity prod.:** 7 bil kWh. **Labor force** (2004): agriculture 18.1%, industry 17.3%, services 64.6%.

Finance: Monetary unit: Dollar (JMD) (Sept. 2007: 68.30 = $1 U.S.). **GDP:** $12.8 bil; **per capita GDP:** $4,600; **GDP growth:** 2.3%. **Imports:** $4.7 bil; U.S. 39.4%, Trinidad and Tobago 14.4%, Venezuela 5.8%. **Exports:** $2.1 bil; U.S. 23.7%, Canada 16.5%, China 15.1%, UK 10.1%, Germany 7.5%, Netherlands 6.4%, Norway 5.9%. **Tourism:** $1.5 bil. **Budget:** $3.2 bil. **Intl. reserves less gold:** $1.54 bil.

Transport: Railroad: Length: 169 mi. **Motor vehicles:** 129,000 pass. cars; 65,200 comm. vehicles. **Civil aviation:** 3.1 bil pass.-mi; 11 airports. **Chief ports:** Kingston, Port Esquivel, Port Kaiser, Port Rhoades, Rocky Point.

Communications: TV sets: 191 per 1,000 pop. **Radios:** 796 per 1,000 pop. **Telephone lines:** 319,000. **Internet:** 1.2 mil users.

Health: Life expect.: 71.4 male; 74.9 female. **Births** (per 1,000 pop.): 20.4. **Deaths** (per 1,000 pop.): 6.6. **Natural inc.:** 1.39%. **Infant mortality** (per 1,000 live births): 15.7. **AIDS rate:** 1.5%.

Education: Compulsory: ages 6-11. **Literacy:** 79.9%.

Major intl. organizations: UN (FAO, IBRD, ILO, IMF, IMO, WHO, WTO), Caricom, the Commonwealth, OAS.

Embassy: 1520 New Hampshire Ave. NW 20036; 452-0660.

Website: www.jis.gov.jm

Jamaica was visited by Columbus, 1494, and ruled by Spain (under whom Arawak Indians died out) until seized by Britain, 1655. Jamaica won independence Aug. 6, 1962. The island's rich musical innovations include ska and reggae. Rastafarianism is an influential religious movement.

In 1974 Jamaica sought an increase in taxes paid by U.S. and Canadian bauxite mines. The socialist government acquired 50% ownership of the companies' Jamaican interests in 1976, and was reelected that year. Rudimentary welfare state measures were passed. Relations with the U.S. improved in the 1980s when Jamaican politics entered a more conservative phase. Violence between government forces and West Kingston slum residents claimed at least 20 lives July 7-10, 2001.

At least 17 died when Hurricane Ivan hit southern Jamaica Sept. 10-11, 2004. Portia Simpson Miller, leader of the People's National Party, became Jamaica's first female prime minister, Mar. 30, 2006. The opposition Jamaica Labour Party won the parliamentary elections of Sept. 3, 2007.

Japan

People: Population: 127,433,494. **Age distrib. (%):** <15: 13.8; 65+: 21. **Pop. density:** 881 per sq mi, 340 per sq km. **Urban:** 65.8%. **Ethnic groups:** Japanese 99%. **Principal language:** Japanese. **Chief religions:** Shinto and Buddhist, observed together by 84%.

Geography: Total area: 145,883 sq mi, 377,835 sq km; **Land area:** 144,689 sq mi, 374,744 sq km. **Location:** Archipelago off E coast of Asia. **Neighbors:** Russia to N, S. Korea to W. **Topography:** Consists of 4 main islands: Honshu ("mainland"), 87,805 sq mi; Hokkaido, 30,144 sq mi; Kyushu, 14,114 sq mi; and Shikoku, 7,049 sq mi. The coast, deeply indented, measures 16,654 mi. The northern islands are continuation of the Sakhalin Mts. The Kunlun range of China continues into southern islands, the ranges merging in Japanese Alps. In a vast transverse fissure crossing Honshu E-W rises a group of volcanoes, mostly extinct or inactive, including 12,388 ft. Mt. Fuji (Fujiyama) near Tokyo. **Capital:** Tokyo, 35,197,000. **Cities (urban aggr.):** Osaka, 11,268,000, (1998 city proper: 2,599,642); Nagoya, 3,179,000; Sapporo, 2,530,000.

Government: Type: Constitutional monarchy with parliamentary democracy. **Head of state:** Emperor Akihito; b. Dec. 23, 1933; in office: Jan. 7, 1989. **Head of gov.:** Prime Min. Yasuo Fukuda; b. July 16, 1936; in office: Sept. 26, 2007. **Local divisions:** 47 prefectures. **Defense budget** (2005): $44.7 bil. **Active troops:** 239,900.

Economy: Industries: motor vehicles, electronic equip., machine tools, steel & nonferrous metals, ships, chemicals, textiles, proc. foods. **Chief crops:** rice, sugar beets, vegetables, fruit. **Natural resources:** fish. **Crude oil reserves:** 58.5 mil bbls. **Arable land:** 12%. **Livestock:** cattle: 4.4 mil; chickens: 280.6 mil; goats: 34,000; pigs: 9.6 mil; sheep: 11,000. **Fish catch:** 4,819,116 metric tons. **Electricity prod.:** 1,024.6 bil kWh. **Labor force** (2004): agriculture 4.6%, industry 27.8%, services 67.7%.

Finance: Monetary unit: Yen (JPY) (Sept. 2007: 115.36 = $1 U.S.). **GDP:** $4.2 tril; **per capita GDP:** $33,100; **GDP growth:** 2.2%. **Imports:** $524.1 bil; China 20.5%, U.S. 12%, Saudi Arabia 6.4%, UAE 5.5%, Australia 4.8%, South Korea 4.7%, Indonesia 4.2%. **Exports:** $590.3 bil; U.S. 22.8%, China 14.3%, South Korea 7.8%, Taiwan 6.8%, Hong Kong 5.6%. **Tourism:** $12.4 bil. **Budget:** $1.6 tril. **Intl. reserves less gold:** $584.74 bil. **Gold:** 24.6 mil oz t. **Consumer prices:** 0.24%.

Transport: Railroad: Length: 14,637 mi. **Motor vehicles:** 56 mil pass. cars; 17 mil comm. vehicles. **Civil aviation:** 91.3 bil pass.-mi; 145 airports. **Chief ports:** Kobe, Nagoya, Osaka, Tokyo.

Communications: TV sets: 719 per 1,000 pop. **Radios:** 956 per 1,000 pop. **Telephone lines:** 55.2 mil. **Daily newspaper circ.:** 566 per 1,000 pop. **Internet:** 87.5 mil users.
Health: Life expect.: 78.7 male; 85.6 female. **Births** (per 1,000 pop.): 8.1. **Deaths** (per 1,000 pop.): 9. **Natural inc.:** −0.09%. **Infant mortality** (per 1,000 live births): 2.8. **AIDS rate:** <0.1%.
Education: Compulsory: ages 6-15. **Literacy:** 99%.
Major intl. organizations: UN and all its specialized agencies, APEC, OECD.
Embassy: 2520 Massachusetts Ave. NW 20008; 238-6700.
Website: www.kantei.go.jp

According to Japanese legend, the empire was founded by Emperor Jimmu, 660 BCE, but earliest records of a unified Japan date from 1,000 years later. Chinese influence was strong in the formation of Japanese civilization. Buddhism was introduced before the 6th cent. CE.

A feudal system, with locally powerful noble families and their samurai warrior retainers, dominated from 1192. Central power was held by successive families of shoguns (military dictators), 1192-1867, until recovered by Emperor Meiji, 1868. The Portuguese and Dutch had minor trade with Japan in the 16th and 17th centuries; U.S. Commodore Matthew C. Perry opened the country to U.S. trade in a treaty ratified 1854. Industrialization was begun in the late 19th cent. Japan fought China, 1894-95, gaining Taiwan. After war with Russia, 1904-05, Russia ceded the southern half of Sakhalin and gave concessions in China. Japan annexed Korea, 1910.

In WWI Japan ousted Germany from Shandong in China and took over German Pacific islands. Japan took Manchuria in 1931 and launched full-scale war in China in 1937. Japan launched war against the U.S. by attacking Pearl Harbor Dec. 7, 1941. The U.S. dropped atomic bombs on Hiroshima, Aug. 6, and Nagasaki, Aug. 9, 1945. Japan surrendered Aug. 14, 1945.

In a new constitution adopted May 3, 1947, Japan renounced the right to wage war; the emperor gave up claims to divinity; the Diet became the sole law-making authority. The U.S. and 48 other non-Communist nations signed a peace treaty and the U.S. a bilateral defense agreement with Japan, in San Francisco Sept. 8, 1951, restoring Japan's sovereignty as of April 28, 1952.

Rebuilding after WWII, Japan emerged as one of the most powerful economies in the world, and as a leader in technology.The U.S. and Western Europe criticized Japan for its restrictive policy on imports, which eventually allowed Japan to accumulate huge trade surpluses.

On June 26, 1968, the U.S. returned to Japanese control the Bonin Isls., Volcano Isls. (including Iwo Jima), and Marcus Isls. On May 15, 1972, Okinawa, the other Ryukyu Isls., and the Daito Isls. were returned by the U.S.; it was agreed the U.S. would continue to maintain military bases on Okinawa.

The Liberal Democratic Party (LDP) governed Japan from the mid-1950s through the early '90s. The Recruit scandal, the nation's worst political scandal since WWII, which involved illegal political donations and stock trading, led to the resignation of LDP Prime Min. Noboru Takeshita in May 1989. Following new political and economic scandals, the LDP was denied a majority in general elections July 18, 1993. On June 29, 1994, Tomiichi Murayama became Japan's first Socialist premier since 1947-48.

An earthquake in the Kobe area in Jan. 1995 claimed more than 5,000 lives, injured nearly 35,000, and caused over $90 bil in property damage. On Mar. 20, a nerve gas attack in the Tokyo subway (blamed on a religious cult) killed 12 and injured thousands. Public anger at the rape of a 12-year-old Okinawa schoolgirl by 3 U.S. servicemen, Sept. 4, led the U.S. to begin reducing its military presence there. Nagano hosted the Winter Olympics, Feb. 7-22, 1998.

With the country mired in a lengthy recession, a series of weak LDP governments led Japan. In Apr. 2001 Junichiro Koizumi, a populist reformer, became LDP leader and prime minister. In Sept. 2002, Koizumi became the first Japanese prime min. to visit N. Korea; during the meeting N. Korean leader Kim Jong Il apologized for abducting Japanese citizens. Five of these abductees returned to Japan in Oct. 2002.

Koizumi's coalition retained power in the elections of Nov. 9, 2003. A commuter train crash at Amagasaki, western Japan, Apr. 25, 2005, killed over 100 people. Voters in legislative elections Sept. 11 gave Koizumi a mandate to restructure the economy. About 600 noncombatant troops were in Iraq Feb. 2004-July 2006, the first time since WWII that Japanese forces served in an overseas war zone.

Shinzo Abe, a Koizumi protégé, succeeded him in Sept. 2006 as LDP leader and prime minister. Scandals and controversies forced the resignation of several cabinet ministers, and Agric. Min. Toshikatsu Matsuoka hanged himself May 28, 2007, after questions were raised about his financial dealings. Elections for the upper house of the Diet, July 29, dealt the LDP a crushing setback. Abe announced his resignation Sept. 12, and was replaced by Yasuo Fukuda, an LDP stalwart.

Jordan
Hashemite Kingdom of Jordan
People: Population: 6,053,193. **Age distrib.** (%): <15: 33; 65+: 4. **Pop. density:** 170 per sq mi, 66 per sq km. **Urban:** 82.3%. **Ethnic groups:** Arab 98%, Armenian 1%, Circassian 1%. **Principal languages:** Arabic (official), English. **Chief religions:** Muslim (official; mostly Sunni) 92%, Christian 6%.
Geography: Total area: 35,637 sq mi, 92,300 sq km; **Land area:** 35,510 sq mi, 91,971 sq km. **Location:** In Middle East. **Neighbors:** Israel, West Bank on W; Saudi Arabia on S; Iraq on E; Syria on N. **Topography:** About 88% is arid. Fertile areas are in W. Only port is on short Aqaba Gulf coast. Country shares Dead Sea (about 1,300 ft below sea level) with Israel. **Capital:** Amman,1,292,000.
Government: Type: Constitutional monarchy. **Head of state:** King Abdullah II; b. Jan. 30, 1962; in office: Feb. 7, 1999. **Head of gov.:** Prime Min. Marouf al-Bakhit; b. 1947; in office: Nov. 27, 2005. **Local divisions:** 12 governorates. **Defense budget:** $1 bil. **Active troops:** 100,500.
Economy: Industries: phosphates, oil refining, cement, potash, light mfg. **Chief crops:** citrus, tomatoes, cucumbers, olives. **Natural resources:** phosphates, potash, shale oil. **Crude oil reserves:** 1 mil bbls. **Arable land:** 3%. **Livestock:** cattle: 67,520; chickens: 25 mil; goats: 473,810; sheep: 2 mil. **Fish catch:** 1,071 metric tons. **Electricity prod.:** 9.1 bil kWh. **Labor force** (2001 est.): agriculture 5%, industry 12.5%, services 82.5%.
Finance: Monetary unit: Dinar (JOD) (Sept. 2007: 0.71 = $1 U.S.). **GDP:** $30 bil; **per capita GDP:** $5,100; **GDP growth:** 6.3%. **Imports:** $10.4 bil; Saudi Arabia 22.9%, Germany 8.1%, China 7.9%, U.S. 5.2%. **Exports:** $4.8 bil; U.S. 25.3%, Iraq 17%, India 8.1%, Saudi Arabia 5.8%, Syria 4.7%. **Tourism:** $1.4 bil. **Budget:** $5.5 bil. **Intl. reserves less gold:** $4.47 bil. **Gold:** 410,000 oz t. **Consumer prices:** 6.25%.
Transport: Railroad: Length: 314 mi. **Motor vehicles:** 396,000 pass. cars; 176,000 comm. vehicles. **Civil aviation:** 2.8 bil pass.-mi; 15 airports. **Chief port:** Al Aqabah.
Communications: TV sets: 83 per 1,000 pop. **Radios:** 271 per 1,000 pop. **Telephone lines:** 614,000. **Daily newspaper circ.:** 74.2 per 1,000 pop. **Internet:** 796,900 users.
Health: Life expect.: 76 male; 81.2 female. **Births** (per 1,000 pop.): 20.7. **Deaths** (per 1,000 pop.): 2.7. **Natural inc.:** 1.8%. **Infant mortality** (per 1,000 live births): 16.2. **AIDS rate:** NA.
Education: Compulsory: ages 6-15. **Literacy:** 91.1%.
Major intl. organizations: UN (FAO, IBRD, ILO, IMF, IMO, WHO, WTO), AL.
Embassy: 3504 International Dr. NW 20008; 966-2664.
Website: www.jordanembassyus.org

From ancient times to 1922 the lands to the east of the Jordan R. were culturally and politically united with the lands to the W. Arabs conquered the area in the 7th cent.; the Ottomans took control in the 16th. Britain's 1920 Palestine Mandate covered both sides of the Jordan. In 1921, Abdullah, son of the ruler of Hejaz in Arabia, was installed by Britain as emir of an autonomous Transjordan, covering two-thirds of Palestine. An independent kingdom was proclaimed, 1946.

During the 1948 Arab-Israeli war the West Bank and East Jerusalem were added to the kingdom, which changed its name to Jordan. All these territories were lost to Israel in the 1967 war, which swelled the number of Arab refugees on the East Bank.

Some 700,000 refugees entered Jordan following Iraq's invasion of Kuwait, Aug. 1990. Jordan was viewed as supporting Iraq during the 1990-91 Persian Gulf crisis.

Jordan and Israel officially agreed, July 25, 1994, to end their state of war; a formal peace treaty was signed Oct. 26. Following a prolonged bout with cancer, King Hussein died Feb. 7, 1999; his eldest son and designated successor immediately assumed the throne as Abdullah II.

Jordanian authorities Apr. 2004 said they had foiled a possible chemical attack against the U.S. embassy and other Amman targets; the plot was traced to Abu Musab al-Zarqawi, a high-ranking Jordanian member of al-Qaeda whom the U.S. accused of leading guerrilla activities in Iraq. Zarqawi was also linked to a rocket attack at Aqaba, Aug. 19, 2005, that narrowly missed a U.S. warship. He was killed in Iraq by a U.S. air strike, June 7, 2006. About 750,000 refugees from the Iraq war were living in Jordan in mid-2007.

Kazakhstan
Republic of Kazakhstan
People: Population: 15,284,929. **Age distrib.** (%): <15: 22.5; 65+: 8.3. **Pop. density:** 15 per sq mi, 6 per sq km. **Urban:** 57.3%. **Ethnic groups:** Kazakh 53%, Russian 30%, Ukrainian 4%, Uzbek 3%, German 2%, Uighur 1%. **Principal languages:** Kazakh (Qazaq, state lang.), Russian (official). **Chief religions:** Muslim 47%, Russian Orthodox 44%.
Geography: Total area: 1,049,155 sq mi, 2,717,300 sq km; **Land area:** 1,030,816 sq mi, 2,669,800 sq km. **Location:** In Central Asia. **Neighbors:** Russia on N; China on E; Kyrgyzstan, Uzbekistan, Turkmenistan on S; Caspian Sea on W. **Topography:** Extends from lower reaches of Volga in Europe to Altay Mts. on Chinese border. **Capital:** Astana, 331,000. **Cities (urban aggr.):** Alma-Ata, 1,156,000.
Government: Type: Republic. **Head of state:** Pres. Nursultan A. Nazarbayev; b. July 6, 1940; in office: Apr. 1990. **Head of gov.:** Prime Min. Karim Masimov; b. office: Jan. 10, 2007. **Local divisions:** 14 oblystar, 3 cities. **Defense budget:** $648 mil. **Active troops:** 65,800.
Economy: Industries: mining and oil producer, agric. machinery, electric motors, constr. materials. **Chief crops:** grain (mostly

spring wheat), cotton. **Natural resources:** oil, nat. gas, coal, iron ore, mang., chrome ore, nickel, cobalt, copper, molybd., lead, zinc, bauxite, gold, uranium. **Crude oil reserves:** 30 bil bbls. **Arable land:** 8%. **Livestock:** cattle: 5.5 mil; chickens: 26.1 mil; goats: 2.2 mil; pigs: 1.3 mil; sheep: 12.2 mil. **Fish catch:** 31,589 metric tons. **Electricity prod.:** 64.2 bil kWh. **Labor force** (2002 est.): agriculture 20%, industry 30%, services 50%.

Finance: Monetary unit: Tenge (KZT) (Sept. 2007: 121.87 = $1 U.S.). **GDP:** $143.1 bil; **per capita GDP:** $9,400; **GDP growth:** 10.6%. **Imports:** $22 bil; Russia 36.8%, China 19.5%, Germany 7.4%. **Exports:** $35.6 bil; Germany 12.4%, Russia 11.6%, China 10.9%, Italy 10.5%, France 7.4%. **Tourism:** $708 mil. **Budget:** $18.1 bil. **Intl. reserves less gold:** $11.80 bil. **Gold:** 2.16 mil oz t. **Consumer prices:** 8.59%.

Transport: Railroad: Length: 8,513 mi. **Motor vehicles:** 1.2 mil pass. cars; 307,000 comm. vehicles. **Civil aviation:** 1.3 bil pass.-mi; 67 airports. **Chief ports:** Aqtau, Atyrau.

Communications: TV sets: 240 per 1,000 pop. **Radios:** 395 per 1,000 pop. **Telephone lines:** 2.9 mil. **Internet:** 1.2 mil users.

Health: Life expect.: 61.9 male; 72.8 female. **Births** (per 1,000 pop.): 16.2. **Deaths** (per 1,000 pop.): 9.4. **Natural inc.:** 0.68%. **Infant mortality** (per 1,000 live births): 27.4. **AIDS rate:** 0.1%.

Education: Compulsory: ages 7-17. **Literacy:** 99.5%.

Major intl. organizations: UN (FAO, IBRD, ILO, IMF, IMO, WHO), CIS, OSCE.

Embassy: 1401 16th St. NW 20036; 232-5488.

Website: www.government.kz

The region came under the Mongols' rule in the 13th cent. and gradually came under Russian rule, 1730-1853. It was admitted to the USSR as a constituent republic in 1936.

Kazakhstan declared independence Dec. 16, 1991. It became an independent state when the Soviet Union dissolved Dec. 26, 1991. The party chief, Nursultan Nazarbayev, was elected president unopposed. He boosted the economy by encouraging Western investment in the oil industry. Dissent was suppressed, and much of the nation's oil wealth was reportedly controlled by the president's family and aides.

Kazakhstan agreed, Feb. 14, 1994, to dismantle nuclear missiles. Private land ownership was legalized Dec. 26, 1995. Astana (formerly Akmola) became the nation's new capital, June 9, 1998. Reelected in 1999 and 2005, Pres. Nazarbayev was authorized to run for an unlimited number of terms under a constitutional amendment passed by parliament May 18, 2007.

Kenya
Republic of Kenya

People: Population: 36,913,721. **Age distrib.** (%): <15: 42.1; 65+: 2.6. **Pop. density:** 168 per sq mi, 65 per sq km. **Urban:** 20.7%. **Ethnic groups:** Kikuyu 22%, Luhya 14%, Luo 13%, Kalenjin 12%, Kamba 11%, Kisii 6%, Meru 6%. **Principal languages:** English, Swahili (both official); numerous indigenous languages. **Chief religions:** Protestant 45%, Roman Catholic 33%, indigenous beliefs 10%, Muslim 10%.

Geography: Total area: 224,962 sq mi, 582,650 sq km; **Land area:** 219,789 sq mi, 569,250 sq km. **Location:** E Africa, on coast of Indian O. **Neighbors:** Uganda on W, Tanzania on S, Somalia on E, Ethiopia on N, Sudan on NW. **Topography:** The northern three-fifths of Kenya is arid. To S, a low coastal area and a plateau varying 3,000-10,000 ft. The Great Rift Valley enters the country N-S, flanked by high mountains. **Capital:** Nairobi, 2,773,000. **Cities (urban aggr.):** Mombasa: 817,000.

Government: Type: Republic. **Head of state and gov.:** Pres. Mwai Kibaki; b. Nov. 15, 1931; in office: Dec. 30, 2002. **Local divisions:** 7 provinces and Nairobi area. **Defense budget:** $455 mil. **Active troops:** 24,120.

Economy: Industries: light consumer goods, agric. proc., oil refining, cement, tourism. **Chief crops:** tea, coffee, corn, wheat, sugarcane, fruit. **Natural resources:** gold, limestone, soda ash, salt barites, rubies, fluorspar, garnets, wildlife, hydropower. **Arable land:** 8%. **Livestock:** cattle: 12.4 mil; chickens: 29.4 mil; goats: 10.1 mil; pigs: 321,000; sheep: 9.3 mil. **Fish catch:** 149,171 metric tons. **Electricity prod.:** 5.5 bil kWh. **Labor force** (2003 est.): agriculture 75%, industry and services 25%.

Finance: Monetary unit: Shilling (KES) (Sept. 2007: 67.02 = $1 U.S.). **GDP:** $41.4 bil; **per capita GDP:** $1,200; **GDP growth:** 5.7%. **Imports:** $6.6 bil; UAE 11.9%, India 8.9%, China 8.4%, Saudi Arabia 8.4%, U.S. 7.1%, South Africa 6.4%, UK 5.4%. **Exports:** $3.6 bil; Uganda 15.8%, UK 10.3%, U.S. 8.2%, Netherlands 7.8%, Tanzania 7.7%. **Tourism:** $495 mil. **Budget:** $5.4 bil. **Intl. reserves less gold:** $1.61 bil. **Consumer prices:** 14.45%.

Transport: Railroad: Length: 1,726 mi. **Motor vehicles:** 308,000 pass. cars; 299,000 comm. vehicles. **Civil aviation:** 2.6 bil pass.-mi; 15 airports. **Chief ports:** Mombasa, Kisumu, Lamu.

Communications: TV sets: 22 per 1,000 pop. **Radios:** 216 per 1,000 pop. **Telephone lines:** 293,400. **Daily newspaper circ.:** 8.3 per 1,000 pop. **Internet:** 2.8 mil users.

Health: Life expect.: 55.2 male; 55.4 female. **Births** (per 1,000 pop.): 38.9. **Deaths** (per 1,000 pop.): 11. **Natural inc.:** 2.8%. **Infant mortality** (per 1,000 live births): 57.4. **AIDS rate:** 6.1%.

Education: Compulsory: ages 6-13. **Literacy:** 73.6%.

Major intl. organizations: UN and all of its specialized agencies, the Commonwealth, AU.

Embassy: 2249 R St. NW 20008; 387-6101.

Website: www.kenya.go.ke

Arab colonies exported spices and slaves from the Kenya coast as early as the 8th cent. Britain obtained control in the 19th cent. Kenya won independence Dec. 12, 1963, 4 years after the end of the violent Mau Mau uprising.

Kenya had steady growth in industry and agriculture under a modified private enterprise system, and enjoyed a relatively free political life. But stability was shaken in 1974-75, with opposition charges of corruption and oppression. Jomo Kenyatta, the country's leader since independence, died Aug. 22, 1978. He was succeeded by his vice president, Daniel arap Moi.

During the first half of the 1990s, Kenya suffered widespread unemployment and high inflation. Tribal clashes in the western provinces claimed thousands of lives and left tens of thousands homeless. Pres. Moi won a 3rd term in Dec. 1992 elections, which were marred by violence and fraud. Clashes in the Mombasa region, Aug. 1997, left more than 40 people dead. Pres. Moi was reelected Dec. 29, in an election plagued by irregularities.

A truck bomb explosion at the U.S. embassy in Nairobi, Aug. 7, 1998, killed more than 200 people and injured about 5,000. The U.S. blamed the attack and a near-simultaneous embassy bombing in Tanzania on al-Qaeda. After a trial in New York City, 4 conspirators were convicted May 29, 2001. In Mombasa, Nov. 28, 2002, terrorists linked with al-Qaeda killed 12 Kenyans and 3 Israeli tourists at an Israeli-owned hotel and narrowly missed shooting down an Israeli-bound jet.

Constitutionally barred from seeking another term, Pres. Moi was succeeded Dec. 30, 2002, by Mwai Kibaki, the candidate of the opposition Democratic Party. Kibaki's top anticorruption official, John Githongo, resigned and fled to the UK in Feb. 2005 after his life was reportedly threatened. Violence triggered by a cattle-rustling raid in northern Kenya July 12, 2005, left 65 people dead. Violence by Mungiki gang members and by police hunting them down claimed at least 100 lives during the first half of 2007.

Kiribati
Republic of Kiribati

People: Population: 107,817. **Age distrib.** (%): <15: 38.2; 65+: 3.4. **Pop. density:** 344 per sq mi, 133 per sq km. **Urban:** 47.4%. **Ethnic groups:** Micronesian 99%. **Principal languages:** English (official), I-Kiribati. **Chief religions:** Roman Catholic 52%, Protestant 40%.

Geography: Total area: 313 sq mi, 811 sq km; **Land area:** 313 sq mi, 811 sq km. **Location:** 33 Micronesian islands (the Gilbert, Line, and Phoenix groups) in mid-Pacific scattered in a 2-mil sq mi chain around the point where the International Date Line formerly cut the Equator. In 1997 the Date Line was moved to follow Kiribati's E border. **Neighbors:** Nearest are Nauru to SW, Tuvalu and Tokelau Isls. to S. **Topography:** Except Banaba (Ocean) Isl., all are low-lying, with soil of coral sand and rock fragments, subject to erratic rainfall. **Capital:** Tarawa, 42,000.

Government: Type: Republic. **Head of state and gov.:** Pres. Anote Tong; b. June 11, 1952; in office: July 10, 2003. **Local divisions:** 3 units, 6 districts.

Economy: Industries: fishing, handicrafts. **Chief crops:** copra, taro, breadfruit, sweet potatoes. **Natural resources:** phosphates. **Arable land:** 3%. **Livestock:** chickens: 460,000; pigs: 12,400. **Fish catch:** 34,012 metric tons. **Electricity prod.:** 10 mil kWh. **Labor force** (2000): agriculture 2.7%, industry 32%, services 65.3%.

Finance: Monetary unit: Australia Dollar (AUD) (Sept. 2007: 1.19 = $1 U.S.). **GDP:** $240 mil; **per capita GDP** (2004 est.): $2,800; **GDP growth** (2005 est.): 0.3%. **Imports** (2004 est.): $62 mil; Australia 33%, Fiji 27.1%, Japan 18.1%, New Zealand 6.9%. **Exports** (2004 est.): $17 mil; U.S. 22.8%, Belgium 21.5%, Japan 14.3%, Samoa 7.8%, Australia 7.5%, Malaysia 6.7%, Taiwan 5.6%. **Tourism:** $3 mil. **Budget** (FY05): $59.7 mil.

Transport: Civil aviation: 3 airports. **Chief port:** Betio.

Communications: TV sets: 23 per 1,000 pop. **Radios:** 341 per 1,000 pop. **Telephone lines** (2004): 4,500. **Internet** (2004): 2,000 users.

Health: Life expect.: 59.4 male; 65.6 female. **Births** (per 1,000 pop.): 30.5. **Deaths** (per 1,000 pop.): 8.1. **Natural inc.:** 2.24%. **Infant mortality** (per 1,000 live births): 46. **AIDS rate:** NA.

Education: Compulsory: ages 6-15. **Literacy:** NA.

Major intl. organizations: UN (FAO, IBRD, ILO, IMF, IMO, WHO), the Commonwealth.

Consulate: 95 Nakolo Pl., Rm. 265, Honolulu, HI 96819; 808-834-6775.

Website: www.state.gov/r/eap/ci/kr/

A British protectorate since 1892, the Gilbert and Ellice Islands colony was completed with the inclusion of the Phoenix Islands, 1937. Tarawa Atoll was the scene of some of the bloodiest fighting in the Pacific during WWII.

Self-rule was granted 1971; the Ellice Islands separated from the colony 1975 and became independent Tuvalu, 1978. Kiribati (pronounced Kiribass) independence was attained July 12, 1979. Under a treaty of friendship the U.S. relinquished its claims to several Line and Phoenix islands, including Christmas (Kiritimati), Canton, and Enderbury. Kiribati was admitted to the UN Sept. 14, 1999.

Korea, North
Democratic People's Republic of Korea

People: Population: 23,301,725. **Age distrib. (%):** <15: 23.3; 65+: 8.5. **Pop. density:** 501 per sq mi, 194 per sq km. **Urban:** 61.6%. **Ethnic group:** Korean. **Principal language:** Korean (official). **Chief religions:** Activities almost non-existent; traditionally Buddhist, Confucianist, Chondogyo.

Geography: Total area: 46,541 sq mi, 120,540 sq km; **Land area:** 46,491 sq mi, 120,410 sq km. **Location:** In northern E Asia. **Neighbors:** China and Russia on N, S. Korea on S. **Topography:** Mountains and hills cover nearly all the country, with narrow valleys and small plains in between. N and E coasts are most rugged areas. **Capital:** Pyongyang, 3,351,000. **Cities (urban aggr.):** Nampo, 1,102,000.

Government: Type: Communist state. **Head of state:** Kim Jong Il; b. Feb. 16, 1942; officially assumed post Oct. 8, 1997. **Head of gov.:** Prem. Kim Yong Il; b. May 2, 1944; in office: Apr. 11, 2007. **Local divisions:** 9 provinces, 4 special cities. **Defense budget:** $2.3 bil. **Active troops:** 1,106,000.

Economy: Industries: armaments, machine building, electric power, chemicals, mining, metallurgy, textiles. **Chief crops:** rice, corn, potatoes, soybeans. **Natural resources:** coal, lead, tungsten, zinc, graphite, magnesite, iron ore, copper, gold, pyrites, salt, fluorspar, hydropower. **Arable land:** 22%. **Livestock:** cattle: 570,000; chickens: 21 mil; goats: 2.7 mil; pigs: 3.2 mil; sheep: 172,000. **Fish catch:** 268,700 metric tons. **Electricity prod.:** 22.2 bil kWh. **Labor force:** agricultural 36%, industry and services 64%.

Finance: Monetary unit: Won (KPW) (Sept. 2007: 142.45 = $1 U.S.). **GDP:** $40 bil; **per capita GDP:** $1,800; **GDP growth:** 1.8%. **Imports** (2005): $2.7 bil; China 42%, South Korea 28%, Russia 9%, Thailand 8%. **Exports** (2005): $1.3 bil; China 35%, South Korea 24%, Thailand 9%, Japan 9%. **Tourism:** $150 mil. **Budget:** NA.

Transport: Railroad: Length: 3,240 mi. **Civil Aviation:** 19.9 mil pass.-mi; 36 airports. **Chief ports:** Chongjin, Haeju, Hungnam, Kimchaek, Kosong, Najin, Nampo, Sinuiju, Sonbong, Songnim, Wonsan.

Communications: TV sets: 55 per 1,000 pop. **Radios:** 146 per 1,000 pop. **Telephone lines** (2005): 980,000.

Health: Life expect.: 69.2 male; 74.8 female. **Births** (per 1,000 pop.): 15.1. **Deaths** (per 1,000 pop.): 7.2. **Natural inc.:** 0.79%. **Infant mortality** (per 1,000 live births): 22.6. **AIDS rate:** NA.

Labor force: agriculture 36%, industry and services 64%.

Education: Compulsory: ages 6-15. **Literacy:** 99%.

Major intl. organizations: UN (FAO, ILO, IMO, WHO).

Permanent UN Representative: 820 Second Ave., 13th Fl., New York, NY 10017; 212-972-3105.

Website: www.korea-dpr.com

The Democratic People's Republic of Korea was founded May 1, 1948, in the zone occupied by Russian troops after WWII. Its armies tried to conquer the south, 1950. After 3 years of fighting, with Chinese and U.S. intervention, a cease-fire was proclaimed.

For the next 4 decades, a hardline Communist regime headed by Kim Il Sung kept tight control over the nation's political, economic, and cultural life. The nation used its abundant mineral and hydroelectric resources to develop its military strength and heavy industry. By the early 1990s, North Korea was widely believed to be developing nuclear weapons. The U.S. and North Korea signed an agreement, Oct. 21, 1994, providing for phased dismantling of North Korea's nuclear development program in return for U.S. energy aid and improved ties with the U.S.

Kim Il Sung died July 8, 1994. He was succeeded by his son, Kim Jong Il. Defections by high officials, a deteriorating economy, and severe food shortages plagued North Korea in the late 1990s.

On Sept. 17, 1999, the U.S. eased travel and trade restrictions on North Korea after Pyongyang agreed to suspend long-range missile testing. A first-ever summit conference in Pyongyang between North and South Korean leaders, June 13-15, 2000, marked an unexpected improvement in relations between the 2 Koreas, and brought an end to many U.S. sanctions. In Sept. 2002, Japanese Prime Min. Junichiro Koizumi became the first Japanese prime minister to visit North Korea; in a landmark summit, the 2 countries agreed to begin normalizing relations.

Pres. George W. Bush, in a speech Jan. 31, 2002, included North Korea with Iraq and Iran as part of an "axis of evil." In Oct. 2002, N. Korea admitted to pursuing a secret nuclear weapons program, in violation of past agreements, and, in Jan. 2003, withdrew from the Nuclear Non-Proliferation Treaty. The U.S. insisted that North Korea dismantle its nuclear weapons program, while North Korea demanded a nonaggression treaty and economic aid from the U.S. Six-nation talks sponsored by China, 2003-04, failed to produce an agreement. A huge explosion in the Ryongchon railway station Apr. 22, 2004, killed 161 people.

North Korea declared Feb. 10, 2005, that it had produced nuclear weapons. North Korean missile tests July 5, 2006, included the long-range Taepodong-2, which failed. The UN Security Council condemned the tests, July 15, but omitted the sanctions threat requested by Japan and the U.S.

In 6-nation talks Feb. 13, 2007, North Korea agreed to begin closing its nuclear facilities, in exchange for 1 mil metric tons of heavy fuel oil. The 2 Koreas resumed direct rail service May 17 for the first time since the Korean War. Floods in Aug. killed at least 600 people and caused extensive damage to homes, livestock, and infrastructure. Chief U.S. negotiator Christopher Hill announced Sept. 2 that North Korea had pledged to reveal and dismantle all nuclear programs by Dec. 31.

Korea, South
Republic of Korea

People: Population: 49,044,790. **Age distrib. (%):** <15: 18.3; 65+: 9.6. **Pop. density:** 1,294 per sq mi, 499 per sq km. **Urban:** 80.8%. **Ethnic group:** Korean. **Principal language:** Korean (official). **Chief religions:** No affiliation 49%, Christian 26%, Buddhist 23%.

Geography: Total area: 38,023 sq mi, 98,480 sq km; **Land area:** 37,911 sq mi, 98,190 sq km. **Location:** In northern E Asia. **Neighbors:** North Korea on N. **Topography:** Mountainous, with a rugged E coast. W and S coasts are deeply indented, with many islands and harbors. **Capital:** Seoul, 9,645,000. **Cities (urban aggr.):** Pusan, 3,554,000; Inch'on, 2,620,000; Taegu, 2,511,000.

Government: Type: Republic. **Head of state:** Pres. Roh Moo Hyun; b. Aug. 6, 1946; in office: Feb. 25, 2003. **Head of gov.:** Prime Min. Han Duck Soo; b. June 18, 1949; in office: Apr. 2, 2007. **Local divisions:** 9 provinces, 7 special cities. **Defense budget:** $23.7 bil. **Active troops:** 687,000.

Economy: Industries: electronics, autos, chemicals, shipbuilding, steel, textiles, clothing, footwear, food proc. **Chief crops:** rice, root crops, barley, vegetables, fruit. **Natural resources:** coal, tungsten, graphite, molybd., lead, hydropower potential. **Arable land:** 17%. **Livestock:** cattle: 2.5 mil; chickens: 119.2 mil; goats: 522,534; pigs: 9.4 mil; sheep: 1,202. **Fish catch:** 2,075,301 metric tons. **Electricity prod.:** 366.2 bil kWh. **Labor force** (2006 est.): agriculture 6.4%, industry 26.4%, services 67.2%.

Finance: Monetary unit: Won (KRW) (Sept. 2007: 928.83 = $1 U.S.). **GDP:** $1.2 tril; **per capita GDP:** $24,500; **GDP growth:** 4.8%. **Imports:** $309.3 bil; Japan 17.4%, China 15.4%, U.S. 11.2%, Saudi Arabia 6.4%. **Exports:** $326 bil; China 24.7%, U.S. 13.1%, Japan 7.5%, Hong Kong 4.2%, Taiwan 4.1%. **Tourism:** $5.7 bil. **Budget:** $201 bil. **Intl. reserves less gold:** $158.79 bil. **Gold:** 420,000 oz t. **Consumer prices:** 2.24%.

Transport: Railroad: Length: 2,157 mi. **Motor vehicles:** 10.6 mil pass. cars; 4.3 mil comm. vehicles. **Civil aviation:** 35.8 mil pass.-mi; 69 airports. **Chief ports:** Inchon, Masan, Pohang, Pusan, Ulsan.

Communications: TV sets: 364 per 1,000 pop. **Radios:** 1,039 per 1,000 pop. **Telephone lines:** 26.9 mil. **Internet:** 34.1 mil users.

Health: Life expect.: 73.8 male; 80.9 female. **Births** (per 1,000 pop.): 9.9. **Deaths** (per 1,000 pop.): 6. **Natural inc.:** 0.39%. **Infant mortality** (per 1,000 live births): 6.1. **AIDS rate:** <0.1%.

Education: Compulsory: ages 6-14. **Literacy:** 97.9%.

Major intl. organizations: UN (FAO, IBRD, ILO, IMF, IMO, WHO, WTO), APEC, OECD.

Embassy: 2320 Massachusetts Ave. NW 20008; 939-5654.

Website: www.korea.net

Korea, once called the Hermit Kingdom, has a recorded history since the 1st cent. BCE. It was united in a kingdom under the Silla Dynasty, 668 CE. It was at times associated with the Chinese empire; the treaty that concluded the Sino-Japanese war of 1894-95 recognized Korea's complete independence. In 1910 Japan forcibly annexed Korea as Chosun.

At the Potsdam conference, July 1945, the 38th parallel was designated as the line dividing the Soviet and the American occupation. Russian troops entered Korea Aug. 10, 1945; U.S. troops entered Sept. 8, 1945.

The South Koreans formed the Republic of Korea in May 1948 with Seoul as the capital. Dr. Syngman Rhee was chosen president. A separate, Communist regime was formed in the north; its army attacked the south in June 1950, initiating the Korean War. UN troops, under U.S. command, supported the S in the war, which ended in an armistice (July 1953) leaving Korea divided by a demilitarized zone (DMZ) along the 38th parallel.

Rhee's authoritarian rule became increasingly unpopular, and a movement spearheaded by college students forced his resignation Apr. 26, 1960. In an army coup May 16, 1961, Gen. Park Chung Hee became chairman of a ruling junta. He was elected president, 1963; a 1972 referendum allowed him to be reelected for an unlimited series of 6-year terms. Park was assassinated by the chief of the Korean CIA, Oct. 26, 1979.

In May 1980, Gen. Chun Doo Hwan, head of military intelligence, ordered the brutal suppression of pro-democracy demonstrations in Kwangju. On July 1, 1987, following weeks of antigovernment protests, some of them violent, Chun agreed to permit election of the next president by direct popular vote and other democratic reforms. In Dec., Roh Tae Woo was elected president. In 1990, the nation's 3 largest political parties merged; some 100,000 students protested the merger as undemocratic.

Pres. Kim Young Sam took office in 1993. Convicted of mutiny, treason, and corruption, Chun was sentenced to death by a Seoul court, Aug. 26, 1996, for his role in the 1979 coup and 1980 Kwangju massacre; Roh received a 22-1/2 year prison sentence. On Dec. 16, Chun's term was reduced to life in prison, and Roh's to 17 years.

The collapse in Jan. 1997 of the Hanbo steel firm triggered a series of corruption scandals. With currency and stock values plummeting, the nation averted default by agreeing, Dec. 4, on a $57 bil bailout from the IMF. Kim Dae Jung, a longtime dissident, won the presidential election Dec. 18. Chun and Roh were released and pardoned Dec. 22, 1997.

At an unprecedented summit meeting in Pyongyang, June 13-15, 2000, Pres. Kim Dae Jung and North Korean leader Kim Jong Il agreed to work for reconciliation and eventual reunification of their 2 countries. On Oct. 13, 2000, Kim Dae Jung was named the winner of the 2000 Nobel Peace Prize. Roh Moo Hyun won a presidential election Dec. 19.

A subway fire in Taegu, Feb. 18, 2003, killed 198 people; the arsonist was given a life term, and 8 subway officials charged with negligence also received prison sentences. Typhoon Maemi battered Pusan and other areas Sept. 12-13, 2003, leaving about 130 people dead and causing at least $4.1 bil in damage.

The National Assembly, Mar. 12, 2004, impeached Pres. Roh Moo Hyun for violating political neutrality and urging voters to support the Uri Party in upcoming legislative elections; voters backed Roh Apr. 15 by electing a Uri majority, and the Constitutional Court May 14 restored Roh to office. The IAEA Sept. 2 said South Korea had acknowledged having secretly processed a small amount of uranium to near weapons-grade level in 2000, violating the Nuclear Non-Proliferation Treaty and a bilateral accord with North Korea.

Ban Ki-Moon, South Korea's foreign minister in 2004-06, took office as UN secretary-general Jan. 1, 2007. The U.S. and South Korea announced a free-trade accord Apr. 2.

As of mid-2007, the U.S. had about 29,000 troops stationed in South Korea, and 1,200 Korean troops were participating in the U.S.-led coalition in Iraq.

Kuwait
State of Kuwait

People: Population: 2,505,559. **Age distrib.** (%): <15: 26.7; 65+: 2.8. **Pop. density:** 364 per sq mi, 141 per sq km. **Urban:** 98.3%. **Ethnic groups:** Arab 80%, South Asian 9%, Iranian 4%. **Principal languages:** Arabic (official), English. **Chief religion:** Muslim (official; Sunni 70%, Shi'a 30%) 85%.

Geography: Total area: 6,880 sq mi, 17,820 sq km; **Land area:** 6,880 sq mi, 17,820 sq km. **Location:** In Middle East, at N end of Persian Gulf. **Neighbors:** Iraq on N, Saudi Arabia on S. **Topography:** Flat, very dry, and extremely hot. **Capital:** Kuwait City, 1,810,000.

Government: Type: Constitutional monarchy. **Head of state:** Emir Sheikh Sabah al-Ahmad al-Jabir as-Sabah; b. June 6, 1929; in office: Jan. 29, 2006. **Head of gov.:** Prime Min. Sheikh Nasser al-Muhammad al-Ahmad as-Sabah; b. 1940; in office: Feb. 7, 2006. **Local divisions:** 5 governorates. **Defense budget:** $4.51 bil. **Active troops:** 15,500.

Economy: Industries: oil, petrochems., desalination, food proc., constr. materials. **Chief crops:** practically none. **Natural resources:** oil, fish, shrimp, nat. gas. **Crude oil reserves:** 101.5 bi bbls. **Arable land:** 1%. **Livestock:** cattle: 28,000; chickens: 32.5 mil; goats: 150,000; sheep: 900,000. **Fish catch:** 5,222 metric tons. **Electricity prod.:** 41.1 bil kWh. **Labor force:** NA.

Finance: Monetary unit: Dinar (KWD) (Sept. 2007: 0.28 = $1 U.S.). **GDP:** $55.9 bil; **per capita GDP:** $23,100; **GDP growth:** 12.6%. **Imports:** $19.1 bil; U.S. 14.1%, Japan 7.8%, Germany 7.7%, Saudi Arabia 6.8%, China 5.7%, UK 5.4%. **Exports:** $56.1 bil; Japan 20.2%, South Korea 16%, Taiwan 11.5%, Singapore 9.6%, U.S. 8.9%, Netherlands 5.1%. **Tourism:** $180 mil. **Budget:** $33.6 bil. **Intl. reserves less gold:** $8.35 bil. **Gold:** 2.54 mil oz t. **Consumer prices:** 3.08%.

Transport: Motor vehicles: 849,000 pass. cars; 172,000 comm. vehicles. **Civil aviation:** 3.9 bil pass.-mi; 4 airports. **Chief port:** Mina al-Ahmadi.

Communications: TV sets: 480 per 1,000 pop. **Radios:** 633 per 1,000 pop. **Telephone lines:** 510,300. **Internet:** 816,700 users.

Health: Life expect.: 76.3 male; 78.5 female. **Births** (per 1,000 pop.): 22. **Deaths** (per 1,000 pop.): 2.4. **Natural inc.:** 1.96%. **Infant mortality** (per 1,000 live births): 9.5. **AIDS rate:** NA.

Education: Compulsory: ages 6-14. **Literacy:** 93.3%.

Major intl. organizations: UN (FAO, IBRD, ILO, IMF, IMO, WHO, WTO), AL, OPEC.

Embassy: 2940 Tilden St. NW 20008; 966-0702.

Website: www.da.gov.kw

Kuwait is ruled by the Sabah dynasty, founded 1759. Britain ran foreign relations and defense from 1899 until independence in 1961. The majority of the population is non-Kuwaiti, with many Palestinians, and cannot vote.

Oil is the fiscal mainstay, providing most of Kuwait's income. Oil pays for free medical care, education, and social security. There are no taxes, except customs duties.

Kuwait was attacked and overrun by Iraqi forces Aug. 2, 1990. The emir and senior members of the ruling family fled to Saudi Arabia to establish a government in exile. On Aug. 28, Iraq announced that Kuwait was its 19th province. Following several weeks of aerial attacks on Iraq and Iraqi forces in Kuwait, a U.S.-led coalition began a ground attack Feb. 23, 1991. By Feb. 27, Iraqi forces were routed and Kuwait liberated.

Former U.S. Pres. George Bush visited Kuwait, Apr. 14-16, 1993. Kuwaiti authorities arrested 14 Iraqis and Kuwaitis for alleg-

edly plotting to assassinate him during his visit; 13 were convicted and sentenced to prison or death, June 4, 1994. Northern Kuwait was used by U.S. and British troops as a staging area prior to the Mar. 2003 invasion of Iraq.

Political rights were extended to women, May 16, 2005; the first female cabinet member was appointed June 12. After Emir Sheikh Jabir al-Ahmad al-Jabir as-Sabah died Jan. 15, 2006, an ailing successor was ousted, and Prime Min. Sheikh Sabah al-Ahmad al-Jabir as-Sabah became the new emir Jan. 29.

Kyrgyzstan
Kyrgyz Republic

People: Population: 5,284,149. **Age distrib.** (%): <15: 30.3; 65+: 6.2. **Pop. density:** 72 per sq mi, 28 per sq km. **Urban:** 35.8%. **Ethnic groups:** Kyrgyz 65%, Uzbek 14%, Russian 13%. **Principal languages:** Kyrgyz, Russian (both official); Uzbek; Dungun. **Chief religions:** Muslim 75%, Russian Orthodox 20%.

Geography: Total area: 76,641 sq mi, 198,500 sq km; **Land area:** 73,861 sq mi, 191,300 sq km. **Location:** In Central Asia. **Neighbors:** Kazakhstan on N, China on E, Uzbekistan on W, Tajikistan on S. **Topography:** Landlocked country nearly covered by Tien Shan and Pamir Mts.; avg. elevation 9,020 ft. A large lake, Issyk-Kul, in NE is 1 mi above sea level. **Capital:** Bishkek, 798,000.

Government: Type: Republic. **Head of state:** Pres. Kurmanbek Bakiyev; b. Aug. 1, 1949; in office: Aug. 14, 2005 (acting from Mar. 25). **Head of gov.:** Prime Min. Almazbek Atambayev; b. Sept. 17, 1956; in office: Mar. 30, 2007. **Local divisions:** 7 oblasts and Bishkek. **Defense budget:** $36.7 mil. **Active troops:** 12,500.

Economy: Industries: small machinery, textiles, food proc., cement, shoes, timber, refrigerators, furniture, electric motors. **Chief crops:** tobacco, cotton, potatoes, vegetables, grapes, fruits & berries. **Natural resources:** hydropower, gold, rare earth metals, coal, oil, nat. gas, nepheline, mercury, bismuth, lead, zinc. **Crude oil reserves:** 40 mil bbls. **Arable land:** 7%. **Livestock:** cattle: 1.1 mil; chickens: 4.3 mil; goats: 814,000; pigs: 77,500; sheep: 3.1 mil. **Fish catch:** 27 metric tons. **Electricity prod.:** 15.2 bil kWh. **Labor force** (2000 est.): agriculture 55%, industry 15%, services 30%.

Finance: Monetary unit: Som (KGS) (Sept. 2007: 37.67 = $1 U.S.). **GDP:** $10.7 bil; **per capita GDP:** $2,100; **GDP growth:** 2.7%. **Imports:** $1.2 bil; China 56.8%, Russia 15.1%, Kazakhstan 8.1%. **Exports:** $701.8 mil; UAE 35.8%, Russia 20.2%, Kazakhstan 13.1%, China 11.8%. **Tourism:** $76 mil. **Budget:** $544.8 mil. **Intl. reserves less gold:** $508 mil. **Gold:** 80,000 oz t. **Consumer prices:** 5.56%.

Transport: Railroad: Length: 292 mi. **Motor vehicles:** 196,000 pass. cars. **Civil aviation:** 231.2 mil pass.-mi; 18 airports. **Chief port:** Ysyk-Kol.

Communications: TV sets: 49 per 1,000 pop. **Radios:** 113 per 1,000 pop. **Telephone lines:** 440,400. **Internet:** 298,100 users.

Health: Life expect.: 64.8 male; 73 female. **Births** (per 1,000 pop.): 23.1. **Deaths** (per 1,000 pop.): 7. **Natural inc.:** 1.61%. **Infant mortality** (per 1,000 live births): 33.4. **AIDS rate:** 0.1%.

Education: Compulsory: ages 7-15. **Literacy:** 98.7%.

Major intl. organizations: UN (FAO, IBRD, ILO, IMF, WHO, WTO), CIS, OSCE.

Embassy: 2360 Massachusetts Ave. NW 20008; 338-5141.

Website: www.president.kg

The region was inhabited around the 13th cent. by the Kyrgyz. It was annexed to Russia, 1864, and became a constituent republic of the USSR in 1936. Kyrgyzstan declared independence Aug. 31, 1991. It became an independent state when the USSR disbanded Dec. 26, 1991.

In power since 1990, Pres. Askar Akayev won a 3rd 5-year term in the Oct. 29, 2000, election. The U.S. military presence in Kyrgyzstan expanded from Dec. 2001. Fraud by Akayev loyalists in parliamentary elections Feb.-Mar. 2005 sparked protests. Akayev fled the country, Mar. 24, and formally resigned, Apr. 4. His interim successor, former Prime Min. Kurmanbek Bakiyev, a leader of the "tulip revolution," won by a landslide in the July 10 presidential vote. A prominent imam, Muhammad Rafik Kamalov, was killed Aug. 6, 2006, in what Kyrgyz security forces described as a shootout with Islamic extremists.

A new constitution limiting presidential powers was enacted Nov. 8, 2006; on Jan. 15, 2007, Bakiyev signed amendments restoring much of his presidential authority. Prime Min. Almazbek Atambayev survived an apparent attempt to poison him, May 11.

Laos
Lao People's Democratic Republic

People: Population: 6,521,998. **Age distrib.** (%): <15: 41.2; 65+: 3.1. **Pop. density:** 73 per sq mi, 28 per sq km. **Urban:** 20.6%. **Ethnic groups:** Lao Loum 68%, Lao Theung 22%, Lao Soung (incl. Hmong and Yao) 9%. **Principal languages:** Lao (official), French, English, various ethnic languages. **Chief religions:** Buddhist 65%, animist and other 33%.

Geography: Total area: 91,429 sq mi, 236,800 sq km; **Land area:** 89,112 sq mi, 230,800 sq km. **Location:** In Indochina Peninsula in SE Asia. **Neighbors:** Myanmar, China on N; Vietnam on E; Cambodia on S; Thailand on W. **Topography:** Landlocked, dominated by jungle. High mountains along E border are source of the E-W rivers slicing across the country to the Mekong R., which defines most of W border. **Capital:** Vientiane, 702,000.

Government: Type: Communist. **Head of state:** Pres. Choummaly Sayasone; b. Mar. 6, 1936; in office: June 8, 2006. **Head of gov.:** Prime Min. Bouasone Bouphavanh; b. June 3, 1954; in office: June 8, 2006. **Local divisions:** 16 provinces, 1 municipality, 1 special zone. **Defense budget:** $13.4 mil. **Active troops:** 29,100.

Economy: Industries: mining, timber, electric power, agric. proc., constr., garments, tourism. **Chief crops:** sweet potatoes, vegetables, corn, coffee, sugarcane. **Natural resources:** timber, hydropower, gypsum, tin, gold, gemstones. **Arable land:** 4%. **Livestock:** cattle: 1.3 mil; chickens: 19.8 mil; goats: 143,000; pigs: 1.8 mil. **Fish catch:** 107,800 metric tons. **Electricity prod.:** 1.7 bil kWh. **Labor force** (2005 est.): agriculture 80%, industry and services 20%.

Finance: Monetary unit: Kip (LAK) (Sept. 2007: 9,622.40 = $1 U.S.). **GDP:** $13.6 bil; **per capita GDP:** $2,100; **GDP growth:** 7.4%. **Imports:** $1.4 bil; Thailand 69%, China 11.4%, Vietnam 5.6%. **Exports:** $982.2 mil; Thailand 42.4%, Vietnam 10%, China 4.2%, Malaysia 4.2%. **Tourism:** $146 mil. **Budget:** $537.4 mil. **Intl. reserves less gold:** $217 mil. **Gold:** 210,000 oz t. **Consumer prices:** 6.8%.

Transport: Civil aviation: 55.9 mil pass.-mi; 9 airports.

Communications: TV sets: 10 per 1,000 pop. **Radios:** 145 per 1,000 pop. **Telephone lines:** 75,300. **Internet:** 25,000 users.

Health: Life expect.: 53.8 male; 58 female. **Births** (per 1,000 pop.): 35. **Deaths** (per 1,000 pop.): 11.3. **Natural inc.:** 2.37%. **Infant mortality** (per 1,000 live births): 81.4. **AIDS rate:** 0.1%.

Education: Compulsory: ages 6-10. **Literacy:** 68.7%.

Major intl. organizations: UN (FAO, IBRD, ILO, IMF, WHO), ASEAN.

Embassy: 2222 S St. NW 20008; 332-6416.

Website: www.tourismlaos.gov.la

Laos became a French protectorate in 1893, but regained independence as a constitutional monarchy July 19, 1949.

Conflicts among neutralist, Communist, and conservative factions created a chaotic political situation. Armed conflict increased after 1960.

The 3 factions formed a coalition government in June 1962, with neutralist Prince Souvanna Phouma as premier. A 14-nation conference in Geneva signed agreements, 1962, guaranteeing neutrality and independence. By 1964 the Pathet Lao had withdrawn from the coalition, and, with aid from North Vietnamese troops, renewed sporadic attacks. U.S. planes bombed the Ho Chi Minh trail, a supply line from North Vietnam to Communist forces in Laos and South Vietnam.

In 1970 the U.S. stepped up air support and military aid. After Pathet Lao military gains, Souvanna Phouma in May 1975 ordered government troops to cease fighting; the Pathet Lao took control. The Lao People's Democratic Republic was proclaimed Dec. 3, 1975.

From the mid-1970s through the 1980s, Laos relied on Vietnam for military and financial aid. Since easing its foreign investment laws in 1988, Laos has attracted more than $5 bil from Thailand, the U.S., and other nations. Laos was admitted to ASEAN on July 23, 1997. The U.S. Congress, Nov. 19, 2004, approved normalization of trade with Laos. The 8th congress of the Communist Party, Mar. 2006, marked the transition to a younger generation of leaders.

Latvia
Republic of Latvia

People: Population: 2,259,810. **Age distrib.** (%): <15: 13.6; 65+: 16.7. **Pop. density:** 92 per sq mi, 36 per sq km. **Urban:** 67.8%. **Ethnic groups:** Latvian 58%, Russian 30%, Belarusian 4%, Ukrainian 3%, Polish 2%, Lithuanian 1%. **Principal languages:** Latvian (official), Russian, Lithuanian. **Chief religions:** Lutheran, Roman Catholic, Russian Orthodox.

Geography: Total area: 24,938 sq mi, 64,589 sq km; **Land area:** 24,552 sq mi, 63,589 sq km. **Location:** E Europe, on Baltic Sea. **Neighbors:** Estonia on N; Lithuania, Belarus on S; Russia on E. **Topography:** Lowland with numerous lakes, marshes, and peat bogs. Principal river, W. Dvina (Daugava), rises in Russia. Glacial hills in E. **Capital:** Riga, 729,000.

Government: Type: Republic. **Head of state:** Pres. Valdis Zatlers; b. Mar. 22, 1955; in office: July 8, 2007. **Head of gov.:** Prime Min. Aigars Kalvitis; b. June 27, 1966; in office: Dec. 2, 2004. **Local divisions:** 26 counties, 7 municipalities. **Defense budget:** $340 mil. **Active troops:** 5,339.

Economy: Industries: vehicles, railroad cars, synthetics, agric. machinery, fertilizers, washing machines. **Chief crops:** grain, sugar beets, potatoes, vegetables. **Natural resources:** peat, limestone, dolomite, hydropower, wood, amber. **Arable land:** 28%. **Livestock:** cattle: 385,200; chickens: 3.5 mil; goats: 14,900; pigs: 427,900; sheep: 41,600. **Fish catch:** 151,160 metric tons. **Electricity prod.:** 4.8 bil kWh. **Labor force** (2005 est.): agriculture 13%, industry 19%, services 68%.

Finance: Monetary unit: Lat (LVL) (Sept. 2007: 0.51 = $1 U.S.). **GDP:** $36.5 bil; **per capita GDP:** $16,000; **GDP growth:** 11.9%. **Imports:** $10.3 bil; Germany 15.4%, Lithuania 13%, Russia 8%, Estonia 7.7%, Poland 7.2%, Finland 5.7%, Sweden 5%. **Exports:** $7 bil; Lithuania 14.1%, Estonia 12.2%, Russia 11.6%, Germany 9.8%, UK 7.7%, Sweden 6.3%. **Tourism:** $341 mil. **Budget:**

$6.5 bil. **Intl. reserves less gold:** $2.89 bil. **Gold:** 250,000 oz t **Consumer prices:** 6.56%.

Transport: Railroad: Length: 1,431 mi. **Motor vehicles** 686,000 pass. cars; 118,000 comm. vehicles. **Civil aviation:** 152.2 mil pass.-mi; 24 airports. **Chief port:** Riga.

Communications: TV sets: 757 per 1,000 pop. **Radios:** 701 per 1,000 pop. **Telephone lines:** 657,400. **Daily newspaper circ.:** 137.8 per 1,000 pop. **Internet:** 1.1 mil users.

Health: Life expect.: 66.4 male; 77.1 female. **Births** (per 1,000 pop.): 9.4. **Deaths** (per 1,000 pop.): 13.6. **Natural inc.:** –0.42%. **Infant mortality** (per 1,000 live births): 9.2. **AIDS rate:** 0.8%.

Education: Compulsory: ages 7-15. **Literacy:** 99.7%.

Major intl. organizations: UN (FAO, IBRD, ILO, IMF, IMO, WHO), EU, NATO, OSCE.

Embassy: 2306 Massachusetts Ave. NW 20008; 328-2840.

Website: www.lv

Prior to 1918, Latvia was occupied by the Russians and Germans. It was an independent republic, 1918-39. The Aug. 1939 Soviet-German agreement assigned Latvia to the Soviet sphere of influence. It was officially accepted as part of the USSR on Aug. 5, 1940. It was overrun by the German army in 1941, but retaken in 1945.

During an abortive Soviet coup, Latvia declared independence, Aug. 21, 1991. The Soviet Union recognized Latvia's independence in Sept. 1991. The last Russian troops in Latvia withdrew by Aug. 31, 1994. Responding to international pressure, Latvian voters on Oct. 3, 1998, eased citizenship laws that had discriminated against some 500,000 ethnic Russians. On June 17, 1999, the legislature elected Vaira Vike-Freiberga as Latvia's first woman president. Latvia joined the EU and NATO in 2004. Latvia ratified a proposed EU constitution, June 2, 2005. A NATO summit conference in Riga, Nov. 28-29, 2006, marked the alliance's first in a former Soviet republic.

Lebanon
Lebanese Republic

People: Population: 3,925,502. **Age distrib.** (%): <15: 26.2; 65+: 7.1. **Pop. density:** 994 per sq mi, 384 per sq km. **Urban:** 86.6%. **Ethnic groups:** Arab 95%, Armenian 4%. **Principal languages:** Arabic (official), French, English, Armenian. **Chief religions:** Muslim 60%, Christian 39%.

Geography: Total area: 4,015 sq mi, 10,400 sq km; **Land area:** 3,950 sq mi, 10,230 sq km. **Location:** In Middle East, at E end of Mediterranean Sea. **Neighbors:** Syria on E, Israel on S. **Topography:** There is a narrow coastal strip, and 2 mountain ranges running N-S enclosing the fertile Beqaa Valley. The Litani R. runs S through the valley, turning W to empty into Mediterranean. **Capital:** Beirut, 1,777,000.

Government: Type: Republic. **Head of state:** Pres. Emile Lahoud; b. Jan. 12, 1936; in office: Nov. 24, 1998. **Head of gov.:** Prime Min. Fouad Siniora; b. 1943; in office: July 19, 2005. **Local divisions:** 6 governorates. **Defense budget:** $663 mil. **Active troops:** 72,100.

Economy: Industries: banking, food proc., jewelry, cement, textiles, mineral & chemical products. **Chief crops:** citrus, grapes, tomatoes, apples, vegetables, potatoes, olives, tobacco. **Natural resources:** limestone, iron ore, salt, water. **Arable land:** 16%. **Livestock:** cattle: 76,900; chickens: 35 mil; goats: 494,700; pigs: 15,000; sheep: 337,300. **Fish catch:** 4,601 metric tons. **Electricity prod.:** 9.6 bil kWh. **Labor force:** NA.

Finance: Monetary unit: Pound (LBP) (Sept. 2007: 1,514.00 = $1 U.S.). **GDP:** $22 bil; **per capita GDP:** $5,700; **GDP growth:** –6.4%. **Imports** (2005 est.): $9.3 bil; Syria 11.4%, Italy 9.6%, U.S. 9.2%, France 7.6%, Germany 5.9%. **Exports:** $1.9 bil (2005 est.): Syria 26.4%, UAE 11.8%, Switzerland 7.9%, Saudi Arabia 5.6%, Turkey 4.4%. **Tourism:** $5.4 bil. **Budget:** $7.4 bil. **Intl. reserves less gold:** $8.89 bil. **Gold:** 9.22 mil oz t.

Transport: Railroad: Length: 249 mi. **Motor vehicles:** 1.4 mil pass. cars; 102,400 comm. vehicles. **Civil aviation:** 1.2 bil pass.-mi; 5 airports. **Chief ports:** Beirut, Chekka, Jounie, Tripoli.

Communications: TV sets: 355 per 1,000 pop. **Radios:** 907 per 1,000 pop. **Telephone lines:** 681,400. **Newspaper circ.:** 63.3 per 1,000 pop. **Internet:** 950,000 users.

Health: Life expect.: 70.7 male; 75.8 female. **Births** (per 1,000 pop.): 18.1. **Deaths** (per 1,000 pop.): 6.1. **Natural inc.:** 1.2%. **Infant mortality** (per 1,000 live births): 23.4. **AIDS rate:** 0.1%.

Education: Compulsory: ages 6-15. **Literacy:** 87.4%.

Major intl. organizations: UN (FAO, IBRD, ILO, IMF, IMO, WHO), AL.

Embassy: 2560 28th St. NW 20008; 939-6300.

Website: www.informs.gov.lb

Formed from 5 former Turkish Empire districts, Lebanon became an independent state Sept. 1, 1920, administered under French mandate 1920-41. French troops withdrew in 1946.

Under the 1943 National Covenant, all public positions were divided among the various religious communities, with Christians in the majority. By the 1970s, Muslims became the majority and demanded a larger political and economic role.

U.S. Marines intervened, May-Oct. 1958, during a Syrian-aided revolt. Continued raids against Israeli civilians, 1970-75, brought Israeli retaliation in southern Lebanon.

An estimated 60,000 were killed and billions of dollars in damage inflicted in a 1975-76 civil war. Palestinian units and leftist Muslims fought against the Maronite militia, the Phalange, and other Christians. Several Arab countries provided political and arms support to the various factions, while Israel aided Christian forces. Up to 15,000 Syrian troops intervened in 1976 to fight Palestinian groups. A cease-fire was mainly policed by Syria.

Israeli forces invaded Lebanon June 6, 1982, attacking strongholds of the Palestine Liberation Organization (PLO). Israeli and Syrian forces engaged in the Bekaa Valley. On Aug. 21, the PLO evacuated west Beirut after massive Israeli bombings there. Israeli troops entered west Beirut following the Sept. 14 assassination of newly elected Lebanese Pres. Bashir Gemayel. On Sept. 16, Lebanese Christian troops entered the Sabra and Shatila refugee camps and massacred hundreds of Palestinian civilians. An agreement May 17, 1983, between Lebanon, Israel, and the U.S. (but not Syria) provided for the withdrawal of Israeli troops; at least 30,000 Syrian troops remained in Lebanon, and Israel held onto a "security zone" in the south.

In 1983, terrorist bombings became a way of life in Beirut as some 50 people were killed in an explosion at the U.S. Embassy, Apr. 18; 241 U.S. servicemen and 58 French soldiers died in separate Islamist suicide attacks, Oct. 23. The 1980s also witnessed kidnappings of U.S., British, French, and Soviet citizens by Islamic militants. All hostages were released by 1992.

A treaty signed May 22, 1991, between Lebanon and Syria recognized Lebanon as a separate state for the first time since the 2 countries gained independence in 1943.

Israeli forces conducted air raids and artillery strikes against guerrilla bases and villages in southern Lebanon, causing over 200,000 to flee their homes July 25-29, 1993. Some 500,000 civilians fled their homes in Apr. 1996 when Israel again struck suspected guerrilla bases in the south. The economy revived in the 1990s, but Syria continued to dominate Lebanon's political affairs. Israel withdrew virtually all its troops from S Lebanon by May 24, 2000, leaving Hezbollah, an Iranian-backed guerrilla group, in control of much of the region.

Rafik al-Hariri, a former prime minister (1992-98, 2000-04), was killed by a truck bomb, Feb. 14, 2005. Many Lebanese blamed Syria, which denied involvement. As anti-Syrian protests mounted, Syria pulled nearly all its troops out of Lebanon, although some intelligence agents may have remained. An anti-Syrian bloc won parliamentary elections held in May and June. A new cabinet, installed July 19, was headed by Fouad Siniora, a friend and aide to Hariri, and included a Hezbollah member.

A rocket attack and border raid by Hezbollah, July 12, 2006, in which 3 Israeli soldiers were killed and 2 captured, triggered a massive escalation of hostilities. Hezbollah, led by Sheikh Hassan Nasrallah, bombarded northern Israel with nearly 4,000 rockets, while Israeli air and ground forces assaulted suspected Hezbollah strongholds in southern Lebanon and southern Beirut. Roads, bridges, and other installations were destroyed, and hundreds of civilians were caught in the crossfire; at least 28 civilians were killed by an Israeli air strike July 30 at Qana, where more than 100 in a UN compound had died from an Israeli artillery barrage 10 years earlier. By Aug. 14, when a UN-sponsored cease-fire took hold, the war dead included nearly 1,150 Lebanese. To enforce the truce, thousands of Lebanese govt. troops began moving into southern Lebanon, and expansion of the small UN force already in Lebanon (UNIFIL) was approved.

Industry Min. Pierre Gemayel, a prominent Christian and critic of Syria, was assassinated Nov. 21, 2006. At an international conference in Paris, Jan. 25, 2007, donor countries pledged more than $7.6 bil in reconstruction aid. UNIFIL had about 13,300 troops in Lebanon at the end of Aug. 2007. After more than 3 months of fighting in which over 400 people died, Lebanese forces Sept. 2 defeated Islamic militants at the Nahr al-Bared Palestinian refugee camp north of Tripoli.

Lesotho
Kingdom of Lesotho

People: Population: 2,125,262. **Age distrib. (%):** <15: 35.7; 65+: 5. **Pop. density:** 181 per sq mi, 70 per sq km. **Urban:** 18.7%. **Ethnic groups:** Sotho 99%. **Principal languages:** Sesotho, English (both official); Zulu; Xhosa. **Chief religions:** Christian 80%, indigenous beliefs 20%.

Geography: Total area: 11,720 sq mi, 30,355 sq km; **Land area:** 11,720 sq mi, 30,355 sq km. **Location:** In southern Africa. **Neighbors:** Completely surrounded by Republic of South Africa. **Topography:** Landlocked and mountainous, altitudes from 5,000 to 11,100 ft. **Capital:** Maseru, 172,000.

Government: Type: Modified constitutional monarchy. **Head of state:** King Letsie III; b. July 17, 1963; in office: Feb. 7, 1996. **Head of gov.:** Prime Min. Pakalitha Mosisili; b. Mar. 14, 1945; in office: May 29, 1998. **Local divisions:** 10 districts. **Defense budget:** $30 mil. **Active troops:** 2,000.

Economy: Industries: food, beverages, textiles, apparel, handicrafts. **Chief crops:** corn, wheat, pulses, sorghum, barley. **Natural resources:** water, diamonds, other minerals. **Arable land:** 11%. **Livestock:** cattle: 650,000; chickens: 1.8 mil; goats: 790,000; pigs: 65,000; sheep: 1 mil. **Fish catch:** 46 metric tons. **Electricity prod.:** 350 mil kWh. **Labor force:** 86% of resident population engaged in subsistence agriculture; roughly 35% of the active male wage earners work in South Africa, industry and services 14%.

Finance: Monetary unit: Loti (LSL) (Sept. 2007: 7.16 = $1 U.S.). **GDP:** $5.3 bil; **per capita GDP:** $2,600; **GDP growth:** 3%. **Imports:** $1.4 bil; U.S. 83.8%, Belgium 12.7%, Canada 2.4%. **Exports:** $779.1 mil; Hong Kong 29.6%, China 24%, Taiwan 22.3%, Germany 5.7%, India 5.5%. **Tourism:** $30 mil. **Budget:** $734.7 mil. **Intl. reserves less gold:** $438 mil. **Consumer prices:** 6.05%.

Transport: Railroad: Length: NA. **Motor vehicles:** NA. **Civil aviation:** 3 airports.

Communications: TV sets: 16 per 1,000 pop. **Radios:** 52 per 1,000 pop. **Telephone lines:** 48,000. **Daily newspaper circ.:** 9 per 1,000 pop. **Internet:** 51,500 users.

Health: Life expect.: 40.7 male; 39.2 female. **Births** (per 1,000 pop.): 24.7. **Deaths** (per 1,000 pop.): 22.5. **Natural inc.:** 0.22%. **Infant mortality** (per 1,000 live births): 79.9. **AIDS rate:** 23.2%.

Education: Compulsory: ages 6-12. **Literacy:** 82.2%.

Major intl. organizations: UN (FOA, IBRD, ILO, IMF, WHO, WTO), the Commonwealth, AU.

Embassy: 2511 Massachusetts Ave. NW 20008; 797-5533.

Website: www.lesotho.gov.ls

Lesotho (once called Basutoland) became a British protectorate in 1868 when Chief Moshesh sought protection against the Boers. Independence came Oct. 4, 1966. Most of Lesotho's GNP is provided by citizens working in South Africa. Livestock raising is the chief industry; diamonds are the chief export.

South Africa imposed a blockade, Jan. 1, 1986, because Lesotho had given sanctuary to anti-apartheid groups. The blockade sparked a Jan. 20 military coup and was lifted, Jan. 25, when the new leaders agreed to expel the rebels.

In Mar. 1990, King Moshoeshoe was exiled by the military government. Letsie III became king Nov. 12. In Mar. 1993, Ntsu Mokhehle, a civilian, was elected prime minister, ending 23 years of military rule. After a series of violent disturbances, the king dismissed the Mokhehle government Aug. 17, 1994; constitutional rule was restored Sept. 14.

Letsie abdicated and Moshoeshoe was reinstated Jan. 25, 1995. Moshoeshoe died in an automobile accident, Jan. 15, 1996. Letsie was reinstated Feb. 7. South Africa and Botswana sent troops Sept. 22, 1998, to help suppress violent antigovernment protests.

According to UN estimates, more than 20% of the adult population has HIV/AIDS.

Liberia
Republic of Liberia

People: Population: 3,195,931. **Age distrib. (%):** <15: 43.6; 65+: 2.7. **Pop. density:** 86 per sq mi, 33 per sq km. **Urban:** 58.1%. **Ethnic groups:** Kpelle, Bassa, Dey, other tribes 95%; Americo-Liberians 2.5%; Caribbean 2.5%. **Principal languages:** English (official); Mande, West Atlantic, Kwa languages. **Chief religions:** Indigenous beliefs 40%, Christian 40%, Muslim 20%.

Geography: Total area: 43,000 sq mi, 111,370 sq km; **Land area:** 37,189 sq mi, 96,320 sq km. **Location:** On SW coast of W Africa. **Neighbors:** Sierra Leone on W, Guinea on N, Côte d'Ivoire on E. **Topography:** Marshy Atlantic coastline rises to low mountains and plateaus in forested interior; 6 major rivers flow in parallel courses to the ocean. **Capital:** Monrovia, 936,000.

Government: Type: Republic. **Head of state and gov.:** Pres. Ellen Johnson-Sirleaf; b. Oct. 29, 1938; in office: Jan. 16, 2006. **Local divisions:** 15 counties. **Defense budget:** NA. **Active troops:** 2,400.

Economy: Industries: rubber & palm oil proc., timber, diamonds. **Chief crops:** rubber, coffee, cocoa, rice, cassava, palm oil, sugarcane, bananas. **Natural resources:** iron ore, timber, diamonds, gold, hydropower. **Arable land:** 3%. **Livestock:** cattle: 36,000; chickens: 5.3 mil; goats: 220,000; pigs: 130,000; sheep: 210,000. **Fish catch:** 10,000 metric tons. **Electricity prod.:** 320 mil kWh. **Labor force** (2000 est.): agriculture 70%, industry 8%, services 22%.

Finance: Monetary unit: Dollar (LRD) (Sept. 2007: 62.50 = $1 U.S.). **GDP:** $2.8 bil; **per capita GDP:** $900; **GDP growth:** 7.8%. **Imports** (2004 est.): $4.8 bil; South Korea 40.2%, Singapore 16%, Japan 13.6%, China 8.7%. **Exports** (2004 est.): $910 mil; Germany 23.4%, South Africa 16.1%, Poland 15.7%, U.S. 11.3%, Spain 11%. **Tourism:** NA. **Budget** (2000 est.): $90.5 mil. **Intl. reserves less gold:** $48 mil.

Transport: Railroad: Length: 304 mi. **Motor vehicles:** 17,100 pass. cars; 12,800 comm. vehicles. **Civil aviation:** 2 airports. **Chief ports:** Buchanan, Monrovia.

Communications: TV sets: 26 per 1,000 pop. **Radios:** 329 per 1,000 pop. **Telephone lines** (2004): 6,900. **Daily newspaper circ.:** 14.2 per 1,000 pop. **Internet** (2003): 1,000 users.

Health: Life expect.: 38.9 male; 41.9 female. **Births** (per 1,000 pop.): 43.8. **Deaths** (per 1,000 pop.): 22.2. **Natural inc.:** 2.15%. **Infant mortality** (per 1,000 live births): 149.7. **AIDS rate:** NA.

Education (2004): Compulsory: ages 6-15. **Literacy:** 51.9%.

Major intl. organizations: UN and most of its specialized agencies, AU.

Embassy: 5201 16th St. NW 20011; 723-0437.

Website: www.emansion.gov.lr

Liberia was founded in 1822 by U.S. black freedmen who settled at Monrovia with the aid of colonization societies. It became a republic July 26, 1847, with a constitution modeled on that of the U.S. Descendants of freedmen dominated politics.

Under Pres. William V. S. Tubman, Liberia was a founding member of the UN in 1945. Tubman died in 1971 and was succeeded by his vice president, William R. Tolbert Jr. Charging rampant corruption, an Army Redemption Council of enlisted men staged a bloody predawn coup, Apr. 12, 1980, in which Pres. Tolbert was killed and replaced as head of state by Sgt. Samuel Doe. In 1985, Doe was chosen president in a disputed election.

A civil war began Dec. 1989. In Sept. 1990, Pres. Doe was captured and put to death. Despite the introduction of peacekeeping forces from several countries, the conflict intensified. Factional fighting devastated Monrovia in Apr. 1996. On Sept. 3, Ruth Perry became modern Africa's first female head of state, leading a transitional government. By then, the civil war had claimed more than 150,000 lives and uprooted over half the population.

Former rebel leader Charles Taylor was elected president July 19, 1997, in Liberia's first national election in 12 years. The UN imposed sanctions May 4, 2001, to punish Liberia for aiding the Revolutionary United Front (RUF) insurgency in Sierra Leone. Taylor declared a state of emergency Feb. 8, 2002, after Liberian rebels launched raids near Monrovia.

A UN-sponsored war crimes tribunal indicted Taylor June 4, 2003, for his role in Sierra Leone. With rebels again threatening Monrovia, Taylor resigned Aug. 11 and went into exile. The UN authorized a 15,000-member peacekeeping force (UNMIL) Sept. 19 to help stabilize the nation. A businessman, Charles Gyude Bryant, was sworn in Oct. 14 to head a power-sharing interim government. Ellen Johnson-Sirleaf won a presidential runoff election Nov. 8, 2005, and took office Jan. 16, 2006. Captured Mar. 29, 2006, while trying to flee Nigeria, Taylor was transferred to the Netherlands; his trial at the Hague began June 4, 2007, but was plagued by delays.

Libya
Great Socialist People's Libyan Arab Jamahiriya

People: Population: 6,036,914. **Age distrib.** (%): <15: 33.4; 65+: 4.2. **Pop. density:** 9 per sq mi, 3 per sq km. **Urban:** 84.8%. **Ethnic groups:** Arab-Berber 97%. **Principal languages:** Arabic (official), Italian, English. **Chief religion:** Muslim (official; mostly Sunni) 97%.

Geography: Total area: 679,362 sq mi, 1,759,540 sq km; **Land area:** 679,362 sq mi, 1,759,540 sq km. **Location:** On Mediterranean coast of N Africa. **Neighbors:** Tunisia, Algeria on W; Niger, Chad on S; Sudan, Egypt on E. **Topography:** Desert and semi-desert regions cover 92% of land, with low mountains in N, higher mountains in S, and a narrow coastal zone. **Capital:** Tripoli, 2,098,000. **Cities (urban aggr.):** Benghazi, 912,000.

Government: Type: Islamic Arabic Socialist "Mass-State." **Head of state and gov.:** Col. Muammar al-Qaddafi; b. Sept. 1942; in power: Sept. 1, 1969. **Local divisions:** 25 municipalities. **Defense budget:** $793 mil. **Active troops:** 76,000.

Economy: Industries: oil, food proc., textiles, handicrafts, cement. **Chief crops:** wheat, barley, olives, dates, citrus, vegetables, peanuts, soybeans. **Natural resources:** oil, nat. gas, gypsum. **Crude oil reserves:** 41.5 bil bbls. **Arable land:** 1%. **Livestock:** cattle: 130,000; chickens: 25 mil; goats: 1.3 mil; sheep: 4.5 mil. **Fish catch:** 46,339 metric tons. **Electricity prod.:** 21.2 bil kWh. **Labor force** (2004 est.): agriculture 17%, industry 23%, services 59%.

Finance: Monetary unit: Dinar (LYD) (Sept. 2007: 1.25 = $1 U.S.). **GDP:** $72.7 bil; **per capita GDP:** $12,300; **GDP growth:** 6.1%. **Imports:** $14.5 bil; Italy 18.8%, Germany 7.8%, China 7.5%, Tunisia 6.2%, France 5.8%, Turkey 5.2%. **Exports:** $37 bil; Italy 37.4%, Germany 14.8%, Spain 7.8%, U.S. 6.2%, France 5.6%, Turkey 5.4%. **Tourism:** $218 mil. **Budget:** $19.3 bil. **Intl. reserves less gold:** $39.41 bil. **Gold:** 4.62 mil oz t.

Transport: Motor vehicles: 552,700 pass. cars; 195,500 comm. vehicles. **Civil aviation:** 512.6 mil pass.-mi; 60 airports. **Chief ports:** Ra's Lanuf, Tripoli.

Communications: TV sets: 139 per 1,000 pop. **Radios:** 259 per 1,000 pop. **Telephone lines:** 483,000. **Daily newspaper circ.:** 14.1 per 1,000 pop. **Internet:** 232,000 users.

Health: Life expect.: 74.6 male; 79.2 female. **Births** (per 1,000 pop.): 26.1. **Deaths** (per 1,000 pop.): 3.5. **Natural inc.:** 2.26%. **Infant mortality** (per 1,000 live births): 22.8. **AIDS rate:** NA.

Education: Compulsory: ages 6-14. **Literacy:** 84.2%.

Major intl. organizations: UN (FAO, IBRD, ILO, IMF, IMO, WHO), AL, AU, OPEC.

Embassy: 2600 Virginia Ave. NW, Ste. 705, 20037; 944-9601. **Website:** www.libyanbureau-dc.org

First settled by Berbers, Libya was ruled in succession by Carthage, Rome, the Vandals, and the Ottomans. Italy ruled from 1912 and Britain and France after WWII. Libya became an independent constitutional monarchy Jan. 2, 1952. In 1969 a junta led by Col. Muammar al-Qaddafi seized power.

Libya and Egypt fought several air and land battles along their border in July 1977. Chad charged Libya with military occupation of its uranium-rich northern region in 1977. Libyan troops were driven from their last major stronghold by Chad forces in 1987.

During the 1980s, Libya was accused of aiding terrorists and violent revolutionary groups. The U.S. charged Qaddafi with ordering the Apr. 5, 1986, bombing of a West Berlin discotheque, which

killed 3, including a U.S. serviceman. In response, the U.S. sent warplanes to attack what it called "terrorist-related targets" in Libya, Apr. 14, including Qaddafi's barracks.

Libyan agents were accused of planting bombs that blew up Pan Am Flight 103 over Lockerbie, Scotland, killing 270 people Dec. 21, 1988, and UTA Flight 772 over Niger, killing 170 people Sept. 19, 1989. The UN imposed sanctions, Apr. 15, 1992, for Libya's failure to cooperate in the Lockerbie and UTA cases.

Libya agreed in 2003 to renounce terrorism and settle compensation cases for the families of the Lockerbie and UTA bombing victims. The UN lifted sanctions, Sept. 12. Secret talks with the U.S. and UK led to Libya's announcement Dec. 19 that it would stop developing nuclear, chemical, and biological weapons and long-range missiles. The U.S. ended most economic sanctions Apr. 23, 2004. Libya pledged Aug. 10 to compensate non-U.S. victims of the 1986 Berlin disco bombing. EU sanctions were lifted Oct. 11, 2004, and the U.S. restored full diplomatic relations May 15, 2006.

Libya signed aid and trade deals with the EU after freeing, July 24, 2007, 5 Bulgarian nurses and a Palestinian doctor held since 1999 on charges they had infected Libyan children with the AIDS virus; human rights groups and the international medical community had protested the detentions.

Liechtenstein
Principality of Liechtenstein

People: Population: 34,247. **Age distrib.** (%): <15: 17.1; 65+: 12.8. **Pop. density:** 552 per sq mi, 214 per sq km. **Urban:** 14.6%. **Ethnic groups:** Alemannic 86%; Italian, Turkish, and other 14%. **Principal languages:** German (official), Alemannic dialect. **Chief religions:** Roman Catholic 76%, Protestant 7%.

Geography: Total area: 62 sq mi, 160 sq km; **Land area:** 62 sq mi, 160 sq km. **Location:** Central Europe, in Alps. **Neighbors:** Switzerland on W, Austria on E. **Topography:** Rhine Valley occupies one-third of country, Alps cover the rest. **Capital:** Vaduz, 5,053.

Government: Type: Hereditary constitutional monarchy. **Head of state:** Prince Hans-Adam II; b Feb. 14, 1945; in office: Nov. 13, 1989. **Head of gov.:** Prime Min.Otmar Hasler; b Sept. 28, 1953; in office: Apr. 5, 2001. **Local divisions:** 11 communes.

Economy: Industries: electronics, metallurgy, textiles, ceramics, pharm., food products, precision instruments, tourism. **Chief crops:** wheat, barley, corn, potatoes. **Natural resources:** hydropower. **Arable land:** 25%. **Livestock:** cattle: 6,000; goats: 280; pigs: 3,000; sheep: 2,900. **Labor force** (2001 est.): agriculture 2%, industry 47%, services 51%.

Finance: Monetary unit: Switzerland Franc (CHF) (Sept. 2007: 1.19 = $1 U.S.). **GDP** (2001 est.): $1.8 bil; **per capita GDP** (1999 est.): $25,000; **GDP growth** (1999 est.): 11%. **Imports** (1996): $917.3 mil; EU, Switzerland. **Exports** (1996): $2.5 bil; EU 62.6% (Germany 24.3%, Austria 9.5%, France 8.9%, Italy 6.6%, UK 4.6%), U.S. 18.9%, Switzerland 15.7%. **Tourism:** NA. **Budget** (1998 est.): $414.1 mil.

Transport: Railroad: Length: 6 mi.

Communications: TV sets: 469 per 1,000 pop. **Radios:** 656 per 1,000 pop. **Telephone lines:** 20,100. **Internet:** 22,000 users.

Health: Life expect.: 76.2 male; 83.4 female. **Births** (per 1,000 pop.): 10. **Deaths** (per 1,000 pop.): 7.3. **Natural inc.:** 0.27%. **Infant mortality** (per 1,000 live births): 4.6. **AIDS rate:** NA.

Education (2003): Compulsory: ages 7-16. **Literacy:** 100%.

Major intl. organizations: UN (WTO), EFTA, OSCE.

Permanent UN Representative: 1300 I St NW, Washington, DC 20005; 202-216-0460.

Embassy: 888 17th St. NW, Ste. 1250, 20006; 331-0590 **Website:** www.liechtenstein.li

Liechtenstein became sovereign in 1806. Austria administered Liechtenstein's ports up to 1920; Switzerland has administered its postal services since 1921. Liechtenstein is united with Switzerland by a customs and monetary union. Taxes are low; many international corporations have headquarters there. Foreign workers comprise 2/3 of the labor force. On Aug. 15, 2004, Prince Hans-Adam II assigned day-to-day responsibilities for running the tiny country to his son, Crown Prince Alois.

Lithuania
Republic of Lithuania

People: Population: 3,575,439. **Age distrib.** (%): <15: 14.9; 65+: 15.8. **Pop. density:** 142 per sq mi, 55 per sq km. **Urban:** 66.6%. **Ethnic groups:** Lithuanian 83%, Polish 7%, Russian 6%. **Principal languages:** Lithuanian (official), Russian, Polish. **Chief religion:** Roman Catholic 79%.

Geography: Total area: 25,174 sq mi, 65,200 sq km. **Land area:** 25,174 sq mi, 65,200 sq km. **Location:** In E Europe, on SE coast of Baltic. **Neighbors:** Latvia on N; Belarus on E, S; Poland, Russia on W. **Topography:** Lowland with hills in W and S; fertile soil; many small lakes and rivers, with marshes espec. in N and W. **Capital:** Vilnius, 553,000.

Government: Type: Republic. **Head of state:** Pres. Valdas Adamkus; b. Nov. 3, 1926; in office: July 12, 2004. **Head of gov.:** Prime Min. Gediminas Kirkilas; b. Aug. 30, 1951; in office: July 4, 2006. **Local divisions:** 10 provinces. **Defense budget:** $353 mil. **Active troops:** 12,010.

Economy: Industries: machine tools, electric motors, large appliances, oil refining, shipbuilding. **Chief crops:** grain, potatoes, sugar beets, flax, vegetables. **Natural resources:** peat. **Crude oil reserves:** 12 mil bbls. **Arable land:** 45%. **Livestock:** cattle: 800,286; chickens: 9.2 mil; goats: 21,984; pigs: 1.1 mil; sheep: 29,208. **Fish catch:** 141,798 metric tons. **Electricity prod.:** 13.5 bil kWh. **Labor force** (2004): agriculture 15.8%, industry 28.2%, services 56%.

Finance: Monetary unit: Litas (LTL) (Sept. 2007: 2.49 = $1 U.S.). **GDP:** $54.9 bil; **per capita GDP:** $15,300; **GDP growth:** 7.5%. **Imports:** $18.3 bil; Russia 24.4%, Germany 14.9%, Poland 9.6%, Latvia 4.8%. **Exports:** $14.6 bil; Russia 12.8%, Latvia 11.1%, Germany 8.7%, Estonia 6.5%, Poland 6%. **Tourism:** $921 mil. **Budget:** $9.8 bil. **Intl. reserves less gold:** $3.76 bil. **Gold:** 190,000 oz t. **Consumer prices:** 3.84%.

Transport: Railroad: Length: 1,100 mi. **Motor vehicles:** 1.3 mil pass. cars; 130,000 comm. vehicles. **Civil aviation:** 245.4 mil pass.-mi; 34 airports. **Chief port:** Klaipeda.

Communications: TV sets: 422 per 1,000 pop. **Radios:** 502 per 1,000 pop. **Telephone lines:** 792,400. **Daily newspaper circ.:** 30.9 per 1,000 pop. **Internet:** 1.1 mil users.

Health: Life expect.: 69.5 male; 79.7 female. **Births** (per 1,000 pop.): 8.9. **Deaths** (per 1,000 pop.): 11.1. **Natural inc.:** −0.22%. **Infant mortality** (per 1,000 live births): 6.7. **AIDS rate:** 0.2%.

Education: Compulsory: ages 7-15. **Literacy:** 99.6%.

Major intl. organizations: UN (FAO, IBRD, ILO, IMF, IMO, WHO, WTO), EU, NATO, OSCE.

Embassy: 4590 MacArthur Blvd. NW, Ste. 200, 20007; 234-5860.

Website: www.president.lt

Lithuania was occupied by the German army, 1914-18. It was annexed by the Soviet Russian army, but the Soviets were overthrown, 1919. Lithuania was a democratic republic until 1926, when the regime was ousted by a coup. In 1939 the Soviet-German treaty assigned most of Lithuania to the Soviet sphere of influence. Lithuania was annexed by the USSR Aug. 3, 1940.

Lithuania formally declared its independence from the Soviet Union Mar. 11, 1990. During an abortive Soviet coup in Aug., the Western nations recognized Lithuania's independence, which was ratified by the Soviet Union in Sept. 1991.

The conservative Homeland Union defeated the former Communists in parliamentary elections Oct.-Nov. 1996. A Lithuanian-American, Valdas Adamkus, won the presidency in a runoff election Jan. 4, 1998. He lost to Rolandas Paksas in a runoff Jan. 5, 2003. After the legislature impeached and removed Paksas from office, Apr. 6, 2004, Adamkus regained the presidency.

Luxembourg
Grand Duchy of Luxembourg

People: Population: 480,222. **Age distrib.** (%): <15: 18.8; 65+: 14.7. **Pop. density:** 481 per sq mi, 186 per sq km. **Urban:** 82.8%. **Ethnic groups:** Mixture of mostly French and German. **Principal languages:** Luxembourgish (national); German, French (both administrative). **Chief religions:** Roman Catholic 87%, other (incl. Protestant, Jewish, and Muslim) 13% .

Geography: Total area: 998 sq mi, 2,586 sq km; **Land area:** 998 sq mi, 2,586 sq km. **Location:** In W Europe. **Neighbors:** Belgium on W, France on S, Germany on E. **Topography:** Heavy forests (Ardennes) cover N. S is a low, open plateau. **Capital:** Luxembourg-Ville, 77,000.

Government: Type: Constitutional monarchy. **Head of state:** Grand Duke Henri; b. Apr. 16, 1955; in office: Oct. 7, 2000. **Head of gov.:** Prime Min. Jean-Claude Juncker; b. Dec. 9, 1954; in office: Jan. 20, 1995. **Local divisions:** 3 districts. **Defense budget:** $260 mil. **Active troops:** 900.

Economy: Industries: banking, iron & steel, food proc., chemicals, metal products, engineering, tires, glass, aluminum. **Chief crops:** wine, grapes, barley, oats, potatoes, wheat, fruits. **Natural resources:** iron ore. **Arable land:** 24%. **Livestock:** cattle: 183,640; chickens: 81.3 mil; goats: 1,950; pigs: 84,151; sheep: 9,644. **Electricity prod.:** 3.2 bil kWh. **Labor force** (2004 est.): agriculture 1%, industry 13%, services 86%.

Finance: Monetary unit: Euro (EUR) (Sept. 2007: 0.72 = $1 U.S.). **GDP:** $33.9 bil; **per capita GDP:** $71,400; **GDP growth:** 6.2%. **Imports:** $24.2 bil; Germany 26.3%, Germany 20.1%, China 16.7%, France 8.5%, UK 5.5%. **Exports:** $19.6 bil; Germany 19.3%, France 15.5%, Italy 9.5%, UK 9.5%, Belgium 8.8%, Spain 5.3%. **Tourism:** $3.6 bil. **Budget:** $19.8 bil. **Intl. reserves less gold:** $145 mil. **Gold:** 70,000 oz t. **Consumer prices:** 2.68%.

Transport: Railroad: Length: 170 mi. **Motor vehicles:** 300,000 pass. cars; 53,000 comm. vehicles. **Civil aviation:** 340.5 mil pass.-mi; 1 airport. **Chief port:** Mertert.

Communications: TV sets: 599 per 1,000 pop. **Radios:** 683 per 1,000 pop. **Telephone lines:** 246,700. **Daily newspaper circ.:** 275.7 per 1,000 pop. **Internet:** 339,000 users.

Health: Life expect.: 75.8 male; 82.5 female. **Births** (per 1,000 pop.): 11.8. **Deaths** (per 1,000 pop.): 8.4. **Natural inc.:** 0.34%. **Infant mortality** (per 1,000 live births): 4.7. **AIDS rate:** 0.2%.

Education: Compulsory: ages 6-15. **Literacy:** 100%.

Major intl. organizations: UN (FAO, IBRD, ILO, IMF, IMO, WHO, WTO), EU, NATO, OECD, OSCE.

Embassy: 2200 Massachusetts Ave. NW 20008; 265-4171.

Website: www.luxembourg-usa.org

Luxembourg, founded about 963, was ruled by Burgundy, Spain, Austria, and France from 1448 to 1815. It left the Germanic Confederation in 1866. Overrun by Germany in 2 world wars, Luxembourg ended its neutrality in 1948, when a customs union with Belgium and Netherlands was adopted.

Luxembourg was one of the 6 founding members (1951) of what became the European Union. Its voters ratified the EU constitution in July 2005.

Macedonia
Former Yugoslav Republic of Macedonia

People: Population: 2,055,915. **Age distrib.** (%): <15: 19.8; 65+: 11.1. **Pop. density:** 214 per sq mi, 83 per sq km. **Urban:** 68.9%. **Ethnic groups:** Macedonian 64%, Albanian 25%, Turkish 4%, Roma 3%, Serb 2%. **Principal languages:** Macedonian (official), Albanian, Turkish, Romani, Serbian. **Chief religions:** Macedonian Orthodox 65%, Muslim 33%.

Geography: Total area: 9,781 sq mi, 25,333 sq km; **Land area:** 9,597 sq mi, 24,856 sq km. **Location:** In SE Europe. **Neighbors:** Bulgaria on E, Greece on S, Albania on W, Serbia on N. **Topography:** Macedonia is a landlocked, mostly mountainous country, with deep river valleys, 3 large lakes; country is bisected by Vardar R. **Capital:** Skopje, 475,000.

Government: Type: Republic. **Head of state:** Pres. Branko Crvenkovski; b. Oct. 12, 1962; in office: May 12, 2004. **Head of gov.:** Prime Min. Nikola Gruevski; b. Aug. 31, 1970; in office: Aug. 27, 2006. **Local divisions:** 123 municipalities. **Defense budget:** $139 mil. **Active troops:** 10,890.

Economy: Industries: mining, textiles, wood products, tobacco, food proc., buses. **Chief crops:** grapes, wine, tobacco, vegetables. **Natural resources:** chromium, lead, zinc, mang., tungsten, nickel, iron ore, asbestos, sulfur, timber. **Arable land:** 22%. **Livestock:** cattle: 248,185; chickens: 2.6 mil; pigs: 195,753; sheep: 1.2 mil. **Fish catch:** 1,114 metric tons. **Electricity prod.:** 6.6 bil kWh. **Labor force** (2006): agriculture 21.7%, industry 32.6%, services 45.7%.

Finance: Monetary unit: Denar (MKD) (Sept. 2007: 44.28 = $1 U.S.). **GDP:** $16.9 bil; **per capita GDP:** $8,300; **GDP growth:** 3.1%. **Imports:** $3.6 bil; Russia 15.1%, Germany 9.8%, Greece 8.5%, Serbia and Montenegro 7.5%, Bulgaria 6.7%, Italy 6%. **Exports:** $2.3 bil; Serbia and Montenegro 23.2%, Germany 15.6%, Greece 15.1%, Italy 9.9%, Bulgaria 5.4%, Croatia 5.2%. **Tourism:** $84 mil. **Budget:** $2.3 bil. **Intl. reserves less gold:** $1.16 bil. **Gold:** 220,000 oz t. **Consumer prices** (2005): 0.04%.

Transport: Railroad: Length: 434 mi. **Motor vehicles:** 300,000 pass. cars; 32,000 comm. vehicles. **Civil aviation:** 174 mil pass.-mi; 10 airports.

Communications: TV sets: 273 per 1,000 pop. **Radios:** 550 per 1,000 pop. **Telephone lines:** 490,900. **Daily newspaper circ.:** 53.5 per 1,000 pop. **Internet:** 268,000 users.

Health: Life expect.: 71.7 male; 76.9 female. **Births** (per 1,000 pop.): 12. **Deaths** (per 1,000 pop.): 8.8. **Natural inc.:** 0.32%. **Infant mortality** (per 1,000 live births): 9.5. **AIDS rate:** <0.1%.

Education: Compulsory: ages 7-14. **Literacy:** 96.1%.

Major intl. organizations: UN (FAO, IBRD, ILO, IMF, IMO, WHO, WTO, OSCE).

Embassy: 1101 30th St. NW, Ste. 302, 20007; 625-4377.

Website: www.vlada.mk

Macedonia was ruled by Muslim Turks from 1389 to 1912. In 1913, the area was incorporated into Serbia, which in 1918 became part of the Kingdom of Serbs, Croats, and Slovenes (later Yugoslavia). In 1946, Macedonia became a constituent republic of Yugoslavia.

Macedonia declared its independence Sept. 8, 1991, and was admitted to the UN in 1993. A UN force was deployed there to deter warring factions in Bosnia from carrying their dispute into other areas of the Balkans. In Feb. 1994 both Russia and the U.S. recognized Macedonia. Greece, which objected to Macedonia's use of what it considered a Hellenic name and symbols, imposed a trade blockade on the landlocked nation; the 2 countries agreed to normalize relations Sept. 13, 1995.

By the end of NATO's air war against Yugoslavia, Mar.-June 1999, Macedonia had a Kosovar refugee population of more than 250,000; over 90% had been repatriated by Sept. 1. Boris Trajkovski, candidate of the ruling center-right coalition, won a presidential runoff vote Nov. 14.

Ethnic Albanian guerrillas launched an offensive Mar. 2001 in NW Macedonia. An accord signed Aug. 13 paved the way for the introduction of a NATO peacekeeping force. A law broadening the rights of ethnic Albanians was enacted Jan. 24, 2002. A 320-member EU force replaced the NATO peacekeepers Mar. 31, 2003. After Trajkovski died in a plane crash Feb. 26, 2004, Prime Min. Branko Crvenkovski won a presidential runoff vote Apr. 28.

Madagascar
Republic of Madagascar

People: Population: 19,448,815. **Age distrib.** (%): <15: 43.9; 65+: 3.1. **Pop. density:** 87 per sq mi, 33 per sq km. **Urban:** 26.8%. **Ethnic groups:** Malayo-Indonesian, Cotiers, French, Indian, Creole, Comoran. **Principal languages:** Malagasy, French (both official). **Chief religions:** Indigenous beliefs 52%, Christian 41%, Muslim 7%.

Geography: Total area: 226,657 sq mi, 587,040 sq km; **Land area:** 224,534 sq mi, 581,540 sq km. **Location:** In Indian O., off SE coast of Africa. **Neighbors:** Comoro Isls. to NW, Mozambique to W. **Topography:** Humid coastal strip in E, fertile valleys in mountainous center plateau region, and a wider coastal strip on W. **Capital:** Antananarivo, 1,585,000.

Government: Type: Republic. **Head of state:** Pres. Marc Ravalomanana; b. Dec. 12, 1949; in office: Feb. 22, 2002. **Head of gov.:** Prime Min. Charles Rabemananjara; b. June 9, 1947; in office: Jan. 25, 2007. **Local divisions:** 6 provinces. **Defense budget:** $300 mil. **Active troops:** 13,500.

Economy: Industries: meat proc., soap, brewing, hides, sugar, textiles, glassware, cement, autos. **Chief crops:** coffee, vanilla, sugarcane, cloves, cocoa, rice, cassava, beans, bananas, peanuts. **Natural resources:** graphite, chromite, coal, bauxite, salt, quartz, tar sands, gemstones, mica, fish, hydropower. **Arable land:** 5%. **Livestock:** cattle: 9.7 mil; chickens: 24 mil; goats: 1.2 mil; pigs: 1.6 mil; sheep: 703,343. **Fish catch:** 144,900 metric tons. **Electricity prod.:** 1.1 bil kWh. **Labor force:** NA.

Finance: Monetary unit: Ariary (MGA) (Sept. 2007: 1,852.95 = $1 U.S.). **GDP:** $17.3 bil; **per capita GDP:** $900; **GDP growth:** 4.7%. **Imports:** $1.5 bil; France 13.4%, China 11.6%, Iran 9%, Mauritius 7.4%, Hong Kong 4.6%. **Exports:** $993.5 mil; France 32%, U.S. 25.3%, Germany 6%, Italy 5%, UK 4.1%. **Tourism:** $105 mil. **Budget:** $1.1 bil. **Intl. reserves less gold:** $388 mil. **Consumer prices:** 10.77%.

Transport: Railroad: Length: 531 mi. **Motor vehicles:** 64,000 pass. cars; 9,100 comm. vehicles. **Civil aviation:** 444.3 mil pass.-mi; 29 airports. **Chief ports:** Antsiranana, Mahajanga, Toamasina, Toliara.

Communications: TV sets: 23 per 1,000 pop. **Radios:** 209 per 1,000 pop. **Telephone lines:** 129,800. **Daily newspaper circ.:** 4.5 per 1,000 pop. **Internet:** 110,000 users.

Health: Life expect.: 60.2 male; 64.1 female. **Births** (per 1,000 pop.): 38.6. **Deaths** (per 1,000 pop.): 8.5. **Natural inc.:** 3.01%. **Infant mortality** (per 1,000 live births): 57. **AIDS rate:** 0.5%.

Education: Compulsory: ages 6-10. **Literacy:** 70.7%.

Major intl. organizations: UN (FAO, IBRD, ILO, IMF, IMO, WHO, WTO), AU.

Embassy: 2374 Massachusetts Ave. NW 20008; 265-5525.

Website: www.assemblee-nationale.mg

Madagascar was settled 2,000 years ago by Malayan-Indonesian people, whose descendants still predominate. A unified kingdom ruled the 18th and 19th centuries. The island became a French protectorate, 1885, and a colony 1896. Independence came June 26, 1960.

Discontent with inflation and French domination led to a coup in 1972. The new regime nationalized French-owned financial interests, closed French bases and a U.S. space-tracking station, and obtained Chinese aid. The government conducted a program of arrests, expulsion of foreigners, and repression of strikes, 1979.

In 1990, Madagascar ended a ban on multiparty politics that had been in place since 1975. Albert Zafy was elected president in 1993, ending the 17-year rule of Adm. Didier Ratsiraka. After Zafy was impeached by the legislature, Madagascar's constitutional court removed him from office, Sept. 5, 1996. Prime Min. Norbert Ratsirahonana then became interim president pending national elections, Nov. 3 and Dec. 29, in which Ratsiraka edged Zafy. A cholera epidemic, exacerbated by cyclones in Feb. and Apr. 2000, claimed at least 1,600 lives.

Marc Ravalomanana won a power struggle with Ratsiraka that followed a disputed presidential election Dec. 16, 2001; he was reelected with a 55% majority Dec. 3, 2006.

Malawi
Republic of Malawi

People: Population: 13,603,181. **Age distrib.** (%): <15: 46.1; 65+: 2.7. **Pop. density:** 374 per sq mi, 145 per sq km. **Urban:** 17.2%. **Ethnic groups:** Chewa, Nyanja, Tumbuka, Yao, Lomwe, Sena, Tonga, Ngoni, Ngonde, Asian, European. **Principal languages:** Chichewa, several African languages. **Chief religions:** Christian 80%, Muslim 13%.

Geography: Total area: 45,745 sq mi, 118,480 sq km; **Land area:** 36,324 sq mi, 94,080 sq km. **Location:** In SE Africa. **Neighbors:** Zambia on W, Mozambique on S and E, Tanzania on N. **Topography:** Malawi stretches 560 mi N-S along Lake Malawi (Lake Nyasa), most of which belongs to Malawi. High plateaus and mountains line the Rift Valley the length of the nation. **Capital:** Lilongwe, 676,000. **Cities** (urban aggr., 1998 est.): Blantyre, 2,000,000.

Government: Type: Republic. **Head of state and gov.:** Pres. Bingu wa Mutharika; b. Feb. 24, 1934; in office: May 24, 2004. **Local divisions:** 3 regions, 26 districts. **Defense budget:** $21 mil. **Active troops:** 5,300

Economy: Industries: tobacco, tea, sugar, wood products, cement, consumer goods. **Chief crops:** tobacco, sugarcane, cotton, tea, corn, potatoes, cassava, sorghum. **Natural resources:** limestone, hydropower, uranium, coal, bauxite. **Arable land:** 21%. **Livestock:** cattle: 750,000; chickens: 15.2 mil; goats: 1.9 mil; pigs: 456,300; sheep: 115,000. **Fish catch:** 59,595 metric tons. **Electricity prod.:** 1.4 bil kWh. **Labor force** (2003 est.): agriculture 90% industry and services 10%.

Finance: Monetary unit: Kiwacha (MWK) (Sept. 2007: 139.59 = $1 U.S.). **GDP:** $8.3 bil; **per capita GDP:** $600; **GDP growth:** 8.5%. **Imports:** $767.9 mil; South Africa 29.3%, Zambia 9.3%, Zimbabwe 7.8%, Mozambique 7.2%, India 6.9%, U.S. 5.4%, Tanzania 5%. **Exports:** $513.1 mil; South Africa 12.9%, Germany 9.9%, Egypt 9.8%, U.S. 9.7%, Mozambique 5.5%, Russia 5.5%. **Tourism:** $24 mil. **Budget:** $895.9 mil. **Intl. reserves less gold:** $89 mil. **Gold:** 10,000 oz t. **Consumer prices:** 13.97%.

Transport: Railroad: Length: 495 mi. **Motor vehicles:** 2,000 pass. cars; 3,000 comm. vehicles. **Civil aviation:** 91.3 mil pass.-mi; 6 airports. **Chief ports:** Chilumba, Chipoka, Monkey Bay, Nkhata Bay, Nkhotakota.

Communications: TV sets: 3 per 1,000 pop. **Radios:** 476 per 1,000 pop. **Telephone lines:** 102,700. **Daily newspaper circ.:** 2.4 per 1,000 pop. **Internet:** 59,700 users.

Health: Life expect.: 43.4 male; 42.6 female. **Births** (per 1,000 pop.): 42.1. **Deaths** (per 1,000 pop.): 18.3. **Natural inc.:** 2.38%. **Infant mortality** (per 1,000 live births): 92.1. **AIDS rate:** 14.1%.

Education: Compulsory: ages 6-13. **Literacy:** 64.1%.

Major intl. organizations: UN (FAO, IBRD, ILO, IMF, IMO, WHO, WTO), the Commonwealth, AU.

Embassy: 2408 Massachusetts Ave. NW 20008; 797-1007.

Website: www.malawi.gov.mw

Bantus came to the land in the 16th cent., Arab slavers in the 19th. The area became the British protectorate Nyasaland in 1891. It became independent July 6, 1964, and a republic in 1966.

After 3 decades as a one-party state under Pres. Hastings Kamuzu Banda, Malawi adopted a new constitution and, in multiparty elections held May 17, 1994, chose a new leader, Bakili Muluzi. Banda was acquitted, Dec. 23, 1995, of complicity in the deaths of 4 political opponents in 1983; he died Nov. 25, 1997.

Bingu wa Muthdrika, candidate of the ruling United Democratic Front, won a disputed presidential election May 20, 2004. In an ongoing power struggle, an effort by Mutharika's former political allies to impeach him was halted by Malawi's Constitutional Court, Oct. 26, 2005. He fired Vice Pres. Cassim Chilumpha but was forced to reinstate him, Feb. 2006; he then had Chilumpha arrested on treason charges, Apr. 28. Former Pres. Muluzi was arrested on corruption charges, July 27, then released 4 days later.

Malaysia

People: Population: 24,821,286. **Age distrib.** (%): <15: 32.2; 65+: 4.8. **Pop. density:** 196 per sq mi, 76 per sq km. **Urban:** 67.3%. **Ethnic groups:** Malay and other indigenous 61%, Chinese 24%, Indian 7%. **Principal languages:** Malay (official), English, Chinese dialects, Tamil, Telugu, Malayalam, Panjabi, Thai; Iban and Kadazan in East. **Chief religions:** Muslim (official) 60%, Buddhist 19%, Christian 9%, Hindu 6%, Confucianist/Taoist 3%.

Geography: Total area: 127,317 sq mi, 329,750 sq km; **Land area:** 126,854 sq mi, 328,550 sq km. **Location:** On SE tip of Asia, plus N coast of the island of Borneo. **Neighbors:** Thailand, Brunei on N; Indonesia on S. **Topography:** Most of W Malaysia is covered by tropical jungle, including the central mountain range that runs N-S through the peninsula. W coast is marshy, the E coast, sandy. E Malaysia has a wide, swampy coastal plain, with interior jungles and mountains. **Capital:** Kuala Lumpur, 1,405,000.

Government: Type: Constitutional monarchy. **Head of state:** Paramount Ruler Al-Wathiqu Billah Tuanku Mizan Zainal Abidin ibni al-Marhum Sultan Mahmud Al-Muktafi Billah Shah; b. Jan. 22, 1962; in office: Dec. 13, 2006. **Head of gov.:** Prime Min. Datuk Seri Abdullah Ahmad Badawi; b. Nov. 26, 1939; in office: Oct. 31, 2003. **Local divisions:** 13 states, 3 federal territories. **Defense budget:** $3.08 bil. **Active troops:** 109,000.

Economy: Industries: rubber & palm oil proc., light mfg., electronics, tin, mining, timber, oil. **Chief crops:** rubber, palm oil, cocoa, rice, coconuts, pepper. **Natural resources:** tin, oil, timber, copper, iron ore, nat. gas, bauxite. **Crude oil reserves:** 3 bil bbls. **Arable land:** 5%. **Livestock:** cattle: 801,000; chickens: 185 mil; goats: 271,000; pigs: 2.2 mil; sheep: 109,000. **Fish catch:** 1,390,017 metric tons. **Electricity prod.:** 82.4 bil kWh. **Labor force** (2005 est.): agriculture 13%, industry 36%, services 51%.

Finance: Monetary unit: Ringgit (MYR) (Sept. 2007: 3.48 = $1 U.S.). **GDP:** $313.8 bil; **per capita GDP:** $12,900; **GDP growth:** 5.9%. **Imports:** $127.3 bil; Japan 13.3%, U.S. 12.6%, China 12.2%, Singapore 11.7%, Thailand 5.5%, Taiwan 5.5%, South Korea 5.4%. **Exports:** $158.7 bil; U.S. 18.8%, Singapore 15.4%, Japan 8.9%, China 7.2%, Thailand 5.3%. **Tourism:** $8.5 bil. **Budget:** $37 bil. **Intl. reserves less gold:** $54.60 bil. **Gold:** 1.17 mil oz t. **Consumer prices:** 3.61%.

Transport: Railroad: Length: 1,174 mi. **Motor vehicles:** 482,000 pass. cars; 53,000 comm. vehicles. **Civil aviation:** 23.9 bil pass.-mi; 37 airports. **Chief ports:** Bintulu, Johor Bahru, Lahad Datu, Lumut, Miri, George Town (Penang).

Communications: TV sets: 174 per 1,000 pop. **Radios:** 434 per 1,000 pop. **Telephone lines:** 4.3 mil. **Daily newspaper circ.:** 95.3 per 1,000 pop. **Internet:** 11.3 mil users.

Health: Life expect.: 70.1 male; 75.7 female. **Births** (per 1,000 pop.): 22.7. **Deaths** (per 1,000 pop.): 5.1. **Natural inc.:** 1.76%. **Infant mortality** (per 1,000 live births): 16.6. **AIDS rate:** 0.5%.

Education: Compulsory: ages 6-11. **Literacy:** 88.7%.

Major intl. organizations: UN (FAO, IBRD, ILO, IMF, IMO, WHO, WTO), APEC, ASEAN, the Commonwealth.

Embassy: 3516 International Ct. NW 20008; 572-9700. **Website:** www.gov.my

European traders appeared in the 16th cent.; Britain established control in 1867. Malaysia was created Sept. 16, 1963. It included Malaya (which had become independent in 1957 after the suppression of Communist rebels), plus the formerly British Singapore, Sabah (N Borneo), and Sarawak (NW Borneo). Singapore was separated in 1965, in order to end tensions between Chinese, the majority in Singapore, and Malays in control of the Malaysian government.

A monarch is elected by a council of hereditary rulers of the Malayan states every 5 years.

Abundant natural resources have bolstered prosperity, and foreign investment has aided industrialization. Work on a new federal capital at Putrajaya, south of Kuala Lumpur, began in 1995. However, sagging stock and currency prices forced the postponement of major development projects in Sept. 1997.

Mahathir bin Mohamad dominated Malaysian politics as prime minister, 1981-2003. His successor, Abdullah Ahmad Badawi, took office Oct. 31, 2003, and led his National Front coalition to a resounding win in parliamentary elections Mar. 21, 2004. The Indian Ocean tsunami of Dec. 26 left at least 68 people dead and 8,000 displaced in Malaysia.

Maldives
Republic of Maldives

People: Population: 369,031. **Age distrib.** (%): <15: 42.9; 65+: 3.1. **Pop. density:** 3,181 per sq mi, 1,230 per sq km. **Urban:** 29.6%. **Ethnic groups:** Dravidian, Sinhalese, Arab. **Principal languages:** Divehi (Sinhala dialect, Arabic script; official), English. **Chief religion:** Muslim (official; mostly Sunni).

Geography: Total area: 116 sq mi, 300 sq km; **Land area:** 116 sq mi, 300 sq km. **Location:** In Indian O., SW of India. **Neighbors:** Nearest is India on N. **Topography:** 19 atolls with 1,190 islands, 198 inhabited. None of the islands are over 5 sq mi in area, and all are nearly flat. **Capital:** Male, 89,000.

Government: Type: Republic. **Head of state and gov.:** Pres. Maumoon Abdul Gayoom; b. Dec. 29, 1937; in office: Nov. 11, 1978. **Local divisions:** 19 atolls and Male capital atoll.

Economy: Industries: fish proc., tourism, shipping, boat building, coconut proc., garments. **Chief crops:** coconuts, corn, sweet potatoes. **Natural resources:** fish. **Arable land:** 13%. **Fish catch:** 185,980 metric tons. **Electricity prod.:** 170 mil kWh. **Labor force** (1995): agriculture 22%, industry 18%, services 60%.

Finance: Monetary unit: Rufiyaa (MVR) (Sept. 2007: 12.80 = $1 U.S.). **GDP:** $2.8 bil; **per capita GDP** (2002 est.): $3,900; **GDP growth:** 18%. **Imports:** $832 mil; Singapore 23.3%, UAE 15.8%, India 11.1%, Malaysia 7.9%, Thailand 7%, Sri Lanka 5.7%. **Exports:** $214 mil; Thailand 32.1%, UK 13.9%, Sri Lanka 11.6%, Japan 10%, France 6.7%, Algeria 6%. **Tourism:** $471 mil. **Budget:** $671 mil. **Intl. reserves less gold:** $154 mil. **Consumer prices:** 0.32%.

Transport: Motor vehicles: 2,000 pass. cars; 1,000 comm. vehicles. **Civil aviation:** 17.4 mil pass.-mi; 2 airports. **Chief ports:** Male, Gan.

Communications: TV sets: 38 per 1,000 pop. **Radios:** 129 per 1,000 pop. **Telephone lines:** 32,500. **Internet:** 20,100 users.

Health: Life expect.: 63.4 male; 66.2 female. **Births** (per 1,000 pop.): 34.2. **Deaths** (per 1,000 pop.): 6.9. **Natural inc.:** 2.73%. **Infant mortality** (per 1,000 live births): 53.3. **AIDS rate:** NA.

Education: Compulsory: ages 6-12. **Literacy:** 96.3%.

Major intl. organizations: UN (FAO, IBRD, IMF, IMO, WHO, WTO), the Commonwealth.

Permanent UN Representative: 800 Second Ave., Ste. 400E, New York, NY 10017; 212-599-6194. **Website:** www.maldivesinfo.gov.mv

A British protectorate since 1887, the nation achieved independence July 26, 1965; long a sultanate, the Maldives became a republic in 1968. Tourism and fishing are the most important sectors of the economy. Pres. Gayoom has held power since 1978; political parties are suppressed. The Indian Ocean tsunami of Dec. 26, 2004, killed at least 82 people and displaced more than 21,600 in Maldives. Rising sea levels threaten the country, which comprises at least 1,200 small, low-lying coral islands.

Mali
Republic of Mali

People: Population: 11,995,402. **Age distrib.** (%): <15: 48.2; 65+: 3.1. **Pop. density:** 25 per sq mi, 10 per sq km. **Urban:** 30.5%. **Ethnic groups:** Mande 50% (Bambara, Malinke, Soninke), Peul 17%, Voltaic 12%, Tuareg and Moor 10%, Songhai 6%. **Principal languages:** French (official); Bambara and other African languages. **Chief religions:** Muslim 90%, indigenous beliefs 9%.

Geography: Total area: 478,767 sq mi, 1,240,000 sq km; **Land area:** 471,045 sq mi, 1,220,000 sq km. **Location:** In interior of W Africa. **Neighbors:** Mauritania, Senegal on W; Guinea, Côte d'Ivoire, Burkina Faso on S; Niger on E; Algeria on N. **Topography:** Landlocked grassy plain in upper basins of the Senegal and Niger rivers, extending N into the Sahara. **Capital:** Bamako, 1,368,000.

Government: Type: Republic. **Head of state:** Pres. Amadou Toumani Touré; b. Nov. 4, 1948; in office: June 8, 2002. **Head of gov.:** Prime Min. Modibo Sidibé; b. Nov. 4, 1952; in office: Sept. 28,

2007. **Local divisions:** 8 regions, 1 capital district. **Defense budget:** $136 mil. **Active troops:** 7,350.

Economy: Industries: food proc., constr., phosphates, gold. **Chief crops:** cotton, millet, rice, corn, vegetables, peanuts. **Natural resources:** gold, phosphates, kaolin, salt, limestone, uranium, hydropower. **Arable land:** 4%. **Livestock:** cattle: 7.7 mil; chickens: 31 mil; goats: 12 mil; pigs: 69,000; sheep: 8.4 mil. **Fish catch:** 101,008 metric tons. **Electricity prod.:** 440 mil kWh. **Labor force** (2001 est.): agriculture 80%, industry and services 20%.

Finance: Monetary unit: CFA BCEAO Franc (XOF) (Sept. 2007: 472.78 = $1 U.S.). **GDP:** $14.8 bil; **per capita GDP:** $1,300; **GDP growth:** 5.1%. **Imports** (2004 est.): $1.9 bil; Senegal 13.8%, France 12.6%, Cote d'Ivoire 10.2%. **Exports** (2004 est.): $323 mil; China 35.6%, Thailand 9.4%, Taiwan 8.1%, Bangladesh 5.3%, Australia 5%. **Tourism:** $130 mil. **Budget** (2002 est.): $828 mil. **Intl. reserves less gold:** $644 mil. **Consumer prices:** 1.54%.

Transport: Railroad: Length: NA. **Motor vehicles:** 18,900 pass. cars; 31,700 comm. vehicles. **Civil aviation** (2001): 80.8 mil pass.-mi; 9 airports. **Chief port:** Koulikoro.

Communications: TV sets: 13 per 1,000 pop. **Radios:** 55 per 1,000 pop. **Telephone lines:** 82,500. **Daily newspaper circ.:** 1.1 per 1,000 pop. **Internet:** 70,000 users.

Health: Life expect.: 47.6 male; 51.5 female. **Births** (per 1,000 pop.): 49.6. **Deaths** (per 1,000 pop.): 16.5. **Natural inc.:** 3.31%. **Infant mortality** (per 1,000 live births): 105.7. **AIDS rate:** 1.7%.

Education: Compulsory: ages 7-16. **Literacy:** 24%.

Major intl. organizations: UN and most of its specialized agencies, AU.

Embassy: 2130 R St. NW 20008; 332-2249. **Website:** www.maliembassy.us

Until the 15th cent. the area was part of the great Mali Empire. Timbuktu (Tombouctou) was a center of Islamic study. French rule was secured, 1898. The Sudanese Rep. and Senegal became independent as the Mali Federation June 20, 1960, but Senegal withdrew, and the Sudanese Rep. was renamed Mali.

Mali signed economic agreements with France and, in 1963, with Senegal. A socialist regime led, 1960-68, by Pres. Modibo Keita, was toppled by a coup. Famine struck in 1973-74, killing as many as 100,000 people. Drought conditions returned in the 1980s.

The military, Mar. 26, 1991, overthrew the government of Pres. Moussa Traoré, who had been in power since 1968. Oumar Konare, a coup leader, was elected president, Apr. 26, 1992. A peace accord between the government and a Tuareg rebel group was signed in June 1994. Konare and his party won a series of flawed elections, Apr.-Aug. 1997. Twice condemned to death for crimes committed in office, Traoré had his sentences commuted to life imprisonment in Dec. 1997 and Sept. 1999.

Amadou Toumani Touré, who led the 1991 coup, was elected president May 12, 2002, and reelected Apr. 29, 2007.

Malta
Republic of Malta

People: Population: 401,880. **Age distrib.** (%): <15: 16.7; 65+: 13.8. **Pop. density:** 3,294 per sq mi, 1,272 per sq km. **Urban:** 95.3%. **Ethnic groups:** Maltese, other Mediterranean. **Principal languages:** Maltese (Semitic dialect), English (both official). **Chief religion:** Roman Catholic (official) 98%.

Geography: Total area: 122 sq mi, 316 sq km; **Land area:** 122 sq mi, 316 sq km. **Location:** In center of Mediterranean Sea. **Neighbors:** Nearest is Italy on N. **Topography:** Isl. of Malta is 95 sq mi; other islands in the group: Gozo, 26 sq mi; Comino, 1 sq mi. Coastline is heavily indented. Low hills cover the interior. **Capital:** Valletta, 210,000.

Government: Type: Parliamentary democracy. **Head of state:** Pres. Edward (Eddie) Fenech-Adami; b. Feb. 7, 1934; in office: Apr. 4, 2004. **Head of gov.:** Prime Min. Lawrence Gonzi; b. July 1, 1953; in office: Mar. 23, 2004. **Local divisions:** 3 regions comprising 67 local councils. **Defense budget:** $42 mil. **Active troops:** 1,609.

Economy: Industries: tourism, electronics, shipbuilding, food & beverages, textiles. **Chief crops:** potatoes, cauliflower, grapes, wheat, barley, tomatoes, citrus. **Natural resources:** limestone, salt. **Arable land:** 31%. **Livestock:** cattle: 19,742; chickens: 1 mil; goats: 6,272; pigs: 73,025; sheep: 14,642. **Fish catch:** 271 metric tons. **Electricity prod.:** 2.1 bil kWh. **Labor force** (2005 est.): agriculture 3%, industry 22%, services 75%.

Finance: Monetary unit: Lira (MTL) (Sept. 2007: 0.31 = $1 U.S.) (will switch to the Euro Jan. 1, 2008). **GDP:** $8.4 bil; **per capita GDP:** $21,000; **GDP growth:** 2.4%. **Imports:** $4.1 bil; Italy 28%, UK 10.5%, France 8.7%, Germany 7.6%, Singapore 6.8%, U.S. 5.6%. **Exports:** $2.4 bil; France 15.3%, Singapore 13.2%, U.S. 13%, Germany 12.5%, UK 9.5%. **Tourism:** $780 mil. **Budget:** $2.7 bil. **Intl. reserves less gold:** $1.98 bil. **Gold:** 10,000 oz t. **Consumer prices:** 2.77%.

Transport: Motor vehicles: 241,000 pass. cars; 56,000 comm. vehicles. **Civil aviation:** 1.4 bil pass.-mi; 1 airport. **Chief ports:** Marsaxlokk, Valletta.

Communications: TV sets: 549 per 1,000 pop. **Radios:** 669 per 1,000 pop. **Telephone lines:** 202,300. **Internet:** 127,200 users.

Health: Life expect.: 77 male; 81.5 female. **Births** (per 1,000 pop.): 10.3. **Deaths** (per 1,000 pop.): 8.2. **Natural inc.:** 0.21%. **Infant mortality** (per 1,000 live births): 3.8. **AIDS rate:** 0.1%.

Education: Compulsory: ages 5-15. **Literacy:** 87.9%.

Major intl. organizations: UN (FAO, IBRD, ILO, IMF, IMO, WHO, WTO), the Commonwealth, EU,OSCE.

Embassy: 2017 Connecticut Ave. NW 20008; 462-3611.

Website: www.gov.mt

Malta was ruled by Phoenicians, Romans, Arabs, Normans, the Knights of Malta, France, and Britain (since 1814). It became independent Sept. 21, 1964. Malta became a republic in 1974. The withdrawal of the last British sailors, Apr. 1, 1979, ended 179 years of British military presence on the island.

From 1971 to 1987 and again from 1996 to 1998, Malta was governed by the socialist Labour Party; the Nationalist Party, which pressed for Malta's entry into the EU, held office 1987-96 and won the elections of Sept. 5, 1998, and Apr. 12, 2003. Malta became a full member of the EU May 1, 2004.

Marshall Islands
Republic of the Marshall Islands

People: Population: 61,815. **Age distrib. (%):** <15: 38.3; 65+: 2.8. **Pop. density:** 885 per sq mi, 342 per sq km. **Urban:** 66.7%.

Ethnic groups: Micronesian. **Principal languages:** English, Marshallese (both official). **Chief religions:** Protestant 55%, Assembly of God 26%, Roman Catholic 8%.

Geography: Total area: 70 sq mi, 181 sq km; **Land area:** 70 sq mi, 181 sq km. **Location:** In N Pacific Ocean; composed of two 800-mi-long parallel chains of coral atolls. **Neighbors:** Nearest are Micronesia to W, Nauru and Kiribati to S. **Topography:** Marshall Islands are low coral limestone and sand islands. **Capital** (2003): Majuro, 25,000.

Government: Type: Republic in free association with the U.S. **Head of state and gov.:** Pres. Kessai Note; b. Aug. 7, 1950; in office: Jan. 10, 2000. **Local divisions:** 33 municipalities.

Economy: Industries: copra, fish, tourism, handicrafts, wood, pearls. **Chief crops:** coconuts, tomatoes, melons, taro, breadfruit, fruits. **Natural resources:** fish, minerals. **Arable land:** 11%. **Fish catch:** 56,664 metric tons. **Labor force:** agriculture 41%, industry 20.9%, services 57.7%.

Finance: Monetary unit: U.S. Dollar (USD). **GDP** (2001 est.): $115 mil; **per capita GDP** (2005 est.): $2,900; **GDP growth** (2005 est.): 3.5%. **Imports** (2000): $54.7 mil; U.S., Japan, Australia, New Zealand, Singapore, Fiji, China, Philippines. **Exports** (2000): $9.1 mil; U.S., Japan, Australia, China. **Tourism:** $4 mil. **Budget** (1999): $40 mil.

Transport: Civil aviation: 22.4 mil pass.-mi; 4 airports. **Chief port:** Majuro.

Communications: Telephone lines (2004): 4,500. **Internet:** 2,200 users.

Health: Life expect.: 68.6 male; 72.7 female. **Births** (per 1,000 pop.): 32.4. **Deaths** (per 1,000 pop.): 4.7. **Natural inc.:** 2.77%. **Infant mortality** (per 1,000 live births): 27.3. **AIDS rate:** NA.

Education: Compulsory: ages 6-14. **Literacy:** 93.7%.

Major intl. organizations: UN (FAO, IBRD, IMF, IMO, WHO).

Embassy: 2433 Massachusetts Ave. NW 20008; 234-5414.

Website: www.rmiembassyus.org

The Marshall Islands were a German possession until WWI and were administered by Japan between the World Wars. After WWII, they were administered as part of the UN Trust Territory of the Pacific Islands by the U.S. From 1946-58, Bikini and Enewetak atolls were used as test sites for the U.S. nuclear weapons program, including the hydrogen bomb.

The Compact of Free Association, ratified by the U.S. on Oct. 21, 1986, gave the islands their independence. In the compact, the U.S. agreed to provide financial aid to the islands, maintain their defense, and compensate victims of nuclear testing; it was renewed Dec. 2003. The Marshall Islands joined the UN Sept. 17, 1991. Amata Kabua, the islands' first and only president since 1979, died Dec. 19, 1996. His cousin Imata Kabua, elected president Jan. 13, 1997, was succeeded by Kessai Note on Jan. 10, 2000; he began a 2nd term Jan. 5, 2004.

Mauritania
Islamic Republic of Mauritania

People: Population: 3,270,065. **Age distrib. (%):** <15: 45.5; 65+: 2.2. **Pop. density:** 8 per sq mi, 3 per sq km. **Urban:** 40.4%. **Ethnic groups:** Mixed Moor/black 40%, Moor 30%, black 30%. **Principal languages:** Arabic (official), Pulaar, Soninke, French, Hassaniya, Wolof. **Chief religion:** Predominantly Muslim (official) 100%.

Geography: Total area: 397,956 sq mi, 1,030,700 sq km; **Land area:** 397,840 sq mi, 1,030,400 sq km. **Location:** In NW Africa. **Neighbors:** Western Sahara on N; Algeria, Mali on E; Senegal on S. **Topography:** Fertile Senegal R. valley in the S gives way to a wide central region of sandy plains and scrub trees. N is arid and extends into the Sahara. **Capital:** Nouakchott, 637,000.

Government: Type: In transition. **Head of state:** Pres. Sidi Mohamed Ould Cheikh Abdallahi; b. 1938; in office: Apr. 19, 20075. **Head of gov.:** Prime Min. Zeine Ould Zeidane; b. 1966; in office: Apr. 20, 2007. **Local divisions:** 12 regions, 1 capital district. **Defense budget:** $17.7 mil. **Active troops:** 15,870.

Economy: Industries: fish proc., iron ore, gypsum. **Chief crops:** dates, millet, sorghum, rice, corn. **Natural resources:** iron ore, gypsum, copper, phosphate, diamonds, gold, oil, fish. **Crude oil reserves:** 100 mil bbls. **Arable land:** 0.2%. **Livestock:** cattle:

1.7 mil; chickens: 4.2 mil; goats: 5.6 mil; sheep: 8.9 mil. **Fish catch:** 247,577 metric tons. **Electricity prod.:** 250 mil kWh. **Labor force** (2001 est.): agriculture 50%, industry 10%, services 40%.

Finance: Monetary unit: Ouguiya (MRO) (Sept. 2007: 251.00 = $1 U.S.). **GDP:** $8.1 bil; **per capita GDP:** $2,600; **GDP growth:** 14.1%. **Imports** (2004 est.): $1.1 bil; France 11.9%, China 8.2%, U.S. 6.8%, Belgium 6.7%, Italy 5.9%, Spain 5.5%. **Exports** (2004 est.): $784 mil; China 26.3%, Italy 11.8%, France 10.2%, Belgium 6.8%, Spain 6.7%, Japan 5.4%. **Tourism:** $11 mil. **Budget** (2002 est.): $378 mil. **Intl. reserves less gold** (2003): $280 mil. **Gold** (2003): 10,000 oz t. **Consumer prices:** 6.24%.

Transport: Railroad: Length: 446 mi. **Motor vehicles:** 12,200 pass. cars; 18,200 comm. vehicles. **Civil aviation:** 30.4 mil pass.-mi; 8 airports. **Chief ports:** Nouadhibou, Nouakchott.

Communications: TV sets: 95 per 1,000 pop. **Radios:** 146 per 1,000 pop. **Telephone lines:** 34,900. **Internet:** 100,000 users.

Health: Life expect.: 51.2 male; 55.9 female. **Births** (per 1,000 pop.): 40.6. **Deaths** (per 1,000 pop.): 11.9. **Natural inc.:** 2.87%. **Infant mortality** (per 1,000 live births): 68.1. **AIDS rate:** 0.7%.

Education: Compulsory: ages 6-14. **Literacy:** 51.2%.

Major intl. organizations: UN (FAO, IBRD, ILO, IMF, IMO, WHO, WTO), AL, AU.

Embassy: 2129 Leroy Pl. NW 20008; 232-5700.

Website: www.mauritania.mr

Mauritania was a French protectorate from 1903. It became independent Nov. 28, 1960, and annexed the south of former Spanish Sahara (now Western Sahara) in 1976. Mauritania signed a peace treaty with the Saharan guerrillas of the Polisario Front, 1979, and renounced its own claim to the region.

Maaouiya Ould Sid Ahmed Taya took power in a military coup in 1984. Taya, a U.S. ally, was toppled in a bloodless coup, Aug. 3, 2005. During Jan.-June 2006, up to 10,000 people tried to emigrate in handmade boats from Mauritania to Spain's Canary Islands; more than 1,700 died. Voters approved a new constitution limiting presidential powers, June 25, 2006; presidential elections, Mar. 11-25, 2007, completed the transition to civilian rule. Major oil finds have recently been developed.

Although slavery has been repeatedly abolished, most recently in 1981, thousands of Mauritanians continued to live under conditions of servitude; legislation mandating prison terms for slaveholders was enacted Aug. 8, 2007.

Mauritius
Republic of Mauritius

People: Population: 1,250,882. **Age distrib. (%):** <15: 23.5; 65+: 6.7. **Pop. density:** 1,596 per sq mi, 616 per sq km. **Urban:** 42.4%. **Ethnic groups:** Indo-Mauritian 68%, Creole 27%, Sino-Mauritian 3%, Franco-Mauritian 2%. **Principal languages:** English (official), French, Bhojpuri. **Chief religions:** Hindu 48%, Roman Catholic 24%, Muslim 17%.

Geography: Total area: 788 sq mi, 2,040 sq km; **Land area:** 784 sq mi, 2,030 sq km. **Location:** In Indian O., 500 mi E of Madagascar. **Neighbors:** Nearest is Madagascar to W. **Topography:** A volcanic island nearly surrounded by coral reefs. A central plateau is encircled by mountain peaks. **Capital:** Port Louis, 146,000.

Government: Type: Republic. **Head of state:** Pres. Anerood Jugnauth; b. Mar. 29, 1930; in office: Oct. 7, 2003. **Head of gov.:** Prime Min.Navinchandra Ramgoolam; b. July 14,1947; in office: July 5, 2005. **Local divisions:** 9 districts, 3 dependencies. **Defense budget:** $18 mil. **Active troops:** None.

Economy: Industries: sugar & food proc., textiles, clothing, chemicals. **Chief crops:** sugarcane, tea, corn, potatoes, bananas. **Natural resources:** fish. **Arable land:** 49%. **Livestock:** cattle: 28,000; chickens: 9.8 mil; goats: 93,000; pigs: 13,000; sheep: 11,500. **Fish catch:** 10,448 metric tons. **Electricity prod.:** 2.1 bil kWh. **Labor force** (1995): agriculture and fishing 14%, construction and industry 36%, transportation and communication 7%, trade, restaurants, hotels 16%, finance 3%, other services 24%.

Finance: Monetary unit: Rupee (MUR) (Sept. 2007: 30.96 = $1 U.S.). **GDP:** $17 bil; **per capita GDP:** $13,700; **GDP growth:** 4.9%. **Imports** (2003): $3.4 bil; France 15.5%, South Africa 8.6%, India 7.4%, China 5.9%, Bahrain 5.6%. **Exports** (2003): $2.3 bil; UK 30.5%, France 15.2%, UAE 10.5%, U.S. 10.3%, Madagascar 7%. **Tourism:** $871 mil. **Budget:** $1.9 bil. **Intl. reserves less gold:** $844 mil. **Gold:** 60,000 oz t. **Consumer prices:** 8.91%.

Transport: Motor vehicles: 115,000 pass. cars; 40,000 comm. vehicles. **Civil aviation:** 3.3 bil pass.-mi; 2 airports. **Chief port:** Port Louis.

Communications: TV sets: 248 per 1,000 pop. **Radios:** 371 per 1,000 pop. **Telephone lines:** 357,300. **Daily newspaper circ.:** 116.4 per 1,000 pop. **Internet:** 182,000 users.

Health: Life expect.: 68.9 male; 76.9 female. **Births** (per 1,000 pop.): 15.3. **Deaths** (per 1,000 pop.): 6.9. **Natural inc.:** 0.84%. **Infant mortality** (per 1,000 live births): 14.1. **AIDS rate:** 0.6%.

Education: Compulsory: ages 6-11. **Literacy:** 84.3%.

Major intl. organizations: UN and all of its specialized agencies, the Commonwealth, AU.

Embassy: 4301 Connecticut Ave. NW, Ste. 441, 20008; 244-1491.

Website: www.gov.mu

Mauritius was uninhabited when settled in 1638 by the Dutch, who introduced sugarcane. France took over in 1721, bringing African slaves. Britain ruled from 1810 to Mar. 12, 1968, bringing Indian workers for the sugar plantations.

Mauritius formally severed its association with the British crown Mar. 12, 1992.

Mexico
United Mexican States

People: Population: 108,700,891. **Age distrib.** (%): <15: 30.1; 65+: 5.9. **Pop. density:** 146 per sq mi, 57 per sq km. **Urban:** 76%. **Ethnic groups:** Mestizo 60%, Amerindian 30%, white 9%. **Principal languages:** Spanish (official), Náhuatl, Maya, Zapotec, Otomi, Mixtec, other indigenous. **Chief religions:** Roman Catholic 76.5%, Protestant 6%.

Geography: Total area: 761,606 sq mi, 1,972,550 sq km; **Land area:** 742,490 sq mi, 1,923,040 sq km. **Location:** in southern N. America. **Neighbors:** U.S. on N, Guatemala and Belize on S. **Topography:** The Sierra Madre Occidental Mts. run NW-SE near the west coast; the Sierra Madre Oriental Mts. run near Gulf of Mexico. They join S of Mexico City. Between the 2 ranges lies the dry central plateau, 5,000 to 8,000 ft alt., rising toward the S, with temperate vegetation. Coastal lowlands are tropical. About 45% of land is arid. **Capital:** Mexico City, 19,411,000. **Cities (urban aggr.):** Guadalajara, 3,968,000 Monterrey, 3,596,000; Puebla, 1,824,000.

Government: Type: Federal republic. **Head of state and gov.:** Pres. Felipe de Jesús Calderón Hinojosa; b. Aug. 18, 1962; in office: Dec. 1, 2006. **Local divisions:** 31 states, 1 federal district. **Defense budget:** $3.22 bil. **Active troops:** 237,800.

Economy: Industries: food & beverages, tobacco, chemicals, iron & steel, oil, mining, textiles, clothing, autos, consumer durables, tourism. **Chief crops:** corn, wheat, soybeans, rice, beans, cotton, coffee, fruit, tomatoes. **Natural resources:** oil, silver, copper, gold, lead, zinc, nat. gas, timber. **Crude oil reserves:** 12.4 bil bbls. **Arable land:** 13%. **Livestock:** cattle: 28.6 mil; chickens: 289.7 mil; goats: 8.9 mil; pigs: 15.4 mil; sheep: 7.5 mil. **Fish catch:** 1,422,344 metric tons. **Electricity prod.:** 222.4 bil kWh. **Labor force** (2003): agriculture 18%, industry 24%, services 58%.

Finance: Monetary unit: Peso (MXN) (Sept. 2007: 11.12 = $1 U.S.). **GDP:** $1.1 tril; **per capita GDP:** $10,700; **GDP growth:** 4.8%. **Imports:** $253.1 bil; U.S. 50%, Japan 4.2%, China 3.9%. **Exports:** $248.8 bil; U.S. 78.7%, Canada 6%, Spain 1.4%. **Tourism:** $11.8 bil. **Budget:** $196.2 bil. **Intl. reserves less gold:** $50.70 bil. **Gold:** 90,000 oz t. **Consumer prices:** 3.63%.

Transport: Railroad: length: 10,913 mi. **Motor vehicles:** 13.4 mil pass. cars; 6.3 mil comm. vehicles. **Civil aviation:** 18 bil pass.-mi; 228 airports. **Chief ports:** Altamira, Manzanillo, Salina Cruz, Tampico, Topolobampo, Veracruz.

Communications: TV sets: 272 per 1,000 pop. **Radios:** 329 per 1,000 pop. **Telephone lines:** 19.9 mil. **Daily newspaper circ.:** 93.5 per 1,000 pop. **Internet:** 18.1 mil users.

Health: Life expect.: 72.8 male; 78.6 female. **Births** (per 1,000 pop.): 20.4. **Deaths** (per 1,000 pop.): 4.8. **Natural inc.:** 1.56%. **Infant mortality** (per 1,000 live births): 19.6. **AIDS rate:** 0.3%.

Education: Compulsory: ages 6-15. **Literacy:** 91.6%.

Major intl. organizations: UN (FAO, IBRD, ILO, IMF, IMO, WHO, WTO), APEC, OAS, OECD.

Embassy: 1911 Pennsylvania Ave. NW 20006; 728-1600.

Website: www.presidencia.gob.mx

Mexico was the site of advanced Indian civilizations. The Mayans, an agricultural people, moved up from Yucatan, built huge stone pyramids, and invented a calendar. The Toltecs were overcome by the Aztecs, who founded Tenochtitlan 1325 CE, now Mexico City. Hernán Cortés, Spanish conquistador, destroyed the Aztec empire, 1519-21. After 3 centuries of Spanish rule the people rose, under Fr. Miguel Hidalgo y Costilla, 1810, Fr. Morelos y Pavón, 1812, and Gen. Agustín Iturbide, who made himself emperor as Agustín I, 1822. A republic was declared in 1823.

Mexican territory extended into the present American Southwest and California until Texas revolted and established a republic in 1836. The U.S.-Mexican War, 1846-48, resulted in the loss by Mexico of the lands north of the Rio Grande.

French arms supported an Austrian archduke on the throne of Mexico as Maximilian I, 1864-67, but pressure from the U.S. forced France to withdraw. Dictatorial rule by Porfirio Díaz, president 1877-80, 1884-1911, led to a period of rebellion and factional fighting. A new constitution, Feb. 5, 1917, brought reform.

The Institutional Revolutionary Party (PRI) dominated politics from 1929 until the late 1990s. Radical opposition, including some guerrilla activity, was contained by strong measures. Some gains in agriculture, industry, and social services were achieved, but much of the work force remained jobless or underemployed. Although prospects brightened with the discovery of vast oil reserves, inflation and a drop in world oil prices aggravated Mexico's economic problems in the 1980s. Mexico reached agreement with the U.S. and Canada on the North American Free Trade Agreement (NAFTA) Aug. 12, 1992; it took effect Jan. 1, 1994.

Guerrillas of the Zapatista National Liberation Army (EZLN) launched an uprising, Jan. 1, 1994, in southern Mexico. A tentative peace accord was reached Mar. 2. The presidential candidate of the governing PRI, Luis Donaldo Colosio Murrieta, was assassinated at a political rally in Tijuana, Mar. 23. The new PRI candidate, Ernesto Zedillo Ponce de León, won election Aug. 21 and was inaugurated Dec. 1, 1994.

An austerity plan and pledges of aid from the U.S. saved Mexico's currency from collapse in early 1995. Popular Revolutionary Army guerrillas launched coordinated attacks on government targets in Aug. 1996. In elections July 6, 1997, the PRI failed to win a congressional majority for the first time since 1929. An armed gang massacred 45 peasants in Chiapas on Dec. 22, 1997.

In the presidential election of July 2, 2000, the PRI lost for the first time in over 7 decades; the winner, Vicente Fox Quesada of the National Action Party (PAN), took office Dec. 1, 2000. Hurricane Wilma hit Cancún Oct. 21, 2005, causing $2 bil damage.

Results of the July 2, 2006, presidential vote gave the PAN candidate, conservative Felipe Calderón Hinojosa, a slim margin over former Mexico City mayor Andrés Manuel López Obrador, nominee of the leftist Democratic Revolutionary Party. Claiming vote fraud, López Obrador and his supporters held massive protests, but Calderón was declared the winner and took office Dec. 1. He launched a crackdown on drug cartels, which were blamed for more than 3,000 killings from Jan. 2006 through June 2007.

As of 2005, an estimated 26.8 mil persons of Mexican ancestry were living in the U.S. More recent estimates of illegal immigrants from Mexico to the U.S. range up to 12 mil or more.

Micronesia
Federated States of Micronesia

People: Population: 107,862. **Age distrib.** (%): <15: 35.9; 65+: 2.9. **Pop. density:** 398 per sq mi, 154 per sq km. **Urban:** 22.3%. **Ethnic groups:** Chuukese 49%, Pohnpeian 24%, Kosraean 6%, Yapese 5%, Yap outer islands 5%. **Principal languages:** English (official), Trukese, Pohnpeian, Yapese, Kosrean, Ulithian, Woleaian, Nukuoro, Kapingamaran. **Chief religions:** Roman Catholic 50%, Protestant 47%.

Geography: Total area: 271 sq mi, 702 sq km; **Land area:** 271 sq mi, 702 sq km. **Location:** Consists of 607 islands in W Pacific Ocean. **Topography:** Includes both high mountainous islands and low coral atolls; volcanic outcroppings on Pohnpei, Kosrae, and Truk. Climate is tropical. **Capital:** Palikir, on Pohnpei, 7,000 (1994 island pop.) 33,372.

Government: Type: Republic in free association with U.S. **Head of state and gov.:** Pres. Emanuel (Manny) Mori; b. Dec. 25, 1948; in office: May 11, 2007. **Local divisions:** 4 states.

Economy: Industries: tourism, constr., fish proc., handicrafts. **Chief crops:** black pepper, tropical fruits & vegetables, coconuts, bananas, cassava, kava, betel nuts, sweet potatoes. **Natural resources:** timber, fish, minerals. **Arable land:** 6%. **Livestock:** cattle: 13,900; chickens: 185,000; goats: 4,000; pigs: 32,000. **Fish catch:** 29,336 metric tons. **Labor force** (2005 est.): agriculture 0.9%, industry 34.4%, services 64.7%; two-thirds are government employees.

Finance: Monetary unit: U.S. Dollar (USD). **GDP** (2002 est.): $277 mil (supplemented by grant aid, ave. perhaps $100 mil a year); **per capita GDP** (2005 est.): $2,300; **GDP growth** (2005 est.): 0.3%. **Imports** (2004): $132.7 mil; U.S., Japan, Hong Kong. **Exports** (2004 est.): $14 mil; Japan, U.S., Guam. **Tourism:** $17 mil. **Budget** (2005 est.): $144.2 mil. **Intl. reserves less gold:** $31 mil.

Transport: Civil aviation: 6 airports. **Chief port:** Tomil Harbor.

Communications: TV sets: 20 per 1,000 pop. **Radios:** 70 per 1,000 pop. **Telephone lines:** 12,400. **Internet:** 16,000 users.

Health: Life expect.: 68.5 male; 72.3 female. **Births** (per 1,000 pop.): 24.1. **Deaths** (per 1,000 pop.): 4.7. **Natural inc.:** 1.95%. **Infant mortality** (per 1,000 live births): 28.2. **AIDS rate:** NA.

Education: Compulsory: ages 6-13. **Literacy:** 89%.

Major intl. organizations: UN (FAO, IBRD, IMF, WHO).

Embassy: 1725 N St. NW 20036; 223-4383.

Website: www.fsmgov.org

The Federated States of Micronesia, formerly known as the Caroline Islands, ruled successively by Spain, Germany, Japan, and the U.S. The nation gained independence under a compact of free association with the U.S., Nov. 1986 and was admitted to the UN, Sept. 17, 1991. Tropical Storm Chata'an July 1-2, 2002, left 47 people dead and over 1,000 homeless in Chuuk. Typhoon Sudal battered Yap Apr. 9, 2004, leaving at least 1,500 homeless.

Moldova
Republic of Moldova

People: Population: 4,328,816. **Age distrib.** (%): <15: 16.5; 65+: 10.9. **Pop. density:** 336 per sq mi, 130 per sq km. **Urban:** 46.7%. **Ethnic groups:** Moldovan/Romanian 78%, Ukrainian 8%, Russian 6%, Gagauz 4%. **Principal languages:** Moldovan (official), Russian, Gagauz (Turkish dialect). **Chief religion:** Eastern Orthodox 98%.

Geography: Total area: 13,067 sq mi, 33,843 sq km; **Land area:** 12,885 sq mi, 33,371 sq km. **Location:** In E Europe. **Neighbors:** Romania on W; Ukraine on N, E, and S. **Topography:** Country is landlocked; mainly hilly plains, with steppelands in S near Black Sea. **Capital:** Chisinau, 598,000.

Government: Type: Republic. **Head of state:** Pres. Vladimir Voronin; b. May 25, 1941; in office: Apr. 7, 2001. **Head of gov.:** Prime Min. Vasile Tarlev; b. Oct. 9, 1963; in office: Apr. 19, 2001. **Local divisions:** 9 counties, 1 municipality, 1 autonomous territory. **Defense budget:** $9.5 mil. **Active troops:** 6,750.

Economy: Industries: food proc., agric. machinery, foundry equip. **Chief crops:** vegetables, fruits, wine, grain, sugar beets, sunflower seed, tobacco. **Natural resources:** lignite, phosphorite, gypsum, limestone. **Arable land:** 55%. **Livestock:** cattle: 310,476; chickens: 22.1 mil; goats: 119,372; pigs: 460,678; sheep: 818,316. **Fish catch:** 5,001 metric tons. **Electricity prod.:** 3.9 bil kWh. **Labor force** (2005 est.): agriculture 40.7%, industry 12.1%, services 47.2%.

Finance: Monetary unit: Leu (MDL) (Sept. 2007: 11.71 = $1 U.S.). **GDP:** $9.1 bil; **per capita GDP:** $2,000; **GDP growth:** 4%. **Imports:** $2.7 bil; Russia 21.9%, Ukraine 17.8%, Romania 9.6%, Germany 9.2%, Italy 6.4%. **Exports:** $1 bil; Russia 22.5%, Germany 12%, Italy 10.9%, Romania 10.5%, Ukraine 9.4%, Belarus 5.6%. **Tourism:** $128 mil. **Budget:** $1.3 bil. **Intl. reserves less gold:** $515 mil. **Consumer prices:** 11.62%.

Transport: Railroad: Length: 707 mi. **Motor vehicles:** 280,000 pass. cars; 5,000 comm. vehicles. **Civil aviation:** 138.6 mil pass.-mi; 6 airports.

Communications: TV sets: 297 per 1,000 pop. **Radios:** 742 per 1,000 pop. **Telephone lines:** 1 mil. **Daily newspaper circ.:** 153.4 per 1,000 pop. **Internet:** 727,700 users.

Health: Life expect.: 66.5 male; 74.1 female. **Births** (per 1,000 pop.): 10.9. **Deaths** (per 1,000 pop.): 10.8. **Natural inc.:** 0.003%. **Infant mortality** (per 1,000 live births): 13.9. **AIDS rate:** 1.1%.

Education: Compulsory: ages 7-15. **Literacy:** 99.1%.

Major intl. organizations: UN (FAO, IBRD, ILO, IMF, IMO, WHO, WTO), CIS, OSCE.

Embassy: 2101 S St. NW 20008; 667-1130.

Website: www.moldova.md

In 1918, Romania annexed all of Bessarabia that Russia had acquired from Turkey in 1812 by the Treaty of Bucharest. In 1924, the Soviet Union established the Moldavian Autonomous Soviet Socialist Republic on the eastern bank of the Dniester. It was merged with the Romanian-speaking districts of Bessarabia in 1940 to form the Moldavian SSR.

During WWII, Romania, allied with Germany, occupied the area. It was recaptured by the USSR in 1944. Moldova declared independence Aug. 27, 1991. It became an independent state when the USSR disbanded Dec. 26, 1991.

Fighting erupted Mar. 1992 in the Trans-Dniester region between Moldovan security forces and Slavic separatists—ethnic Russians and ethnic Ukrainians—who feared Moldova would merge with neighboring Romania. In a plebiscite on Mar. 6, 1994, voters in Moldova supported independence, without unification with Romania.

Defying the Moldovan government, voters in the breakaway Trans-Dniester region held legislative elections and approved a separatist constitution Dec. 24, 1995. A peace accord with Trans-Dniester separatists was signed in Moscow May 8, 1997.

Communists won the most seats in Moldovan parliamentary elections Mar. 22, 1998, but a coalition of three center-right parties formed the government. The Communists gained legislative majorities in elections Feb. 25, 2001, and Mar. 6, 2005. In a referendum Sept. 17, 2006, Trans-Dniester voters overwhelmingly supported independence from Moldova and eventual union with Russia.

Monaco
Principality of Monaco

People: Population: 32,671. **Age distrib.** (%): <15: 15; 65+: 22.7. **Pop. density:** 32,671 per sq mi, 16,336 per sq km. **Urban:** 100.0%. **Ethnic groups:** French 47%, Monegasque 16%, Italian 16%. **Principal languages:** French (official), English, Italian, Monegasque. **Chief religion:** Roman Catholic (official) 90%.

Geography: Total area: <1 sq mi, 2 sq km; **Land area:** <1 sq mi, 2 sq km. **Location:** On NW Mediterranean coast. **Neighbors:** France to W, N, E. **Topography:** Monaco-Ville sits atop a high promontory, the rest of the principality rises from the port up the hillside. **Capital** (2003): Monaco-ville, 34,000.

Government: Type: Constitutional monarchy. **Head of state:** Prince Albert II; b. Mar. 14, 1958; in office: Apr. 6, 2005. **Head of gov.:** Min. of State Jean-Paul Proust; b. Mar. 3, 1940; in office: June 1, 2005. **Local divisions:** 4 quarters.

Economy: Industries: tourism, constr., light industrial products. **Chief crops:** None. **Natural resources:** None. **Fish catch:** 2 metric tons. **Labor force:** NA.

Finance: Monetary unit: Euro (EUR) (Sept. 2007: 0.72 = $1 U.S.). **GDP:** $976.3 mil; **per capita GDP:** $30,000; **GDP growth** (2000 est.): 0.9%. **Tourism:** NA. **Budget** (2005 est.): $920.6 mil.

Transport: Railroad: Length: NA. **Motor vehicles:** 17,000 pass. cars, 4,000 comm. vehicles. **Civil aviation:** 3.7 mil pass.-mi; 1 airport. **Chief port:** Monaco.

Communications: TV sets: 758 per 1,000 pop. **Radios:** 1,030 per 1,000 pop. **Telephone lines:** 34,000. **Internet:** 20,000 users.

Health: Life expect.: 76 male; 83.9 female. **Births** (per 1,000 pop.): 9.1. **Deaths** (per 1,000 pop.): 12.9. **Natural inc.:** −0.38%. **Infant mortality** (per 1,000 live births): 5.3. **AIDS rate:** NA.

Education: Compulsory: ages 6-15. **Literacy:** 99%.

Major intl. organizations: UN (FAO, IMO, WHO), OSCE.

Embassy: 2314 Wyoming Ave. NW 20008; 234-1530.

Website: www.gouv.mc

An independent principality for over 300 years, Monaco has belonged to the House of Grimaldi since 1297, except during the French Revolution. It was placed under the protectorate of Sardinia in 1815, and under France, 1861. The Prince of Monaco was an absolute ruler until the 1911 constitution. Monaco was admitted to the UN on May 28, 1993.

Monaco is noted for its mild climate, magnificent scenery, and elegant casinos. Prince Rainier III, who ruled Monaco from 1949 and turned it into one of Europe's top tourist spots, died Apr. 6, 2005, and was succeeded by his son, Albert II.

Mongolia

People: Population: 2,951,786. **Age distrib.** (%): <15: 28.7; 65+: 3.9. **Pop. density:** 5 per sq mi, 2 per sq km. **Urban:** 56.7%. **Ethnic groups:** Mongol 95%, Turkic 5%. **Principal languages:** Khalkha Mongol, Turkic, Russian. **Chief religion:** Tibetan Buddhist Lamaism 50%.

Geography: Total area: 603,909 sq mi, 1,564,116 sq km; **Location:** In E Central Asia. **Neighbors:** Russia on N, China on E, W, and S. **Topography:** Mostly a high plateau with mountains, salt lakes, and vast grasslands. Arid lands in S are part of the Gobi Desert. **Capital:** Ulaanbaatar, 863,000.

Government: Type: Republic. **Head of state:** Pres. Nambaryn Enkhbayar; b. June 1, 1958; in office: June 24, 2005. **Head of gov.:** Prime. Min. Miyeegombo Enkhbold; b. 1964; in office: Jan. 25, 2006. **Local divisions:** 18 provinces, 3 municipalities. **Defense budget** (2005): $17 mil. **Active troops:** 8,600.

Economy: Industries: constr. materials, mining, oil, food, beverages. **Chief crops:** wheat, barley, vegetables, forage crops. **Natural resources:** oil, coal, copper, molybd., tungsten, phosphates, tin, nickel, zinc, fluorspar, gold, silver, iron. **Arable land:** 1%. **Livestock:** cattle: 2 mil; chickens: 30,000; goats: 13.3 mil; pigs: 6,000; sheep: 12.9 mil. **Fish catch:** 366 metric tons. **Electricity prod.:** 3.3 bil kWh. **Labor force** (2005): agriculture 39.9%, industry 31.4%, services 28.7%.

Finance: Monetary unit: Tughrik (MNT) (Sept. 2007: 1,185.00 = $1 U.S.). **GDP:** $5.9 bil; **per capita GDP:** $2,100; **GDP growth:** 7.5% (official). **Imports** (2005): $916.1 mil (full customs integration with France). **Exports** (2005): $716.3 mil (full customs integration with France). **Tourism:** $185 mil. **Budget** (2005 est.): $634.5 mil. **Intl. reserves less gold:** $616 mil. **Gold:** 210,000 oz t. **Consumer prices:** 5.1%.

Transport: Railroad: Length: 1,125 mi. **Motor vehicles:** NA. **Civil aviation:** 429.4 mil pass.-mi; 12 airports.

Communications: TV sets: 58 per 1,000 pop. **Radios:** 142 per 1,000 pop. **Telephone lines:** 156,000. **Daily newspaper circ.:** 17.6 per 1,000 pop. **Internet:** 268,300 users.

Health: Life expect.: 64.6 male; 69.5 female. **Births** (per 1,000 pop.): 21.1. **Deaths** (per 1,000 pop.): 6.2. **Natural inc.:** 1.49%. **Infant mortality** (per 1,000 live births): 42.7. **AIDS rate:** <0.1%.

Education: Compulsory: ages 7-14. **Literacy:** 97.8%.

Major intl. organizations: UN (FAO, IBRD, ILO, IMF, IMO, WHO, WTO).

Embassy: 2833 M St. NW 20007; 333-7117.

Website: www.pmis.gov.mn

One of the world's oldest countries, Mongolia reached the zenith of its power in the 13th cent. when Genghis Khan and his successors conquered all of China and extended their influence as far west as Hungary and Poland. In later centuries, the empire dissolved and Mongolia became a province of China.

With the advent of the 1911 Chinese revolution, Mongolia, with Russian backing, declared its independence. A Communist regime was established July 11, 1921.

In 1990, the Mongolian Communist Party yielded its monopoly on power but won election in July. A new constitution took effect Feb. 12, 1992. Natsagiyn Bagabandi, a former Communist, won the presidential election of May 18, 1997. A protracted political crisis took a violent turn Oct. 2, 1998, with the murder of Sanjaasuregiyn Zorig, a popular cabinet member seeking to become prime minister. Pres. Bagabandi was reelected May 20, 2001. Nambaryn Enkhbayar, a former prime minister (2000-04), won the presidential election of May 22, 2005.

Mongolia contributed troops to U.S.-led operations in Afghanistan and Iraq. On Nov. 21, 2005, Pres. George W. Bush became the first sitting U.S. president to visit Mongolia.

Montenegro
Republic of Montenegro

People: Population: 684,736. **Age distrib.:** NA. **Pop. density:** 128 per sq mi, 50 per sq km. **Urban:** NA. **Ethnic groups:** Montenegrin 43%, Serbian 32%, Bosniak 8%, Albanian 5%. **Principal languages:** Serbian (official), Bosnian, Albanian, Crotian. **Chief religions:** Orthodox, Muslim, Roman Catholic.

Geography: Total area: 5,415 sq mi, 14,026 sq km; **Land area:** 5,333 sq mi, 13,812 sq km. **Location:** On Balkan Peninsula in SE Europe. **Neighbors:** Bosnia and Herzegovina on N and W; Serbia on E; Albania on SE; Adriatic Sea on SW; Croatia on W. **Topography:** Most terrain is rugged and mountainous, with few arable regions, mostly along the Zeta R.; narrow coastline is highly indented. **Capital** (2003): Podgorica (administrative), 139,724; Cetinje (official).

Government: Type: Republic. **Head of state:** Pres. Filip Vujanovic; b. Sept. 1, 1954; in office: May 22, 2003. **Head of gov.:** Prime. Min. Zeljko Sturanovic; b. Jan. 31, 1960; in office: Nov. 10, 2006. **Local divisions:** 21 municipalities. **Defense budget:** NA. **Active troops:** 7,300.

Economy: Industries: aluminum, steel, consumer goods, tourism, agriculture, animal husbandry. **Chief crops:** grains, tobacco, potatoes, citrus fruits, olives, grapes. **Natural resources:** lignite, bauxite, hydropower, sea salt. **Arable land:** 14%. **Livestock:** cattle: 117,842; chickens: 462,000; pigs: 10,697; sheep: 254,898. **Electricity prod.:** NA. **Labor force** (2004 est.): agriculture 2%, industry 30%, services 68%.

Finance: Monetary unit: Euro (EUR) (Sept. 2007: 0.72 = $1 U.S.). **GDP:** $3.4 bil; **per capita GDP** (2005 est.): $3,800; **GDP growth:** NA. **Imports** (2003): $601.7 mil; Greece 10.2%, Italy 10.2%, Germany 9.6%, Bosnia and Herzegovina 9.2%. **Exports** (2003): $171.3 mil; Switzerland 83.9%, Italy 6.1%, Bosnia and Herzegovina 1.3%. **Tourism:** NA. **Budget** (2005 est.): $11.1 bil (incl. Serbia). **Intl. reserves less gold:** $288 mil. **Gold:** 40,000 oz t.

Transport: Railroad: Length: 155 mi. **Motor vehicles:** NA. **Civil aviation:** 3 airports. **Chief port:** Bar.

Communications: TV sets: NA. **Radios:** NA. **Telephone lines:** 353,300. **Internet:** 266,000 users.

Health: Life expect.: 74.1 male; 80.1 female. **Births** (per 1,000 pop.): 11.2. **Deaths** (per 1,000 pop.): 8.4. **Natural inc.:** 0.28%. **Infant mortality** (per 1,000 live births): 10.6. **AIDS rate:** NA.

Education: Compulsory: ages 7-14. **Literacy:** 96.4%.

Major intl. organizations: UN (FAO, ILO, WHO), OSCE.

Embassy: 1610 New Hampshire Ave. NW 20009; 234-6108.

Website: www.montenegro.yu

Part of the medieval Serbian Kingdom, Montenegro preserved its autonomy for centuries because of its mountainous terrain. It was ruled by Orthodox prince-bishops from the 16th to the 19th centuries, but became a secular principality in 1852. After WWI, it was part of the Kingdom of Serbs, Croats, and Slovenes, later renamed Yugoslavia. Italian forces occupied parts of Montenegro during WWII. In 1945, with the establishment of a federal Yugoslavia under Communist rule, Montenegro became one of 6 constituent republics.

In Apr. 1992, when 4 other republics had declared independence, Montenegro and Serbia reconstituted themselves as the Federal Republic of Yugoslavia. Because of its ties with Serbia, Montenegro was a target of NATO air strikes during the Kosovo war, Mar.-June 1999. The republic sought closer ties with the West, however, and worked to reduce its political and economic dependence on Serbia. Under a charter that took effect Feb. 4, 2003, the name Yugoslavia was dropped in favor of the new union of Serbia and Montenegro. The charter allowed Montenegro to hold a referendum on independence, which passed May 21, 2006, with barely more than the 55% majority required. Montenegro declared independence June 3 and was admitted as a UN member June 28.

Morocco
Kingdom of Morocco

People: Population: 33,757,175. **Age distrib.** (%): <15: 31; 65+: 5.1. **Pop. density:** 196 per sq mi, 76 per sq km. **Urban:** 58.7%. **Ethnic groups:** Arab-Berber 99%. **Principal languages:** Arabic (official), Berber dialects, French. **Chief religion:** Muslim (official) 99%.

Geography: Total area: 172,414 sq mi, 446,550 sq km; **Land area:** 172,317 sq mi, 446,300 sq km. **Location:** On NW coast of Africa. **Neighbors:** Western Sahara on S, Algeria on E, Spain on N. **Topography:** Consists of 5 natural regions: mountain ranges (Riff in the N, Middle Atlas, Upper Atlas, and Anti-Atlas); rich plains in W; alluvial plains in SW; well-cultivated plateaus in the center; a pre-Sahara arid zone extending from SE. **Capital:** Rabat, 1,647,000. **Cities (urban aggr.):** Casablanca, 3,138,000; Fes, 963,000.

Government: Type: Constitutional monarchy. **Head of state:** King Mohammed VI; b. Aug. 21, 1963; in office: July 23, 1999. **Head of gov.:** Prime Min. Abbas El Fassi; b. Sept. 18, 1940; in office: Sept. 19, 2007. **Local divisions:** 16 regions. **Defense budget** (2005): $2 bil. **Active troops:** 200,800.

Economy: Industries: mining, food proc., leather goods, textiles, constr., tourism. **Chief crops:** barley, wheat, citrus, wine, vegetables, olives. **Natural resources:** phosphates, iron ore, mang., lead, zinc, fish, salt. **Crude oil reserves:** 1 mil bbls. **Arable land:** 19%. **Livestock:** cattle: 2.7 mil; chickens: 140 mil; goats: 5.3 mil; pigs: 8,000; sheep: 16.9 mil. **Fish catch:** 934,961 metric tons. **Electricity prod.:** 21.4 bil kWh. **Labor force** (2003 est.): agriculture 40%, industry 15%, services 45%.

Finance: Monetary unit: Dirham (MAD) (Sept. 2007: 8.11 = $1 U.S.). **GDP:** $152.5 bil; **per capita GDP:** $4,600; **GDP growth:** 9.3%. **Imports:** $21.2 bil; France 17.4%, Spain 13.4%, Saudi Arabia 6.9%, China 6.6%, Italy 6.3%, Germany 5.9%. **Exports:** $11.7 bil; France 21.4%, Spain 20.5%, UK 4.9%, Italy 4.7%, India 4.1%. **Tourism:** $4.6 bil. **Budget:** $20.4 bil. **Intl. reserves less gold:** $13.52 bil. **Gold:** 710,000 oz t. **Consumer prices:** 3.28%.

Transport: Railroad: Length: 1,185 mi. **Motor vehicles:** 1.3 mil pass. cars; 444,000 comm. vehicles. **Civil aviation:** 3 bil pass.-mi; 26 airports. **Chief ports:** Agadir, Casablanca, Mohammedia, Safi, Tangier.

Communications: TV sets: 165 per 1,000 pop. **Radios:** 247 per 1,000 pop. **Telephone lines:** 1.3 mil. **Daily newspaper circ.:** 29.1 per 1,000 pop. **Internet:** 6.1 mil users.

Health: Life expect.: 68.9 male; 73.7 female. **Births** (per 1,000 pop.): 21.6. **Deaths** (per 1,000 pop.): 5.5. **Natural inc.:** 1.61%. **Infant mortality** (per 1,000 live births): 38.9. **AIDS rate:** 0.1%.

Education: Compulsory: ages 6-14. **Literacy:** 52.3%.

Major intl. organizations: UN (FAO, IBRD, ILO, IMF, IMO, WHO, WTO), AL.

Embassy: 1601 21st St. NW 20009; 462-7979.

Website: www.mincom.gov.ma

Berbers were the original inhabitants, followed by Carthaginians and Romans. Arabs conquered in 683. In the 11th and 12th centuries, a Berber empire ruled all northwest Africa and most of Spain from Morocco.

Part of Morocco came under Spanish rule in the 19th cent.; France controlled the rest in the early 20th. Tribal uprisings lasted from 1911 to 1933. The country became independent Mar. 2, 1956. Tangier, an internationalized seaport, was turned over to Morocco, 1956. Ifni, a Spanish enclave, was ceded in 1969. Morocco annexed the disputed territory of Western Sahara during the second half of the 1970s.

King Hassan II assumed the throne in 1961, reigning until his death on July 23, 1999; he was immediately succeeded by his eldest son. Political reforms in the 1990s included the establishment of a bicameral legislature in 1997.

Five terrorist attacks in Casablanca May 16, 2003, left about 40 people dead, including 10 suicide bombers; the government blamed Salafia Jihadia, a group connected with al-Qaeda. An earthquake Feb. 24, 2004, killed at least 629 people in the vicinity of al-Hoceima, northern coastal Morocco. Parliamentary elections Sept. 7, 2007, were marred by a turnout of only 37%.

Western Sahara

Western Sahara, formerly the protectorate of Spanish Sahara, is bounded on the N by Morocco, the NE by Algeria, the E and S by Mauritania, and the W by the Atlantic Ocean. Phosphates are the major resource. Population (2007 est.): 382,617; capital: Laayoune (El Aaiún). Area: 102,703 sq mi.

Spain withdrew from its protectorate in Feb. 1976. On Apr. 14, 1976, Morocco annexed over 70,000 sq mi, with the remainder annexed by Mauritania. A guerrilla movement, the Polisario Front, which had proclaimed the region independent Feb. 27, launched attacks with Algerian support. After Mauritania signed a treaty with Polisario on Aug. 5, 1979, Morocco occupied Mauritania's portion of Western Sahara.

After years of bitter fighting, Morocco controlled the main urban areas, but Polisario guerrillas moved freely in the vast, sparsely populated deserts. The 2 sides implemented a cease-fire in 1991, when a UN peacekeeping force was deployed. Former U.S. Sec. of State James A. Baker III served as UN envoy 1997-2004 but was unable to resolve the dispute.

Mozambique
Republic of Mozambique

People: Population: 20,905,585. **Age distrib.** (%): <15: 44.7; 65+: 2.8. **Pop. density:** 69 per sq mi, 27 per sq km. **Urban:** 34.5%. **Ethnic groups:** Shangaan, Chokwe, Manyika, Sena, Makua. **Principal languages:** Portuguese (official), Emakhuwa, Xichangana Elomwe, Cisena. **Chief religions:** Catholic 24%, Muslim 18%, Zionist Christian 18%.

Geography: Total area: 309,496 sq mi, 801,590 sq km; **Land area:** 302,739 sq mi, 784,090 sq km. **Location:** On SE coast of Africa. **Neighbors:** Tanzania on N; Malawi, Zambia, Zimbabwe on W; South Africa, Swaziland on S. **Topography:** Coastal lowlands comprise nearly half the country with plateaus rising in steps to the mountains along W border. **Capital:** Maputo, 1,320,000.

Government: Type: Republic. **Head of state:** Pres. Armando Guebuza; b. Jan. 20, 1943; in office: Feb. 2, 2005. **Head of gov.:** Prime Min. Luisa Diogo; b. Apr. 11, 1958; in office: Feb. 17, 2004. **Local divisions:** 10 provinces and Maputo municipality. **Defense budget:** $58 mil. **Active troops:** 11,200.

Economy: Industries: food, beverages, chemicals, oil products, textiles, cement. **Chief crops:** cotton, cashew nuts, sugarcane, tea, cassava, corn, coconuts, sisal, citrus & tropical fruits. **Natural resources:** coal, titanium, nat. gas, hydropower, tantalum, graphite. **Arable land:** 5%. **Livestock:** cattle: 1.3 mil; chickens: 28 mil; goats: 392,000; pigs: 180,000; sheep: 125,000. **Fish catch:** 43,695 metric tons. **Electricity prod.:** 13.2 bil kWh. **Labor force** (1997 est.): agriculture 81%, industry 6%, services 13%.

Finance: Monetary unit: Metical (MZN) (Sept. 2007: 25.85 = $1 U.S.). **GDP:** $29.2 bil; **per capita GDP:** $1,500; **GDP growth:** 7.9%. **Imports:** $2.8 bil; South Africa 35.9%, Australia 9.4%, China 5%. **Exports:** $2.4 bil; Belgium 29.3%, Italy 22%, Spain 12.7%, China 4.1%. **Tourism:** $95 mil. **Budget:** $1.8 bil. **Intl. reserves less gold:** $768 mil. **Gold:** 100,000 oz t. **Consumer prices:** 13.24%.

Transport: Railroad: Length: 1,941 mi. **Motor vehicles:** 112,000 pass. cars; 40,000 comm. vehicles. **Civil aviation:** 251.7 mil pass.-mi; 22 airports. **Chief ports:** Beira, Maputo, Nacala.

Communications: TV sets: 5 per 1,000 pop. **Radios:** 40 per 1,000 pop. **Telephone lines:** 67,000. **Daily newspaper circ.:** 2.5 per 1,000 pop. **Internet:** 178,000 users.

Health: Life expect.: 41.4 male; 40.4 female. **Births** (per 1,000 pop.): 38.5. **Deaths** (per 1,000 pop.): 20.5. **Natural inc.:** 1.8%. **Infant mortality** (per 1,000 live births): 109.9. **AIDS rate:** 16.1%.

Education: Compulsory: ages 6-12. **Literacy:** 38.7%.

Major intl. organizations: UN (FAO, IBRD, ILO, IMF, IMO, WHO, WTO), the Commonwealth, AU.

Embassy: 1990 M St. NW, Ste. 570, 20036; 293-7146.

Website: www.embamoc-usa.org

The first Portuguese post on the Mozambique coast was established in 1505, on the trade route to the East. Mozambique became independent June 25, 1975, after a 10-year war against Portuguese colonial domination. The 1974 revolution in Portugal had paved the way for the orderly transfer of power to Frelimo (Front for the Liberation of Mozambique). Frelimo took over local administration Sept. 20, 1974.

The new Frelimo government, headed by Pres. Samora Machel, a former guerrilla commander, provided for a gradual transition to a Communist system. Most of the country's whites emigrated. In the 1980s, severe drought and civil war caused famine and heavy loss of life. Pres. Machel was killed in a plane crash just inside the South African border, Oct. 19, 1986. Frelimo formally abandoned Marxist-Leninism in 1989, and a new constitution, effective Nov. 30, 1990, provided for multiparty elections and a free-market economy.

On Oct. 4, 1992, a peace agreement was signed aimed at ending hostilities between the government and the rebel Mozambican National Resistance (MNR). Repatriation of 1.7 mil Mozambican refugees officially ended June 1995. In Mar. 1999 the heaviest floods in 4 decades left nearly 200,000 people stranded. Even worse flooding in Feb.-Mar. 2000 claimed more than 600 lives, displaced over 1 mil people, and devastated the economy. A train crash May 25, 2002, in southern Mozambique killed 196 people. Frelimo retained its hold under Pres. Joaquim Chissano (in office 1986-2005) and his successor, Pres. Armando Guebuza, elected Dec. 1-2, 2004. Flooding of the Zambezi River basin, followed by Cyclone Favio, killed at least 45 people and left more than 170,000 people homeless in Feb. 2007.

Myanmar *(formerly* Burma)
Union of Myanmar

People: Population: 47,373,958. **Age distrib. (%):** <15: 26.1; 65+: 5.3. **Pop. density:** 187 per sq mi, 72 per sq km. **Urban:** 30.6%. **Ethnic groups:** Burman 68%, Shan 9%, Karen 7%, Rakhine 4%. **Principal languages:** Burmese (official), many ethnic minority languages. **Chief religions:** Buddhist 89%, Christian 4%, Muslim 4%, animist 1%.

Geography: Total area: 261,970 sq mi, 678,500 sq km; **Land area:** 253,955 sq mi, 657,740 sq km. **Location:** Between S and SE Asia, on Bay of Bengal. **Neighbors:** Bangladesh, India on W; China, Laos, Thailand on E. **Topography:** Mountains surround Myanmar on W, N, and E, and dense forests cover much of the nation. N-S rivers provide habitable valleys and communications, especially the Irrawaddy, navigable for 900 mi. Country has a tropical monsoon climate. **Capital:** Yangon (Rangoon) 4,107,000. **Cities (urban aggr.):** Mandalay, 924,000.

Government: Type: Military. **Head of state:** Gen. Than Shwe; b. Feb. 2, 1933; in office: Apr. 23, 1992. **Head of gov.:** Lt. Gen. Thein Sein; b. 1945; in office: May 18, 2007 (acting). **Local divisions:** 7 states, 7 divisions. **Defense budget** (2005): $6.23 bil. **Active troops:** 375,000.

Economy: Industries: agric. proc., apparel, wood & wood products, mining, constr. materials. **Chief crops:** rice, pulses, beans, sesame, groundnuts, sugarcane. **Natural resources:** oil, timber, tin, antimony, zinc, copper, tungsten, lead, coal, marble, limestone, gemstones, nat. gas, hydropower. **Crude oil reserves:** 50 mil bbls. **Arable land:** 15%. **Livestock:** cattle: 12.1 mil; chickens: 81.5 mil; goats: 1.8 mil; pigs: 5.7 mil; sheep: 516,832. **Fish catch:** 2,217,466 metric tons. **Electricity prod.:** 5.8 bil kWh. **Labor force** (2001 est.): agriculture 70%, industry 7%, services 23%.

Finance: Monetary unit: Kyat (MMK) (Sept. 2007: 6.42 = $1 U.S.). **GDP:** $85.2 bil; **per capita GDP:** $1,800; **GDP growth:** 3%. **Imports:** $2 bil; China 33.6%, Thailand 21.2%, Singapore 15.7%, Malaysia 4.6%, South Korea 4.1%. **Exports:** $3.6 bil; Thailand 48.4%, India 12.6%, China 5.2%, Japan 5.1%. **Tourism:** $84 mil. **Budget:** $2.4 bil. **Intl. reserves less gold:** $821 mil. **Gold:** 230,000 oz t. **Consumer prices** (2005): 9.37%.

Transport: Railroad: Length: 2,458 mi. **Motor vehicles:** 188,000 pass. cars, 131,000 comm. vehicles. **Civil aviation:** 672.9 mil pass.-mi; 21 airports. **Chief ports:** Moulmein, Rangoon, Sittwe.

Communications: TV sets: 7 per 1,000 pop. **Radios:** 72 per 1,000 pop. **Telephone lines:** 503,900. **Daily newspaper circ.:** 8.7 per 1,000 pop. **Internet:** 93,600 users.

Health: Life expect.: 60.3 male; 64.8 female. **Births** (per 1,000 pop.): 17.5. **Deaths** (per 1,000 pop.): 9.3. **Natural inc.:** 0.82%. **Infant mortality** (per 1,000 live births): 50.7. **AIDS rate:** 1.3%.

Education: Compulsory: ages 5-9. **Literacy:** 89.9%.

Major intl. organizations: UN (FAO, IBRD, ILO, IMF, IMO, WHO, WTO), ASEAN.

Embassy: 2300 S St. NW 20008; 332-3344.

Website: www.myanmar.gov.mm

The Burmese arrived from Tibet before the 9th cent., displacing earlier cultures, and a Buddhist monarchy was established by the 11th. Burma was conquered by the Mongol dynasty of China in 1272, then ruled by Shans as a Chinese tributary, until the 16th cent. Britain subjugated Burma in 3 wars, 1824-84, and ruled the country as part of India until 1937, when it became self-governing. Independence outside the Commonwealth was achieved Jan. 4, 1948.

Gen. Ne Win dominated politics from 1962 to 1988, first as military ruler, then as constitutional president. His regime drove Indians from the civil service and Chinese from commerce. Economic socialization was advanced, isolation from foreign countries enforced. In 1987 Burma, once the richest nation in Southeast Asia, was granted less-developed status by the UN.

Ne Win resigned July 1988, following antigovernment riots. In Sept. the military seized power, under Gen. Saw Maung. In 1989 the country's name was changed to Myanmar.

The first free multiparty elections in 30 years took place May 27, 1990, with the main opposition party winning a decisive victory, but the military refused to hand over power. A key opposition leader, Aung San Suu Kyi, awarded the Nobel Peace Prize in 1991, was held under house arrest, 1989-95, 2000-02, and again from 2003. Because of the regime's poor human rights record and continued harassment of Aung San Suu Kyi and her supporters, the U.S. has imposed sanctions. The Indian Ocean tsunami of Dec. 26, 2004, killed at least 61 people in Myanmar.

The country was admitted to ASEAN July 23, 1997. Yielding to pressure from critics of the regime, Myanmar announced July 26, 2005, that it would forgo its turn to chair ASEAN in 2006. In Sept. 2005 a human rights investigator reported to the UN that Myanmar held more than 1,100 political prisoners, who were subject to torture. Beginning Nov. 6, the government moved to Naypyidaw, a fortified inland capital near Pyinmana.

Public anger over soaring fuel costs in Aug. 2007 triggered new challenges to the military regime. In late Sept., thousands of Buddhist monks led a series of mass protests in Yangon; security forces cracked down by raiding monasteries, arresting monks, and firing on demonstrators. On Sept. 25, the U.S. announced tougher sanctions against junta leaders.

Namibia
Republic of Namibia

People: Population: 2,055,080. **Age distrib. (%):** <15: 37.7; 65+: 3.8. **Pop. density:** 6 per sq mi, 2 per sq km. **Urban:** 35.1%. **Ethnic groups:** Ovambo 50%, Kavangos 9%, Herero 7%, Damara 7%, white 6%, Nama 5%, mixed 7%. **Principal languages:** English (official), Afrikaans, German, Oshivambo, Herero, Nama. **Chief religions:** Lutheran 50%, other Christian 30%, indigenous beliefs 10-20%.

Geography: Total area: 318,696 sq mi, 825,418 sq km; **Land area:** 318,696 sq mi, 825,418 sq km. **Location:** In southern Africa on coast of Atlantic O. **Neighbors:** Angola on N; Botswana, Zambia on E; South Africa on S. **Topography:** Three distinct regions incl. Namib desert along the Atlantic coast, a mountainous central plateau with woodland savanna, and Kalahari desert in E. True forests found in NE. There are 4 rivers, but little other surface water. **Capital:** Windhoek, 289,000.

Government: Type: Republic. **Head of state:** Pres. Hifikepunye Pohamba; b. Aug. 18, 1935; in office: Mar. 21, 2005. **Head of gov.:** Prime Min. Nahas Angula; b. Aug. 22, 1943; in office: Mar. 21, 2005. **Local divisions:** 13 regions. **Defense budget** $184 mil. **Active troops:** 9,200.

Economy: Industries: meatpacking, fish proc., dairy products, mining. **Chief crops:** millet, sorghum, peanuts. **Natural resources:** diamonds, copper, uranium, gold, lead, tin, lithium, cadmium, zinc, salt, vanadium, nat. gas, hydropower, fish. **Arable land:** 1%. **Livestock:** cattle: 2.4 mil; chickens: 3.5 mil; goats: 2.1 mil; pigs: 25,000; sheep: 2.7 mil. **Fish catch:** 552,745 metric tons. **Electricity prod.:** 1.7 bil kWh. **Labor force** (1999 est.): agriculture 47%, industry 20%, services 33%.

Finance: Monetary unit: Dollar (NAD) (Sept. 2007: 7.16 = $1 U.S.). **GDP:** $15.4 bil; **per capita GDP:** $7,600; **GDP growth:** 4.6%. **Imports:** $2.5 bil; South Africa 85.2%, U.S. **Exports:** $2.3 bil; South Africa 33.4%, U.S. 4%. **Tourism:** $405 mil. **Budget:** $2.2 bil. **Intl. reserves less gold:** $299 mil. **Consumer prices:** 5.05%.

Transport: Railroad: Length: 1,480 mi. **Motor vehicles:** NA. **Civil aviation:** 577.9 mil pass.-mi; 21 airports. **Chief ports:** Luderitz, Walvis Bay.

Communications: TV sets: 38 per 1,000 pop. **Radios:** 143 per 1,000 pop. **Telephone lines:** 138,900. **Daily newspaper circ.:** 17.2 per 1,000 pop. **Internet:** 80,600 users.

Health: Life expect.: 44.4 male; 41.8 female. **Births** (per 1,000 pop.): 23.5. **Deaths** (per 1,000 pop.): 19.2. **Natural inc.:** 0.44%. **Infant mortality** (per 1,000 live births): 47.2. **AIDS rate:** 19.6%.

Education: Compulsory: ages 6-15. **Literacy:** 85%.

Major intl. organizations: UN (FAO, IBRD, ILO, IMF, IMO, WHO, WTO), the Commonwealth, AU.

Embassy: 1605 New Hampshire Ave. NW 20009; 986-0540.

Website: www.grnnet.gov.na

Namibia was declared a German protectorate in 1890 and officially called South-West Africa. South Africa seized the territory from Germany in 1915 during WWI; the League of Nations gave South Africa a mandate over the territory in 1920. In 1966, the Marxist South-West Africa People's Organization (SWAPO) launched a guerrilla war for independence. The UN General Assembly named the area Namibia in 1968.

After many years of guerrilla warfare, South Africa, Angola, and Cuba signed a U.S.-mediated agreement Dec. 22, 1988, to end South African administration of Namibia and provide for a cease-fire and transition to independence, in accordance with a 1978 UN plan. A separate accord between Cuba and Angola provided for a phased withdrawal of Cuban troops from Namibia. A constitution providing for multiparty government was adopted Feb. 9, 1990, and Namibia gained independence Mar. 21. SWAPO has remained the dominant political group.

Walvis Bay, the principal deepwater port, had been turned over to South African administration in 1922. It remained in South African hands after independence, but South Africa turned control of the port back to Namibia, as of Mar. 1, 1994. Separatist violence flared in the Caprivi Strip in the late 1990s.

Nauru
Republic of Nauru
People: Population: 13,528. **Age distrib.** (%): <15: 36.4; 65+: 2. **Pop. density:** 1,691 per sq mi, 644 per sq km. **Urban:** 100%. **Ethnic groups:** Nauruan 58%, other Pacific Islander 26%, Chinese 8%, European 8%. **Principal languages:** Nauruan (official), English. **Chief religions:** Protestant 66%, Roman Catholic 33%.

Geography: Total area: 8 sq mi, 21 sq km; **Land area:** 8 sq mi, 21 sq km. **Location:** In W Pacific O. just S of Equator. **Neighbors:** Nearest is Kiribati to E. **Topography:** Mostly a plateau bearing high-grade phosphate deposits, surrounded by a sandy shore and coral reef in concentric rings. **Capital** (2003): Nauru, 13,000.

Government: Type: Republic. **Head of state and gov.:** Pres. Ludwig Scotty; b. June 20, 1948; in office June 22, 2004. **Local divisions:** 14 districts.

Economy: Industries: phosphate mining, offshore banking, coconut products. **Chief crops:** coconuts. **Natural resources:** phosphates, fish. **Livestock:** chickens: 5,000; pigs: 2,800. **Fish catch** 39 metric tons. **Electricity prod.:** 30 mil kWh. **Labor force** (1992): Employed in mining phosphates, public administration, education, and transportation.

Finance: Monetary unit: Australia Dollar (AUD) (Sept. 2007: 1.19 = $1 U.S.). **GDP** (2005 est.): $60 mil; **per capita GDP** (2005 est.): $5,000; **GDP growth:** NA. **Imports** (2004 est.): $20 mil; South Korea 43.8%, Australia 36.2%, U.S. 5.9%, Germany 4.3%. **Exports** (2005 est.): $64,000; South Africa 63.7%, South Korea 7.6%, Canada 6.6%. **Tourism:** NA. **Budget** (2005): $13.5 mil.

Transport: Railroad: Length: 3 mi. **Civil aviation:** 170.9 mil pass.-mi; 1 airport. **Chief port:** Nauru.

Communications: TV sets: 1 per 1,000 pop. **Radios:** 45 per 1,000 pop. **Internet:** 249,400 users.

Health: Life expect.: 59.9 male; 67.2 female. **Births** (per 1,000 pop.): 24.5. **Deaths** (per 1,000 pop.): 6.7. **Natural inc.:** 1.78%. **Infant mortality** (per 1,000 live births): 9.6. **AIDS rate:** NA.

Education: Compulsory: ages 6-16. **Literacy:** NA.

Major intl. organizations: UN (FAO, WHO), the Commonwealth.

Permanent UN Representative: 800 Second Ave., Ste. 400D, New York, NY 10017; 212-937-0074.

Website: www.un.int/nauru

The island was discovered in 1798 by the British but was formally annexed to the German Empire in 1886. After WWI, Nauru became a League of Nations mandate administered by Australia. During WWII the Japanese occupied the island. In 1947 Nauru was made a UN trust territory, administered by Australia. It became an independent republic Jan. 31, 1968, and was admitted to the UN Sept. 14, 1999.

Phosphate exports provided Nauru with per capita revenues that were among the highest in the Third World. Phosphate reserves, however, are nearly depleted, and environmental damage from strip-mining has been severe. Lax banking practices have made Nauru a haven for money laundering; the country has also raised funds by selling passports to noncitizens, possibly to some with terrorist connections. Nauru defaulted on a loan payment for its real estate holdings in Australia and was virtually bankrupt by 2004, when financial reforms were implemented.

Nepal
Kingdom of Nepal
People: Population: 28,901,790. **Age distrib.** (%): <15: 38.3; 65+: 3.8. **Pop. density:** 523 per sq mi, 202 per sq km. **Urban:** 15.8%. **Ethnic groups:** Chhettri 16%, Brahman-Hill 13%, Magar 7%, Tharu 7%, Tamang 6%, Newar 5%, Muslim 4%. **Principal languages:** Nepali (official); about 30 dialects and 12 other languages. **Chief religions:** Hinduism (official) 81%, Buddhism 11%, Muslim 4%.

Geography: Total area: 54,363 sq mi, 140,800 sq km; **Land area:** 52,819 sq mi, 136,800 sq km. **Location:** Astride the Himalaya Mts. **Neighbors:** China on N, India on S. **Topography:** The Himalayas stretch across the N, the hill country with its fertile valleys extends across the center, while S border region is part of the flat, subtropical Ganges Plain. **Capital:** Kathmandu, 815,000.

Government: Type: In transition. **Head of state and gov.:** Girija Prasad Koirala; b. 1925; in office: Jan. 15, 2007, as acting head of state (prime min. from Apr. 30, 2006). **Local divisions:** 5 regions subdivided into 14 zones. **Defense budget:** $139 mil. **Active troops:** 69,000.

Economy: Industries: tourism, carpets, textiles, rice, jute, sugar, oilseed. **Chief crops:** rice, corn, wheat, sugarcane. **Natural resources:** quartz, water, timber, hydropower, lignite, copper, cobalt, iron ore. **Arable land:** 16%. **Livestock:** cattle: 7 mil; chickens: 23.2 mil; goats: 7.4 mil; pigs: 960,827; sheep: 812,085. **Fish catch:**

42,463 metric tons. **Electricity prod.:** 2.4 bil kWh. **Labor force** (2004 est.): agriculture 76%, industry 6%, services 18%.

Finance: Monetary unit: Rupee (NPR) (Sept. 2007: 64.30 = $1 U.S.). **GDP:** $41.2 bil; **per capita GDP:** $1,500; **GDP growth:** 1.9%. **Imports** (2005 est.): $2 bil; India 49%, China 12.4%, UAE 11.7%, Saudi Arabia 5.2%, Kuwait 4.4%. **Exports** (2005 est.): $822 mil; India 59.3%, U.S. 14%, Germany 5.9%. **Tourism:** $230 mil. **Budget** (2007 est.): $1.9 bil. **Intl. reserves less gold** (2005): $1.05 bil. **Gold** (2005): 130,000 oz t. **Consumer prices:** 7.56%.

Transport: Railroad: Length: 37 mi. **Motor vehicles:** 63,500 pass. cars; 72,700 comm. vehicles. **Civil aviation:** 412 mil pass.-mi; 10 airports.

Communications: TV sets: 6 per 1,000 pop. **Radios:** 38 per 1,000 pop. **Telephone lines:** 595,800. **Internet:** 249,400 users.

Health: Life expect.: 60.8 male; 60.3 female. **Births** (per 1,000 pop.): 30.5. **Deaths** (per 1,000 pop.): 9.1. **Natural inc.:** 2.13%. **Infant mortality** (per 1,000 live births): 63.7. **AIDS rate:** 0.5%.

Education: Compulsory: ages 5-9. **Literacy:** 48.6%.

Major intl. organizations: UN (FAO, IBRD, ILO, IMF, IMO, WHO, WTO).

Embassy: 2131 Leroy Pl. NW 20008; 667-4550.

Website: www.nepalgov.gov.np

Nepal was originally a group of petty principalities, the inhabitants of one of which, the Gurkhas, became dominant about 1769. In 1951 King Tribhubana Bir Bikram, member of the Shah family, who had kept the kings virtual prisoners, and established a cabinet system of government.

Virtually closed to the outside world for centuries, Nepal is now linked to India and Pakistan by roads and air service and to Tibet by road. Polygamy, child marriage, and the caste system were officially abolished in 1963.

The government announced the legalization of political parties in 1990. Elections on Nov. 15, 1994, led to the installation of Nepal's first Communist government, which held power until a no-confidence vote Sept. 10, 1995.

Nine members of Nepal's royal family, including King Birendra and Queen Aishwarya, died as the result of a massacre on the night of June 1, 2001. An official inquiry blamed the carnage on a 10th family member, Crown Prince Dipendra, who reportedly shot himself that night and died 3 days later, allowing Birendra's brother Gyanendra Bir Bikram Shah Dev to take the throne.

Citing the government's failure to stop a Maoist insurgency, King Gyanendra assumed absolute authority, Feb. 1, 2005. After weeks of pro-democracy demonstrations, in which police killed at least 12 protesters, the king agreed Apr. 24, 2006, to reinstate parliament, which had not met for 4 years. A new government, led by Prime Min. Girija Prasad Koirala, signed a peace accord with Maoist rebels Nov. 21, ending a decade-long civil war that had claimed 13,000 lives. Under a draft constitution that made Koirala acting head of state, Maoists joined an interim parliament Jan. 15, 2007, and entered the cabinet Apr. 1. The king was stripped of most powers. Maoists quit the government Sept. 18 when other coalition members rejected their demand that the monarchy be abolished before elections scheduled for Nov. 22.

Netherlands
Kingdom of the Netherlands
People: Population: 16,570,613. **Age distrib.** (%): <15: 17.8; 65+: 14.4. **Pop. density:** 1,267 per sq mi, 489 per sq km. **Urban:** 80.2%. **Ethnic groups:** Dutch 83%, other 17% (9% of which are non-Western in origin). **Principal languages:** Dutch, Frisian (both official). **Chief religions:** Roman Catholic 31%, Protestant 21%, Muslim 6%.

Geography: Total area: 16,033 sq mi, 41,526 sq km; **Land area:** 13,082 sq mi, 33,883 sq km. **Location:** In NW Europe on North Sea. **Neighbors:** Germany on E, Belgium on S. **Topography:** Land is flat, an average alt. of 37 ft above sea level, with much land below sea level reclaimed and protected by some 1,500 mi of dikes. Since 1920 the government has been draining the IJsselmeer, formerly the Zuider Zee. **Capital:** Amsterdam (official), 1,147,000; The Hague (administrative, 2003), 705,000. **Cities (urban aggr.):** Rotterdam, 1,101,000.

Government: Type: Parliamentary democracy under a constitutional monarch. **Head of state:** Queen Beatrix; b. Jan. 31, 1938; in office: Apr. 30, 1980. **Head of gov.:** Prime Min. Jan Peter Balkenende; b. May 7, 1956; in office: July 22, 2002. **Seat of govt.:** The Hague. **Local divisions:** 12 provinces. **Defense budget:** $9.95 bil. **Active troops:** 53,130.

Economy: Industries: agro industries, metal & engineering products, electrical machinery & equip., chemicals, oil, constr., microelectronics, fishing. **Chief crops:** grains, potatoes, sugar beets, fruits, vegetables. **Natural resources:** nat. gas, oil. **Crude oil reserves:** 100 mil bbls. **Arable land:** 22%. **Livestock:** cattle: 3.7 mil; chickens: 90 mil; goats: 310,000; pigs: 11.3 mil; sheep: 1.7 mil. **Fish catch:** 617,383 metric tons. **Electricity prod.:** 94.3 bil kWh. **Labor force** (2004 est.): agriculture 2%, industry 19%, services 79%.

Finance: Monetary unit: Euro (EUR) (Sept. 2007: 0.72 = $1 U.S.). **GDP:** $529.1 bil; **per capita GDP:** $32,100; **GDP growth:** 2.9%. **Imports:** $373.8 bil; Germany 17.1%, Belgium 9.5%, China 9.4%, U.S. 7.8%, UK 5.9%, Russia 5.1%. **Exports:** $413.8 bil; Germany 25.5%, Belgium 14%, UK 8.9%, France 8.6%, Italy 5.1%. **Tourism:** $10.4 bil. **Budget:** $306.5 bil. **Intl. reserves less gold:** $7.18 bil. **Gold:** 20.61 mil oz t. **Consumer prices:** 1.14%.

Transport: Railroad: Length: 1,745 mi. **Motor vehicles:** 6.9 mil pass. cars; 1.1 mil comm. vehicles. **Civil aviation:** 42.7 bil pass.-mi; 20 airports. **Chief ports:** Amsterdam, Ijmuiden, Rotterdam.

Communications: TV sets: 540 per 1,000 pop. **Radios:** 980 per 1,000 pop. **Telephone lines:** 7.6 mil. **Daily newspaper circ.:** 279.5 per 1,000 pop. **Internet:** 14.5 mil users.

Health: Life expect.: 76.5 male; 81.8 female. **Births** (per 1,000 pop.): 10.7. **Deaths** (per 1,000 pop.): 8.7. **Natural inc.:** 0.2%. **Infant mortality** (per 1,000 live births): 4.9. **AIDS rate:** 0.2%.

Education: Compulsory: ages 6-18. **Literacy:** 99%.

Major intl. organizations: UN and all of its specialized agencies, EU, NATO, OECD, OSCE.

Embassy: 4200 Linnean Ave. NW 20008; 244-5300.

Website: www.government.nl

Julius Caesar conquered the region in 55 BCE, when it was inhabited by Celtic and Germanic tribes. After the empire of Charlemagne fell apart, the Netherlands (Holland, Belgium, Flanders) split among counts, dukes, and bishops, passed to Burgundy and thence to Spain. William the Silent, prince of Orange, led a confederation of the northern provinces, called Estates, in the Union of Utrecht, 1579; in 1581 they repudiated allegiance to Spain. The rise of the Dutch republic to naval, economic, and artistic eminence came in the 17th cent.

The United Dutch Republic ended 1795 when the French formed the Batavian Republic. Napoleon made his brother Louis king of Holland, 1806; Louis abdicated 1810 when Napoleon annexed Holland. In 1813 the French were expelled. In 1815 the Congress of Vienna formed a kingdom of the Netherlands, including Belgium, under William I. In 1830, the Belgians seceded and formed a separate kingdom.

The constitution, promulgated 1814, and subsequently revised, provides for a hereditary constitutional monarchy.

The Netherlands maintained its neutrality in WWI, but was invaded and brutally occupied by Germany, 1940-45. In 1949, after several years of fighting, the Netherlands granted independence to Indonesia.

The murder May 6, 2002, of right-wing populist leader Pim Fortuyn, 9 days before legislative elections, marked the first political assassination in modern Dutch history. The killing of filmmaker Theo van Gogh, Nov. 2, 2004, by an Islamic extremist also shocked many Dutch. Concerns about immigration contributed to the defeat of a proposed EU constitution by 62% to 38% in a referendum, June 1, 2005.

Netherlands Dependencies

The **Netherlands Antilles**, constitutionally on a level of equality with the Netherlands homeland within the kingdom, consist of 2 groups of islands in the West Indies. **Curaçao** and **Bonaire** are near the coast of Venezuela; **St. Eustatius, Saba,** and the southern part of **St. Maarten** are southeast of Puerto Rico. The northern two-thirds of St. Maarten belongs to French Guadeloupe; the French call the island St. Martin. Total area of the 2 groups is 371 sq mi, incl. Bonaire (111), Curaçao (171), St. Eustatius (8), Saba (5), St. Maarten (Dutch part) (13). St. Maarten suffered extensive damage from Hurricane Luis, Sept. 1995. Total pop. of the Netherlands Antilles (2007 est.) was 223,652. Willemstad, on Curaçao, is the capital. The principal industry is the refining of crude oil from Venezuela. Tourism is also an important industry, as is shipbuilding.

Aruba, about 26 mi west of Curaçao, was separated from the Netherlands Antilles on Jan. 1, 1986; it is an autonomous member of the Netherlands, the same status as the Netherland Antilles. Area: 75 sq mi; pop. (2007 est.): 100,018; capital: Oranjestad. Chief industries are oil refining and tourism.

New Zealand

People: Population: 4,115,771. **Age distrib.** (%): <15: 20.8; 65+: 11.9. **Pop. density:** 40 per sq mi, 15 per sq km. **Urban:** 86.2%. **Ethnic groups:** White 79%, Maori 8%, Asian 6%, Pacific Islander 4%. **Principal languages:** English, Maori (both official). **Chief religions:** Anglican 15%, Roman Catholic 12%.

Geography: Total area: 103,738 sq mi, 268,680 sq km. **Land area:** 103,484 sq mi, 268,021 sq km. **Location:** In SW Pacific O. **Neighbors:** Nearest are Australia on W, Fiji and Tonga on N. **Topography:** Each of the 2 main islands (North and South Isls.) is mainly hilly and mountainous. The E coasts consist of fertile plains, especially the broad Canterbury Plains on South Isl. A volcanic plateau is in center of North Isl. South Isl. has glaciers and 15 peaks over 10,000 ft. **Capital:** Wellington, 346,000. **Cities (urban aggr.):** Auckland, 1,148,000; Christchurch, 331,443.

Government: Type: Parliamentary democracy. **Head of state:** Queen Elizabeth II, represented by Gov.-Gen. Anand Satyanand; b. July 22, 1944; in office: Aug. 23, 2006. **Head of gov.:** Prime Min. Helen Clark; b. Feb. 26, 1950; in office: Dec. 10, 1999. **Local divisions:** 16 regions. **Defense budget:** $1.31 bil. **Active troops:** 8,951.

Economy: Industries: food proc., wood & paper products, textiles, machinery, transp. equip., banking & insurance, tourism, mining. **Chief crops:** wheat, barley, potatoes, pulses, fruits, vegetables. **Natural resources:** nat. gas, iron ore, sand, coal, timber, hydropower, gold, limestone. **Crude oil reserves:** 53 mil bbls.

Arable land: 6%. **Livestock:** cattle: 9.7 mil; chickens: 20.9 mil; goats: 155,000; pigs: 341,465; sheep: 40.1 mil. **Fish catch:** 640,695 metric tons. **Electricity prod.:** 41.6 bil kWh. **Labor force** (1995): agriculture 10%, industry 25%, services 65%.

Finance: Monetary unit: Dollar (NZD) (Sept. 2007: 1.40 = $1 U.S.). **GDP:** $106.9 bil; **per capita GDP:** $26,200; **GDP growth:** 1.5%. **Imports:** $25.2 bil; Australia 20.5%, China 12.3%, U.S. 11.8%, Japan 9.2%, Germany 4.4%, Singapore 4.4%. **Exports:** $23.7 bil; Australia 20.5%, U.S. 13.1%, Japan 10.3%, China 5.4%, UK 4.9%. **Tourism:** $5 bil. **Budget:** $37 bil. **Intl. reserves less gold:** $9.35 bil. **Consumer prices:** 3.36%.

Transport: Railroad: Length: 2,565 mi. **Motor vehicles:** 2.1 mil pass. cars; 472,000 comm. vehicles. **Civil aviation:** 14.5 bil pass.-mi; 45 airports. **Chief ports:** Auckland, Lyttelton, Tauranga, Wellington, Whangarei.

Communications: TV sets: 516 per 1,000 pop. **Radios:** 997 per 1,000 pop. **Telephone lines:** 1.7 mil. **Daily newspaper circ.:** 202.2 per 1,000 pop. **Internet:** 3.2 mil users.

Health: Life expect.: 76 male; 82.1 female. **Births** (per 1,000 pop.): 13.6. **Deaths** (per 1,000 pop.): 7.5. **Natural inc.:** 0.61%. **Infant mortality** (per 1,000 live births): 5.7. **AIDS rate:** 0.1%.

Education: Compulsory: ages 5-16. **Literacy** (2005): 99%.

Major intl. organizations: UN (FAO, IBRD, ILO, IMF, IMO, WHO, WTO), APEC, the Commonwealth, OECD.

Embassy: 37 Observatory Cir. NW 20008; 328-4800.

Website: www.govt.nz

The Maoris, a Polynesian group from the eastern Pacific, reached New Zealand before and during the 14th cent. The first European to sight New Zealand was Dutch navigator Abel Janszoon Tasman, but Maoris refused to allow him to land. British Capt. James Cook explored the coasts, 1769-70.

British sovereignty was proclaimed and Maori land rights were recognized in the Treaty of Waitangi, 1840, with organized settlement beginning in the same year. Representative institutions were granted in 1853. Maori Wars ended in 1870 with British victory. The colony became a dominion in 1907 and gained full independence in 1947. It is a member of the Commonwealth. Maoris make up about 15% of the population; 7 of 120 members of the House of Representatives are directly elected from Maori constituencies, but Maoris may also run in other districts.

A progressive tradition in politics dates back to the 19th cent., when New Zealand was internationally known for social experimentation; much of the nation's economy has been deregulated in recent years. Jenny Shipley of the National Party became the nation's first female prime minister, Dec. 8, 1997. The Labour Party, led by Helen Clark, won the general elections of Nov. 27, 1999, and July 27, 2002.

The legislature legalized prostitution June 2003. In July, New Zealand contributed troops to the Australian-led force in the Solomon Islands. A measure establishing a Supreme Court and ending appeals to the UK Privy Council passed Oct. 14.

Prime Min. Clark, May 4, 2004, survived a no-confidence vote on a plan to nationalize the coastline. The plan was opposed by some Maoris, who claimed it infringed their land rights under the Waitangi Treaty. Clark formed a new coalition government after elections Sept. 17, 2005, that gave the Labour Party a thin plurality.

New Zealand comprises **North Island**, 44,702 sq mi; **South Island**, 58,384 sq mi; **Stewart Island**, 674 sq mi; **Chatham Islands**, 372 sq mi; and several groups of smaller islands.

In 1965, the **Cook Islands** (pop. [2007 est.]: 21,750; area: 91 sq mi, halfway between New Zealand and Hawaii, became self-governing. New Zealand retains responsibility for defense and foreign affairs. **Niue** attained the same status in 1974; it lies 400 mi W (pop. [2007 est.]: 1,492; area: 100 sq mi). Cyclone Heta devastated Niue Jan. 6, 2004. **Tokelau** (pop. [2007 est.]: 1,449; area: 4 sq mi) comprises 3 atolls 300 mi N of Samoa. A referendum on Tokelau self-government, held Feb. 13-15, 2006, failed to gain the required two-third majority.

Ross Dependency, administered by New Zealand since 1923, comprises 160,000 sq mi of Antarctic territory.

Nicaragua

Republic of Nicaragua

People: Population: 5,675,356. **Age distrib.** (%): <15: 35.5; 65+: 3.2. **Pop. density:** 122 per sq mi, 47 per sq km. **Urban:** 59%. **Ethnic groups:** Mestizo 69%, white 17%, black 9%, Amerindian 5%. **Principal languages:** Spanish (official), Miskito; indigenous languages, English on Atlantic coast. **Chief religions:** Roman Catholic 73%, Evangelical 15%.

Geography: Total area: 49,998 sq mi, 129,494 sq km; **Land area:** 46,430 sq mi, 120,254 sq km. **Location:** In Central America. **Neighbors:** Honduras on N, Costa Rica on S. **Topography:** Both Caribbean and Pacific coasts are over 200 mi long. Cordillera Mts., with many volcanic peaks, run NW-SE through middle of the country. Between this and a volcanic range to the E lie Lakes Managua and Nicaragua. **Capital:** Managua, 1,165,000.

Government: Type: Republic. **Head of state and gov.:** Pres. Daniel Ortega Saavedra; b. Nov. 11, 1945; in office Jan. 10, 2007. **Local divisions:** 15 departments, 2 autonomous regions. **Defense budget** (2005): $33.9 mil. **Active troops:** 14,000.

Economy: Industries: food proc., chemicals, machinery & metal products, textiles, clothing, oil refining & distribution, beverages, footwear, wood. **Chief crops:** coffee, bananas, sugarcane, cotton, rice, corn, tobacco, sesame, soya. **Natural resources:** gold, silver, copper, tungsten, lead, zinc, timber, fish. **Arable land:** 15%. **Livestock:** cattle: 3.5 mil; chickens: 18 mil; goats: 7,100; pigs: 123,000; sheep: 4,500. **Fish catch:** 40,897 metric tons. **Electricity prod.:** 2.7 bil kWh. **Labor force** (2006 est.): agriculture 29%, industry 19%, services 52%.

Finance: Monetary unit: Cordoba (NIO) (Sept. 2007: 18.67 = $1 U.S.). **GDP:** $17.3 bil; **per capita GDP:** $3,100; **GDP growth:** 3.7%. **Imports:** $3.2 bil; U.S. 22.6%, Venezuela 10.6%, Costa Rica 7.8%, Mexico 7.3%, Guatemala 6.1%. **Exports:** $1.7 bil; U.S. 66.1%, El Salvador 7%, Honduras 3.9%. **Tourism:** $207 mil. **Budget:** $1.3 bil. **Intl. reserves less gold:** $613 mil. **Gold** (2003): 10,000 oz t. **Consumer prices:** 9.14%.

Transport: Railroad: Length: 4 mi. **Motor vehicles:** 82,200 pass. cars; 107,700 comm. vehicles. **Civil aviation** (2000): 4.7 mil pass.-mi; 11 airports. **Chief ports:** Bluefields, Corinto, El Bluff.

Communications: TV sets: 69 per 1,000 pop. **Radios:** 270 per 1,000 pop. **Telephone lines:** 247,900. **Internet:** 155,000 users.

Health: Life expect.: 68.8 male; 73.1 female. **Births** (per 1,000 pop.): 24.1. **Deaths** (per 1,000 pop.): 4.4. **Natural inc.:** 1.97%. **Infant mortality** (per 1,000 live births): 27.1. **AIDS rate:** 0.2%.

Education: Compulsory: ages 7-12. **Literacy:** 76.7%.

Major intl. organizations: UN and most of its specialized agencies, OAS.

Embassy: 1627 New Hampshire Ave. NW 20009; 939-6570.

Website: www.state.gov/p/wha/ci/nu/

Nicaragua, inhabited by various Indian tribes, was conquered by Spain in 1552. After gaining independence from Spain, 1821, Nicaragua was united for a short period with Mexico, then with the United Provinces of Central America, finally becoming an independent republic, 1838. U.S. Marines occupied the country at times in the early 20th cent., the last time from 1926 to 1933.

Gen. Anastasio Somoza Debayle was elected president in 1967. He resigned in 1972, but was reelected president in 1974. Martial law was imposed in Dec. 1974, after officials were kidnapped by the Marxist Sandinista guerrillas. Violent opposition spread to nearly all classes in 1978; nationwide antigovernment strikes touched off a civil war, which ended when Somoza fled Nicaragua and the Sandinistas took control of Managua in July 1979. Somoza was assassinated in Paraguay, Sept. 17, 1980.

Relations with the U.S. were strained as a result of Nicaragua's aid to leftist guerrillas in El Salvador and U.S. backing of anti-Sandinista contra guerrilla groups. In 1983 the contras launched a major offensive; the Sandinistas imposed rule by decree. In 1985 the U.S. House rejected Pres. Reagan's request for military aid to the contras. The subsequent diversion of funds to the contras from the proceeds of a secret arms sale to Iran caused a major scandal in the U.S.

In a stunning upset, Violeta Barrios de Chamorro defeated Sandinista leader Daniel Ortega Saavedra in national elections, Feb. 25, 1990. Arnoldo Alemán Lacayo, a conservative former mayor of Managua, defeated Ortega in the presidential election of Oct. 20, 1996. Up to 2,000 people died Oct. 30, 1998, in a mudslide caused by rains from Hurricane Mitch.

Drought and a drop in coffee prices plunged Nicaragua into an economic crisis in 2001. Enrique Bolaños Geyer, a conservative businessman, won the presidency that year. The corruption trial of former Pres. Alemán ended with a guilty verdict, Dec. 7, 2003; he was fined $10 mil and sentenced to 20 years in prison. After a medical review, Alemán was allowed to serve the sentence under house arrest. Ortega won the presidential election of Nov. 5, 2006. After taking office Jan. 10, 2007, he irritated the U.S. by cultivating ties with Venezuela and Iran, which offered aid to the financially hard-pressed country. Hurricane Felix, a Category 5 storm that struck Sept. 4, killed more than 100 people.

Niger
Republic of Niger

People: Population: 12,894,865. **Age distrib.** (%): <15: 46.9; 65+: 2.4. **Pop. density:** 26 per sq mi, 10 per sq km. **Urban:** 16.8%. **Ethnic groups:** Haoussa 55%, Djerma Sonrai 21%, Touareg 9%, Peuhl 9%, Kanouri Manga 5%. **Principal languages:** French (official), Hausa, Djerma. **Chief religion:** Muslim 80%.

Geography: Total area: 489,192 sq mi, 1,267,000 sq km; **Land area:** 489,076 sq mi, 1,266,700 sq km. **Location:** In interior of N Africa. **Neighbors:** Libya, Algeria on N; Mali, Burkina Faso on W; Benin, Nigeria on S; Chad on E. **Topography:** Mostly arid desert and mountains. A narrow savanna in S and Niger R. basin in the SW contain most of the population. **Capital:** Niamey, 850,000.

Government: Type: Republic. **Head of state:** Pres. Mamadou Tandja; b. 1938; in office: Dec. 22, 1999. **Head of gov.:** Prime Min. Seyni Oumarou; b. Aug. 9, 1950; in office: June 7, 2007. **Local divisions:** 7 departments, 1 capital district. **Defense budget:** $43 mil. **Active troops:** 5,300.

Economy: Industries: uranium mining, cement, brick, textiles, food proc., chemicals. **Chief crops:** cowpeas, cotton, peanuts, millet, sorghum, cassava, rice. **Natural resources:** uranium, coal, iron ore, tin, phosphates, gold, oil. **Arable land:** 11%. **Livestock:** cattle: 2.4 mil; chickens: 25 mil; goats: 7.7 mil; pigs: 39,500; sheep: 4.9 mil. **Fish catch:** 50,058 metric tons. **Electricity prod.:** 230 mil kWh. **Labor force:** agriculture 90%, industry 6%, services 4%.

Finance: Monetary unit: CFA BCEAO Franc (XOF) (Sept. 2007: 472.78 = $1 U.S.). **GDP:** $12.4 bil; **per capita GDP:** $1,000; **GDP growth:** 3.5%. **Imports** (2004 est.): $588 mil; U.S. 14.2%, France 12.2%, China 7.9%, Nigeria 7.8%, French Polynesia 7.8%, Cote d'Ivoire 5%. **Exports** (2004 est.): $222 mil; France 34.8%, U.S. 26.5%, Nigeria 18.3%, Russia 11.3%. **Tourism:** $28 mil. **Budget** (2002 est.): $320 mil. **Intl. reserves less gold:** $247 mil. **Consumer prices:** 0.04%.

Transport: Motor vehicles: 9,300 pass. cars; 3,800 comm. vehicles. **Civil aviation** (2001): 80.8 mil pass.-mi; 9 airports.

Communications: TV sets: 15 per 1,000 pop. **Radios:** 36 per 1,000 pop. **Telephone lines:** 24,000. **Daily newspaper circ.:** 0.2 per 1,000 pop. **Internet:** 40,000 users.

Health: Life expect.: 44.1 male; 44 female. **Births** (per 1,000 pop.): 50.2. **Deaths** (per 1,000 pop.): 20.6. **Natural inc.:** 2.96%. **Infant mortality** (per 1,000 live births): 116.8. **AIDS rate:** 1.1%.

Education: Compulsory: ages 7-12. **Literacy:** 28.7%.

Major intl. organizations: UN (FAO, IBRD, ILO, IMF, WHO, WTO), AU.

Embassy: 2204 R St. NW 20008; 483-4224.

Website: www.nigerembassyusa.org

Niger was part of ancient and medieval African empires. European explorers reached the area in the late 18th cent. The French colony of Niger was established 1900-22, after the defeat of Tuareg fighters, who had invaded the area from the north a century before. The country became independent Aug. 3, 1960.

In 1993, Niger held its first free and open elections since independence; an opposition leader, Mahamane Ousmane, won the presidency. A peace accord Apr. 24, 1995, ended a Tuareg rebellion that began in 1990. A coup, Jan. 27, 1996, followed by a disputed presidential election in July, left the military in control of Niger. On Apr. 9, 1999, Gen. Ibrahim Bare Mainassara, Niger's president since 1996, was assassinated, apparently by members of his security team. Elections were held Oct. 17 and Nov. 24, 1999, under a new constitution, approved by referendum July 18, that restored civilian rule.

One of the world's poorest countries, Niger experienced severe food shortages in 2005 after locusts and drought ruined the grain harvest. A resurgence of Tuareg rebel activity in June 2007 brought a major government counteroffensive.

Nigeria
Federal Republic of Nigeria

People: 135,031,164. **Age distrib.** (%): <15: 42.2; 65+: 3.1. **Pop. density:** 384 per sq mi, 148 per sq km. **Urban:** 48.2%. **Ethnic groups:** More than 250; Hausa and Fulani 29%, Yoruba 21%, Igbo (Ibo) 18%, Ijaw 10%, Kanuri 4%, Ibibio 4%. **Principal languages:** English (official), Hausa, Yoruba, Igbo (Ibo), Fulani. **Chief religions:** Muslim 50%, Christian 40%, indigenous beliefs 10%.

Geography: Total area: 356,669 sq mi, 923,768 sq km; **Land area:** 351,650 sq mi, 910,768 sq km. **Location:** On S coast of W Africa. **Neighbors:** Benin on W, Niger on N, Chad and Cameroon on E. **Topography:** 4 E-W regions divide Nigeria: a coastal mangrove swamp 10-60 mi wide, a tropical rain forest 50-100 mi wide, a plateau of savanna and open woodland, and semi-desert in N. **Capital:** Abuja, 612,000. **Cities (urban aggr.):** Lagos, 10,886,000; Kano 2,993,000; Ibadan, 2,437,000.

Government: Type: Federal republic. **Head of state and gov.:** Pres. Umaru Musa Yar'Adua; b. 1951; in office: May 29, 2007. **Local divisions:** 36 states, 1 capital territory. **Defense budget:** $768 bil. **Active troops:** 85,000.

Economy: Industries: crude oil, mining, palm oil, peanuts, cotton, rubber. **Chief crops:** cocoa, peanuts, palm oil, corn, rice, sorghum, millet, cassava, yams, rubber. **Natural resources:** nat. gas, oil, tin, columbite, iron ore, coal, limestone, lead, zinc. **Crude oil reserves:** 36.2 bil bbls. **Arable land:** 33%. **Livestock:** cattle: 15.9 mil; chickens: 150.7 mil; goats: 28 mil; pigs: 6.7 mil; sheep: 23 mil. **Fish catch:** 579,537 metric tons. **Electricity prod.:** 22.5 bil kWh. **Labor force** (1999 est.): agriculture 70%, industry 10%, services 20%.

Finance: Monetary unit: Naira (NGN) (Sept. 2007: 125.90 = $1 U.S.). **GDP:** $191.4 bil; **per capita GDP:** $1,500; **GDP growth:** 5.3%. **Imports:** $25.1 bil; China 10.6%, U.S. 8.3%, Netherlands 5.9%, UK 5.7%, France 5.5%. **Exports:** $59 bil; U.S. 49.9%, Spain 8.1%, Brazil 6.3%, France 4.3%. **Tourism:** $21 mil. **Budget:** $19.1 bil. **Intl. reserves less gold:** $28.12 bil. **Gold:** 690,000 oz t. **Consumer prices:** 8.24%.

Transport: Railroad: Length: 2,178 mi. **Motor vehicles:** 2,300 pass. cars; 13,500 comm. vehicles. **Civil aviation:** 396.4 mil pass.-mi; 36 airports. **Chief ports:** Calabar, Lagos, Port Harcourt.

Communications: TV sets: 69 per 1,000 pop. **Radios:** 226 per 1,000 pop. **Telephone lines:** 1.7 mil. **Daily newspaper circ.:** 25.4 per 1,000 pop. **Internet:** 8 mil users.

Health: Life expect.: 46.8 male; 48.1 female. **Births** (per 1,000 pop.): 40.2. **Deaths** (per 1,000 pop.): 16.7. **Natural inc.:** 2.35%. **Infant mortality** (per 1,000 live births): 95.5. **AIDS rate:** 3.9%.

Education: Compulsory: ages 6-14. **Literacy** (2005): 69.1%.

Major intl. organizations: UN (FAO, IBRD, ILO, IMF, IMO, WHO, WTO), the Commonwealth, AU, OPEC.

Embassy: 3519 International Ct. NW 20008; 986-8400.

Website: www.nigeria.gov.ng

Early cultures in Nigeria date back to at least 700 BCE. From the 12th to the 14th centuries, more advanced cultures developed in the Yoruba area, at Ife, and in the north, where Muslim influence prevailed. Portuguese and British slavers appeared from the 15th-16th centuries. Britain seized Lagos, 1861, and gradually extended control inland until 1900. Nigeria became independent Oct. 1, 1960, and a republic Oct. 1, 1963.

On May 30, 1967, the Eastern Region seceded, proclaiming itself the Republic of Biafra, plunging the country into civil war. Casualties in the war were estimated at over 1 mil, including many "Biafrans" (mostly Ibos) who died of starvation despite international efforts to provide relief. The secessionists, after steadily losing ground, capitulated Jan. 12, 1970.

Nigeria emerged as one of the world's leading oil exporters in the 1970s, but much of the revenue has been squandered through corruption and mismanagement. After 13 years of military rule, the nation made a peaceful return to civilian government, Oct. 1979. Military rule resumed, Dec. 31, 1983; a second coup came in 1985.

Headed by Gen. Ibrahim Babangida, the military regime held elections June 12, 1993, but annulled the vote June 23 when it appeared that Moshood Abiola would win. Riots followed and many were killed. Babangida resigned and appointed a civilian to head an interim government, Aug. 26, but that government was ousted Nov. 17 in a coup led by Gen. Sani Abacha. On June 11, 1994, Abiola declared himself president; he was jailed June 23.

Abacha's brutal rule ended June 8, 1998, when he died of an apparent heart attack. Abiola died in prison July 7, as Abacha's successor, Gen. Abdulsalam Abubakar, was reportedly preparing to free him. Abiola's death sparked riots in Lagos and other cities; on July 20, Abubakar promised elections and a return to civilian rule. Olusegun Obasanjo (a former military ruler) won the presidential vote Feb. 27, 1999, Nigeria's first civilian government in 15 years.

An oil fire that exploded from a ruptured pipeline in southern Nigeria, Oct. 17, 1998, killed at least 700 people who were scavenging for fuel. The imposition of strict Islamic law in northern states led to clashes, Jan.-Mar. 2000, in which at least 800 people died. Clashes between Muslims and Christians Sept. 7-12 and Oct. 13-14 claimed an estimated 600 lives; another 200 people died when soldiers went on a rampage in southeast Nigeria Oct. 22-24.

At least 1,000 people were killed Jan. 27, 2002, when an army weapons depot in Lagos exploded; many of the victims drowned in a drainage canal while fleeing the blasts.

By 2002, the strict Islamic legal code of sharia had been adopted by about one-third of Nigeria's 36 states. Controversy over Nigeria's plans to host a Miss World pageant sparked sectarian riots in Kaduna, Nov. 20-24, leaving more than 200 people dead and 1,100 injured. Obasanjo won reelection Apr. 19, 2003.

Christian militia members massacred about 630 Muslims at Yelwa, central Nigeria, May 2, 2004. Although the World Court awarded the oil-rich Bakassi peninsula to Cameroon in 2002 and the handover was scheduled for Sept. 2004, final agreement on a Nigerian troop pullout was not reached until June 12, 2006. Rebel activities in the Niger Delta region in 2006-07 led to cutbacks in Nigeria's petroleum output and upward pressure on worldwide oil prices. Obasanjo's chosen successor, Umaru Musa Yar'Adua, won a landslide victory Apr. 21, 2007, in a presidential election marred by violence and described as "not credible" by international monitors.

Norway
Kingdom of Norway

People: Population: 4,627,926. **Age distrib.** (%): <15: 19; 65+: 14.8. **Pop. density:** 39 per sq mi, 15 per sq km. **Urban:** 77.4%.
Ethnic groups: Norwegian, Sami. **Principal languages:** Norwegian (official), Sami, Finnish. **Chief religion:** Evangelical Lutheran (official) 86%.
Geography: Total area: 125,182 sq mi, 324,220 sq km; **Land area:** 118,865 sq mi, 307,860 sq km. **Location:** W part of Scandinavian peninsula in NW Europe (extends farther north than any European land). **Neighbors:** Sweden, Finland, Russia on E. **Topography:** Highly indented coast is lined with tens of thousands of islands. Mountains and plateaus cover most of the country, which is only 25% forested. **Capital:** Oslo, 802,000.
Government: Type: Hereditary constitutional monarchy. **Head of state:** King Harald V; b. Feb. 21, 1937; in office: Jan. 17, 1991. **Head of gov.:** Prime Min. Jens Stoltenberg; b. Mar. 16, 1959; in office: Oct. 17, 2005. **Local divisions:** 19 provinces. **Defense budget:** \$4.83 bil. **Active troops:** 23,400.
Economy: Industries: oil & gas, food proc., shipbuilding, pulp & paper products, metals, chemicals, timber, mining, textiles, fishing. **Chief crops:** barley, wheat, potatoes. **Natural resources:** oil, copper, nat. gas, pyrites, nickel, iron ore, zinc, lead, fish, timber, hydropower. **Crude oil reserves:** 7.8 bil bbls. **Arable land:** 3%. **Livestock:** cattle: 920,416; chickens: 3.3 mil; goats: 72,468; pigs: 827,489; sheep: 2.4 mil. **Fish catch:** 2,949,570 metric tons. **Electricity prod.:** 135.8 bil kWh. **Labor force** (1995): agriculture, forestry, and fishing 4%, industry 22%, services 74%.
Finance: Monetary unit: Krone (NOK) (Sept. 2007: 5.64 = \$1 U.S.). **GDP:** \$213.6 bil; **per capita GDP:** \$46,300; **GDP growth:** 4.6%. **Imports:** \$59.9 bil; Sweden 15%, Germany 13.5%, Denmark 6.9%, UK 6.4%, China 5.7%, U.S. 5.3%. **Exports:** \$122.6 bil; UK 26.6%, Germany 12.2%, Netherlands 10.4%, France 8.2%, Swe-

den 6.5%, U.S. 5.9%. **Tourism:** \$2.9 bil. **Budget:** \$133.1 bil. **Intl. reserves less gold:** \$37.78 bil. **Gold** (2003): 1.18 mil oz t. **Consumer prices:** 2.33%.
Transport: Railroad: Length: 2,533 mi. **Motor vehicles:** 2 mil pass. cars; 480,000 comm. vehicles. **Civil aviation:** 6.5 bil pass.-mi; 67 airports. **Chief ports:** Bergen, Mo i Rana, Narvik, Oslo.
Communications: TV sets: 653 per 1,000 pop. **Radios:** 917 per 1,000 pop. **Telephone lines:** 2.1 mil. **Daily newspaper circ.:** 569 per 1,000 pop. **Internet:** 4.1 mil users.
Health: Life expect.: 77 male; 82.5 female. **Births** (per 1,000 pop.): 11.3. **Deaths** (per 1,000 pop.): 9.4. **Natural inc.:** 0.19%. **Infant mortality** (per 1,000 live births): 3.6. **AIDS rate:** 0.1%.
Education: Compulsory: ages 6-16. **Literacy:** 100%.
Major intl. organizations: UN and all of its specialized agencies, EFTA, NATO, OECD, OSCE.
Embassy: 2720 34th St. NW 20008; 333-6000.
Website: www.norway.no

The first ruler of Norway was Harald the Fairhaired, who came to power in 872 CE. Between 800 and 1000, Norway's Vikings raided and occupied widely dispersed parts of Europe.

The country was united with Denmark 1381-1814, and with Sweden, 1814-1905. In 1905, the country became independent with Prince Charles of Denmark as king.

Norway remained neutral during WWI. Germany attacked Norway Apr. 9, 1940, and held it until liberation May 8, 1945. The country abandoned its neutrality after the war, and joined NATO. In a referendum Nov. 28, 1994, Norwegian voters rejected European Union membership.

Abundant hydroelectric resources provided the base for industrialization, giving Norway one of the highest living standards in the world. The country is a leading producer and exporter of crude oil, with extensive reserves in the North Sea. Norway's merchant marine is one of the world's largest.

A center-left bloc led by Jens Stoltenberg won parliamentary elections Sept. 12, 2005, and took office Oct. 17.

Svalbard is a group of mountainous islands in the Arctic O., area 23,560 sq mi, pop. (2007 est.) 2,214. The largest, Spitsbergen (formerly called West Spitsbergen), 15,060 sq mi, seat of the governor, is about 370 mi N of Norway. By a treaty signed in Paris, 1920, major European powers recognized the sovereignty of Norway, which incorporated it in 1925.

Jan Mayen, area 146 sq mi, is a volcanic island located about 565 mi W-NW of Norway; it was annexed in 1929.

Oman
Sultanate of Oman

People: Population: 3,204,897. **Age distrib.** (%): <15: 42.7; 65+: 2.7. **Pop. density:** 39 per sq mi, 15 per sq km. **Urban:** 71.5%.
Ethnic groups: Arab, Baluchi, South Asian, African. **Principal languages:** Arabic (official), English, Baluchi, Urdu, Indian dialects. **Chief religion:** Muslim (official; mostly Ibadhi) 75%.
Geography: Total area: 82,031 sq mi, 212,460 sq km; **Land area:** 82,031 sq mi, 212,460 sq km. **Location:** On SE coast of Arabian peninsula. **Neighbors:** United Arab Emirates, Saudi Arabia, Yemen on W. **Topography:** A narrow coastal plain up to 10 mi wide, a range of barren mountains reaching 9,900 ft, and a wide, stony, mostly waterless plateau, avg. alt. 1,000 ft. Also, an exclave at the tip of the Musandam peninsula controls access to the Persian Gulf. **Capital:** Muscat, 565,000.
Government: Type: Absolute monarchy. **Head of state and gov.:** Sultan Qabus bin Said; b. Nov. 18, 1940; in office: July 23, 1970 (also prime min. since Jan. 2, 1972). **Local divisions:** 6 regions and 2 governorates. **Defense budget:** \$3.27 bil. **Active troops:** 41,700.
Economy: Industries: oil, gas, constr., cement, copper. **Chief crops:** dates, limes, bananas, alfalfa, vegetables. **Natural resources:** oil, copper, asbestos, marble, limestone, chromium, gypsum, nat. gas. **Crude oil reserves:** 5.5 bil bbls. **Arable land:** 0.1%. **Livestock:** cattle: 307,580; chickens: 4.2 mil; goats: 1.6 mil; sheep: 358,050. **Fish catch:** 150,744 metric tons. **Electricity prod.:** 11.9 bil kWh. **Labor force:** NA.
Finance: Monetary unit: Rial (OMR) (Sept. 2007: 0.38 = \$1 U.S.). **GDP:** \$44.5 bil; **per capita GDP:** \$14,400; **GDP growth:** 6.6%. **Imports:** \$10.3 bil; UAE 22.4%, Japan 16.4%, U.S. 8.1%, Germany 5.4%, India 4.3%. **Exports:** \$24.7 bil; China 23.7%, South Korea 18%, Japan 10.9%, Thailand 10.7%, South Africa 7.7%, UAE 6.3%. **Tourism:** \$518 mil. **Budget:** \$12.8 bil. **Intl. reserves less gold:** \$3.33 bil. **Consumer prices:** 3.2%.
Transport: Motor vehicles: 324,000 pass. cars; 109,100 comm. vehicles. **Civil aviation:** 3.7 bil pass.-mi; 6 airports. **Chief ports:** Mina' Qabus, Salalah.
Communications: TV sets: 575 per 1,000 pop. **Radios:** 607 per 1,000 pop. **Telephone lines:** 278,300. **Internet:** 319,200 users.
Health: Life expect.: 71.4 male; 76 female. **Births** (per 1,000 pop.): 35.8. **Deaths** (per 1,000 pop.): 3.8. **Natural inc.:** 3.2%. **Infant mortality** (per 1,000 live births): 18.3. **AIDS rate:** NA.
Education: NA. **Literacy:** 81.4%.
Major intl. organizations: UN (FAO, IBRD, ILO, IMF, IMO, WHO, WTO), AL.
Embassy: 2535 Belmont Rd. NW 20008; 387-1980.
Website: www.omanet.com

Oman was originally called Muscat and Oman. A long history of rule by other lands, including Portugal in the 16th cent., ended with the ouster of the Persians in 1744. By the early 19th cent., Muscat and Oman was one of the most important countries in the region, controlling much of the Persian and Pakistani coasts, and also ruling far-away Zanzibar, which was separated in 1861 under British mediation.

British influence was confirmed in a 1951 treaty, and Britain helped suppress an uprising by traditionally rebellious interior tribes against control by Muscat in the 1950s.

On July 23, 1970, Sultan Said bin Taimur was overthrown by his son, who changed the nation's name to Sultanate of Oman.

Oil is the major source of income.

Oman opened its air bases to Western forces following the Iraqi invasion of Kuwait on Aug. 2, 1990, and was a base for U.S. aircraft in the Afghanistan war, 2001. After a secret trial, 31 suspected Islamists received prison sentences, May 2, 2005, for plotting a coup. A free trade agreement with the U.S. was signed Jan. 19, 2006.

Pakistan
Islamic Republic of Pakistan

People: Population: 164,741,924. **Age distrib.** (%): <15: 36.9; 65+: 4.3. **Pop. density:** 548 per sq mi, 212 per sq km. **Urban:** 34.9%. **Ethnic groups:** Punjabi, Sindhi, Pashtun, Balochi, Muhajir. **Principal languages:** English, Urdu (both official); Punjabi; Sindhi; Siraiki; Pashtu; Balochi; Hindko; Brahui; Burushaski. **Chief religions:** Muslim (official; Sunni 77%, Shi'a 20%) 97%.

Geography: Total area: 310,403 sq mi, 803,940 sq km; **Land area:** 300,666 sq mi, 778,720 sq km. **Location:** In W part of South Asia. **Neighbors:** Iran on W, Afghanistan and China on N, India on E. **Topography:** The Indus R. rises in the Hindu Kush and Himalaya Mts. in the N (highest is K2, or Godwin Austen, 28,250 ft, 2nd highest in world), then flows over 1,000 mi through fertile valley and empties into Arabian Sea. Thar Desert, Eastern Plains flank Indus Valley. **Capital:** Islamabad, 736,000. **Cities (urban aggr.):** Karachi, 11,608,000; Lahore, 6,289,000; Faisalabad, 2,494,000.

Government: Type: Republic with strong military influence. **Head of state:** Pres. Pervez Musharraf; b Aug. 11,1943; in office: Oct. 12, 1999 (as pres. from June 20, 2001). **Head of gov.:** Prime Min. Shaukat Aziz; b Mar. 6, 1949; in office: Aug. 28, 2004. **Local divisions:** 4 provinces and 1 capital territory, plus federally administered tribal areas. **Defense budget:** $4.14 bil. **Active troops:** 619,000.

Economy: Industries: textiles, food proc., beverages, constr. materials, clothing, paper products. **Chief crops:** cotton, wheat, rice, sugarcane, fruits. **Natural resources:** nat. gas, oil, coal, iron ore, copper, salt, limestone. **Crude oil reserves:** 289.2 mil bbls. **Arable land:** 24%. **Livestock:** cattle: 25.5 mil; chickens: 162 mil; goats: 61.9 mil; sheep: 25.4 mil. **Fish catch:** 515,095 metric tons. **Electricity prod.:** 89.8 bil kWh. **Labor force** (2004 est.): agriculture 42%, industry 20%, services 38%.

Finance: Monetary unit: Rupee (PKR) (Sept. 2007: 60.60 = $1 U.S.). **GDP:** $437.5 bil; **per capita GDP:** $2,600; **GDP growth:** 6.6%. **Imports:** $26.8 bil; China 13.7%, Saudi Arabia 10.4%, UAE 9.7%, U.S. 6.4%, Japan 5.7%. **Exports:** $19.2 bil; U.S. 21.2%, UAE 9.1%, Afghanistan 7.7%, China 5.4%, UK 5.1%. **Tourism:** $185 mil. **Budget:** $25.7 bil. **Intl. reserves less gold:** $7.67 bil. **Gold:** 2.1 mil oz t. **Consumer prices:** 7.92%.

Transport: Railroad: Length: 5,072 mi. **Motor vehicles:** 1.4 mil pass. cars; 657,000 comm. vehicles. **Civil aviation:** 7.4 bil pass.-mi; 91 airports. **Chief port:** Karachi.

Communications: TV sets: 105 per 1,000 pop. **Radios:** 94 per 1,000 pop. **Telephone lines:** 5.2 mil. **Daily newspaper circ.:** 39.3 per 1,000 pop. **Internet:** 12 mil users.

Health: Life expect.: 62.7 male; 64.8 female. **Births** (per 1,000 pop.): 27.5. **Deaths** (per 1,000 pop.): 8. **Natural inc.:** 1.95%. **Infant mortality** (per 1,000 live births): 68.8. **AIDS rate:** 0.1%.

Education: Compulsory: ages 5-9. **Literacy:** 49.9%.

Major intl. organizations: UN (FAO, IBRD, ILO, IMF, IMO, WHO, WTO), the Commonwealth.

Embassy: 3517 International Ct. NW 20008; 243-6500.

Website: www.pakistan.gov.pk

Pakistan shares the 5,000-year history of the India-Pakistan subcontinent. At present-day Harappa and Mohenjo Daro, the Indus Valley Civilization, with large cities and elaborate irrigation systems, flourished c. 4,000-2,500 BCE. Aryan invaders from the northwest conquered the region around 1,500 BCE, forging the Vedic civilization that dominated the region for over a thousand years. Other invaders from the west followed. The first Arab invasion, 712 CE, introduced Islam. Present-day Pakistan and India were part of the Mogul empire from 1526 to 1857. Muslim power faded by the end of the 19th cent. as the British gained control of the north and northwest areas of the subcontinent.

After WWI, the Muslims of British India began agitation for minority rights in elections. Muhammad Ali Jinnah (1876-1948) was the principal architect of Pakistan. When the British withdrew Aug. 14, 1947, the Islamic majority areas of India acquired self-government as Pakistan, with dominion status in the Commonwealth. Pakistan was divided into 2 sections, West Pakistan and East Pakistan. The 2 areas were nearly 1,000 mi apart on opposite sides of India.

The Awami League, which had sought regional autonomy for East Pakistan for several years, won a majority in Dec. 1970 elections to a constituent assembly. In Mar. 1971, Pakistan's military-dominated government postponed the assembly. Rioting and strikes broke out in the East. On Mar. 25, 1971, government troops launched attacks in the East. The Easterners, aided by India, proclaimed the independent nation of Bangladesh. In months of widespread fighting, countless thousands were killed. Some 10 mil Easterners fled into India. Full-scale war between India and Pakistan had spread to both the East and West fronts by Dec. 3. Pakistan troops in the East surrendered Dec. 16; Pakistan agreed to a cease-fire in the West Dec. 17. On July 3, 1972, Pakistan and India signed a pact agreeing to withdraw troops from their borders and resolve problems peacefully.

Zulfikar Ali Bhutto, leader of the Pakistan People's Party, which had won the most West Pakistan votes in Dec. 1970 elections, became president Dec. 20, 1971. Bhutto was overthrown in a military coup July 1977. Convicted of complicity in a 1974 political murder, he was executed Apr. 4, 1979. Millions of Afghan refugees flooded into Pakistan after the USSR invaded Afghanistan Dec. 1979; by 2007, more than 3 mil refugees had been repatriated, but up to 2.4 mil remained.

Pres. Mohammad Zia ul-Haq was killed when his plane exploded in Aug. 1988. Following Nov. elections, Benazir Bhutto, daughter of Zulfikar Ali Bhutto, was named prime minister, becoming the first woman leader of a Muslim nation. She was accused of corruption and dismissed by the president, Aug. 1990. Bhutto returned to power Oct. 1993 but was dismissed again, Nov. 1996, amid further corruption charges. Responding to nuclear weapons tests by India, Pakistan conducted its own tests in 1998; the U.S. imposed economic sanctions on both countries.

In mid-1999, Muslim infiltrators, apparently including Pakistani troops, seized Indian-held positions in the disputed territory of Kashmir, which witnessed its heaviest fighting in over 2 decades (see Kashmir). After meeting with Pres. Bill Clinton on July 4, Prime Min. Nawaz Sharif agreed to a Pakistani pullback. Growing conflict between Sharif and the military climaxed in his firing on Oct. 12 of army chief Gen. Pervez Musharraf, whose supporters staged a bloodless coup. Musharraf assumed the presidency June 20, 2001.

Following the Sept. 11, 2001, terrorist attacks on the U.S., Pres. Musharraf, Sept. 19, pledged cooperation with the U.S. in fighting Taliban and al-Qaeda militants within its own tribal areas and in neighboring Afghanistan. In return, the U.S. waived its 1998 sanctions and offered Pakistan financial aid and debt relief. A referendum Apr. 30, 2002, extended Musharraf's rule for 5 years; many observers called the vote rigged.

Since 2002, there has been evidence of growing al-Qaeda and Taliban activity within Pakistan. Militants kidnapped *Wall Street Journal* reporter Daniel Pearl Jan. 23, 2002, and eventually killed him; 4 Islamic extremists were convicted July 15. The alleged mastermind of the Sept. 11 attacks, Khalid Sheikh Mohammed, was apprehended in Rawalpindi, Mar. 1, 2003. Islamic extremists carried out bombings in Rawalpindi Dec. 14 and 25, in unsuccessful attempts to assassinate Musharraf. A top al-Qaeda figure implicated in those attempts, Amjad Hussain Farooqi, was killed by security forces in late Sept. 2004.

Accused of selling atomic secrets to Iran, Libya, and North Korea, Pakistan's top nuclear scientist, Abdul Qadeer Khan, made a televised apology, Feb. 4, 2004, and said his actions were unauthorized. He received a pardon from Musharraf Feb. 5. Shaukat Aziz, who survived a suicide bomb attack July 30, was elected prime min. Aug. 27. British ties with Pakistan were frayed by reports that 3 of 4 suspects in the London train and bus bombings, July 7, 2005, were of Pakistani ancestry, and that 2 had recently been to Pakistan. Musharraf pledged July 29 to arrest leaders of banned Islamist groups and to expel foreign students from Islamic schools, or *madrassas*. An earthquake that rocked Pakistan and the Pakistani-held region of Kashmir Oct. 8 , 2005, killed about 80,000 people and left up to 3 mil homeless.

Musharraf's grip appeared to weaken in 2007. On Mar. 9 he suspended Chief Justice Iftikhar Muhammad Chaudhry, who had taken up cases involving the "forced disappearances" of hundreds of detainees; the suspension sparked mass protests by pro-democracy demonstrators and was ruled illegal July 20 by Pakistan's Supreme Court, which reinstated Chaudhry. Musharraf survived an assassination attempt (at least the 4th in 5 years) when gunmen fired on his plane July 6. More than 70 Islamic militants were killed July 10 when government troops raided Islamabad's Red Mosque, an extremist stronghold. The violence spread July 14-19, as at least 160 people died in suicide attacks and bombings after a 10-month-old peace deal broke down between the central govt. and tribal leaders in North Waziristan, a haven for the Taliban and al-Qaeda. With an electoral college scheduled to hold a presidential vote Oct. 6, Musharraf maneuvered to retain power as president, army chief, or both.

Palau
Republic of Palau

People: Population: 20,842. **Age distrib.** (%): <15: 26; 65+: 4.7. **Pop. density:** 118 per sq mi, 46 per sq km. **Urban:** 69.6%. **Ethnic groups:** Palauan (Micronesian/Malayan/Melanesian mix) 70%, Asian 28%, white 2%. **Principal languages:** English (official); Palauan, Sonsorolese, Tobi, Angaur, Japanese (all official in certain states); Chinese. **Chief religions:** Roman Catholic 42%, Protestant 23%, Modekngei 9%, Seventh-Day Adventist 5%.

Geography: Total area: 177 sq mi, 458 sq km; **Land area:** 177 sq mi, 458 sq km. **Location:** Archipelago (26 islands, more than 300 islets) in W Pacific Ocean, about 530 mi SE of the Philippines. **Neighbors:** Micronesia to E, Indonesia to S. **Topography:** A mountainous main island and low coral atolls, usually fringed with large barrier reefs. **Capital:** Melekeok, 391.

Government: Type: Republic. **Head of state and gov.:** Pres. Tommy Esang Remengesau Jr.; b. Feb. 28, 1956; in office: Jan. 19, 2001. **Local divisions:** 16 states.

Economy: Industries: tourism, handicrafts, constr., garment making. **Chief crops:** coconuts, copra, cassava, sweet potatoes. **Natural resources:** timber, gold & other minerals, fish. **Arable land:** 9%. **Fish catch:** 937 metric tons. **Labor force** (1990): agriculture 20%.

Finance: Monetary unit: U.S. Dollar (USD). **GDP** (2004 est.): $124.5 mil (includes U.S. subsidy); **per capita GDP** (2005 est.): $7,600; **GDP growth** (2005 est.): 5.5%. **Imports** (2004 est.): $107.3 mil; U.S., Singapore, Japan, South Korea. **Exports** (2004 est.): $5.9 mil; U.S., Japan, Singapore. **Tourism:** $59 mil. **Budget** (FY04/05 est.): $72.4 mil.

Transport: Civil aviation: 1 airport. **Chief port:** Koror.
Communications: TV sets: 98 per 1,000 pop. **Radios:** 550 per 1,000 pop. **Telephone lines:** NA. **Internet:** NA.
Health: Life expect.: 67.5 male; 74.1 female. **Births** (per 1,000 pop.): 17.7. **Deaths** (per 1,000 pop.): 6.8. **Natural inc.:** 1.09%. **Infant mortality** (per 1,000 live births): 14.1. **AIDS rate:** NA.
Education: Compulsory: ages 6-14. **Literacy:** 92%.
Major intl. organizations: UN (FAO, IBRD, ILO, IMF, WHO).
Embassy: 1700 Pennsylvania Ave. NW, Ste. 400, 20006; 452-6814.
Website: www.palaugov.net

Spain acquired the Palau Islands in 1886 and sold them to Germany in 1899. Japan seized them in 1914. American forces occupied the islands in 1944; in 1947, they became part of the U.S.-administered UN Trust Territory of the Pacific Islands. In 1981 Palau became an autonomous republic; in 1993 the republic ratified a compact of free association with the U.S., which provides financial aid in return for U.S. use of Palauan military facilities over 15 years. Palau became an independent nation on Oct. 1, 1994. Vice Pres. Tommy Remengesau won the presidential election held Nov. 7, 2000, and was reelected Nov. 2, 2004.

Panama
Republic of Panama

People: Population: 3,242,173. **Age distrib.** (%): <15: 30; 65+: 6.4. **Pop. density:** 111 per sq mi, 43 per sq km. **Urban:** 70.8%. **Ethnic groups:** Mestizo 70%, Amerindian-West Indian 14%, white 10%, Amerindian 6%. **Principal languages:** Spanish (official), English. **Chief religions:** Roman Catholic 85%, Protestant 15%.

Geography: Total area: 30,193 sq mi, 78,200 sq km; **Land area:** 29,340 sq mi, 75,990 sq km. **Location:** In Central America. **Neighbors:** Costa Rica on W, Colombia on E. **Topography:** 2 mountain ranges run the length of the isthmus. Tropical rain forests cover the Caribbean coast and E Panama. **Capital:** Panama City, 1,216,000.

Government: Type: Republic. **Head of state and gov.:** Pres. Martin Torrijos Espino; b. July 18, 1963; in office: Sept. 1, 2004. **Local divisions:** 9 provinces, 5 territories. **Defense budget:** $171 mil. **Active troops:** None.

Economy: Industries: constr., oil refining, brewing, constr. materials, sugar milling. **Chief crops:** bananas, rice, corn, coffee, sugarcane. **Natural resources:** copper, mahogany, shrimp, hydropower. **Arable land:** 7%. **Livestock:** cattle: 1.6 mil; chickens: 14.6 mil; goats: 6,300; pigs: 286,200. **Fish catch:** 222,756 metric tons. **Electricity prod.:** 5.7 bil kWh. **Labor force** (1995 est.): agriculture 20.8%, industry 18%, services 61.2%.

Finance: Monetary unit: Balboa (PAB) (Sept. 2007: 1.00 = $1 U.S.). **GDP:** $26 bil; **per capita GDP:** $8,200; **GDP growth:** 8.1%. **Imports:** $9.4 bil; Japan 33.2%, China 16%, U.S. 11.2%, Singapore 11.2%. **Exports:** $8.1 bil; Spain 26.8%, U.S. 18.9%, Italy 5.7%, Germany 5.4%. **Tourism:** $780 mil. **Budget:** $4.5 bil. **Intl. reserves less gold:** $887 mil. **Consumer prices:** 2.1%.

Transport: Railroad: Length: 221 mi. **Motor vehicles:** 245,000 pass. cars; 80,000 comm. vehicles. **Civil aviation:** 2.2 bil pass.-mi; 53 airports. **Chief ports:** Balboa, Cristobal.
Communications: TV sets: 192 per 1,000 pop. **Radios:** 299 per 1,000 pop. **Telephone lines:** 432,900. **Internet:** 220,000 users.
Health: Life expect.: 72.7 male; 77.8 female. **Births** (per 1,000 pop.): 21.5. **Deaths** (per 1,000 pop.): 5.4. **Natural inc.:** 1.6%. **Infant mortality** (per 1,000 live births): 16. **AIDS rate:** 0.9%.
Education: Compulsory: ages 6-11. **Literacy:** 91.9%.
Major intl. organizations: UN (FAO, IBRD, ILO, IMF, IMO, OAS, WHO, WTO).
Embassy: 2862 McGill Terrace NW 20008; 483-1407.
Website: www.visitpanama.com

The coast of Panama was sighted by Rodrigo de Bastidas, sailing with Columbus for Spain in 1501, and was visited by Columbus in 1502. Vasco Nunez de Balboa crossed the isthmus and "discovered" the Pacific Ocean, Sept. 13, 1513. Spanish colonies were ravaged by Francis Drake, 1572-95, and Henry Morgan, 1668-71. Morgan destroyed the old city of Panama which had been founded in 1519. Freed from Spain, Panama joined Colombia in 1821.

Panama declared its independence from Colombia Nov. 3, 1903, with U.S. recognition. In support of Panama, U.S. naval forces deterred action by Colombia. Panama granted use, occupation, and control of the Canal Zone to the U.S. by treaty, ratified Feb. 26, 1904. In 1978, a new treaty provided for a gradual takeover by Panama of the canal, and withdrawal of U.S. troops, to be completed before the end of the century. U.S. payments were substantially increased in the interim.

Pres. Delvalle was ousted by the National Assembly, Feb. 26, 1988, after he tried to fire the head of the Panama Defense Forces, Gen. Manuel Antonio Noriega, who was under U.S. federal indictment on drug charges. U.S. troops invaded Panama Dec. 20, 1989, and Noriega surrendered Jan. 3, 1990.

Mireya Moscoso, widow of former Pres. Arnulfo Arias, was elected president May 2, 1999, becoming Panama's first female head of state. The U.S. handed over control of the Panama Canal to Panama Dec. 31, 1999. Martin Torrijos Espino, son of Brig. Gen. Omar Torrijos Herrera (dictator of Panama, 1968-81), won the presidential election of May 2, 2004. A $5.3-bil plan to widen the canal was approved by national referendum Oct. 22, 2006.

Papua New Guinea
Independent State of Papua New Guinea

People: Population: 5,795,887. **Age distrib.** (%): <15: 37.6; 65+: 3.9. **Pop. density:** 33 per sq mi, 13 per sq km. **Urban:** 13.4%. **Ethnic groups:** Melanesian, Papuan, Negrito, Micronesian, Polynesian. **Principal languages:** Melanesian Pidgin, English, Motu, 820 indigenous languages spoken. **Chief religions:** Indigenous beliefs 34%, Roman Catholic 22%, Protestant 44%.

Geography: Total area: 178,704 sq mi, 462,840 sq km; **Land area:** 174,850 sq mi, 452,860 sq km. **Location:** SE Asia, occupying E half of island of New Guinea and about 600 nearby islands. **Neighbors:** Indonesia (West Irian) on W, Australia on S. **Topography:** Thickly forested mts. cover much of center of the country, with lowlands along the coasts. Included are some islands of Bismarck and Solomon groups, such as Admiralty Isls., New Ireland, New Britain, and Bougainville. **Capital:** Port Moresby, 289,000.

Government: Type: Parliamentary democracy. **Head of state:** Queen Elizabeth II, represented by Gov.-Gen. Sir Paulias Matane; b. 1931; in office: June 29, 2004. **Head of gov.:** Prime Min. Sir Michael Somare; b. Apr. 9, 1936; in office: Aug. 5, 2002. **Local divisions:** 20 provinces. **Defense budget:** $30.2 mil. **Active troops:** 3,100.

Economy: Industries: copra & palm oil proc., wood products, mining. **Chief crops:** coffee, cocoa, copra, palm kernels, tea, sugar, rubber, sweet potatoes. **Natural resources:** gold, copper, silver, nat. gas, timber, oil, fish. **Crude oil reserves:** 240 mil bbls. **Arable land:** 0.5%. **Livestock:** cattle: 91,500; chickens: 4 mil; goats: 2,700; pigs: 1.8 mil; sheep: 7,500. **Fish catch:** 250,280 metric tons. **Electricity prod.:** 3.7 bil kWh. **Labor force:** agriculture 85%.

Finance: Monetary unit: Kina (PGK) (Sept. 2007: 2.93 = $1 U.S.). **GDP:** $15.4 bil; **per capita GDP:** $2,700; **GDP growth:** 3.7%. **Imports:** $1.7 bil; Australia 53%, Singapore 12.8%, China 6%, Japan 4.4%. **Exports:** $4.1 bil; Australia 30.3%, Japan 8.2%, China 5.7%. **Tourism:** $5 mil. **Budget:** $2.2 bil. **Intl. reserves less gold:** $931 mil. **Gold:** 60,000 oz t. **Consumer prices:** 2.87%.

Transport: Motor vehicles: 24,900 pass. cars; 87,800 comm. vehicles. **Civil aviation:** 357.9 mil pass.-mi; 21 airports. **Chief ports:** Kimbe, Lae, Rabaul.
Communications: TV sets: 13 per 1,000 pop. **Radios:** 91 per 1,000 pop. **Telephone lines:** 63,700. **Internet:** 110,000 users.
Health: Life expect.: 63.4 male; 68 female. **Births** (per 1,000 pop.): 28.8. **Deaths** (per 1,000 pop.): 7.1. **Natural inc.:** 2.16%. **Infant mortality** (per 1,000 live births): 48.5. **AIDS rate:** 1.8%.
Education: Compulsory: ages 6-14. **Literacy:** 57.3%.
Major intl. organizations: UN (FAO, IBRD, ILO, IMF, IMO, WHO, WTO), the Commonwealth, APEC.
Embassy: 1779 Massachusetts Ave NW, Ste. 805, 20036; 745-3680.
Website: www.pngonline.gov.pg

Human remains have been found in the interior of New Guinea dating back at least 10,000 years and possibly much earlier. Europeans visited in the 15th cent., but actual land claims did not begin until the 19th cent., when the Dutch took control of the island's western half. The southern half of eastern New Guinea was first claimed by Britain in 1884, and transferred to Australia in 1905. The northern half was claimed by Germany in 1884, but captured in WWI by Australia, which received a League of Nations mandate and then a UN trusteeship over the area. The 2 territories were administered jointly after 1949, gained self-government Dec. 1, 1973, and became independent Sept. 16, 1975.

Secessionist rebels clashed with government forces on Bougainville beginning in 1988; a truce signed Oct. 10, 1997, brought a halt to the fighting, which had claimed some 20,000 lives. The country suffered from a severe drought in 1997. A tsunami killed at least 3,000 people July 17, 1998. A Bougainville autonomy agreement was signed Aug. 30, 2001. Army mutinies were suppressed in Mar. 2001 and Mar. 2002. Sir Michael Somare, the nation's 1st prime minister (1975-80, 1982-85), regained the office in 2002 and was reelected by parliament Aug. 13, 2007.

The country has extensive energy resources; a proposed pipeline would transport natural gas to Queensland, Australia.

HUSSEIN'S FINAL MOMENTS
Saddam Hussein (shown on Iraqi state television) was executed, Dec. 30, 2006. An Iraqi court had sentenced him to death in November for crimes against humanity.

LIFE AFTER IRAQ
U.S. Army Sgt. Chad Rozanski, 21, who lost both legs in a roadside bombing in Iraq, attended a job fair for wounded soldiers in San Antonio, TX, Mar. 27, 2007.

CHANGING OF THE GUARD
Army Gen. David Petraeus (left), commander of multi-national forces in Iraq, greeted outgoing Joint Chiefs Chairman Gen. Peter Pace (right), July 16 in Baghdad. Iraqi soldiers (below) arrested a man in Baqouba, near Baghdad, July 24, a month after U.S. and Iraqi troops launched a new offensive to clear insurgents from the city.

BUSH AND PUTIN'S "LOBSTER SUMMIT"

Pres. Bush and Russian Pres. Vladimir Putin, at the Bush family compound in Kennebunkport, ME, in July 2007, met to resolve tensions over U.S. plans for an eastern European missile shield.

CHINESE GOODS UNDER CLOSE SCRUTINY

Mattel Inc. recalled more than 21 million Chinese-made toys in summer 2007, later taking responsibility for design flaws. Chinese-made goods were also implicated in health scares involving pet food, toothpaste, and other products.

PROTESTERS TURN UP THE HEAT

In Bangkok, Thai protesters demanded action against catastrophic climate change. The Intergovernmental Panel on Climate Change asserted in 2007 that human contributions to greenhouse gas emissions played a significant role in global warming.

NEW AID FOR NORTH KOREA

South Korean workers prepared a shipment of rice for North Korea, which took new steps toward nuclear disarmament in June 2007 in exchange for food and other assistance from its southern neighbor.

BRITAIN AND RUSSIA CLASH OVER MURDER OF EX-SPY

On Dec. 13, 2006, German authorities investigated traces of radiation at a site connected with former Russian spy Alexander Litvinenko (inset, from May 10, 2002), who had died of radiation poisoning in November. In May 2007 British officials accused former KGB operative Andrei Lugovoi of murder, but Russia refused to extradite Lugovoi to face charges.

PARTNERS IN POWER

French Pres. Nicolas Sarkozy, left, greeted British Prime Min. Gordon Brown in Paris, July 20, 2007. At their first meeting since taking office in May and June, respectively, the new leaders pledged cooperation in the fight against terrorism and vowed to bring an end to the "catastrophe" in Darfur.

TERROR ATTACKS RATTLE GREAT BRITAIN

An SUV exploded at the main terminal of Glasgow airport, July 30, 2007, a day after British police defused two car bombs in London's theatre district. The passenger in the SUV, a British-born Iraqi, was charged with conspiring to cause explosions; the driver, an Indian engineer, was hospitalized for severe burns and died Aug. 2.

PALESTINIANS PROTEST AFTER HAMAS TAKEOVER

Supporters of Hamas demanded the reopening of the Rafah Crossing, a gateway between the Gaza Strip and Egypt, in July 2007. The crossing was completely closed by Israeli authorities in June, after Hamas took control of Gaza in fighting that killed at least 100 and wounded more than 500.

CHAVEZ COASTS TO RE-ELECTION

Venezuelan Pres. Hugo Chavez won re-election in Dec. 2006 with more than 60% of the vote. Chavez, who had mocked and challenged Pres. Bush throughout 2006, declared the election a mandate for socialism in Venezuela.

BBC REPORTER SET FREE

After nearly four months in captivity, BBC reporter Alan Johnston (center) was released by the militant Palestinian group Army of Islam after Hamas leader Ismail Haniyeh intervened on his behalf.

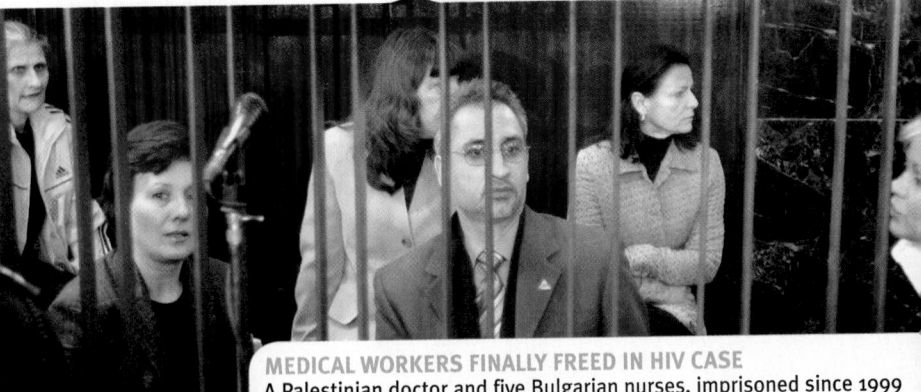

MEDICAL WORKERS FINALLY FREED IN HIV CASE

A Palestinian doctor and five Bulgarian nurses, imprisoned since 1999 for allegedly infecting 438 children in a Libyan hospital with HIV, were convicted in a Libyan court, Dec. 19, 2006. A deal between EU and Libyan officials granted freedom to all six in July 2007. Foreign experts had long asserted that the infections were a result of poor hygiene.

TRIUMPH AT WIMBLEDON

Roger Federer and Venus Williams emerged victorious at Wimbledon, claiming their respective fifth and fourth Wimbledon titles. At the end of the 2007 Grand Slam tournament season, Federer had won 12 career Grand Slams, just two behind Pete Sampras's all-time record.

CONTADOR WINS A TAINTED TOUR

Spain's Alberto Contador won the 2007 Tour de France, which had been plagued by doping allegations. American Floyd Landis was stripped of the 2006 Tour title in Sept. 2007.

BONDS MAKES HIS MARK

On Aug. 7, Barry Bonds smashed his 756th career home run and Hank Aaron's all-time record. Bonds continued to be dogged by allegations of steroid abuse.

SAN ANTONIO BRINGS IT HOME

Tony Parker (top) and the San Antonio
Spurs won the franchise's fourth
championship since 1999, sweeping the
Cleveland Cavaliers (with Sasha Pavlovic,
bottom) in the NBA Finals.

MILESTONES AT SUPER BOWL XLI

Quarterback Peyton Manning (top) led
the Indianapolis Colts to victory over
the Chicago Bears in Super Bowl XLI
and was named Super Bowl MVP. Colts
head coach Tony Dungy (bottom, right)
and Bears head coach Lovie Smith
(bottom, left) were the first black
coaches to take their teams to the
Super Bowl.

FLORIDA CLAIMS DUAL NCAA TITLES
The Florida Gators made history against Ohio State, defeating the Buckeyes to win the NCAA championships in football and basketball. Florida was the first school to capture the NCAA title in both sports in the same year.

BECKHAM BENDS THE RULES
British soccer player David Beckham made his American major league soccer debut, joining the Los Angeles Galaxy amid much fanfare—and with a record-breaking salary deal worth as much as $50 million a year. It was hoped that the superstar midfielder would attract new fans to the fledgling U.S. league.

815

ROBERT ALTMAN
Nov. 20, 2006

INGMAR BERGMAN
July 30, 2007

JAMES BROWN
Dec. 25, 2006

LIZ CLAIBORNE
June 26, 2007

JERRY FALWELL
May 15, 2007

MILTON FRIEDMAN
Nov. 16, 2006

MERV GRIFFIN
Aug. 12, 2007

DON HERBERT (MR. WIZARD)
June 12, 2007

LADY BIRD JOHNSON
July 11, 2007

JACK PALANCE
Nov. 10, 2006

LUCIANO PAVAROTTI
Sept. 6, 2007

ARTHUR SCHLESINGER JR.
Feb. 28, 2007

BEVERLY SILLS
July 2, 2007

ANNA NICOLE SMITH
Feb. 8, 2007

KURT VONNEGUT JR.
Apr. 11, 2007

BORIS YELTSIN
Apr. 23, 2007

Paraguay
Republic of Paraguay

People: Population: 6,669,056. **Age distrib.** (%): <15: 37.2; 65+: 5.1. **Pop. density:** 44 per sq mi, 17 per sq km. **Urban:** 58.5%. **Ethnic groups:** Mestizo 95%. **Principal languages:** Spanish, Guaraní (both official). **Chief religions:** Roman Catholic 90%, Protestant 6%.

Geography: Total area: 157,047 sq mi, 406,750 sq km; **Land area:** 153,398 sq mi, 397,300 sq km. **Location:** Landlocked country in central S. America. **Neighbors:** Bolivia on N, Argentina on S, Brazil on E. **Topography:** Paraguay R. bisects the country. To E are fertile plains, wooded slopes, grasslands. To W is the Gran Chaco plain, with marshes and scrub trees. Extreme W is arid. **Capital:** Asunción, 1,858,000.

Government: Type: Republic. **Head of state and gov.:** Pres. Nicanor Duarte Frutos; b. Oct. 11, 1956; in office: Aug. 15, 2003. **Local divisions:** 17 departments and capital city. **Defense budget** (2005): $58.2 mil. **Active troops:** 10,100.

Economy: Industries: sugar, cement, textiles, beverages, wood products. **Chief crops:** cotton, sugarcane, soybeans, corn, wheat, tobacco, cassava. **Natural resources:** hydropower, timber, iron ore, mang., limestone. **Arable land:** 7%. **Livestock:** cattle: 10 mil; chickens: 17 mil; goats: 155,000; pigs: 1.6 mil; sheep: 500,000. **Fish catch:** 23,100 metric tons. **Electricity prod.:** 50.7 bil kWh. **Labor force:** agriculture 45%.

Finance: Monetary unit: Guaraní (PYG) (Sept. 2007: 4,996.30 = $1 U.S.). **GDP:** $31.3 bil; **per capita GDP:** $4,800; **GDP growth:** 4%. **Imports:** $4.5 bil; China 27%, Brazil 20%, Argentina 13.6%, Japan 8.3%, U.S. 6.4%. **Exports** (2005 est.): $1.7 bil; Uruguay 22%, Brazil 17.2%, Russia 11.9%, Argentina 8.8%, Chile 6.9%. **Tourism:** $82 mil. **Budget:** $1.7 bil. **Intl. reserves less gold:** $1.13 bil. **Gold** (2003): 30,000 oz t. **Consumer prices:** 9.59%.

Transport: Railroad: Length: 22 mi. **Motor vehicles:** 325,000 pass. cars; 50,000 comm. vehicles. **Civil aviation:** 198.8 mil pass.-mi; 12 airports. **Chief ports:** Asunción, Encarnación, Villeta.

Communications: TV sets: 205 per 1,000 pop. **Radios:** 182 per 1,000 pop. **Telephone lines:** 331,100. **Internet:** 260,000 users.

Health: Life expect.: 72.8 male; 78 female. **Births** (per 1,000 pop.): 28.8. **Deaths** (per 1,000 pop.): 4.5. **Natural inc.:** 2.42%. **Infant mortality** (per 1,000 live births): 26.5. **AIDS rate:** 0.4%.

Education (2005): Compulsory: ages 6-14. **Literacy:** 93.5%.

Major intl. organizations: UN (FAO, IBRD, ILO, IMF, IMO, WHO, WTO), OAS.

Embassy: 2400 Massachusetts Ave. NW 20008; 483-6960.

Website: www.paraguayconsulatela.com

The Guaraní Indians were settled farmers speaking a common language before the arrival of Europeans. Visited by Sebastian Cabot in 1527 and settled as a Spanish possession in 1535, Paraguay gained its independence from Spain in 1811. It lost much of its territory to Brazil, Uruguay, and Argentina in the War of the Triple Alliance, 1865-70. Large areas were won from Bolivia in the Chaco War, 1932-35.

Gen. Alfredo Stroessner, who had ruled since 1954, was ousted in a military coup led by Gen. Andrés Rodríguez on Feb. 3, 1989. Rodríguez was elected president May 1. Juan Carlos Wasmosy was elected president May 9, 1993, becoming the nation's first civilian head of state in many years.

A prolonged power struggle involving a popular military leader, Gen. Lino César Oviedo, who was accused of insubordination, culminated in his surrender Dec. 12, 1997. He was freed Aug. 18, 1998, following the inauguration of Pres. Raúl Cubas Grau, Oviedo's successor as Colorado Party nominee.

The assassination of Vice Pres. Luis María Argaña, Mar. 23, 1999, by an unidentified gunman, was widely attributed to Cubas and triggered protests and an impeachment vote; Cubas resigned Mar. 28 and was succeeded by Senate leader Luis Ángel González Macchi. An attempted military coup was suppressed May 18, 2000.

Mass protests over the depressed economy led to the proclamation of a state of emergency July 15, 2002. Nicanor Duarte Frutos won the presidency, Apr. 27, 2003, maintaining 55 years of uninterrupted Colorado Party rule.

Paraguayan authorities blamed a leftist group, Patria Libre, for the Sept. 2004 kidnapping and subsequent murder of Cecilia Cubas, daughter of former Pres. Cubas. Former Pres. González Macchi was convicted of fraud and embezzlement, Dec. 4, 2006, and sentenced to 8 years in prison. Drought and faulty land management practices contributed to wildfires, Sept. 2007, that scorched about 370,000 acres.

Peru
Republic of Peru

People: Population: 28,674,757. **Age distrib.** (%): <15: 30.3; 65+: 5.4. **Pop. density:** 58 per sq mi, 22 per sq km. **Urban:** 72.6%. **Ethnic groups:** Amerindian 45%, mestizo 37%, white 15%. **Principal languages:** Spanish, Quechua (both official); Aymara; minor Amazonian languages. **Chief religion:** Roman Catholic (official) 81%.

Geography: Total area: 496,226 sq mi, 1,285,220 sq km; **Land area:** 494,211 sq mi, 1,280,000 sq km. **Location:** On Pacific coast of S. America. **Neighbors:** Ecuador, Colombia on N; Brazil, Bolivia on E; Chile on S. **Topography:** An arid coastal strip, 10-100 mi wide, supports much of the population thanks to widespread irrigation. The Andes cover 27% of land area. The uplands are well-watered, as are the eastern slopes reaching the Amazon basin, which covers half the country. **Capital:** Lima, 7,186,000. **Cities (urban aggr.):** Arequipa, 819,000; Callao, 424,294.

Government: Type: Republic. **Head of state:** Pres. Alan García; b. May 23, 1949; in office: July 28, 2006. **Head of gov.:** Prime Min. Jorge del Castillo; b. July 2, 1950; in office: July 28, 2006. **Local divisions:** 12 regions, 24 departments, 1 constitutional province. **Defense budget:** $1.1 bil. **Active troops:** 80,000.

Economy: Industries: mining, oil, fishing, textiles, clothing, food proc. **Chief crops:** asparagus, coffee, cotton, sugarcane, rice, potatoes, corn, plantains, grapes, oranges, coca. **Natural resources:** copper, silver, gold, oil, timber, fish, iron ore, coal, phosphate, potash, hydropower, nat. gas. **Crude oil reserves:** 929.6 mil bbls. **Arable land:** 3%. **Livestock:** cattle: 5.2 mil; chickens: 99.3 mil; goats: 2 mil; pigs: 3 mil; sheep: 14.8 mil. **Fish catch:** 9,416,130 metric tons. **Electricity prod.:** 25 bil kWh. **Labor force** (2001): agriculture 9%, industry 18%, services 73%.

Finance: Monetary unit: Nuevo Sol (PEN) (Sept. 2007: 3.14 = $1 U.S.). **GDP:** $186.6 bil; **per capita GDP:** $6,600; **GDP growth:** 8%. **Imports:** $15.4 bil; U.S. 20.1%, Brazil 8.1%, Ecuador 7.5%, China 6.9%, Chile 6.4%, Colombia 6.2%, Argentina 5.2%. **Exports:** $22.7 bil; U.S. 25.6%, China 12%, Canada 8.4%, Chile 5.9%, Japan 5.4%. **Tourism:** $1.2 bil. **Budget:** $25.2 bil. **Intl. reserves less gold:** $11.12 bil. **Gold:** 1.11 mil oz t. **Consumer prices:** 2%.

Transport: Railroad: Length: 2,151 mi. **Motor vehicles:** 906,600 pass. cars; 555,300 comm. vehicles. **Civil aviation:** 1.7 bil pass.-mi; 54 airports. **Chief ports:** Callao, Iquitos, Matarani, Pucallpa.

Communications: TV sets: 147 per 1,000 pop. **Radios:** 273 per 1,000 pop. **Telephone lines:** 2.3 mil. **Daily newspaper circ.:** 22.7 per 1,000 pop. **Internet:** 6.1 mil users.

Health: Life expect.: 68.3 male; 72 female. **Births** (per 1,000 pop.): 20.1. **Deaths** (per 1,000 pop.): 6.2. **Natural inc.:** 1.39%. **Infant mortality** (per 1,000 live births): 30. **AIDS rate:** 0.6%.

Education: Compulsory: ages 6-16. **Literacy:** 87.9%.

Major intl. organizations: UN and all of its specialized agencies, APEC, OAS.

Embassy: 1700 Massachusetts Ave. NW 20036; 833-9860.

Website: www.peru.info

The powerful Inca empire had its seat at Cuzco in the Andes and covered much of S. America. A civil war had weakened the empire when Francisco Pizarro, Spanish conquistador, began raiding Peru for its wealth, 1532. In 1533 he executed the Inca ruler, Atahualpa, and enslaved the people.

Lima was the seat of Spanish viceroys until the Argentine liberator, José de San Martín, captured it in 1821; Spanish forces were ultimately routed by Simón Bolívar, 1824. For much of the 19th cent., the country was governed by military leaders. Chile defeated Peru in the War of the Pacific (1879-83). The first half of the 20th cent. was dominated by rivalry between right-wing groups (allied with the military) and the leftist APRA party.

Peru returned to democratic leadership in 1980 but was plagued by economic problems and by leftist Shining Path (Sendero Luminoso) guerrillas. Conflict between guerrillas and government troops, 1980-2000, killed more than 69,000 people, mostly Andean Indians.

Elected president in June 1990, Alberto Fujimori, the son of Japanese immigrants, dissolved the National Congress, suspended parts of the constitution, and initiated press censorship, Apr. 5, 1992. The leader of Shining Path was captured Sept. 12.

Fujimori won reelection Apr. 9, 1995, but his repressive antiterrorism tactics drew international criticism. A hostage standoff that began Dec. 17, 1996, when leftist Tupac Amaru guerrillas infiltrated a reception at the Japanese ambassador's residence in Lima, ended Apr. 22, 1997, when Peruvian soldiers stormed the embassy, rescuing 71 captives; 1 hostage, 2 soldiers, and all 14 guerrillas were killed.

Fujimori's path to a 3rd term was cleared when his lone remaining challenger withdrew, charging electoral fraud, 6 days before a runoff vote on May 28, 2000. Scandals involving his top aide and intelligence chief, Vladimiro Montesinos, led Fujimori to resign his office Nov. 20 while on a visit to Japan; instead of accepting his resignation, Congress ousted him as "morally unfit."

Alejandro Toledo won a presidential runoff election June 3, 2001. Montesinos was captured in Venezuela June 23; extradited to Peru, he was convicted in a series of criminal trials. Charges were filed Sept. 5, 2001, against the exiled Fujimori, alleging his complicity in the killings by a paramilitary death squad of at least 25 people during 1991-92. Fujimori was arrested in Chile, Nov. 7, 2005, and extradited to Peru, Sept. 22, 2007.

A sagging economy, resurgent rebel activity, and a series of scandals eroded Toledo's popularity during 2003-05. Alan García, whose 1st term as president (1985-90) had ended with the country facing hyperinflation and guerrilla war, won a presidential runoff election June 4, 2006, and took office July 28. An earthquake rocked SW coastal Peru, Aug. 15, 2007, killing more than 500 people and leaving 200,000 homeless.

Philippines
Republic of the Philippines

People: Population: 91,077,287. **Age distrib.** (%): <15: 34.5; 65+: 4.1. **Pop. density:** 791 per sq mi, 305 per sq km. **Urban:** 62.7%. **Ethnic groups:** Tagalog 28%, Cebuano 13%, Ilocano 9%, Bisaya/Binisaya 8%, Hiligaynon Ilonggo 8%, Bikol 6%, other 25%. **Principal languages:** Filipino (based on Tagalog), English (both official); many dialects. **Chief religions:** Roman Catholic 81%, Muslim 5%.

Geography: Total area: 115,831 sq mi, 300,000 sq km; **Land area:** 115,124 sq mi, 298,170 sq km. **Location:** An archipelago off SE coast of Asia. **Neighbors:** Nearest are Malaysia, Indonesia on S; Taiwan on N. **Topography:** The country consists of some 7,100 islands stretching 1,100 mi N-S. About 95% of area and population are on 11 largest islands, which are volcanic, except for the heavily indented coastlines and central plain on Luzon. **Capital:** Manila, 10,686,000. **Cities (urban aggr.):** Quezon City, 2,160,000; Davao, 1,327,000; Cebu 799,000.

Government: Type: Republic. **Head of state and gov.:** Pres. Gloria Macapagal Arroyo; b. Apr. 5, 1947; in office: Jan. 20, 2001. **Local divisions:** 79 provinces. **Defense budget:** $909 mil. **Active troops:** 106,000.

Economy: Industries: textiles, pharm., chemicals, wood products, food proc., electronics. **Chief crops:** sugarcane, coconuts, rice, corn, bananas, cassavas, pineapples. **Natural resources:** timber, oil, nickel, cobalt, silver, gold, salt, copper. **Crude oil reserves:** 138.5 mil bbls. **Arable land:** 19%. **Livestock:** cattle: 2.5 mil; chickens: 134.3 mil; goats: 3.7 mil; pigs: 13 mil; sheep: 30,000. **Fish catch:** 2,803,603 metric tons. **Electricity prod.:** 53.7 bil kWh. **Labor force** (2004 est.): agriculture 36%, industry 15%, services 49%.

Finance: Monetary unit: Peso (PHP) (Sept. 2007: 46.21 = $1 U.S.). **GDP:** $449.8 bil; **per capita GDP:** $5,000; **GDP growth:** 5.4%. **Imports:** $51.6 bil; Japan 15.9%, U.S. 13.7%, China 10.1%, Singapore 8.9%, Taiwan 7.2%, Saudi Arabia 4.8%, S. Korea 4.7%, Hong Kong 4.6%, Thailand 4.6%. **Exports:** $47.2 bil; China 24.5%, U.S. 15.2%, Japan 12.2%, Singapore 8.3%, Hong Kong 7.6%, Malaysia 4.4%, Netherlands 4.5%. **Tourism:** $2 bil. **Budget:** $20.7 bil. **Intl. reserves less gold:** $13.31 bil. **Gold:** 4.62 mil oz t. **Consumer prices:** 6.28%.

Transport: Railroad: Length: 557 mi. **Motor vehicles:** 1.2 mil pass. cars; 302,000 comm. vehicles. **Civil aviation:** 8.6 bil pass.-mi; 83 airports. **Chief ports:** Cebu, Davao, Iloilo, Manila.

Communications: TV sets: 110 per 1,000 pop. **Radios:** 161 per 1,000 pop. **Telephone lines:** 3.4 mil. **Daily newspaper circ.:** 66.1 per 1,000 pop. **Internet:** 4.6 mil users.

Health: Life expect.: 67.6 male; 73.6 female. **Births** (per 1,000 pop.): 24.5. **Deaths** (per 1,000 pop.): 5.4. **Natural inc.:** 1.91%. **Infant mortality** (per 1,000 live births): 22.1. **AIDS rate:** <0.1%.

Education: Compulsory: ages 6-12. **Literacy:** 92.6%.

Major intl. organizations: UN (FAO, IBRD, ILO, IMF, IMO, WHO, WTO), APEC, ASEAN.

Embassy: 1600 Massachusetts Ave. NW 20036; 467-9300.

Website: www.gov.ph

Originally inhabited by Malay peoples, the archipelago was visited by Magellan, 1521. The Spanish founded Manila, 1571. The islands, named for King Philip II of Spain, were ceded by Spain to the U.S. for $20 mil, 1898, following the Spanish-American War. U.S. troops suppressed a guerrilla uprising in a brutal 6-year war, 1899-1905.

Japan attacked the Philippines Dec. 8, 1941, and occupied the islands during WWII. On July 4, 1946, independence was proclaimed in accordance with an act passed by the U.S. Congress in 1934. A republic was established.

The repressive and corrupt regime of Pres. Ferdinand Marcos and his wife, Imelda, ruled the Philippines 1965-86. The assassination of prominent opposition leader Benigno S. Aquino Jr. Aug. 21, 1983, sparked demonstrations calling for Marcos's resignation. Amid allegations of widespread election fraud, Marcos was declared the victor Feb. 16, 1986, over Corazon Aquino, widow of the slain opposition leader. Marcos fled the country Feb. 25, and Corazon Aquino became president.

Her government was plagued by a weak economy, widespread poverty, Communist and Muslim insurgencies, and lukewarm military support. Rebel troops seized military bases and TV stations and bombed the presidential palace, Dec. 1, 1989. Government forces, with U.S. air support, defeated the attempted coup. Aquino endorsed Fidel Ramos in the May 1992 presidential election, which he won. The U.S. vacated the Subic Bay Naval Station in late 1992, ending its long military presence in the Philippines. The government signed a cease-fire agreement, Jan. 30, 1994, with Muslim separatist guerrillas, but some rebels refused to abide by the accord. A new treaty providing for expansion and development of an autonomous Muslim region on Mindanao was signed Sept. 2, 1996, formally ending a rebellion that had claimed more than 120,000 lives since 1972.

Running as a populist, Joseph (Erap) Estrada, a former movie actor, won the presidential election of May 11, 1998. Charged with bribery and corruption, he was impeached Nov. 13, 2000. When the Supreme Court ruled the presidency vacant Jan. 20, 2001, Vice Pres. Gloria Macapagal Arroyo became president.

As part of the war on terrorism, the U.S. assisted Filipino troops in combating Abu Sayyaf, an Islamic guerrilla group responsible for the deaths of more than 400 civilians since 2000. A resurgence of terrorism on Mindanao in 2003 included bombings at Davao's airport, Mar. 4, and ferry terminal, Apr. 2. A mutiny by some 300 troops in Manila, July 27, was suppressed.

Pres. Arroyo won reelection May 10, 2004. Flooding and mudslides from tropical storms, Nov.-Dec. 2004, left at least 1,060 people dead, more than 560 missing, and 880,000 displaced. A landslide on the island of Leyte, Feb. 17, 2006, killed at least 139 people, with 973 missing and presumed dead. Typhoon Durian slammed into the central Philippines Nov. 30, killing at least 720. Former Pres. Estrada was convicted, Sept. 12, 2007, of taking more than $85 mil in bribes and kickbacks while in office.

Poland
Republic of Poland

People: Population: 38,518,241. **Age distrib.** (%): <15: 15.5; 65+: 13.3. **Pop. density:** 328 per sq mi, 127 per sq km. **Urban:** 62.1%. **Ethnic groups:** Polish 97%. **Principal language:** Polish. **Chief religion:** Roman Catholic 90%.

Geography: Total area: 120,728 sq mi, 312,685 sq km; **Land area:** 117,555 sq mi, 304,465 sq km. **Location:** On Baltic Sea in E central Europe. **Neighbors:** Germany on W; Czech Rep., Slovakia on S; Lithuania, Belarus, Ukraine on E; Russia on N. **Topography:** Mostly lowlands forming part of the Northern European Plain. The Carpathian Mts. along S border rise to 8,200 ft. **Capital:** Warsaw, 1,680,000. **Cities:** Lodz, 789,318; Krakow, 758,544.

Government: Type: Republic. **Head of state:** Pres. Lech Kaczynski; b. June 18, 1949; in office: Dec. 23, 2005. **Head of gov.:** Prime Min. Jaroslaw Kaczynski; b. June 18, 1949; in office: July 14, 2006. **Local divisions:** 16 provinces. **Defense budget:** $5.80 bil. **Active troops:** 141,500.

Economy: Industries: machinery, iron & steel, coal, chemicals, shipbuilding, food proc., glass, beverages, textiles. **Chief crops:** potatoes, fruits, vegetables, wheat. **Natural resources:** coal, sulfur, copper, nat. gas, silver, lead, salt. **Crude oil reserves:** 96.4 mil bbls. **Arable land:** 40%. **Livestock:** cattle: 5.6 mil; chickens: 124.9 mil; goats: 130,369; pigs: 18.9 mil; sheep: 300,802. **Fish catch:** 192,854 metric tons. **Electricity prod.:** 146.2 bil kWh. **Labor force** (2002): agriculture 16.1%, industry 29%, services 54.9%.

Finance: Monetary unit: Zloty (PLN) (Sept. 2007: 2.73 = $1 U.S.). **GDP:** $552.4 bil; **per capita GDP:** $14,300; **GDP growth:** 5.8%. **Imports:** $113.2 bil; Germany 28.8%, Russia 9.6%, Italy 6.3%, Netherlands 5.7%, France 5.4%. **Exports:** $110.7 bil; Germany 27.2%, Italy 6.4%, France 6.3%, UK 5.7%, Czech Rep. 5.6%, Russia 4.3%. **Tourism:** $5.8 bil. **Budget:** $71.3 bil. **Intl. reserves less gold:** $30.82 bil. **Gold:** 3.31 mil oz t. **Consumer prices:** 1.11%.

Transport: Railroad: Length: 14,336 mi. **Motor vehicles:** 12 mil pass. cars; 2.5 mil comm. vehicles. **Civil aviation:** 3.4 bil pass.-mi; 83 airports. **Chief ports:** Gdansk, Gdynia, Swinoujscie, Szczecin.

Communications: TV sets: 387 per 1,000 pop. **Radios:** 522 per 1,000 pop. **Telephone lines:** 11.5 mil. **Daily newspaper circ.:** 101.6 per 1,000 pop. **Internet:** 11 mil users.

Health: Life expect.: 71.2 male; 79.4 female. **Births** (per 1,000 pop.): 9.9. **Deaths** (per 1,000 pop.): 9.9. **Natural inc.:** 0%. **Infant mortality** (per 1,000 live births): 7.1. **AIDS rate:** 0.1%.

Education: Compulsory: ages 7-15. **Literacy:** 99.8%.

Major intl. organizations: UN (FAO, IBRD, ILO, IMF, IMO, WHO, WTO), EU, NATO, OECD, OSCE.

Embassy: 2640 16th St. NW 20009; 234-3800.

Website: www.poland.pl

Slavic tribes in the area were converted to Latin Christianity in the 10th cent. Poland was a great power from the 14th to the 17th centuries. In 3 partitions (1772, 1793, 1795) it was apportioned among Prussia, Russia, and Austria. Overrun by the Austro-German armies in WWI, it declared its independence on Nov. 11, 1918, and was recognized as independent by the Treaty of Versailles, June 28, 1919. Large territories to the east were taken in a war with Russia, 1921.

Germany and the USSR invaded Poland Sept. 1-27, 1939, and divided the country. During the war, some 6 mil Polish citizens, half of them Jews, were killed by the Nazis. With Germany's defeat, a Polish government-in-exile in London was recognized by the U.S., but the USSR pressed the claims of a rival group. The election of 1947 was completely dominated by the Communists.

In compensation for 69,860 sq mi ceded to the USSR, in 1945 Poland received approx. 40,000 sq mi of German territory east of the Oder-Neisse line comprising Silesia, Pomerania, West Prussia, and part of East Prussia.

In 12 years of rule by Stalinists, large estates were abolished, industries nationalized, schools secularized, and Roman Catholic prelates jailed. Farm production fell off. Harsh working conditions caused a riot in Poznan, June 28-29, 1956. A new Politburo, committed to a more independent Polish Communism, was named Oct. 1956, with Wladyslaw Gomulka as first secretary of the party. Collectivization of farms was ended. Gomulka agreed to permit religious liberty and religious publications, provided the church kept out of politics.

In Dec. 1970 workers in port cities rioted because of price rises and new incentive wage rules. On Dec. 20 Gomulka resigned as party leader; he was succeeded by Edward Gierek. The rules were dropped and price rises revoked.

After 2 months of labor turmoil had crippled the country, the Polish government, Aug. 30, 1980, met the demands of striking workers at the Lenin Shipyard, Gdansk. Government concessions included the right to form independent trade unions and the right to strike. By

1981, 9.5 mil workers had joined the independent trade union (Solidarity). As Solidarity's demands grew bolder, the government, spurred by fear of Soviet intervention, imposed martial law Dec. 13. Lech Walesa and other Solidarity leaders were arrested.

On Apr. 5, 1989, an accord was reached between the government and opposition factions on political and economic reforms, including free elections. Candidates endorsed by Solidarity swept the parliamentary elections, June 4. Lech Walesa became president Dec. 22, 1990.

A radical economic program designed to transform the economy into a free-market system led to inflation and unemployment. In Sept. 1993, former Communists and other leftists won a majority in the lower house of Parliament. Walesa lost to a former Communist, Aleksander Kwasniewski, in a presidential runoff election, Nov. 19, 1995.

A new constitution was approved by referendum May 25, 1997. Flooding in July caused more than $1 bil in property damage. Solidarity won parliamentary elections held Sept. 21. Poland became a full member of NATO, Mar. 12, 1999. Pres. Kwasniewski was reelected Oct. 8, 2000. Former Communists won a plurality in parliamentary voting Sept. 23, 2001; in elections 4 years later, however, a center-right coalition prevailed.

Poland entered the European Union May 1, 2004. The country, a close U.S. ally, had about 900 troops in Iraq as of mid-2007; more than 1,100 Polish troops were serving in Afghanistan.

Lech Kaczynski, the conservative mayor of Warsaw, won a presidential runoff election Oct. 23, 2005. In July 2006 he appointed his identical twin brother Jaroslaw as prime min. Poland's governing coalition fell apart in 2007, and early elections were scheduled for Oct. 21.

Portugal
Portuguese Republic
People: Population: 10,642,836. **Age distrib.** (%): <15: 16.5; 65+: 17.3. **Pop. density:** 300 per sq mi, 116 per sq km. **Urban:** 57.6%. **Ethnic groups:** Mainly Portuguese. **Principal languages:** Portuguese, Mirandese (both official). **Chief religion:** Roman Catholic 84%.

Geography: Total area: 35,672 sq mi, 92,391 sq km; **Land area:** 35,502 sq mi, 91,951 sq km. **Location:** At SW extreme of Europe. **Neighbors:** Spain on N, E. **Topography:** Portugal N of Tajus R., which bisects country NE-SW, is mountainous, cool and rainy. To the S there are drier, rolling plains, and a warm climate. **Capital:** Lisbon, 2,761,000. **Cities (urban agg.):** Porto, 1,309,000.

Government: Type: Republic. **Head of state:** Pres. Aníbal Cavaco Silva; b. July 15, 1939; in office: Mar. 9, 2006. **Head of gov.:** Prime Min. José Sócrates Carvalho Pinto de Sousa; b. Sept. 6, 1957; in office: Mar. 12, 2005. **Local divisions:** 18 districts, 2 autonomous regions. **Defense budget:** $2.44 bil. **Active troops:** 43,960.

Economy: Industries: textiles, footwear, wood and paper products, metalworking, oil refining, chemicals, fish proc, wine, tourism. **Chief crops:** grain, potatoes, tomatoes, olives, grapes. **Natural resources:** fish, cork, tungsten, iron ore, uranium ore, marble, hydropower. **Arable land:** 17%. **Livestock:** cattle: 1.4 mil; chickens: 36 mil; goats: 551,310; pigs: 2.3 mil; sheep: 3.6 mil. **Fish catch:** 218,242 metric tons. **Electricity prod.:** 43.7 bil kWh. **Labor force** (2001 est.): agriculture 10%, industry 30%, services 60%.

Finance: Monetary unit: Euro (EUR) (Sept. 2007: 0.72 = $1 U.S.). **GDP:** $210.1 bil; **per capita GDP:** $19,800; **GDP growth:** 1.3%. **Imports:** $12.4 bil; France 13.3%, Japan 10.1%, U.S. 9.3%, Italy 8.9%, Germany 7.8%, UK 6.2%, Saudi Arabia 5.7%, S. Korea 4.5%. **Exports:** $33.3 bil; Japan 39.8%, S. Korea 18.6%, Singapore 6.4%, Thailand 4.1%. **Tourism:** $7.9 bil. **Budget:** $93.1 bil. **Intl. reserves less gold:** $1.37 bil. **Gold:** 12.3 mil oz t. **Consumer prices:** 2.74%.

Transport: Railroad: Length: 1,771 mi. **Motor vehicles:** 6 mil pass. cars; 2 mil comm. vehicles. **Civil aviation:** 8.4 bil pass.-mi; 43 airports. **Chief ports:** Leixoes, Lisbon, Setubal.

Communications: TV sets: 567 per 1,000 pop. **Radios:** 306 per 1,000 pop. **Telephone lines:** 4.2 mil. **Daily newspaper circ.:** 102.4 per 1,000 pop. **Internet:** 3.2 mil users.

Health: Life expect.: 74.6 male; 81.4 female. **Births** (per 1,000 pop.): 10.6. **Deaths** (per 1,000 pop.): 10.6. **Natural inc.:** 0.003%. **Infant mortality** (per 1,000 live births): 4.9. **AIDS rate:** 0.4%.

Education: Compulsory: ages 6-14. **Literacy:** 93.8%.

Major intl. organizations: UN (FAO, IBRD, ILO, IMF, IMO, WHO, WTO), EU, NATO, OECD, OSCE.

Embassy: 2125 Kalorama Rd. NW 20008; 328-8610.

Website: www.portugal.gov.pt

Portugal, an independent state since the 12th cent., was a kingdom until a revolution in 1910 drove out King Manoel II and a republic was proclaimed. From 1932 a strong, repressive government was headed by Premier Antonio de Oliveira Salazar. Illness forced his retirement in Sept. 1968.

On Apr. 25, 1974, the government was seized by a military junta led by Gen. Antonio de Spinola, who became president. The new government reached agreements providing independence for Guinea-Bissau, Mozambique, Cape Verde Islands, Angola, and São Tomé and Príncipe. Banks, insurance companies, and other industries were nationalized.

Parliament approved, June 1, 1989, a program to denationalize industries. Portugal returned Macao to China on Dec. 20, 1999. With the economy lagging, opposition Socialists won a majority in elections Feb. 20, 2005. The conservative Aníbal Cavaco Silva, a

former prime min. (1985-95). defeated two Socialist candidates to win the presidential election of Jan. 22, 2006. After a referendum to ease abortion restrictions failed Feb. 11, 2007, because of low turnout, parliament enacted a similar measure.

Azores Islands, in the Atlantic, 740 mi W of Portugal, have an area of 868 sq mi and a pop. (1993 est.) of 238,000. A 1951 agreement gave the U.S. rights to use defense facilities in the Azores. The **Madeira Islands**, 350 mi off the NW coast of Africa, have an area of 306 sq mi and a pop. (1993 est.) of 437,312. Both groups were offered partial autonomy in 1976.

Qatar
State of Qatar
People: Population: 907,229. **Age distrib.** (%): <15: 23.1; 65+: 4. **Pop. density:** 205 per sq mi, 79 per sq km. **Urban:** 95.4%. **Ethnic groups:** Arab 40%, Pakistani 18%, Indian 18%, Iranian 10%. **Principal languages:** Arabic (official), English. **Chief religions:** Muslim 78%, Christian 9%.

Geography: Total area: 4,416 sq mi, 11,437 sq km; **Land area:** 4,416 sq mi, 11,437 sq km. **Location:** Middle East, occupying peninsula on W coast of Persian Gulf. **Neighbors:** Saudi Arabia on S. **Topography:** Mostly flat desert with some limestone ridges; vegetation of any kind is scarce. **Capital:** Doha, 357,000.

Government: Type: Traditional monarchy. **Head of state:** Emir Sheikh Hamad bin Khalifa al Thani; b. 1952; in office: June 27, 1995. **Head of gov.:** Prime Min. Sheikh Hamad bin Jassim bin Jabr al-Thani; b. 1959; in office: Apr. 3, 2007. **Local divisions:** 9 municipalities. **Defense budget:** $2.33 bil. **Active troops:** 12,400.

Economy: Industries: oil prod. & refining, fertilizers, petrochems., constr. materials. **Chief crops:** fruits, vegetables. **Natural resources:** oil, nat. gas, fish. **Crude oil reserves:** 15.2 bil bbls. **Arable land:** 2%. **Livestock:** cattle: 6,565; chickens: 4.5 mil; goats: 152,722; sheep: 111,550. **Fish catch:** 13,946 metric tons. **Electricity prod.:** 13.5 bil kWh. **Labor force:** NA.

Finance: Monetary unit: Riyal (QAR) (Sept. 2007: 3.64 = $1 U.S.). **GDP:** $26.4 bil; **per capita GDP:** $29,800; **GDP growth:** 7.1%. **Imports:** $12.4 bil; France 13.3%, Japan 10.1%, U.S. 9.3%, Italy 8.9%, Germany 7.8%, UK 6.2%, Saudi Arabia 5.7%, S. Korea 4.5%. **Exports:** $33.3 bil; Japan 39.8%, S. Korea 18.6%, Singapore 6.4%, Thailand 4.1%. **Tourism:** $498 mil. **Budget:** $16.9 bil. **Intl. reserves less gold:** $3.58 bil. **Gold:** 20,000 oz t. **Consumer prices:** 11.84%.

Transport: Motor vehicles: 230,100 pass. cars; 109,700 comm. vehicles. **Civil aviation:** 5 bil pass.-mi; 3 airports. **Chief port:** Doha.

Communications: TV sets: 866 per 1,000 pop. **Radios:** 450 per 1,000 pop. **Telephone lines:** 228,300. **Internet:** 289,900 users.

Health: Life expect.: 71.6 male; 76.8 female. **Births** (per 1,000 pop.): 15.6. **Deaths** (per 1,000 pop.): 4.8. **Natural inc.:** 1.07%. **Infant mortality** (per 1,000 live births): 17.5. **AIDS rate:** NA.

Education: Compulsory: ages 6-17. **Literacy:** 89%.

Major intl. organizations: UN (FAO, IBRD, ILO, IMF, IMO, WHO, WTO), AL, OPEC.

Embassy: 2555 M St. NW 20037; 274-1600.

Website: english.mofa.gov.qa

Qatar was under Bahrain's control until the Ottoman Turks took power, 1872 to 1915. In a treaty signed 1916, Qatar gave Great Britain responsibility for its defense and foreign relations. After Britain announced it would remove its military forces from the Persian Gulf area by the end of 1971, Qatar sought a federation with other British-protected states in the area; this failed and Qatar declared itself independent, Sept. 1, 1971. Crown Prince Hamad bin Khalifa ath-Thani ousted his father, Emir Khalifa bin Hamad ath-Thani, June 27, 1995. In municipal elections held Mar. 8, 1999, women participated for the 1st time as candidates and voters.

Oil and natural gas revenues give Qatar a per capita income among the world's highest. Military ties with the U.S. have been expanding; Camp As-Sayliyah, a base near Doha, served as a command center for the U.S.-led invasion of Iraq, Mar. 2003. The influential Arab news network Al-Jazeera is based in Qatar.

Romania
People: Population: 22,276,056. **Age distrib.** (%): <15: 15.6; 65+: 14.7. **Pop. density:** 250 per sq mi, 97 per sq km. **Urban:** 53.7%. **Ethnic groups:** Romanian 90%, Hungarian 7%, Roma 1%. **Principal languages:** Romanian (official), Hungarian, Romani. **Chief religions:** Romanian Orthodox 87%, Protestant 8%, Roman Catholic 5%.

Geography: Total area: 91,699 sq mi, 237,500 sq km; **Land area:** 88,935 sq mi, 230,340 sq km. **Location:** SE Europe, on the Black Sea. **Neighbors:** Moldova on E, Ukraine on N, Hungary and Serbia on W, Bulgaria on S. **Topography:** The Carpathian Mts. encase the north-central Transylvanian plateau. There are wide plains S and E of the mountains, through which flow the lower reaches of the rivers of Danube system. **Capital:** Bucharest, 1,934,000.

Government: Type: Republic. **Head of state:** Pres. Traian Basescu; b. Nov. 4, 1951; in office: Dec. 20, 2004. **Head of gov.:** Prime Min. Calin Constantin Anton Popescu-Tariceanu; b. Jan. 14, 1952; in office: Dec. 29, 2004. **Local divisions:** 41 counties and Bucharest. **Defense budget:** $2.41 bil. **Active troops:** 69,600.

Economy: Industries: textiles & footwear, light machinery, auto assembly, mining, timber. **Chief crops:** wheat, corn, barley, sugar beets, sunflower seed, potatoes, grapes. **Natural resources:** oil, timber, nat. gas, coal, iron ore, salt, hydropower. **Crude oil reserves:** 600 mil bbls. **Arable land:** 39%. **Livestock:** cattle: 2.9 mil; chickens: 86.6 mil; goats: 687,000; pigs: 6.6 mil; sheep: 7.6 mil. **Fish catch:** 13,352 metric tons. **Electricity prod.:** 56.9 bil kWh. **Labor force** (2004): agriculture 31.6%, industry 30.7%, services 37.7%.

Finance: Monetary unit: New Leu (RON) (Sept. 2007: 2.43 = $1 U.S.). **GDP:** $202.2 bil; **per capita GDP:** $9,100; **GDP growth:** 7.7%. **Imports:** $46.5 bil; Germany 16.6%, Italy 12.9%, China 11.3%, Russia 6.1%, Hungary 5.8%, France 5.3%, Austria 4.9%, Turkey 4.3%. **Exports:** $33 bil; Italy 16.1%, Germany 15.3%, Turkey 7.8%, Hungary 6.4%, France 6.3%, Austria 4.7%, UK 4.5%. **Tourism:** $1.1 bil. **Budget:** $39.1 bil. **Intl. reserves less gold:** $18.66 bil. **Gold:** 3.37 mil oz t. **Consumer prices:** 6.58%.

Transport: Railroad: Length: 7,074 mi. **Motor vehicles:** 3.2 mil pass. cars; 526,000 comm. vehicles. **Civil aviation:** 1.1 bil pass.-mi; 25 airports. **Chief ports:** Braila, Constanta.

Communications: TV sets: 312 per 1,000 pop. **Radios:** 335 per 1,000 pop. **Telephone lines:** 4.2 mil. **Internet:** 7 mil users.

Health: Life expect.: 68.4 male; 75.6 female. **Births** (per 1,000 pop.): 10.7. **Deaths** (per 1,000 pop.): 11.8. **Natural inc.:** −0.11%. **Infant mortality** (per 1,000 live births): 24.6. **AIDS rate:** <0.1%.

Education: Compulsory: ages 7-14. **Literacy:** 97.3%.

Major intl. organizations: UN (FAO, IBRD, ILO, IMF, IMO, WHO, WTO), NATO, OSCE.

Embassy: 1607 23rd St. NW 20008; 332-4846.

Website: www.guv.ro

Romania's earliest known people merged with invading Proto-Thracians, preceding by centuries the Dacians. The Dacian kingdom was occupied by Rome, 106-271 CE; people and language were Romanized. The principalities of Wallachia and Moldavia, dominated by Turkey, were united in 1859, became Romania in 1861, and gained recognition as an independent kingdom, 1881.

After WWI, Romania acquired Bessarabia, Bukovina, Transylvania, and Banat. In 1940 it ceded Bessarabia and Northern Bukovina to the USSR, part of southern Dobrudja to Bulgaria, and northern Transylvania to Hungary. In 1941, Prem. Marshal Ion Antonescu led Romania in support of Germany against the USSR. In 1944 he was overthrown, and Romania joined the Allies. After occupation by Soviet troops, a People's Republic was proclaimed, Dec. 30, 1947.

On Aug. 22, 1965, a new constitution proclaimed Romania a Socialist Republic. Pres. Nicolae Ceausescu maintained an independent course in foreign affairs, but his domestic policies were repressive. All industry was state-owned, and state farms and cooperatives owned almost all arable land. Ceausescu's security forces fired on antigovernment demonstrators in Dec. 1989, killing hundreds, but when the army sided with the protesters, his regime fell. Ceausescu and his wife were captured and, following a trial in which they were found guilty of genocide, were executed Dec. 25, 1989.

Former Communists dominated the government in succeeding years. A new constitution providing for a multiparty system took effect Dec. 8, 1991. Many of Romania's state-owned companies were privatized in 1996. The former Communists lost in elections Nov. 3 and Nov. 17, 1996, but made a comeback in balloting Nov. 26 and Dec. 10, 2000. Opposition leader Traian Basescu, the mayor of Bucharest, won a presidential runoff vote, Dec. 12, 2004. Romania became a full NATO member in 2004 and entered the European Union Jan. 1, 2007.

Floods in Jul.-Aug. 2005 left more than 50 people dead. Parliament voted Apr. 19, 2007, to suspend Pres. Basescu, as part of an ongoing political dispute, but 75% of voters in a referendum May 19 refused to support his ouster. Romania, a firm U.S. ally, had about 400 troops in Iraq and 750 in Afghanistan in mid-2007.

Russia
Russian Federation

People: Population: 141,377,752. **Age distrib.** (%): <15: 14.6; 65+: 14.4. **Pop. density:** 22 per sq mi, 8 per sq km. **Urban:** 73%. **Ethnic groups:** Russian 80%, Tatar 4%, Ukrainian 2%. **Principal languages:** Russian (official), many others. **Chief religions:** Russian Orthodox, Muslim.

Geography: Total area: 6,592,772 sq mi, 17,075,200 sq km; **Land area:** 6,562,116 sq mi, 16,995,800 sq km., more than 76% of total area of the former USSR and the largest country in the world. **Location:** Stretches from E Europe across N Asia to the Pacific O. **Neighbors:** Finland, Norway, Estonia, Latvia, Belarus, Ukraine on W; Georgia, Azerbaijan, Kazakhstan, China, Mongolia, N. Korea on S; Kaliningrad exclave bordered by Poland on the S, Lithuania on the N and E. **Topography:** Every type of climate except distinctly tropical. The European portion is a low plain, grassy in S, wooded in N, with Ural Mts. on E, and Caucasus Mts. on S. Urals stretch N-S for 2,500 mi. The Asiatic portion is a vast plain, with mountains on S and in E; tundra covers extreme N, with forest belt below; plains, marshes are in W, desert in SW. **Capital:** Moscow, 10,654,000. **Cities** (urban aggr.): St. Petersburg, 5,312,000; Nizhniy Novgorod, 1,289,000; Novosibirsk, 1,425,000.

Government: Type: Federal republic. **Head of state:** Pres. Vladimir Putin; b. Oct. 7, 1952; in office: May 7, 2000. **Head of gov.:** Prime Min. Viktor Zubkov; b. Sept. 15, 1941; in office: Sept. 14, 2007. **Local divisions:** 7 federal districts incl. 49 provinces, 21 autonomous republics, 6 territories, 1 autonomous region, 10 autonomous districts, 2 federal cities. **Defense budget:** $24.9 bil. **Active troops:** 1,027,000.

Economy: Industries: coal, oil, gas, chemicals, metals; light machinery, shipbuilding; transp., communic. equip., agric. machinery, constr. equip., electric power equip., medical & scientific instruments, consumer durables, textiles. **Chief crops:** grain, sugar beets, sunflower seed, vegetables, fruits. **Natural resources:** oil, nat. gas, coal, minerals, timber. **Crude oil reserve:** 60 bil bbls. **Arable land:** 7%. **Livestock:** cattle: 21.5 mil; chickens: 343 mil; goats: 2.1 mil; pigs: 13.5 mil; sheep: 16.1 mil. **Fish catch:** 3,305,698 metric tons. **Electricity prod.:** 904.4 bil kWh. **Labor force** (2005 est.): agriculture 10.8%, industry 29.1%, services 60.1%.

Finance: Monetary unit: Ruble (RUB) (Sept. 2007: 25.34 = $1 U.S.). **GDP:** $1.7 tril; **per capita GDP:** $12,200; **GDP growth:** 6.7%. **Imports:** $171.5 bil; Germany 13.9%, China 9.7%, Ukraine 7%, Japan 5.9%, S. Korea 5.1%, U.S. 4.8%, France 4.4%, Italy 4.3%. **Exports:** $317.6 bil; Netherlands 12.3%, Italy 8.6%, Germany 8.4%, China 5.4%, Ukraine 5.1%, Turkey 4.9%, Switzerland 4.1%. **Tourism:** $5.5 bil. **Budget:** $157.3 bil. **Intl. reserves less gold:** $196.47 bil. **Gold:** 12.91 mil oz t. **Consumer prices:** 9.68%.

Transport: Railroad: Length: 54,157 mi. **Motor vehicles:** 24.1 mil pass. cars; 4.5 mil comm. vehicles. **Civil aviation:** 33.5 bil pass.-mi; 616 airports. **Chief ports:** Murmansk, Nakhodka, Novorossiysk, Rostov-na-Donu, St. Petersburg, Vanino, Vostochnyy.

Communications: TV sets: 421 per 1,000 pop. **Radios:** 417 per 1,000 pop. **Telephone lines:** 40.1 mil. **Internet:** 25.7 mil users.

Health: Life expect.: 59.1 male; 73 female. **Births** (per 1,000 pop.): 10.9. **Deaths** (per 1,000 pop.): 16. **Natural inc.:** −0.51%. **Infant mortality** (per 1,000 live births): 11.1. **AIDS rate:** 1.1%.

Education: Compulsory: ages 6-15. **Literacy:** 99.4%.

Major intl. organizations: UN (FAO, IBRD, ILO, IMF, IMO, WHO), APEC, CIS, OSCE.

Embassy: 2650 Wisconsin Ave. NW 20007; 298-5700.

Website: www.gov.ru

History. Slavic tribes began migrating into Russia from the west in the 5th cent. First Russian state, founded by Scandinavian chieftains, was established in the 9th cent., centering in Novgorod and Kiev. In the 13th cent. the Mongols overran the country. It recovered under the grand dukes and princes of Muscovy, or Moscow, and by 1480 freed itself from the Mongols. Ivan the Terrible was first formally proclaimed Tsar (1547). Peter the Great (1682-1725) extended the domain and, in 1721, founded the Russian Empire.

Western ideas and the beginnings of modernization spread through the huge Russian empire in the 19th and early 20th centuries. But political evolution failed to keep pace.

Military reverses in the 1905 war with Japan and in WWI led to the breakdown of the Tsarist regime. The 1917 Revolution began in March with a series of sporadic strikes for higher wages by factory workers. A provisional democratic government under Prince Georgi Lvov was established but was quickly followed in May by the second provisional government, led by Alexander Kerensky. The Kerensky government and the freely-elected Constituent Assembly were overthrown in a Communist coup led by Vladimir Ilyich Lenin Nov. 7.

Soviet Union

Lenin's death Jan. 21, 1924, resulted in an internal power struggle from which Joseph Stalin eventually emerged on top. Stalin secured his position at first by exiling opponents, but from the 1930s to 1953, he resorted to a series of "purge" trials, mass executions, and mass exiles to work camps. These measures resulted in millions of deaths, according to most estimates.

Germany and the Soviet Union signed a non-aggression pact Aug. 1939; Germany launched a massive invasion of the Soviet Union, June 1941. A notable heroic episode was the "900 days" siege of Leningrad (now St. Petersburg), lasting to Jan. 1944, and causing a million deaths; the city was never taken. Russian winter counterthrusts, 1941-42 and 1942-43, stopped the German advance. Turning point was the failure of German troops to take and hold Stalingrad (now Volgograd), Sept. 1942 to Feb. 1943. With British and U.S. Lend-Lease aid and sustaining great casualties, the Russians drove the German forces from eastern Europe and the Balkans in the next 2 years.

After Stalin died, Mar. 5, 1953, Nikita Khrushchev was elected first secretary of the Central Committee. In 1956 he condemned Stalin and "de-Stalinization" began.

Under Khrushchev the open antagonism of Poles and Hungarians toward domination by Moscow was brutally suppressed in 1956. He advocated peaceful co-existence with the capitalist countries, but continued arming the Soviet Union with nuclear weapons. He aided the Cuban revolution under Fidel Castro but withdrew Soviet missiles from Cuba during confrontation by U.S. Pres. Kennedy, Sept.-Oct. 1962. Khrushchev was suddenly deposed, Oct. 1964, and replaced by Leonid I. Brezhnev.

In Aug. 1968 Russian, Polish, East German, Hungarian, and Bulgarian military forces invaded Czechoslovakia to put a curb on liberalization policies of the Czech government.

Massive Soviet military aid to North Vietnam in the late 1960s and early 1970s helped assure Communist victories throughout Indo-China. Soviet arms aid and advisers were sent to several African countries in the 1970s.

In Dec. 1979, Soviet forces entered Afghanistan to support that government against rebels. In Apr. 1988, the Soviets agreed to withdraw their troops, ending a futile 8-year war.

Mikhail Gorbachev was chosen gen. secy. of the Communist Party, Mar. 1985. He held 4 summit meetings with U.S. Pres. Ronald Reagan. In 1987 he initiated a program of political and eco nomic reforms, through openness (glasnost) and restructuring (perestroika). Gorbachev faced economic problems as well as ethnic and nationalist unrest in the republics. An apparent coup by Communist hardliners Aug. 1991, was foiled with help from the pres. of the Russian Republic, Boris Yeltsin. On Aug. 24, Gorbachev resigned as leader of the Communist Party. Several republics declared their independence, including Russia, Ukraine, and Kazakhstan. On Aug. 29, the Soviet Parliament voted to suspend all activities of the Communist Party.

The Soviet Union officially broke up Dec. 26, 1991. The Soviet hammer and sickle flying over the Kremlin was lowered and replaced by the flag of Russia, ending the domination of the Communist Party over all areas of national life since 1917.

Russian Federation

Led by Pres. Yeltsin, Russia took steps toward privatization; immediate effects were inflation and a severe economic downturn. In June 1992, Yeltsin and U.S. Pres. George H. W. Bush agreed to massive arms reductions. A power struggle between Yeltsin and the Congress of People's Deputies, which was dominated by conservatives and former Communists, reached a climax Oct. 3, 1993, when anti-Yeltsin forces attacked some facilities in Moscow and broke into the Parliament building. Yeltsin ordered the army to seize the building; about 140 people were killed in the fighting.

Yeltsin remained in power, and in a referendum Dec. 12, 1993, a new constitution was approved. In Dec. 1994 the Russian government sent troops into the breakaway republic of Chechnya. Grozny, the Chechen capital, fell in Feb. 1995 after heavy fighting, but Chechen rebels continued to resist.

Despite poor health, Yeltsin won a presidential runoff election over a Communist opponent, July 3, 1996. On Aug. 14, after rebels embarrassed the Russian military by retaking Grozny, Yeltsin gave his security chief, Alexander Lebed, broad powers to negotiate an end to the Chechnya war. Lebed and Chechen leaders signed a peace accord Aug. 31. On Oct. 17, Yeltsin dismissed Lebed for insubordination. Russian troops remaining in Chechnya were pulled out Jan. 1997. On May 27, Yeltsin signed a "founding act" increasing cooperation with NATO and paving the way for NATO to admit Eastern European nations.

Russia's economic crisis deepened in the late 1990s, heightening tensions between Yeltsin and parliament. Russia moved forcibly in Aug. 1999 to suppress Islamic rebels in Dagestan; the conflict soon spread to neighboring Chechnya, where Russia launched a full-scale assault. A series of 5 bombings in Moscow and Dagestan, which the Russian government attributed to Chechen rebels, killed over 300 people.

Yeltsin unexpectedly resigned Dec. 31, 1999, naming Prime Min. Vladimir Putin as his interim successor. Russian troops took control of Grozny in early Feb. 2000. Putin defeated 10 opponents in a presidential election Mar. 26. The Russian nuclear submarine *Kursk* sank in the Barents Sea Aug. 12, killing 118 sailors.

As Russian forces continued their campaign against Islamic separatists in Chechnya, some 50 Chechen guerrillas seized more than 800 hostages in a Moscow theater, Oct. 23, 2002; 129 hostages and nearly all the guerrillas were killed Oct. 26 when Russian special forces used knockout gas in retaking the theater. Russia, which supported the U.S.-led war in Afghanistan in 2001, sided with France and Germany in blocking UN Security Council endorsement of the U.S.-led invasion of Iraq, Mar. 2003.

Putin's allies won legislative elections, Dec. 7, 2003, and the president was reelected Mar. 14, 2004, with 71% of the vote; international election monitors cited flaws on both occasions. Putin blamed Chechen terrorists for a blast on a Moscow subway car, Feb. 6, that killed at least 39 people. A bomb in Grozny, May 9, killed Chechnya's pro-Moscow president, Akhmad Kadyrov, and at least 6 others. Putin's choice for the Chechen presidency, Maj. Gen. Alu Alkhanov, was elected Aug. 29.

The Chechnya conflict unleashed a wave of terrorism elsewhere during Aug.-Sept. 2004. After taking off the night of Aug. 24 from Moscow's Domodedovo airport, 2 passenger planes exploded in midair, killing 90 people. A suicide bombing in a Moscow subway station Aug. 31 left 11 dead. Chechen rebels Sept. 1 seized control of a school in Beslan, North Ossetia, taking more than 1,100 hostages; Russian troops stormed the school Sept. 3; in the end more than 330 people died, including 186 children. Putin cited the terrorist threat Sept. 13 in proposing a government overhaul that would tighten his control over parliament and regional officeholders.

On Nov. 5, 2004, Russia ratified the Kyoto Protocol, which aims to curb greenhouse gas emissions and global warming. Russian forces killed Chechen rebel leader Aslan Maskhadov, Mar. 8, 2005. Mikhail Khodorkovsky, an oil tycoon whose political agenda had rivaled Putin's, was convicted of fraud and tax evasion, May 31, and sentenced to 9 years in prison. Chechen guerrilla leader Shamil Basayev, who had organized the terrorist attack at Beslan, was killed July 10, 2006. Another Putin opponent, former Russian agent Alexander Litvinenko, was poisoned with radioactive polonium-210 and died in London Nov. 23.

With Russia's economy rising and Putin's popularity soaring because of an oil boom, the nation took a tougher stance toward the West. Putin announced Apr. 26, 2007, that Russia would suspend compliance with a treaty on conventional weapons in Europe. Russia also opposed U.S.-backed plans for a missile-defense system

partly based in Poland and the Czech Rep. Putin shook up his cabinet Sept. 12, in preparation for parliamentary elections, scheduled for Dec. 2; he was constitutionally barred from running in presidential elections, Mar. 2, 2008.

Rwanda
Republic of Rwanda

People: Population: 9,907,509. **Age distrib.** (%): <15: 41.9; 65+: 2.5. **Pop. density:** 1,029 per sq mi, 397 per sq km. **Urban:** 19.3%. **Ethnic groups:** Hutu 84%, Tutsi 15%. **Principal languages:** Kinyarwanda, French, English (all official); Swahili. **Chief religions:** Roman Catholic 57%, Protestant 26%, Adventist 11%, Muslim 5%.

Geography: Total area: 10,169 sq mi, 26,338 sq km; **Land area:** 9,632 sq mi, 24,948 sq km. **Location:** In E central Africa. **Neighbors:** Uganda on N, Congo (formerly Zaire) on W, Burundi on S, Tanzania on E. **Topography:** Grassy uplands and hills cover most of country, with chain of volcanoes in the NW. The source of the Nile R. has been located in headwaters of the Kagera (Akagera) R., SW of Kigali. **Capital:** Kigali, 779,000.

Government: Type: Republic. **Head of state:** Pres. Paul Kagame; b. Oct. 23, 1957; in office: Apr. 22, 2000 (de facto from Mar. 24). **Head of govt.:** Prime Min. Bernard Makuza; b. 1961; in office: Mar. 8, 2000. **Local divisions:** 12 prefectures subdivided into 155 communes. **Defense budget:** $71 mil. **Active troops:** 33,000.

Economy: Industries: cement, agric. products. **Chief crops:** coffee, tea, pyrethrum (insecticide made from chrysanthemums), bananas. **Natural resources:** gold, tin, tungsten, methane, hydropower. **Crude oil reserves:** NA. **Arable land:** 46%. **Livestock:** cattle: 1 mil; chickens: 2 mil; goats: 1.3 mil; pigs: 346,922; sheep: 464,330. **Fish catch:** 8,186 metric tons. **Electricity prod.:** 100 mil kWh. **Labor force:** agriculture 90%, industry and services 10%.

Finance: Monetary unit: Franc (RWF) (Sept. 2007: 547.14 = $1 U.S.). **GDP:** $13.7 bil; **per capita GDP:** $1,600; **GDP growth:** 5.8%. **Imports:** $390.4 mil; Kenya 19.7%, Germany 7.8%, Uganda 6.9%, Belgium 5%. **Exports:** $135.4 mil; China 10.2%, Germany 9.6%, U.S. 4.3%. **Tourism:** $44 mil. **Budget:** $654 mil. **Intl. reserves less gold:** $292 mil. **Consumer prices:** 8.88%.

Transport: Motor vehicles: 10,700 pass. cars; 16,300 comm. vehicles. **Civil aviation:** 4 airports. **Chief ports:** Cyangugu, Gisenyi, Kibuye.

Communications: TV sets: .09 per 1,000 pop. **Radios:** 101 per 1,000 pop. **Telephone lines:** 16,500. **Daily newspaper circ.:** 0.1 per 1,000 pop. **Internet:** 65,000 users.

Health: Life expect.: 47.9 male; 50.2 female. **Births** (per 1,000 pop.): 40.2. **Deaths** (per 1,000 pop.): 14.9. **Natural inc.:** 2.53%. **Infant mortality** (per 1,000 live births): 85.3. **AIDS rate:** 3.1%.

Education: Compulsory: ages 7-12. **Literacy:** 64.9%.

Major intl. organizations: UN (FAO, IBRD, ILO, IMF, WHO, WTO), AU.

Embassy: 1714 New Hampshire Ave. NW 20009; 232-2882. **Website:** www.gov.rw

For centuries, the Tutsi (an extremely tall people) dominated the Hutu (90% of the population). A civil war broke out in 1959 and Tutsi power was ended. Many Tutsi went into exile. Rwanda, which had been part of the Belgian UN trusteeship of Rwanda-Urundi, became independent July 1, 1962.

In 1963 Tutsi exiles invaded in an unsuccessful coup; a large-scale massacre of Tutsi followed. Rivalries among Hutu led to a bloodless coup July 1973 in which Juvénal Habyarimana took power. After an invasion and coup attempt by Tutsi exiles in 1990, a multiparty democracy was established.

Renewed ethnic strife led to an Aug. 1993 peace accord between the government and rebels of the Tutsi-led Rwandan Patriotic Front (RPF). But after Habyarimana and Burundi Pres. Cyprien Ntaryamira were killed Apr. 6, 1994, in a suspicious plane crash, massive violence broke out. More than 1 mil may have died in massacres, mostly of Tutsi by Hutu militias, and in civil warfare as the RPF sought power. About 2 mil Tutsi and Hutu fled to camps in Zaire (now Congo) and other countries, where many died of cholera and other natural causes. French troops under a UN mandate moved into SW Rwanda June 23 to establish a so-called safe zone. The RPF claimed victory, installing a government in July led by a moderate Hutu president. French troops pulled out Aug. 22. A UN peacekeeping mission ended Mar. 8, 1996, but the Rwandan government and a UN-sponsored tribunal in Tanzania continued to gather evidence against those responsible for genocide. More than 1 mil refugees (mostly Hutu) flooded back to Rwanda from Tanzania and Zaire in Nov. and Dec. 1996.

Firing squads in Rwanda on Apr. 24, 1998, executed 22 people convicted of genocide. Former Prime Min. Jean Kambanda pleaded guilty May 1 before the UN tribunal and received a life sentence Sept. 4, 1998. Maj. Gen. Paul Kagame, leader of the RPF, became Rwanda's 1st Tutsi president Apr. 22, 2000.

Rwandans in 2003 approved a new constitution, May 26, reelected Pres. Kagame, Aug. 25, and chose a new parliament, Sept. 29-30. Former Pres. Bizimungu was sentenced to 15 years for embezzlement, June 2004; he was pardoned by Kagame and released, Apr. 6, 2007. Rwanda cut diplomatic ties with France Nov. 24, 2006, after a French judge linked Kagame and his close aides to the deaths in 1994 of Habyarimana and Ntaryamira.

Saint Kitts and Nevis
Federation of Saint Kitts and Nevis

People: Population: 39,349. **Age distrib.** (%): <15: 27.2; 65+: 7.9. **Pop. density:** 390 per sq mi, 151 per sq km. **Urban:** 32.2%. **Ethnic group:** Black, British, Portuguese, Lebanese. **Principal language:** English. **Chief religions:** Anglican, other Protestant, Roman Catholic.

Geography: Total area: 101 sq mi, 261 sq km; **Land area:** 101 sq mi, 261 sq km. **Location:** In N part of the Leeward group of Lesser Antilles in E Caribbean Sea. **Neighbors:** Antigua and Barbuda to E. **Topography:** St. Kitts has forested volcanic slopes; Nevis rises from beaches to central peak. Climate is tropical moderated by sea breezes. **Capital** (2001): Basseterre, 13,033.

Government: Type: Constitutional monarchy. **Head of state:** Queen Elizabeth II, represented by Gov.-Gen. Sir Cuthbert M. Sebastian; b. Oct. 22, 1921; in office: Jan. 1, 1996. **Head of gov.:** Prime Min. Denzil Llewellyn Douglas; b. Jan. 14, 1953; in office: July 7, 1995. **Local divisions:** 14 parishes.

Economy: Industries: sugar proc., tourism, cotton, salt, copra, clothing, footwear, beverages. **Chief crops:** sugarcane, rice, yams, vegetables, bananas. **Arable land:** 19%. **Livestock:** cattle: 4,800; chickens: 70,000; goats: 16,000; pigs: 2,000; sheep: 12,500. **Fish catch:** 450 metric tons. **Electricity prod.:** 130 mil kWh. **Labor force:** NA.

Finance: Monetary unit: East Caribbean Dollar (XCD) (Sept. 2007: 2.67 = $1 U.S.). **GDP:** $726 mil; **per capita GDP** (2005 est.): $8,200; **GDP growth** (2005 est.): 4.9%. **Imports** (2004 est.): $405 mil; U.S. 49.7%, Trinidad and Tobago 13.3%, UK 4.5%. **Exports** (2004 est.): $70 mil; U.S. 64.7%, Canada 9.8%, Netherlands 6.9%. **Tourism:** $107 mil. **Budget** (2003 est.): $128.2 mil. **Intl. reserves less gold:** $59 mil. **Consumer prices** (2005): 1.8%.

Transport: Railroad: Length: 31 mi. **Motor vehicles:** 9,000 pass. cars; 3,000 comm. vehicles. **Civil aviation:** 2 airports. **Chief ports:** Basseterre, Charlestown.

Communications: TV sets: 256 per 1,000 pop. **Radios:** 718 per 1,000 pop. **Telephone lines:** 25,000. **Internet** (2004): 10,000 users.

Health: Life expect.: 69.8 male; 75.7 female. **Births** (per 1,000 pop.): 17.9. **Deaths** (per 1,000 pop.): 8.2. **Natural inc.:** 0.97%. **Infant mortality** (per 1,000 live births): 13.7. **AIDS rate:** NA.

Education: Compulsory: ages 5-16. **Literacy:** 97.8%.

Major intl. organizations: UN (FAO, IBRD, ILO, IMF, IMO, WHO, WTO), Caricom, the Commonwealth, OAS, OECS.

Embassy: 3216 New Mexico Ave. NW 20016; 686-2636.

Website: www.gov.kn

St. Kitts (formerly St. Christopher; known by indigenous peoples as Liamuiga) and Nevis were reached (and named) by Columbus in 1493. They were settled by Britain in 1623, but ownership was disputed with France until 1713. They were part of the Leeward Islands Federation, 1871-1956, and the Federation of the West Indies, 1958-62. The colony achieved self-government as an Associated State of the UK in 1967, and became fully independent Sept. 19, 1983. A secession referendum on Nevis, Aug. 10, 1998, fell short of the two-thirds majority required.

St. Kitts and Nevis is the smallest independent nation in the Western Hemisphere.

Saint Lucia

People: Population: 170,649. **Age distrib.** (%): <15: 29.4; 65+: 5.1. **Pop. density:** 729 per sq mi, 282 per sq km. **Urban:** 27.6%. **Ethnic groups:** Black 83%, mixed 12%, East Indian 2%, white 1%. **Principal languages:** English (official), French patois. **Chief religions:** Roman Catholic 68%, Protestant 18%.

Geography: Total area: 238 sq mi, 616 sq km; **Land area:** 234 sq mi, 606 sq km. **Location:** In E Caribbean, 2nd largest of Windward Isls. **Neighbors:** Martinique to N, St. Vincent to S. **Topography:** Mountainous, volcanic in origin; Soufriere, a volcanic crater, in S. Wooded mountains run N-S to Mt. Gimie, 3,145 ft, with streams through fertile valleys. **Capital:** Castries, 13,000.

Government: Type: Constitutional monarchy. **Head of state:** Queen Elizabeth II, represented by Gov.-Gen. Dame Calliopa Pearlette Louisy; b. June 8, 1946; in office: Sept. 17, 1997. **Head of gov.:** Prime Min. Stephenson King; in office: Sept. 9, 2007 (acting from May 1). May 24, 1997. **Local divisions:** 11 quarters.

Economy: Industries: clothing, electronic components, beverages, cardboard, tourism, lime & coconut proc. **Chief crops:** bananas, coconuts, vegetables, citrus, root crops, cocoa. **Natural resources:** timber, pumice, mineral springs, geothermal areas. **Arable land:** 6%. **Livestock:** cattle: 12,400; chickens: 270,000; goats: 9,800; pigs: 15,000; sheep: 12,500. **Fish catch:** 1,410 metric tons. **Electricity prod.:** 300 mil kWh. **Labor force** (2002 est.): agriculture 21.7%, industry, commerce, and manufacturing 24.7%, services 53.6%.

Finance: Monetary unit: East Caribbean Dollar (XCD) (Sept. 2007: 2.67 = $1 U.S.). **GDP:** $1.8 bil; **per capita GDP** (2005 est.): $4,800; **GDP growth** (2005 est.): 5.1%. **Imports** (2004 est.): $410 mil; U.S. 19.9%, Trinidad and Tobago 14.1%, Italy 11.6%, France 11.1%, UK 6.5%, Argentina 6.4%, Netherlands 5.5%, Venezuela 5.1%. **Exports** (2004 est.): $82 mil; France 69.1%, U.S. 10.1%, UK 8.7%. **Tourism:** $356 mil. **Budget** (2000 est.): $146.7 mil. **Intl. reserves less gold:** $89 mil. **Consumer prices:** 2.34%.

Transport: Motor vehicles: 23,800 pass. cars; 9,800 comm. vehicles. **Civil aviation:** 2 airports. **Chief ports:** Castries, Cul-de-Sac, Vieux-Fort.

Communications: TV sets: 368 per 1,000 pop. **Radios:** 750 per 1,000 pop. **Telephone lines** (2004): 51,100. **Internet:** 55,000 users.

Health: Life expect.: 70.5 male; 77.9 female. **Births** (per 1,000 pop.): 19.3. **Deaths** (per 1,000 pop.): 5. **Natural inc.:** 1.43%. **Infant mortality** (per 1,000 live births): 12.8. **AIDS rate:** NA.

Education: Compulsory: ages 5-15. **Literacy:** 90.1%.

Major intl. organizations: UN (FAO, IBRD, ILO, IMF, IMO, WHO, WTO), Caricom, the Commonwealth, OAS, OECS.

Embassy: 3216 New Mexico Ave. NW 20016; 364-6792.

Website: www.stlucia.gov.lc

St. Lucia was ceded to Britain by France at the Treaty of Paris, 1814. Self-government was granted with the West Indies Act, 1967. Independence was attained Feb. 22, 1979.

Saint Vincent and the Grenadines

People: Population: 118,149. **Age distrib.** (%): <15: 25.9; 65+: 6.5. **Pop. density:** 788 per sq mi, 304 per sq km. **Urban:** 45.9%. **Ethnic groups:** Black 66%, mixed 19%, East Indian 6%, Carib Amerindian 2%. **Principal languages:** English (official), French patois. **Chief religions:** Anglican 47%, Methodist 28%, Roman Catholic 13%.

Geography: Total area: 150 sq mi, 389 sq km; **Land area:** 150 sq mi, 389 sq km. **Location:** In E Caribbean, St. Vincent (133 sq mi) and the northern islets of the Grenadines form a part of Windward chain. **Neighbors:** St. Lucia to N, Barbados to E, Grenada to S. **Topography:** St. Vincent is volcanic, with a ridge of thickly wooded mountains running its length. **Capital:** Kingstown, 26,000.

Government: Constitutional monarchy. **Head of state:** Queen Elizabeth II, represented by Sir Frederick Ballantyne; b. July 5, 1936; in office: Sept. 2, 2002. **Head of gov.:** Prime Min. Ralph Gonsalves; b. Aug. 8, 1946; in office: Mar. 29, 2001. **Local divisions:** 6 parishes.

Economy: Industries: food proc., cement, furniture, clothing, starch. **Chief crops:** bananas, coconuts, sweet potatoes, spices. **Natural resources:** hydropower. **Arable land:** 18%. **Livestock:** cattle: 5,000; chickens: 125,000; goats: 7,200; pigs: 9,150; sheep: 12,000. **Fish catch:** 2,745 metric tons. **Electricity prod.:** 120 mil kWh. **Labor force** (1980 est.): agriculture 26%, industry 17%, services 57%.

Finance: Monetary unit: East Caribbean Dollar (XCD) (Sept. 2007: 2.67 = $1 U.S.). **GDP:** $864 mil; **per capita GDP** (2005 est.): $3,600; **GDP growth** (2005 est.): 4.9%. **Imports** (2004 est.): $225 mil; Singapore 17.5%, Trinidad and Tobago 12.3%, U.S. 11.2%, Italy 11.1%, Spain 9.6%, Turkey 4.6%, Germany 4.4%. **Exports** (2004 est.): $37 mil; France 26.3%, Greece 21.3%, Italy 18.9%, Russia 7.2%, UK 6.9%. **Tourism:** $101 mil. **Budget** (2000 est.): $85.8 mil. **Intl. reserves less gold:** $52 mil. **Consumer prices:** 3.04%.

Transport: Motor vehicles: 11,000 pass. cars; 4,000 comm. vehicles. **Civil aviation:** 5 airports. **Chief port:** Kingstown.

Communications: TV sets: 230 per 1,000 pop. **Radios:** 688 per 1,000 pop. **Telephone lines:** 22,600. **Internet:** 10,000 users.

Health: Life expect.: 72.2 male; 76 female. **Births** (per 1,000 pop.): 16. **Deaths** (per 1,000 pop.): 6. **Natural inc.:** 1.01%. **Infant mortality** (per 1,000 live births): 14. **AIDS rate:** NA.

Education: Compulsory: ages 5-15. **Literacy:** 96%.

Major intl. organizations: UN (FAO, IBRD, ILO, IMF, WHO, WTO), Caricom, the Commonwealth, OAS, OECS.

Embassy: 3216 New Mexico Ave. NW 20016; 364-6730.

Website: www.gov.vc

Columbus landed on St. Vincent on Jan. 22, 1498 (St. Vincent's Day). Britain and France both laid claim to the island in the 17th and 18th centuries; the Treaty of Versailles, 1783, finally ceded it to Britain. Associated State status was granted 1969; independence was attained Oct. 27, 1979.

Samoa *(formerly* Western Samoa)
Independent State of Samoa

People: Population: 214,265. **Age distrib.** (%): <15: 38.1; 65+: 5.6. **Pop. density:** 189 per sq mi, 73 per sq km. **Urban:** 22.4%. **Ethnic groups:** Samoan 93%, Euronesians 7%. **Principal languages:** Samoan (official), English. **Chief religion:** Christian 98%.

Geography: Total area: 1,137 sq mi, 2,944 sq km; **Land area:** 1,133 sq mi, 2,934 sq km. **Location:** In S Pacific O. **Neighbors:** Nearest are Fiji to SW, Tonga to S. **Topography:** Main islands, Savaii (659 sq mi) and Upolu (432 sq mi), both ruggedly mountainous, and small islands Manono and Apolima. **Capital:** Apia, 41,000.

Government: Type: Constitutional monarchy. **Head of state:** Tuiatua Tupua Tamasese Efi; b. Mar. 1, 1938; in office: June 19, 2007. **Head of gov.:** Prime Min. Tuilaepa Sailele Malielegaoi; b. Apr. 14, 1945; in office: Nov. 23, 1998. **Local divisions:** 11 districts.

Economy: Industries: food proc., building materials, auto parts. **Chief crops:** coconuts, bananas, taro, yams. **Natural resources:** timber, fish, hydropower. **Arable land:** 21%. **Livestock:** cattle: 29,000; chickens: 450,000; pigs: 201,000. **Fish catch:** 4,501 metric tons. **Electricity prod.:** 110 mil kWh. **Labor force:** NA.

Finance: Monetary unit: Tala (WST) (Sept. 2007: 2.70 = $1 U.S.). **GDP:** $1.2 bil; **per capita GDP** (2005 est.): $2,100; **GDP growth** (2005 est.): 5.5%. **Imports** (2004 est.): $285 mil; New Zealand 21.4%, Fiji 14.7%, Singapore 13.2%, Australia 8.6%, Japan 8.6%, U.S. 6.2%, Indonesia 5%, China 4.4%. **Exports** (2004 est.): $94 mil; Australia 48.1%, American Samoa 32.6%, U.S.

3.7%. **Tourism:** $77 mil. **Budget** (2005 est.): $78.1 mil. **Intl. reserves less gold:** $61 mil. **Consumer prices:** 3.78%.

Transport: Civil aviation: 173.4 mil pass.-mi; 3 airports. **Chief port:** Apia.

Communications: TV sets: 56 per 1,000 pop. **Radios:** 1,035 per 1,000 pop. **Telephone lines:** 19,500. **Internet:** 8,000 users.

Health: Life expect.: 68.5 male; 74.3 female. **Births** (per 1,000 pop.): 28.3. **Deaths** (per 1,000 pop.): 5.9. **Natural inc.:** 2.24%. **Infant mortality** (per 1,000 live births): 25.9. **AIDS rate:** NA.

Education: Compulsory: ages 5-14. **Literacy:** 98.6%.

Major intl. organizations: UN (FAO, IBRD, ILO, IMF, IMO, WHO), the Commonwealth.

Embassy: 800 Second Ave., Ste. 400J, New York, NY 10017; 212-599-6196.

Website: www.govt.ws

Samoa (formerly known as Western Samoa to distinguish it from American Samoa, a small U.S. territory) was a German colony, 1899 to 1914, when New Zealand landed troops and took over. It became a New Zealand mandate under the League of Nations and, in 1945, a New Zealand UN Trusteeship.

An elected local government took office in Oct. 1959, and the country became fully independent Jan. 1, 1962. Malietoa Tanumafili II, Samoa's head of state since independence, died May 11, 2007, and was succeeded by Tuiatua Tupua Tamasese Efi.

San Marino
Republic of San Marino

People: Population: 29,615. **Age distrib.** (%): <15: 16.8; 65+: 17.1. **Pop. density:** 1,234 per sq mi, 485 per sq km. **Urban:** 97.2%. **Ethnic groups:** Sammarinese, Italian. **Principal language:** Italian (official). **Chief religion:** Roman Catholic.

Geography: Total area: 24 sq mi, 61 sq km; **Land area:** 24 sq mi, 61 sq km. **Location:** In N central Italy near Adriatic coast. **Neighbors:** Completely surrounded by Italy. **Topography:** The country lies on slopes of Mt. Titano. **Capital** (2003): San Marino, 5,000.

Government: Type: Republic. **Heads of state and gov.:** Two co-regents appt. every 6 months. **Local divisions:** 9 castelli.

Economy: Industries: tourism, banking, textiles, electronics, ceramics, cement, wine. **Chief crops:** wheat, grapes, corn, olives. **Natural resources:** building stone. **Arable land:** 17%. **Labor force** (2006 est.): agriculture 0.2%, industry 40.1%, services 59.7%.

Finance: Monetary unit: Euro (EUR) (Sept. 2007: 0.72 = $1 U.S.). **GDP** (2004 est.): $850 mil; **per capita GDP** (2004 est.): $34,100; **GDP growth** (2004 est.): 4.6%. **Imports** (2004): $2 bil. **Exports** (2004): $1.3 bil. **Intl. reserves less gold:** $248 mil. **Tourism:** NA. **Budget** (2004): $672.3 mil. **Intl. reserves less gold:** $326 mil.

Transport: NA.

Communications: TV sets: 875 per 1,000 pop. **Radios:** 1,346 per 1,000 pop. **Internet** (2002): 14,300 users.

Health: Life expect.: 78.3 male; 85.6 female. **Births** (per 1,000 pop.): 9.9. **Deaths** (per 1,000 pop.): 8.3. **Natural inc.:** 0.16%. **Infant mortality** (per 1,000 live births): 5.5. **AIDS rate:** NA.

Education (2003): Compulsory: ages 6-14. **Literacy:** 96%.

Major intl. organizations: UN (FAO, IBRD, ILO, IMF, IMO, WHO), OSCE.

Consulate General: 1899 L St. NW, Ste. 500, 20036; 223-3517.

Website: www.visitsanmarino.com

San Marino claims to be the oldest state in Europe and to have been founded in the 4th cent. A Communist-led coalition ruled 1947-57; a similar coalition ruled 1978-86. San Marino has had a treaty of friendship with Italy since 1862.

São Tomé and Príncipe
Democratic Republic of São Tomé and Príncipe

People: Population: 199,579. **Age distrib.** (%): <15: 47.3; 65+: 3.7. **Pop. density:** 517 per sq mi, 199 per sq km. **Urban:** 58%. **Ethnic groups:** Mestizo, black, Portuguese. **Principal language:** Portuguese (official). **Chief religion:** Roman Catholic 70%.

Geography: Total area: 386 sq mi, 1,001 sq km; **Land area:** 386 sq mi, 1,001 sq km. **Location:** In Gulf of Guinea about 125 miles off W central Africa. **Neighbors:** Gabon, Equatorial Guinea to E. **Topography:** São Tomé and Príncipe islands, part of an extinct volcano chain, are both covered by lush forests and croplands. **Capital:** São Tomé, 57,000.

Government: Type: Republic. **Head of state:** Pres. Fradique Melo de Menezes; b. Mar. 21, 1942; in office: Sept. 3, 2001. **Head of gov.:** Prime Min. Tomé Vera Cruz; in office: Apr. 21, 2006. **Local divisions:** 2 provinces.

Economy: Industries: light constr., textiles, soap, beer; fish proc. **Chief crops:** cocoa, coconuts, palm kernels, copra, cinnamon, pepper, coffee. **Natural resources:** fish, hydropower. **Arable land:** 8%. **Livestock:** cattle: 4,600; chickens: 350,000; goats: 5,000; pigs: 2,500; sheep: 3,000. **Fish catch:** 3,600 metric tons **Electricity prod.:** 20 mil kWh. **Labor force:** Pop. mainly engaged in subsistence agriculture and fishing; shortage of skilled workers.

Finance: Monetary unit: Dobra (STD) (Sept. 2007: 13,695.00 = $1 U.S.). **GDP** (2003 est.): $278 mil; **per capita GDP** (2003 est.): $1,200; **GDP growth:** 4.4%. **Imports:** $48.9 mil; Portugal 48.7%, France 19.8%, U.S. 5.1%, Belgium 4.4%. **Exports:** $9.8 mil; Netherlands 41.9%, Belgium 16.6%, S. Korea 9%, Portugal 8.1%. **Tourism:** $10 mil. **Budget:** $61.4 mil. **Intl. reserves less gold:** $23 mil.

Transport: Civil aviation: 9.3 mil pass.-mi; 2 airports. **Chief port:** São Tomé.

Communications: TV sets: 229 per 1,000 pop. **Radios:** 319 per 1,000 pop. **Telephone lines:** 7,600. **Internet:** 29,000 users.

Health: Life expect.: 66 male; 69.3 female. **Births** (per 1,000 pop.): 39.7. **Deaths** (per 1,000 pop.): 6.3. **Natural inc.:** 3.34%. **Infant mortality** (per 1,000 live births): 40.5. **AIDS rate:** NA.

Education: Compulsory: ages 7-12. **Literacy:** 84.9%.

Major intl. organizations: UN (FAO, IBRD, ILO, IMF, IMO, WHO), AU.

Permanent UN Representative: 400 Park Ave., 7th Fl., New York, NY 10022; 212-317-0533.

Website: www.saotome.st

The islands were discovered in 1471 by the Portuguese, who brought the first settlers—convicts and exiled Jews. Sugar planting was replaced by the slave trade as the chief economic activity until coffee and cocoa were introduced in the 19th cent.

Portugal agreed, 1974, to turn the colony over to the Gabon-based Movement for the Liberation of São Tomé and Príncipe, which proclaimed as first president its East German-trained leader, Manuel Pinto da Costa. Independence came July 12, 1975. Democratic reforms were instituted in 1987. In 1991 Miguel Trovoada won the first free presidential election following da Costa's withdrawal. A military coup that ousted Trovoada Aug. 15, 1995, was reversed a week later after Angolan mediation. Trovoada defeated da Costa in a presidential runoff election, July 21, 1996.

Fradique de Menezes, a wealthy cocoa exporter, easily beat da Costa in the presidential election of July 29, 2001. The government was ousted in a military coup July 16, 2003, but was restored to power a week later and reelected July 30, 2006. The country, long one of the world's poorest, is expected to reap billions of dollars from oil development in the Gulf of Guinea.

Saudi Arabia
Kingdom of Saudi Arabia

People: Population: 27,601,038. **Age distrib.** (%): <15: 38.2; 65+: 2.4. **Pop. density:** 33 per sq mi, 13 per sq km. **Urban:** 81%. **Ethnic groups:** Arab 90%, Afro-Asian 10%. **Principal language:** Arabic (official). **Chief religion:** Muslim (official).

Geography: Total area: 756,985 sq mi, 1,960,582 sq km; **Land area:** 756,985 sq mi, 1,960,582 sq km. **Location:** Occupies most of Arabian Peninsula in Mid-East. **Neighbors:** Kuwait, Iraq, Jordan on N; Yemen, Oman on S; United Arab Emirates, Qatar on E. **Topography:** Bordered by Red Sea on W. The highlands on W, up to 9,000 ft, slope as arid, barren desert to the Persian Gulf on E. **Capital:** Riyadh, 4,193,000. **Cities (urban aggr.):** Jeddah, 2,860,000; Mecca, 1,319,000.

Government: Type: Monarchy with council of ministers. **Head of state and gov.:** King Abdullah bin Abdul Aziz; b. 1924; in office: Aug. 1, 2005. **Local divisions:** 13 provinces. **Defense budget** (2005): $25.4 bil. **Active troops:** 224,500.

Economy: Industries: oil prod. & refining, petrochems., cement, construction, fertilizers, plastics. **Chief crops:** wheat, barley, tomatoes, melons, dates, citrus. **Natural resources:** oil, nat. gas, iron ore, gold, copper. **Crude oil reserves:** 262.3 bil bbls. **Arable land:** 2%. **Livestock:** cattle: 352,000; chickens: 141 mil; goats: 2.2 mil; sheep: 7 mil. **Fish catch:** 74,778 metric tons. **Electricity prod.:** 165.6 bil kWh. **Labor force** (1999 est.): agriculture 12%, industry 25%, services 63%.

Finance: Monetary unit: Riyal (SAR) (Sept. 2007: 3.75 = $1 U.S.). **GDP:** $366.2 bil; **per capita GDP:** $13,600; **GDP growth:** 2.4%. **Imports:** $64.2 bil; U.S. 12.2%, Germany 8.5%, China 7.9%, Japan 7.2%, UK 4.8%, Italy 4.8%. **Exports:** $204.5 bil; Japan 17.6%, U.S. 15.8%, S. Korea 9.6%, China 7.2%, Singapore 4.4%, Taiwan 4.4%. **Tourism:** NA. **Budget:** $107.6 bil. **Intl. reserves less gold:** $18.30 bil. **Gold:** 4.6 mil oz t. **Consumer prices:** 2.21%.

Transport: Railroad: Length: 865 mi. **Motor vehicles:** 9.9 mil pass. cars. **Civil aviation:** 12.9 bil pass.-mi; 73 airports. **Chief ports:** Ad Dammam, Jiddah.

Communications: TV sets: 263 per 1,000 pop. **Radios:** 321 per 1,000 pop. **Telephone lines:** 4 mil. **Internet:** 4.7 mil users.

Health: Life expect.: 73.9 male; 78 female. **Births** (per 1,000 pop.): 29.1. **Deaths** (per 1,000 pop.): 2.6. **Natural inc.:** 2.66%. **Infant mortality** (per 1,000 live births): 12.4. **AIDS rate:** NA.

Education: Compulsory: ages 6-11. **Literacy:** 82.9%.

Major intl. organizations: UN (FAO, IBRD, ILO, IMF, IMO, WHO, WTO), AL, OPEC.

Embassy: 601 New Hampshire Ave. NW 20037; 342-3800.

Website: www.saudi.gov.sa

Before Muhammad, Arabia was divided among numerous warring tribes and small kingdoms. It was united for the first time by Muhammad, in the early 7th cent. His successors conquered the entire Near East and North Africa, bringing Islam and the Arabic language. But Arabia itself soon returned to its former status.

Nejd, in central Arabia, long an independent state and center of the Wahhabi sect, fell under Turkish rule in the 18th cent. In 1913 Ibn Saud, founder of the Saudi dynasty, overthrew the Turks and captured the Turkish province of Hasa in eastern Arabia; he took the Hejaz region in western Arabia in 1925 and most of Asir, in SW Arabia, by 1926. The discovery of oil in the 1930s transformed the nation.

Ibn Saud reigned until his death, Nov. 1953. Subsequent kings have been sons of Ibn Saud. The king exercises authority together with a Council of Ministers. The Islamic religious code is the law of the land. Alcohol and public entertainments are restricted, and women have an inferior legal status.

Saudi Arabia has often allied itself with the U.S. and other Western nations, and billions of dollars of advanced arms have been purchased from Britain, France, and the U.S.; however, Western support for Israel has often strained relations. Saudi units fought against Israel in the 1948 and 1973 Arab-Israeli wars. Beginning with the 1967 Arab-Israeli war, Saudi Arabia provided large annual financial gifts to Egypt; aid was later extended to Syria, Jordan, and Palestinian groups.

King Faisal played a leading role in the 1973-74 Arab oil embargo against the U.S. and other nations. Crown Prince Khalid was proclaimed king on Mar. 25, 1975, after the assassination of Faisal. Fahd became king on June 13, 1982, following Khalid's death.

The Hejaz contains the holy cities of Islam—Medina, where the Mosque of the Prophet enshrines the tomb of Muhammad, and Mecca, his birthplace. More than 2 mil Muslims make pilgrimage to Mecca annually. In 1987, Iranians making a pilgrimage to Mecca clashed with anti-Iranian pilgrims and Saudi police; more than 400 were killed. Some 1,426 Muslim pilgrims died July 2, 1990, in a stampede in a pedestrian tunnel leading to Mecca. Nearly 300 pilgrims were killed in a stampede in Mecca, May 26, 1994. More than 340 pilgrims died in a tent fire near Mecca, Apr. 15, 1997. A stampede at Mina killed more than 250, Feb. 1, 2004; another stampede at Mina killed at least 363 pilgrims, Jan. 12, 2006.

Following Iraq's attack on Kuwait, Aug. 2, 1990, Saudi Arabia accepted the Kuwaiti royal family and more than 400,000 Kuwaiti refugees. King Fahd invited Western and Arab troops to deploy on its soil in support of Saudi defense forces. During the 1991 Persian Gulf War, 28 U.S. soldiers were killed when an Iraqi missile hit their barracks in Dhahran, Feb. 25, 1991. Islamic extremists were blamed for truck bombs that killed 7 (5 from the U.S.) at a military training center in Riyadh, Nov. 13, 1995, and 19 Americans at a base in Dhahran, June 25, 1996.

The presence of 15 Saudis among the 19 al-Qaeda hijackers who took part in the Sept. 11, 2001, attacks on the U.S. raised new tensions between the U.S. and Saudi governments, and some blamed the Saudi government for allowing Muslim extremism to flourish in Saudi Arabia. Policy differences over the Israeli-Palestinian dispute and Iraq (where Saudi jihadists have supported the Sunni cause) were further irritants. The U.S. completed a pullout of its combat forces from Saudi Arabia in Sept. 2003.

Alarmed at guerrilla attacks that killed more than 100 people, mostly foreigners, in Saudi Arabia during 2003-04, the Saudi government stepped up antiterrorist activities in cooperation with the U.S. Islamist candidates on a "golden list" circulated by conservative clerics fared well in municipal council elections, Feb.-Apr. 2005; women were barred from voting in the elections, the country's first since 1963.

King Fahd, on the throne since 1982, died Aug. 1, 2005. He was succeeded by his half-brother, Abdullah, who had in effect ruled the Kingdom since Fahd suffered a stroke in Nov. 1995. Guards thwarted an attack by suicide bombers, Feb. 24, 2006, at the huge Abqaiq oil and gas facility. Security officials, Apr. 27, 2007, announced the arrest of 172 men accused of plotting attacks on oil installations, military posts, and other targets.

Senegal
Republic of Senegal

People: Population: 12,521,851. **Age distrib. (%):** <15: 42; 65+: 3. **Pop. density:** 169 per sq mi, 65 per sq km. **Urban:** 41.6%. **Ethnic groups:** Wolof 43%, Pular 24%, Serer 15%, Jola 4%, Mandinka 3%, Soninke 1%. **Principal languages:** French (official), Wolof, Pulaar, Jola, Mandinka. **Chief religions:** Muslim 94%, Christian 5%.

Geography: Total area: 75,749 sq mi, 196,190 sq km; **Land area:** 74,132 sq mi, 192,000 sq km. **Location:** At W extreme of Africa. **Neighbors:** Mauritania on N, Mali on E, Guinea and Guinea-Bissau on S; surrounds Gambia on three sides. **Topography:** Low rolling plains cover most of Senegal, rising somewhat in SE. Swamp and jungles are in SW. **Capital:** Dakar, 2,159,000.

Government: Type: Republic. **Head of state:** Pres. Abdoulaye Wade; b. May 29, 1926; in office: Apr. 1, 2000. **Head of gov.:** Prime Min. Cheikh Hadjibou Soumaré; b. 1951; in office: June 19, 2007. **Local divisions:** 11 regions. **Defense budget:** $136 mil. **Active troops:** 13,620.

Economy: Industries: food & fish proc., phosphate mining, fertilizer. **Chief crops:** peanuts, millet, corn, sorghum, rice, cotton. **Natural resources:** fish, phosphates, iron ore. **Arable land:** 13%. **Livestock:** cattle: 3.1 mil; chickens: 29.2 mil; goats: 4.3 mil; pigs: 317,814; sheep: 5 mil. **Fish catch:** 405,263 metric tons. **Electricity prod.:** 2.2 bil kWh. **Labor force** (1990 est.): agriculture 77%, industry and services 23%.

Finance: Monetary unit: CFA BCEAO Franc (XOF) (Sept. 2007: 472.78 = $1 U.S.). **GDP:** $21.5 bil; **per capita GDP:** $1,800; **GDP growth:** 2%. **Imports:** $3 bil; France 21.3%, Nigeria 10.6%, UK 8.9%, Netherlands 4.9%, China 4.8%, Brazil 4.1% **Exports:** $1.5 bil; Mali 18.5%, India 14.3%, France 6.9%, Italy 5.1%, The Gambia 5%. **Tourism:** $209 mil. **Intl. reserves less gold:** $887 mil. **Consumer prices:** 2.1%.

Transport: Railroad: Length: 563 mi. **Motor vehicles:** 147,000 pass. cars; 46,000 comm. vehicles. **Civil aviation:** 241.1 mil pass.-mi; 9 airports. **Chief port:** Dakar.

Communications: TV sets: 41 per 1,000 pop. **Radios:** 141 per 1,000 pop. **Telephone lines:** 282,600. **Daily newspaper circ.:** 5.3 per 1,000 pop. **Internet:** 650,000 users.

Health: Life expect.: 55.3 male; 58.1 female. **Births** (per 1,000 pop.): 37.4. **Deaths** (per 1,000 pop.): 11. **Natural inc.:** 2.64%. **Infant mortality** (per 1,000 live births): 60.2. **AIDS rate:** 0.9%.

Education: Compulsory: ages 7-12. **Literacy:** 39.3%.

Major intl. organizations: UN and all of its specialized agencies, AU.

Embassy: 2112 Wyoming Ave. NW 20008; 234-0540.
Website: www.senegal-tourism.com

Portuguese settlers arrived in the 15th cent., but French control grew from the 17th cent. The last independent Muslim state was subdued in 1893. Senegal became an independent republic Aug. 20, 1960, but French political and economic influence remained strong. Senegambia, a loose confederation of Senegal and The Gambia, was established in 1982 but dissolved 7 years later.

Forty years of Socialist Party rule ended when Abdoulaye Wade, leader of the Senegalese Democratic Party, won a presidential runoff election Mar. 19, 2000. A Senegalese ferry capsized off the coast of The Gambia Sept. 26, 2002, killing at least 1,863 people. A peace accord signed Dec. 30, 2004, with separatists in Cassamance Province, S Senegal, sought to end a 22-year insurgency. Pres. Wade was reelected Feb. 25, 2007.

Serbia

People: Population: 10,150,265. **Pop. density:** 298 per sq mi, 115 per sq km. **Urban:** NA. **Ethnic groups:** Serb 83%, Hungarian 4%, Roma 2%. **Principal languages:** Serbian (official), Albanian, Hungarian. **Chief religions:** Orthodox 85%, Roman Catholic 6%, Muslim 3%.

Geography: Total area: 39,518 sq mi, 102,350 sq km; **Land area:** 39,435 sq mi, 102,136 sq km. **Location:** On Balkan Peninsula in SE Europe. **Neighbors:** Croatia, Bosnia and Herzegovina on W; Hungary on N; Romania, Bulgaria on E; Montenegro, Albania, Macedonia on S. **Topography:** Terrain varies widely, with fertile plains drained by Danube and other rivers in N, limestone basins in E, ancient mountains and hills in SE, and very high coastline in Montenegro along SW. **Capital:** Belgrade, 1,106,000.

Government: Type: Republic. **Head of state:** Pres. Boris Tadic; b. Jan. 15, 1958; in office: July 11, 2004. **Head of gov.:** Prime Min. Vojislav Kostunica; b. Mar. 24, 1944; in office: Mar. 3, 2004. **Local divisions:** 1 republic with 2 autonomous provinces. **Defense budget:** $736 mil. **Active troops:** 39,686.

Economy: Industries: aircraft, vehicle, & other machine building; metallurgy, mining, consumer goods, electronics, oil products, chemicals. **Chief crops:** wheat, maize, sugar beets, sunflower. **Natural resources:** oil, gas, coal, antimony, copper, lead, zinc, nickel, gold, pyrite, chrome, hydropower. **Crude oil reserves:** 77.5 mil bbls. **Livestock:** cattle: 1.1 mil; chickens: 17.9 mil; goats: 138,604; pigs: 3.2 mil; sheep: 1.6 mil. **Fish catch:** 7,022 metric tons (incl. Montenegro). **Electricity prod.:** NA. **Labor force** (2002): agriculture 30%, industry 46%, services 24% (not incl. Kosovo and Montenegro).

Finance: Monetary unit: Dinar (RSD) (Sept. 2007: 59.73 = $1 U.S.). **GDP:** $44.8 bil (includes Kosovo); **per capita GDP** (2005 est.): $4,400 (includes Kosovo); **GDP growth** (2005 est.): 5.9% (excludes Kosovo). **Imports** (2005 est.): $10.6 bil (excluding Kosovo). **Exports:** $6.4 bil (excluding Kosovo); Italy 30.1%, Germany 16.6%, Austria 7.4%, Greece 7.1%, France 5.3%, Slovenia 4.2%, U.S. 4.1%. **Tourism:** NA. **Budget** (2005 est.): $11.1 bil (incl. Montenegro). **Intl. reserves less gold:** $7.74 bil. **Gold:** 380,000 oz t.

Transport: Railroad: Length: 2,569 mi. **Motor vehicles:** (incl. Montenegro): 1.6 mil pass. cars; 158,400 comm. vehicles. **Civil aviation:** 16 airports. **Chief ports:** Bar, Novi Sad.

Communications: TV sets: 277 per 1,000 pop. **Radios:** 296 per 1,000 pop. **Telephone lines:** 2.7 mil. **Internet:** 1.4 mil.

Health: Life expect.: 72.5 male; 77.9 female. **Births** (per 1,000 pop.): 12.1. **Deaths** (per 1,000 pop.): 10.7. **Natural inc.:** 0.14%. **Infant mortality** (per 1,000 live births): 12.3. **AIDS rate:** 0.2% (figure is for Serbia and Montenegro).

Education: Compulsory: ages 7-14. **Literacy:** 96.4%.

Major intl. organizations: UN (FAO, IBRD, ILO, IMF, IMO, WHO), OSCE.

Embassy: 2134 Kalorama Rd. NW 20008; 332-0333.
Website: www.gov.yu

Serbia, which had since 1389 been a vassal principality of Turkey, was established as an independent kingdom by the Treaty of Berlin, 1878. After the Balkan wars, Serbia's boundaries were enlarged by the annexation of Old Serbia and Macedonia, 1913.

When the Austro-Hungarian empire collapsed after WWI, the Kingdom of Serbs, Croats, and Slovenes was formed from the former provinces of Croatia, Dalmatia, Bosnia, Herzegovina, Slovenia, Vojvodina, and the independent state of Montenegro. The name became Yugoslavia in 1929.

Nazi Germany invaded in 1941. After the Nazis were driven out in 1945, Yugoslavia became a federal republic, headed by Josip Broz, a Communist, known as Marshal Tito. He rejected Stalin's policy of dictating to all Communist nations, and he accepted economic and military aid from the West. Pres. Tito died May 4, 1980. Yugoslavia held together for a decade, then broke apart. Croatia and Slovenia declared independence in 1991. In Croatia, fighting began between Croats and ethnic Serbs. Serbia sent arms and medical supplies to the Serb rebels in Croatia. Croatian forces clashed with Yugoslav army units and their Serb supporters.

The republics of Serbia and Montenegro proclaimed a new "Federal Republic of Yugoslavia" Apr. 17, 1992. Serbia, under Pres. Slobodan Milosevic, was the main arms supplier to ethnic Serb fighters in Bosnia and Herzegovina. The UN imposed sanctions May 30 on the newly reconstituted Yugoslavia as a means of ending the bloodshed in Bosnia.

A peace agreement initialed in Dayton, OH, Nov. 21, 1995, was signed in Paris, Dec. 14, by Milosevic and leaders of Bosnia and Croatia. In May 1996, a UN tribunal in the Netherlands began trying suspected war criminals from the former Yugoslavia. The UN lifted sanctions against Yugoslavia Oct. 1, 1996, after elections were held in Bosnia. Mass protests erupted when Milosevic refused to accept opposition victories in local elections Nov. 17; non-Communist governments took office in Belgrade and other cities in Feb. 1997. Barred from running for a 3rd term as Serbian president, Milosevic had himself inaugurated as president of Yugoslavia on July 23, 1997.

Defeated in a presidential election Sept. 24, 2000, by opposition leader Vojislav Kostunica, Milosevic initially refused to accept the result. A rising tide of mass demonstrations forced him to resign Oct. 6, and Kostunica was sworn in the next day. Charged with corruption and abuse of power, Milosevic surrendered to Serbian authorities Apr. 1, 2001. He was extradited June 28 to The Hague, Netherlands, where a UN tribunal had indicted him for war crimes. His trial began Feb. 12, 2002, but proceeded slowly. He was found dead in his prison cell Mar. 11, 2006, before a verdict was reached.

A pact to reconstitute Yugoslavia as a new union of Serbia and Montenegro took effect Feb. 4, 2003. Zoran Djindjic, premier of the Republic of Serbia, was assassinated Mar. 12 in Belgrade; the murder triggered a roundup of more than 4,500 people associated with organized crime and the Milosevic regime. Serbia's union with Montenegro disintegrated in 2006, as Montenegrins voted support for separation in a referendum May 21, and Montenegro became an independent republic June 3. A new constitution approved by referendum Oct. 28-29 restated Serbia's claim to the province of Kosovo (see below).

Kosovo: A nominally autonomous province in southern Serbia (4,203 sq mi), with a population of about 2 mil, mostly Albanians. The capital is Pristina. Revoking provincial autonomy, Serbia began ruling Kosovo by force in 1989. Albanian secessionists proclaimed an independent Republic of Kosovo in July 1990. Guerrilla attacks by the Kosovo Liberation Army in 1997 brought a ferocious counteroffensive by Serbian authorities.

Fearful that the Serbs were using "ethnic cleansing" tactics, as they had in Bosnia, the U.S. and its NATO allies sought to pressure the Yugoslav government. When Milosevic refused to comply, NATO launched an air war against Yugoslavia, Mar.-June 1999; the Serbs retaliated by terrorizing the Kosovars and forcing hundreds of thousands to flee, mostly to Albania and Macedonia. A 50,000-member multinational force (KFOR) entered Kosovo in June, and most of the Kosovar refugees had returned by Sept. 1. In the worst fighting there since 1999, Albanians and Serbs clashed in Mar. 2004, killing about 30 people, and injuring 500+, incl. UN/NATO troops.

As of mid-2007, Kosovo was under UN administration (UNMIK), with a NATO-led security force of about 16,000, pending the outcome of negotiations on Kosovo's final status. Legislative and municipal elections were scheduled for Nov. 17.

Vojvodina: A nominally autonomous province in northern Serbia (8,304 sq mi), with a population of about 2 mil, mostly Serbian. The capital is Novi Sad.

Seychelles
Republic of Seychelles
People: Population: 81,895. **Age distrib.** (%): <15: 25.4; 65+: 6.1. **Pop. density:** 465 per sq mi, 180 per sq km. **Urban:** 52.9%. **Ethnic groups:** Mainly Seychellois (mix of French, African, Arab, and Asian). **Principal languages:** English, Creole (both official). **Chief religions:** Roman Catholic 82%, Anglican 6%.

Geography: Total area: 176 sq mi, 455 sq km; **Land area:** 176 sq mi, 455 sq km. **Location:** In Indian O. 700 miles NE of Madagascar. **Neighbors:** Nearest are Madagascar on SW, Somalia on NW. **Topography:** A group of 86 islands, about half of them composed of coral, the other half granite, the latter predominantly mountainous. **Capital** (2004): Victoria 25,500.

Government: Type: Republic. **Head of state and gov.:** Pres. James Michel, b. Aug. 18, 1944; in office: Apr. 14, 2004. **Local divisions:** 23 districts. **Defense budget:** $13 mil. **Active troops:** 200.

Economy: Industries: fishing, tourism, coconut & vanilla proc., rope, boats. **Chief crops:** coconuts, cinnamon, vanilla, sweet potatoes, cassava, bananas. **Natural resources:** fish, copra, cinnamon. **Arable land:** 2%. **Livestock:** cattle: 1,400; chickens: 570,000; goats: 5,150; pigs: 18,500. **Fish catch:** 107,327 metric tons. **Electricity prod.:** 210 mil kWh. **Labor force** (1989): agriculture 10%, industry 19%, services 71%.

Finance: Monetary unit: Rupee (SCR) (Sept. 2007: 6.94 = $1 U.S.). **GDP** (2002 est.): $626 mil; **per capita GDP** (2002 est.): $7,800; **GDP growth:** −1%. **Imports:** $570.6 mil; Saudi Arabia 17.6%, South Africa 9.6%, Spain 8.1%, France 7.5%, Singapore 7.2%; Italy 4.8%, UK 4%. **Exports:** $365.1 mil; UK 26.2%, France 18.1%, Italy 12.6%, Japan 8.5%, Spain 8.3%, Netherlands 4.4%. **Tourism:** $172 mil. **Budget:** $376 mil. **Intl. reserves less gold:**

$75 mil. **Consumer prices:** −0.33%.

Transport: Motor vehicles: 6,200 pass. cars; 2,400 comm. vehicles. **Civil aviation:** 612.7 mil pass.-mi; 8 airports. **Chief port:** Victoria.

Communications: TV sets: 214 per 1,000 pop. **Radios:** 560 per 1,000 pop. **Telephone lines:** 20,700. **Internet:** 29,000 users.

Health: Life expect.: 67 male; 77.9 female. **Births** (per 1,000 pop.): 15.8. **Deaths** (per 1,000 pop.): 6.3. **Natural inc.:** 0.96%. **Infant mortality** (per 1,000 live births): 14.8. **AIDS rate:** NA.

Education: Compulsory: ages 6-15. **Literacy:** 91.8%.

Major intl. organizations: UN (FAO, IBRD, ILO, IMF, IMO, WHO), the Commonwealth, AU.

Embassy: 800 Second Ave., Ste. 400C, New York, NY 10017; 212-687-9766.

Website: www.virtualseychelles.sc

The islands were occupied by France in 1768 and seized by Britain in 1794. Ruled as part of Mauritius from 1814, the Seychelles became a separate colony in 1903. Independence was declared June 29, 1976. The first president was ousted in a coup a year later by a socialist leader, France Albert René. A new constitution, approved June 1993, provided for a multiparty state. After nearly 27 years in power, René resigned Apr. 14, 2004, and was succeeded by Vice Pres. James Michel, who won a full 5-year term in elections July 28-30, 2006.

Sierra Leone
Republic of Sierra Leone
People: Population: 6,144,562. **Age distrib.** (%): <15: 44.8; 65+: 3.2. **Pop. density:** 222 per sq mi, 86 per sq km. **Urban:** 40.7%. **Ethnic groups:** Temne 30%, Mende 30%, other tribes 30%, Creole 10%. **Principal languages:** English (official), Mende, Temne, Krio (Eng. Creole). **Chief religions:** Muslim 60%, indigenous beliefs 30%, Christian 10%.

Geography: Total area: 27,699 sq mi, 71,740 sq km; **Land area:** 27,653 sq mi, 71,620 sq km. **Location:** On W coast of W Africa. **Neighbors:** Guinea on N and E, Liberia on S. **Topography:** The heavily-indented, 210-mi coastline has mangrove swamps. Behind are wooded hills, rising to a plateau and mountains in E. **Capital:** Freetown, 799,000.

Government: Type: Republic. **Head of state and gov.:** Pres. Ernest Bai Koroma; b. Oct. 2, 1953; in office: Sept. 17, 2007. **Local divisions:** 3 provinces, 1 area. **Defense budget:** $27 mil. **Active troops:** 10,500.

Economy: Industries: diamonds, light mfg., oil refining. **Chief crops:** rice, coffee, cocoa, palm kernels & oil, peanuts. **Natural resources:** diamonds, titanium ore, bauxite, iron ore, gold, chromite. **Arable land:** 8%. **Livestock:** cattle: 350,000; chickens: 7.5 mil; goats: 540,000; pigs: 52,000; sheep: 470,000. **Fish catch:** 145,993 metric tons. **Electricity prod.:** 250 mil kWh. **Labor force:** NA.

Finance: Monetary unit: Leone (SLL) (Sept. 2007: 2,935.00 = $1 U.S.). **GDP:** $5.5 bil; **per capita GDP:** $900; **GDP growth:** 7.1%. **Imports** (2004 est.): $531 mil; Cote d'Ivoire 9.7%, U.S. 8.1%, China 8%, UK 7%, Netherlands 5.8%, South Africa 4.7%, India 4.6%, France 4.4%. **Exports** (2004 est.): $185 mil; Belgium 52.2%, U.S. 19.1%, Netherlands 6.8%. **Tourism:** $83 mil. **Budget** (2000 est.): $351 mil. **Intl. reserves less gold:** $122 mil. **Consumer prices:** 9.54%.

Transport: Railroad: Length: NA. **Motor vehicles:** 11,400 pass. cars; 7,800 comm. vehicles. **Civil aviation:** 46 mil pass.-mi; 1 airport. **Chief ports:** Freetown, Pepel.

Communications: TV sets: 13 per 1,000 pop. **Radios:** 274 per 1,000 pop. **Telephone lines** (2004): 24,000. **Internet:** 10,000 users.

Health: Life expect.: 38.4 male; 42.9 female. **Births** (per 1,000 pop.): 45.4. **Deaths** (per 1,000 pop.): 22.6. **Natural inc.:** 2.28%. **Infant mortality** (per 1,000 live births): 158.3. **AIDS rate:** 1.6%.

Education: Compulsory: ages 6-12. **Literacy:** 34.8%.

Major intl. organizations: UN (FAO, IBRD, ILO, IMF, IMO, WHO, WTO), the Commonwealth, AU.

Embassy: 1701 19th St. NW 20009; 939-9261.

Website: www.statehouse-sl.org

Freetown was founded in 1787 by the British government as a haven for freed slaves. Full independence arrived Apr. 27, 1961. Sierra Leone declared itself a republic Apr. 19, 1971. A one-party state approved by referendum in 1978 brought political stability, but mismanagement and corruption plagued the economy.

Mutinous soldiers ousted Pres. Joseph Momoh Apr. 30, 1992. Another coup, Jan. 16, 1996, paved the way for multiparty elections and a return to civilian rule. A peace accord, signed Nov. 30 with the Revolutionary United Front (RUF), brought a temporary halt to a civil war that had claimed over 10,000 lives in 5 years.

A coup on May 25, 1997, was met with widespread international opposition. Armed intervention by Nigeria restored Pres. Ahmad Tejan Kabbah to power on Mar. 10, 1998, but RUF rebels mounted a guerrilla counteroffensive, killing thousands of civilians and mutilating thousands more. The Kabbah government signed a power-sharing agreement with the RUF on July 7, 1999. A UN mission (UNAMSIL) was established in Oct. to help maintain the agreement. The accord collapsed in early May 2000, as RUF guerrillas took more than 500 UN peacekeepers hostage. Rebel leader Foday Sankoh was captured in Freetown May 17. The hostages were freed by the end of May, and 233 more UN personnel behind rebel lines were rescued July 15.

A UN-sponsored disarmament program in 2001 reduced the level of violence. On Jan. 16, 2002, the government and the UN signed an agreement creating the Sierra Leone Special Court to try war crimes that had occurred from Nov. 1996 onwards. Government and rebel leaders declared an official end to the war Jan. 18; by then, the death toll had risen to more than 50,000. Kabbah won the May 14 presidential election.

Sankoh, an indicted war criminal, died in UN custody July 29, 2003. A UN helicopter crashed June 29, 2004, in eastern Sierra Leone, killing all 24 people on board. UNAMSIL, which ended Dec. 31, 2005, was succeeded by UNIOSIL, a UN mission intended to strengthen political institutions. Opposition leader Ernest Bai Koroma won a presidential runoff vote, Sept. 8, 2007.

Singapore
Republic of Singapore

People: Population: 4,553,009. **Age distrib.** (%): <15: 15.2; 65+: 8.5. **Pop. density:** 17,265 per sq mi, 6,666 per sq km. **Urban:** 100.0%. **Ethnic groups:** Chinese 77%, Malay 14%, Indian 8%. **Principal languages:** Cantonese, Mandarin, English, Malay, Hokkien, Teochew, Tamil. **Chief religions:** Buddhist 43%, Muslim 15%, Christian 15%, Taoist 9%.

Geography: Total area: 267 sq mi, 693 sq km; **Land area:** 264 sq mi, 683 sq km. **Location:** Off tip of Malayan Peninsula in SE Asia. **Neighbors:** Nearest are Malaysia on N, Indonesia on S. **Topography:** Singapore is a flat, formerly swampy island. The nation includes 40 nearby islets. **Capital:** Singapore, 4,326,000.

Government: Type: Republic. **Head of state:** Pres. S. R. Nathan; b. July 3, 1924; in office: Sept. 1, 1999. **Head of gov.:** Prime Min. Lee Hsien Loong; b. Feb. 10, 1952; in office: Aug. 12, 2004. **Defense budget:** $6.4 bil. **Active troops:** 72,500.

Economy: Industries: electronics, chemicals, financial services, oil drilling equip., oil refining, rubber proc. **Chief crops:** rubber, copra, fruit, orchids, vegetables. **Natural resources:** fish. **Arable land:** 1%. **Livestock:** cattle: 200; chickens: 2 mil; goats: 600; pigs: 250,000. **Fish catch:** 7,837 metric tons. **Electricity prod.:** 35.9 bil kWh. **Labor force** (2003): manufacturing 18%, construction 6%, transportation and communication 11%, financial, business, and other services 39%, other 26%.

Finance: Monetary unit: Dollar (SGD) (Sept. 2007: 1.51 = $1 U.S.). **GDP:** $141.2 bil; **per capita GDP:** $31,400; **GDP growth:** 7.9%. **Imports:** $246.1 bil; Malaysia 13%, U.S. 12.7%, China 11.4%, Japan 8.3%, Taiwan 6.4%, Indonesia 6.2%, S. Korea 4.4%. **Exports:** $283.6 bil; Malaysia 13.1%, U.S. 10.2%, Hong Kong 10.1%, China 9.7%, Indonesia 9.2%, Japan 5.5%, Thailand 4.2%. **Tourism:** $5.1 bil. **Budget:** $19.9 bil. **Intl. reserves less gold:** $90.58 bil. **Consumer prices:** 0.96%.

Transport: Railroad: Length: NA. **Motor vehicles:** 437,500 pass. cars; 139,600 comm. vehicles. **Civil aviation:** 40.6 bil pass.-mi; 9 airports. **Chief port:** Singapore.

Communications: TV sets: 341 per 1,000 pop. **Radios:** 744 per 1,000 pop. **Telephone lines:** 1.9 mil. **Daily newspaper circ.:** 272.9 per 1,000 pop. **Internet:** 1.7 mil users.

Health: Life expect.: 79.2 male; 84.6 female. **Births** (per 1,000 pop.): 9.2. **Deaths** (per 1,000 pop.): 4.4. **Natural inc.:** 0.48%. **Infant mortality** (per 1,000 live births): 2.3. **AIDS rate:** 0.3%.

Education: Compulsory: ages 6-16. **Literacy:** 92.5%.

Major intl. organizations: UN (IBRD, ILO, IMF, IMO, WHO, WTO), the Commonwealth, APEC, ASEAN.

Embassy: 3501 International Pl. NW 20008; 537-3100.

Website: www.gov.sg

Founded in 1819 by Sir Thomas Stamford Raffles, Singapore was a British colony until 1959, when it became autonomous within the Commonwealth. On Sept. 16, 1963, it joined with Malaya, Sarawak, and Sabah to form the Federation of Malaysia. Tensions between Malayans, dominant in the federation, and ethnic Chinese, dominant in Singapore, led to an accord under which Singapore became a separate nation, Aug. 9, 1965.

Singapore is one of the world's largest ports and a major center of manufacturing, banking, and commerce. Standards in health, education, and housing are generally high. The government, dominated by a single party, has taken strong actions to keep order and suppress dissent.

In Dec. 2001, the government thwarted an alleged plot to blow up the U.S. Embassy; in Sept. 2002, authorities reported arrests of 21 militants identified as members of Jemaah Islamiah, a radical Muslim group active in SE Asia.

Singapore has had only 3 prime mins.: Lee Kuan Yew, who dominated national politics, 1959-90; Goh Chok Tong, 1990-2004; and Lee Kuan Yew's son, Lee Hsien Loong, who took office Aug. 12, 2004. At the White House, July 12, 2005, the prime min. and Pres. George W. Bush signed an agreement tightening U.S.-Singapore defense ties.

Slovakia
Slovak Republic

People: Population: 5,447,502. **Age distrib.** (%): <15: 16.4; 65+: 12.2. **Pop. density:** 289 per sq mi, 112 per sq km. **Urban:** 56.2%. **Ethnic groups:** Slovak 86%, Hungarian 10%, Roma 2%. **Principal languages:** Slovak (official), Hungarian, Roma, Ukrainian. **Chief religions:** Roman Catholic 69%, Protestant 11%.

Geography: Total area: 18,859 sq mi, 48,845 sq km; **Land area:** 18,842 sq mi, 48,800 sq km. **Location:** In E central Europe. **Neighbors:** Poland on N, Hungary on S, Austria and Czech Rep.

on W, Ukraine on E. **Topography:** Mountains (Carpathians) in N, fertile Danube plane in S. **Capital:** Bratislava, 424,000.

Government: Type: Republic. **Head of state:** Pres. Ivan Gasparovic; b. Mar. 27, 1941; in office: June 15, 2004. **Head of gov.:** Prime Min. Robert Fico; b. Sept. 15, 1964; in office: July 4, 2006. **Local divisions:** 8 departments. **Defense budget:** $966 mil. **Active troops:** 15,223.

Economy: Industries: metals; food & beverages; electricity, gas, coke, oil, nuclear fuels. **Chief crops:** grains, potatoes, sugar beets, hops, fruit. **Natural resources:** coal, lignite, iron ore, copper, mang., salt. **Crude oil reserves:** 9 mil bbls. **Arable land:** 29%. **Livestock:** cattle: 527,889; chickens: 13.6 mil; goats: 39,566; pigs: 1.1 mil; sheep: 320,487. **Fish catch:** 2,648 metric tons. **Electricity prod.:** 29.9 bil kWh. **Labor force** (2003): agriculture 5.8%, industry 29.3%, construction 9%, services 55.9%.

Finance: Monetary unit: Koruna (SKK) (Sept. 2007: 24.33 = $1 U.S.). **GDP:** $99.2 bil; **per capita GDP:** $18,200; **GDP growth:** 8.3%. **Imports:** $41.8 bil; Germany 23.6%, Czech Rep. 18.2%, Russia 11%, Hungary 6%, Austria 5.5%, Poland 4.9%, Italy 4.4%. **Exports:** $39.6 bil; Germany 23.7%, Czech Rep. 14.1%, Italy 6.5%, Poland 6.2%, Austria 6%, Hungary 5.8%, France 4.3%, Netherlands 4.2%. **Tourism:** $1.2 bil. **Budget:** $26.1 bil. **Intl. reserves less gold:** $8.41 bil. **Gold:** 1.13 mil oz t. **Consumer prices:** 4.48%.

Transport: Railroad: Length: 2,275 mi. **Motor vehicles:** 1.2 mil pass. cars; 175,000 comm. vehicles. **Civil aviation:** 136.7 mil pass.-mi; 18 airports. **Chief ports:** Bratislava, Komarno.

Communications: TV sets: 418 per 1,000 pop. **Radios:** 967 per 1,000 pop. **Telephone lines:** 1.2 mil. **Daily newspaper circ.:** 130.8 per 1,000 pop. **Internet:** 2.3 mil users.

Health: Life expect.: 71 male; 79.1 female. **Births** (per 1,000 pop.): 10.7. **Deaths** (per 1,000 pop.): 9.5. **Natural inc.:** 0.12%. **Infant mortality** (per 1,000 live births): 7.1. **AIDS rate:** <0.1%.

Education: Compulsory: ages 6-15. **Literacy:** 99.6%.

Major intl. organizations: UN (FAO, IBRD, ILO, IMF, IMO, WHO, WTO), EU, NATO, OECD, OSCE.

Embassy: 3523 International Ct. NW 20008; 237-1054.

Website: www.vlada.gov.sk

Slovakia was originally settled by Illyrian, Celtic, and Germanic tribes and was incorporated into Great Moravia in the 9th cent. It became part of Hungary in the 11th cent. Overrun by Czech Hussites in the 15th cent., it was restored to Hungarian rule in 1526. The Slovaks disassociated themselves from Hungary after WWI and joined the Czechs of Bohemia to form the Republic of Czechoslovakia, Oct. 28, 1918.

Germany invaded Czechoslovakia, 1939, and declared Slovakia independent. Slovakia rejoined Czechoslovakia in 1945. Czechoslovakia split into 2 separate states—the Czech Republic and Slovakia—on Jan. 1, 1993. A prolonged parliamentary standoff left the country without a president for much of 1998.

Prime Min. Vladimir Meciar, a nationalist, suffered a setback in legislative elections Sept. 25-26, 1998, and was defeated in a presidential runoff vote by Rudolf Schuster, May 29, 1999. A center-right coalition governed Slovakia after parliamentary elections Sept. 20-21, 2002. Meciar lost another bid for the presidency to his former ally, Ivan Gasparovic, Apr. 17, 2004. Slovakia became a full member of the EU and NATO in 2004. Robert Fico, a leftist, became prime min. July 4, 2006.

Slovenia
Republic of Slovenia

People: Population: 2,009,245. **Age distrib.** (%): <15: 13.7; 65+: 16. **Pop. density:** 258 per sq mi, 100 per sq km. **Urban:** 51%. **Ethnic groups:** Slovene 83%, Croat 2%, Serb 2%. **Principal languages:** Slovenian (official), Serbo-Croatian. **Chief religion:** Roman Catholic 58%.

Geography: Total area: 7,827 sq mi, 20,273 sq km; **Land area:** 7,780 sq mi, 20,151 sq km. **Location:** In SE Europe. **Neighbors:** Italy on W, Austria on N, Hungary on NE, Croatia on SE, S. **Topography:** Mostly hilly; 42% forested. **Capital:** Ljubljana, 263,000.

Government: Type: Republic. **Head of state:** Pres. Janez Drnovsek; b. May 17, 1950; in office: Dec. 22, 2002. **Head of gov.:** Prime Min. Janez Jansa; b. Sept. 17, 1958; in office: Nov. 9, 2004. **Local divisions:** 183 municipalities, 11 urban municipalities. **Defense budget:** $580 mil. **Active troops:** 6,550.

Economy: Industries: metallurgy, electronics, trucks, electric power equip., wood products, textiles, chemicals, machine tools. **Chief crops:** potatoes, hops, wheat, sugar beets, corn, grapes. **Natural resources:** lignite, lead, zinc, mercury, uranium, silver, hydropower, timber. **Arable land:** 9%. **Livestock:** cattle: 452,517; chickens: 4.8 mil; goats: 25,480; pigs: 547,430; sheep: 129,352. **Fish catch:** 2,759 metric tons. **Electricity prod.:** 14.3 bil kWh. **Labor force** (2004): agriculture 4.8%, industry 39.1%, services 56.1%.

Finance: Monetary unit: Euro (EUR) (Sept. 2007: 0.72 = $1 U.S.). **GDP:** $47 bil; **per capita GDP:** $23,400; **GDP growth:** 5.2%. **Imports:** $23.6 bil; Germany 19.7%, Italy 18.1%, Austria 11.9%, France 6%, Croatia 4.7%. **Exports:** $21.9 bil; Germany 20.1%, Italy 13%, Croatia 9.1%, Austria 8.8%, France 6.5%, Russia 4.4%. **Tourism:** $1.6 bil. **Budget:** $16.4 bil. **Intl. reserves less gold:** $4.68 bil. **Gold:** 160,000 oz t. **Consumer prices:** 2.46%.

Transport: Railroad: Length: 746 mi. **Motor vehicles:** 936,000 pass. cars; 59,000 comm. vehicles. **Civil aviation:** 435 mil pass.-mi; 6 airports. **Chief port:** Koper.

Communications: TV sets: 362 per 1,000 pop. **Radios:** 404

per 1,000 pop. **Telephone lines:** 837,500. **Daily newspaper circ.:** 168.4 per 1,000 pop. **Internet:** 1.3 mil users.

Health: Life expect.: 72.8 male; 80.5 female. **Births** (per 1,000 pop.): 9. **Deaths** (per 1,000 pop.): 10.4. **Natural inc.:** −0.14%. **Infant mortality** (per 1,000 live births): 4.4. **AIDS rate:** <0.1%.

Education: Compulsory: ages 6-14. **Literacy:** 99.7%.

Major intl. organizations: UN (FAO, IBRD, ILO, IMF, IMO, WHO, WTO), EU, NATO, OSCE.

Embassy: 1525 New Hampshire Ave. NW 20036; 667-5363.

Website: e-uprava.gov.si

The Slovenes settled in their current territory during the period from the 6th to the 8th cent. They fell under German domination as early as the 9th cent. Modern Slovenian political history began after 1848 when the Slovenes, who were divided among several Austrian provinces, began their struggle for political and national unification. In 1918 a majority of Slovenes became part of the Kingdom of Serbs, Croats, and Slovenes, later renamed Yugoslavia.

Slovenia declared independence June 25, 1991, and joined the UN May 22, 1992. It attained full membership in the EU and NATO in 2004. Slovenia adopted the euro currency Jan. 1, 2007.

Solomon Islands

People: Population: 566,842. **Age distrib.** (%): <15: 40.7; 65+: 3.3. **Pop. density:** 53 per sq mi, 21 per sq km. **Urban:** 17%. **Ethnic groups:** Melanesian 95%, Polynesian 3%, Micronesian 1%. **Principal languages:** English (official), Melanesian pidgin, 120 indigenous languages. **Chief religions:** Protestant 74%, Roman Catholic 19%.

Geography: Total area: 10,985 sq mi, 28,450 sq km; **Land area:** 10,633 sq mi, 27,540 sq km. **Location:** Melanesian Archipelago in W Pacific O. **Neighbors:** Nearest is Papua New Guinea to W. **Topography:** 10 large volcanic and rugged islands and 4 groups of smaller ones. **Capital:** Honiara, 61,000.

Government: Type: Parliamentary democracy. **Head of state:** Queen Elizabeth II, represented by Gov.-Gen. Sir Nathaniel Waena; b. 1945; in office: July 7, 2004. **Head of gov.:** Prime Min. Manasseh Sogavare; b. 1954; in office: May 4, 2006. **Local divisions:** 9 provinces and Honiara.

Economy: Industries: tuna, mining, timber. **Chief crops:** cocoa beans, coconuts, palm kernels, rice, potatoes. **Natural resources:** fish, timber, gold, bauxite, phosphates, lead, zinc, nickel. **Arable land:** 1%. **Crude oil reserves:** NA. **Livestock:** cattle: 13,500; chickens: 230,000; pigs: 53,000. **Fish catch:** 28,520 metric tons. **Electricity prod.:** 60 mil kWh. **Labor force** (2000 est.): agriculture 75%, industry 5%, services 20%.

Finance: Monetary unit: Dollar (SBD) (Sept. 2007: 7.34 = $1 U.S.). **GDP** (2002 est.): $800 mil; **per capita GDP** (2005 est.): $600; **GDP growth** (2005 est.): 4.4%. **Imports** (2004 est.): $159 mil; Australia 25.2%, Singapore 23.3%, Japan 7.8%, New Zealand 5%, Fiji 4.2%. **Exports** (2004 est.): $171 mil; China 45.2%, S. Korea 13.9%, Japan 8.4%, Philippines 4.5%, Thailand 4.4%. **Tourism:** $4 mil. **Budget** (2003): $75.1 mil. **Intl. reserves less gold:** $69 mil. **Consumer prices** (2005): 7.17%.

Transport: Civil aviation: 36.7 mil pass.-mi; 2 airports. **Chief ports:** Honiara, Yandina.

Communications: TV sets: 16 per 1,000 pop. **Radios:** 141 per 1,000 pop. **Telephone lines:** 7,400. **Internet:** 8,000 users.

Health: Life expect.: 70.6 male; 75.8 female. **Births** (per 1,000 pop.): 29.3. **Deaths** (per 1,000 pop.): 3.9. **Natural inc.:** 2.54%. **Infant mortality** (per 1,000 live births): 20. **AIDS rate:** NA.

Education: NA. **Literacy:** NA.

Major intl. organizations: UN (FAO, IBRD, ILO, IMF, IMO, WHO, WTO), the Commonwealth.

Embassy: 800 Second Ave., Ste. 800L, New York, NY 10017; 212-599-6192.

Website: www.pmc.gov.sb

The Solomon Islands were sighted in 1568 by an expedition from Peru. Britain established a protectorate in the 1890s over most of the group, inhabited by Melanesians. The islands saw major WWII battles. Self-government came Jan. 2, 1976, and independence was formally attained July 7, 1978.

A coup attempt June 5, 2000, sparked factional fighting in Honiara. During the next 3 years, violence, lawlessness, and corruption became widespread. To restore order, a 2,225-member intervention force, led by Australia and authorized by the Pacific Islands Forum, began arriving in Honiara July 24, 2003; nearly all foreign troops had been removed by mid-2005.

Following elections Apr. 5, 2006, parliament's choice of Snyder Rini as prime min. led to 2 days of rioting in Honiara over alleged influence-buying by the ethnic Chinese business community. Rini resigned Apr. 26 rather than face a no-confidence vote, and Manasseh Sogavare replaced him. An earthquake and tsunami Apr. 2, 2007, claimed at least 52 lives.

Somalia

People: Population: 9,118,773. **Age distrib.** (%): <15: 44.4; 65+: 2.6. **Pop. density:** 38 per sq mi, 15 per sq km. **Urban:** 35.2%. **Ethnic groups:** Somali 85%, Bantu and other 15%. **Principal languages:** Somali, Arabic (both official); Italian; English. **Chief religion:** Sunni Muslim (official).

Geography: Total area: 246,201 sq mi, 637,657 sq km; **Land area:** 242,216 sq mi, 627,337 sq km. **Location:** Occupies eastern horn of Africa. **Neighbors:** Djibouti, Ethiopia, Kenya on W. **Topog-**

raphy: The coastline extends for 1,700 mi. Hills cover the N; center and S are flat. **Capital:** Mogadishu, 1,320,000.

Government: Type: In transition. **Head of state:** Pres. Abdullahi Yusuf Ahmed; b. Dec. 15, 1934; in office: Oct. 14, 2004. **Head of gov.:** Prime Min. Ali Muhammad Ghedi; b. 1952; in office: Nov. 3, 2004. **Local divisions:** 18 regions. **Defense budget:** NA. **Active troops:** None.

Economy: Industries: a few light industries, incl. sugar refining, textiles, wireless communication. **Chief crops:** bananas, sorghum, corn, coconuts, rice. **Natural resources:** uranium, iron ore, tin, gypsum, bauxite, copper, salt, nat. gas, oil. **Arable land:** 2%. **Livestock:** cattle: 5.4 mil; chickens: 3.4 mil; goats: 12.7 mil; pigs: 4,200; sheep: 13.1 mil. **Fish catch:** 30,000 metric tons. **Electricity prod.:** 270 mil kWh. **Labor force** (1975): agriculture 71%, industry and services 29%.

Finance: Monetary unit: Shilling (SOS) (Sept. 2007: 1,306.00 = $1 U.S.). **GDP:** $5.3 bil; **per capita GDP:** $600; **GDP growth:** 2.6%. **Imports** (2004 est.): $576 mil; Djibouti 31%, India 8.2%, Kenya 8.1%, Brazil 7.7%, Oman 5.5%, UAE 5.2%, Yemen 5%. **Exports** (2004 est.): $241 mil; Thailand 31.3%, UAE 22.8%, Yemen 14.9%, India 8.5%, Oman 5.4%. **Tourism:** NA. **Budget:** NA.

Transport: Motor vehicles: 12,000 pass. cars; 12,000 comm. vehicles. **Civil aviation:** 7 airports. **Chief ports:** Berbera, Mogadishu.

Communications: TV sets: 14 per 1,000 pop. **Radios:** 47 per 1,000 pop. **Telephone lines:** 100,000. **Internet:** 94,000 users.

Health: Life expect.: 47.1 male; 50.7 female. **Births** (per 1,000 pop.): 44.6. **Deaths** (per 1,000 pop.): 16.3. **Natural inc.:** 2.83%. **Infant mortality** (per 1,000 live births): 113.1. **AIDS rate:** 0.9%.

Education (2004): Compulsory: ages 6-13. **Literacy:** 37.8%.

Major intl. organizations: UN (FAO, IBRD, ILO, IMF, IMO, WHO), AL, AU.

Permanent UN mission: 425 E. 61st St., Ste. 702, New York, NY, 10021; 212-688-9410.

Website: www.state.gov/p/af/ci/so/

British Somaliland (present-day North Somalia) was formed in the 19th cent., as was Italian Somaliland (now central and South Somalia). Italy lost its African colonies in WWII. British Somaliland gained independence, June 26, 1960, and by prearrangement, merged July 1 with the UN Trust Territory of Somalia to create the independent Somali Republic.

On Oct. 16, 1969, Pres. Abdi Rashid Ali Shirmarke was assassinated. On Oct. 21, a military group led by Maj. Gen. Muhammad Siad Barre seized power. In 1970, Barre declared the country a socialist state—the Somali Democratic Republic.

Somalia has laid claim to Ogaden, the huge eastern region of Ethiopia, peopled mostly by Somalis. Ethiopia battled Somali rebels in 1977. Some 11,000 Cuban troops with Soviet arms defeated Somali army troops and ethnic Somali rebels in Ethiopia, 1978. As many as 1.5 mil refugees entered Somalia. Guerrilla fighting in Ogaden continued until 1988, when a peace agreement was reached with Ethiopia.

The civil war intensified again and Barre was forced to flee the capital, Jan. 1991. Fighting between rival factions caused 40,000 casualties in 1991 and 1992, and by mid-1992 the civil war, drought, and banditry combined to produce a famine that threatened some 1.5 mil people with starvation.

In Dec. 1992 the UN accepted a U.S. offer of troops to safeguard food delivery to the starving. The UN took control of the multinational relief effort from the U.S. May 4, 1993. While the operation helped alleviate the famine, there were significant U.S. and other casualties; a failed mission Oct. 3-4 left 18 U.S. troops and more than 500 Somalis dead. The U.S. withdrew its peacekeeping forces Mar. 25, 1994.

When the last UN troops pulled out Mar. 3, 1995, Mogadishu had no functioning central government, and armed factions controlled different regions. By 1999 a joint police force was operating in the capital, but much of the country, especially in southern Somalia, faced continued violence and food shortages. After political and factional leaders signed a peace deal Jan. 29, 2004, a transitional parliament, Somalia's first legislature in 13 yrs, was inaugurated Aug. 22. Meeting in Nairobi, Kenya, the parliament chose Abdullahi Yusuf Ahmed as president; he was sworn in Oct. 14. The Indian Ocean tsunami of Dec. 26, 2004, killed at least 150 people and displaced about 5,000 in Somalia.

Because Mogadishu was held by his rivals, Pres. Yusuf moved, July 26, 2005, to make his transitional capital at Jowhar; an interim parliament convened Feb. 26, 2006, at Baidoa. On June 5, an Islamist militia took over Mogadishu, defeating secular warlords backed by the U.S. The Islamists, calling themselves the Supreme Islamic Courts Council, also held much of the central and southern regions. Pres. Yusuf escaped assassination, Sept. 18, but 8 others died in a car bomb explosion at Baidoa 5 days later.

With aid from Ethiopian troops, transitional govt. forces recaptured Mogadishu in late Dec. 2006. The UN Security Council authorized, Feb. 20, 2007, an African Union peacekeeping mission to Somalia (AMISOM). An upsurge of fighting in Mogadishu, Feb.-Apr., killed hundreds of people and caused 350,000 to flee the capital. Prime Min. Ghedi survived a suicide attack June 3. Clan reconciliation talks, boycotted by the Islamists, were held in Mogadishu July 15-Aug. 30, as violence continued.

South Africa
Republic of South Africa

People: Population: 43,997,828. **Age distrib.** (%): <15: 29.1; 65+: 5.4. **Pop. density:** 93 per sq mi, 36 per sq km. **Urban:** 59.3%. **Ethnic groups:** Black 79%, white 10%, mixed 9%, Indian 3%. **Principal languages:** IsiZulu, IsiXhosa, Afrikaans, Sepedi, English, Setswana, Sesotho, Xitsonga. **Chief religion:** Christian 81%.

Geography: Total area: 471,011 sq mi, 1,219,912 sq km; **Land area:** 471,011 sq mi, 1,219,912 sq km. **Location:** At southern extreme of Africa. **Neighbors:** Namibia, Botswana, Zimbabwe on N; Mozambique, Swaziland on E; surrounds Lesotho. **Topography:** Large interior plateau reaches close to the country's 1,739-mi coastline. There are few major rivers or lakes; rainfall sparse in W, more plentiful in E. **Capitals:** Cape Town (legislative), 3,083,000, Pretoria (administrative), 1,271,000, and Bloemfontein (judicial), 400,000. **Cities (urban aggr.):** Durban, 2,631,000; Johannesburg, 3,254,000; Ekurhuleni, 2,817,000.

Government: Type: Republic. **Head of state and gov.:** Pres. Thabo Mvuyelwa Mbeki; b. June 18, 1942; in office: June 16, 1999. **Local divisions:** 9 provinces. **Defense budget:** $3.3 bil. **Active troops:** 62,334.

Economy: Industries: mining (espec. platinum, gold, chromium), auto assembly, metalworking, machinery, textiles, chemicals, fertilizer, foodstuffs. **Chief crops:** corn, wheat, sugarcane, fruits, vegetables. **Natural resources:** gold, chromium, antimony, coal, iron ore, mang., nickel, phosphates, tin, uranium, diamonds, platinum, copper, vanadium, salt, nat. gas. **Crude oil reserves:** 15 mil bbls. **Arable land:** 12%. **Livestock:** cattle: 13.8 mil; chickens: 125.8 mil; goats: 6.4 mil; pigs: 1.6 mil; sheep: 25 mil. **Fish catch:** 820,750 metric tons. **Electricity prod.:** 228.3 bil kWh. **Labor force** (1999 est.): agriculture 30%, industry 25%, services 45%.

Finance: Monetary unit: Rand (ZAR) (Sept. 2007: 7.16 = $1 U.S.). **GDP:** $587.5 bil; **per capita GDP:** $13,300; **GDP growth:** 5%. **Imports:** $61.5 bil; Germany 12.6%, China 10%, U.S. 7.6%, Japan 6.6%, Saudi Arabia 5.3%, UK 5%. **Exports:** $59.2 bil; Japan 12.1%, U.S. 11.8%, UK 9%, Germany 7.6%, Netherlands 5.3%, China 4%. **Tourism:** $7.3 bil. **Budget:** $75.9 bil. **Intl. reserves less gold:** 15.33 bil. **Gold:** 3.99 mil oz t. **Consumer prices:** 4.64%.

Transport: Railroad: Length: 12,969 mi. **Motor vehicles:** 4 mil pass. cars; 2.2 mil comm. vehicles. **Civil aviation:** 15.3 bil pass.-mi; 146 airports. **Chief ports:** Cape Town, Durban, East London, Port Elizabeth, Richards Bay, Saldanha Bay.

Communications: TV sets: 138 per 1,000 pop. **Radios:** 355 per 1,000 pop. **Telephone lines:** 4.7 mil. **Daily newspaper circ.:** 25.4 per 1,000 pop. **Internet:** 5.1 mil users.

Health: Life expect.: 43.2 male; 41.7 female. **Births** (per 1,000 pop.): 17.9. **Deaths** (per 1,000 pop.): 22.5. **Natural inc.:** −0.45%. **Infant mortality** (per 1,000 live births): 59.4. **AIDS rate:** 18.8%.

Education: Compulsory: ages 7-15. **Literacy:** 82.4%.

Major intl. organizations: UN (FAO, IBRD, ILO, IMF, IMO, WHO, WTO), the Commonwealth, AU.

Embassy: 3051 Massachusetts Ave. NW 20008; 232-4400.
Website: www.gov.za

Bushmen and KhoiKhoi were the original inhabitants. Bantus, including Zulu, Xhosa, Swazi, and Sotho, had occupied the area from northeastern to southern South Africa before the 17th cent.

The Cape of Good Hope area was settled by the Dutch, beginning in the 17th cent. Britain seized the Cape in 1806. Many Dutch trekked north and founded 2 republics, Transvaal and Orange Free State. Diamonds were discovered, 1867, and gold, 1886. The Dutch (Boers) resented encroachments by the British and others; the Anglo-Boer War followed, 1899-1902. Britain won and, effective May 31, 1910, created the Union of South Africa, incorporating 2 British colonies (Cape and Natal) with Transvaal and Orange Free State. After a referendum, the Union became the Republic of South Africa, May 31, 1961, and withdrew from the Commonwealth.

With the election victory of Daniel Malan's National Party in 1948, the policy of separate development of the races, or apartheid, already existing unofficially, became official. Under apartheid, blacks were severely restricted to certain occupations, and paid far lower wages than whites for similar work. Only whites could vote or run for public office. Persons of Asian Indian ancestry and those of mixed race (Coloureds) had limited political rights. In 1959 the government passed acts providing for the eventual creation of several Bantu nations, or Bantustans.

Protests against apartheid were brutally suppressed. At Sharpeville on Mar. 21, 1960, 69 black protesters were killed by government troops. At least 600 persons, mostly Bantus, were killed in 1976 riots protesting apartheid. In 1981, South Africa launched military operations in Angola and Mozambique to combat guerrilla groups. Meanwhile, the apartheid system slowly began to crumble.

In 1986, Nobel Peace Prize winner Bishop Desmond Tutu called for Western nations to apply sanctions against South Africa to force an end to apartheid. Pres. P. W. Botha announced in Apr. the end to the nation's system of racial pass laws and offered blacks an advisory role in government. On May 19, 1986, South Africa attacked 3 neighboring countries—Zimbabwe, Botswana, Zambia—to strike at guerrilla strongholds of the black nationalist African National Congress (ANC). A nationwide state of emergency was declared June 12, giving almost unlimited power to the security forces.

Some 2 mil South African black workers staged a massive strike, June 6-8, 1988. Pres. Botha, head of the government since 1978,

resigned Aug. 14, 1989, and was replaced by F. W. de Klerk. In 1990 the government lifted its ban on the ANC. Black nationalist leader Nelson Mandela was freed Feb. 11 after more than 27 years in prison. In Feb. 1991, Pres. de Klerk pledged to end all apartheid laws.

In 1993 negotiators agreed on basic principles for a new democratic constitution. South Africa's partially self-governing black territories, or "homelands," were dissolved and incorporated into a national system of 9 provinces. In elections Apr. 26-29, 1994, the ANC won 62.7% of the vote, making Mandela president. The National Party won 20.4%. The Inkatha Freedom Party won 10.5% and control of the legislature in a mainly Zulu province. By then, fighting between the ANC and Inkatha (aided, during the apartheid era, by South African defense forces) had killed more than 14,000 people in the Zulu region since the mid-1980s.

In 1995, Mandela appointed a truth commission, led by Desmond Tutu, to document human rights abuses under apartheid. A post-apartheid constitution became law Dec. 10, 1996. The ANC won a landslide victory in elections held June 2, 1999. ANC leader Thabo Mbeki thus became South Africa's second popularly elected president. Led by Mbeki, the ANC won almost 70% of the vote in elections Apr. 14, 2004. In a farewell address before parliament, Nelson Mandela, 85, retired from public life, May 10. South Africa, Nov. 30, 2006, became the 1st country in Africa to legalize same-sex marriage.

Spain
Kingdom of Spain

People: Population: 40,448,191. **Age distrib.** (%): <15: 14.4; 65+: 17.8. **Pop. density:** 210 per sq mi, 81 per sq km. **Urban:** 76.7%. **Ethnic groups:** Castilian, Catalan, Basque, Galician. **Principal languages:** Castilian Spanish (official), Catalan, Galician, Basque. **Chief religion:** Roman Catholic 94%.

Geography: Total area: 194,897 sq mi, 504,782 sq km; **Land area:** 192,874 sq mi, 499,542 sq km. **Location:** In SW Europe. **Neighbors:** Portugal on W; France, Andorra on N; Morocco to S. **Topography:** The interior is a high, arid plateau broken by mountain ranges and river valleys. The NW is heavily watered, the S has lowlands and a Medit. climate. **Capital:** Madrid, 5,608,000. **Cities (urban agg.):** Barcelona, 4,795,000; Valencia, 797,000.

Government: Type: Constitutional monarchy. **Head of state:** King Juan Carlos I de Borbon y Borbon; b. Jan. 5, 1938; in office: Nov. 22, 1975. **Head of gov.:** Prime Min. José Luis Rodríguez Zapatero; b. Aug. 4, 1960; in office: Apr. 17, 2004. **Local divisions:** 17 autonomous communities and 2 autonomous cities. **Defense budget:** $9.13 bil. **Active troops:** 147,255.

Economy: Industries: textiles & apparel, food & beverages, metals, chemicals, shipbuilding, autos, machine tools, tourism. **Chief crops:** grain, vegetables, olives, wine grapes, sugar beets, citrus. **Natural resources:** coal, lignite, iron ore, uranium, mercury, pyrites, fluorspar, gypsum, zinc, lead, tungsten, copper, kaolin, potash, hydropower. **Crude oil reserves:** 150 mil bbls. **Arable land:** 27%. **Livestock:** cattle: 6.5 mil; chickens: 135 mil; goats: 2.8 mil; pigs: 25.1 mil; sheep: 22.5 mil. **Fish catch:** 1,070,720 metric tons. **Electricity prod.:** 270.3 bil kWh. **Labor force** (2004 est.): agriculture 5.3%, industry 30.1%, services 64.6%.

Finance: Monetary unit: Euro (EUR) (Sept. 2007: 0.72 = $1 U.S.). **GDP:** $1.1 tril; **per capita GDP:** $27,400; **GDP growth:** 3.9%. **Imports:** $324.4 bil; Germany 14.7%, France 13.2%, Italy 8.1%, UK 5%, Netherlands 4.8%, China 4.8%. **Exports:** $222.1 bil; France 18.9%, Germany 11%, Portugal 8.9%, Italy 8.6%, UK 7.8%, U.S. 4.5%. **Tourism:** $47.9 bil. **Budget:** $475.3 bil. **Intl. reserves less gold:** $7.19 bil. **Gold:** 13.4 mil oz t. **Consumer prices:** 3.52%.

Transport: Railroad: Length: 9,242 mi. **Motor vehicles:** 19.5 mil pass. cars; 4.7 mil comm. vehicles. **Civil aviation:** 35.8 bil pass.-mi; 96 airports. **Chief ports:** Algeciras, Barcelona, Cartagena, Gijon, Huelva, Tarragona, Valencia.

Communications: TV sets: 555 per 1,000 pop. **Radios:** 331 per 1,000 pop. **Telephone lines:** 18.4 mil. **Daily newspaper circ.:** 98.2 per 1,000 pop. **Internet:** 18.6 mil users.

Health: Life expect.: 76.5 male; 83.3 female. **Births** (per 1,000 pop.): 10. **Deaths** (per 1,000 pop.): 9.8. **Natural inc.:** 0.02%. **Infant mortality** (per 1,000 live births): 4.3. **AIDS rate:** 0.6%.

Education: Compulsory: ages 6-16. **Literacy:** 97.9%.

Major intl. organizations: UN and all of its specialized agencies, EU, NATO, OECD, OSCE.

Embassy: 2375 Pennsylvania Ave. NW 20037; 452-0100.
Website: www.la-moncloa.es

Initially settled by Iberians, Basques, and Celts, Spain was successively ruled (wholly or in part) by Carthage, Rome, and the Visigoths. Muslims invaded Iberia from N Africa in 711. Reconquest of the peninsula by Christians from the N laid the foundations of modern Spain. In 1469 the kingdoms of Aragon and Castile were united by the marriage of Ferdinand II and Isabella I. Moorish rule ended with the fall of Granada, 1492. Spain's large Jewish community was expelled the same year.

Spain obtained a colonial empire with the "discovery" of America by Columbus, 1492, the conquest of Mexico by Cortes, and Peru by Pizarro. It also controlled the Netherlands and parts of Italy and Germany. Spain lost its American colonies in the early 19th cent. It lost Cuba, the Philippines, and Puerto Rico during the Spanish-American War, 1898.

Primo de Rivera became dictator in 1923. King Alfonso XIII revoked the dictatorship, 1930, but was forced to leave the country in 1931. A republic was proclaimed, which disestablished the church, curtailed its privileges, and secularized education. During 1936-39 a Popular Front composed of socialists, Communists, republicans, and anarchists governed Spain.

Army officers under Francisco Franco revolted against the government, 1936. In a destructive 3-year war, in which some 500,000 to 1 mil people died, Franco received massive help and troops from Italy and Germany, while the USSR, France, and Mexico supported the republic. The war ended Mar. 28, 1939. Franco was named caudillo, leader of the nation. Spain was officially neutral in World War II, but its cordial relations with fascist countries caused its exclusion from the UN until 1955.

In July 1969, Franco and the Cortes (Parliament) designated Prince Juan Carlos as the future king and chief of state. After Franco's death, Nov. 20, 1975, Juan Carlos was sworn in as king. In free elections June 1977, moderates and democratic socialists emerged as the largest parties.

In 1981 a coup attempt by right-wing military officers was thwarted by the king. The Socialist Workers' Party, under Felipe González Márquez, won 4 consecutive general elections, from 1982 to 1993, but lost to a coalition of conservative and regional parties in the election of Mar. 3, 1996.

The Popular Party of conservative Prime Min. José María Aznar won a majority in the parliamentary election of Mar. 12, 2000. Aznar, going against Spanish public opinion, openly supported the U.S.-led invasion of Iraq, Mar. 2003.

Four commuter trains were bombed in central Madrid, Mar. 11, 2004, killing 191 people. Aznar's govt. initially blamed the attacks on ETA, but evidence pointed to Islamic extremists angered by Spain's role in Iraq. The opposition Socialist Workers Party won elections 3 days later, and Socialist leader José Luis Rodríguez Zapatero, who became prime min. Apr. 17, fulfilled a campaign pledge to remove all 1,300 Spanish troops from Iraq. Same-sex marriage became legal in Spain, July 3, 2005.

Catalonia and the Basque country were granted autonomy, Jan. 1980, following overwhelming approval in home-rule referendums. Basque extremists, however, pushed for independence. Bombings carried out by the militant Basque separatist group ETA have killed about 800 people since 1968. ETA declared a permanent ceasefire effective Mar. 24, 2006, after which the Spanish govt. agreed to begin formal peace talks. Negotiations broke down after ETA exploded a car bomb killing 2 people at the Madrid airport, Dec. 30, 2006; the Basque militants formally rescinded the truce, June 5, 2007. In Catalonia, voters approved a plan for expanded home-rule powers, June 18, 2006.

The **Balearic Islands** in the W Mediterranean, 1,927 sq mi, are a province of Spain; they include **Majorca** (Mallorca; capital Palma de Mallorca), **Minorca**, **Cabrera**, **Ibiza**, and **Formentera**. The **Canary Islands**, 2,807 sq mi, in the Atlantic W of Morocco, form 2 provinces, and include the islands of **Tenerife**, **Palma**, **Gomera**, **Hierro**, **Grand Canary**, **Fuerteventura**, and **Lanzarote**; Las Palmas and Santa Cruz are thriving ports. More than 1,700 people died trying to get from Mauritania to the Canary Islands in rickety boats, Jan.-June 2006.

Ceuta and **Melilla**, small Spanish enclaves on Morocco's Mediterranean coast, gained limited autonomy in Sept. 1994. Spain has sought the return of Gibraltar, in British hands since 1704.

Sri Lanka
Democratic Socialist Republic of Sri Lanka
People: Population: 20,926,315. **Age distrib. (%):** <15: 24.3; 65+: 7.8. **Pop. density:** 837 per sq mi, 323 per sq km. **Urban:** 15.1%. **Ethnic groups:** Sinhalese 74%, Tamil 9%, Moor 7%. **Principal languages:** Sinhala, Tamil (both official); English. **Chief religions:** Buddhist 69%, Muslim 8%, Hindu 7%, Christian 6%.

Geography: Total area: 25,332 sq mi, 65,610 sq km; **Land area:** 24,996 sq mi, 64,740 sq km. **Location:** In Indian O. off SE coast of India. **Neighbors:** India on NW. **Topography:** Coastal area and N half are flat; S-central area is hilly and mountainous. **Capital:** Colombo, 652,000; Sri Jayewardenepura Kotte (legislative) 117,000.

Government: Type: Republic. **Head of state:** Pres. Mahinda Rajapaksa; b. Nov. 18, 1945; in office: Nov. 19, 2005. **Head of gov.:** Prime Min. Ratnasiri Wickremanayake; b. May 5, 1933; in office: Nov. 21, 2005. **Local divisions:** 9 provinces with 25 districts. **Defense budget:** $686 mil. **Active troops:** 150,900.

Economy: Industries: rubber proc., tea & coconut prod., clothing, cement, oil refining, textiles, tobacco. **Chief crops:** rice, sugarcane, grains, pulses, oilseed, spices, tea, rubber. **Natural resources:** limestone, graphite, mineral sands, gems, phosphates, clay, hydropower. **Arable land:** 14%. **Livestock:** cattle: 1.2 mil; chickens: 13.3 mil; goats: 381,550; pigs: 92,210; sheep: 13,620. **Fish catch:** 163,684 metric tons. **Electricity prod.:** 8.4 bil kWh. **Labor force** (2006 est.): agriculture 34.3%, industry 25.3%, services 40.4%.

Finance: Monetary unit: Rupee (LKR) (Sept. 2007: 113.32 = $1 U.S.). **GDP:** $95.6 bil; **per capita GDP:** $4,700; **GDP growth:** 7.5%. **Imports:** $9.7 bil; India 19.2%, China 10.3%, Singapore 8.6%, Iran 5.6%, Malaysia 5%, Hong Kong 4.1%. **Exports:** $7.1 bil; U.S. 27.7%, UK 11.4%, India 9.4%, Belgium 4.7%, Germany 4%. **Tourism:** $513 mil. **Budget** (2007 est.): $8.4 bil. **Intl. reserves less gold:** $1.89 bil. **Gold:** 170,000 oz t. **Consumer prices:** 13.69%.

Transport: Railroad: Length: 900 mi. **Motor vehicles:** 507,000 pass. cars; 280,000 comm. vehicles. **Civil aviation:** 4.3 bil pass.-mi; 14 airports. **Chief ports:** Colombo, Galle.

Communications: TV sets: 102 per 1,000 pop. **Radios:** 211 per 1,000 pop. **Telephone lines:** 1.9 mil. **Daily newspaper circ.:** 28.8 per 1,000 pop. **Internet:** 428,000 users.

Health: Life expect.: 72.8 male; 76.9 female. **Births** (per 1,000 pop.): 17. **Deaths** (per 1,000 pop.): 6. **Natural inc.:** 1.1%. **Infant mortality** (per 1,000 live births): 19.5. **AIDS rate:** <0.1%.

Education: Compulsory: ages 5-13. **Literacy:** 90.7%.

Major intl. organizations: UN (FAO, IBRD, ILO, IMF, IMO, WHO, WTO), the Commonwealth.

Embassy: 2148 Wyoming Ave. NW 20008; 483-4025.

Website: www.priu.gov.lk

The island was known to the ancient world as Taprobane (Greek for copper-colored) and later as Serendip (from Arabic). Colonists from northern India subdued the indigenous Veddahs about 543 BCE; their descendants, the Buddhist Sinhalese, still form most of the population. Hindu descendants of Tamil immigrants from S India account for about one-fifth of the population.

Parts were occupied by the Portuguese in 1505 and the Dutch in 1658. The British seized the island in 1796. As Ceylon it became an independent member of the Commonwealth in 1948, and the Republic of Sri Lanka May 22, 1972.

Prime Min. Solomon W. R. D. Bandaranaike was assassinated Sept. 25, 1959. His widow, Mrs. Sirimavo Bandaranaike, served as prime min. 1960-65, 1970-77, 1994-2000. In 1971 the nation suffered economic problems and terrorist activities by ultra-leftists, thousands of whom were executed. Massive land reform and nationalization of foreign-owned plantations took place in the mid-1970s.

Tensions between Sinhalese and Tamil separatists erupted into violence in the early 1980s. More than 60,000 died in the civil war, which continued for the next 2 decades; another 20,000, mostly young Tamils, "disappeared" after they were taken into custody by government security forces.

Pres. Ranasinghe Premadasa was assassinated May 1, 1993, by a Tamil rebel. Mrs. Bandaranaike's daughter, Chandrika Bandaranaike Kumaratunga, became prime min. after the Aug. 16, 1994, general elections. Elected president Nov. 9, Kumaratunga appointed her mother prime min. Kumaratunga, who was injured in a suicide bomb attack at a campaign rally Dec. 18, 1999, won a 2nd 6-year term 3 days later. In failing health, Mrs. Bandaranaike resigned Aug. 10 and died Oct. 10, 2000.

Facing a possible no-confidence motion, Pres. Kumaratunga suspended parliament July 10, 2001. Elections Dec. 5 resulted in a victory for the United National Party, headed by Ranil Wickremesinghe. A truce accord intended to bring an end to the civil war was signed Feb. 22, 2002. Severe monsoon flooding in the S and SW, May 2003, killed at least 265 people.

A dispute with Wickremesinghe over how to negotiate with rebel Tamils led Kumaratunga again to suspend parliament, Nov. 4, 2003. Her United People's Freedom Alliance won a plurality in legislative elections Apr. 2, 2004, and formed a coalition govt. The Indian Ocean tsunami of Dec. 26 left more than 31,100 dead, 4,100 missing, and 519,000 displaced in Sri Lanka.

Foreign Min. Lakshman Kadirgamar, a Tamil who took a hard line against the rebels, died Aug. 12, 2005, after he was shot by a sniper. Prime Min. Mahinda Rajapaksa of the United People's Freedom Alliance won the presidential election of Nov. 17. A resurgence of fighting by govt. forces, paramilitary groups, and Tamil rebels beginning in Dec. 2005 claimed more than 4,800 lives by mid-2007.

Sudan
Republic of the Sudan
People: Population: 39,379,358. **Age distrib. (%):** <15: 41.6; 65+: 2.4. **Pop. density:** 43 per sq mi, 17 per sq km. **Urban:** 40.8%. **Ethnic groups:** Black 52%, Arab 39%, Beja 6%. **Principal languages:** Arabic (official), Nubian, Ta Bedawie, Nilotic, Nilo-Hamitic, Sudanic dialects, English. **Chief religions:** Sunni Muslim 70%, indigenous beliefs 25%, Christian 5%.

Geography: Total area: 967,499 sq mi, 2,505,810 sq km; **Land area:** 917,379 sq mi, 2,376,000 sq km. **Location:** At E end of Sahara desert zone. **Neighbors:** Egypt on N; Libya, Chad, Central African Republic on W; Congo, Uganda, Kenya on S; Ethiopia, Eritrea on E. **Topography:** The N consists of Libyan Desert in W, and the mountainous Nubia Desert in E, with narrow Nile valley between. Center contains large, fertile, rainy areas with fields, pasture, and forest. The S has rich soil, heavy rain. **Capital:** Khartoum, 4,518,000.

Government: Type: Republic with strong military influence. **Head of state and gov.:** Pres. Gen. Omar Hassan Ahmad Al-Bashir; b. Jan. 1, 1944; in office: June 30, 1989. **Local divisions:** 26 states. **Defense budget:** $535 mil. **Active troops:** 104,800.

Economy: Industries: oil, cotton ginning, textiles, cement, edible oils, sugar. **Chief crops:** cotton, peanuts, sorghum, millet, wheat, gum arabic, sugarcane. **Natural resources:** oil, iron ore, copper, chromium ore, zinc, tungsten, mica, silver, gold, hydropower. **Crude oil reserves:** 5 bil bbls. **Arable land:** 7%. **Livestock:** cattle: 40.5 mil; chickens: 37 mil; goats: 42.5 mil; sheep: 49.8 mil. **Fish catch:** 63,600 metric tons. **Electricity prod.:** 3.9 bil kWh. **Labor force** (1998 est.): agriculture 80%, industry 7%, services 13%.

Finance: Monetary unit: Dinar (SDD) (Sept. 2007: 203.24 = $1 U.S.). **GDP:** $97.5 bil; **per capita GDP:** $2,400; **GDP growth:** 9.6%. **Imports:** $8.7 bil; China 18.2%, Saudi Arabia 9.2%, UAE

5.8%, Egypt 5.3%, Germany 5.2%, India 4.6%, France 4.1%. **Exports:** $7.5 bil; Japan 49.6%, China 32%, Saudi Arabia 3.1%. **Tourism:** $21 mil. **Budget:** $10.1 bil. **Intl. reserves less gold:** $1.10 bil. **Consumer prices:** 7.2%.

Transport: Railroad: Length: 3,715 mi. **Motor vehicles:** 47,300 pass. cars; 62,500 comm. vehicles. **Civil aviation:** 488.4 mil pass.-mi; 15 airports. **Chief port:** Port Sudan.

Communications: TV sets: 173 per 1,000 pop. **Radios:** 480 per 1,000 pop. **Telephone lines:** 636,900. **Internet:** 3.5 mil users.

Health: Life expect.: 48.2 male; 50 female. **Births** (per 1,000 pop.): 34.9. **Deaths** (per 1,000 pop.): 14.4. **Natural inc.:** 2.05%. **Infant mortality** (per 1,000 live births): 91.8. **AIDS rate:** 1.6%.

Education: Compulsory: ages 6-13. **Literacy:** 60.9%.

Major intl. organizations: UN (FAO, IBRD, ILO, IMF, IMO, WHO), AL, AU.

Embassy: 2210 Massachusetts Ave. NW 20008; 338-8565.

Website: www.state.gov/p/af/ci/su/

Northern Sudan, ancient Nubia, was settled by Egyptians in antiquity. The population was converted to Coptic Christianity in the 6th cent. Arab conquests brought Islam to the area in the 15th cent. In the 1820s Egypt took over Sudan, defeating the last of earlier empires, including the Fung. In the 1880s a revolution was led by Muhammad Ahmad, who called himself the Mahdi (leader of the faithful), and his followers, the dervishes.

In 1898 an Anglo-Egyptian force crushed the Mahdi's successors. In 1951 the Egyptian Parliament abrogated its 1899 and 1936 treaties with Great Britain and amended its constitution to provide for a separate Sudanese constitution. Sudan voted for complete independence effective Jan. 1, 1956. In 1969, a Revolutionary Council took power, but a civilian premier and cabinet were appointed. The government announced it would create a socialist state.

Economic problems plagued the nation in the 1980s and 1990s, aggravated by civil war and influxes of refugees from neighboring countries. After 16 years in office, Pres. Jaafar al-Nimeiry was overthrown in a bloodless coup, Apr. 6, 1985. Sudan held its first democratic parliamentary elections in 18 years in 1986, but the elected government was toppled in a bloodless coup June 30, 1989.

In the mid-1980s, rebels in the S (populated largely by black Christians and followers of tribal religions) took up arms against government domination by northern Sudan, mostly Arab-Muslim. War and related famine cost an estimated 2 mil lives and displaced millions of southerners. In 1993, Amnesty International accused the Sudanese government of "ethnic cleansing."

A new constitution based on Islamic law took effect June 30, 1998. On Aug. 20, in retaliation for bombings in Kenya and Tanzania, U.S. missiles destroyed a Khartoum pharmaceutical plant the U.S. alleged was associated with terrorist activities; independent inquiries later cast some doubt on the U.S. claim.

An accord to end the rebellion in the S was signed Jan. 9, 2005. Under a power-sharing constitution with autonomy for southern Sudan, former rebel leader John Garang became first vice pres., July 9. His death 3 weeks later in a helicopter crash sparked riots in Khartoum and other cities, Aug. 1-3, killing at least 130. A national unity government was installed Sept. 20.

During 2003-07, a rebellion in the Darfur region of western Sudan led to a new crisis. Marauding Arab militias, known as the *janjaweed*, retaliated by attacking black African villagers, looting and burning homes, and killing inhabitants, reportedly in collusion with Sudanese government troops. The African Union sent more than 7,000 peacekeepers, but fighting continued. A peace deal reached with a major rebel faction May 5, 2006, also failed to halt the conflict, which had killed at least 200,000 people and forced more than 2 mil to flee to refugee camps. Rebel and militia activities in both Sudan and Chad led to border clashes and further attacks on civilians. Rebel and civilian casualties in Darfur appeared to decline during Jan.-Aug. 2007, but fighting flared between rival Arab tribes. The UN Security Council voted July 31, 2007, to begin deploying a joint UN-African Union force of up to 26,000 peacekeepers (UNMIS) by the end of the year.

Suriname
Republic of Suriname

People: Population: 470,784. **Age distrib.** (%): <15: 28; 65+: 6.2. **Pop. density:** 8 per sq mi, 3 per sq km. **Urban:** 73.9%. **Ethnic groups:** East Indian 37%, Creole 31%, Javanese 15%, Maroon 10%, Amerindian 2%, Chinese 2%, white 1%. **Principal languages:** Dutch (official), English, Sranang Tongo (Eng. Creole), Hindustani, Javanese. **Chief religions:** Hindu 27%, Protestant 25%, Roman Catholic 23%, Muslim 20%.

Geography: Total area: 63,039 sq mi, 163,270 sq km; **Land area:** 62,344 sq mi, 161,470 sq km. **Location:** On N shore of S. America. **Neighbors:** Guyana on W, Brazil on S, French Guiana on E. **Topography:** A flat Atlantic coast, where dikes permit agriculture. Inland is forest belt; to S, largely unexplored hills cover 75% of country. **Capital:** Paramaribo, 268,000.

Government: Type: Republic. **Head of state and gov.:** Pres. Runaldo Ronald Venetiaan; b. June 18, 1936; in office: Aug. 12, 2000. **Local divisions:** 10 districts. **Defense budget:** $20.5 mil. **Active troops:** 1,840.

Economy: Industries: mining, oil, lumber, food proc., fishing. **Chief crops:** rice, bananas, palm kernels, coconuts, plantains, peanuts. **Natural resources:** timber, hydropower, fish, kaolin, shrimp, bauxite, gold, nickel, copper, platinum, iron ore. **Crude oil reserves:**

111 mil bbls. **Arable land:** 0.4%. **Livestock:** cattle: 137,000; chickens: 3.8 mil; goats: 7,100; pigs: 24,500; sheep: 7,700. **Fish catch:** 40,191 metric tons. **Electricity prod.:** 1.5 bil kWh. **Labor force** (2004): agriculture 8%, industry 14%, services 78%.

Finance: Monetary unit: Dollar (SRD) (Sept. 2007: 2.74 = $1 U.S.). **GDP:** $3.1 bil; **per capita GDP:** $7,100; **GDP growth:** 5%. **Imports** (2004 est.): $750 mil; U.S. 29%, Netherlands 18.6%, Trinidad and Tobago 14.6%, Japan 5%, Brazil 5%, China 4.9%. **Exports** (2004 est.): $881 mil; Norway 24.7%, Canada 16.6%, U.S. 13.6%, Belgium 10.5%, France 9.1%, UAE 7.5%, Iceland 4.5%. **Tourism:** $17 mil. **Budget** (2004): $425.9 mil. **Intl. reserves less gold:** $143 mil. **Gold:** 40,000 oz t. **Consumer prices** (2005): 9.95%.

Transport: Railroad: NA. **Motor vehicles:** 76,000 pass. cars; 29,900 comm. vehicles. **Civil aviation:** 913.4 mil pass.-mi; 5 airports. **Chief port:** Paramaribo.

Communications: TV sets: 241 per 1,000 pop. **Radios:** 728 per 1,000 pop. **Telephone lines:** 81,500. **Daily newspaper circ.:** 67 per 1,000 pop. **Internet:** 32,000 users.

Health: Life expect.: 70.5 male; 76.1 female. **Births** (per 1,000 pop.): 17.3. **Deaths** (per 1,000 pop.): 5.5. **Natural inc.:** 1.18%. **Infant mortality** (per 1,000 live births): 20.1. **AIDS rate:** 1.9%.

Education: Compulsory: ages 6-11. **Literacy:** 89.6%.

Major intl. organizations: UN (FAO, IBRD, ILO, IMF, IMO, WHO, WTO), Caricom, OAS.

Embassy: 4301 Connecticut Ave. NW, Ste. 460, 20008; 244-7488.

Website: www.surinameembassy.org

The Netherlands acquired Suriname in 1667 from Britain, in exchange for New Netherlands (New York). The 1954 Dutch constitution raised the colony to a level of equality with the Netherlands and the Netherlands Antilles. Independence was granted Nov. 25, 1975, despite objections from East Indians. Some 40% of the population (mostly East Indians) immigrated to the Netherlands in the months before independence.

The National Military Council took control of the government Feb. 1982. Civilian rule was restored in 1987, but political turmoil continued until 1992, disrupting the nation's economy. A special assembly, convened after parliament deadlocked, reelected Pres. Runaldo Ronald Venetiaan on Aug. 3, 2005.

Swaziland
Kingdom of Swaziland

People: Population: 1,133,066. **Age distrib.** (%): <15: 40.3; 65+: 3.6. **Pop. density:** 171 per sq mi, 66 per sq km. **Urban:** 24.1%. **Ethnic groups:** African 97%, European 3%. **Principal languages:** English, siSwati (both official). **Chief religions:** Zionist 40%, Roman Catholic 20%, Muslim 10%.

Geography: Total area: 6,704 sq mi, 17,363 sq km; **Land area:** 6,642 sq mi, 17,203 sq km. **Location:** In southern Africa, near Indian O. coast. **Neighbors:** South Africa on N, W, S; Mozambique on E. **Topography:** Descends W-E in broad belts, becoming more arid in low veld region, then rising to plateau in E. **Capitals:** Mbabane (administrative), 73,000; Lobamba (legislative).

Government: Type: Constitutional monarchy. **Head of state:** King Mswati III; b. Apr. 19, 1968; in office: Apr. 25, 1986. **Head of gov.:** Prime Min. Absalom Themba Dlamini; b. Dec. 1, 1950; in office: Nov. 26, 2003. **Local divisions:** 4 districts.

Economy: Industries: coal mining, wood pulp, sugar, soft drinks, textiles, apparel. **Chief crops:** sugarcane, cotton, corn, tobacco, rice, citrus. **Natural resources:** asbestos, coal, clay, cassiterite, hydropower, timber, gold, diamonds, quarry stone, talc. **Arable land:** 10%. **Livestock:** cattle: 580,000; chickens: 3.2 mil; goats: 275,000; pigs: 30,000; sheep: 27,000. **Fish catch:** 70 metric tons. **Electricity prod.:** 460 mil kWh. **Labor force:** NA.

Finance: Monetary unit: Lilangeni (SZL) (Sept. 2007: 7.14 = $1 U.S.). **GDP:** $5.9 bil; **per capita GDP:** $5,200; **GDP growth:** 1.2%. **Imports:** $2.3 bil; South Africa 95.6%, EU 0.9%, Japan 0.9%, Singapore 0.3%. **Exports:** $2.2 bil; South Africa 59.7%, EU 8.8%, U.S. 8.8%, Mozambique 6.2%. **Tourism:** $95 mil. **Budget:** $1 bil. **Intl. reserves less gold:** $248 mil.

Transport: Railroad: Length: 187 mi. **Motor vehicles:** 49,000 pass. cars; 63,000 comm. vehicles. **Civil aviation** (2000): 42.3 mil pass.-mi; 1 airport.

Communications: TV sets: 112 per 1,000 pop. **Radios:** 168 per 1,000 pop. **Telephone lines:** 44,000. **Internet:** 41,600 users.

Health: Life expect.: 31.8 male; 32.6 female. **Births** (per 1,000 pop.): 27. **Deaths** (per 1,000 pop.): 30.4. **Natural inc.:** -0.34%. **Infant mortality** (per 1,000 live births): 70.7. **AIDS rate:** 33.4%.

Education: Compulsory: ages 6-12. **Literacy:** 79.6%.

Major intl. organizations: UN (FAO, IBRD, ILO, IMF, WHO, WTO), the Commonwealth, AU.

Embassy: 1712 New Hampshire Ave. NW 20009; 234-5002.

Website: www.gov.sz

The royal house of Swaziland traces back almost 400 years, and is one of Africa's last ruling dynasties. The Swazis, a Bantu people, were driven to Swaziland from lands to the N by the Zulus in 1820. Their autonomy was later guaranteed by Britain and Transvaal (later part of South Africa), with Britain assuming control after 1903. Independence came Sept. 6, 1968. In 1973 the king repealed the constitution and assumed full powers.

A new constitution banning political parties took effect Oct. 13, 1978. A shrinking economy and the AIDS crisis have fueled student and labor unrest in recent years.

Sweden
Kingdom of Sweden

People: Population: 9,031,088. **Age distrib.** (%): <15: 16.4; 65+: 17.9. **Pop. density:** 57 per sq mi, 22 per sq km. **Urban:** 84.2%. **Ethnic groups:** Swedish 89%, Finnish 2%, Sami and other 9%. **Principal languages:** Swedish (official), Sami, Finnish. **Chief religion:** Lutheran 87%.

Geography: Total area: 173,732 sq mi, 449,964 sq km; **Land area:** 158,663 sq mi, 410,934 sq km. **Location:** On Scandinavian Peninsula in N Europe. **Neighbors:** Norway on W, Denmark on S (across Kattegat), Finland on E. **Topography:** Mountains along NW border cover 25% of Sweden, flat or rolling terrain covers central and southern areas, which include several large lakes. **Capital:** Stockholm, 1,708,000. **Cities (urban aggr.):** Göteborg, 827,000.

Government: Type: Constitutional monarchy. **Head of state:** King Carl XVI Gustaf; b. Apr. 30, 1946; in office: Sept. 19, 1973. **Head of gov.:** Prime Min. Fredrik Reinfeldt; b. Aug. 4, 1965; in office: Oct. 5, 2006. **Local divisions:** 21 counties. **Defense budget:** $5.9 bil. **Active troops:** 27,600.

Economy: Industries: iron & steel, precision equip., wood & paper products, proc. foods, autos. **Chief crops:** barley, wheat, sugar beets. **Natural resources:** zinc, iron ore, lead, copper, silver, timber, uranium, hydropower. **Arable land:** 6%. **Livestock:** cattle: 1.6 mil; chickens: 6.8 mil; pigs: 1.7 mil; sheep: 479,700. **Fish catch:** 262,239 metric tons. **Electricity prod.:** 153.2 bil kWh. **Labor force** (2000 est.): agriculture 2%, industry 24%, services 74%.

Finance: Monetary unit: Krona (SEK) (Sept. 2007: 6.67 = $1 U.S.). **GDP:** $290.6 bil; **per capita GDP:** $32,200; **GDP growth:** 4.7%. **Imports:** $151.8 bil; Germany 17.2%, Denmark 9%, Norway 8.1%, UK 5.9%, Netherlands 5.7%, Finland 5.6%, France 4.5%. **Exports:** $173.9 bil; Germany 9.7%, U.S. 9.2%, Norway 9.1%, UK 7.1%, Denmark 6.8%, Finland 5.9%, France 4.9%, Netherlands 4.7%. **Tourism:** $7.4 bil. **Budget:** $210.5 bil. **Intl. reserves less gold:** $16.47 bil. **Gold:** 5.1 mil oz t. **Consumer prices:** 1.36%.

Transport: Railroad: Length: 7,134 mi. **Motor vehicles:** 4.1 mil pass. cars; 453,400 comm. vehicles. **Civil aviation:** 7.2 bil pass.-mi; 155 airports. **Chief ports:** Göteborg, Malmö, Stockholm.

Communications: TV sets: 551 per 1,000 pop. **Radios:** 932 per 1,000 pop. **Telephone lines:** 5.6 mil. **Daily newspaper circ.:** 409.5 per 1,000 pop. **Internet:** 7 mil users.

Health: Life expect.: 78.4 male; 83 female. **Births** (per 1,000 pop.): 10.2. **Deaths** (per 1,000 pop.): 10.3. **Natural inc.:** −0.01%. **Infant mortality** (per 1,000 live births): 2.8. **AIDS rate:** 0.2%.

Education: Compulsory: ages 7-16. **Literacy:** 99%.

Major intl. organizations: UN and all of its specialized agencies, EU, OECD, OSCE.

Embassy: 901 30th St. NW 20007; 467-2600.

Website: www.sweden.gov.se

The Swedes have lived in present-day Sweden for at least 5,000 years, longer than nearly any other European people. Gothic tribes from Sweden played a major role in the disintegration of the Roman Empire. Other Swedes helped create the first Russian state in the 9th cent.

The Swedes were Christianized from the 11th cent., and a strong centralized monarchy developed. A parliament, the Riksdag, was first called in 1435, the earliest parliament on the European continent, with all classes of society represented.

Swedish independence from rule by Danish kings (dating from 1397) was secured by Gustavus I in a revolt, 1521-23; he built up the government and military and established the Lutheran Church. In the 17th cent. Sweden was a major European power, gaining most of the Baltic seacoast, but its international position subsequently declined. The Napoleonic wars, 1799-1815, in which Sweden acquired Norway (it became independent 1905), were the last in which Sweden participated. Armed neutrality was maintained in both world wars.

More than 4 decades of Social Democratic rule ended in the 1976 parliamentary elections; the party returned to power in the 1982 elections. After Prime Min. Olof Palme was shot to death in Stockholm, Feb. 28, 1986, Ingvar Carlsson took office. Carl Bildt, a non-Socialist, became prime min. Oct. 1991, with a mandate to restore Sweden's economic competitiveness. The Social Democrats returned to power following 1994 elections.

Swedish voters approved membership in the European Union Nov. 13, 1994, and Sweden entered the EU as of Jan. 1, 1995. Carlsson retired and was succeeded by Goran Persson in Mar. 1996. Persson and his Social Democrats led coalition governments after the elections of Sept. 20, 1998, and Sept. 15, 2002. Foreign Min. Anna Lindh died Sept. 11, 2003, after being stabbed in a Stockholm department store. Her killer, Mijailo Mijailovic, was sentenced to life in prison Mar. 2004; an appeals court later deemed him mentally ill and sent him to a psychiatric ward.

Swedish voters Sept. 14, 2003, rejected adoption of the euro currency. Foreign Min. Laila Freivalds resigned Mar. 21, 2006, after press reports cited her role in shutting down an Internet political site that was about to post cartoons of the prophet Muhammad; the caricatures, originally published in Denmark, had already sparked worldwide Muslim protests. A center-right alliance led by Fredrik Reinfeldt defeated the Social Democrats in Sept. 17 elections.

Switzerland
Swiss Confederation

People: Population: 7,554,661. **Age distrib.** (%): <15: 16.1; 65+: 15.8. **Pop. density:** 492 per sq mi, 190 per sq km. **Urban:** 75.2%. **Ethnic groups:** German 65%, French 18%, Italian 10%, Romansch 1%. **Principal languages:** German, French, Italian (all official); Serbo-Croatian; Albanian; Portugese; Spanish; English; Romansch. **Chief religions:** Roman Catholic 42%, Protestant 35%, Muslim 4%.

Geography: Total area: 15,942 sq mi, 41,290 sq km; **Land area:** 15,355 sq mi, 39,770 sq km. **Location:** In Alps Mts. in central Europe. **Neighbors:** France on W; Italy on S; Liechtenstein, Austria on E; Germany on N. **Topography:** The Alps cover 60% of land area; the Jura, near France, 10%. Running between, NE-SW, are midlands, 30%. **Capital:** Bern, 357,000. **Cities (urban aggr.):** Zurich, 1,144,000; Basel, 166,700; Geneva, 398,910.

Government: Type: Federal republic. **Head of state and gov.:** The president is elected by the Federal Assembly to a nonrenewable 1-year term. **Local divisions:** 20 full cantons, 6 half cantons. **Defense budget:** $3.6 bil. **Active troops:** 4,200.

Economy: Industries: machinery, chemicals, watches, textiles, precision instruments. **Chief crops:** grains, fruits, vegetables. **Natural resources:** hydropower, timber, salt. **Arable land:** 10%. **Livestock:** cattle: 1.6 mil; chickens: 7.8 mil; goats: 76,900; pigs: 1.7 mil; sheep: 449,300. **Fish catch:** 2,689 metric tons. **Electricity prod.:** 56.1 bil kWh. **Labor force** (1998): agriculture 4.6%, industry 26.3%, services 69.1%.

Finance: Monetary unit: Franc (CHF) (Sept. 2007: 1.19 = $1 U.S.). **GDP:** $255.5 bil; **per capita GDP:** $34,000; **GDP growth:** 2.7%. **Imports:** $162.3 bil; Germany 27.3%, Italy 10.1%, U.S. 9.1%, France 8.1%, Russia 7.6%, UK 4.9%, Austria 4.1%. **Exports:** $166.3 bil; Germany 21.5%, U.S. 9.5%, France 8.6%, Italy 8.4%, UK 5.3%. **Tourism:** $11 bil. **Budget:** $139.1 bil. **Intl. reserves less gold:** $25.32 bil. **Gold:** 41.48 mil oz t. **Consumer prices:** 1.06%.

Transport: Railroad: Length: 2,848 mi. **Motor vehicles:** 3.7 mil pass. cars; 333,000 comm. vehicles. **Civil aviation:** 14.5 bil pass.-mi; 42 airports. **Chief port:** Basel.

Communications: TV sets: 457 per 1,000 pop. **Radios:** 979 per 1,000 pop. **Telephone lines:** 5 mil. **Daily newspaper circ.:** 371.7 per 1,000 pop. **Internet:** 4.4 mil users.

Health: Life expect.: 77.8 male; 83.6 female. **Births** (per 1,000 pop.): 9.7. **Deaths** (per 1,000 pop.): 8.5. **Natural inc.:** 0.12%. **Infant mortality** (per 1,000 live births): 4.3. **AIDS rate:** 0.4%.

Education: Compulsory: ages 7-15. **Literacy:** 99%.

Major intl. organizations: UN and most of its specialized agencies, EFTA, OECD, OSCE.

Embassy: 2900 Cathedral Ave. NW 20008; 745-7900.

Website: www.admin.ch

Switzerland, the former Roman province of Helvetia, traces its modern history to 1291, when 3 cantons created a defensive league. Other cantons were subsequently admitted to the Swiss Confederation, which obtained its independence from the Holy Roman Empire through the Peace of Westphalia (1648). The cantons were joined under a federal constitution in 1848, with large powers of local control retained by each.

Switzerland has maintained an armed neutrality since 1815 and has not been involved in a foreign war since 1515. It is the seat of many UN and other international agencies but did not become a full member of the UN until Sept. 10, 2002.

Switzerland is a world banking center. Stung by charges that assets seized by the Nazis and deposited in Swiss banks in WWII had not been properly returned, the government announced, Mar. 5, 1997, a $4.7 bil fund to compensate victims of the Holocaust and other catastrophies. Swiss banks agreed Aug. 12, 1998, to pay $1.25 bil in reparations. Abortion was decriminalized by a June 2, 2002 referendum. The rightist Swiss People's Party topped Oct. 2003 parlimentary voting and entered a coalition government. In referendums June 5 and Sept. 25, 2005, voters backed plans harmonizing travel, asylum, law enforcement, and labor policies with the EU; more rights for same-sex couples were also endorsed June 5.

Syria
Syrian Arab Republic

People: Population: 19,314,747. **Age distrib.** (%): <15: 36.5; 65+: 3.3. **Pop. density:** 272 per sq mi, 105 per sq km. **Urban:** 50.6%. **Ethnic groups:** Arab 90%, Kurds, Armenians, other 10%. **Principal languages:** Arabic (official), Kurdish, Armenian, Aramaic, Circassian. **Chief religions:** Sunni Muslim 74%, other Muslims 16%, Christian 10%.

Geography: Total area: 71,498 sq mi, 185,180 sq km; **Land area:** 71,062 sq mi, 184,050 sq km. **Location:** Middle East, at E end of Medit. Sea. **Neighbors:** Lebanon, Israel on W; Jordan on S; Iraq on E; Turkey on N. **Topography:** Syria has a short Medit. coastline, then stretches E and S with fertile lowlands and plains, alternating with mountains and large desert areas. **Capital:** Damascus, 2,272,000. **Cities (urban aggr.):** Aleppo, 2,520,000; Homs, 923,000.

Government: Type: Republic (under military regime). **Head of state:** Pres. Bashar al-Assad; b. Sept. 11, 1965; in office: July 17, 2000. **Head of gov.:** Prime Min. Muhammad Naji al-Otari; b. 1944; in office: Sept. 10, 2003. **Local divisions:** 14 provinces. **Defense budget:** $1.36 bil. **Active troops:** 307,600.

Economy: Industries: oil, textiles, food proc., beverages, tobacco, phosphate mining. **Chief crops:** wheat, barley, cotton, lentils, chickpeas, olives, sugar beets. **Natural resources:** oil, phosphates, chrome, mang., asphalt, iron ore, salt, marble, gypsum, hydropower. **Crude oil reserves:** 2.5 bil bbls. **Arable land:** 25%. **Livestock:** cattle: 1.1 mil; chickens: 23.8 mil; goats: 1.3 mil; sheep: 19.7 mil. **Fish catch:** 16,980 metric tons. **Electricity prod.:** 33 bil kWh. **Labor force** (2003 est.): agriculture 26%, industry 14%, services 60%.

Finance: Monetary unit: Pound (SYP) (Sept. 2007: 51.36 = $1 U.S.). **GDP:** $77.7 bil; **per capita GDP:** $4,100; **GDP growth:** 3.5%. **Imports:** $6.6 bil; Saudi Arabia 12.1%, China 7.7%, Egypt 6.1%, UAE 5.9%, Italy 4.8%, Ukraine 4.7%, Germany 4.7%, Iran 4.4%. **Exports:** $6.9 bil; Iraq 27.4%, Germany 12.2%, Lebanon 9.5%, Italy 6.6%, Egypt 5.3%, Saudi Arabia 4.8%. **Tourism:** $1.8 bil. **Budget:** $9.9 bil. **Intl. reserves less gold:** NA. **Gold:** 830,000 oz t. **Consumer prices:** 10.02%.

Transport: Railroad: Length: 1,685 mi. **Motor vehicles:** 281,000 pass. cars; 394,000 comm. vehicles. **Civil aviation:** 1.1 bil pass.-mi; 26 airports. **Chief ports:** Baniyas, Latakia.

Communications: TV sets: 68 per 1,000 pop. **Radios:** 278 per 1,000 pop. **Telephone lines:** 3.2 mil. **Internet:** 1.5 mil users.

Health: Life expect.: 69.3 male; 72 female. **Births** (per 1,000 pop.): 27.2. **Deaths** (per 1,000 pop.): 4.7. **Natural inc.:** 2.25%. **Infant mortality** (per 1,000 live births): 27.7 **AIDS rate:** NA.

Education: Compulsory: ages 6-14. **Literacy:** 80.8%.

Major intl. organizations: UN (FAO, IBRD, ILO, IMF, IMO, WHO), AL.

Embassy: 2215 Wyoming Ave. NW 20008; 232-6313.

Website: www.syrianembassy.us

Syria was the center of the Seleucid empire, but later became absorbed in the Roman and Arab empires. Ottoman rule prevailed for 4 cents., until the end of WWI.

The state of Syria was formed from former Turkish districts, separated by the Treaty of Sevres, 1920, and divided into the states of Syria and Greater Lebanon. Both were administered under a French League of Nations mandate 1920-41.

Syria was proclaimed a republic by the occupying French Sept. 16, 1941, and exercised full independence Apr. 17, 1946. Syria joined the Arab invasion of Israel in 1948.

Syria joined Egypt Feb. 1958 in the United Arab Republic but seceded Sept. 1961. The Socialist Baath party and military leaders seized power Mar. 1963. The Baath, a pan-Arab organization, became the only legal party. The government has been dominated by the Alawite minority.

In the Arab-Israeli war of June 1967, Israel seized and occupied the Golan Heights, from which Syria had shelled Israeli settlements. On Oct. 6, 1973, Syria joined Egypt in an attack on Israel. Syrian troops entered Lebanon in 1976, during the Lebanese civil war, and remained a strong presence in the country. They fought Palestinian guerrillas and, later, Christian militiamen. Syria sided with Iran during the Iran-Iraq war, 1980-88.

Following Israel's invasion of Lebanon, June 6, 1982, Israeli planes destroyed 17 Syrian antiaircraft missile batteries in the Bekaa Valley, June 9. Some 25 Syrian planes were downed during the engagement. Israel and Syria agreed to a cease-fire June 11. Syria's alleged role in promoting international terrorism led to strained relations with the U.S. and Great Britain.

Syria condemned the Aug. 1990 Iraqi invasion of Kuwait and sent troops to help Allied forces in the Gulf War. In 1991, Syria accepted U.S. proposals for the terms of an Arab-Israeli peace conference. Syria subsequently participated in negotiations with Israel, but progress toward peace was slow.

Former Prime Min. Mahmoud al-Zoubi killed himself May 21, 2000, after being charged with corruption. Hafez al-Assad, president of Syria since 1971, died June 10, 2000, and was succeeded by his son Bashar al-Assad.

Following the invasion of Iraq, Mar. 2003, the U.S. pressured Syria to rein in extremists and deny safe haven to fugitive Iraqi leaders. Israeli planes hit an alleged terrorist camp near Damascus Oct. 4, 2003. The U.S. imposed limited sanctions on Syria, May 11, 2004.

The killing of former Lebanese Prime Min. Rafik al-Hariri by a truck bomb in Beirut, Feb. 14, 2005, was a catalyst for massive anti-Syrian protests in Lebanon. Syria denied responsibility for the blast but pulled nearly all its troops out of Lebanon by Apr. 26; some Syrian intelligence agents may have remained. Syria aided Hezbollah fighters in their conflict with Israel. When Israeli armed forces struck Lebanon, July-Aug. 2006, in an effort to cripple Hezbollah, about 180,000 Lebanese found temporary refuge in Syria. Four suspected Islamic militants stormed the U.S. embassy in Damascus Sept. 12 but were gunned down by Syrian security guards.

In an uncontested referendum, May 27, 2007, Syrian voters confirmed Pres. Bashar al-Assad for another 7-year term. An estimated 1.5 mil Iraqi refugees were living in Syria at midyear. On Sept. 6, Israel bombed a secret site in N Syria where the Israelis reportedly believed Syria and N. Korea were developing a nuclear facility; both countries denied the claim.

Taiwan
Republic of China

People: Population: 22,858,872. **Age distrib.** (%): <15: 17.8; 65+: 10.2. **Pop. density:** 1,835 sq mi, 709 per sq km. **Urban:** NA. **Ethnic groups:** Taiwanese 84%, mainland Chinese 14%, in-

digenous 2%. **Principal languages:** Mandarin Chinese (official), Taiwanese (Min), Hakka dialects. **Chief religions:** Buddhist, Confucian, Taoist 93%; Christian 5%.

Geography: Total area: 13,892 sq mi, 35,980 sq km; **Land area:** 12,456 sq mi, 32,260 sq km. **Location:** Off SE coast of China, between E and S China seas. **Neighbors:** Nearest is China to NW. **Topography:** A mountain range forms backbone of island; the eastern half is very steep and craggy, western slope is flat, fertile, and well cultivated. **Capital:** Taipei, 2,606,000. **Cities:** Kaohsiung, 1,512,677; Taichung, 1,021,292.

Government: Type: Democracy. **Head of state:** Pres. Chen Shui-bian; b. Feb. 18, 1951; in office: May 20, 2000. **Head of gov.:** Prime Min. Chang Chun-hsiung; b. Mar. 23, 1938; in office: May 21, 2007. **Local divisions:** 16 counties, 5 municipalities, 2 special municipalities (Taipei, Kaohsiung). **Defense budget:** $7.73 bil. **Active troops:** 290,000.

Economy: Industries: electronics, oil refining, chemicals, textiles, iron & steel, machinery, cement, food proc. **Chief crops:** rice, corn, vegetables, fruit, tea. **Natural resources:** coal, nat. gas, limestone, marble, asbestos. **Crude oil reserves:** 2.4 mil bbls. **Arable land:** 24%. **Fish catch:** 1,321,999 metric tons. **Electricity prod.:** 210.3 bil kWh. **Labor force** (2005 est.): agriculture 5.5%, industry 36%, services 58.5%.

Finance: Monetary unit: New Dollar (TWD) (Sept. 2007: 33.07 = $1 U.S.). **GDP:** $680.5 bil; **per capita GDP:** $29,500; **GDP growth:** 4.6%. **Imports:** $205.3 bil; Japan 23%, China 11.9%, U.S. 10.9%, S. Korea 7.2%, Saudi Arabia 4.9%. **Exports:** $215 bil; China 22.5%, Hong Kong 15.7%, U.S. 15%, Japan 7.3%. **Tourism:** $5 bil. **Budget:** $77.9 bil. **Intl. reserves less gold:** $176.91 bil.

Transport: Railroad: Length: 1,552 mi. **Motor vehicles:** NA. **Civil aviation:** 38 airports. **Chief ports:** Chijung (Keelung), Hualien, Kaohsiung, Suao, Taichung.

Communications: TV sets: 327 per 1,000 pop. **Radios:** 402 per 1,000 pop. **Telephone lines:** 14.5 mil. **Internet:** 13.2 mil users.

Health: Life expect.: 74.7 male; 80.7 female. **Births** (per 1,000 pop.): 9. **Deaths** (per 1,000 pop.): 6.5. **Natural inc.:** 0.24%. **Infant mortality** (per 1,000 live births): 5.5. **AIDS rate:** NA.

Education: Compulsory: ages 6-14. **Literacy:** 96.1%.

Major intl. organizations: APEC.

Embassy: 4201 Wisconsin Ave. NW 20016; 895-1800.

Website: www.gov.tw

Large-scale Chinese immigration began in the 17th cent. The island came under mainland control after an interval of Dutch rule, 1620-62. Taiwan (also called Formosa) was ruled by Japan 1895-1945. The Kuomintang (Chinese nationalist govt.) fled to Taiwan in 1949 and established the Republic of China under Chiang Kai-shek, who ruled until his death in 1975. The U.S. provided military aid to deter a Communist invasion.

In 1971, the UN expelled Taiwan from its seat and recognized the mainland government. The U.S. officially recognized the People's Republic, Dec. 15, 1978, and severed ties with Taiwan. However, the U.S. and Taiwan have continued a strong trading relationship and maintain contact via quasi-official agencies.

Land reform, government planning, U.S. aid and investment, and free universal education brought huge advances in industry, agriculture, and living standards. In 1987 martial law was lifted after 38 years, and in 1991 the 43-year period of emergency rule ended. Taiwan held its first direct presidential election Mar. 23, 1996. An earthquake on Sept. 21, 1999, killed more than 2,300 people and injured thousands more.

Five decades of Nationalist Party rule ended with the presidential election of Mar. 18, 2000, won by Chen Shui-bian, leader of the pro-independence Democratic Progressive Party. Chen was wounded in an apparent assassination attempt Mar. 19, 2004, one day before he narrowly won a 2nd term as president. Beleaguered by corruption scandals, Chen yielded some of his powers to the prime min., May 31, 2006. Attempts to remove the president June 27 and Oct. 13 failed to gain the required two-thirds majority in the legislature. His wife and 3 presidential aides were indicted Nov. 3 on charges of mishandling govt. funds. Chen is immune from prosecution until his term expires in 2008.

Since 1949, the People's Republic has considered Taiwan a rebel province of the mainland, while, until 1991, Taiwan claimed to be the sole government of both. Beijing and Taipei increased economic cooperation in the 1990s. In 1999, relations between the 2 soured, when Taiwan redefined its relationship with mainland China as "state to state." China has warned that any Taiwan move toward independence could provoke military action.

The **Penghu Isls.** (Pescadores), 49 sq mi, pop. (2006 est.) 91,785, lie between Taiwan and the mainland. **Quemoy**, pop. (2006 est.) 76,491, and **Matsu**, pop. (2006 est.) 9,786, lie just off the mainland.

Tajikistan
Republic of Tajikistan

People: Population: 7,076,598. **Age distrib.** (%): <15: 35; 65+: 3.8. **Pop. density:** 128 per sq mi, 50 per sq km. **Urban:** 24.7%. **Ethnic groups:** Tajik 80%, Uzbek 15%, Russian 1%, Kyrgyz 1%. **Principal languages:** Tajik (official), Russian. **Chief religions:** Sunni Muslim 85%, Shi'a Muslim 5%.

Geography: Total area: 55,251 sq mi, 143,100 sq km; **Land area:** 55,097 sq mi, 142,700 sq km. **Location:** Central Asia. **Neighbors:** Uzbekistan on N and W, Kyrgyzstan on N, China on E,

Afghanistan on S. **Topography:** Mountainous region that contains the Pamirs, Trans-Alai mountain system. **Capital:** Dushanbe, 549,000.

Government: Type: Republic. **Head of state:** Pres. Imomali Rakhmon; b. Oct. 5, 1952; in office: Nov. 6, 1994. **Head of gov.:** Prime Min. Akil Akilov; b. 1944; in office: Jan. 20, 1999. **Local divisions:** 2 viloyats, 1 autonomous viloyat. **Defense budget:** $70.7 mil. **Active troops:** 7,600.

Economy: Industries: metals, chemicals & fertilizers, cement, vegetable oil, machine tools. **Chief crops:** cotton, grain, fruits, grapes, vegetables. **Natural resources:** hydropower, oil, uranium, mercury, lignite, lead, zinc, antimony, tungsten, silver, gold. **Crude oil reserves:** 12 mil bbls. **Arable land:** 7%. **Livestock:** cattle: 1.4 mil; chickens: 3.5 mil; goats: 1.2 mil; pigs: 1,000; sheep: 1.9 mil. **Fish catch:** 210 metric tons. **Electricity prod.:** 16.9 bil kWh. **Labor force** (2000 est.): agriculture 67.2%, industry 7.5%, services 25.3%.

Finance: Monetary unit: Somoni (TJS) (Sept. 2007: 3.44 = $1 U.S.). **GDP:** $9.5 bil; **per capita GDP:** $1,300; **GDP growth:** 7%. **Imports:** $1.5 bil; Russia 21.2%, China 17.2%, Kazakhstan 10.6%, Uzbekistan 9.6%, Azerbaijan 7.3%, Ukraine 5.2%, Turkey 4%. **Exports:** $1.2 bil; Norway 13.9%, Russia 13%, Turkey 12.2%, Uzbekistan 9.4%, U.S. 6.4%, Italy 5.3%, Iran 5.2%, Greece 4.2%. **Tourism:** $1 mil. **Budget:** $622 mil. **Intl. reserves less gold:** $116 mil. **Gold:** 50,000 oz t.

Transport: Railroad: Length: 300 mi. **Motor vehicles:** 117,100 pass. cars; 16,800 comm. vehicles. **Civil aviation:** 530.7 mil pass.-mi; 17 airports.

Communications: TV sets: 328 per 1,000 pop. **Radios:** 143 per 1,000 pop. **Telephone lines:** 280,200. **Internet:** 19,500 users.

Health: Life expect.: 61.6 male; 67.8 female. **Births** (per 1,000 pop.): 27.3. **Deaths** (per 1,000 pop.): 7.1. **Natural inc.:** 2.03%. **Infant mortality** (per 1,000 live births): 43.6. **AIDS rate:** 0.1%.

Education: Compulsory: ages 7-15. **Literacy:** 99.5%.

Major International Organizations: UN (FAO, IBRD, ILO, IMF, WHO), CIS, OSCE.

Embassy: 1005 New Hampshire Ave. NW 20037; 223-6090.

Website: www.tjus.org

There were settled societies in the region from about 3000 BCE. Invaders have included Iranians, Arabs (who converted the population to Islam), Mongols, Uzbeks, Afghans, and Russians. The USSR gained control 1918-25. In 1924, the Tajik ASSR was created within the Uzbek SSR. The Tajik SSR was proclaimed in 1929.

Tajikistan declared independence Sept. 9, 1991. Factional fighting led to the installation of a pro-Communist regime, Jan. 1993. A new constitution establishing a presidential system was approved by referendum Nov. 6, 1994.

Clashes between Muslim rebels, reportedly armed by Afghanistan, and troops loyal to the government (and supported by Russia) claimed an estimated 55,000 lives by mid-1997, despite a series of peace accords. Constitutional changes including legalization of Islamic political parties were approved by referendum Sept. 26, 1999. Pres. Imomali Rakhmonov won a Nov. 6 election called "a farce" by human-rights observers. Voters approved, June 22, 2003, constitutional changes giving Rakhmonov the right to serve as president until 2020. Leading opposition groups boycotted the election of Nov. 6, 2006, again won by Rakhmonov. He changed his name to Rakhmon under a decree that banned Slavic name endings and other Soviet-era practices.

Tanzania
United Republic of Tanzania

People: Population: 39,384,223. **Age distrib. (%):** <15: 43.9; 65+: 2.8. **Pop. density:** 115 per sq mi, 44 per sq km. **Urban:** 24.2%. **Ethnic groups:** Mainland: Bantu 95%; Zanzibar: Arab, African, mixed. **Principal languages:** Swahili, English (both official); Arabic, local languages. **Chief religions:** Christian 30%, Muslim 35%, indigenous beliefs 35%; Zanzibar is 99% Muslim.

Geography: Total area: 364,900 sq mi, 945,087 sq km; **Land area:** 342,101 sq mi, 886,037 sq km. **Location:** On coast of E Africa. **Neighbors:** Kenya, Uganda on N; Rwanda, Burundi, Congo on W; Zambia, Malawi, Mozambique on S. **Topography:** Hot, arid central plateau, surrounded by lake region in W, temperate highlands in N and S, the coastal plains. Mt. Kilimanjaro, 19,340 ft, is highest in Africa. **Capital:** Dodoma, 168,000. **Cities (urban aggr.):** Dar es Salaam, 2,676,000.

Government: Type: Republic. **Head of state:** Pres. Jakaya Mrisho Kikwete; b. Oct. 7, 1950; in office: Dec. 21, 2005. **Head of gov.:** Prime Min. Edward Lowassa; b. Aug. 26, 1953; in office: Dec. 30, 2005. **Local divisions:** 25 regions. **Defense budget:** $137 mil. **Active troops:** 27,000.

Economy: Industries: agric. proc., diamond & gold mining, oil refining, shoes. **Chief crops:** coffee, sisal, tea, cotton, pyrethrum (insecticide from chrysanthemums), cashews. **Natural resources:** hydropower, tin, phosphates, iron ore, coal, diamonds, gemstones, gold, nat. gas, nickel. **Arable land:** 4%. **Livestock:** cattle: 17.7 mil; chickens: 30 mil; goats: 12.6 mil; pigs: 455,000; sheep: 3.5 mil. **Fish catch:** 347,811 metric tons. **Electricity prod.:** 1.9 bil kWh. **Labor force** (2002 est.): agriculture 80%, industry and services 20%.

Finance: Monetary unit: Shilling (TZS) (Sept. 2007: 1,246.00 = $1 U.S.). **GDP:** $29.6 bil; **per capita GDP:** $800; **GDP growth:** 5.8%. **Imports:** $3.6 bil; South Africa 10%, China 9.6%, Kenya 8%, India 6.9%, UAE 6.1%, U.S. 4%. **Exports:** $1.8 bil; China 8.9%, India 8.8%, Netherlands 6.2%, Japan 5.4%, Zambia 4.7%, UAE

4.3%. **Tourism:** $594 mil. **Budget:** $3 bil. **Intl. reserves less gold:** $1.50 bil. **Consumer prices:** 9.12%.

Transport: Railroad: Length: 2,293 mi. **Motor vehicles:** 35,600 pass. cars; 98,800 comm. vehicles. **Civil aviation:** 93.8 mil pass.-mi; 11 airports. **Chief ports:** Dar es Salaam, Mtwara, Zanzibar City.

Communications: TV sets: 21 per 1,000 pop. **Radios:** 280 per 1,000 pop. **Telephone lines:** 157,300. **Internet:** 384,300 users.

Health: Life expect.: 49.4 male; 52 female. **Births** (per 1,000 pop.): 36. **Deaths** (per 1,000 pop.): 13.4. **Natural inc.:** 2.26%. **Infant mortality** (per 1,000 live births): 71.7. **AIDS rate:** 6.5%.

Education: Compulsory: ages 6-12. **Literacy:** 69.4%.

Major intl. organizations: UN and all of its specialized agencies, the Commonwealth, AU.

Embassy: 2139 R St. NW 20008; 939-6125.

Website: www.tanzania.go.tz

The Republic of Tanganyika in East Africa and the island Republic of Zanzibar, off the coast of Tanganyika, both of which had recently gained independence, joined into a single nation, the United Republic of Tanzania, Apr. 26, 1964. Zanzibar retains internal self-government.

Until resigning as president in 1985, Julius K. Nyerere, a former Tanganyikan independence leader, dominated Tanzania's politics, which emphasized government planning and control of the economy, with single-party rule. In 1992 the constitution was amended to establish a multiparty system. Privatization of the economy was undertaken in the 1990s.

At least 500 people died when an overcrowded Tanzanian ferry sank in Lake Victoria, May 21, 1996. About 460,000 Rwandan refugees, mostly Hutu, returned from Tanzania to Rwanda in Dec. 1996. A bomb at the U.S. embassy in Dar-es-Salaam, Aug. 7, 1998, killed 11 people and injured at least 70 others. The U.S. blamed the attack and a near-simultaneous embassy bombing in Kenya on Islamic terrorists associated with Osama bin Laden. After a trial in New York City, 4 conspirators were convicted May 29, 2001.

Former Pres. Nyerere died in London Oct. 14, 1999. President since 1995, Benjamin Mkapa was reelected Oct. 29, 2000. Over 280 people died in a train wreck June 24, 2002, SE of Dodoma. Jakaya Mrisho Kikwete of the ruling Chama Cha Mapinduzi (Party of the Revolution) won the Dec. 14, 2005, presidential election.

Tanganyika. Arab colonization and slaving began in the 8th cent. CE; Portuguese sailors explored the coast by about 1500. Other Europeans followed.

In 1885 Germany established German East Africa of which Tanganyika formed the bulk. It became a League of Nations mandate and, after 1946, a UN trust territory, both under Britain. It became independent Dec. 9, 1961, and a republic within the Commonwealth a year later.

Zanzibar, the Isle of Cloves, lies 23 mi off mainland Tanzania; area 640 sq mi and pop. (2002) 622,459. The island of **Pemba,** 25 mi to the NE, area 380 sq mi and pop. (2002) 362,166 is included in the administration.

Chief industry is cloves and clove oil production, of which Zanzibar and Pemba produce most of the world's supply.

Zanzibar was for centuries the center for Arab slave traders. Portugal ruled the region for 2 centuries until ousted by Arabs around 1700. Zanzibar became a British Protectorate in 1890; independence came Dec. 10, 1963. Revolutionary forces overthrew the Sultan Jan. 12, 1964. The new government ousted Western diplomats and newsmen, slaughtered thousands of Arabs, and nationalized farms. Union with Tanganyika followed.

Thailand
Kingdom of Thailand

People: Population: 65,068,149. **Age distrib. (%):** <15: 21.6; 65+: 8.2. **Pop. density:** 329 per sq mi, 127 per sq km. **Urban:** 32.3%. **Ethnic groups:** Thai 75%, Chinese 14%. **Principal languages:** Thai; English; ethnic, regional dialects. **Chief religions:** Buddhism (official) 95%, Muslim 5%.

Geography: Total area: 198,457 sq mi, 514,000 sq km; **Land area:** 197,596 sq mi, 511,770 sq km. **Location:** On Indochinese and Malayan peninsulas in SE Asia. **Neighbors:** Myanmar on W and N, Laos on N, Cambodia on E, Malaysia on S. **Topography:** A plateau dominates NE third of Thailand, dropping to the fertile alluvial valley of Chao Phraya R. in center. Forested mountains are in N, with narrow fertile valleys. The S peninsula region is covered by rain forests. **Capital:** Bangkok, 6,593,000. **Cities (urban aggr.)** (1999): Chiang-Mai, 160,200

Government: Type: Constitutional monarchy. **Head of state:** King Bhumibol Adulyadej; b. Dec. 5, 1927; in office: June 9, 1946. **Head of gov.:** Prime Min. Surayud Chulanont; b. Aug. 28, 1943; in office: Oct. 1, 2006. **Local divisions:** 76 provinces. **Defense budget:** $2.13 bil. **Active troops:** 306,600.

Economy: Industries: tourism; textiles & garments, agric. proc., beverages, tobacco, cement, light mfg.; electric appliances & components, computers & parts. **Chief crops:** rice, cassava, rubber, corn, sugarcane, coconuts, soybeans. **Natural resources:** tin, rubber, nat. gas, tungsten, tantalum, timber, lead, fish, gypsum, lignite, fluorite. **Crude oil reserves:** 290 mil bbls. **Arable land:** 28%. **Livestock:** cattle: 6 mil; chickens: 203.2 mil; goats: 324,150; pigs: 8.2 mil; sheep: 51,151. **Fish catch:** 3,743,398 metric tons. **Electricity prod.:** 124.6 bil kWh. **Labor force** (2000 est.): agriculture 49%, industry 14%, services 37%.

Finance: Monetary unit: Baht (THB) (Sept. 2007: 32.02 = $1

U.S.). **GDP:** $596.5 bil; **per capita GDP:** $9,200; **GDP growth:** 4.8%. **Imports:** $119.3 bil; Japan 20.1%, China 10.6%, U.S. 6.7%, Malaysia 6.6%, UAE 5.6%, Singapore 4.5%. **Exports:** $123.5 bil; U.S. 15%, Japan 12.7%, China 9%, Singapore 6.4%, Hong Kong 5.5%, Malaysia 5.1%. **Tourism:** $10.1 bil. **Budget:** $40.3 bil. **Intl. reserves less gold:** $43.40 bil. **Gold:** 2.7 mil oz t. **Consumer prices:** 4.64%.

Transport: Railroad: Length: 2,530 mi. **Motor vehicles:** 3 mil pass. cars; 4.4 mil comm. vehicles. **Civil aviation:** 28.2 bil pass.-mi; 66 airports. **Chief ports:** Bangkok, Laem Chabang, Prachuap Port, Si Racha.

Communication: TV sets: 274 per 1,000 pop. **Radios:** 234 per 1,000 pop. **Telephone lines:** 7.1 mil. **Daily newspaper circ.:** 196.9 per 1,000 pop. **Internet:** 8.5 mil users.

Health: Life expect.: 70.2 male; 75 female. **Births** (per 1,000 pop.): 13.7. **Deaths** (per 1,000 pop.): 7.1. **Natural inc.:** 0.66%. **Infant mortality** (per 1,000 live births): 18.9. **AIDS rate:** 1.4%.

Education: Compulsory: ages 6-14. **Literacy:** 92.6%.

Major intl. organizations: UN (FAO, IBRD, ILO, IMF, IMO, WHO, WTO), ASEAN, APEC.

Embassy: 1024 Wisconsin Ave. NW, Ste. 401, 20007; 944-3600.

Website: www.thaigov.go.th

Thais began migrating from southern China during the 11th cent. A unified Thai kingdom was established in 1350. Known as Siam until 1939, Thailand is the only country in SE Asia never taken over by a European power, thanks to King Mongkut and his son King Chulalongkorn. Ruling successively from 1851 to 1910, they modernized the country and signed trade treaties with Britain and France. A bloodless revolution in 1932 limited the monarchy. Thailand was an ally of Japan during WWII and of the U.S. during the postwar period. For decades, the military had a dominant role in governing the country.

A steep downturn in the economy forced Thailand to seek more than $15 bil in emergency international loans in Aug. 1997. A new constitution won legislative approval Sept. 27. By the end of the 1990s, according to UN estimates, more than 750,000 people in Thailand had HIV/AIDS; a nationwide prevention campaign has reduced the number of new infections.

Following elections in Jan. 2001, Thaksin Shinawatra, a wealthy former telecommunications executive, became prime min. On Feb. 1, 2003, Thaksin launched a nationwide crackdown on methamphetamines; human rights observers criticized police tactics in the drug war, which killed more than 2,200 people by Apr. 30. The Indian Ocean tsunami of Dec. 26, 2004, left about 5,400 people dead and over 2,800 missing in Thailand.

Elections Feb. 6, 2005, gave Thaksin's party a huge majority in parliament. He assumed emergency powers July 15 to deal with an Islamic insurgency in southern Thailand; from Jan. 2004 to Aug. 2007, more than 2,400 people (nearly 90% of them civilians) died in the fighting.

Facing rising opposition and accused of benefiting improperly from the sale of his family's telecom business, Thaksin called snap elections for Apr. 2, 2006, 3 years ahead of schedule; the vote, which major parties boycotted, was later ruled unconstitutional. A military junta took power in a bloodless coup Sept. 19. Thaksin's party was disbanded by court order, May 30, 2007, and he and other party officials were banned from politics for 5 years. Voters ratified a new constitution Aug. 19, and elections were set for Dec. 23.

Timor-Leste
(East Timor)
Democratic Republic of Timor-Leste

People: Population: 1,084,971. **Age distrib.** (%): <15: 35.7; 65+: 3.2. **Pop. density:** 187 per sq mi, 72 per sq km. **Urban:** 26.5%. **Ethnic groups:** Austronesian, Papuan. **Principal languages:** Tetum, Portuguese (both official); Indonesian; English; other indigenous languages. **Chief religion:** Roman Catholic 98%.

Geography: Total area: 5,794 sq mi, 15,007 sq km. **Land area:** 5,641 sq mi, 14,609 sq km. **Location:** E half of Timor Isl. in SW Pacific O. **Neighbors:** Indonesia (West Timor) on W. **Topography:** Terrain is rugged, rising to 9,721 ft at Mt. Ramelau. **Capital:** Dili, 156,000.

Government: Type: Republic. **Head of state:** Pres. José Ramos-Horta; b. Dec. 26, 1949; in office: May 20, 2007. **Head of gov.:** Prime Min. Xanana Gusmão; b. June 20, 1946; in office: Aug. 8, 2007. **Local divisions:** 13 districts. **Defense budget:** NA. **Active troops:** 1,250.

Economy: Industries: printing, soap, handicrafts, clothing. **Chief crops:** coffee, rice, corn, cassava, sweet potatoes. **Natural resources:** gold, oil, nat. gas, manu., marble. **Arable land:** 8%. **Livestock:** cattle: 171,000; chickens: 2.2 mil; goats: 80,000; pigs: 346,000; sheep: 25,000. **Fish catch:** 350 metric tons. **Electricity prod.:** NA. **Labor force:** NA.

Finance: Monetary unit: U.S. Dollar (USD). **GDP** (2004 est.): $370 mil; **per capita GDP** (2005 est.): $800; **GDP growth** (2005 est.): 1.8%. **Imports** (2004 est.): $202 mil. **Exports** (2005 est.): $10 mil; Indonesia 100%. **Tourism:** NA. **Budget** (2004 est.): $73 mil.

Transport: Civil aviation: 3 airports. **Chief port:** Dili.

Communication: NA.

Health: Life expect.: 64.3 male; 69 female. **Births** (per 1,000 pop.): 26.8. **Deaths** (per 1,000 pop.): 6.2. **Natural inc.:** 2.06%. **Infant mortality** (per 1,000 live births): 44.5. **AIDS rate:** NA.

Education: Compulsory: ages 7-15. **Literacy:** 58.6%.

Major intl. organizations: UN (FAO, IBRD, ILO, IMF, IMO, WHO).

Embassy: 4201 Connecticut Ave. NW 20008; 966-3202.

Website: www.timor-leste.gov.tl

The collapse of Portuguese rule in East Timor led to an outbreak of factional fighting in Aug. 1975 and an invasion by Indonesia in Dec. Indonesia annexed East Timor as a 27th province in 1976, despite international condemnation. In over 2 decades some 200,000 Timorese died as a result of civil war, famine, and persecution by Indonesian authorities. In a referendum held Aug. 30, 1999, under UN auspices, Timorese voted overwhelmingly for independence. Pro-Indonesian militias then went on a rampage, terrorizing the population. Under pressure, the government allowed entrance of an international peacekeeping force, which began arriving in Sept.; a UN interim administration formally took command Oct. 26, 1999.

Pro-independence forces won elections for a constituent assembly Aug. 30, 2001. Xanana Gusmão, a former guerrilla leader, won the presidential election Apr. 14, 2002. As Timor-Leste, the territory became independent May 20 and entered the UN Sept. 27. A sovereignty dispute with Australia over the oil-rich Timor Sea was resolved in Aug. 2004. Australia and other nations sent peacekeepers to suppress a wave of gang violence that engulfed Dili in May 2006. Pres. José Ramos-Horta, a Nobel laureate, won a presidential runoff vote May 9, 2007. After inconclusive parliamentary elections June 30, Ramos-Horta ended a political deadlock by choosing Gusmão as prime min.

Togo
Togolese Republic

People: Population: 5,701,579. **Age distrib.** (%): <15: 42; 65+: 2.7. **Pop. density:** 272 per sq mi, 105 per sq km. **Urban:** 40.1%. **Ethnic groups:** 37 African tribes; largest are Ewe, Mina, Kabre. **Principal languages:** French (official); Ewe, Mina; Kabye; Dagomba. **Chief religions:** Indigenous beliefs 51%, Christian 29%, Muslim 20%.

Geography: Total area: 21,925 sq mi, 56,785 sq km; **Land area:** 20,998 sq mi, 54,385 sq km. **Location:** On S coast of W Africa. **Neighbors:** Ghana on W, Burkina Faso on N, Benin on E. **Topography:** A range of hills running SW-NE splits Togo into 2 savanna plains regions. **Capital:** Lomé, 1,337,000.

Government: Type: Republic. **Head of state:** Pres. Faure Gnassingbé; b. June 6, 1966; in office: May 4, 2005. **Head of gov.:** Prime Min. Feleti Sevele; b. 1944; in office: Mar. 30, 2006 (acting from Feb. 11). **Local divisions:** 5 regions. **Defense budget:** $35 mil. **Active troops:** 8,550.

Economy: Industries: phosphates mining, agric. proc., cement, handicrafts. **Chief crops:** coffee, cocoa, cotton, yams, cassava, corn. **Natural resources:** phosphates, limestone, marble. **Arable land:** 44%. **Livestock:** cattle: 280,000; chickens: 9 mil; goats: 1.5 mil; pigs: 320,000; sheep: 1.9 mil. **Fish catch:** 29,267 metric tons. **Electricity prod.:** 180 mil kWh. **Labor force** (1998 est.): agriculture 65%, industry 5%, services 30%.

Finance: Monetary unit: CFA BCEAO Franc (XOF) (Sept. 2007: 472.78 = $1 U.S.). **GDP:** $9.3 bil; **per capita GDP:** $1,700; **GDP growth:** 2%. **Imports:** $1.2 bil; China 30.9%, UK 11.3%, France 9.2%, Netherlands 6.1%, Belgium 6%, U.S. 4.8%. **Exports:** $868.4 mil; Ghana 16.7%, Burkina Faso 14.4%, Benin 9.1%, Belgium 6.1%, Mali 5.8%, Germany 5.4%. **Tourism:** $15 mil. **Budget:** $311 mil. **Intl. reserves less gold:** $249 mil. **Consumer prices:** 2.23%.

Transport: Railroad: Length: 353 mi. **Motor vehicles:** 51,400 pass. cars; 24,500 comm. vehicles. **Civil aviation** (2001): 80.8 mil pass.-mi; 2 airports. **Chief port:** Lomé.

Communications: TV sets: 22 per 1,000 pop. **Radios:** 244 per 1,000 pop. **Telephone lines:** 82,100. **Daily newspaper circ.:** 2.2 per 1,000 pop. **Internet:** 320,000 users.

Health: Life expect.: 55.8 male; 60 female. **Births** (per 1,000 pop.): 36.8. **Deaths** (per 1,000 pop.): 9.7. **Natural inc.:** 2.72%. **Infant mortality** (per 1,000 live births): 59.1. **AIDS rate:** 3.2%.

Education: Compulsory: ages 6-15. **Literacy:** 53.2%.

Major intl. organizations: UN (FAO, IBRD, ILO, IMF, IMO, WHO, WTO), AU.

Embassy: 2208 Massachusetts Ave. NW 20008; 234-4212.

Website: www.state.gov/p/af/ci/to/

Togoland was administered by Germany and then by France and Britain. The French sector became the republic of Togo Apr. 27, 1960. In office since 1967, Pres. Gnassingbé Eyadéma was Africa's longest-serving head of state until his death Feb. 5, 2005. His son, Faure Gnassingbé, was immediately installed as president, but other African leaders pressured Togo to hold an election, which Gnassingbé won Apr. 24. Opposition parties disputed the result, and protests led to violent clashes in Lomé.

Tonga
Kingdom of Tonga

People: Population: 116,921. **Age distrib.** (%): <15: 34.6; 65+: 4.2. **Pop. density:** 422 per sq mi, 163 per sq km. **Urban:** 24%. **Ethnic groups:** Polynesian. **Principal languages:** Tongan, English (both official). **Chief religions:** Wesleyan 41%, Roman Catholic 16%, Mormon 14%.

Geography: Total area: 289 sq mi, 748 sq km; **Land area:** 277 sq mi, 718 sq km. **Location:** In western S Pacific O. **Neighbors:** Nearest are Fiji to W, Samoa to NE. **Topography:** Tonga comprises 170 volcanic and coral islands, 36 inhabited. **Capital:** Nuku'alofa, 25,000.

Government: Type: Constitutional monarchy. **Head of state:** King George Tupou V; b. May 4, 1948; in office: Sept. 11, 2006. **Head of gov.:** Prime Min. Prince Ulukalala Lavaka Ata; b. July 12, 1959; in office: Jan. 3, 2000. **Local divisions:** 3 island groups.

Economy: Industries: tourism, fishing. **Chief crops:** squash, coconuts, copra, bananas, vanilla beans, cocoa. **Natural resources:** fish. **Arable land:** 20%. **Livestock:** cattle: 11,250; chickens: 300,000; goats: 12,500; pigs: 81,000. **Fish catch:** 1,901 metric tons. **Electricity prod.:** 40 mil kWh. **Labor force** (1997 est.): agriculture 65%, industry and services 35%.

Finance: Monetary unit: Pa'anga (TOP) (Sept. 2007: 1.92 = $1 U.S.). **GDP** (2004 est.): $178.5 mil; **per capita GDP** (2005 est.): $2,200; **GDP growth** (2005 est.): 2.4%. **Imports** (2004 est.): $122 mil; Fiji 30%, New Zealand 27.5%, U.S. 8.2%, Australia 7.5%, France 5.6%, UK 4.6%. **Exports** (2004 est.): $34 mil; U.S. 41.8%, Japan 29.2%, New Zealand 8.6%, Fiji 4.2%. **Tourism:** $15 mil. **Budget** (2005 est.): $83.9 mil. **Intl. reserves less gold:** $32 mil. **Consumer prices:** 6.44%.

Transport: Motor vehicles: 7,000 pass. cars; 7,000 comm. vehicles. **Civil aviation:** 9.3 mil pass.-mi; 1 airport. **Chief port:** Nuku'alofa.

Communications: TV sets: 61 per 1,000 pop. **Radios:** 663 per 1,000 pop. **Telephone lines:** 13,700. **Internet:** 3,100 users.

Health: Life expect.: 67.6 male; 72.8 female. **Births** (per 1,000 pop.): 23.7. **Deaths** (per 1,000 pop.): 5.2. **Natural inc.:** 1.85%. **Infant mortality** (per 1,000 live births): 12. **AIDS rate:** NA.

Education: Compulsory: ages 6-14. **Literacy:** 98.9%.

Major intl. organizations: UN (FAO, IBRD, ILO, IMF, IMO, WHO), the Commonwealth.

Embassy: 250 E. 51st St., New York, NY 10022; 917-369-1025. **Website:** pmo.gov.to

The islands were first visited by the Dutch in the early 17th cent. A series of civil wars ended in 1845 with establishment of the Tupou dynasty. In 1900 Tonga became a British protectorate. On June 4, 1970, Tonga became independent and a member of the Commonwealth. It joined the UN on Sept. 14, 1999. Prince Tu'ipelehake, a democratic reformer, and his wife Princess Kaimana died July 5, 2006, after a highway accident while visiting California. George Tupou V became king Sept. 11, following the death of his father, Taufa'ahau Tupou IV, who had reigned since 1965.

Trinidad and Tobago
Republic of Trinidad and Tobago

People: Population: 1,056,608. **Age distrib.** (%): <15: 19.5; 65+: 8.9. **Pop. density:** 534 per sq mi, 206 per sq km. **Urban:** 12.2%. **Ethnic groups:** East Indian 40%, black 38%, mixed 21%. **Principal languages:** English (official), Hindi, French, Spanish, Chinese. **Chief religions:** Roman Catholic 26%, Hindu 23%, Protestant 14%, Muslim 6%.

Geography: Total area: 1,980 sq mi, 5,128 sq km; **Land area:** 1,980 sq mi, 5,128 sq km. **Location:** In Caribbean, off E coast of Venezuela. **Neighbors:** Nearest is Venezuela to SW. **Topography:** Three low mountain ranges cross Trinidad E-W, with a well-watered plain between N and central ranges. Parts of E and W coasts are swamps. Tobago, 116 sq mi, lies 20 mi NE. **Capital:** Port-of-Spain, 52,000.

Government: Type: Parliamentary democracy. **Head of state:** Pres. George Maxwell Richards; b. 1931; in office: Mar. 17, 2003. **Head of gov.:** Prime Min. Patrick Augustus Mervyn Manning; b. Aug. 17, 1946; in office: Dec. 24, 2001. **Local divisions:** 8 counties, 3 municipalities, 1 ward. **Defense budget:** NA. **Active troops:** 2,700.

Economy: Industries: oil, chemicals, tourism, food proc. **Chief crops:** cocoa, rice, citrus, coffee, vegetables. **Natural resources:** oil, nat. gas, asphalt. **Crude oil reserves:** 728.3 mil bbls. **Arable land:** 15%. **Livestock:** cattle: 29,000; chickens: 28.2 mil; goats: 59,300; pigs: 43,000; sheep: 3,400. **Fish catch:** 13,414 metric tons. **Electricity prod.:** 6.6 bil kWh. **Labor force** (1997 est.): agriculture 9.5%, manufacturing, mining, and quarrying 14%, construction and utilities 12.4%, services 64.1%.

Finance: Monetary unit: Dollar (TTD) (Sept. 2007: 6.25 = $1 U.S.). **GDP:** $21.1 bil; **per capita GDP:** $19,800; **GDP growth:** 11.9%. **Imports:** $8.8 bil; U.S. 26.9%, Venezuela 14.5%, Brazil 14.2%, Gabon 4.2%, Colombia 4.1%. **Exports:** $12.5 bil; U.S. 60.4%, Jamaica 5.6%, Spain 5.4%. **Tourism:** $341 mil. **Budget:** $5.6 bil. **Intl. reserves less gold:** $4.37 bil. **Gold:** 60,000 oz t. **Consumer prices:** 8.32%.

Transport: Motor vehicles: 229,000 pass. cars; 54,000 comm. vehicles. **Civil aviation:** 1.7 bil pass.-mi; 3 airports. **Chief ports:** Pointe-a-Pierre, Point Lisas, Port-of-Spain.

Communications: TV sets: 337 per 1,000 pop. **Radios:** 532 per 1,000 pop. **Telephone lines:** 325,500. **Internet:** 163,000 users.

Health: Life expect.: 65.9 male; 67.9 female. **Births** (per 1,000 pop.): 13.1. **Deaths** (per 1,000 pop.): 10.8. **Natural inc.:** 0.23%. **Infant mortality** (per 1,000 live births): 24.3. **AIDS rate:** 2.6%.

Education: Compulsory: ages 5-11. **Literacy:** 98.4%.

Major intl. organizations: UN (FAO, IBRD, ILO, IMF, IMO, WHO, WTO), Caricom, the Commonwealth, OAS.

Embassy: 1708 Massachusetts Ave. NW 20036; 467-6490. **Website:** www.gov.tt

Columbus sighted Trinidad in 1498. A British possession since 1802, Trinidad and Tobago won independence Aug. 31, 1962. It became a republic in 1976.

The nation is one of the most prosperous in the Caribbean. Oil production has increased with offshore finds. Middle Eastern oil is refined and exported, mostly to the U.S.

In July 1990, some 120 Muslim extremists captured the Parliament building and TV station and took about 50 hostages, including Prime Min. Arthur N. R. Robinson, who was beaten, shot in the legs, and tied to explosives. After a 6-day siege, the rebels surrendered.

Basdeo Panday, the country's first prime min. of East Indian ancestry, took office Nov. 9, 1995. Robinson became president on Mar. 19, 1997. Patrick Manning of the People's National Movement became prime min. after elections Dec. 10, 2001. George Maxwell Richards, a former university dean, succeeded Robinson as president, Mar. 17, 2003.

Tunisia
Tunisian Republic

People: Population: 10,276,158. **Age distrib.** (%): <15: 24; 65+: 6.9. **Pop. density:** 171 per sq mi, 66 per sq km. **Urban:** 65.3%. **Ethnic groups:** Arab 98%, European 1%, Jewish and other 1%. **Principal languages:** Arabic (official), French prevalent. **Chief religion:** Muslim (official; mostly Sunni) 98%.

Geography: Total area: 63,170 sq mi, 163,610 sq km; **Land area:** 59,985 sq mi, 155,360 sq km. **Location:** On N coast of Africa. **Neighbors:** Algeria on W, Libya on E. **Topography:** The N is wooded and fertile. The central coastal plains are given to grazing and orchards. The S is arid, approaching Sahara Desert. **Capital:** Tunis, 734,000.

Government: Type: Republic. **Head of state:** Pres. Gen. Zine al-Abidine Ben Ali; b. Sept. 3, 1936; in office: Nov. 7, 1987. **Head of gov.:** Prime Min. Mohamed Ghannouchi; b. Aug. 18, 1941; in office: Nov. 17, 1999. **Local divisions:** 24 governorates. **Defense budget:** $443 mil. **Active troops:** 35,300.

Economy: Industries: oil, mining, tourism, textiles, footwear, agribusiness. **Chief crops:** olives, olive oil, grain, tomatoes, citrus fruit, sugar beets, dates, almonds. **Natural resources:** oil, phosphates, iron ore, lead, zinc, salt. **Crude oil reserves:** 400 mil bbls. **Arable land:** 17%. **Livestock:** cattle: 686,320; chickens: 64 mil; goats: 1.4 mil; pigs: 6,000; sheep: 7.2 mil. **Fish catch:** 111,782 metric tons. **Electricity prod.:** 12.9 bil kWh. **Labor force** (1995 est.): agriculture 55%, industry 23%, services 22%.

Finance: Monetary unit: Dinar (TND) (Sept. 2007: 1.27 = $1 U.S.). **GDP:** $89.7 bil; **per capita GDP:** $8,800; **GDP growth:** 5.1%. **Imports:** $13.9 bil; France 24.9%, Italy 21.8%, Germany 9.4%, Spain 4.7%. **Exports:** $11.6 bil; France 28.9%, Italy 20.4%, Germany 8.6%, Spain 6.1%, Libya 4.9%, U.S. 4%. **Tourism:** $2.0 bil. **Budget:** $8.7 bil. **Intl. reserves less gold:** $4.50 bil. **Gold:** 220,000 oz t. **Consumer prices:** 4.49%.

Transport: Railroad: Length: 1,338 mi. **Motor vehicles:** 553,000 pass. cars; 282,000 comm. vehicles. **Civil aviation:** 1.5 bil pass.-mi; 14 airports. **Chief ports:** Tunis, Sfax, Bizerte.

Communications: TV sets: 190 per 1,000 pop. **Radios:** 158 per 1,000 pop. **Telephone lines:** 1.3 mil. **Daily newspaper circ.:** 18.9 per 1,000 pop. **Internet:** 1.3 mil users.

Health: Life expect.: 73.6 male; 77.2 female. **Births** (per 1,000 pop.): 15.5. **Deaths** (per 1,000 pop.): 5.2. **Natural inc.:** 1.04%. **Infant mortality** (per 1,000 live births): 22.9. **AIDS rate:** 0.1%.

Education: Compulsory: ages 6-16. **Literacy:** 74.3%.

Major intl. organizations: UN (FAO, IBRD, ILO, IMF, IMO, WHO, WTO), AL, AU.

Embassy: 1515 Massachusetts Ave. NW 20005; 862-1850. **Website:** www.tunisiaonline.com

Site of ancient Carthage and a former Barbary state under the suzerainty of Turkey, Tunisia became a protectorate of France under a treaty signed May 12, 1881. The nation became independent Mar. 20, 1956, and ended the monarchy the following year. Habib Bourguiba, an independence leader, served as president until 1987, when he was deposed by his prime min., Zine al-Abidine Ben Ali, who then won 4 presidential elections, 1989-2004, all tightly controlled by the ruling party.

Tunisia has actively repressed Islamic fundamentalism. A synagogue blast on Djerba Is., Apr. 11, 2002, apparently set off by al-Qaeda, killed 17 people, including 12 German tourists.

Turkey
Republic of Turkey

People: Population: 71,158,647. **Age distrib.** (%): <15: 24.9; 65+: 6.9. **Pop. density:** 239 per sq mi, 92 per sq km. **Urban:** 67.3%. **Ethnic groups:** Turkish 80%, Kurdish 20%. **Principal languages:** Turkish (official), Kurdish, Dimli, Azeri, Kabardian. **Chief religion:** Muslim 99.8% (mostly Sunni).

Geography: Total area: 301,384 sq mi, 780,580 sq km; **Land area:** 297,592 sq mi, 770,760 sq km. **Location:** Occupies Asia Minor, stretches into continental Europe; borders on Medit. and Black seas. **Neighbors:** Bulgaria, Greece on W; Georgia, Armenia on N; Iran on E; Iraq, Syria on S. **Topography:** Central Turkey has wide plateaus, with hot, dry summers and cold winters. High mountains ring the interior on all but W, with more than 20 peaks over 10,000 ft. Rolling plains are in W; mild, fertile coastal plains are in S, W. **Capital:** Ankara, 3,573,000. **Cities (urban aggr.):** Istanbul, 3,573,000; Izmir, 2,487,000.

Government: Type: Republic. **Head of state:** Pres. Abdullah Gül; b. Oct. 29, 1950; in office: Aug. 28, 2007. **Head of gov.:** Prime

Min. Recep Tayyip Erdogan; b. Feb. 26, 1954; in office: Mar. 14, 2003. **Local divisions:** 81 provinces. **Defense budget:** $8.08 bil. **Active troops:** 514,850.

Economy: Industries: textiles, food proc., autos, mining, steel, oil, constr. **Chief crops:** tobacco, cotton, grain, olives, sugar beets, pulse, citrus. **Natural resources:** antimony, coal, chromium, mercury, copper, borate, sulfur, iron ore, hydropower. **Crude oil reserves:** 300 mil bbls. **Arable land:** 30%. **Livestock:** cattle: 10.5 mil; chickens: 317.5 mil; goats: 6.5 mil; pigs: 1,934; sheep: 25.3 mil. **Fish catch:** 545,673 metric tons. **Electricity prod.:** 154.2 bil kWh. **Labor force** (2004): agriculture 35.9%, industry 22.8%, services 41.2%.

Finance: Monetary unit: New Lira (TRY) (Sept. 2007: 1.26 = $1 U.S.). **GDP:** $635.6 bil; **per capita GDP:** $9,000; **GDP growth:** 5.3%. **Imports:** $120.9 bil; Russia 12.7%, Germany 10.6%, China 7%, Italy 6.3%, France 4.8%, U.S. 4.3%, Iran 4.1%. **Exports:** $85.2 bil; Germany 11.4%, UK 8%, Italy 7.9%, U.S. 5.9%, France 5.4%, Spain 4.3%. **Tourism:** $18.2 bil. **Budget:** $121.6 bil. **Intl. reserves less gold:** $40.60 bil. **Gold:** 3.73 mil oz t. **Consumer prices:** 10.51%.

Transport: Railroad: Length: 5,404 mi. **Motor vehicles:** 5.4 mil pass. cars; 2.4 mil comm. vehicles. **Civil aviation:** 10.2 bil pass.-mi; 89 airports. **Chief ports:** Aliaga, Eregli, Istanbul, Izmir, Kocaeli, Toros.

Communications: TV sets: 328 per 1,000 pop. **Radios:** 510 per 1,000 pop. **Telephone lines:** 19 mil. **Internet:** 12.3 mil users.

Health: Life expect.: 70.4 male; 75.5 female. **Births** (per 1,000 pop.): 16.4. **Deaths** (per 1,000 pop.): 6. **Natural inc.:** 1.04%. **Infant mortality** (per 1,000 live births): 38.3. **AIDS rate:** NA.

Education: Compulsory: ages 6-14. **Literacy:** 87.4%.

Major intl. organizations: UN (FAO, IBRD, ILO, IMF, IMO, WHO, WTO), NATO, OECD, OSCE.

Embassy: 2525 Massachusetts Ave. NW 20008; 612-6700.

Website: www.cankaya.gov.tr

Ancient inhabitants of Turkey were among the world's first agriculturalists. Such civilizations as the Hittite, Phrygian, and Lydian flourished in Asiatic Turkey (Asia Minor), as did much of Greek civilization. After the fall of Rome in the 5th cent., Constantinople (now Istanbul) was the capital of the Byzantine Empire for 1,000 years. It fell in 1453 to Ottoman Turks, who ruled a vast empire for over 400 years.

Just before WWI, Turkey, or the Ottoman Empire, ruled what is now Syria, Lebanon, Iraq, Jordan, Israel, Saudi Arabia, Yemen, and islands in the Aegean Sea. Turkey joined Germany and Austria in WWI, and its defeat resulted in the loss of much territory and the fall of the sultanate. A republic was declared Oct. 29, 1923, with Mustafa Kemal (later Kemal Ataturk) as its first president. Ataturk led Turkey until his death in 1938.

Turkey kept neutral during most of WWII. The country became a full member of NATO in 1952 and remained a Western ally despite domestic political instability. Military coups overthrew civilian governments in 1960 and 1980. Turkey invaded nearby Cyprus July 20, 1974, to prevent that country from being united with Greece; since then, Cyprus has been divided into Greek and Turkish zones.

In recent decades, Turkish governments have contended with Kurdish separatism and the rise of militant Islam. Turkey was a member of the U.S.-led force that ousted Iraq from Kuwait, 1991. In the aftermath of the war, millions of Kurdish refugees fled to Turkey's border to escape Iraqi forces. Turkish offensives against the Kurds caused heavy casualties among guerrillas and civilians. Kurdish militants raided Turkish diplomatic missions in some 25 Western European cities June 24, 1993.

Tansu Ciller officially became Turkey's first woman prime min. July 5, 1993. The Welfare Party, an Islamic group, gained strength in the 1990s but was unable to form a government until June 1996, when it came to power in coalition with Ciller's True Path Party. The pro-Islamic government resigned June 18, 1997, under pressure from the military, which stepped up its campaign against Islamic fundamentalism in 1998.

Kurdish rebel leader Abdullah Öcalan was captured Feb. 15, 1999; convicted of terrorism June 29, he was sentenced to death by a Turkish security court. His organization, the Kurdistan Workers' Party, announced Aug. 5, 1999, that it would abandon its 14-year-old insurgency, in which more than 30,000 people died.

Earthquakes in Apr. and Nov. 1999 killed over 17,000 people. The IMF announced $7.5 bil in emergency loans Dec. 6, 2000, to help Turkey cope with a severe financial crisis. The death penalty was abolished Aug. 3, 2002, and Öcalan's sentence was commuted to life in prison Oct. 3. The Justice and Development Party, an Islamic group headed by Recep Tayyip Erdogan, won elections Nov. 3.

During the U.S.-led invasion of Iraq, Mar.-Apr. 2003, Turkey, a NATO ally, refused to allow coalition forces to launch attacks on N Iraq from Turkish soil. Suicide bombings by Islamic extremists Nov. 15-20, 2003, killed 58 people and wounded about 750 at 2 synagogues, the British consulate, and the offices of a London-based bank, all in Istanbul. Renewed clashes in Mar.-Apr. 2006 between Kurds and Turkish security forces claimed at least 15 lives. Erdogan's party scored a landslide win in national elections, July 22, 2007. Overcoming objections by the military and other secularists, parliament, Aug. 28, chose an Islamic politician, Abdullah Gül, as president.

Turkey has long sought to become a full member of the European Union, but the EU has deferred talks on accession until economic, human rights, and immigration issues are resolved.

Turkmenistan

People: Population: 5,097,028. **Age distrib.** (%): <15: 34.7; 65+: 4.4. **Pop. density:** 27 per sq mi, 10 per sq km. **Urban:** 46.2%. **Ethnic groups:** Turkmen 85%, Uzbek 5%, Russian 4%. **Principal languages:** Turkmen, Russian, Uzbek. **Chief religions:** Muslim 89%, Eastern Orthodox 9%.

Geography: Total area: 188,457 sq mi, 488,100 sq km; **Land area:** 188,457 sq mi, 488,100 sq km. **Location:** Central Asia bordering Caspian Sea. **Neighbors:** Kazakhstan on N; Uzbekistan on N and E; Afghanistan, Iran on S. **Topography:** The Kara Kum Desert occupies 80% of the area. Bordered on W by Caspian Sea. **Capital:** Ashgabat, 711,000.

Government: Type: Republic with authoritarian rule. **Head of state and gov.:** Pres. Gurbanguly Berdymukhammedov; June 29, 1957; in office: Feb. 14, 2007 (acting from Dec. 21, 2006). **Local divisions:** 5 regions. **Defense budget:** $181 mil. **Active troops:** 26,000.

Economy: Industries: nat. gas, oil, oil products, textiles, food proc. **Chief crops:** cotton, grain. **Natural resources:** oil, nat. gas, coal, sulfur, salt. **Crude oil reserves:** 600 mil bbls. **Arable land:** 5%. **Livestock:** cattle: 2.1 mil; chickens: 7.5 mil; goats: 904,000; pigs: 29,000; sheep: 15.7 mil. **Fish catch:** 15,016 metric tons. **Electricity prod.:** 12.1 bil kWh. **Labor force** (2003 est.): agriculture 48.2%, industry 13.8%, services 37%.

Finance: Monetary unit: Manat (TMM) (Sept. 2007: 5,200.05 = $1 U.S.). **GDP:** $42.8 bil; **per capita GDP:** $8,500; **GDP growth:** 6% (IMF estimate). **Imports:** $3.9 bil; UAE 13.6%, Azerbaijan 11.8%, Turkey 9.8%, Ukraine 8%, Russia 8%, Germany 6.8%, Iran 6.7%, China 5.6%. **Exports:** $5.4 bil; Ukraine 47.1%, Iran 16.2%, Azerbaijan 4.3%. **Tourism:** NA. **Budget:** $2.1 bil.

Transport: Railroad: Length: 1,516 mi. **Civil aviation:** 1 bil pass.-mi; 22 airports. **Chief port:** Turkmenbasy.

Communications: TV sets: 198 per 1,000 pop. **Radios:** 289 per 1,000 pop. **Telephone lines:** 398,100. **Daily newspaper circ.:** 6.8 per 1,000 pop. **Internet:** 64,800 users.

Health: Life expect.: 65.2 male; 71.5 female. **Births** (per 1,000 pop.): 25.4. **Deaths** (per 1,000 pop.): 6.2. **Natural inc.:** 1.92%. **Infant mortality** (per 1,000 live births): 53.5. **AIDS rate:** <0.1%.

Education: Compulsory: ages 7-15. **Literacy:** 98.8%.

Major intl. organizations: UN (FAO, IBRD, ILO, IMF, IMO, WHO), CIS, OSCE.

Embassy: 2207 Massachusetts Ave. NW 20008; 588-1500.

Website: www.turkmenistan.gov.tm

The region has been inhabited by Turkic tribes since the 10th cent. It became part of Russian Turkestan in 1881, and a constituent republic of the USSR in 1925. Turkmenistan declared independence Oct. 27, 1991, and became an independent state when the USSR disbanded Dec. 26, 1991.

Extensive oil and gas reserves place Turkmenistan in a favorable economic position. Political power centered around the former Communist party apparatus, and authoritarian Pres. Saparmurad Niyazov (also known as Turkmenbashi) became the object of a personality cult. Niyazov died Dec. 21, 2006, and was succeeded by Gurbanguly Berdymukhammedov; he won the presidential election of Feb. 11, 2007, considered neither free nor fair by international observers.

Tuvalu

People: Population: 11,992. **Age distrib.** (%): <15: 29.8; 65+: 5. **Pop. density:** 1,199 per sq mi, 461 per sq km. **Urban:** 48.1%. **Ethnic group:** Polynesian 96%, Micronesian 4%. **Principal languages:** Tuvaluan, English, Samoan, Kiribati (on Nui). **Chief religion:** Church of Tuvalu (Congregationalist) 97%.

Geography: Total area: 10 sq mi, 26 sq km; **Land area:** 10 sq mi, 26 sq km. **Location:** 9 islands forming NW-SE chain 360 mi long in SW Pacific O. **Neighbors:** Nearest are Kiribati to N, Fiji to S. **Topography:** The islands are all low-lying atolls, nowhere rising more than 15 ft above sea level, composed of coral reefs. **Capital:** Funafuti, 6,000.

Government: Type: Constitutional monarchy, with a parliamentary democracy. **Head of state:** Queen Elizabeth II, represented by Gov.-Gen. Filoimea Telito; in office: Apr. 15, 2005. **Head of gov.:** Prime Min. Apisai Ielemia; in office: Aug. 14, 2006.

Economy: Industries: fishing, tourism, copra. **Chief crops:** coconuts. **Natural resources:** fish. **Livestock:** chickens: 45,000; pigs: 13,500 **Fish catch:** 2,561 metric tons. **Electricity prod.:** NA. **Labor force:** People make a living mainly through exploitation of the sea, reefs, and atolls and from wages sent home by those abroad (mostly workers in the phosphate industry and sailors).

Finance: Monetary unit: Dollar (TVD) (Sept. 2007: 1.19 = $1 U.S.). **GDP** (2002 est.): $14.9 mil; **per capita GDP** (2002 est.): $1,600; **GDP growth** (2002 est.): 1.2%. **Imports** (2004 est.): $9.2 mil; Fiji 46.1%, Japan 18.9%, China 18.2%, Australia 7.7%, New Zealand 4.1%. **Exports** (2004 est.): $1 mil; Germany 60.5%, Italy 20.1%, Fiji 6.9%. **Tourism:** NA. **Budget** (2002 est.): $14.2 mil.

Transport: Civil aviation: 1 airport. **Chief port:** Funafuti.

Communications: TV sets: 9 per 1,000 pop. **Radios:** 364 per 1,000 pop. **Internet** (2002): 1,300 users.

Health: Life expect.: 66.4 male; 71 female. **Births** (per 1,000 pop.): 22.4. **Deaths** (per 1,000 pop.): 7. **Natural inc.:** 1.54%. **Infant mortality** (per 1,000 live births): 18.9. **AIDS rate:** NA.

Education: Compulsory: ages 7-14. **Literacy:** NA.

Major intl. organizations: UN (FAO, ILO, IMO, WHO), the Commonwealth.

UN Mission: 800 Second Ave., Ste. 400D, New York, NY 10017; 212-490-0534.

Website: www.timelesstuvalu.com

The Ellice Islands separated from the British Gilbert and Ellice Islands Colony in 1975 and became Tuvalu; independence came Oct. 1, 1978. In 2000, Tuvalu joined the United Nations.

Uganda
Republic of Uganda

People: Population: 30,262,610. **Age distrib.** (%): <15: 50.2; 65+: 2.2. **Pop. density:** 392 per sq mi, 152 per sq km. **Urban:** 12.6%. **Ethnic groups:** Baganda 17%, Banyakole 10%, Basoga 8%, Bakiga 7%, Iteso 6%, Langi 6%, many others. **Principal languages:** English (official), Swahili, Ganda, Bantu and Nilotic languages, Arabic. **Chief religions:** Roman Catholic 42%, Protestant 42%, Muslim 12%.

Geography: Total area: 91,136 sq mi, 236,040 sq km; **Land area:** 77,108 sq mi, 199,710 sq km. **Location:** In E Central Africa. **Neighbors:** Sudan on N, Congo (formerly Zaire) on W, Rwanda and Tanzania on S, Kenya on E. **Topography:** Most of Uganda is a high plateau 3,000-6,000 ft high, with high Ruwenzori range in W (Mt. Margherita 16,763 ft), volcanoes in SW; NE is arid, W and SW rainy. Lakes Victoria, Edward, Albert form much of borders. **Capital:** Kampala, 1,319,000.

Government: Type: Republic. **Head of state:** Pres. Yoweri Kaguta Museveni; b. Aug. 15, 1944; in office: Jan. 29, 1986. **Head of gov.:** Prime Min. Apolo Nsibambi; b. Nov. 27, 1938; in office: Apr. 5, 1999. **Local divisions:** 56 districts. **Defense budget:** $187 mil. **Active troops:** 45,000.

Economy: Industries: sugar, brewing, tobacco, cotton textiles, cement. **Chief crops:** coffee, tea, cotton, tobacco, cassava, potatoes. **Natural resources:** copper, cobalt, hydropower, limestone, salt. **Arable land:** 22%. **Livestock:** cattle: 7 mil; chickens: 22.8 mil; goats: 8 mil; pigs: 2 mil; sheep: 1.6 mil. **Fish catch:** 427,575 metric tons. **Electricity prod.:** 2 bil kWh. **Labor force** (1999 est.): agriculture 82%, industry 5%, services 13%.

Finance: Monetary unit: Shilling (UGX) (Sept. 2007: 1,754.00 = $1 U.S.). **GDP:** $52.9 bil; **per capita GDP:** $1,900; **GDP growth:** 5.3%. **Imports:** $1.9 bil; Kenya 34.6%, UAE 8.7%, China 7.2%, India 5.6%, South Africa 5.5%. **Exports:** $961.7 mil; Belgium 9.8%, Netherlands 9.2%, France 7.8%, Germany 7.5%, Rwanda 5.5%. **Tourism:** $266 mil. **Budget:** $2 bil. **Intl. reserves less gold:** $1.20 bil. **Consumer prices:** 6.61%.

Transport: Railroad: Length: 773 mi. **Motor vehicles:** 60,000 pass. cars; 96,000 comm. vehicles. **Civil aviation:** 147.3 mil pass.-mi; 5 airports. **Chief ports:** Entebbe, Jinja, Port Bell.

Communications: TV sets: 28 per 1,000 pop. **Radios:** 130 per 1,000 pop. **Telephone lines:** 108,100. **Daily newspaper circ.:** 2.7 per 1,000 pop. **Internet:** 750,000 users.

Health: Life expect.: 50.8 male; 52.7 female. **Births** (per 1,000 pop.): 48.1. **Deaths** (per 1,000 pop.): 12.6. **Natural inc.:** 3.55%. **Infant mortality** (per 1,000 live births): 67.2. **AIDS rate:** 6.7%.

Education: Compulsory: ages 6-12. **Literacy:** 66.8%.

Major intl. organizations: UN (FAO, IBRD, ILO, IMF, WHO, WTO), the Commonwealth, AU.

Embassy: 5911 16th St. NW 20011; 726-7100.

Websites: www.statehouse.go.ug

Britain obtained a protectorate over Uganda in 1894. The country became independent Oct. 9, 1962, and a republic within the Commonwealth a year later. In 1967, the traditional kingdoms, including the powerful Buganda state, were abolished.

Gen. Idi Amin seized power from Prime Min. Milton Obote in 1971. During his 8 years of dictatorial rule, he was responsible for the deaths of up to 300,000 of his opponents. In 1972 he expelled nearly all of Uganda's 45,000 Asians. Tanzanian troops and Ugandan exiles and rebels ousted Amin, Apr. 11, 1979.

Obote held the presidency from Dec. 1980 until his ouster in a military coup July 27, 1985. Guerrilla war and rampant human rights abuses plagued Uganda under Obote's regime.

Conditions improved after Yoweri Museveni took power in Jan. 1986. In 1993 the Buganda and other traditional monarchies were restored, but only for ceremonial purposes. Uganda helped Laurent Kabila seize power in the Congo (formerly Zaire) in 1997 but sent troops in 1998 to aid insurgents seeking his ouster. A withdrawal accord was signed Sept. 6, 2002.

At least 330 members of the Movement for the Restoration of the Ten Commandments of God died in a church fire in Kanungu, Mar. 17, 2000; in all, over 900 deaths were linked to the cult.

Pres. Museveni won reelection Mar. 12, 2001, and Feb. 23, 2006; opponents disputed the latter result, citing what they claimed were trumped-up charges of treason, terrorism, and rape lodged against Museveni's main rival, Kizza Besigye.

An ongoing insurgency in N Uganda has killed more than 100,000 people and forced up to 2 mil to flee. The Lord's Resistance Army, a rebel group, has fought the Museveni govt. since 1986 and has abducted some 30,000 children to serve as soldiers and sex slaves. Peace talks brokered by Sudan began July 2006; as talks continued into 2007, the violence diminished, and many refugees returned to their homes.

Ukraine

People: Population: 46,299,862. **Age distrib.** (%): <15: 14; 65+: 16.3. **Pop. density:** 199 per sq mi, 77 per sq km. **Urban:** 67.8%. **Ethnic groups:** Ukrainian 78%, Russian 17%. **Principal languages:** Ukrainian (official), Russian, Romanian, Polish, Hungarian. **Chief religions:** Ukrainian Orthodox (Kiev patriarchate and Russian patriarchate), Autocephalous Orthodox, Ukrainian Greek Catholic.

Geography: Total area: 233,090 sq mi, 603,700 sq km; **Land area:** 233,090 sq mi, 603,700 sq km. **Location:** In E Europe. **Neighbors:** Belarus on N; Russia on NE and E; Moldova and Romania on SW; Hungary, Slovakia, and Poland on W. **Topography:** Part of the E European plain. Mountainous areas include the Carpathians in the SW and Crimean chain in the S. Arable black soil constitutes a large part of the country. **Capital:** Kiev, 2,672,000. **Cities (urban aggr.):** Kharkov, 1,436,000, Odesa, 1,010,000.

Government: Type: Republic. **Head of state:** Pres. Viktor Andriyovych Yushchenko; b. Feb. 23, 1954; in office: Jan. 23, 2005. **Head of gov.:** Prime Min. Viktor Yanukovych; b. July 9, 1950; in office: Aug. 4, 2006. **Local divisions:** 24 oblasts, 2 municipalities, 1 autonomous republic. **Defense budget:** $1.74 bil. **Active troops:** 187,600.

Economy: Industries: coal, electric power, metals, machinery & transp. equip., chemicals, sugar. **Chief crops:** grain, sugar beets, sunflower seed, vegetables. **Natural resources:** iron ore, coal, mang., nat. gas, oil, salt, sulfur, graphite, titanium, magnesium, kaolin, nickel, mercury, timber. **Crude oil reserves:** 395 mil bbls. **Arable land:** 54%. **Livestock:** cattle: 6.5 mil; chickens: 140.5 mil; goats: 758,000; pigs: 7.1 mil; sheep: 872,000. **Fish catch:** 273,688 metric tons. **Electricity prod.:** 175.4 bil kWh. **Labor force** (1996): agriculture 25%, industry 20%, services 55%.

Finance: Monetary unit: Hryvna (UAH) (Sept. 2007: 5.01 = $1 U.S.). **GDP:** $364.3 bil; **per capita GDP:** $7,800; **GDP growth:** 7.1%. **Imports:** $44.11 bil; Russia 28.4%, Germany 11.7%, Poland 7.6%, China 7.1%, Turkmenistan 5.7%. **Exports:** $38.9 bil; Russia 21.2%, Turkey 6.9%, Italy 6.3%, U.S. 4%. **Tourism:** $1.1 bil. **Budget:** $35.6 bil. **Intl. reserves less gold:** $14.52 bil. **Gold:** 810,000 oz t. **Consumer prices:** 9.08%.

Transport: Railroad: Length: 13,964 mi. **Motor vehicles:** 5.4 mil pass. cars; 917,000 comm. vehicles. **Civil aviation:** 1.5 bil pass.-mi; 193 airports. **Chief ports:** Feodosiya, Kerch, Kherson, Mariupol, Mykolayiv, Odesa.

Communications: TV sets: 433 per 1,000 pop. **Radios:** 882 per 1,000 pop. **Telephone lines:** 12.3 mil. **Daily newspaper circ.:** 174.8 per 1,000 pop. **Internet:** 5.5 mil users.

Health: Life expect.: 62.2 male; 74 female. **Births** (per 1,000 pop.): 9.5. **Deaths** (per 1,000 pop.): 16.1. **Natural inc.:** −0.66%. **Infant mortality** (per 1,000 live births): 9.5. **AIDS rate:** 1.4%.

Education: Compulsory: ages 6-17. **Literacy:** 99.4%.

Major intl. organizations: UN (FAO, IBRD, ILO, IMF, IMO, WHO), CIS, OSCE.

Embassy: 3350 M St. NW 20007; 333-0606.

Website: www.kmu.gov.ua

Ukrainians' Slavic ancestors inhabited modern Ukrainian territory well before the 1st cent. CE. In the 9th cent., the princes of Kiev established a strong state called Kievan Rus, which included much of present-day Ukraine. Internal conflicts led to the disintegration of the Ukrainian state by the 13th cent. Mongol rule was supplanted by Poland and Lithuania in the 14th and 15th centuries. The N Black Sea coast and Crimea came under Turkish control in 1478. Ukrainian Cossacks, starting in the late 16th cent., rebelled against the occupiers of Ukraine: Russia, Poland, and Turkey.

An independent Ukrainian National Republic was proclaimed on Jan. 22, 1918. But in 1921, Ukraine's neighbors occupied and divided Ukrainian territory. In 1922, Ukraine became a constituent republic of the USSR as the Ukrainian SSR. In 1932-33, the Soviet government engineered a famine in eastern Ukraine, resulting in the deaths of 6-7 mil Ukrainians. During WWII the Ukrainian nationalist underground fought both Nazi and Soviet forces. Over 5 mil Ukrainians died in the war. With the reoccupation of Ukraine by Soviet troops in 1944 came a renewed wave of mass arrests, executions, and deportations.

The world's worst nuclear power plant disaster occurred in Chernobyl, Ukraine, in April 1986; many thousands were killed or disabled as a result of the radiation leak. The plant was finally shut down Dec. 15, 2000.

Ukrainian independence was restored in Dec. 1991 with the dissolution of the Soviet Union. In the post-Soviet period Ukraine was burdened with a deteriorating economy. Following a 1994 accord with Russia and the U.S., Ukraine's large nuclear arsenal was transferred to Russia for destruction.

President since 1994, Leonid Kuchma attempted to engineer the election in 2004 of his handpicked successor, Prime Min. Viktor Yanukovych, also favored by Russia. The main challenger, Viktor Yushchenko, a former prime min., was poisoned in Sept. with dioxin, but continued to campaign. Official results of a runoff vote Nov. 21 showed a win for Yanukovych. Yushchenko supporters, calling the election fraudulent, staged massive protests (the "orange revolution"), and the vote was annulled. An election rerun Dec. 26 gave the victory to Yushchenko. Inaugurated Jan. 23, 2005, he dismissed his cabinet Sept. 8, amid allegations of infighting and corruption among his top aides.

Yushchenko's Our Ukraine party fared poorly in parliamentary elections Mar. 26, 2006, and the resurgent Yanukovych, whose party won the vote, returned as prime min. Aug. 4. The two rivals then engaged in a year-long political struggle, with new elections scheduled for Sept. 30, 2007.

A report released Feb. 19, 2007, by the International Organization for Migration estimated that 117,000 Ukrainians had been trafficked abroad as forced laborers or prostitutes since 1991.

United Arab Emirates

People: Population: 4,444,011. **Age distrib.** (%): <15: 20.6; 65+: 0.9. **Pop. density:** 138 per sq mi, 53 per sq km. **Urban:** 76.7%. **Ethnic groups:** Arab and Iranian 42%, Indian 50%. **Principal languages:** Arabic (official), Persian, English, Hindi, Urdu. **Chief religion:** Muslim (official; Shi'a 16%) 96%.

Geography: Total area: 32,000 sq mi, 82,880 sq km; **Land area:** 32,000 sq mi, 82,880 sq km. **Location:** Middle East, on E shore of the Persian Gulf. **Neighbors:** Saudi Arabia on W and S, Oman on E. **Topography:** A barren, flat coastal plain gives way to uninhabited sand dunes on S. Hajar Mts. on E. **Capital:** Abu Dhabi, 597,000. **Cites (urban aggr.):** Dubai 1,330,000.

Government: Type: Federation of emirates. **Head of state:** Pres. Sheikh Khalifa ibn Zaid an-Nahayan; b. 1948; in office: Nov. 3, 2004. **Head of gov.:** Prime Min. Sheikh Muhammad ibn Rashid al-Maktum; b. 1949; in office: Jan. 5, 2006. **Local divisions:** 7 autonomous emirates: Abu Dhabi, Ajman, Dubai, Fujaira, Ras al-Khaimah, Sharjah, Umm al-Qaiwain. **Defense budget:** $2.58 bil. **Active troops:** 50,500.

Economy: Industries: oil, fishing, petrochems., constr. materials, boat building, handicrafts, pearling. **Chief crops:** dates, vegetables, watermelons. **Natural resources:** oil, nat. gas. **Crude oil reserves:** 97.8 bil bbls. **Arable land:** 1%. **Livestock:** cattle: 115,000; chickens: 15 mil; goats: 1.5 mil; sheep: 580,000. **Fish catch:** 90,570 metric tons. **Electricity prod.:** 57.1 bil kWh. **Labor force** (2000 est.): agriculture 7%, industry 15%, services 78%.

Finance: Monetary unit: Dirham (AED) (Sept. 2007: 3.67 = $1 U.S.). **GDP:** $129.5 bil; **per capita GDP:** $49,700; **GDP growth:** 8.9%. **Imports:** $88.9 bil; U.S. 11.4%, China 11%, India 9.8%, Germany 6.2%, Japan 5.8%, UK 5.5%, France 4.1%, Italy 4%. **Exports:** $137.1 bil; Japan 25.9%, S. Korea 10.3%, Thailand 5.9%, India 4.5%. **Tourism:** NA. **Budget:** $35.2 bil. **Intl. reserves less gold:** $18.36 bil.

Transport: Motor vehicles: 794,100 pass. cars; 477,900 comm. vehicles. **Civil aviation:** 25.8 bil pass.-mi; 23 airportss. **Civil aviation:** 25.8 bil pass.-mi; 23 airports. **Chief ports:** Al Fujayrah, Khawr Fakkan, Mina Jabal Ali, Mina Saqr, Mina Zayid.

Communications: TV sets: 309 per 1,000 pop. **Radios:** 355 per 1,000 pop. **Telephone lines:** 1.3 mil. **Internet:** 1.7 mil users.

Health: Life expect.: 73.2 male; 78.4 female. **Births** (per 1,000 pop.): 16.1. **Deaths** (per 1,000 pop.): 2.2. **Natural inc.:** 1.39%. **Infant mortality** (per 1,000 live births): 13.5. **AIDS rate:** NA.

Education: Compulsory: ages 6-14. **Literacy:** 88.7%.

Major intl. organizations: UN (FAO, IBRD, ILO, IMF, IMO, WHO, WTO), AL, OPEC.

Embassy: 3522 International Ct. NW, Ste. 400, 20008; 243-2400.

Website: www.government.ae

The 7 "Trucial Sheikdoms" gave Britain control of defense and foreign relations in the 19th cent. They merged to become an independent state Dec. 2, 1971. The Abu Dhabi Petroleum Co. was fully nationalized in 1975. Oil revenues have made the UAE one of the world's wealthiest countries. International banking, investment, and construction have boomed. Foreigners make up about 85% of the population and nearly all the private work force.

In 2006, emirate-owned Dubai Ports World's management takeover of 6 U.S. ports spurred controversy in the U.S.; the firm pledged to sell the port operations to a wholly American company.

United Kingdom
United Kingdom of Great Britain and Northern Ireland

People: Population: 60,776,238. **Age distrib.** (%): <15: 17.2; 65+: 15.8. **Pop. density:** 652 per sq mi, 252 per sq km. **Urban:** 89.7%. **Ethnic groups:** English 84%, Scottish 9%, Welsh 5%, N. Irish 3%, Black 2%, Indian 2%. **Principal languages:** English (official), Welsh and Scottish Gaelic. **Chief religions:** Christian 72%, Muslim 3%.

Geography: Total area: 94,526 sq mi, 244,820 sq km; **Land area:** 93,278 sq mi, 241,590 sq km. **Location:** Off NW coast of Europe, across English Channel, Strait of Dover, North Sea. **Neighbors:** Ireland to W, France to SE. **Topography:** England is mostly rolling land, rising to Uplands of southern Scotland. Lowlands are in center of Scotland, granite Highlands in N. Coast is heavily indented, especially on W. British Isles have milder climate than N Europe due to Gulf Stream and ample rainfall. Severn, 220 mi, and Thames, 215 mi, are longest rivers. **Capital:** London, 8,505,000. **Cities (urban aggr.):** Birmingham, 2,280,000; Manchester, 2,228,000; West Yorkshire, 1,519,000; Glasgow, 1,159,000.

Government: Type: Constitutional monarchy. **Head of state:** Queen Elizabeth II; b. Apr. 21, 1926; in office: Feb. 6, 1952. **Head of gov.:** Prime Min. Gordon Brown; b. Feb. 20, 1951; in office: June 27, 2007. **Local divisions:** 467 local authorities, including England: 387; Wales: 22; Scotland: 32; Northern Ireland: 26. **Defense budget:** $55.1 bil. **Active troops:** 191,030.

Economy: Industries: machine tools, electric power equip., automotion equip., railroad equip., shipbuilding, aircraft, vehicles, electronics & comm. equip., metals, chemicals, coal, oil. **Chief crops:** cereals, oilseed, potatoes, vegetables. **Natural resources:** coal, oil, nat. gas, iron, limestone, iron ore, salt, clay, chalk, gypsum, lead, silica. **Crude oil reserves:** 3.9 bil bbls. **Arable land:** 23%. **Livestock:** cattle: 10.2 mil; chickens: 158.2 mil; goats: 96,000; pigs: 4.9 mil; sheep: 34.7 mil. **Fish catch:** 842,271 metric tons. **Electricity prod.:** 372.6 bil kWh. **Labor force** (2006 est.): agriculture 1.4%, industry 18.2%, services 80.4%.

Finance: Monetary unit: Pound (GBP) (Sept. 2007: 0.50 = $1 U.S.). **GDP:** $1.9 tril; **per capita GDP:** $31,800; **GDP growth:** 2.8%. **Imports:** $603 bil; Germany 12.8%, U.S. 8.9%, France 6.9%, Netherlands 6.6%, China 5.3%, Norway 4.9%. **Exports:** $468.8 bil; U.S. 13.9%, Germany 10.9%, France 10.4%, Ireland 7.1%, Netherlands 6.3%, Belgium 5.2%. **Tourism:** $28.2 bil. **Budget:** $1 tril. **Intl. reserves less gold:** $27.05 bil. **Gold:** 9.97 mil oz t. **Consumer prices:** 3.19%.

Transport: Railroad: Length: 10,660 mi. **Motor vehicles:** 27.8 mil pass. cars; 3.8 mil comm. vehicles. **Civil aviation:** 103.5 bil pass.-mi; 334 airports. **Chief ports:** Liverpool, London, Southampton.

Communications: TV sets: 661 per 1,000 pop. **Radios:** 1,437 per 1,000 pop. **Telephone lines:** 33.6 mil. **Daily newspaper circ.:** 326.4 per 1,000 pop. **Internet:** 33.5 mil users.

Health: Life expect.: 76.2 male; 81.3 female. **Births** (per 1,000 pop.): 10.7. **Deaths** (per 1,000 pop.): 10.1. **Natural inc.:** 0.06%. **Infant mortality** (per 1,000 live births): 5. **AIDS rate:** 0.2%.

Education: Compulsory: ages 5-16. **Literacy:** 99%.

Major intl. organizations: UN and all of its specialized agencies, the Commonwealth, EU, NATO, OECD, OSCE.

Embassy: 3100 Massachusetts Ave. NW 20008; 588-6500.

Website: www.direct.gov.uk

The United Kingdom of Great Britain and Northern Ireland comprises England, Wales, Scotland, and Northern Ireland.

Queen and Royal Family. The ruling sovereign is Elizabeth II of the House of Windsor, b. Apr. 21, 1926, elder daughter of King George VI. She succeeded to the throne Feb. 6, 1952, and was crowned June 2, 1953. She was married Nov. 20, 1947, to Lt. Philip Mountbatten, b. June 10, 1921, former Prince of Greece. He was created Duke of Edinburgh, and given the title H.R.H., Nov. 19, 1947; he was named Prince of the United Kingdom and Northern Ireland Feb. 22, 1957. Prince Charles Philip Arthur George, b. Nov. 14, 1948, is the Prince of Wales and heir apparent. His first son, William Philip Arthur Louis, b. June 21, 1982, is second in line to the throne.

Parliament is the legislative body for the UK, with certain powers over dependent units. It consists of 2 houses: the **House of Commons** has 646 members, elected by direct ballot and divided as follows: England, 529; Wales, 40; Scotland, 59; Northern Ireland, 18. Following a drastic reduction in 1999 in the number of hereditary peerages, the **House of Lords** (July 2007) comprised 92 hereditary peers, 629 life peers, and 2 archbishops and 24 bishops of the Church of England, for a total of 747.

Resources and Industries. Great Britain's major occupations are manufacturing and trade. Metals and metal-using industries contribute more than 50% of exports. Of about 60 mil acres of land in England, Wales, and Scotland, 46 mil are farmed, of which 17 mil are arable, the rest pastures. Large oil and gas fields have been found in the North Sea. Commercial oil production began in 1975. There are large deposits of coal.

Britain imports all of its cotton, rubber, sulphur, about 80% of its wool, half of its food and iron ore, also certain amounts of paper, tobacco, chemicals. Manufactured goods made from these basic materials have been exported since the industrial age began. Main exports are machinery, chemicals, textiles, clothing, autos and trucks, iron and steel, locomotives, ships, jet aircraft, farm machinery, drugs, radio, TV, radar and navigation equipment, scientific instruments, arms, whisky.

Religion and Education. The Church of England is Protestant Episcopal. The queen is its temporal head, with rights of appointments to archbishoprics, bishoprics, and other offices. There are 2 provinces, Canterbury and York, each headed by an archbishop. The most famous church is Westminster Abbey (1050-1760), site of coronations, tombs of Elizabeth I, Mary, Queen of Scots, kings, poets, and of the Unknown Warrior.

The most celebrated British universities are Oxford and Cambridge, each dating to the 13th cent. There are about 70 other universities.

History. Britain was part of the continent of Europe until about 6,000 BCE, but migration across the English Channel continued long afterward. Celts arrived 2,500 to 3,000 years ago. Their language survives in Welsh and Gaelic enclaves.

England was added to the Roman Empire in 43 CE. After the withdrawal of Roman legions in 410, waves of Jutes, Angles, and Saxons arrived from German lands. They contended with Danish raiders for control from the 8th through 11th centuries. The last successful invasion was by French speaking Normans in 1066, who united the country with their dominions in France.

Opposition by nobles to royal authority forced King John to agree to the Magna Carta in 1215, a guarantee of rights and the rule of law. In the ensuing decades, the foundations of the parliamentary system were laid.

English dynastic claims to large parts of France led to the Hundred Years War, 1338-1453, and the defeat of England. A long civil war, the War of the Roses, lasted 1455-85, and ended with the establishment of the powerful Tudor monarchy. A distinct English civilization flourished. The economy prospered over long periods of domestic peace unmatched in continental Europe. Religious independence was secured when the Church of England was separated from the authority of the pope in 1534.

Under Queen Elizabeth I, England became a major naval power, leading to the founding of colonies in the new world and the expansion of trade with Europe and the Orient. Scotland was united with England when James VI of Scotland was crowned James I of England in 1603.

A struggle between Parliament and the Stuart kings led to a bloody civil war, 1642-49, and the establishment of a republic under the Puritan Oliver Cromwell. The monarchy was restored in 1660, but the "Glorious Revolution" of 1688 confirmed the sovereignty of Parliament: a Bill of Rights was granted 1689.

In the 18th cent., parliamentary rule was strengthened. Technological and entrepreneurial innovations led to the Industrial Revolution. The 13 N. American colonies were lost but replaced by growing empires in Canada and India. Britain's role in the defeat of Napoleon, 1815, strengthened its position as the leading world power.

The extension of the franchise in 1832 and 1867, the formation of trade unions, and the development of universal public education were among the drastic social changes that accompanied the spread of industrialization and urbanization in the 19th cent. Large parts of Africa and Asia were added to the empire during the reign of Queen Victoria, 1837-1901.

Though victorious in WWI, Britain suffered huge casualties and economic dislocation. Ireland became independent in 1921, and independence movements became active in India and other colonies. The country suffered major bombing damage in WWII, but held out against Germany single-handedly for a year after France fell in 1940.

Industrial growth continued in the postwar period, but Britain lost its leadership position to other powers. Labor governments passed socialist programs nationalizing some basic industries and expanding social security. Prime Min. Margaret Thatcher's Conservative government, however, tried to increase the role of private enterprise. In 1987, Thatcher became the first British leader in 160 years to be elected to a 3rd consecutive term as prime min. Falling on unpopular times, she resigned as prime min. in Nov. 1990. Her successor, John Major, led Conservatives to an upset victory at the polls, Apr. 9, 1992.

The UK supported the UN resolutions against Iraq and sent military forces to the Persian Gulf War, 1991. The Channel Tunnel linking Britain to the Continent was inaugurated May 6, 1994.

On May 1, 1997, the Labour Party swept into power in a landslide victory, the largest of any party since 1935. Labour Party leader Tony Blair, 43, became Britain's youngest prime min. since 1812. Diana, Princess of Wales, died in a car crash in Paris, Aug. 31. Britain played a leading role in the NATO air war against Yugoslavia, Mar.-June 1999, and contributed 12,000 troops to the multinational security force in Kosovo (KFOR).

Blair led Labour to another landslide election victory June 7, 2001. After the Sept. 11 attacks on the U.S., Britain took an important role in the U.S.-led war against terrorism. The UK participated in the bombing of Afghanistan that began Oct. 7, 2001; about 7,700 UK troops were serving in Afghanistan in mid-2007.

Overcoming dissent within his own cabinet, Blair committed British troops to the U.S.-led invasion of Iraq, Mar.-Apr. 2003. Forces from the UK (5,500 in Sept. 2007) remained to occupy southern Iraq, with more than 160 casualties reported.

In elections May 5, 2005, Blair became the first Labour prime min. to win 3 consecutive terms, but continued controversy over Iraq reduced his parliamentary majority. Suicide bombings on 3 London underground trains and a bus, July 7, left 56 people dead and hundreds injured; police identified the bombers as 4 British Muslim men (3 of Pakistani origin). British authorities announced Aug. 10, 2006, that they had thwarted a plot to use liquid explosives to blow up passenger aircraft flying between the U.S. and UK. Some 2 dozen suspects were arrested in Britain; many had ties to Pakistan, which assisted in cracking the case.

Blair stepped down June 27, 2007, and was succeeded by Gordon Brown, a Scot who as chancellor of the exchequer (1997-2007) had earned credit for the UK's steady economic performance. Failed car bombings in London, June 29, and at Glasgow Airport Scotland, June 30, led to the arrest in Britain of 7 suspects, mostly foreign-born medical workers. Severe floods June-Aug. in central England caused at least $2 bil in damage.

Wales

The Principality of Wales in western Britain has an area of 8,019 sq mi and a population (2006 est.) of 2,966,000. Cardiff is the capital, pop. (2005 est., city proper) 319,700.

Less than 20% of Wales residents speak English and Welsh; about 32,000 speak Welsh solely. A 1979 referendum rejected, 4-1, the creation of an elected Welsh assembly; a similar proposal passed by a thin margin on Sept. 18, 1997. Elections for the 60-seat assembly were held in 1997, 2003, and 2007.

Early Anglo-Saxon invaders drove Celtic peoples into the mountains of Wales, terming them Waelise (Welsh, or foreign). There they developed a distinct nationality. Members of the ruling house of Gwynedd in the 13th cent. fought England but were crushed, 1283. Edward of Caernarvon, son of Edward I of England, was created Prince of Wales, 1301.

Scotland

Scotland, a kingdom now united with England and Wales in Great Britain, occupies the northern 37% of the main British island, and the Hebrides, Orkney, Shetland, and smaller islands. Length 275 mi, breadth approx. 150 mi, area 30,418 sq mi, pop. (2006 est.) 5,117,000.

The Lowlands, a belt of land approx. 60 mi wide from the Firth of Clyde to the Firth of Forth, divide the farming region of the Southern Uplands from the granite Highlands of the N; they contain 75% of the population and most of the industry. The Highlands, famous for hunting and fishing, have been opened to industry by many hydroelectric power stations.

Edinburgh, pop. (2006 est., city proper) 463,510, is the capital. Glasgow, pop. (2006 est., city proper) 580,690, is Britain's greatest industrial center. It is a shipbuilding complex on the Clyde and an ocean port. Aberdeen, pop. (2006 est.) 202,090, NE of Edinburgh, is a major port, center of granite industry, fish-processing, and North Sea oil exploration. Dundee, pop. (2006 est.) 142,160, NE of Edinburgh, is an industrial and fish-processing center. About 90,000 persons speak Gaelic as well as English.

History. Scotland was called Caledonia by the Romans who battled early Celtic tribes and occupied southern areas from the 1st to the 4th centuries. Missionaries from Britain introduced Christianity in the 4th cent.; St. Columba, an Irish monk, converted most of Scotland in the 6th cent.

The Kingdom of Scotland was founded in 1018. William Wallace and Robert Bruce both defeated English armies 1297 and 1314, respectively.

In 1603 James VI of Scotland, son of Mary, Queen of Scots, succeeded to the throne of England as James I, and effected the Union of the Crowns. In 1707 Scotland received representation in the British Parliament, resulting from the union of former separate Parliaments. Its executive in the British cabinet is the Secretary of State for Scotland. The growing Scottish National Party urges independence. A 1979 referendum on the creation of an elected Scottish assembly was defeated, but a proposal to create a regional legislature with limited taxing authority passed by a landslide Sept. 11, 1997. Elections for the 129-seat parliament were held 1999, 2003, and 2007; in the 2007 vote, Scottish Nationalist candidates upset the Labour Party.

Memorials of Robert Burns, Sir Walter Scott, John Knox, and Mary, Queen of Scots, draw many tourists, as do the beauties of the Trossachs, Loch Katrine, Loch Lomond, and abbey ruins.

Industries. Engineering products are the most important industry, with growing emphasis on office machinery, autos, electronics, and other consumer goods. Oil has been discovered offshore in the North Sea, stimulating on-shore support industries.

Scotland produces fine woolens, worsteds, tweeds, silks, fine linens, and jute. It is known for its special breeds of cattle and sheep. Fisheries have large hauls of herring, cod, whiting. Whisky is the biggest export.

The Hebrides are a group of c. 500 islands, 100 inhabited, off the W coast. The Inner Hebrides include **Skye**, **Mull**, and **Iona**, the last famous for the arrival of St. Columba, 563 CE. The Outer Hebrides include **Lewis** and **Harris**. Industries include sheep raising and weaving. The **Orkney Isls.**, c. 90, are to the NE. The capital is Kirkwall, on Pomona Isl. Fish curing, sheep raising, and weaving are occupations. NE of the Orkneys are the 200 **Shetland Isls.**, 24 inhabited, home of Shetland ponies. The Orkneys and Shetlands are centers for the North Sea oil industry.

Northern Ireland

Northern Ireland was constituted in 1920 from 6 of the 9 counties of Ulster, the NE corner of Ireland. Area 5,452 sq mi, pop. (2006 est.) 1,742,000. Capital and chief industrial center, Belfast, pop. (2006 est., city proper) 267,400.

Industries. Shipbuilding, including large tankers, has long been an important industry, centered in Belfast, the largest port. Linen manufacture is also important, along with apparel, rope, and twine. Growing diversification has added engineering products, synthetic fibers, and electronics. There are large numbers of cattle, hogs, and sheep. Potatoes, poultry, and dairy foods are also produced.

Government. An act of the British Parliament, 1920, divided Northern from Southern Ireland, each with a parliament and government. When Ireland became a dominion, 1921, and later a republic, Northern Ireland chose to remain a part of the United Kingdom. It elects 18 members to the House of Commons.

During 1968-69, large demonstrations were conducted by Roman Catholics who charged they were discriminated against in voting rights, housing, and employment. The Catholics, a minority comprising about a third of the population, demanded abolition of property qualifications for voting in local elections. Violence and terrorism intensified, involving branches of the Irish Republican Army (outlawed in the Irish Republic), Protestant groups, police, and British troops.

A succession of Northern Ireland prime ministers pressed reform programs but failed to satisfy extremists on both sides. Between 1969 and 1994 more than 3,000 were killed in sectarian violence, many in England itself. Britain suspended the Northern Ireland parliament Mar. 30, 1972, and imposed direct British rule. A coalition government was formed in 1973 when moderates won election to a new one-house Assembly. But a Protestant general strike overthrew the government in 1974 and direct rule was resumed.

The agony of Northern Ireland was dramatized in 1981 by the deaths of 10 Irish nationalist hunger strikers in Maze Prison near

Belfast. In 1985 the Hillsborough agreement gave the Rep. of Ireland a voice in the governing of Northern Ireland; the accord was strongly opposed by Ulster loyalists. On Dec. 12, 1993, Britain and Ireland announced a declaration of principles to resolve the Northern Ireland conflict.

A settlement reached on Good Friday, April 10, 1998, provided for restoration of home rule and election of a 108-member assembly with safeguards for minority rights. Both Ireland and Great Britain agreed to give up their constitutional claims on Northern Ireland. The accord was approved May 22 by voters in Northern Ireland and the Irish Republic, and elections to the assembly were held June 25. IRA dissidents seeking to derail the agreement were responsible for a bomb at Omagh Aug. 15 that killed 29 people and injured over 330.

London transferred authority to a Northern Ireland power-sharing government Dec. 2, 1999. Delays in IRA disarmament led to several suspensions of self-government. The IRA stated July 28, 2005, that it had renounced violence and ordered all units to disarm. In response, the British began reducing their military presence in the region. On Sept. 26, an international monitoring group reported that the IRA had apparently scrapped its entire arsenal. The Northern Ireland legislature, suspended for 3 1/2 years, reconvened May 15, 2006. Following elections Mar. 7, 2007, agreement was reached on a power-sharing govt. led by the Protestant Rev. Ian Paisley of the Democratic Unionist Party and the Irish nationalist Martin McGuinness of Sinn Fein.

Education and Religion. Northern Ireland is about 58% Protestant, 42% Roman Catholic. Education is compulsory between the ages of 5 and 16 years.

Channel Islands

The Channel Islands, area 75 sq mi, pop. (2003 est.) 145,000, off the NW coast of France, the only parts of the one-time Dukedom of Normandy belonging to England, are Jersey, Guernsey and the dependencies of Guernsey—Alderney, Brechou, Great Sark, Little Sark, Herm, Jethou and Lihou. Jersey, pop. (2007 est.) 91,321, and Guernsey, pop. (2007 est.) 65,573, have separate legal existences and lieutenant governors named by the Crown. The islands were the only British soil occupied by German troops in WWII.

Isle of Man

The Isle of Man, area 221 sq mi, pop. (2007 est.) 75,831, is in the Irish Sea, 20 mi from Scotland, 30 mi from Cumberland. It is rich in lead and iron. The island has its own laws and a lieutenant governor appointed by the Crown. The Tynwald (legislature) consists of the Legislative Council, partly elected, and House of Keys, elected. Capital: Douglas. Farming, tourism, and fishing (kippers, scallops) are chief occupations. Man is famous for the Manx tailless cat.

Gibraltar

Gibraltar, a dependency on the S coast of Spain, guards the entrance to the Mediterranean. The Rock of Gibraltar has been in British possession since 1704. The Rock is 2.5 mi long, 3/4 of a mi wide and 1,396 ft in height; a narrow isthmus connects it with the mainland. Pop. (2007 est.) 27,967.

Gibraltar has historically been an object of contention between Britain and Spain. Residents voted with near unanimity to remain under British rule, in a 1967 referendum held in pursuance of a UN resolution on decolonization. A new constitution, May 30, 1969, increased Gibraltarian control of domestic affairs (the UK continues to handle defense and internal security matters). Following a 1984 agreement between Britain and Spain, the border, closed by Spain in 1969, was fully reopened in Feb. 1985. A UN General Assembly resolution requested Britain to end Gibraltar's colonial status by Oct. 1, 1996. A plan for the U.K. and Spain to share sovereignty was rejected by Gibraltar voters, Nov. 7, 2002. Residents approved a new constitution Nov. 30, 2006.

British West Indies

Swinging in a vast arc from the coast of Venezuela NE, then N and NW toward Puerto Rico are the Leeward Islands, forming a coral and volcanic barrier sheltering the Caribbean from the open Atlantic. Many of the islands are self-governing British possessions. Universal suffrage was instituted 1951-54; ministerial systems were set up 1956-60.

The **Leeward Isls.** still associated with the UK are **Montserrat**, area 40 sq mi, pop. (2007 est.) 9,538, capital Plymouth; the **British Virgin Isls.**, 59.1 sq mi, pop. (2007 est.) 23,552, capital Road Town; and **Anguilla**, the most northerly of Leeward Islands, 40 sq mi, pop. (2007 est.) 13,677, capital The Valley. Montserrat has been devastated by the Soufrière Hills volcano, which began erupting July 18, 1995.

The three **Cayman Isls.**, a dependency, lie S of Cuba, NW of Jamaica. Pop. (2007 est.) 46,600, most of it on Grand Cayman. It is a free port; in the 1970s Grand Cayman became a tax-free refuge for foreign funds and branches of many Western banks were opened there. Total area 101 sq mi, capital George Town.

The **Turks and Caicos Isls.** are a dependency at the SE end of the Bahama Islands. Of about 30 islands, only 6 are inhabited; area 166 sq mi, pop. (2007 est.) 21,746; capital Grand Turk. Salt, shellfish, and conch shells are the main exports.

Bermuda

Bermuda is a British dependency governed by a royal governor and an assembly, dating from 1620, the oldest legislative body among British dependencies. Capital is Hamilton.

It is a group of about 150 small islands of coral formation, 20 inhabited, comprising 21 sq mi in the western Atlantic, 580 mi E of N. Carolina. Pop. (2007 est.) 66,163 (about 61% of African descent). Pop. density is high.

The U.S. maintains a NASA tracking facility; a U.S. naval air base was closed in 1995.

Tourism is the major industry; Bermuda boasts many resort hotels. Bermuda is also a haven for the offshore insurance industry. Exports include petroleum products, medicine. In a referendum Aug. 15, 1995, voters rejected independence by nearly a 3-to-1 majority.

Hurricane Fabian, the most potent storm to reach Bermuda in 50 years, struck Sept. 5, 2003; 4 people were missing and presumed dead, and damage was estimated at over $300 mil.

South Atlantic

The **Falkland Isls.**, a dependency, lie 300 mi E of the Strait of Magellan at the southern end of S. America.

The Falklands, or Islas Malvinas, include 2 large islands and about 200 smaller ones, area 4,700 sq mi, pop. (2007 est.) 3,105, capital Stanley. The licensing of foreign fishing vessels has become the major source of revenue. Sheep-grazing is a main industry; wool is the principal export. There are indications of large oil and gas deposits. The islands are also claimed by Argentina, though 97% of inhabitants are of British origin. Argentina invaded the islands Apr. 2, 1982. The British responded by sending a task force to the area, landing their main force on the Falklands, May 21, and forcing an Argentine surrender at Port Stanley, June 14. A pact resuming commercial air service with Argentina was signed July 14, 1999.

British Antarctic Territory, south of 60° S lat., formerly a dependency of the Falkland Isls., was made a separate colony in 1962 and includes the **South Shetland Isls.**, the **South Orkneys**, and the Antarctic Peninsula. A chain of meteorological stations is maintained.

South Georgia and the South Sandwich Isls., formerly administered by the Falkland Isls., became a separate dependency in 1985. Total area of 1,507 sq mi. South Georgia with no permanent population, is about 800 mi SE of the Falklands; the South Sandwich Isls. are uninhabited, about 470 mi SE of South Georgia.

St. Helena, an island 1,200 mi off the W coast of Africa and 1,800 mi E of S. America, 160 sq mi and pop. (2007 est.) 7,543. Flax, lace, and rope-making are the chief industries. After Napoleon Bonaparte was defeated at Waterloo the Allies exiled him to St. Helena, where he lived from Oct. 16, 1815, to his death, May 5, 1821. Capital is Jamestown.

Tristan da Cunha is the principal island in a group of islands of volcanic origin, total area 40 sq mi, halfway between the Cape of Good Hope and S. America. A volcanic peak 6,760 ft high erupted in 1961. The 262 inhabitants were removed to England, but most returned in 1963. The islands are dependencies of St. Helena. Pop. (2002) 284.

Ascension is an island of volcanic origin, 34 sq mi in area, 700 mi NW of St. Helena, through which it is administered. It is a communications relay center for Britain, and has a U.S. satellite tracking center. Pop. (2002) was 1,050, half of them communications workers. The island is noted for sea turtles.

British Indian Ocean Territory

Formed Nov. 1965, embracing islands formerly dependencies of Mauritius or Seychelles: the Chagos Archipelago (including Diego Garcia), Aldabra, Farquhar, and Des Roches. The latter 3 were transferred to Seychelles, which became independent in 1976. Area 23 sq mi. No permanent civilian population remains; the U.K. and the U.S. maintain a military presence.

Pacific Ocean

Pitcairn Isl. is in the Pacific, halfway between S. America and Australia. The island was discovered in 1767 by Philip Carteret but was not inhabited until 23 years later when the mutineers of the *Bounty* landed there. The area is 18 sq mi and 2007 pop. was 48. It is a British dependency and is administered by a British High Commissioner in New Zealand and a local Council. The uninhabited islands of **Henderson**, **Ducie**, and **Oeno** are in the Pitcairn group.

United States

United States of America

People: Population: 301,139,947. (incl. 50 states & Dist. of Columbia). (Note: U.S. pop. figures may differ elsewhere in *The World Almanac*.) **Age distrib.** (%): <15: 20.2; 65+: 12.6. **Pop. density:** 85 per sq mi, 33 per sq km. **Urban:** 80.8%. **Ethnic groups:** White 82%, black 13%, Asian 4%, Amerindian and Alaska native 1%. (Hispanic, any race 12.5%.) **Principal languages:** English, Spanish. **Chief religions:** Protestant 52%, Roman Catholic 24%, Mormon 2%, Jewish 1%.

Geography: Total area: 3,718,712 sq mi, 9,631,418 sq km; **Land area:** 3,537,439 sq mi, 9,161,923 sq km. **Topography:** Vast central plain, mountains in W, hills and low mountains in E. **Capital:** Washington, DC, 4,238,000.

Government: Federal republic, strong democratic tradition. **Head of state and gov.:** Pres. George W. Bush; b. July 6, 1946; in office: Jan. 20, 2001. **Local divisions:** 50 states and Dist. of Columbia. **Defense budget:** $535.9 bil. **Active troops:** 1,506,757.

Economy: Industries: oil, steel, motor vehicles, aerospace, telecom., chemicals, electronics, food proc., consumer goods, lumber, mining. **Chief crops:** wheat, corn, fruits, vegetables, cotton. **Natural resources:** coal, copper, lead, molybd., phosphates, uranium, bauxite, gold, iron, mercury, nickel, potash, silver, tungsten, zinc, oil, nat. gas, timber. **Crude oil reserves:** 21.8 bil bbls. **Arable land:** 18%. **Livestock:** cattle: 96.7 mil; chickens: 2.1 bil.; goats: 2.8 mil; pigs: 61.4 mil; sheep: 6.2 mil. **Fish catch:** 5,360,579 metric tons. **Electricity prod.:** 4,062 bil kWh. **Labor force** (2006): farming, forestry, and fishing 0.7%, manufacturing, extraction, transportation, and crafts 22.9%, managerial, professional., and technical 34.9%, sales and office 25%, other services 16.5%.

Finance: Dollar (USD) (Sept. 2007: 1.00 = $1 U.S.). **GDP:** $13.1 tril; **per capita GDP:** $44,000; **GDP growth:** 3.2%. **Imports:** $1.9 tril; Canada 16%, China 15.9%, Mexico 10.4%, Japan 7.9%, Germany 4.8%. **Exports:** $1 tril; Canada 22.2%, Mexico 12.9%, Japan 5.8%, China 5.3%, UK 4.4%. **Tourism:** $93.9 bil. **Budget:** $2.7 tril. **Intl. reserves less gold:** $36.46 bil. **Gold:** 261.5 mil oz t. **Consumer prices:** 3.23%.

Transport: Railroad: Length: 140,806 mi. **Motor vehicles:** 222.7 mil pass. cars; 8.7 mil comm. vehicles. **Civil aviation:** 643.3 bil pass.-mi; 5,119 airports.

Communications: TV sets: 844 per 1,000 pop. **Radios:** 2,116 per 1,000 pop. **Telephone lines:** 172 mil. **Daily newspaper circ.:** 196.3 per 1,000 pop. **Internet:** 208 mil users.

Health: Life expect.: 75.2 male; 81 female. **Births** (per 1,000 pop.): 14.2. **Deaths** (per 1,000 pop.): 8.3. **Natural inc.:** 0.59%. **Infant mortality** (per 1,000 live births): 6.4. **AIDS rate:** 0.6%.

Education: Compulsory: ages 6-17. **Literacy:** 99%.

Major intl. organizations: UN (FAO, IBRD, ILO, IMF, IMO, WHO, WTO), APEC, NATO, OAS, OECD, OSCE.

Website: www.usa.gov

See also U.S. History chapter; Chronology of the Year's Events.

Uruguay
Oriental Republic of Uruguay

People: Population: 3,460,607. **Age distrib.** (%): <15: 23; 65+: 13.2. **Pop. density:** 52 per sq mi, 20 per sq km. **Urban:** 92%. **Ethnic groups:** White 88%, mestizo 8%, black 4%. **Principal languages:** Spanish (official), Portunol/Brazilero (Port.-Span.). **Chief religion:** Roman Catholic 66%.

Geography: Total area: 68,039 sq mi, 176,220 sq km; **Land area:** 67,035 sq mi, 173,620 sq km. **Location:** In southern S. America, on Atlantic O. **Neighbors:** Argentina on W, Brazil on N. **Topography:** Uruguay is composed of rolling, grassy plains and hills, well watered by rivers flowing W to Uruguay R. **Capital:** Montevideo, 1,264,000.

Government: Type: Republic. **Head of state and gov.:** Pres. Tabaré Ramón Vázquez Rosas; b. Jan. 17, 1940; in office: Mar. 1, 2005. **Local divisions:** 19 departments. **Defense budget:** $227 mil. **Active troops:** 25,100.

Economy: Industries: food proc., electrical machinery, transp. equip., oil products, textiles. **Chief crops:** rice, wheat, corn, barley. **Natural resources:** hydropower, minor minerals, fisheries. **Arable land:** 8%. **Livestock:** cattle: 12 mil; chickens: 14 mil; goats: 16,000; pigs: 257,000; sheep: 9.7 mil. **Fish catch:** 125,953 metric tons. **Electricity prod.:** 7.6 bil kWh. **Labor force:** agriculture 14%, industry 16%, services 70%.

Finance: Monetary unit: Peso (UYU) (Sept. 2007: 23.13 = $1 U.S.). **GDP:** $37.5 bil; **per capita GDP:** $10,900; **GDP growth:** 7%. **Imports:** $4.5 bil; Brazil 17.2%, Argentina 16.4%, U.S. 8.9%, Paraguay 7.8%, China 7.5%, Venezuela 5.2%, Nigeria 4.8%. **Exports:** $4 bil; Brazil 14%, U.S. 12.3%, Argentina 8.2%, China 6.1%, Germany 5%, Russia 5%, Mexico 4.3%. **Tourism:** $594 mil. **Budget:** $5.4 bil. **Intl. reserves less gold:** $2.05 bil. **Gold:** 10,000 oz t. **Consumer prices:** 6.4%.

Transport: Railroad: Length: 1,288 mi. **Motor vehicles:** 372,000 pass. cars; 54,000 comm. vehicles. **Civil aviation:** 639.4 mil pass.-mi; 8 airports. **Chief port:** Montevideo.

Communications: TV sets: 531 per 1,000 pop. **Radios:** 603 per 1,000 pop. **Telephone lines:** 987,000. **Internet:** 756,000 users.

Health: Life expect.: 72.7 male; 79.3 female. **Births** (per 1,000 pop.): 14.4. **Deaths** (per 1,000 pop.): 9.2. **Natural inc.:** 0.53%. **Infant mortality** (per 1,000 live births): 12. **AIDS rate:** 0.5%.

Education (2005): Compulsory: ages 6-15. **Literacy:** 96.8%.

Major intl. organizations: UN (FAO, IBRD, ILO, IMF, IMO, WHO, WTO), OAS.

Embassy: 1913 I St. NW 20006; 331-1313.

Website: www.uruwashi.org

Spanish settlers began to supplant the indigenous Charrua Indians in 1624. Portuguese from Brazil arrived later, but Uruguay was attached to the Spanish Viceroyalty of Rio de la Plata in the 18th cent. Rebels fought against Spain beginning in 1810. An independent republic was declared Aug. 25, 1825.

Socialist measures were adopted in the early 1900s. The state retains a dominant role in the power, telephone, railroad, cement, oil-refining, and other industries, although some privatization began in the early 2000s. Uruguay's standard of living remains one of the highest in S. America, and political and labor conditions among the freest. A leftist, Tabaré Vázquez, was elected president Oct. 31, 2004, and took office Mar. 1, 2005.

Uzbekistan
Republic of Uzbekistan

People: Population: 27,780,059. **Age distrib.** (%): <15: 32.4; 65+: 4.8. **Pop. density:** 169 per sq mi, 65 per sq km. **Urban:** 36.7%. **Ethnic groups:** Uzbek 80%, Russian 6%, Tajik 5%, Kazakh 3%, Karakalpak 3%, Tatar 2%. **Principal languages:** Uzbek (official), Russian, Tajik. **Chief religions:** Muslim 88% (mostly Sunni), Eastern Orthodox 9%.

Geography: Total area: 172,742 sq mi, 447,400 sq km; **Land area:** 164,248 sq mi, 425,400 sq km. **Location:** Central Asia. **Neighbors:** Kazakhstan on N and W; Kyrgyzstan, Tajikistan on E; Afghanistan, Turkmenistan on S. **Topography:** Mostly plains and desert. **Capital:** Tashkent, 2,181,000.

Government: Type: Republic with authoritarian rule. **Head of state:** Pres. Islam A. Karimov; b. Jan. 30, 1938; in office: Mar. 24, 1990. **Head of gov.:** Prime Min. Shavkat Mirziyaev; b 1957; in office: Dec. 11, 2003. **Local divisions:** 12 regions, 1 autonomous republic, 1 city. **Defense budget:** $84 mil. **Active troops:** 55,000.

Economy: Industries: textiles, food proc., machine building, metallurgy, nat. gas, chemicals. **Chief crops:** cotton, vegetables, fruits, grain. **Natural resources:** nat. gas, oil, coal, gold, uranium, silver, copper, lead, zinc, tungsten, molybd. **Crude oil reserves:** 594 mil bbls. **Arable land:** 11%. **Livestock:** cattle: 7 mil; chickens: 24.2 mil; goats: 2 mil; pigs: 93,100; sheep: 10 mil. **Fish catch:** 5,425 metric tons. **Electricity prod.:** 45.2 bil kWh. **Labor force** (1995): agriculture 44%, industry 20%, services 36%.

Finance: Monetary unit: Som (UZS) (Sept. 2007: 1,276.28 = $1 U.S.). **GDP:** $55.8 bil; **per capita GDP:** $2,000; **GDP growth:** 7.3%. **Imports:** $4 bil; Russia 27.8%, S. Korea 15.6%, China 10.4%, Kazakhstan 7.3%, Germany 7.1%, Ukraine 4.8%, Turkey 4.5%. **Exports:** $5.5 bil; Russia 23.9%, Poland 11.8%, China 10.5%, Turkey 7.5%, Kazakhstan 6%, Ukraine 4.7%, Bangladesh 4.4%. **Tourism:** $28 mil. **Budget** (FY07 est.): $4.2 bil.

Transport: Railroad: Length: 2,454 mi. **Motor vehicles:** NA. **Civil aviation:** 2.4 bil pass.-mi; 34 airports. **Chief port:** Termiz.

Communications: TV sets: 280 per 1,000 pop. **Radios:** 465 per 1,000 pop. **Telephone lines:** 1.8 mil. **Internet:** 7 mil users.

Health: Life expect.: 61.6 male; 68.6 female. **Births** (per 1,000 pop.): 26.5. **Deaths** (per 1,000 pop.): 7.7. **Natural inc.:** 1.87%. **Infant mortality** (per 1,000 live births): 68.9. **AIDS rate:** 0.2%.

Education: Compulsory: ages 7-15. **Literacy:** 99.3%.

Major intl. organizations: UN (FAO, IBRD, ILO, IMF, WHO), CIS, OSCE.

Embassy: 1746 Massachusetts Ave. NW 20036; 887-5300.

Website: www.gov.uz

The region was overrun by the Mongols under Genghis Khan in 1220. In the 14th cent., Uzbekistan became the center of a native Timurid empire. In later centuries Muslim feudal states emerged. Russian military conquest began in the 19th cent. Uzbek SSR became a Soviet republic in 1925.

Uzbekistan declared independence Aug. 29, 1991. It became an independent republic when the Soviet Union disbanded Dec. 26, 1991. Since then, the authoritarian government of Uzbekistan has been led by a former Communist, Islam A. Karimov.

Attacks by Islamic militants, Mar.-July 2004, killed more than 50 people. In June 2004, Russia's OAO Lukoil signed a $1 bil deal to develop Uzbekistan's natural gas fields. Militants bombed the U.S. and Israeli embassies in Tashkent, July 30.

After armed dissidents at Andizhan, east Uzbekistan, attacked government buildings and freed hundreds of prisoners, May 12-13, 2005, Uzbek security forces opened fire on rebels and unarmed demonstrators, killing many. Karimov then launched a general crackdown on human rights activists. Irritated by U.S. human rights pressures, Karimov ordered the U.S. to vacate an airbase used to support operations in Afghanistan; the U.S. pullout was completed Nov. 21. Meeting in Moscow a week earlier, Karimov and Russian Pres. Vladimir Putin signed a military cooperation agreement. Karimov remained in office following the formal expiration of his presidential term Jan. 22, 2007; new elections were scheduled for Dec. 23.

Vanuatu
Republic of Vanuatu

People: Population: 211,971. **Age distrib.** (%): <15: 31.9; 65+: 3.8. **Pop. density:** 45 per sq mi, 17 per sq km. **Urban:** 23.5%. **Ethnic groups:** Ni-Vanuatu 98%. **Principal languages:** Bislama, English, French (all official); 100+ local languages. **Chief religions:** Presbyterian 31%, Anglican 13%, Roman Catholic 13%, other Christian 14%, indigenous beliefs 6%.

Geography: Total area: 4,710 sq mi, 12,200 sq km; **Land area:** 4,710 sq mi, 12,200 sq km. **Location:** SW Pacific, 1,200 mi. NE of Brisbane, Australia. **Neighbors:** Fiji to E, Solomon Isls. to NW. **Topography:** Dense forest with narrow coastal strips of cultivated land. **Capital:** Port-Vila, 36,000.

Government: Type: Republic. **Head of state:** Pres. Kalkot Mataskelekele; b. 1949; in office: Aug. 16, 2004. **Head of gov.:** Prime Min. Ham Lini; b. 1951; in office: Dec. 11, 2004. **Local divisions:** 6 provinces.

Economy: Industries: food & fish freezing, wood proc., meat canning. **Chief crops:** copra, coconuts, cocoa, coffee, taro, yams. **Natural resources:** mang., timber, fish. **Arable land:** 2%. **Livestock:** cattle: 152,000; chickens: 340,000; goats: 12,000; pigs: 62,000. **Fish catch:** 151,080 metric tons. **Electricity prod.:** 40 mil kWh. **Labor force** (2000 est.): agriculture 65%, industry 5%, services 30%.

Finance: Monetary unit: Vatu (VUV) (Sept. 2007: 95.00 = $1 U.S.). **GDP:** $739 mil; **per capita GDP** (2005 est.): $2,900; **GDP growth** (2005 est.): 6.8%. **Imports** (2004 est.): $117.1 mil; Australia 20%, Japan 19.2%, Singapore 11.7%, New Zealand 8.6%, Fiji 7.5%, China 7.2%, New Caledonia 4.2%. **Exports** (2004 est.): $34.1 mil; Thailand 59%, India 16.5%, Japan 11.3%. **Tourism:** $52 mil. **Budget** (2005 est.): $72.2 mil. **Intl. reserves less gold:** $70 mil. **Consumer prices** (2005): 1.15%.

Transport: Motor vehicles: 6,000 pass. cars; 4,600 comm. vehicles. **Civil aviation:** 109.4 mil pass.-mi; 3 airports. **Chief ports:** Forari, Port-Vila, Santo.

Communications: TV sets: 12 per 1,000 pop. **Radios:** 350 per 1,000 pop. **Telephone lines:** 7,000. **Internet:** 7,500 users.

Health: Life expect.: 61.7 male; 64.8 female. **Births** (per 1,000 pop.): 22.4. **Deaths** (per 1,000 pop.): 7.8. **Natural inc.:** 1.46%. **Infant mortality** (per 1,000 live births): 52.5. **AIDS rate:** NA.

Education: Compulsory: ages 6-12. **Literacy:** 74%.

Major intl. organizations: UN (FAO, IBRD, ILO, IMF, IMO, WHO), the Commonwealth.

Permanent UN mission: 800 Second Ave., Ste. 400B, New York, NY 10017; 212-661-4323.

Website: www.vanuatu.gov.ru

The Anglo-French condominium of the New Hebrides, administered jointly by France and Great Britain since 1906, became the independent Republic of Vanuatu on July 30, 1980. Vanuatu is located in the "Ring of Fire," a zone where earthquakes and volcanic eruptions are frequent.

Vatican City (The Holy See)

People: Population: 821. **Pop. density:** 4,833 per sq mi, 1,866 per sq km. **Urban:** 100%. **Ethnic groups:** Italian, Swiss, other. **Principal languages:** Latin (official), Italian, French, others. **Chief religion:** Roman Catholic.

Geography: Total area: 108.7 acres. **Location:** In Rome, Italy. **Neighbors:** Completely surrounded by Italy. Note: Dignitaries, priests, nuns, guards, and 3,000 lay workers live outside the Vatican.

Finance: Euro (EUR) (Sept. 2007: 0.72 = $1 U.S.). **Budget** (2005): $243 mil.

Labor force: Essentially services with a small amount of industry; dignitaries, priests, nuns, guards, and 3,000 lay workers live outside the Vatican.

Apostolic Nunciature in U.S.: 3339 Massachusetts Ave. NW 20008; 333-7121.

Website: www.vatican.va

The popes for many centuries, with brief interruptions, held temporal sovereignty over mid-Italy (the so-called Papal States), comprising an area of some 16,000 sq mi, with a population in the 19th cent. of more than 3 mil. This territory was incorporated in the new Kingdom of Italy (1861), the sovereignty of the pope being confined to the palaces of the Vatican and the Lateran in Rome and the villa of Castel Gandolfo, by an Italian law, May 13, 1871. This law also guaranteed to the pope and his successors a yearly indemnity of over $620,000. The allowance, however, remained unclaimed.

A Treaty of Conciliation, a concordat, and a financial convention were signed Feb. 11, 1929, by Cardinal Gasparri and Premier Mussolini. The documents established the independent state of Vatican City and gave the Roman Catholic church special status in Italy. The treaty (Lateran Agreement) was made part of the Constitution of Italy (Article 7) in 1947. Italy and the Vatican signed an agreement in 1984 on revisions of the concordat; the accord eliminated Roman Catholicism as the state religion and ended required religious education in Italian schools.

The U.S. restored formal relations in 1984 after the U.S. Congress repealed an 1867 ban on diplomatic relations with the Vatican. The Vatican and Israel agreed to establish formal relations Dec. 30, 1993.

Vatican City includes the Basilica of Saint Peter, the Vatican Palace and Museum covering over 13 acres, the Vatican gardens, and neighboring buildings between Viale Vaticano and the church. Thirteen buildings in Rome, outside the boundaries, enjoy extraterritorial rights; these buildings house congregations or officers necessary for the administration of the Holy See.

The legal system is based on the code of canon law, the apostolic constitutions, and laws especially promulgated for the Vatican City by the pope. The Secretariat of State represents the Holy See in its diplomatic relations. By the Treaty of Conciliation the pope is pledged to a perpetual neutrality unless his mediation is specifically requested. This, however, does not prevent the defense of the Church whenever it is persecuted.

The present sovereign of the State of Vatican City is the Supreme Pontiff Benedict XVI, born Joseph Ratzinger in Marktl am Inn, Germany, Apr. 16, 1927, elected Apr. 19, 2005.

Venezuela

Bolivarian Republic of Venezuela

People: Population: 26,023,528. **Age distrib.** (%): <15: 31.6; 65+: 5.1. **Pop. density:** 76 per sq mi, 30 per sq km. **Urban:** 93.4%. **Ethnic groups:** Spanish, Italian, Portuguese, Arab, German, black, indigenous. **Principal languages:** Spanish (official), indigenous dialects. **Chief religion:** Roman Catholic 96%.

Geography: Total area: 352,145 sq mi, 912,050 sq km; **Land area:** 340,561 sq mi, 882,050 sq km. **Location:** On Carib. coast of S. America. **Neighbors:** Colombia on W, Brazil on S, Guyana on E. **Topography:** Flat coastal plain and Orinoco Delta are bordered by Andes Mts. and hills. Plains, called llanos, extend between mountains and Orinoco. Guiana Highlands and plains are S of Orinoco, which stretches 1,600 mi and drains 80% of country. **Capital:** Caracas, 2,913,000. **Cities (urban aggr.):** Maracaibo, 2,255,000; Valencia, 2,451,000.

Government: Type: Federal republic. **Head of state and gov.:** Pres. Hugo Rafael Chávez Frías; b. July 28, 1954; in office: Feb. 2, 1999. **Local divisions:** 23 states, 1 federal district (Caracas), 1 federal dependency (72 islands). **Defense budget:** $1.68 bil. **Active troops:** 82,300.

Economy: Industries: oil, iron, constr. materials, food proc., textiles, steel, aluminum, auto assembly. **Chief crops:** corn, sorghum, sugarcane, rice, bananas, vegetables, coffee. **Natural resources:** oil, nat. gas, iron ore, gold, bauxite, other minerals, hydropower, diamonds. **Crude oil reserves:** 80 bil bbls. **Arable land:** 3%. **Livestock:** cattle: 16.6 mil; chickens: 110 mil; goats: 1.3 mil; pigs: 3.3 mil; sheep: 525,121. **Fish catch:** 492,210 metric tons. **Electricity prod.:** 99.2 bil kWh. **Labor force** (1997 est.): agriculture 13%, industry 23%, services 64%.

Finance: Monetary unit: Bolivar (VEB) (Sept. 2007: 2,147.30 = $1 U.S.). **GDP:** $186.3 bil **per capita GDP:** $7,200; **GDP growth:** 10.3%. **Imports:** $28.8 bil; U.S. 30.2%, Colombia 10%, Brazil 8.2%, Mexico 6.3%, China 5.7%. **Exports:** $69.2 bil; U.S. 45.8%, Netherlands Antilles 7.5%, China 3.2%. **Tourism:** $641 mil. **Budget:** $52.9 bil. **Intl. reserves less gold:** $19.55 bil. **Gold:** 11.48 mil oz t. **Consumer prices:** 13.66%.

Transport: Railroad: Length: 424 mi. **Motor vehicles:** 2.5 mil pass. cars; 677,000 comm. vehicles. **Civil aviation:** 1.3 bil pass.-mi; 129 airports. **Chief ports:** La Guaira, Maracaibo, Puerto Cabello.

Communications: TV sets: 185 per 1,000 pop. **Radios:** 296 per 1,000 pop. **Telephone lines:** 4.2 mil. **Internet:** 4.1 mil users.

Health: Life expect.: 70.2 male; 76.5 female. **Births** (per 1,000 pop.): 21.2. **Deaths** (per 1,000 pop.): 5.1. **Natural inc.:** 1.61%. **Infant mortality** (per 1,000 live births): 22.5. **AIDS rate:** 0.7%.

Education: Compulsory: ages 6-15. **Literacy:** 93%.

Major intl. organizations: UN (FAO, IBRD, ILO, IMF, IMO, WHO, WTO), OAS, OPEC.

Embassy: 1099 30th St. NW 20007; 342-2214.

Website: www.embavenez-us.org

Columbus first set foot on the S. American continent on the peninsula of Paria, Aug. 1498. Alonso de Ojeda, 1499, was the first European to see Lake Maracaibo. He called the land Venezuela, or Little Venice, because the Indians had houses on stilts. Spanish colonialists dominated Venezuela until Simón Bolívar's victory near Carabobo in June 1821. The republic was formed after secession from the Colombian Federation in 1830. Military strongmen ruled Venezuela for much of its history. Since 1959, the country has had democratically elected governments.

Oil accounts for more than 75% of export earnings and about half of government revenues. Venezuela helped found the Organization of Petroleum Exporting Countries (OPEC) in 1960. The government, Jan. 1, 1976, nationalized the oil industry with compensation. The economy suffered a cash crisis in the 1980s and 1990s as a result of depressed oil revenues. Government attempts to reduce dependence on oil have met with limited success.

An attempted coup by midlevel military officers was thwarted by loyalist troops Feb. 4, 1992. A second coup attempt was thwarted in Nov. Pres. Carlos Andrés Pérez was removed from office on corruption charges, May 1993; he was convicted, May 1996, of mismanaging a $17 mil secret government fund.

A 1992 coup leader, Hugo Chávez, who ran as a populist, was elected president Dec. 6, 1998. Voters on Dec. 15 approved a new constitution greatly increasing his powers.

Popular among the poor, Chávez alienated some middle- and upper-class Venezuelans with his program of economic and political reform, and his foreign policy antagonized the U.S. Gunfire erupted at a mass protest Apr. 11, 2002, in Caracas, killing at least 17 people. Chávez was forced to relinquish power, but when an interim government issued decrees suspending democratic institutions, Chávez loyalists rebelled; the coup fell apart, and the president reclaimed his office Apr. 14. Opponents of Chávez mounted a crippling general strike, Dec. 2002-Feb. 2003, which ended after mediation by the OAS and former U.S. Pres. Jimmy Carter.

Opponents presented petitions with over 3 mil signatures Aug. 20, 2003, demanding a vote to recall Chávez. In a recall referendum held Aug. 15, 2004, and monitored by Carter and the OAS, Chávez won with 59% of the vote. Elections Dec. 4, 2005, boycotted by major opposition parties, strengthened his control over the legislature.

Chávez countered U.S. efforts to isolate him diplomatically and militarily by solidifying ties with other Latin American leftist leaders and with Iran and Russia; an agreement in July 2006 to buy fighter jets and helicopters brought Venezuela's arms purchases from Russia to over $3 bil in 18 months. With the economy surging, Chávez captured a 63% majority in the Dec. 3 presidential election. On Jan. 31, 2007, the legislature granted him the power to rule by decree through mid-2008. He took steps, May 1, to sever ties with the IMF and World Bank, which he said were "dominated by U.S. imperialism," and seized control of the last remaining Venezuelan oil projects held by major U.S. and European firms.

Vietnam
Socialist Republic of Vietnam

People: Population: 85,262,356. **Age distrib.** (%): <15: 26.3; 65+: 5.8. **Pop. density:** 679 per sq mi, 262 per sq km. **Urban:** 26.4%. **Ethnic groups:** Kinh (Viet) 86%, Tay 2%, Thai 2%, Muong 2%. **Principal languages:** Vietnamese (official), French, Chinese, English, Khmer. **Chief religions:** Buddhist, Taoist, Roman Catholic, indigenous beliefs.

Geography: Total area: 127,244 sq mi, 329,560 sq km; **Land area:** 125,622 sq mi, 325,360 sq km. **Location:** SE Asia, on E coast of Indochinese Peninsula. **Neighbors:** China on N; Laos, Cambodia on W. **Topography:** Vietnam is long and narrow, with 1,400-mi coast. About 22% of country is readily arable, including densely settled Red R. valley in N, narrow coastal plains in center, and the wide, often marshy Mekong R. Delta in S. The rest consists of semi-arid plateaus and barren mountains, with some stretches of tropical rain forest. **Capital:** Hanoi, 4,164,000. **Cities** (urban aggr.): Ho Chi Minh City, 5,065,000; Hai Phong, 1,873,000.

Government: Type: Communist. **Head of state:** Pres. Nguyen Minh Triet; b. Oct. 8, 1942; in office: June 27, 2006. **Head of gov.:** Prime Min. Nguyen Tan Dung; b. Nov. 17, 1949; in office: June 27, 2006. **Local divisions:** 58 provinces, 3 cities, 1 capital region. **Defense budget:** $3.43 bil. **Active troops:** 455,000.

Economy: Industries: food proc., garments, shoes, machinery, mining. **Chief crops:** rice, coffee, rubber, cotton, tea, pepper, soybeans, cashews. **Natural resources:** phosphates, coal, mang., bauxite, chromate, oil, nat. gas, timber, hydropower. **Crude oil reserves:** 600 mil bbls. **Arable land:** 20%. **Livestock:** cattle: 6.5 mil; chickens: 150.2 mil; goats: 1.5 mil; pigs: 26.9 mil. **Fish catch:** 3,367,200 metric tons. **Electricity prod.:** 51.3 bil kWh. **Labor force** (2005): agriculture 56.8%, industry 37%, services 6.2%.

Finance: Monetary unit: Dong (VND) (Sept. 2007: 16,275.00 = $1 U.S.). **GDP:** $262.8 bil **per capita GDP:** $3,100; **GDP growth:** 8.2%. **Imports:** $39.2 bil; China 17.2%, Singapore 12.6%, Taiwan 11.2%, Japan 9.5%, S. Korea 9.3%, Thailand 7.1%, Malaysia 4%. **Exports:** $39.9 bil; U.S. 20.7%, Japan 12%, Australia 9.2%, China 5.6%, Germany 4.4%. **Tourism:** NA. **Budget:** $16.6 bil. **Intl. reserves less gold:** $8.90 bil. **Consumer prices** (2005): 8.25%.

Transport: Railroad: Length: 1,616 mi. **Motor vehicles:** 206,000 comm. vehicles. **Civil aviation:** 1.2 bil pass.-mi; 26 airports. **Chief ports:** Haiphong, Ho Chi Minh City.

Communications: TV sets: 184 per 1,000 pop. **Radios:** 107 per 1,000 pop. **Telephone lines:** 15.8 mil. **Daily newspaper circ.:** 5.8 per 1,000 pop. **Internet:** 14.7 mil users.

Health: Life expect.: 68.3 male; 74.1 female. **Births** (per 1,000 pop.): 16.6. **Deaths** (per 1,000 pop.): 6.2. **Natural inc.:** 1.04%. **Infant mortality** (per 1,000 live births): 24.4. **AIDS rate:** 0.5%.

Education: Compulsory: ages 6-14. **Literacy:** 90.3%.

Major intl. organizations: UN (FAO, IBRD, ILO, IMF, IMO, WHO, WTO), APEC, ASEAN.

Embassy: 1233 20th St. NW, Ste. 400, 20036; 861-0737.

Website: www.na.gov.vn

Vietnam's recorded history began in Tonkin before the Christian era. Settled by Viets from central China, Vietnam was held by China, 111 BCE-939 CE, and was a vassal state during subsequent periods. Vietnam defeated the armies of Kublai Khan, 1288. Conquest by France began in 1858 and ended in 1884 with the protectorates of Tonkin and Annam in the N and the colony of Cochin-China in the S.

Japan occupied Vietnam in 1940; nationalist aims gathered force. A number of groups formed the Vietminh (Independence) League, headed by Ho Chi Minh, Communist guerrilla leader. In Aug. 1945 the Vietminh forced out Bao Dai, former emperor of Annam, head of a Japan-sponsored regime. France, seeking to reestablish colonial control, battled Communist and nationalist forces, 1946-54, and was defeated at Dienbienphu, May 8, 1954. Meanwhile, on July 1, 1949, Bao Dai had formed a State of Vietnam, with himself as chief of state, with French approval. China backed Ho Chi Minh.

A cease-fire agreement was signed in Paris Jan. 27, 1973, by the U.S., N. and S. Vietnam, and the Vietcong. It was never implemented. N. Vietnamese forces attacked remaining government outposts in the Central Highlands in the first months of 1975. Government retreats turned into a rout, and the Saigon regime surrendered April 30. N. Vietnam assumed control, and began transforming society along Communist lines. The country was officially reunited July 2, 1976.

Casualties of the war were as follows—Combat deaths: U.S. 47,369; S. Vietnam more than 200,000; other allied forces 5,225. Total U.S. fatalities numbered more than 58,000. Vietnamese civilian casualties were more than 1 mil. The war displaced more than 6.5 mil in S. Vietnam.

Conditions in the region remained unstable after the Vietnam War ended. Heavy fighting with Cambodia took place, 1977-80. Relations with China soured as 140,000 ethnic Chinese left Vietnam charging discrimination; China cut off economic aid. Reacting to Vietnam's invasion of Cambodia, China attacked 4 Vietnamese border provinces, Feb. 1979. Vietnam launched an offensive against Cambodian refugee strongholds along the Thai-Cambodian border in 1985; they also engaged Thai troops.

Vietnam announced reforms aimed at reducing central control of the economy in 1987, as many of the old revolutionary followers of Ho Chi Minh were removed from office.

Citing Hanoi's cooperation in returning remains of U.S. soldiers killed in the Vietnam War, the U.S. announced an end, Feb. 3, 1994, to a 19-year-old U.S. embargo on trade with Vietnam. The U.S. extended full diplomatic recognition to Vietnam July 11, 1995. The Communist Party replaced the country's ill and aging leadership in Sept. 1997.

Floods in central Vietnam, Oct.-Nov. 1999, killed some 550 people and left over 600,000 families homeless. U.S. Pres. Bill Clinton made a historic visit to Vietnam Nov. 17-19, 2000. Nong Duc Manh, a moderate, was named to head the Communist Party Apr. 22, 2001. The U.S. has become Vietnam's top export market, with total annual trade over $6 bil; the 2 countries agreed June 5, 2006, to strengthen defense ties. Communists reputed to be economic reformers took the top govt. leadership posts June 27. Meeting with U.S. Pres. George W. Bush, June 22, 2007, Pres. Nguyen Minh Triet was the first Vietnamese head of state since the Vietnam War to be welcomed at the White House.

Western Samoa

See Samoa.

Yemen
Republic of Yemen

People: Population: 22,230,531. **Age distrib.** (%): <15: 46.3; 65+: 2.6. **Pop. density:** 109 per sq mi, 42 per sq km. **Urban:** 27.3%. **Ethnic groups:** Mainly Arab; Afro-Arab, South Asian, European. **Principal language:** Arabic (official). **Chief religion:** Muslim (incl. Sunni and Shi'a).

Geography: Total area: 203,850 sq mi, 527,970 sq km; **Land area:** 203,850 sq mi, 527,970 sq km. **Location:** Middle East, on S coast of the Arabian Peninsula. **Neighbors:** Saudi Arabia on N, Oman on E. **Topography:** A sandy coastal strip leads to well-watered fertile mountains in interior. **Capital:** Sana'a, 1,801,000.

Government: Type: Republic. **Head of state:** Pres. Ali Abdullah Saleh; b. Mar. 21, 1942; in office: July 17, 1978. **Head of gov.:** Prime Min. Ali Muhammad Mujawar; b. 1953; in office: Apr. 7, 2007. **Local divisions:** 19 governorates and capital region. **Defense budget:** $823 mil. **Active troops:** 66,700.

Economy: Industries: oil prod. & refining, cotton textiles, leather goods, food proc. **Chief crops:** grain, fruits, vegetables, pulses, coffee, cotton. **Natural resources:** oil, fish, salt, marble, coal, gold, lead, nickel, copper. **Crude oil reserves:** 3 bil bbls. **Arable land:** 3%. **Livestock:** cattle: 1.5 mil; chickens: 47.5 mil; goats: 8 mil; sheep: 8.2 mil. **Fish catch:** 263,000 metric tons. **Electricity prod.:** 4.5 bil kWh. **Labor force:** Most people are employed in agriculture and herding; services, construction, industry, and commerce account for less than one-fourth of the labor force.

Finance: Monetary unit: Rial (YER) (Sept. 2007: 198.75 = $1 U.S.). **GDP:** $20.6 bil; **per capita GDP:** $1,000; **GDP growth:** 2.6%. **Imports:** $5 bil; UAE 15.8%, China 12.3%, Saudi Arabia 7.5%, Switzerland 6.4%, Kuwait 5.6%, Malaysia 4%. **Exports:** $8.2 bil; China 29.9%, India 16.6%, Thailand 15.9%, S. Korea 6.4%, U.S. 6.4%, Switzerland 5.2%. **Tourism:** $262 mil. **Budget:** $7 bil. **Intl. reserves less gold:** $4.99 bil. **Gold:** 50,000 oz t. **Consumer prices** (2003): 10.83%.

Transport: Motor vehicles: 346,600 pass. cars; 587,900 comm. vehicles. **Civil aviation:** 1 bil pass.-mi; 16 airports. **Chief ports:** Aden, Nishtun.

Communications: TV sets: 286 per 1,000 pop. **Radios:** 64 per 1,000 pop. **Telephone lines:** 968,400. **Internet:** 270,000 users.

Health: Life expect.: 60.6 male; 64.5 female. **Births** (per 1,000 pop.): 42.7. **Deaths** (per 1,000 pop.): 8.1. **Natural inc.:** 3.46%. **Infant mortality** (per 1,000 live births): 57.9. **AIDS rate:** NA.

Education: Compulsory: ages 6-14. **Literacy:** 54.1%.

Major intl. organizations: UN (FAO, IBRD, ILO, IMF, IMO, WHO), AL.

Embassy: 2319 Wyoming Ave. NW 20008; 965-4760.

Website: www.nic.gov.ye

Yemen's territory once was part of the ancient biblical Kingdom of Sheba, or Saba, a prosperous link in trade between Africa and India. Yemen became independent in 1918, after centuries of Ottoman Turkish rule, but remained politically and economically backward.

Imam Ahmed ruled 1948-62. Army officers headed by Brig. Gen. Abdullah al-Sallal declared the country to be the Yemen Arab Republic, Sept. 1962. Ahmed's heir, the Imam Mohamad al-Badr, fled to the mountains where tribesmen joined royalist forces, aided by the Saudi monarchy. Fighting between royalists and republicans killed about 150,000 people until hostilities ended in 1970.

Meanwhile, South Yemen, formed from the British colony of Aden and the British protectorate of South Arabia, became independent Nov. 1967. A Marxist state and a Soviet ally, it took the name People's Democratic Republic of Yemen in 1970. More than 300,000 Yemenis fled from the S to the N after independence, contributing to 2 decades of hostility between the 2 states that flared into warfare twice in the 1970s.

The 2 countries were formally united May 21, 1990, but regional clan-based rivalries led to full-scale civil war in 1994. Secessionists declared a breakaway state in South Yemen, May 21, 1994, but northern troops captured the former southern capital of Aden in July. A new constitution was approved Sept. 28.

Yemen, the ancestral home of Osama bin Laden, has been caught in a crossfire between the U.S. and Islamic extremists.

While on a refueling stop in Aden, Oct. 12, 2000, the destroyer U.S.S. *Cole* was bombed, leaving 17 Americans dead and more than 3 dozen injured; the U.S. government blamed the attack on terrorists associated with bin Laden. The U.S. sent troops in 2002 to help track down members of al-Qaeda.

A missile fired Nov. 3, 2002, from an unmanned CIA surveillance aircraft killed 6 suspected al-Qaeda members, including an American. Three U.S. missionaries were slain at a Baptist hospital in Jibla, Dec. 30; the gunman, an Islamic militant, was executed Feb. 27, 2006. Clashes beginning in June 2004 between Yemeni government forces and Shiite rebels led by an anti-U.S. cleric, Hussein al-Houthi, left more than 200 people dead. The government announced Sept. 10, 2004, that Yemeni troops had killed al-Houthi. Incumbent Pres. Ali Abdullah Saleh was reelected Sept. 20, 2006.

The Shiite rebellion flared again in early 2007; the insurgents agreed to a truce June 16. A suicide attack blamed on al-Qaeda hit a tourist convoy July 2, killing 8 Spaniards and 2 Yemenis.

Yugoslavia

See Montenegro and Serbia.

Zaire

See Congo.

Zambia
Republic of Zambia

People: Population: 11,477,447. **Age distrib.** (%): <15: 45.7; 65+: 2.4. **Pop. density:** 40 per sq mi, 15 per sq km. **Urban:** 35%. **Ethnic groups:** 70+ groups; largest are Bemba, Tonga, Ngoni, Lozi. **Principal languages:** English (official), Bemba, Kaonda, Lozi, Lunda, Luvale, Nyanja, Tonga, 70 others. **Chief religions:** Christian 50%-75%, Muslim and Hindu 24%-49%.

Geography: Total area: 290,586 sq mi, 752,614 sq km; **Land area:** 285,995 sq mi, 740,724 sq km. **Location:** In S central Africa. **Neighbors:** Congo on N; Tanzania, Malawi, Mozambique on E; Zimbabwe, Namibia on S; Angola on W. **Topography:** Mostly high plateau covered with thick forests and drained by several important rivers, including the Zambezi. **Capital:** Lusaka, 1,260,000.

Government: Type: Republic. **Head of state and gov.:** Pres. Levy Patrick Mwanawasa; b. Sept. 3, 1948; in office: Jan. 2, 2002. **Local divisions:** 9 provinces. **Defense budget:** $231 mil. **Active troops:** 15,100.

Economy: Industries: copper mining & proc., constr., foodstuffs. **Chief crops:** corn, sorghum, rice, peanuts, sunflower seed, vegetables, flowers. **Natural resources:** copper, cobalt, zinc, lead, coal, emeralds, gold, silver, uranium, hydropower. **Arable land:** 7%. **Livestock:** cattle: 2.6 mil; chickens: 30 mil; goats: 1.3 mil; pigs: 340,000; sheep: 150,000. **Fish catch:** 70,125 metric tons. **Electricity prod.:** 8.9 bil kWh. **Labor force:** agriculture 85%, industry 6%, services 9%.

Finance: Monetary unit: Kwacha (ZMK) (Sept. 2007: 3,965.00 = $1 U.S.). **GDP:** $11.6 bil; **per capita GDP:** $1,000; **GDP growth:** 5.8%. **Imports:** $3.1 bil; South Africa 50%, Zimbabwe 5.4%, UAE 4.7%, China 4.4%. **Exports:** $3.9 bil; Switzerland 24.6%, South Africa 10.8%, Thailand 10.3%, China 9.9%, Italy 9%, Democratic Republic of the Congo 5%, Tanzania 4.7%. **Tourism:** NA. **Budget:** $3 bil. **Intl. reserves less gold:** $478 mil. **Consumer prices (2005):** 18.32%.

Transport: Railroad: Length: 1,350 mi. **Motor vehicles:** 3,700 pass. cars; 3,900 comm. vehicles. **Civil aviation:** 8.7 mil pass.-mi; 10 airports. **Chief port:** Mpulungu.

Communications: TV sets: 145 per 1,000 pop. **Radios:** 160 per 1,000 pop. **Telephone lines:** 93,400. **Daily newspaper circ.:** 21.9 per 1,000 pop. **Internet:** 500,000 users.

Health: Life expect.: 38.3 male; 38.5 female. **Births** (per 1,000 pop.): 40.8. **Deaths** (per 1,000 pop.): 21.5. **Natural inc.:** 1.93%. **Infant mortality** (per 1,000 live births): 100.7. **AIDS rate:** 17%.

Education: Compulsory: ages 7-13. **Literacy:** 68%.

Major intl. organizations: UN (FAO, IBRD, ILO, IMF, WHO, WTO), the Commonwealth, AU.

Embassy: 2419 Massachusetts Ave. NW 20008; 265-9717.
Website: www.statehouse.gov.zm

Ruled by the British as Northern Rhodesia, the country became the independent republic of Zambia within the Commonwealth Oct. 24, 1964. Independence leader Kenneth Kaunda governed the country as president, 1964-91. A Zambian government corporation in 1970 took over 51% of 2 foreign-owned copper-mining companies. Privately-held land and other enterprises were nationalized in 1975. In the 1980s and 1990s lowered copper prices hurt the economy and severe drought caused famine.

Food riots erupted in June 1990, as the nation suffered its worst violence since independence. Elections held Oct. 1991 brought an end to Kaunda's one-party rule. The new government sought to sell state enterprises, including the copper industry. Pres. Frederick Chiluba won reelection Nov. 18, 1996, but international observers cited harassment of opposition parties. A coup attempt was suppressed Oct. 28, 1997.

Thwarted in his effort to change the constitution to allow himself to run for a 3rd term, Chiluba endorsed Levy Patrick Mwanawasa, who won a disputed election Dec. 27, 2001. Food shortages threatened more than 2 mil Zambians in 2002; the government refused to distribute shipments of U.S. grain because it was genetically modified. In a hard-fought election, Sept. 28, 2006, Mwanawasa

won a 2nd term. Charged with embezzling state funds while he was president, Chiluba was ordered to pay $58 mil by a British court, June 7, 2007.

The country has made progress in treating HIV/AIDS, which afflicts about 1 mil adults in Zambia.

Zimbabwe
Republic of Zimbabwe

People: Population: 12,311,143. **Age distrib.** (%): <15: 37.2; 65+: 3.5. **Pop. density:** 82 per sq mi, 32 per sq km. **Urban:** 35.9%. **Ethnic groups:** Shona 82%, Ndebele 14%. **Principal languages:** English (official), Shona, Sindebele, many dialects. **Chief religions:** Syncretic (Christian-indigenous mix) 50%, Christian 25%, indigenous beliefs 24%.

Geography: Total area: 150,804 sq mi, 390,580 sq km; **Land area:** 149,294 sq mi, 386,670 sq km. **Location:** In southern Africa. **Neighbors:** Zambia on N, Botswana on W, South Africa on S, Mozambique on E. **Topography:** High plateau country, rising to mountains on E border, sloping down on other borders. **Capital:** Harare, 1,515,000.

Government: Type: Republic. **Head of state and gov.:** Pres. Robert Mugabe; b. Feb. 21, 1924; in office: Dec. 31, 1987. **Local divisions:** 8 provinces, 2 cities. **Defense budget:** $60 mil. **Active troops:** 29,000.

Economy: Industries: mining, steel, wood products, cement, chemicals. **Chief crops:** corn, cotton, tobacco, wheat, coffee. **Natural resources:** coal, chromium ore, asbestos, gold, nickel, copper, iron ore, vanadium, lithium, tin, platinum. **Arable land:** 8%. **Livestock:** cattle: 5.4 mil; chickens: 23 mil; goats: 3 mil; pigs: 610,000; sheep: 610,000. **Fish catch:** 15,452 metric tons. **Electricity prod.:** 10 bil kWh. **Labor force** (1996): agriculture 66%, industry 10%, services 24%.

Finance: Monetary unit: Dollar (ZWD) (Sept. 2007: 30,000.00 = $1 U.S.). **GDP:** $25.4 bil; **per capita GDP:** $2,100; **GDP growth:** -4.4%. **Imports:** $2.1 bil; South Africa 46.1%, China 5.9%, Botswana 4.8%, Zambia 4.1%. **Exports:** $1.8 bil; South Africa 32.3%, China 6.3%, Zambia 6.2%, Japan 5.9%, U.S. 4.9%, Netherlands 4.6%, Italy 4.4%, Germany 4%. **Tourism:** $44 mil. **Budget:** $1.9 bil. **Intl. reserves less gold** (2002): $61 mil. **Gold** (2002): 140,000 oz t. **Consumer prices** (2002): 140.08%.

Transport: Railroad: Length: 1,912 mi. **Motor vehicles:** 598,000 pass. cars; 103,000 comm. vehicles. **Civil aviation:** 271.5 mil pass.-mi; 17 airports. **Chief ports:** Binga, Kariba.

Communications: TV sets: 35 per 1,000 pop. **Radios:** 389 per 1,000 pop. **Telephone lines:** 331,700. **Internet:** 1.2 mil users.

Health: Life expect.: 40.6 male; 38.4 female. **Births** (per 1,000 pop.): 27.7. **Deaths** (per 1,000 pop.): 21.8. **Natural inc.:** 0.6%. **Infant mortality** (per 1,000 live births): 51.1. **AIDS rate:** 20.1%.

Education (2004): Compulsory: ages 6-12. **Literacy:** 89.4%.

Major intl. organizations: UN (FAO, IBRD, ILO, IMF, IMO, WHO, WTO), AU.

Embassy: 1608 New Hampshire Ave. NW 20009; 332-7100.
Website: www.zim.gov.zw

Britain took over the area as Southern Rhodesia in 1923 from the British South Africa Co. (which, under Cecil Rhodes, had conquered it by 1897) and granted internal self-government. Under a 1961 constitution, voting was restricted to keep whites in power. On Nov. 11, 1965, Prime Min. Ian D. Smith announced his country's unilateral declaration of independence.

Britain termed the act illegal and demanded that the country (known as Rhodesia until 1980) broaden voting rights to provide for eventual rule by the black African majority. The UN imposed sanctions and, in May 1968, a trade embargo. Intermittent negotiations between the government and various black nationalist groups failed to prevent increasing guerrilla warfare.

In the country's first universal-franchise election, Apr. 21, 1979, Bishop Abel Muzorewa's United African National Council gained a bare majority of the black-dominated Parliament. A cease-fire was accepted by all parties, Dec. 5. Independence as Zimbabwe was finally achieved Apr. 18, 1980. Robert Mugabe, the nation's 1st prime min., became executive president in 1987.

On Mar. 6, 1992, Mugabe declared a national disaster because of drought and appealed to foreign donors for food, money, and medicine. An economic adjustment program caused widespread hardship. Mugabe was reelected Mar. 1996 after opposition candidates withdrew. A land redistribution campaign launched by Mugabe triggered violent attacks in Apr. 2000 against some white farmers; whites made up less than 1% of the population but held 70% of the land.

International observers criticized Mugabe for relying on fraud and intimidation to win the presidential election of Mar. 9-11, 2002. The EU, the U.S., and the Commonwealth imposed sanctions on the Mugabe regime. Zimbabwe withdrew from the Commonwealth as of Dec. 7, 2003. In May 2005, Mugabe launched Operation Murambatsvina ("Drive out rubbish"), razing shanty dwellings and illegal street markets in urban areas and leaving some 700,000 people homeless. In 2006-07, inflation soared to a yearly rate of 10,000%. With the economy near collapse, Mugabe's increasingly repressive regime cracked down on political opponents, and harassed and arrested thousands of merchants for allegedly violating govt. price controls.

World Population Growth

Although the population of the world in ancient times can only be very roughly estimated, it is believed that there were perhaps 50 mil people in the world in 1000 BCE. The United Nations Population Division estimates a figure of 300 mil for 1 CE; this chart shows estimated population growth from that time onward as estimated by the UN.

While figures for other centuries vary depending on source, all sources indicate that world population began growing more rapidly in the 18th and 19th centuries and grew much more rapidly in the 20th century. According to UN estimates, the world population reached 1 bil in 1804, rose to 2 bil 123 years later, to 3 bil 33 years after that, to 4 bil in 14 years, to 5 bil in 13 years, and to 6 bil in 12 years. The UN estimated the 6 bil figure was reached in 1999. **By mid-2007 the total world population was estimated to be about 6.6 bil.**

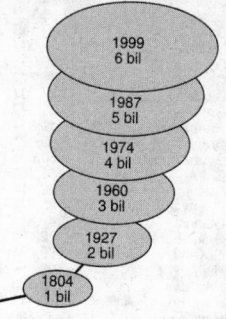

1 CE
300 mil

1250
400 mil

1500
500 mil

1804
1 bil

1927
2 bil

1960
3 bil

1974
4 bil

1987
5 bil

1999
6 bil

Area and Population of the Continents

Source: Population Division/International Programs Center, U.S. Census Bureau, U.S. Dept. of Commerce

Continent or region	AREA[1] (sq km)	AREA[1] (sq mi)	% of Earth	% world total, 2007	POPULATION (est., mid-year)				
					2007	1950	1975	2000	2025[2]
Asia	30,947,538	11,948,911	23.7	60.6	4,001,623,990	1,437,201,723	2,412,691,104	3,677,535,065	4,801,362,124
Africa	29,805,695	11,508,043	22.8	14.2	934,499,752	228,182,746	410,728,579	801,053,965	1,338,002,438
Europe	22,832,064	8,815,509	17.5	11.1	729,871,042	546,415,793	677,127,418	729,623,640	712,205,195
N. America ..	21,327,439	8,234,570	16.3	7.9	522,807,432	220,857,588	346,216,831	485,968,142	618,785,049
S. America ..	17,433,220	6,731,004	13.3	5.8	379,919,602	111,384,890	215,772,736	348,339,764	448,405,592
Oceania, incl. Australia	8,426,635	3,253,542	6.4	0.5	33,552,994	12,476,128	21,220,574	30,744,658	39,790,491
Antarctica[3] ..	14,000,000	5,405,430	10.7	—	—	—	—	—	—
WORLD	144,772,591	55,897,010	100.0	100.0	6,602,274,812	2,556,518,868	4,083,757,242	6,073,265,234	7,958,550,889

(1) Areas are as defined by the U.S. Census Bureau. Area for Europe includes all of Russia. Figures may not add to totals because of rounding. (2) Projected. (3) Antarctica has no indigenous inhabitants; researchers stay for various periods of time.

Current Population and Projections for All Countries and Territories: 2007, 2025, and 2050

Source: Population Division/International Programs Center, U.S. Census Bureau, U.S. Dept. of Commerce

(mid-year figures)

Country/terr.	2007	2025	2050
World	6,602,274,812	7,958,550,889	9,401,550,854
Afghanistan	31,889,923	50,252,227	81,933,479
Albania	3,600,523	3,944,360	4,016,945
Algeria	33,333,216	40,254,833	43,983,870
American Samoa	57,663	51,752	35,129
Andorra	71,822	77,973	69,129
Angola	12,263,596	17,418,643	24,746,652
Anguilla	13,677	15,672	15,921
Antigua and Barbuda	69,481	75,116	69,259
Argentina	40,301,927	45,757,375	48,740,060
Armenia	2,971,650	3,044,164	2,943,441
Aruba	100,018	126,130	150,730
Australia	20,434,176	23,022,980	24,175,783
Austria	8,199,783	8,189,560	7,520,950
Azerbaijan	8,120,247	9,352,531	9,955,428
Bahamas, The	305,655	327,317	324,052
Bahrain	708,573	865,890	973,412
Bangladesh	150,448,339	204,538,715	279,955,405
Barbados	280,946	293,744	274,523
Belarus	9,724,723	9,033,301	7,738,613
Belgium	10,392,226	10,453,261	9,882,599
Belize	294,385	410,468	541,734
Benin	8,078,314	11,911,838	16,356,458
Bermuda	66,163	70,683	66,025
Bhutan	2,327,849	3,294,556	4,653,447
Bolivia	9,119,152	11,369,857	13,772,819
Bosnia and Herzegovina	4,552,198	4,535,296	3,891,669
Botswana	1,815,508	2,165,143	2,385,685
Brazil	190,010,647	217,825,222	228,426,737
Brunei	374,577	498,756	638,157
Bulgaria	7,322,858	6,257,716	4,651,477
Burkina Faso	14,326,203	23,995,152	43,656,786
Burundi	8,390,505	13,912,642	22,852,556
Cambodia	13,995,904	18,966,883	23,965,562
Cameroon	18,060,382	25,522,447	34,908,839
Canada	33,390,141	38,164,606	41,429,579

Country/terr.	2007	2025	2050
Cape Verde	423,613	451,021	380,614
Cayman Islands	46,600	67,308	90,230
Central African Republic	4,369,038	5,486,686	6,502,151
Chad	9,885,661	13,914,726	20,473,601
Chile	16,284,741	18,521,553	19,244,843
China[1]	1,321,851,888	1,453,123,817	1,424,161,948
Colombia	44,379,598	55,270,899	64,977,344
Comoros	711,417	1,128,278	1,837,671
Congo (Kinshasa)	65,751,512	114,263,739	203,039,557
Congo Rep. (Brazzaville)	3,800,610	6,165,891	9,618,358
Cook Islands	21,750	24,025	24,930
Costa Rica	4,133,884	5,074,472	5,696,700
Cote d'Ivoire	18,013,409	24,381,767	32,400,664
Croatia	4,493,312	4,374,007	3,864,201
Cuba	11,394,043	11,649,747	10,540,567
Cyprus	788,457	851,733	841,102
Czech Republic	10,228,744	9,844,275	8,540,221
Denmark	5,468,120	5,697,913	5,575,147
Djibouti	496,374	681,030	993,011
Dominica	72,377	74,374	64,772
Dominican Republic	9,365,818	11,922,144	14,657,962
Ecuador	13,755,680	17,099,305	20,332,088
Egypt	80,335,036	103,573,056	127,563,256
El Salvador	6,948,073	9,135,049	12,110,592
Equatorial Guinea	551,201	768,236	1,063,071
Eritrea	4,906,585	7,244,126	10,164,076
Estonia	1,315,912	1,149,245	861,913
Ethiopia	76,511,887	107,804,235	144,716,331
Faroe Islands	47,511	51,765	53,050
Fiji	918,675	1,153,122	1,447,573
Finland	5,238,460	5,251,272	4,819,615
France	63,718,187	68,521,942	69,809,351
French Guiana	203,321	259,123	317,377
French Polynesia	278,963	344,920	393,533
Gabon	1,454,867	2,059,662	3,221,749

Country/terr.	2007	2025	2050
Gambia, The	1,688,359	2,624,964	4,068,861
Gaza Strip	1,482,405	2,588,747	4,209,026
Georgia	4,646,003	4,341,061	3,784,724
Germany	82,400,996	80,637,451	73,607,121
Ghana	22,931,299	30,536,326	38,735,638
Gibraltar	27,967	28,001	25,617
Greece	10,706,290	10,670,697	10,035,935
Greenland	56,344	56,473	56,644
Grenada	89,971	96,253	87,136
Guadeloupe	456,698	512,604	528,062
Guam	173,456	213,329	242,692
Guatemala	12,728,111	17,564,073	22,995,434
Guernsey	65,573	67,016	60,606
Guinea	9,947,814	15,806,084	28,713,509
Guinea-Bissau	1,472,780	2,061,262	2,894,545
Guyana	769,095	755,884	597,806
Haiti	8,706,497	13,254,108	19,807,275
Honduras	7,483,763	10,004,876	12,641,869
Hong Kong S.A.R.	6,980,412	7,354,531	6,172,725
Hungary	9,956,108	9,437,569	8,374,619
Iceland	301,931	337,632	350,922
India	1,129,866,154	1,448,821,234	1,807,878,574
Indonesia	234,693,997	278,502,882	313,020,847
Iran	65,397,521	76,779,032	81,490,039
Iraq	27,499,638	40,418,381	56,360,779
Ireland	4,109,086	4,842,255	5,396,215
Isle of Man	75,831	81,694	80,131
Israel	6,426,679	7,612,022	8,516,835
Italy	58,147,733	56,234,163	50,389,841
Jamaica	2,780,132	3,128,416	3,499,068
Japan	127,433,494	117,816,135	93,673,826
Jersey	91,231	93,281	84,077
Jordan	6,053,193	8,651,714	11,772,789
Kazakhstan	15,284,929	16,041,146	15,099,700
Kenya	36,913,721	51,261,167	65,175,864
Kiribati	107,817	158,047	235,342
Korea, North	23,301,725	25,755,009	26,363,688
Korea, South	49,044,790	50,560,956	45,224,224
Kuwait	2,505,559	4,175,172	6,374,800
Kyrgyzstan	5,284,149	6,678,722	8,237,623
Laos	6,521,998	9,450,131	13,176,153
Latvia	2,259,810	1,992,516	1,544,073
Lebanon	3,925,502	4,964,025	4,964,025
Lesotho	2,125,262	2,119,170	1,946,586
Liberia	3,195,931	4,753,240	7,091,537
Libya	6,036,914	8,322,662	10,817,176
Liechtenstein	34,247	37,567	35,776
Lithuania	3,575,439	3,355,985	2,787,516
Luxembourg	480,222	586,296	720,603
Macao S.A.R.	456,989	519,108	487,488
Macedonia	2,055,915	2,119,511	1,990,728
Madagascar	19,448,815	32,431,146	56,513,827
Malawi	13,603,181	20,244,055	29,820,957
Malaysia	24,821,286	33,064,523	43,122,397
Maldives	369,031	563,760	815,031
Mali	11,995,402	20,386,013	40,002,414
Malta	401,880	421,239	395,639
Marshall Islands	61,815	83,203	103,092
Martinique	439,202	479,148	478,627
Mauritania	3,270,065	5,291,845	8,635,801
Mauritius	1,250,882	1,406,509	1,451,156
Mayotte	208,783	356,683	592,000
Mexico	108,700,891	130,198,692	147,907,650
Micronesia	107,862	98,879	74,296
Moldova	4,328,816	4,205,616	3,635,357
Monaco	32,671	34,590	32,964
Mongolia	2,951,786	3,725,352	4,340,496
Montenegro	684,736	635,537	577,654
Montserrat	9,538	11,014	11,908
Morocco	33,757,175	42,553,182	50,871,553
Mozambique	20,905,585	28,893,271	41,842,274
Myanmar (Burma)	47,373,958	52,995,497	54,430,334
Namibia	2,055,080	2,061,106	1,795,852
Nauru	13,528	17,887	22,696
Nepal	28,901,790	39,917,760	53,293,874
Netherlands	16,570,613	17,539,636	17,334,090
Netherlands Antilles	223,652	249,361	254,227
New Caledonia	221,943	263,151	290,682
New Zealand	4,115,771	4,672,537	4,842,397
Nicaragua	5,675,356	7,510,206	9,437,504
Niger	12,894,865	20,951,836	34,419,502
Nigeria	135,031,164	206,165,946	356,523,597
Northern Mariana Islands	84,546	116,270	143,132
Norway	4,627,926	4,916,787	4,966,385
Oman	3,204,897	5,294,475	8,337,734
Pakistan	164,741,924	218,495,756	277,554,980
Palau	20,842	24,320	26,300
Panama	3,242,173	4,109,552	5,038,122
Papua New Guinea	5,795,887	8,001,357	10,670,394
Paraguay	6,669,086	9,864,987	14,604,978
Peru	28,674,757	34,476,469	38,300,067
Philippines	91,077,287	118,685,776	147,630,852
Poland	38,518,241	37,349,696	32,084,570
Portugal	10,642,836	10,806,202	9,933,334
Puerto Rico	3,944,259	4,095,850	3,770,496
Qatar	907,229	1,153,966	1,239,216
Réunion	798,094	981,122	1,132,283
Romania	22,276,056	21,260,138	18,678,226
Russia	141,377,752	128,180,396	109,187,353
Rwanda	9,907,509	15,699,855	25,128,735
Saint Helena	7,543	7,868	7,247
Saint Kitts and Nevis	39,349	46,486	52,348
Saint Lucia	170,649	209,064	235,420
Saint Pierre and Miquelon	7,036	7,079	6,355
Saint Vincent and the Grenadines	118,149	118,308	92,335
Samoa	214,265	280,753	428,641
San Marino	29,615	34,565	35,335
São Tomé and Príncipe	199,579	328,825	502,489
Saudi Arabia	27,601,038	35,668,686	49,706,851
Senegal	12,521,851	18,717,375	27,519,852
Serbia	10,150,265	10,027,056	9,274,767
Seychelles	81,895	88,071	89,713
Sierra Leone	6,144,562	9,140,077	13,998,936
Singapore	4,553,009	5,100,929	4,635,110
Slovakia	5,447,502	5,458,581	4,943,616
Slovenia	2,009,245	1,907,560	1,596,947
Solomon Islands	566,842	815,582	1,110,514
Somalia	9,118,773	14,861,596	25,499,605
South Africa	43,997,828	39,905,523	33,002,952
Spain	40,448,191	39,578,066	35,564,293
Sri Lanka	20,926,315	23,707,228	24,920,558
Sudan	39,379,358	57,461,705	88,227,761
Suriname	470,784	560,061	617,249
Swaziland	1,133,066	1,008,990	751,328
Sweden	9,031,088	9,315,507	9,084,788
Switzerland	7,554,661	7,774,334	7,296,092
Syria	19,314,747	26,547,725	34,437,235
Taiwan	22,858,872	23,213,741	20,161,286
Tajikistan	7,076,598	9,510,130	12,132,365
Tanzania	39,384,223	53,427,873	66,843,312
Thailand	65,068,149	70,523,958	69,268,817
Timor-Leste	1,084,971	1,493,841	1,942,734
Togo	5,701,579	8,986,546	14,714,623
Tonga	116,921	150,787	188,340
Trinidad and Tobago	1,056,608	881,713	622,011
Tunisia	10,276,158	11,931,451	12,462,798
Turkey	71,158,647	82,204,623	86,473,786
Turkmenistan	5,097,028	6,501,830	7,591,841
Turks and Caicos Islands	21,746	32,242	42,384
Tuvalu	11,992	15,821	20,018
Uganda	30,262,610	56,744,814	128,007,514
Ukraine	46,299,862	41,037,583	33,573,842
United Arab Emirates	4,444,011	7,063,346	8,018,904
United Kingdom	60,776,238	63,818,586	63,977,435
United States	301,139,947	349,666,199	420,080,587
Uruguay	3,460,067	3,715,772	3,815,368
Uzbekistan	27,780,059	36,947,068	48,597,111
Vanuatu	211,971	263,267	310,486
Vatican City	821	NA	NA
Venezuela	26,023,528	33,188,608	40,255,592
Vietnam	85,262,356	99,977,731	107,772,641
Virgin Islands	108,448	107,559	103,303
Virgin Islands, British	23,552	30,695	34,038
Wallis and Futuna	16,309	18,502	20,434
West Bank	2,535,927	3,882,966	5,580,321
Western Sahara	382,617	616,533	996,674
Yemen	22,230,531	39,696,392	71,278,172
Zambia	11,477,447	14,829,985	18,435,053
Zimbabwe	12,311,143	12,915,433	12,221,257

NA = Not available. (1) Excludes Hong Kong, population 6,980,412, and Macao, population 456,989.

Population of the World's Largest Cities

Source: *World Population Prospects, World Urbanization Prospects*, Dept. of Economic and Social Affairs, UN Population Division

Pop. figures are UN estimates and projections for "urban agglomerations"—i.e., contiguous densely populated urban areas, not demarcated by administrative boundaries, as revised in 2005. Data may differ from figures elsewhere in *The World Almanac*.

Rank[1]	City, country	Pop. (thousands) 2000	Pop. (thousands) 2015[2]	Annual growth (%) 1995-2000	Pop. (thousands) 1975	Total growth (%) 1975-2000	Total growth (%) 2000-15[2]	Pop. of city as percentage of nation's 2000 pop.
1.	Tokyo, Japan	34,450	35,494	0.51	26,615	29.4	3.0	27.1
2.	Mexico City, Mexico	18,066	21,568	1.47	10,690	69.0	19.4	18.1
3.	New York, NY, U.S.	17,846	19,876	1.04	15,880	12.4	11.4	6.3
4.	São Paulo, Brazil	17,099	20,535	1.39	9,614	77.9	20.1	9.8
5.	Mumbai (Bombay), India	16,086	21,869	2.62	7,082	127.1	36.0	1.6
6.	Shanghai, China	13,243	17,225	4.79	7,326	80.8	30.1	1.0
7.	Kolkata (Calcutta), India	13,058	16,980	1.82	7,888	65.5	30.0	1.3
8.	Delhi, India	12,441	18,604	4.18	4,426	181.1	49.5	1.2
9.	Buenos Aires, Argentina	11,847	13,396	1.21	8,745	35.5	13.1	32.1
10.	Los Angeles, CA, U.S.	11,814	13,095	0.82	8,926	32.4	10.8	4.2
11.	Osaka, Japan	11,165	11,309	0.20	9,844	13.4	1.3	8.8
12.	Jakarta, Indonesia	11,065	16,822	3.78	4,813	129.9	52.0	5.3
13.	Rio de Janeiro, Brazil	10,803	12,770	1.20	7,557	43.0	18.2	6.2
14.	Cairo, Egypt	10,391	13,138	1.36	6,450	61.1	26.4	15.4
15.	Beijing, China	9,782	12,850	2.84	6,034	62.1	31.4	0.8

(1) Ranked by 2000 population. (2) Projected.

National Rankings by Population, Area, Population Density, 2007

Source: Population Division/International Programs Center, U.S. Census Bureau, U.S. Dept. of Commerce

As of mid-2007, according to U.S. Census Bureau, the world had an estimated population of 6,602,274,812. China was the most populous nation, with $1/5$ of the world total. India, the second largest, passed the 1-bil mark in 1999. Russia is the largest country in land area.

Largest Populations

Rank	Country	Population
1.	China[1]	1,321,851,888
2.	India	1,129,866,154
3.	United States	301,139,947
4.	Indonesia	234,693,997
5.	Brazil	190,010,647
6.	Pakistan	164,741,924
7.	Bangladesh	150,448,339
8.	Russia	141,377,752
9.	Nigeria	135,031,164
10.	Japan	127,433,494
11.	Mexico	108,700,891
12.	Philippines	91,077,287
13.	Vietnam	85,262,356
14.	Germany	82,400,996
15.	Egypt	80,335,036
16.	Ethiopia	76,511,887
17.	Turkey	71,158,647
18.	Congo, Democratic Republic of the	65,751,512
19.	Iran	65,397,521
20.	Thailand	65,068,149

Smallest Populations

Rank	Country	Population
1.	Vatican City	821
2.	Tuvalu	11,992
3.	Nauru	13,528
4.	Palau	20,842
5.	San Marino	29,615
6.	Monaco	32,671
7.	Liechtenstein	34,247
8.	Saint Kitts and Nevis	39,349
9.	Marshall Islands	61,815
10.	Antigua and Barbuda	69,481
11.	Andorra	71,822
12.	Dominica	72,377
13.	Seychelles	81,895
14.	Grenada	89,971
15.	Kiribati	107,817
16.	Micronesia	107,862
17.	Tonga	116,921
18.	Saint Vincent and the Grenadines	118,149
19.	Saint Lucia	170,649
20.	São Tomé and Príncipe	199,579

Largest Land Areas[2]

Rank	Country	Area (sq mi)	Area (sq km)
1.	Russia	6,562,112	16,995,800
2.	China	3,600,946	9,326,410
3.	United States	3,537,437	9,161,923
4.	Canada	3,511,023	9,093,507
5.	Brazil	3,265,077	8,456,510
6.	Australia	2,941,299	7,617,930
7.	India	1,147,955	2,973,190
8.	Argentina	1,056,642	2,736,690
9.	Kazakhstan	1,030,816	2,669,800
10.	Algeria	919,595	2,381,740

Smallest Land Areas[2]

Rank	Country	Area (sq mi)	Area (sq km)
1.	Vatican City	0.17	0.44
2.	Monaco	1	2
3.	Nauru	8	21
4.	Tuvalu	10	26
5.	San Marino	24	61
6.	Liechtenstein	62	160
7.	Marshall Islands	70	181
8.	Saint Kitts and Nevis	101	261
9.	Maldives	116	300
10.	Malta	122	316

Most Densely Populated[3]

Rank	Country	Persons per sq mi	Persons per sq km
1.	Monaco	32,671.0	16,335.5
2.	Singapore	17,265.4	6,666.2
3.	Vatican City	4,832.7	1,865.9
4.	Malta	3,294.1	1,271.8
5.	Maldives	3,181.3	1,230.1
6.	Bangladesh	2,909.9	1,123.5
7.	Bahrain	2,757.1	1,065.5
8.	Taiwan	1,835.2	708.6
9.	Barbados	1,692.4	651.8
10.	Nauru	1,691.0	644.2

Most Sparsely Populated[3]

Rank	Country	Persons per sq mi	Persons per sq km
1.	Mongolia	4.9	1.9
2.	Namibia	6.4	2.5
3.	Australia	6.9	2.7
4.	Suriname	7.6	2.9
5.	Iceland	7.8	3.0
6.	Botswana	8.0	3.1
7.	Mauritania	8.2	3.2
8.	Libya	8.9	3.4
9.	Canada	9.5	3.7
10.	Guyana	10.1	3.9

(1) Excluding Hong Kong, pop. 6,980,412, and Macao, pop. 456,989. (2) Land area of a country does not include inland water. Rankings by total area, including inland water, may differ from these. For national total area figures, see the country entries in this chapter. (3) Density is calculated here according to land area.

Countries With Highest & Lowest Gross Domestic Product and Per Capita GDP[1]

Source: *The World Factbook 2007*, Central Intelligence Agency

GDP (in millions)				Per Capita GDP[8]			
Highest		**Lowest**		**Highest**		**Lowest**	
1. U.S.	$13,130,000	1. Tuvalu[3]	$15	1. Luxembourg	$71,400	1. Solomon Islands[4]	$600
2. China[2]	10,170,000	2. Nauru[4]	60	2. Equatorial Guinea[4]	50,200	2. Comoros[4]	600
3. Japan	4,218,000	3. Marshall Islands[5]	115	3. United Arab Emirates	49,700	Somalia	600
4. India	4,156,000	4. Palau[6]	125	4. Norway	46,300	Malawi	600
5. Germany	2,630,000	5. Tonga[6]	179	5. Ireland	44,500	5. Burundi	700
6. UK	1,930,000	6. Kiribati	240	6. U.S.	44,000	Dem. Rep. of the Congo	700
7. France	1,891,000	7. Micronesia[3]	277	7. Andorra[7]	38,800	7. Afghanistan[6]	800
8. Italy	1,756,000	8. São Tomé and Principe	278	8. Iceland	38,000	Tanzania	800
9. Russia	1,746,000	9. Timor-Leste[6]	370	9. Denmark	37,000	Timor-Leste[4]	800
10. Brazil	1,655,000	10. Dominica	485	10. Canada	35,600	10. Liberia	900
11. South Korea	1,196,000	11. Seychelles[3]	626	11. Austria	34,600	Madagascar	900
12. Canada	1,178,000	12. St. Kitts and Nevis	726	12. San Marino[6]	34,100	Guinea-Bissau	900
13. Mexico	1,149,000	13. Vanuatu	739	13. Switzerland	34,000	Sierra Leone	900
14. Spain	1,109,000	14. Solomon Islands[3]	800	14. Finland	33,700	14. Djibouti[4]	1,000
15. Indonesia	948,300	15. San Marino[6]	850	15. Australia	33,300	Ethiopia	1,000
16. Taiwan	680,500	16. St. Vincent and the Grenadines	864	16. Japan	33,100	Zambia	1,000
17. Australia	674,600	17. Monaco	976	17. Belgium	33,000	Yemen	1,000
18. Turkey	635,600	18. Grenada	982	18. Sweden	32,200	Niger	1,000
19. Argentina	608,800	19. Antigua and Barbuda	1,145	19. Netherlands	32,100	Eritrea[4]	1,000
20. Iran	599,200	20. St. Lucia	1,179	20. Germany	31,900	20. Benin	1,100

(1) All figures are for 2006, unless otherwise indicated. Data may differ from estimates by the U.S. Bureau of Economic Analysis. International GDP estimates derive from purchasing power parity calculations, which involve the use of intl. dollar price weights applied to quantities of goods and services produced in a given economy. Countries do not include some territories or former territories. (2) Does not include Hong Kong, which had a GDP of $258.8 bil and a per capita GDP of $37,300 in 2006, or Macao, which had a GDP of $10 bil in 2004 and a per capita GDP of $24,300 in 2005. (3) 2002 est. (4) 2005 est. (5) 2001 est. (6) 2004 est. (7) 2005. (8) Per capita GDP calculated using U.S. census population figures for the year each GDP was available.

Gold Reserves of Central Banks and Governments

Source: *International Financial Statistics*, International Monetary Fund

(in million fine troy ounces)

Year end	All countries[1]	United States	China[2]	Canada	France	Germany[3]	Italy	Japan	Nether- lands	Switzer- land	United Kingdom
1975	1,018.71	274.71	NA	21.95	100.93	117.61	82.48	21.11	54.33	83.20	21.03
1980	952.99	264.32	12.80	20.98	81.85	95.18	66.67	24.23	43.94	83.28	18.84
1985	949.39	262.65	12.70	20.11	81.85	95.18	66.67	24.33	43.94	83.28	19.03
1990	939.01	261.91	12.70	14.76	81.85	95.18	66.67	24.23	43.94	83.28	18.94
1995	908.79	261.70	12.70	3.41	81.85	95.18	66.67	24.23	34.77	83.28	18.43
1996	906.10	261.66	12.70	3.09	81.85	95.18	66.67	24.23	34.77	83.28	18.43
1997	890.57	261.64	12.70	3.09	81.89	95.18	66.67	24.23	27.07	83.28	18.42
1998	966.15	261.61	12.70	2.49	102.37	118.98	83.36	24.23	33.83	83.28	23.00
1999	967.07	261.61	12.70	1.81	97.25	111.52	78.83	24.23	31.57	83.28	20.55
2000	952.09	261.61	12.70	1.18	97.25	111.52	78.83	24.55	29.32	77.79	15.67
2001	942.76	262.00	16.10	1.05	97.25	111.13	78.83	24.60	28.44	70.68	11.42
2002	931.18	262.00	19.29	0.60	97.25	110.79	78.83	24.60	27.38	61.62	10.09
2003	913.29	261.55	19.29	0.11	97.25	110.58	78.83	24.60	25.00	52.51	10.07
2004	900.58	261.59	19.29	0.11	95.98	110.38	78.83	24.60	25.00	43.54	10.04
2005	881.69	261.55	19.29	0.11	90.85	110.21	78.83	24.60	22.34	41.48	9.99
2006	867.15	261.50	19.29	0.11	87.44	110.04	78.83	24.60	20.61	41.48	9.97

NA = Not available. (1) Covers IMF members with reported gold holdings. For countries not listed above, see International Monetary Fund's *International Financial Statistics* report. (2) Figures are for mainland China only and do not include Hong Kong or Macao. (3) West Germany prior to 1991.

Consumer Price Changes in Selected Countries, 1975-2006

Source: *International Financial Statistics*, International Monetary Fund

(annual averages)

Country	1975-80	1980-85	1992-93	1993-94	1994-95	1995-96	1996-97	1997-98	1998-99	1999-2000	2000-01	2001-02	2002-03	2003-04	2004-05	2005-06
Canada	8.7	7.4	1.8	0.2	2.2	1.6	1.6	1.0	1.7	2.7	2.3	2.2	2.8	1.8	2.2	2.0
China[1]	NA	NA	14.6	24.2	16.9	8.3	2.8	−.9	−1.4	0.3	0.5	−0.8	1.2	4.0	1.8	1.5
France	10.5	9.6	2.1	1.7	1.8	2.0	1.2	0.7	0.5	1.7	1.6	1.9	2.1	2.1	1.8	1.6
Germany	4.1	3.9	4.1	3.0	1.8	1.5	1.8	1.0	0.6	1.5	2.0	1.4	1.1	1.7	2.0	1.7
Italy	16.3	13.7	4.5	4.0	5.2	4.0	2.0	2.0	1.7	2.5	2.8	2.5	2.7	2.2	2.0	2.1
Japan	6.5	2.7	1.3	0.7	−0.1	0.1	1.7	0.6	−0.3	−0.7	−0.7	−0.9	−0.3	−0.1	−0.3	0.2
Spain	18.6	12.2	4.6	4.7	4.7	3.6	2.0	1.8	2.3	3.4	3.6	3.1	3.0	3.0	3.4	3.5
Sweden	10.5	9.0	4.6	2.2	2.5	0.5	0.5	−0.1	0.5	0.9	2.4	2.2	1.9	0.4	0.5	1.4
Switzerland	2.3	4.3	3.3	0.8	1.8	0.8	0.5	0.1	0.7	1.5	1.0	0.6	0.6	0.8	1.2	1.1
United Kingdom	14.4	7.2	1.6	2.5	3.4	2.4	3.1	3.4	1.6	2.9	1.8	1.6	2.9	3.0	2.8	3.2
United States	8.9	5.5	3.0	2.6	2.8	3.0	2.3	1.6	2.2	3.4	2.8	1.6	2.3	2.7	3.4	3.2

NA = Not available. (1) Figures are for mainland China only and do not include Hong Kong or Macao.

Hourly Compensation Costs[1], by Selected Country, 1975-2005

Source: Bureau of Labor Statistics, U.S. Dept. of Labor

(in U.S. dollars; compensation for production workers in manufacturing)

Country/terr.	1975	1985	1995	2002	2003	2004	2005	Country/terr.	1975	1985	1995	2002	2003	2004	2005
Australia......	5.60	8.18	15.36	15.38	19.79	23.38	24.91	Luxembourg ...	6.22	7.48	23.56	18.71	23.12	26.57	27.68
Austria........	4.50	7.57	25.26	20.71	25.51	28.53	29.42	Mexico........	1.46	1.59	1.70	2.49	2.44	2.44	2.63
Belgium	5.77	8.21	25.67	21.77	26.55	30.01	30.79	New Zealand ...	3.28	4.55	10.35	9.10	11.69	13.65	14.97
Brazil	—	—	2.57	2.74	3.15	4.09		Norway	6.90	10.47	24.84	27.93	32.73	36.41	39.14
Denmark......	6.24	8.10	25.28	24.31	30.22	34.45	35.47	Portugal.......	1.52	1.46	5.09	5.07	6.24	7.02	7.33
Finland.......	4.63	8.20	24.31	21.78	27.10	30.67	31.93	Singapore	0.83	2.52	7.57	6.71	7.18	7.38	7.66
France	4.50	7.48	19.26	17.13	21.14	23.89	24.63	South Korea ...	0.32	1.23	7.28	8.77	9.69	11.13	13.56
Germany[2]....	—	—	30.10	24.22	29.64	32.50	33.00	Spain	2.52	4.64	12.70	11.95	15.01	17.14	17.78
Greece	1.69	3.67	9.07	—	—	—	—	Sri Lanka	0.28	0.28	0.48	0.49	0.51	0.52	—
Hong Kong[3] ...	0.75	1.73	4.80	5.66	5.54	5.51	5.65	Sweden	7.14	9.61	21.68	20.23	25.19	28.42	28.73
Ireland........	3.06	6.00	13.75	15.26	19.09	21.94	22.76	Switzerland	6.03	9.55	28.90	23.77	27.78	30.21	30.50
Israel	2.02	3.65	9.41	11.00	11.62	12.01	12.42	Taiwan........	0.38	1.51	5.99	5.64	5.69	5.98	6.38
Italy..........	4.64	7.56	15.69	14.75	18.11	20.48	21.05	United Kingdom.	3.35	6.22	13.79	18.36	21.33	24.76	25.66
Japan........	2.97	6.27	23.47	18.60	20.26	21.84	21.76	United States...	6.16	12.71	17.17	21.33	22.20	22.82	23.65

— Data not available. **Note:** Previous years' data for some countries have been revised to reflect updated information. (1) Compensation includes all direct pay (including bonuses, etc.), paid benefits, and for some countries, labor taxes. (2) 1975 and 1985 data are for area covered by the former West Germany. 1995-present data are for unified Germany. (3) Part of China since 1997.

Unemployment Rates, by Selected Country, 1970-2006[1]

Source: Bureau of Labor Statistics, U.S. Dept. of Labor

Year	U.S.	Australia	Canada	France	Germany[2]	Italy	Japan	Sweden	UK
1970	4.9	1.7	5.7	2.5	0.5	3.2	1.2	1.5	3.1
1975	8.5	4.9	6.9	4.2	3.4	3.4	1.9	1.6	4.5
1980	7.1	6.1	7.3	6.5	2.8	4.4	2.0	2.0	6.9
1981	7.6	5.8	7.3	7.6	4.0	4.9	2.2	2.5	9.7
1982	9.7	7.2	10.7	8.3	5.6	5.4	2.4	3.1	10.8
1983	9.6	10.0	11.6	8.6	6.9	5.9	2.7	3.5	11.5
1984	7.5	9.0	10.9	10.0	7.1	5.9	2.8	3.1	11.8
1985	7.2	8.3	10.2	10.5	7.2	6.0	2.7	2.8	11.4
1986	7.0	7.9	9.3	10.6	6.6	7.5	2.8	2.6	11.4
1987	6.2	7.9	8.4	10.8	6.3	7.9	2.9	2.2	10.5
1988	5.5	7.0	7.4	10.3	6.3	7.9	2.5	1.9	8.6
1989	5.3	6.0	7.1	9.6	5.7	7.8	2.3	1.6	7.3
1990	5.6	6.7	7.7	8.6	5.0	7.0	2.1	1.8	7.1
1991	6.8	9.3	9.8	9.1	5.6	6.9	2.1	3.1	8.9
1992	7.5	10.5	10.7	10.0	6.7	7.3	2.2	5.6	10.0
1993	6.9	10.6	10.8	11.3	9.0	9.8	2.5	9.4	10.4
1994	6.1	9.4	9.6	11.9	8.5	10.7	2.9	9.6	8.7
1995	5.6	8.2	8.7	11.3	8.2	11.3	3.2	9.1	8.7
1996	5.4	8.2	8.9	11.8	9.0	11.3	3.4	9.9	8.1
1997	4.9	8.3	8.4	11.7	9.9	11.4	3.4	10.1	7.0
1998	4.5	7.7	7.7	11.2	9.3	11.5	4.1	8.4	6.3
1999	4.2	6.9	7.0	10.5	8.5	11.0	4.7	7.1	6.0
2000	4.0	6.3	6.1	9.1	7.8	10.2	4.8	5.8	5.5
2001	4.7	6.8	6.5	8.4	7.9	9.2	5.1	5.0	5.1
2002	5.8	6.4	7.0	8.8	8.6	8.7	5.4	5.1	5.2
2003	6.0	6.1	6.9	9.5	9.3	8.5	5.3	5.8	5.0
2004	5.5	5.5	6.4	9.7	10.3	8.1	4.8	6.6	4.8
2005	5.1	5.1	6.0	9.9	11.2	7.8	4.5	7.7	4.8
2006	4.6	4.9	5.5	9.2	10.3	6.8	4.2	7.0	5.5

Note: Civilian labor force, seasonally adjusted. For the sake of comparisons, U.S. unemployment rate concepts were applied to unemployment data for other countries. Previous years' data for some countries have been revised to reflect updated information. (1) As a result of revisions in survey methodology, there are breaks in the data series for the U.S. (1990, 1994); Australia (1986, 2001); France (1982, 1990); Germany (1983, 1991, 1999, 2005); Italy (1986, 1991, 1993); and Sweden (1987, 2005). Data prior to a survey change are not fully comparable to data after a survey change. (2) For former West Germany only, through 1990; from 1991 on figures are for unified Germany.

Tax Payments in Selected Countries, 2006[1]

Source: *Taxing Wages: 2005/2006*, Organization for Economic Cooperation and Development

(as % of gross wage earnings; ranked by total payment)

Country	Income tax	Social security	Total payment[2]	Country	Income tax	Social security	Total payment[2]
Germany	21.1%	21.7%	42.7%	Greece...............	8.7%	16.0%	24.7%
Belgium	27.8	14.0	41.8	Iceland..............	24.3	0.2	24.5
Denmark............	30.2	10.7	40.9	Canada	16.8	7.4	24.2
Netherlands	13.4	22.7	36.1	Australia	23.7	0.0	23.7
Hungary	19.7	14.3	34.0	United States........	15.7	7.7	23.4
Austria	14.9	18.1	33.0	Czech Republic......	10.0	12.5	22.5
Poland	6.3	25.8	32.2	Slovak Republic......	9.0	13.4	22.4
Sweden	24.1	7.0	31.1	Switzerland	10.8	11.1	21.9
Finland	23.9	6.8	30.7	Portugal.............	10.2	11.0	21.2
Turkey	15.5	15.0	30.5	New Zealand	20.9	0.0	20.9
France	15.6	13.6	29.1	Spain	14.1	6.4	20.5
Norway.............	21.2	7.8	29.0	Japan...............	7.3	12.2	19.5
Luxembourg.........	14.0	13.9	27.9	Ireland..............	9.7	5.1	14.8
Italy...............	18.4	9.2	27.6	Korea...............	3.4	7.2	10.6
United Kingdom	17.6	9.2	26.8	Mexico..............	3.5	1.4	5.0

(1) Does not include taxes not listed, such as sales tax or VAT. Rates shown apply to a single person without children with average earnings. (2) Figures may not add to totals due to rounding.

The World's Refugees, 2006

Source: *World Refugee Survey 2007*, U.S. Committee for Refugees and Immigrants

These estimates are conservative and have been rounded. Totals include individuals granted asylum and those with pending asylum claims as of year-end 2006. Figures generally do not include those who have achieved permanent resettlement. They also do not include Internally Displaced Persons (IDPs), who are displaced within their own country due to persecution or armed conflict and are not protected by international refugee law. The Internal Displacement Monitoring Centre estimated that in 2006, there were 24.5 mil IDPs worldwide, 70%-80% of whom were women and children.

(As of Dec. 31, 2006; only countries estimated to host 50,000 or more refugees are listed. Region totals incl. nations not listed.)

Place of asylum	Origin of most refugees	Number
AFRICA		**3,199,900**
Algeria	Morocco	95,000
Cameroon	Chad, Central African Republic	71,200
Chad	Sudan, Central African Republic	286,800
Congo, Dem. Rep.	Angola, Rwanda, Burundi	208,500
Congo, Rep.	Dem. Rep. of the Congo, Rwanda	60,000
Egypt	Iraq, Former Palestine, Sudan	172,900
Ethiopia	Sudan, Somalia	147,300
Ghana	Liberia, Togo	50,500
Kenya	Somalia, Sudan, Ethiopia	337,700
Rwanda	Dem. Rep. of the Congo	53,100
South Africa	Dem. Rep. of the Congo, Zimbabwe, Somalia	171,400
Sudan	Eritrea, Chad, Ethiopia	296,400
Tanzania	Burundi, Dem. Rep. of the Congo	485,700
Uganda	Sudan, Dem. Rep. of the Congo, Rwanda	277,800
Zambia	Dem. Rep. of the Congo, Angola	120,500
AMERICAS AND THE CARIBBEAN		**648,900**
Ecuador	Colombia	207,500
United States	China, Haiti, Cuba, Somalia	147,200
Venezuela	Colombia	208,500

Place of asylum	Origin of most refugees	Number
EAST ASIA AND THE PACIFIC		**953,500**
China	Vietnam, North Korea	335,400
Malaysia	Philippines, Myanmar	155,700
Thailand	Myanmar, Laos	408,400
SOUTH AND CENTRAL ASIA		**2,914,200**
Bangladesh	Myanmar	178,100
India	China, Nepal, Sri Lanka, Myanmar, Bangladesh, Afghanistan	435,900
Nepal	Bhutan, China	129,600
Pakistan	Afghanistan	2,161,500
EUROPE		**569,200**
Russia	Afghanistan, Georgia	187,400
Serbia	Croatia, Bosnia and Herzegovina	77,900
MIDDLE EAST		**5,931,000**
Gaza Strip	Former Palestine	1,017,000
Iran	Afghanistan, Iraq	1,025,000
Jordan	Iraq, Former Palestine	862,700
Lebanon	Former Palestine, Iraq	294,200
Saudi Arabia	Former Palestine	241,000
Syria	Iraq, Former Palestine	1,329,300
West Bank	Former Palestine	722,000
Yemen	Somalia	96,700
TOTAL		**13,948,800**

Principal Sources of Refugees, 2006

Sources: *World Refugee Survey 2007*, U.S. Committee for Refugees and Immigrants
(as of Dec. 31, 2006)

Afghanistan	3,260,300	Burundi	393,700	Sri Lanka	108,900
Former Palestine	3,036,400	Vietnam	308,000	Nepal	102,500
Iraq	1,687,800	Eritrea	255,400	Rwanda	92,100
Myanmar	693,300	Angola	195,000	Chad	84,800
Sudan	648,000	China	158,700	Ethiopia	77,800
Colombia	453,300	Liberia	141,100	Central African Republic	73,000
Dem. Rep. of the Congo	413,300	Bhutan	119,100	Philippines	69,400
Somalia	410,300	Morocco	116,800	Croatia	57,300

Major Foreign Development Aid Donors, 2005-06

Source: Org. for Economic Cooperation and Development; ranked by percent of GNI (gross national income) in 2006.
In 2006, the U.S. gave the highest total amount of development aid but ranked 22nd by percent of GNI.

Country	ODA[1], as % of GNI 2006	2005	ODA[1] in U.S. dollars (millions) 2006	2005	Country	ODA[1], as % of GNI 2006	2005	ODA[1] in U.S. dollars (millions) 2006	2005
1. Sweden	1.03	0.94	3,967	3,362	13. Germany	0.36	0.36	10,351	10,082
2. Norway	0.89	0.94	2,946	2,786	14. Spain	0.32	0.27	3,801	3,018
Luxembourg	0.89	0.86	291	256	15. Canada	0.30	0.34	3,713	3,756
4. Netherlands	0.81	0.82	5,452	5,115	Australia	0.30	0.25	2,128	1,680
5. Denmark	0.80	0.81	2,234	2,109	17. New Zealand	0.27	0.27	257	274
6. Ireland	0.53	0.42	997	719	18. (G7 nations)	0.26	0.30	75,138	80,492
7. United Kingdom	0.52	0.47	12,607	10,767	19. Japan	0.25	0.28	11,608	13,147
8. Belgium	0.50	0.53	1,968	1,963	20. Portugal	0.21	0.21	391	377
9. Austria	0.48	0.52	1,513	1,573	21. Italy	0.20	0.29	3,672	5,091
10. France	0.47	0.47	10,448	10,026	22. United States	0.17	0.22	22,739	27,622
11. Finland	0.39	0.46	826	902	23. Greece	0.16	0.17	384	384
Switzerland	0.39	0.44	1,647	1,767					

(1) ODA = Official Development Assistance.

Top 10 Recipients of U.S. Development Aid, 2004-05

Source: Development Assistance Committee, Organization for Economic Cooperation and Development
(in millions of U.S. dollars)

Country	Avg. 2004-05	Country	Avg. 2004-05	Country	Avg. 2004-05
1. Iraq	$6,926	5. Ethiopia	$552	8. Palestinian Adm. Areas	$227
2. Afghanistan	1,060	6. Jordan	368	9. Uganda	225
3. Egypt	750	7. Colombia	366	10. Pakistan	224
4. Sudan	575				

Note: Total outlays shared by other recipient nations averaged $10.3 bil over the two-year period.

Estimated HIV Infection and Reported AIDS Cases, Year-End 2006

Source: Joint United Nations Program on HIV/AIDS, World Health Organization

Global HIV prevalence, or the percentage of people living with HIV/AIDS, has leveled off somewhat, due to changes in behavior and prevention programs. The number of people living with HIV/AIDS continues to rise, however, with new cases outpacing the number of HIV/AIDS-related deaths each year. There were an estimated 4.3 mil new cases of HIV/AIDS in 2006; about 2.9 mil adults and children with AIDS died the same year.

At year-end 2006, approximately 39.5 mil worldwide were living with HIV/AIDS, up from 38.6 mil at year-end 2005. 2.3 mil of them were under age 15. In 2006, 40% of new HIV/AIDS infections were in young adults 15-24 years old. Globally, just under half of all adults 15 and older (48%) living with HIV/AIDS are female. In many regions, females are expected to make up a growing percentage of the HIV/AIDS infected population. In sub-Saharan Africa, women already make up 59% of all infected adults.

HIV prevalence has increased most dramatically in East Asia, Eastern Europe, and Central Asia. The total infected population in these regions was 21% higher in 2006 than in 2004. The use of non-sterile equipment by drug users caused an estimated 67% of prevalent HIV/AIDS infections in Eastern Europe and Central Asia. Excluding India, in 2005, 49% of HIV/AIDS infections in South and Southeast Asia were concentrated in sex workers and their clients; in the same region, 22% of those infected were injection drug users.

Sub-Saharan Africa was still by far the worst affected region. About 62.5% of the world's total HIV/AIDS-infected population, or 24.7 mil, live in this region, with the most intense HIV/AIDS epidemic occurring in Swaziland. Other vulnerable populations include racial and ethnic minorities in North America, immigrants and migrants in Western and Central Europe, and young people in Eastern Europe and Central Asia.

Global spending on HIV/AIDS treatment and prevention in 2006 was nearly five times the amount spent in 2001, when $1.6 bil was directed toward HIV/AIDS treatment. The estimated $8.9 bil spent in 2006 still fell short of the $14.9 bil needed to combat HIV/AIDS.

The number of HIV/AIDS cases and deaths are estimated based on all available data, including surveys of pregnant women visiting prenatal clinics, household surveys, monitoring of at-risk population groups, and birth and death records.

Current and New HIV/AIDS Cases and Deaths by Region, Year-End 2006

Region	Current cases[1]	Percent[2]	New cases, 2006	Est. deaths, 2006
Sub-Saharan Africa	24,700,000	62.5	2,800,000	2,100,000
North Africa and Middle East	460,000	1.2	68,000	36,000
South and South-East Asia	7,800,000	19.7	860,000	590,000
East Asia	750,000	1.9	100,000	43,000
Oceania	81,000	0.2	7,100	4,000
Latin America	1,700,000	4.3	140,000	65,000
Caribbean	250,000	0.6	27,000	19,000
Eastern Europe and Central Asia	1,700,000	4.3	270,000	84,000
Western and Central Europe	740,000	1.9	22,000	12,000
North America	1,400,000	3.5	43,000	18,000
WORLD[3]	39,500,000	100.0	4,300,000	2,900,000

(1) Adults (ages 15 and older) and children (under 15) living with HIV/AIDS. (2) Percentage of total number of people worldwide living with HIV/AIDS. (3) Figures may not add to totals because of rounding.

Nuclear Powers of the World

As of Sept. 2007, 8 countries were acknowledged nuclear powers: the **UK, France, China, India, Pakistan, Russia, North Korea,** and the **U.S.** In addition, the Carnegie Endowment for Intl. Peace estimated **Israel** to have a nuclear arsenal of 100-170 warheads. **Iran** was suspected of developing nuclear weapons despite the country's claims that it was focusing on nuclear energy. More than 40 nations have the knowledge or technology needed to produce nuclear weapons. All have signed the Nuclear Non-Proliferation Treaty (NPT) except for Israel, India, and Pakistan. N. Korea withdrew in Jan. 10, 2003, following the country's expelling of Intl. Atomic Energy Agency (IAEA) inspectors in Dec. 2002.

In a draft accord reached at six-party talks with China, Japan, Russia, S. Korea, and the U.S. on Sept. 19, 2005, N. Korea agreed to scrap its nuclear weapons program in exchange for aid. Left unresolved was Pyongyang's continuing demand for international donors to provide light-water nuclear reactors for "peaceful uses."

N. Korea test-fired 7 ballistic missiles, July 5, 2006, and conducted its first-ever nuclear test Oct. 9, 2006. Despite the lack of progress at a new round of six-party talks Dec. 2006, N. Korea agreed to a deal Feb. 13, 2007: in exchange for closing its main nuclear facility and readmitting inspectors as steps toward relinquishing its nuclear weapons program, the country would receive economic aid and diplomatic recognition.

Several countries have abandoned their nuclear ambitions. **South Africa** announced in 1993 that it had built 7 fission weapons (1 was under construction) but had dismantled all of them. In the 1980s, **Argentina** and **Brazil** had active nuclear weapons programs, but they abandoned them by mutual treaty and signed the NPT.

Estimated Numbers of Nuclear Weapons by Country, 1945-2007[1]

Source: Natural Resources Defense Council; Federation of American Scientists; Carnegie Endowment for Intl. Peace; *Bulletin of the Atomic Scientists*

Year	United States	U.S.S.R./ Russia	United Kingdom	France	China	India	Pakistan	Total
1945	6	—	—	—	—	—	—	6
1950	369	5	—	—	—	—	—	374
1960	20,434	1,605	30	—	—	—	—	22,069
1970	26,662	11,643	280	36	75	—	—	38,696
1980	24,304	30,062	350	250	280	—	—	55,246
1990	21,004	37,000	300	505	430	—	—	59,239
1995	12,144	27,000	300	500	400	—	—	40,344
2000	10,577	21,000	185	470	400	—	—	32,632
2007	9,938[2]	15,000[3]	200	350	410	75-110	50-110	27,600

(1) Israel is widely presumed to have a nuclear stockpile, though it has never been declared. (2) Only about 5,163 are considered active or operational. The rest are categorized as responsive (not operationally deployed and in storage) or inactive. (3) Only about 5,670 are considered operational. The rest are believed to be in reserve or marked for dismantlement.

Nuclear Arms Treaties and Negotiations: A Historical Overview

Aug. 5, 1963—Partial (Limited) Test Ban Treaty signed by U.S., USSR, and Britain in Moscow, went into effect Oct. 10, 1963. Prohibited the testing of nuclear weapons in the atmosphere, in outer space, and under water.

Jan. 27, 1967—Treaty on Principles Governing the Activities of States in the Exploration and Use of Outer Space, including the Moon and Other Celestial Bodies (or the **Outer Space Treaty**) opened to signatures, went into effect Oct. 10, 1967. Banned the introduction of nuclear weapons or any other weapons of mass destruction into space.

July 1, 1968—Nuclear Nonproliferation Treaty (NPT) opened to signatures, went into effect Mar. 5, 1970. With the U.S., USSR, and Great Britain as major signers, the treaty limited the spread of nuclear material for military purposes by agreement not to help non-nuclear nations get or make nuclear weapons.

At an NPT review conference in 1995, the treaty was extended indefinitely. As of Sept. 2007, 190 countries were party to the treaty; Israel, India, and Pakistan were not signatories.

May 26, 1972—Strategic Arms Limitation Treaty (SALT I) signed by U.S. and USSR in Moscow. Consists of two agreements: the **Treaty on the Limitation of Anti-Ballistic Missile Systems** (or the **ABM Treaty**) and the **Interim Agreement on Certain Measures with Respect to the Limitation of Strategic Offensive Arms**. The latter agreement imposed a five-year freeze on both testing and deployment of intercontinental ballistic missiles (ICBMs) and submarine-launched ballistic missiles (SLBMs). The ABM Treaty limited antiballistic missiles to two sites of 100 antiballistic missile launchers in each country. (The treaty was amended in 1974 to one site in each country.)

Though SALT I expired in Sept. 1977, the U.S. and USSR agreed to continue to abide by it.

July 3, 1974—Treaty on the Limitation of Underground Nuclear Weapon Tests (or the **Threshold Test Ban Treaty**) signed by U.S. and USSR in Moscow. Limited underground testing of nuclear weapons to 150 kilotons. On May 28, 1976, U.S. and Russia signed the **Peaceful Nuclear Explosions Treaty**, governing explosions occurring outside of weapons test sites. Both treaties entered into force Dec. 11, 1990.

June 18, 1979—Strategic Offensive Arms Limitation Treaty (or **SALT II**) signed by U.S. and USSR in Vienna. Constrained offensive nuclear weapons, limiting each side to 2,400 missile launchers and heavy bombers; ceiling to apply until Jan. 1, 1985. Treaty also set a sub-ceiling of 1,320 ICBMs and SLBMs with multiple warheads on each side. Following Dec. 1979 Soviet invasion of Afghanistan, however, Pres. Jimmy Carter withdrew SALT II from Senate consideration for ratification.

Dec. 8, 1987—Intermediate-Range Nuclear Forces (INF) Treaty signed by U.S. and USSR in Washington, DC. Eliminated all U.S. and Soviet intermediate- and shorter-range nuclear missiles from Europe and Asia. Ratified, with conditions, by U.S. Senate May 27, 1988, and by USSR June 1, 1988. Entered into force June 1, 1988.

July 31, 1991—Strategic Arms Reduction Treaty (START I) signed by USSR and U.S. in Moscow, to reduce strategic offensive arms by about 30% in three phases over seven years. START I was the first treaty to mandate reductions by the superpowers. Treaty was approved by U.S. Senate Oct. 1, 1992.

With the Soviet Union breakup in Dec. 1991, four former republics became independent nations with strategic nuclear weapons—Russia, Ukraine, Kazakhstan, and Belarus. Under the Lisbon Protocol of May 1992, the last three countries agreed in principle to destroy or transfer their nuclear weapons to Russia and to ratify START I. The Russian Supreme Soviet voted for ratification but decided not to provide instruments of ratification until the other three republics ratified START I and acceded to the NPT as non-nuclear nations. Ukraine's signing of the NPT on Dec. 5, 1994, cleared the way for START I.

Jan. 3, 1993—START II signed by U.S. and Russia in Moscow, ratified by the two countries on Jan. 26, 1996, and Apr. 14, 2000, respectively. Called for both sides to reduce their long-range nuclear arsenals to about one-third of their then-current levels within a decade and to disable and dismantle launching systems.

On Sept. 26, 1997, the U.S. and Russia signed an extension that would delay the dismantling of launch systems under START II to Dec. 31, 2007.

Sept. 24, 1996—Comprehensive Test Ban Treaty (CTBT) signed by U.S. and Russia in New York City. The CTBT banned all nuclear weapons tests and other nuclear explosions. It was intended to prevent the nuclear powers from developing more advanced weapons, while limiting the ability of other states to acquire such devices.

As of Sept. 2007, the CTBT had been signed by 177 nations, including China, Russia, and France. It has been ratified by 140, including France, Russia, and the UK but not the U.S. or China. Enters into force after 44 nuclear-capable states ratify it; only 34 of the 44 have done so.

Sept. 26, 1997—Accord amending **ABM Treaty** signed by U.S. and Russia in New York City, allowing for greater flexibility in development of short-range nuclear weapons.

May 24, 2002—Strategic Offensive Reductions Treaty (SORT or Moscow Treaty) signed by U.S. and Russia in Moscow, entered into force June 1, 2003. Committed both countries to cutting nuclear arsenals to 1,700-2,200 warheads each, down from about 6,000, by Dec. 31, 2012. No intermediate timetable established, but joint committee set up for monitoring implementation. Either side allowed to back out with 90 days notice.

June 2002—U.S. formally withdrew from **ABM Treaty**, effective June 13, with intent of developing a defensive missile system. Russia, June 14, announced its withdrawal from **START II**, stating that U.S. withdrawal from the ABM Treaty effectively invalidated START II.

Major International Organizations

African Union (AU), inaugurated July 9, 2002, in Durban, South Africa, following disbanding of the Organization of African Unity, and consisting of the same 53 members, i.e., all countries of Africa except Morocco, which left the OAU after it admitted Western Sahara (Sahrawi Arab Dem. Rep.), a territory claimed by Morocco. The new organization is intended to focus on achieving greater socioeconomic integration and unity among its member states. The founders provided for a peer review committee to oversee member states' adherence to standards of good government, respect for human rights, and financial transparency. The AU's founding document authorized the organization to intervene to stop genocide, war crimes, or human rights abuses within individual member nations. **Headquarters:** Addis Ababa, Ethiopia. **Website:** www.africa-union.org

Asia-Pacific Economic Cooperation (APEC), founded Nov. 1989 as a forum to further cooperation on trade and investment between nations of the region and the rest of the world. Its 21 members are Australia, Brunei, Canada, Chile, China, Hong Kong, Indonesia, Japan, Malaysia, Mexico, New Zealand, Papua New Guinea, Peru, Philippines, Russia, Singapore, South Korea, Taiwan, Thailand, the U.S., and Vietnam. **Headquarters:** Singapore. **Website:** www.apec.org

Association of Southeast Asian Nations (ASEAN), formed Aug. 8, 1967, to promote economic, social, and cultural cooperation and development among states of the Southeast Asian region. Members in 2007 were Brunei, Cambodia, Indonesia, Laos, Malaysia, Myanmar, Philippines, Singapore, Thailand, and Vietnam. **Headquarters:** Jakarta, Indonesia. **Website:** www.aseansec.org

Caribbean Community and Common Market (CARICOM), established Aug. 1, 1973. Its aim is to increase cooperation in economics, health, education, culture, science and technology, and tax administration, as well as the coordination of foreign policy. Members in 2007 were Antigua and Barbuda, The Bahamas, Barbados, Belize, Dominica, Grenada, Guyana, Haiti, Jamaica, Montserrat, Saint Kitts and Nevis, Saint Lucia, Saint Vincent and the Grenadines, Suriname, and Trinidad and Tobago. Associate members in 2007 were Anguilla, Bermuda, British Virgin Islands, Cayman Islands, and Turks and Caicos Islands. **Headquarters:** Georgetown, Guyana. **Website:** www.caricom.org

The Commonwealth, originally called the British Commonwealth of Nations, then the Commonwealth of Nations is an association of nations and dependencies that were once parts of the former British Empire. The British monarch is the symbolic head of the Commonwealth.

There are 53 independent nations in the Commonwealth. As of 2007, regular members included the UK and 15 other nations recognizing the British monarch, represented by a governor-general, as their head of state: Antigua and Barbuda, Australia, The Bahamas, Barbados, Belize, Canada, Grenada, Jamaica, New Zealand, Papua New Guinea, Saint Kitts and Nevis, Saint Lucia, Saint Vincent and the Grenadines, the Solomon Islands, and Tuvalu. Also members in good standing were 36 countries with their own heads of state: Bangladesh, Botswana, Brunei, Cameroon, Cyprus, Dominica, The Gambia, Ghana, Guyana, India, Kenya, Kiribati, Lesotho, Malawi, Malaysia, Maldives, Malta, Mauritius, Mozambique (the only member never part of the British Empire), Namibia, Nauru, Nigeria, Pakistan, Samoa, Seychelles, Sierra Leone, Singapore, South Africa, Sri Lanka, Swaziland, Tanzania, Tonga, Trinidad and Tobago, Uganda, Vanuatu, and Zambia.

Pakistan was suspended from the councils of the Commonwealth in Oct. 1999, following a military coup, but regained its member status Mar. 22, 2004. Zimbabwe was suspended in Mar. 2002, following election and land redistribution controversies; it withdrew from the Commonwealth, Dec. 7, 2003. Fiji's military regime was suspended from the Commonwealth on Dec. 8, 2006. The Commonwealth facilitates consultation among members through meetings of ministers and through a permanent secretariat. **Headquarters:** London, UK. **Website:** www.thecommonwealth.org

Commonwealth of Independent States (CIS), an alliance established in Dec. 1991, made up of former Soviet constituent republics. Members in 2007 were Armenia, Azerbaijan, Belarus, Georgia, Kazakhstan, Kyrgyzstan, Moldova, Russia, Tajikistan, Turkmenistan, Ukraine, and Uzbekistan. Policy is set through coordinating bodies such as the Council of the Heads of States and Council of the Heads of Governments. **Headquarters:** Minsk, Belarus. **Website:** www.cis.minsk.by

European Free Trade Association (EFTA), created May 3, 1960, to promote expansion of free trade. By Dec. 31, 1966, tariffs and quotas between member nations had been eliminated. Members entered into free trade agreements with the EU in 1972 and 1973. In 1992, EFTA and EU agreed to create a single market—with free flow of goods, services, capital, and labor—among nations of the 2 organizations. Members in 2007 were Iceland, Liechtenstein, Norway, and Switzerland. Many former EFTA members are now EU members. **Headquarters:** Geneva, Switzerland. **Website:** www.efta.int

European Union (EU), known as the European Community (EC) until 1994; the name covers 3 organizations with common membership: the European Economic Community (Common Market), the European Coal and Steel Community, and the European Atomic Energy Community (Euratom). A merger of the 3 communities' executives went into effect July 1, 1967. As of Sept. 2007, there were 27 EU members. These included the 12 original members (Belgium, Denmark, France, Germany, Greece, Ireland, Italy, Luxembourg, Netherlands, Portugal, Spain, and UK), 3 states that entered Jan. 1, 1995 (Austria, Finland, Sweden), 10 members that joined on May 1, 2004 (Cyprus, Czech Republic, Estonia, Hungary, Latvia, Lithuania, Malta, Poland, Slovakia, Slovenia), and 2 members that joined Jan. 1, 2007 (Bulgaria, Romania). Some 70 nations in Africa, the Caribbean, and the Pacific are affiliated under the Lomé Convention. **Headquarters:** Brussels, Belgium. **Website:** europa.eu.int

The EU aims to integrate the economies, coordinate social developments, and bring about political union of the member states. The Council of the Union, European Commission, European Parliament, and European Courts of Justice and of Auditors comprise the permanent structure. Effective Dec. 31, 1992, there are no restrictions on the movement of goods, services, capital, workers, and tourists within the EU. There are also common agricultural, fisheries, and nuclear research policies.

Leaders of the member nations (12 at the time), meeting Dec. 9-11, 1991, in Maastricht, the Netherlands, committed the organization to launching a common currency (the euro) by 1999; sought to establish common foreign policies; laid the groundwork for a common defense policy; gave the organization a leading role in social policy (Britain was not included in this plan); pledged increased aid for poorer member nations; and slightly increased the powers of the 567-member European Parliament. The treaties went into effect Nov. 1, 1993, following ratification by all 12 members.

In June 1998 the European Central Bank was established. In Jan. 1999, 11 of the then-15 EU countries began using the euro for some purposes. By Feb. 2002, national currencies in those 11 countries and Greece were removed from circulation and replaced with the euro as the only currency of legal tender. EU peacekeeping forces replaced NATO troops in Macedonia, Mar. 31, 2003, the first such mission for the organization.

As of mid-2007, 16 countries have ratified the EU constitution. After voters in France and the Netherlands rejected ratification in 2005, other EU nations deferred action on the constitution. Turkey, Croatia, and Macedonia were candidate countries. Slovenia adopted the euro on Jan. 1, 2007. Cyprus and Malta will introduce the euro on Jan. 1, 2008.

Group of Eight (G-8), established Sept. 22, 1985; forum of 7 major industrial democracies (Canada, France, Germany, Italy, Japan, the UK, and U.S.) and (later) Russia, which meet periodically to discuss economic and other issues. At its annual summit in May 1998, the name was changed to G-8 from G-7. The 7 were still free to meet without Russia on some issues, especially those relating to global finance. The presidency rotates yearly among members. The 2004 summit was hosted in the U.S. at Sea Island, GA. The 2005 summit was held in Perthshire, Scotland. It was interrupted by the July 7 bombings in London but concluded as scheduled. The 2006 summit was in St. Petersburg, Russia; the 2007 summit in Heiligendamm, Germany; and the 2008 summit will be in Hokkaido, Japan, July 7-9.

International Criminal Police Organization (Interpol), created June 13, 1956, to promote mutual assistance among all police authorities within the limits of the law existing in the different countries. There were 186 members (independent nations), plus 11 sub-bureaus (dependencies) in 2007. **Headquarters:** Lyon, France. **Website:** www.interpol.com

League of Arab States (Arab League), created Mar. 22, 1945. The League promotes economic, social, political, and military cooperation, mediates disputes, and represents Arab states in certain international negotiations. Members in 2007 were Algeria, Bahrain, Comoros, Djibouti, Egypt, Iraq, Jordan, Kuwait, Lebanon, Libya, Mauritania, Morocco, Oman, Palestine (considered an independent state by the League), Qatar, Saudi Arabia, Somalia, Sudan, Syria, Tunisia, United Arab Emirates, and Yemen. **Headquarters:** Cairo, Egypt. **Website:** www.arableagueonline.org

North Atlantic Treaty Organization (NATO), created by treaty (signed Apr. 4, 1949; in effect Aug. 24, 1949). Members in 2007 included Belgium, Bulgaria, Canada, Czech Republic, Denmark, Estonia, France, Germany, Greece, Hungary, Iceland, Italy, Latvia, Lithuania, Luxembourg, Netherlands, Norway, Poland, Portugal, Romania,

Slovakia, Slovenia, Spain, Turkey, UK, and U.S. Of these, 7 states—Bulgaria, Estonia, Latvia, Lithuania, Romania, Slovakia, and Slovenia—joined the alliance in 2004. All are former Warsaw Pact nations from Eastern Europe. That marked the fifth time NATO increased its membership and was the single largest expansion.

Members have agreed to settle disputes by peaceful means, to develop their capacity to resist armed attack, to regard an attack on one as an attack on all, and to take necessary action to repel an attack under Article 51 of the UN Charter. **Headquarters:** Brussels, Belgium. **Website:** www.nato.int

The NATO structure consists of the North Atlantic Council (NAC), the Defense Planning Committee, the Military Committee (realigned in June 2003 and consisting of 2 commands: Allied Command Operations and Allied Command Transformation), the Nuclear Planning Group, and the Canada-U.S. Regional Planning Group. France detached itself from the military command structure in 1966.

With the end of the cold war in the early 1990s, members put greater stress on political action and on creating a rapid deployment force to react to local crises. By the mid-1990s, 27 nations, including Russia and other former Soviet republics, had joined with NATO in the so-called Partnership for Peace (PfP; drafted Dec. 1993), which provided for limited joint military exercises, peace-keeping missions, and information exchange. NATO has proceeded gradually toward extending full membership to former Eastern bloc nations. On Mar. 12, 1999, 3 former Warsaw Pact members, Hungary, Poland, and the Czech Republic, formally became members. NATO and Russia signed a cooperation pact May 28, 2002, forming a NATO-Russia Council, and NATO invited 7 former eastern-bloc nations to join the alliance, Nov. 21.

In Dec. 1995, a NATO-led multinational force (SFOR) was deployed to help keep the peace in Bosnia and Herzegovina; in 1999, another force (KFOR) was deployed in Kosovo.

Following the terrorist attacks on the U.S., the NATO Council agreed, Sept. 12, 2001, to invoke for the first time Article 5 of the treaty, which stipulates mutual defense of alliance members. NATO assumed control of the International Security Assistance Force in Afghanistan (ISAF), Aug. 2003, marking the first time NATO led a mission outside Europe. As of Sept. 2007, ISAF troops from 37 countries numbered over 35,000.

Organization of American States (OAS), formed in Bogotá, Colombia, Apr. 30, 1948. It has a Permanent Council, Inter-American Council for Integral Development, Juridical Committee, and Commission on Human Rights. The Permanent Council can call meetings of foreign ministers to deal with urgent security matters. A General Assembly meets annually.

Members in 2007 were Antigua and Barbuda, Argentina, The Bahamas, Barbados, Belize, Bolivia, Brazil, Canada, Chile, Colombia, Costa Rica, Cuba, Dominica, Dominican Republic, Ecuador, El Salvador, Grenada, Guatemala, Guyana, Haiti, Honduras, Jamaica, Mexico, Nicaragua, Panama, Paraguay, Peru, Saint Kitts and Nevis, Saint Lucia, Saint Vincent and the Grenadines, Suriname, Trinidad and Tobago, U.S., Uruguay, and Venezuela. In 1962, the OAS barred Cuba from participation in activities though it retains membership. **Headquarters:** Washington, DC. **Website:** www.oas.org

Organization for Economic Cooperation and Development (OECD), established Dec. 14, 1960, to promote the economic and social welfare of all its member countries and to stimulate efforts on behalf of developing nations. The OECD also collects and disseminates economic and environmental information. Members in 2007 were Australia, Austria, Belgium, Canada, Czech Republic, Denmark, Finland, France, Germany, Greece, Hungary, Iceland, Ireland, Italy, Japan, Luxembourg, Mexico, Netherlands, New Zealand, Norway, Poland, Portugal, Slovakia, South Korea, Spain, Sweden, Switzerland, Turkey, UK, and the U.S. **Headquarters:** Paris, France. **Website:** www.oecd.org

Organization of Petroleum Exporting Countries (OPEC), created Sept. 14, 1960. This group made up of most—but not all—the major petroleum exporting nations seeks to stabilize the oil market and set world oil prices by controlling production. Members in 2007 were Algeria, Angola, Indonesia, Iran, Iraq, Kuwait, Libya, Nigeria, Qatar, Saudi Arabia, United Arab Emirates, and Venezuela. **Headquarters:** Vienna, Austria. **Website:** www.opec.org

Organization for Security and Cooperation in Europe (OSCE), established in 1972 as the Conference on Security and Cooperation in Europe; name adopted Jan. 1, 1995. The group, formed by NATO and Warsaw Pact members, seeks improved East-West relations through a commitment to nonaggression and human rights as well as cooperation in economics, science and technology, cultural exchange, and environmental protection. There were 56 member states in 2007. **Headquarters:** Vienna, Austria. **Website:** www.osce.org

United Nations

The 62nd regular session of the United Nations General Assembly opened Sept. 18, 2007, attended by world leaders and other delegates from 192 nations.

The UN headquarters is in New York, NY, between First Ave. and Roosevelt Dr. at E. 42nd St. and E. 48th St.

The UN consists of 6 main organs: the General Assembly, Security Council, Secretariat, Economic and Social Council, Trusteeship Council, and the International Court of Justice. The UN family is much larger, encompassing 15 agencies and several programs and bodies.

The UN Dept. of Public Information maintains a news service, available online at www.un.org/news. It also publishes the *UN Chronicle*, available at www.un.org/Pubs/chronicle. The UN has a post office originating its own stamps.

Proposals to establish an organization of nations for maintenance of world peace led to the convening of the United Nations Conference on International Organization in San Francisco, Apr. 25-June 26, 1945, where the UN charter was drawn. It was signed June 26 by 50 nations and by Poland, one of the original 51 members, on Oct. 15, 1945. It went into effect Oct. 24, 1945, upon ratification by the permanent members of the Security Council and a majority of the other signatories.

Purposes. To maintain international peace and security; to develop friendly relations among nations; to achieve international cooperation in solving economic, social, cultural, and humanitarian problems and in promoting respect for human rights and basic freedoms; to be a center for harmonizing the actions of nations in attaining these common ends.

Visitors to the UN. The headquarters are open to the public every day except during the 62nd General Assembly Session, Eid al-Fitr (Oct. 12, 2007), Thanksgiving, Christmas, and New Year's Day. Guided tours are given about every half hour from 9:30 AM to 4:45 PM weekdays; 10 AM to 4:30 PM weekends. The UN is closed weekends in Jan. and Feb.

Groups of 12 or more require reservations and should e-mail unitg@un.org or telephone (212) 963-4440. Children under 5 not permitted on tours.

United Nations Secretaries General

Took office	Secretary, nation	Took office	Secretary, nation
1946	Trygve Lie, Norway	1982	Javier Pérez de Cuéllar, Peru
1953	Dag Hammarskjöld, Sweden	1992	Boutros Boutros-Ghali, Egypt
1961	U Thant, Burma	1997	Kofi Annan, Ghana
1972	Kurt Waldheim, Austria	2007	Ban Ki-moon, South Korea

Six Main Organs of the United Nations

The United Nations consists of 6 principal organs, 15 agencies, and many programs and other bodies. The 6 principal organs are the General Assembly, the Security Council, the Secretariat, the Economic and Social Council, the Trusteeship Council, and the Intl. Court of Justice.

General Assembly. The General Assembly is composed of representatives of all the member nations. Each nation is entitled to one vote. The General Assembly meets in regular annual sessions and in special session when convoked at the request of the Security Council or a majority of UN members. On important questions a two-thirds majority of members present and voting is required; on other questions a simple majority is sufficient.

The General Assembly must approve the UN budget and apportion expenses among members. A member in arrears can lose its vote if the amount of arrears equals or exceeds the amount of the contributions due for the preceding 2 full years. The General Assembly proposed a total budget of $4.19 bil for the 2008-09 biennium. **Website:** www.un.org/ga

Security Council. The Security Council consists of 15 members, 5 with permanent seats. The remaining 10 are elected for 2-year terms by the General Assembly.

The permanent members of the Council are China, France, Russia, United Kingdom, and the United States. Nonpermanent members with terms expiring Dec. 31, 2007, are Republic of Congo, Ghana, Peru, Qatar, and Slovakia; those with terms expiring Dec. 31, 2008, are Belgium, Indonesia, Italy, Panama, and South Africa.

The Security Council has the primary responsibility within the UN for maintaining international peace and security. The Council may investigate any dispute that threatens international peace and security.

Any member of the UN at UN headquarters may, if invited by the Council, participate in its discussions, and a nation not a member of the UN may appear if it is a party to a dispute. Decisions on procedural questions are made by an affirmative vote of 9 members. On all other matters the affirmative vote of 9 members must include the concurring votes of all permanent members (giving them veto power). A party to a dispute must refrain from voting.

The Security Council directs the various peacekeeping forces deployed throughout the world. **Website:** www.un.org/sc

Secretariat. The Secretariat has an international staff of about 8,900 that carries out the day-to-day operations of the UN and is headed by the secretary general. The secretary general is the chief administrative officer of the UN, and is appointed by the General Assembly, on the recommendation of the Security Council, for a 5-year, renewable term. The Secretary General reports to the General Assembly and may bring to the attention of the Security Council any matter that threatens international peace. **Website:** www.un.org/documents/st.htm

Economic and Social Council. The Economic and Social Council consists of 54 members elected by the General Assembly for 3-year terms. The council is responsible for carrying out UN functions with regard to international economic, social, cultural, educational, health, and related matters. It meets once a year. **Website:** www.un.org/esa

Trusteeship Council. Made up of the 5 permanent members of the Security Council. The administration of trust territories was under UN supervision; however, all 11 Trust Territories have attained their right to self-determination. The Council formally suspended its work Nov. 1, 1994. **Website:** www.un.org/documents/tc

International Court of Justice (World Court). The International Court of Justice is the principal judicial organ of the UN. All members are ipso facto parties to the statute of the Court. The Court has jurisdiction over cases the parties submit to it and matters especially provided for in the charter or in treaties. It gives advisory opinions and renders judgments. In disputes between nations, the Court's decisions are binding only between parties concerned and in respect to a particular dispute. If any party to a case fails to heed a judgment, the other party may have recourse to the Security Council.

The 15 judges are elected for 9-year terms by the General Assembly and the Security Council. Retiring judges are eligible for reelection. The Court remains permanently in session, except during vacations. All questions are decided by a majority. The International Court of Justice sits in The Hague, Netherlands. **Website:** www.icj-cij.org

The text of the **UN Charter** may be obtained from the Public Inquiries Unit, Department of Public Information, United Nations, New York, NY 10017. (212) 963-4475. **Website:** www.un.org/aboutun/charter/index.html

Selected Specialized and Related Agencies

These specialized and related agencies are autonomous, with their own memberships and organs, and at the same time have a functional relationship or working agreement with the UN (headquarters), except for UNICEF and UNHCR, which report directly to the Economic and Social Council and to the General Assembly.

Food and Agriculture Organization (FAO) helps developing countries modernize farms, forests, and fisheries; improves food distribution and marketing; and educates on nutrition. (Viale delle Terme di Caracalla, 00100 Rome, Italy) **Website:** www.fao.org

International Atomic Energy Agency (IAEA) aims to promote safe, peaceful uses of atomic energy. (P.O. Box 100, Wagramer Strasse 5, A-1400, Vienna, Austria) **Website:** www.iaea.org

International Civil Aviation Org. (ICAO) promotes international civil aviation standards and regulations. (999 University St., Montreal, Quebec H3C 5H7, Canada) **Website:** www.icao.int

International Fund for Agricultural Development (IFAD) seeks to alleviate poverty in rural areas in developing countries. (Via del Serafico, 107, 00142 Rome, Italy) **Website:** www.ifad.org

International Labor Org. (ILO) aims to promote decent and productive employment practices, the improvement of labor conditions, social security, and vocational training. (4 route des Morillons, CH-1211 Geneva 22, Switzerland) **Website:** www.ilo.org

International Maritime Org. (IMO) aims to promote cooperation on technical matters affecting international shipping. (4 Albert Embankment, London, SE1 7SR, UK) **Website:** www.imo.org

International Monetary Fund (IMF) aims to promote international monetary cooperation, currency stabilization, and the expansion of international trade. (700 19th St. NW, Washington, DC 20431) **Website:** www.imf.org

International Telecommunication Union (ITU) regulates all aspects of global communication, including setting standards for radio, telegraph, telephone, and space radio-communications, and allocating radio frequencies. (Place des Nations, 1211 Geneva 20, Switzerland) **Website:** www.itu.int

Office of the High Commissioner for Human Rights (OHCHR) seeks to uphold human rights standards by monitoring areas of concern, investigating abuses, and working with gov. institutions to improve conditions. (1211 Geneva 10, Switzerland) **Website:** www.ohchr.org

United Nations Children's Fund (UNICEF) provides financial aid and development assistance to programs for children and mothers in developing countries. (3 United Nations Plaza, New York, NY 10017) **Website:** www.unicef.org

United Nations Educational, Scientific, and Cultural Org. (UNESCO) aims to promote collaboration among nations through education, science, and culture. After a 19-yr boycott, the United States rejoined the organization on Sept. 29, 2003. (7, Place de Fontenoy, 75352 Paris 07 SP, France) **Website:** www.unesco.org

United Nations High Commissioner for Refugees (UNHCR) provides essential assistance for refugees. (Case Postale 2500, CH-1211 Genève 2 Dépôt, Switzerland) **Website:** www.unhcr.ch

United Nations Industrial Development Org. (UNIDO) helps developing nations and those in transition pursue sustainable industrial development while promoting international industrial cooperation. (Vienna Intl. Centre, P.O. Box 300, Wagramerstr. 5, A-1400 Vienna, Austria) **Website:** www.unido.org

Universal Postal Union (UPU) aims to perfect postal services and promote international collaboration. (Case Postale 13, 3000 Berne 15, Switzerland) **Website:** www.upu.int

World Bank Group encompasses 2 development institutions and 3 affiliates focused on worldwide poverty reduction. The **International Bank for Reconstruction and Development (IBRD)** provides loans and technical assistance for projects in developing member countries and encourages co-financing for projects from other public and private sources. The **International Development Association (IDA)** provides funds for development projects on concessionary terms to the poorer developing member countries. The **International Finance Corporation (IFC)** promotes the growth of the private sector in developing member countries; encourages the development of local capital markets; and stimulates the international flow of private capital. The **Multilateral Investment Guarantee Agency (MIGA)** promotes investment in developing countries; guarantees investments to protect investors from noncommercial risks, such as nationalization; and advises governments on attracting private investment. The **International Center for Settlement of Investment Disputes (ICSID)** provides conciliation and arbitration services for disputes between foreign investors and host governments that arise out of an investment. (1818 H St. NW, Washington, DC 20433) **Website:** www.worldbank.org

World Health Org. (WHO) aims for the attainment of the highest possible level of health. (Avenue Appia 20, CH-1211 Geneva 27, Switzerland) **Website:** www.who.int

World Intellectual Property Org. (WIPO) seeks to protect, through international cooperation, literary, industrial, scientific, and artistic works. (34, Chemin des Colombettes, 1211 Geneva 20, Switzerland) **Website:** www.wipo.int

World Meteorological Org. (WMO) aims to coordinate and improve world meteorological work. (7bis, Avenue de la Paix, CP 2300, CH-1211 Geneva 2, Switzerland) **Website:** www.wmo.ch

World Tourism Org. (UNWTO) promotes responsible, sustainable, and universally accessible tourism with the aim of fostering economic development and international understanding. (Capitán Haya 42, 28020 Madrid, Spain) **Website:** www.unwto.org

World Trade Org. (WTO) replaces the General Agreement on Tariffs and Trade (GATT). It administers trade agreements and treaties between nations, examines the trade regimes of members, keeps track of various trade measures and statistics, and attempts to settle trade disputes. (Centre William Rappard, Rue de Lausanne 154, CH-1211 Geneva 21, Switzerland) **Website:** www.wto.org

Ongoing UN Peacekeeping Missions, 2007

Source: Dept. of Peacekeeping Operations, United Nations Secretariat, UN

(Year given is the year each mission began operation.)

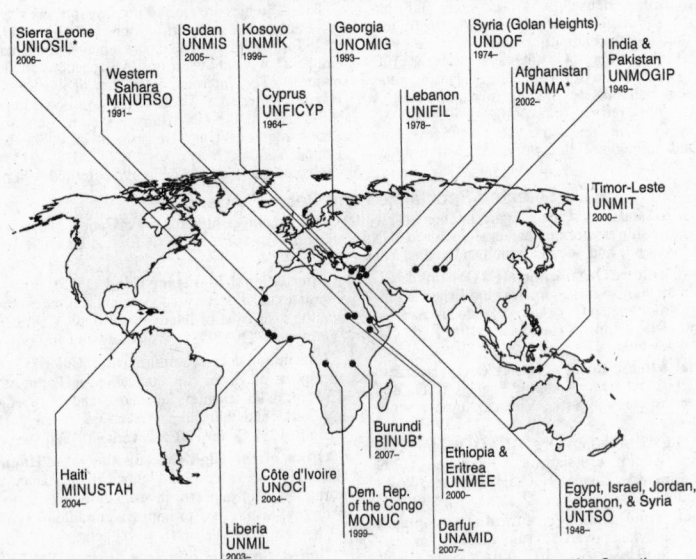

*Political or peacebuilding mission directed and supported by the Dept. of Peacekeeping Operations.

Peacekeeping personnel
As of Aug. 31, 2007

Military personnel and civilian police serving in peacekeeping operations	83,326[1]
Countries contributing military personnel and civilian police	117
International civilian personnel	4,824[1]
Local civilian personnel	11,185[1]
Total number of fatalities in peacekeeping operations since 1948	2,386[2]

(1) Not incl. statistics for 3 special political and/or peacebuilding missions (UNAMA, UNIOSIL, and BINUB). (2) Incl. fatalities for all UN peace operations.

Roster of the United Nations

The 192 members of the United Nations, with the years in which they became members; as of June 2006.

Member	Year	Member	Year	Member	Year	Member	Year
Afghanistan	1946	Dominica	1978	Libya	1955	Saint Vincent and the	1980
Albania	1955	Dominican Republic	1945	Liechtenstein	1990	Grenadines	
Algeria	1962	Ecuador	1945	Lithuania	1991	Samoa (formerly	1976
Andorra	1993	Egypt[3]	1945	Luxembourg	1945	Western Samoa)	
Angola	1976	El Salvador	1945	Macedonia[5]	1993	San Marino	1992
Antigua and Barbuda	1981	Equatorial Guinea	1968	Madagascar	1960	São Tomé and Príncipe	1975
Argentina	1945	Eritrea	1993	Malawi	1964	Saudi Arabia	1945
Armenia	1992	Estonia	1991	Malaysia[6]	1957	Senegal	1960
Australia	1945	Ethiopia	1945	Maldives	1965	Serbia[8,9]	1945
Austria	1955	Fiji	1970	Mali	1960	Seychelles	1976
Azerbaijan	1992	Finland	1955	Malta	1964	Sierra Leone	1961
Bahamas	1973	France	1945	Marshall Islands	1991	Singapore[6]	1965
Bahrain	1971	Gabon	1960	Mauritania	1961	Slovakia[2]	1993
Bangladesh	1974	Gambia, The	1965	Mauritius	1968	Slovenia	1992
Barbados	1966	Georgia	1992	Mexico	1945	Solomon Islands	1978
Belarus	1945	Germany	1973	Micronesia	1991	Somalia	1960
Belgium	1945	Ghana	1957	Moldova	1992	South Africa[10]	1945
Belize	1981	Greece	1945	Monaco	1993	Spain	1955
Benin	1960	Grenada	1974	Mongolia	1961	Sri Lanka	1955
Bhutan	1971	Guatemala	1945	Montenegro[8,9]	2006	Sudan	1956
Bolivia	1945	Guinea	1958	Morocco	1956	Suriname	1975
Bosnia & Herzegovina	1992	Guinea-Bissau	1974	Mozambique	1975	Swaziland	1968
Botswana	1966	Guyana	1966	Myanmar (Burma)	1948	Sweden	1946
Brazil	1945	Haiti	1945	Namibia	1990	Switzerland	2002
Brunei	1984	Honduras	1945	Nauru	1999	Syria[3]	1945
Bulgaria	1955	Hungary	1955	Nepal	1955	Tajikistan	1992
Burkina Faso	1960	Iceland	1946	Netherlands	1945	Tanzania[11]	1961
Burundi	1962	India	1945	New Zealand	1945	Thailand	1946
Cambodia	1955	Indonesia[4]	1950	Nicaragua	1945	Timor-Leste	2002
Cameroon	1960	Iran	1945	Niger	1960	Togo	1960
Canada	1945	Iraq	1945	Nigeria	1960	Tonga	1999
Cape Verde	1975	Ireland	1955	Norway	1945	Trinidad and Tobago	1962
Central African Rep.	1960	Israel	1949	Oman	1971	Tunisia	1956
Chad	1960	Italy	1955	Pakistan	1947	Turkey	1945
Chile	1945	Jamaica	1962	Palau	1994	Turkmenistan	1992
China[1]	1945	Japan	1956	Panama	1945	Tuvalu	2000
Colombia	1945	Jordan	1955	Papua New Guinea	1975	Uganda	1962
Comoros	1975	Kazakhstan	1992	Paraguay	1945	Ukraine	1945
Congo, Democratic	1960	Kenya	1963	Peru	1945	United Arab Emirates	1971
Rep. of the (Zaire)		Kiribati	1999	Philippines	1945	United Kingdom	1945
Congo, Republic of the.	1960	Korea, North	1991	Poland	1945	United States	1945
Costa Rica	1945	Korea, South	1991	Portugal	1955	Uruguay	1945
Côte d'Ivoire	1960	Kuwait	1963	Qatar	1971	Uzbekistan	1992
Croatia	1992	Kyrgyzstan	1992	Romania	1955	Vanuatu	1981
Cuba	1945	Laos	1955	Russia[7]	1945	Venezuela	1945
Cyprus	1960	Latvia	1991	Rwanda	1962	Vietnam	1977
Czech Republic[2]	1993	Lebanon	1945	Saint Kitts and Nevis	1983	Yemen[12]	1947
Denmark	1945	Lesotho	1966	Saint Lucia	1979	Zambia	1964
Djibouti	1977	Liberia	1945			Zimbabwe	1980

(1) The General Assembly voted in 1971 to expel the Chinese government in Taiwan and admit the Beijing government. (2) Czechoslovakia, which split into Czech Republic and Slovakia on Jan. 1, 1993, was a UN member 1945-1992. (3) Egypt and Syria were original members. In 1958, the United Arab Republic was established by a union of Egypt and Syria and continued as one single member of the UN. In 1961, Syria resumed separate membership. (4) Indonesia withdrew from the UN in 1965 and rejoined in 1966. (5) Admitted under the provisional name of The Former Yugoslav Republic of Macedonia. (6) Malaya joined the UN in 1957. In 1963, its name was changed to Malaysia following the accession of Singapore, Sabah, and Sarawak. Singapore became an independent UN member in 1965. (7) The USSR was an original member from 1945. After the USSR's dissolution in 1991, Russia informed the UN it would continue the USSR's membership in the Security Council and all other UN organs with the support of the Commonwealth of Independent States (comprising most of the former Soviet republics). (8) The Socialist Federal Republic of Yugoslavia became a member in 1945. After 4 of its 6 republics (Bosnia and Herzegovina, Croatia, Macedonia, and Slovenia) declared independence in 1991-92, the 2 remaining republics, Montenegro and Serbia, reconstituted themselves as the Federal Republic of Yugoslavia, assuming Yugoslavia's UN seat Apr. 8, 1992. In Sept. 1992, the General Assembly decided the Federal Republic of Yugoslavia could not automatically take the seat of the former Yugoslavia. Membership was granted in Nov. 2000 by a General Assembly vote. In Feb. 2003, Yugoslavia changed its name to Serbia and Montenegro. (9) After Montenegro declared independence in June 2006, Serbia continued the membership of the State Union of Serbia and Montenegro. Montenegro was admitted as a UN member later the same month. (10) In June 1994, the General Assembly admitted the South African delegation after it was suspended from participation in 1974 because of apartheid. (11) Tanganyika was a member from 1961 and Zanzibar from 1963. Following the 1964 ratification of Articles of Union between Tanganyika and Zanzibar, the United Republic of Tanganyika and Zanzibar continued as a single UN member, later changing its name to the United Republic of Tanzania. (12) The Yemen Arab Republic was admitted in 1947; the People's Republic of Yemen, in 1967. The 2 nations merged in 1990. **Note:** Vatican City and China (Taiwan) are not members. Vatican City is a permanent observer. Taiwan's bid for UN membership was rejected for the 15th consecutive year in Sept. 2007.

U.S. Representatives to the United Nations

The U.S. Representative to the United Nations is the chief of the U.S. Mission to the United Nations in New York and holds the rank and status of Ambassador Extraordinary and Plenipotentiary (A.E.P.) Year given is the year each took office.

Year	Representative	Year	Representative	Year	Representative	Year	Representative
1946	Edward R. Stettinius, Jr.	1969	Charles W. Yost	1989	Thomas R. Pickering	2004	John C. Danforth
1946	Herschel V. Johnson (act.)	1971	George H. W. Bush	1992	Edward J. Perkins	2005	Anne W. Patterson (act.)
1947	Warren R. Austin	1973	John A. Scali	1993	Madeleine K. Albright	2005	John R. Bolton
1953	Henry Cabot Lodge, Jr.	1975	Daniel P. Moynihan	1997	Bill Richardson	2006	Alejandro D. Wolff (act.)
1960	James J. Wadsworth	1976	William W. Scranton	1998	A. Peter Burleigh (act.)	2007	Zalmay M. Khalilzad
1961	Adlai E. Stevenson	1977	Andrew Young	1999	Richard C. Holbrooke		
1965	Arthur J. Goldberg	1979	Donald McHenry	2001	James B. Cunningham		
1968	George W. Ball	1981	Jeane J. Kirkpatrick		(act.)		
1968	James Russell Wiggins	1985	Vernon A. Walters	2001	John D. Negroponte		

International Criminal Court (ICC)

The International Criminal Court was created when 120 nations signed the Rome Statute on July 17, 1998. Its mission is to try individuals accused of genocide, war crimes, or other crimes against humanity, as has been undertaken in the past by temporary tribunals. The statute came into force July 1, 2002, 60 days after the 60th nation ratified it. As of Jan. 1, 2007, 104 nations were members of the ICC. China, Japan, Russia, and the U.S., however, had not joined. The U.S. expressed opposition to some provisions of the ICC, mainly regarding liability of its military in peacekeeping situations.

The ICC, unlike the World Court, is not part of the UN, but an independent international agency with its own budget and administration. It consists of 18 judges elected by member nations. An absolute majority of these 18 judges elect 3 from among themselves to serve as president, 1st vice president, and 2nd vice president in 3-year, renewable terms. A Registry handles the nonjudicial aspects of administration. The Office of the Prosecutor reviews, investigates, and, prosecutes cases referred to it by a state or by the UN Security Council.

The ICC prosecutor has opened investigations into the situations in Uganda, the Dem. Rep. of the Congo, Darfur, Sudan, and most recently, the Central African Republic.

Though jurisdiction is limited to member nations, the ICC is a court of last resort. It may also initiate cases involving non-member nations if it deems the country's authorities have not taken steps to investigate or prosecute a case. The ICC is based in The Hague, Netherlands, though it may sit elsewhere. Website: www.icc-cpi.int

Geneva Conventions

The Geneva Conventions are 4 international treaties governing the protection of civilians in time of war, the treatment of prisoners of war, and the care of the wounded and sick in the armed forces. The first convention, covering the sick and wounded in war, was concluded in Geneva, Switzerland, in 1864; it was amended and expanded in 1906. In 1929, two more conventions covering the wounded and prisoners of war were signed. Outrage at the treatment of prisoners and civilians during WWII by some belligerents, notably Germany and Japan, prompted the conclusion, in Aug. 1949, of 4 new conventions. Three of these restated and strengthened the previous conventions, and the fourth codified general principles of international law governing the treatment of civilians in wartime.

The 1949 convention for civilians provided for special safeguards for wounded persons, children under 15 years of age, pregnant women, and the elderly. Discrimination on racial, religious, national, or political grounds was forbidden. Torture, collective punishment, reprisals, unwarranted destruction of property, and forced use of civilians for an occupier's armed forces were also prohibited. Also included was a pledge to treat prisoners humanely, feed them adequately, and deliver relief supplies to them. They were not to be forced to disclose more than minimal information. Two additional protocols were adopted in June 1977 dealing with the protection of victims, especially civilians, in international and non-international armed conflicts.

Most countries have formally accepted all or most of the humanitarian conventions as binding. However, there is no permanent machinery in place to apprehend, try, or punish violators.

Genocide

by Aram A. Schvey, former Crowley Fellow and Adjunct Professor at Fordham University School of Law

Source: Convention on the Prevention and Punishment of the Crime of Genocide, United Nations Treaty Series 277; Rome Statute of the International Criminal Court

The term "genocide" (literally "murder of a race") was coined by Prof. Raphael Lemkin (1900-59) in 1944 and refers to the intentional destruction or attempted destruction of a national, ethnic, racial, or religious group, whether in wartime or peacetime. Genocide is defined as killing members of the group, causing serious bodily harm to members of the group, or otherwise attempting to bring about its destruction, including preventing births or transferring children away from the group. Although the legal definition of genocide does not extend to political groups, the term is often used colloquially to refer to large-scale political violence.

The prohibition against genocide is part of customary international law and is codified in the Convention on the Prevention and Punishment of the Crime of Genocide ("Genocide Convention"), entered into force on Jan. 12, 1951. Today, more than 130 nations, including the U.S., are parties to it. Genocide is also prohibited by the domestic laws of many nations.

The first modern trials for genocide were conducted by the Allies after WWII. Although the charter of the Nuremberg Tribunal (the international court set up to try Nazi war criminals) did not use the term "genocide," its definition of "crimes against humanity" included persecution on racial or religious grounds. More recently, the UN Security Council created ad hoc tribunals to try those responsible for genocide and other serious crimes in the former Yugoslavia and in Rwanda. The International Criminal Court (ICC), which began functioning July 1, 2002, also has jurisdiction to try perpetrators of genocide. In Mar. 2005, the Security Council referred the situation in Darfur, Sudan, to the ICC prosecutor.

Examples of Genocides Since 1900

Year	Event	Location	Est. deaths
1915	Extermination of Armenians by the Young Turks	Turkey/Ottoman Empire	1,000,000+
1930s	Intentional infliction of famine on Ukraine	Soviet Union (Ukraine)	6,000,000-7,000,000
1933-45	Attempted destruction of European Jewry (Holocaust)	Europe	6,000,000
1975-79	Khmer Rouge campaign of extermination under Pol Pot	Cambodia	1,500,000-2,000,000
1988	Anfal Campaign (named by the Iraqi government) against Iraqi Kurds	Iraq	100,000-200,000
1992-95	Ethnic killings during the breakup of Yugoslavia, chiefly Serbs against Bosnian Muslims	Bosnia-Herzegovina, Serbia, Croatia	200,000
1994	Hutu massacre of Tutsis	Rwanda	800,000
2003-present	Rebel group and government-backed Arab militia attacks on non-Arab southern tribes, black population[1]	Darfur region, Sudan	200,000-400,000

Note: Estimates based on historical evidence. The legal definition of "genocide" does not include politically motivated mass killings. Therefore, instances of mass violence against political or class enemies, such as Josef Stalin's purges in the 1930s, which killed some 20 mil Soviets, and Mao Zedong's Cultural Revolution, which killed several mil Chinese, are not included. The mass killings of an estimated 1.7 mil during Cambodia's Khmer Rouge regime are often spoken of as a genocide, despite the fact that many of the murders were politically or class motivated. (1) In Oct. 2004, the UN sec. gen. established a commission to determine whether genocide was occurring in Darfur. Although the commission concluded that the "international offenses ... that have been committed in Darfur may be no less serious and heinous than genocide," it did not term the situation there a genocide.

SPORTS

SPORTS HIGHLIGHTS OF 2007

Led by Troy Smith, their Heisman Trophy-winning quarterback, Ohio State went undefeated during the 2006 college football season. The Buckeyes seemed poised to claim the national title, but the **2007 BCS National Championship Game** (held in Glendale, AZ, on Jan. 8) delivered a shocker: The #2-ranked Florida Gators overwhelmed the heavily favored Buckeyes, 41-14. Florida was not even expected to play for the championship, but the Gators moved up in the rankings when #2 USC was upset by cross-town rival UCLA during the final week of the regular season.

Before 2007, no African American coach had ever taken a team to the Super Bowl, but both contenders in **Super Bowl XLI** were led by black coaches. Playing through the rain in Miami on Feb. 4, Tony Dungy's Indianapolis Colts scored a decisive victory against Lovie Smith's Chicago Bears, winning 29-17. Colts quarterback Peyton Manning turned in a sterling performance to win the game's MVP honors.

Already national champions of college football, the Univ. of Florida achieved a rare feat by also winning the **NCAA men's basketball championship** in Atlanta on April 2. In a bizarre twist, the Gators handed Ohio State losses in the finals of both sports. By taking down the Buckeyes, 84-75, Florida successfully defended its 2006 title. Florida's Corey Brewer was named the most outstanding player of the Men's Final Four.

Cleveland hosted the Final Four of the **NCAA women's basketball tournament.** Tennessee defeated Rutgers in the April 3 final by a score of 59-46. The Lady Vols were led by Candace Parker, who was honored as the Final Four's most outstanding player.

The winner of the 2006 Kentucky Derby, **Barbaro,** died on Jan. 29, 2007. After shattering his leg during the 2006 Preakness, the horse appeared to make an unlikely recovery, but he ultimately succumbed to complications from his catastrophic injury.

Street Sense, the favorite, raced to the winner's circle of the 133rd **Kentucky Derby**. But 2007 did not produce a Triple Crown winner, as Curlin staged a thrilling late surge to edge out Street Sense in the **Preakness**. In the **Belmont Stakes,** Rags to Riches sprinted past Curlin, becoming the first filly to win since 1905.

Baseball salaries continued to climb in 2007. Before the season began, the Boston Red Sox paid more than $51 million for the right to negotiate with Japanese pitcher Daisuke Matsuzaka; they ultimately signed him to a six-year, $52 million contract. After a disastrous start to their season, the New York Yankees signed the veteran Roger Clemens to a prorated $28 million contract, making him the highest-paid pitcher in baseball history. The team later staged a remarkable comeback, but Clemens was not a major factor.

Anaheim won the first **Stanley Cup** in the 14-year history of its NHL franchise on June 6. The Ducks breezed past the Ottawa Senators in the championship series, 4 games to 1, with a decisive 6-2 win on home ice in the final game. Team captain Scott Niedermayer received the Conn Smythe Trophy as the most valuable player of the NHL postseason.

Unheralded Zach Johnson upset Tiger Woods to take the green jacket at **The Masters** on April 8. Angel Cabrera was a surprise winner at the June 17 **U.S. Open,** which was played at Pennsylvania's Oakmont Country Club. On July 22, Padraig Harrington edged out Sergio Garcia to win the **British Open**. But Tiger Woods dominated the golf world for much of 2007, winning the **PGA Championship** at the Southern Hills Country Club in Tulsa, OK, on Aug. 12. Tiger's seven tournament victories in 2007 earned him the inaugural $10 million FedExCup for winning the PGA Tour's new playoff system.

On April 15, baseball celebrated the **60th anniversary of Jackie Robinson's debut** in the major leagues, which broke the sport's color barrier. More than 200 players wore number 42 as a tribute to Robinson.

The San Antonio Spurs completed a sweep of the Cleveland Cavaliers on June 14 to claim their fourth **NBA championship.** Tony Parker became the first European player to be named Finals MVP. In August, the league was roiled by scandal as referee Tim Donaghy pleaded guilty to two felony counts related to organized gambling.

Major League Soccer, eager to attract a wider U.S. audience, began the year with a splash, as the Los Angeles Galaxy signed **David Beckham** to a five-year contract worth some $250 million. Despite the media hoopla surrounding his arrival in July, Beckham's first season was disappointingly marred by injury.

On July 17, a federal grand jury indicted Atlanta Falcons quarterback **Michael Vick** on multiple felony counts for his involvement in an organized dog-fighting ring. Details of the case, including tales of animal cruelty, provoked a storm of protest. In August, Vick accepted a plea bargain, and NFL Commissioner Roger Goodell suspended him indefinitely. Vick was to be sentenced on federal charges in Dec. 2007.

The **Tour de France** descended into near-chaos in July over allegations of doping and cheating. Pre-race favorite Alexander Vinokourov and race leader Michael Rasmussen were both forced to withdraw from competition, and a group of young riders interrupted the race to protest corruption in cycling. The relentless scandals overshadowed the July 29 Tour victory by Spaniard Alberto Contador of the Discovery Channel team. Capping the sad affair in September was the decision by an arbitration panel to formally strip 2006 Tour winner Floyd Landis of his title for doping.

On Aug. 7, San Francisco Giants left fielder Barry Bonds hit the 756th homer of his career, breaking Major League Baseball's **all-time home-run record,** held for 31 years by Hank Aaron. The achievement remained tainted in the eyes of many baseball fans, since Bonds had been dogged by persistent rumors of steroid use. Major League Baseball grappled with the issue of performance-enhancing drugs throughout 2007, as the names of several players were leaked in conjunction with drug investigations. While Tony Gwynn and Cal Ripken Jr., were voted into the Hall of Fame by landslide margins, slugger Mark McGwire was denied a ticket to Cooperstown, presumably on the basis of steroid suspicions.

Roger Federer continued to dominate men's tennis by winning the Australian Open, Wimbledon, and the U.S. Open. But Federer missed out on the Grand Slam by losing the French Open to Rafael Nadal, who won the tournament for the third consecutive year. On the women's side, Serena Williams prevailed in the Australian Open, Venus Williams took the crown at Wimbledon, and Justine Henin emerged victorious at both the French and U.S. Opens.

World Almanac Editors' Picks
Memorable Moments in Sports History Since 1950

Amazing Final Plays

The Shot Heard 'Round the World
Oct. 3, 1951: National League Championship, New York Giants vs. Brooklyn Dodgers

Entering the 3-game playoff series with identical 96-58 records, the Giants and Dodgers took one game each—the Giants winning Game 1 at Ebbets Field; the Dodgers shutting them out in Game 2 at the Polo Grounds. In Game 3, the Dodgers scored one run in the first inning and three more in the eighth; entering the bottom of the ninth, the Giants had only one run on the board. But the team rallied, bringing in one more run and landing two more men on base as third baseman Bobby Thomson stepped up to the plate. He took the first pitch for a strike, then ripped the second into left field, clearing the fence for a three-run, walk-off homer—an unbelievable win for a team that had trailed the Dodgers by 13 1/2 games less than two months earlier.

The Immaculate Reception
Dec. 23, 1972: AFC divisional playoffs, Pittsburgh Steelers vs. Oakland Raiders

With 22 seconds on the clock and no time-outs, facing 4th-and-10 on their own 40-yard line, the Steelers trailed 7-6. Steelers quarterback Terry Bradshaw launched a pass at John "Frenchy" Fuqua, but Raiders safety Jack Tatum knocked Fuqua down just as the ball reached him; the ball bounced backward off the players and was caught by Steelers running back Franco Harris, who ran in the game-winning touchdown with five seconds remaining. Steelers fans swarmed the field while officials debated how to call the play; if the ball bounced off Fuqua, or if it touched the ground before Harris snared it, the reception would be illegal. The Steelers were finally awarded the touchdown, made the conversion, and won the game 13-7.

Secretariat's Record-Breaking Triple Crown
June 9, 1973: The Belmont Stakes

Secretariat kicked off 1973's Triple Crown season by setting a new record at the Kentucky Derby (1:59 2/5), then winning the Preakness by 2 1/2 lengths. Timing errors at the latter delayed the reporting of his official time, listed by Preakness officials as 1:54 2/5. At the Belmont Stakes, Secretariat and Sham, his second-place challenger in the first two races, opened an immediate lead on their competitors—but Secretariat surged even further ahead after the halfway mark. Hitting the stretch, he had a lead of nearly 20 lengths, then opened it even wider before crossing the wire with a still-standing 1 1/2-mile dirt track record of 2:24 (more than 1 2/5 seconds faster than any other horse has run). Later review of race videotapes marked Secretariat's winning lead at an unimaginable 31 lengths.

"The Band is on the Field"
November 20, 1982: Univ. of California v. Stanford

With four seconds left on the clock, Stanford took the lead (20-19) with a field goal. On the last-second kickoff return California players charged down the field, as the Stanford marching band ran out to celebrate. California players shot five lateral passes, ending with Cal's Kevin Moen, who scored the game-winning touchdown by charging through the middle of the band—and knocking down Stanford trombone player Gary Tyrrell.

Strug's One-Legged Vault
July 23, 1996: Summer Olympics, Women's Team Gymnastics

In the final rotation, the U.S. team was leading Russia by a respectable margin—but U.S. gymnast Dominique Moceanu fell on both of her vaults, leading teammate Kerri Strug (and her coaches) to believe that she needed a sensational vault to seal the team's victory. Strug injured her ankle on her first attempt, but limped back to the start and landed her second vault on one foot, picking up a score of 9.712. Final results showed that the U.S. would have won even without Strug's performance.

Embarrassing Moments

Leon Lett (Dallas Cowboys), January 31, 1993

Late in the fourth quarter of Super Bowl XXVII, with an enormous (52-17) Dallas lead over the Buffalo Bills, Lett recovered a fumble and ran for what appeared to be an easy touchdown. As he approached the end zone, he raised his arms in victory—allowing Bills' wide receiver Don Beebe to knock the ball out of his hand, into the end zone, and out of bounds for a touchback.

Jose Canseco (Texas Rangers), May 26, 1993

Playing right field against the Cleveland Indians, Canseco lost a fly ball (hit by Carlos Martinez) in the lights. The ball bounced off Canseco's head and over the wall, for a home run. The Harrisburg Heat pro soccer team jokingly offered Canseco a contract the next day, citing his "great potential for the head ball."

Larry Walker (Montreal Expos), April 24, 1994

Playing the L.A. Dodgers, with one out and a runner on first, Walker caught a fly ball—but thinking it was the third out, he gave the ball to a boy in the stands and started walking to the dugout. When Walker realized his error a few seconds later, the boy handed over the ball, allowing Walker to stop the runner at third.

Mike Tyson (vs. Evander Holyfield), June 28, 1997

In what he later described as retribution for a second-round head butt, Tyson bit off a chunk of Holyfield's right ear, and then attacked Holyfield from behind as he walked to his corner. After a brief delay, referee Mills Lane penalized Tyson two points but allowed the fight to continue—only to stop it again moments later when Tyson ripped an even larger chunk out of Holyfield's left ear, bringing the fight to an ugly close.

"The Super Bowl Shuffle" (Chicago Bears), 1985

Prior to their winning appearance in Super Bowl XX (played in 1986), members of the Chicago Bears, including Walter Payton and William "Refrigerator" Perry, recorded the first-ever rap song and music video performed by a pro sports team. The song garnered a Grammy nomination for best R&B Group Vocal Performance—despite cringe-inducing lines like Willie Gault's "Now I'm as smooth as a chocolate swirl / I dance a little funky, so watch me girl." or Steve Fuller's "I'm not here to feather his ruffle / I just came here to do The Super Bowl Shuffle." Fortunately, the "shufflin' crew" donated the profits from the song and video to charity.

OLYMPICS

2008 Summer Olympic Games

Beijing, China, Aug. 8-24, 2008

In 2008, an estimated 10,708 athletes were expected to compete in 302 events in 28 different sports in the 29th Summer Olympiad. Of the events, 165 were men's, 127 were women's, and 10 were mixed (e.g. mixed doubles in tennis and badminton).

The number of planned events is not substantially different from that of the 2004 Olympiad (301 events), but individual changes have been made to events in various sports. Swimming will include a 10-km long-distance event, known as the marathon, for both men and women. In men's cycling, a BMX (bicycle moto-cross) event is expected to debut. In track and field, women will compete in the 3,000-m steeplechase for the first time.

The official 2008 Olympiad slogan is "One World, One Dream." The Games' official mascots are Fuwa, five distinct characters—with colors inspired by the Olympic rings—whose abbreviated names can be combined to equal the phrase, "Welcome to Beijing," in Mandarin Chinese: *Bei Jing Huan Ying Ni.*

Summer Olympic Games Champions, 1896-2004

(*indicates Olympic record; (w) indicates wind-aided)

The 1980 games were boycotted by 62 nations, including the U.S. The 1984 games were boycotted by the USSR and most Eastern bloc nations. E and W Germany competed separately, 1968-88. The 1992 Unified Team consisted of 12 former Soviet republics. The 1992 Independent Olympic Participants (I.O.P.) were from Serbia, Montenegro, and Macedonia.

Track and Field—Men

100-Meter Run	Time
1896 Thomas Burke, United States	12.0s
1900 Francis W. Jarvis, United States	11.0s
1904 Archie Hahn, United States	11.0s
1908 Reginald Walker, South Africa	10.8s
1912 Ralph Craig, United States	10.8s
1920 Charles Paddock, United States	10.8s
1924 Harold Abrahams, Great Britain	10.6s
1928 Percy Williams, Canada	10.8s
1932 Eddie Tolan, United States	10.3s
1936 Jesse Owens, United States	10.3s
1948 Harrison Dillard, United States	10.3s
1952 Lindy Remigino, United States	10.4s
1956 Bobby Morrow, United States	10.5s
1960 Armin Hary, Germany	10.2s
1964 Bob Hayes, United States	10.0s
1968 Jim Hines, United States	9.95s
1972 Valery Borzov, USSR	10.14s
1976 Hasely Crawford, Trinidad	10.06s
1980 Allan Wells, Great Britain	10.25s
1984 Carl Lewis, United States	9.99s
1988 Carl Lewis, United States	9.92s
1992 Linford Christie, Great Britain	9.96s
1996 Donovan Bailey, Canada	9.84s*
2000 Maurice Greene, United States	9.87s
2004 Justin Gatlin, United States	9.85s

200-Meter Run	Time
1900 Walter Tewksbury, United States	22.2s
1904 Archie Hahn, United States	21.6s
1908 Robert Kerr, Canada	22.6s
1912 Ralph Craig, United States	21.7s
1920 Allan Woodring, United States	22.0s
1924 Jackson Scholz, United States	21.6s
1928 Percy Williams, Canada	21.8s
1932 Eddie Tolan, United States	21.2s
1936 Jesse Owens, United States	20.7s
1948 Mel Patton, United States	21.1s
1952 Andrew Stanfield, United States	20.7s
1956 Bobby Morrow, United States	20.6s
1960 Livio Berruti, Italy	20.5s
1964 Henry Carr, United States	20.3s
1968 Tommie Smith, United States	19.83s
1972 Valeri Borzov, USSR	20.00s
1976 Donald Quarrie, Jamaica	20.23s
1980 Pietro Mennea, Italy	20.19s
1984 Carl Lewis, United States	19.80s
1988 Joe DeLoach, United States	19.75s
1992 Mike Marsh, United States	20.01s
1996 Michael Johnson, United States	19.32s*
2000 Konstantinos Kenteris, Greece	20.09s
2004 Shawn Crawford, United States	19.79s

400-Meter Run	Time
1896 Thomas Burke, United States	54.2s
1900 Maxey Long, United States	49.4s
1904 Harry Hillman, United States	49.2s
1908 Wyndham Halswelle, Great Brit., walkover	50.0s
1912 Charles Reidpath, United States	48.2s
1920 Bevil Rudd, South Africa	49.6s
1924 Eric Liddell, Great Britain	47.6s
1928 Ray Barbuti, United States	47.8s
1932 William Carr, United States	46.2s

400-Meter Run	Time
1936 Archie Williams, United States	46.5s
1948 Arthur Wint, Jamaica	46.2s
1952 George Rhoden, Jamaica	45.9s
1956 Charles Jenkins, United States	46.7s
1960 Otis Davis, United States	44.9s
1964 Michael Larrabee, United States	45.1s
1968 Lee Evans, United States	43.86s
1972 Vincent Matthews, United States	44.66s
1976 Alberto Juantorena, Cuba	44.26s
1980 Viktor Markin, USSR	44.60s
1984 Alonzo Babers, United States	44.27s
1988 Steven Lewis, United States	43.87s
1992 Quincy Watts, United States	43.50s
1996 Michael Johnson, United States	43.49s*
2000 Michael Johnson, United States	43.84s
2004 Jeremy Wariner, United States	44.00s

800-Meter Run	Time
1896 Edwin Flack, Australia	2m.11s
1900 Alfred Tysoe, Great Britain	2m.1.2s
1904 James Lightbody, United States	1m. 56s
1908 Mel Sheppard, United States	1m. 52.8s
1912 James Meredith, United States	1m. 51.9s
1920 Albert Hill, Great Britain	1m. 53.4s
1924 Douglas Lowe, Great Britain	1m. 52.4s
1928 Douglas Lowe, Great Britain	1m. 51.8s
1932 Thomas Hampson, Great Britain	1m. 49.8s
1936 John Woodruff, United States	1m. 52.9s
1948 Mal Whitfield, United States	1m. 49.2s
1952 Mal Whitfield, United States	1m. 49.2s
1956 Thomas Courtney, United States	1m. 47.7s
1960 Peter Snell, New Zealand	1m. 46.3s
1964 Peter Snell, New Zealand	1m. 45.1s
1968 Ralph Doubell, Australia	1m. 44.3s
1972 Dave Wottle, United States	1m. 45.9s
1976 Alberto Juantorena, Cuba	1m. 43.50s
1980 Steve Ovett, Great Britain	1m. 45.40s
1984 Joaquim Cruz, Brazil	1m. 43.00s
1988 Paul Ereng, Kenya	1m. 43.45s
1992 William Tanui, Kenya	1m. 43.66s
1996 Vebjoern Rodal, Norway	1m. 42.58s*
2000 Nils Schumann, Germany	1m. 45.08s
2004 Yuriy Borzakovskiy, Russia	1m. 44.45s

1,500-Meter Run	Time
1896 Edwin Flack, Australia	4m. 33.2s
1900 Charles Bennett, Great Britain	4m. 6.2s
1904 James Lightbody, United States	4m. 5.4s
1908 Mel Sheppard, United States	4m. 3.4s
1912 Arnold Jackson, Great Britain	3m. 56.8s
1920 Albert Hill, Great Britain	4m. 1.8s
1924 Paavo Nurmi, Finland	3m. 53.6s
1928 Harry Larva, Finland	3m. 53.2s
1932 Luigi Beccali, Italy	3m. 51.2s
1936 Jack Lovelock, New Zealand	3m. 47.8s
1948 Henri Eriksson, Sweden	3m. 49.8s
1952 Joseph Barthel, Luxembourg	3m. 45.2s
1956 Ron Delany, Ireland	3m. 41.2s
1960 Herb Elliott, Australia	3m. 35.6s
1964 Peter Snell, New Zealand	3m. 38.1s
1968 Kipchoge Keino, Kenya	3m. 34.9s
1972 Pekka Vasala, Finland	3m. 36.3s
1976 John Walker, New Zealand	3m. 39.17s

1,500-Meter Run	Time
1980 Sebastian Coe, Great Britain	3m. 38.4s
1984 Sebastian Coe, Great Britain	3m. 32.53s
1988 Peter Rono, Kenya	3m. 35.96s
1992 Fermin Cacho Ruiz, Spain	3m. 40.12s
1996 Noureddine Morceli, Algeria	3m. 35.78s
2000 Noah Ngeny, Kenya	3m. 32.07s*
2004 Hicham el-Guerrouj, Morocco	3m. 34.18s

5,000-Meter Run	Time
1912 Hannes Kolehmainen, Finland	14m. 36.6s
1920 Joseph Guillemot, France	14m. 55.6s
1924 Paavo Nurmi, Finlands	14m. 31.2s
1928 Willie Ritola, Finland	14m. 38s
1932 Lauri Lehtinen, Finland	14m. 30s
1936 Gunnar Hockert, Finland	14m. 22.2s
1948 Gaston Reiff, Belgium	14m. 17.6s
1952 Emil Zatopek, Czechoslovakia	14m. 6.6s
1956 Vladimir Kuts, USSR	13m. 39.6s
1960 Murray Halberg, New Zealand	13m. 43.4s
1964 Bob Schul, United States	13m. 48.8s
1968 Mohamed Gammoudi, Tunisia	14m. 05.0s
1972 Lasse Viren, Finland	13m. 26.4s
1976 Lasse Viren, Finland	13m. 24.76s
1980 Miruts Yifter, Ethiopia	13m. 21.0s
1984 Said Aouita, Morocco	13m. 05.59s*
1988 John Ngugi, Kenya	13m. 11.70s
1992 Dieter Baumann, Germany	13m. 12.52s
1996 Venuste Niyongabo, Burundi	13m. 07.96s
2000 Million Wolde, Ethiopia	13m. 35.49s
2004 Hicham el-Guerrouj, Morocco	13m. 14.39s

10,000-Meter Run	Time
1912 Hannes Kolehmainen, Finland	31m. 20.8s
1920 Paavo Nurmi, Finland	31m. 45.8s
1924 Willie Ritola, Finland	30m. 23.2s
1928 Paavo Nurmi, Finland	30m. 18.8s
1932 Janusz Kusocinski, Poland	30m. 11.4s
1936 Ilmari Salminen, Finland	30m. 15.4s
1948 Emil Zatopek, Czechoslovakia	29m. 59.6s
1952 Emil Zatopek, Czechoslovakia	29m. 17.0s
1956 Vladimir Kuts, USSR	28m. 45.6s
1960 Pyotr Bolotnikov, USSR	28m. 32.2s
1964 Billy Mills, United States	28m. 24.4s
1968 Naftali Temu, Kenya	29m. 27.4s
1972 Lasse Viren, Finland	27m. 38.4s
1976 Lasse Viren, Finland	27m. 40.4s
1980 Miruts Yifter, Ethiopia	27m. 42.7s
1984 Alberto Cova, Italy	27m. 47.54s
1988 Brahim Boutaib, Morocco	27m. 21.46s
1992 Khalid Skah, Morocco	27m. 46.70s
1996 Haile Gebrselassie, Ethiopia	27m. 07.34s
2000 Haile Gebrselassie, Ethiopia	27m. 18.20s
2004 Kenenisa Bekele, Ethiopia	27m. 05.10s*

110-Meter Hurdles	Time
1896 Thomas Curtis, United States	17.6s
1900 Alvin Kraenzlein, United States	15.4s
1904 Frederick Schule, United States	16.0s
1908 Forrest Smithson, United States	15.0s
1912 Frederick Kelly, United States	15.1s
1920 Earl Thomson, Canada	14.8s
1924 Daniel Kinsey, United States	15.0s
1928 Sydney Atkinson, South Africa	14.8s
1932 George Saling, United States	14.6s
1936 Forrest Towns, United States	14.2s
1948 William Porter, United States	13.9s
1952 Harrison Dillard, United States	13.7s
1956 Lee Calhoun, United States	13.5s
1960 Lee Calhoun, United States	13.8s
1964 Hayes Jones, United States	13.6s
1968 Willie Davenport, United States	13.33s
1972 Rod Milburn, United States	13.24s
1976 Guy Drut, France	13.30s
1980 Thomas Munkelt, E. Germany	13.39s
1984 Roger Kingdom, United States	13.20s
1988 Roger Kingdom, United States	12.98s
1992 Mark McCoy, Canada	13.12s
1996 Allen Johnson, United States	12.95s
2000 Anier Garcia, Cuba	13.00s
2004 Liu Xiang, China	12.91s*

400-Meter Hurdles	Time
1900 J.W.B. Tewksbury, United States	57.6s
1904 Harry Hillman, United States	53.0s
1908 Charles Bacon, United States	55.0s
1920 Frank Loomis, United States	54.0s
1924 F. Morgan Taylor, United States	52.6s
1928 Lord Burghley, Great Britain	53.4s

400-Meter Hurdles	Time
1932 Robert Tisdall, Ireland	51.7s
1936 Glenn Hardin, United States	52.4s
1948 Roy Cochran, United States	51.1s
1952 Charles Moore, United States	50.8s
1956 Glenn Davis, United States	50.1s
1960 Glenn Davis, United States	49.3s
1964 Rex Cawley, United States	49.6s
1968 Dave Hemery, Great Britain	48.12s
1972 John Akii-Bua, Uganda	47.82s
1976 Edwin Moses, United States	47.64s
1980 Volker Beck, E. Germany	48.70s
1984 Edwin Moses, United States	47.75s
1988 Andre Phillips, United States	47.19s
1992 Kevin Young, United States	46.78s*
1996 Derrick Adkins, United States	47.54s
2000 Angelo Taylor, United States	47.50s
2004 Felix Sanchez, Dominican Republic	47.63s

400-Meter Relay	Time
1912 Great Britain	42.4s
1920 United States	42.2s
1924 United States	41.0s
1928 United States	41.0s
1932 United States	40.0s
1936 United States	39.8s
1948 United States	40.6s
1952 United States	40.1s
1956 United States	39.5s
1960 Germany (U.S. disqualified)	39.5s
1964 United States	39.0s
1968 United States	38.24s
1972 United States	38.19s
1976 United States	38.33s
1980 USSR	38.26s
1984 United States	37.83s
1988 USSR (U.S. disqualified)	38.19s
1992 United States	37.40s*
1996 Canada	37.69s
2000 United States	37.61s
2004 Great Britain	38.07s

1,600-Meter Relay	Time
1908 United States	3m. 29.4s
1912 United States	3m. 16.6s
1920 Great Britain	3m. 22.2s
1924 United States	3m. 16s
1928 United States	3m. 14.2s
1932 United States	3m. 8.2s
1936 Great Britain	3m. 9s
1948 United States	3m. 10.4s
1952 Jamaica	3m. 03.9s
1956 United States	3m. 04.8s
1960 United States	3m. 02.2s
1964 United States	3m. 00.7s
1968 United States	2m. 56.16s
1972 Kenya	2m. 59.8s
1976 United States	2m. 58.65s
1980 USSR	3m. 01.1s
1984 United States	2m. 57.91s
1988 United States	2m. 56.16s
1992 United States	2m. 55.74s*
1996 United States	2m. 55.99s
2000 United States	2m. 56.35s
2004 United States	2m. 55.91s

3,000-Meter Steeplechase	Time
1920 Percy Hodge, Great Britain	10m. 0.4s
1924 Willie Ritola, Finland	9m. 33.6s
1928 Toivo Loukola, Finland	9m. 21.8s
1932 Volmari Iso-Hollo, Finland	10m. 33.4s
(About 3,450 m; extra lap by error.)	
1936 Volmari Iso-Hollo, Finland	9m. 3.8s
1948 Thore Sjoestrand, Sweden	9m. 4.6s
1952 Horace Ashenfelter, United States	8m. 45.4s
1956 Chris Brasher, Great Britain	8m. 41.2s
1960 Zdzislaw Krzyszkowiak, Poland	8m. 34.2s
1964 Gaston Roelants, Belgium	8m. 30.8s
1968 Amos Biwott, Kenya	8m. 51s
1972 Kipchoge Keino, Kenya	8m. 23.6s
1976 Anders Garderud, Sweden	8m. 08.2s
1980 Bronislaw Malinowski, Poland	8m. 09.7s
1984 Julius Korir, Kenya	8m. 11.8s
1988 Julius Kariuki, Kenya	8m. 05.51s*
1992 Matthew Birir, Kenya	8m. 08.84s
1996 Joseph Keter, Kenya	8m. 07.12s
2000 Reuben Kosgei, Kenya	8m. 21.43s
2004 Ezekiel Kemboi, Kenya	8m. 05.81s

20-Kilometer Walk

Year		Time
1956	Leonid Spirin, USSR	1h. 31m. 27.4s
1960	Vladimir Golubnichy, USSR	1h. 33m. 7.2s
1964	Kenneth Mathews, Great Britain	1h. 29m. 34.0s
1968	Vladimir Golubnichy, USSR	1h. 33m. 58.4s
1972	Peter Frenkel, E. Germany	1h. 26m. 42.4s
1976	Daniel Bautista, Mexico	1h. 24m. 40.6s
1980	Maurizio Damilano, Italy	1h. 23m. 35.5s
1984	Ernesto Canto, Mexico	1h. 23m. 13.0s
1988	Josef Pribilinec, Czechoslovakia	1h. 19m. 57.0s
1992	Daniel Plaza Montero, Spain	1h. 21m. 45.0s
1996	Jefferson Perez, Ecuador	1h. 20m. 7s
2000	Robert Korzeniowski, Poland	1h. 18m. 59.0s*
2004	Ivano Brugnetti, Italy	1h. 19m. 40s

50-Kilometer Walk

Year		Time
1932	Thomas W. Green, Great Britain	4h. 50m. 10s
1936	Harold Whitlock, Great Britain	4h. 30m. 41.4s
1948	John Ljunggren, Sweden	4h. 41m. 52s
1952	Giuseppe Dordoni, Italy	4h. 28m. 07.8s
1956	Norman Read, New Zealand	4h. 30m. 42.8s
1960	Donald Thompson, Great Britain	4h. 25m. 30s
1964	Abdon Pamich, Italy	4h. 11m. 12.4s
1968	Christoph Hohne, E. Germany	4h. 20m. 13.6s
1972	Bern Kannenberg, W. Germany	3h. 56m. 11.6s
1980	Hartwig Gauter, E. Germany	3h. 49m. 24.0s
1984	Raul Gonzalez, Mexico	3h. 47m. 26.0s
1988	Vyacheslav Ivanenko, USSR	3h. 38m. 29.0s*
1992	Andrei Perlov, Unified Team	3h. 50m. 13.0s
1996	Robert Korzeniowski, Poland	3h. 43m. 30s
2000	Robert Korzeniowski, Poland	3h. 42m. 22s
2004	Robert Korzeniowski, Poland	3h. 38m. 46s

Marathon

Year		Time
1896	Spiridon Loues, Greece	2h. 58m. 50s
1900	Michel Theato, France	2h. 59m. 45s
1904	Thomas Hicks, United States	3h. 28m. 63s
1908	John J. Hayes, United States	2h. 55m. 18.4s
1912	Kenneth McArthur, South Africa	2h. 36m. 54.8s
1920	Hannes Kolehmainen, Finland	2h. 32m. 35.8s
1924	Albin Stenroos, Finland	2h. 41m. 22.6s
1928	A.B. El Ouafi, France	2h. 32m. 57s
1932	Juan Zabala, Argentina	2h. 31m. 36s
1936	Kijung Son, Japan (Korean)	2h. 29m. 19.2s
1948	Delfo Cabrera, Argentina	2h. 34m. 51.6s
1952	Emil Zatopek, Czechoslovakia	2h. 23m. 03.2s
1956	Alain Mimoun, France	2h. 25m.
1960	Abebe Bikila, Ethiopia	2h. 15m. 16.2s
1964	Abebe Bikila, Ethiopia	2h. 12m. 11.2s
1968	Mamo Wolde, Ethiopia	2h. 20m. 26.4s
1972	Frank Shorter, United States	2h. 12m. 19.8s
1976	Waldemar Cierpinski, E. Germany	2h. 09m. 55s
1980	Waldemar Cierpinski, E. Germany	2h. 11m. 03s
1984	Carlos Lopes, Portugal	2h. 09m. 21s*
1988	Gelindo Bordin, Italy	2h. 10m. 32s
1992	Hwang Young-Cho, S. Korea	2h. 13m. 23s
1996	Josia Thugwane, South Africa	2h. 12m. 36s
2000	Gezahgne Abera, Ethiopia	2h. 10m. 11s
2004	Stefano Baldino, Italy	2h. 10m. 55s

High Jump

1896	Ellery Clark, United States	1.81m.	(5'11¼")
1900	Irving Baxter, United States	1.90m.	(6' 2¾")
1904	Samuel Jones, United States	1.80m.	(5' 11")
1908	Harry Porter, United States	1.90m.	(6' 2¾")
1912	Alma Richards, United States	1.93m.	(6' 4")
1920	Richmond Landon, United States	1.93m.	(6' 4")
1924	Harold Osborn, United States	1.98m.	(6' 6")
1928	Robert W. King, United States	1.94m.	(6' 4¼")
1932	Duncan McNaughton, Canada	1.97m.	(6' 5½")
1936	Cornelius Johnson, United States	2.03m.	(6' 8")
1948	John L. Winter, Australia	1.98m.	(6' 6")
1952	Walter Davis, United States	2.04m.	(6' 8¼")
1956	Charles Dumas, United States	2.12m.	(6' 11½")
1960	Robert Shavlakadze, USSR	2.16m.	(7' 1")
1964	Valery Brumel, USSR	2.18m.	(7' 1¾")
1968	Dick Fosbury, United States	2.24m.	(7' 4¼")
1972	Jüri Tarmak, USSR	2.23m.	(7' 3¾")
1976	Jacek Wszola, Poland	2.25m.	(7' 4½")
1980	Gerd Wessig, E. Germany	2.36m.	(7' 8¾")
1984	Dietmar Mögenburg, W. Germany	2.35m.	(7' 8½")
1988	Hennady Avdeyenko, USSR	2.38m.	(7' 9¾")
1992	Javier Sotomayor Sanabria, Cuba	2.34m.	(7' 8")
1996	Charles Austin, United States	2.39m.	(7' 10")*
2000	Sergey Kliugin, Russia	2.35m.	(7' 8½")
2004	Stefen Holm, Sweden	2.36m.	(7' 9"¾)

Long Jump

1896	Ellery Clark, United States	6.35m.	(20' 10")
1900	Alvin Kraenzlein, United States	7.18m.	(23' 6¾")

Long Jump

1904	Meyer Prinstein, United States	7.34m.	(24' 1")
1908	Frank Irons, United States	7.48m.	(24' 6½")
1912	Albert Gutterson, United States	7.60m.	(24' 11¼")
1920	William Pettersson, Sweden	7.15m.	(23' 5½")
1924	William DeHart Hubbard, U.S.	7.44m.	(24' 5")
1928	Edward B. Hamm, United States	7.73m.	(25' 4½")
1932	Edward Gordon, United States	7.64m.	(25' ¾")
1936	Jesse Owens, United States	8.06m.	(26' 5½")
1948	Willie Steele, United States	7.82m.	(25' 8")
1952	Jerome Biffle, United States	7.57m.	(24' 10")
1956	Gregory Bell, United States	7.83m.	(25' 8¼")
1960	Ralph Boston, United States	8.12m.	(26' 7¾")
1964	Lynn Davies, Great Britain	8.07m.	(26' 5¾")
1968	Bob Beamon, United States	8.90m.	(29' 2½")*
1972	Randy Williams, United States	8.24m.	(27' ½")
1976	Arnie Robinson, United States	8.35m.	(27' 4¾")
1980	Lutz Dombrowski, E. Germany	8.54m.	(28' ¼")
1984	Carl Lewis, United States	8.54m.	(28' ¼")
1988	Carl Lewis, United States	8.72m.	(28' 7½")
1992	Carl Lewis, United States	8.67m.	(28' 5½")
1996	Carl Lewis, United States	8.50m.	(27' 10¾")
2000	Ivan Pedroso, Cuba	8.55m.	(28' ¾")
2004	Dwight Phillips, United States	8.59m.	(28' 2¼")

Triple Jump

1896	James Connolly, United States	13.71m.	(44' 11¾")
1900	Meyer Prinstein, United States	14.47m.	(47' 5¾")
1904	Meyer Prinstein, United States	14.35m.	(47' 1")
1908	Timothy Ahearne, G.B.-Ireland	14.92m.	(48' 11½")
1912	Gustaf Lindblom, Sweden	14.76m.	(48' 5")
1920	Vilho Tuulos, Finland	14.50m.	(47' 7")
1924	Anthony Winter, Australia	15.52m.	(50' 11")
1928	Mikio Oda, Japan	15.21m.	(49' 11")
1932	Chuhei Nambu, Japan	15.72m.	(51' 7")
1936	Naoto Tajima, Japan	16.00m.	(52' 6")
1948	Arne Ahman, Sweden	15.40m.	(50' 6¼")
1952	Adhemar Ferreira da Silva, Brazil	16.22m.	(53' 2¾")
1956	Adhemar Ferreira da Silva, Brazil	16.35m.	(53' 7¾")
1960	Jozef Schmidt, Poland	16.81m.	(55' 1½")
1964	Jozef Schmidt, Poland	16.85m.	(55' 3½")
1968	Viktor Saneyev, USSR	17.39m.	(57' ¾")
1972	Viktor Saneyev, USSR	17.35m.	(56' 11¼")
1976	Viktor Saneyev, USSR	17.29m.	(56' 8¾")
1980	Jaak Uudmae, USSR	17.35m.	(56' 11")
1984	Al Joyner, United States	17.26m.	(56' 7½")
1988	Khristo Markov, Bulgaria	17.61m.	(57' 9½")
1992	Mike Conley, United States	18.17m.	(59' 7½")(w)
1996	Kenny Harrison, United States	18.09m.	(59' 4¼")*
2000	Jonathan Edwards, Britain	17.71m.	(58' 1¼")
2004	Christian Olsson, Sweden	17.79m.	(58' 4 ½")

Discus Throw

1896	Robert Garrett, United States	29.15m.	(95' 7")
1900	Rudolf Bauer, Hungary	36.04m.	(118' 3")
1904	Martin Sheridan, United States	39.28m.	(128' 10")
1908	Martin Sheridan, United States	40.89m.	(134' 1")
1912	Armas Taipale, Finland	45.21m.	(148' 3")
1920	Elmer Niklander, Finland	44.68m.	(146' 7")
1924	Clarence Houser, United States	46.15m.	(151' 4")
1928	Clarence Houser, United States	47.32m.	(155' 3")
1932	John Anderson, United States	49.49m.	(162' 4")
1936	Ken Carpenter, United States	50.48m.	(165' 7")
1948	Adolfo Consolini, Italy	52.78m.	(173' 2")
1952	Sim Iness, United States	55.03m.	(180' 6")
1956	Al Oerter, United States	56.36m.	(184' 11")
1960	Al Oerter, United States	59.18m.	(194' 2")
1964	Al Oerter, United States	61.00m.	(200' 1")
1968	Al Oerter, United States	64.78m.	(212' 6")
1972	Ludvik Danek, Czechoslovakia	64.40m.	(211' 3")
1976	Mac Wilkins, United States	67.50m.	(221' 5")
1980	Viktor Rashchupkin, USSR	66.64m.	(218' 8")
1984	Rolf Dannenberg, W. Germany	66.60m.	(218' 6")
1988	Jurgen Schult, E. Germany	68.82m.	(225' 9")
1992	Romas Ubartas, Lithuania	65.12m.	(213' 8")
1996	Lars Riedel, Germany	69.40m.	(227' 8")
2000	Virgilijus Alekna, Lithuania	69.30m.	(227' 4")
2004	Virgilijus Alekna, Lithuania	69.89m.	(228' 9¾")*

Hammer Throw

1900	John Flanagan, United States	49.73m.	(163' 1")
1904	John Flanagan, United States	51.22m.	(168' 0")
1908	John Flanagan, United States	51.92m.	(170' 4")
1912	Matt McGrath, United States	54.74m.	(179' 7")
1920	Pat Ryan, United States	52.86m.	(173' 5")
1924	Fred Tootell, United States	53.28m.	(174' 10")
1928	Patrick O'Callaghan, Ireland	51.38m.	(168' 7")
1932	Patrick O'Callaghan, Ireland	53.92m.	(176' 11")
1936	Karl Hein, Germany	56.48m.	(185' 4")

Hammer Throw

1948	Imre Németh, Hungary	56.06m. (183' 11")
1952	József Csérmák, Hungary	60.34m. (197' 11")
1956	Harold Connolly, United States	63.18m. (207' 3")
1960	Vasily Rudenkov, USSR	67.10m. (202' 0")
1964	Romuald Klim, USSR	69.74m. (228' 10")
1968	Gyula Zsivótsky, Hungary	73.36m. (240' 8")
1972	Anatoly Bondarchuk, USSR	75.50m. (247' 8")
1976	Yuri Syedykh, USSR	77.52m. (254' 4")
1980	Yuri Syedykh, USSR	81.80m. (268' 4")
1984	Juha Tiainen, Finland	78.08m. (256' 2")
1988	Sergei Litvinov, USSR	84.80m. (278' 2")*
1992	Andrey Abduvaliyev, Unified Team..	82.54m. (270' 9")
1996	Balázs Kiss, Hungary	81.24m. (266' 6")
2000	Szymon Ziolkowski, Poland	80.02m. (262' 6")
2004	Koji Murofushi, Japan	82.91m. (272')

Javelin Throw

1908	Erik Lemming, Sweden	54.82m. (179' 10")
1912	Erik Lemming, Sweden	60.64m. (198' 11")
1920	Jonni Myyrä, Finland	64.78m. (215' 10")
1924	Jonni Myyrä, Finland	62.96m. (206' 7")
1928	Eric Lundkvist, Sweden	66.60m. (218' 6")
1932	Matti Järvinen, Finland	72.70m. (238' 6")
1936	Gerhard Stöck, Germany	71.84m. (235' 8")
1948	Kai Tapio Rautavaara, Finland	69.76m. (228' 11")
1952	Cy Young, United States	73.78m. (242' 1")
1956	Egil Danielsen, Norway	85.70m. (281' 2")
1960	Viktor Tsibulenko, USSR	84.64m. (277' 8")
1964	Pauli Nevala, Finland	82.66m. (271' 2")
1968	Janis Lusis, USSR	90.10m. (295' 7")
1972	Klaus Wolfermann, W. Germany	90.48m. (296' 10")
1976	Miklós Németh, Hungary	94.58m. (310' 4")
1980	Dainis Kula, USSR	91.20m. (299' 2")
1984	Arto Härkönen, Finland	86.76m. (284' 8")
1988	Tapio Korjus, Finland	84.28m. (276' 6")
1992	Jan Zelezny, Czechoslovakia (a)	89.66m. (294' 2")
1996	Jan Zelezny, Czech Republic	88.16m. (289' 3")
2000	Jan Zelezny, Czech Republic	90.17m. (295' 9½")*
2004	Andreas Thorkildsen, Norway	86.50m. (283' 10")

(a) New records were kept after javelin was modified in 1986.

Pole Vault

1896	William Welles Hoyt, United States..	3.30m. (10' 10")
1900	Irving Baxter, United States	3.30m. (10' 10")
1904	Charles Dvorak, United States	3.50m. (11' 6")
1908	A. C. Gilbert, United States; Edward Cooke Jr., United States	3.71m. (12' 2")
1920	Frank Foss, United States	4.09m. (13' 5")
1924	Lee Barnes, United States	3.95m. (12' 11½")
1928	Sabin W. Carr, United States	4.20m. (13' 9¼")
1932	William Miller, United States	4.31m. (14' 1¾")
1936	Earle Meadows, United States	4.35m. (14' 3¼")
1948	Guinn Smith, United States	4.30m. (14' 1¼")
1952	Robert Richards, United States	4.55m. (14' 11¼")
1956	Robert Richards, United States	4.56m. (14' 11½")
1960	Don Bragg, United States	4.70m. (15' 5")
1964	Fred Hansen, United States	5.10m. (16' 8¾")
1968	Bob Seagren, United States	5.40m. (17' 8½")
1972	Wolfgang Nordwig, E. Germany	5.50m. (18' ½")
1976	Tadeusz Slusarski, Poland	5.50m. (18' ½")
1980	Wladyslaw Kozakiewicz, Poland..	5.78m. (18' 11½")
1984	Pierre Quinon, France	5.75m. (18' 10¼")
1988	Sergei Bubka, USSR	5.90m. (19' 4¼")
1992	Maksim Tarassov, Unified Team	5.80m. (19' ¼")
1996	Jean Galfione, France	5.92m. (19' 5")*
2000	Nick Hysong, United States	5.90m. (19' 4¼")
2004	Timothy Mack, United States	5.95m. (19' 6¼")*

16-lb. Shot Put

1896	Robert Garrett, United States	11.22m. (36' 9¾")
1900	Richard Sheldon, United States	14.10m. (46' 3¼")
1904	Ralph Rose, United States	14.81m. (48' 7")
1908	Ralph Rose, United States	14.21m. (46' 7½")
1912	Pat McDonald, United States	15.34m. (50' 4")
1920	Ville Pörhölä, Finland	14.81m. (48' 7¼")
1924	L. Clarence Houser, United States	14.99m. (49' 2¼")
1928	John Kuck, United States	15.87m. (52' ¾")
1932	Leo Sexton, United States	16.00m. (52' 6")
1936	Hans Woellke, Germany	16.20m. (53' 1¾")
1948	Wilbur Thompson, United States	17.12m. (56' 2")
1952	W. Parry O'Brien, United States	17.41m. (57' 1½")
1956	W. Parry O'Brien, United States	18.57m. (60' 11¼")
1960	William Nieder, United States	19.68m. (64' 6¾")
1964	Dallas Long, United States	20.33m. (66' 8½")
1968	Randy Matson, United States	20.54m. (67' 4¾")
1972	Wladyslaw Komar, Poland	21.18m. (69' 6")
1976	Udo Beyer, E. Germany	21.05m. (69' ¾")
1980	Vladimir Kyselyov, USSR	21.35m. (70' ½")

16-lb. Shot Put

1984	Alessandro Andrei, Italy	21.26m. (69' 9")
1988	Ulf Timmermann, E. Germany	22.47m. (73' 8¾")*
1992	Michael Stulce, United States	21.70m. (71' 2½")
1996	Randy Barnes, United States	21.62m. (70' 11¼")
2000	Arsi Harju, Finland	21.29m. (69' 10¼")
2004	Yuriy Bilonog, Ukraine	21.16m. (69' 5¼")

Decathlon (not held 1908)

		Points
1904	Thomas Kiely, Ireland	6,036
1912	Hugo Wieslander, Sweden (a)	7,724.49
1920	Helge Lovland, Norway	6,804.35
1924	Harold Osborn, United States	7,710.77
1928	Paavo Yrjola, Finland	8,053.29
1932	James Bausch, United States	8,462.23
1936	Glenn Morris, United States	7,900
1948	Robert Mathias, United States	7,139
1952	Robert Mathias, United States	7,887
1956	Milton Campbell, United States	7,937
1960	Rafer Johnson, United States	8,392
1964	Willi Holdorf, Germany (b)	7,887
1968	Bill Toomey, United States	8,193
1972	Nikolai Avilov, USSR	8,454
1976	Bruce Jenner, United States	8,617
1980	Daley Thompson, Great Britain	8,495
1984	Daley Thompson, Great Britain (c)	8,798
1988	Christian Schenk, E. Germany	8,488
1992	Robert Zmelik, Czechoslovakia	8,611
1996	Dan O'Brien, United States	8,824
2000	Erki Nool, Estonia	8,641
2004	Roman Sebrle, Czech Republic	8,893*

(a) Jim Thorpe of the U.S. won the 1912 Decathlon with 8,413 pts. but was disqualified and had to return his medals because he had played pro baseball prior to the Olympics. The IOC in 1982 posthumously restored his decathlon and pentathlon golds. (b) Former point systems used prior to 1964. (c) Scoring change effective Apr. 1985; Thompson's readjusted score is 8,847 pts.

Track and Field—Women

100-Meter Run

		Time
1928	Elizabeth Robinson, United States	12.2s
1932	Stella Walsh, Poland (a)	11.9s
1936	Helen Stephens, United States	11.5s
1948	Francina Blankers-Koen, Netherlands.	11.9s
1952	Marjorie Jackson, Australia	11.5s
1956	Betty Cuthbert, Australia	11.5s
1960	Wilma Rudolph, United States	11.0s
1964	Wyomia Tyus, United States	11.4s
1968	Wyomia Tyus, United States	11.07s
1972	Renate Stecher, E. Germany	11.08s
1976	Annegret Richter, W. Germany	11.08s
1980	Lyudmila Kondratyeva, USSR	11.06s
1984	Evelyn Ashford, United States	10.97s
1988	Florence Griffith-Joyner, United States	10.54s (w)
1992	Gail Devers, United States	10.82s
1996	Gail Devers, United States	10.94s
2000	Marion Jones, United States	10.75s
2004	Yuliya Nesterenko, Belarus	10.93s

(a) A 1980 autopsy determined that Walsh was a man.

200-Meter Run

		Time
1948	Francina Blankers-Koen, Netherlands.	24.4s
1952	Marjorie Jackson, Australia	23.7s
1956	Betty Cuthbert, Australia	23.4s
1960	Wilma Rudolph, United States	24.0s
1964	Edith McGuire, United States	23.0s
1968	Irena Szewinska, Poland	22.5s
1972	Renate Stecher, E. Germany	22.40s
1976	Barbel Eckert, E. Germany	22.37s
1980	Barbel Wockel, E. Germany	22.03s
1984	Valerie Brisco-Hooks, United States	21.81s
1988	Florence Griffith-Joyner, United States	21.34s*
1992	Gwen Torrence, United States	21.81s
1996	Marie-Jose Perec, France	22.12s
2000	Marion Jones, United States	21.84s
2004	Veronica Campbell, Jamaica	22.05s

400-Meter Run

		Time
1964	Betty Cuthbert, Australia	52.0s
1968	Colette Besson, France	52.0s
1972	Monika Zehrt, E. Germany	51.08s
1976	Irena Szewinska, Poland	49.29s
1980	Marita Koch, E. Germany	48.88s
1984	Valerie Brisco-Hooks, United States	48.83s
1988	Olga Bryzgina, USSR	48.65s
1992	Marie-Jose Perec, France	48.83s
1996	Marie-Jose Perec, France	48.25s*
2000	Cathy Freeman, Australia	49.11s
2004	Tonique Williams-Darling, Bahamas	49.41s

800-Meter Run

		Time
1928	Lina Radke, Germany	2m. 16.8s
1960	Ludmila Shevtsova, USSR	2m. 4.3s
1964	Ann Packer, Great Britain	2m. 1.1s
1968	Madeline Manning, United States	2m. 0.9s
1972	Hildegard Falck, W. Germany	1m. 58.6s
1976	Tatyana Kazankina, USSR	1m. 54.94s
1980	Nadezhda Olizarenko, USSR	1m. 53.43s*
1984	Doina Melinte, Romania	1m. 57.60s
1988	Sigrun Wodars, E. Germany	1m. 56.10s
1992	Ellen Van Langen, Netherlands	1m. 55.54s
1996	Svetlana Masterkova, Russia	1m. 57.73s
2000	Maria Mutola, Mozambique	1m. 56.15s
2004	Kelly Holmes, Great Britain	1m. 56.38s

1,500-Meter Run

		Time
1972	Lyudmila Bragina, USSR	4m. 01.4s
1976	Tatyana Kazankina, USSR	4m. 05.48s
1980	Tatyana Kazankina, USSR	3m. 56.6s
1984	Gabriella Dorio, Italy	4m. 03.25s
1988	Paula Ivan, Romania	3m. 53.96s*
1992	Hassiba Boulmerka, Algeria	3m. 55.30s
1996	Svetlana Masterkova, Russia	4m. 00.83s
2000	Nouria Benida Merah, Algeria	4m. 05.10s
2004	Kelly Holmes, Great Britain	3m. 57.90s

3,000-Meter Run

		Time
1984	Maricica Puica, Romania	8m. 35.96s
1988	Tatyana Samolenko, USSR	8m. 26.53s*
1992	Elena Romanova, Unified Team	8m. 46.04s

5,000-Meter Run

		Time
1996	Wang Junxia, China	14m. 59.88s
2000	Gabriela Szabo, Romania	14m. 40.79s*
2004	Meseret Defar, Ethiopa	14m. 45.65s

10,000-Meter Run

		Time
1988	Olga Boldarenko, USSR	31m. 44.69s
1992	Derartu Tulu, Ethiopia	31m. 06.02s
1996	Fernanda Ribeiro, Portugal	31m. 01.63s
2000	Derartu Tulu, Ethiopia	30m.17.49s*
2004	Xing Huina, China	30m. 24.36s

100-Meter Hurdles

		Time
1972	Annelie Ehrhardt, E. Germany	12.59s
1976	Johanna Schaller, E. Germany	12.77s
1980	Vera Komisova, USSR	12.56s
1984	Benita Brown-Fitzgerald, United States	12.84s
1988	Jordanka Donkova, Bulgaria	12.38s
1992	Paraskevi Patoulidou, Greece	12.64s
1996	Ludmila Enquist, Sweden	12.58s
2000	Olga Shishigina, Kazakhstan	12.65s
2004	Joanna Hayes, United States	12.37s*

400-Meter Hurdles

		Time
1984	Nawal el Moutawakii, Morocco	54.61s
1988	Debra Flintoff-King, Australia	53.17s
1992	Sally Gunnell, Great Britain	53.23s
1996	Deon Hemmings, Jamaica	52.82s
2000	Irina Privalova, Russia	53.02s
2004	Fani Halkia, Greece	52.82s*

400-Meter Relay

		Time
1928	Canada	48.4s
1932	United States	46.9s
1936	United States	46.9s
1948	Netherlands	47.5s
1952	United States	45.9s
1956	Australia	44.5s
1960	United States	44.5s
1964	Poland	43.6s
1968	United States	42.88s
1972	West Germany	42.81s
1976	East Germany	42.55s
1980	East Germany	41.60s*
1984	United States	41.65s
1988	United States	41.98s
1992	United States	42.11s
1996	United States	41.95s
2000	Bahamas	41.95s
2004	Jamaica	41.73s

1,600-Meter Relay

		Time
1972	East Germany	3m. 23s
1976	East Germany	3m. 19.23s
1980	USSR	3m. 20.02s
1984	United States	3m. 18.29s
1988	USSR	3m. 15.17s*
1992	Unified Team	3m. 20.20s
1996	United States	3m. 20.91s

1,600-Meter Relay

		Time
2000	United States	3m. 22.62s
2004	United States	3m. 19.01s

10-Kilometer Walk

		Time
1992	Chen Yueling, China	44m. 32s
1996	Elena Nikolayeva, Russia	41m. 49s*

20-Kilometer Walk

		Time
2000	Wang Liping, China	1m. 29.05s*
2004	Athanasia Tsoumeleka, Greece	1m. 29.12s

Marathon

		Time
1984	Joan Benoit, United States	2h. 24m. 52s
1988	Rosa Mota, Portugal	2h. 25m. 40s
1992	Valentina Yegorova, Unified Team	2h. 32m. 41s
1996	Fatuma Roba, Ethiopia	2h. 26m. 05s
2000	Naoko Takahashi, Japan	2h. 23m. 14s*
2004	Mizuki Noguchi, Japan	2h. 26m. 20s

High Jump

1928	Ethel Catherwood, Canada	1.59m. (5' 2½")
1932	Jean Shiley, United States	1.65m. (5' 5")
1936	Ibolya Csák, Hungary	1.60m. (5' 3")
1948	Alice Coachman, U. S.	1.68m. (5' 6")
1952	Esther Brand, South Africa	1.67m. (5' 5¾")
1956	Mildred L. McDaniel, U. S.	1.76m. (5' 9¼")
1960	Iolanda Balas, Romania	1.85m. (6' ¾")
1964	Iolanda Balas, Romania	1.90m. (6' 2¾")
1968	Miloslava Resková, Czech.	1.82m. (5' 11½")
1972	Ulrike Meyfarth, W. Germany	1.92m. (6' 3½")
1976	Rosemarie Ackermann, E. Ger.	1.93m. (6' 4")
1980	Sara Simeoni, Italy	1.97m. (6' 5½")
1984	Ulrike Meyfarth, W. Germany	2.02m. (6' 7½")
1988	Louise Ritter, United States	2.03m. (6' 8")
1992	Heike Henkel, Germany	2.02m. (6' 7½")
1996	Stefka Kostadinova, Bulgaria	2.05m. (6' 8¾")*
2000	Yelena Yelesina, Russia	2.01m. (6' 7")
2004	Yelena Slesarenko, Russia	2.06m. (6' 9")*

Long Jump

1948	Olga Gyarmati, Hungary	5.69m. (18' 8")
1952	Yvette Williams, New Zealand	6.24m. (20' 5¼")
1956	Elzbieta Krzeskinska, Poland	6.35m. (20' 10")
1960	Vira Krepkina, USSR	6.37m. (20' 10¾")
1964	Mary Rand, Great Britain	6.76m. (22' 2¼")
1968	Viorica Viscopoleanu, Romania	6.82m. (22' 4½")
1972	Heidemarie Rosendahl, W. Ger.	6.78m. (22' 3")
1976	Angela Voigt, E. Germany	6.72m. (22' ¾")
1980	Tatyana Kolpakova, USSR	7.06m. (23' 2")
1984	Anisoara Cusmir-Stanciu, Rom.	6.96m. (22' 10")
1988	Jackie Joyner-Kersee, United States	7.40m. (24' 3½")*
1992	Heike Drechsler, Germany	7.14m. (23' 5¼")
1996	Chioma Ajunwa, Nigeria	7.12m. (23' 4½")
2000	Heike Drechsler, Germany	6.99m. (22' 11¼")
2004	Tatyana Lebedeva, Russia	7.07m. (23' 2½")

Triple Jump

1996	Inessa Kravets, Ukraine	15.33m. (50' 3½")*
2000	Tereza Marinova, Bulgaria	15.20m. (49' 10½")
2004	Francoise Mbango Etone, Cameroon	15.30m. (50' 2⅓")

Discus Throw

1928	Halina Konopacka, Poland	39.62m. (130' 0")
1932	Lillian Copeland, United States	40.58m. (133' 2")
1936	Gisela Mauermayer, Germany	47.62m. (156' 3")
1948	Micheline Ostermeyer, France	41.92m. (137' 6")
1952	Nina Ponomareva, USSR	51.42m. (168' 8")
1956	Olga Fikotová, Czech.	53.68m. (176' 1")
1960	Nina Ponomareva, USSR	55.10m. (180' 9")
1964	Tamara Press, USSR	57.26m. (187' 10")
1968	Lia Manoliu, Romania	58.28m. (191' 2")
1972	Faina Melnik, USSR	66.62m. (218' 7")
1976	Evelin Jahl, E. Germany	69.00m. (226' 4")
1980	Evelin Jahl, E. Germany	69.96m. (229' 6")
1984	Ria Stalman, Netherlands	65.36m. (214' 5")
1988	Martina Hellmann, E. Germany	72.30m. (237' 2")*
1992	Maritza Martén Garcia, Cuba	70.06m. (229' 10")
1996	Ilke Wyludda, Germany	69.66m. (228' 6")
2000	Ellina Zvereva, Belarus	68.40m. (224' 5")
2004	Natalya Sadova, Russia	67.02m. (219' 9")

Hammer Throw

2000	Kamila Skolimowska, Poland	71.16m. (233' 5¾")*
2004	Olga Kuzenkova, Russia	75.02m. (246' 1")

Pole Vault

2000	Stacy Dragila, United States	4.60m. (15' 1")*
2004	Yelena Isinbayeva, Russia	4.91m. (16' 1⅓")

Shot Put (8 lb., 13 oz.)
1948	Micheline Ostermeyer, France	13.75m. (45' 1½")
1952	Galina Zybina, USSR	15.28m. (50' 1½")
1956	Tamara Tyshkyevich, USSR	16.59m. (54' 5¼")
1960	Tamara Press, USSR	17.32m. (56' 10")
1964	Tamara Press, USSR	18.14m. (59' 6¼")
1968	Margitta Gummel, E. Germany	19.61m. (64' 4")
1972	Nadezhda Chizova, USSR	21.03m. (69' 0")
1976	Ivanka Khristova, Bulgaria	21.16m. (69' 5¼")
1980	Ilona Slupianek, E. Germany	22.41m. (73' 6¼")*
1984	Claudia Losch, W. Germany	20.49m. (67' 2¼")
1988	Natalya Lisovskaya, USSR	22.24m. (72' 11¾")
1992	Svetlana Krivelyova, Unified Team	21.06m. (69' 1¼")
1996	Astrid Kumbernuss, Germany	20.56m. (67' 5½")
2000	Yanina Karolchik, Belarus	20.56m. (67' 5½")
2004	Yumileidi Cumba Jay, Cuba	19.59m. (64' 3¼")

Javelin Throw
1932	"Babe" Didrikson, United States	43.68m. (143' 4")
1936	Tilly Fleischer, Germany	45.18m. (148' 3")
1948	Herma Bauma, Austria	45.56m. (149' 6")
1952	Dana Zátopková, Czech.	50.46m. (165' 7")
1956	Inese Jaunzeme, USSR	53.86m. (176' 8")
1960	Elvira Ozolina, USSR	55.98m. (183' 8")
1964	Mihaela Penes, Romania	60.54m. (198' 7")
1968	Angéla Németh, Hungary	60.36m. (198' 0")
1972	Ruth Fuchs, E. Germany	63.88m. (209' 7")
1976	Ruth Fuchs, E. Germany	65.94m. (216' 4")
1980	Maria Colón Ruenes, Cuba	68.40m. (224' 5")
1984	Tessa Sanderson, Great Britain	69.56m. (228' 2")
1988	Petra Felke, E. Germany	74.68m. (245' 0")
1992	Silke Renke, Germany	68.34m. (224' 2")
1996	Heli Rantanen, Finland	67.94m. (222' 11")
2000	Trine Hattestad, Norway (a)	68.91m. (226' 1")
2004	Osleidys Menendez, Cuba	71.53m. (234' 8")*

(a) New records were kept after javelin was modified in 1999.

Heptathlon
		Points
1984	Glynis Nunn, Australia	6,390
1988	Jackie Joyner-Kersee, United States	7,291*
1992	Jackie Joyner-Kersee, United States	7,044
1996	Ghada Shouaa, Syria	6,780
2000	Denise Lewis, Britain	6,584
2004	Carolina Kluft, Sweden	6,952

Swimming and Diving—Men

50-Meter Freestyle
		Time
1988	Matt Biondi, United States	0:22.14
1992	Aleksandr Popov, Unified Team	0:21.91*
1996	Aleksandr Popov, Russia	0:22.13
2000	Anthony Ervin, United States	0:21.98
2000	Gary Hall Jr., United States	0:21.98
2004	Gary Hall Jr., United States	0:21.93

100-Meter Freestyle
		Time
1896	Alfred Hajos, Hungary	1:22.2
1904	Zoltan de Halmay, Hungary (100 yards)	1:02.8
1908	Charles Daniels, United States	1:05.6
1912	Duke P. Kahanamoku, United States	1:03.4
1920	Duke P. Kahanamoku, United States	1:01.4
1924	John Weissmuller, United States	0:59.0
1928	John Weissmuller, United States	0:58.6
1932	Yasuji Miyazaki, Japan	0:58.2
1936	Ferenc Csik, Hungary	0:57.6
1948	Wally Ris, United States	0:57.3
1952	Clark Scholes, United States	0:57.4
1956	Jon Henricks, Australia	0:55.4
1960	John Devitt, Australia	0:55.2
1964	Don Schollander, United States	0:53.4
1968	Mike Wenden, Australia	0:52.2
1972	Mark Spitz, United States	0:51.22
1976	Jim Montgomery, United States	0:49.99
1980	Jorg Woithe, E. Germany	0:50.40
1984	Rowdy Gaines, United States	0:49.80
1988	Matt Biondi, United States	0:48.63
1992	Aleksandr Popov, Unified Team	0:49.02
1996	Aleksandr Popov, Russia	0:48.74
2000	Pieter van den Hoogenband, Netherlands	0:48.30
2004	Pieter van den Hoogenband, Netherlands	0:48.17

200-Meter Freestyle
		Time
1968	Mike Wenden, Australia	1:55.2
1972	Mark Spitz, United States	1:52.78
1976	Bruce Furniss, United States	1:50.29
1980	Sergei Kopliakov, USSR	1:49.81
1984	Michael Gross, W. Germany	1:47.44
1988	Duncan Armstrong, Australia	1:47.25
1992	Yevgeny Sadovyi, Unified Team	1:46.70
1996	Danyon Loader, New Zealand	1:47.63
2000	Pieter van den Hoogenband, Netherlands	1:45.35
2004	Ian Thorpe, Australia	1:44.71*

400-Meter Freestyle
		Time
1904	C. M. Daniels, United States (440 yards)	6:16.2
1908	Henry Taylor, Great Britain	5:36.8
1912	George Hodgson, Canada	5:24.4
1920	Norman Ross, United States	5:26.8
1924	John Weissmuller, United States	5:04.2
1928	Albert Zorilla, Argentina	5:01.6
1932	Clarence Crabbe, United States	4:48.4
1936	Jack Medica, United States	4:44.5
1948	William Smith, United States	4:41.0
1952	Jean Boiteux, France	4:30.7
1956	Murray Rose, Australia	4:27.3
1960	Murray Rose, Australia	4:18.3
1964	Don Schollander, United States	4:12.2
1968	Mike Burton, United States	4:09.0
1972	Brad Cooper, Australia	4:00.27
1976	Brian Goodell, United States	3:51.93
1980	Vladimir Salnikov, USSR	3:51.31
1984	George DiCarlo, United States	3:51.23
1988	Ewe Dassler, E. Germany	3:46.95
1992	Yevgeny Sadovyi, Unified Team	3:45.00
1996	Danyon Loader, New Zealand	3:47.97
2000	Ian Thorpe, Australia	3:40.59*
2004	Ian Thorpe, Australia	3:43.10

1,500-Meter Freestyle
		Time
1908	Henry Taylor, Great Britain	22:48.4
1912	George Hodgson, Canada	22:00.0
1920	Norman Ross, United States	22:23.2
1924	Andrew Charlton, Australia	20:06.6
1928	Arne Borg, Sweden	19:51.8
1932	Kusuo Kitamura, Japan	19:12.4
1936	Noboru Terada, Japan	19:13.7
1948	James McLane, United States	19:18.5
1952	Ford Konno, United States	18:30.3
1956	Murray Rose, Australia	17:58.9
1960	Jon Konrads, Australia	17:19.6
1964	Robert Windle, Australia	17:01.7
1968	Mike Burton, United States	16:38.9
1972	Mike Burton, United States	15:52.58
1976	Brian Goodell, United States	15:02.40
1980	Vladimir Salnikov, USSR	14:58.27
1984	Michael O'Brien, United States	15:05.20
1988	Vladimir Salnikov, USSR	15:00.40
1992	Kieren Perkins, Australia	14:43.48
1996	Kieren Perkins, Australia	14:56.40
2000	Grant Hackett, Australia	14:48.33
2004	Grant Hackett, Australia	14:43.40*

100-Meter Backstroke
		Time
1904	Walter Brack, Germany (100 yds.)	1:16.8
1908	Arno Bieberstein, Germany	1:24.6
1912	Harry Hebner, United States	1:21.2
1920	Warren Kealoha, United States	1:15.2
1924	Warren Kealoha, United States	1:13.2
1928	George Kojac, United States	1:08.2
1932	Masaji Kiyokawa, Japan	1:08.6
1936	Adolph Kiefer, United States	1:05.9
1948	Allen Stack, United States	1:06.4
1952	Yoshi Oyakawa, United States	1:05.4
1956	David Thiele, Australia	1:02.2
1960	David Thiele, Australia	1:01.9
1968	Roland Matthes, E. Germany	0:58.7
1972	Roland Matthes, E. Germany	0:56.58
1976	John Naber, United States	0:55.49
1980	Bengt Baron, Sweden	0:56.33
1984	Rick Carey, United States	0:55.79
1988	Daichi Suzuki, Japan	0:55.05
1992	Mark Tewksbury, Canada	0:53.98
1996	Jeff Rouse, United States	0:54.10
2000	Lenny Krayzelburg, United States	0:53.72
2004	Aaron Peirsol, United States	0:54.06

200-Meter Backstroke
		Time
1964	Jed Graef, United States	2:10.3
1968	Roland Matthes, E. Germany	2:09.6
1972	Roland Matthes, E. Germany	2:02.82
1976	John Naber, United States	1:59.19
1980	Sandor Wladar, Hungary	2:01.93
1984	Rick Carey, United States	2:00.23
1988	Igor Polianski, USSR	1:59.37
1992	Martin Lopez-Zubero, Spain	1:58.47
1996	Brad Bridgewater, United States	1:58.54
2000	Lenny Krayzelburg, United States	1:56.76
2004	Aaron Peirsol, United States	1:54.95*

100-Meter Breaststroke

Year	Name	Time
1968	Don McKenzie, United States	1:07.79
1972	Nobutaka Taguchi, Japan	1:04.94
1976	John Hencken, United States	1:03.11
1980	Duncan Goodhew, Great Britain	1:03.44
1984	Steve Lundquist, United States	1:01.65
1988	Adrian Moorhouse, Great Britain	1:02.04
1992	Nelson Diebel, United States	1:01.50
1996	Fred Deburghgraeve, Belgium	1:00.60
2000	Domenico Fioravanti, Italy	1:00.46
2004	Kosuke Kitajima, Japan	1:00.08

200-Meter Breaststroke

Year	Name	Time
1908	Frederick Holman, Great Britain	3:09.2
1912	Walter Bathe, Germany	3:01.8
1920	Haken Malmroth, Sweden	3:04.4
1924	Robert Skelton, United States	2:56.6
1928	Yoshiyuki Tsuruta, Japan	2:48.8
1932	Yoshiyuki Tsuruta, Japan	2:45.4
1936	Tetsuo Hamuro, Japan	2:41.5
1948	Joseph Verdeur, United States	2:39.3
1952	John Davies, Australia	2:34.4
1956	Masura Furukawa, Japan	2:34.7
1960	William Mulliken, United States	2:37.4
1964	Ian O'Brien, Australia	2:27.8
1968	Felipe Munoz, Mexico	2:28.7
1972	John Hencken, United States	2:21.55
1976	David Wilkie, Great Britain	2:15.11
1980	Robertas Zhulpa, USSR	2:15.85
1984	Victor Davis, Canada	2:13.34
1988	Jozsef Szabo, Hungary	2:13.52
1992	Mike Barrowman, United States	2:10.16
1996	Norbert Rozsa, Hungary	2:12.57
2000	Domenico Fioravanti, Italy	2:10.87
2004	Kosuke Kitajima, Japan	2:09.44*

100-Meter Butterfly

Year	Name	Time
1968	Doug Russell, United States	0:55.9
1972	Mark Spitz, United States	0:54.27
1976	Matt Vogel, United States	0:54.35
1980	Par Arvidsson, Sweden	0:54.92
1984	Michael Gross, W. Germany	0:53.08
1988	Anthony Nesty, Suriname	0:53.00
1992	Pablo Morales, United States	0:53.32
1996	Denis Pankratov, Russia	0:52.27
2000	Lars Froelander, Sweden	0:52.00
2004	Michael Phelps, United States	0:51.25*

200-Meter Butterfly

Year	Name	Time
1956	William Yorzyk, United States	2:19.3
1960	Michael Troy, United States	2:12.8
1964	Kevin J. Berry, Australia	2:06.6
1968	Carl Robie, United States	2:08.7
1972	Mark Spitz, United States	2:00.70
1976	Mike Bruner, United States	1:59.23
1980	Sergei Fesenko, USSR	1:59.76
1984	Jon Sieben, Australia	1:57.04
1988	Michael Gross, W. Germany	1:56.94
1992	Mel Stewart, United States	1:56.26
1996	Denis Pankratov, Russia	1:56.51
2000	Tom Malchow, United States	1:55.35
2004	Michael Phelps, United States	1:54.04*

200-Meter Individual Medley

Year	Name	Time
1968	Charles Hickcox, United States	2:12.0
1972	Gunnar Larsson, Sweden	2:07.17
1984	Alex Baumann, Canada	2:01.42
1988	Tamas Darnyi, Hungary	2:00.17
1992	Tamas Darnyi, Hungary	2:00.76
1996	Attila Czene, Hungary	1:59.91
2000	Massimiliano Rosolino, Italy	1:58.98
2004	Michael Phelps, United States	1:57.14*

400-Meter Individual Medley

Year	Name	Time
1964	Dick Roth, United States	4:45.4
1968	Charles Hickcox, United States	4:48.4
1972	Gunnar Larsson, Sweden	4:31.98
1976	Rod Strachan, United States	4:23.68
1980	Aleksandr Sidorenko, USSR	4:22.89
1984	Alex Baumann, Canada	4:17.41
1988	Tamas Darnyi, Hungary	4:14.75
1992	Tamas Darnyi, Hungary	4:14.23
1996	Tom Dolan, United States	4:14.90
2000	Tom Dolan, United States	4:11.76
2004	Michael Phelps, United States	4:08.26*

400-Meter Freestyle Relay

Year	Name	Time
1964	United States	3:31.2
1968	United States	3:31.7
1972	United States	3:26.42
1984	United States	3:19.03
1988	United States	3:16.53

400-Meter Freestyle Relay

Year	Name	Time
1992	United States	3:16.74
1996	United States	3:15.41
2000	Australia	3:13.67
2004	South Africa	3:13.17*

800-Meter Freestyle Relay

Year	Name	Time
1908	Great Britain	10:55.6
1912	Australia	10:11.6
1920	United States	10:04.4
1924	United States	9:53.4
1928	United States	9:36.2
1932	Japan	8:58.4
1936	Japan	8:51.5
1948	United States	8:46.0
1952	United States	8:31.1
1956	Australia	8:23.6
1960	United States	8:10.2
1964	United States	7:52.1
1968	United States	7:52.33
1972	United States	7:35.78
1976	United States	7:23.22
1980	USSR	7:23.50
1984	United States	7:15.69
1988	United States	7:12.51
1992	Unified Team	7:11.95
1996	United States	7:14.84
2000	Australia	7:07.05*
2004	United States	7:07.33

400-Meter Medley Relay

Year	Name	Time
1960	United States	4:05.4
1964	United States	3:58.4
1968	United States	3:54.9
1972	United States	3:48.16
1976	United States	3:42.22
1980	Australia	3:45.70
1984	United States	3:39.30
1988	United States	3:36.93
1992	United States	3:36.93
1996	United States	3:34.84
2000	United States	3:33.73
2004	United States	3:30.68*

Springboard Diving

Year	Name	Points
1908	Albert Zurner, Germany	85.50
1912	Paul Guenther, Germany	79.23
1920	Louis Kuehn, U.S	675.40
1924	Albert White, United States	97.46
1928	Pete Desjardins, United States	185.04
1932	Michael Galitzen, United States	161.38
1936	Richard Degener, United States	163.57
1948	Bruce Harlan, United States	163.64
1952	David Browning, United States	205.29
1956	Robert Clotworthy, United States	159.56
1960	Gary Tobian, United States	170.00
1964	Kenneth Sitzberger, United States	159.90
1968	Bernie Wrightson, United States	170.15
1972	Vladimir Vasin, USSR	594.09
1976	Phil Boggs, United States	619.52
1980	Aleksandr Portnov, USSR	905.02
1984	Greg Louganis, United States	754.41
1988	Greg Louganis, United States	730.80
1992	Mark Lenzi, United States	676.53
1996	Xiong Ni, China	701.46
2000	Xiong Ni, China	708.72
2004	Peng Bo, China	787.30

Platform Diving

Year	Name	Points
1904	Dr. G.E. Sheldon, United States	112.75
1908	Hjalmar Johansson, Sweden	183.75
1912	Erik Adlerz, Sweden	73.94
1920	Clarence Pinkston, United States	100.67
1924	Albert White, United States	97.46
1928	Pete Desjardins, United States	98.74
1932	Harold Smith, United States	124.80
1936	Marshall Wayne, United States	113.58
1948	Sammy Lee, United States	130.05
1952	Sammy Lee, United States	156.28
1956	Joaquin Capilla, Mexico	152.44
1960	Robert Webster, United States	165.56
1964	Robert Webster, United States	148.58
1968	Klaus Dibiasi, Italy	164.18
1972	Klaus Dibiasi, Italy	504.12
1976	Klaus Dibiasi, Italy	600.51
1980	Falk Hoffmann, E. Germany	835.65
1984	Greg Louganis, United States	710.91
1988	Greg Louganis, United States	638.61
1992	Sun Shuwei, China	677.31
1996	Dmitri Sautin, Russia	692.34
2000	Tian Liang, China	724.53
2004	Hu Jia, China	748.08

Synchronized Platform	Points
2004 Tian Liang and Yang Jinghui, China	383.88

Synchronized Springboard	Points
2004 Nikolaos Siranidis and Thomas Bimis, Greece	353.34

Swimming and Diving—Women

50-Meter Freestyle	Time
1988 Kristin Otto, E. Germany	0:25.49
1992 Yang Wenyi, China	0:24.76
1996 Amy Van Dyken, United States	0:24.87
2000 Inge de Bruijn, Netherlands	0:24.32
2004 Inge de Bruijn, Netherlands	0:24.58

100-Meter Freestyle	Time
1912 Fanny Durack, Australia	1:22.2
1920 Ethelda Bleibtrey, United States	1:13.6
1924 Ethel Lackie, United States	1:12.4
1928 Albina Osipowich, United States	1:11.0
1932 Helene Madison, United States	1:06.8
1936 Hendrika Mastenbroek, Holland	1:05.9
1948 Greta Andersen, Denmark	1:06.3
1952 Katalin Szoke, Hungary	1:06.8
1956 Dawn Fraser, Australia	1:02.0
1960 Dawn Fraser, Australia	1:01.2
1964 Dawn Fraser, Australia	0:59.5
1968 Jan Henne, United States	1:00.0
1972 Sandra Neilson, United States	0:58.59
1976 Kornelia Ender, E. Germany	0:55.65
1980 Barbara Krause, E. Germany	0:54.79
1984 Carrie Steinseifer, United States	0:55.92
Nancy Hogshead, United States (tie)	0:55.92
1988 Kristin Otto, E. Germany	0:54.93
1992 Zhuang Yong, China	0:54.64
1996 Li Jingyi, China	0:54.50
2000 Inge de Bruijn, Netherlands	0:53.83
2004 Jodie Henry, Australia	0:53.84

200-Meter Freestyle	Time
1968 Debbie Meyer, United States	2:10.5
1972 Shane Gould, Australia	2:03.56
1976 Kornelia Ender, E. Germany	1:59.26
1980 Barbara Krause, E. Germany	1:58.33
1984 Mary Wayte, United States	1:59.23
1988 Heike Friedrich, E. Germany	1:57.65*
1992 Nicole Haislett, United States	1:57.90
1996 Claudia Poll, Costa Rica	1:58.16
2000 Susie O'Neill, Australia	1:58.24
2004 Camelia Potec, Romania	1:58.03

400-Meter Freestyle	Time
1924 Martha Norelius, United States	6:02.2
1928 Martha Norelius, United States	5:42.8
1932 Helene Madison, United States	5:28.5
1936 Hendrika Mastenbroek, Netherlands	5:26.4
1948 Ann Curtis, United States	5:17.8
1952 Valerie Gyenge, Hungary	5:12.1
1956 Lorraine Crapp, Australia	4:54.6
1960 Susan Chris von Saltza, United States	4:50.6
1964 Virginia Duenkel, United States	4:43.3
1968 Debbie Meyer, United States	4:31.8
1972 Shane Gould, Australia	4:19.44
1976 Petra Thuemer, E. Germany	4:09.89
1980 Ines Diers, E. Germany	4:08.76
1984 Tiffany Cohen, United States	4:07.10
1988 Janet Evans, United States	4:03.85*
1992 Dagmar Hase, Germany	4:07.18
1996 Michelle Smith, Ireland	4:07.25
2000 Brooke Bennett, United States	4:05.80
2004 Laure Manaudou, France	4:05.34

800-Meter Freestyle	Time
1968 Debbie Meyer, United States	9:24.0
1972 Keena Rothhammer, United States	8:53.68
1976 Petra Thuemer, E. Germany	8:37.14
1980 Michelle Ford, Australia	8:28.90
1984 Tiffany Cohen, United States	8:24.95
1988 Janet Evans, United States	8:20.20
1992 Janet Evans, United States	8:25.52
1996 Brooke Bennett, United States	8:27.89
2000 Brooke Bennett, United States	8:19.67*
2004 Ai Shibata, Japan	8:24.54

100-Meter Backstroke	Time
1924 Sybil Bauer, United States	1:23.2
1928 Marie Braun, Netherlands	1:22.0
1932 Eleanor Holm, United States	1:19.4
1936 Dina Senff, Netherlands	1:18.9
1948 Karen Harup, Denmark	1:14.4
1952 Joan Harrison, South Africa	1:14.3
1956 Judy Grinham, Great Britain	1:12.9
1960 Lynn Burke, United States	1:09.3
1964 Cathy Ferguson, United States	1:07.7
1968 Kaye Hall, United States	1:06.2
1972 Melissa Belote, United States	1:05.78
1976 Ulrike Richter, E. Germany	1:01.83
1980 Rica Reinisch, E. Germany	1:00.86
1984 Theresa Andrews, United States	1:02.55
1988 Kristin Otto, E. Germany	1:00.89
1992 Krisztina Egerszegi, Hungary	1:00.68
1996 Beth Botsford, United States	1:01.19
2000 Diana Mocanu, Romania	1:00.21
2004 Natalie Coughlin, United States	1:00.37

200-Meter Backstroke	Time
1968 Pokey Watson, United States	2:24.8
1972 Melissa Belote, United States	2:19.19
1976 Ulrike Richter, E. Germany	2:13.43
1980 Rica Reinisch, E. Germany	2:11.77
1984 Jolanda De Rover, Netherlands	2:12.38
1988 Krisztina Egerszegi, Hungary	2:09.29
1992 Krisztina Egerszegi, Hungary	2:07.06*
1996 Krisztina Egerszegi, Hungary	2:07.83
2000 Diana Mocanu, Romania	2:08.16
2004 Kirsty Coventry, Zimbabwe	2:09.19

100-Meter Breaststroke	Time
1968 Djurdjica Bjedov, Yugoslavia	1:15.8
1972 Cathy Carr, United States	1:13.58
1976 Hannelore Anke, E. Germany	1:11.16
1980 Ute Geweniger, E. Germany	1:10.22
1984 Petra Van Staveren, Netherlands	1:09.88
1988 Tania Dangalakova, Bulgaria	1:07.95
1992 Elena Roudkovskaia, Unified Team	1:08.00
1996 Penny Heyns, South Africa	1:07.73
2000 Megan Quann, United States	1:07.05
2004 Luo Xuejuan, China	1:06.64*

200-Meter Breaststroke	Time
1924 Lucy Morton, Great Britain	3:33.2
1928 Hilde Schrader, Germany	3:12.6
1932 Clare Dennis, Australia	3:06.3
1936 Hideko Maehata, Japan	3:03.6
1948 Nelly Van Vliet, Netherlands	2:57.2
1952 Eva Szekely, Hungary	2:51.7
1956 Ursula Happe, Germany	2:53.1
1960 Anita Lonsbrough, Great Britain	2:49.5
1964 Galina Prozumenschikova, USSR	2:46.4
1968 Sharon Wichman, United States	2:44.4
1972 Beverly Whitfield, Australia	2:41.71
1976 Marina Koshevaia, USSR	2:33.35
1980 Lina Kachushite, USSR	2:29.54
1984 Anne Ottenbrite, Canada	2:30.38
1988 Silke Hoerner, E. Germany	2:26.71
1992 Kyoko Iwasaki, Japan	2:26.65
1996 Penny Heyns, South Africa	2:25.41
2000 Agnes Kovacs, Hungary	2:24.35
2004 Amanda Beard, United States	2:23.37*

100-Meter Butterfly	Time
1956 Shelley Mann, United States	1:11.0
1960 Carolyn Schuler, United States	1:09.5
1964 Sharon Stouder, United States	1:04.7
1968 Lynn McClements, Australia	1:05.5
1972 Mayumi Aoki, Japan	1:03.34
1976 Kornelia Ender, E. Germany	1:00.13
1980 Caren Metschuck, E. Germany	1:00.42
1984 Mary T. Meagher, United States	0:59.26
1988 Kristin Otto, E. Germany	0:59.00
1992 Qian Hong, China	0:58.62
1996 Amy Van Dyken, United States	0:59.13
2000 Inge de Bruijn, Netherlands	0:56.61*
2004 Petria Thomas, Australia	0:57.72

200-Meter Butterfly	Time
1968 Ada Kok, Netherlands	2:24.7
1972 Karen Moe, United States	2:15.57
1976 Andrea Pollack, E. Germany	2:11.41
1980 Ines Geissler, E. Germany	2:10.44
1984 Mary T. Meagher, United States	2:06.90
1988 Kathleen Nord, E. Germany	2:09.51
1992 Summer Sanders, United States	2:08.67
1996 Susan O'Neill, Australia	2:07.76
2000 Misty Hyman, United States	2:05.88*
2004 Otylia Jedrzejczak, Poland	2:06.05

200-Meter Individual Medley

		Time
1968	Claudia Kolb, United States	2:24.7
1972	Shane Gould, Australia	2:23.07
1984	Tracy Caulkins, United States	2:12.64
1988	Daniela Hunger, E. Germany	2:12.59
1992	Lin Li, China	2:11.65
1996	Michelle Smith, Ireland	2:13.93
2000	Yana Klochkova, Ukraine	2:10.68*
2004	Yana Klochkova, Ukraine	2:11.14

400-Meter Individual Medley

		Time
1964	Donna de Varona, United States	5:18.7
1968	Claudia Kolb, United States	5:08.5
1972	Gail Neall, Australia	5:02.97
1976	Ulrike Tauber, E. Germany	4:42.77
1980	Petra Schneider, E. Germany	4:36.29
1984	Tracy Caulkins, United States	4:39.24
1988	Janet Evans, United States	4:37.76
1992	Krisztina Egerszegi, Hungary	4:36.54
1996	Michelle Smith, Ireland	4:39.18
2000	Yana Klochkova, Ukraine	4:33.59*
2004	Yana Klochkova, Ukraine	4:34.83

400-Meter Freestyle Relay

		Time
1912	Great Britain	5:52.8
1920	United States	5:11.6
1924	United States	4:58.8
1928	United States	4:47.6
1932	United States	4:38.0
1936	Netherlands	4:36.0
1948	United States	4:29.2
1952	Hungary	4:24.4
1956	Australia	4:17.1
1960	United States	4:08.9
1964	United States	4:03.8
1968	United States	4:02.5
1972	United States	3:55.19
1976	United States	3:44.82
1980	East Germany	3:42.71
1984	United States	3:43.43
1988	East Germany	3:40.63
1992	United States	3:39.46
1996	United States	3:39.29
2000	United States	3:36.61
2004	Australia	3:35.94*

800-Meter Freestyle Relay

		Time
1996	United States	7:59.87
2000	United States	7:57.80
2004	United States	7:53.42*

400-Meter Medley Relay

		Time
1960	United States	4:41.1
1964	United States	4:33.9
1968	United States	4:28.3
1972	United States	4:20.75
1976	East Germany	4:07.95
1980	East Germany	4:06.67

400-Meter Medley Relay

		Time
1984	United States	4:08.34
1988	East Germany	4:03.74
1992	United States	4:02.54
1996	United States	4:02.88
2000	United States	3:58.30
2004	Australia	3:57.32*

Springboard Diving

		Points
1920	Aileen Riggin, United States	539.90
1924	Elizabeth Becker, United States	474.50
1928	Helen Meany, United States	78.62
1932	Georgia Coleman United States	87.52
1936	Marjorie Gestring, United States	89.27
1948	Victoria M. Draves, United States	108.74
1952	Patricia McCormick, United States	147.30
1956	Patricia McCormick, United States	142.36
1960	Ingrid Kramer, Germany	155.81
1964	Ingrid Engel-Kramer, Germany	145.00
1968	Sue Gossick, United States	150.77
1972	Micki King, United States	450.03
1976	Jenni Chandler, United States	506.19
1980	Irina Kalinina, USSR	725.91
1984	Sylvie Bernier, Canada	530.70
1988	Gao Min, China	580.23
1992	Gao Min, China	572.40
1996	Fu Mingxia, China	547.68
2000	Fu Mingxia, China	609.42
2004	Guo Jingjing, China	633.15

Platform Diving

		Points
1912	Greta Johansson, Sweden	39.90
1920	Stefani Fryland-Clausen, Denmark	34.60
1924	Caroline Smith, United States	33.20
1928	Elizabeth B. Pinkston, United States	31.60
1932	Dorothy Poynton, United States	40.26
1936	Dorothy Poynton Hill, United States	33.93
1948	Victoria M. Draves, United States	8.87
1952	Patricia McCormick, United States	79.37
1956	Patricia McCormick, United States	84.85
1960	Ingrid Kramer, Germany	91.28
1964	Lesley Bush, United States	99.80
1968	Milena Duchkova, Czech.	109.59
1972	Ulrika Knape, Sweden	390.00
1976	Elena Vaytsekhouskaya, USSR	406.59
1980	Martina Jaschke, E. Germany	596.25
1984	Zhou Jihong, China	435.51
1988	Xu Yanmei, China	445.20
1992	Fu Mingxia, China	461.43
1996	Fu Mingxia, China	521.58
2000	Laura Wilkinson, United States	543.75
2004	Chantelle Newbery, Australia	590.31

Synchronized Platform

		Points
2004	Lao Lishi and Li Ting, China	352.14

Synchronized Springboard

		Points
2004	Wu Minxia and Guo Jingjing, China	336.90

BOXING

Lt. Flyweight (48 kg/106 lbs)

1968	Francisco Rodriguez, Venezuela
1972	Gyorgy Gedo, Hungary
1976	Jorge Hernandez, Cuba
1980	Shamil Sabyrov, USSR
1984	Paul Gonzalez, United States
1988	Ivailo Hristov, Bulgaria
1992	Rogelio Marcelo, Cuba
1996	Daniel Petrov, Bulgaria
2000	Brahim Asloum, France
2004	Yan Bhartelemy Varela, Cuba

Flyweight (51 kg/112 lbs)

1904	George Finnegan, United States
1920	William Di Gennara, United States
1924	Fidel LaBarba, United States
1928	Antal Kocsis, Hungary
1932	Istvan Enekes, Hungary
1936	Willi Kaiser, Germany
1948	Pascual Perez, Argentina
1952	Nathan Brooks, United States
1956	Terence Spinks, Great Britain
1960	Gyula Torok, Hungary
1964	Fernando Atzori, Italy
1968	Ricardo Delgado, Mexico
1972	Georgi Kostadinov, Bulgaria
1976	Leo Randolph, United States
1980	Peter Lessov, Bulgaria
1984	Steve McCrory, United States
1988	Kim Kwang Sun, S. Korea
1992	Su Choi Choi, N. Korea

1996	Maikro Romero, Cuba
2000	Wijan Ponlid, Thailand
2004	Yuriorkis Gamboa Toledano, Cuba

Bantamweight (54 kg /119 lbs)

1904	Oliver Kirk, United States
1908	A. Henry Thomas, Great Britain
1920	Clarence Walker, South Africa
1924	William Smith, South Africa
1928	Vittorio Tamagnini, Italy
1932	Horace Gwynne, Canada
1936	Ulderico Sergo, Italy
1948	Tibor Csik, Hungary
1952	Pentti Hamalainen, Finland
1956	Wolfgang Behrendt, E. Germany
1960	Oleg Grigoryev, USSR
1964	Takao Sakurai, Japan
1968	Valery Sokolov, USSR
1972	Orlando Martinez, Cuba
1976	Yong-Jo Gu, N. Korea
1980	Juan Hernandez, Cuba
1984	Maurizio Stecca, Italy
1988	Kennedy McKinney, United States
1992	Joel Casamayor, Cuba
1996	Istvan Kovacs, Hungary
2000	Guillermo Rigondeaux, Cuba
2004	Guillermo Rigondeaux, Cuba

Featherweight (57 kg/125 lbs)

1904	Oliver Kirk, United States
1908	Richard Gunn, Great Britain
1920	Paul Fritsch, France

1924	John Fields, United States
1928	Lambertus van Klaveren, Netherlands
1932	Carmelo Robledo, Argentina
1936	Oscar Casanovas, Argentina
1948	Ernesto Formenti, Italy
1952	Jan Zachara, Czechoslovakia
1956	Vladimir Safronov, USSR
1960	Francesco Musso, Italy
1964	Stanislav Stephashkin, USSR
1968	Antonin Roldan, Mexico
1972	Boris Kousnetsov, USSR
1976	Angel Herrera, Cuba
1980	Rudi Fink, E. Germany
1984	Meldrick Taylor, United States
1988	Giovanni Parisi, Italy
1992	Andreas Tews, Germany
1996	Somluck Kamsing, Thailand
2000	Bekzat Sattarkhanov, Kazakhstan
2004	Alexei Tichtchenko, Russia

Lightweight (60 kg/132 lbs)

1904	Harry Spanger, United States
1908	Frederick Grace, Great Britain
1920	Samuel Mosberg, United States
1924	Hans Nielsen, Denmark
1928	Carlo Orlandi, Italy
1932	Lawrence Stevens, South Africa
1936	Imre Harangi, Hungary
1948	Gerald Dreyer, South Africa
1952	Aureliano Bolognesi, Italy
1956	Richard McTaggart, Great Britain

1960	Kazimierz Pazdzior, Poland
1964	Jozef Grudzien, Poland
1968	Ronald Harris, United States
1972	Jan Szczepanski, Poland
1976	Howard Davis, United States
1980	Angel Herrera, Cuba
1984	Pernell Whitaker, United States
1988	Andreas Zuelow, E. Germany
1992	Oscar De La Hoya, United States
1996	Hocine Soltani, Algeria
2000	Mario Kindelan, Cuba
2004	Mario Kindelan, Cuba

Lt. Welterweight (63.5 kg/139 lbs)

1952	Charles Adkins, United States
1956	Vladimir Yengibaryan, USSR
1960	Bohumil Nemecek, Czechoslovakzia
1964	Jerzy Kulej, Poland
1968	Jerzy Kulej, Poland
1972	Ray Seales, United States
1976	Ray Leonard, United States
1980	Patrizio Oliva, Italy
1984	Jerry Page, United States
1988	Viatcheslav Janovski, USSR
1992	Hector Vinent, Cuba
1996	Hector Vinent, Cuba
2000	Mahamadkadyz Abdullaev, Uzbekistan
2004	Manus Boonjumnong, Thailand

Welterweight (67 kg/147 lbs)

1904	Albert Young, United States
1920	Albert Schneider, Canada
1924	Jean Delarge, Belgium
1928	Edward Morgan, New Zealand
1932	Edward Flynn, United States
1936	Sten Suvio, Finland
1948	Julius Torma, Czechoslovakia
1952	Zygmunt Chychia, Poland
1956	Nicolae Linca, Romania
1960	Giovanni Benvenuti, Italy
1964	Marian Kasprzyk, Poland
1968	Manfred Wolke, E. Germany
1972	Emilio Correa, Cuba
1976	Jochen Bachfeld, E. Germany
1980	Andres Aldama, Cuba
1984	Mark Breland, United States
1988	Robert Wangila, Kenya
1992	Michael Carruth, Ireland

1996	Oleg Saitov, Russia
2000	Oleg Saitov, Russia
2004	Artayev Bakhtiyar, Kazakhstan

Lt. Middleweight (71 kg/156 lbs)

1952	Laszlo Papp, Hungary
1956	Laszlo Papp, Hungary
1960	Wilbert McClure, United States
1964	Boris Lagutin, USSR
1968	Boris Lagutin, USSR
1972	Dieter Kottysch, W. Germany
1976	Jerzy Rybicki, Poland
1980	Armando Martinez, Cuba
1984	Frank Tate, United States
1988	Park Si Hun, S. Korea
1992	Juan Lemus, Cuba
1996	David Reid, United States
2000	Yermakhan Ibraimov, Kazakhstan

Middleweight (75 kg/165 lbs)

1904	Charles Mayer, United States
1908	John Douglas, Great Britain
1920	Harry Mallin, Great Britain
1924	Harry Mallin, Great Britain
1928	Piero Toscani, Italy
1932	Carmen Barth, United States
1936	Jean Despeaux, France
1948	Laszlo Papp, Hungary
1952	Floyd Patterson, United States
1956	Gennady Schatkov, USSR
1960	Edward Crook, United States
1964	Valery Popenchenko, USSR
1968	Christopher Finnegan, Great Britain
1972	Vyacheslav Lemechev, USSR
1976	Michael Spinks, United States
1980	Jose Gomez, Cuba
1984	Joon-Sup Shin, S. Korea
1988	Henry Maske, E. Germany
1992	Ariel Hernandez, Cuba
1996	Ariel Hernandez, Cuba
2000	Jorge Gutierrez, Cuba
2004	Gaydarbek Gaydarbekov, Russia

Lt. Heavyweight (81 kg/178 lbs)

1920	Edward Eagan, United States
1924	Harry Mitchell, Great Britain
1928	Victor Avendano, Argentina
1932	David Carstens, South Africa
1936	Roger Michelot, France

1948	George Hunter, South Africa
1952	Norvel Lee, United States
1956	James Boyd, United States
1960	Cassius Clay, United States
1964	Cosimo Pinto, Italy
1968	Dan Poznyak, USSR
1972	Mate Parlov, Yugoslavia
1976	Leon Spinks, United States
1980	Slobodan Kacar, Yugoslavia
1984	Anton Josipovic, Yugoslavia
1988	Andrew Maynard, United States
1992	Torsten May, Germany
1996	Vassili Jirov, Kazakhstan
2000	Alexander Lebziak, Russia
2004	Andre Ward, United States

Heavyweight (91 kg/201 lbs)

1984	Henry Tillman, United States
1988	Ray Mercer, United States
1992	Felix Savon, Cuba
1996	Felix Savon, Cuba
2000	Felix Savon, Cuba
2004	Odlanier Solis Fonte, Cuba

Super Heavyweight (91+ kg/201+ lbs)

(known as heavyweight, 1904-80)

1904	Samuel Berger, United States
1908	Albert Oldham, Great Britain
1920	Ronald Rawson, Great Britain
1924	Otto von Porat, Norway
1928	Arturo Rodriguez Jurado, Argentina
1932	Santiago Lovell, Argentina
1936	Herbert Runge, Germany
1948	Rafael Iglesias, Argentina
1952	H. Edward Sanders, United States
1956	T. Peter Rademacher, United States
1960	Franco De Piccoli, Italy
1964	Joe Frazier, United States
1968	George Foreman, United States
1972	Teofilo Stevenson, Cuba
1976	Teofilo Stevenson, Cuba
1980	Teofilo Stevenson, Cuba
1984	Tyrell Biggs, United States
1988	Lennox Lewis, Canada
1992	Roberto Balado, Cuba
1996	Vladimir Klitchko, Ukraine
2000	Audley Harrison, Britain
2004	Alexander Povetkin, Russia

Winter Olympic Games in 2006—Highlights

Turin (Torino), Italy, Feb. 10-26, 2006

The XX Winter Olympic Games opened Feb. 10, 2006, in Turin—Italy's 4th largest city and the largest ever to host the Winter Game. More than 2,500 athletes from 84 countries competed in 84 medal events over 16 days in Turin. As in 1998 and 2002, Germany led the medal count, with 29, and the U.S. claimed 25 medals, its highest medal count for Winter Games not held in the U.S.

A new rating system was implemented for figure skating events following a scoring controversy in the 2002 games. Favored skaters Sasha Cohen (2006 U.S. champion) and Russian Irina Slutskaya (2005 world champion) fell during their routines and had to settle for silver and bronze, respectively, as Shizuka Arakawa became the first Japanese gold medalist in that event. Speedskater Shani Davis won the men's 1,000-meter event, becoming the first African American to claim gold in a Winter Games individual event. Canadian speedskater Cindy Klassen won the most medals of any athlete in the games, with 1 gold, 2 silver and 2 bronze. The U.S. curling team won bronze—the nation's first curling medal—after defeating Britain. Snowboarding events were dominated by the U.S. as the team won 3 of 6 golds. But the celebrated U.S. alpine ski team, which had given itself the motto "Best in the World," managed to claim just 2 medals in competition (both gold). The Austrian team dominated alpine competition, winning 14 of 30 medals up for grabs. In hockey, the U.S. women's team was upset in a 3-2 shootout in the semifinals by Sweden and had to settle for bronze, while the U.S. men's team did not medal and Sweden defeated Finland for the gold.

2006 Final Medal Standings

	Gold	Silver	Bronze	Total		Gold	Silver	Bronze	Total
Germany	11	12	6	29	Czech Republic	1	2	1	4
United States	9	9	7	25	Estonia	3	0	0	3
Canada	7	10	7	24	Croatia	1	2	0	3
Austria	9	7	7	23	Australia	1	0	1	2
Russia	8	6	8	22	Poland	0	1	1	2
Norway	2	8	9	19	Ukraine	0	0	2	2
Sweden	7	2	5	14	Japan	1	0	0	1
Switzerland	5	4	5	14	Belarus	0	1	0	1
South Korea	6	3	2	11	Great Britain	0	1	0	1
Italy	5	0	6	11	Bulgaria	0	1	0	1
China	2	4	5	11	Slovakia	0	1	0	1
France	3	2	4	9	Latvia	0	0	1	1
Netherlands	3	2	4	9	**TOTAL**	**84**	**84**	**84**	**252**
Finland	0	6	3	9					

Winter Olympic Games Champions, 1924-2006

In 1992, the Unified Team represented the former Soviet republics of Russia, Ukraine, Belarus, Kazakhstan, and Uzbekistan.

Alpine Skiing

Men's Downhill

Year	Champion	Time
1948	Henri Oreiller, France	2:55.0
1952	Zeno Colo, Italy	2:30.8
1956	Toni Sailer, Austria	2:52.2
1960	Jean Vuarnet, France	2:06.0
1964	Egon Zimmermann, Austria	2:18.16
1968	Jean-Claude Killy, France	1:59.85
1972	Bernhard Russi, Switzerland	1:51.43
1976	Franz Klammer, Austria	1:45.73
1980	Leonhard Stock, Austria	1:45.50
1984	Bill Johnson, United States	1:45.49
1988	Pirmin Zurbriggen, Switzerland	1:59.63
1992	Patrick Ortlieb, Austria	1:50.37
1994	Tommy Moe, United States	1:45.75
1998	Jean-Luc Cretier, France	1:50.11
2002	Fritz Strobl, Austria	1:39.13
2006	Antoine Deneriaz, France	1:48.80

Men's Super Giant Slalom

Year	Champion	Time
1988	Franck Piccard, France	1:39.66
1992	Kjetil-Andre Aamodt, Norway	1:13.04
1994	Markus Wasmeier, Germany	1:32.53
1998	Hermann Maier, Austria	1:34.82
2002	Kjetil Andre Aamodt, Norway	1:21.58
2006	Kjetil Andre Aamodt, Norway	1:30.65

Men's Giant Slalom

Year	Champion	Time
1952	Stein Eriksen, Norway	2:25.0
1956	Toni Sailer, Austria	3:00.1
1960	Roger Staub, Switzerland	1:48.3
1964	Francois Bonlieu, France	1:46.71
1968	Jean-Claude Killy, France	3:29.28
1972	Gustavo Thoeni, Italy	3:09.62
1976	Heini Hemmi, Switzerland	3:26.97
1980	Ingemar Stenmark, Sweden	2:40.74
1984	Max Julen, Switzerland	2:41.18
1988	Alberto Tomba, Italy	2:06.37
1992	Alberto Tomba, Italy	2:06.98
1994	Markus Wasmeier, Germany	2:52.46
1998	Hermann Maier, Austria	2:38.51
2002	Stephan Eberharter, Austria	2:23.28
2006	Benjamin Raich, Austria	2:35.00

Men's Slalom

Year	Champion	Time
1948	Edi Reinalter, Switzerland	2:10.3
1952	Othmar Schneider, Austria	2:00.0
1956	Toni Sailer, Austria	3:14.7
1960	Ernst Hinterseer, Austria	2:08.9
1964	Josef Stiegler, Austria	2:11.13
1968	Jean-Claude Killy, France	1:39.73
1972	Francisco Fernandez-Ochoa, Spain	1:49.27
1976	Piero Gros, Italy	2:03.29
1980	Ingemar Stenmark, Sweden	1:44.26
1984	Phil Mahre, United States	1:39.41
1988	Alberto Tomba, Italy	1:39.47
1992	Finn Christian Jagge, Norway	1:44.39
1994	Thomas Stangassinger, Austria	2:02.02
1998	Hans-Petter Buraas, Norway	1:49.31
2002	Jean-Pierre Vidal, France	1:41.06
2006	Benjamin Raich, Austria	1:43.14

Men's Combined

Year	Champion	Time
1936	Franz-Pfnuer, Germany	99.25 (pts.)
1948	Henri Oreiller, France	3.27 (pts.)
1988	Hubert Strolz, Austria	36.55 (pts.)
1992	Josef Polig, Italy	14.58 (pts.)
1994	Lasse Kjus, Norway	3:17.53
1998	Mario Reiter, Austria	3:08.06
2002	Kjetil Andre Aamodt, Norway	3:17.56
2006	Ted Ligety, United States	3:09.35

Women's Downhill

Year	Champion	Time
1948	Hedi Schlunegger, Switzerland	2:28.3
1952	Trude Beiser-Jochum, Austria	1:47.1
1956	Madeleine Berthod, Switzerland	1:40.7
1960	Heidi Biebl, Germany	1:37.6
1964	Christl Haas, Austria	1:55.39
1968	Olga Pall, Austria	1:40.87
1972	Marie-Theres Nadig, Switzerland	1:36.68
1976	Rosi Mittermaier, W. Germany	1:46.16
1980	Annemarie Moser-Proell, Austria	1:37.52
1984	Michela Figini, Switzerland	1:13.36
1988	Marina Kiehl, W. Germany	1:25.86
1992	Kerrin Lee-Gartner, Canada	1:52.55
1994	Katja Seizinger, Germany	1:35.93
1998	Katja Seizinger, Germany	1:28.89
2002	Carole Montillet, France	1:39.56
2006	Michaela Dorfmeister, Austria	1:56.49

Women's Super Giant Slalom

Year	Champion	Time
1988	Sigrid Wolf, Austria	1:19.03
1992	Deborah Compagnoni, Italy	1:21.22
1994	Diann Roffe (Steinrotter), United States	1:22.15
1998	Picabo Street, United States	1:18.02
2002	Daniela Ceccarelli, Italy	1:13.59
2006	Michaela Dorfmeister, Austria	1:32.47

Women's Giant Slalom

Year	Champion	Time
1952	Andrea Mead Lawrence, United States	2:06.8
1956	Ossi Reichert, Germany	1:56.5
1960	Yvonne Ruegg, Switzerland	1:39.9
1964	Marielle Goitschel, France	1:52.24
1968	Nancy Greene, Canada	1:51.97
1972	Marie-Theres Nadig, Switzerland	1:29.90
1976	Kathy Kreiner, Canada	1:29.13
1980	Hanni Wenzel, Liechtenstein (2 runs)	2:41.66
1984	Debbie Armstrong, United States	2:20.98
1988	Vreni Schneider, Switzerland	2:06.49
1992	Pernilla Wiberg, Sweden	2:12.74
1994	Deborah Compagnoni, Italy	2:30.97
1998	Deborah Compagnoni, Italy	2:50.59
2002	Janica Kostelic, Croatia	2:30.01
2006	Julia Mancuso, United States	2:09.19

Women's Slalom

Year	Champion	Time
1948	Gretchen Fraser, United States	1:57.2
1952	Andrea Mead Lawrence, United States	2:10.6
1956	Renee Colliard, Switzerland	1:52.3
1960	Anne Heggtveit, Canada	1:49.6
1964	Christine Goitschel, France	1:29.86
1968	Marielle Goitschel, France	1:25.86
1972	Barbara Ann Cochran, United States	1:31.24
1976	Rosi Mittermaier, W. Germany	1:30.54
1980	Hanni Wenzel, Liechtenstein	1:25.09
1984	Paoletta Magoni, Italy	1:36.47
1988	Vreni Schneider, Switzerland	1:36.69
1992	Petra Kronberger, Austria	1:32.68
1994	Vreni Schneider, Switzerland	1:56.01
1998	Hilde Gerg, Germany	1:32.40
2002	Janica Kostelic, Croatia	1:46.10
2006	Anja Paerson, Sweden	1:29.04

Women's Combined

Year	Champion	Time
1936	Christl Cranz, Germany	97.06 (pts.)
1948	Trude Beiser-Jochum, Austria	6.58 (pts.)
1988	Anita Wachter, Austria	29.25 (pts.)
1992	Petra Kronberger, Austria	2.55 (pts.)
1994	Pernilla Wiberg, Sweden	3:05.16
1998	Katja Seizinger, Germany	2:40.74
2002	Janica Kostelic, Croatia	2:43.28
2006	Janica Kostelic, Croatia	2:51.08

Biathlon

Men's 10 Kilometers

Year	Champion	Time
1980	Frank Ullrich, E. Germany	32:10.69
1984	Eirik Kvalfoss, Norway	30:53.80
1988	Frank-Peter Roetsch, E. Germany	25:08.10
1992	Mark Kirchner, Germany	26:02.30
1994	Serguei Tchepikov, Russia	28:07.00
1998	Ole Einar Bjoerndalen, Norway	27:16.20
2002	Ole Einar Bjoerndalen, Norway	24:51.30
2006	Sven Fischer, Germany	26:11.6

Men's 12.5 Kilometers

Year	Champion	Time
2002	Ole Einar Bjoerndalen, Norway	32:34.6
2006	Vincent Defrasne, France	35:20.2

Men's 15 Kilometers

Year	Champion	Time
2006	Michael Greis, Germany	47:20.0

Men's 20 Kilometers

Year	Champion	Time
1960	Klas Lestander, Sweden	1:33:21.6
1964	Vladimir Melanin, USSR	1:20:26.8
1968	Magnar Solberg, Norway	1:13:45.9
1972	Magnar Solberg, Norway	1:15:55.50
1976	Nikolai Kruglov, USSR	1:14:12.26
1980	Anatoly Aljabiev, USSR	1:08:16.31
1984	Peter Angerer, W. Germany	1:11:52.7
1988	Frank-Peter Roetsch, E. Germany	0:56:33.33
1992	Yevgeny Redkine, Unified Team	0:57:34.4
1994	Serguei Tarasov, Russia	0:57:25.3
1998	Halvard Hanevold, Norway	0:56:16.4
2002	Ole Einar Bjoerndalen, Norway	0:51:03.03
2006	Michael Greis, Germany	0:54:23.0

Men's 30-Kilometer Relay

Year		Time
1968	USSR, Norway, Sweden (40 km)	2:13:02.4
1972	USSR, Finland, E. Germany (40 km)	1:51:44.92
1976	USSR, Finland, E. Germany (40 km)	1:57:55.64
1980	USSR, E. Germany, W. Germany	1:34:03.27
1984	USSR, Norway, W. Germany	1:38:51.70
1988	USSR, W. Germany, Italy	1:22:30.00
1992	Germany, Unified Team, Sweden	1:24:43.50
1994	Germany, Russia, France	1:30:22.1
1998	Norway, Norway, Russia	1:19:43.3
2002	Norway, Germany, France	1:23:42.3
2006	Germany, Russia, France	1:21:51.5

Women's 7.5 Kilometers

Year		Time
1992	Anfissa Restsova, Unified Team	24:29.2
1994	Myriam Bedard, Canada	26:08.8
1998	Galina Koukleva, Russia	23:08.0
2002	Kati Wilhelm, Germany	20:41.4
2006	Florence Baverel-Robert, France	22:31.4

Women's 10 Kilometers

Year		Time
2002	Olga Pyleva, Russia	31:07.7
2006	Kati Wilhelm, Germany	36:43.6

Women's 12.5 Kilometers

Year		Time
2006	Anna Carin Olofsson, Sweden	40:36.5

Women's 15 Kilometers

Year		Time
1992	Antje Misersky, Germany	51:47.2
1994	Myriam Bedard, Canada	52:06.6
1998	Ekaterina Dafovska, Bulgaria	54:52.0
2002	Andrea Henkel, Germany	47:30.0
2006	Svetlana Ishmouratova, Russia	49:24.1

Women's 24-Kilometer Relay

Year		Time
1992	France, Germany, Unified Team (22.5 km)	1:15:55.6
1994	Russia, Germany, France (30 km)	1:47:19.5
1998	Germany, Russia, Norway (30 km)	1:40:13.6
2002	Germany, Norway, Russia (30 km)	1:27:55.0
2006	Russia, Germany, France	1:16:12.5

Bobsledding
(Driver in parentheses)

4-Man Bob

Year		Time
1924	Switzerland (Eduard Scherrer)	5:45.54
1928	United States (William Fiske) (5-man)	3:20.50
1932	United States (William Fiske)	7:53.68
1936	Switzerland (Pierre Musy)	5:19.85
1948	United States (Francis Tyler)	5:20.10
1952	Germany (Andreas Ostler)	5:07.84
1956	Switzerland (Franz Kapus)	5:10.44
1964	Canada (Victor Emery)	4:14.46
1968	Italy (Eugenio Monti) (2 races)	2:17.39
1972	Switzerland (Jean Wicki)	4:43.07
1976	E. Germany (Meinhard Nehmer)	3:40.43
1980	E. Germany (Meinhard Nehmer)	3:59.92
1984	E. Germany (Wolfgang Hoppe)	3:20.22
1988	Switzerland (Ekkehard Fasser)	3:47.51
1992	Austria (Ingo Appelt)	3:53.90
1994	Germany (Wolfgang Hoppe)	3:27.28
1998	Germany II (Christoph Langen)	2:39.41
2002	Germany II (Andre Lange)	3:07.51
2006	Germany (Andre Lange)	3:40.42

2-Man Bob

Year		Time
1932	United States (Hubert Stevens)	8:14.74
1936	United States (Ivan Brown)	5:29.29
1948	Switzerland (F. Endrich)	5:29.20
1952	Germany (Andreas Ostler)	5:24.54
1956	Italy (Dalla Costa)	5:30.14
1964	Great Britain (Anthony Nash)	4:21.90
1968	Italy (Eugenio Monti)	4:41.54
1972	W. Germany (Wolfgang Zimmerer)	4:57.07
1976	E. Germany (Meinhard Nehmer)	3:44.42
1980	Switzerland (Erich Schaerer)	4:09.36
1984	E. Germany (Wolfgang Hoppe)	3:25.56
1988	USSR (Janis Kipours)	3:54.19
1992	Switzerland (Gustav Weber)	4:03.26
1994	Switzerland (Gustav Weber)	3:30.81
1998	Canada (Pierre Lueders), Italy (Guenther Huber) (tie)	3:37.24
2002	Germany II (Christoph Langen)	3:10.11
2006	Germany (Andre Lange)	3:43.38

2-Woman Bob

Year		Time
2002	United States II (Jill Bakken)	1:37.76
2006	Germany (Sandra Kiriasis)	3:49.98

Curling

Men

Year	
1998	Switzerland, Canada, Norway
2002	Norway, Canada, Switzerland
2006	Canada, Finland, United States

Women

Year	
1998	Canada, Denmark, Sweden
2002	Britain, Switzerland, Canada
2006	Sweden, Switzerland, Canada

Figure Skating

Men's Singles

Year	
1908[1]	Ulrich Salchow, Sweden
1920[1]	Gillis Grafstrom, Sweden
1924	Gillis Grafstrom, Sweden
1928	Gillis Grafstrom, Sweden
1932	Karl Schaefer, Austria
1936	Karl Schaefer, Austria
1948	Richard Button, United States
1952	Richard Button, United States
1956	Hayes Alan Jenkins, United States
1960	David W. Jenkins, United States
1964	Manfred Schnelldorfer, Germany
1968	Wolfgang Schwartz, Austria
1972	Ondrej Nepela, Czechoslovakia
1976	John Curry, Great Britain
1980	Robin Cousins, Great Britain
1984	Scott Hamilton, United States
1988	Brian Boitano, United States
1992	Viktor Petrenko, Unified Team
1994	Aleksei Urmanov, Russia
1998	Ilya Kulik, Russia
2002	Alexei Yagudin, Russia
2006	Yevgeny Plushenko, Russia

(1) Event held during Summer Olympic Games.

Women's Singles

Year	
1908[1]	Madge Syers, Great Britain
1920[1]	Magda Julin-Mauroy, Sweden
1924	Herma von Szabo-Planck, Austria
1928	Sonja Henie, Norway
1932	Sonja Henie, Norway
1936	Sonja Henie, Norway
1948	Barbara Ann Scott, Canada
1952	Jeanette Altwegg, Great Britan
1956	Tenley Albright, United States
1960	Carol Heiss, United States
1964	Sjoukje Dijkstra, Netherlands
1968	Peggy Fleming, United States
1972	Beatrix Schuba, Austria
1976	Dorothy Hamill, United States
1980	Anett Poetzsch, E. Germany
1984	Katarina Witt, E. Germany
1988	Katarina Witt, E. Germany
1992	Kristi Yamaguchi, United States
1994	Oksana Baiul, Ukraine
1998	Tara Lipinski, United States
2002	Sarah Hughes, United States
2006	Shizuka Arakawa, Japan

(1) Event was held at Summer Olympics.

Pairs

Year	
1908[1]	Anna Hubler & Heinrich Burger, Germany
1920[1]	Ludovika & Walter Jakobsson, Finland
1924	Helene Engelman & Alfred Berger, Austria
1928	Andree Joly & Pierre Brunet, France
1932	Andree Joly & Pierre Brunet, France
1936	Maxi Herber & Ernst Baier, Germany
1948	Micheline Lannoy & Pierre Baugniet, Belgium
1952	Ria and Paul Falk, Germany
1956	Elisabeth Schwartz & Kurt Oppelt, Austria
1964	Ludmila Beloussova & Oleg Protopopov, USSR
1968	Ludmila Beloussova & Oleg Protopopov, USSR
1972	Irina Rodnina & Alexei Ulanov, USSR
1976	Irina Rodnina & Aleksandr Zaitzev, USSR
1980	Irina Rodnina & Aleksandr Zaitzev, USSR
1984	Elena Valova & Oleg Vassiliev, USSR
1988	Ekaterina Gordeeva & Sergei Grinkov, USSR
1992	Natalia Mishkutienok & Artur Dimitriev, Unified Team
1994	Ekaterina Gordeeva & Sergei Grinkov, Russia
1998	Oksana Kazakova & Artur Dmitriev, Russia
2002	Elena Berezhnaya & Anton Sikharulidze, Russia; Jamie Sale & David Pelletier, Canada (tie)
2006	Tatyana Totmianina & Maxim Marinin, Russia

(1) Event held during Summer Olympic Games.

Ice Dancing

Year	
1976	Ludmila Pakhomova & Aleksandr Gorschkov, USSR
1980	Natalya Linichuk & Gennadi Karponosov, USSR
1984	Jayne Torvill & Christopher Dean, Great Britain
1988	Natalia Bestemianova & Andrei Bukin, USSR
1992	Marina Klimova & Sergei Ponomarenko, Unified Team

Ice Dancing

1994	Pasha Grishuk & Evgeny Platov, Russia
1998	Pasha Grishuk & Evgeny Platov, Russia
2002	Marina Anissina & Gwendal Peizerat, France
2006	Tatyana Navka & Roman Kostomarov, Russia

Freestyle Skiing

Men's Moguls

		Points
1992	Edgar Grospiron, France	25.81
1994	Jean-Luc Brassard, Canada	27.24
1998	Jonny Moseley, United States	26.93
2002	Janne Lahtela, Finland	27.97
2006	Dale Begg-Smith, Australia	26.77

Men's Aerials

		Points
1994	Andreas Schoenbaechler, Switzerland	234.67
1998	Eric Bergoust, United States	255.64
2002	Ales Valenta, Czech Republic	257.02
2006	Xiaopeng Han, China	250.77

Women's Moguls

		Points
1992	Donna Weinbrecht, United States	23.69
1994	Stine Lise Hattestad, Norway	25.97
1998	Tae Satoya, Japan	25.06
2002	Kari Traa, Norway	25.94
2006	Jennifer Heil, Canada	26.50

Women's Aerials

		Points
1994	Lina Tcherjazova, Uzbekistan	166.84
1998	Nikki Stone, United States	193.00
2002	Alisa Camplin, Australia	193.47
2006	Evelyne Leu, Switzerland	202.55

Ice Hockey

Men

1920[1]	Canada, United States, Czechoslovakia
1924	Canada, United States, Great Britain
1928	Canada, Sweden, Switzerland
1932	Canada, United States, Germany
1936	Great Britain, Canada, United States
1948	Canada, Czechoslovakia, Switzerland
1952	Canada, United States, Sweden
1956	USSR, United States, Canada
1960	United States, Canada, USSR
1964	USSR, Sweden, Czechoslovakia
1968	USSR, Czechoslovakia, Canada
1972	USSR, United States, Czechoslovakia
1976	USSR, Czechoslovakia, W. Germany
1980	United States, USSR, Sweden
1984	USSR, Czechoslovakia, Sweden
1988	USSR, Finland, Sweden
1992	Unified Team, Canada, Czechoslovakia
1994	Sweden, Canada, Finland
1998	Czech Republic, Russia, Finland
2002	Canada, United States, Russia
2006	Sweden, Finland, Czech Republic

Women

1998	United States, Canada, Finland
2002	Canada, United States, Sweden
2006	Canada, Sweden, United States

(1) Event held during Summer Olympic Games

Luge

Men's Singles

		Time
1964	Thomas Keohler, E. Germany	3:27.77
1968	Manfred Schmid, Austria	2:52.48
1972	Wolfgang Scheidel, E. Germany	3:27.58
1976	Detlef Guenther, E. Germany	3:27.688
1980	Bernhard Glass, E. Germany	2:54.796
1984	Paul Hildgartner, Italy	3:04.258
1988	Jens Mueller, E. Germany	3:05.548
1992	Georg Hackl, Germany	3:02.363
1994	Georg Hackl, Germany	3:21.571
1998	Georg Hackl, Germany	3:18.436
2002	Armin Zoeggeler, Italy	2:57.941
2006	Armin Zoeggeler, Italy	3:26.088

Women's Singles

		Time
1964	Ortun Enderlein, Germany	3:24.67
1968	Erica Lechner, Italy	2:28.66
1972	Anna M. Muller, E. Germany	2:59.18
1976	Margit Schumann, E. Germany	2:50.621
1980	Vera Zozulya, USSR	2:36.537
1984	Steffi Martin, E. Germany	2:46.570
1988	Steffi Walter, E. Germany	3:03.973
1992	Doris Neuner, Austria	3:06.696
1994	Gerda Weissensteiner, Italy	3:15.517
1998	Silke Kraushaar, Germany	3:23.779
2002	Sylke Otto, Germany	2:52.464
2006	Sylke Otto, Germany	3:07.979

Men's Doubles

		Time
1964	Austria	1:41.62
1968	E. Germany	1:35.85
1972	Italy, E. Germany (tie)	1:28.35
1976	E. Germany	1:25.604
1980	E. Germany	1:19.331
1984	W. Germany	1:23.620
1988	E. Germany	1:31.940
1992	Germany	1:32.053
1994	Italy	1:36.720
1998	Germany	1:41.105
2002	Germany	1:26.082
2006	Austria	1:34.497

Nordic Skiing
Cross-Country Events

Men's Sprint

		Time
2002	Tor Arne Hetland, Norway (1.5 kms)	2:56.9
2006	Bjoern Lind, Sweden (1.3 kms)	2:26.5

Men's Team Sprint

		Time
2006	Bjoern Lind & Thobias Fredriksson, Sweden.	17:02.9

Men's 10 Kilometers (6.2 miles)

		Time
1992	Vegard Ulvang, Norway	27:36.0
1994	Bjoern Daehlie, Norway	24:20.1
1998	Bjoern Daehlie, Norway	27:24.5
2002	Thomas Alsgaard, Norway; Frode Estil, Norway (tie) (a)	49:48.9

(a) Awarded gold after Johann Muehlegg of Spain was stripped of gold for a drug offense.

Men's 15 Kilometers (9.3 miles)

		Time
1924	Thorleif Haug, Norway	1:14:31
1928	Johan Grottumsbraaten, Norway	1:37:01
1932	Sven Utterstrom, Sweden	1:23:07
1936	Erik-August Larsson, Sweden	1:14:38
1948	Martin Lundstrom, Sweden	1:13:50
1952	Hallgeir Brenden, Norway	1:01:34
1956	Hallgeir Brenden, Norway	0:49:39.0
1960	Haakon Brusveen, Norway	0:51:55.5
1964	Eero Maentyranta, Finland	0:50:54.1
1968	Harald Groenningen, Norway	0:47:54.2
1972	Sven-Ake Lundback, Sweden	0:45:28.24
1976	Nikolai Balukov, USSR	0:43:58.47
1980	Thomas Wassberg, Sweden	0:41:57.63
1984	Gunde Svan, Sweden	0:41:25.6
1988	Mikhail Deviatiarov, USSR	0:41:18.9
1992	Bjoern Daehlie, Norway	0:38:01.9
1994	Bjoern Daehlie, Norway	0:35:48.8
1998	Thomas Alsgaard, Norway	1:07:01.7
2002	Andrus Veerpalu, Estonia	0:37:07.4
2006	Andrus Veerpalu, Estonia	0:38:01.3

(Note: approx. 18-km course 1924-1952)

Men's 30 Kilometers (18.6 miles)

		Time
1956	Veikko Hakulinen, Finland	1:44:06.0
1964	Eero Maentyranta, Finland	1:30:50.7
1968	Franco Nones, Italy	1:35:39.2
1972	Vyacheslav Vedenine, USSR	1:36:31.15
1976	Sergei Saveliev, USSR	1:30:29.38
1980	Nikolai Zimyatov, USSR	1:27:02.80
1984	Nikolai Zimyatov, USSR	1:28:56.3
1988	Aleksei Prokourorov, USSR	1:24:26.3
1992	Vegard Ulvang, Norway	1:22:27.8
1994	Thomas Alsgaard, Norway	1:12:26.4
1998	Mika Myllylae, Finland	1:33:55.8
2002	Christian Hoffmann, Austria (a)	1:11:31.0
2006	Eugeni Dementiev, Russia	1:17:00.8

(a) Awarded gold after Johann Muehlegg of Spain was stripped of gold for a drug offense.

Men's 50 Kilometers (31.2 miles)

		Time
1924	Thorleif Haug, Norway	3:44:32.0
1928	Per Erik Hedlund, Sweden	4:52:03.0
1932	Veli Saarinen, Finland	4:28:00.0
1936	Elis Wiklund, Sweden	3:30:11.0
1948	Nils Karlsson, Sweden	3:47:48.0
1952	Veikko Hakulinen, Sweden	3:33:33.0
1956	Sixten Jernberg, Sweden	2:50:27.0
1960	Kalevi Hamalainen, Finland	2:59:06.3
1964	Sixten Jernberg, Sweden	2:43:52.6
1968	Ole Ellefsaeter, Norway	2:28:45.8
1972	Paal Tyldum, Norway	2:43:14.75
1976	Ivar Formo, Norway	2:37:30.05
1980	Nikolai Zimyatov, USSR	2:27:24.60
1984	Thomas Wassberg, Sweden	2:15:55.8
1988	Gunde Svan, Sweden	2:04:30.9
1992	Bjoern Daehlie, Norway	2:03:41.5
1994	Vladimir Smirnov, Kazakhstan	2:07:20.3
1998	Bjoern Daehlie, Norway	2:05:08.2
2002	Mikhail Ivanov, Russia	2:06:20.8
2006	Giorgio di Centa, Italy	2:06:11.8

Men's 40-Kilometer Relay

		Time
1936	Finland, Norway, Sweden	2:41:33.0
1948	Sweden, Finland, Norway	2:32:08.0
1952	Finland, Norway, Sweden	2:20:16.0
1956	USSR, Finland, Sweden	2:15:30.0
1960	Finland, Norway, USSR	2:18:45.6
1964	Sweden, Finland, USSR	2:18:34.6
1968	Norway, Sweden, Finland	2:08:33.5
1972	USSR, Norway, Switzerland	2:04:47.94
1976	Finland, Norway, USSR	2:07:59.72
1980	USSR, Norway, Finland	1:57:03.46
1984	Sweden, USSR, Finland	1:55:06.30
1988	Sweden, USSR, Czechoslovakia	1:43:58.60
1992	Norway, Italy, Finland	1:39:26.00
1994	Italy, Norway, Finland	1:41:15.00
1998	Norway, Italy, Finland	1:40:55.70
2002	Norway, Italy, Germany	1:32:45.5
2006	Italy, Germany, Sweden	1:43:45.7

Women's Sprint

		Time
2002	Julia Tchepalova, Russia (1.5 km)	3:10.6
2006	Chandra Crawford, Canada (1.1. km)	2:12.3

Women's Team Sprint

		Time
2006	Lina Andersson & Anna Dahlberg, Sweden	16:36.9

Women's 5 Kilometers (3.1 miles)

		Time
1964	Claudia Boyarskikh, USSR	17:50.5
1968	Toini Gustafsson, Sweden	16:45.2
1972	Galina Koulacova, USSR	17:00.50
1976	Helena Takalo, Finland	15:48.69
1980	Raisa Smetanina, USSR	15:06.92
1984	Marja-Liisa Haemaelainen, Finland	17:04.0
1988	Marjo Matikainen, Finland	15:04.0
1992	Marjut Lukkarinen, Finland	14:13.8
1994	Ljubov Egorova, Russia	14:08.8
1998	Larissa Lazutina, Russia	17:37.9
2002	Beckie Scott, Canada (a)	25:09.9

(a) Awarded gold after Olga Danilova of Russia was stripped of gold and Larissa Lazutina of Russia was stripped of silver for drug offenses.

Women's 10 Kilometers (6.2 miles)

		Time
1952	Lydia Wideman, Finland	41:40.0
1956	Lyubov Kosyreva, USSR	38:11.0
1960	Maria Gusakova, USSR	39:46.6
1964	Claudia Boyarskikh, USSR	40:24.3
1968	Toini Gustafsson, Sweden	36:46.5
1972	Galina Koulacova, USSR	34:17.82
1976	Raisa Smetanina, USSR	30:13.41
1980	Barbara Petzold, E. Germany	30:31.54
1984	Marja-Liisa Haemaelainen, Finland	31:44.2
1988	Vida Ventsene, USSR	30:08.3
1992	Lyubov Egorova, Unified Team	25:53.7
1994	Lyubov Egorova, Russia	27:30.1
1998	Larissa Lazutina, Russia	46:06.9
2002	Bente Skari, Norway	28:05.6
2006	Kristina Smigun, Estonia	27:51.4

Women's 15 Kilometers (9.3 miles)

		Time
1992	Lyubov Egorova, Unified Team	42:20.8
1994	Manuela Di Centa, Italy	39:44.5
1998	Olga Danilova, Russia	46:55.4
2002	Stefania Belmondo, Italy	39:54.4
2006	Kristina Smigun, Estonia	42:48.7

Women's 30 Kilometers (18.6 miles)

		Time
1992	Stefania Belmondo, Italy	1:22:30.1
1994	Manuela Di Centa, Italy	1:25:41.6
1998	Julija Tchepalova, Russia	1:22:01.5
2002	Gabriella Paruzzi, Italy	1:30:57.1
2006	Katerina Neumannova, Czech Republic	1:22:25.4

Women's 20-Kilometer Relay

		Time
1956	Finland, USSR, Sweden (15 km)	1:09:01.0
1960	Sweden, USSR, Finland (15 km)	1:04:21.4
1964	USSR, Sweden, Finland (15 km)	0:59:20.2
1968	Norway, Sweden, USSR (15 km)	0:57:30.0
1972	USSR, Finland, Norway (15 km)	0:48:46.15
1976	USSR, Finland, E. Germany	1:07:49.75
1980	E. Germany, USSR, Norway	1:02:11.1
1984	Norway, Czechoslovakia, Finland	1:06:49.7
1988	USSR, Norway, Finland	0:59:51.1
1992	United Team, Norway, Italy	0:59:34.8
1994	Russia, Norway, Italy	0:57:12.5
1998	Russia, Norway, Italy	0:55:13.5
2002	Germany, Norway, Switzerland	0:49:30.6
2006	Russia, Germany, Italy	0:54:47.7

Nordic Combined—Men

7.5 Kilometer Nordic Combined

2002	Samppa Lajunen, Finland
2006	Felix Gottwald, Austria

15 Kilometer Nordic Combined

1924	Thorleif Haug, Norway
1928	Johan Grottumsbraaten, Norway
1932	Johan Grottumsbraaten, Norway
1936	Oddbjorn Hagen, Norway
1948	Heikki Hasu, Finland
1952	Simon Slattvik, Norway
1956	Sverre Stenersen, Norway
1960	Georg Thoma, W. Germany
1964	Tormod Knutsen, Norway
1968	Franz Keller, W. Germany
1972	Ulrich Wehling, E. Germany
1976	Ulrich Wehling, E. Germany
1980	Ulrich Wehling, E. Germany
1984	Tom Sandberg, Norway
1988	Hippolyt Kempf, Switzerland
1992	Fabrice Guy, France
1994	Fred Barre Lundberg, Norway
1998	Bjarte Engen Vik, Norway
2002	Samppa Lajunen, Finland
2006	Georg Hettich, Germany

Team Nordic Combined

1988	W. Germany, Switzerland, Austria
1992	Japan, Norway, Austria
1994	Japan, Norway, Switzerland
1998	Norway, Finland, France
2002	Finland, Germany, Austria
2006	Austria, Germany, Finland

Skeleton

Men

		Time
1928	Jennison Heaton, United States	3:01.8
1948	Nino Bibbia, Italy	5:23.2
2002	Jim Shea, United States	1:41.96
2006	Duff Gibson, Canada	1:55.88

Women

		Time
2002	Tristan Gale, United States	1:45.11
2006	Maya Pedersen, Switzerland	1:59.83

Ski Jumping—Men

Normal Hill

		Points
1964	Veikko Kankkonen, Finland	229.9
1968	Jiri Raska, Czechoslovakia	216.5
1972	Yukio Kasaya, Japan	244.2
1976	Hans-Georg Aschenbach, E. Germany	252.0
1980	Toni Innauer, Austria	266.3
1984	Jens Weissflog, E. Germany	215.2
1988	Matti Nykaenen, Finland	230.5
1992	Ernst Vettori, Austria	222.8
1994	Espen Bredesen, Norway	282.0
1998	Jani Soininen, Finland	234.5
2002	Simon Ammann, Switzerland	269.0
2006	Lars Bystoel, Norway	266.5

Large Hill

		Points
1924	Jacob Tullin Thams, Norway	18.960
1928	Alfred Andersen, Norway	19.208
1932	Birger Ruud, Norway	228.1
1936	Birger Ruud, Norway	232.0
1948	Petter Hugsted, Norway	228.1
1952	Arnfinn Bergmann, Norway	226.0
1956	Antti Hyvarinen, Finland	227.0
1960	Helmut Recknagel, E. Germany	227.2
1964	Toralf Engan, Norway	230.7
1968	Vladimir Beloussov, USSR	231.3
1972	Wojciech Fortuna, Poland	219.9
1976	Karl Schnabl, Austria	234.8
1980	Jouko Tormanen, Finland	271.0
1984	Matti Nykaenen, Finland	231.2
1988	Matti Nykaenen, Finland	224.0
1992	Toni Nieminen, Finland	239.5
1994	Jens Weissflog, Germany	274.5
1998	Kazuyoshi Funaki, Japan	272.3
2002	Simon Ammann, Switzerland	281.4
2006	Thomas Morgenstern, Austria	276.9

Team Large Hill

		Points
1988	Finland, Yugoslavia, Norway	634.4
1992	Finland, Austria, Czechoslovakia	644.4
1994	Germany, Japan, Austria	970.1
1998	Japan, Germany, Austria	933.0
2002	Germany, Finland, Slovenia	974.1
2006	Austria, Finland, Norway	984.0

Snowboarding

Men's Parallel Giant Slalom

		Time
1998	Ross Rebagliati, Canada	2:03.96
2002	Philipp Schoch, Switzerland	NA
2006	Philipp Schoch, Switzerland	NA

In 2002, the Giant Slalom became the Parallel Giant Slalom.

Men's Halfpipe

		Points
1998	Gian Simmen, Switzerland	85.2
2002	Ross Powers, United States	46.1
2006	Shaun White, United States	46.8

Men's Snowboard Cross

2006	Seth Wescott, United States

Women's Parallel Giant Slalom

		Time
1998	Karine Ruby, France	2:17.34
2002	Isabelle Blanc, France	NA
2006	Daniela Meuli, Switzerland	NA

In 2002, the Giant Slalom became the Parallel Giant Slalom.

Women's Halfpipe

		Points
1998	Nicola Thost, Germany	74.6
2002	Kelly Clark, United States	47.9
2006	Hannah Teter, United States	46.4

Women's Snowboard Cross

2006	Tanja Frieden, Switzerland

Speed Skating

*indicates Olympic record

Men's 500 Meters

		Time
1924	Charles Jewtraw, United States	0:44.0
1928	Thunberg, Finland & Evensen, Norway (tie)	0:43.4
1932	John A. Shea, United States	0:43.4
1936	Ivar Ballangrud, Norway	0:43.4
1948	Finn Helgesen, Norway	0:43.1
1952	Kenneth Henry, United States	0:43.2
1956	Evgeniy Grishin, USSR	0:40.2
1960	Evgeniy Grishin, USSR	0:40.2
1964	Terry McDermott, United States	0:40.1
1968	Erhard Keller, W. Germany	0:40.3
1972	Erhard Keller, W. Germany	0:39.44
1976	Evgeny Kulikov, USSR	0:39.17
1980	Eric Heiden, United States	0:38.03
1984	Sergei Fokichev, USSR	0:38.19
1988	Uwe-Jens Mey, E. Germany	0:36.45
1992	Uwe-Jens Mey, Germany	0:37.14
1994	Aleksandr Golubev, Russia	0:36.33
1998	Hiroyasu Shimizu, Japan	0:35.59
2002	Casey FitzRandolph, United States	0:34.42*
2006	Joey Cheek, United States	0:34.82

Men's 1,000 Meters

		Time
1976	Peter Mueller, U.S.	1:19.32
1980	Eric Heiden, United States	1:15.18
1984	Gaetan Boucher, Canada	1:15.80
1988	Nikolai Guiliaev, USSR	1:13.03
1992	Olaf Zinke, Germany	1:14.85
1994	Dan Jansen, United States	1:12.43
1998	Ids Postma, Netherlands	1:10.64
2002	Gerard van Velde, Netherlands	1:07.18*
2006	Shani Davis, United States	1:08.89

Men's 1,500 Meters

		Time
1924	Clas Thunberg, Finland	2:20.8
1928	Clas Thunberg, Finland	2:21.1
1932	John A. Shea, United States	2:57.5
1936	Charles Mathiesen, Norway	2:19.2
1948	Sverre Farstad, Norway	2:17.6
1952	Hjalmar Andersen, Norway	2:20.4
1956	Grishin, & Mikhailov, both USSR (tie)	2:08.6
1960	Aas, Norway & Grishin, USSR (tie)	2:10.4
1964	Ants Anston, USSR	2:10.3
1968	Cornetis Verkerk, Netherlands	2:03.4
1972	Ard Schenk, Netherlands	2:02.96
1976	Jan Egil Storholt, Norway	1:59.38
1980	Eric Heiden, United States	1:55.44
1984	Gaetan Boucher, Canada	1:58.36
1988	Andre Hoffmann, E. Germany	1:52.06
1992	Johann Koss, Norway	1:54.81
1994	Johann Koss, Norway	1:51.29
1998	Aadne Sondral, Norway	1:47.87
2002	Derek Parra, United States	1:43.95*
2006	Enrico Fabris, Italy	1:45.97

Men's 5,000 Meters

		Time
1924	Clas Thunberg, Finland	8:39.0
1928	Ivar Ballangrud, Norway	8:50.5
1932	Irving Jaffee, United States	9:40.8
1936	Ivar Ballangrud, Norway	8:19.6
1948	Reidar Liaklev, Norway	8:29.4

Men's 5,000 Meters

		Time
1952	Hjalmar Andersen, Norway	8:10.6
1956	Boris Shilkov, USSR	7:48.7
1960	Viktor Kosichkin, USSR	7:51.3
1964	Knut Johannesen, Norway	7:38.4
1968	F. Anton Maier, Norway	7:22.4
1972	Ard Schenk, Netherlands	7:23.61
1976	Sten Stensen, Norway	7:24.48
1980	Eric Heiden, United States	7:02.29
1984	Sven Tomas Gustafson, Sweden	7:12.28
1988	Tomas Gustafson, Sweden	6:44.63
1992	Geir Karlstad, Norway	6:59.97
1994	Johann Koss, Norway	6:34.96
1998	Gianni Romme, Netherlands	6:22.20
2002	Jochem Uytdehaage, Netherlands	6:14.66*
2006	Chad Hedrick, United States	6:14.68

Men's 10,000 Meters

		Time
1924	Julius Skutnabb, Finland	18:04.8
1928	Event not held because of thawing of ice	
1932	Irving Jaffee, United States	19:13.6
1936	Ivar Ballangrud, Norway	17:24.3
1948	Ake Seyffarth, Sweden	17:26.3
1952	Hjalmar Andersen, Norway	16:45.8
1956	Sigvard Ericsson, Sweden	16:35.9
1960	Knut Johannesen, Norway	15:46.6
1964	Jonny Nilsson, Sweden	15:50.1
1968	Jonny Hoeglin, Sweden	15:23.6
1972	Ard Schenk, Netherlands	15:01.35
1976	Piet Kleine, Netherlands	14:50.59
1980	Eric Heiden, United States	14:28.13
1984	Igor Malkov, USSR	14:39.90
1988	Tomas Gustafson, Sweden	13:48.20
1992	Bart Veldkamp, Netherlands	14:12.12
1994	Johann Koss, Norway	13:30.55
1998	Gianni Romme, Netherlands	13:15.33
2002	Jochem Uytdehaage, Netherlands	12:58.92*
2006	Bob de Jong, Netherlands	13:01.57

Women's 500 Meters

		Time
1960	Helga Haase, Germany	0:45.9
1964	Lydia Skoblikova, USSR	0:45.0
1968	Ludmila Titova, USSR	0:46.1
1972	Anne Henning, United States	0:43.33
1976	Sheila Young, United States	0:42.76
1980	Karin Enke, E. Germany	0:41.78
1984	Christa Rothenburger, E. Germany	0:41.02
1988	Bonnie Blair, United States	0:39.10
1992	Bonnie Blair, United States	0:40.33
1994	Bonnie Blair, United States	0:39.25
1998	Catriona Le May-Doan, Canada	0:38.21
2002	Catriona Le May Doan, Canada	0:37.30*
2006	Svetlana Zhurova, Russia	0:38.23

Women's 1,000 Meters

		Time
1960	Klara Guseva, USSR	1:34.1
1964	Lydia Skoblikova, USSR	1:33.2
1968	Carolina Geijssen, Netherlands	1:32.6
1972	Monika Pflug, W. Germany	1:31.40
1976	Tatiana Averina, USSR	1:28.43
1980	Natalya Petruseva, USSR	1:24.10
1984	Karin Enke, E. Germany	1:21.61
1988	Christa Rothenburger, E. Germany	1:17.65
1992	Bonnie Blair, United States	1:21.90
1994	Bonnie Blair, United States	1:18.74
1998	Marianne Timmer, Netherlands	1:16.51
2002	Chris Witty, United States	1:13.83*
2006	Marianne Timmer, Netherlands	1:16.05

Women's 1,500 Meters

		Time
1960	Lydia Skoblikova, USSR	2:52.2
1964	Lydia Skoblikova, USSR	2:22.6
1968	Kaija Mustonen, Finland	2:22.4
1972	Dianne Holum, United States	2:20.85
1976	Galina Stepanskaya, USSR	2:16.58
1980	Anne Borckink, Netherlands	2:10.95
1984	Karin Enke, E. Germany	2:03.42
1988	Yvonne van Gennip, Netherlands	2:00.68
1992	Jacqueline Boerner, Germany	2:05.87
1994	Emese Hunyady, Austria	2:02.19
1998	Marianne Timmer, Netherlands	1:57.58
2002	Anni Friesinger, Germany	1:54.02*
2006	Cindy Klassen, Canada	1:55.27

Women's 3,000 Meters

		Time
1960	Lydia Skoblikova, USSR	5:14.3
1964	Lydia Skoblikova, USSR	5:14.9
1968	Johanna Schut, Netherlands	4:56.2
1972	Christina Baas-Kaiser, Netherlands	4:52.14
1976	Tatiana Averina, USSR	4:45.19

	Women's 3,000 Meters	Time
1980	Bjoerg Eva Jensen, Norway	4:32.13
1984	Andrea Schoene, E. Germany	4:24.79
1988	Yvonne van Gennip, Netherlands	4:11.94
1992	Gunda Niemann, Germany	4:19.90
1994	Svetlana Bazhanova, Russia	4:17.43
1998	Gunda Niemann-Stirnemann, Germany	4:07.29
2002	Claudia Pechstein, Germany,	3:57.70*
2006	Ireen Wust, Netherlands	4:02.43

	Women's 5,000 Meters	Time
1988	Yvonne van Gennip, Netherlands	7:14.13
1992	Gunda Niemann, Germany	7:31.57
1994	Claudia Pechstein, Germany	7:14.37
1998	Claudia Pechstein, Germany	6:59.61
2002	Claudia Pechstein, Germany	6:46.91*
2006	Clara Hughes, Canada	6:59.07

	Men's Team Pursuit	Time
2006	Italy, Canada, Netherlands	3:44.46

	Women's Team Pursuit	Time
2006	Germany, Canada, Russia	3:01.25

Short-Track Speed Skating
* indicates Olympic record

	Men's 500 Meters	Time
1998	Takafumi Nishitani, Japan	42.862
2002	Marc Gagnon, Canada	41.802*
2006	Apolo Anton Ohno, United States	41.935

	Men's 1,000 Meters	Time
1992	Kim Ki-Hoon, S. Korea	1:30.76
1994	Kim Ki-Hoon, S. Korea	1:34.57
1998	Dong-Sung Kim, S. Korea	1:32.375

	Men's 1,000 Meters	Time
2002	Steven Bradbury, Australia	1:29.109
2006	Hyun-Soo Ahn, S. Korea	1:26.739*

	Men's 1,500 Meters	Time
2002	Apolo Anton Ohno, United States	2:18.541
2006	Hyun-Soo Ahn, S. Korea	2:25.341

	Men's 5,000-Meter Relay	Time
1992	S. Korea, Canada, Japan	7:14.02
1994	Italy, United States, Australia	7:11.74
1998	Canada, S. Korea, China	7:06.075
2002	Canada, Italy, China	6:51.579
2006	S. Korea, Canada, United States	6:43.376*

	Women's 500 Meters	Time
1992	Cathy Turner, United States	47.04
1994	Cathy Turner, United States	45.98
1998	Annie Perreault, Canada	46.568
2002	Yang Yang (A), China	44.187
2006	Meng Wang, China	44.345

	Women's 1,000 Meters	Time
1998	Chun Lee-Kyung, S. Korea	1:42.776
2002	Yang Yang (A), China	1:36.391
2006	Sun-Yu Jin, S. Korea	1:32.859

	Women's 1,500 Meters	Time
2002	Gi-Hyun Ko, S. Korea	2:31.581
2006	Sun-Yu Jin, S. Korea	2:23.494

	Women's 3,000 Meter Relay	Time
1992	Canada, United States, Unified Team	4:36.62
1994	S. Korea, Canada, United States	4:26.64
1998	S. Korea, China, Canada	4:16.26
2002	S. Korea, China, Canada	4:12.793*
2006	S. Korea, Canada, Italy	4:17.040

Olympic Information

The modern Olympic Games, first held in Athens, Greece, in 1896, were the result of efforts by Baron Pierre de Coubertin, a French educator, to promote interest in education and culture and to foster better international understanding through love of athletics. His inspiration was the ancient Greek Olympic Games, most notable of the 4 Panhellenic celebrations. The games were combined patriotic, religious, and athletic festivals held every 4 years. The first such recorded festival was held in 776 BCE, which the Greeks began to keep their calendar by "Olympiads," or 4-year spans between the games.

Baron de Coubertin enlisted 13 nations to send athletes to the first modern Olympics in 1896; now athletes from nearly 200 nations and territories compete in the Summer Olympics. The Winter Olympic Games were started in 1924.

Symbol: Five rings or circles, linked together to represent the sporting friendship of all peoples. They also symbolize 5 geographic areas—Europe, Asia, Africa, Australia, and America. Each ring is a different color—blue, yellow, black, green, or red.

Flag: The symbol of the 5 rings on a plain white background.

Creed: "The most important thing in the Olympic Games is not to win but to take part, just as the most important thing in life is not the triumph but the struggle. The essential thing is not to have conquered but to have fought well."

Motto: "Citius, Altius, Fortius." Latin meaning "swifter, higher, stronger."

Oath: "In the name of all competitors I promise that we will take part in these Olympic Games, respecting and abiding by the rules which govern them, in the true spirit of sportsmanship for the glory of sport and the honor of our teams."

Flame: The modern version of the flame was adopted in 1936. The torch used to kindle it is first lit by the sun's rays at Olympia, Greece, then carried to the site of the Games by relays of runners. Ships and planes are used when necessary.

Sites of Winter Olympic Games

1924	Chamonix, France	1952	Oslo, Norway	1976	Innsbruck, Austria	1998	Nagano, Japan
1928	St. Moritz, Switzerland	1956	Cortina d'Ampezzo, Italy	1980	Lake Placid, NY	2002	Salt Lake City, UT
1932	Lake Placid, NY	1960	Squaw Valley, CA	1984	Sarajevo, Yugoslavia	2006	Turin, Italy
1936	Garmisch-Partenkirchen, Germany	1964	Innsbruck, Austria	1988	Calgary, Canada	2010	Vancouver, B.C., Canada
		1968	Grenoble, France	1992	Albertville, France	2014	Sochi, Russia
1948	St. Moritz, Switzerland	1972	Sapporo, Japan	1994	Lillehammer, Norway		

Sites of Summer Olympic Games

1896	Athens, Greece	1924	Paris, France	1960	Rome, Italy	1988	Seoul, South Korea
1900	Paris, France	1928	Amsterdam, Netherlands	1964	Tokyo, Japan	1992	Barcelona, Spain
1904	St. Louis, MO	1932	Los Angeles, CA	1968	Mexico City, Mexico	1996	Atlanta, GA
1906	Athens, Greece*	1936	Berlin, Germany	1972	Munich, W. Germany	2000	Sydney, Australia
1908	London, England	1948	London, England	1976	Montreal, Canada	2004	Athens, Greece
1912	Stockholm, Sweden	1952	Helsinki, Finland	1980	Moscow, USSR	2008	Beijing, China
1920	Antwerp, Belgium	1956	Melbourne, Australia	1984	Los Angeles, CA	2012	London, England

*Games not recognized by International Olympic Committee. Games VI (1916), XII (1940), and XIII (1944) were not celebrated.

Paralympics

The first Olympic games for the disabled were held in Rome after the 1960 Summer Olympics; use of the name "paralympic" began with the 1964 games in Tokyo. The Paralympics are held by the Olympic host country in the same year and usually the same city or venue. A goal of the Paralympics is to provide elite competition to athletes with functional disabilities that prevent their involvement in the Olympics. In 1976 the first Winter Paralympics were held, in Ornskoldsvik, Sweden.

The IX Paralympic Winter Games were held Mar. 10-19, 2006, in Turin, Italy. About 1,300 athletes from a 39 nations competed in 5 sports including, for the first time, wheelchair curling. Russia won the most medals, with 33, and the most golds, with 13. Ukraine landed at 2nd in the medal count after finishing in 18th place in 2002, with 25 medals. Germany was 3rd, with 18 medals; the U.S. won 12 and was ranked 7th.

The XIII Paralympic Summer Games are scheduled to be held Sept. 6-17, 2008, in Beijing, China. A record 4,000 athletes from 150 nations are expected to compete in 471 events in 20 sports including, for the first time, rowing.

Special Olympics

Special Olympics is an international program of year-round sports training and athletic competition for people with intellectual disabilities. All 50 U.S. states, Washington, DC, and Guam have chapter offices. In addition, there are accredited Special Olympics programs in more than 165 countries. Persons wishing to volunteer or find out more can contact Special Olympics, 1133 19th St. NW, Washington, DC 20036, or access the Special Olympics website at www.specialolympics.org

The 12th Special Olympics World Summer Games were to be held Oct. 2-11, 2007, in Shanghai, China. About 7,500 athletes, 3,500 event officials, and 40,000 volunteers were expected to attend the first Special Olympic World Games outside the U.S. Athletic events included aquatics, athletics (track and field), badminton, bocce, bowling, cycling, equestrian sports, golf, gymnastics (artistic and rhythmic), judo, kayaking, power lifting, rollerskating, table tennis, and tennis. Scheduled team sports were basketball, cricket, dragon boat racing, handball, lion dancing, sailing, soccer, and volleyball.

The 8th Special Olympics World Winter Games were held Feb. 26-Mar. 5, 2005, in Nagano, Japan's Olympic venues. More than 1,800 athletes from 80 countries competed in alpine skiing, cross-country skiing, floor hockey, figure skating, speed skating, snowshoeing, and snowboarding events. The 9th Special Olympics World Winter Games were to be held in Boise, ID, Feb. 6-13, 2009.

TRACK AND FIELD

World Track and Field Outdoor Records

As of Sept. 15, 2007.

The International Association of Athletics Federations, the world body of track and field, recognizes only records in metric distances, except for the mile.

*Pending ratification.

Men's Records

Running

Event	Record	Holder	Country	Date	Where made
100 meters	9.74 s.*	Asafa Powell	Jamaica	Sept. 9, 2007	Rieti, Italy
200 meters	19.32 s.	Michael Johnson	U.S.	Aug. 1, 1996	Atlanta, GA
400 meters	43.18 s.	Michael Johnson	U.S.	Aug. 26, 1999	Seville, Spain
800 meters	1 m., 41.11 s.	Wilson Kipketer	Denmark	Aug. 24, 1997	Cologne, Germany
1,000 meters	2 m., 11.96 s.	Noah Ngeny	Kenya	Sept. 5, 1999	Rieti, Italy
1,500 meters	3 m., 26.00 s.	Hicham El Guerrouj	Morocco	July 14, 1998	Rome, Italy
1 mile	3 m., 43.13 s.	Hicham El Guerrouj	Morocco	July 7, 1999	Rome, Italy
2,000 meters	4 m., 44.79 s.	Hicham El Guerrouj	Morocco	Sept. 7, 1999	Berlin, Germany
3,000 meters	7 m., 20.67 s.	Daniel Komen	Kenya	Sept. 1, 1996	Rieti, Italy
5,000 meters	12 m., 37.35 s.	Kenenisa Bekele	Ethiopia	May 31, 2004	Hengelo, Netherlands
10,000 meters	26 m., 17.53 s.	Kenenisa Bekele	Ethiopia	Aug. 26, 2005	Brussels, Belgium
20,000 meters	56 m., 26.0 s.	Haile Gebrselassie	Ethiopia	June 27, 2007	Ostrava, Czech Rep.
25,000 meters	1 hr., 13 m., 55.8 s.	Toshihiko Seko	Japan	Mar. 22, 1981	Christchurch, NZ
3,000 meter stpl.	7 m., 53.63 s.	Saif Saaeed Shaheen	Qatar	Sept. 3, 2004	Brussels, Belgium
Marathon	2 hr., 4 m., 55 s.	Paul Tergat	Kenya	Sept. 28, 2003	Berlin, Germany

Hurdles

Event	Record	Holder	Country	Date	Where made
110 meters	12.88 s.	Xiang Liu	China	July 11, 2006	Lausanne, Switzerland
400 meters	46.78 s.	Kevin Young	U.S.	Aug. 6, 1992	Barcelona, Spain

Relay Races

Event	Record	Holder	Country	Date	Where made
400 mtrs. (4x100)	37.40 s.	(Marsh, Burrell, Mitchell, Lewis)	U.S.	Aug. 8, 1992	Barcelona, Spain
800 mtrs. (4x200)	1 m., 18.68 s.	(Drummond, Cason, Mitchell, Burrell)	U.S.	Aug. 21, 1993	Stuttgart, Germany
1,600 mtrs. (4x400)	2 m., 54.20 s.	(Marsh, Burrell, Heard, Lewis)	U.S.	Apr. 17, 1994	Walnut, CA
3,200 mtrs. (4x800)	7 m., 02.43 s.	(Young, Pettigrew, Washington, Johnson)	U.S.	July 22, 1998	Long Island, NY
		(Mutua, Yiampoy, Kombich, Bungei)	Kenya	Aug. 25, 2006	Brussels, Belgium

Field Events

Event	Record	Holder	Country	Date	Where made
High jump	2.45m (8' ½")	Javier Sotomayor	Cuba	July 27, 1993	Salamanca, Spain
Long jump	8.95m (29' 4½")	Mike Powell	U.S.	Aug. 30, 1991	Tokyo, Japan
Triple jump	18.29m (60' ¼")	Jonathan Edwards	Gr. Britain	Aug. 7, 1995	Göteborg, Sweden
Pole vault	6.14m (20' 1¾")	Sergei Bubka	Ukraine	July 31, 1994	Sestriere, Italy
16-lb. shot put	23.12m (75' 10¼")	Randy Barnes	U.S.	May 20, 1990	Los Angeles, CA
Discus	74.08m (243' 0")	Juergen Schult	E. Germany	June 6, 1986	Neubrandenburg, Germany
Javelin	98.48m (323' 1")	Jan Zelezny	Czech Rep.	May 25, 1996	Jena, Germany
16-lb. hammer	86.74m (284' 7")	Yuriy Sedykh	USSR	Aug. 30, 1986	Stuttgart, W. Germany
Decathlon	9,026 pts.	Roman Sebrle	Czech Rep.	May 27, 2001	Götzis, Austria

Women's Records

Running

Event	Record	Holder	Country	Date	Where made
100 meters	10.49 s.	Florence Griffith-Joyner	U.S.	July 16, 1988	Indianapolis, IN
200 meters	21.34 s.	Florence Griffith-Joyner	U.S.	Sept. 29, 1988	Seoul, S. Korea
400 meters	47.60 s.	Marita Koch	E. Germany	Oct. 6, 1985	Canberra, Australia
800 meters	1 m., 53.28 s.	Jarmila Kratochvilová	Czechoslovakia	July 26, 1983	Munich, Germany
1,000 meters	2 m., 28.98 s.	Svetlana Masterkova	Russia	Aug. 23, 1996	Brussels, Belgium
1,500 meters	3 m., 50.46 s.	Qu Yunxia	China	Sept. 11, 1993	Beijing, China
1 mile	4 m., 12.56 s.	Svetlana Masterkova	Russia	Aug. 14, 1996	Zurich, Switzerland
2,000 meters	5 m., 25.36 s.	Sonia O'Sullivan	Ireland	July 8, 1994	Edinburgh, Scotland
3,000 meters	8 m., 06.11 s.	Wang Junxia	China	Sept. 13, 1993	Beijing, China

Event	Record	Holder	Country	Date	Where made
3,000 meter stpl.	9 m., 1.59 s.	Gulnara Samitova	Russia	July 4, 2004.	Iraklio, Greece
5,000 meters	14 m., 16.63 s.	Meseret Defar	Ethiopia	June 15, 2007	Oslo, Norway
10,000 meters	29 m., 31.78 s.	Wang Junxia	China	Sept. 8, 1993.	Beijing, China
20,000 meters	1 h., 05m. 26.6 s.	Tegla Loroupe	Kenya.	Sept. 3, 2000.	Borgholzhausen, Germany
30,000 meters	1 h., 45 m., 50 s.	Tegla Loroupe	Kenya.	June 6, 2003.	Warstein, Germany
Marathon	2 h., 15 m., 25 s.	Paula Radcliffe.	Gr. Britain.	April 13, 2003.	London, England

Hurdles

Event	Record	Holder	Country	Date	Where made
100 meters	12.21 s.	Yordanka Donkova	Bulgaria	Aug. 20, 1988.	Stara Zagora, Bulgaria
400 meters	52.34 s.	Yuliya Pechenkina	Russia	Aug. 10, 2003.	Tula, Russia

Relay Races

Event	Record	Holder	Country	Date	Where made
400 mtrs. (4×100)	41.37 s.	(Gladisch, Rieger, Auerswald, Goehr)	E. Germany.	Oct. 6, 1985.	Canberra, Australia
800 mtrs. (4×200)	1 m., 27.46 s.	U.S. "Blue" (Jenkins, Clarke, Richardson, Jamieson)	U.S.	Apr. 29, 2000.	Philadelphia, PA
1,600 mtrs. (4×400)	3 m., 15.17 s.	(Ledovskaya, Nazarova, Pinigina, Bryzgina).	USSR.	Oct. 1, 1988.	Seoul, S. Korea
3,200 mtrs. (4×800)	7 m., 50.17 s.	(Olizarenko, Gurina, Borisova, Podyalovskaya).	USSR.	Aug. 5, 1984.	Moscow, USSR

Field Events

Event	Record	Holder	Country	Date	Where made
High jump	2.09m (6' 10¼")	Stefka Kostadinova	Bulgaria	Aug. 30, 1987.	Rome, Italy
Long jump	7.52m (24' 8¼")	Galina Chistyakova	USSR.	June 11, 1988.	Leningrad, Russia
Triple jump	15.50m (50' 10¼")	Inessa Kravets	Ukraine	Aug. 10, 1995.	Göteborg, Sweden
Pole vault	5.01m (16' 5¼")*	Yelena Isinbayeva	Russia	Aug. 12, 2005.	Helsinki, Finland
Shot put	22.63m (74' 3")	Natalya Lisovskaya	USSR.	June 7, 1987.	Moscow, Russia
Discus	76.80m (252' 0").	Gabriele Reinsch	E. Germany	July 9, 1988.	Neubrandenburg, Germany
Hammer	78.61m (257' 10⅞")*	Tatyana Lysenko	Russia	May 26, 2007	Sochi, Russia
Javelin	71.70m (235' 3").	Osleidys Menéndez	Cuba	Aug. 14, 2005.	Helsinki, Finland
Heptathlon	7,291 pts.	Jackie Joyner-Kersee	U.S.	Sept. 24, 1988.	Seoul, S. Korea

World Track and Field Indoor Records

As of Sept. 15, 2007.

The International Association of Athletics Federations first recognized world indoor track and field records on Jan. 1, 1987. World indoor bests set prior to Jan. 1, 1987, were subject to approval as world records providing they met the IAAF world records criteria, including drug testing. Criteria for indoor and outdoor records are the same, except that a track performance cannot be set on an indoor track longer than 200 meters. (a)=altitude. *Pending ratification.

Men's Records

Event	Record	Holder	Country	Date	Where made
50 meters	5.56 s. (a)	Donovan Bailey	Canada.	Feb. 9, 1996.	Reno, NV
60 meters	6.39 s.	Maurice Greene	U.S.	Mar. 3, 2001.	Atlanta, GA
	6.39 s.	Maurice Greene	U.S.	Feb. 3, 1998.	Madrid, Spain
		Frank Fredericks	Namibia	Feb. 18, 1996.	Lievin, France
200 meters	19.92 s.		U.S.	Mar. 12, 2005.	Fayetteville, AR
400 meters	44.57 s.	Kerron Clement		Mar. 9, 1997.	Paris, France
800 meters	1:42.67 min.	Wilson Kipketer	Denmark.	Feb. 20, 2000.	Birmingham, England
1,000 meters	2:14.96 min.	Wilson Kipketer	Denmark.	Feb. 2, 1997.	Stuttgart, Germany
1,500 meters	3:31.18 min.	Hicham El Guerrouj	Morocco.	Feb. 2, 1997.	Ghent, Belgium
1 mile	3:48.45 min.	Hicham El Guerrouj	Morocco.	Feb. 12, 1997.	Budapest, Hungary
3,000 meters	7:24.90 min.	Daniel Komen	Kenya	Feb. 6, 1998.	Budapest, Hungary
5,000 meters	12:49.60 min.	Kenenisa Bekele	Ethiopia	Feb. 20, 2004.	Birmingham, England
50-meter hurdles	6.25 s.	Mark McKoy	Canada.	Mar. 5, 1986.	Kobe, Japan
60-meter hurdles	7.30 s.	Colin Jackson	Gr. Britain.	Mar. 6, 1994.	Sindelfingen, Germany
High jump	2.43m (7' 11½")	Javier Sotomayor	Cuba.	Mar. 4, 1989.	Budapest, Hungary
Pole vault	6.15m (20' 2")	Sergey Bubka	Ukraine.	Feb. 21, 1993.	Donyetsk, Ukraine
Long jump	8.79m (28' 10¼")	Carl Lewis	U.S.	Jan. 27, 1984.	New York, NY
Triple jump	17.83 (58' 6")	Aliecer Urrutia	Cuba.	Mar. 1, 1997.	Sindelfingen, Germany
		Christian Olsson	Sweden.	Mar. 7, 2004.	Budapest, Hungary
Shot put	22.66m (74' 4¼").	Randy Barnes	U.S.	Jan. 20, 1989.	Los Angeles, CA

Women's Records

Event	Record	Holder	Country	Date	Where made
50 meters	5.96 s.	Irina Privalova	Russia	Feb. 9, 1995.	Madrid, Spain
60 meters	6.92 s.	Irina Privalova	Russia	Feb. 9, 1995.	Madrid, Spain
	6.92 s.	Irina Privalova	Russia	Feb. 11, 1993.	Madrid, Spain
		Merlene Ottey	Jamaica	Feb. 13, 1993.	Lievin, France
200 meters	21.87 s.	Merlene Ottey	Czechoslovakia	Mar. 7, 1982.	Milan, Italy
400 meters	49.59 s.	Jarmila Kratochvílová	Slovenia	Mar. 3, 2002.	Vienna, Austria
800 meters	1:55.82 s.	Jolanda Ceplak	Mozambique.	Feb. 25, 1999.	Stockholm, Sweden
1,000 meters	2:30.94 min.	Maria Mutola	Russia	Feb. 18, 2006.	Moscow, Russia
1,500 meters	3:58.28 min.	Yelena Soboleva	Romania.	Feb. 9, 1990.	E. Rutherford, NJ
1 mile	4:17.14 min.	Doina Melinte	Ethiopia	Jan. 27, 2007.	Stuttgart, Germany
3,000 meters	8:23.72 min.*	Meseret Defar	Ethiopia	Jan. 27, 2007.	Boston, MA
5,000 meters	14:27.42 min.	Tirunesh Dibaba	E. Germany	Feb. 20, 1988.	Berlin, Germany
50-meter hurdles	6.58 s.	Cornelia Oschkenat	USSR.	Feb. 4, 1990.	Chelyabinsk, USSR
60-meter hurdles	7.69 s.	Ludmila Engquist	Sweden	Feb. 4, 2006.	Arnstadt, Germany
High jump	2.08m (6' 10")	Kajsa Bergqvist	Russia	Feb. 10, 2007.	Donetsk, Ukraine
Pole vault	4.93m (16' 2⅛")*	Yelena Isinbayeva	Russia	Feb. 13, 1988.	Vienna, Austria
Long jump	7.37m (24' 2¼")	Heike Drechsler	E. Germany	Mar. 3, 2004.	Budapest, Hungary
Triple jump	15.36m (50' 4¾")	Tatyana Lebedeva	Czechoslovakia	Feb. 19, 1977.	Jablonec, Czechoslovakia
Shot put	22.50m (73' 10")	Helena Fibingerová			

BASEBALL

Bonds Breaks All-Time Home Run Record; Multiple Players Attain Career Milestones; NL Races Go Down to the Wire and Beyond

The Giants' Barry Bonds launched his 756th career home run on Aug. 7, 2007, breaking the record held by Hank Aaron since 1974. Texas Ranger Sammy Sosa, who had not played during the 2006 season, became the fifth player in history to hit 600 career home runs, while the Blue Jays' Frank Thomas, the Yankees' Alex Rodriguez, and the White Sox's Jim Thome joined the 500-home run club. Houston's Craig Biggio recorded his 3,000th hit and Tom Glavine picked up his 300th win.

The Yankees began the season in a slump but mounted a comeback and won the AL Wild Card playoff slot. The Boston Red Sox held on to claim the AL East division title; the Cleveland Indians took the AL Central, ending Detroit's chance for two consecutive postseason appearances; and the Los Angeles Angels of Anaheim easily captured the AL West title.

The New York Mets set a record for the worst late-season collapse in baseball history, and the Phillies claimed the NL East title on the final day of the season. The Cubs surged past the Brewers and the Cardinals to clinch the NL Central. The Diamondbacks were the surprise winners of a heated NL West race, with NL West teams Colorado and San Diego tying for the NL Wild Card. The Rockies took the final postseason spot after defeating the Padres in a thrilling 13-inning one-game playoff.

National League Final Standings, 2007

Eastern Division

	W	L	Pct.	GB	Home	Road	vs. East	vs. Central	vs. West	vs. AL
Philadelphia	89	73	.549	—	47-34	42-39	42-30	25-16	14-20	8-7
New York	88	74	.543	1.0	41-40	47-34	35-37	28-12	17-18	8-7
Atlanta	84	78	.519	5.0	44-37	40-41	39-33	22-20	19-14	4-11
Washington	73	89	.451	16.0	40-41	33-48	32-40	21-18	11-22	9-9
Florida	71	91	.438	18.0	36-45	35-46	32-40	18-20	12-22	9-9

Central Division

	W	L	Pct.	GB	Home	Road	vs. East	vs. Central	vs. West	vs. AL
Chicago	85	77	.525	—	44-37	41-40	15-21	45-34	17-18	8-4
Milwaukee	83	79	.512	2.0	51-30	32-49	16-17	43-36	16-19	8-7
St. Louis	78	84	.481	7.0	43-38	35-46	14-21	43-37	15-17	6-9
Houston	73	89	.451	12.0	42-39	31-50	13-18	35-44	16-18	9-9
Cincinnati	72	90	.444	13.0	39-42	33-48	15-19	36-43	14-17	7-11
Pittsburgh	68	94	.420	17.0	37-44	31-50	13-18	36-44	14-22	5-10

Western Division

	W	L	Pct.	GB	Home	Road	vs. East	vs. Central	vs. West	vs. AL
Arizona	90	72	.556	—	50-31	40-41	24-9	22-20	36-36	8-7
Colorado*	90	73	.552	0.5	51-31	39-42	17-15	20-20	43-30	10-8
San Diego	89	74	.546	1.5	47-34	42-40	17-16	26-16	40-33	6-9
Los Angeles	82	80	.506	8.0	43-38	39-42	20-16	23-16	34-38	5-10
San Francisco	71	91	.438	19.0	39-42	32-49	18-17	20-20	28-44	5-10

* Wild Card team.

American League Final Standings, 2007

Eastern Division

	W	L	Pct.	GB	Home	Road	vs. East	vs. Central	vs. West	vs. NL
Boston	96	66	.593	—	51-30	45-36	42-30	22-13	20-17	12-6
New York*	94	68	.580	2.0	52-29	42-39	39-33	30-11	15-16	10-8
Toronto	83	79	.512	13.0	49-32	34-47	36-36	19-18	18-17	10-8
Baltimore	69	93	.426	27.0	35-46	34-47	34-38	16-19	13-24	6-12
Tampa Bay	66	96	.407	30.0	37-44	29-52	29-43	14-24	16-18	7-11

* Wild Card team.

Central Division

	W	L	Pct.	GB	Home	Road	vs. East	vs. Central	vs. West	vs. NL
Cleveland	96	66	.593	—	52-29	44-37	18-18	48-24	21-15	9-9
Detroit	88	74	.543	8.0	45-36	43-38	20-15	36-36	18-19	14-4
Minnesota	79	83	.488	17.0	41-40	38-43	19-19	28-44	21-13	11-7
Chicago	72	90	.444	24.0	38-43	34-47	17-23	39-33	12-20	4-14
Kansas City	69	93	.426	27.0	35-46	34-47	11-26	29-43	19-16	10-8

Western Division

	W	L	Pct.	GB	Home	Road	vs. East	vs. Central	vs. West	vs. NL
Los Angeles	94	68	.580	—	54-27	40-41	26-18	22-21	32-25	14-4
Seattle	88	74	.543	6.0	49-32	39-42	25-19	23-20	31-26	9-9
Oakland	76	86	.469	18.0	40-41	36-45	21-20	21-25	24-33	10-8
Texas	75	87	.463	19.0	47-34	28-53	20-25	17-25	27-30	11-7

National League Statistics, 2007

(Individual Statistics: Batting—at least 150 at-bats; Pitching—at least 70 innings or 10 saves; *changed teams within NL during season; entry includes statistics for more than 1 team; # changed teams to or from AL during season; entry includes only NL stats)

Team Batting

Team	BA	AB	R	H	HR	RBI
Colorado Rockies	.280	5691	860	1591	171	823
Los Angeles Dodgers	.275	5613	735	1544	129	706
New York Mets	.275	5605	804	1543	177	761
Atlanta Braves	.275	5689	810	1562	176	781
St. Louis Cardinals	.274	5529	725	1513	141	690
Philadelphia Phillies	.274	5688	892	1558	213	850
Chicago Cubs	.271	5643	752	1530	151	711
Cincinnati Reds	.267	5607	783	1496	204	747
Florida Marlins	.267	5627	790	1504	201	749
Pittsburgh Pirates	.263	5569	724	1463	148	694
Milwaukee Brewers	.262	5554	801	1455	231	774
Houston Astros	.260	5605	723	1457	167	700
Washington Nationals	.256	5520	673	1415	123	646
San Francisco Giants	.254	5538	683	1407	131	641
San Diego Padres	.251	5612	741	1408	171	704
Arizona Diamondbacks	.250	5398	712	1350	171	687

Team Pitching

Team	ERA	IP	H	SO	BB	SV
San Diego Padres	3.70	1484.2	1406	1136	474	45
Chicago Cubs	4.04	1446.2	1340	1211	573	39
Atlanta Braves	4.11	1456.1	1442	1106	537	36
Arizona Diamondbacks	4.13	1441.0	1446	1088	546	51
San Francisco Giants	4.19	1453.2	1442	1057	593	37
Los Angeles Dodgers	4.20	1450.0	1443	1184	518	43
New York Mets	4.26	1452.1	1415	1134	570	39
Colorado Rockies	4.32	1472.0	1497	967	504	39
Milwaukee Brewers	4.41	1444.1	1513	1174	507	49
Washington Nationals	4.58	1446.2	1502	931	580	46
St. Louis Cardinals	4.65	1435.2	1514	945	509	34
Houston Astros	4.68	1464.2	1566	1109	510	38
Philadelphia Phillies	4.73	1458.1	1555	1050	558	42
Pittsburgh Pirates	4.93	1447.2	1627	997	518	32
Cincinnati Reds	4.94	1449.2	1605	1068	482	34
Florida Marlins	4.94	1443.2	1617	1142	661	40

Arizona Diamondbacks

BATTERS	AVG	AB	R	H	HR	RBI	SO	SB
O Hudson	.294	517	69	152	10	63	87	10
E Byrnes	.286	626	103	179	21	83	98	50
C Jackson	.284	415	56	118	15	60	50	2
M Reynolds	.279	366	62	102	17	62	129	0
C Tracy	.264	227	30	60	7	35	43	0
C Snyder	.252	326	37	82	13	47	67	0
T Clark	.249	221	31	55	17	51	59	0
S Drew	.238	543	60	129	12	60	100	9
C Young	.237	569	85	135	32	68	141	27
M Montero	.224	214	30	48	10	37	35	0
C Quentin	.214	229	29	49	5	31	54	2

PITCHERS	W-L	ERA	IP	H	BB	SO	SV
J Valverde	1-4	2.66	64.1	46	26	78	47
B Lyon	6-4	2.68	74.0	70	22	40	2
B Webb	18-10	3.01	236.1	209	72	194	0
T Pena	5-4	3.27	85.1	63	31	63	2
D Davis	13-12	4.25	192.2	211	95	144	0
M Owings	8-8	4.30	152.2	146	50	106	0
L Hernandez	11-11	4.93	204.1	247	79	90	0
E Gonzalez	8-4	5.03	102.0	110	28	62	0

Manager-Bob Melvin

Atlanta Braves

BATTERS	AVG	AB	R	H	HR	RBI	SO	SB
M Diaz	.338	358	44	121	12	45	63	4
C Jones	.337	513	108	173	29	102	75	5
E Renteria	.332	494	87	164	12	57	77	11
Y Escobar	.326	319	54	104	5	28	44	5
M Teixeira#	.317	208	38	66	17	56	46	0
J Francoeur	.293	642	84	188	19	105	129	5
K Johnson	.276	521	91	144	16	68	117	9
B McCann	.270	504	51	136	18	92	74	0
W Harris	.270	344	56	93	2	32	71	17
A Jones	.222	572	83	127	26	94	138	5
S Thorman	.216	287	37	62	11	36	70	1

PITCHERS	W-L	ERA	IP	H	BB	SO	SV
P Moylan	5-3	1.80	90.0	65	31	63	1
R Soriano	3-3	3.00	72.0	47	15	70	9
J Smoltz	14-8	3.11	205.2	196	47	197	0
T Hudson	16-10	3.33	224.1	221	53	132	0
B Wickman*	3-4	3.58	50.1	54	21	37	20
C James	11-10	4.24	161.1	164	58	116	0
O Villarreal	2-2	4.24	76.1	75	32	58	1
B Carlyle	8-7	5.21	107.0	117	32	74	0
K Davies	4-8	5.76	86.0	92	44	59	0

Manager-Bobby Cox

Chicago Cubs

BATTERS	AVG	AB	R	H	HR	RBI	SO	SB
D Lee	.317	567	91	180	22	82	114	6
A Ramirez	.310	506	72	157	26	101	66	0
A Soriano	.299	579	97	173	33	70	130	19
M DeRosa	.293	502	64	147	10	72	93	1
J Jones	.285	453	52	129	5	66	70	6
C Floyd	.284	282	40	80	9	45	47	0
M Murton	.281	235	35	66	8	22	39	1
M Fontenot	.278	234	32	65	3	29	43	5
J Kendall#	.270	174	21	47	1	19	15	0
R Theriot	.266	537	80	143	3	45	50	28
F Pie	.215	177	26	38	2	20	43	8

PITCHERS	W-L	ERA	IP	H	BB	SO	SV
B Howry	6-7	3.32	81.1	76	19	72	8
M Wuertz	2-3	3.48	72.1	64	35	79	0
T Lilly	15-8	3.83	207.0	181	55	174	0
R Hill	11-8	3.92	195.0	170	63	183	0
S Marshall	7-8	3.92	103.1	107	35	67	0
C Zambrano	18-13	3.95	216.1	187	101	177	0
J Marquis	12-9	4.60	191.2	190	76	109	0
R Dempster	2-7	4.73	66.2	59	30	55	28

Manager-Lou Piniella

Cincinnati Reds

BATTERS	AVG	AB	R	H	HR	RBI	SO	SB
J Keppinger	.332	241	39	80	5	32	12	2
N Hopper	.329	307	51	101	0	14	33	14
S Hatteberg	.310	361	50	112	10	47	35	0
J Hamilton	.292	298	52	87	19	47	65	3
E Encarnacion	.289	502	66	145	16	76	86	8
B Phillips	.288	650	107	187	30	94	109	32
K Griffey	.277	528	78	146	30	93	99	6
J Valentin	.276	243	19	67	2	34	25	0
A Gonzalez	.272	393	55	107	16	55	75	0
A Dunn	.264	522	101	138	40	106	165	9
R Freel	.245	277	44	68	3	16	47	15
D Ross	.203	311	32	63	17	39	92	0

Pittsburgh / Right column

(Pitchers — Arizona right column top)

PITCHERS	W-L	ERA	IP	H	BB	SO	SV
D Weathers	2-6	3.59	77.2	67	27	48	33
A Harang	16-6	3.73	231.2	213	52	218	0
B Arroyo	9-15	4.23	210.2	232	63	156	0
M Belisle	8-9	5.32	177.2	212	43	125	0

Manager-Jerry Narron, Pete Mackanin

Colorado Rockies

BATTERS	AVG	AB	R	H	HR	RBI	SO	SB
M Holliday	.340	636	120	216	36	137	126	11
T Helton	.320	557	86	178	17	91	74	0
W Taveras	.320	372	64	119	2	24	55	33
G Atkins	.301	605	83	182	25	111	96	3
R Spilborghs	.299	264	40	79	11	51	45	4
T Tulowitzki	.291	609	104	177	24	99	130	7
B Hawpe	.291	516	80	150	29	116	137	0
K Matsui	.288	410	84	118	4	37	69	32
Y Torrealba	.255	396	47	101	8	47	73	2
J Carroll	.225	227	45	51	2	22	34	6
C Iannetta	.218	197	22	43	4	27	58	0

PITCHERS	W-L	ERA	IP	H	BB	SO	SV
M Corpas	4-2	2.08	78.0	63	20	58	19
B Fuentes	3-5	3.08	61.1	46	23	56	20
A Cook	8-7	4.12	166.0	178	44	61	0
J Francis	17-9	4.22	215.1	234	63	165	0
T Buchholz	6-5	4.23	93.2	105	20	61	0
U Jimenez	4-4	4.28	82.0	70	37	68	0
R Lopez	5-4	4.42	79.1	83	21	43	0
J Hirsh	5-7	4.81	112.1	103	48	75	0
J Fogg	10-9	4.94	165.2	194	59	94	0

Manager-Clint Hurdle

Florida Marlins

BATTERS	AVG	AB	R	H	HR	RBI	SO	SB
C Ross	.335	173	35	58	12	39	38	2
H Ramirez	.332	639	125	212	29	81	95	51
M Cabrera	.320	588	91	188	34	119	127	2
J Hermida	.296	429	54	127	18	63	105	3
A Boone	.286	189	27	54	5	28	41	2
M Treanor	.269	171	16	46	4	19	29	0
J Willingham	.265	521	75	138	21	89	122	8
M Jacobs	.265	426	57	113	17	54	101	1
A Amezaga	.263	400	46	105	2	30	52	13
D Uggla	.245	632	113	155	31	88	167	2
T Linden	.245	184	21	45	1	11	59	4
M Olivo	.237	452	43	107	16	60	123	4
J Borchard	.196	179	20	35	4	19	60	4

PITCHERS	W-L	ERA	IP	H	BB	SO	SV
L Gardner	3-4	1.94	74.1	72	18	52	2
K Gregg	0-5	3.54	84.0	63	40	87	32
S Mitre	5-8	4.65	149.0	180	41	80	0
D Willis	10-15	5.17	205.1	241	87	146	0
S Olsen	10-15	5.81	176.2	226	85	133	0
B Kim	10-8	6.08	118.1	131	68	107	0
R VandenHurk	4-6	6.83	81.2	94	48	82	0

Manager-Fredi Gonzalez

Houston Astros

BATTERS	AVG	AB	R	H	HR	RBI	SO	SB
H Pence	.322	456	57	147	17	69	95	11
C Lee	.303	627	93	190	32	119	63	10
M Lamb	.289	311	45	90	11	40	45	0
M Loretta	.287	460	52	132	4	41	41	1
T Wigginton#	.284	169	24	48	6	18	40	2
L Berkman	.278	561	95	156	34	102	125	7
L Scott	.255	369	49	94	18	64	95	3
C Biggio	.251	517	68	130	10	50	112	4
B Ausmus	.235	349	38	82	3	25	74	6
A Everett	.232	220	18	51	2	15	31	4
C Burke	.229	319	39	73	6	28	52	9

PITCHERS	W-L	ERA	IP	H	BB	SO	SV
C Qualls	6-5	3.05	82.2	84	25	78	5
R Oswalt	14-7	3.18	212.0	221	60	154	0
B Lidge	5-3	3.36	67.0	54	30	88	19
W Rodriguez	9-13	4.58	182.2	179	62	158	0
C Sampson	7-8	4.59	121.2	138	30	51	0
D Wheeler#	1-4	5.07	49.2	46	13	56	11
D Borkowski	5-3	5.15	71.2	76	34	63	1
W Williams	8-15	5.27	188.0	216	53	101	0
M Albers	4-11	5.86	110.2	127	50	71	0
J Jennings	2-9	6.45	99.0	119	34	71	0

Manager-Cecil Cooper

Los Angeles Dodgers

BATTERS	AVG	AB	R	H	HR	RBI	SO	SB
M Kemp	.342	292	47	100	10	42	66	10
J Loney	.331	344	41	114	15	67	48	0
J Kent	.302	494	78	149	20	79	61	1
J Pierre	.293	668	96	196	0	41	37	64
R Martin	.293	540	87	158	19	87	89	21
A Ethier	.284	447	50	127	13	64	68	0
N Garciaparra	.283	431	39	122	7	59	41	3
L Gonzalez	.278	464	70	129	15	68	56	6
T Abreu	.271	166	19	45	2	17	21	0
R Furcal	.270	581	87	157	6	47	68	25
W Betemit#	.231	156	22	36	10	26	49	0

PITCHERS	W-L	ERA	IP	H	BB	SO	SV
T Saito	2-1	1.40	64.1	33	13	78	39
J Broxton	4-4	2.85	82.0	69	25	99	2
B Penny	16-4	3.03	208.0	199	73	135	0
C Billingsley	12-5	3.31	147.0	131	64	141	0
R Seanez	6-3	3.79	76.0	78	27	73	1
D Lowe	12-14	3.88	199.1	194	59	147	0
R Wolf	9-6	4.73	102.2	110	39	94	0
M Hendrickson	4-8	5.21	122.2	142	29	92	0
D Wells*	9-9	5.43	157.1	201	42	82	0

Manager-Grady Little

Milwaukee Brewers

BATTERS	AVG	AB	R	H	HR	RBI	SO	SB
R Braun	.324	451	91	146	34	97	112	15
C Hart	.295	505	86	149	24	81	99	23
P Fielder	.288	573	109	165	50	119	121	2
J Estrada	.278	442	40	123	10	54	43	0
J Hardy	.277	592	89	164	26	80	73	2
K Mench	.267	288	39	77	8	37	21	3
G Jenkins	.255	420	45	107	21	64	116	2
B Hall	.254	452	59	115	14	63	128	4
T Graffanino	.238	231	34	55	9	30	44	0
D Miller	.237	186	19	44	4	24	39	1
R Weeks	.235	409	87	96	16	36	116	25
G Gross	.235	183	28	43	7	24	37	3
C Counsell	.220	282	31	62	3	24	47	4

PITCHERS	W-L	ERA	IP	H	BB	SO	SV
F Cordero	0-4	2.98	63.1	52	18	86	44
Y Gallardo	9-5	3.67	110.1	103	37	101	0
S Linebrink*	5-6	3.71	70.1	68	25	50	1
B Sheets	12-5	3.82	141.1	138	37	106	0
C Villanueva	8-5	3.94	114.1	101	53	99	1
J Suppan	12-12	4.62	206.2	243	68	114	0
C Vargas	11-6	5.09	134.1	153	54	107	1
C Capuano	5-12	5.10	150.0	170	54	132	0
D Bush	12-10	5.12	186.1	217	44	134	0

Manager-Ned Yost

New York Mets

BATTERS	AVG	AB	R	H	HR	RBI	SO	SB
M Alou	.341	328	51	112	13	49	30	3
D Wright	.325	604	113	196	30	107	115	34
L Castillo#	.296	199	37	59	1	20	17	10
R Gotay	.295	190	25	56	4	24	42	3
S Green	.291	446	62	130	10	46	62	11
E Chavez	.287	150	20	43	1	17	16	5
J Reyes	.280	681	119	191	12	57	78	78
D Easley	.280	193	24	54	10	26	35	0
C Beltran	.276	554	93	153	33	112	111	23
P Lo Duca	.272	445	46	121	9	54	33	2
L Milledge	.272	184	27	50	7	29	42	3
C Delgado	.258	538	71	139	24	87	118	4
J Conine*	.254	256	25	65	6	37	36	4
J Valentin	.241	166	18	40	3	18	28	2

PITCHERS	W-L	ERA	IP	H	BB	SO	SV
B Wagner	2-2	2.63	68.1	55	22	80	34
A Heilman	7-7	3.03	86.0	72	20	63	1
O Perez	15-10	3.56	177.0	153	79	174	0
O Hernandez	9-5	3.72	147.2	109	64	128	0
J Maine	15-10	3.91	191.0	168	75	180	0
T Glavine	13-8	4.45	200.1	219	64	89	0
J Sosa	9-8	4.47	112.2	109	41	69	0
M Pelfrey	3-8	5.57	72.2	85	39	45	0

Manager-Willie Randolph

Philadelphia Phillies

BATTERS	AVG	AB	R	H	HR	RBI	SO	SB
C Utley	.332	530	104	176	22	103	89	9
A Rowand	.309	612	105	189	27	89	119	6
J Werth	.298	255	43	76	8	49	73	7
J Rollins	.296	716	139	212	30	94	85	41
S Victorino	.281	456	78	128	12	46	62	37
G Dobbs	.272	324	45	88	10	55	67	3
R Howard	.268	529	94	142	47	136	199	1
C Ruiz	.259	374	42	97	6	54	49	6
P Burrell	.256	472	77	121	30	97	120	0
V Helms	.246	280	21	69	5	39	62	0
A Nunez	.234	252	24	59	0	16	48	2

PITCHERS	W-L	ERA	IP	H	BB	SO	SV
C Hamels	15-5	3.39	183.1	163	43	177	0
K Kendrick	10-4	3.87	121.0	129	25	49	0
B Myers	5-7	4.33	68.2	61	27	83	21
K Lohse*	9-12	4.62	192.2	207	57	122	0
J Lieber	3-6	4.73	78.0	91	22	54	0
J Moyer	14-12	5.01	199.1	222	66	133	0
A Eaton	10-10	6.29	161.2	192	71	97	0

Manager-Charlie Manuel

Pittsburgh Pirates

BATTERS	AVG	AB	R	H	HR	RBI	SO	SB
F Sanchez	.304	602	77	183	11	81	76	0
J Wilson	.296	477	67	141	12	56	46	2
X Nady	.278	431	55	120	20	72	101	3
R Doumit	.274	252	33	69	9	32	59	1
A LaRoche*	.272	563	71	153	21	88	131	1
R Paulino	.263	457	56	120	11	55	79	2
N McLouth	.258	329	62	85	13	38	77	22
C Izturis*	.258	314	31	81	0	16	19	3
J Bautista	.254	532	75	135	15	63	101	6
C Duffy	.249	241	31	60	3	22	43	13
J Bay	.247	538	78	133	21	84	141	4
J Castillo	.244	221	18	54	0	24	48	0

PITCHERS	W-L	ERA	IP	H	BB	SO	SV
M Capps	4-7	2.28	79.0	64	16	64	18
I Snell	9-12	3.76	208.0	209	68	177	0
T Gorzelanny	14-10	3.88	201.2	214	68	135	0
S Chacon	5-4	3.94	96.0	95	48	79	1
M Morris*	10-11	4.89	198.2	240	61	102	0
P Maholm	10-15	5.02	177.2	204	49	105	0
S Torres	2-4	5.47	52.2	57	17	45	12
Z Duke	3-8	5.53	107.1	161	25	41	0
T Armas	4-5	6.03	97.0	111	38	73	0

Manager-Jim Tracy

St. Louis Cardinals

BATTERS	AVG	AB	R	H	HR	RBI	SO	SB
S Schumaker	.333	177	19	59	2	19	20	1
A Pujols	.327	565	99	185	32	103	58	2
D Eckstein	.309	434	58	134	3	31	22	10
A Miles	.290	414	55	120	2	32	40	2
S Taguchi	.290	307	48	89	3	30	32	7
B Ryan	.289	180	30	52	4	12	19	7
R Ankiel	.285	172	31	49	11	39	41	1
J Encarnacion	.283	283	43	80	9	47	43	2
Y Molina	.275	353	30	97	6	40	43	1
S Spiezio	.269	223	31	60	4	31	40	0
R Ludwick	.267	303	42	81	14	52	72	4
S Rolen	.265	392	55	104	8	58	56	5
D Duncan	.259	375	51	97	21	70	123	2
J Edmonds	.252	365	39	92	12	53	75	0
G Bennett	.252	155	12	39	2	17	16	1
A Kennedy	.219	279	27	61	3	18	33	6
R Branyan*	.196	163	22	32	10	26	69	1

PITCHERS	W-L	ERA	IP	H	BB	SO	SV
J Isringhausen	4-0	2.48	65.1	42	28	54	32
R Franklin	4-4	3.04	80.0	70	11	44	1
A Wainwright	14-12	3.70	202.0	212	70	136	0
B Thompson	8-6	4.73	129.1	157	40	53	0
B Looper	12-12	4.94	175.0	183	51	87	0
K Wells	7-17	5.70	162.2	186	78	122	0
A Reyes	2-14	6.04	107.1	108	43	74	0

Manager-Tony La Russa

San Diego Padres

BATTERS	AVG	AB	R	H	HR	RBI	SO	SB
J Bard	.285	389	42	111	5	51	58	0
A Gonzalez	.282	646	101	182	30	100	140	0
K Kouzmanoff	.275	484	57	133	18	74	94	1
B Giles	.271	483	72	131	13	51	61	4
K Greene	.254	611	89	155	27	97	128	4
G Blum	.252	330	34	83	5	33	52	0
M Barrett*	.244	344	29	84	9	41	57	2
S Hairston	.243	263	37	64	11	36	55	2
M Cameron	.242	571	88	138	21	78	160	18
J Cruz	.234	256	37	60	6	21	65	6
M Ensberg*	.230	282	47	65	12	39	67	0
M Giles	.229	420	52	96	4	39	82	10
T Sledge	.210	200	22	42	7	23	60	1
J Lane*	.175	171	18	30	8	27	31	1

PITCHERS	W-L	ERA	IP	H	BB	SO	SV
H Bell	6-4	2.02	93.2	60	30	102	2
J Peavy	19-6	2.54	223.1	169	68	240	0
T Hoffman	4-5	2.98	57.1	49	15	44	42
D Brocail	5-1	3.05	76.2	66	24	43	0
C Young	9-8	3.12	173.0	118	72	167	0
C Meredith	5-3	3.50	79.2	94	17	59	0
G Maddux	14-11	4.14	198.0	221	25	104	0
J Germano	7-10	4.46	133.1	133	40	78	0
B Tomko*	4-12	5.55	131.1	149	48	105	0

Manager-Bud Black

San Francisco Giants

BATTERS	AVG	AB	R	H	HR	RBI	SO	SB
R Winn	.300	593	73	178	14	65	85	15
F Lewis	.287	157	34	45	3	19	32	5
D Ortmeier	.287	157	20	45	6	16	41	2
R Davis*	.279	190	32	53	1	9	28	22
B Molina	.276	497	38	137	19	81	53	0
B Bonds	.276	340	75	94	28	66	54	5
K Frandsen	.269	264	26	71	5	31	24	4
D Roberts	.260	396	61	103	2	23	66	31
R Klesko	.260	362	51	94	6	44	68	5
P Feliz	.253	557	61	141	20	72	70	2
R Aurilia	.252	329	40	83	5	33	45	0
O Vizquel	.246	513	54	126	4	51	48	14
R Durham	.218	464	56	101	11	71	75	10
PITCHERS	W-L	ERA		IP	H	BB	SO	SV
B Hennessey	4-5	3.42		68.1	66	23	40	19
K Correia	4-7	3.45		101.2	94	40	80	0
M Cain	7-16	3.65		200.0	173	79	163	0
N Lowry	14-8	3.92		156.0	155	87	87	0
T Lincecum	7-5	4.00		146.1	122	65	150	0
R. Messenger*	2-4	4.20		64.1	85	21	40	1
B Zito	11-13	4.53		196.2	182	83	131	0

Manager-Bruce Bochy

Washington Nationals

BATTERS	AVG	AB	R	H	HR	RBI	SO	SB
C Guzman	.328	174	31	57	2	14	21	2
D Young	.320	460	57	147	13	74	74	0
R Belliard	.290	511	57	148	11	58	72	3
R Church	.272	470	57	128	15	70	107	3
R Zimmerman	.266	653	99	174	24	91	125	4
A Kearns	.266	587	84	156	16	74	106	2
N Logan	.265	325	39	86	0	21	86	23
F Lopez	.245	603	70	148	9	50	109	24
J Flores	.244	180	21	44	4	25	48	0
B Schneider	.235	408	33	96	6	54	56	0
R Fick	.234	197	24	46	2	16	42	0
R Langerhans*#	.170	206	27	35	6	23	79	3
PITCHERS	W-L	ERA		IP	H	BB	SO	SV
C Cordero	3-3	3.36		75.0	75	29	62	37
S Hill	4-5	3.42		97.1	86	25	65	0
J Rauch	8-4	3.61		87.1	75	21	71	4
T Redding	3-6	3.64		84.0	84	38	47	0
S Rivera	4-6	3.68		93.0	88	42	64	3
J Bergmann	6-6	4.45		115.1	99	42	86	0
M Chico	7-9	4.63		167.0	183	74	94	0
M Bacsik	5-8	5.11		118.0	141	29	45	0
J Simontacchi	6-7	6.37		70.2	95	23	42	0

Manager-Manny Acta

American League Team Statistics, 2007

(Individual Statistics: Batting—at least 150 at-bats; Pitching—at least 70 innings or 10 saves; *changed teams within AL during season; entry includes only AL stats)

TEAM BATTING

Team	BA	AB	R	H	HR	RBI
New York Yankees	.290	5717	968	1656	201	929
Detroit Tigers	.287	5757	887	1652	177	857
Seattle Mariners	.287	5684	794	1629	153	754
Los Angeles Angels	.284	5554	822	1578	123	776
Boston Red Sox	.279	5589	867	1561	166	829
Baltimore Orioles	.272	5631	756	1529	142	718
Cleveland Indians	.268	5604	811	1504	178	784
Tampa Bay Rays	.268	5593	782	1500	187	750
Minnesota Twins	.264	5522	718	1460	118	671
Texas Rangers	.263	5555	816	1460	179	768
Kansas City Royals	.261	5534	706	1447	102	660
Toronto Blue Jays	.259	5536	753	1434	165	719
Oakland Athletics	.256	5577	741	1430	171	711
Chicago White Sox	.246	5441	693	1341	190	667

TEAM PITCHING

Team	ERA	IP	H	SO	BB	SV
Boston Red Sox	3.87	1438.2	1350	1149	482	45
Toronto Blue Jays	4.00	1448.2	1383	1067	479	44
Cleveland Indians	4.05	1462.2	1519	1047	410	49
Minnesota Twins	4.15	1436.2	1505	1094	420	38
Los Angeles Angels	4.23	1435.0	1480	1156	477	43
Oakland Athletics	4.28	1448.0	1468	1036	530	36
Kansas City Royals	4.48	1437.1	1547	993	520	36
New York Yankees	4.49	1450.2	1498	1009	578	34
Detroit Tigers	4.57	1447.1	1498	1047	566	44
Seattle Mariners	4.73	1434.1	1578	1020	546	43
Texas Rangers	4.75	1430.0	1525	976	668	42
Chicago White Sox	5.17	1440.2	1556	1015	499	42
Baltimore Orioles	5.17	1438.2	1491	1087	696	30
Tampa Bay Devil Rays	5.53	1429.2	1649	1194	568	28

Baltimore Orioles

BATTERS	AVG	AB	R	H	HR	RBI	SO	SB
N Markakis	.300	637	97	191	23	112	112	18
M Tejada	.296	514	72	152	18	81	55	2
B Roberts	.290	621	103	180	12	57	99	50
A Huff	.280	550	68	154	15	72	87	1
M Mora	.274	467	67	128	14	58	63	3
C Patterson	.269	461	65	124	8	45	65	37
R Hernandez	.258	364	40	94	9	62	59	1
J Payton	.256	434	48	111	7	58	42	5
K Millar	.254	476	63	121	17	63	94	1
J Gibbons	.230	270	28	62	6	28	52	0
P Bako	.205	156	13	32	1	8	50	0
PITCHERS	W-L	ERA		IP	H	BB	SO	SV
E Bedard	13-5	3.16		182.0	141	57	221	0
J Guthrie	7-5	3.70		175.1	165	47	123	0
C Ray	5-6	4.43		42.2	35	18	44	16
S Trachsel	6-8	4.48		140.2	151	69	45	0
D Cabrera	9-18	5.55		204.1	207	108	166	0
B Burres	6-8	5.95		121.0	140	66	96	0

Manager-Sam Perlozzo, Dave Trembley

Boston Red Sox

BATTERS	AVG	AB	R	H	HR	RBI	SO	SB
D Ortiz	.332	549	116	182	35	117	103	3
M Lowell	.324	589	79	191	21	120	71	3
D Pedroia	.317	520	86	165	8	50	42	7
M Ramirez	.296	483	84	143	20	88	92	0
K Youkilis	.288	528	85	152	16	83	105	4
J Drew	.270	466	84	126	11	64	100	4
C Crisp	.268	526	85	141	6	60	84	28
J Varitek	.255	435	57	111	17	68	122	1
A Cora	.246	207	30	51	3	18	23	1
R Clayton	.246	195	24	48	1	12	53	2
J Lugo	.237	570	71	135	8	73	82	33
W Pena	.218	156	18	34	5	17	58	0
E Hinske	.204	186	25	38	6	21	54	3
PITCHERS	W-L	ERA		IP	H	BB	SO	SV
J Papelbon	1-3	1.85		58.1	30	15	84	37
J Beckett	20-7	3.27		200.2	189	40	194	0
E Gagne*	4-2	3.81		52.0	49	21	51	16
C Schilling	9-8	3.87		151.0	165	23	101	0
D Matsuzaka	15-12	4.40		204.2	191	80	201	0
T Wakefield	17-12	4.76		189.0	191	64	110	0
J Tavarez	7-11	5.15		134.2	151	57	77	0

Manager-Terry Francona

Chicago White Sox

BATTERS	AVG	AB	R	H	HR	RBI	SO	SB
R Mackowiak	.278	237	34	66	6	36	53	3
J Thome	.275	432	79	119	35	96	134	0
J Owens	.267	356	44	95	1	17	63	32
A Pierzynski	.263	472	54	124	14	50	66	1
P Konerko	.259	549	71	142	31	90	102	0
J Dye	.254	508	68	129	28	78	107	2
T Iguchi#	.251	327	45	82	6	31	65	8
D Erstad	.248	310	33	77	4	32	44	7
J Fields	.244	373	54	91	23	67	125	1
S Podsednik	.243	214	30	52	2	11	36	12
A Cintron	.243	185	23	45	2	19	35	2
J Uribe	.234	513	55	120	20	68	112	1
D Richar	.230	187	30	43	6	15	33	1
J Crede	.216	167	13	36	4	22	24	0
A Gonzalez	.185	189	17	35	2	11	61	1
PITCHERS	W-L	ERA		IP	H	BB	SO	SV
B Jenks	3-5	2.77		65.0	45	13	56	40
M Buehrle	10-9	3.63		201.0	208	45	115	0
J Vazquez	15-8	3.74		216.2	197	50	213	0
J Garland	10-13	4.23		208.1	219	57	98	0
G Floyd	1-5	5.27		70.0	85	19	49	0
J Danks	6-13	5.50		139.0	160	54	109	0
J Contreras	10-17	5.57		189.0	232	62	113	0

Manager-Ozzie Guillen

Cleveland Indians

BATTERS	AVG	AB	R	H	HR	RBI	SO	SB
V Martinez	.301	562	78	169	25	114	76	0
C Gomez	.297	222	21	66	1	21	26	1
K Lofton*	.296	490	86	145	7	38	51	23
R Garko	.289	484	62	140	21	61	94	1
A Cabrera	.283	159	30	45	3	22	31	0
G Sizemore	.277	628	118	174	24	78	155	33
C Blake	.270	588	81	159	18	78	123	1
J Peralta	.270	574	87	155	21	72	146	0
J Michaels	.270	267	43	72	7	39	50	0
T Hafner	.266	545	80	145	24	100	115	0
F Gutierrez	.266	271	41	72	13	36	77	0
K Shoppach	.261	161	26	42	7	30	56	0
T Nixon	.251	307	30	77	3	31	59	0
J Barfield	.243	420	53	102	3	50	90	0
D Dellucci	.230	178	25	41	4	20	40	0

PITCHERS	W-L	ERA	IP	H	BB	SO	SV
R Betancourt	5-1	1.47	79.1	51	9	80	3
F Carmona	19-8	3.06	215.0	199	61	137	0
C Sabathia	19-7	3.21	241.0	238	37	209	0
J Westbrook	6-9	4.32	152.0	159	55	93	0
P Byrd	15-8	4.59	192.1	239	28	88	0
J Borowski	4-5	5.07	65.2	77	17	58	45
C Lee	5-8	6.29	97.1	112	36	66	0

Manager-Eric Wedge

Detroit Tigers

BATTERS	AVG	AB	R	H	HR	RBI	SO	SB
M Ordonez	.363	595	117	216	28	139	79	4
P Polanco	.341	587	105	200	9	67	30	7
C Granderson	.302	612	122	185	23	74	141	26
C Guillen	.296	564	86	167	21	102	93	13
S Casey	.296	453	40	134	4	54	42	2
I Rodriguez	.281	502	50	141	11	63	96	2
O Infante	.271	166	24	45	2	17	29	4
G Sheffield	.265	494	107	131	25	75	71	22
M Rabelo	.256	168	14	43	1	18	41	0
M Thames	.242	269	37	65	18	54	72	2
B Inge	.236	508	64	120	14	71	150	9
C Monroe	.222	343	47	76	11	55	94	0

PITCHERS	W-L	ERA	IP	H	BB	SO	SV
J Verlander	18-6	3.66	201.2	181	67	183	0
T Jones	1-4	4.26	61.1	64	23	33	38
C Durbin	8-7	4.72	127.2	133	49	66	1
J Grilli	5-3	4.74	79.2	81	32	62	0
N Robertson	9-13	4.76	177.2	199	63	119	0
J Bonderman	11-9	5.01	174.1	193	48	145	0
M Maroth	5-2	5.06	78.1	97	33	28	0

Manager-Jim Leyland

Kansas City Royals

BATTERS	AVG	AB	R	H	HR	RBI	SO	SB
J Gathright	.307	228	28	70	0	19	36	9
M Grudzielanek	.302	453	70	137	6	51	60	1
B Butler	.292	329	38	96	8	52	55	0
R Gload	.288	320	37	92	7	51	39	2
M Teahen	.285	544	78	155	7	60	127	13
T Pena#	.267	509	58	136	2	47	78	5
E German	.264	348	49	92	4	37	60	11
D DeJesus	.260	605	101	157	7	58	83	10
M Sweeney	.260	265	26	69	7	38	29	0
E Brown	.257	366	44	94	6	62	71	12
A Gordon	.247	543	60	134	15	60	137	14
J Buck	.222	347	41	77	18	48	92	0
R Shealy	.221	172	18	38	3	21	53	0
J LaRue	.148	169	14	25	4	13	66	1

PITCHERS	W-L	ERA	IP	H	BB	SO	SV
J Soria	2-3	2.48	69.0	46	19	75	17
G Meche	9-13	3.67	216.0	218	62	156	0
Z Greinke	7-7	3.69	122.0	122	36	106	1
J Peralta	1-3	3.80	87.2	93	19	66	1
B Bannister	12-9	3.87	165.0	156	44	77	0
O Dotel	2-1	3.91	23.0	24	11	29	11
O Perez	8-11	5.57	137.1	178	50	64	0
J De La Rosa	8-12	5.82	130.0	160	53	82	0

Manager-Buddy Bell

Los Angeles Angels of Anaheim

BATTERS	AVG	AB	R	H	HR	RBI	SO	SB
C Figgins	.330	442	81	146	3	58	81	41
V Guerrero	.324	574	89	186	27	125	62	2
H Kendrick	.322	338	55	109	5	39	61	5
O Cabrera	.301	638	101	192	8	86	64	20
G Anderson	.297	417	67	124	16	80	54	1
C Kotchman	.296	443	64	131	11	68	43	2
R Willits	.293	430	74	126	0	34	83	27
M Izturis	.289	336	47	97	6	51	39	7
S Hillenbrand	.254	197	19	50	3	22	18	0
G Matthews	.252	516	79	130	18	72	102	18
M Napoli	.247	219	40	54	10	34	63	5
R Quinlan	.247	178	21	44	3	21	27	3
E Aybar	.237	194	18	46	1	19	32	4
Mathis	.211	171	24	36	4	23	49	0

PITCHERS	W-L	ERA	IP	H	BB	SO	SV
F Rodriguez	5-2	2.81	67.1	50	34	90	40
J Lackey	19-9	3.01	224.0	219	52	179	0
K Escobar	18-7	3.40	195.2	182	66	160	0
S Shields	4-5	3.86	77.0	62	33	77	2
Weaver	13-7	3.91	161.0	178	45	115	0
Moseley	4-3	4.40	92.0	97	27	50	0
Saunders	8-5	4.44	107.1	129	34	69	0
Bootcheck	3-3	4.77	77.1	81	24	56	0
Santana	7-14	5.76	150.0	174	58	126	0
Colon	6-8	6.34	99.1	132	29	76	0

Manager-Mike Scioscia

Minnesota Twins

BATTERS	AVG	AB	R	H	HR	RBI	SO	SB
L Castillo#	.304	349	54	106	0	18	28	9
M Redmond	.294	272	23	80	1	38	23	0
J Mauer	.293	406	62	119	7	60	51	7
T Hunter	.287	600	94	172	28	107	101	18
J Tyner	.286	304	42	87	1	22	26	8
M Cuddyer	.276	547	87	151	16	81	107	5
J Kubel	.273	418	49	114	13	65	79	5
J Morneau	.271	590	84	160	31	111	91	1
J Bartlett	.265	510	75	135	5	43	73	23
J Cirillo	.261	153	18	40	2	21	13	2
A Casilla	.222	189	15	42	0	9	29	11
L Rodriguez	.219	155	18	34	2	12	14	1
N Punto	.210	472	53	99	1	25	90	16

PITCHERS	W-L	ERA	IP	H	BB	SO	SV
J Nathan	4-2	1.88	71.2	54	19	77	37
M Guerrier	2-4	2.35	88.0	71	21	68	1
P Neshek	7-2	2.94	70.1	44	27	74	0
J Santana	15-13	3.33	219.0	183	52	235	0
M Garza	5-7	3.69	83.0	96	32	67	0
C Silva	13-14	4.19	202.0	229	36	89	0
S Baker	9-9	4.26	143.2	162	29	102	0
B Bonser	8-12	5.10	173.0	199	65	136	0
R Ortiz	4-4	5.14	91.0	112	15	44	0

Manager-Ron Gardenhire

New York Yankees

BATTERS	AVG	AB	R	H	HR	RBI	SO	SB
J Posada	.338	506	91	171	20	90	98	2
D Jeter	.322	639	102	206	12	73	100	15
A Rodriguez	.314	583	143	183	54	156	120	24
R Cano	.306	617	93	189	19	97	85	4
A Phillips	.292	185	27	54	2	25	26	0
H Matsui	.285	547	100	156	25	103	73	4
B Abreu	.283	605	123	171	16	101	115	25
D Mientkiewicz	.277	166	26	46	5	24	23	0
M Cabrera	.273	545	66	149	8	73	68	13
J Damon	.270	533	93	144	12	63	79	27
J Molina*	.257	191	18	49	1	19	43	2
J Giambi	.236	254	31	60	14	39	66	1

PITCHERS	W-L	ERA	IP	H	BB	SO	SV
M Rivera	3-4	3.15	71.1	68	12	74	30
C Wang	19-7	3.70	199.1	199	59	104	0
A Pettitte	15-9	4.05	215.1	238	69	141	0
R Clemens	6-6	4.18	99.0	99	31	68	0
L Vizcaino#	8-2	4.30	75.1	66	43	62	0
P Hughes	5-3	4.46	72.2	64	29	58	0
M Mussina	11-10	5.15	152.0	180	35	91	0

Manager-Joe Torre

Oakland Athletics

BATTERS	AVG	AB	R	H	HR	RBI	SO	SB
S Stewart	.290	576	79	167	12	48	60	11
T Buck	.288	285	41	82	7	34	66	4
M Ellis	.276	583	84	161	19	76	94	9
M Piazza	.275	309	33	85	8	44	61	0
N Swisher	.262	539	84	141	22	78	131	3
J Scutaro	.260	338	49	88	7	41	40	2
J Cust	.256	395	61	101	26	82	164	0
K Suzuki	.249	213	27	53	7	39	39	0
E Chavez	.240	341	43	82	15	46	76	4
D Johnson	.236	416	53	98	18	62	77	0
B Crosby	.226	349	40	79	8	31	62	10
J Kendall#	.226	292	24	66	2	22	27	3
M Kotsay	.214	206	20	44	1	20	20	1

PITCHERS	W-L	ERA	IP	H	BB	SO	SV
H Street	5-2	2.88	50.0	35	12	63	16
D Haren	15-9	3.07	222.2	214	55	192	0
J Blanton	14-10	3.95	230.0	240	40	140	0
A Embree	1-2	3.97	68.0	67	19	51	17
L DiNardo	8-10	4.11	131.1	136	50	59	0
C Gaudin	11-13	4.42	199.1	205	100	154	0
D Braden	1-8	6.72	72.1	91	26	55	0

Manager-Bob Geren

Seattle Mariners

BATTERS	AVG	AB	R	H	HR	RBI	SO	SB
I Suzuki	.351	678	111	238	6	68	77	37
J Vidro	.314	548	78	172	6	59	57	0
R Ibanez	.291	573	80	167	21	105	97	0
J Guillen	.290	593	72	172	23	99	118	5
K Johjima	.287	485	52	139	14	61	41	0
W Betancourt	.289	536	72	155	9	67	48	5
W Bloomquist	.277	173	28	48	2	13	35	7
A Beltre	.276	595	87	164	26	99	104	14
B Broussard	.275	240	27	66	7	29	50	2
J Lopez	.252	524	58	132	11	62	64	2
R Sexson	.205	434	56	89	21	63	100	1

PITCHERS	W-L	ERA	IP	H	BB	SO	SV
J Putz	6-1	1.38	71.2	37	13	82	40
F Hernandez	14-7	3.92	190.1	209	53	165	0
M Batista	16-11	4.29	193.0	209	85	133	0
J Washburn	10-15	4.32	193.2	201	67	114	0
C Baek	4-3	5.15	73.1	87	14	49	0
J Weaver	7-13	6.20	146.2	190	35	80	0
H Ramirez	8-7	7.16	98.0	139	42	40	0

Manager-Mike Hargrove, John McLaren

Tampa Bay Devil Rays

BATTERS	AVG	AB	R	H	HR	RBI	SO	SB
C Crawford	.315	584	93	184	11	80	112	50
B Upton	.300	474	86	142	24	82	154	22
D Young	.288	645	65	186	13	93	127	10
B Harris	.286	521	72	149	12	59	96	4
A Iwamura	.285	491	82	140	7	34	114	12
C Pena	.282	490	99	138	46	121	142	1
T Wigginton#	.275	378	47	104	16	49	73	1
J Wilson	.251	263	25	66	2	24	51	6
J Gomes	.244	348	48	85	17	49	126	12
G Norton	.243	202	25	49	4	23	55	1
D Navarro	.227	388	46	88	9	44	67	3
E Dukes	.190	184	27	35	10	21	44	2

PITCHERS	W-L	ERA	IP	H	BB	SO	SV
S Kazmir	13-9	3.48	206.2	196	89	239	0
J Shields	12-8	3.85	215.0	202	36	184	0
G Glover	6-5	4.89	77.1	87	27	51	2
A Reyes	2-4	4.90	60.2	49	21	70	26
E Jackson	5-15	5.76	161.0	195	88	128	0
A Sonnanstine	6-10	5.85	130.2	151	26	97	0
J Hammel	3-5	6.14	85.0	100	40	64	0
C Fossum	5-8	7.70	76.0	109	27	53	0

Manager-Joe Maddon

Texas Rangers

BATTERS	AVG	AB	R	H	HR	RBI	SO	SB
M Young	.315	639	80	201	9	94	107	13
M Byrd	.307	414	60	127	10	70	88	5
M Teixeira#	.297	286	48	85	13	49	66	0
H Blalock	.293	208	32	61	10	33	38	4
I Kinsler	.263	483	96	127	20	61	83	23
F Catalanotto	.260	331	52	86	11	44	37	2
T Metcalf	.255	161	25	41	5	21	41	0
S Sosa	.252	412	53	104	21	92	112	0

BATTERS	AVG	AB	R	H	HR	RBI	SO	SB
J Saltalamacchia#	.251	167	28	42	7	21	47	0
J Botts	.240	167	19	40	2	14	59	1
N Cruz	.235	307	35	72	9	34	87	2
B Wilkerson	.234	338	54	79	20	62	107	4
R Vazquez	.230	300	42	69	8	28	72	1
G Laird	.224	407	48	91	9	47	103	6
J Hairston	.189	159	22	30	3	16	24	5

PITCHERS	W-L	ERA	IP	H	BB	SO	SV
J Benoit	7-4	2.85	82.0	68	28	87	6
C Wilson	2-1	3.03	68.1	50	33	63	12
J Wright	4-5	3.62	77.0	72	41	39	0
K Gabbard*	6-1	4.65	81.1	68	41	55	0
B McCarthy	5-10	4.87	101.2	111	48	59	0
K Millwood	10-14	5.16	172.2	213	67	123	0
K Loe	6-11	5.36	136.0	162	56	78	0
V Padilla	6-10	5.76	120.1	146	50	71	0
R Tejeda	5-9	6.61	95.1	110	60	69	0

Manager-Ron Washington

Toronto Blue Jays

BATTERS	AVG	AB	R	H	HR	RBI	SO	SB
A Rios	.297	643	114	191	24	85	103	17
A Hill	.291	608	87	177	17	78	102	4
M Stairs	.289	357	58	103	21	64	66	2
F Thomas	.277	531	63	147	26	95	94	0
T Glaus	.262	385	60	101	20	62	102	0
J McDonald	.251	327	32	82	1	31	48	7
V Wells	.245	584	85	143	16	80	89	10
G Zaun	.242	331	43	80	10	52	55	0
L Overbay	.240	425	49	102	10	44	78	2
A Lind	.238	290	34	69	11	46	65	1
R Johnson	.236	275	31	65	2	14	54	0

PITCHERS	W-L	ERA	IP	H	BB	SO	SV
J Accardo	4-4	2.14	67.1	51	24	57	30
C Janssen	2-3	2.35	72.2	67	20	39	6
R Halladay	16-7	3.71	225.1	232	48	139	0
A Burnett	10-8	3.75	165.2	131	66	176	0
J Litsch	7-9	3.81	111.0	116	36	50	0
D McGowan	12-10	4.08	169.2	146	61	144	0
S Marcum	12-6	4.13	159.0	149	49	122	1
J Kennedy	4-9	4.42	108.0	115	53	50	0
J Towers	5-10	5.38	107.0	129	22	76	0

Manager-John Gibbons

Major League Leaders in 2007
American League

Batting: Magglio Ordonez, Detroit, .363; Ichiro Suzuki, Seattle, .351; Placido Polanco, Detroit, .341; Jorge Posada, New York, .338; David Ortiz, Boston, .332.

Runs: Alex Rodriguez, New York, 143; Bobby Abreu, New York, 123; Curtis Granderson, Detroit, 122; Grady Sizemore, Cleveland, 118; Magglio Ordonez, Detroit, 117.

Runs Batted In: Alex Rodriguez, New York, 156; Magglio Ordonez, Detroit, 139; Vladimir Guerrero, Los Angeles, 125; Carlos Pena, Tampa Bay, 121; Mike Lowell, Boston, 120.

Hits: Ichiro Suzuki, Seattle, 238; Magglio Ordonez, Detroit, 216; Derek Jeter, New York, 206; Michael Young, Texas, 201; Placido Polanco, Detroit, 200.

Doubles: Magglio Ordonez, Detroit, 54; David Ortiz, Boston, 52; Aaron Hill, Toronto, 47; Vladimir Guerrero, Los Angeles, 45; Torii Hunter, Minnesota, 45.

Triples: Curtis Granderson, Detroit, 23; Akinori Iwamura, Tampa Bay, 10; Carl Crawford, Tampa Bay, 9; David DeJesus, Kansas City, 9; Carlos Guillen, Detroit, 9.

Home Runs: Alex Rodriguez, New York, 54; Carlos Pena, Tampa Bay, 46; David Ortiz, Boston, 35; Jim Thome, Chicago, 35; Paul Konerko, Chicago, 31; Justin Morneau, Minnesota, 31.

Stolen Bases: Carl Crawford, Tampa Bay, 50; Brian Roberts, Baltimore, 50; Chone Figgins, Los Angeles, 41; Corey Patterson, Baltimore, 37; Ichiro Suzuki, Seattle, 37.

Pitching Wins: Josh Beckett, Boston, 20-7; Fausto Carmona, Cleveland, 19-8; John Lackey, Los Angeles, 19-9; C.C. Sabathia, Cleveland, 19-7; Chien-Ming Wang, 19-7.

Earned Run Average: John Lackey, Los Angeles, 3.01; Fausto Carmona, Cleveland, 3.06; Dan Haren, Oakland, 3.07; Erik Bedard, Baltimore, 3.16; C.C. Sabathia, Cleveland, 3.21.

Strikeouts: Scott Kazmir, Tampa Bay, 239; Johan Santana, Minnesota, 235; Erik Bedard, Baltimore, 221; Javier Vazquez, Chicago, 213; C.C. Sabathia, Cleveland, 209.

Saves: Joe Borowski, Cleveland, 45; Bobby Jenks, Chicago, 40; J.J. Putz, Seattle, 40; Francisco Rodriguez, Los Angeles, 40; Todd Jones, Detroit, 38.

National League

Batting: Matt Holliday, Colorado, .340; Chipper Jones, Atlanta, .337; Hanley Ramirez, Florida, .332; Edgar Renteria, Atlanta, .332; Chase Utley, Philadelphia, .332.

Runs: Jimmy Rollins, Philadelphia, 139; Hanley Ramirez, Florida, 125; Matt Holliday, Colorado, 120; Jose Reyes, New York, 119; Dan Uggla, Florida, 113; David Wright, New York, 113.

Runs Batted In: Matt Holliday, Colorado, 137; Ryan Howard, Philadelphia, 136; Miguel Cabrera, Florida, 119; Prince Fielder, Milwaukee, 119; Carlos Lee, Houston, 119.

Hits: Matt Holliday, Colorado, 216; Hanley Ramirez, Florida, 212; Jimmy Rollins, Philadelphia, 212; Juan Pierre, Los Angeles, 196; David Wright, New York, 196.

Doubles: Matt Holliday, Colorado, 50; Dan Uggla, Florida, 49; Hanley Ramirez, Florida, 48; Chase Utley, Philadelphia, 48; Adrian Gonzalez, San Diego, 46.

Triples: Jimmy Rollins, Philadelphia, 20; Jose Reyes, New York, 12; Kelly Johnson, Atlanta, 10; Alfredo Amezaga, Florida, 9; Corey Hart, Milwaukee, 9; Orlando Hudson, Arizona, 9; Hunter Pence, Houston, 9; Dave Roberts, San Francisco, 9.

Home Runs: Prince Fielder, Milwaukee, 50; Ryan Howard, Philadelphia, 47; Adam Dunn, Cincinnati, 40; Matt Holliday, Colorado, 36; Lance Berkman, Houston, 34; Ryan Braun, Milwaukee, 34; Miguel Cabrera, Florida, 34.

Stolen Bases: Jose Reyes, New York, 78; Juan Pierre, Los Angeles, 64; Hanley Ramirez, Florida, 51; Eric Byrnes, Arizona, 50; Jimmy Rollins, Philadelphia, 41.

Pitching Wins: Jake Peavy, San Diego, 19-6; Brandon Webb, Arizona, 18-10; Carlos Zambrano, Chicago, 18-13; Jeff Francis, Colorado, 17-9; Aaron Harang, Cincinnati, 16-6; Tim Hudson, Atlanta, 16-10; Brad Penny, Los Angeles, 16-4.

Earned Run Average: Jake Peavy, San Diego, 2.54; Brandon Webb, Arizona, 3.01; Brad Penny, Los Angeles, 3.03; John Smoltz, Atlanta, 3.11; Chris Young, San Diego, 3.12.

Strikeouts: Jake Peavy, San Diego, 240; Aaron Harang, Cincinnati, 218; John Smoltz, Atlanta, 197; Brandon Webb, Arizona, 194; Rich Hill, Chicago, 183.

Saves: Jose Valverde, Arizona, 47; Francisco Cordero, Milwaukee, 44; Trevor Hoffman, San Diego, 42; Takashi Saito, Los Angeles, 39; Chad Cordero, Washington, 37.

All-Time Major League Single-Season Leaders
(Source: www.mlb.com; *player active in 2007 season; records for "modern" era beginning 1901)

Home Runs
Barry Bonds* (2001)	73
Mark McGwire (1998)	70
Sammy Sosa* (1998)	66
Mark McGwire (1999)	65
Sammy Sosa* (2001)	64

Runs
Babe Ruth (1921)	177
Lou Gehrig (1936)	167
Lou Gehrig (1931)	163
Babe Ruth (1928)	163
Chuck Klein (1930)	158
Babe Ruth (1920, 1927)	158

Hits
Ichiro Suzuki* (2004)	262
George Sisler (1920)	257
Lefty O'Doul (1929)	254
Bill Terry (1930)	254
Al Simmons (1925)	253

Runs Batted In
Hack Wilson (1930)	191
Lou Gehrig (1931)	184
Hank Greenberg (1937)	183
Jimmie Foxx (1938)	175
Lou Gehrig (1927)	175

Batting Average
Nap Lajoie (1901)	.426
Rogers Hornsby (1924)	.424
George Sisler (1922)	.420
Ty Cobb (1911)	.420
Ty Cobb (1912)	.410

Stolen Bases
Rickey Henderson (1982)	130
Lou Brock (1974)	118
Vince Coleman (1985)	110
Vince Coleman (1987)	109
Rickey Henderson (1983)	108

Walks (Batter)
Barry Bonds* (2004)	232
Barry Bonds* (2002)	198
Barry Bonds* (2001)	177
Babe Ruth (1923)	170
Mark McGwire (1998)	162
Ted Williams (1947, 1949)	162

Strikeouts (Batter)
Ryan Howard* (2007)	199
Adam Dunn* (2004)	195
Adam Dunn* (2006)	194
Bobby Bonds (1970)	189
Jose Hernandez* (2002)	188

Earned Run Average
Dutch Leonard (1914)	0.96
Mordecai Brown (1906)	1.04
Bob Gibson (1968)	1.12
Walter Johnson (1913)	1.14
Christy Mathewson (1909)	1.14

Wins
Jack Chesbro (1904)	41
Ed Walsh (1908)	40
Christy Mathewson (1908)	37
Walter Johnson (1913)	36
Joe McGinnity (1904)	35

Strikeouts
Nolan Ryan (1973)	383
Sandy Koufax (1965)	382
Randy Johnson* (2001)	372
Nolan Ryan (1974)	367
Randy Johnson* (1999)	364

Saves
Bobby Thigpen (1990)	57
Eric Gagne* (2003)	55
John Smoltz* (2002)	55
Trevor Hoffman* (1998)	53
Randy Myers (1993)	53
Mariano Rivera* (2004)	53

All-Time Major League Leaders
(Source: www.mlb.com; *player active in 2007 season)

Games
Pete Rose	3,562
Carl Yastrzemski	3,308
Hank Aaron	3,298
Rickey Henderson	3,081
Ty Cobb	3,035
Eddie Murray	3,026
Stan Musial	3,026
Cal Ripken Jr.	3,001
Willie Mays	2,992
Barry Bonds*	2,986

Stolen Bases
Rickey Henderson	1,406
Lou Brock	938
Billy Hamilton	912
Ty Cobb	892
Tim Raines	808
Vince Coleman	752
Eddie Collins	745
Max Carey	738
Honus Wagner	722
Joe Morgan	689

Strikeouts
Nolan Ryan	5,714
Roger Clemens*	4,672
Randy Johnson*	4,616
Steve Carlton	4,136
Bert Blyleven	3,701
Tom Seaver	3,640
Don Sutton	3,574
Gaylord Perry	3,534
Walter Johnson	3,508
Phil Niekro	3,342

At Bats
Pete Rose	14,053
Hank Aaron	12,364
Carl Yastrzemski	11,988
Cal Ripken Jr.	11,551
Ty Cobb	11,429
Eddie Murray	11,336
Robin Yount	11,008
Dave Winfield	11,003
Stan Musial	10,972
Rickey Henderson	10,961

Triples
Sam Crawford	309
Ty Cobb	297
Honus Wagner	252
Jake Beckley	243
Roger Connor	233
Tris Speaker	222
Fred Clarke	220
Dan Brouthers	205
Joe Kelley	194
Paul Waner	191

Saves
Trevor Hoffman*	524
Lee Smith	478
Mariano Rivera*	443
John Franco	424
Dennis Eckersley	390
Jeff Reardon	367
Billy Wagner*	358
Randy Myers	347
Rollie Fingers	341
John Wetteland	330

Runs Batted In
Hank Aaron	2,297
Babe Ruth	2,213
Cap Anson	2,076
Barry Bonds*	1,996
Lou Gehrig	1,995
Stan Musial	1,951
Ty Cobb	1,938
Jimmie Foxx	1,922
Eddie Murray	1,917
Willie Mays	1,903

Batting Average
Ty Cobb	0.367
Rogers Hornsby	0.358
Ed Delahanty	0.346
Tris Speaker	0.345
Billy Hamilton	0.344
Ted Williams	0.344
Dan Brouthers	0.342
Harry Heilmann	0.342
Babe Ruth	0.342
Willie Keeler	0.341
Bill Terry	0.341

Shutouts
Walter Johnson	110
Grover Alexander	90
Christy Mathewson	79
Cy Young	76
Eddie Plank	69
Warren Spahn	63
Nolan Ryan	61
Tom Seaver	61
Bert Blyleven	60
Don Sutton	58

Runs
Rickey Henderson	2,295
Ty Cobb	2,245
Barry Bonds*	2,227
Hank Aaron	2,174
Babe Ruth	2,174
Pete Rose	2,165
Willie Mays	2,062
Cap Anson	1,996
Stan Musial	1,949
Lou Gehrig	1,888

Walks
Barry Bonds*	2,558
Rickey Henderson	2,190
Babe Ruth	2,062
Ted Williams	2,019
Joe Morgan	1,865
Carl Yastrzemski	1,845
Mickey Mantle	1,733
Mel Ott	1,708
Frank Thomas*	1,628
Eddie Yost	1,614

Losses
Cy Young	.316
Jim Galvin	.310
Nolan Ryan	.292
Walter Johnson	.279
Phil Niekro	.274
Gaylord Perry	.265
Don Sutton	.256
Jack Powell	.254
Eppa Rixey	.251
Bert Blyleven	.250

All-Time Home Run Leaders
(Source: www.mlb.com; *player active in 2007 season)

Barry Bonds*	762	Mike Schmidt	548	Eddie Murray	504	Dave Kingman	442	Dale Murphy	398
Hank Aaron	755	Mickey Mantle	536	Lou Gehrig	493	Andre Dawson	438	Joe Carter	396
Babe Ruth	714	Jimmie Foxx	534	Fred McGriff	493	Juan Gonzalez	434	Graig Nettles	390
Willie Mays	660	Willie McCovey	521	Manny Ramirez*	490	Carlos Delgado*	431	Johnny Bench	389
Sammy Sosa*	609	Ted Williams	521	Gary Sheffield*	480	Cal Ripken Jr.	431	Chipper Jones*	386
Ken Griffey Jr.*	593	Alex Rodriguez*	518	Stan Musial	475	Mike Piazza*	427	Dwight Evans	385
Frank Robinson	586	Frank Thomas*	513	Willie Stargell	475	Billy Williams	426	Harold Baines	384
Mark McGwire	583	Ernie Banks	512	Dave Winfield	465	Darrell Evans	414	Larry Walker	383
Harmon Killebrew	573	Ed Mathews	512	Jose Canseco	462	Duke Snider	407	Frank Howard	382
Rafael Palmeiro	569	Mel Ott	511	Carl Yastrzemski	452	Andres Galarraga	399	Jim Rice	382
Reggie Jackson	563	Jim Thome*	507	Jeff Bagwell	449	Al Kaline	399		

Players With 3,000 Major League Hits
(Source: www.mlb.com; *player active in 2007 season)

Pete Rose	4,256	Cap Anson	3,418	Nap Lajoie	3,242	Tony Gwynn	3,141	Lou Brock	3,023
Ty Cobb	4,189	Honus Wagner	3,415	Cal Ripken Jr.	3,184	Dave Winfield	3,110	Rafael Palmeiro	3,020
Hank Aaron	3,771	Paul Molitor	3,319	George Brett	3,154	Craig Biggio*	3,060	Wade Boggs	3,010
Stan Musial	3,630	Eddie Collins	3,315	Paul Waner	3,152	Rickey Henderson	3,055	Al Kaline	3,007
Tris Speaker	3,514	Willie Mays	3,283	Robin Yount	3,142	Rod Carew	3,053	Roberto Clemente	3,000
Carl Yastrzemski	3,419	Eddie Murray	3,255								

50 Home Run Club

Only Mark McGwire and Barry Bonds have ever hit 70 or more home runs in a season. Five players—including Babe Ruth and Roger Maris—have hit 60 or more, a feat Sammy Sosa accomplished for the 3rd time in 2001. Those 5 are at the pinnacle of a select group of players to have hit 50 or more homers in a season. The following list shows each time a player achieved this mark.

HR	Player, team	Year
73	Barry Bonds, San Francisco Giants	2001
70	Mark McGwire, St. Louis Cardinals	1998
66	Sammy Sosa, Chicago Cubs	1998
65	Mark McGwire, St. Louis Cardinals	1999
64	Sammy Sosa, Chicago Cubs	2001
63	Sammy Sosa, Chicago Cubs	1999
61	Roger Maris, N.Y. Yankees	1961
60	Babe Ruth, N.Y. Yankees	1927
59	Babe Ruth, N.Y. Yankees	1921
58	Jimmie Foxx, Philadelphia Athletics	1932
58	Hank Greenberg, Detroit Tigers	1938
58	Ryan Howard, Philadelphia Phillies	2006
58	Mark McGwire, Oakland A's/St. Louis Cardinals	1997
57	Luis Gonzalez, Arizona Diamondbacks	2001
57	Alex Rodriguez, Texas Rangers	2002
56	Hack Wilson, Chicago Cubs	1930
56	Ken Griffey Jr., Seattle Mariners	1997
56	Ken Griffey Jr., Seattle Mariners	1998
54	David Ortiz, Boston Red Sox	2006
54	Babe Ruth, N.Y. Yankees	1920
54	Babe Ruth, N.Y. Yankees	1928

HR	Player, team	Year
54	Ralph Kiner, Pittsburgh Pirates	1949
54	Mickey Mantle, N.Y. Yankees	1961
54	Alex Rodriguez, N.Y. Yankees	2007
52	Mickey Mantle, N.Y. Yankees	1956
52	Willie Mays, San Francisco Giants	1965
52	George Foster, Cincinnati Reds	1977
52	Mark McGwire, Oakland A's	1996
52	Alex Rodriguez, Texas Rangers	2001
52	Jim Thome, Cleveland Indians	2002
51	Andruw Jones, Atlanta Braves	2005
51	Ralph Kiner, Pittsburgh Pirates	1947
51	Johnny Mize, N.Y. Giants	1947
51	Willie Mays, N.Y. Giants	1955
51	Cecil Fielder, Detroit Tigers	1990
50	Jimmie Foxx, Boston Red Sox	1938
50	Albert Belle, Cleveland Indians	1995
50	Brady Anderson, Baltimore Orioles	1996
50	Greg Vaughn, San Diego Padres	1998
50	Sammy Sosa, Chicago Cubs	2000
50	Prince Fielder, Milwaukee Brewers	2007

Pitchers With 300 Major League Wins

(Source: www.mlb.com; *player active in 2007 season)

Cy Young	511	Kid Nichols	361	Eddie Plank	326	Charley Radbourn	309
Walter Johnson	417	Roger Clemens*	354	Nolan Ryan	324	Mickey Welch	307
Grover Alexander	373	Greg Maddux*	347	Don Sutton	324	Tom Glavine*	303
Christy Mathewson	373	Tim Keefe	342	Phil Niekro	318	Lefty Grove	300
Jim Galvin	365	Steve Carlton	329	Gaylord Perry	314	Early Wynn	300
Warren Spahn	363	John Clarkson	328	Tom Seaver	311		

Official Major League Perfect Games Since 1900

Date	Pitcher	Teams
5/5/04	Cy Young	Boston 3 vs. Phil. 0 (AL)
10/2/08	Addie Joss	Clev. 1 vs. Chicago 0 (AL)
4/30/22	Charlie Robertson	Chicago 2 at Detroit 0 (AL)
10/8/56	Don Larsen	N.Y. 2 vs. Brooklyn 0 (AL)*
6/21/64	Jim Bunning	Phil. 6 at N.Y. 0 (NL)
9/9/65	Sandy Koufax	L.A. 1 vs. Chicago 0 (NL)
5/8/68	Catfish Hunter	Oakland 4 vs. Minn. 0 (AL)
5/15/81	Len Barker	Clev. 3 vs. Toronto 0 (AL)

Date	Pitcher	Teams
9/30/84	Mike Witt	Calif.1 at Texas 0 (AL)
9/16/88	Tom Browning	Cincinnati 1 vs. L.A. 0 (NL)
7/28/91	Dennis Martinez	Montreal 2 vs. L.A. 0 (NL)
7/28/94	Kenny Rogers	Texas 4 vs. California 0 (AL)
5/17/98	David Wells	N.Y. 4 vs. Minn. 0 (AL)
7/18/99	David Cone	N.Y. 6 vs. Montreal 0 (AL)
5/18/04	Randy Johnson	Ariz. 2 vs. Atlanta 0 (AL)

*World Series game

Most Career Major League No-Hitters

No.	Pitcher
7	Nolan Ryan
4	Sandy Koufax
3	Larry Corcoran, Bob Feller, Cy Young
2	Jim Bunning, Steve Busby, Carl Erskine, Bob Forsch, Pud Galvin, Ken Holtzman, Randy Johnson, Addie Joss, Dutch Leonard, Jim Maloney, Christy Mathewson, Hideo Nomo, Allie Reynolds, Frank Smith, Warren Spahn, Bill Stoneman, Virgil Trucks, Johnny Vander Meer, Ed Walsh, Don Wilson

Home Run Leaders, by Season

Note: Asterisk (*) indicates the all-time single-season record for each league.

	National League			American League	
Year	Player, Team	HR	Year	Player, Team	HR
1901	Sam Crawford, Cincinnati	16	1901	Napoleon Lajoie, Philadelphia	13
1902	Thomas Leach, Pittsburgh	6	1902	Socks Seybold, Philadelphia	16
1903	James Sheckard, Brooklyn	9	1903	Buck Freeman, Boston	13
1904	Harry Lumley, Brooklyn	9	1904	Harry Davis, Philadelphia	10
1905	Fred Odwell, Cincinnati	9	1905	Harry Davis, Philadelphia	8
1906	Timothy Jordan, Brooklyn	12	1906	Harry Davis, Philadelphia	12
1907	David Brain, Boston	10	1907	Harry Davis, Philadelphia	8
1908	Timothy Jordan, Brooklyn	12	1908	Sam Crawford, Detroit	7
1909	Red Murray, New York	7	1909	Ty Cobb, Detroit	9
1910	Fred Beck, Boston; Frank Schulte, Chicago	10	1910	Jake Stahl, Boston	10
1911	Frank Schulte, Chicago	21	1911	J. Franklin Baker, Philadelphia	9
1912	Henry Zimmerman, Chicago	14	1912	J. Franklin Baker, Philadelphia; Tris Speaker, Boston	10
1913	Gavvy Cravath, Philadelphia	19	1913	J. Franklin Baker, Philadelphia	13
1914	Gavvy Cravath, Philadelphia	19	1914	J. Franklin Baker, Philadelphia	7
1915	Gavvy Cravath, Philadelphia	24	1915	Robert Roth, Chicago-Cleveland	7
1916	Dave Robertson, N.Y.; Fred (Cy) Williams, Chi.	12	1916	Wally Pipp, New York	12
1917	Dave Robertson, N.Y.; Gavvy Cravath, Phi.	12	1917	Wally Pipp, New York	9
1918	Gavvy Cravath, Philadelphia	8	1918	Babe Ruth, Boston; Tilly Walker, Philadelphia	11
1919	Gavvy Cravath, Philadelphia	12	1919	Babe Ruth, Boston	29
1920	Cy Williams, Philadelphia	15	1920	Babe Ruth, New York	54
1921	George Kelly, New York	23	1921	Babe Ruth, New York	59
1922	Rogers Hornsby, St. Louis	42	1922	Ken Williams, St. Louis	39
1923	Cy Williams, Philadelphia	41	1923	Babe Ruth, New York	41

National League			American League		
Year	Player, Team	HR	Year	Player, Team	HR
1924	Jacques Fournier, Brooklyn	27	1924	Babe Ruth, New York	46
1925	Rogers Hornsby, St. Louis	39	1925	Bob Meusel, New York	33
1926	Hack Wilson, Chicago	21	1926	Babe Ruth, New York	47
1927	Hack Wilson, Chicago; Cy Williams, Philadelphia	30	1927	Babe Ruth, New York	60
1928	Hack Wilson, Chicago; Jim Bottomley, St. Louis	31	1928	Babe Ruth, New York	54
1929	Chuck Klein, Philadelphia	43	1929	Babe Ruth, New York	46
1930	Hack Wilson, Chicago	56	1930	Babe Ruth, New York	49
1931	Chuck Klein, Philadelphia	31	1931	Babe Ruth, Lou Gehrig, both New York	46
1932	Chuck Klein, Philadelphia; Mel Ott, New York	38	1932	Jimmie Foxx, Philadelphia	58
1933	Chuck Klein, Philadelphia	28	1933	Jimmie Foxx, Philadelphia	48
1934	Rip Collins, St. Louis; Mel Ott, New York	35	1934	Lou Gehrig, New York	49
1935	Walter Berger, Boston	34	1935	Jimmie Foxx, Philadelphia; Hank Greenberg, Detroit	36
1936	Mel Ott, New York	33	1936	Lou Gehrig, New York	49
1937	Mel Ott, New York; Joe Medwick, St. Louis	31	1937	Joe DiMaggio, New York	46
1938	Mel Ott, New York	36	1938	Hank Greenberg, Detroit	58
1939	John Mize, St. Louis	28	1939	Jimmie Foxx, Boston	35
1940	John Mize, St. Louis	43	1940	Hank Greenberg, Detroit	41
1941	Dolph Camilli, Brooklyn	34	1941	Ted Williams, Boston	37
1942	Mel Ott, New York	30	1942	Ted Williams, Boston	36
1943	Bill Nicholson, Chicago	29	1943	Rudy York, Detroit	34
1944	Bill Nicholson, Chicago	33	1944	Nick Etten, New York	22
1945	Tommy Holmes, Boston	28	1945	Vern Stephens, St. Louis	24
1946	Ralph Kiner, Pittsburgh	23	1946	Hank Greenberg, Detroit	44
1947	Ralph Kiner, Pittsburgh; John Mize, New York	51	1947	Ted Williams, Boston	32
1948	Ralph Kiner, Pittsburgh; John Mize, New York	40	1948	Joe DiMaggio, New York	39
1949	Ralph Kiner, Pittsburgh	54	1949	Ted Williams, Boston	43
1950	Ralph Kiner, Pittsburgh	47	1950	Al Rosen, Cleveland	37
1951	Ralph Kiner, Pittsburgh	42	1951	Gus Zernial, Chicago-Philadelphia	33
1952	Ralph Kiner, Pittsburgh; Hank Sauer, Chicago	37	1952	Larry Doby, Cleveland	32
1953	Ed Mathews, Milwaukee	47	1953	Al Rosen, Cleveland	43
1954	Ted Kluszewski, Cincinnati	49	1954	Larry Doby, Cleveland	32
1955	Willie Mays, New York	51	1955	Mickey Mantle, New York	37
1956	Duke Snider, Brooklyn	43	1956	Mickey Mantle, New York	52
1957	Hank Aaron, Milwaukee	44	1957	Roy Sievers, Washington	42
1958	Ernie Banks, Chicago	47	1958	Mickey Mantle, New York	42
1959	Ed Mathews, Milwaukee	46	1959	Rocky Colavito, Cleve.; Harmon Killebrew, Wash.	42
1960	Ernie Banks, Chicago	41	1960	Mickey Mantle, New York	40
1961	Orlando Cepeda, San Francisco	46	1961	Roger Maris, New York	61*
1962	Willie Mays, San Francisco	49	1962	Harmon Killebrew, Minnesota	48
1963	Hank Aaron, Milwaukee; Willie McCovey, S.F.	44	1963	Harmon Killebrew, Minnesota	45
1964	Willie Mays, San Francisco	47	1964	Harmon Killebrew, Minnesota	49
1965	Willie Mays, San Francisco	52	1965	Tony Conigliaro, Boston	32
1966	Hank Aaron, Atlanta	44	1966	Frank Robinson, Baltimore	49
1967	Hank Aaron, Atlanta	39	1967	Carl Yastrzemski, Boston; Harmon Killebrew, Minn.	44
1968	Willie McCovey, San Francisco	36	1968	Frank Howard, Washington	44
1969	Willie McCovey, San Francisco	45	1969	Harmon Killebrew, Minnesota	49
1970	Johnny Bench, Cincinnati	45	1970	Frank Howard, Washington	44
1971	Willie Stargell, Pittsburgh	48	1971	Bill Melton, Chicago	33
1972	Johnny Bench, Cincinnati	40	1972	Dick Allen, Chicago	37
1973	Willie Stargell, Pittsburgh	44	1973	Reggie Jackson, Oakland	32
1974	Mike Schmidt, Philadelphia	36	1974	Dick Allen, Chicago	32
1975	Mike Schmidt, Philadelphia	38	1975	George Scott, Milwaukee; Reggie Jackson, Oakland	36
1976	Mike Schmidt, Philadelphia	38	1976	Graig Nettles, New York	32
1977	George Foster, Cincinnati	52	1977	Jim Rice, Boston	39
1978	George Foster, Cincinnati	40	1978	Jim Rice, Boston	46
1979	Dave Kingman, Chicago	48	1979	Gorman Thomas, Milwaukee	45
1980	Mike Schmidt, Philadelphia	48	1980	Reggie Jackson, New York; Ben Oglivie, Milwaukee	41
1981	Mike Schmidt, Philadelphia	31	1981	Bobby Grich, California; Tony Armas, Oakland; Dwight Evans, Boston; Eddie Murray, Baltimore	22
1982	Dave Kingman, New York	37	1982	Gorman Thomas, Milwaukee; Reggie Jackson, Cal.	39
1983	Mike Schmidt, Philadelphia	40	1983	Jim Rice, Boston	39
1984	Mike Schmidt, Phi.; Dale Murphy, Atlanta	36	1984	Tony Armas, Boston	43
1985	Dale Murphy, Atlanta	37	1985	Darrell Evans, Detroit	40
1986	Mike Schmidt, Philadelphia	37	1986	Jesse Barfield, Toronto	40
1987	Andre Dawson, Chicago	49	1987	Mark McGwire, Oakland	49
1988	Darryl Strawberry, New York	39	1988	Jose Canseco, Oakland	42
1989	Kevin Mitchell, San Francisco	47	1989	Fred McGriff, Toronto	36
1990	Ryne Sandberg, Chicago	40	1990	Cecil Fielder, Detroit	51
1991	Howard Johnson, New York	38	1991	Cecil Fielder, Detroit; Jose Canseco, Oakland	44
1992	Fred McGriff, San Diego	35	1992	Juan Gonzalez, Texas	43
1993	Barry Bonds, San Francisco	46	1993	Juan Gonzalez, Texas	46
1994	Matt Williams, San Francisco	43	1994	Ken Griffey Jr., Seattle	40
1995	Dante Bichette, Colorado	40	1995	Albert Belle, Cleveland	50
1996	Andres Galarraga, Colorado	47	1996	Mark McGwire, Oakland	52
1997[1]	Larry Walker, Colorado	49	1997[1]	Ken Griffey Jr., Seattle	56
1998	Mark McGwire, St. Louis	70	1998	Ken Griffey Jr., Seattle	56
1999	Mark McGwire, St. Louis	65	1999	Ken Griffey Jr., Seattle	48
2000	Sammy Sosa, Chicago	50	2000	Troy Glaus, Anaheim	47
2001	Barry Bonds, San Francisco	73*	2001	Alex Rodriguez, Texas	52
2002	Sammy Sosa, Chicago	49	2002	Alex Rodriguez, Texas	57
2003	Jim Thome, Philadelphia	47	2003	Alex Rodriguez, Texas	47
2004	Adrian Beltre, Los Angeles	48	2004	Manny Ramirez, Boston	43
2005	Andruw Jones, Atlanta	51	2005	Alex Rodriguez, New York	48
2006	Ryan Howard, Philadelphia	58	2006	David Ortiz, Boston	54
2007	Prince Fielder, Milwaukee	50	2007	Alex Rodriguez, New York	54

1) In 1997, Mark McGwire hit 58 home runs; 34 with the Oakland Athletics (AL) and 24 with the St. Louis Cardinals (NL).

Runs Batted In Leaders, by Season

Note: Asterisk (*) indicates the all-time single-season record for each league since beginning of "modern" era in 1901.

	National League			American League	
Year	Player, Team	RBI	Year	Player, Team	RBI
1907	Sherwood Magee, Philadelphia	85	1907	Ty Cobb, Detroit	116
1908	Honus Wagner, Pittsburgh	109	1908	Ty Cobb, Detroit	108
1909	Honus Wagner, Pittsburgh	100	1909	Ty Cobb, Detroit	107
1910	Sherwood Magee, Philadelphia	123	1910	Sam Crawford, Detroit	120
1911	Frank Schulte, Chicago	121	1911	Ty Cobb, Detroit	144
1912	Henry Zimmerman, Chicago	103	1912	J. Franklin Baker, Philadelphia	133
1913	Gavvy Cravath, Philadelphia	128	1913	J. Franklin Baker, Philadelphia	126
1914	Sherwood Magee, Philadelphia	103	1914	Sam Crawford, Detroit	104
1915	Gavvy Cravath, Philadelphia	115	1915	Sam Crawford, Detroit; Robert Veach, Detroit	112
1916	Henry Zimmerman, Chicago-NewYork	83	1916	Del Pratt, St. Louis	103
1917	Henry Zimmerman, New York	102	1917	Robert Veach, Detroit	103
1918	Sherwood Magee, Philadelphia	76	1918	Robert Veach, Detroit	78
1919	Hi Myers, Boston	73	1919	Babe Ruth, Boston	114
1920	George Kelly, N.Y.; Rogers Hornsby, St. Louis	94	1920	Babe Ruth, New York	137
1921	Rogers Hornsby, St. Louis	126	1921	Babe Ruth, New York	171
1922	Rogers Hornsby, St. Louis	152	1922	Ken Williams, St. Louis	155
1923	Emil Meusel, New York	125	1923	Babe Ruth, New York	131
1924	George Kelly, New York	136	1924	Goose Goslin, Washington	129
1925	Rogers Hornsby, St. Louis	143	1925	Bob Meusel, New York	138
1926	Jim Bottomley, St. Louis	120	1926	Babe Ruth, New York	145
1927	Paul Waner, Pittsburgh	131	1927	Lou Gehrig, New York	175
1928	Jim Bottomley, St. Louis	136	1928	Babe Ruth, New York; Lou Gehrig, New York	142
1929	Hack Wilson, Chicago	159	1929	Al Simmons, Philadelphia	157
1930	Hack Wilson, Chicago	191*	1930	Lou Gehrig, New York	174
1931	Chuck Klein, Philadelphia	121	1931	Lou Gehrig, New York	184*
1932	Don Hurst, Philadelphia	143	1932	Jimmie Foxx, Philadelphia	169
1933	Chuck Klein, Philadelphia	120	1933	Jimmie Foxx, Philadelphia	163
1934	Mel Ott, New York	135	1934	Lou Gehrig, New York	165
1935	Walter Berger, Boston	130	1935	Hank Greenberg, Detroit	170
1936	Joe Medwick, St. Louis	138	1936	Hal Trosky, Cleveland	162
1937	Joe Medwick, St. Louis	154	1937	Hank Greenberg, Detroit	183
1938	Joe Medwick, St. Louis	122	1938	Jimmie Foxx, Boston	175
1939	Frank McCormick, Cincinnati	128	1939	Ted Williams, Boston	145
1940	John Mize, St. Louis	137	1940	Hank Greenberg, Detroit	150
1941	Adolph Camilli, Brooklyn	120	1941	Joe DiMaggio, New York	125
1942	John Mize, New York	110	1942	Ted Williams, Boston	137
1943	Bill Nicholson, Chicago	128	1943	Rudy York, Detroit	118
1944	Bill Nicholson, Chicago	122	1944	Vern Stephens, St. Louis	109
1945	Dixie Walker, Brooklyn	124	1945	Nick Etten, New York	111
1946	Enos Slaughter, St. Louis	130	1946	Hank Greenberg, Detroit	127
1947	John Mize, New York	138	1947	Ted Williams, Boston	114
1948	Stan Musial, St. Louis	131	1948	Joe DiMaggio, New York	155
1949	Ralph Kiner, Pittsburgh	127	1949	Ted Williams, Bos.; Vern Stephens, Bos.	159
1950	Del Ennis, Philadelphia	126	1950	Walt Dropo, Bos.; Vern Stephens, Bos.	144
1951	Monte Irvin, New York	121	1951	Gus Zernial, Chicago-Philadelphia	129
1952	Hank Sauer, Chicago	121	1952	Al Rosen, Cleveland	105
1953	Roy Campanella, Brooklyn	142	1953	Al Rosen, Cleveland	145
1954	Ted Kluszewski, Cincinnati	141	1954	Larry Doby, Cleveland	126
1955	Duke Snider, Brooklyn	136	1955	Ray Boone, Detroit; Jackie Jensen, Boston	116
1956	Stan Musial, St. Louis	109	1956	Mickey Mantle, New York	130
1957	Hank Aaron, Milwaukee	132	1957	Roy Sievers, Washington	114
1958	Ernie Banks, Chicago	129	1958	Jackie Jensen, Boston	122
1959	Ernie Banks, Chicago	143	1959	Jackie Jensen, Boston	112
1960	Hank Aaron, Milwaukee	126	1960	Roger Maris, New York	112
1961	Orlando Cepeda, San Francisco	142	1961	Roger Maris, New York	142
1962	Tommy Davis, Los Angeles	153	1962	Harmon Killebrew, Minnesota	126
1963	Hank Aaron, Milwaukee	130	1963	Dick Stuart, Boston	118
1964	Ken Boyer, St. Louis	119	1964	Brooks Robinson, Baltimore	118
1965	Deron Johnson, Cincinnati	130	1965	Rocky Colavito, Cleveland	108
1966	Hank Aaron, Atlanta	127	1966	Frank Robinson, Baltimore	122
1967	Orlando Cepeda, St. Louis	111	1967	Carl Yastrzemski, Boston	121
1968	Willie McCovey, San Francisco	105	1968	Ken Harrelson, Boston	109
1969	Willie McCovey, San Francisco	126	1969	Harmon Killebrew, Minnesota	140
1970	Johnny Bench, Cincinnati	148	1970	Frank Howard, Washington	126
1971	Joe Torre, St. Louis	137	1971	Harmon Killebrew, Minnesota	119
1972	Johnny Bench, Cincinnati	125	1972	Dick Allen, Chicago	113
1973	Willie Stargell, Pittsburgh	119	1973	Reggie Jackson, Oakland	117
1974	Johnny Bench, Cincinnati	129	1974	Jeff Burroughs, Texas	118
1975	Greg Luzinski, Philadelphia	120	1975	George Scott, Milwaukee	109
1976	George Foster, Cincinnati	121	1976	Lee May, Baltimore	109
1977	George Foster, Cincinnati	149	1977	Larry Hisle, Minnesota	119
1978	George Foster, Cincinnati	120	1978	Jim Rice, Boston	139
1979	Dave Winfield, San Diego	118	1979	Don Baylor, California	139
1980	Mike Schmidt, Philadelphia	121	1980	Cecil Cooper, Milwaukee	122
1981	Mike Schmidt, Philadelphia	91	1981	Eddie Murray, Baltimore	78
1982	Dale Murphy, Atlanta; Al Oliver, Montreal	109	1982	Hal McRae, Kansas City	133
1983	Dale Murphy, Atlanta	121	1983	Cecil Cooper, Milwaukee; Jim Rice, Boston	126
1984	Gary Carter, Montreal; Mike Schmidt, Phi.	106	1984	Tony Armas, Boston	123
1985	Dave Parker, Cincinnati	125	1985	Don Mattingly, New York	145
1986	Mike Schmidt, Philadelphia	119	1986	Joe Carter, Cleveland	121
1987	Andre Dawson, Chicago	137	1987	George Bell, Toronto	134

Year	National League Player, Team	RBI		Year	American League Player, Team	RBI
1988	Will Clark, San Francisco	109		1988	Jose Canseco, Oakland	124
1989	Kevin Mitchell, San Francisco	125		1989	Ruben Sierra, Texas	119
1990	Matt Williams, San Francisco	122		1990	Cecil Fielder, Detroit	132
1991	Howard Johnson, New York	117		1991	Cecil Fielder, Detroit	133
1992	Darren Daulton, Philadelphia	109		1992	Cecil Fielder, Detroit	124
1993	Barry Bonds, San Francisco	123		1993	Albert Belle, Cleveland	129
1994	Jeff Bagwell, Houston	116		1994	Kirby Puckett, Minnesota	112
1995	Dante Bichette, Colorado	128		1995	Albert Belle, Cleveland; Mo Vaughn, Boston	126
1996	Andres Galarraga, Colorado	150		1996	Albert Belle, Cleveland	148
1997	Andres Galarraga, Colorado	140		1997	Ken Griffey Jr., Seattle	147
1998	Sammy Sosa, Chicago	158		1998	Juan Gonzalez, Texas	157
1999	Mark McGwire, St. Louis	147		1999	Manny Ramirez, Cleveland	165
2000	Todd Helton, Colorado	147		2000	Edgar Martinez, Seattle	145
2001	Sammy Sosa, Chicago	160		2001	Bret Boone, Seattle	141
2002	Lance Berkman, Houston	128		2002	Alex Rodriguez, Texas	142
2003	Preston Wilson, Colorado	141		2003	Carlos Delgado, Toronto	145
2004	Vinny Castilla, Colorado	131		2004	Miguel Tejada, Baltimore	150
2005	Andruw Jones, Atlanta	128		2005	David Ortiz, Boston	148
2006	Ryan Howard, Philadelphia	149		2006	David Ortiz, Boston	137
2007	Matt Holliday, Colorado	137		2007	Alex Rodriguez, New York	156

Batting Champions, by Season

Note: Asterisk (*) indicates the all-time single-season record for each league since the beginning of the "modern" era in 1901.

Year	National League Player	Team	Avg.		Year	American League Player	Team	Avg.
1901	Jesse C. Burkett	St. Louis	.382		1901	Napoleon Lajoie	Philadelphia	.426*
1902	Clarence Beaumont	Pittsburgh	.357		1902	Ed Delahanty	Washington	.376
1903	Honus Wagner	Pittsburgh	.355		1903	Napoleon Lajoie	Cleveland	.355
1904	Honus Wagner	Pittsburgh	.349		1904	Napoleon Lajoie	Cleveland	.381
1905	James Seymour	Cincinnati	.377		1905	Elmer Flick	Cleveland	.306
1906	Honus Wagner	Pittsburgh	.339		1906	George Stone	St. Louis	.358
1907	Honus Wagner	Pittsburgh	.350		1907	Ty Cobb	Detroit	.350
1908	Honus Wagner	Pittsburgh	.354		1908	Ty Cobb	Detroit	.324
1909	Honus Wagner	Pittsburgh	.339		1909	Ty Cobb	Detroit	.377
1910	Sherwood Magee	Philadelphia	.331		1910[1]	Ty Cobb	Detroit	.385
1911	Honus Wagner	Pittsburgh	.334		1911	Ty Cobb	Detroit	.420
1912	Henry Zimmerman	Chicago	.372		1912	Ty Cobb	Detroit	.410
1913	Jacob Daubert	Brooklyn	.350		1913	Ty Cobb	Detroit	.390
1914	Jacob Daubert	Brooklyn	.329		1914	Ty Cobb	Detroit	.368
1915	Larry Doyle	New York	.320		1915	Ty Cobb	Detroit	.369
1916	Hal Chase	Cincinnati	.339		1916	Tris Speaker	Cleveland	.386
1917	Edd Roush	Cincinnati	.341		1917	Ty Cobb	Detroit	.383
1918	Zach Wheat	Brooklyn	.335		1918	Ty Cobb	Detroit	.382
1919	Edd Roush	Cincinnati	.321		1919	Ty Cobb	Detroit	.384
1920	Rogers Hornsby	St. Louis	.370		1920	George Sisler	St. Louis	.407
1921	Rogers Hornsby	St. Louis	.397		1921	Harry Heilmann	Detroit	.394
1922	Rogers Hornsby	St. Louis	.401		1922	George Sisler	St. Louis	.420
1923	Rogers Hornsby	St. Louis	.384		1923	Harry Heilmann	Detroit	.403
1924	Rogers Hornsby	St. Louis	.424*		1924	Babe Ruth	New York	.378
1925	Rogers Hornsby	St. Louis	.403		1925	Harry Heilmann	Detroit	.393
1926	Eugene Hargrave	Cincinnati	.353		1926	Henry Manush	Detroit	.378
1927	Paul Waner	Pittsburgh	.380		1927	Harry Heilmann	Detroit	.398
1928	Rogers Hornsby	Boston	.387		1928	Goose Goslin	Washington	.379
1929	Lefty O'Doul	Philadelphia	.398		1929	Lew Fonseca	Cleveland	.369
1930	Bill Terry	New York	.401		1930	Al Simmons	Philadelphia	.381
1931	Chick Hafey	St. Louis	.349		1931	Al Simmons	Philadelphia	.390
1932	Lefty O'Doul	Brooklyn	.368		1932	Dale Alexander	Detroit-Boston	.367
1933	Chuck Klein	Philadelphia	.368		1933	Jimmie Foxx	Philadelphia	.356
1934	Paul Waner	Pittsburgh	.362		1934	Lou Gehrig	New York	.363
1935	Arky Vaughan	Pittsburgh	.385		1935	Buddy Myer	Washington	.349
1936	Paul Waner	Pittsburgh	.373		1936	Luke Appling	Chicago	.388
1937	Joe Medwick	St. Louis	.374		1937	Charlie Gehringer	Detroit	.371
1938	Ernie Lombardi	Cincinnati	.342		1938	Jimmie Foxx	Boston	.349
1939	John Mize	St. Louis	.349		1939	Joe DiMaggio	New York	.381
1940	Debs Garms	Pittsburgh	.355		1940	Joe DiMaggio	New York	.352
1941	Pete Reiser	Brooklyn	.343		1941	Ted Williams	Boston	.406
1942	Ernie Lombardi	Boston	.330		1942	Ted Williams	Boston	.356
1943	Stan Musial	St. Louis	.357		1943	Luke Appling	Chicago	.328
1944	Dixie Walker	Brooklyn	.357		1944	Lou Boudreau	Cleveland	.327
1945	Phil Cavarretta	Chicago	.355		1945	George Stirnweiss	New York	.309
1946	Stan Musial	St. Louis	.365		1946	Mickey Vernon	Washington	.353
1947	Harry Walker	St.L.-Phi.	.363		1947	Ted Williams	Boston	.343
1948	Stan Musial	St. Louis	.376		1948	Ted Williams	Boston	.369
1949	Jackie Robinson	Brooklyn	.342		1949	George Kell	Detroit	.343
1950	Stan Musial	St. Louis	.346		1950	Billy Goodman	Boston	.354
1951	Stan Musial	St. Louis	.355		1951	Ferris Fain	Philadelphia	.344
1952	Stan Musial	St. Louis	.336		1952	Ferris Fain	Philadelphia	.327
1953	Carl Furillo	Brooklyn	.344		1953	Mickey Vernon	Washington	.337
1954	Willie Mays	New York	.345		1954	Roberto Avila	Cleveland	.341
1955	Richie Ashburn	Philadelphia	.338		1955	Al Kaline	Detroit	.340
1956	Hank Aaron	Milwaukee	.328		1956	Mickey Mantle	New York	.353
1957	Stan Musial	St. Louis	.351		1957	Ted Williams	Boston	.388
1958	Richie Ashburn	Philadelphia	.350		1958	Ted Williams	Boston	.328
1959	Hank Aaron	Milwaukee	.355		1959	Harvey Kuenn	Detroit	.353

Year	Player (NL)	Team	Avg.	Year	Player (AL)	Team	Avg.
	National League				**American League**		
1960	Dick Groat	Pittsburgh	.325	1960	Pete Runnels	Boston	.320
1961	Roberto Clemente	Pittsburgh	.351	1961	Norm Cash	Detroit	.361
1962	Tommy Davis	Los Angeles	.346	1962	Pete Runnels	Boston	.326
1963	Tommy Davis	Los Angeles	.326	1963	Carl Yastrzemski	Boston	.321
1964	Roberto Clemente	Pittsburgh	.339	1964	Tony Oliva	Minnesota	.323
1965	Roberto Clemente	Pittsburgh	.329	1965	Tony Oliva	Minnesota	.321
1966	Matty Alou	Pittsburgh	.342	1966	Frank Robinson	Baltimore	.316
1967	Roberto Clemente	Pittsburgh	.357	1967	Carl Yastrzemski	Boston	.326
1968	Pete Rose	Cincinnati	.335	1968	Carl Yastrzemski	Boston	.301
1969	Pete Rose	Cincinnati	.348	1969	Rod Carew	Minnesota	.332
1970	Rico Carty	Atlanta	.366	1970	Alex Johnson	California	.329
1971	Joe Torre	St. Louis	.363	1971	Tony Oliva	Minnesota	.337
1972	Billy Williams	Chicago	.333	1972	Rod Carew	Minnesota	.318
1973	Pete Rose	Cincinnati	.338	1973	Rod Carew	Minnesota	.350
1974	Ralph Garr	Atlanta	.353	1974	Rod Carew	Minnesota	.364
1975	Bill Madlock	Chicago	.354	1975	Rod Carew	Minnesota	.359
1976	Bill Madlock	Chicago	.339	1976	George Brett	Kansas City	.333
1977	Dave Parker	Pittsburgh	.338	1977	Rod Carew	Minnesota	.388
1978	Dave Parker	Pittsburgh	.334	1978	Rod Carew	Minnesota	.333
1979	Keith Hernandez	St. Louis	.344	1979	Fred Lynn	Boston	.333
1980	Bill Buckner	Chicago	.324	1980	George Brett	Kansas City	.390
1981	Bill Madlock	Pittsburgh	.341	1981	Carney Lansford	Boston	.336
1982	Al Oliver	Montreal	.331	1982	Willie Wilson	Kansas City	.332
1983	Bill Madlock	Pittsburgh	.323	1983	Wade Boggs	Boston	.361
1984	Tony Gwynn	San Diego	.351	1984	Don Mattingly	New York	.343
1985	Willie McGee	St. Louis	.353	1985	Wade Boggs	Boston	.368
1986	Tim Raines	Montreal	.334	1986	Wade Boggs	Boston	.357
1987	Tony Gwynn	San Diego	.370	1987	Wade Boggs	Boston	.363
1988	Tony Gwynn	San Diego	.313	1988	Wade Boggs	Boston	.366
1989	Tony Gwynn	San Diego	.336	1989	Kirby Puckett	Minnesota	.339
1990	Willie McGee	St. Louis	.335	1990	George Brett	Kansas City	.329
1991	Terry Pendleton	Atlanta	.319	1991	Julio Franco	Texas	.341
1992	Gary Sheffield	San Diego	.330	1992	Edgar Martinez	Seattle	.343
1993	Andres Galarraga	Colorado	.370	1993	John Olerud	Toronto	.363
1994	Tony Gwynn	San Diego	.394	1994	Paul O'Neill	New York	.359
1995	Tony Gwynn	San Diego	.368	1995	Edgar Martinez	Seattle	.356
1996	Tony Gwynn	San Diego	.353	1996	Alex Rodriguez	Seattle	.358
1997	Tony Gwynn	San Diego	.372	1997	Frank Thomas	Chicago	.347
1998	Larry Walker	Colorado	.363	1998	Bernie Williams	New York	.339
1999	Larry Walker	Colorado	.379	1999	Nomar Garciaparra	Boston	.357
2000	Todd Helton	Colorado	.372	2000	Nomar Garciaparra	Boston	.372
2001	Larry Walker	Colorado	.350	2001	Ichiro Suzuki	Seattle	.350
2002	Barry Bonds	San Francisco	.370	2002	Manny Ramirez	Boston	.349
2003	Albert Pujols	St. Louis	.359	2003	Bill Mueller	Boston	.326
2004	Barry Bonds	San Francisco	.362	2004	Ichiro Suzuki	Seattle	.372
2005	Derrek Lee	Chicago	.335	2005	Michael Young	Texas	.331
2006	Freddy Sanchez	Pittsburgh	.344	2006	Joe Mauer	Minnesota	.347
2007	Matt Holliday	Colorado	.340	2007	Magglio Ordonez	Detroit	.363

(1) Some baseball researchers have concluded that Ty Cobb actually hit .382 in 1910 while Napoleon Lajoie, Cleveland, hit .383.

Earned Run Average Leaders, by Season

Year	Player, team (NL)	G	IP	ERA	Year	Player, team (AL)	G	IP	ERA
	National League					**American League**			
1977	John Candelaria, Pittsburgh	33	231	2.34	1977	Frank Tanana, California	31	241	2.54
1978	Craig Swan, New York	29	207	2.43	1978	Ron Guidry, New York	35	274	1.74
1979	J. R. Richard, Houston	38	292	2.71	1979	Ron Guidry, New York	33	236	2.78
1980	Don Sutton, Los Angeles	32	212	2.21	1980	Rudy May, New York	41	175	2.47
1981	Nolan Ryan, Houston	21	149	1.69	1981	Steve McCatty, Oakland	22	186	2.32
1982	Steve Rogers, Montreal	35	277	2.40	1982	Rick Sutcliffe, Cleveland	34	216	2.96
1983	Atlee Hammaker, San Francisco	23	172	2.25	1983	Rick Honeycutt, Texas	25	174	2.42
1984	Alejandro Pena, Los Angeles	28	199	2.48	1984	Mike Boddicker, Baltimore	34	261	2.79
1985	Dwight Gooden, New York	35	276	1.53	1985	Dave Stieb, Toronto	36	265	2.48
1986	Mike Scott, Houston	37	275	2.22	1986	Roger Clemens, Boston	33	254	2.48
1987	Nolan Ryan, Houston	34	211	2.76	1987	Jimmy Key, Toronto	36	261	2.76
1988	Joe Magrane, St. Louis	24	165	2.18	1988	Allan Anderson, Minnesota	30	202	2.45
1989	Scott Garrelts, San Francisco	30	193	2.28	1989	Bret Saberhagen, Kansas City	36	262	2.16
1990	Danny Darwin, Houston	48	162	2.21	1990	Roger Clemens, Boston	31	228	1.93
1991	Dennis Martinez, Montreal	31	222	2.39	1991	Roger Clemens, Boston	35	271	2.62
1992	Bill Swift, San Francisco	30	164	2.08	1992	Roger Clemens, Boston	32	246	2.41
1993	Greg Maddux, Atlanta	36	267	2.36	1993	Kevin Appier, Kansas City	34	238	2.56
1994	Greg Maddux, Atlanta	25	202	1.56	1994	Steve Ontiveros, Oakland	27	115	2.65
1995	Greg Maddux, Atlanta	28	209	1.63	1995	Randy Johnson, Seattle	30	214	2.48
1996	Kevin Brown, Florida	32	233	1.89	1996	Juan Guzman, Toronto	27	187	2.93
1997	Pedro Martinez, Montrea	31	241	1.90	1997	Roger Clemens, Toronto	34	264	2.05
1998	Greg Maddux, Atlanta	34	251	2.22	1998	Roger Clemens, Toronto	33	234	2.65
1999	Randy Johnson, Arizona	35	271	2.48	1999	Pedro Martinez, Boston	31	213	2.07
2000	Kevin K. Brown, Los Angeles	33	230	2.58	2000	Pedro Martinez, Boston	29	217	1.74
2001	Randy Johnson, Arizona	35	249	2.49	2001	Freddy Garcia, Seattle	34	238	3.05
2002	Randy Johnson, Arizona	35	260	2.32	2002	Pedro Martinez, Boston	30	199	2.26
2003	Jason Schmidt, San Francisco	29	207	2.34	2003	Pedro Martinez, Boston	29	186	2.22
2004	Jake Peavy, San Diego	27	166.1	2.27	2004	Johan Santana, Minnesota	34	228	2.61
2005	Roger Clemens, Houston	32	211.1	1.87	2005	Kevin Millwood, Cleveland	30	192	2.86
2006	Roy Oswalt, Houston	33	220.2	2.98	2006	Johan Santana, Minnesota	34	233.2	2.77
2007	Jake Peavy, San Diego	34	223.1	2.54	2007	John Lackey, Los Angeles	33	224.0	3.01

ERA is computed by multiplying earned runs allowed by 9, then dividing by innings pitched.

Strikeout Leaders, by Season

Note: Asterisk (*) indicates the all-time single-season record for each league.

National League			American League		
Year	Pitcher, Team	SO	Year	Pitcher, Team	SO
1901	Noodles Hahn, Cincinnati	239	1901	Cy Young, Boston	158
1902	Vic Willis, Boston	225	1902	Rube Waddell, Philadelphia	210
1903	Christy Mathewson, New York	267	1903	Rube Waddell, Philadelphia	302
1904	Christy Mathewson, New York	212	1904	Rube Waddell, Philadelphia	349
1905	Christy Mathewson, New York	206	1905	Rube Waddell, Philadelphia	287
1906	Fred Beebe, Chicago-St. Louis	171	1906	Rube Waddell, Philadelphia	196
1907	Christy Mathewson, New York	178	1907	Rube Waddell, Philadelphia	232
1908	Christy Mathewson, New York	259	1908	Ed Walsh, Chicago	269
1909	Orval Overall, Chicago	205	1909	Frank Smith, Chicago	177
1910	Earl Moore, Philadelphia	185	1910	Walter Johnson, Washington	313
1911	Rube Marquard, New York	237	1911	Ed Walsh, Chicago	255
1912	Grover Alexander, Philadelphia	195	1912	Walter Johnson, Washington	303
1913	Tom Seaton, Philadelphia	168	1913	Walter Johnson, Washington	243
1914	Grover Alexander, Philadelphia	214	1914	Walter Johnson, Washington	225
1915	Grover Alexander, Philadelphia	241	1915	Walter Johnson, Washington	203
1916	Grover Alexander, Philadelphia	167	1916	Walter Johnson, Washington	228
1917	Grover Alexander, Philadelphia	201	1917	Walter Johnson, Washington	188
1918	Hippo Vaughn, Chicago	148	1918	Walter Johnson, Washington	162
1919	Hippo Vaughn, Chicago	141	1919	Walter Johnson, Washington	147
1920	Grover Alexander, Chicago	173	1920	Stan Coveleski, Cleveland	133
1921	Burleigh Grimes, Brooklyn	136	1921	Walter Johnson, Washington	143
1922	Dazzy Vance, Brooklyn	134	1922	Urban Shocker, St. Louis	149
1923	Dazzy Vance, Brooklyn	197	1923	Walter Johnson, Washington	130
1924	Dazzy Vance, Brooklyn	262	1924	Walter Johnson, Washington	158
1925	Dazzy Vance, Brooklyn	221	1925	Lefty Grove, Philadelphia	116
1926	Dazzy Vance, Brooklyn	140	1926	Lefty Grove, Philadelphia	194
1927	Dazzy Vance, Brooklyn	184	1927	Lefty Grove, Philadelphia	174
1928	Dazzy Vance, Brooklyn	200	1928	Lefty Grove, Philadelphia	183
1929	Pat Malone, Chicago	166	1929	Lefty Grove, Philadelphia	170
1930	Bill Hallahan, St. Louis	177	1930	Lefty Grove, Philadelphia	209
1931	Bill Hallahan, St. Louis	159	1931	Lefty Grove, Philadelphia	175
1932	Dizzy Dean, St. Louis	191	1932	Red Ruffing, New York	190
1933	Dizzy Dean, St. Louis	199	1933	Lefty Gomez, New York	163
1934	Dizzy Dean, St. Louis	195	1934	Lefty Gomez, New York	158
1935	Dizzy Dean, St. Louis	190	1935	Tommy Bridges, Detroit	163
1936	Van Lingle Mungo, Brooklyn	238	1936	Tommy Bridges, Detroit	175
1937	Carl Hubbell, New York	159	1937	Lefty Gomez, New York	194
1938	Clay Bryant, Chicago	135	1938	Bob Feller, Cleveland	240
1939	Claude Passeau, Philadelphia-Chicago	137	1939	Bob Feller, Cleveland	246
	Bucky Walters, Cincinnati	137			
1940	Kirby Higbe, Philadelphia	137	1940	Bob Feller, Cleveland	261
1941	John Vander Meer, Cincinnati	202	1941	Bob Feller, Cleveland	260
1942	John Vander Meer, Cincinnati	186	1942	Tex Hughson, Boston	113
				Bobo Newsom, Washington	113
1943	John Vander Meer, Cincinnati	174	1943	Allie Reynolds, Cleveland	151
1944	Bill Voiselle, New York	161	1944	Hal Newhouser, Detroit	187
1945	Preacher Roe, Pittsburgh	148	1945	Hal Newhouser, Detroit	212
1946	Johnny Schmitz, Cincinnati	135	1946	Bob Feller, Cleveland	348
1947	Ewell Blackwell, Cincinnati	193	1947	Bob Feller, Cleveland	196
1948	Harry Brecheen, St. Louis	149	1948	Bob Feller, Cleveland	164
1949	Warren Spahn, Boston	151	1949	Virgil Trucks, Detroit	153
1950	Warren Spahn, Boston	191	1950	Bob Lemon, Cleveland	170
1951	Warren Spahn, Boston	164	1951	Vic Raschi, New York	164
	Don Newcombe, Brooklyn	164			
1952	Warren Spahn, Boston	183	1952	Allie Reynolds, New York	160
1953	Robin Roberts, Philadelphia	198	1953	Billy Pierce, Chicago	186
1954	Robin Roberts, Philadelphia	185	1954	Bob Turley, Baltimore	185
1955	Sam Jones, Chicago	198	1955	Herb Score, Cleveland	245
1956	Sam Jones, Chicago	176	1956	Herb Score, Cleveland	263
1957	Jack Sanford, Philadelphia	188	1957	Early Wynn, Cleveland	184
1958	Sam Jones, St. Louis	225	1958	Early Wynn, Chicago	179
1959	Don Drysdale, Los Angeles	242	1959	Jim Bunning, Detroit	201
1960	Don Drysdale, Los Angeles	246	1960	Jim Bunning, Detroit	201
1961	Sandy Koufax, Los Angeles	269	1961	Camilo Pascual, Minnesota	221
1962	Don Drysdale, Los Angeles	232	1962	Camilo Pascual, Minnesota	206
1963	Sandy Koufax, Los Angeles	306	1963	Camilo Pascual, Minnesota	202
1964	Bob Veale, Pittsburgh	250	1964	Al Downing, New York	217
1965	Sandy Koufax, Los Angeles	382*	1965	Sam McDowell, Cleveland	325
1966	Sandy Koufax, Los Angeles	317	1966	Sam McDowell, Cleveland	225
1967	Jim Bunning, Philadelphia	253	1967	Jim Lonborg, Boston	246
1968	Bob Gibson, St. Louis	268	1968	Sam McDowell, Cleveland	283
1969	Ferguson Jenkins, Chicago	273	1969	Sam McDowell, Cleveland	279
1970	Tom Seaver, New York	283	1970	Sam McDowell, Cleveland	304
1971	Tom Seaver, New York	289	1971	Mickey Lolich, Detroit	308
1972	Steve Carlton, Philadelphia	310	1972	Nolan Ryan, California	329
1973	Tom Seaver, New York	251	1973	Nolan Ryan, California	383*
1974	Steve Carlton, Philadelphia	240	1974	Nolan Ryan, California	367
1975	Tom Seaver, New York	243	1975	Frank Tanana, California	269
1976	Tom Seaver, New York	235	1976	Nolan Ryan, California	327
1977	Phil Niekro, Atlanta	262	1977	Nolan Ryan, California	341
1978	J.R. Richard, Houston	303	1978	Nolan Ryan, California	260
1979	J.R. Richard, Houston	313	1979	Nolan Ryan, California	223
1980	Steve Carlton, Philadelphia	286	1980	Len Barker, Cleveland	187
1981	Fernando Valenzuela, Los Angeles	180	1981	Len Barker, Cleveland	127
1982	Steve Carlton, Philadelphia	286	1982	Floyd Bannister, Seattle	209
1983	Steve Carlton, Philadelphia	275	1983	Jack Morris, Detroit	232

	National League			American League	
Year	Pitcher, Team	SO	Year	Pitcher, Team	SO
1984	Dwight Gooden, New York	276	1984	Mark Langston, Seattle	204
1985	Dwight Gooden, New York	268	1985	Bert Blyleven, Cleveland-Minnesota	206
1986	Mike Scott, Houston	306	1986	Mark Langston, Seattle	245
1987	Nolan Ryan, Houston	270	1987	Mark Langston, Seattle	262
1988	Nolan Ryan, Houston	228	1988	Roger Clemens, Boston	291
1989	Jose DeLeon, St. Louis	201	1989	Nolan Ryan, Texas	301
1990	David Cone, New York	233	1990	Nolan Ryan, Texas	232
1991	David Cone, New York	241	1991	Roger Clemens, Boston	241
1992	John Smoltz, Atlanta	215	1992	Randy Johnson, Seattle	241
1993	Jose Rijo, Cincinnati	227	1993	Randy Johnson, Seattle	308
1994	Andy Benes, San Diego	189	1994	Randy Johnson, Seattle	204
1995	Hideo Nomo, Los Angeles	236	1995	Randy Johnson, Seattle	294
1996	John Smoltz, Atlanta	276	1996	Roger Clemens, Boston	257
1997	Curt Schilling, Philadelphia	319	1997	Roger Clemens, Toronto	292
1998	Curt Schilling, Philadelphia	300	1998	Roger Clemens, Toronto	271
1999	Randy Johnson, Arizona	364	1999	Pedro Martinez, Boston	313
2000	Randy Johnson, Arizona	347	2000	Pedro Martinez, Boston	284
2001	Randy Johnson, Arizona	372	2001	Hideo Nomo, Boston	220
2002	Randy Johnson, Arizona	334	2002	Pedro Martinez, Boston	239
2003	Kerry Wood, Chicago	266	2003	Esteban Loaiza, Chicago	207
2004	Randy Johnson, Arizona	290	2004	Johan Santana, Minnesota	265
2005	Jake Peavy, San Diego	216	2005	Johan Santana, Minnesota	238
2006	Aaron Harang, Cincinnati	216	2006	Johan Santana, Minnesota	245
2007	Jake Peavy, San Diego	240	2007	Scott Kazmir, Tampa Bay	239

Victory Leaders by Season

Note: Asterisk (*) indicates the all-time single-season record for each league in the "modern" era beginning in 1901.

	National League			American League	
Year	Pitcher, Team	Wins	Year	Pitcher, Team	Wins
1901	Bill Donavan, Brooklyn	25	1901	Cy Young, Boston	33
1902	Jack Chesbro, Pittsburgh	28	1902	Cy Young, Boston	32
1903	Joe McGinnity, New York	31	1903	Cy Young, Boston	28
1904	Joe McGinnity, New York	35	1904	Jack Chesbro, New York	41*
1905	Christy Mathewson, New York	31	1905	Rube Waddell, Philadelphia	27
1906	Joe McGinnity, New York	27	1906	Al Orth, New York	27
1907	Christy Mathewson, New York	24	1907	Doc White, Chicago	27
1908	Christy Mathewson, New York	37*	1908	Ed Walsh, Chicago	40
1909	Mordecai Brown, Chicago	27	1909	George Mullin, Detroit	29
1910	Christy Mathewson, New York	27	1910	Jack Coombs, Philadelphia	31
1911	Grover Alexander, Chicago	28	1911	Jack Coombs, Philadelphia	28
1912	Rube Marquard, New York	26	1912	Joe Wood, Boston	34
1913	Tom Seaton, Philadelphia	27	1913	Walter Johnson, Washington	36
1914	Grover Alexander, Philadelphia	27	1914	Walter Johnson, Washington	28
1915	Grover Alexander, Philadelphia	31	1915	Walter Johnson, Washington	27
1916	Grover Alexander, Philadelphia	33	1916	Walter Johnson, Washington	25
1917	Grover Alexander, Philadelphia	30	1917	Eddie Cicotte, Chicago	28
1918	Hippo Vaughn, Chicago	22	1918	Walter Johnson, Washington	23
1919	Jesse Barnes, New York	25	1919	Eddie Cicotte, Chicago	29
1920	Grover Alexander, Philadelphia	27	1920	Jim Bagby, Cleveland	31
1921	Burleigh Grimes, Brooklyn	22	1921	Urban Shocker, St. Louis	27
1922	Eppa Rixey, Cincinnati	25	1922	Eddie Rommel, Philadelphia	27
1923	Dolf Luque, Cincinnati	27	1923	George Uhle, Cleveland	26
1924	Dazzy Vance, Brooklyn	28	1924	Walter Johnson, Washington	23
1925	Dazzy Vance, Brooklyn	22	1925	Eddie Rommel, Philadelphia	21
1926	Flint Rhem, St. Louis	20	1926	George Uhle, Cleveland	27
1927	Charlie Root, Chicago	26	1927	Ted Lyons, Chicago	22
1928	Burleigh Grimes, Pittsburgh	25	1928	George Pipgras, New York	24
1929	Pat Malone, Chicago	22	1929	George Earnshaw, Philadelphia	24
1930	Pat Malone, Chicago	20	1930	Lefty Grove, Philadelphia	28
1931	Heine Meine, Pittsburgh	19	1931	Lefty Grove, Philadelphia	31
1932	Lon Warneke, Chicago	22	1932	Alvin Crowder, Washington	26
1933	Carl Hubbell, New York	23	1933	Lefty Grove, Philadelphia	24
1934	Dizzy Dean, St. Louis	30	1934	Lefty Gomez, New York	26
1935	Dizzy Dean, St. Louis	28	1935	Wes Ferrell, Boston	25
1936	Carl Hubbell, New York	26	1936	Tommy Bridges, Detroit	23
1937	Carl Hubbell, New York	22	1937	Lefty Gomez, New York	21
1938	Bill Lee, Chicago	22	1938	Red Ruffing, New York	21
1939	Bucky Walters, Cincinnati	27	1939	Bob Feller, Cleveland	24
1940	Bucky Walters, Cincinnati	22	1940	Bob Feller, Cleveland	27
1941	Whit Wyatt, Brooklyn	22	1941	Bob Feller, Cleveland	25
1942	Mort Cooper, St. Louis	22	1942	Tex Hughson, Boston	22
1943	Rip Sewell, Pittsburgh	21	1943	Dizzy Trout, Detroit	20
1944	Bucky Walters, Cincinnati	23	1944	Hal Newhouser, Detroit	29
1945	Red Barrett, Boston-St. Louis	23	1945	Hal Newhouser, Detroit	25
1946	Howie Pollet, St. Louis	21	1946	Hal Newhouser, Detroit	26
1947	Ewell Blackwell, Cincinnati	22	1947	Bob Feller, Cleveland	20
1948	Johnny Sain, Boston	24	1948	Hal Newhouser, Detroit	21
1949	Warren Spahn, Boston	21	1949	Mel Parnell, Boston	25
1950	Warren Spahn, Boston	21	1950	Bob Lemon, Cleveland	23
1951	Sal Maglie, New York	23	1951	Bob Feller, Cleveland	22
1952	Robin Roberts, Philadelphia	28	1952	Bobby Shantz, Philadelphia	24
1953	Warren Spahn, Milwaukee	23	1953	Bob Porterfield, Washington	22
1954	Robin Roberts, Philadelphia	23	1954	Early Wynn, Cleveland	23
1955	Robin Roberts, Philadelphia	23	1955	Frank Sullivan, Boston	18
1956	Don Newcombe, Brooklyn	27	1956	Frank Lary, Detroit	21
1957	Warren Spahn, Milwaukee	21	1957	Billy Pierce, Chicago	20
1958	Warren Spahn, Milwaukee	22	1958	Bob Turley, New York	21
1959	Warren Spahn, Milwaukee	21	1959	Early Wynn, Chicago	22

	National League			American League	
Year	Pitcher, Team	Wins	Year	Pitcher, Team	Wins
1960	Warren Spahn, Milwaukee	21	1960	Jim Perry, Cleveland	18
1961	Warren Spahn, Milwaukee	21	1961	Whitey Ford, New York	25
1962	Don Drysdale, Los Angeles	25	1962	Ralph Terry, New York	23
1963	Juan Marichal, San Francisco	25	1963	Whitey Ford, New York	24
1964	Larry Jackson, Chicago	24	1964	Gary Peters, Chicago	20
1965	Sandy Koufax, Los Angeles	26	1965	Mudcat (Jim) Grant, Minnesota	21
1966	Sandy Koufax, Los Angeles	27	1966	Jim Kaat, Minnesota	25
1967	Mike McCormick, San Francisco	22	1967	Earl Wilson, Detroit	22
1968	Juan Marichal, San Francisco	26	1968	Denny McLain, Detroit	31
1969	Tom Seaver, New York	25	1969	Denny McLain, Detroit	24
1970	Gaylord Perry, San Francisco	23	1970	Jim Perry, Minnesota	24
1971	Fergie Jenkins, Chicago	24	1971	Mickey Lolich, Detroit	25
1972	Steve Carlton, Philadelphia	27	1972	Wilbur Wood, Chicago	24
1973	Ron Bryant, San Francisco	24	1973	Wilbur Wood, Chicago	24
1974	Phil Niekro, Atlanta	20	1974	Fergie Jenkins, Texas	25
1975	Tom Seaver, New York	22	1975	Jim Palmer, Baltimore	23
1976	Randy Jones, San Diego	22	1976	Jim Palmer, Baltimore	22
1977	Steve Carlton, Philadelphia	23	1977	Jim Palmer, Baltimore	20
1978	Gaylord Perry, San Diego	21	1978	Ron Guidry, New York	25
1979	Phil Niekro, Atlanta	21	1979	Mike Flanagan, Baltimore	23
1980	Steve Carlton, Philadelphia	24	1980	Steve Stone, Baltimore	25
1981	Tom Seaver, Cincinnati	14	1981	Pete Vuckovich, Milwaukee	14
1982	Steve Carlton, Philadelphia	23	1982	La Marr Hoyt, Chicago	19
1983	John Denny, Philadelphia	19	1983	La Marr Hoyt, Chicago	24
1984	Joaquin Andujar, St. Louis	20	1984	Mike Boddicker, Baltimore	20
1985	Dwight Gooden, New York	24	1985	Ron Guidry, New York	22
1986	Fernando Valenzuela, Los Angeles	21	1986	Roger Clemens, Boston	24
1987	Rick Sutcliffe, Chicago	18	1987	Dave Stewart, Oakland; Roger Clemens, Boston	20
1988	Danny Jackson, Cincinnati	23	1988	Frank Viola, Minnesota	24
1989	Mike Scott, Houston	20	1989	Bret Saberhagen, Kansas City	23
1990	Doug Drabek, Pittsburgh	22	1990	Bob Welch, Oakland	27
1991	John Smiley, Pittsburgh	20	1991	Bill Gullickson, Detroit	20
1992	Greg Maddux, Chicago	20	1992	Jack Morris, Toronto	21
1993	Tom Glavine, Atlanta	22	1993	Jack McDowell, Chicago	22
1994	Greg Maddux, Atlanta	16	1994	Jimmy Key, New York	17
1995	Greg Maddux, Atlanta	19	1995	Mike Mussina, Baltimore	19
1996	John Smoltz, Atlanta	24	1996	Andy Pettitte, New York	21
1997	Denny Neagle, Atlanta	20	1997	Roger Clemens, Toronto	21
1998	Tom Glavine, Atlanta	20	1998	Rick Helling, Texas; Roger Clemens, Toronto	20
1999	Mike Hampton, Houston	22	1999	Pedro Martinez, Boston	23
2000	Tom Glavine, Atlanta	21	2000	David Wells, Toronto	20
2001	Matt Morris, St. Louis; Curt Schilling, Arizona	22 22	2001	Mark Mulder, Oakland	21
2002	Randy Johnson, Arizona	24	2002	Barry Zito, Oakland	23
2003	Russ Ortiz, Atlanta	21	2003	Roy Halladay, Toronto	22
2004	Roy Oswalt, Houston	20	2004	Curt Schilling, Boston	21
2005	Dontrelle Willis, Florida	22	2005	Bartolo Colon, Los Angeles	21
2006	Aaron Harang, Cincinnati; Derek Lowe, Los Angeles; Brad Penny, Los Angeles; John Smoltz, Atlanta; Brandon Webb, Arizona; Carlos Zambrano, Chicago	16	2006	Johan Santana, Minnesota; Chien-Ming Wang, New York	19 19
2007	Jake Peavy, San Diego	19	2007	Josh Beckett, Boston	20

Cy Young Award Winners

Year	Player, Team	Year	Player, Team	Year	Player, Team
1956	Don Newcombe, Dodgers	1977	(NL) Steve Carlton, Phillies	1993	(NL) Greg Maddux, Braves
1957	Warren Spahn, Braves		(AL) Sparky Lyle, Yankees		(AL) Jack McDowell, White Sox
1958	Bob Turley, Yankees	1978	(NL) Gaylord Perry, Padres	1994	(NL) Greg Maddux, Braves
1959	Early Wynn, White Sox		(AL) Ron Guidry, Yankees		(AL) David Cone, Royals
1960	Vernon Law, Pirates	1979	(NL) Bruce Sutter, Cubs	1995	(NL) Greg Maddux, Braves
1961	Whitey Ford, Yankees		(AL) Mike Flanagan, Orioles		(AL) Randy Johnson, Mariners
1962	Don Drysdale, Dodgers	1980	(NL) Steve Carlton, Phillies	1996	(NL) John Smoltz, Braves
1963	Sandy Koufax, Dodgers		(AL) Steve Stone, Orioles		(AL) Pat Hentgen, Blue Jays
1964	Dean Chance, Angels	1981	(NL) Fernando Valenzuela, Dodgers	1997	(NL) Pedro Martinez, Expos
1965	Sandy Koufax, Dodgers		(AL) Rollie Fingers, Brewers		(AL) Roger Clemens, Blue Jays
1966	Sandy Koufax, Dodgers	1982	(NL) Steve Carlton, Phillies	1998	(NL) Tom Glavine, Braves
1967	(NL) Mike McCormick, Giants		(AL) Pete Vuckovich, Brewers		(AL) Roger Clemens, Blue Jays
	(AL) Jim Lonborg, Red Sox	1983	(NL) John Denny, Phillies	1999	(NL) Randy Johnson, Diamondbacks
1968	(NL) Bob Gibson, Cardinals		(AL) LaMarr Hoyt, White Sox		(AL) Pedro Martinez, Red Sox
	(AL) Dennis McLain, Tigers	1984	(NL) Rick Sutcliffe, Cubs	2000	(NL) Randy Johnson, Diamondbacks
1969	(NL) Tom Seaver, Mets		(AL) Willie Hernandez, Tigers		(AL) Pedro Martinez, Red Sox
	(AL) (tie) Dennis McLain, Tigers Mike Cuellar, Orioles	1985	(NL) Dwight Gooden, Mets (AL) Bret Saberhagen, Royals	2001	(NL) Randy Johnson, Diamondbacks
1970	(NL) Bob Gibson, Cardinals	1986	(NL) Mike Scott, Astros		(AL) Roger Clemens, Yankees
	(AL) Jim Perry, Twins		(AL) Roger Clemens, Red Sox	2002	(NL) Randy Johnson, Diamondbacks
1971	(NL) Ferguson Jenkins, Cubs	1987	(NL) Steve Bedrosian, Phillies		(AL) Barry Zito, Athletics
	(AL) Vida Blue, Athletics		(AL) Roger Clemens, Red Sox	2003	(NL) Eric Gagne, Dodgers
1972	(NL) Steve Carlton, Phillies	1988	(NL) Orel Hershiser, Dodgers		(AL) Roy Halladay, Blue Jays
	(AL) Gaylord Perry, Indians		(AL) Frank Viola, Twins	2004	(NL) Roger Clemens, Astros
1973	(NL) Tom Seaver, Mets	1989	(NL) Mark Davis, Padres		(AL) Johan Santana, Twins
	(AL) Jim Palmer, Orioles		(AL) Bret Saberhagen, Royals	2005	(NL) Chris Carpenter, Cardinals
1974	(NL) Mike Marshall, Dodgers	1990	(NL) Doug Drabek, Pirates		(AL) Bartolo Colon, Angels
	(AL) Jim (Catfish) Hunter, Athletics		(AL) Bob Welch, Athletics	2006	(NL) Brandon Webb, Arizona
1975	(NL) Tom Seaver, Mets	1991	(NL) Tom Glavine, Braves		(AL) Johan Santana, Minnesota
	(AL) Jim Palmer, Orioles		(AL) Roger Clemens, Red Sox		
1976	(NL) Randy Jones, Padres	1992	(NL) Greg Maddux, Cubs		
	(AL) Jim Palmer, Orioles		(AL) Dennis Eckersley, Athletics		

Most Valuable Players

(As selected by the Baseball Writers' Assoc. of America. Prior to 1931, MVP honors were named by various sources.)

National League

Year	Player, team	Year	Player, team	Year	Player, team
1931	Frank Frisch, St. Louis	1957	Hank Aaron, Milwaukee	1982	Dale Murphy, Atlanta
1932	Chuck Klein, Philadelphia	1958	Ernie Banks, Chicago	1983	Dale Murphy, Atlanta
1933	Carl Hubbell, New York	1959	Ernie Banks, Chicago	1984	Ryne Sandberg, Chicago
1934	Dizzy Dean, St. Louis	1960	Dick Groat, Pittsburgh	1985	Willie McGee, St. Louis
1935	Gabby Hartnett, Chicago	1961	Frank Robinson, Cincinnati	1986	Mike Schmidt, Philadelphia
1936	Carl Hubbell, N.Y.	1962	Maury Wills, L.A.	1987	Andre Dawson, Chicago
1937	Joe Medwick, St. Louis	1963	Sandy Koufax, L.A.	1988	Kirk Gibson, L.A.
1938	Ernie Lombardi, Cincinnati	1964	Ken Boyer, St. Louis	1989	Kevin Mitchell, San Francisco
1939	Bucky Walters, Cincinnati	1965	Willie Mays, San Francisco	1990	Barry Bonds, Pittsburgh
1940	Frank McCormick, Cincinnati	1966	Roberto Clemente, Pittsburgh	1991	Terry Pendleton, Atlanta
1941	Dolph Camilli, Brooklyn	1967	Orlando Cepeda, St. Louis	1992	Barry Bonds, Pittsburgh
1942	Mort Cooper, St. Louis	1968	Bob Gibson, St. Louis	1993	Barry Bonds, San Francisco
1943	Stan Musial, St. Louis	1969	Willie McCovey, San Francisco	1994	Jeff Bagwell, Houston
1944	Martin Marion, St. Louis	1970	Johnny Bench, Cincinnati	1995	Barry Larkin, Cincinnati
1945	Phil Cavarretta, Chicago	1971	Joe Torre, St. Louis	1996	Ken Caminiti, San Diego
1946	Stan Musial, St. Louis	1972	Johnny Bench, Cincinnati	1997	Larry Walker, Colorado
1947	Bob Elliott, Boston	1973	Pete Rose, Cincinnati	1998	Sammy Sosa, Chicago
1948	Stan Musial, St. Louis	1974	Steve Garvey, L.A.	1999	Chipper Jones, Atlanta
1949	Jackie Robinson, Brooklyn	1975	Joe Morgan, Cincinnati	2000	Jeff Kent, San Francisco
1950	Jim Konstanty, Philadelphia	1976	Joe Morgan, Cincinnati	2001	Barry Bonds, San Francisco
1951	Roy Campanella, Brooklyn	1977	George Foster, Cincinnati	2002	Barry Bonds, San Francisco
1952	Hank Sauer, Chicago	1978	(tie) Dave Parker, Pittsburgh	2003	Barry Bonds, San Francisco
1953	Roy Campanella, Brooklyn		Keith Hernandez, St. Louis	2004	Barry Bonds, San Francisco
1954	Willie Mays, N.Y.	1980	Mike Schmidt, Philadelphia	2005	Albert Pujols, St. Louis
1955	Roy Campanella, Brooklyn	1981	Mike Schmidt, Philadelphia	2006	Ryan Howard, Philadelphia
1956	Don Newcombe, Brooklyn				

American League

Year	Player, team	Year	Player, team	Year	Player, team
1931	Lefty Grove, Philadelphia	1957	Mickey Mantle, N.Y.	1982	Robin Yount, Milwaukee
1932	Jimmie Foxx, Philadelphia	1958	Jackie Jensen, Boston	1983	Cal Ripken Jr., Baltimore
1933	Jimmie Foxx, Philadelphia	1959	Nellie Fox, Chicago	1984	Willie Hernandez, Detroit
1934	Mickey Cochrane, Detroit	1960	Roger Maris, N.Y.	1985	Don Mattingly, N.Y.
1935	Hank Greenberg, Detroit	1961	Roger Maris, N.Y.	1986	Roger Clemens, Boston
1936	Lou Gehrig, N.Y.	1962	Mickey Mantle, N.Y.	1987	George Bell, Toronto
1937	Charley Gehringer, Detroit	1963	Elston Howard, N.Y.	1988	Jose Canseco, Oakland
1938	Jimmie Foxx, Boston	1964	Brooks Robinson, Baltimore	1989	Robin Yount, Milwaukee
1939	Joe DiMaggio, N.Y.	1965	Zoilo Versalles, Minnesota	1990	Rickey Henderson, Oakland
1940	Hank Greenberg, Detroit	1966	Frank Robinson, Baltimore	1991	Cal Ripken Jr., Baltimore
1941	Joe DiMaggio, N.Y.	1967	Carl Yastrzemski, Boston	1992	Dennis Eckersley, Oakland
1942	Joe Gordon, N.Y.	1968	Denny McLain, Detroit	1993	Frank Thomas, Chicago
1943	Spurgeon Chandler, N.Y.	1969	Harmon Killebrew, Minnesota	1994	Frank Thomas, Chicago
1944	Hal Newhouser, Detroit	1970	John (Boog) Powell, Baltimore	1995	Mo Vaughn, Boston
1945	Hal Newhouser, Detroit	1971	Vida Blue, Oakland	1996	Juan Gonzalez, Texas
1946	Ted Williams, Boston	1972	Dick Allen, Chicago	1997	Ken Griffey Jr., Seattle
1947	Joe DiMaggio, N.Y.	1973	Reggie Jackson, Oakland	1998	Juan Gonzalez, Texas
1948	Lou Boudreau, Cleveland	1974	Jeff Burroughs, Texas	1999	Ivan Rodriguez, Texas
1949	Ted Williams, Boston	1975	Fred Lynn, Boston	2000	Jason Giambi, Oakland
1950	Phil Rizzuto, N.Y.	1976	Thurman Munson, N.Y.	2001	Ichiro Suzuki, Seattle
1951	Yogi Berra, N.Y.	1977	Rod Carew, Minnesota	2002	Miguel Tejada, Oakland
1952	Bobby Shantz, Philadelphia	1978	Jim Rice, Boston	2003	Alex Rodriguez, Texas
1953	Al Rosen, Cleveland	1979	Don Baylor, California	2004	Vladimir Guerrero, L.A.
1954	Yogi Berra, N.Y.	1980	George Brett, Kansas City	2005	Alex Rodriguez, New York
1955	Yogi Berra, N.Y.	1981	Rollie Fingers, Milwaukee	2006	Justin Morneau, Minnesota
1956	Mickey Mantle, N.Y.				

Rookies of the Year

(As selected by the Baseball Writers' Assoc. of America)

1947—Combined selection—Jackie Robinson, Brooklyn, 1B; 1948—Combined selection—Alvin Dark, Boston, NL, SS

National League

Year	Player, team	Year	Player, team	Year	Player, team
1949	Don Newcombe, Brooklyn, P	1969	Ted Sizemore, L.A., 2B	1988	Chris Sabo, Cincinnati, 3B
1950	Sam Jethroe, Boston, OF	1970	Carl Morton, Montreal, P	1989	Jerome Walton, Chicago, OF
1951	Willie Mays, N.Y., OF	1971	Earl Williams, Atlanta, C	1990	Dave Justice, Atlanta, 1B
1952	Joe Black, Brooklyn, P	1972	Jon Matlack, N.Y., P	1991	Jeff Bagwell, Houston, 1B
1953	Jim Gilliam, Brooklyn, 2B	1973	Gary Matthews, S.F., OF	1992	Eric Karros, L.A., 1B
1954	Wally Moon, St. Louis, OF	1974	Bake McBride, St. Louis, OF	1993	Mike Piazza, L.A., C
1955	Bill Virdon, St. Louis, OF	1975	John Montefusco, S.F., P	1994	Raul Mondesi, L.A., OF
1956	Frank Robinson, Cincinnati, OF	1976	Butch Metzger, San Diego, P	1995	Hideo Nomo, L.A., P
1957	Jack Sanford, Philadelphia, P		(tie) Pat Zachry, Cincinnati, P	1996	Todd Hollandsworth, L.A., OF
1958	Orlando Cepeda, S.F., 1B	1977	Andre Dawson, Montreal, OF	1997	Scott Rolen, Philadelphia, 3B
1959	Willie McCovey, S.F., 1B	1978	Bob Horner, Atlanta, 3B	1998	Kerry Wood, Chicago, P
1960	Frank Howard, L.A., OF	1979	Rick Sutcliffe, L.A., P	1999	Scott Williamson, Cincinnati, P
1961	Billy Williams, Chicago, OF	1980	Steve Howe, L.A., P	2000	Rafael Furcal, Atlanta, SS
1962	Ken Hubbs, Chicago, 2B	1981	Fernando Valenzuela, L.A., P	2001	Albert Pujols, St. Louis, OF
1963	Pete Rose, Cincinnati, 2B	1982	Steve Sax, L.A., 2B	2002	Jason Jennings, Colorado, P
1964	Richie Allen, Philadelphia, 3B	1983	Darryl Strawberry, N.Y., OF	2003	Dontrelle Willis, Florida, P
1965	Jim Lefebvre, L.A., 2B	1984	Dwight Gooden, N.Y., P	2004	Jason Bay, Pittsburgh, OF
1966	Tommy Helms, Cincinnati, 2B	1985	Vince Coleman, St. Louis, OF	2005	Ryan Howard, Philadelphia, 1B
1967	Tom Seaver, N.Y., P	1986	Todd Worrell, St. Louis, P	2006	Hanley Ramirez, Florida, SS
1968	Johnny Bench, Cincinnati, C	1987	Benito Santiago, San Diego, C		

American League

Year	Player, team	Year	Player, team	Year	Player, team
1949	Roy Sievers, St. Louis, OF	1969	Lou Piniella, Kansas City, OF	1988	Walt Weiss, Oakland, SS
1950	Walt Dropo, Boston, 1B	1970	Thurman Munson, N.Y., C	1989	Gregg Olson, Baltimore, P
1951	Gil McDougald, N.Y., 3B	1971	Chris Chambliss, Cleveland, 1B	1990	Sandy Alomar, Jr., Cleveland, C
1952	Harry Byrd, Philadelphia, P	1972	Carlton Fisk, Boston, C	1991	Chuck Knoblauch, Minnesota, 2B
1953	Harvey Kuenn, Detroit, SS	1973	Al Bumbry, Baltimore, OF	1992	Pat Listach, Milwaukee, SS
1954	Bob Grim, N.Y., P	1974	Mike Hargrove, Texas, 1B	1993	Tim Salmon, California, OF
1955	Herb Score, Cleveland, P	1975	Fred Lynn, Boston, OF	1994	Bob Hamelin, Kansas City, DH
1956	Luis Aparicio, Chicago, SS	1976	Mark Fidrych, Detroit, P	1995	Marty Cordova, Minnesota, OF
1957	Tony Kubek, N.Y., IF-OF	1977	Eddie Murray, Baltimore, DH	1996	Derek Jeter, N.Y., SS
1958	Albie Pearson, Washington, OF	1978	Lou Whitaker, Detroit, 2B	1997	Nomar Garciaparra, Boston, SS
1959	Bob Allison, Washington, OF	1979	John Castino, Minnesota, 3B	1998	Ben Grieve, Oakland, OF
1960	Ron Hansen, Baltimore, SS	(tie)	Alfredo Griffin, Toronto, SS	1999	Carlos Beltran, Kansas City, OF
1961	Don Schwall, Boston, P	1980	Joe Charboneau, Cleveland, OF	2000	Kazuhiro Sasaki, Seattle, P
1962	Tom Tresh, N.Y.,IF-OF	1981	Dave Righetti, N.Y., P	2001	Ichiro Suzuki, Seattle, OF
1963	Gary Peters, Chicago, P	1982	Cal Ripken, Jr., Baltimore, SS	2002	Eric Hinske, Toronto, 3B
1964	Tony Oliva, Minnesota, OF	1983	Ron Kittle, Chicago, OF	2003	Angel Berroa, Kansas City, SS
1965	Curt Blefary, Baltimore, OF	1984	Alvin Davis, Seattle, 1B	2004	Bobby Crosby, Oakland, SS
1966	Tommie Agee, Chicago, OF	1985	Ozzie Guillen, Chicago, SS	2005	Huston Street, Oakland, P
1967	Rod Carew, Minnesota, 2B	1986	Jose Canseco, Oakland, OF	2006	Justin Verlander, Detroit, P
1968	Stan Bahnsen, N.Y., P	1987	Mark McGwire, Oakland, 1B		

Rawlings Gold Glove Awards: 2006 and All-Time Leaders

American League

Kenny Rogers, Detroit, P
Ivan Rodriguez, Detroit, C
Mark Teixeira, Texas, 1B
Mark Grudzielanek, Kansas City, 2B
Eric Chavez, Oakland, 3B
Derek Jeter, New York, SS
Torii Hunter, Minnesota, OF
Ichiro Suzuki, Seattle, OF
Vernon Wells, Toronto, OF

National League

Greg Maddux, Los Angeles, P
Brad Ausmus, Houston, C
Albert Pujols, St. Louis, 1B
Orlando Hudson, Arizona, 2B
Scott Rolen, St. Louis, 3B
Omar Vizquel, San Francisco, SS
Carlos Beltran, New York, OF
Mike Cameron, San Diego, OF
Andruw Jones, Atlanta, OF

The following are the players at each position who have won the most Gold Gloves since the award was instituted in 1957.

Position	Player		Player	
Pitcher:	Jim Kaat	16		
	Greg Maddux	16		
Catcher:	Ivan Rodriguez	12		
	Johnny Bench	10		
First base:	Keith Hernandez	11		
	Don Mattingly	9		
Second base:	Roberto Alomar	10		
	Ryne Sandberg	9		
	Bill Mazeroski	8		
	Frank White	8		
Third base:	Brooks Robinson	16		
	Mike Schmidt	10		
Shortstop:	Ozzie Smith	13		
	Omar Vizquel	11		
Outfield:	Roberto Clemente	12		
	Willie Mays	12		
	Al Kaline	10		
	Ken Griffey Jr.	10		

Manager of the Year

Year			Year			Year		
1983	(NL)	Tommy Lasorda, L.A.	1991	(NL)	Bobby Cox, Atlanta	1999	(NL)	Jack McKeon, Cincinnati
	(AL)	Tony La Russa, Chicago		(AL)	Tom Kelly, Minnesota		(AL)	Jimy Williams, Boston
1984	(NL)	Jim Frey, Chicago	1992	(NL)	Jim Leyland, Pittsburgh	2000	(NL)	Dusty Baker, San Francisco
	(AL)	Sparky Anderson, Detroit		(AL)	Tony La Russa, Oakland		(AL)	Jerry Manuel, Chicago
1985	(NL)	Whitey Herzog, St. Louis	1993	(NL)	Dusty Baker, San Francisco	2001	(NL)	Larry Bowa, Philadelphia
	(AL)	Bobby Cox, Toronto		(AL)	Gene Lamont, Chicago		(AL)	Lou Piniella, Seattle
1986	(NL)	Hal Lanier, Houston	1994	(NL)	Felipe Alou, Montreal	2002	(NL)	Tony La Russa, St. Louis
	(AL)	John McNamara, Boston		(AL)	Buck Showalter, N.Y.		(AL)	Mike Scioscia, Anaheim
1987	(NL)	Buck Rodgers, Montreal	1995	(NL)	Don Baylor, Colorado	2003	(NL)	Jack McKeon, Florida
	(AL)	Sparky Anderson, Detroit		(AL)	Lou Piniella, Seattle		(AL)	Tony Pena, Kansas City
1988	(NL)	Tommy Lasorda, L.A.	1996	(NL)	Bruce Bochy, San Diego	2004	(NL)	Bobby Cox, Atlanta
	(AL)	Tony La Russa, Oakland		(AL)	(tie) Joe Torre, N.Y.,		(AL)	Buck Showalter, Texas
1989	(NL)	Don Zimmer, Chicago			Johnny Oates, Texas	2005	(NL)	Bobby Cox, Atlanta
	(AL)	Frank Robinson, Baltimore	1997	(NL)	Dusty Baker, San Francisco		(AL)	Ozzie Guillen, Chicago
1990	(NL)	Jim Leyland, Pittsburgh		(AL)	Davey Johnson, Baltimore	2006	(NL)	Joe Girardi, Florida
	(AL)	Jeff Torborg, Chicago	1998	(NL)	Larry Dierker, Houston		(AL)	Jim Leyland, Detroit
				(AL)	Joe Torre, N.Y.			

Major League Pennant Winners, 1901–1975

	National League						American League				
Year	Winner	Won	Lost	Pct	Manager	Year	Winner	Won	Lost	Pct	Manager
1901	Pittsburgh	90	49	.647	Clarke	1901	Chicago	83	53	.610	Griffith
1902	Pittsburgh	103	36	.741	Clarke	1902	Philadelphia	83	53	.610	Mack
1903	Pittsburgh	91	49	.650	Clarke	1903	Boston	91	47	.659	Collins
1904	New York	106	47	.693	McGraw	1904	Boston	95	59	.617	Collins
1905	New York	105	48	.686	McGraw	1905	Philadelphia	92	56	.622	Mack
1906	Chicago	116	36	.763	Chance	1906	Chicago	93	58	.616	Jones
1907	Chicago	107	45	.704	Chance	1907	Detroit	92	58	.613	Jennings
1908	Chicago	99	55	.643	Chance	1908	Detroit	90	63	.588	Jennings
1909	Pittsburgh	110	42	.724	Clarke	1909	Detroit	98	54	.645	Jennings
1910	Chicago	104	50	.675	Chance	1910	Philadelphia	102	48	.680	Mack
1911	New York	99	54	.647	McGraw	1911	Philadelphia	101	50	.669	Mack
1912	New York	103	48	.682	McGraw	1912	Boston	105	47	.691	Stahl
1913	New York	101	51	.664	McGraw	1913	Philadelphia	96	57	.627	Mack
1914	Boston	94	59	.614	Stallings	1914	Philadelphia	99	53	.651	Mack
1915	Philadelphia	90	62	.592	Moran	1915	Boston	101	50	.669	Carrigan
1916	Brooklyn	94	60	.610	Robinson	1916	Boston	91	63	.591	Carrigan
1917	New York	98	56	.636	McGraw	1917	Chicago	100	54	.649	Rowland
1918	Chicago	84	45	.651	Mitchell	1918	Boston	75	51	.595	Barrow
1919	Cincinnati	96	44	.686	Moran	1919	Chicago	88	52	.629	Gleason
1920	Brooklyn	93	60	.604	Robinson	1920	Cleveland	98	56	.636	Speaker
1921	New York	94	56	.614	McGraw	1921	New York	98	55	.641	Huggins
1922	New York	93	61	.604	McGraw	1922	New York	94	60	.610	Huggins
1923	New York	95	58	.621	McGraw	1923	New York	98	54	.645	Huggins
1924	New York	93	60	.608	McGraw	1924	Washington	92	62	.597	Harris
1925	Pittsburgh	95	58	.621	McKechnie	1925	Washington	96	55	.636	Harris
1926	St. Louis	89	65	.578	Hornsby	1926	New York	91	63	.591	Huggins
1927	Pittsburgh	94	60	.610	Bush	1927	New York	110	44	.714	Huggins
1928	St. Louis	95	59	.617	McKechnie	1928	New York	101	53	.656	Huggins
1929	Chicago	98	54	.645	McCarthy	1929	Philadelphia	104	46	.693	Mack
1930	St. Louis	92	62	.597	Street	1930	Philadelphia	102	52	.662	Mack
1931	St. Louis	101	53	.656	Street	1931	Philadelphia	107	45	.704	Mack
1932	Chicago	90	64	.584	Grimm	1932	New York	107	47	.695	McCarthy

	National League						American League				
Year	Winner	Won	Lost	Pct	Manager	Year	Winner	Won	Lost	Pct	Manager
1933	New York	91	61	.599	Terry	1933	Washington	99	53	.651	Cronin
1934	St. Louis	95	58	.621	Frisch	1934	Detroit	101	53	.656	Cochrane
1935	Chicago	100	54	.649	Grimm	1935	Detroit	93	58	.616	Cochrane
1936	New York	91	62	.597	Terry	1936	New York	102	51	.667	McCarthy
1937	New York	95	57	.625	Terry	1937	New York	102	52	.662	McCarthy
1938	Chicago	89	63	.586	Hartnett	1938	New York	99	53	.651	McCarthy
1939	Cincinnati	97	57	.630	McKechnie	1939	New York	106	45	.702	McCarthy
1940	Cincinnati	100	53	.654	McKechnie	1940	Detroit	90	64	.584	Baker
1941	Brooklyn	100	54	.649	Durocher	1941	New York	101	53	.656	McCarthy
1942	St. Louis	106	48	.688	Southworth	1942	New York	103	51	.669	McCarthy
1943	St. Louis	105	49	.682	Southworth	1943	New York	98	56	.636	McCarthy
1944	St. Louis	105	49	.682	Southworth	1944	St. Louis	89	65	.578	Sewell
1945	Chicago	98	56	.636	Grimm	1945	Detroit	88	65	.575	O'Neill
1946	St. Louis	98	58	.628	Dyer	1946	Boston	104	50	.675	Cronin
1947	Brooklyn	94	60	.610	Shotton	1947	New York	97	57	.630	Harris
1948	Boston	91	62	.595	Southworth	1948	Cleveland	97	58	.626	Boudreau
1949	Brooklyn	97	57	.630	Shotton	1949	New York	97	57	.630	Stengel
1950	Philadelphia	91	63	.591	Sawyer	1950	New York	98	56	.636	Stengel
1951	New York	98	59	.624	Durocher	1951	New York	98	56	.636	Stengel
1952	Brooklyn	96	57	.627	Dressen	1952	New York	95	59	.617	Stengel
1953	Brooklyn	105	49	.682	Dressen	1953	New York	99	52	.656	Stengel
1954	New York	97	57	.630	Durocher	1954	Cleveland	111	43	.721	Lopez
1955	Brooklyn	98	55	.641	Alston	1955	New York	96	58	.623	Stengel
1956	Brooklyn	93	61	.604	Alston	1956	New York	97	57	.630	Stengel
1957	Milwaukee	95	59	.617	Haney	1957	New York	98	56	.636	Stengel
1958	Milwaukee	92	62	.597	Haney	1958	New York	92	62	.597	Stengel
1959	Los Angeles	88	68	.564	Alston	1959	Chicago	94	60	.610	Lopez
1960	Pittsburgh	95	59	.617	Murtaugh	1960	New York	97	57	.630	Stengel
1961	Cincinnati	93	61	.604	Hutchinson	1961	New York	109	53	.673	Houk
1962	San Francisco	103	62	.624	Dark	1962	New York	96	66	.593	Houk
1963	Los Angeles	99	63	.611	Alston	1963	New York	104	57	.646	Houk
1964	St. Louis	93	69	.574	Keane	1964	New York	99	63	.611	Berra
1965	Los Angeles	97	65	.599	Alston	1965	Minnesota	102	60	.630	Mele
1966	Los Angeles	95	67	.586	Alston	1966	Baltimore	97	63	.606	Bauer
1967	St. Louis	101	60	.627	Schoendienst	1967	Boston	92	70	.568	Williams
1968	St. Louis	97	65	.599	Schoendienst	1968	Detroit	103	59	.636	Smith
1969	N.Y. Mets	100	62	.617	Hodges	1969	Baltimore	100	53	.673	Weaver
1970	Cincinnati	102	60	.630	Anderson	1970	Baltimore	108	54	.667	Weaver
1971	Pittsburgh	97	65	.599	Murtaugh	1971	Baltimore	101	57	.639	Weaver
1972	Cincinnati	95	59	.617	Anderson	1972	Oakland	93	62	.600	Williams
1973	N.Y. Mets	82	79	.509	Berra	1973	Oakland	94	68	.580	Williams
1974	Los Angeles	102	60	.630	Alston	1974	Oakland	90	72	.556	Dark
1975	Cincinnati	108	54	.667	Anderson	1975	Boston	97	65	.594	Johnson

Major League Pennant Winners, 1976-2007

National League

		East					West				Pennant
Year	Winner	W	L	Pct	Manager	Winner	W	L	Pct	Manager	Winner
1976	Philadelphia	101	61	.623	Ozark	Cincinnati	102	60	.630	Anderson	Cincinnati
1977	Philadelphia	101	61	.623	Ozark	Los Angeles	98	64	.605	Lasorda	Los Angeles
1978	Philadelphia	90	72	.556	Ozark	Los Angeles	95	67	.586	Lasorda	Los Angeles
1979	Pittsburgh	98	64	.605	Tanner	Cincinnati	90	71	.559	McNamara	Pittsburgh
1980	Philadelphia	91	71	.562	Green	Houston	93	70	.571	Virdon	Philadelphia
1981(a)	Philadelphia	34	21	.618	Green	Los Angeles	36	21	.632	Lasorda	(c)
1981(b)	Montreal	30	23	.566	Williams, Fanning	Houston	33	20	.623	Virdon	Los Angeles
1982	St. Louis	92	70	.568	Herzog	Atlanta	89	73	.549	Torre	St. Louis
1983	Philadelphia	90	72	.556	Corrales, Owens	Los Angeles	91	71	.562	Lasorda	Philadelphia
1984	Chicago	96	65	.596	Frey	San Diego	92	70	.568	Williams	San Diego
1985	St. Louis	101	61	.623	Herzog	Los Angeles	95	67	.586	Lasorda	St. Louis
1986	N.Y. Mets	108	54	.667	Johnson	Houston	96	66	.593	Lanier	New York
1987	St. Louis	95	67	.586	Herzog	San Francisco	90	72	.556	Craig	St. Louis
1988	N.Y. Mets	100	60	.625	Johnson	Los Angeles	94	67	.584	Lasorda	Los Angeles
1989	Chicago	93	69	.571	Zimmer	San Francisco	92	70	.568	Craig	San Francisco
1990	Pittsburgh	95	67	.586	Leyland	Cincinnati	91	71	.562	Piniella	Cincinnati
1991	Pittsburgh	98	64	.605	Leyland	Atlanta	94	68	.580	Cox	Atlanta
1992	Pittsburgh	96	66	.593	Leyland	Atlanta	98	64	.605	Cox	Atlanta
1993	Philadelphia	97	65	.599	Fregosi	Atlanta	104	58	.642	Cox	Philadelphia

Year	Division	Winner	W	L	Pct	Manager	Playoffs	Pennant Winner
1994 (d)	East	Montreal	74	40	.649	Alou		
	Central	Cincinnati	66	48	.579	Johnson		
	West	Los Angeles	58	56	.509	Lasorda		
1995	East	Atlanta	90	54	.625	Cox	Atlanta 3, Colorado* 1	Atlanta
	Central	Cincinnati	85	59	.590	Johnson	Cincinnati 3, Los Angeles 0	
	West	Los Angeles	78	66	.542	Lasorda	Atlanta 4, Cincinnati 0	
1996	East	Atlanta	96	66	.593	Cox	Atlanta 3, Los Angeles* 0	Atlanta
	Central	St. Louis	88	74	.543	La Russa	St. Louis 3, San Diego 0	
	West	San Diego	91	71	.562	Bochy	Atlanta 4, St. Louis 3	
1997	East	Atlanta	101	61	.623	Cox	Atlanta 3, Houston 0	Florida* (e)
	Central	Houston	84	78	.519	Dierker	Florida* 3, San Francisco 0	
	West	San Francisco	90	72	.556	Baker	Florida* 4, Atlanta 2	
1998	East	Atlanta	106	56	.654	Cox	Atlanta 3, Chicago* 0	San Diego
	Central	Houston	102	60	.630	Dierker	San Diego 3, Houston 1	
	West	San Diego	97	64	.602	Bochy	San Diego 4, Atlanta 2	
1999	East	Atlanta	103	59	.636	Cox	Atlanta 3, Houston 1	Atlanta
	Central	Houston	97	65	.599	Dierker	New York* 3, Arizona 1	
	West	Arizona	100	62	.617	Showalter	Atlanta 4, New York 2	
2000	East	Atlanta	95	67	.586	Cox	St. Louis 3, Atlanta 0	New York* (f)
	Central	St. Louis	95	67	.586	La Russa	New York* 3, San Francisco 1	
	West	San Francisco	97	65	.599	Baker	New York* 4, St. Louis 1	

Year	Division	Winner	W	L	Pct	Manager	Playoffs	Pennant Winner
2001	East	Atlanta	88	74	.543	Cox	Atlanta 3, Houston 0	Arizona
	Central	Houston	93	69	.574	Dierker	Arizona 3, St. Louis* 2	
	West	Arizona	92	70	.568	Brenly	Arizona 4, Atlanta 1	
2002	East	Atlanta	101	59	.631	Cox	St. Louis 3, Arizona 0	San Francisco* (g)
	Central	St. Louis	97	65	.599	La Russa	San Francisco* 3, Atlanta 2	
	West	Arizona	98	64	.605	Brenly	San Francisco 4, St. Louis 1	
2003	East	Atlanta	101	61	.623	Cox	Chicago 3, Atlanta 2	Florida*(i)
	Central	Chicago	88	74	.543	Baker	Florida* 3, San Francisco 2	
	West	San Francisco	100	61	.621	Alou	Florida* 4, Chicago 3	
2004	East	Atlanta	96	66	.593	Cox	Houston* 3, Atlanta 2	St. Louis
	Central	St. Louis	105	57	.648	La Russa	St. Louis 3, Dodgers 1	
	West	Los Angeles	93	69	.594	Tracy	St. Louis 4, Houston 3	
2005	East	Atlanta	90	72	.556	Cox	St. Louis 3, San Diego 0	Houston* (j)
	Central	St. Louis	100	62	.617	La Russa	Houston* 3, Atlanta 1	
	West	San Diego	82	80	.506	Bochy	Houston* 4, St. Louis 2	
2006	East	N.Y. Mets	97	65	.599	Randolph	N.Y. Mets 3, Los Angeles* 0	St. Louis
	Central	St. Louis	83	78	.516	La Russa	St. Louis 3, San Diego 1	
	West	San Diego	88	74	.543	Bochy	St. Louis 4, New York 3	
2007	East	Philadelphia	89	73	.549	Manuel	Colorado* 3, Philadelphia 0	
	Central	Chicago	85	77	.525	Piniella	Arizona 3, Chicago 0	
	West	Arizona	90	72	.556	Melvin	Colorado vs. Arizona (m)	

American League

	East					West					Pennant
Year	Winner	W	L	Pct	Manager	Winner	W	L	Pct	Manager	Winner
1976	New York	97	62	.610	Martin	Kansas City	90	72	.556	Herzog	New York
1977	New York	100	62	.617	Martin	Kansas City	102	60	.630	Herzog	New York
1978	New York	100	63	.613	Martin, Lemon	Kansas City	92	70	.568	Herzog	New York
1979	Baltimore	102	57	.642	Weaver	California	88	74	.543	Fregosi	Baltimore
1980	New York	103	59	.636	Howser	Kansas City	97	65	.599	Frey	Kansas City
1981 (a)	New York	34	22	.607	Michael	Oakland	37	23	.617	Martin	(c)
1981 (b)	Milwaukee	31	22	.585	Rodgers	Kansas City	30	23	.566	Frey, Howser	New York
1982	Milwaukee	95	67	.586	Rodgers, Kuenn	California	93	69	.574	Mauch	Milwaukee
1983	Baltimore	98	64	.605	Altobelli	Chicago	99	63	.611	La Russa	Baltimore
1984	Detroit	104	58	.642	Anderson	Kansas City	84	78	.519	Howser	Detroit
1985	Toronto	99	62	.615	Cox	Kansas City	91	71	.562	Howser	Kansas City
1986	Boston	95	66	.590	McNamara	California	92	70	.568	Mauch	Boston
1987	Detroit	98	64	.605	Anderson	Minnesota	85	77	.525	Kelly	Minnesota
1988	Boston	89	73	.549	McNamara, Morgan	Oakland	104	58	.642	La Russa	Oakland
1989	Toronto	89	73	.549	Williams, Gaston	Oakland	99	63	.611	La Russa	Oakland
1990	Boston	88	74	.543	Morgan	Oakland	103	59	.636	La Russa	Oakland
1991	Toronto	91	71	.562	Gaston	Minnesota	95	67	.586	Kelly	Minnesota
1992	Toronto	96	66	.593	Gaston	Oakland	96	66	.593	La Russa	Toronto
1993	Toronto	95	67	.586	Gaston	Chicago	94	68	.580	Lamont	Toronto

Year	Division	Winner	W	L	Pct	Manager	Playoffs	Pennant Winner
1994 (d)	East	New York	70	43	.619	Showalter	—	—
	Central	Chicago	67	46	.593	Lamont		
	West	Texas	52	62	.456	Kennedy		
1995	East	Boston	86	58	.597	Kennedy	Cleveland 3, Boston 0	Cleveland
	Central	Cleveland	100	44	.694	Hargrove	Seattle 3, New York* 2	
	West	Seattle	79	66	.545	Piniella	Cleveland 4, Seattle 2	
1996	East	New York	92	70	.568	Torre	Baltimore* 3, Cleveland 1	New York
	Central	Cleveland	99	62	.615	Hargrove	New York 3, Texas 1	
	West	Texas	90	72	.556	Oates	New York 4, Baltimore* 1	
1997	East	Baltimore	98	64	.605	Johnson	Baltimore 3, Seattle 1	Cleveland
	Central	Cleveland	86	75	.534	Hargrove	Cleveland 3, New York* 2	
	West	Seattle	90	72	.556	Piniella	Cleveland 4, Baltimore 2	
1998	East	New York	114	48	.704	Torre	New York 3, Texas 0	New York
	Central	Cleveland	89	73	.549	Hargrove	Cleveland 3, Boston* 1	
	West	Texas	88	74	.543	Oates	New York 4, Cleveland 2	
1999	East	New York	98	64	.605	Torre	New York 3, Texas 0	New York
	Central	Cleveland	97	65	.599	Hargrove	Boston* 3, Cleveland 2	
	West	Texas	95	67	.586	Oates	New York 4, Boston* 1	
2000	East	New York	87	74	.540	Torre	New York 3, Oakland 2	New York
	Central	Chicago	95	67	.586	Manuel	Seattle* 3, Chicago 0	
	West	Oakland	91	70	.565	Howe	New York 4, Seattle* 2	
2001	East	New York	95	65	.594	Torre	Seattle 3, Cleveland 2	New York
	Central	Cleveland	91	71	.562	Manuel	New York 3, Oakland 2	
	West	Seattle	116	46	.716	Piniella	New York 4, Seattle* 1	
2002	East	New York	103	58	.640	Torre	Anaheim* 3, New York 1	Anaheim* (h)
	Central	Minnesota	94	67	.584	Gardenhire	Minnesota 3, Oakland 2	
	West	Oakland	103	59	.636	Howe	Anaheim* 4, Minnesota 1	
2003	East	New York	101	61	.623	Torre	New York 3, Minnesota 1	New York
	Central	Minnesota	90	72	.556	Gardenhire	Boston* 3, Oakland 2	
	West	Oakland	96	66	.593	Macha	New York 4, Boston* 3	
2004	East	New York	101	61	.623	Torre	New York 3, Minnesota 1	Boston* (k)
	Central	Minnesota	92	70	.568	Gardenhire	Boston* 3, Anaheim 0	
	West	Anaheim	92	70	.568	Scioscia	Boston* 4, New York 3	
2005	East	New York	95	67	.586	Torre	Chicago 3, Boston* 0	Chicago
	Central	Chicago	99	63	.611	Guillen	Los Angeles 3, New York 2	
	West	Los Angeles	95	67	.586	Scioscia	Chicago 4, Los Angeles 1	
2006	East	New York	97	65	.599	Torre	Oakland 3, Minnesota 0	Detroit*(l)
	Central	Minnesota	96	66	.593	Gardenhire	Detroit* 3, N.Y. Yankees 1	
	West	Oakland	93	69	.574	Macha		
2007	East	Boston	96	66	.593	Francona	Boston 3, Los Angeles 0	
	Central	Cleveland	96	66	.593	Wedge	Cleveland 3, New York* 1	
	West	Los Angeles	94	68	.580	Scioscia	Boston vs. Cleveland (m)	

*Wild card team. (a) First half. (b) Second half. (c) Montreal, L.A., N.Y. Yankees, and Oakland won the divisional playoffs. (d) In Aug. 1994, a players' strike began that caused the cancellation of the remainder of the season, the playoffs, and the World Series. Teams listed as division "winners" for 1994 were leading their divisions at the time of the strike. (e) Florida manager: Jim Leyland. (f) New York manager Bobby Valentine. (g) San Francisco manager: Dusty Baker. (h) Anaheim manager: Mike Scioscia. (i) Florida manager: Jack McKeon. (j) Houston manager: Phil Garner. (k) Boston manager: Terry Francona. (l) Detroit manager: Jim Leyland. (m) Not decided at press time.

World Series Results, 1903-2006

1903 Boston AL 5, Pittsburgh NL 3	1938 New York AL 4, Chicago NL 0	1973 Oakland AL 4, New York NL 3
1904 No series	1939 New York AL 4, Cincinnati NL 0	1974 Oakland AL 4, Los Angeles NL 1
1905 New York NL 4, Philadelphia AL 1	1940 Cincinnati NL 4, Detroit AL 3	1975 Cincinnati NL 4, Boston AL 3
1906 Chicago AL 4, Chicago NL 2	1941 New York AL 4, Brooklyn NL 1	1976 Cincinnati NL 4, New York AL 0
1907 Chicago NL 4, Detroit AL 0, 1 tie	1942 St. Louis NL 4, New York AL 1	1977 New York AL 4, Los Angeles NL 2
1908 Chicago NL 4, Detroit AL 1	1943 New York AL 4, St. Louis NL 1	1978 New York AL 4, Los Angeles NL 2
1909 Pittsburgh NL 4, Detroit AL 3	1944 St. Louis NL 4, St. Louis AL 2	1979 Pittsburgh NL 4, Baltimore AL 3
1910 Philadelphia AL 4, Chicago NL 1	1945 Detroit AL 4, Chicago NL 3	1980 Philadelphia NL 4, Kansas City AL 2
1911 Philadelphia AL 4, New York NL 2	1946 St. Louis NL 4, Boston AL 3	1981 Los Angeles NL 4, New York AL 2
1912 Boston AL 4, New York NL 3, 1 tie	1947 New York AL 4, Brooklyn NL 3	1982 St. Louis NL 4, Milwaukee AL 3
1913 Philadelphia AL 4, New York NL 1	1948 Cleveland AL 4, Boston NL 2	1983 Baltimore AL 4, Philadelphia NL 1
1914 Boston NL 4, Philadelphia AL 0	1949 New York AL 4, Brooklyn NL 1	1984 Detroit AL 4, San Diego NL 1
1915 Boston AL 4, Philadelphia NL 1	1950 New York AL 4, Philadelphia NL 0	1985 Kansas City AL 4, St. Louis NL 3
1916 Boston AL 4, Brooklyn NL 1	1951 New York AL 4, New York NL 2	1986 New York NL 4, Boston AL 3
1917 Chicago AL 4, New York NL 2	1952 New York AL 4, Brooklyn NL 3	1987 Minnesota AL 4, St. Louis NL 3
1918 Boston AL 4, Chicago NL 2	1953 New York AL 4, Brooklyn NL 2	1988 Los Angeles NL 4, Oakland AL 1
1919 Cincinnati NL 5, Chicago AL 3	1954 New York NL 4, Cleveland AL 0	1989 Oakland AL 4, San Francisco NL 0
1920 Cleveland AL 5, Brooklyn NL 2	1955 Brooklyn NL 4, New York AL 3	1990 Cincinnati NL 4, Oakland AL 0
1921 New York NL 5, New York AL 3	1956 New York AL 4, Brooklyn NL 3	1991 Minnesota AL 4, Atlanta NL 3
1922 New York NL 4, New York AL 0, 1 tie	1957 Milwaukee NL 4, New York AL 3	1992 Toronto AL 4, Atlanta NL 2
1923 New York AL 4, New York NL 2	1958 New York AL 4, Milwaukee NL 3	1993 Toronto AL 4, Philadelphia NL 2
1924 Washington AL 4, New York NL 3	1959 Los Angeles NL 4, Chicago AL 2	1994 No series
1925 Pittsburgh NL 4, Washington AL 3	1960 Pittsburgh NL 4, New York AL 3	1995 Atlanta NL 4, Cleveland AL 2
1926 St. Louis NL 4, New York AL 3	1961 New York AL 4, Cincinnati NL 1	1996 New York AL 4, Atlanta NL 2
1927 New York AL 4, Pittsburgh NL 0	1962 New York AL 4, San Francisco NL 3	1997 Florida NL 4, Cleveland AL 3
1928 New York AL 4, St. Louis NL 0	1963 Los Angeles NL 4, New York AL 0	1998 New York AL 4, San Diego NL 0
1929 Philadelphia AL 4, Chicago NL 1	1964 St. Louis NL 4, New York AL 3	1999 New York AL 4, Atlanta NL 0
1930 Philadelphia AL 4, St. Louis NL 2	1965 Los Angeles NL 4, Minnesota AL 3	2000 New York AL 4, New York NL 1
1931 St. Louis NL 4, Philadelphia AL 3	1966 Baltimore AL 4, Los Angeles NL 0	2001 Arizona NL 4, New York AL 3
1932 New York AL 4, Chicago NL 0	1967 St. Louis NL 4, Boston AL 3	2002 Anaheim AL 4, San Francisco NL 3
1933 New York NL 4, Washington AL 1	1968 Detroit AL 4, St. Louis NL 3	2003 Florida NL 4, New York AL 2
1934 St. Louis NL 4, Detroit AL 3	1969 New York NL 4, Baltimore AL 1	2004 Boston AL 4, St. Louis NL 0
1935 Detroit AL 4, Chicago NL 2	1970 Baltimore AL 4, Cincinnati NL 1	2005 Chicago AL 4, Houston NL 0
1936 New York AL 4, New York NL 2	1971 Pittsburgh NL 4, Baltimore AL 3	2006 St. Louis NL 4, Detroit AL 1
1937 New York AL 4, New York NL 1	1972 Oakland AL 4, Cincinnati NL 3	

World Series Most Valuable Player

Year	Player, Position, Team	Year	Player, Position, Team	Year	Player, Position, Team
1955	Johnny Podres, P, Brooklyn	1974	Rollie Fingers, P, Oakland	1990	Jose Rijo, P, Cincinnati
1956	Don Larsen, P, New York, AL	1975	Pete Rose, 3B, Cincinnati	1991	Jack Morris, P, Minnesota
1957	Lew Burdette, P, Milwaukee, NL	1976	Johnny Bench, C, Cincinnati	1992	Pat Borders, C, Toronto
1958	Bob Turley, P, NY AL	1977	Reggie Jackson, OF, NY, AL	1993	Paul Molitor, DH, Toronto
1959	Larry Sherry, P, LA	1978	Bucky Dent, SS, NY, AL	1994	no series
1960[1]	Bobby Richardson, 2B, NY, AL	1979	Willie Stargell, 1B, Pittsburgh	1995	Tom Glavine, P, Atlanta
1961	Whitey Ford, P, NY, AL	1980	Mike Schmidt, 3B, Philadelphia	1996	John Wetteland, P, NY, AL
1962	Ralph Terry, P, NY, AL	1981	Ron Cey, 3B, LA	1997	Livan Hernandez, P, Florida
1963	Sandy Koufax, P, Los Angeles, NL		Pedro Guerrero, OF, LA	1998	Scott Brosius, 3B, NY, AL
1964	Bob Gibson, P, St. Louis		Steve Yeager, C, LA	1999	Mariano Rivera, P, NY, AL
1965	Sandy Koufax, P, Los Angeles, NL	1982	Darrell Porter, C, St. Louis	2000	Derek Jeter, SS, NY, AL
1966	Frank Robinson, of, Baltimore	1983	Rick Dempsey, C, Baltimore	2001	Curt Schilling, P, Arizona
1967	Bob Gibson, P, St. Louis	1984	Alan Trammell, SS, Detroit		Randy Johnson, P, Arizona
1968	Mickey Lolich, P, Detroit	1985	Bret Saberhagen, P, Kansas City	2002	Troy Glaus, 3B, Anaheim
1969	Donn Clendenon, 1B, NY, NL	1986	Ray Knight, 3B, NY, NL	2003	Josh Beckett, P, Florida
1970	Brooks Robinson, 3B, Baltimore	1987	Frank Viola, P, Minnesota	2004	Manny Ramirez, OF, Boston
1971	Roberto Clemente, OF, Pittsburgh	1988	Orel Hershiser, P, LA	2005	Jermaine Dye, OF, Chicago
1972	Gene Tenace, C, Oakland	1989	Dave Stewart, P, Oakland	2006	David Eckstein, SS, St. Louis
1973	Reggie Jackson, OF, Oakland				

(1) Bobby Richardson won the MVP although Pittsburgh beat New York.

World Series Won-Lost Records, by Franchise[1]

Team	Wins	Losses	Team	Wins	Losses
New York Yankees	26	13	Florida Marlins	2	0
St. Louis Cardinals	10	8	Toronto Blue Jays	2	0
Philadelphia/Kansas City/Oakland A's	9	5	New York Mets	2	2
Boston Red Sox	7	4	Cleveland Indians	2	3
Brooklyn/Los Angeles Dodgers	6	12	Chicago Cubs	2	8
Pittsburgh Pirates	5	2	LA/California/Anaheim/LA Angels	1	0
Cincinnati Reds	5	4	Arizona Diamondbacks	1	0
New York/San Francisco Giants	5	12	Kansas City Royals	1	1
Detroit Tigers	4	6	Philadelphia Phillies	1	4
Chicago White Sox	3	2	Seattle Pilots/Milwaukee Brewers	0	1
Washington Senators/Minnesota Twins	3	3	San Diego Padres	0	2
St. Louis Browns/Baltimore Orioles	3	4	Houston Astros	0	1
Boston/Milwaukee/Atlanta Braves	3	6			

(1) Through 2006. Figures represent overall series wins, not individual games.

All-Time World Series Career Leaders
(Through 2006)

Batting Leaders

Batter	Hits	AB	Avg.	Batter	Hits	AB	Avg.
1. Bobby Brown	18	41	.439	6. Lou Brock	34	87	.391
2. Paul Molitor	23	55	.418	7. Marquis Grissom	30	77	.390
3. Pepper Martin	23	55	.418	8. Troy Glaus	10	26	.385
4. J.T. Snow	11	27	.407	9. George Brett	19	51	.373
5. Hal McRae	18	45	.400	10. Thurman Munson	25	67	.373

Games Played

Yogi Berra	75
Mickey Mantle	65
Elston Howard	54
Hank Bauer	53
Gil McDougald	53
Phil Rizzuto	52
Joe DiMaggio	51
Frankie Frisch	50
Pee Wee Reese	44
Roger Maris	41
Babe Ruth	41

Hits

Yogi Berra	71
Mickey Mantle	59
Frankie Frisch	58
Joe DiMaggio	54
Hank Bauer	46
PeeWee Reese	46
Phil Rizzuto	45
Gil McDougald	45
Lou Gehrig	43
Elston Howard	42
Babe Ruth	42
Eddie Collins	42

Runs

Mickey Mantle	42
Yogi Berra	41
Babe Ruth	37
Lou Gehrig	30
Joe DiMaggio	27
Derek Jeter	27
Roger Maris	26
Elston Howard	25
Gil McDougald	23
Jackie Robinson	22

Runs Batted In

Mickey Mantle	40
Yogi Berra	39
Lou Gehrig	35
Babe Ruth	33
Joe DiMaggio	30
Bill Skowron	29
Duke Snider	26
Reggie Jackson	24
Hank Bauer	24
Bill Dickey	24
Gil McDougald	24

Home Runs

Mickey Mantle	18
Babe Ruth	15
Yogi Berra	12
Duke Snider	11
Reggie Jackson	10
Lou Gehrig	10
Joe DiMaggio	8
Bill Skowron	8
Frank Robinson	8
Hank Bauer	7
Gil McDougald	7
Goose Goslin	7

Stolen Bases

Lou Brock	14
Eddie Collins	14
Frank Chance	10
Dave Lopes	10
Phil Rizzuto	10
Frank Frisch	9
Honus Wagner	9
Johnny Evers	8
Roberto Alomar	7
Rickey Henderson	7
Pepper Martin	7
Joe Morgan	7
Joe Tinker	7

Pitching Leaders

Games Pitched

Whitey Ford	22
Mariano Rivera	20
Rollie Fingers	16
Jeff Nelson	16
Allie Reynolds	15
Mike Stanton	15
Bob Turley	15
Clay Carroll	14
Clem Labine	13
Mark Wohlers	13
Waite Hoyt	12
Catfish Hunter	12
Art Nehf	12

Wins

Whitey Ford	10
Bob Gibson	7
Allie Reynolds	7
Red Ruffing	7
Chief Bender	6
Lefty Gomez	6
Waite Hoyt	6
Three Finger Brown	5
Jack Coombs	5
Catfish Hunter	5
Herb Pennock	5
Vic Raschi	5
Christy Mathewson	5

Strikeouts

Whitey Ford	94
Bob Gibson	92
Allie Reynolds	62
Sandy Koufax	61
Red Ruffing	61
Chief Bender	59
George Earnshaw	56
John Smoltz	52
Waite Hoyt	49
Christy Mathewson	48

Saves

Mariano Rivera	9
Rollie Fingers	6
Johnny Murphy	4
Allie Reynolds	4
John Wetteland	4
Robb Nen	4

All-Star Baseball Games, 1933-2007

Year	Winner, Score	Host team	Year	Winner, Score	Host team	Year	Winner, Score	Host team
1933*	American, 4-2	Chicago (AL)	1959*	American, 5-3	Los Angeles	1982	National, 4-1	Montreal
1934*	American, 9-7	New York (NL)	1960*	National, 5-3	Kansas City	1983	American, 13-3	Chicago (AL)
1935*	American, 4-1	Cleveland	1960*	National, 6-0	New York (AL)	1984	National, 3-1	San Francisco
1936*	National, 4-3	Boston (NL)	1961*	National, 5-4[3]	San Francisco	1985	National, 6-1	Minnesota
1937*	American, 8-3	Washington	1961*	Called—rain, 1-1	Boston	1986	American, 3-2	Houston
1938*	National, 4-1	Cincinnati	1962*	National, 3-1[3]	Washington	1987	National, 2-0[5]	Oakland
1939*	American, 3-1	New York (AL)	1962*	American, 9-4	Chicago (NL)	1988	American, 2-1	Cincinnati
1940*	National, 4-0	St. Louis (NL)	1963*	National, 5-3	Cleveland	1989	American, 5-3	California
1941*	American, 7-5	Detroit	1964*	National, 7-4	New York (NL)	1990	American, 2-0	Chicago (NL)
1942	American, 3-1	New York (NL)	1965*	National, 6-5	Minnesota	1991	American, 4-2	Toronto
1943	American, 5-3	Philadelphia (AL)	1966*	National, 2-1[3]	St. Louis	1992	American, 13-6	San Diego
1944	National, 7-1	Pittsburgh	1967*	National, 2-1[4]	California	1993	American, 9-3	Baltimore
1945	(Not played)		1968	National, 1-0	Houston	1994	National, 8-7[3]	Pittsburgh
1946*	American, 12-0	Boston (AL)	1969*	National, 9-3	Washington	1995	National, 3-2	Texas
1947*	American, 2-1	Chicago (NL)	1970	National, 5-4[2]	Cincinnati	1996	National, 6-0	Philadelphia
1948*	American, 5-2	St. Louis (AL)	1971	American, 6-4	Detroit	1997	American, 3-1	Cleveland
1949*	American, 11-7	Brooklyn	1972	National, 4-3[3]	Atlanta	1998	American, 13-8	Colorado
1950*	National, 4-3[1]	Chicago (AL)	1973	National, 7-1	Kansas City	1999	American, 4-1	Boston
1951*	National, 8-3	Detroit	1974	National, 7-2	Pittsburgh	2000	American, 6-3	Atlanta
1952*	National, 3-2	Philadelphia (NL)	1975	National, 6-3	Milwaukee	2001	American, 4-1	Seattle
1953*	National, 5-1	Cincinnati	1976	National, 7-1	Philadelphia	2002	Tie, 7-7[6]	Milwaukee
1954*	American, 11-9	Cleveland	1977	National, 7-5	New York (AL)	2003	American, 7-6[7]	Chicago (AL)
1955*	National, 6-5[2]	Milwaukee	1978	National, 7-3	San Diego	2004	American, 9-4	Houston
1956*	National, 7-3	Washington	1979	National, 7-6	Seattle	2005	American, 7-5	Detroit
1957*	American, 6-5	St. Louis	1980	National, 4-2	Los Angeles	2006	American, 3-2	Pittsburgh
1958*	American, 4-3	Baltimore	1981	National, 5-4	Cleveland	2007	American, 5-4	San Francisco
1959*	National, 5-4	Pittsburgh						

*Denotes day game. (1) 14 innings. (2) 12 innings. (3) 10 innings. (4) 15 innings. (5) 13 innings. (6) Commissioner's decision, game called in the 11th inning when both teams ran out of pitchers. (7) Under rule change beginning in 2003, league winning All-Star games earned World Series home-field advantage.

Baseball Stadiums[1]

National League

Team	Stadium (year opened)	Surface	LF	Center	RF	Seating capacity
			Home run distances (ft.)			
Arizona Diamondbacks	Chase Field (1998)	Grass	330	407	334	49,033
Atlanta Braves	Turner Field (1997)	Grass	335	401	330	50,096
Chicago Cubs	Wrigley Field (1914)	Grass	355	400	353	38,902
Cincinnati Reds	Great American Ballpark (2003)	Grass	328	404	325	42,059
Colorado Rockies	Coors Field (1995)	Grass	347	415	350	50,445
Florida Marlins	Dolphins Stadium (1987)	Grass	330	434	345	47,662
Houston Astros	Minute Maid Park (2000)	Grass	315	435	326	40,950
Los Angeles Dodgers	Dodger Stadium (1962)	Grass	330	395	330	56,000
Milwaukee Brewers	Miller Park (2001)	Grass	344	400	345	42,400
New York Mets	Shea Stadium (1964)	Grass	338	410	338	55,601
Philadelphia Phillies	Citizens Bank Park (2004)	Grass	329	401	330	43,500
Pittsburgh Pirates	PNC Park (2001)	Grass	325	399	320	38,365
St. Louis Cardinals	New Busch Stadium (2006)	Grass	336	400	335	46,861
San Diego Padres	PETCO Park (2004)	Grass	334	396	322	42,500
San Francisco Giants	SBC Park (2000)	Grass	335	404	307	41,584
Washington Nationals	Robert F. Kennedy Memorial Stadium (1961)	Grass	335	410	335	56,000

American League

Team	Stadium (year opened)	Surface	LF	Center	RF	Seating capacity
Baltimore Orioles	Oriole Park at Camden Yards (1992)	Grass	333	400	318	48,876
Boston Red Sox	Fenway Park (1912)	Grass	310	420	302	35,095
Chicago White Sox	U.S. Cellular Field (1991)	Grass	330	400	335	47,098
Cleveland Indians	Jacobs Field (1994)	Grass	325	405	325	43,368
Detroit Tigers	Comerica Park (2000)	Grass	345	420	330	40,000
Kansas City Royals	Kauffman Stadium (1973)	Grass	330	410	330	40,793
Los Angeles Angels	Angel Stadium of Anaheim (1966)	Grass	330	406	330	45,050
Minnesota Twins	Hubert H. Humphrey Metrodome (1982)	Artificial	343	408	327	48,678
New York Yankees	Yankee Stadium (1923)	Grass	318	408	314	57,478
Oakland A's	McAfee Coliseum (1968)	Grass	330	400	330	43,662
Seattle Mariners	Safeco Field (1999)	Grass	331	405	327	47,116
Tampa Bay Devil Rays	Tropicana Field (1990)	Artificial	315	404	322	45,000
Texas Rangers	Ameriquest Field in Arlington (1994)	Grass	332	400	325	49,200
Toronto Blue Jays	Rogers Centre (1989)	Artificial	328	400	328	50,516

(1) As of 2007 season. The Washington Nationals expected to open a new ballpark in 2008.

Major League Franchise Shifts and Additions

1953: Boston Braves (NL) became Milwaukee Braves.
1954: St. Louis Browns (AL) became Baltimore Orioles.
1955: Philadelphia Athletics (AL) became Kansas City Athletics.
1958: New York Giants (NL) became San Francisco Giants.
1958: Brooklyn Dodgers (NL) became L.A. Dodgers.
1961: Washington Senators (AL) became Minnesota Twins.
1961: L.A. Angels (renamed California Angels in 1965 and Anaheim Angels in 1997) enfranchised by the American League.
1961: Washington Senators enfranchised by the American League (a new franchise, replacing the former Washington club, whose franchise was moved to Minneapolis-St. Paul).
1962: Houston Colt .45's (renamed the Houston Astros in 1965) enfranchised by the National League.
1962: New York Mets enfranchised by the National League.
1966: Milwaukee Braves (NL) became Atlanta Braves.
1968: Kansas City Athletics (AL) became Oakland Athletics.

1969: Kansas City Royals and Seattle Pilots enfranchised by the American League; Montreal Expos and San Diego Padres enfranchised by the National League.
1970: Seattle Pilots became Milwaukee Brewers.
1971: Washington Senators became Texas Rangers (Dallas-Fort Worth area).
1977: Toronto Blue Jays and Seattle Mariners enfranchised by the American League.
1993: Colorado Rockies (Denver) and Florida Marlins (Miami) enfranchised by the National League.
1998: Tampa Bay Devil Rays began play in the American League; Arizona Diamondbacks (Phoenix) began play in the National League (both teams enfranchised in 1995). Milwaukee Brewers moved from the AL to the NL.
2005: Montreal Expos (NL) became Washington Nationals; Anaheim Angels became Los Angeles Angels of Anaheim.

NCAA Baseball Division I Champions

1947	California	1959	Oklahoma St.	1972	USC	1984	Cal. St.-Fullerton	1996 LSU
1948	Southern California	1960	Minnesota	1973	USC	1985	Miami (FL)	1997 LSU
		1961	USC	1974	USC	1986	Arizona	1998 USC
1949	Texas	1962	Michigan	1975	Texas	1987	Stanford	1999 Miami (FL)
1950	Texas	1963	USC	1976	Arizona	1988	Stanford	2000 LSU
1951	Oklahoma	1964	Minnesota	1977	Arizona St.	1989	Wichita St.	2001 Miami (FL)
1952	Holy Cross	1965	Arizona St.	1978	USC	1990	Georgia	2002 Texas
1953	Michigan	1966	Ohio St.	1979	Cal. St.-Fullerton	1991	LSU	2003 Rice
1954	Missouri	1967	Arizona St.	1980	Arizona	1992	Pepperdine	2004 Cal. St.-Fullerton
1955	Wake Forest	1968	USC	1981	Arizona St.	1993	LSU	2005 Texas
1956	Minnesota	1969	Arizona St.	1982	Miami (FL)	1994	Oklahoma	2006 Oregon State
1957	California	1970	USC	1983	Texas	1995	Cal. St.-Fullerton	2007 Oregon State
1958	USC	1971	USC					

NCAA Women's Softball Division I Champions

1982	UCLA	1988	UCLA	1993	Arizona	1998	Fresno St.	2003 UCLA
1983	Texas A&M	1989	UCLA	1994	Arizona	1999	UCLA	2004 UCLA
1984	UCLA	1990	UCLA	1995	UCLA	2000	Oklahoma	2005 Michigan
1985	UCLA	1991	Arizona	1996	Arizona	2001	Arizona	2006 Arizona
1986	Cal St. Fullerton	1992	UCLA	1997	Arizona	2002	California	2007 Arizona
1987	Texas A&M							

Little League World Series

The Little League World Series is played annually in Williamsport, PA.

Year	Winning team; Losing team	Score	Year	Winning team; Losing team	Score
1947	Williamsport, PA; Lock Haven, PA	16-7	1954	Schenectady, NY; Colton, CA	7-5
1948	Lock Haven, PA; St. Petersburg, FL	6-5	1955	Morrisville, PA; Merchantville, NJ	4-3
1949	Hammonton, NJ; Pensacola, FL	5-0	1956	Roswell, NM; Delaware, NJ	3-1
1950	Houston, TX; Bridgeport, CT	2-1	1957	Mexico; La Mesa, CA	4-0
1951	Stamford, CT; Austin, TX	3-0	1958	Mexico; Kankakee, IL	10-1
1952	Norwalk, CT; Monongahela, PA	4-3	1959	Hamtramck, MI; Auburn, CA	12-0
1953	Birmingham, AL; Schenectady, NY	1-0	1960	Levittown, PA; Ft. Worth, TX	5-0

Year	Winning team; Losing team	Score	Year	Winning team; Losing team	Score
1961	El Cajon, CA; El Campo, TX	4-2	1985	South Korea; Mexico	7-1
1962	San Jose, CA; Kankakee, IL	3-0	1986	Taiwan; Tucson, AZ	12-0
1963	Granada Hills, CA; Stratford, CT	2-1	1987	Chinese Taipei; Irvine, CA	21-1
1964	Staten Island, NY; Mexico	4-0	1988	Chinese Taipei; Pearl City, HI	10-0
1965	Windsor Locks, CT; Ontario, Canada	3-1	1989	Trumbull, CT; Chinese Taipei	5-2
1966	Houston, TX; W. New York, NJ	8-2	1990	Chinese Taipei; Shippensburg, PA	9-0
1967	Tokyo, Japan; Chicago, IL	4-1	1991	Chinese Taipei; Danville, CA	11-0
1968	Osaka, Japan; Richmond, VA	1-0	1992	Long Beach, CA; Philippines*	6-0
1969	Taiwan; Santa Clara, CA	5-0	1993	Long Beach, CA; Panama	3-2
1970	Wayne, NJ; Campbell, CA	2-0	1994	Venezuela; Northridge, CA	4-3
1971	Taiwan; Gary, IN	12-3	1995	Taiwan; Spring, TX	17-3
1972	Taiwan; Hammond, IN	6-0	1996	Taiwan; Cranston, RI	13-3
1973	Taiwan; Tucson, AZ	12-0	1997	Mexico; Mission Viejo, CA	5-4
1974	Taiwan; Red Bluff, CA	12-1	1998	Toms River, NJ; Japan	12-9
1975	Lakewood, NJ; Tampa, FL	4-3	1999	Japan; Phenix City, AL	5-0
1976	Tokyo, Japan; Campbell, CA	10-3	2000	Venezuela; Bellaire, TX	3-2
1977	Taiwan; El Cajon, CA	7-2	2001	Japan; Apopka, FL	2-1
1978	Taiwan; Danville, CA	11-1	2002	Louisville, KY; Japan	1-0
1979	Taiwan; Campbell, CA	2-1	2003	Japan; East Boynton Beach, FL	10-1
1980	Taiwan; Tampa, FL	4-3	2004	Curacao; Conejo Valley of Thousand Oaks, CA	5-2
1981	Taiwan; Tampa, FL	4-2	2005	Ewa Beach HI; Curacao	7-6
1982	Kirkland, WA; Taiwan	6-0	2006	Columbus, GA; Japan	2-1
1983	Marietta, GA; Dominican Rep.	3-1	2007	Macon, GA; Japan	3-2
1984	South Korea; Altamonte Springs, FL	6-2			

*Philippines won 15-4, but was disqualified for using ineligible players. Long Beach was awarded title by forfeit 6-0 (1 run per inning).

National Baseball Hall of Fame and Museum, Cooperstown, NY[1]

#Aaron, Hank (The Hammer)
Alexander, Grover Cleveland (Old Pete)
Alston, Walt
Anderson, Sparky
Anson, Cap
Aparicio, Luis
Appling, Luke
Ashburn, Richie
Averill, Earl
Baker, Frank (Home Run)
Bancroft, Dave
#Banks, Ernie
Barlick, Al
Barrow, Edward G.
Beckley, Jake
Bell, Cool Papa
#Bench, Johnny
Bender, Chief
Berra, Yogi
#Boggs, Wade
Bottomley, Jim
Boudreau, Lou
Bresnahan, Roger
#Brett, George
#Brock, Lou
Brouthers, Dan
Brown, Mordecai (Three Finger)
Brown, Ray
Brown, Willard
Bulkeley, Morgan C.
Bunning, Jim
Burkett, Jesse C.
Campanella, Roy
#Carew, Rod
Carey, Max
#Carlton, Steve
Carter, Gary
Cartwright, Alexander
Cepeda, Orlando
Chadwick, Henry
Chance, Frank
Chandler, Happy
Charleston, Oscar
Chesbro, John
Chylak, Nestor
Clarke, Fred
Clarkson, John
#Clemente, Roberto
Cobb, Ty[2]
Cochrane, Mickey
Collins, Eddie
Collins, James
Combs, Earle
Comiskey, Charles A.

Conlan, Jocko
Connolly, Thomas H.
Connor, Roger
Cooper, Andy
Coveleski, Stan
Crawford, Sam
Cronin, Joe
Cummings, Candy
Cuyler, Kiki
Dandridge, Ray
Davis, George (Gorgeous)
Day, Leon
Dean, Dizzy
Delahanty, Ed
Dickey, Bill
Dihigo, Martín
DiMaggio, Joe
#Doby, Larry
Doerr, Bobby
Drysdale, Don
Duffy, Hugh
Durocher, Leo
#Eckersly, Dennis
Evans, Billy
Evers, John
Ewing, Buck
Faber, Urban (Red)
#Feller, Bob
Ferrell, Rick
Fingers, Rollie
Fisk, Carlton
Flick, Elmer H.
Ford, Whitey
Foster, Andrew (Rube)
Foster, Bill
Fox, Nellie
Foxx, Jimmie
Frick, Ford
Frisch, Frank
Galvin, Pud
#Gehrig, Lou
Gehringer, Charles
#Gibson, Bob
Gibson, Josh
Giles, Warren
Gomez, Lefty
Goslin, Goose
Grant, Frank
Greenberg, Hank
Griffith, Clark
Grimes, Burleigh
Grove, Lefty
#*Gwynn, Tony
Hafey, Chick
Haines, Jesee
Hamilton, Bill
Hanlon, Ned

Harridge, Will
Harris, Bucky
Hartnett, Gabby
Heilmann, Harry
Herman, Billy
Hill, Pete
Hooper, Harry
Hornsby, Rogers
Hoyt, Waite
Hubbard, Cal
Hubbell, Carl
Huggins, Miller
Hulbert, William
Hunter, Catfish
Irvin, Monte
#Jackson, Reggie
Jackson, Travis
Jenkins, Ferguson
Jennings, Hugh
Johnson, Byron (Ban)
Johnson, William (Judy)
Johnson, Walter[2]
Joss, Addie
#Kaline, Al
Keefe, Timothy
Keeler, William
Kell, George
Kelley, Joe
Kelly, George
Kelly, King
Killebrew, Harmon
Kiner, Ralph
Klein, Chuck
Klem, Bill
#Koufax, Sandy
Lajoie, Napoleon
Landis, Kenesaw M.
Lasorda, Tom
Lazzeri, Tony
Lemon, Bob
Leonard, Buck
Lindstrom, Fred
Lloyd, Pop
Lombardi, Ernie
Lopez, Al
Lyons, Ted
Mack, Connie
Mackey, Biz
MacPhail, Larry
MacPhail, Lee
Manley, Effa
#Mantle, Mickey
Manush, Henry
Maranville, Rabbit
Marichal, Juan
Marquard, Rube
Mathews, Eddie
Mathewson, Christy[2]

#Mays, Willie
Mazeroski, Bill
McCarthy, Joe
McCarthy, Thomas
#McCovey, Willie
McGinnity, Joe
McGowan, Bill
McGraw, John
McKechnie, Bill
McPhee, John (Bid)
Medwick, Joe
Mendez, Jose
Mize, Johnny
#Molitor, Paul
#Morgan, Joe
#Murray, Eddie
#Musial, Stan
Newhouser, Hal
Nichols, Kid
Niekro, Phil
O'Rourke, James
Ott, Mel
Paige, Satchel
#Palmer, Jim
Pennock, Herb
Perez, Tony
Perry, Gaylord
Plank, Ed
Pompez, Alex
Posey, Cum
#Puckett, Kirby
Radbourn, Charlie
Reese, Pee Wee
Rice, Sam
Rickey, Branch
#*Ripken, Cal Jr.
Rixey, Eppa
Rizzuto, Phil (Scooter)
Roberts, Robin
#Robinson, Brooks
#Robinson, Frank
#Robinson, Jackie
Robinson, Wilbert
Rogan, Joe (Bullet)
Roush, Edd
Ruffing, Red
Rusie, Amos
#Ruth, Babe[2]
#Ryan, Nolan
Sandberg, Ryne
Santop, Louis
Schalk, Ray
#Schmidt, Mike
Schoendienst, Red
#Seaver, Tom
Selee, Frank
Sewell, Joe
Simmons, Al

Sisler, George
Slaughter, Enos
Smith, Hilton
#Smith, Ozzie
Snider, Duke
#Spahn, Warren
Spalding, Albert
Speaker, Tris
#Stargell, Willie
Stearnes, Norman (Turkey)
Stengel, Casey
Sutter, Bruce
Suttles, Mule
Sutton, Don
Taylor, Ben
Terry, Bill
Thompson, Sam
Tinker, Joe
Torriente, Cristobal
Traynor, Pie
Vance, Dazzy
Vaughan, Arky
Veeck, Bill
Waddell, Rube
Wagner, Honus[2]
Wallace, Roderick (Bobby)
Walsh, Ed
Waner, Lloyd
Waner, Paul
Ward, John
Weaver, Earl
Weiss, George
Welch, Mickey
Wells, Willie
Wheat, Zach
White, Sol
Wilhelm, Hoyt
Wilkinson, J.L.
Williams, Billy
Williams, Joe (Smokey Joe)
#Williams, Ted
Willis, Vic
Wilson, Hack
Wilson, Jud
#Winfield, Dave
Wright, George
Wright, Harry
Wynn, Early
#Yastrzemski, Carl
Yawkey, Tom
Young, Cy
Youngs, Ross
#Yount, Robin

(1) Player must generally be retired for 5 complete seasons before being eligible for induction. (2) Players inducted in 1936 (the year the Hall of Fame began). # Denotes players chosen in first year of Hall of Fame eligibility or under special circumstances earlier. *Denotes 2007 inductees. **Note:** Four players, Babe Ruth (1936), Lou Gehrig (1939), Joe DiMaggio (1955), and Roberto Clemente (1973), were inducted less than 5 years after retirement or, in Clemente's case, death.

NATIONAL BASKETBALL ASSOCIATION

2006-07 Season: Spurs Sweep Cavaliers in Finals; Nowitzki Wins Season MVP; NBA Tests Synthetic Ball

The San Antonio Spurs, June 14, completed a 4-game sweep of the Cleveland Cavaliers to win the 2007 NBA Finals—the franchise's fourth championship, all under head coach Gregg Popovich, since 1999. The Spurs rode strong performances from point guard Tony Parker and center Tim Duncan to win four straight over forward LeBron James and the Cavaliers. The series produced the lowest television ratings in Finals history, and both teams' defense-first mentalities resulted in a sluggish pace. Game 3 was the second-lowest-scoring Finals game in history—a 75-72 Spurs win—and each team broke 90 points only once.

LeBron James's entrance onto the Finals stage was heavily hyped; however, he shot only 4-of-16 and committed 6 turnovers, en route to an 85-76 Game 1 defeat in which the Cavaliers trailed by as many as 18 points. Parker notched 27 points and 7 assists, while Duncan scored 24 and grabbed 13 rebounds. The trend continued in Game 2, as Parker scored 30 points; Duncan had 23 points, 9 rebounds, and 8 assists; and Spurs guard Manu Ginobili had 25 points off the bench, allowing San Antonio to build a 26-point lead by the third quarter and take a 103-92 victory. In Game 4, down 3 games to 0, Cleveland continued to fight. James had 24 points and 10 assists and forward Drew Gooden had 11 points and 11 rebounds, but the Cavaliers could not overcome Parker and Ginobili, who combined for 51 points, 12 rebounds and only 4 turnovers. The Spurs won the game, 83-82, and the series.

Parker averaged 24.5 points per game in the series, earning him Finals MVP honors; Duncan averaged 18.3 points and 11.5 rebounds; and James, falling short of his regular-season stats, averaged 22.0 points and 5.8 turnovers in the series—thanks in part to stellar defensive play by Spurs forward Bruce Bowen. Forward Robert Horry collected his 7th championship ring.

In the regular season, German forward Dirk Nowitzki became the first European-born player to win the NBA regular-season MVP, leading the Dallas Mavericks to a team-record 67 wins. Toronto Raptors head coach Sam Mitchell was named coach of the year after guiding the team to a 20-game improvement (27-55 to 47-35) over the previous season.

Just days before the start of the regular season, legendary Boston Celtics head coach Red Auerbach died at age 89. Auerbach won a record nine national championships and accumulated 938 victories—both NBA records when he retired in 1966—during his 20 years as an NBA head coach.

At the start of the season, the NBA experimented with a new, synthetic ball, replacing the traditional leather ball that had been used for 35 seasons. Many players complained the balls were inferior to their leather predecessors, prompting the league to discontinue use of the new ball on Jan. 1, 2007.

Final Standings, 2006-07 Season
(Playoff seeding in parentheses.)

Eastern Conference	W	L	PCT	GB	Western Conference	W	L	PCT	GB
Atlantic					**Northwest**				
Toronto Raptors (3)	47	35	0.573	0	Utah Jazz (4)	51	31	0.622	0
New Jersey Nets (6)	41	41	0.500	6	Denver Nuggets (6)	45	37	0.549	6
Philadelphia 76ers	35	47	0.427	12	Minnesota Timberwolves	32	49	0.390	18.5
New York Knicks	33	49	0.402	14	Portland Trail Blazers	32	50	0.390	19
Boston Celtics	24	58	0.293	23	Seattle SuperSonics	31	51	0.378	20
Central					**Pacific**				
Detroit Pistons (1)	53	29	0.646	0	Phoenix Suns (2)	61	21	0.744	0
Cleveland Cavaliers (2)	50	32	0.610	3	L.A. Lakers (7)	42	40	0.512	19
Chicago Bulls (5)	49	33	0.598	4	Golden State Warriors (8)	42	40	0.512	19
Indiana Pacers	35	47	0.427	18	L.A. Clippers	40	42	0.488	21
Milwaukee Bucks	28	54	0.341	25	Sacramento Kings	32	49	0.390	28.5
Southeast					**Southwest**				
Miami Heat (4)	44	38	0.537	0	Dallas Mavericks (1)	67	15	0.817	0
Washington Wizards (7)	41	41	0.500	3	San Antonio Spurs (3)	58	24	0.707	9
Orlando Magic (8)	40	42	0.488	4	Houston Rockets (5)	52	30	0.634	15
Charlotte Bobcats	33	49	0.402	11	New Orleans Hornets	39	43	0.476	28
Atlanta Hawks	30	52	0.366	14	Memphis Grizzlies	22	60	0.268	45

2006–07 NBA Regular Season Individual Highs

Minutes, game: 57, Raymond Felton, Charlotte v. L.A. Lakers, Dec. 29; Dirk Nowitzki, Dallas v. Phoenix, Mar. 14

Points, game: 65, Kobe Bryant, L.A. Lakers v. Portland, Mar. 16

Field goals, game: 23, Kobe Bryant, L.A. Lakers v. Portland, Mar. 16

Field goal attempts, game: 45, Kobe Bryant, L.A. Lakers v. Charlotte, Dec. 29

3-pointers, game: 9, Vince Carter, New Jersey v. Memphis, Dec. 11; Mike Miller, Memphis v. Golden State, Jan. 3; Mike Miller, Memphis v. Golden State, Feb. 21; Mike Bibby, Sacramento v. Phoenix, Mar. 23

3-pt. attempts, game: 20, Vince Carter, New Jersey v. Memphis, Dec. 11

Free throws, game: 23, Dwyane Wade, Miami v. Cleveland, Feb. 1

Free throw attempts, game: 27, Gilbert Arenas, Washington v. L.A. Lakers, Dec. 17

Rebounds, game: 27, Ben Wallace, Chicago v. Milwaukee, Dec. 15

Assists, game: 21, Steve Nash, Phoenix v. Cleveland, Jan. 11; Deron Williams, Utah v. Memphis, Jan. 24

Steals, game: 9, Rafer Alston, Houston v. Charlotte, Feb. 10

Blocks, game: 10, Emeka Okafor, Charlotte v. New York, Jan. 12

Minutes, season: 3,195, LeBron James, Cleveland

Off. rebounds, season: 320, Tyson Chandler, New Orleans

Def. rebounds, season: 792, Kevin Garnett, Minnesota

Personal fouls, season: 304, Andris Biedrins, Golden State

2007 NBA Playoff Results

Eastern Conference
Detroit defeated Orlando 4 games to 0
Cleveland defeated Washington 4 games to 0
New Jersey defeated Toronto 4 games to 2
Chicago defeated Miami 4 games to 0
Detroit defeated Chicago 4 games to 2
Cleveland defeated New Jersey 4 games to 2
Cleveland defeated Detroit 4 games to 2

Western Conference
Golden State defeated Dallas 4 games to 2
Phoenix defeated L.A. Lakers 4 games to 1
San Antonio defeated Denver 4 games to 1
Utah defeated Houston 4 games to 3
San Antonio defeated Phoenix 4 games to 2
Utah defeated Golden State 4 games to 1
San Antonio defeated Utah 4 games to 1

Championship
San Antonio defeated Cleveland 4 games to 0 (85-76, 103-92, 75-72, 83-82)

NBA Finals Composite Box Scores

San Antonio	FG M-A	FT M-A	Reb O-T	Ast	Avg	Cleveland	FG M-A	FT M-A	Reb O-T	Ast	Avg
Tony Parker	42-74	10-19	3-20	13	24.5	LeBron James	32-90	20-29	4-28	27	22.0
Tim Duncan	29-65	15-24	16-46	15	18.3	Drew Gooden	22-44	7-8	12-33	1	12.8
Manu Ginobili	18-49	25-30	1-23	10	17.8	Daniel Gibson	18-41	1-1	1-7	10	10.8
Bruce Bowen	8-27	1-4	3-22	5	6.0	Aleksandar Pavlovic	16-44	2-6	4-10	3	9.8
Fabricio Oberto	8-17	1-3	7-17	2	4.3	Zydrunas Ilgauskas	13-37	5-6	18-41	2	7.8
Francisco Elson	6-6	4-5	6-10	0	4.0	Anderson Varejao	10-15	10-16	6-21	3	7.5
Michael Finley	6-23	2-3	1-8	3	3.8	Damon Jones	5-11	3-3	1-5	4	4.5
Brent Barry	4-11	0-0	1-6	2	3.0	Donyell Marshall	5-16	3-4	2-9	5	3.8
Robert Horry	3-9	3-4	4-18	13	3.0	Eric Snow	2-5	1-2	1-4	9	1.3
Jacque Vaughn	4-7	0-0	1-5	4	2.0	Larry Hughes	1-10	0-0	0-5	2	1.0
Beno Udrih	0-0	0-0	0-0	0	0.0	Ira Newble	0-1	0-0	0-1	0	0.0
						Scot Pollard	0-0	0-0	0-0	0	0.0
						Shannon Brown	0-0	0-0	0-0	0	0.0

NBA Finals MVP

1969	Jerry West, Los Angeles	1982	Magic Johnson, Los Angeles
1970	Willis Reed, New York	1983	Moses Malone, Philadelphia
1971	Lew Alcindor (Kareem Abdul-Jabbar), Milwaukee	1984	Larry Bird, Boston
1972	Wilt Chamberlain, Los Angeles	1985	Kareem Abdul-Jabbar, L.A. Lakers
1973	Willis Reed, New York	1986	Larry Bird, Boston
1974	John Havlicek, Boston	1987	Magic Johnson, L.A. Lakers
1975	Rick Barry, Golden State	1988	James Worthy, L.A. Lakers
1976	JoJo White, Boston	1989	Joe Dumars, Detroit
1977	Bill Walton, Portland	1990	Isiah Thomas, Detroit
1978	Wes Unseld, Washington	1991	Michael Jordan, Chicago
1979	Dennis Johnson, Seattle	1992	Michael Jordan, Chicago
1980	Magic Johnson, Los Angeles	1993	Michael Jordan, Chicago
1981	Cedric Maxwell, Boston	1994	Hakeem Olajuwon, Houston

1995	Hakeem Olajuwon, Houston
1996	Michael Jordan, Chicago
1997	Michael Jordan, Chicago
1998	Michael Jordan, Chicago
1999	Tim Duncan, San Antonio
2000	Shaquille O'Neal, L.A. Lakers
2001	Shaquille O'Neal, L.A. Lakers
2002	Shaquille O'Neal, L.A. Lakers
2003	Tim Duncan, San Antonio
2004	Chauncey Billups, Detroit
2005	Tim Duncan, San Antonio
2006	Dwyane Wade, Miami
2007	Tony Parker, San Antonio

NBA Finals All-Time Statistical Leaders

(At the end of the 2007 NBA Finals. *Player active in 2006-07 season.)

Scoring Average (Minimum 10 Games)

	G	FG	FT	Pts	Avg		G	FG	FT	Pts	Avg
Rick Barry	10	138	87	363	36.3	Hakeem Olajuwon	17	187	91	467	27.5
*Shaquille O'Neal	19	253	144	650	34.2	Elgin Baylor	44	442	277	1,161	26.4
Michael Jordan	35	438	258	1,176	33.6	Julius Erving	22	216	128	561	25.5
Jerry West	55	612	455	1,679	30.5	Joe Fulks	11	84	104	272	24.7
Bob Pettit	25	241	227	709	28.4	Clyde Drexler	15	126	108	367	24.5

Games Played

Bill Russell	70
Sam Jones	64
Kareem Abdul-Jabbar	56
Jerry West	55
Tom Heinsohn	52

Rebounds

Bill Russell	1,718
Wilt Chamberlain	862
Elgin Baylor	593
Kareem Abdul-Jabbar	507
Tom Heinsohn	473

Assists

Magic Johnson	584
Bob Cousy	400
Bill Russell	315
Jerry West	306
Dennis Johnson	228

NBA Scoring Leaders

Year	Scoring Champion	Pts	Avg	Year	Scoring Champion	Pts	Avg
1947	Joe Fulks, Philadelphia	1,389	23.2	1978	George Gervin, San Antonio	2,232	27.2
1948	Max Zaslofsky, Chicago	1,007	21.0	1979	George Gervin, San Antonio	2,365	29.6
1949	George Mikan, Minneapolis	1,698	28.3	1980	George Gervin, San Antonio	2,585	33.1
1950	George Mikan, Minneapolis	1,865	27.4	1981	Adrian Dantley, Utah	2,452	30.7
1951	George Mikan, Minneapolis	1,932	28.4	1982	George Gervin, San Antonio	2,551	32.3
1952	Paul Arizin, Philadelphia	1,674	25.4	1983	Alex English, Denver	2,326	28.4
1953	Neil Johnston, Philadelphia	1,564	22.3	1984	Adrian Dantley, Utah	2,418	30.6
1954	Neil Johnston, Philadelphia	1,759	24.4	1985	Bernard King, New York	1,809	32.9
1955	Neil Johnston, Philadelphia	1,631	22.7	1986	Dominique Wilkins, Atlanta	2,366	30.3
1956	Bob Pettit, St. Louis	1,849	25.7	1987	Michael Jordan, Chicago	3,041	37.1
1957	Paul Arizin, Philadelphia	1,817	25.6	1988	Michael Jordan, Chicago	2,868	35.0
1958	George Yardley, Detroit	2,001	27.8	1989	Michael Jordan, Chicago	2,633	32.5
1959	Bob Pettit, St. Louis	2,105	29.2	1990	Michael Jordan, Chicago	2,753	33.6
1960	Wilt Chamberlain, Philadelphia	2,707	37.9	1991	Michael Jordan, Chicago	2,580	31.5
1961	Wilt Chamberlain, Philadelphia	3,033	38.4	1992	Michael Jordan, Chicago	2,404	30.1
1962	Wilt Chamberlain, Philadelphia	4,029	50.4	1993	Michael Jordan, Chicago	2,541	32.6
1963	Wilt Chamberlain, San Francisco	3,586	44.8	1994	David Robinson, San Antonio	2,383	29.8
1964	Wilt Chamberlain, San Francisco	2,948	36.5	1995	Shaquille O'Neal, Orlando	2,315	29.3
1965	Wilt Chamberlain, San Francisco, Phil.	2,534	34.7	1996	Michael Jordan, Chicago	2,465	30.4
1966	Wilt Chamberlain, Philadelphia	2,649	33.5	1997	Michael Jordan, Chicago	2,431	29.6
1967	Rick Barry, San Francisco	2,775	35.6	1998	Michael Jordan, Chicago	2,357	28.7
1968	Dave Bing, Detroit	2,142	27.1	1999	Allen Iverson, Philadelphia	1,284	26.8
1969	Elvin Hayes, San Diego	2,327	28.4	2000	Shaquille O'Neal, L.A. Lakers	2,344	29.7
1970	Jerry West, Los Angeles	2,309	31.2	2001	Allen Iverson, Philadelphia	2,207	31.1
1971	Lew Alcindor (Abdul-Jabbar), Milwaukee	2,596	31.7	2002	Allen Iverson, Philadelphia	1,883	31.4
1972	Kareem Abdul-Jabbar, Milwaukee	2,822	34.8	2003	Tracy McGrady, Orlando	2,407	32.1
1973	Nate Archibald, Kans. City-Omaha	2,719	34.0	2004	Tracy McGrady, Orlando	1,878	28.0
1974	Bob McAdoo, Buffalo	2,261	30.6	2005	Allen Iverson, Philadelphia	2,302	30.7
1975	Bob McAdoo, Buffalo	2,831	34.5	2006	Kobe Bryant, L.A. Lakers	2,832	35.4
1976	Bob McAdoo, Buffalo	2,427	31.1	2007	Kobe Bryant, L.A. Lakers	2,430	31.6
1977	Pete Maravich, New Orleans	2,273	31.1				

NBA Most Valuable Player

1956	Bob Pettit, St. Louis	1961	Bill Russell, Boston	1966	Wilt Chamberlain, Philadelphia
1957	Bob Cousy, Boston	1962	Bill Russell, Boston	1967	Wilt Chamberlain, Philadelphia
1958	Bill Russell, Boston	1963	Bill Russell, Boston	1968	Wilt Chamberlain, Philadelphia
1959	Bob Pettit, St. Louis	1964	Oscar Robertson, Cincinnati	1969	Wes Unseld, Baltimore
1960	Wilt Chamberlain, Philadelphia	1965	Bill Russell, Boston	1970	Willis Reed, New York

1971 Lew Alcindor (Abdul-Jabbar), Milw.	1984 Larry Bird, Boston	1996 Michael Jordan, Chicago
1972 Kareem Abdul-Jabbar, Milwaukee	1985 Larry Bird, Boston	1997 Karl Malone, Utah
1973 Dave Cowens, Boston	1986 Larry Bird, Boston	1998 Michael Jordan, Chicago
1974 Kareem Abdul-Jabbar, Milwaukee	1987 Magic Johnson, L.A. Lakers	1999 Karl Malone, Utah
1975 Bob McAdoo, Buffalo	1988 Michael Jordan, Chicago	2000 Shaquille O'Neal, L.A. Lakers
1976 Kareem Abdul-Jabbar, Los Angeles	1989 Magic Johnson, L.A. Lakers	2001 Allen Iverson, Philadelphia
1977 Kareem Abdul-Jabbar, Los Angeles	1990 Magic Johnson, L.A. Lakers	2002 Tim Duncan, San Antonio
1978 Bill Walton, Portland	1991 Michael Jordan, Chicago	2003 Tim Duncan, San Antonio
1979 Moses Malone, Houston	1992 Michael Jordan, Chicago	2004 Kevin Garnett, Minnesota
1980 Kareem Abdul-Jabbar, Los Angeles	1993 Charles Barkley, Phoenix	2005 Steve Nash, Phoenix
1981 Julius Erving, Philadelphia	1994 Hakeem Olajuwon, Houston	2006 Steve Nash, Phoenix
1982 Moses Malone, Houston	1995 David Robinson, San Antonio	2007 Dirk Nowitzki, Dallas
1983 Moses Malone, Philadelphia		

NBA Champions, 1947-2007

Year	Eastern Conference	Western Conference	Champion	Coach	Runner-Up
	Regular Season			Playoffs	
1947	Washington Capitols	Chicago Stags	Philadelphia	Ed Gottlieb	Chicago
1948	Philadelphia Warriors	St. Louis Bombers	Baltimore	Buddy Jeannette	Philadelphia
1949	Washington Capitols	Rochester	Minneapolis	John Kundla	Washington
1950	Syracuse	Minneapolis	Minneapolis	John Kundla	Syracuse
1951	Philadelphia Warriors	Minneapolis	Rochester	Lester Harrison	New York
1952	Syracuse	Rochester	Minneapolis	John Kundla	New York
1953	New York	Minneapolis	Minneapolis	John Kundla	New York
1954	New York	Minneapolis	Minneapolis	John Kundla	Syracuse
1955	Syracuse	Ft. Wayne	Syracuse	Al Cervi	Ft. Wayne
1956	Philadelphia Warriors	Ft. Wayne	Philadelphia	George Senesky	St. Louis
1957	Boston	St. Louis	Boston	Red Auerbach	St. Louis
1958	Boston	St. Louis	St. Louis	Alex Hannum	Boston
1959	Boston	St. Louis	Boston	Red Auerbach	Minneapolis
1960	Boston	St. Louis	Boston	Red Auerbach	St. Louis
1961	Boston	St. Louis	Boston	Red Auerbach	St. Louis
1962	Boston	Los Angeles	Boston	Red Auerbach	Los Angeles
1963	Boston	Los Angeles	Boston	Red Auerbach	Los Angeles
1964	Boston	San Francisco	Boston	Red Auerbach	San Francisco
1965	Boston	Los Angeles	Boston	Red Auerbach	Los Angeles
1966	Philadelphia	Los Angeles	Boston	Red Auerbach	Los Angeles
1967	Philadelphia	San Francisco	Philadelphia	Alex Hannum	San Francisco
1968	Philadelphia	St. Louis	Boston	Bill Russell	Los Angeles
1969	Baltimore	Los Angeles	Boston	Bill Russell	Los Angeles
1970	New York	Atlanta	New York	Red Holzman	Los Angeles

Year	Atlantic	Central	Midwest	Pacific	Champion	Coach	Runner-Up
1971	New York	Baltimore	Milwaukee	Los Angeles	Milwaukee	Larry Costello	Baltimore
1972	Boston	Baltimore	Milwaukee	Los Angeles	Los Angeles	Bill Sharman	New York
1973	Boston	Baltimore	Milwaukee	Los Angeles	New York	Red Holzman	Los Angeles
1974	Boston	Capital	Milwaukee	Los Angeles	Boston	Tom Heinsohn	Milwaukee
1975	Boston	Washington	Chicago	Golden State	Golden State	Al Attles	Washington
1976	Boston	Cleveland	Milwaukee	Golden State	Boston	Tom Heinsohn	Phoenix
1977	Philadelphia	Houston	Denver	Los Angeles	Portland	Jack Ramsay	Philadelphia
1978	Philadelphia	San Antonio	Denver	Portland	Washington	Dick Motta	Seattle
1979	Washington	San Antonio	Kansas City	Seattle	Seattle	Len Wilkens	Washington
1980	Boston	Atlanta	Milwaukee	Los Angeles	Los Angeles	Paul Westhead	Philadelphia
1981	Boston	Milwaukee	San Antonio	Phoenix	Boston	Bill Fitch	Houston
1982	Boston	Milwaukee	San Antonio	Los Angeles	Los Angeles	Pat Riley	Philadelphia
1983	Philadelphia	Milwaukee	San Antonio	Los Angeles	Philadelphia	Billy Cunningham	Los Angeles
1984	Boston	Milwaukee	Utah	Los Angeles	Boston	K.C. Jones	Los Angeles
1985	Boston	Milwaukee	Denver	L.A. Lakers	L.A. Lakers	Pat Riley	Boston
1986	Boston	Milwaukee	Houston	L.A. Lakers	Boston	K.C. Jones	Houston
1987	Boston	Atlanta	Dallas	L.A. Lakers	L.A. Lakers	Pat Riley	Boston
1988	Boston	Detroit	Denver	L.A. Lakers	L.A. Lakers	Pat Riley	Detroit
1989	New York	Detroit	Utah	L.A. Lakers	Detroit	Chuck Daly	L.A. Lakers
1990	Philadelphia	Detroit	San Antonio	L.A. Lakers	Detroit	Chuck Daly	Portland
1991	Boston	Chicago	San Antonio	Portland	Chicago	Phil Jackson	L.A. Lakers
1992	Boston	Chicago	Utah	Portland	Chicago	Phil Jackson	Portland
1993	New York	Chicago	Houston	Phoenix	Chicago	Phil Jackson	Phoenix
1994	New York	Atlanta	Houston	Seattle	Houston	Rudy Tomjanovich	New York
1995	Orlando	Indiana	San Antonio	Phoenix	Houston	Rudy Tomjanovich	Orlando
1996	Orlando	Chicago	San Antonio	Seattle	Chicago	Phil Jackson	Seattle
1997	Miami	Chicago	Utah	Seattle	Chicago	Phil Jackson	Utah
1998	Miami	Chicago	Utah	L.A. Lakers	Chicago	Phil Jackson	Utah
1999	Miami	Indiana	San Antonio	Portland	San Antonio	Gregg Popovich	New York
2000	Miami	Indiana	Utah	L.A. Lakers	L.A. Lakers	Phil Jackson	Indiana
2001	Philadelphia	Milwaukee	San Antonio	L.A. Lakers	L.A. Lakers	Phil Jackson	Philadelphia
2002	New Jersey	Detroit	San Antonio	Sacramento	L.A. Lakers	Phil Jackson	New Jersey
2003	New Jersey	Detroit	San Antonio	Sacramento	San Antonio	Gregg Popovich	L.A. Lakers
2004	New Jersey	Indiana	Minnesota	L.A. Lakers	Detroit	Larry Brown	L.A. Lakers

Year	Atlantic	Central	Southeast	Northwest	Pacific	Southwest	Champion	Coach	Runner-Up
2005	Boston	Detroit	Miami	Seattle	Phoenix	San Antonio	San Antonio	Gregg Popovich	Detroit
2006	New Jersey	Detroit	Miami	Denver	Phoenix	San Antonio	Miami	Pat Riley	Dallas
2007	Toronto	Detroit	Miami	Utah	Phoenix	Dallas	San Antonio	Gregg Popovich	Cleveland

All-NBA and All-Defensive Teams, 2006-07

All-NBA Team		Position	All-Defensive Team	
First Team	Second Team		First Team	Second Team
Dirk Nowitzki, Dallas	LeBron James, Cleveland	Forward	Bruce Bowen, San Antonio	Tayshaun Prince, Detroit
Tim Duncan, San Antonio	Chris Bosh, Toronto	Forward	Tim Duncan, San Antonio	Kevin Garnett, Minnesota
Amare Stoudemire, Pheonix	Yao Ming, Houston	Center	Marcus Camby, Denver	Ben Wallace, Chicago
Steve Nash, Phoenix	Gilbert Arenas, Washington	Guard	Kobe Bryant, L.A. Lakers	Jason Kidd, New Jersey
Kobe Bryant, L.A. Lakers	Tracy McGrady, Houston	Guard	Raja Bell, Phoenix	Kirk Hinrich, Chicago

NBA Coach of the Year, 1963-2007

Year	Coach	Year	Coach	Year	Coach
1963	Harry Gallatin, St. Louis	1978	Hubie Brown, Atlanta	1993	Pat Riley, New York
1964	Alex Hannum, San Francisco	1979	Cotton Fitzsimmons, Kansas City	1994	Lenny Wilkens, Atlanta
1965	Red Auerbach, Boston	1980	Bill Fitch, Boston	1995	Del Harris, L.A. Lakers
1966	Dolph Schayes, Philadelphia	1981	Jack McKinney, Indiana	1996	Phil Jackson, Chicago
1967	Johnny Kerr, Chicago	1982	Gene Shue, Washington	1997	Pat Riley, Miami
1968	Richie Guerin, St. Louis	1983	Don Nelson, Milwaukee	1998	Larry Bird, Indiana
1969	Gene Shue, Baltimore	1984	Frank Layden, Utah	1999	Mike Dunleavy, Portland
1970	Red Holzman, New York	1985	Don Nelson, Milwaukee	2000	Glenn "Doc" Rivers, Orlando
1971	Dick Motta, Chicago	1986	Mike Fratello, Atlanta	2001	Larry Brown, Philadelphia
1972	Bill Sharman, L.A. Lakers	1987	Mike Schuler, Portland	2002	Rick Carlisle, Detroit
1973	Tom Heinsohn, Boston	1988	Doug Moe, Denver	2003	Gregg Popovich, San Antonio
1974	Ray Scott, Detroit	1989	Cotton Fitzsimmons, Phoenix	2004	Hubie Brown, Memphis
1975	Phil Johnson, Kansas City-Omaha	1990	Pat Riley, L.A. Lakers	2005	Mike D'Antoni, Phoenix
1976	Bill Fitch, Cleveland	1991	Don Chaney, Houston	2006	Avery Johnson, Dallas
1977	Tom Nissalke, Houston	1992	Don Nelson, Golden State	2007	Sam Mitchell, Toronto

NBA Statistical Leaders, 2006-07

Scoring Average
(Minimum 70 games or 1,400 pts)

	G	FG	FT	Pts	Avg
Kobe Bryant, L.A. Lakers	77	813	667	2,430	31.6
Carmelo Anthony, Denver	65	691	459	1,881	28.9
Gilbert Arenas, Washington	74	647	606	2,105	28.4
LeBron James, Cleveland	78	772	489	2,132	27.3
Michael Redd, Milwaukee	53	477	345	1,416	26.7
Ray Allen, Seattle	55	505	279	1,454	26.4
Allen Iverson, Denver-Philadelphia	65	581	485	1,709	26.3
Vince Carter, New Jersey	82	726	462	2,070	25.2
Joe Johnson, Atlanta	57	536	235	1,426	25.0
Tracy McGrady, Houston	71	638	345	1,747	24.6
Dirk Nowitzki, Dallas	78	673	498	1,916	24.6

3-Point Field Goal Percentage
(Minimum 55 3-point field goals made)

	3-FGM	3-FGA	Pct
Jason Kapono, Miami	108	210	0.514
Steve Nash, Phoenix	156	343	0.455
Brent Barry, San Antonio	128	287	0.446
Luther Head, Houston	177	401	0.441
Anthony Parker, Toronto	115	261	0.441
Jason Terry, Dallas	162	370	0.438
Leandro Barbosa, Phoenix	190	438	0.434
Al Harrington, Golden State-Indianapolis	127	293	0.433
Kyle Korver, Philadelphia	132	307	0.430
Eddie House, New Jersey	75	175	0.429

Field Goal Percentage
(Minimum 300 field goals made)

	FGM	FGA	Pct
Mikki Moore, New Jersey	308	506	0.609
Dwight Howard, Orlando	526	873	0.603
Andris Biedrins, Golden State	348	581	0.599
Eddy Curry, New York	585	1,016	0.576
Amare Stoudemire, Phoenix	607	1,055	0.575
Carlos Boozer, Utah	647	1,154	0.561
Andrew Bogut, Milwaukee	348	629	0.553
Ruben Patterson, Milwaukee	475	867	0.548
Tim Duncan, San Antonio	618	1,131	0.546
Samuel Dalembert, Philadelphia	356	658	0.541

Free Throw Percentage
(Minimum 125 free throws made)

	FTM	FTA	Pct
Kyle Korver, Philadelphia	191	209	0.914
Matt Carroll, Charlotte	188	208	0.904
Dirk Nowitzki, Dallas	498	551	0.904
Ray Allen, Seattle	279	309	0.903
Steve Nash, Phoenix	222	247	0.899
Earl Boykins, Milwaukee-Denver	220	245	0.898
Tyronn Lue, Atlanta	144	163	0.883
Chauncey Billups, Detroit	386	437	0.883
Damien Wilkins, Seattle	150	170	0.882
Sam Cassell, L.A. Clippers	160	182	0.879

Rebounds per Game
(Minimum 70 games or 800 rebounds)

	G	Off	Def	Tot	Avg
Kevin Garnett, Minnesota	76	183	792	975	12.8
Tyson Chandler, New Orleans/Oklahoma City	73	320	584	904	12.4
Dwight Howard, Orlando	82	283	725	1,008	12.3
Carlos Boozer, Utah	74	235	632	867	11.7
Marcus Camby, Denver	70	164	652	816	11.7
Ben Wallace, Chicago	77	303	518	821	10.7
Tim Duncan, San Antonio	80	213	632	845	10.6
Shawn Marion, Phoenix	80	172	613	785	9.8
Amare Stoudemire, Phoenix	82	222	564	786	9.6
Elton Brand, L.A. Clippers	80	268	476	744	9.3
Andris Biedrins, Golden State	82	251	511	762	9.3

Assists per Game
(Minimum 70 games or 400 assists)

	G	Ast	Avg
Steve Nash, Phoenix	76	884	11.6
Deron Williams, Utah	80	745	9.3
Jason Kidd, New Jersey	80	736	9.2
Chris Paul, New Orleans/Oklahoma City	64	569	8.9
Baron Davis, Golden State	63	509	8.1
T.J. Ford, Toronto	75	595	7.9
Andre Miller, Philadelphia-Denver	80	625	7.8
Allen Iverson, Denver-Philadelphia	65	468	7.2
Chauncey Billups, Detroit	70	502	7.2
Raymond Felton, Charlotte	78	545	7.0

Steals per Game
(Minimum 70 games or 125 steals)

	G	Stl	Avg
Baron Davis, Golden State	63	135	2.14
Ron Artest, Sacramento	70	149	2.13
Caron Butler, Washington	63	134	2.13
Andre Iguodala, Philadelphia	76	152	2.00
Gerald Wallace, Charlotte	72	144	2.00
Shawn Marion, Phoenix	80	156	1.95
Gilbert Arenas, Washington	74	139	1.88
Monta Ellis, Golden State	77	132	1.71
Rajon Rondo, Boston	78	128	1.64
Jamaal Tinsley, Indianapolis	72	117	1.63

Blocked Shots per Game
(Minimum 70 games or 100 blocked shots)

	G	Blk	Avg
Marcus Camby, Denver	70	231	3.30
Josh Smith, Atlanta	72	207	2.88
Jermaine O'Neal, Indianapolis	69	182	2.64
Emeka Okafor, Charlotte	67	172	2.57
Tim Duncan, San Antonio	80	190	2.38
Alonzo Mourning, Miami	77	178	2.31
Elton Brand, L.A. Clippers	80	179	2.24
Pau Gasol, Memphis	59	126	2.14
Andrei Kirilenko, Utah	70	144	2.06
Ben Wallace, Chicago	77	156	2.03

NBA Defensive Player of the Year

1983	Sidney Moncrief, Milwaukee	1992	David Robinson, San Antonio	2001	Dikembe Mutombo, Philadelphia-Atlanta
1984	Sidney Moncrief, Milwaukee	1993	Hakeem Olajuwon, Houston	2002	Ben Wallace, Detroit
1985	Mark Eaton, Utah	1994	Hakeem Olajuwon, Houston	2003	Ben Wallace, Detroit
1986	Alvin Robertson, San Antonio	1995	Dikembe Mutombo, Denver	2004	Ron Artest, Indiana
1987	Michael Cooper, L.A. Lakers	1996	Gary Payton, Seattle	2005	Ben Wallace, Detroit
1988	Michael Jordan, Chicago	1997	Dikembe Mutombo, Atlanta	2006	Ben Wallace, Detroit
1989	Mark Eaton, Utah	1998	Dikembe Mutombo, Atlanta	2007	Marcus Camby, Denver
1990	Dennis Rodman, Detroit	1999	Alonzo Mourning, Miami		
1991	Dennis Rodman, Detroit	2000	Alonzo Mourning, Miami		

NBA Rookie of the Year

1953	Don Meineke, Ft. Wayne	1972	Sidney Wicks, Portland	1991	Derrick Coleman, New Jersey
1954	Ray Felix, Baltimore	1973	Bob McAdoo, Buffalo	1992	Larry Johnson, Charlotte
1955	Bob Pettit, Milwaukee	1974	Ernie DiGregorio, Buffalo	1993	Shaquille O'Neal, Orlando
1956	Maurice Stokes, Rochester	1975	Keith Wilkes, Golden State	1994	Chris Webber, Golden State
1957	Tom Heinsohn, Boston	1976	Alvan Adams, Phoenix	1995	Grant Hill, Detroit;
1958	Woody Sauldsberry, Philadelphia	1977	Adrian Dantley, Buffalo		Jason Kidd, Dallas (tie)
1959	Elgin Baylor, Minneapolis	1978	Walter Davis, Phoenix	1996	Damon Stoudamire, Toronto
1960	Wilt Chamberlain, Philadelphia	1979	Phil Ford, Kansas City	1997	Allen Iverson, Philadelphia
1961	Oscar Robertson, Cincinnati	1980	Larry Bird, Boston	1998	Tim Duncan, San Antonio
1962	Walt Bellamy, Chicago	1981	Darrell Griffith, Utah	1999	Vince Carter, Toronto
1963	Terry Dischinger, Chicago	1982	Buck Williams, New Jersey	2000	Elton Brand, Chicago;
1964	Jerry Lucas, Cincinnati	1983	Terry Cummings, San Diego		Steve Francis, Houston (tie)
1965	Willis Reed, New York	1984	Ralph Sampson, Houston	2001	Mike Miller, Orlando
1966	Rick Barry, San Francisco	1985	Michael Jordan, Chicago	2002	Pau Gasol, Memphis
1967	Dave Bing, Detroit	1986	Patrick Ewing, New York	2003	Amare Stoudemire, Phoenix
1968	Earl Monroe, Baltimore	1987	Chuck Person, Indiana	2004	LeBron James, Cleveland
1969	Wes Unseld, Baltimore	1988	Mark Jackson, New York	2005	Emeka Okafor, Charlotte
1970	Lew Alcindor (Abdul-Jabbar), Milw.	1989	Mitch Richmond, Golden State	2006	Chris Paul, New Or./Okla. City
1971	Dave Cowens, Boston;	1990	David Robinson, San Antonio	2007	Brandon Roy, Portland
	Geoff Petrie, Portland (tie)				

NBA Sixth Man Award

1983	Bobby Jones, Philadelphia	1992	Detlef Schrempf, Indiana	2000	Rodney Rogers, Phoenix
1984	Kevin McHale, Boston	1993	Clifford Robinson, Portland	2001	Aaron McKie, Philadelphia
1985	Kevin McHale, Boston	1994	Dell Curry, Charlotte	2002	Corliss Williamson, Detroit
1986	Bill Walton, Boston	1995	Anthony Mason, New York	2003	Bobby Jackson, Sacramento
1987	Ricky Pierce, Milwaukee	1996	Toni Kukoc, Chicago	2004	Antawn Jamison, Dallas
1988	Roy Tarpley, Dallas	1997	John Starks, New York	2005	Ben Gordon, Chicago
1989	Eddie Johnson, Phoenix	1998	Danny Manning, Phoenix	2006	Mike Miller, Memphis
1990	Ricky Pierce, Milwaukee	1999	Darrell Armstrong, Orlando	2007	Leandro Barbosa, Phoenix
1991	Detlef Schrempf, Indiana				

2007 NBA Player Draft, First-Round Picks
(Held June 28, 2007)

	Team	Player, College/Team		Team	Player, College/Team
1.	Portland	Greg Oden, Center, Ohio State	16.	Washington	Nick Young, Guard/Forward, Southern California
2.	Seattle	Kevin Durant, Forward, Texas	17.	New Jersey	Sean Williams, Forward/Center, Boston College
3.	Atlanta	Al Horford, Forward/Center, Florida	18.	Golden State	Marco Belinelli, Guard, Italy
4.	Memphis	Mike Conley Jr., Guard, Ohio State	19.	L.A. Lakers	Javaris Crittenton, Guard, Georgia Tech
5.	Boston	Jeff Green, Forward, Georgetown[1]	20.	Miami	Jason Smith, Forward/Center, Colorado State[6]
6.	Milwaukee	Yi Jianlian, Forward, China	21.	Philadelphia[7]	Daequan Cook, Guard, Ohio State[8]
7.	Minnesota	Corey Brewer, Forward, Florida	22.	Charlotte[9]	Jared Dudley, Forward, Boston College
8.	Charlotte	Brandan Wright, Forward, North Carolina[2]	23.	New York[10]	Wilson Chandler, Forward, DePaul
9.	Chicago[3]	Joakim Noah, Forward/Center, Florida	24.	Phoenix[11]	Rudy Fernandez, Guard, Spain[12]
10.	Sacramento	Spencer Hawes, Center, Washington	25.	Utah	Morris Almond, Guard, Rice
11.	Atlanta[4]	Acie Law IV, Guard, Texas A&M	26.	Houston	Aaron Brooks, Guard, Oregon
12.	Philadelphia	Thaddeus Young, Forward, Georgia Tech	27.	Detroit	Arron Afflalo, Guard, UCLA
13.	New Orleans	Julian Wright, Forward, Kansas	28.	San Antonio	Tiago Splitter, Forward, Brazil
14.	Los Angeles	Al Thornton, Forward, Florida State	29.	Phoenix	Alando Tucker, Forward, Wisconsin
15.	Detroit[5]	Rodney Stuckey, Guard, Eastern Washington	30.	Philadelphia[13]	Petteri Koponen, Guard, Finland[14]

(1) Rights traded to Seattle. (2) Rights traded to Golden State. (3) From New York. (4) From Indiana. (5) From Orlando. (6) Rights traded to Philadelphia. (7) From Denver. (8) Rights traded to Miami. (9) From Toronto. (10) From Chicago. (11) From Cleveland. (12) Rights traded to Portland. (13) From Dallas. (14) Rights traded to Portland.

Number-One First-Round NBA Draft Picks, 1966-2007

Year	Team	Player, College/Team	Year	Team	Player, College/Team
1966	New York	Cazzie Russell, Michigan	1987	San Antonio	David Robinson, Navy
1967	Detroit	Jimmy Walker, Providence	1988	L.A. Clippers	Danny Manning, Kansas
1968	San Diego	Elvin Hayes, Houston	1989	Sacramento	Pervis Ellison, Louisville
1969	Milwaukee	Lew Alcindor (Kareem Abdul-Jabbar), UCLA	1990	New Jersey	Derrick Coleman, Syracuse
			1991	Charlotte	Larry Johnson, UNLV
1970	Detroit	Bob Lanier, St. Bonaventure	1992	Orlando	Shaquille O'Neal, LSU
1971	Cleveland	Austin Carr, Notre Dame	1993	Orlando	Chris Webber[2], Michigan
1972	Portland	LaRue Martin, Loyola-Chicago	1994	Milwaukee	Glenn Robinson, Purdue
1973	Philadelphia	Doug Collins, Illinois State	1995	Golden State	Joe Smith, Maryland
1974	Portland	Bill Walton, UCLA	1996	Philadelphia	Allen Iverson, Georgetown
1975	Atlanta	David Thompson[1], N.C. State	1997	San Antonio	Tim Duncan, Wake Forest
1976	Houston	John Lucas, Maryland	1998	L.A. Clippers	Michael Olowokandi, Pacific
1977	Milwaukee	Kent Benson, Indiana	1999	Chicago	Elton Brand, Duke
1978	Portland	Mychal Thompson, Minnesota	2000	New Jersey	Kenyon Martin, Cincinnati
1979	L.A. Lakers	Earvin "Magic" Johnson, Michigan State	2001	Washington	Kwame Brown, Glynn Academy (HS)
1980	Golden State	Joe Barry Carroll, Purdue	2002	Houston	Yao Ming, Shanghai Sharks (China)
1981	Dallas	Mark Aguirre, DePaul	2003	Cleveland	LeBron James, St. Vincent-St. Mary (HS)
1982	L.A. Lakers	James Worthy, North Carolina	2004	Orlando	Dwight Howard, Southwest Atlanta Christian Academy (HS)
1983	Houston	Ralph Sampson, Virginia			
1984	Houston	Akeem Olajuwon, Houston	2005	Milwaukee	Andrew Bogut, Utah
1985	New York	Patrick Ewing, Georgetown	2006	Toronto	Andrea Bargnani, Benneton Treviso (Italy)
1986	Cleveland	Brad Daugherty, North Carolina	2007	Portland	Greg Oden, Ohio State

(1) Signed with Denver of the ABA. (2) Traded to Golden State for rights to Anfernee Hardaway and three future first-round draft choices.

All-Time NBA Statistical Leaders

(At the end of the 2006-07 season. *Player active in 2006-07 season.)

Scoring Average
(Minimum 400 games or 10,000 points)

	G	Pts	Avg
Michael Jordan	1,072	32,292	30.1
Wilt Chamberlain	1,045	31,419	30.1
*Allen Iverson	747	20,824	27.9
Elgin Baylor	846	23,149	27.4
Jerry West	932	25,192	27.0
Bob Pettit	792	20,880	26.4
George Gervin	791	20,708	26.2
*Shaquille O'Neal	981	25,454	25.9
Oscar Robertson	1,040	26,710	25.7
Karl Malone	1,476	36,928	25.0

Field Goal Percentage
(Minimum 2,000 field goals made)

	FGA	FGM	Pct
Artis Gilmore	9,570	5,732	.599
Mark West	4,356	2,528	.580
*Shaquille O'Neal	17,394	10,091	.580
Steve Johnson	4,965	2,841	.572
Darryl Dawkins	6,079	3,477	.572
James Donaldson	5,442	3,105	.571
*Bo Outlaw	3,531	2,003	.567
Jeff Ruland	3,734	2,105	.564
Kareem Abdul-Jabbar	28,307	15,837	.559
Kevin McHale	12,334	6,830	.554

Free Throw Percentage
(Minimum 1,200 free throws made)

	FTA	FTM	Pct
Mark Price	2,362	2,135	.904
Rick Barry	4,243	3,818	.900
*Steve Nash	2,173	1,948	.896
*Peja Stojakovic	2,124	1,895	.892
Calvin Murphy	3,864	3,445	.892
Scott Skiles	1,741	1,548	.889
*Ray Allen	3,582	3,180	.888
Reggie Miller	7,026	6,237	.888
Larry Bird	4,471	3,960	.886
Bill Sharman	3,559	3,143	.883

3-Point Field Goal Percentage
(Minimum 250 3-point field goals made)

	3-FGA	3-FGM	Pct
Steve Kerr	1,599	726	.454
Hubert Davis	1,651	728	.441
Drazen Petrovic	583	255	.437
Tim Legler	603	260	.431
*Steve Nash	2,521	1,073	.426
B. J. Armstrong	1,026	436	.425
*Ben Gordon	1,088	455	.418
*Leandro Barbosa	983	411	.418
Wesley Person	2,754	1,150	.418
*Kyle Korver	1,510	623	.413

Games Played

Robert Parish	1,611
Kareem Abdul-Jabbar	1,560
John Stockton	1,504
Karl Malone	1,476
*Kevin Willis	1,424
Reggie Miller	1,389
*Clifford Robinson	1,380
*Gary Payton	1,335
Moses Malone	1,329
Buck Williams	1,307

Field Goals Attempted

Kareem Abdul-Jabbar	28,307
Karl Malone	26,210
Michael Jordan	24,537
Elvin Hayes	24,272
John Havlicek	23,930
Wilt Chamberlain	23,497
Dominique Wilkins	21,589
Alex English	21,036
Hakeem Olajuwon	20,991
Elgin Baylor	20,171

Points

Kareem Abdul-Jabbar	38,387
Karl Malone	36,928
Michael Jordan	32,292
Wilt Chamberlain	31,419
Moses Malone	27,409
Elvin Hayes	27,313
Hakeem Olajuwon	26,946
Oscar Robertson	26,710
Dominique Wilkins	26,668
John Havlicek	26,395

Minutes Played

Kareem Abdul-Jabbar	57,446
Karl Malone	54,852
Elvin Hayes	50,000
Wilt Chamberlain	47,859
John Stockton	47,764
Reggie Miller	47,619
*Gary Payton	47,117
John Havlicek	46,471
Robert Parish	45,704
Moses Malone	45,071

Field Goals Made

Kareem Abdul-Jabbar	15,837
Karl Malone	13,528
Wilt Chamberlain	12,681
Michael Jordan	12,192
Elvin Hayes	10,976
Hakeem Olajuwon	10,749
Alex English	10,659
John Havlicek	10,513
*Shaquille O'Neal	10,091
Dominique Wilkins	9,963

Rebounds

Wilt Chamberlain	23,924
Bill Russell	21,620
Kareem Abdul-Jabbar	17,440
Elvin Hayes	16,279
Moses Malone	16,212
Karl Malone	14,968
Robert Parish	14,715
Nate Thurmond	14,464
Walt Bellamy	14,241
Wes Unseld	13,769

Personal Fouls

Kareem Abdul-Jabbar	4,657
Karl Malone	4,578
Robert Parish	4,443
Charles Oakley	4,421
Hakeem Olajuwon	4,383
Buck Williams	4,267
Elvin Hayes	4,193
*Clifford Robinson	4,176
*Kevin Willis	4,172
Otis Thorpe	4,146

3-Point Field Goals Attempted

Reggie Miller	6,486
*Ray Allen	4,839
Tim Hardaway	4,345
Nick Van Exel	4,278
Dale Ellis	4,266
*Antoine Walker	4,076
*Eddie Jones	4,031
Vernon Maxwell	3,931
Glen Rice	3,896
Mookie Blaylock	3,816

Assists

John Stockton	15,806
Mark Jackson	10,334
Magic Johnson	10,141
Oscar Robertson	9,887
Isiah Thomas	9,061
*Gary Payton	8,966
*Jason Kidd	8,691
Rod Strickland	7,987
Maurice Cheeks	7,392
Lenny Wilkens	7,211

Blocks

Hakeem Olajuwon	3,830
*Dikembe Mutombo	3,230
Kareem Abdul-Jabbar	3,189
Mark Eaton	3,064
David Robinson	2,954
Patrick Ewing	2,894
Tree Rollins	2,542
*Shaquille O'Neal	2,432
Robert Parish	2,361
*Alonzo Mourning	2,314

3-Point Field Goals Made

Reggie Miller	2,560
*Ray Allen	1,920
Dale Ellis	1,719
Glen Rice	1,559
Tim Hardaway	1,542
Nick Van Exel	1,528
*Eddie Jones	1,512
Dan Majerle	1,360
Mitch Richmond	1,326
*Antoine Walker	1,325

Steals

John Stockton	3,265
Michael Jordan	2,514
*Gary Payton	2,445
Maurice Cheeks	2,310
Scottie Pippen	2,307
Clyde Drexler	2,207
Hakeem Olajuwon	2,162
Alvin Robertson	2,112
Karl Malone	2,085
Mookie Blaylock	2,075

All-Time NBA Regular Season Coaching Victories

(At the end of the 2006-07 season, ranked by wins. *Active through 2006-07 season.)

Coach	W-L	Pct	Coach	W-L	Pct	Coach	W-L	Pct
Lenny Wilkens	1,332-1,155	.536	Dick Motta	935-1,017	.479	John MacLeod	707-657	.518
*Don Nelson	1,232-920	.572	*Phil Jackson	919-393	.700	Red Holzman	696-604	.535
*Pat Riley	1,195-627	.656	Jack Ramsay	864-783	.525	*Mike Fratello	667-548	.549
*Jerry Sloan	1,035-689	.600	Cotton Fitzsimmons	832-775	.518	Chuck Daly	638-437	.593
Larry Brown	1,010-800	.558	*George Karl	829-582	.588	Doug Moe	628-529	.543
Bill Fitch	944-1,106	.460	Gene Shue	784-861	.477	*Gregg Popovich	576-276	.676
Red Auerbach	938-479	.662	*Rick Adelman	752-481	.610			

Basketball Hall of Fame, Springfield, MA

(*2007 inductees. **Enshrined as both a player and coach.)

PLAYERS

Abdul-Jabbar, Kareem
Archibald, Nate
Arizin, Paul
Barkley, Charles
Barlow, Thomas
Barry, Rick
Baylor, Elgin
Beckman, John
Bellamy, Walt
Belov, Sergei
Bing, Dave
Bird, Larry
Blazejowski, Carol
Borgmann, Bennie
Bradley, Bill
Brennan, Joseph
Cervi, Al
Chamberlain, Wilt
Cooper, Charles
Cosic, Kresimir
Cousy, Bob
Cowens, Dave
Crawford, Joan
Cunningham, Billy
Curry, Denise
Dalipagic, Drazen
Davies, Bob
DeBernardi, Forrest
DeBusschere, Dave
Dehnert, Dutch
Donovan, Anne
Drexler, Clyde
Dumars, Joe
Endacott, Paul
English, Alex
Erving, Julius
Foster, Bud
Frazier, Walt
Friedman, Max
Fulks, Joe
Gale, Lauren
Gallatin, Harry
Gates, Pop
Gervin, George
Gola, Tom
Goodrich, Gail
Greer, Hal
Gruenig, Ace
Hagan, Cliff
Hanson, Victor
Harris-Stewart, Lusia
Havlicek, John
Hawkins, Connie
Hayes, Elvin
Haynes, Marques
Heinsohn, Tom
Holman, Nat

Houbregs, Bob
Howell, Bailey
Hyatt, Chuck
Issel, Dan
Jeannette, Harry "Buddy"
Johnson, Earvin "Magic"
Johnson, William
Johnston, Neil
Jones, K.C.
Jones, Sam
Krause, Moose
Kurland, Bob
Lanier, Bob
Lapchick, Joe
Lieberman, Nancy
Lovellette, Clyde
Lucas, Jerry
Luisetti, Angelo "Hank"
Macauley, Ed
Malone, Moses
Maravich, Pete
Marcari, Hortencia
Martin, Slater
McAdoo, Bob
McCracken, Branch
McCracken, Jack
McDermott, Bobby
McGuire, Dick
McHale, Kevin
Meneghin, Dino
Meyers, Ann
Mikan, George
Mikkelsen, Vern
Miller, Cheryl
Monroe, Earl
Murphy, Calvin
Murphy, Charles "Stretch"
Page, Harlan "Pat"
Parish, Robert
Petrovic, Drazen
Pettit, Bob
Phillip, Andy
Pollard, Jim
Ramsay, Frank
Reed, Willis
Risen, Arnie
Robertson, Oscar
Roosma, John
Russell, Bill
Russell, Honey
Schayes, Adolph
Schmidt, Ernest
Schommer, John
Sedran, Barney
Semjonova, Uljana
Steinmetz, Christian
Stokes, Maurice

Thomas, Isiah
Thompson, Cat
Thompson, David
Thurmond, Nate
Twyman, Jack
Unseld, Wes
Vandivier, Robert "Fuzzy"
Wachter, Edward
Walton, Bill
Wanzer, Bobby
West, Jerry
White, Nera
**Wilkens, Lenny
Wilkins, Dominique
Woodard, Lynette
**Wooden, John
Worthy, James
Yardley, George

COACHES

Allen, Forrest C. "Phog"
Anderson, Harold
Auerbach, Red
Auriemma, Geno
Barmore, Leon
Barry, Justin "Sam"
Blood, Ernest
Boeheim, Jim
Brown, Hubert "Hubie"
Brown, Larry
Calhoun, Jim
Cann, Howard
Carlson, Clifford
Carnesecca, Lou
Carnevale, Ben
Carril, Pete
Case, Everett
*Chancellor, Van
Chaney, John
Conradt, Jody
Crum, Denzil "Denny"
Daly, Chuck
Dean, Everett
Diaz-Miguel, Antonio
Diddle, Edgar
Drake, Bruce
*Ferrandiz, Pedro
Gaines, Clarence
Gamba, Sandro
Gardner, James "Jack"
Gill, Slats
Gomelsky, Aleksandr
Gunter, Sue
Hannum, Alex
Harshman, Marv
Haskins, Don
Hickey, Edgar
Hobson, Howard

Holzman, Red
Iba, Hank
*Jackson, Phil
Julian, Alvin
Keaney, Frank
Keogan, George
Knight, Bob
Krzyzewski, Mike
Kundla, John
Lambert, Ward
Litwack, Harry
Loeffler, Kenneth
Lonborg, Dutch
McCutchan, Arad
McGuire, Al
McGuire, Frank
McLendon, John
Meanwell, Dr. Walter
Meyer, Ray
Miller, Ralph
Moore, Billie
Newell, Pete
Nikolic, Aleksandar
*Novosel, Mirko
Olson, Lute
Ramsay, John "Jack"
Rubini, Cesare
Rupp, Adolph
Sachs, Leonard
**Sharman, Bill
Shelton, Everett
Smith, Dean
Summitt, Pat
Taylor, Fred
Thompson, John
Wade, Margaret
Watts, Stan
**Wilkens, Lenny
*Williams, Roy
**Wooden, John
Woolpert, Phil
Wootten, Morgan
Yow, Kay

TEAMS

Buffalo Germans
First Team
Harlem Globetrotters
New York Renaissance
Original Celtics
*Texas Western

REFEREES

Enright, James
Hepbron, George
Hoyt, George
Kennedy, Matthew
Leith, Lloyd
Mihalik, Red
Nucatola, John

Quigley, Ernest
*Rudolph, Marvin "Mendy"
Shirley, J. Dallas
Strom, Earl
Tobey, David
Walsh, David

CONTRIBUTORS

Abbott, Senda Berenson
Bee, Clair
Biasone, Danny
Brown, Walter
Bunn, John
Colangelo, Jerry
Douglas, Bob
Duer, Al
Embry, Wayne
Fagan, Cliff
Fisher, Harry
Fleisher, Larry
Gavitt, David
Gottlieb, Edward
Gulick, Dr. Luther
Harrison, Lester
Hearn, Chick
Hepp, Dr. Ferenc
Hickox, Edward
Hinkle, Tony
Irish, Edward "Ned"
Jones, R. William
Kennedy, Walter
Lemon, Meadowlark
Liston, Emil
Lloyd, Earl
Mokray, Bill
Morgan, Ralph
Morgenweck, Frank
Naismith, Dr. James
Newton, C.M.
O'Brien, John
O'Brien, Larry
Olsen, Harold
Podoloff, Maurice
Porter, Henry V.
Reid, William
Ripley, Elmer
St. John, Lynn
Saperstein, Abe
Schabinger, Arthur
Stagg, Alonzo
Stankovic, Boris
Steitz, Edward
Taylor, Chuck
Teague, Bertha
Tower, Oswald
Trester, Arthur
Wells, Clifford
Wilke, Lou
Zollner, Fred

NBA Home Courts[1]

Team	Name (built)	Capacity
Atlanta	Philips Arena (1999)	18,729
Boston	TD Banknorth Garden[2] (1995)	18,854
Charlotte	Charlotte Bobcats Arena (2005)	19,026
Chicago	United Center (1994)	21,711
Cleveland	Quicken Loans Arena (1994)	20,562
Dallas	American Airlines Center (2001)	19,200
Denver	Pepsi Center (1999)	19,155
Detroit	The Palace of Auburn Hills (1988)	22,076
Golden State	ORACLE Arena[3] (1966)	19,596
Houston	Toyota Center (2003)	18,300
Indiana	Conseco Fieldhouse (1999)	18,345
L.A. Clippers	Staples Center (1999)	18,997
L.A. Lakers	Staples Center (1999)	18,997
Memphis	FedExForum (2004)	18,400
Miami	American Airlines Arena (1999)	19,600
Milwaukee	Bradley Center (1988)	18,717
Minnesota	Target Center (1990)	19,006
New Jersey	Continental Airlines Arena[4] (1981)	19,968
New Orleans[5]	New Orleans Arena (1999)	18,000
New York	Madison Square Garden (IV) (1968)	19,763
Orlando	Amway Arena[6] (1989)	17,451
Philadelphia	Wachovia Center[7] (1996)	20,444
Phoenix	US Airways Center[8] (1992)	18,422
Portland	Rose Garden (1995)	19,980
Sacramento	ARCO Arena (1988)	17,317
San Antonio	AT&T Center[9] (2002)	18,500
Seattle	KeyArena at Seattle Center[10] (1962)	17,072
Toronto	Air Canada Centre (1999)	19,800
Utah	EnergySolutions Arena[11] (1991)	19,911
Washington	Verizon Center[12] (1997)	20,674

(1) At the end of the 2006-07 season. (2) Fleet Center, 1995-2005. (3) Oakland Coliseum Arena, 1966-96; Arena in Oakland, 1997-2006. (4) Brendan Byrne/Meadowlands Arena, 1981-96. (5) Because of damage to New Orleans Arena due to Hurricane Katrina, the Hornets played 35 games in the Ford Center (built 2002; capacity 19,599) in Oklahoma City, OK, 3 games in New Orleans Arena and 3 games at other locations during the 2005-06 season. In 2006-07, the Hornets played 35 games at the Ford Center and 6 games in New Orleans Arena. The Hornets are expected to play all 41 home games in 2007-08 in New Orleans Arena. (6) Orlando Arena, 1989-2000; TD Waterhouse Centre, 2006-07. (7) CoreStates Center, 1996-98; First Union Center, 1998-2003. (8) America West Arena, 1992-2006. (9) SBC Center, 2002-06. (10) Seattle Center Coliseum, 1962-94; renovated, expanded, and renamed in 1995. (11) Delta Center, 1991-2003. (12) MCI Center, 1997-2006.

WOMEN'S PROFESSIONAL BASKETBALL
Phoenix Mercury Overwhelm Detroit Shock for WNBA Title

The Phoenix Mercury defeated the defending champion Detroit Shock, 108-92, in Auburn Hills, MI, in the 5th and deciding game of the 2007 WNBA Finals, Sept. 16. The Mercury were the first team in WNBA history to claim the title on the road. Phoenix took an early lead and went up 20-9 during the middle of the first quarter, and held no less than a 9 point lead for the rest of the game. Phoenix guard Cappie Pondexter, in her second WNBA season, scored 26 points in the final game and was named the WNBA Finals MVP. Mercury coach Paul Westhead, who had coached the Los Angeles Lakers to the NBA championship in 1980, advocated a speedy "run-and-gun" offensive strategy for much of the season, making Phoenix the WNBA's highest scoring team in 2007. The Mercury's strategy contrasted with Detroit's more defense-minded approach, but by halftime, with the score favoring Phoenix 55-43, the teams had set a WNBA Finals record for combined points in a half.

WNBA 2007 Final Standings
x-clinched playoff berth; y-clinched top seed

Eastern Conference	W	L	Pct	GB	Western Conference	W	L	Pct	GB
y-Detroit Shock	24	10	0.706	—	y-Phoenix Mercury	23	11	0.676	—
x-Indiana Fever	21	13	0.618	3.0	x-San Antonio Silver Stars	20	14	0.588	3.0
x-Connecticut Sun	18	16	0.529	6.0	x-Sacramento Monarchs	19	15	0.559	4.0
x-New York Liberty	16	18	0.471	8.0	x-Seattle Storm	17	17	0.500	6.0
Washington Mystics	16	18	0.471	8.0	Houston Comets	13	21	0.382	10.0
Chicago Sky	14	20	0.412	10.0	Minnesota Lynx	10	24	0.294	13.0
					Los Angeles Sparks	10	24	0.294	13.0

2007 WNBA Playoffs
(Playoff seeding in parentheses; conference winner automatically gets top seed)

Eastern Conference
(1) Detroit defeated (4) New York, 2 games to 1
(2) Indiana defeated (3) Connecticut, 2 games to 1
(1) Detroit defeated (2) Indiana, 2 games to 1

Western Conference
(1) Phoenix defeated (4) Seattle, 2 games to 0
(2) San Antonio defeated (3) Sacramento, 2 games to 1
(1) Phoenix defeated (2) San Antonio, 2 games to 0

2007 WNBA Championship
Phoenix defeated Detroit, 3 games to 2 (100-108, 98-70, 83-88, 77-76, 108-92) in the 5-game series.

2007 All-WNBA Teams

First Team	Position	Second Team
Diana Taurasi, Phoenix	Forward	Tamika Catchings, Indiana
Penny Taylor, Phoenix	Forward	Sophia Young, San Antonio
Becky Hammon, San Antonio	Guard	Katie Douglas, Connecticut
Deanna Nolan, Detroit	Guard	Seimone Augustus, Minnesota
Lauren Jackson, Seattle	Center	Tina Thompson, Houston

WNBA Statistical Leaders and Awards in 2007

Minutes played: 1,233, Tina Thompson, Houston
Total points: 769, Seimone Augustus, Minnesota
Points per game: 23.8, Lauren Jackson, Seattle
Highest field goal %: .546, Janel McCarville, New York
Highest 3-pt. field goal %: .451, Jamie Carey, Connecticut
Highest free throw %: .964, Nicole Powell, Sacramento
Total rebounds: 300, Lauren Jackson, Seattle
Rebounds per game: 9.7, Lauren Jackson, Seattle

Total assists: 169, Lindsay Whalen, Connecticut
Assists per game: 5.00, Becky Hammon, San Antonio
Total steals: 75, Loree Moore, New York
Steals per game: 3.14, Tamika Catchings, Indiana
Total blocked shots: 66, Margo Dydek, Connecticut
Coach of the year: Dan Hughes, San Antonio
Defensive player of year: Lauren Jackson, Seattle
Most improved player: Janel McCarville, New York

WNBA Champions, 1997-2007

	Regular Season			Playoffs	
Year	Eastern Conference	Western Conference	Champion	Coach	Opponent
1997	Houston Comets	Phoenix Mercury	Houston	Van Chancellor	New York
1998	Cleveland Rockers	Houston Comets	Houston	Van Chancellor	Phoenix
1999	New York Liberty	Houston Comets	Houston	Van Chancellor	New York
2000	New York Liberty	Los Angeles Sparks	Houston	Van Chancellor	New York
2001	Cleveland Rockers	Los Angeles Sparks	Los Angeles	Michael Cooper	Charlotte
2002	New York Liberty	Los Angeles Sparks	Los Angeles	Michael Cooper	New York
2003	Detroit Shock	Los Angeles Sparks	Detroit	Bill Laimbeer	Los Angeles
2004	Connecticut Sun	Los Angeles Sparks	Seattle	Ann Donovan	Connecticut
2005	Connecticut Sun	Sacramento Monarchs	Sacramento	John Whisenant	Connecticut
2006	Connecticut Sun	Sacramento Monarchs	Detroit	Bill Laimbeer	Sacramento
2007	Detroit Shock	Phoenix Mercury	Phoenix	Paul Westhead	Detroit

WNBA Scoring Leaders

Year	Scoring Champion	Pts	Avg	Year	Scoring Champion	Pts	Avg	Year	Scoring Champion	Pts	Avg
1997	Cynthia Cooper, Houston	.621	22.2	2002	Chamique Holdsclaw, Washington	397	19.9	2005	Sheryl Swoopes, Houston	614	18.6
1998	Cynthia Cooper, Houston	.680	22.7	2003	Lauren Jackson, Seattle	.698	21.2	2006	Diana Taurasi, Phoenix	860	25.3
1999	Cynthia Cooper, Houston	.686	22.1	2004	Lauren Jackson, Seattle	.634	20.5	2007	Seimone Augustus, Minnesota	769	22.6
2000	Sheryl Swoopes, Houston	.643	20.7								
2001	Katie Smith, Minnesota	.739	23.1								

WNBA Finals MVP

Year	Player
1997	Cynthia Cooper, Houston
1998	Cynthia Cooper, Houston
1999	Yolanda Griffith, Sacramento
2000	Sheryl Swoopes, Houston
2001	Lisa Leslie, Los Angeles
2002	Sheryl Swoopes, Houston
2003	Lauren Jackson, Seattle
2004	Lisa Leslie, Los Angeles
2005	Sheryl Swoopes, Houston
2006	Deanna Nolan, Detroit
2007	Cappie Pondexter, Phoenix

WNBA Most Valuable Player

Year	Player
1997	Cynthia Cooper, Houston
1998	Cynthia Cooper, Houston
1999	Cynthia Cooper, Houston
2000	Cynthia Cooper, Houston
2001	Lisa Leslie, Los Angeles
2002	Lisa Leslie, Los Angeles
2003	Ruth Riley, Detroit
2004	Betty Lennox, Seattle
2005	Yolanda Griffith, Sacramento
2006	Lisa Leslie, Los Angeles
2007	Lauren Jackson, Seattle

WNBA Rookie of the Year

Year	Player
1997	no award
1998	Tracy Reid, Charlotte
1999	Chamique Holdsclaw, Washington
2000	Betty Lennox, Minnesota
2001	Jackie Stiles, Portland
2002	Tamika Catchings, Indiana
2003	Cheryl Ford, Detroit
2004	Diana Taurasi, Phoenix
2005	Temeka Johnson, Washington
2006	Seimone Augustus, Minnesota
2007	Armintie Price, Chicago

COLLEGE BASKETBALL

2007 Men's NCAA Tournament: Florida Gators Beat Buckeyes to a Second National Title

The Univ. of Florida Gators defeated the Ohio State Buckeyes, 84-75, to win its second consecutive Division I national basketball title Apr. 2, 2007, in Atlanta, GA. The Gators had also defeated the Buckeyes for the year's football title, making Florida the first Division I school ever to hold simultaneous titles in the two sports. Forty-one-year-old Coach Billy Donovan earned his second NCAA title in his third NCAA Finals appearance as a head coach. Forward Corey Brewer, who scored 13 points and picked up eight rebounds in the final game, was named the Most Outstanding Player of the Final Four.

NCAA Division I Champions

Year	Champion	Coach	Final opponent	Score	Most outstanding player	Site
1939	Oregon	Howard Hobson	Ohio St.	46-33	Jimmy Hull, Ohio St.	Evanston, IL
1940	Indiana	Branch McCracken	Kansas	60-42	Marvin Huffman, Indiana	Kansas City, MO
1941	Wisconsin	Harold Foster	Washington St.	39-34	John Kotz, Wisconsin	Kansas City, MO
1942	Stanford	Everett Dean	Dartmouth	53-38	Howard Dallmar, Stanford	Kansas City, MO
1943	Wyoming	Everett Shelton	Georgetown	46-34	Ken Sailors, Wyoming	New York, NY
1944	Utah	Vadal Peterson	Dartmouth	42-40[1]	Arnold Ferrin, Utah	New York, NY
1945	Oklahoma St.[2]	Henry Iba	NYU	49-45	Bob Kurland, Oklahoma St.	New York, NY
1946	Oklahoma St.[2]	Henry Iba	North Carolina	43-40	Bob Kurland, Oklahoma St.	New York, NY
1947	Holy Cross	Alvin Julian	Oklahoma	58-47	George Kaftan, Holy Cross	New York, NY
1948	Kentucky	Adolph Rupp	Baylor	58-42	Alex Groza, Kentucky	New York, NY
1949	Kentucky	Adolph Rupp	Oklahoma St.	46-36	Alex Groza, Kentucky	Seattle, WA
1950	CCNY	Nat Holman	Bradley	71-68	Irwin Dambrot, CCNY	New York, NY
1951	Kentucky	Adolph Rupp	Kansas St.	68-58	Bill Spivey, Kentucky	Minneapolis, MN
1952	Kansas	Forrest Allen	St. John's	80-63	Clyde Lovellette, Kansas	Seattle, WA
1953	Indiana	Branch McCracken	Kansas	69-68	B.H. Born, Kansas	Kansas City, MO
1954	La Salle	Kenneth Loeffler	Bradley	92-76	Tom Gola, La Salle	Kansas City, MO
1955	San Francisco	Phil Woolpert	La Salle	77-63	Bill Russell, San Francisco	Kansas City, MO
1956	San Francisco	Phil Woolpert	Iowa	83-71	Hal Lear, Temple	Evanston, IL
1957	North Carolina	Frank McGuire	Kansas	54-53[1]	Wilt Chamberlain, Kansas	Kansas City, MO
1958	Kentucky	Adolph Rupp	Seattle	84-72	Elgin Baylor, Seattle	Louisville, KY
1959	California	Pete Newell	West Virginia	71-70	Jerry West, West Virginia	Louisville, KY
1960	Ohio St.	Fred Taylor	California	75-55	Jerry Lucas, Ohio St.	San Francisco, CA
1961	Cincinnati	Edwin Jucker	Ohio St.	70-65[1]	Jerry Lucas, Ohio St.	Kansas City, MO
1962	Cincinnati	Edwin Jucker	Ohio St.	71-59	Paul Hogue, Cincinnati	Louisville, KY
1963	Loyola (IL)	George Ireland	Cincinnati	60-58[1]	Art Heyman, Duke	Louisville, KY
1964	UCLA	John Wooden	Duke	98-83	Walt Hazzard, UCLA	Kansas City, MO
1965	UCLA	John Wooden	Michigan	91-80	Bill Bradley, Princeton	Portland, OR
1966	Texas-El Paso[3]	Don Haskins	Kentucky	72-65	Jerry Chambers, Utah	College Park, MD
1967	UCLA	John Wooden	Dayton	79-64	Lew Alcindor, UCLA	Louisville, KY
1968	UCLA	John Wooden	North Carolina	78-55	Lew Alcindor, UCLA	Los Angeles, CA
1969	UCLA	John Wooden	Purdue	92-72	Lew Alcindor, UCLA	Louisville, KY
1970	UCLA	John Wooden	Jacksonville	80-69	Sidney Wicks, UCLA	College Park, MD
1971	UCLA	John Wooden	Villanova*	68-62	Howard Porter, Villanova*	Houston, TX
1972	UCLA	John Wooden	Florida St.	81-76	Bill Walton, UCLA	Los Angeles, CA
1973	UCLA	John Wooden	Memphis[4]	87-66	Bill Walton, UCLA	St. Louis, MO
1974	North Carolina St.	Norm Sloan	Marquette	76-64	David Thompson, NC St.	Greensboro, NC
1975	UCLA	John Wooden	Kentucky	92-85	Richard Washington, UCLA	San Diego, CA
1976	Indiana	Bob Knight	Michigan	86-68	Kent Benson, Indiana	Philadelphia, PA
1977	Marquette	Al McGuire	North Carolina	67-59	Butch Lee, Marquette	Atlanta, GA
1978	Kentucky	Joe Hall	Duke	94-88	Jack Givens, Kentucky	St. Louis, MO
1979	Michigan St.	Jud Heathcote	Indiana St.	75-64	Magic Johnson, Michigan St.	Salt Lake City, UT
1980	Louisville	Denny Crum	UCLA*	59-54	Darrell Griffith, Louisville	Indianapolis, IN
1981	Indiana	Bob Knight	North Carolina	63-50	Isiah Thomas, Indiana	Philadelphia, PA
1982	North Carolina	Dean Smith	Georgetown	63-62	James Worthy, N. Carolina	New Orleans, LA
1983	North Carolina St.	Jim Valvano	Houston	54-52	Hakeem Olajuwon, Houston	Albuquerque, NM
1984	Georgetown	John Thompson	Houston	84-75	Patrick Ewing, Georgetown	Seattle, WA
1985	Villanova	Rollie Massimino	Georgetown	66-64	Ed Pinckney, Villanova	Lexington, KY
1986	Louisville	Denny Crum	Duke	72-69	Pervis Ellison, Louisville	Dallas, TX
1987	Indiana	Bob Knight	Syracuse	74-73	Keith Smart, Indiana	New Orleans, LA
1988	Kansas	Larry Brown	Oklahoma	83-79	Danny Manning, Kansas	Kansas City, MO
1989	Michigan	Steve Fisher	Seton Hall	80-79[1]	Glen Rice, Michigan	Seattle, WA
1990	UNLV	Jerry Tarkanian	Duke	103-73	Anderson Hunt, UNLV	Denver, CO
1991	Duke	Mike Krzyzewski	Kansas	72-65	Christian Laettner, Duke	Indianapolis, IN
1992	Duke	Mike Krzyzewski	Michigan	71-51	Bobby Hurley, Duke	Minneapolis, MN
1993	North Carolina	Dean Smith	Michigan	77-71	Donald Williams, N. Carolina	New Orleans, LA
1994	Arkansas	Nolan Richardson	Duke	76-72	Corliss Williamson, Arkansas	Charlotte, NC
1995	UCLA	Jim Harrick	Arkansas	89-78	Ed O'Bannon, UCLA	Seattle, WA
1996	Kentucky	Rick Pitino	Syracuse	76-67	Tony Delk, Kentucky	E. Rutherford, NJ
1997	Arizona	Lute Olson	Kentucky	84-79[1]	Miles Simon, Arizona	Indianapolis, IN
1998	Kentucky	Tubby Smith	Utah	78-69	Jeff Sheppard, Kentucky	San Antonio, TX
1999	Connecticut	Jim Calhoun	Duke	77-74	Richard Hamilton, Connecticut	St. Petersburg, FL
2000	Michigan St.	Tom Izzo	Florida	89-76	Mateen Cleaves, Michigan St.	Indianapolis, IN
2001	Duke	Mike Krzyzewski	Arizona	82-72	Shane Battier, Duke	Minneapolis, MN
2002	Maryland	Gary Williams	Indiana	64-52	Juan Dixon, Maryland	Atlanta, GA
2003	Syracuse	Jim Boeheim	Kansas	81-78	Carmelo Anthony, Syracuse	New Orleans, LA
2004	Connecticut	Jim Calhoun	Georgia Tech	82-73	Emeka Okafor, Connecticut	San Antonio, TX
2005	North Carolina	Roy Williams	Illinois	75-70	Sean May, North Carolina	St. Louis, MO
2006	Florida	Billy Donovan	UCLA	73-57	Joakim Noah, Florida	Indianapolis, IN
2007	Florida	Billy Donovan	Ohio State	84-75	Corey Brewer, Florida	Atlanta, GA

*Declared ineligible after the tournament. (1) Overtime. (2) Then known as Oklahoma A&M. (3) Then known as Texas Western. (4) Then known as Memphis State.

Top Division I Career Scorers

(minimum 1,500 points; ranked by average, points per game)

Player, school	Years	Points	Avg	Player, school	Years	Points	Avg
Pete Maravich, LSU	1968-70	3,667	44.2	Dwight Lamar, LA-Lafayette[1]	1972-73	1,862	32.7
Austin Carr, Notre Dame	1969-71	2,560	34.6	Frank Selvy, Furman	1952-54	2,538	32.5
Oscar Robertson, Cincinnati	1958-60	2,973	33.8	Rick Mount, Purdue	1968-70	2,323	32.3
Calvin Murphy, Niagara	1968-70	2,548	33.1	Darrell Floyd, Furman	1954-56	2,281	32.1

(1) Known as SW Louisiana until 1999.

2007 MEN'S NCAA BASKETBALL TOURNAMENT

MIDWEST REGIONALS

(1) Florida 112
(16) Jackson St. 69

Florida 74

(8) Arizona 63
(9) Purdue 72

Purdue 67

Florida 65

(5) Butler 57
(12) Old Dominion 46

Butler 62

Butler 57

(4) Maryland 82
(13) Davidson 70

Maryland 59

Florida 85

(6) Notre Dame 64
(11) Winthrop 74

Winthrop 61

(3) Oregon 58
(14) Miami (OH) 56

Oregon 75

Oregon 76

Florida 76

(7) UNLV 67
(10) Georgia Tech 63

UNLV 74

Oregon 77

(2) Wisconsin 76
(15) TX A&M Corpus Christi 63

Wisconsin 68

UNLV 72

WEST REGIONALS

(1) Kansas 107
(16) Niagara* 67

Kansas 88

(8) Kentucky 67
(9) Villanova 58

Kentucky 76

Kansas 61

(5) Virginia Tech 54
(12) Illinois 52

Virginia Tech 48

Southern Illinois 58

(4) Southern Illinois 61
(13) Holy Cross 51

Southern Illinois 63

Kansas 55

(6) Duke 77
(11) VCU 79

VCU 79

(3) Pittsburgh 79
(14) Wright St. 58

Pittsburgh 84 (OT)

Pittsburgh 55

UCLA 66

(7) Indiana 70
(10) Gonzaga 57

Indiana 49

UCLA 68

(2) UCLA 70
(15) Weber St. 42

UCLA 54

UCLA 64

EAST REGIONALS

(1) North Carolina 86
(16) Eastern Kentucky 65

North Carolina 81

(8) Marquette 49
(9) Michigan St. 61

Michigan St. 67

North Carolina 74

(5) USC 77
(12) Arkansas 60

USC 87

USC 64

(4) Texas 79
(13) New Mexico St. 67

Texas 68

North Carolina 84

(6) Vanderbilt 77
(11) George Washington 44

Vanderbilt 78 (2 OT)

Vanderbilt 65

(3) Washington St. 70
(14) Oral Roberts 54

Washington St. 74

Georgetown 60

(7) Boston College 84
(10) Texas Tech 75

Boston College 55

Georgetown 96 (OT)

(2) Georgetown 80
(15) Belmont 55

Georgetown 62

Georgetown 66

SOUTH REGIONALS

(1) Ohio St. 78
(16) Central Connecticut St. 57

Ohio St. 78

(8) Brigham Young 77
(9) Xavier 79

Xavier 71

Ohio St. 85

(5) Tennessee 121
(12) Long Beach St. 86

Tennessee 77

Tennessee 84

(4) Virginia 84
(13) Albany 57

Virginia 74

Ohio St. 92

(6) Louisville 78
(11) Stanford 58

Louisville 69

Texas A&M 64

(3) Texas A&M 68
(14) Pennsylvania 52

Texas A&M 72

Ohio St. 67

(7) Nevada 77 (OT)
(10) Creighton 71

Nevada 62

Memphis 65

(2) Memphis 73
(15) North Texas 58

Memphis 78

Memphis 76

Florida 84
Ohio St. 75

*Niagara defeated Florida A&M, 77-69, in the opening-round game on March 13.

Men's Final NCAA Division I Conference Standings, 2006-07

(*conference tournament champion)

America East

	Conf W	Conf L	All W	All L
Vermont	15	1	25	8
Albany*	13	3	23	10
Boston Univ.	8	8	12	18
Maine	7	9	12	18
MD Baltimore Co.	7	9	12	19
Binghamton	6	10	13	16
Hartford	6	10	13	18
New Hampshire	6	10	10	20
Stony Brook	4	12	9	20

Atlantic Coast

	Conf W	Conf L	All W	All L
North Carolina*	11	5	31	7
Virginia	11	5	21	11
Maryland	10	6	25	9
Virginia Tech	10	6	22	12
Boston Coll.	10	6	21	12
Duke	8	8	22	11
Georgia Tech	8	8	20	12
Clemson	7	9	25	11
Florida State	7	9	22	13
NC State	5	11	20	16
Wake Forest	5	11	15	16
Miami (FL)	4	12	12	20

Atlantic Sun

	Conf W	Conf L	All W	All L
E. Tennessee St.	16	2	23	10
Belmont*	14	4	23	10
Lipscomb	11	7	18	13
Jacksonville	11	7	15	14
Kennesaw State	9	9	13	18
Mercer	8	10	13	17
Campbell	7	11	14	17
Gardner-Webb	7	11	9	21
Stetson	6	12	11	20
North Florida	1	17	3	26

Atlantic 10

	Conf W	Conf L	All W	All L
Xavier	13	3	25	9
Massachusetts	13	3	24	9
George Washington*	11	5	23	9
Fordham	10	6	18	12
Rhode Island	10	6	19	14
St. Joseph's	9	7	18	14
Dayton	8	8	19	12
St. Louis	8	8	20	13
Charlotte	7	9	14	16
Temple	6	10	12	18
Duquesne	6	10	10	19
Richmond	4	12	8	22
St. Bonaventure	4	12	7	22
La Salle	3	13	10	20

Big East

	Conf W	Conf L	All W	All L
Georgetown*	13	3	30	7
Pittsburgh	12	4	29	8
Louisville	12	4	24	10
Notre Dame	11	5	24	8
Marquette	10	6	24	10
Syracuse	10	6	24	11
West Virginia	9	7	27	9
Villanova	9	7	22	11
DePaul	9	7	20	14
Providence	8	8	18	13
St. John's	9	9	16	15
Connecticut	6	10	17	14
Seton Hall	4	12	13	16
South Florida	3	13	12	18
Rutgers	3	13	10	19
Cincinnati	2	14	11	19

Big Sky[1]

	Conf W	Conf L	All W	All L
Weber State*	11	5	20	12
Northern Arizona	11	5	17	12
Montana	10	6	17	15
Portland State	9	7	19	13
Eastern Wash.	8	8	15	14
Idaho State	8	8	13	17
Montana State	8	8	11	19
Sacramento State	5	11	10	19
Northern Colorado	2	14	4	24

Big South

	Conf W	Conf L	All W	All L
Winthrop*	14	0	29	5
High Point	11	3	22	10
Liberty	8	6	14	17
Coastal Carolina	7	7	15	15
UNC Ashville	6	8	12	19
VMI	5	9	14	19
Radford	3	11	7	22
Charleston Southern	2	12	8	22

Big 10

	Conf W	Conf L	All W	All L
Ohio State*	15	1	35	4
Wisconsin	13	3	30	6
Indiana	10	6	21	11
Illinois	9	7	23	12
Purdue	9	7	22	12
Iowa	9	7	17	14
Michigan State	8	8	23	12
Michigan	8	8	22	13
Minnesota	3	13	9	22
Northwestern	2	14	13	18
Penn State	2	14	11	19

Big 12

	Conf W	Conf L	All W	All L
Kansas*	14	2	33	5
Texas A&M	13	3	27	7
Texas	12	4	25	10
Kansas State	10	6	23	12
Texas Tech	9	7	21	13
Missouri	7	9	18	12
Oklahoma State	6	10	22	13
Nebraska	6	10	17	14
Oklahoma	6	10	16	15
Iowa State	6	10	15	16
Baylor	4	12	15	16
Colorado	3	13	7	20

Big West

	Conf W	Conf L	All W	All L
Long Beach State*	12	2	24	8
Cal. St. Fullerton	9	5	20	10
Cal. Poly.	9	5	19	11
UC Santa Barbara	9	5	17	11
UC Irvine	6	8	15	18
Cal. St. Northridge	5	9	14	17
Pacific	5	9	12	19
UC Riverside	1	13	7	24

Colonial Athletic Association

	Conf W	Conf L	All W	All L
VCU*	16	2	28	7
Old Dominion	15	3	24	9
Hofstra	14	4	22	10
Drexel	13	5	23	9
George Mason	9	9	18	15
Northeastern	9	9	13	19
William & Mary	8	10	15	15
Towson	8	10	15	17
Georgia State	5	13	11	20
UNC Wilmington	4	14	7	22
James Madison	4	14	7	23
Delaware	3	15	5	26

Conference USA

	Conf W	Conf L	All W	All L
Memphis	16	0	33	4
Central Florida	11	5	22	9
Houston	10	6	18	15
Southern Miss.	9	7	20	11
Tulsa	9	7	20	11
Tulane	9	7	17	13
Rice	8	8	16	16
UAB	7	9	15	16
Marshall	7	9	13	19
UTEP	6	10	14	17
Southern Methodist	3	13	14	17
East Carolina	1	15	6	24

Horizon League

	Conf W	Conf L	All W	All L
Wright State*	15	3	23	10
Butler	14	4	29	7
Loyola (IL)	11	7	21	11
Wisc.-Green Bay	9	10	18	15
Youngstown State	8	10	14	17
Illinois-Chicago	8	10	14	18
Detroit	6	11	11	19
Wisc.-Milwaukee	6	11	9	22
Cleveland State	3	14	10	21

Ivy League[2]

	Conf W	Conf L	All W	All L
Penn	13	1	22	9
Yale	10	4	14	13
Cornell	9	5	16	12
Columbia	7	7	16	12
Brown	6	8	11	18
Harvard	5	9	12	16
Dartmouth	4	10	9	18
Princeton	2	12	11	17

Metro Atlantic Athletic

	Conf W	Conf L	All W	All L
Marist	14	4	25	9
Niagara*	13	5	23	12
Siena	12	6	20	12
Loyola (MD)	12	6	18	13
Manhattan	10	8	13	17
Fairfield	10	8	13	19
Rider	9	9	16	15
Canisius	6	12	12	19
St. Peter's	3	15	5	25
Iona	1	17	2	28

Mid-American

East Division

	Conf W	Conf L	All W	All L
Akron	13	3	26	7
Kent State	12	4	21	11
Miami (OH)*	10	6	18	15
Ohio	9	7	19	13
Buffalo	4	12	12	19
Bowling Green	3	13	13	18

West Division

	Conf W	Conf L	All W	All L
Toledo	14	2	19	13
Western Michigan	9	7	16	16
Central Michigan	7	9	13	18
Eastern Michigan	6	10	13	19
Ball State	5	11	9	22
Northern Illinois	4	12	7	23

Mid-Continent

	Conf W	Conf L	All W	All L
Oral Roberts*	12	2	23	11
Oakland	10	4	19	14
Valparaiso	9	5	16	15
Indiana-Purdue	7	7	15	15
Southern Utah	6	8	16	14
Missouri-Kansas City	6	8	12	20
Centenary	3	11	10	21
Western Illinois	3	11	7	23

Mid-Eastern Athletic

	Conf W	Conf L	All W	All L
Delaware State*	16	2	21	13
Florida A&M	12	6	21	14
Hampton	10	8	15	16
North Carolina A&T	10	8	15	17
South Carolina St.	10	8	13	17
Morgan State	10	8	13	18
Norfolk State	10	8	11	19
Coppin State	9	9	12	20
Bethune-Cookman	6	12	9	21
Howard	5	13	9	22
MD-Eastern Shore	1	17	4	27

Missouri Valley

	Conf W	Conf L	All W	All L
Southern Illinois	15	3	29	7
Creighton*	13	5	22	11
Missouri State	12	6	22	11
Bradley	10	8	22	13
Northern Iowa	9	9	18	13
Witchita State	8	10	22	10
Drake	6	12	17	15
Illinois State	6	12	15	16
Evansville	6	12	14	17
Indiana State	5	13	13	18

Mountain West

	Conf W	Conf L	All W	All L
Brigham Young	13	3	25	9
UNLV*	12	4	30	7
Air Force	10	6	26	9
San Diego State	10	6	22	11
Wyoming	7	9	17	15
Colorado State	6	10	17	13
Utah	6	10	11	19
New Mexico	4	12	15	17
TCU	4	12	13	17

Northeast

	Conf W	Conf L	All W	All L
Central Conn. State*	16	2	22	12
Sacred Heart	12	6	18	14
Quinnipiac	11	7	14	15
Robert Morris	9	9	17	11
Fairleigh-Dickinson	9	9	14	16
Mount St. Mary's	9	9	11	21

	Conf. W L	All W L
Wagner	8 10	11 19
Monmouth	7 11	12 18
St. Francis (NY)	7 11	9 22
Long Island	6 12	10 19
St. Francis (PA)	5 13	8 21
Ohio Valley		
Austin Peay	16 4	21 12
Eastern Kentucky*	13 7	21 12
Tennessee Tech	13 7	19 13
Murray State	13 7	16 14
Samford	12 8	16 16
SE Missouri State	9 11	11 20
Morehead State	8 12	12 18
Tennessee State	8 12	12 20
Jacksonville State	7 13	9 21
Eastern Illinois	6 14	10 20
Tennessee-Martin	5 15	8 23
Pacific-10		
UCLA	15 3	30 6
Washington State	13 5	26 8
Oregon*	11 7	29 8
USC	11 7	25 12
Arizona	11 7	20 14
Stanford	10 8	18 13
Washington	8 10	19 13
California	6 12	16 17
Oregon State	3 15	11 21
Arizona State	2 16	8 22
Patriot		
Holy Cross*	13 1	25 9
Bucknell	13 1	22 9
American	7 7	16 14
Lehigh	7 7	12 19
Colgate	5 9	10 19
Army	4 10	15 16
Navy	4 10	14 26
Lafayette	3 11	9 21
Southeastern		
East Division		
Florida*	13 3	35 5
Tennessee	10 6	24 11
Vanderbilt	10 6	22 12
Kentucky	9 7	22 12
Georgia	8 8	19 14
South Carolina	4 12	14 16

	Conf. W L	All W L
West Division		
Mississippi	8 8	21 13
Mississippi State	8 8	21 14
Alabama	7 9	20 12
Arkansas	7 9	21 14
Auburn	7 9	17 15
LSU	5 11	17 15
Southern		
North Division		
Appalachian State	15 3	25 8
UNC Greensboro	12 6	16 14
Western Carolina	8 11	11 20
Chattanooga	7 12	15 18
Elon	5 14	7 23
South Division		
Davidson*	17 1	29 5
Charleston	13 5	22 11
Furman	8 10	15 16
Georgia Southern	8 11	15 16
Wofford	5 14	10 20
Citadel	4 15	7 23
Southland[1]		
East Division		
Northwestern St.	10 6	17 15
McNeese State	9 7	15 17
SE Louisiana	8 8	16 14
Lamar	8 8	15 17
Nicholls State	7 9	8 22
Central Arkansas	4 12	10 20
West Division		
TX A&M-Corp. Christi*	14 2	26 7
Sam Houston State	13 3	21 10
Stephen F. Austin	8 8	16 14
Texas-Arlington	8 8	13 17
Texas State	4 12	9 20
Texas-San Antonio	3 13	7 22
Southwestern Athletic		
Jackson State*	15 6	21 14
Miss. Valley State	15 6	18 16
Grambling	10 9	12 14
Alcorn State	10 9	11 19
Texas Southern	10 10	14 17
Ark.-Pine Bluff	10 10	12 19
Southern	9 10	10 20
Alabama State	8 11	10 20
Prairie View	6 12	8 22
Alabama A&M	4 14	10 20

	Conf. W L	All W L
Sun Belt[1]		
East Division		
South Alabama*	13 5	20 12
Western Kentucky	12 6	22 11
Florida Atlantic	10 8	16 15
Middle Tenn. State	8 10	15 17
Troy	8 10	13 17
Florida Intl.	7 11	12 17
West Division		
Louisiana-Monroe	11 7	18 14
Arkansas State	11 7	18 15
North Texas*	10 8	23 11
New Orleans	9 9	14 17
Arkansas-Little Rock	8 10	13 17
Louisiana-Lafayette	7 11	9 21
Denver	3 15	4 25
West Coast		
Gonzaga*	11 3	23 11
Santa Clara	10 4	21 10
St. Mary's (CA)	8 6	17 15
San Francisco	8 6	13 18
San Diego	6 8	18 14
Loyola Marymount	5 9	13 18
Portland	4 10	9 23
Pepperdine	4 10	8 23
Western Athletic		
Nevada	14 2	29 5
New Mexico State*	11 5	25 9
Fresno State	10 6	22 10
Utah State	9 7	23 12
Hawaii	8 8	18 13
Boise State	8 8	17 14
Louisiana Tech	7 9	10 20
San Jose State	4 12	5 25
Idaho	1 15	4 27
Independents[1,2]		
Utah Valley State	— —	22 7
North Dakota State	— —	20 8
TX Pan American	— —	13 15
I-P Fort Wayne	— —	12 17
Savannah State	— —	11 18
Chicago State	— —	9 20
Longwood	— —	9 22
South Dakota State	— —	6 24
UC Davis	— —	5 23
Winston-Salem	— —	5 24
NJ Tech	— —	5 24

(1) Conference changes in 2006 included: Northern Colorado to Big Sky; Texas A&M-Corpus Christi and Central Arkansas to Southland; Florida Atlantic and Louisiana-Monroe to Sun Belt; Chicago State, Winston-Salem, and NJ Tech became independent. (2) Schools do not participate in a tournament.

All-Time Winningest Division I College Teams by Percentage

(through 2006-07 season)

TEAM	Yrs	Won	Lost	Pct.	TEAM	Yrs	Won	Lost	Pct.	TEAM	Yrs	Won	Lost	Pct.
Kentucky	104	1,948	608	0.762	UCLA	88	1,611	713	0.693	Illinois	102	1,569	824	0.656
N. Carolina	97	1,914	696	0.733	Syracuse	106	1,704	782	0.685	Louisville	93	1,529	816	0.652
UNLV	49	1,010	410	0.711	W. Kentucky	88	1,548	764	0.670	Arizona	102	1,528	829	0.648
Kansas	109	1,906	782	0.709	St. John's-NY	100	1,659	831	0.666	Indiana	107	1,610	876	0.648
Duke	102	1,818	802	0.694	Utah	99	1,595	833	0.657					

Major College Basketball Tournaments

The National Invitation Tournament (NIT), first played in 1938, is the oldest U.S. basketball tournament. The first National Collegiate Athletic Association (NCAA) national championship tournament was played one year later. In Aug. 2005, the NCAA agreed to purchase the NIT from the five New York City-area colleges that had run the NIT, and administer its pre- and post-season tournaments.

National Invitation Tournament Champions

Year	Champion	Year	Champion	Year	Champion	Year	Champion	Year	Champion
1938	Temple	1952	La Salle	1966	Brigham Young	1980	Virginia	1994	Villanova
1939	Long Island Univ.	1953	Seton Hall	1967	Southern Illinois	1981	Tulsa	1995	Virginia Tech
1940	Colorado	1954	Holy Cross	1968	Dayton	1982	Bradley	1996	Nebraska
1941	Long Island Univ.	1955	Duquesne	1969	Temple	1983	Fresno State	1997	Michigan
1942	West Virginia	1956	Louisville	1970	Marquette	1984	Michigan	1998	Minnesota
1943	St. John's	1957	Bradley	1971	North Carolina	1985	UCLA	1999	California
1944	St. John's	1958	Xavier (Ohio)	1972	Maryland	1986	Ohio State	2000	Wake Forest
1945	DePaul	1959	St. John's	1973	Virginia Tech	1987	So. Mississippi	2001	Tulsa
1946	Kentucky	1960	Bradley	1974	Purdue	1988	Connecticut	2002	Memphis
1947	Utah	1961	Providence	1975	Princeton	1989	St. John's	2003	St. John's
1948	St. Louis	1962	Dayton	1976	Kentucky	1990	Vanderbilt	2004	Michigan
1949	San Francisco	1963	Providence	1977	St. Bonaventure	1991	Stanford	2005	South Carolina
1950	CCNY	1964	Bradley	1978	Texas	1992	Virginia	2006	South Carolina
1951	Brigham Young	1965	St. John's	1979	Indiana	1993	Minnesota	2007	West Virginia

John R. Wooden Award

Awarded to the nation's outstanding men's college basketball player by the Los Angeles Athletic Club since 1977; awarded under the same name to women since 2004.

1977 Marques Johnson, UCLA	1989 Sean Elliott, Arizona	2001 Shane Battier, Duke
1978 Phil Ford, North Carolina	1990 Lionel Simmons, La Salle	2002 Jay Williams, Duke
1979 Larry Bird, Indiana State	1991 Larry Johnson, UNLV	2003 T.J. Ford, Texas
1980 Darrell Griffith, Louisville	1992 Christian Laettner, Duke	2004 (M) Jameer Nelson, St. Joseph's; (W)
1981 Danny Ainge, Brigham Young	1993 Calbert Cheaney, Indiana	Alana Beard, Duke
1982 Ralph Sampson, Virginia	1994 Glenn Robinson, Purdue	2005 (M) Andrew Bogut, Utah;
1983 Ralph Sampson, Virginia	1995 Ed O'Bannon, UCLA	(W) Seimone Augustus
1984 Michael Jordan, North Carolina	1996 Marcus Camby, Massachusetts	2006 (M) J.J. Redick, Duke;
1985 Chris Mullin, St. John's	1997 Tim Duncan, Wake Forest	(W) Seimone Augustus
1986 Walter Berry, St. John's	1998 Antawn Jamison, North Carolina	2007 (M) Kevin Durant, Texas;
1987 David Robinson, Navy	1999 Elton Brand, Duke	(W) Candace Parker
1988 Danny Manning, Kansas	2000 Kenyon Martin, Cincinnati	

Most Coaching Victories in the NCAA Tournament Through 2007

(Coaches active in 2006-07 season in bold)

Coach, School(s), First/Last appearance	Wins	Tournaments	Championships
Mike Krzyzewski, Duke, 1984/2007	68	23	3
Dean Smith, North Carolina, 1967/1997	65	27	2
John Wooden, UCLA, 1950/1975	47	16	10
Bob Knight, Indiana, Texas Tech, 1973/2007	45	28	3
Lute Olson, Iowa, Arizona, 1979/2007	46	27	1
Denny Crum, Louisville, 1972/2000	42	23	2
Roy Williams, Kansas, N. Carolina, 1990/2007	45	18	1
Jim Boeheim, Syracuse, 1977/2006	40	25	1
Jim Calhoun, Northeastern, Connecticut, 1981/2006	39	19	2
Eddie Sutton, Creighton, Arkansas, Kentucky, Oklahoma St., 1974/2005	37	25	0

WOMEN'S COLLEGE BASKETBALL

2007 Women's NCAA Tournament: Vols Conquer Knights

The Tennessee Lady Volunteers defeated Rutgers Univ.'s Scarlet Knights, 59-46, to claim the Women's 2007 Division I basketball title Apr. 3, 2007, in Cleveland, OH. Known as defensive powerhouses, both teams combined for the lowest point total in tournament history. Vols Head Coach Pat Summitt tallied her 947th win, by far the most of any men's or women's NCAA Division I team.

NCAA Division I Women's Champions

Year	Champion	Coach	Final opponent	Score	Outstanding player	Site
1982	Louisiana Tech	Sonja Hogg	Cheyney	76-62	Janice Lawrence, La. Tech	Norfolk, VA
1983	USC	Linda Sharp	Louisiana Tech	69-67	Cheryl Miller, USC	Norfolk, VA
1984	USC	Linda Sharp	Tennessee	72-61	Cheryl Miller, USC	Los Angeles, CA
1985	Old Dominion	Marianne Stanley	Georgia	70-65	Tracy Claxton, Old Dominion	Austin, TX
1986	Texas	Jody Conradt	USC	97-81	Clarissa Davis, Texas	Lexington, KY
1987	Tennessee	Pat Summitt	Louisiana Tech	67-44	Tonya Edwards, Tennessee	Austin, TX
1988	Louisiana Tech	Leon Barmore	Auburn	56-54	Erica Westbrooks, La. Tech	Tacoma, WA
1989	Tennessee	Pat Summitt	Auburn	76-60	Bridgette Gordon, Tennessee	Tacoma, WA
1990	Stanford	Tara VanDerveer	Auburn	88-81	Jennifer Azzi, Stanford	Knoxville, TN
1991	Tennessee	Pat Summitt	Virginia	70-67 (OT)	Dawn Staley, Virginia	New Orleans, LA
1992	Stanford	Tara VanDerveer	W. Kentucky	78-62	Molly Goodenbour, Stanford	Los Angeles, CA
1993	Texas Tech	Marsha Sharp	Ohio St.	84-82	Sheryl Swoopes, Texas Tech	Atlanta, GA
1994	North Carolina	Sylvia Hatchell	Louisiana Tech	60-59	Charlotte Smith, North Carolina	Richmond, VA
1995	Connecticut	Geno Auriemma	Tennessee	70-64	Rebecca Lobo, Connecticut	Minneapolis, MN
1996	Tennessee	Pat Summitt	Georgia	83-65	Michelle Marciniak, Tennessee	Charlotte, NC
1997	Tennessee	Pat Summitt	Old Dominion	68-59	Chamique Holdsclaw, Tennessee	Cincinnati, OH
1998	Tennessee	Pat Summitt	Louisiana Tech	93-75	Chamique Holdsclaw, Tennessee	Kansas City, MO
1999	Purdue	Carolyn Peck	Duke	62-45	Ukari Figgs, Purdue	San Jose, CA
2000	Connecticut	Geno Auriemma	Tennessee	71-52	Shea Ralph, Connecticut	Philadelphia, PA
2001	Notre Dame	Muffet McGraw	Purdue	68-66	Ruth Riley, Notre Dame	St. Louis, MO
2002	Connecticut	Geno Auriemma	Oklahoma	82-70	Swin Cash, Connecticut	San Antonio, TX
2003	Connecticut	Geno Auriemma	Tennessee	73-68	Diana Taurasi, Connecticut	Atlanta, GA
2004	Connecticut	Geno Auriemma	Tennessee	70-61	Diana Taurasi, Connecticut	New Orleans, LA
2005	Baylor	Kim Mulkey-Robertson	Michigan State	84-62	Sophia Young, Baylor	Indianapolis, IN
2006	Maryland	Brenda Frese	Duke	78-75 (OT)	Laura Harper, Maryland	Boston, MA
2007	Tennessee	Pat Summitt	Rutgers	59-46	Candace Parker, Tennessee	Cleveland, OH

Wade Trophy

Awarded by National Assn. for Girls and Women in Sport for character, leadership, and player performance.

Year	Player, school	Year	Player, school	Year	Player, school
1978	Carol Blazejowski, Montclair St.	1988	Teresa Weatherspoon, Louisiana Tech	1998	Ticha Penicheiro, Old Dominion
1979	Nancy Lieberman, Old Dominion	1989	Clarissa Davis, Texas	1999	Stephanie White-McCarty, Purdue
1980	Nancy Lieberman, Old Dominion	1990	Jennifer Azzi, Stanford	2000	Edwina Brown, Texas
1981	Lynette Woodard, Kansas	1991	Daedra Charles, Tennessee	2001	Jackie Stiles, SW Missouri St.
1982	Pam Kelly, Louisiana Tech	1992	Susan Robinson, Penn St.	2002	Sue Bird, Connecticut
1983	LaTaunya Pollard, Long Beach St.	1993	Karen Jennings, Nebraska	2003	Diana Taurasi, Connecticut
1984	Janice Lawrence, Louisiana Tech	1994	Carol Ann Shudlick, Minnesota	2004	Alana Beard, Duke
1985	Cheryl Miller, USC	1995	Rebecca Lobo, Connecticut	2005	Seimone Augustus, LSU
1986	Kamie Ethridge, Texas	1996	Jennifer Rizzotti, Connecticut	2006	Seimone Augustus, LSU
1987	Shelly Pennefeather, Villanova	1997	DeLisha Milton, Florida	2007	Candace Parker, Tennessee

Top Division I Women's Career Scorers

(Through 2006-07 season. Minimum 1,500 points; ranked by average.)

Player, school	Years	Points	Avg	Player, school	Years	Points	Avg
Patricia Hoskins, Miss. Valley St.	1985-89	3,122	28.4	Andrea Congreaves, Mercer	1989-93	2,796	25.9
Sandra Hodge, New Orleans	1981-84	2,860	26.7	Cindy Blodgett, Maine	1994-98	3,005	25.5
Jackie Stiles, Missouri St.	1997-2001	3,393	26.3	Valorie Whiteside, Appalachian St.	1984-88	2,944	25.4
Lorri Bauman, Drake	1981-84	3,115	26.0				

2007 WOMEN'S NCAA BASKETBALL TOURNAMENT

DALLAS REGIONAL

(1) North Carolina 95
(16) Prairie View 38
    North Carolina 60
(8) California 59
(9) Notre Dame 62
    Notre Dame 51
        North Carolina 70

(5) George Washington 76
(12) Boise St. 67
    George Washington 59
(4) Texas A&M 58
(13) Texas-Arlington 50
    Texas A&M 47
        George Washington 56

           North Carolina 84

(6) Iowa St. 79
(11) Washington 60
    Iowa St. 56
(3) Georgia 53
(14) Belmont 36
    Georgia 76
        Georgia 65

           North Carolina 50

(7) Georgia Tech 55
(10) DePaul 54
    Georgia Tech 63
(2) Purdue 63
(15) Oral Roberts 42
    Purdue 76
        Purdue 78

        Purdue 72

DAYTON REGIONAL

(1) Tennessee 76
(16) Drake 37
    Tennessee 68
(8) Pittsburgh 71
(9) James Madison 61
    Pittsburgh 54
        Tennessee 65

(5) Middle Tennessee St. 85
(12) Gonzaga 46
    Middle Tennessee St. 59
(4) Ohio St. 63
(13) Marist 67
    Marist 73
        Marist 46

        Tennessee 98

           Tennessee 56

(6) Marquette 87
(11) LA Lafayette 58
    Marquette 47
(3) Oklahoma 74
(14) Southeast Missouri St. 60
    Oklahoma 78
        Oklahoma 82

(7) Mississippi 88
(10) TCU 74
    Mississippi 89
(2) Maryland 89
(15) Harvard 65
    Maryland 78
        Mississippi 90

        Mississippi 62

           Tennessee 59
           Rutgers 46

FRESNO REGIONAL

(1) Connecticut 82
(16) Maryland-Baltimore Co.
    Connecticut 94
(8) New Mexico 52
(9) Wisconsin-Green Bay 59
    Wisconsin-Green Bay 70
        Connecticut 78

(5) Baylor 68
(12) Chattanooga 55
    Baylor 72
(4) North Carolina St. 84
(13) Robert Morris 52
    North Carolina St. 78 (OT)
        North Carolina St. 71

        Connecticut 50

(6) Xavier 52
(11) West Virginia 65
    West Virginia 43
(3) LSU 77
(14) UNC Asheville 39
    LSU 49
        LSU 55

           LSU 35

(7) Old Dominion 75
(10) Florida St. 85
    Florida St. 68
(2) Stanford 96
(15) Idaho St. 58
    Stanford 61
        Florida St. 43

        LSU 73

GREENSBORO REGIONAL

(1) Duke 81
(16) Holy Cross 44
    Duke 62
(8) Temple 64
(9) Nebraska 61
    Temple 52
        Duke 52

(5) Michigan St. 69
(12) Delaware 58
    Michigan St. 57
(4) Rutgers 77
(13) East Carolina 34
    Rutgers 70
        Rutgers 53

        Rutgers 64

(6) Louisville 80
(11) Brigham Young 54
    Louisville 58
(3) Arizona St. 57
(14) UC Riverside 50
    Arizona St. 67
        Arizona St. 67

        Rutgers 59

(7) Bowling Green 70
(10) Oklahoma St. 66
    Bowling Green 59
(2) Vanderbilt 62
(15) Delaware St. 47
    Vanderbilt 56
        Bowling Green 49

        Arizona St. 45

NATIONAL FOOTBALL LEAGUE
NFL 2006-2007: Colts Win Championship; Tomlinson and Rookies Set New Records

The Indianapolis Colts beat the Chicago Bears, 29-17, on Feb. 4, 2007, in Miami, FL, to win Super Bowl XLI. In the regular season, San Diego Chargers running back LaDainian Tomlinson, the 2006 NFL MVP, broke Paul Hornung's 46-year-old NFL record for points scored in a season, with 186. Tomlinson also set the record for total touchdowns in a season with 31, and rushing touchdowns in a season with 28. Chicago Bears rookie defensive back Devin Hester set a new NFL record for returns for touchdowns in a season with six. Hester's return of a missed field goal tied the NFL record for the longest distance covered on a single play, 108 yards. Reggie Bush of the New Orleans Saints set the record for passes caught by a rookie running back with 88, surpassing Earl Cooper's record of 83.

Final 2006 Standings

American Football Conference

	W	L	T	Pct	Pts	Opp	Div
East Division							
New England	12	4	0	.750	385	237	4-2
*N.Y. Jets	10	6	0	.625	316	295	4-2
Buffalo	7	9	0	.438	300	311	3-3
Miami	6	10	0	.375	260	283	1-5
North Division							
Baltimore	13	3	0	.812	353	201	5-1
Cincinnati	8	8	0	.500	373	331	4-2
Pittsburgh	8	8	0	.500	353	315	3-3
Cleveland	4	12	0	.250	238	356	0-6
South Division							
Indianapolis	12	4	0	.750	427	360	3-3
Tennessee	8	8	0	.500	324	400	4-2
Jacksonville	8	8	0	.500	371	274	2-4
Houston	6	10	0	.375	267	366	3-3
West Division							
San Diego	14	2	0	.875	492	303	5-1
*Kansas City	9	7	0	.562	331	315	4-2
Denver	9	7	0	.562	319	305	3-3
Oakland	2	14	0	.125	168	332	0-6

National Football Conference

	W	L	T	Pct	Pts	Opp	Div
East Division							
Philadelphia	10	6	0	.625	398	328	5-1
*Dallas	9	7	0	.562	425	350	2-4
*N.Y. Giants	8	8	0	.500	355	362	4-2
Washington	5	11	0	.312	307	376	1-5
North Division							
Chicago	13	3	0	.812	427	255	5-1
Green Bay	8	8	0	.500	301	366	5-1
Minnesota	6	10	0	.375	282	327	2-4
Detroit	3	13	0	.188	305	398	0-6
South Division							
New Orleans	10	6	0	.625	413	322	4-2
Carolina	8	8	0	.500	270	305	5-1
Atlanta	7	9	0	.438	292	328	3-3
Tampa Bay	4	12	0	.250	211	353	0-6
West Division							
Seattle	9	7	0	.562	335	341	3-3
St. Louis	8	8	0	.500	367	381	2-4
San Francisco	7	9	0	.438	298	412	3-3
Arizona	5	11	0	.312	314	389	4-2

* Wild card team.

AFC Playoffs—Indianapolis 23, Kansas City 8; New England 37, N.Y. Jets 16; Indianapolis 15, Baltimore 6; New England 24, San Diego 21; Indianapolis 38, New England 34

NFC Playoffs—Seattle 21, Dallas 20; Philadelphia 23, N.Y. Giants 20; New Orleans 27, Philadelphia 24; Chicago 27, Seattle 24 (OT); Chicago 39, New Orleans 14

2006 NFL Individual Leaders
American Football Conference

PASSING	Att	Comp	Pct Comp	Yds	Yds/Att	Long	TDs	Pct TD	Ints	Rating
Peyton Manning, Indianapolis	557	362	65.0%	4,397	7.89	68	31	5.6%	9	101.0
Damon Huard, Kansas City	244	148	60.7%	1,878	7.70	78	11	4.5%	1	98.0
Carson Palmer, Cincinnati	520	324	62.3%	4,035	7.76	74	28	5.4%	13	93.9
Philip Rivers, San Diego	460	284	61.7%	3,388	7.37	57	22	4.8%	9	92.0
Tom Brady, New England	516	319	61.8%	3,529	6.84	62	24	4.7%	12	87.9
J.P. Losman, Buffalo	429	268	62.5%	3,051	7.11	83	19	4.4%	14	84.9
Chad Pennington, N.Y. Jets	485	313	64.5%	3,352	6.91	71	17	3.5%	16	82.6
Steve McNair, Baltimore	468	295	63.0%	3,050	6.52	87	16	3.4%	12	82.1
David Carr, Houston	442	302	68.3%	2,767	6.26	53	11	2.5%	11	82.1
David Garrard, Jacksonville	241	145	60.2%	1,735	7.20	49	10	4.1%	9	80.5

RUSHING YARDS	Yds	Att	Avg	Long	TD
LaDainian Tomlinson, San Diego	1,815	348	5.2	85	28
Larry Johnson, Kansas City	1,789	416	4.3	47	17
Willie Parker, Pittsburgh	1,494	337	4.4	76	13
Rudi Johnson, Cincinnati	1,309	341	3.8	22	12
Travis Henry, Tennessee	1,211	270	4.5	70	7
Fred Taylor, Jacksonville	1,146	231	5.0	76	5
Jamal Lewis, Baltimore	1,132	314	3.6	52	9
Joseph Addai, Indianapolis	1,081	226	4.8	41	7
Tatum Bell, Denver	1,025	233	4.4	51	2
Ronnie Brown, Miami	1,008	241	4.2	47	5

RECEIVING	Rec	Yds	Avg	Long	TD
Andre Johnson, Houston	103	1,147	11.1	53	5
Marvin Harrison, Indianapolis	95	1,366	14.4	68	12
Laveranues Coles, N.Y. Jets	91	1,098	12.1	58	6
T.J. Houshmandzadeh, Cincinnati	90	1,081	12.0	40	9
Kellen Winslow, Cleveland	89	875	9.8	40	3
Chad Johnson, Cincinnati	87	1,369	15.7	74	7
Reggie Wayne, Indianapolis	86	1,310	15.2	51	9
Lee Evans, Buffalo	82	1,292	15.8	83	8
Jerricho Cotchery, N.Y. Jets	82	961	11.7	71	6
Hines Ward, Pittsburgh	74	975	13.2	70	6

SCORING—KICKERS	PAT	FG	Long	Pts
Nate Kaeding, San Diego	58/58	26/29	54	136
Matt Stover, Baltimore	37/37	28/30	52	121
Josh Scobee, Jacksonville	41/41	26/32	48	119
Jason Elam, Denver	34/34	27/29	51	115
Olindo Mare, Miami	22/22	26/36	52	100

SCORING—NON-KICKERS	TD	Rush	Rec	2-PT	Pts
LaDainian Tomlinson, San Diego	31	28	3	0	186
Larry Johnson, Kansas City	19	17	2	0	114
Maurice Jones-Drew, Jacksonville	17	13	2	0	96
Willie Parker, Pittsburgh	16	13	3	0	96
Corey Dillon, New England	13	13	0	0	78

INTERCEPTIONS	No.	Yds	Avg	Long	TD
Champ Bailey, Denver	10	162	16.2	70	1
Asante Samuel, New England	10	120	12.0	33	0
Nnamdi Asomugha, Oakland	8	59	7.4	24	1
Rashean Mathis, Jacksonville	8	146	18.3	55	0
Kevin Kaesviharn, Cincinnati	6	24	4.0	22	0
Chris McAlister, Baltimore	6	121	20.2	60	2
Daven Holly, Cleveland	5	127	25.4	57	1
Chris Hope, Tennessee	5	105	21.0	61	1
Sean Jones, Cleveland	5	46	9.2	19	0
Dawan Landry, Baltimore	5	101	20.2	37	1
Ed Reed, Baltimore	5	70	14.0	37	1

KICKOFF RETURNS	No.	Yds	Avg	Long	TD
Justin Miller, N.Y. Jets	46	1,304	28.3	103	2
Laurence Maroney, New England	28	783	28.0	77	0
Maurice Jones-Drew, Jacksonville	31	860	27.7	93	1
Michael Turner, San Diego	36	954	26.5	58	0
Terrence McGee, Buffalo	52	1,355	26.1	88	0
Adam "Pacman" Jones, Tennessee	20	521	26.1	70	0

PUNT RETURNS	No.	Yds	Avg	LG	TD
Adam "Pacman" Jones, Tennessee	34	440	12.9	90	3
Roscoe Parrish, Buffalo	32	364	11.4	82	1
Dennis Northcutt, Cleveland	28	312	11.1	81	0
Kevin Faulk, New England	31	330	10.6	43	0
B.J. Sams, Baltimore	29	307	10.6	65	0

PUNTING	No.	Yds	Long	Avg
Shane Lechler, Oakland	77	3,660	67	47.5
Kyle Larson, Cincinnati	77	3,428	67	44.5
Hunter Smith, Indianapolis	47	2,085	61	44.4
Dustin Colquitt, Kansas City	71	3,145	72	44.3
Ben Graham, N.Y. Jets	72	3,182	69	44.2

Sacks: Shawne Merriman, San Diego, 17.0; Aaron Schobel, Buffalo, 14.0; Jason Taylor, Miami, 13.5; Trevor Pryce, Baltimore, 13.0; Shaun Phillips, San Diego, 11.5; Adalius Thomas, Baltimore, 11.0; Kamerion Wimbley, Cleveland, 11.0; Derrick Burgess, Oakland, 11.0; Robert Geathers, Cincinnati, 10.5; Bobby McCray, Jacksonville, 10.0; Warren Sapp, Oakland, 10.0.

National Football Conference

PASSING	Att	Comp	Pct Comp	Yds	Yds/Att	Long	TD	Pct TD	Int	Rating
Drew Brees, New Orleans	554	356	64.3%	4,418	7.97	86	26	4.7%	11	96.2
Donovan McNabb, Philadelphia	316	180	57.0%	2,647	8.38	87	18	5.7%	6	95.5
Tony Romo, Dallas	337	220	65.3%	2,903	8.61	56	19	5.6%	13	95.1
Marc Bulger, St. Louis	588	370	62.9%	4,301	7.31	67	24	4.1%	8	92.9
Mark Brunell, Washington	260	162	62.3%	1,789	6.88	74	8	3.1%	4	86.5
Jake Delhomme, Carolina	431	263	61.0%	2,805	6.51	72	17	3.9%	11	82.6
Jon Kitna, Detroit	596	372	62.4%	4,208	7.06	60	21	3.5%	22	79.9
Eli Manning, N.Y. Giants	522	301	57.7%	3,244	6.21	55	24	4.6%	18	77.0
Matt Hasselbeck, Seattle	371	210	56.6%	2,442	6.58	72	18	4.9%	15	76.0
Michael Vick, Atlanta	388	204	52.6%	2,474	6.38	55	20	5.2%	13	75.7

RUSHING YARDS	Yds	Att	Avg	Long	TD
Frank Gore, San Francisco	1,695	312	5.4	72	8
Tiki Barber, N.Y. Giants	1,662	327	5.1	55	5
Steven Jackson, St. Louis	1,528	346	4.4	59	13
Brian Westbrook, Philadelphia	1,217	240	5.1	71	7
Chester Taylor, Minnesota	1,216	303	4.0	95	6
Thomas Jones, Chicago	1,210	296	4.1	30	6
Edgerrin James, Arizona	1,159	337	3.4	18	6
Ladell Betts, Washington	1,154	245	4.7	26	4
Warrick Dunn, Atlanta	1,140	286	4.0	90	4
Julius Jones, Dallas	1,084	267	4.1	77	4

RECEPTIONS	Rec	Yds	Avg	Long	TD
Mike Furrey, Detroit	98	1,086	11.1	31	6
Torry Holt, St. Louis	93	1,188	12.8	67	10
Donald Driver, Green Bay	92	1,295	14.1	82	8
Steven Jackson, St. Louis	90	806	9.0	63	3
Reggie Bush, New Orleans	88	742	8.4	74	2
Terrell Owens, Dallas	85	1,180	13.9	56	13
Anquan Boldin, Arizona	83	1,203	14.5	64	4
Steve Smith, Carolina	83	1,166	14.0	72	8
Roy Williams, Detroit	82	1,310	16.0	60	7
Brian Westbrook, Philadelphia	77	699	9.1	52	4

SCORING—KICKERS	PAT	FG	Long	Pts
Robbie Gould, Chicago	47/47	32/36	49	143
Jeff Wilkins, St. Louis	35/35	32/37	53	131
Jason Hanson, Detroit	30/30	29/33	53	117
Joe Nedney, San Francisco	29/29	29/35	51	116
Neil Rackers, Arizona	32/32	28/37	50	116

SCORING—NON-KICKERS	TD	Rush	Rec	2 Pt	Pts
Marion Barber, Dallas	16	14	2	0	96
Steven Jackson, St. Louis	16	13	3	0	96
Terrell Owens, Dallas	13	0	13	1	80
Brian Westbrook, Philadelphia	11	7	4	0	66
Deuce McAllister, New Orleans	10	10	0	0	66

INTERCEPTIONS	No.	Yds	Avg	Long	TD
Charles Woodson, Green Bay	8	61	7.6	23	1
Walt Harris, San Francisco	8	84	10.5	42	1
Lito Sheppard, Philadelphia	6	157	26.2	102	1
Roy Williams, Dallas	5	33	6.6	27	0
Ricky Manning, Chicago	5	113	22.6	54	1
Charles Tillman, Chicago	5	32	6.4	13	0
Brian Dawkins, Philadelphia	4	38	9.5	38	0
Adrian Wilson, Arizona	4	146	36.5	99	1
Darren Sharper, Minnesota	4	10	2.5	10	0
Dwight Smith, Minnesota	4	81	20.3	47	0
Antoine Winfield, Minnesota	4	33	8.3	26	1
DeAngelo Hall, Atlanta	4	131	32.8	60	1

KICKOFF RETURNS	No.	Yds	Avg	Long	TD
Devin Hester, Chicago	20	528	26.4	96	2
Miles Austin, Dallas	29	753	26.0	37	0
Tyson Thompson, Dallas	21	546	26.0	41	0
Maurice Hicks, San Francisco	57	1,428	25.1	64	0
Nate Burleson, Seattle	26	643	24.7	50	0
Michael Lewis, New Orleans	37	914	24.7	51	0

PUNT RETURNS	No.	Yds	Avg	Long	TD
Devin Hester, Chicago	47	600	12.8	84	3
Eddie Drummond, Detroit	28	296	10.6	40	0
Troy Walters, Arizona	24	250	10.4	37	0
Terence Newman, Dallas	20	202	10.1	56	1
Mewelde Moore, Minnesota	36	365	10.1	71	1

PUNTING	No.	Yds	Long	Avg
Mat McBriar, Dallas	56	2,697	75	48.2
Jason Baker, Carolina	98	4,483	70	45.7
Ryan Plackemeier, Seattle	84	3,778	72	45.0
Nick Harris, Detroit	66	2,967	67	45.0
Scott Player, Arizona	66	2,965	58	44.9

Sacks: Aaron Kampman, Green Bay, 15.5; Julius Peppers, Carolina, 13.0; Leonard Little, St. Louis, 13.0; Mark Anderson, Chicago, 12.0; DeMarcus Ware, Dallas, 11.5; Will Smith, New Orleans, 10.5; Julian Peterson, Seattle, 10.0; Chike Okeafor, Arizona, 8.5; Trent Cole, Philadelphia, 8.0; Karlos Dansby, Arizona, 8.0; Cory Redding, Detroit, 8.0.

Super Bowl XLI: Indianapolis 29, Chicago 17

The Indianapolis Colts on Feb. 4, 2007, defeated the Chicago Bears, 29-17, at Dolphin Stadium in Miami, FL, to win Super Bowl XLI. It was the franchise's second Super Bowl win—their first came in 1971 as the Baltimore Colts. Colts coach Tony Dungy and Bears coach Lovie Smith made NFL history by being the first African American head coaches to lead teams to the Super Bowl. In winning, Dungy became the first African American to lead a team to a Super Bowl victory.

Peyton Manning of the Colts, two-time winner of the NFL MVP award, was named Super Bowl MVP, after completing 25 of 38 passes for 247 yards and a touchdown. Colts kicker Adam Vinatieri, who kicked three field goals and two extra points, set a record for the most career points for a kicker in the Super Bowl with 34, and the most field goals with seven.

Score by Quarters

Team	1	2	3	4	Total
Indianapolis	6	10	6	7	29
Chicago	14	0	3	0	17

Scoring

Chicago — Devin Hester 92 yd. kickoff return (Gould PAT)

Indianapolis — Reggie Wayne 53 yd. pass from Peyton Manning (No PAT)

Chicago — Muhsin Muhammad 4 yd. pass from Rex Grossman (Gould PAT)

Indianapolis — Adam Vinatieri 29 yd. field goal

Indianapolis — Dominic Rhodes 1 yd. run (Vinatieri PAT)

Indianapolis — Adam Vinatieri 24 yd. field goal

Indianapolis — Adam Vinatieri 20 yd. field goal

Chicago — Robbie Gould 44 yd. field goal

Indianapolis — Kelvin Hayden 56 yd. interception return (Vinatieri PAT)

Individual Statistics

Rushing — Indianapolis: Rhodes 21-113, 1 TD; Addai 19-77; Clark 1-1; Manning 1-0. Chicago: Jones 15-112; Grossman 2-0; Benson 2- -1.

Passing — Indianapolis: Peyton Manning 25-38, 247 yds, 1 TD, 1 Int. Chicago: Rex Grossman 20-28, 165 yds, 1 TD, 2 Int.

Receiving — Indianapolis: Addai 10-66; Harrison 5-59; Clark 4-36; Wayne 2-61, 1 TD; Fletcher 2-9; Rhodes 1-8; Utecht 1-8. Chicago: Clark 6-64; Berrian 4-38; Jones 4-18; Muhammad 3-35, 1 TD; McKie 2-8; Davis 1-2.

Team Statistics	Colts	Bears
1st downs	24	11
Total net yards	430	265
Rushes-yards	42-191	19-111
Passing yards, net	239	154
Punt returns-yards	3-42	1-3
Kickoff returns-yards	4-89	6-138
Interception return-yards	2-94	1-6
Field goals made-attempts	3-4	1-1
Att.-comp.-int.	38-25-1	28-20-2
Sacked-yards lost	1-8	1-11
Punts-average	4-40.5	5-45.2
Fumbles-lost	2-2	4-3
Penalties-yards	6-40	4-35
Time of possession	38:04	21:56

Attendance — 74,512   **Game Length** — 3:31

Super Bowl Results

	Year	Winner	Loser	Winning coach	Site
I	1967	*Green Bay Packers, 35	Kansas City Chiefs, 10	Vince Lombardi	Memorial Coliseum, Los Angeles, C
II	1968	Green Bay Packers, 33	*Oakland Raiders, 14	Vince Lombardi	Orange Bowl, Miami, FL
III	1969	*New York Jets, 16	Baltimore Colts, 7	Weeb Ewbank	Orange Bowl, Miami, FL
IV	1970	Kansas City Chiefs, 23	*Minnesota Vikings, 7	Hank Stram	Tulane Stadium, New Orleans, LA
V	1971	Baltimore Colts, 16	*Dallas Cowboys, 13	Don McCafferty	Orange Bowl, Miami, FL
VI	1972	Dallas Cowboys, 24	*Miami Dolphins, 3	Tom Landry	Tulane Stadium, New Orleans, LA
VII	1973	*Miami Dolphins, 14	Washington Redskins, 7	Don Shula	Memorial Coliseum, Los Angeles, C
VIII	1974	*Miami Dolphins, 24	Minnesota Vikings, 7	Don Shula	Rice Stadium, Houston, TX
IX	1975	*Pittsburgh Steelers, 16	Minnesota Vikings, 6	Chuck Noll	Tulane Stadium, New Orleans, LA
X	1976	Pittsburgh Steelers, 21	*Dallas Cowboys, 17	Chuck Noll	Orange Bowl, Miami, FL
XI	1977	*Oakland Raiders, 32	Minnesota Vikings, 14	John Madden	Rose Bowl, Pasadena, CA
XII	1978	*Dallas Cowboys, 27	Denver Broncos, 10	Tom Landry	Superdome, New Orleans, LA
XIII	1979	Pittsburgh Steelers, 35	*Dallas Cowboys, 31	Chuck Noll	Orange Bowl, Miami, FL
XIV	1980	Pittsburgh Steelers, 31	*Los Angeles Rams, 19	Chuck Noll	Rose Bowl, Pasadena, CA
XV	1981	Oakland Raiders, 27	*Philadelphia Eagles, 10	Tom Flores	Superdome, New Orleans, LA
XVI	1982	*San Francisco 49ers, 26	Cincinnati Bengals, 21	Bill Walsh	Silverdome, Pontiac, MI
XVII	1983	Washington Redskins, 27	*Miami Dolphins, 17	Joe Gibbs	Rose Bowl, Pasadena, CA
XVIII	1984	*Los Angeles Raiders, 38	Washington Redskins, 9	Tom Flores	Tampa Stadium, FL
XIX	1985	*San Francisco 49ers, 38	Miami Dolphins, 16	Bill Walsh	Stanford Stadium, Stanford, CA
XX	1986	*Chicago Bears, 46	New England Patriots, 10	Mike Ditka	Superdome, New Orleans, LA
XXI	1987	New York Giants, 39	*Denver Broncos, 20	Bill Parcells	Rose Bowl, Pasadena, CA
XXII	1988	*Washington Redskins, 42	Denver Broncos, 10	Joe Gibbs	Jack Murphy Stadium, San Diego, C
XXIII	1989	*San Francisco 49ers, 20	Cincinnati Bengals, 16	Bill Walsh	Joe Robbie Stadium, Miami, FL
XXIV	1990	San Francisco 49ers, 55	*Denver Broncos, 10	George Seifert	Superdome, New Orleans, LA
XXV	1991	New York Giants, 20	*Buffalo Bills, 19	Bill Parcells	Tampa Stadium, FL
XXVI	1992	*Washington Redskins, 37	Buffalo Bills, 24	Joe Gibbs	Metrodome, Minneapolis, MN
XXVII	1993	Dallas Cowboys, 52	*Buffalo Bills, 17	Jimmy Johnson	Rose Bowl, Pasadena, CA
XXVIII	1994	*Dallas Cowboys, 30	Buffalo Bills, 13	Jimmy Johnson	Georgia Dome, Atlanta, GA
XXIX	1995	*San Francisco 49ers, 49	San Diego Chargers, 26	George Seifert	Joe Robbie Stadium, Miami, FL
XXX	1996	*Dallas Cowboys, 27	Pittsburgh Steelers, 17	Barry Switzer	Sun Devil Stadium, Tempe, AZ
XXXI	1997	Green Bay Packers, 35	*New England Patriots, 21	Mike Holmgren	Superdome, New Orleans, LA
XXXII	1998	Denver Broncos, 31	*Green Bay Packers, 24	Mike Shanahan	Qualcomm Stadium, San Diego, CA
XXXIII	1999	Denver Broncos, 34	*Atlanta Falcons, 19	Mike Shanahan	Pro Player Stadium, Miami, FL
XXXIV	2000	*St. Louis Rams, 23	Tennessee Titans, 16	Dick Vermeil	Georgia Dome, Atlanta, GA
XXXV	2001	Baltimore Ravens, 34	*New York Giants, 7	Brian Billick	Raymond James Stad., Tampa, FL
XXXVI	2002	New England Patriots, 20	*St. Louis Rams, 17	Bill Belichick	Superdome, New Orleans, LA
XXXVII	2003	*Tampa Bay Buccaneers, 48	Oakland Raiders, 21	Jon Gruden	Qualcomm Stadium, San Diego, CA
XXXVIII	2004	New England Patriots, 32	*Carolina Panthers, 29	Bill Belichick	Reliant Stadium, Houston, TX
XXXIX	2005	New England Patriots, 24	*Philadelphia Eagles, 21	Bill Belichick	Alltel Stadium, Jacksonville, FL
XL	2006	Pittsburgh Steelers, 21	*Seattle Seahawks, 10	Bill Cowher	Ford Field, Detroit, MI
XLI	2007	Indianapolis Colts, 29	*Chicago Bears, 17	Tony Dungy	Dolphin Stadium, Miami, FL

*Team that won the coin toss. All teams that won the toss elected to receive.

Future Super Bowl Sites

(Information subject to change.)

No.	Site	Date	No.	Site	Date
XLII	University of Phoenix Stadium, Glendale, AZ	Feb. 3, 2008	XLIV	Dolphin Stadium, Miami, FL	Feb. 2010
XLIII	Raymond James Stadium, Tampa, FL	Feb. 1, 2009	XLV	New Dallas Cowboys Stadium, Arlington, TX	Feb. 2011

Super Bowl Single-Game Statistical Leaders

Passing Yards

	Year	Att/Comp	Yds	TDs
Kurt Warner, Rams	2000	45/24	414	2
Kurt Warner, Rams	2002	44/28	365	1
Donovon McNabb, Eagles	2005	51/30	357	3
Joe Montana, 49ers	1989	36/23	357	2

Receiving Yards

	Year	Recept.	Yds	TDs
Jerry Rice, 49ers	1989	11	215	1
Ricky Sanders, Redskins	1988	9	193	2
Isaac Bruce, Rams	2000	6	162	1

Rushing Yards

	Year	Attempts	Yds	TDs
Timmy Smith, Redskins	1988	22	204	2
Marcus Allen, Raiders	1984	20	191	2
John Riggins, Redskins	1983	38	166	1

Passing Touchdowns

	Year	Att/Comp	Yds	TDs
Steve Young, 49ers	1995	36/24	325	6
Joe Montana, 49ers	1990	29/22	297	5
Troy Aikman, Cowboys	1993	30/22	273	4
Doug Williams, Redskins	1988	29/18	340	4
Terry Bradshaw, Steelers	1979	30/17	318	4

Scoring

	Year	Points	
Terrell Davis, Broncos	1998	18	3 TDs
Jerry Rice, 49ers	1995	18	3 TDs
Ricky Watters, 49ers	1995	18	3 TDs
Jerry Rice, 49ers	1990	18	3 TDs
Roger Craig, 49ers	1985	18	3 TDs
Don Chandler, Packers	1968	15	4 FG, 3PATs

Super Bowl MVPs

1967	Bart Starr, Green Bay	1981	Jim Plunkett, Oakland	1995	Steve Young, San Francisco
1968	Bart Starr, Green Bay	1982	Joe Montana, San Francisco	1996	Larry Brown, Dallas
1969	Joe Namath, N.Y. Jets	1983	John Riggins, Washington	1997	Desmond Howard, Green Bay
1970	Len Dawson, Kansas City	1984	Marcus Allen, L.A. Raiders	1998	Terrell Davis, Denver
1971	Chuck Howley, Dallas	1985	Joe Montana, San Francisco	1999	John Elway, Denver
1972	Roger Staubach, Dallas	1986	Richard Dent, Chicago	2000	Kurt Warner, St. Louis
1973	Jake Scott, Miami	1987	Phil Simms, N.Y. Giants	2001	Ray Lewis, Baltimore
1974	Larry Csonka, Miami	1988	Doug Williams, Washington	2002	Tom Brady, New England
1975	Franco Harris, Pittsburgh	1989	Jerry Rice, San Francisco	2003	Dexter Jackson, Tampa Bay
1976	Lynn Swann, Pittsburgh	1990	Joe Montana, San Francisco	2004	Tom Brady, New England
1977	Fred Biletnikoff, Oakland	1991	Ottis Anderson, N.Y. Giants	2005	Deion Branch, New England
1978	Randy White, Harvey Martin, Dallas	1992	Mark Rypien, Washington	2006	Hines Ward, Pittsburgh
1979	Terry Bradshaw, Pittsburgh	1993	Troy Aikman, Dallas	2007	Peyton Manning, Indianapolis
1980	Terry Bradshaw, Pittsburgh	1994	Emmitt Smith, Dallas		

The Sporting News 2006 NFL All-Pro Team

Offense—Quarterback: Drew Brees, New Orleans. Running Backs: LaDainian Tomlinson, San Diego; Larry Johnson, Kansas City. Wide Receivers: Marvin Harrison, Indianapolis; Chad Johnson, Cincinnati. Tight End: Antonio Gates, San Diego. Tackles: Walter Jones, Seattle; Jonathan Ogden, Baltimore. Guards: Steve Hutchinson, Minnesota; Shawn Andrews, Philadelphia. Center: Olin Kreutz, Chicago.

Defense—Linebackers: Brian Urlacher, Chicago; Shawne Merriman, San Diego; Lance Briggs, Chicago. Defensive Ends: Jason Taylor, Miami; Julius Peppers, Carolina. Defensive Tackles: Jamal Williams, San Diego; Kevin Williams, Minnesota. Cornerbacks: Champ Bailey, Denver; Rashean Mathis, Jacksonville. Safeties: Ed Reed, Baltimore; Adrian Wilson, Arizona.

Special Teams—Kicker: Robbie Gould, Chicago. Punter: Brian Moorman, Buffalo. Kick Returner: Justin Miller, N.Y. Jets. Punt Returner: Devin Hester, Chicago.

First-Round Selections in the 2007 NFL Draft

Team	Player	Pos	College	Team	Player	Pos	College
1. Oakland	Russell, JaMarcus	QB	LSU	17. Denver[4]	Moss, Jarvis	DE	Florida
2. Detroit	Johnson, Calvin	WR	Georgia Tech	18. Cincinnati	Hall, Leon	CB	Michigan
3. Cleveland	Thomas, Joe	OT	Wisconsin	19. Tennessee	Griffin, Michael	FS	Texas
4. Tampa Bay	Adams, Gaines	DE	Clemson	20. N.Y. Giants	Ross, Aaron	CB	Texas
5. Arizona	Brown, Levi	OT	Penn State	21. Jacksonville[5]	Nelson, Reggie	FS	Florida
6. Washington	Landry, LaRon	FS	LSU	22. Cleveland[6]	Quinn, Brady	QB	Notre Dame
7. Minnesota	Peterson, Adrian	RB	Oklahoma	23. Kansas City	Bowe, Dwayne	WR	LSU
8. Atlanta[1]	Anderson, Jamaal	DE	Arkansas	24. New England[7]	Meriweather, Brandon	FS	Miami (FL)
9. Miami	Ginn Jr., Ted	WR	Ohio State	25. Carolina[8]	Beason, Jon	OLB	Miami (FL)
10. Houston[2]	Okoye, Amobi	DT	Louisville	26. Dallas[9]	Spencer, Anthony	DE	Purdue
11. San Francisco	Willis, Patrick	ILB	Mississippi	27. New Orleans	Meachem, Robert	WR	Tennessee
12. Buffalo	Lynch, Marshawn	RB	California	28. San Francisco[10]	Staley, Joe	OT	Central Michigan
13. St. Louis	Carriker, Adam	DE	Nebraska	29. Baltimore	Grubbs, Ben	G	Auburn
14. N.Y. Jets[3]	Revis, Darrelle	CB	Pittsburgh	30. San Diego	Davis, Craig	WR	LSU
15. Pittsburgh	Timmons, Lawrence	OLB	Florida State	31. Chicago	Olsen, Greg	TE	Miami (FL)
16. Green Bay	Harrell, Justin	DT	Tennessee	32. Indianapolis	Gonzalez, Anthony	WR	Ohio State

(1) From Houston. (2) From Atlanta. (3) From Carolina. (4) From Jacksonville. (5) From Denver. (6) From Dallas. (7) From Seattle. (8) From N.Y. Jets. (9) From Philadelphia. (10) From New England.

Number One NFL Draft Choices, 1936-2007

Year	Team	Player, Pos., College	Year	Team	Player, Pos., College
1936	Philadelphia	Jay Berwanger, HB, Chicago	1972	Buffalo	Walt Patulski, DE, Notre Dame
1937	Philadelphia	Sam Francis, FB, Nebraska	1973	Houston	John Matuszak, DE, Tampa
1938	Cleveland Rams	Corbett Davis, FB, Indiana	1974	Dallas	Ed "Too Tall" Jones, DE, Tenn. St.
1939	Chicago Cards	Ki Aldrich, C, TCU	1975	Atlanta	Steve Bartkowski, QB, Cal.
1940	Chicago Cards	George Cafego, HB, Tennessee	1976	Tampa Bay	Lee Roy Selmon, DE, Oklahoma
1941	Chicago Bears	Tom Harmon, HB, Michigan	1977	Tampa Bay	Ricky Bell, RB, USC
1942	Pittsburgh	Bill Dudley, HB, Virginia	1978	Houston	Earl Campbell, RB, Texas
1943	Detroit	Frank Sinkwich, HB, Georgia	1979	Buffalo	Tom Cousineau, LB, Ohio St.
1944	Boston Yanks	Angelo Bertelli, QB, Notre Dame	1980	Detroit	Billy Sims, RB, Oklahoma
1945	Chicago Cards	Charley Trippi, HB, Georgia	1981	New Orleans	George Rogers, RB, S. Carolina
1946	Boston Yanks	Frank Dancewicz, QB, Notre Dame	1982	New England	Kenneth Sims, DT, Texas
1947	Chicago Bears	Bob Fenimore, HB, Okla. A&M	1983	Baltimore Colts	John Elway, QB, Stanford
1948	Washington	Harry Gilmer, QB, Alabama	1984	New England	Irving Fryar, WR, Nebraska
1949	Philadelphia	Chuck Bednarik, C, Penn	1985	Buffalo	Bruce Smith, DE, Va. Tech
1950	Detroit	Leon Hart, E, Notre Dame	1986	Tampa Bay	Bo Jackson, RB, Auburn
1951	N.Y. Giants	Kyle Rote, HB, SMU	1987	Tampa Bay	Vinny Testaverde, QB, Miami (FL)
1952	L.A. Rams	Bill Wade, QB, Vanderbilt	1988	Atlanta	Aundray Bruce, LB, Auburn
1953	San Francisco	Harry Babcock, E, Georgia	1989	Dallas	Troy Aikman, QB, UCLA
1954	Cleveland	Bobby Garrett, QB, Stanford	1990	Indianapolis	Jeff George, QB, Illinois
1955	Baltimore Colts	George Shaw, QB, Oregon	1991	Dallas	Russell Maryland, DL, Miami (FL)
1956	Pittsburgh	Gary Glick, DB, Col. A&M	1992	Indianapolis	Steve Emtman, DL, Washington
1957	Green Bay	Paul Hornung, QB, Notre Dame	1993	New England	Drew Bledsoe, QB, Washington St.
1958	Chicago Cards	King Hill, QB, Rice	1994	Cincinnati	Dan Wilkinson, DT, Ohio St.
1959	Green Bay	Randy Duncan, QB, Iowa	1995	Cincinnati	Ki-Jana Carter, RB, Penn State
1960	L.A. Rams	Billy Cannon, HB, LSU	1996	N.Y. Jets	Keyshawn Johnson, WR, USC
1961	Minnesota	Tommy Mason, HB, Tulane	1997	St. Louis	Orlando Pace, T, Ohio St.
1962	Washington	Ernie Davis, HB, Syracuse	1998	Indianapolis	Peyton Manning, QB, Tennessee
1963	L.A. Rams	Terry Baker, QB, Oregon St.	1999	Cleveland	Tim Couch, QB, Kentucky
1964	San Francisco	Dave Parks, E, Texas Tech	2000	Cleveland	Courtney Brown, DE, Penn State
1965	N.Y. Giants	Tucker Frederickson, HB, Auburn	2001	Atlanta	Michael Vick, QB, Virginia Tech
1966	Atlanta	Tommy Nobis, LB, Texas	2002	Houston	David Carr, QB, Fresno St.
1967	Baltimore Colts	Bubba Smith, DT, Michigan St.	2003	Cincinnati	Carson Palmer, QB, USC
1968	Minnesota	Ron Yary, T, USC	2004	San Diego	Eli Manning, QB, Mississippi
1969	Buffalo	O.J. Simpson, RB, USC	2005	San Francisco	Alex D. Smith, QB, Utah
1970	Pittsburgh	Terry Bradshaw, QB, La.Tech	2006	Houston	Mario Williams, DE, NC State
1971	New England	Jim Plunkett, QB, Stanford	2007	Oakland	JaMarcus Russell, QB, LSU

American Football League Champions 1960-1969

Year	Eastern Division	Western Division	Championship
1960	Houston Oilers (10-4-0)	Los Angeles Chargers (10-4-0)	Houston 24, Los Angeles 16
1961	Houston Oilers (10-3-1)	San Diego Chargers (12-2-0)	Houston 10, San Diego 3
1962	Houston Oilers (11-3-0)	Dallas Texans (11-3-0)	Dallas 20, Houston 17 (2 overtimes)
1963	Boston Patriots (7-6-1) (a)	San Diego Chargers (11-3-0)	San Diego 51, Boston 10
1964	Buffalo Bills (12-2-0)	San Diego Chargers (8-5-1)	Buffalo 20, San Diego 7
1965	Buffalo Bills (10-3-1)	San Diego Chargers (9-2-3)	Buffalo 23, San Diego 0
1966	Buffalo Bills (9-4-1)	Kansas City Chiefs (11-2-1)	Kansas City 31, Buffalo 7
1967	Houston Oilers (9-4-1)	Oakland Raiders (13-1-0)	Oakland 40, Houston 7
1968	New York Jets (11-3-0)	Oakland Raiders (12-2-0) (b)	New York 27, Oakland 23
1969	New York Jets (10-4-0)	Oakland Raiders (12-1-1)	Kansas City 17, Oakland 7 (c)

(a) Defeated Buffalo Bills in divisional playoff. (b) Defeated Kansas City Chiefs in divisional playoff. (c) Kansas City defeated N.Y. Jets and Oakland Raiders defeated Houston Oilers in divisional playoffs.

National Football League Champions 1933-1969

Year	East Winner (W-L-T)	West Winner (W-L-T)	Championship
1933	New York Giants (11-3-0)	Chicago Bears (10-2-1)	Chicago Bears 23, New York 21
1934	New York Giants (8-5-0)	Chicago Bears (13-0-0)	New York 30, Chicago Bears 13
1935	New York Giants (9-3-0)	Detroit Lions (7-3-2)	Detroit 26, New York 7
1936	Boston Redskins (7-5-0)	Green Bay Packers (10-1-1)	Green Bay 21, Boston 6
1937	Washington Redskins (8-3-0)	Chicago Bears (9-1-1)	Washington 28, Chicago Bears 21
1938	New York Giants (8-2-1)	Green Bay Packers (8-3-0)	New York 23, Green Bay 17
1939	New York Giants (9-1-1)	Green Bay Packers (9-2-0)	Green Bay 27, New York 0
1940	Washington Redskins (9-2-0)	Chicago Bears (8-3-0)	Chicago Bears 73, Washington 0
1941	New York Giants (8-3-0)	Chicago Bears (10-1-1)(a)	Chicago Bears 37, New York 9
1942	Washington Redskins (10-1-1)	Chicago Bears (11-0-0)	Washington 14, Chicago Bears 6
1943	Washington Redskins (6-3-1)	Chicago Bears (8-1-1)	Chicago Bears, 41, Washington 21
1944	New York Giants (8-1-1)	Green Bay Packers (8-2-0)	Green Bay 14, New York 7
1945	Washington Redskins (8-2-0)	Cleveland Rams (9-1-0)	Cleveland 15, Washington 14
1946	New York Giants (7-3-1)	Chicago Bears (8-2-1)	Chicago Bears 24, New York 14
1947	Philadelphia Eagles (8-4-0)(a)	Chicago Cardinals (9-3-0)	Chicago Cardinals 28, Philadelphia 21
1948	Philadelphia Eagles (9-2-1)	Chicago Cardinals (11-1-0)	Philadelphia 7, Chicago Cardinals 0
1949	Philadelphia Eagles (11-1-0)	Los Angeles Rams (8-2-2)	Philadelphia 14, Los Angeles 0
1950	Cleveland Browns (10-2-0)(a)	Los Angeles Rams (9-3-0) (a)	Cleveland 30, Los Angeles 28
1951	Cleveland Browns (11-1-0)	Los Angeles Rams (8-4-0)	Los Angeles 24, Cleveland 17
1952	Cleveland Browns (8-4-0)	Detroit Lions (9-3-0)(a)	Detroit 17, Cleveland 7
1953	Cleveland Browns (11-1-0)	Detroit Lions (10-2-0)	Detroit 17, Cleveland 16
1954	Cleveland Browns (9-3-0)	Detroit Lions (9-2-1)	Cleveland 56, Detroit 10
1955	Cleveland Browns (9-2-1)	Los Angeles Rams (8-3-1)	Cleveland 38, Los Angeles 14
1956	New York Giants (8-3-1)	Chicago Bears (9-2-1)	New York 47, Chicago Bears 7
1957	Cleveland Browns (9-2-1)	Detroit Lions (8-4-0)(a)	Detroit 59, Cleveland 14
1958	New York Giants (9-3-0)(a)	Baltimore Colts (9-3-0)	Baltimore 23, New York 17 (b)
1959	New York Giants (10-2-0)	Baltimore Colts (9-3-0)	Baltimore 31, New York 16
1960	Philadelphia Eagles (10-2-0)	Green Bay Packers (8-4-0)	Philadelphia 17, Green Bay 13
1961	New York Giants (10-3-1)	Green Bay Packers (11-3-0)	Green Bay 37, New York 0
1962	New York Giants (12-2-0)	Green Bay Packers (13-1-0)	Green Bay 16, New York 7
1963	New York Giants (11-3-0)	Chicago Bears (11-1-2)	Chicago 14, New York 10
1964	Cleveland Browns (10-3-1)	Baltimore Colts (12-2-0)	Cleveland 27, Baltimore 0
1965	Cleveland Browns (11-3-0)	Green Bay Packers (10-3-1)(a)	Green Bay 23, Cleveland 12
1966	Dallas Cowboys (10-3-1)	Green Bay Packers (12-2-0)	Green Bay 34, Dallas 27
1967	Dallas Cowboys (9-5-0)	Green Bay Packers (9-4-1)	Green Bay 21, Dallas 17
1968	Cleveland Browns (10-4-0)	Baltimore Colts (13-1-0)	Baltimore 34, Cleveland 0
1969	Cleveland Browns (10-3-1)	Minnesota Vikings (12-2-0)	Minnesota 27, Cleveland 7

(a) Won divisional playoff. (b) Won at 8:15 of sudden death overtime period.

NFL Divisional Champions and Wild Cards 1970-1995

The American Football League and National Football League officially merged in 1966. At the beginning of the 1970 season, the two leagues became the AFC and NFC conferences in the new NFL. Regular-season records are in parentheses.

American Football Conference

Year	Eastern	Central	Western	Wild Card
1970	Baltimore Colts (11-2-1)	Cincinnati Bengals (8-6-0)	Oakland Raiders (8-4-2)	Miami Dolphins (10-4-0)
1971	Miami Dolphins (10-3-1)	Cleveland Browns (9-5-0)	Kansas City Chiefs (10-3-1)	Baltimore Colts (10-4-0)
1972	Miami Dolphins (14-0-0)	Pittsburgh Steelers (11-3-0)	Oakland Raiders (10-3-1)	Cleveland Browns (10-4-0)
1973	Miami Dolphins (12-2-0)	Cincinnati Bengals (10-4-0)	Oakland Raiders (9-4-1)	Cincinnati Bengals (10-4-0)
1974	Miami Dolphins (11-3-0)	Pittsburgh Steelers (10-3-1)	Oakland Raiders (12-2-0)	Buffalo Bills (9-5-0)
1975	Baltimore Colts (10-4-0)	Pittsburgh Steelers (12-2-0)	Oakland Raiders (11-3-0)	Cincinnati Bengals (11-3-0)
1976	Baltimore Colts (11-3-0)	Pittsburgh Steelers (10-4-0)	Oakland Raiders (13-1-0)	New England Patriots (11-3-0)
1977	Baltimore Colts (10-4-0)	Pittsburgh Steelers (9-5-0)	Denver Broncos (12-2-0)	Oakland Raiders (11-3-0)
1978	New England Patriots (11-5-0)	Pittsburgh Steelers (14-2-0)	Denver Broncos (10-6-0)	Houston Oilers (10-6-0) Miami Dolphins (11-5-0)
1979	Miami Dolphins (10-6-0)	Pittsburgh Steelers (12-4-0)	San Diego Chargers (12-4-0)	Houston Oilers (11-5-0) Denver Broncos (10-6-0)
1980	Buffalo Bills (11-5-0)	Cleveland Browns (11-5-0)	San Diego Chargers (11-5-0)	Houston Oilers (11-5-0) Oakland Raiders (11-5-0)
1981	Miami Dolphins (11-4-1)	Cincinnati Bengals (12-4-0)	San Diego Chargers (10-6-0)	Buffalo Bills (10-6-0) N.Y. Jets (10-5-1)
1982	Strike abbreviated season. See note.			
1983	Miami Dolphins (12-4-0)	Pittsburgh Steelers (10-6-0)	L.A. Raiders (12-4-0)	Denver Broncos (9-7-0) Seattle Seahawks (9-7-0)
1984	Miami Dolphins (14-2-0)	Pittsburgh Steelers (9-7-0)	Denver Broncos (13-3-0)	L.A. Raiders (11-5-0) Seattle Seahawks (12-4-0)
1985	Miami Dolphins (12-4-0)	Cleveland Browns (8-8-0)	L.A. Raiders (12-4-0)	New England Patriots (11-5-0) N.Y. Jets (11-5-0)
1986	New England Patriots (11-5-0)	Cleveland Browns (12-4-0)	Denver Broncos (11-5-0)	K.C. Chiefs (10-6-0) N.Y. Jets (10-6-0)
1987	Indianapolis Colts (9-6-0)	Cleveland Browns (10-5-0)	Denver Broncos (12-4-0)	Houston Oilers (9-6-0) Seattle Seahawks (9-6-0)
1988	Buffalo Bills (12-4-0)	Cincinnati Bengals (12-4-0)	Seattle Seahawks (9-7-0)	Cleveland Browns (10-6-0) Houston Oilers (10-6-0)
1989	Buffalo Bills (9-7-0)	Cleveland Browns (9-6-1)	Denver Broncos (11-5-0)	Houston Oilers (9-7-0) Pittsburgh Steelers (9-7-0)
1990	Buffalo Bills (13-3-0)	Cincinnati Bengals (9-7-0)	L.A. Raiders (12-4-0)	Houston Oilers (9-7-0) Kansas City Chiefs (11-5-0) Miami Dolphins (12-4-0)
1991	Buffalo Bills (13-3-0)	Houston Oilers (11-5-0)	Denver Broncos (12-4-0)	Kansas City Chiefs (11-5-0) Miami Dolphins (12-4-0) N.Y. Jets (8-8-0)

American Football Conference

Year	Eastern	Central	Western	Wild Card
1992	Miami Dolphins (11-5-0)	Pittsburgh Steelers (11-5-0)	San Diego Chargers (11-5-0)	Buffalo Bills (11-5-0)
				Houston Oilers (10-6-0)
				Kansas City Chiefs (10-6-0)
1993	Buffalo Bills (12-4-0)	Houston Oilers (12-4-0)	Kansas City Chiefs (11-5-0)	Denver Broncos (9-7-0)
				L.A. Raiders (10-6-0)
				Pittsburgh Steelers (9-7-0)
1994	Miami Dolphins (10-6-0)	Pittsburgh Steelers (12-4-0)	San Diego Chargers (11-5-0)	Cleveland Browns (11-5-0)
				Kansas City Chiefs (9-7-0)
				New England Patriots (10-6-0)
1995	Buffalo Bills (10-6-0)	Pittsburgh Steelers (11-5-0)	Kansas City Chiefs (13-3-0)	Miami Dolphins (9-7-0)
				Indianapolis Colts (9-7-0)
				San Diego Chargers (9-7-0)

National Football Conference

Year	Eastern	Central	Western	Wild Card
1970	Dallas Cowboys (10-4-0)	Minnesota Vikings (12-2-0)	San Francisco 49ers (10-3-1)	Detroit Lions (10-4-0)
1971	Dallas Cowboys (11-3-0)	Minnesota Vikings (11-3-0)	San Francisco 49ers (9-5-0)	Washington Redskins (9-4-1)
1972	Washington Redskins (11-3-0)	Green Bay Packers (10-4-0)	San Francisco 49ers (8-5-1)	Dallas Cowboys (10-4-0)
1973	Dallas Cowboys (10-4-0)	Minnesota Vikings (12-2-0)	L.A. Rams (12-2-0)	Washington Redskins (10-4-0)
1974	St. Louis Cardinals (10-4-0)	Minnesota Vikings (10-4-0)	L.A. Rams (10-4-0)	Washington Redskins (10-4-0)
1975	St. Louis Cardinals (11-3-0)	Minnesota Vikings (12-2-0)	L.A. Rams (12-2-0)	Dallas Cowboys (10-4-0)
1976	Dallas Cowboys (11-3-0)	Minnesota Vikings (11-2-1)	L.A. Rams (10-3-1)	Washington Redskins (10-4-0)
1977	Dallas Cowboys (12-2-0)	Minnesota Vikings (9-5-0)	L.A. Rams (10-4-0)	Chicago Bears (9-5-0)
1978	Dallas Cowboys (12-4-0)	Minnesota Vikings (8-7-1)	L.A. Rams (12-4-0)	Atlanta Falcons (9-7-0)
				Philadelphia Eagles (9-7-0)
1979	Dallas Cowboys (11-5-0)	Tampa Bay Buccaneers (10-6-0)	L.A. Rams (9-7-0)	Chicago Bears (10-6-0)
				Philadelphia Eagles (11-5-0)
1980	Philadelphia Eagles (12-4-0)	Minnesota Vikings (9-7-0)	Atlanta Falcons (12-4-0)	Dallas Cowboys (12-4-0)
				L.A. Rams (11-5-0)
1981	Dallas Cowboys (12-4-0)	Tampa Bay Buccaneers (9-7-0)	San Francisco 49ers (13-3-0)	N.Y. Giants (9-7-0)
				Philadelphia Eagles (10-6-0)
1982	Strike abbreviated season. See note.			
1983	Washington Redskins (14-2-0)	Detroit Lions (9-7-0)	San Francisco 49ers (10-6-0)	Dallas Cowboys (12-4-0)
				L.A. Rams (9-7-0)
1984	Washington Redskins (11-5-0)	Chicago Bears (10-6-0)	San Francisco 49ers (15-1-0)	L.A. Rams (10-6-0)
				N.Y. Giants (9-7-0)
1985	Dallas Cowboys (10-6-0)	Chicago Bears (15-1-0)	L.A. Rams (11-5-0)	N.Y. Giants (10-6-0)
				San Francisco 49ers (10-6-0)
1986	N.Y. Giants (14-2-0)	Chicago Bears (14-2-0)	San Francisco 49ers (10-5-1)	L.A. Rams (10-6-0)
				Washington Redskins (12-4-0)
1987	Washington Redskins (11-4-0)	Chicago Bears (11-4-0)	San Francisco 49ers (13-2-0)	Minnesota Vikings (8-7-0)
				New Orleans Saints (12-3-0)
1988	Philadelphia Eagles (10-6-0)	Chicago Bears (12-4-0)	San Francisco 49ers (10-6-0)	L.A. Rams (10-6-0)
				Minnesota Vikings (11-5-0)
1989	N.Y. Giants (12-4-0)	Minnesota Vikings (10-6-0)	San Francisco 49ers (14-2-0)	L.A. Rams (11-5-0)
				Philadelphia Eagles (11-5-0)
1990	N.Y. Giants (13-3-0)	Chicago Bears (11-5-0)	San Francisco 49ers (14-2-0)	New Orleans Saints (8-8-0)
				Philadelphia Eagles (10-6-0)
				Washington Redskins (10-6-0)
1991	Washington Redskins (14-2-0)	Detroit Lions (12-4-0)	New Orleans Saints (11-5-0)	Atlanta Falcons (10-6-0)
				Chicago Bears (11-5-0)
				Dallas Cowboys (11-5-0)
1992	Dallas Cowboys (13-3-0)	Minnesota Vikings (11-5-0)	San Francisco 49ers (14-2-0)	New Orleans Saints (12-4-0)
				Philadelphia Eagles (11-5-0)
				Washington Redskins (9-7-0)
1993	Dallas Cowboys (12-4-0)	Detroit Lions (10-6-0)	San Francisco 49ers (10-6-0)	Green Bay Packers (9-7-0)
				Minnesota Vikings (9-7-0)
				N.Y. Giants (11-5-0)
1994	Dallas Cowboys (12-4-0)	Minnesota Vikings (10-6-0)	San Francisco 49ers (13-3-0)	Chicago Bears (9-7-0)
				Detroit Lions (9-7-0)
				Green Bay Packers (9-7-0)
1995	Dallas Cowboys (12-4-0)	Green Bay Packers (11-5-0)	San Francisco 49ers (11-5-0)	Philadelphia Eagles (10-6-0)
				Detroit Lions (10-6-0)
				Atlanta Falcons (9-7-0)

Note: A strike shortened the 1982 season from 16 to 9 games. The top 8 teams in each conference played in a tournament to determine the conference champion. AFC—Miami Dolphins, New England Patriots, L.A. Raiders, Cleveland Browns, N.Y. Jets, Cincinnati Bengals, San Diego Chargers, Pittsburgh Steelers. NFC—Washington Redskins, Detroit Lions, Green Bay Packers, St. Louis Cardinals, Dallas Cowboys, Tampa Bay Buccaneers, Minnesota Vikings, Atlanta Falcons.

NFL Playoff Results, 1996-2006

Year	Conference	Division	Winner (W-L-T)	Playoffs (a)	Year
1996	American	Eastern	New England Patriots (11-5-0)	Jacksonville* 30, Denver 27	1996
		Central	Pittsburgh Steelers (10-6-0)	New England 28, Pittsburgh 3	
		Western	Denver Broncos (13-3-0)	New England 20, Jacksonville* 6	
	National	Eastern	Dallas Cowboys (10-6-0)	Green Bay 35, San Francisco* 14	
		Central	Green Bay Packers (13-3-0)	Carolina 26, Dallas 17	
		Western	Carolina Panthers (12-4-0)	Green Bay 30, Carolina 13	
1997	American	Eastern	New England Patriots (10-6-0)	Pittsburgh 7, New England 6	1997
		Central	Pittsburgh Steelers (11-5-0)	Denver* 14, Kansas City 10	
		Western	Kansas City Chiefs (13-3-0)	Denver* 24, Pittsburgh 21	
	National	Eastern	New York Giants (10-5-1)	San Francisco 38, Minnesota* 22	
		Central	Green Bay Packers (13-3-0)	Green Bay 21, Tampa Bay* 7	
		Western	San Francisco 49ers (13-3-0)	Green Bay 23, San Francisco 10	

Year	Conference	Division	Winner (W-L-T)	Playoffs (a)	Year
1998	American	Eastern	N.Y. Jets (12-4-0)	Denver 38, Miami* 3	1998
		Central	Jacksonville Jaguars (11-5-0)	N.Y. Jets 34, Jacksonville 24	
		Western	Denver Broncos (14-2-0)	Denver 23, N.Y. Jets 10	
	National	Eastern	Dallas Cowboys (10-6-0)	Atlanta 20, San Francisco* 18	
		Central	Minnesota Vikings (15-1-0)	Minnesota 41, Arizona* 21	
		Western	Atlanta Falcons (14-2-0)	Atlanta 30, Minnesota 27 (OT)	
1999	American	Eastern	Indianapolis Colts (13-3-0)	Jacksonville 62, Miami* 7	1999
		Central	Jacksonville Jaguars (14-2-0)	Tennessee* 19, Indianapolis 16	
		Western	Seattle Seahawks (9-7-0)	Tennessee* 33, Jacksonville 14	
	National	Eastern	Washington Redskins (10-6-0)	Tampa Bay 14, Washington 13	
		Central	Tampa Bay Buccaneers (11-5-0)	St. Louis 49, Minnesota* 37	
		Western	St. Louis Rams (13-3-0)	St. Louis 11, Tampa Bay 6	
2000	American	Eastern	Miami Dolphins (11-5-0)	Oakland 27, Miami 0	2000
		Central	Tennessee Titans (13-3-0)	Baltimore* 24, Tennessee 10	
		Western	Oakland Raiders (12-4-0)	Baltimore* 16, Oakland 3	
	National	Eastern	N.Y. Giants (12-4-0)	Minnesota 34, New Orleans 16	
		Central	Minnesota Vikings (11-5-0)	N.Y. Giants 20, Philadelphia* 10	
		Western	New Orleans Saints (10-6-0)	N.Y. Giants 41, Minnesota 0	
2001	American	Eastern	New England Patriots (11-5-0)	New England 16, Oakland 13	2001
		Central	Pittsburgh Steelers (13-3-0)	Pittsburgh 27, Baltimore 10	
		Western	Oakland Raiders (10-6-0)	New England 24, Pittsburgh 17	
	National	Eastern	Philadelphia Eagles (11-5-0)	Philadelphia 33, Chicago 19	
		Central	Chicago Bears (13-3-0)	St. Louis 45, Green Bay* 17	
		Western	St. Louis Rams (14-2-0)	St. Louis 29, Philadelphia 24	
2002	American	East	N.Y. Jets (9-7-0)		2002
		North	Pittsburgh Steelers (10-5-1)	Oakland 30, N.Y. Jets 10	
		South	Tennessee Titans (11-5-0)	Tennessee 34, Pittsburgh 31	
		West	Oakland Raiders (11-5-0)	Oakland 41, Tennessee 24	
	National	East	Philadelphia Eagles (12-4-0)		
		North	Green Bay Packers (12-4-0)	Philadelphia 20, Atlanta* 6	
		South	Tampa Bay Buccaneers (12-4-0)	Tampa Bay 31, San Francisco 6	
		West	San Francisco 49ers (10-6-0)	Tampa Bay 27, Philadelphia 10	
2003	American	East	New England Patriots (14-2-0)		2003
		North	Baltimore Ravens (10-6-0)	Indianapolis 38, Kansas City 31	
		South	Indianapolis Colts (12-4-0)	New England 24, Tennessee* 14	
		West	Kansas City Chiefs (13-3-0)	New England 24, Indianapolis 14	
	National	East	Philadelphia Eagles (12-4-0)		
		North	Green Bay Packers (10-6-0)	Carolina 29, St. Louis 23	
		South	Carolina Panthers (11-5-0)	Philadelphia 20, Green Bay 17	
		West	St. Louis Rams (12-4-0)	Carolina 14, Philadelphia 3	
2004	American	East	New England Patriots (14-2-0)		2004
		North	Pittsburgh Steelers (15-1-0)	Pittsburgh 20, N.Y. Jets 17* (OT)	
		South	Indianapolis Colts (12-4-0)	New England 20, Indianapolis 3	
		West	San Diego Chargers (12-4-0)	New England 41, Pittsburgh 27	
	National	East	Philadelphia Eagles (13-3-0)		
		North	Green Bay Packers (10-6-0)	Atlanta 47, St. Louis* 17	
		South	Atlanta Falcons (11-5-0)	Philidelphia 27, Minnesota* 14	
		West	Seattle Seahawks (9-7-0)	Philidelphia 27, Atlanta 10	
2005	American	East	New England Patriots (10-6-0)		2005
		North	Cincinnati Bengals (11-5-0)	Denver 27, New England 13	
		South	Indianapolis Colts (14-2-0)	Pittsburgh* 21, Indianapolis 18	
		West	Denver Broncos (13-3-0)	Pittsburgh* 34, Denver 17	
	National	East	N.Y Giants (11-5-0)		
		North	Chicago Bears (11-5-0)	Seattle 20, Washington* 10	
		South	Tampa Bay Buccaneers (11-5-0)	Carolina* 29, Chicago 21	
		West	Seattle Seahawks (13-3-0)	Seattle 34, Carolina* 14	
2006	American	East	New England Patriots (12-4-0)		2006
		North	Baltimore Ravens (13-3-0)	Indianapolis 15, Baltimore 6	
		South	Indianapolis Colts (12-4-0)	New England 24, San Diego 21	
		West	San Diego Chargers (14-2-0)	Indianapolis 38, New England 34	
	National	East	Philadelphia Eagles (10-6-0)		
		North	Chicago Bears (13-3-0)	New Orleans 27, Philadelphia 24	
		South	New Orleans Saints (10-6-0)	Chicago 27, Seattle 24 (OT)	
		West	Seattle Seahawks (9-7-0)	Chicago 39, New Orleans 14	

*Wild card team. (a) Only the final 2 conference playoff rounds are shown.

American Football Conference Leaders

(American Football League, 1960-69)

Player, team	Att	Com	YG	TD	Year	Player, team	Rec.	YG	TD
	Passing[1]						Receptions		
Jack Kemp, L.A. Chargers	406	211	3,018	20	1960	Lionel Taylor, Denver	92	1,235	12
George Blanda, Houston	362	187	3,330	36	1961	Lionel Taylor, Denver	100	1,176	4
Len Dawson, Dallas Texans	310	189	2,759	29	1962	Lionel Taylor, Denver	77	908	4
Tobin Rote, San Diego	286	170	2,510	20	1963	Lionel Taylor, Denver	78	1,101	10
Len Dawson, Kansas City	354	199	2,879	30	1964	Charley Hennigan, Houston	101	1,546	8
John Hadl, San Diego	348	174	2,798	20	1965	Lionel Taylor, Denver	85	1,131	6
Len Dawson, Kansas City	284	159	2,527	26	1966	Lance Alworth, San Diego	73	1,383	13
Daryle Lamonica, Oakland	425	220	3,228	30	1967	George Sauer, N.Y. Jets	75	1,189	6
Len Dawson, Kansas City	224	131	2,109	17	1968	Lance Alworth, San Diego	68	1,312	10
Greg Cook, Cincinnati	197	106	1,854	15	1969	Lance Alworth, San Diego	64	1,003	4
Daryle Lamonica, Oakland	356	179	2,516	22	1970	Marlin Briscoe, Buffalo	57	1,036	8
Bob Griese, Miami	263	145	2,089	19	1971	Fred Biletnikoff, Oakland	61	929	9
Earl Morrall, Miami	150	83	1,360	11	1972	Fred Biletnikoff, Oakland	58	802	7
Ken Stabler, Oakland	260	163	1,997	14	1973	Fred Willis, Houston	57	371	1
Ken Anderson, Cincinnati	328	213	2,667	18	1974	Lydell Mitchell, Baltimore Colts	72	544	2
Ken Anderson, Cincinnati	377	228	3,169	21	1975	Reggie Rucker, Cleveland	60	770	3
						Lydell Mitchell, Baltimore Colts	60	554	4
Ken Stabler, Oakland	291	194	2,737	27	1976	MacArthur Lane, Kansas City	66	686	1

Passing[1]

Player, team	Att	Com	YG	TD	Year
Bob Griese, Miami	307	180	2,252	22	1977
Terry Bradshaw, Pittsburgh	368	207	2,915	28	1978
Dan Fouts, San Diego	530	332	4,082	24	1979
Brian Sipe, Cleveland	554	337	4,132	30	1980
Ken Anderson, Cincinnati	479	300	3,754	29	1981
Ken Anderson, Cincinnati	309	218	2,495	12	1982
Dan Marino, Miami	296	173	2,210	20	1983
Dan Marino, Miami	564	362	5,084	48	1984
Ken O'Brien, N.Y. Jets	488	297	3,888	25	1985
Dan Marino, Miami	623	378	4,746	44	1986
Bernie Kosar, Cleveland	389	241	3,033	22	1987
Boomer Esiason, Cincinnati	388	223	3,572	28	1988
Boomer Esiason, Cincinnati	455	258	3,525	28	1989
Jim Kelly, Buffalo	346	219	2,829	24	1990
Jim Kelly, Buffalo	474	304	3,844	33	1991
Warren Moon, Houston	346	224	2,521	18	1992
John Elway, Denver	551	348	4,030	25	1993
Dan Marino, Miami	615	385	4,453	30	1994
Jim Harbaugh, Indianapolis	314	200	2,575	17	1995
John Elway, Denver	466	287	3,328	26	1996
Mark Brunell, Jacksonville	435	264	3,281	18	1997
Vinny Testaverde, N.Y. Jets	421	259	3,256	29	1998
Peyton Manning, Indianapolis	533	331	4,135	26	1999
Brian Griese, Denver	336	216	2,688	19	2000
Rich Gannon, Oakland	549	361	3,828	27	2001
Chad Pennington, N.Y. Jets	399	275	3,120	22	2002
Steve McNair, Tennessee	400	250	3,215	24	2003
Peyton Manning, Indianapolis	497	336	4,557	49	2004
Peyton Manning, Indianapolis	453	305	3,747	28	2005
Peyton Manning, Indianapolis	557	362	4,397	31	2006

Receptions

Year	Player, team	Rec.	YG	TD
1977	Lydell Mitchell, Baltimore Colts	71	620	4
1978	Steve Largent, Seattle	71	1,168	8
1979	Joe Washington, Baltimore Colts	82	750	3
1980	Kellen Winslow, San Diego	89	1,290	9
1981	Kellen Winslow, San Diego	88	1,075	10
1982	Kellen Winslow, San Diego	54	721	6
1983	Todd Christensen, L.A. Raiders	92	1,247	12
1984	Ozzie Newsome, Cleveland	89	1,001	5
1985	Lionel James, San Diego	86	1,027	6
1986	Todd Christensen, L.A. Raiders	95	1,153	8
1987	Al Toon, N.Y. Jets	68	976	5
1988	Al Toon, N.Y. Jets	93	1,067	5
1989	Andre Reed, Buffalo	88	1,312	6
1990	Haywood Jeffires, Houston	74	1,048	8
1990	Drew Hill, Houston	74	1,019	5
1991	Haywood Jeffires, Houston	100	1,181	7
1992	Haywood Jeffires, Houston	90	913	9
1993	Reggie Langhorne, Indianapolis	85	1,038	3
1994	Ben Coates, New England	96	1,174	7
1995	Carl Pickens, Cincinnati	99	1,234	17
1996	Carl Pickens, Cincinnati	100	1,180	12
1997	Tim Brown, Oakland	104	1,408	5
1998	O.J. McDuffie, Miami	90	1,050	7
1999	Jimmy Smith, Jacksonville	116	1,636	6
2000	Marvin Harrison, Indianapolis	102	1,413	14
2001	Rod Smith, Denver	113	1,343	11
2002	Marvin Harrison, Indianapolis	143	1,722	11
2003	LaDainian Tomlinson, San Diego	100	725	4
2004	Tony Gonzalez, Kansas City	102	1,258	7
2005	Chad Johnson, Cincinnati	97	1,432	9
2006	Andre Johnson, Houston	103	1,147	5

Scoring

Player, team	TD	PAT	FG	Pts	Year
Gene Mingo, Denver	6	33	18	123	1960
Gino Cappelletti, Boston	8	48	17	147	1961
Gene Mingo, Denver	4	32	27	137	1962
Gino Cappelletti, Boston	2	35	22	113	1963
Gino Cappelletti, Boston	7	36	25	155	1964
Gino Cappelletti, Boston	9	27	17	132	1965
Gino Cappelletti, Boston	6	35	16	119	1966
George Blanda, Oakland	0	56	20	116	1967
Jim Turner, N.Y. Jets	0	43	34	145	1968
Jim Turner, N.Y. Jets	0	33	32	129	1969
Jan Stenerud, Kansas City	0	26	30	116	1970
Garo Yepremian, Miami	0	33	28	117	1971
Bobby Howfield, N.Y. Jets	0	40	27	121	1972
Roy Gerela, Pittsburgh	0	36	29	123	1973
Roy Gerela, Pittsburgh	0	33	20	93	1974
O.J. Simpson, Buffalo	23	0	0	138	1975
Toni Linhart, Baltimore Colts	0	49	20	109	1976
Errol Mann, Oakland	0	39	20	99	1977
Pat Leahy, N.Y. Jets	0	41	22	107	1978
John Smith, New England	0	46	23	115	1979
John Smith, New England	0	51	26	129	1980
Jim Breech, Cincinnati	0	49	22	115	1981
Nick Lowery, Kansas City	0	37	26	115	
Marcus Allen, L.A. Raiders	14	0	0	84	1982
Gary Anderson, Pittsburgh	0	38	27	119	1983
Gary Anderson, Pittsburgh	0	45	24	117	1984
Gary Anderson, Pittsburgh	0	40	33	139	1985
Tony Franklin, New England	0	44	32	140	1986
Jim Breech, Cincinnati	0	25	24	97	1987
Scott Norwood, Buffalo	0	33	32	129	1988
David Treadwell, Denver	0	39	27	120	1989
Nick Lowery, Kansas City	0	37	34	139	1990
Pete Stoyanovich, Miami	0	28	31	121	1991
Pete Stoyanovich, Miami	0	34	30	124	1992
Jeff Jaeger, L.A. Raiders	0	27	35	132	1993
John Carney, San Diego	0	33	34	135	1994
Norm Johnson, Pittsburgh	0	39	34	141	1995
Cary Blanchard, Indianapolis	0	27	36	135	1996
Mike Hollis, Jacksonville	0	41	31	134	1997
Steve Christie, Buffalo	0	41	33	140	1998
Mike Vanderjagt, Indianapolis	0	43	34	145	1999
Matt Stover, Baltimore	0	30	35	135	2000
Mike Vanderjagt, Indianapolis	0	41	28	125	2001
Priest Holmes, Kansas City	24	0	0	144	2002
Priest Holmes, Kansas City	27	0	0	162	2003
Adam Vinatieri, New England	0	48	31	141	2004
Shayne Graham, Cincinnati	0	47	28	131	2005
LaDainian Tomlinson, San Diego	31	0	0	186	2006

Rushing

Year	Player, team	Yds	Att	TD
1960	Abner Haynes, Dallas Texans	875	156	9
1961	Billy Cannon, Houston	948	200	6
1962	Cookie Gilchrist, Buffalo	1,096	214	13
1963	Clem Daniels, Oakland	1,099	215	3
1964	Cookie Gilchrist, Buffalo	981	230	6
1965	Paul Lowe, San Diego	1,121	222	7
1966	Jim Nance, Boston	1,458	299	11
1967	Jim Nance, Boston	1,216	269	7
1968	Paul Robinson, Cincinnati	1,023	238	8
1969	Dickie Post, San Diego	873	182	6
1970	Floyd Little, Denver	901	209	3
1971	Floyd Little, Denver	1,133	284	6
1972	O.J. Simpson, Buffalo	1,251	292	6
1973	O.J. Simpson, Buffalo	2,003	332	12
1974	Otis Armstrong, Denver	1,407	263	9
1975	O.J. Simpson, Buffalo	1,817	329	16
1976	O.J. Simpson, Buffalo	1,503	290	8
1977	Mark van Eeghen, Oakland	1,273	324	7
1978	Earl Campbell, Houston	1,450	302	13
1979	Earl Campbell, Houston	1,697	368	19
1980	Earl Campbell, Houston	1,934	373	13
1981	Earl Campbell, Houston	1,376	361	10
1982	Freeman McNeil, N.Y. Jets	786	151	6
1983	Curt Warner, Seattle	1,449	335	13
1984	Earnest Jackson, San Diego	1,179	296	8
1985	Marcus Allen, L.A. Raiders	1,759	380	11
1986	Curt Warner, Seattle	1,481	319	13
1987	Eric Dickerson, L.A. Rams-Ind.	1,288*	283	6
1988	Eric Dickerson, Indianapolis	1,659	388	14
1989	Christian Okoye, Kansas City	1,480	370	12
1990	Thurman Thomas, Buffalo	1,297	271	11
1991	Thurman Thomas, Buffalo	1,407	288	7
1992	Barry Foster, Pittsburgh	1,690	390	11
1993	Thurman Thomas, Buffalo	1,315	355	6
1994	Chris Warren, Seattle	1,545	333	9
1995	Curtis Martin, New England	1,487	368	14
1996	Terrell Davis, Denver	1,538	345	13
1997	Terrell Davis, Denver	1,750	369	15
1998	Terrell Davis, Denver	2,008	392	21
1999	Edgerrin James, Indianapolis	1,553	369	13
2000	Edgerrin James, Indianapolis	1,709	387	13
2001	Priest Holmes, Kansas City	1,555	327	8
2002	Ricky Williams, Miami	1,853	383	16
2003	Jamal Lewis, Baltimore	2,066	387	14
2004	Curtis Martin, N.Y. Jets	1,697	371	12
2005	Larry Johnson, Kansas City	1,750	336	20
2006	LaDainian Tomlinson, San Diego	1,815	348	28

*Includes 277 yards after being traded to NFC; 1,011 yards led AFC. (1) Based on quarterback rating points.

National Football Conference Leaders

(National Football League, 1960-69)

Passing[1] Player, team	Att	Com	YG	TD	Year	Receptions Player, team	Rec	YG	TD
Milt Plum, Cleveland	250	151	2,297	21	1960	Raymond Berry, Baltimore Colts	74	1,298	10
Milt Plum, Cleveland	302	177	2,416	18	1961	Jim Phillips, L.A. Rams	78	1,092	5
Bart Starr, Green Bay	285	178	2,438	12	1962	Bobby Mitchell, Washington	72	1,384	11
Y.A. Tittle, N.Y. Giants	367	221	3,145	36	1963	Bobby Joe Conrad, St. Louis Cardinals	73	967	10
Bart Starr, Green Bay	272	163	2,144	15	1964	Johnny Morris, Chicago	93	1,200	10
Rudy Bukich, Chicago	312	176	2,641	20	1965	Dave Parks, San Francisco	80	1,344	12
Bart Starr, Green Bay	251	156	2,257	14	1966	Charley Taylor, Washington	72	1,119	12
Sonny Jurgensen, Washington	508	288	3,747	31	1967	Charley Taylor, Washington	70	990	9
Earl Morrall, Baltimore Colts	317	182	2,909	26	1968	Clifton McNeil, San Francisco	71	994	7
Sonny Jurgensen, Washington	442	274	3,102	22	1969	Dan Abramowicz, New Orleans	73	1,015	7
John Brodie, San Francisco	378	223	2,941	24	1970	Dick Gordon, Chicago	71	1,026	13
Roger Staubach, Dallas	211	126	1,882	15	1971	Bob Tucker, N.Y. Giants	59	791	4
Norm Snead, N.Y. Giants	325	196	2,307	17	1972	Harold Jackson, Philadelphia	62	1,048	4
Roger Staubach, Dallas	286	179	2,428	23	1973	Harold Carmichael, Philadelphia	67	1,116	9
Sonny Jurgensen, Washington	167	107	1,185	11	1974	Charles Young, Philadelphia	63	696	3
Fran Tarkenton, Minnesota	425	273	2,994	25	1975	Chuck Foreman, Minnesota	73	691	9
James Harris, L.A. Rams	158	91	1,460	8	1976	Drew Pearson, Dallas	58	806	6
Roger Staubach, Dallas	361	210	2,620	18	1977	Ahmad Rashad, Minnesota	51	681	2
Roger Staubach, Dallas	413	231	3,190	25	1978	Rickey Young, Minnesota	88	704	5
Roger Staubach, Dallas	461	267	3,586	27	1979	Ahmad Rashad, Minnesota	80	1,156	9
Ron Jaworski, Philadelphia	451	257	3,529	27	1980	Earl Cooper, San Francisco	83	567	4
Joe Montana, San Francisco	488	311	3,565	19	1981	Dwight Clark, San Francisco	85	1,105	4
Joe Thiesmann, Washington	252	161	2,033	13	1982	Dwight Clark, San Francisco	60	913	5
Steve Bartkowski, Atlanta	432	274	3,167	22	1983	Roy Green, St. Louis Cardinals	78	1,227	14
						Charlie Brown, Washington	78	1,225	8
						Earnest Gray, N.Y. Giants	78	1,139	5
Joe Montana, San Francisco	432	279	3,630	28	1984	Art Monk, Washington	106	1,372	7
Joe Montana, San Francisco	494	303	3,653	27	1985	Roger Craig, San Francisco	92	1,016	6
Tommy Kramer, Minnesota	372	208	3,000	24	1986	Jerry Rice, San Francisco	86	1,570	15
Joe Montana, San Francisco	398	266	3,054	31	1987	J.T. Smith, St. Louis Cardinals	91	1,117	8
Wade Wilson, Minnesota	332	204	2,746	15	1988	Henry Ellard, L.A. Rams	86	1,414	10
Joe Montana, San Francisco	386	271	3,521	26	1989	Sterling Sharpe, Green Bay	90	1,423	12
Phil Simms, N.Y. Giants	311	184	2,284	15	1990	Jerry Rice, San Francisco	100	1,502	13
Steve Young, San Francisco	279	180	2,517	17	1991	Michael Irvin, Dallas	93	1,523	8
Steve Young, San Francisco	402	268	3,465	25	1992	Sterling Sharpe, Green Bay	108	1,461	13
Steve Young, San Francisco	462	314	4,023	29	1993	Sterling Sharpe, Green Bay	112	1,274	11
Steve Young, San Francisco	461	324	3,969	35	1994	Cris Carter, Minnesota	122	1,256	7
Brett Favre, Green Bay	570	359	4,413	38	1995	Herman Moore, Detroit	123	1,686	14
Steve Young, San Francisco	316	214	2,410	14	1996	Jerry Rice, San Francisco	108	1,254	8
Steve Young, San Francisco	356	241	3,029	19	1997	Herman Moore, Detroit	104	1,293	8
Randall Cunningham, Minnesota	425	259	3,704	34	1998	Frank Sanders, Arizona	89	1,145	3
Kurt Warner, St. Louis	499	325	4,353	41	1999	Muhsin Muhammad, Carolina	96	1,253	8
Trent Green, St. Louis	240	145	2,063	16	2000	Muhsin Muhammad, Carolina	102	1,183	6
Kurt Warner, St. Louis	546	375	4,830	36	2001	Keyshawn Johnson, Tampa Bay	106	1,266	1
Brad Johnson, Tampa Bay	451	281	3,049	22	2002	Randy Moss, Minnesota	106	1,347	7
Daunte Culpepper, Minnesota	454	295	3,479	25	2003	Torry Holt, St. Louis	117	1,696	12
Daunte Culpepper, Minnesota	548	379	4,717	39	2004	Joe Horn, New Orleans	94	1,399	11
						Torry Holt, St. Louis	94	1,372	10
Matt Hasselbeck, Seattle	449	294	3,459	24	2005	Steve Smith, Carolina	103	1,563	12
						Larry Fitzgerald, Arizona	103	1,409	10
Drew Brees, New Orleans	554	356	4,418	26	2006	Mike Furrey, Detroit	98	1,086	6

Scoring Player, team	TD	PAT	FG	Pts	Year	Rushing Player, team	Yds	Att	TD
Paul Hornung, Green Bay	15	41	15	176	1960	Jim Brown, Cleveland	1,257	215	9
Paul Hornung, Green Bay	10	41	15	146	1961	Jim Brown, Cleveland	1,408	305	8
Jim Taylor, Green Bay	19	0	0	114	1962	Jim Taylor, Green Bay	1,474	272	19
Don Chandler, N.Y. Giants	0	52	18	106	1963	Jim Brown, Cleveland	1,863	291	12
Lenny Moore, Baltimore Colts	20	0	0	120	1964	Jim Brown, Cleveland	1,446	280	7
Gale Sayers, Chicago	22	0	0	132	1965	Jim Brown, Cleveland	1,544	289	17
Bruce Gossett, L.A. Rams	0	29	28	113	1966	Gale Sayers, Chicago	1,231	229	8
Jim Bakken, St. Louis Cardinals	0	36	27	117	1967	Leroy Kelly, Cleveland	1,205	235	11
Leroy Kelly, Cleveland	20	0	0	120	1968	Leroy Kelly, Cleveland	1,239	248	16
Fred Cox, Minnesota	0	43	26	121	1969	Gale Sayers, Chicago	1,032	236	8
Fred Cox, Minnesota	0	35	30	125	1970	Larry Brown, Washington	1,125	237	5
Curt Knight, Washington	0	27	29	114	1971	John Brockington, Green Bay	1,105	216	4
Chester Marcol, Green Bay	0	29	33	128	1972	Larry Brown, Washington	1,216	285	8
David Ray, L.A. Rams	0	40	30	130	1973	John Brockington, Green Bay	1,144	265	3
Chester Marcol, Green Bay	0	19	25	94	1974	Lawrence McCutcheon, L.A. Rams	1,109	236	3
Chuck Foreman, Minnesota	22	0	0	132	1975	Jim Otis, St. Louis Cardinals	1,076	269	5
Mark Moseley, Washington	0	31	22	97	1976	Walter Payton, Chicago	1,390	311	13
Walter Payton, Chicago	16	0	0	96	1977	Walter Payton, Chicago	1,852	339	14
Frank Corral, L.A. Rams	0	31	29	118	1978	Walter Payton, Chicago	1,395	333	11
Mark Moseley, Washington	0	39	25	114	1979	Walter Payton, Chicago	1,610	369	14
Ed Murray, Detroit	0	35	27	116	1980	Walter Payton, Chicago	1,460	317	6
Ed Murray, Detroit	0	46	25	121	1981	George Rogers, New Orleans	1,674	378	13
Rafael Septien, Dallas	0	40	27	121					
Wendell Tyler, L.A. Rams	13	0	0	78	1982	Tony Dorsett, Dallas	745	177	5
Mark Moseley, Washington	0	62	33	161	1983	Eric Dickerson, L.A. Rams	1,808	390	18
Ray Wersching, San Francisco	0	56	25	131	1984	Eric Dickerson, L.A. Rams	2,105	379	14
Kevin Butler, Chicago	0	51	31	144	1985	Gerald Riggs, Atlanta	1,719	397	10

Player, team	TD	PAT	FG	Pts	Year	Player, team	Yds	Att	TD
Kevin Butler, Chicago	0	36	28	120	1986	Eric Dickerson, L.A. Rams	1,821	404	11
Jerry Rice, San Francisco	23	0	0	138	1987	Charles White, L.A. Rams	1,374	324	11
Mike Cofer, San Francisco	0	40	27	121	1988	Herschel Walker, Dallas	1,514	361	5
Mike Cofer, San Francisco	0	49	29	136	1989	Barry Sanders, Detroit	1,470	280	14
Chip Lohmiller, Washington	0	41	30	131	1990	Barry Sanders, Detroit	1,304	255	13
Chip Lohmiller, Washington	0	56	31	149	1991	Emmitt Smith, Dallas	1,563	365	12
Morten Andersen, New Orleans	0	33	29	120	1992	Emmitt Smith, Dallas	1,713	373	18
Chip Lohmiller, Washington	0	30	30	120					
Jason Hanson, Detroit	0	28	34	130	1993	Emmitt Smith, Dallas	1,486	283	9
Fuad Reveiz, Minnesota	0	30	34	132	1994	Barry Sanders, Detroit	1,883	331	7
Emmitt Smith, Dallas	22	0	0	132					
Emmitt Smith, Dallas	25	0	0	150	1995	Emmitt Smith, Dallas	1,773	377	25
John Kasay, Carolina	0	34	37	145	1996	Barry Sanders, Detroit	1,553	307	11
Richie Cunningham, Dallas	0	24	34	126	1997	Barry Sanders, Detroit	2,053	335	11
Gary Anderson, Minnesota	0	59	35	164	1998	Jamal Anderson, Atlanta	1,846	410	14
Jeff Wilkins, St. Louis	0	64	20	124	1999	Stephen Davis, Washington	1,405	290	17
Marshall Faulk, St. Louis	26	0	0	156	2000	Robert Smith, Minnesota	1,521	295	7
Marshall Faulk, St. Louis	21	0	0	128	2001	Stephen Davis, Washington	1,432	356	5
Jay Feely, Atlanta	0	42	32	138	2002	Deuce McAllister, New Orleans	1,388	325	13
Jeff Wilkins, St. Louis	0	46	39	163	2003	Ahman Green, Green Bay	1,883	355	15
David Akers, Philadelphia	0	41	27	122	2004	Shaun Alexander, Seattle	1,696	353	16
Shaun Alexander, Seattle	28	0	0	168	2005	Shaun Alexander, Seattle	1,880	370	27
Robbie Gould, Chicago	0	47	32	143	2006	Frank Gore, San Francisco	1,695	312	8

(1) Based on quarterback rating points.

NFL MVP, Defensive Player of the Year, and Rookie of the Year

The Most Valuable Player and Defensive Player of the Year are two of many awards given out annually by the Associated Press. Rookie of the Year is one of many awards given out annually by *The Sporting News*. Many other organizations give out annual awards honoring the NFL's best players.

Most Valuable Player

1957 Jim Brown, Cleveland	1974 Ken Stabler, Oakland	1992 Steve Young, San Francisco
1958 Gino Marchetti, Baltimore Colts	1975 Fran Tarkenton, Minnesota	1993 Emmitt Smith, Dallas
1959 Charley Conerly, N.Y. Giants	1976 Bert Jones, Baltimore	1994 Steve Young, San Francisco
1960 (tie) Norm Van Brocklin, Philadelphia; Joe Schmidt, Detroit	1977 Walter Payton, Chicago	1995 Brett Favre, Green Bay
	1978 Terry Bradshaw, Pittsburgh	1996 Brett Favre, Green Bay
1961 Paul Hornung, Green Bay	1979 Earl Campbell, Houston	1997 (tie) Brett Favre, Green Bay; Barry Sanders, Detroit
1962 Jim Taylor, Green Bay	1980 Brian Sipe, Cleveland	
1963 Y.A. Tittle, N.Y. Giants	1981 Ken Anderson, Cincinnati	1998 Terrell Davis, Denver
1964 John Unitas, Baltimore Colts	1982 Mark Moseley, Washington	1999 Kurt Warner, St. Louis
1965 Jim Brown, Cleveland	1983 Joe Theismann, Washington	2000 Marshall Faulk, St. Louis
1966 Bart Starr, Green Bay	1984 Dan Marino, Miami	2001 Kurt Warner, St. Louis
1967 John Unitas, Baltimore Colts	1985 Marcus Allen, L.A. Raiders	2002 Rich Gannon, Oakland
1968 Earl Morrall, Baltimore Colts	1986 Lawrence Taylor, N.Y. Giants	2003 (tie) Peyton Manning, Indianapolis; Steve McNair, Tennessee
1969 Roman Gabriel, L.A. Rams	1987 John Elway, Denver	
1970 John Brodie, San Francisco	1988 Boomer Esiason, Cincinnati	2004 Peyton Manning, Indianapolis
1971 Alan Page, Minnesota	1989 Joe Montana, San Francisco	2005 Shaun Alexander, Seattle
1972 Larry Brown, Washington	1990 Joe Montana, San Francisco	2006 LaDainian Tomlinson, San Diego
1973 O.J. Simpson, Buffalo	1991 Thurman Thomas, Buffalo	

Defensive Player of the Year

1966 Larry Wilson, St. Louis	1980 Lester Hayes, Oakland	1993 Bruce Smith, Buffalo
1967 Deacon Jones, Los Angeles	1981 Joe Klecko, N.Y. Jets	1994 Deion Sanders, San Francisco
1968 Deacon Jones, Los Angeles	1982 Mark Gastineau, N.Y. Jets	1995 Bryce Paup, Buffalo
1969 Dick Butkus, Chicago	1983 Jack Lambert, Pittsburgh	1996 Bruce Smith, Buffalo
1970 Dick Butkus, Chicago	1984 Mike Haynes, L.A. Raiders	1997 Dana Stubblefield, San Francisco
1971 Carl Eller, Minnesota	1985 (tie) Howie Long, L.A. Raiders; Andre Tippett, New England	1998 Reggie White, Green Bay
1972 Joe Greene, Pittsburgh		1999 Warren Sapp, Tampa Bay
1973 Alan Page, Minnesota	1986 Lawrence Taylor, N.Y. Giants	2000 Ray Lewis, Baltimore
1974 Joe Greene, Pittsburgh	1987 Reggie White, Philadelphia	2001 Michael Strahan, N.Y. Giants
1975 Curley Culp, Houston	1988 Mike Singletary, Chicago	2002 Derrick Brooks, Tampa Bay
1976 Jerry Sherk, Cleveland	1989 Tim Harris, Green Bay	2003 Ray Lewis, Baltimore
1977 Harvey Martin, Dallas	1990 Bruce Smith, Buffalo	2004 Ed Reed, Baltimore
1978 Randy Gradishar, Denver	1991 Pat Swilling, New Orleans	2005 Brian Urlacher, Chicago
1979 Lee Roy Selmon, Tampa Bay	1992 Junior Seau, San Diego	2006 Jason Taylor, Miami

Rookie of the Year

1964 Charley Taylor, Washington	1976 NFC: Sammy White, Minnesota	1990 Richmond Webb, Miami
1965 Gale Sayers, Chicago	AFC: Mike Haynes, New England	1991 Mike Croel, Denver
1966 Tommy Nobis, Atlanta	1977 NFC: Tony Dorsett, Dallas	1992 Santana Dotson, Tampa Bay
1967 Mel Farr, Detroit	AFC: A. J. Duhe, Miami	1993 Jerome Bettis, L.A. Rams
1968 Earl McCullouch, Detroit	1978 NFC: Al Baker, Detroit	1994 Marshall Faulk, Indianapolis
1969 Calvin Hill, Dallas	AFC: Earl Campbell, Houston	1995 Curtis Martin, New England
1970 NFC: Bruce Taylor, San Francisco	1979 NFC: Ottis Anderson, St. Louis	1996 Eddie George, Houston
AFC: Dennis Shaw, Buffalo	AFC: Jerry Butler, Buffalo	1997 Warrick Dunn, Tampa Bay
1971 NFC: John Brockington, Green Bay	1980 Billy Sims, Detroit	1998 Randy Moss, Minnesota
AFC: Jim Plunkett, New England	1981 George Rogers, New Orleans	1999 Edgerrin James, Indianapolis
1972 NFC: Chester Marcol, Green Bay	1982 Marcus Allen, L.A. Raiders	2000 Brian Urlacher, Chicago
AFC: Franco Harris, Pittsburgh	1983 Dan Marino, Miami	2001 Kendrell Bell, Pittsburgh
1973 NFC: Chuck Foreman, Minnesota	1984 Louis Lipps, Pittsburgh	2002 Clinton Portis, Denver
1973 AFC: Boobie Clark, Cincinnati	1985 Eddie Brown, Cincinnati	2003 Anquan Boldin, Arizona
1974 NFC: Wilbur Jackson, San Francisco	1986 Rueben Mayes, New Orleans	2004 Ben Roethlisberger, Pittsburgh
AFC: Don Woods, San Diego	1987 Robert Awalt, St. Louis	2005 Carnell "Cadillac" Williams, Tampa Bay
1975 NFC: Steve Bartkowski, Atlanta	1988 Keith Jackson, Philadelphia	2006 Vince Young, Tennessee
AFC: Robert Brazile, Houston	1989 Barry Sanders, Detroit	

All-Time Professional (NFL and AFL) Football Records

(at the end of the 2006 season; *active in 2006; (a) includes AFL statistics.)

Leading Lifetime Scorers

Player	Yrs.	TD	PAT	FG	Total
Morten Anderson*	24	0	825	540	2,445
Gary Anderson*	23	0	820	538	2,434
George Blanda (a)	26	9	942	335	2,002
John Carney*	19	0	510	413	1,749
Norm Johnson	18	0	638	366	1,736
Matt Stover*	16	0	491	408	1,715
Nick Lowery	18	0	562	383	1,711
Jan Stenerud (a)	19	0	580	373	1,699
Jason Elam*	14	0	568	368	1,672
Lou Groza (a)	21	1	810	264	1,608
Eddie Murray	19	0	538	352	1,594
Al Del Greco	17	0	543	347	1,584
Jason Hanson*	15	0	469	356	1,537
Steve Christie	15	0	468	336	1,476
Pat Leahy	18	0	558	304	1,470
Jim Turner (a)	16	1	521	304	1,439
Matt Bahr	17	0	522	300	1,422
John Kasay*	15	0	403	334	1,405
Mark Moseley	16	0	482	300	1,382
Jim Bakken	17	0	534	282	1,380

Leading Lifetime Touchdown Scorers

Player	Yrs.	Rush	Rec.	Ret.	TD
Jerry Rice	20	10	197	1	208
Emmitt Smith	15	164	11	0	175
Marcus Allen	16	123	21	1	145
Marshall Faulk*	12	100	36	0	136
Cris Carter	16	0	130	1	131
Jim Brown	9	106	20	0	126
Walter Payton	13	110	15	0	125
Marvin Harrison*	11	0	122	0	122
Terrell Owens*	11	2	101	0	116
John Riggins	11	104	12	0	116
Lenny Moore	12	63	48	2	113
LaDainian Tomlinson	6	100	11	0	111
Barry Sanders	10	99	10	0	109
Shaun Alexander*	7	96	11	0	107
Tim Brown	17	1	100	4	105
Don Hutson	11	3	99	3	105
Randy Moss*	9	0	101	1	102
Steve Largent	14	1	100	0	101
Franco Harris	13	91	9	0	100
Curtis Martin*	11	90	10	0	100

Most Points, Season — 186, LaDainian Tomlinson, San Diego Chargers (31 TDs).
Most Points, Game — 40, Ernie Nevers, Chicago Cardinals vs. Chicago Bears, Nov. 28, 1929 (6 TDs, 4 PATs).
Most Touchdowns, Season — 28, Shaun Alexander, Seattle Seahawks, 2005.
Most Touchdowns, Game — 6, Ernie Nevers, Chicago Cardinals vs. Chicago Bears, Nov. 28, 1929 (6 rushing); Dub Jones, Cleveland Browns vs. Chicago Bears, Nov. 25, 1951 (4 rushing, 2 pass receptions); Gale Sayers, Chicago Bears vs. San Francisco 49ers, Dec. 12, 1965 (4 rushing, 1 pass reception, 1 punt return).
Most Points After TD, Season — 66, Uwe von Schamann, Miami Dolphins, 1984.
Most Consecutive Points After TD — 371, Jason Elam, Denver Broncos, 1993-2002.
Most Field Goals, Season — 40, Neil Rackers, Arizona Cardinals, 2005.
Most Field Goals, Game — 7, Jim Bakken, St. Louis Cardinals vs. Pittsburgh Steelers, Sept. 24, 1967; Rich Karlis, Minnesota Vikings vs. L.A. Rams, Nov. 5, 1989 (OT); Chris Boniol, Dallas Cowboys vs. Green Bay Packers, Nov. 18, 1996; Billy Cundiff, Dallas Cowboys vs. N.Y. Giants, Sept. 15, 2003 (OT).
Most Field Goals, Career — 540, Morton Anderson, New Orleans Saints-Atlanta Falcons-N.Y. Giants-Kansas City Chiefs-Minnesota Vikings, 1982-2006.
Longest Field Goal — 63 yds., Tom Dempsey, New Orleans Saints vs. Detroit Lions, Nov. 8, 1970; Jason Elam, Denver Broncos vs. Jacksonville Jaguars, Oct. 25, 1998.

Defensive Records

Most Interceptions, Career — 81, Paul Krause, Washington Redskins-Minnesota Vikings, 1964-79.
Most Interceptions, Season — 14, Dick "Night Train" Lane, L. A. Rams, 1952.
Most Touchdowns, Career — 12, Rod Woodson, Pittsburgh Steelers-San Francisco 49ers-Baltimore Ravens-Oakland Raiders, 1987-2003.
Most Touchdowns, Season — 4, Ken Houston, Houston Oilers, 1971; Jim Kearney, Kansas City Chiefs, 1972; Eric Allen, Philadelphia Eagles, 1993.
Most Sacks, Career (Since 1982) — 200, Bruce Smith, Buffalo Bills-Washington Redskins, 1985-2003.
Most Sacks, Season (Since 1982) — 22.5, Michael Strahan, N.Y. Giants, 2001.
Most Sacks, Game (Since 1982) — 7, Derrick Thomas, Kansas City Chiefs vs. Seattle Seahawks, Nov. 11, 1990.

Leading Lifetime Rushers

(ranked by rushing yards)

Player	Yrs.	Att.	Yards	Avg.	Long	TD
Emmitt Smith	15	4,409	18,355	4.2	75	164
Walter Payton	13	3,838	16,726	4.4	76	110
Barry Sanders	10	3,062	15,269	5.0	85	99
Curtis Martin*	11	3,518	14,101	4.0	70	90
Jerome Bettis	13	3,479	13,662	3.9	71	91
Eric Dickerson	11	2,996	13,259	4.4	85	90
Tony Dorsett	12	2,936	12,739	4.3	99	77
Jim Brown	9	2,359	12,312	5.2	80	106
Marshall Faulk*	12	2,836	12,279	4.3	71	100
Marcus Allen	16	3,022	12,243	4.1	61	123
Franco Harris	13	2,949	12,120	4.1	75	91
Thurman Thomas	13	2,877	12,074	4.2	80	65
John Riggins	14	2,916	11,352	3.9	66	104
Corey Dillon*	10	2,618	11,241	4.3	96	82
O.J. Simpson (a)	11	2,404	11,236	4.7	94	61
Ricky Watters	10	2,622	10,643	4.1	57	78
Tiki Barber	10	2,217	10,449	4.7	95	55
Eddie George	9	2,865	10,441	3.6	76	68
Edgerrin James*	8	2,525	10,385	4.1	72	70
Ottis Anderson	14	2,562	10,273	4.0	76	81

Most Yards Gained, Season — 2,105, Eric Dickerson, L.A. Rams, 1984.
Most Yards Gained, Game — 295, Jamal Lewis, Baltimore Ravens vs. Cleveland Browns, Sept. 14, 2003.
Most Touchdowns Rushing, Career — 164, Emmitt Smith, Dallas Cowboys-Arizona Cardinals, 1990-2004.
Most Touchdowns Rushing, Season — 28, LaDainian Tomlinson, San Diego Chargers, 2006.
Most Touchdowns Rushing, Game — 6, Ernie Nevers, Chicago Cardinals vs. Chicago Bears, Nov. 28, 1929.
Most Rushing Attempts, Game — 45, Jamie Morris, Washington Redskins vs. Cincinnati Bengals, Dec. 17, 1988 (OT).
Longest Run From Scrimmage — 99 yds., Tony Dorsett, Dallas Cowboys vs. Minnesota Vikings, Jan. 3, 1983 (TD).

Leading Lifetime Receivers

(ranked by number of receptions)

Player	Yrs.	No.	Yards	Avg.	Long	TD
Jerry Rice	20	1,549	22,895	14.8	96	197
Cris Carter	16	1,101	13,899	12.6	80	130
Tim Brown	17	1,094	14,934	13.7	80	100
Marvin Harrison*	11	1,022	13,697	13.4	80	122
Andre Reed	16	951	13,198	13.9	83	87
Art Monk	16	940	12,721	13.5	79	68
Isaac Bruce*	13	887	13,376	15.1	80	80
Jimmy Smith	12	862	12,287	14.3	75	67
Keenan McCardell	15	861	11,117	12.9	76	62
Irving Fryar	17	851	12,785	15.0	80	84
Rod Smith*	12	849	11,389	13.4	85	68
Larry Centers	14	827	6,797	8.2	54	28
Steve Largent	14	819	13,089	16.0	74	100
Shannon Sharpe	14	815	10,060	12.3	82	62
Henry Ellard	16	814	13,777	16.9	81	65
Keyshawn Johnson*	11	814	10,571	13.0	76	64
Terrell Owens*	11	801	11,715	14.6	91	114
Marshall Faulk*	12	767	6,875	9.0	85	36
James Lofton	16	764	14,004	18.3	80	75
Michael Irvin	12	750	11,904	15.9	87	65
Charlie Joiner (a)	18	750	12,146	16.2	87	65

Most Yards Gained, Career — 22,895, Jerry Rice, San Francisco 49ers-Oakland Raiders-Seattle Seahawks, 1985-2004.
Most Yards Gained, Season — 1,848, Jerry Rice, San Francisco 49ers, 1995.
Most Yards Gained, Game — 336, Willie "Flipper" Anderson, L. A. Rams vs. New Orleans, Nov. 26, 1989 (OT).

Most Pass Receptions, Season — 143, Marvin Harrison, Indianapolis Colts, 2002.
Most Pass Receptions, Game — 20, Terrell Owens, San Francisco 49ers vs. Chicago Bears, Dec. 17, 2000 (283 yards).
Most Touchdown Receptions, Career — 197, Jerry Rice, San Francisco 49ers-Oakland Raiders-Seattle Seahawks, 1985-2004.
Most Touchdown Receptions, Season — 22, Jerry Rice, San Francisco 49ers, 1987.
Most Touchdown Receptions, Game — 5, Bob Shaw, Chicago Cardinals vs. Baltimore Colts, Oct. 2, 1950; Kellen Winslow, San Diego Chargers vs. Oakland Raiders, Nov. 22, 1981; Jerry Rice, San Francisco 49ers vs. Atlanta Falcons, Oct. 14, 1990.

Leading Lifetime Passers
(minimum 1,500 attempts; ranked by quarterback rating points)

Player	Yrs.	Att.	Comp.	Yards	TD	Int.	Pts.[1]
Steve Young	15	4,149	2,667	33,124	232	107	96.8
Peyton Manning*	9	4,890	3,131	37,586	275	139	94.4
Kurt Warner*	9	2,508	1,645	20,591	125	83	93.8
Joe Montana	15	5,391	3,409	40,551	273	139	92.3
Marc Bulger*	5	2,106	1,357	16,233	95	59	91.3
Daunte Culpepper*	8	2,741	1,759	21,091	137	89	90.8
Chad Pennington*	7	1,659	1,080	11,973	72	46	89.3
Tom Brady*	7	3,064	1,896	21,564	147	78	88.4
Drew Brees*	6	2,363	1,481	16,766	106	64	87.5
Trent Green*	9	3,527	2,143	26,963	157	101	87.5
Jeff Garcia*	8	2,973	1,811	20,385	136	73	86.4
Dan Marino	17	8,358	4,967	61,361	420	252	86.4
Donovan McNabb*	8	3,259	1,898	22,080	152	72	85.2
Matt Hasselbeck*	8	2,576	1,552	18,367	114	72	85.1
Brett Favre*	16	8,223	5,021	57,500	414	273	85.1
Rich Gannon	16	4,206	2,533	28,743	180	104	84.7
Brian Griese*	9	2,350	1,481	16,564	104	80	84.5
Jim Kelly	11	4,779	2,874	35,467	237	175	84.5
Mark Brunell*	13	4,594	2,738	31,826	182	106	84.5
Jake Delhomme*	6	1,936	1,151	13,965	92	63	84.0

(1) Rating points based on performances in the following categories: percentage of completions, percentage of touchdown passes, percentage of interceptions, and average gain per pass attempt.
Most Yards Gained, Career — 61,361, Dan Marino, Miami Dolphins, 1983-99.
Most Yards Gained, Season — 5,084, Dan Marino, Miami Dolphins, 1984.
Most Yards Gained, Game — 554, Norm Van Brocklin, L. A. Rams vs. N.Y. Yanks, Sept. 28, 1951 (27 completions in 41 attempts).
Most Touchdowns Passing, Career — 420, Dan Marino, Miami Dolphins, 1983-99.
Most Touchdowns Passing, Season — 49, Peyton Manning, Indianapolis Colts, 2004.
Most Touchdowns Passing, Game — 7, Sid Luckman, Chicago Bears vs. N.Y. Giants, Nov. 14, 1943; Adrian Burk, Philadelphia Eagles vs. Washington Redskins, Oct. 17, 1954; George Blanda, Houston Oilers vs. N.Y. Titans, Nov. 19, 1961; Y.A. Tittle, N.Y. Giants vs. Washington Redskins, Oct. 28, 1962; Joe Kapp, Minnesota Vikings vs. Baltimore Colts, Sept. 28, 1969.
Most Passes Completed, Career — 5,021, Brett Favre, Atlanta Falcons-Green Bay Packers, 1991-2006.
Most Passes Completed, Season — 418, Rich Gannon, Oakland Raiders, 2002.
Most Passes Completed, Game — 45, Drew Bledsoe, New England Patriots vs. Minnesota Vikings, Nov. 13, 1994 (OT).

All-Time NFL Coaching Victories
(at end of 2005 season; ranked by overall career wins; *active in 2006)

Coach	Team	Yrs.	Regular Season				Overall			
			W	L	T	Pct.	W	L	T	Pct.
Don Shula	Colts, Dolphins	33	328	156	6	0.677	347	173	6	0.666
George Halas	Bears	40	318	148	31	0.682	324	151	31	0.682
Tom Landry	Cowboys	29	250	162	6	0.607	270	178	6	0.603
Earl "Curly" Lambeau	Packers, Cardinals, Redskins	33	226	132	22	0.631	229	134	22	0.631
Chuck Noll	Steelers	23	193	148	1	0.566	209	156	1	0.572
Marty Schottenheimer*	Browns, Chiefs, Redskins, Chargers	21	200	126	1	0.613	205	139	1	0.596
Dan Reeves	Broncos, Giants, Falcons	23	190	165	2	0.535	201	174	2	0.536
Chuck Knox	Rams, Bills, Seahawks	22	186	147	1	0.558	193	158	1	0.550
Bill Parcells*	Giants, Patriots, Jets, Cowboys	19	172	130	1	0.569	183	138	1	0.570
Paul Brown	Browns, Bengals	21	166	100	6	0.624	170	108	6	0.612
Bud Grant	Vikings	18	158	96	5	0.621	168	108	5	0.608
Joe Gibbs*	Redskins	15	145	87	0	0.625	162	93	0	0.635
Bill Cowher	Steelers	15	149	90	1	0.598	161	99	1	0.619
Mike Holmgren*	Packers, Seahawks	15	147	93	0	0.613	159	103	0	0.607
Marv Levy	Chiefs, Bills	17	143	112	0	0.561	154	120	0	0.562
Steve Owen	Giants	23	151	100	17	0.602	153	108	17	0.586
Mike Shanahan*	Raiders, Broncos	14	131	81	0	0.618	139	86	0	0.618
Hank Stram	Chiefs, Saints	17	131	97	10	0.574	136	100	10	0.576
Weeb Ewbank	Colts, Jets	20	130	129	7	0.502	134	130	7	0.508
Mike Ditka	Bears, Saints	14	121	95	0	0.560	127	101	0	0.557

NFL Stadiums[1]

Team—Stadium, Location, Surface (Year Built)	Capacity
Bears—Soldier Field[2], Chicago, IL, G (1924)	61,500
Bengals—Paul Brown Stad., Cincinnati, OH, A (2000)	65,600
Bills—Ralph Wilson Stad., Orchard Park, NY, A (1973)	73,967
Broncos—Invesco Field at Mile High, Denver, CO, G (2001)	76,125
Browns—Cleveland Browns Stad., Cleveland, OH, G (1999)	73,200
Buccaneers—Raymond James Stad., Tampa, FL, G (1998)	65,647
Cardinals—University of Phoenix Stad., Glendale, AZ, G (2006)	63,000
Chargers—Qualcomm Stad.[3], San Diego, CA, G (1967)	71,500
Chiefs—Arrowhead Stad., Kansas City, MO, G (1972)	79,451
Colts—RCA Dome[4], Indianapolis, IN, A (1983)	57,890
Cowboys—Texas Stad.[5], Irving, TX, A (1971)	65,675
Dolphins—Dolphin Stad.[5], Miami Gardens, FL, G (1987)	75,192
Eagles—Lincoln Financial Field, Philadelphia, PA, G (2003)	68,532
Falcons—Georgia Dome, Atlanta, GA, A (1992)	71,228
49ers—Monster Park[6], San Francisco, CA, G (1960)	69,734

Team—Stadium, Location, Surface (Year Built)	Capacity
Giants—Giants Stad., E. Rutherford, NJ, A (1976)	80,242
Jaguars—Jacksonville Municipal Stad.[7], Jacksonville, FL, G (1946)	67,164
Jets—Giants Stad., E. Rutherford, NJ, A (1976)	80,242
Lions—Ford Field, Detroit, MI, A (2002)	65,000
Packers—Lambeau Field[8], Green Bay, WI, G (1957)	72,515
Panthers—Bank of America Stad.[9], Charlotte, NC, G (1996)	73,400
Patriots—Gillette Stad., Foxboro, MA, A (2002)	68,756
Raiders—McAfee Coliseum[10], Oakland, CA, G (1966)	63,132
Rams—Edward Jones Dome[11], St. Louis, MO, A (1995)	66,000
Ravens—M & T Bank Stad.[12], Baltimore, MD, A (1998)	70,107
Redskins—FedEx Field[13], Landover, MD, G (1997)	91,000
Saints—Louisiana Superdome, New Orleans, LA (1975)	69,703
Seahawks—Qwest Field[14], Seattle, WA, A (2002)	67,000
Steelers—Heinz Field, Pittsburgh, PA, A (2001)	64,450
Texans—Reliant Stadium, Houston, TX, G (2002)	69,500
Titans—The Coliseum[15], Nashville, TN, G (1999)	67,000
Vikings—Hubert H. Humphrey Metrodome, Minn., MN, A (1982)	63,000

G=Grass. A=Artificial turf. (1) As of the start of the 2007 season. (2) Renovation in 2002 replaced interior of stadium (3) Formerly San Diego Stadium (1967-80), San Diego Jack Murphy Stadium (1981-97). (4) Formerly the Hoosier Dome (1983-94) (5) Formerly Joe Robbie Stadium (1987-96); Pro Player Stadium (1996-2005). (6) Formerly Candlestick Park (1960-94); 3Com Park at Candlestick Point (1995-2004). (7) Formerly ALLTEL Stadium (1997-2007), Jacksonville Municipal Stadium (1946-97). (8) Formerly City Stadium (1957-65). Renovation completed in 2003, added 11,625 seats. (9) Formerly Ericsson Stadium (1996-2003). (10) Formerly Oakland/Alameda County Coliseum until 1998; Network Associates Coliseum until 2005. (11) Formerly Trans World Dome (1995-2001); full name: Edward Jones Dome at America's Center. (12) Formerly PSINet Stadium (1998-2002); Ravens Stadium (2002-03). (13) Formerly Jack Kent Cooke Stadium (1997-99). (14) Formerly Seahawks Stadium (2002-04). (15) Formerly Adelphia Col. (1999-2002).

National Football League Franchise Origins

(founding year, league; home stadium location; subsequent history)

Arizona Cardinals—1920, American Professional Football Association (APFA)[1]. Chicago, 1920-59; St. Louis, 1960-87; Tempe, AZ, 1988-2005; Glendale, AZ, 2006-present.
Atlanta Falcons—1966, NFL. Atlanta, 1966-present.
Baltimore Ravens—1996, NFL. Baltimore, 1996-present.
Buffalo Bills—1960, American Football League (AFL)[2]. Buffalo, 1960-72; Orchard Park, NY, 1973-present.
Carolina Panthers—1995, NFL. Clemson, SC, 1995; Charlotte, NC, 1996-present.
Chicago Bears—1920 APFA. Decatur, IL, 1920; Chicago, 1921-present.
Cincinnati Bengals—1968, AFL. Cincinnati, 1968-present.
Cleveland Browns—1946, All-America Football Conference (AAFC)[3]. Cleveland, 1946-95; 1999-present.
Dallas Cowboys—1960, NFL. Dallas, 1960-70; Irving, TX, 1971-present.
Denver Broncos—1960, AFL. Denver, 1960-present.
Detroit Lions—1930, NFL. Portsmouth, OH, 1930-33; Detroit, 1934-74; Pontiac, MI, 1975-2001; Detroit, 2002-present.
Green Bay Packers—1921, APFA. Green Bay, WI, 1921-present.
Houston Texans—2002, NFL. Houston, 2002-present.
Indianapolis Colts—1953, NFL. Baltimore, 1953-83; Indianapolis, 1984-present.
Jacksonville Jaguars—1995, NFL. Jacksonville, FL, 1995-present.
Kansas City Chiefs—1960, AFL. Dallas, 1960-62; Kansas City, MO, 1963-present.
Miami Dolphins—1966, AFL. Miami, 1966-2002; Miami Gardens, FL, 2003-present.
Minnesota Vikings—1961, NFL. Bloomington, MN, 1961-81; Minneapolis, 1982-present.
New England Patriots—1960, AFL. Boston, 1960-70; Foxboro, MA, 1971-present.
New Orleans Saints—1967, NFL. New Orleans, 1967-2004; Baton Rouge and San Antonio, 2005; New Orleans, 2006-present.
New York Giants—1925, NFL. New York, 1925-73; 1975; New Haven, CT, 1973-74; E. Rutherford, NJ, 1976-present.
New York Jets—1960, AFL. New York, 1960-83; E. Rutherford, NJ, 1984-present.
Oakland Raiders—1960, AFL. San Francisco 1960-61; Oakland, CA, 1962-81; Los Angeles, 1982-94; Oakland, CA, 1995-present.
Philadelphia Eagles—1933, NFL. Philadelphia, 1933-present.
Pittsburgh Steelers—1933, NFL. Pittsburgh, 1933-present.
St. Louis Rams—1937, NFL. Cleveland, 1936-45; Los Angeles, 1946-79; Anaheim, 1980-94; St. Louis, 1995-present.
San Diego Chargers—1960, AFL. Los Angeles, 1960; San Diego, 1961-present.
Seattle Seahawks—1976, NFL. Seattle, 1976-present.
San Francisco 49ers—1946, AAFC. San Francisco, 1946-present.
Tampa Bay Buccaneers—1976, NFL. Tampa, 1976-present.
Tennessee Titans—1960, AFL. Houston, 1969-96; Memphis, 1997; Nashville, 1998-present.
Washington Redskins—1932, NFL. Boston, 1932-36; Washington, DC, 1937-96; Landover, MD, 1997-present.
(1) The American Professional Football Association (APFA) was formed in 1920 to standardize the rules of professional football. In 1922, the name was changed to the National Football League. (2) The most successful of 4 separate leagues called the "American Football League" (1926; 1936-37; 1940-41, 1960-69). Congress approved an NFL/AFL merger in 1966. Baltimore, Cleveland, and Pittsburgh agreed to join the 10 incoming AFL teams to form the American Football Conference. The NFL began play in 1970 with 26 teams. (3)   The   All-America Football Conference, 1946-49. In 1950, 3 of its teams joined the NFL (Baltimore, Cleveland, and San Francisco). The Baltimore franchise failed, but the NFL awarded the city a 2nd one, also called the Colts, in 1953.

Pro Football Hall of Fame, Canton, Ohio

(Asterisks indicate 2007 inductees)

Herb Adderley
Troy Aikman
George Allen
Marcus Allen
Lance Alworth
Doug Atkins
Morris "Red" Badgro
Lem Barney
Cliff Battles
Sammy Baugh
Chuck Bednarik
Bert Bell
Bobby Bell
Raymond Berry
Elvin Bethea
Charles Bidwill
Fred Biletnikoff
George Blanda
Mel Blount
Terry Bradshaw
Bob Brown
Jim Brown
Paul Brown
Roosevelt Brown
Willie Brown
Buck Buchanan
Nick Buoniconti
Dick Butkus
Earl Campbell
Tony Canadeo
Joe Carr
Harry Carson
Dave Casper
Guy Chamberlin
Jack Christiansen
Earl "Dutch" Clark
George Connor
Jim Conzelman
Lou Creekmur
Larry Csonka
Al Davis
Willie Davis
Len Dawson
Joe DeLamielleure
Eric Dickerson
Dan Dierdorf
Mike Ditka
Art Donovan
Tony Dorsett

John "Paddy" Driscoll
Bill Dudley
Glen "Turk" Edwards
Carl Eller
John Elway
Weeb Ewbank
Tom Fears
Jim Finks
Ray Flaherty
Len Ford
Dr. Daniel Fortmann
Dan Fouts
Benny Friedman
Frank Gatski
Bill George
Joe Gibbs
Frank Gifford
Sid Gillman
Otto Graham
Red Grange
Bud Grant
Joe Greene
Forrest Gregg
Bob Griese
Lou Groza
George Guyon
Jack Ham
Dan Hampton
John Hannah
Franco Harris
Mike Haynes
Ed Healey
Mel Hein
Ted Hendricks
Wilbur "Pete" Henry
Arnold Herber
Bill Hewitt
*Gene Hickerson
Clarke Hinkle
Elroy "Crazylegs" Hirsch
Paul Hornung
Ken Houston
Cal Hubbard
Sam Huff
Lamar Hunt
Don Hutson
*Michael Irvin
Jimmy Johnson

John Henry Johnson
Charlie Joiner
David "Deacon" Jones
Stan Jones
Henry Jordan
Sonny Jurgensen
Jim Kelly
Leroy Kelly
Walt Kiesling
Frank "Bruiser" Kinard
Paul Krause
Earl "Curly" Lambeau
Jack Lambert
Tom Landry
Dick "Night Train" Lane
Jim Langer
Willie Lanier
Steve Largent
Yale Lary
Dante Lavelli
Bobby Layne
Alphonse "Tuffy" Leemans
Marv Levy
Bob Lilly
Larry Little
James Lofton
Vince Lombardi
Howie Long
Ronnie Lott
Sid Luckman
Roy "Link" Lyman
Tom Mack
John Mackey
John Madden
Tim Mara
Wellington Mara
Gino Marchetti
Dan Marino
George Preston
   Marshall
*Bruce Mathews
Ollie Matson
Don Maynard
George McAfee
Mike McCormack
Tommy McDonald
Hugh McElhenny
Johnny "Blood" McNally

Mike Michalske
Wayne Millner
Bobby Mitchell
Ron Mix
Joe Montana
Warren Moon
Lenny Moore
Marion Motley
Mike Munchak
Anthony Munoz
George Musso
Bronko Nagurski
Joe Namath
Earle "Greasy" Neale
Ernie Nevers
Ozzie Newsome
Ray Nitschke
Chuck Noll
Leo Nomellini
Merlin Olsen
Jim Otto
Steve Owen
Alan Page
Clarence "Ace" Parker
Jim Parker
Walter Payton
Joe Perry
Pete Pihos
Fritz Pollard
Hugh "Shorty" Ray
Dan Reeves
Mel Renfro
John Riggins
Jim Ringo
Andy Robustelli
Art Rooney
Dan Rooney
Pete Rozelle
Bob St. Clair
Barry Sanders
*Charlie Sanders
Gale Sayers
Joe Schmidt
Tex Schramm
Lee Roy Selmon
Billy Shaw
Art Shell
Don Shula

O.J. Simpson
Mike Singletary
Jackie Slater
Jackie Smith
John Stallworth
Bart Starr
Roger Staubach
Ernie Stautner
Jan Stenerud
Dwight Stephenson
Hank Stram
Ken Strong
Joe Stydahar
Lynn Swann
Fran Tarkenton
Charley Taylor
Jim Taylor
Lawrence "LT" Taylor
*Thurman Thomas
Jim Thorpe
Y.A. Tittle
George Trafton
Charley Trippi
Emlen Tunnell
Clyde "Bulldog" Turner
Johnny Unitas
Gene Upshaw
Norm Van Brocklin
Steve Van Buren
Doak Walker
Bill Walsh
Paul Warfield
Bob Waterfield
Mike Webster
Arnie Weinmeister
*Roger Wehrli
Randy White
Reggie White
Dave Wilcox
Bill Willis
Larry Wilson
Kellen Winslow
Alex Wojciechowicz
Willie Wood
Rayfield Wright
Ron Yary
Steve Young
Jack Youngblood

COLLEGE FOOTBALL
Gators Topple Buckeyes to Claim BCS Championship

The Univ. of Florida Gators upset the Ohio State Buckeyes, 41-14, to win the Bowl Championship Series (BCS) Championship Game Jan. 8, 2007, in Glendale, AZ. Florida, coached by Urban Meyer, overcame an early Buckeye lead and kept Ohio State from scoring during the second half. Buckeye quarterback Troy Smith, the 2006 Heisman winner, threw for just 35 yards with one interception, while Florida quarterback Chris Leak completed 25 of 36 passes for 212 yards and one touchdown. With their win, the Gators, who were ranked second in the national polls prior to the game, silenced vocal critics of their selection to the championship game, though several prominent names in college football continued to call for a playoff system to replace the complicated BCS selection process.

National College Football Champions, 1936-2006

The official champion, as determined by the BCS National Championship game, is listed for 2006. For years preceding 2006, the unofficial champion, as selected by the AP poll of writers and USA Today/ESPN (until 1991, UPI; 1991-1996 USA Today/CNN) poll of coaches, is listed. Where the polls disagreed, both teams are listed (AP winner first). The AP poll started in 1936; the UPI poll in 1950.

1936	Minnesota	1951	Tennessee	1966	Notre Dame	1980	Georgia
1937	Pittsburgh	1952	Michigan St.	1967	USC	1981	Clemson
1938	Texas Christian	1953	Maryland	1968	Ohio St.	1982	Penn St.
1939	Texas A&M	1954	Ohio St., UCLA	1969	Texas	1983	Miami (FL)
1940	Minnesota	1955	Oklahoma	1970	Nebraska, Texas	1984	Brigham Young
1941	Minnesota	1956	Oklahoma	1971	Nebraska	1985	Oklahoma
1942	Ohio St.	1957	Auburn, Ohio St.	1972	USC	1986	Penn St.
1943	Notre Dame	1958	Louisiana St.	1973	Notre Dame,	1987	Miami (FL)
1944	Army	1959	Syracuse		Alabama	1988	Notre Dame
1945	Army	1960	Minnesota	1974	Oklahoma, USC	1989	Miami (FL)
1946	Notre Dame	1961	Alabama	1975	Oklahoma	1990	Colorado,
1947	Notre Dame	1962	USC	1976	Pittsburgh		GA Tech
1948	Michigan	1963	Texas	1977	Notre Dame	1991	Miami (FL),
1949	Notre Dame	1964	Alabama	1978	Alabama, USC		Washington
1950	Oklahoma	1965	Alabama, Mich. St.	1979	Alabama	1992	Alabama
						1993	Florida St.
						1994	Nebraska
						1995	Nebraska
						1996	Florida
						1997	Michigan,
							Nebraska
						1998	Tennessee
						1999	Florida St.
						2000	Oklahoma
						2001	Miami (FL)
						2002	Ohio State
						2003	LSU, USC
						2004	USC
						2005	Texas
						2006	Florida

2006 Final Standings

Bowl Championship Series		Associated Press Poll		Coaches' Poll[1]	
Rank, Team	**Rank, Team**	**Rank, Team**	**Rank, Team**	**Rank, Team**	**Rank, Team**
1. Ohio State	14. Wake Forest	1. Florida	14. California	1. Florida	14. California
2. Florida	15. Virginia Tech	2. Ohio State	15. Arkansas	2. Ohio State	15. Brigham Young
3. Michigan	16. Rutgers	3. LSU	16. Brigham Young	3. LSU	16. Arkansas
4. LSU	17. Tennessee	4. USC	17. Notre Dame	4. USC	17. Wake Forest
5. USC	18. California	5. Boise State	18. Wake Forest	5. Wisconsin	18. Virginia Tech
6. Louisville	19. Texas	6. Louisville	19. Virginia Tech	6. Boise State	19. Notre Dame
7. Wisconsin	20. Brigham Young	7. Wisconsin	20. Boston College	7. Louisville	20. Boston College
8. Boise State	21. Texas A&M	8. Michigan	21. TCU	8. Auburn	21. Oregon State
9. Auburn	22. Oregon State	9. Auburn	22. Oregon State	9. Michigan	22. TCU
10. Oklahoma	23. Nebraska	10. West Virginia	23. Tennessee	10. West Virginia	23. Georgia
11. Notre Dame	24. Boston College	11. Oklahoma	24. Hawaii	11. Oklahoma	24. Penn State
12. Arkansas	25. UCLA	12. Rutgers	25. Penn State	12. Rutgers	25. Tennessee
13. West Virginia		13. Texas		13. Texas	

Note: BCS Poll is as of Dec. 3, 2006. AP and Coaches' Polls are final after bowl games. The American Football Coaches Assn. prohibits coaches from voting for schools on major NCAA probation. (1) Sponsored by USA Today.

Annual Results of Major Bowl Games

(Dates indicate year the game was played; bowl games are generally played in late December or early January.)

Rose Bowl, Pasadena, CA

1902	(Jan.) Michigan 49, Stanford 0	1947	Illinois 45, UCLA 14	1978	Washington 27, Michigan 20
1916	Washington St. 14, Brown 0	1948	Michigan 49, USC 0	1979	USC 17, Michigan 10
1917	Oregon 14, Pennsylvania 0	1949	Northwestern 20, California 14	1980	USC 17, Ohio St. 16
1918-19	Service teams	1950	Ohio St. 17, California 14	1981	Michigan 23, Washington 6
1920	Harvard 7, Oregon 6	1951	Michigan 14, California 6	1982	Washington 28, Iowa 0
1921	California 28, Ohio St. 0	1952	Illinois 40, Stanford 7	1983	UCLA 24, Michigan 14
1922	Wash. & Jeff. 0, California 0	1953	USC 7, Wisconsin 0	1984	UCLA 45, Illinois 9
1923	USC 14, Penn St. 3	1954	Mich. St. 28, UCLA 20	1985	USC 20, Ohio St. 17
1924	Navy 14, Washington 14	1955	Ohio St. 20, USC 7	1986	UCLA 45, Iowa 28
1925	Notre Dame 27, Stanford 10	1956	Mich. St. 17, UCLA 14	1987	Arizona St. 22, Michigan 15
1926	Alabama 20, Washington 19	1957	Iowa 35, Oregon St. 19	1988	Mich. St. 20, USC 17
1927	Alabama 7, Stanford 7	1958	Ohio St. 10, Oregon 7	1989	Michigan 22, USC 14
1928	Stanford 7, Pittsburgh 6	1959	Iowa 38, California 12	1990	USC 17, Michigan 10
1929	Georgia Tech 8, California 7	1960	Washington 44, Wisconsin 8	1991	Washington 46, Iowa 34
1930	USC 47, Pittsburgh 14	1961	Washington 17, Minnesota 7	1992	Washington 34, Michigan 14
1931	Alabama 24, Wash. St. 0	1962	Minnesota 21, UCLA 3	1993	Michigan 38, Washington 31
1932	USC 21, Tulane 12	1963	USC 42, Wisconsin 37	1994	Wisconsin 21, UCLA 16
1933	USC 35, Pittsburgh 0	1964	Illinois 17, Washington 7	1995	Penn St. 38, Oregon 20
1934	Columbia 7, Stanford 0	1965	Michigan 34, Oregon St. 7	1996	USC 41, Northwestern 32
1935	Alabama 29, Stanford 13	1966	UCLA 14, Mich. St. 12	1997	Ohio St. 20, Arizona St. 17
1936	Stanford 7, SMU 0	1967	Purdue 14, USC 13	1998	Michigan 21, Wash. St. 16
1937	Pittsburgh 21, Washington 0	1968	USC 14, Indiana 3	1999	Wisconsin 38, UCLA 31
1938	California 13, Alabama 0	1969	Ohio St. 27, USC 16	2000	Wisconsin 17, Stanford 9
1939	USC 7, Duke 3	1970	USC 10, Michigan 3	2001	Washington 34, Purdue 24
1940	USC 14, Tennessee 0	1971	Stanford 27, Ohio St. 17	2002	Miami (FL) 37, Nebraska 14
1941	Stanford 21, Nebraska 13	1972	Stanford 13, Michigan 12	2003	Oklahoma, 34, Washington St. 14
1942*	Oregon St. 20, Duke 16	1973	USC 42, Ohio St. 17	2004	USC 28, Michigan 14
1943	Georgia 9, UCLA 0	1974	Ohio St. 42, USC 21	2005	Texas 38, Michigan 37
1944	USC 29, Washington 0	1975	USC 18, Ohio St. 17	2006	Texas 41, USC 38
1945	USC 25, Tennessee 0	1976	UCLA 23, Ohio St. 10	2007	USC 32, Michigan 18
1946	Alabama 34, USC 14	1977	USC 14, Michigan 6		

*Played in Durham, NC.

Orange Bowl, Miami, FL

1935 (Jan.) Bucknell 26, Miami (FL) 0	1960 Georgia 14, Missouri 0	1985 Washington 28, Oklahoma 17
1936 Catholic U. 20, Mississippi 19	1961 Missouri 21, Navy 14	1986 Oklahoma 25, Penn St. 10
1937 Duquesne 13, Mississippi St. 12	1962 LSU 25, Colorado 7	1987 Oklahoma 42, Arkansas 8
1938 Auburn 6, Michigan St. 0	1963 Alabama 17, Oklahoma 0	1988 Miami (FL) 20, Oklahoma 14
1939 Tennessee 17, Oklahoma 0	1964 Nebraska 13, Auburn 7	1989 Miami (FL) 23, Nebraska 3
1940 Georgia Tech 21, Missouri 7	1965 Texas 21, Alabama 17	1990 Notre Dame 21, Colorado 6
1941 Mississippi St. 14, Georgetown 7	1966 Alabama 39, Nebraska 28	1991 Colorado 10, Notre Dame 9
1942 Georgia 40, TCU 26	1967 Florida 27, Georgia Tech 12	1992 Miami (FL) 22, Nebraska 0
1943 Alabama 37, Boston Coll. 21	1968 Oklahoma 26, Tennessee 24	1993 Florida St. 27, Nebraska 14
1944 LSU 19, Texas A&M 14	1969 Penn St. 15, Kansas 14	1994 Florida St. 18, Nebraska 16
1945 Tulsa 26, Georgia Tech 12	1970 Penn St. 10, Missouri 3	1995 Nebraska 24, Miami (FL) 17
1946 Miami (FL) 13, Holy Cross 6	1971 Nebraska 17, LSU 12	1996 Florida St. 31, Notre Dame 26
1947 Rice 8, Tennessee 0	1972 Nebraska 38, Alabama 6	1996 (Dec.) Nebraska 41,
1948 Georgia Tech 20, Kansas 14	1973 Nebraska 40, Notre Dame 6	Virginia Tech 21
1949 Texas 41, Georgia 28	1974 Penn St. 16, LSU 9	1998 (Jan.) Nebraska 42, Tennessee 17
1950 Santa Clara 21, Kentucky 13	1975 Notre Dame 13, Alabama 11	1999 Florida 31, Syracuse 10
1951 Clemson 15, Miami (FL) 14	1976 Oklahoma 14, Michigan 6	2000 Michigan 35, Alabama 34 (OT)
1952 Georgia Tech 17, Baylor 14	1977 Ohio St. 27, Colorado 10	2001 Oklahoma 13, Florida St. 2
1953 Alabama 61, Syracuse 6	1978 Arkansas 31, Oklahoma 6	2002 Florida 56, Maryland 23
1954 Oklahoma 7, Maryland 0	1979 Oklahoma 31, Nebraska 24	2003 USC 38, Iowa 17
1955 Duke 34, Nebraska 7	1980 Oklahoma 24, Florida St. 7	2004 Miami 16, Florida State 14
1956 Oklahoma 20, Maryland 6	1981 Oklahoma 18, Florida St. 17	2005 USC 55, Oklahoma 19
1957 Colorado 27, Clemson 21	1982 Clemson 22, Nebraska 15	2006 Penn St. 26, Florida St. 23 (3 OT)
1958 Oklahoma 48, Duke 21	1983 Nebraska 21, LSU 20	2007 Louisville 24, Wake Forest 13
1959 Oklahoma 21, Syracuse 6	1984 Miami (FL) 31, Nebraska 30	

Sugar Bowl, New Orleans, LA

1935 (Jan.) Tulane 20, Temple 14	1960 Mississippi 21, LSU 0	1984 Auburn 9, Michigan 7
1936 TCU 3, LSU 2	1961 Mississippi 14, Rice 6	1985 Nebraska 28, LSU 10
1937 Santa Clara 21, LSU 14	1962 Alabama 10, Arkansas 3	1986 Tennessee 35, Miami (FL) 7
1938 Santa Clara 6, LSU 0	1963 Mississippi 17, Arkansas 13	1987 Nebraska 30, LSU 15
1939 TCU 15, Carnegie Tech 7	1964 Alabama 12, Mississippi 7	1988 Syracuse 16, Auburn 16
1940 Texas A&M 14, Tulane 13	1965 LSU 13, Syracuse 10	1989 Florida St. 13, Auburn 7
1941 Boston Col. 19, Tennessee 13	1966 Missouri 20, Florida 18	1990 Miami (FL) 33, Alabama 25
1942 Fordham 2, Missouri 0	1967 Alabama 34, Nebraska 7	1991 Tennessee 23, Virginia 22
1943 Tennessee 14, Tulsa 7	1968 LSU 20, Wyoming 13	1992 Notre Dame 39, Florida 28
1944 Georgia Tech 20, Tulsa 18	1969 Arkansas 16, Georgia 2	1993 Alabama 34, Miami (FL) 13
1945 Duke 29, Alabama 26	1970 Mississippi 27, Arkansas 22	1994 Florida 41, West Virginia 7
1946 Oklahoma A&M 33, St. Mary's 13	1971 Tennessee 34, Air Force 13	1995 Florida St. 23, Florida 17
1947 Georgia 20, N. Carolina 10	1972 Oklahoma 40, Auburn 22	1995 (Dec.) Virginia Tech 28, Texas 10
1948 Texas 27, Alabama 7	1972 (Dec.) Oklahoma 14, Penn St. 0	1997 (Jan.) Florida 52, Florida St. 20
1949 Oklahoma 14, N. Carolina 6	1973 Notre Dame 24, Alabama 23	1998 Florida St. 31, Ohio St. 14
1950 Oklahoma 35, LSU 0	1974 Nebraska 13, Florida 10	1999 Ohio St. 24, Texas A&M 14
1951 Kentucky 13, Oklahoma 7	1975 Alabama 13, Penn St. 6	2000 Florida St. 46, Virginia Tech 29
1952 Maryland 28, Tennessee 13	1977 (Jan.) Pittsburgh 27, Georgia 3	2001 Miami (FL) 37, Florida 20
1953 Georgia Tech 24, Mississippi 7	1978 Alabama 35, Ohio St. 6	2002 LSU 47, Illinois 34
1954 Georgia Tech 42, West Virginia 19	1979 Alabama 14, Penn St. 7	2003 Georgia 26, Florida St. 13
1955 Navy 21, Mississippi 0	1980 Alabama 24, Arkansas 9	2004 LSU 21, Oklahoma 14
1956 Georgia Tech 7, Pittsburgh 0	1981 Georgia 17, Notre Dame 10	2005 Auburn 16, Virginia Tech 13
1957 Baylor 13, Tennessee 7	1982 Pittsburgh 24, Georgia 20	2006 West Virginia 38, Georgia 35*
1958 Mississippi 39, Texas 7	1983 Penn St. 27, Georgia 23	2007 LSU 41, Notre Dame 14
1959 LSU 7, Clemson 0		

*Played in Atlanta, GA.

Chick-fil-A Bowl, Atlanta, GA

(Known as the Peach Bowl, 1968-1997; Chick-fil-A Peach Bowl, 1998-2005.)

1968 (Dec.) LSU 31, Florida St. 27	1981 (Dec.) W. Virginia 26, Florida 6	1995 (Jan.) N. Carolina St. 28, Miss. St. 24
1969 W. Virginia 14, S. Carolina 3	1982 Iowa 28, Tennessee 22	1995 (Dec.) Virginia 34, Georgia 27
1970 Arizona St. 48, N. Carolina 26	1983 Florida St. 28, N. Carolina 3	1996 LSU 10, Clemson 7
1971 Mississippi 41, Georgia Tech 18	1984 Virginia 27, Purdue 24	1998 (Jan.) Auburn 21, Clemson 17
1972 N. Carolina St. 49, W. Virginia 13	1985 Army 31, Illinois 29	1998 (Dec.) Georgia 35, Virginia 33
1973 Georgia 17, Maryland 16	1986 Va. Tech 25, N. Carolina St. 24	1999 Mississippi St. 27, Clemson 7
1974 Vanderbilt 6, Texas Tech 6	1988 (Jan.) Tennessee 28, Indiana 22	2000 LSU 28, Georgia Tech 14
1975 W. Virginia 13, N. Carolina St. 10	1988 (Dec.) N. Carolina St. 28, Iowa 23	2001 North Carolina 16, Auburn 10
1976 Kentucky 21, N. Carolina 0	1989 Syracuse 19, Georgia 18	2002 Maryland 30, Tennessee 3
1977 N. Carolina 24, Iowa St. 14	1990 Auburn 27, Indiana 23	2003 Clemson 27, Tennessee 14
1978 Purdue 41, Georgia Tech. 21	1992 (Jan.) E. Carolina 37, NC St. 34	2004 Miami (FL) 27, Florida 10
1979 Baylor 24, Clemson 18	1993 N. Carolina 21, Mississippi St. 17	2005 LSU 40, Miami (FL) 3
1981 (Jan.) Miami (FL) 20, Virginia Tech 10	1993 (Dec.) Clemson 14, Kentucky 13	2006 Georgia 31, Virginia Tech 24

Cotton Bowl, Dallas, TX

1937 (Jan.) TCU 16, Marquette 6	1958 Navy 20, Rice 7	1979 Notre Dame 35, Houston 34
1938 Rice 28, Colorado 14	1959 TCU 0, Air Force 0	1980 Houston 17, Nebraska 14
1939 St. Mary's 20, Texas Tech 13	1960 Syracuse 23, Texas 14	1981 Alabama 30, Baylor 2
1940 Clemson 6, Boston Coll. 3	1961 Duke 7, Arkansas 6	1982 Texas 14, Alabama 12
1941 Texas A&M 13, Fordham 12	1962 Texas 12, Mississippi 7	1983 SMU 7, Pittsburgh 3
1942 Alabama 29, Texas A&M 21	1963 LSU 13, Texas 0	1984 Georgia 10, Texas 9
1943 Texas 14, Georgia Tech 7	1964 Texas 28, Navy 6	1985 Boston Coll. 45, Houston 28
1944 Randolph Field 7, Texas 7	1965 Arkansas 10, Nebraska 7	1986 Texas A&M 36, Auburn 16
1945 Oklahoma A&M 34, TCU 0	1966 LSU 14, Arkansas 7	1987 Ohio St. 28, Texas A&M 12
1946 Texas 40, Missouri 27	1966 (Dec.) Georgia 24, SMU 9	1988 Texas A&M 35, Notre Dame 10
1947 Arkansas 0, LSU 0	1968 (Jan.) Texas A&M 20, Alabama 16	1989 UCLA 17, Arkansas 3
1948 SMU 13, Penn St. 13	1969 Texas 36, Tennessee 13	1990 Tennessee 31, Arkansas 27
1949 SMU 21, Oregon 13	1970 Texas 21, Notre Dame 17	1991 Miami (FL) 46, Texas 3
1950 Rice 27, North Carolina 13	1971 Notre Dame 24, Texas 11	1992 Florida St. 10, Texas A&M 2
1951 Tennessee 20, Texas 14	1972 Penn St. 30, Texas 6	1993 Notre Dame 28, Texas A&M 3
1952 Kentucky 20, TCU 7	1973 Texas 17, Alabama 13	1994 Notre Dame 24, Texas A&M 21
1953 Texas 16, Tennessee 0	1974 Nebraska 19, Texas 3	1995 USC. 55, Texas Tech 14
1954 Rice 28, Alabama 6	1975 Penn St. 41, Baylor 20	1996 Colorado 38, Oregon 6
1955 Georgia Tech 14, Arkansas 6	1976 Arkansas 31, Georgia 10	1997 Brigham Young 19, Kansas St. 15
1956 Mississippi 14, TCU 13	1977 Houston 30, Maryland 21	1998 UCLA 29, Texas A&M 23
1957 TCU 28, Syracuse 27	1978 Notre Dame 38, Texas 10	1999 Texas 38, Mississippi St. 11

2000 Arkansas 27, Texas 6
2001 Kansas St. 35, Tennessee 21
2002 Oklahoma 10, Arkansas 3

2003 Texas 35, LSU 20
2004 Mississippi 31, Oklahoma St. 28
2005 Tennessee 38, Texas A&M 7

2006 Alabama 13, Texas Tech 10
2007 Auburn 17, Nebraska 14

Capital One Bowl, Orlando, FL
(Florida Citrus Bowl 1984-2002, Tangerine Bowl, 1947-1983)

1947 (Jan.) Catawba 31, Maryville 6
1948 Catawba 7, Marshall 0
1949 Murray St. 21, Sul Ross St. 21
1950 St. Vincent 7, Emory & Henry 6
1951 Morris Harvey 35, Emory & Henry 14
1952 Stetson 35, Arkansas St. 20
1953 East Texas St. 33, Tenn. Tech 0
1954 East Texas St. 7, Arkansas St. 7
1955 Neb.-Omaha 7, E. Kentucky 6
1956 Juniata 6, Missouri Valley 6
1957 West Texas St. 20, So. Miss. 13
1958 East Texas St. 10, So. Miss. 9
1958 (Dec.) East Texas St. 26, Missouri Valley 7
1960 (Jan.) Middle Tennessee 21, Presbyterian 12
1960 (Dec.) Citadel 27, Tenn. Tech 0
1961 Lamar 21, Middle Tennessee 14
1962 Houston 49, Miami (OH) 21
1963 Western Ky. 27, Coast Guard 0
1964 E. Carolina 14, Massachusetts 13

1965 E. Carolina 31, Maine 0
1966 Morgan St. 14, West Chester 6
1967 Tenn.-Martin 25, West Chester 8
1968 Richmond 49, Ohio U. 42
1969 Toledo 56, Davidson 33
1970 Toledo 40, William & Mary 12
1971 Toledo 28, Richmond 3
1972 Tampa 21, Kent St. 18
1973 Miami (OH) 16, Florida 7
1974 Miami 21, Georgia 10
1975 Miami (OH) 20, S. Carolina 7
1976 Okla. St. 49, Brigham Young 21
1977 Florida St. 40, Texas Tech 17
1978 N. Carolina St. 30, Pittsburgh 17
1979 LSU 34, Wake Forest 10
1980 Florida 35, Maryland 20
1981 Missouri 19, So. Mississippi 17
1982 Auburn 33, Boston College 26
1983 Tennessee 30, Maryland 23
1984 Georgia 17, Florida St. 17
1985 Ohio St. 10, Brigham Young 7

1987 (Jan.) Auburn 16, USC 7
1988 Clemson 35, Penn St. 10
1989 Clemson 13, Oklahoma 6
1990 Illinois 31, Virginia 21
1991 Georgia Tech 45, Nebraska 21
1992 California 37, Clemson 13
1993 Georgia 21, Ohio St. 14
1994 Penn St. 31, Tennessee 13
1995 Alabama 24, Ohio St. 17
1996 Tennessee 20, Ohio St. 14
1997 Tennessee 48, Northwestern 28
1998 Florida 21, Penn St. 6
1999 Michigan 45, Arkansas 31
2000 Michigan St. 37, Florida 34
2001 Michigan 31, Auburn 28
2002 Tennessee 45, Michigan 17
2003 Auburn 13, Penn St. 9
2004 Georgia 34, Purdue 27 (OT)
2005 Iowa 30, LSU 25
2006 Wisconsin 24, Auburn 10
2007 Wisconsin 17, Arkansas 14

Fiesta Bowl, Glendale, AZ*

1984 Ohio St. 28, Pittsburgh 23
1985 UCLA 39, Miami (FL) 37
1986 Michigan 27, Nebraska 23
1987 Penn St. 14, Miami (FL) 10
1988 Florida St. 31, Nebraska 28
1989 Notre Dame 34, W. Virginia 21
1990 Florida St. 41, Nebraska 17
1991 Louisville 34, Alabama 7
1992 Penn St. 42, Tennessee 17
1993 Syracuse 26, Colorado 22
1994 Arizona 29, Miami (FL) 0
1995 Colorado 41, Notre Dame 24

1996 Nebraska 62, Florida 24
1997 Penn St. 38, Texas 15
1997 (Dec.) Kansas St. 35, Syracuse 18
1999 (Jan.) Tennessee 23, Florida St. 16
2000 Nebraska 31, Tennessee 21
2001 Oregon St. 41, Notre Dame 9
2002 Oregon 38, Colorado 16
2003 Ohio St. 31, Miami 24 (2 OT)
2004 Ohio St. 35, Kansas St. 28
2005 Utah 35, Pittsburgh 7
2006 Ohio St. 34, Notre Dame 20
2007 Boise St. 43, Oklahoma 42 (OT)

1971 (Dec.) Arizona St. 45, Florida St. 38
1972 Arizona St. 49, Missouri 35
1973 Arizona St. 28, Pittsburgh 7
1974 Okla. St. 16, Brigham Young 6
1975 Arizona St. 17, Nebraska 14
1976 Oklahoma 41, Wyoming 7
1977 Penn St. 42, Arizona St. 30
1978 UCLA 10, Arkansas 10
1979 Pittsburgh 16, Arizona 10
1980 Penn St. 31, Ohio St. 19
1982 (Jan.) Penn St. 26, USC 10
1983 Arizona St. 32, Oklahoma 21
*Played in Tempe, AZ, 1971-2006.

Gator Bowl, Jacksonville, FL

1946 (Jan.) Wake Forest 26, S. Carolina 14
1947 Oklahoma 34, N. Carolina St. 13
1948 Maryland 20, Georgia 20
1949 Clemson 24, Missouri 23
1950 Maryland 20, Missouri 7
1951 Wyoming 20, Washington & Lee 7
1952 Miami 14, Clemson 0
1953 Florida 14, Tulsa 13
1954 Texas Tech 35, Auburn 13
1954 (Dec.) Auburn 33, Baylor 13
1955 Vanderbilt 25, Auburn 13
1956 Georgia Tech 21, Pittsburgh 14
1957 Tennessee 3, Texas A&M 0
1958 Mississippi 7, Florida 3
1960 (Jan.) Arkansas 14, Georgia Tech 7
1960 (Dec.) Florida 13, Baylor 12
1961 Penn St. 30, Georgia Tech 15
1962 Florida 17, Penn St. 7
1963 N. Carolina 35, Air Force 0
1965 (Jan.) Florida St. 36, Okla.19
1965 (Dec.) GA Tech 31, Texas Tech 21

1966 Tennessee 18, Syracuse 12
1967 Penn St. 17, Florida St. 17
1968 Missouri 35, Alabama 10
1969 Florida 14, Tennessee 13
1971 (Jan.) Auburn 35, Mississippi 28
1971 (Dec.) Georgia 7, N. Carolina 3
1972 Auburn 24, Colorado 3
1973 Texas Tech 28, Tennessee 19
1974 Auburn 27, Texas 3
1975 Maryland 13, Florida 0
1976 Notre Dame 20, Penn St. 9
1977 Pittsburgh 34, Clemson 3
1978 Clemson 17, Ohio St. 15
1979 N. Carolina 17, Michigan 15
1980 Pittsburgh 37, S. Carolina 9
1981 N. Carolina 31, Arkansas 27
1982 Florida St. 31, West Virginia 12
1983 Florida 14, Iowa 6
1984 Oklahoma St. 21, S. Carolina 14
1985 Florida St. 34, Oklahoma St. 23
1986 Clemson 27, Stanford 21

1987 LSU 30, S. Carolina 13
1989 (Jan.) Georgia 34, Michigan St. 27
1989 (Dec.) Clemson 27, W. Virginia 7
1991 (Jan.) Michigan 35, Mississippi 3
1991 (Dec.) Oklahoma 48, Virginia 14
1992 Florida 27, N. Carolina St. 10
1993 Alabama 24, N. Carolina 10
1994 Tennessee 45, Virginia Tech 23
1996 (Jan.) Syracuse 41, Clemson 0
1997 N. Carolina 20, W. Virginia 13
1998 N. Carolina 42, Virginia Tech 3
1999 Georgia Tech 35, Notre Dame 28
2000 Miami (FL) 28, Georgia Tech 13
2001 Virginia Tech 41, Clemson 20
2002 Florida St. 30, Virginia Tech 17
2003 N. Carolina St. 28, Notre Dame 6
2004 Maryland 41, West Virginia 7
2005 Florida St. 30, West Virginia 18
2006 Virginia Tech 35, Louisville 24
2007 West Virginia 38, Georgia Tech 35

Liberty Bowl, Memphis, TN

1959 (Dec.) Penn St. 7, Alabama 0
1960 Penn St. 41, Oregon 12
1961 Syracuse 15, Miami (FL) 14
1962 Oregon St. 6, Villanova 0
1963 Mississippi St. 16, N. Carolina St. 12
1964 Utah 32, West Virginia 6
1965 Mississippi 13, Auburn 7
1966 Miami (FL) 14, Virginia Tech 7
1967 N. Carolina St. 14, Georgia 7
1968 Mississippi 34, Virginia Tech 17
1969 Colorado 47, Alabama 33
1970 Tulane 17, Colorado 3
1971 Tennessee 14, Arkansas 13
1972 Georgia Tech 31, Iowa St. 30
1973 N. Carolina St. 31, Kansas 18
1974 Tennessee 7, Maryland 3

1975 USC 20, Texas A&M 0
1976 Alabama 36, UCLA 6
1977 Nebraska 21, N. Carolina 17
1978 Missouri 20, LSU 15
1979 Penn St. 9, Tulane 6
1980 Purdue 28, Missouri 25
1981 Ohio St. 31, Navy 28
1982 Alabama 21, Illinois 15
1983 Notre Dame 19, Boston Coll. 18
1984 Auburn 21, Arkansas 15
1985 Baylor 21, LSU 7
1986 Tennessee 21, Minnesota 14
1987 Georgia 20, Arkansas 17
1988 Indiana 34, S. Carolina 10
1989 Mississippi 42, Air Force 29
1990 Air Force 23, Ohio St. 11

1991 Air Force 38, Mississippi St. 15
1992 Mississippi 13, Air Force 0
1993 Louisville 18, Michigan St. 7
1994 Illinois 30, East Carolina 0
1995 East Carolina 19, Stanford 13
1996 Syracuse 30, Houston 17
1997 So. Mississippi 41, Pittsburgh 7
1998 Tulane 41, Brigham Young 27
1999 So. Mississippi 23, Colorado St. 17
2000 Colorado St. 22, Louisville 17
2001 Louisville 28, BYU 10
2002 TCU 17, Colorado St. 3
2003 Utah 17, So. Mississippi 0
2004 Louisville 44, Boise St. 40
2005 Tulsa 31, Fresno St. 24
2006 South Carolina 44, Houston 36

Sun Bowl, El Paso, TX
(Known as the John Hancock Bowl, 1989-93.)

1936 (Jan.) Hardin-Simmons 14, New Mexico St. 14
1937 Hardin-Simmons 34, Texas Mines 6
1938 West Virginia 7, Texas Tech 6
1939 Utah 26, New Mexico 0
1940 Catholic U. 0, Arizona St. 0

1941 Western Reserve 26, Arizona St. 13
1942 Tulsa 6, Texas Tech 0
1943 2d Air Force 13, Hardin-Simmons 7
1944 Southwestern (TX) 7, New Mexico 0
1945 Southwestern (TX) 35, Univ. of Mexico 0

1946 New Mexico 34, Denver 24
1947 Cincinnati 18, Virginia Tech 6
1948 Miami (OH) 13, Texas Tech 12
1949 West Virginia 21, Texas Mines 12
1950 Texas Western 33, Georgetown 20
1951 West Texas St. 14, Cincinnati 13

1952 Texas Tech 25, Pacific (CA) 14	1970 Georgia Tech. 17, Texas Tech 9	1988 Alabama 29, Army 28
1953 Pacific (CA) 26, S. Mississippi 7	1971 LSU 33, Iowa St. 15	1989 Pittsburgh 31, Texas A&M 28
1954 Texas Western 37, S. Miss. 14	1972 North Carolina 32, Texas Tech 28	1990 Michigan St. 17, USC 16
1955 Texas Western 47, Florida St. 20	1973 Missouri 34, Auburn 17	1991 UCLA 6, Illinois 3
1956 Wyoming 21, Texas Tech 14	1974 Mississippi St. 26,	1992 Baylor 20, Arizona 15
1957 Geo. Washington 13, TX Western 0	North Carolina 24	1993 Oklahoma 41, Texas Tech 10
1958 Louisville 34, Drake 20	1975 Pittsburgh 33, Kansas 19	1994 Texas 35, North Carolina 31
1958 (Dec.) Wyoming 14, Hardin-Simmons 6	1977 (Jan.) Texas A&M 37, Florida 14	1995 Iowa 38, Washington 18
1959 New Mexico St. 28, N. Texas St. 8	1977 (Dec.) Stanford 24, LSU 14	1996 Stanford 38, Michigan St. 0
1960 New Mexico St. 20, Utah St. 13	1978 Texas 42, Maryland 0	1997 Arizona St. 17, Iowa 7
1961 Villanova 17, Wichita 9	1979 Washington 14, Texas 7	1998 TCU 28, USC 19
1962 West Texas St. 15, Ohio U. 14	1980 Nebraska 31, Mississippi St. 17	1999 Oregon 24, Minnesota 20
1963 Oregon 21, SMU 14	1981 Oklahoma 40, Houston 14	2000 Wisconsin 21, UCLA 20
1964 Georgia 7, Texas Tech 0	1982 North Carolina 26, Texas 10	2001 Washington St. 33, Purdue 27
1965 Texas Western 13, TCU 12	1983 Alabama 28, SMU 7	2002 Purdue 34, Washington 24
1966 Wyoming 28, Florida St. 20	1984 Maryland 28, Tennessee 27	2003 Minnesota 31, Oregon 30
1967 UTEP 14, Mississippi 7	1985 Georgia 13, Arizona 13	2004 Arizona St. 27, Purdue 23
1968 Auburn 34, Arizona 10	1986 Alabama 28, Washington 6	2005 UCLA 50, Northwestern 39
1969 Nebraska 45, Georgia 6	1987 Oklahoma St. 35, West Virginia 33	2006 Oregon St. 39, Missouri 38

Other Bowl Results, Late 2006–Early 2007

Alamo Bowl, San Antonio, TX: Texas 26, Iowa 24
Armed Forces (fmr. Fort Worth) Bowl, Ft. Worth, TX: Utah 25, Tulsa 13
Champs Sports Bowl, Orlando, FL: Maryland 24, Purdue 7
Meineke Car Care Bowl, Charlotte, NC: Boston College 25, Navy 24
Emerald Bowl, San Francisco, CA: Florida St. 44, UCLA 27
GMAC Bowl, Mobile, AL: Southern Mississippi 28, Ohio 7
Hawaii Bowl, Honolulu, HI: Hawaii 41, Arizona St. 24
Holiday Bowl, San Diego, CA: California 45, Texas A&M 10
Independence Bowl, Shreveport, LA: Oklahoma St. 34, Alabama 31
Insight Bowl, Tempe, AZ: Texas Tech 44, Minnesota 41 (OT)
International Bowl, Toronto, Ontario: Cincinnati 27, Western Michigan 24

Las Vegas Bowl: BYU 38, Oregon 8
Motor City Bowl, Detroit, MI: Central Michigan 31, Middle Tennessee 14
MPC Computers Bowl, Boise, ID: Miami (FL) 21, Nevada 20
Music City Bowl, Nashville, TN: Kentucky 28, Clemson 20
New Mexico Bowl, Albuquerque, NM: San Jose St. 20, New Mexico 12
New Orleans Bowl: Troy 41, Rice 17
Outback Bowl, Tampa, FL: Penn St. 20, Tennessee 10
PapaJohns.com Bowl, Birmingham, AL: South Florida 24, East Carolina 7
Poinsettia Bowl, San Diego, CA: TCU 37, Northern Illinois 7
Texas (fmr. Houston) Bowl, Houston, TX: Rutgers 37, Kansas St. 10

All-Time NCAA Division I-A Statistical Leaders

(At end of 2006 season. Prior to 2002, postseason games were not included in NCAA final football statistics or records. Beginning with the 2002 season, all postseason games were included. Career rushing yards per game rankings do not include active players.)

Career Rushing Yards

Player, team	Yrs.	Carries	Yds.	Avg.
Ron Dayne, Wisconsin	1996-99	1,115	6,397	5.74
Ricky Williams, Texas	1995-98	1,011	6,279	6.21
Tony Dorsett, Pittsburgh	1973-76	1,074	6,082	5.66
DeAngelo Williams, Memphis	2002-05	969	6,026	6.22
Charles White, USC	1976-79	1,023	5,598	5.47

Career Rushing Yards/Game (min. 2,500 yds.)

Player, team	Yrs.	Carries	Yds.	Avg./Game
Ed Marinaro, Cornell	1969-71	918	4,715	174.6
O.J. Simpson, USC	1967-68	621	3,124	164.4
Herschel Walker, Georgia	1980-82	994	5,259	159.4
Garrett Wolfe, N. Illinois	2004-06	807	5,164	156.5
LeShon Johnson, N. Illinois	1992-93	592	3,314	150.6

Career Passing Yards

Player, team	Yrs.	Comp./Att.	Yds.
Timmy Chang, Hawaii	2000-04	1,388/2,436	17,072
Ty Detmer, BYU	1988-91	958/1,530	15,031
Kevin Kolb, Houston	2003-06	964/1,565	12,964
Tim Rattay, Louisiana Tech	1997-99	1,015/1,552	12,746
Chris Redman, Louisville	1996-99	1,031/1,679	12,541

Career Receiving Yards

Player, team	Yrs.	Rec.	Yds.	Avg.
Trevor Insley, Nevada	1996-99	298	5,005	16.8
Marcus Harris, Wyoming	1993-96	259	4,518	17.4
Ryan Yarborough, Wyoming	1990-93	229	4,357	19.0
Troy Edwards, Louisiana Tech	1996-98	280	4,352	15.5
Aaron Turner, Pacific (CA)	1989-92	266	4,345	16.3

All-Time Team Won-Lost Records[*]

	Years	Won	Lost	Tied	Total	Pct.		Years	Won	Lost	Tied	Total	Pct.
Michigan	127	860	282	36	1,178	.745	Miami (FL)	80	532	297	19	848	.639
Notre Dame	118	821	269	42	1,132	.744	LSU	113	680	376	47	1,103	.638
Texas	114	810	313	33	1,156	.715	Miami (OH)	118	641	362	44	1,047	.633
Oklahoma[1]	112	768	292	53	1,113	.714	Auburn	114	667	384	47	1,098	.629
Ohio St.	117	786	301	53	1,140	.713	Washington	117	646	379	50	1,075	.624
Alabama	112	780	308	43	1,131	.709	Florida	100	619	368	40	1,027	.622
Nebraska	117	803	326	40	1,169	.704	South Fla. (2000)	10	70	43	0	113	.619
USC	114	743	300	54	1,097	.702	Arizona St.	94	530	324	24	878	.617
Tennessee	110	761	316	53	1,130	.697	Colorado	117	652	412	36	1,100	.609
Boise St. (1996)	39	317	140	2	459	.693	Central Michigan	106	542	342	36	920	.609
Penn St.	120	780	343	41	1,164	.688	Texas A&M	112	648	419	48	1,115	.603
Florida St.	60	443	211	17	671	.673	UCLA	88	528	344	37	909	.601
Georgia	113	702	379	54	1,135	.642							

[*]As of 2006 season. Includes records as senior college only. Bowl and playoff games are included, and each tie game is computed as half won and half lost. Teams listed with years in parentheses indicates reclassification to Division I-A (FBS). The year in parentheses is the first year of Division I-A (FBS) membership. Tiebreaker rule began with 1996 season. (1) Includes 2005 season, which Oklahoma was ordered to remove from its record books after "failure to monitor" player employment. An appeal was pending as of July 2007.

Heisman Trophy Winners

Awarded annually to the nation's outstanding college football player by the Downtown Athletic Club.

1935 Jay Berwanger, Chicago, HB	1947 John Lujack, Notre Dame, QB	1959 Billy Cannon, LSU, HB
1936 Larry Kelley, Yale, E	1948 Doak Walker, SMU, HB	1960 Joe Bellino, Navy, HB
1937 Clinton Frank, Yale, HB	1949 Leon Hart, Notre Dame, E	1961 Ernest Davis, Syracuse, HB
1938 David O'Brien, Texas Christian, QB	1950 Vic Janowicz, Ohio St., HB	1962 Terry Baker, Oregon St., QB
1939 Nile Kinnick, Iowa, HB	1951 Richard Kazmaier, Princeton, HB	1963 Roger Staubach, Navy, QB
1940 Tom Harmon, Michigan, HB	1952 Billy Vessels, Oklahoma, HB	1964 John Huarte, Notre Dame, QB
1941 Bruce Smith, Minnesota, HB	1953 John Lattner, Notre Dame, HB	1965 Mike Garrett, USC, HB
1942 Frank Sinkwich, Georgia, HB	1954 Alan Ameche, Wisconsin, FB	1966 Steve Spurrier, Florida, QB
1943 Angelo Bertelli, Notre Dame, QB	1955 Howard Cassady, Ohio St., HB	1967 Gary Beban, UCLA, QB
1944 Leslie Horvath, Ohio St., QB	1956 Paul Hornung, Notre Dame, QB	1968 O. J. Simpson, USC, RB
1945 Felix Blanchard, Army, FB	1957 John Crow, Texas A & M, HB	1969 Steve Owens, Oklahoma, RB
1946 Glenn Davis, Army, HB	1958 Pete Dawkins, Army, HB	1970 Jim Plunkett, Stanford, QB

1971 Pat Sullivan, Auburn, QB	1983 Mike Rozier, Nebraska, RB	1995 Eddie George, Ohio St., RB
1972 Johnny Rodgers, Nebraska, RB-WR	1984 Doug Flutie, Boston College, QB	1996 Danny Wuerffel, Florida, QB
1973 John Cappelletti, Penn St., RB	1985 Bo Jackson, Auburn, RB	1997 Charles Woodson, Michigan, CB
1974 Archie Griffin, Ohio St., RB	1986 Vinny Testaverde, Miami, QB	1998 Ricky Williams, Texas, RB
1975 Archie Griffin, Ohio St., RB	1987 Tim Brown, Notre Dame, WR	1999 Ron Dayne, Wisconsin, RB
1976 Tony Dorsett, Pittsburgh, RB	1988 Barry Sanders, Oklahoma St., RB	2000 Chris Weinke, Florida St., QB
1977 Earl Campbell, Texas, RB	1989 Andre Ware, Houston, QB	2001 Eric Crouch, Nebraska, QB
1978 Billy Sims, Oklahoma, RB	1990 Ty Detmer, BYU, QB	2002 Carson Palmer, USC, QB
1979 Charles White, USC, RB	1991 Desmond Howard, Michigan, WR	2003 Jason White, Oklahoma, QB
1980 George Rogers, S. Carolina, RB	1992 Gino Torretta, Miami, QB	2004 Matt Leinart, USC, QB
1981 Marcus Allen, USC, RB	1993 Charlie Ward, Florida St., QB	2005 Reggie Bush, USC, RB
1982 Herschel Walker, Georgia, RB	1994 Rashaan Salaam, Colorado, RB	2006 Troy Smith, Ohio State, QB

All-Time Division I-A Coaching Victories

Bobby Bowden 366	Bo Schembechler 234	Dana X. Bible 198	John Heisman 185
Joe Paterno 363	Hayden Fry 232	Dan McGugin 197	Johnny Majors 185
Paul "Bear" Bryant . . . 323	Jess Neely 207	**Jim Tressel** 197	Darrell Royal 184
Glenn "Pop" Warner . . . 319	Warren Woodson 203	Fielding Yost 196	Gil Dobie 180
Amos Alonzo Stagg . . . 314	Don Nehlen 202	Howard Jones 194	Jackie Sherrill 180
LaVell Edwards 257	Eddie Anderson 201	John Cooper 192	Carl Snavely 180
Tom Osborne 255	Vince Dooley 201	John Vaught 190	Jerry Claiborne 179
Lou Holtz 249	Jim Sweeney 200	George Welsh 189	Ben Schwartzwalder 178
Woody Hayes 238	**Frank Beamer** 198		

Coaches active in 2006 shown in bold. Total victories through Jan. 9, 2007, including bowl games. John Gagliardi of St. John's Univ. (MN) (Div. III) holds the record for most college football victories, with 443.

College Football Coach of the Year

The Division I-A Coach of the Year has been selected by the American Football Coaches Assn. since 1935 and selected by the Football Writers Assn. of America since 1957. When polls disagree, both winners are indicated.

1935 Lynn Waldorf, Northwestern	1965 Tommy Prothro, UCLA (AFCA);	1984 LaVell Edwards, Brigham Young
1936 Dick Harlow, Harvard	Duffy Daugherty, Mich. St. (FWAA)	1985 Fisher De Berry, Air Force
1937 Edward Mylin, Lafayette	1966 Tom Cahill, Army	1986 Joe Paterno, Penn St.
1938 Bill Kern, Carnegie Tech	1967 John Pont, Indiana	1987 Dick MacPherson, Syracuse
1939 Eddie Anderson, Iowa	1968 Joe Paterno, Penn.St. (AFCA);	1988 Don Nehlen, W. Virginia (AFCA);
1940 Clark Shaughnessy, Stanford	Woody Hayes, Ohio St. (FWAA)	Lou Holtz, Notre Dame (FWAA)
1941 Frank Leahy, Notre Dame	1969 Bo Schembechler, Michigan	1989 Bill McCartney, Colorado
1942 Bill Alexander, Georgia Tech	1970 Charles McClendon, LSU, & Darrell	1990 Bobby Ross, Georgia Tech
1943 Amos Alonzo Stagg, Pacific	Royal, Texas (AFCA);	1991 Don James, Washington
1944 Carroll Widdoes, Ohio St.	Alex Agase, Northwestern (FWAA)	1992 Gene Stallings, Alabama
1945 Bo McMillin, Indiana	1971 Paul "Bear" Bryant, Alabama	1993 Barry Alvarez, Wisconsin (AFCA);
1946 Earl "Red" Blaik, Army	(AFCA); Bob Devaney, Nebraska	Terry Bowden, Auburn (FWAA)
1947 Fritz Crisler, Michigan	(FWAA)	1994 Tom Osborne, Nebraska (AFCA);
1948 Bennie Oosterbaan, Michigan	1972 John McKay, USC	Rich Brooks, Oregon (FWAA)
1949 Bud Wilkinson, Oklahoma	1973 Paul "Bear" Bryant, Alabama	1995 Gary Barnett, Northwestern
1950 Charlie Caldwell, Princeton	(AFCA); Johnny Majors, Pittsburgh	1996 Bruce Snyder, Arizona St.
1951 Chuck Taylor, Stanford	(FWAA)	1997 Mike Price, Washington St.
1952 Biggie Munn, Michigan St.	1974 Grant Teaff, Baylor	1998 Phillip Fulmer, Tennessee
1953 Jim Tatum, Maryland	1975 Frank Kush, Arizona St. (AFCA);	1999 Frank Beamer, Virginia Tech
1954 Henry "Red" Sanders, UCLA	Woody Hayes, Ohio St. (FWAA)	2000 Bob Stoops, Oklahoma
1955 Duffy Daugherty, Michigan St.	1976 Johnny Majors, Pittsburgh	2001 Larry Coker, Miami (FL) & Ralph
1956 Bowden Wyatt, Tennessee	1977 Don James, Washington (AFCA);	Friedgen, Maryland (AFCA); Ralph
1957 Woody Hayes, Ohio St.	Lou Holtz, Arkansas (FWAA)	Friedgen, Maryland (FWAA)
1958 Paul Dietzel, LSU	1978 Joe Paterno, Penn St.	2002 Jim Tressel, Ohio St.
1959 Ben Schwartzwalder, Syracuse	1979 Earle Bruce, Ohio St.	2003 Pete Carroll, USC (AFCA); Nick
1960 Murray Warmath, Minnesota	1980 Vince Dooley, Georgia	Saban, LSU (FWAA)
1961 Paul "Bear" Bryant, Ala. (AFCA);	1981 Danny Ford, Clemson	2004 Tommy Tuberville, Auburn (AFCA);
Darrell Royal, Texas (FWAA)	1982 Joe Paterno, Penn St.	Urban Meyer, Utah (FWAA)
1962 John McKay, USC	1983 Ken Hatfield, Air Force (AFCA);	2005 Joe Paterno, Penn State (AFCA);
1963 Darrell Royal, Texas	Howard Schnellenberger,	Charlie Weis, Notre Dame (FWAA)
1964 Ara Parseghian, Notre Dame, &	Miami (FL) (FWAA)	2006 Jim Grobe, Wake Forest (AFCA);
Frank Broyles, Arkansas (AFCA);		Greg Schiano, Rutgers (FWAA)
Ara Parseghian (FWAA)		

NCAA Div. I-A (FBS) Football Conference Champions (1980-2006)

Atlantic Coast		Big Ten	Big West
1980 North Carolina	2003 Florida St.	1989 Michigan	1980 Long Beach St.
1981 Clemson	2004 Virginia Tech	1990 Iowa, Ill., Mich.,	1981 San Jose St.
1982 Clemson	2005 Florida St.	Mich. St.	1982 Fresno St.
1983 Maryland	2006 Wake Forest	1991 Michigan	1983 Cal St.-Fullerton
1984 Maryland	**Big 12**	1992 Michigan	1984 Cal St.-Fullerton
1985 Maryland	1996 Texas	1993 Ohio St., Wisconsin	1985 Fresno St.
1986 Clemson	1997 Nebraska	1994 Penn St.	1986 San Jose St.
1987 Clemson	1998 Texas A&M	1995 Northwestern	1987 San Jose St.
1988 Clemson	1999 Nebraska	1996 Ohio St.,	1988 Fresno St.
1989 Virginia, Duke	2000 Oklahoma	Northwestern	1989 Fresno St.
1990 Georgia Tech	2001 Colorado	1997 Michigan	1990 San Jose St.
1991 Clemson	2002 Oklahoma	1998 Ohio St.,	1991 San Jose St.,
1992 Florida St.	2003 Kansas St.	Wisconsin,	Fresno St.
1993 Florida St.	2004 Oklahoma	Michigan	1992 Nevada
1994 Florida St.	2005 Texas	1999 Wisconsin	1993 SW Louisiana, Utah
1995 Virginia, Florida St.	2006 Oklahoma	2000 Michigan,	St.
1996 Florida St.	**Big East**	Northwestern,	1994 Nevada, SW
1997 Florida St.	1991 Miami (FL),	Purdue	Louisiana, UNLV
1998 Florida St.,	Syracuse	2001 Illinois	1995 Nevada
Georgia Tech	1992 Miami (FL)	2002 Iowa, Ohio St.	1996 Nevada, Utah St.
1999 Florida St.	1993 West Virginia	2003 Michigan	1997 Nevada, Utah St.
2000 Florida St.	1994 Miami (FL)	2004 Iowa, Michigan	1998 Idaho
2001 Maryland	1995 Virginia Tech, Miami	2005 Penn St., Ohio St.	1999 Boise St.
2002 Florida St.	(FL)	2006 Ohio St.	2000 Boise St.
	1996 Virginia Tech, Miami		
	(FL), Syracuse		
	1997 Syracuse		
	1998 Syracuse		
	1999 Virginia Tech		
	2000 Miami (FL)		
	2001 Miami (FL)		
	2002 Miami (FL)		
	2003 Miami (FL)		
	2004 Pittsburgh,		
	W. Virginia, Boston,		
	Syracuse		
	2005 West Virginia		
	2006 Louisville		

Conference USA
1996 So. Mississippi, Houston
1997 So. Mississippi
1998 Tulane
1999 So. Mississippi
2000 Louisville
2001 Louisville
2002 Cincinnati, TCU
2003 So. Mississippi
2004 Louisville
2005 Tulsa
2006 Houston

Mid-American Athletic
1980 Central Michigan
1981 Toledo
1982 Bowling Green
1983 Northern Illinois
1984 Toledo
1985 Bowling Green
1986 Miami (OH)
1987 E. Michigan
1988 W. Michigan
1989 Ball St.
1990 Central Michigan
1991 Bowling Green
1992 Bowling Green
1993 Ball St.
1994 Central Michigan
1995 Toledo
1996 Ball St.
1997 Marshall

1998 Marshall
1999 Marshall
2000 Marshall
2001 Toledo
2002 Marshall
2003 Miami (OH)
2004 Toledo
2005 Akron
2006 Central Michigan

Mountain West
1999 BYU, Colorado St., Utah
2000 Colorado St.
2001 BYU
2002 Colorado St.
2003 Utah
2004 Utah
2005 TCU
2006 BYU, TCU

Pacific Ten
1980 Washington
1981 Washington
1982 UCLA
1983 UCLA
1984 USC
1985 USC
1986 Arizona St.
1987 UCLA, USC
1988 USC
1989 USC
1990 Washington
1991 Washington

1992 Washington, Stanford
1993 UCLA, Arizona, USC
1994 Oregon
1995 USC, Washington
1996 Arizona St.
1997 Washington St., UCLA
1998 UCLA
1999 Stanford
2000 Washington, Oregon St., Oregon
2001 Oregon
2002 USC, Washington St.
2003 USC
2004 USC
2005 USC
2006 California, USC

Southeastern
1980 Georgia
1981 Georgia, Alabama
1982 Georgia
1983 Auburn
1984 Florida (title vacated)
1985 Tennessee
1986 LSU
1987 Auburn
1988 Auburn, LSU
1989 Ala., Tenn., Auburn
1990 Tennessee

1991 Florida
1992 Alabama
1993 Florida
1994 Florida
1995 Florida
1996 Florida
1997 Tennessee
1998 Tennessee
1999 Alabama
2000 Florida
2001 LSU
2002 Georgia
2003 LSU
2004 Auburn
2005 Georgia
2006 Florida

Sun Belt
2001 Middle Tenn. St., North Texas
2002 North Texas
2003 North Texas
2004 North Texas
2005 Arkansas St., LA-Lafayette, LA-Monroe
2006 Middle Tenn. St., Troy

Western Athletic
1980 Brigham Young (BYU)
1981 Brigham Young

1982 Brigham Young
1983 Brigham Young
1984 Brigham Young
1985 BYU, Air Force
1986 San Diego St.
1987 Wyoming
1988 Wyoming
1989 Brigham Young
1990 Brigham Young
1991 Brigham Young
1992 Hawaii, BYU, Fresno St.
1993 Wyoming, Fresno St., BYU
1994 Colorado St.
1995 Colorado St., Air Force, Utah, BYU
1996 Brigham Young
1997 Colorado St.
1998 Air Force
1999 Fresno St., Hawaii, TCU
2000 Texas Christian, UTEP
2001 Louisiana Tech
2002 Boise State
2003 Boise State
2004 Boise State
2005 Boise State, Nevada
2006 Boise State

NCAA Div. I-AA (FCS) Football Conference Champions (1990-2006)

Atlantic 10
1990 Massachusetts
1991 Delaware, Villanova
1992 Delaware
1993 Boston U.
1994 New Hampshire
1995 Delaware
1996 William & Mary
1997 Villanova
1998 Richmond
1999 J. Madison, Mass.
2000 Delaware, Richmond
2001 Hofstra, Maine, Villanova, Will. & Mary
2002 Maine, Northeastern
2003 Delaware, Mass.
2004 Delaware, J. Madison, New Hampshire, William & Mary
2005 New Hampshire, Richmond
2006 Massachusetts

Big Sky
1990 Nevada
1991 Nevada
1992 Idaho, Eastern Wash.
1993 Montana
1994 Boise St.
1995 Montana
1996 Montana
1997 Eastern Wash.
1998 Montana
1999 Montana
2000 Montana
2001 Montana
2002 Idaho St., Montana, Montana St.
2003 Montana St., Montana, No. Arizona
2004 Montana, Eastern Wash.
2005 Eastern Wash., Montana, Montana St.
2006 Montana

Big South
2002 Gardner-Webb
2003 Gardner-Webb
2004 Coastal Carolina

2005 Coastal Carolina, Charleston Southern
2006 Coastal Carolina

Gateway
1990 Northern Iowa
1991 Northern Iowa
1992 Northern Iowa
1993 Northern Iowa
1994 Northern Iowa
1995 N. Iowa, Eastern Ill.
1996 Northern Iowa
1997 Western Illinois
1998 Western Illinois
1999 Illinois St.
2000 Western Illinois
2001 Northern Iowa
2002 W. Illinois, W. Kentucky
2003 No. Iowa, So. Illinois
2004 So. Illinois
2005 No. Iowa, So. Illinois, Youngstown St.
2006 Youngstown St.

Great West
2004 Cal. Poly
2005 Cal. Poly, UC Davis
2006 North Dakota St.

Ivy League
1990 Cornell, Dartmouth
1991 Dartmouth
1992 Dartmouth, Princeton
1993 Penn
1994 Penn
1995 Princeton
1996 Dartmouth
1997 Harvard
1998 Penn
1999 Brown, Yale
2000 Penn
2001 Harvard
2002 Pennsylvania
2003 Pennsylvania
2004 Harvard
2005 Brown
2006 Yale, Princeton

Metro Atlantic
1993 Iona
1994 Marist, St. John's (NY)
1995 Duquesne
1996 Duquesne
1997 Georgetown

1998 Fairfield, Georgetown
1999 Duquesne
2000 Duquesne
2001 Duquesne
2002 Duquesne
2003 Duquesne
2004 Duquesne
2005 Duquesne
2006 Duquesne, Marist

Mid-Eastern Athletic
1990 Florida A&M
1991 North Carolina A&T
1992 North Carolina A&T
1993 Howard
1994 South Carolina St.
1995 Florida A&M
1996 Florida A&M
1997 Hampton
1998 Florida A&M, Hampton
1999 North Carolina A&T
2000 Florida A&M
2001 Florida A&M
2002 Bethune-Cookman
2003 North Carolina A&T
2004 Hampton, South Carolina St.
2005 Hampton
2006 Hampton

Northeast
1996 R. Morris, Monmouth
1997 Robert Morris
1998 R. Morris, Monmouth
1999 Robert Morris
2000 Robert Morris
2001 Sacred Heart
2002 Albany (NY)
2003 Albany, Monmouth
2004 Central Conn. St., Monmouth
2005 Central Conn. St., Stony Brook
2006 Monmouth (NJ)

Ohio Valley
1990 E. Kentucky., Middle Tenn.
1991 Eastern Kentucky
1992 Middle Tennessee
1993 Eastern Kentucky
1994 Eastern Kentucky
1995 Murray St.
1996 Murray St.

1997 Eastern Kentucky
1998 Tennessee St.
1999 Tennessee St.
2000 Western Kentucky
2001 Eastern Illinois
2002 E. Illinois, Murray St.
2003 Jacksonville St.
2004 Jacksonville St.
2005 Eastern Illinois
2006 E. Illinois, Tenn.-Martin

Patriot
1990 Holy Cross
1991 Holy Cross
1992 Lafayette
1993 Lehigh
1994 Lafayette
1995 Lehigh
1996 Bucknell
1997 Colgate
1998 Lehigh
1999 Colgate, Lehigh
2000 Lehigh
2001 Lehigh
2002 Colgate, Fordham
2003 Colgate
2004 Lafayette, Lehigh
2005 Colgate, Lafayette
2006 Lafayette, Lehigh

Pioneer
1993 Dayton
1994 Dayton, Butler
1995 Drake
1996 Dayton
1997 Dayton
1998 Drake
1999 Dayton
2000 Dayton, Drake, Valparaiso
2001 Dayton
2002 Dayton
2003 Valparaiso
2004 Drake
2005 San Diego
2006 San Diego

Southern
1990 Furman
1991 Appalachian St.
1992 Citadel
1993 Georgia Southern
1994 Marshall
1995 Appalachian St.
1996 Marshall

1997 Georgia Southern
1998 Georgia Southern
1999 Appalachian St., GA Southern, Furman
2000 Georgia Southern
2001 Georgia Southern
2002 Georgia Southern
2003 Wofford
2004 Furman, GA Southern
2005 Appalachian St.
2006 Appalachian St.

Southland
1990 La.-Monroe
1991 McNeese St.
1992 La.-Monroe
1993 McNeese St.
1994 North Texas
1995 McNeese St.
1996 Troy St.
1997 McNeese St., Northwestern St.
1998 Northwestern St.
1999 Troy St., S. F. Austin
2000 Troy St.
2001 Sam Houston St., McNeese St.
2002 McNeese St.
2003 McNeese St.
2004 Northwestern St., Sam Houston St.
2005 Texas St., Nicholls St.
2006 McNeese St.

Southwestern Athletic
1990 Jackson St.
1991 Alabama St.
1992 Alcorn St.
1993 Southern
1994 Grambling St., Alcorn St.
1995 Jackson St.
1996 Jackson St.
1997 Southern
1998 Southern
1999 Southern
2000 Grambling St.
2001 Grambling St.
2002 Grambling St.
2003 Southern
2004 Alabama St.
2005 Grambling St.
2006 Alabama A&M

Selected NCAA Division I Football Teams

(W-L records in last column are for 2006-07 season and include bowl games and playoff games. Conferences and coaches listed are as of July 2007.)

Team	Nickname	Team colors	Conference	Coach	(W-L)
Air Force	Falcons	Blue & silver	Mountain West	Troy Calhoun	4-8
Akron	Zips	Blue & gold	Mid-American	J.D. Brookhart	5-7
Alabama	Crimson Tide	Crimson & white	Southeastern	Nick Saban	6-7
*Appalachian State	Mountaineers	Black & gold	Southern	Jerry Moore	14-1
Arizona	Wildcats	Cardinal & navy	Pacific Ten	Mike Stoops	6-6
Arizona State	Sun Devils	Maroon & gold	Pacific Ten	Dennis Erickson	7-6
Arkansas	Razorbacks	Cardinal & white	Southeastern	Houston Nutt	10-4
Arkansas State	Indians	Scarlet & black	Sun Belt	Steve Roberts	6-6
Army	Black Knights	Black, gold, gray	Independent	Stan Brock	3-9
Auburn	Tigers	Burnt orange & navy	Southeastern	Tommy Tuberville	11-2
Ball State	Cardinals	Cardinal & white	Mid-American	Brady Hoke	5-7
Baylor	Bears	Green & gold	Big Twelve	Guy Morriss	4-8
Boise State	Broncos	Blue & orange	Western Athletic	Chris Petersen	13-0
Boston College	Eagles	Maroon & gold	Atlantic Coast	Jeff Jagodzinski	10-3
Bowling Green	Falcons	Orange & brown	Mid-American	Gregg Brandon	4-8
Brigham Young (BYU)	Cougars	Dark blue & white	Mountain West	Bronco Mendenhall	11-2
*Brown	Bears	Brown, cardinal, white	Ivy League	Phil Estes	3-7
California	Golden Bears	Blue & gold	Pacific Ten	Jeff Tedford	10-3
Central Michigan	Chippewas	Maroon & gold	Mid-American	Butch Jones	10-4
Cincinnati	Bearcats	Red & black	Big East	Brian Kelly	8-5
*Citadel	Bulldogs	Blue & white	Southern	Kevin Higgins	5-6
Clemson	Tigers	Burnt orange & purple	Atlantic Coast	Tommy Bowden	8-5
*Colgate	Red Raiders	Maroon, gray, & white	Patriot League	Dick Biddle	4-7
Colorado	Buffaloes	Silver, gold, & black	Big Twelve	Dan Hawkins	2-10
Colorado State	Rams	Green & gold	Mountain West	Sonny Lubick	4-8
*Columbia	Lions	Columbia blue & white	Ivy League	Norries Wilson	5-5
Connecticut	Huskies	Blue & white	Big East	Randy Edsall	4-8
*Cornell	Big Red	Carnelian & white	Ivy League	Jim Knowles	5-5
*Dartmouth	Big Green	Dartmouth green & white	Ivy League	Buddy Teevens	2-8
*Delaware	Fightin' Blue Hens	Blue & gold	Atlantic Ten	K.C. Keeler	5-6
*Delaware State	Hornets	Red & blue	Mid-Eastern Athletic	Alton Lavan	8-3
Duke	Blue Devils	Royal blue & white	Atlantic Coast	Ted Roof	0-12
East Carolina	Pirates	Purple & gold	Conference USA	Skip Holtz	7-6
*Eastern Illinois	Panthers	Blue & gray	Ohio Valley	Bob Spoo	8-5
*Eastern Kentucky	Colonels	Maroon & white	Ohio Valley	Danny Hope	6-5
Eastern Michigan	Eagles	Dark green & white	Mid-American	Jeff Genyk	1-11
*Eastern Washington	Eagles	Red & white	Big Sky	Paul Wulff	3-8
Florida	Gators	Orange & blue	Southeastern	Urban Meyer	13-1
*Florida A&M	Rattlers	Orange & green	Mid-Eastern Athletic	Rubin Carter	7-4
Florida State	Seminoles	Garnet & gold	Atlantic Coast	Bobby Bowden	7-6
Fresno State	Bulldogs	Red & blue	Western Athletic	Pat Hill	4-8
*Furman	Paladins	Purple & white	Southern	Bobby Lamb	8-4
Georgia	Bulldogs	Red & black	Southeastern	Mark Richt	9-4
*Georgia Southern	Eagles	Blue & white	Southern	Chris Hatcher	3-8
Georgia Tech	Yellow Jackets	Old gold & white	Atlantic Coast	Chan Gailey	9-5
*Grambling State	Tigers	Black & gold	Southwestern Athletic	Rod Broadway	3-8
*Harvard	Crimson	Crimson & white	Ivy League	Tim Murphy	7-3
Hawaii	Warriors	Green, black, white, silver	Western Athletic	June Jones	11-3
*Holy Cross	Crusaders	Royal purple	Patriot League	Tom Gilmore	4-7
Houston	Cougars	Scarlet & white	Conference USA	Art Briles	10-4
*Howard	Bison	Blue, red & white	Mid-Eastern Athletic	Carey Bailey	5-6
*Idaho	Vandals	Silver & gold	Western Athletic	Robb Akey	4-8
*Idaho State	Bengals	Orange & black	Big Sky	John Zamberlin	2-9
Illinois	Fighting Illini	Orange & blue	Big Ten	Ron Zook	2-10
*Illinois State	Redbirds	Red & white	Gateway	Denver Johnson	9-4
Indiana	Hoosiers	Cream & crimson	Big Ten	Bill Lynch	5-7
*Indiana State	Sycamores	Blue & white	Gateway	Lou West	1-10
Iowa	Hawkeyes	Old gold & black	Big Ten	Kirk Ferentz	6-7
Iowa State	Cyclones	Cardinal & gold	Big Twelve	Gene Chizik	4-8
*Jackson State	Tigers	Blue & white	Southwestern Athletic	Rick Comegy	5-5
*James Madison	Dukes	Purple & gold	Atlantic Ten	Mickey Matthews	9-3
Kansas	Jayhawks	Crimson & blue	Big Twelve	Mark Mangino	6-6
Kansas State	Wildcats	Royal purple	Big Twelve	Ron Prince	7-6
Kent State	Golden Flashes	Navy blue & gold	Mid-American	Doug Martin	6-6
Kentucky	Wildcats	Blue & white	Southeastern	Rich Brooks	8-5
*Lafayette	Leopards	Maroon & white	Patriot League	Frank Tavani	6-6
*Lehigh	Mountain Hawks	Brown & white	Patriot League	Andy Coen	6-5
*Liberty	Flames	Red, white, blue	Big South	Danny Rocco	6-5
Louisiana-Lafayette	Ragin' Cajuns	Vermilion & white	Sun Belt	Rickey Bustle	6-6
Louisiana-Monroe	Warhawks	Maroon & gold	Sun Belt	Charlie Weatherbie	4-8
Louisiana State (LSU)	Fighting Tigers	Purple & gold	Southeastern	Les Miles	11-2
Louisiana Tech	Bulldogs	Red & blue	Western Athletic	Derek Dooley	3-10
Louisville	Cardinals	Red, black & white	Big East	Steve Kragthrope	12-1
*Maine	Black Bears	Blue & white	Atlantic Ten	Jack Cosgrove	6-5
Marshall	Thundering Herd	Kelly green & white	Conference USA	Mark Snyder	5-7
Maryland	Terrapins	Red, white, black, gold	Atlantic Coast	Ralph Friedgen	9-4
*Massachusetts	Minutemen	Maroon & white	Atlantic Ten	Don Brown	13-2
*McNeese State	Cowboys	Blue & gold	Southland	Matt Viator	7-5
Memphis	Tigers	Blue & gray	Conference USA	Tommy West	2-10
Miami (Florida)	Hurricanes	Orange, green & white	Atlantic Coast	Randy Shannon	7-6
Miami (Ohio)	RedHawks	Red & white	Mid-American	Shane Montgomery	2-10
Michigan	Wolverines	Maize & blue	Big Ten	Lloyd Carr	11-2
Michigan State	Spartans	Green & white	Big Ten	Mark Dantonio	4-8
Mid. Tennessee State	Blue Raiders	Royal blue & white	Sun Belt	Rick Stockstill	7-6
Minnesota	Golden Gophers	Maroon & gold	Big Ten	Tim Brewster	6-7
Mississippi	Rebels	Cardinal red & navy blue	Southeastern	Ed Orgeron	4-8
Mississippi State	Bulldogs	Maroon & white	Southeastern	Sylvester Croom	3-9
Mississippi Valley State	Delta Devils	Forest green & white	Southwestern Athletic	Willie Totten	6-5

Team	Nickname	Team colors	Conference	Coach	(W-L)
Missouri	Tigers	Old gold & black	Big Twelve	Gary Pinkel	8-5
*Montana	Grizzlies	Copper, silver & gold	Big Sky	Bobby Hauck	12-2
*Montana State	Bobcats	Blue & gold	Big Sky	Rob Ash	8-5
*Morehead State	Eagles	Blue & gold	Pioneer	Matt Ballard	2-9
*Morgan State	Bears	Blue & orange	Mid-Eastern Athletic	Donald Hill-Eley	1-10
*Murray State	Racers	Navy blue & gold	Ohio Valley	Matt Griffin	4-7
Navy	Midshipmen	Navy blue & gold	Independent	Paul Johnson	9-4
Nebraska	Cornhuskers	Scarlet & cream	Big Twelve	Bill Callahan	9-5
Nevada	Wolf Pack	Cobalt blue & silver	Western Athletic	Chris Ault	8-5
Nev.-Las Vegas (UNLV)	Rebels	Scarlet & gray	Mountain West	Mike Sanford	2-10
*New Hampshire	Wildcats	Blue & white	Atlantic Ten	Sean McDonnell	9-4
New Mexico	Lobos	Cherry & silver	Mountain West	Rocky Long	6-7
New Mexico State	Aggies	Crimson & white	Western Athletic	Hal Mumme	4-8
*Nicholls State	Colonels	Red & gray	Southland	Jay Thomas	4-7
North Carolina	Tar Heels	Carolina blue & white	Atlantic Coast	Butch Davis	3-9
North Carolina State	Wolfpack	Red & white	Atlantic Coast	Tom O'Brien	3-9
North Texas	Mean Green	Green & white	Sun Belt	Todd Dodge	3-9
*Northeastern	Huskies	Red & black	Atlantic Ten	Rocky Hager	5-6
*Northern Arizona	Lumberjacks	Blue, gold & sage	Big Sky	Jerome Souers	6-5
*Northern Illinois	Huskies	Cardinal & black	Mid-American	Joe Novak	7-6
*Northern Iowa	Panthers	Purple & gold	Gateway	Mark Farley	7-4
Northwestern	Wildcats	Purple & white	Big Ten	Pat Fitzgerald	4-8
*Northwestern State	Demons	Purple, white, & orange	Southland	Scott Stoker	4-7
Notre Dame	Fighting Irish	Gold & blue	Independent	Charlie Weis	10-3
Ohio	Bobcats	Hunter green & white	Mid-American	Frank Solich	9-5
Ohio State	Buckeyes	Scarlet & gray	Big Ten	Jim Tressel	12-1
Oklahoma	Sooners	Crimson & cream	Big Twelve	Bob Stoops	11-3
Oklahoma State	Cowboys	Orange & black	Big Twelve	Mike Gundy	7-6
Oregon	Ducks	Green & yellow	Pacific Ten	Mike Bellotti	7-6
Oregon State	Beavers	Orange & black	Pacific Ten	Mike Riley	10-4
Penn State	Nittany Lions	Blue & white	Big Ten	Joe Paterno	9-4
*Pennsylvania	Quakers	Red & blue	Ivy League	Al Bagnoli	5-5
Pittsburgh	Panthers	Blue & gold	Big East	Dave Wannstedt	6-6
*Princeton	Tigers	Orange & black	Ivy League	Roger Hughes	9-1
Purdue	Boilermakers	Old gold & black	Big Ten	Joe Tiller	8-6
*Rhode Island	Rams	Keaney blue, dark blue & white	Atlantic Ten	Tim Stowers	4-7
Rice	Owls	Blue & gray	Conference USA	David Bailiff	7-6
*Richmond	Spiders	Red & blue	Atlantic Ten	Dave Clawson	6-5
Rutgers	Scarlet Knights	Scarlet	Big East	Greg Schiano	11-2
*Sam Houston State	Bearkats	Orange & white	Southland	Todd Whitten	6-5
*Samford	Bulldogs	Red & blue	Ohio Valley	Pat Sullivan	3-8
San Diego State	Aztecs	Scarlet & black	Mountain West	Chuck Long	3-9
San Jose State	Spartans	Gold & blue	Western Athletic	Dick Tomey	9-4
South Carolina	Gamecocks	Garnet & black	Southeastern	Steve Spurrier	8-5
*South Carolina State	Bulldogs	Garnet & blue	Mid-Eastern Athletic	Oliver Pough	7-4
*SE Missouri State	Redhawks	Red & black	Ohio Valley	Tony Samuel	4-7
Southern California (USC)	Trojans	Cardinal & gold	Pacific Ten	Pete Carroll	11-2
South Florida	Bulls	Green & gold	Big East	Jim Leavitt	9-4
*Southern Illinois	Salukis	Maroon & white	Gateway	Jerry Kill	9-4
*Southern Methodist (SMU)	Mustangs	Crimson & blue	Conference USA	Phil Bennett	6-6
Southern Mississippi	Golden Eagles	Black & gold	Conference USA	Jeff Bower	9-5
*Stephen F. Austin	Lumberjacks	Red & white	Southland	Jim Harbaugh	1-11
Stanford	Cardinal	Purple, white & red	Pacific Ten	J.C. Harper	4-7
Syracuse	Orange	Orange	Big East	Greg Robinson	4-8
Temple	Owls	Cherry & white	Independent	Al Golden	1-11
Tennessee	Volunteers	Orange & white	Southeastern	Phillip Fulmer	9-4
*Tennessee-Martin	Skyhawks	Orange, white & blue	Ohio Valley	Jason Simpson	9-3
*Tennessee State	Tigers	Royal blue & white	Ohio Valley	James Webster	6-5
*Tennessee Tech	Golden Eagles	Purple & gold	Ohio Valley	Watson Brown	4-7
Texas	Longhorns	Burnt orange & white	Big Twelve	Mack Brown	10-3
Texas A&M	Aggies	Maroon & white	Big Twelve	Dennis Franchione	9-4
Texas Christian (TCU)	Horned Frogs	Purple & white	Mountain West	Gary Patterson	11-2
*Texas Southern	Tigers	Maroon & gray	Southwestern Athletic	Steve Wilson	3-8
*Texas State	Bobcats	Maroon & gold	Southland	Brad Wright	5-6
Texas Tech	Red Raiders	Scarlet & black	Big Twelve	Mike Leach	8-5
Toledo	Rockets	Midnight blue & gold	Mid-American	Tom Amstutz	5-7
Troy	Trojans	Cardinal, black & silver	Sun Belt	Larry Blakeney	8-5
Tulane	Green Wave	Olive green & sky blue	Conference USA	Bob Toledo	4-8
Tulsa	Golden Hurricane	Blue & crimson	Conference USA	Todd Graham	8-5
UCLA	Bruins	Blue & gold	Pacific Ten	Karl Dorrell	7-6
Utah	Utes	Crimson & white	Mountain West	Kyle Whittingham	8-5
Utah State	Aggies	Navy blue & white	Western Athletic	Brent Guy	1-11
UTEP (Texas-El Paso)	Miners	Orange, blue, white & silver	Conference USA	Mike Price	5-7
Vanderbilt	Commodores	Black & gold	Southeastern	Bobby Johnson	4-8
*Villanova	Wildcats	Blue & white	Atlantic Ten	Andy Talley	6-5
Virginia	Cavaliers	Orange & navy blue	Atlantic Coast	Al Groh	5-7
Virginia Tech	Hokies	Burnt orange & maroon	Atlantic Coast	Frank Beamer	10-3
Wake Forest	Demon Deacons	Old gold & black	Atlantic Coast	Jim Grobe	11-3
Washington	Huskies	Purple & gold	Pacific Ten	Tyrone Willingham	5-7
Washington State	Cougars	Crimson & gray	Pacific Ten	Bill Doba	6-6
*Weber State	Wildcats	Royal purple & white	Big Sky	Ron McBride	4-7
West Virginia	Mountaineers	Old gold & blue	Big East	Rich Rodriguez	11-2
*Western Carolina	Catamounts	Purple & gold	Southern	Kent Briggs	2-9
*Western Illinois	Leathernecks	Purple & gold	Gateway	Don Patterson	5-6
*Western Kentucky	Hilltoppers	Red & white	Gateway	David Elson	6-5
Western Michigan	Broncos	Brown & gold	Mid-American	Bill Cubit	8-5
*William & Mary	Tribe	Green, gold & silver	Atlantic Coast	Jimmye Laycock	3-8
Wisconsin	Badgers	Cardinal & white	Big Ten	Bret Bielema	12-1
Wyoming	Cowboys	Brown & gold	Mountain West	Joe Glenn	6-6
*Yale	Bulldogs, Elis	Yale blue & white	Ivy League	Jack Siedlecki	8-2
*Youngstown State	Penguins	Red & white	Gateway	Jon Heacock	11-3

* Football Championship Subdivision (FCS) team (formerly known as I-AA) as of the end of the 2006 regular season.

NATIONAL HOCKEY LEAGUE

2006-2007: The Cup Goes West; Brodeur, Crosby Set Records

The Anaheim Ducks defeated the Ottawa Senators in the Stanley Cup Finals in game 5 at Anaheim on June 6, 2007. It was Anaheim's first Stanley Cup in its 14-season history. It was Ottawa's first championship appearance since 1927. The Ducks became the first West Coast team to win the Cup since NHL clubs began competing exclusively in 1927. (The Victoria Cougars, a Western Canada Hockey League team, won in 1925.) Ducks defenseman Scott Niedermayer was awarded the Conn Smythe Trophy as MVP of the NHL postseason.

Sophomore center Sidney Crosby of Pittsburgh led the NHL with 120 points and received both the Hart and Pearson MVP awards. He broke Wayne Gretzky's record as the youngest player to score 200 career points on Mar. 2 at 19 years, 207 days. New Jersey's veteran goaltender Martin Brodeur set the single-season record of 48 wins on Apr. 5.

Final NHL Standings 2006-2007

(Playoff seeding in parentheses; division winners automatically seeded 1, 2, or 3; teams tied at the end of regulation time are each awarded 1 point, an additional point is awarded to the overtime winner)

Eastern Conference

Atlantic Division	W	L	OTL	GF	GA	PTS
New Jersey Devils (2)	49	24	9	216	201	107
Pittsburgh Penguins (5)	47	24	11	277	246	105
New York Rangers (6)	42	30	10	242	216	94
New York Islanders (8)	40	30	12	248	240	92
Philadelphia Flyers	22	48	12	214	303	56

Northeast Division	W	L	OTL	GF	GA	PTS
Buffalo Sabres (1)	53	22	7	308	242	113
Ottawa Senators (4)	48	25	9	288	222	105
Toronto Maple Leafs	40	31	11	258	269	91
Montreal Canadiens	42	34	6	245	256	90
Boston Bruins	35	41	6	219	289	76

Southeast Division	W	L	OTL	GF	GA	PTS
Atlanta Thrashers (3)	43	28	11	246	245	97
Tampa Bay Lightning (7)	44	33	5	253	261	93
Carolina Hurricanes	40	34	8	241	253	88
Florida Panthers	35	31	16	247	257	86
Washington Capitals	28	40	14	235	286	70

Western Conference

Central Division	W	L	OTL	GF	GA	PTS
Detroit Red Wings (1)	50	19	13	254	199	113
Nashville Predators (4)	51	23	8	272	212	110
St. Louis Blues	34	35	13	214	254	81
Columbus Blue Jackets	33	42	7	201	249	73
Chicago Blackhawks	31	42	9	201	258	71

Northwest Division	W	L	OTL	GF	GA	PTS
Vancouver Canucks (3)	49	26	7	222	201	105
Minnesota Wild (7)	48	26	8	235	191	104
Calgary Flames (8)	43	29	10	258	226	96
Colorado Avalanche	44	31	7	272	251	95
Edmonton Oilers	32	43	7	195	248	71

Pacific Division	W	L	OTL	GF	GA	PTS
Anaheim Ducks (2)	48	20	14	258	208	110
San Jose Sharks (5)	51	26	5	258	199	107
Dallas Stars (6)	50	25	7	226	197	107
Los Angeles Kings	27	41	14	227	283	68
Phoenix Coyotes	31	46	5	216	284	67

2007 Stanley Cup Playoff Results

Eastern Conference

Buffalo defeated N.Y. Islanders 4 games to 1
New Jersey defeated Tampa Bay 4 games to 2
N.Y. Rangers defeated Atlanta 4 games to 0
Ottawa defeated Pittsburgh 4 games to 1
Buffalo defeated N.Y. Rangers 4 games to 2
Ottawa defeated New Jersey 4 games to 1
Ottawa defeated Buffalo 4 games to 1

Western Conference

Detroit defeated Calgary 4 games to 2
Anaheim defeated Minnesota 4 games to 1
San Jose defeated Nashville 4 games to 1
Vancouver defeated Dallas 4 games to 3
Detroit defeated San Jose 4 games to 2
Anaheim defeated Vancouver 4 games to 1
Anaheim defeated Detroit 4 games to 2

Finals

Anaheim defeated Ottawa 4 games to 1 [3-2, 1-0, 3-5, 3-2, 6-2]

Stanley Cup Champions Since 1927

Year	Champion	Coach	Final opponent	Year	Champion	Coach	Final opponent
1927	Ottawa	Dave Gill	Boston	1957	Montreal	Toe Blake	Boston
1928	N.Y. Rangers	Lester Patrick	Montreal Maroons	1958	Montreal	Toe Blake	Boston
1929	Boston	Cy Denneny	N.Y. Rangers	1959	Montreal	Toe Blake	Toronto
1930	Montreal	Cecil Hart	Boston	1960	Montreal	Toe Blake	Toronto
1931	Montreal	Cecil Hart	Chicago	1961	Chicago	Rudy Pilous	Detroit
1932	Toronto	Dick Irvin	N.Y. Rangers	1962	Toronto	Punch Imlach	Chicago
1933	N.Y. Rangers	Lester Patrick	Toronto	1963	Toronto	Punch Imlach	Detroit
1934	Chicago	Tommy Gorman	Detroit	1964	Toronto	Punch Imlach	Detroit
1935	Montreal Maroons	Tommy Gorman	Toronto	1965	Montreal	Toe Blake	Chicago
1936	Detroit	Jack Adams	Toronto	1966	Montreal	Toe Blake	Detroit
1937	Detroit	Jack Adams	N.Y. Rangers	1967	Toronto	Punch Imlach	Montreal
1938	Chicago	Bill Stewart	Toronto	1968	Montreal	Toe Blake	St. Louis
1939	Boston	Art Ross	Toronto	1969	Montreal	Claude Ruel	St. Louis
1940	N.Y. Rangers	Frank Boucher	Toronto	1970	Boston	Harry Sinden	St. Louis
1941	Boston	Cooney Weiland	Detroit	1971	Montreal	Al MacNeil	Chicago
1942	Toronto	Hap Day	Detroit	1972	Boston	Tom Johnson	N.Y. Rangers
1943	Detroit	Jack Adams	Boston	1973	Montreal	Scotty Bowman	Chicago
1944	Montreal	Dick Irvin	Chicago	1974	Philadelphia	Fred Shero	Boston
1945	Toronto	Hap Day	Detroit	1975	Philadelphia	Fred Shero	Buffalo
1946	Montreal	Dick Irvin	Boston	1976	Montreal	Scotty Bowman	Philadelphia
1947	Toronto	Hap Day	Montreal	1977	Montreal	Scotty Bowman	Boston
1948	Toronto	Hap Day	Detroit	1978	Montreal	Scotty Bowman	Boston
1949	Toronto	Hap Day	Detroit	1979	Montreal	Scotty Bowman	N.Y. Rangers
1950	Detroit	Tommy Ivan	N.Y. Rangers	1980	N.Y. Islanders	Al Arbour	Philadelphia
1951	Toronto	Joe Primeau	Montreal	1981	N.Y. Islanders	Al Arbour	Minnesota
1952	Detroit	Tommy Ivan	Montreal	1982	N.Y. Islanders	Al Arbour	Vancouver
1953	Montreal	Dick Irvin	Boston	1983	N.Y. Islanders	Al Arbour	Edmonton
1954	Detroit	Tommy Ivan	Montreal	1984	Edmonton	Glen Sather	N.Y. Islanders
1955	Detroit	Jimmy Skinner	Montreal	1985	Edmonton	Glen Sather	Philadelphia
1956	Montreal	Toe Blake	Detroit	1986	Montreal	Jean Perron	Calgary
				1987	Edmonton	Glen Sather	Philadelphia

Year	Champion	Coach	Final opponent	Year	Champion	Coach	Final opponent
1988	Edmonton	Glen Sather	Boston	1998	Detroit	Scotty Bowman	Washington
1989	Calgary	Terry Crisp	Montreal	1999	Dallas	Ken Hitchcock	Buffalo
1990	Edmonton	John Muckler	Boston	2000	New Jersey	Larry Robinson	Dallas
1991	Pittsburgh	Bob Johnson	Minnesota	2001	Colorado	Bob Hartley	New Jersey
1992	Pittsburgh	Scotty Bowman	Chicago	2002	Detroit	Scotty Bowman	Carolina
1993	Montreal	Jacques Demers	Los Angeles	2003	New Jersey	Pat Burns	Anaheim
1994	N.Y. Rangers	Mike Keenan	Vancouver	2004	Tampa Bay	John Tortorella	Calgary
1995	New Jersey	Jacques Lemaire	Detroit	2005	No competition		
1996	Colorado	Marc Crawford	Florida	2006	Carolina	Peter Laviolette	Edmonton
1997	Detroit	Scotty Bowman	Philadelphia	2007	Anaheim	Randy Carlyle	Ottawa

Most NHL Goals in a Season

Player	Team	Season	Goals	Player	Team	Season	Goals
Wayne Gretzky	Edmonton	1981-82	92	Jari Kurri	Edmonton	1984-85	71
Wayne Gretzky	Edmonton	1983-84	87	Brett Hull	St. Louis	1991-92	70
Brett Hull	St. Louis	1990-91	86	Mario Lemieux	Pittsburgh	1987-88	70
Mario Lemieux	Pittsburgh	1988-89	85	Mario Lemieux	Pittsburgh	1988-89	70
Phil Esposito	Boston	1970-71	76	Bernie Nicholls	Los Angeles	1978-79	69
Alexander Mogilny	Buffalo	1992-93	76	Mike Bossy	N.Y. Islanders	1978-79	69
Teemu Selanne	Winnipeg	1992-93	76	Mario Lemieux	Pittsburgh	1992-93	69
Wayne Gretzky	Edmonton	1984-85	73	Mario Lemieux	Pittsburgh	1995-96	69
Brett Hull	St. Louis	1989-90	72	Mike Bossy	N.Y. Islanders	1980-81	68
Wayne Gretzky	Edmonton	1982-83	71	Phil Esposito	Boston	1973-74	68
				Jari Kurri	Edmonton	1985-86	68

All-Time Regular Season Leading Scorers

Player	Goals	Assists	Points	Player	Goals	Assists	Points	Player	Goals	Assists	Points
Wayne Gretzky	894	1,963	2,857	Phil Esposito	717	873	1,590	Adam Oates	341	1,079	1,420
Mark Messier	694	1,193	1,887	Joe Sakic*	610	979	1,589	Doug Gilmour	450	964	1,414
Gordie Howe	801	1,049	1,850	Ray Bourque	410	1,169	1,579	Dale Hawerchuk	518	891	1,409
Ron Francis	549	1,249	1,798	Paul Coffey	396	1,135	1,531	Jari Kurri	601	797	1,398
Marcel Dionne	731	1,040	1,771	Jaromir Jagr*	621	907	1,528	Luc Robitaille	668	726	1,394
Steve Yzerman	692	1,063	1,755	Stan Mikita	541	926	1,467	Brett Hull	741	650	1,391
Mario Lemieux	690	1,033	1,723	Bryan Trottier	524	901	1,425				

Note: Through end of 2006-2007 season. *Active in the 2006-2007 season.

Hart Memorial Trophy (MVP)

1927 Herb Gardiner, Montreal	1953 Gordie Howe, Detroit	1980 Wayne Gretzky, Edmonton
1928 Howie Morenz, Montreal	1954 Al Rollins, Chicago	1981 Wayne Gretzky, Edmonton
1929 Roy Worters, N.Y. Americans	1955 Ted Kennedy, Toronto	1982 Wayne Gretzky, Edmonton
1930 Nels Stewart, Montreal Maroons	1956 Jean Beliveau, Montreal	1983 Wayne Gretzky, Edmonton
1931 Howie Morenz, Montreal	1957 Gordie Howe, Detroit	1984 Wayne Gretzky, Edmonton
1932 Howie Morenz, Montreal	1958 Gordie Howe, Detroit	1985 Wayne Gretzky, Edmonton
1933 Eddie Shore, Boston	1959 Andy Bathgate, N.Y. Rangers	1986 Wayne Gretzky, Edmonton
1934 Aurel Joliat, Montreal	1960 Gordie Howe, Detroit	1987 Wayne Gretzky, Edmonton
1935 Eddie Shore, Boston	1961 Bernie Geoffrion, Montreal	1988 Mario Lemieux, Pittsburgh
1936 Eddie Shore, Boston	1962 Jacques Plante, Montreal	1989 Wayne Gretzky, Los Angeles
1937 Babe Siebert, Montreal	1963 Gordie Howe, Detroit	1990 Mark Messier, Edmonton
1938 Eddie Shore, Boston	1964 Jean Beliveau, Montreal	1991 Brett Hull, St. Louis
1939 Toe Blake, Montreal	1965 Bobby Hull, Chicago	1992 Mark Messier, N.Y. Rangers
1940 Ebbie Goodfellow, Detroit	1966 Bobby Hull, Chicago	1993 Mario Lemieux, Pittsburgh
1941 Bill Cowley, Boston	1967 Stan Mikita, Chicago	1994 Sergei Fedorov, Detroit
1942 Tom Anderson, Brooklyn Americans	1968 Stan Mikita, Chicago	1995 Eric Lindros, Philadelphia
1943 Bill Cowley, Boston	1969 Phil Esposito, Boston	1996 Mario Lemieux, Pittsburgh
1944 Babe Pratt, Toronto	1970 Bobby Orr, Boston	1997 Dominik Hasek, Buffalo
1945 Elmer Lach, Montreal	1971 Bobby Orr, Boston	1998 Dominik Hasek, Buffalo
1946 Max Bentley, Chicago	1972 Bobby Orr, Boston	1999 Jaromir Jagr, Pittsburgh
1947 Maurice Richard, Montreal	1973 Bobby Clarke, Philadelphia	2000 Chris Pronger, St. Louis
1948 Buddy O'Connor, N.Y. Rangers	1974 Phil Esposito, Boston	2001 Joe Sakic, Colorado
1949 Sid Abel, Detroit	1975 Bobby Clarke, Philadelphia	2002 Jose Theodore, Montreal
1950 Chuck Rayner, N.Y. Rangers	1976 Bobby Clarke, Philadelphia	2003 Peter Forsberg, Colorado
1951 Milt Schmidt, Boston	1977 Guy Lafleur, Montreal	2004 Martin St. Louis, Tampa Bay
1952 Gordie Howe, Detroit	1978 Guy Lafleur, Montreal	2006 Joe Thornton, San Jose
	1979 Bryan Trottier, N.Y. Islanders	2007 Sidney Crosby, Pittsburgh

Conn Smythe Trophy (MVP in Playoffs)

1965 Jean Beliveau, Montreal	1979 Bob Gainey, Montreal	1993 Patrick Roy, Montreal
1966 Roger Crozier, Detroit	1980 Bryan Trottier, N.Y. Islanders	1994 Brian Leetch, N.Y. Rangers
1967 Dave Keon, Toronto	1981 Butch Goring, N.Y. Islanders	1995 Claude Lemieux, New Jersey
1968 Glenn Hall, St. Louis	1982 Mike Bossy, N.Y. Islanders	1996 Joe Sakic, Colorado
1969 Serge Savard, Montreal	1983 Billy Smith, N.Y. Islanders	1997 Mike Vernon, Detroit
1970 Bobby Orr, Boston	1984 Mark Messier, Edmonton	1998 Steve Yzerman, Detroit
1971 Ken Dryden, Montreal	1985 Wayne Gretzky, Edmonton	1999 Joe Nieuwendyk, Dallas
1972 Bobby Orr, Boston	1986 Patrick Roy, Montreal	2000 Scott Stevens, New Jersey
1973 Yvan Cournoyer, Montreal	1987 Ron Hextall, Philadelphia	2001 Patrick Roy, Colorado
1974 Bernie Parent, Philadelphia	1988 Wayne Gretzky, Edmonton	2002 Nicklas Lidstrom, Detroit
1975 Bernie Parent, Philadelphia	1989 Al MacInnis, Calgary	2003 Jean-Sebastien Giguere, Anaheim
1976 Reg Leach, Philadelphia	1990 Bill Ranford, Edmonton	2004 Brad Richards, Tampa Bay
1977 Guy Lafleur, Montreal	1991 Mario Lemieux, Pittsburgh	2006 Cam Ward, Carolina
1978 Larry Robinson, Montreal	1992 Mario Lemieux, Pittsburgh	2007 Scott Niedermayer, Anaheim

Calder Memorial Trophy (Rookie of the Year)

1933 Carl Voss, Detroit	1958 Frank Mahovlich, Toronto	1983 Steve Larmer, Chicago
1934 Russ Blinco, Montreal Maroons	1959 Ralph Backstrom, Montreal	1984 Tom Barrasso, Buffalo
1935 Dave Schriner, N.Y. Americans	1960 Bill Hay, Chicago	1985 Mario Lemieux, Pittsburgh
1936 Mike Karakas, Chicago	1961 Dave Keon, Toronto	1986 Gary Suter, Calgary
1937 Syl Apps, Toronto	1962 Bobby Rousseau, Montreal	1987 Luc Robitaille, Los Angeles
1938 Cully Dahlstrom, Chicago	1963 Kent Douglas, Toronto	1988 Joe Nieuwendyk, Calgary
1939 Frank Brimsek, Boston	1964 Jacques Laperriere, Montreal	1989 Brian Leetch, N.Y. Rangers
1940 Kilby MacDonald, N.Y. Rangers	1965 Roger Crozier, Detroit	1990 Sergei Makarov, Calgary
1941 John Quilty, Montreal	1966 Brit Selby, Toronto	1991 Ed Belfour, Chicago
1942 Grant Warwick, N.Y. Rangers	1967 Bobby Orr, Boston	1992 Pavel Bure, Vancouver
1943 Gaye Stewart, Toronto	1968 Derek Sanderson, Boston	1993 Teemu Selanne, Winnipeg
1944 Gus Bodnar, Toronto	1969 Danny Grant, Minnesota	1994 Martin Brodeur, New Jersey
1945 Frank McCool, Toronto	1970 Tony Esposito, Chicago	1995 Peter Forsberg, Quebec
1946 Edgar Laprade, N.Y. Rangers	1971 Gilbert Perreault, Buffalo	1996 Daniel Alfredsson, Ottawa
1947 Howie Meeker, Toronto	1972 Ken Dryden, Montreal	1997 Bryan Berard, N.Y. Islanders
1948 Jim McFadden, Detroit	1973 Steve Vickers, N.Y. Rangers	1998 Sergei Samsonov, Boston
1949 Pentti Lund, N.Y. Rangers	1974 Denis Potvin, N.Y. Islanders	1999 Chris Drury, Colorado
1950 Jack Gelineau, Boston	1975 Eric Vail, Atlanta	2000 Scott Gomez, New Jersey
1951 Terry Sawchuk, Detroit	1976 Bryan Trottier, N.Y. Islanders	2001 Evgeni Nabokov, San Jose
1952 Bernie Geoffrion, Montreal	1977 Willi Plett, Atlanta	2002 Dany Heatley, Atlanta
1953 Gump Worsley, N.Y. Rangers	1978 Mike Bossy, N.Y. Islanders	2003 Barret Jackman, St. Louis
1954 Camille Henry, N.Y. Rangers	1979 Bobby Smith, Minnesota	2004 Andrew Raycroft, Boston
1955 Ed Litzenberger, Chicago	1980 Ray Bourque, Boston	2006 Alexander Overchkin, Washington
1956 Glenn Hall, Detroit	1981 Peter Stastny, Quebec	2007 Evgeni Malkin, Pittsburgh
1957 Larry Regan, Boston	1982 Dale Hawerchuk, Winnipeg	

Lady Byng Memorial Trophy (Most Gentlemanly Player)

1925 Frank Nighbor, Ottawa	1953 Red Kelly, Detroit	1980 Wayne Gretzky, Edmonton
1926 Frank Nighbor, Ottawa	1954 Red Kelly, Detroit	1981 Rick Kehoe, Pittsburgh
1927 Billy Burch, N.Y. Americans	1955 Sid Smith, Toronto	1982 Rick Middleton, Boston
1928 Frank Boucher, N.Y. Rangers	1956 Earl Reibel, Detroit	1983 Mike Bossy, N.Y. Islanders
1929 Frank Boucher, N.Y. Rangers	1957 Andy Hebenton, N.Y. Rangers	1984 Mike Bossy, N.Y. Islanders
1930 Frank Boucher, N.Y. Rangers	1958 Camille Henry, N.Y. Rangers	1985 Jari Kurri, Edmonton
1931 Frank Boucher, N.Y. Rangers	1959 Alex Delvecchio, Detroit	1986 Mike Bossy, N.Y. Islanders
1932 Joe Primeau, Toronto	1960 Don McKenney, Boston	1987 Joe Mullen, Calgary
1933 Frank Boucher, N.Y. Rangers	1961 Red Kelly, Toronto	1988 Mats Naslund, Montreal
1934 Frank Boucher, N.Y. Rangers	1962 Dave Keon, Toronto	1989 Joe Mullen, Calgary
1935 Frank Boucher, N.Y. Rangers	1963 Dave Keon, Toronto	1990 Brett Hull, St. Louis
1936 Doc Romnes, Chicago	1964 Ken Wharram, Chicago	1991 Wayne Gretzky, Los Angeles
1937 Marty Barry, Detroit	1965 Bobby Hull, Chicago	1992 Wayne Gretzky, Los Angeles
1938 Gordie Drillon, Toronto	1966 Alex Delvecchio, Detroit	1993 Pierre Turgeon, N.Y. Islanders
1939 Clint Smith, N.Y. Rangers	1967 Stan Mikita, Chicago	1994 Wayne Gretzky, Los Angeles
1940 Bobby Bauer, Boston	1968 Stan Mikita, Chicago	1995 Ron Francis, Pittsburgh
1941 Bobby Bauer, Boston	1969 Alex Delvecchio, Detroit	1996 Paul Kariya, Anaheim
1942 Syl Apps, Toronto	1970 Phil Goyette, St. Louis	1997 Paul Kariya, Anaheim
1943 Max Bentley, Chicago	1971 John Bucyk, Boston	1998 Ron Francis, Pittsburgh
1944 Clint Smith, Chicago	1972 Jean Ratelle, N.Y. Rangers	1999 Wayne Gretzky, N.Y. Rangers
1945 Bill Mosienko, Chicago	1973 Gil Perreault, Buffalo	2000 Pavol Demitra, St. Louis
1946 Toe Blake, Montreal	1974 John Bucyk, Boston	2001 Joe Sakic, Colorado
1947 Bobby Bauer, Boston	1975 Marcel Dionne, Detroit	2002 Ron Francis, Carolina
1948 Buddy O'Connor, N.Y. Rangers	1976 Jean Ratelle, N.Y.R.-Boston	2003 Alexander Mogilny, Toronto
1949 Bill Quackenbush, Detroit	1977 Marcel Dionne, Los Angeles	2004 Brad Richards, Tampa Bay
1950 Edgar Laprade, N.Y. Rangers	1978 Butch Goring, Los Angeles	2006 Pavel Datsyuk, Detroit
1951 Red Kelly, Detroit	1979 Bob MacMillan, Atlanta	2007 Pavel Datsyuk, Detroit
1952 Sid Smith, Toronto		

James Norris Memorial Trophy (Outstanding Defenseman)

1954 Red Kelly, Detroit	1972 Bobby Orr, Boston	1990 Ray Bourque, Boston
1955 Doug Harvey, Montreal	1973 Bobby Orr, Boston	1991 Ray Bourque, Boston
1956 Doug Harvey, Montreal	1974 Bobby Orr, Boston	1992 Brian Leetch, N.Y. Rangers
1957 Doug Harvey, Montreal	1975 Bobby Orr, Boston	1993 Chris Chelios, Chicago
1958 Doug Harvey, Montreal	1976 Denis Potvin, N.Y. Islanders	1994 Ray Bourque, Boston
1959 Tom Johnson, Montreal	1977 Larry Robinson, Montreal	1995 Paul Coffey, Detroit
1960 Doug Harvey, Montreal	1978 Denis Potvin, N.Y. Islanders	1996 Chris Chelios, Chicago
1961 Doug Harvey, Montreal	1979 Denis Potvin, N.Y. Islanders	1997 Brian Leetch, N.Y. Rangers
1962 Doug Harvey, N.Y. Rangers	1980 Larry Robinson, Montreal	1998 Rob Blake, Los Angeles
1963 Pierre Pilote, Chicago	1981 Randy Carlyle, Pittsburgh	1999 Al MacInnis, St. Louis
1964 Pierre Pilote, Chicago	1982 Doug Wilson, Chicago	2000 Chris Pronger, St. Louis
1965 Pierre Pilote, Chicago	1983 Rod Langway, Washington	2001 Nicklas Lidstrom, Detroit
1966 Jacques Laperriere, Montreal	1984 Rod Langway, Washington	2002 Nicklas Lidstrom, Detroit
1967 Harry Howell, N.Y. Rangers	1985 Paul Coffey, Edmonton	2003 Nicklas Lidstrom, Detroit
1968 Bobby Orr, Boston	1986 Paul Coffey, Edmonton	2004 Scott Niedermayer, New Jersey
1969 Bobby Orr, Boston	1987 Ray Bourque, Boston	2006 Nicklas Lidstrom, Detroit
1970 Bobby Orr, Boston	1988 Ray Bourque, Boston	2007 Nicklas Lidstrom, Detroit
1971 Bobby Orr, Boston	1989 Chris Chelios, Montreal	

Art Ross Trophy (Leading Points Scorer)

Trophy first awarded in 1948. Prior years list NHL scoring leader.

1927 Bill Cook, N.Y. Rangers	1932 Harvey Jackson, Toronto	1937 Dave Schriner, N.Y. Americans
1928 Howie Morenz, Montreal	1933 Bill Cook, N.Y. Rangers	1938 Gordie Drillon, Toronto
1929 Ace Bailey, Toronto	1934 Charlie Conacher, Toronto	1939 Toe Blake, Montreal
1930 Cooney Weiland, Boston	1935 Charlie Conacher, Toronto	1940 Milt Schmidt, Boston
1931 Howie Morenz, Montreal	1936 Dave Schriner, N.Y. Americans	1941 Bill Cowley, Boston

1942 Bryan Hextall, N.Y. Rangers	1964 Stan Mikita, Chicago	1986 Wayne Gretzky, Edmonton
1943 Doug Bentley, Chicago	1965 Stan Mikita, Chicago	1987 Wayne Gretzky, Edmonton
1944 Herbie Cain, Boston	1966 Bobby Hull, Chicago	1988 Mario Lemieux, Pittsburgh
1945 Elmer Lach, Montreal	1967 Stan Mikita, Chicago	1989 Mario Lemieux, Pittsburgh
1946 Max Bentley, Chicago	1968 Stan Mikita, Chicago	1990 Wayne Gretzky, Los Angeles
1947 Max Bentley, Chicago	1969 Phil Esposito, Boston	1991 Wayne Gretzky, Los Angeles
1948 Elmer Lach, Montreal	1970 Bobby Orr, Boston	1992 Mario Lemieux, Pittsburgh
1949 Roy Conacher, Chicago	1971 Phil Esposito, Boston	1993 Mario Lemieux, Pittsburgh
1950 Ted Lindsay, Detroit	1972 Phil Esposito, Boston	1994 Wayne Gretzky, Los Angeles
1951 Gordie Howe, Detroit	1973 Phil Esposito, Boston	1995 Jaromir Jagr, Pittsburgh
1952 Gordie Howe, Detroit	1974 Phil Esposito, Boston	1996 Mario Lemieux, Pittsburgh
1953 Gordie Howe, Detroit	1975 Bobby Orr, Boston	1997 Mario Lemieux, Pittsburgh
1954 Gordie Howe, Detroit	1976 Guy Lafleur, Montreal	1998 Jaromir Jagr, Pittsburgh
1955 Bernie Geoffrion, Montreal	1977 Guy Lafleur, Montreal	1999 Jaromir Jagr, Pittsburgh
1956 Jean Beliveau, Montreal	1978 Guy Lafleur, Montreal	2000 Jaromir Jagr, Pittsburgh
1957 Gordie Howe, Detroit	1979 Bryan Trottier, N.Y. Islanders	2001 Jaromir Jagr, Pittsburgh
1958 Dickie Moore, Montreal	1980 Marcel Dionne, Los Angeles	2002 Jarome Iginla, Calgary
1959 Dickie Moore, Montreal	1981 Wayne Gretzky, Edmonton	2003 Peter Forsberg, Colorado
1960 Bobby Hull, Chicago	1982 Wayne Gretzky, Edmonton	2004 Martin St. Louis, Tampa Bay
1961 Bernie Geoffrion, Montreal	1983 Wayne Gretzky, Edmonton	2006 Joe Thornton, San Jose
1962 Bobby Hull, Chicago	1984 Wayne Gretzky, Edmonton	2007 Sidney Crosby, Pittsburgh
1963 Gordie Howe, Detroit	1985 Wayne Gretzky, Edmonton	

Vezina Trophy (Outstanding Goalie)*

1927 George Hainsworth, Montreal	1955 Terry Sawchuk, Detroit	1981 Sevigny, Larocque, Herron,
1928 George Hainsworth, Montreal	1956 Jacques Plante, Montreal	Montreal
1929 George Hainsworth, Montreal	1957 Jacques Plante, Montreal	1982 Bill Smith, N.Y. Islanders
1930 Tiny Thompson, Boston	1958 Jacques Plante, Montreal	1983 Pete Peeters, Boston
1931 Roy Worters, N.Y. Americans	1959 Jacques Plante, Montreal	1984 Tom Barrasso, Buffalo
1932 Charlie Gardiner, Chicago	1960 Jacques Plante, Montreal	1985 Pelle Lindbergh, Philadelphia
1933 Tiny Thompson, Boston	1961 Johnny Bower, Toronto	1986 John Vanbiesbrouck, N.Y. Rangers
1934 Charlie Gardiner, Chicago	1962 Jacques Plante, Montreal	1987 Ron Hextall, Philadelphia
1935 Lorne Chabot, Chicago	1963 Glenn Hall, Chicago	1988 Grant Fuhr, Edmonton
1936 Tiny Thompson, Boston	1964 Charlie Hodge, Montreal	1989 Patrick Roy, Montreal
1937 Normie Smith, Detroit	1965 Sawchuk, Bower, Toronto	1990 Patrick Roy, Montreal
1938 Tiny Thompson, Boston	1966 Worsley, Hodge, Montreal	1991 Ed Belfour, Chicago
1939 Frank Brimsek, Boston	1967 Hall, DeJordy, Chicago	1992 Patrick Roy, Montreal
1940 Dave Kerr, N.Y. Rangers	1968 Worsley, Vachon, Montreal	1993 Ed Belfour, Chicago
1941 Turk Broda, Toronto	1969 Hall, Plante, St. Louis	1994 Dominik Hasek, Buffalo
1942 Frank Brimsek, Boston	1970 Tony Esposito, Chicago	1995 Dominik Hasek, Buffalo
1943 Johnny Mowers, Detroit	1971 Giacomin, Villemure, N.Y. Rangers	1996 Jim Carey, Washington
1944 Bill Durnan, Montreal	1972 Esposito, Smith, Chicago	1997 Dominik Hasek, Buffalo
1945 Bill Durnan, Montreal	1973 Ken Dryden, Montreal	1998 Dominik Hasek, Buffalo
1946 Bill Durnan, Montreal	1974 Bernie Parent, Philadelphia;	1999 Dominik Hasek, Buffalo
1947 Bill Durnan, Montreal	Tony Esposito, Chicago	2000 Olaf Kolzig, Washington
1948 Turk Broda, Toronto	1975 Bernie Parent, Philadelphia	2001 Dominik Hasek, Buffalo
1949 Bill Durnan, Montreal	1976 Ken Dryden, Montreal	2002 Jose Theodore, Montreal
1950 Bill Durnan, Montreal	1977 Dryden, Larocque, Montreal	2003 Martin Brodeur, New Jersey
1951 Al Rollins, Toronto	1978 Dryden, Larocque, Montreal	2004 Martin Brodeur, New Jersey
1952 Terry Sawchuk, Detroit	1979 Dryden, Larocque, Montreal	2006 Miikka Kiprusoff, Calgary
1953 Terry Sawchuk, Detroit	1980 Sauve, Edwards, Buffalo	2007 Martin Brodeur, New Jersey
1954 Harry Lumley, Toronto		

*Before 1982, awarded to the goalie or goalies who played a minimum of 25 games for the team that allowed the fewest goals; since 1982, awarded to the outstanding goalie, as determined by a vote of NHL general managers.

NHL Home Ice[1]

Team	Name (built)	Capacity	Team	Name (built)	Capacity
Anaheim	Honda Center[2] (1993)	17,174	Nashville	Sommet Center[10] (1997)	17,113
Atlanta	Philips Arena (1999)	18,750	New Jersey	Continental Airlines Arena[11]	
Boston	TD Banknorth Garden[3] (1995)	17,565		(1981)	19,040
Buffalo	HSBC Arena[4] (1996)	18,690	N.Y. Islanders	Nassau Veterans Memorial Col.	
Calgary	Pengrowth Saddledome[5] (1983)	19,289		(1972)	16,234
Carolina	RBC Center[6] (1999)	18,176	N.Y. Rangers	Madison Square Garden (1968)	18,200
Chicago	United Center (1994)	20,500	Ottawa	Scotiabank Place[12] (1996)	19,153
Colorado	Pepsi Center (1999)	18,007	Philadelphia	Wachovia Center[13] (1996)	19,519
Columbus	Nationwide Arena (2000)	18,500	Phoenix	Jobing.com Arena[14] (2003)	17,653
Dallas	American Airlines Center (2001)	18,532	Pittsburgh	Mellon Arena[15] (1961)	17,132
Detroit	Joe Louis Arena (1979)	20,066	St. Louis	Scottrade Center[16] (1994)	21,000
Edmonton	Rexall Place[7] (1974)	16,839	San Jose	HP Pavilion[17] (1993)	17,483
Florida	BankAtlantic Center[8] (1998)	19,250	Tampa Bay	St. Pete Times Forum[18] (1996)	19,758
Los Angeles	Staples Center (1999)	18,118	Toronto	Air Canada Centre (1999)	18,800
Minnesota	Xcel Energy Arena (2000)	18,064	Vancouver	General Motors Place (1995)	18,630
Montreal	Le Centre Bell[9] (1996)	21,273	Washington	Verizon Center[19] (1997)	18,277

(1) At the end of the 2006-07 season. (2) The Arrowhead Pond of Anaheim, 1993-2006. (3) Fleet Center 1995-2005. (4) Marine Midland Arena, 1996-2000. (5) Olympic Saddledome, 1983-96; Canadian Airlines Saddledome, 1996-2000. (6) Entertainment & Sports Arena, 1999-2002. (7) Northlands Col., 1974-79; Edmonton Col., 1979-98; Skyreach Centre, 1998-2003. (8) National Car Rental Center, 1998-2002; Office Depot Center, 2002-05. (9) Le Centre Molson, 1996-2002. (10) Nashville Arena, 1997-99; Gaylord Entertainment Center, 1999-2007. (11) Brendan Byrne/Meadowlands Arena, 1981-96. (12) Corel Centre, 1996-2006. (13) CoreStates Center, 1996-98; First Union Center, 1998-2003. (14) Glendale Arena, 2003-06. (15) Civic Arena, 1961-99. (16) Kiel Center, 1994-2000; Savvis Center, 2000-06. (17) San Jose Arena, 1993-2001; Compaq Center, 2001-02. (18) Ice Palace, 1996-2002. (19) MCI Center, 1997-2006.

Hockey Hall of Fame, Toronto, Ontario
(2007 inductees have an asterisk*)

PLAYERS

Abel, Sid
Adams, Jack
Apps, Syl
Armstrong, George
Bailey, Ace
Bain, Dan
Baker, Hobey
Barber, Bill
Barry, Marty
Bathgate, Andy
Bauer, Bobby
Beliveau, Jean
Benedict, Clint
Bentley, Doug
Bentley, Max
Blake, Toe
Boivin, Leo
Boon, Dickie
Bossy, Mike
Bouchard, Butch
Boucher, Frank
Boucher, George
Bourque, Ray
Bower, Johnny
Bowie, Dubbie
Brimsek, Frank
Broadbent, Punch
Broda, Turk
Bucyk, John
Burch, Billy
Cameron, Harry
Cheevers, Gerry
Clancy, King
Clapper, Dit
Clarke, Bobby
Cleghorn, Sprague
Coffey, Paul
Colville, Neil
Conacher, Charlie
Conacher, Lionel
Conacher, Roy
Connell, Alex
Cook, Bill
Cook, Bun
Coulter, Art
Cournoyer, Yvan
Cowley, Bill
Crawford, Rusty
Darragh, Jack
Davidson, Scotty
Day, Hap
Delvecchio, Alex
Denneny, Cy
Dionne, Marcel
Drillon, Gordie
Drinkwater, Graham
Dryden, Ken
Duff, Terrance "Dick"
Dumart, Woody
Dunderdale, Tommy
Durnan, Bill
Dutton, Red
Dye, Babe
Esposito, Phil
Esposito, Tony
Farrel, Arthur
Federko, Bernie
Fetisov, Viacheslav
Flaman, Fernie
Foyston, Frank
*Francis, Ron
Fredrickson, Frank
Fuhr, Grant
Gadsby, Bill
Gainey, Bob
Gardiner, Chuck
Gardiner, Herb
Gardiner, Jimmy
Gartner, Mike
Geoffrion, Bernie
Gerard, Eddie
Giacomin, Eddie
Gilbert, Rod
Gillies, Clark
Gilmour, Billy
Goheen, Moose
Goodfellow, Ebbie
Goulet, Michel
Grant, Mike
Green, Shorty
Gretzky, Wayne
Griffis, Si
Hainsworth, George
Hall, Glenn
Hall, Joe
Harvey, Doug
Hawerchuk, Dale
Hay, George
Hern, Riley
Hextall, Bryan
Holmes, Hap
Hooper, Tom
Horner, Red
Horton, Tim
Howe, Gordie
Howe, Syd
Howell, Harry
Hull, Bobby
Hutton, Bouse
Hyland, Harry
Irvin, Dick
Jackson, Busher
Johnson, Ching
Johnson, Ernie
Johnson, Tom
Joliat, Aurel
Keats, Duke
Kelly, Red
Kennedy, Ted
Keon, Dave
Kharlamov, Valeri
Kurri, Jari
Lach, Elmer
Lafleur, Guy
LaFontaine, Pat
Lalonde, Newsy
Langway, Rod
Laperriere, Jacques
Lapointe, Guy
Laprade, Edgar
Laviolette, Jack
LeSueur, Percy
Lehman, Hughie
Lemaire, Jacques
Lemieux, Mario
Lewis, Herbie
Lindsay, Ted
Lumley, Harry
*MacInnis, Al
MacKay, Mickey
Mahovlich, Frank
Malone, Joe
Mantha, Sylvio
Marshall, Jack
Maxwell, Fred
McDonald, Lanny
McGee, Frank
McGimsie, Billy
McNamara, George
*Messier, Mark
Mikita, Stan
Moore, Dickie
Moran, Paddy
Morenz, Howie
Mosienko, Bill
Mullen, Joe
Murphy, Larry
Neely, Cam
Nighbor, Frank
Noble, Reg
O'Connor, Buddy
Oliver, Harry
Olmstead, Bert
Orr, Bobby
Parent, Bernie
Park, Brad
Patrick, Lester
Patrick, Lynn
Perreault, Gilbert
Phillips, Tom
Pilote, Pierre
Pitre, Didier
Plante, Jacques
Potvin, Denis
Pratt, Babe
Primeau, Joe
Pronovost, Marcel
Pulford, Bob
Pulford, Harvey
Quackenbush, Bill
Rankin, Frank
Ratelle, Jean
Rayner, Chuck
Reardon, Kenny
Richard, Henri
Richard, Maurice
Richardson, George
Roberts, Gordie
Robinson, Larry
Ross, Art
Roy, Patrick
Russel, Blair
Russell, Ernie
Ruttan, Jack
Salming, Borje
Savard, Denis
Savard, Serge
Sawchuk, Terry
Scanlan, Fred
Schmidt, Milt
Schriner, Sweeney
Seibert, Earl
Seibert, Oliver
Shore, Eddie
Shutt, Steve
Siebert, Babe
Simpson, Joe
Sittler, Darryl
Smith, Alf
Smith, Billy
Smith, Clint
Smith, Hooley
Smith, Tommy
Stanley, Allan
Stanley, Barney
Stastny, Peter
*Stevens, Ronald Scott
Stewart, Jack
Stewart, Nels
Stuart, Bruce
Stuart, Hod
Taylor, Cyclone
Thompson, Tiny
Tretiak, Vladislav
Trihey, Harry
Trottier, Bryan
Ullman, Norm
Vezina, Georges
Walker, Jack
Walsh, Marty
Watson, Harry (Moose)
Watson, Harry Percival
Weiland, Cooney
Westwick, Harry
Whitcroft, Fred
Wilson, Phat
Worsley, Gump
Worters, Roy
Juckes, Gordon
Kilpatrick, John
Kilrea, Brian
Knox, Seymour
Leader, Al
LeBel, Robert
Lockhart, Thomas
Loicq, Paul
Mariucci, John
Mathers, Frank
McLaughlin, Frederic
Milford, Jake
Molson, Sen. Hartland
Morrison, Ian "Scotty"
Murray, Pere Athol
Neilson, Roger
Nelson, Francis
Norris, Bruce
Norris, James
Norris, James Sr.
Northey, William
O'Brien, J. Ambrose
O'Neill, Brian Francis
Page, Frederick
Patrick, Craig
Patrick, Frank
Pickard, Allan

BUILDERS

Adams, Charles
Adams, Weston
Ahearn, Bunny
Ahearn, Frank
Allan, Sir Montagu
Allen, Keith
Arbour, Al
Ballard, Harold
Bauer, Father David
Bickell, J.P.
Bowman, Scotty
Brooks, Herbert
Brown, George
Brown, Walter
Buckland, Frank
Bush, Walter, Jr.
Butterfield, Jack
Calder, Frank
Campbell, Angus
Campbell, Clarence
Cattarinich, Joseph
Costello, Murray
Dandurand, Leo
Dilio, Frank
Dudley, George
Dunn, James
Fletcher, Cliff
Francis, Emile
Gibson, Jack
Gorman, Tommy
*Gregory, Jim
Griffiths, Frank
Hanley, Bill
Hay, Charles
Hendy, Jim
Hewitt, Foster
Hewitt, William
Hotchkiss, Harley
Hume, Fred
Ilitch, Mike
Imlach, Punch
Ivan, Tommy
Jennings, William
Johnson, Bob
Pilous, Rudy
Poile, Bud
Pollock, Sam
Raymond, Sen. Donat
Robertson, John Ross
Robinson, Claude
Ross, Phillip
Sabetzki, Gunther
Sather, Glen
Selke, Frank
Sinden, Harry
Smith, Frank
Smythe, Conn
Snider, Ed
Stanley, Lord (of Preston)
Sutherland, Capt. James T.
Tarasov, Anatoli
Torrey, Bill
Turner, Lloyd
Tutt, William
Voss, Carl
Waghorne, Fred
Wirtz, Arthur
Wirtz, Bill
Ziegler, John A., Jr.

REFEREES AND LINESMEN

Armstrong, Neil
Ashley, John
Chadwick, Bill
D'Amico, John
Elliott, Chaucer
Hayes, George
Hewiston, Bobby
Ion, Mickey
Pavelich, Matt
Rodden, Mike
Smeaton, Cooper
Storey, Red
Udvari, Frank
Van Hellemond, Andy

NCAA Hockey Champions

1948 Michigan	1960 Denver	1972 Boston Univ.	1984 Bowling Green	1996 Michigan
1949 Boston College	1961 Denver	1973 Wisconsin	1985 Rensselaer	1997 North Dakota
1950 Colorado College	1962 Michigan Tech	1974 Minnesota	1986 Michigan State	1998 Michigan
1951 Michigan	1963 North Dakota	1975 Michigan Tech	1987 North Dakota	1999 Maine
1952 Michigan	1964 Michigan	1976 Minnesota	1988 Lake Superior St.	2000 North Dakota
1953 Michigan	1965 Michigan Tech	1977 Wisconsin	1989 Harvard	2001 Boston College
1954 Rensselaer	1966 Michigan State	1978 Boston Univ.	1990 Wisconsin	2002 Minnesota
1955 Michigan	1967 Cornell	1979 Minnesota	1991 N. Michigan	2003 Minnesota
1956 Michigan	1968 Denver	1980 North Dakota	1992 Lake Superior St.	2004 Denver
1957 Colorado College	1969 Denver	1981 Wisconsin	1993 Maine	2005 Denver
1958 Denver	1970 Cornell	1982 North Dakota	1994 Lake Superior St.	2006 Wisconsin
1959 North Dakota	1971 Boston Univ.	1983 Wisconsin	1995 Boston Univ.	2007 Michigan State

SOCCER

Germany Defeats Brazil for 2007 Women's World Cup Title

Germany successfully defended its Women's World Cup title Sept. 30, 2007, defeating Brazil 2-0 at Hongkou Stadium in Shanghai, China. Germany set several records along the way, outscoring their opponents 21-0. With the help of stellar performances by goalkeeper Nadine Angerer, Germany became the first team in World Cup history to completely shut out its opponents in tournament play. Led by coach Silvia Neid, the team was also the first women's soccer team in history to successfully defend its title at the World Cup. Brazilian superstar midfielder Marta scored 7 goals during the tournament and, despite her team's defeat, won both the Golden Ball, which is given to the tournament's best player, and the Golden Shoe, which is given to its top scorer.

The No. 1-ranked U.S. team had suffered a disappointing end to its 51-game undefeated streak, as they lost 4-0 to Brazil in the semifinals Sept. 27, 2007, in Hangzhou, China. U.S. coach Greg Ryan made the widely-criticized decision to start the more experienced 36-year-old Briana Scurry in place of goalkeeper Hope Solo, and U.S. midfielder Leslie Osborne headed a goal in on her own team. The U.S. was able to come back to win the match against Norway, 4-1, for third place Sept. 30.

2007 First Round Standings

Group A	W	L	T	GF	GA	Pts	Group C	W	L	T	GF	GA	Pts
Germany	2	0	1	13	0	7	Norway	2	0	1	10	4	7
England	1	0	2	8	3	5	Australia	1	0	2	7	4	5
Japan	1	1	1	3	4	4	Canada	1	1	1	7	4	4
Argentina	0	3	0	1	18	0	Ghana	0	3	0	3	15	0

Group B	W	L	T	GF	GA	Pts	Group D	W	L	T	GF	GA	Pts
USA	2	0	1	5	2	7	Brazil	3	0	0	10	0	9
North Korea	1	1	1	5	4	4	China	2	1	0	5	6	6
Sweden	1	1	1	3	4	4	Denmark	1	2	0	4	3	3
Nigeria	0	2	1	1	4	1	New Zealand	0	3	0	0	9	0

First Round Women's World Cup Results

Sept. 10, 2007
Germany 11, Argentina 0 (A)

Sept. 11, 2007
Japan 2, England 2 (A)
U.S. 2, North Korea 2 (B)
Nigeria 1, Sweden 1 (B)

Sept. 12, 2007
Ghana 1, Australia 4 (C)
Norway 2, Canada 1 (C)
New Zealand 0, Brazil 5 (D)
China 3, Denmark 2 (D)

Sept. 14, 2007
Argentina 0, Japan 1 (A)
England 0, Germany 0 (A)
Sweden 0, U.S. 2 (B)
North Korea 2, Nigeria 0 (B)

Sept. 15, 2007
Canada 4, Ghana 0 (C)
Australia 1, Norway 1 (C)
Denmark 2, New Zealand 0 (D)
Brazil 4, China 0 (D)

Sept. 17, 2007
England 6, Argentina 1 (A)
Germany 2, Japan 0 (A)

Sept. 18, 2007
North Korea 1, Sweden 2 (B)
Nigeria 0, U.S. 1 (B)

Sept. 20, 2007
Australia 2, Canada 2 (C)
Norway 7, Ghana 2 (C)
Brazil 1, Denmark 0 (D)
China 2, New Zealand 0 (D)

Final Round Results

Sept. 22: Wuhan, China
Germany 3, North Korea 0

Sept. 23: Wuhan, China
Norway 1, China 0

Sept. 26: Tianjin, China
Germany 3, Norway 0

Sept. 22: Tianjin, China
U.S. 3, England 0

Sept. 27: Hangzhou, China
U.S. 0, Brazil 4

Sept. 30: Shanghai, China
Germany 2, Brazil 0

Sept. 23: Tianjin, China
Brazil 3, Australia 2

Third Place Final
Sept. 30: Shanghai, China
Norway 1, U.S. 4

Women's World Cup, 1991-2007

Year	Winner	Final Opponent	Score	Site	Third Place
1991	U.S.	Norway	2-1	China	Germany
1995	Norway	Germany	2-0	Sweden	U.S.
1999	U.S.	China	0-0*	Pasadena, CA	Brazil
2003	Germany	Sweden	2-1 (OT)	Carson, CA	U.S.
2007	Germany	Brazil	2-0	China	U.S.

* U.S. 5-4, penalty kicks

Italy Wins 2006 FIFA World Cup

Italy defeated France, 5-3 on penalty kicks July 9, after a 1-1 draw continued through 30 minutes of extra time, to win the final match of the 2006 World Cup in Berlin, Germany. The tournament set records for the total number of yellow cards (345) and red cards (28) issued by referees, including France midfielder Zinedine Zidane's red card, received for head-butting Italy's Marco Materazzi in the chest in the Final. Italy, coached by Marcello Lippi and captained by defender Fabio Cannavaro, won its fourth World Cup. Zidane nevertheless received the Golden Ball award as the tournament's best player. German striker Miroslav Klose, who scored 5 goals during the tournament—including the 80th-minute goal that tied Germany's quarterfinal match, enabling the home team to win in penalty kicks—was awarded the Golden Boot as the tournament's top scorer.

First Round Results

Group A	W	L	T	GF	GA	Pts
Germany	3	0	0	8	2	9
Ecuador	2	1	0	5	3	6
Poland	1	2	0	2	4	3
Costa Rica	0	3	0	3	9	0

Group B	W	L	T	GF	GA	Pts
England	2	0	1	5	2	7
Sweden	1	0	2	3	2	5
Paraguay	1	2	0	2	2	3
Trinidad and Tobago	0	2	1	0	4	1

Group C	W	L	T	GF	GA	Pts
Argentina	2	0	1	8	1	7
Netherlands	2	0	1	3	1	7
Côte d'Ivoire	1	2	0	5	6	3
Serbia and Montenegro	0	3	0	2	10	0

Group D	W	L	T	GF	GA	Pts
Portugal	3	0	0	5	1	9
Mexico	1	1	1	4	3	4
Angola	0	1	2	1	2	2
Iran	0	2	1	2	6	1

Group E	W	L	T	GF	GA	Pts
Italy	2	0	1	5	1	7
Ghana	2	1	0	4	3	6
Czech Republic	1	2	0	3	4	3
USA	0	2	1	2	6	1

Group F	W	L	T	GF	GA	Pts
Brazil	3	0	0	7	1	9
Australia	1	1	1	5	5	4
Croatia	0	1	2	2	3	2
Japan	0	2	1	2	7	1

Group F	W	L	T	GF	GA	Pts
Switzerland	2	0	1	4	0	7
France	1	0	2	3	1	5
Korea Republic	1	1	1	3	4	4
Togo	0	3	0	1	6	0

Group G	W	L	T	GF	GA	Pts
Spain	3	0	0	8	1	9
Ukraine	2	1	0	5	4	6
Tunisia	0	2	1	3	6	1
Saudi Arabia	0	2	1	2	7	1

Final Round Results

June 24: Munich
Germany 2, Sweden 0

June 24: Leipzig
Argentina 2, Mexico 1 (extra time)

June 30: Berlin
Germany 1, Argentina 1
(Germany won 4-2 in penalty kicks)

June 26: Kaiserslautern
Italy 1, Australia 0

June 26: Cologne
Ukraine 0, Switzerland 0
(Ukraine won 3-0 in penalty kicks)

June 30: Hamburg
Italy 3, Ukraine 0

July 4: Dortmund
Italy 2, Germany 0 (extra time)

June 25: Stuttgart
England 1, Ecuador 0

June 25: Nuremberg
Portugal 1, Netherlands 0

July 1: Gelsenkirchen
Portugal 0, England 0
(Portugal won 3-1 in penalty kicks)

June 27: Dortmund
Brazil 3, Ghana 0

June 27: Hanover
France 3, Spain 1

July 1: Frankfurt
France 1, Brazil 0

July 5: Munich
France 1, Portugal 0

July 9: Berlin
Italy 1, France 1
(Italy won 5-3 in penalty kicks)

Third Place Final
July 8: Stuttgart
Germany 3, Portugal 1

Men's World Cup, 1930-2006

Year	Winner	Final opponent	Score	Site	Year	Winner	Final opponent	Score	Site
1930	Uruguay	Argentina	4-2	Uruguay	1974	W. Germany	Netherlands	2-1	W. Germany
1934	Italy	Czechoslovakia	2-1*	Italy	1978	Argentina	Netherlands	3-1*	Argentina
1938	Italy	Hungary	4-2	France	1982	Italy	W. Germany	3-1	Spain
1950	Uruguay	Brazil	2-1	Brazil	1986	Argentina	W. Germany	3-2	Mexico
1954	W. Germany	Hungary	3-2	Switzerland	1990	W. Germany	Argentina	1-0	Italy
1958	Brazil	Sweden	5-2	Sweden	1994	Brazil	Italy	0-0¹	U.S.
1962	Brazil	Czechoslovakia	3-1	Chile	1998	France	Brazil	3-0	France
1966	England	W. Germany	4-2*	England	2002	Brazil	Germany	2-0	Japan/S. Korea
1970	Brazil	Italy	4-1	Mexico	2006	Italy	France	1-1²	Germany

Extra time. (1) Brazil won 3-2 on penalty kicks. (2) Italy won 5-3 on penalty kicks.

Major League Soccer

The Houston Dynamo won the Major League Soccer (MLS) championship on Nov. 12, 2006, with a victory over the New England Revolution at Pizza Hut Park in Frisco, TX. The match was long and grueling; neither team scored until the 113th minute, in the game's 2nd overtime period, when New England broke the stalemate. Houston forward Brian Ching, who was named the game's most valuable player, headed in a goal just over a minute later to tie. Ultimately, the game was decided in Houston's favor, 4-3, in five rounds of penalty kicks.

Major League Soccer had announced Nov. 11, 2006, a new policy nicknamed the "Beckham Rule" that allowed each team to exceed the salary cap for one specifically designated player. The rule was designed to attract players of a higher caliber, such as David Beckham, to the fledgling league. Beckham signed a 5-year contract with the Los Angeles Galaxy Jan. 11, 2007, for a record-breaking $250 mil.

Major League Soccer (MLS) Cup Champions, 1996-2006

Year	Winner	Final opponent	Score	Site	MVP
1996	D.C. United	Los Angeles Galaxy	3-2 (OT)	Foxboro, MA	Marco Etcheverry
1997	D.C. United	Colorado Rapids	2-1	Washington, DC	Jaime Moreno
1998	Chicago Fire	D.C. United	2-0	Pasadena, CA	Peter Nowak
1999	D.C. United	Los Angeles Galaxy	2-0	Foxboro, MA	Ben Olsen
2000	Kansas City Wizards	Chicago Fire	1-0	Washington, DC	Tony Meola
2001	San Jose Earthquakes	Los Angeles Galaxy	2-1 (OT)	Columbus, OH	Dwayne DeRosario
2002	Los Angeles Galaxy	New England Revolution	1-0 (OT)	Foxboro, MA	Carlos Ruiz
2003	San Jose Earthquakes	Chicago Fire	4-2	Carson, CA	Landon Donovan
2004	D.C. United	Kansas City Wizards	3-2	Carson, CA	Alecko Eskandarian
2005	Los Angeles Galaxy	New England Revolution	1-0 (OT)	Frisco, TX	Guillermo Ramirez
2006	Houston Dynamo	New England Revolution	1-1 (4-3)*	Frisco, TX	Brian Ching

*Match decided in penalty kicks (shootout score in parentheses).

NCAA Soccer Champions, 1982-2006

Year[1]	Men	Women	Year[1]	Men	Women
1982	Indiana	North Carolina	1995	Wisconsin	Notre Dame
1983	Indiana	North Carolina	1996	St. John's (NY)	North Carolina
1984	Clemson	North Carolina	1997	UCLA	North Carolina
1985	UCLA	George Mason	1998	Indiana	Florida
1986	Duke	North Carolina	1999	Indiana	North Carolina
1987	Clemson	North Carolina	2000	Connecticut	North Carolina
1988	Indiana	North Carolina	2001	North Carolina	Santa Clara
1989	Santa Clara (tie, 2 OT) Virginia	North Carolina	2002	UCLA	Portland
1990	UCLA	North Carolina	2003	Indiana	North Carolina
1991	Virginia	North Carolina	2004	Indiana	Notre Dame
1992	Virginia	North Carolina	2005	Maryland	Portland
1993	Virginia	North Carolina	2006	UC Santa Barbara	North Carolina
1994	Virginia	North Carolina			

(1) NCAA Championships began in 1959 for men, in 1982 for women.

UEFA Championship League Winners and Runners-Up, 1956-2007

Year	Winner	Runner Up	Score	Year	Winner	Runner Up	Score
1956	Real Madrid	Reims	4-3	1982	Villa	Bayern Munich	1-0
1957	Real Madrid	Fiorentina	2-0	1983	Hamburg	Juventus	1-0
1958	Real Madrid	AC Milan	3-2#	1984	Liverpool	Roma	1-1 (4-2)*
1959	Real Madrid	Reims	2-0	1985	Juventus	Liverpool	1-0
1960	Real Madrid	Eintracht	7-3	1986	Steaua	Barcelona	0-0 (2-0)*
1961	Benfica	Barcelona	3-2	1987	Porto	Bayern Munich	2-1
1962	Benfica	Real Madrid	5-3	1988	PSV	Benfica	0-0 (6-5)*
1963	AC Milan	Benfica	2-1	1989	AC Milan	Steaua	4-0
1964	Inter Milan	Real Madrid	3-1	1990	AC Milan	Benfica	1-0
1965	Inter Milan	Benfica	1-0	1991	Crvena zvezda	Marseille	0-0 (5-3)*
1966	Real Madrid	Partizan	2-1	1992	Barcelona	Sampdoria	1-0#
1967	Celtic	Inter Milan	2-1	1993	Marseille	AC Milan	1-0
1968	Man. United	Benfica	4-1#	1994	AC Milan	Barcelona	4-0
1969	AC Milan	Ajax	4-1	1995	Ajax	AC Milan	1-0
1970	Feyenoord	Celtic	2-1#	1996	Juventus	Ajax	1-1 (4-2)*
1971	Ajax	Panathinaikos	2-0	1997	Dortmund	Juventus	3-1
1972	Ajax	Inter Milan	2-0	1998	Real Madrid	Juventus	1-0
1973	Ajax	Juventus	1-0	1999	Man. United	Bayern Munich	2-1
1974	Bayern Munich	Atlético	5-1[1]	2000	Real Madrid	Valencia	3-0
1975	Bayern Munich	Leeds	2-0	2001	Bayern Munich	Valencia	1-1 (5-4)*
1976	Bayern Munich	St-Etienne	1-0	2002	Real Madrid	Leverkusen	2-1
1977	Liverpool	Mönchen-gladbach	3-1	2003	AC Milan	Juventus	0-0 (3-2)*
1978	Liverpool	Club Brugge	1-0	2004	Porto	Monaco	3-0
1979	Notts Forest	Malmö	1-0	2005	Liverpool	AC Milan	3-3 (3-2)*
1980	Notts Forest	Hamburg	1-0	2006	Barcelona	Arsenal	2-1
1981	Liverpool	Real Madrid	1-0	2007	AC Milan	Liverpool	2-1

*Match decided in penalty kicks (shootout score in parentheses). (#) Match decided in extra time. (1) Aggregate score. First game 1-1; 4-0.

European Championships, 1960-2004

The final rounds of the 2008 UEFA European Championships will be jointly hosted by Austria and Switzerland, and were scheduled to open June 7, 2008, in Basel, Switzerland, with the final match to be played at Ernst Happle Stadium in Vienna, Austria, on June 29, 2008.

Year	Winner	Final opponent	Score	Site
1960	USSR	Yugoslavia	2-1 (extra time)	France
1964	Spain	USSR	2-1	Spain
1968	Italy	Yugoslavia	2-0	Italy
1972	W. Germany	USSR	3-0	Belgium
1976	Czechoslovakia	W. Germany	2-2 (Czech. won 5-3 on pens.)	Yugoslavia
1980	W. Germany	Belgium	2-1	Italy
1984	France	Spain	2-0	France
1988	Netherlands	USSR	2-0	W. Germany
1992	Denmark	Germany	2-0	Sweden
1996	Germany	Czech Rep.	2-1 (extra time)	England
2000	France	Italy	2-1 (extra time)	Belgium/Neth.
2004	Greece	Portugal	1-0	Portugal

GOLF

Men's All-Time Major Professional Championship Leaders
(Through the 2007 season; *active PGA player in 2007; (a)=amateur.)

Player	Masters	U.S. Open	British Open	PGA	Total
Jack Nicklaus	1963, '65-66, '72, '75, '86	1962, '67, '72, '80	1966, '70, '78	1963, '71, '73, '75, '80	18
Tiger Woods*	1997, 2001-02, 2005	2000, 2002	2000, 2005-06	1999, 2000, 2006-07	13
Walter Hagen	—	1914, '19	1922, '24, '28-29	1921, '24-27	11
Ben Hogan	1951, '53	1948, '50-51, '53	1953	1946, '48	9
Gary Player	1961, '74, '78	1965	1959, '68, '74	1962, '72	9
Tom Watson*	1977, '81	1982	1975, '77, '80, '82-83	—	8
Bobby Jones (a)	—	1923, '26, '29-30	1926-27, '30	—	7
Arnold Palmer	1958, '60, '62, '64	1960	1961-62	—	7
Gene Sarazen	1935	1922, '32	1932	1922-23, '33	7
Sam Snead	1949, '52, '54	—	1946	1942, '49, '51	7
Harry Vardon	—	1900	1896, '98-99, 1903, '11, '14	—	7
Nick Faldo	1989-90, '96	—	1987, '90, '92	—	6
Lee Trevino	—	1968, '71	1971-72	1974, '84	6

Professional Golfers' Association Leading Money Winners, by Year

Year	Player	Earnings	Year	Player	Earnings	Year	Player	Earnings
1946	Ben Hogan	$42,556	1967	Jack Nicklaus	$188,988	1987	Curtis Strange	$925,941
1947	Jimmy Demaret	27,936	1968	Billy Casper	205,168	1988	Curtis Strange	1,147,644
1948	Ben Hogan	36,812	1969	Frank Beard	175,223	1989	Tom Kite	1,395,278
1949	Sam Snead	31,593	1970	Lee Trevino	157,037	1990	Greg Norman	1,165,477
1950	Sam Snead	35,758	1971	Jack Nicklaus	244,490	1991	Corey Pavin	979,430
1951	Lloyd Mangrum	26,088	1972	Jack Nicklaus	320,542	1992	Fred Couples	1,344,188
1952	Julius Boros	37,032	1973	Jack Nicklaus	308,362	1993	Nick Price	1,478,557
1953	Lew Worsham	34,002	1974	Johnny Miller	353,201	1994	Nick Price	1,499,927
1954	Bob Toski	65,819	1975	Jack Nicklaus	323,149	1995	Greg Norman	1,654,959
1955	Julius Boros	65,121	1976	Jack Nicklaus	266,438	1996	Tom Lehman	1,780,159
1956	Ted Kroll	72,835	1977	Tom Watson	310,653	1997	Tiger Woods	2,066,833
1957	Dick Mayer	65,835	1978	Tom Watson	362,429	1998	David Duval	2,591,031
1958	Arnold Palmer	42,407	1979	Tom Watson	462,636	1999	Tiger Woods	6,616,585
1959	Art Wall, Jr.	53,167	1980	Tom Watson	530,808	2000	Tiger Woods	9,188,321
1960	Arnold Palmer	75,262	1981	Tom Kite	375,699	2001	Tiger Woods	5,687,777
1961	Gary Player	64,540	1982	Craig Stadler	446,462	2002	Tiger Woods	6,912,625
1962	Arnold Palmer	81,448	1983	Hal Sutton	426,668	2003	Vijay Singh	7,573,907
1963	Arnold Palmer	128,230	1984	Tom Watson	476,260	2004	Vijay Singh	10,905,166
1964	Jack Nicklaus	113,284	1985	Curtis Strange	542,321	2005	Tiger Woods	10,628,024
1965	Jack Nicklaus	140,752	1986	Greg Norman	653,296	2006	Tiger Woods	11,141,827
1966	Billy Casper	121,944						

Masters Golf Tournament Winners

Year	Winner	Year	Winner	Year	Winner	Year	Winner	Year	Winner
1934	Horton Smith	1951	Ben Hogan	1966	Jack Nicklaus	1980	Seve Ballesteros	1994	Jose Maria Olazabal
1935	Gene Sarazen	1952	Sam Snead	1967	Gay Brewer, Jr.	1981	Tom Watson	1995	Ben Crenshaw
1936	Horton Smith	1953	Ben Hogan	1968	Bob Goalby	1982	Craig Stadler	1996	Nick Faldo
1937	Byron Nelson	1954	Sam Snead	1969	George Archer	1983	Seve Ballesteros	1997	Tiger Woods
1938	Henry Picard	1955	Cary Middlecoff	1970	Billy Casper	1984	Ben Crenshaw	1998	Mark O'Meara
1939	Ralph Guldahl	1956	Jack Burke	1971	Charles Coody	1985	Bernhard Langer	1999	Jose Maria Olazabal
1940	Jimmy Demaret	1957	Doug Ford	1972	Jack Nicklaus	1986	Jack Nicklaus	2000	Vijay Singh
1941	Craig Wood	1958	Arnold Palmer	1973	Tommy Aaron	1987	Larry Mize	2001	Tiger Woods
1942	Byron Nelson	1959	Art Wall Jr.	1974	Gary Player	1988	Sandy Lyle	2002	Tiger Woods
1943-45	not played	1960	Arnold Palmer	1975	Jack Nicklaus	1989	Nick Faldo	2003	Mike Weir
1946	Herman Keiser	1961	Gary Player	1976	Ray Floyd	1990	Nick Faldo	2004	Phil Mickelson
1947	Jimmy Demaret	1962	Arnold Palmer	1977	Tom Watson	1991	Ian Woosnam	2005	Tiger Woods
1948	Claude Harmon	1963	Jack Nicklaus	1978	Gary Player	1992	Fred Couples	2006	Phil Mickelson
1949	Sam Snead	1964	Arnold Palmer	1979	Fuzzy Zoeller	1993	Bernhard Langer	2007	Zach Johnson
1950	Jimmy Demaret	1965	Jack Nicklaus						

United States Open Winners
(First contested in 1895)

Year	Winner	Year	Winner	Year	Winner	Year	Winner	Year	Winner
1934	Olin Dutra	1952	Julius Boros	1966	Billy Casper	1980	Jack Nicklaus	1994	Ernie Els
1935	Sam Parks, Jr.	1953	Ben Hogan	1967	Jack Nicklaus	1981	David Graham	1995	Corey Pavin
1936	Tony Manero	1954	Ed Furgol	1968	Lee Trevino	1982	Tom Watson	1996	Steve Jones
1937	Ralph Guldahl	1955	Jack Fleck	1969	Orville Moody	1983	Larry Nelson	1997	Ernie Els
1938	Ralph Guldahl	1956	Cary Middlecoff	1970	Tony Jacklin	1984	Fuzzy Zoeller	1998	Lee Janzen
1939	Byron Nelson	1957	Dick Mayer	1971	Lee Trevino	1985	Andy North	1999	Payne Stewart
1940	Lawson Little	1958	Tommy Bolt	1972	Jack Nicklaus	1986	Ray Floyd	2000	Tiger Woods
1941	Craig Wood	1959	Billy Casper	1973	Johnny Miller	1987	Scott Simpson	2001	Retief Goosen
1943-45	not played	1960	Arnold Palmer	1974	Hale Irwin	1988	Curtis Strange	2002	Tiger Woods
1946	Lloyd Mangrum	1961	Gene Littler	1975	Lou Graham	1989	Curtis Strange	2003	Jim Furyk
1947	L. Worsham	1962	Jack Nicklaus	1976	Jerry Pate	1990	Hale Irwin	2004	Retief Goosen
1948	Ben Hogan	1963	Julius Boros	1977	Hubert Green	1991	Payne Stewart	2005	Michael Campbell
1949	Cary Middlecoff	1964	Ken Venturi	1978	Andy North	1992	Tom Kite	2006	Geoff Ogilvy
1950	Ben Hogan	1965	Gary Player	1979	Hale Irwin	1993	Lee Janzen	2007	Angel Cabrera
1951	Ben Hogan								

British Open Winners
(First contested in 1860)

Year	Winner	Year	Winner	Year	Winner	Year	Winner	Year	Winner
1934	Henry Cotton	1953	Ben Hogan	1967	Roberto de Vicenzo	1981	Bill Rogers	1995	John Daly
1935	Alf Perry	1954	Peter Thomson	1968	Gary Player	1982	Tom Watson	1996	Tom Lehman
1936	Alf Padgham	1955	Peter Thomson	1969	Tony Jacklin	1983	Tom Watson	1997	Justin Leonard
1937	T.H. Cotton	1956	Peter Thomson	1970	Jack Nicklaus	1984	Seve Ballesteros	1998	Mark O'Meara
1938	R.A. Whitcombe	1957	Bobby Locke	1971	Lee Trevino	1985	Sandy Lyle	1999	Paul Lawrie
1939	Richard Burton	1958	Peter Thomson	1972	Lee Trevino	1986	Greg Norman	2000	Tiger Woods
1943-45	not played	1959	Gary Player	1973	Tom Weiskopf	1987	Nick Faldo	2001	David Duval
1946	Sam Snead	1960	Kel Nagle	1974	Gary Player	1988	Seve Ballesteros	2002	Ernie Els
1947	Fred Daly	1961	Arnold Palmer	1975	Tom Watson	1989	Mark Calcavecchia	2003	Ben Curtis
1948	Henry Cotton	1962	Arnold Palmer	1976	Johnny Miller	1990	Nick Faldo	2004	Todd Hamilton
1949	Bobby Locke	1963	Bob Charles	1977	Tom Watson	1991	Ian Baker-Finch	2005	Tiger Woods
1950	Bobby Locke	1964	Tony Lema	1978	Jack Nicklaus	1992	Nick Faldo	2006	Tiger Woods
1951	Max Faulkner	1965	Peter Thomson	1979	Seve Ballesteros	1993	Greg Norman	2007	Padraig Harrington
1952	Bobby Locke	1966	Jack Nicklaus	1980	Tom Watson	1994	Nick Price		

PGA Championship Winners
(First contested in 1916)

Year	Winner	Year	Winner	Year	Winner	Year	Winner	Year	Winner
1934	Paul Runyan	1949	Sam Snead	1964	Bob Nichols	1979	David Graham	1994	Nick Price
1935	Johnny Revolta	1950	Chandler Harper	1965	Dave Marr	1980	Jack Nicklaus	1995	Steve Elkington
1936	Denny Shute	1951	Sam Snead	1966	Al Geiberger	1981	Larry Nelson	1996	Mark Brooks
1937	Denny Shute	1952	James Turnesa	1967	Don January	1982	Ray Floyd	1997	Davis Love III
1938	Paul Runyan	1953	Walter Burkemo	1968	Julius Boros	1983	Hal Sutton	1998	Vijay Singh
1939	Henry Picard	1954	Melvin Harbert	1969	Ray Floyd	1984	Lee Trevino	1999	Tiger Woods
1940	Byron Nelson	1955	Doug Ford	1970	Dave Stockton	1985	Hubert Green	2000	Tiger Woods
1941	Victor Ghezzi	1956	Jack Burke	1971	Jack Nicklaus	1986	Bob Tway	2001	David Toms
1942	Sam Snead	1957	Lionel Hebert	1972	Gary Player	1987	Larry Nelson	2002	Rich Beem
1943	not played	1958	Dow Finsterwald	1973	Jack Nicklaus	1988	Jeff Sluman	2003	Shaun Micheel
1944	Bob Hamilton	1959	Bob Rosburg	1974	Lee Trevino	1989	Payne Stewart	2004	Vijay Singh
1945	Byron Nelson	1960	Jay Hebert	1975	Jack Nicklaus	1990	Wayne Grady	2005	Phil Mickelson
1946	Ben Hogan	1961	Jerry Barber	1976	Dave Stockton	1991	John Daly	2006	Tiger Woods
1947	Jim Ferrier	1962	Gary Player	1977	Lanny Wadkins	1992	Nick Price	2007	Tiger Woods
1948	Ben Hogan	1963	Jack Nicklaus	1978	John Mahaffey	1993	Paul Azinger		

FedExCup, 2007

The inaugural FedExCup was clinched by Tiger Woods on Sept. 16, 2007, with his win at The Tour Championship at East Lake Golf Club in Atlanta, GA.

The FedExCup, a season-long competition with points awarded by finishing rank in each tournament, divides the PGA Tour into a regular season lasting 33 weeks, combined with a 4-week-long playoff. The FedExCup winner also claims a $10 million prize.

Women's All-Time Major Professional Championship Leaders
(Through the 2007 season; *active in 2007 LPGA season.)

Player	Nabisco[1]	LPGA	U.S. Women's Open	du Maurier/ British Open[2]	Titleholders[3]	Western Open[4]	Total
Patty Berg	—	—	1946	—	1937-39, '48, '53, '55, '57	1941, '43, '48, '51, '55, '57-58	15
Mickey Wright	—	1958, '60-61, '63	1958-59, '61, '64	—	1961-62	1962-63, '66	13
Louise Suggs	—	1957	1949, '52	—	1946, '54, '56, '59	1946-47, '49, '53	11
Babe Zaharias	—	—	1948, '50, '54	—	1947, '50, '52	1940, '44-45, '50	10
Annika Sorenstam*	2001-02, '05	2003-05	1995-96, 2006	2003	—	—	10
Betsy Rawls	—	1959, '69	1951, '53, '57, '60	—	—	1952, '59	8
Juli Inkster*	1984, '89	1999, 2000	1999, 2002	1984	—	—	7
Karrie Webb*	2000, 2006	2001	2000-01	1999, 2002	—	—	7
Pat Bradley	1986	1986	1981	1980, '85-86	—	—	6
Betsy King	1987, '90, '97	1992	1989-90	—	—	—	6
Patty Sheehan	1996	1983-84, '93	1992, '94	—	—	—	6
Kathy Whitworth	—	1967, '71, '75	—	—	1965-66	1967	6

(1) Nabisco Championship, formerly Nabisco Dinah Shore (1982-99), designated major in 1983. (2) In 2001, the British Open replaced the du Maurier Classic as the LPGA's 4th major. (3) Titleholders Championship was a major from 1930 to 1972. (4) Western Open was a major from 1937 to 1967.

Ladies Professional Golf Association Leading Money Winners

Year	Player	Earnings	Year	Player	Earnings	Year	Player	Earnings
1954	Patty Berg	$16,011	1972	Kathy Whitworth	$65,063	1990	Beth Daniel	$863,578
1955	Patty Berg	16,492	1973	Kathy Whitworth	82,854	1991	Pat Bradley	763,118
1956	Marlene Hagge	20,235	1974	JoAnne Carner	87,094	1992	Dottie Mochrie	693,335
1957	Patty Berg	16,272	1975	Sandra Palmer	94,805	1993	Betsy King	595,992
1958	Beverly Hanson	12,629	1976	Judy Rankin	150,734	1994	Laura Davies	687,201
1959	Betsy Rawls	26,774	1977	Judy Rankin	122,890	1995	Annika Sorenstam	666,533
1960	Louise Suggs	16,892	1978	Nancy Lopez	189,813	1996	Karrie Webb	1,002,000
1961	Mickey Wright	22,236	1979	Nancy Lopez	215,987	1997	Annika Sorenstam	1,236,789
1962	Mickey Wright	21,641	1980	Beth Daniel	231,000	1998	Annika Sorenstam	1,092,748
1963	Mickey Wright	31,269	1981	Beth Daniel	206,977	1999	Karrie Webb	1,591,959
1964	Mickey Wright	29,800	1982	JoAnne Carner	310,399	2000	Karrie Webb	1,876,853
1965	Kathy Whitworth	28,658	1983	JoAnne Carner	291,404	2001	Annika Sorenstam	2,105,868
1966	Kathy Whitworth	33,517	1984	Betsy King	266,771	2002	Annika Sorenstam	2,863,904
1967	Kathy Whitworth	32,937	1985	Nancy Lopez	416,472	2003	Annika Sorenstam	2,029,506
1968	Kathy Whitworth	48,379	1986	Pat Bradley	492,021	2004	Annika Sorenstam	2,544,707
1969	Carol Mann	49,152	1987	Ayako Okamoto	466,034	2005	Annika Sorenstam	2,588,240
1970	Kathy Whitworth	30,235	1988	Sherri Turner	347,255	2006	Lorena Ochoa	2,592,872
1971	Kathy Whitworth	41,181	1989	Betsy King	654,132			

Kraft Nabisco Championship Winners[1]

Year	Winner	Year	Winner	Year	Winner	Year	Winner	Year	Winner
1983	Amy Alcott	1989	Juli Inkster	1995	Nanci Bowen	2000	Karrie Webb	2004	Grace Park
1984	Juli Inkster	1990	Betsy King	1996	Patty Sheehan	2001	Annika Sorenstam	2005	Annika Sorenstam
1985	Alice Miller	1991	Amy Alcott	1997	Betsy King	2002	Annika Sorenstam	2006	Karrie Webb
1986	Pat Bradley	1992	Dottie Pepper	1998	Pat Hurst	2003	Patricia Meunier-Lebouc	2007	Morgan Pressel
1987	Betsy King	1993	Helen Alfredsson	1999	Dottie Pepper				
1988	Amy Alcott	1994	Donna Andrews						

1) Formerly the Colgate Dinah Shore (1972-81), the Nabisco Dinah Shore (1982-99), the Nabisco Championship (2000-01). Designated as a major championship in 1983.

LPGA Championship Winners

Year	Winner	Year	Winner	Year	Winner	Year	Winner	Year	Winner
1955	Beverly Hanson	1966	Gloria Ehret	1977	Chako Higuchi	1988	Sherri Turner	1998	Se Ri Pak
1956	Marlene Hagge	1967	Kathy Whitworth	1978	Nancy Lopez	1989	Nancy Lopez	1999	Juli Inkster
1957	Louise Suggs	1968	Sandra Post	1979	Donna Caponi	1990	Beth Daniel	2000	Juli Inkster
1958	Mickey Wright	1969	Betsy Rawls	1980	Sally Little	1991	Meg Mallon	2001	Karrie Webb
1959	Betsy Rawls	1970	Shirley Englehorn	1981	Donna Caponi	1992	Betsy King	2002	Se Ri Pak
1960	Mickey Wright	1971	Kathy Whitworth	1982	Jan Stephenson	1993	Patty Sheehan	2003	Annika Sorenstam
1961	Mickey Wright	1972	Kathy Ahern	1983	Patty Sheehan	1994	Laura Davies	2004	Annika Sorenstam
1962	Judy Kimball	1973	Mary Mills	1984	Patty Sheehan	1995	Kelly Robbins	2005	Annika Sorenstam
1963	Mickey Wright	1974	Sandra Haynie	1985	Nancy Lopez	1996	Laura Davies	2006	Se Ri Pak
1964	Mary Mills	1975	Kathy Whitworth	1986	Pat Bradley	1997	Chris Johnson	2007	Suzann Pettersen
1965	Sandra Haynie	1976	Betty Burfeindt	1987	Jane Geddes				

U.S. Women's Open Winners

Year	Winner	Year	Winner	Year	Winner	Year	Winner	Year	Winner
1946	Patty Berg	1960	Betsy Rawls	1971	JoAnne Carner	1982	Janet Alex	1995	Annika Sorenstam
1947	Betty Jameson	1961	Mickey Wright	1972	Susie Maxwell Berning	1983	Jan Stephenson	1996	Annika Sorenstam
1948	Babe Zaharias	1962	Murle Lindstrom			1984	Hollis Stacy	1997	Alison Nicholas
1949	Louise Suggs	1963	Mary Mills	1973	Susie Maxwell Berning	1985	Kathy Baker	1998	Se Ri Pak
1950	Babe Zaharias	1964	Mickey Wright			1986	Jane Geddes	1999	Juli Inkster
1951	Betsy Rawls	1965	Carol Mann	1974	Sandra Haynie	1987	Laura Davies	2000	Karrie Webb
1952	Louise Suggs	1966	Sandra Spuzich	1975	Sandra Palmer	1988	Liselotte Neumann	2001	Karrie Webb
1953	Betsy Rawls	1967	Catherine Lacoste (amateur)	1976	JoAnne Carner	1989	Betsy King	2002	Juli Inkster
1954	Babe Zaharias			1977	Hollis Stacy	1990	Betsy King	2003	Hilary Lunke
1955	Fay Crocker	1968	Susie Maxwell Berning	1978	Hollis Stacy	1991	Meg Mallon	2004	Meg Mallon
1956	Mrs. K. Cornelius			1979	Jerilyn Britz	1992	Patty Sheehan	2005	Birdie Kim
1957	Betsy Rawls	1969	Donna Caponi	1980	Amy Alcott	1993	Lauri Merten	2006	Annika Sorenstam
1958	Mickey Wright	1970	Donna Caponi	1981	Pat Bradley	1994	Patty Sheehan	2007	Cristie Kerr
1959	Mickey Wright								

Women's British Open Winners[1]

Year	Winner	Year	Winner	Year	Winner	Year	Winner	Year	Winner
1979	Amy Alcott	1985	Pat Bradley	1991	Nancy Scranton	1997	Colleen Walker	2003	Annika Sorenstam
1980	Pat Bradley	1986	Pat Bradley	1992	Sherri Steinhauer	1998	Brandie Burton	2004	Karen Stupples
1981	Jan Stephenson	1987	Jody Rosenthal	1993	Brandie Burton	1999	Karrie Webb	2005	Jeong Jang
1982	Sandra Haynie	1988	Sally Little	1994	Martha Nause	2000	Meg Mallon	2006	Sherri Steinhauer
1983	Hollis Stacy	1989	Tammie Green	1995	Jenny Lidback	2001	Se Ri Pak	2007	Lorena Ochoa
1984	Juli Inkster	1990	Cathy Johnston	1996	Laura Davies	2002	Karrie Webb		

1) First held as the Ladies' British Open in 1976; became the LPGA's 4th major championship in 2001, replacing the du Maurier Classic. Winners listed 1979-2000 are for the du Maurier Classic (Peter Jackson Classic, 1979-82).

International Golf

Ryder Cup

Began as a biennial team competition between pro golfers from the U.S. and Great Britain. The British team was expanded in 1973 to include players from Ireland and in 1979 from the rest of Europe. The Ryder Cup moved to even years after being postponed following the terrorist attacks of Sept. 11, 2001. Europe routed the Americans for its 3rd-straight victory at the 2006 match up, Sept. 22-24 at the K Club in Straffan, Ireland. The 2008 Ryder Cup was scheduled to be held Sept. 19-21 at the Valhalla Golf Club in Louisville, KY.

Year	Winner	Year	Winner	Year	Winner	Year	Winner
1927	U.S., 9½-2½	1953	U.S., 6½-5½	1971	U.S., 18½-13½	1989	Draw, 14-14
1929	Britain-Ireland, 7-5	1955	U.S., 8-4	1973	U.S., 19-13	1991	U.S., 14½-13½
1931	U.S., 9-3	1957	Britain-Ireland, 7½-4½	1975	U.S., 21-11	1993	U.S., 15-13
1933	Britain, 6½-5½	1959	U.S., 8½-3½	1977	U.S., 12½-7½	1995	Europe, 14½-13½
1935	U.S., 9-3	1961	U.S., 14½-9½	1979	U.S., 17-11	1997	Europe, 14½-13½
1937	U.S., 8-4	1963	U.S., 23-9	1981	U.S., 18½-9½	1999	U.S., 14½-13½
1939-45	Not played	1965	U.S., 19½-12½	1983	U.S., 14½-13½	2002	Europe, 15½-12½
1947	U.S., 11-1	1967	U.S., 23½-8½	1985	Europe, 16½-11½	2004	Europe, 18½-9½
1949	U.S., 7-5	1969	Draw, 16-16	1987	Europe, 15-13	2006	Europe, 18½-9½
1951	U.S., 9½-2½						

Solheim Cup

Began in 1990 as a biennial team competition between pro women golfers from Europe and the U.S. Competition moved to odd years in 2003 to alternate with the Ryder Cup, which had been postponed and moved to even years after the Sept. 2001 terrorist attacks. In 2007, the U.S. team defeated the European team at Halmstad Golfklubb in Sweden, after trailing the Europeans 8½ to 7½ leading into the final day of play. The next Solheim Cup was scheduled to be played at Rich Harvest Farms course in Sugar Grove, IL, in 2009.

Year	Winner	Year	Winner	Year	Winner	Year	Winner
1990	U.S., 11½-4½	1996	U.S., 17-11	2002	U.S., 15½-12½	2005	U.S., 15½-12½
1992	Europe, 11½-6½	1998	U.S., 16-12	2003	Europe, 17½-12½	2007	U.S., 16-12
1994	U.S., 13-7	2000	Europe, 14½-11½				

TENNIS
Australian Open Singles Champions, 1969–2007
(First contested 1905 for men, 1922 for women. Became an Open Championship in 1969.)
*2 tournaments held in 1977 (Jan. & Dec.). **In 1986 tournament moved to Jan. 1987; no championship in 1986.

Men's Singles / Women's Singles

Year	Champion (Men)	Final Opponent (Men)	Year	Champion (Women)	Final Opponent (Women)
1969	Rod Laver	Andres Gimeno	1969	Margaret Smith Court	Billie Jean King
1970	Arthur Ashe	Dick Crealy	1970	Margaret Smith Court	Kerry Melville Reid
1971	Ken Rosewall	Arthur Ashe	1971	Margaret Smith Court	Evonne Goolagong
1972	Ken Rosewall	Mal Anderson	1972	Virginia Wade	Evonne Goolagong
1973	John Newcombe	Onny Parun	1973	Margaret Smith Court	Evonne Goolagong
1974	Jimmy Connors	Phil Dent	1974	Evonne Goolagong	Chris Evert
1975	John Newcombe	Jimmy Connors	1975	Evonne Goolagong	Martina Navratilova
1976	Mark Edmondson	John Newcombe	1976	Evonne Goolagong	Renata Tomanova
1977*	Roscoe Tanner	Guillermo Vilas	1977*	Kerry Reid	Dianne Balestrat
	Vitas Gerulaitis	John Lloyd		Evonne Goolagong	Helen Gourlay
1978	Guillermo Vilas	John Marks	1978	Chris O'Neill	Betsy Nagelsen
1979	Guillermo Vilas	John Sadri	1979	Barbara Jordan	Sharon Walsh
1980	Brian Teacher	Kim Warwick	1980	Hana Mandlikova	Wendy Turnbull
1981	Johan Kriek	Steve Denton	1981	Martina Navratilova	Chris Evert Lloyd
1982	Johan Kriek	Steve Denton	1982	Chris Evert Lloyd	Martina Navratilova
1983	Mats Wilander	Ivan Lendl	1983	Martina Navratilova	Kathy Jordan
1984	Mats Wilander	Kevin Curren	1984	Chris Evert Lloyd	Helena Sukova
1985**	Stefan Edberg	Mats Wilander	1985**	Martina Navratilova	Chris Evert Lloyd
1987	Stefan Edberg	Pat Cash	1987	Hana Mandlikova	Martina Navratilova
1988	Mats Wilander	Pat Cash	1988	Steffi Graf	Chris Evert
1989	Ivan Lendl	Miloslav Mecir	1989	Steffi Graf	Helena Sukova
1990	Ivan Lendl	Stefan Edberg	1990	Steffi Graf	Mary Joe Fernandez
1991	Boris Becker	Ivan Lendl	1991	Monica Seles	Jana Novotna
1992	Jim Courier	Stefan Edberg	1992	Monica Seles	Mary Joe Fernandez
1993	Jim Courier	Stefan Edberg	1993	Monica Seles	Steffi Graf
1994	Pete Sampras	Todd Martin	1994	Steffi Graf	Arantxa Sánchez Vicario
1995	Andre Agassi	Pete Sampras	1995	Mary Pierce	Arantxa Sánchez Vicario
1996	Boris Becker	Michael Chang	1996	Monica Seles	Anke Huber
1997	Pete Sampras	Carlos Moya	1997	Martina Hingis	Mary Pierce.
1998	Petr Korda	Marcelo Rios	1998	Martina Hingis	Conchita Martínez
1999	Yevgeny Kafelnikov	Thomas Enqvist	1999	Martina Hingis	Amelie Mauresmo
2000	Andre Agassi	Yevgeny Kafelnikov	2000	Lindsay Davenport	Martina Hingis
2001	Andre Agassi	Arnaud Clement	2001	Jennifer Capriati	Martina Hingis
2002	Thomas Johansson	Marat Safin	2002	Jennifer Capriati	Martina Hingis
2003	Andre Agassi	Rainer Schuettler	2003	Serena Williams	Venus Williams
2004	Roger Federer	Marat Safin	2004	Justine Henin	Kim Clijsters
2005	Marat Safin	Lleyton Hewitt	2005	Serena Williams	Lindsay Davenport
2006	Roger Federer	Marcos Baghdatis	2006	Amelie Mauresmo	Justine Henin
2007	Roger Federer	Fernando Gonzalez	2007	Serena Williams	Maria Sharapova

French Open (Roland Garros) Singles Champions, 1968–2007
(First contested 1891 for men, 1897 for women. Became an Open Championship in 1968.)

Men's Singles / Women's Singles

Year	Champion (Men)	Final Opponent (Men)	Year	Champion (Women)	Final Opponent (Women)
1968	Ken Rosewall	Rod Laver	1968	Nancy Richey	Ann Jones
1969	Rod Laver	Ken Rosewall	1969	Margaret Smith Court	Ann Jones
1970	Jan Kodes	Zeljko Franulovic	1970	Margaret Smith Court	Helga Niessen
1971	Jan Kodes	Ilie Nastase	1971	Evonne Goolagong	Helen Gourlay
1972	Andres Gimeno	Patrick Proisy	1972	Billie Jean King	Evonne Goolagong
1973	Ilie Nastase	Nikki Pilic	1973	Margaret Smith Court	Chris Evert
1974	Bjorn Borg	Manuel Orantes	1974	Chris Evert	Olga Morozova
1975	Bjorn Borg	Guillermo Vilas	1975	Chris Evert	Martina Navratilova
1976	Adriano Panatta	Harold Solomon	1976	Sue Barker	Renata Tomanova
1977	Guillermo Vilas	Brian Gottfried	1977	Mima Jausovec	Florenza Mihai
1978	Bjorn Borg	Guillermo Vilas	1978	Virginia Ruzici	Mima Jausovec
1979	Bjorn Borg	Victor Pecci	1979	Chris Evert Lloyd	Wendy Turnbull
1980	Bjorn Borg	Vitas Gerulaitis	1980	Chris Evert Lloyd	Virginia Ruzici
1981	Bjorn Borg	Ivan Lendl	1981	Hana Mandlikova	Sylvia Hanika
1982	Mats Wilander	Guillermo Vilas	1982	Martina Navratilova	Andrea Jaeger
1983	Yannick Noah	Mats Wilander	1983	Chris Evert Lloyd	Mima Jausovec
1984	Ivan Lendl	John McEnroe	1984	Martina Navratilova	Chris Evert Lloyd
1985	Mats Wilander	Ivan Lendl	1985	Chris Evert Lloyd	Martina Navratilova
1986	Ivan Lendl	Mikael Pernfors	1986	Chris Evert Lloyd	Martina Navratilova
1987	Ivan Lendl	Mats Wilander	1987	Steffi Graf	Martina Navratilova
1988	Mats Wilander	Henri Leconte	1988	Steffi Graf	Natalia Zvereva
1989	Michael Chang	Stefan Edberg	1989	Arantxa Sánchez Vicario	Steffi Graf
1990	Andres Gomez	Andre Agassi	1990	Monica Seles	Steffi Graf
1991	Jim Courier	Andre Agassi	1991	Monica Seles	Arantxa Sánchez Vicario
1992	Jim Courier	Petr Korda	1992	Monica Seles	Steffi Graf
1993	Sergi Bruguera	Jim Courier	1993	Steffi Graf	Mary Joe Fernandez
1994	Sergi Bruguera	Alberto Berasategui	1994	Arantxa Sánchez Vicario	Mary Pierce
1995	Thomas Muster	Michael Chang	1995	Steffi Graf	Arantxa Sánchez Vicario
1996	Yevgeny Kafelnikov	Michael Stich	1996	Steffi Graf	Arantxa Sánchez Vicario
1997	Gustavo Kuerten	Sergei Bruguera	1997	Iva Majoli	Martina Hingis
1998	Carlos Moya	Alex Corretja	1998	Arantxa Sánchez Vicario	Monica Seles
1999	Andre Agassi	Andrei Medvedev	1999	Steffi Graf	Martina Hingis
2000	Gustavo Kuerten	Magnus Norman	2000	Mary Pierce	Conchita Martinez
2001	Gustavo Kuerten	Alex Corretja	2001	Jennifer Capriati	Kim Clijsters
2002	Albert Costa	Juan Carlos Ferrero	2002	Serena Williams	Venus Williams
2003	Juan Carlos Ferrero	Martin Verkerk	2003	Justine Henin	Kim Clijsters
2004	Gaston Gaudio	Guillermo Coria	2004	Anastasia Myskina	Elena Dementieva
2005	Rafael Nadal	Mariano Puerta	2005	Justine Henin	Mary Pierce
2006	Rafael Nadal	Roger Federer	2006	Justine Henin	Svetlana Kuznetsova
2007	Rafael Nadal	Roger Federer	2007	Justine Henin	Ana Ivanovic

U.S. Open Champions, 1925-2007

(Became an Open Championship in 1970.)

Men's Singles
(First contested 1881)

Year	Champion	Final Opponent
1925	Bill Tilden	William Johnston
1926	Rene Lacoste	Jean Borotra
1927	Rene Lacoste	Bill Tilden
1928	Henri Cochet	Francis Hunter
1929	Bill Tilden	Francis Hunter
1930	John Doeg	Francis Shields
1931	H. Ellsworth Vines	George Lott
1932	H. Ellsworth Vines	Henri Cochet
1933	Fred Perry	John Crawford
1934	Fred Perry	Wilmer Allison
1935	Wilmer Allison	Sidney Wood
1936	Fred Perry	Don Budge
1937	Don Budge	Baron G. von Cramm
1938	Don Budge	C. Gene Mako
1939	Robert Riggs	S. Welby Van Horn
1940	Don McNeill	Robert Riggs
1941	Robert Riggs	F. L. Kovacs
1942	F. R. Schroeder Jr.	Frank Parker
1943	Joseph Hunt	Jack Kramer
1944	Frank Parker	William Talbert
1945	Frank Parker	William Talbert
1946	Jack Kramer	Thomas Brown Jr.
1947	Jack Kramer	Frank Parker
1948	Pancho Gonzales	Eric Sturgess
1949	Pancho Gonzales	F. R. Schroeder Jr.
1950	Arthur Larsen	Herbert Flam
1951	Frank Sedgman	E. Victor Seixas Jr.
1952	Frank Sedgman	Gardnar Mulloy
1953	Tony Trabert	E. Victor Seixas Jr.
1954	E. Victor Seixas Jr.	Rex Hartwig
1955	Tony Trabert	Ken Rosewall
1956	Ken Rosewall	Lewis Hoad
1957	Malcolm Anderson	Ashley Cooper
1958	Ashley Cooper	Malcolm Anderson
1959	Neale A. Fraser	Alejandro Olmedo
1960	Neale A. Fraser	Rod Laver
1961	Roy Emerson	Rod Laver
1962	Rod Laver	Roy Emerson
1963	Rafael Osuna	F. A. Froehling 3rd
1964	Roy Emerson	Fred Stolle
1965	Manuel Santana	Cliff Drysdale
1966	Fred Stolle	John Newcombe
1967	John Newcombe	Clark Graebner
1968	Arthur Ashe	Tom Okker
1969	Rod Laver	Tony Roche
1970	Ken Rosewall	Tony Roche
1971	Stan Smith	Jan Kodes
1972	Ilie Nastase	Arthur Ashe
1973	John Newcombe	Jan Kodes
1974	Jimmy Connors	Ken Rosewall
1975	Manuel Orantes	Jimmy Connors
1976	Jimmy Connors	Bjorn Borg
1977	Guillermo Vilas	Jimmy Connors
1978	Jimmy Connors	Bjorn Borg
1979	John McEnroe	Vitas Gerulaitis
1980	John McEnroe	Bjorn Borg
1981	John McEnroe	Bjorn Borg
1982	Jimmy Connors	Ivan Lendl
1983	Jimmy Connors	Ivan Lendl
1984	John McEnroe	Ivan Lendl
1985	Ivan Lendl	John McEnroe
1986	Ivan Lendl	Miloslav Mecir
1987	Ivan Lendl	Mats Wilander
1988	Mats Wilander	Ivan Lendl
1989	Boris Becker	Ivan Lendl
1990	Pete Sampras	Andre Agassi
1991	Stefan Edberg	Jim Courier
1992	Stefan Edberg	Pete Sampras
1993	Pete Sampras	Cedric Pioline
1994	Andre Agassi	Michael Stich
1995	Pete Sampras	Andre Agassi
1996	Pete Sampras	Michael Chang
1997	Patrick Rafter	Greg Rusedski
1998	Patrick Rafter	Mark Philippoussis
1999	Andre Agassi	Todd Martin
2000	Marat Safin	Pete Sampras
2001	Lleyton Hewitt	Pete Sampras
2002	Pete Sampras	Andre Agassi
2003	Andy Roddick	Juan Carlos Ferrero
2004	Roger Federer	Lleyton Hewitt
2005	Roger Federer	Andre Agassi
2006	Roger Federer	Andy Roddick
2007	Roger Federer	Novak Djokovic

Women's Singles
(First contested 1887)

Year	Champion	Final Opponent
1925	Helen Willis	Kathleen McKane
1926	Molla B. Mallory	Elizabeth Ryan
1927	Helen Wills	Betty Nuthall
1928	Helen Wills	Helen Jacobs
1929	Helen Wills	M. Watson
1930	Betty Nuthall	L. A. Harper
1931	Helen Wills Moody	E. B. Whittingstall
1932	Helen Jacobs	Carolin A. Babcock
1933	Helen Jacobs	Helen Wills Moody
1934	Helen Jacobs	Sarah H. Palfrey
1935	Helen Jacobs	Sarah Palfrey Fabyan
1936	Alice Marble	Helen Jacobs
1937	Anita Lizana	Jadwiga Jedrzejowska
1938	Alice Marble	Nancye Wynne
1939	Alice Marble	Helen Jacobs
1940	Alice Marble	Helen Jacobs
1941	Sarah Palfrey Cooke	Pauline Betz
1942	Pauline Betz	Louise Brough
1943	Pauline Betz	Louise Brough
1944	Pauline Betz	Margaret Osborne
1945	Sarah Palfrey Cooke	Pauline Betz
1946	Pauline Betz	Doris Hart
1947	Louise Brough	Margaret Osborne
1948	Margaret Osborne duPont	Louise Brough
1949	Margaret Osborne duPont	Doris Hart
1950	Margaret Osborne duPont	Doris Hart
1951	Maureen Connolly	Shirley Fry
1952	Maureen Connolly	Doris Hart
1953	Maureen Connolly	Doris Hart
1954	Doris Hart	Louise Brough
1955	Doris Hart	Patricia Ward
1956	Shirley Fry	Althea Gibson
1957	Althea Gibson	Louise Brough
1958	Althea Gibson	Darlene Hard
1959	Maria Bueno	Christine Truman
1960	Darlene Hard	Maria Bueno
1961	Darlene Hard	Ann Haydon
1962	Margaret Smith	Darlene Hard
1963	Maria Bueno	Margaret Smith
1964	Maria Bueno	Carole Graebner
1965	Margaret Smith	Billie Jean Moffitt
1966	Maria Bueno	Nancy Richey
1967	Billie Jean King	Ann Haydon Jones
1968	Virginia Wade	Billie Jean King
1969	Margaret Smith Court	Nancy Richey
1970	Margaret Smith Court	Rosemary Casals
1971	Billie Jean King	Rosemary Casals
1972	Billie Jean King	Kerry Melville
1973	Margaret Smith Court	Evonne Goolagong
1974	Billie Jean King	Evonne Goolagong
1975	Chris Evert	Evonne Goolagong
1976	Chris Evert	Evonne Goolagong
1977	Chris Evert	Wendy Turnbull
1978	Chris Evert	Pam Shriver
1979	Tracy Austin	Chris Evert Lloyd
1980	Chris Evert Lloyd	Hana Mandlikova
1981	Tracy Austin	Martina Navratilova
1982	Chris Evert Lloyd	Hana Mandlikova
1983	Martina Navratilova	Chris Evert Lloyd
1984	Martina Navratilova	Chris Evert Lloyd
1985	Hana Mandlikova	Martina Navratilova
1986	Martina Navratilova	Helena Sukova
1987	Martina Navratilova	Steffi Graf
1988	Steffi Graf	Gabriela Sabatini
1989	Steffi Graf	Martina Navratilova
1990	Gabriela Sabatini	Steffi Graf
1991	Monica Seles	Martina Navratilova
1992	Monica Seles	Arantxa Sanchez Vicario
1993	Steffi Graf	Helena Sukova
1994	Arantxa Sanchez Vicario	Steffi Graf
1995	Steffi Graf	Monica Seles
1996	Steffi Graf	Monica Seles
1997	Martina Hingis	Venus Williams
1998	Lindsay Davenport	Martina Hingis
1999	Serena Williams	Martina Hingis
2000	Venus Williams	Lindsay Davenport
2001	Venus Williams	Serena Williams
2002	Serena Williams	Venus Williams
2003	Justine Henin	Kim Clijsters
2004	Svetlana Kuznetsova	Elena Dementieva
2005	Kim Clijsters	Mary Pierce
2006	Maria Sharapova	Justine Henin
2007	Justine Henin	Svetlana Kuznetsova

All-England Champions, Wimbledon, 1925-2007

(First contested 1877 for men, 1884 for women. Became an Open Championship in 1968. Not held 1940-45.)

	Men's Singles			Women's Singles	
Year	Champion	Final Opponent	Year	Champion	Final Opponent
1925	Rene Lacoste	Jean Borotra	1925	Suzanne Lenglen	Joan Fry
1926	Jean Borotra	Howard Kinsey	1926	Kathleen McKane Godfree	Lili de Alvarez
1927	Henri Cochet	Jean Borotra	1927	Helen Wills	Lili de Alvarez
1928	Rene Lacoste	Henri Cochet	1928	Helen Wills	Lili de Alvarez
1929	Henri Cochet	Jean Borotra	1929	Helen Wills	Helen Jacobs
1930	Bill Tilden	Wilmer Allison	1930	Helen Wills Moody	Elizabeth Ryan
1931	Sidney B. Wood	Francis X. Shields	1931	Cilly Aussem	Hilde Kranwinkel
1932	Ellsworth Vines	Henry Austin	1932	Helen Wills Moody	Helen Jacobs
1933	Jack Crawford	Ellsworth Vines	1933	Helen Wills Moody	Dorothy Round
1934	Fred Perry	Jack Crawford	1934	Dorothy Round	Helen Jacobs
1935	Fred Perry	Gottfried von Cramm	1935	Helen Wills Moody	Helen Jacobs
1936	Fred Perry	Gottfried von Cramm	1936	Helen Jacobs	Hilde Kranwinkel Sperling
1937	Donald Budge	Gottfried von Cramm	1937	Dorothy Round	Jadwiga Jedrzejowska
1938	Donald Budge	Henry Austin	1938	Helen Wills Moody	Helen Jacobs
1939	Bobby Riggs	Elwood Cooke	1939	Alice Marble	Kay Stammers
1946	Yvon Petra	Geoff E. Brown	1946	Pauline Betz	Louise Brough
1947	Jack Kramer	Tom P. Brown	1947	Margaret Osborne	Doris Hart
1948	Bob Falkenburg	John Bromwich	1948	Louise Brough	Doris Hart
1949	Ted Schroeder	Jaroslav Drobny	1949	Louise Brough	Margaret Osborne duPont
1950	Budge Patty	Frank Sedgman	1950	Louise Brough	Margaret Osborne duPont
1951	Dick Savitt	Ken McGregor	1951	Doris Hart	Shirley Fry
1952	Frank Sedgman	Jaroslav Drobny	1952	Maureen Connolly	Louise Brough
1953	Vic Seixas	Kurt Nielsen	1953	Maureen Connolly	Doris Hart
1954	Jaroslav Drobny	Ken Rosewall	1954	Maureen Connolly	Louise Brough
1955	Tony Trabert	Kurt Nielsen	1955	Louise Brough	Beverly Fleitz
1956	Lew Hoad	Ken Rosewall	1956	Shirley Fry	Angela Buxton
1957	Lew Hoad	Ashley Cooper	1957	Althea Gibson	Darlene Hard
1958	Ashley Cooper	Neale Fraser	1958	Althea Gibson	Angela Mortimer
1959	Alex Olmedo	Rod Laver	1959	Maria Bueno	Darlene Hard
1960	Neale Fraser	Rod Laver	1960	Maria Bueno	Sandra Reynolds
1961	Rod Laver	Chuck McKinley	1961	Angela Mortimer	Christine Truman
1962	Rod Laver	Martin Mulligan	1962	Karen Hantze-Susman	Vera Sukova
1963	Chuck McKinley	Fred Stolle	1963	Margaret Smith	Billie Jean Moffitt
1964	Roy Emerson	Fred Stolle	1964	Maria Bueno	Margaret Smith
1965	Roy Emerson	Fred Stolle	1965	Margaret Smith	Maria Bueno
1966	Manuel Santana	Dennis Ralston	1966	Billie Jean King	Maria Bueno
1967	John Newcombe	Wilhelm Bungert	1967	Billie Jean King	Ann Haydon Jones
1968	Rod Laver	Tony Roche	1968	Billie Jean King	Judy Tegart
1969	Rod Laver	John Newcombe	1969	Ann Haydon-Jones	Billie Jean King
1970	John Newcombe	Ken Rosewall	1970	Margaret Smith Court	Billie Jean King
1971	John Newcombe	Stan Smith	1971	Evonne Goolagong	Margaret Smith Court
1972	Stan Smith	Ilie Nastase	1972	Billie Jean King	Evonne Goolagong
1973	Jan Kodes	Alex Metreveli	1973	Billie Jean King	Chris Evert
1974	Jimmy Connors	Ken Rosewall	1974	Chris Evert	Olga Morozova
1975	Arthur Ashe	Jimmy Connors	1975	Billie Jean King	Evonne Goolagong Cawley
1976	Bjorn Borg	Ilie Nastase	1976	Chris Evert	Evonne Goolagong Cawley
1977	Bjorn Borg	Jimmy Connors	1977	Virginia Wade	Betty Stove
1978	Bjorn Borg	Jimmy Connors	1978	Martina Navratilova	Chris Evert
1979	Bjorn Borg	Roscoe Tanner	1979	Martina Navratilova	Chris Evert Lloyd
1980	Bjorn Borg	John McEnroe	1980	Evonne Goolagong	Chris Evert Lloyd
1981	John McEnroe	Bjorn Borg	1981	Chris Evert Lloyd	Hana Mandlikova
1982	Jimmy Connors	John McEnroe	1982	Martina Navratilova	Chris Evert Lloyd
1983	John McEnroe	Chris Lewis	1983	Martina Navratilova	Andrea Jaeger
1984	John McEnroe	Jimmy Connors	1984	Martina Navratilova	Chris Evert Lloyd
1985	Boris Becker	Kevin Curren	1985	Martina Navratilova	Chris Evert Lloyd
1986	Boris Becker	Ivan Lendl	1986	Martina Navratilova	Hana Mandlikova
1987	Pat Cash	Ivan Lendl	1987	Martina Navratilova	Steffi Graf
1988	Stefan Edberg	Boris Becker	1988	Steffi Graf	Martina Navratilova
1989	Boris Becker	Stefan Edberg	1989	Steffi Graf	Martina Navratilova
1990	Stefan Edberg	Boris Becker	1990	Martina Navratilova	Zina Garrison
1991	Michael Stich	Boris Becker	1991	Steffi Graf	Gabriela Sabatini
1992	Andre Agassi	Goran Ivanisevic	1992	Steffi Graf	Monica Seles
1993	Pete Sampras	Jim Courier	1993	Steffi Graf	Jana Novotna
1994	Pete Sampras	Goran Ivanisevic	1994	Conchita Martinez	Martina Navratilova
1995	Pete Sampras	Boris Becker	1995	Steffi Graf	Arantxa Sánchez Vicario
1996	Richard Krajicek	MaliVai Washington	1996	Steffi Graf	Arantxa Sánchez Vicario
1997	Pete Sampras	Cedric Pioline	1997	Martina Hingis	Jana Novotna
1998	Pete Sampras	Goran Ivanisevic	1998	Jana Novotna	Nathalie Tauziat
1999	Pete Sampras	Andre Agassi	1999	Lindsay Davenport	Steffi Graf
2000	Pete Sampras	Patrick Rafter	2000	Venus Williams	Lindsay Davenport
2001	Goran Ivanisevic	Patrick Rafter	2001	Venus Williams	Justine Henin
2002	Lleyton Hewitt	David Nalbandian	2002	Serena Williams	Venus Williams
2003	Roger Federer	Mark Philippoussis	2003	Serena Williams	Venus Williams
2004	Roger Federer	Andy Roddick	2004	Maria Sharapova	Serena Williams
2005	Roger Federer	Andy Roddick	2005	Venus Williams	Lindsay Davenport
2006	Roger Federer	Rafael Nadal	2006	Amelie Mauresmo	Justine Henin
2007	Roger Federer	Rafael Nadal	2007	Venus Williams	Marion Bartoli

Davis Cup, 1900-2006

Year	Result	Year	Result	Year	Result
1900	U.S. 3, British Isles 0	1936	Great Britain 3, Australia 2	1974	South Africa (default by India)
1901	Not held	1937	U.S. 4, Great Britain 1	1975	Sweden 3, Czechoslovakia 2
1902	U.S. 3, British Isles 2	1938	U.S. 3, Australia 2	1976	Italy 4, Chile 1
1903	British Isles 4, U.S. 1	1939	Australia 3, U.S. 2	1977	Australia 3, Italy 1
1904	British Isles 5, Belgium 0	1940-45	Not held	1978	U.S. 4, Great Britain 1
1905	British Isles 5, U.S. 0	1946	U.S. 5, Australia 0	1979	U.S. 5, Italy 0
1906	British Isles 5, U.S. 0	1947	U.S. 4, Australia 1	1980	Czechoslovakia 4, Italy 1
1907	Australia 3, British Isles 2	1948	U.S. 5, Australia 0	1981	U.S. 3, Argentina 1
1908	Australasia 3, U.S. 2	1949	U.S. 4, Australia 1	1982	U.S. 4, France, 1
1909	Australasia 5, U.S. 0	1950	Australia 4, U.S. 1	1983	Australia 3, Sweden 2
1910	Not held	1951	Australia 3, U.S. 2	1984	Sweden 4, U.S. 1
1911	Australasia 5, U.S. 0	1952	Australia 4, U.S. 1	1985	Sweden 3, W. Germany 2
1912	British Isles 3, Australasia 2	1953	Australia 3, U.S. 2	1986	Australia 3, Sweden 2
1913	U.S. 3, British Isles 2	1954	U.S. 3, Australia 2	1987	Sweden 5, India 0
1914	Australasia 3, U.S. 2	1955	Australia 5, U.S. 0	1988	W. Germany 4, Sweden 1
1915-18	Not held	1956	Australia 5, U.S. 0	1989	W. Germany 3, Sweden 2
1919	Australasia 4, British Isles 1	1957	Australia 3, U.S. 2	1990	U.S. 3, Australia 2
1920	U.S. 5, Australasia 0	1958	U.S. 3, Australia 2	1991	France 3, U.S. 1
1921	U.S. 5, Japan 0	1959	Australia 3, U.S. 2	1992	U.S. 3, Switzerland 1
1922	U.S. 4, Australasia 1	1960	Australia 4, Italy 1	1993	Germany 4, Australia 1
1923	U.S. 4, Australasia 1	1961	Australia 5, Italy 0	1994	Sweden 4, Russia 1
1924	U.S. 5, Australasia 0	1962	Australia 5, Mexico 0	1995	U.S. 3, Russia 2
1925	U.S. 5, France 0	1963	U.S. 3, Australia 2	1996	France 3, Sweden 2
1926	U.S. 4, France 1	1964	Australia 3, U.S. 2	1997	Sweden 5, U.S. 0
1927	France 3, U.S. 2	1965	Australia 4, Spain 1	1998	Sweden 4, Italy 1
1928	France 4, U.S. 1	1966	Australia 4, India 1	1999	Australia 3, France 2
1929	France 3, U.S. 2	1967	Australia 4, Spain 1	2000	Spain 3, Australia 1
1930	France 4, U.S. 1	1968	U.S. 4, Australia	2001	France 3, Australia 2
1931	France 3, Great Britain 2	1969	U.S. 5, Romania 0	2002	Russia 3, France 2
1932	France 3, U.S. 2	1970	U.S. 5, W. Germany 0	2003	Australia 3, Spain 1
1933	Great Britain 3, France 2	1971	U.S. 3, Romania 2	2004	Spain 3, U.S. 2
1934	Great Britain 4, U.S. 1	1972*	U.S. 3, Romania 2	2005	Croatia 3, Slovakia 2
1935	Great Britain 5, U.S. 0	1973	Australia 5, U.S. 0	2006	Russia 3, Argentina 2

The challenge round format, which guaranteed the previous year's winner a spot in the finals at home, was eliminated in 1972.

All-Time Grand Slam Singles Titles Leaders

Men	Australian Open	French Open[2]	Wimbledon	U.S. Open	Total
Pete Sampras	1994, '97	—	1993-95, 1997-2000	1990, '93, '95-96, 2002	14
Roger Federer[1]	2004, 2006-07	—	2003-07	2004-07	12
Roy Emerson	1961, '63-67	1963, '67	1964-65	1961, '64	12
Bjorn Borg	—	1974-75, 1978-81	1976-80	—	11
Rod Laver	1960, '62, '69	1962, '69	1961-62, '68-69	1962, '69	11
Bill Tilden	—	—	1920-21, '30	1920-25, '29	10
Andre Agassi	1995, 2000, '01, '03	1999	1992	1994, '99	8
Jimmy Connors	1974	—	1974, '82	1974, '76, '78, '82-83	8
Ivan Lendl	1989-90	1984, '86-87	—	1985-87	8
Fred Perry	1934	1935	1934-36	1933-34, '36	8
Ken Rosewall	1953, '55, '71-72	1953, '68	—	1956, '70	8
Women					
Margaret Smith Court	1960-66, '69-71, '73	1962, '64, '69-70, '73	1963, '65, '70	1962, '65, '69-70, '73	24
Steffi Graf	1988-90, '94	1987-88, '93, '95-96, '99	1988-89, '91-93, '95-96	1988-89, '93, '95-96	22
Helen Wills Moody	—	1928-30, '32	1927-30, '32-33, '35, '38	1923-25, '27-29, '31	19
Chris Evert Lloyd	1982, '84	1974-75, '79-80, '83, '85-86	1974, '76, '81	1975-78, '80, '82	18
Martina Navratilova	1981, '83, '85	1982, '84	1978-79, '82-87, '90	1983-84, '86-87	18
Billie Jean King	1968	1972	1966-68, '72-73, '75	1967, '71-72, '74	12
Suzanne Lenglen	—	1920-23, '25-26	1919-23, '25	—	12
Maureen Connolly	1953	1953-54	1952-54	1951-53	9
Monica Seles	1991-93, '96	1990-92	—	1991-92	9

1) Active player in 2006. (2) Prior to 1925, French Open entry was limited to members of French clubs.

RIFLE AND PISTOL CHAMPIONSHIPS

Source: National Rifle Association

NRA Bianchi Cup National Action Pistol Championships in 2007

Action Pistol: Doug Koenig, Alburtis, PA, 1920-185X

Woman Action Pistol: Julie Goloski, Endfield, CT 1903-139X

Junior Action Pistol: Matthew Harriman, Australia, 1900-148X

National Outdoor Rifle and Pistol Championships in 2007

Pistol: GYSG Brian H. Zins, USMC, Quantico, VA, 2640-115X

Civilian Pistol: Steve F. Reiter, Tucson, AZ, 2621-106X

Woman Pistol: Kimberly Holbart, New Philadelphia, OH, 2535-76X

Smallbore Rifle Prone: LTC Robert E. Harbison, U.S. Army, Columbus, GA, 6397-542X

Civilian Smallbore Rifle Prone: Kenneth M. Benyo, Macungie, PA, 6392-515X

Woman Smallbore Rifle Prone: Reya Kempley, Minden, NV, 6387-474X

Smallbore Rifle NRA 3-Position: SGT Shane M. Barnhart, U.S. Army, Phenix City, AL, 2267-74X

Civilian Smallbore Rifle NRA 3-Position: Abby Fong, New York, NY, 2252-71X

Woman Smallbore Rifle NRA 3-Position: Abby Fong, New York, NY, 2252-71X

High Power Rifle: Carl R. Bernosky, Ashland, PA, 1787-89X

Civilian High Power Rifle: Carl R. Bernosky, Ashland, PA, 1787-89X

Woman High Power Rifle: GYSG Julia L. Watson, USMC, West Jordan, UT, 1762-55X

High Power Rifle Long Range: John L. Whidden, Nashville, GA, 1241-68X

Woman High Power Rifle Long Range: Nancy H. Tompkins, Prescott, AZ, 1226-65X

National Indoor Rifle and Pistol Championships in 2007

Smallbore Rifle 4-Position: Vincent Pestilli, Lebanon, PA, 798-58X
Woman Smallbore Rifle 4-Position: Michelle Bohren, Taylor, MI, 797-69X
Smallbore Rifle NRA 3-Position: Abby Fong, New York, NY, 1181-72X
Woman Smallbore Rifle NRA 3-Position: Abby Fong, New York, NY, 1181-72X
International Smallbore Rifle: Abby Fong, New York, NY, 1181-78X
Woman International Smallbore Rifle: Abby Fong, New York, NY, 1181-78X
Air Rifle: Elisha LaFond, Spokane, WA, 588-20X
Woman Air Rifle: Elisha LaFond, Spokane, WA, 588-20X

Conventional Pistol: James Henderson, Columbus, GA, 892-39X
Woman Conventional Pistol: Victoria Hendrickson, Battle Ground, WA, 866-18X
International Free Pistol: John Zurek, Phoenix, AZ, 566-50X
Woman International Free Pistol: Kathy Chatterton, Glen Rock, NJ, 503-20X
International Standard Pistol: John Bickar, Portola Valley, WA, 579-50X
Woman International Standard Pistol: Ashley Davis, S. Jordan, UT, 525-20X
Air Pistol: Daryl Szarenski, Seale, AL, 577-50X
Woman Air Pistol: Brenda Martin Shinn, Riverside, CA, 566-20X

AUTO RACING
Indianapolis 500 Winners, 1911-2007
(At Indianapolis Motor Speedway in Indianapolis, IN)

Year	Winner, Car[1]	MPH[2]	Year	Winner, Car[1]	MPH
1911	Ray Harroun, Marmon	74.602	1962	Rodger Ward, Watson-Offy	140.293
1912	Joe Dawson, National	78.719	1963	Parnelli Jones, Watson-Offy	143.137
1913	Jules Goux, Peugeot	75.933	1964	A.J. Foyt Jr., Watson-Offy	147.350
1914	Rene Thomas, Delage	82.474	1965	Jim Clark, Lotus-Ford	150.686
1915	Ralph DePalma, Mercedes	89.840	1966	Graham Hill, Lola-Ford	144.317
1916	Dario Resta, Peugeot	84.001	1967	A.J. Foyt Jr., Coyote-Ford	151.207
1917-18—Not held			1968	Bobby Unser, Eagle-Offy	152.882
1919	Howdy Wilcox, Peugeot	88.050	1969	Mario Andretti, Hawk-Ford	156.867
1920	Gaston Chevrolet, Frontenac	88.618	1970	Al Unser, P.J. Colt-Ford	155.749
1921	Tommy Milton, Frontenac	89.621	1971	Al Unser, P.J. Colt-Ford	157.735
1922	Jimmy Murphy, Duesenberg-Miller	94.484	1972	Mark Donohue, McLaren-Offy	162.962
1923	Tommy Milton, Miller	90.954	1973	Gordon Johncock, Eagle-Offy	159.036
1924	L.L. Corum-Joe Boyer, Duesenberg	98.234	1974	Johnny Rutherford, McLaren-Offy	158.589
1925	Peter DePaolo, Duesenberg	101.127	1975	Bobby Unser, Eagle-Offy	149.213
1926	Frank Lockhart, Miller	95.904	1976	Johnny Rutherford, McLaren-Offy	148.725
1927	George Souders, Duesenberg	97.545	1977	A.J. Foyt Jr., Coyote-Foyt	161.331
1928	Louie Meyer, Miller	99.482	1978	Al Unser, Lola-Cosworth	161.363
1929	Ray Keech, Miller	97.585	1979	Rick Mears, Penske-Cosworth	158.899
1930	Billy Arnold, Summers-Miller	100.448	1980	Johnny Rutherford, Chaparral-Cosworth	142.862
1931	Louis Schneider, Stevens-Miller	96.629	1981	Bobby Unser, Penske-Cosworth	139.084
1932	Fred Frame, Wetteroth-Miller	104.144	1982	Gordon Johncock, Wildcat-Cosworth	162.029
1933	Louie Meyer, Miller	104.162	1983	Tom Sneva, March-Cosworth	162.117
1934	Bill Cummings, Miller	104.863	1984	Rick Mears, March-Cosworth	163.612
1935	Kelly Petillo, Wetteroth-Offy	106.240	1985	Danny Sullivan, March-Cosworth	152.982
1936	Louie Meyer, Stevens-Miller	109.069	1986	Bobby Rahal, March-Cosworth	170.722
1937	Wilbur Shaw, Shaw-Offy	113.580	1987	Al Unser, March-Cosworth	162.175
1938	Floyd Roberts, Wetteroth-Miller	117.200	1988	Rick Mears, Penske-Chevy Indy V8	144.809
1939	Wilbur Shaw, Maserati	115.035	1989	Emerson Fittipaldi, Penske-Chevy Indy V8	167.581
1940	Wilbur Shaw, Maserati	114.277	1990	Arie Luyendyk, Lola-Chevy Indy V8	185.981
1941	Floyd Davis-Mauri Rose, Wetteroth-Offy	115.117	1991	Rick Mears, Penske-Chevy Indy V8	176.457
1942-45—Not held			1992	Al Unser Jr., Galmer-Chevy Indy V8A	134.477
1946	George Robson, Adams-Sparks	114.820	1993	Emerson Fittipaldi, Penske-Chevy Indy V8C	157.207
1947	Mauri Rose, Deidt-Offy	116.338	1994	Al Unser Jr., Penske-Mercedes Benz	160.872
1948	Mauri Rose, Deidt-Offy	119.814	1995	Jacques Villeneuve, Reynard-Ford Cosworth XB	153.616
1949	Bill Holland, Deidt-Offy	121.327	1996	Buddy Lazier, Reynard-Ford Cosworth	147.956
1950	Johnnie Parsons, Kurtis-Offy	124.002	1997	Arie Luyendyk, G Force-Aurora	145.827
1951	Lee Wallard, Kurtis-Offy	126.244	1998	Eddie Cheever, Dallara-Aurora	145.155
1952	Troy Ruttman, Kuzma-Offy	128.922	1999	Kenny Brack, Dallara-Aurora	153.176
1953	Bill Vukovich, KK500A-Offy	128.740	2000	Juan Montoya, G Force-Aurora	167.607
1954	Bill Vukovich, KK500A-Offy	130.840	2001	Helio Castroneves, Reynard-Honda	131.294
1955	Bob Sweikert, KK500C-Offy	128.213	2002	Helio Castroneves, Reynard-Honda	166.499
1956	Pat Flaherty, Watson-Offy	128.490	2003	Gil de Ferran, G Force-Toyota	156.291
1957	Sam Hanks, Salih-Offy	135.601	2004	Buddy Rice, G Force-Honda	138.518
1958	Jimmy Bryan, Salih-Offy	133.791	2005	Dan Wheldon, Dallara-Honda	157.603
1959	Rodger Ward, Watson-Offy	135.857	2006	Sam Hornish Jr., Dallara-Honda	157.085
1960	Jim Rathmann, Watson-Offy	138.767	2007	Dario Franchitti, Dallara-Honda	151.774
1961	A.J. Foyt Jr., Trevis-Offy	139.130			

(1) Chassis-Engine. (2) Average speed. *Race record. **Note:** The race was less than 500 mi in the following years: 1916 (300 mi), 1926 (400 mi), 1950 (345 mi), 1973 (332.5 mi), 1975 (435 mi), 1976 (255 mi), 2004 (450 mi), 2007 (415 mi).

Champ Car World Series Vanderbilt Cup Winners, 1959-2006

(U.S. Auto Club Champions prior to 1979; Championship Auto Racing Teams [CART] Champions, 1979-2003; Champ Car World Series Champion, 2004-present. The Vanderbilt Cup became the series' championship trophy in 2000.)

Year	Driver	Year	Driver	Year	Driver	Year	Driver	Year	Driver
1959	Roger Ward	1969	Mario Andretti	1979	Rick Mears	1989	Emerson Fittipaldi	1998	Alex Zanardi
1960	A. J. Foyt	1970	Al Unser	1980	Johnny Rutherford	1990	Al Unser Jr.	1999	Juan Montoya
1961	A. J. Foyt	1971	Joe Leonard	1981	Rick Mears	1991	Michael Andretti	2000	Gil de Ferran
1962	Rodger Ward	1972	Joe Leonard	1982	Rick Mears	1992	Bobby Rahal	2001	Gil de Ferran
1963	A. J. Foyt	1973	Roger McCluskey	1983	Al Unser	1993	Nigel Mansell	2002	Cristiano da Matta
1964	A. J. Foyt	1974	Bobby Unser	1984	Mario Andretti	1994	Al Unser Jr.	2003	Paul Tracy
1965	Mario Andretti	1975	A. J. Foyt	1985	Al Unser	1995	Jacques Villeneuve	2004	Sebastien Bourdais
1966	Mario Andretti	1976	Gordon Johncock	1986	Bobby Rahal	1996	Jimmy Vasser	2005	Sebastien Bourdais
1967	A. J. Foyt	1977	Tom Sneva	1987	Bobby Rahal	1997	Alex Zanardi	2006	Sebastien Bourdais
1968	Bobby Unser	1978	Tom Sneva	1988	Danny Sullivan				

Indy Racing League (IRL) Winners, 1996-2006

(The Indy Racing League was begun in 1994 by a break-away group of CART drivers; its first championship was awarded in 1996)

Year	Driver	Year	Driver	Year	Driver	Year	Driver	Year	Driver
1996	(tie) Scott Sharp,	1998	Kenny Brack	2001	Sam Hornish Jr.	2003	Scott Dixon	2005	Dan Wheldon
	Buzz Calkins	1999	Greg Ray	2002	Sam Hornish Jr.	2004	Tony Kanaan	2006	Sam Hornish Jr.
1997	Tony Stewart	2000	Buddy Lazier						

NASCAR Racing
Nextel Cup Champions, 1949-2006

(Strictly Stock, 1949; Grand National, 1950-1970; Winston Cup 1971-2003)

Year	Driver	Year	Driver	Year	Driver	Year	Driver	Year	Driver
1949	Red Byron	1961	Ned Jarrett	1973	Benny Parsons	1985	Darrell Waltrip	1997	Jeff Gordon
1950	Bill Rexford	1962	Joe Weatherly	1974	Richard Petty	1986	Dale Earnhardt	1998	Jeff Gordon
1951	Herb Thomas	1963	Joe Weatherly	1975	Richard Petty	1987	Dale Earnhardt	1999	Dale Jarrett
1952	Tim Flock	1964	Richard Petty	1976	Cale Yarborough	1988	Bill Elliott	2000	Bobby Labonte
1953	Herb Thomas	1965	Ned Jarrett	1977	Cale Yarborough	1989	Rusty Wallace	2001	Jeff Gordon
1954	Lee Petty	1966	David Pearson	1978	Cale Yarborough	1990	Dale Earnhardt	2002	Tony Stewart
1955	Tim Flock	1967	Richard Petty	1979	Richard Petty	1991	Dale Earnhardt	2003	Matt Kenseth
1956	Buck Baker	1968	David Pearson	1980	Dale Earnhardt	1992	Alan Kulwicki	2004	Kurt Busch
1957	Buck Baker	1969	David Pearson	1981	Darrell Waltrip	1993	Dale Earnhardt	2005	Tony Stewart
1958	Lee Petty	1970	Bobby Isaac	1982	Darrell Waltrip	1994	Dale Earnhardt	2006	Jimmie Johnson
1959	Lee Petty	1971	Richard Petty	1983	Bobby Allison	1995	Jeff Gordon		
1960	Rex White	1972	Richard Petty	1984	Terry Labonte	1996	Terry Labonte		

NASCAR Rookie of the Year, 1958-2006

Year	Driver	Year	Driver	Year	Driver	Year	Driver	Year	Driver
1958	Shorty Rollins	1968	Pete Hamilton	1978	Ronnie Thomas	1988	Ken Bouchard	1998	Kenny Irwin
1959	Richard Petty	1969	Dick Brooks	1979	Dale Earnhardt	1989	Dick Trickle	1999	Tony Stewart
1960	David Pearson	1970	Bill Dennis	1980	Jody Riley	1990	Rob Moroso	2000	Matt Kenseth
1961	Woodie Wilson	1971	Walter Ballard	1981	Ron Bouchard	1991	Bobby Hamilton	2001	Kevin Harvick
1962	Tom Cox	1972	Larry Smith	1982	Geoff Bodine	1992	Jimmy Hensley	2002	Ryan Newman
1963	Billy Wade	1973	Lennie Pond	1983	Sterling Marlin	1993	Jeff Gordon	2003	Jamie McMurray
1964	Doug Cooper	1974	Earl Ross	1984	Rusty Wallace	1994	Jeff Burton	2004	Kasey Kahne
1965	Sam McQuagg	1975	Bruce Hill	1985	Ken Schrader	1995	Ricky Craven	2005	Kyle Busch
1966	James Hylton	1976	Skip Manning	1986	Alan Kulwicki	1996	Johnny Benson	2006	Denny Hamlin
1967	Donnie Allison	1977	Ricky Rudd	1987	Davey Allison	1997	Mike Skinner		

Daytona 500 Winners, 1959-2007

(At Daytona International Speedway in Daytona Beach, FL)

Year	Driver, car	Avg. MPH	Year	Driver, car	Avg. MPH	Year	Driver, car	Avg. MPH
1959	Lee Petty, Oldsmobile	135.521	1976	David Pearson, Mercury	152.181	1992	Davey Allison, Ford	160.256
1960	Junior Johnson, Chevrolet	124.740	1977	Cale Yarborough, Chevrolet	153.218	1993	Dale Jarrett, Chevrolet	154.972
1961	Marvin Panch, Pontiac	149.601	1978	Bobby Allison, Ford	159.730	1994	Sterling Marlin, Chevrolet	156.931
1962	Fireball Roberts, Pontiac	152.529	1979	Richard Petty, Oldsmobile	143.977	1995	Sterling Marlin, Chevrolet	141.710
1963	Tiny Lund, Ford	151.566	1980	Buddy Baker, Oldsmobile	177.602	1996	Dale Jarrett, Ford	154.308
1964	Richard Petty, Plymouth	154.334	1981	Richard Petty, Buick	169.651	1997	Jeff Gordon, Chevrolet	148.295
1965	Fred Lorenzen, Ford (a)	141.539	1982	Bobby Allison, Buick	153.991	1998	Dale Earnhardt, Chevrolet	172.712
1966	Richard Petty, Plymouth (b)	160.627	1983	Cale Yarborough, Pontiac	155.979	1999	Jeff Gordon, Chevrolet	161.551
1967	Mario Andretti, Ford	146.926	1984	Cale Yarborough, Chevrolet	150.994	2000	Dale Jarrett, Ford	155.669
1968	Cale Yarborough, Mercury	143.251	1985	Bill Elliott, Ford	172.265	2001	Michael Waltrip, Chevrolet	161.783
1969	LeeRoy Yarbrough, Ford	160.875	1986	Geoff Bodine, Chevrolet	148.124	2002	Ward Burton, Dodge	142.971
1970	Pete Hamilton, Plymouth	149.601	1987	Bill Elliott, Ford	176.263	2003	Michael Waltrip, Chevrolet (d)	133.870
1971	Richard Petty, Plymouth	144.456	1988	Bobby Allison, Buick	137.531	2004	Dale Earnhardt Jr., Chevrolet	156.345
1972	A. J. Foyt, Mercury	161.550	1989	Darrell Waltrip, Chevrolet	148.466	2005	Jeff Gordon, Chevrolet	135.173
1973	Richard Petty, Dodge	157.205	1990	Derrike Cope, Chevrolet	165.761	2006	Jimmie Johnson, Chevrolet	142.667
1974	Richard Petty, Dodge (c)	140.894	1991	Ernie Irvan, Chevrolet	148.148	2007	Kevin Harvick, Chevrolet	149.335
1975	Benny Parsons, Chevrolet	153.649						

(a) 322.5 mi. (b) 495 mi. (c) 450 mi. (d) 272.5 mi.

Coca-Cola 600 Winners, 1960-2007

(At Lowe's Motor Speedway in Concord, NC. Known as World 600, 1960-85. *=rain-shortened.)

Year	Driver, car	Avg. MPH	Year	Driver, car	Avg. MPH	Year	Driver, car	Avg. MPH
1960	Joe Lee Johnson, Chevrolet	107.735	1976	David Pearson, Mercury	137.352	1992	Dale Earnhardt, Chevrolet	132.980
1961	David Pearson, Pontiac	111.633	1977	Richard Petty, Dodge	137.676	1993	Dale Earnhardt, Chevrolet	145.504
1962	Nelson Stacy, Ford	125.552	1978	Darrell Waltrip, Chevrolet	138.355	1994	Jeff Gordon, Chevrolet	139.445
1963	Fred Lorenzen, Ford	132.418	1979	Darrell Waltrip, Chevrolet	136.674	1995	Bobby Labonte, Chevrolet	151.952
1964	Jim Paschal, Plymouth	125.772	1980	Benny Parsons, Chevrolet	119.265	1996	Dale Jarrett, Ford	147.581
1965	Fred Lorenzen, Ford	121.772	1981	Bobby Allison, Buick	129.326	1997	Jeff Gordon, Chevrolet*	136.745
1966	Marvin Panch, Plymouth	135.042	1982	Neil Bonnett, Ford	130.058	1998	Jeff Gordon, Chevrolet	136.424
1967	Jim Paschal, Plymouth	135.832	1983	Neil Bonnett, Chevrolet	140.707	1999	Jeff Burton, Ford	151.367
1968	Buddy Baker, Dodge*	104.207	1984	Bobby Allison, Buick	129.233	2000	Matt Kenseth, Ford	142.640
1969	LeeRoy Yarbrough, Mercury	134.361	1985	Darrell Waltrip, Chevrolet	141.807	2001	Jeff Burton, Ford	138.107
1970	Donnie Allison, Ford	129.680	1986	Dale Earnhardt, Chevrolet	140.406	2002	Mark Martin, Ford	137.729
1971	Bobby Allison, Mercury	140.422	1987	Kyle Petty, Ford	131.483	2003	Jimmie Johnson, Chevrolet*	126.198
1972	Buddy Baker, Dodge	142.255	1988	Darrell Waltrip, Chevrolet	124.460	2004	Jimmie Johnson, Chevrolet	142.763
1973	Buddy Baker, Dodge	134.890	1989	Darrell Waltrip, Chevrolet	144.077	2005	Jimmie Johnson, Chevrolet	114.698
1974	David Pearson, Mercury	135.720	1990	Rusty Wallace, Pontiac	137.650	2006	Kasey Kahne, Dodge	128.840
1975	Richard Petty, Dodge	145.327	1991	Davey Allison, Ford	138.951	2007	Casey Mears, Chevrolet	130.222

Allstate Brickyard 400 Winners, 1994-2007

(At Indianapolis Motor Speedway in Indianapolis, IN)

Year	Driver, car	Avg. MPH	Year	Driver, car	Avg. MPH	Year	Driver, car	Avg. MPH
1994	Jeff Gordon, Chevrolet	131.977	1999	Dale Jarrett, Ford	148.194	2004	Jeff Gordon, Chevrolet	115.037
1995	Dale Earnhardt, Chevrolet	155.206	2000	Bobby Labonte, Pontiac	155.912	2005	Tony Stewart, Chevrolet	118.782
1996	Dale Jarrett, Ford	139.508	2001	Jeff Gordon, Chevrolet	130.790	2006	Jimmie Johnson, Chevrolet	137.180
1997	Ricky Rudd, Ford	130.814	2002	Bill Elliott, Dodge	125.033	2007	Tony Stewart, Chevrolet	117.379
1998	Jeff Gordon, Chevrolet	126.772	2003	Kevin Harvick, Chevrolet	134.554			

Sharpie 500 Winners, 1961-2007

(At Bristol Motor Speedway in Bristol, TN. Known as the Volunteer 500, 1961-75, '78-79; Volunteer 400, 1976-77; Busch 500, 1980-90; Bud 500, 1991-93; Goody's 500, 1994-99; goracing.com 500, 2000. * = rain-shortened)

Year	Driver, car	Avg. MPH	Year	Driver, car	Avg. MPH	Year	Driver, car	Avg. MPH
1961	Jack Smith, Pontiac	68.37	1977	Cale Yarborough, Chevrolet	79.726	1993	Mark Martin, Ford	88.172
1962	Bobby Johns, Pontiac	73.32	1978	Cale Yarborough, Oldsmobile	88.628	1994	Rusty Wallace, Ford	91.363
1963	Fred Lorenzen, Ford	74.844	1979	Darrell Waltrip, Chevrolet	91.493	1995	Terry Labonte, Chevrolet	81.979
1964	Fred Lorenzen, Ford	78.044	1980	Cale Yarborough, Chevrolet	86.973	1996	Rusty Wallace, Ford	91.267
1965	Ned Jarrett, Ford	61.826	1981	Darrell Waltrip, Buick	84.723	1997	Dale Jarrett, Ford	80.013
1966	Paul Goldsmith, Plymouth	77.963	1982	Darrell Waltrip, Buick	94.318	1998	Mark Martin, Ford	86.949
1967	Richard Petty, Plymouth	78.705	1983	Darrell Waltrip, Chevrolet*	89.43	1999	Dale Earnhardt, Chevrolet	91.276
1968	David Pearson, Ford	76.31	1984	Terry Labonte, Chevrolet	85.365	2000	Rusty Wallace, Ford	85.394
1969	David Pearson, Ford	79.737	1985	Dale Earnhardt, Chevrolet	81.388	2001	Tony Stewart, Pontiac	85.106
1970	Bobby Allison, Dodge	84.88	1986	Darrell Waltrip, Chevrolet	86.934	2002	Jeff Gordon, Chevrolet	77.097
1971	Charlie Glotzbach, Chevrolet	101.074	1987	Dale Earnhardt, Chevrolet	90.373	2003	Kurt Busch, Ford	77.421
1972	Bobby Allison, Chevrolet	92.735	1988	Dale Earnhardt, Chevrolet	78.775	2004	Dale Earnhardt Jr., Chevrolet	8.538
1973	Benny Parsons, Chevrolet	91.342	1989	Darrell Waltrip, Chevrolet	85.554	2005	Matt Kenseth, Ford	84.678
1974	Cale Yarborough, Chevrolet	75.43	1990	Ernie Irvan, Chevrolet	91.782	2006	Matt Kenseth, Ford	90.025
1975	Richard Petty, Dodge	97.016	1991	Alan Kulwicki, Ford	82.028	2007	Carl Edwards, Ford	89.006
1976	Cale Yarborough, Chevrolet	99.175	1992	Darrell Waltrip, Chevrolet	91.198			

NASCAR Nextel All-Star Race, 1985-2007

(at Lowe's Motor Speedway in Concord, NC. Known as The Winston, 1985-2003; The Winston Select, 1995-96.)

Year	Driver	Year	Driver	Year	Driver
1985	Darrell Waltrip, Chevrolet	1993	Dale Earnhardt, Chevrolet	2001	Jeff Gordon, Chevrolet
1986	Bill Elliott, Ford	1994	Geoffrey Bodine, Ford	2002	Ryan Newman, Ford
1987	Dale Earnhardt, Chevrolet	1995	Jeff Gordon, Chevrolet	2003	Jimmie Johnson, Chevrolet
1988	Terry Labonte, Chevrolet	1996	Michael Waltrip, Chevrolet	2004	Matt Kenseth, Ford
1989	Rusty Wallace, Ford	1997	Jeff Gordon, Chevrolet	2005	Mark Martin, Ford
1990	Dale Earnhardt, Chevrolet	1998	Mark Martin, Ford	2006	Jimmie Johnson, Chevrolet
1991	Davey Allison, Ford	1999	Terry Labonte, Chevrolet	2007	Kevin Harvick, Chevrolet
1992	Davey Allison, Ford	2000	Dale Earnhardt Jr., Chevrolet		

Formula One Racing
World Grand Prix Champions, 1950-2006

Year	Driver	Year	Driver	Year	Driver
1950	Nino Farini, Italy	1969	Jackie Stewart, Scotland	1988	Ayrton Senna, Brazil
1951	Juan Manuel Fangio, Argentina	1970	Jochen Rindt, Austria	1989	Alain Prost, France
1952	Alberto Ascari, Italy	1971	Jackie Stewart, Scotland	1990	Ayrton Senna, Brazil
1953	Alberto Ascari, Italy	1972	Emerson Fittipaldi, Brazil	1991	Ayrton Senna, Brazil
1954	Juan Manuel Fangio, Argentina	1973	Jackie Stewart, Scotland	1992	Nigel Mansell, Britain
1955	Juan Manuel Fangio, Argentina	1974	Emerson Fittipaldi, Brazil	1993	Alain Prost, France
1956	Juan Manuel Fangio, Argentina	1975	Niki Lauda, Austria	1994	Michael Schumacher, Germany
1957	Juan Manuel Fangio, Argentina	1976	James Hunt, England	1995	Michael Schumacher, Germany
1958	Mike Hawthorne, England	1977	Niki Lauda, Austria	1996	Damon Hill, England
1959	Jack Brabham, Australia	1978	Mario Andretti, United States	1997	Jacques Villeneuve, Canada
1960	Jack Brabham, Australia	1979	Jody Scheckter, South Africa	1998	Mika Hakkinen, Finland
1961	Phil Hill, United States	1980	Alan Jones, Australia	1999	Mika Hakkinen, Finland
1962	Graham Hill, England	1981	Nelson Piquet, Brazil	2000	Michael Schumacher, Germany
1963	Jim Clark, Scotland	1982	Keke Rosberg, Finland	2001	Michael Schumacher, Germany
1964	John Surtees, England	1983	Nelson Piquet, Brazil	2002	Michael Schumacher, Germany
1965	Jim Clark, Scotland	1984	Niki Lauda, Austria	2003	Michael Schumacher, Germany
1966	Jack Brabham, Australia	1985	Alain Prost, France	2004	Michael Schumacher, Germany
1967	Denis Hulme, New Zealand	1986	Alain Prost, France	2005	Fernando Alonso, Spain
1968	Graham Hill, England	1987	Nelson Piquet, Brazil	2006	Fernando Alonso, Spain

2007 Le Mans 24 Hours Race

The Audi No. 1 Team—led by drivers Frank Biela and Marco Werner (Germany) and Emanuele Pirro (Italy)—won the 75th Le Mans 24 Hours Race on June 17, 2007. Audi No. 1 finished with 369 laps, a full ten laps better than the 2nd-place finisher. The same trio of drivers had made up the winning Le Mans team the previous year. Despite rainy conditions late in the race, the diesel-engine-powered Audi R10 TDI won the endurance race for the second consecutive year. Audi teams have won 7 of the last 8 Le Mans 24 Hours Races. Porsche and Ferrari are the only cars to have won at Le Mans more than Audi.

Notable One-Mile Land Speed Records

Andy Green, a Royal Air Force pilot, broke the sound barrier and set the first supersonic world speed record on land, Oct. 15, 1997, in Black Rock Desert, NV. Green, driving a car built by Richard Noble, had 2 runs at an average speed of 763.035 mph, as calculated under the rules of the Fédération Internationale de l'Automobile (FIA). This record and speed exceeded the speed of sound, calculated at 751.251 mph for that place and time.

Date	Driver	Car	MPH	Date	Driver	Car	MPH
1/26/1906	Marriott	Stanley (Steam)	127.659	11/19/37	Eyston	Thunderbolt 1	311.42
3/16/10	Oldfield	Benz	131.724	9/16/38	Eyston	Thunderbolt 1	357.5
4/23/11	Burman	Benz	141.732	8/23/39	Cobb	Railton	368.9
2/12/19	DePalma	Packard	149.875	9/16/47	Cobb	Railton-Mobil	394.2
4/27/20	Milton	Dusenberg	155.046	8/05/63	Breedlove	Spirit of America	407.45
4/28/26	Parry-Thomas	Thomas Spl.	170.624	10/27/64	Arfons	Green Monster	536.71
3/29/27	Seagrave	Sunbeam	203.790	11/15/65	Breedlove	Spirit of America	600.601
4/22/28	Keech	White Triplex	207.552	10/23/70	Gabelich	Blue Flame	622.407
3/11/29	Seagrave	Irving-Napier	231.446	10/09/79	Barrett	Budweiser Rocket	638.637*
2/05/31	Campbell	Napier-Campbell	246.086	10/04/83	Noble	Thrust 2	633.468
2/24/32	Campbell	Napier-Campbell	253.96	9/25/97	Green	Thrust SSC	714.144
2/22/33	Campbell	Napier-Campbell	272.109	10/15/97	Green	Thrust SSC	763.035
9/03/35	Campbell	Bluebird Special	301.13				

*Not recognized as official by sanctioning bodies.

BOXING

There are many boxing governing bodies, including the World Boxing Council, World Boxing Assn., International Boxing Fed., World Boxing Org., U.S. Boxing Assn., N. American Boxing Fed., and European Boxing Union. All have their own champions and divisions.

International Boxing Hall of Fame 2007 Inductees

Source: International Boxing Hall of Fame, 1 Hall of Fame Dr., Canastota, NY 13032. www.ibhof.com

Modern . . . . Roberto Duran, 103-16-0 (70 KOs)	Ricardo Lopez, 50-5-1 (37 KOs)	Pernell Whitaker, 40-4-1 (17 KOs)
Old-Timer . . . . . George Godfrey, 97-20-3 (80 KOs)	Pedro Montanez, 92-7-4 (54 KOs)	Kid Norfolk, 80-16-2 (31 KOs)
Pioneer . . . . Young Barney Aaron	Dick Curtis	
Non-participant . . Amilcar Brusa (Trainer)	Cuco Conde (Manager/Matchmaker)	Jose Sulalman (Administrator)
Observer . . . . TAD Dorgan (Newspaper Cartoonist)	LeRoy Nelman (Artist)	

Champions by Classes*

Class (weight limit)	WBA	WBC	IBF
Heavyweight.	Ruslan Chagaev, Uzbekistan	Oleg Maskaev, Kazakhstan	Wladimir Klitschko, Ukraine
Cruiserweight (200 lb)	Jean Marc Mormeck, France[1]	Jean Marc Mormeck, France	Steve Cunningham, U.S.
Light Heavyweight (175 lb) . . .	Stipe Drews, Croatia	Chad Dawson, U.S.	Clinton Woods, England
Super Middleweight (168 lb) . .	Mikkel Kessler, Denmark[2]	Mikkel Kessler, Denmark	Alejandro Berrio, Colombia
Middleweight (160 lb)	Felix Sturm, Germany	Kelly Pavlik, U.S.	Arthur Abraham, Germany
Jr. Middleweight (154 lb)	Joachim Alcine, Canada	Vernon Forrest, U.S.	Cory Spinks, U.S.
Welterweight (147 lb)	Miguel Cotto, Puerto Rico	Floyd Mayweather Jr., U.S.	Kermit Cintron, Puerto Rico
Jr. Welterweight (140 lb)	Gavin Rees, Wales.	Junior Witter, England	Paul Malignaggi, U.S.
Lightweight (135 lb)	Juan Diaz, U.S.	David Diaz, U.S.	Julio Cesar Diaz, U.S.
Jr. Lightweight (130 lb).	Edwin Valero, Venezuela	Juan Manuel Marquez, Mexico	Mzonke Fana, South Africa
Featherweight (126 lb)	Chris John, Indonesia	Jorge Linares, Venezuela	Robert Guerrero, U.S.
Jr. Featherweight (122 lb) . . .	Celestino Caballero, Panama	Israel Vazquez, Mexico	Steve Molitor, Canada
Bantamweight (118 lb)	Wladimir Sidorenko, Ukraine	Hozumi Hasegawa, Japan	Joseph Agbeko, Ghana
Jr. Bantamweight (115 lb) . . .	Alexander Muñoz, Venezuela	Cristian Mijares, Mexico	Vacant
Flyweight (112 lb)	Takefumi Sakata, Japan.	Daisuke Naito, Japan	Nonito Donaire, Philippines
Jr. Flyweight (108 lb)	Juan Carlos Reveco, Argentina	Edgar Sosa, Mexico	Ulises Solis, Mexico
Strawweight (105 lb)	Yutaka Niida, Japan.	Eagle Kyowa, Japan	Florante Condes, Philippines

*As of Oct. 1, 2007. **Note:** Interim champions not listed. The WBA and WBC designate certain title holders as "Super World Champs" (listed above) and permit concurrent "World" champions in those classes. Following are the "World" champions: (1) Virgil Hill, U.S., cruiserweight. (2) Anthony Mundine, Australia, super middleweight.

Ring Champions by Years

International Boxing Hall of Fame inductees in *italics*.

(*abandoned the title or was stripped of it; IBF champions listed only for heavyweight division)

Heavyweights

1882-1892	*John L. Sullivan* (a)
1892-1897	*James J. Corbett* (b)
1897-1899	*Bob Fitzsimmons*
1899-1905	*James J. Jeffries** (c)
1905-1906	*Marvin Hart*
1906-1908	*Tommy Burns*
1908-1915	*Jack Johnson*
1915-1919	*Jess Willard*
1919-1926	*Jack Dempsey*
1926-1928	*Gene Tunney**
1928-1930	Vacant
1930-1932	*Max Schmeling*
1932-1933	*Jack Sharkey*
1933-1934	Primo Carnera
1934-1935	Max Baer
1935-1937	*James J. Braddock*
1937-1949	*Joe Louis**
1949-1951	*Ezzard Charles*
1951-1952	Joe Walcott
1952-1956	*Rocky Marciano**
1956-1959	*Floyd Patterson*
1959-1960	*Ingemar Johansson*
1960-1962	*Floyd Patterson*
1962-1964	*Sonny Liston*
1964-1967	*Cassius Clay (Muhammad Ali)* (d)
1970-1973	*Joe Frazier*
1973-1974	*George Foreman*
1974-1978	*Muhammad Ali*

1978-1979	*Muhammad Ali** (WBA)
1978	Leon Spinks (WBC*/WBA) (e); Ken Norton (WBC)
1978-1983	Larry Holmes* (WBC) (f)
1979-1980	John Tate (WBA)
1980-1982	Mike Weaver (WBA)
1982-1983	Michael Dokes (WBA)
1983-1984	Gerrie Coetzee (WBA)
1983-1985	Larry Holmes (IBF) (f)
1984	Tim Witherspoon (WBC)
1984-1985	Greg Page (WBA)
1984-1986	Pinklon Thomas (WBC)
1985-1986	Tony Tubbs (WBA)
1985-1987	*Michael Spinks** (IBF)
1986	Tim Witherspoon (WBA); Trevor Berbick (WBC)
1986-1987	Mike Tyson (WBC); James "Bonecrusher" Smith (WBA)
1987	Tony Tucker (IBF)
1987-1990	Mike Tyson (WBC/WBA/IBF)
1990	"Buster" Douglas (WBA/WBC/IBF)
1990-1992	Evander Holyfield (WBA/WBC/IBF)
1992-1993	Riddick Bowe (WBA/IBF/WBC*)
1992-1994	Lennox Lewis (WBC)

1993-1994	Evander Holyfield (WBA/IBF)
1994	Michael Moorer (WBA/IBF)
1994-1995	Oliver McCall (WBC); George Foreman (WBA*/IBF*)
1995	Frans Botha* (IBF)
1995-1996	Bruce Seldon (WBA); Frank Bruno (WBC)
1996	Mike Tyson (WBC*/WBA)
1996-1997	Michael Moorer (IBF)
1996-1999	Evander Holyfield (WBA/IBF)
1997-2001	Lennox Lewis (WBC)
1999-2001	Lennox Lewis (WBA*/WBC/IBF)
2000-2001	Evander Holyfield (WBA)
2001-2003	John Ruiz (WBA)
2001	Hasim Rahman (WBC/IBF)
2001-2002	Lennox Lewis (IBF*)
2001-2004	Lennox Lewis (WBC)
2002-2006	Chris Byrd (IBF)
2003	Roy Jones Jr. (WBA*)
2004-2005	John Ruiz (WBA)(g); Vitali Klitschko (WBC*)
2005-2006	Hasim Rahman (WBC)
2005-2007	Nicolay Valuev (WBA)
2006-2007	Oleg Maskaev (WBC); Wladimir Klitschko (IBF)
2007	Ruslan Chagaev (WBA)

(a) London Prize Ring (bare knuckle champion). (b) First Marquis of Queensberry champion. (c) Jeffries vacated title (1905), designated Marvin Hart and Jack Root as logical contenders. Hart defeated Root in 12 rounds (1905), in turn was defeated by Tommy Burns (1906), who claimed the title. Jack Johnson def. Burns (1908) and was recognized as champ. Johnson won the title by defeating Jeffries in the latter's attempted comeback (1910). (d) Title declared vacant by the WBA and others in 1967 after Ali refused military induction. Joe Frazier recognized as champ by 6 states, Mexico, and S. America. Jimmy Ellis declared champ by the WBA. Frazier KOd Ellis, Feb. 16, 1970. (e) After Spinks defeated Ali, the WBC recognized Ken Norton as champ. Ali defeated Spinks in 1978 rematch for WBA title, retired in 1979. (f) Holmes relinquished WBC title in Dec. 1983, to fight as champ of the new IBF. (g) James Toney defeated Ruiz April 30, 2005 to claim the title, but it was rescinded when Toney tested positive for steroids.

Light Heavyweights

1903	Jack Root, George Gardner
1903-1905	Bob Fitzsimmons
1905-1912	Philadelphia Jack O'Brien*
1912-1916	Jack Dillon
1916-1920	Battling Levinsky
1920-1922	George Carpentier
1922-1923	Battling Siki
1923-1925	Mike McTigue
1925-1926	Paul Berlenbach
1926-1927	Jack Delaney*
1927-1929	Tommy Loughran*
1930-1934	Maxie Rosenbloom
1934-1935	Bob Olin
1935-1939	John Henry Lewis*
1939	Melio Bettina
1939-1941	Billy Conn*
1941	Anton Christoforidis (won NBA title)
1941-1948	Gus Lesnevich, Freddie Mills
1948-1950	Freddie Mills
1950-1952	Joey Maxim
1952-1962	Archie Moore
1962-1963	Harold Johnson
1963-1965	Willie Pastrano
1965-1966	Jose Torres
1966-1968	Dick Tiger
1968-1974	Bob Foster*
1974-1977	John Conteh (WBC)
1974-1978	Victor Galindez (WBA)
1977-1978	Miguel Cuello (WBC)
1978	Mate Parlov (WBC)
1978-1979	Mike Rossman (WBA); Marvin Johnson (WBC)
1979-1981	Matthew Saad Muhammad (WBC)
1979-1980	Marvin Johnson (WBA)
1980-1981	Eddie Mustafa Muhammad (WBA)
1981-1983	Michael Spinks (WBA); Dwight Muhammed-Qawi Braxton (WBC)
1983-1985	Michael Spinks*
1985-1986	J. B. Williamson (WBC)
1986-1987	Marvin Johnson (WBA); Dennis Andries (WBC)
1987	Leslie Stewart (WBA)
1987-1991	Virgil Hill (WBA)
1987	Thomas Hearns* (WBC)
1987-1988	Don Lalonde (WBC)
1988	Sugar Ray Leonard* (WBC)
1989	Dennis Andries (WBC)
1989-1990	Jeff Harding (WBC)
1990-1991	Dennis Andries (WBC)
1991-1994	Jeff Harding (WBC)
1991-1992	Thomas Hearns (WBA)
1992	Iran Barkley* (WBA)
1992-1997	Virgil Hill (WBA)
1994-1995	Mike McCallum (WBC)
1995-1996	Fabrice Tiozzo* (WBC)
1996-1997	Roy Jones Jr. (WBC)
1997	Montell Griffin (WBC); Roy Jones Jr. (WBC); Darius Michalczewski* (WBA)
1997-1998	Lou Del Valle (WBA)
1998-2003	Roy Jones Jr. (WBA*, WBC*)
2003	Mehdi Sahnoune (WBA); Antonio Tarver (WBC)
2003-04	Roy Jones Jr. (WBA/WBC*)
2004	Antonio Tarver (WBC)
2004-2006	Fabrice Tiozzo (WBA)
2005-2007	Tomasz Adamek (WBC)
2006-2007	Silvio Branco (WBA)
2007	Chad Dawson (WBC); Stipe Drews (WBA)

Middleweights

1884-1891	Jack "Nonpareil" Dempsey
1891-1897	Bob Fitzsimmons*
1897-1907	Tommy Ryan*
1907-1908	Stanley Ketchel, Billy Papke
1908-1910	Stanley Ketchel
1911-1913	vacant
1913	Frank Klaus; George Chip
1914-1917	Al McCoy
1917-1920	Mike O'Dowd
1920-1923	Johnny Wilson
1923-1926	Harry Greb
1926-1931	Tiger Flowers; Mickey Walker
1931-1932	Gorilla Jones (NBA)
1932-1937	Marcel Thil
1938	Al Hostak (NBA); Solly Krieger (NBA)
1939-1940	Al Hostak (NBA)
1941-1947	Tony Zale
1947-1948	Rocky Graziano
1948	Tony Zale; Marcel Cerdan
1949-1951	Jake LaMotta
1951	Ray Robinson; Randy Turpin; Ray Robinson*
1953-1955	Carl (Bobo) Olson
1955-1957	Ray Robinson
1957	Gene Fullmer; Ray Robinson
1957-1958	Carmen Basilio
1958	Ray Robinson
1959	Gene Fullmer (NBA); Ray Robinson (NY)
1960	Gene Fullmer (NBA); Paul Pender (NY and MA)
1961	Gene Fullmer (NBA); Terry Downes (NY, MA, Europe)
1962	Gene Fullmer (NBA); Dick Tiger (NBA); Paul Pender (NY and MA)*
1963	Dick Tiger (universal)
1963-1965	Joey Giardello
1965-1966	Dick Tiger
1966-1967	Emile Griffith
1967	Nino Benvenuti
1967-1968	Emile Griffith
1968-1970	Nino Benvenuti
1970-1977	Carlos Monzon*
1977-1978	Rodrigo Valdez
1978-1979	Hugo Corro
1979-1980	Vito Antuofermo
1980	Alan Minter
1980-1987	Marvin Hagler
1987	Sugar Ray Leonard* (WBC)
1987-1989	Sumbu Kalambay (WBA)
1987-1988	Thomas Hearns (WBC)
1988-1989	Iran Barkley (WBC)
1989-1991	Roberto Duran* (WBC)
1989-1991	Mike McCallum (WBA)
1990-1993	Julian Jackson (WBC)
1992-1993	Reggie Johnson (WBA)
1993-1995	Gerald McClellan* (WBC)
1993-1994	John David Jackson (WBA)
1994-1997	Jorge Castro (WBA)
1995	Julian Jackson (WBC)
1995-1996	Quincy Taylor (WBC); Shinji Takehara (WBA)
1996-1998	Keith Holmes (WBC)
1996-1997	William Joppy (WBA)
1997	Julio Cesar Green (WBA)
1998-2001	William Joppy (WBA)
1998-1999	Hassine Cherifi (WBC)
1999-2001	Keith Holmes (WBC)
2001	Felix Trinidad (WBA)
2001-2005	Bernard Hopkins (WBC, WBA)
2005-2006	Jermain Taylor (WBA)
2005-2007	Jermain Taylor (WBC)
2006-2007	Javier Castillejo (WBA) (a)
2007	Felix Sturm (WBA); Kelly Pavlik (WBC)

(a) Castillejo lost title to Mariano Carrera Dec. 2, 2006, but regained it Feb. 23, 2007, after Carrera tested positive for steroids.

Welterweights

1892-1894	Mysterious Billy Smith
1894-1896	Tommy Ryan
1896	Kid McCoy*
1900	Rube Ferns; Matty Matthews
1901	Rube Ferns
1901-1904	Joe Walcott
1904-1906	Dixie Kid; Joe Walcott; Honey Mellody
1907-1911	Mike Sullivan
1911-1915	Vacant
1915-1919	Ted Lewis
1919-1922	Jack Britton
1922-1926	Mickey Walker
1926	Pete Latzo
1927-1929	Joe Dundee
1929	Jackie Fields
1930	Jack Thompson; Tommy Freeman
1931	Tommy Freeman; Jack Thompson; Lou Brouillard
1932	Jackie Fields
1933	Young Corbett; Jimmy McLarnin
1934	Barney Ross; Jimmy McLarnin
1935-1938	Barney Ross
1938-1940	Henry Armstrong
1940-1941	Fritzie Zivic
1941-1946	Fred Cochrane
1946	Marty Servo*
1946-1951	Ray Robinson* (a)
1951	Johnny Bratton (NBA)
1951-1954	Kid Gavilan
1954-1955	Johnny Saxton
1955	Tony De Marco
1955-1956	Carmen Basilio
1956	Johnny Saxton
1956-1957	Carmen Basilio*
1958	Virgil Akins
1958-1960	Don Jordan
1960-1961	Benny Paret
1961	Emile Griffith
1961-1962	Benny Paret
1962-1963	Emile Griffith
1963	Luis Rodriguez
1963-1966	Emile Griffith*
1966-1969	Curtis Cokes
1969-1970	Jose Napoles
1970-1971	Billy Backus
1971-1975	Jose Napoles
1975-1976	John Stracey (WBC); Angel Espada (WBA)

1976-1979	*Carlos Palomino* (WBC)
1976-1980	*Jose "Pepino" Cuevas* (WBA)
1979	*Wilfred Benitez* (WBC)
1979-1980	*Sugar Ray Leonard* (WBC)
1980	*Roberto Duran* (WBC)
1980-1981	Thomas Hearns (WBA)
1980-1982	Sugar Ray Leonard*
1983-1985	Donald Curry (WBA); Milton McCrory (WBC)
1985-1986	Donald Curry
1986-1987	Lloyd Honeyghan (WBC)
1987	Mark Breland (WBA)
1987-1988	Marlon Starling (WBA); Jorge Vaca (WBC)
1988-1989	Tomas Molinares (WBA); Lloyd Honeyghan (WBC)
1989-1990	Marlon Starling (WBC); Mark Breland (WBA)
1990-1991	Maurice Blocker (WBC); Aaron Davis (WBA)
1991	Simon Brown (WBC)
1991-1992	Meldrick Taylor (WBA)
1991-1993	Buddy McGirt (WBC)
1992-1994	Crisanto Espana (WBA)
1993-1997	*Pernell Whitaker* (WBC)
1994-1998	Ike Quartey (WBA*)
1997-1999	Oscar De La Hoya (WBC*)
1998	James Page (WBA*)
1999-2000	Felix Trinidad (WBC*)
2000	Oscar De La Hoya (WBC*)
2000-2002	Shane Mosley (WBC)
2001-2002	Andrew Lewis (WBA)
2002	Ricardo Mayorga (WBA)
2002-2003	Vernon Forrest (WBC)
2003	Ricardo Mayorga (WBA, WBC)
2003-2005	Cory Spinks (WBA, WBC)
2005-2006	Zab Judah (WBA, WBC)
2006	Ricky Hatton (WBA); Carlos Baldomir (WBC)
2006-2007	Floyd Mayweather Jr.(WBC); Miguel Cotto (WBA)

(a) Robinson gained the title by defeating Tommy Bell in an elimination agreed to by the New York Commission and the National Boxing Association. Both claimed Robinson waived his title when he won the middleweight crown from LaMotta in 1951.

Lightweights

1896-1899	*Kid Lavigne*
1899-1902	Frank Erne
1902-1908	Joe Gans
1908-1910	Battling Nelson
1910-1912	*Ad Wolgast*
1912-1914	Willie Ritchie
1914-1917	Freddie Welsh
1917-1925	Benny Leonard*
1925	Jimmy Goodrich; Rocky Kansas
1926-1930	*Sammy Mandell*
1930	Al Singer ; Tony Canzoneri
1930-1933	Tony Canzoneri
1933-1935	*Barney Ross**
1935-1936	Tony Canzoneri
1936-1938	Lou Ambers
1938	*Henry Armstrong*
1939	*Lou Ambers*
1940	*Lew Jenkins*
1941-1943	*Sammy Angott*
1944	S. Angott (NBA); J. Zurita (NBA)
1945-1951	Ike Williams (NBA: later universal)
1951-1952	*James Carter*
1952	Lauro Salas; *James Carter*
1953-1954	*James Carter*
1954	Paddy De Marco; *James Carter*
1955	James Carter; Bud Smith
1956	Bud Smith; Joe Brown
1956-1962	Joe Brown
1962-1965	*Carlos Ortiz*
1965	*Ismael Laguna*
1965-1968	*Carlos Ortiz*
1968-1969	Teo Cruz
1969-1970	Mando Ramos
1970	*Ismael Laguna*
1970-1972	Ken Buchanan (WBA)
1971-1972	Pedro Carrasco (WBC)
1972-1979	Roberto Duran* (WBA)
1972	Mando Ramos (WBC); Chango Carmona (WBC)
1972-1974	Rodolfo Gonzalez (WBC)
1974-1976	Ishimatsu Suzuki (WBC)
1976-1978	Esteban De Jesus (WBC)
1979-1981	Jim Watt (WBC)
1979-1980	Ernesto Espana (WBA)
1980-1981	Hilmer Kenty (WBA)
1981	Sean O'Grady (WBA); Claude Noel (WBA)
1981-1983	*Alexis Arguello** (WBC)
1981-1982	Arturo Frias (WBA)
1982-1984	Ray Mancini (WBA)
1983-1984	*Edwin Rosario* (WBC)
1984-1986	Livingstone Bramble (WBA)
1984-1985	Jose Luis Ramirez (WBC)
1985-1986	Hector (Macho) Camacho (WBC)
1986-1987	*Edwin Rosario* (WBA)
1987-1988	Julio Cesar Chavez (WBA); Jose Luis Ramirez (WBC)
1988-1989	Julio Cesar Chavez (WBA, WBC)
1989-1990	Edwin Rosario (WBA); Pernell Whitaker (WBC)
1990	Juan Nazario (WBA)
1990-1992	Pernell Whitaker*
1992	Joey Gamache (WBA)
1992-1996	Miguel Angel Gonzalez* (WBC)
1992-1993	Tony Lopez (WBA)
1993	Dingaan Thobela (WBA)
1993-1998	Orzubek Nazarov (WBA)
1996-1997	Jean-Baptiste Mendy (WBC)
1997-1998	Steve Johnston (WBC)
1998-1999	Jean-Baptiste Mendy (WBA); Cesar Bazan (WBC)
1999	Julian Lorcy (WBA); Stefano Zoff (WBA)
1999-2000	Gilberto Serrano (WBA); Steve Johnston (WBC)
2000-2001	Takanori Hatakeyama (WBA)
2000-2002	Jose Luis Castillo (WBC)
2001	Julien Lorcy (WBA)
2001-2002	Raul Balbi (WBA)
2002-2003	Leonard Dorin (WBA)
2002-2004	Floyd Mayweather (WBC)
2004	Lakva Sim (WBA)
2004-2005	Jose Luis Castillo (WBA)
2004-2007	Juan Diaz (WBA)
2005-2006	Diego Corrales (WBC)
2006	Joel Casamayor (WBA)
2006-2007	David Diaz (WBC)

Featherweights

1892-1900	*George Dixon* (disputed)
1900-1901	Terry McGovern; Young Corbett*
1901-1912	*Abe Attell*
1912-1923	*Johnny Kilbane*
1923	Eugene Criqui; Johnny Dundee
1923-1925	*Johnny Dundee**
1925-1927	*Kid Kaplan**
1927-1928	Benny Bass; Tony Canzoneri
1928-1929	Andre Routis
1929-1932	*Battling Battalino**
1932-1934	Tommy Paul (NBA)
1933-1936	*Freddie Miller*
1936-1937	Petey Sarron
1937-1938	*Henry Armstrong**
1938-1940	Joey Archibald
1940-1941	Harry Jeffra
1942-1948	*Willie Pep*
1948-1949	Sandy Saddler
1949-1950	*Willie Pep*
1950-1957	*Sandy Saddler**
1957-1959	Hogan (Kid) Bassey
1959-1963	Davey Moore
1963-1964	Sugar Ramos
1964-1967	*Vicente Saldivar**
1968	Paul Rojas (WBA)
1968-1969	Jose Legra (WBC)
1968-1971	Shozo Saijyo (WBA)
1969-1970	Johnny Famechon (WBC)
1970	*Vicente Salvidar* (WBC)
1970-1972	Kuniaki Shibata (WBC)
1971-1972	Antonio Gomez (WBA)
1972	Clemente Sanchez* (WBC)
1972-1974	*Ernesto Marcel** (WBA)
1972-1973	Jose Legra (WBC)
1973-1974	*Eder Jofre** (WBC)
1974	*Ruben Olivares* (WBA)
1974-1975	*Bobby Chacon* (WBC)
1974-1976	Alexis Arguello* (WBA)
1975	*Ruben Olivares* (WBA)
1975-1976	David Kotey (WBC)
1976-1980	Danny Lopez (WBC)
1977	Rafael Ortega (WBA)
1977-1978	Cecilio Lastra (WBA)
1978-1985	*Eusebio Pedroza* (WBA)
1980-1982	*Salvador Sanchez** (WBC)
1982-1984	Juan LaPorte (WBC)
1984	*Wilfredo Gomez* (WBC)
1984-1988	Azumah Nelson (WBC)
1985-1986	Barry McGuigan (WBA)
1986-1987	Steve Cruz (WBA)
1987-1991	Antonio Esparragoza (WBA)
1988-1990	Jeff Fenech* (WBC)
1990-1991	Marcos Villasana (WBC)
1991-1993	Park Yung Kyun (WBA); Paul Hodkinson (WBC)
1993	Goyo Vargas (WBC)
1993-1995	Kevin Kelley (WBC)
1993-1996	Eloy Rojas (WBA)
1995	Alejandro Gonzalez (WBC)
1995-1996	Manuel Medina (WBC)
1995-1999	Luisito Espinosa (WBC)
1996-1997	Wilfredo Vasquez* (WBA)
1998	Freddie Norwood (WBA)
1998-1999	Antonio Ceremeno (WBA)
1999	Cesar Soto (WBC); Naseem Hamed* (WBC); Freddie Norwood (WBA)
2000-2001	Guty Espadas (WBC)
2000-2003	Derrick Gainer (WBA)
2001-2004	Erik Morales (WBC)(a)
2003-2006	Juan Manuel Marquez (WBA)
2004-2006	In-jin Chi (WBC)
2006-2007	Chris John (WBA)
2006	Takashi Koshimoto (WBC)
2006	Rodolfo Lopez (WBC)
2006-2007	In-jin Chi (WBC)
2007	Jorge Linares (WBC)

(a) Marco Antonio Barrera won unan. decision over Morales, June 22, 2002, but refused WBC title. Morales regained WBC title with unan. decision over Paulie Ayala, Nov. 16, 2002. Morales moved up to Junior Lightweight div. in 2004.

History of Title-Changing Heavyweight Championship Bouts

1889: July 8, John L. Sullivan def. Jake Kilrain, 75, Richburg, MS.

1892: Sept. 7, James J. Corbett def. John L. Sullivan, 21, New Orleans.

1897: Mar. 17, Bob Fitzsimmons def. James J. Corbett, 14, Carson City, NV.

1899: June 9, James J. Jeffries def. Bob Fitzsimmons, 11, Coney Island, NY. (Jeffries retired as champion in 1905.)

1905: July 3, Marvin Hart KOd Jack Root, 12, Reno, NV. (Jeffries refereed, gave title to Hart. Jack O'Brien also claimed the title.)

1906: Feb. 23, Tommy Burns def. Marvin Hart, 20, Los Angeles.

1908: Dec. 26, Jack Johnson KOd Tommy Burns, 14, Sydney, Australia. (Police halted contest.)

1915: April 5, Jess Willard KOd Jack Johnson, 26, Havana.

1919: July 4, Jack Dempsey KOd Jess Willard, Toledo. (Willard failed to answer bell for 4th round.)

1926: Sept. 23, Gene Tunney def. Jack Dempsey, 10, Philadelphia. (Tunney retired as champion in 1928.)

1930: June 12, Max Schmeling def. Jack Sharkey, 4, NY. (Resulted in the election of a successor to Tunney.)

1932: June 21, Jack Sharkey def. Max Schmeling, 15, NY.

1933: June 29, Primo Carnera KOd Jack Sharkey, 6, NY.

1934: June 14, Max Baer KOd Primo Carnera, 11, NY.

1935: June 13, James J. Braddock def. Max Baer, 15, NY.

1937: June 22, Joe Louis KOd James J. Braddock, 8, Chicago. (Louis retired as champion in 1949.)

1949: June 22, Ezzard Charles def. Joe Walcott, 15, Chicago; NBA recognition only.

1951: July 18, Joe Walcott KOd Ezzard Charles, 7, Pittsburgh.

1952: Sept. 23, Rocky Marciano KOd Joe Walcott, 13, Philadelphia. (Marciano retired as champion in 1956.)

1956: Nov. 30, Floyd Patterson KOd Archie Moore, 5, Chicago.

1959: June 26, Ingemar Johansson KOd Floyd Patterson, 3, NY.

1960: June 20, Floyd Patterson KOd Ingemar Johansson, 5, NY.

1962: Sept. 25, Sonny Liston KOd Floyd Patterson, 1, Chicago.

1964: Feb. 25, Cassius Clay (Muhammad Ali) KOd Sonny Liston, 7, Miami Beach, FL. (In 1967, Ali was stripped of his title by the WBA and others for military service.)

1970: Feb. 16, Joe Frazier KOd Jimmy Ellis, 5, NY. (Frazier def. Ali in 15 rounds, Mar. 8, 1971, in NY.)

1973: Jan. 22, George Foreman KOd Joe Frazier, 2, Jamaica.

1974: Oct. 30, Muhammad Ali KOd George Foreman, 8, Kinshasa, Zaire.

1978: Feb. 15, Leon Spinks def. Muhammad Ali, 15, Las Vegas. (WBC recognized Ken Norton as champion after Spinks refused to fight him before his rematch with Ali.); June 9, (WBC) Larry Holmes def. Ken Norton, 15, Las Vegas; Sept. 15, (WBA) Muhammad Ali def. Leon Spinks, 15, New Orleans. (Ali retired as champion in 1979.)

1979: Oct. 20, (WBA) John Tate def. Gerrie Coetzee, 15, Pretoria, South Africa.

1980: Mar. 31, (WBA) Mike Weaver KOd John Tate, 15, Knoxville.

1982: Dec. 10, (WBA) Michael Dokes KOd Mike Weaver, 1, Las Vegas.

1983: Sept. 23, (WBA) Gerrie Coetzee KOd Michael Dokes, 10, Richfield, OH; in Dec., Larry Holmes relinquished the WBC title and was named champion of the newly formed IBF.

1984: Mar. 9, (WBC) Tim Witherspoon def. Greg Page, 12, Las Vegas; Aug. 31, (WBC) Pinklon Thomas def. Tim Witherspoon, 12, Las Vegas; Dec. 2, (WBA) Greg Page KOd Gerrie Coetzee, 8, Sun City, Bophuthatswana, South Africa.

1985: Apr. 29, (WBA) Tony Tubbs def. Greg Page, 15, Buffalo; Sept. 21, (IBF) Michael Spinks def. Larry Holmes, 15, Las Vegas. (Spinks relinquished title in Feb. 1987.)

1986: Jan. 17, (WBA) Tim Witherspoon def. Tony Tubbs, 15, Atlanta, GA; Mar. 23, (WBC) Trevor Berbick def. Pinklon Thomas, 12, Miami; Nov. 22, (WBC) Mike Tyson KOd Trevor Berbick, 2, Las Vegas; Dec. 12, (WBA) James "Bonecrusher" Smith KOd Tim Witherspoon, 1, NY.

1987: Mar. 7, (WBA, WBC) Mike Tyson def. James "Bonecrusher" Smith, 12, Las Vegas; May 30, (IBF) Tony Tucker KOd James "Buster" Douglas, 10, Las Vegas; Aug. 1, (WBA, WBC, IBF) Mike Tyson def. Tony Tucker, 12, Las Vegas. (Tyson became undisputed champion.)

1990: Feb. 11, (WBA, WBC, IBF) James "Buster" Douglas KOd Mike Tyson, 10, Tokyo; Oct. 25, (WBA, WBC, IBF) Evander Holyfield KOd James "Buster" Douglas, 3, Las Vegas.

1992: Nov. 13, (WBA, WBC, IBF) Riddick Bowe def. Evander Holyfield, 12, Las Vegas. (Lennox Lewis was later named WBC champion when Bowe refused to fight him.)

1993: Nov. 6, (WBA, IBF) Evander Holyfield def. Riddick Bowe, 12, Las Vegas.

1994: Apr. 22, (WBA, IBF) Michael Moorer def. Evander Holyfield, 12, Las Vegas; Sept. 24, (WBC) Oliver McCall KOd Lennox Lewis, 2, London; Nov. 5, (WBA, IBF) George Foreman KOd Michael Moorer, 10, Las Vegas. (In Mar. 1995, Foreman was stripped of the WBA title; he relinquished the IBF title in June.)

1995: Sept. 2, (WBC) Frank Bruno def. Oliver McCall, 12, London; Dec. 9, (IBF) Frans Botha def. Axel Schulz, 12, Las Vegas. (Botha was subsequently stripped of title.)

1996: Mar. 16, (WBC) Mike Tyson KOd Frank Bruno, 3, Las Vegas; June 22, (IBF) Michael Moorer def. Axel Schulz, 12, Dortmund, Germany; Sept. 7, (WBA, WBC) Mike Tyson KOd Bruce Seldon, 1, Las Vegas. (Tyson was subsequently stripped of WBC title.); Nov. 9, (WBA) Evander Holyfield KOd Mike Tyson, 11, Las Vegas.

1997: Feb. 7, (WBC) Lennox Lewis KOd Oliver McCall, 5, Las Vegas; Nov. 8, (IBF) Evander Holyfield def. Michael Moorer, 8, Las Vegas.

1999: Nov. 13, (WBA, WBC, IBF) Lennox Lewis def. Evander Holyfield, 12, Las Vegas. (Lewis became undisputed champion. In April 2000, Lewis was stripped of the WBA title.)

2000: Aug. 12, (WBA) Evander Holyfield def. John Ruiz, 12, Las Vegas.

2001: Mar. 3, (WBA) John Ruiz def. Evander Holyfield, 12, Las Vegas; Apr. 21, (WBC, IBF) Hasim Rahman KOd Lennox Lewis, 5, Brakpan, South Africa; Nov. 17, (WBC, IBF) Lennox Lewis KOd Hasim Rahman, 4, Las Vegas.

2002: Dec. 14, (IBF) Chris Byrd def. Evander Holyfield, 12, Atl. City.

2003: Mar. 1, (WBA) Roy Jones Jr. def. John Ruiz, 12, Las Vegas.

2004: Feb. 20, (WBA) Ruiz gained title when Roy Jones, Jr. relinquished it; Apr. 24, (WBC) Vitali Klitschko TKOd Corrie Sanders, 8, Los Angeles, to win title vacated when champ Lennox Lewis retired in Feb.

2005: Apr. 30, (WBA) James Toney def. John Ruiz, 12, NYC (Toney tested positive for steroids; title returned to Ruiz); Nov. 9, (WBC) Hasim Rahman gained title when Vitali Klitschko retired; Dec. 17, (WBA) Nicolay Valuev def. John Ruiz, 12, Berlin, Ger.

2006: Aug. 12, (WBC) Oleg Maskaev TKOd Hasim Rahman, 12, Las Vegas.; Apr. 22, (IBF) Wladimir Klitschko TKOd Chris Byrd, 7, Mannheim, Ger.

2007: Apr. 14, (WBA) Ruslan Chagaev def. Nicolay Valuev, 12, Stuttgart, Ger.

Other International Hall of Famers

Modern	Old-Timer		
Fred Apostoli	Beau Jack	Baby Arizmendi	Harry Harris	Kid Norfolk
Jackie (Kid Berg)	Nicolino Locche	Jimmy Barry	Pete Herman	Billy Petrolle
Jimmy Bivins	Duilio Loi	Panama Al Brown	Peter Jackson	Tom Sharkey
Charley Burley	Richardo Lopez	Kid Chocolate	Joe Jeanette	Jimmy Slattery
Miguel Canto	Bob Montgomery	Joe Choynski	Fidel LaBarba	Freddie Steele
Michael Carbajal	Terry Norris	Johnny Coulon	Sam Langford	Young Stribling
Antonio Cervantes	Manuel Ortiz	Les Darcy	Benny Lynch	Charles "Bud" Taylor
Jeff Chandler	Laszlo Papp	Jim Driscoll	Joe Lynch	Lew Tendler
Gabriel (Flash) Elorde	Pascual Perez	Sixto Escobar	Jack McAuliffe	Pancho Villa
Khosai Galaxy	Aaron Pryor	Frankie Genaro	Packey McFarland	Jimmy Wilde
Humberto Gonzalez	Chalky Wright	Mike Gibbons	Sam McVey	Kid Williams
Billy Graham	Daniel Zaragoza	Tommy Gibbons	Charley Mitchell	Harry Wills
Masahiko (Fighting)	Carlos Zarate	George Godfrey	Pedro Montanez	Midget Wolgast
Harada		Young Griffo	Owen Moran	Teddy Yarosz

THOROUGHBRED RACING

Triple Crown Winners

Since 1920, colts have carried 126 lb. in Triple Crown events; fillies, 121 lb.

(Kentucky Derby, Preakness, and Belmont Stakes)

Year	Horse	Jockey	Trainer	Year	Horse	Jockey	Trainer
1919	Sir Barton	J. Loftus	H. G. Bedwell	1946	Assault	W. Mehrtens	M. Hirsch
1930	Gallant Fox	E. Sande	J. Fitzsimmons	1948	Citation	E. Arcaro	H. A. Jones
1935	Omaha	W. Sanders	J. Fitzsimmons	1973	Secretariat	R. Turcotte	L. Laurin
1937	War Admiral	C. Kurtsinger	G. Conway	1977	Seattle Slew	J. Cruguet	W. H. Turner Jr.
1941	Whirlaway	E. Arcaro	B. A. Jones	1978	Affirmed	S. Cauthen	L. S. Barrera
1943	Count Fleet	J. Longden	G. D. Cameron				

Kentucky Derby

Churchill Downs, Louisville, KY; inaug. 1875; distance 1-1/4 mi; 1-1/2 mi until 1896. 3-year-olds.

Best time: 1:59 2/5, by Secretariat, 1973; 2007 time: 2:02.17.

Year	Winner	Jockey	Year	Winner	Jockey	Year	Winner	Jockey
1875	Aristides	O. Lewis	1920	Paul Jones	T. Rice	1964	Northern Dancer	W. Hartack
1876	Vagrant	R. Swim	1921	Behave Yourself	C. Thompson	1965	Lucky Debonair	W. Shoemaker
1877	Baden Baden	W. Walker	1922	Morvich	A. Johnson	1966	Kauai King	D. Brumfield
1878	Day Star	Carter	1923	Zev	E. Sande	1967	Proud Clarion	R. Ussery
1879	Lord Murphy	C. Schauer	1924	Black Gold	J. D. Mooney	1968	Dancer's Image#	R. Ussery
1880	Fonso	G. Lewis	1925	Flying Ebony	E. Sande	1969	Majestic Prince	W. Hartack
1881	Hindoo	J. McLaughlin	1926	Bubbling Over	A. Johnson	1970	Dust Commander	M. Manganello
1882	Apollo	B. Hurd	1927	Whiskery	L. McAtee	1971	Canonero II	G. Avila
1883	Leonatus	W. Donohue	1928	Reigh Count	C. Lang	1972	Riva Ridge	R. Turcotte
1884	Buchanan	I. Murphy	1929	Clyde Van Dusen	L. McAtee	1973	Secretariat	R. Turcotte
1885	Joe Cotton	E. Henderson	1930	Gallant Fox	E. Sande	1974	Cannonade	A. Cordero
1886	Ben Ali	P. Duffy	1931	Twenty Grand	C. Kurtsinger	1975	Foolish Pleasure	J. Vasquez
1887	Montrose	I. Lewis	1932	Burgoo King	E. James	1976	Bold Forbes	A. Cordero
1888	Macbeth II	G. Covington	1933	Brokers Tip	D. Meade	1977	Seattle Slew	J. Cruguet
1889	Spokane	T. Kiley	1934	Cavalcade	M. Garner	1978	Affirmed	S. Cauthen
1890	Riley	I. Murphy	1935	Omaha	W. Saunders	1979	Spectacular Bid	R. Franklin
1891	Kingman	I. Murphy	1936	Bold Venture	I. Hanford	1980	Genuine Risk*	J. Vasquez
1892	Azra	A. Clayton	1937	War Admiral	C. Kurtsinger	1981	Pleasant Colony	J. Velasquez
1893	Lookout	E. Kunze	1938	Lawrin	E. Arcaro	1982	Gato del Sol	E. Delahoussaye
1894	Chant	F. Goodale	1939	Johnstown	J. Stout	1983	Sunny's Halo	E. Delahoussaye
1895	Halma	J. Perkins	1940	Gallahadion	C. Bierman	1984	Swale	L. Pincay
1896	Ben Brush	W. Simms	1941	Whirlaway	E. Arcaro	1985	Spend a Buck	A. Cordero
1897	Typhoon II	F. Garner	1942	Shut Out	W. D. Wright	1986	Ferdinand	W. Shoemaker
1898	Plaudit	W. Simms	1943	Count Fleet	J. Longden	1987	Alysheba	C. McCarron
1899	Manuel	F. Taral	1944	Pensive	C. McCreary	1988	Winning Colors*	G. Stevens
1900	Lieut. Gibson	J. Boland	1945	Hoop, Jr.	E. Arcaro	1989	Sunday Silence	P. Valenzuela
1901	His Eminence	J. Winkfield	1946	Assault	W. Mehrtens	1990	Unbridled	C. Perret
1902	Alan-a-Dale	J. Winkfield	1947	Jet Pilot	E. Guerin	1991	Strike the Gold	C. Antley
1903	Judge Himes	H. Booker	1948	Citation	E. Arcaro	1992	Lil E. Tee	P. Day
1904	Elwood	F. Prior	1949	Ponder	S. Brooks	1993	Sea Hero	J. Bailey
1905	Agile	J. Martin	1950	Middleground	W. Boland	1994	Go for Gin	C. McCarron
1906	Sir Huon	R. Troxler	1951	Count Turf	C. McCreary	1995	Thunder Gulch	G. Stevens
1907	Pink Star	A. Minder	1952	Hill Gail	E. Arcaro	1996	Grindstone	J. Bailey
1908	Stone Street	A. Pickens	1953	Dark Star	H. Moreno	1997	Silver Charm	G. Stevens
1909	Wintergreen	V. Powers	1954	Determine	R. York	1998	Real Quiet	K. Desormeaux
1910	Donau	F. Herbert	1955	Swaps	W. Shoemaker	1999	Charismatic	C. Antley
1911	Meridian	G. Archibald	1956	Needles	D. Erb	2000	Fusaichi Pegasus	K. Desormeaux
1912	Worth	C.H. Shilling	1957	Iron Liege	W. Hartack	2001	Monarchos	J. Chavez
1913	Donerail	R. Goose	1958	Tim Tam	I. Valenzuela	2002	War Emblem	V. Espinoza
1914	Old Rosebud	J. McCabe	1959	Tomy Lee	W. Shoemaker	2003	Funny Cide	J. Santos
1915	Regret*	J. Notter	1960	Venetian Way	W. Hartack	2004	Smarty Jones	S. Elliot
1916	George Smith	J. Loftus	1961	Carry Back	J. Sellers	2005	Giacomo	M. Smith
1917	Omar Khayyam	C. Borel	1962	Decidedly	W. Hartack	2006	Barbaro	E. Prado
1918	Exterminator	W. Knapp	1963	Chateaugay	B. Baeza	2007	Street Sense	C. Borel
1919	Sir Barton	J. Loftus						

*Regret, Genuine Risk, and Winning Colors are the only fillies to have won the Derby. # Dancer's Image was disqualified from purse money after tests disclosed that he had run with a pain-killing drug, phenylbutazone, in his system. All wagers were paid on Dancer's Image. Forward Pass was awarded first place money. Only two jockeys have won the Kentucky Derby 5 times: Eddie Arcaro, 1938, 1941, 1948, and 1952; and Bill Hartack, 1957, 1960, 1962, 1964, and 1969. It was won 4 times by Willie Shoemaker, 1955, 1959, 1965, and 1986; and 3 times by each of 4 jockeys: Isaac Murphy, 1884, 1890, and 1891; Earle Sande, 1923, 1925, and 1930; Angel Cordero, 1974, 1976, and 1985; and Gary Stevens, 1988, 1995, and 1997.

Fastest Winning Times for the Kentucky Derby

(Kentucky Derby times measured in fifths of a second according to tradition.)

Time	Horse	Jockey	Year	Time	Horse	Jockey	Year
1m. 59 2/5 s.	Secretariat	Ron Turcotte	1973	2m. 1 1/5 s.	Thunder Gulch	Gary Stevens	1995
1m. 59 4/5 s.	Monarchos	Jorge Chavez	2001		Affirmed	Steve Cauthen	1978
2m.	Northern Dancer	Bill Hartack	1964		Lucky Debonair	Bill Shoemaker	1965
2m. 1/5 s.	Spend a Buck	Angel Cordero Jr.	1985	2m. 1 2/5 s.	Whirlaway	Eddie Arcaro	1941
2m. 2/5 s.	Decidedly	Bill Hartack	1962		Barbaro	Edgar Prado	2006
2m. 3/5 s.	Proud Clarion	Robert Ussery	1967	2m. 1 3/5 s.	Bold Forbes	Angel Cordero Jr.	1976
2m. 1 s.	Funny Cide	Jose Santos	2003		Hill Gail	Eddie Arcaro	1952
	War Emblem	Victor Espinoza	2002		Middleground	William Boland	1950
	Fusaichi Pegasus	Kent Desormeaux	2000				
	Grindstone	Jerry Bailey	1996				

Preakness Stakes

Pimlico Race Course, Baltimore, MD; inaug. 1873; distance 1-3/16 mi. 3-year-olds.
Best time: 1:53 2/5, by Tank's Prospect (1985), and Louis Quatorze (1996), and Curlin (2007).

Year	Winner	Jockey	Year	Winner	Jockey	Year	Winner	Jockey
1873	Survivor	G. Barbee	1920	Man o' War	C. Kummer	1965	Tom Rolfe	R. Turcotte
1874	Culpepper	M. Donohue	1921	Broomspun	F. Coltiletti	1966	Kauai King	D. Brumfield
1875	Tom Ochiltree	L. Hughes	1922	Pillory	L. Morris	1967	Damascus	W. Shoemaker
1876	Shirley	G. Barbee	1923	Vigil	B. Marinelli	1968	Forward Pass	I. Valenzuela
1877	Cloverbrook	C. Holloway	1924	Nellie Morse	J. Merimee	1969	Majestic Prince	W. Hartack
1878	Duke of Magenta	C. Holloway	1925	Coventry	C. Kummer	1970	Personality	E. Belmonte
1879	Harold	L. Hughes	1926	Display	J. Malben	1971	Canonero II	G. Avila
1880	Grenada	L. Hughes	1927	Bostonian	A. Abel	1972	Bee Bee Bee	E. Nelson
1881	Saunterer	W. Costello	1928	Victorian	R. Workman	1973	Secretariat	R. Turcotte
1882	Vanguard	W. Costello	1929	Dr. Freeland	L. Schaefer	1974	Little Current	M. Rivera
1883	Jacobus	G. Barbee	1930	Gallant Fox	E. Sande	1975	Master Derby	D. McHargue
1884	Knight of Ellerslie	S. H. Fisher	1931	Mate	G. Ellis	1976	Elocutionist	J. Lively
1885	Tecumseh	J. McLaughlin	1932	Burgoo King	E. James	1977	Seattle Slew	J. Cruguet
1886	The Bard	S. H. Fisher	1933	Head Play	C. Kurtsinger	1978	Affirmed	S. Cauthen
1887	Dunboyne	W. Donohue	1934	High Quest	R. Jones	1979	Spectacular Bid	R. Franklin
1888	Refund	F. Littlefield	1935	Omaha	W. Saunders	1980	Codex	A. Cordero
1889	Buddhist	G. Anderson	1936	Bold Venture	G. Woolf	1981	Pleasant Colony	J. Velasquez
1890	Montague	W. Martin	1937	War Admiral	C. Kurtsinger	1982	Aloma's Ruler	J. Kaenel
1894	Assignee	F. Taral	1938	Dauber	M. Peters	1983	Deputed	D. Miller
1895	Belmar	F. Taral	1939	Challedon	G. Seabo		Testamony	
1896	Margrave	H. Griffin	1940	Bimelech	F.A. Smith	1984	Gate Dancer	A. Cordero
1897	Paul Kauvar	C. Thorpe	1941	Whirlaway	E. Arcaro	1985	Tank's Prospect	P. Day
1898	Sly Fox	W. Simms	1942	Alsab	B. James	1986	Snow Chief	A. Solis
1899	Half Time	R. Clawson	1943	Count Fleet	J. Longden	1987	Alysheba	C. McCarron
1900	Hindus	H. Spencer	1944	Pensive	C. McCreary	1988	Risen Star	E. Delahoussaye
1901	The Parader	F. Landry	1945	Polynesian	W.D. Wright	1989	Sunday Silence	P. Valenzuela
1902	Old England	L. Jackson	1946	Assault	W. Mehrtens	1990	Summer Squall	P. Day
1903	Flocarline	W. Gannon	1947	Faultless	D. Dodson	1991	Hansel	J. Bailey
1904	Bryn Mawr	E. Hildebrand	1948	Citation	E. Arcaro	1992	Pine Bluff	C. McCarron
1905	Cairngorm	W. Davis	1949	Capot	T. Atkinson	1993	Prairie Bayou	M. Smith
1906	Whimsical	W. Miller	1950	Hill Prince	E. Arcaro	1994	Tabasco Cat	P. Day
1907	Don Enrique	G. Mountain	1951	Bold	E. Arcaro	1995	Timber Country	P. Day
1908	Royal Tourist	E. Dugan	1952	Blue Man	C. McCreary	1996	Louis Quatorze	P. Day
1909	Effendi	W. Doyle	1953	Native Dancer	E. Guerin	1997	Silver Charm	G. Stevens
1910	Layminster	R. Estep	1954	Hasty Road	J. Adams	1998	Real Quiet	K. Desormeaux
1911	Watervale	E. Dugan	1955	Nashua	E. Arcaro	1999	Charismatic	C. Antley
1912	Colonel Holloway	C. Turner	1956	Fabius	W. Hartack	2000	Red Bullet	J. Bailey
1913	Buskin	J. Butwell	1957	Bold Ruler	E. Arcaro	2001	Point Given	G. Stevens
1914	Holiday	A. Schuttinger	1958	Tim Tam	I. Valenzuela	2002	War Emblem	V. Espinoza
1915	Rhine Maiden	D. Hoffman	1959	Royal Orbit	W. Harmatz	2003	Funny Cide	J. Santos
1916	Damrosch	L. McAtee	1960	Bally Ache	R. Ussery	2004	Smarty Jones	S. Elliot
1917	Kalitan	E. Haynes	1961	Carry Back	J. Sellers	2005	Afleet Alex	J. Rose
1918*	War Cloud	J. Loftus	1962	Greek Money	J.L. Rotz	2006	Bernardini	J. Castellano
	Jack Hare Jr	C. Peak	1963	Candy Spots	W. Shoemaker	2007	Curlin	R. Albarado
1919	Sir Barton	J. Loftus	1964	Northern Dancer	W. Hartack			

*Horses ran in 2 divisions.

Belmont Stakes

Belmont Park, Elmont, NY; inaug. 1867; distance 1-1/2 mi. 3-year-olds. Best time: 2:24, Secretariat, 1973; 2006 time: 2:28.74.

Year	Winner	Jockey	Year	Winner	Jockey	Year	Winner	Jockey
1867	Ruthless	J. Gilpatrick	1904	Delhi	G. Odom	1943	Count Fleet	J. Longden
1868	General Duke	R. Swim	1905	Tanya	E. Hildebrand	1944	Bounding Home	G. L. Smith
1869	Fenian	C. Miller	1906	Burgomaster	L. Lyne	1945	Pavot	E. Arcaro
1870	Kingfisher	W. Dick	1907	Peter Pan	G. Mountain	1946	Assault	W. Mehrtens
1871	Harry Bassett	W. Miller	1908	Colin	J. Notter	1947	Phalanx	R. Donoso
1872	Joe Daniels	J. Rowe	1909	Joe Madden	E. Dugan	1948	Citation	E. Arcaro
1873	Springbok	J. Rowe	1910	Sweep	J. Butwell	1949	Capot	T. Atkinson
1874	Saxon	G. Barbee	1913	Prince Eugene	R. Troxler	1950	Middleground	W. Boland
1875	Calvin	R. Swim	1914	Luke McLuke	M. Buxton	1951	Counterpoint	D. Gorman
1876	Algerine	W. Donohue	1915	The Finn	G. Byrne	1952	One Count	E. Arcaro
1877	Cloverbrook	C. Holloway	1916	Friar Rock	E. Haynes	1953	Native Dancer	E. Guerin
1878	Duke of Magenta	L. Hughes	1917	Hourless	J. Butwell	1954	High Gun	E. Guerin
1879	Spendthrift	S. Evans	1918	Johren	F. Robinson	1955	Nashua	E. Arcaro
1880	Grenada	L. Hughes	1919	Sir Barton	J. Loftus	1956	Needles	D. Erb
1881	Saunterer	T. Costello	1920	Man o' War	C. Kummer	1957	Gallant Man	W. Shoemaker
1882	Forester	J. McLaughlin	1921	Grey Lag	E. Sande	1958	Cavan	P. Anderson
1883	George Kinney	J. McLaughlin	1922	Pillory	C. H. Miller	1959	Sword Dancer	W. Shoemaker
1884	Panique	J. McLaughlin	1923	Zev	E. Sande	1960	Celtic Ash	W. Hartack
1885	Tyrant	P. Duffy	1924	Mad Play	E. Sande	1961	Sherluck	B. Baeza
1886	Inspector	J. McLaughlin	1925	American Flag	A. Johnson	1962	Jaipur	W. Shoemaker
1887	Hanover	J. McLaughlin	1926	Crusader	A. Johnson	1963	Chateaugay	B. Baeza
1888	Sir Dixon	J. McLaughlin	1927	Chance Shot	E. Sande	1964	Quadrangle	M. Ycaza
1889	Eric	W. Hayward	1928	Vito	C. Kummer	1965	Hail to All	J. Sellers
1890	Burlington	S. Barnes	1929	Blue Larkspur	M. Garner	1966	Amberoid	W. Boland
1891	Foxford	E. Garrison	1930	Gallant Fox	E. Sande	1967	Damascus	W. Shoemaker
1892	Patron	W. Hayward	1931	Twenty Grand	C. Kurtsinger	1968	Stage Door Johnny	H. Gustines
1893	Comanche	W. Simms	1932	Faireno	T. Malley	1969	Arts and Letters	B. Baeza
1894	Henry of Navarre	W. Simms	1933	Hurryoff	M. Garner	1970	High Echelon	J. L. Rotz
1895	Belmar	F. Taral	1934	Peace Chance	W. D. Wright	1971	Pass Catcher	W. Blum
1896	Hastings	H. Griffin	1935	Omaha	W. Saunders	1972	Riva Ridge	R. Turcotte
1897	Scottish Chieftain	J. Scherrer	1936	Granville	J. Stout	1973	Secretariat	R. Turcotte
1898	Bowling Brook	F. Littlefield	1937	War Admiral	C. Kurtsinger	1974	Little Current	M. Rivera
1899	Jean Bereaud	R. R. Clawson	1938	Pasteurized	J. Stout	1975	Avatar	W. Shoemaker
1900	Ildrim	N. Turner	1939	Johnstown	J. Stout	1976	Bold Forbes	A. Cordero
1901	Commando	H. Spencer	1940	Bimelech	F.A. Smith	1977	Seattle Slew	J. Cruguet
1902	Masterman	J. Bullman	1941	Whirlaway	E. Arcaro	1978	Affirmed	S. Cauthen
1903	Africander	J. Bullman	1942	Shut Out	E. Arcaro	1979	Coastal	R. Hernandez

Year	Winner	Jockey	Year	Winner	Jockey	Year	Winner	Jockey
1980	Temperence Hill	E. Maple	1990	Go and Go	M. Kinane	1999	Lemon Drop Kid	J. Santos
1981	Summing	G. Martens	1991	Hansel	J. Bailey	2000	Commendable	P. Day
1982	Conquistador Cielo	L. Pincay	1992	A.P. Indy	E. Delahoussaye	2001	Point Given	G. Stevens
1983	Caveat	L. Pincay	1993	Colonial Affair	J. Krone	2002	Sarava	E. Prado
1984	Swale	L. Pincay	1994	Tabasco Cat	P. Day	2003	Empire Maker	J. Bailey
1985	Creme Fraiche	E. Maple	1995	Thunder Gulch	G. Stevens	2004	Birdstone	E. Prado
1986	Danzig Connection	M. McCarron	1996	Editor's Note	R. Douglas	2005	Afleet Alex	J. Rose
1987	Bet Twice	C. Perret	1997	Touch Gold	C. McCarron	2006	Jazil	F. Jara
1988	Risen Star	E. Delahoussaye	1998	Victory Gallop	G. Stevens	2007	Rags to Riches	J. Velazquez
1989	Easy Goer	P. Day						

Annual Leading Jockey — Money Won[1]
(as of Dec. 19, 2006)

Year	Jockey	Earnings	Year	Jockey	Earnings	Year	Jockey	Earnings
1957	Bill Hartack	$3,060,501	1974	Laffit Pincay, Jr.	$4,251,060	1991	Chris McCarron	$14,441,083
1958	Willie Shoemaker	2,961,693	1975	Braulio Baeza	3,695,198	1992	Kent Desormeaux	14,193,006
1959	Willie Shoemaker	2,843,133	1976	Angel Cordero, Jr.	4,709,500	1993	Mike Smith	14,024,815
1960	Willie Shoemaker	2,123,961	1977	Steve Cauthen	6,151,750	1994	Mike Smith	15,979,820
1961	Willie Shoemaker	2,690,819	1978	Darrel McHargue	6,029,885	1995	Jerry Bailey	16,311,876
1962	Willie Shoemaker	2,916,844	1979	Laffit Pincay, Jr.	8,193,535	1996	Jerry Bailey	19,465,376
1963	Willie Shoemaker	2,526,925	1980	Chris McCarron	7,663,300	1997	Jerry Bailey	18,320,743
1964	Willie Shoemaker	2,649,553	1981	Chris McCarron	8,397,604	1998	Gary Stevens	19,622,855
1965	Braulio Baeza	2,582,702	1982	Angel Cordero, Jr.	9,483,590	1999	Pat Day	18,092,845
1966	Braulio Baeza	2,951,022	1983	Angel Cordero, Jr.	10,116,697	2000	Pat Day	17,479,838
1967	Braulio Baeza	3,088,888	1984	Chris McCarron	12,045,813	2001	Jerry Bailey	22,597,720
1968	Braulio Baeza	2,835,108	1985	Laffit Pincay, Jr.	13,353,299	2002	Jerry Bailey	22,871,814
1969	Jorge Velasquez	2,542,315	1986	Jose Santos	11,329,297	2003	Jerry Bailey	22,829,570
1970	Laffit Pincay, Jr.	2,626,526	1987	Jose Santos	12,375,433	2004	John R. Velazquez	22,248,661
1971	Laffit Pincay, Jr.	3,784,377	1988	Jose Santos	14,877,298	2005	John R. Velazquez	20,770,272
1972	Laffit Pincay, Jr.	3,225,827	1989	Jose Santos	13,838,389	2006	Edgar Prado	19,604,413
1973	Laffit Pincay, Jr.	4,093,492	1990	Gary Stevens	13,881,198			

(1) Total earnings for all horses that jockey raced in year listed; does not reflect jockey's earnings.

Breeders' Cup World Thoroughbred Championships

The Breeders' Cup was inaugurated in 1984 and consists of 7 races at one track on one day late in the year to determine Thoroughbred racing's champion contenders. It has been held at the following locations:

Year	Location	Year	Location	Year	Location	Year	Location
1984	Hollywood Park, CA	1990	Belmont Park, NY	1996	Woodbine Racetrack, Ontario	2001	Belmont Park, NY
1985	Aqueduct Racetrack, NY	1991	Churchill Downs, KY			2002	Arlington Park, IL
1986	Santa Anita Park, CA	1992	Gulfstream Park, FL	1997	Hollywood Park, CA	2003	Santa Anita Park, CA
1987	Hollywood Park, CA	1993	Santa Anita Park, CA	1998	Churchill Downs, KY	2004	Lone Star Park, TX
1988	Churchill Downs, KY	1994	Churchill Downs, KY	1999	Gulfstream Park, FL	2005	Belmont Park, NY
1989	Gulfstream Park, FL	1995	Belmont Park, NY	2000	Churchill Downs, KY	2006	Monmouth Park, NJ

Juvenile
Distances: 1 mi 1984-85, 1987; 1-1/16 mi 1986 and since 1988

Year	Horse	Jockey	Year	Horse	Jockey	Year	Horse	Jockey
1984	Chief's Crown	D. MacBeth	1992	Gilded Time	C. McCarron	2000	Macho Uno	J. Bailey
1985	Tasso	L. Pincay, Jr.	1993	Brocco	G. Stevens	2001	Johannesburg	M. Kinane
1986	Capote	L. Pincay, Jr.	1994	Timber Country	P. Day	2002	Vindication	M. Smith
1987	Success Express	J. Santos	1995	Unbridled's Song	M. Smith	2003	Action This Day	D. Flores
1588	Is It True	L. Pincay, Jr.	1996	Boston Harbor	J. Bailey	2004	Wilko	F. Dettori
1989	Rhythm	C. Perret	1997	Favorite Trick	P. Day	2005	Stevie Wonderboy	G. Gomez
1990	Fly So Free	J. Santos	1998	Answer Lively	J. Bailey	2006	Street Sense	C. Borel
1991	Arazi	P. Valenzuela	1999	Anees	G. Stevens			

Juvenile Fillies
Distances: 1 mi 1984-85, 1987; 1-1/16 mi 1986 and since 1988

Year	Horse	Jockey	Year	Horse	Jockey	Year	Horse	Jockey
1984	*Outstandingly	W. Guerra	1992	Eliza	P. Valenzuela	2000	Caressing	J. Velazquez
1985	Twilight Ridge	J. Velasquez	1993	Phone Chatter	L. Pincay, Jr.	2001	Tempera	D. Flores
1986	Brave Raj	P. Valenzuela	1994	Flanders	P. Day	2002	Storm Flag Flying	J. Velazquez
1987	Epitome	P. Day	1995	My Flag	J. Bailey	2003	Halfbridled	J. Krone
1988	Open Mind	A. Cordero, Jr.	1996	Storm Song	C. Perret	2004	Sweet Catomine	C. Nakatani
1989	Go for Wand	R. Romero	1997	Countess Diana	S. Sellers	2005	Folklore	E. Prado
1990	Meadow Star	J. Santos	1998	Silverbulletday	G. Stevens	2006	Dreaming of Anna	R. Douglas
1991	Pleasant Stage	E. Delahoussaye	1999	Cash Run	J. Bailey			

*By disqualification.

Sprint
Distance: 6 furlongs

Year	Horse	Jockey	Year	Horse	Jockey	Year	Horse	Jockey
1984	Eillo	C. Perret	1992	Thirty Slews	E. Delahoussaye	2000	Kona Gold	A. Solis
1985	Precisionist	C. McCarron	1993	Cardmania	E. Delahoussaye	2001	Squirtle Squirt	J. Bailey
1986	Smile	J. Vasquez	1994	Cherokee Run	M. Smith	2002	Orientate	J. Bailey
1987	Very Subtle	P. Valenzuela	1995	Desert Stormer	K. Desormeaux	2003	Cajun Beat	C. Velasquez
1988	Gulch	A. Cordero, Jr.	1996	Lit De Justice	C. Nakatani	2004	Speightstown	J. Velazquez
1989	Dancing Spree	A. Cordero, Jr.	1997	Elmhurst	C. Nakatani	2005	Silver Train	E. Prado
1990	Safely Kept	C. Perret	1998	Reraise	C. Nakatani	2006	Thor's Echo	C. Nakatani
1991	Sheikh Albadou	P. Eddery	1999	Artax	J. Chaves			

Mile

Year	Horse	Jockey	Year	Horse	Jockey	Year	Horse	Jockey
1984	Royal Heroine	F. Toro	1992	Lure	M. Smith	2000	War Chant	G. Stevens
1985	Cozzene	W. Guerra	1993	Lure	M. Smith	2001	Val Royal	J. Valdivia Jr.
1986	Last Tycoon	Y. St-Martin	1994	Barathea	L. Dettori	2002	Domedriver	T. Thulliez
1987	Miesque	F. Head	1995	Ridgewood Pearl	J. Murtagh	2003	Six Perfections	J. Bailey
1988	Miesque	F. Head	1996	Da Hoss	G. Stevens	2004	Singletary	D. Flores
1989	Steinlen	J. Santos	1997	Spinning World	C. Asmussen	2005	Artie Schiller	G. Gomez
1990	Royal Academy	L. Piggott	1998	Da Hoss	J. Velazquez	2006	Miesque's Approval	E. Castro
1991	Opening Verse	P. Valenzuela	1999	Silic	C. Nakatani			

Filly & Mare Turf

Distances: 1-3/8 mi 1999-2000, 2004, 2006; 1-1/4 mi 2001-03, 2005

Year	Horse	Jockey	Year	Horse	Jockey	Year	Horse	Jockey
1999	Soaring Softly	J. Bailey	2002	Starine	J. Velazquez	2005	Intercontinental	R. Bejarano
2000	Perfect Sting	J. Bailey	2003	Islington	K. Fallon	2006	Ouija Board (GB)	F. Dettori
2001	Banks Hill	O. Peslier	2004	Ouija Board	K. Fallon			

Distaff

Distances: 1-1/4 mi 1984-87; 1-1/8 mi since 1988

Year	Horse	Jockey	Year	Horse	Jockey	Year	Horse	Jockey
1984	Princess Rooney	E. Delahoussaye	1992	Paseana	C. McCarron	2000	Spain	V. Espinoza
1985	Life's Magic	A. Cordero, Jr.	1993	Hollywood Wildcat	E. Delahoussaye	2001	Unbridled Elaine	P. Day
1986	Lady's Secret	P. Day	1994	One Dreamer	G. Stevens	2002	Azeri	M. Smith
1987	Sacahuista	R. Romero	1995	Inside Information	M. Smith	2003	Adoration	P. Valenzuela
1988	Personal Ensign	R. Romero	1996	Jewel Princess	C. Nakatani	2004	Ashado	J. Velazquez
1989	Bayakoa	L. Pincay, Jr.	1997	Ajina	M. Smith	2005	Pleasant Home	C. Velasquez
1990	Bayakoa	L. Pincay, Jr.	1998	Escena	G. Stevens	2006	Round Pond	E. Prado
1991	Dance Smartly	P. Day	1999	Beautiful Pleasure	J. Chaves			

Turf

Distance: 1-1/2 mi

Year	Horse	Jockey	Year	Horse	Jockey	Year	Horse	Jockey
1984	Lashkari	Y. St-Martin	1992	Fraise	P. Valenzuela	2000	Kalanisi	J. Murtagh
1985	Pebbles	P. Eddery	1993	Kotashaan	K. Desormeaux	2001	Fantastic Light	L. Dettori
1986	Manila	J. Santos	1994	Tikkanen	M. Smith	2002	High Chaparral	M. Kinane
1987	Theatrical	P. Day	1995	Northern Spur	C. McCarron	2003	(tie) High Chaparral	M. Kinane
1988	Great Communicator	R. Sibille	1996	Pilsudski	W. Swinburn		Johar	A. Solis
1989	Prized	E. Delahoussaye	1997	Chief Bearhart	J. Santos	2004	Better Talk Now	R. Dominguez
1990	In The Wings	G. Stevens	1998	Buck's Boy	S. Sellers	2005	Shirocco	C. Soumillon
1991	Miss Alleged	E. Legrix	1999	Daylami	L. Dettori	2006	Red Rocks	F. Dettori

Classic

Distance: 1-1/4 mi

Year	Horse	Jockey	Year	Horse	Jockey	Year	Horse	Jockey
1984	Wild Again	P. Day	1992	A.P. Indy	E. Delahoussaye	2000	Tiznow	C. McCarron
1985	Proud Truth	J. Velasquez	1993	Arcangues	J. Bailey	2001	Tiznow	C. McCarron
1986	Skywalker	L. Pincay, Jr.	1994	Concern	J. Bailey	2002	Volponi	P. Johnson
1987	Ferdinand	W. Shoemaker	1995	Cigar	J. Bailey	2003	Pleasantly Perfect	A. Solis
1988	Alysheba	C. McCarron	1996	Alphabet Soup	C. McCarron	2004	Ghostzapper	J. Castellano
1989	Sunday Silence	C. McCarron	1997	Skip Away	M. Smith	2005	Saint Liam	J. Bailey
1990	Unbridled	P. Day	1998	Awesome Again	P. Day	2006	Invasor	F. Jara
1991	Black Tie Affair	J. Bailey	1999	Cat Thief	P. Day			

Eclipse Awards

The Eclipse Awards, honoring the Horse of the Year and other champions of the sport, began in 1971 and are sponsored by the *Daily Racing Form*, the National Thoroughbred Racing Association, and the National Turf Writers Assn. Prior to 1971, the DRF (1936-70) and the TRA (1950-70) issued separate selections for Horse of the Year.

Eclipse Awards for 2006

Horse of the Year: Invasor
2-year-old male: Street Sense
2-year-old female: Dreaming of Anna
3-year-old male: Bernardini
3-year-old female: Wait a While
Older female: (4-year-olds & up) Fleet Indian

Older male: (4-year-olds & up) Invasor
Male turf horse: Miesque's Approval
Female turf horse: Ouija Board
Sprinter: Thor's Echo
Steeplechase horse: McDynamo
Trainer: Todd Pletcher

Jockey: Edgar Prado
Apprentice jockey: Julien Leparoux
Breeder: Adena Springs
Owner: Roy and Gretchen Jackson, Lael Stables; Sheik Mohammed bin Rashid al-Maktoum, Darley Stables

Horse of the Year

Year	Horse	Year	Horse	Year	Horse	Year	Horse
1936	Granville	1954	Native Dancer	1970	Fort Marcy (DRF)	1988	Alysheba
1937	War Admiral	1955	Nashua		Personality (TRA)	1989	Sunday Silence
1938	Seabiscuit	1956	Swaps	1971	Ack Ack	1990	Criminal Type
1939	Challedon	1957	Bold Ruler (DRF)	1972	Secretariat	1991	Black Tie Affair
1940	Challedon		Dedicate (TRA)	1973	Secretariat	1992	A.P. Indy
1941	Whirlaway	1958	Round Table	1974	Forego	1993	Kotashaan
1942	Whirlaway	1959	Sword Dancer	1975	Forego	1994	Holy Bull
1943	Count Fleet	1960	Kelso	1976	Forego	1995	Cigar
1944	Twilight Tear	1961	Kelso	1977	Seattle Slew	1996	Cigar
1945	Busher	1962	Kelso	1978	Affirmed	1997	Favorite Trick
1946	Assault	1963	Kelso	1979	Affirmed	1998	Skip Away
1947	Armed	1964	Kelso	1980	Spectacular Bid	1999	Charismatic
1948	Citation	1965	Roman Brother (DRF)	1981	John Henry	2000	Tiznow
1949	Capot		Moccasin (TRA)	1982	Conquistador Cielo	2001	Point Given
1950	Hill Prince	1966	Buckpasser	1983	All Along	2002	Azeri
1951	Counterpoint	1967	Damascus	1984	John Henry	2003	Mineshaft
1952	One Count (DRF)	1968	Dr. Fager	1985	Spend A Buck	2004	Ghostzapper
	Native Dancer (TRA)	1969	Arts and Letters	1986	Lady's Secret	2005	Saint Liam
1953	Tom Fool			1987	Ferdinand	2006	Invasor

HARNESS RACING
Harness Horse of the Year

(Chosen by the U.S. Trotting Assn. and the U.S. Harness Writers Assn.)

Year	Horse	Year	Horse	Year	Horse	Year	Horse
1947	Victory Song	1955	Scott Frost	1963	Speedy Scot	1971	Albatross
1948	Rodney	1956	Scott Frost	1964	Bret Hanover	1972	Albatross
1949	Good Time	1957	Torpid	1965	Bret Hanover	1973	Sir Dalrae
1950	Proximity	1958	Emily's Pride	1966	Bret Hanover	1974	Delmonica Hanover
1951	Pronto Don	1959	Bye Bye Byrd	1967	Nevele Pride	1975	Savoir
1952	Good Time	1960	Adios Butler	1968	Nevele Pride	1976	Keystone Ore
1953	Hi Lo's Forbes	1961	Adios Butler	1969	Nevele Pride	1977	Green Speed
1954	Stenographer	1962	Su Mac Lad	1970	Fresh Yankee	1978	Abercrombie

Year	Winner	Year	Winner	Year	Winner
1979	Niatross	1986	Forrest Skipper	1993	Staying Together	2000	Gallo Blue Chip
1980	Niatross	1987	Mack Lobell	1994	Cam's Card Shark	2001	Bunny Lake
1981	Fan Hanover	1988	Mack Lobell	1995	CR Kay Suzie	2002	Real Desire
1982	Cam Fella	1989	Matt's Scooter	1996	Continentalvictory	2003	No Pan Intended
1983	Cam Fella	1990	Beach Towel	1997	Malabar Man	2004	Rainbow Blue
1984	Fancy Crown	1991	Precious Bunny	1998	Moni Maker	2005	Rocknroll Hanover
1985	Nihilator	1992	Artsplace	1999	Moni Maker	2006	Glidemaster

The Hambletonian (3-year-old trotters)

Year	Winner	Driver	Year	Winner	Driver
1965	Egyptian Candor	Del Cameron	1986	Nuclear Kosmos	Ulf Thoresen
1966	Kerry Way	Frank Ervin	1987	Mack Lobell	John Campbell
1967	Speedy Streak	Del Cameron	1988	Armbro Goal	John Campbell
1968	Nevele Pride	Stanley Dancer	1989	Park Avenue Joe	Ron Waples
1969	Lindy's Pride	Howard Beissinger	1990	Harmonious	John Campbell
1970	Timothy T	John Simpson Sr.	1991	Giant Victory	Jack Moiseyev
1971	Speedy Crown	Howard Beissinger	1992	Alf Palema	Mickey McNicholl
1972	Super Bowl	Stanley Dancer	1993	American Winner	Ron Pierce
1973	Flirth	Ralph Baldwin	1994	Victory Dream	Michel Lachance
1974	Christopher T	Bill Haughton	1995	Tagliabue	John Campbell
1975	Bonefish	Stanley Dancer	1996	Continental-victory	Michel Lachance
1976	Steve Lobell	Bill Haughton	1997	Malabar Man	Malvern Burroughs
1977	Green Speed	Bill Haughton	1998	Muscles Yankee	John Campbell
1978	Speedy Somolli	Howard Beissinger	1999	Self Possessed	Mike Lachance
1979	Legend Hanover	George Sholty	2000	Yankee Paco	Trevor Ritchie
1980	Burgomeister	Bill Haughton	2001	Scarlet Knight	Stefan Melander
1981	Shiaway St. Pat	Ray Remmen	2002	Chip Chip Hooray	Eric Ledford
1982	Speed Bowl	Tommy Haughton	2003	Amigo Hall	Mike Lachance
1983	Duenna	Stanley Dancer	2004	Windsong's Legacy	Trond Smedshammer
1984	Historic Freight	Ben Webster	2005	Vivid Photo	Roger Hammer
1985	Prakas	Bill O'Donnell	2006	Glidemaster	John Campbell

BOWLING
Professional Bowlers Association
PBA Tournament of Champions, 1965-2007[1]

Year	Winner	Year	Winner	Year	Winner	Year	Winner
1965	Billy Hardwick	1975	Dave Davis	1985	Mark Williams	1996	Dave D'Entremont
1966	Wayne Zahn	1976	Marshall Holman	1986	Marshall Holman	1997	John Gant
1967	Jim Stefanich	1977	Mike Berlin	1987	Pete Weber	1998	Bryan Goebel
1968	Dave Davis	1978	Earl Anthony	1988	Mark Williams	1999	Jason Couch
1969	Jim Godman	1979	George Pappas	1989	Del Ballard, Jr.	2000	Jason Couch
1970	Don Johnson	1980	Wayne Webb	1990	Dave Ferraro	2002	Jason Couch
1971	Johnny Petraglia	1981	Steve Cook	1991	David Ozio	2003	Patrick Healey Jr.
1972	Mike Durbin	1982	Mike Durbin	1992	Marc McDowell	2005	Steve Jaros
1973	Jim Godman	1983	Joe Berardi	1993	George Branham, 3rd	2006	Chris Barnes
1974	Earl Anthony	1984	Mike Durbin	1994	Norm Duke	2007	Tommy Jones

(1) No tournament held in 2001; the tournament now takes place in Apr. at the end of the PBA season (previously held in Dec.).

PBA Leading Money Winners

Total winnings are from PBA, ABC Masters, and BPAA All-Star tournaments only and do not include numerous other tournaments or earnings from special television shows and matches. In 2001, the PBA began an Oct.-Apr. season schedule. After 2000, year shown is the season ended.

Year	Bowler	Amount	Year	Bowler	Amount	Year	Bowler	Amount
1962	Don Carter	$49,972	1977	Mark Roth	$105,583	1992	Marc McDowell	$174,215
1963	Dick Weber	46,333	1978	Mark Roth	134,500	1993	Walter Ray Williams Jr.	296,370
1964	Bob Strampe	33,592	1979	Mark Roth	124,517	1994	Norm Duke	273,753
1965	Dick Weber	47,674	1980	Wayne Webb	116,700	1995	Mike Aulby	219,792
1966	Wayne Zahn	54,720	1981	Earl Anthony	164,735	1996	Walter Ray Williams Jr.	241,330
1967	Dave Davis	54,165	1982	Earl Anthony	134,760	1997	Walter Ray Williams Jr.	240,544
1968	Jim Stefanich	67,377	1983	Earl Anthony	135,605	1998	Walter Ray Williams Jr.	238,225
1969	Billy Hardwick	64,160	1984	Mark Roth	158,712	1999	Parker Bohn III	240,912
1970	Mike McGrath	52,049	1985	Mike Aulby	201,200	2000	Norm Duke	143,325
1971	Johnny Petraglia	85,065	1986	Walter Ray Williams Jr.	145,550	2002	Parker Bohn III	245,200
1972	Don Johnson	56,648	1987	Pete Weber	175,491	2003	Walter Ray Williams Jr.	419,700
1973	Don McCune	69,000	1988	Brian Voss	225,485	2004	Mika Koivuniemi	238,590
1974	Earl Anthony	99,585	1989	Mike Aulby	298,237	2005	Patrick Allen	350,740
1975	Earl Anthony	107,585	1990	Amleto Monacelli	204,775	2006	Tommy Jones	301,700
1976	Earl Anthony	110,833	1991	David Ozio	225,585	2007	Doug Kent	200,530

Leading PBA Averages by Year

Year	Bowler	Average	Year	Bowler	Average	Year	Bowler	Average
1962	Don Carter	212.84	1977	Mark Roth	218.17	1992	Dave Ferraro	219.70
1963	Billy Hardwick	210.34	1978	Mark Roth	219.83	1993	Walter Ray Williams Jr.	222.98
1964	Ray Bluth	210.51	1979	Mark Roth	221.66	1994	Norm Duke	222.83
1965	Dick Weber	211.89	1980	Earl Anthony	218.53	1995	Mike Aulby	225.49
1966	Wayne Zahn	208.66	1981	Mark Roth	216.69	1996	Walter Ray Williams Jr.	225.37
1967	Wayne Zahn	212.34	1982	Marshall Holman	212.84	1997	Walter Ray Williams Jr.	222.00
1968	Jim Stefanich	211.89	1983	Earl Anthony	216.64	1998	Walter Ray Williams Jr.	226.13
1969	Bill Hardwick	212.95	1984	Marshall Holman	213.91	1999	Parker Bohn III	228.04
1970	Nelson Burton Jr.	214.90	1985	Mark Baker	213.71	2000	Chris Barnes	220.93
1971	Don Johnson	213.97	1986	John Gant	214.37	2002	Parker Bohn III	221.54
1972	Don Johnson	215.29	1987	Marshall Holman	216.80	2003	Walter Ray Williams Jr.	224.94
1973	Earl Anthony	215.79	1988	Mark Roth	218.03	2004	Mika Koivuniemi	222.73
1974	Earl Anthony	219.39	1989	Pete Weber	215.43	2005	Walter Ray Williams Jr.	227.07
1975	Earl Anthony	219.06	1990	Amleto Monacelli	218.15	2006	Norm Duke	224.29
1976	Mark Roth	215.97	1991	Norm Duke	218.20	2007	Norm Duke	228.47

United States Bowling Congress

Formed Jan. 1, 2005, from a merger of the American Bowling Congress, Women's International Bowling Congress, the Young American Bowling Alliance, and USA Bowling. Before 2006, certified games and champions are for ABC only.

Most Certified 300 Games — Men
Note: As of Sept. 24, 2007.

Joe Jimenez, Saginaw, MI 88	Gordon Childers, Benton, AR 76	Warren Tam Wasson, Garland, TX . . 66
Chris Hayward, Toledo, OH 87	Jerry Kessler, Dayton, OH. 75	Randy Choat, Ladue, MO. 64
Jeff Carter, Springfield, IL. 86	Jack Kurent, Luzerne, PA 73	Leonard Reynoldt, Catskill, NY. 64
Jim Hosier, Wayne, NJ. 86	Ron Krippelcz, St. Louis 71	Ricky Fuller, Springfield, OH 64
John Delp III, West Lawn, PA. 85	Jim Tomek Jr., Camp Hill, PA 71	Robert Faragon, Albany, NY 63
Dean Wolf, Reading, PA 84	David Bingham, Brainard, NY 67	Jeff Jensen, Wichita, KS. 63
Frank Massengale Jr., Hixon, TN. . . . 82	John Chacko Jr., Larksville, PA. 66	Rick Graham, Lancaster, PA 63
Jeff Ripic, Endicott, NY. . . . . . /. . . . 81	Dale Strike, Saginaw, MI. 66	Shannon Buchan, Waterloo, IA 63

USBC Masters Tournament Champions

Year	Winner	Year	Winner	Year	Winner
1980	Neil Burton, St. Louis, MO	1990	Chris Warren, Dallas, TX	1999	Brian Boghosian, Middletown, CT
1981	Randy Lightfoot, St. Charles, MO	1991	Doug Kent, Canandaigua, NY	2000	Mlka Koivuniemi, Finland
1982	Joe Berardi, Brooklyn, NY	1992	Ken Johnson, N. Richmond Hills, TX	2001	Parker Bohn III, Jackson, NJ
1983	Mike Lastowski, Havre de Grace, MD	1993	Norm Duke, Oklahoma City, OK	2002	Brett Wolfe, Reno, NV
1984	Earl Anthony, Dublin, CA	1994	Steve Fehr, Cincinnati, OH	2003	Bryon Smith, Roseburg, OR
1985	Steve Wunderlich, St. Louis, MO	1995	Mike Aulby, Indianapolis, IN	2004	Walter Ray Williams Jr., FL (Jan.);
1986	Mark Fahy, Chicago, IL	1996	Ernie Schlegel, Vancouver, WA		Danny Wiseman, MD (Oct.)
1987	Rick Steelsmith, Wichita, KS	1997	Jason Queen, Decatur, IL	2005	Mike Scroggins, Amarillo, TX
1988	Del Ballard Jr., Richardson, TX	1998	Mike Aulby, Indianapolis, IN	2006	Doug Kent, Newark, NY
1989	Mike Aulby, Indianapolis, IN				

Open Champions, 2007

Regular Singles: Chip Aki, Nicholasville, KY
Regular Doubles: Jonathan Masur, West Orange, NJ & Jeffrey Butler, Garfield, NJ
Regular All-Events: Mike Rose Jr., West Henrietta, NY
Regular Team: Lava Lanes, Medford, OR
Team All-Events: Browning Pontiac, Eminence, KY

Classified Singles: Lenny Boogaard, Osakis, MN
Classified Doubles: Frank Smyle Jr., Reeder, ND & Jesse Smyle, Bowman, ND
Classified All-Events: Samuel Murray, Toccoa, GA
Classified Team: Roberts Repair, Pontiac, IL

USBC Queens and Open Champions, 2007
Note: Formerly WIBC Queens.

Queens Tournament: Kelly Kulick, Union, NJ
Classic Singles: Tiffany Stanbrough, Oklahoma City, OK
Classic Doubles: Liz Johnson, Cheektowaga, NY & Susan Jeziorski, Buffalo, NY
Classic All-Events: Wendy Macperson, Henderson, NV

Classic Team: Ebonite Bowlers Map, Roseville, CA
Div. I Singles: Lil Holguin, Las Cruces, NM
Div. I Doubles: Kandace Little & Celeste Reynolds, Bronx, NY
Div. I All-Events: LaVonnie Giles, Waldorf, MD
Div. I Team: Ladies on the Roll I, Alexandria, VA

Most Certified 300 Games — Women
Note: As of Sept. 24, 2007.

Altramese Webb, Detroit, MI 42	Tammy Jones, Decatur, IL 26	Mandy Wilson, Dayton, OH 21
Jodi Musto, Schenectady, NY 37	Anne-Marie Duggan, Edmond, OK 25	Jackie Mitskavich 21
Tish Johnson, Panorama City, CA 36	Jeanette Menacho, Sacramento, CA 24	Tiffany Stanbrough, Oklahoma City, OK 19
Marianne DiRupo, Succasunna, NJ . . . 31		Kim Adler, Palm City, FL 18
Dede Davidson, Woodland Hills, CA . . 30	Jeanne Naccarato, Tacoma, WA 23	Cindy Coburn-Carroll, Tonawanda, NY . 18
Shannon Duplantis, New Orleans, LA . 29	Cheryl Daniels, Detroit, MI 22	Charita Williams, Indianapolis, IN. 18
Leanne Hulsenberg, Roseville, CA . . . 28	Jodi Hughes, Greenville, SC 21	Liz Johnson, Cheektowaga, NY 18
Aleta Sill, Dearborn, MI 27	Carolyn Dorin-Ballard, N. Richland Hills, TX 21	Jodi Woessner, Oregon, OH 18
Debbie McMullen, Denver, CO. 27		

CHESS
World Chess Champions

Sources: U.S. Chess Federation; International Chess Federation (FIDE)
Official world champions since the title was first used are as follows:

1886-1894	Wilhelm Steinitz, Austria	1972-1975	Bobby Fischer, U.S. (b)
1894-1921	Emanuel Lasker, Germany	1975-1985	Anatoly Karpov, USSR
1921-1927	Jose R. Capablanca, Cuba	1985-2000	Garry Kasparov, USSR/Russia (c)
1927-1935	Alexander Alekhine, France	1993-1999	Anatoly Karpov, Russia (FIDE)
1935-1937	Max Euwe, Netherlands	1999-2000	Alexander Khalifman, Russia (FIDE)
1937-1946	Alexander Alekhine, France (a)	2000-02	Viswanathan Anand, India (FIDE)
1948-1957	Mikhail Botvinnik, USSR	2000-06	Vladimir Kramnik, Russia (classical) (d, e)
1957-1958	Vassily Smyslov, USSR	2002-04	Ruslan Ponomariov, Ukraine (FIDE)
1958-1959	Mikhail Botvinnik, USSR	2004-05	Rustam Kasimdzhanov, Uzbekistan (FIDE)
1960-1961	Mikhail Tal, USSR	2005-06	Veselin Topalov, Bulgaria (FIDE)
1961-1963	Mikhail Botvinnik, USSR	2006-07	Vladimir Kramnik, Russia (e)
1963-1969	Tigran Petrosian, USSR	2007-	Vishwanathan Anand
1969-1972	Boris Spassky, USSR		

(a) After Alekhine died in 1946, the title was vacant until 1948, when Botvinnik won the 1st world championship event sanctioned by FIDE. (b) Defaulted championship after refusing to accept FIDE rules for a championship match, Apr. 1975. (c) Kasparov broke with FIDE, Feb. 26, 1993. FIDE stripped Kasparov of his FIDE title Mar. 23. Kasparov then defeated Nigel Short of Great Britain in a world championship match played Sept.-Oct. 1993 under the auspices of a new organization the two had founded, the Professional Chess Association. FIDE held a replacement championship match between Anatoly Karpov (Russia) and Jan Timman (the Netherlands), which Karpov won in Nov. 1993. The PCA folded in 1995, but Kasparov was still considered the "classical" world champion. (d) In Nov. 2000, Vladimir Kramnik (Russia) defeated Garry Kasparov (Russia), for the classical world championship title in London. (e) Vladimir Kramnik, the classical world champion since 2000, and Veselin Topalov, FIDE champion since 2005, met at the world chess championship match in Elista, Russia, to compete for a unified championship, which Kramnik won Oct. 13, 2006. **Further information:** www.fide.com

FIGURE SKATING
U.S. and World Individual Champions, 1952-2007

U.S. Champions			World Champions	
MEN	**WOMEN**	**YEAR**	**MEN**	**WOMEN**
Dick Button	Tenley Albright	1952	Dick Button, U.S.	Jacqueline du Bief, France
Hayes Jenkins	Tenley Albright	1953	Hayes Jenkins, U.S.	Tenley Albright, U.S.
Hayes Jenkins	Tenley Albright	1954	Hayes Jenkins, U.S.	Gundi Busch, W. Germany
Hayes Jenkins	Tenley Albright	1955	Hayes Jenkins, U.S.	Tenley Albright, U.S.
Hayes Jenkins	Tenley Albright	1956	Hayes Jenkins, U.S.	Carol Heiss, U.S.
Dave Jenkins	Carol Heiss	1957	Dave Jenkins, U.S.	Carol Heiss, U.S.
Dave Jenkins	Carol Heiss	1958	Dave Jenkins, U.S.	Carol Heiss, U.S.
Dave Jenkins	Carol Heiss	1959	Dave Jenkins, U.S.	Carol Heiss, U.S.
Dave Jenkins	Carol Heiss	1960	Alain Giletti, France	Carol Heiss, U.S.
Bradley Lord	Laurence Owen	1961	none	none
Monty Hoyt	Barbara Roles Pursley	1962	Don Jackson, Canada	Sjoukje Dijkstra, Netherlands
Tommy Litz	Lorraine Hanlon	1963	Don McPherson, Canada	Sjoukje Dijkstra, Netherlands
Scott Allen	Peggy Fleming	1964	Manfred Schnelldorfer, W. Germany	Sjoukje Dijkstra, Netherlands
Gary Visconti	Peggy Fleming	1965	Alain Calmat, France	Petra Burka, Canada
Scott Allen	Peggy Fleming	1966	Emmerich Danzer, Austria	Peggy Fleming, U.S.
Gary Visconti	Peggy Fleming	1967	Emmerich Danzer, Austria	Peggy Fleming, U.S.
Tim Wood	Peggy Fleming	1968	Emmerich Danzer, Austria	Peggy Fleming, U.S.
Tim Wood	Janet Lynn	1969	Tim Wood, U.S.	Gabriele Seyfert, E. Germany
Tim Wood	Janet Lynn	1970	Tim Wood, U.S.	Gabriele Seyfert, E. Germany
John Misha Petkevich	Janet Lynn	1971	Ondrej Nepela, Czechoslovakia	Beatrix Schuba, Austria
Ken Shelley	Janet Lynn	1972	Ondrej Nepela, Czechoslovakia	Beatrix Schuba, Austria
Gordon McKellen, Jr.	Janet Lynn	1973	Ondrej Nepela, Czechoslovakia	Karen Magnussen, Canada
Gordon McKellen, Jr.	Dorothy Hamill	1974	Jan Hoffmann, E. Germany	Christine Errath, E. Germany
Gordon McKellen, Jr.	Dorothy Hamill	1975	Sergei Volkov, USSR	Dianne de Leeuw, Neth.-U.S.
Terry Kubicka	Dorothy Hamill	1976	John Curry, Gr. Britain	Dorothy Hamill, U.S.
Charles Tickner	Linda Fratianne	1977	Vladimir Kovalev, USSR	Linda Fratianne, U.S.
Charles Tickner	Linda Fratianne	1978	Charles Tickner, U.S.	Anett Poetzsch, E. Germany
Charles Tickner	Linda Fratianne	1979	Vladimir Kovalev, USSR	Linda Fratianne, U.S.
Charles Tickner	Linda Fratianne	1980	Jan Hoffmann, E. Germany	Anett Poetzsch, E. Germany
Scott Hamilton	Elaine Zayak	1981	Scott Hamilton, U.S.	Denise Biellmann, Switzerland
Scott Hamilton	Rosalynn Sumners	1982	Scott Hamilton, U.S.	Elaine Zayak, U.S.
Scott Hamilton	Rosalynn Sumners	1983	Scott Hamilton, U.S.	Rosalynn Sumners, U.S.
Scott Hamilton	Rosalynn Sumners	1984	Scott Hamilton, U.S.	Katarina Witt, E. Germany
Brian Boitano	Tiffany Chin	1985	Aleksandr Fadeev, USSR	Katarina Witt, E. Germany
Brian Boitano	Debi Thomas	1986	Brian Boitano, U.S.	Debi Thomas, U.S.
Brian Boitano	Jill Trenary	1987	Brian Orser, Canada	Katarina Witt, E. Germany
Brian Boitano	Debi Thomas	1988	Brian Boitano, U.S.	Katarina Witt, E. Germany
Christopher Bowman	Jill Trenary	1989	Kurt Browning, Canada	Midori Ito, Japan
Todd Eldredge	Jill Trenary	1990	Kurt Browning, Canada	Jill Trenary, U.S.
Todd Eldredge	Tonya Harding	1991	Kurt Browning, Canada	Kristi Yamaguchi, U.S.
Christopher Bowman	Kristi Yamaguchi	1992	Viktor Petrenko, Ukraine	Kristi Yamaguchi, U.S.
Scott Davis	Nancy Kerrigan	1993	Kurt Browning, Canada	Oksana Baiul, Ukraine
Scott Davis	vacant[1]	1994	Elvis Stojko, Canada	Yuka Sato, Japan
Todd Eldredge	Nicole Bobek	1995	Elvis Stojko, Canada	Chen Lu, China
Rudy Galindo	Michelle Kwan	1996	Todd Eldredge, U.S.	Michelle Kwan, U.S.
Todd Eldredge	Tara Lipinski	1997	Elvis Stojko, Canada	Tara Lipinski, U.S.
Todd Eldredge	Michelle Kwan	1998	Alexei Yagudin, Russia	Michelle Kwan, U.S.
Michael Weiss	Michelle Kwan	1999	Alexei Yagudin, Russia	Maria Butyrskaya, Russia
Michael Weiss	Michelle Kwan	2000	Alexei Yagudin, Russia	Michelle Kwan, U.S.
Timothy Goebel	Michelle Kwan	2001	Yevgeny Plushenko, Russia	Michelle Kwan, U.S.
Todd Eldredge	Michelle Kwan	2002	Alexei Yagudin, Russia	Irina Slutskaya, Russia
Michael Weiss	Michelle Kwan	2003	Yevgeny Plushenko, Russia	Michelle Kwan, U.S.
Johnny Weir	Michelle Kwan	2004	Yevgeny Plushenko, Russia	Shizuka Arakawa, Japan
Johnny Weir	Michelle Kwan	2005	Stephane Lambiel, Switzerland	Irina Slutskaya, Russia
Johnny Weir	Sasha Cohen	2006	Stephane Lambiel, Switzerland	Kimmie Meissner, U.S.
Evan Lysacek	Kimmie Meissner	2007	Brian Joubert, France	Miki Ando, Japan

(1) Tonya Harding was stripped of title.

SKIING
World Cup Alpine Champions, 1967-2007

Men

1967	Jean Claude Killy, France	1994	Kjetil Andre Aamodt, Norway
1968	Jean Claude Killy, France	1995	Alberto Tomba, Italy
1969	Karl Schranz, Austria	1996	Lasse Kjus, Norway
1970	Karl Schranz, Austria	1997	Luc Alphand, France
1971	Gustavo Thoeni, Italy	1998	Hermann Maier, Austria
1972	Gustavo Thoeni, Italy	1999	Lasse Kjus, Norway
1973	Gustavo Thoeni, Italy	2000	Hermann Maier, Austria
1974	Piero Gros, Italy	2001	Hermann Maier, Austria
1975	Gustavo Thoeni, Italy	2002	Stephan Eberharter, Austria
1976	Ingemar Stenmark, Sweden	2003	Stephan Eberharter, Austria
1977	Ingemar Stenmark, Sweden	2004	Hermann Maier, Austria
1978	Ingemar Stenmark, Sweden	2005	Bode Miller, U.S.
1979	Peter Luescher, Switzerland	2006	Benjamin Raich, Austria
1980	Andreas Wenzel, Liechtenstein	2007	Aksel Lund Svindal, Norway
1981	Phil Mahre, U.S.		
1982	Phil Mahre, U.S.		
1983	Phil Mahre, U.S.		
1984	Pirmin Zurbriggen, Switzerland		
1985	Marc Girardelli, Luxembourg		
1986	Marc Girardelli, Luxembourg		
1987	Pirmin Zurbriggen, Switzerland		
1988	Pirmin Zurbriggen, Switzerland		
1989	Marc Girardelli, Luxembourg		
1990	Pirmin Zurbriggen, Switzerland		
1991	Marc Girardelli, Luxembourg		
1992	Paul Accola, Switzerland		
1993	Marc Girardelli, Luxembourg		

Women

1967	Nancy Greene, Canada
1968	Nancy Greene, Canada
1969	Gertrud Gabl, Austria
1970	Michele Jacot, France
1971	Annemarie Proell, Austria
1972	Annemarie Proell, Austria
1973	Annemarie Proell, Austria
1974	Annemarie Proell, Austria
1975	Annemarie Proell, Austria
1976	Rose Mittermaier, W. Germany
1977	Lise-Marie Morerod, Switzerland
1978	Hanni Wenzel, Liechtenstein
1979	Annemarie Proell Moser, Austria
1980	Hanni Wenzel, Liechtenstein
1981	Marie-Theres Nadig, Switzerland
1982	Erika Hess, Switzerland
1983	Tamara McKinney, U.S.
1984	Erika Hess, Switzerland
1985	Michela Figini, Switzerland
1986	Maria Walliser, Switzerland
1987	Maria Walliser, Switzerland
1988	Michela Figini, Switzerland
1989	Vreni Schneider, Switzerland
1990	Petra Kronberger, Austria
1991	Petra Kronberger, Austria
1992	Petra Kronberger, Austria
1993	Anita Wachter, Austria
1994	Vreni Schneider, Switzerland
1995	Vreni Schneider, Switzerland
1996	Katja Seizinger, Germany
1997	Pernilla Wiberg, Sweden
1998	Katja Seizinger, Germany
1999	Alexandra Meissnitzer, Austria
2000	Renate Goetschl, Austria
2001	Janica Kostelic, Croatia
2002	Michaela Dorfmeister, Austria
2003	Janica Kostelic, Croatia
2004	Anja Paerson, Sweden
2005	Anja Paerson, Sweden
2006	Janica Kostelic, Croatia
2007	Nicole Hosp, Austria

WRESTLING
NCAA Division I Wrestling Champions, 1964-2007

Year	Champion	Year	Champion	Year	Champion	Year	Champion	Year	Champion
1964	Oklahoma State	1973	Iowa State	1982	Iowa	1991	Iowa	2000	Iowa
1965	Iowa State	1974	Oklahoma	1983	Iowa	1992	Iowa	2001	Minnesota
1966	Oklahoma State	1975	Iowa	1984	Iowa	1993	Iowa	2002	Minnesota
1967	Michigan State	1976	Iowa	1985	Iowa	1994	Oklahoma State	2003	Oklahoma State
1968	Oklahoma State	1977	Iowa State	1986	Iowa	1995	Iowa	2004	Oklahoma State
1969	Iowa State	1978	Iowa	1987	Iowa State	1996	Iowa	2005	Oklahoma State
1970	Iowa State	1979	Iowa	1988	Arizona State	1997	Iowa	2006	Oklahoma State
1971	Oklahoma State	1980	Iowa	1989	Oklahoma State	1998	Iowa	2007	Minnesota
1972	Iowa State	1981	Iowa	1990	Oklahoma State	1999	Iowa		

CYCLING
2007 Tour de France

Spain's Alberto Contador won the 104th Tour de France on July 29, 2007, completing the 2,205-mi race in 91 hours, 26 sec. The 2007 Tour began July 7 in London, England, and ended 20 stages later in Paris, France. The 24-year-old Contador, racing with the Discovery Channel team, was the youngest Tour winner since Jan Ullrich (1997). Contador's victory, just 23 sec. ahead of Australian cyclist Cadel Evans, marked the narrowest margin of victory since 1989, when Greg Lemond beat Laurent Fignon to the yellow jersey by just 8 sec.

The 2007 Tour, still shadowed by 2006 victor Floyd Landis's ongoing appeal of a positive drug test taken during the 2006 race, was again plagued by doping allegations. Alexandre Vinokourov, who had been the pre-race favorite, Cristian Moreni, and Patrik Sinkewitz failed drug tests during the Tour. Michael Rasmussen, who had been leading the race since July 15, was withdrawn by his Rabobank team after the 16th stage on July 25, over having missed 4 out-of-competition drug tests and lying about his whereabouts in the lead up to the Tour.

Tour de France Winners, 1980-2007

Year	Winner	Year	Winner	Year	Winner	Year	Winner
1980	Zoop Zoetemelk, The Netherlands	1987	Stephen Roche, Ireland	1994	Miguel Indurain, Spain	2001	Lance Armstrong, U.S.
		1988	Pedro Delgado, Spain	1995	Miguel Indurain, Spain	2002	Lance Armstrong, U.S.
1981	Bernard Hinault, France	1989	Greg LeMond, U.S.	1996	Bjarne Riis, Denmark	2003	Lance Armstrong, U.S.
1982	Bernard Hinault, France	1990	Greg LeMond, U.S.	1997	Jan Ullrich, Germany	2004	Lance Armstrong, U.S.
1983	Laurent Fignon, France	1991	Miguel Indurain, Spain	1998	Marco Pantani, Italy	2005	Lance Armstrong, U.S.
1984	Laurent Fignon, France	1992	Miguel Indurain, Spain	1999	Lance Armstrong, U.S.	2006	Oscar Pereiro, Spain*
1985	Bernard Hinault, France	1993	Miguel Indurain, Spain	2000	Lance Armstrong, U.S.	2007	Alberto Contador, Spain
1986	Greg LeMond, U.S.						

*Floyd Landis, U.S., was stripped of the title for doping Sept. 20, 2007. As of Sept. 30, 2007, Landis had not yet decided whether to appeal the ruling.

LACROSSE
NCAA Division I Lacrosse Champions 1982-2007

Year[1]	Men	Women	Year[1]	Men	Women	Year[1]	Men	Women
1982	North Carolina	Massachusetts	1991	North Carolina	Virginia	2000	Syracuse	Maryland
1983	Syracuse	Delaware	1992	Princeton	Maryland	2001	Princeton	Maryland
1984	Johns Hopkins	Temple	1993	Syracuse	Virginia	2002	Syracuse	Princeton
1985	Johns Hopkins	New Hampshire	1994	Princeton	Princeton	2003	Virginia	Princeton
1986	North Carolina	Maryland	1995	Syracuse	Maryland	2004	Syracuse	Virginia
1987	Johns Hopkins	Penn St.	1996	Princeton	Maryland	2005	Johns Hopkins	Northwestern
1988	Syracuse	Temple	1997	Princeton	Maryland	2006	Virginia	Northwestern
1989	Syracuse	Penn St.	1998	Princeton	Maryland	2007	Johns Hopkins	Northwestern
1990	vacated	Harvard	1999	Virginia	Maryland			

(1) NCAA Championships began in 1971 for men, in 1982 for women.

SWIMMING
World Swimming Records

Long course (50 m), as of Apr. 1, 2007.

Men's Records

Distance	Time	Holder	Country	Where made	Date
Freestyle					
50 meters	0:21.64	Alexander Popov	Russia	Moscow, Russia	June 16, 2000
100 meters	0:47.84	Pieter van den Hoogenband	Netherlands	Sydney, Australia	Sept. 19, 2000
200 meters	1:43.86	Michael Phelps	U.S.	Melbourne, Australia	Mar. 27, 2007
400 meters	3:40.08	Ian Thorpe	Australia	Manchester, England	July 30, 2002
800 meters	7:38.65	Grant Hackett	Australia	Montreal, Canada	July 27, 2005
1,500 meters	14:34.56	Grant Hackett	Australia	Fukuoka, Japan	July 29, 2001
Breaststroke					
50 meters	0:27.18	Oleg Lisogor	Ukraine	Berlin, Germany	Aug. 2, 2002
100 meters	0:59.13	Brendan Hansen	U.S.	Irvine CA	Aug. 1, 2006
200 meters	2:08.50	Brendan Hansen	U.S.	Victoria, Canada	Aug. 20, 2006
Butterfly					
50 meters	0:22.96	Roland Schoeman	Russia	Montreal, Canada	July 25, 2005
100 meters	0:50.40	Ian Crocker	U.S.	Montreal, Canada	July 30, 2005
200 meters	1:52.09	Michael Phelps	U.S.	Melbourne, Australia	Mar. 28, 2007
Backstroke					
50 meters	0:24.80	Thomas Rupprath	Germany	Barcelona, Spain	July 27, 2003
100 meters	0:52.98	Aaron Peirsol	U.S.	Melbourne, Australia	Mar. 27, 2007
200 meters	1:54.32	Ryan Lochte	U.S.	Melbourne, Australia	Mar 30, 2007
Individual Medley					
200 meters	1:54.98	Michael Phelps	U.S.	Melbourne, Australia	Mar. 29, 2007
400 meters	4:06.22	Michael Phelps	U.S.	Melbourne, Australia	Apr. 1, 2007
Medley Relay					
400 m. (4×100)	3:30.68	Peirsol, Hansen, Crocker, Lezak	U.S.	Athens, Greece	Aug. 21, 2004
Freestyle Relays					
400 m. (4×100)	3:12.46	Phelps, Walker, Jones, Lezak	U.S.	Victoria, Canada	Aug. 19, 2006
800 m. (4×200)	7:03.24	Phelps, Lochte, Keller, Vanderkaay	U.S.	Melbourne, Australia	Mar. 30, 2007

Women's Records

Freestyle

Distance	Time	Holder	Country	Where made	Date
50 meters	0:24.13	Inge de Bruijn	Netherlands	Sydney, Australia	Sept. 22, 2000
100 meters	0:53.30	Britta Steffen	Germany	Budapest, Hungary	Aug. 2, 2006
200 meters	1:55.52	Laure Manaudou	France	Melbourne, Australia	Mar. 28, 2007
400 meters	4:02.13	Laure Manaudou	France	Budapest, Hungary	Aug. 6, 2006
800 meters	8:16.22	Janet Evans	U.S.	Tokyo, Japan	Aug. 20, 1989
1,500 meters	15:42.54	Kate Ziegler	U.S.	Mission Viejo, CA	June 17, 2007

Breaststroke

50 meters	0:30.31	Jade Edmistone	Australia	Melbourne, Australia	Jan. 30, 2006
100 meters	1:05.09	Leisel Jones	Australia	Melbourne, Australia	Mar. 17, 2006
200 meters	2:20.54	Leisel Jones	Australia	Melbourne, Australia	Feb. 1, 2006

Butterfly

50 meters	0:25.46	Therese Alshammar	Sweden	Barcelona, Spain	June 13, 2007
100 meters	0:56.61	Inge de Bruijn	Netherlands	Sydney, Australia	Sept. 17, 2000
200 meters	2:05.40	Jessicah Schipper	Australia	Victoria, Canada	Aug. 17, 2006

Backstroke

50 meters	0:28.16	Leila Vaziri	U.S.	Melbourne, Australia	Mar. 28, 2007
100 meters	0:59.44	Natalie Coughlin	U.S.	Melbourne, Australia	Mar. 27, 2007
200 meters	2:06.62	Kristina Egerszegi	Hungary	Athens, Greece	Aug. 25, 1991

Individual Medley

200 meters	2:09.72	Yanyan Wu	China	Shanghai, China	Oct. 17, 1997
400 meters	4:32.89	Katie Hoff	U.S.	Melbourne, Australia	Apr. 1, 2007

Freestyle Relays

400 m. (4×100)	3:35.22	Dallmann, Goetz, Steffen, Liebs	Germany	Budapest, Hungary	July 31, 2006
800 m. (4×200)	7:50.09	Vollmer, Coughlin, Nymeyer, Hoff	U.S.	Melbourne, Australia	Mar. 29, 2007

Medley Relay

400 m. (4×100)	3:55.74	Seebohm, Jones, Schipper, Lenton	Australia	Melbourne, Australia	Mar. 31, 2007

YACHTING
The America's Cup

In the 32nd America's Cup, the Swiss boat *Alinghi* defended its title against *Emirates Team New Zealand*, 5-2, in a best-of-nine series held in the Mediterranean Sea off the coast of Valencia, Spain, in June-July 2007. Owned by Swiss businessman Ernesto Bertarelli, who also served as the yacht's strategist, *Alinghi* was skippered by New Zealander Brad Butterworth. Russell Coutts, who had skippered the *Alinghi* to victory in 2003, reportedly had been fired after clashing with Bertarelli in 2004. Unlike the last 3 Cups, which had been swept handily, the 2007 event had the two teams struggling for an edge up through the 4th race. The *Alinghi* won the 7th and final race by just 1 second—the closest margin of victory in the history of the America's Cup.

Competition for the America's Cup grew out of the first contest to establish a world yachting championship, one of the carnival features of the London Exposition of 1851. The race covered a 60-mile course around the Isle of Wight; the prize was a cup worth about $500, donated by the Royal Yacht Squadron of England, known as the "America's Cup" because it was first won by the U.S. yacht *America*. It was held by American yachts until 1983.

Winners of the America's Cup, 1851-2007

1851	America	1958	Columbia defeated Sceptre, England (4-0)
1870	Magic defeated Cambria, England (1-0)	1962	Weatherly defeated Gretel, Australia (4-1)
1871	Columbia (first three races) and Sappho (last two races) defeated Livonia, England (4-1)	1964	Constellation defeated Sovereign, England (4-0)
1876	Madeline defeated Countess of Dufferin, Canada (2-0)	1967	Intrepid defeated Dame Pattie, Australia (4-0)
1881	Mischief defeated Atalanta, Canada (2-0)	1970	Intrepid defeated Gretel II, Australia (4-1)
1885	Puritan defeated Genesta, England (2-0)	1974	Courageous defeated Southern Cross, Australia (4-0)
1886	Mayflower defeated Galatea, England (2-0)	1977	Courageous defeated Australia, Australia (4-0)
1887	Volunteer defeated Thistle, Scotland (2-0)	1980	Freedom defeated Australia, Australia (4-1)
1893	Vigilant defeated Valkyrie II, England (3-0)	1983	Australia II, Australia, defeated Liberty (4-3)
1895	Defender defeated Valkyrie III, England (3-0)	1987	Stars & Stripes defeated Kookaburra III, Australia (4-0)
1899	Columbia defeated Shamrock, England (3-0)	1988	Stars & Stripes defeated New Zealand, New Zealand (2-0)
1901	Columbia defeated Shamrock II, England (3-0)	1992	America[3] defeated Il Moro di Venezia, Italy (4-1)
1903	Reliance defeated Shamrock III, England (3-0)	1995	Black Magic 1, New Zealand, defeated Young America (5-0)
1920	Resolute defeated Shamrock IV, England (3-2)	2000	New Zealand, NZ, defeated Luna Rossa, Italy (5-0)
1930	Enterprise defeated Shamrock V, England (3-0)	2003	Alinghi, Switzerland, defeated Team New Zealand, NZ (5-0)
1934	Rainbow defeated Endeavour, England (4-2)	2007	Alinghi, Switzerland, defeated Emirates Team New Zealand, NZ (5-0)
1937	Ranger defeated Endeavour II, England (4-0)		

DOGS
Westminster Kennel Club, 1989-2007

Year	Best-in-show	Breed	Owner(s)
1989	Ch. Royal Tudor's Wild As The Wind	Doberman	Sue & Art Kemp, Richard & Carolyn Vida, Beth Wilhite
1990	Ch. Wendessa Crown Prince	Pekingese	Ed Jenner
1991	Ch. Whisperwind on a Carousel	Poodle	Joan & Frederick Hartsock
1992	Ch. Registry's Lonesome Dove	Fox Terrier	Marion & Sam Lawrence
1993	Ch. Salilyn's Condor	English Springer Spaniel	Donna & Roger Herzig
1994	Ch. Chidley Willum	Norwich Terrier	Ruth Cooper & Patricia Lussier
1995	Ch. Gaelforce Post Script	Scottish Terrier	Dr. Vandra Huber & Dr. Joe Kinnarney
1996	Ch. Clussexx Country Sunrise	Clumber Spaniel	Judith & Richard Zaleski
1997	Ch. Parsifal Di Casa Netzer	Standard Schnauzer	Rita Holloway & Gabrio Del Torre
1998	Ch. Fairewood Frolic	Norwich Terrier	Sandina Kennels
1999	Ch. Loteki Supernatural Being	Papillon	John Oulton
2000	Ch. Salilyn 'N Erin's Shameless	English Springer Spaniel	Carl Blain, Fran Sunseri, & Julia Gasow
2001	Ch. Special Times Just Right	Bichons Frises	Cecilia Ruggles, E. McDonald, & F. Werneck
2002	Ch. Surrey Spice Girl	Poodle (Miniature)	Ron L. & Barbara Scott
2003	Ch. Torum's Scarf Michael	Kerry Blue Terrier	Marilu Hanson
2004	Ch. Darbydale's All Rise Pouchcove	Newfoundland	Peggy Helming & Carol A. Bernard Bergmann
2005	Ch. Kan-Point's VJK Autumn Roses	German Shorthaired Pointer	Linda & Richard Stark, Carol Cronk, Valerie Nunes-Atkinson
2006	Ch. Rocky Top's Sundance Kid	Bull Terrier (colored)	Barbara Bishop, W. F. Poole, N. Shepherd, & R. P. Poole
2007	Ch. Felicity's Diamond Jim	English Springer Spaniel	Teresa & Allen Patton, Ruth Dehmel, D. Hadsall

2006 Iditarod Trail Sled Dog Race

Lance Mackey won the 35th annual Iditarod Trail Sled Dog Race from Anchorage to Nome, Alaska, Mar. 14, 2007. The 36-year-old Mackey, who finished the 1,131-mile course along the southern Iditarod route in 9 days, 5 hours, 8 minutes, and 41 seconds, became (after his father and brother) the third in his family to win the world's most grueling sled dog race. The 2008 race was scheduled to begin Mar. 1 in Anchorage and follow the 1,112-mile northern route to Nome.

MARATHONS
World Marathon Majors

Five of the world's leading marathons (Berlin, Boston, Chicago, London, and New York) agreed Jan. 23, 2006, to form a series called the World Marathon Majors. Marathon runners will be awarded points relative to their finish in each race in the series, and in Olympic and other world championship marathons. The male and female runners with the most points at the end of each 2-year cycle will win $500,000. The first series began with the Boston Marathon in Apr. 2006, and runs through the completion of the New York Marathon in Nov. 2007.

Boston Marathon Winners, 1972-2007
All times in hour:minute:second format. *Course records

Men's Winner	Time	Year	Women's Winner	Time
Olavi Suomalainen, Finland	2:15:39	1972	Nina Kuscsik, U.S.	3:10:26
Jon Anderson, U.S.	2:16:03	1973	Jacqueline Hansen, U.S.	3:05:59
Neil Cusack, Ireland	2:13:39	1974	Michiko Gorman, U.S.	2:47:11
Bill Rodgers, U.S.	2:09:55	1975	Liane Winter, West Germany	2:42:24
Jack Fultz, U.S.	2:20:19	1976	Kim Merritt, U.S.	2:47:10
Jerome Drayton, Canada	2:14:46	1977	Michiko Gorman, U.S.	2:48:33
Bill Rodgers, U.S.	2:10:13	1978	Gayle S. Barron, U.S.	2:44:52
Bill Rodgers, U.S.	2:09:27	1979	Joan Benoit, U.S.	2:35:15
Bill Rodgers, U.S.	2:12:11	1980	Jacqueline Gareau, Canada	2:34:28
Toshihiko Seko, Japan	2:09:26	1981	Allison Roe, N. Zealand	2:26:46
Alberto Salazar, U.S.	2:08:52	1982	Charlotte Teske, West Germany	2:29:33
Greg Meyer, U.S.	2:09:00	1983	Joan Benoit, U.S.	2:22:43
Geoff Smith, Great Britain	2:10:34	1984	Lorraine Moller, New Zealand	2:29:28
Geoff Smith, Great Britain	2:14:05	1985	Lisa Larsen Weidenbach, U.S.	2:34:06
Robert de Castella, Australia	2:07:51	1986	Ingrid Kristiansen, Norway	2:24:55
Toshihiko Seko, Japan	2:11:50	1987	Rosa Mota, Portugal	2:25:21
Ibrahim Hussein, Kenya	2:08:43	1988	Rosa Mota, Portugal	2:24:30
Abebe Mekonnen, Ethiopia	2:09:06	1989	Ingrid Kristiansen, Norway	2:24:33
Gelindo Bordin, Italy	2:08:19	1990	Rosa Mota, Portugal	2:25:24
Ibrahim Hussein, Kenya	2:11:06	1991	Wanda Panfil, Poland	2:24:18
Ibrahim Hussein, Kenya	2:08:14	1992	Olga Markova, Russia	2:23:43
Cosmas Ndeti, Kenya	2:09:33	1993	Olga Markova, Russia	2:25:27
Cosmas Ndeti, Kenya	2:07:15	1994	Uta Pippig, Germany	2:21:45
Cosmas Ndeti, Kenya	2:09:22	1995	Uta Pippig, Germany	2:25:11
Moses Tanui, Kenya	2:09:15	1996	Uta Pippig, Germany	2:27:12
Lameck Aguta, Kenya	2:10:34	1997	Fatuma Roba, Ethiopia	2:26:23
Moses Tanui, Kenya	2:07:34	1998	Fatuma Roba, Ethiopia	2:23:21
Joseh Chebet, Kenya	2:09:52	1999	Fatuma Roba, Ethiopia	2:23:25
Elijah Lagat, Kenya	2:09:47	2000	Catherine Ndereba, Kenya	2:26:11
Lee Bong-ju, S. Korea	2:09:43	2001	Catherine Ndereba, Kenya	2:23:53
Rodgers Rop, Kenya	2:09:02	2002	Margaret Okayo, Kenya	2:20:43*
Robert K. Cheruiyot, Kenya	2:10:11	2003	Svetlana Zakharova, Russia	2:25:20
Timothy Cherigat, Kenya	2:10:37	2004	Catherine Ndereba, Kenya	2:24:27
Hailu Negussie, Ethiopia	2:11:45	2005	Catherine Ndereba, Kenya	2:25:13
Robert Cheruiyot, Kenya	2:07:14*	2006	Rita Jeptoo, Kenya	2:23:38
Robert Cheruiyot, Kenya	2:14:13	2007	Lidiya Grigoryeva, Russia	2:29:18

Boston Marathon Winners, 1897-1971
The 1st Boston Marathon was held in 1897. Women were officially accepted into the race in 1972.

Year	Winner	Time	Year	Winner	Time
1897	John J. McDermott, New York	2:55:10	1930	Clarence DeMar, Massachusetts	2:34:48
1898	Ronald J. MacDonald, Canada	2:42:00	1931	James P. Henigan, Massachusetts	2:46:45
1899	Lawrence Brignolia, Massachusetts	2:39:44	1932	Paul DeBruyn, Germany	2:33:36
1900	John Caffery, Canada	2:29:23	1933	Leslie S. Pawson, Rhode Island	2:31:01
1901	John Caffery, Canada	2:43:12	1934	Dave Komonen, Canada	2:32:53
1902	Sammy Mellor, New York	2:41:29	1935	John A. Kelley, Massachusetts	2:32:07
1903	John Lorden, Massachusetts	2:38:04	1936	Ellison M. Brown, Rhode Island	2:33:40
1904	Michael Spring, New York	2:38:04	1937	Walter Young, Canada	2:33:20
1905	Frederick Lorz, New York	2:38:25	1938	Leslie S. Pawson, Rhode Island	2:35:34
1906	Tim Ford, Massachusetts	2:45:45	1939	Ellison M. Brown, Rhode Island	2:28:51
1907	Thomas Longboat, Canada	2:24:24	1940	Gerard Cote, Canada	2:28:28
1908	Thomas Morrissey, New York	2:25:43	1941	Leslie S. Pawson, Rhode Island	2:30:38
1909	Henri Renaud, New Hampshire	2:53:36	1942	Joe Smith, Massachusetts	2:26:51
1910	Fred Cameron, Canada	2:28:52	1943	Gerard Cote, Canada	2:28:25
1911	Clarence DeMar, Massachusetts	2:21:39	1944	Gerard Cote, Canada	2:31:50
1912	Michael Ryan, New York	2:21:18	1945	John A. Kelley, Massachusetts	2:30:40
1913	Fritz Carlson, Minnesota	2:25:14	1946	Stylianos Kyriakides, Greece	2:29:27
1914	James Duffy, Canada	2:25:14	1947	Yun Bok Suh, Korea	2:25:39
1915	Edouard Fabre, Canada	2:31:41	1948	Gerard Cote, Canada	2:31:02
1916	Arthur Roth, Massachusetts	2:27:16	1949	Karl Leandersson, Sweden	2:31:50
1917	Bill Kennedy, New York	2:28:37	1950	Kee Yong Ham, Korea	2:32:39
1918	Military Relay, Camp Devens	—	1951	Shigeki Tanaka, Japan	2:27:45
1919	Carl Linder, Massachusetts	2:29:13	1952	Doroteo Flores, Guatemala	2:31:53
1920	Peter Trivoulides, New York	2:29:31	1953	Keizo Yamada, Japan	2:18:51
1921	Frank Zuna, New York	2:18:57	1954	Veikko Karvonen, Finland	2:20:39
1922	Clarence DeMar, Massachusetts	2:18:10	1955	Hideo Hamamura, Japan	2:18:22
1923	Clarence DeMar, Massachusetts	2:23:47	1956	Antti Viskari, Finland	2:14:14
1924	Clarence DeMar, Massachusetts	2:29:40	1957	John J. Kelley, Connecticut	2:20:05
1925	Charles Mellor, Illinois	2:33:00	1958	Franjo Mihalic, Yugoslavia	2:25:54
1926	John C. Miles, Canada	2:25:40	1959	Eino Oksanen, Finland	2:22:42
1927	Clarence DeMar, Massachusetts	2:40:22	1960	Paavo Kotila, Finland	2:20:54
1928	Clarence DeMar, Massachusetts	2:37:07	1961	Eino Oksanen, Finland	2:23:39
1929	John C. Miles, Canada	2:33:08	1962	Eino Oksanen, Finland	2:23:48

Year	Winner	Time		Year	Winner	Time
1963	Aurele Vandendriessche, Belgium	2:18:58		1968	Amby Burfoot, Connecticut	2:22:17
1964	Aurele Vandendriessche, Belgium	2:19:59		1969	Yoshiaki Unetani, Japan	2:13:49
1965	Morio Shigematsu, Japan	2:16:33		1970	Ron Hill, Great Britain	2:10:30
1966	Kenji Kemihara, Japan	2:17:11		1971	Alvaro Mejia, Colombia	2:18:45
1967	David McKenzie, New Zealand	2:15:45				

New York City Marathon Winners, 1970-2006
All time in hour:minute:second format; *Course records.

Men's Winner	Time	Year	Women's Winner	Time
Gary Muhrcke, U.S.	2:31:38	1970	no finisher	—
Norman Higgins, U.S.	2:22:54	1971	Beth Bonner, U.S.	2:55:22
Sheldon Karlin, U.S.	2:27:52	1972	Nina Kuscsik, U.S.	3:08:41
Tom Fleming, U.S.	2:19:25	1973	Nina Kuscsik, U.S.	2:57:07
Norbert Sander, U.S.	2:26:30	1974	Katherine Switzer, U.S.	3:07:29
Tom Fleming, U.S.	2:19:27	1975	Kim Merritt, U.S.	2:46:14
Bill Rodgers, U.S.	2:10:10	1976	Miki Gorman, U.S.	2:39:11
Bill Rodgers, U.S.	2:11:28	1977	Miki Gorman, U.S.	2:43:10
Bill Rodgers, U.S.	2:12:12	1978	Grete Waitz, Norway	2:32:30
Bill Rodgers, U.S.	2:11:42	1979	Grete Waitz, Norway	2:27:33
Alberto Salazar, U.S.	2:09:41	1980	Grete Waitz, Norway	2:25:42
Alberto Salazar, U.S.	2:08:13	1981	Allison Roe, New Zealand	2:25:29
Alberto Salazar, U.S.	2:09:29	1982	Grete Waitz, Norway	2:27:14
Rod Dixon, New Zealand	2:08:59	1983	Grete Waitz, Norway	2:27:00
Orlando Pizzolato, Italy	2:14:53	1984	Grete Waitz, Norway	2:29:30
Orlando Pizzolato, Italy	2:11:34	1985	Grete Waitz, Norway	2:28:34
Gianni Poli, Italy	2:11:06	1986	Grete Waitz, Norway	2:28:06
Ibrahim Hussein, Kenya	2:11:01	1987	Priscilla Welch, England	2:30:17
Steve Jones, Great Britain	2:08:20	1988	Grete Waitz, Norway	2:28:07
Juma Ikangaa, Tanzania	2:08:01	1989	Ingrid Kristiansen, Norway	2:25:30
Douglas Wakiihuri, Kenya	2:12:39	1990	Wanda Panfil, Poland	2:30:45
Salvador Garcia, Mexico	2:09:28	1991	Liz McColgan, Great Britain	2:27:32
Willie Mtolo, South Africa	2:09:29	1992	Lisa Ondieki, Australia	2:24:40
Andres Espinosa, Mexico	2:10:04	1993	Uta Pippig, Germany	2:26:24
German Silva, Mexico	2:11:21	1994	Tegla Loroupe, Kenya	2:27:37
German Silva, Mexico	2:11:00	1995	Tegla Loroupe, Kenya	2:28:06
Giacomo Leone, Italy	2:09:54	1996	Anuta Catuna, Romania	2:28:43
John Kagwe, Kenya	2:08:12	1997	F. Rochat-Moser, Switzerland	2:28:43
John Kagwe, Kenya	2:08:45	1998	Franca Fiacconi, Italy	2:25:17
Joseph Chebet, Kenya	2:09:14	1999	Adriana Fernandez, Mexico	2:25:06
Abdelkhader El Mouaziz, Morocco	2:10:09	2000	Ludmila Petrova, Russia	2:25:45
Tesfaye Jifar, Ethiopia	2:07:43*	2001	Margaret Okayo, Kenya	2:24:21
Rodgers Rop, Kenya	2:08:07	2002	Joyce Chepchumba, Kenya	2:25:56
Martin Lel, Kenya	2:10:30	2003	Margaret Okayo, Kenya	2:22:31*
Hendrik Ramaala, South Africa	2:09:28	2004	Paula Radcliffe, England	2:23:10
Paul Tergat, Kenya	2:09:30	2005	Jelena Prokopcuka, Latvia	2:24:41
Marilson Gomes dos Santos, Brazil	2:09:58	2006	Jelena Prokopcuka, Latvia	2:25:05

Other Marathon Results in 2007

Los Angeles Marathon: Mar. 4. *Men:* Fred Mogaka, Kenya, 2:17:14. *Women:* Ramilia Burangolova, Russia, 2:37:54.

Paris Marathon: Apr. 9. *Men:* Mubarak Shami, Qatar, 2:07:19. *Women:* Tafa Magarsa, Ethiopia, 2:25:07.

Rotterdam Marathon: Apr. 15. *Men:* Joshua Chelanga, Kenya, 2:08:21. *Women:* Hiromi Ominami, Japan, 2:26:37.

London Marathon: Apr. 22. *Men:* Martin Lel, Kenya, 2:07:41. *Women:* Chunxiu Zhou, China, 2:20:38.

Berlin Marathon: Sept. 29. *Men:* Haile Gebrselassie, Ethiopia, 2:04:26. *Women:* Gete Wami, Ethiopia, 2:23:17.

Chicago Marathon: Oct. 7. *Men:* Patrick Ivuti, Kenya, 2:11:11. *Women:* Berhane Adere, Ethiopia, 2:33:49

Ironman Triathlon World Championships

The Ironman Triathlon World Championships—a 2.4-mile ocean swim, 112-mile bike ride, and 26.2-mile run—are held annually at Kailua-Kona, Hawaii. On Oct. 21, 2006, the men's race was won by Germany's Normann Stadler in 8:11:56. American Michellie Jones won the women's race with a time of 9:18:31.

All times in hour:minute:second format. *Course records.

Men's Winner	Time	Year	Women's Winner	Time
Gordon Haller, U.S.	11:46:58	1978	no finisher	—
Tom Warren, U.S.	11:15:56	1979	Lyn Lemaire, U.S.	12:55:00
Dave Scott, U.S.	9:24:33	1980	Robin Beck, U.S.	11:21:24
John Howard, U.S.	9:38:29	1981	Linda Sweeney, U.S.	12:00:32
Dave Scott, U.S.	9:08:23	1982	Julie Leach, U.S.	10:54:08
Dave Scott, U.S.	9:05:57	1983	Sylviane Puntous, Canada	10:43:36
Dave Scott, U.S	8:54:20	1984	Sylviane Puntous, Canada	10:25:13
Scott Tinley, U.S.	8:50:54	1985	Joanne Ernst, U.S.	10:25:22
Dave Scott, U.S.	8:28:37	1986	Paula Newby-Fraser, Zimbabwe	9:49:14
Dave Scott, U.S.	8:34:13	1987	Erin Baker, New Zealand	9:35:25
Scott Molina, U.S.	8:31:00	1988	Paula Newby-Fraser, Zimbabwe	9:01:01
Mark Allen, U.S.	8:09:15	1989	Paula Newby-Fraser, Zimbabwe	9:00:56
Mark Allen, U.S.	8:28:17	1990	Erin Baker, New Zealand	9:13:42
Mark Allen, U.S.	8:18:32	1991	Paula Newby-Fraser, Zimbabwe	9:07:52
Mark Allen, U.S.	8:09:08	1992	Paula Newby-Fraser, Zimbabwe	8:55:28*
Mark Allen, U.S.	8:07:45	1993	Paula Newby-Fraser, Zimbabwe	8:58:23
Greg Welch, Australia	8:20:27	1994	Paula Newby-Fraser, Zimbabwe	9:20:14
Mark Allen, U.S.	8:20:34	1995	Karen Smyers, U.S.	9:16:46
Luc Van Lierde, Belgium	8:04:08*	1996	Paula Newby-Fraser, Zimbabwe	9:06:49
Thomas Hellriegel, Germany	8:33:01	1997	Heather Fuhr, Canada	9:31:43
Peter Reid, Canada	8:24:20	1998	Natascha Badmann, Switz.	9:24:16
Luc Van Lierde, Belgium	8:17:17	1999	Lori Bowden, U.S.	9:13:02
Peter Reid, Canada	8:21:01	2000	Natascha Badmann, Switz.	9:26:16
Timothy Deboom, U.S.	8:31:18	2001	Natascha Badmann, Switz.	9:28:37
Timothy Deboom, U.S.	8:29:56	2002	Natascha Badmann, Switz.	9:07:54
Peter Reid, Canada	8:22:35	2003	Lori Bowden, Canada	9:11:55
Normann Stadler, Germany	8:33:29	2004	Natascha Badmann, Switz.[1]	9:50:04
Faris al-Sultan, Germany	8:14:17	2005	Natascha Badmann, Switz.	9:09:30
Normann Stadler, Germany	8:11:56	2006	Michellie Jones, U.S.	9:18:31

(1) First-place finisher Nina Kraft (Germany) admitted to using performance enhancing drugs and was disqualified, Nov. 15, 2004.

SULLIVAN AWARD

James E. Sullivan Memorial Trophy Winners

The James E. Sullivan Memorial Trophy, named after the former president of the Amateur Athletic Union (AAU) and inaugurated in 1930, is awarded annually by the AAU to the athlete who "by his or her performance, example and influence as an amateur, has done the most during the year to advance the cause of sportsmanship."

Year	Winner	Sport	Year	Winner	Sport	Year	Winner	Sport
1930	Bobby Jones	Golf	1957	Bobby Joe Morrow	Track	1984	Greg Louganis	Diving
1931	Barney Berlinger	Track	1958	Glenn Davis	Track	1985	Joan Benoit	
1932	Jim Bausch	Track	1959	Parry O'Brien	Track		Samuelson	Marathon
1933	Glenn Cunningham	Track	1960	Rafer Johnson	Track	1986	Jackie Joyner-Kersee	Track
1934	Bill Bonthron	Track	1961	Wilma Rudolph Ward	Track	1987	Jim Abbott	Baseball
1935	Lawson Little	Golf	1962	James Beatty	Track	1988	Florence Griffith Joyner	Track
1936	Glenn Morris	Track	1963	John Pennel	Track	1989	Janet Evans	Swimming
1937	Don Budge	Tennis	1964	Don Schollander	Swimming	1990	John Smith	Wrestling
1938	Don Lash	Track	1965	Bill Bradley	Basketball	1991	Mike Powell	Track
1939	Joe Burk	Rowing	1966	Jim Ryun	Track	1992	Bonnie Blair	Speed Skatin
1940	Greg Rice	Track	1967	Randy Matson	Track	1993	Charlie Ward	Football,
1941	Leslie MacMitchell	Track	1968	Debbie Meyer	Swimming			Basketball
1942	Cornelius Warmerdam	Track	1969	Bill Toomey	Track	1994	Dan Jansen	Speed Skatin
1943	Gilbert Dodds	Track	1970	John Kinsella	Swimming	1995	Bruce Baumgartner	Wrestling
1944	Ann Curtis	Swimming	1971	Mark Spitz	Swimming	1996	Michael Johnson	Track
1945	Doc Blanchard	Football	1972	Frank Shorter	Track	1997	Peyton Manning	Football
1946	Arnold Tucker	Football	1973	Bill Walton	Basketball	1998	Chamique Holdsclaw	Basketball
1947	John Kelly Jr.	Rowing	1974	Rick Wohlhutter	Track	1999	Coco Miller and	
1948	Robert Mathias	Track	1975	Tim Shaw	Swimming		Kelly Miller	Basketball
1949	Dick Button	Skating	1976	Bruce Jenner	Track	2000	Rulon Gardner	Wrestling
1950	Fred Wilt	Track	1977	John Naber	Swimming	2001	Michelle Kwan	Figure Skatir
1951	Rev. Robert Richards	Track	1978	Tracy Caulkins	Swimming	2002	Sarah Hughes	Figure Skatir
1952	Horace Ashenfelter	Track	1979	Kurt Thomas	Gymnastics	2003	Michael Phelps	Swimming
1953	Dr. Sammy Lee	Diving	1980	Eric Heiden	Speed Skating	2004	Paul Hamm	Gymnastics
1954	Mal Whitfield	Track	1981	Carl Lewis	Track	2005	J. J. Redick	Basketball
1955	Harrison Dillard	Track	1982	Mary Decker	Track	2006	Jessica Long	Swimming
1956	Patricia McCormick	Diving	1983	Edwin Moses	Track			(paralympics

FISHING

Selected IGFA Saltwater & Freshwater All-Tackle World Records

Source: International Game Fish Association; based on records granted as of Oct. 15, 2006

Saltwater Fish Records

Species	Weight	Where caught	Date	Angler
Albacore	88 lbs. 2 oz.	Canary Islands, Spain	Nov. 19, 1977	Siegfried Dickemann
Amberjack, greater	155 lbs. 12 oz.	Bermuda	Aug. 16, 1992	Larry Trott
Barracuda, great	85 lbs.	Christmas Island, Kiribati	Apr. 11, 1992	John Helfrich
Barracuda, Mexican	22 lbs. 8 oz.	Pinas Bay, Panama	Nov. 11, 2005	Frank Ibarra
Barracuda, Pacific	26 lbs. 8 oz.	Playa Matapalo, Costa Rica	Jan. 3, 1999	Doug Hettinger
Bass, barred sand	13 lbs. 3 oz.	Huntington Beach, CA	Aug. 29, 1988	Robert Halal
Bass, black sea	10 lbs. 4 oz.	Virginia Beach, VA	Jan. 1, 2000	Allan Paschall
Bass, giant sea	563 lbs. 8 oz.	Anacapa Island, CA	Aug. 20, 1968	James McAdam Jr.
Bass, striped	78 lbs. 8 oz.	Atlantic City, NJ	Sept. 21, 1982	Albert McReynolds
Bluefish	31 lbs. 12 oz.	Hatteras, NC	Jan. 30, 1972	James Hussey
Bonefish	19 lbs.	Zululand, South Africa	May 26, 1962	Brian Batchelor
Bonito, Atlantic	18 lbs. 4 oz.	Faial Island, Azores	July 8, 1953	D. Higgs
Bonito, Pacific	21 lbs. 5 oz.	181 Spot, CA	Oct. 19, 2003	Kim Larson
Cabezon	23 lbs.	Juan De Fuca Strait, WA	Aug. 4, 1990	Wesley Hunter
Cobia	135 lbs. 9 oz.	Shark Bay, Australia	July 9, 1985	Peter Goulding
Cod, Atlantic	98 lbs. 12 oz.	Isle of Shoals, NH	June 8, 1969	Alphonse Bielevich
Cod, Pacific	38 lbs. 9 oz.	Kawashiro, Kamoenai, Hokkaido, Japan	Jan. 16, 2005	Atsunori Takahira
Conger	133 lbs. 4 oz.	Berry Head, S. Devon, England	June 5, 1995	Vic Evans
Dolphinfish	87 lbs.	Papagallo Gulf, Costa Rica	Sept. 25, 1976	Manuel Salazar
Drum, black	113 lbs. 1 oz.	Lewes, DE	Sept. 15, 1975	Gerald Townsend
Drum, red	94 lbs. 2 oz.	Avon, NC	Nov. 7, 1984	David Deuel
Eel, American	9 lbs. 4 oz.	Cape May, NJ	Nov. 9, 1995	Jeff Pennick
Eel, marbled	36 lbs. 1 oz.	Hazelmere Dam, South Africa	June 10, 1984	Ferdie Van Nooten
Flounder, southern	20 lbs. 9 oz.	Nassau Sound, FL	Dec. 23, 1983	Larenza Mungin
Flounder, summer	22 lbs. 7 oz.	Montauk, NY	Sept. 15, 1975	Charles Nappi
Grouper, Goliath	680 lbs.	Fernandina Beach, FL	May 20, 1961	Lynn Joyner
Grouper, Warsaw	436 lbs. 12 oz.	Gulf of Mexico, Destin, FL	Dec. 22, 1985	Steve Haeusler
Halibut, Atlantic	418 lbs. 13 oz.	Vannaya Troms, Norway	July 28, 2004	Thomas Nielsen
Halibut, California	58 lbs. 9 oz.	Santa Rosa Island, CA	June 26, 1999	Roger W. Borrell
Halibut, Pacific	459 lbs.	Dutch Harbor, AK	June 11, 1996	Jack Tragis
Jack, crevalle	58 lbs. 6 oz.	Barra do Kwanza, Angola	Dec. 10, 2000	Nuno Abohbot
Jack, horse-eye	29 lbs. 8 oz.	Ascencion Island, South Atlantic	May 28, 1993	Mike Hanson
Jack, Pacific crevalle	39 lbs.	Playa Zancudo, Costa Rica	Mar. 3, 1997	Ingrid Callaghan
Kawakawa	29 lbs.	Clarion Island, Mexico	Dec. 17, 1986	Ronald Nakamura
Lingcod	77 lbs. 3 oz.	Homer, AK	July 5, 2006	Kindal Murry
Mackerel, cero	17 lbs. 2 oz.	Islamorada, FL	Apr. 5, 1986	G. Michael Mills
Mackerel, king	93 lbs.	San Juan, PR	Apr. 18, 1999	Steve Perez Graulau
Mackerel, Spanish	13 lbs.	Ocracoke Inlet, NC	Nov. 4, 1987	Robert Cranton
Marlin, Atlantic blue	1,402 lbs. 2 oz.	Vitoria, Brazil	Feb. 29, 1992	Paulo Amorim
Marlin, black	1,560 lbs.	Cabo Blanco, Peru	Aug. 4, 1953	Alfred Glassell Jr.
Marlin, Pacific blue	1,376 lbs.	Kaaiwi Pt., Kona, HI	May 31, 1982	Jay deBeaubien
Marlin, striped	494 lbs.	Tutukaka, New Zealand	Jan. 16, 1986	Bill Boniface
Marlin, white	181 lbs. 14 oz.	Vitoria, Brazil	Dec. 8, 1979	Evandro Coser
Permit	60 lbs.	Ilha do Mel, Paranagua, Brazil	Dec. 14, 2002	Renato Fiedler
Pollack, European	27 lbs. 6 oz.	Salcombe, Devon, England	Jan. 16, 1986	Robert Milkins
Pollock	50 lbs.	Salstraumen, Norway	Nov. 30, 1995	Thor-Magnus Lekang
Pompano, African	50 lbs. 8 oz.	Daytona Beach, FL	Apr. 21, 1990	Tom Sargent
Roosterfish	114 lbs.	La Paz, Baja Cal., Mexico	June 1, 1960	Abe Sackheim

Species	Weight	Where caught	Date	Angler
Runner, blue	11 lbs. 2 oz.	Dauphin Isl., AL	June 28, 1997	Stacey Moiren
Runner, rainbow	37 lbs. 9 oz.	Clarion Island, Mexico	Nov. 21, 1991	Tom Pfleger
Sailfish, Atlantic	141 lbs. 1 oz.	Luanda, Angola	Feb. 19, 1994	Alfredo de Sousa Neves
Sailfish, Pacific	221 lbs.	Santa Cruz Island, Ecuador	Feb. 12, 1947	Carl Stewart
Seabass, white	83 lbs. 12 oz.	San Felipe, Mexico	Mar. 31, 1953	Lyal Baumgardner
Seatrout, spotted	17 lbs. 7 oz.	Ft. Pierce, FL	May 11, 1995	Craig Carson
Shark, bigeye thresher	802 lbs.	Tutukaka, New Zealand	Feb. 8, 1981	Dianne North
Shark, bignose	369 lbs. 14 oz.	Markham R., Papua New Guinea	Oct. 23, 1993	Lester Rohrlach
Shark, blue	528 lbs.	Montauk Point, NY	Aug. 9, 2001	Joe Seidel
Shark, great hammerhead	1280 lbs.	Boca Grande, FL	May 23, 2006	Bucky Dennis
Shark, Greenland	1,708 lbs. 9 oz.	Trondheimsfjord, Norway	Oct. 18, 1987	Terje Nordtvedt
Shark, porbeagle	507 lbs.	Caithness, Scotland	Mar. 9, 1993	Christopher Bennett
Shark, shortfin mako	1,221 lbs.	Chatham, MA	July 21, 2001	Luke Sweeney
Shark, tiger	1,780 lbs.	Cherry Grove, SC	June 14, 1964	Walter Maxwell
Shark, white	2,664 lbs.	Ceduna, Australia	Apr. 21, 1959	Alfred Dean
Sheepshead	21 lbs. 4 oz.	New Orleans, LA	Apr. 16, 1982	Wayne Desselle
Skipjack, black	26 lbs.	Thetis Bank, Baja Cal., Mexico	Oct. 23, 1991	Clifford Hamaishi
Snapper, cubera	121 lbs. 8 oz.	Cameron, LA	July 5, 1982	Mike Hebert
Snapper, red	50 lbs. 4 oz.	Gulf of Mexico, LA	June 23, 1996	Capt. Doc Kennedy
Snook, common	53 lbs. 10 oz.	Parismina Ranch, Costa Rica	Oct. 18, 1978	Gilbert Ponzi
Spearfish, Mediterranean	90 lbs. 13 oz.	Madeira Island, Portugal	June 2, 1980	Joseph Larkin
Swordfish	1,182 lbs.	Iquique, Chile	May 7, 1953	Louis Marron
Tarpon	286 lbs. 9 oz.	Rubane, Guinea-Bissau	Mar. 20, 2003	Max Domecq
Tautog	25 lbs.	Ocean City, NJ	Jan. 20, 1998	Anthony Monica
Trevally, bigeye	31 lbs. 8 oz.	Poivre Isl., Seychelles	Apr. 23, 1997	Les Sampson
Trevally, giant	160 lbs. 7 oz.	Tokara, Kagoshima, Japan	May 22, 2006	Keiki Hamasaki
Tuna, Atlantic bigeye	392 lbs. 6 oz.	Canary Islands, Spain	July 25, 1996	Dieter Vogel
Tuna, blackfin	49 lbs. 6 oz.	Marathon, FL	April 6, 2006	Capt. Matthew E. Pullen
Tuna, bluefin	1,496 lbs.	Aulds Cove, Nova Scotia	Oct. 26, 1979	Ken Fraser
Tuna, longtail	79 lbs. 2 oz.	Montague Isl., Australia	Apr. 12, 1982	Tim Simpson
Tuna, Pacific bigeye	435 lbs.	Cabo Blanco, Peru	Apr. 17, 1957	Dr. Russel Lee
Tuna, skipjack	45 lbs. 4 oz.	Flathead Bank, Baja Cal., Mexico	Nov. 16, 1996	Brian Evans
Tuna, southern bluefin	348 lbs. 5 oz.	Whakatane, New Zealand	Jan. 16, 1981	Rex Wood
Tuna, yellowfin	388 lbs. 12 oz.	San Benedicto Island, Mexico	Apr. 1, 1977	Curt Wiesenhutter
Tunny, little	35 lbs. 2 oz.	Cap de Garde, Algeria	Dec. 14, 1988	Jean Chatard
Wahoo	184 lbs.	Cabo San Lucas., Mexico	July 29, 2005	Sara Hayward
Weakfish	19 lbs. 2 oz.	Jones Beach Inlet, NY	Oct. 11, 1984	Dennis Rooney
		Delaware Bay, DE	May 20, 1989	William Thomas
Yellowtail, California	92 lbs. 1 oz.	Guadelupe Isl., Mexico	Aug. 4, 2004	Kevin Pfeif
Yellowtail, southern	114 lbs. 10 oz.	Tauranga, New Zealand	Feb. 5, 1984	Mike Godfrey
		White Island, New Zealand	Jan. 9, 1987	David Lugton

Freshwater Fish Records

Species	Weight	Where caught	Date	Angler
Barramundi	83 lbs. 7 oz.	Lake Tinaroo, N. Queensland, Australia	Sept. 23, 1999	David Powell
Bass, largemouth	22 lbs. 4 oz.	Montgomery Lake, GA	June 2, 1932	George Perry
Bass, rock	3 lbs.	York River, Ontario	Aug. 1, 1974	Peter Gulgin
	3 lbs.	Lake Erie, PA	June 18, 1998	Herbert Ratner Jr.
Bass, shoal	8 lbs. 12 oz.	Apalachicola River, FL	Jan. 28, 1995	Carl Davis
Bass, smallmouth	11 lbs. 15 oz.	Dale Hollow Lake, TN	July 9, 1955	David Hayes
Bass, white	6 lbs. 13 oz.	Lake Orange, VA	July 31, 1989	Ronald Sprouse
Bass, whiterock	27 lbs. 5 oz.	Greers Ferry Lake, AR	April 24, 1997	Jerald Shaum
Bass, yellow	2 lbs. 9 oz.	Duck River, Waverly, TN	Feb. 27, 1998	John Chappell
Bluegill	4 lbs. 12 oz.	Ketona Lake, AL	Apr. 9, 1950	T. Hudson
Bowfin	21 lbs. 8 oz.	Florence, SC	Jan. 29, 1980	Robert Harmon
Bream	13 lbs. 3 oz.	Hagbyan Creek, Sweden	May 11, 1984	Luis Killan Rasmussen
Buffalo, bigmouth	70 lbs. 5 oz.	Bastrop, LA	Apr. 21, 1980	Delbert Sisk
Buffalo, black	63 lbs. 6 oz.	Mississippi River, IA	Aug. 14, 1999	Jim Winters
Buffalo, smallmouth	82 lbs. 3 oz.	Athens Lake, AL	June 6, 1993	Randy Collins
Bullhead, brown	6 lbs. 5 oz.	Lake Mahopac, NY	Sept. 8, 2002	Ray Lawrence
Bullhead, yellow	4 lbs. 15 oz.	Ogeechee R., GA	Oct. 12, 2003	Glenn Settles
Burbot	18 lbs. 11 oz.	Angenmanalren, Sweden	Oct. 22, 1996	Margit Agren
Carp, common	75 lbs. 11 oz.	Lac de St. Cassien, France	May 21, 1987	Leo van der Gugten
Catfish, blue	124 lbs.	Mississippi R., IL	May 21, 2005	Timothy Pruitt
Catfish, channel	58 lbs.	Santee-Cooper Res., SC	July 7, 1964	W. B. Whaley
Catfish, flathead	123 lbs.	Independence, KS	May 14, 1998	Ken Paulie
Catfish, white	19 lbs. 5 oz.	Oakdale, CA	May 7, 2005	Russell Price
Char, Arctic	32 lbs. 9 oz.	Tree River, Canada	July 30, 1981	Jeffrey Ward
Crappie, white	5 lbs. 3 oz.	Enid Dam, MS	July 31, 1957	Fred Bright
Dolly Varden	20 lbs. 14 oz.	Wulik R., AK	July 7, 2001	Raz Reid
Dorado	55 lbs. 11 oz.	Uruguay R., Concordia, Argentina	Jan. 11, 2006	Andre L.S. de Botton
Drum, freshwater	54 lbs. 8 oz.	Nickajack Lake, TN	Apr. 20, 1972	Benny Hull
Gar, alligator	279 lbs.	Rio Grande, TX	Dec. 2, 1951	Bill Valverde
Gar, Florida	10 lbs.	Everglades, FL	Jan. 28, 2002	Herbert Ratner Jr.
Gar, longnose	50 lbs. 5 oz.	Trinity River, TX	July 30, 1954	Townsend Miller
Gar, shortnose	5 lbs. 12 oz.	Rend Lake, IL	July 16, 1995	Donna Willmert
Gar, spotted	9 lbs. 12 oz.	Lake Mexia, TX	Apr. 7, 1994	Rick Rivard
Grayling, Arctic	5 lbs. 15 oz.	Katseyedie River, NT	Aug. 16, 1967	Jeanne Branson
Inconnu	53 lbs.	Pah River, AK	Aug. 20, 1986	Lawrence Hudnall
Kokanee	9 lbs. 6 oz.	Okanagan Lake, BC	June 18, 1988	Norm Kuhn
Muskellunge	67 lbs. 8 oz.	Lake Court Oreilles, WI	July 24, 1949	Cal Johnson
Muskellunge, tiger	51 lbs. 3 oz.	Lac Vieux-Desert, MI	July 16, 1919	John Knobla
Perch, Nile	230 lbs.	Lake Nasser, Egypt	Dec. 20, 2000	William Toth
Perch, white	3 lbs. 1 oz.	Forest Hill Park, NJ	May 6, 1989	Edward Tango
Perch, yellow	4 lbs. 3 oz.	Bordentown, NJ	May, 1865	Dr. C. C. Abbot
Pickerel, chain	9 lbs. 6 oz.	Homerville, GA	Feb. 17, 1961	Baxley McQuaig Jr.
Pike, northern	55 lbs. 1 oz.	Lake of Grefeern, W. Germany	Oct. 16, 1986	Lothar Louis
Redhorse, greater	9 lbs. 3 oz.	Salmon River, Pulaski, NY	May 11, 1985	Jason Wilson
Redhorse, silver	11 lbs. 7 oz.	Plum Creek, WI	May 29, 1985	Neal Long

Species	Weight	Where caught	Date	Angler
Salmon, Atlantic	79 lbs. 2 oz.	Tana River, Norway	Jan. 1, 1928	Henrik Henriksen
Salmon, chinook	97 lbs. 4 oz.	Kenai River, AK	May 17, 1985	Les Anderson
Salmon, chum	35 lbs.	Edye Pass, BC	July 11, 1995	Todd Johansson
Salmon, coho	33 lbs. 4 oz.	Salmon River, Pulaski, NY	Sept. 27, 1989	Jerry Lifton
Salmon, pink	14 lbs. 13 oz.	Monroe, WA	Sept. 30, 2001	Alexander Minerich
Salmon, sockeye	15 lbs. 3 oz.	Kenai River, AK	Aug. 9, 1987	Stan Roach
Sauger	8 lbs. 12 oz.	Lake Sakakawea, ND	Oct. 6, 1971	Mike Fischer
Shad, American	11 lbs. 4 oz.	Connecticut River, MA	May 19, 1986	Bob Thibodo
Sturgeon, beluga	224 lbs. 13 oz.	Guryev, Kazakhstan	May 3, 1993	Merete Lehne
Sturgeon, white	468 lbs.	Benicia, CA	July 9, 1983	Joey Pallotta III
Sunfish, green	2 lbs. 2 oz.	Stockton Lake, MO	June 18, 1971	Paul Dilley
Sunfish, redbreast	1 lb. 12 oz.	Suwannee River, FL	May 29, 1984	Alvin Buchanan
Sunfish, redear	5 lbs. 7 oz.	Diverson Canal, SC	Nov. 6, 1998	Amos Gay
Tigerfish, giant	97 lbs.	Zaire River, Kinshasa, Zaire (Congo)	July 9, 1988	Raymond Houtmans
Tilapia, Nile	13 lbs. 3 oz.	Antelope Isl., Kariba, Zimbabwe	July 5, 2002	Sarel van Rooyen
Trout, Apache	5 lb. 3 oz.	Apache Res., AZ	May 29, 1991	John Baldwin
Trout, brook	14 lbs. 8 oz.	Nipigon River, ON	July 1916	Dr. W. J. Cook
Trout, bull	32 lbs.	Lake Pend Oreille, ID	Oct. 27, 1949	N. L. Higgins
Trout, cutthroat	41 lbs.	Pyramid Lake, NV	Dec. 1925	John Skimmerhorn
Trout, golden	11 lbs.	Cooks Lake, WY	Aug. 5, 1948	Charles Reed
Trout, lake	72 lbs.	Great Bear Lake, NT	Aug. 19, 1995	Lloyd Bull
Trout, rainbow	42 lbs. 2 oz.	Bell Island, AK	June 22, 1970	David White
Trout, tiger	20 lbs. 13 oz.	Lake Michigan, WI	Aug. 12, 1978	Pete Friedland
Walleye	25 lbs.	Old Hickory Lake, TN	Aug. 2, 1960	Mabry Harper
Warmouth	2 lbs. 7 oz.	Yellow River, Holt, FL	Oct. 19, 1985	Tony Dempsey
Whitefish, lake	14 lbs. 6 oz.	Meaford, ON	May 21, 1984	Dennis Laycock
Whitefish, mountain	5 lbs. 8 oz.	Elbow River, Calgary, AB	Aug. 1, 1995	Randy Woo
Whitefish, round	6 lbs.	Putahow R., MB	June 14, 1984	Allan Ristori
Zander	25 lbs. 2 oz.	Trosa, Sweden	June 12, 1986	Harry Lee Tennison

DIRECTORY OF SPORTS ORGANIZATIONS
Major League Baseball
Office of the Commissioner, 245 Park Ave., 31st Fl., New York, NY 10167. **Website:** www.mlb.com

American League

Baltimore Orioles
333 W. Camden St.
Baltimore, MD 21201

Boston Red Sox
4 Yawkey Way
Boston, MA 02215

Chicago White Sox
333 W. 35th St.
Chicago, IL 60616

Cleveland Indians
2401 Ontario St.
Cleveland, OH 44115-4003

Detroit Tigers
2100 Woodward Ave.
Detroit, MI 48201

Kansas City Royals
One Royal Way
Kansas City, MO 64129

Los Angeles Angels of Anaheim
2000 Gene Autry Way
Anaheim, CA 92806

Minnesota Twins
34 Kirby Puckett Place
Minneapolis, MN 55415

New York Yankees
161st St. and River Ave.
Bronx, NY 10451

Oakland Athletics
7000 Coliseum Way
Oakland, CA 94621

Seattle Mariners
P.O. Box 4100
Seattle, WA 98194

Tampa Bay Devil Rays
One Tropicana Dr.
St. Petersburg, FL 33705

Texas Rangers
1000 Ballpark Way
Arlington, TX 76011

Toronto Blue Jays
One Blue Jays Way, Ste. 3200
Toronto, ON M5V 1J1

Arizona Diamondbacks
401 E. Jefferson St.
Phoenix, AZ 85004

Atlanta Braves
755 Hank Aaron Drive
Atlanta, GA 30315

National League

Chicago Cubs
1060 W. Addison St.
Chicago, IL 60613

Cincinnati Reds
100 Main St.
Cincinnati, OH 45202

Colorado Rockies
2001 Blake St.
Denver, CO 80205

Florida Marlins
2267 Dan Marino Blvd.
Miami, FL 33056

Houston Astros
501 Crawford St.
Houston, TX 77002

Los Angeles Dodgers
1000 Elysian Park Ave.
Los Angeles, CA 90012

Milwaukee Brewers
One Brewers Way
Milwaukee, WI 53214

New York Mets
123-01 Roosevelt Ave.
Flushing, NY 11368

Philadelphia Phillies
One Citizens Bank Way
Philadelphia, PA 19148

Pittsburgh Pirates
115 Federal St.
Pittsburgh, PA 15212

St. Louis Cardinals
700 Clark St.
St. Louis, MO 63102

San Diego Padres
100 Park Blvd.
San Diego, CA 92101

San Francisco Giants
24 Willie Mays Plaza
San Francisco, CA 94107

Washington Nationals
2400 E. Capitol St. SE
Washington, DC 20003

Note: The Washington Nationals expected to open a new ballpark in 2008.

National Basketball Association
League Office, Olympic Tower, 645 5th Ave., New York, NY 10022. **Website:** www.nba.com

Atlanta Hawks
101 Marietta St. SW, Ste. 1900
Atlanta, GA 30303

Boston Celtics
226 Causeway St.
Boston, MA 02114

Charlotte Bobcats
333 E. Trade St.
Charlotte, NC 28202

Chicago Bulls
1901 W. Madison St.
Chicago, IL 60612

Cleveland Cavaliers
One Center Court
Cleveland, OH 44115

Dallas Mavericks
2909 Taylor St.
Dallas, TX 75226

Denver Nuggets
1000 Chopper Circle
Denver, CO 80204

Detroit Pistons
Five Championship Dr.
Auburn Hills, MI 48326

Golden State Warriors
1011 Broadway
Oakland, CA 94607

Houston Rockets
1510 Polk St.
Houston, TX 77002

Indiana Pacers
125 S. Pennsylvania St.
Indianapolis, IN 46204

Los Angeles Clippers
1111 S. Figueroa St.,
Ste. 1100
Los Angeles, CA 90015

Los Angeles Lakers
555 N. Nash St.
El Segundo, CA 90245

Memphis Grizzlies
191 Beale St.
Memphis, TN 38103

Miami Heat
601 Biscayne Blvd.
Miami, FL 33132

Milwaukee Bucks
1001 N. 4th St.
Milwaukee, WI 53203

Minnesota Timberwolves
600 1st Ave. North
Minneapolis, MN 55403

New Jersey Nets
390 Murray Hill Parkway
E. Rutherford, NJ 07073

New Orleans Hornets
1250 Poydras St., Fl. 19
New Orleans, LA 70113

New York Knickerbockers
Two Pennsylvania Plaza
New York, NY 10121

Orlando Magic
8701 Maitland Summit Blvd.
Orlando, FL 32810

Philadelphia 76ers
3601 S. Broad St.
Philadelphia, PA 19148

Phoenix Suns
201 E. Jefferson St.
Phoenix, AZ 85004

Portland Trail Blazers
One Center Ct., Ste. 200
Portland, OR 97227

Sacramento Kings
One Sports Parkway
Sacramento, CA 95834

San Antonio Spurs
One AT&T Center
San Antonio, TX 78219

Seattle SuperSonics
305 Harrison St.
Seattle, WA 98109

Toronto Raptors
40 Bay St.
Toronto, ON M5J 2X2

Utah Jazz
301 W. South Temple
Salt Lake City, UT 84101

Washington Wizards
601 F St. NW
Washington, DC 20004

National Hockey League

League Headquarters, 1251 Ave. of the Americas, 47th Fl., New York, NY 10020. **Website:** www.nhl.com

Anaheim Ducks
2695 E. Katella Ave.
Anaheim, CA 92806

Atlanta Thrashers
Centennial Tower
101 Marietta St. NW, Ste. 1900
Atlanta, GA 30303

Boston Bruins
100 Legends Way
Boston, MA 02114

Buffalo Sabres
One Seymour H. Knox III Plaza
Buffalo, NY 14203

Calgary Flames
P.O. Box 1540, Station M
Calgary, AB T2P 3B9

Carolina Hurricanes
1400 Edwards Mill Rd.
Raleigh, NC 27607

Chicago Blackhawks
1901 W. Madison St.
Chicago, IL 60612

Colorado Avalanche
1000 Chopper Circle
Denver, CO 80204

Columbus Blue Jackets
200 W. Nationwide Blvd.
Columbus, OH 43215

Dallas Stars
2601 Avenue of the Stars
Frisco, TX 75034

Detroit Red Wings
600 Civic Center Dr.
Detroit, MI 48226

Edmonton Oilers
11230 110 St.
Edmonton, AB T5G 3H7

Florida Panthers
One Panther Parkway
Sunrise, FL 33323

Los Angeles Kings
1111 S. Figueroa St.
Los Angeles, CA 90015

Minnesota Wild
317 Washington St.
St. Paul, MN 55102

Montreal Canadiens
1275 St. Antonie St. W
Montreal, QC H3C 5L2

Nashville Predators
501 Broadway
Nashville, TN 37203

New Jersey Devils
P.O. Box 504
E. Rutherford, NJ 07073

New York Islanders
1255 Hempstead Tpke.
Uniondale, NY 11553

New York Rangers
Two Pennsylvania Plaza
New York, NY 10121

Ottawa Senators
1000 Palladium Dr.
Ottawa, ON K2V 1A5

Philadelphia Flyers
3601 South Broad St.
Philadelphia, PA 19148

Phoenix Coyotes
6751 N. White Out Way, #200
Glendale, AZ 85301

Pittsburgh Penguins
66 Mario Lemieux Place
Pittsburgh, PA 15219

St. Louis Blues
1401 Clark Ave.
St. Louis, MO 63103

San Jose Sharks
525 W. Santa Clara St.
San Jose, CA 95113

Tampa Bay Lightning
401 Channelside Dr.
Tampa, FL 33602

Toronto Maple Leafs
40 Bay St., Ste. 400
Toronto, ON M5J 2X2

Vancouver Canucks
800 Griffiths Way
Vancouver, BC V6B 6G1

Washington Capitals
627 Glebe Rd., Ste. 850
Arlington, VA 22203

National Football League

League Office, 280 Park Ave., New York, NY 10017 **Website:** www.nfl.com

Arizona Cardinals
P.O. Box 888
Phoenix AZ 85001

Atlanta Falcons
4400 Falcon Parkway
Flowery Branch, GA 30542

Baltimore Ravens
1101 Russel St.
Baltimore, MD 21230

Buffalo Bills
One Bills Drive
Orchard Park, NY 14127

Carolina Panthers
800 S. Mint St.
Charlotte, NC 28202

Chicago Bears
1000 Football Dr.
Lake Forest, IL 60045

Cincinnati Bengals
One Paul Brown Stadium
Cincinnati, OH 45202

Cleveland Browns
100 Alfred Lerner Way
Cleveland, OH 44114

Dallas Cowboys
2401 E. Airport Fwy.
Irving, TX 75062

Denver Broncos
13655 Broncos Pkwy.
Englewood, CO 80112

Detroit Lions
222 Republic Dr.
Allen Park, MI 48101

Green Bay Packers
1265 Lombardi Ave.
Green Bay, WI 54304

Houston Texans
Two Reliant Park
Houston, TX 77054

Indianapolis Colts
7001 W. 56th St.
Indianapolis, IN 46254

Jacksonville Jaguars
One Stadium Place
Jacksonville, FL 32202

Kansas City Chiefs
One Arrowhead Drive
Kansas City, MO 64129

Miami Dolphins
7500 SW 30th St.
Davie, FL 33314

Minnesota Vikings
9520 Viking Dr.
Eden Prairie, MN 55344

New England Patriots
One Patriot Pl.
Foxboro, MA 02035

New Orleans Saints
1500 Podyras St.
New Orleans, LA 70112

New York Giants
Giants Stadium
E. Rutherford, NJ 07073

New York Jets
1000 Fulton Ave.
Hempstead, NY 11550

Oakland Raiders
1220 Harbor Bay Pkwy.
Alameda, CA 94502

Philadelphia Eagles
One NovaCare Way
Philadelphia, PA 19145

Pittsburgh Steelers
100 Art Rooney Ave.
Pittsburgh, PA 15212

St. Louis Rams
One Rams Way
St. Louis, MO 63045

San Diego Chargers
4020 Murphy Canyon Rd.
San Diego, CA 92123

San Francisco 49ers
4949 Centennial Blvd.
Santa Clara, CA 95054

Seattle Seahawks
800 Occidental Ave. South,
Ste. 200
Seattle, WA 98134

Tampa Bay Buccaneers
One Buccaneer Place
Tampa, FL 33607

Tennessee Titans
One Titans Way
Nashville, TN 37213

Washington Redskins
21300 Redskin Park Dr.
Ashburn, VA 20147

Other North American Sports Organizations

Amateur Athletic Union,
P.O. Box 22409,
Lake Buena Vista, FL 32830
www.aausports.org

Amateur Softball Assn.
2801 NE 50th St.
Oklahoma City, OK 73111
www.softball.org

American Kennel Club
260 Madison Ave.
New York, NY 10016
www.akc.org

Canadian Football League
50 Wellington St. E., 3rd Fl.
Toronto, Ont. M5E 1C8
www.cfl.ca

CART (Championship Auto
Racing Teams)
5350 Lakeview Pkwy. S. Dr.
Indianapolis, IN 46268
www.champcarworld
series.com

Intl. Game Fish Assn.
300 Gulf Stream Way
Dania Beach, FL 33004
www.igfa.org

LPGA
100 International Golf Dr.
Daytona Beach, FL 32124
www.lpga.com

Little League Baseball
PO Box 3485
Williamsport, PA 17701
www.littleleague.org

Major League Soccer
420 5th Ave., 7th Fl.
New York, NY 10018
www.mlsnet.com

NASCAR
P.O. Box 2875
Daytona Beach, FL 32120
www.nascar.com

NCAA
700 W. Washington St.
P.O. Box 6222
Indianapolis, IN 46206
www.ncaa.org

National Rifle Assn.
11250 Waples Mill Rd.
Fairfax, VA 22030
www.nra.org

Pro Bowlers Assn.
719 2nd Ave., Ste. 701
Seattle, WA 98104
www.pbatour.com

PGA
112 PGA Tour Blvd.
Ponte Vedra Beach, FL 32082
www.pga.com

Pro Rodeo Cowboys Assn.
101 Pro Rodeo Dr.
Colorado Springs, CO 80919
www.prorodeo.org

Special Olympics
1133 19th St. NW
Washington, DC 20036
www.specialolympics.org

Thoroughbred Racing Assn.
420 Fair Hill Dr.
Elkton, MD 21921
www.tra-online.com

USA Rugby
2500 Arapahoe Ave.
Boulder, CO 80302
www.usarugby.org

USA Swimming
One Olympic Plaza
Colorado Springs, CO 80909
www.usa-swimming.org

USA Track & Field
One RCA Dome, Ste. 140
Indianapolis, IN 46225
www.usatf.org

U.S. Auto Club
4910 W. 16th St.
Speedway, IN 46224
www.usacracing.com

U.S. Bowling Congress
5301 S. 76th St.
Greendale, WI 53129
www.bowl.com

U.S. Equestrian Federation
4047 Iron Works Pkwy.
Lexington, KY 40511
www.usef.org

U.S. Figure Skating Assn.
20 First St.
Colorado Springs, CO 80906
www.usfigureskating.org

U.S. Olympic Committee
One Olympic Plaza
Colorado Springs, CO 80909
www.usoc.org

U.S. Ski and Snowboard Assn.
1500 Kearns Blvd.
P.O. Box 100
Park City, UT 84060
www.ussa.org

U.S. Soccer Federation
1801 S. Prairie Ave.
Chicago, IL 60616
www.ussoccer.com

U.S. Tennis Assn.
70 W. Red Oak Lane
White Plains, NY 10604
www.usta.com

U.S. Trotting Assn.
750 Michigan Ave.
Columbus, OH 43215
www.ustrotting.com

WNBA
Olympic Tower
645 5th Ave.
New York, NY 10022
www.wnba.com

NOTABLE SPORTS PERSONALITIES

Henry (Hank) Aaron, b. 1934, Milwaukee-Atlanta outfielder; hit record 755 home runs, led NL 4 times; record 2,297 RBI.

Kareem Abdul-Jabbar, b. 1947, Milwaukee, L.A. Lakers center; MVP 6 times; all-time leading NBA scorer, 38,387 points.

Freddy Adu, b. 1989, D.C. United midfielder; youngest player ever to play in the MLS at 14 years, 308 days, in 2004.

Andre Agassi, b. 1970, won: Wimbledon, '92; U.S. Open, '94, '99, '99; Aust. Open, '95, 2000-01, 2003; French Open, '99.

Troy Aikman, b. 1966, quarterback; led Dallas Cowboys to Super Bowl wins in 1993-94, 1996; Super Bowl MVP, 1993.

Amy Alcott, b. 1956, golfer; 29 career wins (5 majors), inducted into World Golf Hall of Fame in 1999.

Shaun Alexander, b. 1977, Seattle Seahawks running back; NFL record for touchdowns in a season, 28.

Grover Cleveland "Pete" Alexander, 1887-1950, pitcher; won 373 NL games; pitched 16 shutouts, 1916.

Muhammad Ali, b. 1942, 3-time heavyweight champion.

Fernando Alonso, b. 1981, Spanish Formula 1 racer; youngest ever to win a World Grand Prix championship, 2005.

Gary Anderson, b. 1959, kicker; NFL's career points leader, with 2,434 through the end of the 2003 season.

Sparky Anderson, b. 1934, only manager to win World Series in the NL (Cincinnati, 1975-76) and the AL (Detroit, 1984).

Mario Andretti, b. 1940, race-car driver; won Daytona 500 (1967), Indy 500 (1969); Formula 1 world title (1978).

Earl Anthony, 1938-2001, bowler; won record 6 PBA Championships (1973-75, 1981-83), 41 career PBA tournaments.

Eddie Arcaro, 1916-97, only jockey to win racing's Triple Crown twice, 1941,1948; rode to 4,779 wins in his career.

Lance Armstrong, b. 1971, cyclist; record 7-time winner of the Tour de France (1999-2005).

Arthur Ashe, 1943-93, tennis player; won U.S. Open (1968); Wimbledon (1975); died of AIDS.

Evelyn Ashford, b. 1957, sprinter; won 100m gold (1984) and silver (1988); member of 5 U.S. Olympic teams (1976-1992).

Red Auerbach, 1917-2006, coached Boston to 9 NBA titles.

Tracy Austin, b. 1962: youngest player to win U.S. Open tennis title (age 16 in 1979), 2-time AP Female Athlete of the Year.

Ernie Banks, b. 1931, Chicago Cubs slugger; hit 512 NL homers; twice MVP; never played in World Series.

Roger Bannister, b. 1929, British physician; ran first sub 4-minute mile, May 6, 1954 (3 min. 59.4 sec.).

Charles Barkley, b. 1963, NBA MVP, 1993; 4th player ever to surpass 20,000 pts, 10,000 rebounds, and 4,000 assists.

Rick Barry, b. 1944: NBA scoring leader, 1967; ABA, 1969.

Sammy Baugh, b. 1914: Washington Redskins quarterback; held numerous records upon retirement after 16 seasons.

Elgin Baylor, b. 1934, L.A. Lakers forward; 11-time all-star.

Bob Beamon, b. 1946, Olympic long jump gold medalist in 1968; world record jump of 29' 2½" stood until 1991.

Boris Becker, b. 1967, German tennis star; won U.S. Open 1989; Wimbledon champ 3 times.

David Beckham, b. 1975, English soccer star; captain of 2002 World Cup team; joined Los Angeles Galaxy, 2007, with record-breaking $250 million contract.

Bill Belichick, b. 1952, NFL coach; led New England Patriots to 3 Super Bowl wins (2001, 2003, 2004); best all-time post-season coaching record; fined $500,000 in 2007 for violating rules about videotaping the opposing sideline.

Jean Beliveau, b. 1931, Montreal Canadiens center; scored 507 goals; twice MVP.

Johnny Bench, b. 1947, Cincinnati Reds catcher; MVP twice; led league in home runs twice, RBIs 3 times.

Patty Berg, 1918-2006, won more than 80 golf tournaments; AP Woman Athlete of the Year 3 times.

Chris Berman, b. 1955, sportscaster and anchor for ESPN.

Yogi Berra, b. 1925, Yankee catcher (1946-63); 3-time MVP.

Abebe Bikila, 1932-73, Ethiopian runner; won consecutive Olympic marathon gold medals in 1960 (barefoot) and 1964.

Matt Biondi, b. 1965, swimmer; won 5 golds, 1988 Olympics.

Larry Bird, b. 1956, Boston Celtics forward (1979-92); NBA MVP, 1984-86; 1998 coach of the year with Indiana Pacers.

Bonnie Blair, b. 1964, speed skater; won 5 individual gold medals in 3 Olympics (1988, '92, '94).

George Blanda, b. 1927, quarterback, kicker; 26 years as active player, scored 2,002 career points.

Fanny Blankers-Koen, 1918-2004, track; won 4 golds in 1948 Olympics.

Wade Boggs, b. 1958, AL batting champ, 1983, 1985-88; reached 3,000 career hits, 1999 (3,010).

Barry Bonds, b. 1964, outfielder; hit record 73 homers in 2001; NL MVP 1990, 1992-93, 2001-04; 1st all-time in HRs (762).

Björn Borg, b. 1956, led Sweden to first Davis Cup, 1975; Wimbledon champion 5 times.

Ray Bourque, b. 1960, Boston defenseman,1979-2000; 5-time Norris Trophy winner; won Stanley Cup with Colorado, 2001.

Bill Bradley, b. 1943, All-America at Princeton; led N.Y. Knicks to 2 NBA titles (1970, '73); U.S. senator, 1979-97.

Donald Bradman, 1908-2001, Australian widely regarded as the greatest cricketer ever; set several batting records.

Terry Bradshaw, b. 1948, quarterback; led Pittsburgh to 4 Super Bowl wins (1975-76, 1979-80); NFL MVP, 1978.

Tom Brady, b. 1977, quarterback; led New England Patriots to 3 Super Bowl titles, 2002, 2004, 2005; MVP 2002, 2004.

Christine Brennan, b. 1958, sports journalist for *USA Today*, radio and television commentator, specializing in figure skating.

George Brett, b. 1953, Kansas City Royals infielder; led AL in batting, 1976, 1980, 1990; MVP, 1980.

Lou Brock, b. 1939, St. Louis Cardinals outfielder; stole NL single-season record 118 bases, 1974; led NL 8 times.

Jim Brown, b. 1936, Clev. fullback; 12,312 career yds.; 2-time Associated Press MVP.

Paul Brown, 1908-91, football owner, coach; led eponymous Cleveland Browns to 3 NFL championships.

Kobe Bryant, b. 1978, guard; won 3 straight titles with Lakers (2000-02); leading NBA scorer, 2005-06 and 2006-07.

Paul "Bear" Bryant, 1913-83, college football coach with 323 wins; led Alabama to 5 national titles (1961, '64, '65, '78, '79).

Sergei Bubka, b. 1963, Ukrainian pole vaulter; first to clear 20 feet; gold medal, 1988 Olympics.

Don Budge, 1915-2000, won numerous amateur and pro tennis titles; Grand Slam, 1938.

Reggie Bush, b. 1985, New Orleans Saints running back drafted 2nd overall in 2006; helped USC to 2 National Titles (2003-04); Heisman Trophy winner (2005).

Dick Butkus, b. 1942, Chicago Bears linebacker; twice chosen NFL defensive player of the year.

Dick Button, b. 1929, figure skater; won 1948, 1952 Olympic gold medals; world titlist, 1948-52.

Walter Camp, 1859-1925, Yale football player, coach, athletic director; established many rules for modern football.

Roy Campanella, 1921-93, Hall of Fame catcher for the Brooklyn Dodgers (1948-57); 3-time NL MVP.

Earl Campbell, b. 1955, NFL running back; MVP 1978-79.

Jose Canseco, b. 1964, outfielder; led Oakland A's to the World Series, 1988; wrote book about steroids in baseball, 2005.

Eric Cantona, b. 1966, French soccer star; Manchester United 1992-97; named Premier League Overseas Player of the Decade (to mark the 1st 10 years of the Premiere League, 1993-2003) in 2003.

Jennifer Capriati, b. 1976, won Aust. (2001-02) and French Opens (2001), at 14 in 1990 was youngest top-10 player.

Rod Carew, b. 1945, AL infielder; 7 batting titles, 1977 MVP.

Steve Carlton, b. 1944, NL pitcher; won 20 games 6 times, Cy Young award 4 times; 4,136 career strikeouts.

Pete Carroll, b. 1951, college football coach; coached the USC Trojans to 2 championships (2003-4).

Billy Casper, b. 1931, PGA Player of the Year 3 times; U.S. Open champ twice.

Wilt Chamberlain, 1936-99, center; was NBA leading scorer 7 times, MVP 4 times; scored 100 pts. in a game, 1962.

Fred Chapman, 1872-1957, pitcher, Philadelphia A's; became the youngest ever U.S. pro athlete on July 22, 1887 when he pitched against the Cleveland Spiders; he was 14 years, 7 months, 29 days old.

Bobby Clarke, b. 1949, Philadelphia Flyers center; led team to 2 Stanley Cup championships; MVP 3 times.

Roger Clemens, b. 1962, pitcher; 1986 AL MVP; only 7-time Cy Young winner (1986-87, '91, '97-98, 2001, '04); twice recorded record 20 Ks in a game; 354 wins, 4,672 Ks (2nd all-time).

Roberto Clemente, 1934-72, Pittsburgh Pirates outfielder; won 4 batting titles; MVP, 1966; killed in plane crash.

Ty Cobb, 1886-1961, Detroit Tigers outfielder; had record .367 lifetime batting average, 12 batting titles.

Sebastian Coe, b. 1956, British runner; won Olympic 1,500m gold medal and 800m silver medal in 1980 and 1984.

Nadia Comaneci, b. 1961, Romanian gymnast; won 3 gold medals, achieved 7 perfect scores, 1976 Olympics.

Maureen Connolly, 1934-69, won tennis Grand Slam, 1953; AP Woman-Athlete-of-the-Year 3 times.

Jimmy Connors, b. 1952, tennis; 5 U.S. titles, 2 Wimbledon.

Cynthia Cooper, b. 1963, basketball; 4-time MVP of the WNBA finals and 2-time league MVP for the Houston Comets.

James J. Corbett, 1866-1933, heavyweight champion, 1892-97; credited with being the first "scientific" boxer.

Angel Cordero Jr., b. 1942, jockey; leading money winner, 1976, 1982-83; rode 3 Kentucky Derby winners.

Margaret Smith Court, b. 1942, Australian tennis great; won 24 Grand Slam events.

Bob Cousy, b. 1928, Boston guard; 6 NBA titles; 1957 MVP.

Mark Cuban, b. 1958, Dallas Mavericks owner; known for outspoken criticism of NBA.

Al Davis, b. 1929, Oakland Raiders owner and former coach.

Bjoern Daehlie, b. 1967, Norwegian cross-country skier; won record 8 Winter Olympic gold medals.

Lindsay Davenport, b. 1976, tennis; won Olympic gold (1996), U.S. Open (1998), Wimbledon (1999), Aust. Open (2000).

Dizzy Dean, 1910-74, pitcher; St. Louis Cardinals' "Gashouse Gang" in the 30s.

Mary Decker Slaney, b. 1958, runner; has held 6 separate American records from the 800m to 10,000m.

Frank Deford, b. 1938, senior contributing writer for *Sports Illustrated*, author and commentator.

Oscar De La Hoya, b. 1972, won IBF lightweight (1995); WBC super lightweight (1996) and welterweight (1997, 2000) titles.

Donna de Varona, b. 1947, 2 Olympic swimming golds,1964; 1st female sportscaster at a major network (ABC), 1965.

Jack Dempsey, 1895-1983, heavyweight champ, 1919-26.

Gail Devers, b. 1966, Olympic 100m gold medalist, 1992, '96.

Eric Dickerson, b. 1960, NFL record 2,105 rushing yds.,1984.

Joe DiMaggio, 1914-99, N.Y. Yankees outfielder; hit safely in record 56 consecutive games, 1941; AL MVP 3 times.

Tony Dorsett, b. 1954, Heisman winner who led the Dallas Cowboys to an NFL title in his rookie year (1977).

Tim Duncan, b. 1976, San Antonio center; 3-time NBA Finals MVP (1999, 2003, 2005); NBA MVP, 2002-03.

Roberto Duran, b. 1951, Panamanian boxer, held titles at 3 weights; lost 1980 "no mas" fight to Sugar Ray Leonard.

Leo Durocher, 1905-91, manager; won 3 NL pennants (Brooklyn-1941, N.Y. Giants-1951, '54) and 1954 World Series.

Dale Earnhardt, 1951-2001, 7-time NASCAR Winston Cup champ; died in a last-lap crash at 2001 Daytona 500.

Stefan Edberg, b. 1966, Swedish tennis player; U.S. Open champ, 1991, 1992; Wimbledon champ, 1988, 1990.

Gertrude Ederle, 1906-2003, first woman to swim English Channel, broke existing men's record, 1926.

Teresa Edwards, b. 1964, basketball; 5-time Olympian; gold medalist in 1984, '88, '96, 2000 and bronze medal in 1992.

Hicham El Guerrouj, b. 1974, Moroccan runner; holds world records in mile (3:43.13) and 1,500m (3:26); won gold medals in 1,500m and 5,000m in 2004 Olympics.

John Elway, b. 1960, quarterback; led Denver Broncos to 2 Super Bowl wins, 1998, 1999; regular-season MVP, 1987.

Julius "Dr. J" Erving, b. 1950, 3-time ABA MVP, 1981 NBA MVP.

Phil Esposito, b. 1942, NHL scoring leader 5 times.

Janet Evans, b. 1971, 4 Olympic swimming golds, 1988-92.

Lee Evans, b. 1947, Olympic 400m gold medalist in 1968 with a 43.86 sec. world record not broken until 1988.

Chris Evert, b. 1954, U.S. Open tennis champ 6 times, Wimbledon champ 3 times.

Ray Ewry, 1873-1937, track-and-field star; won 8 gold medals, 1900, 1904, and 1908 Olympics.

Nick Faldo, b. 1957, British golfer; won Masters, British Open 3 times each.

Juan Manuel Fangio, 1911-95, Argentinian; 5-time World Grand Prix driving champ (1951, 1954-57).

Marshall Faulk, b. 1973, 2000 NFL MVP; scored then-record 26 TDs in 2001; 3-time Off. Player of the Year (1999-2001).

Brett Favre, b. 1969, quarterback; led Green Bay to Super Bowl win, 1997; NFL MVP, 1995, 1996; co-MVP, 1997.

Roger Federer, b. 1981, Swiss tennis star; won Aust. Open (2004, 2006-07), Wimbledon (2003-07), U.S. Open (2004-07).

Bob Feller, b. 1918, Cleveland Indians pitcher; won 266 games; pitched 3 no-hitters, 12 one-hitters.

Rollie Fingers, b. 1946, pitcher; 341 career saves; AL MVP, Cy Young Award, 1981; World Series MVP, 1974.

Peggy Fleming, b. 1948, world figure skating champion, 1966-68; gold medalist, 1968 Olympics.

Whitey Ford, b. 1928, N.Y. Yankees pitcher; won record 10 World Series games.

George Foreman, b. 1949, heavyweight champion, 1973-74, 1994-95; at 45, the oldest to win a heavyweight title.

Dick Fosbury, b. 1947, high jumper; won 1968 Olympic gold medal; developed the "Fosbury Flop."

Jimmie Foxx, 1907-67, Red Sox, Athletics slugger; MVP 3 times; triple crown, 1933.

A.J. Foyt, b. 1935, won Indy 500 4 times; U.S. Auto Club champ 7 times.

Joe Frazier, b. 1944, heavyweight champion, 1970-73.

Walt Frazier, b. 1945, Hall of Fame guard for N.Y. Knicks' NBA championship teams (1970, '73).

Peter Gammons, b. 1945, sportswriter for ESPN, named to Major League Baseball Hall of Fame.

Lou Gehrig, 1903-41, N.Y. Yankees 1st baseman; MVP, 1927, 1936; triple crown, 1934; AL record 184 RBIs, 1931; played in 2,130 straight games (1925-39), a record that stood until 1995.

Althea Gibson,1927-2003, 2-time U.S. and Wimbledon champ.

Bob Gibson, b. 1935, St. Louis Cardinals pitcher; won Cy Young award twice; struck out 3,117 batters.

Josh Gibson, 1911-47, Hall of Fame catcher; known as "Babe Ruth of the Negro Leagues"; credited with as many as 84 homers in 1 season and about 800 in his career.

Marc Girardelli, b. 1963, skier (Lux.); won 5 World Cup titles.

Raul Gonzalez, b. 1977, Spanish soccer player; led Real Madrid to 3 Champions League titles 1998, 2000, 2002.

Jeff Gordon, b. 1971, race car driver; youngest to win NASCAR title 4 times (1995, 1997-98, 2001).

Steffi Graf, b. 1969, German; won tennis Grand Slam, 1988; U.S. champ 5 times; Wimbledon champ 7 times.

Otto Graham, 1921-2003, Cleveland quarterback; 4-time all-pro.

Red Grange, 1903-91, All-American at Univ. of Illinois, 1923-25; played for Chicago Bears, 1925-35.

"Mean" Joe Greene, b. 1946, Pittsburgh Steelers lineman; twice NFL outstanding defensive player.

Wayne Gretzky, b. 1961, top scorer in NHL history with record 894 goals, 1,963 assists, 2,857 points; MVP, 1980-87, 1989.

Bob Griese, b. 1945, All-Pro quarterback; led Miami Dolphins to 17-0 season (1972) and 2 Super Bowl titles (1973-74).

Ken Griffey Jr., b. 1969, outfielder; led AL in homers 1994, 1997-1999; 1997 AL MVP; 10 gold gloves.

Archie Griffin, b. 1954, Ohio State running back; only 2-time winner of the Heisman Trophy (1974-75).

Florence Griffith Joyner, 1959-98, sprinter; won 3 gold medals at 1988 Olympics; world and Olympic record for 100m.

Lefty Grove, 1900-75, pitcher; won 300 AL games.

Vladimir Guerrero, b. 1976, Dominican right fielder for Los Angeles Angels; 2004 American League MVP award.

Janet Guthrie, b. 1938, 1st woman driver in Indy 500 (1977).

Tony Gwynn, b. 1960, 8-time NL batting champ, 1984, 1987-89, 1994-97; 3,141 career hits.

Walter Hagen, 1892-1969, golfer; 5 PGA, 4 British Open titles.

Mika Hakkinen, b. 1968, Finnish Formula One racing driver; Formula One champion 1998, 1999.

George Halas, 1895-1983, founder/player/coach of Chicago Bears; won 6 NFL championships as a coach.

Dorothy Hamill, b. 1956, figure skater; gold medalist at the Olympics and World championships in 1976.

Scott Hamilton, b. 1958, U.S. and world figure skating champion, 1981-84; Olympic gold medalist, 1984.

Mia Hamm, b. 1972, led U.S. to World Cup (1991, '99) and Olympic ('96, 2004) titles; most career internat. goals (144).

Franco Harris, b. 1950, running back; 4 Super Bowls with Steelers (1975-76, 1979-80); 1,000+ yds. in a season 8 times.

Marvin Harrison, b. 1972, Indianapolis Colts wide receiver; holds NFL record for single-season receptions, 143, 2002

Bill Hartack, b. 1932, jockey; rode 5 Kentucky Derby winners.

Dominik Hasek, b. 1965, NHL goaltender; won Vezina Trophy, 1994-95, 1997-99, 2001; NHL MVP, 1997-98.

John Havlicek, b. 1940, Boston Celtics forward; scored 26,395 career pts.

Eric Heiden, b. 1958, speed skater; won 5 Olympic golds, 1980.

Rickey Henderson, b. 1958, outfielder; 1990 AL MVP; record 130 stolen bases, 1982; all-time leader in steals, runs.

Sonja Henie, 1912-69, Norwegian world champion figure skater, 1927-36; Olympic gold medalist, 1928, 1932, 1936.

Martina Hingis, b. 1980, Swiss; won Aust. and U.S. Opens, Wimbledon; youngest No. 1 player (16 yrs., 6 m.), 1997.

Trevor Hoffman, b. 1967; San Diego Padres relief pitcher; set a new all-time career saves record in 2006 with 482.

Ben Hogan, 1912-97, golfer; won 4 U.S. Open titles, 2 PGA Championships, 2 Masters.

Chamique Holdsclaw, b. 1977, L.A. Sparks forward.

Evander Holyfield, b. 1962, 4-time heavyweight champion.

Rogers Hornsby, 1896-1963, NL 2nd baseman; batted record .424 in 1924; twice won triple crown.

Paul Hornung, b. 1935, Green Bay Packers running back, placekicker; scored record 176 points, 1960.

Ryan Howard, b. 1979, first baseman for Philadelphia Phillies, known for his hitting; 2006 National League MVP award.

Gordie Howe, b. 1928, hockey forward; NHL MVP 6 times; scored 801 goals in 26 NHL seasons.

Carl Hubbell, 1903-88, N.Y. Giants pitcher; 20-game winner 5 consecutive years, 1933-37.

Bobby Hull, b. 1939, NHL all-star 10 times; MVP, 1965-66.

Brett Hull, b. 1964: St. Louis Blues forward; led NHL in goals, 1990-92; MVP, 1991.

Catfish Hunter, 1946-99, pitched perfect game, 1968; 20-game winner 5 times.

Don Hutson, 1913-97, Packers receiver; caught 99 TD passes; 2-time NFL MVP.

Juli Inkster, b. 1960, Hall of Fame golfer; 2nd to win all 4 of LPGA's modern majors; won 7 career major titles.

Phil Jackson, b. 1945, won 9 NBA titles as coach of Bulls and Lakers; 1973 title as a player with N.Y Knicks.

Reggie Jackson, b. 1946, slugger; led AL in home runs 4 times; MVP, 1973; hit 5 World Series home runs, 1977.

"Shoeless" Joe Jackson, 1889-1951, outfielder; 3rd highest career batting average (.356); one of the "Black Sox" banned for allegedly throwing 1919 World Series.

Jaromir Jagr, b. 1972, Czech hockey player; NHL MVP in 1999; Art Ross Trophy (leading scorer) 1995, 1998-2001.

Lebron James, b. 1984, Cleveland Cavaliers forward; won Rookie of the Year, 2004.

Ron Jaworski, b. 1951, former NFL quarterback (1974-89), NFL analyst on ESPN.

Sally Jenkins, b. 1960, sports journalist and writer for *The Washington Post.*

Bruce Jenner, b. 1949, Olympic decathlon gold medalist, 1976.

Lynn Jennings, b. 1960, runner; 3-time World and 9-time U.S. cross country champ; bronze at 1992 Olympics (10,000m).

Derek Jeter, b. 1974, shortstop; 8-time All-Star; led NY Yankees to 4 World Series titles; World Series MVP, 2000.

Earvin "Magic" Johnson, b. 1959, NBA MVP, 1987, 1989, 1990; Playoff MVP, 1980, 1982, 1987; 2nd in career assists.

Jack Johnson, 1878-1946, heavyweight champion, 1908-15.

Michael Johnson, b. 1967, 5-time Olympic gold medalist (1996, 2000); world and Olympic record, 200m and 400m.

Randy Johnson, b. 1963, 5-time Cy Young winner; strikeout leader: 1992-95, 1999-2004; 4,616 strikeouts (3rd all-time); pitched perfect game, 2004.

Walter Johnson, 1887-1946, Washington Senators pitcher; won 416 games; record 110 shutouts.

Bobby Jones, 1902-71, won golf's Grand Slam, 1930; U.S. Amateur champ 5 times, U.S. Open champ 4 times.

Cobi Jones, b. 1970, soccer; most U.S. national team appearances with 164.

David "Deacon" Jones, b. 1938, 5-time All-Pro with L.A. Rams (1965-69); "sack" specialist credited with inventing the term.

Marion Jones, b. 1975, 2000 Olympic 100m, 200m, 1,600m relay gold medalist, bronze in long jump and 400m relay.

Roy Jones Jr., b. 1969, light heavyweight champ, 1999-2004.

Michael Jordan, b. 1963, guard; leading NBA scorer, 1987-93, 1996-98; MVP, 1988, 1991-92, '96, '98; playoff MVP, 1991-93, 1996-98; ESPN Athlete of the Century.

Dorothy Kamenshek, b. 1925, led Rockford (IL) Peaches to 4 All-American Girls Baseball League titles in the 1940s.

Kasey Keller, b. 1969, U.S. goalkeeper; U.S. record for most career international victories, 39.

Jackie Joyner-Kersee, b. 1962, Olympic gold medalist in heptathlon (1988,'92) and long jump (1988).

Harmon Killebrew, b. 1936, Minnesota Twins slugger; led AL in home runs 6 times; 573 lifetime.

Jean Claude Killy, b. 1943, French skier; 3 Olympic golds, 1968.

Ralph Kiner, b. 1922, Pittsburgh Pirates slugger; led NL in home runs 7 consecutive years, 1946-52.

Billie Jean King, b. 1943, U.S. singles champ 4 times; Wimbledon champ 6 times; beat Bobby Riggs, 1973.

Peter King, b. 1957, senior writer for *Sports Illustrated.*

Bob Knight, b. 1940, basketball coach; led Indiana U. to NCAA title in 1976, '81, '87.

Olga Korbut, b. 1955, Soviet gymnast; 3 1972 Olympic golds.

Sandy Koufax, b. 1935, 3-time Cy Young winner; lowest ERA in NL, 1962-66; pitched 4 no-hitters, one a perfect game.

Ingrid Kristiansen, b. 1956, Norwegian; only runner to have held world records in 5,000m, 10,000m, and marathon.

Julie Krone, b. 1963, winningest female jockey; only woman to ride a winner in a Triple Crown race (Belmont, 1993).

Michelle Kwan, b. 1980, figure skater; 9 U.S. and 5 World titles; silver medalist at 1998 Olympics, bronze in 2002.

Guy Lafleur, b. 1951, 3-time NHL scoring leader; 1977-78 MVP.

Alexi Lalas, b. 1970, soccer player; first American to play in Italian League Serie A.

Kenesaw Mountain Landis, 1866-1944, 1st commissioner of baseball (1920-44); banned the 8 "Black Sox" involved in fixing 1919 World Series.

Tom Landry, 1924-2000, Dallas Cowboys head coach, 1960-88; won 2 Super Bowls (1972, '78); 3rd in career wins (270).

Dick "Night Train" Lane, 1928-2002, Hall of Fame defensive back, intercepted an NFL season record 14 passes (1952).

Don Larsen, b. 1929, As N.Y. Yankee, pitched only World Series perfect game, Oct. 8, 1956—a 2-0 win over Brooklyn.

Rod Laver, b. 1938, Australian; won tennis Grand Slam twice, 1962, 1969; Wimbledon champ 4 times.

Mario Lemieux, b. 1965, 6-time NHL leading scorer; MVP, 1988, 1993, 1996; playoff MVP, 1991-92.

Greg Lemond, b. 1961, cyclist; 3-time Tour de France winner (1986, '89-90); first American to win the event.

Ivan Lendl, b. 1960, Czech; U.S. Open tennis champ, 1985-87.

Sugar Ray Leonard, b. 1956: boxer; held titles in 5 different weight classes.

Carl Lewis, b. 1961, track-and-field star; won 9 Olympic gold medals in sprinting and the long jump.

Lennox Lewis, b. 1965, Brit.; heavyweight champ, 1997-2004.

Ray Lewis, b. 1975, linebacker for the Baltimore Ravens; Super Bowl XXXV MVP.

Tara Lipinski, b. 1982, youngest figure skater to win U.S. and world championships, 1997, and Winter Olympic gold, 1998.

Vince Lombardi, 1913-70, Green Bay Packers coach; led team to 5 NFL championships and 2 Super Bowl victories.

Nancy Lopez, b. 1957, Hall of Fame golfer; 4-time LPGA Player of the Year, 3-time winner of the LPGA Championship.

Greg Louganis, b. 1960, won Olympic gold medals in both springboard and platform diving, 1984, 1988.

Joe Louis, 1914-81, heavyweight champion, 1937-49.

Sid Luckman, 1916-98, Chicago Bears quarterback; led team to 4 NFL championships; MVP, 1943.

Connie Mack, 1862-1956, Philadelphia Athletics manager, 1901-50; won 9 pennants, 5 championships.

John Madden, b. 1936, won Super Bowl as coach of the Oakland Raiders (1977); NFL TV analyst since 1982.

Greg Maddux, b. 1966, NL pitcher, won 4 consecutive Cy Young awards, 1992-95; 333 career wins.

Karl Malone, b. 1963, Utah Jazz, L.A. Laker forward; MVP, 1997, 1999; 14-time All-Star; 36,928 career points (2nd all-time).

Moses Malone, b. 1955, NBA center; MVP, 1979, 1982-83.

Peyton Manning, b. 1976, Indianapolis Colts quarterback; NFL MVP, 2004; Super Bowl XLI MVP; NFL single-season record 49 TD passes, 121.1 passer rating, 2004.

Mickey Mantle, 1931-95, N.Y. Yankees outfielder; triple crown, 1956; 18 World Series home runs; MVP 3 times.

Diego Maradona, b. 1960, soccer player; led Argentina to World Cup in 1986.

"Pistol" Pete Maravich, 1947-88, guard; scored NCAA record 44.2 ppg during collegiate career; led NBA in scoring, 1977.

Rocky Marciano, 1923-69, heavyweight champion, 1952-56; retired undefeated.

Dan Marino, b. 1961, Miami quarterback; NFL record 5,084 yds passing and 48 TDs, 1984; career leader, TDs, yds passing.

Roger Maris, 1934-85, N.Y. Yankees outfielder; hit AL record 61 home runs, 1961; MVP, 1960 and 1961.

Curtis Martin, b. 1973: Jets running back; 5-time Pro-Bowler; 4th all-time in rushing yards with 14,101.

Eddie Mathews, 1931-2001, Milwaukee-Atlanta Braves 3rd baseman; hit 512 career home runs.

Christy Mathewson, 1880-1925, pitcher; won 373 games.

Bob Mathias, 1930-2006, decathlon gold, 1948, 1952 Olympics.

Willie Mays, b. 1931, N.Y.-S.F. Giants center fielder; hit 660 home runs, led NL 4 times; had 3,283 hits; twice MVP.

Willie McCovey, b. 1938, S.F. Giants slugger; hit 521 home runs; led NL 3 times; MVP, 1969.

John McEnroe, b. 1959, U.S. Open tennis champ, 1979-81, 1984; Wimbledon champ, 1981, 1983-84.

John McGraw, 1873-1934, N.Y. Giants manager; led team to 10 pennants, 3 championships.

Mark McGwire, b. 1963, hit then-record 70 home runs in 1998; 583 career home runs (8th).

Tamara McKinney, b. 1962, 1st U.S. skier to win overall Alpine World Cup championship (1983).

Andrea Mead Lawrence, b. 1932, skier; only woman to win 2 gold medals in alpine skiing at one Olympics (1952).

Mark Messier, b. 1961, center; NHL MVP, 1990, 1992; Conn Smythe Trophy, 1984.

Debbie Meyer, b. 1952, 1st swimmer to win 3 individual Olympic golds (1968).

Al Michaels, b. 1944, *Monday Night Football* announcer, 5 time Outstanding Sports Personality Emmy winner.

George Mikan, 1924-2005, Minn. Lakers center; considered the best basketball player of the first half of the 20th century.

Stan Mikita, b. 1940, Chicago Blackhawks center; led NHL in scoring 4 times; MVP twice.

Billy Mills, b. 1938, runner; upset winner of the 1964 Olympic 10,000m; only American man ever to win the event.

Yao Ming, b. 1980, Chinese center for the Houston Rockets, one of the tallest in NBA at 7'6".

Joe Montana, b. 1956, S.F. 49ers quarterback; Super Bowl MVP, 1982, 1985, 1990.

Archie Moore, 1913-98, light-heavyweight champ, 1952-62.

Howie Morenz, 1902-37, Montreal Canadiens forward; considered best hockey player of first half of the 20th century.

Edwin Moses, b. 1955, undefeated in 122 consecutive 400m hurdles races, 1977-87; Olympic gold medalist, 1976, '84.

Shirley Muldowney, b. 1940, 1st woman to race National Hot Rod Assoc. Top Fuel dragsters; 3-time NHRA points champ.

Eddie Murray, b. 1956, 3rd player to combine 3,000+ hits with 500+ home runs.

Stan Musial, b. 1920, St. Louis Cardinals star; won 7 NL batting titles; MVP 3 times.

Bronko Nagurski, 1908-90, Chicago Bears fullback and tackle; gained more than 4,000 yds. rushing.

Joe Namath, b. 1943, Jets quarterback; 1969 Super Bowl MVP.

Steve Nash, b. 1974, Phoenix Suns point guard; NBA MVP, in 2005, 2006.

Martina Navratilova, b. 1956, Wimbledon champ 9 times, U.S. Open champ 1983-84, 1986-87.

Byron Nelson, b. 1912-2006, won 11 consecutive golf tournaments in 1945; twice Masters and PGA titlist.

Ernie Nevers, 1903-76, Stanford football star; selected as best college fullback to play between 1919-69.

Paula Newby-Fraser, b. 1972, 8-time Ironman Triathlon World Champ; holds women's course record.

John Newcombe, b. 1943, Australian; twice U.S. Open tennis champ; Wimbledon titlist 3 times.

Jack Nicklaus, b. 1940, PGA Player of the Year, 1967, 1972; leading money winner 8 times; won 18 majors (6 Masters).

Chuck Noll, b. 1932, Pittsburgh coach; won 4 Super Bowls.

Paavo Nurmi, 1897-1973, Finnish distance runner; won 6 Olympic gold medals, 1920, 1924, 1928.

Al Oerter, 1936-2007, discus thrower; won gold medal at 4 consecutive Olympics, 1956-68.

Hakeem Olajuwon, b. 1963, Houston center; NBA MVP, 1994, playoffs MVP, 1994-95; career blocked shots leader.

Barney Oldfield, 1878-1946, pioneer auto racer; was first to drive a car 60 mph (1903).

Shaquille O'Neal, b. 1972, center; led L.A. Lakers to NBA titles, 2000-2002; and Miami Heat to NBA title, 2006; Finals MVP 2000, 2002; NBA MVP 2000 .

Magglio Ordonez, b. 1974, Venezuelan right fielder for the Detroit Tigers.

Bobby Orr, b. 1948, Boston Bruins defenseman; 8-time Norris Trophy winner; led NHL in scoring twice, assists 5 times.

Mel Ott, 1909-1958, N.Y. Giants rightfielder; hit 511 home runs; led NL 6 times.

Jesse Owens, 1913-1980, track and field; 4 1936 Olympic golds.

Terrell Owens, b. 1973: Dallas Cowboys wide receiver; NFL record for single-game receptions with 20 in 2000.

Satchel Paige, 1906-1982, pitcher; starred in Negro leagues, 1924-48; entered major leagues at age 42.

Arnold Palmer, b. 1929, golf's first $1 million winner; won 4 Masters, 2 British Opens.

Jim Palmer, b. 1945, Baltimore Orioles pitcher; won Cy Young award 3 times; 20-game winner 8 times.

Joe Paterno, b. 1926, football coach; 2nd-most wins in NCAA Div. I-A (343 through 2004); led Penn St. to titles, 1982, 1986.

Danica Patrick, b. 1982, racecar driver; 4th woman to race at Indy 500, and 1st to lead (2005).

Floyd Patterson, 1935-2006, 2-time heavyweight champion; first to ever regain the title after losing it.

Walter Payton, 1954-1999, Chicago Bears running back; most rushing yards in NFL history; top NFC rusher, 1976-80.

Pelé (Edson Arantes do Nascimento), b. 1940, Brazilian soccer player; led Brazil to 3 World Cups (1958, '62, '70); scored 1,281 goals.

Bob Pettit, b. 1932, first NBA player to score 20,000 points; twice NBA scoring leader.

Richard Petty, b. 1937, NASCAR national champ 7 times; 7-time Daytona 500 winner.

Michael Phelps, b. 1985, swimmer; won 8 medals (6 gold, 2 bronze) at 2004 Olympics; 7 gold medals at 2007 World Championships in Melbourne, Australia; holds 6 world records.

Picabo Street, b. 1971, skier; Olympic World Cup downhill champion (1995-96); Olympic super G gold medalist, 1998.

Laffit Pincay Jr., b. 1946, jockey; leading money-winner, 1970-74, 1979, 1985.

Jacques Plante, 1929-86, NHL goaltender; 7 Vezina trophies; first goalie to wear a mask in a game.

Gary Player, b. 1935, South African golfer; won 3 Masters, 3 British Opens, 2 PGA Championships, and the U.S. Open.

Steve Prefontaine, 1951-75, runner; 1st to win 4 NCAA titles in same event (5,000m, 1970-73); died in auto accident.

Kirby Puckett, 1960-2006, Minnesota Twins center fielder (1984-95); led team to World Series titles in 1987 and 1991.

Albert Pujols, b. 1980, St. Louis first baseman; NL MVP, 2005.

Paula Radcliffe, b. 1973, British runner; set marathon world record of 2:15:25 in London, 2003.

Kimi Räikkönen, b. 1979, Finnish Formula One race car driver, currently driving for Scuderia Ferrari.

Manny Ramirez, b. 1972, Boston Red Sox slugger; 2004 World Series champs.

Willis Reed, b. 1942, N.Y. Knicks center; MVP, 1970; playoff MVP, 1970, 1973.

Mary Lou Retton, b. 1968, gymnast; won all-around gold medal at 1984 Olympics; also won 2 silvers and 2 bronzes.

José Reyes, b. 1983, Dominican shortstop for the New York Mets; 2006-07 All-Star.

Claudio Reyna, b. 1973, midfielder; U.S. National Team; named to the FIFA World Cup All-Star team in 2002.

Jerry Rice, b. 1962, receiver; 1989 Super Bowl MVP; NFL record for career touchdowns (208) and receptions (1,549).

Maurice Richard, 1921-2000, Montreal Canadiens forward; scored 544 regular season goals, 82 playoff goals.

Branch Rickey, 1881-1965, MLB executive; helped break baseball's color barrier, 1947; initiated farm system, 1919.

Cal Ripken Jr., b. 1960, Baltimore shortstop; AL MVP 1983, 1991; most consecutive games played (2,632).

Mariano Rivera, b. 1969: relief pitcher; helped NY Yankees to 4 World Series titles; World Series MVP, 1999; all-time MLB leader in post-season saves with 34.

Oscar Robertson, b. 1938, NBA guard; averaged career 25.7 points per game; 4th in career assists (9,887); MVP, 1964.

Brooks Robinson, b. 1937, Baltimore Orioles 3rd baseman; played in 4 World Series; MVP, 1964; 16 gold gloves.

Frank Robinson, b. 1935, MVP in both NL and AL; triple crown, 1966; 586 career home runs; first black manager in majors.

Jackie Robinson, 1919-72, broke baseball's color barrier with Brooklyn Dodgers, 1947; MVP, 1949.

Sugar Ray Robinson, 1920-89, boxer; middleweight champion 5 times, welterweight champion.

Knute Rockne, 1888-1931, Notre Dame football coach, 1918-31; revolutionized game by stressing forward pass.

Bill Rodgers, b. 1947, runner; won Boston and New York City marathons 4 time each, 1975-80.

Alex Rodriguez, b. 1975, New York Yankees third baseman; A.L. MVP in 2003 and 2005; 11-time All Star.

Juan "Chi Chi" Rodriguez, b. 1935, champion golfer; 8 PGA tour wins and 22 Champions tour wins.

Ben Roethlisberger, b. 1982, quarterback, led Pittsburgh Steelers to Super Bowl, 2005; youngest Super Bowl winning quarterback with Pittsburgh Steelers in 2005.

Ronaldinho, b. 1980, soccer midfielder; led Brazil to World Cup Finals in 2006; FIFA World Player of the Year, 2004, 2005.

Ronaldo (Ronaldo Luiz Nazario de Lima), b. 1976, soccer forward; led Brazil to 2002 World Cup title; 3-time FIFA world player of the year (1996-97, 2002); most World Cup goals, 15.

Art Rooney, 1901-88, famous NFL owner, bought Pittsburgh Pirates in 1933, renamed Steelers in 1940.

Pete Rose, b. 1941, won 3 NL batting titles; hit in 44 consecutive games, 1978; most career hits, 4,256; banned for gambling, 1989; admitted betting on his team, 2004.

Ken Rosewall, b. 1934, Australian tennis player; 2-time U.S. champ, 8 Grand Slam singles titles.

Patrick Roy, b. 1965, Montreal-Colorado goalie; only 3-time NHL Playoffs MVP (Conn Smythe Trophy), 1986, '93, 2001.

Wilma Rudolph, 1940-94, sprinter; won 3 1960 Olympic golds.

Adolph Rupp, 1901-77, NCAA basketball coach; led Kentucky to 4 national titles, 1948-49, 1951, 1958.

Bill Russell, b. 1934, Boston Celtics center; led team to 11 NBA titles; MVP 5 times; first black coach of major pro sports team.

Babe Ruth, 1895-1948, N.Y. Yankees outfielder; hit 60 home runs, 1927; 714 lifetime (2d all-time); led AL 12 times.

Johnny Rutherford, b. 1938, auto racer; won 3 Indy 500s.

Nolan Ryan, b. 1947, pitcher; holds season (383), career (5,714) strikeout records; won 324 games (7 no-hitters).

Pete Sampras, b. 1971, tennis star; 1st man in Open era to win 7 Wimbledons; most career Grand Slam wins (14).

Joan Benoit Samuelson, b. 1968, won 1st Olympic women's marathon (1984), Boston Marathon (1979, '83).

Barry Sanders, b. 1968, rushed for 2,053 yards in 1997; led NFL in rushing, 1990, 1994, 1996, 1997.

Gale Sayers, b. 1943, Chicago back; twice led NFL in rushing.

Mike Schmidt, b. 1949, Phillies 3rd baseman; led NL in home runs 8 times; 548 lifetime; NL MVP, 1980, 1981, 1986.

Michael Schumacher, b. 1969, German race-car driver; 7-time Formula 1 world champ (1994-95, 2000-2004).

Tom Seaver, b. 1944, pitcher; won NL Cy Young award 3 times; won 311 major league games.

Monica Seles, b. 1973, tennis; won U.S. ('91-92), Aust. ('91-93, '96), French ('90-92) Opens; stabbed on court by fan, 1993.

Maria Sharapova, b.1987, Russian tennis star; won Wimbledon 2004, U.S. Open 2006; Australian and French Opens, 2007.

Patty Sheehan, b. 1956, Hall of Fame golfer; 3 LPGA Championships (1983-84, '93).

Willie Shoemaker, 1931-2003, jockey; rode 4 Kentucky Derby and 5 Belmont Stakes winners; leading career money winner.

Frank Shorter, b. 1947, runner, only American to win men's Olympic marathon (1972) since 1908; silver medalist in 1976.

Don Shula, b. 1930, all-time winningest NFL coach (347 games).

Al Simmons, 1902-56, AL outfielder; lifetime .334 batting avg.

Bill Simmons, b. 1969, columnist for *Page 2* on ESPN.com known as "The Sports Guy."

O.J. Simpson, b. 1947, running back; rushed for 2,003 yds., 1973; AFC leading rusher 4 times; acquitted of murder, 1995.

George Sisler, 1893-1973, St. Louis Browns 1st baseman; had then-record 257 hits, 1920; batted .340 lifetime.

Dean Smith, b. 1931, basketball coach; most career Division I wins (879); led North Carolina to 2 NCAA titles (1982, '93).

Emmitt Smith, b. 1969, running back; NFL and Super Bowl MVP, 1993; third-season winner on TV's "Dancing With the Stars."

Conn Smythe, 1895-1980, won 7 Stanley Cups as Toronto GM (1929-1961); playoff MVP award named in his honor.

Sam Snead, 1912-2002, PGA and Masters champ 3 times each, record 82 PGA tournament victories.

Annika Sorenstam, b. 1970, Swedish golfer; set LPGA 18-hole record of 59 (–13) and 72-hole record of 27-under-par, 2001; won 10 LPGA majors, including career Grand Slam.

Sammy Sosa, b. 1968, Rangers designated hitter; 66 homers, NL MVP, 1998; 1st to hit 60+ homers 3 times (1998, 1999, 2001).

Warren Spahn, 1921-2003, pitcher; won 363 NL games; 20-game winner 13 times; Cy Young award, 1957.

Tris Speaker, 1888-1958, AL outfielder; batted .345 over 22 seasons; hit record 793 career doubles.

Mark Spitz, b. 1950, swimmer; won 7 golds at 1972 Olympics.

Amos Alonzo Stagg, 1862-1965, football innovator; Univ. of Chicago football coach for 41 years, 5 undefeated seasons.

Bart Starr, b. 1934, Green Bay Packers quarterback; led team to 5 NFL titles and 2 Super Bowl victories.

Roger Staubach, b. 1942, Dallas Cowboys quarterback; leading NFC passer 5 times.

Casey Stengel, 1890-1975, managed Yankees to 10 pennants, 7 championships, 1949-60.

Jackie Stewart, b. 1939, Scot auto racer; 27 Grand Prix wins.

John Stockton, b. 1962, Utah Jazz guard; NBA career leader in assists, steals; NBA assists leader, 1988-96.

Louise Suggs, b. 1923, golfer; U.S. Women's Open champ., 1949, '52; 11 major victories, ranks 3rd all-time.

John L. Sullivan, 1858-1918, last bareknuckle heavyweight champion, 1882-1892.

Pat Summitt, b. 1952, women's basketball coach; led Tennessee Lady Vols to 7 NCAA titles (1987, '89, '91, '96-98, 2007).

Ichiro Suzuki, b. 1973, Japanese center fielder for the Seattle Mariners; Pacific League MVP, 1994, 1995, 1996; American League MVP, 2001.

Fran Tarkenton, b. 1940, Minnesota, N.Y. Giants quarterback; 3rd in career TD passes (342); 1975 Player of the Year.

Lawrence Taylor, b. 1959, linebacker; led N.Y. Giants to 2 Super Bowl titles; played in 10 Pro Bowls.

Jenny Thompson, b. 1973, swimmer; most decorated U.S. female Olympian; 12 medals (8 gold) in 1992, '96, 2000, '04.

Daley Thompson, b. 1958, British decathlete; Olympic gold medalist in 1980, '84.

Jim Thorpe, 1888-1953, football All-America, 1911, 1912; won pentathlon and decathlon, 1912 Olympics.

Bill Tilden, 1893-1953, won 7 U.S. tennis titles, 3 Wimbledon.

Y. A. Tittle, b. 1926, N.Y. Giants quarterback; MVP, 1961, 1963.

Alberto Tomba "La Bomba", b. 1966, Italian skier; 5 Olympic alpine medals (3 golds, 2 silver) in 1988, 1992.

LaDainian "L.T." Tomlinson, b. 1979, running back for the San Diego Chargers; NFL records for single season touchdowns (31), rushing touchdowns (28) & most points scored in a single season (186).

Lee Trevino, b. 1939, golfer; won U.S., British Open twice.

Bryan Trottier, b. 1956, Islanders, Penguins center for 6 Stanley Cup champs.

Gene Tunney, 1897-1978, heavyweight champion, 1926-28.

Mike Tyson, b. 1966, undisputed heavyweight champ, 1987-1990; at 20, youngest to win a heavyweight title (WBC, 1986).

Wyomia Tyus, b. 1945, Olympic 100m gold medalist, 1964, '68.

Johnny Unitas, 1933-2002, Baltimore Colts quarterback; passed for more than 40,000 yds; MVP, 1957, 1967.

Al Unser, b. 1939, Indy 500 winner 5 times.

Bobby Unser, b. 1934, Indy 500 winner 3 times.

Brian Urlacher, b.1978, Chicago Bears linebacker; Defensive Rookie of the Year, 2000; 5-time Pro Bowler.

Norm Van Brocklin, 1926-83, quarterback; passed for game record 554 yds., 1951; MVP, 1960.

Amy Van Dyken, b. 1973, swimmer, first American woman to win 4 gold medals in one Olympics (1996).

Michael Vick, b. 1960, quarterback for the Atlanta Falcons, suspended and convicted (2007) of illegal dog fighting and gambling activities.

Lasse Viren, b. 1949, Finnish runner; Olympic 5,000m and 10,000m gold medalist in 1972 and 1976.

Dwyane Wade, b.1982, guard; led Miami Heat to NBA title in 2006; finals MVP 2006.

Honus Wagner, 1874-1955, Pirates shortstop; 8 NL batting titles.

Grete Waitz, b. 1953, Norwegian; 9-time winner of the New York City Marathon (1978-80, 1982-86, '88).

"Jersey" Joe Walcott, 1914-94, boxer; became heavyweight champion at age 37, 1951-52.

Bill Walton, b. 1952, center; led Portland Trail Blazers to 1977 NBA title; MVP, 1978; NBA TV commentator.

Kurt Warner, b. 1971, Rams, Giants, Cardinals quarterback; NFL MVP 1999, 2001; Super Bowl MVP, 2000.

Tom Watson, b. 1949, golfer; 6-time PGA Player of the Year, won 5 British Opens, 2 Masters, U.S. Open.

Karrie Webb, b. 1974, Australian golfer; youngest woman (26 yrs. 6 mos.) to win career Grand Slam, 1999-2001.

Johnny Weissmuller, 1903-84, swimmer; won 52 national championships, 5 Olympic gold medals; set 67 world records.

Jerry West, b. 1938, L.A. Lakers guard; had career average 27 points per game; first team all-star 10 times.

Byron "Whizzer" White, 1917-2002, running back; led NCAA in scoring and rushing at Colorado (1937); led NFL in rushing twice (1938, '40); Supreme Court justice, 1962-93.

Kathy Whitworth, b. 1939, 7-time LPGA Player of the Year (1966-69, 1971-73); 88 tour wins most on LPGA or PGA tour.

Michelle Wie, b. 1989, golfer; in 2002 became youngest-ever qualifier for an LPGA event; turned pro at age 15.

Michael Wilbon, b. 1958, sportswriter and columnist for *The Washington Post* and ESPN.

Lenny Wilkens, b. 1937, winningest coach in NBA history; in Hall of Fame as player and coach.

Serena Williams, b. 1981, tennis; Wimbledon (2002, 2003), U.S. Open champ; Australian Open (2003, 2005, 2007); French Open (2002).

Ted Williams, 1918-2002, Boston Red Sox outfielder; won 6 batting titles, 2 triple crowns; hit .406 in 1941.

Venus Williams, b. 1980, champ at Wimbledon (2000, 2001, 2005, 2007), Australian Open (2003), French Open (2002).

Helen Wills Moody, 1905-98, tennis star; won U.S. Open 7 times, Wimbledon 8 times.

Katarina Witt, b. 1965, German figure skater; won Olympic gold medal, 1984, 1988; world champ, 1984-84, 1987-88.

John Wooden, b. 1910, UCLA basketball coach; 10 NCAA titles.

Tiger Woods, b. 1975, golfer; youngest to win career Grand Slam, at age 24 (1997-2000); 13 career major titles.

Mickey Wright, b. 1935, golfer; won LPGA and U.S. Open championship 4 times; 82 career wins, including 13 majors.

Eric Wynalda, b. 1969, soccer; all-time leading U.S. international goal scorer with 33.

Kristi Yamaguchi, b. 1971, figure skater; won national, world, and Olympic titles in 1992.

Carl Yastrzemski, b. 1939, Boston Red Sox slugger; won 3 batting titles; triple crown, 1967.

Cy Young, 1867-1955, pitcher; won record 511 games.

Steve Young, b. 1961, 49ers quarterback; led NFL in passing, 1991-94, 1996, 1997; Super Bowl MVP, 1995.

Vince Young, b. 1983, quarterback for the Tennessee Titans.

Babe Didrikson Zaharias, 1911-56, all-around athlete; 3 track & field medals (2 golds), 1932 Olympics; won 10 golf majors; also played baseball; 6-time AP Female Athlete of the Year.

Emil Zátopek, 1922-2000, Czech runner; won 3 gold medals at 1952 Olympics (5,000m, 10,000m, and marathon).

Zinedine Zidane, b. 1972, soccer midfielder; led France to 1998 World Cup title; named top player in 2006; 3-time FIFA world player of the year (1998, 2000, 2003).

GENERAL INDEX

Note: Page numbers in **boldface** indicate key reference. Page numbers in *italics* indicate photos.

SPORTS QUICK REFERENCE INDEX

FOR COMPLETE INDEX, SEE PAGES 979-1007.